Encyclopedia of Environmental Information Sources

**GALE
ENVIRONMENTAL
LIBRARY**

Encyclopedia of Environmental Information Sources

A Subject Guide to About 34,000 Print and Other Sources of
Information on All Aspects of the Environment

Includes: Abstracting and Indexing Services, Almanacs and Yearbooks,
Bibliographies, Directories, Encyclopedias and Dictionaries, General Works,
Governmental Organizations, Handbooks and Manuals, Online Data Bases,
Periodicals and Newsletters, Research Centers and Institutes, Statistics
Sources, and Trade Associations and Professional Societies

Sarojini Balachandran, Editor

 *Gale Research Inc.* • *DETROIT* • *WASHINGTON, D.C.* • *LONDON*

Sarojini Balachandran, *Editor*

Gale Research Inc. Staff

Lawrence W. Baker, *Senior Developmental Editor*
Donna Wood, *Coordinating Editor*
Jennifer Mossman, *Contributing Editor*
Jacqueline L. Longe and Kelle S. Sisung, *Associate Editors*
Erin E. Holmberg, Matt Merta, Gerda Sherk,
and Bradford J. Wood, *Assistant Editors*

Mary Beth Trimper, *Production Director*
Mary Kelley, *Production Assistant*

Cynthia D. Baldwin, *Art Director*
Bernadette M. Gornie, *Graphic Designer*

Theresa Rocklin, *Supervisor of Systems and Programming*
John Italiano, *Programmer*

Benita L. Spight, *Editorial Data Entry Supervisor*
Gwendolyn Tucker, *Data Entry Group Leader*
Frances L. Monroe and Constance J. Wells, *Data Entry Associates*

∞™ The paper used in this publication meets the minimum requirements of American National Standard for Information Sciences-Permanence Paper for Printed Library Materials, ANSI Z39.48-1984.

♻ This book is printed on recycled paper that meets Environmental Protection Agency Standards.

Copyright © 1993
Gale Research Inc.
835 Penobscot Bldg.
Detroit, MI 48226-4094

Library of Congress Cataloging-in-Publication Data
Encyclopedia of environmental information sources/edited by Sarojini Balachandran. p. cm.
ISBN 0-8103-8568-6: $125.00
1. Environmental protection—Bibliography. 2. Ecology—Bibliography.
3. Conservation of natural resources—Bibliography.
I. Balachandran, Sarojini. Z5863.P7E54 1993 [TD170]   92-10925
016.3637—dc20   CIP

Printed in the United States of America

Published simultaneously in the United Kingdom
by Gale Research International Limited
(An affiliated company of Gale Research Inc.)

The trademark **ITP** is used under license.

Contents

Highlights

34,000 Citations
1100 Topics
Many Additional Topics Covered by Cross-References
2 Arrangements

Environmental issues are addressed constantly in newspapers, magazines, and news broadcasts. Sometimes, the reports are confusing, and we are left with only a part of the story or many unanswered questions. And since all of us have a stake in our world, we often want, and need, to know more.

The Encyclopedia of Environmental Information Sources (EEIS) provides a place to search for facts, opinions, practical advice, etc.

About 1100 environmental subjects are covered by 13 different types of information sources such as encyclopedias and dictionaries, online data bases, and research centers.

The 2 arrangements of the data serve many users - the subject arrangement allows access to information for specific topics while the "Sources Cited" section provides quick and easy access to information for users having a particular source or organization in mind.

The topics included run the gamut from often-explored issues such as air pollution, global warming, and radon to more obscure topics such as buffer species, integrated pest management, and teratogenic agents.

Regardless of the level of your interest or expertise, you will find sources of information that meet your specific need. Citations include both live and print sources and range from highly technical reports to practical consumer-oriented guides.

A Word about Gale and the Environment

We at Gale would like to take this opportunity to publicly affirm our commitment to preserving the environment. Our commitment encompasses not only a zeal to publish information helpful to a variety of people pursuing environmental goals, but also a rededication to creating a safe and healthy workplace for our employees.

In our effort to make responsible use of natural resources, we are publishing all books in the Gale Environmental Library on recycled paper. Our Production Department is continually researching ways to use environmentally safe inks and manufacturing technologies for all Gale books.

In our quest to become better environmental citizens, we've organized a task force representing all operating functions within Gale. With the complete backing of Gale senior management, the task force reviews our current practices and, using the Valdez Principles* as a starting point, makes recommendations that will help us to: reduce waste, make wise use of energy and sustainable use of natural resources, reduce health and safety risks to our employees, and finally, should we cause any damage or injury, take full responsibility.

We look forward to becoming the best environmental citizens we can be and hope that you, too, have joined in the cause of caring for our fragile planet.

The Employees of Gale Research, Inc.

---

* The Valdez Principles were set forth in 1989 by the Coalition for Environmentally Responsible Economics (CERES). The Principles serve as guidelines for companies concerned with improving their environmental behavior. For a copy of the Valdez Principles, write to CERES at 711 Atlantic Avenue, 5th Floor, Boston, MA 02111.

Introduction

The protection and preservation of our fragile environment have, in recent years, become matters of global concern. Problems like acid rain, climate change, and global warming, once the exclusive preserve of fringe movements, are now at the forefront of mainstream political campaigns in this country and abroad. The choice between economic growth and rational utilization of dwindling natural resources is critical to policy makers and affects future generations. The scientific community and the public at large are eager to make decisions based on all available information. Luckily, the environment is an area where the supply of information has kept pace with the demand.

One thing that distinguishes this field of study from a number of others is its interdisciplinary nature. It encompasses not only physical and life sciences but also a number of areas in the social sciences. Included in its scope are agriculture, biology, botany, chemistry, engineering, geology, medicine, and physics as well as economics, accounting, and law. The amount of information available on this multifaceted topic may baffle the average information seeker. It is precisely this issue which is addressed by the *Encyclopedia of Environmental Information Sources (EEIS)*. *EEIS* meets the specific needs of many different users by serving as a starting point of research and by comprehensively covering diverse sources of information, organized in a ready reference format.

Methodology

There are a number of bibliographies focusing on the very broad aspects of environment such as global warming, air pollution, etc. The *Encyclopedia of Environmental Information Sources* goes beyond the conventional bibliographies and offers a search tool that concentrates on very specific and narrowly defined topics. To support this approach, a comprehensive and detailed list of topics was compiled by going through standard textbooks, dictionaries, encyclopedias and handbooks as well as periodical literature covering all aspects of environmental studies. These terms are supplemented by numerous "see" and "see also" references.

Extensive research was required to gather the sources of information on the approximately 1100 topics included in this publication. Only the most recent sources, generally published between the late 1980s and 1992, have been cited. However, if a source is considered a classic or has made a landmark contribution, it has also been included. In compiling the list of sources to be cited, all efforts have been made to check the online catalogs of some major academic libraries, publishers' brochures, recent bibliographies, and other sources including bibliographic data bases like OCLC, as well as indexing sources such as *PAIS Bulletin, American Statistics Index* and *Statistical Reference Index*.

Arrangement

Under each topic, entries are arranged by type of source. A complete list of the type of sources cited, represented as subheadings in *EEIS*, is outlined below, in the sequence in which they appear (although not all types are listed for every subject).

Abstracting and Indexing Services
Almanacs and Yearbooks
Bibliographies
Directories
Encyclopedias and Dictionaries
General Works
Governmental Organizations
Handbooks and Manuals
Online Data Bases
Periodicals and Newsletters
Research Centers and Institutes

Many of the online data bases included are available through one or more of the following major information vendors:

BRS Information Technologies
8000 Westpark Dr.
McLean, VA 22102
(800) 456-7248

Pergamon ORBIT Infoline Inc.
8000 Westpark Dr.
McLean, VA 22102
(800) 289-4277

STN International
Karlsruhe Service Center
PO Box 2465
D-7500 Karlsruhe 1, Germany
07-247-824566

DIALOG Information Services
3460 Hillview Ave.
Palo Alto, CA 94304
(800) 3-DIALOG

If the user has a specific title, organization, or service in mind and requires contact information, an alphabetical list of all sources cited in *EEIS* follows the subject arrangement. Every attempt has been made to include current contact information; but in a few cases, the research was not successful. Known information has been included and the source may be available through a library, regardless of the status of the producer.

Available in Electronic Formats

Diskette/Magnetic Tape. The *Encyclopedia* is available for licensing on magnetic tape or diskette in a fielded format. Either the complete database or a custom selection of entries may be ordered. The data base is available for internal data processing and nonpublishing purposes only. For more information, call 800-877-GALE.

Acknowledgments

In completing this project, I received a tremendous amount of help from a number of people. My special thanks are due to several editors at Gale Research, especially Don Boyden and Larry Baker, for their helpful suggestions and editorial assistance. I thank Chris Anderson of the University of Illinois Library for his computer expertise which he so willingly shared. Last but not least are the data entry people like Sandra Krone, Lisa Walker, Amber McDaniel, Deanna Hanson, Tim Stewart, and Michelle Feese. Without their assistance, this project would have taken much longer to complete.

Suggestions Welcome

Considerable care has been taken to keep errors and inconsistencies to a minimum, but they no doubt will occur. It would be appreciated if users would send to the editor any information, suggestions, comments, or corrections that might improve future editions. Please address remarks to:

Editor
Encyclopedia of Environmental Information Sources
Gale Research Inc.
835 Penobscot Bldg.
Detroit, MI 48226-4094

User's Guide

Entries are arranged alphabetically by **1** subject, and further subdivided by **2** type of source, and by **3** publication title or organization name. Complete citations are provided for each information source. Citations for publications include title, author or editor, publisher's name and address, telephone number, publication date or frequency, and a brief annotation. For data bases, citations include data base name, producer, producer's address, and telephone number. Citations for governmental and other organizations include name, address, and telephone number. For example:

---

1 ACOUSTICS

2 DIRECTORIES

> **3** *Lead Acoustical Products and Suppliers.* 295 Madison Ave., New York, NY 10017. (212) 578-4750. Annual.
>
> *National Council of Acoustical Consultants-Directory.* 66 Morris Ave., Springfield, NJ 07081. (201) 379-1100. Biennial.

ENCYCLOPEDIAS AND DICTIONARIES

> *Encyclopedia of Physical Science and Technology.* Robert A. Meyers, ed. Academic Press, c/o Harcourt Brace Jovanovich Inc., 6277 Sea Harbor Dr., Orlando, FL 32887. (800) 346-8648. Fifteen volumes. Dictionary of engineering, technology and physical sciences.

TRADE ASSOCIATIONS AND PROFESSIONAL SOCIETIES

> Acoustical Society of America. 500 Sunnyside Blvd., Woodbury, NY 11797. (516) 349-7800.
>
> National Association of Noise Control Officials, 53 Cubberly Rd., Trenton, NJ 08690. (609) 984-4161.
>
> National Council of Acoustical Consultants. 66 Morris Ave., Springfield, NJ 07081. (201) 379-1100.

"Outline of Contents" Speeds Access to Topics

For the most efficient use of *EEIS,* do not go directly to the text to look up the topic on which information is sought. Instead, consult the extensive Outline of Contents, where it is possible to determine the exact wording that has been used and to be guided by cross-references to related topics.

"Sources Cited" Arrangement

All of the sources cited under all of the subject headings are arranged alphabetically with each entry in this section containing exactly the same data as in the by subject portion of *EEIS* - contact information and a brief annotation. For example:

Sources Cited

Earth Work. The Student Conservation Association Inc., PO Box 550, Charlestown, NH 03603-0550. (603) 826-4301. 1991- . Monthly. Articles focus on the people, agencies, and the nonprofit organizations that protect our parks, refuges, forests and other lands. Carries a special feature entitled JobScan which provides the most comprehensive listing of natural resource and environmental job opportunities anywhere.

Earthright. H. Patricia Hynes. St. Martin's Press, 175 5th Ave., New York, NY 10010. (212) 674-5151. 1990. Guide to practical ways to resolve problems with pesticides, water pollution, garbage disposal, the ozone layer and global warming.

Eco-Warriors: Understanding the Radical Environmental Movement. Rik Scarce. Noble Pr., 111 E. Chestnut, Suite 48A, Chicago, IL 60611 (312) 880-0439. 1990. Recounts escapades pf pro-ecology sabotage by self-styled eco-warriors.

Ecological Society of America. Arizona State University, Center for Environmental Studies, Tempe, AZ 85287. (602) 965-3000.

Ecophilosophy: A Field Guide to the Literature. Donald Edward David. R. & E. Miles Publishers, International Sales, PO Box 1916, San Pedro, CA 90733. 1989.

Edwards Aquifer Research and Data Center. 248 Freeman Bldg., Southwest Texas State University, San Marco, TX, 78666-4616. (512) 245-2329.

In a few cases, the entire range of information normally provided may not have been available. All the information gathered, however, has been included.

Outline of Contents

Encyclopedia of Environmental Information Sources

A

A HORIZON

See: SOIL SCIENCE

ABATEMENT

See: POLLUTION CONTROL

ABORTION

See: POPULATION

ABSORPTION

See also: CHEMICAL CONTAMINATION; SOIL CONTAMINATION

ABSTRACTING AND INDEXING SERVICES

Abstracts of Air and Water Conservation Literature. American Petroleum Institute. Central Abstracting and Indexing Service, 275 Madison Avenue, New York, New York 10016. 1972.

Applied Science and Technology Index. H.W. Wilson Co., 950 University Ave., Bronx, New York 10452. (800) 367-6770. Formerly Industrial Arts Index.

Biological Abstracts. BIOSIS, 2100 Arch St., Philadelphia, Pennsylvania 19103-1399. (215) 587-4800. 1927-.

Energy Information Abstracts Annual 1987 in Retrospect. EIC/Intelligence Inc., 121 Chanlon Rd., New Providence, New Jersey 07974. (908) 464-6800. 1988. Annual. Cumulative edition of the monthly Energy Information Abstracts. Monitors sources in the field of energy including the scientific, technical and business journal literature, conference and symposia proceedings, corporate, government and academic reports.

Food Science and Technology Abstracts. International Food Information Service, c/o National Food Laboratory, 6363 Clark Ave., Dublin, California 94568. (800) 336-3782. 1969-.

Metals Abstracts. ASM International, 9639 Kinsman, Materials Park, Ohio 44073. (216) 338-5151. 1968-. Published jointly by the Institute of Metals, London and the American Society for Metals. Formed by the Union of Metallurgical Abstracts and Review of Metal Literature.

Physics Briefs. Physikalische Berichte. Physik Verlag, Pappapelallee 3, Postfach 101161, Weinheim, Germany D-6940. 1979-. Semimonthly. In English. Volumes for 1979- issued by the Deutsche Physikalische Gesellschaft and the Fachinformationszentrum Energie Physik, Mathematik in cooperation with the American Institute of Physics.

Pollution Abstracts. Cambridge Scientific Abstracts, 5161 River Rd., Bethesda, Maryland 20816. (301) 961-6750. Six/year. Indexes worldwide technical literature on environmental pollution. Covers air pollution, marine and freshwater pollution, sewage and wastewater treatment, waste management, toxicology and health, noise pollution, radiation, land pollution, and environmental policies, programs, legislation, and education. Also available online.

Science Citation Index. Institute for Scientific Information, 3501 Market St., Philadelphia, Pennsylvania 19104. 1961-.

BIBLIOGRAPHIES

Chemical Engineering Bibliography. Martyn S. Ray. Noyes Publications, 120 Mill Rd., Park Ridge, New Jersey 07656. (201) 391-8484. Contains 20,000 references from 40 journals published over the period 1967-1988. Some of the topics covered include: energy conservation, environmental management, biotechnology, plant operations, absorption and cooling towers, membrane separation and other chemical engineering areas.

Directory of Published Proceedings. Interdok Corp., 173 Halstead Ave., Harrison, New York 10528. (914) 835-3506. 1990. Monthly. This is a listing of published proceedings including the series SEMTE (Science/Medicine/Engineering/Technology) and the series SSH (Social Science/Humanities).

ENCYCLOPEDIAS AND DICTIONARIES

Cambridge Dictionary of Biology. Peter M. B. Walker. Cambridge University Press, 40 W. 20th St., New York, New York 10011. (212) 924-3900 or (800) 227-0247. 1989. Includes 10,000 terms in zoology, botany, biochemistry, molecular biology and genetics. Previously published under the title Chambers Biology Dictionary.

A Concise Dictionary of Biology. Elizabeth Martin, ed. Oxford University Press, 200 Madison Ave., New York, New York 10016. (212) 679-7300 or (800) 334-4249. 1990. New edition. Derived from the Concise Science Dictionary, published in 1984.

Dictionary of Colloid and Surface Science. Paul Becher. Marcel Dekker, Inc., 270 Madison Ave., New York, New

York 10016. (212) 696-9000; (800) 228-1160. 1990. Dictionary deals with the areas of colloids, surface chemistry, and the physics and technology involved with surfaces.

Encyclopedia of Chemical Processing and Design. John J. Mcketta and W. A. Cunningham. Marcel Dekker, Inc., 270 Madison Ave., New York, New York 10016. (212) 696-9000; (800) 228-1160. 1992. Thirty-eight volumes.

Encyclopedia of Physics. Rita G. Lerner and George L. Trigg. VCH Publishers, 303 NW 12th Ave., Deerfield Beach, Florida 33442-1788. (305) 428-5566. 1991. Second edition.

Encyclopedia of Polymer Science and Engineering. Herman F. Mark, et al., eds. John Wiley & Sons, Inc., 605 3rd Ave., New York, New York 10158-0012. (212) 850-6000. 1985-. Seventeen volumes and two supplements.

Kirk-Othmer Encyclopedia of Chemical Technology. J. I. Kroschwitz, ed. John Wiley & Sons, Inc., 605 3rd Ave., New York, New York 10158-0012. (212) 850-6000. 1992-. All articles in the new edition have been rewritten and updated adding new subjects such as biotechnology, computer topics, analytical techniques and instrumentation, environmental concerns, fuels and energy, inorganic and solid state chemistry; composite materials and material science in general, and pharmaceuticals. Also available online.

McGraw-Hill Encyclopedia of Science and Technology. McGraw-Hill, 1221 Avenue of the Americas, New York, New York 10020. (212) 512-2000 or (800) 262-4729. 1992. Seventh edition. Issued in multiple volumes including index. Includes all science and technology broad subject areas.

The Nutrition and Health Encyclopedia. David F. Tver and Percy Russell. Van Nostrand Reinhold, 115 5th Ave., New York, New York 10003. (212) 254-3232. 1989.

Van Nostrand's Scientific Encyclopedia. Glenn D. Considine, ed. Van Nostrand Reinhold, 115 5th Ave., New York, New York 10003. (212) 254-3232. 1983. Sixth edition. Includes all broad subject areas in science.

GENERAL WORKS

Adsorption Technology for Air and Water Pollution Control. Kenneth E. Noll. Lewis Publishers, 200 Corporate Blvd. NW, Boca Raton, Florida 33431. (407) 994-0555 or (800)272-7737. 1991. Contains useful information on adsorption technology which can be applied in both air and water pollution.

Skin Penetration; Hazardous Chemicals at Work. Philippe Grandjean. Taylor & Francis, 79 Madison Ave., New York, New York 10016. (212) 725-1999 or (800) 821-8312. 1990. Mechanisms of percutaneous absorption and methods of evaluating its significance. Reviews different classes of chemicals, emphasizing those considered major skin hazards.

HANDBOOKS AND MANUALS

Absorption Engineering. Motoyuki Suzuki. Elsevier Science Publishing Co., 655 Avenue of the Americas, New York, New York 10010. (212) 984-5800. 1990.

ONLINE DATA BASES

BIOSIS Previews. BIOSIS, 2100 Arch St., Philadelphia, Pennsylvania 19103-1399. (215) 587-4800. Largest and most comprehensive database of research in the life sciences. Contains citations for nearly 9000 primary research journals, monographs, reviews, symposia, preliminary reports, semi-popular journals, selected institutional reports, government reports and research communications.

Kirk-Othmer Encyclopedia of Chemical Technology. John Wiley & Sons, Inc., 605 3rd Ave., 5th Floor, New York, New York 10158. (212) 850-6000. Online version of the publication of the same name.

PERIODICALS AND NEWSLETTERS

The Journal of Biological Chemistry. American Society of Biological Chemists, 428 E. Preston St., Baltimore, Maryland 21202. Three times a month. Biological, agricultural, and energy aspects of the environment.

TRADE ASSOCIATIONS AND PROFESSIONAL SOCIETIES

Institute for Polyacrylate Absorbents. 1330 Connecticut Ave., N.W., Suite 300, Washington, District of Columbia 20036. (202) 659-0060.

ABSTRACTION EFFECT
See: HYDROLOGY

ACARICIDES
See: PESTICIDES

ACCELERATORS
See: RADIOLOGICAL APPLICATIONS

ACCIDENTS
See: DISASTERS

ACCIDENTS, TRANSPORTATION
See also: CHEMICAL CONTAMINATION; NUCLEAR ACCIDENTS

ABSTRACTING AND INDEXING SERVICES

Abstracts of Air and Water Conservation Literature. American Petroleum Institute. Central Abstracting and Indexing Service, 275 Madison Avenue, New York, New York 10016. 1972.

Applied Science and Technology Index. H.W. Wilson Co., 950 University Ave., Bronx, New York 10452. (800) 367-6770. Formerly Industrial Arts Index.

Pollution Abstracts. Cambridge Scientific Abstracts, 5161 River Rd., Bethesda, Maryland 20816. (301) 961-6750.

Six/year. Indexes worldwide technical literature on environmental pollution. Covers air pollution, marine and freshwater pollution, sewage and wastewater treatment, waste management, toxicology and health, noise pollution, radiation, land pollution, and environmental policies, programs, legislation, and education. Also available online.

Science Citation Index. Institute for Scientific Information, 3501 Market St., Philadelphia, Pennsylvania 19104. 1961-.

BIBLIOGRAPHIES

Directory of Published Proceedings. Interdok Corp., 173 Halstead Ave., Harrison, New York 10528. (914) 835-3506. 1990. Monthly. This is a listing of published proceedings including the series SEMTE (Science/Medicine/Engineering/Technology) and the series SSH (Social Science/Humanities).

ONLINE DATA BASES

PressNet Environmental Reports. Chemical Information Systems, Inc., 7215 York Rd., Baltimore, Maryland 21212. (301) 321-8440.

ACCLIMATION

See: ACCLIMATIZATION

ACCLIMATIZATION

See also: BIOGEOGRAPHY; HARDINESS; HIBERNATION

ABSTRACTING AND INDEXING SERVICES

Applied Ecology Abstracts Studies in Renewable Natural Resources. Information Retrieval Ltd., 1911 Jefferson Davis Highway, Arlington, Virginia 22202. 1975-. Monthly.

ASFA Aquaculture Abstracts. Cambridge Scientific Abstracts, Inc., 5161 River Rd., Bethesda, Maryland 20816. (301) 961-6750. 1984.

Biological Abstracts. BIOSIS, 2100 Arch St., Philadelphia, Pennsylvania 19103-1399. (215) 587-4800. 1927-.

Biological and Agricultural Index. H.W. Wilson Co., 950 University Ave., Bronx, New York 10452. (800) 367-6770. 1916-. Monthly.

Ecological Abstracts. Geo Abstracts Ltd. Elsevier Applied Science, Crown House, Linton Rd., Barking, England IG 11 8JU. 1974-. Derived from over 600 leading ecological and environmental journals, plus books, conference proceedings, reports and theses.

Ecology Abstracts. Cambridge Scientific Abstracts, 5161 River Rd., Bethesda, Maryland 20816. (301) 961-6750. Monthly.

Environment Index. Environment Information Center, Index Research Department, 124 E. 39th St., New York, New York 10016. 1971-. Annual.

Environmental Information Connection–EIC. Planning Information Program, Dept. of Urban and Regional Planning, University of Illinois, 1003 West Nevada, Urbana, Illinois 61801. (217) 333-1369. Also available online.

Environmental Periodicals Bibliography. Environmental Studies Institute, International Academy at Santa Barbara, 800 Garden St., Suite D, Santa Barbara, California 93101. (805) 965-5010. Also available online.

Ergonomics Abstracts. Taylor & Francis, 4 John St., London, England WC1N 2ET. 1990-. Bimonthly. Provides details on recent additions to the international literature on human factors in human-machine systems and physical environmental influences.

General Science Index. H. W. Wilson Co., 950 University Ave., Bronx, New York 10452. 1978-. Monthly, also issued in annual cumulation. Cumulative subject index to English language periodicals in the subject fields of astronomy, botany, chemistry, earth science, environment and conservation, food and nutrition, genetics, mathematics, medicine and health, microbiology, oceanography, physics, physiology and zoology.

Geographical Abstracts. London School of Economics, Dept. of Geography, Regency House, 34 Duke St., London, England 1966-. Continued by Geo Abstracts issued in 6 parts: Pt. A. Landforms and the quaternary; Pt. B. Biogeography and Climatology; Pt. C. Economic geography; Pt. D. Social geography and cartography; Pt. E. Sedimentology; Pt. F. Regional and community planning.

Index to Scientific Book Contents. Institute for Scientific Information, 3501 Market St., Philadelphia, Pennsylvania 19104. (800) 523-1857. 1985-. Annual. Gives contents of science books published.

Multimedia Index to Ecology. National Information Center for Educational Media, University of Southern California, Los Angeles, California 90007.

Science Citation Index. Institute for Scientific Information, 3501 Market St., Philadelphia, Pennsylvania 19104. 1961-.

BIBLIOGRAPHIES

Directory of Published Proceedings. Interdok Corp., 173 Halstead Ave., Harrison, New York 10528. (914) 835-3506. 1990. Monthly. This is a listing of published proceedings including the series SEMTE (Science/Medicine/Engineering/Technology) and the series SSH (Social Science/Humanities).

EPA Publications Bibliography. U.S. Environmental Protection Agency, Library Systems Branch, 401 M St., SW, Washington, District of Columbia 20460. (202) 260-2090. Quarterly.

ENCYCLOPEDIAS AND DICTIONARIES

Encyclopedia of Human Biology. Renato Dulbecco, ed. Academic Press, c/o Harcourt Brace Jovanovich Inc., 6277 Sea Harbor Dr., Orlando, Florida 32887. (800) 346-8648. 1991. Eight volumes.

McGraw-Hill Encyclopedia of Science and Technology. McGraw-Hill, 1221 Avenue of the Americas, New York, New York 10020. (212) 512-2000 or (800) 262-4729. 1992. Seventh edition. Issued in multiple volumes including index. Includes all science and technology broad subject areas.

The New York Times Encyclopedic Dictionary of the Environment. Paul Sarnoff. Quadrangle Books, New York, New York 1971. Focuses on state-of-the-art methods of pollution control, abatement, prevention and removal.

GENERAL WORKS

Adaptations to Climatic Changes. P. Revet, ed. Karger, 26 W. Avon Rd., Box 529, Farmington, Connecticut 06085. (203) 675-7834. 1987. Issued by the "8th Conference of the European Society for Comparative Physiology and Biochemistry, Strasbourg, August 31-September 2, 1986."

The Changing Climate: Responses of the Natural Fauna and Flora. Michael J. Ford. G. Allen and Unwin, 8 Winchester Pl., Winchester, Massachusetts 01890. (617) 729-0830. 1982. Describes the climate changes and the acclimatization of the flora and fauna.

Ecology of Biological Invasions of North America and Hawaii. H. G. Baker, et al. Springer-Verlag, 175 5th Ave., New York, New York 10010. (212) 460-1500; (800) 777-4643. 1986.

Environmental and Metabolic Animal Physiology. C. Ladd Prosser, ed. John Wiley & Sons, Inc., Wiley-Liss Division, 605 3rd Ave., New York, New York 10158-0012. (212) 850-6000. 1991. 4th ed. Focuses on the various aspects of adaptive physiology, including environmental, biochemical, and regulatory topics. Examines the theory of adaptation, water and ions, temperature and hydrostatic pressure, nutrition, digestion, nitrogen metabolism, and energy transfer, respiration, O2 and CO2 transport and circulation.

Human Performance Physiology and Environmental Medicine at Terrestrial Extremes. Kent B. Pandolf, et al., eds. WCB Brown and Benchmark Pr., 2460 Kerper Blvd., Dubuque, Iowa 52001. (800) 338-5578. 1988. Includes the most current information available on the physiological and medical responses to heat, cold, altitude, poor air quality and hyperbaric conditions.

Man and Animals in Hot Environments. Douglas Leslie Ingram. Springer-Verlag, 175 5th Ave., New York, New York 10010. (212) 460-1500; (800) 777-4643. 1975. Describes the physiological effect of heat on man and animals. Includes extensive bibliography.

Man at High Altitude: the Pathophysiology of Acclimatization and Adaptation. Donald Heath and David Reid Williams. Churchill Livingstone, Inc., 650 Avenue of the Americas, New York, New York 10011. (212) 206-5000. 1981.

Physiological Plant Ecology. O. L. Lange, et al., eds. Springer-Verlag, 175 5th Ave., New York, New York 10010. (212) 460-1500; (800) 777-4643. 1981-1983. Contents: Volume 1 - Responses to the physical environment; Volume 2 - Water relations and carbon assimilation; Volume 3 - Responses to the chemical and biological environment; Volume 4 - Ecosystem processes (mineral cycling, productivity, and man's influence).

Responses of Plants to Environmental Stresses. J. Levitt. Academic Press, c/o Harcourt Brace Jovanovich Inc., 6277 Sea Harbor Dr., Orlando, Florida 32887. (800) 346-8648. 1980. 2nd ed. Volume 1 covers chilling, freezing and high temperature. Volume 2 contains water, radiation, salt, and other stresses.

Stress Responses in Plants: Adaptation and Acclimation Mechanisms. Ruth G. Alscher. Wiley-Liss, 605 3rd Ave., New York, New York 10158-0012. (212) 850-6000. 1990. Effect of stress on plant adaptation and acclimatization.

ONLINE DATA BASES

Enviro/Energyline Abstracts Plus. R. R. Bowker Co., 121 Chanlon Rd., New Providence, New Jersey 07974. (908) 464-6800.

Environmental Periodicals Bibliography. National Information Services Corp., Ste. 6, Wyman Towers, 3100 St. Paul St., Baltimore, Maryland 21218. (410)243-0797. Online version of abstract of same name.

PERIODICALS AND NEWSLETTERS

Journal of Applied Physiology. American Physiology Society, 9650 Rockville Pike, Bethesda, Maryland 20814-3991. Monthly. Covers physiological aspects of exercise, adaption, respiration, and exertion.

The Journal of Biological Chemistry. American Society of Biological Chemists, 428 E. Preston St., Baltimore, Maryland 21202. Three times a month. Biological, agricultural, and energy aspects of the environment.

RESEARCH CENTERS AND INSTITUTES

University of Wyoming, Red Buttes Environmental Biology Laboratory. Box 3166, University Station, Laramie, Wyoming 82071. (307) 745-8504.

TRADE ASSOCIATIONS AND PROFESSIONAL SOCIETIES

American Institute of Biomedical Climatology. 1023 Welsh Rd., Philadelphia, Pennsylvania 19115. (215) 673-8368.

ACID MINE DRAINAGE
See: ACID WASTE

ACID POLLUTION OF RIVERS, LAKES, ETC.
See also: ACID PRECIPITATION; WATER POLLUTION

ABSTRACTING AND INDEXING SERVICES

Abstracts of Air and Water Conservation Literature. American Petroleum Institute. Central Abstracting and Indexing Service, 275 Madison Avenue, New York, New York 10016. 1972.

Applied Ecology Abstracts Studies in Renewable Natural Resources. Information Retrieval Ltd., 1911 Jefferson Davis Highway, Arlington, Virginia 22202. 1975-. Monthly.

Biological Abstracts. BIOSIS, 2100 Arch St., Philadelphia, Pennsylvania 19103-1399. (215) 587-4800. 1927-.

Biological and Agricultural Index. H.W. Wilson Co., 950 University Ave., Bronx, New York 10452. (800) 367-6770. 1916-. Monthly.

Biology Digest. Data Courier, Plexus Pub Inc., 143 Old Marlton Pike, Medford, New Jersey 08055. 1974-. Monthly. Abstracts biology periodicals.

Bulletin Signaletique: Eau et Assainissement, Pollution Atmospherique, Droit des Pollutions. Centre de Documentation, Centre National de la Recherche Scientifique, 15, quai Anatole France, Paris, France 75700. (1) 45 55 92 25. 1983-. Monthly. Indexes pollution periodicals including water, atmospheric and related pollutions.

Chemical Abstracts. Chemical Abstracts Service, 2540 Olentangy River Rd., PO Box 3012, Columbus, Ohio 43210. (800) 848-6533. 1907-.

Ecological Abstracts. Geo Abstracts Ltd. Elsevier Applied Science, Crown House, Linton Rd., Barking, England IG 11 8JU. 1974-. Derived from over 600 leading ecological and environmental journals, plus books, conference proceedings, reports and theses.

Ecology Abstracts. Cambridge Scientific Abstracts, 5161 River Rd., Bethesda, Maryland 20816. (301) 961-6750. Monthly.

Environment Index. Environment Information Center, Index Research Department, 124 E. 39th St., New York, New York 10016. 1971-. Annual.

Environmental Information Connection-EIC. Planning Information Program, Dept. of Urban and Regional Planning, University of Illinois, 1003 West Nevada, Urbana, Illinois 61801. (217) 333-1369. Also available online.

Environmental Periodicals Bibliography. Environmental Studies Institute, International Academy at Santa Barbara, 800 Garden St., Suite D, Santa Barbara, California 93101. (805) 965-5010. Also available online.

ERDA Research Abstracts. U.S. ERDA Technical Information Center, Box 62, Oak Ridge, Tennessee 37830.

General Science Index. H. W. Wilson Co., 950 University Ave., Bronx, New York 10452. 1978-. Monthly, also issued in annual cumulation. Cumulative subject index to English language periodicals in the subject fields of astronomy, botany, chemistry, earth science, environment and conservation, food and nutrition, genetics, mathematics, medicine and health, microbiology, oceanography, physics, physiology and zoology.

Multimedia Index to Ecology. National Information Center for Educational Media, University of Southern California, Los Angeles, California 90007.

Pollution Abstracts. Cambridge Scientific Abstracts, 5161 River Rd., Bethesda, Maryland 20816. (301) 961-6750. Six/year. Indexes worldwide technical literature on environmental pollution. Covers air pollution, marine and freshwater pollution, sewage and wastewater treatment, waste management, toxicology and health, noise pollution, radiation, land pollution, and environmental policies, programs, legislation, and education. Also available online.

Science Citation Index. Institute for Scientific Information, 3501 Market St., Philadelphia, Pennsylvania 19104. 1961-.

BIBLIOGRAPHIES

Bibliography and Index of Geology. American Geological Institute, 4220 King St., Alexandria, Virginia 22302. Monthly. Includes environmental geology and hydrogeology.

Current Contents. Agriculture, Biology and Environmental Sciences. Institute for Scientific Information, 3501 Market St., Philadelphia, Pennsylvania 19104. (800) 523-1857. 1973-. Previous title: Current Contents. Agricultural, Food & Veterinary Sciences. Gives the table of contents of periodicals in the fields of agriculture, biology, environmental and related areas.

Directory of Published Proceedings. Interdok Corp., 173 Halstead Ave., Harrison, New York 10528. (914) 835-3506. 1990. Monthly. This is a listing of published proceedings including the series SEMTE (Science/Medicine/Engineering/Technology) and the series SSH (Social Science/Humanities).

EPA Publications Bibliography. U.S. Environmental Protection Agency, Library Systems Branch, 401 M St., SW, Washington, District of Columbia 20460. (202) 260-2090. Quarterly.

ENCYCLOPEDIAS AND DICTIONARIES

The Encyclopedia of Geochemistry and Environmental Sciences. Rhodes Whitmore Fairbridge. Van Nostrand Reinhold Co., 115 5th Ave., New York, New York 10003. (212) 254-3232. 1972.

Grzimek's Encyclopedia of Ecology. Bernhard Grzimek. Van Nostrand Reinhold, 115 5th Ave., New York, New York 10003. (212) 254-3232. 1976.

McGraw-Hill Encyclopedia of Environmental Science. Sybil P. Parker. McGraw-Hill Science & Engineering Books, 11 W. 19th St., New York, New York 10011. (212) 337-6010. 1980. Covers ecology, man's influence on nature, and environmental protection.

McGraw-Hill Encyclopedia of Science and Technology. McGraw-Hill, 1221 Avenue of the Americas, New York, New York 10020. (212) 512-2000 or (800) 262-4729. 1992. Seventh edition. Issued in multiple volumes including index. Includes all science and technology broad subject areas.

North American Reference Encyclopedia of Ecology and Pollution. William White. North American Pub. Co., 401 N. Broad St., Philadelphia, Pennsylvania 19108. (215) 238-5300. 1972.

Van Nostrand's Scientific Encyclopedia. Glenn D. Considine, ed. Van Nostrand Reinhold, 115 5th Ave., New York, New York 10003. (212) 254-3232. 1983. Sixth edition. Includes all broad subject areas in science.

GENERAL WORKS

Acidic Deposition and Aquatic Ecosystems. D. F. Charles and S. Christie, eds. Springer-Verlag, 175 5th Ave., New York, New York 10010. (212) 460-1500. 1991. Comprehensive integrated synthesis of available information on current and potential effects of acidic precipitation on lakes and streams in different geographic regions of the U.S. Examines the current status of water chemistry.

Acidic Deposition and Forest Soils. Dan Binkley. Springer-Verlag, 175 Fifth Ave., New York, New York 10010.

(212) 460-1500 or (800) 777-4643. 1990. Environmental aspects of acid deposition, forest soils and soil acidity.

Industrial Environmental Control. A. M. Springer. John Wiley & Sons, Inc., 605 3rd Ave., New York, New York 10158-0012. (212) 850-6000. 1986. Covers in great detail all the basic information regarding industrial pollution and its treatment.

Magill's Survey of Science. Earth Science Series. Frank N. Magill. Salem Press, PO Box 50062, Pasadena, California 91105. 1990-. Five volumes. Includes information on earth's crust, hot spots and volcanic island chains, physical properties of minerals, rock magnetism, physical properties of rocks, and index.

Restoring Acid Waters. G. Howells. Elsevier Science Publishing Co., 655 Avenue of the Americas, New York, New York 10010. (212) 984-5800. 1992. Detailed and comprehensive accounts of pre-liming conditions, liming techniques employed, post-liming changes in water quality and fish restoration.

The Surface Water Acidification Programme. B. J. Mason, ed. Cambridge University Press, 40 W. 20th St., New York, New York 10011. (212) 924-3900; (800) 227-0247. 1991. Proceedings of the final Conference of the Surface Water Acidification Programme, held at the Royal Society in March 1990. Deals with the acid pollution of rivers and lakes and presents research results on watersheds in Great Britain and Scandinavia.

HANDBOOKS AND MANUALS

Handbook of Methods for Acid Deposition Studies: Field Methods for Surface Water Chemistry. D. J. Chaloud, et al. U.S. Environmental Protection Agency, Office of Modeling, Monitoring Systems, and Quality Assurance, 401 M St., SW, Washington, District of Columbia 20460. (202) 260-2090. 1990-.

ONLINE DATA BASES

BIOSIS Previews. BIOSIS, 2100 Arch St., Philadelphia, Pennsylvania 19103-1399. (215) 587-4800. Largest and most comprehensive database of research in the life sciences. Contains citations for nearly 9000 primary research journals, monographs, reviews, symposia, preliminary reports, semi-popular journals, selected institutional reports, government reports and research communications.

Chemical Abstracts-CA. Chemical Abstracts Service, 2540 Olentangy River Rd., P.O. Box 3012, Columbus, Ohio 43210. (800) 848-6533 or (614) 421-3600. Information sources include 9000 journals, patents from 27 countries, two industrial property organizations, new books, conference proceedings, and government research reports.

Enviro/Energyline Abstracts Plus. R. R. Bowker Co., 121 Chanlon Rd., New Providence, New Jersey 07974. (908) 464-6800.

Environmental Periodicals Bibliography. National Information Services Corp., Ste. 6, Wyman Towers, 3100 St. Paul St., Baltimore, Maryland 21218. (410)243-0797. Online version of abstract of same name.

Monthly Catalog of United States Government Publications. U.S. G.P.O., Supt. of Docs., PO Box 371954, Pittsburgh, Pennsylvania 15250-7954. (202) 512-0000.

National Technical Information Service. U.S. Department of Commerce, National Technical Information Service, Office of Data Base Services, 5285 Port Royal Rd., Springfield, Virginia 22161. (703) 487-4807. Bibliographic database of government sponsored research and technical reports.

PressNet Environmental Reports. Chemical Information Systems, Inc., 7215 York Rd., Baltimore, Maryland 21212. (301) 321-8440.

PERIODICALS AND NEWSLETTERS

Waste Disposal and Pollution Control. Wakeman/Walworth, P.O. Box 1939, New Haven, Connecticut 06509. (203) 562-8518. Monthly. Covers air and water pollution, toxic waste, and acid rain.

ACID PRECIPITATION

See also: FOG; WEATHER

ABSTRACTING AND INDEXING SERVICES

Abstracts of Air and Water Conservation Literature. American Petroleum Institute. Central Abstracting and Indexing Service, 275 Madison Avenue, New York, New York 10016. 1972.

Acid Rain Abstracts. EIC/Intelligence Inc., 121 Chanlon Rd., New Providence, New Jersey 07974. (908) 464-6800. Bimonthly.

Acid Rain Abstracts Annual. Bowker A & I Publishing, 121 Chanlon Rd., New Providence, New Jersey 07974. (908) 464-6800. 1990-. Annual. Includes key retrospective research issues covered in the year. The book identifies and locates timely information in areas of rapidly developing science and technology as well as social and government policy issues. Each annual edition also contains two articles that highlight key issues and events of the year covered.

Applied Ecology Abstracts Studies in Renewable Natural Resources. Information Retrieval Ltd., 1911 Jefferson Davis Highway, Arlington, Virginia 22202. 1975-. Monthly.

Applied Science and Technology Index. H.W. Wilson Co., 950 University Ave., Bronx, New York 10452. (800) 367-6770. Formerly Industrial Arts Index.

ASFA Aquaculture Abstracts. Cambridge Scientific Abstracts, Inc., 5161 River Rd., Bethesda, Maryland 20816. (301) 961-6750. 1984.

Biological Abstracts. BIOSIS, 2100 Arch St., Philadelphia, Pennsylvania 19103-1399. (215) 587-4800. 1927-.

Biological and Agricultural Index. H.W. Wilson Co., 950 University Ave., Bronx, New York 10452. (800) 367-6770. 1916-. Monthly.

Bulletin Signaletique: Eau et Assainissement, Pollution Atmospherique, Droit des Pollutions. Centre de Documentation, Centre National de la Recherche Scientifique, 15, quai Anatole France, Paris, France 75700. (1) 45 55 92 25. 1983-. Monthly. Indexes pollution periodicals including water, atmospheric and related pollutions.

Chemical Abstracts. Chemical Abstracts Service, 2540 Olentangy River Rd., PO Box 3012, Columbus, Ohio 43210. (800) 848-6533. 1907-.

Ecological Abstracts. Geo Abstracts Ltd. Elsevier Applied Science, Crown House, Linton Rd., Barking, England IG 11 8JU. 1974-. Derived from over 600 leading ecological and environmental journals, plus books, conference proceedings, reports and theses.

Ecology Abstracts. Cambridge Scientific Abstracts, 5161 River Rd., Bethesda, Maryland 20816. (301) 961-6750. Monthly.

Environment Periodicals Bibliography. Environmental Studies Institute, International Academy at Santa Barbara, 800 Garden St., Suite D, Santa Barbara, California 993101. (805) 965-5010. 6 issues plus a cumulative annual index. Indexes journal articles relevant to environmental issues. Includes broad subject areas such as: air, energy, land resources, agriculture, marine and fresh water resources, water pollution, water management, effluents, sewage and pollution, nutrition and health, acid rain. Covers over 350 journal titles.

The Environmental Index. UMI Data Courier, 620 South Third St., Louisville, Kentucky 40202-2475. (800) 626-2823 or (502) 583-4111. 1992. Quarterly updates. Provides citations to articles in nearly 1,000 U.S. publications including New York Times, USA Today, and other popular journals like Time, Newsweek, Consumer Reports, Environment, Business Week and National Geographic. Covers topics such as global warming, overflowing landfills, waste management companies, city-wide recycling program, green consumers, buildings with asbestos, rivers full of toxins and other environmental issues.

General Science Index. H. W. Wilson Co., 950 University Ave., Bronx, New York 10452. 1978-. Monthly, also issued in annual cumulation. Cumulative subject index to English language periodicals in the subject fields of astronomy, botany, chemistry, earth science, environment and conservation, food and nutrition, genetics, mathematics, medicine and health, microbiology, oceanography, physics, physiology and zoology.

Geographical Abstracts. London School of Economics, Dept. of Geography, Regency House, 34 Duke St., London, England 1966-. Continued by Geo Abstracts issued in 6 parts: Pt. A. Landforms and the quaternary; Pt. B. Biogeography and Climatology; Pt. C. Economic geography; Pt. D. Social geography and cartography; Pt. E. Sedimentology; Pt. F. Regional and community planning.

Green Engineering: A Current Awareness Bulletin. Institution of Mechanical Engineers, 1 Birdcage Walk, Westminster, London, England SW1H 9JJ. 71973 1266/7. 1991. Monthly. Covers acid rain, aerosol technology, biotechnology chlorofluorocarbons, chemical and process engineering, environmental protection, energy conservation, energy generation, greenhouse effect, materials, pollution, recycling, waste disposal, and other environmental topics.

Health and Environmental Effects of Acid Rain: An Abstracted Literature Collection, 1966-1979. Nancy S. Dale. Federation of American Societies for Experimental Biology, 9650 Rockville Pike, Bethesda, Maryland 20814. (301) 530-7000. 1980. Prepared in cooperation with the National Library of Medicine as a response to the chemical crises project of the Federation of American Societies for Experimental Biology. Covers the years 1966-1979.

Index to Scientific Book Contents. Institute for Scientific Information, 3501 Market St., Philadelphia, Pennsylvania 19104. (800) 523-1857. 1985-. Annual. Gives contents of science books published.

Multimedia Index to Ecology. National Information Center for Educational Media, University of Southern California, Los Angeles, California 90007.

Pollution Abstracts. Cambridge Scientific Abstracts, 5161 River Rd., Bethesda, Maryland 20816. (301) 961-6750. Six/year. Indexes worldwide technical literature on environmental pollution. Covers air pollution, marine and freshwater pollution, sewage and wastewater treatment, waste management, toxicology and health, noise pollution, radiation, land pollution, and environmental policies, programs, legislation, and education. Also available online.

Science Citation Index. Institute for Scientific Information, 3501 Market St., Philadelphia, Pennsylvania 19104. 1961-.

BIBLIOGRAPHIES

Acid Precipitation. Sandra Hicks, ed. Technical Information Center, U.S. Dept. of Energy, National Technical Information Service, 5285 Port Royal Rd., Springfield, Virginia 37831. (703) 487-4650. 1983. Annual. Distributed in microfiche by the U.S. Dept. of Energy, Technical Information Center, #EDB-500200 and DE83 008750.

Acid Precipitation: A Bibliography; A Compilation of Worldwide Literature. U.S. Department of Energy, Technical Information Center, PO Box 62, Oak Ridge, Tennessee 37831. (615) 576-1223. 1983.

Acid Precipitation: An Annotated Bibliography. Denise A. Wiltshire and Margaret L. Evans. Department of the Interior, U.S. Geological Survey, Distribution Branch, Text Products Section, 119 National Center, Reston, Virginia 22092. (703) 648-4460. 1984. Geological Survey circular 923.

Acid Rain. Pauline Hollman. Library of Congress, Science and Technology Division, Science Reference Section, Washington, District of Columbia (202) 738-3238. 1986. This is part of LC Science Trace Bulletin ISSN 0090-5232 TB 86-11. It supersedes TB 80-13. Shipping list no. 87-92-P.

Acid Rain. Robert W. Lockerby. Vance Bibliographies, 112 N. Charter St., PO Box 229, Monticello, Illinois 61856. (217) 762-3831. 1982. Public Administration series–Bibliography: P-928.

Acid Rain, 1980-1984: A Selected Bibliography. P. J. Koshy. Vance Bibliographies, 112 North Charter St., PO Box 229, Monticello, Illinois 61856. (217) 762-3831. 1986. Public Administration series–Bibliography: P1881

Acid Rain 1983-85. Sheldon Cheney. U.S. Department of Agriculture, National Agricultural Library, 10301 Baltimore Blvd., Beltsville, Maryland 20705-2351. (301) 504-5755. 1985. Part of Quick Bibliography series, #NAL-BIBL QB 86-23. The database searched is AGRICOLA and it updates QB 83-18. Shipping list 86-10-P.

Acid Rain, 1986. Sheldon Cheney. U.S. Department of Agriculture, National Agricultural Library, 10301 Baltimore Blvd., Beltsville, Maryland 20705-2351. (301) 504-

5755. 1987. Irregular. Includes 223 citations. Quick Bibliography series: NAL-BIBL QB 87-11. It updates an earlier bibliography, QB 86-23.

Acid Rain: A Bibliography of Canadian Federal and Provincial Government Documents. Albert H. Joy. Meckler, 11 Ferry Ln., W., Westport, Connecticut 06880. (203) 226-6967. 1991. Contains Canadian Federal and provincial government documents. Includes bibliographical references and index. Approximately 1,100 documents covering diverse topics including environmental effects, air and atmospheric processes, socioeconomic aspects, and migration and corrective measures.

Acid Rain: A Bibliography of Research Annotated for Easy Access. Harry G. Stopp, Jr. Scarecrow Press, 52 Liberty St., Box 4167, Metuchen, New Jersey 08840. (201) 548-8600 or (800) 537-7107. 1985.

Acid Rain: A Legal and Political Perspective. Karen Fair Harrell. Vance Bibliographies, 112 N. Charter St., PO Box 229, Monticello, Illinois 61856. (217) 762-3831. 1983. Public Administration series–Bibliography: P-1319

Acid Rain: An Annotated Bibliography of Selected References. University of Central Florida, Orlando, Florida 32816. 1980. Library bibliography series no. 8.

Acid Rain and Dry Deposition. Larry W. Canter. Lewis Publishers, 200 Corporate Blvd. NW, Boca Raton, Florida 33431. (407) 994-0555 or (800)272-7737. 1986.

Acid Rain and the Environment, 1980-1984. Penny Farmer. Technical Communications, British Lib. Sci. Inf. Services, 100 High Ave., Letchworth, England SG6 3RR. 1984. Reviews a selection of the literature on acid rain. Current and projected research are summarized.

Acid Rain and the Environment, 1984-1988. Lesley Grayson, comp. and ed. Technical Communications, British Lib. Sci. Inf. Services, 100 High Ave., Letchworth, England SG6 3RR. 1989. Updates the 1980-84 edition.

Acid Rain Bibliography. Charlene S. Sayers. U.S. Environmental Protection Agency, 401 M St. SW, Washington, District of Columbia 20460. (202) 260-2090. 1983. Part of EPA bibliography series no. EPA-840-83-022

Acid Rain: Effects, Measurement and Monitoring, 1980. Tennessee Valley Authority, Technical Library. Tennessee Valley Authority, 400 W. Summit Hill Dr., Knoxville, Tennessee 37902. (615) 632-2101. 1977. TVA bibliography, no. 1535 supplement

Acid Rain: Impacts on Agriculture, 1975-1982. Sheldon Cheney. U.S. Department of Agriculture, National Agricultural Library, 10301 Baltimore Blvd., Beltsville, Maryland 20705-2351. (301) 504-5755. 1983. National Agricultural Library Quick Bibliography series 83-18. It updates QB 81-29.

Acid Rain in Canada: A Selected Bibliography. John Miletich. CPL Bibliographies, 1313 E. 60th St., Chicago, Illinois 60637-2897. (312) 942-2163. 1983. Council of Planning Librarians Bibliography No. 124.

Acid Rain: Industrial Pollution. Elaine Gray. Council of Planning Librarians, 1313 E. 60th St., Chicago, Illinois 60637-2897. (312) 942-2163. 1988. Part of Council of Planning Librarians Bibliography Series no. 223.

Acid Rain: January 1987-March 1990. Sheldon Cheney. U.S. Department of Agriculture, National Agricultural Library, 10301 Baltimore Blvd., Beltsville, Maryland

20705-2351. (301) 504-5755. 1990. Contains 417 citations from AGRICOLA and is Quick Bibliography series QB 90-54. Includes an index.

Acid Rain: Measurement and Monitoring, 1970-1976. Tennessee Valley Authority, Technical Library. Tennessee Valley Authority, 400 W. Summit Hill Dr., Knoxville, Tennessee 37902. (615) 632-2101. 1977. TVA bibliography, no. 1535

Acid Rain Publications by the U.S. Fish and Wildlife Service. Rita F. Villella. U.S. Department of the Interior, Fish and Wildlife Service, Washington, District of Columbia 20240. (202) 208-5634. 1989. Part of Air Pollution and Acid Rain Report no. 28. Also part of Biological Report 80 (40.28).

Acid Rain: Suggested Background Readings. Air Resources Information Clearinghouse, 99 Court St., Rochester, New York 14604. (716) 546-3796.

Bibliography and Index of Geology. American Geological Institute, 4220 King St., Alexandria, Virginia 22302. Monthly. Includes environmental geology and hydrogeology.

Directory of Published Proceedings. Interdok Corp., 173 Halstead Ave., Harrison, New York 10528. (914) 835-3506. 1990. Monthly. This is a listing of published proceedings including the series SEMTE (Science/Medicine/Engineering/Technology) and the series SSH (Social Science/Humanities).

Effects of Air Pollution and Acid Rain on Agriculture. Joseph R. Barse, Walter Ferguson, and Virgil Whetzel. U.S. Department of Agriculture, Economic Research Service, Natural Resources Division, 14th St. and Independence Ave. S.W., Washington, District of Columbia (202) 447-7454. 1985. Series no. ERS Staff Report: No AGES 850702. It is distributed to depository libraries in microfiche. The bibliography is annotated. It is also available to the research community outside the United States for limited distribution.

International Bibliography of Acid Rain, 1977-1986. BIOSIS, 2100 Arch St., Philadelphia, Pennsylvania 19103-1399. (215) 587-4800. 1987. Contains more than 3,900 references to literature dating from 1977 through 1986.

New Publications of the Geological Survey. U.S. Department of the Interior, Geological Survey, 119 National Center, Reston, Virginia 22092. (703) 648-4460. 1984-. Monthly. Bibliography of geological publications and related government documents published by the Geological Survey.

Separation and Purification Methods. Marcel Dekker, Inc., 270 Madison Ave., New York, New York 10016. (212) 696-9000. 1972. Technology of separation and chemical purification.

DIRECTORIES

Acid Rain Foundation Speakers Bureau Directory. Acid Rain Foundation, Inc., 1410 Varsity Dr., Raleigh, North Carolina 27606. (919) 828-9443.

Acid Rain Resources Directory. Acid Rain Foundation, 1410 Varsity Dr., Raleigh, North Carolina 27606-2010. (919) 828-9443. 1986. Irregular. Third edition. Lists state, national, and international governments, public and private companies, corporations and organizations actively involved in the subject area of acid rain.

Directory of Global Climate Change Organizations. Janet Wright. National Agricultural Library, 10301 Baltimore Blvd., Beltsville, Maryland 20705. (301) 504-5755. 1991. Identifies organizations that provide information regarding global climate change issues to the general public.

International Directory of Acid Deposition Researchers. National Technical Information Service, 5285 Port Royal Rd., Springfield, Virginia 22161. (703) 487-4650. Irregular.

Operating Research Plan. Interagency Task Force on Acid Precipitation. The Task Force, Washington, District of Columbia 1984. Volume One covers research framework. Volume Two contains an inventory of research under the National Acid Precipitation Assessment Program.

ENCYCLOPEDIAS AND DICTIONARIES

The Encyclopedia of Climatology. John E. Oliver and Rhodes W. Fairbridge, eds. Van Nostrand Reinhold, 115 5th Ave., New York, New York 10003. (212) 254-3232. 1987. Belongs in the series Encyclopedia of Earth Sciences, v.11.

Grzimek's Encyclopedia of Ecology. Bernhard Grzimek. Van Nostrand Reinhold, 115 5th Ave., New York, New York 10003. (212) 254-3232. 1976.

McGraw-Hill Encyclopedia of Environmental Science. Sybil P. Parker. McGraw-Hill Science & Engineering Books, 11 W. 19th St., New York, New York 10011. (212) 337-6010. 1980. Covers ecology, man's influence on nature, and environmental protection.

McGraw-Hill Encyclopedia of Science and Technology. McGraw-Hill, 1221 Avenue of the Americas, New York, New York 10020. (212) 512-2000 or (800) 262-4729. 1992. Seventh edition. Issued in multiple volumes including index. Includes all science and technology broad subject areas.

North American Reference Encyclopedia of Ecology and Pollution. William White. North American Pub. Co., 401 N. Broad St., Philadelphia, Pennsylvania 19108. (215) 238-5300. 1972.

Ullmanns Encyclopedia of Industrial Chemistry. Hans Jurgen Arpe and Wolfgang Gerhartz, eds. VCH Publishers, 303 NW 12th Ave., Deerfield Beach, Florida 33442-1788. (305) 428-5566. 1990. Designed to keep up with the broad spectrum of chemical technology. Thirty-six volumes of the encyclopedia have been divided into two sets: the 28 A volumes contain alphabetically arranged articles on chemicals, product groups, processes and technological concepts; and the 8 B volumes are compendia of basic knowledge in industrial chemistry.

Van Nostrand's Scientific Encyclopedia. Glenn D. Considine, ed. Van Nostrand Reinhold, 115 5th Ave., New York, New York 10003. (212) 254-3232. 1983. Sixth edition. Includes all broad subject areas in science.

Vocabulaire sur les Precipitations Acides et la Pollution Atmosphrique. Vocabulary of Acid Precipitation and Air Pollution Denis Rivard. Dept. of the Secretary of State of Canada, 200 W. Rene Levesque, Tower West, Rm 401, Montreal, Quebec, Canada H2Z 1X4. (514) 283-0289. 1987.

GENERAL WORKS

Acid Politics: Environmental and Energy Policies in Britain and Germany. S. Boehmer-Christiansen and J. Skea. Belhaven Press, 136 S. Broadway, Irvington, New York 10533. (914) 591-9111. 1991. Studies the differences in Britain's and Germany's recognition of and policy reaction to the acid rain issue to exemplify the different political attitudes to "green" issues between the two countries.

Acid Precipitation. Springer-Verlag, 175 5th Ave., New York, New York 10010. (212) 460-1500; (800) 777-4643. 1989-. 5 volume set. Deals with various aspects of acidic precipitations such as: biological and ecological effects; sources, deposition and canopy interactions; soils aquatic processes and lake acidification. Also includes case studies and an international overview and assessment.

Acid Rain. Michael Bright. Gloucester Press, 95 Madison Ave., New York, New York 10016. (212) 447-7788. 1991. Describes what acid rain is, what causes it, and how it affects the environment. Also examines ways in which pollution levels can be reduced or minimized.

Acid Rain: A Student's First Sourcebook. Beth Ann Kyle and Mary Deardorff. U.S. Environmental Protection Agency, Office of Environmental Processes and Effects Research, Office of Research and Development, 401 M St. SW, Washington, District of Columbia 20460. (202) 260-2090. 1990.

Acid Rain: A Survey of Data and Current Analyses. U.S. G.P.O., Washington, District of Columbia 20401. (202) 521-0000. 1984.

Acid Rain and Emissions Trading: Implementing a Market Approach to Pollution Control. Roger K. Raufer and Stephen L. Feldman. Rowman & Littlefield, Publishers, Inc., 8705 Bollman Pl., Savage, Maryland 20763. (301) 306-0400. 1987. Methodological approach to the acid rain issue whereby emissions trading could be performed through a controlled leasing policy instead of outright trades. A comprehensive examination of the concerns surrounding the implementation of the market approach for dealing with acid rain.

Acid Rain and Ozone Layer Depletion. Jutta Brunnee. Transnational Publishers, PO Box 7282, Ardsley-on-Hudson, New York 10503. (914) 693-0089. 1988. International law and regulation relating to air pollution.

The Acid Rain Controversy. James L. Regens and Robert W. Rycroft. University of Pittsburgh Press, 127 N. Bellefield Ave., Pittsburgh, Pennsylvania 15260. (412) 624-4110. 1988. Examines various aspects of the U.S. government's response to the problem. Covers the emergence of acid rain as a public policy issue. Also covers acid rain's causes, effects, severity, control technologies, economic costs and benefits and alternatives for financing emissions control.

The Acid Rain Debate: Scientific, Economic, and Political Dimensions. Ernest J. Yanarella and Randal H. Ihara. Westview, 6065 Mission Gorge Rd., Suite 425, San Diego, California 92120. 1985. Examines public policy issues relating to the environment, with special reference to acid rain in the U.S., Canada and Europe.

Acidic Deposition and Aquatic Ecosystems. D. F. Charles and S. Christie, eds. Springer-Verlag, 175 5th Ave., New York, New York 10010. (212) 460-1500. 1991. Comprehensive integrated synthesis of available information on current and potential effects of acidic precipitation on lakes and streams in different geographic regions of the U.S. Examines the current status of water chemistry.

Acidic Deposition and Forest Soils. Dan Binkley. Springer-Verlag, 175 Fifth Ave., New York, New York 10010. (212) 460-1500 or (800) 777-4643. 1990. Environmental aspects of acid deposition, forest soils and soil acidity.

Air Pollution, Acid Rain, and the Future of Forests. Sandra Postel. Worldwatch Institute, 1776 Massachusetts Ave., N.W., Washington, District of Columbia 20036-1904. 1984.

The Changing Atmosphere: A Global Challenge. John Firor. Yale University Press, 302 Temple St., 92 A Yale Sta., New Haven, Connecticut 06520. (203) 432-0960. 1990. Examines three atmospheric problems: Acid rain, ozone depletion, and climate heating.

The Environment: Problems and Solutions. Stuart Bruchey, ed. Garland Publishing, Inc., 1000A Sherman Ave., Hamden, Connecticut 06514. (203) 281-4487. 1991. Topics covered: forested wetlands and agriculture, the political economy of smog in southern California, environmental limits to growth in world agriculture, the tradeoff between cost and risk in hazardous waste management, and the protection of groundwater from agricultural pollution.

Environment, Resources, and Conservation. Susan Owens and Peter L. Owens. Cambridge University Press, 40 W 20th St., New York, New York 10011. (212) 924-3900 or (800) 227-0247. 1991. The book studies three cases illuminating problems and policy responses at three levels of geographic scale–international, national, and local. The case of acid rain is used to illustrate a pollution problem with international dimensions; the British coal industry is analyzed as an example of national nonrenewable resource depletion; and renewable wetland ecosystem management illustrates a local concern by analyzing conservation measures.

Environmental Engineering and Sanitation. Joseph A. Salvato. John Wiley & Sons, Inc., 605 3rd Ave., New York, New York 10158-0012. (212) 850-6000. 1992. 3d ed. Applies principles of sanitary science and engineering to sanitation and environmental health. It includes design, construction, maintenance, and operations of sanitation plants and structures. Provides state-of-the-art information on environmental factors associated with chronic and non-infectious diseases; environmental engineering planning and impact analysis; waste management and control; food sanitation; administration of health and sanitation programs; acid rain; noise control; campground sanitation, etc.

Global Air Pollution: Problems for the 1990s. Howard Bridgman. Belhaven Press, 136 S. Broadway, Irvington, New York 10533. (914) 591-9111. 1990. Addresses the environmental problems caused by human activities resulting in change and deterioration of the earth's atmosphere.

Magill's Survey of Science. Earth Science Series. Frank N. Magill. Salem Press, PO Box 50062, Pasadena, California 91105. 1990-. Five volumes. Includes information on earth's crust, hot spots and volcanic island chains, physical properties of minerals, rock magnetism, physical properties of rocks, and index.

Separation and Purification. Edmond S. Perry. John Wiley & Sons, Inc., 605 3rd Ave., New York, New York

10158-0012. (212) 850-6000. 1978. Techniques of chemistry and separation technology.

The Surface Water Acidification Programme. B. J. Mason, ed. Cambridge University Press, 40 W. 20th St., New York, New York 10011. (212) 924-3900; (800) 227-0247. 1991. Proceedings of the final Conference of the Surface Water Acidification Programme, held at the Royal Society in March 1990. Deals with the acid pollution of rivers and lakes and presents research results on watersheds in Great Britain and Scandinavia.

Treatment Technologies. Environment Protection Agency. Government Institutes, Inc., 4 Research Pl., Ste. 200, Rockville, Maryland 20850. (301)921-2300. 1991. 2nd ed. Provides a clear explanation of 24 treatment technologies and evaluates the effectiveness of the design and operations of each type of treatment. This new edition has more supporting numerical data, examples for a better understanding of the technology and an updated reference for specific industrial wastes.

Troubled Skies, Troubled Waters: The Story of Acid Rain. Jon R. Loma. Viking, 375 Hudson St., New York, New York 10014. (212) 366-2000 or (800) 631-3577. 1984.

Ultrapurity; Methods and Techniques. Marcel Dekker, Inc., 270 Madison Ave., New York, New York 10016. (212) 696-9000. 1972. Purification of chemicals and chemical storage.

Waste Management: Towards A Sustainable Society. Om Prakash Kharbanda and E. A. Stallworthy. Auburn House, 14 Dedham St., Dover, Massachusetts 02030-0658. (505) 785-2220; (800) 223-2665. 1990. Describes the generation of various types of hazardous and nonhazardous wastes, with a whole chapter devoted to acid rain.

World on Fire: Saving the Endangered Earth. George J. Mitchell. Scribner Educational Publishers, 866 3d Ave., New York, New York 10022. (212) 702-2000; (800) 257-5755. 1991. Discusses the problems entailed with the issues of greenhouse effect, acid rain, the rift in the stratosphere ozone layer, and the destruction of tropical rain forests.

GOVERNMENTAL ORGANIZATIONS

U.S. Environmental Protection Agency: Office of Environmental Engineering and Technology. 401 M St., S.W., Washington, District of Columbia 20460. (202) 382-2600.

HANDBOOKS AND MANUALS

Acid Rain 1986: A Handbook for States and Provinces. Acid Rain Foundation, 1410 Varsity Dr., Raleigh, North Carolina 27606-2010. (919) 828-9443. 1986. Proceedings of Wingspread Conference sponsored by the Johnson Foundation Inc., dealing with environmental aspects of acid rain in the United States.

Acid Rain Information Book. David V. Bubenick. Noyes Publications, 120 Mill Rd., Park Ridge, New Jersey 07656. (201) 391-8484. 2nd ed.

The Acid Rain Sourcebook. Thomas C. Elliott and Robert G. Schwieger, eds. McGraw-Hill Science & Engineering Books, 11 W. 19th St., New York, New York 10011. (212) 337-6010. 1984. Organized under several sections dealing with the acid rain problem and legislative solutions; International mitigation programs; U.S. programs;

emission reduction before, during, and after contamination; and engineering solutions under development. Text is based on papers presented at the first International Conference on Acid Rain held in Washington, DC, on March 27-28, 1984.

Clean Air Handbook. Government Institutes, Inc., 4 Research Pl., Ste. 200, Rockville, Maryland 20850. (301) 921-2300. Analyzes the requirements of the Clean Air Act and its 1990 amendments, as well as what can be expected in terms of new regulation.

Purification of Laboratory Chemicals. Douglas Dalzell Perrin. Pergamon Microforms International, Inc., Fairview Park, Elmsford, New York 10523. (914) 592-7720. Deals with chemical purification technology.

ONLINE DATA BASES

Acid Rain. R. R. Bowker Co., Bowker Electronic Publishing, 121 Chanlon Rd., New Providence, New Jersey 07974. (800) 521-8110.

Aerometric Information Retrieval System. U.S. Environmental Protection Agency, Office of Air Quality Planning and Standards, National Air Data Branch, 401 M St. SW, Washington, District of Columbia 20460. (202) 260-2090. Contains data reported by more than 5000 air monitoring stations located throughout the United States.

Air Pollution Technical Information Center File. U.S. Environmental Protection Agency, Library Services Office, Air Information Center (MD-35), 401 M St. SW, Washington, District of Columbia 20460. (202) 260-2090. Citations and abstracts of the world's literature on air quality and air pollution prevention and control.

AREAL-RTP Acid Rain System–SAD. U.S. Environmental Protection Agency, MD 75, Research Triangle Park, North Carolina 27711. (919) 541-2184. Data collected during the course of a study of acid precipitations in the United States, Canada, and other foreign countries.

BIOSIS Previews. BIOSIS, 2100 Arch St., Philadelphia, Pennsylvania 19103-1399. (215) 587-4800. Largest and most comprehensive database of research in the life sciences. Contains citations for nearly 9000 primary research journals, monographs, reviews, symposia, preliminary reports, semi-popular journals, selected institutional reports, government reports and research communications.

CAS Source Index–CASSI. Chemical Abstracts Service, 2540 Olentangy River Rd., P.O. Box 3012, Columbus, Ohio 43210. (800) 848-6533 or (614) 421-3600. A listing of bibliographic and library holdings information for scientific and technical primary literature relevant to the chemical sciences.

Chemical Abstracts–CA. Chemical Abstracts Service, 2540 Olentangy River Rd., P.O. Box 3012, Columbus, Ohio 43210. (800) 848-6533 or (614) 421-3600. Information sources include 9000 journals, patents from 27 countries, two industrial property organizations, new books, conference proceedings, and government research reports.

Chemical Collection System/Request Tracking–CCS/RTS. U.S. Environmental Protection Agency, Office of Pesticides and Toxic Substances, 401 M St., SW, Washington, District of Columbia 20460. (202) 260-2090. Contains information on various properties of a number of chemicals including environmental effects, test and analysis methods, and health effects. Available from EPA.

Chemical Dictionary Online–CHEMLINE. Chemical Abstracts Service, 2540 Olentangy River Rd., Columbus, Ohio 43210. (614) 421-3600 or (800) 848-6533. Part of MEDLINE of the National Library of Medicine (NLM). File of 900,000 names for chemical substances, representing 450,000 unique compounds. It contains such information as Chemical Abstracts (CA) Service Registry Numbers, molecular formulas, preferred chemical nomenclature, and generic and ring structure information. Available on NLM's ELHILL system.

Chemical Exposure. Science Applications International Corp., Health & Environmental Information, P.O. Box 2501, Oak Ridge, Tennessee 37831. (615) 482-9031. Database of chemicals that have been identified in both human tissues and body fluids and in feral and food animals. Contains reference to journal articles, conferences, and reports. Covers the whole fields of information related to human and animal exposure to food, air, and water contaminants and pharmaceuticals. Its records include information on chemical properties, formulas, tissues measured, analytical method used, demographics and more. Available on DIALOG.

Enviroline. R. R. Bowker Co., Bowker Electronic Publishing, 121 Chanlon Rd., New Providence, New Jersey 07974. (800) 521-8110.

Environment Week. NewsNet, Inc., 945 Haverford Rd., Bryn Mawr, Pennsylvania 19010. (800) 345-1301. Online version of periodical of same name.

Global Environmental Change Report. Cutter Information Corp., 37 Broadway, Arlington, Massachusetts 02174-5539. (617) 648-8700. Online access to environmental issues worldwide, including global warming, ozone depletion, deforestation, and acid rain. Online version of periodical of the same name.

Monthly Catalog of United States Government Publications. U.S. G.P.O., Supt. of Docs., PO Box 371954, Pittsburgh, Pennsylvania 15250-7954. (202) 512-0000.

National Technical Information Service. U.S. Department of Commerce, National Technical Information Service, Office of Data Base Services, 5285 Port Royal Rd., Springfield, Virginia 22161. (703) 487-4807. Bibliographic database of government sponsored research and technical reports.

PressNet Environmental Reports. Chemical Information Systems, Inc., 7215 York Rd., Baltimore, Maryland 21212. (301) 321-8440.

PERIODICALS AND NEWSLETTERS

Acid Precipitation. National Technical Information Service, 5285 Port Royal Rd., Springfield, Virginia 22161. (703) 487-4650. Monthly. Abstracts and indexes information on deposition transport and effects of acid precipitation.

Acid Precipitation Digest. Acid Rain Information Clearinghouse, Center for Environmental Information, 46 Prince St., Rochester, New York 14607. (716) 271-3550. Monthly. A summary of current news, research, and events related to acidic deposition and transboundary air pollution, atmospheric science, aquatic and terrestrial biology and chemistry, forestry and agriculture, materials science and engineering, and pollutants emissions and control.

Atmospheric Environment. Pergamon Microforms International, Inc., Fairview Park, Elmsford, New York 10523. (914) 592-7720. 1966-. Publishes papers on all aspects of man's interactions with his atmospheric environment, including the administrative, economic and political aspects of these interactions. Air pollution research and its applications are covered, taking into account changes in the atmospheric flow patterns, temperature distributions and chemical constitution caused by natural and artificial variations in the earth's surface.

City Sierran. Sierra Club-NYC Group, 625 Broadway, 2nd Fl., New York, New York 10012. (212) 473-7841. 1984-. Quarterly. Reports environmental news to Sierra Club members in New York City. Writers are activists and experts on acid rain, pollution, toxic wastes, recycling, endangered species, etc.

Environment Week. King Communications Group, Inc., 627 National Press Bldg., Washington, District of Columbia 20045. (202) 638-4260. Weekly. Covers acid rain, solid waste and disposal, clean coal, nuclear and hazardous waste. Also available online.

Global Environmental Change Report. Cutter Information Corp., 37 Broadway, Arlington, Massachusetts 02174-5539. (617) 648-8700. Biweekly. Focus on global warming, ozone depletion, deforestation, and acid rain. Also available online.

Probe Post. Pollution Probe Foundation, 12 Madison Ave., Toronto, Ontario, Canada M5R 2S1. (416) 926-1647. Quarterly. Acid rain, toxic waste, renewable energy, deep ecology, land use, and greenhouse effect.

Waste Disposal and Pollution Control. Wakeman/Walworth, P.O. Box 1939, New Haven, Connecticut 06509. (203) 562-8518. Monthly. Covers air and water pollution, toxic waste, and acid rain.

Water, Air, and Soil Pollution. Kluwer Academic Publishers, 101 Philip Dr., Assinippi Park, Norwell, Massachusetts 02061. (617) 871-6600. Bimonthly. Covers water, soil, and air pollution. This is an international journal on environmental pollution dealing with all types of pollution including acid rain.

RESEARCH CENTERS AND INSTITUTES

Center for Earth and Environmental Science. State University of New York, Plattsburgh, New York 12901.

Center for Environmental Sciences. University of Colorado-Denver, P.O. Box 173364, Denver, Colorado 80217-3364. (303) 5556-4277.

Laboratory for Environmental Studies. Ohio Agricultural R & D Center, Ohio State University, Madison, Ohio 44691. (216) 263-3720.

Mississippi State University, Research Center. John C. Stennis Space Center, Stennis Space Center, Mississippi 39529-6000. (601) 688-3227.

Vineyard Environmental Research Institute. RFD 862, Martha's Vineyard Airport, Tisbury, Massachusetts 02568. (508) 693-4632.

STATISTICS SOURCES

Air Pollution and Acid Rain Reports. National Technical Information Service, 5285 Port Royal Rd., Springfield, Virginia 22161. (703) 487-4650. Annual. Air pollution and acid rain environmental effects and controls.

Environmental Quality. Council on Environmental Quality. U.S. G.P.O., Washington, District of Columbia 20401. (202) 512-0000. Annual.

World Resources. World Resources Institute. 1709 New York Ave., N.W., Washington, District of Columbia 20006. (202) 638-6300. Annual. Statistical and textual analysis of world's natural resources and the effects of growth-caused environmental pollution.

TRADE ASSOCIATIONS AND PROFESSIONAL SOCIETIES

Alliance for Acid Rain Control. 444 N. Capitol St., Suite 526, Washington, District of Columbia 20001. (202) 624-5475.

Canada-United States Environmental Council. c/o Defenders of Wildlife, 1244 19th St., N.W., Washington, District of Columbia 20036. (202) 659-9510.

The Izaak Walton League of America. 1401 Wilson Boulevard, Level B, Arlington, Virginia 22209. (703) 528-1818.

Threshold, International Center for Environmental Renewal. Drawer CU, Bisbee, Arizona 85603. (602) 432-7353.

ACID RAIN

See: ACID PRECIPITATION

ACID WASTE

ABSTRACTING AND INDEXING SERVICES

Abstracts of Air and Water Conservation Literature. American Petroleum Institute. Central Abstracting and Indexing Service, 275 Madison Avenue, New York, New York 10016. 1972.

Applied Ecology Abstracts Studies in Renewable Natural Resources. Information Retrieval Ltd., 1911 Jefferson Davis Highway, Arlington, Virginia 22202. 1975-. Monthly.

Biological Abstracts. BIOSIS, 2100 Arch St., Philadelphia, Pennsylvania 19103-1399. (215) 587-4800. 1927-.

Chemical Abstracts. Chemical Abstracts Service, 2540 Olentangy River Rd., PO Box 3012, Columbus, Ohio 43210. (800) 848-6533. 1907-.

Ecological Abstracts. Geo Abstracts Ltd. Elsevier Applied Science, Crown House, Linton Rd., Barking, England IG 11 8JU. 1974-. Derived from over 600 leading ecological and environmental journals, plus books, conference proceedings, reports and theses.

Environment Abstracts. Bowker A & I Publishing, 121 Chanlon Rd., New Providence, New Jersey 07974. (908) 464-6800. 1974-.

Environment Index. Environment Information Center, Index Research Department, 124 E. 39th St., New York, New York 10016. 1971-. Annual.

Environmental Information Connection–EIC. Planning Information Program, Dept. of Urban and Regional Planning, University of Illinois, 1003 West Nevada, Urbana, Illinois 61801. (217) 333-1369. Also available online.

Environmental Periodicals Bibliography. Environmental Studies Institute, International Academy at Santa Barbara, 800 Garden St., Suite D, Santa Barbara, California 93101. (805) 965-5010. Also available online.

General Science Index. H. W. Wilson Co., 950 University Ave., Bronx, New York 10452. 1978-. Monthly, also issued in annual cumulation. Cumulative subject index to English language periodicals in the subject fields of astronomy, botany, chemistry, earth science, environment and conservation, food and nutrition, genetics, mathematics, medicine and health, microbiology, oceanography, physics, physiology and zoology.

Geographical Abstracts. London School of Economics, Dept. of Geography, Regency House, 34 Duke St., London, England 1966-. Continued by Geo Abstracts issued in 6 parts: Pt. A. Landforms and the quaternary; Pt. B. Biogeography and Climatology; Pt. C. Economic geography; Pt. D. Social geography and cartography; Pt. E. Sedimentology; Pt. F. Regional and community planning.

Multimedia Index to Ecology. National Information Center for Educational Media, University of Southern California, Los Angeles, California 90007.

Pollution Abstracts. Cambridge Scientific Abstracts, 5161 River Rd., Bethesda, Maryland 20816. (301) 961-6750. Six/year. Indexes worldwide technical literature on environmental pollution. Covers air pollution, marine and freshwater pollution, sewage and wastewater treatment, waste management, toxicology and health, noise pollution, radiation, land pollution, and environmental policies, programs, legislation, and education. Also available online.

BIBLIOGRAPHIES

Acid Mine Water. U.S. Department of the Interior, Office of Water Research and Technology, Water Resources Scientific Information Center, 1849 C. St. NW, Washington, District of Columbia 20240. (202) 208-3171.

Directory of Published Proceedings. Interdok Corp., 173 Halstead Ave., Harrison, New York 10528. (914) 835-3506. 1990. Monthly. This is a listing of published proceedings including the series SEMTE (Science/Medicine/Engineering/Technology) and the series SSH (Social Science/Humanities).

EPA Publications Bibliography. U.S. Environmental Protection Agency, Library Systems Branch, 401 M St., SW, Washington, District of Columbia 20460. (202) 260-2090. Quarterly.

Mine Drainage Bibliography. V.E. Gleason. National Technical Information Service, 5285 Port Royal Rd., Springfield, Virginia 22161. (703) 487-4650. Formation and effects of acid mine drainage; erosion and sedimentation; sediment control technology effects of coal mining on ground water quality and on hydrology; and drainage from coal storage piles.

ENCYCLOPEDIAS AND DICTIONARIES

The Agriculture Dictionary. Ray V. Herren and Roy L. Donahue. Delmar Publishers Inc., 2 Computer Dr. W., Albany, New York 12212. (518) 459-1150. 1991. Covers all the agricultural areas including acid rain, acid mine drainage, food additives, agricultural engineering, conservation of the natural resources, microorganisms, triticale and other related topics.

Van Nostrand's Scientific Encyclopedia. Glenn D. Considine, ed. Van Nostrand Reinhold, 115 5th Ave., New York, New York 10003. (212) 254-3232. 1983. Sixth edition. Includes all broad subject areas in science.

GENERAL WORKS

Acid Deposition. Allan H. Legge. Lewis Publishers, 2000 Corporate Blvd., N.W., Boca Raton, Florida 33431. (407) 994-0555 or (800) 272-7737. 1990. Acidic deposition is described in great detail using the results of a major holistic, interdisciplinary research program carried out with scientific input from both the U.S. and Canada.

Acid Precipitation. Springer-Verlag, 175 5th Ave., New York, New York 10010. (212) 460-1500; (800) 777-4643. 1989-. 5 volume set. Deals with various aspects of acidic precipitations such as: biological and ecological effects; sources, deposition and canopy interactions; soils aquatic processes and lake acidification. Also includes case studies and an international overview and assessment.

Concentrated Mine Drainage Disposal into Sewage Treatment Systems. Environmental Protection Agency, 401 M St. SW, Washington, District of Columbia 20460. (202) 382-5480. 1971. Covers acid mine drainage and sewage purification.

Stopping Acid Mine Drainage: A New Approach. West Virginia Geological and Economic Survey, PO Box 879, Morgantown, West Virginia 26507. (304) 594-2331. 1985.

The Surface Water Acidification Programme. B. J. Mason, ed. Cambridge University Press, 40 W. 20th St., New York, New York 10011. (212) 924-3900; (800) 227-0247. 1991. Proceedings of the final Conference of the Surface Water Acidification Programme, held at the Royal Society in March 1990. Deals with the acid pollution of rivers and lakes and presents research results on watersheds in Great Britain and Scandinavia.

HANDBOOKS AND MANUALS

Design Manual: Neutralization of Acid Mine Drainage. U.S. Environmental Protection Agency, Office of Research and Development, Industrial Environmental Research Laboratory, 26 W. Martin Luther King Dr., Cincinnati, Ohio 45268. (513) 569-7931. 1983. Acid mine drainage and the chemistry of neutralization.

Handbook of Methods for Acid Deposition Studies: Field Methods for Surface Water Chemistry. D. J. Chaloud, et al. U.S. Environmental Protection Agency, Office of Modeling, Monitoring Systems, and Quality Assurance, 401 M St., SW, Washington, District of Columbia 20460. (202) 260-2090. 1990-.

In-line Aeration and Treatment of Acid Mine Drainage. U.S. Department of the Interior, Bureau of Mines, 810 7th St. NW, Washington, District of Columbia 20241. (202) 501-9649. 1984. Water and oxidation methods.

ONLINE DATA BASES

BIOSIS Previews. BIOSIS, 2100 Arch St., Philadelphia, Pennsylvania 19103-1399. (215) 587-4800. Largest and most comprehensive database of research in the life sciences. Contains citations for nearly 9000 primary research journals, monographs, reviews, symposia, preliminary reports, semi-popular journals, selected institutional reports, government reports and research communications.

CAS Source Index–CASSI. Chemical Abstracts Service, 2540 Olentangy River Rd., P.O. Box 3012, Columbus, Ohio 43210. (800) 848-6533 or (614) 421-3600. A listing of bibliographic and library holdings information for scientific and technical primary literature relevant to the chemical sciences.

Chemical Abstracts-CA. Chemical Abstracts Service, 2540 Olentangy River Rd., P.O. Box 3012, Columbus, Ohio 43210. (800) 848-6533 or (614) 421-3600. Information sources include 9000 journals, patents from 27 countries, two industrial property organizations, new books, conference proceedings, and government research reports.

Enviro/Energyline Abstracts Plus. R. R. Bowker Co., 121 Chanlon Rd., New Providence, New Jersey 07974. (908) 464-6800.

Environmental Periodicals Bibliography. National Information Services Corp., Ste. 6, Wyman Towers, 3100 St. Paul St., Baltimore, Maryland 21218. (410)243-0797. Online version of abstract of same name.

Monthly Catalog of United States Government Publications. U.S. G.P.O., Supt. of Docs., PO Box 371954, Pittsburgh, Pennsylvania 15250-7954. (202) 512-0000.

National Technical Information Service. U.S. Department of Commerce, National Technical Information Service, Office of Data Base Services, 5285 Port Royal Rd., Springfield, Virginia 22161. (703) 487-4807. Bibliographic database of government sponsored research and technical reports.

PERIODICALS AND NEWSLETTERS

Applied and Environmental Microbiology Journal. American Society for Microbiology, 1325 Massachusetts Avenue N.W., Washington, District of Columbia 20005. (202) 737-3600. Monthly. Articles on industrial and food microbiology and ecological studies.

Environmental Science and Technology. American Chemical Society, 1155 16th St. N.W., Washington, District of Columbia 20036. (800) 227-5558. 1967-. Monthly. Contains research articles on various aspects of environmental chemistry, interpretative articles by invited experts and commentary on the scientific aspects of environmental management.

Journal of Fish Biology. Academic Press, c/o Harcourt Brace Jovanovich Inc., 6277 Sea Harbor Dr., Orlando, Florida 32887. (800) 346-8648. Quarterly.

ACIDITY

See: pH

ACIDOPHILIC

See: ACIDS

ACIDS

See also: PH

ABSTRACTING AND INDEXING SERVICES

Abstracts of Air and Water Conservation Literature. American Petroleum Institute. Central Abstracting and Indexing Service, 275 Madison Avenue, New York, New York 10016. 1972.

Biological Abstracts. BIOSIS, 2100 Arch St., Philadelphia, Pennsylvania 19103-1399. (215) 587-4800. 1927-.

Chemical Abstracts. Chemical Abstracts Service, 2540 Olentangy River Rd., PO Box 3012, Columbus, Ohio 43210. (800) 848-6533. 1907-.

Ecological Abstracts. Geo Abstracts Ltd. Elsevier Applied Science, Crown House, Linton Rd., Barking, England IG 11 8JU. 1974-. Derived from over 600 leading ecological and environmental journals, plus books, conference proceedings, reports and theses.

Engineering Index. The Engineering Index Inc., 345 E. 47th St., New York, New York 10017. 1962-.

Environment Abstracts. Bowker A & I Publishing, 121 Chanlon Rd., New Providence, New Jersey 07974. (908) 464-6800. 1974-.

Environment Index. Environment Information Center, Index Research Department, 124 E. 39th St., New York, New York 10016. 1971-. Annual.

Environmental Information Connection–EIC. Planning Information Program, Dept. of Urban and Regional Planning, University of Illinois, 1003 West Nevada, Urbana, Illinois 61801. (217) 333-1369. Also available online.

Environmental Periodicals Bibliography. Environmental Studies Institute, International Academy at Santa Barbara, 800 Garden St., Suite D, Santa Barbara, California 93101. (805) 965-5010. Also available online.

Food Science and Technology Abstracts. International Food Information Service, c/o National Food Laboratory, 6363 Clark Ave., Dublin, California 94568. (800) 336-3782. 1969-.

General Science Index. H. W. Wilson Co., 950 University Ave., Bronx, New York 10452. 1978-. Monthly, also issued in annual cumulation. Cumulative subject index to English language periodicals in the subject fields of astronomy, botany, chemistry, earth science, environment and conservation, food and nutrition, genetics, mathematics, medicine and health, microbiology, oceanography, physics, physiology and zoology.

Pollution Abstracts. Cambridge Scientific Abstracts, 5161 River Rd., Bethesda, Maryland 20816. (301) 961-6750. Six/year. Indexes worldwide technical literature on environmental pollution. Covers air pollution, marine and freshwater pollution, sewage and wastewater treatment, waste management, toxicology and health, noise pollution, radiation, land pollution, and environmental poli-

cies, programs, legislation, and education. Also available online.

Science Citation Index. Institute for Scientific Information, 3501 Market St., Philadelphia, Pennsylvania 19104. 1961-.

BIBLIOGRAPHIES

EPA Publications Bibliography. U.S. Environmental Protection Agency, Library Systems Branch, 401 M St., SW, Washington, District of Columbia 20460. (202) 260-2090. Quarterly.

ENCYCLOPEDIAS AND DICTIONARIES

The Agriculture Dictionary. Ray V. Herren and Roy L. Donahue. Delmar Publishers Inc., 2 Computer Dr. W., Albany, New York 12212. (518) 459-1150. 1991. Covers all the agricultural areas including acid rain, acid mine drainage, food additives, agricultural engineering, conservation of the natural resources, microorganisms, triticale and other related topics.

The Concise Russian-English Chemical Glossary: Acids, Esters, Ethers, and Salts. James F. Shipp. Wychwood Press, PO Box 10, College Park, Maryland 20740. 1983. Lists four of the basic substances commonly occurring in chemical and environmental literature: acids, esters, ethers and salts.

Van Nostrand's Scientific Encyclopedia. Glenn D. Considine, ed. Van Nostrand Reinhold, 115 5th Ave., New York, New York 10003. (212) 254-3232. 1983. Sixth edition. Includes all broad subject areas in science.

GENERAL WORKS

Acidity Functions. Colin H. Rochester. Academic Press, c/o Harcourt Brace Jovanovich Inc., 6277 Sea Harbor Dr., Orlando, Florida 32887. (800) 346-8648. 1970. Deals with acid-base equilibrium, acids and solution chemistry.

Caution, Inorganic Metal Cleaners Can Be Dangerous. National Institute for Occupational Safety and Health. U.S. Department of Health and Human Services, National Institute for Occupational Safety and Health, 200 Independence Ave. SW, Washington, District of Columbia 20201. (202)619-1296. 1975.

HANDBOOKS AND MANUALS

Handbook of Acid-Proof Construction. Friedrich Karl Flacke. VCH Publishers, 303 NW 12th Ave., Deerfield Beach, Florida 33442-1788. (305) 428-5566. 1985. Details the equipment and supplies used in chemical plants and how corrosion affects them.

Nucleic Acid Sequences Handbook. Christian Gautier. Greenwood Publishing Group, Inc., 88 Post Rd., W., P. O. Box 5007, Westport, Connecticut 06881. (203) 226-3571. 1981-.

ONLINE DATA BASES

AGRICOLA. U.S. Department of Agriculture, Office of Public Affairs, 14 Independence Ave., S.W., Washington, District of Columbia 20250. (202) 447-7454.

BIOSIS Previews. BIOSIS, 2100 Arch St., Philadelphia, Pennsylvania 19103-1399. (215) 587-4800. Largest and most comprehensive database of research in the life sciences. Contains citations for nearly 9000 primary research journals, monographs, reviews, symposia, preliminary reports, semi-popular journals, selected institutional reports, government reports and research communications.

CAS Source Index–CASSI. Chemical Abstracts Service, 2540 Olentangy River Rd., P.O. Box 3012, Columbus, Ohio 43210. (800) 848-6533 or (614) 421-3600. A listing of bibliographic and library holdings information for scientific and technical primary literature relevant to the chemical sciences.

Chemest. Technical Database Services, Inc., 10 Columbus Circle, New York, New York 10019. (212) 245-0044. Covers methods of estimating 11 important properties: water solubility, soil adsorption coefficient, bioconcentration factor, acid dissociation constant, activity coefficient, boiling point, vapor pressure, water volatilization rate, Henry's Law Constant, melting point, and liquid viscosity.

Chemical Abstracts-CA. Chemical Abstracts Service, 2540 Olentangy River Rd., P.O. Box 3012, Columbus, Ohio 43210. (800) 848-6533 or (614) 421-3600. Information sources include 9000 journals, patents from 27 countries, two industrial property organizations, new books, conference proceedings, and government research reports.

Computerized Engineering Index–COMPENDEX. Engineering Information Inc., 345 E. 47th St., New York, New York 10017. (212) 705-7600.

Enviro/Energyline Abstracts Plus. R. R. Bowker Co., 121 Chanlon Rd., New Providence, New Jersey 07974. (908) 464-6800.

Environmental Periodicals Bibliography. National Information Services Corp., Ste. 6, Wyman Towers, 3100 St. Paul St., Baltimore, Maryland 21218. (410)243-0797. Online version of abstract of same name.

STATISTICS SOURCES

Acrylic Acid Markets. FIND/SVP, 625 Avenue of the Americas, New York, New York 10011. (212) 645-4500. 1991. U.S. capacity, production, foreign trade and demand for acrylic acid, as well as acrylate esters and acrylic acid polymers.

Mineral Acids. FIND/SVP, 625 Avenue of the Americas, New York, New York 10011. (212) 645-4500. 1991. Historical data and forecasts of demand and market for sulfuric; phosphoric; nitric; hydrochloric; and hydrofluoric.

ACOUSTIC MEASUREMENTS

See: ACOUSTICS

ACOUSTIC SOUNDING

See: ACOUSTICS

ACOUSTICS

ABSTRACTING AND INDEXING SERVICES

Acoustics Abstracts. Multi-Science Publishing Co. Ltd., 107 High St., Brentwood, England CM14 4RX. (0277) 224632. Monthly. Covers the world's major periodical literature, conference proceedings, unpublished reports, and book notices on acoustics.

Applied Science and Technology Index. H.W. Wilson Co., 950 University Ave., Bronx, New York 10452. (800) 367-6770. Formerly Industrial Arts Index.

Civil Engineering Hydraulic Abstracts. BHRA Fluid Engineering, Air Science Co., PO Box 143, Corning, New York 14830. (607) 962-5591. Monthly. Abstracts of periodicals that publish in the areas of hydraulic engineering and other related topics.

Engineering Index. The Engineering Index Inc., 345 E. 47th St., New York, New York 10017. 1962-.

Environment Abstracts. Bowker A & I Publishing, 121 Chanlon Rd., New Providence, New Jersey 07974. (908) 464-6800. 1974-.

Environment Index. Environment Information Center, Index Research Department, 124 E. 39th St., New York, New York 10016. 1971-. Annual.

Environmental Information Connection–EIC. Planning Information Program, Dept. of Urban and Regional Planning, University of Illinois, 1003 West Nevada, Urbana, Illinois 61801. (217) 333-1369. Also available online.

Environmental Periodicals Bibliography. Environmental Studies Institute, International Academy at Santa Barbara, 800 Garden St., Suite D, Santa Barbara, California 93101. (805) 965-5010. Also available online.

General Science Index. H. W. Wilson Co., 950 University Ave., Bronx, New York 10452. 1978-. Monthly, also issued in annual cumulation. Cumulative subject index to English language periodicals in the subject fields of astronomy, botany, chemistry, earth science, environment and conservation, food and nutrition, genetics, mathematics, medicine and health, microbiology, oceanography, physics, physiology and zoology.

Index to Scientific Book Contents. Institute for Scientific Information, 3501 Market St., Philadelphia, Pennsylvania 19104. (800) 523-1857. 1985-. Annual. Gives contents of science books published.

Physics Briefs. Physikalische Berichte. Physik Verlag, Pappapelallee 3, Postfach 101161, Weinheim, Germany D-6940. 1979-. Semimonthly. In English. Volumes for 1979- issued by the Deutsche Physikalische Gesellschaft and the Fachinformationszentrum Energie Physik, Mathematik in cooperation with the American Institute of Physics.

Pollution Abstracts. Cambridge Scientific Abstracts, 5161 River Rd., Bethesda, Maryland 20816. (301) 961-6750. Six/year. Indexes worldwide technical literature on environmental pollution. Covers air pollution, marine and freshwater pollution, sewage and wastewater treatment, waste management, toxicology and health, noise pollution, radiation, land pollution, and environmental policies, programs, legislation, and education. Also available online.

Science Citation Index. Institute for Scientific Information, 3501 Market St., Philadelphia, Pennsylvania 19104. 1961-.

BIBLIOGRAPHIES

EPA Publications Bibliography. U.S. Environmental Protection Agency, Library Systems Branch, 401 M St., SW, Washington, District of Columbia 20460. (202) 260-2090. Quarterly.

DIRECTORIES

Acoustical Contractors. 5711 S. 86th Circle, Omaha, Nebraska 68127. (402) 593-4600. Annual.

Acoustical Society of America–Biennial Membership List. Acoustical Society of America, 500 Sunnyside Blvd., Woodbury, New York 11797. (516) 349-7800.

Lead Acoustical Products and Suppliers. 295 Madison Ave., New York, New York 10017. (212) 578-4750. Annual.

National Council of Acoustical Consultants–Directory. 66 Morris Ave., Springfield, New Jersey 07081. (201) 379-1100. Biennial.

ENCYCLOPEDIAS AND DICTIONARIES

Encyclopedia of Physical Science and Technology. Robert A. Meyers, ed. Academic Press, c/o Harcourt Brace Jovanovich Inc., 6277 Sea Harbor Dr., Orlando, Florida 32887. (800) 346-8648. Dictionary of engineering, technology and physical sciences.

Encyclopedia of Physics. Rita G. Lerner and George L. Trigg. VCH Publishers, 303 NW 12th Ave., Deerfield Beach, Florida 33442-1788. (305) 428-5566. 1991. Second edition.

McGraw-Hill Encyclopedia of Science and Technology. McGraw-Hill, 1221 Avenue of the Americas, New York, New York 10020. (212) 512-2000 or (800) 262-4729. 1992. Seventh edition. Issued in multiple volumes including index. Includes all science and technology broad subject areas.

Van Nostrand's Scientific Encyclopedia. Glenn D. Considine, ed. Van Nostrand Reinhold, 115 5th Ave., New York, New York 10003. (212) 254-3232. 1983. Sixth edition. Includes all broad subject areas in science.

HANDBOOKS AND MANUALS

Handbook of Acoustical Measurements and Noise Control. Cyril M. Harris. McGraw-Hill Science & Engineering Books, 11 W. 19th St., New York, New York 10011. (212) 337-6010. 1991.

Tables of Physical and Chemical Constants and Some Mathematical Functions. G. W. C. Kaye, et al. Longman Group Ltd., Longman House, Burnt Mill, Harlow, England CM20 2J6. 0279 426721. 1988. Fifteenth edition. Includes tables on mechanical properties, density, elasticity, viscosity, surface tension, temperature and heat. Also covers radiation, optics, chemistry, electrochemistry, astrophysics, and chemical thermodynamics.

ONLINE DATA BASES

Computerized Engineering Index–COMPENDEX. Engineering Information Inc., 345 E. 47th St., New York, New York 10017. (212) 705-7600.

Enviro/Energyline Abstracts Plus. R. R. Bowker Co., 121 Chanlon Rd., New Providence, New Jersey 07974. (908) 464-6800.

Environmental Periodicals Bibliography. National Information Services Corp., Ste. 6, Wyman Towers, 3100 St. Paul St., Baltimore, Maryland 21218. (410)243-0797. Online version of abstract of same name.

Noise Levels. Canadian Centre for Occupational Health & Safety, 250 Main St., East, Hamilton, Ontario, Canada L8N 1H6. (800) 263-8276.

PERIODICALS AND NEWSLETTERS

Applied Acoustics. Elsevier Science Publishing Co., 655 Avenue of the Americas, New York, New York 10010. (212) 989-5800. Quarterly. Acoustics of musical instruments and of sound propagation through the atmosphere and underwater.

The Journal of the Acoustical Society of America. American Institute of Physics for the Acoustical Society of America, 500 Sunnyside Boulevard, Woodbury, New York 11797-2999. (516) 349-7800. Monthly.

Vibrations. National Association of Noise Control Officials, 53 Cubberly Rd., Trenton, New Jersey 08690. (609) 984-4161. Monthly. Covers technical advancements in the environmental noise control area.

STATISTICS SOURCES

World Resources. World Resources Institute. 1709 New York Ave., N.W., Washington, District of Columbia 20006. (202) 638-6300. Annual. Statistical and textual analysis of world's natural resources and the effects of growth-caused environmental pollution.

TRADE ASSOCIATIONS AND PROFESSIONAL SOCIETIES

Acoustical Society of America. 500 Sunnyside Blvd., Woodbury, New York 11797. (516) 349-7800.

Institute of Environmental Sciences. 940 E. Northwest Hwy., Mount Prospect, Illinois 60056. (708) 255-1561.

National Association of Noise Control Officials. 53 Cubberly Rd., Trenton, New Jersey 08690. (609) 984-4161.

National Council of Acoustical Consultants. 66 Morris Ave., Springfield, New Jersey 07081. (201) 379-1100.

Noise Control Products and Materials Association. 104 Cresta Verde Dr., Rolling Hills, California 90274. (213) 377-9958.

Vibration Institute. 6262 S. Kingery Hwy., Suite 212, Willowbrook, Illinois 60514. (708) 654-2254.

ACTIVATED CARBON

See also: FILTRATION; WASTEWATER TREATMENT

ABSTRACTING AND INDEXING SERVICES

Abstracts of Air and Water Conservation Literature. American Petroleum Institute. Central Abstracting and Indexing Service, 275 Madison Avenue, New York, New York 10016. 1972.

Applied Ecology Abstracts Studies in Renewable Natural Resources. Information Retrieval Ltd., 1911 Jefferson Davis Highway, Arlington, Virginia 22202. 1975-. Monthly.

Applied Science and Technology Index. H.W. Wilson Co., 950 University Ave., Bronx, New York 10452. (800) 367-6770. Formerly Industrial Arts Index.

Biological Abstracts. BIOSIS, 2100 Arch St., Philadelphia, Pennsylvania 19103-1399. (215) 587-4800. 1927-.

Chemical Abstracts. Chemical Abstracts Service, 2540 Olentangy River Rd., PO Box 3012, Columbus, Ohio 43210. (800) 848-6533. 1907-.

Ecological Abstracts. Geo Abstracts Ltd. Elsevier Applied Science, Crown House, Linton Rd., Barking, England IG 11 8JU. 1974-. Derived from over 600 leading ecological and environmental journals, plus books, conference proceedings, reports and theses.

Environment Abstracts. Bowker A & I Publishing, 121 Chanlon Rd., New Providence, New Jersey 07974. (908) 464-6800. 1974-.

Environment Index. Environment Information Center, Index Research Department, 124 E. 39th St., New York, New York 10016. 1971-. Annual.

Environmental Information Connection–EIC. Planning Information Program, Dept. of Urban and Regional Planning, University of Illinois, 1003 West Nevada, Urbana, Illinois 61801. (217) 333-1369. Also available online.

Environmental Periodicals Bibliography. Environmental Studies Institute, International Academy at Santa Barbara, 800 Garden St., Suite D, Santa Barbara, California 93101. (805) 965-5010. Also available online.

General Science Index. H. W. Wilson Co., 950 University Ave., Bronx, New York 10452. 1978-. Monthly, also issued in annual cumulation. Cumulative subject index to English language periodicals in the subject fields of astronomy, botany, chemistry, earth science, environment and conservation, food and nutrition, genetics, mathematics, medicine and health, microbiology, oceanography, physics, physiology and zoology.

Index to Scientific Book Contents. Institute for Scientific Information, 3501 Market St., Philadelphia, Pennsylvania 19104. (800) 523-1857. 1985-. Annual. Gives contents of science books published.

Metals Abstracts. ASM International, 9639 Kinsman, Materials Park, Ohio 44073. (216) 338-5151. 1968-. Published jointly by the Institute of Metals, London and the American Society for Metals. Formed by the Union of Metallurgical Abstracts and Review of Metal Literature.

Multimedia Index to Ecology. National Information Center for Educational Media, University of Southern California, Los Angeles, California 90007.

Pollution Abstracts. Cambridge Scientific Abstracts, 5161 River Rd., Bethesda, Maryland 20816. (301) 961-6750.

Six/year. Indexes worldwide technical literature on environmental pollution. Covers air pollution, marine and freshwater pollution, sewage and wastewater treatment, waste management, toxicology and health, noise pollution, radiation, land pollution, and environmental policies, programs, legislation, and education. Also available online.

Science Citation Index. Institute for Scientific Information, 3501 Market St., Philadelphia, Pennsylvania 19104. 1961-.

BIBLIOGRAPHIES

EPA Publications Bibliography. U.S. Environmental Protection Agency, Library Systems Branch, 401 M St., SW, Washington, District of Columbia 20460. (202) 260-2090. Quarterly.

ENCYCLOPEDIAS AND DICTIONARIES

Encyclopedia of Physics. Rita G. Lerner and George L. Trigg. VCH Publishers, 303 NW 12th Ave., Deerfield Beach, Florida 33442-1788. (305) 428-5566. 1991. Second edition.

McGraw-Hill Encyclopedia of Science and Technology. McGraw-Hill, 1221 Avenue of the Americas, New York, New York 10020. (212) 512-2000 or (800) 262-4729. 1992. Seventh edition. Issued in multiple volumes including index. Includes all science and technology broad subject areas.

Van Nostrand's Scientific Encyclopedia. Glenn D. Considine, ed. Van Nostrand Reinhold, 115 5th Ave., New York, New York 10003. (212) 254-3232. 1983. Sixth edition. Includes all broad subject areas in science.

GENERAL WORKS

Activated Charcoal: Antidotal and Other Medical Uses. David O. Cooney. Marcel Dekker, Inc., 270 Madison Ave., New York, New York 10016. (212) 696-9000; (800) 228-1160. 1980. Therapeutic use of activated carbon, specifically as an antidote.

Drinking Water and Groundwater Remediation Cost Evaluation: Granular Activated Carbon. Robert M. Clark and Jeffrey Q. Adams. Lewis Publishers, 2000 Corporate Blvd. N.W., Boca Raton, Florida 33431. (800) 272-7737. 1991. Shows GAC costs and performance forthe remediation of hazardous waste sites or drinking watertreatment. Compares the cost of the technology against other available technologies.

Toxicity Reduction in Industrial Effluents. Perry W. Lanford, et al. Van Nostrand Reinhold, 115 5th Ave., New York, New York 10003. (212) 254-3232. 1990. Overview of aquatic toxicology and toxicity reduction. Specific treatment technologies that can be used to reduce toxicity, such as aerobic and anaerobic biological treatment, air and steam stripping of volatile organics, granulated carbon absorption, powdered activated carbon treatment and chemical oxidation, are discussed in detail.

HANDBOOKS AND MANUALS

Tables of Physical and Chemical Constants and Some Mathematical Functions. G. W. C. Kaye, et al. Longman Group Ltd., Longman House, Burnt Mill, Harlow, England CM20 2J6. 0279 426721. 1988. Fifteenth edition. Includes tables on mechanical properties, density, elasticity, viscosity, surface tension, temperature and heat. Also covers radiation, optics, chemistry, electrochemistry, astrophysics, and chemical thermodynamics.

ONLINE DATA BASES

BIOSIS Previews. BIOSIS, 2100 Arch St., Philadelphia, Pennsylvania 19103-1399. (215) 587-4800. Largest and most comprehensive database of research in the life sciences. Contains citations for nearly 9000 primary research journals, monographs, reviews, symposia, preliminary reports, semi-popular journals, selected institutional reports, government reports and research communications.

CAS Source Index–CASSI. Chemical Abstracts Service, 2540 Olentangy River Rd., P.O. Box 3012, Columbus, Ohio 43210. (800) 848-6533 or (614) 421-3600. A listing of bibliographic and library holdings information for scientific and technical primary literature relevant to the chemical sciences.

Chemical Abstracts-CA. Chemical Abstracts Service, 2540 Olentangy River Rd., P.O. Box 3012, Columbus, Ohio 43210. (800) 848-6533 or (614) 421-3600. Information sources include 9000 journals, patents from 27 countries, two industrial property organizations, new books, conference proceedings, and government research reports.

Enviro/Energyline Abstracts Plus. R. R. Bowker Co., 121 Chanlon Rd., New Providence, New Jersey 07974. (908) 464-6800.

Environmental Periodicals Bibliography. National Information Services Corp., Ste. 6, Wyman Towers, 3100 St. Paul St., Baltimore, Maryland 21218. (410)243-0797. Online version of abstract of same name.

ACTIVATED SILICA

ABSTRACTING AND INDEXING SERVICES

Abstracts of Air and Water Conservation Literature. American Petroleum Institute. Central Abstracting and Indexing Service, 275 Madison Avenue, New York, New York 10016. 1972.

Applied Ecology Abstracts Studies in Renewable Natural Resources. Information Retrieval Ltd., 1911 Jefferson Davis Highway, Arlington, Virginia 22202. 1975-. Monthly.

Applied Science and Technology Index. H.W. Wilson Co., 950 University Ave., Bronx, New York 10452. (800) 367-6770. Formerly Industrial Arts Index.

Chemical Abstracts. Chemical Abstracts Service, 2540 Olentangy River Rd., PO Box 3012, Columbus, Ohio 43210. (800) 848-6533. 1907-.

General Science Index. H. W. Wilson Co., 950 University Ave., Bronx, New York 10452. 1978-. Monthly, also issued in annual cumulation. Cumulative subject index to English language periodicals in the subject fields of astronomy, botany, chemistry, earth science, environment and conservation, food and nutrition, genetics, mathematics, medicine and health, microbiology, oceanography, physics, physiology and zoology.

Multimedia Index to Ecology. National Information Center for Educational Media, University of Southern California, Los Angeles, California 90007.

Science Citation Index. Institute for Scientific Information, 3501 Market St., Philadelphia, Pennsylvania 19104. 1961-.

ENCYCLOPEDIAS AND DICTIONARIES

Encyclopedia of Physics. Rita G. Lerner and George L. Trigg. VCH Publishers, 303 NW 12th Ave., Deerfield Beach, Florida 33442-1788. (305) 428-5566. 1991. Second edition.

Van Nostrand's Scientific Encyclopedia. Glenn D. Considine, ed. Van Nostrand Reinhold, 115 5th Ave., New York, New York 10003. (212) 254-3232. 1983. Sixth edition. Includes all broad subject areas in science.

HANDBOOKS AND MANUALS

Tables of Physical and Chemical Constants and Some Mathematical Functions. G. W. C. Kaye, et al. Longman Group Ltd., Longman House, Burnt Mill, Harlow, England CM20 2J6. 0279 426721. 1988. Fifteenth edition. Includes tables on mechanical properties, density, elasticity, viscosity, surface tension, temperature and heat. Also covers radiation, optics, chemistry, electrochemistry, astrophysics, and chemical thermodynamics.

ONLINE DATA BASES

CAS Source Index–CASSI. Chemical Abstracts Service, 2540 Olentangy River Rd., P.O. Box 3012, Columbus, Ohio 43210. (800) 848-6533 or (614) 421-3600. A listing of bibliographic and library holdings information for scientific and technical primary literature relevant to the chemical sciences.

Chemical Abstracts-CA. Chemical Abstracts Service, 2540 Olentangy River Rd., P.O. Box 3012, Columbus, Ohio 43210. (800) 848-6533 or (614) 421-3600. Information sources include 9000 journals, patents from 27 countries, two industrial property organizations, new books, conference proceedings, and government research reports.

ACTIVATED SLUDGE

See also: SEWAGE TREATMENT

ABSTRACTING AND INDEXING SERVICES

Abstracts of Air and Water Conservation Literature. American Petroleum Institute. Central Abstracting and Indexing Service, 275 Madison Avenue, New York, New York 10016. 1972.

Applied Ecology Abstracts Studies in Renewable Natural Resources. Information Retrieval Ltd., 1911 Jefferson Davis Highway, Arlington, Virginia 22202. 1975-. Monthly.

Applied Science and Technology Index. H.W. Wilson Co., 950 University Ave., Bronx, New York 10452. (800) 367-6770. Formerly Industrial Arts Index.

Biological Abstracts. BIOSIS, 2100 Arch St., Philadelphia, Pennsylvania 19103-1399. (215) 587-4800. 1927-.

Biotechnology Research Abstracts. Cambridge Scientific Abstracts, 5161 River Rd., Bethesda, Maryland 20816. (301) 961-6750. Monthly. Includes such broad areas as genetic intervention, biochemical genetics, and microbiological techniques.

Bulletin Signaletique: Eau et Assainissement, Pollution Atmospherique, Droit des Pollutions. Centre de Documentation, Centre National de la Recherche Scientifique, 15, quai Anatole France, Paris, France 75700. (1) 45 55 92 25. 1983-. Monthly. Indexes pollution periodicals including water, atmospheric and related pollutions.

Chemical Abstracts. Chemical Abstracts Service, 2540 Olentangy River Rd., PO Box 3012, Columbus, Ohio 43210. (800) 848-6533. 1907-.

Ecological Abstracts. Geo Abstracts Ltd. Elsevier Applied Science, Crown House, Linton Rd., Barking, England IG 11 8JU. 1974-. Derived from over 600 leading ecological and environmental journals, plus books, conference proceedings, reports and theses.

Engineering Index. The Engineering Index Inc., 345 E. 47th St., New York, New York 10017. 1962-.

Environment Abstracts. Bowker A & I Publishing, 121 Chanlon Rd., New Providence, New Jersey 07974. (908) 464-6800. 1974-.

Environment Index. Environment Information Center, Index Research Department, 124 E. 39th St., New York, New York 10016. 1971-. Annual.

Environmental Information Connection–EIC. Planning Information Program, Dept. of Urban and Regional Planning, University of Illinois, 1003 West Nevada, Urbana, Illinois 61801. (217) 333-1369. Also available online.

Environmental Periodicals Bibliography. Environmental Studies Institute, International Academy at Santa Barbara, 800 Garden St., Suite D, Santa Barbara, California 93101. (805) 965-5010. Also available online.

General Science Index. H. W. Wilson Co., 950 University Ave., Bronx, New York 10452. 1978-. Monthly, also issued in annual cumulation. Cumulative subject index to English language periodicals in the subject fields of astronomy, botany, chemistry, earth science, environment and conservation, food and nutrition, genetics, mathematics, medicine and health, microbiology, oceanography, physics, physiology and zoology.

Index to Scientific Book Contents. Institute for Scientific Information, 3501 Market St., Philadelphia, Pennsylvania 19104. (800) 523-1857. 1985-. Annual. Gives contents of science books published.

Multimedia Index to Ecology. National Information Center for Educational Media, University of Southern California, Los Angeles, California 90007.

Pollution Abstracts. Cambridge Scientific Abstracts, 5161 River Rd., Bethesda, Maryland 20816. (301) 961-6750. Six/year. Indexes worldwide technical literature on environmental pollution. Covers air pollution, marine and freshwater pollution, sewage and wastewater treatment, waste management, toxicology and health, noise pollution, radiation, land pollution, and environmental policies, programs, legislation, and education. Also available online.

Science Citation Index. Institute for Scientific Information, 3501 Market St., Philadelphia, Pennsylvania 19104. 1961-.

BIBLIOGRAPHIES

Directory of Published Proceedings. Interdok Corp., 173 Halstead Ave., Harrison, New York 10528. (914) 835-3506. 1990. Monthly. This is a listing of published proceedings including the series SEMTE (Science/Medicine/Engineering/Technology) and the series SSH (Social Science/Humanities).

EPA Publications Bibliography. U.S. Environmental Protection Agency, Library Systems Branch, 401 M St., SW, Washington, District of Columbia 20460. (202) 260-2090. Quarterly.

ENCYCLOPEDIAS AND DICTIONARIES

McGraw-Hill Encyclopedia of Science and Technology. McGraw-Hill, 1221 Avenue of the Americas, New York, New York 10020. (212) 512-2000 or (800) 262-4729. 1992. Seventh edition. Issued in multiple volumes including index. Includes all science and technology broad subject areas.

The New York Times Encyclopedic Dictionary of the Environment. Paul Sarnoff. Quadrangle Books, New York, New York 1971. Focuses on state-of-the-art methods of pollution control, abatement, prevention and removal.

Van Nostrand's Scientific Encyclopedia. Glenn D. Considine, ed. Van Nostrand Reinhold, 115 5th Ave., New York, New York 10003. (212) 254-3232. 1983. Sixth edition. Includes all broad subject areas in science.

HANDBOOKS AND MANUALS

Water Treatment Handbook. Degremont s.a., 184, ave. du 18-Juin-1940, Rueil-Malmaison, France F-92500. 1991. Sixth edition. Part 1 is a general survey of water and its action on the materials with which it comes into contact, and theoretical principles of separation and correction processes used in water treatment. Part 2 describes the process and the treatment plant beginning with the separation process.

ONLINE DATA BASES

BIOSIS Previews. BIOSIS, 2100 Arch St., Philadelphia, Pennsylvania 19103-1399. (215) 587-4800. Largest and most comprehensive database of research in the life sciences. Contains citations for nearly 9000 primary research journals, monographs, reviews, symposia, preliminary reports, semi-popular journals, selected institutional reports, government reports and research communications.

Chemical Abstracts-CA. Chemical Abstracts Service, 2540 Olentangy River Rd., P.O. Box 3012, Columbus, Ohio 43210. (800) 848-6533 or (614) 421-3600. Information sources include 9000 journals, patents from 27 countries, two industrial property organizations, new books, conference proceedings, and government research reports.

Computerized Engineering Index–COMPENDEX. Engineering Information Inc., 345 E. 47th St., New York, New York 10017. (212) 705-7600.

Enviro/Energyline Abstracts Plus. R. R. Bowker Co., 121 Chanlon Rd., New Providence, New Jersey 07974. (908) 464-6800.

Environmental Periodicals Bibliography. National Information Services Corp., Ste. 6, Wyman Towers, 3100 St. Paul St., Baltimore, Maryland 21218. (410)243-0797. Online version of abstract of same name.

Monthly Catalog of United States Government Publications. U.S. G.P.O., Supt. of Docs., PO Box 371954, Pittsburgh, Pennsylvania 15250-7954. (202) 512-0000.

National Technical Information Service. U.S. Department of Commerce, National Technical Information Service, Office of Data Base Services, 5285 Port Royal Rd., Springfield, Virginia 22161. (703) 487-4807. Bibliographic database of government sponsored research and technical reports.

PressNet Environmental Reports. Chemical Information Systems, Inc., 7215 York Rd., Baltimore, Maryland 21212. (301) 321-8440.

ACUTE TOXICITY
See: TOXICITY

ADAPTATION
See: ACCLIMATIZATION

ADENOSINE TRIPHOSPHATE
See also: METABOLISM

ABSTRACTING AND INDEXING SERVICES

Biological Abstracts. BIOSIS, 2100 Arch St., Philadelphia, Pennsylvania 19103-1399. (215) 587-4800. 1927-.

Chemical Abstracts. Chemical Abstracts Service, 2540 Olentangy River Rd., PO Box 3012, Columbus, Ohio 43210. (800) 848-6533. 1907-.

Ecological Abstracts. Geo Abstracts Ltd. Elsevier Applied Science, Crown House, Linton Rd., Barking, England IG 11 8JU. 1974-. Derived from over 600 leading ecological and environmental journals, plus books, conference proceedings, reports and theses.

Ecology Abstracts. Cambridge Scientific Abstracts, 5161 River Rd., Bethesda, Maryland 20816. (301) 961-6750. Monthly.

Microbiology Abstracts. Section A. Industrial and Applied Microbiology. Cambridge Scientific Abstracts, 5161 River Rd., Bethesda, Maryland 20816. (301) 961-6750. 1972-.

Science Citation Index. Institute for Scientific Information, 3501 Market St., Philadelphia, Pennsylvania 19104. 1961-.

ENCYCLOPEDIAS AND DICTIONARIES

Dictionary of Colloid and Surface Science. Paul Becher. Marcel Dekker, Inc., 270 Madison Ave., New York, New

York 10016. (212) 696-9000; (800) 228-1160. 1990. Dictionary deals with the areas of colloids, surface chemistry, and the physics and technology involved with surfaces.

Encyclopedia of Human Biology. Renato Dulbecco, ed. Academic Press, c/o Harcourt Brace Jovanovich Inc., 6277 Sea Harbor Dr., Orlando, Florida 32887. (800) 346-8648. 1991. Eight volumes.

The Nutrition and Health Encyclopedia. David F. Tver and Percy Russell. Van Nostrand Reinhold, 115 5th Ave., New York, New York 10003. (212) 254-3232. 1989.

GENERAL WORKS

Biomass Determination–a New Technique for Activated Sludge Control. U.S. Environmental Protection Agency, 401 M St. SW, Washington, District of Columbia 20460. (202) 260-2090. 1972. Includes an analysis of sewage sludge analysis by biomass determination. Also describes sewage disposal.

Cell ATP. William A. Bridger. John Wiley & Sons, Inc., 605 3rd Ave., New York, New York 10158-0012. (212) 850-6000. 1983. Discusses the metabolism of adenosine triphosphate including cell metabolism.

Magill's Survey of Science. Life Science Series. Frank N. Magill, ed. Salem Press, PO Box 50062, Pasadena, California 91105. 1991. Six volumes. Contents: v.1. A-Central and peripheral nervous system functions; v.2. Central metabolism regulation - eukaryotic transcriptional control; v.3. Positive and negative eukaryotic transcriptional control - mammalian hormones; v.4. Hormones and behavior - muscular contraction; v.5. Muscular contraction and relaxation - sexual reproduction in plants; v.6. Reproductive behavior and mating - X inactivation and the Lyon hypothesis.

Muscles, Molecules and Movement: An Essay in the Contraction of Muscles. J. R. Bendall. Heinemann Educational, Hanover St., Portsmouth, New Hampshire 03801-3959. (603) 431-7894. 1969. Discusses muscle proteins and also the effects of adenosine triphosphate.

ONLINE DATA BASES

BIOSIS Previews. BIOSIS, 2100 Arch St., Philadelphia, Pennsylvania 19103-1399. (215) 587-4800. Largest and most comprehensive database of research in the life sciences. Contains citations for nearly 9000 primary research journals, monographs, reviews, symposia, preliminary reports, semi-popular journals, selected institutional reports, government reports and research communications.

CAS Source Index–CASSI. Chemical Abstracts Service, 2540 Olentangy River Rd., P.O. Box 3012, Columbus, Ohio 43210. (800) 848-6533 or (614) 421-3600. A listing of bibliographic and library holdings information for scientific and technical primary literature relevant to the chemical sciences.

Chemical Abstracts-CA. Chemical Abstracts Service, 2540 Olentangy River Rd., P.O. Box 3012, Columbus, Ohio 43210. (800) 848-6533 or (614) 421-3600. Information sources include 9000 journals, patents from 27 countries, two industrial property organizations, new books, conference proceedings, and government research reports.

Chemical Abstracts Chemical Name Directory-CHEM-NAME. Chemical Abstracts Service, 2540 Olentangy River Rd., P.O. Box 3012, Columbus, Ohio 43210. (800) 848-6533 or (614) 421-3600. Listing of chemical substances in a dictionary type file. The Chemical Abstracts (CAS) Registry Number, molecular formula, Chemical Abstracts (CA) Substance Index Name, available synonyms, ring data and other chemical substance information is given for each entry.

Monthly Catalog of United States Government Publications. U.S. G.P.O., Supt. of Docs., PO Box 371954, Pittsburgh, Pennsylvania 15250-7954. (202) 512-0000.

National Technical Information Service. U.S. Department of Commerce, National Technical Information Service, Office of Data Base Services, 5285 Port Royal Rd., Springfield, Virginia 22161. (703) 487-4807. Bibliographic database of government sponsored research and technical reports.

ADHESION

See also: BIOFOULING; TRANSPIRATION

ABSTRACTING AND INDEXING SERVICES

Applied Science and Technology Index. H.W. Wilson Co., 950 University Ave., Bronx, New York 10452. (800) 367-6770. Formerly Industrial Arts Index.

ASFA Aquaculture Abstracts. Cambridge Scientific Abstracts, Inc., 5161 River Rd., Bethesda, Maryland 20816. (301) 961-6750. 1984.

Biological Abstracts. BIOSIS, 2100 Arch St., Philadelphia, Pennsylvania 19103-1399. (215) 587-4800. 1927-.

Environment Abstracts. Bowker A & I Publishing, 121 Chanlon Rd., New Providence, New Jersey 07974. (908) 464-6800. 1974-.

Environment Index. Environment Information Center, Index Research Department, 124 E. 39th St., New York, New York 10016. 1971-. Annual.

Environmental Information Connection–EIC. Planning Information Program, Dept. of Urban and Regional Planning, University of Illinois, 1003 West Nevada, Urbana, Illinois 61801. (217) 333-1369. Also available online.

Environmental Periodicals Bibliography. Environmental Studies Institute, International Academy at Santa Barbara, 800 Garden St., Suite D, Santa Barbara, California 93101. (805) 965-5010. Also available online.

Metals Abstracts. ASM International, 9639 Kinsman, Materials Park, Ohio 44073. (216) 338-5151. 1968-. Published jointly by the Institute of Metals, London and the American Society for Metals. Formed by the Union of Metallurgical Abstracts and Review of Metal Literature.

Science Citation Index. Institute for Scientific Information, 3501 Market St., Philadelphia, Pennsylvania 19104. 1961-.

BIBLIOGRAPHIES

Adhesion and Adhesives. Y. Y. Liu. Library of Congress, Science and Technology Division, Reference Section, Washington, District of Columbia 20540. (202) 738-3238. 1979. LC tracer bullet TB 79-1.

EPA Publications Bibliography. U.S. Environmental Protection Agency, Library Systems Branch, 401 M St., SW, Washington, District of Columbia 20460. (202) 260-2090. Quarterly.

DIRECTORIES

Adhesives Age Directory. 6255 Barfield Rd., Atlanta, Georgia 30328. (404) 256-9800. Annual.

ENCYCLOPEDIAS AND DICTIONARIES

Encyclopedia of Human Biology. Renato Dulbecco, ed. Academic Press, c/o Harcourt Brace Jovanovich Inc., 6277 Sea Harbor Dr., Orlando, Florida 32887. (800) 346-8648. 1991. Eight volumes.

Encyclopedia of Polymer Science and Engineering. Herman F. Mark, et al., eds. John Wiley & Sons, Inc., 605 3rd Ave., New York, New York 10158-0012. (212) 850-6000. 1985-. Seventeen volumes and two supplements.

McGraw-Hill Encyclopedia of Science and Technology. McGraw-Hill, 1221 Avenue of the Americas, New York, New York 10020. (212) 512-2000 or (800) 262-4729. 1992. Seventh edition. Issued in multiple volumes including index. Includes all science and technology broad subject areas.

Van Nostrand's Scientific Encyclopedia. Glenn D. Considine, ed. Van Nostrand Reinhold, 115 5th Ave., New York, New York 10003. (212) 254-3232. 1983. Sixth edition. Includes all broad subject areas in science.

GENERAL WORKS

Plastics: America's Packaging Dilemma. Nancy A. Wolf and Ellen D. Feldman. Island Press, 1718 Connecticut Ave. N.W., Ste. 300, Washington, District of Columbia 20009. (202) 232-7933. 1991. Source books on plastics deal with packaging, building materials, consumer goods, electrical products, transportation, industrial machinery, adhesives, legislative and regulatory issues. Also covers the controversies over plastics incineration, degradability, and recyclability.

HANDBOOKS AND MANUALS

The Infrared Spectra Handbook of Adhesives and Sealants. Sadtler Research Laboratories, 3316 Spring Garden St., Philadelphia, Pennsylvania 19104. (215)382-7800. 1988. Contains 520 adhesives and sealants.

ONLINE DATA BASES

BIOSIS Previews. BIOSIS, 2100 Arch St., Philadelphia, Pennsylvania 19103-1399. (215) 587-4800. Largest and most comprehensive database of research in the life sciences. Contains citations for nearly 9000 primary research journals, monographs, reviews, symposia, preliminary reports, semi-popular journals, selected institutional reports, government reports and research communications.

Enviro/Energyline Abstracts Plus. R. R. Bowker Co., 121 Chanlon Rd., New Providence, New Jersey 07974. (908) 464-6800.

Environmental Periodicals Bibliography. National Information Services Corp., Ste. 6, Wyman Towers, 3100 St. Paul St., Baltimore, Maryland 21218. (410)243-0797. Online version of abstract of same name.

PERIODICALS AND NEWSLETTERS

The Journal of Adhesion. Gordon and Breach Science Publishers, Inc., 270 8th Ave., New York, New York 10011. (212) 206-8900. Quarterly. Phenomenon of adhesion and its practical applications.

Journal of Adhesion Science and Technology. VNU Science Press, VSP BV., PO Box 346, Zeist, Netherlands 3700 A H. (03404)25790. Quarterly. Focus on theories of adhesion; surface energetics; fracture mechanics. Development and application of surface-sensitive methods to study adhesion phenomena, and other related topics.

Treatise on Adhesion and Adhesives. Marcel Dekker, Inc., 270 Madison Ave., New York, New York 10016. (212) 696-9000; (800) 228-1160. Irregular. Each volume is devoted to a special topic in adhesion and adhesives.

STATISTICS SOURCES

Adhesives/Sealants Guide. FIND/SVP, 625 Avenue of the Americas, New York, New York 10011. (212) 645-4500. 1990. Analyzes the structure of the U.S. adhesives and sealants industry and covers the overall outlook to 1994.

TRADE ASSOCIATIONS AND PROFESSIONAL SOCIETIES

Adhesion Society. c/o T.L. St. Clair, M.S. 226, NASA-Langely Research Center, Hamptong, Virginia 23665. (804) 864-4273.

ADIPOSE TISSUE

See also: BODY FAT; HIBERNATION; METABOLISM

ABSTRACTING AND INDEXING SERVICES

Biological Abstracts. BIOSIS, 2100 Arch St., Philadelphia, Pennsylvania 19103-1399. (215) 587-4800. 1927-.

Ecology Abstracts. Cambridge Scientific Abstracts, 5161 River Rd., Bethesda, Maryland 20816. (301) 961-6750. Monthly.

Science Citation Index. Institute for Scientific Information, 3501 Market St., Philadelphia, Pennsylvania 19104. 1961-.

ENCYCLOPEDIAS AND DICTIONARIES

Encyclopedia of Human Biology. Renato Dulbecco, ed. Academic Press, c/o Harcourt Brace Jovanovich Inc., 6277 Sea Harbor Dr., Orlando, Florida 32887. (800) 346-8648. 1991. Eight volumes.

McGraw-Hill Encyclopedia of Science and Technology. McGraw-Hill, 1221 Avenue of the Americas, New York, New York 10020. (212) 512-2000 or (800) 262-4729. 1992. Seventh edition. Issued in multiple volumes in-

cluding index. Includes all science and technology broad subject areas.

GENERAL WORKS

Monitoring Human Tissues for Toxic Substances. National Academy Press, 2101 Constitution Ave. N.W., PO Box 285, Washington, District of Columbia 20418. (202) 334-3313. 1991. Evaluates the National Human Monitoring Program.

ONLINE DATA BASES

BIOSIS Previews. BIOSIS, 2100 Arch St., Philadelphia, Pennsylvania 19103-1399. (215) 587-4800. Largest and most comprehensive database of research in the life sciences. Contains citations for nearly 9000 primary research journals, monographs, reviews, symposia, preliminary reports, semi-popular journals, selected institutional reports, government reports and research communications.

ADSORPTION

ABSTRACTING AND INDEXING SERVICES

Abstracts of Air and Water Conservation Literature. American Petroleum Institute. Central Abstracting and Indexing Service, 275 Madison Avenue, New York, New York 10016. 1972.

Air Pollution Technical Publications of the United States Environmental Protection Agency. U.S. Environmental Protection Agency, Mail Drop 75, Research Triangle Park, North Carolina 27711. (919) 541-2184. 1976. Quarterly.

Applied Science and Technology Index. H.W. Wilson Co., 950 University Ave., Bronx, New York 10452. (800) 367-6770. Formerly Industrial Arts Index.

ASFA Aquaculture Abstracts. Cambridge Scientific Abstracts, Inc., 5161 River Rd., Bethesda, Maryland 20816. (301) 961-6750. 1984.

Biological Abstracts. BIOSIS, 2100 Arch St., Philadelphia, Pennsylvania 19103-1399. (215) 587-4800. 1927-.

Chemical Abstracts. Chemical Abstracts Service, 2540 Olentangy River Rd., PO Box 3012, Columbus, Ohio 43210. (800) 848-6533. 1907-.

Ecological Abstracts. Geo Abstracts Ltd. Elsevier Applied Science, Crown House, Linton Rd., Barking, England IG 11 8JU. 1974-. Derived from over 600 leading ecological and environmental journals, plus books, conference proceedings, reports and theses.

Environment Abstracts. Bowker A & I Publishing, 121 Chanlon Rd., New Providence, New Jersey 07974. (908) 464-6800. 1974-.

Environment Index. Environment Information Center, Index Research Department, 124 E. 39th St., New York, New York 10016. 1971-. Annual.

Environmental Information Connection–EIC. Planning Information Program, Dept. of Urban and Regional Planning, University of Illinois, 1003 West Nevada, Urbana, Illinois 61801. (217) 333-1369. Also available online.

Environmental Periodicals Bibliography. Environmental Studies Institute, International Academy at Santa Barbara, 800 Garden St., Suite D, Santa Barbara, California 93101. (805) 965-5010. Also available online.

Food Science and Technology Abstracts. International Food Information Service, c/o National Food Laboratory, 6363 Clark Ave., Dublin, California 94568. (800) 336-3782. 1969-.

Index to Scientific Book Contents. Institute for Scientific Information, 3501 Market St., Philadelphia, Pennsylvania 19104. (800) 523-1857. 1985-. Annual. Gives contents of science books published.

Metals Abstracts. ASM International, 9639 Kinsman, Materials Park, Ohio 44073. (216) 338-5151. 1968-. Published jointly by the Institute of Metals, London and the American Society for Metals. Formed by the Union of Metallurgical Abstracts and Review of Metal Literature.

Pollution Abstracts. Cambridge Scientific Abstracts, 5161 River Rd., Bethesda, Maryland 20816. (301) 961-6750. Six/year. Indexes worldwide technical literature on environmental pollution. Covers air pollution, marine and freshwater pollution, sewage and wastewater treatment, waste management, toxicology and health, noise pollution, radiation, land pollution, and environmental policies, programs, legislation, and education. Also available online.

Science Citation Index. Institute for Scientific Information, 3501 Market St., Philadelphia, Pennsylvania 19104. 1961-.

BIBLIOGRAPHIES

EPA Publications Bibliography. U.S. Environmental Protection Agency, Library Systems Branch, 401 M St., SW, Washington, District of Columbia 20460. (202) 260-2090. Quarterly.

ENCYCLOPEDIAS AND DICTIONARIES

Concise Encyclopedia of Solid State Physics. Rita G. Lerner and George L. Trigg. Addison-Wesley Longman, Rte. 128, Reading, Massachusetts 01867. (617) 944-3700. 1983. "Articles chosen for this volume have been selected from the encyclopedia of physics."

Dictionary of Colloid and Surface Science. Paul Becher. Marcel Dekker, Inc., 270 Madison Ave., New York, New York 10016. (212) 696-9000; (800) 228-1160. 1990. Dictionary deals with the areas of colloids, surface chemistry, and the physics and technology involved with surfaces.

Encyclopedia of Chemical Processing and Design. John J. Mcketta and W. A. Cunningham. Marcel Dekker, Inc., 270 Madison Ave., New York, New York 10016. (212) 696-9000; (800) 228-1160. 1992. Thirty-eight volumes.

Encyclopedia of Human Biology. Renato Dulbecco, ed. Academic Press, c/o Harcourt Brace Jovanovich Inc., 6277 Sea Harbor Dr., Orlando, Florida 32887. (800) 346-8648. 1991. Eight volumes.

Encyclopedia of Physical Science and Technology. Robert A. Meyers, ed. Academic Press, c/o Harcourt Brace Jovanovich Inc., 6277 Sea Harbor Dr., Orlando, Florida 32887. (800) 346-8648. Dictionary of engineering, technology and physical sciences.

Encyclopedia of Physics. Rita G. Lerner and George L. Trigg. VCH Publishers, 303 NW 12th Ave., Deerfield Beach, Florida 33442-1788. (305) 428-5566. 1991. Second edition.

Kirk-Othmer Encyclopedia of Chemical Technology. J. I. Kroschwitz, ed. John Wiley & Sons, Inc., 605 3rd Ave., New York, New York 10158-0012. (212) 850-6000. 1992-. All articles in the new edition have been rewritten and updated adding new subjects such as biotechnology, computer topics, analytical techniques and instrumentation, environmental concerns, fuels and energy, inorganic and solid state chemistry; composite materials and material science in general, and pharmaceuticals. Also available online.

The New York Times Encyclopedic Dictionary of the Environment. Paul Sarnoff. Quadrangle Books, New York, New York 1971. Focuses on state-of-the-art methods of pollution control, abatement, prevention and removal.

Van Nostrand's Scientific Encyclopedia. Glenn D. Considine, ed. Van Nostrand Reinhold, 115 5th Ave., New York, New York 10003. (212) 254-3232. 1983. Sixth edition. Includes all broad subject areas in science.

GENERAL WORKS

Adsorption Studies Evaluating Codisposal of Coal Gasification Ash with PAH-Containing Wastewater Sludges. John William Kilmer. University of Illinois at Urbana-Champaign, Urbana, Illinois 61801. 1986.

Adsorption Technology for Air and Water Pollution Control. Kenneth E. Noll. Lewis Publishers, 200 Corporate Blvd. NW, Boca Raton, Florida 33431. (407) 994-0555 or (800)272-7737. 1991. Contains useful information on adsorption technology which can be applied in both air and water pollution.

Guidelines for Mastering the Properties of Molecular Sieves. Plenum Press, 233 Spring St., New York, New York 10013-1578. (212) 620-8000. Relationship between the physiochemical properties of zeolitic systems and their low dimensionality.

Influence and Removal of Organics in Drinking Water. Joel Mallevialle and Mel Suffet. Lewis Publishers, 2000 Corporate Blvd., N.W., Boca Raton, Florida 33431. (407) 994-0555 or (800) 272-7737. 1992. Includes fundamentals and applications of adsorption phenomena, different aspects of coagulation process, recent developments in oxidations and disinfection and new technologies.

Toxicity Reduction in Industrial Effluents. Perry W. Lanford, et al. Van Nostrand Reinhold, 115 5th Ave., New York, New York 10003. (212) 254-3232. 1990. Overview of aquatic toxicology and toxicity reduction. Specific treatment technologies that can be used to reduce toxicity, such as aerobic and anaerobic biological treatment, air and steam stripping of volatile organics, granulated carbon absorption, powdered activated carbon treatment and chemical oxidation, are discussed in detail.

Treatment Technologies. Environment Protection Agency. Government Institutes, Inc., 4 Research Pl., Ste. 200, Rockville, Maryland 20850. (301)921-2300. 1991. 2nd ed. Provides a clear explanation of 24 treatment technologies and evaluates the effectiveness of the design and operations of each type of treatment. This new edition has more supporting numerical data, examples for a better understanding of the technology and an updated reference for specific industrial wastes.

ONLINE DATA BASES

BIOSIS Previews. BIOSIS, 2100 Arch St., Philadelphia, Pennsylvania 19103-1399. (215) 587-4800. Largest and most comprehensive database of research in the life sciences. Contains citations for nearly 9000 primary research journals, monographs, reviews, symposia, preliminary reports, semi-popular journals, selected institutional reports, government reports and research communications.

CAS Source Index–CASSI. Chemical Abstracts Service, 2540 Olentangy River Rd., P.O. Box 3012, Columbus, Ohio 43210. (800) 848-6533 or (614) 421-3600. A listing of bibliographic and library holdings information for scientific and technical primary literature relevant to the chemical sciences.

Chemest. Technical Database Services, Inc., 10 Columbus Circle, New York, New York 10019. (212) 245-0044. Covers methods of estimating 11 important properties: water solubility, soil adsorption coefficient, bioconcentration factor, acid dissociation constant, activity coefficient, boiling point, vapor pressure, water volatilization rate, Henry's Law Constant, melting point, and liquid viscosity.

Chemical Abstracts-CA. Chemical Abstracts Service, 2540 Olentangy River Rd., P.O. Box 3012, Columbus, Ohio 43210. (800) 848-6533 or (614) 421-3600. Information sources include 9000 journals, patents from 27 countries, two industrial property organizations, new books, conference proceedings, and government research reports.

Enviro/Energyline Abstracts Plus. R. R. Bowker Co., 121 Chanlon Rd., New Providence, New Jersey 07974. (908) 464-6800.

Environmental Fate Databases. Syracuse Research Cooperation, Merrill Lane, Syracuse, New York 13210. (312) 426-3200. Environmental fate of chemicals.

Environmental Periodicals Bibliography. National Information Services Corp., Ste. 6, Wyman Towers, 3100 St. Paul St., Baltimore, Maryland 21218. (410)243-0797. Online version of abstract of same name.

Kirk-Othmer Encyclopedia of Chemical Technology. John Wiley & Sons, Inc., 605 3rd Ave., 5th Floor, New York, New York 10158. (212) 850-6000. Online version of the publication of the same name.

PERIODICALS AND NEWSLETTERS

Adsorption Science & Technology. Multi-Science Publishing Co. Ltd., 107 High St., Brentwood, Essex, England CM14 4RX. 0277-224632.

The Journal of Biological Chemistry. American Society of Biological Chemists, 428 E. Preston St., Baltimore, Maryland 21202. Three times a month. Biological, agricultural, and energy aspects of the environment.

RESEARCH CENTERS AND INSTITUTES

Michigan Technological University, Environmental Engineering Center for Water and Waste Management. 1400 Townsend Rd., Houghton, Michigan 49931. (906) 487-2194.

ADULTERATION
See: FOOD SCIENCE

AERATED LAGOONS
See: AERATION

AERATION
See also: SEWAGE TREATMENT; WASTEWATER TREATMENT

ABSTRACTING AND INDEXING SERVICES

Abstracts of Air and Water Conservation Literature. American Petroleum Institute. Central Abstracting and Indexing Service, 275 Madison Avenue, New York, New York 10016. 1972.

Applied Science and Technology Index. H.W. Wilson Co., 950 University Ave., Bronx, New York 10452. (800) 367-6770. Formerly Industrial Arts Index.

ASFA Aquaculture Abstracts. Cambridge Scientific Abstracts, Inc., 5161 River Rd., Bethesda, Maryland 20816. (301) 961-6750. 1984.

Biological Abstracts. BIOSIS, 2100 Arch St., Philadelphia, Pennsylvania 19103-1399. (215) 587-4800. 1927-.

Biological and Agricultural Index. H.W. Wilson Co., 950 University Ave., Bronx, New York 10452. (800) 367-6770. 1916-. Monthly.

Civil Engineering Hydraulic Abstracts. BHRA Fluid Engineering, Air Science Co., PO Box 143, Corning, New York 14830. (607) 962-5591. Monthly. Abstracts of periodicals that publish in the areas of hydraulic engineering and other related topics.

Ecological Abstracts. Geo Abstracts Ltd. Elsevier Applied Science, Crown House, Linton Rd., Barking, England IG 11 8JU. 1974-. Derived from over 600 leading ecological and environmental journals, plus books, conference proceedings, reports and theses.

Engineering Index. The Engineering Index Inc., 345 E. 47th St., New York, New York 10017. 1962-.

Environment Abstracts. Bowker A & I Publishing, 121 Chanlon Rd., New Providence, New Jersey 07974. (908) 464-6800. 1974-.

Environment Index. Environment Information Center, Index Research Department, 124 E. 39th St., New York, New York 10016. 1971-. Annual.

Environmental Information Connection–EIC. Planning Information Program, Dept. of Urban and Regional Planning, University of Illinois, 1003 West Nevada, Urbana, Illinois 61801. (217) 333-1369. Also available online.

Environmental Periodicals Bibliography. Environmental Studies Institute, International Academy at Santa Barbara, 800 Garden St., Suite D, Santa Barbara, California 93101. (805) 965-5010. Also available online.

Index to Scientific Book Contents. Institute for Scientific Information, 3501 Market St., Philadelphia, Pennsylvania 19104. (800) 523-1857. 1985-. Annual. Gives contents of science books published.

Pollution Abstracts. Cambridge Scientific Abstracts, 5161 River Rd., Bethesda, Maryland 20816. (301) 961-6750. Six/year. Indexes worldwide technical literature on environmental pollution. Covers air pollution, marine and freshwater pollution, sewage and wastewater treatment, waste management, toxicology and health, noise pollution, radiation, land pollution, and environmental policies, programs, legislation, and education. Also available online.

Science Citation Index. Institute for Scientific Information, 3501 Market St., Philadelphia, Pennsylvania 19104. 1961-.

BIBLIOGRAPHIES

Directory of Published Proceedings. Interdok Corp., 173 Halstead Ave., Harrison, New York 10528. (914) 835-3506. 1990. Monthly. This is a listing of published proceedings including the series SEMTE (Science/Medicine/Engineering/Technology) and the series SSH (Social Science/Humanities).

EPA Publications Bibliography. U.S. Environmental Protection Agency, Library Systems Branch, 401 M St., SW, Washington, District of Columbia 20460. (202) 260-2090. Quarterly.

ENCYCLOPEDIAS AND DICTIONARIES

Cambridge Encyclopedia of Life Sciences. A. E. Friday and David S. Ingram. Cambridge University Press, 40 W 20th St., New York, New York 10011. (212) 924-3900 or (800) 227-0247. 1985. Includes all topics under biology and ecology.

The Encyclopedia of Soil Science. Rhodes W. Fairbridge. Academic Press, c/o Harcourt Brace Jovanovich Inc., 6277 Sea Harbor Dr., Orlando, Florida 32887. (800) 346-8648. 1979-. Includes soil physics, soil chemistry, soil biology, soil fertility and plant nutrition, soil genesis, classification and cartography.

McGraw-Hill Encyclopedia of Environmental Science. Sybil P. Parker. McGraw-Hill Science & Engineering Books, 11 W. 19th St., New York, New York 10011. (212) 337-6010. 1980. Covers ecology, man's influence on nature, and environmental protection.

McGraw-Hill Encyclopedia of Science and Technology. McGraw-Hill, 1221 Avenue of the Americas, New York, New York 10020. (212) 512-2000 or (800) 262-4729. 1992. Seventh edition. Issued in multiple volumes including index. Includes all science and technology broad subject areas.

HANDBOOKS AND MANUALS

In-line Aeration and Treatment of Acid Mine Drainage. U.S. Department of the Interior, Bureau of Mines, 810 7th St. NW, Washington, District of Columbia 20241. (202) 501-9649. 1984. Water and oxidation methods.

ONLINE DATA BASES

BIOSIS Previews. BIOSIS, 2100 Arch St., Philadelphia, Pennsylvania 19103-1399. (215) 587-4800. Largest and

most comprehensive database of research in the life sciences. Contains citations for nearly 9000 primary research journals, monographs, reviews, symposia, preliminary reports, semi-popular journals, selected institutional reports, government reports and research communications.

Computerized Engineering Index–COMPENDEX. Engineering Information Inc., 345 E. 47th St., New York, New York 10017. (212) 705-7600.

Enviro/Energyline Abstracts Plus. R. R. Bowker Co., 121 Chanlon Rd., New Providence, New Jersey 07974. (908) 464-6800.

Environmental Periodicals Bibliography. National Information Services Corp., Ste. 6, Wyman Towers, 3100 St. Paul St., Baltimore, Maryland 21218. (410)243-0797. Online version of abstract of same name.

TRADE ASSOCIATIONS AND PROFESSIONAL SOCIETIES

American Institute of Chemical Engineers. 345 East 47th St., New York, New York 10017. (212) 705-7338.

American Institute of Chemists. 7315 Wisconsin Ave., Bethesda, Maryland 20814. (301) 652-2447.

AEROBIC RESPIRATION

See: RESPIRATION

AEROBIC SYSTEMS

ABSTRACTING AND INDEXING SERVICES

Abstracts of Air and Water Conservation Literature. American Petroleum Institute. Central Abstracting and Indexing Service, 275 Madison Avenue, New York, New York 10016. 1972.

Air Pollution Technical Publications of the United States Environmental Protection Agency. U.S. Environmental Protection Agency, Mail Drop 75, Research Triangle Park, North Carolina 27711. (919) 541-2184. 1976. Quarterly.

Applied Ecology Abstracts Studies in Renewable Natural Resources. Information Retrieval Ltd., 1911 Jefferson Davis Highway, Arlington, Virginia 22202. 1975-. Monthly.

Biological Abstracts. BIOSIS, 2100 Arch St., Philadelphia, Pennsylvania 19103-1399. (215) 587-4800. 1927-.

Biotechnology Research Abstracts. Cambridge Scientific Abstracts, 5161 River Rd., Bethesda, Maryland 20816. (301) 961-6750. Monthly. Includes such broad areas as genetic intervention, biochemical genetics, and microbiological techniques.

Ecological Abstracts. Geo Abstracts Ltd. Elsevier Applied Science, Crown House, Linton Rd., Barking, England IG 11 8JU. 1974-. Derived from over 600 leading ecological and environmental journals, plus books, conference proceedings, reports and theses.

Environment Abstracts. Bowker A & I Publishing, 121 Chanlon Rd., New Providence, New Jersey 07974. (908) 464-6800. 1974-.

Environment Index. Environment Information Center, Index Research Department, 124 E. 39th St., New York, New York 10016. 1971-. Annual.

Environmental Information Connection–EIC. Planning Information Program, Dept. of Urban and Regional Planning, University of Illinois, 1003 West Nevada, Urbana, Illinois 61801. (217) 333-1369. Also available online.

Environmental Periodicals Bibliography. Environmental Studies Institute, International Academy at Santa Barbara, 800 Garden St., Suite D, Santa Barbara, California 93101. (805) 965-5010. Also available online.

Multimedia Index to Ecology. National Information Center for Educational Media, University of Southern California, Los Angeles, California 90007.

Pollution Abstracts. Cambridge Scientific Abstracts, 5161 River Rd., Bethesda, Maryland 20816. (301) 961-6750. Six/year. Indexes worldwide technical literature on environmental pollution. Covers air pollution, marine and freshwater pollution, sewage and wastewater treatment, waste management, toxicology and health, noise pollution, radiation, land pollution, and environmental policies, programs, legislation, and education. Also available online.

Science Citation Index. Institute for Scientific Information, 3501 Market St., Philadelphia, Pennsylvania 19104. 1961-.

BIBLIOGRAPHIES

EPA Publications Bibliography. U.S. Environmental Protection Agency, Library Systems Branch, 401 M St., SW, Washington, District of Columbia 20460. (202) 260-2090. Quarterly.

ONLINE DATA BASES

BIOSIS Previews. BIOSIS, 2100 Arch St., Philadelphia, Pennsylvania 19103-1399. (215) 587-4800. Largest and most comprehensive database of research in the life sciences. Contains citations for nearly 9000 primary research journals, monographs, reviews, symposia, preliminary reports, semi-popular journals, selected institutional reports, government reports and research communications.

Enviro/Energyline Abstracts Plus. R. R. Bowker Co., 121 Chanlon Rd., New Providence, New Jersey 07974. (908) 464-6800.

Environmental Periodicals Bibliography. National Information Services Corp., Ste. 6, Wyman Towers, 3100 St. Paul St., Baltimore, Maryland 21218. (410)243-0797. Online version of abstract of same name.

TRADE ASSOCIATIONS AND PROFESSIONAL SOCIETIES

Anthracite Industry Association. 1275 K St., N.W., Suite 1000, Washington, District of Columbia 20005. (202) 289-3223.

National Coal Association. 1130 17th St., N.W., Washington, District of Columbia 20036. (202) 463-2625.

AEROSOL SIZE

See: AEROSOLS

AEROSOL SPRAY CANS

See also: CHLOROFLUOROCARBONS; OZONE LAYER

ABSTRACTING AND INDEXING SERVICES

Abstracts of Air and Water Conservation Literature. American Petroleum Institute. Central Abstracting and Indexing Service, 275 Madison Avenue, New York, New York 10016. 1972.

Applied Science and Technology Index. H.W. Wilson Co., 950 University Ave., Bronx, New York 10452. (800) 367-6770. Formerly Industrial Arts Index.

Ecological Abstracts. Geo Abstracts Ltd. Elsevier Applied Science, Crown House, Linton Rd., Barking, England IG 11 8JU. 1974-. Derived from over 600 leading ecological and environmental journals, plus books, conference proceedings, reports and theses.

Environment Abstracts. Bowker A & I Publishing, 121 Chanlon Rd., New Providence, New Jersey 07974. (908) 464-6800. 1974-.

Environment Index. Environment Information Center, Index Research Department, 124 E. 39th St., New York, New York 10016. 1971-. Annual.

Environmental Information Connection–EIC. Planning Information Program, Dept. of Urban and Regional Planning, University of Illinois, 1003 West Nevada, Urbana, Illinois 61801. (217) 333-1369. Also available online.

Environmental Periodicals Bibliography. Environmental Studies Institute, International Academy at Santa Barbara, 800 Garden St., Suite D, Santa Barbara, California 93101. (805) 965-5010. Also available online.

Science Citation Index. Institute for Scientific Information, 3501 Market St., Philadelphia, Pennsylvania 19104. 1961-.

BIBLIOGRAPHIES

EPA Publications Bibliography. U.S. Environmental Protection Agency, Library Systems Branch, 401 M St., SW, Washington, District of Columbia 20460. (202) 260-2090. Quarterly.

ONLINE DATA BASES

Enviro/Energyline Abstracts Plus. R. R. Bowker Co., 121 Chanlon Rd., New Providence, New Jersey 07974. (908) 464-6800.

Environmental Periodicals Bibliography. National Information Services Corp., Ste. 6, Wyman Towers, 3100 St. Paul St., Baltimore, Maryland 21218. (410)243-0797. Online version of abstract of same name.

PressNet Environmental Reports. Chemical Information Systems, Inc., 7215 York Rd., Baltimore, Maryland 21212. (301) 321-8440.

TRADE ASSOCIATIONS AND PROFESSIONAL SOCIETIES

American Institute of Chemical Engineers. 345 East 47th St., New York, New York 10017. (212) 705-7338.

American Institute of Chemists. 7315 Wisconsin Ave., Bethesda, Maryland 20814. (301) 652-2447.

AEROSOLS

See also: AIR POLLUTION

ABSTRACTING AND INDEXING SERVICES

Abstracts of Air and Water Conservation Literature. American Petroleum Institute. Central Abstracting and Indexing Service, 275 Madison Avenue, New York, New York 10016. 1972.

Air Pollution Titles. Pennsylvania State University, Center for Air Environmental Studies, 226 Fenske Laboratory, University Park, Pennsylvania 16802. (814) 865-1415. 1965. Bibliographic guide to current research literature on air environment, including monitoring and control of air pollution, health effects, effects on agriculture, forests, toxic air contaminants, and global atmospheric pro cases.

Air Pollution Translations. A Bibliography With Abstracts. U.S. Environmental Protection Agency, MD 75, Research Triangle Park, North Carolina 27711. (919) 541-2184. 1969.

Biological Abstracts. BIOSIS, 2100 Arch St., Philadelphia, Pennsylvania 19103-1399. (215) 587-4800. 1927-.

Biological and Agricultural Index. H.W. Wilson Co., 950 University Ave., Bronx, New York 10452. (800) 367-6770. 1916-. Monthly.

Bulletin Signaletique: Eau et Assainissement, Pollution Atmospherique, Droit des Pollutions. Centre de Documentation, Centre National de la Recherche Scientifique, 15, quai Anatole France, Paris, France 75700. (1) 45 55 92 25. 1983-. Monthly. Indexes pollution periodicals including water, atmospheric and related pollutions.

Chemical Abstracts. Chemical Abstracts Service, 2540 Olentangy River Rd., PO Box 3012, Columbus, Ohio 43210. (800) 848-6533. 1907-.

Engineering Index. The Engineering Index Inc., 345 E. 47th St., New York, New York 10017. 1962-.

Environment Abstracts. Bowker A & I Publishing, 121 Chanlon Rd., New Providence, New Jersey 07974. (908) 464-6800. 1974-.

Environment Index. Environment Information Center, Index Research Department, 124 E. 39th St., New York, New York 10016. 1971-. Annual.

Environmental Information Connection–EIC. Planning Information Program, Dept. of Urban and Regional Planning, University of Illinois, 1003 West Nevada, Urbana, Illinois 61801. (217) 333-1369. Also available online.

Environmental Periodicals Bibliography. Environmental Studies Institute, International Academy at Santa Barbara, 800 Garden St., Suite D, Santa Barbara, California 93101. (805) 965-5010. Also available online.

General Science Index. H. W. Wilson Co., 950 University Ave., Bronx, New York 10452. 1978-. Monthly, also issued in annual cumulation. Cumulative subject index to English language periodicals in the subject fields of astronomy, botany, chemistry, earth science, environment and conservation, food and nutrition, genetics, mathematics, medicine and health, microbiology, oceanography, physics, physiology and zoology.

Green Engineering: A Current Awareness Bulletin. Institution of Mechanical Engineers, 1 Birdcage Walk, Westminster, London, England SW1H 9JJ. 71973 1266/7. 1991. Monthly. Covers acid rain, aerosol technology, biotechnology chlorofluorocarbons, chemical and process engineering, environmental protection, energy conservation, energy generation, greenhouse effect, materials, pollution, recycling, waste disposal, and other environmental topics.

Physics Briefs. Physikalische Berichte. Physik Verlag, Pappapelallee 3, Postfach 101161, Weinheim, Germany D-6940. 1979-. Semimonthly. In English. Volumes for 1979- issued by the Deutsche Physikalische Gesellschaft and the Fachinformationszentrum Energie Physik, Mathematik in cooperation with the American Institute of Physics.

Pollution Abstracts. Cambridge Scientific Abstracts, 5161 River Rd., Bethesda, Maryland 20816. (301) 961-6750. Six/year. Indexes worldwide technical literature on environmental pollution. Covers air pollution, marine and freshwater pollution, sewage and wastewater treatment, waste management, toxicology and health, noise pollution, radiation, land pollution, and environmental policies, programs, legislation, and education. Also available online.

Science Citation Index. Institute for Scientific Information, 3501 Market St., Philadelphia, Pennsylvania 19104. 1961-.

BIBLIOGRAPHIES

Directory of Published Proceedings. Interdok Corp., 173 Halstead Ave., Harrison, New York 10528. (914) 835-3506. 1990. Monthly. This is a listing of published proceedings including the series SEMTE (Science/Medicine/Engineering/Technology) and the series SSH (Social Science/Humanities).

EPA Publications Bibliography. U.S. Environmental Protection Agency, Library Systems Branch, 401 M St., SW, Washington, District of Columbia 20460. (202) 260-2090. Quarterly.

DIRECTORIES

Aerosol Age–Buyer's Guide Issue. 389 Passaic Ave., Fairfield, New Jersey 07006. (201) 227-5151. Annual.

Gale Environmental Sourcebook. Karen Hill. Gale Research Co., 835 Penobscot Bldg., Detroit, Michigan 48226-4094. (313) 961-2242. Contacts, information sources, or general information on environmental topics.

ENCYCLOPEDIAS AND DICTIONARIES

A Dictionary of Air Pollution Terms. Air & Waste Management Association, P.O. Box 2861, Pittsburgh, Pennsylvania 15230. (412) 233-3444. 1989.

Dictionary of Microbiology and Molecular Biology. Paul Singleton and Diana Sainsbury. John Wiley & Sons, Inc., 605 3rd Ave., New York, New York 10158-0012. (212) 850-6000. 1987. Second edition. Comprehensive dictionary with "classical descriptive aspects of microbiology to current developments in related areas of bioenergetics, biochemistry and molecular biology." Entries give synonyms, cross references, and references to pertinent works. Miscellaneous appendixes. Bibliography.

Encyclopedia of Chemical Processing and Design. John J. Mcketta and W. A. Cunningham. Marcel Dekker, Inc., 270 Madison Ave., New York, New York 10016. (212) 696-9000; (800) 228-1160. 1992. Thirty-eight volumes.

The Encyclopedia of Climatology. John E. Oliver and Rhodes W. Fairbridge, eds. Van Nostrand Reinhold, 115 5th Ave., New York, New York 10003. (212) 254-3232. 1987. Belongs in the series Encyclopedia of Earth Sciences, v.11.

The Encyclopedia of Geochemistry and Environmental Sciences. Rhodes Whitmore Fairbridge. Van Nostrand Reinhold Co., 115 5th Ave., New York, New York 10003. (212) 254-3232. 1972.

Encyclopedia of Human Biology. Renato Dulbecco, ed. Academic Press, c/o Harcourt Brace Jovanovich Inc., 6277 Sea Harbor Dr., Orlando, Florida 32887. (800) 346-8648. 1991. Eight volumes.

Kirk-Othmer Encyclopedia of Chemical Technology. J. I. Kroschwitz, ed. John Wiley & Sons, Inc., 605 3rd Ave., New York, New York 10158-0012. (212) 850-6000. 1992-. All articles in the new edition have been rewritten and updated adding new subjects such as biotechnology, computer topics, analytical techniques and instrumentation, environmental concerns, fuels and energy, inorganic and solid state chemistry; composite materials and material science in general, and pharmaceuticals. Also available online.

McGraw-Hill Encyclopedia of Environmental Science. Sybil P. Parker. McGraw-Hill Science & Engineering Books, 11 W. 19th St., New York, New York 10011. (212) 337-6010. 1980. Covers ecology, man's influence on nature, and environmental protection.

McGraw-Hill Encyclopedia of Science and Technology. McGraw-Hill, 1221 Avenue of the Americas, New York, New York 10020. (212) 512-2000 or (800) 262-4729. 1992. Seventh edition. Issued in multiple volumes including index. Includes all science and technology broad subject areas.

GENERAL WORKS

Aerosol Sampling: Science and Practice. J. H. Vincent. John Wiley & Sons, Inc., 605 3rd Ave., New York, New York 10158-0012. (212) 850-6000. 1989. Details the sampling of aerosols with a "real world" approach. Makes the connection between theory and practice.

Air Monitoring for Toxic Exposure. Shirley A. Ness. Van Nostrand Reinhold, 115 5th Ave., New York, New York 10003. (212) 354-3232. 1991. Explains the procedures for evaluating potentially harmful exposure to people from hazardous materials including chemicals, radon and bioaerosols. Presents practical information on how to perform air sampling, collect biological and bulk samples, evaluate dermal exposures, and determine the advantages and limitations of a given method.

Effects of Aerosols and Surface Shadowing on Bidirectional Reflectance Measurements of Deserts Microform. David E. Bowker. National Aeronautics and Space Administration, Scientific and Technical Information Office, 5285 Port Royal Rd., Springfield, Virginia 22161. (703) 487-4805. 1987. NASA technical paper; #2756.

Indoor Air Pollution: Radon, Bioaerosols, and VOCs. Jack G. Kay, et al. Lewis Publishers, 2000 Corporate Blvd., N.W., Boca Raton, Florida 33431. (407) 994-0555 or (800) 272-7737. 1991. Consists of two parts: Overview of the ACS Symposium on Indoor Air Pollution, and Radon overview

Radioactive Aerosols. A. C. Chamberlin. Cambridge University Press, 40 W 20th St., New York, New York 10011. (212) 924-3900; (800) 227-0247. 1991. Describes radioactive gases and particles which are dispersed in the environment, either from natural causes or following nuclear test and accidental emissions.

HANDBOOKS AND MANUALS

Aerosol Science. Pergamon Microforms International, Inc., Fairview Park, Elmsford, New York 10523. (914) 592-7720. 1991. Radioactive pollution of the atmosphere, nuclear reactor accidents and radioactive aerosols.

Handbook on Aerosols. National Defense Research Committee. Atomic Energy Commission, Washington, District of Columbia 20555. (301) 492-7000. 1950.

ONLINE DATA BASES

BIOSIS Previews. BIOSIS, 2100 Arch St., Philadelphia, Pennsylvania 19103-1399. (215) 587-4800. Largest and most comprehensive database of research in the life sciences. Contains citations for nearly 9000 primary research journals, monographs, reviews, symposia, preliminary reports, semi-popular journals, selected institutional reports, government reports and research communications.

Chemical Abstracts-CA. Chemical Abstracts Service, 2540 Olentangy River Rd., P.O. Box 3012, Columbus, Ohio 43210. (800) 848-6533 or (614) 421-3600. Information sources include 9000 journals, patents from 27 countries, two industrial property organizations, new books, conference proceedings, and government research reports.

Computerized Engineering Index–COMPENDEX. Engineering Information Inc., 345 E. 47th St., New York, New York 10017. (212) 705-7600.

Enviro/Energyline Abstracts Plus. R. R. Bowker Co., 121 Chanlon Rd., New Providence, New Jersey 07974. (908) 464-6800.

Environmental Periodicals Bibliography. National Information Services Corp., Ste. 6, Wyman Towers, 3100 St. Paul St., Baltimore, Maryland 21218. (410)243-0797. Online version of abstract of same name.

Kirk-Othmer Encyclopedia of Chemical Technology. John Wiley & Sons, Inc., 605 3rd Ave., 5th Floor, New York, New York 10158. (212) 850-6000. Online version of the publication of the same name.

PressNet Environmental Reports. Chemical Information Systems, Inc., 7215 York Rd., Baltimore, Maryland 21212. (301) 321-8440.

PERIODICALS AND NEWSLETTERS

Aerosol Review. Grampion Press, London, England Annual.

Aerosol Science and Technology. Elsevier Science Publishing Co., 655 Avenue of the Americas, New York, New York 10010. (212) 989-5800. 1982-. Bimonthly. Journal of American Association for Aerosol Research dealing with aerosol filtration and effects on climate, etc.

Annual Report of the Inhalation Toxicology Research Institute. Inhalation Toxicology Research Institute. Lovelace Biomedical and Environmental Research Institute, 5285 Port Royal Rd., Springfield, Virginia 22161. (703) 487-4650. 1972/73-. Annual. Deals with aerosols, poisonous gases and radioactive substances. Describes the impact on inhalation of these hazardous substances.

Water, Air, and Soil Pollution. Kluwer Academic Publishers, 101 Philip Dr., Assinippi Park, Norwell, Massachusetts 02061. (617) 871-6600. Bimonthly. Covers water, soil, and air pollution. This is an international journal on environmental pollution dealing with all types of pollution including acid rain.

RESEARCH CENTERS AND INSTITUTES

Air Pollution Research Laboratory. University of Florida, 408 Black Hall, Gainsville, Florida 32611. (904) 392-0845.

STATISTICS SOURCES

Acid Aerosols Issue Paper: Health Effects and Aerometrics. U.S. Environmental Protection Agency. U.S. G.P.O., Washington, District of Columbia 20401. (202) 512-0000. 1989. Data from 1930 to present on airborne compounds resulting from fossil fuel burning.

Aerosols. FIND/SVP, 625 Avenue of the Americas, New York, New York 10011. (212) 645-4500. 1990.

Environmental Data Compendium. OECD Publications and Information Center, 2001 L St., N.W., Suite 700, Washington, District of Columbia 20036. (202) 785-6323. 1989.

Environmental Indicators. OECD Publications and Information Center, 2001 L St., N.W., Suite 700, Washington, District of Columbia 20036. (202) 785-6323. 1991.

Environmental Quality. Council on Environmental Quality. U.S. G.P.O., Washington, District of Columbia 20401. (202) 512-0000. Annual.

The State of the Environment. OECD Publications and Information Center, 2001 L St., N.W., Suite 700, Washington, District of Columbia 20036. (202) 785-6323. 1991.

TRADE ASSOCIATIONS AND PROFESSIONAL SOCIETIES

American Association for Aerosol Research. 4330 East West Hwy., Ste. 1117, Bethesda, Maryland 20814. (301) 718-6508.

American Association for Aerosol Research Indoor Environment Program. Lawrence Berkeley Library, 1 Cyclotron Rd., Berkeley, California 94720. (919) 541-6736. Prog. 90-3058

American Institute of Chemical Engineers. 345 East 47th St., New York, New York 10017. (212) 705-7338.

American Institute of Chemists. 7315 Wisconsin Ave., Bethesda, Maryland 20814. (301) 652-2447.

Industrial Chemical Research Association. 1811 Monroe St., Dearborn, Michigan 48124. (313) 563-0360.

National Aerosol Association. 584 Bellerive Dr., Suite 3D, Annapolis, Maryland 21401. (301) 974-4472.

AFFORESTATION

See also: FOREST MANAGEMENT; LAND USE

ABSTRACTING AND INDEXING SERVICES

Applied Ecology Abstracts Studies in Renewable Natural Resources. Information Retrieval Ltd., 1911 Jefferson Davis Highway, Arlington, Virginia 22202. 1975-. Monthly.

Biological Abstracts. BIOSIS, 2100 Arch St., Philadelphia, Pennsylvania 19103-1399. (215) 587-4800. 1927-.

Ecological Abstracts. Geo Abstracts Ltd. Elsevier Applied Science, Crown House, Linton Rd., Barking, England IG 11 8JU. 1974-. Derived from over 600 leading ecological and environmental journals, plus books, conference proceedings, reports and theses.

Environment Abstracts. Bowker A & I Publishing, 121 Chanlon Rd., New Providence, New Jersey 07974. (908) 464-6800. 1974-.

Environment Index. Environment Information Center, Index Research Department, 124 E. 39th St., New York, New York 10016. 1971-. Annual.

Environmental Information Connection–EIC. Planning Information Program, Dept. of Urban and Regional Planning, University of Illinois, 1003 West Nevada, Urbana, Illinois 61801. (217) 333-1369. Also available online.

Environmental Periodicals Bibliography. Environmental Studies Institute, International Academy at Santa Barbara, 800 Garden St., Suite D, Santa Barbara, California 93101. (805) 965-5010. Also available online.

General Science Index. H. W. Wilson Co., 950 University Ave., Bronx, New York 10452. 1978-. Monthly, also issued in annual cumulation. Cumulative subject index to English language periodicals in the subject fields of astronomy, botany, chemistry, earth science, environment and conservation, food and nutrition, genetics, mathematics, medicine and health, microbiology, oceanography, physics, physiology and zoology.

Multimedia Index to Ecology. National Information Center for Educational Media, University of Southern California, Los Angeles, California 90007.

Science Citation Index. Institute for Scientific Information, 3501 Market St., Philadelphia, Pennsylvania 19104. 1961-.

BIBLIOGRAPHIES

EPA Publications Bibliography. U.S. Environmental Protection Agency, Library Systems Branch, 401 M St., SW, Washington, District of Columbia 20460. (202) 260-2090. Quarterly.

ENCYCLOPEDIAS AND DICTIONARIES

McGraw-Hill Encyclopedia of Environmental Science. Sybil P. Parker. McGraw-Hill Science & Engineering Books, 11 W. 19th St., New York, New York 10011. (212) 337-6010. 1980. Covers ecology, man's influence on nature, and environmental protection.

ONLINE DATA BASES

BIOSIS Previews. BIOSIS, 2100 Arch St., Philadelphia, Pennsylvania 19103-1399. (215) 587-4800. Largest and most comprehensive database of research in the life sciences. Contains citations for nearly 9000 primary research journals, monographs, reviews, symposia, preliminary reports, semi-popular journals, selected institutional reports, government reports and research communications.

CRIS/USDA. U.S. Department of Agriculture, Cooperative State Research Service, Current Research Information System, National Agricultural Library Building, 5th Fl., 10301 Baltimore Blvd., Beltsville, Maryland 20705. (301) 344-3850. Agricultural, food and nutrition, and forestry research projects.

Enviro/Energyline Abstracts Plus. R. R. Bowker Co., 121 Chanlon Rd., New Providence, New Jersey 07974. (908) 464-6800.

Environmental Periodicals Bibliography. National Information Services Corp., Ste. 6, Wyman Towers, 3100 St. Paul St., Baltimore, Maryland 21218. (410)243-0797. Online version of abstract of same name.

STATISTICS SOURCES

U.S. Forest Planting Report. U.S. Department of Agriculture, Forest Service, 14 Independence Ave. SW, Washington, District of Columbia 20250. (202) 447-7454. Annual. Covers afforestation, strip mining and reclamation of land in the United States.

AFLATIONS

ABSTRACTING AND INDEXING SERVICES

Biological Abstracts. BIOSIS, 2100 Arch St., Philadelphia, Pennsylvania 19103-1399. (215) 587-4800. 1927-.

Science Citation Index. Institute for Scientific Information, 3501 Market St., Philadelphia, Pennsylvania 19104. 1961-.

ENCYCLOPEDIAS AND DICTIONARIES

McGraw-Hill Encyclopedia of Science and Technology. McGraw-Hill, 1221 Avenue of the Americas, New York, New York 10020. (212) 512-2000 or (800) 262-4729. 1992. Seventh edition. Issued in multiple volumes including index. Includes all science and technology broad subject areas.

ONLINE DATA BASES

BIOSIS Previews. BIOSIS, 2100 Arch St., Philadelphia, Pennsylvania 19103-1399. (215) 587-4800. Largest and most comprehensive database of research in the life sciences. Contains citations for nearly 9000 primary research journals, monographs, reviews, symposia, preliminary reports, semi-popular journals, selected institutional reports, government reports and research communications.

AFLOTOXINS

ABSTRACTING AND INDEXING SERVICES

Abstracts of Air and Water Conservation Literature. American Petroleum Institute. Central Abstracting and Indexing Service, 275 Madison Avenue, New York, New York 10016. 1972.

Biological Abstracts. BIOSIS, 2100 Arch St., Philadelphia, Pennsylvania 19103-1399. (215) 587-4800. 1927-.

Chemical Abstracts. Chemical Abstracts Service, 2540 Olentangy River Rd., PO Box 3012, Columbus, Ohio 43210. (800) 848-6533. 1907-.

Food Science and Technology Abstracts. International Food Information Service, c/o National Food Laboratory, 6363 Clark Ave., Dublin, California 94568. (800) 336-3782. 1969-.

Science Citation Index. Institute for Scientific Information, 3501 Market St., Philadelphia, Pennsylvania 19104. 1961-.

Selected Abstracts on Aflatoxins and other Mycotoxins Carcinogenesis. U.S. Dept. of Health Education and Welfare. National Technical Information Service, 5285 Port Royal Rd., Springfield, Virginia 22161. (703) 487-4650. 1978. Prepared for the ICRDB Program by the Cancer Information Dissemination and Analysis Center for Carcinogenesis Information.

BIBLIOGRAPHIES

Aflatoxin Contamination. Rebecca Thompson. U.S. Department of Agriculture, National Agriculture Library, 10301 Baltimore Blvd., Beltsville, Maryland 20705-2351. (301) 504-5755. 1989.

ENCYCLOPEDIAS AND DICTIONARIES

Dictionary of Microbiology and Molecular Biology. Paul Singleton and Diana Sainsbury. John Wiley & Sons, Inc., 605 3rd Ave., New York, New York 10158-0012. (212) 850-6000. 1987. Second edition. Comprehensive dictionary with "classical descriptive aspects of microbiology to current developments in related areas of bioenergetics, biochemistry and molecular biology." Entries give synonyms, cross references, and references to pertinent works. Miscellaneous appendixes. Bibliography.

Encyclopedia of Human Biology. Renato Dulbecco, ed. Academic Press, c/o Harcourt Brace Jovanovich Inc., 6277 Sea Harbor Dr., Orlando, Florida 32887. (800) 346-8648. 1991. Eight volumes.

GENERAL WORKS

Aflatoxins: Chemical and Biological Aspects. John Godfrey Heathcote and J. R. Hibbert. Elsevier Science Publishing Co., 655 Avenue of the Americas, New York, New York 10010. (212) 989-5800. 1978. Discusses the properties of aflatoxins, their toxicology and physiological effects.

Microbial Toxins in Focus and Feeds. Albert E. Pohland, et al., eds. Plenum Press, 233 Spring St., New York, New York 10013. (212) 620-8000; (800) 221-9369. 1990. Proceedings of a Symposium on Cellular and Molecular Mode of Action of Selected Microbial Toxins in Foods and Feeds, Oct. 31- Nov. 2, 1988, Chevy Chase, MD.

HANDBOOKS AND MANUALS

Handbook of Toxic Fungal Metabolites. Richard J. Cole and Richard H. Cox. Academic Press, c/o Harcourt Brace Jovanovich Inc., 6277 Sea Harbor Dr., Orlando, Florida 32887. (800) 346-8648. Oriented toward fungal metabolites that elicit a toxic response in vertebrate animals. Also includes metabolites that show little or no known acute toxicity.

ONLINE DATA BASES

BIOSIS Previews. BIOSIS, 2100 Arch St., Philadelphia, Pennsylvania 19103-1399. (215) 587-4800. Largest and most comprehensive database of research in the life sciences. Contains citations for nearly 9000 primary research journals, monographs, reviews, symposia, preliminary reports, semi-popular journals, selected institutional reports, government reports and research communications.

Chemical Abstracts-CA. Chemical Abstracts Service, 2540 Olentangy River Rd., P.O. Box 3012, Columbus, Ohio 43210. (800) 848-6533 or (614) 421-3600. Information sources include 9000 journals, patents from 27 countries, two industrial property organizations, new books, conference proceedings, and government research reports.

Chemical Carcinogenesis Research Information System–CCRIS. National Library of Medicine, 8600 Rockville Pike, Bethesda, Maryland 20894. (800) 638-8480. Individual assay results and test conditions for 1,451 chemicals in the areas of carcinogenicity, mutagenicity, tumor promotion, and cocarcinogenicity.

AFTERBURNER
See: POLLUTION CONTROL

AGENT ORANGE
See also: DIOXIN

ABSTRACTING AND INDEXING SERVICES

Abstracts of Air and Water Conservation Literature. American Petroleum Institute. Central Abstracting and Indexing Service, 275 Madison Avenue, New York, New York 10016. 1972.

Air Pollution Technical Publications of the United States Environmental Protection Agency. U.S. Environmental Protection Agency, Mail Drop 75, Research Triangle Park, North Carolina 27711. (919) 541-2184. 1976. Quarterly.

Applied Ecology Abstracts Studies in Renewable Natural Resources. Information Retrieval Ltd., 1911 Jefferson

Davis Highway, Arlington, Virginia 22202. 1975-. Monthly.

Biological Abstracts. BIOSIS, 2100 Arch St., Philadelphia, Pennsylvania 19103-1399. (215) 587-4800. 1927-.

Biological and Agricultural Index. H.W. Wilson Co., 950 University Ave., Bronx, New York 10452. (800) 367-6770. 1916-. Monthly.

Bulletin Signaletique: Eau et Assainissement, Pollution Atmospherique, Droit des Pollutions. Centre de Documentation, Centre National de la Recherche Scientifique, 15, quai Anatole France, Paris, France 75700. (1) 45 55 92 25. 1983-. Monthly. Indexes pollution periodicals including water, atmospheric and related pollutions.

Ecological Abstracts. Geo Abstracts Ltd. Elsevier Applied Science, Crown House, Linton Rd., Barking, England IG 11 8JU. 1974-. Derived from over 600 leading ecological and environmental journals, plus books, conference proceedings, reports and theses.

Environment Abstracts. Bowker A & I Publishing, 121 Chanlon Rd., New Providence, New Jersey 07974. (908) 464-6800. 1974-.

Environment Index. Environment Information Center, Index Research Department, 124 E. 39th St., New York, New York 10016. 1971-. Annual.

Environmental Information Connection–EIC. Planning Information Program, Dept. of Urban and Regional Planning, University of Illinois, 1003 West Nevada, Urbana, Illinois 61801. (217) 333-1369. Also available online.

Environmental Periodicals Bibliography. Environmental Studies Institute, International Academy at Santa Barbara, 800 Garden St., Suite D, Santa Barbara, California 93101. (805) 965-5010. Also available online.

General Science Index. H. W. Wilson Co., 950 University Ave., Bronx, New York 10452. 1978-. Monthly, also issued in annual cumulation. Cumulative subject index to English language periodicals in the subject fields of astronomy, botany, chemistry, earth science, environment and conservation, food and nutrition, genetics, mathematics, medicine and health, microbiology, oceanography, physics, physiology and zoology.

Index to Scientific Book Contents. Institute for Scientific Information, 3501 Market St., Philadelphia, Pennsylvania 19104. (800) 523-1857. 1985-. Annual. Gives contents of science books published.

Multimedia Index to Ecology. National Information Center for Educational Media, University of Southern California, Los Angeles, California 90007.

Pollution Abstracts. Cambridge Scientific Abstracts, 5161 River Rd., Bethesda, Maryland 20816. (301) 961-6750. Six/year. Indexes worldwide technical literature on environmental pollution. Covers air pollution, marine and freshwater pollution, sewage and wastewater treatment, waste management, toxicology and health, noise pollution, radiation, land pollution, and environmental policies, programs, legislation, and education. Also available online.

Science Citation Index. Institute for Scientific Information, 3501 Market St., Philadelphia, Pennsylvania 19104. 1961-.

BIBLIOGRAPHIES

Agent Orange and Vietnam: An Annotated Bibliography. Scarecrow Press, 52 Liberty St., Metuchen, New Jersey 08840. (908) 548-8600. Ethical and political aspects of man's relationship to the environment.

Agent Orange Dioxin, TCDD. Trellis C. Wright. Library of Congress, Science and Technology Division, Reference Section, Washington, District of Columbia 20540. (202) 738-3238. 1979.

Current Contents. Agriculture, Biology and Environmental Sciences. Institute for Scientific Information, 3501 Market St., Philadelphia, Pennsylvania 19104. (800) 523-1857. 1973-. Previous title: Current Contents. Agricultural, Food & Veterinary Sciences. Gives the table of contents of periodicals in the fields of agriculture, biology, environmental and related areas.

EPA Publications Bibliography. U.S. Environmental Protection Agency, Library Systems Branch, 401 M St., SW, Washington, District of Columbia 20460. (202) 260-2090. Quarterly.

ENCYCLOPEDIAS AND DICTIONARIES

Grzimek's Encyclopedia of Ecology. Bernhard Grzimek. Van Nostrand Reinhold, 115 5th Ave., New York, New York 10003. (212) 254-3232. 1976.

McGraw-Hill Encyclopedia of Environmental Science. Sybil P. Parker. McGraw-Hill Science & Engineering Books, 11 W. 19th St., New York, New York 10011. (212) 337-6010. 1980. Covers ecology, man's influence on nature, and environmental protection.

McGraw-Hill Encyclopedia of Science and Technology. McGraw-Hill, 1221 Avenue of the Americas, New York, New York 10020. (212) 512-2000 or (800) 262-4729. 1992. Seventh edition. Issued in multiple volumes including index. Includes all science and technology broad subject areas.

North American Reference Encyclopedia of Ecology and Pollution. William White. North American Pub. Co., 401 N. Broad St., Philadelphia, Pennsylvania 19108. (215) 238-5300. 1972.

Van Nostrand's Scientific Encyclopedia. Glenn D. Considine, ed. Van Nostrand Reinhold, 115 5th Ave., New York, New York 10003. (212) 254-3232. 1983. Sixth edition. Includes all broad subject areas in science.

ONLINE DATA BASES

BIOSIS Previews. BIOSIS, 2100 Arch St., Philadelphia, Pennsylvania 19103-1399. (215) 587-4800. Largest and most comprehensive database of research in the life sciences. Contains citations for nearly 9000 primary research journals, monographs, reviews, symposia, preliminary reports, semi-popular journals, selected institutional reports, government reports and research communications.

CAS Source Index–CASSI. Chemical Abstracts Service, 2540 Olentangy River Rd., P.O. Box 3012, Columbus, Ohio 43210. (800) 848-6533 or (614) 421-3600. A listing of bibliographic and library holdings information for scientific and technical primary literature relevant to the chemical sciences.

CERCLIS. Chemical Information Systems, Inc., 7215 York Rd., Baltimore, Maryland 21212. (301) 321-8440. Information on hazardous waste disposal sites that have either been listed by the EPA on the National Priority List (NPL) or nominated for consideration for the NPL.

Chemical Carcinogenesis Research Information System–CCRIS. National Library of Medicine, 8600 Rockville Pike, Bethesda, Maryland 20894. (800) 638-8480. Individual assay results and test conditions for 1,451 chemicals in the areas of carcinogenicity, mutagenicity, tumor promotion, and cocarcinogenicity.

Enviro/Energyline Abstracts Plus. R. R. Bowker Co., 121 Chanlon Rd., New Providence, New Jersey 07974. (908) 464-6800.

Environmental Periodicals Bibliography. National Information Services Corp., Ste. 6, Wyman Towers, 3100 St. Paul St., Baltimore, Maryland 21218. (410)243-0797. Online version of abstract of same name.

Monthly Catalog of United States Government Publications. U.S. G.P.O., Supt. of Docs., PO Box 371954, Pittsburgh, Pennsylvania 15250-7954. (202) 512-0000.

National Technical Information Service. U.S. Department of Commerce, National Technical Information Service, Office of Data Base Services, 5285 Port Royal Rd., Springfield, Virginia 22161. (703) 487-4807. Bibliographic database of government sponsored research and technical reports.

PERIODICALS AND NEWSLETTERS

Agent Orange Review: Information for Veterans Who Served in Vietnam. Veterans Administration, Washington, District of Columbia Quarterly. Medical care of veterans related to Agent Orange.

AGRIBUSINESS
See: AGRONOMICS AND AGRIBUSINESS

AGRICULTURAL CHEMICALS
See also: AGRICULTURE; FERTILIZERS; PESTICIDES

ABSTRACTING AND INDEXING SERVICES

Abstracts of Air and Water Conservation Literature. American Petroleum Institute. Central Abstracting and Indexing Service, 275 Madison Avenue, New York, New York 10016. 1972.

Applied Ecology Abstracts Studies in Renewable Natural Resources. Information Retrieval Ltd., 1911 Jefferson Davis Highway, Arlington, Virginia 22202. 1975-. Monthly.

Biological Abstracts. BIOSIS, 2100 Arch St., Philadelphia, Pennsylvania 19103-1399. (215) 587-4800. 1927-.

Biological and Agricultural Index. H.W. Wilson Co., 950 University Ave., Bronx, New York 10452. (800) 367-6770. 1916-. Monthly.

Bulletin Signaletique: Eau et Assainissement, Pollution Atmospherique, Droit des Pollutions. Centre de Documentation, Centre National de la Recherche Scientifique, 15, quai Anatole France, Paris, France 75700. (1) 45 55 92 25. 1983-. Monthly. Indexes pollution periodicals including water, atmospheric and related pollutions.

Chemical Abstracts. Chemical Abstracts Service, 2540 Olentangy River Rd., PO Box 3012, Columbus, Ohio 43210. (800) 848-6533. 1907-.

Ecological Abstracts. Geo Abstracts Ltd. Elsevier Applied Science, Crown House, Linton Rd., Barking, England IG 11 8JU. 1974-. Derived from over 600 leading ecological and environmental journals, plus books, conference proceedings, reports and theses.

Environment Abstracts. Bowker A & I Publishing, 121 Chanlon Rd., New Providence, New Jersey 07974. (908) 464-6800. 1974-.

Environment Index. Environment Information Center, Index Research Department, 124 E. 39th St., New York, New York 10016. 1971-. Annual.

Environmental Information Connection–EIC. Planning Information Program, Dept. of Urban and Regional Planning, University of Illinois, 1003 West Nevada, Urbana, Illinois 61801. (217) 333-1369. Also available online.

Environmental Periodicals Bibliography. Environmental Studies Institute, International Academy at Santa Barbara, 800 Garden St., Suite D, Santa Barbara, California 93101. (805) 965-5010. Also available online.

General Science Index. H. W. Wilson Co., 950 University Ave., Bronx, New York 10452. 1978-. Monthly, also issued in annual cumulation. Cumulative subject index to English language periodicals in the subject fields of astronomy, botany, chemistry, earth science, environment and conservation, food and nutrition, genetics, mathematics, medicine and health, microbiology, oceanography, physics, physiology and zoology.

Geographical Abstracts. London School of Economics, Dept. of Geography, Regency House, 34 Duke St., London, England 1966-. Continued by Geo Abstracts issued in 6 parts: Pt. A. Landforms and the quaternary; Pt. B. Biogeography and Climatology; Pt. C. Economic geography; Pt. D. Social geography and cartography; Pt. E. Sedimentology; Pt. F. Regional and community planning.

Index to Scientific Book Contents. Institute for Scientific Information, 3501 Market St., Philadelphia, Pennsylvania 19104. (800) 523-1857. 1985-. Annual. Gives contents of science books published.

Multimedia Index to Ecology. National Information Center for Educational Media, University of Southern California, Los Angeles, California 90007.

Pesticide Index. H. Kidd and D. Hartley, eds. Royal Society of Chemistry, c/o CRC Press, 2000 Corporate Blvd. N.W., Boca Raton, Florida 33431-9868. (800) 272-7737. 1988. A quick guide to chemical, common and trade names of pesticides and related crop-protection products world-wide. About 800 active-ingredients are included with about 25,000 trade names of pesticides containing these ingredients.

Pesticides Abstracts. U.S. Environmental Protection Agency, Office of Pesticides Programs, 345 Curtland, Atlanta, Georgia 30365. (404) 347-2864. 1981. Monthly.

Formerly: Health Aspects of Pesticides Abstracts Bulletin.

Science Citation Index. Institute for Scientific Information, 3501 Market St., Philadelphia, Pennsylvania 19104. 1961-.

BIBLIOGRAPHIES

Annotated Bibliography of Literature on Flue Gas Conditioning. U.S. Environmental Protection Agency, Division of Stationary Source Enforcement. U.S. Environmental Protection Agency, 401 M St., SW, Washington, District of Columbia (202) 260-2090. 1981. Covers flue gases and fly ash.

Current Contents. Agriculture, Biology and Environmental Sciences. Institute for Scientific Information, 3501 Market St., Philadelphia, Pennsylvania 19104. (800) 523-1857. 1973-. Previous title: Current Contents. Agricultural, Food & Veterinary Sciences. Gives the table of contents of periodicals in the fields of agriculture, biology, environmental and related areas.

Directory of Published Proceedings. Interdok Corp., 173 Halstead Ave., Harrison, New York 10528. (914) 835-3506. 1990. Monthly. This is a listing of published proceedings including the series SEMTE (Science/Medicine/Engineering/Technology) and the series SSH (Social Science/Humanities).

EPA Publications Bibliography. U.S. Environmental Protection Agency, Library Systems Branch, 401 M St., SW, Washington, District of Columbia 20460. (202) 260-2090. Quarterly.

DIRECTORIES

European Directory of Agrochemical Products. H. Kidd and D. James, eds. Royal Society of Chemistry, c/o CRC Press, 2000 Corporate Blvd. N.W., Boca Raton, Florida 33431-9868. (800) 272-7737. 1990. Provides comprehensive information on over 26,000 agrochemical products currently manufactured, marketed or used in 25 European countries.

Gale Environmental Sourcebook. Karen Hill. Gale Research Co., 835 Penobscot Bldg., Detroit, Michigan 48226-4094. (313) 961-2242. Contacts, information sources, or general information on environmental topics.

ENCYCLOPEDIAS AND DICTIONARIES

Dictionary of Environmental Engineering and Related Sciences: English-Spanish, Spanish-English. Jose T. Villate. Ediciones Universal, 3090 SW 8th St., Miami, Florida 33135. (305) 642-3355. 1979.

Encyclopedia of Environmental Science and Engineering. J.R. Pfafflin. Gordon and Breach Science Publishers, Inc., 270 8th Ave., New York, New York 10011. (212) 206-8900. 1992.

Encyclopedia of Physical Science and Technology. Robert A. Meyers, ed. Academic Press, c/o Harcourt Brace Jovanovich Inc., 6277 Sea Harbor Dr., Orlando, Florida 32887. (800) 346-8648. Dictionary of engineering, technology and physical sciences.

Grzimek's Encyclopedia of Ecology. Bernhard Grzimek. Van Nostrand Reinhold, 115 5th Ave., New York, New York 10003. (212) 254-3232. 1976.

McGraw-Hill Encyclopedia of Science and Technology. McGraw-Hill, 1221 Avenue of the Americas, New York, New York 10020. (212) 512-2000 or (800) 262-4729. 1992. Seventh edition. Issued in multiple volumes including index. Includes all science and technology broad subject areas.

North American Reference Encyclopedia of Ecology and Pollution. William White. North American Pub. Co., 401 N. Broad St., Philadelphia, Pennsylvania 19108. (215) 238-5300. 1972.

Van Nostrand's Scientific Encyclopedia. Glenn D. Considine, ed. Van Nostrand Reinhold, 115 5th Ave., New York, New York 10003. (212) 254-3232. 1983. Sixth edition. Includes all broad subject areas in science.

GENERAL WORKS

Beneath the Bottom Line: Agricultural Approaches to Reduce Agrichemical Contamination of Groundwater. Office of Technology Assessment, U.S. Congress, Washington, District of Columbia 20510-8025. (202) 224-8996. 1991. Identifies ways to minimize contamination of ground water by agricultural chemicals.

Chemical Concepts in Pollutant Behavior. Ian J. Tinsley. John Wiley & Sons, Inc., 605 3rd Ave., New York, New York 10158-0012. (212) 850-6000. 1979.

Chemistry, Agriculture and the Environment. Mervyn L. Richardson. Royal Society of Chemistry, Thomas Graham House, Science Park, Milton Rd., Cambridge, England CB4 4WF. 44(0)223420066. 1991. Provides an overview of the chemical pollution of the environment caused by modern agricultural practices worldwide, and describes the effects of agrochemicals used in intensive animal and crop production on the air, water, soil, plants, and animals including humans. Also available through CRC Press.

Crop Protection Chemicals. B. G. Lever. E. Horwood, 1230 Avenue of the Americas, New York, New York 10020. (212) 698-7000; (800) 223-2348. 1990. Overview of crop protection technology. Traces the evolution of pest control as an integral part of crop production. Focuses on the requirements of governments and society regarding the safety of products to users, food consumers and the environment.

The Ecology of a Garden: The First Fifteen Years. Jennifer Owen. Cambridge University Press, 40 W. 20th St., New York, New York 10011. (212) 924-3900; (800) 227-0247. 1991.

Managing Resistance to Agrochemicals: From Fundamental Research to Practical Strategies. Maurice B. Green, et al., eds. American Chemical Society, 1155 16th St. N.W., Washington, District of Columbia 20036. (800) 227-5558. 1990. A compilation of chapters written by some of the foremost scientists in pesticide and pest management research today.

MSDS Reference for Crop Protection Chemicals. John Wiley & Sons, Inc., 605 3rd Ave., New York, New York 10158-0012. (212) 850-6000. 1990. 3d ed. Covering over 650 brand name pesticides and related products from 19 manufacturers, their reference reproduces the manufacturers' information exactly, in a standardized typeset format.

Multivariate Methods in Drug and Agrochemical Research. David W. Salt and Martyn G. Ford. E. Horwood,

1230 Avenue of the Americas, New York, New York 10020. (212) 698-7000; (800) 223-2348. 1990. Comprehensive reference that provides users with the scope and application of multivariate analysis for researchers in the agrochemical and drug industries.

Regulation of Agrochemicals: A Driving Force in Their Evolution. Gino J. Marco, et al., eds. American Chemical Society, 1155 16th St. N.W., Washington, District of Columbia 20036. (800) 227-5558. 1991. Agrochemicals and the regulatory process before 1970, subsequent regulations and their impact on pesticide chemistry.

Synthesis and Chemistry of Agrochemicals II. Don R. Baker, et al., eds. American Chemical Society, 1155 16th St. N.W., Washington, District of Columbia 20036. (202) 872-4600; (800) 227-5558. 1991. Trends in synthesis and chemistry of agrochemicals.

HANDBOOKS AND MANUALS

Agricultural Chemicals. William Thomas Thomson. Thomson Publications, Box 9335, Fresno, California 93791. (209) 435-2163. 1991. Book 1: Insecticides and acaricides. Book 2: Herbicides. Book 3: Fumigants, growth regulators, repellents and rodenticides. Book 4: Fungicides.

Agricultural Chemicals Hazard Response Handbook. Euan Wallace. Agro-Research Enterprises, P.O. Box 264, Haverlock North, New Zealand 64-70-65-950. 1987. Agricultural chemicals and related compounds are listed by trade names in alphabetical order, coupled to the common names or the abbreviated names of the active ingredient contained in the trade-named product.

The Agrochemicals Handbook. H. Kidd and D. Hartlet, eds. Royal Society of Chemistry, c/o CRC Press, 2000 Corporate Blvd., N.W., Boca Raton, Florida 33431-9868. (800) 272-7737. 1991. 3rd ed. Contains comprehensive worldwide information and data on substances which are active components of agriculture chemical products currently used in crop protection and pest control.

Crop Protection Chemical Reference. Chemical and Pharmaceutical Press/Wiley, 605 3rd Ave., New York, New York 10158-0012. (212) 850-6000. 1991. 7th ed. Updated annual edition of a standard reference on label information on crop protection chemicals contains the complete text of some 540 product labels, which provide detailed information concerning what products can be used to treat a certain crop for certain problems, using what quantities of the chemical and under what restrictions and precautions. Appendices provide useful information on such matters as coding required when transporting products, safety practices, calibrations, etc.

European Directory of Agrochemical Products. Royal Society of Chemistry, Thomas Graham House, Science Park, Milton Rd., Cambridge, England CB4 4WF. 1990. 4th ed. Volume 1: Fungicides. Volume 2: Herbicides. Volume 3: Insecticides. Volume 4: Growth regulators including rodenticides; molluscicides; nematicides; repellents and synerists.

Farm Chemical Handbook. Meister Publishing Co., 37733 Euclid Ave., Willoughby, Ohio 44094. (216) 942-2000. Annual. Covers fertilizers and manures.

Turf and Ornamental Chemicals Reference. John Wiley & Sons, Inc., 605 3rd Ave., New York, New York 10158-0012. (212) 850-6000. 1990. Provides with a consolidated and fully cross-indexed set of chemical product labels and material safety data sheets (MSDA's) in one easily accessible source. Products are indexed in 6 separate color coded indexes as follows: Brand name quick reference; manufacturer; product category; common and chemical name; and plant and site use and pet use.

ONLINE DATA BASES

BIOSIS Previews. BIOSIS, 2100 Arch St., Philadelphia, Pennsylvania 19103-1399. (215) 587-4800. Largest and most comprehensive database of research in the life sciences. Contains citations for nearly 9000 primary research journals, monographs, reviews, symposia, preliminary reports, semi-popular journals, selected institutional reports, government reports and research communications.

CAS Source Index–CASSI. Chemical Abstracts Service, 2540 Olentangy River Rd., P.O. Box 3012, Columbus, Ohio 43210. (800) 848-6533 or (614) 421-3600. A listing of bibliographic and library holdings information for scientific and technical primary literature relevant to the chemical sciences.

CERCLIS. Chemical Information Systems, Inc., 7215 York Rd., Baltimore, Maryland 21212. (301) 321-8440. Information on hazardous waste disposal sites that have either been listed by the EPA on the National Priority List (NPL) or nominated for consideration for the NPL.

Chemical Abstracts-CA. Chemical Abstracts Service, 2540 Olentangy River Rd., P.O. Box 3012, Columbus, Ohio 43210. (800) 848-6533 or (614) 421-3600. Information sources include 9000 journals, patents from 27 countries, two industrial property organizations, new books, conference proceedings, and government research reports.

Chemical Business Newsbase. Royal Society of Chemistry, Thomas Graham House, Science Park, Milton Rd., Cambridge, England CB4 4WF. 44 (223) 420066.

Chemical Carcinogenesis Research Information System–CCRIS. National Library of Medicine, 8600 Rockville Pike, Bethesda, Maryland 20894. (800) 638-8480. Individual assay results and test conditions for 1,451 chemicals in the areas of carcinogenicity, mutagenicity, tumor promotion, and cocarcinogenicity.

Chemical Collection System/Request Tracking–CCS/RTS. U.S. Environmental Protection Agency, Office of Pesticides and Toxic Substances, 401 M St., SW, Washington, District of Columbia 20460. (202) 260-2090. Contains information on various properties of a number of chemicals including environmental effects, test and analysis methods, and health effects. Available from EPA.

Chemical Dictionary Online–CHEMLINE. Chemical Abstracts Service, 2540 Olentangy River Rd., Columbus, Ohio 43210. (614) 421-3600 or (800) 848-6533. Part of MEDLINE of the National Library of Medicine (NLM). File of 900,000 names for chemical substances, representing 450,000 unique compounds. It contains such information as Chemical Abstracts (CA) Service Registry Numbers, molecular formulas, preferred chemical nomenclature, and generic and ring structure information. Available on NLM's ELHILL system.

Chemical Exposure. Science Applications International Corp., Health & Environmental Information, P.O. Box 2501, Oak Ridge, Tennessee 37831. (615) 482-9031.

Database of chemicals that have been identified in both human tissues and body fluids and in feral and food animals. Contains reference to journal articles, conferences, and reports. Covers the whole fields of information related to human and animal exposure to food, air, and water contaminants and pharmaceuticals. Its records include information on chemical properties, formulas, tissues measured, analytical method used, demographics and more. Available on DIALOG.

Chemical Industry Notes–CHEMSIS. Chemical Abstracts Service, PO Box 3012, 2540 Olentangy River, Columbus, Ohio 43210. (614) 421-3600 or (800) 848-6533. Contains citations to business-oriented literature relating to the chemical processing industries. Includes pricing, production, products and processes, corporate and government activities, facilities and people from more than 80 worldwide business periodicals published since 1974. Available on DIALOG and ORBIT.

Current Research Information System–CRIS/USDA. U.S. Department of Agriculture, National Agricultural Library, 10301 Baltimore Blvd., 5th Floor, Beltsville, Maryland 20705-2351. (301) 504-5755. Looks at current research projects in agriculture and allied sciences covering the biological, physical, social and behavioral sciences related to agriculture.

Enviro/Energyline Abstracts Plus. R. R. Bowker Co., 121 Chanlon Rd., New Providence, New Jersey 07974. (908) 464-6800.

Environmental Periodicals Bibliography. National Information Services Corp., Ste. 6, Wyman Towers, 3100 St. Paul St., Baltimore, Maryland 21218. (410)243-0797. Online version of abstract of same name.

Farmer's Own Network for Education. Rodale Institute, 222 Main St., Emmaus, Pennsylvania 18098. (215) 967-5171. Efforts/results of farmers who have cut chemical use, diversified their farms, and adopted other regenerative agricultural techniques.

Monthly Catalog of United States Government Publications. U.S. G.P.O., Supt. of Docs., PO Box 371954, Pittsburgh, Pennsylvania 15250-7954. (202) 512-0000.

National Technical Information Service. U.S. Department of Commerce, National Technical Information Service, Office of Data Base Services, 5285 Port Royal Rd., Springfield, Virginia 22161. (703) 487-4807. Bibliographic database of government sponsored research and technical reports.

PERIODICALS AND NEWSLETTERS

Agrichemical Age Magazine. HBJ Farm Publications, 731 Market Street, San Francisco, California 94103-2011. (415) 495-3340. Eleven times a year. Use and application of agricultural chemicals.

Clean Water Report. Business Publishers, Inc., 951 Pershing Dr., Silver Spring, Maryland 20910-4464. (301) 587-6300. 1964-. Biweekly. Key information source for environmental professionals, covering the important issues: groundwater, drinking water, wastewater treatment, drought, wetlands, coastal protection, dioxin, non-point source pollution, agrichemical contamination, cleanup versus prevention issues, and related topics.

Communications in Soil Science and Plant Analysis. M. Dekker, 270 Madison Ave., New York, New York 10016. (212) 696-9000; (800) 228-1160. 1970-.

Farm Chemicals Magazine. Meister Publishing Co., 37733 Euclid Avenue, Willoughby, Ohio 44094. (216) 942-2000. Monthly. Covers the production, marketing and application of fertilizers and crop protection chemicals.

The Journal of Biological Chemistry. American Society of Biological Chemists, 428 E. Preston St., Baltimore, Maryland 21202. Three times a month. Biological, agricultural, and energy aspects of the environment.

Journal of Pesticide Science. Elsevier Science Publishing Co., Journal Information Center, 655 Avenue of the Americas, New York, New York 10010. (212) 989-5800. Quarterly. Pesticide science in general, agrochemistry and chemistry of biologically active natural products.

RESEARCH CENTERS AND INSTITUTES

Advanced Sciences Research and Development Corporation. P.O. Box 127, Lakemont, Georgia 30552. (404) 782-2092.

STATISTICS SOURCES

Environmental Data Compendium. OECD Publications and Information Center, 2001 L St., N.W., Suite 700, Washington, District of Columbia 20036. (202) 785-6323. 1989.

Environmental Indicators. OECD Publications and Information Center, 2001 L St., N.W., Suite 700, Washington, District of Columbia 20036. (202) 785-6323. 1991.

Environmental Quality. Council on Environmental Quality. U.S. G.P.O., Washington, District of Columbia 20401. (202) 512-0000. Annual.

The Market for Agricultural Chemicals. FIND/SVP, 625 Avenue of the Americas, New York, New York 10011. (212) 645-4500. 1990. Covers the markets for three types of agricultural chemicals: fertilizers, pesticide and natural and biotechnology products.

The State of the Environment. OECD Publications and Information Center, 2001 L St., N.W., Suite 700, Washington, District of Columbia 20036. (202) 785-6323. 1991.

TRADE ASSOCIATIONS AND PROFESSIONAL SOCIETIES

American Society of Agricultural Engineers. 2950 Niles Rd., St Joseph, Michigan 49085. (616) 429-0300.

National Agricultural Chemicals Association. 1155 15th St., N.W., Madison Building, Suite 900, Washington, District of Columbia 20005. (202) 296-1585.

Regenerative Agriculture Association. 222 Main St., Emmaus, Pennsylvania 18098. (215) 967-5171.

Western Agricultural Chemicals Association. 930 G St., Suite 210, Sacramento, California 95815. (916) 446-9222.

AGRICULTURAL CONSERVATION

See also: SOIL CONSERVATION

ABSTRACTING AND INDEXING SERVICES

Applied Ecology Abstracts Studies in Renewable Natural Resources. Information Retrieval Ltd., 1911 Jefferson Davis Highway, Arlington, Virginia 22202. 1975-. Monthly.

Biological Abstracts. BIOSIS, 2100 Arch St., Philadelphia, Pennsylvania 19103-1399. (215) 587-4800. 1927-.

Biological and Agricultural Index. H.W. Wilson Co., 950 University Ave., Bronx, New York 10452. (800) 367-6770. 1916-. Monthly.

Ecological Abstracts. Geo Abstracts Ltd. Elsevier Applied Science, Crown House, Linton Rd., Barking, England IG 11 8JU. 1974-. Derived from over 600 leading ecological and environmental journals, plus books, conference proceedings, reports and theses.

Environment Abstracts. Bowker A & I Publishing, 121 Chanlon Rd., New Providence, New Jersey 07974. (908) 464-6800. 1974-.

Environment Index. Environment Information Center, Index Research Department, 124 E. 39th St., New York, New York 10016. 1971-. Annual.

Environmental Information Connection–EIC. Planning Information Program, Dept. of Urban and Regional Planning, University of Illinois, 1003 West Nevada, Urbana, Illinois 61801. (217) 333-1369. Also available online.

Environmental Periodicals Bibliography. Environmental Studies Institute, International Academy at Santa Barbara, 800 Garden St., Suite D, Santa Barbara, California 93101. (805) 965-5010. Also available online.

Index to Scientific Book Contents. Institute for Scientific Information, 3501 Market St., Philadelphia, Pennsylvania 19104. (800) 523-1857. 1985-. Annual. Gives contents of science books published.

Multimedia Index to Ecology. National Information Center for Educational Media, University of Southern California, Los Angeles, California 90007.

BIBLIOGRAPHIES

Current Contents. Agriculture, Biology and Environmental Sciences. Institute for Scientific Information, 3501 Market St., Philadelphia, Pennsylvania 19104. (800) 523-1857. 1973-. Previous title: Current Contents. Agricultural, Food & Veterinary Sciences. Gives the table of contents of periodicals in the fields of agriculture, biology, environmental and related areas.

Directory of Published Proceedings. Interdok Corp., 173 Halstead Ave., Harrison, New York 10528. (914) 835-3506. 1990. Monthly. This is a listing of published proceedings including the series SEMTE (Science/Medicine/Engineering/Technology) and the series SSH (Social Science/Humanities).

EPA Publications Bibliography. U.S. Environmental Protection Agency, Library Systems Branch, 401 M St., SW, Washington, District of Columbia 20460. (202) 260-2090. Quarterly.

ENCYCLOPEDIAS AND DICTIONARIES

Cambridge Encyclopedia of Life Sciences. A. E. Friday and David S. Ingram. Cambridge University Press, 40 W 20th St., New York, New York 10011. (212) 924-3900 or (800) 227-0247. 1985. Includes all topics under biology and ecology.

Dictionary of Environmental Engineering and Related Sciences: English-Spanish, Spanish-English. Jose T. Villate. Ediciones Universal, 3090 SW 8th St., Miami, Florida 33135. (305) 642-3355. 1979.

Encyclopedia of Environmental Science and Engineering. J.R. Pfafflin. Gordon and Breach Science Publishers, Inc., 270 8th Ave., New York, New York 10011. (212) 206-8900. 1992.

McGraw-Hill Encyclopedia of Science and Technology. McGraw-Hill, 1221 Avenue of the Americas, New York, New York 10020. (212) 512-2000 or (800) 262-4729. 1992. Seventh edition. Issued in multiple volumes including index. Includes all science and technology broad subject areas.

Van Nostrand's Scientific Encyclopedia. Glenn D. Considine, ed. Van Nostrand Reinhold, 115 5th Ave., New York, New York 10003. (212) 254-3232. 1983. Sixth edition. Includes all broad subject areas in science.

GENERAL WORKS

Room to Grow. Diana Stevenson. Office of Planning and Research, 1400 10th St., Sacramento, California 95814. (916)322-2318. 1983. Issues in agricultural land conservation and conversion.

HANDBOOKS AND MANUALS

Agricultural Resource Conservation Program: For State and Country Offices, Short Reference. U.S. Department of Agriculture, Agricultural Stabilization and Conservation Service, 14 Independence Ave., SW, Washington, District of Columbia 20250. (202) 447-7454. Guide to local conservation in the United States.

ONLINE DATA BASES

Current Research Information System–CRIS/USDA. U.S. Department of Agriculture, National Agricultural Library, 10301 Baltimore Blvd., 5th Floor, Beltsville, Maryland 20705-2351. (301) 504-5755. Looks at current research projects in agriculture and allied sciences covering the biological, physical, social and behavioral sciences related to agriculture.

Enviro/Energyline Abstracts Plus. R. R. Bowker Co., 121 Chanlon Rd., New Providence, New Jersey 07974. (908) 464-6800.

Environmental Periodicals Bibliography. National Information Services Corp., Ste. 6, Wyman Towers, 3100 St. Paul St., Baltimore, Maryland 21218. (410)243-0797. Online version of abstract of same name.

Monthly Catalog of United States Government Publications. U.S. G.P.O., Supt. of Docs., PO Box 371954, Pittsburgh, Pennsylvania 15250-7954. (202) 512-0000.

National Technical Information Service. U.S. Department of Commerce, National Technical Information Service, Office of Data Base Services, 5285 Port Royal Rd., Springfield, Virginia 22161. (703) 487-4807. Bibliographic database of government sponsored research and technical reports.

AGRICULTURAL COOLING SYSTEMS
See: COOLING SYSTEMS

AGRICULTURAL DRAINAGE
See: SOIL SCIENCE

AGRICULTURAL ECOLOGY
See also: AGRICULTURAL CONSERVATION

ABSTRACTING AND INDEXING SERVICES

Applied Ecology Abstracts Studies in Renewable Natural Resources. Information Retrieval Ltd., 1911 Jefferson Davis Highway, Arlington, Virginia 22202. 1975-. Monthly.

Biological Abstracts. BIOSIS, 2100 Arch St., Philadelphia, Pennsylvania 19103-1399. (215) 587-4800. 1927-.

Biological and Agricultural Index. H.W. Wilson Co., 950 University Ave., Bronx, New York 10452. (800) 367-6770. 1916-. Monthly.

Bulletin Signaletique: Eau et Assainissement, Pollution Atmospherique, Droit des Pollutions. Centre de Documentation, Centre National de la Recherche Scientifique, 15, quai Anatole France, Paris, France 75700. (1) 45 55 92 25. 1983-. Monthly. Indexes pollution periodicals including water, atmospheric and related pollutions.

Current Advances in Ecological and Environmental Science. Pergamon Microforms International, Inc., Fairview Park, Elmsford, New York 10523. (914) 592-7720. 1989-. Monthly. Current literature searching service includingjournals, reports, abstracts, etc. This service is available online as part of the CABS database on the hosts BRS and ORBIT search service.

Ecological Abstracts. Geo Abstracts Ltd. Elsevier Applied Science, Crown House, Linton Rd., Barking, England IG 11 8JU. 1974-. Derived from over 600 leading ecological and environmental journals, plus books, conference proceedings, reports and theses.

Ecology Abstracts. Cambridge Scientific Abstracts, 5161 River Rd., Bethesda, Maryland 20816. (301) 961-6750. Monthly.

Environment Abstracts. Bowker A & I Publishing, 121 Chanlon Rd., New Providence, New Jersey 07974. (908) 464-6800. 1974-.

Environment Index. Environment Information Center, Index Research Department, 124 E. 39th St., New York, New York 10016. 1971-. Annual.

Environmental Information Connection–EIC. Planning Information Program, Dept. of Urban and Regional Planning, University of Illinois, 1003 West Nevada, Urbana, Illinois 61801. (217) 333-1369. Also available online.

Environmental Periodicals Bibliography. Environmental Studies Institute, International Academy at Santa Barbara, 800 Garden St., Suite D, Santa Barbara, California 93101. (805) 965-5010. Also available online.

General Science Index. H. W. Wilson Co., 950 University Ave., Bronx, New York 10452. 1978-. Monthly, also issued in annual cumulation. Cumulative subject index to English language periodicals in the subject fields of astronomy, botany, chemistry, earth science, environment and conservation, food and nutrition, genetics, mathematics, medicine and health, microbiology, oceanography, physics, physiology and zoology.

Geographical Abstracts. London School of Economics, Dept. of Geography, Regency House, 34 Duke St., London, England 1966-. Continued by Geo Abstracts issued in 6 parts: Pt. A. Landforms and the quaternary; Pt. B. Biogeography and Climatology; Pt. C. Economic geography; Pt. D. Social geography and cartography; Pt. E. Sedimentology; Pt. F. Regional and community planning.

Index to Scientific Book Contents. Institute for Scientific Information, 3501 Market St., Philadelphia, Pennsylvania 19104. (800) 523-1857. 1985-. Annual. Gives contents of science books published.

Multimedia Index to Ecology. National Information Center for Educational Media, University of Southern California, Los Angeles, California 90007.

ALMANACS AND YEARBOOKS

Developments in Agricultural and Managed Forest Ecology. Elsevier Science Publishing Co., 655 Avenue of the Americas, New York, New York 10010. (212) 984-5800. Annual.

BIBLIOGRAPHIES

Current Contents. Agriculture, Biology and Environmental Sciences. Institute for Scientific Information, 3501 Market St., Philadelphia, Pennsylvania 19104. (800) 523-1857. 1973-. Previous title: Current Contents. Agricultural, Food & Veterinary Sciences. Gives the table of contents of periodicals in the fields of agriculture, biology, environmental and related areas.

Directory of Published Proceedings. Interdok Corp., 173 Halstead Ave., Harrison, New York 10528. (914) 835-3506. 1990. Monthly. This is a listing of published proceedings including the series SEMTE (Science/Medicine/Engineering/Technology) and the series SSH (Social Science/Humanities).

EPA Publications Bibliography. U.S. Environmental Protection Agency, Library Systems Branch, 401 M St., SW, Washington, District of Columbia 20460. (202) 260-2090. Quarterly.

ENCYCLOPEDIAS AND DICTIONARIES

Dictionary of Environmental Engineering and Related Sciences: English-Spanish, Spanish-English. Jose T. Villate. Ediciones Universal, 3090 SW 8th St., Miami, Florida 33135. (305) 642-3355. 1979.

Encyclopedia of Environmental Science and Engineering. J.R. Pfafflin. Gordon and Breach Science Publishers, Inc., 270 8th Ave., New York, New York 10011. (212) 206-8900. 1992.

The Encyclopedia of Geochemistry and Environmental Sciences. Rhodes Whitmore Fairbridge. Van Nostrand Reinhold Co., 115 5th Ave., New York, New York 10003. (212) 254-3232. 1972.

Grzimek's Encyclopedia of Ecology. Bernhard Grzimek. Van Nostrand Reinhold, 115 5th Ave., New York, New York 10003. (212) 254-3232. 1976.

McGraw-Hill Encyclopedia of Environmental Science. Sybil P. Parker. McGraw-Hill Science & Engineering Books, 11 W. 19th St., New York, New York 10011. (212) 337-6010. 1980. Covers ecology, man's influence on nature, and environmental protection.

McGraw-Hill Encyclopedia of Science and Technology. McGraw-Hill, 1221 Avenue of the Americas, New York, New York 10020. (212) 512-2000 or (800) 262-4729. 1992. Seventh edition. Issued in multiple volumes including index. Includes all science and technology broad subject areas.

North American Reference Encyclopedia of Ecology and Pollution. William White. North American Pub. Co., 401 N. Broad St., Philadelphia, Pennsylvania 19108. (215) 238-5300. 1972.

Van Nostrand's Scientific Encyclopedia. Glenn D. Considine, ed. Van Nostrand Reinhold, 115 5th Ave., New York, New York 10003. (212) 254-3232. 1983. Sixth edition. Includes all broad subject areas in science.

GENERAL WORKS

Agricultural Ecology. Joy Tivy. John Wiley & Sons, Inc., 605 3rd Ave., New York, New York 10158-0012. (212) 850-6000. 1990. Analyzes the nature of relationships between crops, livestock, and the biophysical environment, and the extent to which man has modified the products and environment to suit his own needs.

ONLINE DATA BASES

Current Research Information System–CRIS/USDA. U.S. Department of Agriculture, National Agricultural Library, 10301 Baltimore Blvd., 5th Floor, Beltsville, Maryland 20705-2351. (301) 504-5755. Looks at current research projects in agriculture and allied sciences covering the biological, physical, social and behavioral sciences related to agriculture.

Enviro/Energyline Abstracts Plus. R. R. Bowker Co., 121 Chanlon Rd., New Providence, New Jersey 07974. (908) 464-6800.

Environmental Periodicals Bibliography. National Information Services Corp., Ste. 6, Wyman Towers, 3100 St. Paul St., Baltimore, Maryland 21218. (410)243-0797. Online version of abstract of same name.

Monthly Catalog of United States Government Publications. U.S. G.P.O., Supt. of Docs., PO Box 371954, Pittsburgh, Pennsylvania 15250-7954. (202) 512-0000.

National Technical Information Service. U.S. Department of Commerce, National Technical Information Service, Office of Data Base Services, 5285 Port Royal Rd., Springfield, Virginia 22161. (703) 487-4807. Bibliographic database of government sponsored research and technical reports.

AGRICULTURAL ENGINEERING

ABSTRACTING AND INDEXING SERVICES

Agricultural Engineering Abstracts. C. A. B. International, 845 North Park Ave., Tucson, Arizona 85719. (602) 621-7897 or (800) 528-4841. 1976-. Monthly. Informs about significant research developments in agricultural engineering and instrumentation. Some of the topics scanned for the abstracts include mechanical power, crop production, crop harvesting and threshing, crop processing and storage, aquaculture, land improvement, protected cultivation, handling and transport, and farm buildings and equipment.

Biological Abstracts. BIOSIS, 2100 Arch St., Philadelphia, Pennsylvania 19103-1399. (215) 587-4800. 1927-.

Biological and Agricultural Index. H.W. Wilson Co., 950 University Ave., Bronx, New York 10452. (800) 367-6770. 1916-. Monthly.

Chemical Abstracts. Chemical Abstracts Service, 2540 Olentangy River Rd., PO Box 3012, Columbus, Ohio 43210. (800) 848-6533. 1907-.

Environment Abstracts. Bowker A & I Publishing, 121 Chanlon Rd., New Providence, New Jersey 07974. (908) 464-6800. 1974-.

Environment Index. Environment Information Center, Index Research Department, 124 E. 39th St., New York, New York 10016. 1971-. Annual.

Environmental Information Connection–EIC. Planning Information Program, Dept. of Urban and Regional Planning, University of Illinois, 1003 West Nevada, Urbana, Illinois 61801. (217) 333-1369. Also available online.

Environmental Periodicals Bibliography. Environmental Studies Institute, International Academy at Santa Barbara, 800 Garden St., Suite D, Santa Barbara, California 93101. (805) 965-5010. Also available online.

Index to Scientific Book Contents. Institute for Scientific Information, 3501 Market St., Philadelphia, Pennsylvania 19104. (800) 523-1857. 1985-. Annual. Gives contents of science books published.

BIBLIOGRAPHIES

Bibliography of Agricultural Engineering Books. Carl W. Hall. American Society of Agricultural Engineers, 2950 Niles Rd., St. Joseph, Michigan 49085-9659. (616) 429-0300. 1976.

Current Contents. Agriculture, Biology and Environmental Sciences. Institute for Scientific Information, 3501 Market St., Philadelphia, Pennsylvania 19104. (800) 523-1857. 1973-. Previous title: Current Contents. Agricultural, Food & Veterinary Sciences. Gives the table of contents of periodicals in the fields of agriculture, biology, environmental and related areas.

Directory of Published Proceedings. Interdok Corp., 173 Halstead Ave., Harrison, New York 10528. (914) 835-3506. 1990. Monthly. This is a listing of published proceedings including the series SEMTE (Science/Medicine/Engineering/Technology) and the series SSH (Social Science/Humanities).

EPA Publications Bibliography. U.S. Environmental Protection Agency, Library Systems Branch, 401 M St., SW, Washington, District of Columbia 20460. (202) 260-2090. Quarterly.

Keyguide to Information Sources in Agricultural Engineering. Bryan Morgan. Mansell Publishing Ltd., 387 Park Ave. S., 5th Fl., New York, New York 10016. (212) 779-1822. 1985.

List of Publications on Agricultural Engineering Subjects. University of Illinois, Dept. of Agricultural Engineering, Urbana, Illinois 61801. 1964.

Ten-Year List of Publications on Agricultural Engineering Subjects. University of Illinois, Agricultural Engineering Dept., Urbana, Illinois 61801. 1973.

DIRECTORIES

Agricultural Information Resource Centers, a World Directory 1990. Rita C. Fisher. IAALD World Directory Working Group, 716 W. Indiana Ave., Urbana, Illinois 61801-4836. (217) 333-7687. 1990. Includes 3,971 information resource centers that have agriculture related collection and/or information services.

ENCYCLOPEDIAS AND DICTIONARIES

Agrartechnik: Mehrsprachen-Bildworterbuch. Agricultural Engineering: Multilingual Illustrated Dictionary Magraf Scientific Publishers, Weikersheim, Germany 1987.

The Agriculture Dictionary. Ray V. Herren and Roy L. Donahue. Delmar Publishers Inc., 2 Computer Dr. W., Albany, New York 12212. (518) 459-1150. 1991. Covers all the agricultural areas including acid rain, acid mine drainage, food additives, agricultural engineering, conservation of the natural resources, microorganisms, triticale and other related topics.

Dictionary of Agricultural and Food Engineering. Arthur W. Farrall. Interstate Publishers, 510 N. Vermillion St., PO Box 50, Danville, Illinois 61834-0050. (217) 446-0500. 1979.

Dictionary of Environmental Engineering and Related Sciences: English-Spanish, Spanish-English. Jose T. Villate. Ediciones Universal, 3090 SW 8th St., Miami, Florida 33135. (305) 642-3355. 1979.

Encyclopedia of Environmental Science and Engineering. J.R. Pfafflin. Gordon and Breach Science Publishers, Inc., 270 8th Ave., New York, New York 10011. (212) 206-8900. 1992.

Encyclopedia of Physical Science and Technology. Robert A. Meyers, ed. Academic Press, c/o Harcourt Brace Jovanovich Inc., 6277 Sea Harbor Dr., Orlando, Florida 32887. (800) 346-8648. Dictionary of engineering, technology and physical sciences.

McGraw-Hill Encyclopedia of Science and Technology. McGraw-Hill, 1221 Avenue of the Americas, New York, New York 10020. (212) 512-2000 or (800) 262-4729. 1992. Seventh edition. Issued in multiple volumes including index. Includes all science and technology broad subject areas.

GENERAL WORKS

Agricultural Engineering Conference 1990. EA Books/Accents Pubs., 1990. Conference sponsored by the Insti-

tute of Engineers, Australia and co-sponsored by the American Society of Agricultural Engineers, held in Toowoomba, Australia, November 1990. Topics cover a wide range of agricultural engineering topics, including soil and water, processing of biological materials, structures and environment, power and machinery, systems and modeling, instrumentation and measurement, education, and international perspectives.

Environmental and Functional Engineering of Agricultural Buildings. Henry J. Barre. Van Nostrand Reinhold, 115 5th Ave., New York, New York 10003. (212) 254-3232. 1988.

Genetic Engineering of Plants: An Agricultural Perspective. Isune Kosuge. Plenum Press, 233 Spring St., New York, New York 10013-1578. (212) 620-8000. 1983. Plant breeding techniques and plant genetic engineering.

ONLINE DATA BASES

Chemical Abstracts-CA. Chemical Abstracts Service, 2540 Olentangy River Rd., P.O. Box 3012, Columbus, Ohio 43210. (800) 848-6533 or (614) 421-3600. Information sources include 9000 journals, patents from 27 countries, two industrial property organizations, new books, conference proceedings, and government research reports.

Current Research Information System–CRIS/USDA. U.S. Department of Agriculture, National Agricultural Library, 10301 Baltimore Blvd., 5th Floor, Beltsville, Maryland 20705-2351. (301) 504-5755. Looks at current research projects in agriculture and allied sciences covering the biological, physical, social and behavioral sciences related to agriculture.

Enviro/Energyline Abstracts Plus. R. R. Bowker Co., 121 Chanlon Rd., New Providence, New Jersey 07974. (908) 464-6800.

Environmental Periodicals Bibliography. National Information Services Corp., Ste. 6, Wyman Towers, 3100 St. Paul St., Baltimore, Maryland 21218. (410)243-0797. Online version of abstract of same name.

Monthly Catalog of United States Government Publications. U.S. G.P.O., Supt. of Docs., PO Box 371954, Pittsburgh, Pennsylvania 15250-7954. (202) 512-0000.

National Technical Information Service. U.S. Department of Commerce, National Technical Information Service, Office of Data Base Services, 5285 Port Royal Rd., Springfield, Virginia 22161. (703) 487-4807. Bibliographic database of government sponsored research and technical reports.

PressNet Environmental Reports. Chemical Information Systems, Inc., 7215 York Rd., Baltimore, Maryland 21212. (301) 321-8440.

PERIODICALS AND NEWSLETTERS

Agricultural Engineering Magazine. American Society of Agricultural Engineers, 2950 Niles Road, St Joseph, Michigan 49085. (616) 429-0300. Bimonthly. Irrigation and other large scale projects with environmental significance.

Journal of Agricultural Engineering Research. Academic Press, c/o Harcourt Brace Jovanovich Inc., 6277 Sea Harbor Dr., Orlando, Florida 32887. (800) 346-8648. Eight times a year.

AGRICULTURAL LAND

See: FARMLAND

AGRICULTURAL POLLUTION

ABSTRACTING AND INDEXING SERVICES

Abstracts of Air and Water Conservation Literature. American Petroleum Institute. Central Abstracting and Indexing Service, 275 Madison Avenue, New York, New York 10016. 1972.

Agrindex. AGRIS Coordinating Center, Via delle Terme di Caracalla, Rome, Italy I-00100. 61 0181-FA01. 1975-.

Applied Ecology Abstracts Studies in Renewable Natural Resources. Information Retrieval Ltd., 1911 Jefferson Davis Highway, Arlington, Virginia 22202. 1975-. Monthly.

Aqualine Abstracts. Water Research Centre. c/o Pergamon Microforms International, Inc., Fairview Park, Elmsford, New York 10523. (914) 592-7720. 1927-. Contains some 8,000 records annually on water and wastewater technology. Covers all aspects of water, wastewater, associated engineering services and the aquatic environment. Over 600 periodicals, as well as books, reports and conference proceedings and other publications from water related institutions worldwide are scanned. Also available online.

ASFA Aquaculture Abstracts. Cambridge Scientific Abstracts, Inc., 5161 River Rd., Bethesda, Maryland 20816. (301) 961-6750. 1984.

Biological Abstracts. BIOSIS, 2100 Arch St., Philadelphia, Pennsylvania 19103-1399. (215) 587-4800. 1927-.

Biological and Agricultural Index. H.W. Wilson Co., 950 University Ave., Bronx, New York 10452. (800) 367-6770. 1916-. Monthly.

Bulletin Signaletique: Eau et Assainissement, Pollution Atmospherique, Droit des Pollutions. Centre de Documentation, Centre National de la Recherche Scientifique, 15, quai Anatole France, Paris, France 75700. (1) 45 55 92 25. 1983-. Monthly. Indexes pollution periodicals including water, atmospheric and related pollutions.

Ecological Abstracts. Geo Abstracts Ltd. Elsevier Applied Science, Crown House, Linton Rd., Barking, England IG 11 8JU. 1974-. Derived from over 600 leading ecological and environmental journals, plus books, conference proceedings, reports and theses.

Ecology Abstracts. Cambridge Scientific Abstracts, 5161 River Rd., Bethesda, Maryland 20816. (301) 961-6750. Monthly.

Environment Abstracts. Bowker A & I Publishing, 121 Chanlon Rd., New Providence, New Jersey 07974. (908) 464-6800. 1974-.

Environment Index. Environment Information Center, Index Research Department, 124 E. 39th St., New York, New York 10016. 1971-. Annual.

Environmental Information Connection–EIC. Planning Information Program, Dept. of Urban and Regional Planning, University of Illinois, 1003 West Nevada, Urbana, Illinois 61801. (217) 333-1369. Also available online.

Environmental Periodicals Bibliography. Environmental Studies Institute, International Academy at Santa Barbara, 800 Garden St., Suite D, Santa Barbara, California 93101. (805) 965-5010. Also available online.

General Science Index. H. W. Wilson Co., 950 University Ave., Bronx, New York 10452. 1978-. Monthly, also issued in annual cumulation. Cumulative subject index to English language periodicals in the subject fields of astronomy, botany, chemistry, earth science, environment and conservation, food and nutrition, genetics, mathematics, medicine and health, microbiology, oceanography, physics, physiology and zoology.

Index to Scientific Book Contents. Institute for Scientific Information, 3501 Market St., Philadelphia, Pennsylvania 19104. (800) 523-1857. 1985-. Annual. Gives contents of science books published.

Multimedia Index to Ecology. National Information Center for Educational Media, University of Southern California, Los Angeles, California 90007.

Pollution Abstracts. Cambridge Scientific Abstracts, 5161 River Rd., Bethesda, Maryland 20816. (301) 961-6750. Six/year. Indexes worldwide technical literature on environmental pollution. Covers air pollution, marine and freshwater pollution, sewage and wastewater treatment, waste management, toxicology and health, noise pollution, radiation, land pollution, and environmental policies, programs, legislation, and education. Also available online.

BIBLIOGRAPHIES

Current Contents. Agriculture, Biology and Environmental Sciences. Institute for Scientific Information, 3501 Market St., Philadelphia, Pennsylvania 19104. (800) 523-1857. 1973-. Previous title: Current Contents. Agricultural, Food & Veterinary Sciences. Gives the table of contents of periodicals in the fields of agriculture, biology, environmental and related areas.

Directory of Published Proceedings. Interdok Corp., 173 Halstead Ave., Harrison, New York 10528. (914) 835-3506. 1990. Monthly. This is a listing of published proceedings including the series SEMTE (Science/Medicine/Engineering/Technology) and the series SSH (Social Science/Humanities).

EPA Publications Bibliography. U.S. Environmental Protection Agency, Library Systems Branch, 401 M St., SW, Washington, District of Columbia 20460. (202) 260-2090. Quarterly.

ENCYCLOPEDIAS AND DICTIONARIES

Dictionary of Environmental Engineering and Related Sciences: English-Spanish, Spanish-English. Jose T. Villate. Ediciones Universal, 3090 SW 8th St., Miami, Florida 33135. (305) 642-3355. 1979.

Encyclopedia of Environmental Science and Engineering. J.R. Pfafflin. Gordon and Breach Science Publishers, Inc., 270 8th Ave., New York, New York 10011. (212) 206-8900. 1992.

The Encyclopedia of Geochemistry and Environmental Sciences. Rhodes Whitmore Fairbridge. Van Nostrand

Reinhold Co., 115 5th Ave., New York, New York 10003. (212) 254-3232. 1972.

McGraw-Hill Encyclopedia of Environmental Science. Sybil P. Parker. McGraw-Hill Science & Engineering Books, 11 W. 19th St., New York, New York 10011. (212) 337-6010. 1980. Covers ecology, man's influence on nature, and environmental protection.

McGraw-Hill Encyclopedia of Science and Technology. McGraw-Hill, 1221 Avenue of the Americas, New York, New York 10020. (212) 512-2000 or (800) 262-4729. 1992. Seventh edition. Issued in multiple volumes including index. Includes all science and technology broad subject areas.

Van Nostrand's Scientific Encyclopedia. Glenn D. Considine, ed. Van Nostrand Reinhold, 115 5th Ave., New York, New York 10003. (212) 254-3232. 1983. Sixth edition. Includes all broad subject areas in science.

GENERAL WORKS

Chemical Concepts in Pollutant Behavior. Ian J. Tinsley. John Wiley & Sons, Inc., 605 3rd Ave., New York, New York 10158-0012. (212) 850-6000. 1979.

The Environment: Problems and Solutions. Stuart Bruchey, ed. Garland Publishing, Inc., 1000A Sherman Ave., Hamden, Connecticut 06514. (203) 281-4487. 1991. Topics covered: forested wetlands and agriculture, the political economy of smog in southern California, environmental limits to growth in world agriculture, the tradeoff between cost and risk in hazardous waste management, and the protection of groundwater from agricultural pollution.

Environmental Impacts of Agricultural Production Activities. Larry W. Canter. Lewis Publishers, 200 Corporate Blvd. NW, Boca Raton, Florida 33431. (407) 994-0555 or (800)272-7737. Volume in general deals with agricultural production technologies and its environmental impacts. It includes case studies and has chapters that separately deal with water and soil impacts; air quality impacts; noise and solid waste impacts. Most importantly it evaluates emerging agricultural technologies and includes a bibliography on the subject.

ONLINE DATA BASES

BIOSIS Previews. BIOSIS, 2100 Arch St., Philadelphia, Pennsylvania 19103-1399. (215) 587-4800. Largest and most comprehensive database of research in the life sciences. Contains citations for nearly 9000 primary research journals, monographs, reviews, symposia, preliminary reports, semi-popular journals, selected institutional reports, government reports and research communications.

CRIS/USDA. U.S. Department of Agriculture, Cooperative State Research Service, Current Research Information System, National Agricultural Library Building, 5th Fl., 10301 Baltimore Blvd., Beltsville, Maryland 20705. (301) 344-3850. Agricultural, food and nutrition, and forestry research projects.

Enviro/Energyline Abstracts Plus. R. R. Bowker Co., 121 Chanlon Rd., New Providence, New Jersey 07974. (908) 464-6800.

Environmental Periodicals Bibliography. National Information Services Corp., Ste. 6, Wyman Towers, 3100 St.

Paul St., Baltimore, Maryland 21218. (410)243-0797. Online version of abstract of same name.

Monthly Catalog of United States Government Publications. U.S. G.P.O., Supt. of Docs., PO Box 371954, Pittsburgh, Pennsylvania 15250-7954. (202) 512-0000.

National Technical Information Service. U.S. Department of Commerce, National Technical Information Service, Office of Data Base Services, 5285 Port Royal Rd., Springfield, Virginia 22161. (703) 487-4807. Bibliographic database of government sponsored research and technical reports.

PressNet Environmental Reports. Chemical Information Systems, Inc., 7215 York Rd., Baltimore, Maryland 21212. (301) 321-8440.

RESEARCH CENTERS AND INSTITUTES

Statewide Air Pollution Research Center. University of California, Riverside, Riverside, California 92521. (714) 787-5124.

TRADE ASSOCIATIONS AND PROFESSIONAL SOCIETIES

American Society of Agricultural Engineers. 2950 Niles Rd., St Joseph, Michigan 49085. (616) 429-0300.

AGRICULTURAL RUNOFF
See: RUNOFF

AGRICULTURAL WASTES
See: WASTE DISPOSAL

AGRICULTURE
See also: CROPS; FARMLAND; ORGANIC GARDENING AND FARMING; SOIL SCIENCE

ABSTRACTING AND INDEXING SERVICES

Abstracts of Air and Water Conservation Literature. American Petroleum Institute. Central Abstracting and Indexing Service, 275 Madison Avenue, New York, New York 10016. 1972.

Agrindex. AGRIS Coordinating Center, Via delle Terme di Caracalla, Rome, Italy I-00100. 61 0181-FA01. 1975-.

Applied Ecology Abstracts Studies in Renewable Natural Resources. Information Retrieval Ltd., 1911 Jefferson Davis Highway, Arlington, Virginia 22202. 1975-. Monthly.

ASFA Aquaculture Abstracts. Cambridge Scientific Abstracts, Inc., 5161 River Rd., Bethesda, Maryland 20816. (301) 961-6750. 1984.

Biological Abstracts. BIOSIS, 2100 Arch St., Philadelphia, Pennsylvania 19103-1399. (215) 587-4800. 1927-.

Biological and Agricultural Index. H.W. Wilson Co., 950 University Ave., Bronx, New York 10452. (800) 367-6770. 1916-. Monthly.

C. A. B. International Serials Checklist. C. A. B. International, Wallingford, England OX10 8DE. 44 0491 32111. 1988. Periodical literature relating to agriculture.

Civil Engineering Hydraulic Abstracts. BHRA Fluid Engineering, Air Science Co., PO Box 143, Corning, New York 14830. (607) 962-5591. Monthly. Abstracts of periodicals that publish in the areas of hydraulic engineering and other related topics.

Ecological Abstracts. Geo Abstracts Ltd. Elsevier Applied Science, Crown House, Linton Rd., Barking, England IG 11 8JU. 1974-. Derived from over 600 leading ecological and environmental journals, plus books, conference proceedings, reports and theses.

Environment Abstracts. Bowker A & I Publishing, 121 Chanlon Rd., New Providence, New Jersey 07974. (908) 464-6800. 1974-.

Environment Index. Environment Information Center, Index Research Department, 124 E. 39th St., New York, New York 10016. 1971-. Annual.

Environmental Information Connection–EIC. Planning Information Program, Dept. of Urban and Regional Planning, University of Illinois, 1003 West Nevada, Urbana, Illinois 61801. (217) 333-1369. Also available online.

Environmental Periodicals Bibliography. Environmental Studies Institute, International Academy at Santa Barbara, 800 Garden St., Suite D, Santa Barbara, California 93101. (805) 965-5010. Also available online.

Food Science and Technology Abstracts. International Food Information Service, c/o National Food Laboratory, 6363 Clark Ave., Dublin, California 94568. (800) 336-3782. 1969-.

General Science Index. H. W. Wilson Co., 950 University Ave., Bronx, New York 10452. 1978-. Monthly, also issued in annual cumulation. Cumulative subject index to English language periodicals in the subject fields of astronomy, botany, chemistry, earth science, environment and conservation, food and nutrition, genetics, mathematics, medicine and health, microbiology, oceanography, physics, physiology and zoology.

Geographical Abstracts. London School of Economics, Dept. of Geography, Regency House, 34 Duke St., London, England 1966-. Continued by Geo Abstracts issued in 6 parts: Pt. A. Landforms and the quaternary; Pt. B. Biogeography and Climatology; Pt. C. Economic geography; Pt. D. Social geography and cartography; Pt. E. Sedimentology; Pt. F. Regional and community planning.

Index to Scientific Book Contents. Institute for Scientific Information, 3501 Market St., Philadelphia, Pennsylvania 19104. (800) 523-1857. 1985-. Annual. Gives contents of science books published.

Multimedia Index to Ecology. National Information Center for Educational Media, University of Southern California, Los Angeles, California 90007.

Pollution Abstracts. Cambridge Scientific Abstracts, 5161 River Rd., Bethesda, Maryland 20816. (301) 961-6750. Six/year. Indexes worldwide technical literature on environmental pollution. Covers air pollution, marine and freshwater pollution, sewage and wastewater treatment, waste management, toxicology and health, noise pollution, radiation, land pollution, and environmental poli-

cies, programs, legislation, and education. Also available online.

Science Citation Index. Institute for Scientific Information, 3501 Market St., Philadelphia, Pennsylvania 19104. 1961-.

BIBLIOGRAPHIES

Agricultural and Animal Sciences Journals and Serials: An Analytical Guide. Richard D. Jensen. Greenwood Publishing Group, Inc., 88 Post Rd. W., PO Box 5007, Westport, Connecticut 06881. (212) 226-3571. 1986.

Agricultural Periodicals Published in Canada. Dorothy Mary Duke. Canada Dept. of Agriculture, Canada 1962.

CAB Serials Checklist. The Bureaux, Slough, England 1983. A consolidated list of the serials regularly scanned by the commonwealth agricultural bureaux with a guide to their location.

Current Contents. Agriculture, Biology and Environmental Sciences. Institute for Scientific Information, 3501 Market St., Philadelphia, Pennsylvania 19104. (800) 523-1857. 1973-. Previous title: Current Contents. Agricultural, Food & Veterinary Sciences. Gives the table of contents of periodicals in the fields of agriculture, biology, environmental and related areas.

Directory of Published Proceedings. Interdok Corp., 173 Halstead Ave., Harrison, New York 10528. (914) 835-3506. 1990. Monthly. This is a listing of published proceedings including the series SEMTE (Science/Medicine/Engineering/Technology) and the series SSH (Social Science/Humanities).

EPA Publications Bibliography. U.S. Environmental Protection Agency, Library Systems Branch, 401 M St., SW, Washington, District of Columbia 20460. (202) 260-2090. Quarterly.

Guide to Sources for Agricultural and Biological Research. University of California Press, 2120 Berkeley Way, Berkeley, California (415) 642-4262; (800) 822-6657. 1981.

Integrated Pest Management. Jayne T. Maclean. National Agricultural Library, 10301 Baltimore Blvd., Beltsville, Maryland 20705-2351. (301) 504-5755. 1985.

Serial Publications Indexed in Bibliography of Agriculture. National Agricultural Library, 10301 Baltimore Blvd., Washington, District of Columbia 20705-2351. (301) 504-5755. 1963.

DIRECTORIES

Agricultural Information Resource Centers, a World Directory 1990. Rita C. Fisher. IAALD World Directory Working Group, 716 W. Indiana Ave., Urbana, Illinois 61801-4836. (217) 333-7687. 1990. Includes 3,971 information resource centers that have agriculture related collection and/or information services.

Directory of Environmental Scientists in Agriculture. Roland D. Hauck. Council for Agricultural Science and Technology, Memorial Union, Iowa State University, Ames, Iowa 50011. 1979. Second edition. Special publication no.6. Pt.1 is organized by environmental topics which the scientists included in this directory are qualified to discuss. pt.2. lists administrators and liaison officers of state and federal research, extension, and regulatory organizations. pt.3. alphabetical listing of the scientists with address and telephone numbers.

Food and Agriculture Organization of the United Nations. CN Index of Agricultural Research Institutions in Europe. AGRIS Coordinating Center, Via delle Terme di Caracalla, Rome, Italy I-00100. Directory of agriculture and agricultural experiment stations.

Healthy Harvest II: A Directory of Sustainable Agriculture and Horticulture Organizations 1987-1988. Susan J. Sanzone, et al., eds. Potomac Valley Press, Suite 105, 1424 16th St. NW, Washington, District of Columbia 20036. 1987.

SATIVA Opportunities Directory. Society for Agricultural Training through Integrated Voluntary Activities, Route 2, Viola, Wisconsin 54664. (608) 625-2217. Annual. Training programs and work opportunities in organic farming and homesteading.

Who's Who in World Agriculture. Longman Group Ltd., 6th Floor, Westgate House, The High, Harlow, England CM20 1NE. 1985. Second edition. Profiles 12,000 senior agricultural and veterinary scientists.

ENCYCLOPEDIAS AND DICTIONARIES

The Agricultural Handbook: A Guide to Terminology. Martin Whitley, et al. BSP Professional Books, 3 Cambridge Center, Suite 208, Cambridge, Massachusetts 02142. 1988. Provides an introductory reference source of definitions and explanations for agricultural terms. All areas of agriculture are covered including animal and crop production, farm management, policy and institutions.

The Agriculture Dictionary. Ray V. Herren and Roy L. Donahue. Delmar Publishers Inc., 2 Computer Dr. W., Albany, New York 12212. (518) 459-1150. 1991. Covers all the agricultural areas including acid rain, acid mine drainage, food additives, agricultural engineering, conservation of the natural resources, microorganisms, triticale and other related topics.

Dictionary of Agriculture. Gunther Haensch and G. H. Deanton. Elsevier Science Publishing Co., 655 Avenue of the Americas, New York, New York 10010. (212) 984-5800. 1986.

Elsevier's Dictionary of Horticultural and Agricultural Plant Production in Ten Languages. Elsevier Science Publishing Co., 655 Avenue of Americas, New York, New York 10010. (212) 989-5800. 1990. Language of the text: English, Dutch, French, German, Danish, Swedish, Italian, Spanish, Portuguese and Latin.

Encyclopedia of Human Biology. Renato Dulbecco, ed. Academic Press, c/o Harcourt Brace Jovanovich Inc., 6277 Sea Harbor Dr., Orlando, Florida 32887. (800) 346-8648. 1991. Eight volumes.

The Encyclopedia of Soil Science. Rhodes W. Fairbridge. Academic Press, c/o Harcourt Brace Jovanovich Inc., 6277 Sea Harbor Dr., Orlando, Florida 32887. (800) 346-8648. 1979-. Includes soil physics, soil chemistry, soil biology, soil fertility and plant nutrition, soil genesis, classification and cartography.

The Marshall Cavendish Encyclopedia of Gardening. Marshall Cavendish, 58 Old Compton St., London, England W1V 5PA. 01-734 6710. 1971. Seven volumes. Encyclopedic treatment of garden plants and advise on how to grow them.

McGraw-Hill Encyclopedia of Environmental Science. Sybil P. Parker. McGraw-Hill Science & Engineering Books, 11 W. 19th St., New York, New York 10011. (212) 337-6010. 1980. Covers ecology, man's influence on nature, and environmental protection.

McGraw-Hill Encyclopedia of Science and Technology. McGraw-Hill, 1221 Avenue of the Americas, New York, New York 10020. (212) 512-2000 or (800) 262-4729. 1992. Seventh edition. Issued in multiple volumes including index. Includes all science and technology broad subject areas.

GENERAL WORKS

Agricultural Ecology. Joy Tivy. John Wiley & Sons, Inc., 605 3rd Ave., New York, New York 10158-0012. (212) 850-6000. 1990. Analyzes the nature of relationships between crops, livestock, and the biophysical environment, and the extent to which man has modified the products and environment to suit his own needs.

Agriculture and Natural Resources: Planning for Educational Priorities for the Twenty-First Century. Wava G. Haney, ed. Conservation of Natural Resources, 5500 Central Ave., Boulder, Colorado 80301. 1991. A volume in the Social Behavior and Natural Resources Series. Text details the priorities in planning for the 21st century while conserving natural resources and the environment.

Agroecology: Researching the Ecological Basis for Sustainable Agriculture. Stephen R. Gliessman, ed. Springer-Verlag, 175 5th Ave., New York, New York 10010. (212) 460-1500; (800) 777-4643. 1990. Demonstrates in a series of international case studies how to combine the more production-oriented focus of the agronomist with the more systems-oriented viewpoint of the ecologist. Methodology for evaluating and quantifying agroecosystem is presented.

The Biodynamic Farm. Herbert H. Koepf. Anthroposophic Press, RR 4 Box 94 A1, Hudson, New York 12534. (518) 851-2054. 1989. Deals with agricultural ecology and with the conservation of natural resources.

Biologically Active Natural Products: Potential Use in Agriculture. Horace G. Culter and Richard B. Russell, eds. American Chemical Society, 1155 16th St. N.W., Washington, District of Columbia 20036. (202) 872-4600; (800) 227-5558. 1988. Describes natural products and their potential use in agriculture.

Chemistry, Agriculture and the Environment. Mervyn L. Richardson. Royal Society of Chemistry, Thomas Graham House, Science Park, Milton Rd., Cambridge, England CB4 4WF. 44(0)223420066. 1991. Provides an overview of the chemical pollution of the environment caused by modern agricultural practices worldwide, and describes the effects of agrochemicals used in intensive animal and crop production on the air, water, soil, plants, and animals including humans. Also available through CRC Press.

Climate Change and World Agriculture. Martin Parry. Earthscan Pub. Ltd., 3 Endsleigh St., London, England WC1H ODD. (071)388-2117. 1990. Describes the effects on agriculture, estimating the impacts on plant and animal growth and looking at the geographical limits to different types of farming.

Controlling Toxic Substances in Agricultural Drainage. U.S. Committee on Irrigation and Drainage, PO Box 15326, Denver, Colorado 80215. 1990. Looks at current technology on toxic substances and water treatment processes and techniques.

Ecological Fruit Production in the North. Bart Hall-Beyer, and Jean Richard. B. Hall-Beyer, RR #3, Scotstown, Quebec, Canada J0B 3J0. 1983. Deals with the production of tree fruits and small fruits in North America. Discusses methods of ecological agriculture.

The Ecology of a Garden: The First Fifteen Years. Jennifer Owen. Cambridge University Press, 40 W. 20th St., New York, New York 10011. (212) 924-3900; (800) 227-0247. 1991.

The Ecology of the Ancient Greek World. Robert Sallares. Cornell University Press, 124 Roberts Place, Ithaca, New York 14850. 1991. Synthesis of ancient history and biological or physical anthropology. Includes chapters on demography and on agriculture in ancient Greece and Egypt. Also includes extensive notes and bibliographies.

Environmental Aspects of Applied Biology. Association of Applied Biologists, Institute of Horticultural Research, Littlehampton, England BN17 6LP. 1988. Volume 1 contains environmental impacts of crop protection and practices within the agricultural ecosystem (crop protection topics). Volume 2 includes environmental aspects of post-harvest practices, the plant response to the combined stresses of pollution, climate and soil conditions, and the straw problem. Includes bibliographies.

The Environmental Gardener: The Solution to Pollution for Lawns and Gardens. Laurence Sombke. MasterMedia, 17 E. 89th St., New York, New York 10128. (212) 348-2020. 1991.

Farming in Nature's Image. Judith A. Soule. Island Press, 1718 Connecticut Ave. N.W., Suite 300, Washington, District of Columbia 20009. (202) 232-7933. 1992. Gives a detailed look into the pioneering work of the Land Institute, the leading educational and research organization for sustainable agriculture.

Farming on the Edge: Saving Family Farms in Marin County, California. John Hart. University of California Press, 2120 Berkeley Way, Berkeley, California 94720. (415) 642-4262; (800) 822-6657. 1991. Case study in successful land-use planning.

Farms of Tomorrow. Trauger Groh. Bio-Dynamic Farming and Gardening Association, PO Box 550, Kimberton, Pennsylvania 19442. (215) 935-7797. 1990. Describes a new approach to farming called community supported agriculture (CSA). It is built upon the solid foundation of organic and biodynamic cultivation, but it focuses on the social and economic conditions that make farming possible.

Federal Lands: A Guide to Planning, Management, and State Revenues. Sally K. Fairfax. Island Press, 1718 Connecticut Ave. N.W., Suite 300, Washington, District of Columbia 20009. (202) 232-7933. 1987. Comprehensive reference on the management and allocation of revenues from public lands.

From the Land. Nancy P. Pittman, ed. Island Press, 1718 Connecticut Ave. N.W., Suite 300, Washington, District of Columbia 20009. (202) 232-7933. 1988. Anthology comes from 13 years of the Land–a journal of conservation writings from the '40s and '50s. Through fiction, essay, poetry, and philosophy we learn how our small farms have given way to today's agribusiness.

Grass Productivity. A. Voisin. Island Press, 1718 Connecticut Ave. N.W., Suite 300, Washington, District of Columbia 20009. (202) 232-7933. 1988. Textbook of scientific information concerning every aspect of management "where the cow and the grass meet." Voisin's "rational grazing" method maximizes productivity in both grass and cattle operations.

The New Organic Grower. Eliot Coleman. Chelsea Green Publishing, PO Box 130, Post Mills, Vermont 05058-0130. (802) 333-9073. 1989. Covers crop rotation, green manures, tillage, seeding, transplanting, cultivation, and garden pests.

Pastures: Their Ecology and Management. R. H. M. Langer, ed. Oxford University Press, 200 Madison Ave., New York, New York 10016. (212) 679-7300; (800) 334-4249. 1990. Covers such areas as the grasslands of New Zealand, pasture plants, pasture as an ecosystem, pasture establishment, soil fertility, management, assessment, livestock production, animal disorders, high country pastures, hay or silage, seed production, weeds, pests, and plant diseases.

Paying the Farm Bill: U.S. Agricultural Policy and the Transition to Sustainable Agriculture. Paul Faeth, et al. World Resources Institute, 1709 New York Ave. N.W., Washington, District of Columbia 20006. (800) 822-0504. 1991. Demonstrates that resource conserving agricultural systems are environmentally and economically superior to conventional systems over the long term.

Plowman's Folly. Edward H. Faulkner. Island Press, 1718 Connecticut Ave. N.W., Suite 300, Washington, District of Columbia 20009. (202) 232-7933. 1987.

Saving the Tropical Forests. Judith Gradwohl and Russell Greenberg. Island Press, 1718 Connecticut Ave. N.W., Suite 300, Washington, District of Columbia 20009. (202) 232-7933. 1988. Sourcebook about the causes and effects of tropical deforestation, with case studies, examples of sustainable agriculture and forestry, and a section on the restoration of tropical rain forests.

Shattering: Food, Politics, and the Loss of Genetic Diversity. Cary Fowler. University of Arizona Press, 1230 N. Park, No. 102, Tucson, Arizona 85719. (602) 621-1441. 1990. Reviews the development of genetic diversity over 10,000 years of human agriculture and its loss in our lifetimes.

Solar Energy in Agriculture. Blaine F. Parker, ed. Elsevier Science Publishing Co., 655 Avenue of the Americas, New York, New York 10010. (212) 989-5800. 1991.

Stray Voltages in Agriculture: Workshop. American Society of Agricultural Engineers, 2950 Niles Rd., St. Joseph, Michigan 49085-9659. (616) 429-0300. 1983. Includes the effects of stray voltage on animals, source of stray voltage, diagnostic procedures for detection and measurement and treatments or corrective procedure for stray voltage problem. The workshop was sponsored by the National Rural Electric Cooperative Association in Minneapolis, MN.

Towards Sustainable Agricultural Development. Michael D. Young. Belhaven Press, 136 S. Broadway, Irvington, New York 10533. (914) 591-9111. 1991. Organisation of Economic Cooperation and Development commissioned experts to examine how sustainability can be achieved for food, industrial crops, and livestock in the developed and developing world. This report provides some sources on the current world status of sustainable agriculture.

Trees, Why Do You Wait? America's Changing Rural Culture. Richard Critchfield. Island Press, 1718 Connecticut Ave. N.W., Suite 300, Washington, District of Columbia 20009. (202) 232-7933. 1991. Oral history chronicling the changes taking place in rural America.

The Violence of Green Revolution. Vandana Shiva. Humanities Pr. Intl., 171 1st Ave., Atlantic Highlands, New Jersey 07716-1289. (201) 872-1441; (800) 221-3845. 1991.

GOVERNMENTAL ORGANIZATIONS

Information Division: Statistical Reporting Service. Room 209, JSM Building, 15th and Independence Ave., S.W., Washington, District of Columbia 20250. (202) 447-4230.

National Agricultural Library. Route 1, Beltsville, Maryland 20705. (301) 344-4348.

HANDBOOKS AND MANUALS

Agricultural Chemicals Hazard Response Handbook. Euan Wallace. Agro-Research Enterprises, P.O. Box 264, Haverlock North, New Zealand 64-70-65-950. 1987. Agricultural chemicals and related compounds are listed by trade names in alphabetical order, coupled to the common names or the abbreviated names of the active ingredient contained in the trade-named product.

The Agricultural Notebook. Primrose McConnell; R. J. Halley, ed. Butterworth-Heinemann, 80 Montvale Ave., Stoneham, Massachusetts 02180. (617) 438-8464 or (800) 366-2665. 1982. Seventeenth edition. Includes data on the business of farming. Topics discussed include soils, drainage, crop physiology, crop nutrition, arable crops, grassland, trees on the farm, weed control, diseases of crops, pests of crops, grain preservation and storage, animal production, farm equipment, farm management, agricultural law, health and safety, and agricultural computers.

CRC Handbook of Data on Organic Compounds. Robert C. Weast. CRC Press, 2000 Corporate Blvd. N.W., Boca Raton, Florida 33431. (800) 272-7737. 1985.

CRC Handbook of Mass Spectra of Environmental Contaminants. R.A. Hites. CRC Press, 2000 Corporate Blvd. N.W., Boca Raton, Florida 33431. (800) 272-7737. 1985. Pollutants spectra and mass spectrometry.

Handbook of Environmental Data on Organic Chemicals. Karel Verschueren. Van Nostrand Reinhold, 115 5th Ave., New York, New York 10003. (212) 254-3232. 1983. Covers individual substances as well as mixtures and preparations. The profiles include: properties, air pollution factors, water pollution factors, and biological effects.

Integrated Pest Management. ANR Publications, University of California, 6701 San Pablo Ave., Oakland, California 94608-1239. (510) 642-2431. 1990-. Irregular. Provides and orderly, scientifically based system for diagnosing, recording, evaluating, preventing, and treating pest problems in a variety of crops.

Permaculture: A Practical Guide for a Sustainable Future. B. C. Mollison. Island Press, 1718 Connecticut Ave. N.W., Suite 300, Washington, District of Columbia 20009. (202) 232-7933. 1990.

ONLINE DATA BASES

AGRICOLA. U.S. Department of Agriculture, Office of Public Affairs, 14 Independence Ave., S.W., Washington, District of Columbia 20250. (202) 447-7454.

AGRIS. Food and Agriculture Organization of the United Nations, Via delle Terme di Caracalla, Rome, Italy 00100. 61 0181-FA01.

BioPatents. BIOSIS, 2100 Arch St., Philadelphia, Pennsylvania 19103. (800) 523-4806.

Bioprocessing Technology. Mead Data Central, Inc., P.O. Box 933, Dayton, Ohio 45401. (800) 227-4908.

BIOSIS Previews. BIOSIS, 2100 Arch St., Philadelphia, Pennsylvania 19103-1399. (215) 587-4800. Largest and most comprehensive database of research in the life sciences. Contains citations for nearly 9000 primary research journals, monographs, reviews, symposia, preliminary reports, semi-popular journals, selected institutional reports, government reports and research communications.

Cambridge Scientific Abstracts Life Science–CSAL. Cambridge Scientific Abstracts, 5161 River Rd., Bethesda, Maryland 20816. (301) 961-6750. Provides access to the following abstracting services: "Life Sciences Collection," "Aquatic Sciences and Fisheries Abstracts," "Oceanic Abstracts," and "Pollution Abstracts."

CRIS/USDA. U.S. Department of Agriculture, Cooperative State Research Service, Current Research Information System, National Agricultural Library Building, 5th Fl., 10301 Baltimore Blvd., Beltsville, Maryland 20705. (301) 344-3850. Agricultural, food and nutrition, and forestry research projects.

Current Contents Search. Institute for Scientific Information, 3501 Market St., Philadelphia, Pennsylvania 19104. (800) 523-1857.

Enviro/Energyline Abstracts Plus. R. R. Bowker Co., 121 Chanlon Rd., New Providence, New Jersey 07974. (908) 464-6800.

Environmental Periodicals Bibliography. National Information Services Corp., Ste. 6, Wyman Towers, 3100 St. Paul St., Baltimore, Maryland 21218. (410)243-0797. Online version of abstract of same name.

Farmer's Own Network for Education. Rodale Institute, 222 Main St., Emmaus, Pennsylvania 18098. (215) 967-5171. Efforts/results of farmers who have cut chemical use, diversified their farms, and adopted other regenerative agricultural techniques.

Life Sciences from NTIS. National Technical Information Center for the Utilization of Federal Technology, 5285 Port Royal Rd., Springfield, Virginia 22161. (703) 487-4650.

Monthly Catalog of United States Government Publications. U.S. G.P.O., Supt. of Docs., PO Box 371954, Pittsburgh, Pennsylvania 15250-7954. (202) 512-0000.

National Technical Information Service. U.S. Department of Commerce, National Technical Information Service, Office of Data Base Services, 5285 Port Royal Rd., Springfield, Virginia 22161. (703) 487-4807. Bibliographic database of government sponsored research and technical reports.

SCISEARCH. Institute for Scientific Information, University City Science Center, 3501 Market St., Philadelphia, Pennsylvania 19104. (215) 386-0100.

PERIODICALS AND NEWSLETTERS

Agrarian Advocate. California Action Network, Box 464, Davis, California 95617. (916) 756-8518. 1978-. Quarterly. Includes issues of concern to rural California residents such as groundwater pollution, pesticides, and sustainable agriculture.

Agricultural Engineering Magazine. American Society of Agricultural Engineers, 2950 Niles Road, St Joseph, Michigan 49085. (616) 429-0300. Bimonthly. Irrigation and other large scale projects with environmental significance.

Agriculture, Ecosystems & Environment. Elsevier Science Publishing Co., 655 Avenue of the Americas, New York, New York 10010. (212) 989-5800. Eight times a year. This journal is concerned with the interaction of methods of agricultural production, ecosystems and the environment.

Agro-Ecosystems. Elsevier Science Publishing Co., 655 Avenue of the Americas, New York, New York 10010. (212) 989-5800. 1982-. Quarterly. Journal of International Association for Ecology featuring ecological interactions between agricultural and managed forest systems.

Fertilizer Research: An International Journal on Fertilizer Use and Technology. Kluwer Academic Publishers, 101 Philip Dr., Assinippi Park, Norwell, Massachusetts 02061. (617) 871-6600. Monthly. Soils, soil fertility, soil chemistry, crop and animal production and husbandry, crop quality and environment.

Hilgardia: A Journal of Agricultural Science. California Agricultural Experiment Station, 2120 University Ave., Berkeley, California 94720. 1925-.

Journal of Agricultural and Food Chemistry. American Chemical Society, 1155 16th St. N.W., Washington, District of Columbia 20036. (202) 872-4600; (800) 227-5558. 1953-. Monthly. Contains documentation of significant advances in the science of agriculture and food chemistry.

Journal of Environmental Quality. American Society of Agronomy, 677 S. Segoe Rd., Madison, Wisconsin 53711-1086. (608) 273-8080. 1972-. Quarterly. Reports and brief reviews of agricultural ecology, environmental engineering and pollution.

Land Improvement Contractors of America News. LICA Service Corp., LICA News, 1300 Maybrook Dr., Maybrook, Illinois 60153. Monthly. Deals with erosion control, land use and improvement.

Technical Paper-Agricultural Experiment Station. University of California Press, 2120 Berkeley Way, Berkeley, California 94720. (510) 642-4247. 1924-. Monthly (irregularly).

RESEARCH CENTERS AND INSTITUTES

Coolidge Center for Environmental Leadership. 1675 Massachusetts Ave., Suite 4, Cambridge, Massachusetts 02138. (617) 864-5085.

Institute for Alternative Agriculture. 9200 Edmonston Rd., Suite 117, Greenbelt, Maryland 20770. (301) 441-8777.

Jamie Whitten Delta States Research Center. PO Box 225, Stoneville, Mississippi 3877-0225. (601) 686-5231.

Michigan State University, W.K. Kellogg Forest. 7060 N. 42nd St., Augusta, Michigan 49012. (616) 731-4597.

Reynolds Homestead Agricultural Experiment Station. Virginia Polytech Institute and State University, PO Box 70, Critz, Virginia 24082. (703) 694-4135.

U.S. Forest Service, Forestry Sciences Laboratory. Forest Hill Road, Houghton, Michigan 49931. (906) 482-6303.

U.S. Forest Service, Shrub Sciences Laboratory. 735 N. 500 E., Provo, Utah 84606. (801) 377-5717.

University of Arizona, Environmental Research Laboratory. Tucson International Airport, 2601 East Airport Drive, Tucson, Arizona 85706. (602) 741-1990.

University of Illinois, Water Resources Center. 2535 Hydrosystems Laboratory, 205 North Matthews Avenue, Urbana, Illinois 61801. (217) 333-0536.

University of Maine, Cooperative Forestry Research Unit. College of Forest Resources, Orono, Maine 04469. (207) 581-2893.

University of Nebraska-Lincoln, Water Center. 103 Natural Resources Hall, Lincoln, Nebraska 68503-0844. (402) 472-3305.

University of Puerto Rico, Central Analytical Laboratory. P.O. Box 21360, Rio Piedras, Puerto Rico 00928. (809) 767-9705.

World Resources Institute. 1709 New York Ave., N.W., Washington, District of Columbia 20006. (202) 638-6300.

STATISTICS SOURCES

Agricultural Conservation Program Statistical Summary. U.S. Agricultural Stabilization and Conservation Service, Dept. of Agriculture, Washington, District of Columbia 20013. (202) 512-0000. Annual. Deals with soil erosion control, water conservation, water quality and costs by state and county.

Alternative Agriculture. National Academy of Sciences, National Research Council, 2101 Constitution Ave., NW, Washington, District of Columbia 20418. (202) 334-2000. 1989. Economic potential of alternative farming systems, methods that emphasize natural processes, limited pesticide use, and conservation of resources.

World Resources. World Resources Institute. 1709 New York Ave., N.W., Washington, District of Columbia 20006. (202) 638-6300. Annual. Statistical and textual analysis of world's natural resources and the effects of growth-caused environmental pollution.

TRADE ASSOCIATIONS AND PROFESSIONAL SOCIETIES

Agricultural Cooperative Development International. 50 F St., N.W., Suite 900, Washington, District of Columbia 20001. (202) 638-4661.

Agricultural Research Institute. 9650 Rockville Pike, Bethesda, Maryland 20814. (301) 530-7122.

American Association for the Advancement of Science. 1333 H St., N.W., Washington, District of Columbia 20005. (202) 326-6400.

American Society of Agricultural Consultants. Enterprise Center, 8301 Greensboro Dr., Suite 260, McLean, Virginia 22102. (703) 356-2455.

American Society of Agricultural Engineers. 2950 Niles Rd., St Joseph, Michigan 49085. (616) 429-0300.

Association for Arid Land Studies. c/o International Center for Arid and Semi-Arid Land Studies, Texas Tech. University, P.O. Box 41036, Lubbock, Texas 79409-1036. (806) 742-2218.

Center for International Development and Environment. 1709 New York Ave., N.W., Washington, District of Columbia 20006. (202) 462-0900.

CONCERN, Inc. 1794 Columbia Rd, NW, Washington, District of Columbia 20009. (202) 328-8160.

Council for Agricultural Science & Technology. 137 Lynn Ave., Ames, Iowa 50010. (515) 292-2125.

Crop Science Society of America. 677 S. Segoe Rd., Madison, Wisconsin 53711. (608) 273-8080.

Food and Agriculture Organization. Liaison Office for North America, 1001 22nd St., N.W., Washington, District of Columbia 20437. (202) 653-2402.

Friends of the Earth. 218 D St., SE, Washington, District of Columbia 20003. (202) 544-2600.

The Izaak Walton League of America. 1401 Wilson Boulevard, Level B, Arlington, Virginia 22209. (703) 528-1818.

The Jessie Smith Noyes Foundation. 16 E. 34th St., New York, New York 10016. (212) 684-6577.

Land Improvement Contractors of America. P.O. Box 9, 1300 Maybrook Dr., Maywood, Illinois 60153. (708) 344-0700.

National Agricultural Aviation Association. 1005 E St., S.E., Washington, District of Columbia 20003. (202) 546-5722.

National Agricultural Chemicals Association. 1155 15th St., N.W., Madison Building, Suite 900, Washington, District of Columbia 20005. (202) 296-1585.

National Association of Agricultural Employees. c/o Eric White, Box B, U.S. Aid Bridgetown, FPO Miami, Florida 34054.

National Association of County Agricultural Agents. 1575 Northside Dr., 200 ATC, Ste. 170, Atlanta, Georgia 30318. (404) 730-7004.

National Association of State Departments of Agriculture. 1616 H St., N.W., Suite 704, Washington, District of Columbia 20006. (202) 628-1566.

National Farmers Union. 10065 E. Harvard Ave., Denver, Colorado 80231. (303) 337-5500.

National Future Farmers of America. P.O. Box 15160, National FFA Center, Alexandria, Virginia 22309. (703) 360-3600.

National Gardening Association. 180 Flynn Ave., Burlington, Vermont 05401. (802) 863-1308.

Native Seeds/Search. 2509 N. Campbell Ave., No. 325, Tucson, Arizona 85719. (602) 327-9123.

New Alchemy Institute. 237 Hatchville Rd., East Falmouth, Massachusetts 02536. (508) 564-6301.

Peace Corps. 1990 K St., N.W., Washington, District of Columbia 20526. (800) 424-8580.

Rural Advancement Fund International (*RAFI-USA*). P.O. Box 655, Pittsboro, North Carolina 27312. (919) 542-1396.

AGRICULTURE, SLASH & BURN (SWIDDEN)

See also: FOREST MANAGEMENT

ABSTRACTING AND INDEXING SERVICES

Agrindex. AGRIS Coordinating Center, Via delle Terme di Caracalla, Rome, Italy I-00100. 61 0181-FA01. 1975-.

Applied Ecology Abstracts Studies in Renewable Natural Resources. Information Retrieval Ltd., 1911 Jefferson Davis Highway, Arlington, Virginia 22202. 1975-. Monthly.

Biological Abstracts. BIOSIS, 2100 Arch St., Philadelphia, Pennsylvania 19103-1399. (215) 587-4800. 1927-.

Biological and Agricultural Index. H.W. Wilson Co., 950 University Ave., Bronx, New York 10452. (800) 367-6770. 1916-. Monthly.

Environment Abstracts. Bowker A & I Publishing, 121 Chanlon Rd., New Providence, New Jersey 07974. (908) 464-6800. 1974-.

Environment Index. Environment Information Center, Index Research Department, 124 E. 39th St., New York, New York 10016. 1971-. Annual.

Environmental Information Connection–EIC. Planning Information Program, Dept. of Urban and Regional Planning, University of Illinois, 1003 West Nevada, Urbana, Illinois 61801. (217) 333-1369. Also available online.

Environmental Periodicals Bibliography. Environmental Studies Institute, International Academy at Santa Barbara, 800 Garden St., Suite D, Santa Barbara, California 93101. (805) 965-5010. Also available online.

Index to Scientific Book Contents. Institute for Scientific Information, 3501 Market St., Philadelphia, Pennsylvania 19104. (800) 523-1857. 1985-. Annual. Gives contents of science books published.

Multimedia Index to Ecology. National Information Center for Educational Media, University of Southern California, Los Angeles, California 90007.

BIBLIOGRAPHIES

Current Contents. Agriculture, Biology and Environmental Sciences. Institute for Scientific Information, 3501 Market St., Philadelphia, Pennsylvania 19104. (800) 523-1857. 1973-. Previous title: Current Contents. Agricultural, Food & Veterinary Sciences. Gives the table of contents of periodicals in the fields of agriculture, biology, environmental and related areas.

EPA Publications Bibliography. U.S. Environmental Protection Agency, Library Systems Branch, 401 M St., SW, Washington, District of Columbia 20460. (202) 260-2090. Quarterly.

List of Periodicals and Serials in the Forestry Library. Commonwealth Forestry Association, c/o Oxford Forestry Institute, Oxford, England OX1 3RB. 1968. Covers agriculture and forests and forestry.

Phosphorus in Agriculture. C. A. B. International, 845 North Park Ave., Tucson, Arizona 85719. (602) 621-7897 or (800) 528-4841. 1991. Two volumes. Contains 1,100 citations.

ENCYCLOPEDIAS AND DICTIONARIES

McGraw-Hill Encyclopedia of Environmental Science. Sybil P. Parker. McGraw-Hill Science & Engineering Books, 11 W. 19th St., New York, New York 10011. (212) 337-6010. 1980. Covers ecology, man's influence on nature, and environmental protection.

McGraw-Hill Encyclopedia of Science and Technology. McGraw-Hill, 1221 Avenue of the Americas, New York, New York 10020. (212) 512-2000 or (800) 262-4729. 1992. Seventh edition. Issued in multiple volumes including index. Includes all science and technology broad subject areas.

GENERAL WORKS

Agricultural and Environmental Policies: Opportunities for Integration. OECD Publications and Information Center, 2001 L St. N.W., Suite 700, Washington, District of Columbia 20036. (202) 785-OECD. 1989. Describes a broad range of approaches by OECD countries to integrating environmental and agricultural policies and argues that eventual cuts in economic support for agriculture and withdrawal of land from production could produce important benefits for the environment.

Feeding Tomorrow's World. Albert Sasson. Centre for Agriculture and Rural Cooperation and UNESCO, 7 Place de Fontenoy, Paris, France 1990. Analyzes Green Revolution and biotechnological revolution and tries to answer other pressing questions through a pluridisciplinary approach to human nutrition and food production. Synthesizes the scientific, economic, socioeconomic and environmental aspects of nutrition throughout the world.

ONLINE DATA BASES

BIOSIS Previews. BIOSIS, 2100 Arch St., Philadelphia, Pennsylvania 19103-1399. (215) 587-4800. Largest and most comprehensive database of research in the life sciences. Contains citations for nearly 9000 primary research journals, monographs, reviews, symposia, preliminary reports, semi-popular journals, selected institutional reports, government reports and research communications.

Cambridge Scientific Abstracts Life Science–CSAL. Cambridge Scientific Abstracts, 5161 River Rd., Bethesda, Maryland 20816. (301) 961-6750. Provides access to the following abstracting services: "Life Sciences Collection," "Aquatic Sciences and Fisheries Abstracts," "Oceanic Abstracts," and "Pollution Abstracts."

CRIS/USDA. U.S. Department of Agriculture, Cooperative State Research Service, Current Research Information System, National Agricultural Library Building, 5th Fl., 10301 Baltimore Blvd., Beltsville, Maryland 20705. (301) 344-3850. Agricultural, food and nutrition, and forestry research projects.

Current Research Information System–CRIS/USDA. U.S. Department of Agriculture, National Agricultural Library, 10301 Baltimore Blvd., 5th Floor, Beltsville, Maryland 20705-2351. (301) 504-5755. Looks at current research projects in agriculture and allied sciences covering the biological, physical, social and behavioral sciences related to agriculture.

Enviro/Energyline Abstracts Plus. R. R. Bowker Co., 121 Chanlon Rd., New Providence, New Jersey 07974. (908) 464-6800.

Environmental Periodicals Bibliography. National Information Services Corp., Ste. 6, Wyman Towers, 3100 St. Paul St., Baltimore, Maryland 21218. (410)243-0797. Online version of abstract of same name.

Monthly Catalog of United States Government Publications. U.S. G.P.O., Supt. of Docs., PO Box 371954, Pittsburgh, Pennsylvania 15250-7954. (202) 512-0000.

National Technical Information Service. U.S. Department of Commerce, National Technical Information Service, Office of Data Base Services, 5285 Port Royal Rd., Springfield, Virginia 22161. (703) 487-4807. Bibliographic database of government sponsored research and technical reports.

PressNet Environmental Reports. Chemical Information Systems, Inc., 7215 York Rd., Baltimore, Maryland 21212. (301) 321-8440.

SCISEARCH. Institute for Scientific Information, University City Science Center, 3501 Market St., Philadelphia, Pennsylvania 19104. (215) 386-0100.

TRADE ASSOCIATIONS AND PROFESSIONAL SOCIETIES

American Institute of Biological Sciences. 730 11th St., N.W., Washington, District of Columbia 20001-4521. (202) 628-1500.

American Society of Agricultural Engineers. 2950 Niles Rd., St Joseph, Michigan 49085. (616) 429-0300.

AGRONOMICS AND AGRIBUSINESS

ABSTRACTING AND INDEXING SERVICES

Agrindex. AGRIS Coordinating Center, Via delle Terme di Caracalla, Rome, Italy I-00100. 61 0181-FA01. 1975-.

Biological Abstracts. BIOSIS, 2100 Arch St., Philadelphia, Pennsylvania 19103-1399. (215) 587-4800. 1927-.

Biological and Agricultural Index. H.W. Wilson Co., 950 University Ave., Bronx, New York 10452. (800) 367-6770. 1916-. Monthly.

Current Advances in Plant Science. Pergamon Microforms International, Inc., Fairview Park, Elmsford, New York 10523. (914) 592-7720. 1984-. Monthly. Current literature searching service including journals, reports, abstracts, etc. This service is available online as part of the CABS database on the hosts BRS and ORBIT search service.

Environment Abstracts. Bowker A & I Publishing, 121 Chanlon Rd., New Providence, New Jersey 07974. (908) 464-6800. 1974-.

Environment Index. Environment Information Center, Index Research Department, 124 E. 39th St., New York, New York 10016. 1971-. Annual.

Environmental Information Connection–EIC. Planning Information Program, Dept. of Urban and Regional Planning, University of Illinois, 1003 West Nevada, Urbana, Illinois 61801. (217) 333-1369. Also available online.

Environmental Periodicals Bibliography. Environmental Studies Institute, International Academy at Santa Barbara, 800 Garden St., Suite D, Santa Barbara, California 93101. (805) 965-5010. Also available online.

General Science Index. H. W. Wilson Co., 950 University Ave., Bronx, New York 10452. 1978-. Monthly, also issued in annual cumulation. Cumulative subject index to English language periodicals in the subject fields of astronomy, botany, chemistry, earth science, environment and conservation, food and nutrition, genetics, mathematics, medicine and health, microbiology, oceanography, physics, physiology and zoology.

Index to Scientific Book Contents. Institute for Scientific Information, 3501 Market St., Philadelphia, Pennsylvania 19104. (800) 523-1857. 1985-. Annual. Gives contents of science books published.

Science Citation Index. Institute for Scientific Information, 3501 Market St., Philadelphia, Pennsylvania 19104. 1961-.

BIBLIOGRAPHIES

Current Contents. Agriculture, Biology and Environmental Sciences. Institute for Scientific Information, 3501 Market St., Philadelphia, Pennsylvania 19104. (800) 523-1857. 1973-. Previous title: Current Contents. Agricultural, Food & Veterinary Sciences. Gives the table of contents of periodicals in the fields of agriculture, biology, environmental and related areas.

Directory of Published Proceedings. Interdok Corp., 173 Halstead Ave., Harrison, New York 10528. (914) 835-3506. 1990. Monthly. This is a listing of published proceedings including the series SEMTE (Science/Medicine/Engineering/Technology) and the series SSH (Social Science/Humanities).

EPA Publications Bibliography. U.S. Environmental Protection Agency, Library Systems Branch, 401 M St., SW, Washington, District of Columbia 20460. (202) 260-2090. Quarterly.

DIRECTORIES

Agricultural Information Resource Centers, a World Directory 1990. Rita C. Fisher. IAALD World Directory Working Group, 716 W. Indiana Ave., Urbana, Illinois 61801-4836. (217) 333-7687. 1990. Includes 3,971 information resource centers that have agriculture related collection and/or information services.

ENCYCLOPEDIAS AND DICTIONARIES

Encyclopedia of Human Biology. Renato Dulbecco, ed. Academic Press, c/o Harcourt Brace Jovanovich Inc., 6277 Sea Harbor Dr., Orlando, Florida 32887. (800) 346-8648. 1991. Eight volumes.

The Encyclopedia of Soil Science. Rhodes W. Fairbridge. Academic Press, c/o Harcourt Brace Jovanovich Inc.,

6277 Sea Harbor Dr., Orlando, Florida 32887. (800) 346-8648. 1979-. Includes soil physics, soil chemistry, soil biology, soil fertility and plant nutrition, soil genesis, classification and cartography.

McGraw-Hill Encyclopedia of Science and Technology. McGraw-Hill, 1221 Avenue of the Americas, New York, New York 10020. (212) 512-2000 or (800) 262-4729. 1992. Seventh edition. Issued in multiple volumes including index. Includes all science and technology broad subject areas.

Van Nostrand's Scientific Encyclopedia. Glenn D. Considine, ed. Van Nostrand Reinhold, 115 5th Ave., New York, New York 10003. (212) 254-3232. 1983. Sixth edition. Includes all broad subject areas in science.

GENERAL WORKS

Agroecology: Researching the Ecological Basis for Sustainable Agriculture. Stephen R. Gliessman, ed. Springer-Verlag, 175 5th Ave., New York, New York 10010. (212) 460-1500; (800) 777-4643. 1990. Demonstrates in a series of international case studies how to combine the more production-oriented focus of the agronomist with the more systems-oriented viewpoint of the ecologist. Methodology for evaluating and quantifying agroecosystem is presented.

From the Land. Nancy P. Pittman, ed. Island Press, 1718 Connecticut Ave. N.W., Suite 300, Washington, District of Columbia 20009. (202) 232-7933. 1988. Anthology comes from 13 years of the Land–a journal of conservation writings from the '40s and '50s. Through fiction, essay, poetry, and philosophy we learn how our small farms have given way to today's agribusiness.

GOVERNMENTAL ORGANIZATIONS

Information Division: Statistical Reporting Service. Room 209, JSM Building, 15th and Independence Ave., S.W., Washington, District of Columbia 20250. (202) 447-4230.

ONLINE DATA BASES

AGRICOLA. U.S. Department of Agriculture, Office of Public Affairs, 14 Independence Ave., S.W., Washington, District of Columbia 20250. (202) 447-7454.

BIOSIS Previews. BIOSIS, 2100 Arch St., Philadelphia, Pennsylvania 19103-1399. (215) 587-4800. Largest and most comprehensive database of research in the life sciences. Contains citations for nearly 9000 primary research journals, monographs, reviews, symposia, preliminary reports, semi-popular journals, selected institutional reports, government reports and research communications.

Cambridge Scientific Abstracts Life Science–CSAL. Cambridge Scientific Abstracts, 5161 River Rd., Bethesda, Maryland 20816. (301) 961-6750. Provides access to the following abstracting services: "Life Sciences Collection," "Aquatic Sciences and Fisheries Abstracts," "Oceanic Abstracts," and "Pollution Abstracts."

CRIS/USDA. U.S. Department of Agriculture, Cooperative State Research Service, Current Research Information System, National Agricultural Library Building, 5th Fl., 10301 Baltimore Blvd., Beltsville, Maryland 20705. (301) 344-3850. Agricultural, food and nutrition, and forestry research projects.

Enviro/Energyline Abstracts Plus. R. R. Bowker Co., 121 Chanlon Rd., New Providence, New Jersey 07974. (908) 464-6800.

Environmental Periodicals Bibliography. National Information Services Corp., Ste. 6, Wyman Towers, 3100 St. Paul St., Baltimore, Maryland 21218. (410)243-0797. Online version of abstract of same name.

Monthly Catalog of United States Government Publications. U.S. G.P.O., Supt. of Docs., PO Box 371954, Pittsburgh, Pennsylvania 15250-7954. (202) 512-0000.

National Technical Information Service. U.S. Department of Commerce, National Technical Information Service, Office of Data Base Services, 5285 Port Royal Rd., Springfield, Virginia 22161. (703) 487-4807. Bibliographic database of government sponsored research and technical reports.

SCISEARCH. Institute for Scientific Information, University City Science Center, 3501 Market St., Philadelphia, Pennsylvania 19104. (215) 386-0100.

PERIODICALS AND NEWSLETTERS

News & Notes. National Food & Energy Council, Inc., 409 Vandiver W., Suite 202, Columbia, Missouri 65202. (314) 875-7155. Bimonthly. Efficient use and management of electricity on farms and assurance of continuing energy for the food system.

RESEARCH CENTERS AND INSTITUTES

Institute for Alternative Agriculture. 9200 Edmonston Rd., Suite 117, Greenbelt, Maryland 20770. (301) 441-8777.

University of Hawaii at Manoa, Water Resources Research Center. 2540 Dole Street, Honolulu, Hawaii 96822. (808) 956-7847.

TRADE ASSOCIATIONS AND PROFESSIONAL SOCIETIES

American Agricultural Economics Association. 80 Heady Hall, Iowa State University, Ames, Iowa 50011-1070. (515) 294-8700.

American Society of Agricultural Engineers. 2950 Niles Rd., St Joseph, Michigan 49085. (616) 429-0300.

American Society of Agronomy. 677 South Segoe Rd., Madison, Wisconsin 53711. (608) 273-8080.

Chamber of Commerce of the United States. 1615 H St., N.W., Washington, District of Columbia 20062. (202) 659-6000.

AIR ANALYSIS
See: AIR QUALITY

AIR CHEMISTRY
See: AIR QUALITY

AIR CONDITIONING
See also: FREON; OZONE LAYER; REFRIGERATION

ABSTRACTING AND INDEXING SERVICES

Air Pollution Technical Publications of the United States Environmental Protection Agency. U.S. Environmental Protection Agency, Mail Drop 75, Research Triangle Park, North Carolina 27711. (919) 541-2184. 1976. Quarterly.

Applied Science and Technology Index. H.W. Wilson Co., 950 University Ave., Bronx, New York 10452. (800) 367-6770. Formerly Industrial Arts Index.

Biological Abstracts. BIOSIS, 2100 Arch St., Philadelphia, Pennsylvania 19103-1399. (215) 587-4800. 1927-.

Engineering Index. The Engineering Index Inc., 345 E. 47th St., New York, New York 10017. 1962-.

Environment Abstracts. Bowker A & I Publishing, 121 Chanlon Rd., New Providence, New Jersey 07974. (908) 464-6800. 1974-.

Environment Index. Environment Information Center, Index Research Department, 124 E. 39th St., New York, New York 10016. 1971-. Annual.

Environmental Information Connection–EIC. Planning Information Program, Dept. of Urban and Regional Planning, University of Illinois, 1003 West Nevada, Urbana, Illinois 61801. (217) 333-1369. Also available online.

Environmental Periodicals Bibliography. Environmental Studies Institute, International Academy at Santa Barbara, 800 Garden St., Suite D, Santa Barbara, California 93101. (805) 965-5010. Also available online.

Physics Briefs. Physikalische Berichte. Physik Verlag, Pappapelallee 3, Postfach 101161, Weinheim, Germany D-6940. 1979-. Semimonthly. In English. Volumes for 1979- issued by the Deutsche Physikalische Gesellschaft and the Fachinformationszentrum Energie Physik, Mathematik in cooperation with the American Institute of Physics.

Science Citation Index. Institute for Scientific Information, 3501 Market St., Philadelphia, Pennsylvania 19104. 1961-.

BIBLIOGRAPHIES

EPA Publications Bibliography. U.S. Environmental Protection Agency, Library Systems Branch, 401 M St., SW, Washington, District of Columbia 20460. (202) 260-2090. Quarterly.

Natural Ventilation, Passive Cooling, and Human Comfort in Buildings: A Comprehensive Technical Bibliography. The Associates, Washington, District of Columbia

DIRECTORIES

Air Conditioning, Heating & Refrigeration News. Directory Issue. Business News Publishing Co., PO Box 2600, Troy, Michigan 48007. (313) 362-3700 or (800) 247-2160. Annual.

Automobile Air Conditioning Equipment Directory. 5711 S. 86th Circle, Omaha, Nebraska 68127. (402) 593-4600. Annual.

Gale Environmental Sourcebook. Karen Hill. Gale Research Co., 835 Penobscot Bldg., Detroit, Michigan 48226-4094. (313) 961-2242. Contacts, information sources, or general information on environmental topics.

Heating-Plumbing Air Conditioning–Buyers' Guide Issue. 1450 Don Mills Rd., Don Mills, Ontario, Canada M3B 2X7. (416) 445-6641. Annual.

Heating, Ventilating, Refrigeration & Air Conditioning Year Book and Daily Buyers' Guide. 34 Palace Court, ESCA House, Bayswater, England W2 4JG. (71) 292488. Annual.

National Council on Refrigeration Sales Association–Membership Directory. c/o Fernley & Fernley, Inc., 1900 Arch St., Philadelphia, Pennsylvania 19103. (215) 564-3484. Annual.

Who's Who in the Plumbing-Heating-Cooling Industry. National Association of Plumbing-Heating-Cooling Contractors, 180 S. Washington St., P.O. Box 6808, Falls Church, Virginia 22046. (703) 237-8100.

ENCYCLOPEDIAS AND DICTIONARIES

Dictionary of Refrigeration and Air Conditioning. K. M. Booth. Elsevier Science Publishing Co., 655 Avenue of the Americas, New York, New York 10010. (212) 989-5800. 1970.

Encyclopedia of Physical Science and Technology. Robert A. Meyers, ed. Academic Press, c/o Harcourt Brace Jovanovich Inc., 6277 Sea Harbor Dr., Orlando, Florida 32887. (800) 346-8648. Dictionary of engineering, technology and physical sciences.

McGraw-Hill Encyclopedia of Science and Technology. McGraw-Hill, 1221 Avenue of the Americas, New York, New York 10020. (212) 512-2000 or (800) 262-4729. 1992. Seventh edition. Issued in multiple volumes including index. Includes all science and technology broad subject areas.

GENERAL WORKS

Heating, Cooling, Lighting. John Wiley & Sons, Inc., 605 3rd Ave., New York, New York 10158-0012. (212) 850-6000. 1991.

ONLINE DATA BASES

BIOSIS Previews. BIOSIS, 2100 Arch St., Philadelphia, Pennsylvania 19103-1399. (215) 587-4800. Largest and most comprehensive database of research in the life sciences. Contains citations for nearly 9000 primary research journals, monographs, reviews, symposia, preliminary reports, semi-popular journals, selected institutional reports, government reports and research communications.

Computerized Engineering Index–COMPENDEX. Engineering Information Inc., 345 E. 47th St., New York, New York 10017. (212) 705-7600.

Enviro/Energyline Abstracts Plus. R. R. Bowker Co., 121 Chanlon Rd., New Providence, New Jersey 07974. (908) 464-6800.

Environmental Periodicals Bibliography. National Information Services Corp., Ste. 6, Wyman Towers, 3100 St. Paul St., Baltimore, Maryland 21218. (410)243-0797. Online version of abstract of same name.

IBSEDEX. Building Services Research & Information Association, Old Bracknell Lane West, Bracknell, Berkshire, England RG12 4AH. 44 (344) 426511.

PERIODICALS AND NEWSLETTERS

Energy and Housing Report. Business Publishers, Inc., 951 Pershing Dr., Silver Spring, Maryland 20910. (301) 587-6300. Monthly. Energy conservation problems; developments in home energy products.

STATISTICS SOURCES

Air Conditioning, Heating, and Refrigeration News: 1990 Statistical Panorama. Business News Publishing Co., PO Box 2600, Troy, Michigan 48007. (313) 362-3700; (800) 247-2160. Shipments of air conditioning, refrigeration, home heating, and related products.

Environmental Data Compendium. OECD Publications and Information Center, 2001 L St., N.W., Suite 700, Washington, District of Columbia 20036. (202) 785-6323. 1989.

Environmental Indicators. OECD Publications and Information Center, 2001 L St., N.W., Suite 700, Washington, District of Columbia 20036. (202) 785-6323. 1991.

Environmental Quality. Council on Environmental Quality. U.S. G.P.O., Washington, District of Columbia 20401. (202) 512-0000. Annual.

News Release From The Air-Conditioning and Refrigeration Institute. Air Conditioning and Refrigeration Institute, 1501 Wilson Blvd., Suite 600, Arlington, Virginia 22209. Monthly. Unitary air conditioner/heat pump domestic shipments.

The State of the Environment. OECD Publications and Information Center, 2001 L St., N.W., Suite 700, Washington, District of Columbia 20036. (202) 785-6323. 1991.

TRADE ASSOCIATIONS AND PROFESSIONAL SOCIETIES

Air-Conditioning and Refrigeration Institute. 1501 Wilson Blvd., 6th Fl., Arlington, Virginia 22209. (703) 524-8800.

Air Cooled Heat Exchanger Manufacturers Association. 25 N. Broadway, Tarrytown, New York 10591. (914) 332-0040.

American Society of Heating, Refrigerating and Air-Conditioning Engineers. 1791 Tullie Circle, N.E., Atlanta, Georgia 30329. (404) 636-8400.

Association of Refrigerant and Desuperheating Manufacturing. P.O. Box 180458, Casselberry, Florida 32718. (407) 260-1313.

Automotive Refrigeration Products Institute. 5100 Forbes Blvd., Lanham, Maryland 20706. (301) 731-5195.

Commercial Refrigerator Manufacturers. 1101 Connecticut Ave., N.W., Suite 700, Washington, District of Columbia 20036. (202) 857-1145.

National Environmental Balancing Bureau. 8224 Old Courthouse Rd., Vienna, Virginia 19103. (215) 564-3484.

Refrigerating Engineers and Technicians Association. c/o Smith-Bucklin Associates, 401 N. Michigan Ave., Chicago, Illinois 60611. (312) 644-6610.

AIR CURTAIN
See: AIR QUALITY

AIR MONITORING
See: POLLUTION CONTROL

AIR POLLUTION
See also: ACID PRECIPITATION; AEROSOLS; AIR QUALITY; EMISSIONS; ENVIRONMENTAL CONDITION; GLOBAL WARMING; PARTICULATES; POLLUTION; SMOG

ABSTRACTING AND INDEXING SERVICES

Abstracts of Air and Water Conservation Literature. American Petroleum Institute. Central Abstracting and Indexing Service, 275 Madison Avenue, New York, New York 10016. 1972.

Air Pollution Technical Publications of the United States Environmental Protection Agency. U.S. Environmental Protection Agency, Mail Drop 75, Research Triangle Park, North Carolina 27711. (919) 541-2184. 1976. Quarterly.

Air Pollution Titles. Pennsylvania State University, Center for Air Environmental Studies, 226 Fenske Laboratory, University Park, Pennsylvania 16802. (814) 865-1415. 1965. Bibliographic guide to current research literature on air environment, including monitoring and control of air pollution, health effects, effects on agriculture, forests, toxic air contaminants, and global atmospheric pro cases.

Air Pollution Translations. A Bibliography With Abstracts. U.S. Environmental Protection Agency, MD 75, Research Triangle Park, North Carolina 27711. (919) 541-2184. 1969.

Applied Ecology Abstracts Studies in Renewable Natural Resources. Information Retrieval Ltd., 1911 Jefferson Davis Highway, Arlington, Virginia 22202. 1975-. Monthly.

Applied Science and Technology Index. H.W. Wilson Co., 950 University Ave., Bronx, New York 10452. (800) 367-6770. Formerly Industrial Arts Index.

Biological Abstracts. BIOSIS, 2100 Arch St., Philadelphia, Pennsylvania 19103-1399. (215) 587-4800. 1927-.

Biological and Agricultural Index. H.W. Wilson Co., 950 University Ave., Bronx, New York 10452. (800) 367-6770. 1916-. Monthly.

Bulletin Signaletique: Eau et Assainissement, Pollution Atmospherique, Droit des Pollutions. Centre de Documentation, Centre National de la Recherche Scientifique, 15, quai Anatole France, Paris, France 75700. (1) 45 55 92 25. 1983-. Monthly. Indexes pollution periodicals including water, atmospheric and related pollutions.

Chemical Abstracts. Chemical Abstracts Service, 2540 Olentangy River Rd., PO Box 3012, Columbus, Ohio 43210. (800) 848-6533. 1907-.

Ecological Abstracts. Geo Abstracts Ltd. Elsevier Applied Science, Crown House, Linton Rd., Barking, England IG 11 8JU. 1974-. Derived from over 600 leading ecological and environmental journals, plus books, conference proceedings, reports and theses.

Ecology Abstracts. Cambridge Scientific Abstracts, 5161 River Rd., Bethesda, Maryland 20816. (301) 961-6750. Monthly.

Environment Abstracts. Bowker A & I Publishing, 121 Chanlon Rd., New Providence, New Jersey 07974. (908) 464-6800. 1974-.

Environment Index. Environment Information Center, Index Research Department, 124 E. 39th St., New York, New York 10016. 1971-. Annual.

Environmental Information Connection-EIC. Planning Information Program, Dept. of Urban and Regional Planning, University of Illinois, 1003 West Nevada, Urbana, Illinois 61801. (217) 333-1369. Also available online.

Environmental Periodicals Bibliography. Environmental Studies Institute, International Academy at Santa Barbara, 800 Garden St., Suite D, Santa Barbara, California 93101. (805) 965-5010. Also available online.

General Science Index. H. W. Wilson Co., 950 University Ave., Bronx, New York 10452. 1978-. Monthly, also issued in annual cumulation. Cumulative subject index to English language periodicals in the subject fields of astronomy, botany, chemistry, earth science, environment and conservation, food and nutrition, genetics, mathematics, medicine and health, microbiology, oceanography, physics, physiology and zoology.

Green Engineering: A Current Awareness Bulletin. Institution of Mechanical Engineers, 1 Birdcage Walk, Westminster, London, England SW1H 9JJ. 71973 1266/7. 1991. Monthly. Covers acid rain, aerosol technology, biotechnology chlorofluorocarbons, chemical and process engineering, environmental protection, energy conservation, energy generation, greenhouse effect, materials, pollution, recycling, waste disposal, and other environmental topics.

Index to Scientific Book Contents. Institute for Scientific Information, 3501 Market St., Philadelphia, Pennsylvania 19104. (800) 523-1857. 1985-. Annual. Gives contents of science books published.

Multimedia Index to Ecology. National Information Center for Educational Media, University of Southern California, Los Angeles, California 90007.

Pollution Abstracts. Cambridge Scientific Abstracts, 5161 River Rd., Bethesda, Maryland 20816. (301) 961-6750. Six/year. Indexes worldwide technical literature on environmental pollution. Covers air pollution, marine and freshwater pollution, sewage and wastewater treatment, waste management, toxicology and health, noise pollution, radiation, land pollution, and environmental policies, programs, legislation, and education. Also available online.

Science Citation Index. Institute for Scientific Information, 3501 Market St., Philadelphia, Pennsylvania 19104. 1961-.

ALMANACS AND YEARBOOKS

Air Pollution. Arthur C. Stern, ed. Academic Press, c/o Harcourt Brace Jovanovich Inc., 6277 Sea Harbor Dr., Orlando, Florida 32887. (800) 346-8648. Annual.

Gale Environmental Almanac. Russ Hoyle. Gale Research Inc., 835 Penobscot Bldg., Detroit, Michigan 48226-4094. (313) 961-2242. 1993. Focuses on the U.S. and Canada, although worldwide and transboundary issues are discussed.

BIBLIOGRAPHIES

Adverse Effects of Air Pollutants. Lillian Sheridan. ABBE Publishers Association of Washington DC, 4111 Gallows Rd., Annandale, Virginia 22003-1862. 1985. Medical subject analysis and research bibliography.

Bibliography and Index of Geology. American Geological Institute, 4220 King St., Alexandria, Virginia 22302. Monthly. Includes environmental geology and hydrogeology.

Current Contents. Agriculture, Biology and Environmental Sciences. Institute for Scientific Information, 3501 Market St., Philadelphia, Pennsylvania 19104. (800) 523-1857. 1973-. Previous title: Current Contents. Agricultural, Food & Veterinary Sciences. Gives the table of contents of periodicals in the fields of agriculture, biology, environmental and related areas.

Directory of Published Proceedings. Interdok Corp., 173 Halstead Ave., Harrison, New York 10528. (914) 835-3506. 1990. Monthly. This is a listing of published proceedings including the series SEMTE (Science/Medicine/Engineering/Technology) and the series SSH (Social Science/Humanities).

Environmental Pollution. National Technical Information Service, 5285 Port Royal Road, Springfield, Virginia 22161. (703) 487-4650. Monthly.

EPA Publications Bibliography. U.S. Environmental Protection Agency, Library Systems Branch, 401 M St., SW, Washington, District of Columbia 20460. (202) 260-2090. Quarterly.

Indoor Air: Reference Bibliography. U.S. Environmental Protection Agency, 401 M St., S.W., Washington, District of Columbia 20460. (202) 260-2090.

List of Publications Sent to Government Depository Libraries. U.S. National Commission on Air Quality, Washington, District of Columbia 1980.

Receptor Model Source Composition Library. U.S. Environmental Protection Agency, MD 75, Research Triangle Park, North Carolina 27711. (919) 541-2184. 1984. Covers air management technology, monitoring and data analysis.

DIRECTORIES

Air and Waste Management Association Directory and Resource Book. Air and Waste Management Association, PO Box 2861, Pittsburgh, Pennsylvania 15230. (412) 232-3444. Annual.

Air Risk Information Support Center: Assistance for State and Local Agencies. U.S. Environmental Protection Agency, Public Information Center, 401 M St., SW, Washington, District of Columbia 20460. (202) 260-2090. 1988.

Canadian Environmental Directory. Canadian Almanac & Directory Publishing Co. Ltd., 134 Adelaide St. E., Ste. 27, Toronto, Ontario, Canada M5C 1K9. (416) 362-4088. 1992. Includes individuals, agencies, firms, and associations.

Directory of Environmental Information Sources. Thomas F. P. Sullivan, ed. Government Institutes, Inc., 4 Research Pl., Ste. 200, Rockville, Maryland 20850. (301) 921-2300. 1992. 3d ed.

Ecological Society of America Bulletin–Directory of Members Issue. Ecological Society of America, c/o Dr. Duncan Patten, Center for Environmental Studies, Arizona State University, Tempe, Arizona 85287. (602) 965-3000.

Environmental Hazards Air Pollution: A Reference Handbook. ABC-CLIO, PO Box 1911, Santa Barbara, California 93116-1911. (805) 968-1911.

Gale Environmental Sourcebook. Karen Hill. Gale Research Co., 835 Penobscot Bldg., Detroit, Michigan 48226-4094. (313) 961-2242. Contacts, information sources, or general information on environmental topics.

The Green Encyclopedia. Irene Franck, David Brownstone. Prentice-Hall, Rte. 9W, Englewood Cliffs, New York 07632. (201) 592-2000. 1992. Covers environmental organizations.

Journal of the Air Pollution Control Association Directory Issue. Air Pollution Control Association, P.O. Box 2861, Pittsburgh, Pennsylvania 15230. (412) 232-3444. Annual.

Who's Who in Environmental Engineering. American Academy of Environmental Engineers, 132 Holiday Court, Suite 206, Annapolis, Maryland 21401. (301) 266-3311. 1980. Annual. Directory of environmental engineers who are certified by the academy.

ENCYCLOPEDIAS AND DICTIONARIES

A Dictionary of Air Pollution Terms. Air & Waste Management Association, P.O. Box 2861, Pittsburgh, Pennsylvania 15230. (412) 233-3444. 1989.

Dictionary of Environmental Engineering and Related Sciences: English-Spanish, Spanish-English. Jose T. Villate. Ediciones Universal, 3090 SW 8th St., Miami, Florida 33135. (305) 642-3355. 1979.

A Dictionary of Environmental Quotations. Barbara K. Rodes and Rice Odell. Simon and Schuster, 15 Columbus Circle, New York, New York 10023. (212) 373-7342. 1992. Collection of nearly 3000 quotations arranged by topic, such as air, noise, energy, nature, pollution, forests, oceans, and other subjects on the environment.

Dictionary of Environmental Science and Technology. Andrew Porteous. John Wiley & Sons, Inc., 605 3rd Ave., New York, New York 10158-0012. (212) 850-6000. 1992.

Encyclopedia of Chemical Processing and Design. John J. Mcketta and W. A. Cunningham. Marcel Dekker, Inc., 270 Madison Ave., New York, New York 10016. (212) 696-9000; (800) 228-1160. 1992. Thirty-eight volumes.

The Encyclopedia of Climatology. John E. Oliver and Rhodes W. Fairbridge, eds. Van Nostrand Reinhold, 115 5th Ave., New York, New York 10003. (212) 254-3232. 1987. Belongs in the series Encyclopedia of Earth Sciences, v.11.

Encyclopedia of Environmental Control Technology. Paul N. Cheremisinoff, ed. Gulf Publishing Co., Book Division, PO Box 2608, Houston, Texas 77252. (713) 529-4301 or (800) 231-6275. 1992. Volume 1: Thermal Treatment of Hazardous Wastes; volume 2: Air Pollution Control; volume 3: Wastewater Treatment Technology; volume 4: Hazardous Waste Containment and Treatment; volumes 5 through 8 in progress. Provides in-depth coverage of specialized topics related to environmental and industrial pollution control problems and state-of-the-art information on technology and research as well as projections of future trends in the field.

Encyclopedia of Environmental Science and Engineering. J.R. Pfafflin. Gordon and Breach Science Publishers, Inc., 270 8th Ave., New York, New York 10011. (212) 206-8900. 1992.

Encyclopedia of Environmental Studies. William Ashworth. Facts on File, Inc., 460 Park Ave. S., New York, New York 10016. (212) 683-2244. 1991.

The Encyclopedia of Geochemistry and Environmental Sciences. Rhodes Whitmore Fairbridge. Van Nostrand Reinhold Co., 115 5th Ave., New York, New York 10003. (212) 254-3232. 1972.

Encyclopedia of Human Biology. Renato Dulbecco, ed. Academic Press, c/o Harcourt Brace Jovanovich Inc., 6277 Sea Harbor Dr., Orlando, Florida 32887. (800) 346-8648. 1991. Eight volumes.

Encyclopedia of Physical Science and Technology. Robert A. Meyers, ed. Academic Press, c/o Harcourt Brace Jovanovich Inc., 6277 Sea Harbor Dr., Orlando, Florida 32887. (800) 346-8648. Dictionary of engineering, technology and physical sciences.

Environmental Encyclopedia. William P. Cunningham, Terence Ball, et. al. Gale Research Inc., 835 Penobscot Bldg., Detroit, Michigan 48226-4094. (313) 961-2242. 1993.

Kirk-Othmer Encyclopedia of Chemical Technology. J. I. Kroschwitz, ed. John Wiley & Sons, Inc., 605 3rd Ave., New York, New York 10158-0012. (212) 850-6000. 1992-. All articles in the new edition have been rewritten and updated adding new subjects such as biotechnology, computer topics, analytical techniques and instrumentation, environmental concerns, fuels and energy, inorganic and solid state chemistry; composite materials and material science in general, and pharmaceuticals. Also available online.

McGraw-Hill Encyclopedia of Environmental Science. Sybil P. Parker. McGraw-Hill Science & Engineering Books, 11 W. 19th St., New York, New York 10011. (212) 337-6010. 1980. Covers ecology, man's influence on nature, and environmental protection.

McGraw-Hill Encyclopedia of Science and Technology. McGraw-Hill, 1221 Avenue of the Americas, New York, New York 10020. (212) 512-2000 or (800) 262-4729. 1992. Seventh edition. Issued in multiple volumes including index. Includes all science and technology broad subject areas.

The New York Times Encyclopedic Dictionary of the Environment. Paul Sarnoff. Quadrangle Books, New York, New York 1971. Focuses on state-of-the-art methods of pollution control, abatement, prevention and removal.

GENERAL WORKS

Acute Lethality Data for Ontario's Petroleum Refinery Effluents Covering the Period from December 1988 to May 1989. Ontario Ministry of Environment, c/o National Technical Information Service, 5285 Port Royal Rd., Springfield, Virginia 22161. (703) 487-4650. 1990. Order number MIC-91-02537 LDM.

Acute Lethality Data for Ontario's Petroleum Refinery Effluents covering the Period June 1989 to November 1989. J. T. Lee. Ontario Ministry of the Environment, c/o National Technical Information Service, 5285 Port Royal Rd., Springfield, Virginia 22161. (703) 487-4650. 1989. Order number MIC-91-02523 LDM.

Adsorption Technology for Air and Water Pollution Control. Kenneth E. Noll. Lewis Publishers, 200 Corporate Blvd. NW, Boca Raton, Florida 33431. (407) 994-0555 or (800)272-7737. 1991. Contains useful information on adsorption technology which can be applied in both air and water pollution.

Aerosol Sampling: Science and Practice. J. H. Vincent. John Wiley & Sons, Inc., 605 3rd Ave., New York, New York 10158-0012. (212) 850-6000. 1989. Details the sampling of aerosols with a "real world" approach. Makes the connection between theory and practice.

Air Emissions from Municipal Solid Waste Landfills. Environmental Protection Agency. National Technical Information Service, 5285 Port Royal Rd., Springfield, Virginia 22161. (703) 487-4650. 1991. Background information for proposed standards and guidelines. Order number PB91-197061LDM.

Air Monitoring for Toxic Exposure. Shirley A. Ness. Van Nostrand Reinhold, 115 5th Ave., New York, New York 10003. (212) 354-3232. 1991. Explains the procedures for evaluating potentially harmful exposure to people from hazardous materials including chemicals, radon and bioaerosols. Presents practical information on how to perform air sampling, collect biological and bulk samples, evaluate dermal exposures, and determine the advantages and limitations of a given method.

Air Pollution, Acid Rain, and the Future of Forests. Sandra Postel. Worldwatch Institute, 1776 Massachusetts Ave., N.W., Washington, District of Columbia 20036-1904. 1984.

Air Pollution Control. Howard E. Hesketh. Technomic Publishing Co., 851 New Holland Ave., Box 3535, Lancaster, Pennsylvania 17604. (717) 291-5609. 1991. Presents both theory and application data. Provides a background relevant to behavior theories and control techniques for capturing gaseous and particulate air pollutants.

Air Pollution Modeling; Theories, Computational Methods, and Available Software. Paolo Zannetti. Van Nostrand Reinhold, 115 5th Ave., New York, New York 10003. (212) 254-3232. 1990. Introduces relevant historical and recently developed examples of modeling techniques for traditional problems including point source dispersion, plume rise, windfield estimation, and surface deposition.

Air Pollution's Toll on Forests and Crops. James J. MacKenzie and Mohamed T. El-Ashry, eds. Yale University Press, 92 A Yale St., 302 Temple St., New Haven, Connecticut 06520. (203) 432-0960. 1992. Proposes an integrated strategy to reduce pollution levels based on improved energy efficiency, abatement technology, and the use of nonfossil energy technologies. This strategy takes into account other critical problems such as increasing oil imports, failure to attain clean air goals in U.S. cities, and the greenhouse effect.

Air Quality. Lewis Publishers, 200 Corporate Blvd. NW, Boca Raton, Florida 33431. (407) 994-0555 or (800)272-7737. 2nd edition. Air pollution and control, stratosphere O3 depletion, global warming, and indoor air pollution.

Air Toxics and Risk Assessment. Edward J. Calabrese and Elaina M. Kenyon. Lewis Publishers, 200 Corporate Blvd. NW, Boca Raton, Florida 33431. (407) 994-0555 or (800)272-7737. 1991. Does risk assessments for more than 110 chemicals that are confirmed or probable air toxics. All chemicals are analyzed with a scientifically sound methodology to assess public health risks.

Analyses of Hazardous Substances in Air. A. Kettrup, ed. VCH Publishers, 303 NW 12th Ave., Deerfield Beach, Florida 33442-1788. (305) 428-5566. 1991. Proceedings from the Commission for the Investigation of Health Hazards of Chemical Compounds in the Work Area. Included are 16 analytical methods for determining organic compounds and heavy metals in the air of work areas by high pressure liquid chromatography, gas chromatography, infrared spectroscopy and atomic absorption spectrometry.

Atmospheric Motion and Air Pollution: An Introduction for Students of Engineering and Science. Richard A. Dobbins. John Wiley & Sons, Inc., 605 3rd Ave., New York, New York 10158-0012. (212) 850-6000. 1979. Atmospheric diffusion and circulation.

Beneficial Use of Waste Solids. Water Pollution Control Federation, 601 Wythe St., Alexandria, Virginia 22314-9990. (703) 684-2400. 1989. Topics in recycling examined by the Task Force on the beneficial use of waste solids.

Car Trouble. James J. MacKenzie, et al. World Resources Institute, 1709 New York Ave., N.W., Washington, District of Columbia 20006. 1992. Reviews the technical options for air purification, cleaner fuels, more flexible transportation systems, and more intelligent city planning, among others.

The Clean Air Act Amendments of 1990: Summary Materials. U.S. Environmental Protection Agency, Office of Air and Radiation, 401 M St. SW, Washington, District of Columbia 20460. (202) 260-2090. 1990.

Comparative Dosimetry of Radon in Mines and Homes. Commission on Life Science, National Research Council. National Academy Press, 2101 Constitution Ave. N.W., PO Box 285, Washington, District of Columbia 20418. (202) 334-3313. 1991.

Countermeasures to Airborne Hazardous Chemicals. J. M. Holmes and C. H. Byers. Noyes Publications, 120 Mill Rd., Park Ridge, New Jersey 07656. (201) 391-8484. 1990. Presents a study of major incidents involving the release of hazardous chemicals and reviews the entire spectrum of activities, recommends appropriate action and gives technical guidance.

Detecting the Climatic Effects of Increasing Carbon Dioxide. National Technical Information Service, 5285 Port Royal Rd., Springfield, Virginia 22161. (703) 487-4650. Carbon dioxide and air pollution measurement.

Efficiency in Environmental Regulation: A Benefit-Cost Analysis of Alternative Approaches. Kluwer Academic Publishers, 101 Philip Dr., Assinippi Park, Norwell, Massachusetts 02061-0358. (617) 871-6600. Quantitative assessment of the efficiency of the EPA's regulation of conventional air and water pollutants from the pulp and paper industry.

Emission Control in Electricity Generation and Industry. OECD Publications and Information Center, 2001 L St., N.W., Suite 700, Washington, District of Columbia 20036. (202) 785-OECD. 1989. Describes progress in IEA countries in reducing the impact of fossil fuel burning on the environment; systems in place for SO2 and NOx control; economic and energy security implications of the various emissions control strategies; of more rational use of energy; the development of combined heat and power and district heating.

Emissions from Combustion Processes–Origin, Measurement, Control. R. E. Clement and R. O. Kagel, eds. Lewis Publishers, 2000 Corporate Blvd., N.W., Boca Raton, Florida 33431. (407) 994-0555 or (800) 272-7737. 1990. Topics discussed include all aspects of combustion from the mechanics, formation, and disposal to emission abatement and risk assessment.

The End of Nature. Bill McKibben. Anchor Books, 666 5th Ave., New York, New York 10103. (212) 765-6500; (800) 223-6834. 1990.

Energy and the Environment. J. Dunderdale, ed. Royal Society of Chemistry, c/o CRC Press, 2000 Corporate Blvd. N.W., Boca Raton, Florida 33431-9868. (800) 272-7737. 1990. Compares the environmental impact of the various energy producing and using processes. The book covers the types and quantities of pollutants produced by these processes, looks at the interaction of these pollutants with the atmosphere, and reviews the use of renewable sources as possible alternatives.

Environmental Indicators. OECD Publication and Information Center, 2001 L St. N.W., Suite 700, Washington, District of Columbia 20036. (202) 785-OECD. 1991. Comprehensive assessments of environmental issues in industrialized countries. Charts the progress achieved over the past 20 years, and points to problems still remaining and sets an agenda of environmental issues to be dealt with in the 1990s.

Environmental Issues: An Anthology of 1989. Thomas W. Joyce, ed. TAPPI Press, Technology Park/Atlanta, PO Box 105113, Atlanta, Georgia 30348. (404) 446-1400. 1990. Contains 39 papers on environmental, safety and occupational health concerns from 11 TAPPI, CPPA and AIChE meetings held during 1989. Also included is a literature review of over 200 papers published in 1989.

Environmental Pollution. Inderscience Enterprises Ltd., World Trade Center Bldg., 110 Avenue Louis Casai, Case Postale 306, Geneva-Airport, Switzerland CH-1215. (44) 908-314248. 1991. Special issue of the International Journal of Environment and Pollution. Proceedings of the 1st International Conference on Environmental Pollution held at the Congress Centre, Lisbon, April 15-19, 1991.

Environmental Pollution and Control. P. Aarne Vesiling, et al. Butterworth-Heinemann, 80 Montvale Ave., Stoneham, Massachusetts 02180. (617) 438-8468; (800) 366-2665. 1990. Describes the more important aspects of environmental engineering science and technology.

The Environmental Sourcebook. Edith Carol Stein. Lyons & Burford, 31 W. 21st St., New York, New York 10010. (212) 620-9580. 1992. Provides information on 11 specific environmental issues, including population; agriculture; energy; climate and atmosphere; biodiversity; water; oceans; solid waste; hazardous substances and waste; endangered lands; and development.

Environmental Viewpoints. Marie Lazzari. Gale Research Inc., 835 Penobscot Bldg., Detroit, Michigan 48226-4094. (313) 961-2242. 1992.

Escaping the Heat Trap. Irving Mintzer and William R. Moomaw. World Resources Institute, 1709 New York Ave. N.W., Washington, District of Columbia 20006. (800) 822-0504. 1991. Report is based on a series of scenarios developed using WRI's Model of Warming Commitment. Investigates the potential of societies to dramatically limit the rate of future greenhouse gas buildup and reduce to zero annual commitment to global warming.

Estimating Costs of Air Pollution Control. William M. Vatavuk. Lewis Publishers, 2000 Corporate Blvd., N.W., Boca Raton, Florida 33431. (407) 994-0555 or (800) 272-7737. 1990. Deals with information to select, size, and estimate budget/study level capital and annual costs for a variety of air pollution control equipment.

Gas Chromatography in Air Pollution Analysis. Viktor G. Berezkin and Yuri S. Drugov. Elsevier Science Publishing Co., 655 Avenue of the Americas, New York, New York 10010. (212) 989-5800. 1991.

Gaseous Pollutants: Characterization and Cycling. Jerome O. Nriagu, ed. J. Wiley, 605 3rd Ave., New York, New York 10158-0012. (800) CALL-WILEY. 1992. Focuses on various methods of sampling and analyzing gaseous pollutants in the atmosphere with emphasis on understanding the chemical and physical processes that occur.

Greenhouse Effect: Life on a Warmer Planet. Rebecca Johnson. Carolina Biological Supply Company, 2700 York Rd., Burlington, North Carolina 27215. (919) 584-0381. 1990. Discusses the effects of what may be the most serious environmental problem ever. Suggests steps everyone can take to reduce the impact of global warming.

Greenhouse Warming: Negotiating a Global Regime. Jessica Tuchman Mathews, ed. World Resources Institute, 1709 New York Ave. N.W., Washington, District of Columbia 20006. (800) 822-0504. 1991. Offers specific suggestions for formulating, implementing, and enforcing a global regime to combat greenhouse warming.

Hazardous Waste TSDF: Background Information for Proposed RCRA Air Emission Standards. National Technical Information Service, 5285 Port Royal Rd., Springfield, Virginia 22161. (703) 487-4650. 1991.

Health Effects of Airborne Particles. Harvard University, 79 John F. Kennedy St., Cambridge, Massachusetts 02130.

The Hole in the Sky: Man's Threat to the Ozone Layer. John R. Gribbin. Bantam Books, 666 5th Ave., New York, New York 10103. (212) 765-6500; (800) 223-6834. 1988. Scientific revelations about the ozone layer and global warming.

Human Exposure Assessment for Airborne Pollutants: Advances and Opportunities. National Research Council (U.S.) Board of Environmental Studies and Toxicology. National Academy of Sciences, 2101 Constitution Ave. NW., Washington, District of Columbia 20418. (202) 334-2000 or (800) 624-6242. 1991. Provides a technical account of the principles and methodology of exposure assessment applied to air pollutants. Also provides valuable information for students on how to study air pollutant exposure and health effects through questionnaires, through air sampling, and through modeling.

Ill Winds. James J. Mackenzie. State University of New York Press, State University Plaza, Albany, New York 12246. (518) 472-5000. 1988. Airborne pollution's toll on trees and crops.

Implementation Strategy for the Clean Air Act Amendments of 1990. U.S. Environmental Protection Agency, Office of Air and Radiation, 401 M St. SW, Washington, District of Columbia 20460. (202) 260-2090. 1991.

Indoor Air Pollution: A Health Perspective. Jonathan M. Samet and John D. Spengler. Johns Hopkins University Press, 701 W. 40th St., Ste. 275, Baltimore, Maryland 21211. (212) 516-6900. 1991. Explores the relationship between air pollution and health. Provides a wealth of useful information including epidemiologic results and standards or requirements that influence air quality both indoor and out.

Indoor Air Pollution Control. Thad Godish. Lewis Publishers, 2000 Corporate Blvd., N.W., Boca Raton, Florida 33431. (407) 994-0555 or (800) 272-7737. 1989. Provides practical information and data needed for indoor air pollution control. Deals with how to conduct indoor air quality investigations in both residences and public access buildings; indoor air quality mitigation practice, and case histories.

Indoor Air Pollution: Radon, Bioaerosols, and VOCs. Jack G. Kay, et al. Lewis Publishers, 2000 Corporate Blvd., N.W., Boca Raton, Florida 33431. (407) 994-0555 or (800) 272-7737. 1991. Consists of two parts: Overview of the ACS Symposium on Indoor Air Pollution, and Radon overview

Indoor Air Quality. Bradford O. Brooks. CRC Press, 2000 Corporate Blvd. N.W., Boca Raton, Florida 33431. (800) 272-7737. 1991. Traces history in context of indoor air quality, measurement, quality improvement and regulations and current philosophy of litigation.

Indoor Air Quality Control Techniques: Radon, Formaldehyde, Combustion Products. W.J. Fisk. Noyes Publications, 120 Mill Rd., Park Ridge, New Jersey 07656. (201) 391-8484. 1987. Air quality in the United States.

Industrial Environmental Control. A. M. Springer. John Wiley & Sons, Inc., 605 3rd Ave., New York, New York 10158-0012. (212) 850-6000. 1986. Covers in great detail all the basic information regarding industrial pollution and its treatment.

Industrial Waste Gases: Utilization and Minimization. RCG/Hagler Bailly Inc. Technomic Publishing Co., 851 New Holland Ave., Box 3535, Lancaster, Pennsylvania 17604. (717) 291-5609. 1990. Also released under title Industrial Waste Gas Management. Deals with factory and trade waste and the effluents that are released into the atmosphere.

International Environmental Information Sources. Pira, Randalls Rd., Leatherhead, England KT22 7RU. 0372 376161. 1990. Contains valuable business and technical contacts for environmental information sources worldwide. Information sources cover the following subjects: Air, noise, water and land pollution; waste control and disposal; recycling; energy recovery; nature conservation. Informational sources include associations, research organizations, legislative/regulatory agencies, directories, statistics, on-line databases, magazines and news letters in 24 countries.

Large Power Plant Effluent Study. Francis A. Schiermeier. U.S. National Air Pollution Control Administration, Raleigh, North Carolina 1970. Electric power plants and air pollution in the United States.

Locating and Estimating Air Emissions from Sources of Carbon Tetrachloride [microform]. U.S. Environmental Protection Agency, 401 M St., SW, MD 75, Research Triangle Park, North Carolina 27711. (919) 541-2184. 1984.

Locating and Estimating Air Emissions from Sources of Chloroform. U.S. Environmental Protection Agency, Office of Air and Radiation, MD 75, Research Triangle Park, North Carolina 27711. (919) 541-2184. 1984.

The Long-Range Atmospheric Transport of Natural and Containment Substances. Anthony H. Knap. Kluwer Academic Publishers, 101 Philip Dr., Assinippi Pk., Norwell, Massachusetts 02061. (617) 871-6600. Transport of sulphur and nitrogen, organic compounds, mineral aerosols and trace elements.

Magill's Survey of Science. Earth Science Series. Frank N. Magill. Salem Press, PO Box 50062, Pasadena, California 91105. 1990-. Five volumes. Includes information on earth's crust, hot spots and volcanic island chains, physical properties of minerals, rock magnetism, physical properties of rocks, and index.

Meteorology of Air Pollution: Implications for the Environment and Its Future. R. S. Scorer. E. Horwood, 66 Wood Lane End, Hemel Hempstead, England HP2 4RG. 1990. Discusses methods of air pollution measurement and future expectations.

Methods for Assessing Exposure of Human and Non-Human Biota. R. G. Tardiff and B. D. Goldstein, eds. John Wiley & Sons, Inc., 605 3rd Ave., New York, New York 10158-0012. (212) 850-6000. 1991. Provides a critical and collective evaluation of approaches to chemical exposure assessment.

National Inventory of Sources and Emissions of Carbon Dioxide. A.P. Jaques. Environmental Canada, 425 St. Joseph Blvd., 3rd Fl., Hull, Quebec, Canada K1A OH3. (613) 953-5921. 1987. Covers environmental aspects of carbon dioxide.

Natural Gas Applications for Air Pollution Control. Nelson E. Hay. Fairmont Press, 700 Indian Trail, Lilburn, Georgia 30247. (404) 925-9388. 1987. Natural gas-induced air pollution.

Occupational Exposure Limits for Airborne Toxic Substances. International Labour Office, 49 Sheridan Ave., Albany, New York 12210. (518) 436-9686. 1991.

Particle Technology. Chapman & Hall, 29 W. 35th St., New York, New York 10001-2291. (212) 244-3336. 1990. Preparation, separation, mixing, agglomeration, crushing, storing, and conveying of particulate matter and bulk solids.

Political Economy of Smog in Southern California. Jeffry Fawcett. Garland Publishers, 136 Madison Ave., New York, New York 10016. (212) 686-7492; (800) 627-6273. 1990.

Population Dynamics of Forest Insects. VCH Publishers, 303 NW 12th Ave., Deerfield Beach, Florida 33442-1788. (305) 428-5566. 1990. Reviews the current research from an international Congress of delegates which covers population models, pest management and insect natural enemy interaction on forest insects. Topics include the effects of industrial air pollutants and acid rain as well as reviews of the biology and population dynamics of most major forest insects.

The Practitioner's Approach to Indoor Air Quality Investigations. American Industrial Hygiene Association, 345 White Pond Dr., Akron, Ohio 44320. (216) 873-2442. 1990. Presents pragmatic advice for approaching and conducting an investigation and describes the range and causes of complaints that fall into categories of acute to subchronic adverse health effects.

Prediction and Regulation of Air Pollution. M. E. Berlyand. Kluwer Academic Publishers, 101 Philip Dr., Assinippi Park, Norwell, Massachusetts 02061-0358. (617) 871-6600. 1991. Revised and updated version of Prognoz i regulirovanie, 1985.

A Primer on Greenhouse Effect Gases. Donald J. Wuebbles and Jae Edmonds. Lewis Publishers, 200 Corporate Blvd. NW, Boca Raton, Florida 33431. (407) 994-0555 or (800)272-7737. 1991. Brings together the most current information available on greenhouse gases. Reveals information critical to developing an understanding of the role of energy and atmospheric chemical and radiative processes in determining atmospheric concentrations of greenhouse gases.

Principles of Air Pollution Meteorology. T. J. Lyons and W. D. Scott. CRC Press, 2000 Corporate Blvd., N.W., Boca Raton, Florida 33431. (800) 272-7737. 1990. Describes atmospheric boundary layer, atmospheric diffusion, pollutants and their properties, and environmental monitoring and impact.

Principles of Air Toxics. Roger D. Griffin. Lewis Publishers, 2000 Corporate Blvd., N.W., Boca Raton, Florida 33431. (407) 994-0555 or (800) 272-7737. 1991. Includes health effects of air pollutants, meteorology, pollutant transport and dispersion, types and definitions, sources and emissions, air emission characteristics, control and mitigation approaches, stationary source control technology, mobile source control, ambient air quality, and regulatory approaches.

Radioactive Aerosols. A. C. Chamberlin. Cambridge University Press, 40 W 20th St., New York, New York 10011. (212) 924-3900; (800) 227-0247. 1991. Describes radioactive gases and particles which are dispersed in the environment, either from natural causes or following nuclear test and accidental emissions.

Radon in the Environment. M. Wilkening. Elsevier Science Publishing Co., 655 Avenue of the Americas, New York, New York 10010. (212) 989-5800. 1990. Describes the discovery of radon, its characteristics, and sources in the environment methods of control, as well as possible health effects.

A Reference Guide to Clean Air. Cass Sandak. Carolina Biological Supply Company, 2700 York Rd., Burlington, North Carolina 27215. (919) 584-0381. 1990. A collection of references and a glossary.

The Satellite as Microscope. R. S. Scorer. E. Horwood, 66 Wood Lane End, Hemel Hempstead, England HP2 4RG. 1990. Describes the use of artificial satellites in air pollution control.

Serious Reduction of Hazardous Waste: Summary. Congress of the U.S., c/o U.S. Government Printing Office, Office of Technology Assessment, N. Capitol & H Sts. NW, Washington, District of Columbia 20401. (202) 512-0000. 1986. Deals with waste reduction from factories and air pollution control.

Sources for the Future. Wallace Oates. Resources for the Future, 1616 P St., NW, Washington, District of Columbia 20036. (202) 328-5086. Examines emissions taxes, abatement subsides, and transferable emission permits in a national, regional, and global context.

The Statehouse Effect: State Policies to Cool the Greenhouse. Daniel A. Lashof and Eric L. Washburn. Natural Resources Defense Council, 40 W. 20th St., New York, New York 10011. (212) 727-2700. 1990. Discusses the need for states to take the initiative in controlling CO2 emissions. Details the sources of greenhouse gases and explains how greenhouse emissions can be reduced through energy efficiency, renewable energy strategies, recycling, and taxation and reforms in transportation, agriculture and forests.

Stones in a Glass House: CFCs and Ozone Depletion. Douglas G. Cogan. Investor Responsibility Research Center, 1755 Massachusetts Ave., NW, Suite 600, Washington, District of Columbia 20036. (202) 234-7500. 1988. Environmental aspects of air pollution.

Survey of Carbon Tetrachloride Emission Sources. National Technical Information Service, 5285 Port Royal Rd., Springfield, Virginia 22161. (703) 487-4650. 1985.

Techniques for Measuring Indoor Air. John Y. Yocom and Sharon M. McCarthy. John Wiley & Sons, Inc., 605 3rd Ave., New York, New York 10158-0012. (212) 850-6000. 1991. Addresses the recent, rapid expansion of interest in indoor air quality and its contribution to total human exposure to air pollutants by presenting past and present developments and also the directions that the field seems to be taking.

Toxic Air Pollution–A Comprehensive Study of Non-Criteria Air Pollutants. Paul J. Lioy and Joan M. Daisey. Lewis Publishers, 2000 Corporate Blvd., N.W., Boca Raton, Florida 33431. (407) 994-0555 or (800) 272-7737. 1987. Provides historical data base of ambient toxic air pollution measurements for future trend analysis, assessment of total exposure and indoor air pollution relationships.

A Who's Who of American Ozone Depleters: A Guide to 3,014 Factories Emitting Three Ozone-Depleting Chemicals. Natural Resources Defense Council, 40 W. 20th St., New York, New York 10011. (212) 727-2700. 1990.

World Guide to Environmental Issues and Organizations. Peter Brackley. Longman Group Ltd., Longman House, Burnt Mill, Harlow, Essex, England CM20 2J6. (0279) 426721. 1991.

HANDBOOKS AND MANUALS

Clean Air Handbook. Government Institutes, Inc., 4 Research Pl., Ste. 200, Rockville, Maryland 20850. (301) 921-2300. Analyzes the requirements of the Clean Air Act and its 1990 amendments, as well as what can be expected in terms of new regulation.

The Engineer's Clean Air Handbook. P. D. Osborn. Butterworth-Heinemann, Linacre House, Jordan Hill, Oxford, England OX2 8DP. (0865) 310366. 1989. Deals with the causes of various types of air pollution and the complicated nature of many of the pollutants. Also describes methods and necessary instrumentation for pollution removal. Includes a list of useful references.

Environmental Statistics Handbook: Europe. Allan Foster, Oksana Newman. Gale Research Inc., 835 Penobscot Bldg., Detroit, Michigan 48226-4094. (313) 961-2242. 1993.

Guide for Air Pollution Episode Avoidance. U.S. G.P.O., Washington, District of Columbia 20401. (202) 512-0000. 1971.

Indoor Air Quality Design Guidebook. Milton Meckler. Fairmont Press, 700 Indian Trail, Lilburn, Georgia 30247. (404) 925-9388. 1991. Air cleaning systems, the carbon dioxide method, health lead/lag procedure, desiccants, contaminant absorption, effects of sick buildings, assessment of measurement techniques, indoor air quality simulation with computer models, and system design and maintenance techniques. Also available through the Association of Energy Engineers.

Managing Indoor Air Quality. Shirely J. Hansen. The Association of Energy Engineers, 4025 Pleasantdale Rd., Suite 420, Atlanta, Georgia 30340. (404) 925-9558. 1991. Includes readily applicable air quality control measures and preventive strategies that can head off the economic and legal problems.

Respiratory Protection: A Manual and Guideline. American Industrial Hygiene Association, 345 White Pond Dr., PO Box 8390, Akron, Ohio 44320. (216) 873-2442. 1991. 2d ed. Provides practical guidelines for establishing and managing respiratory protection programs. Presents guidelines for establishing chemical cartridge field service life policies and audit criteria for evaluating respiratory protection programs. Contains validated qualitative life-testing protocols, new equipment for quantitative respiratory protection, and information on use and testing of supplied-air suits.

ONLINE DATA BASES

Aerometric Information Retrieval System. U.S. Environmental Protection Agency, Office of Air Quality Planning and Standards, National Air Data Branch, 401 M St. SW, Washington, District of Columbia 20460. (202) 260-2090. Contains data reported by more than 5000 air monitoring stations located throughout the United States.

Air Pollution Technical Information Center File. U.S. Environmental Protection Agency, Library Services Office, Air Information Center (MD-35), 401 M St. SW, Washington, District of Columbia 20460. (202) 260-2090. Citations and abstracts of the world's literature on air quality and air pollution prevention and control.

Air Toxics Report. Business Publishers, Inc., 951 Pershing Dr., Silver Spring, Maryland 20910. (301) 587-6300. Online version of periodical of the same name.

Air/Water Pollution Report. NewsNet, Inc., 945 Haverford Rd., Bryn Mawr, Pennsylvania 19010. (800) 345-1301. Online version of periodical of same name.

Applied Social Sciences Index & Abstracts. Bowker-Saur Ltd. Abstracts & Indexes, 59/60 Grosvenor St., London, England W1X 9DA. 44(71)493-5841.

APTIC. U.S. Environmental Protection Agency, CIS Project, 401 M St., S.W., Washington, District of Columbia 20460. (202) 260-2090.

BIOSIS Previews. BIOSIS, 2100 Arch St., Philadelphia, Pennsylvania 19103-1399. (215) 587-4800. Largest and most comprehensive database of research in the life sciences. Contains citations for nearly 9000 primary research journals, monographs, reviews, symposia, preliminary reports, semi-popular journals, selected institutional reports, government reports and research communications.

Cambridge Scientific Abstracts Life Science–CSAL. Cambridge Scientific Abstracts, 5161 River Rd., Bethesda, Maryland 20816. (301) 961-6750. Provides access to the following abstracting services: "Life Sciences Collection," "Aquatic Sciences and Fisheries Abstracts," "Oceanic Abstracts," and "Pollution Abstracts."

Chemical Abstracts-CA. Chemical Abstracts Service, 2540 Olentangy River Rd., P.O. Box 3012, Columbus, Ohio 43210. (800) 848-6533 or (614) 421-3600. Information sources include 9000 journals, patents from 27 countries, two industrial property organizations, new books, conference proceedings, and government research reports.

Concentrations of Indoor Pollutants–CIP. CIP Database Coordinator, Building 90, Rm 3058, Lawrence Berkeley Lab., 1 Cyclotron Rd., Berkeley, California 94720. (415) 486-6591. Contains field data from studies monitoring indoor air quality in occupied buildings in U.S. and Canada.

Enviro/Energyline Abstracts Plus. R. R. Bowker Co., 121 Chanlon Rd., New Providence, New Jersey 07974. (908) 464-6800.

Enviroline. R. R. Bowker Co., Bowker Electronic Publishing, 121 Chanlon Rd., New Providence, New Jersey 07974. (800) 521-8110.

Environment Reporter. Bureau of National Affairs, 1231 25th St., N.W., Rm. 215, Washington, District of Columbia 20037. (800) 372-1033. Online version of periodical of the same name.

Environmental Bibliography. Environmental Studies Institute, International Academy at Santa Barbara, 800 Garden St., Ste. D, Santa Barbara, California 93101. (805) 965-5010. International periodical literature dealing with environmental topics such as air pollution, water treatment, energy conservation, noise abatement, soil mechanics, wildlife preservation, and chemical wastes.

Environmental Periodicals Bibliography. National Information Services Corp., Ste. 6, Wyman Towers, 3100 St. Paul St., Baltimore, Maryland 21218. (410)243-0797. Online version of abstract of same name.

Kirk-Othmer Encyclopedia of Chemical Technology. John Wiley & Sons, Inc., 605 3rd Ave., 5th Floor, New York, New York 10158. (212) 850-6000. Online version of the publication of the same name.

Monthly Catalog of United States Government Publications. U.S. G.P.O., Supt. of Docs., PO Box 371954, Pittsburgh, Pennsylvania 15250-7954. (202) 512-0000.

National Technical Information Service. U.S. Department of Commerce, National Technical Information Service, Office of Data Base Services, 5285 Port Royal Rd., Springfield, Virginia 22161. (703) 487-4807. Bibliographic database of government sponsored research and technical reports.

PressNet Environmental Reports. Chemical Information Systems, Inc., 7215 York Rd., Baltimore, Maryland 21212. (301) 321-8440.

PERIODICALS AND NEWSLETTERS

Air and Water Pollution Control. Bureau of National Affairs, 1231 25th St. N.W., Washington, District of Columbia 20037. (202) 452-4200. 1986-. Biweekly. Review of developments in pollution laws, regulations and trends in government and industry.

Air Currents. Bay Area Air Quality Management District, 939 Ellis St., San Francisco, California 94109. (415) 771-6000. 1959-. Monthly. Describes regulation changes and other information of interest to the air pollution control community.

Air Pollution Control. Bureau of National Affairs, 1231 25th St. NW, Washington, District of Columbia 20037. (202) 452-4200. Biweekly. A reference and advisory service on the control of air pollution, designed to meet the information needs of individuals responsible for complying with EPA and state air pollution control regulations.

Air Toxics Report. Business Publishers, Inc., 951 Pershing Dr., Silver Spring, Maryland 20910-4464. (301) 587-6300. 1988-. Monthly. Directed towards organizations and facilities that are or may be affected by regulations under the Clean Air Act and National Emission Standards for Hazardous Air Pollutants, with articles on government regulation, studies, compliance, violations and legal actions. Also available online.

Air/Water Pollution Report. Business Publishers, Inc., 951 Pershing Dr., Silver Spring, Maryland 20910-4464. (301) 587-6300. 1963-. Weekly. Reports on the hard news and in-depth features for practical use by environmental managers. It keeps readers informed on the latest news from government and industry. Also available online.

ALAPCO Washington Update. Association of Local Air Pollution Control Officials, 444 North Capitol Street, NW, Washington, District of Columbia 20001. (202) 624-7864. Monthly. Air pollution control in Washington, DC.

American Industrial Hygiene Association Journal. American Industrial Hygiene Association, 345 White Pond Drive, Akron, Ohio 44320. (216) 873-2442. Monthly. Reports relating to occupational and environmental health hazards.

APCA Messenger. Mid Atlantic States Section, Air and Waste Management Assn., Box 2861, Pittsburgh, Pennsylvania 15230. (412) 621-1090. 1970-. Three times a year.

Applied and Environmental Microbiology Journal. American Society for Microbiology, 1325 Massachusetts Avenue N.W., Washington, District of Columbia 20005. (202) 737-3600. Monthly. Articles on industrial and food microbiology and ecological studies.

Atmospheric Environment. Pergamon Microforms International, Inc., Fairview Park, Elmsford, New York 10523. (914) 592-7720. 1966-. Publishes papers on all aspects of man's interactions with his atmospheric environment, including the administrative, economic and political aspects of these interactions. Air pollution research and its applications are covered, taking into account changes in the atmospheric flow patterns, temperature distributions and chemical constitution caused by natural and artificial variations in the earth's surface.

B. C. Sportsmen. British Columbia Wildlife Federation, 5659 176th St., Surrey, British Columbia, Canada V3S 4C5. Quarterly.

Bulletin of Environmental Contamination and Toxicology. Springer-Verlag, 175 5th Ave., New York, New York 10010. (212) 460-1500; (800) 777-4643. 1966-. Frequency varies. Disseminates advances and discoveries in the areas of soil, air and food contamination and pollution.

CA Selects: Air Pollution (Books and Reviews). Chemical Abstracts Services, 2540 Olentangy River Rd., Box 3012, Columbus, Ohio 43210. (800) 848-6533. Biweekly. Abstracts on pollution in the atmosphere by fixed and mobile sources; effects of air pollution on animals and vegetation.

California Air Environment. Statewide Air Pollution Research Center, University of California, Riverside, California 92502. 1969-. Quarterly.

California Air Resources Board Bulletin. California Air Resources Board, 1102 Q. St., Sacramento, California 95814. (916) 322-2990. 1962-. Monthly. Government newsletter concerning Air Resources Board activities, and air pollution control news.

Ecological Society of America Bulletin. Ecological Society of America, Center of Environmental Studies, Arizona State University, Tempe, Arizona 85287-1201. (602) 965-3000. Quarterly. Study of living things in relation to their environments.

Ecology. Ecological Society of America, Center of Environmental Studies, Arizona State University, Tempe, Arizona 85287-1201. (602) 965-3000. Bimonthly. Information on the study of living things.

Ecology USA. Business Publishers, Inc., 951 Pershing Dr., Silver Spring, Maryland 20910-4464. (301) 587-6300. 1972-. Biweekly. Contains all the legislation, regulation, and litigation affecting efforts to conserve and protect America's unique environmental and ecological heritage.

Environment Ohio. Ohio Environmental Protection Agency, PO Box 1049, Columbus, Ohio 43216. (614) 644-2160. Bimonthly. Air, water, land pollution, and public water supply.

Environment Reporter. Bureau of National Affairs, 1231 25th St. NW, Washington, District of Columbia 20037. (800) 372-1033. Weekly. Issues of pollution control and environmental activity. Also available online.

Environmental Health Letter. Business Publishers, Inc., 951 Pershing Dr., Silver Spring, Maryland 20910-4464.

(301) 587-6300. 1961-. Biweekly. Covers areas such as: indoor air, asbestos health effects, toxic substances testing, health problems at wastewater plants, risk-based sludge rules, medical waste, developmental toxicity risk assessment, animal carcinogen tests, pesticide risk, air toxics, aerospace chemicals, lead, radionuclide emissions, state right-to-know statutes, and incinerator emissions.

Environmental Pollution. Applied Science Publications, PO Box 5399, New York, New York 10163. (718) 756-6440. 1987-.

Environmental Pollution & Control. National Technical Information Service, 5285 Port Royal Rd., Springfield, Virginia 22161. (703) 487-4650. Weekly. Covers air, noise, solid waste, water pollution, radiation, environmental health and safety, pesticide pollution and control.

Environmental Protection Magazine. Stevens Publishing Co., 225 New Road, PO Box 2604, Waco, Texas 76702-2573. (817) 776-9000. Air and water pollution, wastewater and hazardous materials.

Environmental Resources Research Institute, Newsletter. Environmental Resources Research Institute, Pennsylvania State University, University Park, Pennsylvania 16802. (814) 863-0291. Quarterly. Land, water, air, and mining.

Environmental Toxicology and Chemistry. Society of Environmental Toxicology and Chemistry. Pergamon Microforms International, Inc., Fairview Park, Elmsford, New York 10523. (914) 592-7720. 1981-. Monthly. Contains information on environmental toxicology, and chemistry, including the application of science to hazard assessment.

EPA Journal. U.S. Environmental Protection Agency, 401 M St., S.W., A-107, Washington, District of Columbia 20460. (202) 382-4393. Bimonthly. Air and water pollution, pesticides, noise, solid waste.

Global Climate Change Digest. Elsevier Science Publishing Co., 655 Avenue of the Americas, New York, New York 10010. (212) 984-5800. Monthly. Topics dealing with ozone depletion and the large-scale climatic changes linked to industrial activity, industrial by-products, and man-made substances.

Gold Dust. McIlvaine Co., 2970 Maria Ave., Northbrook, Illinois 60062. (708) 272-0010. Monthly. Air pollution control & equipment service companies.

Indoor Air Review. IAQ Pub. Inc., 5335 Wisconsin Ave., NW., Suite 440, Washington, District of Columbia 20015. (202) 686-2626. 1991. Monthly. Gives the latest news and information on the topic of indoor air quality. Special sections are devoted to updates of legislation, research and development, technology, liability and insurance issues, state and federal governments reports, industry and business forecasts and reports, meetings, conferences, training, standards and accreditation.

INFORM Reports. INFORM Inc., 381 Park Ave., So., New York, New York 10016. (212) 689-4040. Quarterly. INFORM is a nonprofit environmental research & education organization for the preservation and conservation of natural resources and public health.

Journal of Air and Waste Management Association. Air and Waste Management Association, P.O. Box 2861, Pittsburgh, Pennsylvania 15230. (412) 232-3444. Monthly. Current events in air pollution control and hazardous wastes.

Journal of Atmospheric Sciences. American Meteorology Society, 45 Beacon Street, Boston, Massachusetts 02108. (617) 227-2425. Biweekly. Articles on the atmosphere of the earth and other planets.

Journal of Environmental Engineering. American Society for Civil Engineers, 345 East 47th Street, New York, New York 10017. (212) 705-7496. Bimonthly. Covers problems in the environment and sanitation.

Journal of Environmental Health. National Environmental Health Association, 720 South Colorado Boulevard, Suite 970, Denver, Colorado 80222. (303) 756-9090. Bimonthly. Covers phases in environmental health.

Multinational Environmental Outlook. Business Publishers, Inc., 951 Pershing Dr., Silver Spring, Maryland 20910-4464. (301) 587-6300. 1974-. Biweekly. Covers developments in world environmental problems such as acid rain, deforestation, soil erosion, overfishing, threats to health, animal extinction, population growth, diminishing water supply and other related matters. Also available online.

National Air Toxics Information Clearinghouse Newsletter. National Air Toxic Information Clearinghouse, P.O. Box 13000, Research Triangle Park, North Carolina 27709. (919) 541-9100. Bimonthly. Covers noncriteria pollutant emissions.

Pollution Engineering. Cahners Publishing Co., 249 W. 17th St., New York, New York 10011. (212) 645-0067. 1969-. Monthly.

Pollution Equipment News. Rimbach Publishing, Inc., 8650 Babcock Boulevard, Pittsburgh, Pennsylvania 15237. (412) 364-5366. Bimonthly. Covers new products, techniques, and literature.

Sign Control News. Scenic America, 216 7th St. SE, Washington, District of Columbia 20003. (202) 546-1100. Bimonthly.

Virginair. Virginia State Air Pollution Control Board, Room 1106, 9th St., Office Bldg., Richmond, Virginia 23219. 1972-. Quarterly.

Washington Update. Association of Local Air Pollution Control Officials, 444 N. Capitol St, NW, Suite 306, Washington, District of Columbia 20001. (202) 624-7864. Monthly. Congressional and Environmental Protection Agency activities, and current issues related to air pollution.

Water, Air, and Soil Pollution. Kluwer Academic Publishers, 101 Philip Dr., Assinippi Park, Norwell, Massachusetts 02061. (617) 871-6600. Bimonthly. Covers water, soil, and air pollution. This is an international journal on environmental pollution dealing with all types of pollution including acid rain.

Wet Scrubber Newsletter. McIlvaine Co., 2970 Maria Ave., Northbrook, Illinois 60062. (708) 272-0010. 1974-. Monthly.

RESEARCH CENTERS AND INSTITUTES

Air Pollution Research Laboratory. University of Florida, 408 Black Hall, Gainsville, Florida 32611. (904) 392-0845.

Air Quality Group. University of California, Davis, Crocker Nuclear Laboratories, Davis, California 95616. (510) 752-1124.

Center for Air Pollution Impact and Trend Analysis. Washington University, Campus Box 1124, 319 Urbauer, St. Louis, Missouri 63130. (314) 889-6099.

Cooling Tower Institute. 530 Wells Fargo Dr., Suite 113, Houston, Texas 77273. (713) 583-4087.

Environmental Engineering Science Research Laboratory. University of Florida, College of Engineering, 217 Black Hall, Gainesville, Florida 32611. (904) 392-0841.

Environmental Research Institute for Hazardous Materials and Wastes. University of Connecticut, Rt. 44, Langley Bldg., Box U210, Storrs, Connecticut 06269-3210. (203) 486-4015.

New Jersey Institute of Technology, Air Pollution Research Laboratory. 323 Martin Luther King Boulevard, Newark, New Jersey 07102. (201) 596-3459.

University of Michigan, Michigan Atmospheric Deposition Laboratory. 2126 Space Research Building, Ann Arbor, Michigan 48109-2143. (313) 763-6213.

USDA National Sedimentation Laboratory. P.O.Box 1157, Oxford, Missouri 38655. (601) 232-2900.

STATISTICS SOURCES

Air Pollution and Acid Rain Reports. National Technical Information Service, 5285 Port Royal Rd., Springfield, Virginia 22161. (703) 487-4650. Annual. Air pollution and acid rain environmental effects and controls.

America in the 21st Century: The Demographic Dimension: Environmental Concerns. Population Reference Bureau, P.O. Box 96152, Washington, District of Columbia 20090-6152. Distribution of pollution by source.

Environmental Data Compendium. OECD Publications and Information Center, 2001 L St., N.W., Suite 700, Washington, District of Columbia 20036. (202) 785-6323. 1989.

Environmental Indicators. OECD Publications and Information Center, 2001 L St., N.W., Suite 700, Washington, District of Columbia 20036. (202) 785-6323. 1991.

Environmental Quality. Council on Environmental Quality. U.S. G.P.O., Washington, District of Columbia 20401. (202) 512-0000. Annual.

National Air Pollutant Emission Estimates. U.S. Environmental Protection Agency, 401 M St., S.W., Washington, District of Columbia 20460. (202) 260-2090. Annual. Estimates of nationwide emissions of particulates, sulfur oxides, nitrogen oxides, volatile organic compounds, carbon monoxide, and lead, by source.

OECD Environmental Data Compendium 1989. OECD Publications and Information Center, 2001 L St. N.W., Suite 700, Washington, District of Columbia 20036. (202) 785-OECD. 1989. Provides statistical data for OECD countries on air pollution, water pollution, the marine environment, land use, forests, wildlife, solid waste, noise and radioactivity. Also provides data on the underlying pressures on the environment such as energy use, transportation, industrial activity and agriculture.

Progress in the Prevention and Control of Air Pollution. U.S. Environmental Protection Agency. National Technical Information Service, Springfield, Virginia 22161. (703) 487-4650. Annual. Covers air quality trends and control of radon, suspended particulates, sulfur and nitrogen oxides, carbon monoxide, ozone and lead.

The State of the Environment. OECD Publications and Information Center, 2001 L St., N.W., Suite 700, Washington, District of Columbia 20036. (202) 785-6323. 1991.

Statistical Record of the Environment. Arsen J. Darnay. Gale Research Inc., 835 Penobscot Bldg., Detroit, Michigan 48226-4094. (313) 961-2242. 1992.

Toxic Air Pollutant Emission Factors. U.S. Environmental Protection Agency. National Technical Information Service, Springfield, Virginia 22161. (703) 487-4650. 1990. Irregular. Data on emissions by source, SIC code, combustion material and pollutant process.

Trends '90: A Compendium of Data on Global Change. Thomas A. Boden, et al. Carbon Dioxide Information Analysis Center, Environmental Sciences Division, Oak Ridge National Laboratory, Oak Ridge, Tennessee 37831-6335. 1990. Source of frequently used global change data. Includes estimates of global and national CO2 emissions from the burning of fossil fuels and from the production of cement and other pollutants.

TRADE ASSOCIATIONS AND PROFESSIONAL SOCIETIES

Air and Waste Management Association. Box 2861, Pittsburgh, Pennsylvania 15230. (412) 232-3444.

Air Resources Information Clearinghouse. 99 Court St., Rochester, New York 14604. (716) 546-3796.

Alliance for Responsible Chlorofluorocarbon Policy. 1901 N. Fort Myer Dr., Suite 1200, Rosslyn, Virginia 22209. (703) 243-0344.

American Association for Aerosol Research Indoor Environment Program. Lawrence Berkeley Library, 1 Cyclotron Rd., Berkeley, California 94720. (919) 541-6736. Prog. 90-3058

American Institute of Chemical Engineers. 345 East 47th St., New York, New York 10017. (212) 705-7338.

American Institute of Chemists. 7315 Wisconsin Ave., Bethesda, Maryland 20814. (301) 652-2447.

American Welding Institute. 10628 Dutchtown Rd., Knoxville, Tennessee 37932. (615) 675-2150.

American Welding Society. P.O. Box 351040, 550 LeJeune Rd., N.W., Miami, Florida 33135. (305) 443-9353.

Association of Local Air Pollution Control Officials. 444 North Capitol St., N.W., Washington, District of Columbia 20001 (202) 624-7864.

Association of New Jersey Environmental Commissions. PO Box 157, 300 Mendham Rd., Mendham, New Jersey 07945. (201) 539-7547.

Automotive Industry Action Group. 20200 Lahser, Suite 200, Southfield, Michigan 48075. (313) 358-3570.

Center for Environmental Information, Inc. 99 Court St., Rochester, New York 14604. (716) 546-3796.

Ecological Society of America. Arizona State University, Center for Environmental Studies, Tempe, Arizona 85287. (602) 965-3000.

Industrial Gas Clearing Institute. 1707 L St., N.W., Suite 570, Washington, District of Columbia 20036. (202) 457-0911.

INFORM. 381 Park Avenue S., New York, New York 10016. (212) 689-4040.

International Society for Ecological Modeling/North American Chapter. Water Quality Division, South Florida Water Management District, PO Box 24680, West Palm Beach, Florida 33416. (407) 686-8800.

Kids for a Clean Environment. P.O. Box 158254, Nashville, Tennessee 37215. (615) 331-0708.

Manufacturers of Emission Controls Association. 1707 L St., N.W., Suite 570, Washington, District of Columbia 20036. (202) 296-4797.

National Air Toxics Information Clearinghouse. Research Triangle Park, North Carolina 27711. (919) 541-0850.

State and Territorial Air Pollution Program Administrators. 444 North Capitol St., Washington, District of Columbia 20001. (202) 624-7864.

Welding Research Council. 345 E. 47th St., New York, New York 10017. (212) 705-7956.

AIR POLLUTION EQUIPMENT
See: TECHNOLOGY AND THE ENVIRONMENT

AIR POLLUTION INCIDENTS
See: AIR POLLUTION

AIR POLLUTION INDEX
See: AIR POLLUTION

AIR POLLUTION INDICATORS
See also: AIR POLLUTION

ABSTRACTING AND INDEXING SERVICES

Abstracts of Air and Water Conservation Literature. American Petroleum Institute. Central Abstracting and Indexing Service, 275 Madison Avenue, New York, New York 10016. 1972.

Air Pollution Technical Publications of the United States Environmental Protection Agency. U.S. Environmental Protection Agency, Mail Drop 75, Research Triangle Park, North Carolina 27711. (919) 541-2184. 1976. Quarterly.

Air Pollution Titles. Pennsylvania State University, Center for Air Environmental Studies, 226 Fenske Laboratory, University Park, Pennsylvania 16802. (814) 865-1415. 1965. Bibliographic guide to current research literature on air environment, including monitoring and control of air pollution, health effects, effects on agriculture, forests, toxic air contaminants, and global atmospheric pro cases.

Air Pollution Translations. A Bibliography With Abstracts. U.S. Environmental Protection Agency, MD 75, Research Triangle Park, North Carolina 27711. (919) 541-2184. 1969.

Biological Abstracts. BIOSIS, 2100 Arch St., Philadelphia, Pennsylvania 19103-1399. (215) 587-4800. 1927-.

Engineering Index. The Engineering Index Inc., 345 E. 47th St., New York, New York 10017. 1962-.

Environment Abstracts. Bowker A & I Publishing, 121 Chanlon Rd., New Providence, New Jersey 07974. (908) 464-6800. 1974-.

Environment Index. Environment Information Center, Index Research Department, 124 E. 39th St., New York, New York 10016. 1971-. Annual.

Environmental Information Connection–EIC. Planning Information Program, Dept. of Urban and Regional Planning, University of Illinois, 1003 West Nevada, Urbana, Illinois 61801. (217) 333-1369. Also available online.

Environmental Periodicals Bibliography. Environmental Studies Institute, International Academy at Santa Barbara, 800 Garden St., Suite D, Santa Barbara, California 93101. (805) 965-5010. Also available online.

Geographical Abstracts. London School of Economics, Dept. of Geography, Regency House, 34 Duke St., London, England 1966-. Continued by Geo Abstracts issued in 6 parts: Pt. A. Landforms and the quaternary; Pt. B. Biogeography and Climatology; Pt. C. Economic geography; Pt. D. Social geography and cartography; Pt. E. Sedimentology; Pt. F. Regional and community planning.

Pollution Abstracts. Cambridge Scientific Abstracts, 5161 River Rd., Bethesda, Maryland 20816. (301) 961-6750. Six/year. Indexes worldwide technical literature on environmental pollution. Covers air pollution, marine and freshwater pollution, sewage and wastewater treatment, waste management, toxicology and health, noise pollution, radiation, land pollution, and environmental policies, programs, legislation, and education. Also available online.

Science Citation Index. Institute for Scientific Information, 3501 Market St., Philadelphia, Pennsylvania 19104. 1961-.

Selected References on Environmental Quality as It Relates to Health. National Library of Medicine, 8600 Rockville Pike, Bethesda, Maryland 20894. (800) 638-8480. 1977.

BIBLIOGRAPHIES

EPA Publications Bibliography. U.S. Environmental Protection Agency, Library Systems Branch, 401 M St., SW, Washington, District of Columbia 20460. (202) 260-2090. Quarterly.

ONLINE DATA BASES

BIOSIS Previews. BIOSIS, 2100 Arch St., Philadelphia, Pennsylvania 19103-1399. (215) 587-4800. Largest and most comprehensive database of research in the life sciences. Contains citations for nearly 9000 primary research journals, monographs, reviews, symposia, preliminary reports, semi-popular journals, selected institutional reports, government reports and research communications.

Computerized Engineering Index–COMPENDEX. Engineering Information Inc., 345 E. 47th St., New York, New York 10017. (212) 705-7600.

CRIS/USDA. U.S. Department of Agriculture, Cooperative State Research Service, Current Research Information System, National Agricultural Library Building, 5th Fl., 10301 Baltimore Blvd., Beltsville, Maryland 20705. (301) 344-3850. Agricultural, food and nutrition, and forestry research projects.

Enviro/Energyline Abstracts Plus. R. R. Bowker Co., 121 Chanlon Rd., New Providence, New Jersey 07974. (908) 464-6800.

Environmental Periodicals Bibliography. National Information Services Corp., Ste. 6, Wyman Towers, 3100 St. Paul St., Baltimore, Maryland 21218. (410)243-0797. Online version of abstract of same name.

RESEARCH CENTERS AND INSTITUTES

State University of New York College of Environmental Science and Forestry. Roosevelt Wildlife Institute, Syracuse, New York 13210. (315) 470-6741.

TRADE ASSOCIATIONS AND PROFESSIONAL SOCIETIES

American Institute of Chemical Engineers. 345 East 47th St., New York, New York 10017. (212) 705-7338.

American Institute of Chemists. 7315 Wisconsin Ave., Bethesda, Maryland 20814. (301) 652-2447.

Association of Local Air Pollution Control Officials. 444 North Capitol St., N.W., Washington, District of Columbia 20001 (202) 624-7864.

State and Territorial Air Pollution Program Administrators. 444 North Capitol St., Washington, District of Columbia 20001. (202) 624-7864.

AIR POLLUTION, INDOORS

See also: AIR POLLUTION

ABSTRACTING AND INDEXING SERVICES

Abstracts of Air and Water Conservation Literature. American Petroleum Institute. Central Abstracting and Indexing Service, 275 Madison Avenue, New York, New York 10016. 1972.

Air Pollution Technical Publications of the United States Environmental Protection Agency. U.S. Environmental Protection Agency, Mail Drop 75, Research Triangle Park, North Carolina 27711. (919) 541-2184. 1976. Quarterly.

Air Pollution Titles. Pennsylvania State University, Center for Air Environmental Studies, 226 Fenske Laboratory, University Park, Pennsylvania 16802. (814) 865-1415. 1965. Bibliographic guide to current research literature on air environment, including monitoring and control of air pollution, health effects, effects on agriculture, forests, toxic air contaminants, and global atmospheric pro cases.

Air Pollution Translations. A Bibliography With Abstracts. U.S. Environmental Protection Agency, MD 75, Research Triangle Park, North Carolina 27711. (919) 541-2184. 1969.

Biological Abstracts. BIOSIS, 2100 Arch St., Philadelphia, Pennsylvania 19103-1399. (215) 587-4800. 1927-.

Bulletin Signaletique: Eau et Assainissement, Pollution Atmospherique, Droit des Pollutions. Centre de Documentation, Centre National de la Recherche Scientifique, 15, quai Anatole France, Paris, France 75700. (1) 45 55 92 25. 1983-. Monthly. Indexes pollution periodicals including water, atmospheric and related pollutions.

Ecology Abstracts. Cambridge Scientific Abstracts, 5161 River Rd., Bethesda, Maryland 20816. (301) 961-6750. Monthly.

Environment Abstracts. Bowker A & I Publishing, 121 Chanlon Rd., New Providence, New Jersey 07974. (908) 464-6800. 1974-.

Environment Index. Environment Information Center, Index Research Department, 124 E. 39th St., New York, New York 10016. 1971-. Annual.

Environmental Information Connection–EIC. Planning Information Program, Dept. of Urban and Regional Planning, University of Illinois, 1003 West Nevada, Urbana, Illinois 61801. (217) 333-1369. Also available online.

Environmental Periodicals Bibliography. Environmental Studies Institute, International Academy at Santa Barbara, 800 Garden St., Suite D, Santa Barbara, California 93101. (805) 965-5010. Also available online.

General Science Index. H. W. Wilson Co., 950 University Ave., Bronx, New York 10452. 1978-. Monthly, also issued in annual cumulation. Cumulative subject index to English language periodicals in the subject fields of astronomy, botany, chemistry, earth science, environment and conservation, food and nutrition, genetics, mathematics, medicine and health, microbiology, oceanography, physics, physiology and zoology.

Geographical Abstracts. London School of Economics, Dept. of Geography, Regency House, 34 Duke St., London, England 1966-. Continued by Geo Abstracts issued in 6 parts: Pt. A. Landforms and the quaternary; Pt. B. Biogeography and Climatology; Pt. C. Economic geography; Pt. D. Social geography and cartography; Pt. E. Sedimentology; Pt. F. Regional and community planning.

Pollution Abstracts. Cambridge Scientific Abstracts, 5161 River Rd., Bethesda, Maryland 20816. (301) 961-6750. Six/year. Indexes worldwide technical literature on environmental pollution. Covers air pollution, marine and freshwater pollution, sewage and wastewater treatment, waste management, toxicology and health, noise pollution, radiation, land pollution, and environmental policies, programs, legislation, and education. Also available online.

Science Citation Index. Institute for Scientific Information, 3501 Market St., Philadelphia, Pennsylvania 19104. 1961-.

Selected References on Environmental Quality as It Relates to Health. National Library of Medicine, 8600 Rockville Pike, Bethesda, Maryland 20894. (800) 638-8480. 1977.

BIBLIOGRAPHIES

Current Contents. Agriculture, Biology and Environmental Sciences. Institute for Scientific Information, 3501 Market St., Philadelphia, Pennsylvania 19104. (800) 523-1857. 1973-. Previous title: Current Contents. Agricultural, Food & Veterinary Sciences. Gives the table of contents of periodicals in the fields of agriculture, biology, environmental and related areas.

EPA Publications Bibliography. U.S. Environmental Protection Agency, Library Systems Branch, 401 M St., SW, Washington, District of Columbia 20460. (202) 260-2090. Quarterly.

Indoor Air: Reference Bibliography. U.S. Environmental Protection Agency, 401 M St., S.W., Washington, District of Columbia 20460. (202) 260-2090.

ENCYCLOPEDIAS AND DICTIONARIES

Dictionary of Environmental Engineering and Related Sciences: English-Spanish, Spanish-English. Jose T. Villate. Ediciones Universal, 3090 SW 8th St., Miami, Florida 33135. (305) 642-3355. 1979.

Encyclopedia of Environmental Science and Engineering. J.R. Pfafflin. Gordon and Breach Science Publishers, Inc., 270 8th Ave., New York, New York 10011. (212) 206-8900. 1992.

McGraw-Hill Encyclopedia of Environmental Science. Sybil P. Parker. McGraw-Hill Science & Engineering Books, 11 W. 19th St., New York, New York 10011. (212) 337-6010. 1980. Covers ecology, man's influence on nature, and environmental protection.

McGraw-Hill Encyclopedia of Science and Technology. McGraw-Hill, 1221 Avenue of the Americas, New York, New York 10020. (212) 512-2000 or (800) 262-4729. 1992. Seventh edition. Issued in multiple volumes including index. Includes all science and technology broad subject areas.

GENERAL WORKS

Indoor Air Pollution: A Health Perspective. Jonathan M. Samet and John D. Spengler. Johns Hopkins University Press, 701 W. 40th St., Ste. 275, Baltimore, Maryland 21211. (212) 516-6900. 1991. Explores the relationship between air pollution and health. Provides a wealth of useful information including epidemiologic results and standards or requirements that influence air quality both indoor and out.

Indoor Air Pollution Control. Thad Godish. Lewis Publishers, 2000 Corporate Blvd., N.W., Boca Raton, Florida 33431. (407) 994-0555 or (800) 272-7737. 1989. Provides practical information and data needed for indoor air pollution control. Deals with how to conduct indoor air quality investigations in both residences and public access buildings; indoor air quality mitigation practice, and case histories.

Indoor Air Pollution: Radon, Bioaerosols, and VOCs. Jack G. Kay, et al. Lewis Publishers, 2000 Corporate Blvd., N.W., Boca Raton, Florida 33431. (407) 994-0555 or (800) 272-7737. 1991. Consists of two parts: Overview of the ACS Symposium on Indoor Air Pollution, and Radon overview

Legal Responses to Indoor Air Pollution. Frank B. Cross. Quorum Books, Div. of Greenwood Publishing Group, Inc., 88 Post Rd. W., Box 5007, Westport, Connecticut 06881. (203) 226-3571. 1990. Examines the under-recognized risks of indoor air pollution and the shortcomings of regulatory and judicial responses to these risks.

HANDBOOKS AND MANUALS

Managing Indoor Air Quality. Shirely J. Hansen. The Association of Energy Engineers, 4025 Pleasantdale Rd., Suite 420, Atlanta, Georgia 30340. (404) 925-9558. 1991. Includes readily applicable air quality control measures and preventive strategies that can head off the economic and legal problems.

ONLINE DATA BASES

AGRICOLA. U.S. Department of Agriculture, Office of Public Affairs, 14 Independence Ave., S.W., Washington, District of Columbia 20250. (202) 447-7454.

AGRIS. Food and Agriculture Organization of the United Nations, Via delle Terme di Caracalla, Rome, Italy 00100. 61 0181-FA01.

BIOSIS Previews. BIOSIS, 2100 Arch St., Philadelphia, Pennsylvania 19103-1399. (215) 587-4800. Largest and most comprehensive database of research in the life sciences. Contains citations for nearly 9000 primary research journals, monographs, reviews, symposia, preliminary reports, semi-popular journals, selected institutional reports, government reports and research communications.

Concentrations of Indoor Pollutants–CIP. CIP Database Coordinator, Building 90, Rm 3058, Lawrence Berkeley Lab., 1 Cyclotron Rd., Berkeley, California 94720. (415) 486-6591. Contains field data from studies monitoring indoor air quality in occupied buildings in U.S. and Canada.

CRIS/USDA. U.S. Department of Agriculture, Cooperative State Research Service, Current Research Information System, National Agricultural Library Building, 5th Fl., 10301 Baltimore Blvd., Beltsville, Maryland 20705. (301) 344-3850. Agricultural, food and nutrition, and forestry research projects.

Enviro/Energyline Abstracts Plus. R. R. Bowker Co., 121 Chanlon Rd., New Providence, New Jersey 07974. (908) 464-6800.

Environmental Periodicals Bibliography. National Information Services Corp., Ste. 6, Wyman Towers, 3100 St. Paul St., Baltimore, Maryland 21218. (410)243-0797. Online version of abstract of same name.

Monthly Catalog of United States Government Publications. U.S. G.P.O., Supt. of Docs., PO Box 371954, Pittsburgh, Pennsylvania 15250-7954. (202) 512-0000.

National Technical Information Service. U.S. Department of Commerce, National Technical Information Service, Office of Data Base Services, 5285 Port Royal Rd., Springfield, Virginia 22161. (703) 487-4807. Biblio-

graphic database of government sponsored research and technical reports.

PressNet Environmental Reports. Chemical Information Systems, Inc., 7215 York Rd., Baltimore, Maryland 21212. (301) 321-8440.

PERIODICALS AND NEWSLETTERS

Indoor Air Review. IAQ Pub. Inc., 5335 Wisconsin Ave., NW., Suite 440, Washington, District of Columbia 20015. (202) 686-2626. 1991. Monthly. Gives the latest news and information on the topic of indoor air quality. Special sections are devoted to updates of legislation, research and development, technology, liability and insurance issues, state and federal governments reports, industry and business forecasts and reports, meetings, conferences, training, standards and accreditation.

Indoor Environment. S. Karger Publishing, Inc., 26 West Avon Rd., PO Box 529, Farmington, Connecticut 06085. Bimonthly. The quality of the indoor environment at home and in the workplace, building design, materials, ventilation and air conditioning, and chemistry.

Indoor Pollution Law Report. Leader Publications, New York Law Publishing Co., 111 Eighth Ave., New York, New York 10011. (212) 463-5709. Monthly.

Indoor Pollution News. Buraff Publications, 1350 Connecticut Ave., NW, Suite 100, Washington, District of Columbia 20036. (202) 862-0990. Biweekly. Air quality in buildings (including radon, formaldehyde, solvents and asbestos) or other air pollutions, such as lead in pipes.

STATISTICS SOURCES

Air Contaminants: Permissible Exposure Limits. U.S. Occupational Safety and Health Administration. U.S. G.P.O., Washington, District of Columbia 20401. (202) 512-0000. 1989. Irregular. Data on OSHA legal limits on occupational air contaminants.

Airliner Cabin Environment: Contaminant, Measurements, Health Risks, and Mitigation Options. U.S. G.P.O, Washington, District of Columbia 20402-9325. (202) 512-0000. 1990. Cabin air quality tests conducted on smoking and nonsmoking flights for smoke-related contaminants (nicotine, respirable suspended particles, carbon monoxide) as well as ozone carbon dioxide, and various bacteria and fungi.

Stat/EPA Indoor Radon Survey. U.S. G.P.O., Washington, District of Columbia 20401. (202) 512-0000. Annual. Indoor radon levels in houses in selected states.

Trends '90: A Compendium of Data on Global Change. Thomas A. Boden, et al. Carbon Dioxide Information Analysis Center, Environmental Sciences Division, Oak Ridge National Laboratory, Oak Ridge, Tennessee 37831-6335. 1990. Source of frequently used global change data. Includes estimates of global and national CO_2 emissions from the burning of fossil fuels and from the production of cement and other pollutants.

AIR PURIFICATION, NATURAL

See: AIR POLLUTION

AIR QUALITY

See also: AIR POLLUTION; EMISSIONS

ABSTRACTING AND INDEXING SERVICES

Abstracts of Air and Water Conservation Literature. American Petroleum Institute. Central Abstracting and Indexing Service, 275 Madison Avenue, New York, New York 10016. 1972.

Air Pollution Technical Publications of the United States Environmental Protection Agency. U.S. Environmental Protection Agency, Mail Drop 75, Research Triangle Park, North Carolina 27711. (919) 541-2184. 1976. Quarterly.

Air Pollution Titles. Pennsylvania State University, Center for Air Environmental Studies, 226 Fenske Laboratory, University Park, Pennsylvania 16802. (814) 865-1415. 1965. Bibliographic guide to current research literature on air environment, including monitoring and control of air pollution, health effects, effects on agriculture, forests, toxic air contaminants, and global atmospheric pro cases.

Air Pollution Translations. A Bibliography With Abstracts. U.S. Environmental Protection Agency, MD 75, Research Triangle Park, North Carolina 27711. (919) 541-2184. 1969.

Biological Abstracts. BIOSIS, 2100 Arch St., Philadelphia, Pennsylvania 19103-1399. (215) 587-4800. 1927-.

Bulletin Signaletique: Eau et Assainissement, Pollution Atmospherique, Droit des Pollutions. Centre de Documentation, Centre National de la Recherche Scientifique, 15, quai Anatole France, Paris, France 75700. (1) 45 55 92 25. 1983-. Monthly. Indexes pollution periodicals including water, atmospheric and related pollutions.

Ecology Abstracts. Cambridge Scientific Abstracts, 5161 River Rd., Bethesda, Maryland 20816. (301) 961-6750. Monthly.

Environment Abstracts. Bowker A & I Publishing, 121 Chanlon Rd., New Providence, New Jersey 07974. (908) 464-6800. 1974-.

Environment Index. Environment Information Center, Index Research Department, 124 E. 39th St., New York, New York 10016. 1971-. Annual.

Environmental Information Connection–EIC. Planning Information Program, Dept. of Urban and Regional Planning, University of Illinois, 1003 West Nevada, Urbana, Illinois 61801. (217) 333-1369. Also available online.

Environmental Periodicals Bibliography. Environmental Studies Institute, International Academy at Santa Barbara, 800 Garden St., Suite D, Santa Barbara, California 93101. (805) 965-5010. Also available online.

General Science Index. H. W. Wilson Co., 950 University Ave., Bronx, New York 10452. 1978-. Monthly, also issued in annual cumulation. Cumulative subject index to English language periodicals in the subject fields of astronomy, botany, chemistry, earth science, environment and conservation, food and nutrition, genetics, mathematics, medicine and health, microbiology, oceanography, physics, physiology and zoology.

Geographical Abstracts. London School of Economics, Dept. of Geography, Regency House, 34 Duke St., London, England 1966-. Continued by Geo Abstracts issued in 6 parts: Pt. A. Landforms and the quaternary; Pt. B. Biogeography and Climatology; Pt. C. Economic geography; Pt. D. Social geography and cartography; Pt. E. Sedimentology; Pt. F. Regional and community planning.

Index to Scientific Book Contents. Institute for Scientific Information, 3501 Market St., Philadelphia, Pennsylvania 19104. (800) 523-1857. 1985-. Annual. Gives contents of science books published.

Pollution Abstracts. Cambridge Scientific Abstracts, 5161 River Rd., Bethesda, Maryland 20816. (301) 961-6750. Six/year. Indexes worldwide technical literature on environmental pollution. Covers air pollution, marine and freshwater pollution, sewage and wastewater treatment, waste management, toxicology and health, noise pollution, radiation, land pollution, and environmental policies, programs, legislation, and education. Also available online.

Science Citation Index. Institute for Scientific Information, 3501 Market St., Philadelphia, Pennsylvania 19104. 1961-.

ALMANACS AND YEARBOOKS

Gale Environmental Almanac. Russ Hoyle. Gale Research Inc., 835 Penobscot Bldg., Detroit, Michigan 48226-4094. (313) 961-2242. 1993. Focuses on the U.S. and Canada, although worldwide and transboundary issues are discussed.

Steam-Electric Plant Air and Water Quality Control Data for the Year Ended...Summary Report. Federal Energy Regulatory Commission, Office of Electrical Power Regulation, 825 N. Capitol St. NE, Washington, District of Columbia 20426. (202) 208-0200. 1969-1973. Covers electric power-plants, air quality, and water quality.

The Weather Almanac. Frank E. Bair, ed. Gale Research Co., 835 Penobscot Bldg., Detroit, Michigan 48226-4094. (313) 961-2242. 1992. Sixth edition. A reference guide to weather, climate, and air quality in the United States and its key cities, compromising statistics, principles, and terminology.

BIBLIOGRAPHIES

Acid Rain: A Bibliography of Canadian Federal and Provincial Government Documents. Albert H. Joy. Meckler, 11 Ferry Ln., W., Westport, Connecticut 06880. (203) 226-6967. 1991. Contains Canadian Federal and provincial government documents. Includes bibliographical references and index. Approximately 1,100 documents covering diverse topics including environmental effects, air and atmospheric processes, socioeconomic aspects, and migration and corrective measures.

Current Contents. Agriculture, Biology and Environmental Sciences. Institute for Scientific Information, 3501 Market St., Philadelphia, Pennsylvania 19104. (800) 523-1857. 1973-. Previous title: Current Contents. Agricultural, Food & Veterinary Sciences. Gives the table of contents of periodicals in the fields of agriculture, biology, environmental and related areas.

EPA Publications Bibliography. U.S. Environmental Protection Agency, Library Systems Branch, 401 M St., SW,

Washington, District of Columbia 20460. (202) 260-2090. Quarterly.

Receptor Model Source Composition Library. U.S. Environmental Protection Agency, MD 75, Research Triangle Park, North Carolina 27711. (919) 541-2184. 1984. Covers air management technology, monitoring and data analysis.

DIRECTORIES

Canadian Environmental Directory. Canadian Almanac & Directory Publishing Co. Ltd., 134 Adelaide St. E., Ste. 27, Toronto, Ontario, Canada M5C 1K9. (416) 362-4088. 1992. Includes individuals, agencies, firms, and associations.

Gale Environmental Sourcebook. Karen Hill. Gale Research Co., 835 Penobscot Bldg., Detroit, Michigan 48226-4094. (313) 961-2242. Contacts, information sources, or general information on environmental topics.

ENCYCLOPEDIAS AND DICTIONARIES

Clean Air Act: A Primer and Glossary. Clean Air Working Group, 818 Connecticut Ave., NW, Suite 900, Washington, District of Columbia 20006. (202) 857-0370. 1990.

Dictionary of Environmental Engineering and Related Sciences: English-Spanish, Spanish-English. Jose T. Villate. Ediciones Universal, 3090 SW 8th St., Miami, Florida 33135. (305) 642-3355. 1979.

Dictionary of the Environment. Michael Allaby. New York University Press, 70 Washington Sq. S., New York, New York 10012. (212) 998-2575. 1989.

Encyclopedia of Environmental Science and Engineering. J.R. Pfafflin. Gordon and Breach Science Publishers, Inc., 270 8th Ave., New York, New York 10011. (212) 206-8900. 1992.

Encyclopedia of Environmental Studies. William Ashworth. Facts on File, Inc., 460 Park Ave. S., New York, New York 10016. (212) 683-2244. 1991.

The Encyclopedia of Geochemistry and Environmental Sciences. Rhodes Whitmore Fairbridge. Van Nostrand Reinhold Co., 115 5th Ave., New York, New York 10003. (212) 254-3232. 1972.

Encyclopedia of Human Biology. Renato Dulbecco, ed. Academic Press, c/o Harcourt Brace Jovanovich Inc., 6277 Sea Harbor Dr., Orlando, Florida 32887. (800) 346-8648. 1991. Eight volumes.

Encyclopedia of Physical Science and Technology. Robert A. Meyers, ed. Academic Press, c/o Harcourt Brace Jovanovich Inc., 6277 Sea Harbor Dr., Orlando, Florida 32887. (800) 346-8648. Dictionary of engineering, technology and physical sciences.

Enumeration of Scientific Terms and Concepts Used in the Establishment of National Ambient Air Quality Standards. Patricia A. Porter. U.S. National Commission on Air Quality, Washington, District of Columbia 1980. Terminology of air quality.

Environmental Encyclopedia. William P. Cunningham, Terence Ball, et. al. Gale Research Inc., 835 Penobscot Bldg., Detroit, Michigan 48226-4094. (313) 961-2242. 1993.

McGraw-Hill Encyclopedia of Environmental Science. Sybil P. Parker. McGraw-Hill Science & Engineering Books, 11 W. 19th St., New York, New York 10011. (212) 337-6010. 1980. Covers ecology, man's influence on nature, and environmental protection.

The New York Times Encyclopedic Dictionary of the Environment. Paul Sarnoff. Quadrangle Books, New York, New York 1971. Focuses on state-of-the-art methods of pollution control, abatement, prevention and removal.

GENERAL WORKS

Aerosol Sampling: Science and Practice. J. H. Vincent. John Wiley & Sons, Inc., 605 3rd Ave., New York, New York 10158-0012. (212) 850-6000. 1989. Details the sampling of aerosols with a "real world" approach. Makes the connection between theory and practice.

Air Emissions from Municipal Solid Waste Landfills. Environmental Protection Agency. National Technical Information Service, 5285 Port Royal Rd., Springfield, Virginia 22161. (703) 487-4650. 1991. Background information for proposed standards and guidelines. Order number PB91-197061LDM.

Air Monitoring for Toxic Exposure. Shirley A. Ness. Van Nostrand Reinhold, 115 5th Ave., New York, New York 10003. (212) 354-3232. 1991. Explains the procedures for evaluating potentially harmful exposure to people from hazardous materials including chemicals, radon and bioaerosols. Presents practical information on how to perform air sampling, collect biological and bulk samples, evaluate dermal exposures, and determine the advantages and limitations of a given method.

Air Pollution Control. Howard E. Hesketh. Technomic Publishing Co., 851 New Holland Ave., Box 3535, Lancaster, Pennsylvania 17604. (717) 291-5609. 1991. Presents both theory and application data. Provides a background relevant to behavior theories and control techniques for capturing gaseous and particulate air pollutants.

Air Pollution Emission Standards and Guidelines for Municipal Waste Combustors: Economic Analysis of Materials Separation Requirement. B. J. Morton, et al. National Technical Information Service, 5285 Port Royal Rd., Springfield, Virginia 22161. (703) 487-4650. 1990. Final report prepared by the Research Triangle Institute for the Center for Economics Research.

Air Quality. Lewis Publishers, 200 Corporate Blvd. NW, Boca Raton, Florida 33431. (407) 994-0555 or (800)272-7737. 2nd edition. Air pollution and control, stratosphere O3 depletion, global warming, and indoor air pollution.

Atmospheric Chemistry: Models and Predictions for Climate and Air Quality. C. S. Sloane and T. W. Tesche. Lewis Publishers, 2000 Corporate Blvd., N.W., Boca Raton, Florida 33431. (407) 994-0555 or (800) 272-7737. 1991. Discusses the chemistry of stratospheric ozone depletion and its impact and related topics.

The Clean Air Act Amendments of 1990: Summary Materials. U.S. Environmental Protection Agency, Office of Air and Radiation, 401 M St. SW, Washington, District of Columbia 20460. (202) 260-2090. 1990.

Clean Air Act Policy Compendium. Government Institutes, Inc., 4 Research Pl., Ste. 200, Rockville, Maryland

20850. (301) 921-2300. 1985. Gives detailed insight into both compliance and enforcement of the Clean Air Act.

Comparative Dosimetry of Radon in Mines and Homes. Commission on Life Science, National Research Council. National Academy Press, 2101 Constitution Ave. N.W., PO Box 285, Washington, District of Columbia 20418. (202) 334-3313. 1991.

The Environmental Sourcebook. Edith Carol Stein. Lyons & Burford, 31 W. 21st St., New York, New York 10010. (212) 620-9580. 1992. Provides information on 11 specific environmental issues, including population; agriculture; energy; climate and atmosphere; biodiversity; water; oceans; solid waste; hazardous substances and waste; endangered lands; and development.

Environmental Viewpoints. Marie Lazzari. Gale Research Inc., 835 Penobscot Bldg., Detroit, Michigan 48226-4094. (313) 961-2242. 1992.

Escaping the Heat Trap. Irving Mintzer and William R. Moomaw. World Resources Institute, 1709 New York Ave. N.W., Washington, District of Columbia 20006. (800) 822-0504. 1991. Report is based on a series of scenarios developed using WRI's Model of Warming Commitment. Investigates the potential of societies to dramatically limit the rate of future greenhouse gas buildup and reduce to zero annual commitment to global warming.

Gas Chromatography in Air Pollution Analysis. Viktor G. Berezkin and Yuri S. Drugov. Elsevier Science Publishing Co., 655 Avenue of the Americas, New York, New York 10010. (212) 989-5800. 1991.

Greenhouse Gas Emissions–The Energy Dimension. OECD Publications and Information Center, 2001 L St., N.W., Suite 700, Washington, District of Columbia 20036. (202) 785-OECD. Source for a comprehensive discussion on the relationship between energy use and greenhouse emissions as they relate to the energy used by geographical and regional sectors.

Implementation Strategy for the Clean Air Act Amendments of 1990. U.S. Environmental Protection Agency, Office of Air and Radiation, 401 M St. SW, Washington, District of Columbia 20460. (202) 260-2090. 1991.

Indoor Air Pollution: Radon, Bioaerosols, and VOCs. Jack G. Kay, et al. Lewis Publishers, 2000 Corporate Blvd., N.W., Boca Raton, Florida 33431. (407) 994-0555 or (800) 272-7737. 1991. Consists of two parts: Overview of the ACS Symposium on Indoor Air Pollution, and Radon overview

Indoor Air Quality. Bradford O. Brooks. CRC Press, 2000 Corporate Blvd. N.W., Boca Raton, Florida 33431. (800) 272-7737. 1991. Traces history in context of indoor air quality, measurement, quality improvement and regulations and current philosophy of litigation.

Indoor Air Quality Control Techniques: Radon, Formaldehyde, Combustion Products. W.J. Fisk. Noyes Publications, 120 Mill Rd., Park Ridge, New Jersey 07656. (201) 391-8484. 1987. Air quality in the United States.

Industrial Ventilation Workbook; Indoor Air Quality Workbook; Laboratory Ventilation Workbook. American Industrial Hygiene Association, 345 White Pond Dr., Akron, Ohio 44320. (216) 873-2442. 1990-1991. Includes expanded coverage of introductory concepts through advanced materials and discussions of the state-of-the-art hood and duct design, loss factors, dilution ventilation,

etc. Also describes HVAC in simple understandable terms. The Lab workbook describes lab hood exhaust systems and associated HVAC systems.

Industrial Waste Gases: Utilization and Minimization. RCG/Hagler Bailly Inc. Technomic Publishing Co., 851 New Holland Ave., Box 3535, Lancaster, Pennsylvania 17604. (717) 291-5609. 1990. Also released under title Industrial Waste Gas Management. Deals with factory and trade waste and the effluents that are released into the atmosphere.

Legal Responses to Indoor Air Pollution. Frank B. Cross. Quorum Books, Div. of Greenwood Publishing Group, Inc., 88 Post Rd. W., Box 5007, Westport, Connecticut 06881. (203) 226-3571. 1990. Examines the under-recognized risks of indoor air pollution and the shortcomings of regulatory and judicial responses to these risks.

Minding the Carbon Store: Weighing U.S. Forestry Strategies to Slow Global Warming. Mark C. Trexler. World Resources Institute, 1709 New York Ave. N.W., Washington, District of Columbia 20006. (800) 833 0504. 1991. Assesses the strengths and weaknesses of each of the major domestic forestry options, including their costs and carbon benefits.

The New York Environment Book. Eric A. Goldstein. Island Press, 1718 Connecticut Ave. N.W., Suite 300, Washington, District of Columbia 20009. (202) 232-7933. 1990. Provides an in-depth analysis of New York City's environment. The five areas surveyed are: solid waste disposal, hazardous substances, water pollution, air quality, and drinking water quality. Discusses past cleanup efforts, and offers an agenda for the future. Describes and analyzes the general environment of urban areas, and offers solutions for their special environmental problems.

Occupational Exposure Limits for Airborne Toxic Substances. International Labour Office, 49 Sheridan Ave., Albany, New York 12210. (518) 436-9686. 1991.

Planning Pollution Prevention: Anticipatory Controls Over Air Pollution Sources. Christopher Wood. Heinemann Newnes, Halley Court, Jordan Hill, Oxford, England OX2 8EJ. 1991. Presents a comparative evaluation of two very different approaches to environmental regulation: the British controls based on 'best practicable means' and the American controls based upon air quality standards.

The Practitioner's Approach to Indoor Air Quality Investigations. American Industrial Hygiene Association, 345 White Pond Dr., Akron, Ohio 44320. (216) 873-2442. 1990. Presents pragmatic advice for approaching and conducting an investigation and describes the range and causes of complaints that fall into categories of acute to subchronic adverse health effects.

Prediction and Regulation of Air Pollution. M. E. Berlyand. Kluwer Academic Publishers, 101 Philip Dr., Assinippi Park, Norwell, Massachusetts 02061-0358. (617) 871-6600. 1991. Revised and updated version of Prognoz i regulirovanie, 1985.

A Primer on Greenhouse Effect Gases. Donald J. Wuebbles and Jae Edmonds. Lewis Publishers, 200 Corporate Blvd. NW, Boca Raton, Florida 33431. (407) 994-0555 or (800)272-7737. 1991. Brings together the most current information available on greenhouse gases. Reveals information critical to developing an understanding of the role of energy and atmospheric chemical and radiative processes in determining atmospheric concentrations of greenhouse gases.

Radiation Exposure and Occupational Risks. G. Keller, et al. Springer-Verlag, 175 5th Ave., New York, New York 10010. (212) 460-1500; (800) 777-4643. 1990. Discusses radiation exposure injuries in the workplace and prevention.

Radioactive Aerosols. A. C. Chamberlin. Cambridge University Press, 40 W 20th St., New York, New York 10011. (212) 924-3900; (800) 227-0247. 1991. Describes radioactive gases and particles which are dispersed in the environment, either from natural causes or following nuclear test and accidental emissions.

A Reference Guide to Clean Air. Cass Sandak. Carolina Biological Supply Company, 2700 York Rd., Burlington, North Carolina 27215. (919) 584-0381. 1990. A collection of references and a glossary.

The State of the Earth Atlas. Joni Seger, ed. Touchstone/ Simon and Schuster, Rockefeller Center, 1230 Avenue of the Americas, New York, New York 10020. 1990. Deals with environmental issues such as air quality, urban sprawl, toxic waste, tropical forests and tourism from a socioeconomic perspective.

The Statehouse Effect: State Policies to Cool the Greenhouse. Daniel A. Lashof and Eric L. Washburn. Natural Resources Defense Council, 40 W. 20th St., New York, New York 10011. (212) 727-2700. 1990. Discusses the need for states to take the initiative in controlling CO_2 emissions. Details the sources of greenhouse gases and explains how greenhouse emissions can be reduced through energy efficiency, renewable energy strategies, recycling, and taxation and reforms in transportation, agriculture and forests.

Techniques for Measuring Indoor Air. John Y. Yocom and Sharon M. McCarthy. John Wiley & Sons, Inc., 605 3rd Ave., New York, New York 10158-0012. (212) 850-6000. 1991. Addresses the recent, rapid expansion of interest in indoor air quality and its contribution to total human exposure to air pollutants by presenting past and present developments and also the directions that the field seems to be taking.

Technological Responses to the Greenhouse Effect. George Thurlow, ed. Elsevier Science Publishing Co., 655 Avenue of the Americas, New York, New York 10010. (212) 989-5800. 1990. Watt Committee on Energy (London) working with 23 British experts has reported on various greenhouse gases, their sources and sinks, followed by an analysis of the release of these gases in "energy conversion" primarily in electric power production.

World Guide to Environmental Issues and Organizations. Peter Brackley. Longman Group Ltd., Longman House, Burnt Mill, Harlow, Essex, England CM20 2J6. (0279) 426721. 1991.

World on Fire: Saving the Endangered Earth. George J. Mitchell. Scribner Educational Publishers, 866 3d Ave., New York, New York 10022. (212) 702-2000; (800) 257-5755. 1991. Discusses the problems entailed with the issues of greenhouse effect, acid rain, the rift in the stratosphere ozone layer, and the destruction of tropical rain forests.

GOVERNMENTAL ORGANIZATIONS

Department of Environmental Quality: Air Quality. Administrator, Air Quality Division, Herschler Building, Cheyenne, Wyoming (307) 777-7391.

Environmental Protection Agency: Office of Atmospheric and Indoor Air Programs. Waterside West Building, 401 M St., S.W., Washington, District of Columbia 20460. (202) 382-7404.

National Weather Service. 8060 13th St., Silver Spring, Maryland 20910. (301) 443-8910.

U.S. Environmental Protection Agency: Air Emission Factor Clearinghouse. Research Triangle Park, North Carolina 27711. (919) 541-0888.

U.S. Environmental Protection Agency: Air Risk Information Support Center. Research Triangle Park, North Carolina 27711. (919) 541-0888.

U.S. Environmental Protection Agency: Assistant Administrator for Enforcement. 401 M St., S.W., Washington, District of Columbia 20460. (202) 382-4134.

U.S. Environmental Protection Agency: Office of Air Quality Planning and Standards. Research Triangle Park, North Carolina 27711. (919) 541-5615.

U.S. Environmental Protection Agency: Office of Mobile Services. 401 M St., S.W., Washington, District of Columbia 20460. (202) 382-7645.

HANDBOOKS AND MANUALS

Clean Air Handbook. Government Institutes, Inc., 4 Research Pl., Ste. 200, Rockville, Maryland 20850. (301) 921-2300. Analyzes the requirements of the Clean Air Act and its 1990 amendments, as well as what can be expected in terms of new regulation.

The Engineer's Clean Air Handbook. P. D. Osborn. Butterworth-Heinemann, Linacre House, Jordan Hill, Oxford, England OX2 8DP. (0865) 310366. 1989. Deals with the causes of various types of air pollution and the complicated nature of many of the pollutants. Also describes methods and necessary instrumentation for pollution removal. Includes a list of useful references.

Environmental Statistics Handbook: Europe. Allan Foster, Oksana Newman. Gale Research Inc., 835 Penobscot Bldg., Detroit, Michigan 48226-4094. (313) 961-2242. 1993.

Indoor Air Quality Design Guidebook. Milton Meckler. Fairmont Press, 700 Indian Trail, Lilburn, Georgia 30247. (404) 925-9388. 1991. Air cleaning systems, the carbon dioxide method, health lead/lag procedure, desiccants, contaminant absorption, effects of sick buildings, assessment of measurement techniques, indoor air quality simulation with computer models, and system design and maintenance techniques. Also available through the Association of Energy Engineers.

Managing Indoor Air Quality. Shirely J. Hansen. The Association of Energy Engineers, 4025 Pleasantdale Rd., Suite 420, Atlanta, Georgia 30340. (404) 925-9558. 1991. Includes readily applicable air quality control measures and preventive strategies that can head off the economic and legal problems.

Standard Handbook of Environmental Engineering. Robert A. Corbitt. McGraw-Hill, 1221 Ave. of the Americas, New York, New York 10020. (212) 512-2000 or (800)

262-4729. 1990. Hands-on reference to understand environmental engineering technology. Covers air quality control, water supply, wastewater disposal, waste management, stormwater and hazardous wastes.

ONLINE DATA BASES

Aerometric Information Retrieval System. U.S. Environmental Protection Agency, Office of Air Quality Planning and Standards, National Air Data Branch, 401 M St. SW, Washington, District of Columbia 20460. (202) 260-2090. Contains data reported by more than 5000 air monitoring stations located throughout the United States.

Air Pollution Technical Information Center File. U.S. Environmental Protection Agency, Library Services Office, Air Information Center (MD-35), 401 M St. SW, Washington, District of Columbia 20460. (202) 260-2090. Citations and abstracts of the world's literature on air quality and air pollution prevention and control.

Air Toxics Report. Business Publishers, Inc., 951 Pershing Dr., Silver Spring, Maryland 20910. (301) 587-6300. Online version of periodical of the same name.

BIOSIS Previews. BIOSIS, 2100 Arch St., Philadelphia, Pennsylvania 19103-1399. (215) 587-4800. Largest and most comprehensive database of research in the life sciences. Contains citations for nearly 9000 primary research journals, monographs, reviews, symposia, preliminary reports, semi-popular journals, selected institutional reports, government reports and research communications.

Concentrations of Indoor Pollutants–CIP. CIP Database Coordinator, Building 90, Rm 3058, Lawrence Berkeley Lab., 1 Cyclotron Rd., Berkeley, California 94720. (415) 486-6591. Contains field data from studies monitoring indoor air quality in occupied buildings in U.S. and Canada.

Enviro/Energyline Abstracts Plus. R. R. Bowker Co., 121 Chanlon Rd., New Providence, New Jersey 07974. (908) 464-6800.

Environmental Periodicals Bibliography. National Information Services Corp., Ste. 6, Wyman Towers, 3100 St. Paul St., Baltimore, Maryland 21218. (410)243-0797. Online version of abstract of same name.

International Air Data Base. U.S. Environmental Protection Agency, Office of Monitoring Systems and Quality Assurance, 401 M St., S.W., Washington, District of Columbia 20460. (202) 260-2090. Ambient air data from the World Health Organization and precipitation data from the World Meteorological Organization.

Monthly Catalog of United States Government Publications. U.S. G.P.O., Supt. of Docs., PO Box 371954, Pittsburgh, Pennsylvania 15250-7954. (202) 512-0000.

National Technical Information Service. U.S. Department of Commerce, National Technical Information Service, Office of Data Base Services, 5285 Port Royal Rd., Springfield, Virginia 22161. (703) 487-4807. Bibliographic database of government sponsored research and technical reports.

PressNet Environmental Reports. Chemical Information Systems, Inc., 7215 York Rd., Baltimore, Maryland 21212. (301) 321-8440.

PERIODICALS AND NEWSLETTERS

Air Currents. Bay Area Air Quality Management District, 939 Ellis St., San Francisco, California 94109. (415) 771-6000. 1959-. Monthly. Describes regulation changes and other information of interest to the air pollution control community.

Air Pollution Control. Bureau of National Affairs, 1231 25th St. NW, Washington, District of Columbia 20037. (202) 452-4200. Biweekly. A reference and advisory service on the control of air pollution, designed to meet the information needs of individuals responsible for complying with EPA and state air pollution control regulations.

Air Quality Digest. South Coast Air Quality Management District, 9150 Flair Dr., El Monet, California 91731. (818) 572-6200. 1971-. Quarterly. Reports developments of significance in air pollution control. Centers on program administered by LA County ARCD.

Air Toxics Report. Business Publishers, Inc., 951 Pershing Dr., Silver Spring, Maryland 20910-4464. (301) 587-6300. 1988-. Monthly. Directed towards organizations and facilities that are or may be affected by regulations under the Clean Air Act and National Emission Standards for Hazardous Air Pollutants, with articles on government regulation, studies, compliance, violations and legal actions. Also available online.

ALAPCO Washington Update. Association of Local Air Pollution Control Officials, 444 North Capitol Street, NW, Washington, District of Columbia 20001. (202) 624-7864. Monthly. Air pollution control in Washington, DC.

Atmospheric Environment. Pergamon Microforms International, Inc., Fairview Park, Elmsford, New York 10523. (914) 592-7720. 1966-. Publishes papers on all aspects of man's interactions with his atmospheric environment, including the administrative, economic and political aspects of these interactions. Air pollution research and its applications are covered, taking into account changes in the atmospheric flow patterns, temperature distributions and chemical constitution caused by natural and artificial variations in the earth's surface.

Clean Air News. Industrial Gas Cleaning Institute, 1707 L St. N.W., #570, Washington, District of Columbia 20036. (202) 457-0911. 1960-. Bimonthly. Industrial air pollution control.

Clean Air Permits. Thompson Publishing Group, 1725 K St., N.W., Suite 200, Washington, District of Columbia 20006. (202) 872-4000. Monthly. Manager's guide to the 1990 Clean Air Act.

Clean Air Report. National Environmental Development Assn., 1440 New York Ave., NW, Suite 300, Washington, District of Columbia 20005. (202) 638-1230. Quarterly.

ENFO. 1251-B Miller Ave., Winter Park, Florida 32789-4827. (407) 644-5377. Bimonthly. Water resources, parks, wildlife air quality, growth management, government and private actions.

Environmental Defense Fund Letter. Environmental Defense Fund, 257 Park Avenue South, New York, New York 10010. (212) 505-2100. 1971-. Bimonthly. Environmental issues of concern.

Environmental Health Letter. Business Publishers, Inc., 951 Pershing Dr., Silver Spring, Maryland 20910-4464.

(301) 587-6300. 1961-. Biweekly. Covers areas such as: indoor air, asbestos health effects, toxic substances testing, health problems at wastewater plants, risk-based sludge rules, medical waste, developmental toxicity risk assessment, animal carcinogen tests, pesticide risk, air toxics, aerospace chemicals, lead, radionuclide emissions, state right-to-know statutes, and incinerator emissions.

Indoor Air Review. IAQ Pub. Inc., 5335 Wisconsin Ave., NW., Suite 440, Washington, District of Columbia 20015. (202) 686-2626. 1991. Monthly. Gives the latest news and information on the topic of indoor air quality. Special sections are devoted to updates of legislation, research and development, technology, liability and insurance issues, state and federal governments reports, industry and business forecasts and reports, meetings, conferences, training, standards and accreditation.

Indoor Environment. S. Karger Publishing, Inc., 26 West Avon Rd., PO Box 529, Farmington, Connecticut 06085. Bimonthly. The quality of the indoor environment at home and in the workplace, building design, materials, ventilation and air conditioning, and chemistry.

Indoor Pollution News. Buraff Publications, 1350 Connecticut Ave., NW, Suite 100, Washington, District of Columbia 20036. (202) 862-0990. Biweekly. Air quality in buildings (including radon, formaldehyde, solvents and asbestos) or other air pollutions, such as lead in pipes.

Journal of Atmospheric Sciences. American Meteorology Society, 45 Beacon Street, Boston, Massachusetts 02108. (617) 227-2425. Biweekly. Articles on the atmosphere of the earth and other planets.

Journal of Environmental Health. National Environmental Health Association, 720 South Colorado Boulevard, Suite 970, Denver, Colorado 80222. (303) 756-9090. Bimonthly. Covers phases in environmental health.

National Air Toxics Information Clearinghouse Newsletter. National Air Toxic Information Clearinghouse, P.O. Box 13000, Research Triangle Park, North Carolina 27709. (919) 541-9100. Bimonthly. Covers noncriteria pollutant emissions.

New Jersey Air, Water, & Waste Management Times. New Jersey State Department of Health, Division of Clean Air & Water, John Fitch Plaza, Trenton, New Jersey 08625. Bimonthly.

Pollution Control Newsletter. Arizona State Dept. of Health Services, Bureau of Air Quality Control, 1740 W. Adams St., Phoenix, Arizona 85007. (602) 542-1000. Eight times a year.

RESEARCH CENTERS AND INSTITUTES

Air Quality Group. University of California, Davis, Crocker Nuclear Laboratories, Davis, California 95616. (510) 752-1124.

STATISTICS SOURCES

Annual Report of the Surface Air Sampling Program. National Technical Information Service, 5285 Port Royal Rd., Springfield, Virginia 22161. (703) 487-4650. Annual. Results of the Environmental Measurements Laboratory (EML) sampling program for radionucleides in surface air, by month and week, used to study the

effects of nuclear weapons testing and other nuclear events.

Environmental Data Compendium. OECD Publications and Information Center, 2001 L St., N.W., Suite 700, Washington, District of Columbia 20036. (202) 785-6323. 1989.

Environmental Indicators. OECD Publications and Information Center, 2001 L St., N.W., Suite 700, Washington, District of Columbia 20036. (202) 785-6323. 1991.

Environmental Quality. Council on Environmental Quality. U.S. G.P.O., Washington, District of Columbia 20401. (202) 512-0000. Annual.

National Air Quality and Emissions Trends Report. U.S. Environmental Protection Agency, 401 M St., S.W., Washington, District of Columbia 20460. (202) 260-2090. Annual. Status of air pollution in selected MSAs, 10 EPA regions, and nationwide for each pollutant, pollutant concentrations, and average annual emissions by source (transportation, fuel combustion, industrial processes, and solid waste).

Portable Electric Air Cleaners/Purifiers. FIND/SVP, 625 Avenue of the Americas, New York, New York 10011. (212) 645-4500. 1991. Projects ownership incidence and the market size of portable electric oil cleaners/purifiers, delineated brand shares, prices paid, types of filtration, types of outlet.

The State of the Environment. OECD Publications and Information Center, 2001 L St., N.W., Suite 700, Washington, District of Columbia 20036. (202) 785-6323. 1991.

Statistical Record of the Environment. Arsen J. Darnay. Gale Research Inc., 835 Penobscot Bldg., Detroit, Michigan 48226-4094. (313) 961-2242. 1992.

Trends '90: A Compendium of Data on Global Change. Thomas A. Boden, et al. Carbon Dioxide Information Analysis Center, Environmental Sciences Division, Oak Ridge National Laboratory, Oak Ridge, Tennessee 37831-6335. 1990. Source of frequently used global change data. Includes estimates of global and national CO_2 emissions from the burning of fossil fuels and from the production of cement and other pollutants.

World Resources. World Resources Institute. 1709 New York Ave., N.W., Washington, District of Columbia 20006. (202) 638-6300. Annual. Statistical and textual analysis of world's natural resources and the effects of growth-caused environmental pollution.

TRADE ASSOCIATIONS AND PROFESSIONAL SOCIETIES

Air and Waste Management Association. Box 2861, Pittsburgh, Pennsylvania 15230. (412) 232-3444.

Air Resources Information Clearinghouse. 99 Court St., Rochester, New York 14604. (716) 546-3796.

American Institute of Chemical Engineers. 345 East 47th St., New York, New York 10017. (212) 705-7338.

American Institute of Chemists. 7315 Wisconsin Ave., Bethesda, Maryland 20814. (301) 652-2447.

Association of Local Air Pollution Control Officials. 444 North Capitol St., N.W., Washington, District of Columbia 20001 (202) 624-7864.

Association of New Jersey Environmental Commissions. PO Box 157, 300 Mendham Rd., Mendham, New Jersey 07945. (201) 539-7547.

Center for Clean Air Policy. 444 N. Capitol St., Suite 526, Washington, District of Columbia 20001. (202) 624-7709.

Center for Environmental Information, Inc. 99 Court St., Rochester, New York 14604. (716) 546-3796.

Clean Air Working Group. 818 Connecticut Ave., N.W., Suite 900, Washington, District of Columbia 20006. (202) 857-0370.

Environmental Defense Fund. 257 Park Ave., S., New York, New York 10010. (212) 505-2100. Non-profit organization that was established more than 20 years ago. Its goals are to protect the earth's environment by providing lasting solutions to global environmental problems.

Industrial Gas Clearing Institute. 1707 L St., N.W., Suite 570, Washington, District of Columbia 20036. (202) 457-0911.

Intersociety Committee on Methods for Air Sampling and Analysis. 12113 Shropshire Blvd., Austin, Texas 78753. (512) 835-5118.

National Air Transportation Association. 4226 King St., Alexandria, Virginia 22302. (703) 845-9000.

National Clean Air Coalition. 1400 16th St., N.W., Washington, District of Columbia 20036. (202) 797-5496.

State and Territorial Air Pollution Program Administrators. 444 North Capitol St., Washington, District of Columbia 20001. (202) 624-7864.

United States Public Interest Research Group. 215 Pennsylvania Ave., SE, Washington, District of Columbia 20003. (202) 546-9707.

AIR QUALITY CRITERIA, PROGRAMS, STANDARDS

See: AIR QUALITY

AIR SAMPLING

ABSTRACTING AND INDEXING SERVICES

Abstracts of Air and Water Conservation Literature. American Petroleum Institute. Central Abstracting and Indexing Service, 275 Madison Avenue, New York, New York 10016. 1972.

Air Pollution Technical Publications of the United States Environmental Protection Agency. U.S. Environmental Protection Agency, Mail Drop 75, Research Triangle Park, North Carolina 27711. (919) 541-2184. 1976. Quarterly.

Air Pollution Titles. Pennsylvania State University, Center for Air Environmental Studies, 226 Fenske Laboratory, University Park, Pennsylvania 16802. (814) 865-1415. 1965. Bibliographic guide to current research literature on air environment, including monitoring and control of air pollution, health effects, effects on agricul-

ture, forests, toxic air contaminants, and global atmospheric pro cases.

Air Pollution Translations. A Bibliography With Abstracts. U.S. Environmental Protection Agency, MD 75, Research Triangle Park, North Carolina 27711. (919) 541-2184. 1969.

Applied Ecology Abstracts Studies in Renewable Natural Resources. Information Retrieval Ltd., 1911 Jefferson Davis Highway, Arlington, Virginia 22202. 1975-. Monthly.

Applied Science and Technology Index. H.W. Wilson Co., 950 University Ave., Bronx, New York 10452. (800) 367-6770. Formerly Industrial Arts Index.

Biological Abstracts. BIOSIS, 2100 Arch St., Philadelphia, Pennsylvania 19103-1399. (215) 587-4800. 1927-.

Bulletin Signaletique: Eau et Assainissement, Pollution Atmospherique, Droit des Pollutions. Centre de Documentation, Centre National de la Recherche Scientifique, 15, quai Anatole France, Paris, France 75700. (1) 45 55 92 25. 1983-. Monthly. Indexes pollution periodicals including water, atmospheric and related pollutions.

Chemical Abstracts. Chemical Abstracts Service, 2540 Olentangy River Rd., PO Box 3012, Columbus, Ohio 43210. (800) 848-6533. 1907-.

Ecological Abstracts. Geo Abstracts Ltd. Elsevier Applied Science, Crown House, Linton Rd., Barking, England IG 11 8JU. 1974-. Derived from over 600 leading ecological and environmental journals, plus books, conference proceedings, reports and theses.

Ecology Abstracts. Cambridge Scientific Abstracts, 5161 River Rd., Bethesda, Maryland 20816. (301) 961-6750. Monthly.

Environment Abstracts. Bowker A & I Publishing, 121 Chanlon Rd., New Providence, New Jersey 07974. (908) 464-6800. 1974-.

Environment Index. Environment Information Center, Index Research Department, 124 E. 39th St., New York, New York 10016. 1971-. Annual.

Environmental Information Connection–EIC. Planning Information Program, Dept. of Urban and Regional Planning, University of Illinois, 1003 West Nevada, Urbana, Illinois 61801. (217) 333-1369. Also available online.

Environmental Periodicals Bibliography. Environmental Studies Institute, International Academy at Santa Barbara, 800 Garden St., Suite D, Santa Barbara, California 93101. (805) 965-5010. Also available online.

General Science Index. H. W. Wilson Co., 950 University Ave., Bronx, New York 10452. 1978-. Monthly, also issued in annual cumulation. Cumulative subject index to English language periodicals in the subject fields of astronomy, botany, chemistry, earth science, environment and conservation, food and nutrition, genetics, mathematics, medicine and health, microbiology, oceanography, physics, physiology and zoology.

Multimedia Index to Ecology. National Information Center for Educational Media, University of Southern California, Los Angeles, California 90007.

Pollution Abstracts. Cambridge Scientific Abstracts, 5161 River Rd., Bethesda, Maryland 20816. (301) 961-6750. Six/year. Indexes worldwide technical literature on envi-

ronmental pollution. Covers air pollution, marine and freshwater pollution, sewage and wastewater treatment, waste management, toxicology and health, noise pollution, radiation, land pollution, and environmental policies, programs, legislation, and education. Also available online.

Science Citation Index. Institute for Scientific Information, 3501 Market St., Philadelphia, Pennsylvania 19104. 1961-.

Selected References on Environmental Quality as It Relates to Health. National Library of Medicine, 8600 Rockville Pike, Bethesda, Maryland 20894. (800) 638-8480. 1977.

BIBLIOGRAPHIES

EPA Publications Bibliography. U.S. Environmental Protection Agency, Library Systems Branch, 401 M St., SW, Washington, District of Columbia 20460. (202) 260-2090. Quarterly.

GENERAL WORKS

Advances in Air Sampling. Lewis Publishers, 2000 Corporate Blvd., N.W., Boca Raton, Florida 33431. (407) 994-0555 or (800) 272-7737. 1988. Summary of the ACGIH Symposium on Advances in Air Sampling held February 16-18, 1987 at Pacific Grove, California. Includes topics such as particle size selective sampling, sampling gases and vapors for analysis, real-time aerosol samplers, and sampling strategy.

Aerosol Sampling: Science and Practice. J. H. Vincent. John Wiley & Sons, Inc., 605 3rd Ave., New York, New York 10158-0012. (212) 850-6000. 1989. Details the sampling of aerosols with a "real world" approach. Makes the connection between theory and practice.

Air Monitoring for Toxic Exposure. Shirley A. Ness. Van Nostrand Reinhold, 115 5th Ave., New York, New York 10003. (212) 354-3232. 1991. Explains the procedures for evaluating potentially harmful exposure to people from hazardous materials including chemicals, radon and bioaerosols. Presents practical information on how to perform air sampling, collect biological and bulk samples, evaluate dermal exposures, and determine the advantages and limitations of a given method.

Compilation of EPA's Sampling and Analysis Methods. William Mueller, et al. Lewis Publishers, 2000 Corporate Blvd., N.W., Boca Raton, Florida 33431. (407) 994-0555 or (800) 272-7737. 1991. Aids with rapid searching of sampling and analytical method summaries. More than 650 method/analytical summaries from the database are included in this volume.

Gaseous Pollutants: Characterization and Cycling. Jerome O. Nriagu, ed. J. Wiley, 605 3rd Ave., New York, New York 10158-0012. (800) CALL-WILEY. 1992. Focuses on various methods of sampling and analyzing gaseous pollutants in the atmosphere with emphasis on understanding the chemical and physical processes that occur.

Industrial Environmental Control. A. M. Springer. John Wiley & Sons, Inc., 605 3rd Ave., New York, New York 10158-0012. (212) 850-6000. 1986. Covers in great detail all the basic information regarding industrial pollution and its treatment.

Meteorology of Air Pollution: Implications for the Environment and Its Future. R. S. Scorer. E. Horwood, 66 Wood Lane End, Hemel Hempstead, England HP2 4RG. 1990. Discusses methods of air pollution measurement and future expectations.

Methods of Air Sampling and Analysis. James P. Lodge, Jr. Lewis Publishers, 2000 Corporate Blvd., N.W., Boca Raton, Florida 33431. (407) 994-0555 or (800) 272-7737. 1989. Third edition. Includes all contaminants analyzed or monitored with a given method. Includes information on how to deal with indoor and outdoor air pollution, industrial hygiene, and other related topics.

HANDBOOKS AND MANUALS

The Engineer's Clean Air Handbook. P. D. Osborn. Butterworth-Heinemann, Linacre House, Jordan Hill, Oxford, England OX2 8DP. (0865) 310366. 1989. Deals with the causes of various types of air pollution and the complicated nature of many of the pollutants. Also describes methods and necessary instrumentation for pollution removal. Includes a list of useful references.

Managing Indoor Air Quality. Shirely J. Hansen. The Association of Energy Engineers, 4025 Pleasantdale Rd., Suite 420, Atlanta, Georgia 30340. (404) 925-9558. 1991. Includes readily applicable air quality control measures and preventive strategies that can head off the economic and legal problems.

ONLINE DATA BASES

Air Toxics Report. Business Publishers, Inc., 951 Pershing Dr., Silver Spring, Maryland 20910. (301) 587-6300. Online version of periodical of the same name.

BIOSIS Previews. BIOSIS, 2100 Arch St., Philadelphia, Pennsylvania 19103-1399. (215) 587-4800. Largest and most comprehensive database of research in the life sciences. Contains citations for nearly 9000 primary research journals, monographs, reviews, symposia, preliminary reports, semi-popular journals, selected institutional reports, government reports and research communications.

Chemical Abstracts-CA. Chemical Abstracts Service, 2540 Olentangy River Rd., P.O. Box 3012, Columbus, Ohio 43210. (800) 848-6533 or (614) 421-3600. Information sources include 9000 journals, patents from 27 countries, two industrial property organizations, new books, conference proceedings, and government research reports.

Concentrations of Indoor Pollutants–CIP. CIP Database Coordinator, Building 90, Rm 3058, Lawrence Berkeley Lab., 1 Cyclotron Rd., Berkeley, California 94720. (415) 486-6591. Contains field data from studies monitoring indoor air quality in occupied buildings in U.S. and Canada.

Enviro/Energyline Abstracts Plus. R. R. Bowker Co., 121 Chanlon Rd., New Providence, New Jersey 07974. (908) 464-6800.

Environmental Periodicals Bibliography. National Information Services Corp., Ste. 6, Wyman Towers, 3100 St. Paul St., Baltimore, Maryland 21218. (410)243-0797. Online version of abstract of same name.

Monthly Catalog of United States Government Publications. U.S. G.P.O., Supt. of Docs., PO Box 371954, Pittsburgh, Pennsylvania 15250-7954. (202) 512-0000.

National Technical Information Service. U.S. Department of Commerce, National Technical Information Service, Office of Data Base Services, 5285 Port Royal Rd., Springfield, Virginia 22161. (703) 487-4807. Bibliographic database of government sponsored research and technical reports.

PERIODICALS AND NEWSLETTERS

Air Pollution Monitoring and Sampling Newsletter. McIlvaine Co., 2970 Maria Ave., Northbrook, Illinois 60062. (708) 272-0010. 1980-. Monthly. Information on air pollution monitoring and sampling equipment and service.

Air Toxics Report. Business Publishers, Inc., 951 Pershing Dr., Silver Spring, Maryland 20910-4464. (301) 587-6300. 1988-. Monthly. Directed towards organizations and facilities that are or may be affected by regulations under the Clean Air Act and National Emission Standards for Hazardous Air Pollutants, with articles on government regulation, studies, compliance, violations and legal actions. Also available online.

ALAPCO Washington Update. Association of Local Air Pollution Control Officials, 444 North Capitol Street, NW, Washington, District of Columbia 20001. (202) 624-7864. Monthly. Air pollution control in Washington, DC.

Atmospheric Environment. Pergamon Microforms International, Inc., Fairview Park, Elmsford, New York 10523. (914) 592-7720. 1966-. Publishes papers on all aspects of man's interactions with his atmospheric environment, including the administrative, economic and political aspects of these interactions. Air pollution research and its applications are covered, taking into account changes in the atmospheric flow patterns, temperature distributions and chemical constitution caused by natural and artificial variations in the earth's surface.

TRADE ASSOCIATIONS AND PROFESSIONAL SOCIETIES

Air and Waste Management Association. Box 2861, Pittsburgh, Pennsylvania 15230. (412) 232-3444.

Association of Local Air Pollution Control Officials. 444 North Capitol St., N.W., Washington, District of Columbia 20001 (202) 624-7864.

Association of New Jersey Environmental Commissions. PO Box 157, 300 Mendham Rd., Mendham, New Jersey 07945. (201) 539-7547.

Center for Environmental Information, Inc. 99 Court St., Rochester, New York 14604. (716) 546-3796.

State and Territorial Air Pollution Program Administrators. 444 North Capitol St., Washington, District of Columbia 20001. (202) 624-7864.

AIR-SEA INTERACTION
See: OCEAN-ATMOSPHERE INTERACTION

AIRCRAFT NOISE
See: NOISE POLLUTION

AIRPLANE EMISSIONS
See: AIR QUALITY

AIRPORTS

ABSTRACTING AND INDEXING SERVICES

Engineering Index. The Engineering Index Inc., 345 E. 47th St., New York, New York 10017. 1962-.

Science Citation Index. Institute for Scientific Information, 3501 Market St., Philadelphia, Pennsylvania 19104. 1961-.

ONLINE DATA BASES

Computerized Engineering Index–COMPENDEX. Engineering Information Inc., 345 E. 47th St., New York, New York 10017. (212) 705-7600.

TRADE ASSOCIATIONS AND PROFESSIONAL SOCIETIES

National Air Transportation Association. 4226 King St., Alexandria, Virginia 22302. (703) 845-9000.

ALABAMA ENVIRONMENTAL AGENCIES

GOVERNMENTAL ORGANIZATIONS

Conservation and Natural Resources Department: Fish and Wildlife. Commissioner, 64 North Union St., Room 702, Montgomery, Alabama 36130. (205) 242-3465.

Conservation and Natural Resources Department: Natural Resources. Commissioner, 64 North Union St., Room 702, Montgomery, Alabama 36130. (205) 242-3486.

Department of Agriculture and Industry: Pesticide Registration. Director, Division of Agricultural Chemistry and Plant/Plant Industry, PO Box 3336, 1445 Federal Dr., Montgomery, Alabama 36193. (205) 261-2656.

Department of Labor: Occupational Safety. Assistant Commissioner, 64 North Union St., Room 600, Montgomery, Alabama 36130.

Environmental Health Administration: Environmental Protection. Director, Room 251, State Office Building, Montgomery, Alabama 36130. (205) 242-5004.

Environmental Management Department: Air Quality. Chief, Air Division, 1751 Congressman W. L. Dickinson Dr., Montgomery, Alabama 36130. (205) 271-7861.

Environmental Management Department: Coastal Zone Management. Chief of Field Operations, 1751 Congressman W. L. Dickinson Dr., Montgomery, Alabama 36130. (205) 271-7700.

Environmental Management Department: Emergency Preparedness and Community Right-to-Know. Chief of Operations, Emergency Response Commission, 1751 Congressman W. L. Dickinson Dr., Montgomery, Alabama 36109. (205) 271-7700.

Environmental Management Department: Hazardous Waste Management. Chief, Hazardous Waste Branch,

Land Division, 1751 Congressman W.L. Dickinson Dr., Montgomery, Alabama 36130. (205) 271-7736.

Environmental Management Department: Water Quality. Acting Director, Water Quality, 1751 Congressman W.L. Dickinson Dr., Montgomery, Alabama 36130. (205) 271-7823.

Environmental Management Division: Solid Waste Management. Chief, Division of Solid Waste, 1751 Congressman W.L. Dickinson Dr., Montgomery, Alabama 36130. (205) 271-7823.

Waste Minimization and Pollution Prevention. Director, Hazardous Material Management and Resource Recovery Program, PO Box 872203, Tuscaloosa, Alabama 35487-0203. (205) 348-8401.

ALABAMA ENVIRONMENTAL LEGISLATION

GENERAL WORKS

Alabama Law Handbook. Government Institutes, Inc., 4 Research Pl., Ste. 200, Rockville, Maryland 20850. (301) 921-2300. 1990.

ALAR

See: FOOD SCIENCE

ALASKA ENVIRONMENTAL AGENCIES

GOVERNMENTAL ORGANIZATIONS

Department of Environmental Conservation: Pesticide Registration. Director, Environmental Health, 3132 Channel Dr., Room 135, Juneau, Alaska 99811. (907) 465-2696.

Department of Fish and Game: Fish and Wildlife. Commissioner, PO Box 3-2000, Juneau, Alaska 99802-2000. (907) 465-4100.

Department of Labor: Occupational Safety. Deputy Director, Occupational Safety and Health Division, PO Box 1149, Juneau, Alaska 99802. (907) 465-4855.

Department of Natural Resources: Natural Resources. Commissioner, PO Box M, Juneau, Alaska 99802. (907) 465-2400.

Department of Natural Resources: Underground Storage Tanks. Petroleum Manager, PO Box 7034, Anchorage, Alaska 99510-0734. (907) 561-2020.

Emergency Response Commission: Emergency Preparedness and Community Right-to-Know. Chair, PO Box O, Juneau, Alaska 99811. (907) 465-2600.

Environmental Conservation Department: Air Quality. Chief, Air and Hazardous Waste Management Science, PO Box O, Juneau, Alaska 99811-1800. (907) 465-2666.

Environmental Conservation Department: Environmental Protection. Commissioner, PO Box O, Juneau, Alaska 99811-1800. (907) 465-4100.

Environmental Conservation Department: Groundwater Management. Chief, Water Quality Management, PO Box O, Juneau, Alaska 99811-1800. (907) 465-2634.

Environmental Conservation Department: Hazardous Waste Management. Chief, Hazardous Waste Management Section, PO Box O, Juneau, Alaska 99811-1800. (907) 465-2666.

Environmental Conservation Department: Solid Waste Management. Chief, Hazardous Waste Management Section, PO Box O, Juneau, Alaska 99811-1800. (907) 465-2666.

Environmental Conservation Department: Water Quality. Chief, Water Quality Management, PO Box O, Juneau, Alaska 99811. (907) 465-2634.

Office of the Governor: Coastal Zone Management. Director, Division of Governmental Coordination, PO Box AW, Juneau, Alaska 99811. (907) 762-4355.

Waste Reduction Assistance Program: Waste Minimization and Pollution Program. Executive Director, 431 West Seventh Ave., Anchorage, Alaska 99501. (907) 276-2864.

ALASKA ENVIRONMENTAL LEGISLATION

GENERAL WORKS

The Alaska Conservation Directory. Alaska Conservation Foundation, 430 W. 7th Ave.,Ste. 215, Anchorage, Alaska 99501. (907) 276-1917. 1990.

ALBUMIN

See also: NUTRITION

ABSTRACTING AND INDEXING SERVICES

ASFA Aquaculture Abstracts. Cambridge Scientific Abstracts, Inc., 5161 River Rd., Bethesda, Maryland 20816. (301) 961-6750. 1984.

Biological Abstracts. BIOSIS, 2100 Arch St., Philadelphia, Pennsylvania 19103-1399. (215) 587-4800. 1927-.

Environment Abstracts. Bowker A & I Publishing, 121 Chanlon Rd., New Providence, New Jersey 07974. (908) 464-6800. 1974-.

Environment Index. Environment Information Center, Index Research Department, 124 E. 39th St., New York, New York 10016. 1971-. Annual.

Environmental Information Connection–EIC. Planning Information Program, Dept. of Urban and Regional Planning, University of Illinois, 1003 West Nevada, Urbana, Illinois 61801. (217) 333-1369. Also available online.

Environmental Periodicals Bibliography. Environmental Studies Institute, International Academy at Santa Barbara, 800 Garden St., Suite D, Santa Barbara, California 93101. (805) 965-5010. Also available online.

Food Science and Technology Abstracts. International Food Information Service, c/o National Food Laboratory, 6363 Clark Ave., Dublin, California 94568. (800) 336-3782. 1969-.

General Science Index. H. W. Wilson Co., 950 University Ave., Bronx, New York 10452. 1978-. Monthly, also issued in annual cumulation. Cumulative subject index to English language periodicals in the subject fields of astronomy, botany, chemistry, earth science, environment and conservation, food and nutrition, genetics, mathematics, medicine and health, microbiology, oceanography, physics, physiology and zoology.

Genetics Abstracts. Cambridge Scientific Abstracts, 5161 River Rd., Bethesda, Maryland 20816. (301) 961-6750. 1968-. Monthly. Formerly published by Information Retrieval Ltd., London England. Published by Cambridge Scientific Abstracts since 1982.

Index to Scientific Book Contents. Institute for Scientific Information, 3501 Market St., Philadelphia, Pennsylvania 19104. (800) 523-1857. 1985-. Annual. Gives contents of science books published.

Science Citation Index. Institute for Scientific Information, 3501 Market St., Philadelphia, Pennsylvania 19104. 1961-.

BIBLIOGRAPHIES

EPA Publications Bibliography. U.S. Environmental Protection Agency, Library Systems Branch, 401 M St., SW, Washington, District of Columbia 20460. (202) 260-2090. Quarterly.

ENCYCLOPEDIAS AND DICTIONARIES

Encyclopedia of Human Biology. Renato Dulbecco, ed. Academic Press, c/o Harcourt Brace Jovanovich Inc., 6277 Sea Harbor Dr., Orlando, Florida 32887. (800) 346-8648. 1991. Eight volumes.

Macmillan Dictionary of Toxicology. Ernest Hodgson, et al. Van Nostrand Reinhold, 115 5th Ave., New York, New York 10003. (212) 254-3232. 1988. Intended as a "starting point" to the literature of toxicology. American spelling is used with cross references to British version of words. Contains a list of references. Signed entries give explanatory definitions and cross references.

The Nutrition and Health Encyclopedia. David F. Tver and Percy Russell. Van Nostrand Reinhold, 115 5th Ave., New York, New York 10003. (212) 254-3232. 1989.

Van Nostrand's Scientific Encyclopedia. Glenn D. Considine, ed. Van Nostrand Reinhold, 115 5th Ave., New York, New York 10003. (212) 254-3232. 1983. Sixth edition. Includes all broad subject areas in science.

ONLINE DATA BASES

BIOSIS Previews. BIOSIS, 2100 Arch St., Philadelphia, Pennsylvania 19103-1399. (215) 587-4800. Largest and most comprehensive database of research in the life sciences. Contains citations for nearly 9000 primary research journals, monographs, reviews, symposia, preliminary reports, semi-popular journals, selected institutional reports, government reports and research communications.

Enviro/Energyline Abstracts Plus. R. R. Bowker Co., 121 Chanlon Rd., New Providence, New Jersey 07974. (908) 464-6800.

Environmental Periodicals Bibliography. National Information Services Corp., Ste. 6, Wyman Towers, 3100 St. Paul St., Baltimore, Maryland 21218. (410)243-0797. Online version of abstract of same name.

SCISEARCH. Institute for Scientific Information, University City Science Center, 3501 Market St., Philadelphia, Pennsylvania 19104. (215) 386-0100.

ALCOHOL AS FUEL

ABSTRACTING AND INDEXING SERVICES

Environment Abstracts. Bowker A & I Publishing, 121 Chanlon Rd., New Providence, New Jersey 07974. (908) 464-6800. 1974-.

Environment Index. Environment Information Center, Index Research Department, 124 E. 39th St., New York, New York 10016. 1971-. Annual.

Environmental Information Connection–EIC. Planning Information Program, Dept. of Urban and Regional Planning, University of Illinois, 1003 West Nevada, Urbana, Illinois 61801. (217) 333-1369. Also available online.

Environmental Periodicals Bibliography. Environmental Studies Institute, International Academy at Santa Barbara, 800 Garden St., Suite D, Santa Barbara, California 93101. (805) 965-5010. Also available online.

General Science Index. H. W. Wilson Co., 950 University Ave., Bronx, New York 10452. 1978-. Monthly, also issued in annual cumulation. Cumulative subject index to English language periodicals in the subject fields of astronomy, botany, chemistry, earth science, environment and conservation, food and nutrition, genetics, mathematics, medicine and health, microbiology, oceanography, physics, physiology and zoology.

BIBLIOGRAPHIES

Alcohol Fuels. Vivian O. Sammons. Library of Congress, Science and Technology Division, Reference Section, Washington, District of Columbia 1980.

Directory of Published Proceedings. Interdok Corp., 173 Halstead Ave., Harrison, New York 10528. (914) 835-3506. 1990. Monthly. This is a listing of published proceedings including the series SEMTE (Science/Medicine/Engineering/Technology) and the series SSH (Social Science/Humanities).

EPA Publications Bibliography. U.S. Environmental Protection Agency, Library Systems Branch, 401 M St., SW, Washington, District of Columbia 20460. (202) 260-2090. Quarterly.

Gasohol: Energy from Agriculture. Robert W. Lockerby. Vance Bibliographies, PO Box 229, 112 N. Charter St., Monticello, Illinois 61856. (217) 762-3831. 1980.

Gasohol-One Answer to the Energy Crisis. Joseph Lee Cook. Vance Bibliographies, PO Box 229, 112 N. Charter St., Monticello, Illinois 61856. (217) 762-3831. 1979.

Gasohol Sourcebook: Literature Survey and Abstracts. N. P. Cheremisinoff and P. N. Cheremisinoff. Ann Arbor Science, 230 Collingwood, PO Box 1425, Ann Arbor, Michigan 48106. 1981. Volume includes: biotechnology and bioconversion; ethanol and methanol production;

automotive and other fuels; production of chemical feedstocks; and economics of alcohol production.

A Selected Bibliography on Alcohol Fuels. Solar Energy Research Institute, 1617 Cole Blvd., Golden, Colorado 80401. 1982. Covers literature written about biomass derived ethyl and methyl alcohols, including production processes, economics, use as fuel, engine conversion, feedstocks, financing, government regulations, coproducts, environmental effects and safety. The main focus is on alcohol fuels.

GENERAL WORKS

Alcohol as a Fuel for Farm and Construction Equipment. G.L. Borman. National Technical Information Service, 5285 Port Royal Rd., Springfield, Virginia 22161. (703) 487-4650. 1982. Fuels utilization by farm and construction equipment.

Ethyl Alcohol Production and Use as a Motor Fuel. Noyes Publications, 120 Mill Rd., Park Ridge, New Jersey 07656. (201) 391-8484. 1979. Patents relating to alcohol.

The Forbidden Fuel. Hal Bernton. Boyd Griffin, 714 Stratfield Rd., Fairfield, Connecticut 06432. (203) 335-0229. 1982. Power alcohol in the twentieth century.

Fuel from Farms. National Agricultural Library. National Technical Information Service, 5285 Port Royal Rd., Springfield, Virginia 22161. (703) 487-4650. 1982. A guide to small-scale ethanol production, and biomass energy.

HANDBOOKS AND MANUALS

Ethanol Fuels Reference Guide. Technical Information Branch, Solar Energy Research Institute, 1617 Cole Blvd., Golden, Colorado 80401. 1982. A decision-maker's guide to ethanol fuels like biomass energy and gasohol.

The Manual for the Home and Farm Production of Alcohol Fuel. Stephen W. Mathewson. Ten Speed Press, P.O. Box 7123, Berkeley, California 94707. (800) 841-2665. 1980.

The Mother Earth News Alcohol Fuel Handbook. Michael R. Kerley. Mother Earth News, PO Box 801, Arden, North Carolina 28704-0801. (704) 693-0211. 1980.

ONLINE DATA BASES

Enviro/Energyline Abstracts Plus. R. R. Bowker Co., 121 Chanlon Rd., New Providence, New Jersey 07974. (908) 464-6800.

Environmental Periodicals Bibliography. National Information Services Corp., Ste. 6, Wyman Towers, 3100 St. Paul St., Baltimore, Maryland 21218. (410)243-0797. Online version of abstract of same name.

ALCOHOL DEHYDROGENASE

See also: ALCOHOLS

ABSTRACTING AND INDEXING SERVICES

Biological Abstracts. BIOSIS, 2100 Arch St., Philadelphia, Pennsylvania 19103-1399. (215) 587-4800. 1927-.

Environment Abstracts. Bowker A & I Publishing, 121 Chanlon Rd., New Providence, New Jersey 07974. (908) 464-6800. 1974-.

Environment Index. Environment Information Center, Index Research Department, 124 E. 39th St., New York, New York 10016. 1971-. Annual.

Environmental Information Connection-EIC. Planning Information Program, Dept. of Urban and Regional Planning, University of Illinois, 1003 West Nevada, Urbana, Illinois 61801. (217) 333-1369. Also available online.

Environmental Periodicals Bibliography. Environmental Studies Institute, International Academy at Santa Barbara, 800 Garden St., Suite D, Santa Barbara, California 93101. (805) 965-5010. Also available online.

Genetics Abstracts. Cambridge Scientific Abstracts, 5161 River Rd., Bethesda, Maryland 20816. (301) 961-6750. 1968-. Monthly. Formerly published by Information Retrieval Ltd., London England. Published by Cambridge Scientific Abstracts since 1982.

BIBLIOGRAPHIES

EPA Publications Bibliography. U.S. Environmental Protection Agency, Library Systems Branch, 401 M St., SW, Washington, District of Columbia 20460. (202) 260-2090. Quarterly.

ENCYCLOPEDIAS AND DICTIONARIES

McGraw-Hill Encyclopedia of Science and Technology. McGraw-Hill, 1221 Avenue of the Americas, New York, New York 10020. (212) 512-2000 or (800) 262-4729. 1992. Seventh edition. Issued in multiple volumes including index. Includes all science and technology broad subject areas.

Van Nostrand's Scientific Encyclopedia. Glenn D. Considine, ed. Van Nostrand Reinhold, 115 5th Ave., New York, New York 10003. (212) 254-3232. 1983. Sixth edition. Includes all broad subject areas in science.

ONLINE DATA BASES

BIOSIS Previews. BIOSIS, 2100 Arch St., Philadelphia, Pennsylvania 19103-1399. (215) 587-4800. Largest and most comprehensive database of research in the life sciences. Contains citations for nearly 9000 primary research journals, monographs, reviews, symposia, preliminary reports, semi-popular journals, selected institutional reports, government reports and research communications.

Enviro/Energyline Abstracts Plus. R. R. Bowker Co., 121 Chanlon Rd., New Providence, New Jersey 07974. (908) 464-6800.

Environmental Periodicals Bibliography. National Information Services Corp., Ste. 6, Wyman Towers, 3100 St. Paul St., Baltimore, Maryland 21218. (410)243-0797. Online version of abstract of same name.

ALCOHOLS

ABSTRACTING AND INDEXING SERVICES

Applied Science and Technology Index. H.W. Wilson Co., 950 University Ave., Bronx, New York 10452. (800) 367-6770. Formerly Industrial Arts Index.

Biological Abstracts. BIOSIS, 2100 Arch St., Philadelphia, Pennsylvania 19103-1399. (215) 587-4800. 1927-.

Chemical Abstracts. Chemical Abstracts Service, 2540 Olentangy River Rd., PO Box 3012, Columbus, Ohio 43210. (800) 848-6533. 1907-.

Energy Information Abstracts Annual 1987 in Retrospect. EIC/Intelligence Inc., 121 Chanlon Rd., New Providence, New Jersey 07974. (908) 464-6800. 1988. Annual. Cumulative edition of the monthly Energy Information Abstracts. Monitors sources in the field of energy including the scientific, technical and business journal literature, conference and symposia proceedings, corporate, government and academic reports.

Environment Abstracts. Bowker A & I Publishing, 121 Chanlon Rd., New Providence, New Jersey 07974. (908) 464-6800. 1974-.

Environment Index. Environment Information Center, Index Research Department, 124 E. 39th St., New York, New York 10016. 1971-. Annual.

Environmental Information Connection–EIC. Planning Information Program, Dept. of Urban and Regional Planning, University of Illinois, 1003 West Nevada, Urbana, Illinois 61801. (217) 333-1369. Also available online.

Environmental Periodicals Bibliography. Environmental Studies Institute, International Academy at Santa Barbara, 800 Garden St., Suite D, Santa Barbara, California 93101. (805) 965-5010. Also available online.

Food Science and Technology Abstracts. International Food Information Service, c/o National Food Laboratory, 6363 Clark Ave., Dublin, California 94568. (800) 336-3782. 1969-.

General Science Index. H. W. Wilson Co., 950 University Ave., Bronx, New York 10452. 1978-. Monthly, also issued in annual cumulation. Cumulative subject index to English language periodicals in the subject fields of astronomy, botany, chemistry, earth science, environment and conservation, food and nutrition, genetics, mathematics, medicine and health, microbiology, oceanography, physics, physiology and zoology.

Index to Scientific Book Contents. Institute for Scientific Information, 3501 Market St., Philadelphia, Pennsylvania 19104. (800) 523-1857. 1985-. Annual. Gives contents of science books published.

BIBLIOGRAPHIES

EPA Publications Bibliography. U.S. Environmental Protection Agency, Library Systems Branch, 401 M St., SW, Washington, District of Columbia 20460. (202) 260-2090. Quarterly.

A Selected Bibliography on Alcohol Fuels. Solar Energy Research Institute, 1617 Cole Blvd., Golden, Colorado 80401. 1982. Covers literature written about biomass derived ethyl and methyl alcohols, including production

processes, economics, use as fuel, engine conversion, feedstocks, financing, government regulations, coproducts, environmental effects and safety. The main focus is on alcohol fuels.

ENCYCLOPEDIAS AND DICTIONARIES

Dictionary of Microbiology and Molecular Biology. Paul Singleton and Diana Sainsbury. John Wiley & Sons, Inc., 605 3rd Ave., New York, New York 10158-0012. (212) 850-6000. 1987. Second edition. Comprehensive dictionary with "classical descriptive aspects of microbiology to current developments in related areas of bioenergetics, biochemistry and molecular biology." Entries give synonyms, cross references, and references to pertinent works. Miscellaneous appendixes. Bibliography.

Encyclopedia of Chemical Processing and Design. John J. Mcketta and W. A. Cunningham. Marcel Dekker, Inc., 270 Madison Ave., New York, New York 10016. (212) 696-9000; (800) 228-1160. 1992. Thirty-eight volumes.

Encyclopedia of Human Biology. Renato Dulbecco, ed. Academic Press, c/o Harcourt Brace Jovanovich Inc., 6277 Sea Harbor Dr., Orlando, Florida 32887. (800) 346-8648. 1991. Eight volumes.

Kirk-Othmer Encyclopedia of Chemical Technology. J. I. Kroschwitz, ed. John Wiley & Sons, Inc., 605 3rd Ave., New York, New York 10158-0012. (212) 850-6000. 1992-. All articles in the new edition have been rewritten and updated adding new subjects such as biotechnology, computer topics, analytical techniques and instrumentation, environmental concerns, fuels and energy, inorganic and solid state chemistry; composite materials and material science in general, and pharmaceuticals. Also available online.

McGraw-Hill Encyclopedia of Science and Technology. McGraw-Hill, 1221 Avenue of the Americas, New York, New York 10020. (212) 512-2000 or (800) 262-4729. 1992. Seventh edition. Issued in multiple volumes including index. Includes all science and technology broad subject areas.

The Nutrition and Health Encyclopedia. David F. Tver and Percy Russell. Van Nostrand Reinhold, 115 5th Ave., New York, New York 10003. (212) 254-3232. 1989.

Van Nostrand's Scientific Encyclopedia. Glenn D. Considine, ed. Van Nostrand Reinhold, 115 5th Ave., New York, New York 10003. (212) 254-3232. 1983. Sixth edition. Includes all broad subject areas in science.

ONLINE DATA BASES

BIOSIS Previews. BIOSIS, 2100 Arch St., Philadelphia, Pennsylvania 19103-1399. (215) 587-4800. Largest and most comprehensive database of research in the life sciences. Contains citations for nearly 9000 primary research journals, monographs, reviews, symposia, preliminary reports, semi-popular journals, selected institutional reports, government reports and research communications.

CAS Source Index–CASSI. Chemical Abstracts Service, 2540 Olentangy River Rd., P.O. Box 3012, Columbus, Ohio 43210. (800) 848-6533 or (614) 421-3600. A listing of bibliographic and library holdings information for scientific and technical primary literature relevant to the chemical sciences.

Chemical Abstracts-CA. Chemical Abstracts Service, 2540 Olentangy River Rd., P.O. Box 3012, Columbus, Ohio 43210. (800) 848-6533 or (614) 421-3600. Information sources include 9000 journals, patents from 27 countries, two industrial property organizations, new books, conference proceedings, and government research reports.

Enviro/Energyline Abstracts Plus. R. R. Bowker Co., 121 Chanlon Rd., New Providence, New Jersey 07974. (908) 464-6800.

Environmental Periodicals Bibliography. National Information Services Corp., Ste. 6, Wyman Towers, 3100 St. Paul St., Baltimore, Maryland 21218. (410)243-0797. Online version of abstract of same name.

Kirk-Othmer Encyclopedia of Chemical Technology. John Wiley & Sons, Inc., 605 3rd Ave., 5th Floor, New York, New York 10158. (212) 850-6000. Online version of the publication of the same name.

PERIODICALS AND NEWSLETTERS

Alcohol and Health Research World. National Institute on Alcohol Abuse and Alcoholism. U.S. G.P.O., Washington, District of Columbia 20401. (202) 512-0000. Quarterly. Research articles on prevention and treatment of alcoholism.

STATISTICS SOURCES

Alcohol Health and Research World. U.S. G.P.O, Washington, District of Columbia 20402-9325. (202) 512-0000. Quarterly. Original research on treatment and prevention of alcoholism and alcohol abuse.

TRADE ASSOCIATIONS AND PROFESSIONAL SOCIETIES

American Institute of Chemical Engineers. 345 East 47th St., New York, New York 10017. (212) 705-7338.

American Institute of Chemists. 7315 Wisconsin Ave., Bethesda, Maryland 20814. (301) 652-2447.

ALDEHYDE DEHYDROGENASES

ABSTRACTING AND INDEXING SERVICES

Biological Abstracts. BIOSIS, 2100 Arch St., Philadelphia, Pennsylvania 19103-1399. (215) 587-4800. 1927-.

Chemical Abstracts. Chemical Abstracts Service, 2540 Olentangy River Rd., PO Box 3012, Columbus, Ohio 43210. (800) 848-6533. 1907-.

Environment Abstracts. Bowker A & I Publishing, 121 Chanlon Rd., New Providence, New Jersey 07974. (908) 464-6800. 1974-.

Environment Index. Environment Information Center, Index Research Department, 124 E. 39th St., New York, New York 10016. 1971-. Annual.

Environmental Information Connection–EIC. Planning Information Program, Dept. of Urban and Regional Planning, University of Illinois, 1003 West Nevada, Urbana, Illinois 61801. (217) 333-1369. Also available online.

Environmental Periodicals Bibliography. Environmental Studies Institute, International Academy at Santa Barbara, 800 Garden St., Suite D, Santa Barbara, California 93101. (805) 965-5010. Also available online.

Science Citation Index. Institute for Scientific Information, 3501 Market St., Philadelphia, Pennsylvania 19104. 1961-.

BIBLIOGRAPHIES

EPA Publications Bibliography. U.S. Environmental Protection Agency, Library Systems Branch, 401 M St., SW, Washington, District of Columbia 20460. (202) 260-2090. Quarterly.

ENCYCLOPEDIAS AND DICTIONARIES

Encyclopedia of Human Biology. Renato Dulbecco, ed. Academic Press, c/o Harcourt Brace Jovanovich Inc., 6277 Sea Harbor Dr., Orlando, Florida 32887. (800) 346-8648. 1991. Eight volumes.

McGraw-Hill Encyclopedia of Science and Technology. McGraw-Hill, 1221 Avenue of the Americas, New York, New York 10020. (212) 512-2000 or (800) 262-4729. 1992. Seventh edition. Issued in multiple volumes including index. Includes all science and technology broad subject areas.

ONLINE DATA BASES

BIOSIS Previews. BIOSIS, 2100 Arch St., Philadelphia, Pennsylvania 19103-1399. (215) 587-4800. Largest and most comprehensive database of research in the life sciences. Contains citations for nearly 9000 primary research journals, monographs, reviews, symposia, preliminary reports, semi-popular journals, selected institutional reports, government reports and research communications.

CAS Source Index–CASSI. Chemical Abstracts Service, 2540 Olentangy River Rd., P.O. Box 3012, Columbus, Ohio 43210. (800) 848-6533 or (614) 421-3600. A listing of bibliographic and library holdings information for scientific and technical primary literature relevant to the chemical sciences.

Chemical Abstracts-CA. Chemical Abstracts Service, 2540 Olentangy River Rd., P.O. Box 3012, Columbus, Ohio 43210. (800) 848-6533 or (614) 421-3600. Information sources include 9000 journals, patents from 27 countries, two industrial property organizations, new books, conference proceedings, and government research reports.

Enviro/Energyline Abstracts Plus. R. R. Bowker Co., 121 Chanlon Rd., New Providence, New Jersey 07974. (908) 464-6800.

Environmental Periodicals Bibliography. National Information Services Corp., Ste. 6, Wyman Towers, 3100 St. Paul St., Baltimore, Maryland 21218. (410)243-0797. Online version of abstract of same name.

TRADE ASSOCIATIONS AND PROFESSIONAL SOCIETIES

American Institute of Chemical Engineers. 345 East 47th St., New York, New York 10017. (212) 705-7338.

American Institute of Chemists. 7315 Wisconsin Ave., Bethesda, Maryland 20814. (301) 652-2447.

ALDEHYDES

See also: AIR POLLUTION, INDOORS; WATER POLLUTION

ABSTRACTING AND INDEXING SERVICES

Biological Abstracts. BIOSIS, 2100 Arch St., Philadelphia, Pennsylvania 19103-1399. (215) 587-4800. 1927-.

Chemical Abstracts. Chemical Abstracts Service, 2540 Olentangy River Rd., PO Box 3012, Columbus, Ohio 43210. (800) 848-6533. 1907-.

Environment Abstracts. Bowker A & I Publishing, 121 Chanlon Rd., New Providence, New Jersey 07974. (908) 464-6800. 1974-.

Environment Index. Environment Information Center, Index Research Department, 124 E. 39th St., New York, New York 10016. 1971-. Annual.

Environmental Information Connection–EIC. Planning Information Program, Dept. of Urban and Regional Planning, University of Illinois, 1003 West Nevada, Urbana, Illinois 61801. (217) 333-1369. Also available online.

Environmental Periodicals Bibliography. Environmental Studies Institute, International Academy at Santa Barbara, 800 Garden St., Suite D, Santa Barbara, California 93101. (805) 965-5010. Also available online.

Food Science and Technology Abstracts. International Food Information Service, c/o National Food Laboratory, 6363 Clark Ave., Dublin, California 94568. (800) 336-3782. 1969-.

General Science Index. H. W. Wilson Co., 950 University Ave., Bronx, New York 10452. 1978-. Monthly, also issued in annual cumulation. Cumulative subject index to English language periodicals in the subject fields of astronomy, botany, chemistry, earth science, environment and conservation, food and nutrition, genetics, mathematics, medicine and health, microbiology, oceanography, physics, physiology and zoology.

Index to Scientific Book Contents. Institute for Scientific Information, 3501 Market St., Philadelphia, Pennsylvania 19104. (800) 523-1857. 1985-. Annual. Gives contents of science books published.

INIS Atomindex. International Atomic Energy Agency, Wagramerstrasse 5, Vienna, Austria A-1400. 222 23606198. 1988-. Semiannual. Abstracts nuclear energy and nuclear physics topics from journals, conferences, technical reports and other related publications. Issued in 6 parts: Personal Author, Corporate Entry, Subject, Report, Standard Patent, Conference (by place), Conference (by date).

Pollution Abstracts. Cambridge Scientific Abstracts, 5161 River Rd., Bethesda, Maryland 20816. (301) 961-6750. Six/year. Indexes worldwide technical literature on environmental pollution. Covers air pollution, marine and freshwater pollution, sewage and wastewater treatment, waste management, toxicology and health, noise pollution, radiation, land pollution, and environmental policies, programs, legislation, and education. Also available online.

Science Citation Index. Institute for Scientific Information, 3501 Market St., Philadelphia, Pennsylvania 19104. 1961-.

BIBLIOGRAPHIES

EPA Publications Bibliography. U.S. Environmental Protection Agency, Library Systems Branch, 401 M St., SW, Washington, District of Columbia 20460. (202) 260-2090. Quarterly.

ENCYCLOPEDIAS AND DICTIONARIES

McGraw-Hill Encyclopedia of Science and Technology. McGraw-Hill, 1221 Avenue of the Americas, New York, New York 10020. (212) 512-2000 or (800) 262-4729. 1992. Seventh edition. Issued in multiple volumes including index. Includes all science and technology broad subject areas.

Van Nostrand's Scientific Encyclopedia. Glenn D. Considine, ed. Van Nostrand Reinhold, 115 5th Ave., New York, New York 10003. (212) 254-3232. 1983. Sixth edition. Includes all broad subject areas in science.

ONLINE DATA BASES

BIOSIS Previews. BIOSIS, 2100 Arch St., Philadelphia, Pennsylvania 19103-1399. (215) 587-4800. Largest and most comprehensive database of research in the life sciences. Contains citations for nearly 9000 primary research journals, monographs, reviews, symposia, preliminary reports, semi-popular journals, selected institutional reports, government reports and research communications.

CAS Source Index–CASSI. Chemical Abstracts Service, 2540 Olentangy River Rd., P.O. Box 3012, Columbus, Ohio 43210. (800) 848-6533 or (614) 421-3600. A listing of bibliographic and library holdings information for scientific and technical primary literature relevant to the chemical sciences.

Chemical Abstracts-CA. Chemical Abstracts Service, 2540 Olentangy River Rd., P.O. Box 3012, Columbus, Ohio 43210. (800) 848-6533 or (614) 421-3600. Information sources include 9000 journals, patents from 27 countries, two industrial property organizations, new books, conference proceedings, and government research reports.

Enviro/Energyline Abstracts Plus. R. R. Bowker Co., 121 Chanlon Rd., New Providence, New Jersey 07974. (908) 464-6800.

Environmental Periodicals Bibliography. National Information Services Corp., Ste. 6, Wyman Towers, 3100 St. Paul St., Baltimore, Maryland 21218. (410)243-0797. Online version of abstract of same name.

ALDICARB

See: TOXICITY

ALDRINS

See also: CARCINOGENS; PESTICIDES

ABSTRACTING AND INDEXING SERVICES

Applied Ecology Abstracts Studies in Renewable Natural Resources. Information Retrieval Ltd., 1911 Jefferson

Davis Highway, Arlington, Virginia 22202. 1975-. Monthly.

Biological Abstracts. BIOSIS, 2100 Arch St., Philadelphia, Pennsylvania 19103-1399. (215) 587-4800. 1927-.

Chemical Abstracts. Chemical Abstracts Service, 2540 Olentangy River Rd., PO Box 3012, Columbus, Ohio 43210. (800) 848-6533. 1907-.

Environment Abstracts. Bowker A & I Publishing, 121 Chanlon Rd., New Providence, New Jersey 07974. (908) 464-6800. 1974-.

Environment Index. Environment Information Center, Index Research Department, 124 E. 39th St., New York, New York 10016. 1971-. Annual.

Environmental Information Connection–EIC. Planning Information Program, Dept. of Urban and Regional Planning, University of Illinois, 1003 West Nevada, Urbana, Illinois 61801. (217) 333-1369. Also available online.

Environmental Periodicals Bibliography. Environmental Studies Institute, International Academy at Santa Barbara, 800 Garden St., Suite D, Santa Barbara, California 93101. (805) 965-5010. Also available online.

Index to Scientific Book Contents. Institute for Scientific Information, 3501 Market St., Philadelphia, Pennsylvania 19104. (800) 523-1857. 1985-. Annual. Gives contents of science books published.

Multimedia Index to Ecology. National Information Center for Educational Media, University of Southern California, Los Angeles, California 90007.

Pollution Abstracts. Cambridge Scientific Abstracts, 5161 River Rd., Bethesda, Maryland 20816. (301) 961-6750. Six/year. Indexes worldwide technical literature on environmental pollution. Covers air pollution, marine and freshwater pollution, sewage and wastewater treatment, waste management, toxicology and health, noise pollution, radiation, land pollution, and environmental policies, programs, legislation, and education. Also available online.

Science Citation Index. Institute for Scientific Information, 3501 Market St., Philadelphia, Pennsylvania 19104. 1961-.

BIBLIOGRAPHIES

Aldrin and Endrin in Water: A Bibliography. National Technical Information Service, 5285 Port Royal Rd., Springfield, Virginia 22161. (703) 487-4650. 1972. Water Resources Scientific Information Center Bibliography series, WRSIC 72-203.

EPA Publications Bibliography. U.S. Environmental Protection Agency, Library Systems Branch, 401 M St., SW, Washington, District of Columbia 20460. (202) 260-2090. Quarterly.

ENCYCLOPEDIAS AND DICTIONARIES

Encyclopedia of Trademarks and Synonyms. H. Bennett, ed. Chemical Publishing Co., 80 Eighth Ave., New York, New York 10011. (212) 255-1950. 1981. Three volumes. Includes chemical compounds, compositions consisting of one or more chemicals and other products. Also included are abbreviated names and WHO free names.

McGraw-Hill Encyclopedia of Science and Technology. McGraw-Hill, 1221 Avenue of the Americas, New York, New York 10020. (212) 512-2000 or (800) 262-4729. 1992. Seventh edition. Issued in multiple volumes including index. Includes all science and technology broad subject areas.

The New York Times Encyclopedic Dictionary of the Environment. Paul Sarnoff. Quadrangle Books, New York, New York 1971. Focuses on state-of-the-art methods of pollution control, abatement, prevention and removal.

Van Nostrand's Scientific Encyclopedia. Glenn D. Considine, ed. Van Nostrand Reinhold, 115 5th Ave., New York, New York 10003. (212) 254-3232. 1983. Sixth edition. Includes all broad subject areas in science.

ONLINE DATA BASES

BIOSIS Previews. BIOSIS, 2100 Arch St., Philadelphia, Pennsylvania 19103-1399. (215) 587-4800. Largest and most comprehensive database of research in the life sciences. Contains citations for nearly 9000 primary research journals, monographs, reviews, symposia, preliminary reports, semi-popular journals, selected institutional reports, government reports and research communications.

CAS Source Index–CASSI. Chemical Abstracts Service, 2540 Olentangy River Rd., P.O. Box 3012, Columbus, Ohio 43210. (800) 848-6533 or (614) 421-3600. A listing of bibliographic and library holdings information for scientific and technical primary literature relevant to the chemical sciences.

Chemical Abstracts-CA. Chemical Abstracts Service, 2540 Olentangy River Rd., P.O. Box 3012, Columbus, Ohio 43210. (800) 848-6533 or (614) 421-3600. Information sources include 9000 journals, patents from 27 countries, two industrial property organizations, new books, conference proceedings, and government research reports.

Chemical Abstracts Chemical Name Directory-CHEM-NAME. Chemical Abstracts Service, 2540 Olentangy River Rd., P.O. Box 3012, Columbus, Ohio 43210. (800) 848-6533 or (614) 421-3600. Listing of chemical substances in a dictionary type file. The Chemical Abstracts (CAS) Registry Number, molecular formula, Chemical Abstracts (CA) Substance Index Name, available synonyms, ring data and other chemical substance information is given for each entry.

Chemical Carcinogenesis Research Information System–CCRIS. National Library of Medicine, 8600 Rockville Pike, Bethesda, Maryland 20894. (800) 638-8480. Individual assay results and test conditions for 1,451 chemicals in the areas of carcinogenicity, mutagenicity, tumor promotion, and cocarcinogenicity.

Enviro/Energyline Abstracts Plus. R. R. Bowker Co., 121 Chanlon Rd., New Providence, New Jersey 07974. (908) 464-6800.

Environmental Periodicals Bibliography. National Information Services Corp., Ste. 6, Wyman Towers, 3100 St. Paul St., Baltimore, Maryland 21218. (410)243-0797. Online version of abstract of same name.

The Merck Index Online. Merck & Company, Inc., Box 2000, Building 86-0900, Rahway, New Jersey 07065-0900. (201) 855-4558.

SCISEARCH. Institute for Scientific Information, University City Science Center, 3501 Market St., Philadelphia, Pennsylvania 19104. (215) 386-0100.

PERIODICALS AND NEWSLETTERS

The Merck Index. Merck Co., Inc., Box 2000, Rahway, New Jersey 07065. (201) 855-4558. Data on chemicals, drugs, and biological substances.

ALFISOL

See: SOIL SCIENCE

ALGAE

ABSTRACTING AND INDEXING SERVICES

Abstracts of Air and Water Conservation Literature. American Petroleum Institute. Central Abstracting and Indexing Service, 275 Madison Avenue, New York, New York 10016. 1972.

Algae Abstracts: A Guide to the Literature. IFI/Plenum, 233 Spring St., New York, New York 10013. (800) 221-9369. Covers algology, water pollution and eutrophication.

Applied Ecology Abstracts Studies in Renewable Natural Resources. Information Retrieval Ltd., 1911 Jefferson Davis Highway, Arlington, Virginia 22202. 1975-. Monthly.

Aqualine Abstracts. Water Research Centre. c/o Pergamon Microforms International, Inc., Fairview Park, Elmsford, New York 10523. (914) 592-7720. 1927-. Contains some 8,000 records annually on water and wastewater technology. Covers all aspects of water, wastewater, associated engineering services and the aquatic environment. Over 600 periodicals, as well as books, reports and conference proceedings and other publications from water related institutions worldwide are scanned. Also available online.

ASFA Aquaculture Abstracts. Cambridge Scientific Abstracts, Inc., 5161 River Rd., Bethesda, Maryland 20816. (301) 961-6750. 1984.

Biological Abstracts. BIOSIS, 2100 Arch St., Philadelphia, Pennsylvania 19103-1399. (215) 587-4800. 1927-.

Biological and Agricultural Index. H.W. Wilson Co., 950 University Ave., Bronx, New York 10452. (800) 367-6770. 1916-. Monthly.

Biotechnology Research Abstracts. Cambridge Scientific Abstracts, 5161 River Rd., Bethesda, Maryland 20816. (301) 961-6750. Monthly. Includes such broad areas as genetic intervention, biochemical genetics, and microbiological techniques.

Ecological Abstracts. Geo Abstracts Ltd. Elsevier Applied Science, Crown House, Linton Rd., Barking, England IG 11 8JU. 1974-. Derived from over 600 leading ecological and environmental journals, plus books, conference proceedings, reports and theses.

Ecology Abstracts. Cambridge Scientific Abstracts, 5161 River Rd., Bethesda, Maryland 20816. (301) 961-6750. Monthly.

Environment Abstracts. Bowker A & I Publishing, 121 Chanlon Rd., New Providence, New Jersey 07974. (908) 464-6800. 1974-.

Environment Index. Environment Information Center, Index Research Department, 124 E. 39th St., New York, New York 10016. 1971-. Annual.

Environmental Information Connection–EIC. Planning Information Program, Dept. of Urban and Regional Planning, University of Illinois, 1003 West Nevada, Urbana, Illinois 61801. (217) 333-1369. Also available online.

Environmental Periodicals Bibliography. Environmental Studies Institute, International Academy at Santa Barbara, 800 Garden St., Suite D, Santa Barbara, California 93101. (805) 965-5010. Also available online.

Food Science and Technology Abstracts. International Food Information Service, c/o National Food Laboratory, 6363 Clark Ave., Dublin, California 94568. (800) 336-3782. 1969-.

General Science Index. H. W. Wilson Co., 950 University Ave., Bronx, New York 10452. 1978-. Monthly, also issued in annual cumulation. Cumulative subject index to English language periodicals in the subject fields of astronomy, botany, chemistry, earth science, environment and conservation, food and nutrition, genetics, mathematics, medicine and health, microbiology, oceanography, physics, physiology and zoology.

Genetics Abstracts. Cambridge Scientific Abstracts, 5161 River Rd., Bethesda, Maryland 20816. (301) 961-6750. 1968-. Monthly. Formerly published by Information Retrieval Ltd., London England. Published by Cambridge Scientific Abstracts since 1982.

INIS Atomindex. International Atomic Energy Agency, Wagramerstrasse 5, Vienna, Austria A-1400. 222 23606198. 1988-. Semiannual. Abstracts nuclear energy and nuclear physics topics from journals, conferences, technical reports and other related publications. Issued in 6 parts: Personal Author, Corporate Entry, Subject, Report, Standard Patent, Conference (by place), Conference (by date).

Multimedia Index to Ecology. National Information Center for Educational Media, University of Southern California, Los Angeles, California 90007.

Pollution Abstracts. Cambridge Scientific Abstracts, 5161 River Rd., Bethesda, Maryland 20816. (301) 961-6750. Six/year. Indexes worldwide technical literature on environmental pollution. Covers air pollution, marine and freshwater pollution, sewage and wastewater treatment, waste management, toxicology and health, noise pollution, radiation, land pollution, and environmental policies, programs, legislation, and education. Also available online.

Science Citation Index. Institute for Scientific Information, 3501 Market St., Philadelphia, Pennsylvania 19104. 1961-.

BIBLIOGRAPHIES

Current Contents. Agriculture, Biology and Environmental Sciences. Institute for Scientific Information, 3501 Market St., Philadelphia, Pennsylvania 19104. (800) 523-1857. 1973-. Previous title: Current Contents. Agricultural, Food & Veterinary Sciences. Gives the table of

contents of periodicals in the fields of agriculture, biology, environmental and related areas.

EPA Publications Bibliography. U.S. Environmental Protection Agency, Library Systems Branch, 401 M St., SW, Washington, District of Columbia 20460. (202) 260-2090. Quarterly.

ENCYCLOPEDIAS AND DICTIONARIES

Cambridge Encyclopedia of Life Sciences. A. E. Friday and David S. Ingram. Cambridge University Press, 40 W 20th St., New York, New York 10011. (212) 924-3900 or (800) 227-0247. 1985. Includes all topics under biology and ecology.

Dictionary of Microbiology and Molecular Biology. Paul Singleton and Diana Sainsbury. John Wiley & Sons, Inc., 605 3rd Ave., New York, New York 10158-0012. (212) 850-6000. 1987. Second edition. Comprehensive dictionary with "classical descriptive aspects of microbiology to current developments in related areas of bioenergetics, biochemistry and molecular biology." Entries give synonyms, cross references, and references to pertinent works. Miscellaneous appendixes. Bibliography.

Encyclopedia of Human Biology. Renato Dulbecco, ed. Academic Press, c/o Harcourt Brace Jovanovich Inc., 6277 Sea Harbor Dr., Orlando, Florida 32887. (800) 346-8648. 1991. Eight volumes.

The Encyclopedia of Soil Science. Rhodes W. Fairbridge. Academic Press, c/o Harcourt Brace Jovanovich Inc., 6277 Sea Harbor Dr., Orlando, Florida 32887. (800) 346-8648. 1979-. Includes soil physics, soil chemistry, soil biology, soil fertility and plant nutrition, soil genesis, classification and cartography.

Grzimek's Encyclopedia of Ecology. Bernhard Grzimek. Van Nostrand Reinhold, 115 5th Ave., New York, New York 10003. (212) 254-3232. 1976.

McGraw-Hill Encyclopedia of Environmental Science. Sybil P. Parker. McGraw-Hill Science & Engineering Books, 11 W. 19th St., New York, New York 10011. (212) 337-6010. 1980. Covers ecology, man's influence on nature, and environmental protection.

McGraw-Hill Encyclopedia of Science and Technology. McGraw-Hill, 1221 Avenue of the Americas, New York, New York 10020. (212) 512-2000 or (800) 262-4729. 1992. Seventh edition. Issued in multiple volumes including index. Includes all science and technology broad subject areas.

North American Reference Encyclopedia of Ecology and Pollution. William White. North American Pub. Co., 401 N. Broad St., Philadelphia, Pennsylvania 19108. (215) 238-5300. 1972.

Van Nostrand's Scientific Encyclopedia. Glenn D. Considine, ed. Van Nostrand Reinhold, 115 5th Ave., New York, New York 10003. (212) 254-3232. 1983. Sixth edition. Includes all broad subject areas in science.

GENERAL WORKS

The Biology of Seaweeds. Christopher S. Lobban. Blackwell Scientific Publications, 3 Cambridge Ctr., Ste. 208, Boston, Massachusetts 02142. (617) 225-0401. 1981. Topics in botany with special reference to marine algae.

Environmental Role of Nitrogen-Fixing Blue-Green Algae and Asymbiotic Bacteria. U. Granhall. Swedish Natural Science Research Council, P.O. Box 6711, Stockholm, Sweden S-113 85. 08-15-1580. 1978. Deals with nitrogen-fixing microorganisms, nitrogen-fixing algae and cyanobacteria.

Magill's Survey of Science. Life Science Series. Frank N. Magill, ed. Salem Press, PO Box 50062, Pasadena, California 91105. 1991. Six volumes. Contents: v.1. A-Central and peripheral nervous system functions; v.2. Central metabolism regulation - eukaryotic transcriptional control; v.3. Positive and negative eukaryotic transcriptional control - mammalian hormones; v.4. Hormones and behavior - muscular contraction; v.5. Muscular contraction and relaxation - sexual reproduction in plants; v.6. Reproductive behavior and mating - X inactivation and the Lyon hypothesis.

Microbial Enzymes in Aquatic Environments. Ryszard J. Chrost. Springer-Varlag, 175 5th Ave., New York, New York 10010. (212) 460-1500. 1991. Brings together studies on enzymatic degradation processes from disciplines as diverse as water and sediment research, bacterial and algal aquatic ecophysiology, eutrophication, nutrient cycling, and biogeochemistry, in both freshwater and marine ecosystem.

HANDBOOKS AND MANUALS

Handbook of Protoctista. Lynn Margulis. Jones and Bartlett Publishers, 20 Park Plaza, Boston, Massachusetts 02116. (617) 482-5243. 1990. The structure, cultivation, habitats, and life histories of the eukaryotic microorganisms and their descendants exclusive of animals, plants, and fungi. A guide to the algae, ciliates, foraminifera, sporazoa, water molds, slime molds, and the other protoctists.

Methods for Toxicity Tests of Single Substances and Liquid Complex Wastes With Marine Unicellular Algae. Gerald E. Walsh. Environmental Protection Agency, U.S. Environmental Research Laboratory, 401 M St. SW, Washington, District of Columbia 20460. (202) 260-2090. 1988. Deals with the impact of factory and trade waste on the marine environment, especially on algae and other biological forms.

ONLINE DATA BASES

BIOSIS Previews. BIOSIS, 2100 Arch St., Philadelphia, Pennsylvania 19103-1399. (215) 587-4800. Largest and most comprehensive database of research in the life sciences. Contains citations for nearly 9000 primary research journals, monographs, reviews, symposia, preliminary reports, semi-popular journals, selected institutional reports, government reports and research communications.

Cambridge Scientific Abstracts Life Science–CSAL. Cambridge Scientific Abstracts, 5161 River Rd., Bethesda, Maryland 20816. (301) 961-6750. Provides access to the following abstracting services: "Life Sciences Collection," "Aquatic Sciences and Fisheries Abstracts," "Oceanic Abstracts," and "Pollution Abstracts."

Enviro/Energyline Abstracts Plus. R. R. Bowker Co., 121 Chanlon Rd., New Providence, New Jersey 07974. (908) 464-6800.

Environmental Periodicals Bibliography. National Information Services Corp., Ste. 6, Wyman Towers, 3100 St. Paul St., Baltimore, Maryland 21218. (410)243-0797. Online version of abstract of same name.

SCISEARCH. Institute for Scientific Information, University City Science Center, 3501 Market St., Philadelphia, Pennsylvania 19104. (215) 386-0100.

RESEARCH CENTERS AND INSTITUTES

Marine Biotechnology Center. University of California, Santa Barbara, Marine Science Institute, Santa Barbara, California 93106. (805) 893-3765.

University of Maine, Center for Marine Studies. 14 Coburn Hall, Orono, Maine 04469. (207) 581-1435.

University of Montana, Flathead Lake Biological Station. 311 Bio Station Lane, Polson, Montana 59860. (406) 982-3301.

University of North Carolina at Chapel Hill, Herbarium. 401 Coker Hall 010A, CB 3280, Chapel Hill, North Carolina 27599-3280. (919) 962-6931.

University of North Carolina at Wilmington, NOAA National Undersea Research Center. 7205 Wrightsville Avenue, Wilmington, North Carolina 28403. (919) 256-5133.

University of Texas at Austin, Culture Collection of Algae. Department of Botany, Austin, Texas 78713. (512) 471-4019.

University of Wisconsin-Madison, Marine Studies Centers. Department of Botany, 132 Birge Hall, Madison, Wisconsin 53706. (608) 262-1057.

TRADE ASSOCIATIONS AND PROFESSIONAL SOCIETIES

American Society of Naturalists. Department of Ecology and Evolation, State University of New York, Stony Brook, New York 11794. (516) 632-8589.

ALGAL BLOOMS

See: ALGAE

ALGICIDE RESIDUES

See: ALGICIDES

ALGICIDES

See also: PESTICIDES; WATER TREATMENT

ABSTRACTING AND INDEXING SERVICES

Abstracts of Air and Water Conservation Literature. American Petroleum Institute. Central Abstracting and Indexing Service, 275 Madison Avenue, New York, New York 10016. 1972.

ASFA Aquaculture Abstracts. Cambridge Scientific Abstracts, Inc., 5161 River Rd., Bethesda, Maryland 20816. (301) 961-6750. 1984.

Biological Abstracts. BIOSIS, 2100 Arch St., Philadelphia, Pennsylvania 19103-1399. (215) 587-4800. 1927-.

Biological and Agricultural Index. H.W. Wilson Co., 950 University Ave., Bronx, New York 10452. (800) 367-6770. 1916-. Monthly.

Ecological Abstracts. Geo Abstracts Ltd. Elsevier Applied Science, Crown House, Linton Rd., Barking, England IG 11 8JU. 1974-. Derived from over 600 leading ecological and environmental journals, plus books, conference proceedings, reports and theses.

Environment Abstracts. Bowker A & I Publishing, 121 Chanlon Rd., New Providence, New Jersey 07974. (908) 464-6800. 1974-.

Environment Index. Environment Information Center, Index Research Department, 124 E. 39th St., New York, New York 10016. 1971-. Annual.

Environmental Information Connection–EIC. Planning Information Program, Dept. of Urban and Regional Planning, University of Illinois, 1003 West Nevada, Urbana, Illinois 61801. (217) 333-1369. Also available online.

Environmental Periodicals Bibliography. Environmental Studies Institute, International Academy at Santa Barbara, 800 Garden St., Suite D, Santa Barbara, California 93101. (805) 965-5010. Also available online.

Index to Scientific Book Contents. Institute for Scientific Information, 3501 Market St., Philadelphia, Pennsylvania 19104. (800) 523-1857. 1985-. Annual. Gives contents of science books published.

Pollution Abstracts. Cambridge Scientific Abstracts, 5161 River Rd., Bethesda, Maryland 20816. (301) 961-6750. Six/year. Indexes worldwide technical literature on environmental pollution. Covers air pollution, marine and freshwater pollution, sewage and wastewater treatment, waste management, toxicology and health, noise pollution, radiation, land pollution, and environmental policies, programs, legislation, and education. Also available online.

Science Citation Index. Institute for Scientific Information, 3501 Market St., Philadelphia, Pennsylvania 19104. 1961-.

BIBLIOGRAPHIES

Current Contents. Agriculture, Biology and Environmental Sciences. Institute for Scientific Information, 3501 Market St., Philadelphia, Pennsylvania 19104. (800) 523-1857. 1973-. Previous title: Current Contents. Agricultural, Food & Veterinary Sciences. Gives the table of contents of periodicals in the fields of agriculture, biology, environmental and related areas.

EPA Publications Bibliography. U.S. Environmental Protection Agency, Library Systems Branch, 401 M St., SW, Washington, District of Columbia 20460. (202) 260-2090. Quarterly.

ENCYCLOPEDIAS AND DICTIONARIES

McGraw-Hill Encyclopedia of Environmental Science. Sybil P. Parker. McGraw-Hill Science & Engineering Books, 11 W. 19th St., New York, New York 10011. (212) 337-6010. 1980. Covers ecology, man's influence on nature, and environmental protection.

McGraw-Hill Encyclopedia of Science and Technology. McGraw-Hill, 1221 Avenue of the Americas, New York, New York 10020. (212) 512-2000 or (800) 262-4729.

1992. Seventh edition. Issued in multiple volumes including index. Includes all science and technology broad subject areas.

The New York Times Encyclopedic Dictionary of the Environment. Paul Sarnoff. Quadrangle Books, New York, New York 1971. Focuses on state-of-the-art methods of pollution control, abatement, prevention and removal.

ONLINE DATA BASES

BIOSIS Previews. BIOSIS, 2100 Arch St., Philadelphia, Pennsylvania 19103-1399. (215) 587-4800. Largest and most comprehensive database of research in the life sciences. Contains citations for nearly 9000 primary research journals, monographs, reviews, symposia, preliminary reports, semi-popular journals, selected institutional reports, government reports and research communications.

Chemical Carcinogenesis Research Information System–CCRIS. National Library of Medicine, 8600 Rockville Pike, Bethesda, Maryland 20894. (800) 638-8480. Individual assay results and test conditions for 1,451 chemicals in the areas of carcinogenicity, mutagenicity, tumor promotion, and cocarcinogenicity.

Chemical Collection System/Request Tracking–CCS/RTS. U.S. Environmental Protection Agency, Office of Pesticides and Toxic Substances, 401 M St., SW, Washington, District of Columbia 20460. (202) 260-2090. Contains information on various properties of a number of chemicals including environmental effects, test and analysis methods, and health effects. Available from EPA.

Chemical Dictionary Online–CHEMLINE. Chemical Abstracts Service, 2540 Olentangy River Rd., Columbus, Ohio 43210. (614) 421-3600 or (800) 848-6533. Part of MEDLINE of the National Library of Medicine (NLM). File of 900,000 names for chemical substances, representing 450,000 unique compounds. It contains such information as Chemical Abstracts (CA) Service Registry Numbers, molecular formulas, preferred chemical nomenclature, and generic and ring structure information. Available on NLM's ELHILL system.

Chemical Exposure. Science Applications International Corp., Health & Environmental Information, P.O. Box 2501, Oak Ridge, Tennessee 37831. (615) 482-9031. Database of chemicals that have been identified in both human tissues and body fluids and in feral and food animals. Contains reference to journal articles, conferences, and reports. Covers the whole fields of information related to human and animal exposure to food, air, and water contaminants and pharmaceuticals. Its records include information on chemical properties, formulas, tissues measured, analytical method used, demographics and more. Available on DIALOG.

Enviro/Energyline Abstracts Plus. R. R. Bowker Co., 121 Chanlon Rd., New Providence, New Jersey 07974. (908) 464-6800.

Environmental Periodicals Bibliography. National Information Services Corp., Ste. 6, Wyman Towers, 3100 St. Paul St., Baltimore, Maryland 21218. (410)243-0797. Online version of abstract of same name.

PressNet Environmental Reports. Chemical Information Systems, Inc., 7215 York Rd., Baltimore, Maryland 21212. (301) 321-8440.

SCISEARCH. Institute for Scientific Information, University City Science Center, 3501 Market St., Philadelphia, Pennsylvania 19104. (215) 386-0100.

ALIPHATICS

ABSTRACTING AND INDEXING SERVICES

Biological Abstracts. BIOSIS, 2100 Arch St., Philadelphia, Pennsylvania 19103-1399. (215) 587-4800. 1927-.

Biological and Agricultural Index. H.W. Wilson Co., 950 University Ave., Bronx, New York 10452. (800) 367-6770. 1916-. Monthly.

Chemical Abstracts. Chemical Abstracts Service, 2540 Olentangy River Rd., PO Box 3012, Columbus, Ohio 43210. (800) 848-6533. 1907-.

Environment Abstracts. Bowker A & I Publishing, 121 Chanlon Rd., New Providence, New Jersey 07974. (908) 464-6800. 1974-.

Environment Index. Environment Information Center, Index Research Department, 124 E. 39th St., New York, New York 10016. 1971-. Annual.

Environmental Information Connection–EIC. Planning Information Program, Dept. of Urban and Regional Planning, University of Illinois, 1003 West Nevada, Urbana, Illinois 61801. (217) 333-1369. Also available online.

Environmental Periodicals Bibliography. Environmental Studies Institute, International Academy at Santa Barbara, 800 Garden St., Suite D, Santa Barbara, California 93101. (805) 965-5010. Also available online.

Pollution Abstracts. Cambridge Scientific Abstracts, 5161 River Rd., Bethesda, Maryland 20816. (301) 961-6750. Six/year. Indexes worldwide technical literature on environmental pollution. Covers air pollution, marine and freshwater pollution, sewage and wastewater treatment, waste management, toxicology and health, noise pollution, radiation, land pollution, and environmental policies, programs, legislation, and education. Also available online.

Science Citation Index. Institute for Scientific Information, 3501 Market St., Philadelphia, Pennsylvania 19104. 1961-.

BIBLIOGRAPHIES

EPA Publications Bibliography. U.S. Environmental Protection Agency, Library Systems Branch, 401 M St., SW, Washington, District of Columbia 20460. (202) 260-2090. Quarterly.

ENCYCLOPEDIAS AND DICTIONARIES

McGraw-Hill Encyclopedia of Science and Technology. McGraw-Hill, 1221 Avenue of the Americas, New York, New York 10020. (212) 512-2000 or (800) 262-4729. 1992. Seventh edition. Issued in multiple volumes including index. Includes all science and technology broad subject areas.

Van Nostrand's Scientific Encyclopedia. Glenn D. Considine, ed. Van Nostrand Reinhold, 115 5th Ave., New

York, New York 10003. (212) 254-3232. 1983. Sixth edition. Includes all broad subject areas in science.

HANDBOOKS AND MANUALS

Chemistry of Carbon Compounds: A Modern Comprehensive Treatise. M. F. Ansell, ed. Elsevier Science Publishing Co., 655 Avenue of the Americas, New York, New York 10010. (212) 984-5800. Irregular.

ONLINE DATA BASES

BIOSIS Previews. BIOSIS, 2100 Arch St., Philadelphia, Pennsylvania 19103-1399. (215) 587-4800. Largest and most comprehensive database of research in the life sciences. Contains citations for nearly 9000 primary research journals, monographs, reviews, symposia, preliminary reports, semi-popular journals, selected institutional reports, government reports and research communications.

Chemical Abstracts-CA. Chemical Abstracts Service, 2540 Olentangy River Rd., P.O. Box 3012, Columbus, Ohio 43210. (800) 848-6533 or (614) 421-3600. Information sources include 9000 journals, patents from 27 countries, two industrial property organizations, new books, conference proceedings, and government research reports.

Chemical Carcinogenesis Research Information System-CCRIS. National Library of Medicine, 8600 Rockville Pike, Bethesda, Maryland 20894. (800) 638-8480. Individual assay results and test conditions for 1,451 chemicals in the areas of carcinogenicity, mutagenicity, tumor promotion, and cocarcinogenicity.

Enviro/Energyline Abstracts Plus. R. R. Bowker Co., 121 Chanlon Rd., New Providence, New Jersey 07974. (908) 464-6800.

Environmental Periodicals Bibliography. National Information Services Corp., Ste. 6, Wyman Towers, 3100 St. Paul St., Baltimore, Maryland 21218. (410)243-0797. Online version of abstract of same name.

ALKALINITY

See: pH

ALKALINIZATION OF SOILS

See also: EROSION; IRRIGATION; RESERVOIRS; SOIL SCIENCE; WATER MANAGEMENT

ABSTRACTING AND INDEXING SERVICES

Biological and Agricultural Index. H.W. Wilson Co., 950 University Ave., Bronx, New York 10452. (800) 367-6770. 1916-. Monthly.

Environment Abstracts. Bowker A & I Publishing, 121 Chanlon Rd., New Providence, New Jersey 07974. (908) 464-6800. 1974-.

Environment Index. Environment Information Center, Index Research Department, 124 E. 39th St., New York, New York 10016. 1971-. Annual.

Environmental Information Connection-EIC. Planning Information Program, Dept. of Urban and Regional Planning, University of Illinois, 1003 West Nevada, Urbana, Illinois 61801. (217) 333-1369. Also available online.

Environmental Periodicals Bibliography. Environmental Studies Institute, International Academy at Santa Barbara, 800 Garden St., Suite D, Santa Barbara, California 93101. (805) 965-5010. Also available online.

General Science Index. H. W. Wilson Co., 950 University Ave., Bronx, New York 10452. 1978-. Monthly, also issued in annual cumulation. Cumulative subject index to English language periodicals in the subject fields of astronomy, botany, chemistry, earth science, environment and conservation, food and nutrition, genetics, mathematics, medicine and health, microbiology, oceanography, physics, physiology and zoology.

Index to Scientific Book Contents. Institute for Scientific Information, 3501 Market St., Philadelphia, Pennsylvania 19104. (800) 523-1857. 1985-. Annual. Gives contents of science books published.

INIS Atomindex. International Atomic Energy Agency, Wagramerstrasse 5, Vienna, Austria A-1400. 222 23606198. 1988-. Semiannual. Abstracts nuclear energy and nuclear physics topics from journals, conferences, technical reports and other related publications. Issued in 6 parts: Personal Author, Corporate Entry, Subject, Report, Standard Patent, Conference (by place), Conference (by date).

Science Citation Index. Institute for Scientific Information, 3501 Market St., Philadelphia, Pennsylvania 19104. 1961-.

BIBLIOGRAPHIES

EPA Publications Bibliography. U.S. Environmental Protection Agency, Library Systems Branch, 401 M St., SW, Washington, District of Columbia 20460. (202) 260-2090. Quarterly.

ENCYCLOPEDIAS AND DICTIONARIES

Dictionary of Alkaloids. J. Buckingham Southon. Chapman & Hall, 29 West 35th St., New York, New York 10001-2291. (212) 244-3336. 1989.

Encyclopedia of Chemical Processing and Design. John J. Mcketta and W. A. Cunningham. Marcel Dekker, Inc., 270 Madison Ave., New York, New York 10016. (212) 696-9000; (800) 228-1160. 1992. Thirty-eight volumes.

The Encyclopedia of Geochemistry and Environmental Sciences. Rhodes Whitmore Fairbridge. Van Nostrand Reinhold Co., 115 5th Ave., New York, New York 10003. (212) 254-3232. 1972.

Kirk-Othmer Encyclopedia of Chemical Technology. J. I. Kroschwitz, ed. John Wiley & Sons, Inc., 605 3rd Ave., New York, New York 10158-0012. (212) 850-6000. 1992-. All articles in the new edition have been rewritten and updated adding new subjects such as biotechnology, computer topics, analytical techniques and instrumentation, environmental concerns, fuels and energy, inorganic and solid state chemistry; composite materials and material science in general, and pharmaceuticals. Also available online.

McGraw-Hill Encyclopedia of Environmental Science. Sybil P. Parker. McGraw-Hill Science & Engineering Books, 11 W. 19th St., New York, New York 10011. (212) 337-6010. 1980. Covers ecology, man's influence on nature, and environmental protection.

McGraw-Hill Encyclopedia of Science and Technology. McGraw-Hill, 1221 Avenue of the Americas, New York, New York 10020. (212) 512-2000 or (800) 262-4729. 1992. Seventh edition. Issued in multiple volumes including index. Includes all science and technology broad subject areas.

Van Nostrand's Scientific Encyclopedia. Glenn D. Considine, ed. Van Nostrand Reinhold, 115 5th Ave., New York, New York 10003. (212) 254-3232. 1983. Sixth edition. Includes all broad subject areas in science.

ONLINE DATA BASES

Enviro/Energyline Abstracts Plus. R. R. Bowker Co., 121 Chanlon Rd., New Providence, New Jersey 07974. (908) 464-6800.

Environmental Periodicals Bibliography. National Information Services Corp., Ste. 6, Wyman Towers, 3100 St. Paul St., Baltimore, Maryland 21218. (410)243-0797. Online version of abstract of same name.

Kirk-Othmer Encyclopedia of Chemical Technology. John Wiley & Sons, Inc., 605 3rd Ave., 5th Floor, New York, New York 10158. (212) 850-6000. Online version of the publication of the same name.

SCISEARCH. Institute for Scientific Information, University City Science Center, 3501 Market St., Philadelphia, Pennsylvania 19104. (215) 386-0100.

ALLERGIES

See also: AIR POLLUTION; ASTHMA

ABSTRACTING AND INDEXING SERVICES

Air Pollution Titles. Pennsylvania State University, Center for Air Environmental Studies, 226 Fenske Laboratory, University Park, Pennsylvania 16802. (814) 865-1415. 1965. Bibliographic guide to current research literature on air environment, including monitoring and control of air pollution, health effects, effects on agriculture, forests, toxic air contaminants, and global atmospheric pro cases.

Air Pollution Translations. A Bibliography With Abstracts. U.S. Environmental Protection Agency, MD 75, Research Triangle Park, North Carolina 27711. (919) 541-2184. 1969.

Biological Abstracts. BIOSIS, 2100 Arch St., Philadelphia, Pennsylvania 19103-1399. (215) 587-4800. 1927-.

Environment Abstracts. Bowker A & I Publishing, 121 Chanlon Rd., New Providence, New Jersey 07974. (908) 464-6800. 1974-.

Environment Index. Environment Information Center, Index Research Department, 124 E. 39th St., New York, New York 10016. 1971-. Annual.

Environmental Information Connection–EIC. Planning Information Program, Dept. of Urban and Regional Planning, University of Illinois, 1003 West Nevada, Urbana, Illinois 61801. (217) 333-1369. Also available online.

Environmental Periodicals Bibliography. Environmental Studies Institute, International Academy at Santa Barbara, 800 Garden St., Suite D, Santa Barbara, California 93101. (805) 965-5010. Also available online.

Pollution Abstracts. Cambridge Scientific Abstracts, 5161 River Rd., Bethesda, Maryland 20816. (301) 961-6750. Six/year. Indexes worldwide technical literature on environmental pollution. Covers air pollution, marine and freshwater pollution, sewage and wastewater treatment, waste management, toxicology and health, noise pollution, radiation, land pollution, and environmental policies, programs, legislation, and education. Also available online.

Science Citation Index. Institute for Scientific Information, 3501 Market St., Philadelphia, Pennsylvania 19104. 1961-.

BIBLIOGRAPHIES

EPA Publications Bibliography. U.S. Environmental Protection Agency, Library Systems Branch, 401 M St., SW, Washington, District of Columbia 20460. (202) 260-2090. Quarterly.

DIRECTORIES

Allergy Products Directory. Allergy Publications, Inc., Box 640, Menlo Park, California 94026. (415) 322-1663.

American Academy of Allergy & Immunology–Membership Directory. American Academy of Allergy & Immunology, 611 E. Wells St., Milwaukee, Wisconsin 53202. (414) 272-6071.

ENCYCLOPEDIAS AND DICTIONARIES

Encyclopedia of Allergy and Environmental Illness: A Self-Help Approach. Ellen Rothera. Sterling Pub. Co., 387 Park Ave, South, New York, New York 10016-8810. (212) 532-7160 or (800) 367-9692. 1991. Presents the problem of multiple environmental allergies and deals with allergic reactions to such things as foods, food additives, household cleaners, molds, cooking gas, and air pollution.

Encyclopedia of Human Biology. Renato Dulbecco, ed. Academic Press, c/o Harcourt Brace Jovanovich Inc., 6277 Sea Harbor Dr., Orlando, Florida 32887. (800) 346-8648. 1991. Eight volumes.

McGraw-Hill Encyclopedia of Science and Technology. McGraw-Hill, 1221 Avenue of the Americas, New York, New York 10020. (212) 512-2000 or (800) 262-4729. 1992. Seventh edition. Issued in multiple volumes including index. Includes all science and technology broad subject areas.

The Nutrition and Health Encyclopedia. David F. Tver and Percy Russell. Van Nostrand Reinhold, 115 5th Ave., New York, New York 10003. (212) 254-3232. 1989.

Van Nostrand's Scientific Encyclopedia. Glenn D. Considine, ed. Van Nostrand Reinhold, 115 5th Ave., New York, New York 10003. (212) 254-3232. 1983. Sixth edition. Includes all broad subject areas in science.

GENERAL WORKS

Magill's Survey of Science. Life Science Series. Frank N. Magill, ed. Salem Press, PO Box 50062, Pasadena, California 91105. 1991. Six volumes. Contents: v.1. A-Central and peripheral nervous system functions; v.2. Central metabolism regulation - eukaryotic transcriptional control; v.3. Positive and negative eukaryotic transcriptional control - mammalian hormones; v.4. Hormones and behavior - muscular contraction; v.5. Muscular contraction and relaxation - sexual reproduction in plants; v.6. Reproductive behavior and mating - X inactivation and the Lyon hypothesis.

ONLINE DATA BASES

BIOSIS Previews. BIOSIS, 2100 Arch St., Philadelphia, Pennsylvania 19103-1399. (215) 587-4800. Largest and most comprehensive database of research in the life sciences. Contains citations for nearly 9000 primary research journals, monographs, reviews, symposia, preliminary reports, semi-popular journals, selected institutional reports, government reports and research communications.

Enviro/Energyline Abstracts Plus. R. R. Bowker Co., 121 Chanlon Rd., New Providence, New Jersey 07974. (908) 464-6800.

Environmental Periodicals Bibliography. National Information Services Corp., Ste. 6, Wyman Towers, 3100 St. Paul St., Baltimore, Maryland 21218. (410)243-0797. Online version of abstract of same name.

PressNet Environmental Reports. Chemical Information Systems, Inc., 7215 York Rd., Baltimore, Maryland 21212. (301) 321-8440.

SCISEARCH. Institute for Scientific Information, University City Science Center, 3501 Market St., Philadelphia, Pennsylvania 19104. (215) 386-0100.

TRADE ASSOCIATIONS AND PROFESSIONAL SOCIETIES

American Academy of Otolaryngic Allergy. 8455 Colesville Rd., Suite 745, Silver Spring, Maryland 20910-9998. (301) 588-1800.

American Allergy Association. P.O. Box 7273, Menlo Park, California 94026. (415) 322-1663.

American Board of Allergy and Immunology. University City Science Center, 3624 Market St., Philadelphia, Pennsylvania 19104. (215) 349-9466.

American College of Allergy and Immunology. 800 E. Northwest Hwy., Suite 1080, Palatine, Illinois 60067. (708) 359-2800.

American In-Vitro Allergy/Immunology Society. P.O. Box 459, Lake Jackson, Texas 77566. (409) 297-5636.

Asthma and Allergy Foundation of America. 1717 Massachusetts Ave., Suite 305, Washington, District of Columbia 20036. (202) 265-0265.

ALLUVIUM

See: EROSION

ALPINE TUNDRAS

See also: BIOMES; ECOSYSTEMS; TUNDRA BIOMES

ABSTRACTING AND INDEXING SERVICES

Applied Ecology Abstracts Studies in Renewable Natural Resources. Information Retrieval Ltd., 1911 Jefferson Davis Highway, Arlington, Virginia 22202. 1975-. Monthly.

Biological and Agricultural Index. H.W. Wilson Co., 950 University Ave., Bronx, New York 10452. (800) 367-6770. 1916-. Monthly.

Ecological Abstracts. Geo Abstracts Ltd. Elsevier Applied Science, Crown House, Linton Rd., Barking, England IG 11 8JU. 1974-. Derived from over 600 leading ecological and environmental journals, plus books, conference proceedings, reports and theses.

Ecology Abstracts. Cambridge Scientific Abstracts, 5161 River Rd., Bethesda, Maryland 20816. (301) 961-6750. Monthly.

Environment Abstracts. Bowker A & I Publishing, 121 Chanlon Rd., New Providence, New Jersey 07974. (908) 464-6800. 1974-.

Environment Index. Environment Information Center, Index Research Department, 124 E. 39th St., New York, New York 10016. 1971-. Annual.

Environmental Information Connection–EIC. Planning Information Program, Dept. of Urban and Regional Planning, University of Illinois, 1003 West Nevada, Urbana, Illinois 61801. (217) 333-1369. Also available online.

Environmental Periodicals Bibliography. Environmental Studies Institute, International Academy at Santa Barbara, 800 Garden St., Suite D, Santa Barbara, California 93101. (805) 965-5010. Also available online.

Geographical Abstracts. London School of Economics, Dept. of Geography, Regency House, 34 Duke St., London, England 1966-. Continued by Geo Abstracts issued in 6 parts: Pt. A. Landforms and the quaternary; Pt. B. Biogeography and Climatology; Pt. C. Economic geography; Pt. D. Social geography and cartography; Pt. E. Sedimentology; Pt. F. Regional and community planning.

Multimedia Index to Ecology. National Information Center for Educational Media, University of Southern California, Los Angeles, California 90007.

Science Citation Index. Institute for Scientific Information, 3501 Market St., Philadelphia, Pennsylvania 19104. 1961-.

BIBLIOGRAPHIES

EPA Publications Bibliography. U.S. Environmental Protection Agency, Library Systems Branch, 401 M St., SW, Washington, District of Columbia 20460. (202) 260-2090. Quarterly.

ENCYCLOPEDIAS AND DICTIONARIES

Cambridge Encyclopedia of Life Sciences. A. E. Friday and David S. Ingram. Cambridge University Press, 40 W

20th St., New York, New York 10011. (212) 924-3900 or (800) 227-0247. 1985. Includes all topics under biology and ecology.

McGraw-Hill Encyclopedia of Environmental Science. Sybil P. Parker. McGraw-Hill Science & Engineering Books, 11 W. 19th St., New York, New York 10011. (212) 337-6010. 1980. Covers ecology, man's influence on nature, and environmental protection.

McGraw-Hill Encyclopedia of Science and Technology. McGraw-Hill, 1221 Avenue of the Americas, New York, New York 10020. (212) 512-2000 or (800) 262-4729. 1992. Seventh edition. Issued in multiple volumes including index. Includes all science and technology broad subject areas.

ONLINE DATA BASES

Enviro/Energyline Abstracts Plus. R. R. Bowker Co., 121 Chanlon Rd., New Providence, New Jersey 07974. (908) 464-6800.

Environmental Periodicals Bibliography. National Information Services Corp., Ste. 6, Wyman Towers, 3100 St. Paul St., Baltimore, Maryland 21218. (410)243-0797. Online version of abstract of same name.

SCISEARCH. Institute for Scientific Information, University City Science Center, 3501 Market St., Philadelphia, Pennsylvania 19104. (215) 386-0100.

ALTERNATE ENERGY SOURCES

See: RENEWABLE ENERGY RESOURCES

ALTERNATE PREY SPECIES

See: BUFFER SPECIES

ALTERNATIVE FUELS

ABSTRACTING AND INDEXING SERVICES

Environment Abstracts. Bowker A & I Publishing, 121 Chanlon Rd., New Providence, New Jersey 07974. (908) 464-6800. 1974-.

Environment Index. Environment Information Center, Index Research Department, 124 E. 39th St., New York, New York 10016. 1971-. Annual.

Environmental Information Connection–EIC. Planning Information Program, Dept. of Urban and Regional Planning, University of Illinois, 1003 West Nevada, Urbana, Illinois 61801. (217) 333-1369. Also available online.

Environmental Periodicals Bibliography. Environmental Studies Institute, International Academy at Santa Barbara, 800 Garden St., Suite D, Santa Barbara, California 93101. (805) 965-5010. Also available online.

ERDA Research Abstracts. U.S. ERDA Technical Information Center, Box 62, Oak Ridge, Tennessee 37830.

General Science Index. H. W. Wilson Co., 950 University Ave., Bronx, New York 10452. 1978-. Monthly, also

issued in annual cumulation. Cumulative subject index to English language periodicals in the subject fields of astronomy, botany, chemistry, earth science, environment and conservation, food and nutrition, genetics, mathematics, medicine and health, microbiology, oceanography, physics, physiology and zoology.

Highway Research Abstracts. Transportation Research Board, National Research Council, 2101 Constitution Ave. NW., Washington, District of Columbia 20418. 1931-. Monthly. Provides information about highway and nonrail mass transit. It also deals with related environmental issues such as energy and environment, environmental design, climate, safety, human factors, and soils.

Index to Scientific Book Contents. Institute for Scientific Information, 3501 Market St., Philadelphia, Pennsylvania 19104. (800) 523-1857. 1985-. Annual. Gives contents of science books published.

Physics Briefs. Physikalische Berichte. Physik Verlag, Pappapelallee 3, Postfach 101161, Weinheim, Germany D-6940. 1979-. Semimonthly. In English. Volumes for 1979- issued by the Deutsche Physikalische Gesellschaft and the Fachinformationszentrum Energie Physik, Mathematik in cooperation with the American Institute of Physics.

ALMANACS AND YEARBOOKS

Gale Environmental Almanac. Russ Hoyle. Gale Research Inc., 835 Penobscot Bldg., Detroit, Michigan 48226-4094. (313) 961-2242. 1993. Focuses on the U.S. and Canada, although worldwide and transboundary issues are discussed.

BIBLIOGRAPHIES

Directory of Published Proceedings. Interdok Corp., 173 Halstead Ave., Harrison, New York 10528. (914) 835-3506. 1990. Monthly. This is a listing of published proceedings including the series SEMTE (Science/Medicine/Engineering/Technology) and the series SSH (Social Science/Humanities).

EPA Publications Bibliography. U.S. Environmental Protection Agency, Library Systems Branch, 401 M St., SW, Washington, District of Columbia 20460. (202) 260-2090. Quarterly.

A Selected Bibliography on Alcohol Fuels. Solar Energy Research Institute, 1617 Cole Blvd., Golden, Colorado 80401. 1982. Covers literature written about biomass derived ethyl and methyl alcohols, including production processes, economics, use as fuel, engine conversion, feedstocks, financing, government regulations, coproducts, environmental effects and safety. The main focus is on alcohol fuels.

DIRECTORIES

Canadian Environmental Directory. Canadian Almanac & Directory Publishing Co. Ltd., 134 Adelaide St. E., Ste. 27, Toronto, Ontario, Canada M5C 1K9. (416) 362-4088. 1992. Includes individuals, agencies, firms, and associations.

The Green Encyclopedia. Irene Franck, David Brownstone. Prentice-Hall, Rte. 9W, Englewood Cliffs, New York 07632. (201) 592-2000. 1992. Covers environmental organizations.

ENCYCLOPEDIAS AND DICTIONARIES

Dictionary of Environmental Engineering and Related Sciences: English-Spanish, Spanish-English. Jose T. Villate. Ediciones Universal, 3090 SW 8th St., Miami, Florida 33135. (305) 642-3355. 1979.

Dictionary of Environmental Science and Technology. Andrew Porteous. John Wiley & Sons, Inc., 605 3rd Ave., New York, New York 10158-0012. (212) 850-6000. 1992.

Dictionary of the Environment. Michael Allaby. New York University Press, 70 Washington Sq. S., New York, New York 10012. (212) 998-2575. 1989.

Encyclopedia of Environmental Science and Engineering. J.R. Pfafflin. Gordon and Breach Science Publishers, Inc., 270 8th Ave., New York, New York 10011. (212) 206-8900. 1992.

Encyclopedia of Physical Science and Technology. Robert A. Meyers, ed. Academic Press, c/o Harcourt Brace Jovanovich Inc., 6277 Sea Harbor Dr., Orlando, Florida 32887. (800) 346-8648. Dictionary of engineering, technology and physical sciences.

Environmental Encyclopedia. William P. Cunningham, Terence Ball, et. al. Gale Research Inc., 835 Penobscot Bldg., Detroit, Michigan 48226-4094. (313) 961-2242. 1993.

McGraw-Hill Encyclopedia of Science and Technology. McGraw-Hill, 1221 Avenue of the Americas, New York, New York 10020. (212) 512-2000 or (800) 262-4729. 1992. Seventh edition. Issued in multiple volumes including index. Includes all science and technology broad subject areas.

GENERAL WORKS

Alternative Fuels: Chemical Energy Resources. E.M. Goodger. John Wiley & Sons, Inc., 605 3rd Ave., New York, New York (212) 850-6000. 1980. Covers synthetic fuels.

Alternative Fuels Research Guidebook. Michael E. Crouse. U.S. Department of Energy, 1000 Independence Ave. SW, Washington, District of Columbia 20585. (202) 252-1760. 1985. Fuel characterization, instrumentation, engine and vehicle testing.

Alternative Transportation Fuels. Daniel Sperling. Quorum Books, Div. of Greenwood Press, Inc., 88 Post Rd. W., Box 5007, Westport, Connecticut 06881. (203) 226-3571. 1989. An environmental and energy solution involving synthetic fuels.

Emergency Fuels Utilization Guidebook: Alternative Fuels Utilization Program. National Technical Information Service, 5285 Port Royal Rd., Springfield, Virginia 22161. (703) 487-4650. 1980.

The Environmental Sourcebook. Edith Carol Stein. Lyons & Burford, 31 W. 21st St., New York, New York 10010. (212) 620-9580. 1992. Provides information on 11 specific environmental issues, including population; agriculture; energy; climate and atmosphere; biodiversity; water; oceans; solid waste; hazardous substances and waste; endangered lands; and development.

Environmental Viewpoints. Marie Lazzari. Gale Research Inc., 835 Penobscot Bldg., Detroit, Michigan 48226-4094. (313) 961-2242. 1992.

Replacing Gasoline: Alternative Fuels for Light-Duty Vehicles. Congress of the U.S., c/o U.S. Government Printing Office, Office of Technology Assesment, N. Capitol & H Sts. NW, Washington, District of Columbia 20401. (202) 512-0000. 1990. Gives information on alternatives to standard gasoline. Some of the alternatives are: electricity, hydrogen, compressed natural gas, liquified natural gas, liquid propane gas, methanol, ethanol, and reformulated gasoline.

World Guide to Environmental Issues and Organizations. Peter Brackley. Longman Group Ltd., Longman House, Burnt Mill, Harlow, Essex, England CM20 2J6. (0279) 426721. 1991.

HANDBOOKS AND MANUALS

Environmental Statistics Handbook: Europe. Allan Foster, Oksana Newman. Gale Research Inc., 835 Penobscot Bldg., Detroit, Michigan 48226-4094. (313) 961-2242. 1993.

ONLINE DATA BASES

Enviro/Energyline Abstracts Plus. R. R. Bowker Co., 121 Chanlon Rd., New Providence, New Jersey 07974. (908) 464-6800.

Environmental Periodicals Bibliography. National Information Services Corp., Ste. 6, Wyman Towers, 3100 St. Paul St., Baltimore, Maryland 21218. (410)243-0797. Online version of abstract of same name.

Monthly Catalog of United States Government Publications. U.S. G.P.O., Supt. of Docs., PO Box 371954, Pittsburgh, Pennsylvania 15250-7954. (202) 512-0000.

National Technical Information Service. U.S. Department of Commerce, National Technical Information Service, Office of Data Base Services, 5285 Port Royal Rd., Springfield, Virginia 22161. (703) 487-4807. Bibliographic database of government sponsored research and technical reports.

PressNet Environmental Reports. Chemical Information Systems, Inc., 7215 York Rd., Baltimore, Maryland 21212. (301) 321-8440.

STATISTICS SOURCES

Statistical Record of the Environment. Arsen J. Darnay. Gale Research Inc., 835 Penobscot Bldg., Detroit, Michigan 48226-4094. (313) 961-2242. 1992.

ALUM

ABSTRACTING AND INDEXING SERVICES

Environment Abstracts. Bowker A & I Publishing, 121 Chanlon Rd., New Providence, New Jersey 07974. (908) 464-6800. 1974-.

Environment Index. Environment Information Center, Index Research Department, 124 E. 39th St., New York, New York 10016. 1971-. Annual.

Environmental Information Connection-EIC. Planning Information Program, Dept. of Urban and Regional Planning, University of Illinois, 1003 West Nevada,

Urbana, Illinois 61801. (217) 333-1369. Also available online.

Environmental Periodicals Bibliography. Environmental Studies Institute, International Academy at Santa Barbara, 800 Garden St., Suite D, Santa Barbara, California 93101. (805) 965-5010. Also available online.

Science Citation Index. Institute for Scientific Information, 3501 Market St., Philadelphia, Pennsylvania 19104. 1961-.

BIBLIOGRAPHIES

EPA Publications Bibliography. U.S. Environmental Protection Agency, Library Systems Branch, 401 M St., SW, Washington, District of Columbia 20460. (202) 260-2090. Quarterly.

ENCYCLOPEDIAS AND DICTIONARIES

McGraw-Hill Encyclopedia of Science and Technology. McGraw-Hill, 1221 Avenue of the Americas, New York, New York 10020. (212) 512-2000 or (800) 262-4729. 1992. Seventh edition. Issued in multiple volumes including index. Includes all science and technology broad subject areas.

ONLINE DATA BASES

CAS Source Index–CASSI. Chemical Abstracts Service, 2540 Olentangy River Rd., P.O. Box 3012, Columbus, Ohio 43210. (800) 848-6533 or (614) 421-3600. A listing of bibliographic and library holdings information for scientific and technical primary literature relevant to the chemical sciences.

Chemical Carcinogenesis Research Information System–CCRIS. National Library of Medicine, 8600 Rockville Pike, Bethesda, Maryland 20894. (800) 638-8480. Individual assay results and test conditions for 1,451 chemicals in the areas of carcinogenicity, mutagenicity, tumor promotion, and cocarcinogenicity.

Enviro/Energyline Abstracts Plus. R. R. Bowker Co., 121 Chanlon Rd., New Providence, New Jersey 07974. (908) 464-6800.

Environmental Periodicals Bibliography. National Information Services Corp., Ste. 6, Wyman Towers, 3100 St. Paul St., Baltimore, Maryland 21218. (410)243-0797. Online version of abstract of same name.

ALUMINUM
See: METALS AND METALLURGY

AMARANTH
See: CROPS

AMBIENT AIR
See: AIR QUALITY

AMBIENT WATER
See: WATER QUALITY

AMERICIUM
See: ELEMENTS

AMINO ACIDS

ABSTRACTING AND INDEXING SERVICES

ASFA Aquaculture Abstracts. Cambridge Scientific Abstracts, Inc., 5161 River Rd., Bethesda, Maryland 20816. (301) 961-6750. 1984.

Biological Abstracts. BIOSIS, 2100 Arch St., Philadelphia, Pennsylvania 19103-1399. (215) 587-4800. 1927-.

Biotechnology Research Abstracts. Cambridge Scientific Abstracts, 5161 River Rd., Bethesda, Maryland 20816. (301) 961-6750. Monthly. Includes such broad areas as genetic intervention, biochemical genetics, and microbiological techniques.

Chemical Abstracts. Chemical Abstracts Service, 2540 Olentangy River Rd., PO Box 3012, Columbus, Ohio 43210. (800) 848-6533. 1907-.

Current Advances in Plant Science. Pergamon Microforms International, Inc., Fairview Park, Elmsford, New York 10523. (914) 592-7720. 1984-. Monthly. Current literature searching service including journals, reports, abstracts, etc. This service is available online as part of the CABS database on the hosts BRS and ORBIT search service.

Ecology Abstracts. Cambridge Scientific Abstracts, 5161 River Rd., Bethesda, Maryland 20816. (301) 961-6750. Monthly.

Environment Abstracts. Bowker A & I Publishing, 121 Chanlon Rd., New Providence, New Jersey 07974. (908) 464-6800. 1974-.

Environment Index. Environment Information Center, Index Research Department, 124 E. 39th St., New York, New York 10016. 1971-. Annual.

Environmental Information Connection–EIC. Planning Information Program, Dept. of Urban and Regional Planning, University of Illinois, 1003 West Nevada, Urbana, Illinois 61801. (217) 333-1369. Also available online.

Environmental Periodicals Bibliography. Environmental Studies Institute, International Academy at Santa Barbara, 800 Garden St., Suite D, Santa Barbara, California 93101. (805) 965-5010. Also available online.

Food Science and Technology Abstracts. International Food Information Service, c/o National Food Laboratory, 6363 Clark Ave., Dublin, California 94568. (800) 336-3782. 1969-.

Pollution Abstracts. Cambridge Scientific Abstracts, 5161 River Rd., Bethesda, Maryland 20816. (301) 961-6750. Six/year. Indexes worldwide technical literature on environmental pollution. Covers air pollution, marine and freshwater pollution, sewage and wastewater treatment,

waste management, toxicology and health, noise pollution, radiation, land pollution, and environmental policies, programs, legislation, and education. Also available online.

Science Citation Index. Institute for Scientific Information, 3501 Market St., Philadelphia, Pennsylvania 19104. 1961-.

BIBLIOGRAPHIES

Bibliography and Index of Geology. American Geological Institute, 4220 King St., Alexandria, Virginia 22302. Monthly. Includes environmental geology and hydrogeology.

EPA Publications Bibliography. U.S. Environmental Protection Agency, Library Systems Branch, 401 M St., SW, Washington, District of Columbia 20460. (202) 260-2090. Quarterly.

ENCYCLOPEDIAS AND DICTIONARIES

The Dictionary of Cell Biology. J. M. Lackie and J. A. T. Dow, eds. Academic Press, c/o Harcourt Brace Jovanovich Inc., 6277 Sea Harbor Dr., Orlando, Florida 32887. (800) 346-8648. 1989. Covers the broad subject area of cell biology including lipid, vitamins, amino acid, lectins, proteins, and other related topics.

Encyclopedia of Chemical Processing and Design. John J. Mcketta and W. A. Cunningham. Marcel Dekker, Inc., 270 Madison Ave., New York, New York 10016. (212) 696-9000; (800) 228-1160. 1992. Thirty-eight volumes.

Encyclopedia of Human Biology. Renato Dulbecco, ed. Academic Press, c/o Harcourt Brace Jovanovich Inc., 6277 Sea Harbor Dr., Orlando, Florida 32887. (800) 346-8648. 1991. Eight volumes.

Kirk-Othmer Encyclopedia of Chemical Technology. J. I. Kroschwitz, ed. John Wiley & Sons, Inc., 605 3rd Ave., New York, New York 10158-0012. (212) 850-6000. 1992-. All articles in the new edition have been rewritten and updated adding new subjects such as biotechnology, computer topics, analytical techniques and instrumentation, environmental concerns, fuels and energy, inorganic and solid state chemistry; composite materials and material science in general, and pharmaceuticals. Also available online.

Life Sciences on File. Diagram Group. Facts on File, Inc., 460 Park Ave. S., New York, New York 10016. (212) 683-2244. 1986. Encyclopedia of pictorial collection in life sciences. Deals with all major topics in life sciences including ecology.

McGraw-Hill Encyclopedia of Science and Technology. McGraw-Hill, 1221 Avenue of the Americas, New York, New York 10020. (212) 512-2000 or (800) 262-4729. 1992. Seventh edition. Issued in multiple volumes including index. Includes all science and technology broad subject areas.

The Nutrition and Health Encyclopedia. David F. Tver and Percy Russell. Van Nostrand Reinhold, 115 5th Ave., New York, New York 10003. (212) 254-3232. 1989.

Van Nostrand's Scientific Encyclopedia. Glenn D. Considine, ed. Van Nostrand Reinhold, 115 5th Ave., New York, New York 10003. (212) 254-3232. 1983. Sixth edition. Includes all broad subject areas in science.

GENERAL WORKS

Magill's Survey of Science. Earth Science Series. Frank N. Magill. Salem Press, PO Box 50062, Pasadena, California 91105. 1990-. Five volumes. Includes information on earth's crust, hot spots and volcanic island chains, physical properties of minerals, rock magnetism, physical properties of rocks, and index.

HANDBOOKS AND MANUALS

Complete Guide to Vitamins, Minerals and Supplements. H. Winter Griffith. Fisher Books, 3499 N. Campbell Ave., Suite 909, Tucson, Arizona 85712. (602) 325-5263. 1988. Includes name, brand name, reasons to use, who should use, recommended daily allowance, and other related data in the form of a chart.

ONLINE DATA BASES

BIOSIS Previews. BIOSIS, 2100 Arch St., Philadelphia, Pennsylvania 19103-1399. (215) 587-4800. Largest and most comprehensive database of research in the life sciences. Contains citations for nearly 9000 primary research journals, monographs, reviews, symposia, preliminary reports, semi-popular journals, selected institutional reports, government reports and research communications.

CAS Source Index–CASSI. Chemical Abstracts Service, 2540 Olentangy River Rd., P.O. Box 3012, Columbus, Ohio 43210. (800) 848-6533 or (614) 421-3600. A listing of bibliographic and library holdings information for scientific and technical primary literature relevant to the chemical sciences.

Chemical Abstracts-CA. Chemical Abstracts Service, 2540 Olentangy River Rd., P.O. Box 3012, Columbus, Ohio 43210. (800) 848-6533 or (614) 421-3600. Information sources include 9000 journals, patents from 27 countries, two industrial property organizations, new books, conference proceedings, and government research reports.

Enviro/Energyline Abstracts Plus. R. R. Bowker Co., 121 Chanlon Rd., New Providence, New Jersey 07974. (908) 464-6800.

Environmental Periodicals Bibliography. National Information Services Corp., Ste. 6, Wyman Towers, 3100 St. Paul St., Baltimore, Maryland 21218. (410)243-0797. Online version of abstract of same name.

Kirk-Othmer Encyclopedia of Chemical Technology. John Wiley & Sons, Inc., 605 3rd Ave., 5th Floor, New York, New York 10158. (212) 850-6000. Online version of the publication of the same name.

SCISEARCH. Institute for Scientific Information, University City Science Center, 3501 Market St., Philadelphia, Pennsylvania 19104. (215) 386-0100.

PERIODICALS AND NEWSLETTERS

Biogenic Amines. Pergamon Microforms International, Inc., Fairview Park, Elmsford, New York 10523. (914) 592-7720. 1984-. Bimonthly. Journal including of all aspects of research on biogenic amines and amino acid transmitters, their relating compounds and their interaction phenomena.

The Journal of Biological Chemistry. American Society of Biological Chemists, 428 E. Preston St., Baltimore,

Maryland 21202. Three times a month. Biological, agricultural, and energy aspects of the environment.

RESEARCH CENTERS AND INSTITUTES

Bioanalytical Center. Washington State University, Troy Hall, Pullman, Washington 99164. (509) 335-5126.

Sheldon Biotechnology Centre. McGill University, 3773 University St., Montreal, Quebec, Canada H3A 2B4. (514) 398-3998.

AMMONIA AND AMMONIUM COMPOUNDS

ABSTRACTING AND INDEXING SERVICES

ASFA Aquaculture Abstracts. Cambridge Scientific Abstracts, Inc., 5161 River Rd., Bethesda, Maryland 20816. (301) 961-6750. 1984.

Biotechnology Research Abstracts. Cambridge Scientific Abstracts, 5161 River Rd., Bethesda, Maryland 20816. (301) 961-6750. Monthly. Includes such broad areas as genetic intervention, biochemical genetics, and microbiological techniques.

Chemical Abstracts. Chemical Abstracts Service, 2540 Olentangy River Rd., PO Box 3012, Columbus, Ohio 43210. (800) 848-6533. 1907-.

Ecology Abstracts. Cambridge Scientific Abstracts, 5161 River Rd., Bethesda, Maryland 20816. (301) 961-6750. Monthly.

Environment Abstracts. Bowker A & I Publishing, 121 Chanlon Rd., New Providence, New Jersey 07974. (908) 464-6800. 1974-.

Environment Index. Environment Information Center, Index Research Department, 124 E. 39th St., New York, New York 10016. 1971-. Annual.

Environmental Information Connection–EIC. Planning Information Program, Dept. of Urban and Regional Planning, University of Illinois, 1003 West Nevada, Urbana, Illinois 61801. (217) 333-1369. Also available online.

Environmental Periodicals Bibliography. Environmental Studies Institute, International Academy at Santa Barbara, 800 Garden St., Suite D, Santa Barbara, California 93101. (805) 965-5010. Also available online.

Science Citation Index. Institute for Scientific Information, 3501 Market St., Philadelphia, Pennsylvania 19104. 1961-.

BIBLIOGRAPHIES

EPA Publications Bibliography. U.S. Environmental Protection Agency, Library Systems Branch, 401 M St., SW, Washington, District of Columbia 20460. (202) 260-2090. Quarterly.

ENCYCLOPEDIAS AND DICTIONARIES

Encyclopedia of Chemical Processing and Design. John J. Mcketta and W. A. Cunningham. Marcel Dekker, Inc., 270 Madison Ave., New York, New York 10016. (212) 696-9000; (800) 228-1160. 1992. Thirty-eight volumes.

Kirk-Othmer Encyclopedia of Chemical Technology. J. I. Kroschwitz, ed. John Wiley & Sons, Inc., 605 3rd Ave., New York, New York 10158-0012. (212) 850-6000. 1992-. All articles in the new edition have been rewritten and updated adding new subjects such as biotechnology, computer topics, analytical techniques and instrumentation, environmental concerns, fuels and energy, inorganic and solid state chemistry; composite materials and material science in general, and pharmaceuticals. Also available online.

McGraw-Hill Encyclopedia of Science and Technology. McGraw-Hill, 1221 Avenue of the Americas, New York, New York 10020. (212) 512-2000 or (800) 262-4729. 1992. Seventh edition. Issued in multiple volumes including index. Includes all science and technology broad subject areas.

ONLINE DATA BASES

CAS Source Index–CASSI. Chemical Abstracts Service, 2540 Olentangy River Rd., P.O. Box 3012, Columbus, Ohio 43210. (800) 848-6533 or (614) 421-3600. A listing of bibliographic and library holdings information for scientific and technical primary literature relevant to the chemical sciences.

Chemical Abstracts-CA. Chemical Abstracts Service, 2540 Olentangy River Rd., P.O. Box 3012, Columbus, Ohio 43210. (800) 848-6533 or (614) 421-3600. Information sources include 9000 journals, patents from 27 countries, two industrial property organizations, new books, conference proceedings, and government research reports.

Chemical Abstracts Chemical Name Directory-CHEMNAME. Chemical Abstracts Service, 2540 Olentangy River Rd., P.O. Box 3012, Columbus, Ohio 43210. (800) 848-6533 or (614) 421-3600. Listing of chemical substances in a dictionary type file. The Chemical Abstracts (CAS) Registry Number, molecular formula, Chemical Abstracts (CA) Substance Index Name, available synonyms, ring data and other chemical substance information is given for each entry.

Enviro/Energyline Abstracts Plus. R. R. Bowker Co., 121 Chanlon Rd., New Providence, New Jersey 07974. (908) 464-6800.

Environmental Periodicals Bibliography. National Information Services Corp., Ste. 6, Wyman Towers, 3100 St. Paul St., Baltimore, Maryland 21218. (410)243-0797. Online version of abstract of same name.

Kirk-Othmer Encyclopedia of Chemical Technology. John Wiley & Sons, Inc., 605 3rd Ave., 5th Floor, New York, New York 10158. (212) 850-6000. Online version of the publication of the same name.

AMORPHIZATION
See: IRRADIATION

ANAEROBIC LAGOONS
See: WASTE TREATMENT

ANAEROBIC RESPIRATION

See: RESPIRATION

ANILIDES AND ANILINES

See also: DYES

ABSTRACTING AND INDEXING SERVICES

Biological Abstracts. BIOSIS, 2100 Arch St., Philadelphia, Pennsylvania 19103-1399. (215) 587-4800. 1927-.

Environment Abstracts. Bowker A & I Publishing, 121 Chanlon Rd., New Providence, New Jersey 07974. (908) 464-6800. 1974-.

Environment Index. Environment Information Center, Index Research Department, 124 E. 39th St., New York, New York 10016. 1971-. Annual.

Environmental Information Connection-EIC. Planning Information Program, Dept. of Urban and Regional Planning, University of Illinois, 1003 West Nevada, Urbana, Illinois 61801. (217) 333-1369. Also available online.

Environmental Periodicals Bibliography. Environmental Studies Institute, International Academy at Santa Barbara, 800 Garden St., Suite D, Santa Barbara, California 93101. (805) 965-5010. Also available online.

Science Citation Index. Institute for Scientific Information, 3501 Market St., Philadelphia, Pennsylvania 19104. 1961-.

BIBLIOGRAPHIES

Directory of Published Proceedings. Interdok Corp., 173 Halstead Ave., Harrison, New York 10528. (914) 835-3506. 1990. Monthly. This is a listing of published proceedings including the series SEMTE (Science/Medicine/Engineering/Technology) and the series SSH (Social Science/Humanities).

EPA Publications Bibliography. U.S. Environmental Protection Agency, Library Systems Branch, 401 M St., SW, Washington, District of Columbia 20460. (202) 260-2090. Quarterly.

ENCYCLOPEDIAS AND DICTIONARIES

McGraw-Hill Encyclopedia of Science and Technology. McGraw-Hill, 1221 Avenue of the Americas, New York, New York 10020. (212) 512-2000 or (800) 262-4729. 1992. Seventh edition. Issued in multiple volumes including index. Includes all science and technology broad subject areas.

HANDBOOKS AND MANUALS

Tables of Physical and Chemical Constants and Some Mathematical Functions. G. W. C. Kaye, et al. Longman Group Ltd., Longman House, Burnt Mill, Harlow, England CM20 2J6. 0279 426721. 1988. Fifteenth edition. Includes tables on mechanical properties, density, elasticity, viscosity, surface tension, temperature and heat. Also covers radiation, optics, chemistry, electrochemistry, astrophysics, and chemical thermodynamics.

ONLINE DATA BASES

BIOSIS Previews. BIOSIS, 2100 Arch St., Philadelphia, Pennsylvania 19103-1399. (215) 587-4800. Largest and most comprehensive database of research in the life sciences. Contains citations for nearly 9000 primary research journals, monographs, reviews, symposia, preliminary reports, semi-popular journals, selected institutional reports, government reports and research communications.

CAS Source Index-CASSI. Chemical Abstracts Service, 2540 Olentangy River Rd., P.O. Box 3012, Columbus, Ohio 43210. (800) 848-6533 or (614) 421-3600. A listing of bibliographic and library holdings information for scientific and technical primary literature relevant to the chemical sciences.

Chemical Collection System/Request Tracking-CCS/RTS. U.S. Environmental Protection Agency, Office of Pesticides and Toxic Substances, 401 M St., SW, Washington, District of Columbia 20460. (202) 260-2090. Contains information on various properties of a number of chemicals including environmental effects, test and analysis methods, and health effects. Available from EPA.

Chemical Dictionary Online-CHEMLINE. Chemical Abstracts Service, 2540 Olentangy River Rd., Columbus, Ohio 43210. (614) 421-3600 or (800) 848-6533. Part of MEDLINE of the National Library of Medicine (NLM). File of 900,000 names for chemical substances, representing 450,000 unique compounds. It contains such information as Chemical Abstracts (CA) Service Registry Numbers, molecular formulas, preferred chemical nomenclature, and generic and ring structure information. Available on NLM's ELHILL system.

Chemical Exposure. Science Applications International Corp., Health & Environmental Information, P.O. Box 2501, Oak Ridge, Tennessee 37831. (615) 482-9031. Database of chemicals that have been identified in both human tissues and body fluids and in feral and food animals. Contains reference to journal articles, conferences, and reports. Covers the whole fields of information related to human and animal exposure to food, air, and water contaminants and pharmaceuticals. Its records include information on chemical properties, formulas, tissues measured, analytical method used, demographics and more. Available on DIALOG.

Enviro/Energyline Abstracts Plus. R. R. Bowker Co., 121 Chanlon Rd., New Providence, New Jersey 07974. (908) 464-6800.

Environmental Periodicals Bibliography. National Information Services Corp., Ste. 6, Wyman Towers, 3100 St. Paul St., Baltimore, Maryland 21218. (410)243-0797. Online version of abstract of same name.

SCISEARCH. Institute for Scientific Information, University City Science Center, 3501 Market St., Philadelphia, Pennsylvania 19104. (215) 386-0100.

TRADE ASSOCIATIONS AND PROFESSIONAL SOCIETIES

Aniline Association. 1330 Connecticut Ave., N.W., Washington, District of Columbia 20036. (202) 659-0060.

Substituted Anilines Task Force. 1330 Connecticut Ave., N.W., Suite 300, Washington, District of Columbia 20036. (202) 659-0060.

ANIMAL ECOLOGY

ABSTRACTING AND INDEXING SERVICES

Index to Scientific Book Contents. Institute for Scientific Information, 3501 Market St., Philadelphia, Pennsylvania 19104. (800) 523-1857. 1985-. Annual. Gives contents of science books published.

ENCYCLOPEDIAS AND DICTIONARIES

The Encyclopedia of Animal Ecology. Peter D. Moore. Facts on File, Inc., 460 Park Ave. S., New York, New York 10016. (212) 683-2244. 1987.

GENERAL WORKS

Comparative Ecology of Microorganisms and Macroorganisms. John H. Andrews. Springer-Verlag, 175 5th Ave., New York, New York 10010. (212) 460-1500. 1991. Constructs a format in which to compare the ecologies of large and small plant and animal organisms. Examines the differences between the sizes, and explores what similarities or parallels can be identified, and where they don't seem to exist. The ideas are illustrated by applying evolutionary principles to the individual organism.

A Guide to the Study of Animal Ecology. Charles Christopher Adams. Arno Press, PO Box 958, Salem, New Hampshire 03079. (603) 669-5933. 1977.

ONLINE DATA BASES

Current Research Information System–CRIS/USDA. U.S. Department of Agriculture, National Agricultural Library, 10301 Baltimore Blvd., 5th Floor, Beltsville, Maryland 20705-2351. (301) 504-5755. Looks at current research projects in agriculture and allied sciences covering the biological, physical, social and behavioral sciences related to agriculture.

PERIODICALS AND NEWSLETTERS

The Journal of Animal Ecology. Blackwell Scientific Publications, PO Box 87, Oxford, England OX2 0DT. 44 0865 791155. Three times a year.

ANIMAL FEED

See also: LIVESTOCK

ABSTRACTING AND INDEXING SERVICES

Biological Abstracts. BIOSIS, 2100 Arch St., Philadelphia, Pennsylvania 19103-1399. (215) 587-4800. 1927-.

Biological and Agricultural Index. H.W. Wilson Co., 950 University Ave., Bronx, New York 10452. (800) 367-6770. 1916-. Monthly.

Ecological Abstracts. Geo Abstracts Ltd. Elsevier Applied Science, Crown House, Linton Rd., Barking, England IG 11 8JU. 1974-. Derived from over 600 leading ecological and environmental journals, plus books, conference proceedings, reports and theses.

General Science Index. H. W. Wilson Co., 950 University Ave., Bronx, New York 10452. 1978-. Monthly, also issued in annual cumulation. Cumulative subject index to English language periodicals in the subject fields of astronomy, botany, chemistry, earth science, environment and conservation, food and nutrition, genetics, mathematics, medicine and health, microbiology, oceanography, physics, physiology and zoology.

Index to Scientific Book Contents. Institute for Scientific Information, 3501 Market St., Philadelphia, Pennsylvania 19104. (800) 523-1857. 1985-. Annual. Gives contents of science books published.

Pollution Abstracts. Cambridge Scientific Abstracts, 5161 River Rd., Bethesda, Maryland 20816. (301) 961-6750. Six/year. Indexes worldwide technical literature on environmental pollution. Covers air pollution, marine and freshwater pollution, sewage and wastewater treatment, waste management, toxicology and health, noise pollution, radiation, land pollution, and environmental policies, programs, legislation, and education. Also available online.

BIBLIOGRAPHIES

Current Contents. Agriculture, Biology and Environmental Sciences. Institute for Scientific Information, 3501 Market St., Philadelphia, Pennsylvania 19104. (800) 523-1857. 1973-. Previous title: Current Contents. Agricultural, Food & Veterinary Sciences. Gives the table of contents of periodicals in the fields of agriculture, biology, environmental and related areas.

ENCYCLOPEDIAS AND DICTIONARIES

The Encyclopedia of Animal Ecology. Peter D. Moore. Facts on File, Inc., 460 Park Ave. S., New York, New York 10016. (212) 683-2244. 1987.

McGraw-Hill Encyclopedia of Science and Technology. McGraw-Hill, 1221 Avenue of the Americas, New York, New York 10020. (212) 512-2000 or (800) 262-4729. 1992. Seventh edition. Issued in multiple volumes including index. Includes all science and technology broad subject areas.

GENERAL WORKS

Feed from Animal Wastes: State of Knowledge. Z.O. Muller. Food and Agriculture Organization of the United Nations, Via delle Terme di Caralla, Rome, Italy 00100. 61 0181-FA01. 1980.

Microbial Toxins in Focus and Feeds. Albert E. Pohland, et al., eds. Plenum Press, 233 Spring St., New York, New York 10013. (212) 620-8000; (800) 221-9369. 1990. Proceedings of a Symposium on Cellular and Molecular Mode of Action of Selected Microbial Toxins in Foods and Feeds, Oct. 31- Nov. 2, 1988, Chevy Chase, MD.

HANDBOOKS AND MANUALS

Feed from Animal Wastes: Feeding Manual. Z.O. Muller. Food and Agriculture Organization of the United Nations, Via delle Terme di Caracalla, Rome, Italy 00100. 61 0181-FA01. 1982. Organic wastes as feed and animal waste.

ONLINE DATA BASES

BIOSIS Previews. BIOSIS, 2100 Arch St., Philadelphia, Pennsylvania 19103-1399. (215) 587-4800. Largest and most comprehensive database of research in the life sciences. Contains citations for nearly 9000 primary research journals, monographs, reviews, symposia, preliminary reports, semi-popular journals, selected institutional reports, government reports and research communications.

Current Research Information System–CRIS/USDA. U.S. Department of Agriculture, National Agricultural Library, 10301 Baltimore Blvd., 5th Floor, Beltsville, Maryland 20705-2351. (301) 504-5755. Looks at current research projects in agriculture and allied sciences covering the biological, physical, social and behavioral sciences related to agriculture.

Monthly Catalog of United States Government Publications. U.S. G.P.O., Supt. of Docs., PO Box 371954, Pittsburgh, Pennsylvania 15250-7954. (202) 512-0000.

National Technical Information Service. U.S. Department of Commerce, National Technical Information Service, Office of Data Base Services, 5285 Port Royal Rd., Springfield, Virginia 22161. (703) 487-4807. Bibliographic database of government sponsored research and technical reports.

PERIODICALS AND NEWSLETTERS

Animal Feed Science and Technology. Elsevier Science Publishing Co., 655 Avenue of the Americas, New York, New York 10010. (212) 984-5800.

ANIMAL RIGHTS MOVEMENT

ABSTRACTING AND INDEXING SERVICES

Applied Ecology Abstracts Studies in Renewable Natural Resources. Information Retrieval Ltd., 1911 Jefferson Davis Highway, Arlington, Virginia 22202. 1975-. Monthly.

Ecological Abstracts. Geo Abstracts Ltd. Elsevier Applied Science, Crown House, Linton Rd., Barking, England IG 11 8JU. 1974-. Derived from over 600 leading ecological and environmental journals, plus books, conference proceedings, reports and theses.

Multimedia Index to Ecology. National Information Center for Educational Media, University of Southern California, Los Angeles, California 90007.

GENERAL WORKS

The Thee Generation: Reflections on the Coming Revolution. Tom Regan. Temple University Press, 1601 N. Broad St., Philadelphia, Pennsylvania 19122. (215) 787-8787. 1991. Topics in animal rights and ecology.

ONLINE DATA BASES

Monthly Catalog of United States Government Publications. U.S. G.P.O., Supt. of Docs., PO Box 371954, Pittsburgh, Pennsylvania 15250-7954. (202) 512-0000.

National Technical Information Service. U.S. Department of Commerce, National Technical Information Service, Office of Data Base Services, 5285 Port Royal Rd., Springfield, Virginia 22161. (703) 487-4807. Bibliographic database of government sponsored research and technical reports.

PERIODICALS AND NEWSLETTERS

Animal Welfare Institute Quarterly. Animal Welfare Institute, Box 3650, Washington, District of Columbia 20007. (202) 337-2333. 1951-. Quarterly. Promotes the reduction of total pain and fear inflicted on animals by man.

Animals' Agenda. Animal Rights Networks, 456 Monroe Tpke., Monroe, Connecticut 06468. (203) 452-9543. 1979-. Ten times a year. Magazine of animal rights and ecology. Featured are a wide range of subjects about humanity's exploitation of animals and the environment.

Animals International. World Society for the Protection of Animals, 29 Perkins St., PO Box 190, Boston, Massachusetts 02130. (617) 522-7000. Monthly. Programs and issues related to animal protection and wildlife conservation.

Anthrozoos. University Press of New England, 17 1/2 Lebanon St., Hanover, New Hampshire 03755. (603) 643-7100. 1987-. Quarterly. A multidisciplinary journal on the interactions of people, animals, and environment.

Educational Materials for Animal Rights. International Society for Animal Rights, Inc., 421 S. State St., Clarks Summit, Pennsylvania 18411. (717) 586-2200. Annual.

International Society for Animal Rights Support. International Society for Animal Rights, Inc., 421 S. State St., Clarks Summit, Pennsylvania 18411. (717) 586-2200. Bimonthly.

Mainstream. Animal Protection Institute of America, 2831 Frutridge Rd., PO Box 22505, Sacramento, California 95822. (916) 731-5521. Quarterly. Covers animal welfare problems.

One World. Trans-Species Unlimited, Box 1553, Williamsport, Pennsylvania 17703. (717) 322-3252. Irregular. Vegetarianism and animal rights.

TRADE ASSOCIATIONS AND PROFESSIONAL SOCIETIES

Animal Protection Institute of America. 2831 Fruitridge Road, P.O. Box 22505, Sacramento, California 95822. (916) 731-5521.

Animal Rights International. PO Box 214, Planetarium Station, New York, New York 10024. (212) 873-3674.

Animal Rights League of America. PO Box 474, New Albany, Ohio 43054. (614) 855-2494.

Animal Welfare Institute. P.O. Box 3650, Georgetown Sta., Washington, District of Columbia 20007. (202) 337-2333.

Friends of Animals, Inc. Box 1244, Norwalk, Connecticut 06856. (203) 866-5223.

Fund for Animals, Inc. 200 W. 57th St., New York, New York 10019. (212) 246-2096.

Humane Society of the United States. 2100 L St., NW, Washington, District of Columbia 20037. (202) 452-1100.

International Society of Animal Rights. 421 S. State St., Clark's Summit, Pennsylvania 18411. (715) 586-2200.

National Animal Damage Control Association. Rte. 1, Box 37, Shell Lake, Wisconsin 54871. (715) 468-2038.

National Trappers Association. P.O. Box 3667, Bloomington, Illinois 61702. (309) 829-2422.

People for Ethical Treatment of Animals. Box 42516, Washington, District of Columbia 20015. (301) 770-7444.

Society for Animal Protective Legislation. PO Box 3719, Georgetown Station, Washington, District of Columbia 20007. (202) 337-2334.

United States Animal Health Association. P.O. Box K227, 1610 Forest Ave., Ste. 114, Richmond, Virginia 23228. (804) 266-3275.

World Society for the Protection of Animals. 29 Perkins St., PO Box 190, Boston, Massachusetts 02130. (617) 522-7000.

ANIMAL WASTES

See also: METHANE; WASTE-TO-ENERGY SYSTEMS; WASTE TREATMENT

ABSTRACTING AND INDEXING SERVICES

Applied Ecology Abstracts Studies in Renewable Natural Resources. Information Retrieval Ltd., 1911 Jefferson Davis Highway, Arlington, Virginia 22202. 1975-. Monthly.

Biological Abstracts. BIOSIS, 2100 Arch St., Philadelphia, Pennsylvania 19103-1399. (215) 587-4800. 1927-.

Biological and Agricultural Index. H.W. Wilson Co., 950 University Ave., Bronx, New York 10452. (800) 367-6770. 1916-. Monthly.

Bulletin Signaletique: Eau et Assainissement, Pollution Atmospherique, Droit des Pollutions. Centre de Documentation, Centre National de la Recherche Scientifique, 15, quai Anatole France, Paris, France 75700. (1) 45 55 92 25. 1983-. Monthly. Indexes pollution periodicals including water, atmospheric and related pollutions.

Ecological Abstracts. Geo Abstracts Ltd. Elsevier Applied Science, Crown House, Linton Rd., Barking, England IG 11 8JU. 1974-. Derived from over 600 leading ecological and environmental journals, plus books, conference proceedings, reports and theses.

Environment Abstracts. Bowker A & I Publishing, 121 Chanlon Rd., New Providence, New Jersey 07974. (908) 464-6800. 1974-.

Environment Index. Environment Information Center, Index Research Department, 124 E. 39th St., New York, New York 10016. 1971-. Annual.

Environmental Information Connection–EIC. Planning Information Program, Dept. of Urban and Regional Planning, University of Illinois, 1003 West Nevada, Urbana, Illinois 61801. (217) 333-1369. Also available online.

Environmental Periodicals Bibliography. Environmental Studies Institute, International Academy at Santa Barbara, 800 Garden St., Suite D, Santa Barbara, California 93101. (805) 965-5010. Also available online.

Index to Scientific Book Contents. Institute for Scientific Information, 3501 Market St., Philadelphia, Pennsylvania 19104. (800) 523-1857. 1985-. Annual. Gives contents of science books published.

Multimedia Index to Ecology. National Information Center for Educational Media, University of Southern California, Los Angeles, California 90007.

Pollution Abstracts. Cambridge Scientific Abstracts, 5161 River Rd., Bethesda, Maryland 20816. (301) 961-6750. Six/year. Indexes worldwide technical literature on environmental pollution. Covers air pollution, marine and freshwater pollution, sewage and wastewater treatment, waste management, toxicology and health, noise pollution, radiation, land pollution, and environmental policies, programs, legislation, and education. Also available online.

BIBLIOGRAPHIES

Bibliography of Livestock Waste Management. U.S. Government Printing Office, Washington, District of Columbia 20402-9325. (202) 783-3238. 1972. Covers agricultural and animal waste, manure handling, and feedlots.

Current Contents. Agriculture, Biology and Environmental Sciences. Institute for Scientific Information, 3501 Market St., Philadelphia, Pennsylvania 19104. (800) 523-1857. 1973-. Previous title: Current Contents. Agricultural, Food & Veterinary Sciences. Gives the table of contents of periodicals in the fields of agriculture, biology, environmental and related areas.

EPA Publications Bibliography. U.S. Environmental Protection Agency, Library Systems Branch, 401 M St., SW, Washington, District of Columbia 20460. (202) 260-2090. Quarterly.

ENCYCLOPEDIAS AND DICTIONARIES

The Encyclopedia of Animal Ecology. Peter D. Moore. Facts on File, Inc., 460 Park Ave. S., New York, New York 10016. (212) 683-2244. 1987.

McGraw-Hill Encyclopedia of Environmental Science. Sybil P. Parker. McGraw-Hill Science & Engineering Books, 11 W. 19th St., New York, New York 10011. (212) 337-6010. 1980. Covers ecology, man's influence on nature, and environmental protection.

McGraw-Hill Encyclopedia of Science and Technology. McGraw-Hill, 1221 Avenue of the Americas, New York, New York 10020. (212) 512-2000 or (800) 262-4729. 1992. Seventh edition. Issued in multiple volumes including index. Includes all science and technology broad subject areas.

GENERAL WORKS

Effluents from Livestock. J. K. R. Gasser, et al., eds. Applied Science Publications, PO Box 5399, New York, New York 10163. (718) 756-6440. 1980. Proceedings of a seminar to discuss work carried out within the EEC under the programme Effluents from Intensive Livestock, organized by Prof. H. Vetter and held at Bad Zwischenahn, 2-5 October, 1979.

Livestock Waste, a Renewable Resource. American Society of Agricultural Engineers, 2950 Niles Rd., St. Joseph,

Michigan 49085-9659. (616) 429-0300. 1981. Papers presented at the 4th International Symposium on Livestock Wastes, Amarillo, TX, 1980. Topics covered include: processing manure for feed, methane production, land application, lagoons, runoff, odors, economics, stabilization, treatment, collection and transport, storage and solid-liquid separation.

ONLINE DATA BASES

BIOSIS Previews. BIOSIS, 2100 Arch St., Philadelphia, Pennsylvania 19103-1399. (215) 587-4800. Largest and most comprehensive database of research in the life sciences. Contains citations for nearly 9000 primary research journals, monographs, reviews, symposia, preliminary reports, semi-popular journals, selected institutional reports, government reports and research communications.

Current Research Information System–CRIS/USDA. U.S. Department of Agriculture, National Agricultural Library, 10301 Baltimore Blvd., 5th Floor, Beltsville, Maryland 20705-2351. (301) 504-5755. Looks at current research projects in agriculture and allied sciences covering the biological, physical, social and behavioral sciences related to agriculture.

Enviro/Energyline Abstracts Plus. R. R. Bowker Co., 121 Chanlon Rd., New Providence, New Jersey 07974. (908) 464-6800.

Environmental Periodicals Bibliography. National Information Services Corp., Ste. 6, Wyman Towers, 3100 St. Paul St., Baltimore, Maryland 21218. (410)243-0797. Online version of abstract of same name.

Monthly Catalog of United States Government Publications. U.S. G.P.O., Supt. of Docs., PO Box 371954, Pittsburgh, Pennsylvania 15250-7954. (202) 512-0000.

National Technical Information Service. U.S. Department of Commerce, National Technical Information Service, Office of Data Base Services, 5285 Port Royal Rd., Springfield, Virginia 22161. (703) 487-4807. Bibliographic database of government sponsored research and technical reports.

SCISEARCH. Institute for Scientific Information, University City Science Center, 3501 Market St., Philadelphia, Pennsylvania 19104. (215) 386-0100.

RESEARCH CENTERS AND INSTITUTES

Lawrence Berkeley Laboratory, Chemical Biodynamics Division. One Cyclotron Road, Berkeley, California 94720. (415) 486-4355.

STATISTICS SOURCES

Journal of the American Veterinary Medical Association. American Veterinary Medical Association, 930 N. Meacham Rd., Schaumburg, Illinois 60196-1074. Semimonthly. Professional developments, research and clinical reports.

ANIMALS

See: DOMESTIC ANIMALS

ANODIC STRIPPING VOLTAMMETRY

ABSTRACTING AND INDEXING SERVICES

Biological Abstracts. BIOSIS, 2100 Arch St., Philadelphia, Pennsylvania 19103-1399. (215) 587-4800. 1927-.

Chemical Abstracts. Chemical Abstracts Service, 2540 Olentangy River Rd., PO Box 3012, Columbus, Ohio 43210. (800) 848-6533. 1907-.

Environment Abstracts. Bowker A & I Publishing, 121 Chanlon Rd., New Providence, New Jersey 07974. (908) 464-6800. 1974-.

Environment Index. Environment Information Center, Index Research Department, 124 E. 39th St., New York, New York 10016. 1971-. Annual.

Environmental Information Connection–EIC. Planning Information Program, Dept. of Urban and Regional Planning, University of Illinois, 1003 West Nevada, Urbana, Illinois 61801. (217) 333-1369. Also available online.

Environmental Periodicals Bibliography. Environmental Studies Institute, International Academy at Santa Barbara, 800 Garden St., Suite D, Santa Barbara, California 93101. (805) 965-5010. Also available online.

Science Citation Index. Institute for Scientific Information, 3501 Market St., Philadelphia, Pennsylvania 19104. 1961-.

BIBLIOGRAPHIES

EPA Publications Bibliography. U.S. Environmental Protection Agency, Library Systems Branch, 401 M St., SW, Washington, District of Columbia 20460. (202) 260-2090. Quarterly.

ENCYCLOPEDIAS AND DICTIONARIES

Encyclopedia of Physical Science and Technology. Robert A. Meyers, ed. Academic Press, c/o Harcourt Brace Jovanovich Inc., 6277 Sea Harbor Dr., Orlando, Florida 32887. (800) 346-8648. Dictionary of engineering, technology and physical sciences.

McGraw-Hill Encyclopedia of Science and Technology. McGraw-Hill, 1221 Avenue of the Americas, New York, New York 10020. (212) 512-2000 or (800) 262-4729. 1992. Seventh edition. Issued in multiple volumes including index. Includes all science and technology broad subject areas.

ONLINE DATA BASES

BIOSIS Previews. BIOSIS, 2100 Arch St., Philadelphia, Pennsylvania 19103-1399. (215) 587-4800. Largest and most comprehensive database of research in the life sciences. Contains citations for nearly 9000 primary research journals, monographs, reviews, symposia, preliminary reports, semi-popular journals, selected institutional reports, government reports and research communications.

Chemical Abstracts-CA. Chemical Abstracts Service, 2540 Olentangy River Rd., P.O. Box 3012, Columbus, Ohio 43210. (800) 848-6533 or (614) 421-3600. Information sources include 9000 journals, patents from 27 countries, two industrial property organizations, new

books, conference proceedings, and government research reports.

Enviro/Energyline Abstracts Plus. R. R. Bowker Co., 121 Chanlon Rd., New Providence, New Jersey 07974. (908) 464-6800.

Environmental Periodicals Bibliography. National Information Services Corp., Ste. 6, Wyman Towers, 3100 St. Paul St., Baltimore, Maryland 21218. (410)243-0797. Online version of abstract of same name.

ANTARCTIC

See also: BIOMES; ECOSYSTEMS; INTERNATIONAL TREATIES; MINERAL EXPLORATION; OZONE LAYER; WHALING

ABSTRACTING AND INDEXING SERVICES

Applied Ecology Abstracts Studies in Renewable Natural Resources. Information Retrieval Ltd., 1911 Jefferson Davis Highway, Arlington, Virginia 22202. 1975-. Monthly.

Biological Abstracts. BIOSIS, 2100 Arch St., Philadelphia, Pennsylvania 19103-1399. (215) 587-4800. 1927-.

Ecological Abstracts. Geo Abstracts Ltd. Elsevier Applied Science, Crown House, Linton Rd., Barking, England IG 11 8JU. 1974-. Derived from over 600 leading ecological and environmental journals, plus books, conference proceedings, reports and theses.

Environment Abstracts. Bowker A & I Publishing, 121 Chanlon Rd., New Providence, New Jersey 07974. (908) 464-6800. 1974-.

Environment Index. Environment Information Center, Index Research Department, 124 E. 39th St., New York, New York 10016. 1971-. Annual.

Environmental Information Connection–EIC. Planning Information Program, Dept. of Urban and Regional Planning, University of Illinois, 1003 West Nevada, Urbana, Illinois 61801. (217) 333-1369. Also available online.

Environmental Periodicals Bibliography. Environmental Studies Institute, International Academy at Santa Barbara, 800 Garden St., Suite D, Santa Barbara, California 93101. (805) 965-5010. Also available online.

General Science Index. H. W. Wilson Co., 950 University Ave., Bronx, New York 10452. 1978-. Monthly, also issued in annual cumulation. Cumulative subject index to English language periodicals in the subject fields of astronomy, botany, chemistry, earth science, environment and conservation, food and nutrition, genetics, mathematics, medicine and health, microbiology, oceanography, physics, physiology and zoology.

Index to Scientific Book Contents. Institute for Scientific Information, 3501 Market St., Philadelphia, Pennsylvania 19104. (800) 523-1857. 1985-. Annual. Gives contents of science books published.

Multimedia Index to Ecology. National Information Center for Educational Media, University of Southern California, Los Angeles, California 90007.

Science Citation Index. Institute for Scientific Information, 3501 Market St., Philadelphia, Pennsylvania 19104. 1961-.

BIBLIOGRAPHIES

Directory of Published Proceedings. Interdok Corp., 173 Halstead Ave., Harrison, New York 10528. (914) 835-3506. 1990. Monthly. This is a listing of published proceedings including the series SEMTE (Science/Medicine/Engineering/Technology) and the series SSH (Social Science/Humanities).

EPA Publications Bibliography. U.S. Environmental Protection Agency, Library Systems Branch, 401 M St., SW, Washington, District of Columbia 20460. (202) 260-2090. Quarterly.

ENCYCLOPEDIAS AND DICTIONARIES

McGraw-Hill Encyclopedia of Environmental Science. Sybil P. Parker. McGraw-Hill Science & Engineering Books, 11 W. 19th St., New York, New York 10011. (212) 337-6010. 1980. Covers ecology, man's influence on nature, and environmental protection.

McGraw-Hill Encyclopedia of Science and Technology. McGraw-Hill, 1221 Avenue of the Americas, New York, New York 10020. (212) 512-2000 or (800) 262-4729. 1992. Seventh edition. Issued in multiple volumes including index. Includes all science and technology broad subject areas.

Van Nostrand's Scientific Encyclopedia. Glenn D. Considine, ed. Van Nostrand Reinhold, 115 5th Ave., New York, New York 10003. (212) 254-3232. 1983. Sixth edition. Includes all broad subject areas in science.

GENERAL WORKS

Southern Exposure: Deciding Antarctica's Future. Lee A. Kimball. World Resources Institute, 1709 New York Ave. N.W., Washington, District of Columbia 20006. (800) 822-0504. 1990. Reviews Antarctica's importance from a global perspective.

GOVERNMENTAL ORGANIZATIONS

National Science Foundation. 1800 G St., N.W., Washington, District of Columbia 20550. (202) 357-9498.

ONLINE DATA BASES

Arctic Science and Technology Information System. Arctic Institute of North America, University of Calgary, 2500 University Dr., N.W., Calgary, Alberta, Canada T2N 1N4. (403) 220-4036.

BIOSIS Previews. BIOSIS, 2100 Arch St., Philadelphia, Pennsylvania 19103-1399. (215) 587-4800. Largest and most comprehensive database of research in the life sciences. Contains citations for nearly 9000 primary research journals, monographs, reviews, symposia, preliminary reports, semi-popular journals, selected institutional reports, government reports and research communications.

Cold. U.S. Army Corps of Engineers, Cold Regions Research and Engineering Laboratory, 22 Lyme Rd., Hanover, New Hampshire 03755-1290. (603) 646-4221.

Cold Regions. Library of Congress, Science & Technology Division, Cold Regions Bibliography Project, Washington, District of Columbia 20540. (202) 707-1181.

Enviro/Energyline Abstracts Plus. R. R. Bowker Co., 121 Chanlon Rd., New Providence, New Jersey 07974. (908) 464-6800.

Environmental Periodicals Bibliography. National Information Services Corp., Ste. 6, Wyman Towers, 3100 St. Paul St., Baltimore, Maryland 21218. (410)243-0797. Online version of abstract of same name.

Monthly Catalog of United States Government Publications. U.S. G.P.O., Supt. of Docs., PO Box 371954, Pittsburgh, Pennsylvania 15250-7954. (202) 512-0000.

National Technical Information Service. U.S. Department of Commerce, National Technical Information Service, Office of Data Base Services, 5285 Port Royal Rd., Springfield, Virginia 22161. (703) 487-4807. Bibliographic database of government sponsored research and technical reports.

SCISEARCH. Institute for Scientific Information, University City Science Center, 3501 Market St., Philadelphia, Pennsylvania 19104. (215) 386-0100.

TRADE ASSOCIATIONS AND PROFESSIONAL SOCIETIES

The Antarctica Project. 218 D St., S.E., Washington, District of Columbia 20003. (202) 544-2600.

Arctic Institute of North America. 2500 University Dr., N.W., University of Calgary, Calgary, Alberta, Canada T2N 1N4. (403) 220-7515.

International Antarctic Glaciological Project. Geophysical and Polar Research Center, University of Wisconsin, Madison, Wisconsin 53706. (608) 262-1921.

U.S. Antarctic Research Program. Polar Information Program, National Science Foundation, Washington, District of Columbia 20550. (202) 357-7817.

ANTHRACITE

See: COAL

ANTIBIOTICS

See also: BACTERIA; FUNGI

ABSTRACTING AND INDEXING SERVICES

Biological Abstracts. BIOSIS, 2100 Arch St., Philadelphia, Pennsylvania 19103-1399. (215) 587-4800. 1927-.

Environment Abstracts. Bowker A & I Publishing, 121 Chanlon Rd., New Providence, New Jersey 07974. (908) 464-6800. 1974-.

Environment Index. Environment Information Center, Index Research Department, 124 E. 39th St., New York, New York 10016. 1971-. Annual.

Environmental Information Connection–EIC. Planning Information Program, Dept. of Urban and Regional Planning, University of Illinois, 1003 West Nevada,

Urbana, Illinois 61801. (217) 333-1369. Also available online.

Environmental Periodicals Bibliography. Environmental Studies Institute, International Academy at Santa Barbara, 800 Garden St., Suite D, Santa Barbara, California 93101. (805) 965-5010. Also available online.

Food Science and Technology Abstracts. International Food Information Service, c/o National Food Laboratory, 6363 Clark Ave., Dublin, California 94568. (800) 336-3782. 1969-.

General Science Index. H. W. Wilson Co., 950 University Ave., Bronx, New York 10452. 1978-. Monthly, also issued in annual cumulation. Cumulative subject index to English language periodicals in the subject fields of astronomy, botany, chemistry, earth science, environment and conservation, food and nutrition, genetics, mathematics, medicine and health, microbiology, oceanography, physics, physiology and zoology.

Pollution Abstracts. Cambridge Scientific Abstracts, 5161 River Rd., Bethesda, Maryland 20816. (301) 961-6750. Six/year. Indexes worldwide technical literature on environmental pollution. Covers air pollution, marine and freshwater pollution, sewage and wastewater treatment, waste management, toxicology and health, noise pollution, radiation, land pollution, and environmental policies, programs, legislation, and education. Also available online.

Science Citation Index. Institute for Scientific Information, 3501 Market St., Philadelphia, Pennsylvania 19104. 1961-.

BIBLIOGRAPHIES

EPA Publications Bibliography. U.S. Environmental Protection Agency, Library Systems Branch, 401 M St., SW, Washington, District of Columbia 20460. (202) 260-2090. Quarterly.

ENCYCLOPEDIAS AND DICTIONARIES

Dictionary of Antibiotics and Related Substances. Chapman & Hall, 29 West 35th St., New York, New York 10001-2291. (212) 244-3336. 1988.

Dictionary of Biotechnology. J. Coombs. Elsevier Science Publishing Co., 655 Avenue of the Americas, New York, New York 10010. (212) 984-5800. 1986. Areas covered in this dictionary include: fermentation; brewing; vaccines; plant tissue; culture; antibiotic production; production and use of enzymes; biomass; byproduct recovery and effluent treatment; equipment; processes; micro-organisms and biochemicals.

Encyclopedia of Human Biology. Renato Dulbecco, ed. Academic Press, c/o Harcourt Brace Jovanovich Inc., 6277 Sea Harbor Dr., Orlando, Florida 32887. (800) 346-8648. 1991. Eight volumes.

Encyclopedia of Terpenoids. John S. Glasby. John Wiley & Sons, Inc., 605 3rd Ave., New York, New York 10158-0012. (212) 850-6000. 1982. Two volumes. Compendium of organic compounds found in nature, embracing a wide range of substances from the simple monoterpenoids to the highly complex triterpenoids and cartenoids, which are used in perfumes, antibiotics, cytotoxic agents and antifeedeants. Covers literature to the end of 1979.

McGraw-Hill Encyclopedia of Science and Technology. McGraw-Hill, 1221 Avenue of the Americas, New York, New York 10020. (212) 512-2000 or (800) 262-4729. 1992. Seventh edition. Issued in multiple volumes including index. Includes all science and technology broad subject areas.

ONLINE DATA BASES

BIOSIS Previews. BIOSIS, 2100 Arch St., Philadelphia, Pennsylvania 19103-1399. (215) 587-4800. Largest and most comprehensive database of research in the life sciences. Contains citations for nearly 9000 primary research journals, monographs, reviews, symposia, preliminary reports, semi-popular journals, selected institutional reports, government reports and research communications.

Enviro/Energyline Abstracts Plus. R. R. Bowker Co., 121 Chanlon Rd., New Providence, New Jersey 07974. (908) 464-6800.

Environmental Periodicals Bibliography. National Information Services Corp., Ste. 6, Wyman Towers, 3100 St. Paul St., Baltimore, Maryland 21218. (410)243-0797. Online version of abstract of same name.

ANTIDOTE

See: TOXICOLOGY

ANTIFUNGAL

See: FUNGICIDES

ANTIMONY

See: METALS AND METALLURGY

APHIDS

See also: INSECTS; INSECTICIDES

ABSTRACTING AND INDEXING SERVICES

Applied Ecology Abstracts Studies in Renewable Natural Resources. Information Retrieval Ltd., 1911 Jefferson Davis Highway, Arlington, Virginia 22202. 1975-. Monthly.

Biological Abstracts. BIOSIS, 2100 Arch St., Philadelphia, Pennsylvania 19103-1399. (215) 587-4800. 1927-.

Biological and Agricultural Index. H.W. Wilson Co., 950 University Ave., Bronx, New York 10452. (800) 367-6770. 1916-. Monthly.

Ecological Abstracts. Geo Abstracts Ltd. Elsevier Applied Science, Crown House, Linton Rd., Barking, England IG 11 8JU. 1974-. Derived from over 600 leading ecological and environmental journals, plus books, conference proceedings, reports and theses.

Environment Abstracts. Bowker A & I Publishing, 121 Chanlon Rd., New Providence, New Jersey 07974. (908) 464-6800. 1974-.

Environment Index. Environment Information Center, Index Research Department, 124 E. 39th St., New York, New York 10016. 1971-. Annual.

Environmental Information Connection–EIC. Planning Information Program, Dept. of Urban and Regional Planning, University of Illinois, 1003 West Nevada, Urbana, Illinois 61801. (217) 333-1369. Also available online.

Environmental Periodicals Bibliography. Environmental Studies Institute, International Academy at Santa Barbara, 800 Garden St., Suite D, Santa Barbara, California 93101. (805) 965-5010. Also available online.

General Science Index. H. W. Wilson Co., 950 University Ave., Bronx, New York 10452. 1978-. Monthly, also issued in annual cumulation. Cumulative subject index to English language periodicals in the subject fields of astronomy, botany, chemistry, earth science, environment and conservation, food and nutrition, genetics, mathematics, medicine and health, microbiology, oceanography, physics, physiology and zoology.

Multimedia Index to Ecology. National Information Center for Educational Media, University of Southern California, Los Angeles, California 90007.

Science Citation Index. Institute for Scientific Information, 3501 Market St., Philadelphia, Pennsylvania 19104. 1961-.

BIBLIOGRAPHIES

EPA Publications Bibliography. U.S. Environmental Protection Agency, Library Systems Branch, 401 M St., SW, Washington, District of Columbia 20460. (202) 260-2090. Quarterly.

ENCYCLOPEDIAS AND DICTIONARIES

McGraw-Hill Encyclopedia of Science and Technology. McGraw-Hill, 1221 Avenue of the Americas, New York, New York 10020. (212) 512-2000 or (800) 262-4729. 1992. Seventh edition. Issued in multiple volumes including index. Includes all science and technology broad subject areas.

Van Nostrand's Scientific Encyclopedia. Glenn D. Considine, ed. Van Nostrand Reinhold, 115 5th Ave., New York, New York 10003. (212) 254-3232. 1983. Sixth edition. Includes all broad subject areas in science.

ONLINE DATA BASES

BIOSIS Previews. BIOSIS, 2100 Arch St., Philadelphia, Pennsylvania 19103-1399. (215) 587-4800. Largest and most comprehensive database of research in the life sciences. Contains citations for nearly 9000 primary research journals, monographs, reviews, symposia, preliminary reports, semi-popular journals, selected institutional reports, government reports and research communications.

Enviro/Energyline Abstracts Plus. R. R. Bowker Co., 121 Chanlon Rd., New Providence, New Jersey 07974. (908) 464-6800.

Environmental Periodicals Bibliography. National Information Services Corp., Ste. 6, Wyman Towers, 3100 St. Paul St., Baltimore, Maryland 21218. (410)243-0797. Online version of abstract of same name.

SCISEARCH. Institute for Scientific Information, University City Science Center, 3501 Market St., Philadelphia, Pennsylvania 19104. (215) 386-0100.

APPROPRIATE TECHNOLOGY

See also: TECHNOLOGY AND THE ENVIRONMENT

ABSTRACTING AND INDEXING SERVICES

Applied Science and Technology Index. H.W. Wilson Co., 950 University Ave., Bronx, New York 10452. (800) 367-6770. Formerly Industrial Arts Index.

Environment Abstracts. Bowker A & I Publishing, 121 Chanlon Rd., New Providence, New Jersey 07974. (908) 464-6800. 1974-.

Environment Index. Environment Information Center, Index Research Department, 124 E. 39th St., New York, New York 10016. 1971-. Annual.

Environmental Information Connection–EIC. Planning Information Program, Dept. of Urban and Regional Planning, University of Illinois, 1003 West Nevada, Urbana, Illinois 61801. (217) 333-1369. Also available online.

Environmental Periodicals Bibliography. Environmental Studies Institute, International Academy at Santa Barbara, 800 Garden St., Suite D, Santa Barbara, California 93101. (805) 965-5010. Also available online.

Science Citation Index. Institute for Scientific Information, 3501 Market St., Philadelphia, Pennsylvania 19104. 1961-.

BIBLIOGRAPHIES

EPA Publications Bibliography. U.S. Environmental Protection Agency, Library Systems Branch, 401 M St., SW, Washington, District of Columbia 20460. (202) 260-2090. Quarterly.

ENCYCLOPEDIAS AND DICTIONARIES

Dictionary of Environmental Engineering and Related Sciences: English-Spanish, Spanish-English. Jose T. Villate. Ediciones Universal, 3090 SW 8th St., Miami, Florida 33135. (305) 642-3355. 1979.

Encyclopedia of Environmental Science and Engineering. J.R. Pfafflin. Gordon and Breach Science Publishers, Inc., 270 8th Ave., New York, New York 10011. (212) 206-8900. 1992.

Encyclopedia of Physical Science and Technology. Robert A. Meyers, ed. Academic Press, c/o Harcourt Brace Jovanovich Inc., 6277 Sea Harbor Dr., Orlando, Florida 32887. (800) 346-8648. Dictionary of engineering, technology and physical sciences.

ONLINE DATA BASES

Enviro/Energyline Abstracts Plus. R. R. Bowker Co., 121 Chanlon Rd., New Providence, New Jersey 07974. (908) 464-6800.

Environmental Periodicals Bibliography. National Information Services Corp., Ste. 6, Wyman Towers, 3100 St. Paul St., Baltimore, Maryland 21218. (410)243-0797. Online version of abstract of same name.

SCISEARCH. Institute for Scientific Information, University City Science Center, 3501 Market St., Philadelphia, Pennsylvania 19104. (215) 386-0100.

TRADE ASSOCIATIONS AND PROFESSIONAL SOCIETIES

American Institute of Chemical Engineers. 345 East 47th St., New York, New York 10017. (212) 705-7338.

American Institute of Chemists. 7315 Wisconsin Ave., Bethesda, Maryland 20814. (301) 652-2447.

AQUACULTURE

See also: CRAYFISH; FISH AND FISHERIES; SHRIMP AND SHRIMP FISHERIES

ABSTRACTING AND INDEXING SERVICES

Agricultural Engineering Abstracts. C. A. B. International, 845 North Park Ave., Tucson, Arizona 85719. (602) 621-7897 or (800) 528-4841. 1976-. Monthly. Informs about significant research developments in agricultural engineering and instrumentation. Some of the topics scanned for the abstracts include mechanical power, crop production, crop harvesting and threshing, crop processing and storage, aquaculture, land improvement, protected cultivation, handling and transport, and farm buildings and equipment.

Applied Ecology Abstracts Studies in Renewable Natural Resources. Information Retrieval Ltd., 1911 Jefferson Davis Highway, Arlington, Virginia 22202. 1975-. Monthly.

Aqualine Abstracts. Water Research Centre. c/o Pergamon Microforms International, Inc., Fairview Park, Elmsford, New York 10523. (914) 592-7720. 1927-. Contains some 8,000 records annually on water and wastewater technology. Covers all aspects of water, wastewater, associated engineering services and the aquatic environment. Over 600 periodicals, as well as books, reports and conference proceedings and other publications from water related institutions worldwide are scanned. Also available online.

Aquatic Sciences and Fisheries Abstracts. Cambridge Scientific Abstracts, 5161 River Rd., Bethesda, Maryland 20816. (301) 961-6750. Monthly. Compiled by the United Nations Dept. of Economic and Social Affairs, the Food and Agriculture Organization of the United Nations and the Intergovernmental Oceanographic Commission with the collaboration of other agencies. Includes the broad subject areas of ecology, fisheries, marine biology, public policy, aquatic biology, and aquatic ecology.

ASFA Aquaculture Abstracts. Cambridge Scientific Abstracts, Inc., 5161 River Rd., Bethesda, Maryland 20816. (301) 961-6750. 1984.

Biological Abstracts. BIOSIS, 2100 Arch St., Philadelphia, Pennsylvania 19103-1399. (215) 587-4800. 1927-.

Biological and Agricultural Index. H.W. Wilson Co., 950 University Ave., Bronx, New York 10452. (800) 367-6770. 1916-. Monthly.

Biology Digest. Data Courier, Plexus Pub Inc., 143 Old Marlton Pike, Medford, New Jersey 08055. 1974-. Monthly. Abstracts biology periodicals.

Biotechnology Research Abstracts. Cambridge Scientific Abstracts, 5161 River Rd., Bethesda, Maryland 20816. (301) 961-6750. Monthly. Includes such broad areas as genetic intervention, biochemical genetics, and microbiological techniques.

Ecological Abstracts. Geo Abstracts Ltd. Elsevier Applied Science, Crown House, Linton Rd., Barking, England IG 11 8JU. 1974-. Derived from over 600 leading ecological and environmental journals, plus books, conference proceedings, reports and theses.

Ecology Abstracts. Cambridge Scientific Abstracts, 5161 River Rd., Bethesda, Maryland 20816. (301) 961-6750. Monthly.

Environment Abstracts. Bowker A & I Publishing, 121 Chanlon Rd., New Providence, New Jersey 07974. (908) 464-6800. 1974-.

Environment Index. Environment Information Center, Index Research Department, 124 E. 39th St., New York, New York 10016. 1971-. Annual.

Environmental Information Connection–EIC. Planning Information Program, Dept. of Urban and Regional Planning, University of Illinois, 1003 West Nevada, Urbana, Illinois 61801. (217) 333-1369. Also available online.

Environmental Periodicals Bibliography. Environmental Studies Institute, International Academy at Santa Barbara, 800 Garden St., Suite D, Santa Barbara, California 93101. (805) 965-5010. Also available online.

Fisheries Review. U.S. Fish and Wildlife Service. U.S. G.P.O., Washington, District of Columbia 20401. (202) 512-0000. Quarterly. Abstracting service dealing with fisheries and ichthyology.

General Science Index. H. W. Wilson Co., 950 University Ave., Bronx, New York 10452. 1978-. Monthly, also issued in annual cumulation. Cumulative subject index to English language periodicals in the subject fields of astronomy, botany, chemistry, earth science, environment and conservation, food and nutrition, genetics, mathematics, medicine and health, microbiology, oceanography, physics, physiology and zoology.

Index to Scientific Book Contents. Institute for Scientific Information, 3501 Market St., Philadelphia, Pennsylvania 19104. (800) 523-1857. 1985-. Annual. Gives contents of science books published.

Multimedia Index to Ecology. National Information Center for Educational Media, University of Southern California, Los Angeles, California 90007.

Science Citation Index. Institute for Scientific Information, 3501 Market St., Philadelphia, Pennsylvania 19104. 1961-.

Sea Grant Abstracts. National Sea Grant Depository, Pell Laboratory Bldg., Bay Campus, University of Rhode Island, Narragansett, Rhode Island 02882. (401) 792-

6114. 1986-. Quarterly. Published by the National Sea Grant Programs, this collection includes annual reports, serials and newsletters, charts and maps.

BIBLIOGRAPHIES

Current Contents. Agriculture, Biology and Environmental Sciences. Institute for Scientific Information, 3501 Market St., Philadelphia, Pennsylvania 19104. (800) 523-1857. 1973-. Previous title: Current Contents. Agricultural, Food & Veterinary Sciences. Gives the table of contents of periodicals in the fields of agriculture, biology, environmental and related areas.

Directory of Published Proceedings. Interdok Corp., 173 Halstead Ave., Harrison, New York 10528. (914) 835-3506. 1990. Monthly. This is a listing of published proceedings including the series SEMTE (Science/Medicine/Engineering/Technology) and the series SSH (Social Science/Humanities).

EPA Publications Bibliography. U.S. Environmental Protection Agency, Library Systems Branch, 401 M St., SW, Washington, District of Columbia 20460. (202) 260-2090. Quarterly.

An Interdisciplinary Bibliography of Freshwater Crayfishes. C. W. Hart, Jr. and Janice Clark. Smithsonian Institution Press, 470 L'Enfant Plaza, No. 7100, Washington, District of Columbia 20560. (800) 782-4612. 1987.

Water Quality in Agriculture. National Agricultural Library, 10301 Baltimore Blvd., Beltsville, Maryland 20705-2351. (301) 504-5755. 1990.

DIRECTORIES

The North American Directory of Aquaculture. Kevin Gordon, ed. Kevgor Aquasystems, PO Box 48851, 595 Burrard St., Vancouver, British Columbia, Canada V7X 1A8. (604) 681-2377. 1989/1990. Annual. Lists buyers and sellers of seafood in general. Includes participation listings, province/state listings, company listings, and future conferences.

ENCYCLOPEDIAS AND DICTIONARIES

Cambridge Encyclopedia of Life Sciences. A. E. Friday and David S. Ingram. Cambridge University Press, 40 W 20th St., New York, New York 10011. (212) 924-3900 or (800) 227-0247. 1985. Includes all topics under biology and ecology.

Illustrated Encyclopedia of Science and the Future. Mike Biscare, et al., ed. Marshall Cavendish, 58 Old Compton St., London, England 0W1V5 PA. 01-734 6710. 1983. Twenty volumes. Each volume has 5 sections: Frontiers, Electronics in Action, Medical Science, Military Technology, and Resources.

McGraw-Hill Encyclopedia of Environmental Science. Sybil P. Parker. McGraw-Hill Science & Engineering Books, 11 W. 19th St., New York, New York 10011. (212) 337-6010. 1980. Covers ecology, man's influence on nature, and environmental protection.

McGraw-Hill Encyclopedia of Science and Technology. McGraw-Hill, 1221 Avenue of the Americas, New York, New York 10020. (212) 512-2000 or (800) 262-4729. 1992. Seventh edition. Issued in multiple volumes in-

cluding index. Includes all science and technology broad subject areas.

Van Nostrand's Scientific Encyclopedia. Glenn D. Considine, ed. Van Nostrand Reinhold, 115 5th Ave., New York, New York 10003. (212) 254-3232. 1983. Sixth edition. Includes all broad subject areas in science.

GENERAL WORKS

Aquaculture Techniques: Water Use and Discharge Quality. George W. Klontz. Idaho Water Research Institute, University of Idaho, Moscow, Idaho 83843. Covers aquaculture techniques, fish culture, and effluent quality.

Biomass Production Anaerobic Digestion and Nutrient Recycling of Small Benthic or Floating Seaweeds. John H. Ryther. National Technical Information Service, 5285 Port Royal Rd., Springfield, Virginia 22161. (703) 487-4650. Environmental aspects of aquaculture.

ONLINE DATA BASES

AGRIS. Food and Agriculture Organization of the United Nations, Via delle Terme di Caracalla, Rome, Italy 00100. 61 0181-FA01.

Aquaculture. National Oceanic and Atmospheric Administration, National Environmental Data Referral Service, 1825 Connecticut Ave., N.W., Washington, District of Columbia 20235. (202) 673-5548.

Aqualine. Water Research Center, Medmenham Laboratory, Marlow, Buckinghamshire, England SL7 2HD. Literature on water and wastewater technology.

AQUAREF. Environment Canada, WATDOC, Inland Waters Directorate, Ottawa, Ontario, Canada K1A OH3. (819) 997-2324.

BIOSIS Previews. BIOSIS, 2100 Arch St., Philadelphia, Pennsylvania 19103-1399. (215) 587-4800. Largest and most comprehensive database of research in the life sciences. Contains citations for nearly 9000 primary research journals, monographs, reviews, symposia, preliminary reports, semi-popular journals, selected institutional reports, government reports and research communications.

Cambridge Scientific Abstracts Life Science–CSAL. Cambridge Scientific Abstracts, 5161 River Rd., Bethesda, Maryland 20816. (301) 961-6750. Provides access to the following abstracting services: "Life Sciences Collection," "Aquatic Sciences and Fisheries Abstracts," "Oceanic Abstracts," and "Pollution Abstracts."

Current Research Information System–CRIS/USDA. U.S. Department of Agriculture, National Agricultural Library, 10301 Baltimore Blvd., 5th Floor, Beltsville, Maryland 20705-2351. (301) 504-5755. Looks at current research projects in agriculture and allied sciences covering the biological, physical, social and behavioral sciences related to agriculture.

Enviro/Energyline Abstracts Plus. R. R. Bowker Co., 121 Chanlon Rd., New Providence, New Jersey 07974. (908) 464-6800.

Environmental Periodicals Bibliography. National Information Services Corp., Ste. 6, Wyman Towers, 3100 St. Paul St., Baltimore, Maryland 21218. (410)243-0797. Online version of abstract of same name.

FISHNET. Aquatic Data Center, 1100 Gentry St., North Kansas City, Missouri 64116. (816) 842-5936.

Life Sciences from NTIS. National Technical Information Center for the Utilization of Federal Technology, 5285 Port Royal Rd., Springfield, Virginia 22161. (703) 487-4650.

Monthly Catalog of United States Government Publications. U.S. G.P.O., Supt. of Docs., PO Box 371954, Pittsburgh, Pennsylvania 15250-7954. (202) 512-0000.

National Technical Information Service. U.S. Department of Commerce, National Technical Information Service, Office of Data Base Services, 5285 Port Royal Rd., Springfield, Virginia 22161. (703) 487-4807. Bibliographic database of government sponsored research and technical reports.

SCISEARCH. Institute for Scientific Information, University City Science Center, 3501 Market St., Philadelphia, Pennsylvania 19104. (215) 386-0100.

RESEARCH CENTERS AND INSTITUTES

Aquatic Research Institute. 2242 Davis Court, Hayward, California 94545. (415) 782-4058.

Auburn University, International Center for Aquaculture. Auburn, Alabama 36849-5124. (205) 826-4786.

Connecticut Sea Grant College Program. University of Connecticut at Avery Point, 1084 Schennecossett Rd., Groton, Connecticut 06340. (203) 445-5108.

Murray State University, Handcock Biological Station. Murray, Kentucky 42071. (502) 474-2272.

Ohio State University, Franz Theodore Stone Laboratory. 1541 Research Center, 1314 Kinnear Road, Columbus, Ohio 43212. (614) 292-8949.

Ohio State University, Ohio Sea Grant College Program. 1541 Research Center, 1314 Kinnear Road, Columbus, Ohio 43212. (614) 292-8949.

Rhode Island Sea Grant Marine Advisory Service. Narragansett Bay Campus, University of Rhode Island, Narragansett, Rhode Island 02882. (401) 792-6211.

Robert J. Bernard Biological Field Station. Claremont McKenna College, Claremont, California 91711. (714) 621-5425.

Rutgers University, Fisheries and Aquaculture Technology Extension Center. P.O. Box 231, New Brunswick, New Jersey 08903. (908) 932-8959.

Sea Grant College Program. University of Delaware, 196 South College Avenue, Newark, Delaware 19716. (302) 451-8182.

Texas A&M University, Sea Grant College Program. 1716 Briarcrest Dr., Ste. 702, College Station, Texas 77802. (409) 845-3854.

University of Alaska Fairbanks, Alaska Sea Grant College Program. 138 Irving II, Fairbanks, Alaska 99775-5040. (907) 474-7086.

University of Alaska Fairbanks, Seward Marine Center. P.O.Box 730, Seward, Alaska 99664. (907) 224-5261.

University of Arizona, Environmental Research Laboratory. Tucson International Airport, 2601 East Airport Drive, Tucson, Arizona 85706. (602) 741-1990.

University of Hawaii at Manoa Hawaii Institute of Marine Biology. Coconut Island, P.O. Box 1346, Kaneohe, Hawaii 96744-1346. (808) 236-7401.

University of Maine, Center for Marine Studies. 14 Coburn Hall, Orono, Maine 04469. (207) 581-1435.

University of Maine, Maine Sea Grant College Program. 14 Coburn Hall, University of Maine, Orono, Maine 04469-0114. (207) 581-1435.

University of Maryland, Center for Environmental and Estuarine Studies. Center Operations, Horn Point, P.O.Box 775, Cambridge, Maryland 21613. (410) 228-9250.

University of Minnesota, Bell Museum of Natural History. 10 Church St., S.E., Minneapolis, Minnesota 55455. (612) 624-4112.

University of Minnesota, Minnesota Sea Grant College Program. 1518 Cleveland Ave., Ste. 302, St. Paul, Minnesota 55108. (612) 625-9288.

University of New Hampshire, Anadromous Fish and Aquatic Invertebrate Research Facility. Marine Institute, Department of Zoology, Durham, New Hampshire 03824. (603) 862-2103.

University of Puerto Rico, Sea Grant College Program. Department of Marine Sciences, P.O. Box 5000, Mayaguez, Puerto Rico 00681-5000. (809) 832-3585.

University of Southern California, Fish Harbor Marine Research Laboratory. 820 South Seaside Avenue, Terminal Island, California 90731. (310) 830-4570.

University of Texas at Austin, Brues-Wheeler-Sellards Archives for Entomology and Paleoentomology. Texas Memorial Museum, 2400 Trinity Street, Austin, Texas 78705. (512) 471-4823.

TRADE ASSOCIATIONS AND PROFESSIONAL SOCIETIES

American Petroleum Institute. 1220 L St., N.W., Washington, District of Columbia 20005. (202) 682-8000.

Future Fisherman Foundation. 1250 Grove Ave., Ste. 300, Barrington, Illinois 60010. (708) 381-4061.

Hydroponic Society of America. P.O. Box 6067, Concord, California 94524. (415) 682-4193.

International Aquaculture Foundation. 2440 Virginia Ave., N.W., No. D305, Washington, District of Columbia 20037. (202) 785-8215.

Sea Grant Association. c/o Dr. Christopher F. D'Elia, Maryland Sea Grant College, 1123 Taliaferro Hall, UMCP, College Park, Maryland 20742. (301) 405-6371.

World Aquaculture Society. 143 J.M. Parker Coliseum, Louisiana State University, Baton Rouge, Louisiana 70803. (504) 388-3137.

AQUARIUMS

See also: AQUATIC ECOSYSTEMS

ABSTRACTING AND INDEXING SERVICES

Applied Ecology Abstracts Studies in Renewable Natural Resources. Information Retrieval Ltd., 1911 Jefferson Davis Highway, Arlington, Virginia 22202. 1975-. Monthly.

Biological Abstracts. BIOSIS, 2100 Arch St., Philadelphia, Pennsylvania 19103-1399. (215) 587-4800. 1927-.

Biological and Agricultural Index. H.W. Wilson Co., 950 University Ave., Bronx, New York 10452. (800) 367-6770. 1916-. Monthly.

Ecological Abstracts. Geo Abstracts Ltd. Elsevier Applied Science, Crown House, Linton Rd., Barking, England IG 11 8JU. 1974-. Derived from over 600 leading ecological and environmental journals, plus books, conference proceedings, reports and theses.

Ecology Abstracts. Cambridge Scientific Abstracts, 5161 River Rd., Bethesda, Maryland 20816. (301) 961-6750. Monthly.

Environment Abstracts. Bowker A & I Publishing, 121 Chanlon Rd., New Providence, New Jersey 07974. (908) 464-6800. 1974-.

Environment Index. Environment Information Center, Index Research Department, 124 E. 39th St., New York, New York 10016. 1971-. Annual.

Environmental Information Connection–EIC. Planning Information Program, Dept. of Urban and Regional Planning, University of Illinois, 1003 West Nevada, Urbana, Illinois 61801. (217) 333-1369. Also available online.

Environmental Periodicals Bibliography. Environmental Studies Institute, International Academy at Santa Barbara, 800 Garden St., Suite D, Santa Barbara, California 93101. (805) 965-5010. Also available online.

General Science Index. H. W. Wilson Co., 950 University Ave., Bronx, New York 10452. 1978-. Monthly, also issued in annual cumulation. Cumulative subject index to English language periodicals in the subject fields of astronomy, botany, chemistry, earth science, environment and conservation, food and nutrition, genetics, mathematics, medicine and health, microbiology, oceanography, physics, physiology and zoology.

Multimedia Index to Ecology. National Information Center for Educational Media, University of Southern California, Los Angeles, California 90007.

Science Citation Index. Institute for Scientific Information, 3501 Market St., Philadelphia, Pennsylvania 19104. 1961-.

BIBLIOGRAPHIES

EPA Publications Bibliography. U.S. Environmental Protection Agency, Library Systems Branch, 401 M St., SW, Washington, District of Columbia 20460. (202) 260-2090. Quarterly.

ENCYCLOPEDIAS AND DICTIONARIES

The Aquarium Encyclopedia. Gunther Sterba. MIT Press, 55 Hayward St., Cambridge, Massachusetts 02142. (617) 253-2884 or (800) 356-0343. 1983.

Dr. Axelrod's Atlas of Freshwater Aquarium Fishes. H. R. Axelrod, ed. TFH Publications, 1 TFH Plaza, Neptune City, New Jersey 07753. (908) 988-8400. 1989. Third edition. Identifies fish, their common names, scientific name, range, habitat, water condition, size and food requirement. Includes colored illustrations and 4500 photos in full color.

Dr. Burgess's Atlas of Marine Aquarium Fishes. W. E. Burgess, et al. TFH Publications, 1 TFH Plaza, Neptune City, New Jersey 07753. (908) 988-8400. 1988. Pictorial aid for identification of marine fishes. More than 400 photos in full color are included. Also includes scientific name and common name, food habits, size and habitat.

The Encyclopedia of Animal Ecology. Peter D. Moore. Facts on File, Inc., 460 Park Ave. S., New York, New York 10016. (212) 683-2244. 1987.

McGraw-Hill Encyclopedia of Environmental Science. Sybil P. Parker. McGraw-Hill Science & Engineering Books, 11 W. 19th St., New York, New York 10011. (212) 337-6010. 1980. Covers ecology, man's influence on nature, and environmental protection.

McGraw-Hill Encyclopedia of Science and Technology. McGraw-Hill, 1221 Avenue of the Americas, New York, New York 10020. (212) 512-2000 or (800) 262-4729. 1992. Seventh edition. Issued in multiple volumes including index. Includes all science and technology broad subject areas.

Van Nostrand's Scientific Encyclopedia. Glenn D. Considine, ed. Van Nostrand Reinhold, 115 5th Ave., New York, New York 10003. (212) 254-3232. 1983. Sixth edition. Includes all broad subject areas in science.

ONLINE DATA BASES

BIOSIS Previews. BIOSIS, 2100 Arch St., Philadelphia, Pennsylvania 19103-1399. (215) 587-4800. Largest and most comprehensive database of research in the life sciences. Contains citations for nearly 9000 primary research journals, monographs, reviews, symposia, preliminary reports, semi-popular journals, selected institutional reports, government reports and research communications.

Cambridge Scientific Abstracts Life Science–CSAL. Cambridge Scientific Abstracts, 5161 River Rd., Bethesda, Maryland 20816. (301) 961-6750. Provides access to the following abstracting services: "Life Sciences Collection," "Aquatic Sciences and Fisheries Abstracts," "Oceanic Abstracts," and "Pollution Abstracts."

Current Research Information System–CRIS/USDA. U.S. Department of Agriculture, National Agricultural Library, 10301 Baltimore Blvd., 5th Floor, Beltsville, Maryland 20705-2351. (301) 504-5755. Looks at current research projects in agriculture and allied sciences covering the biological, physical, social and behavioral sciences related to agriculture.

Enviro/Energyline Abstracts Plus. R. R. Bowker Co., 121 Chanlon Rd., New Providence, New Jersey 07974. (908) 464-6800.

Environmental Periodicals Bibliography. National Information Services Corp., Ste. 6, Wyman Towers, 3100 St. Paul St., Baltimore, Maryland 21218. (410)243-0797. Online version of abstract of same name.

Monthly Catalog of United States Government Publications. U.S. G.P.O., Supt. of Docs., PO Box 371954, Pittsburgh, Pennsylvania 15250-7954. (202) 512-0000.

National Technical Information Service. U.S. Department of Commerce, National Technical Information Service, Office of Data Base Services, 5285 Port Royal Rd., Springfield, Virginia 22161. (703) 487-4807. Bibliographic database of government sponsored research and technical reports.

SCISEARCH. Institute for Scientific Information, University City Science Center, 3501 Market St., Philadelphia, Pennsylvania 19104. (215) 386-0100.

AQUATIC BIOMES

See also: AQUATIC ECOSYSTEMS

GENERAL WORKS

Cache la Poudre: The Natural History of Rocky Mountain River. Howard Ensign Evans and Mary Alice Evans. University Press of Colorado, PO Box 849, Niwot, Colorado 80544. (303) 530-5337. 1991. Includes a summary of the ecological and cultural values of the river corridor. Describes the corridor's flora, fauna, geology, insects, people and history.

Wetland Creation and Restoration: The Status of the Science. Jon A. Kusler and Mary E. Kentula, eds. Island Press, 1718 Connecticut Ave. N.W., Suite 300, Washington, District of Columbia 20009. (202) 232-7933. 1990. Eighty papers from leading scientists and technicians draw upon important new information and provide assessment by region of the capacity to implement a goal of no-net-loss of wetlands.

Wetlands: A Threatened Landscape. Michael Williams. B. Blackwell, 3 Cambridge Ctr., Suite 208, Cambridge, Massachusetts 02142. (617) 225-0401. 1990. Explores the evolution and composition of wetlands and their physical and biological dynamics, considers the impact of agriculture, industry, urbanization, and recreation upon them, and examines what steps we are taking and what steps should be considered to manage and preserve wetlands.

Wetlands: Mitigating and Regulating Development Impacts. David Salvesen. The Urban Land Institute, 1090 Vermont Ave. N.W., Washington, District of Columbia 20005. (202) 289-8500; (800) 237-9196. 1990. Presents the latest examination of the conflicts surrounding development of wetlands. Explains both federal and state wetland regulations. Included is an up-to-date review of important wetlands case law and a detailed look at six of the toughest state programs.

PERIODICALS AND NEWSLETTERS

Applied and Environmental Microbiology Journal. American Society for Microbiology, 1325 Massachusetts Avenue N.W., Washington, District of Columbia 20005. (202) 737-3600. Monthly. Articles on industrial and food microbiology and ecological studies.

RESEARCH CENTERS AND INSTITUTES

Oregon State University, Oak Creek Laboratory of Biology. Department of Fisheries and Wildlife, 104 Nash Hall, Corvallis, Oregon 97331. (503) 737-3503.

University of Iowa, Iowa Lakeside Laboratory. R.R. 2, Box 305, Milford, Iowa 51351. (712) 337-3669.

University of Kansas, John H. Nelson Environmental Study Area. Division of Biological Sciences, Lawrence, Kansas 66045. (913) 864-3236.

University of Louisville, Water Resource Laboratory. Louisville, Kentucky 40292. (502) 588-6731.

University of Michigan, School of Natural Resources, Research Service. 430 East University, Ann Arbor, Michigan 48109. (313) 764-6823.

University of Minnesota, Cedar Creek Natural History Area. 2660 Fawn Lake Drive NE, Bethel, Minnesota 55005. (612) 434-5131.

University of Oklahoma, Aquatic Biology Center. Zoology Department, 730 Van Vleet Oval, Norman, Oklahoma 73019. (405) 325-1058.

AQUATIC COMMUNITIES

See also: AQUATIC ECOSYSTEMS; FRESHWATER ECOSYSTEMS; MARINE ENVIRONMENTS AND ECOSYSTEMS

ABSTRACTING AND INDEXING SERVICES

Abstracts of Air and Water Conservation Literature. American Petroleum Institute. Central Abstracting and Indexing Service, 275 Madison Avenue, New York, New York 10016. 1972.

Fisheries Review. U.S. Fish and Wildlife Service. U.S. G.P.O., Washington, District of Columbia 20401. (202) 512-0000. Quarterly. Abstracting service dealing with fisheries and ichthyology.

Pollution Abstracts. Cambridge Scientific Abstracts, 5161 River Rd., Bethesda, Maryland 20816. (301) 961-6750. Six/year. Indexes worldwide technical literature on environmental pollution. Covers air pollution, marine and freshwater pollution, sewage and wastewater treatment, waste management, toxicology and health, noise pollution, radiation, land pollution, and environmental policies, programs, legislation, and education. Also available online.

GENERAL WORKS

Aquatic Toxicology. Jerome O. Nriagu. John Wiley & Sons, Inc., 605 3rd Ave., New York, New York 10158-0012. (212) 850-6000. 1989.

Carcinogenic, Mutagenic, and Teratogenic Marine Pollutants. Portfolio Publishing Co., P.O. Box 7802, The Woodlands, Texas 77381. (713) 363-3577. 1990. Effects of marine pollution on aquatic organisms as well as human beings.

Life History and Ecology of the Slider Turtle. J. Whitfield Gibbons. Smithsonian Institution Press, 470 L'Enfant Plaza #7100, Washington, District of Columbia 20560. (800) 782-4612. 1990. Deals with all that is known about a species, its taxonomic status and genetics, reproduction and growth, population structure and demography, population ecology, and bioenergetics.

Turtles of the World. Carl H. Ernst and Roger W. Barbour. Smithsonian Institution Press, 470 L'Enfant Plaza #7100, Washington, District of Columbia 20560. (800) 782-4612. 1989. Comprehensive coverage of the world's 257 turtle species.

Wetland Creation and Restoration: The Status of the Science. Jon A. Kusler and Mary E. Kentula, eds. Island

Press, 1718 Connecticut Ave. N.W., Suite 300, Washington, District of Columbia 20009. (202) 232-7933. 1990. Eighty papers from leading scientists and technicians draw upon important new information and provide assessment by region of the capacity to implement a goal of no-net-loss of wetlands.

PERIODICALS AND NEWSLETTERS

Aquasphere. New England Aquarium, Central Wharf, Boston, Massachusetts 02110. (617) 742-8830. 1963. Articles on any subject related to the world of water. Emphasis on ecology, environment, and aquatic animals.

Aquatic Toxicology. Elsevier Science Publishing Co., 655 Avenue of the Americas, New York, New York 10010. (212) 989-5800. 1981-. 6/year.

Ecology USA. Business Publishers, Inc., 951 Pershing Dr., Silver Spring, Maryland 20910-4464. (301) 587-6300. 1972-. Biweekly. Contains all the legislation, regulation, and litigation affecting efforts to conserve and protect America's unique environmental and ecological heritage.

Facets of Freshwater. Freshwater Biological Research Foundation, 2500 Shadywood Rd., Box 90, Navarre, Minnesota 55392. (612) 471-8407. 1970-. Quarterly. Topics in freshwater biological research.

RESEARCH CENTERS AND INSTITUTES

University of Kansas, Museum of Natural History. Dyche Hall, Lawrence, Kansas 66045. (913) 864-4541.

TRADE ASSOCIATIONS AND PROFESSIONAL SOCIETIES

American Institute of Biological Sciences. 730 11th St., N.W., Washington, District of Columbia 20001-4521. (202) 628-1500.

American Society of Naturalists. Department of Ecology and Evolation, State University of New York, Stony Brook, New York 11794. (516) 632-8589.

AQUATIC ECOSYSTEMS

See also: ECOSYSTEMS; FRESHWATER ECOSYSTEMS; MARINE ENVIRONMENT AND ECOSYSTEMS; WETLANDS

ABSTRACTING AND INDEXING SERVICES

Abstracts of Air and Water Conservation Literature. American Petroleum Institute. Central Abstracting and Indexing Service, 275 Madison Avenue, New York, New York 10016. 1972.

Applied Ecology Abstracts Studies in Renewable Natural Resources. Information Retrieval Ltd., 1911 Jefferson Davis Highway, Arlington, Virginia 22202. 1975-. Monthly.

Aqualine Abstracts. Water Research Centre. c/o Pergamon Microforms International, Inc., Fairview Park, Elmsford, New York 10523. (914) 592-7720. 1927-. Contains some 8,000 records annually on water and wastewater technology. Covers all aspects of water, wastewater, associated engineering services and the aquatic environment. Over 600 periodicals, as well as books, reports and conference proceedings and other

publications from water related institutions worldwide are scanned. Also available online.

Aquatic Sciences and Fisheries Abstracts. Cambridge Scientific Abstracts, 5161 River Rd., Bethesda, Maryland 20816. (301) 961-6750. Monthly. Compiled by the United Nations Dept. of Economic and Social Affairs, the Food and Agriculture Organization of the United Nations and the Intergovernmental Oceanographic Commission with the collaboration of other agencies. Includes the broad subject areas of ecology, fisheries, marine biology, public policy, aquatic biology, and aquatic ecology.

ASFA Aquaculture Abstracts. Cambridge Scientific Abstracts, Inc., 5161 River Rd., Bethesda, Maryland 20816. (301) 961-6750. 1984.

Biological Abstracts. BIOSIS, 2100 Arch St., Philadelphia, Pennsylvania 19103-1399. (215) 587-4800. 1927-.

Biological and Agricultural Index. H.W. Wilson Co., 950 University Ave., Bronx, New York 10452. (800) 367-6770. 1916-. Monthly.

Biology Digest. Data Courier, Plexus Pub Inc., 143 Old Marlton Pike, Medford, New Jersey 08055. 1974-. Monthly. Abstracts biology periodicals.

Biotechnology Research Abstracts. Cambridge Scientific Abstracts, 5161 River Rd., Bethesda, Maryland 20816. (301) 961-6750. Monthly. Includes such broad areas as genetic intervention, biochemical genetics, and microbiological techniques.

Current Advances in Ecological and Environmental Science. Pergamon Microforms International, Inc., Fairview Park, Elmsford, New York 10523. (914) 592-7720. 1989-. Monthly. Current literature searching service includingjournals, reports, abstracts, etc. This service is available online as part of the CABS database on the hosts BRS and ORBIT search service.

Ecological Abstracts. Geo Abstracts Ltd. Elsevier Applied Science, Crown House, Linton Rd., Barking, England IG 11 8JU. 1974-. Derived from over 600 leading ecological and environmental journals, plus books, conference proceedings, reports and theses.

Ecology Abstracts. Cambridge Scientific Abstracts, 5161 River Rd., Bethesda, Maryland 20816. (301) 961-6750. Monthly.

Environment Abstracts. Bowker A & I Publishing, 121 Chanlon Rd., New Providence, New Jersey 07974. (908) 464-6800. 1974-.

Environment Index. Environment Information Center, Index Research Department, 124 E. 39th St., New York, New York 10016. 1971-. Annual.

Environmental Information Connection–EIC. Planning Information Program, Dept. of Urban and Regional Planning, University of Illinois, 1003 West Nevada, Urbana, Illinois 61801. (217) 333-1369. Also available online.

Environmental Periodicals Bibliography. Environmental Studies Institute, International Academy at Santa Barbara, 800 Garden St., Suite D, Santa Barbara, California 93101. (805) 965-5010. Also available online.

Fisheries Review. U.S. Fish and Wildlife Service. U.S. G.P.O., Washington, District of Columbia 20401. (202) 512-0000. Quarterly. Abstracting service dealing with fisheries and ichthyology.

General Science Index. H. W. Wilson Co., 950 University Ave., Bronx, New York 10452. 1978-. Monthly, also issued in annual cumulation. Cumulative subject index to English language periodicals in the subject fields of astronomy, botany, chemistry, earth science, environment and conservation, food and nutrition, genetics, mathematics, medicine and health, microbiology, oceanography, physics, physiology and zoology.

Index to Scientific Book Contents. Institute for Scientific Information, 3501 Market St., Philadelphia, Pennsylvania 19104. (800) 523-1857. 1985-. Annual. Gives contents of science books published.

INIS Atomindex. International Atomic Energy Agency, Wagramerstrasse 5, Vienna, Austria A-1400. 222 23606198. 1988-. Semiannual. Abstracts nuclear energy and nuclear physics topics from journals, conferences, technical reports and other related publications. Issued in 6 parts: Personal Author, Corporate Entry, Subject, Report, Standard Patent, Conference (by place), Conference (by date).

Multimedia Index to Ecology. National Information Center for Educational Media, University of Southern California, Los Angeles, California 90007.

Pollution Abstracts. Cambridge Scientific Abstracts, 5161 River Rd., Bethesda, Maryland 20816. (301) 961-6750. Six/year. Indexes worldwide technical literature on environmental pollution. Covers air pollution, marine and freshwater pollution, sewage and wastewater treatment, waste management, toxicology and health, noise pollution, radiation, land pollution, and environmental policies, programs, legislation, and education. Also available online.

Science Citation Index. Institute for Scientific Information, 3501 Market St., Philadelphia, Pennsylvania 19104. 1961-.

Sea Grant Abstracts. National Sea Grant Depository, Pell Laboratory Bldg., Bay Campus, University of Rhode Island, Narragansett, Rhode Island 02882. (401) 792-6114. 1986-. Quarterly. Published by the National Sea Grant Programs, this collection includes annual reports, serials and newsletters, charts and maps.

BIBLIOGRAPHIES

Current Contents. Agriculture, Biology and Environmental Sciences. Institute for Scientific Information, 3501 Market St., Philadelphia, Pennsylvania 19104. (800) 523-1857. 1973-. Previous title: Current Contents. Agricultural, Food & Veterinary Sciences. Gives the table of contents of periodicals in the fields of agriculture, biology, environmental and related areas.

Directory of Published Proceedings. Interdok Corp., 173 Halstead Ave., Harrison, New York 10528. (914) 835-3506. 1990. Monthly. This is a listing of published proceedings including the series SEMTE (Science/Medicine/Engineering/Technology) and the series SSH (Social Science/Humanities).

EPA Publications Bibliography. U.S. Environmental Protection Agency, Library Systems Branch, 401 M St., SW, Washington, District of Columbia 20460. (202) 260-2090. Quarterly.

DIRECTORIES

Ecological Society of America Bulletin–Directory of Members Issue. Ecological Society of America, c/o Dr. Duncan Patten, Center for Environmental Studies, Arizona State University, Tempe, Arizona 85287. (602) 965-3000.

ENCYCLOPEDIAS AND DICTIONARIES

Cambridge Encyclopedia of Life Sciences. A. E. Friday and David S. Ingram. Cambridge University Press, 40 W 20th St., New York, New York 10011. (212) 924-3900 or (800) 227-0247. 1985. Includes all topics under biology and ecology.

The Encyclopedia of Animal Ecology. Peter D. Moore. Facts on File, Inc., 460 Park Ave. S., New York, New York 10016. (212) 683-2244. 1987.

Grzimek's Encyclopedia of Ecology. Bernhard Grzimek. Van Nostrand Reinhold, 115 5th Ave., New York, New York 10003. (212) 254-3232. 1976.

McGraw-Hill Encyclopedia of Environmental Science. Sybil P. Parker. McGraw-Hill Science & Engineering Books, 11 W. 19th St., New York, New York 10011. (212) 337-6010. 1980. Covers ecology, man's influence on nature, and environmental protection.

McGraw-Hill Encyclopedia of Science and Technology. McGraw-Hill, 1221 Avenue of the Americas, New York, New York 10020. (212) 512-2000 or (800) 262-4729. 1992. Seventh edition. Issued in multiple volumes including index. Includes all science and technology broad subject areas.

North American Reference Encyclopedia of Ecology and Pollution. William White. North American Pub. Co., 401 N. Broad St., Philadelphia, Pennsylvania 19108. (215) 238-5300. 1972.

Van Nostrand's Scientific Encyclopedia. Glenn D. Considine, ed. Van Nostrand Reinhold, 115 5th Ave., New York, New York 10003. (212) 254-3232. 1983. Sixth edition. Includes all broad subject areas in science.

GENERAL WORKS

Acidic Deposition and Aquatic Ecosystems. D. F. Charles and S. Christie, eds. Springer-Verlag, 175 5th Ave., New York, New York 10010. (212) 460-1500. 1991. Comprehensive integrated synthesis of available information on current and potential effects of acidic precipitation on lakes and streams in different geographic regions of the U.S. Examines the current status of water chemistry.

Alternatives in Regulated River Management. J. A. Gore and G. E. Petts, eds. CRC Press, 2000 Corporate Blvd. N.W., Boca Raton, Florida 33431. (800) 272-7737. 1989. Provides an alternative to the emphasis on ecological effects of river regulation and is a source of alternatives for managerial decision making.

Aquatic Chemistry Concepts. James F. Pankow. Lewis Publishers, 2000 Corporate Blvd., N.W., Boca Raton, Florida 33431. (407) 994-0555 or (800) 272-7737. 1991. A basic book on water chemistry and the concepts accompanying it. Discusses thermodynamic principles, quantitative equilibrium calculations, pH as a master variable, titration of acids and bases, and other related areas.

Aquatic Toxicology. Jerome O. Nriagu. John Wiley & Sons, Inc., 605 3rd Ave., New York, New York 10158-0012. (212) 850-6000. 1989.

Better Trout Habitat. Christopher J. Hunter. Island Press, 1718 Connecticut Ave. N.W., Suite 300, Washington, District of Columbia 20009. (202) 232-7933. 1991. Explains the physical, chemical and biological needs of trout, and shows how climate, geology, vegetation, and flowing water all help to create trout habitats. Book includes 14 detailed case studies of successful trout stream restoration projects.

The Biology of Particles in Aquatic Systems. Roger S. Wotton, ed. CRC Press, 2000 Corporate Blvd. N.W., Boca Raton, Florida 33431. (407) 994-0555; (800) 272-7737. 1990. Discusses the classification of particulate and dissolved material and sampling for these materials.

Cache la Poudre: The Natural History of Rocky Mountain River. Howard Ensign Evans and Mary Alice Evans. University Press of Colorado, PO Box 849, Niwot, Colorado 80544. (303) 530-5337. 1991. Includes a summary of the ecological and cultural values of the river corridor. Describes the corridor's flora, fauna, geology, insects, people and history.

Chemical Kinetics and Process Dynamics in Aquatic Systems. Patrick L. Brezonik. Lewis Publishers, 2000 Corporate Blvd., N.W., Boca Raton, Florida 33431. (407) 994-0555 or (800) 272-7737. 1993. Discusses natural waters as nonequilibrium systems, rate expressions for chemical reactions, reactors, mass transport and process models.

Ecological Processes and Cumulative Impacts Illustrated by Bottomland Harwood Wetland Ecosystems. James G. Gosselink, et al. Lewis Publishers, 2000 Corporate Blvd., N.W., Boca Raton, Florida 33431. (407) 994-0555 or (800) 272-7737. 1990. Covers the ecological processes in bottomland hardwood forests and relates these processes to human activities.

The Ecology and Management of Aquatic Terrestrial Ecotones. R. J. Naiman and H. Decamps, eds. Parthenon Pub., Casterton Hall, Carnforth, England LA6 2LA. 1990.

Ecosystems Experiments. H. A. Mooney, et al., eds. John Wiley & Sons, Inc., 605 3rd Ave., New York, New York 10158-0012. (212) 850-6000. 1991. Explores the potential ecosystem experimentation as a tool for understanding and predicting changes in the biosphere. Areas investigated include deforestation, desertification, El Nino phenomenon, acid rain, watersheds, wetlands, and aquatic and climatic changes.

Ecosystems of Florida. Ronald L. Myers and John J. Ewel, eds. Central Florida University, Dist. by Univ. Presses of Florida, 15 N.W. 15th St., Gainesville, Florida 32603. (904) 392-1351. 1990. Presents an ecosystem setting with geology, geography and soils, climate, and 13 ecosystems in a broad human context of historical biogeography and current human influences. Also presents community vulnerability and management techniques and issues in conservation.

Life History and Ecology of the Slider Turtle. J. Whitfield Gibbons. Smithsonian Institution Press, 470 L'Enfant Plaza #7100, Washington, District of Columbia 20560. (800) 782-4612. 1990. Deals with all that is known about a species, its taxonomic status and genetics, reproduction and growth, population structure and demography, population ecology, and bioenergetics.

Long-Term Ecological Research: An International Perspective. Paul G. Risser, ed. John Wiley & Sons, Inc., 605 3rd Ave., New York, New York 10158-0012. (212) 850-6000. 1991. Describes and analyzes research programs in various ecosystems such as temperate forests, arid steppes, deserts, temperate and tropical grasslands, aquatic systems from countries including Scotland, Kenya, USA, Australia, Canada, Germany, and France.

Microbial Enzymes in Aquatic Environments. Ryszard J. Chrost. Springer-Varlag, 175 5th Ave., New York, New York 10010. (212) 460-1500. 1991. Brings together studies on enzymatic degradation processes from disciplines as diverse as water and sediment research, bacterial and algal aquatic ecophysiology, eutrophication, nutrient cycling, and biogeochemistry, in both freshwater and marine ecosystem.

Pollution: Causes, Effects and Control. Roy Michael Harrison. Royal Society of Chemistry, c/o CRC Press, 2000 Corporate Blvd. N.W., Boca Raton, Florida 33431. (800) 272-7737. 1990. 2nd ed. Deals with environmental pollution and its associated problems and legal ramifications.

Restoring Acid Waters. G. Howells. Elsevier Science Publishing Co., 655 Avenue of the Americas, New York, New York 10010. (212) 984-5800. 1992. Detailed and comprehensive accounts of pre-liming conditions, liming techniques employed, post-liming changes in water quality and fish restoration.

Toxicological Risk in Aquatic Ecosystems. Steven M. Bartell, et al. Lewis Publishers, 2000 Corporate Blvd., N.W., Boca Raton, Florida 33431. (407) 994-0555 or (800) 272-7737. 1991. Describes the development, application, and analysis of a methodology for forecasting probable effects of toxic chemicals on the production dynamics of a generalized aquatic ecosystem.

Turtles of the World. Carl H. Ernst and Roger W. Barbour. Smithsonian Institution Press, 470 L'Enfant Plaza #7100, Washington, District of Columbia 20560. (800) 782-4612. 1989. Comprehensive coverage of the world's 257 turtle species.

The Uses of Ecology: Lake Washington and Beyond. W. T. Edmondson. University of Washington Press, PO Box 50096, Seattle, Washington 98145-5096. (206) 543-4050; (800) 441-4115. 1991. Author delivered most of the contents of this book as a Danz lecture at the University of Washington. Gives an account of the pollution and recovery of Lake Washington and describes how communities worked and applied lessons learned from Lake Washington cleanup. Includes extensive documentation and bibliographies.

Wetlands: A Threatened Landscape. Michael Williams. B. Blackwell, 3 Cambridge Ctr., Suite 208, Cambridge, Massachusetts 02142. (617) 225-0401. 1990. Explores the evolution and composition of wetlands and their physical and biological dynamics, considers the impact of agriculture, industry, urbanization, and recreation upon them, and examines what steps we are taking and what steps should be considered to manage and preserve wetlands.

Wetlands: Mitigating and Regulating Development Impacts. David Salvesen. The Urban Land Institute, 1090 Vermont Ave. N.W., Washington, District of Columbia 20005. (202) 289-8500; (800) 237-9196. 1990. Presents the latest examination of the conflicts surrounding development of wetlands. Explains both federal and state wetland regulations. Included is an up-to-date review of important wetlands case law and a detailed look at six of the toughest state programs.

Wetlands of North America. William A. Niering. Thomasson-Grant, 1 Morton Dr., Suite 500, Charlottesville, Virginia 22901. (804) 977-1780 or (800) 999-1780. 1991. Deals with wetlands ecology and the methods of its preservation.

HANDBOOKS AND MANUALS

Handbook of Acute Toxicity of Chemicals to Fish and Aquatic Invertebrates. Waynon W. Johnson and Mack T. Finley. U.S. Department of the Interior, Fish and Wildlife Service, Washington, District of Columbia 20240. (202) 208-5634. 1980. Fisheries Research Laboratory, 1965-78; Resource publication/U.S. Fish and Wildlife Service, no. 137.

ONLINE DATA BASES

BIOSIS Previews. BIOSIS, 2100 Arch St., Philadelphia, Pennsylvania 19103-1399. (215) 587-4800. Largest and most comprehensive database of research in the life sciences. Contains citations for nearly 9000 primary research journals, monographs, reviews, symposia, preliminary reports, semi-popular journals, selected institutional reports, government reports and research communications.

Cambridge Scientific Abstracts Life Science–CSAL. Cambridge Scientific Abstracts, 5161 River Rd., Bethesda, Maryland 20816. (301) 961-6750. Provides access to the following abstracting services: "Life Sciences Collection," "Aquatic Sciences and Fisheries Abstracts," "Oceanic Abstracts," and "Pollution Abstracts."

Current Research Information System–CRIS/USDA. U.S. Department of Agriculture, National Agricultural Library, 10301 Baltimore Blvd., 5th Floor, Beltsville, Maryland 20705-2351. (301) 504-5755. Looks at current research projects in agriculture and allied sciences covering the biological, physical, social and behavioral sciences related to agriculture.

Enviro/Energyline Abstracts Plus. R. R. Bowker Co., 121 Chanlon Rd., New Providence, New Jersey 07974. (908) 464-6800.

Environmental Periodicals Bibliography. National Information Services Corp., Ste. 6, Wyman Towers, 3100 St. Paul St., Baltimore, Maryland 21218. (410)243-0797. Online version of abstract of same name.

Life Sciences from NTIS. National Technical Information Center for the Utilization of Federal Technology, 5285 Port Royal Rd., Springfield, Virginia 22161. (703) 487-4650.

Monthly Catalog of United States Government Publications. U.S. G.P.O., Supt. of Docs., PO Box 371954, Pittsburgh, Pennsylvania 15250-7954. (202) 512-0000.

National Technical Information Service. U.S. Department of Commerce, National Technical Information Service, Office of Data Base Services, 5285 Port Royal Rd., Springfield, Virginia 22161. (703) 487-4807. Bibliographic database of government sponsored research and technical reports.

SCISEARCH. Institute for Scientific Information, University City Science Center, 3501 Market St., Philadelphia, Pennsylvania 19104. (215) 386-0100.

PERIODICALS AND NEWSLETTERS

Applied and Environmental Microbiology Journal. American Society for Microbiology, 1325 Massachusetts Avenue N.W., Washington, District of Columbia 20005. (202) 737-3600. Monthly. Articles on industrial and food microbiology and ecological studies.

Aquasphere. New England Aquarium, Central Wharf, Boston, Massachusetts 02110. (617) 742-8830. 1963. Articles on any subject related to the world of water. Emphasis on ecology, environment, and aquatic animals.

Aquatic Toxicology. Elsevier Science Publishing Co., 655 Avenue of the Americas, New York, New York 10010. (212) 989-5800. 1981-. 6/year.

Ecological Monographs. Business Office of the Ecological Society of America, Center of Environmental Studies, Arizona State University, Tempe, Arizona 85287-1201. (602) 965-3000. Quarterly. Scientific journal of ecological issues.

Ecological Society of America Bulletin. Ecological Society of America, Center of Environmental Studies, Arizona State University, Tempe, Arizona 85287-1201. (602) 965-3000. Quarterly. Study of living things in relation to their environments.

Ecology. Ecological Society of America, Center of Environmental Studies, Arizona State University, Tempe, Arizona 85287-1201. (602) 965-3000. Bimonthly. Information on the study of living things.

Ecology USA. Business Publishers, Inc., 951 Pershing Dr., Silver Spring, Maryland 20910-4464. (301) 587-6300. 1972-. Biweekly. Contains all the legislation, regulation, and litigation affecting efforts to conserve and protect America's unique environmental and ecological heritage.

Environmental Biology of Fishes. Dr. W. Junk Publishers, Postbus 163, Dordrecht, Netherlands 3300 AD. 1976-.

Facets of Freshwater. Freshwater Biological Research Foundation, 2500 Shadywood Rd., Box 90, Navarre, Minnesota 55392. (612) 471-8407. 1970-. Quarterly. Topics in freshwater biological research.

Geojourney. Florida Department of Natural Resources, 3900 Commonwealth Blvd., Tallahassee, Florida 32303. (904) 488-1234. 1980-. Quarterly. Covers activities on resource management, marine resources, parks and recreation, and subjects related to fishing, boating and all uses of Florida's natural resources.

Hydrobiological Journal. John Wiley & Sons, Inc., Periodicals Division, 605 Third Ave., New York, New York 10158-0012. (212) 850-6000. Six times a year. Deals with fisheries in various water resources.

The Journal of Biological Chemistry. American Society of Biological Chemists, 428 E. Preston St., Baltimore, Maryland 21202. Three times a month. Biological, agricultural, and energy aspects of the environment.

Journal of Shoreline Management. Elsevier Science Publishing Co., 655 Avenue of the Americas, New York, New York 10010. (212) 989-5800. Two issues a year. Deals

with coastal ecology, coastal zone management, and ocean and shoreline management.

RESEARCH CENTERS AND INSTITUTES

Alaska Cooperative Fishery and Wildlife Research Unit. 138 Arctic Health Research Unit, University of Alaska-Fairbanks, Fairbanks, Alaska 99775-0110. (907) 474-7661.

Albion College, Whitehouse Nature Center. Albion, Michigan 49224. (517) 629-2030.

Alice L. Kibbe Life Science Station. Western Illinois University, Department of Biological Sciences, Macomb, Illinois 61455. (309) 298-1553.

Aquatic Station. Southwest Texas State University, H. M. Freeman Aquatic Biology Building, San Marcos, Texas 78666-4616. (512) 245-2284.

Archbold Biological Station. P.O. Box 2057, Lake Placid, Florida 33852. (813) 465-2571.

Auburn University, Alabama Cooperative Fish and Wildlife Research Unit. 331 Funchess Hall, Auburn, Alabama 36849. (205) 844-4796.

Benedict Estuarine Research Laboratory. Academy of Natural Sciences, Benedict Avenue, Benedict, Maryland 20612. (301) 274-3134.

Center for Aquatic Plants. University of Florida, 7922 N.W. 71st Street, Gainesville, Florida 32606. (904) 392-1799.

Center for Limnology. University of Colorado-Boulder, Department of EPO Biology, Boulder, Colorado 80309-0334. (303) 492-6379.

Institute of Biomedical Aquatic Studies. University of Florida, Box J-144, Gainesville, Florida 32610. (904) 392-0921.

Michigan State University, Department of Fisheries and Wildlife. East Lansing, Michigan 48824. (517) 353-0647.

Osborn Laboratories of Marine Sciences. New York Aquarium, Boardwalk and West 8th, Brooklyn, New York 11224. (718) 265-3400.

Scripps Institution of Oceanography, Scripps Aquarium-Museum. University of California, San Diego, 8602 La Jolla Shores Drive, La Jolla, California 92093-6933. (619) 534-4084.

Sea Grant College Program. University of Delaware, 196 South College Avenue, Newark, Delaware 19716. (302) 451-8182.

U.S. Forest Service, Aquatic Ecosystem Analysis Laboratory. 105 Page, Brigham Young University, Provo, Utah 84602. (801) 378-4928.

University of Idaho, Idaho Cooperative Fish and Wildlife Research Unit. College of Forestry, Wildlife and Range Sciences, Moscow, Idaho 83843. (208) 885-6336.

University of Maine, Migratory Fish Research Institute. Department of Zoology, Orono, Maine 04469. (207) 581-2548.

University of Michigan, Biological Station. Pellston, Michigan 49769. (616) 539-8406.

University of Michigan, Center for Great Lakes and Aquatic Sciences. 2200 Bonisteel Boulevard, Ann Arbor, Michigan 48109-2099. (313) 763-3515.

University of Minnesota, Cedar Creek Natural History Area. 2660 Fawn Lake Drive NE, Bethel, Minnesota 55005. (612) 434-5131.

University of Minnesota, Lake Itasca Forestry and Biological Station. Post Office, Lake Itasca, Minnesota 56460. (218) 266-3345.

University of Nevada-Las Vegas, Environmental Research Center. 4505 S. Maryland Parkway, Las Vegas, Nevada 89154-4009. (702) 739-3382.

University of Notre Dame, Environmental Research Center. Department of Biological Sciences, Notre Dame, Indiana 46556. (219) 239-7186.

University of Oklahoma, Aquatic Biology Center. Zoology Department, 730 Van Vleet Oval, Norman, Oklahoma 73019. (405) 325-1058.

University of Oklahoma, Aquatic Ecology and Fisheries Research Center. 730 Van Vleet Oval, Room 314, Richards Hall, Norman, Oklahoma 73019. (405) 325-4821.

University of Pittsburgh, Pymatuning Laboratory of Ecology. R.R. #1, Box 7, Linesville, Pennsylvania 16424. (814) 683-5813.

University of Tennessee at Knoxville, Water Resources Research Center. Knoxville, Tennessee 37996. (615) 974-2151.

University of Wisconsin-Madison, Center for Biotic Systems. 1042 WARF Office Building, 610 Walnut Street, Madison, Wisconsin 53705. (608) 262-9937.

University of Wisconsin-Madison, Center for Limnology. 680 North Park Street, Madison, Wisconsin 53706. (608) 262-3014.

University of Wisconsin-Milwaukee, Center for Great Lakes Studies. Milwaukee, Wisconsin 53201. (414) 649-3000.

University of Wisconsin-Milwaukee, Herbarium. Department of Biological Sciences, Box 413, Milwaukee, Wisconsin 53201. (414) 229-6728.

University of Wisconsin-Stevens Point, Wisconsin Cooperative Fishery Research Unit. College of Natural Resources, Stevens Point, Wisconsin 54481. (715) 346-2178.

University of Wyoming, Red Buttes Environmental Biology Laboratory. Box 3166, University Station, Laramie, Wyoming 82071. (307) 745-8504.

Upper Cumberland Biological Station at Tech Aqua. Tennessee Technological University, Box 5063, Edison, New Jersey 38505. (615) 372-3129.

Utah State University, Bear Lake Biological Laboratory. c/o Department of Fisheries and Wildlife, Logan, Utah 84322-5210. (801) 753-2459.

Utah State University, Ecology Center. Logan, Utah 84322-5200. (801) 750-2555.

STATISTICS SOURCES

Ecology: Community Profiles. U.S. Fish and Wildlife Service. National Technical Information Service, 5285 Port Royal Road, Springfield, Virginia 22161. (703) 487-4650. Irregular. Data on coastal and inland ecosystems, including wetlands, tidal-flats, near-shore seagrasses, sand dunes, drilling platforms, oyster reefs, estuaries, rivers and streams.

TRADE ASSOCIATIONS AND PROFESSIONAL SOCIETIES

American Institute of Biological Sciences. 730 11th St., N.W., Washington, District of Columbia 20001-4521. (202) 628-1500.

American Society of Naturalists. Department of Ecology and Evolation, State University of New York, Stony Brook, New York 11794. (516) 632-8589.

Aquatic Plant Management Society. P.O. Box 2695, Washington, District of Columbia 20013. (301) 330-8831.

Ecological Society of America. Arizona State University, Center for Environmental Studies, Tempe, Arizona 85287. (602) 965-3000.

Sea Grant Association. c/o Dr. Christopher F. D'Elia, Maryland Sea Grant College, 1123 Taliaferro Hall, UMCP, College Park, Maryland 20742. (301) 405-6371.

AQUATIC PESTICIDES

See: PESTICIDES

AQUATIC PLANTS

See: AQUATIC ECOSYSTEMS

AQUATIC WEED CONTROL

See also: AQUATIC ECOSYSTEMS; WETLANDS

ABSTRACTING AND INDEXING SERVICES

Abstracts of Air and Water Conservation Literature. American Petroleum Institute. Central Abstracting and Indexing Service, 275 Madison Avenue, New York, New York 10016. 1972.

Applied Ecology Abstracts Studies in Renewable Natural Resources. Information Retrieval Ltd., 1911 Jefferson Davis Highway, Arlington, Virginia 22202. 1975-. Monthly.

Aquatic Sciences and Fisheries Abstracts. Cambridge Scientific Abstracts, 5161 River Rd., Bethesda, Maryland 20816. (301) 961-6750. Monthly. Compiled by the United Nations Dept. of Economic and Social Affairs, the

Food and Agriculture Organization of the United Nations and the Intergovernmental Oceanographic Commission with the collaboration of other agencies. Includes the broad subject areas of ecology, fisheries, marine biology, public policy, aquatic biology, and aquatic ecology.

Biological Abstracts. BIOSIS, 2100 Arch St., Philadelphia, Pennsylvania 19103-1399. (215) 587-4800. 1927-.

Biological and Agricultural Index. H.W. Wilson Co., 950 University Ave., Bronx, New York 10452. (800) 367-6770. 1916-. Monthly.

Ecological Abstracts. Geo Abstracts Ltd. Elsevier Applied Science, Crown House, Linton Rd., Barking, England IG 11 8JU. 1974-. Derived from over 600 leading ecological and environmental journals, plus books, conference proceedings, reports and theses.

Ecology Abstracts. Cambridge Scientific Abstracts, 5161 River Rd., Bethesda, Maryland 20816. (301) 961-6750. Monthly.

Environment Abstracts. Bowker A & I Publishing, 121 Chanlon Rd., New Providence, New Jersey 07974. (908) 464-6800. 1974-.

Environment Index. Environment Information Center, Index Research Department, 124 E. 39th St., New York, New York 10016. 1971-. Annual.

Environmental Information Connection–EIC. Planning Information Program, Dept. of Urban and Regional Planning, University of Illinois, 1003 West Nevada, Urbana, Illinois 61801. (217) 333-1369. Also available online.

Environmental Periodicals Bibliography. Environmental Studies Institute, International Academy at Santa Barbara, 800 Garden St., Suite D, Santa Barbara, California 93101. (805) 965-5010. Also available online.

General Science Index. H. W. Wilson Co., 950 University Ave., Bronx, New York 10452. 1978-. Monthly, also issued in annual cumulation. Cumulative subject index to English language periodicals in the subject fields of astronomy, botany, chemistry, earth science, environment and conservation, food and nutrition, genetics, mathematics, medicine and health, microbiology, oceanography, physics, physiology and zoology.

Index to Scientific Book Contents. Institute for Scientific Information, 3501 Market St., Philadelphia, Pennsylvania 19104. (800) 523-1857. 1985-. Annual. Gives contents of science books published.

Multimedia Index to Ecology. National Information Center for Educational Media, University of Southern California, Los Angeles, California 90007.

Pesticides Abstracts. U.S. Environmental Protection Agency, Office of Pesticides Programs, 345 Curtland, Atlanta, Georgia 30365. (404) 347-2864. 1981. Monthly. Formerly: Health Aspects of Pesticides Abstracts Bulletin.

Science Citation Index. Institute for Scientific Information, 3501 Market St., Philadelphia, Pennsylvania 19104. 1961-.

Weed Abstracts. C. A. B. International, 845 North Park Ave., Tucson, Arizona 85719. (602) 621-7897 or (800) 528-4841. 1954-. Monthly. Abstracts the world literature on weeds, weed control and allied subjects.

BIBLIOGRAPHIES

Current Contents. Agriculture, Biology and Environmental Sciences. Institute for Scientific Information, 3501 Market St., Philadelphia, Pennsylvania 19104. (800) 523-1857. 1973-. Previous title: Current Contents. Agricultural, Food & Veterinary Sciences. Gives the table of contents of periodicals in the fields of agriculture, biology, environmental and related areas.

EPA Publications Bibliography. U.S. Environmental Protection Agency, Library Systems Branch, 401 M St., SW, Washington, District of Columbia 20460. (202) 260-2090. Quarterly.

New Publications of the Geological Survey. U.S. Department of the Interior, Geological Survey, 119 National Center, Reston, Virginia 22092. (703) 648-4460. 1984-. Monthly. Bibliography of geological publications and related government documents published by the Geological Survey.

ENCYCLOPEDIAS AND DICTIONARIES

McGraw-Hill Encyclopedia of Environmental Science. Sybil P. Parker. McGraw-Hill Science & Engineering Books, 11 W. 19th St., New York, New York 10011. (212) 337-6010. 1980. Covers ecology, man's influence on nature, and environmental protection.

McGraw-Hill Encyclopedia of Science and Technology. McGraw-Hill, 1221 Avenue of the Americas, New York, New York 10020. (212) 512-2000 or (800) 262-4729. 1992. Seventh edition. Issued in multiple volumes including index. Includes all science and technology broad subject areas.

Van Nostrand's Scientific Encyclopedia. Glenn D. Considine, ed. Van Nostrand Reinhold, 115 5th Ave., New York, New York 10003. (212) 254-3232. 1983. Sixth edition. Includes all broad subject areas in science.

GENERAL WORKS

Aquatic Toxicology. Jerome O. Nriagu. John Wiley & Sons, Inc., 605 3rd Ave., New York, New York 10158-0012. (212) 850-6000. 1989.

ONLINE DATA BASES

BIOSIS Previews. BIOSIS, 2100 Arch St., Philadelphia, Pennsylvania 19103-1399. (215) 587-4800. Largest and most comprehensive database of research in the life sciences. Contains citations for nearly 9000 primary research journals, monographs, reviews, symposia, preliminary reports, semi-popular journals, selected institutional reports, government reports and research communications.

Cambridge Scientific Abstracts Life Science–CSAL. Cambridge Scientific Abstracts, 5161 River Rd., Bethesda, Maryland 20816. (301) 961-6750. Provides access to the following abstracting services: "Life Sciences Collection," "Aquatic Sciences and Fisheries Abstracts," "Oceanic Abstracts," and "Pollution Abstracts."

Current Research Information System–CRIS/USDA. U.S. Department of Agriculture, National Agricultural Library, 10301 Baltimore Blvd., 5th Floor, Beltsville, Maryland 20705-2351. (301) 504-5755. Looks at current research projects in agriculture and allied sciences covering the biological, physical, social and behavioral sciences related to agriculture.

Enviro/Energyline Abstracts Plus. R. R. Bowker Co., 121 Chanlon Rd., New Providence, New Jersey 07974. (908) 464-6800.

Environmental Periodicals Bibliography. National Information Services Corp., Ste. 6, Wyman Towers, 3100 St. Paul St., Baltimore, Maryland 21218. (410)243-0797. Online version of abstract of same name.

Monthly Catalog of United States Government Publications. U.S. G.P.O., Supt. of Docs., PO Box 371954, Pittsburgh, Pennsylvania 15250-7954. (202) 512-0000.

National Technical Information Service. U.S. Department of Commerce, National Technical Information Service, Office of Data Base Services, 5285 Port Royal Rd., Springfield, Virginia 22161. (703) 487-4807. Bibliographic database of government sponsored research and technical reports.

SCISEARCH. Institute for Scientific Information, University City Science Center, 3501 Market St., Philadelphia, Pennsylvania 19104. (215) 386-0100.

RESEARCH CENTERS AND INSTITUTES

Auburn University, Water Resources Research Institute. 202 Hargis Hall, Auburn University, Alabama 36849-5124. (205) 844-5080.

University of North Texas, Institute of Applied Sciences. P.O. Box 13078, Denton, Texas 76203. (817) 565-2694.

University of Tennessee at Knoxville, Water Resources Research Center. Knoxville, Tennessee 37996. (615) 974-2151.

TRADE ASSOCIATIONS AND PROFESSIONAL SOCIETIES

American Institute of Biological Sciences. 730 11th St., N.W., Washington, District of Columbia 20001-4521. (202) 628-1500.

American Society of Naturalists. Department of Ecology and Evolation, State University of New York, Stony Brook, New York 11794. (516) 632-8589.

AQUEDUCTS

See also: DAMS; IRRIGATION; RESERVOIRS; WATER USES

ABSTRACTING AND INDEXING SERVICES

Abstracts of Air and Water Conservation Literature. American Petroleum Institute. Central Abstracting and Indexing Service, 275 Madison Avenue, New York, New York 10016. 1972.

Applied Science and Technology Index. H.W. Wilson Co., 950 University Ave., Bronx, New York 10452. (800) 367-6770. Formerly Industrial Arts Index.

Aqualine Abstracts. Water Research Centre. c/o Pergamon Microforms International, Inc., Fairview Park, Elmsford, New York 10523. (914) 592-7720. 1927-. Contains some 8,000 records annually on water and wastewater technology. Covers all aspects of water, wastewater, associated engineering services and the

aquatic environment. Over 600 periodicals, as well as books, reports and conference proceedings and other publications from water related institutions worldwide are scanned. Also available online.

Biological and Agricultural Index. H.W. Wilson Co., 950 University Ave., Bronx, New York 10452. (800) 367-6770. 1916-. Monthly.

Engineering Index. The Engineering Index Inc., 345 E. 47th St., New York, New York 10017. 1962-.

Science Citation Index. Institute for Scientific Information, 3501 Market St., Philadelphia, Pennsylvania 19104. 1961-.

ENCYCLOPEDIAS AND DICTIONARIES

Dictionary of Environmental Engineering and Related Sciences: English-Spanish, Spanish-English. Jose T. Villate. Ediciones Universal, 3090 SW 8th St., Miami, Florida 33135. (305) 642-3355. 1979.

Encyclopedia of Environmental Science and Engineering. J.R. Pfafflin. Gordon and Breach Science Publishers, Inc., 270 8th Ave., New York, New York 10011. (212) 206-8900. 1992.

Encyclopedia of Physical Science and Technology. Robert A. Meyers, ed. Academic Press, c/o Harcourt Brace Jovanovich Inc., 6277 Sea Harbor Dr., Orlando, Florida 32887. (800) 346-8648. Dictionary of engineering, technology and physical sciences.

McGraw-Hill Encyclopedia of Environmental Science. Sybil P. Parker. McGraw-Hill Science & Engineering Books, 11 W. 19th St., New York, New York 10011. (212) 337-6010. 1980. Covers ecology, man's influence on nature, and environmental protection.

McGraw-Hill Encyclopedia of Science and Technology. McGraw-Hill, 1221 Avenue of the Americas, New York, New York 10020. (212) 512-2000 or (800) 262-4729. 1992. Seventh edition. Issued in multiple volumes including index. Includes all science and technology broad subject areas.

ONLINE DATA BASES

Computerized Engineering Index–COMPENDEX. Engineering Information Inc., 345 E. 47th St., New York, New York 10017. (212) 705-7600.

Monthly Catalog of United States Government Publications. U.S. G.P.O., Supt. of Docs., PO Box 371954, Pittsburgh, Pennsylvania 15250-7954. (202) 512-0000.

National Technical Information Service. U.S. Department of Commerce, National Technical Information Service, Office of Data Base Services, 5285 Port Royal Rd., Springfield, Virginia 22161. (703) 487-4807. Bibliographic database of government sponsored research and technical reports.

SCISEARCH. Institute for Scientific Information, University City Science Center, 3501 Market St., Philadelphia, Pennsylvania 19104. (215) 386-0100.

AQUIFERS

See also: HYDROLOGY; WATER USES; WATER WELLS; WETLANDS

ABSTRACTING AND INDEXING SERVICES

Abstracts of Air and Water Conservation Literature. American Petroleum Institute. Central Abstracting and Indexing Service, 275 Madison Avenue, New York, New York 10016. 1972.

Aqualine Abstracts. Water Research Centre. c/o Pergamon Microforms International, Inc., Fairview Park, Elmsford, New York 10523. (914) 592-7720. 1927-. Contains some 8,000 records annually on water and wastewater technology. Covers all aspects of water, wastewater, associated engineering services and the aquatic environment. Over 600 periodicals, as well as books, reports and conference proceedings and other publications from water related institutions worldwide are scanned. Also available online.

Biological Abstracts. BIOSIS, 2100 Arch St., Philadelphia, Pennsylvania 19103-1399. (215) 587-4800. 1927-.

Biological and Agricultural Index. H.W. Wilson Co., 950 University Ave., Bronx, New York 10452. (800) 367-6770. 1916-. Monthly.

Civil Engineering Hydraulic Abstracts. BHRA Fluid Engineering, Air Science Co., PO Box 143, Corning, New York 14830. (607) 962-5591. Monthly. Abstracts of periodicals that publish in the areas of hydraulic engineering and other related topics.

Ecological Abstracts. Geo Abstracts Ltd. Elsevier Applied Science, Crown House, Linton Rd., Barking, England IG 11 8JU. 1974-. Derived from over 600 leading ecological and environmental journals, plus books, conference proceedings, reports and theses.

Engineering Index. The Engineering Index Inc., 345 E. 47th St., New York, New York 10017. 1962-.

Environment Abstracts. Bowker A & I Publishing, 121 Chanlon Rd., New Providence, New Jersey 07974. (908) 464-6800. 1974-.

Environment Index. Environment Information Center, Index Research Department, 124 E. 39th St., New York, New York 10016. 1971-. Annual.

Environmental Information Connection–EIC. Planning Information Program, Dept. of Urban and Regional Planning, University of Illinois, 1003 West Nevada, Urbana, Illinois 61801. (217) 333-1369. Also available online.

Environmental Periodicals Bibliography. Environmental Studies Institute, International Academy at Santa Barbara, 800 Garden St., Suite D, Santa Barbara, California 93101. (805) 965-5010. Also available online.

General Science Index. H. W. Wilson Co., 950 University Ave., Bronx, New York 10452. 1978-. Monthly, also issued in annual cumulation. Cumulative subject index to English language periodicals in the subject fields of astronomy, botany, chemistry, earth science, environment and conservation, food and nutrition, genetics, mathematics, medicine and health, microbiology, oceanography, physics, physiology and zoology.

Mineralogical Abstracts. Mineralogical Society, 41 Queen's Gate, London, England SW7 5HR. 71 5847916. Quarterly. Abstracts of journal articles, conferences, technical reports and specialized books in the areas of minerals, clay minerals, economic minerals, ore deposits, environmental studies, experimental mineralogy, gem-

stones, geochemistry, petrology, lunar and planetary studies and other related areas in mineralogy.

Pollution Abstracts. Cambridge Scientific Abstracts, 5161 River Rd., Bethesda, Maryland 20816. (301) 961-6750. Six/year. Indexes worldwide technical literature on environmental pollution. Covers air pollution, marine and freshwater pollution, sewage and wastewater treatment, waste management, toxicology and health, noise pollution, radiation, land pollution, and environmental policies, programs, legislation, and education. Also available online.

Science Citation Index. Institute for Scientific Information, 3501 Market St., Philadelphia, Pennsylvania 19104. 1961-.

BIBLIOGRAPHIES

EPA Publications Bibliography. U.S. Environmental Protection Agency, Library Systems Branch, 401 M St., SW, Washington, District of Columbia 20460. (202) 260-2090. Quarterly.

ENCYCLOPEDIAS AND DICTIONARIES

Cambridge Encyclopedia of Life Sciences. A. E. Friday and David S. Ingram. Cambridge University Press, 40 W 20th St., New York, New York 10011. (212) 924-3900 or (800) 227-0247. 1985. Includes all topics under biology and ecology.

McGraw-Hill Encyclopedia of Science and Technology. McGraw-Hill, 1221 Avenue of the Americas, New York, New York 10020. (212) 512-2000 or (800) 262-4729. 1992. Seventh edition. Issued in multiple volumes including index. Includes all science and technology broad subject areas.

Van Nostrand's Scientific Encyclopedia. Glenn D. Considine, ed. Van Nostrand Reinhold, 115 5th Ave., New York, New York 10003. (212) 254-3232. 1983. Sixth edition. Includes all broad subject areas in science.

ONLINE DATA BASES

BIOSIS Previews. BIOSIS, 2100 Arch St., Philadelphia, Pennsylvania 19103-1399. (215) 587-4800. Largest and most comprehensive database of research in the life sciences. Contains citations for nearly 9000 primary research journals, monographs, reviews, symposia, preliminary reports, semi-popular journals, selected institutional reports, government reports and research communications.

Computerized Engineering Index–COMPENDEX. Engineering Information Inc., 345 E. 47th St., New York, New York 10017. (212) 705-7600.

Enviro/Energyline Abstracts Plus. R. R. Bowker Co., 121 Chanlon Rd., New Providence, New Jersey 07974. (908) 464-6800.

Environmental Periodicals Bibliography. National Information Services Corp., Ste. 6, Wyman Towers, 3100 St. Paul St., Baltimore, Maryland 21218. (410)243-0797. Online version of abstract of same name.

Monthly Catalog of United States Government Publications. U.S. G.P.O., Supt. of Docs., PO Box 371954, Pittsburgh, Pennsylvania 15250-7954. (202) 512-0000.

National Technical Information Service. U.S. Department of Commerce, National Technical Information Service, Office of Data Base Services, 5285 Port Royal Rd., Springfield, Virginia 22161. (703) 487-4807. Bibliographic database of government sponsored research and technical reports.

SCISEARCH. Institute for Scientific Information, University City Science Center, 3501 Market St., Philadelphia, Pennsylvania 19104. (215) 386-0100.

TRADE ASSOCIATIONS AND PROFESSIONAL SOCIETIES

American Institute of Chemical Engineers. 345 East 47th St., New York, New York 10017. (212) 705-7338.

American Institute of Chemists. 7315 Wisconsin Ave., Bethesda, Maryland 20814. (301) 652-2447.

ARABLE LAND

See: AGRICULTURE

ARBOREAL

See also: FOREST ECOSYSTEMS; FORESTS

ABSTRACTING AND INDEXING SERVICES

Biological Abstracts. BIOSIS, 2100 Arch St., Philadelphia, Pennsylvania 19103-1399. (215) 587-4800. 1927-.

Biological and Agricultural Index. H.W. Wilson Co., 950 University Ave., Bronx, New York 10452. (800) 367-6770. 1916-. Monthly.

Ecological Abstracts. Geo Abstracts Ltd. Elsevier Applied Science, Crown House, Linton Rd., Barking, England IG 11 8JU. 1974-. Derived from over 600 leading ecological and environmental journals, plus books, conference proceedings, reports and theses.

Environment Abstracts. Bowker A & I Publishing, 121 Chanlon Rd., New Providence, New Jersey 07974. (908) 464-6800. 1974-.

Environment Index. Environment Information Center, Index Research Department, 124 E. 39th St., New York, New York 10016. 1971-. Annual.

Environmental Information Connection–EIC. Planning Information Program, Dept. of Urban and Regional Planning, University of Illinois, 1003 West Nevada, Urbana, Illinois 61801. (217) 333-1369. Also available online.

Environmental Periodicals Bibliography. Environmental Studies Institute, International Academy at Santa Barbara, 800 Garden St., Suite D, Santa Barbara, California 93101. (805) 965-5010. Also available online.

Science Citation Index. Institute for Scientific Information, 3501 Market St., Philadelphia, Pennsylvania 19104. 1961-.

BIBLIOGRAPHIES

Current Contents. Agriculture, Biology and Environmental Sciences. Institute for Scientific Information, 3501 Market St., Philadelphia, Pennsylvania 19104. (800) 523-1857. 1973-. Previous title: Current Contents. Agricultural, Food & Veterinary Sciences. Gives the table of contents of periodicals in the fields of agriculture, biology, environmental and related areas.

EPA Publications Bibliography. U.S. Environmental Protection Agency, Library Systems Branch, 401 M St., SW, Washington, District of Columbia 20460. (202) 260-2090. Quarterly.

ENCYCLOPEDIAS AND DICTIONARIES

McGraw-Hill Encyclopedia of Environmental Science. Sybil P. Parker. McGraw-Hill Science & Engineering Books, 11 W. 19th St., New York, New York 10011. (212) 337-6010. 1980. Covers ecology, man's influence on nature, and environmental protection.

McGraw-Hill Encyclopedia of Science and Technology. McGraw-Hill, 1221 Avenue of the Americas, New York, New York 10020. (212) 512-2000 or (800) 262-4729. 1992. Seventh edition. Issued in multiple volumes including index. Includes all science and technology broad subject areas.

ONLINE DATA BASES

BIOSIS Previews. BIOSIS, 2100 Arch St., Philadelphia, Pennsylvania 19103-1399. (215) 587-4800. Largest and most comprehensive database of research in the life sciences. Contains citations for nearly 9000 primary research journals, monographs, reviews, symposia, preliminary reports, semi-popular journals, selected institutional reports, government reports and research communications.

Cambridge Scientific Abstracts Life Science–CSAL. Cambridge Scientific Abstracts, 5161 River Rd., Bethesda, Maryland 20816. (301) 961-6750. Provides access to the following abstracting services: "Life Sciences Collection," "Aquatic Sciences and Fisheries Abstracts," "Oceanic Abstracts," and "Pollution Abstracts."

Enviro/Energyline Abstracts Plus. R. R. Bowker Co., 121 Chanlon Rd., New Providence, New Jersey 07974. (908) 464-6800.

Environmental Periodicals Bibliography. National Information Services Corp., Ste. 6, Wyman Towers, 3100 St. Paul St., Baltimore, Maryland 21218. (410)243-0797. Online version of abstract of same name.

RESEARCH CENTERS AND INSTITUTES

Bartlett Arboretum. University of Connecticut, 151 Brookdale Rd., Stamford, Connecticut 06903. (203) 322-6971.

TRADE ASSOCIATIONS AND PROFESSIONAL SOCIETIES

International Society of Arboriculture. P.O. Box 908, 303 W. University Ave., Urbana, Illinois 61801. (217) 328-2032.

National Arbor Day Foundation. 100 Arbor Ave., Nebraska City, Nebraska 68410. (402) 474-5655.

ARCHAEOLOGY

ABSTRACTING AND INDEXING SERVICES

Biological Abstracts. BIOSIS, 2100 Arch St., Philadelphia, Pennsylvania 19103-1399. (215) 587-4800. 1927-.

Environment Abstracts. Bowker A & I Publishing, 121 Chanlon Rd., New Providence, New Jersey 07974. (908) 464-6800. 1974-.

Environment Index. Environment Information Center, Index Research Department, 124 E. 39th St., New York, New York 10016. 1971-. Annual.

Environmental Information Connection–EIC. Planning Information Program, Dept. of Urban and Regional Planning, University of Illinois, 1003 West Nevada, Urbana, Illinois 61801. (217) 333-1369. Also available online.

Environmental Periodicals Bibliography. Environmental Studies Institute, International Academy at Santa Barbara, 800 Garden St., Suite D, Santa Barbara, California 93101. (805) 965-5010. Also available online.

Science Citation Index. Institute for Scientific Information, 3501 Market St., Philadelphia, Pennsylvania 19104. 1961-.

BIBLIOGRAPHIES

EPA Publications Bibliography. U.S. Environmental Protection Agency, Library Systems Branch, 401 M St., SW, Washington, District of Columbia 20460. (202) 260-2090. Quarterly.

ENCYCLOPEDIAS AND DICTIONARIES

McGraw-Hill Encyclopedia of Science and Technology. McGraw-Hill, 1221 Avenue of the Americas, New York, New York 10020. (212) 512-2000 or (800) 262-4729. 1992. Seventh edition. Issued in multiple volumes including index. Includes all science and technology broad subject areas.

ONLINE DATA BASES

BIOSIS Previews. BIOSIS, 2100 Arch St., Philadelphia, Pennsylvania 19103-1399. (215) 587-4800. Largest and most comprehensive database of research in the life sciences. Contains citations for nearly 9000 primary research journals, monographs, reviews, symposia, preliminary reports, semi-popular journals, selected institutional reports, government reports and research communications.

Enviro/Energyline Abstracts Plus. R. R. Bowker Co., 121 Chanlon Rd., New Providence, New Jersey 07974. (908) 464-6800.

Environmental Periodicals Bibliography. National Information Services Corp., Ste. 6, Wyman Towers, 3100 St. Paul St., Baltimore, Maryland 21218. (410)243-0797. Online version of abstract of same name.

RESEARCH CENTERS AND INSTITUTES

University of Georgia, Zooarchaelogy Laboratory. Baldwin Hall, Athens, Georgia 30602. (404) 542-3922.

University of Nevada-Las Vegas, Marjorie Barrick Museum of Natural History. Las Vegas, Nevada 89154. (702) 739-3381.

TRADE ASSOCIATIONS AND PROFESSIONAL SOCIETIES

The Archaeological Conservancy. 415 Orchard Dr., Santa Fe, New Mexico 87501. (505) 982-3278.

ARCHITECTURE AND ENERGY CONSERVATION

ABSTRACTING AND INDEXING SERVICES

Applied Ecology Abstracts Studies in Renewable Natural Resources. Information Retrieval Ltd., 1911 Jefferson Davis Highway, Arlington, Virginia 22202. 1975-. Monthly.

Applied Science and Technology Index. H.W. Wilson Co., 950 University Ave., Bronx, New York 10452. (800) 367-6770. Formerly Industrial Arts Index.

Engineering Index. The Engineering Index Inc., 345 E. 47th St., New York, New York 10017. 1962-.

Environment Abstracts. Bowker A & I Publishing, 121 Chanlon Rd., New Providence, New Jersey 07974. (908) 464-6800. 1974-.

Environment Index. Environment Information Center, Index Research Department, 124 E. 39th St., New York, New York 10016. 1971-. Annual.

Environmental Information Connection–EIC. Planning Information Program, Dept. of Urban and Regional Planning, University of Illinois, 1003 West Nevada, Urbana, Illinois 61801. (217) 333-1369. Also available online.

Environmental Periodicals Bibliography. Environmental Studies Institute, International Academy at Santa Barbara, 800 Garden St., Suite D, Santa Barbara, California 93101. (805) 965-5010. Also available online.

General Science Index. H. W. Wilson Co., 950 University Ave., Bronx, New York 10452. 1978-. Monthly, also issued in annual cumulation. Cumulative subject index to English language periodicals in the subject fields of astronomy, botany, chemistry, earth science, environment and conservation, food and nutrition, genetics, mathematics, medicine and health, microbiology, oceanography, physics, physiology and zoology.

Multimedia Index to Ecology. National Information Center for Educational Media, University of Southern California, Los Angeles, California 90007.

Science Citation Index. Institute for Scientific Information, 3501 Market St., Philadelphia, Pennsylvania 19104. 1961-.

BIBLIOGRAPHIES

Alternative Sources of Energy. Barbara K. Harrah. Scarecrow Press, 52 Liberty St., Metuchen, New Jersey 08840. (908) 548-8600. 1975. A bibliography of solar, geothermal, wind, and tidal energy, and environmental architecture.

Current Perspectives on Energy Conservation in Architecture: A Selected Bibliography. Robert Bartlett Harmon. Vance Bibliographies, PO Box 229, 112 N. Charter St., Monticello, Illinois 61856. (217) 762-3831. 1980.

Directory of Published Proceedings. Interdok Corp., 173 Halstead Ave., Harrison, New York 10528. (914) 835-3506. 1990. Monthly. This is a listing of published proceedings including the series SEMTE (Science/Medicine/Engineering/Technology) and the series SSH (Social Science/Humanities).

EPA Publications Bibliography. U.S. Environmental Protection Agency, Library Systems Branch, 401 M St., SW, Washington, District of Columbia 20460. (202) 260-2090. Quarterly.

Landscape Architecture and Energy Conservation. Coppa & Avery Consultants. Vance Bibliographies, PO Box 229, 112 N. Charter St., Monticello, Illinois 61856. (217) 762-3831. 1980.

Solar Energy in Housing and Architecture: A Bibliography. Kathleen Ann Lodl. Vance Bibliographies, PO Box 229, 112 N. Charter St., Monticello, Illinois 61856. (217) 762-3831. 1987.

ENCYCLOPEDIAS AND DICTIONARIES

Dictionary of Environmental Engineering and Related Sciences: English-Spanish, Spanish-English. Jose T. Villate. Ediciones Universal, 3090 SW 8th St., Miami, Florida 33135. (305) 642-3355. 1979.

A Dictionary of Landscape: A Dictionary of Terms Used in the Description of the World's Land Surface. George A. Goulty. Avebury Technical, c/o Gower, Gower House, Croft Rd., Aldershot, England GU11 3HR. (0252) 331551. 1991. Earth sciences dictionary. Covers architecture, building construction, horticulture, and town planning.

Encyclopedia of Environmental Science and Engineering. J.R. Pfafflin. Gordon and Breach Science Publishers, Inc., 270 8th Ave., New York, New York 10011. (212) 206-8900. 1992.

Encyclopedia of Physical Science and Technology. Robert A. Meyers, ed. Academic Press, c/o Harcourt Brace Jovanovich Inc., 6277 Sea Harbor Dr., Orlando, Florida 32887. (800) 346-8648. Dictionary of engineering, technology and physical sciences.

McGraw-Hill Encyclopedia of Environmental Science. Sybil P. Parker. McGraw-Hill Science & Engineering Books, 11 W. 19th St., New York, New York 10011. (212) 337-6010. 1980. Covers ecology, man's influence on nature, and environmental protection.

McGraw-Hill Encyclopedia of Science and Technology. McGraw-Hill, 1221 Avenue of the Americas, New York, New York 10020. (212) 512-2000 or (800) 262-4729. 1992. Seventh edition. Issued in multiple volumes including index. Includes all science and technology broad subject areas.

GENERAL WORKS

The Design Connection. Ralph W. Crump. Van Nostrand Reinhold, 115 5th Ave., New York, New York 10003. (212) 254-3232. 1981. Energy and technology in architecture.

Energy and Architecture. Christopher Flavin. Worldwatch Institute, 1776 Massachusetts Ave. NW, Washington, District of Columbia 20036. 1980. Solar energy and conservation potential.

Solar Primer One: Solar Energy in Architecture: A Guide for the Designer. Quinton M. Bradley. SOLARC, 2300 Cliff Dr., Newport Beach, California 92263. (714)631-3182. 1975. Architecture and solar radiation, and energy conservation.

Sun/Earth: Alternative Energy Design for Architecture. Richard L. Crowther. Van Nostrand Reinhold, 115 Fifth Ave., New York, New York 10003. (212) 254-3232. 1983. Renewable energy sources and energy conservation in dwellings.

The Windmill: Architecture and Energy. Carole Cable. Vance Bibliographies, PO Box 229, 112 N. Charter St., Monticello, Illinois 61856. (217) 762-3831. 1983.

ONLINE DATA BASES

Computerized Engineering Index–COMPENDEX. Engineering Information Inc., 345 E. 47th St., New York, New York 10017. (212) 705-7600.

Enviro/Energyline Abstracts Plus. R. R. Bowker Co., 121 Chanlon Rd., New Providence, New Jersey 07974. (908) 464-6800.

Environmental Periodicals Bibliography. National Information Services Corp., Ste. 6, Wyman Towers, 3100 St. Paul St., Baltimore, Maryland 21218. (410)243-0797. Online version of abstract of same name.

ARCTIC ECOLOGY

ABSTRACTING AND INDEXING SERVICES

Applied Ecology Abstracts Studies in Renewable Natural Resources. Information Retrieval Ltd., 1911 Jefferson Davis Highway, Arlington, Virginia 22202. 1975-. Monthly.

Biological and Agricultural Index. H.W. Wilson Co., 950 University Ave., Bronx, New York 10452. (800) 367-6770. 1916-. Monthly.

Ecological Abstracts. Geo Abstracts Ltd. Elsevier Applied Science, Crown House, Linton Rd., Barking, England IG 11 8JU. 1974-. Derived from over 600 leading ecological and environmental journals, plus books, conference proceedings, reports and theses.

Ecology Abstracts. Cambridge Scientific Abstracts, 5161 River Rd., Bethesda, Maryland 20816. (301) 961-6750. Monthly.

Environment Abstracts. Bowker A & I Publishing, 121 Chanlon Rd., New Providence, New Jersey 07974. (908) 464-6800. 1974-.

Environment Index. Environment Information Center, Index Research Department, 124 E. 39th St., New York, New York 10016. 1971-. Annual.

Environmental Information Connection–EIC. Planning Information Program, Dept. of Urban and Regional Planning, University of Illinois, 1003 West Nevada, Urbana, Illinois 61801. (217) 333-1369. Also available online.

Environmental Periodicals Bibliography. Environmental Studies Institute, International Academy at Santa Barbara, 800 Garden St., Suite D, Santa Barbara, California 93101. (805) 965-5010. Also available online.

General Science Index. H. W. Wilson Co., 950 University Ave., Bronx, New York 10452. 1978-. Monthly, also issued in annual cumulation. Cumulative subject index to English language periodicals in the subject fields of astronomy, botany, chemistry, earth science, environment and conservation, food and nutrition, genetics, mathematics, medicine and health, microbiology, oceanography, physics, physiology and zoology.

Multimedia Index to Ecology. National Information Center for Educational Media, University of Southern California, Los Angeles, California 90007.

BIBLIOGRAPHIES

Current Contents. Agriculture, Biology and Environmental Sciences. Institute for Scientific Information, 3501 Market St., Philadelphia, Pennsylvania 19104. (800) 523-1857. 1973-. Previous title: Current Contents. Agricultural, Food & Veterinary Sciences. Gives the table of contents of periodicals in the fields of agriculture, biology, environmental and related areas.

Directory of Published Proceedings. Interdok Corp., 173 Halstead Ave., Harrison, New York 10528. (914) 835-3506. 1990. Monthly. This is a listing of published proceedings including the series SEMTE (Science/Medicine/Engineering/Technology) and the series SSH (Social Science/Humanities).

EPA Publications Bibliography. U.S. Environmental Protection Agency, Library Systems Branch, 401 M St., SW, Washington, District of Columbia 20460. (202) 260-2090. Quarterly.

ENCYCLOPEDIAS AND DICTIONARIES

Cambridge Encyclopedia of Life Sciences. A. E. Friday and David S. Ingram. Cambridge University Press, 40 W 20th St., New York, New York 10011. (212) 924-3900 or (800) 227-0247. 1985. Includes all topics under biology and ecology.

Grzimek's Encyclopedia of Ecology. Bernhard Grzimek. Van Nostrand Reinhold, 115 5th Ave., New York, New York 10003. (212) 254-3232. 1976.

McGraw-Hill Encyclopedia of Science and Technology. McGraw-Hill, 1221 Avenue of the Americas, New York, New York 10020. (212) 512-2000 or (800) 262-4729. 1992. Seventh edition. Issued in multiple volumes including index. Includes all science and technology broad subject areas.

North American Reference Encyclopedia of Ecology and Pollution. William White. North American Pub. Co., 401 N. Broad St., Philadelphia, Pennsylvania 19108. (215) 238-5300. 1972.

Van Nostrand's Scientific Encyclopedia. Glenn D. Considine, ed. Van Nostrand Reinhold, 115 5th Ave., New York, New York 10003. (212) 254-3232. 1983. Sixth edition. Includes all broad subject areas in science.

GENERAL WORKS

Arctic Animal Ecology. Hermann Remmert. Springer-Verlag, 175 5th Ave., New York, New York 10010. (212) 460-1500. 1980. Animal ecology in the Arctic regions.

Arctic Arthropods. H.V. Danks. Entomological Society of Canada, 393 Winston Ave., Ottawa, Ontario, Canada K2A 1Y8. (613) 725-2619. 1981.

Vegetation and Production Ecology of the Alaskan Arctic Tundra. Larry L. Tieszen. Springer-Verlag, 175 5th Ave., New York, New York 10010. (212) 460-1500. 1978. Primary productivity, tundra ecology, and tundra flora.

ONLINE DATA BASES

Enviro/Energyline Abstracts Plus. R. R. Bowker Co., 121 Chanlon Rd., New Providence, New Jersey 07974. (908) 464-6800.

Environmental Periodicals Bibliography. National Information Services Corp., Ste. 6, Wyman Towers, 3100 St. Paul St., Baltimore, Maryland 21218. (410)243-0797. Online version of abstract of same name.

SCISEARCH. Institute for Scientific Information, University City Science Center, 3501 Market St., Philadelphia, Pennsylvania 19104. (215) 386-0100.

ARCTIC TUNDRAS

See also: BIOMES; ECOSYSTEMS; TUNDRA BIOMES

ABSTRACTING AND INDEXING SERVICES

Applied Ecology Abstracts Studies in Renewable Natural Resources. Information Retrieval Ltd., 1911 Jefferson Davis Highway, Arlington, Virginia 22202. 1975-. Monthly.

Biological Abstracts. BIOSIS, 2100 Arch St., Philadelphia, Pennsylvania 19103-1399. (215) 587-4800. 1927-.

Biological and Agricultural Index. H.W. Wilson Co., 950 University Ave., Bronx, New York 10452. (800) 367-6770. 1916-. Monthly.

Ecological Abstracts. Geo Abstracts Ltd. Elsevier Applied Science, Crown House, Linton Rd., Barking, England IG 11 8JU. 1974-. Derived from over 600 leading ecological and environmental journals, plus books, conference proceedings, reports and theses.

Environment Abstracts. Bowker A & I Publishing, 121 Chanlon Rd., New Providence, New Jersey 07974. (908) 464-6800. 1974-.

Environment Index. Environment Information Center, Index Research Department, 124 E. 39th St., New York, New York 10016. 1971-. Annual.

Environmental Information Connection–EIC. Planning Information Program, Dept. of Urban and Regional Planning, University of Illinois, 1003 West Nevada, Urbana, Illinois 61801. (217) 333-1369. Also available online.

Environmental Periodicals Bibliography. Environmental Studies Institute, International Academy at Santa Barbara, 800 Garden St., Suite D, Santa Barbara, California 93101. (805) 965-5010. Also available online.

General Science Index. H. W. Wilson Co., 950 University Ave., Bronx, New York 10452. 1978-. Monthly, also issued in annual cumulation. Cumulative subject index to English language periodicals in the subject fields of astronomy, botany, chemistry, earth science, environment and conservation, food and nutrition, genetics, mathematics, medicine and health, microbiology, oceanography, physics, physiology and zoology.

Index to Scientific Book Contents. Institute for Scientific Information, 3501 Market St., Philadelphia, Pennsylvania 19104. (800) 523-1857. 1985-. Annual. Gives contents of science books published.

Multimedia Index to Ecology. National Information Center for Educational Media, University of Southern California, Los Angeles, California 90007.

Science Citation Index. Institute for Scientific Information, 3501 Market St., Philadelphia, Pennsylvania 19104. 1961-.

BIBLIOGRAPHIES

EPA Publications Bibliography. U.S. Environmental Protection Agency, Library Systems Branch, 401 M St., SW, Washington, District of Columbia 20460. (202) 260-2090. Quarterly.

DIRECTORIES

Arctic Environmental Data Directory. Diane Weixler and A.C. Brown. U.S. Geological Survey, National Center, 12201 Sunrise Valley Drive, Reston, Virginia 22092. (703) 648-4460. 1990.

ENCYCLOPEDIAS AND DICTIONARIES

McGraw-Hill Encyclopedia of Science and Technology. McGraw-Hill, 1221 Avenue of the Americas, New York, New York 10020. (212) 512-2000 or (800) 262-4729. 1992. Seventh edition. Issued in multiple volumes including index. Includes all science and technology broad subject areas.

Van Nostrand's Scientific Encyclopedia. Glenn D. Considine, ed. Van Nostrand Reinhold, 115 5th Ave., New York, New York 10003. (212) 254-3232. 1983. Sixth edition. Includes all broad subject areas in science.

ONLINE DATA BASES

BIOSIS Previews. BIOSIS, 2100 Arch St., Philadelphia, Pennsylvania 19103-1399. (215) 587-4800. Largest and most comprehensive database of research in the life sciences. Contains citations for nearly 9000 primary research journals, monographs, reviews, symposia, preliminary reports, semi-popular journals, selected institutional reports, government reports and research communications.

Cambridge Scientific Abstracts Life Science-CSAL. Cambridge Scientific Abstracts, 5161 River Rd., Bethesda, Maryland 20816. (301) 961-6750. Provides access to the following abstracting services: "Life Sciences Collection," "Aquatic Sciences and Fisheries Abstracts," "Oceanic Abstracts," and "Pollution Abstracts."

Enviro/Energyline Abstracts Plus. R. R. Bowker Co., 121 Chanlon Rd., New Providence, New Jersey 07974. (908) 464-6800.

Environmental Periodicals Bibliography. National Information Services Corp., Ste. 6, Wyman Towers, 3100 St. Paul St., Baltimore, Maryland 21218. (410)243-0797. Online version of abstract of same name.

SCISEARCH. Institute for Scientific Information, University City Science Center, 3501 Market St., Philadelphia, Pennsylvania 19104. (215) 386-0100.

RESEARCH CENTERS AND INSTITUTES

Alaska Cooperative Fishery and Wildlife Research Unit. 138 Arctic Health Research Unit, University of Alaska-Fairbanks, Fairbanks, Alaska 99775-0110. (907) 474-7661.

U.S. Arctic Research Commission. Geophysical Institute, University of Alaska, Fairbanks, Alaska 99775-0800. (202) 371-9631.

University of Alaska Anchorage, Arctic Environmental Information and Data Center. 707 A Street, Anchorage, Alaska 99501. (907) 257-2733.

University of Alaska Fairbanks, Institute of Arctic Biology. Fairbanks, Alaska 99775. (907) 474-7648.

STATISTICS SOURCES

Glaciological Data. U.S. National Environmental Satellite, Data and Info Service. U.S. G.P.O., Washington, District of Columbia 20401. (202) 512-0000. Irregular. Covers occurrence, properties, processes, and effects of snow, ice and glaciers.

TRADE ASSOCIATIONS AND PROFESSIONAL SOCIETIES

American Society of Naturalists. Department of Ecology and Evolation, State University of New York, Stony Brook, New York 11794. (516) 632-8589.

AREA COMPARISONS

ABSTRACTING AND INDEXING SERVICES

Environment Abstracts. Bowker A & I Publishing, 121 Chanlon Rd., New Providence, New Jersey 07974. (908) 464-6800. 1974-.

Environment Index. Environment Information Center, Index Research Department, 124 E. 39th St., New York, New York 10016. 1971-. Annual.

Environmental Information Connection-EIC. Planning Information Program, Dept. of Urban and Regional Planning, University of Illinois, 1003 West Nevada, Urbana, Illinois 61801. (217) 333-1369. Also available online.

Environmental Periodicals Bibliography. Environmental Studies Institute, International Academy at Santa Barbara, 800 Garden St., Suite D, Santa Barbara, California 93101. (805) 965-5010. Also available online.

Index to Scientific Book Contents. Institute for Scientific Information, 3501 Market St., Philadelphia, Pennsylvania 19104. (800) 523-1857. 1985-. Annual. Gives contents of science books published.

BIBLIOGRAPHIES

EPA Publications Bibliography. U.S. Environmental Protection Agency, Library Systems Branch, 401 M St., SW, Washington, District of Columbia 20460. (202) 260-2090. Quarterly.

ENCYCLOPEDIAS AND DICTIONARIES

Dictionary of Environmental Engineering and Related Sciences: English-Spanish, Spanish-English. Jose T. Villate. Ediciones Universal, 3090 SW 8th St., Miami, Florida 33135. (305) 642-3355. 1979.

Encyclopedia of Environmental Science and Engineering. J.R. Pfafflin. Gordon and Breach Science Publishers, Inc., 270 8th Ave., New York, New York 10011. (212) 206-8900. 1992.

ONLINE DATA BASES

Enviro/Energyline Abstracts Plus. R. R. Bowker Co., 121 Chanlon Rd., New Providence, New Jersey 07974. (908) 464-6800.

Environmental Periodicals Bibliography. National Information Services Corp., Ste. 6, Wyman Towers, 3100 St. Paul St., Baltimore, Maryland 21218. (410)243-0797. Online version of abstract of same name.

ARID ZONES

See also: AGRICULTURE; DESERTS; GRASSLAND BIOME

ABSTRACTING AND INDEXING SERVICES

Applied Ecology Abstracts Studies in Renewable Natural Resources. Information Retrieval Ltd., 1911 Jefferson Davis Highway, Arlington, Virginia 22202. 1975-. Monthly.

Biological and Agricultural Index. H.W. Wilson Co., 950 University Ave., Bronx, New York 10452. (800) 367-6770. 1916-. Monthly.

Ecological Abstracts. Geo Abstracts Ltd. Elsevier Applied Science, Crown House, Linton Rd., Barking, England IG 11 8JU. 1974-. Derived from over 600 leading ecological and environmental journals, plus books, conference proceedings, reports and theses.

Ecology Abstracts. Cambridge Scientific Abstracts, 5161 River Rd., Bethesda, Maryland 20816. (301) 961-6750. Monthly.

Environment Abstracts. Bowker A & I Publishing, 121 Chanlon Rd., New Providence, New Jersey 07974. (908) 464-6800. 1974-.

Environment Index. Environment Information Center, Index Research Department, 124 E. 39th St., New York, New York 10016. 1971-. Annual.

Environmental Information Connection–EIC. Planning Information Program, Dept. of Urban and Regional Planning, University of Illinois, 1003 West Nevada, Urbana, Illinois 61801. (217) 333-1369. Also available online.

Environmental Periodicals Bibliography. Environmental Studies Institute, International Academy at Santa Barba-

ra, 800 Garden St., Suite D, Santa Barbara, California 93101. (805) 965-5010. Also available online.

General Science Index. H. W. Wilson Co., 950 University Ave., Bronx, New York 10452. 1978-. Monthly, also issued in annual cumulation. Cumulative subject index to English language periodicals in the subject fields of astronomy, botany, chemistry, earth science, environment and conservation, food and nutrition, genetics, mathematics, medicine and health, microbiology, oceanography, physics, physiology and zoology.

Multimedia Index to Ecology. National Information Center for Educational Media, University of Southern California, Los Angeles, California 90007.

Science Citation Index. Institute for Scientific Information, 3501 Market St., Philadelphia, Pennsylvania 19104. 1961-.

BIBLIOGRAPHIES

Directory of Published Proceedings. Interdok Corp., 173 Halstead Ave., Harrison, New York 10528. (914) 835-3506. 1990. Monthly. This is a listing of published proceedings including the series SEMTE (Science/Medicine/Engineering/Technology) and the series SSH (Social Science/Humanities).

EPA Publications Bibliography. U.S. Environmental Protection Agency, Library Systems Branch, 401 M St., SW, Washington, District of Columbia 20460. (202) 260-2090. Quarterly.

World Desertification: Cause and Effect, A Literature Review and Annotated Bibliography. Wade C. Sherbrooke. University of Arizona, Office of Arid Land Studies, 1230 N. Park, # 102, Tucson, Arizona 85719. (602) 621-1441. 1973.

DIRECTORIES

Arid Lands Research Institutions: A World Directory. Barbara S. Hutchinson. Allerton Press, Inc., 150 5th Ave., New York, New York 10011. (212) 924-3950. 1988. 3d ed.

ENCYCLOPEDIAS AND DICTIONARIES

The Encyclopedia of Climatology. John E. Oliver and Rhodes W. Fairbridge, eds. Van Nostrand Reinhold, 115 5th Ave., New York, New York 10003. (212) 254-3232. 1987. Belongs in the series Encyclopedia of Earth Sciences, v.11.

McGraw-Hill Encyclopedia of Environmental Science. Sybil P. Parker. McGraw-Hill Science & Engineering Books, 11 W. 19th St., New York, New York 10011. (212) 337-6010. 1980. Covers ecology, man's influence on nature, and environmental protection.

McGraw-Hill Encyclopedia of Science and Technology. McGraw-Hill, 1221 Avenue of the Americas, New York, New York 10020. (212) 512-2000 or (800) 262-4729. 1992. Seventh edition. Issued in multiple volumes including index. Includes all science and technology broad subject areas.

GENERAL WORKS

Ecotoxicology and Climate. Philippe Bordeaux, et al., eds. John Wiley & Sons, Inc., 605 3rd Ave., New York,

New York 10158-0012. (212) 850-6000. 1989. Describes environmental chemistry of toxic pollutants in hot and cold climates. Includes bibliographical references and an index.

Effects of Aerosols and Surface Shadowing on Bidirectional Reflectance Measurements of Deserts Microform. David E. Bowker. National Aeronautics and Space Administration, Scientific and Technical Information Office, 5285 Port Royal Rd., Springfield, Virginia 22161. (703) 487-4805. 1987. NASA technical paper; #2756.

United States Sources of Information in the Area of Decertification. United States. U.S. Environmental Protection Agency, Assistant Administrator for Planning and Management, Office of Administration, Washington, District of Columbia 1977.

GOVERNMENTAL ORGANIZATIONS

Office of Environmental Affairs: Bureau of Reclamation. 18th and C St., N.W., Washington, District of Columbia 20240. (202) 343-4662.

ONLINE DATA BASES

Enviro/Energyline Abstracts Plus. R. R. Bowker Co., 121 Chanlon Rd., New Providence, New Jersey 07974. (908) 464-6800.

Environmental Periodicals Bibliography. National Information Services Corp., Ste. 6, Wyman Towers, 3100 St. Paul St., Baltimore, Maryland 21218. (410)243-0797. Online version of abstract of same name.

SCISEARCH. Institute for Scientific Information, University City Science Center, 3501 Market St., Philadelphia, Pennsylvania 19104. (215) 386-0100.

PERIODICALS AND NEWSLETTERS

Arid Lands Newsletter. University of Arizona, 845 N. Park Ave., Tucson, Arizona 85719. (602) 621-1955. 1975-. Semiannually. Brief articles on world desert problems.

Arid Soil Research and Rehabilitation. Taylor & Francis, 1900 Frost Rd., Ste. 101, Bristol, Pennsylvania 19007. (215) 785-5800. Quarterly. Scientific studies on desert, arid, and semi-arid soil research and recovery.

Journal of Arid Environmentals. Academic Press, c/o Harcourt Brace Jovanovich Inc., 6277 Sea Harbor Dr., Orlando, Florida 32887. (800) 346-8648. Quarterly. Ecology of deserts and arid zones.

RESEARCH CENTERS AND INSTITUTES

Aridland Watershed Management Research Unit. 2000 East Allen Road, Tucson, Arizona 85719. (602) 629-6381.

ARIDLANDS. University of Arizona, Office of Arid Lands Studies, Tucson, Arizona 85719. (602) 621-1955.

Texas Tech University, International Center for Arid and Semiarid Land Studies. P.O. Box 4620, Lubbock, Texas 79409. (806) 742-2218.

University of Nevada-Reno, Desert Research Institute, Biological Sciences Center. P.O. Box 60220, Reno, Nevada 89506. (702) 673-7321.

University of Nevada-Reno, Desert Research Institute, Energy and Environmental Engineering Center. P.O. Box 60220, Reno, Nevada 89506. (702) 677-3107.

TRADE ASSOCIATIONS AND PROFESSIONAL SOCIETIES

Association for Arid Land Studies. c/o International Center for Arid and Semi-Arid Land Studies, Texas Tech. University, P.O. Box 41036, Lubbock, Texas 79409-1036. (806) 742-2218.

ARIZONA ENVIRONMENTAL AGENCIES

GOVERNMENTAL ORGANIZATIONS

Department of Environmental Quality: Air Quality. Director, 2005 North Central, Room 701, Phoenix, Arizona 85004. (602) 257-2308.

Department of Environmental Quality: Environmental Protection. Director, 2005 North Central, Room 701, Phoenix, Arizona 85004. (602) 257-6917.

Department of Environmental Quality: Solid Waste Management. Director, 2005 North Central, Room 701, Phoenix, Arizona 85004. (602) 257-6917.

Department of Environmental Quality: Water Quality. Director, 2005 North Central, Room 701, Phoenix, Arizona 85004. (602) 257-2305.

Department of Health Services: Underground Storage Tanks. Director, 1740 W. Adams St., Room 407, Phoenix, Arizona 85007. (602) 542-1024.

Department of Water Resources: Groundwater Management. Director, 15 S. 15th Ave., Phoenix, Arizona 85007. (602) 542-1540.

Emergency Response Commission: Emergency Preparedness and Community Right-to-Know. Division of Emergency Services, Building 341, 5036 East McDowell Rd., Phoenix, Arizona 85008. (602) 231-6326.

Game and Fish Department: Fish and Wildlife. Director, 2221 W. Greenway Rd., Phoenix, Arizona 85023. (602) 942-3000.

Industrial Commission: Occupational Safety. Director, 800 W. Washington, Phoenix, Arizona 85007. (602) 542-4411.

Office of State Chemist: Pesticide Registration. State Chemist, PO Box 1586, Phoenix, Arizona 85211-1586. (602) 833-5442.

State Land Commissioner and Forester: Natural Resources. 1616 West Adams St., Room 329, Phoenix, Arizona 85007. (602) 542-4621.

U.S. EPA Region 9: Pollution Prevention. Deputy Director, Hazardous Waste, 215 Fremont St., San Francisco, California 94105. (415) 556-6322.

ARIZONA ENVIRONMENTAL LEGISLATION

GENERAL WORKS

Arizona Environmental Law Letter. Lee Smith Publishers & Printers, Nashville, Tennessee

Arizona Laws Relating to Environmental Quality. Michie Co., PO Box 7587, Charlottesville, Virginia 22906. (804) 972-7600. 1990.

ARKANSAS ENVIRONMENTAL AGENCIES

GOVERNMENTAL ORGANIZATIONS

Department of Arkansas Heritage: Natural Resources. Director, 225 East Markham St., #200, Little Rock, Arkansas 72201. (501) 371-1639.

Department of Labor: Emergency Preparedness and Community Right-to-Know. Depository of Documents, 10421 West Markham, Little Rock, Arkansas 72205. (501) 681-4534.

Department of Labor: Occupational Safety. Director, 10421 W. Markham, #100, Little Rock, Arkansas 72205. (501) 682-4500.

Department of Pollution Control and Ecology: Air Quality. Director, 8001 National Dr., Little Rock, Arkansas 72219. (501) 562-7444.

Department of Pollution Control and Ecology: Environmental Protection. Director, 8001 National Dr., Little Rock, Arkansas 72219. (501) 570-2121.

Department of Pollution Control and Ecology: Hazardous Waste Management. Director, 8001 National Dr., Little Rock, Arkansas 72219. (501) 570-2872.

Department of Pollution Control and Ecology: Solid Waste Management. Director, 8001 National Dr., Little Rock, Arkansas 72219. (501) 570-2858.

Department of Pollution Control and Ecology: Underground Storage Tanks. 8001 National Dr., Little Rock, Arkansas 72219. (501) 562-7444.

Department of Pollution Control and Ecology: Waste Minimization and Pollution Prevention. Directors, Solid Waste & Hazardous Waste Division, 1 Capitol Mall, Little Rock, Arkansas 72201. (501) 562-7444.

Department of Pollution Control and Ecology: Water Quality. Director, 8001 National Dr., Little Rock, Arkansas 72219. (501) 570-2114.

Game and Fish Commission: Fish and Wildlife. Director, #2 Natural Resources Dr., Little Rock, Arkansas 72205. (501) 223-6305.

State Plant Board: Pesticide Registration. Director, Division of Feeds, Fertilizer and Pesticides, PO Box 1069, Little Rock, Arkansas 72205. (501) 225-1598.

ARKANSAS ENVIRONMENTAL LEGISLATION

GENERAL WORKS

Arkansas Handbook on Environmental Laws. Government Institutes, Inc., 4 Research Pl., Ste. 200, Rockville, Maryland 20850. (301) 921-2300. 1990.

AROMATIC AMINES

See also: AIR POLLUTION

ABSTRACTING AND INDEXING SERVICES

Air Pollution Titles. Pennsylvania State University, Center for Air Environmental Studies, 226 Fenske Laboratory, University Park, Pennsylvania 16802. (814) 865-1415. 1965. Bibliographic guide to current research literature on air environment, including monitoring and control of air pollution, health effects, effects on agriculture, forests, toxic air contaminants, and global atmospheric pro cases.

Air Pollution Translations. A Bibliography With Abstracts. U.S. Environmental Protection Agency, MD 75, Research Triangle Park, North Carolina 27711. (919) 541-2184. 1969.

Biological Abstracts. BIOSIS, 2100 Arch St., Philadelphia, Pennsylvania 19103-1399. (215) 587-4800. 1927-.

Chemical Abstracts. Chemical Abstracts Service, 2540 Olentangy River Rd., PO Box 3012, Columbus, Ohio 43210. (800) 848-6533. 1907-.

Environment Abstracts. Bowker A & I Publishing, 121 Chanlon Rd., New Providence, New Jersey 07974. (908) 464-6800. 1974-.

Environment Index. Environment Information Center, Index Research Department, 124 E. 39th St., New York, New York 10016. 1971-. Annual.

Environmental Information Connection–EIC. Planning Information Program, Dept. of Urban and Regional Planning, University of Illinois, 1003 West Nevada, Urbana, Illinois 61801. (217) 333-1369. Also available online.

Environmental Periodicals Bibliography. Environmental Studies Institute, International Academy at Santa Barbara, 800 Garden St., Suite D, Santa Barbara, California 93101. (805) 965-5010. Also available online.

Science Citation Index. Institute for Scientific Information, 3501 Market St., Philadelphia, Pennsylvania 19104. 1961-.

BIBLIOGRAPHIES

EPA Publications Bibliography. U.S. Environmental Protection Agency, Library Systems Branch, 401 M St., SW, Washington, District of Columbia 20460. (202) 260-2090. Quarterly.

ENCYCLOPEDIAS AND DICTIONARIES

McGraw-Hill Encyclopedia of Environmental Science. Sybil P. Parker. McGraw-Hill Science & Engineering Books, 11 W. 19th St., New York, New York 10011. (212) 337-6010. 1980. Covers ecology, man's influence on nature, and environmental protection.

McGraw-Hill Encyclopedia of Science and Technology. McGraw-Hill, 1221 Avenue of the Americas, New York, New York 10020. (212) 512-2000 or (800) 262-4729. 1992. Seventh edition. Issued in multiple volumes including index. Includes all science and technology broad subject areas.

Van Nostrand's Scientific Encyclopedia. Glenn D. Considine, ed. Van Nostrand Reinhold, 115 5th Ave., New York, New York 10003. (212) 254-3232. 1983. Sixth edition. Includes all broad subject areas in science.

ONLINE DATA BASES

BIOSIS Previews. BIOSIS, 2100 Arch St., Philadelphia, Pennsylvania 19103-1399. (215) 587-4800. Largest and most comprehensive database of research in the life sciences. Contains citations for nearly 9000 primary research journals, monographs, reviews, symposia, preliminary reports, semi-popular journals, selected institutional reports, government reports and research communications.

CAS Source Index–CASSI. Chemical Abstracts Service, 2540 Olentangy River Rd., P.O. Box 3012, Columbus, Ohio 43210. (800) 848-6533 or (614) 421-3600. A listing of bibliographic and library holdings information for scientific and technical primary literature relevant to the chemical sciences.

Chemical Abstracts-CA. Chemical Abstracts Service, 2540 Olentangy River Rd., P.O. Box 3012, Columbus, Ohio 43210. (800) 848-6533 or (614) 421-3600. Information sources include 9000 journals, patents from 27 countries, two industrial property organizations, new books, conference proceedings, and government research reports.

Chemical Carcinogenesis Research Information System–CCRIS. National Library of Medicine, 8600 Rockville Pike, Bethesda, Maryland 20894. (800) 638-8480. Individual assay results and test conditions for 1,451 chemicals in the areas of carcinogenicity, mutagenicity, tumor promotion, and cocarcinogenicity.

Chemical Collection System/Request Tracking–CCS/RTS. U.S. Environmental Protection Agency, Office of Pesticides and Toxic Substances, 401 M St., SW, Washington, District of Columbia 20460. (202) 260-2090. Contains information on various properties of a number of chemicals including environmental effects, test and analysis methods, and health effects. Available from EPA.

Chemical Dictionary Online–CHEMLINE. Chemical Abstracts Service, 2540 Olentangy River Rd., Columbus, Ohio 43210. (614) 421-3600 or (800) 848-6533. Part of MEDLINE of the National Library of Medicine (NLM). File of 900,000 names for chemical substances, representing 450,000 unique compounds. It contains such information as Chemical Abstracts (CA) Service Registry Numbers, molecular formulas, preferred chemical nomenclature, and generic and ring structure information. Available on NLM's ELHILL system.

Chemical Exposure. Science Applications International Corp., Health & Environmental Information, P.O. Box 2501, Oak Ridge, Tennessee 37831. (615) 482-9031. Database of chemicals that have been identified in both human tissues and body fluids and in feral and food animals. Contains reference to journal articles, conferences, and reports. Covers the whole fields of information related to human and animal exposure to food, air, and water contaminants and pharmaceuticals. Its records include information on chemical properties, formulas, tissues measured, analytical method used, demographics and more. Available on DIALOG.

Enviro/Energyline Abstracts Plus. R. R. Bowker Co., 121 Chanlon Rd., New Providence, New Jersey 07974. (908) 464-6800.

Environmental Periodicals Bibliography. National Information Services Corp., Ste. 6, Wyman Towers, 3100 St. Paul St., Baltimore, Maryland 21218. (410)243-0797. Online version of abstract of same name.

AROMATIC HYDROCARBONS

See also: AIR POLLUTION

ABSTRACTING AND INDEXING SERVICES

Air Pollution Titles. Pennsylvania State University, Center for Air Environmental Studies, 226 Fenske Laboratory, University Park, Pennsylvania 16802. (814) 865-1415. 1965. Bibliographic guide to current research literature on air environment, including monitoring and control of air pollution, health effects, effects on agriculture, forests, toxic air contaminants, and global atmospheric pro cases.

Air Pollution Translations. A Bibliography With Abstracts. U.S. Environmental Protection Agency, MD 75, Research Triangle Park, North Carolina 27711. (919) 541-2184. 1969.

Biological Abstracts. BIOSIS, 2100 Arch St., Philadelphia, Pennsylvania 19103-1399. (215) 587-4800. 1927-.

Biological and Agricultural Index. H.W. Wilson Co., 950 University Ave., Bronx, New York 10452. (800) 367-6770. 1916-. Monthly.

Chemical Abstracts. Chemical Abstracts Service, 2540 Olentangy River Rd., PO Box 3012, Columbus, Ohio 43210. (800) 848-6533. 1907-.

Ecology Abstracts. Cambridge Scientific Abstracts, 5161 River Rd., Bethesda, Maryland 20816. (301) 961-6750. Monthly.

Environment Abstracts. Bowker A & I Publishing, 121 Chanlon Rd., New Providence, New Jersey 07974. (908) 464-6800. 1974-.

Environment Index. Environment Information Center, Index Research Department, 124 E. 39th St., New York, New York 10016. 1971-. Annual.

Environmental Information Connection–EIC. Planning Information Program, Dept. of Urban and Regional Planning, University of Illinois, 1003 West Nevada, Urbana, Illinois 61801. (217) 333-1369. Also available online.

|

Environmental Periodicals Bibliography. Environmental Studies Institute, International Academy at Santa Barbara, 800 Garden St., Suite D, Santa Barbara, California 93101. (805) 965-5010. Also available online.

Index to Scientific Book Contents. Institute for Scientific Information, 3501 Market St., Philadelphia, Pennsylvania 19104. (800) 523-1857. 1985-. Annual. Gives contents of science books published.

Science Citation Index. Institute for Scientific Information, 3501 Market St., Philadelphia, Pennsylvania 19104. 1961-.

BIBLIOGRAPHIES

EPA Publications Bibliography. U.S. Environmental Protection Agency, Library Systems Branch, 401 M St., SW, Washington, District of Columbia 20460. (202) 260-2090. Quarterly.

ENCYCLOPEDIAS AND DICTIONARIES

McGraw-Hill Encyclopedia of Science and Technology. McGraw-Hill, 1221 Avenue of the Americas, New York, New York 10020. (212) 512-2000 or (800) 262-4729. 1992. Seventh edition. Issued in multiple volumes including index. Includes all science and technology broad subject areas.

ONLINE DATA BASES

BIOSIS Previews. BIOSIS, 2100 Arch St., Philadelphia, Pennsylvania 19103-1399. (215) 587-4800. Largest and most comprehensive database of research in the life sciences. Contains citations for nearly 9000 primary research journals, monographs, reviews, symposia, preliminary reports, semi-popular journals, selected institutional reports, government reports and research communications.

CAS Source Index-CASSI. Chemical Abstracts Service, 2540 Olentangy River Rd., P.O. Box 3012, Columbus, Ohio 43210. (800) 848-6533 or (614) 421-3600. A listing of bibliographic and library holdings information for scientific and technical primary literature relevant to the chemical sciences.

Chemical Abstracts-CA. Chemical Abstracts Service, 2540 Olentangy River Rd., P.O. Box 3012, Columbus, Ohio 43210. (800) 848-6533 or (614) 421-3600. Information sources include 9000 journals, patents from 27 countries, two industrial property organizations, new books, conference proceedings, and government research reports.

Chemical Carcinogenesis Research Information System-CCRIS. National Library of Medicine, 8600 Rockville Pike, Bethesda, Maryland 20894. (800) 638-8480. Individual assay results and test conditions for 1,451 chemicals in the areas of carcinogenicity, mutagenicity, tumor promotion, and cocarcinogenicity.

Chemical Collection System/Request Tracking-CCS/RTS. U.S. Environmental Protection Agency, Office of Pesticides and Toxic Substances, 401 M St., SW, Washington, District of Columbia 20460. (202) 260-2090. Contains information on various properties of a number of chemicals including environmental effects, test and analysis methods, and health effects. Available from EPA.

Chemical Dictionary Online-CHEMLINE. Chemical Abstracts Service, 2540 Olentangy River Rd., Columbus, Ohio 43210. (614) 421-3600 or (800) 848-6533. Part of MEDLINE of the National Library of Medicine (NLM). File of 900,000 names for chemical substances, representing 450,000 unique compounds. It contains such information as Chemical Abstracts (CA) Service Registry Numbers, molecular formulas, preferred chemical nomenclature, and generic and ring structure information. Available on NLM's ELHILL system.

Chemical Exposure. Science Applications International Corp., Health & Environmental Information, P.O. Box 2501, Oak Ridge, Tennessee 37831. (615) 482-9031. Database of chemicals that have been identified in both human tissues and body fluids and in feral and food animals. Contains reference to journal articles, conferences, and reports. Covers the whole fields of information related to human and animal exposure to food, air, and water contaminants and pharmaceuticals. Its records include information on chemical properties, formulas, tissues measured, analytical method used, demographics and more. Available on DIALOG.

Enviro/Energyline Abstracts Plus. R. R. Bowker Co., 121 Chanlon Rd., New Providence, New Jersey 07974. (908) 464-6800.

Environmental Periodicals Bibliography. National Information Services Corp., Ste. 6, Wyman Towers, 3100 St. Paul St., Baltimore, Maryland 21218. (410)243-0797. Online version of abstract of same name.

ARSENATES

See: ARSENIC

ARSENIC

See also: HAZARDOUS WASTES; METALS AND METALLURGY; PESTICIDES; TOXICITY; WASTE DISPOSAL

ABSTRACTING AND INDEXING SERVICES

Biological Abstracts. BIOSIS, 2100 Arch St., Philadelphia, Pennsylvania 19103-1399. (215) 587-4800. 1927-.

Chemical Abstracts. Chemical Abstracts Service, 2540 Olentangy River Rd., PO Box 3012, Columbus, Ohio 43210. (800) 848-6533. 1907-.

Ecology Abstracts. Cambridge Scientific Abstracts, 5161 River Rd., Bethesda, Maryland 20816. (301) 961-6750. Monthly.

Environment Abstracts. Bowker A & I Publishing, 121 Chanlon Rd., New Providence, New Jersey 07974. (908) 464-6800. 1974-.

Environment Index. Environment Information Center, Index Research Department, 124 E. 39th St., New York, New York 10016. 1971-. Annual.

Environmental Information Connection-EIC. Planning Information Program, Dept. of Urban and Regional Planning, University of Illinois, 1003 West Nevada, Urbana, Illinois 61801. (217) 333-1369. Also available online.

Environmental Periodicals Bibliography. Environmental Studies Institute, International Academy at Santa Barbara, 800 Garden St., Suite D, Santa Barbara, California 93101. (805) 965-5010. Also available online.

General Science Index. H. W. Wilson Co., 950 University Ave., Bronx, New York 10452. 1978-. Monthly, also issued in annual cumulation. Cumulative subject index to English language periodicals in the subject fields of astronomy, botany, chemistry, earth science, environment and conservation, food and nutrition, genetics, mathematics, medicine and health, microbiology, oceanography, physics, physiology and zoology.

Index to Scientific Book Contents. Institute for Scientific Information, 3501 Market St., Philadelphia, Pennsylvania 19104. (800) 523-1857. 1985-. Annual. Gives contents of science books published.

Science Citation Index. Institute for Scientific Information, 3501 Market St., Philadelphia, Pennsylvania 19104. 1961-.

BIBLIOGRAPHIES

Directory of Published Proceedings. Interdok Corp., 173 Halstead Ave., Harrison, New York 10528. (914) 835-3506. 1990. Monthly. This is a listing of published proceedings including the series SEMTE (Science/Medicine/Engineering/Technology) and the series SSH (Social Science/Humanities).

EPA Publications Bibliography. U.S. Environmental Protection Agency, Library Systems Branch, 401 M St., SW, Washington, District of Columbia 20460. (202) 260-2090. Quarterly.

ENCYCLOPEDIAS AND DICTIONARIES

Encyclopedia of Chemical Processing and Design. John J. Mcketta and W. A. Cunningham. Marcel Dekker, Inc., 270 Madison Ave., New York, New York 10016. (212) 696-9000; (800) 228-1160. 1992. Thirty-eight volumes.

Kirk-Othmer Encyclopedia of Chemical Technology. J. I. Kroschwitz, ed. John Wiley & Sons, Inc., 605 3rd Ave., New York, New York 10158-0012. (212) 850-6000. 1992-. All articles in the new edition have been rewritten and updated adding new subjects such as biotechnology, computer topics, analytical techniques and instrumentation, environmental concerns, fuels and energy, inorganic and solid state chemistry; composite materials and material science in general, and pharmaceuticals. Also available online.

McGraw-Hill Encyclopedia of Environmental Science. Sybil P. Parker. McGraw-Hill Science & Engineering Books, 11 W. 19th St., New York, New York 10011. (212) 337-6010. 1980. Covers ecology, man's influence on nature, and environmental protection.

McGraw-Hill Encyclopedia of Science and Technology. McGraw-Hill, 1221 Avenue of the Americas, New York, New York 10020. (212) 512-2000 or (800) 262-4729. 1992. Seventh edition. Issued in multiple volumes including index. Includes all science and technology broad subject areas.

Van Nostrand's Scientific Encyclopedia. Glenn D. Considine, ed. Van Nostrand Reinhold, 115 5th Ave., New York, New York 10003. (212) 254-3232. 1983. Sixth edition. Includes all broad subject areas in science.

HANDBOOKS AND MANUALS

Tables of Physical and Chemical Constants and Some Mathematical Functions. G. W. C. Kaye, et al. Longman Group Ltd., Longman House, Burnt Mill, Harlow, England CM20 2J6. 0279 426721. 1988. Fifteenth edition. Includes tables on mechanical properties, density, elasticity, viscosity, surface tension, temperature and heat. Also covers radiation, optics, chemistry, electrochemistry, astrophysics, and chemical thermodynamics.

ONLINE DATA BASES

BIOSIS Previews. BIOSIS, 2100 Arch St., Philadelphia, Pennsylvania 19103-1399. (215) 587-4800. Largest and most comprehensive database of research in the life sciences. Contains citations for nearly 9000 primary research journals, monographs, reviews, symposia, preliminary reports, semi-popular journals, selected institutional reports, government reports and research communications.

CAS Source Index–CASSI. Chemical Abstracts Service, 2540 Olentangy River Rd., P.O. Box 3012, Columbus, Ohio 43210. (800) 848-6533 or (614) 421-3600. A listing of bibliographic and library holdings information for scientific and technical primary literature relevant to the chemical sciences.

Chemical Abstracts-CA. Chemical Abstracts Service, 2540 Olentangy River Rd., P.O. Box 3012, Columbus, Ohio 43210. (800) 848-6533 or (614) 421-3600. Information sources include 9000 journals, patents from 27 countries, two industrial property organizations, new books, conference proceedings, and government research reports.

Chemical Abstracts Chemical Name Directory-CHEMNAME. Chemical Abstracts Service, 2540 Olentangy River Rd., P.O. Box 3012, Columbus, Ohio 43210. (800) 848-6533 or (614) 421-3600. Listing of chemical substances in a dictionary type file. The Chemical Abstracts (CAS) Registry Number, molecular formula, Chemical Abstracts (CA) Substance Index Name, available synonyms, ring data and other chemical substance information is given for each entry.

Chemical Carcinogenesis Research Information System-CCRIS. National Library of Medicine, 8600 Rockville Pike, Bethesda, Maryland 20894. (800) 638-8480. Individual assay results and test conditions for 1,451 chemicals in the areas of carcinogenicity, mutagenicity, tumor promotion, and cocarcinogenicity.

Chemical Collection System/Request Tracking-CCS/RTS. U.S. Environmental Protection Agency, Office of Pesticides and Toxic Substances, 401 M St., SW, Washington, District of Columbia 20460. (202) 260-2090. Contains information on various properties of a number of chemicals including environmental effects, test and analysis methods, and health effects. Available from EPA.

Chemical Dictionary Online-CHEMLINE. Chemical Abstracts Service, 2540 Olentangy River Rd., Columbus, Ohio 43210. (614) 421-3600 or (800) 848-6533. Part of MEDLINE of the National Library of Medicine (NLM). File of 900,000 names for chemical substances, representing 450,000 unique compounds. It contains such information as Chemical Abstracts (CA) Service Registry Numbers, molecular formulas, preferred chemical no-

menclature, and generic and ring structure information. Available on NLM's ELHILL system.

Chemical Exposure. Science Applications International Corp., Health & Environmental Information, P.O. Box 2501, Oak Ridge, Tennessee 37831. (615) 482-9031. Database of chemicals that have been identified in both human tissues and body fluids and in feral and food animals. Contains reference to journal articles, conferences, and reports. Covers the whole fields of information related to human and animal exposure to food, air, and water contaminants and pharmaceuticals. Its records include information on chemical properties, formulas, tissues measured, analytical method used, demographics and more. Available on DIALOG.

Enviro/Energyline Abstracts Plus. R. R. Bowker Co., 121 Chanlon Rd., New Providence, New Jersey 07974. (908) 464-6800.

Environmental Periodicals Bibliography. National Information Services Corp., Ste. 6, Wyman Towers, 3100 St. Paul St., Baltimore, Maryland 21218. (410)243-0797. Online version of abstract of same name.

Kirk-Othmer Encyclopedia of Chemical Technology. John Wiley & Sons, Inc., 605 3rd Ave., 5th Floor, New York, New York 10158. (212) 850-6000. Online version of the publication of the same name.

ARTHROPODS

See also: CRAYFISH; ECOSYSTEMS; INSECTS; SHRIMP AND SHRIMP FISHERIES; SOIL ORGANISMS

ABSTRACTING AND INDEXING SERVICES

Applied Ecology Abstracts Studies in Renewable Natural Resources. Information Retrieval Ltd., 1911 Jefferson Davis Highway, Arlington, Virginia 22202. 1975-. Monthly.

Biological Abstracts. BIOSIS, 2100 Arch St., Philadelphia, Pennsylvania 19103-1399. (215) 587-4800. 1927-.

Biological and Agricultural Index. H.W. Wilson Co., 950 University Ave., Bronx, New York 10452. (800) 367-6770. 1916-. Monthly.

Ecological Abstracts. Geo Abstracts Ltd. Elsevier Applied Science, Crown House, Linton Rd., Barking, England IG 11 8JU. 1974-. Derived from over 600 leading ecological and environmental journals, plus books, conference proceedings, reports and theses.

Ecology Abstracts. Cambridge Scientific Abstracts, 5161 River Rd., Bethesda, Maryland 20816. (301) 961-6750. Monthly.

Environment Abstracts. Bowker A & I Publishing, 121 Chanlon Rd., New Providence, New Jersey 07974. (908) 464-6800. 1974-.

Environment Index. Environment Information Center, Index Research Department, 124 E. 39th St., New York, New York 10016. 1971-. Annual.

Environmental Information Connection–EIC. Planning Information Program, Dept. of Urban and Regional Planning, University of Illinois, 1003 West Nevada, Urbana, Illinois 61801. (217) 333-1369. Also available online.

Environmental Periodicals Bibliography. Environmental Studies Institute, International Academy at Santa Barbara, 800 Garden St., Suite D, Santa Barbara, California 93101. (805) 965-5010. Also available online.

General Science Index. H. W. Wilson Co., 950 University Ave., Bronx, New York 10452. 1978-. Monthly, also issued in annual cumulation. Cumulative subject index to English language periodicals in the subject fields of astronomy, botany, chemistry, earth science, environment and conservation, food and nutrition, genetics, mathematics, medicine and health, microbiology, oceanography, physics, physiology and zoology.

Index to Scientific Book Contents. Institute for Scientific Information, 3501 Market St., Philadelphia, Pennsylvania 19104. (800) 523-1857. 1985-. Annual. Gives contents of science books published.

Multimedia Index to Ecology. National Information Center for Educational Media, University of Southern California, Los Angeles, California 90007.

Science Citation Index. Institute for Scientific Information, 3501 Market St., Philadelphia, Pennsylvania 19104. 1961-.

BIBLIOGRAPHIES

EPA Publications Bibliography. U.S. Environmental Protection Agency, Library Systems Branch, 401 M St., SW, Washington, District of Columbia 20460. (202) 260-2090. Quarterly.

ENCYCLOPEDIAS AND DICTIONARIES

McGraw-Hill Encyclopedia of Environmental Science. Sybil P. Parker. McGraw-Hill Science & Engineering Books, 11 W. 19th St., New York, New York 10011. (212) 337-6010. 1980. Covers ecology, man's influence on nature, and environmental protection.

McGraw-Hill Encyclopedia of Science and Technology. McGraw-Hill, 1221 Avenue of the Americas, New York, New York 10020. (212) 512-2000 or (800) 262-4729. 1992. Seventh edition. Issued in multiple volumes including index. Includes all science and technology broad subject areas.

Van Nostrand's Scientific Encyclopedia. Glenn D. Considine, ed. Van Nostrand Reinhold, 115 5th Ave., New York, New York 10003. (212) 254-3232. 1983. Sixth edition. Includes all broad subject areas in science.

GENERAL WORKS

Magill's Survey of Science. Life Science Series. Frank N. Magill, ed. Salem Press, PO Box 50062, Pasadena, California 91105. 1991. Six volumes. Contents: v.1. A-Central and peripheral nervous system functions; v.2. Central metabolism regulation - eukaryotic transcriptional control; v.3. Positive and negative eukaryotic transcriptional control - mammalian hormones; v.4. Hormones and behavior - muscular contraction; v.5. Muscular contraction and relaxation - sexual reproduction in plants; v.6. Reproductive behavior and mating - X inactivation and the Lyon hypothesis.

ONLINE DATA BASES

BIOSIS Previews. BIOSIS, 2100 Arch St., Philadelphia, Pennsylvania 19103-1399. (215) 587-4800. Largest and

most comprehensive database of research in the life sciences. Contains citations for nearly 9000 primary research journals, monographs, reviews, symposia, preliminary reports, semi-popular journals, selected institutional reports, government reports and research communications.

Enviro/Energyline Abstracts Plus. R. R. Bowker Co., 121 Chanlon Rd., New Providence, New Jersey 07974. (908) 464-6800.

Environmental Periodicals Bibliography. National Information Services Corp., Ste. 6, Wyman Towers, 3100 St. Paul St., Baltimore, Maryland 21218. (410)243-0797. Online version of abstract of same name.

ARTIFICIAL DESTRATIFICATION

ABSTRACTING AND INDEXING SERVICES

Biological Abstracts. BIOSIS, 2100 Arch St., Philadelphia, Pennsylvania 19103-1399. (215) 587-4800. 1927-.

Environment Abstracts. Bowker A & I Publishing, 121 Chanlon Rd., New Providence, New Jersey 07974. (908) 464-6800. 1974-.

Environment Index. Environment Information Center, Index Research Department, 124 E. 39th St., New York, New York 10016. 1971-. Annual.

Environmental Information Connection–EIC. Planning Information Program, Dept. of Urban and Regional Planning, University of Illinois, 1003 West Nevada, Urbana, Illinois 61801. (217) 333-1369. Also available online.

Environmental Periodicals Bibliography. Environmental Studies Institute, International Academy at Santa Barbara, 800 Garden St., Suite D, Santa Barbara, California 93101. (805) 965-5010. Also available online.

Science Citation Index. Institute for Scientific Information, 3501 Market St., Philadelphia, Pennsylvania 19104. 1961-.

BIBLIOGRAPHIES

EPA Publications Bibliography. U.S. Environmental Protection Agency, Library Systems Branch, 401 M St., SW, Washington, District of Columbia 20460. (202) 260-2090. Quarterly.

ONLINE DATA BASES

BIOSIS Previews. BIOSIS, 2100 Arch St., Philadelphia, Pennsylvania 19103-1399. (215) 587-4800. Largest and most comprehensive database of research in the life sciences. Contains citations for nearly 9000 primary research journals, monographs, reviews, symposia, preliminary reports, semi-popular journals, selected institutional reports, government reports and research communications.

Enviro/Energyline Abstracts Plus. R. R. Bowker Co., 121 Chanlon Rd., New Providence, New Jersey 07974. (908) 464-6800.

Environmental Periodicals Bibliography. National Information Services Corp., Ste. 6, Wyman Towers, 3100 St.

Paul St., Baltimore, Maryland 21218. (410)243-0797. Online version of abstract of same name.

ASBESTOS

See also: CARCINOGENS; HAZARDOUS WASTE

ABSTRACTING AND INDEXING SERVICES

Abstracts of Air and Water Conservation Literature. American Petroleum Institute. Central Abstracting and Indexing Service, 275 Madison Avenue, New York, New York 10016. 1972.

Applied Science and Technology Index. H.W. Wilson Co., 950 University Ave., Bronx, New York 10452. (800) 367-6770. Formerly Industrial Arts Index.

Biological Abstracts. BIOSIS, 2100 Arch St., Philadelphia, Pennsylvania 19103-1399. (215) 587-4800. 1927-.

Chemical Abstracts. Chemical Abstracts Service, 2540 Olentangy River Rd., PO Box 3012, Columbus, Ohio 43210. (800) 848-6533. 1907-.

Civil Engineering Hydraulic Abstracts. BHRA Fluid Engineering, Air Science Co., PO Box 143, Corning, New York 14830. (607) 962-5591. Monthly. Abstracts of periodicals that publish in the areas of hydraulic engineering and other related topics.

Environment Abstracts. Bowker A & I Publishing, 121 Chanlon Rd., New Providence, New Jersey 07974. (908) 464-6800. 1974-.

Environment Index. Environment Information Center, Index Research Department, 124 E. 39th St., New York, New York 10016. 1971-. Annual.

Environmental Information Connection–EIC. Planning Information Program, Dept. of Urban and Regional Planning, University of Illinois, 1003 West Nevada, Urbana, Illinois 61801. (217) 333-1369. Also available online.

Environmental Periodicals Bibliography. Environmental Studies Institute, International Academy at Santa Barbara, 800 Garden St., Suite D, Santa Barbara, California 93101. (805) 965-5010. Also available online.

General Science Index. H. W. Wilson Co., 950 University Ave., Bronx, New York 10452. 1978-. Monthly, also issued in annual cumulation. Cumulative subject index to English language periodicals in the subject fields of astronomy, botany, chemistry, earth science, environment and conservation, food and nutrition, genetics, mathematics, medicine and health, microbiology, oceanography, physics, physiology and zoology.

Index to Scientific Book Contents. Institute for Scientific Information, 3501 Market St., Philadelphia, Pennsylvania 19104. (800) 523-1857. 1985-. Annual. Gives contents of science books published.

Science Citation Index. Institute for Scientific Information, 3501 Market St., Philadelphia, Pennsylvania 19104. 1961-.

BIBLIOGRAPHIES

Asbestos and Silicate Pollution: Citations from the Engineering Index Data Base. Diane M. Cavagnaro. National

Technical Information Service, 5285 Port Royal Rd., Springfield, Virginia 22161. (703) 487-4650. 1980. Deals with asbestos pollution and silicate pollution and their effects on the environment.

Asbestos in Air. Federation of American Societies for Experimental Biology, 9650 Rockville Pike, Bethesda, Maryland 20814. (301) 530-7000. 1980. Bibliography of environmental aspects of asbestos.

Asbestos Toxicity. Geraldine Nowak. National Institutes of Health, Department of Health and Human Services, 8600 Rockville Pike, Bethesda, Maryland 20894. (301) 496-6308. 1977.

Bibliography and Index of Geology. American Geological Institute, 4220 King St., Alexandria, Virginia 22302. Monthly. Includes environmental geology and hydrogeology.

Directory of Published Proceedings. Interdok Corp., 173 Halstead Ave., Harrison, New York 10528. (914) 835-3506. 1990. Monthly. This is a listing of published proceedings including the series SEMTE (Science/Medicine/Engineering/Technology) and the series SSH (Social Science/Humanities).

EPA Publications Bibliography. U.S. Environmental Protection Agency, Library Systems Branch, 401 M St., SW, Washington, District of Columbia 20460. (202) 260-2090. Quarterly.

DIRECTORIES

Gale Environmental Sourcebook. Karen Hill. Gale Research Co., 835 Penobscot Bldg., Detroit, Michigan 48226-4094. (313) 961-2242. Contacts, information sources, or general information on environmental topics.

Reference Directory to Asbestos Removal Contractors, Consultants and Laboratories. Rimbach Publishing, Inc., 8650 Babcock Blvd., Pittsburgh, Pennsylvania 15237. (412) 364-5366.

ENCYCLOPEDIAS AND DICTIONARIES

Dictionary of Civil Engineering. John S. Scott. Halsted Press, Division of J. Wiley, 605 3rd Ave., New York, New York 10158. (212) 850-6000. 1981. Third edition.

Encyclopedia of Chemical Processing and Design. John J. Mcketta and W. A. Cunningham. Marcel Dekker, Inc., 270 Madison Ave., New York, New York 10016. (212) 696-9000; (800) 228-1160. 1992. Thirty-eight volumes.

Encyclopedia of Human Biology. Renato Dulbecco, ed. Academic Press, c/o Harcourt Brace Jovanovich Inc., 6277 Sea Harbor Dr., Orlando, Florida 32887. (800) 346-8648. 1991. Eight volumes.

Glossary of Geology. Robert Latimer Bates and Julia A. Jackson, eds. American Geological Institute, 4220 King St., Alexandria, Virginia 22302-1507. (703) 379-2480 or (800) 336-4764. 1987. Third edition.

Kirk-Othmer Encyclopedia of Chemical Technology. J. I. Kroschwitz, ed. John Wiley & Sons, Inc., 605 3rd Ave., New York, New York 10158-0012. (212) 850-6000. 1992-. All articles in the new edition have been rewritten and updated adding new subjects such as biotechnology, computer topics, analytical techniques and instrumentation, environmental concerns, fuels and energy, inorganic and solid state chemistry; composite materials and

material science in general, and pharmaceuticals. Also available online.

McGraw-Hill Encyclopedia of Science and Technology. McGraw-Hill, 1221 Avenue of the Americas, New York, New York 10020. (212) 512-2000 or (800) 262-4729. 1992. Seventh edition. Issued in multiple volumes including index. Includes all science and technology broad subject areas.

McGraw-Hill Encyclopedia of the Geological Sciences. Sybil P. Parker, ed. McGraw-Hill, 1221 Avenue of the Americas, New York, New York 10020. (212) 512-2000 or (800) 262-4729. 1988. Second edition. Published previously in the McGraw-Hill Encyclopedia of Science and Technology.

Van Nostrand's Scientific Encyclopedia. Glenn D. Considine, ed. Van Nostrand Reinhold, 115 5th Ave., New York, New York 10003. (212) 254-3232. 1983. Sixth edition. Includes all broad subject areas in science.

GENERAL WORKS

Asbestos Engineering, Management and Control. Ken Cherry. Lewis Publishers, 2000 Corporate Blvd., N.W., Boca Raton, Florida 33431. (407) 994-0555 or (800) 272-7737. 1988. Details of major legal issues and cost estimating methods. Also includes every aspect of abatement work from initial survey through final cleanup. In addition medical aspects, respirator use, training, sample contracts and other topics coupled with a practical approach are covered.

Asbestos: the Hazardous Fiber. Melvin A. Bernade. CRC Press, 2000 Corporate Blvd. N.W., Boca Raton, Florida 33431. (800) 272-7737. 1990. An overview of the state-of-the-art of asbestos and its problems in the environment.

How Serious is the Threat of Asbestos?. Institute of Real Estate Management, PO Box 109025, Chicago, Illinois 60610-9025. (312) 661-1953. 1989. Harvard Symposium on Health Aspects of Exposure to Asbestos in Buildings.

Magill's Survey of Science. Earth Science Series. Frank N. Magill. Salem Press, PO Box 50062, Pasadena, California 91105. 1990-. Five volumes. Includes information on earth's crust, hot spots and volcanic island chains, physical properties of minerals, rock magnetism, physical properties of rocks, and index.

Safety in the Use of Asbestos. International Labour Office, 49 Sheridan Ave., Albany, New York 12210. (518) 436-9686. 1990. An ILO code of practice. The first part of the code includes monitoring in the work place, preventive measures, the protection and supervision of the workers' health, and the packaging, handling, transport and disposal of asbestos waste. More detailed guidance on the limitation of exposure to asbestos in specific activities is given in the second part of the code, which includes sections on mining and milling, asbestos cement, textiles, friction materials, and the removal of asbestos-containing materials.

TAPPI Environmental Conference Proceedings, Seattle, WA, April 9-11, 1990. TAPPI Press, Technology Park/Atlanta, PO Box 105113, Atlanta, Georgia 30348. (404) 446-1400. 1990. Contains 11 papers presented at the conference covering industrial pollution and its remedies.

ONLINE DATA BASES

Asbestos Abatement: Risks & Responsibilities. Bureau of National Affairs, BNA PLUS, 1231 25th Street, N.W., Rm. 215, Washington, District of Columbia 20037. (800) 452-7773.

Asbestos Control Report. Business Publishers, Inc., 951 Pershing Dr., Silver Spring, Maryland 20910-4464. (301) 587-6300. Covers industry ramifications of the Asbestos Hazard Emergency Response Act of 1986, with technical information on control techniques, worksite health and safety. Online version of periodical of the same name.

Asbestos Information System–AIS. U.S. Environmental Protection Agency, Office of Pesticides and Toxic Substances, 401 M St., SW, Washington, District of Columbia 20460. (202) 260-2090. Information on asbestos including chemical use, exposure, manufacturing, the human population, and environmental releases.

BIOSIS Previews. BIOSIS, 2100 Arch St., Philadelphia, Pennsylvania 19103-1399. (215) 587-4800. Largest and most comprehensive database of research in the life sciences. Contains citations for nearly 9000 primary research journals, monographs, reviews, symposia, preliminary reports, semi-popular journals, selected institutional reports, government reports and research communications.

Buraff Asbestos Abatement Report. Buraff Publications, 1350 Connecticut Ave., N.W., Washington, District of Columbia 20036. (202) 862-0990.

CERCLIS. Chemical Information Systems, Inc., 7215 York Rd., Baltimore, Maryland 21212. (301) 321-8440. Information on hazardous waste disposal sites that have either been listed by the EPA on the National Priority List (NPL) or nominated for consideration for the NPL.

Chemical Abstracts-CA. Chemical Abstracts Service, 2540 Olentangy River Rd., P.O. Box 3012, Columbus, Ohio 43210. (800) 848-6533 or (614) 421-3600. Information sources include 9000 journals, patents from 27 countries, two industrial property organizations, new books, conference proceedings, and government research reports.

Enviro/Energyline Abstracts Plus. R. R. Bowker Co., 121 Chanlon Rd., New Providence, New Jersey 07974. (908) 464-6800.

Environmental Periodicals Bibliography. National Information Services Corp., Ste. 6, Wyman Towers, 3100 St. Paul St., Baltimore, Maryland 21218. (410)243-0797. Online version of abstract of same name.

Kirk-Othmer Encyclopedia of Chemical Technology. John Wiley & Sons, Inc., 605 3rd Ave., 5th Floor, New York, New York 10158. (212) 850-6000. Online version of the publication of the same name.

PERIODICALS AND NEWSLETTERS

Andrews School Asbestos Alert. Andrews Publications, Inc., PO Box 200, Edgemont, Pennsylvania 19028. (215) 353-2565. Monthly. Legal proceedings, construction, and medical problems relating to exposure to asbestos in schools.

Asbestos Abatement Report. Buraff Publications, 1350 Connecticut Ave. N.W., Washington, District of Columbia 20036. (202) 862-0990. 1987-. Biweekly. News about developments in asbestos control.

Asbestos Control Report. Business Publishers, Inc., 951 Pershing Drive, Silver Spring, Maryland 20910-4464. (301) 587-6300. Biweekly. Information on asbestos control techniques, research, and regulations. Also available online.

Asbestos Information Association of North American Newsletter. Asbestos Information Association/North America, 1745 Jefferson Davis Highway, Suite 509, Arlington, Virginia 22202. (703) 979-1150. Monthly. Issues pertaining to asbestos and health.

Asbestos Issues. PH Publishing, Inc., 760 Whalers Way Sta., 100-A., Fort Collins, Colorado 80525. (303) 229-0029. 1988-. Monthly. Provides coverage of the asbestos control field. Improves awareness of management issues and informs readers of risks, insurance, etc.

Environmental Health Letter. Business Publishers, Inc., 951 Pershing Dr., Silver Spring, Maryland 20910-4464. (301) 587-6300. 1961-. Biweekly. Covers areas such as: indoor air, asbestos health effects, toxic substances testing, health problems at wastewater plants, risk-based sludge rules, medical waste, developmental toxicity risk assessment, animal carcinogen tests, pesticide risk, air toxics, aerospace chemicals, lead, radionuclide emissions, state right-to-know statutes, and incinerator emissions.

STATISTICS SOURCES

Control of Asbestos Exposure During Brake Drum Service. U.S. G.P.O, Washington, District of Columbia 20402-9325. (202) 512-0000. Annual. Airborne asbestos control technologies used in the motor vehicle brake drum service industry.

Environmental Data Compendium. OECD Publications and Information Center, 2001 L St., N.W., Suite 700, Washington, District of Columbia 20036. (202) 785-6323. 1989.

Environmental Indicators. OECD Publications and Information Center, 2001 L St., N.W., Suite 700, Washington, District of Columbia 20036. (202) 785-6323. 1991.

Environmental Quality. Council on Environmental Quality. U.S. G.P.O., Washington, District of Columbia 20401. (202) 512-0000. Annual.

The State of the Environment. OECD Publications and Information Center, 2001 L St., N.W., Suite 700, Washington, District of Columbia 20036. (202) 785-6323. 1991.

TRADE ASSOCIATIONS AND PROFESSIONAL SOCIETIES

American Institute of Chemical Engineers. 345 East 47th St., New York, New York 10017. (212) 705-7338.

American Institute of Chemists. 7315 Wisconsin Ave., Bethesda, Maryland 20814. (301) 652-2447.

Asbestos Information Association of North America. 1745 Jefferson Davis Highway, Suite 509, Arlington, Virginia 22202. (703) 979-1150.

Association of Asbestos Cement Pipe Producers. 1745 Jefferson Davis Hwy., Suite 509, Arlington, Virginia 22202. (703) 979-1026.

International Association of Heat & Frost Insulators & Asbestos Workers. 1300 Connecticut Ave., N.W., Suite

505, Washington, District of Columbia 20036. (202) 785-2388.

National Asbestos Council. 1777 N.E. Expressway, Suite 150, Atlanta, Georgia 30329. (404) 633-2622.

ASH

See also: INCINERATION; VOLCANOES

ABSTRACTING AND INDEXING SERVICES

Biological Abstracts. BIOSIS, 2100 Arch St., Philadelphia, Pennsylvania 19103-1399. (215) 587-4800. 1927-.

Environment Abstracts. Bowker A & I Publishing, 121 Chanlon Rd., New Providence, New Jersey 07974. (908) 464-6800. 1974-.

Environment Index. Environment Information Center, Index Research Department, 124 E. 39th St., New York, New York 10016. 1971-. Annual.

Environmental Information Connection–EIC. Planning Information Program, Dept. of Urban and Regional Planning, University of Illinois, 1003 West Nevada, Urbana, Illinois 61801. (217) 333-1369. Also available online.

Environmental Periodicals Bibliography. Environmental Studies Institute, International Academy at Santa Barbara, 800 Garden St., Suite D, Santa Barbara, California 93101. (805) 965-5010. Also available online.

General Science Index. H. W. Wilson Co., 950 University Ave., Bronx, New York 10452. 1978-. Monthly, also issued in annual cumulation. Cumulative subject index to English language periodicals in the subject fields of astronomy, botany, chemistry, earth science, environment and conservation, food and nutrition, genetics, mathematics, medicine and health, microbiology, oceanography, physics, physiology and zoology.

Index to Scientific Book Contents. Institute for Scientific Information, 3501 Market St., Philadelphia, Pennsylvania 19104. (800) 523-1857. 1985-. Annual. Gives contents of science books published.

Pollution Abstracts. Cambridge Scientific Abstracts, 5161 River Rd., Bethesda, Maryland 20816. (301) 961-6750. Six/year. Indexes worldwide technical literature on environmental pollution. Covers air pollution, marine and freshwater pollution, sewage and wastewater treatment, waste management, toxicology and health, noise pollution, radiation, land pollution, and environmental policies, programs, legislation, and education. Also available online.

Science Citation Index. Institute for Scientific Information, 3501 Market St., Philadelphia, Pennsylvania 19104. 1961-.

BIBLIOGRAPHIES

EPA Publications Bibliography. U.S. Environmental Protection Agency, Library Systems Branch, 401 M St., SW, Washington, District of Columbia 20460. (202) 260-2090. Quarterly.

DIRECTORIES

Gale Environmental Sourcebook. Karen Hill. Gale Research Co., 835 Penobscot Bldg., Detroit, Michigan 48226-4094. (313) 961-2242. Contacts, information sources, or general information on environmental topics.

ONLINE DATA BASES

BIOSIS Previews. BIOSIS, 2100 Arch St., Philadelphia, Pennsylvania 19103-1399. (215) 587-4800. Largest and most comprehensive database of research in the life sciences. Contains citations for nearly 9000 primary research journals, monographs, reviews, symposia, preliminary reports, semi-popular journals, selected institutional reports, government reports and research communications.

Enviro/Energyline Abstracts Plus. R. R. Bowker Co., 121 Chanlon Rd., New Providence, New Jersey 07974. (908) 464-6800.

Environmental Periodicals Bibliography. National Information Services Corp., Ste. 6, Wyman Towers, 3100 St. Paul St., Baltimore, Maryland 21218. (410)243-0797. Online version of abstract of same name.

PERIODICALS AND NEWSLETTERS

Ash at Work. American Coal Ash Association, 1000 16th Street, NW, Suite 507, Washington, District of Columbia 20036. (202) 659-2303. Quarterly. Information on fly ash from the combustion of coal.

STATISTICS SOURCES

Environmental Data Compendium. OECD Publications and Information Center, 2001 L St., N.W., Suite 700, Washington, District of Columbia 20036. (202) 785-6323. 1989.

Environmental Indicators. OECD Publications and Information Center, 2001 L St., N.W., Suite 700, Washington, District of Columbia 20036. (202) 785-6323. 1991.

Environmental Quality. Council on Environmental Quality. U.S. G.P.O., Washington, District of Columbia 20401. (202) 512-0000. Annual.

The State of the Environment. OECD Publications and Information Center, 2001 L St., N.W., Suite 700, Washington, District of Columbia 20036. (202) 785-6323. 1991.

ASPHALT

ABSTRACTING AND INDEXING SERVICES

Applied Science and Technology Index. H.W. Wilson Co., 950 University Ave., Bronx, New York 10452. (800) 367-6770. Formerly Industrial Arts Index.

Civil Engineering Hydraulic Abstracts. BHRA Fluid Engineering, Air Science Co., PO Box 143, Corning, New York 14830. (607) 962-5591. Monthly. Abstracts of periodicals that publish in the areas of hydraulic engineering and other related topics.

Environment Abstracts. Bowker A & I Publishing, 121 Chanlon Rd., New Providence, New Jersey 07974. (908) 464-6800. 1974-.

Environment Index. Environment Information Center, Index Research Department, 124 E. 39th St., New York, New York 10016. 1971-. Annual.

Environmental Information Connection–EIC. Planning Information Program, Dept. of Urban and Regional Planning, University of Illinois, 1003 West Nevada, Urbana, Illinois 61801. (217) 333-1369. Also available online.

Environmental Periodicals Bibliography. Environmental Studies Institute, International Academy at Santa Barbara, 800 Garden St., Suite D, Santa Barbara, California 93101. (805) 965-5010. Also available online.

General Science Index. H. W. Wilson Co., 950 University Ave., Bronx, New York 10452. 1978-. Monthly, also issued in annual cumulation. Cumulative subject index to English language periodicals in the subject fields of astronomy, botany, chemistry, earth science, environment and conservation, food and nutrition, genetics, mathematics, medicine and health, microbiology, oceanography, physics, physiology and zoology.

Index to Scientific Book Contents. Institute for Scientific Information, 3501 Market St., Philadelphia, Pennsylvania 19104. (800) 523-1857. 1985-. Annual. Gives contents of science books published.

Science Citation Index. Institute for Scientific Information, 3501 Market St., Philadelphia, Pennsylvania 19104. 1961-.

BIBLIOGRAPHIES

EPA Publications Bibliography. U.S. Environmental Protection Agency, Library Systems Branch, 401 M St., SW, Washington, District of Columbia 20460. (202) 260-2090. Quarterly.

DIRECTORIES

Asphalt/Asphalt Products Directory. 5711 S. 86th Circle, Omaha, Nebraska 68127. (402) 593-4600.

Asphalt Emulsion Manufacturers Association–Membership Directory. Three Church Circle, Suite 250, Annapolis, Maryland 21401. (301) 267-0023. Annual.

Asphalt Paving Technologists. 1404 Concordia Ave., St. Paul, Minnesota 55104. (612) 642-1350. Annual.

ENCYCLOPEDIAS AND DICTIONARIES

Dictionary of Civil Engineering. John S. Scott. Halsted Press, Division of J. Wiley, 605 3rd Ave., New York, New York 10158. (212) 850-6000. 1981. Third edition.

Encyclopedia of Chemical Processing and Design. John J. Mcketta and W. A. Cunningham. Marcel Dekker, Inc., 270 Madison Ave., New York, New York 10016. (212) 696-9000; (800) 228-1160. 1992. Thirty-eight volumes.

Glossary of Geology. Robert Latimer Bates and Julia A. Jackson, eds. American Geological Institute, 4220 King St., Alexandria, Virginia 22302-1507. (703) 379-2480 or (800) 336-4764. 1987. Third edition.

Kirk-Othmer Encyclopedia of Chemical Technology. J. I. Kroschwitz, ed. John Wiley & Sons, Inc., 605 3rd Ave., New York, New York 10158-0012. (212) 850-6000. 1992-. All articles in the new edition have been rewritten and updated adding new subjects such as biotechnology, computer topics, analytical techniques and instrumentation, environmental concerns, fuels and energy, inorganic and solid state chemistry; composite materials and material science in general, and pharmaceuticals. Also available online.

McGraw-Hill Encyclopedia of Science and Technology. McGraw-Hill, 1221 Avenue of the Americas, New York, New York 10020. (212) 512-2000 or (800) 262-4729. 1992. Seventh edition. Issued in multiple volumes including index. Includes all science and technology broad subject areas.

McGraw-Hill Encyclopedia of the Geological Sciences. Sybil P. Parker, ed. McGraw-Hill, 1221 Avenue of the Americas, New York, New York 10020. (212) 512-2000 or (800) 262-4729. 1988. Second edition. Published previously in the McGraw-Hill Encyclopedia of Science and Technology.

GENERAL WORKS

Asphalt Emulsions. Harold W. Muncy, ed. ASTM, 1916 Race St., Philadelphia, Pennsylvania 19103-1187. (215) 299-5400. 1990. Presents practical information on asphalt emulsions technology, from laboratory methods, to mix designs, to application of materials.

ONLINE DATA BASES

CERCLIS. Chemical Information Systems, Inc., 7215 York Rd., Baltimore, Maryland 21212. (301) 321-8440. Information on hazardous waste disposal sites that have either been listed by the EPA on the National Priority List (NPL) or nominated for consideration for the NPL.

Enviro/Energyline Abstracts Plus. R. R. Bowker Co., 121 Chanlon Rd., New Providence, New Jersey 07974. (908) 464-6800.

Environmental Periodicals Bibliography. National Information Services Corp., Ste. 6, Wyman Towers, 3100 St. Paul St., Baltimore, Maryland 21218. (410)243-0797. Online version of abstract of same name.

Kirk-Othmer Encyclopedia of Chemical Technology. John Wiley & Sons, Inc., 605 3rd Ave., 5th Floor, New York, New York 10158. (212) 850-6000. Online version of the publication of the same name.

TRADE ASSOCIATIONS AND PROFESSIONAL SOCIETIES

American Institute of Chemical Engineers. 345 East 47th St., New York, New York 10017. (212) 705-7338.

American Institute of Chemists. 7315 Wisconsin Ave., Bethesda, Maryland 20814. (301) 652-2447.

Asphalt Recycling & Reclaiming Association. 3 Church Cir., Suite 250, Annapolis, Maryland 21401. (301) 267-0023.

Association of Asphalt Paving Technologists. 1404 Concordia Ave., St. Paul, Minnesota 55104. (612) 642-1350.

Flexible Pavements. P.O. Box 16186, Columbus, Ohio 43216. (614) 221-5402.

National Asphalt Pavement Association. Calvert Bldg., Suite 620, 6811 Kenilworth Ave., Riverdale, Maryland 20737. (301) 779-4880.

ASSAY METHOD

See also: NUTRITION

ABSTRACTING AND INDEXING SERVICES

Biological Abstracts. BIOSIS, 2100 Arch St., Philadelphia, Pennsylvania 19103-1399. (215) 587-4800. 1927-.

Environment Abstracts. Bowker A & I Publishing, 121 Chanlon Rd., New Providence, New Jersey 07974. (908) 464-6800. 1974-.

Environment Index. Environment Information Center, Index Research Department, 124 E. 39th St., New York, New York 10016. 1971-. Annual.

Environmental Information Connection–EIC. Planning Information Program, Dept. of Urban and Regional Planning, University of Illinois, 1003 West Nevada, Urbana, Illinois 61801. (217) 333-1369. Also available online.

Environmental Periodicals Bibliography. Environmental Studies Institute, International Academy at Santa Barbara, 800 Garden St., Suite D, Santa Barbara, California 93101. (805) 965-5010. Also available online.

General Science Index. H. W. Wilson Co., 950 University Ave., Bronx, New York 10452. 1978-. Monthly, also issued in annual cumulation. Cumulative subject index to English language periodicals in the subject fields of astronomy, botany, chemistry, earth science, environment and conservation, food and nutrition, genetics, mathematics, medicine and health, microbiology, oceanography, physics, physiology and zoology.

Science Citation Index. Institute for Scientific Information, 3501 Market St., Philadelphia, Pennsylvania 19104. 1961-.

BIBLIOGRAPHIES

EPA Publications Bibliography. U.S. Environmental Protection Agency, Library Systems Branch, 401 M St., SW, Washington, District of Columbia 20460. (202) 260-2090. Quarterly.

ENCYCLOPEDIAS AND DICTIONARIES

Van Nostrand's Scientific Encyclopedia. Glenn D. Considine, ed. Van Nostrand Reinhold, 115 5th Ave., New York, New York 10003. (212) 254-3232. 1983. Sixth edition. Includes all broad subject areas in science.

ONLINE DATA BASES

BIOSIS Previews. BIOSIS, 2100 Arch St., Philadelphia, Pennsylvania 19103-1399. (215) 587-4800. Largest and most comprehensive database of research in the life sciences. Contains citations for nearly 9000 primary research journals, monographs, reviews, symposia, preliminary reports, semi-popular journals, selected institutional reports, government reports and research communications.

Enviro/Energyline Abstracts Plus. R. R. Bowker Co., 121 Chanlon Rd., New Providence, New Jersey 07974. (908) 464-6800.

Environmental Periodicals Bibliography. National Information Services Corp., Ste. 6, Wyman Towers, 3100 St. Paul St., Baltimore, Maryland 21218. (410)243-0797. Online version of abstract of same name.

ASSIMILATION

See also: WATER PURIFICATION; NUTRITION

ABSTRACTING AND INDEXING SERVICES

Abstracts of Air and Water Conservation Literature. American Petroleum Institute. Central Abstracting and Indexing Service, 275 Madison Avenue, New York, New York 10016. 1972.

Biological Abstracts. BIOSIS, 2100 Arch St., Philadelphia, Pennsylvania 19103-1399. (215) 587-4800. 1927-.

Environment Abstracts. Bowker A & I Publishing, 121 Chanlon Rd., New Providence, New Jersey 07974. (908) 464-6800. 1974-.

Environment Index. Environment Information Center, Index Research Department, 124 E. 39th St., New York, New York 10016. 1971-. Annual.

Environmental Information Connection–EIC. Planning Information Program, Dept. of Urban and Regional Planning, University of Illinois, 1003 West Nevada, Urbana, Illinois 61801. (217) 333-1369. Also available online.

Environmental Periodicals Bibliography. Environmental Studies Institute, International Academy at Santa Barbara, 800 Garden St., Suite D, Santa Barbara, California 93101. (805) 965-5010. Also available online.

General Science Index. H. W. Wilson Co., 950 University Ave., Bronx, New York 10452. 1978-. Monthly, also issued in annual cumulation. Cumulative subject index to English language periodicals in the subject fields of astronomy, botany, chemistry, earth science, environment and conservation, food and nutrition, genetics, mathematics, medicine and health, microbiology, oceanography, physics, physiology and zoology.

Science Citation Index. Institute for Scientific Information, 3501 Market St., Philadelphia, Pennsylvania 19104. 1961-.

BIBLIOGRAPHIES

EPA Publications Bibliography. U.S. Environmental Protection Agency, Library Systems Branch, 401 M St., SW, Washington, District of Columbia 20460. (202) 260-2090. Quarterly.

ONLINE DATA BASES

BIOSIS Previews. BIOSIS, 2100 Arch St., Philadelphia, Pennsylvania 19103-1399. (215) 587-4800. Largest and most comprehensive database of research in the life sciences. Contains citations for nearly 9000 primary research journals, monographs, reviews, symposia, preliminary reports, semi-popular journals, selected institutional reports, government reports and research communications.

Enviro/Energyline Abstracts Plus. R. R. Bowker Co., 121 Chanlon Rd., New Providence, New Jersey 07974. (908) 464-6800.

Environmental Periodicals Bibliography. National Information Services Corp., Ste. 6, Wyman Towers, 3100 St. Paul St., Baltimore, Maryland 21218. (410)243-0797. Online version of abstract of same name.

TRADE ASSOCIATIONS AND PROFESSIONAL SOCIETIES

American Institute of Chemical Engineers. 345 East 47th St., New York, New York 10017. (212) 705-7338.

American Institute of Chemists. 7315 Wisconsin Ave., Bethesda, Maryland 20814. (301) 652-2447.

ASTHMA

See also: AIR POLLUTION; ALLERGIES

ABSTRACTING AND INDEXING SERVICES

Environment Abstracts. Bowker A & I Publishing, 121 Chanlon Rd., New Providence, New Jersey 07974. (908) 464-6800. 1974-.

Environment Index. Environment Information Center, Index Research Department, 124 E. 39th St., New York, New York 10016. 1971-. Annual.

Environmental Information Connection–EIC. Planning Information Program, Dept. of Urban and Regional Planning, University of Illinois, 1003 West Nevada, Urbana, Illinois 61801. (217) 333-1369. Also available online.

Environmental Periodicals Bibliography. Environmental Studies Institute, International Academy at Santa Barbara, 800 Garden St., Suite D, Santa Barbara, California 93101. (805) 965-5010. Also available online.

Science Citation Index. Institute for Scientific Information, 3501 Market St., Philadelphia, Pennsylvania 19104. 1961-.

Selected References on Environmental Quality as It Relates to Health. National Library of Medicine, 8600 Rockville Pike, Bethesda, Maryland 20894. (800) 638-8480. 1977.

BIBLIOGRAPHIES

EPA Publications Bibliography. U.S. Environmental Protection Agency, Library Systems Branch, 401 M St., SW, Washington, District of Columbia 20460. (202) 260-2090. Quarterly.

ENCYCLOPEDIAS AND DICTIONARIES

McGraw-Hill Encyclopedia of Science and Technology. McGraw-Hill, 1221 Avenue of the Americas, New York, New York 10020. (212) 512-2000 or (800) 262-4729. 1992. Seventh edition. Issued in multiple volumes including index. Includes all science and technology broad subject areas.

The Nutrition and Health Encyclopedia. David F. Tver and Percy Russell. Van Nostrand Reinhold, 115 5th Ave., New York, New York 10003. (212) 254-3232. 1989.

Van Nostrand's Scientific Encyclopedia. Glenn D. Considine, ed. Van Nostrand Reinhold, 115 5th Ave., New York, New York 10003. (212) 254-3232. 1983. Sixth edition. Includes all broad subject areas in science.

ONLINE DATA BASES

Enviro/Energyline Abstracts Plus. R. R. Bowker Co., 121 Chanlon Rd., New Providence, New Jersey 07974. (908) 464-6800.

Environmental Periodicals Bibliography. National Information Services Corp., Ste. 6, Wyman Towers, 3100 St. Paul St., Baltimore, Maryland 21218. (410)243-0797. Online version of abstract of same name.

ATMOSPHERE

ABSTRACTING AND INDEXING SERVICES

Abstracts of Air and Water Conservation Literature. American Petroleum Institute. Central Abstracting and Indexing Service, 275 Madison Avenue, New York, New York 10016. 1972.

Air Pollution Technical Publications of the United States Environmental Protection Agency. U.S. Environmental Protection Agency, Mail Drop 75, Research Triangle Park, North Carolina 27711. (919) 541-2184. 1976. Quarterly.

Air Pollution Titles. Pennsylvania State University, Center for Air Environmental Studies, 226 Fenske Laboratory, University Park, Pennsylvania 16802. (814) 865-1415. 1965. Bibliographic guide to current research literature on air environment, including monitoring and control of air pollution, health effects, effects on agriculture, forests, toxic air contaminants, and global atmospheric pro cases.

Air Pollution Translations. A Bibliography With Abstracts. U.S. Environmental Protection Agency, MD 75, Research Triangle Park, North Carolina 27711. (919) 541-2184. 1969.

Applied Science and Technology Index. H.W. Wilson Co., 950 University Ave., Bronx, New York 10452. (800) 367-6770. Formerly Industrial Arts Index.

Civil Engineering Hydraulic Abstracts. BHRA Fluid Engineering, Air Science Co., PO Box 143, Corning, New York 14830. (607) 962-5591. Monthly. Abstracts of periodicals that publish in the areas of hydraulic engineering and other related topics.

Ecological Abstracts. Geo Abstracts Ltd. Elsevier Applied Science, Crown House, Linton Rd., Barking, England IG 11 8JU. 1974-. Derived from over 600 leading ecological and environmental journals, plus books, conference proceedings, reports and theses.

Ecology Abstracts. Cambridge Scientific Abstracts, 5161 River Rd., Bethesda, Maryland 20816. (301) 961-6750. Monthly.

Environment Abstracts. Bowker A & I Publishing, 121 Chanlon Rd., New Providence, New Jersey 07974. (908) 464-6800. 1974-.

Environment Index. Environment Information Center, Index Research Department, 124 E. 39th St., New York, New York 10016. 1971-. Annual.

Environmental Information Connection–EIC. Planning Information Program, Dept. of Urban and Regional Planning, University of Illinois, 1003 West Nevada, Urbana, Illinois 61801. (217) 333-1369. Also available online.

Environmental Periodicals Bibliography. Environmental Studies Institute, International Academy at Santa Barbara, 800 Garden St., Suite D, Santa Barbara, California 93101. (805) 965-5010. Also available online.

General Science Index. H. W. Wilson Co., 950 University Ave., Bronx, New York 10452. 1978-. Monthly, also issued in annual cumulation. Cumulative subject index to English language periodicals in the subject fields of astronomy, botany, chemistry, earth science, environment and conservation, food and nutrition, genetics, mathematics, medicine and health, microbiology, oceanography, physics, physiology and zoology.

Index to Scientific Book Contents. Institute for Scientific Information, 3501 Market St., Philadelphia, Pennsylvania 19104. (800) 523-1857. 1985-. Annual. Gives contents of science books published.

Meteorological and Geoastrophysical Abstracts. American Meteorological Society, 45 Beacon St., Boston, Massachusetts 02108. (617) 227-2425.

Physics Briefs. Physikalische Berichte. Physik Verlag, Pappapelallee 3, Postfach 101161, Weinheim, Germany D-6940. 1979-. Semimonthly. In English. Volumes for 1979- issued by the Deutsche Physikalische Gesellschaft and the Fachinformationszentrum Energie Physik, Mathematik in cooperation with the American Institute of Physics.

Science Citation Index. Institute for Scientific Information, 3501 Market St., Philadelphia, Pennsylvania 19104. 1961-.

BIBLIOGRAPHIES

Acid Rain: A Bibliography of Canadian Federal and Provincial Government Documents. Albert H. Joy. Meckler, 11 Ferry Ln., W., Westport, Connecticut 06880. (203) 226-6967. 1991. Contains Canadian Federal and provincial government documents. Includes bibliographical references and index. Approximately 1,100 documents covering diverse topics including environmental effects, air and atmospheric processes, socioeconomic aspects, and migration and corrective measures.

Bibliography and Index of Geology. American Geological Institute, 4220 King St., Alexandria, Virginia 22302. Monthly. Includes environmental geology and hydrogeology.

Carbon Dioxide and Climate: A Bibliography. National Technical Information Service, 5285 Port Royal Rd., Springfield, Virginia 22161. (703) 487-4650. 1981.

Directory of Published Proceedings. Interdok Corp., 173 Halstead Ave., Harrison, New York 10528. (914) 835-3506. 1990. Monthly. This is a listing of published proceedings including the series SEMTE (Science/Medicine/Engineering/Technology) and the series SSH (Social Science/Humanities).

EPA Publications Bibliography. U.S. Environmental Protection Agency, Library Systems Branch, 401 M St., SW, Washington, District of Columbia 20460. (202) 260-2090. Quarterly.

ENCYCLOPEDIAS AND DICTIONARIES

The Encyclopedia of Atmospheric Sciences and Astrogeology. Rhodes Whitmore Fairbridge. Reinhold Pub. Co., 115 5th Ave., New York, New York 10003. (212) 254-3232. 1967.

The Encyclopedia of Climatology. John E. Oliver and Rhodes W. Fairbridge, eds. Van Nostrand Reinhold, 115 5th Ave., New York, New York 10003. (212) 254-3232. 1987. Belongs in the series Encyclopedia of Earth Sciences, v.11.

Encyclopedia of Physics. Rita G. Lerner and George L. Trigg. VCH Publishers, 303 NW 12th Ave., Deerfield Beach, Florida 33442-1788. (305) 428-5566. 1991. Second edition.

McGraw-Hill Encyclopedia of Environmental Science. Sybil P. Parker. McGraw-Hill Science & Engineering Books, 11 W. 19th St., New York, New York 10011. (212) 337-6010. 1980. Covers ecology, man's influence on nature, and environmental protection.

McGraw-Hill Encyclopedia of Science and Technology. McGraw-Hill, 1221 Avenue of the Americas, New York, New York 10020. (212) 512-2000 or (800) 262-4729. 1992. Seventh edition. Issued in multiple volumes including index. Includes all science and technology broad subject areas.

The New York Times Encyclopedic Dictionary of the Environment. Paul Sarnoff. Quadrangle Books, New York, New York 1971. Focuses on state-of-the-art methods of pollution control, abatement, prevention and removal.

Van Nostrand's Scientific Encyclopedia. Glenn D. Considine, ed. Van Nostrand Reinhold, 115 5th Ave., New York, New York 10003. (212) 254-3232. 1983. Sixth edition. Includes all broad subject areas in science.

GENERAL WORKS

Air Pollution Modeling; Theories, Computational Methods, and Available Software. Paolo Zannetti. Van Nostrand Reinhold, 115 5th Ave., New York, New York 10003. (212) 254-3232. 1990. Introduces relevant historical and recently developed examples of modeling techniques for traditional problems including point source dispersion, plume rise, windfield estimation, and surface deposition.

Atmospheric Transmission, Emission, and Scattering. Thomas G. Kyle. Pergamon Microforms International Inc., Fairview Park, Elmsford, New York 10523. (914) 592-7720.

The Carbon Cycle and Atmospheric CO2: Natural Variations, Archean to Present. E.T. Sundquist. American Geophysical Union, 2000 Florida Ave. N.W., Washington, District of Columbia 20009. (202) 462-6900. 1985. Deals with carbon cycle, atmospheric carbon dioxide, and paleothermometry.

Carbon Dioxide and Other Greenhouse Gases. Kluwer Academic Publishers, 101 Philip Dr., Assinippi Pk,

Norwell, Massachusetts 02061. (617) 871-6600. Looks at environmental aspects of greenhouse effects.

Carbon Dioxide: Friend or Foe?. IBR Press, 631 E. Laguana Dr., Tempe, Arizona 85282. (802) 966-8693. An inquiry into the climatic and agricultural consequences of the rapidly rising CO2 content of earth's atmosphere.

Carbon Dioxide Review. Oxford University Press, 200 Madison Ave., New York, New York 10016. (212) 679-7300. 1982. Cites atmospheric carbon dioxide research.

Carbon Dioxide, the Greenhouse Effect, and Climate. John R. Justus. U.S. G.P.O., Washington, District of Columbia 20401. (202) 521-0000. 1984.

The Changing Atmosphere: A Global Challenge. John Firor. Yale University Press, 302 Temple St., 92 A Yale Sta., New Haven, Connecticut 06520. (203) 432-0960. 1990. Examines three atmospheric problems: Acid rain, ozone depletion, and climate heating.

Chlorofluoromethanes and the Stratosphere. Robert D. Hudson, ed. National Technical Information Service, 5285 Port Royal Rd., Springfield, Virginia 22161. (703) 487-4650. 1977.

Climates of the States. Gale Research Inc., 835 Penobscot Bldg., Detroit, Michigan 48226-4094. (313) 961-2242. 1986. State-by-state summaries of climate based on first order weather reporting stations for the period 1951-1980.

Detecting the Climatic Effects of Increasing Carbon Dioxide. National Technical Information Service, 5285 Port Royal Rd., Springfield, Virginia 22161. (703) 487-4650. Carbon dioxide and air pollution measurement.

Energy and Climate Change. Lewis Publishers, 2000 Corporate Blvd., N.W., Boca Raton, Florida 33431. (407) 994-0555 or (800) 272-7737. 1990. Includes energy scenarios, cost and risk analysis, energy emissions, atmospheric chemistry, and climate effects.

Environment in Peril. Anthony B. Wolbarst, ed. Smithsonian Institution Press, 470 L'Enfant Plaza, No. 7100, Washington, District of Columbia 20560. (800) 782-4612. 1991. Brings together in one volume the primary concerns of eleven of the world's leaders in conservation, ecology and public policy. Broad environmental issues covered are: ozone depletion, overpopulation, global warming, thinning forests, extinction of species, spreading deserts, toxic chemicals, and various pollutants.

The Greenhouse Effect and Ozone Layer. Philip Neal. Dryad, 15 Sherman Ave., Takoma Park, Maryland 20912. (301) 891-3729. 1989. Covers atmospheric carbon dioxide and effects of carbon dioxide on climate.

Halocarbons: Environmental Effects of Chlorofluoromethane Release. National Research Council. Committee on Impacts of Stratospheric Change. National Academy of Sciences, 2101 Constitution Ave., NW, Washington, District of Columbia 20418. (202) 334-2000. 1976.

The Long-Range Atmospheric Transport of Natural and Containment Substances. Anthony H. Knap. Kluwer Academic Publishers, 101 Philip Dr., Assinippi Pk., Norwell, Massachusetts 02061. (617) 871-6600. Transport of sulphur and nitrogen, organic compounds, mineral aerosols and trace elements.

Magill's Survey of Science. Earth Science Series. Frank N. Magill. Salem Press, PO Box 50062, Pasadena, California 91105. 1990-. Five volumes. Includes information on

earth's crust, hot spots and volcanic island chains, physical properties of minerals, rock magnetism, physical properties of rocks, and index.

Organic Chemistry of the Earth's Atmosphere. Valerii A. Isidorov. Springer-Verlag, 175 5th Ave., New York, New York 10010. (212) 460-1500; (800) 777-4643. 1990. Describes the composition of atmosphere; distribution of organic components in space and time; natural sources; human- created sources; atmosphere organic reactions methods of analysis.

Ozone. Kathryn Gay. Franklin Watts, 387 Park Ave. S., New York, New York 10016. (212) 686-7070. 1989. Environmental aspects of chlorofluorocarbons.

The Potential Effects of Global Climate Change on the United States. Joel B. Smith and Dennis A. Tirpak, eds. Hemisphere Publishing Co., 79 Madison Ave., Suite 1110, New York, New York 10016. (212) 725-1999; (800) 821-8312. 1990. Addresses the effects of climate change in vital areas such as water resources, agriculture, sea levels and forests. Also focuses on wetlands, human health, rivers and lakes and analyzes policy options for mitigating the effects of global warming.

Present State of Knowledge of the Upper Atmosphere. R.T. Watson. National Aeronautics and Space Administration, Scientific and Technical Information Office, 5285 Port Royal Rd., Springfield, Virginia 22161. (703) 487-4805. 1988. Atmospheric ozone and atmospheric chemistry.

A Primer on Greenhouse Effect Gases. Donald J. Wuebbles and Jae Edmonds. Lewis Publishers, 200 Corporate Blvd. NW, Boca Raton, Florida 33431. (407) 994-0555 or (800)272-7737. 1991. Brings together the most current information available on greenhouse gases. Reveals information critical to developing an understanding of the role of energy and atmospheric chemical and radiative processes in determining atmospheric concentrations of greenhouse gases.

Projecting the Climatic Effects of Increasing Carbon Dioxide. Michael C. MacCracken. National Technical Information Service, 5285 Port Royal Rd., Springfield, Virginia 22161. (703) 487-4650. 1985.

Prospects for Future Climate: A Special US/USSR Report on Climate and Climate Change. Michael C. MacCracken, et al. Lewis Publishers, 2000 Corporate Blvd., N.W., Boca Raton, Florida 33431. (407) 994-0555 or (800) 272-7737. 1990. Describes the effects of the increasing concentration of greenhouse gases and the potential for climate change and impact on agriculture and hydrology. Projections are based on insights from both numerical models and empirical methods.

Radon in the Environment. M. Wilkening. Elsevier Science Publishing Co., 655 Avenue of the Americas, New York, New York 10010. (212) 989-5800. 1990. Describes the discovery of radon, its characteristics, and sources in the environment methods of control, as well as possible health effects.

Stones in a Glass House: CFCs and Ozone Depletion. Douglas G. Cogan. Investor Responsibility Research Center, 1755 Massachusetts Ave., NW, Suite 600, Washington, District of Columbia 20036. (202) 234-7500. 1988. Environmental aspects of air pollution.

Techniques for Measuring Indoor Air. John Y. Yocom and Sharon M. McCarthy. John Wiley & Sons, Inc., 605 3rd Ave., New York, New York 10158-0012. (212) 850-

6000. 1991. Addresses the recent, rapid expansion of interest in indoor air quality and its contribution to total human exposure to air pollutants by presenting past and present developments and also the directions that the field seems to be taking.

Weather of U.S. Cities. Frank E. Bair. Gale Research Inc., 835 Penobscot Bldg., Detroit, Michigan 48226-4094. (313) 961-2242. 1992. Compilation of U.S. government weather data on 281 cities and weather observation stations.

A Who's Who of American Ozone Depleters: A Guide to 3,014 Factories Emitting Three Ozone-Depleting Chemicals. Natural Resources Defense Council, 40 W. 20th St., New York, New York 10011. (212) 727-2700. 1990.

GOVERNMENTAL ORGANIZATIONS

Environmental Protection Agency: Office of Atmospheric and Indoor Air Programs. Waterside West Building, 401 M St., S.W., Washington, District of Columbia 20460. (202) 382-7404.

National Science Foundation. 1800 G St., N.W., Washington, District of Columbia 20550. (202) 357-9498.

HANDBOOKS AND MANUALS

The Engineer's Clean Air Handbook. P. D. Osborn. Butterworth-Heinemann, Linacre House, Jordan Hill, Oxford, England OX2 8DP. (0865) 310366. 1989. Deals with the causes of various types of air pollution and the complicated nature of many of the pollutants. Also describes methods and necessary instrumentation for pollution removal. Includes a list of useful references.

Handbook of Geophysics and the Space Environment. Adolph S. Jursa, ed. Air Force Geophysics Laboratory, Air Force Systems Command, United States Air Force, c/o National Technical Information Service, 5285 Port Royal Rd., Springfield, Virginia 22161. (703) 487-4650. 1985. Two volumes. Broad subject areas covered are space, atmosphere, and terrestrial environment. Includes topics such as solar radiation, sunspots, solar wind, geomagnetic fields, radiation belts, cosmic radiation, atmospheric gases, etc.

ONLINE DATA BASES

Enviro/Energyline Abstracts Plus. R. R. Bowker Co., 121 Chanlon Rd., New Providence, New Jersey 07974. (908) 464-6800.

Environmental Periodicals Bibliography. National Information Services Corp., Ste. 6, Wyman Towers, 3100 St. Paul St., Baltimore, Maryland 21218. (410)243-0797. Online version of abstract of same name.

Monthly Catalog of United States Government Publications. U.S. G.P.O., Supt. of Docs., PO Box 371954, Pittsburgh, Pennsylvania 15250-7954. (202) 512-0000.

National Technical Information Service. U.S. Department of Commerce, National Technical Information Service, Office of Data Base Services, 5285 Port Royal Rd., Springfield, Virginia 22161. (703) 487-4807. Bibliographic database of government sponsored research and technical reports.

Real-Time Atmospheric Monitoring. Kavouras, Inc., 6301 34th Ave. S, Minneapolis, Minnesota 554540. (612) 726-9515.

SCISEARCH. Institute for Scientific Information, University City Science Center, 3501 Market St., Philadelphia, Pennsylvania 19104. (215) 386-0100.

PERIODICALS AND NEWSLETTERS

Atmosphere. Friends of the Earth, 701-251 Laurier Ave. W., Ste. 701, Ottawa, Ontario, Canada K1P 5J6. (613) 230-3352. 1988-. Quarterly. News and developments on stratospheric ozone depletion and ozone protection measures.

Atmospheric Environment. Pergamon Microforms International, Inc., Fairview Park, Elmsford, New York 10523. (914) 592-7720. 1966-. Publishes papers on all aspects of man's interactions with his atmospheric environment, including the administrative, economic and political aspects of these interactions. Air pollution research and its applications are covered, taking into account changes in the atmospheric flow patterns, temperature distributions and chemical constitution caused by natural and artificial variations in the earth's surface.

Earth Science. American Geological Institute, 4220 King Street, Alexandria, Virginia 22302. (703) 379-2480. Quarterly. Covers geological issues.

Global Climate Change Digest. Elsevier Science Publishing Co., 655 Avenue of the Americas, New York, New York 10010. (212) 984-5800. Monthly. Topics dealing with ozone depletion and the large-scale climatic changes linked to industrial activity, industrial by-products, and man-made substances.

Journal of Atmospheric Sciences. American Meteorology Society, 45 Beacon Street, Boston, Massachusetts 02108. (617) 227-2425. Biweekly. Articles on the atmosphere of the earth and other planets.

RESEARCH CENTERS AND INSTITUTES

Centre for Atmospheric Chemistry. York University, 4700 Keele St., Downsview, Ontario, Canada M3J 1P3. (416) 736-5586.

Statewide Air Pollution Research Center. University of California, Riverside, Riverside, California 92521. (714) 787-5124.

University of Miami, Cooperative Institute for Marine and Atmospheric Studies. 4600 Rickenbacker Causeway, Miami, Florida 33149. (305) 361-4159.

University of Miami, Rosenstiel School of Marine and Atmospheric Science. 4600 Rickenbacker Causeway, Miami, Florida 33149. (305) 361-4000.

University of Michigan, Michigan Atmospheric Deposition Laboratory. 2126 Space Research Building, Ann Arbor, Michigan 48109-2143. (313) 763-6213.

University of Wyoming, High Altitude Balloon Research Group. Physics and Astronomy Department, Box 3905, Laramie, Wyoming 82071. (307) 766-4323.

Utah State University, Utah Water Research Laboratory. Logan, Utah 84322-8200. (801) 750-3200.

STATISTICS SOURCES

Trends '90: A Compendium of Data on Global Change. Thomas A. Boden, et al. Carbon Dioxide Information Analysis Center, Environmental Sciences Division, Oak

Ridge National Laboratory, Oak Ridge, Tennessee 37831-6335. 1990. Source of frequently used global change data. Includes estimates of global and national CO_2 emissions from the burning of fossil fuels and from the production of cement and other pollutants.

World Resources. World Resources Institute. 1709 New York Ave., N.W., Washington, District of Columbia 20006. (202) 638-6300. Annual. Statistical and textual analysis of world's natural resources and the effects of growth-caused environmental pollution.

TRADE ASSOCIATIONS AND PROFESSIONAL SOCIETIES

Alliance for Responsible Chlorofluorocarbon Policy. 1901 N. Fort Myer Dr., Suite 1200, Rosslyn, Virginia 22209. (703) 243-0344.

American Association for the Advancement of Science. 1333 H St., N.W., Washington, District of Columbia 20005. (202) 326-6400.

Association of Local Air Pollution Control Officials. 444 North Capitol St., N.W., Washington, District of Columbia 20001 (202) 624-7864.

Greenpeace. 1436 U St., NW, Washington, District of Columbia 20009. (202) 462-1177.

National Center for Atmospheric Research. National Science Foundation, 1800 G. St., N.W., Room 520, Washington, District of Columbia 20550. (202) 357-9498.

University Corporation for Atmospheric Research. P.O. Box 3000, Boulder, Colorado 80307-3000. (303) 497-1650.

ATMOSPHERIC DIFFUSION

ABSTRACTING AND INDEXING SERVICES

Abstracts of Air and Water Conservation Literature. American Petroleum Institute. Central Abstracting and Indexing Service, 275 Madison Avenue, New York, New York 10016. 1972.

Air Pollution Technical Publications of the United States Environmental Protection Agency. U.S. Environmental Protection Agency, Mail Drop 75, Research Triangle Park, North Carolina 27711. (919) 541-2184. 1976. Quarterly.

Air Pollution Titles. Pennsylvania State University, Center for Air Environmental Studies, 226 Fenske Laboratory, University Park, Pennsylvania 16802. (814) 865-1415. 1965. Bibliographic guide to current research literature on air environment, including monitoring and control of air pollution, health effects, effects on agriculture, forests, toxic air contaminants, and global atmospheric pro cases.

Air Pollution Translations. A Bibliography With Abstracts. U.S. Environmental Protection Agency, MD 75, Research Triangle Park, North Carolina 27711. (919) 541-2184. 1969.

Applied Science and Technology Index. H.W. Wilson Co., 950 University Ave., Bronx, New York 10452. (800) 367-6770. Formerly Industrial Arts Index.

Environment Abstracts. Bowker A & I Publishing, 121 Chanlon Rd., New Providence, New Jersey 07974. (908) 464-6800. 1974-.

Environment Index. Environment Information Center, Index Research Department, 124 E. 39th St., New York, New York 10016. 1971-. Annual.

Environmental Information Connection–EIC. Planning Information Program, Dept. of Urban and Regional Planning, University of Illinois, 1003 West Nevada, Urbana, Illinois 61801. (217) 333-1369. Also available online.

Environmental Periodicals Bibliography. Environmental Studies Institute, International Academy at Santa Barbara, 800 Garden St., Suite D, Santa Barbara, California 93101. (805) 965-5010. Also available online.

General Science Index. H. W. Wilson Co., 950 University Ave., Bronx, New York 10452. 1978-. Monthly, also issued in annual cumulation. Cumulative subject index to English language periodicals in the subject fields of astronomy, botany, chemistry, earth science, environment and conservation, food and nutrition, genetics, mathematics, medicine and health, microbiology, oceanography, physics, physiology and zoology.

Meteorological and Geoastrophysical Abstracts. American Meteorological Society, 45 Beacon St., Boston, Massachusetts 02108. (617) 227-2425.

Physics Briefs. Physikalische Berichte. Physik Verlag, Pappapelallee 3, Postfach 101161, Weinheim, Germany D-6940. 1979-. Semimonthly. In English. Volumes for 1979- issued by the Deutsche Physikalische Gesellschaft and the Fachinformationszentrum Energie Physik, Mathematik in cooperation with the American Institute of Physics.

Science Citation Index. Institute for Scientific Information, 3501 Market St., Philadelphia, Pennsylvania 19104. 1961-.

BIBLIOGRAPHIES

EPA Publications Bibliography. U.S. Environmental Protection Agency, Library Systems Branch, 401 M St., SW, Washington, District of Columbia 20460. (202) 260-2090. Quarterly.

ENCYCLOPEDIAS AND DICTIONARIES

McGraw-Hill Encyclopedia of Science and Technology. McGraw-Hill, 1221 Avenue of the Americas, New York, New York 10020. (212) 512-2000 or (800) 262-4729. 1992. Seventh edition. Issued in multiple volumes including index. Includes all science and technology broad subject areas.

Van Nostrand's Scientific Encyclopedia. Glenn D. Considine, ed. Van Nostrand Reinhold, 115 5th Ave., New York, New York 10003. (212) 254-3232. 1983. Sixth edition. Includes all broad subject areas in science.

GENERAL WORKS

Atmospheric Chemistry: Models and Predictions for Climate and Air Quality. C. S. Sloane and T. W. Tesche. Lewis Publishers, 2000 Corporate Blvd., N.W., Boca Raton, Florida 33431. (407) 994-0555 or (800) 272-7737. 1991. Discusses the chemistry of stratospheric ozone depletion and its impact and related topics.

Atmospheric Diffusion. Frank Pasquill. Halsted Press, 605 3rd Ave., New York, New York 10158. (212) 850-6000. 1983.

Atmospheric Motion and Air Pollution: An Introduction for Students of Engineering and Science. Richard A. Dobbins. John Wiley & Sons, Inc., 605 3rd Ave., New York, New York 10158-0012. (212) 850-6000. 1979. Atmospheric diffusion and circulation.

Long Range Transport of Pesticides. David A. Kurtz. Lewis Publishers, 2000 Corporate Blvd., N.W., Boca Raton, Florida 33431. (407) 994-0555 or (800) 272-7737. 1990. Presents the latest vital information on long range transport of pesticides. Includes sources of pesticides from lakes, oceans, and soil, circulation on global and regional basis, deposition, and fate of pesticides.

HANDBOOKS AND MANUALS

Handbook on Atmospheric Diffusion. Steven R. Hanna. Technical Information Center, U.S. Dept. of Energy, PO Box 62, Oak Ridge, Tennessee 37831. (615)576-2268. 1982. Includes cooling towers, climatic factors, and smoke plumes.

ONLINE DATA BASES

Enviro/Energyline Abstracts Plus. R. R. Bowker Co., 121 Chanlon Rd., New Providence, New Jersey 07974. (908) 464-6800.

Environmental Periodicals Bibliography. National Information Services Corp., Ste. 6, Wyman Towers, 3100 St. Paul St., Baltimore, Maryland 21218. (410)243-0797. Online version of abstract of same name.

SCISEARCH. Institute for Scientific Information, University City Science Center, 3501 Market St., Philadelphia, Pennsylvania 19104. (215) 386-0100.

PERIODICALS AND NEWSLETTERS

Atmospheric Environment. Pergamon Microforms International, Inc., Fairview Park, Elmsford, New York 10523. (914) 592-7720. 1966-. Publishes papers on all aspects of man's interactions with his atmospheric environment, including the administrative, economic and political aspects of these interactions. Air pollution research and its applications are covered, taking into account changes in the atmospheric flow patterns, temperature distributions and chemical constitution caused by natural and artificial variations in the earth's surface.

ATMOSPHERIC TURBIDITY

See also: AIR POLLUTION; AIR QUALITY; ATMOSPHERE

ABSTRACTING AND INDEXING SERVICES

Abstracts of Air and Water Conservation Literature. American Petroleum Institute. Central Abstracting and Indexing Service, 275 Madison Avenue, New York, New York 10016. 1972.

Air Pollution Technical Publications of the United States Environmental Protection Agency. U.S. Environmental Protection Agency, Mail Drop 75, Research Triangle Park, North Carolina 27711. (919) 541-2184. 1976. Quarterly.

Air Pollution Titles. Pennsylvania State University, Center for Air Environmental Studies, 226 Fenske Laboratory, University Park, Pennsylvania 16802. (814) 865-1415. 1965. Bibliographic guide to current research literature on air environment, including monitoring and control of air pollution, health effects, effects on agriculture, forests, toxic air contaminants, and global atmospheric pro cases.

Air Pollution Translations. A Bibliography With Abstracts. U.S. Environmental Protection Agency, MD 75, Research Triangle Park, North Carolina 27711. (919) 541-2184. 1969.

Applied Science and Technology Index. H.W. Wilson Co., 950 University Ave., Bronx, New York 10452. (800) 367-6770. Formerly Industrial Arts Index.

Biological Abstracts. BIOSIS, 2100 Arch St., Philadelphia, Pennsylvania 19103-1399. (215) 587-4800. 1927-.

Ecological Abstracts. Geo Abstracts Ltd. Elsevier Applied Science, Crown House, Linton Rd., Barking, England IG 11 8JU. 1974-. Derived from over 600 leading ecological and environmental journals, plus books, conference proceedings, reports and theses.

Environment Abstracts. Bowker A & I Publishing, 121 Chanlon Rd., New Providence, New Jersey 07974. (908) 464-6800. 1974-.

Environment Index. Environment Information Center, Index Research Department, 124 E. 39th St., New York, New York 10016. 1971-. Annual.

Environmental Information Connection–EIC. Planning Information Program, Dept. of Urban and Regional Planning, University of Illinois, 1003 West Nevada, Urbana, Illinois 61801. (217) 333-1369. Also available online.

Environmental Periodicals Bibliography. Environmental Studies Institute, International Academy at Santa Barbara, 800 Garden St., Suite D, Santa Barbara, California 93101. (805) 965-5010. Also available online.

General Science Index. H. W. Wilson Co., 950 University Ave., Bronx, New York 10452. 1978-. Monthly, also issued in annual cumulation. Cumulative subject index to English language periodicals in the subject fields of astronomy, botany, chemistry, earth science, environment and conservation, food and nutrition, genetics, mathematics, medicine and health, microbiology, oceanography, physics, physiology and zoology.

Meteorological and Geoastrophysical Abstracts. American Meteorological Society, 45 Beacon St., Boston, Massachusetts 02108. (617) 227-2425.

Physics Briefs. Physikalische Berichte. Physik Verlag, Pappapelallee 3, Postfach 101161, Weinheim, Germany D-6940. 1979-. Semimonthly. In English. Volumes for 1979- issued by the Deutsche Physikalische Gesellschaft and the Fachinformationszentrum Energie Physik, Mathematik in cooperation with the American Institute of Physics.

Science Citation Index. Institute for Scientific Information, 3501 Market St., Philadelphia, Pennsylvania 19104. 1961-.

BIBLIOGRAPHIES

EPA Publications Bibliography. U.S. Environmental Protection Agency, Library Systems Branch, 401 M St., SW, Washington, District of Columbia 20460. (202) 260-2090. Quarterly.

ENCYCLOPEDIAS AND DICTIONARIES

The Encyclopedia of Atmospheric Sciences and Astrogeology. Rhodes Whitmore Fairbridge. Reinhold Pub. Co., 115 5th Ave., New York, New York 10003. (212) 254-3232. 1967.

The Encyclopedia of Climatology. John E. Oliver and Rhodes W. Fairbridge, eds. Van Nostrand Reinhold, 115 5th Ave., New York, New York 10003. (212) 254-3232. 1987. Belongs in the series Encyclopedia of Earth Sciences, v.11.

McGraw-Hill Encyclopedia of Science and Technology. McGraw-Hill, 1221 Avenue of the Americas, New York, New York 10020. (212) 512-2000 or (800) 262-4729. 1992. Seventh edition. Issued in multiple volumes including index. Includes all science and technology broad subject areas.

GENERAL WORKS

Envirosoft 86. P. Zanetti, ed. Computational Mechanics Inc., 25 Bridge St., Billerica, Massachusetts 01821. 1986. Environmental software part of the proceedings of the International Conference on Development and Applications of Computer Techniques to Environmental Studies, Los Angeles, 1986.

Envirosoft 88: Computer Techniques in Environmental Studies. P. Zannetti, ed. Computational Mechanics Inc., 25 Bridge St., Billerica, Massachusetts 01821. (508) 667-5841. 1988. Proceedings of the 2nd International Conference, Envirosoft 88, covering the development and application of computer techniques to environmental problems.

Organic Chemistry of the Earth's Atmosphere. Valerii A. Isidorov. Springer-Verlag, 175 5th Ave., New York, New York 10010. (212) 460-1500; (800) 777-4643. 1990. Describes the composition of atmosphere; distribution of organic components in space and time; natural sources; human- created sources; atmosphere organic reactions methods of analysis.

Prospects for Future Climate: A Special US/USSR Report on Climate and Climate Change. Michael C. MacCracken, et al. Lewis Publishers, 2000 Corporate Blvd., N.W., Boca Raton, Florida 33431. (407) 994-0555 or (800) 272-7737. 1990. Describes the effects of the increasing concentration of greenhouse gases and the potential for climate change and impact on agriculture and hydrology. Projections are based on insights from both numerical models and empirical methods.

Radon in the Environment. M. Wilkening. Elsevier Science Publishing Co., 655 Avenue of the Americas, New York, New York 10010. (212) 989-5800. 1990. Describes the discovery of radon, its characteristics, and sources in the environment methods of control, as well as possible health effects.

Techniques for Measuring Indoor Air. John Y. Yocom and Sharon M. McCarthy. John Wiley & Sons, Inc., 605 3rd Ave., New York, New York 10158-0012. (212) 850-6000. 1991. Addresses the recent, rapid expansion of interest in indoor air quality and its contribution to total human exposure to air pollutants by presenting past and present developments and also the directions that the field seems to be taking.

HANDBOOKS AND MANUALS

The Engineer's Clean Air Handbook. P. D. Osborn. Butterworth-Heinemann, Linacre House, Jordan Hill, Oxford, England OX2 8DP. (0865) 310366. 1989. Deals with the causes of various types of air pollution and the complicated nature of many of the pollutants. Also describes methods and necessary instrumentation for pollution removal. Includes a list of useful references.

ONLINE DATA BASES

BIOSIS Previews. BIOSIS, 2100 Arch St., Philadelphia, Pennsylvania 19103-1399. (215) 587-4800. Largest and most comprehensive database of research in the life sciences. Contains citations for nearly 9000 primary research journals, monographs, reviews, symposia, preliminary reports, semi-popular journals, selected institutional reports, government reports and research communications.

Enviro/Energyline Abstracts Plus. R. R. Bowker Co., 121 Chanlon Rd., New Providence, New Jersey 07974. (908) 464-6800.

Environmental Periodicals Bibliography. National Information Services Corp., Ste. 6, Wyman Towers, 3100 St. Paul St., Baltimore, Maryland 21218. (410)243-0797. Online version of abstract of same name.

Monthly Catalog of United States Government Publications. U.S. G.P.O., Supt. of Docs., PO Box 371954, Pittsburgh, Pennsylvania 15250-7954. (202) 512-0000.

National Technical Information Service. U.S. Department of Commerce, National Technical Information Service, Office of Data Base Services, 5285 Port Royal Rd., Springfield, Virginia 22161. (703) 487-4807. Bibliographic database of government sponsored research and technical reports.

SCISEARCH. Institute for Scientific Information, University City Science Center, 3501 Market St., Philadelphia, Pennsylvania 19104. (215) 386-0100.

PERIODICALS AND NEWSLETTERS

Atmospheric Environment. Pergamon Microforms International, Inc., Fairview Park, Elmsford, New York 10523. (914) 592-7720. 1966-. Publishes papers on all aspects of man's interactions with his atmospheric environment, including the administrative, economic and political aspects of these interactions. Air pollution research and its applications are covered, taking into account changes in the atmospheric flow patterns, temperature distributions and chemical constitution caused by natural and artificial variations in the earth's surface.

Journal of Atmospheric Sciences. American Meteorology Society, 45 Beacon Street, Boston, Massachusetts 02108. (617) 227-2425. Biweekly. Articles on the atmosphere of the earth and other planets.

RESEARCH CENTERS AND INSTITUTES

Baylor University, Institute of Environmental Studies. B.U. Box 7266, Waco, Texas 76798-7266. (817) 755-3406.

TRADE ASSOCIATIONS AND PROFESSIONAL SOCIETIES

American Institute of Biomedical Climatology. 1023 Welsh Rd., Philadelphia, Pennsylvania 19115. (215) 673-8368.

University Corporation for Atmospheric Research. P.O. Box 3000, Boulder, Colorado 80307-3000. (303) 497-1650.

ATOMIC ABSORPTION

ABSTRACTING AND INDEXING SERVICES

Applied Science and Technology Index. H.W. Wilson Co., 950 University Ave., Bronx, New York 10452. (800) 367-6770. Formerly Industrial Arts Index.

Biological Abstracts. BIOSIS, 2100 Arch St., Philadelphia, Pennsylvania 19103-1399. (215) 587-4800. 1927-.

Chemical Abstracts. Chemical Abstracts Service, 2540 Olentangy River Rd., PO Box 3012, Columbus, Ohio 43210. (800) 848-6533. 1907-.

Environment Abstracts. Bowker A & I Publishing, 121 Chanlon Rd., New Providence, New Jersey 07974. (908) 464-6800. 1974-.

Environment Index. Environment Information Center, Index Research Department, 124 E. 39th St., New York, New York 10016. 1971-. Annual.

Environmental Information Connection–EIC. Planning Information Program, Dept. of Urban and Regional Planning, University of Illinois, 1003 West Nevada, Urbana, Illinois 61801. (217) 333-1369. Also available online.

Environmental Periodicals Bibliography. Environmental Studies Institute, International Academy at Santa Barbara, 800 Garden St., Suite D, Santa Barbara, California 93101. (805) 965-5010. Also available online.

General Science Index. H. W. Wilson Co., 950 University Ave., Bronx, New York 10452. 1978-. Monthly, also issued in annual cumulation. Cumulative subject index to English language periodicals in the subject fields of astronomy, botany, chemistry, earth science, environment and conservation, food and nutrition, genetics, mathematics, medicine and health, microbiology, oceanography, physics, physiology and zoology.

Physics Briefs. Physikalische Berichte. Physik Verlag, Pappapelallee 3, Postfach 101161, Weinheim, Germany D-6940. 1979-. Semimonthly. In English. Volumes for 1979- issued by the Deutsche Physikalische Gesellschaft and the Fachinformationszentrum Energie Physik, Mathematik in cooperation with the American Institute of Physics.

Pollution Abstracts. Cambridge Scientific Abstracts, 5161 River Rd., Bethesda, Maryland 20816. (301) 961-6750. Six/year. Indexes worldwide technical literature on environmental pollution. Covers air pollution, marine and freshwater pollution, sewage and wastewater treatment, waste management, toxicology and health, noise pollution, radiation, land pollution, and environmental policies, programs, legislation, and education. Also available online.

Science Citation Index. Institute for Scientific Information, 3501 Market St., Philadelphia, Pennsylvania 19104. 1961-.

BIBLIOGRAPHIES

EPA Publications Bibliography. U.S. Environmental Protection Agency, Library Systems Branch, 401 M St., SW, Washington, District of Columbia 20460. (202) 260-2090. Quarterly.

ENCYCLOPEDIAS AND DICTIONARIES

Encyclopedia of Physical Science and Technology. Robert A. Meyers, ed. Academic Press, c/o Harcourt Brace Jovanovich Inc., 6277 Sea Harbor Dr., Orlando, Florida 32887. (800) 346-8648. Dictionary of engineering, technology and physical sciences.

Encyclopedia of Physics. Rita G. Lerner and George L. Trigg. VCH Publishers, 303 NW 12th Ave., Deerfield Beach, Florida 33442-1788. (305) 428-5566. 1991. Second edition.

McGraw-Hill Encyclopedia of Science and Technology. McGraw-Hill, 1221 Avenue of the Americas, New York, New York 10020. (212) 512-2000 or (800) 262-4729. 1992. Seventh edition. Issued in multiple volumes including index. Includes all science and technology broad subject areas.

ONLINE DATA BASES

BIOSIS Previews. BIOSIS, 2100 Arch St., Philadelphia, Pennsylvania 19103-1399. (215) 587-4800. Largest and most comprehensive database of research in the life sciences. Contains citations for nearly 9000 primary research journals, monographs, reviews, symposia, preliminary reports, semi-popular journals, selected institutional reports, government reports and research communications.

Chemical Abstracts-CA. Chemical Abstracts Service, 2540 Olentangy River Rd., P.O. Box 3012, Columbus, Ohio 43210. (800) 848-6533 or (614) 421-3600. Information sources include 9000 journals, patents from 27 countries, two industrial property organizations, new books, conference proceedings, and government research reports.

Enviro/Energyline Abstracts Plus. R. R. Bowker Co., 121 Chanlon Rd., New Providence, New Jersey 07974. (908) 464-6800.

Environmental Periodicals Bibliography. National Information Services Corp., Ste. 6, Wyman Towers, 3100 St. Paul St., Baltimore, Maryland 21218. (410)243-0797. Online version of abstract of same name.

TRADE ASSOCIATIONS AND PROFESSIONAL SOCIETIES

American Society of Naturalists. Department of Ecology and Evolation, State University of New York, Stony Brook, New York 11794. (516) 632-8589.

ATOMIC ENERGY

See: NUCLEAR POWER

ATOMIC PILES

See: REACTORS

ATRAZINE

See: PESTICIDES

ATTRACTANTS

See: BIOLOGICAL CONTROL

AUTOCLAVE REACTORS

See: REACTORS

AUTOMOBILE EMISSIONS

See: EMISSIONS

AUTOMOBILE FUEL ECONOMY

See: FUELS

AUTOMOBILE NOISE

See: NOISE POLLUTION

AUTOMOBILE SCRAP

See: AUTOMOBILES

AUTOMOBILES

ABSTRACTING AND INDEXING SERVICES

Applied Science and Technology Index. H.W. Wilson Co., 950 University Ave., Bronx, New York 10452. (800) 367-6770. Formerly Industrial Arts Index.

Engineering Index. The Engineering Index Inc., 345 E. 47th St., New York, New York 10017. 1962-.

General Science Index. H. W. Wilson Co., 950 University Ave., Bronx, New York 10452. 1978-. Monthly, also issued in annual cumulation. Cumulative subject index to English language periodicals in the subject fields of astronomy, botany, chemistry, earth science, environment and conservation, food and nutrition, genetics, mathematics, medicine and health, microbiology, oceanography, physics, physiology and zoology.

Pollution Abstracts. Cambridge Scientific Abstracts, 5161 River Rd., Bethesda, Maryland 20816. (301) 961-6750. Six/year. Indexes worldwide technical literature on environmental pollution. Covers air pollution, marine and freshwater pollution, sewage and wastewater treatment, waste management, toxicology and health, noise pollution, radiation, land pollution, and environmental policies, programs, legislation, and education. Also available online.

Transportation Research News. National Academy of Science, Transportation Research Board, Box 289, Washington, District of Columbia 20055. (202) 334-3213. 1982. Monthly.

ENCYCLOPEDIAS AND DICTIONARIES

Encyclopedia of Physical Science and Technology. Robert A. Meyers, ed. Academic Press, c/o Harcourt Brace Jovanovich Inc., 6277 Sea Harbor Dr., Orlando, Florida 32887. (800) 346-8648. Dictionary of engineering, technology and physical sciences.

Encyclopedia of Physics. Rita G. Lerner and George L. Trigg. VCH Publishers, 303 NW 12th Ave., Deerfield Beach, Florida 33442-1788. (305) 428-5566. 1991. Second edition.

McGraw-Hill Encyclopedia of Environmental Science. Sybil P. Parker. McGraw-Hill Science & Engineering Books, 11 W. 19th St., New York, New York 10011. (212) 337-6010. 1980. Covers ecology, man's influence on nature, and environmental protection.

McGraw-Hill Encyclopedia of Science and Technology. McGraw-Hill, 1221 Avenue of the Americas, New York, New York 10020. (212) 512-2000 or (800) 262-4729. 1992. Seventh edition. Issued in multiple volumes including index. Includes all science and technology broad subject areas.

GENERAL WORKS

Automobile Catalytic Converters. Kathleen C. Taylor. Agency for Toxic Substances and Disease Registry, U.S. Public Health Service, 1600 Clifton Rd. NE, Atlanta, Georgia 30333. (404) 452-4111. 1984.

Emissions: Misfueling, Catalytic Deactivation and Alternative Catalyst. Society of Automotive Engineers, 400 Commonwealth Dr., Warrendale, Pennsylvania 15096. (412) 776-4841. 1985. Automobile catalytic converters, internal combustion engines, spark ignition, and alternative fuels.

GOVERNMENTAL ORGANIZATIONS

U.S. Environmental Protection Agency: Office of Mobile Services. 401 M St., S.W., Washington, District of Columbia 20460. (202) 382-7645.

HANDBOOKS AND MANUALS

Aftermath Catalytic Convertors: Guide to Their Purchase, Installation, and Use. Illinois Environmental Protection Agency, 2200 Churchill Rd., P.O. Box 19276, Springfield, Illinois 62794-9276. (217) 782-2829. 1989.

ONLINE DATA BASES

Computerized Engineering Index–COMPENDEX. Engineering Information Inc., 345 E. 47th St., New York, New York 10017. (212) 705-7600.

Transportation Research Information Service–TRIS. Transportation Research Board, Box 289, Washington, District of Columbia 20055. (202) 334-3213.

STATISTICS SOURCES

World Resources. World Resources Institute. 1709 New York Ave., N.W., Washington, District of Columbia 20006. (202) 638-6300. Annual. Statistical and textual analysis of world's natural resources and the effects of growth-caused environmental pollution.

TRADE ASSOCIATIONS AND PROFESSIONAL SOCIETIES

SAE. 400 Commonwealth Dr., Warrendale, Pennsylvania 15096-0001. (412) 776-4841.

Transportation Research Board. Box 289, Washington, District of Columbia 20055. (202) 334-3213.

AUTOTROPHIC

See also: CHEMOSYNTHESIS; ECOSYSTEMS; NUTRITION; PHOTOSYNTHESIS; PLANTS

ABSTRACTING AND INDEXING SERVICES

Biological Abstracts. BIOSIS, 2100 Arch St., Philadelphia, Pennsylvania 19103-1399. (215) 587-4800. 1927-.

General Science Index. H. W. Wilson Co., 950 University Ave., Bronx, New York 10452. 1978-. Monthly, also issued in annual cumulation. Cumulative subject index to English language periodicals in the subject fields of astronomy, botany, chemistry, earth science, environment and conservation, food and nutrition, genetics, mathematics, medicine and health, microbiology, oceanography, physics, physiology and zoology.

Index to Scientific Book Contents. Institute for Scientific Information, 3501 Market St., Philadelphia, Pennsylvania 19104. (800) 523-1857. 1985-. Annual. Gives contents of science books published.

Science Citation Index. Institute for Scientific Information, 3501 Market St., Philadelphia, Pennsylvania 19104. 1961-.

ENCYCLOPEDIAS AND DICTIONARIES

McGraw-Hill Encyclopedia of Environmental Science. Sybil P. Parker. McGraw-Hill Science & Engineering Books, 11 W. 19th St., New York, New York 10011. (212) 337-6010. 1980. Covers ecology, man's influence on nature, and environmental protection.

McGraw-Hill Encyclopedia of Science and Technology. McGraw-Hill, 1221 Avenue of the Americas, New York, New York 10020. (212) 512-2000 or (800) 262-4729. 1992. Seventh edition. Issued in multiple volumes including index. Includes all science and technology broad subject areas.

ONLINE DATA BASES

BIOSIS Previews. BIOSIS, 2100 Arch St., Philadelphia, Pennsylvania 19103-1399. (215) 587-4800. Largest and most comprehensive database of research in the life sciences. Contains citations for nearly 9000 primary research journals, monographs, reviews, symposia, preliminary reports, semi-popular journals, selected institutional reports, government reports and research communications.

Monthly Catalog of United States Government Publications. U.S. G.P.O., Supt. of Docs., PO Box 371954, Pittsburgh, Pennsylvania 15250-7954. (202) 512-0000.

National Technical Information Service. U.S. Department of Commerce, National Technical Information Service, Office of Data Base Services, 5285 Port Royal Rd., Springfield, Virginia 22161. (703) 487-4807. Bibliographic database of government sponsored research and technical reports.

AVALANCHES

ABSTRACTING AND INDEXING SERVICES

Environment Abstracts. Bowker A & I Publishing, 121 Chanlon Rd., New Providence, New Jersey 07974. (908) 464-6800. 1974-.

Environment Index. Environment Information Center, Index Research Department, 124 E. 39th St., New York, New York 10016. 1971-. Annual.

Environmental Information Connection–EIC. Planning Information Program, Dept. of Urban and Regional Planning, University of Illinois, 1003 West Nevada, Urbana, Illinois 61801. (217) 333-1369. Also available online.

Environmental Periodicals Bibliography. Environmental Studies Institute, International Academy at Santa Barbara, 800 Garden St., Suite D, Santa Barbara, California 93101. (805) 965-5010. Also available online.

General Science Index. H. W. Wilson Co., 950 University Ave., Bronx, New York 10452. 1978-. Monthly, also issued in annual cumulation. Cumulative subject index to English language periodicals in the subject fields of astronomy, botany, chemistry, earth science, environment and conservation, food and nutrition, genetics, mathematics, medicine and health, microbiology, oceanography, physics, physiology and zoology.

Science Citation Index. Institute for Scientific Information, 3501 Market St., Philadelphia, Pennsylvania 19104. 1961-.

BIBLIOGRAPHIES

Bibliography and Index of Geology. American Geological Institute, 4220 King St., Alexandria, Virginia 22302. Monthly. Includes environmental geology and hydrogeology.

EPA Publications Bibliography. U.S. Environmental Protection Agency, Library Systems Branch, 401 M St., SW, Washington, District of Columbia 20460. (202) 260-2090. Quarterly.

ENCYCLOPEDIAS AND DICTIONARIES

McGraw-Hill Encyclopedia of Science and Technology. McGraw-Hill, 1221 Avenue of the Americas, New York, New York 10020. (212) 512-2000 or (800) 262-4729. 1992. Seventh edition. Issued in multiple volumes including index. Includes all science and technology broad subject areas.

GENERAL WORKS

Magill's Survey of Science. Earth Science Series. Frank N. Magill. Salem Press, PO Box 50062, Pasadena, California 91105. 1990-. Five volumes. Includes information on earth's crust, hot spots and volcanic island chains, physical properties of minerals, rock magnetism, physical properties of rocks, and index.

ONLINE DATA BASES

Enviro/Energyline Abstracts Plus. R. R. Bowker Co., 121 Chanlon Rd., New Providence, New Jersey 07974. (908) 464-6800.

Environmental Periodicals Bibliography. National Information Services Corp., Ste. 6, Wyman Towers, 3100 St. Paul St., Baltimore, Maryland 21218. (410)243-0797. Online version of abstract of same name.

AVIAN ECOLOGY

See also: ECOSYSTEMS

ABSTRACTING AND INDEXING SERVICES

Applied Ecology Abstracts Studies in Renewable Natural Resources. Information Retrieval Ltd., 1911 Jefferson Davis Highway, Arlington, Virginia 22202. 1975-. Monthly.

Biology Digest. Data Courier, Plexus Pub Inc., 143 Old Marlton Pike, Medford, New Jersey 08055. 1974-. Monthly. Abstracts biology periodicals.

Current Advances in Ecological and Environmental Science. Pergamon Microforms International, Inc., Fairview Park, Elmsford, New York 10523. (914) 592-7720. 1989-. Monthly. Current literature searching service includingjournals, reports, abstracts, etc. This service is available online as part of the CABS database on the hosts BRS and ORBIT search service.

Ecological Abstracts. Geo Abstracts Ltd. Elsevier Applied Science, Crown House, Linton Rd., Barking, England IG 11 8JU. 1974-. Derived from over 600 leading ecological and environmental journals, plus books, conference proceedings, reports and theses.

Environment Abstracts. Bowker A & I Publishing, 121 Chanlon Rd., New Providence, New Jersey 07974. (908) 464-6800. 1974-.

Environment Index. Environment Information Center, Index Research Department, 124 E. 39th St., New York, New York 10016. 1971-. Annual.

Environmental Information Connection–EIC. Planning Information Program, Dept. of Urban and Regional Planning, University of Illinois, 1003 West Nevada,

Urbana, Illinois 61801. (217) 333-1369. Also available online.

Environmental Periodicals Bibliography. Environmental Studies Institute, International Academy at Santa Barbara, 800 Garden St., Suite D, Santa Barbara, California 93101. (805) 965-5010. Also available online.

General Science Index. H. W. Wilson Co., 950 University Ave., Bronx, New York 10452. 1978-. Monthly, also issued in annual cumulation. Cumulative subject index to English language periodicals in the subject fields of astronomy, botany, chemistry, earth science, environment and conservation, food and nutrition, genetics, mathematics, medicine and health, microbiology, oceanography, physics, physiology and zoology.

Index to Scientific Book Contents. Institute for Scientific Information, 3501 Market Sts., Philadelphia, Pennsylvania 19104. (800) 523-1857. 1985-. Annual. Gives contents of science books published.

Multimedia Index to Ecology. National Information Center for Educational Media, University of Southern California, Los Angeles, California 90007.

BIBLIOGRAPHIES

Directory of Published Proceedings. Interdok Corp., 173 Halstead Ave., Harrison, New York 10528. (914) 835-3506. 1990. Monthly. This is a listing of published proceedings including the series SEMTE (Science/Medicine/Engineering/Technology) and the series SSH (Social Science/Humanities).

EPA Publications Bibliography. U.S. Environmental Protection Agency, Library Systems Branch, 401 M St., SW, Washington, District of Columbia 20460. (202) 260-2090. Quarterly.

ENCYCLOPEDIAS AND DICTIONARIES

The Encyclopedia of Animal Ecology. Peter D. Moore. Facts on File, Inc., 460 Park Ave. S., New York, New York 10016. (212) 683-2244. 1987.

Examining Your Environment. Daniel F. Wentworth. Holt, Rinehart & Winston of Canada, 55 Horner Ave., Toronto, Ontario, Canada M8Z 4X6. 1971-1976. Ecology program designed for use in grades 4-8 covering astronomy, birds, dandelions, ecology, mapping, miniclimates, pollution, running water, small animals, snow, ice, and trees.

Grzimek's Encyclopedia of Ecology. Bernhard Grzimek. Van Nostrand Reinhold, 115 5th Ave., New York, New York 10003. (212) 254-3232. 1976.

McGraw-Hill Encyclopedia of Environmental Science. Sybil P. Parker. McGraw-Hill Science & Engineering Books, 11 W. 19th St., New York, New York 10011. (212) 337-6010. 1980. Covers ecology, man's influence on nature, and environmental protection.

McGraw-Hill Encyclopedia of Science and Technology. McGraw-Hill, 1221 Avenue of the Americas, New York, New York 10020. (212) 512-2000 or (800) 262-4729. 1992. Seventh edition. Issued in multiple volumes including index. Includes all science and technology broad subject areas.

North American Reference Encyclopedia of Ecology and Pollution. William White. North American Pub. Co., 401

N. Broad St., Philadelphia, Pennsylvania 19108. (215) 238-5300. 1972.

GENERAL WORKS

Avian Ecology. Christopher M. Perrins. Chapman & Hall, 29 W. 35th St., New York, New York 10001-2291. (212) 244-3336. 1983.

Ecological Aspects of Social Evolution. Daniel I. Rubenstein. Princeton University Press, 41 Williams St., Princeton, New Jersey 08540. (609) 258-4900. 1986. Behavior of birds and mammals.

The Ecology of Bird Communities. John A. Wiens. Cambridge University Press, 40 W. 20th St., New York, New York 10011. (212) 924-3900. 1989. Foundations, patterns, processes, and variations in birds.

HANDBOOKS AND MANUALS

Distribution and Taxonomy of Birds of the World. Charles G. Sibley and Burt L. Monroe. Yale University Press, 92 A Yale Station, 302 Temple St., New Haven, Connecticut 06520. (203) 432-0960. 1990. An up-to-date delineation of the present distribution of the species of birds arranged in a classification based primarily on evidence of phytogenetic relationships from comparison of the DNAs. Includes a list of scientific and English names of species.

New Generation Guide to the Birds of Britain and Europe. Christopher Perrins, ed. University of Texas Press, PO Box 7819, Austin, Texas 78713-7819. (512) 471-7233 or (800) 252-3206. 1987.

ONLINE DATA BASES

Enviro/Energyline Abstracts Plus. R. R. Bowker Co., 121 Chanlon Rd., New Providence, New Jersey 07974. (908) 464-6800.

Environmental Periodicals Bibliography. National Information Services Corp., Ste. 6, Wyman Towers, 3100 St. Paul St., Baltimore, Maryland 21218. (410)243-0797. Online version of abstract of same name.

Monthly Catalog of United States Government Publications. U.S. G.P.O., Supt. of Docs., PO Box 371954, Pittsburgh, Pennsylvania 15250-7954. (202) 512-0000.

National Technical Information Service. U.S. Department of Commerce, National Technical Information Service, Office of Data Base Services, 5285 Port Royal Rd., Springfield, Virginia 22161. (703) 487-4807. Bibliographic database of government sponsored research and technical reports.

SCISEARCH. Institute for Scientific Information, University City Science Center, 3501 Market St., Philadelphia, Pennsylvania 19104. (215) 386-0100.

PERIODICALS AND NEWSLETTERS

Blue Goose Flyer. National Wildlife Refuge, Box 124, Winona, Minnesota 55987. (612) 447-5586. 1975-. Quarterly. Wildlife refuge system management news.

Duckological. Ducks Unlimited, 1 Waterfowl Way, Long Grove, Illinois 60047. (708) 438-4300. Bimonthly. Protection of ducks.

East End Environment. Southampton College, Natural Science Division, Southampton, New York 11968. 1970-. Quarterly.

Massachusetts Audubon Newsletter. Massachusetts Audubon Society, S. Great Rd., Lincoln, Massachusetts 01773. (617) 259-9500. 1962-. Ten times a year.

New Hampshire Audubon News. Audubon Society of New Hampshire, 3 Silk Farm Rd., Concord, New Hampshire 03301. 1966-. Monthly.

TRADE ASSOCIATIONS AND PROFESSIONAL SOCIETIES

American Association of Avian Pathologists. University of Pennsylvania, New Bolton Center, Kennett Square, Pennsylvania 19348. (215) 444-4282.

Association of Field Ornithologists, Inc. c/o Elissa Landre, Broadmoor Wildlife Sanctuary, Massachusetts Audubon Society, 280 Eliot St., South Natick, Massachusetts 01760. (508) 655-2296.

Ducks Unlimited. 1 Waterfowl Way, Long Grove, Illinois 60047. (708) 438-4300.

Inland Bird Banding Association. RD 2, Box 26, Wisner, Nebraska 68791. (402) 529-6679.

National Audubon Society. 950 Third Ave., New York, New York 10022. (212) 832-3200.

North American Bluebird Society. Box 6295, Silver Spring, Maryland 20906. (301) 384-2798.

North American Falconers Association. 820 Jay Pl., Berthoud, Colorado 80513.

AVICIDES

See: PESTICIDES

B

BACKGROUND RADIATION
See: RADIATION, NATURAL

BACTERIA
See also: DISEASE CARRIERS; ECOSYSTEMS; FOOD SCIENCE; MICROORGANISMS; NUTRITION; WASTE MANAGEMENT

ABSTRACTING AND INDEXING SERVICES

Applied Ecology Abstracts Studies in Renewable Natural Resources. Information Retrieval Ltd., 1911 Jefferson Davis Highway, Arlington, Virginia 22202. 1975-. Monthly.

Aqualine Abstracts. Water Research Centre. c/o Pergamon Microforms International, Inc., Fairview Park, Elmsford, New York 10523. (914) 592-7720. 1927-. Contains some 8,000 records annually on water and wastewater technology. Covers all aspects of water, wastewater, associated engineering services and the aquatic environment. Over 600 periodicals, as well as books, reports and conference proceedings and other publications from water related institutions worldwide are scanned. Also available online.

ASFA Aquaculture Abstracts. Cambridge Scientific Abstracts, Inc., 5161 River Rd., Bethesda, Maryland 20816. (301) 961-6750. 1984.

Biological Abstracts. BIOSIS, 2100 Arch St., Philadelphia, Pennsylvania 19103-1399. (215) 587-4800. 1927-.

Biological and Agricultural Index. H.W. Wilson Co., 950 University Ave., Bronx, New York 10452. (800) 367-6770. 1916-. Monthly.

Biology Digest. Data Courier, Plexus Pub Inc., 143 Old Marlton Pike, Medford, New Jersey 08055. 1974-. Monthly. Abstracts biology periodicals.

Biotechnology Research Abstracts. Cambridge Scientific Abstracts, 5161 River Rd., Bethesda, Maryland 20816. (301) 961-6750. Monthly. Includes such broad areas as genetic intervention, biochemical genetics, and microbiological techniques.

Ecological Abstracts. Geo Abstracts Ltd. Elsevier Applied Science, Crown House, Linton Rd., Barking, England IG 11 8JU. 1974-. Derived from over 600 leading ecological and environmental journals, plus books, conference proceedings, reports and theses.

Ecology Abstracts. Cambridge Scientific Abstracts, 5161 River Rd., Bethesda, Maryland 20816. (301) 961-6750. Monthly.

Environment Abstracts. Bowker A & I Publishing, 121 Chanlon Rd., New Providence, New Jersey 07974. (908) 464-6800. 1974-.

Environment Index. Environment Information Center, Index Research Department, 124 E. 39th St., New York, New York 10016. 1971-. Annual.

Environmental Information Connection–EIC. Planning Information Program, Dept. of Urban and Regional Planning, University of Illinois, 1003 West Nevada, Urbana, Illinois 61801. (217) 333-1369. Also available online.

Environmental Periodicals Bibliography. Environmental Studies Institute, International Academy at Santa Barbara, 800 Garden St., Suite D, Santa Barbara, California 93101. (805) 965-5010. Also available online.

Food Science and Technology Abstracts. International Food Information Service, c/o National Food Laboratory, 6363 Clark Ave., Dublin, California 94568. (800) 336-3782. 1969-.

Forestry Abstracts. C. A. B. International, Wallingford, England OX10 8DE. (0491) 3211. 1939/40-. Monthly. Journal of abstracts of journal articles, conferences, technical reports in the subject areas of: silviculture, forest mensuration and management, physical environment, fire, plant biology, genetics and breeding, mycology and pathology, game and wildlife, fish, protection of forests and other related matter.

General Science Index. H. W. Wilson Co., 950 University Ave., Bronx, New York 10452. 1978-. Monthly, also issued in annual cumulation. Cumulative subject index to English language periodicals in the subject fields of astronomy, botany, chemistry, earth science, environment and conservation, food and nutrition, genetics, mathematics, medicine and health, microbiology, oceanography, physics, physiology and zoology.

Microbiology Abstracts. Section A. Industrial and Applied Microbiology. Cambridge Scientific Abstracts, 5161 River Rd., Bethesda, Maryland 20816. (301) 961-6750. 1972-.

Multimedia Index to Ecology. National Information Center for Educational Media, University of Southern California, Los Angeles, California 90007.

Pollution Abstracts. Cambridge Scientific Abstracts, 5161 River Rd., Bethesda, Maryland 20816. (301) 961-6750. Six/year. Indexes worldwide technical literature on environmental pollution. Covers air pollution, marine and

freshwater pollution, sewage and wastewater treatment, waste management, toxicology and health, noise pollution, radiation, land pollution, and environmental policies, programs, legislation, and education. Also available online.

Science Citation Index. Institute for Scientific Information, 3501 Market St., Philadelphia, Pennsylvania 19104. 1961-.

BIBLIOGRAPHIES

Current Contents. Agriculture, Biology and Environmental Sciences. Institute for Scientific Information, 3501 Market St., Philadelphia, Pennsylvania 19104. (800) 523-1857. 1973-. Previous title: Current Contents. Agricultural, Food & Veterinary Sciences. Gives the table of contents of periodicals in the fields of agriculture, biology, environmental and related areas.

Directory of Published Proceedings. Interdok Corp., 173 Halstead Ave., Harrison, New York 10528. (914) 835-3506. 1990. Monthly. This is a listing of published proceedings including the series SEMTE (Science/Medicine/Engineering/Technology) and the series SSH (Social Science/Humanities).

EPA Publications Bibliography. U.S. Environmental Protection Agency, Library Systems Branch, 401 M St., SW, Washington, District of Columbia 20460. (202) 260-2090. Quarterly.

ENCYCLOPEDIAS AND DICTIONARIES

Cambridge Encyclopedia of Life Sciences. A. E. Friday and David S. Ingram. Cambridge University Press, 40 W 20th St., New York, New York 10011. (212) 924-3900 or (800) 227-0247. 1985. Includes all topics under biology and ecology.

A Dictionary of Genetics. Robert C. King and William A. Stansfield. Oxford University Press, 200 Madison Ave., New York, New York 10016. (212) 679-7300 or (800) 334-4249. 1991. Fourth edition. Includes 7,100 definitions with 250 illustrations. Also includes bibliography of major sources.

Dictionary of Genetics and Cell Biology. Norman Maclean. New York University Press, 70 Washington Sq. S., New York, New York 10012. (212) 998-2575. 1987. Includes the subject areas of cytology and genetics.

Encyclopedia of Human Biology. Renato Dulbecco, ed. Academic Press, c/o Harcourt Brace Jovanovich Inc., 6277 Sea Harbor Dr., Orlando, Florida 32887. (800) 346-8648. 1991. Eight volumes.

Encyclopedic Dictionary of Genetics: With German Term Equivalents and Extensive German/English Index. R. C. King and W. D. Stansfield. VCH Publishers, 303 NW 12th Ave., Deerfield Beach, Florida 33442-1788. (305) 428-5566. 1990. 4th ed. Revised edition of: A Dictionary of Genetics, third edition.

McGraw-Hill Encyclopedia of Environmental Science. Sybil P. Parker. McGraw-Hill Science & Engineering Books, 11 W. 19th St., New York, New York 10011. (212) 337-6010. 1980. Covers ecology, man's influence on nature, and environmental protection.

McGraw-Hill Encyclopedia of Science and Technology. McGraw-Hill, 1221 Avenue of the Americas, New York, New York 10020. (212) 512-2000 or (800) 262-4729.

1992. Seventh edition. Issued in multiple volumes including index. Includes all science and technology broad subject areas.

The Nutrition and Health Encyclopedia. David F. Tver and Percy Russell. Van Nostrand Reinhold, 115 5th Ave., New York, New York 10003. (212) 254-3232. 1989.

Van Nostrand's Scientific Encyclopedia. Glenn D. Considine, ed. Van Nostrand Reinhold, 115 5th Ave., New York, New York 10003. (212) 254-3232. 1983. Sixth edition. Includes all broad subject areas in science.

GENERAL WORKS

Bacteria. L. R. Hill and B. E. Kirsop, eds. Cambridge University Press, 40 W. 20th St., New York, New York 10011. (212) 924-3900; (800) 227-0247. 1991. Directory and collection of bacteria type specimens.

Bacteria in Nature. Edward R. Leadbetter. Plenum Press, 233 Spring St., New York, New York 10013-1578. (212) 620-8000. 1989.

Bacteria in Their Natural Environments. Madilyn Fletcher, ed. Academic Press Ltd., 24-28 Oval Rd., London, England NW1 7DX. (071) 2674466. 1985.

Bacterial Genetic Systems. Jeffrey H. Miller, ed. Academic Press, c/o Harcourt Brace Jovanovich Inc., 6277 Sea Harbor Dr., Orlando, Florida 32887. (800) 346-8648. 1991. A volume in the Methods in Enzymology series, no. 204.

Bacterial Toxins. W. E. Van Heyningen. Charles C. Thomas Publisher, 2600 S. First St., Springfield, Illinois 62794-9265. (217) 789-8980. Covers bacterial toxins and antitoxins.

Biodegradability of Organic Substances in the Aquatic Environment. Pavel Pitter, et al. CRC Press, 2000 Corporate Blvd. N.W., Boca Raton, Florida 33431. (800) 272-7737. 1990. Explains the principles and theories of biodegradation, primarily from an ecological standpoint. Current techniques used to evaluate the biodegradability of individual chemicals are reviewed.

Biofouling and Biocorrosion in Industrial Water Systems. Hans C. Flemming, ed. Springer-Verlag, 175 5th Ave., New York, New York 10010. (212) 460-1500. 1991.

Dentrification in Soil and Sediment. Niels Peter Revsbech and Jan Sorensen, eds. Plenum Press, 233 Spring St., New York, New York 10013-1578. (212) 620-8000; (800) 221-9369. 1991. The process, its measurement, and its significance are analyzed in 20 papers from a June 1989 symposium in Ahrus, Denmark. Topics included are: biochemistry, genetics, ecophysiology, and the emission of nitrogen-oxygen compounds.

Environmental Role of Nitrogen-Fixing Blue-Green Algae and Asymbiotic Bacteria. U. Granhall. Swedish Natural Science Research Council, P.O. Box 6711, Stockholm, Sweden S-113 85. 08-15-1580. 1978. Deals with nitrogen-fixing microorganisms, nitrogen-fixing algae and cyanobacteria.

Molecular Strategies of Pathogens and Host Plants. Suresh S. Patil, et al., eds. Springer-Verlag, 175 5th Ave, New York, New York 10010. (212) 460-1500. 1991. Papers from an April seminar in Honolulu discusses the molecular interactions between plant pathogens and their hosts, considering the strategies of various bacteria and fungi, the plant's response, and an approach to breeding disease-resistant plants.

Nitrification. J.I. Prosser, ed. IRL, Southfield Rd., Eynsham, Oxford, England OX8 1JJ. (0865) 88283. 1987.

Report on the Design and Operation of a Full-Scale Anaerobic Dairy Manure Digester: Final Report. Elizabeth Coppinger, et al. U.S. Department of Energy, Solar Energy Research Institute, 5285 Port Royal Rd., Springfield, Virginia 22161. (703) 487-4650. 1979.

Sewage and the Bacterial Purification of Sewage. Samuel Rideal. John Wiley & Sons, Inc., 605 3rd Ave., New York, New York 10158-0012. (212) 850-6000. 1906. Publication on sewage purification with illustrations and colored plates.

ONLINE DATA BASES

BIOSIS Previews. BIOSIS, 2100 Arch St., Philadelphia, Pennsylvania 19103-1399. (215) 587-4800. Largest and most comprehensive database of research in the life sciences. Contains citations for nearly 9000 primary research journals, monographs, reviews, symposia, preliminary reports, semi-popular journals, selected institutional reports, government reports and research communications.

Biotechnology Abstracts. Derwent Publications Ltd., 6845 Elm St., McLean, Virginia 22101. (703) 790-0400. Includes material on genetic manipulation, biochemical engineering, fermentation, biocatalysis, cell hybridization, in vitro plant propagation and industrial waste management.

Cambridge Scientific Abstracts Life Science–CSAL. Cambridge Scientific Abstracts, 5161 River Rd., Bethesda, Maryland 20816. (301) 961-6750. Provides access to the following abstracting services: "Life Sciences Collection," "Aquatic Sciences and Fisheries Abstracts," "Oceanic Abstracts," and "Pollution Abstracts."

Current Research Information System–CRIS/USDA. U.S. Department of Agriculture, National Agricultural Library, 10301 Baltimore Blvd., 5th Floor, Beltsville, Maryland 20705-2351. (301) 504-5755. Looks at current research projects in agriculture and allied sciences covering the biological, physical, social and behavioral sciences related to agriculture.

Enviro/Energyline Abstracts Plus. R. R. Bowker Co., 121 Chanlon Rd., New Providence, New Jersey 07974. (908) 464-6800.

Environmental Periodicals Bibliography. National Information Services Corp., Ste. 6, Wyman Towers, 3100 St. Paul St., Baltimore, Maryland 21218. (410)243-0797. Online version of abstract of same name.

Monthly Catalog of United States Government Publications. U.S. G.P.O., Supt. of Docs., PO Box 371954, Pittsburgh, Pennsylvania 15250-7954. (202) 512-0000.

National Technical Information Service. U.S. Department of Commerce, National Technical Information Service, Office of Data Base Services, 5285 Port Royal Rd., Springfield, Virginia 22161. (703) 487-4807. Bibliographic database of government sponsored research and technical reports.

SCISEARCH. Institute for Scientific Information, University City Science Center, 3501 Market St., Philadelphia, Pennsylvania 19104. (215) 386-0100.

PERIODICALS AND NEWSLETTERS

Applied and Environmental Microbiology Journal. American Society for Microbiology, 1325 Massachusetts Avenue N.W., Washington, District of Columbia 20005. (202) 737-3600. Monthly. Articles on industrial and food microbiology and ecological studies.

Biodegradation. Kluwer Academic Publishers, 101 Philip Dr., Assinippi Park, Norwell, Massachusetts 02061-0358. (617) 871-6600. 1990-. Quarterly. Covers all aspects of science pertaining to the detoxification, recycling, amelioration or treatment of waste materials and pollutants by naturally occurring microbial strains, associations, or recombinant microorganisms.

CMI Descriptions of Pathogenic Fungi and Bacteria. Commonwealth Mycological Institute, Ferry Lane, Kew, Richmond, England TW9 3AF. 1964-. Four sets a year.

The Journal of Applied Bacteriology. Academic Press, c/o Harcourt Brace Jovanovich Inc., 6277 Sea Harbor Dr., Orlando, Florida 32887. (800) 346-8648. Monthly. Deals with agricultural, biological and environmental aspects of bacteriology.

RESEARCH CENTERS AND INSTITUTES

Michigan State University, Microbial Ecology Center. 540 Plant and Soil Sciences Building, East Lansing, Michigan 48824-1325. (517) 353-9021.

Rockefeller University, Laboratory of Microbiology. 1230 York Avenue, New York, New York 10021-6399. (212) 570-8277.

Southeastern Massachusetts University, Southeastern New England Clinical Microbiology Research Group. North Dartmouth, Massachusetts 02747. (508) 999-8320.

University of Iowa, University Large Scale Fermentation Facility. Department of Microbiology, Iowa City, Iowa 52242. (319) 335-7780.

University of Oregon, Institute of Molecular Biology. Eugene, Oregon 97403. (503) 686-5151.

Virginia Polytechnic Institute and State University, Anaerobe Laboratory. Department of Anaerobic Microbiology, Blacksburg, Virginia 24061-0305. (703) 231-6935.

TRADE ASSOCIATIONS AND PROFESSIONAL SOCIETIES

American Society of Naturalists. Department of Ecology and Evolation, State University of New York, Stony Brook, New York 11794. (516) 632-8589.

BACTERICIDES

See also: ANTIBIOTICS; PESTICIDES

ABSTRACTING AND INDEXING SERVICES

Applied Ecology Abstracts Studies in Renewable Natural Resources. Information Retrieval Ltd., 1911 Jefferson Davis Highway, Arlington, Virginia 22202. 1975-. Monthly.

Biological Abstracts. BIOSIS, 2100 Arch St., Philadelphia, Pennsylvania 19103-1399. (215) 587-4800. 1927-.

Biological and Agricultural Index. H.W. Wilson Co., 950 University Ave., Bronx, New York 10452. (800) 367-6770. 1916-. Monthly.

Biology Digest. Data Courier, Plexus Pub Inc., 143 Old Marlton Pike, Medford, New Jersey 08055. 1974-. Monthly. Abstracts biology periodicals.

Environment Abstracts. Bowker A & I Publishing, 121 Chanlon Rd., New Providence, New Jersey 07974. (908) 464-6800. 1974-.

Environment Index. Environment Information Center, Index Research Department, 124 E. 39th St., New York, New York 10016. 1971-. Annual.

Environmental Information Connection-EIC. Planning Information Program, Dept. of Urban and Regional Planning, University of Illinois, 1003 West Nevada, Urbana, Illinois 61801. (217) 333-1369. Also available online.

Environmental Periodicals Bibliography. Environmental Studies Institute, International Academy at Santa Barbara, 800 Garden St., Suite D, Santa Barbara, California 93101. (805) 965-5010. Also available online.

General Science Index. H. W. Wilson Co., 950 University Ave., Bronx, New York 10452. 1978-. Monthly, also issued in annual cumulation. Cumulative subject index to English language periodicals in the subject fields of astronomy, botany, chemistry, earth science, environment and conservation, food and nutrition, genetics, mathematics, medicine and health, microbiology, oceanography, physics, physiology and zoology.

Index to Scientific Book Contents. Institute for Scientific Information, 3501 Market St., Philadelphia, Pennsylvania 19104. (800) 523-1857. 1985-. Annual. Gives contents of science books published.

Multimedia Index to Ecology. National Information Center for Educational Media, University of Southern California, Los Angeles, California 90007.

Pesticides Abstracts. U.S. Environmental Protection Agency, Office of Pesticides Programs, 345 Curtland, Atlanta, Georgia 30365. (404) 347-2864. 1981. Monthly. Formerly: Health Aspects of Pesticides Abstracts Bulletin.

Science Citation Index. Institute for Scientific Information, 3501 Market St., Philadelphia, Pennsylvania 19104. 1961-.

BIBLIOGRAPHIES

Current Contents. Agriculture, Biology and Environmental Sciences. Institute for Scientific Information, 3501 Market St., Philadelphia, Pennsylvania 19104. (800) 523-1857. 1973-. Previous title: Current Contents. Agricultural, Food & Veterinary Sciences. Gives the table of contents of periodicals in the fields of agriculture, biology, environmental and related areas.

EPA Publications Bibliography. U.S. Environmental Protection Agency, Library Systems Branch, 401 M St., SW, Washington, District of Columbia 20460. (202) 260-2090. Quarterly.

ENCYCLOPEDIAS AND DICTIONARIES

Cambridge Encyclopedia of Life Sciences. A. E. Friday and David S. Ingram. Cambridge University Press, 40 W

20th St., New York, New York 10011. (212) 924-3900 or (800) 227-0247. 1985. Includes all topics under biology and ecology.

Encyclopedia of Human Biology. Renato Dulbecco, ed. Academic Press, c/o Harcourt Brace Jovanovich Inc., 6277 Sea Harbor Dr., Orlando, Florida 32887. (800) 346-8648. 1991. Eight volumes.

McGraw-Hill Encyclopedia of Environmental Science. Sybil P. Parker. McGraw-Hill Science & Engineering Books, 11 W. 19th St., New York, New York 10011. (212) 337-6010. 1980. Covers ecology, man's influence on nature, and environmental protection.

McGraw-Hill Encyclopedia of Science and Technology. McGraw-Hill, 1221 Avenue of the Americas, New York, New York 10020. (212) 512-2000 or (800) 262-4729. 1992. Seventh edition. Issued in multiple volumes including index. Includes all science and technology broad subject areas.

Van Nostrand's Scientific Encyclopedia. Glenn D. Considine, ed. Van Nostrand Reinhold, 115 5th Ave., New York, New York 10003. (212) 254-3232. 1983. Sixth edition. Includes all broad subject areas in science.

HANDBOOKS AND MANUALS

The Agrochemicals Handbook. H. Kidd and D. Hartlet, eds. Royal Society of Chemistry, c/o CRC Press, 2000 Corporate Blvd., N.W., Boca Raton, Florida 33431-9868. (800) 272-7737. 1991. 3rd ed. Contains comprehensive worldwide information and data on substances which are active components of agriculture chemical products currently used in crop protection and pest control.

ONLINE DATA BASES

BIOSIS Previews. BIOSIS, 2100 Arch St., Philadelphia, Pennsylvania 19103-1399. (215) 587-4800. Largest and most comprehensive database of research in the life sciences. Contains citations for nearly 9000 primary research journals, monographs, reviews, symposia, preliminary reports, semi-popular journals, selected institutional reports, government reports and research communications.

Cambridge Scientific Abstracts Life Science-CSAL. Cambridge Scientific Abstracts, 5161 River Rd., Bethesda, Maryland 20816. (301) 961-6750. Provides access to the following abstracting services: "Life Sciences Collection," "Aquatic Sciences and Fisheries Abstracts," "Oceanic Abstracts," and "Pollution Abstracts."

Chemical Collection System/Request Tracking-CCS/RTS. U.S. Environmental Protection Agency, Office of Pesticides and Toxic Substances, 401 M St., SW, Washington, District of Columbia 20460. (202) 260-2000. Contains information on various properties of a number of chemicals including environmental effects, test and analysis methods, and health effects. Available from EPA.

Chemical Dictionary Online-CHEMLINE. Chemical Abstracts Service, 2540 Olentangy River Rd., Columbus, Ohio 43210. (614) 421-3600 or (800) 848-6533. Part of MEDLINE of the National Library of Medicine (NLM). File of 900,000 names for chemical substances, representing 450,000 unique compounds. It contains such information as Chemical Abstracts (CA) Service Registry Numbers, molecular formulas, preferred chemical no-

menclature, and generic and ring structure information. Available on NLM's ELHILL system.

Chemical Exposure. Science Applications International Corp., Health & Environmental Information, P.O. Box 2501, Oak Ridge, Tennessee 37831. (615) 482-9031. Database of chemicals that have been identified in both human tissues and body fluids and in feral and food animals. Contains reference to journal articles, conferences, and reports. Covers the whole fields of information related to human and animal exposure to food, air, and water contaminants and pharmaceuticals. Its records include information on chemical properties, formulas, tissues measured, analytical method used, demographics and more. Available on DIALOG.

Enviro/Energyline Abstracts Plus. R. R. Bowker Co., 121 Chanlon Rd., New Providence, New Jersey 07974. (908) 464-6800.

Environmental Periodicals Bibliography. National Information Services Corp., Ste. 6, Wyman Towers, 3100 St. Paul St., Baltimore, Maryland 21218. (410)243-0797. Online version of abstract of same name.

Monthly Catalog of United States Government Publications. U.S. G.P.O., Supt. of Docs., PO Box 371954, Pittsburgh, Pennsylvania 15250-7954. (202) 512-0000.

National Technical Information Service. U.S. Department of Commerce, National Technical Information Service, Office of Data Base Services, 5285 Port Royal Rd., Springfield, Virginia 22161. (703) 487-4807. Bibliographic database of government sponsored research and technical reports.

SCISEARCH. Institute for Scientific Information, University City Science Center, 3501 Market St., Philadelphia, Pennsylvania 19104. (215) 386-0100.

BAIT-BLOCK METHOD

See: PEST CONTROL

BALLISTIC SEPARATORS

See: COMPOST

BARIUM

See also: ELEMENTS

ABSTRACTING AND INDEXING SERVICES

Applied Science and Technology Index. H.W. Wilson Co., 950 University Ave., Bronx, New York 10452. (800) 367-6770. Formerly Industrial Arts Index.

Biological Abstracts. BIOSIS, 2100 Arch St., Philadelphia, Pennsylvania 19103-1399. (215) 587-4800. 1927-.

Chemical Abstracts. Chemical Abstracts Service, 2540 Olentangy River Rd., PO Box 3012, Columbus, Ohio 43210. (800) 848-6533. 1907-.

INIS Atomindex. International Atomic Energy Agency, Wagramerstrasse 5, Vienna, Austria A-1400. 222 23606198. 1988-. Semiannual. Abstracts nuclear energy and nuclear physics topics from journals, conferences, technical reports and other related publications. Issued in 6 parts: Personal Author, Corporate Entry, Subject, Report, Standard Patent, Conference (by place), Conference (by date).

Pollution Abstracts. Cambridge Scientific Abstracts, 5161 River Rd., Bethesda, Maryland 20816. (301) 961-6750. Six/year. Indexes worldwide technical literature on environmental pollution. Covers air pollution, marine and freshwater pollution, sewage and wastewater treatment, waste management, toxicology and health, noise pollution, radiation, land pollution, and environmental policies, programs, legislation, and education. Also available online.

Science Citation Index. Institute for Scientific Information, 3501 Market St., Philadelphia, Pennsylvania 19104. 1961-.

ENCYCLOPEDIAS AND DICTIONARIES

Encyclopedia of Chemical Processing and Design. John J. Mcketta and W. A. Cunningham. Marcel Dekker, Inc., 270 Madison Ave., New York, New York 10016. (212) 696-9000; (800) 228-1160. 1992. Thirty-eight volumes.

Encyclopedia of Electrochemistry of Elements. A. J. Bard. Marcel Dekker, Inc., 270 Madison Ave., New York, New York 10016. (212) 696-9000 or (800) 228-1160. Encyclopedic treatment of the subject area of electrochemistry and related subjects.

Encyclopedia of Human Biology. Renato Dulbecco, ed. Academic Press, c/o Harcourt Brace Jovanovich Inc., 6277 Sea Harbor Dr., Orlando, Florida 32887. (800) 346-8648. 1991. Eight volumes.

Kirk-Othmer Encyclopedia of Chemical Technology. J. I. Kroschwitz, ed. John Wiley & Sons, Inc., 605 3rd Ave., New York, New York 10158-0012. (212) 850-6000. 1992-. All articles in the new edition have been rewritten and updated adding new subjects such as biotechnology, computer topics, analytical techniques and instrumentation, environmental concerns, fuels and energy, inorganic and solid state chemistry; composite materials and material science in general, and pharmaceuticals. Also available online.

McGraw-Hill Encyclopedia of Science and Technology. McGraw-Hill, 1221 Avenue of the Americas, New York, New York 10020. (212) 512-2000 or (800) 262-4729. 1992. Seventh edition. Issued in multiple volumes including index. Includes all science and technology broad subject areas.

ONLINE DATA BASES

BIOSIS Previews. BIOSIS, 2100 Arch St., Philadelphia, Pennsylvania 19103-1399. (215) 587-4800. Largest and most comprehensive database of research in the life sciences. Contains citations for nearly 9000 primary research journals, monographs, reviews, symposia, preliminary reports, semi-popular journals, selected institutional reports, government reports and research communications.

Chemical Abstracts-CA. Chemical Abstracts Service, 2540 Olentangy River Rd., P.O. Box 3012, Columbus, Ohio 43210. (800) 848-6533 or (614) 421-3600. Information sources include 9000 journals, patents from 27 countries, two industrial property organizations, new

books, conference proceedings, and government research reports.

Chemical Abstracts Chemical Name Directory-CHEM-NAME. Chemical Abstracts Service, 2540 Olentangy River Rd., P.O. Box 3012, Columbus, Ohio 43210. (800) 848-6533 or (614) 421-3600. Listing of chemical substances in a dictionary type file. The Chemical Abstracts (CAS) Registry Number, molecular formula, Chemical Abstracts (CA) Substance Index Name, available synonyms, ring data and other chemical substance information is given for each entry.

Kirk-Othmer Encyclopedia of Chemical Technology. John Wiley & Sons, Inc., 605 3rd Ave., 5th Floor, New York, New York 10158. (212) 850-6000. Online version of the publication of the same name.

BATTERIES

See also: LEAD; POWER GENERATION; SOLAR CELLS; WASTE MANAGEMENT

ABSTRACTING AND INDEXING SERVICES

Applied Science and Technology Index. H.W. Wilson Co., 950 University Ave., Bronx, New York 10452. (800) 367-6770. Formerly Industrial Arts Index.

Engineering Index. The Engineering Index Inc., 345 E. 47th St., New York, New York 10017. 1962-.

General Science Index. H. W. Wilson Co., 950 University Ave., Bronx, New York 10452. 1978-. Monthly, also issued in annual cumulation. Cumulative subject index to English language periodicals in the subject fields of astronomy, botany, chemistry, earth science, environment and conservation, food and nutrition, genetics, mathematics, medicine and health, microbiology, oceanography, physics, physiology and zoology.

ENCYCLOPEDIAS AND DICTIONARIES

Encyclopedia of Chemical Processing and Design. John J. Mcketta and W. A. Cunningham. Marcel Dekker, Inc., 270 Madison Ave., New York, New York 10016. (212) 696-9000; (800) 228-1160. 1992. Thirty-eight volumes.

Encyclopedia of Physical Science and Technology. Robert A. Meyers, ed. Academic Press, c/o Harcourt Brace Jovanovich Inc., 6277 Sea Harbor Dr., Orlando, Florida 32887. (800) 346-8648. Dictionary of engineering, technology and physical sciences.

Kirk-Othmer Encyclopedia of Chemical Technology. J. I. Kroschwitz, ed. John Wiley & Sons, Inc., 605 3rd Ave., New York, New York 10158-0012. (212) 850-6000. 1992-. All articles in the new edition have been rewritten and updated adding new subjects such as biotechnology, computer topics, analytical techniques and instrumentation, environmental concerns, fuels and energy, inorganic and solid state chemistry; composite materials and material science in general, and pharmaceuticals. Also available online.

McGraw-Hill Encyclopedia of Science and Technology. McGraw-Hill, 1221 Avenue of the Americas, New York, New York 10020. (212) 512-2000 or (800) 262-4729. 1992. Seventh edition. Issued in multiple volumes in-

cluding index. Includes all science and technology broad subject areas.

Van Nostrand's Scientific Encyclopedia. Glenn D. Considine, ed. Van Nostrand Reinhold, 115 5th Ave., New York, New York 10003. (212) 254-3232. 1983. Sixth edition. Includes all broad subject areas in science.

ONLINE DATA BASES

Battery & EV Technology. Business Communications Company, Inc., 25 Van Zant St., Norwalk, Connecticut 06855. (203) 853-4266. Applications in the battery and electric vehicle industries.

Computerized Engineering Index–COMPENDEX. Engineering Information Inc., 345 E. 47th St., New York, New York 10017. (212) 705-7600.

Kirk-Othmer Encyclopedia of Chemical Technology. John Wiley & Sons, Inc., 605 3rd Ave., 5th Floor, New York, New York 10158. (212) 850-6000. Online version of the publication of the same name.

PERIODICALS AND NEWSLETTERS

Newsletter. Association of Battery Recyclers, Sanders Lead Co. Corp., Sanders Rd., PO Drawer 707, Troy, Alabama 36081. (205) 566-1563. Bimonthly.

STATISTICS SOURCES

The Dry Cell Battery Market. FIND/SVP, 625 Avenue of the Americas, New York, New York 10011. (212) 645-4500. 1990. Analyzes the $3 billion dry-cell battery market and its four major product categories–carbon zinc, alkaline, rechargeable and lithium ultralife batteries.

BAYS

See also: ESTUARIES; WATER POLLUTION; WETLANDS

ABSTRACTING AND INDEXING SERVICES

Applied Ecology Abstracts Studies in Renewable Natural Resources. Information Retrieval Ltd., 1911 Jefferson Davis Highway, Arlington, Virginia 22202. 1975-. Monthly.

Biological Abstracts. BIOSIS, 2100 Arch St., Philadelphia, Pennsylvania 19103-1399. (215) 587-4800. 1927-.

Civil Engineering Hydraulic Abstracts. BHRA Fluid Engineering, Air Science Co., PO Box 143, Corning, New York 14830. (607) 962-5591. Monthly. Abstracts of periodicals that publish in the areas of hydraulic engineering and other related topics.

Ecological Abstracts. Geo Abstracts Ltd. Elsevier Applied Science, Crown House, Linton Rd., Barking, England IG 11 8JU. 1974-. Derived from over 600 leading ecological and environmental journals, plus books, conference proceedings, reports and theses.

Ecology Abstracts. Cambridge Scientific Abstracts, 5161 River Rd., Bethesda, Maryland 20816. (301) 961-6750. Monthly.

Environment Abstracts. Bowker A & I Publishing, 121 Chanlon Rd., New Providence, New Jersey 07974. (908) 464-6800. 1974-.

Environment Index. Environment Information Center, Index Research Department, 124 E. 39th St., New York, New York 10016. 1971-. Annual.

Environmental Information Connection–EIC. Planning Information Program, Dept. of Urban and Regional Planning, University of Illinois, 1003 West Nevada, Urbana, Illinois 61801. (217) 333-1369. Also available online.

Environmental Periodicals Bibliography. Environmental Studies Institute, International Academy at Santa Barbara, 800 Garden St., Suite D, Santa Barbara, California 93101. (805) 965-5010. Also available online.

Multimedia Index to Ecology. National Information Center for Educational Media, University of Southern California, Los Angeles, California 90007.

Oceanic Abstracts. UMI Data Courier, 620 S. 3rd St., Louisville, Kentucky 40202. (800) 626-2823. Formerly: Oceanic Index and Oceanic Citation Journal.

Pollution Abstracts. Cambridge Scientific Abstracts, 5161 River Rd., Bethesda, Maryland 20816. (301) 961-6750. Six/year. Indexes worldwide technical literature on environmental pollution. Covers air pollution, marine and freshwater pollution, sewage and wastewater treatment, waste management, toxicology and health, noise pollution, radiation, land pollution, and environmental policies, programs, legislation, and education. Also available online.

Science Citation Index. Institute for Scientific Information, 3501 Market St., Philadelphia, Pennsylvania 19104. 1961-.

BIBLIOGRAPHIES

EPA Publications Bibliography. U.S. Environmental Protection Agency, Library Systems Branch, 401 M St., SW, Washington, District of Columbia 20460. (202) 260-2090. Quarterly.

ENCYCLOPEDIAS AND DICTIONARIES

The Encyclopedia of Beaches and Coastal Environments. Maurice L. Schwartz. Hutchinson Ross Pub. Co., Stroudsburg, Pennsylvania 1982.

The Encyclopedia of Geochemistry and Environmental Sciences. Rhodes Whitmore Fairbridge. Van Nostrand Reinhold Co., 115 5th Ave., New York, New York 10003. (212) 254-3232. 1972.

McGraw-Hill Encyclopedia of Science and Technology. McGraw-Hill, 1221 Avenue of the Americas, New York, New York 10020. (212) 512-2000 or (800) 262-4729. 1992. Seventh edition. Issued in multiple volumes including index. Includes all science and technology broad subject areas.

Van Nostrand's Scientific Encyclopedia. Glenn D. Considine, ed. Van Nostrand Reinhold, 115 5th Ave., New York, New York 10003. (212) 254-3232. 1983. Sixth edition. Includes all broad subject areas in science.

ONLINE DATA BASES

BIOSIS Previews. BIOSIS, 2100 Arch St., Philadelphia, Pennsylvania 19103-1399. (215) 587-4800. Largest and most comprehensive database of research in the life sciences. Contains citations for nearly 9000 primary research journals, monographs, reviews, symposia, preliminary reports, semi-popular journals, selected institutional reports, government reports and research communications.

Enviro/Energyline Abstracts Plus. R. R. Bowker Co., 121 Chanlon Rd., New Providence, New Jersey 07974. (908) 464-6800.

Environmental Periodicals Bibliography. National Information Services Corp., Ste. 6, Wyman Towers, 3100 St. Paul St., Baltimore, Maryland 21218. (410)243-0797. Online version of abstract of same name.

Monthly Catalog of United States Government Publications. U.S. G.P.O., Supt. of Docs., PO Box 371954, Pittsburgh, Pennsylvania 15250-7954. (202) 512-0000.

National Technical Information Service. U.S. Department of Commerce, National Technical Information Service, Office of Data Base Services, 5285 Port Royal Rd., Springfield, Virginia 22161. (703) 487-4807. Bibliographic database of government sponsored research and technical reports.

Oceanic Abstracts. Cambridge Scientific Abstracts, 5161 River Rd., Bethesda, Maryland 20816. (301) 961-6750. Online access.

SCISEARCH. Institute for Scientific Information, University City Science Center, 3501 Market St., Philadelphia, Pennsylvania 19104. (215) 386-0100.

BEACHES

See also: MARINE POLLUTION

ABSTRACTING AND INDEXING SERVICES

Applied Ecology Abstracts Studies in Renewable Natural Resources. Information Retrieval Ltd., 1911 Jefferson Davis Highway, Arlington, Virginia 22202. 1975-. Monthly.

Biological Abstracts. BIOSIS, 2100 Arch St., Philadelphia, Pennsylvania 19103-1399. (215) 587-4800. 1927-.

Civil Engineering Hydraulic Abstracts. BHRA Fluid Engineering, Air Science Co., PO Box 143, Corning, New York 14830. (607) 962-5591. Monthly. Abstracts of periodicals that publish in the areas of hydraulic engineering and other related topics.

Ecological Abstracts. Geo Abstracts Ltd. Elsevier Applied Science, Crown House, Linton Rd., Barking, England IG 11 8JU. 1974-. Derived from over 600 leading ecological and environmental journals, plus books, conference proceedings, reports and theses.

Ecology Abstracts. Cambridge Scientific Abstracts, 5161 River Rd., Bethesda, Maryland 20816. (301) 961-6750. Monthly.

Environment Abstracts. Bowker A & I Publishing, 121 Chanlon Rd., New Providence, New Jersey 07974. (908) 464-6800. 1974-.

Environment Index. Environment Information Center, Index Research Department, 124 E. 39th St., New York, New York 10016. 1971-. Annual.

Environmental Information Connection–EIC. Planning Information Program, Dept. of Urban and Regional Planning, University of Illinois, 1003 West Nevada, Urbana, Illinois 61801. (217) 333-1369. Also available online.

Environmental Periodicals Bibliography. Environmental Studies Institute, International Academy at Santa Barbara, 800 Garden St., Suite D, Santa Barbara, California 93101. (805) 965-5010. Also available online.

Index to Scientific Book Contents. Institute for Scientific Information, 3501 Market St., Philadelphia, Pennsylvania 19104. (800) 523-1857. 1985-. Annual. Gives contents of science books published.

Multimedia Index to Ecology. National Information Center for Educational Media, University of Southern California, Los Angeles, California 90007.

Oceanic Abstracts. UMI Data Courier, 620 S. 3rd St., Louisville, Kentucky 40202. (800) 626-2823. Formerly: Oceanic Index and Oceanic Citation Journal.

Pollution Abstracts. Cambridge Scientific Abstracts, 5161 River Rd., Bethesda, Maryland 20816. (301) 961-6750. Six/year. Indexes worldwide technical literature on environmental pollution. Covers air pollution, marine and freshwater pollution, sewage and wastewater treatment, waste management, toxicology and health, noise pollution, radiation, land pollution, and environmental policies, programs, legislation, and education. Also available online.

Science Citation Index. Institute for Scientific Information, 3501 Market St., Philadelphia, Pennsylvania 19104. 1961-.

BIBLIOGRAPHIES

Bibliography and Index of Geology. American Geological Institute, 4220 King St., Alexandria, Virginia 22302. Monthly. Includes environmental geology and hydrogeology.

EPA Publications Bibliography. U.S. Environmental Protection Agency, Library Systems Branch, 401 M St., SW, Washington, District of Columbia 20460. (202) 260-2090. Quarterly.

ENCYCLOPEDIAS AND DICTIONARIES

The Encyclopedia of Beaches and Coastal Environments. Maurice L. Schwartz. Hutchinson Ross Pub. Co., Stroudsburg, Pennsylvania 1982.

The Encyclopedia of Geochemistry and Environmental Sciences. Rhodes Whitmore Fairbridge. Van Nostrand Reinhold Co., 115 5th Ave., New York, New York 10003. (212) 254-3232. 1972.

The Encyclopedia of Oceanography. Rhodes Whitmore Fairbridge. Reinhold Pub. Co., 115 5th Ave., New York, New York 10003. (212) 254-3232. 1966.

Illustrated Encyclopedia of Science and the Future. Mike Biscare, et al., ed. Marshall Cavendish, 58 Old Compton St., London, England 0W1V5 PA. 01-734 6710. 1983. Twenty volumes. Each volume has 5 sections: Frontiers,

Electronics in Action, Medical Science, Military Technology, and Resources.

McGraw-Hill Encyclopedia of Science and Technology. McGraw-Hill, 1221 Avenue of the Americas, New York, New York 10020. (212) 512-2000 or (800) 262-4729. 1992. Seventh edition. Issued in multiple volumes including index. Includes all science and technology broad subject areas.

GENERAL WORKS

Ecology of Sandy Shores. A. C. Brown and A. Mclachlan. Elsevier Science Publishing Co., 655 Avenue of the Americas, New York, New York 10010. (212) 989-5800. 1990. Deals with the biological study of sandy beaches.

Magill's Survey of Science. Earth Science Series. Frank N. Magill. Salem Press, PO Box 50062, Pasadena, California 91105. 1990-. Five volumes. Includes information on earth's crust, hot spots and volcanic island chains, physical properties of minerals, rock magnetism, physical properties of rocks, and index.

ONLINE DATA BASES

BIOSIS Previews. BIOSIS, 2100 Arch St., Philadelphia, Pennsylvania 19103-1399. (215) 587-4800. Largest and most comprehensive database of research in the life sciences. Contains citations for nearly 9000 primary research journals, monographs, reviews, symposia, preliminary reports, semi-popular journals, selected institutional reports, government reports and research communications.

Enviro/Energyline Abstracts Plus. R. R. Bowker Co., 121 Chanlon Rd., New Providence, New Jersey 07974. (908) 464-6800.

Environmental Periodicals Bibliography. National Information Services Corp., Ste. 6, Wyman Towers, 3100 St. Paul St., Baltimore, Maryland 21218. (410)243-0797. Online version of abstract of same name.

Monthly Catalog of United States Government Publications. U.S. G.P.O., Supt. of Docs., PO Box 371954, Pittsburgh, Pennsylvania 15250-7954. (202) 512-0000.

National Technical Information Service. U.S. Department of Commerce, National Technical Information Service, Office of Data Base Services, 5285 Port Royal Rd., Springfield, Virginia 22161. (703) 487-4807. Bibliographic database of government sponsored research and technical reports.

Oceanic Abstracts. Cambridge Scientific Abstracts, 5161 River Rd., Bethesda, Maryland 20816. (301) 961-6750. Online access.

PressNet Environmental Reports. Chemical Information Systems, Inc., 7215 York Rd., Baltimore, Maryland 21212. (301) 321-8440.

SCISEARCH. Institute for Scientific Information, University City Science Center, 3501 Market St., Philadelphia, Pennsylvania 19104. (215) 386-0100.

PERIODICALS AND NEWSLETTERS

American Shore and Beach Preservation Association Newsletter. American Shore and Beach Preservation Association, PO Box 279, Middletown, California 95461. (707) 987-2385. 1955-. Quarterly.

Newsletter. American Shore and Beach Preservation Association, PO Box 279, Middletown, California 95461. (707) 987-2385. Quarterly. Coastal management projects, news, conservation issues, and government policies.

TRADE ASSOCIATIONS AND PROFESSIONAL SOCIETIES

American Littoral Society. Sandy Hook, Highlands, New Jersey 07732. (908) 291-0055.

American Shore and Beach Preservation Association. P.O. 279, Middletown, California 95461. (707) 987-2385.

Barrier Islands Coalition. 40 W. 20th St., 11th Fl., New York, New York 10011. (212) 727-2700.

BEARING CAPACITY
See: SOIL SCIENCE

BED LOAD
See: STREAMS

BEHAVIOR, ENVIRONMENTAL

ABSTRACTING AND INDEXING SERVICES

Biological Abstracts. BIOSIS, 2100 Arch St., Philadelphia, Pennsylvania 19103-1399. (215) 587-4800. 1927-.

Biological and Agricultural Index. H.W. Wilson Co., 950 University Ave., Bronx, New York 10452. (800) 367-6770. 1916-. Monthly.

Ecological Abstracts. Geo Abstracts Ltd. Elsevier Applied Science, Crown House, Linton Rd., Barking, England IG 11 8JU. 1974-. Derived from over 600 leading ecological and environmental journals, plus books, conference proceedings, reports and theses.

Environment Abstracts. Bowker A & I Publishing, 121 Chanlon Rd., New Providence, New Jersey 07974. (908) 464-6800. 1974-.

Environment Index. Environment Information Center, Index Research Department, 124 E. 39th St., New York, New York 10016. 1971-. Annual.

Environmental Information Connection–EIC. Planning Information Program, Dept. of Urban and Regional Planning, University of Illinois, 1003 West Nevada, Urbana, Illinois 61801. (217) 333-1369. Also available online.

Environmental Periodicals Bibliography. Environmental Studies Institute, International Academy at Santa Barbara, 800 Garden St., Suite D, Santa Barbara, California 93101. (805) 965-5010. Also available online.

Index to Scientific Book Contents. Institute for Scientific Information, 3501 Market St., Philadelphia, Pennsylvania 19104. (800) 523-1857. 1985-. Annual. Gives contents of science books published.

Pollution Abstracts. Cambridge Scientific Abstracts, 5161 River Rd., Bethesda, Maryland 20816. (301) 961-6750. Six/year. Indexes worldwide technical literature on environmental pollution. Covers air pollution, marine and freshwater pollution, sewage and wastewater treatment, waste management, toxicology and health, noise pollution, radiation, land pollution, and environmental policies, programs, legislation, and education. Also available online.

Science Citation Index. Institute for Scientific Information, 3501 Market St., Philadelphia, Pennsylvania 19104. 1961-.

BIBLIOGRAPHIES

EPA Publications Bibliography. U.S. Environmental Protection Agency, Library Systems Branch, 401 M St., SW, Washington, District of Columbia 20460. (202) 260-2090. Quarterly.

ENCYCLOPEDIAS AND DICTIONARIES

McGraw-Hill Encyclopedia of Science and Technology. McGraw-Hill, 1221 Avenue of the Americas, New York, New York 10020. (212) 512-2000 or (800) 262-4729. 1992. Seventh edition. Issued in multiple volumes including index. Includes all science and technology broad subject areas.

Van Nostrand's Scientific Encyclopedia. Glenn D. Considine, ed. Van Nostrand Reinhold, 115 5th Ave., New York, New York 10003. (212) 254-3232. 1983. Sixth edition. Includes all broad subject areas in science.

ONLINE DATA BASES

BIOSIS Previews. BIOSIS, 2100 Arch St., Philadelphia, Pennsylvania 19103-1399. (215) 587-4800. Largest and most comprehensive database of research in the life sciences. Contains citations for nearly 9000 primary research journals, monographs, reviews, symposia, preliminary reports, semi-popular journals, selected institutional reports, government reports and research communications.

Cambridge Scientific Abstracts Life Science–CSAL. Cambridge Scientific Abstracts, 5161 River Rd., Bethesda, Maryland 20816. (301) 961-6750. Provides access to the following abstracting services: "Life Sciences Collection," "Aquatic Sciences and Fisheries Abstracts," "Oceanic Abstracts," and "Pollution Abstracts."

Enviro/Energyline Abstracts Plus. R. R. Bowker Co., 121 Chanlon Rd., New Providence, New Jersey 07974. (908) 464-6800.

Environmental Periodicals Bibliography. National Information Services Corp., Ste. 6, Wyman Towers, 3100 St. Paul St., Baltimore, Maryland 21218. (410)243-0797. Online version of abstract of same name.

SCISEARCH. Institute for Scientific Information, University City Science Center, 3501 Market St., Philadelphia, Pennsylvania 19104. (215) 386-0100.

BENDIOCARB

ABSTRACTING AND INDEXING SERVICES

Biological Abstracts. BIOSIS, 2100 Arch St., Philadelphia, Pennsylvania 19103-1399. (215) 587-4800. 1927-.

Biological and Agricultural Index. H.W. Wilson Co., 950 University Ave., Bronx, New York 10452. (800) 367-6770. 1916-. Monthly.

Environment Abstracts. Bowker A & I Publishing, 121 Chanlon Rd., New Providence, New Jersey 07974. (908) 464-6800. 1974-.

Environment Index. Environment Information Center, Index Research Department, 124 E. 39th St., New York, New York 10016. 1971-. Annual.

Environmental Information Connection–EIC. Planning Information Program, Dept. of Urban and Regional Planning, University of Illinois, 1003 West Nevada, Urbana, Illinois 61801. (217) 333-1369. Also available online.

Environmental Periodicals Bibliography. Environmental Studies Institute, International Academy at Santa Barbara, 800 Garden St., Suite D, Santa Barbara, California 93101. (805) 965-5010. Also available online.

Science Citation Index. Institute for Scientific Information, 3501 Market St., Philadelphia, Pennsylvania 19104. 1961-.

BIBLIOGRAPHIES

EPA Publications Bibliography. U.S. Environmental Protection Agency, Library Systems Branch, 401 M St., SW, Washington, District of Columbia 20460. (202) 260-2090. Quarterly.

ENCYCLOPEDIAS AND DICTIONARIES

Encyclopedia of Trademarks and Synonyms. H. Bennett, ed. Chemical Publishing Co., 80 Eighth Ave., New York, New York 10011. (212) 255-1950. 1981. Three volumes. Includes chemical compounds, compositions consisting of one or more chemicals and other products. Also included are abbreviated names and WHO free names.

ONLINE DATA BASES

BIOSIS Previews. BIOSIS, 2100 Arch St., Philadelphia, Pennsylvania 19103-1399. (215) 587-4800. Largest and most comprehensive database of research in the life sciences. Contains citations for nearly 9000 primary research journals, monographs, reviews, symposia, preliminary reports, semi-popular journals, selected institutional reports, government reports and research communications.

Chemical Abstracts Chemical Name Directory-CHEM-NAME. Chemical Abstracts Service, 2540 Olentangy River Rd., P.O. Box 3012, Columbus, Ohio 43210. (800) 848-6533 or (614) 421-3600. Listing of chemical substances in a dictionary type file. The Chemical Abstracts (CAS) Registry Number, molecular formula, Chemical Abstracts (CA) Substance Index Name, available synonyms, ring data and other chemical substance information is given for each entry.

Chemical Carcinogenesis Research Information System–CCRIS. National Library of Medicine, 8600 Rockville Pike, Bethesda, Maryland 20894. (800) 638-8480. Individual assay results and test conditions for 1,451 chemicals in the areas of carcinogenicity, mutagenicity, tumor promotion, and cocarcinogenicity.

Enviro/Energyline Abstracts Plus. R. R. Bowker Co., 121 Chanlon Rd., New Providence, New Jersey 07974. (908) 464-6800.

Environmental Periodicals Bibliography. National Information Services Corp., Ste. 6, Wyman Towers, 3100 St. Paul St., Baltimore, Maryland 21218. (410)243-0797. Online version of abstract of same name.

BENOMYL

ABSTRACTING AND INDEXING SERVICES

Biological Abstracts. BIOSIS, 2100 Arch St., Philadelphia, Pennsylvania 19103-1399. (215) 587-4800. 1927-.

Biological and Agricultural Index. H.W. Wilson Co., 950 University Ave., Bronx, New York 10452. (800) 367-6770. 1916-. Monthly.

Biotechnology Research Abstracts. Cambridge Scientific Abstracts, 5161 River Rd., Bethesda, Maryland 20816. (301) 961-6750. Monthly. Includes such broad areas as genetic intervention, biochemical genetics, and microbiological techniques.

Ecology Abstracts. Cambridge Scientific Abstracts, 5161 River Rd., Bethesda, Maryland 20816. (301) 961-6750. Monthly.

Environment Abstracts. Bowker A & I Publishing, 121 Chanlon Rd., New Providence, New Jersey 07974. (908) 464-6800. 1974-.

Environment Index. Environment Information Center, Index Research Department, 124 E. 39th St., New York, New York 10016. 1971-. Annual.

Environmental Information Connection–EIC. Planning Information Program, Dept. of Urban and Regional Planning, University of Illinois, 1003 West Nevada, Urbana, Illinois 61801. (217) 333-1369. Also available online.

Environmental Periodicals Bibliography. Environmental Studies Institute, International Academy at Santa Barbara, 800 Garden St., Suite D, Santa Barbara, California 93101. (805) 965-5010. Also available online.

Pollution Abstracts. Cambridge Scientific Abstracts, 5161 River Rd., Bethesda, Maryland 20816. (301) 961-6750. Six/year. Indexes worldwide technical literature on environmental pollution. Covers air pollution, marine and freshwater pollution, sewage and wastewater treatment, waste management, toxicology and health, noise pollution, radiation, land pollution, and environmental policies, programs, legislation, and education. Also available online.

Science Citation Index. Institute for Scientific Information, 3501 Market St., Philadelphia, Pennsylvania 19104. 1961-.

BIBLIOGRAPHIES

EPA Publications Bibliography. U.S. Environmental Protection Agency, Library Systems Branch, 401 M St., SW, Washington, District of Columbia 20460. (202) 260-2090. Quarterly.

ENCYCLOPEDIAS AND DICTIONARIES

Encyclopedia of Trademarks and Synonyms. H. Bennett, ed. Chemical Publishing Co., 80 Eighth Ave., New York, New York 10011. (212) 255-1950. 1981. Three volumes. Includes chemical compounds, compositions consisting of one or more chemicals and other products. Also included are abbreviated names and WHO free names.

ONLINE DATA BASES

BIOSIS Previews. BIOSIS, 2100 Arch St., Philadelphia, Pennsylvania 19103-1399. (215) 587-4800. Largest and most comprehensive database of research in the life sciences. Contains citations for nearly 9000 primary research journals, monographs, reviews, symposia, preliminary reports, semi-popular journals, selected institutional reports, government reports and research communications.

Cambridge Scientific Abstracts Life Science–CSAL. Cambridge Scientific Abstracts, 5161 River Rd., Bethesda, Maryland 20816. (301) 961-6750. Provides access to the following abstracting services: "Life Sciences Collection," "Aquatic Sciences and Fisheries Abstracts," "Oceanic Abstracts," and "Pollution Abstracts."

Chemical Carcinogenesis Research Information System–CCRIS. National Library of Medicine, 8600 Rockville Pike, Bethesda, Maryland 20894. (800) 638-8480. Individual assay results and test conditions for 1,451 chemicals in the areas of carcinogenicity, mutagenicity, tumor promotion, and cocarcinogenicity.

Enviro/Energyline Abstracts Plus. R. R. Bowker Co., 121 Chanlon Rd., New Providence, New Jersey 07974. (908) 464-6800.

Environmental Periodicals Bibliography. National Information Services Corp., Ste. 6, Wyman Towers, 3100 St. Paul St., Baltimore, Maryland 21218. (410)243-0797. Online version of abstract of same name.

BENTHIC COMMUNITIES

See: BENTHOS

BENTHIC ECOLOGY

See also: AQUATIC ECOSYSTEMS; BENTHOS

ABSTRACTING AND INDEXING SERVICES

Ecological Abstracts. Geo Abstracts Ltd. Elsevier Applied Science, Crown House, Linton Rd., Barking, England IG 11 8JU. 1974-. Derived from over 600 leading ecological and environmental journals, plus books, conference proceedings, reports and theses.

General Science Index. H. W. Wilson Co., 950 University Ave., Bronx, New York 10452. 1978-. Monthly, also issued in annual cumulation. Cumulative subject index to English language periodicals in the subject fields of astronomy, botany, chemistry, earth science, environment and conservation, food and nutrition, genetics, mathematics, medicine and health, microbiology, oceanography, physics, physiology and zoology.

Index to Scientific Book Contents. Institute for Scientific Information, 3501 Market St., Philadelphia, Pennsylvania 19104. (800) 523-1857. 1985-. Annual. Gives contents of science books published.

BIBLIOGRAPHIES

Directory of Published Proceedings. Interdok Corp., 173 Halstead Ave., Harrison, New York 10528. (914) 835-3506. 1990. Monthly. This is a listing of published proceedings including the series SEMTE (Science/Medicine/Engineering/Technology) and the series SSH (Social Science/Humanities).

ENCYCLOPEDIAS AND DICTIONARIES

McGraw-Hill Encyclopedia of Environmental Science. Sybil P. Parker. McGraw-Hill Science & Engineering Books, 11 W. 19th St., New York, New York 10011. (212) 337-6010. 1980. Covers ecology, man's influence on nature, and environmental protection.

The New York Times Encyclopedic Dictionary of the Environment. Paul Sarnoff. Quadrangle Books, New York, New York 1971. Focuses on state-of-the-art methods of pollution control, abatement, prevention and removal.

PERIODICALS AND NEWSLETTERS

The Journal of Biological Chemistry. American Society of Biological Chemists, 428 E. Preston St., Baltimore, Maryland 21202. Three times a month. Biological, agricultural, and energy aspects of the environment.

TRADE ASSOCIATIONS AND PROFESSIONAL SOCIETIES

North American Benthological Society. c/o Cheryl R. Black, Savannah River Ecology Laboratory, Drawer E, Aiken, South Carolina 29802. (803) 925-7425.

BENTHOS

ABSTRACTING AND INDEXING SERVICES

Applied Ecology Abstracts Studies in Renewable Natural Resources. Information Retrieval Ltd., 1911 Jefferson Davis Highway, Arlington, Virginia 22202. 1975-. Monthly.

Biological Abstracts. BIOSIS, 2100 Arch St., Philadelphia, Pennsylvania 19103-1399. (215) 587-4800. 1927-.

Biological and Agricultural Index. H.W. Wilson Co., 950 University Ave., Bronx, New York 10452. (800) 367-6770. 1916-. Monthly.

Biology Digest. Data Courier, Plexus Pub Inc., 143 Old Marlton Pike, Medford, New Jersey 08055. 1974-. Monthly. Abstracts biology periodicals.

Ecological Abstracts. Geo Abstracts Ltd. Elsevier Applied Science, Crown House, Linton Rd., Barking, England IG 11 8JU. 1974-. Derived from over 600 leading ecological and environmental journals, plus books, conference proceedings, reports and theses.

Ecology Abstracts. Cambridge Scientific Abstracts, 5161 River Rd., Bethesda, Maryland 20816. (301) 961-6750. Monthly.

Environment Abstracts. Bowker A & I Publishing, 121 Chanlon Rd., New Providence, New Jersey 07974. (908) 464-6800. 1974-.

Environment Index. Environment Information Center, Index Research Department, 124 E. 39th St., New York, New York 10016. 1971-. Annual.

Environmental Information Connection–EIC. Planning Information Program, Dept. of Urban and Regional Planning, University of Illinois, 1003 West Nevada, Urbana, Illinois 61801. (217) 333-1369. Also available online.

Environmental Periodicals Bibliography. Environmental Studies Institute, International Academy at Santa Barbara, 800 Garden St., Suite D, Santa Barbara, California 93101. (805) 965-5010. Also available online.

General Science Index. H. W. Wilson Co., 950 University Ave., Bronx, New York 10452. 1978-. Monthly, also issued in annual cumulation. Cumulative subject index to English language periodicals in the subject fields of astronomy, botany, chemistry, earth science, environment and conservation, food and nutrition, genetics, mathematics, medicine and health, microbiology, oceanography, physics, physiology and zoology.

Index to Scientific Book Contents. Institute for Scientific Information, 3501 Market St., Philadelphia, Pennsylvania 19104. (800) 523-1857. 1985-. Annual. Gives contents of science books published.

Multimedia Index to Ecology. National Information Center for Educational Media, University of Southern California, Los Angeles, California 90007.

Pollution Abstracts. Cambridge Scientific Abstracts, 5161 River Rd., Bethesda, Maryland 20816. (301) 961-6750. Six/year. Indexes worldwide technical literature on environmental pollution. Covers air pollution, marine and freshwater pollution, sewage and wastewater treatment, waste management, toxicology and health, noise pollution, radiation, land pollution, and environmental policies, programs, legislation, and education. Also available online.

Science Citation Index. Institute for Scientific Information, 3501 Market St., Philadelphia, Pennsylvania 19104. 1961-.

BIBLIOGRAPHIES

EPA Publications Bibliography. U.S. Environmental Protection Agency, Library Systems Branch, 401 M St., SW, Washington, District of Columbia 20460. (202) 260-2090. Quarterly.

ENCYCLOPEDIAS AND DICTIONARIES

Cambridge Encyclopedia of Life Sciences. A. E. Friday and David S. Ingram. Cambridge University Press, 40 W 20th St., New York, New York 10011. (212) 924-3900 or (800) 227-0247. 1985. Includes all topics under biology and ecology.

The Encyclopedia of Animal Ecology. Peter D. Moore. Facts on File, Inc., 460 Park Ave. S., New York, New York 10016. (212) 683-2244. 1987.

Grzimek's Encyclopedia of Ecology. Bernhard Grzimek. Van Nostrand Reinhold, 115 5th Ave., New York, New York 10003. (212) 254-3232. 1976.

McGraw-Hill Encyclopedia of Environmental Science. Sybil P. Parker. McGraw-Hill Science & Engineering Books, 11 W. 19th St., New York, New York 10011. (212) 337-6010. 1980. Covers ecology, man's influence on nature, and environmental protection.

McGraw-Hill Encyclopedia of Science and Technology. McGraw-Hill, 1221 Avenue of the Americas, New York, New York 10020. (212) 512-2000 or (800) 262-4729. 1992. Seventh edition. Issued in multiple volumes including index. Includes all science and technology broad subject areas.

The New York Times Encyclopedic Dictionary of the Environment. Paul Sarnoff. Quadrangle Books, New York, New York 1971. Focuses on state-of-the-art methods of pollution control, abatement, prevention and removal.

North American Reference Encyclopedia of Ecology and Pollution. William White. North American Pub. Co., 401 N. Broad St., Philadelphia, Pennsylvania 19108. (215) 238-5300. 1972.

Van Nostrand's Scientific Encyclopedia. Glenn D. Considine, ed. Van Nostrand Reinhold, 115 5th Ave., New York, New York 10003. (212) 254-3232. 1983. Sixth edition. Includes all broad subject areas in science.

GENERAL WORKS

Ecology and Paleoecology of Benthic Foraminifera. John Williams Murray. John Wiley & Sons, Inc., 605 3rd Ave., New York, New York (212) 850-6000. 1991.

Ecology of Marine Benthos. Bruce C. Coull. University of South Carolina Press, Columbia, South Carolina 29208. (803) 777-5243. 1977. Papers on marine science, marine biological and coastal research.

The Ecology of Marine Sediments. John S. Gray. Cambridge University Press, 40 W. 20th St., New York, New York 10011. (212) 924-3900. 1981. An introduction to the structure and function of benthic communities.

The Living Ocean. Boyce Thorne-Miller. Island Press, 1718 Connecticut Ave. N.W., Suite 300, Washington, District of Columbia 20009. (202) 232-7933. 1991. Discusses all marine ecosystems, including coastal benthic, shore systems, estuaries, wetlands, and coral reefs, coastal pelagic, deep-sea benthic, hydrothermal vents and others.

Microbial Mats. Yehuda Cohen. American Society of Microbiology, 1325 Massachusetts Ave. NW, Washington, District of Columbia 20005. (202) 737-3600. 1989. Physiological ecology of benthic microbial communities.

Sublittoral Ecology. R. Earll. Oxford University Press, Inc., 200 Madison Ave., New York, New York 10016. (212) 679-7300. 1983. The ecology of the shadow sublittoral benthos.

ONLINE DATA BASES

BIOSIS Previews. BIOSIS, 2100 Arch St., Philadelphia, Pennsylvania 19103-1399. (215) 587-4800. Largest and most comprehensive database of research in the life sciences. Contains citations for nearly 9000 primary research journals, monographs, reviews, symposia, preliminary reports, semi-popular journals, selected institutional reports, government reports and research communications.

Cambridge Scientific Abstracts Life Science–CSAL. Cambridge Scientific Abstracts, 5161 River Rd., Bethesda, Maryland 20816. (301) 961-6750. Provides access to the following abstracting services: "Life Sciences Collection," "Aquatic Sciences and Fisheries Abstracts," "Oceanic Abstracts," and "Pollution Abstracts."

Current Research Information System–CRIS/USDA. U.S. Department of Agriculture, National Agricultural Library, 10301 Baltimore Blvd., 5th Floor, Beltsville, Maryland 20705-2351. (301) 504-5755. Looks at current research projects in agriculture and allied sciences covering the biological, physical, social and behavioral sciences related to agriculture.

Enviro/Energyline Abstracts Plus. R. R. Bowker Co., 121 Chanlon Rd., New Providence, New Jersey 07974. (908) 464-6800.

Environmental Periodicals Bibliography. National Information Services Corp., Ste. 6, Wyman Towers, 3100 St. Paul St., Baltimore, Maryland 21218. (410)243-0797. Online version of abstract of same name.

SCISEARCH. Institute for Scientific Information, University City Science Center, 3501 Market St., Philadelphia, Pennsylvania 19104. (215) 386-0100.

RESEARCH CENTERS AND INSTITUTES

Benedict Estuarine Research Laboratory. Academy of Natural Sciences, Benedict Avenue, Benedict, Maryland 20612. (301) 274-3134.

University of Maine, Ira C. Darling Center for Research Teaching and Service. Walpole, Maine 04573. (207) 563-3146.

University of Texas at Austin, Marine Science Institute. Port Aransas, Texas 78373. (512) 749-6711.

TRADE ASSOCIATIONS AND PROFESSIONAL SOCIETIES

American Littoral Society. Sandy Hook, Highlands, New Jersey 07732. (908) 291-0055.

American Society of Naturalists. Department of Ecology and Evolation, State University of New York, Stony Brook, New York 11794. (516) 632-8589.

Bigelow Laboratory for Ocean Sciences, Division of Northeast Research Foundation, Inc. Mckown Point, West Boothbay Harbor, Maine 04575. (207) 633-2173.

North American Benthological Society. c/o Cheryl R. Black, Savannah River Ecology Laboratory, Drawer E, Aiken, South Carolina 29802. (803) 925-7425.

BENZENE

See also: CARCINOGENS; HAZARDOUS WASTES; MUTAGENIC AGENTS; TOXIC POLLUTANTS; WATER POLLUTION

ABSTRACTING AND INDEXING SERVICES

Biological Abstracts. BIOSIS, 2100 Arch St., Philadelphia, Pennsylvania 19103-1399. (215) 587-4800. 1927-.

Chemical Abstracts. Chemical Abstracts Service, 2540 Olentangy River Rd., PO Box 3012, Columbus, Ohio 43210. (800) 848-6533. 1907-.

Environment Abstracts. Bowker A & I Publishing, 121 Chanlon Rd., New Providence, New Jersey 07974. (908) 464-6800. 1974-.

Environment Index. Environment Information Center, Index Research Department, 124 E. 39th St., New York, New York 10016. 1971-. Annual.

Environmental Information Connection–EIC. Planning Information Program, Dept. of Urban and Regional Planning, University of Illinois, 1003 West Nevada, Urbana, Illinois 61801. (217) 333-1369. Also available online.

Environmental Periodicals Bibliography. Environmental Studies Institute, International Academy at Santa Barbara, 800 Garden St., Suite D, Santa Barbara, California 93101. (805) 965-5010. Also available online.

Science Citation Index. Institute for Scientific Information, 3501 Market St., Philadelphia, Pennsylvania 19104. 1961-.

BIBLIOGRAPHIES

Benzene Toxicology. S. Jackson. U.S. Department of Health and Human Services, Public Health Services, National Institutes of Health, 9000 Rockville Pike, Bethesda, Maryland 20892. (301) 496-4000. 1980.

Directory of Published Proceedings. Interdok Corp., 173 Halstead Ave., Harrison, New York 10528. (914) 835-3506. 1990. Monthly. This is a listing of published proceedings including the series SEMTE (Science/Medicine/Engineering/Technology) and the series SSH (Social Science/Humanities).

EPA Publications Bibliography. U.S. Environmental Protection Agency, Library Systems Branch, 401 M St., SW, Washington, District of Columbia 20460. (202) 260-2090. Quarterly.

ENCYCLOPEDIAS AND DICTIONARIES

Encyclopedia of Chemical Processing and Design. John J. Mcketta and W. A. Cunningham. Marcel Dekker, Inc., 270 Madison Ave., New York, New York 10016. (212) 696-9000; (800) 228-1160. 1992. Thirty-eight volumes.

Kirk-Othmer Encyclopedia of Chemical Technology. J. I. Kroschwitz, ed. John Wiley & Sons, Inc., 605 3rd Ave., New York, New York 10158-0012. (212) 850-6000. 1992-. All articles in the new edition have been rewritten and updated adding new subjects such as biotechnology, computer topics, analytical techniques and instrumentation, environmental concerns, fuels and energy, inorganic and solid state chemistry; composite materials and material science in general, and pharmaceuticals. Also available online.

McGraw-Hill Encyclopedia of Environmental Science. Sybil P. Parker. McGraw-Hill Science & Engineering Books, 11 W. 19th St., New York, New York 10011. (212) 337-6010. 1980. Covers ecology, man's influence on nature, and environmental protection.

McGraw-Hill Encyclopedia of Science and Technology. McGraw-Hill, 1221 Avenue of the Americas, New York, New York 10020. (212) 512-2000 or (800) 262-4729. 1992. Seventh edition. Issued in multiple volumes in-

cluding index. Includes all science and technology broad subject areas.

GENERAL WORKS

National Emissions Standards for Hazardous Air Pollutants, Benzene Emissions. U.S. Environmental Protection Agency, 401 M St., S.W., Washington, District of Columbia 20460. (202) 260-2090. 1989.

ONLINE DATA BASES

BIOSIS Previews. BIOSIS, 2100 Arch St., Philadelphia, Pennsylvania 19103-1399. (215) 587-4800. Largest and most comprehensive database of research in the life sciences. Contains citations for nearly 9000 primary research journals, monographs, reviews, symposia, preliminary reports, semi-popular journals, selected institutional reports, government reports and research communications.

Chemical Abstracts-CA. Chemical Abstracts Service, 2540 Olentangy River Rd., P.O. Box 3012, Columbus, Ohio 43210. (800) 848-6533 or (614) 421-3600. Information sources include 9000 journals, patents from 27 countries, two industrial property organizations, new books, conference proceedings, and government research reports.

Chemical Collection System/Request Tracking–CCS/RTS. U.S. Environmental Protection Agency, Office of Pesticides and Toxic Substances, 401 M St., SW, Washington, District of Columbia 20460. (202) 260-2090. Contains information on various properties of a number of chemicals including environmental effects, test and analysis methods, and health effects. Available from EPA.

Chemical Dictionary Online–CHEMLINE. Chemical Abstracts Service, 2540 Olentangy River Rd., Columbus, Ohio 43210. (614) 421-3600 or (800) 848-6533. Part of MEDLINE of the National Library of Medicine (NLM). File of 900,000 names for chemical substances, representing 450,000 unique compounds. It contains such information as Chemical Abstracts (CA) Service Registry Numbers, molecular formulas, preferred chemical nomenclature, and generic and ring structure information. Available on NLM's ELHILL system.

Chemical Exposure. Science Applications International Corp., Health & Environmental Information, P.O. Box 2501, Oak Ridge, Tennessee 37831. (615) 482-9031. Database of chemicals that have been identified in both human tissues and body fluids and in feral and food animals. Contains reference to journal articles, conferences, and reports. Covers the whole fields of information related to human and animal exposure to food, air, and water contaminants and pharmaceuticals. Its records include information on chemical properties, formulas, tissues measured, analytical method used, demographics and more. Available on DIALOG.

Dewitt Petrochemical Newsletter. DeWitt and Company, 16800 Greenspoint Park, North Atrium Suite 120, Houston, Texas 77060. (713) 875-5525.

Enviro/Energyline Abstracts Plus. R. R. Bowker Co., 121 Chanlon Rd., New Providence, New Jersey 07974. (908) 464-6800.

Environmental Periodicals Bibliography. National Information Services Corp., Ste. 6, Wyman Towers, 3100 St.

Paul St., Baltimore, Maryland 21218. (410)243-0797. Online version of abstract of same name.

Kirk-Othmer Encyclopedia of Chemical Technology. John Wiley & Sons, Inc., 605 3rd Ave., 5th Floor, New York, New York 10158. (212) 850-6000. Online version of the publication of the same name.

SCISEARCH. Institute for Scientific Information, University City Science Center, 3501 Market St., Philadelphia, Pennsylvania 19104. (215) 386-0100.

BENZENE HEXACHLORIDE

See: BENZENE

BENZO-A-PYRENE

ABSTRACTING AND INDEXING SERVICES

Biological Abstracts. BIOSIS, 2100 Arch St., Philadelphia, Pennsylvania 19103-1399. (215) 587-4800. 1927-.

Chemical Abstracts. Chemical Abstracts Service, 2540 Olentangy River Rd., PO Box 3012, Columbus, Ohio 43210. (800) 848-6533. 1907-.

Environment Abstracts. Bowker A & I Publishing, 121 Chanlon Rd., New Providence, New Jersey 07974. (908) 464-6800. 1974-.

Environment Index. Environment Information Center, Index Research Department, 124 E. 39th St., New York, New York 10016. 1971-. Annual.

Environmental Information Connection–EIC. Planning Information Program, Dept. of Urban and Regional Planning, University of Illinois, 1003 West Nevada, Urbana, Illinois 61801. (217) 333-1369. Also available online.

Environmental Periodicals Bibliography. Environmental Studies Institute, International Academy at Santa Barbara, 800 Garden St., Suite D, Santa Barbara, California 93101. (805) 965-5010. Also available online.

Science Citation Index. Institute for Scientific Information, 3501 Market St., Philadelphia, Pennsylvania 19104. 1961-.

BIBLIOGRAPHIES

EPA Publications Bibliography. U.S. Environmental Protection Agency, Library Systems Branch, 401 M St., SW, Washington, District of Columbia 20460. (202) 260-2090. Quarterly.

HANDBOOKS AND MANUALS

FDA Food Additives Analytical Manual. C. Warner, et al., eds. Association of Official Analytical Chemists, 2200 Wilson Blvd., Suite 400-P, Arlington, Virginia 22201-3301. (703) 522-3032. 1983-1987. 2 vols. Provides methodology for determining compliance with food additive regulations. Contains analytical methods that have been evaluated by the FDA or found to operate satisfactorily in at least two laboratories.

ONLINE DATA BASES

BIOSIS Previews. BIOSIS, 2100 Arch St., Philadelphia, Pennsylvania 19103-1399. (215) 587-4800. Largest and most comprehensive database of research in the life sciences. Contains citations for nearly 9000 primary research journals, monographs, reviews, symposia, preliminary reports, semi-popular journals, selected institutional reports, government reports and research communications.

CAS Source Index–CASSI. Chemical Abstracts Service, 2540 Olentangy River Rd., P.O. Box 3012, Columbus, Ohio 43210. (800) 848-6533 or (614) 421-3600. A listing of bibliographic and library holdings information for scientific and technical primary literature relevant to the chemical sciences.

Chemical Abstracts-CA. Chemical Abstracts Service, 2540 Olentangy River Rd., P.O. Box 3012, Columbus, Ohio 43210. (800) 848-6533 or (614) 421-3600. Information sources include 9000 journals, patents from 27 countries, two industrial property organizations, new books, conference proceedings, and government research reports.

Chemical Abstracts Chemical Name Directory-CHEM-NAME. Chemical Abstracts Service, 2540 Olentangy River Rd., P.O. Box 3012, Columbus, Ohio 43210. (800) 848-6533 or (614) 421-3600. Listing of chemical substances in a dictionary type file. The Chemical Abstracts (CAS) Registry Number, molecular formula, Chemical Abstracts (CA) Substance Index Name, available synonyms, ring data and other chemical substance information is given for each entry.

Chemical Carcinogenesis Research Information System–CCRIS. National Library of Medicine, 8600 Rockville Pike, Bethesda, Maryland 20894. (800) 638-8480. Individual assay results and test conditions for 1,451 chemicals in the areas of carcinogenicity, mutagenicity, tumor promotion, and cocarcinogenicity.

Chemical Collection System/Request Tracking–CCS/RTS. U.S. Environmental Protection Agency, Office of Pesticides and Toxic Substances, 401 M St., SW, Washington, District of Columbia 20460. (202) 260-2090. Contains information on various properties of a number of chemicals including environmental effects, test and analysis methods, and health effects. Available from EPA.

Chemical Exposure. Science Applications International Corp., Health & Environmental Information, P.O. Box 2501, Oak Ridge, Tennessee 37831. (615) 482-9031. Database of chemicals that have been identified in both human tissues and body fluids and in feral and food animals. Contains reference to journal articles, conferences, and reports. Covers the whole fields of information related to human and animal exposure to food, air, and water contaminants and pharmaceuticals. Its records include information on chemical properties, formulas, tissues measured, analytical method used, demographics and more. Available on DIALOG.

Enviro/Energyline Abstracts Plus. R. R. Bowker Co., 121 Chanlon Rd., New Providence, New Jersey 07974. (908) 464-6800.

Environmental Periodicals Bibliography. National Information Services Corp., Ste. 6, Wyman Towers, 3100 St. Paul St., Baltimore, Maryland 21218. (410)243-0797. Online version of abstract of same name.

BERYLLIUM

See: AIR POLLUTION

BEST AVAILABLE TECHNOLOGY

See: TECHNOLOGY AND THE ENVIRONMENT

BEST PRACTICAL TECHNOLOGY

See: TECHNOLOGY AND THE ENVIRONMENT

BEVERAGES

See: FOOD SCIENCE

BICYCLES

See: TRANSPORTATION

BIOACCUMULATION

See also: ECOSYSTEMS; NUTRITION; PCBS; TOXIC POLLUTANTS

ABSTRACTING AND INDEXING SERVICES

Applied Ecology Abstracts Studies in Renewable Natural Resources. Information Retrieval Ltd., 1911 Jefferson Davis Highway, Arlington, Virginia 22202. 1975-. Monthly.

ASFA Aquaculture Abstracts. Cambridge Scientific Abstracts, Inc., 5161 River Rd., Bethesda, Maryland 20816. (301) 961-6750. 1984.

Biological Abstracts. BIOSIS, 2100 Arch St., Philadelphia, Pennsylvania 19103-1399. (215) 587-4800. 1927-.

Biological and Agricultural Index. H.W. Wilson Co., 950 University Ave., Bronx, New York 10452. (800) 367-6770. 1916-. Monthly.

Biology Digest. Data Courier, Plexus Pub Inc., 143 Old Marlton Pike, Medford, New Jersey 08055. 1974-. Monthly. Abstracts biology periodicals.

Biotechnology Research Abstracts. Cambridge Scientific Abstracts, 5161 River Rd., Bethesda, Maryland 20816. (301) 961-6750. Monthly. Includes such broad areas as genetic intervention, biochemical genetics, and microbiological techniques.

Current Advances in Ecological and Environmental Science. Pergamon Microforms International, Inc., Fairview Park, Elmsford, New York 10523. (914) 592-7720. 1989-. Monthly. Current literature searching service including-journals, reports, abstracts, etc. This service is available online as part of the CABS database on the hosts BRS and ORBIT search service.

Ecological Abstracts. Geo Abstracts Ltd. Elsevier Applied Science, Crown House, Linton Rd., Barking, England IG 11 8JU. 1974-. Derived from over 600 leading ecological

and environmental journals, plus books, conference proceedings, reports and theses.

Ecology Abstracts. Cambridge Scientific Abstracts, 5161 River Rd., Bethesda, Maryland 20816. (301) 961-6750. Monthly.

Environment Abstracts. Bowker A & I Publishing, 121 Chanlon Rd., New Providence, New Jersey 07974. (908) 464-6800. 1974-.

Environment Index. Environment Information Center, Index Research Department, 124 E. 39th St., New York, New York 10016. 1971-. Annual.

Environmental Information Connection–EIC. Planning Information Program, Dept. of Urban and Regional Planning, University of Illinois, 1003 West Nevada, Urbana, Illinois 61801. (217) 333-1369. Also available online.

Environmental Periodicals Bibliography. Environmental Studies Institute, International Academy at Santa Barbara, 800 Garden St., Suite D, Santa Barbara, California 93101. (805) 965-5010. Also available online.

General Science Index. H. W. Wilson Co., 950 University Ave., Bronx, New York 10452. 1978-. Monthly, also issued in annual cumulation. Cumulative subject index to English language periodicals in the subject fields of astronomy, botany, chemistry, earth science, environment and conservation, food and nutrition, genetics, mathematics, medicine and health, microbiology, oceanography, physics, physiology and zoology.

Index to Scientific Book Contents. Institute for Scientific Information, 3501 Market St., Philadelphia, Pennsylvania 19104. (800) 523-1857. 1985-. Annual. Gives contents of science books published.

Multimedia Index to Ecology. National Information Center for Educational Media, University of Southern California, Los Angeles, California 90007.

Pollution Abstracts. Cambridge Scientific Abstracts, 5161 River Rd., Bethesda, Maryland 20816. (301) 961-6750. Six/year. Indexes worldwide technical literature on environmental pollution. Covers air pollution, marine and freshwater pollution, sewage and wastewater treatment, waste management, toxicology and health, noise pollution, radiation, land pollution, and environmental policies, programs, legislation, and education. Also available online.

Science Citation Index. Institute for Scientific Information, 3501 Market St., Philadelphia, Pennsylvania 19104. 1961-.

BIBLIOGRAPHIES

Current Contents. Agriculture, Biology and Environmental Sciences. Institute for Scientific Information, 3501 Market St., Philadelphia, Pennsylvania 19104. (800) 523-1857. 1973-. Previous title: Current Contents. Agricultural, Food & Veterinary Sciences. Gives the table of contents of periodicals in the fields of agriculture, biology, environmental and related areas.

Directory of Published Proceedings. Interdok Corp., 173 Halstead Ave., Harrison, New York 10528. (914) 835-3506. 1990. Monthly. This is a listing of published proceedings including the series SEMTE (Science/Medicine/Engineering/Technology) and the series SSH (Social Science/Humanities).

EPA Publications Bibliography. U.S. Environmental Protection Agency, Library Systems Branch, 401 M St., SW, Washington, District of Columbia 20460. (202) 260-2090. Quarterly.

ENCYCLOPEDIAS AND DICTIONARIES

Cambridge Encyclopedia of Life Sciences. A. E. Friday and David S. Ingram. Cambridge University Press, 40 W 20th St., New York, New York 10011. (212) 924-3900 or (800) 227-0247. 1985. Includes all topics under biology and ecology.

Encyclopedia of Human Biology. Renato Dulbecco, ed. Academic Press, c/o Harcourt Brace Jovanovich Inc., 6277 Sea Harbor Dr., Orlando, Florida 32887. (800) 346-8648. 1991. Eight volumes.

McGraw-Hill Encyclopedia of Environmental Science. Sybil P. Parker. McGraw-Hill Science & Engineering Books, 11 W. 19th St., New York, New York 10011. (212) 337-6010. 1980. Covers ecology, man's influence on nature, and environmental protection.

McGraw-Hill Encyclopedia of Science and Technology. McGraw-Hill, 1221 Avenue of the Americas, New York, New York 10020. (212) 512-2000 or (800) 262-4729. 1992. Seventh edition. Issued in multiple volumes including index. Includes all science and technology broad subject areas.

Van Nostrand's Scientific Encyclopedia. Glenn D. Considine, ed. Van Nostrand Reinhold, 115 5th Ave., New York, New York 10003. (212) 254-3232. 1983. Sixth edition. Includes all broad subject areas in science.

GENERAL WORKS

Inorganic Contaminants of Surface Water; Research and Monitoring Priorities. James W. Moore. Springer-Verlag, 175 Fifth Ave., New York, New York 10010. (212) 460-1500 or (800) 777-4643. 1991. Inorganic contaminants of surface water in terms of production, sources, and residues, chemistry, bioaccualtion, toxic effects to aquatic organisms, health effects and drinking water.

ONLINE DATA BASES

BIOSIS Previews. BIOSIS, 2100 Arch St., Philadelphia, Pennsylvania 19103-1399. (215) 587-4800. Largest and most comprehensive database of research in the life sciences. Contains citations for nearly 9000 primary research journals, monographs, reviews, symposia, preliminary reports, semi-popular journals, selected institutional reports, government reports and research communications.

Cambridge Scientific Abstracts Life Science–CSAL. Cambridge Scientific Abstracts, 5161 River Rd., Bethesda, Maryland 20816. (301) 961-6750. Provides access to the following abstracting services: "Life Sciences Collection," "Aquatic Sciences and Fisheries Abstracts," "Oceanic Abstracts," and "Pollution Abstracts."

Current Research Information System–CRIS/USDA. U.S. Department of Agriculture, National Agricultural Library, 10301 Baltimore Blvd., 5th Floor, Beltsville, Maryland 20705-2351. (301) 504-5755. Looks at current research projects in agriculture and allied sciences covering the biological, physical, social and behavioral sciences related to agriculture.

Enviro/Energyline Abstracts Plus. R. R. Bowker Co., 121 Chanlon Rd., New Providence, New Jersey 07974. (908) 464-6800.

Environmental Fate Databases. Syracuse Research Cooperation, Merrill Lane, Syracuse, New York 13210. (312) 426-3200. Environmental fate of chemicals.

Environmental Periodicals Bibliography. National Information Services Corp., Ste. 6, Wyman Towers, 3100 St. Paul St., Baltimore, Maryland 21218. (410)243-0797. Online version of abstract of same name.

Monthly Catalog of United States Government Publications. U.S. G.P.O., Supt. of Docs., PO Box 371954, Pittsburgh, Pennsylvania 15250-7954. (202) 512-0000.

National Technical Information Service. U.S. Department of Commerce, National Technical Information Service, Office of Data Base Services, 5285 Port Royal Rd., Springfield, Virginia 22161. (703) 487-4807. Bibliographic database of government sponsored research and technical reports.

SCISEARCH. Institute for Scientific Information, University City Science Center, 3501 Market St., Philadelphia, Pennsylvania 19104. (215) 386-0100.

PERIODICALS AND NEWSLETTERS

Analytical Biochemistry. Academic Press, 111 Fifth Ave., New York, New York 10003. (800) 346-8648. Covers biological and chemical topics relating to the environment.

The Journal of Biological Chemistry. American Society of Biological Chemists, 428 E. Preston St., Baltimore, Maryland 21202. Three times a month. Biological, agricultural, and energy aspects of the environment.

RESEARCH CENTERS AND INSTITUTES

University of Wisconsin-Superior, Center for Lake Superior Environmental Studies. 1800 Grand Avenue, Superior, Wisconsin 54880. (715) 394-8315.

BIOASSAY

ABSTRACTING AND INDEXING SERVICES

Applied Ecology Abstracts Studies in Renewable Natural Resources. Information Retrieval Ltd., 1911 Jefferson Davis Highway, Arlington, Virginia 22202. 1975-. Monthly.

ASFA Aquaculture Abstracts. Cambridge Scientific Abstracts, Inc., 5161 River Rd., Bethesda, Maryland 20816. (301) 961-6750. 1984.

Biological Abstracts. BIOSIS, 2100 Arch St., Philadelphia, Pennsylvania 19103-1399. (215) 587-4800. 1927-.

Biological and Agricultural Index. H.W. Wilson Co., 950 University Ave., Bronx, New York 10452. (800) 367-6770. 1916-. Monthly.

Biology Digest. Data Courier, Plexus Pub Inc., 143 Old Marlton Pike, Medford, New Jersey 08055. 1974-. Monthly. Abstracts biology periodicals.

Biotechnology Research Abstracts. Cambridge Scientific Abstracts, 5161 River Rd., Bethesda, Maryland 20816.

(301) 961-6750. Monthly. Includes such broad areas as genetic intervention, biochemical genetics, and microbiological techniques.

Ecological Abstracts. Geo Abstracts Ltd. Elsevier Applied Science, Crown House, Linton Rd., Barking, England IG 11 8JU. 1974-. Derived from over 600 leading ecological and environmental journals, plus books, conference proceedings, reports and theses.

Ecology Abstracts. Cambridge Scientific Abstracts, 5161 River Rd., Bethesda, Maryland 20816. (301) 961-6750. Monthly.

Environment Abstracts. Bowker A & I Publishing, 121 Chanlon Rd., New Providence, New Jersey 07974. (908) 464-6800. 1974-.

Environment Index. Environment Information Center, Index Research Department, 124 E. 39th St., New York, New York 10016. 1971-. Annual.

Environmental Information Connection–EIC. Planning Information Program, Dept. of Urban and Regional Planning, University of Illinois, 1003 West Nevada, Urbana, Illinois 61801. (217) 333-1369. Also available online.

Environmental Periodicals Bibliography. Environmental Studies Institute, International Academy at Santa Barbara, 800 Garden St., Suite D, Santa Barbara, California 93101. (805) 965-5010. Also available online.

General Science Index. H. W. Wilson Co., 950 University Ave., Bronx, New York 10452. 1978-. Monthly, also issued in annual cumulation. Cumulative subject index to English language periodicals in the subject fields of astronomy, botany, chemistry, earth science, environment and conservation, food and nutrition, genetics, mathematics, medicine and health, microbiology, oceanography, physics, physiology and zoology.

Multimedia Index to Ecology. National Information Center for Educational Media, University of Southern California, Los Angeles, California 90007.

Pollution Abstracts. Cambridge Scientific Abstracts, 5161 River Rd., Bethesda, Maryland 20816. (301) 961-6750. Six/year. Indexes worldwide technical literature on environmental pollution. Covers air pollution, marine and freshwater pollution, sewage and wastewater treatment, waste management, toxicology and health, noise pollution, radiation, land pollution, and environmental policies, programs, legislation, and education. Also available online.

BIBLIOGRAPHIES

Current Contents. Agriculture, Biology and Environmental Sciences. Institute for Scientific Information, 3501 Market St., Philadelphia, Pennsylvania 19104. (800) 523-1857. 1973-. Previous title: Current Contents. Agricultural, Food & Veterinary Sciences. Gives the table of contents of periodicals in the fields of agriculture, biology, environmental and related areas.

EPA Publications Bibliography. U.S. Environmental Protection Agency, Library Systems Branch, 401 M St., SW, Washington, District of Columbia 20460. (202) 260-2090. Quarterly.

ENCYCLOPEDIAS AND DICTIONARIES

Cambridge Encyclopedia of Life Sciences. A. E. Friday and David S. Ingram. Cambridge University Press, 40 W 20th St., New York, New York 10011. (212) 924-3900 or (800) 227-0247. 1985. Includes all topics under biology and ecology.

A Dictionary of Genetics. Robert C. King and William A. Stansfield. Oxford University Press, 200 Madison Ave., New York, New York 10016. (212) 679-7300 or (800) 334-4249. 1991. Fourth edition. Includes 7,100 definitions with 250 illustrations. Also includes bibliography of major sources.

Dictionary of Genetics and Cell Biology. Norman Maclean. New York University Press, 70 Washington Sq. S., New York, New York 10012. (212) 998-2575. 1987. Includes the subject areas of cytology and genetics.

Dictionary of Microbiology and Molecular Biology. Paul Singleton and Diana Sainsbury. John Wiley & Sons, Inc., 605 3rd Ave., New York, New York 10158-0012. (212) 850-6000. 1987. Second edition. Comprehensive dictionary with "classical descriptive aspects of microbiology to current developments in related areas of bioenergetics, biochemistry and molecular biology." Entries give synonyms, cross references, and references to pertinent works. Miscellaneous appendixes. Bibliography.

Encyclopedic Dictionary of Genetics: With German Term Equivalents and Extensive German/English Index. R. C. King and W. D. Stansfield. VCH Publishers, 303 NW 12th Ave., Deerfield Beach, Florida 33442-1788. (305) 428-5566. 1990. 4th ed. Revised edition of: A Dictionary of Genetics, third edition.

McGraw-Hill Encyclopedia of Environmental Science. Sybil P. Parker. McGraw-Hill Science & Engineering Books, 11 W. 19th St., New York, New York 10011. (212) 337-6010. 1980. Covers ecology, man's influence on nature, and environmental protection.

McGraw-Hill Encyclopedia of Science and Technology. McGraw-Hill, 1221 Avenue of the Americas, New York, New York 10020. (212) 512-2000 or (800) 262-4729. 1992. Seventh edition. Issued in multiple volumes including index. Includes all science and technology broad subject areas.

Van Nostrand's Scientific Encyclopedia. Glenn D. Considine, ed. Van Nostrand Reinhold, 115 5th Ave., New York, New York 10003. (212) 254-3232. 1983. Sixth edition. Includes all broad subject areas in science.

GENERAL WORKS

Automated Biomonitoring: Living Sensors as Environmental Monitors. D. Gruber. John Wiley & Sons, Inc., 605 3rd Ave., New York, New York 10158. (212) 850-6000. 1988. Papers presented deal with conceptual and historical issues of biological early warning systems. Studies using fish as sensors are presented as well as studies using other biological sensors. Not limited to water quality monitoring alone.

Bioassay of Endrin for Possible Carcinogenicity. National Cancer Institute, Div. of Cancer Cause and Prevention, Carcinogenesis Testing Program, NIH Bldg. 31, Room 10A 24, 9030 Old Georgetown Rd., Bethesda, Maryland 20892. (301) 496-7403. 1978.

Bioassay of Fenthion for Possible Carcinogenicity. Department of Health and Human Services, 200 Independence Ave. SW, Washington, District of Columbia 20201. (202) 619-0257. 1979. Covers carcinogens and organophosphorus compounds and toxicology of insecticides.

Bioassay of Hexachlorophene for Possible Carcinogenicity. National Cancer Institute, Cancer Cause and Prevention Division, 9030 Old Georgetown Rd., Bethesda, Maryland 20892. (301) 496-7403. 1978.

Bioassay of Malathion for Possible Carcinogenicity. National Cancer Institute, Division of Cancer Cause and Prevention, 9030 Old Georgetown Rd., Bethesda, Maryland 20892. (301) 496-7403. 1979. Adverse effects of malathion and carcinogens.

Microcomputers in Environmental Biology. J. N. R. Jeffers, ed. Parthenon Pub., Casterton Hall, Carnforth, England LA6 2LA. Lancs. 1991. Contains extensive lists of programs written specially to show the ways in which microcomputers can be most usefully employed in the analysis of experiments and surveys, the analysis of multivariate data, radio tagging and the analysis of animal movement, and in modeling complex systems.

HANDBOOKS AND MANUALS

Handbook of Toxicology. W. Thomas Shier and Dietrich Mebs. Marcel Dekker, Inc., 270 Madison Ave., New York, New York 10016. (212) 696-9000; (800) 228-1160. 1990. Covers most toxins for which sufficient research has been done to clearly establish the identity and characteristics of the toxin.

ONLINE DATA BASES

BIOSIS Previews. BIOSIS, 2100 Arch St., Philadelphia, Pennsylvania 19103-1399. (215) 587-4800. Largest and most comprehensive database of research in the life sciences. Contains citations for nearly 9000 primary research journals, monographs, reviews, symposia, preliminary reports, semi-popular journals, selected institutional reports, government reports and research communications.

Cambridge Scientific Abstracts Life Science–CSAL. Cambridge Scientific Abstracts, 5161 River Rd., Bethesda, Maryland 20816. (301) 961-6750. Provides access to the following abstracting services: "Life Sciences Collection," "Aquatic Sciences and Fisheries Abstracts," "Oceanic Abstracts," and "Pollution Abstracts."

Chemest. Technical Database Services, Inc., 10 Columbus Circle, New York, New York 10019. (212) 245-0044. Covers methods of estimating 11 important properties: water solubility, soil adsorption coefficient, bioconcentration factor, acid dissociation constant, activity coefficient, boiling point, vapor pressure, water volatilization rate, Henry's Law Constant, melting point, and liquid viscosity.

Current Research Information System–CRIS/USDA. U.S. Department of Agriculture, National Agricultural Library, 10301 Baltimore Blvd., 5th Floor, Beltsville, Maryland 20705-2351. (301) 504-5755. Looks at current research projects in agriculture and allied sciences covering the biological, physical, social and behavioral sciences related to agriculture.

Enviro/Energyline Abstracts Plus. R. R. Bowker Co., 121 Chanlon Rd., New Providence, New Jersey 07974. (908) 464-6800.

Environmental Periodicals Bibliography. National Information Services Corp., Ste. 6, Wyman Towers, 3100 St. Paul St., Baltimore, Maryland 21218. (410)243-0797. Online version of abstract of same name.

SCISEARCH. Institute for Scientific Information, University City Science Center, 3501 Market St., Philadelphia, Pennsylvania 19104. (215) 386-0100.

PERIODICALS AND NEWSLETTERS

Analytical Biochemistry. Academic Press, 111 Fifth Ave., New York, New York 10003. (800) 346-8648. Covers biological and chemical topics relating to the environment.

The Journal of Biological Chemistry. American Society of Biological Chemists, 428 E. Preston St., Baltimore, Maryland 21202. Three times a month. Biological, agricultural, and energy aspects of the environment.

RESEARCH CENTERS AND INSTITUTES

University of Michigan, Biophysics Research Division. Institute of Science and Technology, 2200 Bonisteel Boulevard, Ann Arbor, Michigan 48109-2099. (313) 764-5218.

TRADE ASSOCIATIONS AND PROFESSIONAL SOCIETIES

American Institute of Biological Sciences. 730 11th St., N.W., Washington, District of Columbia 20001-4521. (202) 628-1500.

American Society of Naturalists. Department of Ecology and Evolation, State University of New York, Stony Brook, New York 11794. (516) 632-8589.

Federation of American Societies for Experimental Biology. 9650 Rockville Pike, Bethesda, Maryland 20814. (301) 530-7090.

BIOAVAILABILITY

See: NUTRITION

BIOCHEMICAL OXYGEN DEMAND

See also: AQUATIC ECOSYSTEMS; BIOLOGICAL OXYGEN DEMAND; WATER QUALITY

ABSTRACTING AND INDEXING SERVICES

Applied Ecology Abstracts Studies in Renewable Natural Resources. Information Retrieval Ltd., 1911 Jefferson Davis Highway, Arlington, Virginia 22202. 1975-. Monthly.

ASFA Aquaculture Abstracts. Cambridge Scientific Abstracts, Inc., 5161 River Rd., Bethesda, Maryland 20816. (301) 961-6750. 1984.

Biological Abstracts. BIOSIS, 2100 Arch St., Philadelphia, Pennsylvania 19103-1399. (215) 587-4800. 1927-.

Biological and Agricultural Index. H.W. Wilson Co., 950 University Ave., Bronx, New York 10452. (800) 367-6770. 1916-. Monthly.

Biology Digest. Data Courier, Plexus Pub Inc., 143 Old Marlton Pike, Medford, New Jersey 08055. 1974-. Monthly. Abstracts biology periodicals.

Ecological Abstracts. Geo Abstracts Ltd. Elsevier Applied Science, Crown House, Linton Rd., Barking, England IG 11 8JU. 1974-. Derived from over 600 leading ecological and environmental journals, plus books, conference proceedings, reports and theses.

Environment Abstracts. Bowker A & I Publishing, 121 Chanlon Rd., New Providence, New Jersey 07974. (908) 464-6800. 1974-.

Environment Index. Environment Information Center, Index Research Department, 124 E. 39th St., New York, New York 10016. 1971-. Annual.

Environmental Information Connection–EIC. Planning Information Program, Dept. of Urban and Regional Planning, University of Illinois, 1003 West Nevada, Urbana, Illinois 61801. (217) 333-1369. Also available online.

Environmental Periodicals Bibliography. Environmental Studies Institute, International Academy at Santa Barbara, 800 Garden St., Suite D, Santa Barbara, California 93101. (805) 965-5010. Also available online.

General Science Index. H. W. Wilson Co., 950 University Ave., Bronx, New York 10452. 1978-. Monthly, also issued in annual cumulation. Cumulative subject index to English language periodicals in the subject fields of astronomy, botany, chemistry, earth science, environment and conservation, food and nutrition, genetics, mathematics, medicine and health, microbiology, oceanography, physics, physiology and zoology.

Multimedia Index to Ecology. National Information Center for Educational Media, University of Southern California, Los Angeles, California 90007.

Pollution Abstracts. Cambridge Scientific Abstracts, 5161 River Rd., Bethesda, Maryland 20816. (301) 961-6750. Six/year. Indexes worldwide technical literature on environmental pollution. Covers air pollution, marine and freshwater pollution, sewage and wastewater treatment, waste management, toxicology and health, noise pollution, radiation, land pollution, and environmental policies, programs, legislation, and education. Also available online.

Science Citation Index. Institute for Scientific Information, 3501 Market St., Philadelphia, Pennsylvania 19104. 1961-.

BIBLIOGRAPHIES

Biochemical Oxygen Demand. National Technical Information Service, 5285 Port Royal Rd., Springfield, Virginia 22161. (703) 487-4650. 1973.

Directory of Published Proceedings. Interdok Corp., 173 Halstead Ave., Harrison, New York 10528. (914) 835-3506. 1990. Monthly. This is a listing of published proceedings including the series SEMTE (Science/Medicine/Engineering/Technology) and the series SSH (Social Science/Humanities).

EPA Publications Bibliography. U.S. Environmental Protection Agency, Library Systems Branch, 401 M St., SW, Washington, District of Columbia 20460. (202) 260-2090. Quarterly.

ENCYCLOPEDIAS AND DICTIONARIES

Cambridge Encyclopedia of Life Sciences. A. E. Friday and David S. Ingram. Cambridge University Press, 40 W 20th St., New York, New York 10011. (212) 924-3900 or (800) 227-0247. 1985. Includes all topics under biology and ecology.

Dictionary of Genetics and Cell Biology. Norman Maclean. New York University Press, 70 Washington Sq. S., New York, New York 10012. (212) 998-2575. 1987. Includes the subject areas of cytology and genetics.

McGraw-Hill Encyclopedia of Environmental Science. Sybil P. Parker. McGraw-Hill Science & Engineering Books, 11 W. 19th St., New York, New York 10011. (212) 337-6010. 1980. Covers ecology, man's influence on nature, and environmental protection.

GENERAL WORKS

Principles of Water Quality Management. William Wesley Eckenfelder. CBI, Boston, Massachusetts 1980.

HANDBOOKS AND MANUALS

Technical Guidance Manual for Performing Waste Load Allocations. U.S. Environmental Protection Agency, 401 M St., S.W., Washington, District of Columbia 20460. (202) 260-2090. 1984-.

ONLINE DATA BASES

BIOSIS Previews. BIOSIS, 2100 Arch St., Philadelphia, Pennsylvania 19103-1399. (215) 587-4800. Largest and most comprehensive database of research in the life sciences. Contains citations for nearly 9000 primary research journals, monographs, reviews, symposia, preliminary reports, semi-popular journals, selected institutional reports, government reports and research communications.

Current Research Information System–CRIS/USDA. U.S. Department of Agriculture, National Agricultural Library, 10301 Baltimore Blvd., 5th Floor, Beltsville, Maryland 20705-2351. (301) 504-5755. Looks at current research projects in agriculture and allied sciences covering the biological, physical, social and behavioral sciences related to agriculture.

Enviro/Energyline Abstracts Plus. R. R. Bowker Co., 121 Chanlon Rd., New Providence, New Jersey 07974. (908) 464-6800.

Environmental Periodicals Bibliography. National Information Services Corp., Ste. 6, Wyman Towers, 3100 St. Paul St., Baltimore, Maryland 21218. (410)243-0797. Online version of abstract of same name.

SCISEARCH. Institute for Scientific Information, University City Science Center, 3501 Market St., Philadelphia, Pennsylvania 19104. (215) 386-0100.

Solid Waste Report. NewsNet, Inc., 945 Haverford Rd., Bryn Mawr, Pennsylvania 19010. (800) 345-1301. Online version of the periodical of the same name.

PERIODICALS AND NEWSLETTERS

The Journal of Biological Chemistry. American Society of Biological Chemists, 428 E. Preston St., Baltimore,

Maryland 21202. Three times a month. Biological, agricultural, and energy aspects of the environment.

RESEARCH CENTERS AND INSTITUTES

Rockefeller University, Laboratory of Biochemistry and Molecular Biology. 1230 York Avenue, New York, New York 10021-6399. (212) 570-8000.

Rockefeller University, Laboratory of Organic Chemistry and Physical Biochemistry. 1230 York Ave, New York, New York 10021-6399. (212) 570-8264.

Syracuse University, Biological Research Laboratories. 130 College Place, Syracuse, New York 13210. (315) 423-3186.

University of Michigan, Biochemical Engineering Laboratory. Department of Chemical Engineering, Ann Arbor, Michigan 48109. (313) 763-1178.

TRADE ASSOCIATIONS AND PROFESSIONAL SOCIETIES

American Institute of Biological Sciences. 730 11th St., N.W., Washington, District of Columbia 20001-4521. (202) 628-1500.

BIOCIDES

See also: PESTICIDES

ABSTRACTING AND INDEXING SERVICES

Applied Ecology Abstracts Studies in Renewable Natural Resources. Information Retrieval Ltd., 1911 Jefferson Davis Highway, Arlington, Virginia 22202. 1975-. Monthly.

Biological Abstracts. BIOSIS, 2100 Arch St., Philadelphia, Pennsylvania 19103-1399. (215) 587-4800. 1927-.

Biological and Agricultural Index. H.W. Wilson Co., 950 University Ave., Bronx, New York 10452. (800) 367-6770. 1916-. Monthly.

Environment Abstracts. Bowker A & I Publishing, 121 Chanlon Rd., New Providence, New Jersey 07974. (908) 464-6800. 1974-.

Environment Index. Environment Information Center, Index Research Department, 124 E. 39th St., New York, New York 10016. 1971-. Annual.

Environmental Information Connection–EIC. Planning Information Program, Dept. of Urban and Regional Planning, University of Illinois, 1003 West Nevada, Urbana, Illinois 61801. (217) 333-1369. Also available online.

Environmental Periodicals Bibliography. Environmental Studies Institute, International Academy at Santa Barbara, 800 Garden St., Suite D, Santa Barbara, California 93101. (805) 965-5010. Also available online.

General Science Index. H. W. Wilson Co., 950 University Ave., Bronx, New York 10452. 1978-. Monthly, also issued in annual cumulation. Cumulative subject index to English language periodicals in the subject fields of astronomy, botany, chemistry, earth science, environment and conservation, food and nutrition, genetics,

mathematics, medicine and health, microbiology, oceanography, physics, physiology and zoology.

Index to Scientific Book Contents. Institute for Scientific Information, 3501 Market St., Philadelphia, Pennsylvania 19104. (800) 523-1857. 1985-. Annual. Gives contents of science books published.

Multimedia Index to Ecology. National Information Center for Educational Media, University of Southern California, Los Angeles, California 90007.

Science Citation Index. Institute for Scientific Information, 3501 Market St., Philadelphia, Pennsylvania 19104. 1961-.

BIBLIOGRAPHIES

Current Contents. Agriculture, Biology and Environmental Sciences. Institute for Scientific Information, 3501 Market St., Philadelphia, Pennsylvania 19104. (800) 523-1857. 1973-. Previous title: Current Contents. Agricultural, Food & Veterinary Sciences. Gives the table of contents of periodicals in the fields of agriculture, biology, environmental and related areas.

EPA Publications Bibliography. U.S. Environmental Protection Agency, Library Systems Branch, 401 M St., SW, Washington, District of Columbia 20460. (202) 260-2090. Quarterly.

ENCYCLOPEDIAS AND DICTIONARIES

Cambridge Encyclopedia of Life Sciences. A. E. Friday and David S. Ingram. Cambridge University Press, 40 W 20th St., New York, New York 10011. (212) 924-3900 or (800) 227-0247. 1985. Includes all topics under biology and ecology.

McGraw-Hill Encyclopedia of Environmental Science. Sybil P. Parker. McGraw-Hill Science & Engineering Books, 11 W. 19th St., New York, New York 10011. (212) 337-6010. 1980. Covers ecology, man's influence on nature, and environmental protection.

McGraw-Hill Encyclopedia of Science and Technology. McGraw-Hill, 1221 Avenue of the Americas, New York, New York 10020. (212) 512-2000 or (800) 262-4729. 1992. Seventh edition. Issued in multiple volumes including index. Includes all science and technology broad subject areas.

GENERAL WORKS

Environmental Fact Sheet: Mercury Biocides in Paint. U.S. Environmental Protection Agency, Office of Pesticides and Toxic Substances, 401 M St. SW, Washington, District of Columbia 20460. (202) 260-2090. 1990.

ONLINE DATA BASES

BIOSIS Previews. BIOSIS, 2100 Arch St., Philadelphia, Pennsylvania 19103-1399. (215) 587-4800. Largest and most comprehensive database of research in the life sciences. Contains citations for nearly 9000 primary research journals, monographs, reviews, symposia, preliminary reports, semi-popular journals, selected institutional reports, government reports and research communications.

CERCLIS. Chemical Information Systems, Inc., 7215 York Rd., Baltimore, Maryland 21212. (301) 321-8440.

Information on hazardous waste disposal sites that have either been listed by the EPA on the National Priority List (NPL) or nominated for consideration for the NPL.

Chemical Carcinogenesis Research Information System–CCRIS. National Library of Medicine, 8600 Rockville Pike, Bethesda, Maryland 20894. (800) 638-8480. Individual assay results and test conditions for 1,451 chemicals in the areas of carcinogenicity, mutagenicity, tumor promotion, and cocarcinogenicity.

Chemical Collection System/Request Tracking–CCS/RTS. U.S. Environmental Protection Agency, Office of Pesticides and Toxic Substances, 401 M St., SW, Washington, District of Columbia 20460. (202) 260-2090. Contains information on various properties of a number of chemicals including environmental effects, test and analysis methods, and health effects. Available from EPA.

Chemical Dictionary Online–CHEMLINE. Chemical Abstracts Service, 2540 Olentangy River Rd., Columbus, Ohio 43210. (614) 421-3600 or (800) 848-6533. Part of MEDLINE of the National Library of Medicine (NLM). File of 900,000 names for chemical substances, representing 450,000 unique compounds. It contains such information as Chemical Abstracts (CA) Service Registry Numbers, molecular formulas, preferred chemical nomenclature, and generic and ring structure information. Available on NLM's ELHILL system.

Chemical Exposure. Science Applications International Corp., Health & Environmental Information, P.O. Box 2501, Oak Ridge, Tennessee 37831. (615) 482-9031. Database of chemicals that have been identified in both human tissues and body fluids and in feral and food animals. Contains reference to journal articles, conferences, and reports. Covers the whole fields of information related to human and animal exposure to food, air, and water contaminants and pharmaceuticals. Its records include information on chemical properties, formulas, tissues measured, analytical method used, demographics and more. Available on DIALOG.

Enviro/Energyline Abstracts Plus. R. R. Bowker Co., 121 Chanlon Rd., New Providence, New Jersey 07974. (908) 464-6800.

Environmental Periodicals Bibliography. National Information Services Corp., Ste. 6, Wyman Towers, 3100 St. Paul St., Baltimore, Maryland 21218. (410)243-0797. Online version of abstract of same name.

SCISEARCH. Institute for Scientific Information, University City Science Center, 3501 Market St., Philadelphia, Pennsylvania 19104. (215) 386-0100.

PERIODICALS AND NEWSLETTERS

The Journal of Biological Chemistry. American Society of Biological Chemists, 428 E. Preston St., Baltimore, Maryland 21202. Three times a month. Biological, agricultural, and energy aspects of the environment.

Marine Biology. Springer-Verlag, 175 5th Ave., New York, New York 10010. (212) 461-1500; (800) 777-4643. Sixteen/year. Life in oceans and coastal waters.

TRADE ASSOCIATIONS AND PROFESSIONAL SOCIETIES

American Institute of Biological Sciences. 730 11th St., N.W., Washington, District of Columbia 20001-4521. (202) 628-1500.

BIOCONVERSION

ABSTRACTING AND INDEXING SERVICES

Applied Ecology Abstracts Studies in Renewable Natural Resources. Information Retrieval Ltd., 1911 Jefferson Davis Highway, Arlington, Virginia 22202. 1975-. Monthly.

Biodeterioration Research Titles. Biodeterioration Information Centre, University of Aston in Birmingham, Birmingham, England

Biological Abstracts. BIOSIS, 2100 Arch St., Philadelphia, Pennsylvania 19103-1399. (215) 587-4800. 1927-.

Biological and Agricultural Index. H.W. Wilson Co., 950 University Ave., Bronx, New York 10452. (800) 367-6770. 1916-. Monthly.

Biology Digest. Data Courier, Plexus Pub Inc., 143 Old Marlton Pike, Medford, New Jersey 08055. 1974-. Monthly. Abstracts biology periodicals.

Ecological Abstracts. Geo Abstracts Ltd. Elsevier Applied Science, Crown House, Linton Rd., Barking, England IG 11 8JU. 1974-. Derived from over 600 leading ecological and environmental journals, plus books, conference proceedings, reports and theses.

Energy Information Abstracts Annual 1987 in Retrospect. EIC/Intelligence Inc., 121 Chanlon Rd., New Providence, New Jersey 07974. (908) 464-6800. 1988. Annual. Cumulative edition of the monthly Energy Information Abstracts. Monitors sources in the field of energy including the scientific, technical and business journal literature, conference and symposia proceedings, corporate, government and academic reports.

Environment Abstracts. Bowker A & I Publishing, 121 Chanlon Rd., New Providence, New Jersey 07974. (908) 464-6800. 1974-.

Environment Index. Environment Information Center, Index Research Department, 124 E. 39th St., New York, New York 10016. 1971-. Annual.

Environmental Information Connection–EIC. Planning Information Program, Dept. of Urban and Regional Planning, University of Illinois, 1003 West Nevada, Urbana, Illinois 61801. (217) 333-1369. Also available online.

Environmental Periodicals Bibliography. Environmental Studies Institute, International Academy at Santa Barbara, 800 Garden St., Suite D, Santa Barbara, California 93101. (805) 965-5010. Also available online.

General Science Index. H. W. Wilson Co., 950 University Ave., Bronx, New York 10452. 1978-. Monthly, also issued in annual cumulation. Cumulative subject index to English language periodicals in the subject fields of astronomy, botany, chemistry, earth science, environment and conservation, food and nutrition, genetics, mathematics, medicine and health, microbiology, oceanography, physics, physiology and zoology.

Multimedia Index to Ecology. National Information Center for Educational Media, University of Southern California, Los Angeles, California 90007.

Science Citation Index. Institute for Scientific Information, 3501 Market St., Philadelphia, Pennsylvania 19104. 1961-.

BIBLIOGRAPHIES

Current Contents. Agriculture, Biology and Environmental Sciences. Institute for Scientific Information, 3501 Market St., Philadelphia, Pennsylvania 19104. (800) 523-1857. 1973-. Previous title: Current Contents. Agricultural, Food & Veterinary Sciences. Gives the table of contents of periodicals in the fields of agriculture, biology, environmental and related areas.

EPA Publications Bibliography. U.S. Environmental Protection Agency, Library Systems Branch, 401 M St., SW, Washington, District of Columbia 20460. (202) 260-2090. Quarterly.

Gasohol Sourcebook: Literature Survey and Abstracts. N. P. Cheremisinoff and P. N. Cheremisinoff. Ann Arbor Science, 230 Collingwood, PO Box 1425, Ann Arbor, Michigan 48106. 1981. Volume includes: biotechnology and bioconversion; ethanol and methanol production; automotive and other fuels; production of chemical feedstocks; and economics of alcohol production.

ENCYCLOPEDIAS AND DICTIONARIES

Cambridge Encyclopedia of Life Sciences. A. E. Friday and David S. Ingram. Cambridge University Press, 40 W 20th St., New York, New York 10011. (212) 924-3900 or (800) 227-0247. 1985. Includes all topics under biology and ecology.

McGraw-Hill Encyclopedia of Environmental Science. Sybil P. Parker. McGraw-Hill Science & Engineering Books, 11 W. 19th St., New York, New York 10011. (212) 337-6010. 1980. Covers ecology, man's influence on nature, and environmental protection.

McGraw-Hill Encyclopedia of Science and Technology. McGraw-Hill, 1221 Avenue of the Americas, New York, New York 10020. (212) 512-2000 or (800) 262-4729. 1992. Seventh edition. Issued in multiple volumes including index. Includes all science and technology broad subject areas.

Van Nostrand's Scientific Encyclopedia. Glenn D. Considine, ed. Van Nostrand Reinhold, 115 5th Ave., New York, New York 10003. (212) 254-3232. 1983. Sixth edition. Includes all broad subject areas in science.

GENERAL WORKS

Bioconversion of Waste Materials to Industrial Products. A. M. Martin, ed. Elsevier Science Publishing Co., 655 Avenue of the Americas, New York, New York 10010. (212) 984-5800. 1991. Biodegradation of refuse, refuse disposal and recycling of materials.

Extractive Bioconversions. Marcel Dekker, Inc., 270 Madison Ave., New York, New York 10016. (212) 696-9000; (800) 228-1160. Integration of downstream processing and bioconversion, separation technologies, cultivation of eukaryotic and prokaryotic cells, and the separation of the bioproducts.

Solar Energy Application, Bioconversion and Synfuels. T. Nejat Veziroglu, ed. Nova Science Publishers Inc., 283 Commack Rd., Suite 300, Commack, New York 11725-3401. (516) 499-3103; (516) 499-3106. 1990. Deals with solar energy applications such as heating and cooking, energy transmission, photovoltaics and industrial applications. Also includes chapters on bioconversion and synfuels.

ONLINE DATA BASES

BIOSIS Previews. BIOSIS, 2100 Arch St., Philadelphia, Pennsylvania 19103-1399. (215) 587-4800. Largest and most comprehensive database of research in the life sciences. Contains citations for nearly 9000 primary research journals, monographs, reviews, symposia, preliminary reports, semi-popular journals, selected institutional reports, government reports and research communications.

Cambridge Scientific Abstracts Life Science–CSAL. Cambridge Scientific Abstracts, 5161 River Rd., Bethesda, Maryland 20816. (301) 961-6750. Provides access to the following abstracting services: "Life Sciences Collection," "Aquatic Sciences and Fisheries Abstracts," "Oceanic Abstracts," and "Pollution Abstracts."

Current Research Information System–CRIS/USDA. U.S. Department of Agriculture, National Agricultural Library, 10301 Baltimore Blvd., 5th Floor, Beltsville, Maryland 20705-2351. (301) 504-5755. Looks at current research projects in agriculture and allied sciences covering the biological, physical, social and behavioral sciences related to agriculture.

Enviro/Energyline Abstracts Plus. R. R. Bowker Co., 121 Chanlon Rd., New Providence, New Jersey 07974. (908) 464-6800.

Environmental Periodicals Bibliography. National Information Services Corp., Ste. 6, Wyman Towers, 3100 St. Paul St., Baltimore, Maryland 21218. (410)243-0797. Online version of abstract of same name.

Monthly Catalog of United States Government Publications. U.S. G.P.O., Supt. of Docs., PO Box 371954, Pittsburgh, Pennsylvania 15250-7954. (202) 512-0000.

National Technical Information Service. U.S. Department of Commerce, National Technical Information Service, Office of Data Base Services, 5285 Port Royal Rd., Springfield, Virginia 22161. (703) 487-4807. Bibliographic database of government sponsored research and technical reports.

PERIODICALS AND NEWSLETTERS

Analytical Biochemistry. Academic Press, 111 Fifth Ave., New York, New York 10003. (800) 346-8648. Covers biological and chemical topics relating to the environment.

BioScience Journal. American Institute of Biological Sciences, 730 11th Street, Nw, Washington, District of Columbia 20001-4521. (202) 628-1500. Eleven times a year. Current research, feature articles, book reviews, and new products.

The Journal of Biological Chemistry. American Society of Biological Chemists, 428 E. Preston St., Baltimore, Maryland 21202. Three times a month. Biological, agricultural, and energy aspects of the environment.

Marine Biology. Springer-Verlag, 175 5th Ave., New York, New York 10010. (212) 461-1500; (800) 777-4643. Sixteen/year. Life in oceans and coastal waters.

TRADE ASSOCIATIONS AND PROFESSIONAL SOCIETIES

American Institute of Biological Sciences. 730 11th St., N.W., Washington, District of Columbia 20001-4521. (202) 628-1500.

BIODEGRADABLE

See also: BACTERIA; COMPOSTING; MICROORGANISMS; RECYCLING; WASTE DISPOSAL

ABSTRACTING AND INDEXING SERVICES

Applied Ecology Abstracts Studies in Renewable Natural Resources. Information Retrieval Ltd., 1911 Jefferson Davis Highway, Arlington, Virginia 22202. 1975-. Monthly.

ASFA Aquaculture Abstracts. Cambridge Scientific Abstracts, Inc., 5161 River Rd., Bethesda, Maryland 20816. (301) 961-6750. 1984.

Biodeterioration Abstracts. Farnham Royal, Slough, England SL2 3BN. Quarterly.

Biodeterioration Research Titles. Biodeterioration Information Centre, University of Aston in Birmingham, Birmingham, England

Biological Abstracts. BIOSIS, 2100 Arch St., Philadelphia, Pennsylvania 19103-1399. (215) 587-4800. 1927-.

Biological and Agricultural Index. H.W. Wilson Co., 950 University Ave., Bronx, New York 10452. (800) 367-6770. 1916-. Monthly.

Biology Digest. Data Courier, Plexus Pub Inc., 143 Old Marlton Pike, Medford, New Jersey 08055. 1974-. Monthly. Abstracts biology periodicals.

Biotechnology Research Abstracts. Cambridge Scientific Abstracts, 5161 River Rd., Bethesda, Maryland 20816. (301) 961-6750. Monthly. Includes such broad areas as genetic intervention, biochemical genetics, and microbiological techniques.

Current Advances in Ecological and Environmental Science. Pergamon Microforms International, Inc., Fairview Park, Elmsford, New York 10523. (914) 592-7720. 1989-. Monthly. Current literature searching service includingjournals, reports, abstracts, etc. This service is available online as part of the CABS database on the hosts BRS and ORBIT search service.

Ecological Abstracts. Geo Abstracts Ltd. Elsevier Applied Science, Crown House, Linton Rd., Barking, England IG 11 8JU. 1974-. Derived from over 600 leading ecological and environmental journals, plus books, conference proceedings, reports and theses.

Ecology Abstracts. Cambridge Scientific Abstracts, 5161 River Rd., Bethesda, Maryland 20816. (301) 961-6750. Monthly.

Environment Abstracts. Bowker A & I Publishing, 121 Chanlon Rd., New Providence, New Jersey 07974. (908) 464-6800. 1974-.

Environment Index. Environment Information Center, Index Research Department, 124 E. 39th St., New York, New York 10016. 1971-. Annual.

Environmental Information Connection–EIC. Planning Information Program, Dept. of Urban and Regional Planning, University of Illinois, 1003 West Nevada, Urbana, Illinois 61801. (217) 333-1369. Also available online.

Environmental Periodicals Bibliography. Environmental Studies Institute, International Academy at Santa Barba-

ra, 800 Garden St., Suite D, Santa Barbara, California 93101. (805) 965-5010. Also available online.

General Science Index. H. W. Wilson Co., 950 University Ave., Bronx, New York 10452. 1978-. Monthly, also issued in annual cumulation. Cumulative subject index to English language periodicals in the subject fields of astronomy, botany, chemistry, earth science, environment and conservation, food and nutrition, genetics, mathematics, medicine and health, microbiology, oceanography, physics, physiology and zoology.

Multimedia Index to Ecology. National Information Center for Educational Media, University of Southern California, Los Angeles, California 90007.

Pollution Abstracts. Cambridge Scientific Abstracts, 5161 River Rd., Bethesda, Maryland 20816. (301) 961-6750. Six/year. Indexes worldwide technical literature on environmental pollution. Covers air pollution, marine and freshwater pollution, sewage and wastewater treatment, waste management, toxicology and health, noise pollution, radiation, land pollution, and environmental policies, programs, legislation, and education. Also available online.

Science Citation Index. Institute for Scientific Information, 3501 Market St., Philadelphia, Pennsylvania 19104. 1961-.

BIBLIOGRAPHIES

Biodegradation of Oil Spills: Citations from the NTIS Bibliographic Database. National Technical Information Service, 5285 Port Royal Road, Springfield, Virginia 22161. (703) 487-4650. 1990.

Biodegradation of Toxic Wastes: Citations from the Energy Database. National Technical Information Service, 5285 Port Royal Road, Springfield, Virginia 22161. (703) 487-4650. 1990.

Current Contents. Agriculture, Biology and Environmental Sciences. Institute for Scientific Information, 3501 Market St., Philadelphia, Pennsylvania 19104. (800) 523-1857. 1973-. Previous title: Current Contents. Agricultural, Food & Veterinary Sciences. Gives the table of contents of periodicals in the fields of agriculture, biology, environmental and related areas.

Directory of Published Proceedings. Interdok Corp., 173 Halstead Ave., Harrison, New York 10528. (914) 835-3506. 1990. Monthly. This is a listing of published proceedings including the series SEMTE (Science/Medicine/Engineering/Technology) and the series SSH (Social Science/Humanities).

EPA Publications Bibliography. U.S. Environmental Protection Agency, Library Systems Branch, 401 M St., SW, Washington, District of Columbia 20460. (202) 260-2090. Quarterly.

DIRECTORIES

Gale Environmental Sourcebook. Karen Hill. Gale Research Co., 835 Penobscot Bldg., Detroit, Michigan 48226-4094. (313) 961-2242. Contacts, information sources, or general information on environmental topics.

ENCYCLOPEDIAS AND DICTIONARIES

Cambridge Encyclopedia of Life Sciences. A. E. Friday and David S. Ingram. Cambridge University Press, 40 W 20th St., New York, New York 10011. (212) 924-3900 or (800) 227-0247. 1985. Includes all topics under biology and ecology.

Dictionary of Genetics and Cell Biology. Norman Maclean. New York University Press, 70 Washington Sq. S., New York, New York 10012. (212) 998-2575. 1987. Includes the subject areas of cytology and genetics.

Dictionary of Microbiology and Molecular Biology. Paul Singleton and Diana Sainsbury. John Wiley & Sons, Inc., 605 3rd Ave., New York, New York 10158-0012. (212) 850-6000. 1987. Second edition. Comprehensive dictionary with "classical descriptive aspects of microbiology to current developments in related areas of bioenergetics, biochemistry and molecular biology." Entries give synonyms, cross references, and references to pertinent works. Miscellaneous appendixes. Bibliography.

McGraw-Hill Encyclopedia of Environmental Science. Sybil P. Parker. McGraw-Hill Science & Engineering Books, 11 W. 19th St., New York, New York 10011. (212) 337-6010. 1980. Covers ecology, man's influence on nature, and environmental protection.

The New York Times Encyclopedic Dictionary of the Environment. Paul Sarnoff. Quadrangle Books, New York, New York 1971. Focuses on state-of-the-art methods of pollution control, abatement, prevention and removal.

Van Nostrand's Scientific Encyclopedia. Glenn D. Considine, ed. Van Nostrand Reinhold, 115 5th Ave., New York, New York 10003. (212) 254-3232. 1983. Sixth edition. Includes all broad subject areas in science.

GENERAL WORKS

Bioconversion of Waste Materials to Industrial Products. A. M. Martin, ed. Elsevier Science Publishing Co., 655 Avenue of the Americas, New York, New York 10010. (212) 984-5800. 1991. Biodegradation of refuse, refuse disposal and recycling of materials.

Biodegradability of Organic Substances in the Aquatic Environment. Pavel Pitter, et al. CRC Press, 2000 Corporate Blvd. N.W., Boca Raton, Florida 33431. (800) 272-7737. 1990. Explains the principles and theories of biodegradation, primarily from an ecological standpoint. Current techniques used to evaluate the biodegradability of individual chemicals are reviewed.

Biodegradation of PCBs Sorbed to Sewage Sludge Lagoon Sediments in an Aerobic Digester. William Amdor Chantry. University of Wisconsin Press, 114 N. Murray St., Madison, Wisconsin 53715. (608) 262-8782. 1989.

Biosynthesis and Biodegradation of Cellulose. Candace H. Haigler and Paul J. Weimer. Marcel Dekker, Inc., 270 Madison Ave., New York, New York 10016. (212) 696-9000; (800) 228-1160. 1991. Brings together knowledge of both the synthesis and degradation of cellulose.

Degradable Materials: Perspectives, Issues, and Opportunities. Sumner A. Barenberg, et al. CRC Press, 2000 Corporate Blvd. N.W., Boca Raton, Florida 33431. (800) 272-7737. 1990. State-of-the-art of degradable materials including plastics.

Degradation of Synthetic Organic Molecules in the Biosphere. National Academy of Sciences, 2101 Constitution Ave. N.W., Washington, District of Columbia 20418. (202) 334-2000. 1972. Proceedings of conference, San

Francisco, CA, June 12-13, 1971, under the aegis of the National Research Council.

Enhanced Biodegradation of Pesticides in the Environment. Kenneth D. Racke and Joel R. Coats, eds. American Chemical Society, 1155 16th St. N.W., Washington, District of Columbia 20036. (202) 872-4600; (800) 227-5558. 1990. Discusses pesticides in the soil, microbial ecosystems, and the effects of long term application of herbicides on the soil.

Pesticide Transformation Products: Fate and Significance in the Environment: Papers. L. Somasundaram and Joel R. Coats, eds. American Chemical Society, 1155 16th St. N.W., Washington, District of Columbia 20036. (202) 872-4600; (800) 227-5558. 1991. The significance and impact of pesticide products on the environment is discussed.

Treatment Potential for 56 EPA Listed Hazardous Chemicals in Soil. Ronald C. Sims, et al. Robert S. Kerr Environmental Research Laboratory, U.S. Environmental Protection Agency, PO Box 1198, Ada, Oklahoma 74820. (405) 332-8800. 1988.

HANDBOOKS AND MANUALS

Handbook of Environmental Degradation Rates. Philip H. Howard, et al. Lewis Publishers, 2000 Corporate Blvd., N.W., Boca Raton, Florida 33431. (407) 994-0555 or (800) 272-7737. 1991. Provides rate constant and half-life ranges for various processes and combines them into ranges for different media (air, groundwater, surface water, soils) which can be directly entered into various models.

ONLINE DATA BASES

BIOSIS Previews. BIOSIS, 2100 Arch St., Philadelphia, Pennsylvania 19103-1399. (215) 587-4800. Largest and most comprehensive database of research in the life sciences. Contains citations for nearly 9000 primary research journals, monographs, reviews, symposia, preliminary reports, semi-popular journals, selected institutional reports, government reports and research communications.

Cambridge Scientific Abstracts Life Science–CSAL. Cambridge Scientific Abstracts, 5161 River Rd., Bethesda, Maryland 20816. (301) 961-6750. Provides access to the following abstracting services: "Life Sciences Collection," "Aquatic Sciences and Fisheries Abstracts," "Oceanic Abstracts," and "Pollution Abstracts."

Current Research Information System–CRIS/USDA. U.S. Department of Agriculture, National Agricultural Library, 10301 Baltimore Blvd., 5th Floor, Beltsville, Maryland 20705-2351. (301) 504-5755. Looks at current research projects in agriculture and allied sciences covering the biological, physical, social and behavioral sciences related to agriculture.

Enviro/Energyline Abstracts Plus. R. R. Bowker Co., 121 Chanlon Rd., New Providence, New Jersey 07974. (908) 464-6800.

Environmental Fate Databases. Syracuse Research Cooperation, Merrill Lane, Syracuse, New York 13210. (312) 426-3200. Environmental fate of chemicals.

Environmental Periodicals Bibliography. National Information Services Corp., Ste. 6, Wyman Towers, 3100 St.

Paul St., Baltimore, Maryland 21218. (410)243-0797. Online version of abstract of same name.

Monthly Catalog of United States Government Publications. U.S. G.P.O., Supt. of Docs., PO Box 371954, Pittsburgh, Pennsylvania 15250-7954. (202) 512-0000.

National Technical Information Service. U.S. Department of Commerce, National Technical Information Service, Office of Data Base Services, 5285 Port Royal Rd., Springfield, Virginia 22161. (703) 487-4807. Bibliographic database of government sponsored research and technical reports.

SCISEARCH. Institute for Scientific Information, University City Science Center, 3501 Market St., Philadelphia, Pennsylvania 19104. (215) 386-0100.

PERIODICALS AND NEWSLETTERS

Biodegradation. Kluwer Academic Publishers, 101 Philip Dr., Assinippi Park, Norwell, Massachusetts 02061-0358. (617) 871-6600. 1990-. Quarterly. Covers all aspects of science pertaining to the detoxification, recycling, amelioration or treatment of waste materials and pollutants by naturally occurring microbial strains, associations, or recombinant microorganisms.

The Journal of Biological Chemistry. American Society of Biological Chemists, 428 E. Preston St., Baltimore, Maryland 21202. Three times a month. Biological, agricultural, and energy aspects of the environment.

RESEARCH CENTERS AND INSTITUTES

University of Minnesota, Gray Freshwater Biological Institute. P.O. Box 100, Navarre, Minnesota 55392. (612) 471-8476.

University of Tennessee at Knoxville, Center for Environmental Biotechnology. 10515 Research Drive, Knoxville, Tennessee 37932. (615) 675-9450.

Utah State University, Biotechnology Center. Logan, Utah 84322-4430. (801) 750-2730.

STATISTICS SOURCES

Environmental Data Compendium. OECD Publications and Information Center, 2001 L St., N.W., Suite 700, Washington, District of Columbia 20036. (202) 785-6323. 1989.

Environmental Indicators. OECD Publications and Information Center, 2001 L St., N.W., Suite 700, Washington, District of Columbia 20036. (202) 785-6323. 1991.

Environmental Quality. Council on Environmental Quality. U.S. G.P.O., Washington, District of Columbia 20401. (202) 512-0000. Annual.

The State of the Environment. OECD Publications and Information Center, 2001 L St., N.W., Suite 700, Washington, District of Columbia 20036. (202) 785-6323. 1991.

Strategic Planning for Waste Minimization. FIND/SVP, 625 Avenue of the Americas, New York, New York 10011. (212) 645-4500. 1990.

TRADE ASSOCIATIONS AND PROFESSIONAL SOCIETIES

American Institute of Biological Sciences. 730 11th St., N.W., Washington, District of Columbia 20001-4521. (202) 628-1500.

BIOFILTRATION

See also: SEWAGE DISPOSAL; WASTEWATER TREATMENT

GENERAL WORKS

Guidelines for Mastering the Properties of Molecular Sieves. Plenum Press, 233 Spring St., New York, New York 10013-1578. (212) 620-8000. Relationship between the physiochemical properties of zeolitic systems and their low dimensionality.

New Developments in Industrial Wastewater Treatment. Aysen Turkman, ed. Kluwer Academic Publishers, 101 Philip Dr., Assinippi Park, Norwell, Massachusetts 02061-0358. (617) 871-6600. 1991. NATO Advanced Research Workshop, Oct-Nov. 1989.

Trihalomethane Removal by Coagulation Techniques in a Softening Process. U.S. Environmental Protection Agency, Municipal Environmental Research Laboratory, 26 W. Martin Luther King Dr., Cincinnati, Ohio 45268. (513) 569-7931. 1983. Sewage purification through chlorination.

HANDBOOKS AND MANUALS

Water Treatment Handbook. Degremont s.a., 184, ave. du 18-Juin-1940, Rueil-Malmaison, France F-92500. 1991. Sixth edition. Part 1 is a general survey of water and its action on the materials with which it comes into contact, and theoretical principles of separation and correction processes used in water treatment. Part 2 describes the process and the treatment plant beginning with the separation process.

BIOFOULING

See also: BACTERIA; MICROORGANISMS

ABSTRACTING AND INDEXING SERVICES

Applied Ecology Abstracts Studies in Renewable Natural Resources. Information Retrieval Ltd., 1911 Jefferson Davis Highway, Arlington, Virginia 22202. 1975-. Monthly.

Biodeterioration Abstracts. Farnham Royal, Slough, England SL2 3BN. Quarterly.

Biodeterioration Research Titles. Biodeterioration Information Centre, University of Aston in Birmingham, Birmingham, England

Biological Abstracts. BIOSIS, 2100 Arch St., Philadelphia, Pennsylvania 19103-1399. (215) 587-4800. 1927-.

Biological and Agricultural Index. H.W. Wilson Co., 950 University Ave., Bronx, New York 10452. (800) 367-6770. 1916-. Monthly.

Biology Digest. Data Courier, Plexus Pub Inc., 143 Old Marlton Pike, Medford, New Jersey 08055. 1974-. Monthly. Abstracts biology periodicals.

Bulletin Signaletique: Eau et Assainissement, Pollution Atmospherique, Droit des Pollutions. Centre de Documentation, Centre National de la Recherche Scientifique, 15, quai Anatole France, Paris, France 75700. (1) 45 55 92 25. 1983-. Monthly. Indexes pollution periodicals including water, atmospheric and related pollutions.

Ecological Abstracts. Geo Abstracts Ltd. Elsevier Applied Science, Crown House, Linton Rd., Barking, England IG 11 8JU. 1974-. Derived from over 600 leading ecological and environmental journals, plus books, conference proceedings, reports and theses.

Environment Abstracts. Bowker A & I Publishing, 121 Chanlon Rd., New Providence, New Jersey 07974. (908) 464-6800. 1974-.

Environment Index. Environment Information Center, Index Research Department, 124 E. 39th St., New York, New York 10016. 1971-. Annual.

Environmental Information Connection–EIC. Planning Information Program, Dept. of Urban and Regional Planning, University of Illinois, 1003 West Nevada, Urbana, Illinois 61801. (217) 333-1369. Also available online.

Environmental Periodicals Bibliography. Environmental Studies Institute, International Academy at Santa Barbara, 800 Garden St., Suite D, Santa Barbara, California 93101. (805) 965-5010. Also available online.

General Science Index. H. W. Wilson Co., 950 University Ave., Bronx, New York 10452. 1978-. Monthly, also issued in annual cumulation. Cumulative subject index to English language periodicals in the subject fields of astronomy, botany, chemistry, earth science, environment and conservation, food and nutrition, genetics, mathematics, medicine and health, microbiology, oceanography, physics, physiology and zoology.

Multimedia Index to Ecology. National Information Center for Educational Media, University of Southern California, Los Angeles, California 90007.

BIBLIOGRAPHIES

Current Contents. Agriculture, Biology and Environmental Sciences. Institute for Scientific Information, 3501 Market St., Philadelphia, Pennsylvania 19104. (800) 523-1857. 1973-. Previous title: Current Contents. Agricultural, Food & Veterinary Sciences. Gives the table of contents of periodicals in the fields of agriculture, biology, environmental and related areas.

EPA Publications Bibliography. U.S. Environmental Protection Agency, Library Systems Branch, 401 M St., SW, Washington, District of Columbia 20460. (202) 260-2090. Quarterly.

ENCYCLOPEDIAS AND DICTIONARIES

Cambridge Encyclopedia of Life Sciences. A. E. Friday and David S. Ingram. Cambridge University Press, 40 W 20th St., New York, New York 10011. (212) 924-3900 or (800) 227-0247. 1985. Includes all topics under biology and ecology.

McGraw-Hill Encyclopedia of Environmental Science. Sybil P. Parker. McGraw-Hill Science & Engineering

Books, 11 W. 19th St., New York, New York 10011. (212) 337-6010. 1980. Covers ecology, man's influence on nature, and environmental protection.

Van Nostrand's Scientific Encyclopedia. Glenn D. Considine, ed. Van Nostrand Reinhold, 115 5th Ave., New York, New York 10003. (212) 254-3232. 1983. Sixth edition. Includes all broad subject areas in science.

GENERAL WORKS

Biofouling and Biocorrosion in Industrial Water Systems. Hans C. Flemming, ed. Springer-Verlag, 175 5th Ave., New York, New York 10010. (212) 460-1500. 1991.

ONLINE DATA BASES

BIOSIS Previews. BIOSIS, 2100 Arch St., Philadelphia, Pennsylvania 19103-1399. (215) 587-4800. Largest and most comprehensive database of research in the life sciences. Contains citations for nearly 9000 primary research journals, monographs, reviews, symposia, preliminary reports, semi-popular journals, selected institutional reports, government reports and research communications.

Cambridge Scientific Abstracts Life Science–CSAL. Cambridge Scientific Abstracts, 5161 River Rd., Bethesda, Maryland 20816. (301) 961-6750. Provides access to the following abstracting services: "Life Sciences Collection," "Aquatic Sciences and Fisheries Abstracts," "Oceanic Abstracts," and "Pollution Abstracts."

Enviro/Energyline Abstracts Plus. R. R. Bowker Co., 121 Chanlon Rd., New Providence, New Jersey 07974. (908) 464-6800.

Environmental Periodicals Bibliography. National Information Services Corp., Ste. 6, Wyman Towers, 3100 St. Paul St., Baltimore, Maryland 21218. (410)243-0797. Online version of abstract of same name.

Monthly Catalog of United States Government Publications. U.S. G.P.O., Supt. of Docs., PO Box 371954, Pittsburgh, Pennsylvania 15250-7954. (202) 512-0000.

National Technical Information Service. U.S. Department of Commerce, National Technical Information Service, Office of Data Base Services, 5285 Port Royal Rd., Springfield, Virginia 22161. (703) 487-4807. Bibliographic database of government sponsored research and technical reports.

SCISEARCH. Institute for Scientific Information, University City Science Center, 3501 Market St., Philadelphia, Pennsylvania 19104. (215) 386-0100.

PERIODICALS AND NEWSLETTERS

Biofouling. Harwood Academic Publishers, PO Box 786, Cooper Sta., New York, New York 10276. (212) 206-8900. Quarterly.

The Journal of Biological Chemistry. American Society of Biological Chemists, 428 E. Preston St., Baltimore, Maryland 21202. Three times a month. Biological, agricultural, and energy aspects of the environment.

RESEARCH CENTERS AND INSTITUTES

Center for Interfacial Microbial Process Engineering. Montana State University, College of Engineering, 409

Cobleigh Hall, Bozeman, Montana 59717-0007. (406) 994-4770.

TRADE ASSOCIATIONS AND PROFESSIONAL SOCIETIES

American Institute of Biological Sciences. 730 11th St., N.W., Washington, District of Columbia 20001-4521. (202) 628-1500.

BIOFUEL

See also: POWER GENERATION; WASTE-TO-ENERGY SYSTEMS

ABSTRACTING AND INDEXING SERVICES

Biological Abstracts. BIOSIS, 2100 Arch St., Philadelphia, Pennsylvania 19103-1399. (215) 587-4800. 1927-.

Biological and Agricultural Index. H.W. Wilson Co., 950 University Ave., Bronx, New York 10452. (800) 367-6770. 1916-. Monthly.

Biology Digest. Data Courier, Plexus Pub Inc., 143 Old Marlton Pike, Medford, New Jersey 08055. 1974-. Monthly. Abstracts biology periodicals.

Environment Abstracts. Bowker A & I Publishing, 121 Chanlon Rd., New Providence, New Jersey 07974. (908) 464-6800. 1974-.

Environment Index. Environment Information Center, Index Research Department, 124 E. 39th St., New York, New York 10016. 1971-. Annual.

Environmental Information Connection–EIC. Planning Information Program, Dept. of Urban and Regional Planning, University of Illinois, 1003 West Nevada, Urbana, Illinois 61801. (217) 333-1369. Also available online.

Environmental Periodicals Bibliography. Environmental Studies Institute, International Academy at Santa Barbara, 800 Garden St., Suite D, Santa Barbara, California 93101. (805) 965-5010. Also available online.

General Science Index. H. W. Wilson Co., 950 University Ave., Bronx, New York 10452. 1978-. Monthly, also issued in annual cumulation. Cumulative subject index to English language periodicals in the subject fields of astronomy, botany, chemistry, earth science, environment and conservation, food and nutrition, genetics, mathematics, medicine and health, microbiology, oceanography, physics, physiology and zoology.

Geographical Abstracts. London School of Economics, Dept. of Geography, Regency House, 34 Duke St., London, England 1966-. Continued by Geo Abstracts issued in 6 parts: Pt. A. Landforms and the quaternary; Pt. B. Biogeography and Climatology; Pt. C. Economic geography; Pt. D. Social geography and cartography; Pt. E. Sedimentology; Pt. F. Regional and community planning.

BIBLIOGRAPHIES

Biogas and Alcohols from Biomass: January 1986-September 1990. Jean A. Larson. National Agricultural Library, 10301 Baltimore Blvd., Beltsville, Maryland 20705-2351. (301) 504-5755. 1990. Covers biogas and biomass chemicals.

Current Contents. Agriculture, Biology and Environmental Sciences. Institute for Scientific Information, 3501 Market St., Philadelphia, Pennsylvania 19104. (800) 523-1857. 1973-. Previous title: Current Contents. Agricultural, Food & Veterinary Sciences. Gives the table of contents of periodicals in the fields of agriculture, biology, environmental and related areas.

Directory of Published Proceedings. Interdok Corp., 173 Halstead Ave., Harrison, New York 10528. (914) 835-3506. 1990. Monthly. This is a listing of published proceedings including the series SEMTE (Science/Medicine/Engineering/Technology) and the series SSH (Social Science/Humanities).

EPA Publications Bibliography. U.S. Environmental Protection Agency, Library Systems Branch, 401 M St., SW, Washington, District of Columbia 20460. (202) 260-2090. Quarterly.

ENCYCLOPEDIAS AND DICTIONARIES

Cambridge Encyclopedia of Life Sciences. A. E. Friday and David S. Ingram. Cambridge University Press, 40 W 20th St., New York, New York 10011. (212) 924-3900 or (800) 227-0247. 1985. Includes all topics under biology and ecology.

Dictionary of Microbiology and Molecular Biology. Paul Singleton and Diana Sainsbury. John Wiley & Sons, Inc., 605 3rd Ave., New York, New York 10158-0012. (212) 850-6000. 1987. Second edition. Comprehensive dictionary with "classical descriptive aspects of microbiology to current developments in related areas of bioenergetics, biochemistry and molecular biology." Entries give synonyms, cross references, and references to pertinent works. Miscellaneous appendixes. Bibliography.

McGraw-Hill Encyclopedia of Environmental Science. Sybil P. Parker. McGraw-Hill Science & Engineering Books, 11 W. 19th St., New York, New York 10011. (212) 337-6010. 1980. Covers ecology, man's influence on nature, and environmental protection.

McGraw-Hill Encyclopedia of Science and Technology. McGraw-Hill, 1221 Avenue of the Americas, New York, New York 10020. (212) 512-2000 or (800) 262-4729. 1992. Seventh edition. Issued in multiple volumes including index. Includes all science and technology broad subject areas.

Van Nostrand's Scientific Encyclopedia. Glenn D. Considine, ed. Van Nostrand Reinhold, 115 5th Ave., New York, New York 10003. (212) 254-3232. 1983. Sixth edition. Includes all broad subject areas in science.

HANDBOOKS AND MANUALS

International Bio-Energy Directory and Handbook. P. F. Bente, Jr. , ed. The Bio-Energy Council, Suite 825 A, 1625 Eye St. NW, Washington, District of Columbia 20006. 1984.

ONLINE DATA BASES

BIOSIS Previews. BIOSIS, 2100 Arch St., Philadelphia, Pennsylvania 19103-1399. (215) 587-4800. Largest and most comprehensive database of research in the life sciences. Contains citations for nearly 9000 primary research journals, monographs, reviews, symposia, preliminary reports, semi-popular journals, selected institu-

tional reports, government reports and research communications.

Enviro/Energyline Abstracts Plus. R. R. Bowker Co., 121 Chanlon Rd., New Providence, New Jersey 07974. (908) 464-6800.

Environmental Periodicals Bibliography. National Information Services Corp., Ste. 6, Wyman Towers, 3100 St. Paul St., Baltimore, Maryland 21218. (410)243-0797. Online version of abstract of same name.

Monthly Catalog of United States Government Publications. U.S. G.P.O., Supt. of Docs., PO Box 371954, Pittsburgh, Pennsylvania 15250-7954. (202) 512-0000.

National Technical Information Service. U.S. Department of Commerce, National Technical Information Service, Office of Data Base Services, 5285 Port Royal Rd., Springfield, Virginia 22161. (703) 487-4807. Bibliographic database of government sponsored research and technical reports.

SCISEARCH. Institute for Scientific Information, University City Science Center, 3501 Market St., Philadelphia, Pennsylvania 19104. (215) 386-0100.

PERIODICALS AND NEWSLETTERS

Biomass and Bioenergy. Pergamon Microforms International, Inc., Fairview Park, Elmsford, New York 10523. (914) 592-7720. 1991-. Monthly. Key areas covered by this journal are: Biomass-sources, energy, crop production processes, genetic improvements, composition; biological residues: wastes from agricultural production and forestry, processing industries, and municipal sources; bioenergy processes: fermentations, thermochemical conversions, liquid and gaseous fuels, and petrochemical substitutes; bioenergy utilization: direct combustion gasification, electricity production, chemical processes, and by-product remediation. Also includes environmental management and economic aspects of biomass and bioenergy.

STATISTICS SOURCES

Estimates of Biofuels Consumption in the U.S. U.S. G.P.O, Washington, District of Columbia 20402-9325. (202) 512-0000. 1990. Consumption of energy from biofuels, including wood, solid waste, and ethanol. Waste energy types include mass burning, manufacturing wastes, refuse derived fuel and methane gas form landfills.

TRADE ASSOCIATIONS AND PROFESSIONAL SOCIETIES

American Institute of Biological Sciences. 730 11th St., N.W., Washington, District of Columbia 20001-4521. (202) 628-1500.

BIOGEOCHEMISTRY

ABSTRACTING AND INDEXING SERVICES

Applied Ecology Abstracts Studies in Renewable Natural Resources. Information Retrieval Ltd., 1911 Jefferson Davis Highway, Arlington, Virginia 22202. 1975-. Monthly.

Biodeterioration Research Titles. Biodeterioration Information Centre, University of Aston in Birmingham, Birmingham, England

Biological Abstracts. BIOSIS, 2100 Arch St., Philadelphia, Pennsylvania 19103-1399. (215) 587-4800. 1927-.

Biological and Agricultural Index. H.W. Wilson Co., 950 University Ave., Bronx, New York 10452. (800) 367-6770. 1916-. Monthly.

Biology Digest. Data Courier, Plexus Pub Inc., 143 Old Marlton Pike, Medford, New Jersey 08055. 1974-. Monthly. Abstracts biology periodicals.

Chemical Abstracts. Chemical Abstracts Service, 2540 Olentangy River Rd., PO Box 3012, Columbus, Ohio 43210. (800) 848-6533. 1907-.

Current Advances in Ecological and Environmental Science. Pergamon Microforms International, Inc., Fairview Park, Elmsford, New York 10523. (914) 592-7720. 1989-. Monthly. Current literature searching service includingjournals, reports, abstracts, etc. This service is available online as part of the CABS database on the hosts BRS and ORBIT search service.

Ecological Abstracts. Geo Abstracts Ltd. Elsevier Applied Science, Crown House, Linton Rd., Barking, England IG 11 8JU. 1974-. Derived from over 600 leading ecological and environmental journals, plus books, conference proceedings, reports and theses.

Ecology Abstracts. Cambridge Scientific Abstracts, 5161 River Rd., Bethesda, Maryland 20816. (301) 961-6750. Monthly.

Environment Abstracts. Bowker A & I Publishing, 121 Chanlon Rd., New Providence, New Jersey 07974. (908) 464-6800. 1974-.

Environment Index. Environment Information Center, Index Research Department, 124 E. 39th St., New York, New York 10016. 1971-. Annual.

Environmental Information Connection–EIC. Planning Information Program, Dept. of Urban and Regional Planning, University of Illinois, 1003 West Nevada, Urbana, Illinois 61801. (217) 333-1369. Also available online.

Environmental Periodicals Bibliography. Environmental Studies Institute, International Academy at Santa Barbara, 800 Garden St., Suite D, Santa Barbara, California 93101. (805) 965-5010. Also available online.

General Science Index. H. W. Wilson Co., 950 University Ave., Bronx, New York 10452. 1978-. Monthly, also issued in annual cumulation. Cumulative subject index to English language periodicals in the subject fields of astronomy, botany, chemistry, earth science, environment and conservation, food and nutrition, genetics, mathematics, medicine and health, microbiology, oceanography, physics, physiology and zoology.

Geographical Abstracts. London School of Economics, Dept. of Geography, Regency House, 34 Duke St., London, England 1966-. Continued by Geo Abstracts issued in 6 parts: Pt. A. Landforms and the quaternary; Pt. B. Biogeography and Climatology; Pt. C. Economic geography; Pt. D. Social geography and cartography; Pt. E. Sedimentology; Pt. F. Regional and community planning.

Multimedia Index to Ecology. National Information Center for Educational Media, University of Southern California, Los Angeles, California 90007.

Pollution Abstracts. Cambridge Scientific Abstracts, 5161 River Rd., Bethesda, Maryland 20816. (301) 961-6750. Six/year. Indexes worldwide technical literature on environmental pollution. Covers air pollution, marine and freshwater pollution, sewage and wastewater treatment, waste management, toxicology and health, noise pollution, radiation, land pollution, and environmental policies, programs, legislation, and education. Also available online.

Science Citation Index. Institute for Scientific Information, 3501 Market St., Philadelphia, Pennsylvania 19104. 1961-.

BIBLIOGRAPHIES

Current Contents. Agriculture, Biology and Environmental Sciences. Institute for Scientific Information, 3501 Market St., Philadelphia, Pennsylvania 19104. (800) 523-1857. 1973-. Previous title: Current Contents. Agricultural, Food & Veterinary Sciences. Gives the table of contents of periodicals in the fields of agriculture, biology, environmental and related areas.

Directory of Published Proceedings. Interdok Corp., 173 Halstead Ave., Harrison, New York 10528. (914) 835-3506. 1990. Monthly. This is a listing of published proceedings including the series SEMTE (Science/Medicine/Engineering/Technology) and the series SSH (Social Science/Humanities).

EPA Publications Bibliography. U.S. Environmental Protection Agency, Library Systems Branch, 401 M St., SW, Washington, District of Columbia 20460. (202) 260-2090. Quarterly.

New Publications of the Geological Survey. U.S. Department of the Interior, Geological Survey, 119 National Center, Reston, Virginia 22092. (703) 648-4460. 1984-. Monthly. Bibliography of geological publications and related government documents published by the Geological Survey.

ENCYCLOPEDIAS AND DICTIONARIES

Cambridge Encyclopedia of Life Sciences. A. E. Friday and David S. Ingram. Cambridge University Press, 40 W 20th St., New York, New York 10011. (212) 924-3900 or (800) 227-0247. 1985. Includes all topics under biology and ecology.

McGraw-Hill Encyclopedia of Environmental Science. Sybil P. Parker. McGraw-Hill Science & Engineering Books, 11 W. 19th St., New York, New York 10011. (212) 337-6010. 1980. Covers ecology, man's influence on nature, and environmental protection.

McGraw-Hill Encyclopedia of Science and Technology. McGraw-Hill, 1221 Avenue of the Americas, New York, New York 10020. (212) 512-2000 or (800) 262-4729. 1992. Seventh edition. Issued in multiple volumes including index. Includes all science and technology broad subject areas.

Van Nostrand's Scientific Encyclopedia. Glenn D. Considine, ed. Van Nostrand Reinhold, 115 5th Ave., New York, New York 10003. (212) 254-3232. 1983. Sixth edition. Includes all broad subject areas in science.

GENERAL WORKS

Atmospheric Carbon Dioxide and the Global Carbon Cycle. U.S. Department of Energy, Office of Energy Research, Carbon Dioxide Research Division, 1000 Independence Ave., S.W., Washington, District of Columbia 20535. (202) 252-1760. Research on atmospheric carbon dioxide.

Biogeochemical Processes at the Land-Sea Boundary. Pierre Lasserre. Elsevier Science Publishing Co., 655 Avenue of the Americas, New York, New York 10010. (212) 989-5800. 1988. Covers biogeochemical cycles, and seashore and coastal ecology.

Biogeochemistry: An Analysis of Global Change. William H. Schlesinger. Academic Press, c/o Harcourt Brace Jovanovich Inc., 6277 Sea Harbor Dr., Orlando, Florida 32887. (800) 346-8648. 1991. Examines global changes that have occurred and are occurring in our water, air, and on land, relates them to the global cycles of water, carbon, nitrogen, phosphorous, and sulfur.

Biogeochemistry of Major World Rivers. Egon T. Degens, et al. John Wiley & Sons, Inc., 605 3rd Ave., New York, New York 10158-0012. (212) 850-6000. 1991.

The Biogeochemistry of Mercury in the Environment. J.O. Nriagu. Elsevier Science Publishing Co., 655 Avenue of the Americas, New York, New York 10010. (212) 984-5800. 1979. Environmental aspects and toxicology of mercury.

Carbon Nitrogen Sulfur: Human Interference in Grand Biospheric Cycles. Vaclay Smil. Plenum Press, 233 Spring St., New York, New York 10013-1578. (212) 620-8000. 1985.

The Challenging Carbon Cycle: A Global Analysis. Springer-Verlag, 175 Fifth Ave., New York, New York 10010. (212) 460-1500. 1986. Looks at environmental aspects of carbon cycle, biogeochemistry.

Cycles of Soil: Carbon, Nitrogen, Phosphorus, Sulfur, Micronutrients. F.J. Stevenson. John Wiley & Sons Inc., 605 3rd Ave., New York, New York 10158-0012. (212) 850-6000. 1986.

Diversity of Environmental Biogeochemistry. J. Berthelin, ed. Elsevier Science Publishing Co., 655 Avenue of the Americas, New York, New York 10010. (212) 989-5800. 1991.

Environmental Biogeochemistry. R. Hallberg. Publishing House/FRN, P.O. Box 6711, Stockholm, Sweden S-113 85. 08-15-1580. 1983. Biogeochemistry and environmental engineering.

Environmental Chemistry and Toxicology of Aluminum. Timothy E. Lewis. Lewis Publishers, 2000 Corporate Blvd., N.W., Boca Raton, Florida 33431. (407) 994-0555 or (800) 272-7737. 1989. Examines the sources, fate, transport, and health effects of aluminum in aquatic and terrestrial environments. Also includes the latest advances in the study of aluminum in the environment; toxicity research–aquatic and terrestrial biota; neurotoxicity and possible links to Alzheimer's disease; different forms of aluminum in soils and soil water; coordination chemistry; specification and analytical methods.

Environmental Combination by Lead and Other Heavy Metals. University of Illinois, Institute for Environmental Studies, Urbana, Illinois 61801. 1977.

Facets of Modern Biogeochemistry. V. Ittekkott, et al. Springer-Verlag, 175 5th Ave., New York, New York 10010. (212) 460-1500; (800) 777-4643. 1990. Deals with the geochemistry of marine sediments and related areas.

HANDBOOKS AND MANUALS

The Environmental Chemistry of Aluminum. Garrison Sposito. CRC Press, 2000 Corporate Blvd. N.W., Boca Raton, Florida 33431. (800) 272-7737. 1989. Environmental aspects of aluminum content in water, soil and acid deposition.

The Handbook of Environmental Chemistry. O. Hutzinger. Springer-Verlag, 175 5th Ave., New York, New York 10010. (212) 460-1500. Irregular. Distribution and equilibria between environmental compartments, pathways, thermodynamics and kinetics.

Reactions and Processes. P.B. Barraclough. Springer-Verlag, 175 5th Ave., New York, New York 10010. (212) 460-1500. 1988. Covers natural environment and the biological cycles, reaction and processes, anthropogenic compounds, air and water pollution.

ONLINE DATA BASES

BIOSIS Previews. BIOSIS, 2100 Arch St., Philadelphia, Pennsylvania 19103-1399. (215) 587-4800. Largest and most comprehensive database of research in the life sciences. Contains citations for nearly 9000 primary research journals, monographs, reviews, symposia, preliminary reports, semi-popular journals, selected institutional reports, government reports and research communications.

CAS Source Index–CASSI. Chemical Abstracts Service, 2540 Olentangy River Rd., P.O. Box 3012, Columbus, Ohio 43210. (800) 848-6533 or (614) 421-3600. A listing of bibliographic and library holdings information for scientific and technical primary literature relevant to the chemical sciences.

Chemical Abstracts-CA. Chemical Abstracts Service, 2540 Olentangy River Rd., P.O. Box 3012, Columbus, Ohio 43210. (800) 848-6533 or (614) 421-3600. Information sources include 9000 journals, patents from 27 countries, two industrial property organizations, new books, conference proceedings, and government research reports.

Enviro/Energyline Abstracts Plus. R. R. Bowker Co., 121 Chanlon Rd., New Providence, New Jersey 07974. (908) 464-6800.

Environmental Periodicals Bibliography. National Information Services Corp., Ste. 6, Wyman Towers, 3100 St. Paul St., Baltimore, Maryland 21218. (410)243-0797. Online version of abstract of same name.

Monthly Catalog of United States Government Publications. U.S. G.P.O., Supt. of Docs., PO Box 371954, Pittsburgh, Pennsylvania 15250-7954. (202) 512-0000.

National Technical Information Service. U.S. Department of Commerce, National Technical Information Service, Office of Data Base Services, 5285 Port Royal Rd., Springfield, Virginia 22161. (703) 487-4807. Bibliographic database of government sponsored research and technical reports.

SCISEARCH. Institute for Scientific Information, University City Science Center, 3501 Market St., Philadelphia, Pennsylvania 19104. (215) 386-0100.

PERIODICALS AND NEWSLETTERS

Analytical Biochemistry. Academic Press, 111 Fifth Ave., New York, New York 10003. (800) 346-8648. Covers biological and chemical topics relating to the environment.

Ecological Applications. Ecological Society of America, Center for Environmental Studies, Arizona State University, Tempe, Arizona 85287. (602) 965-3000. 1991-. Quarterly. Emphasizes the application of basic ecological concepts to a wide range of problems.

The Journal of Biological Chemistry. American Society of Biological Chemists, 428 E. Preston St., Baltimore, Maryland 21202. Three times a month. Biological, agricultural, and energy aspects of the environment.

Marine Biology. Springer-Verlag, 175 5th Ave., New York, New York 10010. (212) 461-1500; (800) 777-4643. Sixteen/year. Life in oceans and coastal waters.

TRADE ASSOCIATIONS AND PROFESSIONAL SOCIETIES

American Institute of Biological Sciences. 730 11th St., N.W., Washington, District of Columbia 20001-4521. (202) 628-1500.

American Institute of Chemical Engineers. 345 East 47th St., New York, New York 10017. (212) 705-7338.

American Institute of Chemists. 7315 Wisconsin Ave., Bethesda, Maryland 20814. (301) 652-2447.

BIOGEOGRAPHY

See also: CLIMATE

ABSTRACTING AND INDEXING SERVICES

Applied Ecology Abstracts Studies in Renewable Natural Resources. Information Retrieval Ltd., 1911 Jefferson Davis Highway, Arlington, Virginia 22202. 1975-. Monthly.

ASFA Aquaculture Abstracts. Cambridge Scientific Abstracts, Inc., 5161 River Rd., Bethesda, Maryland 20816. (301) 961-6750. 1984.

Biological Abstracts. BIOSIS, 2100 Arch St., Philadelphia, Pennsylvania 19103-1399. (215) 587-4800. 1927-.

Biological and Agricultural Index. H.W. Wilson Co., 950 University Ave., Bronx, New York 10452. (800) 367-6770. 1916-. Monthly.

Biology Digest. Data Courier, Plexus Pub Inc., 143 Old Marlton Pike, Medford, New Jersey 08055. 1974-. Monthly. Abstracts biology periodicals.

Current Advances in Ecological and Environmental Science. Pergamon Microforms International, Inc., Fairview Park, Elmsford, New York 10523. (914) 592-7720. 1989-. Monthly. Current literature searching service including journals, reports, abstracts, etc. This service is available online as part of the CABS database on the hosts BRS and ORBIT search service.

Ecological Abstracts. Geo Abstracts Ltd. Elsevier Applied Science, Crown House, Linton Rd., Barking, England IG 11 8JU. 1974-. Derived from over 600 leading ecological and environmental journals, plus books, conference proceedings, reports and theses.

Ecology Abstracts. Cambridge Scientific Abstracts, 5161 River Rd., Bethesda, Maryland 20816. (301) 961-6750. Monthly.

Environment Abstracts. Bowker A & I Publishing, 121 Chanlon Rd., New Providence, New Jersey 07974. (908) 464-6800. 1974-.

Environment Index. Environment Information Center, Index Research Department, 124 E. 39th St., New York, New York 10016. 1971-. Annual.

Environmental Information Connection-EIC. Planning Information Program, Dept. of Urban and Regional Planning, University of Illinois, 1003 West Nevada, Urbana, Illinois 61801. (217) 333-1369. Also available online.

Environmental Periodicals Bibliography. Environmental Studies Institute, International Academy at Santa Barbara, 800 Garden St., Suite D, Santa Barbara, California 93101. (805) 965-5010. Also available online.

General Science Index. H. W. Wilson Co., 950 University Ave., Bronx, New York 10452. 1978-. Monthly, also issued in annual cumulation. Cumulative subject index to English language periodicals in the subject fields of astronomy, botany, chemistry, earth science, environment and conservation, food and nutrition, genetics, mathematics, medicine and health, microbiology, oceanography, physics, physiology and zoology.

Multimedia Index to Ecology. National Information Center for Educational Media, University of Southern California, Los Angeles, California 90007.

Pollution Abstracts. Cambridge Scientific Abstracts, 5161 River Rd., Bethesda, Maryland 20816. (301) 961-6750. Six/year. Indexes worldwide technical literature on environmental pollution. Covers air pollution, marine and freshwater pollution, sewage and wastewater treatment, waste management, toxicology and health, noise pollution, radiation, land pollution, and environmental policies, programs, legislation, and education. Also available online.

Science Citation Index. Institute for Scientific Information, 3501 Market St., Philadelphia, Pennsylvania 19104. 1961-.

BIBLIOGRAPHIES

Bibliography and Index of Geology. American Geological Institute, 4220 King St., Alexandria, Virginia 22302. Monthly. Includes environmental geology and hydrogeology.

Current Contents. Agriculture, Biology and Environmental Sciences. Institute for Scientific Information, 3501 Market St., Philadelphia, Pennsylvania 19104. (800) 523-1857. 1973-. Previous title: Current Contents. Agricultural, Food & Veterinary Sciences. Gives the table of contents of periodicals in the fields of agriculture, biology, environmental and related areas.

Directory of Published Proceedings. Interdok Corp., 173 Halstead Ave., Harrison, New York 10528. (914) 835-3506. 1990. Monthly. This is a listing of published proceedings including the series SEMTE (Science/Medicine/Engineering/Technology) and the series SSH (Social Science/Humanities).

EPA Publications Bibliography. U.S. Environmental Protection Agency, Library Systems Branch, 401 M St., SW, Washington, District of Columbia 20460. (202) 260-2090. Quarterly.

New Publications of the Geological Survey. U.S. Department of the Interior, Geological Survey, 119 National Center, Reston, Virginia 22092. (703) 648-4460. 1984-. Monthly. Bibliography of geological publications and related government documents published by the Geological Survey.

DIRECTORIES

Ecological Society of America Bulletin–Directory of Members Issue. Ecological Society of America, c/o Dr. Duncan Patten, Center for Environmental Studies, Arizona State University, Tempe, Arizona 85287. (602) 965-3000.

Raise the Stakes–North America Plus Issue. Planet Drum Foundation, Box 31251, San Francisco, California 94131. (415) 285-6556.

ENCYCLOPEDIAS AND DICTIONARIES

Cambridge Dictionary of Biology. Peter M. B. Walker. Cambridge University Press, 40 W. 20th St., New York, New York 10011. (212) 924-3900 or (800) 227-0247. 1989. Includes 10,000 terms in zoology, botany, biochemistry, molecular biology and genetics. Previously published under the title Chambers Biology Dictionary.

Cambridge Encyclopedia of Life Sciences. A. E. Friday and David S. Ingram. Cambridge University Press, 40 W 20th St., New York, New York 10011. (212) 924-3900 or (800) 227-0247. 1985. Includes all topics under biology and ecology.

A Concise Dictionary of Biology. Elizabeth Martin, ed. Oxford University Press, 200 Madison Ave., New York, New York 10016. (212) 679-7300 or (800) 334-4249. 1990. New edition. Derived from the Concise Science Dictionary, published in 1984.

A Dictionary of Genetics. Robert C. King and William A. Stansfield. Oxford University Press, 200 Madison Ave., New York, New York 10016. (212) 679-7300 or (800) 334-4249. 1991. Fourth edition. Includes 7,100 definitions with 250 illustrations. Also includes bibliography of major sources.

Dictionary of Genetics and Cell Biology. Norman Maclean. New York University Press, 70 Washington Sq. S., New York, New York 10012. (212) 998-2575. 1987. Includes the subject areas of cytology and genetics.

The Encyclopedia of Animal Ecology. Peter D. Moore. Facts on File, Inc., 460 Park Ave. S., New York, New York 10016. (212) 683-2244. 1987.

Encyclopedic Dictionary of Genetics: With German Term Equivalents and Extensive German/English Index. R. C. King and W. D. Stansfield. VCH Publishers, 303 NW 12th Ave., Deerfield Beach, Florida 33442-1788. (305) 428-5566. 1990. 4th ed. Revised edition of: A Dictionary of Genetics, third edition.

Life Sciences on File. Diagram Group. Facts on File, Inc., 460 Park Ave. S., New York, New York 10016. (212) 683-2244. 1986. Encyclopedia of pictorial collection in

life sciences. Deals with all major topics in life sciences including ecology.

McGraw-Hill Encyclopedia of Environmental Science. Sybil P. Parker. McGraw-Hill Science & Engineering Books, 11 W. 19th St., New York, New York 10011. (212) 337-6010. 1980. Covers ecology, man's influence on nature, and environmental protection.

McGraw-Hill Encyclopedia of Science and Technology. McGraw-Hill, 1221 Avenue of the Americas, New York, New York 10020. (212) 512-2000 or (800) 262-4729. 1992. Seventh edition. Issued in multiple volumes including index. Includes all science and technology broad subject areas.

Van Nostrand's Scientific Encyclopedia. Glenn D. Considine, ed. Van Nostrand Reinhold, 115 5th Ave., New York, New York 10003. (212) 254-3232. 1983. Sixth edition. Includes all broad subject areas in science.

GENERAL WORKS

Agroecology: Researching the Ecological Basis for Sustainable Agriculture. Stephen R. Gliessman, ed. Springer-Verlag, 175 5th Ave., New York, New York 10010. (212) 460-1500; (800) 777-4643. 1990. Demonstrates in a series of international case studies how to combine the more production-oriented focus of the agronomist with the more systems-oriented viewpoint of the ecologist. Methodology for evaluating and quantifying agroecosystem is presented.

Biogeography. Joy Tivy. Longman Publishing Group, 10 Bonk St., White Plains, New York 10606. (914) 993-5000. 1982. A study of plants in the ecosphere and phytogeography.

The Biogeography of Ground Beetles. G. R. Noonan, et al., eds. VCH Publishers, 303 NW 12th Ave., Deerfield Beach, Florida 33442-1788. (305) 428-5566. 1991. Book summarizes knowledge about the biogeography of ground beetles of mountains and islands. It describes a diverse group of ecologically divergent species from areas of special interest to biogeographers.

Climates of the States. Gale Research Inc., 835 Penobscot Bldg., Detroit, Michigan 48226-4094. (313) 961-2242. 1986. State-by-state summaries of climate based on first order weather reporting stations for the period 1951-1980.

Ecology of Arable Land. Olof Andersen, et al., eds. Munksgaard International, PO Box 2148, Copenhagen K, Denmark DK-1016. 1990. Investigates and synthesizes the contributions of the soil organisms and nitrogen and carbon circulation in four contrasting cropping systems. Also looks into future challenges of agroecosystem research.

Ecosystems of Florida. Ronald L. Myers and John J. Ewel, eds. Central Florida University, Dist. by Univ. Presses of Florida, 15 N.W. 15th St., Gainesville, Florida 32603. (904) 392-1351. 1990. Presents an ecosystem setting with geology, geography and soils, climate, and 13 ecosystems in a broad human context of historical biogeography and current human influences. Also presents community vulnerability and management techniques and issues in conservation.

Environmental Change in Iceland: Past and Present. Judith K. Maizels and Chris Caseldine, eds. Kluwer Academic Publishers, 101 Philip Dr., Assinippi Park,

Norwell, Massachusetts 02061. (617) 871-6600. 1991. Describes the glacial landforms and paleoclimatology in Iceland. Volume 7 of the Glaciology and Quaternary Geology Series.

Human Performance Physiology and Environmental Medicine Atterrestrial Extremes. Kent B. Pandolf, et al., eds. WCB Brown and Benchmark Pr., 2460 Kerper Blvd., Dubuque, Iowa 52001. (800) 338-5578. 1988. Includes the most current information available on the physiological and medical responses to heat, cold, altitude, poor air quality and hyperbaric conditions.

Magill's Survey of Science. Earth Science Series. Frank N. Magill. Salem Press, PO Box 50062, Pasadena, California 91105. 1990-. Five volumes. Includes information on earth's crust, hot spots and volcanic island chains, physical properties of minerals, rock magnetism, physical properties of rocks, and index.

Nature Reserves: Island Theory and Conservation Practice. Craig L. Shafer. Smithsonian Institution Press, 470 L'Enfant Plaza, No. 7100, Washington, District of Columbia 20560. (800) 782-4612. 1991. Encompasses ecology, biogeography, evolutionary biology, genetics, paleobiology, as well as legal, social, and economic issues.

Preserving Communities and Corridors. Gay Mackintosh, ed. Defenders of Wildlife, 1244 19th St. N.W., Washington, District of Columbia 20036. (202) 659-9510. 1989.

Weather of U.S. Cities. Frank E. Bair. Gale Research Inc., 835 Penobscot Bldg., Detroit, Michigan 48226-4094. (313) 961-2242. 1992. Compilation of U.S. government weather data on 281 cities and weather observation stations.

ONLINE DATA BASES

BIOSIS Previews. BIOSIS, 2100 Arch St., Philadelphia, Pennsylvania 19103-1399. (215) 587-4800. Largest and most comprehensive database of research in the life sciences. Contains citations for nearly 9000 primary research journals, monographs, reviews, symposia, preliminary reports, semi-popular journals, selected institutional reports, government reports and research communications.

Cambridge Scientific Abstracts Life Science–CSAL. Cambridge Scientific Abstracts, 5161 River Rd., Bethesda, Maryland 20816. (301) 961-6750. Provides access to the following abstracting services: "Life Sciences Collection," "Aquatic Sciences and Fisheries Abstracts," "Oceanic Abstracts," and "Pollution Abstracts."

Enviro/Energyline Abstracts Plus. R. R. Bowker Co., 121 Chanlon Rd., New Providence, New Jersey 07974. (908) 464-6800.

Environmental Periodicals Bibliography. National Information Services Corp., Ste. 6, Wyman Towers, 3100 St. Paul St., Baltimore, Maryland 21218. (410)243-0797. Online version of abstract of same name.

Monthly Catalog of United States Government Publications. U.S. G.P.O., Supt. of Docs., PO Box 371954, Pittsburgh, Pennsylvania 15250-7954. (202) 512-0000.

National Technical Information Service. U.S. Department of Commerce, National Technical Information Service, Office of Data Base Services, 5285 Port Royal Rd., Springfield, Virginia 22161. (703) 487-4807. Bibliographic database of government sponsored research and technical reports.

SCISEARCH. Institute for Scientific Information, University City Science Center, 3501 Market St., Philadelphia, Pennsylvania 19104. (215) 386-0100.

PERIODICALS AND NEWSLETTERS

The American Naturalist. Americana Society of Naturalists, Business Sciences, University of Kansas, Lawrence, Kansas 66045. (913) 864-3763. Monthly. Contains information by professionals of the biological sciences.

BioScience Journal. American Institute of Biological Sciences, 730 11th Street, Nw, Washington, District of Columbia 20001-4521. (202) 628-1500. Eleven times a year. Current research, feature articles, book reviews, and new products.

Ecological Monographs. Business Office of the Ecological Society of America, Center of Environmental Studies, Arizona State University, Tempe, Arizona 85287-1201. (602) 965-3000. Quarterly. Scientific journal of ecological issues.

Ecological Society of America Bulletin. Ecological Society of America, Center of Environmental Studies, Arizona State University, Tempe, Arizona 85287-1201. (602) 965-3000. Quarterly. Study of living things in relation to their environments.

Ecomod. ISEM–North America Chapter, Water Quality Division, South Florida Water Management District, P.O. Box 24608, West Palm Beach, Florida 33416. (407) 686-8800. Monthly. Current events in ecological and environmental modeling.

Global Ecology and Biogeography Letter. Blackwell Scientific Publications, 3 Cambridge Ctr., Suite 208, Cambridge, Massachusetts 02142. (617) 225-0401. 1991. Bimonthly. Global Ecology and Biogeography Letters is a sister publication of Journal of Biogeography and is only available with a subscription to the Journal. Provides a fast-track outlet for short research papers, news items, editorials, and book reviews. Topics related to the major scientific concerns of our present era, such as global warming, world sea-level rises, environmental acidification, development and conservation, biodiversity, and important new theories and themes in biogeography and ecology.

Journal of Applied Meteorology. American Meteorological Society, 45 Beacon Street, Boston, Massachusetts 02108. (617) 227-2425. Monthly. Articles on the relationship between weather and environment.

Journal of Biogeography. Blackwell Scientific Publications Inc., 3 Cambridge Ctr., Suite 208, Cambridge, Massachusetts 02142. (617) 225-0401.

The Journal of Biological Chemistry. American Society of Biological Chemists, 428 E. Preston St., Baltimore, Maryland 21202. Three times a month. Biological, agricultural, and energy aspects of the environment.

Marine Biology. Springer-Verlag, 175 5th Ave., New York, New York 10010. (212) 461-1500; (800) 777-4643. Sixteen/year. Life in oceans and coastal waters.

Nature and Resources. Elsevier Science Publishing Co., 655 Avenue of the Americas, New York, New York 10010. (212) 989-5800. 1965-. Quarterly. Provides in-depth reviews of contemporary environmental issues from an international perspective.

RESEARCH CENTERS AND INSTITUTES

Ohio State University, Museum of Zoology. 1315 Kinnear Rd., Columbus, Ohio 43212. (614) 422-8560.

Shippensburg University, Vertebrate Museum. Franklin Science Center, Shippensburg, Pennsylvania 17257. (714) 532-1407.

University of Massachusetts, Museum of Zoology. Department of Zoology, Amherst, Massachusetts 01003. (413) 545-2287.

University of Michigan, Museum of Zoology. 1082 University Museums, Ann Arbor, Michigan 48109. (313) 764-0476.

University of Nebraska-Lincoln, Harold W. Manter Laboratory of Parasitology. W529 Nebraska Hall West, Lincoln, Nebraska 68588-0514. (402) 472-3334.

University of Texas at El Paso, Laboratory for Environmental Biology. Department of Biology, EL Paso, Texas 79968. (915) 747-5164.

TRADE ASSOCIATIONS AND PROFESSIONAL SOCIETIES

American Institute of Biological Sciences. 730 11th St., N.W., Washington, District of Columbia 20001-4521. (202) 628-1500.

American Institute of Biomedical Climatology. 1023 Welsh Rd., Philadelphia, Pennsylvania 19115. (215) 673-8368.

American Society of Naturalists. Department of Ecology and Evolation, State University of New York, Stony Brook, New York 11794. (516) 632-8589.

Ecological Society of America. Arizona State University, Center for Environmental Studies, Tempe, Arizona 85287. (602) 965-3000.

International Bio-Environmental Foundation. 15300 Ventura Blvd., Suite 405, Sherman Oaks, California 91403. (818) 907-5483.

BIOINDICATORS

See also: BIOMONITORING; BIOSENSORS

ABSTRACTING AND INDEXING SERVICES

Applied Ecology Abstracts Studies in Renewable Natural Resources. Information Retrieval Ltd., 1911 Jefferson Davis Highway, Arlington, Virginia 22202. 1975-. Monthly.

Biological Abstracts. BIOSIS, 2100 Arch St., Philadelphia, Pennsylvania 19103-1399. (215) 587-4800. 1927-.

Biological and Agricultural Index. H.W. Wilson Co., 950 University Ave., Bronx, New York 10452. (800) 367-6770. 1916-. Monthly.

Biology Digest. Data Courier, Plexus Pub Inc., 143 Old Marlton Pike, Medford, New Jersey 08055. 1974-. Monthly. Abstracts biology periodicals.

Ecological Abstracts. Geo Abstracts Ltd. Elsevier Applied Science, Crown House, Linton Rd., Barking, England IG 11 8JU. 1974-. Derived from over 600 leading ecological

and environmental journals, plus books, conference proceedings, reports and theses.

Environment Abstracts. Bowker A & I Publishing, 121 Chanlon Rd., New Providence, New Jersey 07974. (908) 464-6800. 1974-.

Environment Index. Environment Information Center, Index Research Department, 124 E. 39th St., New York, New York 10016. 1971-. Annual.

Environmental Information Connection–EIC. Planning Information Program, Dept. of Urban and Regional Planning, University of Illinois, 1003 West Nevada, Urbana, Illinois 61801. (217) 333-1369. Also available online.

Environmental Periodicals Bibliography. Environmental Studies Institute, International Academy at Santa Barbara, 800 Garden St., Suite D, Santa Barbara, California 93101. (805) 965-5010. Also available online.

General Science Index. H. W. Wilson Co., 950 University Ave., Bronx, New York 10452. 1978-. Monthly, also issued in annual cumulation. Cumulative subject index to English language periodicals in the subject fields of astronomy, botany, chemistry, earth science, environment and conservation, food and nutrition, genetics, mathematics, medicine and health, microbiology, oceanography, physics, physiology and zoology.

Multimedia Index to Ecology. National Information Center for Educational Media, University of Southern California, Los Angeles, California 90007.

Pollution Abstracts. Cambridge Scientific Abstracts, 5161 River Rd., Bethesda, Maryland 20816. (301) 961-6750. Six/year. Indexes worldwide technical literature on environmental pollution. Covers air pollution, marine and freshwater pollution, sewage and wastewater treatment, waste management, toxicology and health, noise pollution, radiation, land pollution, and environmental policies, programs, legislation, and education. Also available online.

Science Citation Index. Institute for Scientific Information, 3501 Market St., Philadelphia, Pennsylvania 19104. 1961-.

BIBLIOGRAPHIES

Current Contents. Agriculture, Biology and Environmental Sciences. Institute for Scientific Information, 3501 Market St., Philadelphia, Pennsylvania 19104. (800) 523-1857. 1973-. Previous title: Current Contents. Agricultural, Food & Veterinary Sciences. Gives the table of contents of periodicals in the fields of agriculture, biology, environmental and related areas.

Directory of Published Proceedings. Interdok Corp., 173 Halstead Ave., Harrison, New York 10528. (914) 835-3506. 1990. Monthly. This is a listing of published proceedings including the series SEMTE (Science/Medicine/Engineering/Technology) and the series SSH (Social Science/Humanities).

EPA Publications Bibliography. U.S. Environmental Protection Agency, Library Systems Branch, 401 M St., SW, Washington, District of Columbia 20460. (202) 260-2090. Quarterly.

ENCYCLOPEDIAS AND DICTIONARIES

Cambridge Encyclopedia of Life Sciences. A. E. Friday and David S. Ingram. Cambridge University Press, 40 W 20th St., New York, New York 10011. (212) 924-3900 or (800) 227-0247. 1985. Includes all topics under biology and ecology.

McGraw-Hill Encyclopedia of Environmental Science. Sybil P. Parker. McGraw-Hill Science & Engineering Books, 11 W. 19th St., New York, New York 10011. (212) 337-6010. 1980. Covers ecology, man's influence on nature, and environmental protection.

McGraw-Hill Encyclopedia of Science and Technology. McGraw-Hill, 1221 Avenue of the Americas, New York, New York 10020. (212) 512-2000 or (800) 262-4729. 1992. Seventh edition. Issued in multiple volumes including index. Includes all science and technology broad subject areas.

Van Nostrand's Scientific Encyclopedia. Glenn D. Considine, ed. Van Nostrand Reinhold, 115 5th Ave., New York, New York 10003. (212) 254-3232. 1983. Sixth edition. Includes all broad subject areas in science.

GENERAL WORKS

Automated Biomonitoring: Living Sensors as Environmental Monitors. D. Gruber. John Wiley & Sons, Inc., 605 3rd Ave., New York, New York 10158. (212) 850-6000. 1988. Papers presented deal with conceptual and historical issues of biological early warning systems. Studies using fish as sensors are presented as well as studies using other biological sensors. Not limited to water quality monitoring alone.

Bioindications of Chemical Radioactive Pollution. D. A. Krivolutsky. Lewis Publishers, 2000 Corporate Blvd. N.W., Boca Raton, Florida 33431. (800) 272-7737. 1991. Part of the Advances in Science and Technology in the USSR series.

ONLINE DATA BASES

BIOSIS Previews. BIOSIS, 2100 Arch St., Philadelphia, Pennsylvania 19103-1399. (215) 587-4800. Largest and most comprehensive database of research in the life sciences. Contains citations for nearly 9000 primary research journals, monographs, reviews, symposia, preliminary reports, semi-popular journals, selected institutional reports, government reports and research communications.

Cambridge Scientific Abstracts Life Science–CSAL. Cambridge Scientific Abstracts, 5161 River Rd., Bethesda, Maryland 20816. (301) 961-6750. Provides access to the following abstracting services: "Life Sciences Collection," "Aquatic Sciences and Fisheries Abstracts," "Oceanic Abstracts," and "Pollution Abstracts."

Enviro/Energyline Abstracts Plus. R. R. Bowker Co., 121 Chanlon Rd., New Providence, New Jersey 07974. (908) 464-6800.

Environmental Periodicals Bibliography. National Information Services Corp., Ste. 6, Wyman Towers, 3100 St. Paul St., Baltimore, Maryland 21218. (410)243-0797. Online version of abstract of same name.

Monthly Catalog of United States Government Publications. U.S. G.P.O., Supt. of Docs., PO Box 371954, Pittsburgh, Pennsylvania 15250-7954. (202) 512-0000.

National Technical Information Service. U.S. Department of Commerce, National Technical Information Service, Office of Data Base Services, 5285 Port Royal Rd., Springfield, Virginia 22161. (703) 487-4807. Bibliographic database of government sponsored research and technical reports.

SCISEARCH. Institute for Scientific Information, University City Science Center, 3501 Market St., Philadelphia, Pennsylvania 19104. (215) 386-0100.

PERIODICALS AND NEWSLETTERS

The Journal of Biological Chemistry. American Society of Biological Chemists, 428 E. Preston St., Baltimore, Maryland 21202. Three times a month. Biological, agricultural, and energy aspects of the environment.

TRADE ASSOCIATIONS AND PROFESSIONAL SOCIETIES

American Institute of Biological Sciences. 730 11th St., N.W., Washington, District of Columbia 20001-4521. (202) 628-1500.

BIOLOGICAL COMMUNITIES

See also: AVIAN ECOLOGY; ECOSYSTEMS

ABSTRACTING AND INDEXING SERVICES

Applied Ecology Abstracts Studies in Renewable Natural Resources. Information Retrieval Ltd., 1911 Jefferson Davis Highway, Arlington, Virginia 22202. 1975-. Monthly.

Biological Abstracts. BIOSIS, 2100 Arch St., Philadelphia, Pennsylvania 19103-1399. (215) 587-4800. 1927-.

Biological and Agricultural Index. H.W. Wilson Co., 950 University Ave., Bronx, New York 10452. (800) 367-6770. 1916-. Monthly.

Biology Digest. Data Courier, Plexus Pub Inc., 143 Old Marlton Pike, Medford, New Jersey 08055. 1974-. Monthly. Abstracts biology periodicals.

Current Advances in Ecological and Environmental Science. Pergamon Microforms International, Inc., Fairview Park, Elmsford, New York 10523. (914) 592-7720. 1989-. Monthly. Current literature searching service includingjournals, reports, abstracts, etc. This service is available online as part of the CABS database on the hosts BRS and ORBIT search service.

Ecological Abstracts. Geo Abstracts Ltd. Elsevier Applied Science, Crown House, Linton Rd., Barking, England IG 11 8JU. 1974-. Derived from over 600 leading ecological and environmental journals, plus books, conference proceedings, reports and theses.

Environment Abstracts. Bowker A & I Publishing, 121 Chanlon Rd., New Providence, New Jersey 07974. (908) 464-6800. 1974-.

Environment Index. Environment Information Center, Index Research Department, 124 E. 39th St., New York, New York 10016. 1971-. Annual.

Environmental Information Connection–EIC. Planning Information Program, Dept. of Urban and Regional Planning, University of Illinois, 1003 West Nevada,

Urbana, Illinois 61801. (217) 333-1369. Also available online.

Environmental Periodicals Bibliography. Environmental Studies Institute, International Academy at Santa Barbara, 800 Garden St., Suite D, Santa Barbara, California 93101. (805) 965-5010. Also available online.

General Science Index. H. W. Wilson Co., 950 University Ave., Bronx, New York 10452. 1978-. Monthly, also issued in annual cumulation. Cumulative subject index to English language periodicals in the subject fields of astronomy, botany, chemistry, earth science, environment and conservation, food and nutrition, genetics, mathematics, medicine and health, microbiology, oceanography, physics, physiology and zoology.

Multimedia Index to Ecology. National Information Center for Educational Media, University of Southern California, Los Angeles, California 90007.

BIBLIOGRAPHIES

Current Contents. Agriculture, Biology and Environmental Sciences. Institute for Scientific Information, 3501 Market St., Philadelphia, Pennsylvania 19104. (800) 523-1857. 1973-. Previous title: Current Contents. Agricultural, Food & Veterinary Sciences. Gives the table of contents of periodicals in the fields of agriculture, biology, environmental and related areas.

EPA Publications Bibliography. U.S. Environmental Protection Agency, Library Systems Branch, 401 M St., SW, Washington, District of Columbia 20460. (202) 260-2090. Quarterly.

ENCYCLOPEDIAS AND DICTIONARIES

Cambridge Encyclopedia of Life Sciences. A. E. Friday and David S. Ingram. Cambridge University Press, 40 W 20th St., New York, New York 10011. (212) 924-3900 or (800) 227-0247. 1985. Includes all topics under biology and ecology.

McGraw-Hill Encyclopedia of Environmental Science. Sybil P. Parker. McGraw-Hill Science & Engineering Books, 11 W. 19th St., New York, New York 10011. (212) 337-6010. 1980. Covers ecology, man's influence on nature, and environmental protection.

McGraw-Hill Encyclopedia of Science and Technology. McGraw-Hill, 1221 Avenue of the Americas, New York, New York 10020. (212) 512-2000 or (800) 262-4729. 1992. Seventh edition. Issued in multiple volumes including index. Includes all science and technology broad subject areas.

Van Nostrand's Scientific Encyclopedia. Glenn D. Considine, ed. Van Nostrand Reinhold, 115 5th Ave., New York, New York 10003. (212) 254-3232. 1983. Sixth edition. Includes all broad subject areas in science.

GENERAL WORKS

Biodiversity. E. O. Wilson. National Academy Press, 2101 Constitution Ave. N.W., PO Box 285, Washington, District of Columbia 20418. (202) 334-3313. 1988.

Research Priorities for Conservation Biology. Michael E. Soulfe and Kathryn A. Kohm, eds. Island Press, 1718 Connecticut Ave. N.W., Suite 300, Washington, District of Columbia 20009. (202) 232-7933. 1989. Proposes an urgent research agenda to improve our understanding and preservation of biological diversity.

ONLINE DATA BASES

BIOSIS Previews. BIOSIS, 2100 Arch St., Philadelphia, Pennsylvania 19103-1399. (215) 587-4800. Largest and most comprehensive database of research in the life sciences. Contains citations for nearly 9000 primary research journals, monographs, reviews, symposia, preliminary reports, semi-popular journals, selected institutional reports, government reports and research communications.

Biotechnology Abstracts. Derwent Publications Ltd., 6845 Elm St., McLean, Virginia 22101. (703) 790-0400. Includes material on genetic manipulation, biochemical engineering, fermentation, biocatalysis, cell hybridization, in vitro plant propagation and industrial waste management.

Cambridge Scientific Abstracts Life Science–CSAL. Cambridge Scientific Abstracts, 5161 River Rd., Bethesda, Maryland 20816. (301) 961-6750. Provides access to the following abstracting services: "Life Sciences Collection," "Aquatic Sciences and Fisheries Abstracts," "Oceanic Abstracts," and "Pollution Abstracts."

Enviro/Energyline Abstracts Plus. R. R. Bowker Co., 121 Chanlon Rd., New Providence, New Jersey 07974. (908) 464-6800.

Environmental Periodicals Bibliography. National Information Services Corp., Ste. 6, Wyman Towers, 3100 St. Paul St., Baltimore, Maryland 21218. (410)243-0797. Online version of abstract of same name.

Monthly Catalog of United States Government Publications. U.S. G.P.O., Supt. of Docs., PO Box 371954, Pittsburgh, Pennsylvania 15250-7954. (202) 512-0000.

National Technical Information Service. U.S. Department of Commerce, National Technical Information Service, Office of Data Base Services, 5285 Port Royal Rd., Springfield, Virginia 22161. (703) 487-4807. Bibliographic database of government sponsored research and technical reports.

SCISEARCH. Institute for Scientific Information, University City Science Center, 3501 Market St., Philadelphia, Pennsylvania 19104. (215) 386-0100.

TRADE ASSOCIATIONS AND PROFESSIONAL SOCIETIES

American Institute of Biological Sciences. 730 11th St., N.W., Washington, District of Columbia 20001-4521. (202) 628-1500.

BIOLOGICAL CONTAMINATION

ABSTRACTING AND INDEXING SERVICES

Aqualine Abstracts. Water Research Centre. c/o Pergamon Microforms International, Inc., Fairview Park, Elmsford, New York 10523. (914) 592-7720. 1927-. Contains some 8,000 records annually on water and wastewater technology. Covers all aspects of water, wastewater, associated engineering services and the aquatic environment. Over 600 periodicals, as well as books, reports and conference proceedings and other

publications from water related institutions worldwide are scanned. Also available online.

Biodeterioration Abstracts. Farnham Royal, Slough, England SL2 3BN. Quarterly.

Biodeterioration Research Titles. Biodeterioration Information Centre, University of Aston in Birmingham, Birmingham, England

Biological Abstracts. BIOSIS, 2100 Arch St., Philadelphia, Pennsylvania 19103-1399. (215) 587-4800. 1927-.

Biological and Agricultural Index. H.W. Wilson Co., 950 University Ave., Bronx, New York 10452. (800) 367-6770. 1916-. Monthly.

Biology Digest. Data Courier, Plexus Pub Inc., 143 Old Marlton Pike, Medford, New Jersey 08055. 1974-. Monthly. Abstracts biology periodicals.

Current Advances in Ecological and Environmental Science. Pergamon Microforms International, Inc., Fairview Park, Elmsford, New York 10523. (914) 592-7720. 1989-. Monthly. Current literature searching service including journals, reports, abstracts, etc. This service is available online as part of the CABS database on the hosts BRS and ORBIT search service.

Ecological Abstracts. Geo Abstracts Ltd. Elsevier Applied Science, Crown House, Linton Rd., Barking, England IG 11 8JU. 1974-. Derived from over 600 leading ecological and environmental journals, plus books, conference proceedings, reports and theses.

Environment Abstracts. Bowker A & I Publishing, 121 Chanlon Rd., New Providence, New Jersey 07974. (908) 464-6800. 1974-.

Environment Index. Environment Information Center, Index Research Department, 124 E. 39th St., New York, New York 10016. 1971-. Annual.

Environmental Information Connection–EIC. Planning Information Program, Dept. of Urban and Regional Planning, University of Illinois, 1003 West Nevada, Urbana, Illinois 61801. (217) 333-1369. Also available online.

Environmental Periodicals Bibliography. Environmental Studies Institute, International Academy at Santa Barbara, 800 Garden St., Suite D, Santa Barbara, California 93101. (805) 965-5010. Also available online.

General Science Index. H. W. Wilson Co., 950 University Ave., Bronx, New York 10452. 1978-. Monthly, also issued in annual cumulation. Cumulative subject index to English language periodicals in the subject fields of astronomy, botany, chemistry, earth science, environment and conservation, food and nutrition, genetics, mathematics, medicine and health, microbiology, oceanography, physics, physiology and zoology.

BIBLIOGRAPHIES

Current Contents. Agriculture, Biology and Environmental Sciences. Institute for Scientific Information, 3501 Market St., Philadelphia, Pennsylvania 19104. (800) 523-1857. 1973-. Previous title: Current Contents. Agricultural, Food & Veterinary Sciences. Gives the table of contents of periodicals in the fields of agriculture, biology, environmental and related areas.

EPA Publications Bibliography. U.S. Environmental Protection Agency, Library Systems Branch, 401 M St., SW,

Washington, District of Columbia 20460. (202) 260-2090. Quarterly.

ENCYCLOPEDIAS AND DICTIONARIES

Cambridge Encyclopedia of Life Sciences. A. E. Friday and David S. Ingram. Cambridge University Press, 40 W 20th St., New York, New York 10011. (212) 924-3900 or (800) 227-0247. 1985. Includes all topics under biology and ecology.

McGraw-Hill Encyclopedia of Environmental Science. Sybil P. Parker. McGraw-Hill Science & Engineering Books, 11 W. 19th St., New York, New York 10011. (212) 337-6010. 1980. Covers ecology, man's influence on nature, and environmental protection.

McGraw-Hill Encyclopedia of Science and Technology. McGraw-Hill, 1221 Avenue of the Americas, New York, New York 10020. (212) 512-2000 or (800) 262-4729. 1992. Seventh edition. Issued in multiple volumes including index. Includes all science and technology broad subject areas.

Van Nostrand's Scientific Encyclopedia. Glenn D. Considine, ed. Van Nostrand Reinhold, 115 5th Ave., New York, New York 10003. (212) 254-3232. 1983. Sixth edition. Includes all broad subject areas in science.

GENERAL WORKS

Aging and Environmental Toxicology: Biological and Behavioral Perspectives. Ralph L. Cooper, Jerome M. Goldman, and Thomas J. Harbin. Johns Hopkins University Press, 701 W. 40th St., Ste. 275, Baltimore, Maryland 21211. (410) 516-6900. 1991. Physiological aspects of adaptation.

Biologic Environmental Protection by Design. David Wann. Johnson Books, PO Box 990, Boulder, Colorado 80306. (800) 662-2665. 1990. Provides a compendium of ideas and strategies for various environmental problems.

Biomarkers of Environmental Contamination. John F. McCarthy and Lee R. Shugart. Lewis Publishers, 2000 Corporate Blvd., Boca Raton, Florida 33431. (800) 272-7737. 1990. Reviews the use of biological markers in animals and plants as an innovative approach to evaluating the ecological and physiological effects of environmental contamination.

ONLINE DATA BASES

BIOSIS Previews. BIOSIS, 2100 Arch St., Philadelphia, Pennsylvania 19103-1399. (215) 587-4800. Largest and most comprehensive database of research in the life sciences. Contains citations for nearly 9000 primary research journals, monographs, reviews, symposia, preliminary reports, semi-popular journals, selected institutional reports, government reports and research communications.

Biotechnology Abstracts. Derwent Publications Ltd., 6845 Elm St., McLean, Virginia 22101. (703) 790-0400. Includes material on genetic manipulation, biochemical engineering, fermentation, biocatalysis, cell hybridization, in vitro plant propagation and industrial waste management.

Enviro/Energyline Abstracts Plus. R. R. Bowker Co., 121 Chanlon Rd., New Providence, New Jersey 07974. (908) 464-6800.

Enviroline. R. R. Bowker Co., Bowker Electronic Publishing, 121 Chanlon Rd., New Providence, New Jersey 07974. (800) 521-8110.

Environmental Bibliography. Environmental Studies Institute, International Academy at Santa Barbara, 800 Garden St., Ste. D, Santa Barbara, California 93101. (805) 965-5010. International periodical literature dealing with environmental topics such as air pollution, water treatment, energy conservation, noise abatement, soil mechanics, wildlife preservation, and chemical wastes.

Environmental Periodicals Bibliography. National Information Services Corp., Ste. 6, Wyman Towers, 3100 St. Paul St., Baltimore, Maryland 21218. (410)243-0797. Online version of abstract of same name.

Monthly Catalog of United States Government Publications. U.S. G.P.O., Supt. of Docs., PO Box 371954, Pittsburgh, Pennsylvania 15250-7954. (202) 512-0000.

National Technical Information Service. U.S. Department of Commerce, National Technical Information Service, Office of Data Base Services, 5285 Port Royal Rd., Springfield, Virginia 22161. (703) 487-4807. Bibliographic database of government sponsored research and technical reports.

SCISEARCH. Institute for Scientific Information, University City Science Center, 3501 Market St., Philadelphia, Pennsylvania 19104. (215) 386-0100.

PERIODICALS AND NEWSLETTERS

BioScience Journal. American Institute of Biological Sciences, 730 11th Street, Nw, Washington, District of Columbia 20001-4521. (202) 628-1500. Eleven times a year. Current research, feature articles, book reviews, and new products.

Ecological Monographs. Business Office of the Ecological Society of America, Center of Environmental Studies, Arizona State University, Tempe, Arizona 85287-1201. (602) 965-3000. Quarterly. Scientific journal of ecological issues.

The Journal of Biological Chemistry. American Society of Biological Chemists, 428 E. Preston St., Baltimore, Maryland 21202. Three times a month. Biological, agricultural, and energy aspects of the environment.

RESEARCH CENTERS AND INSTITUTES

New Mexico State University, Center for Biochemical Engineering Research. Department of Chemical Engineering, Box 30001, Dept. 3805, Las Cruces, New Mexico 88003-0001. (505) 646-1214.

University of Miami, Research Collections. Department of Biology, Coral Gables, Florida 33124. (305) 284-3973.

TRADE ASSOCIATIONS AND PROFESSIONAL SOCIETIES

American Institute of Biological Sciences. 730 11th St., N.W., Washington, District of Columbia 20001-4521. (202) 628-1500.

American Institute of Biomedical Climatology. 1023 Welsh Rd., Philadelphia, Pennsylvania 19115. (215) 673-8368.

International Bio-Environmental Foundation. 15300 Ventura Blvd., Suite 405, Sherman Oaks, California 91403. (818) 907-5483.

BIOLOGICAL CONTROL

See also: INSECTS; INTEGRATED PEST MANAGEMENT; ORGANIC GARDENING AND FARMING

ABSTRACTING AND INDEXING SERVICES

AgBiotech News and Information. C. A. B. International, 845 North Park Ave., Tucson, Arizona 85719. (602) 621-7897 or (800) 528-4841. 1989-. Bimonthly. Includes news items on topics such as research, companies, products, patents, books, education, diary, people, equipment, and legal issues. Also reviews articles and conference reports. Abstracts journal articles, reports, conferences, and books. Also includes biological control, bioenvironmental interactions and stress resistance and genetics.

Applied Ecology Abstracts Studies in Renewable Natural Resources. Information Retrieval Ltd., 1911 Jefferson Davis Highway, Arlington, Virginia 22202. 1975-. Monthly.

Biodeterioration Abstracts. Farnham Royal, Slough, England SL2 3BN. Quarterly.

Biodeterioration Research Titles. Biodeterioration Information Centre, University of Aston in Birmingham, Birmingham, England

Biological Abstracts. BIOSIS, 2100 Arch St., Philadelphia, Pennsylvania 19103-1399. (215) 587-4800. 1927-.

Biological and Agricultural Index. H.W. Wilson Co., 950 University Ave., Bronx, New York 10452. (800) 367-6770. 1916-. Monthly.

Biology Digest. Data Courier, Plexus Pub Inc., 143 Old Marlton Pike, Medford, New Jersey 08055. 1974-. Monthly. Abstracts biology periodicals.

Biotechnology Research Abstracts. Cambridge Scientific Abstracts, 5161 River Rd., Bethesda, Maryland 20816. (301) 961-6750. Monthly. Includes such broad areas as genetic intervention, biochemical genetics, and microbiological techniques.

Bulletin Signaletique: Eau et Assainissement, Pollution Atmospherique, Droit des Pollutions. Centre de Documentation, Centre National de la Recherche Scientifique, 15, quai Anatole France, Paris, France 75700. (1) 45 55 92 25. 1983-. Monthly. Indexes pollution periodicals including water, atmospheric and related pollutions.

Current Advances in Ecological and Environmental Science. Pergamon Microforms International, Inc., Fairview Park, Elmsford, New York 10523. (914) 592-7720. 1989-. Monthly. Current literature searching service including journals, reports, abstracts, etc. This service is available online as part of the CABS database on the hosts BRS and ORBIT search service.

Ecological Abstracts. Geo Abstracts Ltd. Elsevier Applied Science, Crown House, Linton Rd., Barking, England IG 11 8JU. 1974-. Derived from over 600 leading ecological and environmental journals, plus books, conference proceedings, reports and theses.

Ecology Abstracts. Cambridge Scientific Abstracts, 5161 River Rd., Bethesda, Maryland 20816. (301) 961-6750. Monthly.

Environment Abstracts. Bowker A & I Publishing, 121 Chanlon Rd., New Providence, New Jersey 07974. (908) 464-6800. 1974-.

Environment Index. Environment Information Center, Index Research Department, 124 E. 39th St., New York, New York 10016. 1971-. Annual.

Environmental Information Connection–EIC. Planning Information Program, Dept. of Urban and Regional Planning, University of Illinois, 1003 West Nevada, Urbana, Illinois 61801. (217) 333-1369. Also available online.

Environmental Periodicals Bibliography. Environmental Studies Institute, International Academy at Santa Barbara, 800 Garden St., Suite D, Santa Barbara, California 93101. (805) 965-5010. Also available online.

General Science Index. H. W. Wilson Co., 950 University Ave., Bronx, New York 10452. 1978-. Monthly, also issued in annual cumulation. Cumulative subject index to English language periodicals in the subject fields of astronomy, botany, chemistry, earth science, environment and conservation, food and nutrition, genetics, mathematics, medicine and health, microbiology, oceanography, physics, physiology and zoology.

Multimedia Index to Ecology. National Information Center for Educational Media, University of Southern California, Los Angeles, California 90007.

Pollution Abstracts. Cambridge Scientific Abstracts, 5161 River Rd., Bethesda, Maryland 20816. (301) 961-6750. Six/year. Indexes worldwide technical literature on environmental pollution. Covers air pollution, marine and freshwater pollution, sewage and wastewater treatment, waste management, toxicology and health, noise pollution, radiation, land pollution, and environmental policies, programs, legislation, and education. Also available online.

Science Citation Index. Institute for Scientific Information, 3501 Market St., Philadelphia, Pennsylvania 19104. 1961-.

BIBLIOGRAPHIES

Current Contents. Agriculture, Biology and Environmental Sciences. Institute for Scientific Information, 3501 Market St., Philadelphia, Pennsylvania 19104. (800) 523-1857. 1973-. Previous title: Current Contents. Agricultural, Food & Veterinary Sciences. Gives the table of contents of periodicals in the fields of agriculture, biology, environmental and related areas.

Directory of Published Proceedings. Interdok Corp., 173 Halstead Ave., Harrison, New York 10528. (914) 835-3506. 1990. Monthly. This is a listing of published proceedings including the series SEMTE (Science/Medicine/Engineering/Technology) and the series SSH (Social Science/Humanities).

EPA Publications Bibliography. U.S. Environmental Protection Agency, Library Systems Branch, 401 M St., SW, Washington, District of Columbia 20460. (202) 260-2090. Quarterly.

Integrated Pest Management. Jayne T. Maclean. National Agricultural Library, 10301 Baltimore Blvd., Beltsville, Maryland 20705-2351. (301) 504-5755. 1985.

ENCYCLOPEDIAS AND DICTIONARIES

Cambridge Encyclopedia of Life Sciences. A. E. Friday and David S. Ingram. Cambridge University Press, 40 W 20th St., New York, New York 10011. (212) 924-3900 or (800) 227-0247. 1985. Includes all topics under biology and ecology.

Dictionary of Microbiology and Molecular Biology. Paul Singleton and Diana Sainsbury. John Wiley & Sons, Inc., 605 3rd Ave., New York, New York 10158-0012. (212) 850-6000. 1987. Second edition. Comprehensive dictionary with "classical descriptive aspects of microbiology to current developments in related areas of bioenergetics, biochemistry and molecular biology." Entries give synonyms, cross references, and references to pertinent works. Miscellaneous appendixes. Bibliography.

McGraw-Hill Encyclopedia of Environmental Science. Sybil P. Parker. McGraw-Hill Science & Engineering Books, 11 W. 19th St., New York, New York 10011. (212) 337-6010. 1980. Covers ecology, man's influence on nature, and environmental protection.

McGraw-Hill Encyclopedia of Science and Technology. McGraw-Hill, 1221 Avenue of the Americas, New York, New York 10020. (212) 512-2000 or (800) 262-4729. 1992. Seventh edition. Issued in multiple volumes including index. Includes all science and technology broad subject areas.

Van Nostrand's Scientific Encyclopedia. Glenn D. Considine, ed. Van Nostrand Reinhold, 115 5th Ave., New York, New York 10003. (212) 254-3232. 1983. Sixth edition. Includes all broad subject areas in science.

GENERAL WORKS

Biological Control by Natural Enemies. Paul Debach and David Rosen. Cambridge University Press, 40 W. 20th St., New York, New York 10011. (212) 924-3900. 1991. Second edition. Traces the historical background of biological control and examines in detail some of the most famous examples of the discovery of natural enemies and their implementation as active successful biological control agents.

Biotechnology and Food Safety. Donald D. Bills. Butterworth-Heinemann, 80 Montvale Ave., Stoneham, Massachusetts 02180. (617) 438-8464. Natural control of microorganisms, detection of microorganisms, relation of the biological control of pests to food safety, and ingredients and food safety.

Biotechnology for Biological Control of Pests and Vectors. Karl Maramorosch. CRC Press, 2000 Corporate Blvd. N.W., Boca Raton, Florida 33431. (407) 994-0555; (800) 272-7737. 1991.

Critical Issues in Biological Control. Simon Fraser, et al., eds. VCH Publishers, 303 NW 12th Ave., Deerfield Beach, Florida 33442-1788. (305) 428-5566. 1990. Analyzes the current concerns about the risks that synthetic pesticides pose to the environment and human health. As a potentially powerful forum of pest control that has few environmental disadvantages, biological control is an attractive alternative which has increased the urgency for more research into non-chemical methods of crop and food production.

Microbial Control of Weeds. David O. TeBeest, ed. Chapman & Hall, 29 W. 35th St., New York, New York 10001-2291. (212) 244-3336. 1991. Summarizes the progress that has been made over the last 20 years in the biological control of weeds.

Tortricid Pests: Their Biology, Natural Enemies, and Control. L.P.S. van der Geest. Elsevier Science Publishing Co., 655 Avenue of the Americas, New York, New York 10010. (212) 989-5800. 1991.

Treatment Technologies. Environment Protection Agency. Government Institutes, Inc., 4 Research Pl., Ste. 200, Rockville, Maryland 20850. (301)921-2300. 1991. 2nd ed. Provides a clear explanation of 24 treatment technologies and evaluates the effectiveness of the design and operations of each type of treatment. This new edition has more supporting numerical data, examples for a better understanding of the technology and an updated reference for specific industrial wastes.

HANDBOOKS AND MANUALS

Integrated Pest Management. ANR Publications, University of California, 6701 San Pablo Ave., Oakland, California 94608-1239. (510) 642-2431. 1990-. Irregular. Provides and orderly, scientifically based system for diagnosing, recording, evaluating, preventing, and treating pest problems in a variety of crops.

ONLINE DATA BASES

BIOSIS Previews. BIOSIS, 2100 Arch St., Philadelphia, Pennsylvania 19103-1399. (215) 587-4800. Largest and most comprehensive database of research in the life sciences. Contains citations for nearly 9000 primary research journals, monographs, reviews, symposia, preliminary reports, semi-popular journals, selected institutional reports, government reports and research communications.

Cambridge Scientific Abstracts Life Science–CSAL. Cambridge Scientific Abstracts, 5161 River Rd., Bethesda, Maryland 20816. (301) 961-6750. Provides access to the following abstracting services: "Life Sciences Collection," "Aquatic Sciences and Fisheries Abstracts," "Oceanic Abstracts," and "Pollution Abstracts."

Enviro/Energyline Abstracts Plus. R. R. Bowker Co., 121 Chanlon Rd., New Providence, New Jersey 07974. (908) 464-6800.

Environmental Periodicals Bibliography. National Information Services Corp., Ste. 6, Wyman Towers, 3100 St. Paul St., Baltimore, Maryland 21218. (410)243-0797. Online version of abstract of same name.

Monthly Catalog of United States Government Publications. U.S. G.P.O., Supt. of Docs., PO Box 371954, Pittsburgh, Pennsylvania 15250-7954. (202) 512-0000.

National Technical Information Service. U.S. Department of Commerce, National Technical Information Service, Office of Data Base Services, 5285 Port Royal Rd., Springfield, Virginia 22161. (703) 487-4807. Bibliographic database of government sponsored research and technical reports.

SCISEARCH. Institute for Scientific Information, University City Science Center, 3501 Market St., Philadelphia, Pennsylvania 19104. (215) 386-0100.

PERIODICALS AND NEWSLETTERS

Journal of Pesticide Science. Elsevier Science Publishing Co., Journal Information Center, 655 Avenue of the Americas, New York, New York 10010. (212) 989-5800. Quarterly. Pesticide science in general, agrochemistry and chemistry of biologically active natural products.

TRADE ASSOCIATIONS AND PROFESSIONAL SOCIETIES

American Institute of Biological Sciences. 730 11th St., N.W., Washington, District of Columbia 20001-4521. (202) 628-1500.

American Institute of Biomedical Climatology. 1023 Welsh Rd., Philadelphia, Pennsylvania 19115. (215) 673-8368.

American Society for Biochemistry and Molecular Biology. 9650 Rockville Pike, Bethesda, Maryland 20814. (301) 530-7145.

BIOLOGICAL DIVERSITY

See also: CORAL REEF ECOLOGY; ECOSYSTEMS

ABSTRACTING AND INDEXING SERVICES

Applied Ecology Abstracts Studies in Renewable Natural Resources. Information Retrieval Ltd., 1911 Jefferson Davis Highway, Arlington, Virginia 22202. 1975-. Monthly.

Aqualine Abstracts. Water Research Centre. c/o Pergamon Microforms International, Inc., Fairview Park, Elmsford, New York 10523. (914) 592-7720. 1927-. Contains some 8,000 records annually on water and wastewater technology. Covers all aspects of water, wastewater, associated engineering services and the aquatic environment. Over 600 periodicals, as well as books, reports and conference proceedings and other publications from water related institutions worldwide are scanned. Also available online.

Biological Abstracts. BIOSIS, 2100 Arch St., Philadelphia, Pennsylvania 19103-1399. (215) 587-4800. 1927-.

Biological and Agricultural Index. H.W. Wilson Co., 950 University Ave., Bronx, New York 10452. (800) 367-6770. 1916-. Monthly.

Biology Digest. Data Courier, Plexus Pub Inc., 143 Old Marlton Pike, Medford, New Jersey 08055. 1974-. Monthly. Abstracts biology periodicals.

Ecological Abstracts. Geo Abstracts Ltd. Elsevier Applied Science, Crown House, Linton Rd., Barking, England IG 11 8JU. 1974-. Derived from over 600 leading ecological and environmental journals, plus books, conference proceedings, reports and theses.

Environment Abstracts. Bowker A & I Publishing, 121 Chanlon Rd., New Providence, New Jersey 07974. (908) 464-6800. 1974-.

Environment Index. Environment Information Center, Index Research Department, 124 E. 39th St., New York, New York 10016. 1971-. Annual.

Environmental Information Connection–EIC. Planning Information Program, Dept. of Urban and Regional Planning, University of Illinois, 1003 West Nevada, Urbana, Illinois 61801. (217) 333-1369. Also available online.

Environmental Periodicals Bibliography. Environmental Studies Institute, International Academy at Santa Barbara, 800 Garden St., Suite D, Santa Barbara, California 93101. (805) 965-5010. Also available online.

General Science Index. H. W. Wilson Co., 950 University Ave., Bronx, New York 10452. 1978-. Monthly, also issued in annual cumulation. Cumulative subject index to English language periodicals in the subject fields of astronomy, botany, chemistry, earth science, environment and conservation, food and nutrition, genetics, mathematics, medicine and health, microbiology, oceanography, physics, physiology and zoology.

Multimedia Index to Ecology. National Information Center for Educational Media, University of Southern California, Los Angeles, California 90007.

ALMANACS AND YEARBOOKS

Environmental Almanac. World Resources Institute. Houghton Mifflin, 1 Beacon St., Boston, Massachusetts 02108. (617) 725-5000; (800) 225-3362. 1991. Covers consumer products, energy, endangered species, food safety, global warming, solid wastes, toxics, wetlands and other related areas. Also included are the names and addresses of the chief environmental executives for all 50 states.

BIBLIOGRAPHIES

Biological Diversity: A Selected Bibliography. Beth Clewis. Vance Bibliographies, PO Box 229, 112 N. Charter St., Monticello, Illinois 61856. (217) 762-3831. 1990.

Current Contents. Agriculture, Biology and Environmental Sciences. Institute for Scientific Information, 3501 Market St., Philadelphia, Pennsylvania 19104. (800) 523-1857. 1973-. Previous title: Current Contents. Agricultural, Food & Veterinary Sciences. Gives the table of contents of periodicals in the fields of agriculture, biology, environmental and related areas.

EPA Publications Bibliography. U.S. Environmental Protection Agency, Library Systems Branch, 401 M St., SW, Washington, District of Columbia 20460. (202) 260-2090. Quarterly.

DIRECTORIES

Coral Reefs of the World. Susan M. Wells. World Conservation Union, IUCN Publications Services Unit, 181a Huntingdon Rd., Cambridge, England CB3 0DJ. (0223) 277894. 1991. Catalogues for the first time the significant coral reefs of the world, their geographical context and ecology, their current condition and status in legislation, and prescriptions for their conservation and sustainable use.

Ecological Society of America Bulletin–Directory of Members Issue. Ecological Society of America, c/o Dr. Duncan

Patten, Center for Environmental Studies, Arizona State University, Tempe, Arizona 85287. (602) 965-3000.

ENCYCLOPEDIAS AND DICTIONARIES

Cambridge Encyclopedia of Life Sciences. A. E. Friday and David S. Ingram. Cambridge University Press, 40 W 20th St., New York, New York 10011. (212) 924-3900 or (800) 227-0247. 1985. Includes all topics under biology and ecology.

The Encyclopedia of Animal Ecology. Peter D. Moore. Facts on File, Inc., 460 Park Ave. S., New York, New York 10016. (212) 683-2244. 1987.

McGraw-Hill Encyclopedia of Environmental Science. Sybil P. Parker. McGraw-Hill Science & Engineering Books, 11 W. 19th St., New York, New York 10011. (212) 337-6010. 1980. Covers ecology, man's influence on nature, and environmental protection.

McGraw-Hill Encyclopedia of Science and Technology. McGraw-Hill, 1221 Avenue of the Americas, New York, New York 10020. (212) 512-2000 or (800) 262-4729. 1992. Seventh edition. Issued in multiple volumes including index. Includes all science and technology broad subject areas.

Van Nostrand's Scientific Encyclopedia. Glenn D. Considine, ed. Van Nostrand Reinhold, 115 5th Ave., New York, New York 10003. (212) 254-3232. 1983. Sixth edition. Includes all broad subject areas in science.

GENERAL WORKS

Ancient Forests of the Pacific Northwest. Elliot A. Norse. Island Press, 1718 Connecticut Ave. N.W., Suite 300, Washington, District of Columbia 20009. (202) 232-7933. 1990. Comprehensive assessment of the biological value of the ancient forests, information about how logging and atmospheric changes threaten the forests, and convincing arguments that replicated ecosystems are too weak to support biodiversity.

Balancing on the Brink of Extinction: The Endangered Species Act and Lessons for the Future. Kathryn A. Kohm, ed. Island Press, 1718 Connecticut Ave. N.W., Suite 300, Washington, District of Columbia 20009. (202) 232-7933. 1991. Twenty essays providing an overview of the law's conception and history and its potential for protecting the remaining endangered species.

Biodiversity. E. O. Wilson. National Academy Press, 2101 Constitution Ave. N.W., PO Box 285, Washington, District of Columbia 20418. (202) 334-3313. 1988.

Biodiversity in Sub-Saharan Africa and Its Islands. Simon N. Stuart, et al. International Union for Conservation of Nature and Natural Resources, Avenue du Mont-Blanc, Gland, Switzerland CH-1196. 1990. Contains a broadly based environmental strategy and outlines actions that are necessary at political, economic, social, ecological, biological, and developmental levels. Focuses on the conservation of wild species and natural ecosystems.

Biodiversity: Scientific Issues and Collaborative Research Proposals. Otto T. Solbrig. UNESCO, 7, place de Fontenoy, Paris, France F-75700. (331) 45 68 40 67. 1991. MAB Digest 9. Overview of key scientific issues and questions related to biological diversity and its functional significance.

Biological Conservation. David W. Ehrenfeld. Holt, Rinehart and Winston, 6277 Sea Harbor Dr., Orlando, Florida 32887. (407) 345-2500. 1970.

Comparative Analysis of Ecosystems Patterns, Mechanisms, and Theories. Jonathan Cole, ed. Springer-Verlag, 175 5th Ave., New York, New York 10010. (212) 460-1500; (800) 777-4643. 1991. Includes papers from a conference held in Milbrook, New York, 1989.

Conserving the World's Biological Diversity. Jeffrey A. McNeely, et al. World Resources Institute, 1709 New York Ave. N.W., Washington, District of Columbia 20006. (800) 822-0504. 1990. Provides a clear concise and well illustrated guide to the meaning and importance of biological diversity. Discusses a broad range of practical approaches to biodiversity preservation, including policy changes, integrated land-use management, species and habitat protection, and pollution control.

Down by the River: The Impact of Federal Water Projects and Policies on Biological Diversity. Constance Elizabeth Hunt with Verne Huser. Island Press, 1718 Connecticut Ave. N.W., Suite 300, Washington, District of Columbia 20009. (202) 232-7933. 1988. Presents case studies of development projects on seven river systems, including the Columbia, the Delaware, the Missouri, and the rivers of Maine ,to illustrate their effect on biological diversity.

Drowning the National Heritage: Climate Change and Coastal Biodiversity in the United States. Walter V. C. Reid and Mark C. Trexler. World Resources Institute, 1709 New York Ave. N.W., Washington, District of Columbia 20006. (800) 822 0504. 1991. Examines erosion, flooding, and salt-water intrusion into groundwater, rivers, bays, and estuaries as well as receding coastlines and altered coastal current and upwelling patterns. Evaluates various policy responses and recommends specific changes to protect the biological wealth of these vital ecosystems.

The Ecology and Management of Aquatic Terrestrial Ecotones. R. J. Naiman and H. Decamps, eds. Parthenon Pub., Casterton Hall, Carnforth, England LA6 2LA. 1990.

Ecology of Biological Invasions of North America and Hawaii. H. G. Baker, et al. Springer-Verlag, 175 5th Ave., New York, New York 10010. (212) 460-1500; (800) 777-4643. 1986.

Economics and Biological Diversity: Developing and Using Economic Incentives to Conserve Biological Resources. Jeffrey A. McNeely. Pinter Pub., 136 S. Broadway, Irvington, New York 10533. (914) 591-9111. 1991. Explains how economic incentives can be applied to conservation while complementing development efforts.

Elton's Ecologists: A History of the Bureau of Animal Population. Peter Crowcroft. University of Chicago Press, 5801 Ellis Ave., 4th Fl., Chicago, Illinois 60637. (312) 702-7700. 1991. The story of a smallish university department chronicles an enterprise that appreciably shaped the history of ecology during the mid-decades of the 20th century.

The Expandable Future. Richard J. Tobin. Duke University Press, College Sta., Box 6697, Durham, North Carolina 27708. (919) 684-2173. 1990. Politics and the protection of biological diversity.

GAIA: A New Look at Life on Earth. J. E. Lovelock. Oxford University Press, 200 Madison Ave., New York, New York 10016. (212) 679-7300; (800) 334-4249. 1988.

Explores the idea that life on earth functions as a single organism which actually defines and maintains conditions necessary for its survival.

Investing in Biological Diversity: U.S. Research and Conservation Efforts in Developing Countries. Janet A. Abramovitz. World Resources Institute, 1709 New York Ave. N.W., Washington, District of Columbia 20006. (800) 822-0504. 1991. Analyzes funding for 1,093 projects in 100 developing countries. Special features of the report include multiyear funding comparisons by region and country, type of conservation activity, funder, and implementor. Also examines the funding for areas identified as priorities for biodiversity conservation.

Keeping Options Alive: The Scientific Basis for Conserving Biodiversity. Walter V. C. Reid and Kenton R. Miller. World Resources Institute, 1709 New York Ave. N.W., Washington, District of Columbia 20006. (800) 822-0504. 1989. Examines the fundamental questions and recommends policies based on the best available scientific information for conserving biodiversity.

Landscape Linkages and Biodiversity. Wendy E. Hudson, ed. Island Press, 1718 Connecticut Ave. N.W., Suite 300, Washington, District of Columbia 20009. (202) 232-7933. 1991. Explains biological diversity conservation, focusing on the need for protecting large areas of the most diverse ecosystems, and connecting these ecosystems with land corridors to allow species to move among them more easily.

The Living Ocean. Boyce Thorne-Miller. Island Press, 1718 Connecticut Ave. N.W., Suite 300, Washington, District of Columbia 20009. (202) 232-7933. 1991. Discusses all marine ecosystems, including coastal benthic, shore systems, estuaries, wetlands, and coral reefs, coastal pelagic, deep-sea benthic, hydrothermal vents and others.

Magill's Survey of Science. Life Science Series. Frank N. Magill, ed. Salem Press, PO Box 50062, Pasadena, California 91105. 1991. Six volumes. Contents: v.1. A-Central and peripheral nervous system functions; v.2. Central metabolism regulation - eukaryotic transcriptional control; v.3. Positive and negative eukaryotic transcriptional control - mammalian hormones; v.4. Hormones and behavior - muscular contraction; v.5. Muscular contraction and relaxation - sexual reproduction in plants; v.6. Reproductive behavior and mating - X inactivation and the Lyon hypothesis.

On the Brink of Extinction: Conserving the Diversity of Life. Edward C. Wolf. Worldwatch Institute, 1776 Massachusetts Ave., N.W., Washington, District of Columbia 20036-1904. 1987.

Plant-Animal Interactions; Evolutionary Ecology in Tropical and Temperate Regions. Peter W. Price, et al. John Wiley & Sons, Inc., 605 3rd Ave., New York, New York 10158-0012. (212) 850-6000. 1991. Comprises a comparative analysis of the existing ecological systems of temperate and tropical regions.

Preserving the Global Environment: The Challenge of Shared Leadership. Jessica Tuchman Mathews, ed. World Resources Institute, 1709 New York Ave. N.W., Washington, District of Columbia 20006. (800) 822-0504. 1990. Includes findings on population growth, deforestation and the loss of biological diversity, the ozone layer, energy and climate change, economics, and other critical trends spell out new approaches to international cooperation and regulation in response to the shift from traditional security concerns to a focus on collective global security.

Race to Save the Tropics. Robert Goodland, ed. Island Press, 1718 Connecticut Ave. N.W., Suite 300, Washington, District of Columbia 20009. (202) 232-7933. 1990. Documents the conflict between economic development and protection of biological diversity in tropical countries.

Research Priorities for Conservation Biology. Michael E. Soulfe and Kathryn A. Kohm, eds. Island Press, 1718 Connecticut Ave. N.W., Suite 300, Washington, District of Columbia 20009. (202) 232-7933. 1989. Proposes an urgent research agenda to improve our understanding and preservation of biological diversity.

Saving America's Wildlife. Thomas R. Dunlap. Princeton University Press, 41 Williams St., Princeton, New Jersey 08540. (609) 258-4900. 1988. Explores how we have deepened our commitment to and broadened the scope of animal conservation through the 1980s.

Silent Spring. Rachel Carson. Carolina Biological Supply Company, 2700 York Rd., Burlington, North Carolina 27215. (919) 584-0381. 1987.

Species Conservation: A Population Biological Approach. A. Seitz, ed. Birkhauser Verlag, 675 Massachusetts Ave., Cambridge, Massachusetts 02139. (800) 777-4643. 1991.

Subantarctic Macquarie Island: Environment and Biology. P. M. Selkirk, et al. Cambridge University Press, 40 W. 20th St., New York, New York 10011. (212) 924-3900; (800) 227-0247. 1990. Review of environmental and biologic research on the Macquarie Island. It presents summary of studies done in the last 15 years by Australian scientists. Contains a sequence of 12 chapters that concern the island's discovery and history; situation in the Southern ocean; tectonics and geology; landforms and Quaternary history; vegetation; lakes; birds; mammals; anthropoids; microbiology; near shore environments; and human impact.

Tropical Resources: Ecology and Development. Jose I. Furtado, et al., eds. Harwood Academic Publishers, PO Box 786, Cooper Sta., New York, New York 10276. (212) 206-8900. 1990. Overview of global tropical resources, both terrestrial and aquatic. Subjects discussed include forest resources, wildlife resources, general land use, pasture resources, economic development, fisheries, marine resources, and aquaculture.

Vertebrate Ecology in Northern Neotropics. John F. Esenberg, ed. Smithsonian Institution Press, 470 L'Enfant Plaza, No. 7100, Washington, District of Columbia 20560. (800) 782-4612. 1979. Comparison of faunas found in tropical forests covering several mammalian species, including the red howler monkey, crab-eating fox, cebus monkey, and the didelphid marsupials.

Wetlands: A Threatened Landscape. Michael Williams. B. Blackwell, 3 Cambridge Ctr., Suite 208, Cambridge, Massachusetts 02142. (617) 225-0401. 1990. Explores the evolution and composition of wetlands and their physical and biological dynamics, considers the impact of agriculture, industry, urbanization, and recreation upon them, and examines what steps we are taking and what steps should be considered to manage and preserve wetlands.

Wildlife Extinction. Charles L. Cadieux. Stone Wall Pr., 1241 30th St. N.W., Washington, District of Columbia 20007. (202) 333-1860. 1991. Presents a worldwide picture of animals in danger of extinction and addresses

controversial issues such as exploding human population, the role of zoos and wildlife parks, hunting and poaching.

Wildlife, Forests, and Forestry. Malcolm L. Hunter, Jr. Prentice Hall, Rte 9W, Englewood Cliffs, New Jersey 07632. (201) 592-2000. 1990. Presents new ideas that will form the basis of forest wildlife management in years to come. It looks at the costs of managing wildlife, as well as national policies on forest wildlife management and quantitative techniques for measuring diversity.

Wildlife of the Florida Keys: A Natural History. James D. Lazell, Jr. Island Press, 1718 Connecticut Ave. N.W., Suite 300, Washington, District of Columbia 20009. (202) 232-7933. 1989. Identifies habits, behaviors, and histories of most of the species indigenous to the Keys.

Wildlife Reserves and Corridors in the Urban Environment. Lowell W. Adams. National Institute for Urban Wildlife, 10921 Trotting Ridge Way, Columbia, Maryland 21044. (301) 596-3311. 1989. Reviews the knowledge base on wildlife habitat reserves and corridors in urban and urbanizing areas. Provides guidelines and approaches to ecological landscape planning and wildlife conservation in these regions.

HANDBOOKS AND MANUALS

The Global Ecology Handbook: What You Can Do about the Environmental Crisis. Walter H. Corson, ed. The Global Tomorrow Coalition, Beacon Pr., 25 Beacon St., Boston, Massachusetts 02108-2800. (617) 742-2110. 1990. Covers environment, energy policy, population growth and other issues. It includes chapters on tropical rain forests, garbage, oceans and coasts, global warming, population growth, agriculture, biological diversity, fresh water, hazardous wastes, and environment and development.

The Official World Wildlife Fund Guide to Endangered Species of North America. David W. Lowe, ed. Beacham Publishing, Inc., 2100 S. St. NW, Washington, District of Columbia 20008. (202) 234-0877. 1990. Two volumes. Guide to endangered plants and animals. Describes 540 endangered or threatened species including their habitat, behavior and, recovery. Includes: directories of the Offices of the U.S. Fish and Wildlife Service, Offices ofthe National Marine Fisheries Service, State Heritage Programs, Bureau of Land Management Offices, National Forest Service Offices, National Wildlife Refuges, Canadian agencies, and state offices.

ONLINE DATA BASES

BIOSIS Previews. BIOSIS, 2100 Arch St., Philadelphia, Pennsylvania 19103-1399. (215) 587-4800. Largest and most comprehensive database of research in the life sciences. Contains citations for nearly 9000 primary research journals, monographs, reviews, symposia, preliminary reports, semi-popular journals, selected institutional reports, government reports and research communications.

Biotechnology Abstracts. Derwent Publications Ltd., 6845 Elm St., McLean, Virginia 22101. (703) 790-0400. Includes material on genetic manipulation, biochemical engineering, fermentation, biocatalysis, cell hybridization, in vitro plant propagation and industrial waste management.

Cambridge Scientific Abstracts Life Science–CSAL. Cambridge Scientific Abstracts, 5161 River Rd., Bethesda,

Maryland 20816. (301) 961-6750. Provides access to the following abstracting services: "Life Sciences Collection," "Aquatic Sciences and Fisheries Abstracts," "Oceanic Abstracts," and "Pollution Abstracts."

Enviro/Energyline Abstracts Plus. R. R. Bowker Co., 121 Chanlon Rd., New Providence, New Jersey 07974. (908) 464-6800.

Environmental Periodicals Bibliography. National Information Services Corp., Ste. 6, Wyman Towers, 3100 St. Paul St., Baltimore, Maryland 21218. (410)243-0797. Online version of abstract of same name.

Monthly Catalog of United States Government Publications. U.S. G.P.O., Supt. of Docs., PO Box 371954, Pittsburgh, Pennsylvania 15250-7954. (202) 512-0000.

National Technical Information Service. U.S. Department of Commerce, National Technical Information Service, Office of Data Base Services, 5285 Port Royal Rd., Springfield, Virginia 22161. (703) 487-4807. Bibliographic database of government sponsored research and technical reports.

SCISEARCH. Institute for Scientific Information, University City Science Center, 3501 Market St., Philadelphia, Pennsylvania 19104. (215) 386-0100.

PERIODICALS AND NEWSLETTERS

The American Naturalist. Americana Society of Naturalists, Business Sciences, University of Kansas, Lawrence, Kansas 66045. (913) 864-3763. Monthly. Contains information by professionals of the biological sciences.

Biological Conservation. Applied Science Publishers, 655 Avenue of the Americas, PO Box 5399, New York, New York 10163. (718) 756-6440. Quarterly. Conservation of biological and allied natural resources, plants and animals and their habitats.

Earth First! Journal in Defense of Wilderness and Biodiversity. Earth First!, PO Box 5176, Missoula, Montana 59806. Eight/year.

Ecological Monographs. Business Office of the Ecological Society of America, Center of Environmental Studies, Arizona State University, Tempe, Arizona 85287-1201. (602) 965-3000. Quarterly. Scientific journal of ecological issues.

Ecological Society of America Bulletin. Ecological Society of America, Center of Environmental Studies, Arizona State University, Tempe, Arizona 85287-1201. (602) 965-3000. Quarterly. Study of living things in relation to their environments.

Ecology. Ecological Society of America, Center of Environmental Studies, Arizona State University, Tempe, Arizona 85287-1201. (602) 965-3000. Bimonthly. Information on the study of living things.

Ecology USA. Business Publishers, Inc., 951 Pershing Dr., Silver Spring, Maryland 20910-4464. (301) 587-6300. 1972-. Biweekly. Contains all the legislation, regulation, and litigation affecting efforts to conserve and protect America's unique environmental and ecological heritage.

Ecosphere. Forum International, 91 Gregory Ln., Ste. 21, Pleasant Hill, California 94523. (510) 671-2900. Bimonthly. Eco-development, ecology, ecosystems, interface between culture-environment-tourism.

Global Ecology and Biogeography Letter. Blackwell Scientific Publications, 3 Cambridge Ctr., Suite 208, Cambridge, Massachusetts 02142. (617) 225-0401. 1991. Bimonthly. Global Ecology and Biogeography Letters is a sister publication of Journal of Biogeography and is only available with a subscription to the Journal. Provides a fast-track outlet for short research papers, news items, editorials, and book reviews. Topics related to the major scientific concerns of our present era, such as global warming, world sea-level rises, environmental acidification, development and conservation, biodiversity, and important new theories and themes in biogeography and ecology.

Human Ecology Forum. New York State College of Human Ecology, Cornell University, Martha Van Rensselaer Hall, Ithaca, New York 14853. Quarterly.

Human Factors. Human Factors Society, Publications Division, Box 1369, Santa Monica, California 90406-1369. (310) 394-1811. Bimonthly. Deals with human engineering and human factors.

International Journal of Biosocial and Medical Research. Life Sciences Press, P.O. Box 1174, Takoma, Washington 98401-1174. (206) 922-0442. Semiannual. Deals with psychological and psychobiological aspects of environments.

Journal of Biogeography. Blackwell Scientific Publications Inc., 3 Cambridge Ctr., Suite 208, Cambridge, Massachusetts 02142. (617) 225-0401.

Marine Biology. Springer-Verlag, 175 5th Ave., New York, New York 10010. (212) 461-1500; (800) 777-4643. Sixteen/year. Life in oceans and coastal waters.

RESEARCH CENTERS AND INSTITUTES

World Resources Institute. 1709 New York Ave., N.W., Washington, District of Columbia 20006. (202) 638-6300.

STATISTICS SOURCES

Global Biodiversity 1992: Status of the Earth's Living Resources. World Conservation Monitoring Centre. World Conservation Union, IUCN Publications Services Unit, 181a Huntingdon Road, Cambridge, England CB3 0DJ. (0223) 277894. Describes diversity at the genetic, species, and ecosystem levels; the trends and rates of change; "in situ" and "ex situ" management; the benefits and values of biodiversity; gap analysis for data priorities; and data requirements for monitoring.

World Resources. World Resources Institute. 1709 New York Ave., N.W., Washington, District of Columbia 20006. (202) 638-6300. Annual. Statistical and textual analysis of world's natural resources and the effects of growth-caused environmental pollution.

TRADE ASSOCIATIONS AND PROFESSIONAL SOCIETIES

American Institute of Biological Sciences. 730 11th St., N.W., Washington, District of Columbia 20001-4521. (202) 628-1500.

American Nature Study Society. 5881 Cold Brook Rd., Homer, New York 13077. (607) 749-3655.

Earth First!. PO Box 5176, Missoula, Montana 59806.

Ecological Society of America. Arizona State University, Center for Environmental Studies, Tempe, Arizona 85287. (602) 965-3000.

Elmwood Institute. P.O. Box 5805, Berkeley, California 94705. (510) 845-4595.

Sierra Club. 100 Bush St., San Francisco, California 94104. (415) 291-1600.

BIOLOGICAL INDICATORS

ABSTRACTING AND INDEXING SERVICES

Applied Ecology Abstracts Studies in Renewable Natural Resources. Information Retrieval Ltd., 1911 Jefferson Davis Highway, Arlington, Virginia 22202. 1975-. Monthly.

Aqualine Abstracts. Water Research Centre. c/o Pergamon Microforms International, Inc., Fairview Park, Elmsford, New York 10523. (914) 592-7720. 1927-. Contains some 8,000 records annually on water and wastewater technology. Covers all aspects of water, wastewater, associated engineering services and the aquatic environment. Over 600 periodicals, as well as books, reports and conference proceedings and other publications from water related institutions worldwide are scanned. Also available online.

Biological Abstracts. BIOSIS, 2100 Arch St., Philadelphia, Pennsylvania 19103-1399. (215) 587-4800. 1927-.

Biological and Agricultural Index. H.W. Wilson Co., 950 University Ave., Bronx, New York 10452. (800) 367-6770. 1916-. Monthly.

Biology Digest. Data Courier, Plexus Pub Inc., 143 Old Marlton Pike, Medford, New Jersey 08055. 1974-. Monthly. Abstracts biology periodicals.

Environment Abstracts. Bowker A & I Publishing, 121 Chanlon Rd., New Providence, New Jersey 07974. (908) 464-6800. 1974-.

Environment Index. Environment Information Center, Index Research Department, 124 E. 39th St., New York, New York 10016. 1971-. Annual.

Environmental Information Connection–EIC. Planning Information Program, Dept. of Urban and Regional Planning, University of Illinois, 1003 West Nevada, Urbana, Illinois 61801. (217) 333-1369. Also available online.

Environmental Periodicals Bibliography. Environmental Studies Institute, International Academy at Santa Barbara, 800 Garden St., Suite D, Santa Barbara, California 93101. (805) 965-5010. Also available online.

General Science Index. H. W. Wilson Co., 950 University Ave., Bronx, New York 10452. 1978-. Monthly, also issued in annual cumulation. Cumulative subject index to English language periodicals in the subject fields of astronomy, botany, chemistry, earth science, environment and conservation, food and nutrition, genetics, mathematics, medicine and health, microbiology, oceanography, physics, physiology and zoology.

Multimedia Index to Ecology. National Information Center for Educational Media, University of Southern California, Los Angeles, California 90007.

BIBLIOGRAPHIES

Current Contents. Agriculture, Biology and Environmental Sciences. Institute for Scientific Information, 3501 Market St., Philadelphia, Pennsylvania 19104. (800) 523-1857. 1973-. Previous title: Current Contents. Agricultural, Food & Veterinary Sciences. Gives the table of contents of periodicals in the fields of agriculture, biology, environmental and related areas.

EPA Publications Bibliography. U.S. Environmental Protection Agency, Library Systems Branch, 401 M St., SW, Washington, District of Columbia 20460. (202) 260-2090. Quarterly.

ENCYCLOPEDIAS AND DICTIONARIES

Cambridge Encyclopedia of Life Sciences. A. E. Friday and David S. Ingram. Cambridge University Press, 40 W 20th St., New York, New York 10011. (212) 924-3900 or (800) 227-0247. 1985. Includes all topics under biology and ecology.

McGraw-Hill Encyclopedia of Environmental Science. Sybil P. Parker. McGraw-Hill Science & Engineering Books, 11 W. 19th St., New York, New York 10011. (212) 337-6010. 1980. Covers ecology, man's influence on nature, and environmental protection.

McGraw-Hill Encyclopedia of Science and Technology. McGraw-Hill, 1221 Avenue of the Americas, New York, New York 10020. (212) 512-2000 or (800) 262-4729. 1992. Seventh edition. Issued in multiple volumes including index. Includes all science and technology broad subject areas.

ONLINE DATA BASES

BIOSIS Previews. BIOSIS, 2100 Arch St., Philadelphia, Pennsylvania 19103-1399. (215) 587-4800. Largest and most comprehensive database of research in the life sciences. Contains citations for nearly 9000 primary research journals, monographs, reviews, symposia, preliminary reports, semi-popular journals, selected institutional reports, government reports and research communications.

Enviro/Energyline Abstracts Plus. R. R. Bowker Co., 121 Chanlon Rd., New Providence, New Jersey 07974. (908) 464-6800.

Environmental Periodicals Bibliography. National Information Services Corp., Ste. 6, Wyman Towers, 3100 St. Paul St., Baltimore, Maryland 21218. (410)243-0797. Online version of abstract of same name.

Monthly Catalog of United States Government Publications. U.S. G.P.O., Supt. of Docs., PO Box 371954, Pittsburgh, Pennsylvania 15250-7954. (202) 512-0000.

National Technical Information Service. U.S. Department of Commerce, National Technical Information Service, Office of Data Base Services, 5285 Port Royal Rd., Springfield, Virginia 22161. (703) 487-4807. Bibliographic database of government sponsored research and technical reports.

SCISEARCH. Institute for Scientific Information, University City Science Center, 3501 Market St., Philadelphia, Pennsylvania 19104. (215) 386-0100.

BIOLOGICAL OXIDATION

ABSTRACTING AND INDEXING SERVICES

Applied Ecology Abstracts Studies in Renewable Natural Resources. Information Retrieval Ltd., 1911 Jefferson Davis Highway, Arlington, Virginia 22202. 1975-. Monthly.

Biodeterioration Abstracts. Farnham Royal, Slough, England SL2 3BN. Quarterly.

Biodeterioration Research Titles. Biodeterioration Information Centre, University of Aston in Birmingham, Birmingham, England

Biological Abstracts. BIOSIS, 2100 Arch St., Philadelphia, Pennsylvania 19103-1399. (215) 587-4800. 1927-.

Biological and Agricultural Index. H.W. Wilson Co., 950 University Ave., Bronx, New York 10452. (800) 367-6770. 1916-. Monthly.

Biology Digest. Data Courier, Plexus Pub Inc., 143 Old Marlton Pike, Medford, New Jersey 08055. 1974-. Monthly. Abstracts biology periodicals.

Current Advances in Ecological and Environmental Science. Pergamon Microforms International, Inc., Fairview Park, Elmsford, New York 10523. (914) 592-7720. 1989-. Monthly. Current literature searching service including journals, reports, abstracts, etc. This service is available online as part of the CABS database on the hosts BRS and ORBIT search service.

Ecological Abstracts. Geo Abstracts Ltd. Elsevier Applied Science, Crown House, Linton Rd., Barking, England IG 11 8JU. 1974-. Derived from over 600 leading ecological and environmental journals, plus books, conference proceedings, reports and theses.

Environment Abstracts. Bowker A & I Publishing, 121 Chanlon Rd., New Providence, New Jersey 07974. (908) 464-6800. 1974-.

Environment Index. Environment Information Center, Index Research Department, 124 E. 39th St., New York, New York 10016. 1971-. Annual.

Environmental Information Connection-EIC. Planning Information Program, Dept. of Urban and Regional Planning, University of Illinois, 1003 West Nevada, Urbana, Illinois 61801. (217) 333-1369. Also available online.

Environmental Periodicals Bibliography. Environmental Studies Institute, International Academy at Santa Barbara, 800 Garden St., Suite D, Santa Barbara, California 93101. (805) 965-5010. Also available online.

Multimedia Index to Ecology. National Information Center for Educational Media, University of Southern California, Los Angeles, California 90007.

Pollution Abstracts. Cambridge Scientific Abstracts, 5161 River Rd., Bethesda, Maryland 20816. (301) 961-6750. Six/year. Indexes worldwide technical literature on environmental pollution. Covers air pollution, marine and freshwater pollution, sewage and wastewater treatment, waste management, toxicology and health, noise pollution, radiation, land pollution, and environmental policies, programs, legislation, and education. Also available online.

BIBLIOGRAPHIES

Current Contents. Agriculture, Biology and Environmental Sciences. Institute for Scientific Information, 3501 Market St., Philadelphia, Pennsylvania 19104. (800) 523-1857. 1973-. Previous title: Current Contents. Agricultural, Food & Veterinary Sciences. Gives the table of contents of periodicals in the fields of agriculture, biology, environmental and related areas.

EPA Publications Bibliography. U.S. Environmental Protection Agency, Library Systems Branch, 401 M St., SW, Washington, District of Columbia 20460. (202) 260-2090. Quarterly.

ENCYCLOPEDIAS AND DICTIONARIES

Cambridge Encyclopedia of Life Sciences. A. E. Friday and David S. Ingram. Cambridge University Press, 40 W 20th St., New York, New York 10011. (212) 924-3900 or (800) 227-0247. 1985. Includes all topics under biology and ecology.

McGraw-Hill Encyclopedia of Environmental Science. Sybil P. Parker. McGraw-Hill Science & Engineering Books, 11 W. 19th St., New York, New York 10011. (212) 337-6010. 1980. Covers ecology, man's influence on nature, and environmental protection.

ONLINE DATA BASES

BIOSIS Previews. BIOSIS, 2100 Arch St., Philadelphia, Pennsylvania 19103-1399. (215) 587-4800. Largest and most comprehensive database of research in the life sciences. Contains citations for nearly 9000 primary research journals, monographs, reviews, symposia, preliminary reports, semi-popular journals, selected institutional reports, government reports and research communications.

Biotechnology Abstracts. Derwent Publications Ltd., 6845 Elm St., McLean, Virginia 22101. (703) 790-0400. Includes material on genetic manipulation, biochemical engineering, fermentation, biocatalysis, cell hybridization, in vitro plant propagation and industrial waste management.

Cambridge Scientific Abstracts Life Science-CSAL. Cambridge Scientific Abstracts, 5161 River Rd., Bethesda, Maryland 20816. (301) 961-6750. Provides access to the following abstracting services: "Life Sciences Collection," "Aquatic Sciences and Fisheries Abstracts," "Oceanic Abstracts," and "Pollution Abstracts."

Enviro/Energyline Abstracts Plus. R. R. Bowker Co., 121 Chanlon Rd., New Providence, New Jersey 07974. (908) 464-6800.

Environmental Periodicals Bibliography. National Information Services Corp., Ste. 6, Wyman Towers, 3100 St. Paul St., Baltimore, Maryland 21218. (410)243-0797. Online version of abstract of same name.

SCISEARCH. Institute for Scientific Information, University City Science Center, 3501 Market St., Philadelphia, Pennsylvania 19104. (215) 386-0100.

BIOLOGICAL OXYGEN DEMAND (BOD)

See also: AQUATIC ECOSYSTEMS; EUTROPHICATION; FISH AND FISHERIES; WATER QUALITY

ABSTRACTING AND INDEXING SERVICES

Applied Ecology Abstracts Studies in Renewable Natural Resources. Information Retrieval Ltd., 1911 Jefferson Davis Highway, Arlington, Virginia 22202. 1975-. Monthly.

Biological Abstracts. BIOSIS, 2100 Arch St., Philadelphia, Pennsylvania 19103-1399. (215) 587-4800. 1927-.

Biological and Agricultural Index. H.W. Wilson Co., 950 University Ave., Bronx, New York 10452. (800) 367-6770. 1916-. Monthly.

Biology Digest. Data Courier, Plexus Pub Inc., 143 Old Marlton Pike, Medford, New Jersey 08055. 1974-. Monthly. Abstracts biology periodicals.

Current Advances in Ecological and Environmental Science. Pergamon Microforms International, Inc., Fairview Park, Elmsford, New York 10523. (914) 592-7720. 1989-. Monthly. Current literature searching service including-journals, reports, abstracts, etc. This service is available online as part of the CABS database on the hosts BRS and ORBIT search service.

Ecological Abstracts. Geo Abstracts Ltd. Elsevier Applied Science, Crown House, Linton Rd., Barking, England IG 11 8JU. 1974-. Derived from over 600 leading ecological and environmental journals, plus books, conference proceedings, reports and theses.

Environment Abstracts. Bowker A & I Publishing, 121 Chanlon Rd., New Providence, New Jersey 07974. (908) 464-6800. 1974-.

Environment Index. Environment Information Center, Index Research Department, 124 E. 39th St., New York, New York 10016. 1971-. Annual.

Environmental Information Connection–EIC. Planning Information Program, Dept. of Urban and Regional Planning, University of Illinois, 1003 West Nevada, Urbana, Illinois 61801. (217) 333-1369. Also available online.

Environmental Periodicals Bibliography. Environmental Studies Institute, International Academy at Santa Barbara, 800 Garden St., Suite D, Santa Barbara, California 93101. (805) 965-5010. Also available online.

Multimedia Index to Ecology. National Information Center for Educational Media, University of Southern California, Los Angeles, California 90007.

BIBLIOGRAPHIES

EPA Publications Bibliography. U.S. Environmental Protection Agency, Library Systems Branch, 401 M St., SW, Washington, District of Columbia 20460. (202) 260-2090. Quarterly.

ENCYCLOPEDIAS AND DICTIONARIES

McGraw-Hill Encyclopedia of Environmental Science. Sybil P. Parker. McGraw-Hill Science & Engineering Books, 11 W. 19th St., New York, New York 10011. (212) 337-6010. 1980. Covers ecology, man's influence on nature, and environmental protection.

McGraw-Hill Encyclopedia of Science and Technology. McGraw-Hill, 1221 Avenue of the Americas, New York, New York 10020. (212) 512-2000 or (800) 262-4729. 1992. Seventh edition. Issued in multiple volumes in-cluding index. Includes all science and technology broad subject areas.

Van Nostrand's Scientific Encyclopedia. Glenn D. Considine, ed. Van Nostrand Reinhold, 115 5th Ave., New York, New York 10003. (212) 254-3232. 1983. Sixth edition. Includes all broad subject areas in science.

ONLINE DATA BASES

BIOSIS Previews. BIOSIS, 2100 Arch St., Philadelphia, Pennsylvania 19103-1399. (215) 587-4800. Largest and most comprehensive database of research in the life sciences. Contains citations for nearly 9000 primary research journals, monographs, reviews, symposia, preliminary reports, semi-popular journals, selected institutional reports, government reports and research communications.

Enviro/Energyline Abstracts Plus. R. R. Bowker Co., 121 Chanlon Rd., New Providence, New Jersey 07974. (908) 464-6800.

Environmental Periodicals Bibliography. National Information Services Corp., Ste. 6, Wyman Towers, 3100 St. Paul St., Baltimore, Maryland 21218. (410)243-0797. Online version of abstract of same name.

SCISEARCH. Institute for Scientific Information, University City Science Center, 3501 Market St., Philadelphia, Pennsylvania 19104. (215) 386-0100.

RESEARCH CENTERS AND INSTITUTES

St. Joseph's University, Organic Synthesis Research Laboratory. 5600 City Ave., Philadelphia, Pennsylvania 19131. (215) 660-1788.

BIOLOGICAL PURIFICATION

See: BIOLOGICAL TREATMENT

BIOLOGICAL TREATMENT

See also: WASTEWATER TREATMENT

ABSTRACTING AND INDEXING SERVICES

Applied Ecology Abstracts Studies in Renewable Natural Resources. Information Retrieval Ltd., 1911 Jefferson Davis Highway, Arlington, Virginia 22202. 1975-. Monthly.

Aqualine Abstracts. Water Research Centre. c/o Pergamon Microforms International, Inc., Fairview Park, Elmsford, New York 10523. (914) 592-7720. 1927-. Contains some 8,000 records annually on water and wastewater technology. Covers all aspects of water, wastewater, associated engineering services and the aquatic environment. Over 600 periodicals, as well as books, reports and conference proceedings and other publications from water related institutions worldwide are scanned. Also available online.

Biodeterioration Abstracts. Farnham Royal, Slough, England SL2 3BN. Quarterly.

Biodeterioration Research Titles. Biodeterioration Information Centre, University of Aston in Birmingham, Birmingham, England

Biological Abstracts. BIOSIS, 2100 Arch St., Philadelphia, Pennsylvania 19103-1399. (215) 587-4800. 1927-.

Biological and Agricultural Index. H.W. Wilson Co., 950 University Ave., Bronx, New York 10452. (800) 367-6770. 1916-. Monthly.

Biology Digest. Data Courier, Plexus Pub Inc., 143 Old Marlton Pike, Medford, New Jersey 08055. 1974-. Monthly. Abstracts biology periodicals.

Bulletin Signaletique: Eau et Assainissement, Pollution Atmospherique, Droit des Pollutions. Centre de Documentation, Centre National de la Recherche Scientifique, 15, quai Anatole France, Paris, France 75700. (1) 45 55 92 25. 1983-. Monthly. Indexes pollution periodicals including water, atmospheric and related pollutions.

Civil Engineering Hydraulic Abstracts. BHRA Fluid Engineering, Air Science Co., PO Box 143, Corning, New York 14830. (607) 962-5591. Monthly. Abstracts of periodicals that publish in the areas of hydraulic engineering and other related topics.

Current Advances in Ecological and Environmental Science. Pergamon Microforms International, Inc., Fairview Park, Elmsford, New York 10523. (914) 592-7720. 1989-. Monthly. Current literature searching service includingjournals, reports, abstracts, etc. This service is available online as part of the CABS database on the hosts BRS and ORBIT search service.

Ecological Abstracts. Geo Abstracts Ltd. Elsevier Applied Science, Crown House, Linton Rd., Barking, England IG 11 8JU. 1974-. Derived from over 600 leading ecological and environmental journals, plus books, conference proceedings, reports and theses.

Environment Abstracts. Bowker A & I Publishing, 121 Chanlon Rd., New Providence, New Jersey 07974. (908) 464-6800. 1974-.

Environment Index. Environment Information Center, Index Research Department, 124 E. 39th St., New York, New York 10016. 1971-. Annual.

Environmental Information Connection–EIC. Planning Information Program, Dept. of Urban and Regional Planning, University of Illinois, 1003 West Nevada, Urbana, Illinois 61801. (217) 333-1369. Also available online.

Environmental Periodicals Bibliography. Environmental Studies Institute, International Academy at Santa Barbara, 800 Garden St., Suite D, Santa Barbara, California 93101. (805) 965-5010. Also available online.

General Science Index. H. W. Wilson Co., 950 University Ave., Bronx, New York 10452. 1978-. Monthly, also issued in annual cumulation. Cumulative subject index to English language periodicals in the subject fields of astronomy, botany, chemistry, earth science, environment and conservation, food and nutrition, genetics, mathematics, medicine and health, microbiology, oceanography, physics, physiology and zoology.

Index to Scientific Book Contents. Institute for Scientific Information, 3501 Market St., Philadelphia, Pennsylvania 19104. (800) 523-1857. 1985-. Annual. Gives contents of science books published.

Multimedia Index to Ecology. National Information Center for Educational Media, University of Southern California, Los Angeles, California 90007.

Pollution Abstracts. Cambridge Scientific Abstracts, 5161 River Rd., Bethesda, Maryland 20816. (301) 961-6750. Six/year. Indexes worldwide technical literature on environmental pollution. Covers air pollution, marine and freshwater pollution, sewage and wastewater treatment, waste management, toxicology and health, noise pollution, radiation, land pollution, and environmental policies, programs, legislation, and education. Also available online.

Science Citation Index. Institute for Scientific Information, 3501 Market St., Philadelphia, Pennsylvania 19104. 1961-.

BIBLIOGRAPHIES

Current Contents. Agriculture, Biology and Environmental Sciences. Institute for Scientific Information, 3501 Market St., Philadelphia, Pennsylvania 19104. (800) 523-1857. 1973-. Previous title: Current Contents. Agricultural, Food & Veterinary Sciences. Gives the table of contents of periodicals in the fields of agriculture, biology, environmental and related areas.

Directory of Published Proceedings. Interdok Corp., 173 Halstead Ave., Harrison, New York 10528. (914) 835-3506. 1990. Monthly. This is a listing of published proceedings including the series SEMTE (Science/Medicine/Engineering/Technology) and the series SSH (Social Science/Humanities).

EPA Publications Bibliography. U.S. Environmental Protection Agency, Library Systems Branch, 401 M St., SW, Washington, District of Columbia 20460. (202) 260-2090. Quarterly.

ENCYCLOPEDIAS AND DICTIONARIES

McGraw-Hill Encyclopedia of Environmental Science. Sybil P. Parker. McGraw-Hill Science & Engineering Books, 11 W. 19th St., New York, New York 10011. (212) 337-6010. 1980. Covers ecology, man's influence on nature, and environmental protection.

McGraw-Hill Encyclopedia of Science and Technology. McGraw-Hill, 1221 Avenue of the Americas, New York, New York 10020. (212) 512-2000 or (800) 262-4729. 1992. Seventh edition. Issued in multiple volumes including index. Includes all science and technology broad subject areas.

Van Nostrand's Scientific Encyclopedia. Glenn D. Considine, ed. Van Nostrand Reinhold, 115 5th Ave., New York, New York 10003. (212) 254-3232. 1983. Sixth edition. Includes all broad subject areas in science.

GENERAL WORKS

Forest Industry Wastewaters Biological Treatment. A. A. O. Luonsi and P. K. Rantala, eds. Pergamon Microforms International, Inc., Fairview Park, Elmsford, New York 10523. (914) 592-7720. 1988. First volume of the proceedings of an IAWPRC Symposium held at the University of Technology, Finland, June 9-12, 1987. Includes a wide range of research and practical results in the field of biological treatment of various pulp and paper mill effluents and sludges. Includes reports from various parts of the world including discussions on the choice of internal and external measures in pollution control.

TAPPI Environmental Conference Proceedings, Seattle, WA, April 9-11, 1990. TAPPI Press, Technology Park/ Atlanta, PO Box 105113, Atlanta, Georgia 30348. (404) 446-1400. 1990. Contains 11 papers presented at the conference covering industrial pollution and its remedies.

Toxicity Reduction in Industrial Effluents. Perry W. Lanford, et al. Van Nostrand Reinhold, 115 5th Ave., New York, New York 10003. (212) 254-3232. 1990. Overview of aquatic toxicology and toxicity reduction. Specific treatment technologies that can be used to reduce toxicity, such as aerobic and anaerobic biological treatment, air and steam stripping of volatile organics, granulated carbon absorption, powdered activated carbon treatment and chemical oxidation, are discussed in detail.

HANDBOOKS AND MANUALS

Water Treatment Handbook. Degremont s.a., 184, ave. du 18-Juin-1940, Rueil-Malmaison, France F-92500. 1991. Sixth edition. Part 1 is a general survey of water and its action on the materials with which it comes into contact, and theoretical principles of separation and correction processes used in water treatment. Part 2 describes the process and the treatment plant beginning with the separation process.

ONLINE DATA BASES

Enviro/Energyline Abstracts Plus. R. R. Bowker Co., 121 Chanlon Rd., New Providence, New Jersey 07974. (908) 464-6800.

Environmental Periodicals Bibliography. National Information Services Corp., Ste. 6, Wyman Towers, 3100 St. Paul St., Baltimore, Maryland 21218. (410)243-0797. Online version of abstract of same name.

Monthly Catalog of United States Government Publications. U.S. G.P.O., Supt. of Docs., PO Box 371954, Pittsburgh, Pennsylvania 15250-7954. (202) 512-0000.

National Technical Information Service. U.S. Department of Commerce, National Technical Information Service, Office of Data Base Services, 5285 Port Royal Rd., Springfield, Virginia 22161. (703) 487-4807. Bibliographic database of government sponsored research and technical reports.

PressNet Environmental Reports. Chemical Information Systems, Inc., 7215 York Rd., Baltimore, Maryland 21212. (301) 321-8440.

SCISEARCH. Institute for Scientific Information, University City Science Center, 3501 Market St., Philadelphia, Pennsylvania 19104. (215) 386-0100.

PERIODICALS AND NEWSLETTERS

Analytical Biochemistry. Academic Press, 111 Fifth Ave., New York, New York 10003. (800) 346-8648. Covers biological and chemical topics relating to the environment.

The Bioremediation Report. Bioremediation Report, 2330 Circadian Way, Santa Rosa, California 95407. (707) 576-6222. Monthly. Devoted solely to new technical and business developments in the field of bioremediation. Incudes profiles of companies that are applying bioremediation successfully; articles on technologies; a calendar of forthcoming meetings; and summaries of recent developments.

Bioresource Technology. Elsevier Science Publishing Co., 655 Avenue of the Americas, New York, New York 10010. (212) 989-5800. Monthly. Disseminates knowledge in the related areas of biomass, biological waste treatment, bioscience systems analysis and in the technologies associated with production or conversion.

The Journal of Biological Chemistry. American Society of Biological Chemists, 428 E. Preston St., Baltimore, Maryland 21202. Three times a month. Biological, agricultural, and energy aspects of the environment.

RESEARCH CENTERS AND INSTITUTES

Lehigh University, Bioprocessing Institute. 111 Research Drive, Mountaintop Campus, Bethlehem, Pennsylvania 18015. (215) 758-4258.

TRADE ASSOCIATIONS AND PROFESSIONAL SOCIETIES

American Institute of Biological Sciences. 730 11th St., N.W., Washington, District of Columbia 20001-4521. (202) 628-1500.

BIOLUMINESCENCE

See: MARINE ENVIRONMENT AND ECOSYSTEMS

BIOMARKER

See also: BIOMONITORING; ENVIRONMENTAL QUALITY; POLLUTION CONTROL

ABSTRACTING AND INDEXING SERVICES

Applied Ecology Abstracts Studies in Renewable Natural Resources. Information Retrieval Ltd., 1911 Jefferson Davis Highway, Arlington, Virginia 22202. 1975-. Monthly.

Biological Abstracts. BIOSIS, 2100 Arch St., Philadelphia, Pennsylvania 19103-1399. (215) 587-4800. 1927-.

Biological and Agricultural Index. H.W. Wilson Co., 950 University Ave., Bronx, New York 10452. (800) 367-6770. 1916-. Monthly.

Biology Digest. Data Courier, Plexus Pub Inc., 143 Old Marlton Pike, Medford, New Jersey 08055. 1974-. Monthly. Abstracts biology periodicals.

Current Advances in Ecological and Environmental Science. Pergamon Microforms International, Inc., Fairview Park, Elmsford, New York 10523. (914) 592-7720. 1989-. Monthly. Current literature searching service includingjournals, reports, abstracts, etc. This service is available online as part of the CABS database on the hosts BRS and ORBIT search service.

Ecological Abstracts. Geo Abstracts Ltd. Elsevier Applied Science, Crown House, Linton Rd., Barking, England IG 11 8JU. 1974-. Derived from over 600 leading ecological and environmental journals, plus books, conference proceedings, reports and theses.

Environment Abstracts. Bowker A & I Publishing, 121 Chanlon Rd., New Providence, New Jersey 07974. (908) 464-6800. 1974-.

Environment Index. Environment Information Center, Index Research Department, 124 E. 39th St., New York, New York 10016. 1971-. Annual.

Environmental Information Connection–EIC. Planning Information Program, Dept. of Urban and Regional Planning, University of Illinois, 1003 West Nevada, Urbana, Illinois 61801. (217) 333-1369. Also available online.

Environmental Periodicals Bibliography. Environmental Studies Institute, International Academy at Santa Barbara, 800 Garden St., Suite D, Santa Barbara, California 93101. (805) 965-5010. Also available online.

General Science Index. H. W. Wilson Co., 950 University Ave., Bronx, New York 10452. 1978-. Monthly, also issued in annual cumulation. Cumulative subject index to English language periodicals in the subject fields of astronomy, botany, chemistry, earth science, environment and conservation, food and nutrition, genetics, mathematics, medicine and health, microbiology, oceanography, physics, physiology and zoology.

Index to Scientific Book Contents. Institute for Scientific Information, 3501 Market St., Philadelphia, Pennsylvania 19104. (800) 523-1857. 1985-. Annual. Gives contents of science books published.

Multimedia Index to Ecology. National Information Center for Educational Media, University of Southern California, Los Angeles, California 90007.

Science Citation Index. Institute for Scientific Information, 3501 Market St., Philadelphia, Pennsylvania 19104. 1961-.

BIBLIOGRAPHIES

Bibliography and Index of Geology. American Geological Institute, 4220 King St., Alexandria, Virginia 22302. Monthly. Includes environmental geology and hydrogeology.

Current Contents. Agriculture, Biology and Environmental Sciences. Institute for Scientific Information, 3501 Market St., Philadelphia, Pennsylvania 19104. (800) 523-1857. 1973-. Previous title: Current Contents. Agricultural, Food & Veterinary Sciences. Gives the table of contents of periodicals in the fields of agriculture, biology, environmental and related areas.

Directory of Published Proceedings. Interdok Corp., 173 Halstead Ave., Harrison, New York 10528. (914) 835-3506. 1990. Monthly. This is a listing of published proceedings including the series SEMTE (Science/Medicine/Engineering/Technology) and the series SSH (Social Science/Humanities).

EPA Publications Bibliography. U.S. Environmental Protection Agency, Library Systems Branch, 401 M St., SW, Washington, District of Columbia 20460. (202) 260-2090. Quarterly.

ENCYCLOPEDIAS AND DICTIONARIES

Cambridge Encyclopedia of Life Sciences. A. E. Friday and David S. Ingram. Cambridge University Press, 40 W 20th St., New York, New York 10011. (212) 924-3900 or

(800) 227-0247. 1985. Includes all topics under biology and ecology.

McGraw-Hill Encyclopedia of Environmental Science. Sybil P. Parker. McGraw-Hill Science & Engineering Books, 11 W. 19th St., New York, New York 10011. (212) 337-6010. 1980. Covers ecology, man's influence on nature, and environmental protection.

Van Nostrand's Scientific Encyclopedia. Glenn D. Considine, ed. Van Nostrand Reinhold, 115 5th Ave., New York, New York 10003. (212) 254-3232. 1983. Sixth edition. Includes all broad subject areas in science.

GENERAL WORKS

Biologic Markers of Air-Pollution Stress and Damage in Forests. National Academy Press, 2101 Constitution Ave, NW, PO Box 285, Washington, District of Columbia 20418. (202) 334-3313. 1989.

Biomarkers, Genetics, and Cancer. Hoda Anton-Guirgis. Van Nostrand Reinhold, 115 5th Ave., New York, New York 10003. (212) 254-3232. 1985. Covers genetic markers and familial & genetic neoplasms.

Biomarkers of Environmental Contamination. John F. McCarthy and Lee R. Shugart. Lewis Publishers, 2000 Corporate Blvd., Boca Raton, Florida 33431. (800) 272-7737. 1990. Reviews the use of biological markers in animals and plants as an innovative approach to evaluating the ecological and physiological effects of environmental contamination.

Biomarkers: The 10 Determinants of Aging You Can Control. William Evans. Simon & Schuster, 1230 Avenue of the Americas, New York, New York 10020. (212) 689-7000. 1991. Covers longevity, aging and health.

Geochemical Biomarkers. T. F. Yen. Hardwood Academic Publishers, PO Box 786, Cooper Station, New York, New York 10276. (212) 206-8900. 1988. Topics in organic geochemistry and biological markers.

Magill's Survey of Science. Earth Science Series. Frank N. Magill. Salem Press, PO Box 50062, Pasadena, California 91105. 1990-. Five volumes. Includes information on earth's crust, hot spots and volcanic island chains, physical properties of minerals, rock magnetism, physical properties of rocks, and index.

ONLINE DATA BASES

BIOSIS Previews. BIOSIS, 2100 Arch St., Philadelphia, Pennsylvania 19103-1399. (215) 587-4800. Largest and most comprehensive database of research in the life sciences. Contains citations for nearly 9000 primary research journals, monographs, reviews, symposia, preliminary reports, semi-popular journals, selected institutional reports, government reports and research communications.

Biotechnology Abstracts. Derwent Publications Ltd., 6845 Elm St., McLean, Virginia 22101. (703) 790-0400. Includes material on genetic manipulation, biochemical engineering, fermentation, biocatalysis, cell hybridization, in vitro plant propagation and industrial waste management.

Enviro/Energyline Abstracts Plus. R. R. Bowker Co., 121 Chanlon Rd., New Providence, New Jersey 07974. (908) 464-6800.

Environmental Periodicals Bibliography. National Information Services Corp., Ste. 6, Wyman Towers, 3100 St. Paul St., Baltimore, Maryland 21218. (410)243-0797. Online version of abstract of same name.

Monthly Catalog of United States Government Publications. U.S. G.P.O., Supt. of Docs., PO Box 371954, Pittsburgh, Pennsylvania 15250-7954. (202) 512-0000.

National Technical Information Service. U.S. Department of Commerce, National Technical Information Service, Office of Data Base Services, 5285 Port Royal Rd., Springfield, Virginia 22161. (703) 487-4807. Bibliographic database of government sponsored research and technical reports.

SCISEARCH. Institute for Scientific Information, University City Science Center, 3501 Market St., Philadelphia, Pennsylvania 19104. (215) 386-0100.

PERIODICALS AND NEWSLETTERS

Analytical Biochemistry. Academic Press, 111 Fifth Ave., New York, New York 10003. (800) 346-8648. Covers biological and chemical topics relating to the environment.

TRADE ASSOCIATIONS AND PROFESSIONAL SOCIETIES

American Institute of Biological Sciences. 730 11th St., N.W., Washington, District of Columbia 20001-4521. (202) 628-1500.

BIOMASS

See also: AGRICULTURE; ECOSYSTEMS; FUELS; NUTRITION; POWER GENERATION

ABSTRACTING AND INDEXING SERVICES

Applied Ecology Abstracts Studies in Renewable Natural Resources. Information Retrieval Ltd., 1911 Jefferson Davis Highway, Arlington, Virginia 22202. 1975-. Monthly.

ASFA Aquaculture Abstracts. Cambridge Scientific Abstracts, Inc., 5161 River Rd., Bethesda, Maryland 20816. (301) 961-6750. 1984.

Biological Abstracts. BIOSIS, 2100 Arch St., Philadelphia, Pennsylvania 19103-1399. (215) 587-4800. 1927-.

Biological and Agricultural Index. H.W. Wilson Co., 950 University Ave., Bronx, New York 10452. (800) 367-6770. 1916-. Monthly.

Biology Digest. Data Courier, Plexus Pub Inc., 143 Old Marlton Pike, Medford, New Jersey 08055. 1974-. Monthly. Abstracts biology periodicals.

Biotechnology Research Abstracts. Cambridge Scientific Abstracts, 5161 River Rd., Bethesda, Maryland 20816. (301) 961-6750. Monthly. Includes such broad areas as genetic intervention, biochemical genetics, and microbiological techniques.

Current Advances in Ecological and Environmental Science. Pergamon Microforms International, Inc., Fairview Park, Elmsford, New York 10523. (914) 592-7720. 1989-. Monthly. Current literature searching service includingjournals, reports, abstracts, etc. This service is available

online as part of the CABS database on the hosts BRS and ORBIT search service.

Ecological Abstracts. Geo Abstracts Ltd. Elsevier Applied Science, Crown House, Linton Rd., Barking, England IG 11 8JU. 1974-. Derived from over 600 leading ecological and environmental journals, plus books, conference proceedings, reports and theses.

Ecology Abstracts. Cambridge Scientific Abstracts, 5161 River Rd., Bethesda, Maryland 20816. (301) 961-6750. Monthly.

Energy from Biomass and Municipal Wastes. National Technical Information Service, 5285 Port Royal Rd., Springfield, Virginia 22161. (703) 487-4650. Monthly. Biomass production, conversion, and utilization for energy.

Environment Abstracts. Bowker A & I Publishing, 121 Chanlon Rd., New Providence, New Jersey 07974. (908) 464-6800. 1974-.

Environment Index. Environment Information Center, Index Research Department, 124 E. 39th St., New York, New York 10016. 1971-. Annual.

Environmental Information Connection–EIC. Planning Information Program, Dept. of Urban and Regional Planning, University of Illinois, 1003 West Nevada, Urbana, Illinois 61801. (217) 333-1369. Also available online.

Environmental Periodicals Bibliography. Environmental Studies Institute, International Academy at Santa Barbara, 800 Garden St., Suite D, Santa Barbara, California 93101. (805) 965-5010. Also available online.

ERDA Research Abstracts. U.S. ERDA Technical Information Center, Box 62, Oak Ridge, Tennessee 37830.

Food Science and Technology Abstracts. International Food Information Service, c/o National Food Laboratory, 6363 Clark Ave., Dublin, California 94568. (800) 336-3782. 1969-.

General Science Index. H. W. Wilson Co., 950 University Ave., Bronx, New York 10452. 1978-. Monthly, also issued in annual cumulation. Cumulative subject index to English language periodicals in the subject fields of astronomy, botany, chemistry, earth science, environment and conservation, food and nutrition, genetics, mathematics, medicine and health, microbiology, oceanography, physics, physiology and zoology.

Index to Scientific Book Contents. Institute for Scientific Information, 3501 Market St., Philadelphia, Pennsylvania 19104. (800) 523-1857. 1985-. Annual. Gives contents of science books published.

Multimedia Index to Ecology. National Information Center for Educational Media, University of Southern California, Los Angeles, California 90007.

Pollution Abstracts. Cambridge Scientific Abstracts, 5161 River Rd., Bethesda, Maryland 20816. (301) 961-6750. Six/year. Indexes worldwide technical literature on environmental pollution. Covers air pollution, marine and freshwater pollution, sewage and wastewater treatment, waste management, toxicology and health, noise pollution, radiation, land pollution, and environmental policies, programs, legislation, and education. Also available online.

Science Citation Index. Institute for Scientific Information, 3501 Market St., Philadelphia, Pennsylvania 19104. 1961-.

BIBLIOGRAPHIES

Current Contents. Agriculture, Biology and Environmental Sciences. Institute for Scientific Information, 3501 Market St., Philadelphia, Pennsylvania 19104. (800) 523-1857. 1973-. Previous title: Current Contents. Agricultural, Food & Veterinary Sciences. Gives the table of contents of periodicals in the fields of agriculture, biology, environmental and related areas.

Directory of Published Proceedings. Interdok Corp., 173 Halstead Ave., Harrison, New York 10528. (914) 835-3506. 1990. Monthly. This is a listing of published proceedings including the series SEMTE (Science/Medicine/Engineering/Technology) and the series SSH (Social Science/Humanities).

EPA Publications Bibliography. U.S. Environmental Protection Agency, Library Systems Branch, 401 M St., SW, Washington, District of Columbia 20460. (202) 260-2090. Quarterly.

A Selected Bibliography on Alcohol Fuels. Solar Energy Research Institute, 1617 Cole Blvd., Golden, Colorado 80401. 1982. Covers literature written about biomass derived ethyl and methyl alcohols, including production processes, economics, use as fuel, engine conversion, feedstocks, financing, government regulations, coproducts, environmental effects and safety. The main focus is on alcohol fuels.

DIRECTORIES

Biomass Directory. Stockton Press, 257 Park Ave. S, New York, New York 10010. (212) 673-4400 or (800)221-2123.

Directory of Biomass Installations in 13 Southeastern States. Philip C. Badger. Southeastern Regional Biomass Energy Program, Tennessee Valley Authority, CEB 1C, Muscle Shoals, Alabama 35660. (205) 386-3086. 1986. Irregular. Energy and alcohol and methane production facilities in Alabama, Arkansas, Florida, Georgia, Kentucky, Louisiana, Missouri, Mississippi, North Carolina, South Carolina, Tennessee, Virginia, and West Virginia.

Directory of Intermediate Biomass Energy Combustion Equipment. Council of Great Lake Governors, 310 S. Michigan, 10th Fl., Chicago, Illinois 60604. (312) 427-0092.

Great Lakes Region Biomass Energy Facilities Directory. Council of Great Lakes Governors, 310 S. Michigan, 10th Fl., Chicago, Illinois 60604. (312) 427-0092.

ENCYCLOPEDIAS AND DICTIONARIES

Cambridge Encyclopedia of Life Sciences. A. E. Friday and David S. Ingram. Cambridge University Press, 40 W 20th St., New York, New York 10011. (212) 924-3900 or (800) 227-0247. 1985. Includes all topics under biology and ecology.

Dictionary of Biotechnology. J. Coombs. Elsevier Science Publishing Co., 655 Avenue of the Americas, New York, New York 10010. (212) 984-5800. 1986. Areas covered in this dictionary include: fermentation; brewing; vaccines; plant tissue; culture; antibiotic production; produc-

tion and use of enzymes; biomass; byproduct recovery and effluent treatment; equipment; processes; micro-organisms and biochemicals.

Encyclopedia of Human Biology. Renato Dulbecco, ed. Academic Press, c/o Harcourt Brace Jovanovich Inc., 6277 Sea Harbor Dr., Orlando, Florida 32887. (800) 346-8648. 1991. Eight volumes.

Energy Terminology: A Multilingual Glossary. Pergamon Microforms International, Inc., Fairview Park, Elmsford, New York 10523. (914) 592-7720. 1986. Second edition. Contains 1500 defined terms and concepts related to the field of energy together with an index of several thousand undefined keywords used in the definitions of these terms and concepts. Contents appear in four languages: English, French, German and Spanish.

Kaiman's Encyclopedia of Energy Topics. Lee Kaiman and J. Masloff. Environmental Design and Research Center, 26799 Elena Rd., Los Altos Hills, California 94022. 1983. Two volumes. Coverage of topics range from natural energy sources that are renewable to nonrenewable, and the application of these energy sources.

McGraw-Hill Encyclopedia of Environmental Science. Sybil P. Parker. McGraw-Hill Science & Engineering Books, 11 W. 19th St., New York, New York 10011. (212) 337-6010. 1980. Covers ecology, man's influence on nature, and environmental protection.

McGraw-Hill Encyclopedia of Science and Technology. McGraw-Hill, 1221 Avenue of the Americas, New York, New York 10020. (212) 512-2000 or (800) 262-4729. 1992. Seventh edition. Issued in multiple volumes including index. Includes all science and technology broad subject areas.

Van Nostrand's Scientific Encyclopedia. Glenn D. Considine, ed. Van Nostrand Reinhold, 115 5th Ave., New York, New York 10003. (212) 254-3232. 1983. Sixth edition. Includes all broad subject areas in science.

GENERAL WORKS

Bioenergy and the Environment. Janos Pasztor and Lars A. Kristoferson, eds. Westview Press, 5500 Central Ave., Boulder, Colorado 80301. (303) 444-3541. 1990. Includes 14 contributions which addresses issues such as the demand for biomass fuels including wood, charcoal, agricultural residues, and alcohol.

Bioenvironmental Systems. Donald L. Wise, ed. CRC Press, 2000 Corporate Blvd. N.W., Boca Raton, Florida 33431. (407) 994-0555; (800) 272-7737. 1987. 4 vols.

Biomass, Catalysts and Liquid Fuels. Technomic Publishing Co., 851 New Holland Ave., Box 3535, Lancaster, Pennsylvania 17604. (717) 291-5609.

Biomass Determination–a New Technique for Activated Sludge Control. U.S. Environmental Protection Agency, 401 M St. SW, Washington, District of Columbia 20460. (202) 260-2090. 1972. Includes an analysis of sewage sludge analysis by biomass determination. Also describes sewage disposal.

Biomass Production Anaerobic Digestion and Nutrient Recycling of Small Benthic or Floating Seaweeds. John H. Ryther. National Technical Information Service, 5285 Port Royal Rd., Springfield, Virginia 22161. (703) 487-4650. Environmental aspects of aquaculture.

Biomass Yields and Geography of Large Marine Ecosystems. Kenneth Sherman. Westview Press, 5500 Central AVe., Boulder, Colorado 80301. (303) 444-3541. 1989. Environmental aspects of marine pollution, marine productivity, and marine ecology.

Environmental Biotechnology. A. Balaozej and V. Prnivarovna, eds. Elsevier Science Publishing Co., 655 Avenue of the Americas, New York, New York 10010. (212) 989-5800. 1991. Proceedings of the International Symposium on Biotechnology, Bratislava, Czechoslovakia, June 27-29, 1990.

Global Biomass Burning. Joel S. Levine. MIT Press, 55 Hayward St., Cambridge, Massachusetts 02142. (617) 253-2884 or (800) 356-0343. 1991. Atmospheric, climatic, and biospheric implications.

Success and Dominance in Ecosystems. Edward O. Wilson. Ecology Institute, Nordbunte 23, Oldendorf/Luhe, Germany 1990. Proposes that the success of a species is measured by its evolutionary longevity and its dominance by its ability to dominate or control the appropriation of biomass and energy in ecosystems. Explores how and why social insects, representing only 2 percent of insect species but accounting for one-half of insect biomass, became the ecological center of terrestrial ecosystems. Much of the social insects success is attributed to their ability to function as highly structured superorganisms.

Vertebrate Ecology in Northern Neotropics. John F. Esenberg, ed. Smithsonian Institution Press, 470 L'Enfant Plaza, No. 7100, Washington, District of Columbia 20560. (800) 782-4612. 1979. Comparison of faunas found in tropical forests covering several mammalian species, including the red howler monkey, crab-eating fox, cebus monkey, and the didelphid marsupials.

HANDBOOKS AND MANUALS

Biomass Handbook. Osamu Kitani and Carl W. Hall. Gordon and Breach Science Publishers, Inc., 270 8th Ave., New York, New York 10011. (212) 206-8900. 1989. Provides knowledge of biomass and related systems. Includes biomass development from the biotechnology point of view as well as recent facts on biomass.

Energy Deskbook. Samuel Glasstone. Van Nostrand Reinhold, 115 5th Ave., New York, New York 10020. (212) 254-3232. 1983. Single volume reference covering all energy resources.

Sourcebook of Methods of Analysis for Biomass and Biomass Conversion Processes. T. A. Milne, et al. Elsevier Applied Science, 655 Avenue of the Americas, New York, New York 10010. 1990. Presents titles and abstracts of methods relevant to biomass conversion, from analyzing feedstocks to evaluating the performance of biofuels.

ONLINE DATA BASES

BIOSIS Previews. BIOSIS, 2100 Arch St., Philadelphia, Pennsylvania 19103-1399. (215) 587-4800. Largest and most comprehensive database of research in the life sciences. Contains citations for nearly 9000 primary research journals, monographs, reviews, symposia, preliminary reports, semi-popular journals, selected institutional reports, government reports and research communications.

Biotechnology Abstracts. Derwent Publications Ltd., 6845 Elm St., McLean, Virginia 22101. (703) 790-0400. Includes material on genetic manipulation, biochemical engineering, fermentation, biocatalysis, cell hybridization, in vitro plant propagation and industrial waste management.

Cambridge Scientific Abstracts Life Science–CSAL. Cambridge Scientific Abstracts, 5161 River Rd., Bethesda, Maryland 20816. (301) 961-6750. Provides access to the following abstracting services: "Life Sciences Collection," "Aquatic Sciences and Fisheries Abstracts," "Oceanic Abstracts," and "Pollution Abstracts."

Current Research Information System–CRIS/USDA. U.S. Department of Agriculture, National Agricultural Library, 10301 Baltimore Blvd., 5th Floor, Beltsville, Maryland 20705-2351. (301) 504-5755. Looks at current research projects in agriculture and allied sciences covering the biological, physical, social and behavioral sciences related to agriculture.

Enviro/Energyline Abstracts Plus. R. R. Bowker Co., 121 Chanlon Rd., New Providence, New Jersey 07974. (908) 464-6800.

Environmental Periodicals Bibliography. National Information Services Corp., Ste. 6, Wyman Towers, 3100 St. Paul St., Baltimore, Maryland 21218. (410)243-0797. Online version of abstract of same name.

Monthly Catalog of United States Government Publications. U.S. G.P.O., Supt. of Docs., PO Box 371954, Pittsburgh, Pennsylvania 15250-7954. (202) 512-0000.

National Technical Information Service. U.S. Department of Commerce, National Technical Information Service, Office of Data Base Services, 5285 Port Royal Rd., Springfield, Virginia 22161. (703) 487-4807. Bibliographic database of government sponsored research and technical reports.

Olsen's Biomass Energy Report. G. V. Olsen Associates, 170 Broadway, Room 201, New York, New York 10038. (212) 866-5034. Literature relating to biodegradable renewable energy sources and uses.

PressNet Environmental Reports. Chemical Information Systems, Inc., 7215 York Rd., Baltimore, Maryland 21212. (301) 321-8440.

SCISEARCH. Institute for Scientific Information, University City Science Center, 3501 Market St., Philadelphia, Pennsylvania 19104. (215) 386-0100.

PERIODICALS AND NEWSLETTERS

Biomass and Bioenergy. Pergamon Microforms International, Inc., Fairview Park, Elmsford, New York 10523. (914) 592-7720. 1991-. Monthly. Key areas covered by this journal are: Biomass-sources, energy, crop production processes, genetic improvements, composition; biological residues: wastes from agricultural production and forestry, processing industries, and municipal sources; bioenergy processes: fermentations, thermochemical conversions, liquid and gaseous fuels, and petrochemical substitutes; bioenergy utilization: direct combustion gasification, electricity production, chemical processes, and by-product remediation. Also includes environmental management and economic aspects of biomass and bioenergy.

Biomass Bulletin. Multi-Science Publishing Co. Ltd., 107 High Street, Brentwood, Essex, England CM14 4RX. 0277-224632. Quarterly.

Bioresource Technology. Elsevier Science Publishing Co., 655 Avenue of the Americas, New York, New York 10010. (212) 989-5800. Monthly. Disseminates knowledge in the related areas of biomass, biological waste treatment, bioscience systems analysis and in the technologies associated with production or conversion.

RESEARCH CENTERS AND INSTITUTES

Biomass Energy Research Association. 1825 K St., N.W., Suite 503, Washington, District of Columbia 20006. (202) 785-2856.

Biomass Research Center. University of Arkansas, Fayetteville, Arkansas 72701. (501) 575-6299.

Lawrence Berkeley Laboratory, Chemical Biodynamics Division. One Cyclotron Road, Berkeley, California 94720. (415) 486-4355.

U.S. Forest Service, Forest Engineering Research Project. George W. Andrews Forestry Sciences Laboratory, Auburn University, Devall Street, Auburn, Alabama 36849. (205) 826-8700.

University of Alaska Fairbanks, Institute of Arctic Biology. Fairbanks, Alaska 99775. (907) 474-7648.

STATISTICS SOURCES

Ecology: Community Profiles. U.S. Fish and Wildlife Service. National Technical Information Service, 5285 Port Royal Road, Springfield, Virginia 22161. (703) 487-4650. Irregular. Data on coastal and inland ecosystems, including wetlands, tidal-flats, near-shore seagrasses, sand dunes, drilling platforms, oyster reefs, estuaries, rivers and streams.

World Forest Biomass and Primary Production Data. Melvin G. R. Cannell. Academic Press, c/o Harcourt Brace Jovanovich Inc., 6277 Sea Harbor Dr., Orlando, Florida 32887. (800) 346-8648. 1982. Statistics of fuelwood and biomass energy.

TRADE ASSOCIATIONS AND PROFESSIONAL SOCIETIES

American Institute of Biological Sciences. 730 11th St., N.W., Washington, District of Columbia 20001-4521. (202) 628-1500.

BIOMES

See also: BIOGEOGRAPHY; CLIMATE; ECOSYSTEMS

ABSTRACTING AND INDEXING SERVICES

Applied Ecology Abstracts Studies in Renewable Natural Resources. Information Retrieval Ltd., 1911 Jefferson Davis Highway, Arlington, Virginia 22202. 1975-. Monthly.

Biological Abstracts. BIOSIS, 2100 Arch St., Philadelphia, Pennsylvania 19103-1399. (215) 587-4800. 1927-.

Biological and Agricultural Index. H.W. Wilson Co., 950 University Ave., Bronx, New York 10452. (800) 367-6770. 1916-. Monthly.

Biology Digest. Data Courier, Plexus Pub Inc., 143 Old Marlton Pike, Medford, New Jersey 08055. 1974-. Monthly. Abstracts biology periodicals.

Current Advances in Ecological and Environmental Science. Pergamon Microforms International, Inc., Fairview Park, Elmsford, New York 10523. (914) 592-7720. 1989-. Monthly. Current literature searching service including journals, reports, abstracts, etc. This service is available online as part of the CABS database on the hosts BRS and ORBIT search service.

Ecological Abstracts. Geo Abstracts Ltd. Elsevier Applied Science, Crown House, Linton Rd., Barking, England IG 11 8JU. 1974-. Derived from over 600 leading ecological and environmental journals, plus books, conference proceedings, reports and theses.

Ecology Abstracts. Cambridge Scientific Abstracts, 5161 River Rd., Bethesda, Maryland 20816. (301) 961-6750. Monthly.

Environment Abstracts. Bowker A & I Publishing, 121 Chanlon Rd., New Providence, New Jersey 07974. (908) 464-6800. 1974-.

Environment Index. Environment Information Center, Index Research Department, 124 E. 39th St., New York, New York 10016. 1971-. Annual.

Environmental Information Connection–EIC. Planning Information Program, Dept. of Urban and Regional Planning, University of Illinois, 1003 West Nevada, Urbana, Illinois 61801. (217) 333-1369. Also available online.

Environmental Periodicals Bibliography. Environmental Studies Institute, International Academy at Santa Barbara, 800 Garden St., Suite D, Santa Barbara, California 93101. (805) 965-5010. Also available online.

General Science Index. H. W. Wilson Co., 950 University Ave., Bronx, New York 10452. 1978-. Monthly, also issued in annual cumulation. Cumulative subject index to English language periodicals in the subject fields of astronomy, botany, chemistry, earth science, environment and conservation, food and nutrition, genetics, mathematics, medicine and health, microbiology, oceanography, physics, physiology and zoology.

Index to Scientific Book Contents. Institute for Scientific Information, 3501 Market St., Philadelphia, Pennsylvania 19104. (800) 523-1857. 1985-. Annual. Gives contents of science books published.

Multimedia Index to Ecology. National Information Center for Educational Media, University of Southern California, Los Angeles, California 90007.

Science Citation Index. Institute for Scientific Information, 3501 Market St., Philadelphia, Pennsylvania 19104. 1961-.

BIBLIOGRAPHIES

Bibliography and Index of Geology. American Geological Institute, 4220 King St., Alexandria, Virginia 22302. Monthly. Includes environmental geology and hydrogeology.

Current Contents. Agriculture, Biology and Environmental Sciences. Institute for Scientific Information, 3501 Market St., Philadelphia, Pennsylvania 19104. (800) 523-1857. 1973-. Previous title: Current Contents. Agricultural, Food & Veterinary Sciences. Gives the table of contents of periodicals in the fields of agriculture, biology, environmental and related areas.

Directory of Published Proceedings. Interdok Corp., 173 Halstead Ave., Harrison, New York 10528. (914) 835-3506. 1990. Monthly. This is a listing of published proceedings including the series SEMTE (Science/Medicine/Engineering/Technology) and the series SSH (Social Science/Humanities).

EPA Publications Bibliography. U.S. Environmental Protection Agency, Library Systems Branch, 401 M St., SW, Washington, District of Columbia 20460. (202) 260-2090. Quarterly.

DIRECTORIES

Ecological Society of America Bulletin–Directory of Members Issue. Ecological Society of America, c/o Dr. Duncan Patten, Center for Environmental Studies, Arizona State University, Tempe, Arizona 85287. (602) 965-3000.

ENCYCLOPEDIAS AND DICTIONARIES

Cambridge Encyclopedia of Life Sciences. A. E. Friday and David S. Ingram. Cambridge University Press, 40 W 20th St., New York, New York 10011. (212) 924-3900 or (800) 227-0247. 1985. Includes all topics under biology and ecology.

A Dictionary of Genetics. Robert C. King and William A. Stansfield. Oxford University Press, 200 Madison Ave., New York, New York 10016. (212) 679-7300 or (800) 334-4249. 1991. Fourth edition. Includes 7,100 definitions with 250 illustrations. Also includes bibliography of major sources.

Dictionary of Genetics and Cell Biology. Norman Maclean. New York University Press, 70 Washington Sq. S., New York, New York 10012. (212) 998-2575. 1987. Includes the subject areas of cytology and genetics.

The Encyclopedia of Animal Ecology. Peter D. Moore. Facts on File, Inc., 460 Park Ave. S., New York, New York 10016. (212) 683-2244. 1987.

Encyclopedic Dictionary of Genetics: With German Term Equivalents and Extensive German/English Index. R. C. King and W. D. Stansfield. VCH Publishers, 303 NW 12th Ave., Deerfield Beach, Florida 33442-1788. (305) 428-5566. 1990. 4th ed. Revised edition of: A Dictionary of Genetics, third edition.

Life Sciences on File. Diagram Group. Facts on File, Inc., 460 Park Ave. S., New York, New York 10016. (212) 683-2244. 1986. Encyclopedia of pictorial collection in life sciences. Deals with all major topics in life sciences including ecology.

McGraw-Hill Encyclopedia of Environmental Science. Sybil P. Parker. McGraw-Hill Science & Engineering Books, 11 W. 19th St., New York, New York 10011. (212) 337-6010. 1980. Covers ecology, man's influence on nature, and environmental protection.

McGraw-Hill Encyclopedia of Science and Technology. McGraw-Hill, 1221 Avenue of the Americas, New York, New York 10020. (212) 512-2000 or (800) 262-4729.

1992. Seventh edition. Issued in multiple volumes including index. Includes all science and technology broad subject areas.

Van Nostrand's Scientific Encyclopedia. Glenn D. Considine, ed. Van Nostrand Reinhold, 115 5th Ave., New York, New York 10003. (212) 254-3232. 1983. Sixth edition. Includes all broad subject areas in science.

GENERAL WORKS

Bacteria in Nature. Edward R. Leadbetter. Plenum Press, 233 Spring St., New York, New York 10013-1578. (212) 620-8000. 1989.

Bacteria in Their Natural Environments. Madilyn Fletcher, ed. Academic Press Ltd., 24-28 Oval Rd., London, England NW1 7DX. (071) 2674466. 1985.

Biological Conservation. David W. Ehrenfeld. Holt, Rinehart and Winston, 6277 Sea Harbor Dr., Orlando, Florida 32887. (407) 345-2500. 1970.

Ecology of Biological Invasions of North America and Hawaii. H. G. Baker, et al. Springer-Verlag, 175 5th Ave., New York, New York 10010. (212) 460-1500; (800) 777-4643. 1986.

Ecosystems Experiments. H. A. Mooney, et al., eds. John Wiley & Sons, Inc., 605 3rd Ave., New York, New York 10158-0012. (212) 850-6000. 1991. Explores the potential ecosystem experimentation as a tool for understanding and predicting changes in the biosphere. Areas investigated include deforestation, desertification, El Nino phenomenon, acid rain, watersheds, wetlands, and aquatic and climatic changes.

Elton's Ecologists: A History of the Bureau of Animal Population. Peter Crowcroft. University of Chicago Press, 5801 Ellis Ave., 4th Fl., Chicago, Illinois 60637. (312) 702-7700. 1991. The story of a smallish university department chronicles an enterprise that appreciably shaped the history of ecology during the mid-decades of the 20th century.

Ground Beetles: Their Role in Ecological and Environmental Studies. Nigel E. Stork, ed. VCH Publishers, 303 NW 12th Ave., Deerfield Beach, Florida 33442-1788. (305) 428-5566. 1990. Summarizes the latest advances in the use of beetles in a range of ecological studies.

Human Performance Physiology and Environmental Medicine Atterrestrial Extremes. Kent B. Pandolf, et al., eds. WCB Brown and Benchmark Pr., 2460 Kerper Blvd., Dubuque, Iowa 52001. (800) 338-5578. 1988. Includes the most current information available on the physiological and medical responses to heat, cold, altitude, poor air quality and hyperbaric conditions.

Large Marine Ecosystems: Patterns, Processes, and Yields. Kenneth Sherman, et al., eds. American Association for the Advancement of Science, 1333 H St. N.W., 8th Flr., Washington, District of Columbia 20005. (202) 326-6400. 1990. Deals with the conservation and management of vitally important components of the ecosphere.

Long-Term Ecological Research: An International Perspective. Paul G. Risser, ed. John Wiley & Sons, Inc., 605 3rd Ave., New York, New York 10158-0012. (212) 850-6000. 1991. Describes and analyzes research programs in various ecosystems such as temperate forests, arid steppes, deserts, temperate and tropical grasslands, aquatic systems from countries including Scotland, Kenya, USA, Australia, Canada, Germany, and France.

Magill's Survey of Science. Earth Science Series. Frank N. Magill. Salem Press, PO Box 50062, Pasadena, California 91105. 1990-. Five volumes. Includes information on earth's crust, hot spots and volcanic island chains, physical properties of minerals, rock magnetism, physical properties of rocks, and index.

Magill's Survey of Science. Life Science Series. Frank N. Magill, ed. Salem Press, PO Box 50062, Pasadena, California 91105. 1991. Six volumes. Contents: v.1. A-Central and peripheral nervous system functions; v.2. Central metabolism regulation - eukaryotic transcriptional control; v.3. Positive and negative eukaryotic transcriptional control - mammalian hormones; v.4. Hormones and behavior - muscular contraction; v.5. Muscular contraction and relaxation - sexual reproduction in plants; v.6. Reproductive behavior and mating - X inactivation and the Lyon hypothesis.

Managing Marine Environments. Richard A. Kenchington. Taylor & Francis, 1900 Frost Rd., Ste. 101, Bristol, Pennsylvania 19007. (215) 785-5800. 1990. Contemporary issues of multiple-use planning and management of marine environments and natural resources.

Microcomputers in Environmental Biology. J. N. R. Jeffers, ed. Parthenon Pub., Casterton Hall, Carnforth, England LA6 2LA. Lancs. 1991. Contains extensive lists of programs written specially to show the ways in which microcomputers can be most usefully employed in the analysis of experiments and surveys, the analysis of multivariate data, radio tagging and the analysis of animal movement, and in modeling complex systems.

The Next One Hundred Years: Shaping the Fate of Our Living Earth. Jonathan Weiner. Bantam Books, 666 5th Ave., New York, New York 10103. (212) 765-6500; (800) 223-6834. 1991. Explores the following issues: the greenhouse effect, deforestation, the destruction of the ozone layer, the human population explosion and the onset of mass extinctions.

Nitrification. J.I. Prosser, ed. IRL, Southfield Rd., Eynsham, Oxford, England OX8 1JJ. (0865) 88283. 1987.

Pastures: Their Ecology and Management. R. H. M. Langer, ed. Oxford University Press, 200 Madison Ave., New York, New York 10016. (212) 679-7300; (800) 334-4249. 1990. Covers such areas as the grasslands of New Zealand, pasture plants, pasture as an ecosystem, pasture establishment, soil fertility, management, assessment, livestock production, animal disorders, high country pastures, hay or silage, seed production, weeds, pests, and plant diseases.

Preserving Communities and Corridors. Gay Mackintosh, ed. Defenders of Wildlife, 1244 19th St. N.W., Washington, District of Columbia 20036. (202) 659-9510. 1989.

Rain Forest Regeneration and Management. G. Pompa, et al., eds. Parthenon Group Inc., 120 Mill Rd., Park Ridge, New Jersey 07656. (201) 391-6796. 1991. Explores the management implications of present scientific knowledge on rain forest generation. Providing case studies.

Seabirds of the Farallon Islands: Ecology, Dynamics, and Structure of an Upwelling-System Community. David G. Ainley and Robert J. Boekelheide, eds. Stanford University, Stanford, California 94305-2235. (415) 723-9434. 1990. History of seabird populations at the Farallons, a general discussion of patterns in the marine environment, and the general feeding ecology of Farallon seabirds.

Southern Exposure: Deciding Antarctica's Future. Lee A. Kimball. World Resources Institute, 1709 New York Ave. N.W., Washington, District of Columbia 20006. (800) 822-0504. 1990. Reviews Antarctica's importance from a global perspective.

Subantarctic Macquarie Island: Environment and Biology. P. M. Selkirk, et al. Cambridge University Press, 40 W. 20th St., New York, New York 10011. (212) 924-3900; (800) 227-0247. 1990. Review of environmental and biologic research on the Macquarie Island. It presents summary of studies done in the last 15 years by Australian scientists. Contains a sequence of 12 chapters that concern the island's discovery and history; situation in the Southern ocean; tectonics and geology; landforms and Quaternary history; vegetation; lakes; birds; mammals; anthropoids; microbiology; near shore environments; and human impact.

Tropical Forest and Its Environment. Kenneth Alan Longman. Longman Scientific & Technical, 1560 Broadway, New York, New York 10036. (212) 819-5400. 1990. Rain forest and tropical ecology, ecosystems, and cycles.

Where Have All the Birds Gone?. John Terborgh. Princeton University Press, 41 Williams St., Princeton, New Jersey 08540. (609) 258-4900. 1989. Includes topics such as: population monitoring, ecological consequences of fragmentation, evolution of migration, social and territorial behaviors of wintering songbirds.

Wildlife Extinction. Charles L. Cadieux. Stone Wall Pr., 1241 30th St. N.W., Washington, District of Columbia 20007. (202) 333-1860. 1991. Presents a worldwide picture of animals in danger of extinction and addresses controversial issues such as exploding human population, the role of zoos and wildlife parks, hunting and poaching.

HANDBOOKS AND MANUALS

The Global Ecology Handbook: What You Can Do about the Environmental Crisis. Walter H. Corson, ed. The Global Tomorrow Coalition, Beacon Pr., 25 Beacon St., Boston, Massachusetts 02108-2800. (617) 742-2110. 1990. Covers environment, energy policy, population growth and other issues. It includes chapters on tropical rain forests, garbage, oceans and coasts, global warming, population growth, agriculture, biological diversity, fresh water, hazardous wastes, and environment and development.

ONLINE DATA BASES

BIOSIS Previews. BIOSIS, 2100 Arch St., Philadelphia, Pennsylvania 19103-1399. (215) 587-4800. Largest and most comprehensive database of research in the life sciences. Contains citations for nearly 9000 primary research journals, monographs, reviews, symposia, preliminary reports, semi-popular journals, selected institutional reports, government reports and research communications.

Biotechnology Abstracts. Derwent Publications Ltd., 6845 Elm St., McLean, Virginia 22101. (703) 790-0400. Includes material on genetic manipulation, biochemical engineering, fermentation, biocatalysis, cell hybridization, in vitro plant propagation and industrial waste management.

Cambridge Scientific Abstracts Life Science–CSAL. Cambridge Scientific Abstracts, 5161 River Rd., Bethesda, Maryland 20816. (301) 961-6750. Provides access to the following abstracting services: "Life Sciences Collection," "Aquatic Sciences and Fisheries Abstracts," "Oceanic Abstracts," and "Pollution Abstracts."

Enviro/Energyline Abstracts Plus. R. R. Bowker Co., 121 Chanlon Rd., New Providence, New Jersey 07974. (908) 464-6800.

Environmental Periodicals Bibliography. National Information Services Corp., Ste. 6, Wyman Towers, 3100 St. Paul St., Baltimore, Maryland 21218. (410)243-0797. Online version of abstract of same name.

Monthly Catalog of United States Government Publications. U.S. G.P.O., Supt. of Docs., PO Box 371954, Pittsburgh, Pennsylvania 15250-7954. (202) 512-0000.

National Technical Information Service. U.S. Department of Commerce, National Technical Information Service, Office of Data Base Services, 5285 Port Royal Rd., Springfield, Virginia 22161. (703) 487-4807. Bibliographic database of government sponsored research and technical reports.

SCISEARCH. Institute for Scientific Information, University City Science Center, 3501 Market St., Philadelphia, Pennsylvania 19104. (215) 386-0100.

PERIODICALS AND NEWSLETTERS

Biological Conservation. Applied Science Publishers, 655 Avenue of the Americas, PO Box 5399, New York, New York 10163. (718) 756-6440. Quarterly. Conservation of biological and allied natural resources, plants and animals and their habitats.

BioScience Journal. American Institute of Biological Sciences, 730 11th Street, Nw, Washington, District of Columbia 20001-4521. (202) 628-1500. Eleven times a year. Current research, feature articles, book reviews, and new products.

Ecological Applications. Ecological Society of America, Center for Environmental Studies, Arizona State University, Tempe, Arizona 85287. (602) 965-3000. 1991-. Quarterly. Emphasizes the application of basic ecological concepts to a wide range of problems.

Ecological Society of America Bulletin. Ecological Society of America, Center of Environmental Studies, Arizona State University, Tempe, Arizona 85287-1201. (602) 965-3000. Quarterly. Study of living things in relation to their environments.

Ecology. Ecological Society of America, Center of Environmental Studies, Arizona State University, Tempe, Arizona 85287-1201. (602) 965-3000. Bimonthly. Information on the study of living things.

Ecology USA. Business Publishers, Inc., 951 Pershing Dr., Silver Spring, Maryland 20910-4464. (301) 587-6300. 1972-. Biweekly. Contains all the legislation, regulation, and litigation affecting efforts to conserve and protect America's unique environmental and ecological heritage.

Ecomod. ISEM–North America Chapter, Water Quality Division, South Florida Water Management District, P.O. Box 24608, West Palm Beach, Florida 33416. (407) 686-8800. Monthly. Current events in ecological and environmental modeling.

Estuaries. Chesapeake Biological Laboratory, 1 William St., Solomons, Maryland 20688-0038. (410) 326-4281. Quarterly. Journal of the Estuarine Research Federation dealing with estuaries and estuarine biology.

Journal of Applied Meteorology. American Meteorological Society, 45 Beacon Street, Boston, Massachusetts 02108. (617) 227-2425. Monthly. Articles on the relationship between weather and environment.

Marine Biology. Springer-Verlag, 175 5th Ave., New York, New York 10010. (212) 461-1500; (800) 777-4643. Sixteen/year. Life in oceans and coastal waters.

Nature and Resources. Elsevier Science Publishing Co., 655 Avenue of the Americas, New York, New York 10010. (212) 989-5800. 1965-. Quarterly. Provides in-depth reviews of contemporary environmental issues from an international perspective.

RESEARCH CENTERS AND INSTITUTES

University of Miami, Research Collections. Department of Biology, Coral Gables, Florida 33124. (305) 284-3973.

TRADE ASSOCIATIONS AND PROFESSIONAL SOCIETIES

American Institute of Biological Sciences. 730 11th St., N.W., Washington, District of Columbia 20001-4521. (202) 628-1500.

American Society of Naturalists. Department of Ecology and Evolation, State University of New York, Stony Brook, New York 11794. (516) 632-8589.

Center for Conservation Biology. Department of Biological Sciences, Stanford University, Stanford, California 94305. (415) 723-5924.

Ecological Society of America. Arizona State University, Center for Environmental Studies, Tempe, Arizona 85287. (602) 965-3000.

International Bio-Environmental Foundation. 15300 Ventura Blvd., Suite 405, Sherman Oaks, California 91403. (818) 907-5483.

Monteverde Institute. Tropical Biology Program, Council on International Educational Exchange, 205 E. 42nd St., New York, New York 10017.

BIOMETRY

See also: FISH AND WILDLIFE MANAGEMENT

ABSTRACTING AND INDEXING SERVICES

Applied Ecology Abstracts Studies in Renewable Natural Resources. Information Retrieval Ltd., 1911 Jefferson Davis Highway, Arlington, Virginia 22202. 1975-. Monthly.

ASFA Aquaculture Abstracts. Cambridge Scientific Abstracts, Inc., 5161 River Rd., Bethesda, Maryland 20816. (301) 961-6750. 1984.

Biological Abstracts. BIOSIS, 2100 Arch St., Philadelphia, Pennsylvania 19103-1399. (215) 587-4800. 1927-.

Biological and Agricultural Index. H.W. Wilson Co., 950 University Ave., Bronx, New York 10452. (800) 367-6770. 1916-. Monthly.

Biology Digest. Data Courier, Plexus Pub Inc., 143 Old Marlton Pike, Medford, New Jersey 08055. 1974-. Monthly. Abstracts biology periodicals.

Ecological Abstracts. Geo Abstracts Ltd. Elsevier Applied Science, Crown House, Linton Rd., Barking, England IG 11 8JU. 1974-. Derived from over 600 leading ecological and environmental journals, plus books, conference proceedings, reports and theses.

Environment Abstracts. Bowker A & I Publishing, 121 Chanlon Rd., New Providence, New Jersey 07974. (908) 464-6800. 1974-.

Environment Index. Environment Information Center, Index Research Department, 124 E. 39th St., New York, New York 10016. 1971-. Annual.

Environmental Information Connection–EIC. Planning Information Program, Dept. of Urban and Regional Planning, University of Illinois, 1003 West Nevada, Urbana, Illinois 61801. (217) 333-1369. Also available online.

Environmental Periodicals Bibliography. Environmental Studies Institute, International Academy at Santa Barbara, 800 Garden St., Suite D, Santa Barbara, California 93101. (805) 965-5010. Also available online.

General Science Index. H. W. Wilson Co., 950 University Ave., Bronx, New York 10452. 1978-. Monthly, also issued in annual cumulation. Cumulative subject index to English language periodicals in the subject fields of astronomy, botany, chemistry, earth science, environment and conservation, food and nutrition, genetics, mathematics, medicine and health, microbiology, oceanography, physics, physiology and zoology.

Index to Scientific Book Contents. Institute for Scientific Information, 3501 Market St., Philadelphia, Pennsylvania 19104. (800) 523-1857. 1985-. Annual. Gives contents of science books published.

Multimedia Index to Ecology. National Information Center for Educational Media, University of Southern California, Los Angeles, California 90007.

Science Citation Index. Institute for Scientific Information, 3501 Market St., Philadelphia, Pennsylvania 19104. 1961-.

BIBLIOGRAPHIES

Current Contents. Agriculture, Biology and Environmental Sciences. Institute for Scientific Information, 3501 Market St., Philadelphia, Pennsylvania 19104. (800) 523-1857. 1973-. Previous title: Current Contents. Agricultural, Food & Veterinary Sciences. Gives the table of contents of periodicals in the fields of agriculture, biology, environmental and related areas.

EPA Publications Bibliography. U.S. Environmental Protection Agency, Library Systems Branch, 401 M St., SW, Washington, District of Columbia 20460. (202) 260-2090. Quarterly.

ENCYCLOPEDIAS AND DICTIONARIES

Cambridge Encyclopedia of Life Sciences. A. E. Friday and David S. Ingram. Cambridge University Press, 40 W

20th St., New York, New York 10011. (212) 924-3900 or (800) 227-0247. 1985. Includes all topics under biology and ecology.

McGraw-Hill Encyclopedia of Environmental Science. Sybil P. Parker. McGraw-Hill Science & Engineering Books, 11 W. 19th St., New York, New York 10011. (212) 337-6010. 1980. Covers ecology, man's influence on nature, and environmental protection.

McGraw-Hill Encyclopedia of Science and Technology. McGraw-Hill, 1221 Avenue of the Americas, New York, New York 10020. (212) 512-2000 or (800) 262-4729. 1992. Seventh edition. Issued in multiple volumes including index. Includes all science and technology broad subject areas.

Van Nostrand's Scientific Encyclopedia. Glenn D. Considine, ed. Van Nostrand Reinhold, 115 5th Ave., New York, New York 10003. (212) 254-3232. 1983. Sixth edition. Includes all broad subject areas in science.

GENERAL WORKS

Parameter Estimation in Ecology. O. Richter and D. Sondgerath. VCH Publishers, 303 NW 12th Ave., Deerfield Beach, Florida 33442-1788. (305) 428-5566. 1990. Brings together the different aspects of biological modelling, in particular ecological modelling using both stochastic and deterministic models.

Primary Productivity of the Biosphere. Helmut Lieth. Springer-Verlag, 175 5th Ave., New York, New York 10010. (212) 460-1500. 1975. Covers biometry and ecology.

Principles and Measurements in Environmental Biology. F. I. Woodward and J. E. Sheehy. Butterworth-Heinemann, 80 Montvale Ave., Stoneham, Massachusetts 02180. (617) 438-8464. 1983.

ONLINE DATA BASES

BIOSIS Previews. BIOSIS, 2100 Arch St., Philadelphia, Pennsylvania 19103-1399. (215) 587-4800. Largest and most comprehensive database of research in the life sciences. Contains citations for nearly 9000 primary research journals, monographs, reviews, symposia, preliminary reports, semi-popular journals, selected institutional reports, government reports and research communications.

Enviro/Energyline Abstracts Plus. R. R. Bowker Co., 121 Chanlon Rd., New Providence, New Jersey 07974. (908) 464-6800.

Environmental Periodicals Bibliography. National Information Services Corp., Ste. 6, Wyman Towers, 3100 St. Paul St., Baltimore, Maryland 21218. (410)243-0797. Online version of abstract of same name.

Monthly Catalog of United States Government Publications. U.S. G.P.O., Supt. of Docs., PO Box 371954, Pittsburgh, Pennsylvania 15250-7954. (202) 512-0000.

National Technical Information Service. U.S. Department of Commerce, National Technical Information Service, Office of Data Base Services, 5285 Port Royal Rd., Springfield, Virginia 22161. (703) 487-4807. Bibliographic database of government sponsored research and technical reports.

SCISEARCH. Institute for Scientific Information, University City Science Center, 3501 Market St., Philadelphia, Pennsylvania 19104. (215) 386-0100.

TRADE ASSOCIATIONS AND PROFESSIONAL SOCIETIES

American Institute of Biological Sciences. 730 11th St., N.W., Washington, District of Columbia 20001-4521. (202) 628-1500.

American Society of Naturalists. Department of Ecology and Evolation, State University of New York, Stony Brook, New York 11794. (516) 632-8589.

BIOMONITORING

See also: BIOMARKER; ENVIRONMENTAL QUALITY; POLLUTION CONTROL

ABSTRACTING AND INDEXING SERVICES

Applied Ecology Abstracts Studies in Renewable Natural Resources. Information Retrieval Ltd., 1911 Jefferson Davis Highway, Arlington, Virginia 22202. 1975-. Monthly.

Biological Abstracts. BIOSIS, 2100 Arch St., Philadelphia, Pennsylvania 19103-1399. (215) 587-4800. 1927-.

Biological and Agricultural Index. H.W. Wilson Co., 950 University Ave., Bronx, New York 10452. (800) 367-6770. 1916-. Monthly.

Biology Digest. Data Courier, Plexus Pub Inc., 143 Old Marlton Pike, Medford, New Jersey 08055. 1974-. Monthly. Abstracts biology periodicals.

Ecological Abstracts. Geo Abstracts Ltd. Elsevier Applied Science, Crown House, Linton Rd., Barking, England IG 11 8JU. 1974-. Derived from over 600 leading ecological and environmental journals, plus books, conference proceedings, reports and theses.

Ecology Abstracts. Cambridge Scientific Abstracts, 5161 River Rd., Bethesda, Maryland 20816. (301) 961-6750. Monthly.

Environment Abstracts. Bowker A & I Publishing, 121 Chanlon Rd., New Providence, New Jersey 07974. (908) 464-6800. 1974-.

Environment Index. Environment Information Center, Index Research Department, 124 E. 39th St., New York, New York 10016. 1971-. Annual.

Environmental Information Connection–EIC. Planning Information Program, Dept. of Urban and Regional Planning, University of Illinois, 1003 West Nevada, Urbana, Illinois 61801. (217) 333-1369. Also available online.

Environmental Periodicals Bibliography. Environmental Studies Institute, International Academy at Santa Barbara, 800 Garden St., Suite D, Santa Barbara, California 93101. (805) 965-5010. Also available online.

General Science Index. H. W. Wilson Co., 950 University Ave., Bronx, New York 10452. 1978-. Monthly, also issued in annual cumulation. Cumulative subject index to English language periodicals in the subject fields of astronomy, botany, chemistry, earth science, environment and conservation, food and nutrition, genetics,

mathematics, medicine and health, microbiology, oceanography, physics, physiology and zoology.

Index to Scientific Book Contents. Institute for Scientific Information, 3501 Market St., Philadelphia, Pennsylvania 19104. (800) 523-1857. 1985-. Annual. Gives contents of science books published.

Multimedia Index to Ecology. National Information Center for Educational Media, University of Southern California, Los Angeles, California 90007.

Science Citation Index. Institute for Scientific Information, 3501 Market St., Philadelphia, Pennsylvania 19104. 1961-.

BIBLIOGRAPHIES

Current Contents. Agriculture, Biology and Environmental Sciences. Institute for Scientific Information, 3501 Market St., Philadelphia, Pennsylvania 19104. (800) 523-1857. 1973-. Previous title: Current Contents. Agricultural, Food & Veterinary Sciences. Gives the table of contents of periodicals in the fields of agriculture, biology, environmental and related areas.

Directory of Published Proceedings. Interdok Corp., 173 Halstead Ave., Harrison, New York 10528. (914) 835-3506. 1990. Monthly. This is a listing of published proceedings including the series SEMTE (Science/Medicine/Engineering/Technology) and the series SSH (Social Science/Humanities).

EPA Publications Bibliography. U.S. Environmental Protection Agency, Library Systems Branch, 401 M St., SW, Washington, District of Columbia 20460. (202) 260-2090. Quarterly.

ENCYCLOPEDIAS AND DICTIONARIES

Cambridge Encyclopedia of Life Sciences. A. E. Friday and David S. Ingram. Cambridge University Press, 40 W 20th St., New York, New York 10011. (212) 924-3900 or (800) 227-0247. 1985. Includes all topics under biology and ecology.

McGraw-Hill Encyclopedia of Environmental Science. Sybil P. Parker. McGraw-Hill Science & Engineering Books, 11 W. 19th St., New York, New York 10011. (212) 337-6010. 1980. Covers ecology, man's influence on nature, and environmental protection.

Van Nostrand's Scientific Encyclopedia. Glenn D. Considine, ed. Van Nostrand Reinhold, 115 5th Ave., New York, New York 10003. (212) 254-3232. 1983. Sixth edition. Includes all broad subject areas in science.

GENERAL WORKS

Biomarkers of Environmental Contamination. John F. McCarthy and Lee R. Shugart. Lewis Publishers, 2000 Corporate Blvd., Boca Raton, Florida 33431. (800) 272-7737. 1990. Reviews the use of biological markers in animals and plants as an innovative approach to evaluating the ecological and physiological effects of environmental contamination.

Environmental Monitoring, Restoration, and Assessment: What Have We Learned?. Handord Symposium on Health and Environment, 28th, 1989, Richmond, WA. Battelle Press, 505 King Ave., Columbus, Ohio 43201. (614) 424-6393. 1990. Evaluates some of the monitoring and assessment programs that have been conducted or are currently in place. Focuses on radiological monitoring and its expenditures.

Methods for Assessing Exposure of Human and Non-Human Biota. R. G. Tardiff and B. D. Goldstein, eds. John Wiley & Sons, Inc., 605 3rd Ave., New York, New York 10158-0012. (212) 850-6000. 1991. Provides a critical and collective evaluation of approaches to chemical exposure assessment.

Monitoring Human Tissues for Toxic Substances. National Academy Press, 2101 Constitution Ave. N.W., PO Box 285, Washington, District of Columbia 20418. (202) 334-3313. 1991. Evaluates the National Human Monitoring Program.

Reviews of Environmental Contamination and Toxicology: v. 120. George W. Ware, ed. Springer-Verlag, 175 5th Ave., New York, New York 10010. (212) 460-1500; (800) 777-4643. 1991. Covers organochlorine pesticides and polychlorinated biphenyls in human adipose tissue, pesticide residues in foods imported into the U.S., and selected trace elements and the use of biomonitors in subtropical and tropical marine ecosystems.

GOVERNMENTAL ORGANIZATIONS

Office of Public Affairs: Fish and Wildlife Service. 18th and C St., N.W., Washington, District of Columbia 20240. (202) 343-5634.

ONLINE DATA BASES

BIOSIS Previews. BIOSIS, 2100 Arch St., Philadelphia, Pennsylvania 19103-1399. (215) 587-4800. Largest and most comprehensive database of research in the life sciences. Contains citations for nearly 9000 primary research journals, monographs, reviews, symposia, preliminary reports, semi-popular journals, selected institutional reports, government reports and research communications.

Enviro/Energyline Abstracts Plus. R. R. Bowker Co., 121 Chanlon Rd., New Providence, New Jersey 07974. (908) 464-6800.

Environmental Periodicals Bibliography. National Information Services Corp., Ste. 6, Wyman Towers, 3100 St. Paul St., Baltimore, Maryland 21218. (410)243-0797. Online version of abstract of same name.

Monthly Catalog of United States Government Publications. U.S. G.P.O., Supt. of Docs., PO Box 371954, Pittsburgh, Pennsylvania 15250-7954. (202) 512-0000.

National Technical Information Service. U.S. Department of Commerce, National Technical Information Service, Office of Data Base Services, 5285 Port Royal Rd., Springfield, Virginia 22161. (703) 487-4807. Bibliographic database of government sponsored research and technical reports.

SCISEARCH. Institute for Scientific Information, University City Science Center, 3501 Market St., Philadelphia, Pennsylvania 19104. (215) 386-0100.

PERIODICALS AND NEWSLETTERS

Analytical Biochemistry. Academic Press, 111 Fifth Ave., New York, New York 10003. (800) 346-8648. Covers biological and chemical topics relating to the environment.

BioScience Journal. American Institute of Biological Sciences, 730 11th Street, Nw, Washington, District of Columbia 20001-4521. (202) 628-1500. Eleven times a year. Current research, feature articles, book reviews, and new products.

Ecomod. ISEM–North America Chapter, Water Quality Division, South Florida Water Management District, P.O. Box 24608, West Palm Beach, Florida 33416. (407) 686-8800. Monthly. Current events in ecological and environmental modeling.

RESEARCH CENTERS AND INSTITUTES

University of Virginia, Center for Bioprocess/Product Development. Department of Chemical Engineering, Thornton Hall, Charlottesville, Virginia 22901. (804) 924-6278.

TRADE ASSOCIATIONS AND PROFESSIONAL SOCIETIES

American Institute of Biological Sciences. 730 11th St., N.W., Washington, District of Columbia 20001-4521. (202) 628-1500.

American Society of Naturalists. Department of Ecology and Evolation, State University of New York, Stony Brook, New York 11794. (516) 632-8589.

BIONUCLEONICS

ABSTRACTING AND INDEXING SERVICES

Applied Ecology Abstracts Studies in Renewable Natural Resources. Information Retrieval Ltd., 1911 Jefferson Davis Highway, Arlington, Virginia 22202. 1975-. Monthly.

Biological Abstracts. BIOSIS, 2100 Arch St., Philadelphia, Pennsylvania 19103-1399. (215) 587-4800. 1927-.

Biological and Agricultural Index. H.W. Wilson Co., 950 University Ave., Bronx, New York 10452. (800) 367-6770. 1916-. Monthly.

Biology Digest. Data Courier, Plexus Pub Inc., 143 Old Marlton Pike, Medford, New Jersey 08055. 1974-. Monthly. Abstracts biology periodicals.

Environment Abstracts. Bowker A & I Publishing, 121 Chanlon Rd., New Providence, New Jersey 07974. (908) 464-6800. 1974-.

Environment Index. Environment Information Center, Index Research Department, 124 E. 39th St., New York, New York 10016. 1971-. Annual.

Environmental Information Connection–EIC. Planning Information Program, Dept. of Urban and Regional Planning, University of Illinois, 1003 West Nevada, Urbana, Illinois 61801. (217) 333-1369. Also available online.

Environmental Periodicals Bibliography. Environmental Studies Institute, International Academy at Santa Barbara, 800 Garden St., Suite D, Santa Barbara, California 93101. (805) 965-5010. Also available online.

General Science Index. H. W. Wilson Co., 950 University Ave., Bronx, New York 10452. 1978-. Monthly, also issued in annual cumulation. Cumulative subject index to English language periodicals in the subject fields of astronomy, botany, chemistry, earth science, environment and conservation, food and nutrition, genetics, mathematics, medicine and health, microbiology, oceanography, physics, physiology and zoology.

Multimedia Index to Ecology. National Information Center for Educational Media, University of Southern California, Los Angeles, California 90007.

BIBLIOGRAPHIES

Current Contents. Agriculture, Biology and Environmental Sciences. Institute for Scientific Information, 3501 Market St., Philadelphia, Pennsylvania 19104. (800) 523-1857. 1973-. Previous title: Current Contents. Agricultural, Food & Veterinary Sciences. Gives the table of contents of periodicals in the fields of agriculture, biology, environmental and related areas.

EPA Publications Bibliography. U.S. Environmental Protection Agency, Library Systems Branch, 401 M St., SW, Washington, District of Columbia 20460. (202) 260-2090. Quarterly.

ENCYCLOPEDIAS AND DICTIONARIES

Cambridge Encyclopedia of Life Sciences. A. E. Friday and David S. Ingram. Cambridge University Press, 40 W 20th St., New York, New York 10011. (212) 924-3900 or (800) 227-0247. 1985. Includes all topics under biology and ecology.

ONLINE DATA BASES

Enviro/Energyline Abstracts Plus. R. R. Bowker Co., 121 Chanlon Rd., New Providence, New Jersey 07974. (908) 464-6800.

Environmental Periodicals Bibliography. National Information Services Corp., Ste. 6, Wyman Towers, 3100 St. Paul St., Baltimore, Maryland 21218. (410)243-0797. Online version of abstract of same name.

SCISEARCH. Institute for Scientific Information, University City Science Center, 3501 Market St., Philadelphia, Pennsylvania 19104. (215) 386-0100.

BIOSENSORS

ABSTRACTING AND INDEXING SERVICES

AgBiotech News and Information. C. A. B. International, 845 North Park Ave., Tucson, Arizona 85719. (602) 621-7897 or (800) 528-4841. 1989-. Bimonthly. Includes news items on topics such as research, companies, products, patents, books, education, diary, people, equipment, and legal issues. Also reviews articles and conference reports. Abstracts journal articles, reports, conferences, and books. Also includes biological control, bioenvironmental interactions and stress resistance and genetics.

Applied Ecology Abstracts Studies in Renewable Natural Resources. Information Retrieval Ltd., 1911 Jefferson Davis Highway, Arlington, Virginia 22202. 1975-. Monthly.

Biological Abstracts. BIOSIS, 2100 Arch St., Philadelphia, Pennsylvania 19103-1399. (215) 587-4800. 1927-.

Biological and Agricultural Index. H.W. Wilson Co., 950 University Ave., Bronx, New York 10452. (800) 367-6770. 1916-. Monthly.

Biology Digest. Data Courier, Plexus Pub Inc., 143 Old Marlton Pike, Medford, New Jersey 08055. 1974-. Monthly. Abstracts biology periodicals.

Biotechnology Research Abstracts. Cambridge Scientific Abstracts, 5161 River Rd., Bethesda, Maryland 20816. (301) 961-6750. Monthly. Includes such broad areas as genetic intervention, biochemical genetics, and microbiological techniques.

Ecological Abstracts. Geo Abstracts Ltd. Elsevier Applied Science, Crown House, Linton Rd., Barking, England IG 11 8JU. 1974-. Derived from over 600 leading ecological and environmental journals, plus books, conference proceedings, reports and theses.

Ecology Abstracts. Cambridge Scientific Abstracts, 5161 River Rd., Bethesda, Maryland 20816. (301) 961-6750. Monthly.

Environment Abstracts. Bowker A & I Publishing, 121 Chanlon Rd., New Providence, New Jersey 07974. (908) 464-6800. 1974-.

Environment Index. Environment Information Center, Index Research Department, 124 E. 39th St., New York, New York 10016. 1971-. Annual.

Environmental Information Connection–EIC. Planning Information Program, Dept. of Urban and Regional Planning, University of Illinois, 1003 West Nevada, Urbana, Illinois 61801. (217) 333-1369. Also available online.

Environmental Periodicals Bibliography. Environmental Studies Institute, International Academy at Santa Barbara, 800 Garden St., Suite D, Santa Barbara, California 93101. (805) 965-5010. Also available online.

Food Science and Technology Abstracts. International Food Information Service, c/o National Food Laboratory, 6363 Clark Ave., Dublin, California 94568. (800) 336-3782. 1969-.

General Science Index. H. W. Wilson Co., 950 University Ave., Bronx, New York 10452. 1978-. Monthly, also issued in annual cumulation. Cumulative subject index to English language periodicals in the subject fields of astronomy, botany, chemistry, earth science, environment and conservation, food and nutrition, genetics, mathematics, medicine and health, microbiology, oceanography, physics, physiology and zoology.

Index to Scientific Book Contents. Institute for Scientific Information, 3501 Market St., Philadelphia, Pennsylvania 19104. (800) 523-1857. 1985-. Annual. Gives contents of science books published.

Multimedia Index to Ecology. National Information Center for Educational Media, University of Southern California, Los Angeles, California 90007.

Science Citation Index. Institute for Scientific Information, 3501 Market St., Philadelphia, Pennsylvania 19104. 1961-.

BIBLIOGRAPHIES

Current Contents. Agriculture, Biology and Environmental Sciences. Institute for Scientific Information, 3501 Market St., Philadelphia, Pennsylvania 19104. (800) 523-

1857. 1973-. Previous title: Current Contents. Agricultural, Food & Veterinary Sciences. Gives the table of contents of periodicals in the fields of agriculture, biology, environmental and related areas.

EPA Publications Bibliography. U.S. Environmental Protection Agency, Library Systems Branch, 401 M St., SW, Washington, District of Columbia 20460. (202) 260-2090. Quarterly.

ENCYCLOPEDIAS AND DICTIONARIES

Cambridge Encyclopedia of Life Sciences. A. E. Friday and David S. Ingram. Cambridge University Press, 40 W 20th St., New York, New York 10011. (212) 924-3900 or (800) 227-0247. 1985. Includes all topics under biology and ecology.

McGraw-Hill Encyclopedia of Environmental Science. Sybil P. Parker. McGraw-Hill Science & Engineering Books, 11 W. 19th St., New York, New York 10011. (212) 337-6010. 1980. Covers ecology, man's influence on nature, and environmental protection.

Van Nostrand's Scientific Encyclopedia. Glenn D. Considine, ed. Van Nostrand Reinhold, 115 5th Ave., New York, New York 10003. (212) 254-3232. 1983. Sixth edition. Includes all broad subject areas in science.

GENERAL WORKS

Bioinstrumentation and Biosensors. Donald L. Wise, ed. Marcel Dekker, Inc., 270 Madison Ave., New York, New York 10016. (212) 696-9000; (800) 228-1160. 1991. Presents novel biotechnology-based microelectronic instruments, such as those used for detection of very low levels of hazardous chemicals, as well as new medical diagnostic instruments.

Biosensors. Elizabeth A. H. Hall. Prentice Hall, Rte. 9W, Englewood Cliffs, New Jersey 07632. (201) 592-2000; (800) 634-2863. 1991. A basic theoretical and practical approach to understanding of biosensors.

ONLINE DATA BASES

BIOSIS Previews. BIOSIS, 2100 Arch St., Philadelphia, Pennsylvania 19103-1399. (215) 587-4800. Largest and most comprehensive database of research in the life sciences. Contains citations for nearly 9000 primary research journals, monographs, reviews, symposia, preliminary reports, semi-popular journals, selected institutional reports, government reports and research communications.

Enviro/Energyline Abstracts Plus. R. R. Bowker Co., 121 Chanlon Rd., New Providence, New Jersey 07974. (908) 464-6800.

Environmental Periodicals Bibliography. National Information Services Corp., Ste. 6, Wyman Towers, 3100 St. Paul St., Baltimore, Maryland 21218. (410)243-0797. Online version of abstract of same name.

SCISEARCH. Institute for Scientific Information, University City Science Center, 3501 Market St., Philadelphia, Pennsylvania 19104. (215) 386-0100.

PERIODICALS AND NEWSLETTERS

Ecomod. ISEM–North America Chapter, Water Quality Division, South Florida Water Management District,

P.O. Box 24608, West Palm Beach, Florida 33416. (407) 686-8800. Monthly. Current events in ecological and environmental modeling.

Marine Biology. Springer-Verlag, 175 5th Ave., New York, New York 10010. (212) 461-1500; (800) 777-4643. Sixteen/year. Life in oceans and coastal waters.

BIOSPHERES

ABSTRACTING AND INDEXING SERVICES

Applied Ecology Abstracts Studies in Renewable Natural Resources. Information Retrieval Ltd., 1911 Jefferson Davis Highway, Arlington, Virginia 22202. 1975-. Monthly.

Aqualine Abstracts. Water Research Centre. c/o Pergamon Microforms International, Inc., Fairview Park, Elmsford, New York 10523. (914) 592-7720. 1927-. Contains some 8,000 records annually on water and wastewater technology. Covers all aspects of water, wastewater, associated engineering services and the aquatic environment. Over 600 periodicals, as well as books, reports and conference proceedings and other publications from water related institutions worldwide are scanned. Also available online.

Biological Abstracts. BIOSIS, 2100 Arch St., Philadelphia, Pennsylvania 19103-1399. (215) 587-4800. 1927-.

Biological and Agricultural Index. H.W. Wilson Co., 950 University Ave., Bronx, New York 10452. (800) 367-6770. 1916-. Monthly.

Biology Digest. Data Courier, Plexus Pub Inc., 143 Old Marlton Pike, Medford, New Jersey 08055. 1974-. Monthly. Abstracts biology periodicals.

Current Advances in Ecological and Environmental Science. Pergamon Microforms International, Inc., Fairview Park, Elmsford, New York 10523. (914) 592-7720. 1989-. Monthly. Current literature searching service includingjournals, reports, abstracts, etc. This service is available online as part of the CABS database on the hosts BRS and ORBIT search service.

Ecological Abstracts. Geo Abstracts Ltd. Elsevier Applied Science, Crown House, Linton Rd., Barking, England IG 11 8JU. 1974-. Derived from over 600 leading ecological and environmental journals, plus books, conference proceedings, reports and theses.

Ecology Abstracts. Cambridge Scientific Abstracts, 5161 River Rd., Bethesda, Maryland 20816. (301) 961-6750. Monthly.

Environment Abstracts. Bowker A & I Publishing, 121 Chanlon Rd., New Providence, New Jersey 07974. (908) 464-6800. 1974-.

Environment Index. Environment Information Center, Index Research Department, 124 E. 39th St., New York, New York 10016. 1971-. Annual.

Environmental Information Connection–EIC. Planning Information Program, Dept. of Urban and Regional Planning, University of Illinois, 1003 West Nevada, Urbana, Illinois 61801. (217) 333-1369. Also available online.

Environmental Periodicals Bibliography. Environmental Studies Institute, International Academy at Santa Barba-

ra, 800 Garden St., Suite D, Santa Barbara, California 93101. (805) 965-5010. Also available online.

General Science Index. H. W. Wilson Co., 950 University Ave., Bronx, New York 10452. 1978-. Monthly, also issued in annual cumulation. Cumulative subject index to English language periodicals in the subject fields of astronomy, botany, chemistry, earth science, environment and conservation, food and nutrition, genetics, mathematics, medicine and health, microbiology, oceanography, physics, physiology and zoology.

Geographical Abstracts. London School of Economics, Dept. of Geography, Regency House, 34 Duke St., London, England 1966-. Continued by Geo Abstracts issued in 6 parts: Pt. A. Landforms and the quaternary; Pt. B. Biogeography and Climatology; Pt. C. Economic geography; Pt. D. Social geography and cartography; Pt. E. Sedimentology; Pt. F. Regional and community planning.

Index to Scientific Book Contents. Institute for Scientific Information, 3501 Market St., Philadelphia, Pennsylvania 19104. (800) 523-1857. 1985-. Annual. Gives contents of science books published.

Multimedia Index to Ecology. National Information Center for Educational Media, University of Southern California, Los Angeles, California 90007.

Pollution Abstracts. Cambridge Scientific Abstracts, 5161 River Rd., Bethesda, Maryland 20816. (301) 961-6750. Six/year. Indexes worldwide technical literature on environmental pollution. Covers air pollution, marine and freshwater pollution, sewage and wastewater treatment, waste management, toxicology and health, noise pollution, radiation, land pollution, and environmental policies, programs, legislation, and education. Also available online.

Science Citation Index. Institute for Scientific Information, 3501 Market St., Philadelphia, Pennsylvania 19104. 1961-.

BIBLIOGRAPHIES

Bibliography and Index of Geology. American Geological Institute, 4220 King St., Alexandria, Virginia 22302. Monthly. Includes environmental geology and hydrogeology.

Bibliography on the International Network of Biosphere Reserves. U.S. MAB Coordinating Committee for Biosphere Reserves. United States Man and the Biosphere Program, Available from National Technical Information Service, 5285 Port Royal Rd., Springfield, Virginia 22161. (703) 487-4650. 1990.

Current Contents. Agriculture, Biology and Environmental Sciences. Institute for Scientific Information, 3501 Market St., Philadelphia, Pennsylvania 19104. (800) 523-1857. 1973-. Previous title: Current Contents. Agricultural, Food & Veterinary Sciences. Gives the table of contents of periodicals in the fields of agriculture, biology, environmental and related areas.

Directory of Published Proceedings. Interdok Corp., 173 Halstead Ave., Harrison, New York 10528. (914) 835-3506. 1990. Monthly. This is a listing of published proceedings including the series SEMTE (Science/Medicine/Engineering/Technology) and the series SSH (Social Science/Humanities).

EPA Publications Bibliography. U.S. Environmental Protection Agency, Library Systems Branch, 401 M St., SW, Washington, District of Columbia 20460. (202) 260-2090. Quarterly.

DIRECTORIES

Gale Environmental Sourcebook. Karen Hill. Gale Research Co., 835 Penobscot Bldg., Detroit, Michigan 48226-4094. (313) 961-2242. Contacts, information sources, or general information on environmental topics.

United Nations List of National Parks and Protected Areas. World Conservation Monitoring Centre. World Conservation Union, IUCN Publications Services Unit, 181a Huntingdon Road, Cambridge, England CB3 0DJ. (0223) 277894. 1990. Standard list of national parks and other protected areas. Includes lists of world heritage sites, biosphere reserves and wetlands of international importance.

ENCYCLOPEDIAS AND DICTIONARIES

Cambridge Encyclopedia of Life Sciences. A. E. Friday and David S. Ingram. Cambridge University Press, 40 W 20th St., New York, New York 10011. (212) 924-3900 or (800) 227-0247. 1985. Includes all topics under biology and ecology.

A Dictionary of Genetics. Robert C. King and William A. Stansfield. Oxford University Press, 200 Madison Ave., New York, New York 10016. (212) 679-7300 or (800) 334-4249. 1991. Fourth edition. Includes 7,100 definitions with 250 illustrations. Also includes bibliography of major sources.

Dictionary of Genetics and Cell Biology. Norman Maclean. New York University Press, 70 Washington Sq. S., New York, New York 10012. (212) 998-2575. 1987. Includes the subject areas of cytology and genetics.

The Encyclopedia of Animal Ecology. Peter D. Moore. Facts on File, Inc., 460 Park Ave. S., New York, New York 10016. (212) 683-2244. 1987.

Encyclopedia of Human Biology. Renato Dulbecco, ed. Academic Press, c/o Harcourt Brace Jovanovich Inc., 6277 Sea Harbor Dr., Orlando, Florida 32887. (800) 346-8648. 1991. Eight volumes.

Encyclopedic Dictionary of Genetics: With German Term Equivalents and Extensive German/English Index. R. C. King and W. D. Stansfield. VCH Publishers, 303 NW 12th Ave., Deerfield Beach, Florida 33442-1788. (305) 428-5566. 1990. 4th ed. Revised edition of: A Dictionary of Genetics, third edition.

McGraw-Hill Encyclopedia of Environmental Science. Sybil P. Parker. McGraw-Hill Science & Engineering Books, 11 W. 19th St., New York, New York 10011. (212) 337-6010. 1980. Covers ecology, man's influence on nature, and environmental protection.

McGraw-Hill Encyclopedia of Science and Technology. McGraw-Hill, 1221 Avenue of the Americas, New York, New York 10020. (212) 512-2000 or (800) 262-4729. 1992. Seventh edition. Issued in multiple volumes including index. Includes all science and technology broad subject areas.

The New York Times Encyclopedic Dictionary of the Environment. Paul Sarnoff. Quadrangle Books, New York, New York 1971. Focuses on state-of-the-art methods of pollution control, abatement, prevention and removal.

Van Nostrand's Scientific Encyclopedia. Glenn D. Considine, ed. Van Nostrand Reinhold, 115 5th Ave., New York, New York 10003. (212) 254-3232. 1983. Sixth edition. Includes all broad subject areas in science.

GENERAL WORKS

Agricultural Ecology. Joy Tivy. John Wiley & Sons, Inc., 605 3rd Ave., New York, New York 10158-0012. (212) 850-6000. 1990. Analyzes the nature of relationships between crops, livestock, and the biophysical environment, and the extent to which man has modified the products and environment to suit his own needs.

Biosphere 2: The Human Experiment. John Allen. Viking, 375 Hudson St., New York, New York 10014. (212) 366-2000. 1991.

Carbon Dioxide: Friend or Foe?. IBR Press, 631 E. Laguana Dr., Tempe, Arizona 85282. (802) 966-8693. An inquiry into the climatic and agricultural consequences of the rapidly rising CO_2 content of earth's atmosphere.

Chemistry, Agriculture and the Environment. Mervyn L. Richardson. Royal Society of Chemistry, Thomas Graham House, Science Park, Milton Rd., Cambridge, England CB4 4WF. 44(0)223420066. 1991. Provides an overview of the chemical pollution of the environment caused by modern agricultural practices worldwide, and describes the effects of agrochemicals used in intensive animal and crop production on the air, water, soil, plants, and animals including humans. Also available through CRC Press.

The Colorado Front Range: A Century of Ecological Change. University of Utah Press, 401 Kendall D. Graff Building, Salt Lake City, Utah 84112. (801) 581-7274. 1991.

Debt-for-Nature Exchanges and Biosphere Reserves: Experiences and Potential. Peter Dogse and Bernd von Droste. UNESCO, 7, place de Fontenoy, Paris, France F-75700. (331) 45 68 40 67. 1990. MAB Digest 6.

The Dream of the Earth. Thomas Berry. Sierra Club Books, 100 Bush St., San Francisco, California 94104. (415) 291-1600. 1988. Describes the ecological fate from a species perspective.

Ecology for Beginners. Stephen Croall. Pantheon Books, 201 E 50th St., New York, New York 10022. (212) 751-2600. 1981. The story of man's struggle with the environment.

Ecosystems Experiments. H. A. Mooney, et al., eds. John Wiley & Sons, Inc., 605 3rd Ave., New York, New York 10158-0012. (212) 850-6000. 1991. Explores the potential ecosystem experimentation as a tool for understanding and predicting changes in the biosphere. Areas investigated include deforestation, desertification, El Nino phenomenon, acid rain, watersheds, wetlands, and aquatic and climatic changes.

GAIA: A New Look at Life on Earth. J. E. Lovelock. Oxford University Press, 200 Madison Ave., New York, New York 10016. (212) 679-7300; (800) 334-4249. 1988. Explores the idea that life on earth functions as a single organism which actually defines and maintains conditions necessary for its survival.

GAIA, an Atlas of Planet Management. Norman Myers. Anchor Pr./Doubleday, 666 5th Ave., New York, New York 10103. (212) 765-6500; (800) 223-6834. Resource atlas including a wealth of data on the environment with text by authoritative environmentalists.

General Energetics; Energy in the Biosphere and Civilization. Vaclav Smil. John Wiley & Sons, Inc., 605 3rd Ave., New York, New York 10158-0012. (212) 850-6000. 1991. Provides an integrated framework for analyzing planetary energetics (solar radiation and gemorphic processes), bioenergetics (photosynthesis), and human energetics (metabolism and thermoregulation) traced from hunting-gathering and agricultural societies through modern day industrial civilization, concluding with the impact of modern energy use on environment and society.

International Co-ordinating Council of the Programme on Man and the Biosphere, 11th session. Final Report. UNESCO, 7, place de Fontenoy, Paris, France F-75700. (331) 45 68 40 67. 1990. MAB Report series no. 62. Report of the Council session held in Paris 12-16, November 1990.

Long-Term Ecological Research: An International Perspective. Paul G. Risser, ed. John Wiley & Sons, Inc., 605 3rd Ave., New York, New York 10158-0012. (212) 850-6000. 1991. Describes and analyzes research programs in various ecosystems such as temperate forests, arid steppes, deserts, temperate and tropical grasslands, aquatic systems from countries including Scotland, Kenya, USA, Australia, Canada, Germany, and France.

Magill's Survey of Science. Earth Science Series. Frank N. Magill. Salem Press, PO Box 50062, Pasadena, California 91105. 1990-. Five volumes. Includes information on earth's crust, hot spots and volcanic island chains, physical properties of minerals, rock magnetism, physical properties of rocks, and index.

Magill's Survey of Science. Life Science Series. Frank N. Magill, ed. Salem Press, PO Box 50062, Pasadena, California 91105. 1991. Six volumes. Contents: v.1. A-Central and peripheral nervous system functions; v.2. Central metabolism regulation - eukaryotic transcriptional control; v.3. Positive and negative eukaryotic transcriptional control - mammalian hormones; v.4. Hormones and behavior - muscular contraction; v.5. Muscular contraction and relaxation - sexual reproduction in plants; v.6. Reproductive behavior and mating - X inactivation and the Lyon hypothesis.

Man Belongs to the Earth. International Co-operation in Environmental Research, UNESCO's Man and the Biosphere Programme. UNESCO, 7, place de Fontenoy, Paris, France F-75700. (331) 45 68 40 67. 1988. Provides an account of the MAB programme as it stood in 1987.

Mind and Nature: A Necessary Unit. Gregory Bateson. Bantam Books, 666 5th Ave., New York, New York 10103. (212) 765-6500; (800) 223-6834. 1988. Reveals the pattern which connects man and nature.

The Next One Hundred Years: Shaping the Fate of Our Living Earth. Jonathan Weiner. Bantam Books, 666 5th Ave., New York, New York 10103. (212) 765-6500; (800) 223-6834. 1991. Explores the following issues: the greenhouse effect, deforestation, the destruction of the ozone layer, the human population explosion and the onset of mass extinctions.

Patterns of Primary Production in the Biosphere. Helmut F. H. Lieth. Van Nostrand Reinhold, Information Services, 115 5th Ave., New York, New York 10003. (212) 254-3232. 1978.

Planet under Stress: The Challenge of Global Change. Constance Mungall and Digby J. McLaren, eds. Oxford University Press, 200 Madison Ave., New York, New York 10016. (212) 679-7300; (800) 334-4249. 1991.

Remote Sensing of Biosphere Functioning. Springer-Verlag, 175 5th Ave., New York, New York 10010. (212) 460-1500. 1990. Ecological studies relating to biosphere sensing and biological aspects of remote sensing.

Terrestrial and Aquatic Ecosystems: Perturbation and Recovery. Oscar Ravera, ed. E. Horwood, 1230 Avenue of the Americas, New York, New York 10020. (800) 223-2348. 1991. Presented at the 5th European Ecological Symposium held at Siena, Italy in 1989. Some of the topics included: biological responses to the changing ecosystem; anthropogenic perturbations of the community and ecosystem; restoration of degraded ecosystems; environmental management and strategies.

Trace Elements in Soils and Plants. Alina Kabata-Pendias and Henryk Pendias. CRC Press, 2000 Corporate Blvd. N.W., Boca Raton, Florida 33431. (800) 272-7737. 1991. 2d ed. Discusses the pollution of air, water, soil and plants, all about soil processes, and the involvement of trace elements in the soil and plants.

Waste Management: Towards A Sustainable Society. Om Prakash Kharbanda and E. A. Stallworthy. Auburn House, 14 Dedham St., Dover, Massachusetts 02030-0658. (505) 785-2220; (800) 223-2665. 1990. Describes the generation of various types of hazardous and nonhazardous wastes, with a whole chapter devoted to acid rain.

ONLINE DATA BASES

BIOSIS Previews. BIOSIS, 2100 Arch St., Philadelphia, Pennsylvania 19103-1399. (215) 587-4800. Largest and most comprehensive database of research in the life sciences. Contains citations for nearly 9000 primary research journals, monographs, reviews, symposia, preliminary reports, semi-popular journals, selected institutional reports, government reports and research communications.

Biotechnology Abstracts. Derwent Publications Ltd., 6845 Elm St., McLean, Virginia 22101. (703) 790-0400. Includes material on genetic manipulation, biochemical engineering, fermentation, biocatalysis, cell hybridization, in vitro plant propagation and industrial waste management.

Enviro/Energyline Abstracts Plus. R. R. Bowker Co., 121 Chanlon Rd., New Providence, New Jersey 07974. (908) 464-6800.

Environmental Periodicals Bibliography. National Information Services Corp., Ste. 6, Wyman Towers, 3100 St. Paul St., Baltimore, Maryland 21218. (410)243-0797. Online version of abstract of same name.

Monthly Catalog of United States Government Publications. U.S. G.P.O., Supt. of Docs., PO Box 371954, Pittsburgh, Pennsylvania 15250-7954. (202) 512-0000.

National Technical Information Service. U.S. Department of Commerce, National Technical Information Service, Office of Data Base Services, 5285 Port Royal Rd., Springfield, Virginia 22161. (703) 487-4807. Bibliographic database of government sponsored research and technical reports.

SCISEARCH. Institute for Scientific Information, University City Science Center, 3501 Market St., Philadelphia, Pennsylvania 19104. (215) 386-0100.

PERIODICALS AND NEWSLETTERS

BioScience Journal. American Institute of Biological Sciences, 730 11th Street, Nw, Washington, District of Columbia 20001-4521. (202) 628-1500. Eleven times a year. Current research, feature articles, book reviews, and new products.

Biosphere. International Society for Environmental Education, Ohio State University, 210 Kottman Hall, 2021 Coffey Rd., Columbus, Ohio 43210. (614) 292-2265. Three times a year. International environmental education.

Canadian Society of Environmental Biologists Newsletter. Canadian Society of Environmental Biologists, PO Box 962, Sta. F, Toronto, Ontario, Canada M4Y 2N9. 1962-. Quarterly.

Catalyst: Economics for the Living Earth. Catalyst Investing in Social Change, 64 Main St., Montpelier, Vermont 05602. (802) 223-7943. 1983-. Quarterly. Discusses grassroots enterprises working for social change and a humane economy. Focuses on ecological balance, articles on forest destruction, energy issues, native peoples issues and community- based economics.

Chemosphere: Chemistry, Biology and Toxicology as Related to Environmental Problems. Pergamon Microforms International, Inc., Fairview Park, Elmsford, New York 10523. (914) 592-7720. 1970-. Offers maximum dissemination of investigations related to the health and safety of every aspect of life. Environmental protection encompasses a very wide field and relies on scientific research in chemistry, biology, physics, toxicology and inter-related disciplines.

Earthwatch Magazine. Earthwatch Expeditions, 680 Mt. Auburn St., Box 403, Watertown, Massachusetts 02272. (617) 926-8200. Bimonthly. Worldwide research expeditions, endangered species, cultures, and world health.

Ecological Applications. Ecological Society of America, Center for Environmental Studies, Arizona State University, Tempe, Arizona 85287. (602) 965-3000. 1991-. Quarterly. Emphasizes the application of basic ecological concepts to a wide range of problems.

Ecologist. MIT Press, 55 Hayward St., Cambridge, Massachusetts 02142. (617) 253-2889. Bimonthly. Man's impact on the biosphere and social, economic and political barriers.

Ecomod. ISEM–North America Chapter, Water Quality Division, South Florida Water Management District, P.O. Box 24608, West Palm Beach, Florida 33416. (407) 686-8800. Monthly. Current events in ecological and environmental modeling.

Man and the Biosphere Series. J. N. R. Jeffers, ed. Parthenon Pub., Casterton Hall, Carnforth, England LA6 2LA. (05242) 72084. 1990-. Contents: v.1. The Control of Eutrophication of Lakes and Reservoirs; v.2. An Amazonian Rain Forest; v.3. Exploiting the Tropical Rain Forest; v.4. The Ecology and Management of Aquatic-Terrestrial Ecotones; v.5. Sustainable Development and Environmental Management of Small Islands; v.6. Rain Forest Regeneration and Management; v.7. Reproductive Ecology of Tropical Forest Plants; v.8. Redevelopment of Degraded Ecosystems; v.9. Pastoralism in Transition.

Marine Biology. Springer-Verlag, 175 5th Ave., New York, New York 10010. (212) 461-1500; (800) 777-4643. Sixteen/year. Life in oceans and coastal waters.

RESEARCH CENTERS AND INSTITUTES

University of Michigan, Biophysics Research Division. Institute of Science and Technology, 2200 Bonisteel Boulevard, Ann Arbor, Michigan 48109-2099. (313) 764-5218.

STATISTICS SOURCES

Environmental Data Compendium. OECD Publications and Information Center, 2001 L St., N.W., Suite 700, Washington, District of Columbia 20036. (202) 785-6323. 1989.

Environmental Indicators. OECD Publications and Information Center, 2001 L St., N.W., Suite 700, Washington, District of Columbia 20036. (202) 785-6323. 1991.

Environmental Quality. Council on Environmental Quality. U.S. G.P.O., Washington, District of Columbia 20401. (202) 512-0000. Annual.

The State of the Environment. OECD Publications and Information Center, 2001 L St., N.W., Suite 700, Washington, District of Columbia 20036. (202) 785-6323. 1991.

World Resources. World Resources Institute. 1709 New York Ave., N.W., Washington, District of Columbia 20006. (202) 638-6300. Annual. Statistical and textual analysis of world's natural resources and the effects of growth-caused environmental pollution.

TRADE ASSOCIATIONS AND PROFESSIONAL SOCIETIES

American Institute of Biological Sciences. 730 11th St., N.W., Washington, District of Columbia 20001-4521. (202) 628-1500.

American Society of Naturalists. Department of Ecology and Evolation, State University of New York, Stony Brook, New York 11794. (516) 632-8589.

Earthwatch. 680 Mt. Auburn St., P.O. Box 403, Watertown, Massachusetts 02272. (617) 926-8200.

Monteverde Institute. Tropical Biology Program, Council on International Educational Exchange, 205 E. 42nd St., New York, New York 10017.

BIOSTABILIZER

See also: AERATION; COMPOSTING

ABSTRACTING AND INDEXING SERVICES

Applied Ecology Abstracts Studies in Renewable Natural Resources. Information Retrieval Ltd., 1911 Jefferson Davis Highway, Arlington, Virginia 22202. 1975-. Monthly.

Biological Abstracts. BIOSIS, 2100 Arch St., Philadelphia, Pennsylvania 19103-1399. (215) 587-4800. 1927-.

Biological and Agricultural Index. H.W. Wilson Co., 950 University Ave., Bronx, New York 10452. (800) 367-6770. 1916-. Monthly.

Biology Digest. Data Courier, Plexus Pub Inc., 143 Old Marlton Pike, Medford, New Jersey 08055. 1974-. Monthly. Abstracts biology periodicals.

Ecological Abstracts. Geo Abstracts Ltd. Elsevier Applied Science, Crown House, Linton Rd., Barking, England IG 11 8JU. 1974-. Derived from over 600 leading ecological and environmental journals, plus books, conference proceedings, reports and theses.

Environment Abstracts. Bowker A & I Publishing, 121 Chanlon Rd., New Providence, New Jersey 07974. (908) 464-6800. 1974-.

Environment Index. Environment Information Center, Index Research Department, 124 E. 39th St., New York, New York 10016. 1971-. Annual.

Environmental Information Connection–EIC. Planning Information Program, Dept. of Urban and Regional Planning, University of Illinois, 1003 West Nevada, Urbana, Illinois 61801. (217) 333-1369. Also available online.

Environmental Periodicals Bibliography. Environmental Studies Institute, International Academy at Santa Barbara, 800 Garden St., Suite D, Santa Barbara, California 93101. (805) 965-5010. Also available online.

General Science Index. H. W. Wilson Co., 950 University Ave., Bronx, New York 10452. 1978-. Monthly, also issued in annual cumulation. Cumulative subject index to English language periodicals in the subject fields of astronomy, botany, chemistry, earth science, environment and conservation, food and nutrition, genetics, mathematics, medicine and health, microbiology, oceanography, physics, physiology and zoology.

Index to Scientific Book Contents. Institute for Scientific Information, 3501 Market St., Philadelphia, Pennsylvania 19104. (800) 523-1857. 1985-. Annual. Gives contents of science books published.

Multimedia Index to Ecology. National Information Center for Educational Media, University of Southern California, Los Angeles, California 90007.

BIBLIOGRAPHIES

Current Contents. Agriculture, Biology and Environmental Sciences. Institute for Scientific Information, 3501 Market St., Philadelphia, Pennsylvania 19104. (800) 523-1857. 1973-. Previous title: Current Contents. Agricultural, Food & Veterinary Sciences. Gives the table of contents of periodicals in the fields of agriculture, biology, environmental and related areas.

Directory of Published Proceedings. Interdok Corp., 173 Halstead Ave., Harrison, New York 10528. (914) 835-3506. 1990. Monthly. This is a listing of published proceedings including the series SEMTE (Science/Medicine/Engineering/Technology) and the series SSH (Social Science/Humanities).

EPA Publications Bibliography. U.S. Environmental Protection Agency, Library Systems Branch, 401 M St., SW,

Washington, District of Columbia 20460. (202) 260-2090. Quarterly.

ENCYCLOPEDIAS AND DICTIONARIES

Cambridge Encyclopedia of Life Sciences. A. E. Friday and David S. Ingram. Cambridge University Press, 40 W 20th St., New York, New York 10011. (212) 924-3900 or (800) 227-0247. 1985. Includes all topics under biology and ecology.

McGraw-Hill Encyclopedia of Environmental Science. Sybil P. Parker. McGraw-Hill Science & Engineering Books, 11 W. 19th St., New York, New York 10011. (212) 337-6010. 1980. Covers ecology, man's influence on nature, and environmental protection.

Van Nostrand's Scientific Encyclopedia. Glenn D. Considine, ed. Van Nostrand Reinhold, 115 5th Ave., New York, New York 10003. (212) 254-3232. 1983. Sixth edition. Includes all broad subject areas in science.

ONLINE DATA BASES

BIOSIS Previews. BIOSIS, 2100 Arch St., Philadelphia, Pennsylvania 19103-1399. (215) 587-4800. Largest and most comprehensive database of research in the life sciences. Contains citations for nearly 9000 primary research journals, monographs, reviews, symposia, preliminary reports, semi-popular journals, selected institutional reports, government reports and research communications.

Enviro/Energyline Abstracts Plus. R. R. Bowker Co., 121 Chanlon Rd., New Providence, New Jersey 07974. (908) 464-6800.

Environmental Periodicals Bibliography. National Information Services Corp., Ste. 6, Wyman Towers, 3100 St. Paul St., Baltimore, Maryland 21218. (410)243-0797. Online version of abstract of same name.

Monthly Catalog of United States Government Publications. U.S. G.P.O., Supt. of Docs., PO Box 371954, Pittsburgh, Pennsylvania 15250-7954. (202) 512-0000.

National Technical Information Service. U.S. Department of Commerce, National Technical Information Service, Office of Data Base Services, 5285 Port Royal Rd., Springfield, Virginia 22161. (703) 487-4807. Bibliographic database of government sponsored research and technical reports.

SCISEARCH. Institute for Scientific Information, University City Science Center, 3501 Market St., Philadelphia, Pennsylvania 19104. (215) 386-0100.

TRADE ASSOCIATIONS AND PROFESSIONAL SOCIETIES

American Institute of Biological Sciences. 730 11th St., N.W., Washington, District of Columbia 20001-4521. (202) 628-1500.

BIOTA

See also: BIOGEOGRAPHY; BIOLOGICAL COMMUNITIES; ECOSYSTEMS; POPULATION DYNAMICS

ABSTRACTING AND INDEXING SERVICES

Applied Ecology Abstracts Studies in Renewable Natural Resources. Information Retrieval Ltd., 1911 Jefferson Davis Highway, Arlington, Virginia 22202. 1975-. Monthly.

Biological Abstracts. BIOSIS, 2100 Arch St., Philadelphia, Pennsylvania 19103-1399. (215) 587-4800. 1927-.

Biological and Agricultural Index. H.W. Wilson Co., 950 University Ave., Bronx, New York 10452. (800) 367-6770. 1916-. Monthly.

Biology Digest. Data Courier, Plexus Pub Inc., 143 Old Marlton Pike, Medford, New Jersey 08055. 1974-. Monthly. Abstracts biology periodicals.

Ecological Abstracts. Geo Abstracts Ltd. Elsevier Applied Science, Crown House, Linton Rd., Barking, England IG 11 8JU. 1974-. Derived from over 600 leading ecological and environmental journals, plus books, conference proceedings, reports and theses.

Environment Abstracts. Bowker A & I Publishing, 121 Chanlon Rd., New Providence, New Jersey 07974. (908) 464-6800. 1974-.

Environment Index. Environment Information Center, Index Research Department, 124 E. 39th St., New York, New York 10016. 1971-. Annual.

Environmental Information Connection–EIC. Planning Information Program, Dept. of Urban and Regional Planning, University of Illinois, 1003 West Nevada, Urbana, Illinois 61801. (217) 333-1369. Also available online.

Environmental Periodicals Bibliography. Environmental Studies Institute, International Academy at Santa Barbara, 800 Garden St., Suite D, Santa Barbara, California 93101. (805) 965-5010. Also available online.

General Science Index. H. W. Wilson Co., 950 University Ave., Bronx, New York 10452. 1978-. Monthly, also issued in annual cumulation. Cumulative subject index to English language periodicals in the subject fields of astronomy, botany, chemistry, earth science, environment and conservation, food and nutrition, genetics, mathematics, medicine and health, microbiology, oceanography, physics, physiology and zoology.

Index to Scientific Book Contents. Institute for Scientific Information, 3501 Market St., Philadelphia, Pennsylvania 19104. (800) 523-1857. 1985-. Annual. Gives contents of science books published.

Multimedia Index to Ecology. National Information Center for Educational Media, University of Southern California, Los Angeles, California 90007.

Pollution Abstracts. Cambridge Scientific Abstracts, 5161 River Rd., Bethesda, Maryland 20816. (301) 961-6750. Six/year. Indexes worldwide technical literature on environmental pollution. Covers air pollution, marine and freshwater pollution, sewage and wastewater treatment, waste management, toxicology and health, noise pollution, radiation, land pollution, and environmental policies, programs, legislation, and education. Also available online.

Science Citation Index. Institute for Scientific Information, 3501 Market St., Philadelphia, Pennsylvania 19104. 1961-.

BIBLIOGRAPHIES

Current Contents. Agriculture, Biology and Environmental Sciences. Institute for Scientific Information, 3501 Market St., Philadelphia, Pennsylvania 19104. (800) 523-1857. 1973-. Previous title: Current Contents. Agricultural, Food & Veterinary Sciences. Gives the table of contents of periodicals in the fields of agriculture, biology, environmental and related areas.

Directory of Published Proceedings. Interdok Corp., 173 Halstead Ave., Harrison, New York 10528. (914) 835-3506. 1990. Monthly. This is a listing of published proceedings including the series SEMTE (Science/Medicine/Engineering/Technology) and the series SSH (Social Science/Humanities).

EPA Publications Bibliography. U.S. Environmental Protection Agency, Library Systems Branch, 401 M St., SW, Washington, District of Columbia 20460. (202) 260-2090. Quarterly.

DIRECTORIES

Gale Environmental Sourcebook. Karen Hill. Gale Research Co., 835 Penobscot Bldg., Detroit, Michigan 48226-4094. (313) 961-2242. Contacts, information sources, or general information on environmental topics.

ENCYCLOPEDIAS AND DICTIONARIES

Cambridge Encyclopedia of Life Sciences. A. E. Friday and David S. Ingram. Cambridge University Press, 40 W 20th St., New York, New York 10011. (212) 924-3900 or (800) 227-0247. 1985. Includes all topics under biology and ecology.

McGraw-Hill Encyclopedia of Environmental Science. Sybil P. Parker. McGraw-Hill Science & Engineering Books, 11 W. 19th St., New York, New York 10011. (212) 337-6010. 1980. Covers ecology, man's influence on nature, and environmental protection.

McGraw-Hill Encyclopedia of Science and Technology. McGraw-Hill, 1221 Avenue of the Americas, New York, New York 10020. (212) 512-2000 or (800) 262-4729. 1992. Seventh edition. Issued in multiple volumes including index. Includes all science and technology broad subject areas.

GENERAL WORKS

Methods for Assessing Exposure of Human and Non-Human Biota. R. G. Tardiff and B. D. Goldstein, eds. John Wiley & Sons, Inc., 605 3rd Ave., New York, New York 10158-0012. (212) 850-6000. 1991. Provides a critical and collective evaluation of approaches to chemical exposure assessment.

GOVERNMENTAL ORGANIZATIONS

National Science Foundation. 1800 G St., N.W., Washington, District of Columbia 20550. (202) 357-9498.

ONLINE DATA BASES

BIOSIS Previews. BIOSIS, 2100 Arch St., Philadelphia, Pennsylvania 19103-1399. (215) 587-4800. Largest and most comprehensive database of research in the life sciences. Contains citations for nearly 9000 primary research journals, monographs, reviews, symposia, pre-liminary reports, semi-popular journals, selected institutional reports, government reports and research communications.

Enviro/Energyline Abstracts Plus. R. R. Bowker Co., 121 Chanlon Rd., New Providence, New Jersey 07974. (908) 464-6800.

Environmental Periodicals Bibliography. National Information Services Corp., Ste. 6, Wyman Towers, 3100 St. Paul St., Baltimore, Maryland 21218. (410)243-0797. Online version of abstract of same name.

Monthly Catalog of United States Government Publications. U.S. G.P.O., Supt. of Docs., PO Box 371954, Pittsburgh, Pennsylvania 15250-7954. (202) 512-0000.

National Technical Information Service. U.S. Department of Commerce, National Technical Information Service, Office of Data Base Services, 5285 Port Royal Rd., Springfield, Virginia 22161. (703) 487-4807. Bibliographic database of government sponsored research and technical reports.

SCISEARCH. Institute for Scientific Information, University City Science Center, 3501 Market St., Philadelphia, Pennsylvania 19104. (215) 386-0100.

STATISTICS SOURCES

Ecology: Community Profiles. U.S. Fish and Wildlife Service. National Technical Information Service, 5285 Port Royal Road, Springfield, Virginia 22161. (703) 487-4650. Irregular. Data on coastal and inland ecosystems, including wetlands, tidal-flats, near-shore seagrasses, sand dunes, drilling platforms, oyster reefs, estuaries, rivers and streams.

Environmental Data Compendium. OECD Publications and Information Center, 2001 L St., N.W., Suite 700, Washington, District of Columbia 20036. (202) 785-6323. 1989.

Environmental Indicators. OECD Publications and Information Center, 2001 L St., N.W., Suite 700, Washington, District of Columbia 20036. (202) 785-6323. 1991.

Environmental Quality. Council on Environmental Quality. U.S. G.P.O., Washington, District of Columbia 20401. (202) 512-0000. Annual.

The State of the Environment. OECD Publications and Information Center, 2001 L St., N.W., Suite 700, Washington, District of Columbia 20036. (202) 785-6323. 1991.

World Resources. World Resources Institute. 1709 New York Ave., N.W., Washington, District of Columbia 20006. (202) 638-6300. Annual. Statistical and textual analysis of world's natural resources and the effects of growth-caused environmental pollution.

TRADE ASSOCIATIONS AND PROFESSIONAL SOCIETIES

American Institute of Biological Sciences. 730 11th St., N.W., Washington, District of Columbia 20001-4521. (202) 628-1500.

American Society of Naturalists. Department of Ecology and Evolation, State University of New York, Stony Brook, New York 11794. (516) 632-8589.

BIOTECHNOLOGY

See also: AGRICULTURE; CROPS; FOOD SCIENCE;
MICROORGANISMS

ABSTRACTING AND INDEXING SERVICES

AgBiotech News and Information. C. A. B. International,
845 North Park Ave., Tucson, Arizona 85719. (602) 621-
7897 or (800) 528-4841. 1989-. Bimonthly. Includes news
items on topics such as research, companies, products,
patents, books, education, diary, people, equipment, and
legal issues. Also reviews articles and conference reports.
Abstracts journal articles, reports, conferences, and
books. Also includes biological control, bioenvironmental interactions and stress resistance and genetics.

*Applied Ecology Abstracts Studies in Renewable Natural
Resources.* Information Retrieval Ltd., 1911 Jefferson
Davis Highway, Arlington, Virginia 22202. 1975-.
Monthly.

Applied Science and Technology Index. H.W. Wilson Co.,
950 University Ave., Bronx, New York 10452. (800) 367-
6770. Formerly Industrial Arts Index.

ASFA Aquaculture Abstracts. Cambridge Scientific Abstracts, Inc., 5161 River Rd., Bethesda, Maryland 20816.
(301) 961-6750. 1984.

Biodeterioration Abstracts. Farnham Royal, Slough, England SL2 3BN. Quarterly.

Biodeterioration Research Titles. Biodeterioration Information Centre, University of Aston in Birmingham,
Birmingham, England

Biological Abstracts. BIOSIS, 2100 Arch St., Philadelphia, Pennsylvania 19103-1399. (215) 587-4800. 1927-.

Biological and Agricultural Index. H.W. Wilson Co., 950
University Ave., Bronx, New York 10452. (800) 367-
6770. 1916-. Monthly.

Biology Digest. Data Courier, Plexus Pub Inc., 143 Old
Marlton Pike, Medford, New Jersey 08055. 1974-.
Monthly. Abstracts biology periodicals.

Biotechnology Research Abstracts. Cambridge Scientific
Abstracts, 5161 River Rd., Bethesda, Maryland 20816.
(301) 961-6750. Monthly. Includes such broad areas as
genetic intervention, biochemical genetics, and microbiological techniques.

*Current Advances in Ecological and Environmental Sci-
ence.* Pergamon Microforms International, Inc., Fairview
Park, Elmsford, New York 10523. (914) 592-7720. 1989-.
Monthly. Current literature searching service includingjournals, reports, abstracts, etc. This service is available
online as part of the CABS database on the hosts BRS
and ORBIT search service.

Ecological Abstracts. Geo Abstracts Ltd. Elsevier Applied
Science, Crown House, Linton Rd., Barking, England IG
11 8JU. 1974-. Derived from over 600 leading ecological
and environmental journals, plus books, conference
proceedings, reports and theses.

Environment Abstracts. Bowker A & I Publishing, 121
Chanlon Rd., New Providence, New Jersey 07974. (908)
464-6800. 1974-.

Environment Index. Environment Information Center,
Index Research Department, 124 E. 39th St., New York,
New York 10016. 1971-. Annual.

Environmental Information Connection–EIC. Planning
Information Program, Dept. of Urban and Regional
Planning, University of Illinois, 1003 West Nevada,
Urbana, Illinois 61801. (217) 333-1369. Also available
online.

Environmental Periodicals Bibliography. Environmental
Studies Institute, International Academy at Santa Barbara, 800 Garden St., Suite D, Santa Barbara, California
93101. (805) 965-5010. Also available online.

Food Science and Technology Abstracts. International
Food Information Service, c/o National Food Laboratory, 6363 Clark Ave., Dublin, California 94568. (800) 336-
3782. 1969-.

General Science Index. H. W. Wilson Co., 950 University
Ave., Bronx, New York 10452. 1978-. Monthly, also
issued in annual cumulation. Cumulative subject index
to English language periodicals in the subject fields of
astronomy, botany, chemistry, earth science, environment and conservation, food and nutrition, genetics,
mathematics, medicine and health, microbiology, oceanography, physics, physiology and zoology.

Green Engineering: A Current Awareness Bulletin. Institution of Mechanical Engineers, 1 Birdcage Walk, Westminster, London, England SW1H 9JJ. 71973 1266/7.
1991. Monthly. Covers acid rain, aerosol technology,
biotechnology chlorofluorocarbons, chemical and process
engineering, environmental protection, energy conservation, energy generation, greenhouse effect, materials,
pollution, recycling, waste disposal, and other environmental topics.

Index to Scientific Book Contents. Institute for Scientific
Information, 3501 Market St., Philadelphia, Pennsylvania 19104. (800) 523-1857. 1985-. Annual. Gives contents of science books published.

Multimedia Index to Ecology. National Information
Center for Educational Media, University of Southern
California, Los Angeles, California 90007.

Science Citation Index. Institute for Scientific Information, 3501 Market St., Philadelphia, Pennsylvania 19104.
1961-.

Sea Grant Abstracts. National Sea Grant Depository, Pell
Laboratory Bldg., Bay Campus, University of Rhode
Island, Narragansett, Rhode Island 02882. (401) 792-
6114. 1986-. Quarterly. Published by the National Sea
Grant Programs, this collection includes annual reports,
serials and newsletters, charts and maps.

Telegen Reporter Annual. Bowker A & I Publishing. 245
W 17th St., New York, New York 10011. 1989. Provides
up-to-date reviews of the pharmaceutical, agricultural,
industrial and energy applications of the products, processes, and markets of genetic engineering and biotechnology. Also addresses economic, social, regulatory,
patent, and public policy issues. This annual cumulation
abstracts and indexes information from scientific, technical, and business journals, conference and symposium
proceedings, and academic government,and corporate
reports.

BIBLIOGRAPHIES

Chemical Engineering Bibliography. Martyn S. Ray. Noyes Publications, 120 Mill Rd., Park Ridge, New Jersey 07656. (201) 391-8484. Contains 20,000 references from 40 journals published over the period 1967-1988. Some of the topics covered include: energy conservation, environmental management, biotechnology, plant operations, absorption and cooling towers, membrane separation and other chemical engineering areas.

Current Contents. Agriculture, Biology and Environmental Sciences. Institute for Scientific Information, 3501 Market St., Philadelphia, Pennsylvania 19104. (800) 523-1857. 1973-. Previous title: Current Contents. Agricultural, Food & Veterinary Sciences. Gives the table of contents of periodicals in the fields of agriculture, biology, environmental and related areas.

Directory of Published Proceedings. Interdok Corp., 173 Halstead Ave., Harrison, New York 10528. (914) 835-3506. 1990. Monthly. This is a listing of published proceedings including the series SEMTE (Science/Medicine/Engineering/Technology) and the series SSH (Social Science/Humanities).

EPA Publications Bibliography. U.S. Environmental Protection Agency, Library Systems Branch, 401 M St., SW, Washington, District of Columbia 20460. (202) 260-2090. Quarterly.

Gasohol Sourcebook: Literature Survey and Abstracts. N. P. Cheremisinoff and P. N. Cheremisinoff. Ann Arbor Science, 230 Collingwood, PO Box 1425, Ann Arbor, Michigan 48106. 1981. Volume includes: biotechnology and bioconversion; ethanol and methanol production; automotive and other fuels; production of chemical feedstocks; and economics of alcohol production.

Information Sources in Biotechnology. A. Crafts-Lighty. Stockton Press, New York, New York 10010. (212) 673-4400. 1986. Describes information sources in the field of biotechnology.

DIRECTORIES

Agricultural Information Resource Centers, a World Directory 1990. Rita C. Fisher. IAALD World Directory Working Group, 716 W. Indiana Ave., Urbana, Illinois 61801-4836. (217) 333-7687. 1990. Includes 3,971 information resource centers that have agriculture related collection and/or information services.

BioScan: The Biotechnology Corporate Directory Service. Oryx Press, 4041 N. Central at Indian School Rd., Ste. 700, Phoenix, Arizona 85012-3397. (602) 265-2651.

The Biotechnology Directory. J. Coombs and Y. R. Alston. Stockton Press, 257 Park Ave. S., New York, New York 10010. (212) 673-4400. 1992. Provides information on more than 10,000 companies, research centers, and academic institutions involved in new and established technologies, more than 2500 of which are in U.S. and Canada. There are 500 product codes to locate companies and a useful index of organizations.

Biotechnology Engineers: Biographical Directory. OMEC International, Inc., 727 15th St.,N.W., Washington, District of Columbia 20005. (202) 639-8900.

Biotechnology Guide Japan. Stockton Press, 257 Park Ave. S, New York, New York 10010. (212) 673-4400 or (800) 221-2123. 1990. Source of Who's Who and What's What in Japanese biotechnology industry.

Directory of Biotechnology Centers. North Carolina Biotechnology Center, 79 Alexander Dr., P.O. Box 13547, Research Triangle Park, North Carolina 27709-3547. (919) 541-9366.

Federal Biotechnology Funding Sources. Oskar R. Zaborsky and B. K. Young. OMEC International Inc., 727 15th St., NW, Washington, District of Columbia 20005. (202) 639-8400. 1984.

Federal Biotechnology Information Resources Directory. OMEC International Inc., 727 15th St. NW, Washington, District of Columbia 20005. (202) 639-8400. 1987. Directory of federal government information resources relevant to biotechnology. Covers federal programs and provides comprehensive access to federal information resources in biotechnology.

Federal Biotechnology Programs Directory. OMEC International Inc., 727 15th St., NW, Washington, District of Columbia 20005. (202) 639-8400. 1987. Describes federal programs relevant to biotechnology. Provides composite information gleaned from various sources such as program announcements, annual reports, reports to Congress, and OMEC International Inc. extensive contact files.

ENCYCLOPEDIAS AND DICTIONARIES

Biotechnology Glossary. Elsevier Science Publishing Co., 655 Avenue of the Americas, New York, New York 10010. (212) 989-5800. 1990. Glossary originally conceived as an aid to translators faced with technical texts relating to biotechnology. Text in nine languages including English, French, German, Italian, Nedelandse, Dansk, Spanish, Portuguese, and Greek. Deals with sections on molecular biology, physiology, biochemistry, and biochemical techniques, genetic engineering, enzymology, pharmacology, immunology, plant genetics, biomass, and scientific and technical applications.

Cambridge Encyclopedia of Life Sciences. A. E. Friday and David S. Ingram. Cambridge University Press, 40 W 20th St., New York, New York 10011. (212) 924-3900 or (800) 227-0247. 1985. Includes all topics under biology and ecology.

Dictionary of Biotechnology. J. Coombs. Elsevier Science Publishing Co., 655 Avenue of the Americas, New York, New York 10010. (212) 984-5800. 1986. Areas covered in this dictionary include: fermentation; brewing; vaccines; plant tissue; culture; antibiotic production; production and use of enzymes; biomass; byproduct recovery and effluent treatment; equipment; processes; micro-organisms and biochemicals.

Dictionary of Biotechnology English-German. W. Babel, et al., ed. Elsevier Science Publishing Co., 655 Avenue of the Americas, New York, New York 10010. (212) 984-5800. 1989. Presents over 7300 terms in the area of biotechnology from many academic disciplines and treats biotechnology as more than just a bioscience.

Dictionary of Biotechnology in English-Japanese and German. R. Schmid and Saburo Fukui. Springer Verlag, 175 5th Ave., New York, New York 10010. (212) 460-1500 or (800) 777-4643. 1986.

Dictionary of Environmental Engineering and Related Sciences: English-Spanish, Spanish-English. Jose T. Villate. Ediciones Universal, 3090 SW 8th St., Miami, Florida 33135. (305) 642-3355. 1979.

A Dictionary of Genetics. Robert C. King and William A. Stansfield. Oxford University Press, 200 Madison Ave., New York, New York 10016. (212) 679-7300 or (800) 334-4249. 1991. Fourth edition. Includes 7,100 definitions with 250 illustrations. Also includes bibliography of major sources.

Dictionary of Genetics and Cell Biology. Norman Maclean. New York University Press, 70 Washington Sq. S., New York, New York 10012. (212) 998-2575. 1987. Includes the subject areas of cytology and genetics.

Encyclopedia of Environmental Science and Engineering. J.R. Pfafflin. Gordon and Breach Science Publishers, Inc., 270 8th Ave., New York, New York 10011. (212) 206-8900. 1992.

Encyclopedic Dictionary of Genetics: With German Term Equivalents and Extensive German/English Index. R. C. King and W. D. Stansfield. VCH Publishers, 303 NW 12th Ave., Deerfield Beach, Florida 33442-1788. (305) 428-5566. 1990. 4th ed. Revised edition of: A Dictionary of Genetics, third edition.

McGraw-Hill Encyclopedia of Environmental Science. Sybil P. Parker. McGraw-Hill Science & Engineering Books, 11 W. 19th St., New York, New York 10011. (212) 337-6010. 1980. Covers ecology, man's influence on nature, and environmental protection.

McGraw-Hill Encyclopedia of Science and Technology. McGraw-Hill, 1221 Avenue of the Americas, New York, New York 10020. (212) 512-2000 or (800) 262-4729. 1992. Seventh edition. Issued in multiple volumes including index. Includes all science and technology broad subject areas.

Van Nostrand's Scientific Encyclopedia. Glenn D. Considine, ed. Van Nostrand Reinhold, 115 5th Ave., New York, New York 10003. (212) 254-3232. 1983. Sixth edition. Includes all broad subject areas in science.

GENERAL WORKS

Assessing Ecological Risks of Biotechnology. Lev R. Ginzburg. Butterworth-Heinemann, 80 Montvale Ave., Stoneham, Massachusetts 02180. (617) 438-8464; (800) 366-2665. 1991. Presents an analysis of the ecological risk associated with genetically engineered microorganisms, organisms that, through gene splicing, have obtained additional genetic information.

Bacteria. L. R. Hill and B. E. Kirsop, eds. Cambridge University Press, 40 W. 20th St., New York, New York 10011. (212) 924-3900; (800) 227-0247. 1991. Directory and collection of bacteria type specimens.

Biocatalysis; Fundamentals of Enzyme Deactivation Kinetics. Ajit Sadana. Prentice Hall, Rte. 9 W., Englewood Cliffs, New Jersey 07632. (201) 592-2000; (800) 634-2863. 1991. Focuses on the chemical kinetics of enzymes in bioreactions as used in the biotechnology and chemical industries.

Biocatalysts for Industry. Jonathan S. Dordick, ed. Plenum Press, 233 Spring St., New York, New York 10013-1578. (212) 620-8000; (800) 221-9369. 1991. Contributed papers address the applications of enzymes or whole cells to carry out selective transformations of commercial importance, as biocatalysts in the food, pharmaceutical, and chemical industries. Includes general uses of biocatalysts, biocatalysts without chemical competition, emerg-

ing biocatalysts for conventional chemical processing, and future directions of biocatalysts.

Bioenvironmental Systems. Donald L. Wise, ed. CRC Press, 2000 Corporate Blvd. N.W., Boca Raton, Florida 33431. (407) 994-0555; (800) 272-7737. 1987. 4 vols.

Biotechnological Innovations in Food Processing. Butterworth-Heinemann, 80 Montvale Ave., Stoneham, Massachusetts 02180. (617) 438-8464. 1991.

Biotechnological Slurry Process for the Decontamination of Excavated Polluted Soils. R. Kleijintjens. National Technical Information Service, 5285 Port Royal Rd., Springfield, Virginia 22161. (703) 487-4650. 1991.

Biotechnology and Food Safety. Donald D. Bills. Butterworth-Heinemann, 80 Montvale Ave., Stoneham, Massachusetts 02180. (617) 438-8464. Natural control of microorganisms, detection of microorganisms, relation of the biological control of pests to food safety, and ingredients and food safety.

Biotechnology Application in Hazardous Waste Treatment. Gordon Lewandowski. Engineering Foundation, 345 E. 47th St., New York, New York 10017. (212) 705-7835. 1989. Trends in hazardous waste treatment using biotechnological methods.

Biotechnology for Biological Control of Pests and Vectors. Karl Maramorosch. CRC Press, 2000 Corporate Blvd. N.W., Boca Raton, Florida 33431. (407) 994-0555; (800) 272-7737. 1991.

Environmental Biotechnology. A. Balaozej and V. Prnivarovna, eds. Elsevier Science Publishing Co., 655 Avenue of the Americas, New York, New York 10010. (212) 989-5800. 1991. Proceedings of the International Symposium on Biotechnology, Bratislava, Czechoslovakia, June 27-29, 1990.

Environmental Biotechnology for Waste Treatment. Gary S. Sayler, et al., eds. Plenum Press, 233 Spring St., New York, New York 10013-1578. (212) 620-8000. 1991. Symposium on Environmental Biotechnology: Moving from the Flask to the Field. Knoxville, TN, 1990.

Feeding Tomorrow's World. Albert Sasson. Centre for Agriculture and Rural Cooperation and UNESCO, 7 Place de Fontenoy, Paris, France 1990. Analyzes Green Revolution and biotechnological revolution and tries to answer other pressing questions through a pluridisciplinary approach to human nutrition and food production. Synthesizes the scientific, economic, socioeconomic and environmental aspects of nutrition throughout the world.

From Clone to Clinic. D.J.A. Crommelin, ed. Kluwer Academic Publishers, 101 Philip Dr., Assinippi Pk., Norwell, Massachusetts 02061. (617) 871-6600. 1990.

Innovation and Environmental Risk. Lewis Roberts and Albert Wheale. Belhaven Press, 136 S. Broadway, Irvington, New York 10533. (914) 591-9111. 1991. Debates public policies and scientific issues concerning environmental problems. Stresses energy, radiological protection, biotechnology and the role of the media.

Magill's Survey of Science. Life Science Series. Frank N. Magill, ed. Salem Press, PO Box 50062, Pasadena, California 91105. 1991. Six volumes. Contents: v.1. A-Central and peripheral nervous system functions; v.2. Central metabolism regulation - eukaryotic transcriptional control; v.3. Positive and negative eukaryotic transcriptional control - mammalian hormones; v.4. Hor-

mones and behavior - muscular contraction; v.5. Muscular contraction and relaxation - sexual reproduction in plants; v.6. Reproductive behavior and mating - X inactivation and the Lyon hypothesis.

Managing Environmental Risks. Air & Waste Management Association, PO Box 2861, Pittsburgh, Pennsylvania 15230. (412) 232-3444. 1990. Papers presented at the Air & Waste Management Association International Specialty Conference, held in October 1989 in Quebec City, contains topics such as risks related to hazardous waste sites, chemical contaminants, and biotechnology.

Protein Production by Biotechnology. T. J. R. Harris, ed. Elsevier Science Publishing Co., 655 Avenue of the Americas, New York, New York 10010. (212) 984-5800. 1990. Describes the use of recombinant DNA techniques to produce proteins of therapeutic or other importance.

Protein Purification: Design and Scale Up of Downstreams Processing. Scott M. Wheelwright. Oxford University Press, 200 Madison Ave., New York, New York 10016. (212) 679-7300; (800) 334-4249. 1991.

Secondary Metabolism in Microorganisms, Plants and Animals. Martin Luckner. Springer-Verlag, 175 5th Ave., New York, New York 10010. (212) 460-1500. 1990. Includes reviews of the latest results on the biosynthesis for age and degradation of secondary metabolites and characteristics of compounds of specialized cells from all groups of organisms. Has new chapters on: the transport of secondary compounds with the producer organism; the significance of colored and toxic secondary products; and on the improvement of secondary product biosynthesis by genetical means.

HANDBOOKS AND MANUALS

Biochemical Engineering and Biotechnology Handbook. Bernard Atkinson and Ferda Mavituna. Stockton Press, 257 Park Ave. S., New York, New York 10010. (212) 673-4400. 1991. Second edition. Features an increased emphasis on biotechnology. Includes data for the pharmaceutical industry, dairy and beverage industries, and the treatment of effluent water.

Biomass Handbook. Osamu Kitani and Carl W. Hall. Gordon and Breach Science Publishers, Inc., 270 8th Ave., New York, New York 10011. (212) 206-8900. 1989. Provides knowledge of biomass and related systems. Includes biomass development from the biotechnology point of view as well as recent facts on biomass.

Biotechnology and the Environment. J. Gibbs, et al. Stockton Press, 257 Park Ave. S, New York, New York 10010. (212) 673-4400 or (800) 221-2123. 1987. Overview of the regulatory legislation in biotechnology.

Enzyme Handbook. D. Schomburg and M. Salzmann, eds. Springer-Verlag, 175 5th Ave., New York, New York 10010. (212) 460-1500; (800) 777-4643. 1990. The enzymes are arranged in accord with the 1984 Enzyme Commission list of enzymes and follow-up supplements. Information contained for each enzyme is organized in seven basic sections.

Japanese Biotechnology. R. T. Yuan and M. Dibner. Stockton Press, 257 Park Ave. S, New York, New York 10010. (212) 673-4400 or (800) 221-2123. 1991. Comprehensive study of the development of biotechnology in Japan. Covers a broad spectrum of topics including government policy, the biological R & D establishment,

industrial activities in biotechnology, technological transfer, and finance.

ONLINE DATA BASES

AGRICOLA. U.S. Department of Agriculture, Office of Public Affairs, 14 Independence Ave., S.W., Washington, District of Columbia 20250. (202) 447-7454.

BioPatents. BIOSIS, 2100 Arch St., Philadelphia, Pennsylvania 19103. (800) 523-4806.

Bioprocessing Technology. Mead Data Central, Inc., P.O. Box 933, Dayton, Ohio 45401. (800) 227-4908.

BIOQUIP. DECHEMA Deutsche Gesellschaft fuer Chemisches Apparatewesen, Chemische Technik und Biotechnologie e.V., I & D Information Systems and Databanks, Theodor-Heuss-Allee 25, 6000 Frankfurt am Main 97, Germany 970146. 49 (69) 7564-248.

BIOREP. Royal Netherlands Academy of Arts & Sciences, Kloveniersburgwal 29, Amsterdam, Netherlands 1011 JV. 31 (20) 222902.

BIOSIS Previews. BIOSIS, 2100 Arch St., Philadelphia, Pennsylvania 19103-1399. (215) 587-4800. Largest and most comprehensive database of research in the life sciences. Contains citations for nearly 9000 primary research journals, monographs, reviews, symposia, preliminary reports, semi-popular journals, selected institutional reports, government reports and research communications.

BIOTECH Business. NewsNet, Inc., 945 Haverford Rd., Bryn Mawr, Pennsylvania 19010. (800) 345-1301.

Biotechnologie-Informations-Knoten fuer Europa. Gesellschaft fuer Biotechnologische Forschung mbH, Mascheroder Weg 1, Braunschweig-Stoeckheim, Germany 49 (531) 6181-640.

Biotechnology Abstracts. Derwent Publications Ltd., 6845 Elm St., McLean, Virginia 22101. (703) 790-0400. Includes material on genetic manipulation, biochemical engineering, fermentation, biocatalysis, cell hybridization, in vitro plant propagation and industrial waste management.

Biotechnology Newswatch. McGraw-Hill Science & Engineering Books, 11 W. 19th St., New York, New York 10011. (212) 337-6010.

Bioworld. BioWorld, 217 S. B St., San Mateo, California 94401-9805. (800) 879-8790. Bioworld is a division of Bio Publishing, Inc.

Chemical Engineering and Biotechnology Abstracts–CEBA. Orbit Search Service, Maxwell Online Inc., 8000 W. Park Dr., McLean, Virginia 22102. (703) 442-0900 or (800) 456-7248. Monthly. Covers theoretical, practical and commercial material on all aspects of processing safety, and the environment. Also covers process and reaction engineering, measurement and process control, environmental protection and safety, plant design and equipment used in chemical engineering and biotechnology. More than 400 of the world's major primary chemical and process engineering journals are scanned to compile the database. Available from ORBIT.

Directory of Biotechnology Information Resources. National Library of Medicine, Specialized Information Services Division, 8600 Rockville Pike, Bethesda, Maryland 20894. (301) 496-6531.

EMBL Nucleotide Sequence Database. European Molecular Biology Laboratory, EMBL Data Library, Meyerhofstrasse 1, 6900 Heidelberg, Germany 49 (6221) 387258.

Enviro/Energyline Abstracts Plus. R. R. Bowker Co., 121 Chanlon Rd., New Providence, New Jersey 07974. (908) 464-6800.

Environmental Periodicals Bibliography. National Information Services Corp., Ste. 6, Wyman Towers, 3100 St. Paul St., Baltimore, Maryland 21218. (410)243-0797. Online version of abstract of same name.

Life Sciences from NTIS. National Technical Information Center for the Utilization of Federal Technology, 5285 Port Royal Rd., Springfield, Virginia 22161. (703) 487-4650.

Monthly Catalog of United States Government Publications. U.S. G.P.O., Supt. of Docs., PO Box 371954, Pittsburgh, Pennsylvania 15250-7954. (202) 512-0000.

National Technical Information Service. U.S. Department of Commerce, National Technical Information Service, Office of Data Base Services, 5285 Port Royal Rd., Springfield, Virginia 22161. (703) 487-4807. Bibliographic database of government sponsored research and technical reports.

PressNet Environmental Reports. Chemical Information Systems, Inc., 7215 York Rd., Baltimore, Maryland 21212. (301) 321-8440.

SCISEARCH. Institute for Scientific Information, University City Science Center, 3501 Market St., Philadelphia, Pennsylvania 19104. (215) 386-0100.

PERIODICALS AND NEWSLETTERS

AIChE Journal. American Institute of Chemical Engineers, 345 East 47th Street, New York, New York 10017. (212) 705-7338. Monthly. Papers on all areas of chemical engineering.

Applied Microbiology and Biotechnology. Springer International, 44 Hartz Way, Seacaucus, New Jersey 07094. (201) 348-4033. Six times a year. Covers biotechnology, biochemical engineering, applied genetics and regulation, applied microbial and cell physiology, food biotechnology, and environmental biotechnology.

BioScience Journal. American Institute of Biological Sciences, 730 11th Street, Nw, Washington, District of Columbia 20001-4521. (202) 628-1500. Eleven times a year. Current research, feature articles, book reviews, and new products.

Biotechnology and Bioengineering. John Wiley & Sons, Inc., 605 3rd Ave., New York, New York 10158. (212) 850-6000. Monthly. Aerobic and anaerobic processes, systems involving biofilms, algal systems, detoxification and bioremediation and genetic aspects, biosensors, and cellular systems.

Genetic Engineering Letter. Environews, Inc., 952 National Press Bldg., Washington, District of Columbia 20045. (202) 662-7299. Twice a month. Covers developments in the field of biotechnology.

Insecticide and Acaricide Tests. Entomological Society of America, 9301 Annapolis Rd., Lanham, Maryland 20706-3115. (301) 731-4538. Irregular.

International Journal of Biotechnology. Inderscience Enterprises Ltd., World Trade Center Building, 110 Avenue Louis Casai, Case Postale 306, Geneva-Aeroport, Switzerland CH 1215. (44) 908-314248. Quarterly. Authoritative source of information in the field of biotechnology which establishes channels of communication between policy makers, executives in industry.

The Journal of Biological Chemistry. American Society of Biological Chemists, 428 E. Preston St., Baltimore, Maryland 21202. Three times a month. Biological, agricultural, and energy aspects of the environment.

Nature and Resources. Elsevier Science Publishing Co., 655 Avenue of the Americas, New York, New York 10010. (212) 989-5800. 1965-. Quarterly. Provides indepth reviews of contemporary environmental issues from an international perspective.

Waste Management Research and Education Institute Newsletter. Waste Management Research and Education Institute, University of Tennessee at Knoxville, 327 S. Stadium Hall, Knoxville, Tennessee 37996-0710. (615) 974-4251. Quarterly. Environmental biotechnology research.

RESEARCH CENTERS AND INSTITUTES

American Type Culture Collection. 12301 Parklawn Drive, Rockville, Maryland 20852. (301) 881-2600.

Arkansas Biotechnology Center. University of Arkansas, Biomass Research Center, Fayetteville, Arkansas 72701. (501) 575-2651.

Biotechnology Center. University of Connecticut, 184 Auditorium Rd., Storrs, Connecticut 06269-3149. (203) 486-5011.

Connecticut Sea Grant College Program. University of Connecticut at Avery Point, 1084 Schennecossett Rd., Groton, Connecticut 06340. (203) 445-5108.

Environmental Research Foundation. PO Box 3541, Princeton, New Jersey 08543-3541. (609) 683-0707.

Lehigh University, Center for Molecular Bioscience and Biotechnology. Mountaintop Campus, Building 111, Bethlehem, Pennsylvania 18015. (215) 758-5426.

Marine Biotechnology Center. University of California, Santa Barbara, Marine Science Institute, Santa Barbara, California 93106. (805) 893-3765.

Marine Science Institute. University of California, Santa Barbara, Santa Barbara, California 93106. (805) 893-3764.

Mary B. Trotten Center for Biosystematics Technology. University of Nebraska, 436 Nebraska Hall, Lincoln, Nebraska 68588-0514. (402) 472-6606.

Massachusetts Institute of Technology Biotechnology Process Engineering Center. Room 20A-207, Cambridge, Massachusetts 02139. (617) 253-0805.

North Carolina State University, Pulp and Paper Laboratory. College of Forest Resources, Box 8005, Raleigh, North Carolina 247695. (919) 737-2888.

Ohio State University, Biotechnology Center. Rightmire Hall, 1060 Carmack Road, Columbus, Ohio 43210. (614) 292-5670.

Ohio University, Edison Animal Biotechnology Center. West Green, Athens, Ohio 45701. (614) 593-4713.

Oregon State University, Center for Gene Research and Biotechnology. Cordley 3096, Corvallis, Oregon 97331. (503) 737-3347.

Pennsylvania State University, Bioprocessing Resource Center. Biotechnology Institute, 519 Wartik Laboratory, University Park, Pennsylvania 16802. (814) 863-3650.

Rockefeller University, Laboratory of Biochemistry and Molecular Biology. 1230 York Avenue, New York, New York 10021-6399. (212) 570-8000.

Sheldon Biotechnology Centre. McGill University, 3773 University St., Montreal, Quebec, Canada H3A 2B4. (514) 398-3998.

State University of New York at Buffalo, Center for Applied Molecular Biology and Immunology. Vice President of Sponsored Programs, Department of Biochemistry, Cary Hall, Buffalo, New York 14260. (716) 636-3321.

State University of New York at Plattsburg, In Vitro Cell Biology and Biotechnology Program. Department of Biological Science, Plattsburg, New York 12901. (518) 846-7144.

University of Illinois, Biotechnology Center. 105 Observatory, 901 South Matthews, Urbana, Illinois 61801. (217) 333-1695.

University of Maryland, Bioprocess Scale-Up Facility. Engineering Research Center, College Park, Maryland 20742. (301) 405-3908.

University of Maryland, Center of Marine Biotechnology. 600 East Lombard Street, Baltimore, Maryland 21202. (301) 783-4800.

University of Michigan, Biochemical Engineering Laboratory. Department of Chemical Engineering, Ann Arbor, Michigan 48109. (313) 763-1178.

University of Minnesota, Institute for Advanced Studies In Biological Process Technology. 240 Gortner Laboratory, 1479 Gortner Avenue, St. Paul, Minnesota 55108. (612) 624-6774.

University of Nebraska-Lincoln, Center for Biotechnology. 101 Manter Hall, Lincoln, Nebraska 68588-0159. (402) 472-2635.

University of Tennessee at Knoxville, Center for Environmental Biotechnology. 10515 Research Drive, Knoxville, Tennessee 37932. (615) 675-9450.

University of Tennessee at Knoxville, Waste Management Research and Education Institute. 327 South Stadium Hall, Knoxville, Tennessee 37996-0710. (615) 974-4251.

University of Wisconsin-Madison, Biology & Biomaterial Specimen Preparation Laboratory. Room B22, Veterinary Science Building, 1665 Linden Drive, Madison, Wisconsin 53706. (608) 263-3952.

University of Wisconsin-Madison, Biotechnology Center. 1710 University Avenue, Madison, Wisconsin 53705. (608) 262-8606.

Utah State University, Biotechnology Center. Logan, Utah 84322-4430. (801) 750-2730.

Virginia Polytechnic Institute and State University, Anaerobe Laboratory. Department of Anaerobic Microbiology, Blacksburg, Virginia 24061-0305. (703) 231-6935.

Virginia Polytechnic Institute and State University, Biobased Materials Technology Development Center. Thomas M. Brooks Forest Products Center, Blacksburg, Virginia 24061-0503. (703) 231-4403.

STATISTICS SOURCES

Biotechnology Perspective. FIND/SVP, 625 Avenue of the Americas, New York, New York 10011. (212) 645-4500. 1991. Analyzes 1990 sales and indicates companies receiving the most revenues from product sales and R&D.

TRADE ASSOCIATIONS AND PROFESSIONAL SOCIETIES

Association of Biotechnology Companies. 1666 Connecticut Ave. N.W., Suite 330, Washington, District of Columbia 20009-1039. (202) 234-3330.

Association of Bituminous Contractors. 1747 Pennsylvania Ave. N.W., Suite 1050, Washington, District of Columbia 20006. (202) 785-4440.

Industrial Biotechnology Association. 1625 K St., N.W., Suite 1100, Washington, District of Columbia 20006-1604. (202) 857-0244.

BIOTIC COMMUNITIES

See also: PLANT COMMUNITIES

ABSTRACTING AND INDEXING SERVICES

Applied Ecology Abstracts Studies in Renewable Natural Resources. Information Retrieval Ltd., 1911 Jefferson Davis Highway, Arlington, Virginia 22202. 1975-. Monthly.

Biological and Agricultural Index. H.W. Wilson Co., 950 University Ave., Bronx, New York 10452. (800) 367-6770. 1916-. Monthly.

Biology Digest. Data Courier, Plexus Pub Inc., 143 Old Marlton Pike, Medford, New Jersey 08055. 1974-. Monthly. Abstracts biology periodicals.

Ecological Abstracts. Geo Abstracts Ltd. Elsevier Applied Science, Crown House, Linton Rd., Barking, England IG 11 8JU. 1974-. Derived from over 600 leading ecological and environmental journals, plus books, conference proceedings, reports and theses.

Environment Abstracts. Bowker A & I Publishing, 121 Chanlon Rd., New Providence, New Jersey 07974. (908) 464-6800. 1974-.

Environment Index. Environment Information Center, Index Research Department, 124 E. 39th St., New York, New York 10016. 1971-. Annual.

Environmental Information Connection–EIC. Planning Information Program, Dept. of Urban and Regional Planning, University of Illinois, 1003 West Nevada, Urbana, Illinois 61801. (217) 333-1369. Also available online.

Environmental Periodicals Bibliography. Environmental Studies Institute, International Academy at Santa Barbara, 800 Garden St., Suite D, Santa Barbara, California 93101. (805) 965-5010. Also available online.

General Science Index. H. W. Wilson Co., 950 University Ave., Bronx, New York 10452. 1978-. Monthly, also issued in annual cumulation. Cumulative subject index to English language periodicals in the subject fields of astronomy, botany, chemistry, earth science, environment and conservation, food and nutrition, genetics, mathematics, medicine and health, microbiology, oceanography, physics, physiology and zoology.

Index to Scientific Book Contents. Institute for Scientific Information, 3501 Market St., Philadelphia, Pennsylvania 19104. (800) 523-1857. 1985-. Annual. Gives contents of science books published.

Multimedia Index to Ecology. National Information Center for Educational Media, University of Southern California, Los Angeles, California 90007.

Sea Grant Abstracts. National Sea Grant Depository, Pell Laboratory Bldg., Bay Campus, University of Rhode Island, Narragansett, Rhode Island 02882. (401) 792-6114. 1986-. Quarterly. Published by the National Sea Grant Programs, this collection includes annual reports, serials and newsletters, charts and maps.

BIBLIOGRAPHIES

Current Contents. Agriculture, Biology and Environmental Sciences. Institute for Scientific Information, 3501 Market St., Philadelphia, Pennsylvania 19104. (800) 523-1857. 1973-. Previous title: Current Contents. Agricultural, Food & Veterinary Sciences. Gives the table of contents of periodicals in the fields of agriculture, biology, environmental and related areas.

EPA Publications Bibliography. U.S. Environmental Protection Agency, Library Systems Branch, 401 M St., SW, Washington, District of Columbia 20460. (202) 260-2090. Quarterly.

ENCYCLOPEDIAS AND DICTIONARIES

Cambridge Encyclopedia of Life Sciences. A. E. Friday and David S. Ingram. Cambridge University Press, 40 W 20th St., New York, New York 10011. (212) 924-3900 or (800) 227-0247. 1985. Includes all topics under biology and ecology.

McGraw-Hill Encyclopedia of Environmental Science. Sybil P. Parker. McGraw-Hill Science & Engineering Books, 11 W. 19th St., New York, New York 10011. (212) 337-6010. 1980. Covers ecology, man's influence on nature, and environmental protection.

McGraw-Hill Encyclopedia of Science and Technology. McGraw-Hill, 1221 Avenue of the Americas, New York, New York 10020. (212) 512-2000 or (800) 262-4729. 1992. Seventh edition. Issued in multiple volumes including index. Includes all science and technology broad subject areas.

GENERAL WORKS

Ecological Communities. Donald R. Strong. Princeton University Press, 41 Williams St., Princeton, New Jersey 08540. (609) 258-4900. 1984. Conceptual issues and the evidence relating to biotic communities.

Ecological Systems of the Geo-Biosphere. Heinrich Walter. Springer-Verlag, 175 5th Ave., New York, New York 10010. (212) 460-1500. 1985-. Ecological principles in global perspective and tropical and subtropical zono-biomes.

Habitat Structure. Susan S. Bell. Chapman & Hall, 29 W. 35th St., New York, New York 10001-2291. (212) 244-3336. 1991. The physical arrangement of objects in space, animal population, biotic communities and habitat ecology.

A Hierarchial Concept of Ecosystems. R.V. O'Neill. Princeton University Press, 41 Williams St., Princeton, New Jersey 08540. (609) 258-4900. 1986. Covers population biology including ecology and biotic communities.

The Natural Selection of Populations and Communities. David Sloan Wilson. Benjamin/Cummings Publishing Co., 390 Bridge Pkwy., Redwood City, California 94065. (415) 594-4400. 1980. Evolutionary biology, biotic communities and population genetics.

Plant-Animal Interactions; Evolutionary Ecology in Tropical and Temperate Regions. Peter W. Price, et al. John Wiley & Sons, Inc., 605 3rd Ave., New York, New York 10158-0012. (212) 850-6000. 1991. Comprises a comparative analysis of the existing ecological systems of temperate and tropical regions.

Systems Ecology. Howard T. Odum. John Wiley & Sons, Inc., 605 3rd Ave., New York, New York (212) 850-6000. 1983. Simulation methods in ecology and biotic communities and bioenergetics.

Theories of Populations in Biological Communities. F.B. Christiansen. Springer-Verlag, 175 5th Ave., New York, New York 10010. (212) 460-1500. 1977. Ecological studies in biotic communities and population biology.

HANDBOOKS AND MANUALS

Description of the Ecoregions of the United States. Robert G. Bailey. Forest Service, U.S. Dept. of Agriculture, PO Box 96090, Washington, District of Columbia 20090. (202) 720-3760. 1980. Biotic communities in the United States.

ONLINE DATA BASES

Enviro/Energyline Abstracts Plus. R. R. Bowker Co., 121 Chanlon Rd., New Providence, New Jersey 07974. (908) 464-6800.

Environmental Periodicals Bibliography. National Information Services Corp., Ste. 6, Wyman Towers, 3100 St. Paul St., Baltimore, Maryland 21218. (410)243-0797. Online version of abstract of same name.

Monthly Catalog of United States Government Publications. U.S. G.P.O., Supt. of Docs., PO Box 371954, Pittsburgh, Pennsylvania 15250-7954. (202) 512-0000.

National Technical Information Service. U.S. Department of Commerce, National Technical Information Service, Office of Data Base Services, 5285 Port Royal Rd., Springfield, Virginia 22161. (703) 487-4807. Bibliographic database of government sponsored research and technical reports.

SCISEARCH. Institute for Scientific Information, University City Science Center, 3501 Market St., Philadelphia, Pennsylvania 19104. (215) 386-0100.

PERIODICALS AND NEWSLETTERS

Evolutionary Ecology. Chapman & Hall, 2-6 Boundary Row, London, England SE1 8HN. 1987-. Evolution of biotic communities and ecology.

BIOTOPES

See: ECOSYSTEMS

BIRDS

See: ORNITHOLOGY

BITUMINOUS COAL

See: COAL

BLAST FURNACES

See: FURNACES

BLOOD ANALYSIS

ABSTRACTING AND INDEXING SERVICES

ASFA Aquaculture Abstracts. Cambridge Scientific Abstracts, Inc., 5161 River Rd., Bethesda, Maryland 20816. (301) 961-6750. 1984.

Biological Abstracts. BIOSIS, 2100 Arch St., Philadelphia, Pennsylvania 19103-1399. (215) 587-4800. 1927-.

Pollution Abstracts. Cambridge Scientific Abstracts, 5161 River Rd., Bethesda, Maryland 20816. (301) 961-6750. Six/year. Indexes worldwide technical literature on environmental pollution. Covers air pollution, marine and freshwater pollution, sewage and wastewater treatment, waste management, toxicology and health, noise pollution, radiation, land pollution, and environmental policies, programs, legislation, and education. Also available online.

Science Citation Index. Institute for Scientific Information, 3501 Market St., Philadelphia, Pennsylvania 19104. 1961-.

ENCYCLOPEDIAS AND DICTIONARIES

Encyclopedia of Human Biology. Renato Dulbecco, ed. Academic Press, c/o Harcourt Brace Jovanovich Inc., 6277 Sea Harbor Dr., Orlando, Florida 32887. (800) 346-8648. 1991. Eight volumes.

McGraw-Hill Encyclopedia of Science and Technology. McGraw-Hill, 1221 Avenue of the Americas, New York, New York 10020. (212) 512-2000 or (800) 262-4729. 1992. Seventh edition. Issued in multiple volumes including index. Includes all science and technology broad subject areas.

The Nutrition and Health Encyclopedia. David F. Tver and Percy Russell. Van Nostrand Reinhold, 115 5th Ave., New York, New York 10003. (212) 254-3232. 1989.

GENERAL WORKS

Coagulation and Lipids. CRC Press, 2000 Corporate Blvd. N.W., Boca Raton, Florida 33431. (800) 272-7737. 1989. Physiological effect of phospholipids.

Magill's Survey of Science. Life Science Series. Frank N. Magill, ed. Salem Press, PO Box 50062, Pasadena, California 91105. 1991. Six volumes. Contents: v.1. A-Central and peripheral nervous system functions; v.2. Central metabolism regulation - eukaryotic transcriptional control; v.3. Positive and negative eukaryotic transcriptional control - mammalian hormones; v.4. Hormones and behavior - muscular contraction; v.5. Muscular contraction and relaxation - sexual reproduction in plants; v.6. Reproductive behavior and mating - X inactivation and the Lyon hypothesis.

Monitoring Human Tissues for Toxic Substances. National Academy Press, 2101 Constitution Ave. N.W., PO Box 285, Washington, District of Columbia 20418. (202) 334-3313. 1991. Evaluates the National Human Monitoring Program.

Progress in Chemical Fibrinolysis. Raven Press, 1185 Ave. of the Americas, New York, New York 10036. (212) 930-9500.

ONLINE DATA BASES

BIOSIS Previews. BIOSIS, 2100 Arch St., Philadelphia, Pennsylvania 19103-1399. (215) 587-4800. Largest and most comprehensive database of research in the life sciences. Contains citations for nearly 9000 primary research journals, monographs, reviews, symposia, preliminary reports, semi-popular journals, selected institutional reports, government reports and research communications.

MEDITEC. FIZ Technik, Ostbahnhofstrasse 13, Postfach 600547, Frankfurt, Germany D-6000. 49 (69) 4308-225.

Membrane & Separation Technology News. NewsNet, Inc., 945 Haverford Rd., Bryn Mawr, Pennsylvania 19010. (800) 345-1301.

TRADE ASSOCIATIONS AND PROFESSIONAL SOCIETIES

American Institute of Biological Sciences. 730 11th St., N.W., Washington, District of Columbia 20001-4521. (202) 628-1500.

BLOOD LEAD LEVEL

See: BLOOD ANALYSIS

BLOOM

See: ALGAE

BOD

See: BIOCHEMICAL OXYGEN DEMAND

BODY FAT

See also: ADIPOSE TISSUE; HIBERNATION

ABSTRACTING AND INDEXING SERVICES

Biological Abstracts. BIOSIS, 2100 Arch St., Philadelphia, Pennsylvania 19103-1399. (215) 587-4800. 1927-.

Environment Abstracts. Bowker A & I Publishing, 121 Chanlon Rd., New Providence, New Jersey 07974. (908) 464-6800. 1974-.

Environment Index. Environment Information Center, Index Research Department, 124 E. 39th St., New York, New York 10016. 1971-. Annual.

Environmental Information Connection–EIC. Planning Information Program, Dept. of Urban and Regional Planning, University of Illinois, 1003 West Nevada, Urbana, Illinois 61801. (217) 333-1369. Also available online.

Environmental Periodicals Bibliography. Environmental Studies Institute, International Academy at Santa Barbara, 800 Garden St., Suite D, Santa Barbara, California 93101. (805) 965-5010. Also available online.

General Science Index. H. W. Wilson Co., 950 University Ave., Bronx, New York 10452. 1978-. Monthly, also issued in annual cumulation. Cumulative subject index to English language periodicals in the subject fields of astronomy, botany, chemistry, earth science, environment and conservation, food and nutrition, genetics, mathematics, medicine and health, microbiology, oceanography, physics, physiology and zoology.

Index to Scientific Book Contents. Institute for Scientific Information, 3501 Market St., Philadelphia, Pennsylvania 19104. (800) 523-1857. 1985-. Annual. Gives contents of science books published.

Science Citation Index. Institute for Scientific Information, 3501 Market St., Philadelphia, Pennsylvania 19104. 1961-.

BIBLIOGRAPHIES

EPA Publications Bibliography. U.S. Environmental Protection Agency, Library Systems Branch, 401 M St., SW, Washington, District of Columbia 20460. (202) 260-2090. Quarterly.

DIRECTORIES

Carbon & High Performance Fibres Directory. Box 51305, Raleigh, North Carolina 27609. (919) 847-0262. Irregular.

ENCYCLOPEDIAS AND DICTIONARIES

Van Nostrand's Scientific Encyclopedia. Glenn D. Considine, ed. Van Nostrand Reinhold, 115 5th Ave., New York, New York 10003. (212) 254-3232. 1983. Sixth edition. Includes all broad subject areas in science.

ONLINE DATA BASES

BIOSIS Previews. BIOSIS, 2100 Arch St., Philadelphia, Pennsylvania 19103-1399. (215) 587-4800. Largest and most comprehensive database of research in the life sciences. Contains citations for nearly 9000 primary research journals, monographs, reviews, symposia, preliminary reports, semi-popular journals, selected institutional reports, government reports and research communications.

Enviro/Energyline Abstracts Plus. R. R. Bowker Co., 121 Chanlon Rd., New Providence, New Jersey 07974. (908) 464-6800.

Environmental Periodicals Bibliography. National Information Services Corp., Ste. 6, Wyman Towers, 3100 St. Paul St., Baltimore, Maryland 21218. (410)243-0797. Online version of abstract of same name.

SCISEARCH. Institute for Scientific Information, University City Science Center, 3501 Market St., Philadelphia, Pennsylvania 19104. (215) 386-0100.

TRADE ASSOCIATIONS AND PROFESSIONAL SOCIETIES

American Institute of Biological Sciences. 730 11th St., N.W., Washington, District of Columbia 20001-4521. (202) 628-1500.

BOGS

See also: FENS; WETLANDS

ABSTRACTING AND INDEXING SERVICES

Applied Ecology Abstracts Studies in Renewable Natural Resources. Information Retrieval Ltd., 1911 Jefferson Davis Highway, Arlington, Virginia 22202. 1975-. Monthly.

Biological Abstracts. BIOSIS, 2100 Arch St., Philadelphia, Pennsylvania 19103-1399. (215) 587-4800. 1927-.

Environment Abstracts. Bowker A & I Publishing, 121 Chanlon Rd., New Providence, New Jersey 07974. (908) 464-6800. 1974-.

Environment Index. Environment Information Center, Index Research Department, 124 E. 39th St., New York, New York 10016. 1971-. Annual.

Environmental Information Connection–EIC. Planning Information Program, Dept. of Urban and Regional Planning, University of Illinois, 1003 West Nevada, Urbana, Illinois 61801. (217) 333-1369. Also available online.

Environmental Periodicals Bibliography. Environmental Studies Institute, International Academy at Santa Barbara, 800 Garden St., Suite D, Santa Barbara, California 93101. (805) 965-5010. Also available online.

General Science Index. H. W. Wilson Co., 950 University Ave., Bronx, New York 10452. 1978-. Monthly, also issued in annual cumulation. Cumulative subject index to English language periodicals in the subject fields of astronomy, botany, chemistry, earth science, environment and conservation, food and nutrition, genetics, mathematics, medicine and health, microbiology, oceanography, physics, physiology and zoology.

Multimedia Index to Ecology. National Information Center for Educational Media, University of Southern California, Los Angeles, California 90007.

Science Citation Index. Institute for Scientific Information, 3501 Market St., Philadelphia, Pennsylvania 19104. 1961-.

BIBLIOGRAPHIES

EPA Publications Bibliography. U.S. Environmental Protection Agency, Library Systems Branch, 401 M St., SW, Washington, District of Columbia 20460. (202) 260-2090. Quarterly.

ONLINE DATA BASES

BIOSIS Previews. BIOSIS, 2100 Arch St., Philadelphia, Pennsylvania 19103-1399. (215) 587-4800. Largest and most comprehensive database of research in the life sciences. Contains citations for nearly 9000 primary research journals, monographs, reviews, symposia, preliminary reports, semi-popular journals, selected institutional reports, government reports and research communications.

Enviro/Energyline Abstracts Plus. R. R. Bowker Co., 121 Chanlon Rd., New Providence, New Jersey 07974. (908) 464-6800.

Environmental Periodicals Bibliography. National Information Services Corp., Ste. 6, Wyman Towers, 3100 St. Paul St., Baltimore, Maryland 21218. (410)243-0797. Online version of abstract of same name.

SCISEARCH. Institute for Scientific Information, University City Science Center, 3501 Market St., Philadelphia, Pennsylvania 19104. (215) 386-0100.

BOILING WATER REACTORS

See: REACTORS

BOOMS

See: OIL SPILLS

BORON

See: ELEMENTS

BOTANICAL ECOLOGY

ABSTRACTING AND INDEXING SERVICES

Applied Ecology Abstracts Studies in Renewable Natural Resources. Information Retrieval Ltd., 1911 Jefferson Davis Highway, Arlington, Virginia 22202. 1975-. Monthly.

Biological and Agricultural Index. H.W. Wilson Co., 950 University Ave., Bronx, New York 10452. (800) 367-6770. 1916-. Monthly.

Current Advances in Ecological and Environmental Science. Pergamon Microforms International, Inc., Fairview Park, Elmsford, New York 10523. (914) 592-7720. 1989-. Monthly. Current literature searching service includingjournals, reports, abstracts, etc. This service is available online as part of the CABS database on the hosts BRS and ORBIT search service.

Ecological Abstracts. Geo Abstracts Ltd. Elsevier Applied Science, Crown House, Linton Rd., Barking, England IG 11 8JU. 1974-. Derived from over 600 leading ecological and environmental journals, plus books, conference proceedings, reports and theses.

Ecology Abstracts. Cambridge Scientific Abstracts, 5161 River Rd., Bethesda, Maryland 20816. (301) 961-6750. Monthly.

Environment Abstracts. Bowker A & I Publishing, 121 Chanlon Rd., New Providence, New Jersey 07974. (908) 464-6800. 1974-.

Environment Index. Environment Information Center, Index Research Department, 124 E. 39th St., New York, New York 10016. 1971-. Annual.

Environmental Information Connection–EIC. Planning Information Program, Dept. of Urban and Regional Planning, University of Illinois, 1003 West Nevada, Urbana, Illinois 61801. (217) 333-1369. Also available online.

Environmental Periodicals Bibliography. Environmental Studies Institute, International Academy at Santa Barbara, 800 Garden St., Suite D, Santa Barbara, California 93101. (805) 965-5010. Also available online.

Forestry Abstracts. C. A. B. International, Wallingford, England OX10 8DE. (0491) 3211. 1939/40-. Monthly. Journal of abstracts of journal articles, conferences, technical reports in the subject areas of: silviculture, forest mensuration and management, physical environment, fire, plant biology, genetics and breeding, mycology and pathology, game and wildlife, fish, protection of forests and other related matter.

General Science Index. H. W. Wilson Co., 950 University Ave., Bronx, New York 10452. 1978-. Monthly, also issued in annual cumulation. Cumulative subject index to English language periodicals in the subject fields of astronomy, botany, chemistry, earth science, environment and conservation, food and nutrition, genetics, mathematics, medicine and health, microbiology, oceanography, physics, physiology and zoology.

Herbage Abstracts. C. A. B. International, 845 North Park Ave., Tucson, Arizona 85719. (602) 621-7897 or (800) 528-4841. 1931-. Monthly. Covers management, productivity and economics of grasslands, rangelands and fodder crops, grassland ecology, seed production, toxic plants, land use and farming systems, weed control, agricultural meteorology, and other related areas.

Multimedia Index to Ecology. National Information Center for Educational Media, University of Southern California, Los Angeles, California 90007.

BIBLIOGRAPHIES

EPA Publications Bibliography. U.S. Environmental Protection Agency, Library Systems Branch, 401 M St., SW, Washington, District of Columbia 20460. (202) 260-2090. Quarterly.

Phreatophytes; A Bibliography. Patricia Paylore. Water Resources Scientific Information Center, Washington, District of Columbia 1974.

ENCYCLOPEDIAS AND DICTIONARIES

Cambridge Encyclopedia of Life Sciences. A. E. Friday and David S. Ingram. Cambridge University Press, 40 W 20th St., New York, New York 10011. (212) 924-3900 or (800) 227-0247. 1985. Includes all topics under biology and ecology.

Elsevier's Dictionary of Wild and Cultivated Plants in Latin, English, French, Italian, Dutch, and German. W. E. Clason. Elsevier Science Publishing Co., 655 Avenue of the Americas, New York, New York 10010. (212) 989-5800. 1989. This dictionary consists of the scientific names of wild and cultivated plants found in Europe.

The Marshall Cavendish Illustrated Encyclopedia of Plants and Earth Sciences. Marshall Cavendish Corp., 2415 Jerusalem Ave., North Bellmore, New York 11710. (516) 826-4200. 1988.

McGraw-Hill Encyclopedia of Environmental Science. Sybil P. Parker. McGraw-Hill Science & Engineering Books, 11 W. 19th St., New York, New York 10011. (212) 337-6010. 1980. Covers ecology, man's influence on nature, and environmental protection.

McGraw-Hill Encyclopedia of Science and Technology. McGraw-Hill, 1221 Avenue of the Americas, New York, New York 10020. (212) 512-2000 or (800) 262-4729. 1992. Seventh edition. Issued in multiple volumes including index. Includes all science and technology broad subject areas.

Role of Environment Factors. R. P. Pharis, et al. Springer-Verlag, 175 5th Ave., New York, New York 10010. (212) 460-1500 or (800) 777-4643. 1985. Encyclopedia of plant physiology.

Van Nostrand's Scientific Encyclopedia. Glenn D. Considine, ed. Van Nostrand Reinhold, 115 5th Ave., New York, New York 10003. (212) 254-3232. 1983. Sixth edition. Includes all broad subject areas in science.

GENERAL WORKS

Biogeography. Joy Tivy. Longman Publishing Group, 10 Bonk St., White Plains, New York 10606. (914) 993-5000. 1982. A study of plants in the ecosphere and phytogeography.

Comparative Ecology of Microorganisms and Macroorganisms. John H. Andrews. Springer-Verlag, 175 5th Ave., New York, New York 10010. (212) 460-1500. 1991. Constructs a format in which to compare the ecologies of large and small plant and animal organisms. Examines the differences between the sizes, and explores what similarities or parallels can be identified, and where they don't seem to exist. The ideas are illustrated by applying evolutionary principles to the individual organism.

Environment and Plant Ecology. John Wiley & Sons Inc., 605 3rd Ave., New York, New York 10158-0012. (212) 850-6000. 1982. Topics in botanical ecology.

Man's Impact on Vegetation. Kluwer Academic Publishers, 101 Philip Dr., Assinippi Park, Norwell, Canada 02061. (617) 871-6600. 1983. Man's influence on nature and botanical ecology.

Micromolar Evolution, Systematics, and Ecology. Otto Richard Gottlieb. Springer-Verlag, 175 5th Ave., New York, New York 10010. (212) 460-1500. 1982. Evolution of plants, plant chemotaxonomy, botanical chemistry, classification, and ecology of botany.

Responses of Plants to Environmental Stresses. J. Levitt. Academic Press, c/o Harcourt Brace Jovanovich Inc., 6277 Sea Harbor Dr., Orlando, Florida 32887. (800) 346-8648. 1980. 2nd ed. Volume 1 covers chilling, freezing and high temperature. Volume 2 contains water, radiation, salt, and other stresses.

ONLINE DATA BASES

Enviro/Energyline Abstracts Plus. R. R. Bowker Co., 121 Chanlon Rd., New Providence, New Jersey 07974. (908) 464-6800.

Environmental Periodicals Bibliography. National Information Services Corp., Ste. 6, Wyman Towers, 3100 St. Paul St., Baltimore, Maryland 21218. (410)243-0797. Online version of abstract of same name.

SCISEARCH. Institute for Scientific Information, University City Science Center, 3501 Market St., Philadelphia, Pennsylvania 19104. (215) 386-0100.

PERIODICALS AND NEWSLETTERS

Aquatic Botany. Elsevier, Box 211, Amsterdam, Netherlands 1000 AE. (020) 5803-911. Monthly. Covers aquatic plants and ecology.

BOTANICAL PESTICIDES

See: PESTICIDES

BOTTLED WATER

See: WATER QUALITY

BOTULISM

See: FOOD POISONING

BRACKISH WATER

See: ESTUARIES

BREEDER REACTORS

See: REACTORS

BREWERIES

See also: MICROORGANISMS; WASTEWATER TREATMENT

ABSTRACTING AND INDEXING SERVICES

Applied Ecology Abstracts Studies in Renewable Natural Resources. Information Retrieval Ltd., 1911 Jefferson Davis Highway, Arlington, Virginia 22202. 1975-. Monthly.

Biological Abstracts. BIOSIS, 2100 Arch St., Philadelphia, Pennsylvania 19103-1399. (215) 587-4800. 1927-.

General Science Index. H. W. Wilson Co., 950 University Ave., Bronx, New York 10452. 1978-. Monthly, also issued in annual cumulation. Cumulative subject index to English language periodicals in the subject fields of astronomy, botany, chemistry, earth science, environment and conservation, food and nutrition, genetics, mathematics, medicine and health, microbiology, oceanography, physics, physiology and zoology.

Multimedia Index to Ecology. National Information Center for Educational Media, University of Southern California, Los Angeles, California 90007.

ENCYCLOPEDIAS AND DICTIONARIES

Dictionary of Biotechnology. J. Coombs. Elsevier Science Publishing Co., 655 Avenue of the Americas, New York, New York 10010. (212) 984-5800. 1986. Areas covered in this dictionary include: fermentation; brewing; vaccines; plant tissue; culture; antibiotic production; production and use of enzymes; biomass; byproduct recovery and effluent treatment; equipment; processes; micro-organisms and biochemicals.

McGraw-Hill Encyclopedia of Science and Technology. McGraw-Hill, 1221 Avenue of the Americas, New York, New York 10020. (212) 512-2000 or (800) 262-4729. 1992. Seventh edition. Issued in multiple volumes including index. Includes all science and technology broad subject areas.

ONLINE DATA BASES

BIOSIS Previews. BIOSIS, 2100 Arch St., Philadelphia, Pennsylvania 19103-1399. (215) 587-4800. Largest and most comprehensive database of research in the life sciences. Contains citations for nearly 9000 primary research journals, monographs, reviews, symposia, preliminary reports, semi-popular journals, selected institutional reports, government reports and research communications.

TRADE ASSOCIATIONS AND PROFESSIONAL SOCIETIES

American Institute of Biological Sciences. 730 11th St., N.W., Washington, District of Columbia 20001-4521. (202) 628-1500.

American Institute of Chemical Engineers. 345 East 47th St., New York, New York 10017. (212) 705-7338.

American Institute of Chemists. 7315 Wisconsin Ave., Bethesda, Maryland 20814. (301) 652-2447.

BROMASILS

See: PESTICIDES

BROMIDES

See also: ELEMENTS

ABSTRACTING AND INDEXING SERVICES

Chemical Abstracts. Chemical Abstracts Service, 2540 Olentangy River Rd., PO Box 3012, Columbus, Ohio 43210. (800) 848-6533. 1907-.

General Science Index. H. W. Wilson Co., 950 University Ave., Bronx, New York 10452. 1978-. Monthly, also issued in annual cumulation. Cumulative subject index to English language periodicals in the subject fields of astronomy, botany, chemistry, earth science, environment and conservation, food and nutrition, genetics, mathematics, medicine and health, microbiology, oceanography, physics, physiology and zoology.

Pollution Abstracts. Cambridge Scientific Abstracts, 5161 River Rd., Bethesda, Maryland 20816. (301) 961-6750. Six/year. Indexes worldwide technical literature on environmental pollution. Covers air pollution, marine and freshwater pollution, sewage and wastewater treatment, waste management, toxicology and health, noise pollution, radiation, land pollution, and environmental policies, programs, legislation, and education. Also available online.

Science Citation Index. Institute for Scientific Information, 3501 Market St., Philadelphia, Pennsylvania 19104. 1961-.

ENCYCLOPEDIAS AND DICTIONARIES

McGraw-Hill Encyclopedia of Science and Technology. McGraw-Hill, 1221 Avenue of the Americas, New York, New York 10020. (212) 512-2000 or (800) 262-4729. 1992. Seventh edition. Issued in multiple volumes including index. Includes all science and technology broad subject areas.

ONLINE DATA BASES

CAS Source Index–CASSI. Chemical Abstracts Service, 2540 Olentangy River Rd., P.O. Box 3012, Columbus, Ohio 43210. (800) 848-6533 or (614) 421-3600. A listing of bibliographic and library holdings information for scientific and technical primary literature relevant to the chemical sciences.

Chemical Abstracts-CA. Chemical Abstracts Service, 2540 Olentangy River Rd., P.O. Box 3012, Columbus, Ohio 43210. (800) 848-6533 or (614) 421-3600. Information sources include 9000 journals, patents from 27 countries, two industrial property organizations, new books, conference proceedings, and government research reports.

BROMINES

See also: ELEMENTS

ABSTRACTING AND INDEXING SERVICES

Biological Abstracts. BIOSIS, 2100 Arch St., Philadelphia, Pennsylvania 19103-1399. (215) 587-4800. 1927-.

Chemical Abstracts. Chemical Abstracts Service, 2540 Olentangy River Rd., PO Box 3012, Columbus, Ohio 43210. (800) 848-6533. 1907-.

General Science Index. H. W. Wilson Co., 950 University Ave., Bronx, New York 10452. 1978-. Monthly, also

issued in annual cumulation. Cumulative subject index to English language periodicals in the subject fields of astronomy, botany, chemistry, earth science, environment and conservation, food and nutrition, genetics, mathematics, medicine and health, microbiology, oceanography, physics, physiology and zoology.

Science Citation Index. Institute for Scientific Information, 3501 Market St., Philadelphia, Pennsylvania 19104. 1961-.

ENCYCLOPEDIAS AND DICTIONARIES

Encyclopedia of Electrochemistry of Elements. A. J. Bard. Marcel Dekker, Inc., 270 Madison Ave., New York, New York 10016. (212) 696-9000 or (800) 228-1160. Encyclopedic treatment of the subject area of electrochemistry and related subjects.

McGraw-Hill Encyclopedia of Science and Technology. McGraw-Hill, 1221 Avenue of the Americas, New York, New York 10020. (212) 512-2000 or (800) 262-4729. 1992. Seventh edition. Issued in multiple volumes including index. Includes all science and technology broad subject areas.

ONLINE DATA BASES

BIOSIS Previews. BIOSIS, 2100 Arch St., Philadelphia, Pennsylvania 19103-1399. (215) 587-4800. Largest and most comprehensive database of research in the life sciences. Contains citations for nearly 9000 primary research journals, monographs, reviews, symposia, preliminary reports, semi-popular journals, selected institutional reports, government reports and research communications.

CAS Source Index–CASSI. Chemical Abstracts Service, 2540 Olentangy River Rd., P.O. Box 3012, Columbus, Ohio 43210. (800) 848-6533 or (614) 421-3600. A listing of bibliographic and library holdings information for scientific and technical primary literature relevant to the chemical sciences.

Chemical Abstracts-CA. Chemical Abstracts Service, 2540 Olentangy River Rd., P.O. Box 3012, Columbus, Ohio 43210. (800) 848-6533 or (614) 421-3600. Information sources include 9000 journals, patents from 27 countries, two industrial property organizations, new books, conference proceedings, and government research reports.

BRONCHIAL CONSTRICTION

See: ASTHMA

BROWN COAL

See: COAL

BUFFER SPECIES

ABSTRACTING AND INDEXING SERVICES

Applied Ecology Abstracts Studies in Renewable Natural Resources. Information Retrieval Ltd., 1911 Jefferson Davis Highway, Arlington, Virginia 22202. 1975-. Monthly.

Biological Abstracts. BIOSIS, 2100 Arch St., Philadelphia, Pennsylvania 19103-1399. (215) 587-4800. 1927-.

Environment Abstracts. Bowker A & I Publishing, 121 Chanlon Rd., New Providence, New Jersey 07974. (908) 464-6800. 1974-.

Environment Index. Environment Information Center, Index Research Department, 124 E. 39th St., New York, New York 10016. 1971-. Annual.

Environmental Information Connection–EIC. Planning Information Program, Dept. of Urban and Regional Planning, University of Illinois, 1003 West Nevada, Urbana, Illinois 61801. (217) 333-1369. Also available online.

Environmental Periodicals Bibliography. Environmental Studies Institute, International Academy at Santa Barbara, 800 Garden St., Suite D, Santa Barbara, California 93101. (805) 965-5010. Also available online.

Index to Scientific Book Contents. Institute for Scientific Information, 3501 Market St., Philadelphia, Pennsylvania 19104. (800) 523-1857. 1985-. Annual. Gives contents of science books published.

Multimedia Index to Ecology. National Information Center for Educational Media, University of Southern California, Los Angeles, California 90007.

Science Citation Index. Institute for Scientific Information, 3501 Market St., Philadelphia, Pennsylvania 19104. 1961-.

BIBLIOGRAPHIES

EPA Publications Bibliography. U.S. Environmental Protection Agency, Library Systems Branch, 401 M St., SW, Washington, District of Columbia 20460. (202) 260-2090. Quarterly.

ENCYCLOPEDIAS AND DICTIONARIES

McGraw-Hill Encyclopedia of Environmental Science. Sybil P. Parker. McGraw-Hill Science & Engineering Books, 11 W. 19th St., New York, New York 10011. (212) 337-6010. 1980. Covers ecology, man's influence on nature, and environmental protection.

McGraw-Hill Encyclopedia of Science and Technology. McGraw-Hill, 1221 Avenue of the Americas, New York, New York 10020. (212) 512-2000 or (800) 262-4729. 1992. Seventh edition. Issued in multiple volumes including index. Includes all science and technology broad subject areas.

ONLINE DATA BASES

BIOSIS Previews. BIOSIS, 2100 Arch St., Philadelphia, Pennsylvania 19103-1399. (215) 587-4800. Largest and most comprehensive database of research in the life sciences. Contains citations for nearly 9000 primary research journals, monographs, reviews, symposia, preliminary reports, semi-popular journals, selected institutional reports, government reports and research communications.

Enviro/Energyline Abstracts Plus. R. R. Bowker Co., 121 Chanlon Rd., New Providence, New Jersey 07974. (908) 464-6800.

Environmental Periodicals Bibliography. National Information Services Corp., Ste. 6, Wyman Towers, 3100 St. Paul St., Baltimore, Maryland 21218. (410)243-0797. Online version of abstract of same name.

SCISEARCH. Institute for Scientific Information, University City Science Center, 3501 Market St., Philadelphia, Pennsylvania 19104. (215) 386-0100.

BUILDING CODES

See: BUILDINGS, ENVIRONMENTAL ENGINEERING OF

BUILDING DESIGN

See: BUILDINGS, ENVIRONMENTAL ENGINEERING OF

BUILDINGS, ENVIRONMENTAL ENGINEERING OF

See also: SANITARY ENGINEERING; URBAN DESIGN PLANNING

ABSTRACTING AND INDEXING SERVICES

Applied Science and Technology Index. H.W. Wilson Co., 950 University Ave., Bronx, New York 10452. (800) 367-6770. Formerly Industrial Arts Index.

Energy Information Abstracts Annual 1987 in Retrospect. EIC/Intelligence Inc., 121 Chanlon Rd., New Providence, New Jersey 07974. (908) 464-6800. 1988. Annual. Cumulative edition of the monthly Energy Information Abstracts. Monitors sources in the field of energy including the scientific, technical and business journal literature, conference and symposia proceedings, corporate, government and academic reports.

Engineering Index. The Engineering Index Inc., 345 E. 47th St., New York, New York 10017. 1962-.

Index to Scientific Book Contents. Institute for Scientific Information, 3501 Market St., Philadelphia, Pennsylvania 19104. (800) 523-1857. 1985-. Annual. Gives contents of science books published.

BIBLIOGRAPHIES

Directory of Published Proceedings. Interdok Corp., 173 Halstead Ave., Harrison, New York 10528. (914) 835-3506. 1990. Monthly. This is a listing of published proceedings including the series SEMTE (Science/Medicine/Engineering/Technology) and the series SSH (Social Science/Humanities).

Environmental Engineering. Mary A. Vance. Vance Bibliographies, PO Box 229, 112 N. Charter St., Monticello, Illinois 61856. (217) 762-3831. 1983.

Environmental Systems Library. Washington, District of Columbia 1963-1979. Consists of design and installation manuals and worksheets published by the National

Environmental Systems Contractors Association and the Air Conditioning Contractors of America.

Natural Ventilation, Passive Cooling, and Human Comfort in Buildings: A Comprehensive Technical Bibliography. The Associates, Washington, District of Columbia

ENCYCLOPEDIAS AND DICTIONARIES

Dictionary of Environmental Engineering and Related Sciences: English-Spanish, Spanish-English. Jose T. Villate. Ediciones Universal, 3090 SW 8th St., Miami, Florida 33135. (305) 642-3355. 1979.

Elsevier's Dictionary of Building Construction. James Maclean. Elsevier Science Publishing Co., 655 Avenue of the Americas, New York, New York 10010. (212) 989-5800. 1989. Terms cover the basic vocabulary of the building construction industry, with particular emphasis on mechanical and electrical services.

Encyclopedia of Building and Construction Terms. Hugh Brooks. Prentice Hall, Rte. 9W, Englewood Cliffs, New Jersey 07632. (201) 592-2000 or (800) 634-2863. 1983. Includes construction terminology. Also contains index by function, list of construction associations classed under their functions and general conditions of the contract for construction.

Encyclopedia of Energy-Efficient Building Design. Kaiman Lee. Environmental Design & Research Center, 26799 Elena Rd., Los Altos Hills, California 94022. 1977. Covers architecture and energy consumption, designs and plans, and environmental engineering of buildings.

Encyclopedia of Environmental Science and Engineering. J.R. Pfafflin. Gordon and Breach Science Publishers, Inc., 270 8th Ave., New York, New York 10011. (212) 206-8900. 1992.

Encyclopedia of Physical Science and Technology. Robert A. Meyers, ed. Academic Press, c/o Harcourt Brace Jovanovich Inc., 6277 Sea Harbor Dr., Orlando, Florida 32887. (800) 346-8648. Dictionary of engineering, technology and physical sciences.

McGraw-Hill Encyclopedia of Environmental Science. Sybil P. Parker. McGraw-Hill Science & Engineering Books, 11 W. 19th St., New York, New York 10011. (212) 337-6010. 1980. Covers ecology, man's influence on nature, and environmental protection.

McGraw-Hill Encyclopedia of Science and Technology. McGraw-Hill, 1221 Avenue of the Americas, New York, New York 10020. (212) 512-2000 or (800) 262-4729. 1992. Seventh edition. Issued in multiple volumes including index. Includes all science and technology broad subject areas.

Means Illustrated Construction Dictionary. Kornelis Smit, ed. R. S. Means Co., 100 Construction Plaza, PO Box 800, Kingston, Massachusetts 02364-0800. (617) 747-1270. 1991. Focuses on every-day language used by the construction trades and professions in the United States. Includes illustrations.

GENERAL WORKS

Environment Control for Animals and Plants. Louis D. Albright. American Society of Agricultural Engineers, 2950 Niles Rd., St. Joseph, Michigan 49085-9659. (616) 429-0300. 1990. Deals with the physical aspects of environmental control with some attention to biological factors relevant to successful environment control. Includes 10 executable computer programs that allow the user to explore design options.

Environmental Engineering and Sanitation. Joseph A. Salvato. John Wiley & Sons, Inc., 605 3rd Ave., New York, New York 10158-0012. (212) 850-6000. 1992. 3d ed. Applies principles of sanitary science and engineering to sanitation and environmental health. It includes design, construction, maintenance, and operations of sanitation plants and structures. Provides state-of-the-art information on environmental factors associated with chronic and non-infectious diseases; environmental engineering planning and impact analysis; waste management and control; food sanitation; administration of health and sanitation programs; acid rain; noise control; campground sanitation, etc.

Environmental Physics in Construction. Granada, 717 E. Jericho Tpke., Ste. 281, Huntington Station, New York 11746. 1982. Applications in architectural design.

Intelligent Buildings. Michelle D. Gouin. Dow Jones-Irwin, Homewood, Illinois 1986. Strategies for technology and architecture in office buildings .

Noise Control in Building Services. Pergamon Microforms International, Inc., Fairview Park, Elmsford, New York 10523. (914) 592-7720. 1988. Soundproofing techniques in buildings.

State of the Art of Energy-Efficiency: Future Directions. Edward Vine and Drury Crawley, eds. University-Wide Energy Research Group, University of California, 2120 Berkeley Way, Berkeley, California 94720. (415) 642-4262; (800) 822-6657. 1991. Practical compilation of energy-efficient technologies and programs, resource planning, and data collection and analysis for buildings, which account for more than half of all U.S. energy.

HANDBOOKS AND MANUALS

Building Design and Construction Handbook. Frank S. Merritt. McGraw-Hill, 1221 Avenue of the Americas, New York, New York 10020. (212) 512-2000 or (800) 262-4729. 1982. Compendium of current building design and construction practices. Data for selection of building materials and construction methods are included.

Engineering Manual. Robert H. Perry. McGraw-Hill Science & Engineering Books, New York, New York 1976. A practical reference of design methods and data in building systems, chemical, civil, electrical, mechanical, and environmental engineering and energy conservation.

Environmental Science Handbook for Architects and Builders. S.V. Szokolay. John Wiley & Sons, Inc., 605 3rd Ave., New York, New York 10158-0012. (212) 850-6000. 1980. Topics in the environmental engineering of buildings.

Noise, Buildings, and People. Derek J. Croome. Pergamon Microforms International, Inc., Fairview Park, Elmsford, New York 10523. (914) 592-7720. 1977. Soundproofing techniques in buildings.

ONLINE DATA BASES

Computerized Engineering Index–COMPENDEX. Engineering Information Inc., 345 E. 47th St., New York, New York 10017. (212) 705-7600.

Enquete Annuelle d'Entreprises dans l'Industrie. McGraw-Hill Science & Engineering Books, 11 W. 19th St., New York, New York 10011. (212) 337-6010.

Monthly Catalog of United States Government Publications. U.S. G.P.O., Supt. of Docs., PO Box 371954, Pittsburgh, Pennsylvania 15250-7954. (202) 512-0000.

National Technical Information Service. U.S. Department of Commerce, National Technical Information Service, Office of Data Base Services, 5285 Port Royal Rd., Springfield, Virginia 22161. (703) 487-4807. Bibliographic database of government sponsored research and technical reports.

TRADE ASSOCIATIONS AND PROFESSIONAL SOCIETIES

American Society of Civil Engineers. 345 East 47th St., New York, New York 10017. (212) 705-7496.

National Institute of Building Sciences. 1201 L. St., N.W., Suite 400, Washington, District of Columbia 20005. (202) 289-7800.

BUILT ENVIRONMENT
See: CULTURAL RESOURCES

BULKING CAUSE
See: WASTEWATER TREATMENT

BURIAL GROUND (GRAVE YARD)
See: RADIOACTIVE WASTE STORAGE

BURNED AREAS
See: FORESTS

BURNING
See: AIR POLLUTION

BUS TRANSPORTATION
See: TRANSPORTATION

BUTANE
See also: FUELS

ABSTRACTING AND INDEXING SERVICES

Applied Science and Technology Index. H.W. Wilson Co., 950 University Ave., Bronx, New York 10452. (800) 367-6770. Formerly Industrial Arts Index.

Chemical Abstracts. Chemical Abstracts Service, 2540 Olentangy River Rd., PO Box 3012, Columbus, Ohio 43210. (800) 848-6533. 1907-.

Environment Abstracts. Bowker A & I Publishing, 121 Chanlon Rd., New Providence, New Jersey 07974. (908) 464-6800. 1974-.

Environment Index. Environment Information Center, Index Research Department, 124 E. 39th St., New York, New York 10016. 1971-. Annual.

Environmental Information Connection–EIC. Planning Information Program, Dept. of Urban and Regional Planning, University of Illinois, 1003 West Nevada, Urbana, Illinois 61801. (217) 333-1369. Also available online.

Environmental Periodicals Bibliography. Environmental Studies Institute, International Academy at Santa Barbara, 800 Garden St., Suite D, Santa Barbara, California 93101. (805) 965-5010. Also available online.

ERDA Research Abstracts. U.S. ERDA Technical Information Center, Box 62, Oak Ridge, Tennessee 37830.

General Science Index. H. W. Wilson Co., 950 University Ave., Bronx, New York 10452. 1978-. Monthly, also issued in annual cumulation. Cumulative subject index to English language periodicals in the subject fields of astronomy, botany, chemistry, earth science, environment and conservation, food and nutrition, genetics, mathematics, medicine and health, microbiology, oceanography, physics, physiology and zoology.

Science Citation Index. Institute for Scientific Information, 3501 Market St., Philadelphia, Pennsylvania 19104. 1961-.

BIBLIOGRAPHIES

EPA Publications Bibliography. U.S. Environmental Protection Agency, Library Systems Branch, 401 M St., SW, Washington, District of Columbia 20460. (202) 260-2090. Quarterly.

ENCYCLOPEDIAS AND DICTIONARIES

McGraw-Hill Encyclopedia of Science and Technology. McGraw-Hill, 1221 Avenue of the Americas, New York, New York 10020. (212) 512-2000 or (800) 262-4729. 1992. Seventh edition. Issued in multiple volumes including index. Includes all science and technology broad subject areas.

Van Nostrand's Scientific Encyclopedia. Glenn D. Considine, ed. Van Nostrand Reinhold, 115 5th Ave., New York, New York 10003. (212) 254-3232. 1983. Sixth edition. Includes all broad subject areas in science.

ONLINE DATA BASES

CAS Source Index–CASSI. Chemical Abstracts Service, 2540 Olentangy River Rd., P.O. Box 3012, Columbus, Ohio 43210. (800) 848-6533 or (614) 421-3600. A listing of bibliographic and library holdings information for scientific and technical primary literature relevant to the chemical sciences.

Chemical Abstracts-CA. Chemical Abstracts Service, 2540 Olentangy River Rd., P.O. Box 3012, Columbus, Ohio 43210. (800) 848-6533 or (614) 421-3600. Information sources include 9000 journals, patents from 27 countries, two industrial property organizations, new books, conference proceedings, and government research reports.

Enviro/Energyline Abstracts Plus. R. R. Bowker Co., 121 Chanlon Rd., New Providence, New Jersey 07974. (908) 464-6800.

Environmental Periodicals Bibliography. National Information Services Corp., Ste. 6, Wyman Towers, 3100 St. Paul St., Baltimore, Maryland 21218. (410)243-0797. Online version of abstract of same name.

TRADE ASSOCIATIONS AND PROFESSIONAL SOCIETIES

National Propane Gas Association. 1600 Eisenhower Ln., Lisle, Illinois 60532. (708) 515-0600.

C

C14 DATING

See also: RADIOCARBON DATING

ABSTRACTING AND INDEXING SERVICES

Applied Science and Technology Index. H.W. Wilson Co., 950 University Ave., Bronx, New York 10452. (800) 367-6770. Formerly Industrial Arts Index.

Biological Abstracts. BIOSIS, 2100 Arch St., Philadelphia, Pennsylvania 19103-1399. (215) 587-4800. 1927-.

Chemical Abstracts. Chemical Abstracts Service, 2540 Olentangy River Rd., PO Box 3012, Columbus, Ohio 43210. (800) 848-6533. 1907-.

Ecology Abstracts. Cambridge Scientific Abstracts, 5161 River Rd., Bethesda, Maryland 20816. (301) 961-6750. Monthly.

Engineering Index. The Engineering Index Inc., 345 E. 47th St., New York, New York 10017. 1962-.

Environment Abstracts. Bowker A & I Publishing, 121 Chanlon Rd., New Providence, New Jersey 07974. (908) 464-6800. 1974-.

Environment Index. Environment Information Center, Index Research Department, 124 E. 39th St., New York, New York 10016. 1971-. Annual.

Environmental Information Connection–EIC. Planning Information Program, Dept. of Urban and Regional Planning, University of Illinois, 1003 West Nevada, Urbana, Illinois 61801. (217) 333-1369. Also available online.

Environmental Periodicals Bibliography. Environmental Studies Institute, International Academy at Santa Barbara, 800 Garden St., Suite D, Santa Barbara, California 93101. (805) 965-5010. Also available online.

General Science Index. H. W. Wilson Co., 950 University Ave., Bronx, New York 10452. 1978-. Monthly, also issued in annual cumulation. Cumulative subject index to English language periodicals in the subject fields of astronomy, botany, chemistry, earth science, environment and conservation, food and nutrition, genetics, mathematics, medicine and health, microbiology, oceanography, physics, physiology and zoology.

Index to Scientific Book Contents. Institute for Scientific Information, 3501 Market St., Philadelphia, Pennsylvania 19104. (800) 523-1857. 1985-. Annual. Gives contents of science books published.

INIS Atomindex. International Atomic Energy Agency, Wagramerstrasse 5, Vienna, Austria A-1400. 222 23606198. 1988-. Semiannual. Abstracts nuclear energy and nuclear physics topics from journals, conferences, technical reports and other related publications. Issued in 6 parts: Personal Author, Corporate Entry, Subject, Report, Standard Patent, Conference (by place), Conference (by date).

Physics Briefs. Physikalische Berichte. Physik Verlag, Pappapelallee 3, Postfach 101161, Weinheim, Germany D-6940. 1979-. Semimonthly. In English. Volumes for 1979- issued by the Deutsche Physikalische Gesellschaft and the Fachinformationszentrum Energie Physik, Mathematik in cooperation with the American Institute of Physics.

Science Citation Index. Institute for Scientific Information, 3501 Market St., Philadelphia, Pennsylvania 19104. 1961-.

BIBLIOGRAPHIES

Directory of Published Proceedings. Interdok Corp., 173 Halstead Ave., Harrison, New York 10528. (914) 835-3506. 1990. Monthly. This is a listing of published proceedings including the series SEMTE (Science/Medicine/Engineering/Technology) and the series SSH (Social Science/Humanities).

EPA Publications Bibliography. U.S. Environmental Protection Agency, Library Systems Branch, 401 M St., SW, Washington, District of Columbia 20460. (202) 260-2090. Quarterly.

ENCYCLOPEDIAS AND DICTIONARIES

Cambridge Encyclopedia of Life Sciences. A. E. Friday and David S. Ingram. Cambridge University Press, 40 W 20th St., New York, New York 10011. (212) 924-3900 or (800) 227-0247. 1985. Includes all topics under biology and ecology.

The Encyclopedia of Climatology. John E. Oliver and Rhodes W. Fairbridge, eds. Van Nostrand Reinhold, 115 5th Ave., New York, New York 10003. (212) 254-3232. 1987. Belongs in the series Encyclopedia of Earth Sciences, v.11.

The Encyclopedia of Geochemistry and Environmental Sciences. Rhodes Whitmore Fairbridge. Van Nostrand Reinhold Co., 115 5th Ave., New York, New York 10003. (212) 254-3232. 1972.

Glossary of Geology. Robert Latimer Bates and Julia A. Jackson, eds. American Geological Institute, 4220 King St., Alexandria, Virginia 22302-1507. (703) 379-2480 or (800) 336-4764. 1987. Third edition.

McGraw-Hill Encyclopedia of Science and Technology. McGraw-Hill, 1221 Avenue of the Americas, New York, New York 10020. (212) 512-2000 or (800) 262-4729. 1992. Seventh edition. Issued in multiple volumes including index. Includes all science and technology broad subject areas.

McGraw-Hill Encyclopedia of the Geological Sciences. Sybil P. Parker, ed. McGraw-Hill, 1221 Avenue of the Americas, New York, New York 10020. (212) 512-2000 or (800) 262-4729. 1988. Second edition. Published previously in the McGraw-Hill Encyclopedia of Science and Technology.

Van Nostrand's Scientific Encyclopedia. Glenn D. Considine, ed. Van Nostrand Reinhold, 115 5th Ave., New York, New York 10003. (212) 254-3232. 1983. Sixth edition. Includes all broad subject areas in science.

ONLINE DATA BASES

BIOSIS Previews. BIOSIS, 2100 Arch St., Philadelphia, Pennsylvania 19103-1399. (215) 587-4800. Largest and most comprehensive database of research in the life sciences. Contains citations for nearly 9000 primary research journals, monographs, reviews, symposia, preliminary reports, semi-popular journals, selected institutional reports, government reports and research communications.

CAS Source Index–CASSI. Chemical Abstracts Service, 2540 Olentangy River Rd., P.O. Box 3012, Columbus, Ohio 43210. (800) 848-6533 or (614) 421-3600. A listing of bibliographic and library holdings information for scientific and technical primary literature relevant to the chemical sciences.

Chemical Abstracts-CA. Chemical Abstracts Service, 2540 Olentangy River Rd., P.O. Box 3012, Columbus, Ohio 43210. (800) 848-6533 or (614) 421-3600. Information sources include 9000 journals, patents from 27 countries, two industrial property organizations, new books, conference proceedings, and government research reports.

Chemical Engineering and Biotechnology Abstracts–CEBA. Orbit Search Service, Maxwell Online Inc., 8000 W. Park Dr., McLean, Virginia 22102. (703) 442-0900 or (800) 456-7248. Monthly. Covers theoretical, practical and commercial material on all aspects of processing safety, and the environment. Also covers process and reaction engineering, measurement and process control, environmental protection and safety, plant design and equipment used in chemical engineering and biotechnology. More than 400 of the world's major primary chemical and process engineering journals are scanned to compile the database. Available from ORBIT.

Computerized Engineering Index–COMPENDEX. Engineering Information Inc., 345 E. 47th St., New York, New York 10017. (212) 705-7600.

Enviro/Energyline Abstracts Plus. R. R. Bowker Co., 121 Chanlon Rd., New Providence, New Jersey 07974. (908) 464-6800.

Environmental Periodicals Bibliography. National Information Services Corp., Ste. 6, Wyman Towers, 3100 St. Paul St., Baltimore, Maryland 21218. (410)243-0797. Online version of abstract of same name.

CADMIUM
See: ELEMENTS

CAFFEINE

ABSTRACTING AND INDEXING SERVICES

Biological Abstracts. BIOSIS, 2100 Arch St., Philadelphia, Pennsylvania 19103-1399. (215) 587-4800. 1927-.

Biological and Agricultural Index. H.W. Wilson Co., 950 University Ave., Bronx, New York 10452. (800) 367-6770. 1916-. Monthly.

Environment Abstracts. Bowker A & I Publishing, 121 Chanlon Rd., New Providence, New Jersey 07974. (908) 464-6800. 1974-.

Environment Index. Environment Information Center, Index Research Department, 124 E. 39th St., New York, New York 10016. 1971-. Annual.

Environmental Information Connection–EIC. Planning Information Program, Dept. of Urban and Regional Planning, University of Illinois, 1003 West Nevada, Urbana, Illinois 61801. (217) 333-1369. Also available online.

Environmental Periodicals Bibliography. Environmental Studies Institute, International Academy at Santa Barbara, 800 Garden St., Suite D, Santa Barbara, California 93101. (805) 965-5010. Also available online.

Food Science and Technology Abstracts. International Food Information Service, c/o National Food Laboratory, 6363 Clark Ave., Dublin, California 94568. (800) 336-3782. 1969-.

General Science Index. H. W. Wilson Co., 950 University Ave., Bronx, New York 10452. 1978-. Monthly, also issued in annual cumulation. Cumulative subject index to English language periodicals in the subject fields of astronomy, botany, chemistry, earth science, environment and conservation, food and nutrition, genetics, mathematics, medicine and health, microbiology, oceanography, physics, physiology and zoology.

Index to Scientific Book Contents. Institute for Scientific Information, 3501 Market St., Philadelphia, Pennsylvania 19104. (800) 523-1857. 1985-. Annual. Gives contents of science books published.

Science Citation Index. Institute for Scientific Information, 3501 Market St., Philadelphia, Pennsylvania 19104. 1961-.

BIBLIOGRAPHIES

Caffeine: A Medical and Scientific Subject Analysis and Research Index with Bibliography. Hanna U. Tyler. ABBE Publishers Association of Washington DC, 4111 Gallows Rd., Annandale, Virginia 22003-1862. Bibliography of caffeine toxicology and caffeine habits and their physiological effects.

EPA Publications Bibliography. U.S. Environmental Protection Agency, Library Systems Branch, 401 M St., SW, Washington, District of Columbia 20460. (202) 260-2090. Quarterly.

ENCYCLOPEDIAS AND DICTIONARIES

Encyclopedia of Human Biology. Renato Dulbecco, ed. Academic Press, c/o Harcourt Brace Jovanovich Inc., 6277 Sea Harbor Dr., Orlando, Florida 32887. (800) 346-8648. 1991. Eight volumes.

McGraw-Hill Encyclopedia of Science and Technology. McGraw-Hill, 1221 Avenue of the Americas, New York, New York 10020. (212) 512-2000 or (800) 262-4729. 1992. Seventh edition. Issued in multiple volumes including index. Includes all science and technology broad subject areas.

The Nutrition and Health Encyclopedia. David F. Tver and Percy Russell. Van Nostrand Reinhold, 115 5th Ave., New York, New York 10003. (212) 254-3232. 1989.

Van Nostrand's Scientific Encyclopedia. Glenn D. Considine, ed. Van Nostrand Reinhold, 115 5th Ave., New York, New York 10003. (212) 254-3232. 1983. Sixth edition. Includes all broad subject areas in science.

GENERAL WORKS

Caffeine. LeRoy Werley. University of North Carolina, P.O. Box 2288, Chapel Hill, North Carolina 27515-2288. 1981.

The Caffeine Book. Frances Sheridan Goulart. Mead Publishing Corp., 1515 S. Commerce St., Las Vegas, Nevada 81902-2703. (702) 387-8750. 1984.

Caffeine: Perspectives from Recent Research. P.B. Dews, ed. Springer-Verlag, 175 5th Ave., New York, New York 10010. (212) 460-1500. 1984.

The Health Effects of Caffeine. American Council on Science and Health. The Council, Summit, New Jersey 1981.

HANDBOOKS AND MANUALS

FDA Food Additives Analytical Manual. C. Warner, et al., eds. Association of Official Analytical Chemists, 2200 Wilson Blvd., Suite 400-P, Arlington, Virginia 22201-3301. (703) 522-3032. 1983-1987. 2 vols. Provides methodology for determining compliance with food additive regulations. Contains analytical methods that have been evaluated by the FDA or found to operate satisfactorily in at least two laboratories.

ONLINE DATA BASES

BIOSIS Previews. BIOSIS, 2100 Arch St., Philadelphia, Pennsylvania 19103-1399. (215) 587-4800. Largest and most comprehensive database of research in the life sciences. Contains citations for nearly 9000 primary research journals, monographs, reviews, symposia, preliminary reports, semi-popular journals, selected institutional reports, government reports and research communications.

Enviro/Energyline Abstracts Plus. R. R. Bowker Co., 121 Chanlon Rd., New Providence, New Jersey 07974. (908) 464-6800.

Environmental Periodicals Bibliography. National Information Services Corp., Ste. 6, Wyman Towers, 3100 St. Paul St., Baltimore, Maryland 21218. (410)243-0797. Online version of abstract of same name.

PressNet Environmental Reports. Chemical Information Systems, Inc., 7215 York Rd., Baltimore, Maryland 21212. (301) 321-8440.

TRADE ASSOCIATIONS AND PROFESSIONAL SOCIETIES

National Campground Owners Association. 11307 Sunset Hills Rd., Ste. B7, Reston, Virginia 22090. (703) 471-0143.

CALCIUM

See also: ELEMENTS; METABOLISM; NUTRITION; SOIL SCIENCE

ABSTRACTING AND INDEXING SERVICES

Applied Science and Technology Index. H.W. Wilson Co., 950 University Ave., Bronx, New York 10452. (800) 367-6770. Formerly Industrial Arts Index.

Biological Abstracts. BIOSIS, 2100 Arch St., Philadelphia, Pennsylvania 19103-1399. (215) 587-4800. 1927-.

Biotechnology Research Abstracts. Cambridge Scientific Abstracts, 5161 River Rd., Bethesda, Maryland 20816. (301) 961-6750. Monthly. Includes such broad areas as genetic intervention, biochemical genetics, and microbiological techniques.

Chemical Abstracts. Chemical Abstracts Service, 2540 Olentangy River Rd., PO Box 3012, Columbus, Ohio 43210. (800) 848-6533. 1907-.

Ecology Abstracts. Cambridge Scientific Abstracts, 5161 River Rd., Bethesda, Maryland 20816. (301) 961-6750. Monthly.

Environment Abstracts. Bowker A & I Publishing, 121 Chanlon Rd., New Providence, New Jersey 07974. (908) 464-6800. 1974-.

Environment Index. Environment Information Center, Index Research Department, 124 E. 39th St., New York, New York 10016. 1971-. Annual.

Environmental Information Connection–EIC. Planning Information Program, Dept. of Urban and Regional Planning, University of Illinois, 1003 West Nevada, Urbana, Illinois 61801. (217) 333-1369. Also available online.

Environmental Periodicals Bibliography. Environmental Studies Institute, International Academy at Santa Barbara, 800 Garden St., Suite D, Santa Barbara, California 93101. (805) 965-5010. Also available online.

Food Science and Technology Abstracts. International Food Information Service, c/o National Food Laboratory, 6363 Clark Ave., Dublin, California 94568. (800) 336-3782. 1969-.

General Science Index. H. W. Wilson Co., 950 University Ave., Bronx, New York 10452. 1978-. Monthly, also issued in annual cumulation. Cumulative subject index to English language periodicals in the subject fields of astronomy, botany, chemistry, earth science, environment and conservation, food and nutrition, genetics, mathematics, medicine and health, microbiology, oceanography, physics, physiology and zoology.

Index to Scientific Book Contents. Institute for Scientific Information, 3501 Market St., Philadelphia, Pennsylvania 19104. (800) 523-1857. 1985-. Annual. Gives contents of science books published.

Physics Briefs. Physikalische Berichte. Physik Verlag, Pappapelallee 3, Postfach 101161, Weinheim, Germany D-6940. 1979-. Semimonthly. In English. Volumes for 1979- issued by the Deutsche Physikalische Gesellschaft and the Fachinformationszentrum Energie Physik, Mathematik in cooperation with the American Institute of Physics.

Pollution Abstracts. Cambridge Scientific Abstracts, 5161 River Rd., Bethesda, Maryland 20816. (301) 961-6750. Six/year. Indexes worldwide technical literature on environmental pollution. Covers air pollution, marine and freshwater pollution, sewage and wastewater treatment, waste management, toxicology and health, noise pollution, radiation, land pollution, and environmental policies, programs, legislation, and education. Also available online.

Science Citation Index. Institute for Scientific Information, 3501 Market St., Philadelphia, Pennsylvania 19104. 1961-.

BIBLIOGRAPHIES

EPA Publications Bibliography. U.S. Environmental Protection Agency, Library Systems Branch, 401 M St., SW, Washington, District of Columbia 20460. (202) 260-2090. Quarterly.

ENCYCLOPEDIAS AND DICTIONARIES

Encyclopedia of Chemical Processing and Design. John J. Mcketta and W. A. Cunningham. Marcel Dekker, Inc., 270 Madison Ave., New York, New York 10016. (212) 696-9000; (800) 228-1160. 1992. Thirty-eight volumes.

Encyclopedia of Electrochemistry of Elements. A. J. Bard. Marcel Dekker, Inc., 270 Madison Ave., New York, New York 10016. (212) 696-9000 or (800) 228-1160. Encyclopedic treatment of the subject area of electrochemistry and related subjects.

Encyclopedia of Human Biology. Renato Dulbecco, ed. Academic Press, c/o Harcourt Brace Jovanovich Inc., 6277 Sea Harbor Dr., Orlando, Florida 32887. (800) 346-8648. 1991. Eight volumes.

Kirk-Othmer Encyclopedia of Chemical Technology. J. I. Kroschwitz, ed. John Wiley & Sons, Inc., 605 3rd Ave., New York, New York 10158-0012. (212) 850-6000. 1992-. All articles in the new edition have been rewritten and updated adding new subjects such as biotechnology, computer topics, analytical techniques and instrumentation, environmental concerns, fuels and energy, inorganic and solid state chemistry; composite materials and material science in general, and pharmaceuticals. Also available online.

McGraw-Hill Encyclopedia of Science and Technology. McGraw-Hill, 1221 Avenue of the Americas, New York, New York 10020. (212) 512-2000 or (800) 262-4729. 1992. Seventh edition. Issued in multiple volumes including index. Includes all science and technology broad subject areas.

The Nutrition and Health Encyclopedia. David F. Tver and Percy Russell. Van Nostrand Reinhold, 115 5th

Ave., New York, New York 10003. (212) 254-3232. 1989.

Van Nostrand's Scientific Encyclopedia. Glenn D. Considine, ed. Van Nostrand Reinhold, 115 5th Ave., New York, New York 10003. (212) 254-3232. 1983. Sixth edition. Includes all broad subject areas in science.

GENERAL WORKS

Calcium, Cell Cycles, and Cancer. James F. Whitfield. CRC Press, 2000 Corporate Blvd. N.W., Boca Raton, Florida 33431. (800) 272-7737. 1990.

Calcium Channels: Structure and Function. New York Academy of Sciences, Marketing Dept., 2E 63rd St., New York, New York 10021. (212) 838-0230. 1989.

Calcium in Biological Systems. Ronald P. Rubin. Plenum Press, 233 Spring St., New York, New York 10013-1578. (212) 620-8000. 1985. Covers calcification and calcium channel blockers.

Calcium, Membranes, Aging, and Alzheimer's Disease. New York Academy of Sciences, Marketing Dept., 2E 63rd St., New York, New York 10021. (212) 838-0230. 1989. Discusses calcium in the body.

The Role of Calcium in Biological Systems. CRC Press, 2000 Corporate Blvd. N.W., Boca Raton, Florida 33431. (800) 272-7737. 1982-.

The Role of Calcium in Drug Action. Pergamon Microforms International Inc., Fairview Park, Elmsford, New York 10523. (914) 592-7720. 1987. Calcium, agonists and their therapeutic use.

Techniques in Calcium Research. M.V. Thomas. Academic Press, c/o Harcourt Brace Jovanovich Inc., 6277 Sea Harbor Dr., Orlando, Florida 32887. (800) 346-8648. 1982. Calcium analysis and physiological effect.

HANDBOOKS AND MANUALS

Tables of Physical and Chemical Constants and Some Mathematical Functions. G. W. C. Kaye, et al. Longman Group Ltd., Longman House, Burnt Mill, Harlow, England CM20 2J6. 0279 426721. 1988. Fifteenth edition. Includes tables on mechanical properties, density, elasticity, viscosity, surface tension, temperature and heat. Also covers radiation, optics, chemistry, electrochemistry, astrophysics, and chemical thermodynamics.

ONLINE DATA BASES

BIOSIS Previews. BIOSIS, 2100 Arch St., Philadelphia, Pennsylvania 19103-1399. (215) 587-4800. Largest and most comprehensive database of research in the life sciences. Contains citations for nearly 9000 primary research journals, monographs, reviews, symposia, preliminary reports, semi-popular journals, selected institutional reports, government reports and research communications.

CAS Source Index–CASSI. Chemical Abstracts Service, 2540 Olentangy River Rd., P.O. Box 3012, Columbus, Ohio 43210. (800) 848-6533 or (614) 421-3600. A listing of bibliographic and library holdings information for scientific and technical primary literature relevant to the chemical sciences.

Chemical Abstracts-CA. Chemical Abstracts Service, 2540 Olentangy River Rd., P.O. Box 3012, Columbus,

Ohio 43210. (800) 848-6533 or (614) 421-3600. Information sources include 9000 journals, patents from 27 countries, two industrial property organizations, new books, conference proceedings, and government research reports.

Chemical Engineering and Biotechnology Abstracts–CEBA. Orbit Search Service, Maxwell Online Inc., 8000 W. Park Dr., McLean, Virginia 22102. (703) 442-0900 or (800) 456-7248. Monthly. Covers theoretical, practical and commercial material on all aspects of processing safety, and the environment. Also covers process and reaction engineering, measurement and process control, environmental protection and safety, plant design and equipment used in chemical engineering and biotechnology. More than 400 of the world's major primary chemical and process engineering journals are scanned to compile the database. Available from ORBIT.

Enviro/Energyline Abstracts Plus. R. R. Bowker Co., 121 Chanlon Rd., New Providence, New Jersey 07974. (908) 464-6800.

Environmental Periodicals Bibliography. National Information Services Corp., Ste. 6, Wyman Towers, 3100 St. Paul St., Baltimore, Maryland 21218. (410)243-0797. Online version of abstract of same name.

Kirk-Othmer Encyclopedia of Chemical Technology. John Wiley & Sons, Inc., 605 3rd Ave., 5th Floor, New York, New York 10158. (212) 850-6000. Online version of the publication of the same name.

PERIODICALS AND NEWSLETTERS

Cell Calcium. Churchill Livingstone, Inc., 650 Avenue of the Americas, New York, New York 10011. (212) 206-5000. Bimonthly. The international interdisciplinary forum for research on calcium.

CALIFORNIA ENVIRONMENTAL AGENCIES

GOVERNMENTAL ORGANIZATIONS

Coastal Commission: Coastal Zone Management. Chairman, 631 Howard St., 4th Floor, San Francisco, California 94105. (415) 543-8555.

Department of Conservation: Natural Resources. Director, 1416 Ninth St., Room 1320, Sacramento, California 95814. (916) 322-1080.

Department of Environmental Affairs: Air Quality. Secretary, 1102 Q St., Sacramento, California 95814. (916) 322-5840.

Department of Environmental Affairs: Environmental Protection. Secretary, 1102 Q St., Sacramento, California 95814. (916) 322-5840.

Department of Fish and Game: Fish and Wildlife. Director, 1416 Ninth St., 12th Floor, Sacramento, California 95814. (916) 445-3535.

Department of Food and Agriculture: Pesticide Registration. Associate Director, Division of Pest Management, Environmental Protection and Worker Safety, PO Box 942871, Sacramento, California 94271-0001. (916) 322-6315.

Department of Industrial Relations: Occupational Safety. Chief, Occupational Safety and Health, 525 Golden Gate Ave., San Francisco, California 94102. (415) 557-1946.

Department of Water Resources: Groundwater Management. Chief, Planning Division, 1416 9th St., Sacramento, California 95814. (916) 445-9610.

Environmental Affairs Agency: Hazardous Waste Management. Chairman, Waste Management Board, 1020 Ninth St., Suite 300, Sacramento, California 95814. (916) 322-3330.

Environmental Affairs Agency: Solid Waste Management. Chairman, Waste Management Board, 1020 Ninth St., Suite 300, Sacramento, California 95814. (916) 322-3330.

Office of Environmental Affairs: Emergency Preparedness and Community Right-to-Know. Section 313 Reports, PO Box 2815, Sacramento, California 95832. (916) 427-4287.

Toxic Substances Control Program: Waste Minimization and Pollution Prevention. Supervising Waste Management Engineer, Alternative Technology Division, 714/744 P St., Sacramento, California 94234-7320. (916) 322-5347.

Water Resources Control Board: Water Quality. Chief, Division of Water Quality, 901 P St., PO Box 100, Sacramento, California 95801. (916) 445-9552.

CALIFORNIA ENVIRONMENTAL LEGISLATION

GENERAL WORKS

California Environmental Law Handbook. Government Institutes, Inc., 4 Research Pl., Ste. 200, Rockville, Maryland 20850. (301) 921-2300. 1991.

CALORIES
See: NUTRITION

CANCER RISKS
See: CARCINOGENS

CANDU REACTORS
See: REACTORS

CANISTER CORROSION
See: RADIOACTIVE WASTES

CAR POOLS
See: TRANSPORTATION

CARBAMATE PESTICIDES

See: PESTICIDES

CARBARYL

See: INSECTICIDES

CARBOHYDRATES

See: NUTRITION

CARBON

See also: ELEMENTS; METABOLISM

ABSTRACTING AND INDEXING SERVICES

Applied Science and Technology Index. H.W. Wilson Co., 950 University Ave., Bronx, New York 10452. (800) 367-6770. Formerly Industrial Arts Index.

Biological Abstracts. BIOSIS, 2100 Arch St., Philadelphia, Pennsylvania 19103-1399. (215) 587-4800. 1927-.

Chemical Abstracts. Chemical Abstracts Service, 2540 Olentangy River Rd., PO Box 3012, Columbus, Ohio 43210. (800) 848-6533. 1907-.

Ecology Abstracts. Cambridge Scientific Abstracts, 5161 River Rd., Bethesda, Maryland 20816. (301) 961-6750. Monthly.

Engineering Index. The Engineering Index Inc., 345 E. 47th St., New York, New York 10017. 1962-.

Environment Abstracts. Bowker A & I Publishing, 121 Chanlon Rd., New Providence, New Jersey 07974. (908) 464-6800. 1974-.

Environment Index. Environment Information Center, Index Research Department, 124 E. 39th St., New York, New York 10016. 1971-. Annual.

Environmental Information Connection–EIC. Planning Information Program, Dept. of Urban and Regional Planning, University of Illinois, 1003 West Nevada, Urbana, Illinois 61801. (217) 333-1369. Also available online.

Environmental Periodicals Bibliography. Environmental Studies Institute, International Academy at Santa Barbara, 800 Garden St., Suite D, Santa Barbara, California 93101. (805) 965-5010. Also available online.

Index to Scientific Book Contents. Institute for Scientific Information, 3501 Market St., Philadelphia, Pennsylvania 19104. (800) 523-1857. 1985-. Annual. Gives contents of science books published.

Metals Abstracts. ASM International, 9639 Kinsman, Materials Park, Ohio 44073. (216) 338-5151. 1968-. Published jointly by the Institute of Metals, London and the American Society for Metals. Formed by the Union of Metallurgical Abstracts and Review of Metal Literature.

Physics Briefs. Physikalische Berichte. Physik Verlag, Pappapelallee 3, Postfach 101161, Weinheim, Germany D-6940. 1979-. Semimonthly. In English. Volumes for 1979- issued by the Deutsche Physikalische Gesellschaft and the Fachinformationszentrum Energie Physik, Mathematik in cooperation with the American Institute of Physics.

Pollution Abstracts. Cambridge Scientific Abstracts, 5161 River Rd., Bethesda, Maryland 20816. (301) 961-6750. Six/year. Indexes worldwide technical literature on environmental pollution. Covers air pollution, marine and freshwater pollution, sewage and wastewater treatment, waste management, toxicology and health, noise pollution, radiation, land pollution, and environmental policies, programs, legislation, and education. Also available online.

Science Citation Index. Institute for Scientific Information, 3501 Market St., Philadelphia, Pennsylvania 19104. 1961-.

BIBLIOGRAPHIES

EPA Publications Bibliography. U.S. Environmental Protection Agency, Library Systems Branch, 401 M St., SW, Washington, District of Columbia 20460. (202) 260-2090. Quarterly.

ENCYCLOPEDIAS AND DICTIONARIES

Encyclopedia of Physics. Rita G. Lerner and George L. Trigg. VCH Publishers, 303 NW 12th Ave., Deerfield Beach, Florida 33442-1788. (305) 428-5566. 1991. Second edition.

Life Sciences on File. Diagram Group. Facts on File, Inc., 460 Park Ave. S., New York, New York 10016. (212) 683-2244. 1986. Encyclopedia of pictorial collection in life sciences. Deals with all major topics in life sciences including ecology.

McGraw-Hill Encyclopedia of Science and Technology. McGraw-Hill, 1221 Avenue of the Americas, New York, New York 10020. (212) 512-2000 or (800) 262-4729. 1992. Seventh edition. Issued in multiple volumes including index. Includes all science and technology broad subject areas.

Van Nostrand's Scientific Encyclopedia. Glenn D. Considine, ed. Van Nostrand Reinhold, 115 5th Ave., New York, New York 10003. (212) 254-3232. 1983. Sixth edition. Includes all broad subject areas in science.

GENERAL WORKS

Minding the Carbon Store: Weighing U.S. Forestry Strategies to Slow Global Warming. Mark C. Trexler. World Resources Institute, 1709 New York Ave. N.W., Washington, District of Columbia 20006. (800) 833 0504. 1991. Assesses the strengths and weaknesses of each of the major domestic forestry options, including their costs and carbon benefits.

HANDBOOKS AND MANUALS

Chemistry of Carbon Compounds: A Modern Comprehensive Treatise. M. F. Ansell, ed. Elsevier Science Publishing Co., 655 Avenue of the Americas, New York, New York 10010. (212) 984-5800. Irregular.

Tables of Physical and Chemical Constants and Some Mathematical Functions. G. W. C. Kaye, et al. Longman Group Ltd., Longman House, Burnt Mill, Harlow, England CM20 2J6. 0279 426721. 1988. Fifteenth edition. Includes tables on mechanical properties, density, elasticity, viscosity, surface tension, temperature and heat. Also covers radiation, optics, chemistry, electrochemistry, astrophysics, and chemical thermodynamics.

ONLINE DATA BASES

BIOSIS Previews. BIOSIS, 2100 Arch St., Philadelphia, Pennsylvania 19103-1399. (215) 587-4800. Largest and most comprehensive database of research in the life sciences. Contains citations for nearly 9000 primary research journals, monographs, reviews, symposia, preliminary reports, semi-popular journals, selected institutional reports, government reports and research communications.

Chemical Abstracts-CA. Chemical Abstracts Service, 2540 Olentangy River Rd., P.O. Box 3012, Columbus, Ohio 43210. (800) 848-6533 or (614) 421-3600. Information sources include 9000 journals, patents from 27 countries, two industrial property organizations, new books, conference proceedings, and government research reports.

Computerized Engineering Index–COMPENDEX. Engineering Information Inc., 345 E. 47th St., New York, New York 10017. (212) 705-7600.

Enviro/Energyline Abstracts Plus. R. R. Bowker Co., 121 Chanlon Rd., New Providence, New Jersey 07974. (908) 464-6800.

Environmental Periodicals Bibliography. National Information Services Corp., Ste. 6, Wyman Towers, 3100 St. Paul St., Baltimore, Maryland 21218. (410)243-0797. Online version of abstract of same name.

PERIODICALS AND NEWSLETTERS

Carbon. Pergamon Microforms International, Inc., Fairview Park, Elmsford, New York 10523. (914) 592-7720. Monthly. Covers environmental aspects of carbon.

Topics in Carbon-13 NMR Spectroscopy. John Wiley & Sons Inc., 605 3rd Ave., New York, New York 10158-0012. (212) 850-6000. 1974-. Irregular.

STATISTICS SOURCES

Ecology: Community Profiles. U.S. Fish and Wildlife Service. National Technical Information Service, 5285 Port Royal Road, Springfield, Virginia 22161. (703) 487-4650. Irregular. Data on coastal and inland ecosystems, including wetlands, tidal-flats, near-shore seagrasses, sand dunes, drilling platforms, oyster reefs, estuaries, rivers and streams.

TRADE ASSOCIATIONS AND PROFESSIONAL SOCIETIES

American Institute of Chemical Engineers. 345 East 47th St., New York, New York 10017. (212) 705-7338.

American Institute of Chemists. 7315 Wisconsin Ave., Bethesda, Maryland 20814. (301) 652-2447.

CARBON, ACTIVATED

See also: FILTRATION; WASTEWATER TREATMENT

ABSTRACTING AND INDEXING SERVICES

Applied Science and Technology Index. H.W. Wilson Co., 950 University Ave., Bronx, New York 10452. (800) 367-6770. Formerly Industrial Arts Index.

Biological Abstracts. BIOSIS, 2100 Arch St., Philadelphia, Pennsylvania 19103-1399. (215) 587-4800. 1927-.

Engineering Index. The Engineering Index Inc., 345 E. 47th St., New York, New York 10017. 1962-.

Environment Abstracts. Bowker A & I Publishing, 121 Chanlon Rd., New Providence, New Jersey 07974. (908) 464-6800. 1974-.

Environment Index. Environment Information Center, Index Research Department, 124 E. 39th St., New York, New York 10016. 1971-. Annual.

Environmental Information Connection–EIC. Planning Information Program, Dept. of Urban and Regional Planning, University of Illinois, 1003 West Nevada, Urbana, Illinois 61801. (217) 333-1369. Also available online.

Environmental Periodicals Bibliography. Environmental Studies Institute, International Academy at Santa Barbara, 800 Garden St., Suite D, Santa Barbara, California 93101. (805) 965-5010. Also available online.

General Science Index. H. W. Wilson Co., 950 University Ave., Bronx, New York 10452. 1978-. Monthly, also issued in annual cumulation. Cumulative subject index to English language periodicals in the subject fields of astronomy, botany, chemistry, earth science, environment and conservation, food and nutrition, genetics, mathematics, medicine and health, microbiology, oceanography, physics, physiology and zoology.

Index to Scientific Book Contents. Institute for Scientific Information, 3501 Market St., Philadelphia, Pennsylvania 19104. (800) 523-1857. 1985-. Annual. Gives contents of science books published.

Physics Briefs. Physikalische Berichte. Physik Verlag, Pappapelallee 3, Postfach 101161, Weinheim, Germany D-6940. 1979-. Semimonthly. In English. Volumes for 1979- issued by the Deutsche Physikalische Gesellschaft and the Fachinformationszentrum Energie Physik, Mathematik in cooperation with the American Institute of Physics.

Science Citation Index. Institute for Scientific Information, 3501 Market St., Philadelphia, Pennsylvania 19104. 1961-.

BIBLIOGRAPHIES

EPA Publications Bibliography. U.S. Environmental Protection Agency, Library Systems Branch, 401 M St., SW, Washington, District of Columbia 20460. (202) 260-2090. Quarterly.

ENCYCLOPEDIAS AND DICTIONARIES

Dictionary of Environmental Engineering and Related Sciences: English-Spanish, Spanish-English. Jose T. Villate. Ediciones Universal, 3090 SW 8th St., Miami, Florida 33135. (305) 642-3355. 1979.

Encyclopedia of Chemical Processing and Design. John J. Mcketta and W. A. Cunningham. Marcel Dekker, Inc., 270 Madison Ave., New York, New York 10016. (212) 696-9000; (800) 228-1160. 1992. Thirty-eight volumes.

Encyclopedia of Environmental Science and Engineering. J.R. Pfafflin. Gordon and Breach Science Publishers, Inc., 270 8th Ave., New York, New York 10011. (212) 206-8900. 1992.

Encyclopedia of Physics. Rita G. Lerner and George L. Trigg. VCH Publishers, 303 NW 12th Ave., Deerfield Beach, Florida 33442-1788. (305) 428-5566. 1991. Second edition.

Kirk-Othmer Encyclopedia of Chemical Technology. J. I. Kroschwitz, ed. John Wiley & Sons, Inc., 605 3rd Ave., New York, New York 10158-0012. (212) 850-6000. 1992-. All articles in the new edition have been rewritten and updated adding new subjects such as biotechnology, computer topics, analytical techniques and instrumentation, environmental concerns, fuels and energy, inorganic and solid state chemistry; composite materials and material science in general, and pharmaceuticals. Also available online.

McGraw-Hill Encyclopedia of Environmental Science. Sybil P. Parker. McGraw-Hill Science & Engineering Books, 11 W. 19th St., New York, New York 10011. (212) 337-6010. 1980. Covers ecology, man's influence on nature, and environmental protection.

McGraw-Hill Encyclopedia of Science and Technology. McGraw-Hill, 1221 Avenue of the Americas, New York, New York 10020. (212) 512-2000 or (800) 262-4729. 1992. Seventh edition. Issued in multiple volumes including index. Includes all science and technology broad subject areas.

Van Nostrand's Scientific Encyclopedia. Glenn D. Considine, ed. Van Nostrand Reinhold, 115 5th Ave., New York, New York 10003. (212) 254-3232. 1983. Sixth edition. Includes all broad subject areas in science.

ONLINE DATA BASES

BIOSIS Previews. BIOSIS, 2100 Arch St., Philadelphia, Pennsylvania 19103-1399. (215) 587-4800. Largest and most comprehensive database of research in the life sciences. Contains citations for nearly 9000 primary research journals, monographs, reviews, symposia, preliminary reports, semi-popular journals, selected institutional reports, government reports and research communications.

CAS Source Index–CASSI. Chemical Abstracts Service, 2540 Olentangy River Rd., P.O. Box 3012, Columbus, Ohio 43210. (800) 848-6533 or (614) 421-3600. A listing of bibliographic and library holdings information for scientific and technical primary literature relevant to the chemical sciences.

Computerized Engineering Index–COMPENDEX. Engineering Information Inc., 345 E. 47th St., New York, New York 10017. (212) 705-7600.

Enviro/Energyline Abstracts Plus. R. R. Bowker Co., 121 Chanlon Rd., New Providence, New Jersey 07974. (908) 464-6800.

Environmental Periodicals Bibliography. National Information Services Corp., Ste. 6, Wyman Towers, 3100 St. Paul St., Baltimore, Maryland 21218. (410)243-0797. Online version of abstract of same name.

Kirk-Othmer Encyclopedia of Chemical Technology. John Wiley & Sons, Inc., 605 3rd Ave., 5th Floor, New York, New York 10158. (212) 850-6000. Online version of the publication of the same name.

CARBON DIOXIDE

See also: COMBUSTION; GREENHOUSE EFFECT; RESPIRATION

ABSTRACTING AND INDEXING SERVICES

Air Pollution Technical Publications of the United States Environmental Protection Agency. U.S. Environmental Protection Agency, Mail Drop 75, Research Triangle Park, North Carolina 27711. (919) 541-2184. 1976. Quarterly.

Air Pollution Titles. Pennsylvania State University, Center for Air Environmental Studies, 226 Fenske Laboratory, University Park, Pennsylvania 16802. (814) 865-1415. 1965. Bibliographic guide to current research literature on air environment, including monitoring and control of air pollution, health effects, effects on agriculture, forests, toxic air contaminants, and global atmospheric pro cases.

Air Pollution Translations. A Bibliography With Abstracts. U.S. Environmental Protection Agency, MD 75, Research Triangle Park, North Carolina 27711. (919) 541-2184. 1969.

Applied Science and Technology Index. H.W. Wilson Co., 950 University Ave., Bronx, New York 10452. (800) 367-6770. Formerly Industrial Arts Index.

Biological Abstracts. BIOSIS, 2100 Arch St., Philadelphia, Pennsylvania 19103-1399. (215) 587-4800. 1927-.

Biotechnology Research Abstracts. Cambridge Scientific Abstracts, 5161 River Rd., Bethesda, Maryland 20816. (301) 961-6750. Monthly. Includes such broad areas as genetic intervention, biochemical genetics, and microbiological techniques.

Bulletin Signaletique: Eau et Assainissement, Pollution Atmospherique, Droit des Pollutions. Centre de Documentation, Centre National de la Recherche Scientifique, 15, quai Anatole France, Paris, France 75700. (1) 45 55 92 25. 1983-. Monthly. Indexes pollution periodicals including water, atmospheric and related pollutions.

Chemical Abstracts. Chemical Abstracts Service, 2540 Olentangy River Rd., PO Box 3012, Columbus, Ohio 43210. (800) 848-6533. 1907-.

Ecological Abstracts. Geo Abstracts Ltd. Elsevier Applied Science, Crown House, Linton Rd., Barking, England IG 11 8JU. 1974-. Derived from over 600 leading ecological and environmental journals, plus books, conference proceedings, reports and theses.

Ecology Abstracts. Cambridge Scientific Abstracts, 5161 River Rd., Bethesda, Maryland 20816. (301) 961-6750. Monthly.

Energy Information Abstracts Annual 1987 in Retrospect. EIC/Intelligence Inc., 121 Chanlon Rd., New Providence, New Jersey 07974. (908) 464-6800. 1988. Annual. Cumulative edition of the monthly Energy Information Abstracts. Monitors sources in the field of energy including the scientific, technical and business journal literature, conference and symposia proceedings, corporate, government and academic reports.

Environment Abstracts. Bowker A & I Publishing, 121 Chanlon Rd., New Providence, New Jersey 07974. (908) 464-6800. 1974-.

Environment Index. Environment Information Center, Index Research Department, 124 E. 39th St., New York, New York 10016. 1971-. Annual.

Environmental Information Connection–EIC. Planning Information Program, Dept. of Urban and Regional Planning, University of Illinois, 1003 West Nevada, Urbana, Illinois 61801. (217) 333-1369. Also available online.

Environmental Periodicals Bibliography. Environmental Studies Institute, International Academy at Santa Barbara, 800 Garden St., Suite D, Santa Barbara, California 93101. (805) 965-5010. Also available online.

General Science Index. H. W. Wilson Co., 950 University Ave., Bronx, New York 10452. 1978-. Monthly, also issued in annual cumulation. Cumulative subject index to English language periodicals in the subject fields of astronomy, botany, chemistry, earth science, environment and conservation, food and nutrition, genetics, mathematics, medicine and health, microbiology, oceanography, physics, physiology and zoology.

Index to Scientific Book Contents. Institute for Scientific Information, 3501 Market St., Philadelphia, Pennsylvania 19104. (800) 523-1857. 1985-. Annual. Gives contents of science books published.

Physics Briefs. Physikalische Berichte. Physik Verlag, Pappapelallee 3, Postfach 101161, Weinheim, Germany D-6940. 1979-. Semimonthly. In English. Volumes for 1979- issued by the Deutsche Physikalische Gesellschaft and the Fachinformationszentrum Energie Physik, Mathematik in cooperation with the American Institute of Physics.

Pollution Abstracts. Cambridge Scientific Abstracts, 5161 River Rd., Bethesda, Maryland 20816. (301) 961-6750. Six/year. Indexes worldwide technical literature on environmental pollution. Covers air pollution, marine and freshwater pollution, sewage and wastewater treatment, waste management, toxicology and health, noise pollution, radiation, land pollution, and environmental policies, programs, legislation, and education. Also available online.

Science Citation Index. Institute for Scientific Information, 3501 Market St., Philadelphia, Pennsylvania 19104. 1961-.

BIBLIOGRAPHIES

Carbon Dioxide and Climate: A Bibliography. National Technical Information Service, 5285 Port Royal Rd., Springfield, Virginia 22161. (703) 487-4650. 1981.

EPA Publications Bibliography. U.S. Environmental Protection Agency, Library Systems Branch, 401 M St., SW, Washington, District of Columbia 20460. (202) 260-2090. Quarterly.

DIRECTORIES

Gale Environmental Sourcebook. Karen Hill. Gale Research Co., 835 Penobscot Bldg., Detroit, Michigan 48226-4094. (313) 961-2242. Contacts, information sources, or general information on environmental topics.

ENCYCLOPEDIAS AND DICTIONARIES

Cambridge Encyclopedia of Life Sciences. A. E. Friday and David S. Ingram. Cambridge University Press, 40 W 20th St., New York, New York 10011. (212) 924-3900 or (800) 227-0247. 1985. Includes all topics under biology and ecology.

Encyclopedia of Chemical Processing and Design. John J. Mcketta and W. A. Cunningham. Marcel Dekker, Inc., 270 Madison Ave., New York, New York 10016. (212) 696-9000; (800) 228-1160. 1992. Thirty-eight volumes.

Encyclopedia of Human Biology. Renato Dulbecco, ed. Academic Press, c/o Harcourt Brace Jovanovich Inc., 6277 Sea Harbor Dr., Orlando, Florida 32887. (800) 346-8648. 1991. Eight volumes.

Kirk-Othmer Encyclopedia of Chemical Technology. J. I. Kroschwitz, ed. John Wiley & Sons, Inc., 605 3rd Ave., New York, New York 10158-0012. (212) 850-6000. 1992-. All articles in the new edition have been rewritten and updated adding new subjects such as biotechnology, computer topics, analytical techniques and instrumentation, environmental concerns, fuels and energy, inorganic and solid state chemistry; composite materials and material science in general, and pharmaceuticals. Also available online.

McGraw-Hill Encyclopedia of Environmental Science. Sybil P. Parker. McGraw-Hill Science & Engineering Books, 11 W. 19th St., New York, New York 10011. (212) 337-6010. 1980. Covers ecology, man's influence on nature, and environmental protection.

McGraw-Hill Encyclopedia of Science and Technology. McGraw-Hill, 1221 Avenue of the Americas, New York, New York 10020. (212) 512-2000 or (800) 262-4729. 1992. Seventh edition. Issued in multiple volumes including index. Includes all science and technology broad subject areas.

Ullmanns Encyclopedia of Industrial Chemistry. Hans Jurgen Arpe and Wolfgang Gerhartz, eds. VCH Publishers, 303 NW 12th Ave., Deerfield Beach, Florida 33442-1788. (305) 428-5566. 1990. Designed to keep up with the broad spectrum of chemical technology. Thirty-six volumes of the encyclopedia have been divided into two sets: the 28 A volumes contain alphabetically arranged articles on chemicals, product groups, processes and technological concepts; and the 8 B volumes are compendia of basic knowledge in industrial chemistry.

Van Nostrand's Scientific Encyclopedia. Glenn D. Considine, ed. Van Nostrand Reinhold, 115 5th Ave., New York, New York 10003. (212) 254-3232. 1983. Sixth edition. Includes all broad subject areas in science.

GENERAL WORKS

Atmospheric Carbon Dioxide and the Global Carbon Cycle. U.S. Department of Energy, Office of Energy Research, Carbon Dioxide Research Division, 1000 Independence Ave., S.W., Washington, District of Columbia 20535. (202) 252-1760. Research on atmospheric carbon dioxide.

Biophysics and Physiology of Carbon Dioxide. C. Bauer. Springer-Verlag, 175 Fifth Ave., New York, New York 10010. (212) 460-1500. Carbon dioxide in the body.

Can We Delay a Greenhouse Warming?. U.S. G.P.O., Washington, District of Columbia 20401. (202) 512-0000. The effectiveness and feasibility of options to slow a build-up of carbon dioxide in the atmosphere.

The Carbon Cycle and Atmospheric CO2: Natural Variations, Archean to Present. E.T. Sundquist. American Geophysical Union, 2000 Florida Ave. N.W., Washington, District of Columbia 20009. (202) 462-6900. 1985. Deals with carbon cycle, atmospheric carbon dioxide, and paleothermometry.

Carbon Dioxide and Global Change: Earth in Transition. Sherwood B. Idso. IBR Press, 631 E. Laguna Dr., Tempe, Arizona 85282. (602) 966-8693. 1989. Discusses environmental aspects of greenhouse effect.

Carbon Dioxide and Other Greenhouse Gases. Kluwer Academic Publishers, 101 Philip Dr., Assinippi Pk, Norwell, Massachusetts 02061. (617) 871-6600. Looks at environmental aspects of greenhouse effects.

Carbon Dioxide: Friend or Foe?. IBR Press, 631 E. Laguana Dr., Tempe, Arizona 85282. (802) 966-8693. An inquiry into the climatic and agricultural consequences of the rapidly rising CO2 content of earth's atmosphere.

Carbon Dioxide Review. Oxford University Press, 200 Madison Ave., New York, New York 10016. (212) 679-7300. 1982. Cites atmospheric carbon dioxide research.

Carbon Dioxide, the Climate and Man. John R. Gribbin. International Institute for Environment and Development, 3 Endsleigh St., London, England CB2 1ER. 1981. Influence on nature of atmospheric carbon dioxide.

Carbon Dioxide, the Greenhouse Effect, and Climate. John R. Justus. U.S. G.P.O., Washington, District of Columbia 20401. (202) 521-0000. 1984.

Carbon Monoxide. R. W. Cargill. Pergamon Microforms International, Inc., Fairview Park, Elmsford, New York 10523. (914) 592-7720. 1990. Contains tabulated collections and critical evaluations of original data for the solubility of carbon monoxide in a variety of liquid solvents.

The Challenging Carbon Cycle: A Global Analysis. Springer-Verlag, 175 Fifth Ave., New York, New York 10010. (212) 460-1500. 1986. Looks at environmental aspects of carbon cycle, biogeochemistry.

Climatic Change and Society: Consequences of Increasing Atmospheric Carbon Dioxide. Westview Press, 5500 Central Ave., Boulder, Colorado 80301. (303) 444-3541. 1982. Social aspects of climatic changes.

Detecting the Climatic Effects of Increasing Carbon Dioxide. National Technical Information Service, 5285 Port Royal Rd., Springfield, Virginia 22161. (703) 487-4650. Carbon dioxide and air pollution measurement.

Direct Effects of Increasing Carbon Dioxide on Vegetation. National Technical Information Service, 5285 Port Royal Rd., Springfield, Virginia 22161. (703) 487-4650. Covers carbon dioxide, vegetation and climate.

Driving Forces: Motor Vehicle Trends and Their Implications for Global Warming, Energy Strategies, and Transportation. James J. MacKenzie and Michael P. Walsh. World Resources Institute, 1709 New York Ave., Washington, District of Columbia 20006. (800) 822-0504. 1990. Overview of new-vehicle fuel efficiency, reductions in air pollution emissions, and overall improvements in transportation and land-use as they relate to global warming planning. Also available through State University of New York Press.

Energy and Climate Change. Lewis Publishers, 2000 Corporate Blvd., N.W., Boca Raton, Florida 33431. (407) 994-0555 or (800) 272-7737. 1990. Includes energy scenarios, cost and risk analysis, energy emissions, atmospheric chemistry, and climate effects.

Global Air Pollution: Problems for the 1990s. Howard Bridgman. Belhaven Press, 136 S. Broadway, Irvington, New York 10533. (914) 591-9111. 1990. Addresses the environmental problems caused by human activities resulting in change and deterioration of the earth's atmosphere.

Global Energy Futures and the Carbon Dioxide Problem. Council on Environmental Quality, Old Executive Office Bldg., Rm. 154, Washington, District of Columbia 20500. (202) 395-5080. 1981. Fossil fuels and energy policy.

The Greenhouse Effect and Ozone Layer. Philip Neal. Dryad, 15 Sherman Ave., Takoma Park, Maryland 20912. (301) 891-3729. 1989. Covers atmospheric carbon dioxide and effects of carbon dioxide on climate.

Magill's Survey of Science. Life Science Series. Frank N. Magill, ed. Salem Press, PO Box 50062, Pasadena, California 91105. 1991. Six volumes. Contents: v.1. A-Central and peripheral nervous system functions; v.2. Central metabolism regulation - eukaryotic transcriptional control; v.3. Positive and negative eukaryotic transcriptional control - mammalian hormones; v.4. Hormones and behavior - muscular contraction; v.5. Muscular contraction and relaxation - sexual reproduction in plants; v.6. Reproductive behavior and mating - X inactivation and the Lyon hypothesis.

Man-made Carbon Dioxide and Climatic Change. Geo Abstracts Ltd., c/o Elsevier Science Pub., Crown House, Linton Rd., Barking, England IG11 8JU. 1983.

Minding the Carbon Store: Weighing U.S. Forestry Strategies to Slow Global Warming. Mark C. Trexler. World Resources Institute, 1709 New York Ave. N.W., Washington, District of Columbia 20006. (800) 833 0504. 1991. Assesses the strengths and weaknesses of each of the major domestic forestry options, including their costs and carbon benefits.

National Inventory of Sources and Emissions of Carbon Dioxide. A.P. Jaques. Environmental Canada, 425 St. Joseph Blvd., 3rd Fl., Hull, Quebec, Canada K1A OH3. (613) 953-5921. 1987. Covers environmental aspects of carbon dioxide.

Projecting the Climatic Effects of Increasing Carbon Dioxide. Michael C. MacCracken. National Technical Information Service, 5285 Port Royal Rd., Springfield, Virginia 22161. (703) 487-4650. 1985.

The Statehouse Effect: State Policies to Cool the Greenhouse. Daniel A. Lashof and Eric L. Washburn. Natural Resources Defense Council, 40 W. 20th St., New York, New York 10011. (212) 727-2700. 1990. Discusses the need for states to take the initiative in controlling CO2 emissions. Details the sources of greenhouse gases and explains how greenhouse emissions can be reduced through energy efficiency, renewable energy strategies, recycling, and taxation and reforms in transportation, agriculture and forests.

HANDBOOKS AND MANUALS

Master Index for the Carbon Dioxide Research State-of-the-Art Report. Michael P. Farrell. U.S. Department of Energy, Carbon Dioxide Research Division, Washington, District of Columbia 1987. Covers atmospheric carbon dioxide and the global carbon cycle and the effects of increasing carbon dioxide on vegetation the climate.

ONLINE DATA BASES

BIOSIS Previews. BIOSIS, 2100 Arch St., Philadelphia, Pennsylvania 19103-1399. (215) 587-4800. Largest and most comprehensive database of research in the life sciences. Contains citations for nearly 9000 primary research journals, monographs, reviews, symposia, preliminary reports, semi-popular journals, selected institutional reports, government reports and research communications.

CAS Source Index–CASSI. Chemical Abstracts Service, 2540 Olentangy River Rd., P.O. Box 3012, Columbus, Ohio 43210. (800) 848-6533 or (614) 421-3600. A listing of bibliographic and library holdings information for scientific and technical primary literature relevant to the chemical sciences.

Chemical Abstracts-CA. Chemical Abstracts Service, 2540 Olentangy River Rd., P.O. Box 3012, Columbus, Ohio 43210. (800) 848-6533 or (614) 421-3600. Information sources include 9000 journals, patents from 27 countries, two industrial property organizations, new books, conference proceedings, and government research reports.

Enviro/Energyline Abstracts Plus. R. R. Bowker Co., 121 Chanlon Rd., New Providence, New Jersey 07974. (908) 464-6800.

Environmental Periodicals Bibliography. National Information Services Corp., Ste. 6, Wyman Towers, 3100 St. Paul St., Baltimore, Maryland 21218. (410)243-0797. Online version of abstract of same name.

Kirk-Othmer Encyclopedia of Chemical Technology. John Wiley & Sons, Inc., 605 3rd Ave., 5th Floor, New York, New York 10158. (212) 850-6000. Online version of the publication of the same name.

SCISEARCH. Institute for Scientific Information, University City Science Center, 3501 Market St., Philadelphia, Pennsylvania 19104. (215) 386-0100.

PERIODICALS AND NEWSLETTERS

Atmospheric Environment. Pergamon Microforms International, Inc., Fairview Park, Elmsford, New York 10523. (914) 592-7720. 1966-. Publishes papers on all aspects of man's interactions with his atmospheric environment, including the administrative, economic and political aspects of these interactions. Air pollution research and its applications are covered, taking into account changes in the atmospheric flow patterns, temperature distributions and chemical constitution caused by natural and artificial variations in the earth's surface.

Carbon. Pergamon Microforms International, Inc., Fairview Park, Elmsford, New York 10523. (914) 592-7720. Monthly. Covers environmental aspects of carbon.

STATISTICS SOURCES

Carbon Dioxide Effects: Research and Assessment Program. National Technical Information Service, 5285 Port Royal Rd., Springfield, Virginia 22161. (703) 487-4650. 1990. Covers the effects of increasing atmospheric carbon dioxide on the physical environment and living organisms.

Environmental Data Compendium. OECD Publications and Information Center, 2001 L St., N.W., Suite 700, Washington, District of Columbia 20036. (202) 785-6323. 1989.

Environmental Indicators. OECD Publications and Information Center, 2001 L St., N.W., Suite 700, Washington, District of Columbia 20036. (202) 785-6323. 1991.

Environmental Quality. Council on Environmental Quality. U.S. G.P.O., Washington, District of Columbia 20401. (202) 512-0000. Annual.

The State of the Environment. OECD Publications and Information Center, 2001 L St., N.W., Suite 700, Washington, District of Columbia 20036. (202) 785-6323. 1991.

Trends '90: A Compendium of Data on Global Change. Thomas A. Boden, et al. Carbon Dioxide Information Analysis Center, Environmental Sciences Division, Oak Ridge National Laboratory, Oak Ridge, Tennessee 37831-6335. 1990. Source of frequently used global change data. Includes estimates of global and national CO2 emissions from the burning of fossil fuels and from the production of cement and other pollutants.

World Resources. World Resources Institute. 1709 New York Ave., N.W., Washington, District of Columbia 20006. (202) 638-6300. Annual. Statistical and textual analysis of world's natural resources and the effects of growth-caused environmental pollution.

CARBON MONOXIDE

See also: AIR POLLUTION; COMBUSTION; GREENHOUSE EFFECT

ABSTRACTING AND INDEXING SERVICES

Air Pollution Technical Publications of the United States Environmental Protection Agency. U.S. Environmental Protection Agency, Mail Drop 75, Research Triangle Park, North Carolina 27711. (919) 541-2184. 1976. Quarterly.

Air Pollution Titles. Pennsylvania State University, Center for Air Environmental Studies, 226 Fenske Laboratory, University Park, Pennsylvania 16802. (814) 865-1415. 1965. Bibliographic guide to current research literature on air environment, including monitoring and control of air pollution, health effects, effects on agriculture, forests, toxic air contaminants, and global atmospheric pro cases.

Air Pollution Translations. A Bibliography With Abstracts. U.S. Environmental Protection Agency, MD 75,

Research Triangle Park, North Carolina 27711. (919) 541-2184. 1969.

Applied Science and Technology Index. H.W. Wilson Co., 950 University Ave., Bronx, New York 10452. (800) 367-6770. Formerly Industrial Arts Index.

Biological Abstracts. BIOSIS, 2100 Arch St., Philadelphia, Pennsylvania 19103-1399. (215) 587-4800. 1927-.

Biological and Agricultural Index. H.W. Wilson Co., 950 University Ave., Bronx, New York 10452. (800) 367-6770. 1916-. Monthly.

Bulletin Signaletique: Eau et Assainissement, Pollution Atmospherique, Droit des Pollutions. Centre de Documentation, Centre National de la Recherche Scientifique, 15, quai Anatole France, Paris, France 75700. (1) 45 55 92 25. 1983-. Monthly. Indexes pollution periodicals including water, atmospheric and related pollutions.

Chemical Abstracts. Chemical Abstracts Service, 2540 Olentangy River Rd., PO Box 3012, Columbus, Ohio 43210. (800) 848-6533. 1907-.

Ecology Abstracts. Cambridge Scientific Abstracts, 5161 River Rd., Bethesda, Maryland 20816. (301) 961-6750. Monthly.

Environment Abstracts. Bowker A & I Publishing, 121 Chanlon Rd., New Providence, New Jersey 07974. (908) 464-6800. 1974-.

Environment Index. Environment Information Center, Index Research Department, 124 E. 39th St., New York, New York 10016. 1971-. Annual.

Environmental Information Connection–EIC. Planning Information Program, Dept. of Urban and Regional Planning, University of Illinois, 1003 West Nevada, Urbana, Illinois 61801. (217) 333-1369. Also available online.

Environmental Periodicals Bibliography. Environmental Studies Institute, International Academy at Santa Barbara, 800 Garden St., Suite D, Santa Barbara, California 93101. (805) 965-5010. Also available online.

General Science Index. H. W. Wilson Co., 950 University Ave., Bronx, New York 10452. 1978-. Monthly, also issued in annual cumulation. Cumulative subject index to English language periodicals in the subject fields of astronomy, botany, chemistry, earth science, environment and conservation, food and nutrition, genetics, mathematics, medicine and health, microbiology, oceanography, physics, physiology and zoology.

Index to Scientific Book Contents. Institute for Scientific Information, 3501 Market St., Philadelphia, Pennsylvania 19104. (800) 523-1857. 1985-. Annual. Gives contents of science books published.

Physics Briefs. Physikalische Berichte. Physik Verlag, Pappapelallee 3, Postfach 101161, Weinheim, Germany D-6940. 1979-. Semimonthly. In English. Volumes for 1979- issued by the Deutsche Physikalische Gesellschaft and the Fachinformationszentrum Energie Physik, Mathematik in cooperation with the American Institute of Physics.

Pollution Abstracts. Cambridge Scientific Abstracts, 5161 River Rd., Bethesda, Maryland 20816. (301) 961-6750. Six/year. Indexes worldwide technical literature on environmental pollution. Covers air pollution, marine and freshwater pollution, sewage and wastewater treatment, waste management, toxicology and health, noise pollution, radiation, land pollution, and environmental policies, programs, legislation, and education. Also available online.

Science Citation Index. Institute for Scientific Information, 3501 Market St., Philadelphia, Pennsylvania 19104. 1961-.

BIBLIOGRAPHIES

EPA Publications Bibliography. U.S. Environmental Protection Agency, Library Systems Branch, 401 M St., SW, Washington, District of Columbia 20460. (202) 260-2090. Quarterly.

DIRECTORIES

Gale Environmental Sourcebook. Karen Hill. Gale Research Co., 835 Penobscot Bldg., Detroit, Michigan 48226-4094. (313) 961-2242. Contacts, information sources, or general information on environmental topics.

ENCYCLOPEDIAS AND DICTIONARIES

Cambridge Encyclopedia of Life Sciences. A. E. Friday and David S. Ingram. Cambridge University Press, 40 W 20th St., New York, New York 10011. (212) 924-3900 or (800) 227-0247. 1985. Includes all topics under biology and ecology.

Encyclopedia of Human Biology. Renato Dulbecco, ed. Academic Press, c/o Harcourt Brace Jovanovich Inc., 6277 Sea Harbor Dr., Orlando, Florida 32887. (800) 346-8648. 1991. Eight volumes.

McGraw-Hill Encyclopedia of Science and Technology. McGraw-Hill, 1221 Avenue of the Americas, New York, New York 10020. (212) 512-2000 or (800) 262-4729. 1992. Seventh edition. Issued in multiple volumes including index. Includes all science and technology broad subject areas.

The New York Times Encyclopedic Dictionary of the Environment. Paul Sarnoff. Quadrangle Books, New York, New York 1971. Focuses on state-of-the-art methods of pollution control, abatement, prevention and removal.

Van Nostrand's Scientific Encyclopedia. Glenn D. Considine, ed. Van Nostrand Reinhold, 115 5th Ave., New York, New York 10003. (212) 254-3232. 1983. Sixth edition. Includes all broad subject areas in science.

GENERAL WORKS

Carbon Monoxide. R. W. Cargill. Pergamon Microforms International, Inc., Fairview Park, Elmsford, New York 10523. (914) 592-7720. 1990. Contains tabulated collections and critical evaluations of original data for the solubility of carbon monoxide in a variety of liquid solvents.

Carbon Monoxide, the Silent Killer. Charles C. Thomas Publishers, 2600 S. First St., Springfield, Illinois 62794-9265. (217) 789-8980. Covers physiological effects and toxicology of carbon monoxide.

New Trends in CO Activation. L. Guczi, ed. Elsevier Science Publishing Co., 655 Avenue of the Americas, New York, New York 10010. (212) 989-5800. 1991.

ONLINE DATA BASES

BIOSIS Previews. BIOSIS, 2100 Arch St., Philadelphia, Pennsylvania 19103-1399. (215) 587-4800. Largest and most comprehensive database of research in the life sciences. Contains citations for nearly 9000 primary research journals, monographs, reviews, symposia, preliminary reports, semi-popular journals, selected institutional reports, government reports and research communications.

Chemical Abstracts-CA. Chemical Abstracts Service, 2540 Olentangy River Rd., P.O. Box 3012, Columbus, Ohio 43210. (800) 848-6533 or (614) 421-3600. Information sources include 9000 journals, patents from 27 countries, two industrial property organizations, new books, conference proceedings, and government research reports.

Enviro/Energyline Abstracts Plus. R. R. Bowker Co., 121 Chanlon Rd., New Providence, New Jersey 07974. (908) 464-6800.

Environmental Periodicals Bibliography. National Information Services Corp., Ste. 6, Wyman Towers, 3100 St. Paul St., Baltimore, Maryland 21218. (410)243-0797. Online version of abstract of same name.

SCISEARCH. Institute for Scientific Information, University City Science Center, 3501 Market St., Philadelphia, Pennsylvania 19104. (215) 386-0100.

PERIODICALS AND NEWSLETTERS

Atmospheric Environment. Pergamon Microforms International, Inc., Fairview Park, Elmsford, New York 10523. (914) 592-7720. 1966-. Publishes papers on all aspects of man's interactions with his atmospheric environment, including the administrative, economic and political aspects of these interactions. Air pollution research and its applications are covered, taking into account changes in the atmospheric flow patterns, temperature distributions and chemical constitution caused by natural and artificial variations in the earth's surface.

STATISTICS SOURCES

Environmental Data Compendium. OECD Publications and Information Center, 2001 L St., N.W., Suite 700, Washington, District of Columbia 20036. (202) 785-6323. 1989.

Environmental Indicators. OECD Publications and Information Center, 2001 L St., N.W., Suite 700, Washington, District of Columbia 20036. (202) 785-6323. 1991.

Environmental Quality. Council on Environmental Quality. U.S. G.P.O., Washington, District of Columbia 20401. (202) 512-0000. Annual.

Ozone and Carbon Monoxide Air Quality Design Values. U.S. G.P.O., Washington, District of Columbia 20401. (202) 512-0000. Annual. National Ambient Air Quality Standards for Ozone and Carbon Monoxide Concentrations.

Progress in the Prevention and Control of Air Pollution. U.S. Environmental Protection Agency. National Technical Information Service, Springfield, Virginia 22161. (703) 487-4650. Annual. Covers air quality trends and control of radon, suspended particulates, sulfur and nitrogen oxides, carbon monoxide, ozone and lead.

The State of the Environment. OECD Publications and Information Center, 2001 L St., N.W., Suite 700, Washington, District of Columbia 20036. (202) 785-6323. 1991.

CARBON TETRACHLORIDE

See also: TOXIC POLLUTANTS

ABSTRACTING AND INDEXING SERVICES

Air Pollution Technical Publications of the United States Environmental Protection Agency. U.S. Environmental Protection Agency, Mail Drop 75, Research Triangle Park, North Carolina 27711. (919) 541-2184. 1976. Quarterly.

Applied Science and Technology Index. H.W. Wilson Co., 950 University Ave., Bronx, New York 10452. (800) 367-6770. Formerly Industrial Arts Index.

Chemical Abstracts. Chemical Abstracts Service, 2540 Olentangy River Rd., PO Box 3012, Columbus, Ohio 43210. (800) 848-6533. 1907-.

Environment Abstracts. Bowker A & I Publishing, 121 Chanlon Rd., New Providence, New Jersey 07974. (908) 464-6800. 1974-.

Environment Index. Environment Information Center, Index Research Department, 124 E. 39th St., New York, New York 10016. 1971-. Annual.

Environmental Information Connection-EIC. Planning Information Program, Dept. of Urban and Regional Planning, University of Illinois, 1003 West Nevada, Urbana, Illinois 61801. (217) 333-1369. Also available online.

Environmental Periodicals Bibliography. Environmental Studies Institute, International Academy at Santa Barbara, 800 Garden St., Suite D, Santa Barbara, California 93101. (805) 965-5010. Also available online.

General Science Index. H. W. Wilson Co., 950 University Ave., Bronx, New York 10452. 1978-. Monthly, also issued in annual cumulation. Cumulative subject index to English language periodicals in the subject fields of astronomy, botany, chemistry, earth science, environment and conservation, food and nutrition, genetics, mathematics, medicine and health, microbiology, oceanography, physics, physiology and zoology.

Index to Scientific Book Contents. Institute for Scientific Information, 3501 Market St., Philadelphia, Pennsylvania 19104. (800) 523-1857. 1985-. Annual. Gives contents of science books published.

Physics Briefs. Physikalische Berichte. Physik Verlag, Pappapelallee 3, Postfach 101161, Weinheim, Germany D-6940. 1979-. Semimonthly. In English. Volumes for 1979- issued by the Deutsche Physikalische Gesellschaft and the Fachinformationszentrum Energie Physik, Mathematik in cooperation with the American Institute of Physics.

Science Citation Index. Institute for Scientific Information, 3501 Market St., Philadelphia, Pennsylvania 19104. 1961-.

BIBLIOGRAPHIES

EPA Publications Bibliography. U.S. Environmental Protection Agency, Library Systems Branch, 401 M St., SW, Washington, District of Columbia 20460. (202) 260-2090. Quarterly.

DIRECTORIES

Gale Environmental Sourcebook. Karen Hill. Gale Research Co., 835 Penobscot Bldg., Detroit, Michigan 48226-4094. (313) 961-2242. Contacts, information sources, or general information on environmental topics.

ENCYCLOPEDIAS AND DICTIONARIES

McGraw-Hill Encyclopedia of Environmental Science. Sybil P. Parker. McGraw-Hill Science & Engineering Books, 11 W. 19th St., New York, New York 10011. (212) 337-6010. 1980. Covers ecology, man's influence on nature, and environmental protection.

McGraw-Hill Encyclopedia of Science and Technology. McGraw-Hill, 1221 Avenue of the Americas, New York, New York 10020. (212) 512-2000 or (800) 262-4729. 1992. Seventh edition. Issued in multiple volumes including index. Includes all science and technology broad subject areas.

Ullmanns Encyclopedia of Industrial Chemistry. Hans Jurgen Arpe and Wolfgang Gerhartz, eds. VCH Publishers, 303 NW 12th Ave., Deerfield Beach, Florida 33442-1788. (305) 428-5566. 1990. Designed to keep up with the broad spectrum of chemical technology. Thirty-six volumes of the encyclopedia have been divided into two sets: the 28 A volumes contain alphabetically arranged articles on chemicals, product groups, processes and technological concepts; and the 8 B volumes are compendia of basic knowledge in industrial chemistry.

Van Nostrand's Scientific Encyclopedia. Glenn D. Considine, ed. Van Nostrand Reinhold, 115 5th Ave., New York, New York 10003. (212) 254-3232. 1983. Sixth edition. Includes all broad subject areas in science.

GENERAL WORKS

Ambient Water Quality Criteria for Carbon Tetrachloride. Office of Water Regulations and Standards. U.S. Environmental Protection Agency, 401 M St., SW, Washington, District of Columbia 20460. (202) 260-2090. 1980.

Chloroform, Carbon Tetrachloride, and Other Halomethanes. National Academy of Sciences, 2101 Constitution Ave, N.W., Washington, District of Columbia 20418. (202) 334-2000. 1978.

Criteria for a Recommended Standard: Occupational Exposure to Carbon Tetrachloride. National Institute for Occupational Safety and Health, 1600 Clifton Rd. NE, Atlanta, Georgia 30333. (404) 639-3286. 1976.

Health Assessment Document for Carbon Tetrachloride. U.S. Environmental Protection Agency, 401 M St., SW, Washington, District of Columbia 20460. (202) 260-2090. 1984.

Locating and Estimating Air Emissions from Sources of Carbon Tetrachloride [microform]. U.S. Environmental Protection Agency, 401 M St., SW, MD 75, Research Triangle Park, North Carolina 27711. (919) 541-2184. 1984.

Survey of Carbon Tetrachloride Emission Sources. National Technical Information Service, 5285 Port Royal Rd., Springfield, Virginia 22161. (703) 487-4650. 1985.

A Who's Who of American Ozone Depleters: A Guide to 3,014 Factories Emitting Three Ozone-Depleting Chemicals. Natural Resources Defense Council, 40 W. 20th St., New York, New York 10011. (212) 727-2700. 1990.

ONLINE DATA BASES

CAS Source Index–CASSI. Chemical Abstracts Service, 2540 Olentangy River Rd., P.O. Box 3012, Columbus, Ohio 43210. (800) 848-6533 or (614) 421-3600. A listing of bibliographic and library holdings information for scientific and technical primary literature relevant to the chemical sciences.

CERCLIS. Chemical Information Systems, Inc., 7215 York Rd., Baltimore, Maryland 21212. (301) 321-8440. Information on hazardous waste disposal sites that have either been listed by the EPA on the National Priority List (NPL) or nominated for consideration for the NPL.

Chemical Abstracts-CA. Chemical Abstracts Service, 2540 Olentangy River Rd., P.O. Box 3012, Columbus, Ohio 43210. (800) 848-6533 or (614) 421-3600. Information sources include 9000 journals, patents from 27 countries, two industrial property organizations, new books, conference proceedings, and government research reports.

Enviro/Energyline Abstracts Plus. R. R. Bowker Co., 121 Chanlon Rd., New Providence, New Jersey 07974. (908) 464-6800.

Environmental Periodicals Bibliography. National Information Services Corp., Ste. 6, Wyman Towers, 3100 St. Paul St., Baltimore, Maryland 21218. (410)243-0797. Online version of abstract of same name.

SCISEARCH. Institute for Scientific Information, University City Science Center, 3501 Market St., Philadelphia, Pennsylvania 19104. (215) 386-0100.

STATISTICS SOURCES

Environmental Data Compendium. OECD Publications and Information Center, 2001 L St., N.W., Suite 700, Washington, District of Columbia 20036. (202) 785-6323. 1989.

Environmental Indicators. OECD Publications and Information Center, 2001 L St., N.W., Suite 700, Washington, District of Columbia 20036. (202) 785-6323. 1991.

Environmental Quality. Council on Environmental Quality. U.S. G.P.O., Washington, District of Columbia 20401. (202) 512-0000. Annual.

The State of the Environment. OECD Publications and Information Center, 2001 L St., N.W., Suite 700, Washington, District of Columbia 20036. (202) 785-6323. 1991.

TRADE ASSOCIATIONS AND PROFESSIONAL SOCIETIES

American Institute of Chemical Engineers. 345 East 47th St., New York, New York 10017. (212) 705-7338.

American Institute of Chemists. 7315 Wisconsin Ave., Bethesda, Maryland 20814. (301) 652-2447.

CARBOXYHEMOGLOBIN

See: BLOOD ANALYSIS

CARCINOGENS

See also: INSECTICIDES; MUTAGENIC AGENTS (MUTAGENS); PESTICIDES

ABSTRACTING AND INDEXING SERVICES

Air Pollution Technical Publications of the United States Environmental Protection Agency. U.S. Environmental Protection Agency, Mail Drop 75, Research Triangle Park, North Carolina 27711. (919) 541-2184. 1976. Quarterly.

Applied Ecology Abstracts Studies in Renewable Natural Resources. Information Retrieval Ltd., 1911 Jefferson Davis Highway, Arlington, Virginia 22202. 1975-. Monthly.

ASFA Aquaculture Abstracts. Cambridge Scientific Abstracts, Inc., 5161 River Rd., Bethesda, Maryland 20816. (301) 961-6750. 1984.

Biological Abstracts. BIOSIS, 2100 Arch St., Philadelphia, Pennsylvania 19103-1399. (215) 587-4800. 1927-.

Biological and Agricultural Index. H.W. Wilson Co., 950 University Ave., Bronx, New York 10452. (800) 367-6770. 1916-. Monthly.

Chemical Abstracts. Chemical Abstracts Service, 2540 Olentangy River Rd., PO Box 3012, Columbus, Ohio 43210. (800) 848-6533. 1907-.

Ecological Abstracts. Geo Abstracts Ltd. Elsevier Applied Science, Crown House, Linton Rd., Barking, England IG 11 8JU. 1974-. Derived from over 600 leading ecological and environmental journals, plus books, conference proceedings, reports and theses.

Environment Abstracts. Bowker A & I Publishing, 121 Chanlon Rd., New Providence, New Jersey 07974. (908) 464-6800. 1974-.

Environment Index. Environment Information Center, Index Research Department, 124 E. 39th St., New York, New York 10016. 1971-. Annual.

Environmental Information Connection–EIC. Planning Information Program, Dept. of Urban and Regional Planning, University of Illinois, 1003 West Nevada, Urbana, Illinois 61801. (217) 333-1369. Also available online.

Environmental Periodicals Bibliography. Environmental Studies Institute, International Academy at Santa Barbara, 800 Garden St., Suite D, Santa Barbara, California 93101. (805) 965-5010. Also available online.

General Science Index. H. W. Wilson Co., 950 University Ave., Bronx, New York 10452. 1978-. Monthly, also issued in annual cumulation. Cumulative subject index to English language periodicals in the subject fields of astronomy, botany, chemistry, earth science, environment and conservation, food and nutrition, genetics, mathematics, medicine and health, microbiology, oceanography, physics, physiology and zoology.

Index to Scientific Book Contents. Institute for Scientific Information, 3501 Market St., Philadelphia, Pennsylvania 19104. (800) 523-1857. 1985-. Annual. Gives contents of science books published.

Multimedia Index to Ecology. National Information Center for Educational Media, University of Southern California, Los Angeles, California 90007.

Pesticides Abstracts. U.S. Environmental Protection Agency, Office of Pesticides Programs, 345 Curtland, Atlanta, Georgia 30365. (404) 347-2864. 1981. Monthly. Formerly: Health Aspects of Pesticides Abstracts Bulletin.

Pollution Abstracts. Cambridge Scientific Abstracts, 5161 River Rd., Bethesda, Maryland 20816. (301) 961-6750. Six/year. Indexes worldwide technical literature on environmental pollution. Covers air pollution, marine and freshwater pollution, sewage and wastewater treatment, waste management, toxicology and health, noise pollution, radiation, land pollution, and environmental policies, programs, legislation, and education. Also available online.

Science Citation Index. Institute for Scientific Information, 3501 Market St., Philadelphia, Pennsylvania 19104. 1961-.

Selected Abstracts on Aflatoxins and other Mycotoxins Carcinogenesis. U.S. Dept. of Health Education and Welfare. National Technical Information Service, 5285 Port Royal Rd., Springfield, Virginia 22161. (703) 487-4650. 1978. Prepared for the ICRDB Program by the Cancer Information Dissemination and Analysis Center for Carcinogenesis Information.

Selected References on Environmental Quality as It Relates to Health. National Library of Medicine, 8600 Rockville Pike, Bethesda, Maryland 20894. (800) 638-8480. 1977.

Selected Water Abstracts on Dioxins and Dibenzofurans in Carcinogenesis, 1980-1986. Anthony J. Girardi. National Cancer Institute, U. S. Dept. of Health and Human Services, Public Health Service, National Institutes of Health, Washington, District of Columbia 20402-9325. (202) 783-3238. 1987.

BIBLIOGRAPHIES

Current Contents. Agriculture, Biology and Environmental Sciences. Institute for Scientific Information, 3501 Market St., Philadelphia, Pennsylvania 19104. (800) 523-1857. 1973-. Previous title: Current Contents. Agricultural, Food & Veterinary Sciences. Gives the table of contents of periodicals in the fields of agriculture, biology, environmental and related areas.

Degradation of Chemical Carcinogens: An Annotated Bibliography. M.W. Slein. Van Nostrand Reinhold, 115 Fifth Ave., New York, New York 10003. (212) 254-3232. 1980.

Directory of Published Proceedings. Interdok Corp., 173 Halstead Ave., Harrison, New York 10528. (914) 835-3506. 1990. Monthly. This is a listing of published proceedings including the series SEMTE (Science/Medicine/Engineering/Technology) and the series SSH (Social Science/Humanities).

EPA Publications Bibliography. U.S. Environmental Protection Agency, Library Systems Branch, 401 M St., SW,

Washington, District of Columbia 20460. (202) 260-2090. Quarterly.

Selected Abstracts on Short-Term Test Systems for Potential Mutagens and Carcinogens. Vincent F. Simmon. National Technical Information Service, 5285 Port Royal Rd., Springfield, Virginia 22161. (703) 487-4650. 1981.

DIRECTORIES

American Cancer Society Cancer Book. Doubleday & Company, Inc., 666 Fifth Ave., New York, New York 10103. (212) 765-6500.

Choices: Realistic Alternatives in Cancer Treatment. Avon Books, 105 Madison Ave., New York, New York 10016. (212) 481-5600.

Directory of On-Going Research in Cancer Epidemiology. International Agency for Research on Cancer, 150, Cours Albert Thomas, Cedex 08, Lyons, France F-69372. 78 72738485.

Gale Environmental Sourcebook. Karen Hill. Gale Research Co., 835 Penobscot Bldg., Detroit, Michigan 48226-4094. (313) 961-2242. Contacts, information sources, or general information on environmental topics.

PDQ. International Cancer Information Center, National Cancer Institute, R.A. Bloch Building, Bethesda, Maryland 20892. (301) 496-7403.

ENCYCLOPEDIAS AND DICTIONARIES

Cambridge Encyclopedia of Life Sciences. A. E. Friday and David S. Ingram. Cambridge University Press, 40 W 20th St., New York, New York 10011. (212) 924-3900 or (800) 227-0247. 1985. Includes all topics under biology and ecology.

Encyclopedia of Human Biology. Renato Dulbecco, ed. Academic Press, c/o Harcourt Brace Jovanovich Inc., 6277 Sea Harbor Dr., Orlando, Florida 32887. (800) 346-8648. 1991. Eight volumes.

Handbook of Hazardous Chemicals and Carcinogens. Marshall Sittig. Noyes Publications, 120 Mill Rd., Park Ridge, New Jersey 07656. (201) 391-8484. 1985.

Handbook of Toxic and Hazardous Chemicals and Carcinogens. Marshall Sittig. Noyes Publications, 120 Mill Rd., Park Ridge, New Jersey 07656. (201) 391-8484. 1991.

McGraw-Hill Encyclopedia of Environmental Science. Sybil P. Parker. McGraw-Hill Science & Engineering Books, 11 W. 19th St., New York, New York 10011. (212) 337-6010. 1980. Covers ecology, man's influence on nature, and environmental protection.

McGraw-Hill Encyclopedia of Science and Technology. McGraw-Hill, 1221 Avenue of the Americas, New York, New York 10020. (212) 512-2000 or (800) 262-4729. 1992. Seventh edition. Issued in multiple volumes including index. Includes all science and technology broad subject areas.

Van Nostrand's Scientific Encyclopedia. Glenn D. Considine, ed. Van Nostrand Reinhold, 115 5th Ave., New York, New York 10003. (212) 254-3232. 1983. Sixth edition. Includes all broad subject areas in science.

GENERAL WORKS

Annual Report on Carcinogens. Summary. U.S. Department of Health and Human Services, Public Health Service, 9000 Rockville Pike, Bethesda, Maryland 20892. (301) 496-4000. Annual.

Bioassay of Endrin for Possible Carcinogenicity. National Cancer Institute, Div. of Cancer Cause and Prevention, Carcinogenesis Testing Program, NIH Bldg. 31, Room 10A 24, 9030 Old Georgetown Rd., Bethesda, Maryland 20892. (301) 496-7403. 1978.

Bioassay of Fenthion for Possible Carcinogenicity. Department of Health and Human Services, 200 Independence Ave. SW, Washington, District of Columbia 20201. (202) 619-0257. 1979. Covers carcinogens and organophosphorus compounds and toxicology of insecticides.

Bioassay of Hexachlorophene for Possible Carcinogenicity. National Cancer Institute, Cancer Cause and Prevention Division, 9030 Old Georgetown Rd., Bethesda, Maryland 20892. (301) 496-7403. 1978.

Bioassay of Malathion for Possible Carcinogenicity. National Cancer Institute, Division of Cancer Cause and Prevention, 9030 Old Georgetown Rd., Bethesda, Maryland 20892. (301) 496-7403. 1979. Adverse effects of malathion and carcinogens.

Biological Effects of Heavy Metals. E. C. Foulkes. CRC Press, 2000 Corporate Blvd. N.W., Boca Raton, Florida 33431. (800) 272-7737. 1990. Two volumes. Reviews general mechanisms of metal carcinogenesis. It illustrates this effect by detailed reference to some specific metals, including Cd, Co and Ni. The material illustrates the common threads running through the field of metal carcinogenesis.

CA Selects: Carcinogens, Mutagens & Teratogens. Chemical Abstracts Services, 2540 Olentangy River Rd., Columbus, Ohio 43210. (800) 848-6533. Irregular.

Calcium, Cell Cycles, and Cancer. James F. Whitfield. CRC Press, 2000 Corporate Blvd. N.W., Boca Raton, Florida 33431. (800) 272-7737. 1990.

Cancer Control Objectives for the Nation: 1985-2000. National Cancer Institute, 9030 Old Georgetown Rd., Bethesda, Maryland 20892. (301) 496-7403. 1986.

Carcinogenic, Mutagenic, and Teratogenic Marine Pollutants. Portfolio Publishing Co., P.O. Box 7802, The Woodlands, Texas 77381. (713) 363-3577. 1990. Effects of marine pollution on aquatic organisms as well as human beings.

Carcinogenic Risk Assessment. Curtis C. Travis. Plenum Press, 233 Spring St., New York, New York 10013-1578. (212) 620-8000; (800) 221-9369. 1988.

Carcinogenically-Active Chemicals: A Reference Guide. Richard J. Lewis, Sr. Global Professional Publications, 2805 McGraw Ave., PO Box 19539, Irvine, California 92713-9539. (800) 854-7179. 1990. Includes 3,400 verified or suspected carcinogens, classified as confirmed, suspected, or questionable.

Carcinogenicity and Pesticides. Nancy N. Ragsdale and Robert E. Menzer, eds. American Chemical Society, 1155 16th St. N.W., Washington, District of Columbia 20036. (202) 872-4600; (800) 227-5558. 1989. Discusses the role of structure activity relationship analysis in evaluation of pesticides for potential carcinogenicity. Also traces the background, pesticide regulations, assessment of hazard and risk, and epidemiological studies of cancer and pesticide exposure.

Carcinogens and Mutagens in the Environment. Hans F. Stich, ed. CRC Press, 2000 Corporate Blvd. N.W., Boca Raton, Florida 33431. (800) 272-7737. 1982-. Naturally occurring compounds, endogenous modulation.

Carcinogens in Industry and the Environment. James M. Sontag, ed. M. Dekker, 270 Madison Ave., New York, New York 10016. (212) 696-9000. 1981. Environmentally induced diseases and industrial hygiene.

Handbook of Carcinogen Testing. Harry A. Milman. Noyes Publications, 120 Mill Rd., Park Ridge, New Jersey 07656. (201) 391-8484. 1985. Biological assay, carcinogens and carcinogenicity testing.

Identifying and Regulating Carcinogens. M. Dekker, 270 Madison Ave., New York, New York 10016. (212) 696-9000. 1989. Health risk assessment and testing.

In Search of Safety: Chemicals and Cancer Risk. J. D. Graham. Harvard University Press, 79 Garden St., Cambridge, Massachusetts 02138. (617) 495-2600. 1988.

Measurement Techniques for Carcinogenic Agents in Workplace Air. Royal Society of Chemistry, c/o CRC Press, 2000 Corporate Blvd. N.W., Boca Raton, Florida 33431-9868. (800) 272-7737. 1989. Covers 31 substances with known or suspended carcinogenic properties and describes recommended analytical methods for each substance when present in workplace air. It provides information including CAS Registry number, synonyms, manufacture, uses and determination (with recommended sampling and measuring procedures, and performance characteristics), plus a review of other methods used.

Microbial Toxins in Focus and Feeds. Albert E. Pohland, et al., eds. Plenum Press, 233 Spring St., New York, New York 10013. (212) 620-8000; (800) 221-9369. 1990. Proceedings of a Symposium on Cellular and Molecular Mode of Action of Selected Microbial Toxins in Foods and Feeds, Oct. 31- Nov. 2, 1988, Chevy Chase, MD.

Occupational Exposure to Silica and Cancer Risk. L. Simonato, et al., eds. International Agency for Research on Cancer, Distributed by Oxford Univ. Press, 200 Madison Ave., New York, New York 10016. (212) 679-7300. 1990. IARC Scientific Publications: No. 97. Deals with toxicology of silica in the workplace and the incidents of cancer.

Safe Handling of Chemical Carcinogens, Mutagens, and Highly Toxic Substances. Douglas B. Walters, ed. Ann Arbor Science, 230 Collingwood, Ann Arbor, Michigan 48106. 1980-. Prevention and control of occupational accidents.

Safety in the Use of Asbestos. International Labour Office, 49 Sheridan Ave., Albany, New York 12210. (518) 436-9686. 1990. An ILO code of practice. The first part of the code includes monitoring in the work place, preventive measures, the protection and supervision of the workers' health, and the packaging, handling, transport and disposal of asbestos waste. More detailed guidance on the limitation of exposure to asbestos in specific activities is given in the second part of the code, which includes sections on mining and milling, asbestos cement, textiles, friction materials, and the removal of asbestos-containing materials.

Survey of Chemicals Tested for Carcinogenicity. Science Resource Center, Kensington, Maryland 1976. Entries from scientific literature from approximately 1913 to 1973, reporting on groups of animals treated with any chemical compounds and subsequently examined for tumors.

Survey of Compounds Which Have Been Tested for Carcinogenic Activity. National Cancer Institute. National Institutes of Health, National Cancer Institute, 9000 Rockville Pike, Bethesda, Maryland 20892. (301) 496-4000. 1976. Series of books with extracted data from scientific literature regarding the test of chemical compounds in experimental animals. Over 4,500 compounds are identified.

Suspected Carcinogens: A Subfile of the NIOSH Toxic Substance List. Herbert E. Christensen and Thomas T. Luginbyh, eds. U.S. Department of Health and Human Services, 200 Independence Ave. SW, Washington, District of Columbia 20201. (202) 619-0257. 1975.

Toxicological Profile for Chloroform. National Technical Information Service, 5285 Port Royal Rd., Springfield, Virginia 22161. (703) 487-4650. 1989.

HANDBOOKS AND MANUALS

Cancer Sourcebook: Basic Information on Cancer Types, Symptoms, Diagnostic Methods, and Treatments. Frank E. Bair, ed. Omnigraphics, Inc., 2500 Penobscot Bldg., Detroit, Michigan 48226. (313) 961-1340. 1990. Includes statistics of cancer occurrences worldwide and the risks associated with known carcinogens and activities.

CRC Handbook of Identified Carcinogens and Noncarcinogens: Carcinogenicity-Mutagenicity Database. Jean V. Soderman, ed. CRC Press, 2000 Corporate Blvd. N.W., Boca Raton, Florida 33431. (800) 272-7737. 1982.

Handbook of Carcinogens and Hazardous Substances: Chemical and Trace Analysis. Malcolm C. Bowman, ed. M. Dekker, 270 Madison Ave., New York, New York 10016. (212) 696-9000. 1982. Alkylating agents, aromatic amines and azo compounds, estrogens, mycotoxins, N-nitrosamines and n-nitroso compounds, pesticides and related substances and hydrocarbons.

Handbook of Toxicology. W. Thomas Shier and Dietrich Mebs. Marcel Dekker, Inc., 270 Madison Ave., New York, New York 10016. (212) 696-9000; (800) 228-1160. 1990. Covers most toxins for which sufficient research has been done to clearly establish the identity and characteristics of the toxin.

ONLINE DATA BASES

BIOSIS Previews. BIOSIS, 2100 Arch St., Philadelphia, Pennsylvania 19103-1399. (215) 587-4800. Largest and most comprehensive database of research in the life sciences. Contains citations for nearly 9000 primary research journals, monographs, reviews, symposia, preliminary reports, semi-popular journals, selected institutional reports, government reports and research communications.

Cancerlit. U.S. National Institutes of Health, National Eye Institute, Building 31, Rm. 6A32, Bethesda, Maryland 20892. (301) 496-5248.

Cancerquest Online. CDC AIDS Weekly/NCI Cancer Weekly, 206 Roger St, N.E., Suite 104, Atlanta, Georgia 30317. (404) 377-8895.

CAS Source Index–CASSI. Chemical Abstracts Service, 2540 Olentangy River Rd., P.O. Box 3012, Columbus, Ohio 43210. (800) 848-6533 or (614) 421-3600. A listing of bibliographic and library holdings information for scientific and technical primary literature relevant to the chemical sciences.

CERCLIS. Chemical Information Systems, Inc., 7215 York Rd., Baltimore, Maryland 21212. (301) 321-8440. Information on hazardous waste disposal sites that have either been listed by the EPA on the National Priority List (NPL) or nominated for consideration for the NPL.

CESARS. State of Michigan, Department of Natural Resources, Great Lakes & Environmental Assessment Section, P.O. Box 30028, Lansing, Michigan 45909. (517) 373-2190.

Chemical Abstracts-CA. Chemical Abstracts Service, 2540 Olentangy River Rd., P.O. Box 3012, Columbus, Ohio 43210. (800) 848-6533 or (614) 421-3600. Information sources include 9000 journals, patents from 27 countries, two industrial property organizations, new books, conference proceedings, and government research reports.

Chemical Carcinogenesis Research Information System–CCRIS. National Library of Medicine, 8600 Rockville Pike, Bethesda, Maryland 20894. (800) 638-8480. Individual assay results and test conditions for 1,451 chemicals in the areas of carcinogenicity, mutagenicity, tumor promotion, and cocarcinogenicity.

Chemical Collection System/Request Tracking–CCS/RTS. U.S. Environmental Protection Agency, Office of Pesticides and Toxic Substances, 401 M St., SW, Washington, District of Columbia 20460. (202) 260-2090. Contains information on various properties of a number of chemicals including environmental effects, test and analysis methods, and health effects. Available from EPA.

Chemical Dictionary Online–CHEMLINE. Chemical Abstracts Service, 2540 Olentangy River Rd., Columbus, Ohio 43210. (614) 421-3600 or (800) 848-6533. Part of MEDLINE of the National Library of Medicine (NLM). File of 900,000 names for chemical substances, representing 450,000 unique compounds. It contains such information as Chemical Abstracts (CA) Service Registry Numbers, molecular formulas, preferred chemical nomenclature, and generic and ring structure information. Available on NLM's ELHILL system.

Chemical Evaluation Search and Retrieval System. Michigan State Department of Natural Resources, Surface Water Quality Division, Great Lakes and Environmental Assessment Section, Knapp's Office Center, PO Box 30028, Lansing, Michigan 48909. (517) 373-2190. Covers toxicology information on compounds of environmental concern, providing acute and chronic toxicity data for aquatic and terrestrial life as well as information on carcinogenicity, mutagenicity, and reproductive and developmental effects, bioconcentration, and environmental fate.

Chemical Exposure. Science Applications International Corp., Health & Environmental Information, P.O. Box 2501, Oak Ridge, Tennessee 37831. (615) 482-9031. Database of chemicals that have been identified in both human tissues and body fluids and in feral and food animals. Contains reference to journal articles, conferences, and reports. Covers the whole fields of information related to human and animal exposure to food, air,

and water contaminants and pharmaceuticals. Its records include information on chemical properties, formulas, tissues measured, analytical method used, demographics and more. Available on DIALOG.

CLINPROT: CLINical cancer PROTocols. U.S. National Institutes of Health, National Eye Institute, Building 31, Rm. 6A32, Bethesda, Maryland 20892. (301) 496-5248.

Enviro/Energyline Abstracts Plus. R. R. Bowker Co., 121 Chanlon Rd., New Providence, New Jersey 07974. (908) 464-6800.

Environmental Periodicals Bibliography. National Information Services Corp., Ste. 6, Wyman Towers, 3100 St. Paul St., Baltimore, Maryland 21218. (410)243-0797. Online version of abstract of same name.

Medical Toxicology and Environmental Health. Department of Health and Social Security, Medical Toxiclology & Environmental Health Division, Hannibal House, Rm. 719, Elephant and Castle, London, England SE1 6TE. 44 (71) 972-2162.

The Merck Index Online. Merck & Company, Inc., Box 2000, Building 86-0900, Rahway, New Jersey 07065-0900. (201) 855-4558.

Monthly Catalog of United States Government Publications. U.S. G.P.O., Supt. of Docs., PO Box 371954, Pittsburgh, Pennsylvania 15250-7954. (202) 512-0000.

National Technical Information Service. U.S. Department of Commerce, National Technical Information Service, Office of Data Base Services, 5285 Port Royal Rd., Springfield, Virginia 22161. (703) 487-4807. Bibliographic database of government sponsored research and technical reports.

NCI Cancer Weekly. CANCERQUEST, 206 Rogers St., N.E., suite 104, Atlanta, Georgia 30317. (404) 377-8895.

PressNet Environmental Reports. Chemical Information Systems, Inc., 7215 York Rd., Baltimore, Maryland 21212. (301) 321-8440.

SCISEARCH. Institute for Scientific Information, University City Science Center, 3501 Market St., Philadelphia, Pennsylvania 19104. (215) 386-0100.

PERIODICALS AND NEWSLETTERS

Asbestos Control Report. Business Publishers, Inc., 951 Pershing Drive, Silver Spring, Maryland 20910-4464. (301) 587-6300. Biweekly. Information on asbestos control techniques, research, and regulations. Also available online.

Asbestos Information Association of North American Newsletter. Asbestos Information Association/North America, 1745 Jefferson Davis Highway, Suite 509, Arlington, Virginia 22202. (703) 979-1150. Monthly. Issues pertaining to asbestos and health.

The Journal of Biological Chemistry. American Society of Biological Chemists, 428 E. Preston St., Baltimore, Maryland 21202. Three times a month. Biological, agricultural, and energy aspects of the environment.

Journal of Environmental Science and Health. Marcel Dekker, Inc., 270 Madison Ave., New York, New York 10016. (212) 696-9000. Bimonthly. Concerns pesticides, food contaminants, chemical carcinogens, and agricultural wastes.

Journal of the National Cancer Institute. National Institute of Health. U.S. G.P.O., Washington, District of Columbia 20401. (202) 512-0000. Semi-monthly. Covers epidemiology and biochemistry of cancer.

The Merck Index. Merck Co., Inc., Box 2000, Rahway, New Jersey 07065. (201) 855-4558. Data on chemicals, drugs, and biological substances.

RESEARCH CENTERS AND INSTITUTES

Laboratory of Chemical Biodynamics. University of California, Berkeley, Berkeley, California 64720. (415) 486-4311.

STATISTICS SOURCES

Cancer Facts and Figures. American Cancer Society, 1599 Clifton Rd., NE, Atlanta, Georgia 30329. Annual. Discusses cancer incidence and mortality, by state, country, and sex; and survival rates.

Cancer in Populations Living Near Nuclear Facilities. U.S. G.P.O., Washington, District of Columbia 20401. (202) 512-0000. 1990.

Cancer Statistics Review. U.S. G.P.O., Washington, District of Columbia 20401. (202) 512-0000. Annual. Cancer incidence, deaths, and relative survival rates.

Environmental Data Compendium. OECD Publications and Information Center, 2001 L St., N.W., Suite 700, Washington, District of Columbia 20036. (202) 785-6323. 1989.

Environmental Indicators. OECD Publications and Information Center, 2001 L St., N.W., Suite 700, Washington, District of Columbia 20036. (202) 785-6323. 1991.

Environmental Quality. Council on Environmental Quality. U.S. G.P.O., Washington, District of Columbia 20401. (202) 512-0000. Annual.

The Market for Cancer Therapeutics and Diagnostics. FIND/SVP, 625 Avenue of the Americas, New York, New York 10011. (212) 645-4500. 1991/92.

The State of the Environment. OECD Publications and Information Center, 2001 L St., N.W., Suite 700, Washington, District of Columbia 20036. (202) 785-6323. 1991.

TRADE ASSOCIATIONS AND PROFESSIONAL SOCIETIES

American Association for Cancer Education. Box 700, UAB Station, Birmingham, Alabama 35294. (205) 934-3054.

American Cancer Society. 1599 Clifton Rd., N.E., Atlanta, Georgia 30329. (404) 320-3333.

American Heart Association. 7320 Greenville Ave., Dallas, Texas 75231. (214) 373-6300.

American Industrial Health Council. 1330 Connecticut Ave., N.W., Suite 300, Washington, District of Columbia 20036. (202) 659-0060.

American Industrial Hygiene Association. 345 White Pond Dr., PO Box 8390, Akron, Ohio 44320. (216) 873-2442.

American Institute of Biological Sciences. 730 11th St., N.W., Washington, District of Columbia 20001-4521. (202) 628-1500.

Asbestos Information Association of North America. 1745 Jefferson Davis Highway, Suite 509, Arlington, Virginia 22202. (703) 979-1150.

Association of American Cancer Institutes. 666 Elm St., Buffalo, New York 14263. (716) 845-3028.

United Cancer Council. 4010 W. 86th St., Suite H, Indianapolis, Indiana 46268. (317) 879-9900.

CARDBOARD
See: PAPER

CARRYING CAPACITY
See: ECOSYSTEMS

CATALYSTS
See also: ENZYMES

ABSTRACTING AND INDEXING SERVICES

Applied Science and Technology Index. H.W. Wilson Co., 950 University Ave., Bronx, New York 10452. (800) 367-6770. Formerly Industrial Arts Index.

Biological Abstracts. BIOSIS, 2100 Arch St., Philadelphia, Pennsylvania 19103-1399. (215) 587-4800. 1927-.

Biotechnology Research Abstracts. Cambridge Scientific Abstracts, 5161 River Rd., Bethesda, Maryland 20816. (301) 961-6750. Monthly. Includes such broad areas as genetic intervention, biochemical genetics, and microbiological techniques.

Chemical Abstracts. Chemical Abstracts Service, 2540 Olentangy River Rd., PO Box 3012, Columbus, Ohio 43210. (800) 848-6533. 1907-.

Energy Information Abstracts Annual 1987 in Retrospect. EIC/Intelligence Inc., 121 Chanlon Rd., New Providence, New Jersey 07974. (908) 464-6800. 1988. Annual. Cumulative edition of the monthly Energy Information Abstracts. Monitors sources in the field of energy including the scientific, technical and business journal literature, conference and symposia proceedings, corporate, government and academic reports.

Environment Abstracts. Bowker A & I Publishing, 121 Chanlon Rd., New Providence, New Jersey 07974. (908) 464-6800. 1974-.

Environment Index. Environment Information Center, Index Research Department, 124 E. 39th St., New York, New York 10016. 1971-. Annual.

Environmental Information Connection–EIC. Planning Information Program, Dept. of Urban and Regional Planning, University of Illinois, 1003 West Nevada, Urbana, Illinois 61801. (217) 333-1369. Also available online.

Environmental Periodicals Bibliography. Environmental Studies Institute, International Academy at Santa Barbara, 800 Garden St., Suite D, Santa Barbara, California 93101. (805) 965-5010. Also available online.

General Science Index. H. W. Wilson Co., 950 University Ave., Bronx, New York 10452. 1978-. Monthly, also issued in annual cumulation. Cumulative subject index to English language periodicals in the subject fields of astronomy, botany, chemistry, earth science, environment and conservation, food and nutrition, genetics, mathematics, medicine and health, microbiology, oceanography, physics, physiology and zoology.

Index to Scientific Book Contents. Institute for Scientific Information, 3501 Market St., Philadelphia, Pennsylvania 19104. (800) 523-1857. 1985-. Annual. Gives contents of science books published.

BIBLIOGRAPHIES

EPA Publications Bibliography. U.S. Environmental Protection Agency, Library Systems Branch, 401 M St., SW, Washington, District of Columbia 20460. (202) 260-2090. Quarterly.

Molybdenum Catalyst Bibliography. Climax Molybdenum Co., 101 Merritt 7 Corporate Park, Norvalk, Connecticut 06851. (203) 845-3000. Irregular. Bibliography of catalysts.

ENCYCLOPEDIAS AND DICTIONARIES

Cambridge Encyclopedia of Life Sciences. A. E. Friday and David S. Ingram. Cambridge University Press, 40 W 20th St., New York, New York 10011. (212) 924-3900 or (800) 227-0247. 1985. Includes all topics under biology and ecology.

Concise Encyclopedia of Solid State Physics. Rita G. Lerner and George L. Trigg. Addison-Wesley Longman, Rte. 128, Reading, Massachusetts 01867. (617) 944-3700. 1983. "Articles chosen for this volume have been selected from the encyclopedia of physics."

Dictionary of Colloid and Surface Science. Paul Becher. Marcel Dekker, Inc., 270 Madison Ave., New York, New York 10016. (212) 696-9000; (800) 228-1160. 1990. Dictionary deals with the areas of colloids, surface chemistry, and the physics and technology involved with surfaces.

Encyclopedia of Chemical Processing and Design. John J. Mcketta and W. A. Cunningham. Marcel Dekker, Inc., 270 Madison Ave., New York, New York 10016. (212) 696-9000; (800) 228-1160. 1992. Thirty-eight volumes.

Encyclopedia of Human Biology. Renato Dulbecco, ed. Academic Press, c/o Harcourt Brace Jovanovich Inc., 6277 Sea Harbor Dr., Orlando, Florida 32887. (800) 346-8648. 1991. Eight volumes.

Encyclopedia of Industrial Chemical Additives. Michael and Irene Ash. Chemical Publishing Co., 80 Eighth Ave., New York, New York 10011. (212) 255-1950. 1984-87. Four volumes. Comprehensive compilation of tradename products that function as additives in enhancing the properties of various major industrial products.

Kirk-Othmer Encyclopedia of Chemical Technology. J. I. Kroschwitz, ed. John Wiley & Sons, Inc., 605 3rd Ave., New York, New York 10158-0012. (212) 850-6000. 1992-. All articles in the new edition have been rewritten and updated adding new subjects such as biotechnology, computer topics, analytical techniques and instrumentation, environmental concerns, fuels and energy, inorganic and solid state chemistry; composite materials and

material science in general, and pharmaceuticals. Also available online.

McGraw-Hill Encyclopedia of Science and Technology. McGraw-Hill, 1221 Avenue of the Americas, New York, New York 10020. (212) 512-2000 or (800) 262-4729. 1992. Seventh edition. Issued in multiple volumes including index. Includes all science and technology broad subject areas.

Ullmanns Encyclopedia of Industrial Chemistry. Hans Jurgen Arpe and Wolfgang Gerhartz, eds. VCH Publishers, 303 NW 12th Ave., Deerfield Beach, Florida 33442-1788. (305) 428-5566. 1990. Designed to keep up with the broad spectrum of chemical technology. Thirty-six volumes of the encyclopedia have been divided into two sets: the 28 A volumes contain alphabetically arranged articles on chemicals, product groups, processes and technological concepts; and the 8 B volumes are compendia of basic knowledge in industrial chemistry.

GENERAL WORKS

Biocatalysts for Industry. Jonathan S. Dordick, ed. Plenum Press, 233 Spring St., New York, New York 10013-1578. (212) 620-8000; (800) 221-9369. 1991. Contributed papers address the applications of enzymes or whole cells to carry out selective transformations of commercial importance, as biocatalysts in the food, pharmaceutical, and chemical industries. Includes general uses of biocatalysts, biocatalysts without chemical competition, emerging biocatalysts for conventional chemical processing, and future directions of biocatalysts.

Biomass, Catalysts and Liquid Fuels. Technomic Publishing Co., 851 New Holland Ave., Box 3535, Lancaster, Pennsylvania 17604. (717) 291-5609.

Catalyst Deactivation. Calvin H. Bartholomew and John B. Butt, eds. Elsevier Science Publishing Co., 655 Avenue of the Americas, New York, New York 10010. (212) 989-5800. 1991. Proceedings of the fifth International Symposium, Evanston, IL, June 24-26, 1991.

Catalyst Design: Progress and Perspectives. John Wiley & Sons, Inc., 605 Third Ave., New York, New York 10158-0012. (212) 850-6000.

Catalyst Manufacture: Laboratory and Commercial Preparations. Marcel Dekker, Inc., 270 Madison Ave., New York, New York 10016. (212) 696-9000.

Characterization of Heterogeneous Catalysts. Francis Delannay. Marcel Dekker, Inc., 270 Madison Ave., New York, New York 10016. (212) 696-9000. 1984.

Design of Industrial Catalysts. Elsevier Science Publishing Co., 655 Avenue of the Americas, New York, New York 10010. (212) 989-5800.

Guidelines for Mastering the Properties of Molecular Sieves. Plenum Press, 233 Spring St., New York, New York 10013-1578. (212) 620-8000. Relationship between the physiochemical properties of zeolitic systems and their low dimensionality.

Introduction to Characterization and Testing of Catalysts. Academic Press, c/o Harcourt Brace Jovanovich Inc., 6277 Sea Harbor Dr., Orlando, Florida 32887. (800) 346-8648. Analysis and industrial applications of catalysts.

Polymeric Reagents and Catalysts. American Chemical Society, 1155 16th St. N.W., Washington, District of

Columbia 20036. (800) 227-5558. Covers chemical tests and reagents, polymers and polymerization.

HANDBOOKS AND MANUALS

Handbook of Catalyst Manufacture. Noyes Publications, 120 Mill Rd., Park Ridge, New Jersey 07656. (201) 391-8484. Contains patents of catalysts.

ONLINE DATA BASES

BIOSIS Previews. BIOSIS, 2100 Arch St., Philadelphia, Pennsylvania 19103-1399. (215) 587-4800. Largest and most comprehensive database of research in the life sciences. Contains citations for nearly 9000 primary research journals, monographs, reviews, symposia, preliminary reports, semi-popular journals, selected institutional reports, government reports and research communications.

CAS Source Index–CASSI. Chemical Abstracts Service, 2540 Olentangy River Rd., P.O. Box 3012, Columbus, Ohio 43210. (800) 848-6533 or (614) 421-3600. A listing of bibliographic and library holdings information for scientific and technical primary literature relevant to the chemical sciences.

Chemical Abstracts-CA. Chemical Abstracts Service, 2540 Olentangy River Rd., P.O. Box 3012, Columbus, Ohio 43210. (800) 848-6533 or (614) 421-3600. Information sources include 9000 journals, patents from 27 countries, two industrial property organizations, new books, conference proceedings, and government research reports.

Enviro/Energyline Abstracts Plus. R. R. Bowker Co., 121 Chanlon Rd., New Providence, New Jersey 07974. (908) 464-6800.

Environmental Periodicals Bibliography. National Information Services Corp., Ste. 6, Wyman Towers, 3100 St. Paul St., Baltimore, Maryland 21218. (410)243-0797. Online version of abstract of same name.

Kirk-Othmer Encyclopedia of Chemical Technology. John Wiley & Sons, Inc., 605 3rd Ave., 5th Floor, New York, New York 10158. (212) 850-6000. Online version of the publication of the same name.

Monthly Catalog of United States Government Publications. U.S. G.P.O., Supt. of Docs., PO Box 371954, Pittsburgh, Pennsylvania 15250-7954. (202) 512-0000.

National Technical Information Service. U.S. Department of Commerce, National Technical Information Service, Office of Data Base Services, 5285 Port Royal Rd., Springfield, Virginia 22161. (703) 487-4807. Bibliographic database of government sponsored research and technical reports.

SCISEARCH. Institute for Scientific Information, University City Science Center, 3501 Market St., Philadelphia, Pennsylvania 19104. (215) 386-0100.

PERIODICALS AND NEWSLETTERS

Applied Catalysts. Elsevier Science Publishing Co., 655 Avenue of the Americas, New York, New York 10010. (212) 989-5800. Bimonthly. An international journal devoted to catalytic science and its applications.

Catalyst: Economics for the Living Earth. Catalyst Investing in Social Change, 64 Main St., Montpelier, Vermont 05602. (802) 223-7943. 1983-. Quarterly. Discusses grassroots enterprises working for social change and a humane economy. Focuses on ecological balance, articles on forest destruction, energy issues, native peoples issues and community- based economics.

Catalyst for Environmental Quality. Catalyst for Environmental/Energy, New York, New York

RESEARCH CENTERS AND INSTITUTES

Catalysis Society. c/o Dr. William J. Linn, E.I. DuPont, P.O. Box 80402, Wilmington, Delaware 80402. (302) 695-4655.

Utah State University, Center for Bio-Catalysis Science and Technology. Logan, Utah 84322-4630. (801) 750-2033.

TRADE ASSOCIATIONS AND PROFESSIONAL SOCIETIES

American Institute of Biological Sciences. 730 11th St., N.W., Washington, District of Columbia 20001-4521. (202) 628-1500.

American Institute of Chemical Engineers. 345 East 47th St., New York, New York 10017. (212) 705-7338.

American Institute of Chemists. 7315 Wisconsin Ave., Bethesda, Maryland 20814. (301) 652-2447.

Organic Reactions Catalysis Society. c/o R.L. Augustine, Dept. of Chemistry, Seton Hall University, South Orange, New Jersey 07079. (201) 761-9033.

CATALYTIC CONVERTERS

See also: AIR POLLUTION; EMISSIONS

ABSTRACTING AND INDEXING SERVICES

Applied Science and Technology Index. H.W. Wilson Co., 950 University Ave., Bronx, New York 10452. (800) 367-6770. Formerly Industrial Arts Index.

Engineering Index. The Engineering Index Inc., 345 E. 47th St., New York, New York 10017. 1962-.

Environment Abstracts. Bowker A & I Publishing, 121 Chanlon Rd., New Providence, New Jersey 07974. (908) 464-6800. 1974-.

Environment Index. Environment Information Center, Index Research Department, 124 E. 39th St., New York, New York 10016. 1971-. Annual.

Environmental Information Connection–EIC. Planning Information Program, Dept. of Urban and Regional Planning, University of Illinois, 1003 West Nevada, Urbana, Illinois 61801. (217) 333-1369. Also available online.

Environmental Periodicals Bibliography. Environmental Studies Institute, International Academy at Santa Barbara, 800 Garden St., Suite D, Santa Barbara, California 93101. (805) 965-5010. Also available online.

ERDA Research Abstracts. U.S. ERDA Technical Information Center, Box 62, Oak Ridge, Tennessee 37830.

General Science Index. H. W. Wilson Co., 950 University Ave., Bronx, New York 10452. 1978-. Monthly, also

issued in annual cumulation. Cumulative subject index to English language periodicals in the subject fields of astronomy, botany, chemistry, earth science, environment and conservation, food and nutrition, genetics, mathematics, medicine and health, microbiology, oceanography, physics, physiology and zoology.

Index to Scientific Book Contents. Institute for Scientific Information, 3501 Market St., Philadelphia, Pennsylvania 19104. (800) 523-1857. 1985-. Annual. Gives contents of science books published.

Pollution Abstracts. Cambridge Scientific Abstracts, 5161 River Rd., Bethesda, Maryland 20816. (301) 961-6750. Six/year. Indexes worldwide technical literature on environmental pollution. Covers air pollution, marine and freshwater pollution, sewage and wastewater treatment, waste management, toxicology and health, noise pollution, radiation, land pollution, and environmental policies, programs, legislation, and education. Also available online.

Science Citation Index. Institute for Scientific Information, 3501 Market St., Philadelphia, Pennsylvania 19104. 1961-.

BIBLIOGRAPHIES

EPA Publications Bibliography. U.S. Environmental Protection Agency, Library Systems Branch, 401 M St., SW, Washington, District of Columbia 20460. (202) 260-2090. Quarterly.

ENCYCLOPEDIAS AND DICTIONARIES

Dictionary of Environmental Engineering and Related Sciences: English-Spanish, Spanish-English. Jose T. Villate. Ediciones Universal, 3090 SW 8th St., Miami, Florida 33135. (305) 642-3355. 1979.

Encyclopedia of Environmental Science and Engineering. J.R. Pfafflin. Gordon and Breach Science Publishers, Inc., 270 8th Ave., New York, New York 10011. (212) 206-8900. 1992.

Encyclopedia of Physical Science and Technology. Robert A. Meyers, ed. Academic Press, c/o Harcourt Brace Jovanovich Inc., 6277 Sea Harbor Dr., Orlando, Florida 32887. (800) 346-8648. Dictionary of engineering, technology and physical sciences.

Kaiman's Encyclopedia of Energy Topics. Lee Kaiman and J. Masloff. Environmental Design and Research Center, 26799 Elena Rd., Los Altos Hills, California 94022. 1983. Two volumes. Coverage of topics range from natural energy sources that are renewable to nonrenewable, and the application of these energy sources.

McGraw-Hill Encyclopedia of Science and Technology. McGraw-Hill, 1221 Avenue of the Americas, New York, New York 10020. (212) 512-2000 or (800) 262-4729. 1992. Seventh edition. Issued in multiple volumes including index. Includes all science and technology broad subject areas.

Van Nostrand's Scientific Encyclopedia. Glenn D. Considine, ed. Van Nostrand Reinhold, 115 5th Ave., New York, New York 10003. (212) 254-3232. 1983. Sixth edition. Includes all broad subject areas in science.

GENERAL WORKS

Automobile Catalytic Converters. Kathleen C. Taylor. Agency for Toxic Substances and Disease Registry, U.S. Public Health Service, 1600 Clifton Rd. NE, Atlanta, Georgia 30333. (404) 452-4111. 1984.

Emissions: Misfueling, Catalytic Deactivation and Alternative Catalyst. Society of Automotive Engineers, 400 Commonwealth Dr., Warrendale, Pennsylvania 15096. (412) 776-4841. 1985. Automobile catalytic converters, internal combustion engines, spark ignition, and alternative fuels.

New Trends in CO Activation. L. Guczi, ed. Elsevier Science Publishing Co., 655 Avenue of the Americas, New York, New York 10010. (212) 989-5800. 1991.

HANDBOOKS AND MANUALS

Aftermath Catalytic Convertors: Guide to Their Purchase, Installation, and Use. Illinois Environmental Protection Agency, 2200 Churchill Rd., P.O. Box 19276, Springfield, Illinois 62794-9276. (217) 782-2829. 1989.

ONLINE DATA BASES

CERCLIS. Chemical Information Systems, Inc., 7215 York Rd., Baltimore, Maryland 21212. (301) 321-8440. Information on hazardous waste disposal sites that have either been listed by the EPA on the National Priority List (NPL) or nominated for consideration for the NPL.

Chemical Engineering and Biotechnology Abstracts–CEBA. Orbit Search Service, Maxwell Online Inc., 8000 W. Park Dr., McLean, Virginia 22102. (703) 442-0900 or (800) 456-7248. Monthly. Covers theoretical, practical and commercial material on all aspects of processing safety, and the environment. Also covers process and reaction engineering, measurement and process control, environmental protection and safety, plant design and equipment used in chemical engineering and biotechnology. More than 400 of the world's major primary chemical and process engineering journals are scanned to compile the database. Available from ORBIT.

Computerized Engineering Index–COMPENDEX. Engineering Information Inc., 345 E. 47th St., New York, New York 10017. (212) 705-7600.

Enviro/Energyline Abstracts Plus. R. R. Bowker Co., 121 Chanlon Rd., New Providence, New Jersey 07974. (908) 464-6800.

Environmental Periodicals Bibliography. National Information Services Corp., Ste. 6, Wyman Towers, 3100 St. Paul St., Baltimore, Maryland 21218. (410)243-0797. Online version of abstract of same name.

Los Angeles Catalytic Study–LACS. U.S. Environmental Protection Agency, Office of Monitoring Systems and Quality Assurance, 401 M St., S.W., Washington, District of Columbia 20460. (202) 260-2090.

Monthly Catalog of United States Government Publications. U.S. G.P.O., Supt. of Docs., PO Box 371954, Pittsburgh, Pennsylvania 15250-7954. (202) 512-0000.

National Technical Information Service. U.S. Department of Commerce, National Technical Information Service, Office of Data Base Services, 5285 Port Royal Rd., Springfield, Virginia 22161. (703) 487-4807. Biblio-

graphic database of government sponsored research and technical reports.

CATTLE

See: LIVESTOCK

CAUSTIC SODA

See: SODIUM HYDROXIDE

CELLS

See also: CARCINOGENS; GENETICS; METABOLISM; MUTAGENIC AGENTS; NUTRITION; RESPIRATION; TERATOGENIC AGENTS; TOXICITY

ABSTRACTING AND INDEXING SERVICES

ASFA Aquaculture Abstracts. Cambridge Scientific Abstracts, Inc., 5161 River Rd., Bethesda, Maryland 20816. (301) 961-6750. 1984.

Biological Abstracts. BIOSIS, 2100 Arch St., Philadelphia, Pennsylvania 19103-1399. (215) 587-4800. 1927-.

Biological and Agricultural Index. H.W. Wilson Co., 950 University Ave., Bronx, New York 10452. (800) 367-6770. 1916-. Monthly.

Biotechnology Research Abstracts. Cambridge Scientific Abstracts, 5161 River Rd., Bethesda, Maryland 20816. (301) 961-6750. Monthly. Includes such broad areas as genetic intervention, biochemical genetics, and microbiological techniques.

Current Advances in Plant Science. Pergamon Microforms International, Inc., Fairview Park, Elmsford, New York 10523. (914) 592-7720. 1984-. Monthly. Current literature searching service including journals, reports, abstracts, etc. This service is available online as part of the CABS database on the hosts BRS and ORBIT search service.

Environment Abstracts. Bowker A & I Publishing, 121 Chanlon Rd., New Providence, New Jersey 07974. (908) 464-6800. 1974-.

Environment Index. Environment Information Center, Index Research Department, 124 E. 39th St., New York, New York 10016. 1971-. Annual.

Environmental Information Connection–EIC. Planning Information Program, Dept. of Urban and Regional Planning, University of Illinois, 1003 West Nevada, Urbana, Illinois 61801. (217) 333-1369. Also available online.

Environmental Periodicals Bibliography. Environmental Studies Institute, International Academy at Santa Barbara, 800 Garden St., Suite D, Santa Barbara, California 93101. (805) 965-5010. Also available online.

Food Science and Technology Abstracts. International Food Information Service, c/o National Food Laboratory, 6363 Clark Ave., Dublin, California 94568. (800) 336-3782. 1969-.

General Science Index. H. W. Wilson Co., 950 University Ave., Bronx, New York 10452. 1978-. Monthly, also issued in annual cumulation. Cumulative subject index to English language periodicals in the subject fields of astronomy, botany, chemistry, earth science, environment and conservation, food and nutrition, genetics, mathematics, medicine and health, microbiology, oceanography, physics, physiology and zoology.

Genetics Abstracts. Cambridge Scientific Abstracts, 5161 River Rd., Bethesda, Maryland 20816. (301) 961-6750. 1968-. Monthly. Formerly published by Information Retrieval Ltd., London England. Published by Cambridge Scientific Abstracts since 1982.

Index to Scientific Book Contents. Institute for Scientific Information, 3501 Market St., Philadelphia, Pennsylvania 19104. (800) 523-1857. 1985-. Annual. Gives contents of science books published.

Pollution Abstracts. Cambridge Scientific Abstracts, 5161 River Rd., Bethesda, Maryland 20816. (301) 961-6750. Six/year. Indexes worldwide technical literature on environmental pollution. Covers air pollution, marine and freshwater pollution, sewage and wastewater treatment, waste management, toxicology and health, noise pollution, radiation, land pollution, and environmental policies, programs, legislation, and education. Also available online.

Science Citation Index. Institute for Scientific Information, 3501 Market St., Philadelphia, Pennsylvania 19104. 1961-.

BIBLIOGRAPHIES

EPA Publications Bibliography. U.S. Environmental Protection Agency, Library Systems Branch, 401 M St., SW, Washington, District of Columbia 20460. (202) 260-2090. Quarterly.

ENCYCLOPEDIAS AND DICTIONARIES

The Dictionary of Cell Biology. J. M. Lackie and J. A. T. Dow, eds. Academic Press, c/o Harcourt Brace Jovanovich Inc., 6277 Sea Harbor Dr., Orlando, Florida 32887. (800) 346-8648. 1989. Covers the broad subject area of cell biology including lipid, vitamins, amino acid, lectins, proteins, and other related topics.

A Dictionary of Genetics. Robert C. King and William A. Stansfield. Oxford University Press, 200 Madison Ave., New York, New York 10016. (212) 679-7300 or (800) 334-4249. 1991. Fourth edition. Includes 7,100 definitions with 250 illustrations. Also includes bibliography of major sources.

Dictionary of Genetics and Cell Biology. Norman Maclean. New York University Press, 70 Washington Sq. S., New York, New York 10012. (212) 998-2575. 1987. Includes the subject areas of cytology and genetics.

Dictionary of Microbiology and Molecular Biology. Paul Singleton and Diana Sainsbury. John Wiley & Sons, Inc., 605 3rd Ave., New York, New York 10158-0012. (212) 850-6000. 1987. Second edition. Comprehensive dictionary with "classical descriptive aspects of microbiology to current developments in related areas of bioenergetics, biochemistry and molecular biology." Entries give synonyms, cross references, and references to pertinent works. Miscellaneous appendixes. Bibliography.

Encyclopedia of Human Biology. Renato Dulbecco, ed. Academic Press, c/o Harcourt Brace Jovanovich Inc., 6277 Sea Harbor Dr., Orlando, Florida 32887. (800) 346-8648. 1991. Eight volumes.

Encyclopedic Dictionary of Genetics: With German Term Equivalents and Extensive German/English Index. R. C. King and W. D. Stansfield. VCH Publishers, 303 NW 12th Ave., Deerfield Beach, Florida 33442-1788. (305) 428-5566. 1990. 4th ed. Revised edition of: A Dictionary of Genetics, third edition.

Life Sciences on File. Diagram Group. Facts on File, Inc., 460 Park Ave. S., New York, New York 10016. (212) 683-2244. 1986. Encyclopedia of pictorial collection in life sciences. Deals with all major topics in life sciences including ecology.

McGraw-Hill Encyclopedia of Science and Technology. McGraw-Hill, 1221 Avenue of the Americas, New York, New York 10020. (212) 512-2000 or (800) 262-4729. 1992. Seventh edition. Issued in multiple volumes including index. Includes all science and technology broad subject areas.

GENERAL WORKS

Biocatalysts for Industry. Jonathan S. Dordick, ed. Plenum Press, 233 Spring St., New York, New York 10013-1578. (212) 620-8000; (800) 221-9369. 1991. Contributed papers address the applications of enzymes or whole cells to carry out selective transformations of commercial importance, as biocatalysts in the food, pharmaceutical, and chemical industries. Includes general uses of biocatalysts, biocatalysts without chemical competition, emerging biocatalysts for conventional chemical processing, and future directions of biocatalysts.

Calcium, Membranes, Aging, and Alzheimer's Disease. New York Academy of Sciences, Marketing Dept., 2E 63rd St., New York, New York 10021. (212) 838-0230. 1989. Discusses calcium in the body.

Cell ATP. William A. Bridger. John Wiley & Sons, Inc., 605 3rd Ave., New York, New York 10158-0012. (212) 850-6000. 1983. Discusses the metabolism of adenosine triphosphate including cell metabolism.

Magill's Survey of Science. Life Science Series. Frank N. Magill, ed. Salem Press, PO Box 50062, Pasadena, California 91105. 1991. Six volumes. Contents: v.1. A-Central and peripheral nervous system functions; v.2. Central metabolism regulation - eukaryotic transcriptional control; v.3. Positive and negative eukaryotic transcriptional control - mammalian hormones; v.4. Hormones and behavior - muscular contraction; v.5. Muscular contraction and relaxation - sexual reproduction in plants; v.6. Reproductive behavior and mating - X inactivation and the Lyon hypothesis.

Secondary Metabolism in Microorganisms, Plants and Animals. Martin Luckner. Springer-Verlag, 175 5th Ave., New York, New York 10010. (212) 460-1500. 1990. Includes reviews of the latest results on the biosynthesis for age and degradation of secondary metabolites and characteristics of compounds of specialized cells from all groups of organisms. Has new chapters on: the transport of secondary compounds with the producer organism; the significance of colored and toxic secondary products; and on the improvement of secondary product biosynthesis by genetical means.

Understanding Cell Toxicology: Principles and Practice. Erik Walum, Kjell Stenberg and Dag Jenssen. E. Horwood, 200 Old Tappan Rd., Old Tappan, New Jersey 07675. (800) 223-2348. 1990. Surveys the uses of mammalian cell assays to evaluate the toxic actions of chemical and physical agents.

ONLINE DATA BASES

BIOSIS Previews. BIOSIS, 2100 Arch St., Philadelphia, Pennsylvania 19103-1399. (215) 587-4800. Largest and most comprehensive database of research in the life sciences. Contains citations for nearly 9000 primary research journals, monographs, reviews, symposia, preliminary reports, semi-popular journals, selected institutional reports, government reports and research communications.

Biotechnology Abstracts. Derwent Publications Ltd., 6845 Elm St., McLean, Virginia 22101. (703) 790-0400. Includes material on genetic manipulation, biochemical engineering, fermentation, biocatalysis, cell hybridization, in vitro plant propagation and industrial waste management.

Chemical Engineering and Biotechnology Abstracts–CEBA. Orbit Search Service, Maxwell Online Inc., 8000 W. Park Dr., McLean, Virginia 22102. (703) 442-0900 or (800) 456-7248. Monthly. Covers theoretical, practical and commercial material on all aspects of processing safety, and the environment. Also covers process and reaction engineering, measurement and process control, environmental protection and safety, plant design and equipment used in chemical engineering and biotechnology. More than 400 of the world's major primary chemical and process engineering journals are scanned to compile the database. Available from ORBIT.

Enviro/Energyline Abstracts Plus. R. R. Bowker Co., 121 Chanlon Rd., New Providence, New Jersey 07974. (908) 464-6800.

Environmental Periodicals Bibliography. National Information Services Corp., Ste. 6, Wyman Towers, 3100 St. Paul St., Baltimore, Maryland 21218. (410)243-0797. Online version of abstract of same name.

PERIODICALS AND NEWSLETTERS

Trends in Cell Biology. Elsevier Science Publishing Co., 655 Avenue of the Americas, New York, New York 10010. (212) 984-5800. Monthly. Includes current opinion in the field such as comments, letters and also includes headlines and short subject reviews as well as book reviews. A calendar events and the job trends are also outlined.

RESEARCH CENTERS AND INSTITUTES

American Type Culture Collection. 12301 Parklawn Drive, Rockville, Maryland 20852. (301) 881-2600.

Brandeis University, Photobiology Group. Biology Department, Waltham, Massachusetts 02254. (617) 736-2685.

Cell Regulation Group. University of Calgary, Medical Biochemistry, Faculty of Medicine, 330 Hospital Dr., N.W., Calgary, Alberta, Canada T2N 4N1. (403) 220-3018.

Developmental Biology Center. University of California, Irvine, Irvine, California 92717. (714) 856-5957.

New York University, Laboratory of Cellular Biology. Biology Department, 109 Main Building, Washington Square, New York, New York 10003. (212) 998-820.

Rockefeller University. 1230 York Ave., New York, New York 10021-6399. (212) 570-7661.

Rockefeller University, Laboratory of Cell Biology. 1230 York Avenue, New York, New York 10021-6399. (212) 570-8770.

Rockefeller University, Laboratory of Neurobiology and Behavior. 1230 York Ave., New York, New York 10021-6399. (212) 570-8666.

Rutgers University, Center for Agricultural Molecular Biology. Cook College, P.O. Box 231, New Brunswick, New Jersey 08903. (908) 932-8165.

State University of New York at Plattsburg, In Vitro Cell Biology and Biotechnology Program. Department of Biological Science, Plattsburg, New York 12901. (518) 846-7144.

University of Iowa, University Large Scale Fermentation Facility. Department of Microbiology, Iowa City, Iowa 52242. (319) 335-7780.

University of Miami, Institute for Molecular Cellular Evolution. 12500 SW 152 Street, Miami, Florida 33177. (305) 284-7366.

University of Michigan, Cell Biology Laboratories. Department of Anatomy & Cell Biology, 4747 Medical Science II, Box 0616, 1301 Catherine Road, Ann Arbor, Michigan 48109. (313) 764-4360.

University of New Hampshire, Coastal Marine Laboratory. Department of Zoology, Durham, New Hampshire 03824. (603) 862-2100.

University of Oregon, Institute of Molecular Biology. Eugene, Oregon 97403. (503) 686-5151.

University of Oregon, Program in Cellular Biology. Institute of Molecular Biology, Eugene, Oregon 97403. (503) 346-5151.

University of Texas at Austin, Cell Research Institute. Austin, Texas 78713-7640. (512) 471-1431.

University of Texas Health Science Center at Houston, Cryobiology Research Center. 3606 A. Suite 1, Research Forest Drive, Woodlands, Texas 77381. (713) 221-8000.

University of Virginia, Center for Bioprocess/Product Development. Department of Chemical Engineering, Thornton Hall, Charlottesville, Virginia 22901. (804) 924-6278.

University of Wisconsin-Madison, Center for the Study of Nitrogen Fixation. 420 Henry Mall, Department of Biochemistry, Madison, Wisconsin 53706. (608) 262-6859.

University of Wisconsin-Madison, Drosophila Mutagenesis Laboratory. Zoology Department, Madison, Wisconsin 53706. (608) 263-7875.

University of Wisconsin-Madison, Integrated Microscopy Resource for Biomedical Research. Animal Science Building, 1675 Observatory Drive, Madison, Wisconsin 53706. (608) 263-6288.

University of Wisconsin-Madison, Laboratory of Molecular Biology. 1525 Linden Drive, Madison, Wisconsin 53706. (608) 262-3203.

TRADE ASSOCIATIONS AND PROFESSIONAL SOCIETIES

American Institute of Biological Sciences. 730 11th St., N.W., Washington, District of Columbia 20001-4521. (202) 628-1500.

CEMENT

ABSTRACTING AND INDEXING SERVICES

Applied Science and Technology Index. H.W. Wilson Co., 950 University Ave., Bronx, New York 10452. (800) 367-6770. Formerly Industrial Arts Index.

Environment Abstracts. Bowker A & I Publishing, 121 Chanlon Rd., New Providence, New Jersey 07974. (908) 464-6800. 1974-.

Environment Index. Environment Information Center, Index Research Department, 124 E. 39th St., New York, New York 10016. 1971-. Annual.

Environmental Information Connection–EIC. Planning Information Program, Dept. of Urban and Regional Planning, University of Illinois, 1003 West Nevada, Urbana, Illinois 61801. (217) 333-1369. Also available online.

Environmental Periodicals Bibliography. Environmental Studies Institute, International Academy at Santa Barbara, 800 Garden St., Suite D, Santa Barbara, California 93101. (805) 965-5010. Also available online.

General Science Index. H. W. Wilson Co., 950 University Ave., Bronx, New York 10452. 1978-. Monthly, also issued in annual cumulation. Cumulative subject index to English language periodicals in the subject fields of astronomy, botany, chemistry, earth science, environment and conservation, food and nutrition, genetics, mathematics, medicine and health, microbiology, oceanography, physics, physiology and zoology.

BIBLIOGRAPHIES

Cements Research Progress. American Ceramic Society, 757 Brookside Plaza Dr., Westerville, Ohio 43081. (614) 890-4700. Annual. Bibliography of cement manufacturing.

Comprehensive Bibliography of Cement and Concrete, 1925-1947. Floyd O. Slate. Purdue University Press, 1131 S. Campus Cts.-B, Lafayette, Indiana 47907. (317) 494-2038. 1952.

EPA Publications Bibliography. U.S. Environmental Protection Agency, Library Systems Branch, 401 M St., SW, Washington, District of Columbia 20460. (202) 260-2090. Quarterly.

History of Concrete, 30 B.C. to 1926 A.D.: Annotated. American Concrete Institute, 22400 W. Seven Mile Rd., P.O. Box 19150, Detroit, Michigan 48219. (313) 532-2600. 1982.

DIRECTORIES

American Cement Directory. 123 S. Third St., Allentown, Pennsylvania 18105. (215) 434-5191. Annual.

Concrete Contractors Directory. 5711 S. 86th Circle, Omaha, Nebraska 68127. (402) 593-4600. Annual.

Concrete Products–Wholesale. 5711 S. 86th Circle, Omaha, Nebraska 68127. (402) 593-4600. Annual.

Concrete–Ready Mix Directory. 5711 S. 86th Circle, Omaha, Nebraska 68127. (402) 593-4600. Annual.

World Cement Directory. European Cement Association, 2 rue Saint-Charles, Cedex 15, Paris, France F-75740. 1 45792866. 1961-. Annual.

ENCYCLOPEDIAS AND DICTIONARIES

Dictionary of Civil Engineering. John S. Scott. Halsted Press, Division of J. Wiley, 605 3rd Ave., New York, New York 10158. (212) 850-6000. 1981. Third edition.

Dictionary of Environmental Engineering and Related Sciences: English-Spanish, Spanish-English. Jose T. Villate. Ediciones Universal, 3090 SW 8th St., Miami, Florida 33135. (305) 642-3355. 1979.

Encyclopedia of Environmental Science and Engineering. J.R. Pfafflin. Gordon and Breach Science Publishers, Inc., 270 8th Ave., New York, New York 10011. (212) 206-8900. 1992.

McGraw-Hill Encyclopedia of Science and Technology. McGraw-Hill, 1221 Avenue of the Americas, New York, New York 10020. (212) 512-2000 or (800) 262-4729. 1992. Seventh edition. Issued in multiple volumes including index. Includes all science and technology broad subject areas.

HANDBOOKS AND MANUALS

Cement-Data-Book. Walter H. Duda. Bauverlag, Wittelsbacherstr. 10, Postfach 1460, Wiesbaden, Germany D-6200. 1977. Covers process engineering in the cement industry, including methods of calculation, formulas, diagrams, numerical tables.

Cement Engineers' Handbook. Otto Labahn. Bauverlag, Wittelsbacherstr. 10, Postfach 1460, Weisbaden, Germany D-6200. 1983.

Cement Manufacturer's Handbook. Kurt E. Peray. Chemical Publishing Co., 80 Eighth Ave., New York, New York 10011. (212) 255-1950. 1979.

ONLINE DATA BASES

Enviro/Energyline Abstracts Plus. R. R. Bowker Co., 121 Chanlon Rd., New Providence, New Jersey 07974. (908) 464-6800.

Environmental Periodicals Bibliography. National Information Services Corp., Ste. 6, Wyman Towers, 3100 St. Paul St., Baltimore, Maryland 21218. (410)243-0797. Online version of abstract of same name.

PERIODICALS AND NEWSLETTERS

Advances in Cement Research. Scholium International, Inc., 99 Seaview Blvd., Port Washington, New York 11050-4610. (516) 484-3290. Covers fundamentals of cement science.

Cement and Concrete Research. Pergamon Microforms International, Inc., Fairview Pk., Elmsford, New York 10523. (914) 592-7720.

Cement, Concrete and Aggregates. American Society for Testing and Materials, 1916 S. Race St., Philadelphia, Pennsylvania 19103. (215) 299-5585. Semiannual. Covers cement, concrete and other building materials.

TRADE ASSOCIATIONS AND PROFESSIONAL SOCIETIES

American Concrete Institute. P.O. Box 19150, Detroit, Michigan 48219. (303) 532-2600.

National Concrete Masonry Association. P.O. Box 781, Herndon, Virginia 22070. (703) 435-4900.

National Precast Association. 825 E. 64th St., Indianapolis, Indiana 46220. (317) 253-0486.

National Ready Mixed Concrete Association. 900 Spring St., Silver Springs, Maryland 20910. (301) 587-1400.

Portland Cement Association. 5320 Old Orchard Rd., Skokie, Illinois 60077. (708) 966-6200.

Reinforced Concrete Research Council. 205 N. Mathews Ave., Urbana, Illinois 61801. (217) 333-7384.

Structural Cement-Fiber Products Association. 5028 Wisconsin Ave., N.W., Washington, District of Columbia 20016. (301) 961-9800.

CERIUM
See: ELEMENTS

CESIUM
See: ELEMENTS

CFCS
See: CHLOROFLUOROCARBONS

CHAIN REACTIONS
See: REACTORS

CHANNEL GEOMETRY
See: HYDROLOGY

CHANNELIZATION
See also: DAMS; ECOSYSTEMS; FLOODS; IRRIGATION; STREAMS; WATER POLLUTION

ABSTRACTING AND INDEXING SERVICES

Biological Abstracts. BIOSIS, 2100 Arch St., Philadelphia, Pennsylvania 19103-1399. (215) 587-4800. 1927-.

General Science Index. H. W. Wilson Co., 950 University Ave., Bronx, New York 10452. 1978-. Monthly, also issued in annual cumulation. Cumulative subject index to English language periodicals in the subject fields of astronomy, botany, chemistry, earth science, environment and conservation, food and nutrition, genetics, mathematics, medicine and health, microbiology, oceanography, physics, physiology and zoology.

Science Citation Index. Institute for Scientific Information, 3501 Market St., Philadelphia, Pennsylvania 19104. 1961-.

BIBLIOGRAPHIES

Bibliography and Index of Geology. American Geological Institute, 4220 King St., Alexandria, Virginia 22302. Monthly. Includes environmental geology and hydrogeology.

Current Contents. Agriculture, Biology and Environmental Sciences. Institute for Scientific Information, 3501 Market St., Philadelphia, Pennsylvania 19104. (800) 523-1857. 1973-. Previous title: Current Contents. Agricultural, Food & Veterinary Sciences. Gives the table of contents of periodicals in the fields of agriculture, biology, environmental and related areas.

ENCYCLOPEDIAS AND DICTIONARIES

Dictionary of Environmental Engineering and Related Sciences: English-Spanish, Spanish-English. Jose T. Villate. Ediciones Universal, 3090 SW 8th St., Miami, Florida 33135. (305) 642-3355. 1979.

Encyclopedia of Environmental Science and Engineering. J.R. Pfafflin. Gordon and Breach Science Publishers, Inc., 270 8th Ave., New York, New York 10011. (212) 206-8900. 1992.

The Encyclopedia of Geochemistry and Environmental Sciences. Rhodes Whitmore Fairbridge. Van Nostrand Reinhold Co., 115 5th Ave., New York, New York 10003. (212) 254-3232. 1972.

McGraw-Hill Encyclopedia of Environmental Science. Sybil P. Parker. McGraw-Hill Science & Engineering Books, 11 W. 19th St., New York, New York 10011. (212) 337-6010. 1980. Covers ecology, man's influence on nature, and environmental protection.

McGraw-Hill Encyclopedia of Science and Technology. McGraw-Hill, 1221 Avenue of the Americas, New York, New York 10020. (212) 512-2000 or (800) 262-4729. 1992. Seventh edition. Issued in multiple volumes including index. Includes all science and technology broad subject areas.

GENERAL WORKS

Magill's Survey of Science. Earth Science Series. Frank N. Magill. Salem Press, PO Box 50062, Pasadena, California 91105. 1990-. Five volumes. Includes information on earth's crust, hot spots and volcanic island chains, physical properties of minerals, rock magnetism, physical properties of rocks, and index.

ONLINE DATA BASES

BIOSIS Previews. BIOSIS, 2100 Arch St., Philadelphia, Pennsylvania 19103-1399. (215) 587-4800. Largest and most comprehensive database of research in the life sciences. Contains citations for nearly 9000 primary research journals, monographs, reviews, symposia, preliminary reports, semi-popular journals, selected institutional reports, government reports and research communications.

SCISEARCH. Institute for Scientific Information, University City Science Center, 3501 Market St., Philadelphia, Pennsylvania 19104. (215) 386-0100.

PERIODICALS AND NEWSLETTERS

Waste Treatment Technology News. Business Communications Company, Inc., 25 Van Zant Street, Norwalk, Connecticut 06855. (203) 853-4266. Monthly. Covers effective management and handling of hazardous wastes.

CHARCOAL

See: FILTRATION

CHECK DAMS

See: DAMS

CHELATING AGENTS

See also: FERTILIZERS

ABSTRACTING AND INDEXING SERVICES

Biological Abstracts. BIOSIS, 2100 Arch St., Philadelphia, Pennsylvania 19103-1399. (215) 587-4800. 1927-.

Environment Abstracts. Bowker A & I Publishing, 121 Chanlon Rd., New Providence, New Jersey 07974. (908) 464-6800. 1974-.

Environment Index. Environment Information Center, Index Research Department, 124 E. 39th St., New York, New York 10016. 1971-. Annual.

Environmental Information Connection–EIC. Planning Information Program, Dept. of Urban and Regional Planning, University of Illinois, 1003 West Nevada, Urbana, Illinois 61801. (217) 333-1369. Also available online.

Environmental Periodicals Bibliography. Environmental Studies Institute, International Academy at Santa Barbara, 800 Garden St., Suite D, Santa Barbara, California 93101. (805) 965-5010. Also available online.

General Science Index. H. W. Wilson Co., 950 University Ave., Bronx, New York 10452. 1978-. Monthly, also issued in annual cumulation. Cumulative subject index to English language periodicals in the subject fields of astronomy, botany, chemistry, earth science, environment and conservation, food and nutrition, genetics, mathematics, medicine and health, microbiology, oceanography, physics, physiology and zoology.

Pollution Abstracts. Cambridge Scientific Abstracts, 5161 River Rd., Bethesda, Maryland 20816. (301) 961-6750. Six/year. Indexes worldwide technical literature on environmental pollution. Covers air pollution, marine and freshwater pollution, sewage and wastewater treatment,

waste management, toxicology and health, noise pollution, radiation, land pollution, and environmental policies, programs, legislation, and education. Also available online.

Science Citation Index. Institute for Scientific Information, 3501 Market St., Philadelphia, Pennsylvania 19104. 1961-.

BIBLIOGRAPHIES

Current Contents. Agriculture, Biology and Environmental Sciences. Institute for Scientific Information, 3501 Market St., Philadelphia, Pennsylvania 19104. (800) 523-1857. 1973-. Previous title: Current Contents. Agricultural, Food & Veterinary Sciences. Gives the table of contents of periodicals in the fields of agriculture, biology, environmental and related areas.

EPA Publications Bibliography. U.S. Environmental Protection Agency, Library Systems Branch, 401 M St., SW, Washington, District of Columbia 20460. (202) 260-2090. Quarterly.

ENCYCLOPEDIAS AND DICTIONARIES

McGraw-Hill Encyclopedia of Environmental Science. Sybil P. Parker. McGraw-Hill Science & Engineering Books, 11 W. 19th St., New York, New York 10011. (212) 337-6010. 1980. Covers ecology, man's influence on nature, and environmental protection.

McGraw-Hill Encyclopedia of Science and Technology. McGraw-Hill, 1221 Avenue of the Americas, New York, New York 10020. (212) 512-2000 or (800) 262-4729. 1992. Seventh edition. Issued in multiple volumes including index. Includes all science and technology broad subject areas.

GENERAL WORKS

Bypassing Bypass: The New Technique of Chelation Therapy. Elmer M. Cranton. Stein and Day, New York, New York 1984. Therapeutic use of ethylenediaminetetraacetic acid.

Chelated Mineral Nutrition in Plants, Animals, and Man. Charles C. Thomas Publishers, 2600 S. First, Springfield, Illinois 62794-9265. (217) 789-8980. 217-789-8980.

Chelates in Nutrition. F. Howard Kratzer. CRC Press, 2000 Corporate Blvd. N.W., Boca Raton, Florida 33431. (800) 272-7737. 1986. Mineral in human nutrition and chelation therapy.

Chelating Agents and Metal Chelates. Academic Press, c/o Harcourt Brace Jovanovich Inc., 6277 Sea Harbor Dr., Orlando, Florida 32887. (800) 346-8648. 1964. Organic chemistry and chelating agents.

Conversations on Chelation and Mineral Nutrition. H. DeWayne Ashmead. Keats Publishing, Inc., P.O. Box 876, New Canaan, Connecticut 06840. (203) 966-8721. 1989.

ONLINE DATA BASES

BIOSIS Previews. BIOSIS, 2100 Arch St., Philadelphia, Pennsylvania 19103-1399. (215) 587-4800. Largest and most comprehensive database of research in the life sciences. Contains citations for nearly 9000 primary research journals, monographs, reviews, symposia, pre-

liminary reports, semi-popular journals, selected institutional reports, government reports and research communications.

CERCLIS. Chemical Information Systems, Inc., 7215 York Rd., Baltimore, Maryland 21212. (301) 321-8440. Information on hazardous waste disposal sites that have either been listed by the EPA on the National Priority List (NPL) or nominated for consideration for the NPL.

Enviro/Energyline Abstracts Plus. R. R. Bowker Co., 121 Chanlon Rd., New Providence, New Jersey 07974. (908) 464-6800.

Environmental Periodicals Bibliography. National Information Services Corp., Ste. 6, Wyman Towers, 3100 St. Paul St., Baltimore, Maryland 21218. (410)243-0797. Online version of abstract of same name.

PERIODICALS AND NEWSLETTERS

Chelates in Analytical Chemistry. M. Dekker, 270 Madison Ave., New York, New York 10016. (212) 696-9000. Annual. Chemical tests and reagents.

TRADE ASSOCIATIONS AND PROFESSIONAL SOCIETIES

American Institute of Biological Sciences. 730 11th St., N.W., Washington, District of Columbia 20001-4521. (202) 628-1500.

American Institute of Chemical Engineers. 345 East 47th St., New York, New York 10017. (212) 705-7338.

American Institute of Chemists. 7315 Wisconsin Ave., Bethesda, Maryland 20814. (301) 652-2447.

CHEMICAL CONTAMINATION

See also: FOOD CONTAMINATION; POLLUTION; WATER QUALITY

ABSTRACTING AND INDEXING SERVICES

Applied Ecology Abstracts Studies in Renewable Natural Resources. Information Retrieval Ltd., 1911 Jefferson Davis Highway, Arlington, Virginia 22202. 1975-. Monthly.

Aqualine Abstracts. Water Research Centre. c/o Pergamon Microforms International, Inc., Fairview Park, Elmsford, New York 10523. (914) 592-7720. 1927-. Contains some 8,000 records annually on water and wastewater technology. Covers all aspects of water, wastewater, associated engineering services and the aquatic environment. Over 600 periodicals, as well as books, reports and conference proceedings and other publications from water related institutions worldwide are scanned. Also available online.

ASFA Aquaculture Abstracts. Cambridge Scientific Abstracts, Inc., 5161 River Rd., Bethesda, Maryland 20816. (301) 961-6750. 1984.

Biological and Agricultural Index. H.W. Wilson Co., 950 University Ave., Bronx, New York 10452. (800) 367-6770. 1916-. Monthly.

Bulletin Signaletique: Eau et Assainissement, Pollution Atmospherique, Droit des Pollutions. Centre de Documentation, Centre National de la Recherche Scientifique,

15, quai Anatole France, Paris, France 75700. (1) 45 55 92 25. 1983-. Monthly. Indexes pollution periodicals including water, atmospheric and related pollutions.

Ecological Abstracts. Geo Abstracts Ltd. Elsevier Applied Science, Crown House, Linton Rd., Barking, England IG 11 8JU. 1974-. Derived from over 600 leading ecological and environmental journals, plus books, conference proceedings, reports and theses.

Environment Abstracts. Bowker A & I Publishing, 121 Chanlon Rd., New Providence, New Jersey 07974. (908) 464-6800. 1974-.

Environment Index. Environment Information Center, Index Research Department, 124 E. 39th St., New York, New York 10016. 1971-. Annual.

Environmental Information Connection–EIC. Planning Information Program, Dept. of Urban and Regional Planning, University of Illinois, 1003 West Nevada, Urbana, Illinois 61801. (217) 333-1369. Also available online.

Environmental Periodicals Bibliography. Environmental Studies Institute, International Academy at Santa Barbara, 800 Garden St., Suite D, Santa Barbara, California 93101. (805) 965-5010. Also available online.

Ergonomics Abstracts. Taylor & Francis, 4 John St., London, England WC1N 2ET. 1990-. Bimonthly. Provides details on recent additions to the international literature on human factors in human-machine systems and physical environmental influences.

General Science Index. H. W. Wilson Co., 950 University Ave., Bronx, New York 10452. 1978-. Monthly, also issued in annual cumulation. Cumulative subject index to English language periodicals in the subject fields of astronomy, botany, chemistry, earth science, environment and conservation, food and nutrition, genetics, mathematics, medicine and health, microbiology, oceanography, physics, physiology and zoology.

INIS Atomindex. International Atomic Energy Agency, Wagramerstrasse 5, Vienna, Austria A-1400. 222 23606198. 1988-. Semiannual. Abstracts nuclear energy and nuclear physics topics from journals, conferences, technical reports and other related publications. Issued in 6 parts: Personal Author, Corporate Entry, Subject, Report, Standard Patent, Conference (by place), Conference (by date).

Multimedia Index to Ecology. National Information Center for Educational Media, University of Southern California, Los Angeles, California 90007.

Pesticides Abstracts. U.S. Environmental Protection Agency, Office of Pesticides Programs, 345 Curtland, Atlanta, Georgia 30365. (404) 347-2864. 1981. Monthly. Formerly: Health Aspects of Pesticides Abstracts Bulletin.

Pollution Abstracts. Cambridge Scientific Abstracts, 5161 River Rd., Bethesda, Maryland 20816. (301) 961-6750. Six/year. Indexes worldwide technical literature on environmental pollution. Covers air pollution, marine and freshwater pollution, sewage and wastewater treatment, waste management, toxicology and health, noise pollution, radiation, land pollution, and environmental policies, programs, legislation, and education. Also available online.

Science Citation Index. Institute for Scientific Information, 3501 Market St., Philadelphia, Pennsylvania 19104. 1961-.

Selected References on Environmental Quality as It Relates to Health. National Library of Medicine, 8600 Rockville Pike, Bethesda, Maryland 20894. (800) 638-8480. 1977.

BIBLIOGRAPHIES

Chemical Spills: A Bibliography. Vance Bibliographies, PO Box 229, 112 N. Charter St., Monticello, Illinois 61856. (217) 762-3831. Looks at hazardous substances and environmental chemistry.

Directory of Published Proceedings. Interdok Corp., 173 Halstead Ave., Harrison, New York 10528. (914) 835-3506. 1990. Monthly. This is a listing of published proceedings including the series SEMTE (Science/Medicine/Engineering/Technology) and the series SSH (Social Science/Humanities).

EPA Publications Bibliography. U.S. Environmental Protection Agency, Library Systems Branch, 401 M St., SW, Washington, District of Columbia 20460. (202) 260-2090. Quarterly.

ENCYCLOPEDIAS AND DICTIONARIES

Common Synonyms for Chemicals Listed Under Section 313 of the Emergency Planning and Community Right to Know Act. Washington, District of Columbia 1991. Toxic chemical release inventory, glossary of synonyms, covering hazardous substances and chemicals.

Compendium of Hazardous Chemicals in Schools and Colleges. Forum for Scientific Excellence. J. B. Lippincott, 227 E. Washington Sq., Philadelphia, Pennsylvania 19105. (215) 238-4200; (800) 982-4377. 1990. Encyclopedia of more than 950 hazardous chemicals found in academic institutions. Contains all the data necessary for identifying these chemicals and their hazardous effects.

Dictionary of Environmental Engineering and Related Sciences: English-Spanish, Spanish-English. Jose T. Villate. Ediciones Universal, 3090 SW 8th St., Miami, Florida 33135. (305) 642-3355. 1979.

Encyclopedia of Environmental Science and Engineering. J.R. Pfafflin. Gordon and Breach Science Publishers, Inc., 270 8th Ave., New York, New York 10011. (212) 206-8900. 1992.

Grzimek's Encyclopedia of Ecology. Bernhard Grzimek. Van Nostrand Reinhold, 115 5th Ave., New York, New York 10003. (212) 254-3232. 1976.

McGraw-Hill Encyclopedia of Environmental Science. Sybil P. Parker. McGraw-Hill Science & Engineering Books, 11 W. 19th St., New York, New York 10011. (212) 337-6010. 1980. Covers ecology, man's influence on nature, and environmental protection.

McGraw-Hill Encyclopedia of Science and Technology. McGraw-Hill, 1221 Avenue of the Americas, New York, New York 10020. (212) 512-2000 or (800) 262-4729. 1992. Seventh edition. Issued in multiple volumes including index. Includes all science and technology broad subject areas.

North American Reference Encyclopedia of Ecology and Pollution. William White. North American Pub. Co., 401

N. Broad St., Philadelphia, Pennsylvania 19108. (215) 238-5300. 1972.

Ullmanns Encyclopedia of Industrial Chemistry. Hans Jurgen Arpe and Wolfgang Gerhartz, eds. VCH Publishers, 303 NW 12th Ave., Deerfield Beach, Florida 33442-1788. (305) 428-5566. 1990. Designed to keep up with the broad spectrum of chemical technology. Thirty-six volumes of the encyclopedia have been divided into two sets: the 28 A volumes contain alphabetically arranged articles on chemicals, product groups, processes and technological concepts; and the 8 B volumes are compendia of basic knowledge in industrial chemistry.

Van Nostrand's Scientific Encyclopedia. Glenn D. Considine, ed. Van Nostrand Reinhold, 115 5th Ave., New York, New York 10003. (212) 254-3232. 1983. Sixth edition. Includes all broad subject areas in science.

GENERAL WORKS

Analyses of Hazardous Substances in Air. A. Kettrup, ed. VCH Publishers, 303 NW 12th Ave., Deerfield Beach, Florida 33442-1788. (305) 428-5566. 1991. Proceedings from the Commission for the Investigation of Health Hazards of Chemical Compounds in the Work Area. Included were 16 analytical methods for determining organic compounds and heavy metals in the air of work areas by high pressure liquid chromatography, gas chromatography, infrared spectroscopy and atomic absorption spectrometry.

Analyses of Hazardous Substances in Biological Materials. J. Angere, ed. VCH Publishers, 303 NW 12th Ave., Deerfield Beach, Florida 33442-1788. (305) 428-5566. 1991. Discusses industrial hygiene and the various toxic substances involved.

Biomarkers of Environmental Contamination. John F. McCarthy and Lee R. Shugart. Lewis Publishers, 2000 Corporate Blvd., Boca Raton, Florida 33431. (800) 272-7737. 1990. Reviews the use of biological markers in animals and plants as an innovative approach to evaluating the ecological and physiological effects of environmental contamination.

Catalyst Deactivation. Calvin H. Bartholomew and John B. Butt, eds. Elsevier Science Publishing Co., 655 Avenue of the Americas, New York, New York 10010. (212) 989-5800. 1991. Proceedings of the fifth International Symposium, Evanston, IL, June 24-26, 1991.

Chemical Contamination and Its Victims: Medical Remedies, Legal Redress, and Public Policy. David W. Schnare, ed. Greenwood Publishing Group, Inc., 88 Post Rd., W., Box 5007, Westport, Connecticut 06881. (203) 226-3571. 1989. Covers toxicology, hazardous waste, and liability for hazardous substances pollution damages.

Chemical Contamination in the Human Environment. Morton Lippmann. Oxford University Press, 200 Madison Ave., New York, New York 10016. (212) 679-7300. 1979. Deals with pollution and environmental health.

Chemical Hazard Communication Guidebook: OSHA, EPA, and DOT Requirements. Andrew B. Waldo and Richard D. Hinds. PennWell Books, PO Box 21288, Tulsa, Oklahoma 74121. (918) 831-9421; (800) 752-9764. 1991. Covers how to comply with hazard communication requirements applicable to chemicals in the workplace, how to meet reporting responsibilities imposed by emergency planning and community right to know requirements and how to comply with restrictions on the transportation of hazardous materials.

Chemical Hazards in the Workplace. Ronald M. Scott. Lewis Publishers, 200 Corporate Blvd. NW, Boca Raton, Florida 33431. (407) 994-0555 or (800)272-7737. 1989. Presents basics of toxicology. Reports a sampling of the accumulated knowledge of the hazards of specific compounds in the workplace. Also discusses the federal regulatory agencies charged with worker protection and the specific practices involved in maintaining safety and regulatory compliance.

Chemical Spill Uncertainty Analysis. W. J. Shields. Electric Power Research Institute, 3412 Hillview Ave., Palo Alto, California 94304. (415) 965-4081. 1989. Covers mathematical models to deal with chemical spills.

Classification of Floating CHRIS Chemicals for the Development of a Spill Response Manual. A. T. Szhula. National Technical Information Service, 5285 Port Royal Rd, Springfield, Virginia 22161. (703) 487-4650. Covers classification of chemical spills.

Controlling Chemical Hazards: Fundamentals of the Management of Toxic Chemicals. Raymond P. Cote and Peter G. Wells, eds. Unwin Hyman, 77/85 Fulham Palace Rd., London, England W6 8JB. 081 741 7070. 1991. Gives an overview of the properties, fate of, and dilemmas involving hazardous chemicals.

Cutting Chemical Wastes. David J. Sarokin, et al. INFORM, 381 Park Ave. S., New York, New York 10016. (212) 689-4040. 1985. Describes the activities of 29 organic chemical plants that are trying to reduce hazardous chemical wastes.

Ecotoxicology and Climate. Philippe Bordeaux, et al., eds. John Wiley & Sons, Inc., 605 3rd Ave., New York, New York 10158-0012. (212) 850-6000. 1989. Describes environmental chemistry of toxic pollutants in hot and cold climates. Includes bibliographical references and an index.

Environment in Peril. Anthony B. Wolbarst, ed. Smithsonian Institution Press, 470 L'Enfant Plaza, No. 7100, Washington, District of Columbia 20560. (800) 782-4612. 1991. Brings together in one volume the primary concerns of eleven of the world's leaders in conservation, ecology and public policy. Broad environmental issues covered are: ozone depletion, overpopulation, global warming, thinning forests, extinction of species, spreading deserts, toxic chemicals, and various pollutants.

Environmental Biotechnology: Reducing Risks from Environmental Chemicals through Biotechnology. Gilbert S. Omenn. Plenum Press, 233 Spring St., New York, New York 10013-1578. (212) 620-8000. Covers environmental aspects of the chemical and biological treatment of sewage.

Environmental Chemistry: Australian Perspective. Greg Laidler. Longman Cheshire, South Melbourne, Australia 1991.

Environmental Fact Sheet: The Delaney Paradox and Negligible Risk. U.S. Environmental Protection Agency, Office of Pesticides and Toxic Substances, 401 M St. SW, Washington, District of Columbia 20460. (202) 260-2090. 1990.

Governmental Management of Chemical Risk. Rae Zimmerman. Lewis Publishers, 2000 Corporate Blvd., N.W., Boca Raton, Florida 33431. (407) 994-0555 or (800) 272-

7737. 1990. Covers managerial, legal and financial strategies that are or can be employed to manage the health risks posed by technology.

Hazard Assessment of Chemicals. Academic Press, c/o Harcourt Brace Jovanovich Inc., 6277 Sea Harbor Dr., Orlando, Florida 32887. (800) 346-8648. 1981-. Annually. Presents comprehensive authoritative reviews of new and significant developments in the area of hazard assessment of chemicals or chemical classes.

Hazards in the Chemical Laboratory. L. Bretherick, ed. Royal Society of Chemistry, c/o CRC Press, 2000 Corporate Blvd. N.W., Boca Raton, Florida 33431-9868. (800) 272-7737. 1986. 4th ed. Handbook of safety practices, measures and toxic effects for laboratories handling dangerous chemicals.

Human Health Risks from Chemical Exposure: The Great Lakes Ecosystem. R. Warren Flint. Lewis Publishers, 2000 Corporate Blvd., N.W., Boca Raton, Florida 33431. (407) 994-0555 or (800) 272-7737. 1991. Gives background on toxic chemicals in the Great Lakes. Also describes the toxicology and environmental chemistry of exposure to toxic chemicals, environmental and wildlife toxicology, epidemiology, public health and other related areas.

Immunoassays for Trace Chemical Analysis; Monitoring Toxic Chemicals in Humans, Food, and the Environment. Martin Vandelaan, et al. American Chemical Society, 1155 16th St., N.W., Washington, District of Columbia 20036. (202) 872-4600; (800) 227-5558. Deals with the use of immunoassays as alternative methods for conducting sampling for chemical residues in food and the environment, for natural toxins, and for monitoring human exposure to toxic chemicals.

Inorganic Contaminants of Surface Water; Research and Monitoring Priorities. James W. Moore. Springer-Verlag, 175 Fifth Ave., New York, New York 10010. (212) 460-1500 or (800) 777-4643. 1991. Inorganic contaminants of surface water in terms of production, sources, and residues, chemistry, bioaccumulation, toxic effects to aquatic organisms, health effects and drinking water.

Managing Environmental Risks. Air & Waste Management Association, PO Box 2861, Pittsburgh, Pennsylvania 15230. (412) 232-3444. 1990. Papers presented at the Air & Waste Management Association International Specialty Conference, held in October 1989 in Quebec City, contains topics such as risks related to hazardous waste sites, chemical contaminants, and biotechnology.

Methods for Assessing Exposure of Human and Non-Human Biota. R. G. Tardiff and B. D. Goldstein, eds. John Wiley & Sons, Inc., 605 3rd Ave., New York, New York 10158-0012. (212) 850-6000. 1991. Provides a critical and collective evaluation of approaches to chemical exposure assessment.

Pesticide Transformation Products: Fate and Significance in the Environment: Papers. L. Somasundaram and Joel R. Coats, eds. American Chemical Society, 1155 16th St. N.W., Washington, District of Columbia 20036. (202) 872-4600; (800) 227-5558. 1991. The significance and impact of pesticide products on the environment is discussed.

Prevention of Major Industrial Accidents. International Labour Office, 49 Sheridan Ave., Albany, New York 12210. (518) 436-9686. 1992. Provides guidance in setting up an administrative, legal and technical system for the control of installations producing, storing or using hazardous substances. Covers siting, analysis of risks, prevention, safe operation, emergency planning, and the duties and responsibilities of all those involved.

Proctor and Hughes' Chemical Hazards of the Workplace. G. J. Hathaway, et al. Global Professional Publications, 2805 McGraw Ave., PO Box 19539, Irvine, California 92713-9539. (800) 854-7179. 1991. Third edition. Includes 100 new chemicals and the new 1991 Threshold Limit Values. Gives a practical easy-to-use introduction to toxicology and hazards of over 600 chemicals most likely to be encountered in the workplace.

Response Manual for Combatting Spills of Floating Hazardous CHRIS Chemicals. National Technical Information Service, 5285 Port Royal Rd., Springfield, Virginia 22161. (703) 487-4650. Covers chemical spills, hazardous substance accidents, and marine pollution.

Risk Assessment for the Chemical Process Industries. Stone & Webster Engineering Corp. Global Professional Publications, 2805 McGraw Ave., PO Box 19539, Irvine, California 92713-9539. (800) 854-7179. 1991. Covers the performance and supervision of safety studies for chemical, petrochemical, and other process industries. Also includes hazard identification and assessment embraces methods for both detecting hazards and determining root causes.

Risk Assessment of Chemicals in the Environment. M. L. Richardson, ed. Royal Society of Chemistry, c/o CRC Press, 2000 Corporate Blvd. N.W., Boca Raton, Florida 33431-9868. (800) 272-7737. 1990. Covers both chemical and radioactive risk acceptance approaches to the control of chemical disasters, etc.

A Science of Impurity: Water Analysis in Nineteenth Century Britain. Christopher Hamlin. University of California Press, Berkeley, California 94720. (510) 642-4247. 1990. Presents a series of biographies of scientists and government officials responsible for London's water quality during a period of pressing need and sparse scientific knowledge. Also presents some chemical information, placing chemical and epidemiological concepts in perspective, which is needed to grasp the inconsistencies of water analysis in 19th-century Britain.

Silent Spring. Rachel Carson. Carolina Biological Supply Company, 2700 York Rd., Burlington, North Carolina 27215. (919) 584-0381. 1987.

Skin Penetration; Hazardous Chemicals at Work. Philippe Grandjean. Taylor & Francis, 79 Madison Ave., New York, New York 10016. (212) 725-1999 or (800) 821-8312. 1990. Mechanisms of percutaneous absorption and methods of evaluating its significance. Reviews different classes of chemicals, emphasizing those considered major skin hazards.

Toxic Chemical Releases and Your "Right-To-Know". U.S. Environmental Protection Agency, 401 M St. SW, Washington, District of Columbia 20460. (202) 260-2090. 1988.

Toxic Politics: Responding to Chemical Disasters. Cornell University Press, 124 Roberts Place, Ithaca, New York 14850. 1991.

Toxics in the Community: National and Local Perspectives. U.S. Environmental Protection Agency, Offices of Pesticides and Toxic Substances, 401 M St. SW, Washington, District of Columbia 20460. (202) 260-2090. 1990.

The Toxics Release Inventory: Executive Summary. U.S. Environmental Protection Agency, Office of Pesticides and Toxic Substances, 401 M St. SW, Washington, District of Columbia 20460. (202) 260-2090. 1989.

Wildlife Toxicology. Tony J. Peterle. Van Nostrand Reinhold, 115 5th Ave., New York, New York 10003. (212) 354-3232. 1991. Presents an historical overview of the toxicology problem and summarizes the principal laws, testing protocols, and roles of leading U.S. federal agencies, especially EPA. Examines state and local issues, monitoring programs, and contains an unique section on the regulation of toxic substances overseas.

Workplace Environmental Exposure Level Guide. American Industrial Hygiene Association, 345 White Pond Dr., Akron, Ohio 44320. (216) 873-2442. 1991-. Includes guidelines for benzophenone, butyraldehyde, sodium hypochlorite, and vinylcyclohexene.

HANDBOOKS AND MANUALS

Bretherick's Handbook of Reactive Chemical Hazards. L. Bretherick. Butterworth-Heinemann, 80 Montvale Ave., Stoneham, Massachusetts 02180. (617) 438-8464; (800) 366-2665. 1990. Lists compounds or elements in order by Hill chemical formula: to aid verification, the International Union of Pure and Applied Chemistry systematic name and the Chemical Abstracts Service Registry Number are recorded. Also lists chemicals that react in some violent fashion with the main chemical cited. A brief description of the type of reaction and citations to the literature in which the reaction was reported are included.

Chemical Information Manual. Government Institutes, Inc., 4 Research Pl., Ste. 200, Rockville, Maryland 20850. (301) 921-2300. 1991. Handbook presenting a variety of useful data on each chemical substances, including proper identification, OSHA exposure limits, description and physical properties, carcinogenic status, health effects and toxicology, sampling and analysis.

CHRIS: A Condensed Guide to Chemical Hazards. Washington, District of Columbia 1985. Covers chemical hazard response information system.

Concise Manual of Chemical and Environmental Safety in Schools and Colleges. Forum for Scientific Excellence. J. B. Lippincott, 227 E. Washington Sq., Philadelphia, Pennsylvania 19105. (215) 238-4200; (800) 982-4377. 1991.

CRC Handbook of Radiation Chemistry. Yoneho Tabata, ed. CRC Press, 2000 Corporate Blvd. N.W., Boca Raton, Florida 33431. (800) 272-7737. 1991. Covers broad fields from basic to applied in radiation chemistry and its related fields.

Groundwater Chemicals Desk Reference. John H. Montgomery. Lewis Publishers, 2000 Corporate Blvd. NW, Boca Raton, Florida 33431. (407) 994-0555 or (800)272-7737. 1990. Protection and remediation of the groundwater environment. Includes profiles of chemical compounds promulgated by the EPA under the Clean Water Act of 1977.

Groundwater Chemicals Desk Reference, Volume II. John Montgomery. Lewis Publishers, 2000 Corporate Blvd., N.W., Boca Raton, Florida 33431. (407) 994-0555 or (800) 272-7737. 1991. Contains abbreviations, symbols, chemicals, conversion factors, CAS index, RTECS number index empirical formula, and synonym index.

Handbook of Environmental Degradation Rates. Philip H. Howard, et al. Lewis Publishers, 2000 Corporate Blvd., N.W., Boca Raton, Florida 33431. (407) 994-0555 or (800) 272-7737. 1991. Provides rate constant and half-life ranges for various processes and combines them into ranges for different media (air, groundwater, surface water, soils) which can be directly entered into various models.

The Hazardous Chemicals on File Collection. Craig T. Norback. Facts on File, Inc., 460 Park Ave. S., New York, New York 10016. (212) 683-2244. A guide for the general public seeking up-to-date, authoritative information on the characteristics of, and protection against, hazardous materials in the workplace

Household Hazards: a Guide to Detoxifying Your Home. League of Women Voters of Albany County, 119 Washington Ave., Albany, New York 12207. 1988. Covers household supplies and appliances safety measures.

How to Respond to Hazardous Chemical Spills. W. Unterberg, et al. Noyes Publications, 120 Mill Rd., Park Ridge, New Jersey 07656. (201) 391-8484. 1988. Reference manual of countermeasures is designed to assist responders to spills of hazardous substances.

Laboratory Chemical Standards: The Complete OSHA Compliance Manual. Bureau of National Affairs, 1231 25th St. N.W., Washington, District of Columbia 20037. (800) 372-1033. 1990. OSHA's new lab standard applies to laboratories that use hazardous chemicals and requires a written plan that satisfies federal guidelines.

Manual for Preventing Spills of Hazardous Substances at Fixed Facilities. Hemisphere Publishing Co., 79 Madison Ave., Suite 1110, New York, New York 10016. (212) 725-1999. Environmental monitoring of chemical spills and hazardous substances.

NIOSH Pocket Guide to Chemical Hazards. National Institute for Occupational Safety and Health, 1600 Clifton Rd. NE, Atlanta, Georgia 30333. (404) 639-3286. 1990. Presents sources of general industrial hygiene and medical surveillance information for workers, employees and others. Presents key information and data in an abbreviated format for 398 individual chemicals or chemical types.

Solvents in Common Use: Health Risks to Workers. Royal Society of Chemistry, c/o CRC Press, 2000 Corporate Blvd. N.W., Boca Raton, Florida 33431-9868. (800) 272-7737. 1988. 1st reprint 1990. Handbook contains essential information on ten of the most commonly used solvents.

Suspect Chemicals Sourcebook. Roytech Publications, Inc., 7910 Woodmont Ave., Ste. 902, Bethesda, Maryland 20814. (301) 654-4281. 1985-. Includes: chemical name index, CAS registry numbers; OSHA Chemical Hazard chemical name; Summary and full text of OSHA Chemical Hazard Communication Standard and history and overview. Also available online.

Where Did That Chemical Go? A Practical Guide to Chemical Fate and Transport in the Environment. Ronald E. Ney. Van Nostrand Reinhold, 115 Fifth Ave., New York, New York 10003. (212) 254-3232. 1990. Offers predictive techniques for determining what happens to a chemical once it is accidently released, or intentionally placed, in air, water, soil, plants, and animals.

ONLINE DATA BASES

Asbestos Information System–AIS. U.S. Environmental Protection Agency, Office of Pesticides and Toxic Substances, 401 M St., SW, Washington, District of Columbia 20460. (202) 260-2090. Information on asbestos including chemical use, exposure, manufacturing, the human population, and environmental releases.

Chem-Bank. SilverPlatter Information, Inc., 37 Walnut St., Wellesley Hills, Massachusetts 02181. 617-239-0306. Registry of Toxic Effects of Chemical Substances; Oil and Hazardous Materials Technical Assistance Data System; Chemical Hazard Response Information System; and the Toxic Substances Control Act Initial Inventory.

Chemical Carcinogenesis Research Information System–CCRIS. National Library of Medicine, 8600 Rockville Pike, Bethesda, Maryland 20894. (800) 638-8480. Individual assay results and test conditions for 1,451 chemicals in the areas of carcinogenicity, mutagenicity, tumor promotion, and cocarcinogenicity.

Chemical Collection System/Request Tracking–CCS/RTS. U.S. Environmental Protection Agency, Office of Pesticides and Toxic Substances, 401 M St., SW, Washington, District of Columbia 20460. (202) 260-2090. Contains information on various properties of a number of chemicals including environmental effects, test and analysis methods, and health effects. Available from EPA.

Chemical Dictionary Online–CHEMLINE. Chemical Abstracts Service, 2540 Olentangy River Rd., Columbus, Ohio 43210. (614) 421-3600 or (800) 848-6533. Part of MEDLINE of the National Library of Medicine (NLM). File of 900,000 names for chemical substances, representing 450,000 unique compounds. It contains such information as Chemical Abstracts (CA) Service Registry Numbers, molecular formulas, preferred chemical nomenclature, and generic and ring structure information. Available on NLM's ELHILL system.

Chemical Engineering. McGraw-Hill Science & Engineering Books, 11 W. 19th St., New York, New York 10011. (212) 337-6010. Online version of periodical of the same name.

Chemical Exposure. Science Applications International Corp., Health & Environmental Information, P.O. Box 2501, Oak Ridge, Tennessee 37831. (615) 482-9031. Database of chemicals that have been identified in both human tissues and body fluids and in feral and food animals. Contains reference to journal articles, conferences, and reports. Covers the whole fields of information related to human and animal exposure to food, air, and water contaminants and pharmaceuticals. Its records include information on chemical properties, formulas, tissues measured, analytical method used, demographics and more. Available on DIALOG.

Chemical Information File. OSHA Salt Lake City Analytical Laboratory, 1781 S. 300 W., Salt Lake City, Utah 84165-0200. (801) 524-5287. Database is part of the OSHA Computerized Information System (OCIS) and contains chemical substances found in the workplace with current information on identification, exposure limits, compliance sampling methods, and analytical methods.

Chemical Regulation Reporter. Bureau of National Affairs, BNA PLUS, 1231 25th St., N.W., Room 215, Washington, District of Columbia 20037. (800) 452-7773. Online version of periodicals of the same name.

Chemical Regulations and Guidelines System–CRGS. Network Management, 11242 Waples Mill Rd., Fairfax, Virginia 22030. (703) 359-9400. Maintains bibliographical information on the state of regulatory material, October 1982 to the present, on control of selected chemical substances or classes. It contains U.S. Statutes, promulgated regulations, available government standards and guidelines, and support documents. CRGS follows the regulatory cycle and includes a reference to each document including main documents and revisions in the Federal Register. Available on DIALOG.

Enviro/Energyline Abstracts Plus. R. R. Bowker Co., 121 Chanlon Rd., New Providence, New Jersey 07974. (908) 464-6800.

Enviroline. R. R. Bowker Co., Bowker Electronic Publishing, 121 Chanlon Rd., New Providence, New Jersey 07974. (800) 521-8110.

Environmental Bibliography. Environmental Studies Institute, International Academy at Santa Barbara, 800 Garden St., Ste. D, Santa Barbara, California 93101. (805) 965-5010. International periodical literature dealing with environmental topics such as air pollution, water treatment, energy conservation, noise abatement, soil mechanics, wildlife preservation, and chemical wastes.

Environmental Health News. Occupational Health Services, Inc., 450 7th Ave., New York, New York 10123. (212) 967-1100. Online access to court decisions, regulatory changes, and medical and scientific news related to hazardous substances.

Environmental Periodicals Bibliography. National Information Services Corp., Ste. 6, Wyman Towers, 3100 St. Paul St., Baltimore, Maryland 21218. (410)243-0797. Online version of abstract of same name.

Epidemiology Information System. Oak Ridge National Laboratory, Toxicology Information Response Center, Building 2001, P.O. Box 2008, Oak Ridge, Tennessee 37831-6050. (615) 576-1746.

HADB. National Library of Medicine, Toxicology Information Program, 8600 Rockville Pike, Bethesda, Maryland 20894. (800) 638-8480.

HAZINF. University of Alberta, Department of Chemistry, Edmonton, Alberta, Canada T6G 2G2. (403) 432-3254.

Information System for Hazardous Organics in Water. U.S. Environmental Protection Agency, Office of Pesticides & Toxic Substances, 401 M St., S.W., Washington, District of Columbia 20460. (202) 260-2090.

Integrated Risk Information System - IRIS. US Environomental Protection Agency. Toxicology Data Network (TOXNET), 8600 Rockville Pike, Bethesda, Maryland 20894. (301) 496-1131. Quarterly. Effects of chemicals on human health and information on reference doses and carcinogen assessments.

Medical Toxicology and Environmental Health. Department of Health and Social Security, Medical Toxiclology & Environmental Health Division, Hannibal House, Rm. 719, Elephant and Castle, London, England SE1 6TE. 44 (71) 972-2162.

Monthly Catalog of United States Government Publications. U.S. G.P.O., Supt. of Docs., PO Box 371954, Pittsburgh, Pennsylvania 15250-7954. (202) 512-0000.

National Technical Information Service. U.S. Department of Commerce, National Technical Information Service, Office of Data Base Services, 5285 Port Royal Rd., Springfield, Virginia 22161. (703) 487-4807. Bibliographic database of government sponsored research and technical reports.

PressNet Environmental Reports. Chemical Information Systems, Inc., 7215 York Rd., Baltimore, Maryland 21212. (301) 321-8440.

Registry of Toxic Effects of Chemical Substances–Online1. US Department of Health and Human Services, National Institute for Occupational Safety and Health, Washington, District of Columbia 20402-9325. (202) 783-3238. Tests on chemical substances: Substance Identification, Toxicity/Biomedical Effects, Toxicology and Carcinogenicity Review, and Exposure Standards and Regulations.

REPRORISK System. Micromedex, Inc., 600 Grant St., Denver, Colorado 80203. (800) 525-9083 or (303) 831-1400. Reproductive risks to females and males caused by drugs, chemicals, and physical and environmental agents. Includes the Teratogen Information System (TERIS), which deals with the teratogenicity of over 700 drugs and environmental agents that affect a fetus. One of the additional modules under development is the REPRO-TEXT database, containing a ranking system for reproductive hazards and the general toxicity of over 600 chemicals, emphasizing chronic occupational exposures.

Suspect Chemicals Sourcebook. Roytech Publications, Inc., 7910 Woodmont Ave., Ste. 902, Bethesda, Maryland 20814. (301) 654-4281. References to U.S. federal regulations and precautionary data pertaining to the manufacture, sale, storage, use, and transportation of more than 5,000 industrial chemical substances. Online version of handbook of the same name.

PERIODICALS AND NEWSLETTERS

Applied and Environmental Microbiology Journal. American Society for Microbiology, 1325 Massachusetts Avenue N.W., Washington, District of Columbia 20005. (202) 737-3600. Monthly. Articles on industrial and food microbiology and ecological studies.

Bulletin of Environmental Contamination and Toxicology. Springer-Verlag, 175 5th Ave., New York, New York 10010. (212) 460-1500; (800) 777-4643. 1966-. Frequency varies. Disseminates advances and discoveries in the areas of soil, air and food contamination and pollution.

ChemEcology. Chemical Manufacturers Association, 2501 M St. NW, Washington, District of Columbia 20037. (202) 887-1100. Monthly. Articles on how the chemical industry deals with environmental issues.

Chemical & Engineering News. American Chemical Society, 1155 16th St. N.W., Washington, District of Columbia 20036. (800) 227-5558. Weekly. Cites technical and business developments in the chemical process industry.

Chemical Engineering. McGraw-Hill Science & Engineering Books, 11 W. 19th St., New York, New York 10011. (212) 337-6010. Monthly. Articles on new engineering techniques and equipment. Also available online.

Chemical Regulation Reporter. Bureau of National Affairs, 1231 25th St. NW, Washington, District of Columbia 20037. (202) 452-4200. Weekly. Periodical covering legislative, regulatory, and industry action affecting controls on pesticides. Also available online.

Community and Worker Right-to-Know News. Thompson Publishing Group, 1725 K St. NW, Washington, District of Columbia 20006. (800) 424-2959. Bimonthly. Reports on chemical disclosure requirements and industrial liability.

Drug and Chemical Toxicology. Marcel Dekker, Inc., 270 Madison Ave., New York, New York 10016. (212) 696-9000. Quarterly. Covers safety evaluations of drugs and chemicals.

Ecotoxicology and Environmental Safety. Academic Press, c/o Harcourt Brace Jovanovich Inc., 6277 Sea Harbor Dr., Orlando, Florida 32887. (800) 346-8648. 1977-. Bimonthly.

Environmental Health News. University of Washington, School of Public Health, Dept. of Environmental Health, Seattle, Washington 98195. (206) 543-3222. Quarterly. Occupational health, air pollution and safety.

Environmental Toxicology and Chemistry. Society of Environmental Toxicology and Chemistry. Pergamon Microforms International, Inc., Fairview Park, Elmsford, New York 10523. (914) 592-7720. 1981-. Monthly. Contains information on environmental toxicology, and chemistry, including the application of science to hazard assessment.

Focus. Hazardous Materials Control Research Institute, 9300 Columbia Blvd, Silver Spring, Maryland 20910-1702. (301) 587-9390. Monthly. Covers hazardous materials technology and legislation.

Food and Chemical Toxicology. Pergamon Microforms International Inc., Fairview Park, Elmsford, New York 10523. (914) 592-7720. Monthly. Information and risks of food and chemicals.

HAZCHEM Alert. Van Nostrand Reinhold, 115 Fifth Ave., New York, New York 10003. (212) 254-3232. Biweekly. Covers hazardous chemical news and information.

Journal of Environmental Science and Health. Marcel Dekker, Inc., 270 Madison Ave., New York, New York 10016. (212) 696-9000. Bimonthly. Concerns pesticides, food contaminants, chemical carcinogens, and agricultural wastes.

Oil and Chemical Pollution. Elsevier Science Publishing Co., 655 Avenue of the Americas, New York, New York 10010. (212) 989-5800. Technology of spills and clean-ups.

Waste Age. National Solid Waste Management Association, 1730 Rhode Island Avenue, NW, Ste. 1000, Washington, District of Columbia 20036. (202) 659-4613. Monthly. Covers control and use of solid, hazardous and liquid wastes.

TRADE ASSOCIATIONS AND PROFESSIONAL SOCIETIES

American Chemical Society. 1155 16th St., N.W., Washington, District of Columbia 20036. (202) 872-4600.

Chemical Manufacturers Association. 2501 M St., N.W., Washington, District of Columbia 20037. (202) 887-1100.

Chemical Waste Transportation Council. 1730 Rhode Island Ave., N.W., Suite 1000, Washington, District of Columbia 20036. (202) 659-4613.

Oil, Chemical, & Atomic Workers International Union. Box 2812, Denver, Colorado 80201. (303) 987-2229.

Pulp Chemicals Association. P.O. Box 105113, Atlanta, Georgia 30348. (404) 446-1290.

Rachel Carson Council. 8940 Jones Mill Rd., Chevy Chase, Maryland 20815. (301) 652-1877.

Society of Toxicology. 1101 14th St., N.W., Suite 1100, Washington, District of Columbia 20005. (202) 371-1393.

CHEMICAL CONTROLS

See: PESTICIDES

CHEMICAL INDICATOR

See also: WATER QUALITY

ABSTRACTING AND INDEXING SERVICES

Biological Abstracts. BIOSIS, 2100 Arch St., Philadelphia, Pennsylvania 19103-1399. (215) 587-4800. 1927-.

Environment Abstracts. Bowker A & I Publishing, 121 Chanlon Rd., New Providence, New Jersey 07974. (908) 464-6800. 1974-.

Environment Index. Environment Information Center, Index Research Department, 124 E. 39th St., New York, New York 10016. 1971-. Annual.

Environmental Information Connection–EIC. Planning Information Program, Dept. of Urban and Regional Planning, University of Illinois, 1003 West Nevada, Urbana, Illinois 61801. (217) 333-1369. Also available online.

Environmental Periodicals Bibliography. Environmental Studies Institute, International Academy at Santa Barbara, 800 Garden St., Suite D, Santa Barbara, California 93101. (805) 965-5010. Also available online.

General Science Index. H. W. Wilson Co., 950 University Ave., Bronx, New York 10452. 1978-. Monthly, also issued in annual cumulation. Cumulative subject index to English language periodicals in the subject fields of astronomy, botany, chemistry, earth science, environment and conservation, food and nutrition, genetics, mathematics, medicine and health, microbiology, oceanography, physics, physiology and zoology.

Index to Scientific Book Contents. Institute for Scientific Information, 3501 Market St., Philadelphia, Pennsylvania 19104. (800) 523-1857. 1985-. Annual. Gives contents of science books published.

BIBLIOGRAPHIES

EPA Publications Bibliography. U.S. Environmental Protection Agency, Library Systems Branch, 401 M St., SW, Washington, District of Columbia 20460. (202) 260-2090. Quarterly.

ENCYCLOPEDIAS AND DICTIONARIES

Dictionary of Environmental Engineering and Related Sciences: English-Spanish, Spanish-English. Jose T. Villate. Ediciones Universal, 3090 SW 8th St., Miami, Florida 33135. (305) 642-3355. 1979.

Encyclopedia of Environmental Science and Engineering. J.R. Pfafflin. Gordon and Breach Science Publishers, Inc., 270 8th Ave., New York, New York 10011. (212) 206-8900. 1992.

McGraw-Hill Encyclopedia of Environmental Science. Sybil P. Parker. McGraw-Hill Science & Engineering Books, 11 W. 19th St., New York, New York 10011. (212) 337-6010. 1980. Covers ecology, man's influence on nature, and environmental protection.

ONLINE DATA BASES

BIOSIS Previews. BIOSIS, 2100 Arch St., Philadelphia, Pennsylvania 19103-1399. (215) 587-4800. Largest and most comprehensive database of research in the life sciences. Contains citations for nearly 9000 primary research journals, monographs, reviews, symposia, preliminary reports, semi-popular journals, selected institutional reports, government reports and research communications.

Chemical Collection System/Request Tracking–CCS/RTS. U.S. Environmental Protection Agency, Office of Pesticides and Toxic Substances, 401 M St., SW, Washington, District of Columbia 20460. (202) 260-2090. Contains information on various properties of a number of chemicals including environmental effects, test and analysis methods, and health effects. Available from EPA.

Chemical Dictionary Online–CHEMLINE. Chemical Abstracts Service, 2540 Olentangy River Rd., Columbus, Ohio 43210. (614) 421-3600 or (800) 848-6533. Part of MEDLINE of the National Library of Medicine (NLM). File of 900,000 names for chemical substances, representing 450,000 unique compounds. It contains such information as Chemical Abstracts (CA) Service Registry Numbers, molecular formulas, preferred chemical nomenclature, and generic and ring structure information. Available on NLM's ELHILL system.

Chemical Exposure. Science Applications International Corp., Health & Environmental Information, P.O. Box 2501, Oak Ridge, Tennessee 37831. (615) 482-9031. Database of chemicals that have been identified in both human tissues and body fluids and in feral and food animals. Contains reference to journal articles, conferences, and reports. Covers the whole fields of information related to human and animal exposure to food, air, and water contaminants and pharmaceuticals. Its records include information on chemical properties, formulas, tissues measured, analytical method used, demographics and more. Available on DIALOG.

Enviro/Energyline Abstracts Plus. R. R. Bowker Co., 121 Chanlon Rd., New Providence, New Jersey 07974. (908) 464-6800.

Environmental Periodicals Bibliography. National Information Services Corp., Ste. 6, Wyman Towers, 3100 St. Paul St., Baltimore, Maryland 21218. (410)243-0797. Online version of abstract of same name.

TRADE ASSOCIATIONS AND PROFESSIONAL SOCIETIES

American Chemical Society. 1155 16th St., N.W., Washington, District of Columbia 20036. (202) 872-4600.

CHEMICAL OXYGEN DEMAND

See also: BIOLOGICAL OXYGEN DEMAND; WATER POLLUTION; WATER QUALITY

ABSTRACTING AND INDEXING SERVICES

Biological Abstracts. BIOSIS, 2100 Arch St., Philadelphia, Pennsylvania 19103-1399. (215) 587-4800. 1927-.

General Science Index. H. W. Wilson Co., 950 University Ave., Bronx, New York 10452. 1978-. Monthly, also issued in annual cumulation. Cumulative subject index to English language periodicals in the subject fields of astronomy, botany, chemistry, earth science, environment and conservation, food and nutrition, genetics, mathematics, medicine and health, microbiology, oceanography, physics, physiology and zoology.

Index to Scientific Book Contents. Institute for Scientific Information, 3501 Market St., Philadelphia, Pennsylvania 19104. (800) 523-1857. 1985-. Annual. Gives contents of science books published.

Pollution Abstracts. Cambridge Scientific Abstracts, 5161 River Rd., Bethesda, Maryland 20816. (301) 961-6750. Six/year. Indexes worldwide technical literature on environmental pollution. Covers air pollution, marine and freshwater pollution, sewage and wastewater treatment, waste management, toxicology and health, noise pollution, radiation, land pollution, and environmental policies, programs, legislation, and education. Also available online.

BIBLIOGRAPHIES

Current Contents. Agriculture, Biology and Environmental Sciences. Institute for Scientific Information, 3501 Market St., Philadelphia, Pennsylvania 19104. (800) 523-1857. 1973-. Previous title: Current Contents. Agricultural, Food & Veterinary Sciences. Gives the table of contents of periodicals in the fields of agriculture, biology, environmental and related areas.

ENCYCLOPEDIAS AND DICTIONARIES

McGraw-Hill Encyclopedia of Environmental Science. Sybil P. Parker. McGraw-Hill Science & Engineering Books, 11 W. 19th St., New York, New York 10011. (212) 337-6010. 1980. Covers ecology, man's influence on nature, and environmental protection.

Van Nostrand's Scientific Encyclopedia. Glenn D. Considine, ed. Van Nostrand Reinhold, 115 5th Ave., New York, New York 10003. (212) 254-3232. 1983. Sixth edition. Includes all broad subject areas in science.

ONLINE DATA BASES

BIOSIS Previews. BIOSIS, 2100 Arch St., Philadelphia, Pennsylvania 19103-1399. (215) 587-4800. Largest and most comprehensive database of research in the life sciences. Contains citations for nearly 9000 primary research journals, monographs, reviews, symposia, preliminary reports, semi-popular journals, selected institutional reports, government reports and research communications.

Monthly Catalog of United States Government Publications. U.S. G.P.O., Supt. of Docs., PO Box 371954, Pittsburgh, Pennsylvania 15250-7954. (202) 512-0000.

National Technical Information Service. U.S. Department of Commerce, National Technical Information Service, Office of Data Base Services, 5285 Port Royal Rd., Springfield, Virginia 22161. (703) 487-4807. Bibliographic database of government sponsored research and technical reports.

TRADE ASSOCIATIONS AND PROFESSIONAL SOCIETIES

American Chemical Society. 1155 16th St., N.W., Washington, District of Columbia 20036. (202) 872-4600.

American Institute of Biological Sciences. 730 11th St., N.W., Washington, District of Columbia 20001-4521. (202) 628-1500.

CHEMICAL PRECIPITATION
See: ACID PRECIPITATION

CHEMICAL PURIFICATION
See: ACID PRECIPITATION

CHEMICAL RESIDUES
See: CHEMICAL CONTAMINATION

CHEMICAL SPILLS
See: CHEMICAL CONTAMINATION

CHEMICAL STORAGE

ABSTRACTING AND INDEXING SERVICES

Chemical Abstracts. Chemical Abstracts Service, 2540 Olentangy River Rd., PO Box 3012, Columbus, Ohio 43210. (800) 848-6533. 1907-.

Engineering Index. The Engineering Index Inc., 345 E. 47th St., New York, New York 10017. 1962-.

Environment Abstracts. Bowker A & I Publishing, 121 Chanlon Rd., New Providence, New Jersey 07974. (908) 464-6800. 1974-.

Environment Index. Environment Information Center, Index Research Department, 124 E. 39th St., New York, New York 10016. 1971-. Annual.

Environmental Information Connection–EIC. Planning Information Program, Dept. of Urban and Regional Planning, University of Illinois, 1003 West Nevada, Urbana, Illinois 61801. (217) 333-1369. Also available online.

Environmental Periodicals Bibliography. Environmental Studies Institute, International Academy at Santa Barbara, 800 Garden St., Suite D, Santa Barbara, California 93101. (805) 965-5010. Also available online.

BIBLIOGRAPHIES

EPA Publications Bibliography. U.S. Environmental Protection Agency, Library Systems Branch, 401 M St., SW, Washington, District of Columbia 20460. (202) 260-2090. Quarterly.

ENCYCLOPEDIAS AND DICTIONARIES

Ullmanns Encyclopedia of Industrial Chemistry. Hans Jurgen Arpe and Wolfgang Gerhartz, eds. VCH Publishers, 303 NW 12th Ave., Deerfield Beach, Florida 33442-1788. (305) 428-5566. 1990. Designed to keep up with the broad spectrum of chemical technology. Thirty-six volumes of the encyclopedia have been divided into two sets: the 28 A volumes contain alphabetically arranged articles on chemicals, product groups, processes and technological concepts; and the 8 B volumes are compendia of basic knowledge in industrial chemistry.

GENERAL WORKS

Ultrapurity; Methods and Techniques. Marcel Dekker, Inc., 270 Madison Ave., New York, New York 10016. (212) 696-9000. 1972. Purification of chemicals and chemical storage.

HANDBOOKS AND MANUALS

Handbook of Acid-Proof Construction. Friedrich Karl Flacke. VCH Publishers, 303 NW 12th Ave., Deerfield Beach, Florida 33442-1788. (305) 428-5566. 1985. Details the equipment and supplies used in chemical plants and how corrosion affects them.

ONLINE DATA BASES

CAS Source Index–CASSI. Chemical Abstracts Service, 2540 Olentangy River Rd., P.O. Box 3012, Columbus, Ohio 43210. (800) 848-6533 or (614) 421-3600. A listing of bibliographic and library holdings information for scientific and technical primary literature relevant to the chemical sciences.

Chemical Abstracts-CA. Chemical Abstracts Service, 2540 Olentangy River Rd., P.O. Box 3012, Columbus, Ohio 43210. (800) 848-6533 or (614) 421-3600. Information sources include 9000 journals, patents from 27 countries, two industrial property organizations, new books, conference proceedings, and government research reports.

Computerized Engineering Index–COMPENDEX. Engineering Information Inc., 345 E. 47th St., New York, New York 10017. (212) 705-7600.

Enviro/Energyline Abstracts Plus. R. R. Bowker Co., 121 Chanlon Rd., New Providence, New Jersey 07974. (908) 464-6800.

Environmental Periodicals Bibliography. National Information Services Corp., Ste. 6, Wyman Towers, 3100 St. Paul St., Baltimore, Maryland 21218. (410)243-0797. Online version of abstract of same name.

Suspect Chemicals Sourcebook. Roytech Publications, Inc., 7910 Woodmont Ave., Ste. 902, Bethesda, Maryland 20814. (301) 654-4281. References to U.S. federal regulations and precautionary data pertaining to the manufacture, sale, storage, use, and transportation of more than 5,000 industrial chemical substances. Online version of handbook of the same name.

PERIODICALS AND NEWSLETTERS

Chemical Times & Trends. Chemical Specialties Manufacturers Association, 1913 Eye Street, NW, Washington, District of Columbia 20006. (202) 872-8110. Quarterly. Discusses trends in manufacturing/selling of industrial, household, and personal care products.

Chemist. American Institute of Chemists, 7315 Wisconsin Avenue, Bethesda, Maryland 20814. (301) 652-2447. Monthly. Covers topics of professional interest to chemists and chemical engineers.

TRADE ASSOCIATIONS AND PROFESSIONAL SOCIETIES

American Chemical Society. 1155 16th St., N.W., Washington, District of Columbia 20036. (202) 872-4600.

American Institute of Chemical Engineers. 345 East 47th St., New York, New York 10017. (212) 705-7338.

American Institute of Chemists. 7315 Wisconsin Ave., Bethesda, Maryland 20814. (301) 652-2447.

CHEMICAL TREATMENTS
See: PESTICIDES

CHEMICAL WASTES
See also: HAZARDOUS WASTES

ABSTRACTING AND INDEXING SERVICES

Applied Ecology Abstracts Studies in Renewable Natural Resources. Information Retrieval Ltd., 1911 Jefferson Davis Highway, Arlington, Virginia 22202. 1975-. Monthly.

Biological and Agricultural Index. H.W. Wilson Co., 950 University Ave., Bronx, New York 10452. (800) 367-6770. 1916-. Monthly.

Chemical Abstracts. Chemical Abstracts Service, 2540 Olentangy River Rd., PO Box 3012, Columbus, Ohio 43210. (800) 848-6533. 1907-.

Environment Abstracts. Bowker A & I Publishing, 121 Chanlon Rd., New Providence, New Jersey 07974. (908) 464-6800. 1974-.

Environment Index. Environment Information Center, Index Research Department, 124 E. 39th St., New York, New York 10016. 1971-. Annual.

Environmental Information Connection–EIC. Planning Information Program, Dept. of Urban and Regional Planning, University of Illinois, 1003 West Nevada, Urbana, Illinois 61801. (217) 333-1369. Also available online.

Environmental Periodicals Bibliography. Environmental Studies Institute, International Academy at Santa Barbara, 800 Garden St., Suite D, Santa Barbara, California 93101. (805) 965-5010. Also available online.

General Science Index. H. W. Wilson Co., 950 University Ave., Bronx, New York 10452. 1978-. Monthly, also issued in annual cumulation. Cumulative subject index to English language periodicals in the subject fields of astronomy, botany, chemistry, earth science, environment and conservation, food and nutrition, genetics, mathematics, medicine and health, microbiology, oceanography, physics, physiology and zoology.

Index to Scientific Book Contents. Institute for Scientific Information, 3501 Market St., Philadelphia, Pennsylvania 19104. (800) 523-1857. 1985-. Annual. Gives contents of science books published.

Multimedia Index to Ecology. National Information Center for Educational Media, University of Southern California, Los Angeles, California 90007.

Pollution Abstracts. Cambridge Scientific Abstracts, 5161 River Rd., Bethesda, Maryland 20816. (301) 961-6750. Six/year. Indexes worldwide technical literature on environmental pollution. Covers air pollution, marine and freshwater pollution, sewage and wastewater treatment, waste management, toxicology and health, noise pollution, radiation, land pollution, and environmental policies, programs, legislation, and education. Also available online.

BIBLIOGRAPHIES

Current Contents. Agriculture, Biology and Environmental Sciences. Institute for Scientific Information, 3501 Market St., Philadelphia, Pennsylvania 19104. (800) 523-1857. 1973-. Previous title: Current Contents. Agricultural, Food & Veterinary Sciences. Gives the table of contents of periodicals in the fields of agriculture, biology, environmental and related areas.

Directory of Published Proceedings. Interdok Corp., 173 Halstead Ave., Harrison, New York 10528. (914) 835-3506. 1990. Monthly. This is a listing of published proceedings including the series SEMTE (Science/Medicine/Engineering/Technology) and the series SSH (Social Science/Humanities).

EPA Publications Bibliography. U.S. Environmental Protection Agency, Library Systems Branch, 401 M St., SW, Washington, District of Columbia 20460. (202) 260-2090. Quarterly.

DIRECTORIES

Directory of Chemical Waste Transporters. Chemical Waste Transport Institute. National Solid Waste Management Association, 1730 Rhode Island Ave. N.W., Suite 1000, Washington, District of Columbia 20036. (202) 659-4613. 1989.

Synthetic Organic Chemicals: U.S. Production and Sales. United States International Trade Commission, 500 E St., S.W., Washington, District of Columbia 20436. (202) 523-0161.

Water Environment & Technology–Buyer's Guide and Yearbook. Water Pollution Control Federation, 601 Wythe St., Alexandria, Virginia 22314-1994. (703) 684-2400.

ENCYCLOPEDIAS AND DICTIONARIES

McGraw-Hill Encyclopedia of Environmental Science. Sybil P. Parker. McGraw-Hill Science & Engineering Books, 11 W. 19th St., New York, New York 10011. (212) 337-6010. 1980. Covers ecology, man's influence on nature, and environmental protection.

Ullmanns Encyclopedia of Industrial Chemistry. Hans Jurgen Arpe and Wolfgang Gerhartz, eds. VCH Publishers, 303 NW 12th Ave., Deerfield Beach, Florida 33442-1788. (305) 428-5566. 1990. Designed to keep up with the broad spectrum of chemical technology. Thirty-six volumes of the encyclopedia have been divided into two sets: the 28 A volumes contain alphabetically arranged articles on chemicals, product groups, processes and technological concepts; and the 8 B volumes are compendia of basic knowledge in industrial chemistry.

GENERAL WORKS

Inside the Poison Trade. Coronet/MTI Film & Video, 108 Wilmot Rd., Deerfield, Illinois 60015. 1990. This video shows what the Greenpeace organization is doing to stop chemical waste export to Africa, as well as the efforts of other organizations.

HANDBOOKS AND MANUALS

Bretherick's Handbook of Reactive Chemical Hazards. L. Bretherick. Butterworth-Heinemann, 80 Montvale Ave., Stoneham, Massachusetts 02180. (617) 438-8464; (800) 366-2665. 1990. Lists compounds or elements in order by Hill chemical formula: to aid verification, the International Union of Pure and Applied Chemistry systematic name and the Chemical Abstracts Service Registry Number are recorded. Also lists chemicals that react in some violent fashion with the main chemical cited. A brief description of the type of reaction and citations to the literature in which the reaction was reported are included.

Synthetic Organic Chemicals. U.S. G.P.O., Washington, District of Columbia 20401. (202) 512-0000. 1967. An annual publication on production and sales in the U.S. for all synthetic organic chemicals produced commercially. About 800 chemicals and 800 manufacturers are included in the USITC surveys, but because of confidentiality requirements only parts of the data are published. U.S. Tariff Commission acts under the provisions of Section 332 of the Tariff Act of 1930, as amended.

ONLINE DATA BASES

CAS Source Index–CASSI. Chemical Abstracts Service, 2540 Olentangy River Rd., P.O. Box 3012, Columbus, Ohio 43210. (800) 848-6533 or (614) 421-3600. A listing of bibliographic and library holdings information for scientific and technical primary literature relevant to the chemical sciences.

Chem-Bank. SilverPlatter Information, Inc., 37 Walnut St., Wellesley Hills, Massachusetts 02181. 617-239-0306. Registry of Toxic Effects of Chemical Substances; Oil and Hazardous Materials Technical Assistance Data

System; Chemical Hazard Response Information System; and the Toxic Substances Control Act Initial Inventory.

Chemical Abstracts-CA. Chemical Abstracts Service, 2540 Olentangy River Rd., P.O. Box 3012, Columbus, Ohio 43210. (800) 848-6533 or (614) 421-3600. Information sources include 9000 journals, patents from 27 countries, two industrial property organizations, new books, conference proceedings, and government research reports.

Chemical Collection System/Request Tracking–CCS/ RTS. U.S. Environmental Protection Agency, Office of Pesticides and Toxic Substances, 401 M St., SW, Washington, District of Columbia 20460. (202) 260-2090. Contains information on various properties of a number of chemicals including environmental effects, test and analysis methods, and health effects. Available from EPA.

Chemical Dictionary Online–CHEMLINE. Chemical Abstracts Service, 2540 Olentangy River Rd., Columbus, Ohio 43210. (614) 421-3600 or (800) 848-6533. Part of MEDLINE of the National Library of Medicine (NLM). File of 900,000 names for chemical substances, representing 450,000 unique compounds. It contains such information as Chemical Abstracts (CA) Service Registry Numbers, molecular formulas, preferred chemical nomenclature, and generic and ring structure information. Available on NLM's ELHILL system.

Chemical Exposure. Science Applications International Corp., Health & Environmental Information, P.O. Box 2501, Oak Ridge, Tennessee 37831. (615) 482-9031. Database of chemicals that have been identified in both human tissues and body fluids and in feral and food animals. Contains reference to journal articles, conferences, and reports. Covers the whole fields of information related to human and animal exposure to food, air, and water contaminants and pharmaceuticals. Its records include information on chemical properties, formulas, tissues measured, analytical method used, demographics and more. Available on DIALOG.

Enviro/Energyline Abstracts Plus. R. R. Bowker Co., 121 Chanlon Rd., New Providence, New Jersey 07974. (908) 464-6800.

Environmental Periodicals Bibliography. National Information Services Corp., Ste. 6, Wyman Towers, 3100 St. Paul St., Baltimore, Maryland 21218. (410)243-0797. Online version of abstract of same name.

Monthly Catalog of United States Government Publications. U.S. G.P.O., Supt. of Docs., PO Box 371954, Pittsburgh, Pennsylvania 15250-7954. (202) 512-0000.

National Technical Information Service. U.S. Department of Commerce, National Technical Information Service, Office of Data Base Services, 5285 Port Royal Rd., Springfield, Virginia 22161. (703) 487-4807. Bibliographic database of government sponsored research and technical reports.

SCISEARCH. Institute for Scientific Information, University City Science Center, 3501 Market St., Philadelphia, Pennsylvania 19104. (215) 386-0100.

PERIODICALS AND NEWSLETTERS

Ecotoxicology and Environmental Safety. Academic Press, c/o Harcourt Brace Jovanovich Inc., 6277 Sea Harbor Dr., Orlando, Florida 32887. (800) 346-8648. 1977-. Bimonthly.

Synthetic Organic Chemical Manufacturers Association Newsletter. Synthetic Organic Chemical Manufacturers Association, 1330 Connecticut Avenue, NW, Washington, District of Columbia 20036. (202) 659-0060. Bi-weekly. Covers trade, environmental and safety issues.

RESEARCH CENTERS AND INSTITUTES

Statewide Air Pollution Research Center. University of California, Riverside, Riverside, California 92521. (714) 787-5124.

TRADE ASSOCIATIONS AND PROFESSIONAL SOCIETIES

American Chemical Society. 1155 16th St., N.W., Washington, District of Columbia 20036. (202) 872-4600.

American Institute of Biological Sciences. 730 11th St., N.W., Washington, District of Columbia 20001-4521. (202) 628-1500.

Chemical Waste Transportation Council. 1730 Rhode Island Ave., N.W., Suite 1000, Washington, District of Columbia 20036. (202) 659-4613.

Institute of Chemical Waste Management. 1730 Rhode Island Ave., N.W., Suite 1000, Washington, District of Columbia 20036. (202) 659-4613.

International Society of Chemical Ecology. University of South Florida, Dept. of Biology, Tampa, Florida 33620. (813) 974-2336.

Pulp Chemicals Association. P.O. Box 105113, Atlanta, Georgia 30348. (404) 446-1290.

Synthetic Organic Chemical Manufacturers Association. 1330 Connecticut Ave., N.W., Suite 300, Washington, District of Columbia 20036. (202) 659-0060.

CHEMICAL WEAPONS

ABSTRACTING AND INDEXING SERVICES

Chemical Abstracts. Chemical Abstracts Service, 2540 Olentangy River Rd., PO Box 3012, Columbus, Ohio 43210. (800) 848-6533. 1907-.

Index to Scientific Book Contents. Institute for Scientific Information, 3501 Market St., Philadelphia, Pennsylvania 19104. (800) 523-1857. 1985-. Annual. Gives contents of science books published.

ENCYCLOPEDIAS AND DICTIONARIES

McGraw-Hill Encyclopedia of Science and Technology. McGraw-Hill, 1221 Avenue of the Americas, New York, New York 10020. (212) 512-2000 or (800) 262-4729. 1992. Seventh edition. Issued in multiple volumes including index. Includes all science and technology broad subject areas.

HANDBOOKS AND MANUALS

Destruction of Chemical Weapons and Defense Equipment to Prevent Enemy Use. Headquarters, Dept. of the Army, Washington, District of Columbia 20310. (202)

695-6153. 1992. Deals with demolition in the military and explosive ordnance disposal.

ONLINE DATA BASES

CAS Source Index–CASSI. Chemical Abstracts Service, 2540 Olentangy River Rd., P.O. Box 3012, Columbus, Ohio 43210. (800) 848-6533 or (614) 421-3600. A listing of bibliographic and library holdings information for scientific and technical primary literature relevant to the chemical sciences.

CERCLIS. Chemical Information Systems, Inc., 7215 York Rd., Baltimore, Maryland 21212. (301) 321-8440. Information on hazardous waste disposal sites that have either been listed by the EPA on the National Priority List (NPL) or nominated for consideration for the NPL.

Chemical Abstracts-CA. Chemical Abstracts Service, 2540 Olentangy River Rd., P.O. Box 3012, Columbus, Ohio 43210. (800) 848-6533 or (614) 421-3600. Information sources include 9000 journals, patents from 27 countries, two industrial property organizations, new books, conference proceedings, and government research reports.

Life Sciences from NTIS. National Technical Information Center for the Utilization of Federal Technology, 5285 Port Royal Rd., Springfield, Virginia 22161. (703) 487-4650.

TRADE ASSOCIATIONS AND PROFESSIONAL SOCIETIES

American Chemical Society. 1155 16th St., N.W., Washington, District of Columbia 20036. (202) 872-4600.

CHEMICALS (ORGANIC, INORGANIC, AND SYNTHETIC)

See also: INDUSTRIAL CHEMICALS

ABSTRACTING AND INDEXING SERVICES

Biological Abstracts. BIOSIS, 2100 Arch St., Philadelphia, Pennsylvania 19103-1399. (215) 587-4800. 1927-.

Chemical Abstracts. Chemical Abstracts Service, 2540 Olentangy River Rd., PO Box 3012, Columbus, Ohio 43210. (800) 848-6533. 1907-.

Index to Scientific Book Contents. Institute for Scientific Information, 3501 Market St., Philadelphia, Pennsylvania 19104. (800) 523-1857. 1985-. Annual. Gives contents of science books published.

ALMANACS AND YEARBOOKS

Registry of Toxic Effects of Chemical Substances. Doris V. Sweet, ed. U.S. Department of Health and Human Services, National Institute for Occupational Safety and Health, Washington, District of Columbia 20402-9325. (202) 783-3238. 1988. Contains information on over 35,000 chemicals.

DIRECTORIES

Blue Book and Catalog Edition of Soap and Chemical Specialties. McNairr-Dorland Co., 101 W. 31st, New York, New York 10001. 1955-. Annually.

Chem Sources–International. Directories Publishing Co., Box 1824, Clemson, South Carolina 29633. (803) 646-7840.

Chemcyclopedia. American Chemical Society, 1155 16th St. N.W., Washington, District of Columbia 20036. (800) 227-5558.

Chemical Engineering Catalog. 600 Summer St., Stamford, Connecticut 06904. (203) 348-7531. Annual.

Chemical Guide to the United States. Noyes Publications, 120 Mill Rd., Park Ridge, New Jersey 07656. (201) 391-8484.

Chemical Week–Financial Survey of the 300 Largest Companies in the U.S. Chemical Process Industries Issue. 816 7th Ave., New York, New York 10019. (212) 586-3430. Annual.

Chemical Wholesalers Directory. American Business Directories, Inc., 5711 S. 86th Circle, Omaha, Nebraska 68127. (402) 593-4600.

Chemicals Directory. Kevin R. Fitzgerald. Cahners Publishing Co., 249 W. 17th St., New York, New York 10011. (212) 645-0067. 1991. Covers manufacturers and suppliers of chemicals and raw materials, containers and packaging, transportation services and storage facilities, and environmental services companies.

Directory of Chemical Producers. Chemical Information Services, Inc., Stanford Research Institute, Menlo Park, California 94305-2235. 1973-. Lists both plants and products for 1,300 companies and approximately 10,000 commercial chemicals. Some information on capacity, process, and raw materials is included for major chemicals.

Directory of World Chemical Producers. Chemical Information Services, Inc., PO Box 8344, University Station, Dallas, Texas 75205. (214) 340-4345. 1991. Contains 48,355 alphabetically listed product titles (including cross-references), manufactured by 5,152 chemical producers in 60 countries on five continents.

Fine Chemicals Directory. Molecular Design Ltd., 2132 Farrallon Dr., San Leandro, California 94577. (415) 895-1313.

OPD Chemical Buyer's Directory. Chemical Marketing Reporter, Schnell Pub. Co., 80 Broad St., New York, New York 10004-2203. (212) 248-4177. 1992. Seventy-ninth edition. Known as the "Green Book", this buyer's directory includes an index of chemical suppliers, branch offices, a glossary, an 800 phone directory for quick supplier reference. Also includes the chemfile folio of company catalogs, chemicals and related materials listings, and other related data.

Synthetic Organic Chemicals: U.S. Production and Sales. United States International Trade Commission, 500 E St., S.W., Washington, District of Columbia 20436. (202) 523-0161.

ENCYCLOPEDIAS AND DICTIONARIES

Chem Address Book. F. W. Derz, ed. Walter De Gruyter, New York, New York 1974. Includes over 180000 names (synonyms) in alphabetical order for chemical compounds and chemicals, radioactive labelled compounds, isotopes, dyes, polymers, etc. and their molecular formulas.

Chem Sources–USA. Chemical Sources International Inc., PO Box 1884, Ormond Beach, Florida 32175-1884. Annual. Includes chemical nomenclature of some 130,000 chemicals of all classifications, trade name index, classified/trade name, company directory, and company index. Also includes paid advertising.

Compendium of Hazardous Chemicals in Schools and Colleges. Forum for Scientific Excellence. J. B. Lippincott, 227 E. Washington Sq., Philadelphia, Pennsylvania 19105. (215) 238-4200; (800) 982-4377. 1990. Encyclopedia of more than 950 hazardous chemicals found in academic institutions. Contains all the data necessary for identifying these chemicals and their hazardous effects.

The Condensed Chemical Dictionary. Gessner G. Hawley. Van Nostrand Reinhold, 115 5th Ave., New York, New York 10003. (212) 254-3232. 1981. 10th ed.

Hazardous Chemicals Desk Reference. Richard J. Lewis. Van Nostrand Reinhold, 115 Fifth Ave., New York, New York 10003. (212) 254-3232. 1991. Information on the hazardous properties of some 5500 chemicals commonly encountered in industry, laboratories, environment, and the workplace.

Kirk-Othmer Encyclopedia of Chemical Technology. J. I. Kroschwitz, ed. John Wiley & Sons, Inc., 605 3rd Ave., New York, New York 10158-0012. (212) 850-6000. 1992-. All articles in the new edition have been rewritten and updated adding new subjects such as biotechnology, computer topics, analytical techniques and instrumentation, environmental concerns, fuels and energy, inorganic and solid state chemistry; composite materials and material science in general, and pharmaceuticals. Also available online.

Ullmanns Encyclopedia of Industrial Chemistry. Hans Jurgen Arpe and Wolfgang Gerhartz, eds. VCH Publishers, 303 NW 12th Ave., Deerfield Beach, Florida 33442-1788. (305) 428-5566. 1990. Designed to keep up with the broad spectrum of chemical technology. Thirty-six volumes of the encyclopedia have been divided into two sets: the 28 A volumes contain alphabetically arranged articles on chemicals, product groups, processes and technological concepts; and the 8 B volumes are compendia of basic knowledge in industrial chemistry.

GENERAL WORKS

Fundamentals of Laboratory Safety: Physical Hazards in the Academic Laboratory. William J. Mahn. Van Nostrand Reinhold, 115 5th Ave., New York, New York 10003. (212) 254-3232. 1991. Discusses safety methods in chemical laboratories, accident prevention and the various hazardous materials in use in the labs.

Organic Chemistry of the Earth's Atmosphere. Valerii A. Isidorov. Springer-Verlag, 175 5th Ave., New York, New York 10010. (212) 460-1500; (800) 777-4643. 1990. Describes the composition of atmosphere; distribution of organic components in space and time; natural sources; human- created sources; atmosphere organic reactions methods of analysis.

Public Policy for Chemicals: National and International Issues. Conservation Foundation, 1250 24th St., NW, Washington, District of Columbia 20037. (202) 293-

4800. 1980. Legal aspects of chemicals and hazardous substances.

Sources of Ignition: Flammability Characteristics of Chemicals and Products. John Bond. Butterworth-Heinemann, 80 Montvale Ave., Stoneham, Massachusetts 02180. (617) 438-8464; (800) 366-2665. 1991.

Supplier Notification Requirements. U.S. Environmental Protection Agency, Office of Pesticides and Toxic Substances, 401 M St., SW, Washington, District of Columbia 20460. (202) 260-2090. 1990. Legal aspects of reporting on chemicals and hazardous wastes.

Survey of Chemicals Tested for Carcinogenicity. Science Resource Center, Kensington, Maryland 1976. Entries from scientific literature from approximately 1913 to 1973, reporting on groups of animals treated with any chemical compounds and subsequently examined for tumors.

Treatment Potential for 56 EPA Listed Hazardous Chemicals in Soil. Ronald C. Sims, et al. Robert S. Kerr Environmental Research Laboratory, U.S. Environmental Protection Agency, PO Box 1198, Ada, Oklahoma 74820. (405) 332-8800. 1988.

GOVERNMENTAL ORGANIZATIONS

National Science Foundation. 1800 G St., N.W., Washington, District of Columbia 20550. (202) 357-9498.

HANDBOOKS AND MANUALS

Bretherick's Handbook of Reactive Chemical Hazards. L. Bretherick. Butterworth-Heinemann, 80 Montvale Ave., Stoneham, Massachusetts 02180. (617) 438-8464; (800) 366-2665. 1990. Lists compounds or elements in order by Hill chemical formula: to aid verification, the International Union of Pure and Applied Chemistry systematic name and the Chemical Abstracts Service Registry Number are recorded. Also lists chemicals that react in some violent fashion with the main chemical cited. A brief description of the type of reaction and citations to the literature in which the reaction was reported are included.

Catalog Handbook of Fine Chemicals. Aldrich Chemical Co., 1001 W. St. Paul Ave., Milwaukee, Wisconsin 53233. (414) 273-3850 or (800) 558-9160. 1990/1991. Contains more than 27,000 products of which over 4,000 are new. Includes: chemicals, equipment, glassware, books, software, research products, bulk quantities, new products, custom synthesis and rare chemicals.

Chemical Economics Handbook. SRI International, 333 Rovenswood Ave., Menlo Park, California 14025-3493. (415) 859-4771. 1983-. 33 vols. Provides an in-depth evaluation of the present and future economic status of major chemical substances

Chemical Information Manual. Government Institutes, Inc., 4 Research Pl., Ste. 200, Rockville, Maryland 20850. (301) 921-2300. 1991. Handbook presenting a variety of useful data on each chemical substances, including proper identification, OSHA exposure limits, description and physical properties, carcinogenic status, health effects and toxicology, sampling and analysis.

Chemical Products Desk Reference. Michael and Irene Ash. Chemical Publishing Co., 80 Eighth Ave., New York, New York 10011. (212) 255-1950. Contains over

32,000 entries of currently marketed commercial chemical trademark products.

Concise Manual of Chemical and Environmental Safety in Schools and Colleges. Forum for Scientific Excellence. J. B. Lippincott, 227 E. Washington Sq., Philadelphia, Pennsylvania 19105. (215) 238-4200; (800) 982-4377. 1991.

Crop Protection Chemical Reference. Chemical and Pharmaceutical Press/Wiley, 605 3rd Ave., New York, New York 10158-0012. (212) 850-6000. 1991. 7th ed. Updated annual edition of a standard reference on label information on crop protection chemicals contains the complete text of some 540 product labels, which provide detailed information concerning what products can be used to treat a certain crop for certain problems, using what quantities of the chemical and under what restrictions and precautions. Appendices provide useful information on such matters as coding required when transporting products, safety practices, calibrations, etc.

Cross-Reference Index of Hazardous Chemicals, Synonyms, and CAS Registry Numbers. The Forum for Scientific Excellence. J. B. Lippincott, 227 E. Washington Sq., Philadelphia, Pennsylvania 19105. (215) 238-4200; (800) 982-4377. 1990. Contains more than 50,000 synonyms for the hazardous chemicals and environmental pollutants identified. Comprehensive resource title available for properly identifying common names, chemical names and product names associated with these chemicals.

Economic Analysis of Proposed Revised Effluent Guidelines and Standards for the Inorganic Chemicals Industry. National Technical Information Service, 5285 Port Royal Rd., Springfield, Virginia 22161. (703) 487-4650. 1980. Covers effluent quality and sewage purification technology.

Groundwater Chemicals Desk Reference. John H. Montgomery. Lewis Publishers, 2000 Corporate Blvd. NW, Boca Raton, Florida 33431. (407) 994-0555 or (800)272-7737. 1990. Protection and remediation of the groundwater environment. Includes profiles of chemical compounds promulgated by the EPA under the Clean Water Act of 1977.

Handbook of Chemical Property Estimation Methods. Warren J. Lyman, et al. McGraw-Hill Science & Engineering Books, 11 W. 19th St., New York, New York 10011. (212) 337-6010. 1982.

Handbook of Chemistry and Physics. CRC Press, 2000 Corporate Blvd. N.W., Boca Raton, Florida 33431. (800) 272-7737. Annually.

Handbook of Environmental Data on Organic Chemicals. Karel Verschueren. Van Nostrand Reinhold, 115 5th Ave., New York, New York 10003. (212) 254-3232. 1983. Covers individual substances as well as mixtures and preparations. The profiles include: properties, air pollution factors, water pollution factors, and biological effects.

Hazardous Materials Spills Emergency Handbook. American Water Works Association, 6666 W. Quincy Ave., Denver, Colorado 80235. (303) 794-7711. Covers chemical safety measures, water pollution, and water purification.

Purification of Laboratory Chemicals. Douglas Dalzell Perrin. Pergamon Microforms International, Inc., Fair-

view Park, Elmsford, New York 10523. (914) 592-7720. Deals with chemical purification technology.

Suspect Chemicals Sourcebook. Roytech Publications, Inc., 7910 Woodmont Ave., Ste. 902, Bethesda, Maryland 20814. (301) 654-4281. 1985-. Includes: chemical name index, CAS registry numbers; OSHA Chemical Hazard chemical name; Summary and full text of OSHA Chemical Hazard Communication Standard and history and overview. Also available online.

Synthetic Organic Chemicals. U.S. G.P.O., Washington, District of Columbia 20401. (202) 512-0000. 1967. An annual publication on production and sales in the U.S. for all synthetic organic chemicals produced commercially. About 800 chemicals and 800 manufacturers are included in the USITC surveys, but because of confidentiality requirements only parts of the data are published. U.S. Tariff Commission acts under the provisions of Section 332 of the Tariff Act of 1930, as amended.

Turf and Ornamental Chemicals Reference. John Wiley & Sons, Inc., 605 3rd Ave., New York, New York 10158-0012. (212) 850-6000. 1990. Provides with a consolidated and fully cross-indexed set of chemical product labels and material safety data sheets (MSDA's) in one easily accessible source. Products are indexed in 6 separate color coded indexes as follows: Brand name quick reference; manufacturer; product category; common and chemical name; and plant and site use and pet use.

Where Did That Chemical Go? A Practical Guide to Chemical Fate and Transport in the Environment. Ronald E. Ney. Van Nostrand Reinhold, 115 Fifth Ave., New York, New York 10003. (212) 254-3232. 1990. Offers predictive techniques for determining what happens to a chemical once it is accidently released, or intentionally placed, in air, water, soil, plants, and animals.

ONLINE DATA BASES

Aqua II. Institution of Chemical Engineers, PPDS Department, George E. Davis Building, 165-171 Railway Terrace, Rugby, England CV21 3HQ. 44 (788) 78214.

BAKER. St. Baker Inc., 222 Red School Lane, Phillipsburg, New Jersey 08865. (201) 859-2151.

Beilstein Online. Beilstein Institute, Varrentrappstrasse 40-42, 6000 Frankfurt am Main 90, Germany 49 (69) 79171.

BIOSIS Previews. BIOSIS, 2100 Arch St., Philadelphia, Pennsylvania 19103-1399. (215) 587-4800. Largest and most comprehensive database of research in the life sciences. Contains citations for nearly 9000 primary research journals, monographs, reviews, symposia, preliminary reports, semi-popular journals, selected institutional reports, government reports and research communications.

CA Search. Chemical Abstracts Service, 2540 Olentangy River Rd., P.O. Box 3012, Columbus, Ohio 43210. (800) 848-6533.

CAB Abstracts. C. A. B. International, Wallingford, England OX11 8DE. 44 (491) 32111.

CASREACT. Chemical Abstracts Service, 2540 Olentangy River Rd., P.O. Box 3012, Columbus, Ohio 43210. (800) 848-6533.

CASSI. Chemical Abstracts Service, 2540 Olentangy River Rd., P.O. Box 3012, Columbus, Ohio 43210. (800) 848-6533.

CEH On-Line. SRI International, Chemical Economics Handbook Program, 333 Ravenwood Ave., Menlo Park, California 14025. (415) 859-5039.

CEHINDEX. SRI International, Chemical Economics Handbook Program, 333 Ravenwood Ave., Menlo Park, California 14025. (415) 859-5039.

CERCLIS. Chemical Information Systems, Inc., 7215 York Rd., Baltimore, Maryland 21212. (301) 321-8440. Information on hazardous waste disposal sites that have either been listed by the EPA on the National Priority List (NPL) or nominated for consideration for the NPL.

CESARS. State of Michigan, Department of Natural Resources, Great Lakes & Environmental Assessment Section, P.O. Box 30028, Lansing, Michigan 45909. (517) 373-2190.

Chem-Bank. SilverPlatter Information, Inc., 37 Walnut St., Wellesley Hills, Massachusetts 02181. 617-239-0306. Registry of Toxic Effects of Chemical Substances; Oil and Hazardous Materials Technical Assistance Data System; Chemical Hazard Response Information System; and the Toxic Substances Control Act Initial Inventory.

CHEM-INTELL–Chemical Trade and Production Statistics Database. Chemical Intelligence Services, 39A Bowling Green Lane, London, England EC1R. OBJ 44 (71) 833-3812.

Chemical Abstracts-CA. Chemical Abstracts Service, 2540 Olentangy River Rd., P.O. Box 3012, Columbus, Ohio 43210. (800) 848-6533 or (614) 421-3600. Information sources include 9000 journals, patents from 27 countries, two industrial property organizations, new books, conference proceedings, and government research reports.

Chemical Age Project File. MBC Information Services Ltd., Paulton House, 8 Shepherdess Walk, London, England N1 7LB. 44 (71) 490-0049.

Chemical Collection System/Request Tracking–CCS/RTS. U.S. Environmental Protection Agency, Office of Pesticides and Toxic Substances, 401 M St., SW, Washington, District of Columbia 20460. (202) 260-2090. Contains information on various properties of a number of chemicals including environmental effects, test and analysis methods, and health effects. Available from EPA.

Chemical Dictionary Online–CHEMLINE. Chemical Abstracts Service, 2540 Olentangy River Rd., Columbus, Ohio 43210. (614) 421-3600 or (800) 848-6533. Part of MEDLINE of the National Library of Medicine (NLM). File of 900,000 names for chemical substances, representing 450,000 unique compounds. It contains such information as Chemical Abstracts (CA) Service Registry Numbers, molecular formulas, preferred chemical nomenclature, and generic and ring structure information. Available on NLM's ELHILL system.

Chemical Engineering. McGraw-Hill Science & Engineering Books, 11 W. 19th St., New York, New York 10011. (212) 337-6010. Online version of periodical of the same name.

Chemical Engineering and Biotechnology Abstracts–CEBA. Orbit Search Service, Maxwell Online Inc., 8000 W. Park Dr., McLean, Virginia 22102. (703) 442-0900 or (800) 456-7248. Monthly. Covers theoretical, practical and commercial material on all aspects of processing safety, and the environment. Also covers process and reaction engineering, measurement and process control, environmental protection and safety, plant design and equipment used in chemical engineering and biotechnology. More than 400 of the world's major primary chemical and process engineering journals are scanned to compile the database. Available from ORBIT.

Chemical Exposure. Science Applications International Corp., Health & Environmental Information, P.O. Box 2501, Oak Ridge, Tennessee 37831. (615) 482-9031. Database of chemicals that have been identified in both human tissues and body fluids and in feral and food animals. Contains reference to journal articles, conferences, and reports. Covers the whole fields of information related to human and animal exposure to food, air, and water contaminants and pharmaceuticals. Its records include information on chemical properties, formulas, tissues measured, analytical method used, demographics and more. Available on DIALOG.

Chemical Hazard Response Information System–CHRIS. U.S. Coast Guard. Office of Research and Development, 2100 2d St., NW., Rm. 5410 C, Washington, District of Columbia 20593. (202) 783-3238. Contains information needed to respond to emergencies that occur during the transport of hazardous chemicals, as well as information that can help prevent emergency situations. Each of the approximately 1,300 records include information on physical and chemical properties, health and fire hazards, labeling, chemical reactivity, hazard classification and water pollution. Available on CIS and on Microdex's TOMES Plus series.

Chemical Industry Notes–CHEMSIS. Chemical Abstracts Service, PO Box 3012, 2540 Olentangy River, Columbus, Ohio 43210. (614) 421-3600 or (800) 848-6533. Contains citations to business-oriented literature relating to the chemical processing industries. Includes pricing, production, products and processes, corporate and government activities, facilities and people from more than 80 worldwide business periodicals published since 1974. Available on DIALOG and ORBIT.

Chemical Information File. OSHA Salt Lake City Analytical Laboratory, 1781 S. 300 W., Salt Lake City, Utah 84165-0200. (801) 524-5287. Database is part of the OSHA Computerized Information System (OCIS) and contains chemical substances found in the workplace with current information on identification, exposure limits, compliance sampling methods, and analytical methods.

Chemical Regulation Reporter. Bureau of National Affairs, BNA PLUS, 1231 25th St., N.W., Room 215, Washington, District of Columbia 20037. (800) 452-7773. Online version of periodicals of the same name.

Chemical Substance Control. Bureau of National Affairs, BNA PLUS, 1231 25th ST., N.W., Rm. 215, Washington, District of Columbia 20037. (800) 452-7773. Online version of periodical of the same name.

Chemical Week. Chemical Week Associates, 816 7th Ave., New York, New York 10019. (212) 586-3430. Online version of periodical of the same name.

ChemQuest. Molecular Design Ltd., 2132 Farrallon Dr., San Leandro, California 94577. (415) 895-1313.

CHEMTRAN. ChemShare Corporation, P.O. Box 1885, Houston, Texas 77251. (713) 627-8945.

CJACS: Chemical Journals of the American Chemical Society. American Chemical Society, 1155 16th St. N.W., Washington, District of Columbia 20036. (800) 227-5558.

CJAOAC: Chemical Journals of the Association of Official Analytical Chemists. Association of Official Analytical Chemists, 2200 Wilson Blvd., Suite 400-P, Arlington, Virginia 22201-3301. (703) 522-3032.

CJELSEVIER. Elsevier Science Publishing Co., Excerpta Medica, Molemverf 1, 1014 AG Amsterdam, Netherlands 31 (20) 5803507.

Current Contents Search. Institute for Scientific Information, 3501 Market St., Philadelphia, Pennsylvania 19104. (800) 523-1857.

EMIS. TECNON (U.K.) Limited, 12 Calico House, Plantation Wharf, York Place, Battersea, London, England SW11 3TN. 44 (71) 924-3955.

Environmental Fate Databases. Syracuse Research Cooperation, Merrill Lane, Syracuse, New York 13210. (312) 426-3200. Environmental fate of chemicals.

*F*A*C*T: Facility for the Analysis of Chemical Thermodynamics.* Thermfact, Ltd., 447 Berwick Ave., Mont-Royal, Quebec, Canada H3R 1Z8.

Fine Chemical Database. Chemron, Inc., 3038 Orchard Hill, San Antonio, Texas 78230-3057. (512) 493-2247.

Global Indexing System. U.S. Environmental Protection Agency, 401 M St., S.W., Washington, District of Columbia 20460. (202) 260-2090. International information on various qualities of chemicals.

Gmelin Formula Index. Gmelin Institut fuer Anorganische Chemie der Max-Planck- Gellschaft zur Foerderung der Wissenschaften, Varrentrappstrasse 40-42, Frankfurt, Germany D-6000. 49 (69) 7917-577.

HODOC: Handbook of Data on Organic Compounds. CRC Press, 2000 Corporate Blvd. N.W., Boca Raton, Florida 33431. (800) 727-7737.

Inorganic Crystal Structure Database. Institute of Inorganic Chemistry, University of Bonn, Gerhard-Domagk-Strasse-1, Bonn 1, Germany D-5300. 49 (228) 732657.

IRSS. U.S. Environmental Protection Agency, CIS Project, 401 M St., S.w., Washington, District of Columbia 20460. (202) 260-2090.

KEMI-INFO. Danish National Institute of Occupational Health, Produktregestret, Lerso Parkalle 105, Copenhagen 0, Denmark 45 (31) 299711.

Kirk-Othmer Encyclopedia of Chemical Technology. John Wiley & Sons, Inc., 605 3rd Ave., 5th Floor, New York, New York 10158. (212) 850-6000. Online version of the publication of the same name.

The Merck Index Online. Merck & Company, Inc., Box 2000, Building 86-0900, Rahway, New Jersey 07065-0900. (201) 855-4558.

POLYMAT. Deutsches Kunststoff-Institut, Schlossgartenstrasse 6, D-6100 Darmstadt, Germany 49 (6151) 162106.

REPRORISK System. Micromedex, Inc., 600 Grant St., Denver, Colorado 80203. (800) 525-9083 or (303) 831-

1400. Reproductive risks to females and males caused by drugs, chemicals, and physical and environmental agents. Includes the Teratogen Information System (TERIS), which deals with the teratogenicity of over 700 drugs and environmental agents that affect a fetus. One of the additional modules under development is the REPRO-TEXT database, containing a ranking system for reproductive hazards and the general toxicity of over 600 chemicals, emphasizing chronic occupational exposures.

Suspect Chemicals Sourcebook. Roytech Publications, Inc., 7910 Woodmont Ave., Ste. 902, Bethesda, Maryland 20814. (301) 654-4281. References to U.S. federal regulations and precautionary data pertaining to the manufacture, sale, storage, use, and transportation of more than 5,000 industrial chemical substances. Online version of handbook of the same name.

PERIODICALS AND NEWSLETTERS

Analytical Chemistry. American Chemical Society, 1155 16th St. N.W., Washington, District of Columbia 20036. (800) 227-5558. 1929-. Bimonthly. Articles for chemists, life scientists and engineers.

Chemical Engineering. McGraw-Hill Science & Engineering Books, 11 W. 19th St., New York, New York 10011. (212) 337-6010. Monthly. Articles on new engineering techniques and equipment. Also available online.

Chemical Regulation Reporter. Bureau of National Affairs, 1231 25th St. NW, Washington, District of Columbia 20037. (202) 452-4200. Weekly. Periodical covering legislative, regulatory, and industry action affecting controls on pesticides. Also available online.

Chemical Substances Control. Bureau of National Affairs, 1231 25th St. NW, Washington, District of Columbia 20037. (202) 452-4200. Biweekly. Periodical covering regulatory compliance and management of chemicals. Also available online.

Chemical Week. Chemical Week Associates, 816 7th Ave., New York, New York 10019. (212) 586-3430. Online version of the periodical of the same name.

Chemist. American Institute of Chemists, 7315 Wisconsin Avenue, Bethesda, Maryland 20814. (301) 652-2447. Monthly. Covers topics of professional interest to chemists and chemical engineers.

Journal of Analytical Toxicology. Preston Publications, PO Box 48312, 7800 Merrimac, Niles, Illinois 60648. (708) 965-0566. Bimonthly. Articles on industrial toxicology, environmental pollution and pharmaceuticals.

Journal of Chemical Ecology. Plenum Press, 233 Spring St., New York, New York 10013-1578. (212) 620-8000. Monthly. Articles on the origin, function, and significance of natural chemicals.

The Merck Index. Merck Co., Inc., Box 2000, Rahway, New Jersey 07065. (201) 855-4558. Data on chemicals, drugs, and biological substances.

Synthetic Organic Chemical Manufacturers Association Newsletter. Synthetic Organic Chemical Manufacturers Association, 1330 Connecticut Avenue, NW, Washington, District of Columbia 20036. (202) 659-0060. Biweekly. Covers trade, environmental and safety issues.

STATISTICS SOURCES

Fine Chemicals. FIND/SVP, 625 Avenue of the Americas, New York, New York 10011. (212) 645-4500. 1990.

TRADE ASSOCIATIONS AND PROFESSIONAL SOCIETIES

American Chemical Society. 1155 16th St., N.W., Washington, District of Columbia 20036. (202) 872-4600.

American Council on Science and Health. 1995 Broadway, 16th Floor, New York, New York 10023. (212) 362-7044.

American Institute of Chemical Engineers. 345 East 47th St., New York, New York 10017. (212) 705-7338.

American Institute of Chemists. 7315 Wisconsin Ave., Bethesda, Maryland 20814. (301) 652-2447.

Association of Official Analytical Chemists. 2200 Wilson Blvd., Suite 400, Arlington, Virginia 22201-3301. (703) 522-3032.

Chemical Manufacturers Association. 2501 M St., N.W., Washington, District of Columbia 20037. (202) 887-1100.

Chemical Referral Center. c/o Chemical Manufacturers Association, 2501 M St., N.W., Washington, District of Columbia 20037. (202) 887-1100.

International Society of Chemical Ecology. University of South Florida, Dept. of Biology, Tampa, Florida 33620. (813) 974-2336.

Petrochemical Energy Group. 1100 15th St., N.W., Suite 1200, Washington, District of Columbia 20005. (202) 452-1880.

Synthetic Organic Chemical Manufacturers Association. 1330 Connecticut Ave., N.W., Suite 300, Washington, District of Columbia 20036. (202) 659-0060.

CHEMILUMINESCENCE

ABSTRACTING AND INDEXING SERVICES

Applied Ecology Abstracts Studies in Renewable Natural Resources. Information Retrieval Ltd., 1911 Jefferson Davis Highway, Arlington, Virginia 22202. 1975-. Monthly.

Applied Science and Technology Index. H.W. Wilson Co., 950 University Ave., Bronx, New York 10452. (800) 367-6770. Formerly Industrial Arts Index.

Biological Abstracts. BIOSIS, 2100 Arch St., Philadelphia, Pennsylvania 19103-1399. (215) 587-4800. 1927-.

Biological and Agricultural Index. H.W. Wilson Co., 950 University Ave., Bronx, New York 10452. (800) 367-6770. 1916-. Monthly.

Chemical Abstracts. Chemical Abstracts Service, 2540 Olentangy River Rd., PO Box 3012, Columbus, Ohio 43210. (800) 848-6533. 1907-.

General Science Index. H. W. Wilson Co., 950 University Ave., Bronx, New York 10452. 1978-. Monthly, also issued in annual cumulation. Cumulative subject index to English language periodicals in the subject fields of astronomy, botany, chemistry, earth science, environ-ment and conservation, food and nutrition, genetics, mathematics, medicine and health, microbiology, oceanography, physics, physiology and zoology.

Index to Scientific Book Contents. Institute for Scientific Information, 3501 Market St., Philadelphia, Pennsylvania 19104. (800) 523-1857. 1985-. Annual. Gives contents of science books published.

Multimedia Index to Ecology. National Information Center for Educational Media, University of Southern California, Los Angeles, California 90007.

Pollution Abstracts. Cambridge Scientific Abstracts, 5161 River Rd., Bethesda, Maryland 20816. (301) 961-6750. Six/year. Indexes worldwide technical literature on environmental pollution. Covers air pollution, marine and freshwater pollution, sewage and wastewater treatment, waste management, toxicology and health, noise pollution, radiation, land pollution, and environmental policies, programs, legislation, and education. Also available online.

Science Citation Index. Institute for Scientific Information, 3501 Market St., Philadelphia, Pennsylvania 19104. 1961-.

ENCYCLOPEDIAS AND DICTIONARIES

Encyclopedia of Human Biology. Renato Dulbecco, ed. Academic Press, c/o Harcourt Brace Jovanovich Inc., 6277 Sea Harbor Dr., Orlando, Florida 32887. (800) 346-8648. 1991. Eight volumes.

Encyclopedia of Physics. Rita G. Lerner and George L. Trigg. VCH Publishers, 303 NW 12th Ave., Deerfield Beach, Florida 33442-1788. (305) 428-5566. 1991. Second edition.

McGraw-Hill Encyclopedia of Science and Technology. McGraw-Hill, 1221 Avenue of the Americas, New York, New York 10020. (212) 512-2000 or (800) 262-4729. 1992. Seventh edition. Issued in multiple volumes including index. Includes all science and technology broad subject areas.

GENERAL WORKS

Cellular Chemiluminescence. CRC Press, 2000 Corporate Blvd. N.W., Boca Raton, Florida 33431. (800) 272-7737. 1987.

Chemiluminescence: Principles and Applications in Biology and Medicine. CCH Publishers, Inc., 220 E. 23rd St., Suite 909, New York, New York 10010-4606. (212) 683-8333. 1988.

ONLINE DATA BASES

BIOSIS Previews. BIOSIS, 2100 Arch St., Philadelphia, Pennsylvania 19103-1399. (215) 587-4800. Largest and most comprehensive database of research in the life sciences. Contains citations for nearly 9000 primary research journals, monographs, reviews, symposia, preliminary reports, semi-popular journals, selected institutional reports, government reports and research communications.

Chemical Abstracts-CA. Chemical Abstracts Service, 2540 Olentangy River Rd., P.O. Box 3012, Columbus, Ohio 43210. (800) 848-6533 or (614) 421-3600. Information sources include 9000 journals, patents from 27 countries, two industrial property organizations, new

books, conference proceedings, and government research reports.

Chemical Collection System/Request Tracking–CCS/ RTS. U.S. Environmental Protection Agency, Office of Pesticides and Toxic Substances, 401 M St., SW, Washington, District of Columbia 20460. (202) 260-2090. Contains information on various properties of a number of chemicals including environmental effects, test and analysis methods, and health effects. Available from EPA.

Chemical Dictionary Online–CHEMLINE. Chemical Abstracts Service, 2540 Olentangy River Rd., Columbus, Ohio 43210. (614) 421-3600 or (800) 848-6533. Part of MEDLINE of the National Library of Medicine (NLM). File of 900,000 names for chemical substances, representing 450,000 unique compounds. It contains such information as Chemical Abstracts (CA) Service Registry Numbers, molecular formulas, preferred chemical nomenclature, and generic and ring structure information. Available on NLM's ELHILL system.

Chemical Exposure. Science Applications International Corp., Health & Environmental Information, P.O. Box 2501, Oak Ridge, Tennessee 37831. (615) 482-9031. Database of chemicals that have been identified in both human tissues and body fluids and in feral and food animals. Contains reference to journal articles, conferences, and reports. Covers the whole fields of information related to human and animal exposure to food, air, and water contaminants and pharmaceuticals. Its records include information on chemical properties, formulas, tissues measured, analytical method used, demographics and more. Available on DIALOG.

SCISEARCH. Institute for Scientific Information, University City Science Center, 3501 Market St., Philadelphia, Pennsylvania 19104. (215) 386-0100.

PERIODICALS AND NEWSLETTERS

CA Selects: Chemiluminescence. Chemical Abstracts Services, 2540 Olentangy River Rd., Box 3012, Columbus, Ohio 43210. (800) 848-6533. Biweekly.

CHEMISTRY, ENVIRONMENTAL

HANDBOOKS AND MANUALS

Handbook of Environmental Data on Organic Chemicals. Karel Verschueren. Van Nostrand Reinhold, 115 5th Ave., New York, New York 10003. (212) 254-3232. 1983. Covers individual substances as well as mixtures and preparations. The profiles include: properties, air pollution factors, water pollution factors, and biological effects.

ONLINE DATA BASES

Chemical Hazard Response Information System–CHRIS. U.S. Coast Guard. Office of Research and Development, 2100 2d St., NW., Rm. 5410 C, Washington, District of Columbia 20593. (202) 783-3238. Contains information needed to respond to emergencies that occur during the transport of hazardous chemicals, as well as information that can help prevent emergency situations. Each of the

approximately 1,300 records include information on physical and chemical properties, health and fire hazards, labeling, chemical reactivity, hazard classification and water pollution. Available on CIS and on Microdex's TOMES Plus series.

Environmental Fate Databases. Syracuse Research Cooperation, Merrill Lane, Syracuse, New York 13210. (312) 426-3200. Environmental fate of chemicals.

TRADE ASSOCIATIONS AND PROFESSIONAL SOCIETIES

National Institute for Chemical Studies. 2300 MacCorkle Ave., S.E., Charleston, West Virginia 25304. (304) 346-6264.

CHEMOSYNTHESIS

See also: AUTOTROPHIC; ECOSYSTEMS; NUTRITION

ABSTRACTING AND INDEXING SERVICES

Applied Ecology Abstracts Studies in Renewable Natural Resources. Information Retrieval Ltd., 1911 Jefferson Davis Highway, Arlington, Virginia 22202. 1975-. Monthly.

Biological Abstracts. BIOSIS, 2100 Arch St., Philadelphia, Pennsylvania 19103-1399. (215) 587-4800. 1927-.

Chemical Abstracts. Chemical Abstracts Service, 2540 Olentangy River Rd., PO Box 3012, Columbus, Ohio 43210. (800) 848-6533. 1907-.

General Science Index. H. W. Wilson Co., 950 University Ave., Bronx, New York 10452. 1978-. Monthly, also issued in annual cumulation. Cumulative subject index to English language periodicals in the subject fields of astronomy, botany, chemistry, earth science, environment and conservation, food and nutrition, genetics, mathematics, medicine and health, microbiology, oceanography, physics, physiology and zoology.

Index to Scientific Book Contents. Institute for Scientific Information, 3501 Market St., Philadelphia, Pennsylvania 19104. (800) 523-1857. 1985-. Annual. Gives contents of science books published.

Multimedia Index to Ecology. National Information Center for Educational Media, University of Southern California, Los Angeles, California 90007.

ENCYCLOPEDIAS AND DICTIONARIES

McGraw-Hill Encyclopedia of Environmental Science. Sybil P. Parker. McGraw-Hill Science & Engineering Books, 11 W. 19th St., New York, New York 10011. (212) 337-6010. 1980. Covers ecology, man's influence on nature, and environmental protection.

McGraw-Hill Encyclopedia of Science and Technology. McGraw-Hill, 1221 Avenue of the Americas, New York, New York 10020. (212) 512-2000 or (800) 262-4729. 1992. Seventh edition. Issued in multiple volumes including index. Includes all science and technology broad subject areas.

ONLINE DATA BASES

BIOSIS Previews. BIOSIS, 2100 Arch St., Philadelphia, Pennsylvania 19103-1399. (215) 587-4800. Largest and most comprehensive database of research in the life sciences. Contains citations for nearly 9000 primary research journals, monographs, reviews, symposia, preliminary reports, semi-popular journals, selected institutional reports, government reports and research communications.

CAS Source Index–CASSI. Chemical Abstracts Service, 2540 Olentangy River Rd., P.O. Box 3012, Columbus, Ohio 43210. (800) 848-6533 or (614) 421-3600. A listing of bibliographic and library holdings information for scientific and technical primary literature relevant to the chemical sciences.

Chemical Abstracts-CA. Chemical Abstracts Service, 2540 Olentangy River Rd., P.O. Box 3012, Columbus, Ohio 43210. (800) 848-6533 or (614) 421-3600. Information sources include 9000 journals, patents from 27 countries, two industrial property organizations, new books, conference proceedings, and government research reports.

PERIODICALS AND NEWSLETTERS

Chemoecology. Thieme Medical Publishers, 381 Park Ave. S., New York, New York 10016. (212) 683-5088. Quarterly. Topics in environmental chemistry.

The Journal of Biological Chemistry. American Society of Biological Chemists, 428 E. Preston St., Baltimore, Maryland 21202. Three times a month. Biological, agricultural, and energy aspects of the environment.

CHLORDANE

See: INSECTICIDES

CHLORIDES

See: CHLORINE

CHLORINATED HYDROCARBONS

See: HYDROCARBONS

CHLORINATION

See also: WASTEWATER TREATMENT; WATER
PURIFICATION

ABSTRACTING AND INDEXING SERVICES

Applied Science and Technology Index. H.W. Wilson Co., 950 University Ave., Bronx, New York 10452. (800) 367-6770. Formerly Industrial Arts Index.

Biological Abstracts. BIOSIS, 2100 Arch St., Philadelphia, Pennsylvania 19103-1399. (215) 587-4800. 1927-.

Biological and Agricultural Index. H.W. Wilson Co., 950 University Ave., Bronx, New York 10452. (800) 367-6770. 1916-. Monthly.

Bulletin Signaletique: Eau et Assainissement, Pollution Atmospherique, Droit des Pollutions. Centre de Documentation, Centre National de la Recherche Scientifique, 15, quai Anatole France, Paris, France 75700. (1) 45 55 92 25. 1983-. Monthly. Indexes pollution periodicals including water, atmospheric and related pollutions.

Chemical Abstracts. Chemical Abstracts Service, 2540 Olentangy River Rd., PO Box 3012, Columbus, Ohio 43210. (800) 848-6533. 1907-.

Engineering Index. The Engineering Index Inc., 345 E. 47th St., New York, New York 10017. 1962-.

Environment Abstracts. Bowker A & I Publishing, 121 Chanlon Rd., New Providence, New Jersey 07974. (908) 464-6800. 1974-.

Environment Index. Environment Information Center, Index Research Department, 124 E. 39th St., New York, New York 10016. 1971-. Annual.

Environmental Information Connection–EIC. Planning Information Program, Dept. of Urban and Regional Planning, University of Illinois, 1003 West Nevada, Urbana, Illinois 61801. (217) 333-1369. Also available online.

Environmental Periodicals Bibliography. Environmental Studies Institute, International Academy at Santa Barbara, 800 Garden St., Suite D, Santa Barbara, California 93101. (805) 965-5010. Also available online.

General Science Index. H. W. Wilson Co., 950 University Ave., Bronx, New York 10452. 1978-. Monthly, also issued in annual cumulation. Cumulative subject index to English language periodicals in the subject fields of astronomy, botany, chemistry, earth science, environment and conservation, food and nutrition, genetics, mathematics, medicine and health, microbiology, oceanography, physics, physiology and zoology.

Index to Scientific Book Contents. Institute for Scientific Information, 3501 Market St., Philadelphia, Pennsylvania 19104. (800) 523-1857. 1985-. Annual. Gives contents of science books published.

Pollution Abstracts. Cambridge Scientific Abstracts, 5161 River Rd., Bethesda, Maryland 20816. (301) 961-6750. Six/year. Indexes worldwide technical literature on environmental pollution. Covers air pollution, marine and freshwater pollution, sewage and wastewater treatment, waste management, toxicology and health, noise pollution, radiation, land pollution, and environmental policies, programs, legislation, and education. Also available online.

Science Citation Index. Institute for Scientific Information, 3501 Market St., Philadelphia, Pennsylvania 19104. 1961-.

BIBLIOGRAPHIES

Current Contents. Agriculture, Biology and Environmental Sciences. Institute for Scientific Information, 3501 Market St., Philadelphia, Pennsylvania 19104. (800) 523-1857. 1973-. Previous title: Current Contents. Agricultural, Food & Veterinary Sciences. Gives the table of contents of periodicals in the fields of agriculture, biology, environmental and related areas.

Directory of Published Proceedings. Interdok Corp., 173 Halstead Ave., Harrison, New York 10528. (914) 835-3506. 1990. Monthly. This is a listing of published proceedings including the series SEMTE (Science/Medicine/Engineering/Technology) and the series SSH (Social Science/Humanities).

EPA Publications Bibliography. U.S. Environmental Protection Agency, Library Systems Branch, 401 M St., SW, Washington, District of Columbia 20460. (202) 260-2090. Quarterly.

ENCYCLOPEDIAS AND DICTIONARIES

Cambridge Encyclopedia of Life Sciences. A. E. Friday and David S. Ingram. Cambridge University Press, 40 W 20th St., New York, New York 10011. (212) 924-3900 or (800) 227-0247. 1985. Includes all topics under biology and ecology.

Dictionary of Environmental Engineering and Related Sciences: English-Spanish, Spanish-English. Jose T. Villate. Ediciones Universal, 3090 SW 8th St., Miami, Florida 33135. (305) 642-3355. 1979.

Encyclopedia of Environmental Science and Engineering. J.R. Pfafflin. Gordon and Breach Science Publishers, Inc., 270 8th Ave., New York, New York 10011. (212) 206-8900. 1992.

Encyclopedia of Physics. Rita G. Lerner and George L. Trigg. VCH Publishers, 303 NW 12th Ave., Deerfield Beach, Florida 33442-1788. (305) 428-5566. 1991. Second edition.

McGraw-Hill Encyclopedia of Environmental Science. Sybil P. Parker. McGraw-Hill Science & Engineering Books, 11 W. 19th St., New York, New York 10011. (212) 337-6010. 1980. Covers ecology, man's influence on nature, and environmental protection.

McGraw-Hill Encyclopedia of Science and Technology. McGraw-Hill, 1221 Avenue of the Americas, New York, New York 10020. (212) 512-2000 or (800) 262-4729. 1992. Seventh edition. Issued in multiple volumes including index. Includes all science and technology broad subject areas.

Van Nostrand's Scientific Encyclopedia. Glenn D. Considine, ed. Van Nostrand Reinhold, 115 5th Ave., New York, New York 10003. (212) 254-3232. 1983. Sixth edition. Includes all broad subject areas in science.

GENERAL WORKS

AWWA Standard for Liquid Chlorine: American National Standard. American National Standards Institute. American Water Works Association, 6666 W. Quincy Ave., Denver, Colorado 80235. (303) 794-7711. 1987.

Environmental Impact and Health Effects of Wastewater Chlorination. Gary R. Brenniman. Institute of Natural Resources, Chicago, Illinois 1981. Physiological and environmental aspects of chlorination.

Guidance Manual for Compliance with the Filtration and Disinfection Requirements for Public Water Systems Using Surface Water Sources. American Water Works Association, 6666 W. Quincy Ave., Denver, Colorado 80235. (303) 794-7711. 1991.

Health Effects Due to the Cessation of Chlorination of Wastewater Treatment Plant Effluent. Janet A. Holden. Institute of Natural Resources, Chicago, Illinois 1981.

HANDBOOKS AND MANUALS

The Handbook of Chlorination. George Clifford White. Van Nostrand Reinhold Co., 115 Fifth Ave., New York, New York 10003. (212) 254-3232. 1986. Water purification through chlorination.

ONLINE DATA BASES

BIOSIS Previews. BIOSIS, 2100 Arch St., Philadelphia, Pennsylvania 19103-1399. (215) 587-4800. Largest and most comprehensive database of research in the life sciences. Contains citations for nearly 9000 primary research journals, monographs, reviews, symposia, preliminary reports, semi-popular journals, selected institutional reports, government reports and research communications.

CAS Source Index–CASSI. Chemical Abstracts Service, 2540 Olentangy River Rd., P.O. Box 3012, Columbus, Ohio 43210. (800) 848-6533 or (614) 421-3600. A listing of bibliographic and library holdings information for scientific and technical primary literature relevant to the chemical sciences.

CERCLIS. Chemical Information Systems, Inc., 7215 York Rd., Baltimore, Maryland 21212. (301) 321-8440. Information on hazardous waste disposal sites that have either been listed by the EPA on the National Priority List (NPL) or nominated for consideration for the NPL.

Chemical Abstracts-CA. Chemical Abstracts Service, 2540 Olentangy River Rd., P.O. Box 3012, Columbus, Ohio 43210. (800) 848-6533 or (614) 421-3600. Information sources include 9000 journals, patents from 27 countries, two industrial property organizations, new books, conference proceedings, and government research reports.

Chemical Collection System/Request Tracking–CCS/RTS. U.S. Environmental Protection Agency, Office of Pesticides and Toxic Substances, 401 M St., SW, Washington, District of Columbia 20460. (202) 260-2090. Contains information on various properties of a number of chemicals including environmental effects, test and analysis methods, and health effects. Available from EPA.

Chemical Dictionary Online–CHEMLINE. Chemical Abstracts Service, 2540 Olentangy River Rd., Columbus, Ohio 43210. (614) 421-3600 or (800) 848-6533. Part of MEDLINE of the National Library of Medicine (NLM). File of 900,000 names for chemical substances, representing 450,000 unique compounds. It contains such information as Chemical Abstracts (CA) Service Registry Numbers, molecular formulas, preferred chemical nomenclature, and generic and ring structure information. Available on NLM's ELHILL system.

Chemical Exposure. Science Applications International Corp., Health & Environmental Information, P.O. Box 2501, Oak Ridge, Tennessee 37831. (615) 482-9031. Database of chemicals that have been identified in both human tissues and body fluids and in feral and food animals. Contains reference to journal articles, conferences, and reports. Covers the whole fields of information related to human and animal exposure to food, air, and water contaminants and pharmaceuticals. Its records include information on chemical properties, formulas, tissues measured, analytical method used, demographics and more. Available on DIALOG.

Computerized Engineering Index–COMPENDEX. Engineering Information Inc., 345 E. 47th St., New York, New York 10017. (212) 705-7600.

Enviro/Energyline Abstracts Plus. R. R. Bowker Co., 121 Chanlon Rd., New Providence, New Jersey 07974. (908) 464-6800.

Environmental Periodicals Bibliography. National Information Services Corp., Ste. 6, Wyman Towers, 3100 St. Paul St., Baltimore, Maryland 21218. (410)243-0797. Online version of abstract of same name.

Monthly Catalog of United States Government Publications. U.S. G.P.O., Supt. of Docs., PO Box 371954, Pittsburgh, Pennsylvania 15250-7954. (202) 512-0000.

National Technical Information Service. U.S. Department of Commerce, National Technical Information Service, Office of Data Base Services, 5285 Port Royal Rd., Springfield, Virginia 22161. (703) 487-4807. Bibliographic database of government sponsored research and technical reports.

PressNet Environmental Reports. Chemical Information Systems, Inc., 7215 York Rd., Baltimore, Maryland 21212. (301) 321-8440.

TRADE ASSOCIATIONS AND PROFESSIONAL SOCIETIES

American Chemical Society. 1155 16th St., N.W., Washington, District of Columbia 20036. (202) 872-4600.

American Institute of Biological Sciences. 730 11th St., N.W., Washington, District of Columbia 20001-4521. (202) 628-1500.

American Institute of Chemical Engineers. 345 East 47th St., New York, New York 10017. (212) 705-7338.

American Institute of Chemists. 7315 Wisconsin Ave., Bethesda, Maryland 20814. (301) 652-2447.

CHLORINE

See also: ELEMENTS; WATER PURIFICATION

ABSTRACTING AND INDEXING SERVICES

Engineering Index. The Engineering Index Inc., 345 E. 47th St., New York, New York 10017. 1962-.

Environment Abstracts. Bowker A & I Publishing, 121 Chanlon Rd., New Providence, New Jersey 07974. (908) 464-6800. 1974-.

Environment Index. Environment Information Center, Index Research Department, 124 E. 39th St., New York, New York 10016. 1971-. Annual.

Environmental Information Connection–EIC. Planning Information Program, Dept. of Urban and Regional Planning, University of Illinois, 1003 West Nevada, Urbana, Illinois 61801. (217) 333-1369. Also available online.

Environmental Periodicals Bibliography. Environmental Studies Institute, International Academy at Santa Barbara, 800 Garden St., Suite D, Santa Barbara, California 93101. (805) 965-5010. Also available online.

Food Science and Technology Abstracts. International Food Information Service, c/o National Food Laboratory, 6363 Clark Ave., Dublin, California 94568. (800) 336-3782. 1969-.

Physics Briefs. Physikalische Berichte. Physik Verlag, Pappapelallee 3, Postfach 101161, Weinheim, Germany D-6940. 1979-. Semimonthly. In English. Volumes for 1979- issued by the Deutsche Physikalische Gesellschaft and the Fachinformationszentrum Energie Physik, Mathematik in cooperation with the American Institute of Physics.

Science Citation Index. Institute for Scientific Information, 3501 Market St., Philadelphia, Pennsylvania 19104. 1961-.

BIBLIOGRAPHIES

EPA Publications Bibliography. U.S. Environmental Protection Agency, Library Systems Branch, 401 M St., SW, Washington, District of Columbia 20460. (202) 260-2090. Quarterly.

ENCYCLOPEDIAS AND DICTIONARIES

Encyclopedia of Electrochemistry of Elements. A. J. Bard. Marcel Dekker, Inc., 270 Madison Ave., New York, New York 10016. (212) 696-9000 or (800) 228-1160. Encyclopedic treatment of the subject area of electrochemistry and related subjects.

McGraw-Hill Encyclopedia of Environmental Science. Sybil P. Parker. McGraw-Hill Science & Engineering Books, 11 W. 19th St., New York, New York 10011. (212) 337-6010. 1980. Covers ecology, man's influence on nature, and environmental protection.

McGraw-Hill Encyclopedia of Science and Technology. McGraw-Hill, 1221 Avenue of the Americas, New York, New York 10020. (212) 512-2000 or (800) 262-4729. 1992. Seventh edition. Issued in multiple volumes including index. Includes all science and technology broad subject areas.

Van Nostrand's Scientific Encyclopedia. Glenn D. Considine, ed. Van Nostrand Reinhold, 115 5th Ave., New York, New York 10003. (212) 254-3232. 1983. Sixth edition. Includes all broad subject areas in science.

GENERAL WORKS

The Chemistry of Chlorine and Chlorination. Frank Nickols. State of Illinois Environmental Protection Agency, 2200 Churchill Rd., Springfield, Illinois 62706. (217) 782-2829. 1990.

Incinerating Municipal and Industrial Waste; Fireside Problems and Prospects for Improvement. Richard W. Bryers. Hemisphere, 79 Madison Ave., Suite 1110, New York, New York 10016. (212) 725-1999; (800) 821-8312. 1991. Addresses the causes and possible cures for corrosion and deposits due to impurities in the combustion of industrial and municipal refuse.

HANDBOOKS AND MANUALS

Is Your Water Safe to Drink?. Raymond Gabler. Consumer Union U.S., New York, New York 1988. Health, microbial, inorganic, and organic hazards in drinking water, chlorination, bottled water, and water shortages.

ONLINE DATA BASES

Computerized Engineering Index–COMPENDEX. Engineering Information Inc., 345 E. 47th St., New York, New York 10017. (212) 705-7600.

Enviro/Energyline Abstracts Plus. R. R. Bowker Co., 121 Chanlon Rd., New Providence, New Jersey 07974. (908) 464-6800.

Environmental Periodicals Bibliography. National Information Services Corp., Ste. 6, Wyman Towers, 3100 St. Paul St., Baltimore, Maryland 21218. (410)243-0797. Online version of abstract of same name.

RESEARCH CENTERS AND INSTITUTES

The Chlorine Institute. 2001 L St., N.W., Suite 506, Washington, District of Columbia 20036. (202) 775-2790.

STATISTICS SOURCES

Chemical Retorts. FIND/SVP, 625 Avenue of the Americas, New York, New York 10011. (212) 645-4500. 1991. Profiles the collapse of selected commodity petrochemical margins including, VCM, PVC, ethylene, polyethylene and chlorine.

TRADE ASSOCIATIONS AND PROFESSIONAL SOCIETIES

American Chemical Society. 1155 16th St., N.W., Washington, District of Columbia 20036. (202) 872-4600.

American Institute of Biological Sciences. 730 11th St., N.W., Washington, District of Columbia 20001-4521. (202) 628-1500.

American Institute of Chemical Engineers. 345 East 47th St., New York, New York 10017. (212) 705-7338.

American Institute of Chemists. 7315 Wisconsin Ave., Bethesda, Maryland 20814. (301) 652-2447.

Methyl Chloride Industry Alliance. c/o Latham and Watkins, 1001 Pennsylvania Ave., N.W., #130, Washington, District of Columbia 20004. (202) 637-2200.

CHLORINE CONTENT CHAMBER

See: WASTEWATER TREATMENT

CHLOROFLUOROCARBONS (CFCS)

See also: AIR POLLUTION; ATMOSPHERE; OZONE LAYER

ABSTRACTING AND INDEXING SERVICES

Abstracts of Air and Water Conservation Literature. American Petroleum Institute. Central Abstracting and Indexing Service, 275 Madison Avenue, New York, New York 10016. 1972.

Applied Ecology Abstracts Studies in Renewable Natural Resources. Information Retrieval Ltd., 1911 Jefferson Davis Highway, Arlington, Virginia 22202. 1975-. Monthly.

Biological Abstracts. BIOSIS, 2100 Arch St., Philadelphia, Pennsylvania 19103-1399. (215) 587-4800. 1927-.

Biological and Agricultural Index. H.W. Wilson Co., 950 University Ave., Bronx, New York 10452. (800) 367-6770. 1916-. Monthly.

Bulletin Signaletique: Eau et Assainissement, Pollution Atmospherique, Droit des Pollutions. Centre de Documentation, Centre National de la Recherche Scientifique, 15, quai Anatole France, Paris, France 75700. (1) 45 55 92 25. 1983-. Monthly. Indexes pollution periodicals including water, atmospheric and related pollutions.

Environment Abstracts. Bowker A & I Publishing, 121 Chanlon Rd., New Providence, New Jersey 07974. (908) 464-6800. 1974-.

Environment Index. Environment Information Center, Index Research Department, 124 E. 39th St., New York, New York 10016. 1971-. Annual.

Environmental Information Connection–EIC. Planning Information Program, Dept. of Urban and Regional Planning, University of Illinois, 1003 West Nevada, Urbana, Illinois 61801. (217) 333-1369. Also available online.

Environmental Periodicals Bibliography. Environmental Studies Institute, International Academy at Santa Barbara, 800 Garden St., Suite D, Santa Barbara, California 93101. (805) 965-5010. Also available online.

General Science Index. H. W. Wilson Co., 950 University Ave., Bronx, New York 10452. 1978-. Monthly, also issued in annual cumulation. Cumulative subject index to English language periodicals in the subject fields of astronomy, botany, chemistry, earth science, environment and conservation, food and nutrition, genetics, mathematics, medicine and health, microbiology, oceanography, physics, physiology and zoology.

Green Engineering: A Current Awareness Bulletin. Institution of Mechanical Engineers, 1 Birdcage Walk, Westminster, London, England SW1H 9JJ. 71973 1266/7. 1991. Monthly. Covers acid rain, aerosol technology, biotechnology chlorofluorocarbons, chemical and process engineering, environmental protection, energy conservation, energy generation, greenhouse effect, materials, pollution, recycling, waste disposal, and other environmental topics.

Index to Scientific Book Contents. Institute for Scientific Information, 3501 Market St., Philadelphia, Pennsylvania 19104. (800) 523-1857. 1985-. Annual. Gives contents of science books published.

Multimedia Index to Ecology. National Information Center for Educational Media, University of Southern California, Los Angeles, California 90007.

BIBLIOGRAPHIES

Bibliography and Index of Geology. American Geological Institute, 4220 King St., Alexandria, Virginia 22302. Monthly. Includes environmental geology and hydrogeology.

CFCs & the Polyurethane Industry: A Compilation of Technical Publications. Society of the Plastics Industry, Polyurethane Division, 355 Lexington Ave., New York, New York 10017. (212)351-5425. 1992. Bibliography of plastic foams, chlorofluorocarbons and polyurethanes.

Current Contents. Agriculture, Biology and Environmental Sciences. Institute for Scientific Information, 3501 Market St., Philadelphia, Pennsylvania 19104. (800) 523-1857. 1973-. Previous title: Current Contents. Agricultural, Food & Veterinary Sciences. Gives the table of contents of periodicals in the fields of agriculture, biology, environmental and related areas.

Directory of Published Proceedings. Interdok Corp., 173 Halstead Ave., Harrison, New York 10528. (914) 835-3506. 1990. Monthly. This is a listing of published proceedings including the series SEMTE (Science/Medicine/Engineering/Technology) and the series SSH (Social Science/Humanities).

EPA Publications Bibliography. U.S. Environmental Protection Agency, Library Systems Branch, 401 M St., SW, Washington, District of Columbia 20460. (202) 260-2090. Quarterly.

DIRECTORIES

Gale Environmental Sourcebook. Karen Hill. Gale Research Co., 835 Penobscot Bldg., Detroit, Michigan 48226-4094. (313) 961-2242. Contacts, information sources, or general information on environmental topics.

ENCYCLOPEDIAS AND DICTIONARIES

Cambridge Encyclopedia of Life Sciences. A. E. Friday and David S. Ingram. Cambridge University Press, 40 W 20th St., New York, New York 10011. (212) 924-3900 or (800) 227-0247. 1985. Includes all topics under biology and ecology.

Grzimek's Encyclopedia of Ecology. Bernhard Grzimek. Van Nostrand Reinhold, 115 5th Ave., New York, New York 10003. (212) 254-3232. 1976.

McGraw-Hill Encyclopedia of Environmental Science. Sybil P. Parker. McGraw-Hill Science & Engineering Books, 11 W. 19th St., New York, New York 10011. (212) 337-6010. 1980. Covers ecology, man's influence on nature, and environmental protection.

McGraw-Hill Encyclopedia of Science and Technology. McGraw-Hill, 1221 Avenue of the Americas, New York, New York 10020. (212) 512-2000 or (800) 262-4729. 1992. Seventh edition. Issued in multiple volumes including index. Includes all science and technology broad subject areas.

North American Reference Encyclopedia of Ecology and Pollution. William White. North American Pub. Co., 401 N. Broad St., Philadelphia, Pennsylvania 19108. (215) 238-5300. 1972.

Van Nostrand's Scientific Encyclopedia. Glenn D. Considine, ed. Van Nostrand Reinhold, 115 5th Ave., New York, New York 10003. (212) 254-3232. 1983. Sixth edition. Includes all broad subject areas in science.

GENERAL WORKS

Alternative Formulations and Packaging to Reduce Use of Chlorofluorocarbons. Thomas P. Nelson. Noyes Publications, 120 Mill Rd., Park Ridge, New Jersey 07656. (201) 391-8484. 1990. Pressure packaging and aerosol propellants.

The Economics of Managing Chlorofluorocarbons: Stratospheric Ozone and Climatic Issues. Johns Hopkins Uni-

versity Press, 701 W. 40th St., Suite 275, Baltimore, Maryland 21211. (410) 516-6900. 1982.

Fully Halogenated Chlorofluorocarbons. World Health Organization, Ave. Appia, Geneva, Switzerland CH-1211. (518) 436-9686. 1990. Environmental aspects of chlorofluorocarbons.

Magill's Survey of Science. Earth Science Series. Frank N. Magill. Salem Press, PO Box 50062, Pasadena, California 91105. 1990-. Five volumes. Includes information on earth's crust, hot spots and volcanic island chains, physical properties of minerals, rock magnetism, physical properties of rocks, and index.

Ozone. Kathryn Gay. Franklin Watts, 387 Park Ave. S., New York, New York 10016. (212) 686-7070. 1989. Environmental aspects of chlorofluorocarbons.

Ozone Crisis: The 15-Year Evolution of a Sudden Global Emergency. Sharon L. Roan. John Wiley & Sons, Inc., 605 3rd Ave., New York, New York 10158-0012. (212) 850-6000. 1989. Chronicles the experiences of F. Sherwood Rowland and Mario Molina, the scientists who first made the ozone depletion discovery.

Ozone Depletion: Health and Environmental Consequences. John Wiley & Sons, Inc., 605 3rd Ave., New York, New York 10158-0012. (212) 850-6000. 1989.

The Ozone Layer. Jane Duden. Crestwood House, Inc., c/o Macmillan Publishing Co., Front & Brown Streets, Riverside, New Jersey 08075. (609) 461-6500. 1990. Describes the ozone layer and its important function in protecting the earth from dangerous ultraviolet rays. Also examines the threats posed to the ozone layer by chlorofluorocarbons and other pollutants.

Present State of Knowledge of the Upper Atmosphere. R.T. Watson. National Aeronautics and Space Administration, Scientific and Technical Information Office, 5285 Port Royal Rd., Springfield, Virginia 22161. (703) 487-4805. 1988. Atmospheric ozone and atmospheric chemistry.

Stones in a Glass House: CFCs and Ozone Depletion. Douglas G. Cogan. Investor Responsibility Research Center, 1755 Massachusetts Ave., NW, Suite 600, Washington, District of Columbia 20036. (202) 234-7500. 1988. Environmental aspects of air pollution.

A Who's Who of American Ozone Depleters: A Guide to 3,014 Factories Emitting Three Ozone-Depleting Chemicals. Natural Resources Defense Council, 40 W. 20th St., New York, New York 10011. (212) 727-2700. 1990.

GOVERNMENTAL ORGANIZATIONS

Environmental Protection Agency: Office of Atmospheric and Indoor Air Programs. Waterside West Building, 401 M St., S.W., Washington, District of Columbia 20460. (202) 382-7404.

HANDBOOKS AND MANUALS

The CFC Handbook. Carl Salas. Fairmont Press, 700 Indian Trail, Lilburn, Georgia 30247. (404) 925-9388. 1990. Discusses use of chlorofluorocarbons (CFCs), CFC recycling, reclamation and reuse for refrigeration.

Guide to Refrigeration CFCs. Carl Salas and Marianne Salas. The American Association of Energy Engineers, 4025 Pleasantdale Rd., Suite 420, Atlanta, Georgia 30340. (404) 925-9558. 1992. Information needed to assess CFC-related alternatives, requirements and restrictions is included. The information presented will enable to assess how the mandated phase out of chlorofluocarbons will impact operations.

Power Generation, Energy Management and Environmental Sourcebook. Marilyn Jackson. The Association of Energy Engineers, 4025 Pleasantdale Rd., Suite 420, Atlanta, Georgia 30340. (404) 925-9558. 1992. Includes practical solutions to energy and environmental problems.

ONLINE DATA BASES

BIOSIS Previews. BIOSIS, 2100 Arch St., Philadelphia, Pennsylvania 19103-1399. (215) 587-4800. Largest and most comprehensive database of research in the life sciences. Contains citations for nearly 9000 primary research journals, monographs, reviews, symposia, preliminary reports, semi-popular journals, selected institutional reports, government reports and research communications.

CERCLIS. Chemical Information Systems, Inc., 7215 York Rd., Baltimore, Maryland 21212. (301) 321-8440. Information on hazardous waste disposal sites that have either been listed by the EPA on the National Priority List (NPL) or nominated for consideration for the NPL.

Chemical Abstracts Chemical Name Directory-CHEM-NAME. Chemical Abstracts Service, 2540 Olentangy River Rd., P.O. Box 3012, Columbus, Ohio 43210. (800) 848-6533 or (614) 421-3600. Listing of chemical substances in a dictionary type file. The Chemical Abstracts (CAS) Registry Number, molecular formula, Chemical Abstracts (CA) Substance Index Name, available synonyms, ring data and other chemical substance information is given for each entry.

Chemical Carcinogenesis Research Information System–CCRIS. National Library of Medicine, 8600 Rockville Pike, Bethesda, Maryland 20894. (800) 638-8480. Individual assay results and test conditions for 1,451 chemicals in the areas of carcinogenicity, mutagenicity, tumor promotion, and cocarcinogenicity.

Enviro/Energyline Abstracts Plus. R. R. Bowker Co., 121 Chanlon Rd., New Providence, New Jersey 07974. (908) 464-6800.

Environmental Periodicals Bibliography. National Information Services Corp., Ste. 6, Wyman Towers, 3100 St. Paul St., Baltimore, Maryland 21218. (410)243-0797. Online version of abstract of same name.

Monthly Catalog of United States Government Publications. U.S. G.P.O., Supt. of Docs., PO Box 371954, Pittsburgh, Pennsylvania 15250-7954. (202) 512-0000.

National Technical Information Service. U.S. Department of Commerce, National Technical Information Service, Office of Data Base Services, 5285 Port Royal Rd., Springfield, Virginia 22161. (703) 487-4807. Bibliographic database of government sponsored research and technical reports.

PressNet Environmental Reports. Chemical Information Systems, Inc., 7215 York Rd., Baltimore, Maryland 21212. (301) 321-8440.

SCISEARCH. Institute for Scientific Information, University City Science Center, 3501 Market St., Philadelphia, Pennsylvania 19104. (215) 386-0100.

STATISTICS SOURCES

CFCs & Replacements. FIND/SVP, 625 Avenue of the Americas, New York, New York 10011. (212) 645-4500. 1991. Assesses the U.S. market for chlorofluorocarbon compounds (CFCs), with a special focus on CFC replacements.

Chlorofluorocarbons. FIND/SVP, 625 Avenue of the Americas, New York, New York 10011. (212) 645-4500. 1991. Markets for commercial fluorine compounds as represented by the chlorofluorocarbons, fluoropolymers, fluoroelastomers, membranes, hydrogen fluoride, other inorganic and organic chemicals containing fluorine, and the alternatives to CFCs.

Environmental Data Compendium. OECD Publications and Information Center, 2001 L St., N.W., Suite 700, Washington, District of Columbia 20036. (202) 785-6323. 1989.

Environmental Indicators. OECD Publications and Information Center, 2001 L St., N.W., Suite 700, Washington, District of Columbia 20036. (202) 785-6323. 1991.

Environmental Quality. Council on Environmental Quality. U.S. G.P.O., Washington, District of Columbia 20401. (202) 512-0000. Annual.

The State of the Environment. OECD Publications and Information Center, 2001 L St., N.W., Suite 700, Washington, District of Columbia 20036. (202) 785-6323. 1991.

World Resources. World Resources Institute. 1709 New York Ave., N.W., Washington, District of Columbia 20006. (202) 638-6300. Annual. Statistical and textual analysis of world's natural resources and the effects of growth-caused environmental pollution.

TRADE ASSOCIATIONS AND PROFESSIONAL SOCIETIES

Alliance for Responsible Chlorofluorocarbon Policy. 1901 N. Fort Myer Dr., Suite 1200, Rosslyn, Virginia 22209. (703) 243-0344.

American Chemical Society. 1155 16th St., N.W., Washington, District of Columbia 20036. (202) 872-4600.

American Institute of Chemical Engineers. 345 East 47th St., New York, New York 10017. (212) 705-7338.

American Institute of Chemists. 7315 Wisconsin Ave., Bethesda, Maryland 20814. (301) 652-2447.

CHLOROFLUOROMETHANES

ABSTRACTING AND INDEXING SERVICES

Biological Abstracts. BIOSIS, 2100 Arch St., Philadelphia, Pennsylvania 19103-1399. (215) 587-4800. 1927-.

Biological and Agricultural Index. H.W. Wilson Co., 950 University Ave., Bronx, New York 10452. (800) 367-6770. 1916-. Monthly.

Environment Abstracts. Bowker A & I Publishing, 121 Chanlon Rd., New Providence, New Jersey 07974. (908) 464-6800. 1974-.

Environment Index. Environment Information Center, Index Research Department, 124 E. 39th St., New York, New York 10016. 1971-. Annual.

Environmental Information Connection–EIC. Planning Information Program, Dept. of Urban and Regional Planning, University of Illinois, 1003 West Nevada, Urbana, Illinois 61801. (217) 333-1369. Also available online.

Environmental Periodicals Bibliography. Environmental Studies Institute, International Academy at Santa Barbara, 800 Garden St., Suite D, Santa Barbara, California 93101. (805) 965-5010. Also available online.

General Science Index. H. W. Wilson Co., 950 University Ave., Bronx, New York 10452. 1978-. Monthly, also issued in annual cumulation. Cumulative subject index to English language periodicals in the subject fields of astronomy, botany, chemistry, earth science, environment and conservation, food and nutrition, genetics, mathematics, medicine and health, microbiology, oceanography, physics, physiology and zoology.

Index to Scientific Book Contents. Institute for Scientific Information, 3501 Market St., Philadelphia, Pennsylvania 19104. (800) 523-1857. 1985-. Annual. Gives contents of science books published.

Science Citation Index. Institute for Scientific Information, 3501 Market St., Philadelphia, Pennsylvania 19104. 1961-.

BIBLIOGRAPHIES

Current Contents. Agriculture, Biology and Environmental Sciences. Institute for Scientific Information, 3501 Market St., Philadelphia, Pennsylvania 19104. (800) 523-1857. 1973-. Previous title: Current Contents. Agricultural, Food & Veterinary Sciences. Gives the table of contents of periodicals in the fields of agriculture, biology, environmental and related areas.

EPA Publications Bibliography. U.S. Environmental Protection Agency, Library Systems Branch, 401 M St., SW, Washington, District of Columbia 20460. (202) 260-2090. Quarterly.

ENCYCLOPEDIAS AND DICTIONARIES

McGraw-Hill Encyclopedia of Environmental Science. Sybil P. Parker. McGraw-Hill Science & Engineering Books, 11 W. 19th St., New York, New York 10011. (212) 337-6010. 1980. Covers ecology, man's influence on nature, and environmental protection.

Van Nostrand's Scientific Encyclopedia. Glenn D. Considine, ed. Van Nostrand Reinhold, 115 5th Ave., New York, New York 10003. (212) 254-3232. 1983. Sixth edition. Includes all broad subject areas in science.

GENERAL WORKS

Halocarbons: Environmental Effects of Chlorofluoromethane Release. National Research Council. Committee on Impacts of Stratospheric Change. National Academy of Sciences, 2101 Constitution Ave., NW, Washington, District of Columbia 20418. (202) 334-2000. 1976.

ONLINE DATA BASES

BIOSIS Previews. BIOSIS, 2100 Arch St., Philadelphia, Pennsylvania 19103-1399. (215) 587-4800. Largest and most comprehensive database of research in the life sciences. Contains citations for nearly 9000 primary research journals, monographs, reviews, symposia, preliminary reports, semi-popular journals, selected institutional reports, government reports and research communications.

CERCLIS. Chemical Information Systems, Inc., 7215 York Rd., Baltimore, Maryland 21212. (301) 321-8440. Information on hazardous waste disposal sites that have either been listed by the EPA on the National Priority List (NPL) or nominated for consideration for the NPL.

Chemical Abstracts Chemical Name Directory-CHEM-NAME. Chemical Abstracts Service, 2540 Olentangy River Rd., P.O. Box 3012, Columbus, Ohio 43210. (800) 848-6533 or (614) 421-3600. Listing of chemical substances in a dictionary type file. The Chemical Abstracts (CAS) Registry Number, molecular formula, Chemical Abstracts (CA) Substance Index Name, available synonyms, ring data and other chemical substance information is given for each entry.

ChemQuest. Molecular Design Ltd., 2132 Farrallon Dr., San Leandro, California 94577. (415) 895-1313.

Enviro/Energyline Abstracts Plus. R. R. Bowker Co., 121 Chanlon Rd., New Providence, New Jersey 07974. (908) 464-6800.

Environmental Periodicals Bibliography. National Information Services Corp., Ste. 6, Wyman Towers, 3100 St. Paul St., Baltimore, Maryland 21218. (410)243-0797. Online version of abstract of same name.

Monthly Catalog of United States Government Publications. U.S. G.P.O., Supt. of Docs., PO Box 371954, Pittsburgh, Pennsylvania 15250-7954. (202) 512-0000.

National Technical Information Service. U.S. Department of Commerce, National Technical Information Service, Office of Data Base Services, 5285 Port Royal Rd., Springfield, Virginia 22161. (703) 487-4807. Bibliographic database of government sponsored research and technical reports.

TRADE ASSOCIATIONS AND PROFESSIONAL SOCIETIES

American Chemical Society. 1155 16th St., N.W., Washington, District of Columbia 20036. (202) 872-4600.

CHLOROFORM

See also: CARCINOGENS; TOXICITY; WATER PURIFICATION

ABSTRACTING AND INDEXING SERVICES

Biological Abstracts. BIOSIS, 2100 Arch St., Philadelphia, Pennsylvania 19103-1399. (215) 587-4800. 1927-.

General Science Index. H. W. Wilson Co., 950 University Ave., Bronx, New York 10452. 1978-. Monthly, also issued in annual cumulation. Cumulative subject index to English language periodicals in the subject fields of astronomy, botany, chemistry, earth science, environment and conservation, food and nutrition, genetics, mathematics, medicine and health, microbiology, oceanography, physics, physiology and zoology.

Index to Scientific Book Contents. Institute for Scientific Information, 3501 Market St., Philadelphia, Pennsylvania 19104. (800) 523-1857. 1985-. Annual. Gives contents of science books published.

Science Citation Index. Institute for Scientific Information, 3501 Market St., Philadelphia, Pennsylvania 19104. 1961-.

BIBLIOGRAPHIES

Health Aspects of Chloroform. National Technical Information Center, 5285 Port Royal Rd., Springfield, Virginia 22161. (703) 487-4650. 1977.

ENCYCLOPEDIAS AND DICTIONARIES

Cambridge Encyclopedia of Life Sciences. A. E. Friday and David S. Ingram. Cambridge University Press, 40 W 20th St., New York, New York 10011. (212) 924-3900 or (800) 227-0247. 1985. Includes all topics under biology and ecology.

McGraw-Hill Encyclopedia of Environmental Science. Sybil P. Parker. McGraw-Hill Science & Engineering Books, 11 W. 19th St., New York, New York 10011. (212) 337-6010. 1980. Covers ecology, man's influence on nature, and environmental protection.

Van Nostrand's Scientific Encyclopedia. Glenn D. Considine, ed. Van Nostrand Reinhold, 115 5th Ave., New York, New York 10003. (212) 254-3232. 1983. Sixth edition. Includes all broad subject areas in science.

GENERAL WORKS

Chloroform, Carbon Tetrachloride, and Other Halomethanes. National Academy of Sciences, 2101 Constitution Ave, N.W., Washington, District of Columbia 20418. (202) 334-2000. 1978.

Health Assessment Document for Chloroform. U.S. Environmental Protection Agency, Office of Research and Development, MD 75, Research Triangle Park, North Carolina 27711. (919) 541-2184. 1985.

Locating and Estimating Air Emissions from Sources of Chloroform. U.S. Environmental Protection Agency, Office of Air and Radiation, MD 75, Research Triangle Park, North Carolina 27711. (919) 541-2184. 1984.

TAPPI Environmental Conference Proceedings, Seattle, WA, April 9-11, 1990. TAPPI Press, Technology Park/Atlanta, PO Box 105113, Atlanta, Georgia 30348. (404) 446-1400. 1990. Contains 11 papers presented at the conference covering industrial pollution and its remedies.

Toxicological Profile for Chloroform. National Technical Information Service, 5285 Port Royal Rd., Springfield, Virginia 22161. (703) 487-4650. 1989.

HANDBOOKS AND MANUALS

FDA Food Additives Analytical Manual. C. Warner, et al., eds. Association of Official Analytical Chemists, 2200 Wilson Blvd., Suite 400-P, Arlington, Virginia 22201-3301. (703) 522-3032. 1983-1987. 2 vols. Provides methodology for determining compliance with food additive regulations. Contains analytical methods that have been evaluated by the FDA or found to operate satisfactorily in at least two laboratories.

ONLINE DATA BASES

BIOSIS Previews. BIOSIS, 2100 Arch St., Philadelphia, Pennsylvania 19103-1399. (215) 587-4800. Largest and most comprehensive database of research in the life sciences. Contains citations for nearly 9000 primary research journals, monographs, reviews, symposia, preliminary reports, semi-popular journals, selected institutional reports, government reports and research communications.

CERCLIS. Chemical Information Systems, Inc., 7215 York Rd., Baltimore, Maryland 21212. (301) 321-8440. Information on hazardous waste disposal sites that have either been listed by the EPA on the National Priority List (NPL) or nominated for consideration for the NPL.

SCISEARCH. Institute for Scientific Information, University City Science Center, 3501 Market St., Philadelphia, Pennsylvania 19104. (215) 386-0100.

CHLOROPHENOLS

ABSTRACTING AND INDEXING SERVICES

Biological Abstracts. BIOSIS, 2100 Arch St., Philadelphia, Pennsylvania 19103-1399. (215) 587-4800. 1927-.

Chemical Abstracts. Chemical Abstracts Service, 2540 Olentangy River Rd., PO Box 3012, Columbus, Ohio 43210. (800) 848-6533. 1907-.

General Science Index. H. W. Wilson Co., 950 University Ave., Bronx, New York 10452. 1978-. Monthly, also issued in annual cumulation. Cumulative subject index to English language periodicals in the subject fields of astronomy, botany, chemistry, earth science, environment and conservation, food and nutrition, genetics, mathematics, medicine and health, microbiology, oceanography, physics, physiology and zoology.

Index to Scientific Book Contents. Institute for Scientific Information, 3501 Market St., Philadelphia, Pennsylvania 19104. (800) 523-1857. 1985-. Annual. Gives contents of science books published.

Science Citation Index. Institute for Scientific Information, 3501 Market St., Philadelphia, Pennsylvania 19104. 1961-.

ENCYCLOPEDIAS AND DICTIONARIES

McGraw-Hill Encyclopedia of Environmental Science. Sybil P. Parker. McGraw-Hill Science & Engineering Books, 11 W. 19th St., New York, New York 10011. (212) 337-6010. 1980. Covers ecology, man's influence on nature, and environmental protection.

Van Nostrand's Scientific Encyclopedia. Glenn D. Considine, ed. Van Nostrand Reinhold, 115 5th Ave., New York, New York 10003. (212) 254-3232. 1983. Sixth edition. Includes all broad subject areas in science.

GENERAL WORKS

Ambient Water Quality Criteria for 2, 4-Dichlorophenol. U. S. Environmental Protection Agency. National Technical Information Service, 5285 Port Royal Rd., Springfield, Virginia 22161. (703) 487-4650. 1980. Describes the regulations and standards criteria set by the EPA.

Chlorophenols Other than Pentachlorophenol. World Health Organization, Ave. Appia, Geneva, Switzerland CH-1211. (518) 436-9686. 1989.

NTP Technical Report on the Toxicology and Carcinogenesis Studies of Two Pentachlorophenol Technical-Grade Mixtures. National Toxicology Program, U.S. Dept. of Health and Human Services, 9000 Rockville Pike, Research Triangle Park, North Carolina 20892. (301)496-4000. 1989.

Pentachlorophenol Health and Safety Guide. World Health Organization, Ave. Appia, Geneva, Switzerland CH-1221. (518) 436-9686. 1989.

HANDBOOKS AND MANUALS

Pentachlorophenol. World Health Organization, Ave. Appia, Geneva, Switzerland CH-1211. (518) 436-9686. 1987.

ONLINE DATA BASES

BIOSIS Previews. BIOSIS, 2100 Arch St., Philadelphia, Pennsylvania 19103-1399. (215) 587-4800. Largest and most comprehensive database of research in the life sciences. Contains citations for nearly 9000 primary research journals, monographs, reviews, symposia, preliminary reports, semi-popular journals, selected institutional reports, government reports and research communications.

Chemical Abstracts-CA. Chemical Abstracts Service, 2540 Olentangy River Rd., P.O. Box 3012, Columbus, Ohio 43210. (800) 848-6533 or (614) 421-3600. Information sources include 9000 journals, patents from 27 countries, two industrial property organizations, new books, conference proceedings, and government research reports.

Chemical Abstracts Chemical Name Directory-CHEMNAME. Chemical Abstracts Service, 2540 Olentangy River Rd., P.O. Box 3012, Columbus, Ohio 43210. (800) 848-6533 or (614) 421-3600. Listing of chemical substances in a dictionary type file. The Chemical Abstracts (CAS) Registry Number, molecular formula, Chemical Abstracts (CA) Substance Index Name, available synonyms, ring data and other chemical substance information is given for each entry.

Chemical Carcinogenesis Research Information System-CCRIS. National Library of Medicine, 8600 Rockville Pike, Bethesda, Maryland 20894. (800) 638-8480. Individual assay results and test conditions for 1,451 chemicals in the areas of carcinogenicity, mutagenicity, tumor promotion, and cocarcinogenicity.

SCISEARCH. Institute for Scientific Information, University City Science Center, 3501 Market St., Philadelphia, Pennsylvania 19104. (215) 386-0100.

TRADE ASSOCIATIONS AND PROFESSIONAL SOCIETIES

American Chemical Society. 1155 16th St., N.W., Washington, District of Columbia 20036. (202) 872-4600.

CHLOROPHYLL

See also: PHOTOSYNTHESIS

ABSTRACTING AND INDEXING SERVICES

Biological Abstracts. BIOSIS, 2100 Arch St., Philadelphia, Pennsylvania 19103-1399. (215) 587-4800. 1927-.

Ecology Abstracts. Cambridge Scientific Abstracts, 5161 River Rd., Bethesda, Maryland 20816. (301) 961-6750. Monthly.

General Science Index. H. W. Wilson Co., 950 University Ave., Bronx, New York 10452. 1978-. Monthly, also issued in annual cumulation. Cumulative subject index to English language periodicals in the subject fields of astronomy, botany, chemistry, earth science, environment and conservation, food and nutrition, genetics, mathematics, medicine and health, microbiology, oceanography, physics, physiology and zoology.

Index to Scientific Book Contents. Institute for Scientific Information, 3501 Market St., Philadelphia, Pennsylvania 19104. (800) 523-1857. 1985-. Annual. Gives contents of science books published.

Science Citation Index. Institute for Scientific Information, 3501 Market St., Philadelphia, Pennsylvania 19104. 1961-.

ENCYCLOPEDIAS AND DICTIONARIES

Encyclopedia of Human Biology. Renato Dulbecco, ed. Academic Press, c/o Harcourt Brace Jovanovich Inc., 6277 Sea Harbor Dr., Orlando, Florida 32887. (800) 346-8648. 1991. Eight volumes.

McGraw-Hill Encyclopedia of Environmental Science. Sybil P. Parker. McGraw-Hill Science & Engineering Books, 11 W. 19th St., New York, New York 10011. (212) 337-6010. 1980. Covers ecology, man's influence on nature, and environmental protection.

Van Nostrand's Scientific Encyclopedia. Glenn D. Considine, ed. Van Nostrand Reinhold, 115 5th Ave., New York, New York 10003. (212) 254-3232. 1983. Sixth edition. Includes all broad subject areas in science.

ONLINE DATA BASES

BIOSIS Previews. BIOSIS, 2100 Arch St., Philadelphia, Pennsylvania 19103-1399. (215) 587-4800. Largest and most comprehensive database of research in the life sciences. Contains citations for nearly 9000 primary research journals, monographs, reviews, symposia, preliminary reports, semi-popular journals, selected institutional reports, government reports and research communications.

Cambridge Scientific Abstracts Life Science-CSAL. Cambridge Scientific Abstracts, 5161 River Rd., Bethesda, Maryland 20816. (301) 961-6750. Provides access to the following abstracting services: "Life Sciences Collection," "Aquatic Sciences and Fisheries Abstracts," "Oceanic Abstracts," and "Pollution Abstracts."

TRADE ASSOCIATIONS AND PROFESSIONAL SOCIETIES

American Institute of Biological Sciences. 730 11th St., N.W., Washington, District of Columbia 20001-4521. (202) 628-1500.

CHLOROSIS

ABSTRACTING AND INDEXING SERVICES

Biological Abstracts. BIOSIS, 2100 Arch St., Philadelphia, Pennsylvania 19103-1399. (215) 587-4800. 1927-.

Chemical Abstracts. Chemical Abstracts Service, 2540 Olentangy River Rd., PO Box 3012, Columbus, Ohio 43210. (800) 848-6533. 1907-.

General Science Index. H. W. Wilson Co., 950 University Ave., Bronx, New York 10452. 1978-. Monthly, also issued in annual cumulation. Cumulative subject index to English language periodicals in the subject fields of astronomy, botany, chemistry, earth science, environment and conservation, food and nutrition, genetics, mathematics, medicine and health, microbiology, oceanography, physics, physiology and zoology.

Index to Scientific Book Contents. Institute for Scientific Information, 3501 Market St., Philadelphia, Pennsylvania 19104. (800) 523-1857. 1985-. Annual. Gives contents of science books published.

Science Citation Index. Institute for Scientific Information, 3501 Market St., Philadelphia, Pennsylvania 19104. 1961-.

ENCYCLOPEDIAS AND DICTIONARIES

Van Nostrand's Scientific Encyclopedia. Glenn D. Considine, ed. Van Nostrand Reinhold, 115 5th Ave., New York, New York 10003. (212) 254-3232. 1983. Sixth edition. Includes all broad subject areas in science.

ONLINE DATA BASES

BIOSIS Previews. BIOSIS, 2100 Arch St., Philadelphia, Pennsylvania 19103-1399. (215) 587-4800. Largest and most comprehensive database of research in the life sciences. Contains citations for nearly 9000 primary research journals, monographs, reviews, symposia, preliminary reports, semi-popular journals, selected institutional reports, government reports and research communications.

Chemical Abstracts-CA. Chemical Abstracts Service, 2540 Olentangy River Rd., P.O. Box 3012, Columbus, Ohio 43210. (800) 848-6533 or (614) 421-3600. Information sources include 9000 journals, patents from 27 countries, two industrial property organizations, new books, conference proceedings, and government research reports.

TRADE ASSOCIATIONS AND PROFESSIONAL SOCIETIES

American Institute of Biological Sciences. 730 11th St., N.W., Washington, District of Columbia 20001-4521. (202) 628-1500.

CHOLESTEROL

See: NUTRITION

CHOLINESTERASE

See also: ENZYMES; INSECTICIDES; PESTICIDES

ABSTRACTING AND INDEXING SERVICES

Biological Abstracts. BIOSIS, 2100 Arch St., Philadelphia, Pennsylvania 19103-1399. (215) 587-4800. 1927-.

General Science Index. H. W. Wilson Co., 950 University Ave., Bronx, New York 10452. 1978-. Monthly, also issued in annual cumulation. Cumulative subject index to English language periodicals in the subject fields of astronomy, botany, chemistry, earth science, environment and conservation, food and nutrition, genetics, mathematics, medicine and health, microbiology, oceanography, physics, physiology and zoology.

Index to Scientific Book Contents. Institute for Scientific Information, 3501 Market St., Philadelphia, Pennsylvania 19104. (800) 523-1857. 1985-. Annual. Gives contents of science books published.

Science Citation Index. Institute for Scientific Information, 3501 Market St., Philadelphia, Pennsylvania 19104. 1961-.

ENCYCLOPEDIAS AND DICTIONARIES

Encyclopedia of Human Biology. Renato Dulbecco, ed. Academic Press, c/o Harcourt Brace Jovanovich Inc., 6277 Sea Harbor Dr., Orlando, Florida 32887. (800) 346-8648. 1991. Eight volumes.

McGraw-Hill Encyclopedia of Environmental Science. Sybil P. Parker. McGraw-Hill Science & Engineering Books, 11 W. 19th St., New York, New York 10011. (212) 337-6010. 1980. Covers ecology, man's influence on nature, and environmental protection.

Van Nostrand's Scientific Encyclopedia. Glenn D. Considine, ed. Van Nostrand Reinhold, 115 5th Ave., New York, New York 10003. (212) 254-3232. 1983. Sixth edition. Includes all broad subject areas in science.

ONLINE DATA BASES

BIOSIS Previews. BIOSIS, 2100 Arch St., Philadelphia, Pennsylvania 19103-1399. (215) 587-4800. Largest and most comprehensive database of research in the life sciences. Contains citations for nearly 9000 primary research journals, monographs, reviews, symposia, preliminary reports, semi-popular journals, selected institutional reports, government reports and research communications.

Chemical Carcinogenesis Research Information System–CCRIS. National Library of Medicine, 8600 Rockville Pike, Bethesda, Maryland 20894. (800) 638-8480. Individual assay results and test conditions for 1,451 chemicals in the areas of carcinogenicity, mutagenicity, tumor promotion, and cocarcinogenicity.

Monthly Catalog of United States Government Publications. U.S. G.P.O., Supt. of Docs., PO Box 371954, Pittsburgh, Pennsylvania 15250-7954. (202) 512-0000.

National Technical Information Service. U.S. Department of Commerce, National Technical Information Service, Office of Data Base Services, 5285 Port Royal Rd., Springfield, Virginia 22161. (703) 487-4807. Bibliographic database of government sponsored research and technical reports.

SCISEARCH. Institute for Scientific Information, University City Science Center, 3501 Market St., Philadelphia, Pennsylvania 19104. (215) 386-0100.

TRADE ASSOCIATIONS AND PROFESSIONAL SOCIETIES

American Institute of Biological Sciences. 730 11th St., N.W., Washington, District of Columbia 20001-4521. (202) 628-1500.

CHROMATES

ABSTRACTING AND INDEXING SERVICES

Biological Abstracts. BIOSIS, 2100 Arch St., Philadelphia, Pennsylvania 19103-1399. (215) 587-4800. 1927-.

Engineering Index. The Engineering Index Inc., 345 E. 47th St., New York, New York 10017. 1962-.

General Science Index. H. W. Wilson Co., 950 University Ave., Bronx, New York 10452. 1978-. Monthly, also issued in annual cumulation. Cumulative subject index to English language periodicals in the subject fields of astronomy, botany, chemistry, earth science, environment and conservation, food and nutrition, genetics, mathematics, medicine and health, microbiology, oceanography, physics, physiology and zoology.

Science Citation Index. Institute for Scientific Information, 3501 Market St., Philadelphia, Pennsylvania 19104. 1961-.

ENCYCLOPEDIAS AND DICTIONARIES

McGraw-Hill Encyclopedia of Science and Technology. McGraw-Hill, 1221 Avenue of the Americas, New York, New York 10020. (212) 512-2000 or (800) 262-4729. 1992. Seventh edition. Issued in multiple volumes including index. Includes all science and technology broad subject areas.

Ullmanns Encyclopedia of Industrial Chemistry. Hans Jurgen Arpe and Wolfgang Gerhartz, eds. VCH Publishers, 303 NW 12th Ave., Deerfield Beach, Florida 33442-1788. (305) 428-5566. 1990. Designed to keep up with the broad spectrum of chemical technology. Thirty-six volumes of the encyclopedia have been divided into two sets: the 28 A volumes contain alphabetically arranged articles on chemicals, product groups, processes and technological concepts; and the 8 B volumes are compendia of basic knowledge in industrial chemistry.

Van Nostrand's Scientific Encyclopedia. Glenn D. Considine, ed. Van Nostrand Reinhold, 115 5th Ave., New York, New York 10003. (212) 254-3232. 1983. Sixth edition. Includes all broad subject areas in science.

ONLINE DATA BASES

BIOSIS Previews. BIOSIS, 2100 Arch St., Philadelphia, Pennsylvania 19103-1399. (215) 587-4800. Largest and most comprehensive database of research in the life sciences. Contains citations for nearly 9000 primary research journals, monographs, reviews, symposia, preliminary reports, semi-popular journals, selected institutional reports, government reports and research communications.

CAS Source Index–CASSI. Chemical Abstracts Service, 2540 Olentangy River Rd., P.O. Box 3012, Columbus, Ohio 43210. (800) 848-6533 or (614) 421-3600. A listing of bibliographic and library holdings information for

scientific and technical primary literature relevant to the chemical sciences.

Chemical Collection System/Request Tracking–CCS/RTS. U.S. Environmental Protection Agency, Office of Pesticides and Toxic Substances, 401 M St., SW, Washington, District of Columbia 20460. (202) 260-2090. Contains information on various properties of a number of chemicals including environmental effects, test and analysis methods, and health effects. Available from EPA.

Chemical Dictionary Online–CHEMLINE. Chemical Abstracts Service, 2540 Olentangy River Rd., Columbus, Ohio 43210. (614) 421-3600 or (800) 848-6533. Part of MEDLINE of the National Library of Medicine (NLM). File of 900,000 names for chemical substances, representing 450,000 unique compounds. It contains such information as Chemical Abstracts (CA) Service Registry Numbers, molecular formulas, preferred chemical nomenclature, and generic and ring structure information. Available on NLM's ELHILL system.

Chemical Exposure. Science Applications International Corp., Health & Environmental Information, P.O. Box 2501, Oak Ridge, Tennessee 37831. (615) 482-9031. Database of chemicals that have been identified in both human tissues and body fluids and in feral and food animals. Contains reference to journal articles, conferences, and reports. Covers the whole fields of information related to human and animal exposure to food, air, and water contaminants and pharmaceuticals. Its records include information on chemical properties, formulas, tissues measured, analytical method used, demographics and more. Available on DIALOG.

Computerized Engineering Index–COMPENDEX. Engineering Information Inc., 345 E. 47th St., New York, New York 10017. (212) 705-7600.

TRADE ASSOCIATIONS AND PROFESSIONAL SOCIETIES

American Chemical Society. 1155 16th St., N.W., Washington, District of Columbia 20036. (202) 872-4600.

CHROMATOGRAPHY

ABSTRACTING AND INDEXING SERVICES

Biological Abstracts. BIOSIS, 2100 Arch St., Philadelphia, Pennsylvania 19103-1399. (215) 587-4800. 1927-.

Engineering Index. The Engineering Index Inc., 345 E. 47th St., New York, New York 10017. 1962-.

Environment Abstracts. Bowker A & I Publishing, 121 Chanlon Rd., New Providence, New Jersey 07974. (908) 464-6800. 1974-.

Environment Index. Environment Information Center, Index Research Department, 124 E. 39th St., New York, New York 10016. 1971-. Annual.

Environmental Information Connection–EIC. Planning Information Program, Dept. of Urban and Regional Planning, University of Illinois, 1003 West Nevada, Urbana, Illinois 61801. (217) 333-1369. Also available online.

Environmental Periodicals Bibliography. Environmental Studies Institute, International Academy at Santa Barba-

ra, 800 Garden St., Suite D, Santa Barbara, California 93101. (805) 965-5010. Also available online.

Food Science and Technology Abstracts. International Food Information Service, c/o National Food Laboratory, 6363 Clark Ave., Dublin, California 94568. (800) 336-3782. 1969-.

General Science Index. H. W. Wilson Co., 950 University Ave., Bronx, New York 10452. 1978-. Monthly, also issued in annual cumulation. Cumulative subject index to English language periodicals in the subject fields of astronomy, botany, chemistry, earth science, environment and conservation, food and nutrition, genetics, mathematics, medicine and health, microbiology, oceanography, physics, physiology and zoology.

Physics Briefs. Physikalische Berichte. Physik Verlag, Pappapelallee 3, Postfach 101161, Weinheim, Germany D-6940. 1979-. Semimonthly. In English. Volumes for 1979- issued by the Deutsche Physikalische Gesellschaft and the Fachinformationszentrum Energie Physik, Mathematik in cooperation with the American Institute of Physics.

Pollution Abstracts. Cambridge Scientific Abstracts, 5161 River Rd., Bethesda, Maryland 20816. (301) 961-6750. Six/year. Indexes worldwide technical literature on environmental pollution. Covers air pollution, marine and freshwater pollution, sewage and wastewater treatment, waste management, toxicology and health, noise pollution, radiation, land pollution, and environmental policies, programs, legislation, and education. Also available online.

Science Citation Index. Institute for Scientific Information, 3501 Market St., Philadelphia, Pennsylvania 19104. 1961-.

BIBLIOGRAPHIES

Bibliography of Liquid Column Chromatography, 1971-1973, and Survey of Applications. Elsevier Science Publishing Co., 655 Avenue of the Americas, New York, New York 10010. (212) 984-5800. 1976.

EPA Publications Bibliography. U.S. Environmental Protection Agency, Library Systems Branch, 401 M St., SW, Washington, District of Columbia 20460. (202) 260-2090. Quarterly.

ENCYCLOPEDIAS AND DICTIONARIES

A Dictionary of Chromatography. Macmillan Publishing Co., 866 Third Ave., New York, New York 10022. (212) 702-2000. 1982.

Encyclopedia of Human Biology. Renato Dulbecco, ed. Academic Press, c/o Harcourt Brace Jovanovich Inc., 6277 Sea Harbor Dr., Orlando, Florida 32887. (800) 346-8648. 1991. Eight volumes.

Encyclopedia of Physical Science and Technology. Robert A. Meyers, ed. Academic Press, c/o Harcourt Brace Jovanovich Inc., 6277 Sea Harbor Dr., Orlando, Florida 32887. (800) 346-8648. Dictionary of engineering, technology and physical sciences.

Encyclopedia of Physics. Rita G. Lerner and George L. Trigg. VCH Publishers, 303 NW 12th Ave., Deerfield Beach, Florida 33442-1788. (305) 428-5566. 1991. Second edition.

McGraw-Hill Encyclopedia of Science and Technology. McGraw-Hill, 1221 Avenue of the Americas, New York, New York 10020. (212) 512-2000 or (800) 262-4729. 1992. Seventh edition. Issued in multiple volumes including index. Includes all science and technology broad subject areas.

Technical Dictionary of Chromatography. Pergamon Microforms International Inc., Fairview Park, Elmsford, New York 10523. (914) 592-7720. 1970.

Van Nostrand's Scientific Encyclopedia. Glenn D. Considine, ed. Van Nostrand Reinhold, 115 5th Ave., New York, New York 10003. (212) 254-3232. 1983. Sixth edition. Includes all broad subject areas in science.

GENERAL WORKS

Advances in Separation Technologies. Technical Insights, PO Box 1304, Fort Lee, New Jersey 07024-9967. (201) 568-4744. 1988.

ASTM Standards on Chromatography. ASTM, 1916 Race St., Philadelphia, Pennsylvania 19103-1187. (215) 299-5400. 1989. Gas chromatography, liquid chromatography, thin-layer chromatography and stearic exclusion chromatography.

Chromatographic Analysis of Pharmaceuticals. Marcel Dekker, Inc., 270 Madison Ave., New York, New York 10016. (212) 696-9000; (800) 228-1160. Analysis of drugs.

Chromatography of Environmental Hazards. Elsevier Science Publishing Co., 655 Avenue of the Americas, New York, New York 10010. (212) 984-5800. Covers carcinogens, mutagens, and teratogens, metals, gaseous and industrial pollutants, pesticides, and drugs of abuse.

Environmental Problem Solving Using Gas and Liquid Chromatography. Elsevier Science Publishing Co., 655 Avenue of the Americas, New York, New York 10010. (212) 984-5800. Covers environmental chemistry and chromatographic analysis.

Gas Chromatography in Air Pollution Analysis. Viktor G. Berezkin and Yuri S. Drugov. Elsevier Science Publishing Co., 655 Avenue of the Americas, New York, New York 10010. (212) 989-5800. 1991.

Introduction of High Performance Liquid Chromatography. John Wiley & Sons, Inc., 605 Third Ave., New York, New York 10158-0012. (212) 850-0660.

Liquid Chromatography/Mass Spectrometry: Applications in Agricultural, Pharmaceutical and Environmental Chemistry. Mark A. Brown, ed. American Chemical Society, 1155 16th St. N.W., Washington, District of Columbia 20036. (202) 872-4600; (800) 227-5558. 1990. Review of the development of LC/MS techniques for enhancing structural information for high-performance LC/MS.

Magill's Survey of Science. Life Science Series. Frank N. Magill, ed. Salem Press, PO Box 50062, Pasadena, California 91105. 1991. Six volumes. Contents: v.1. A-Central and peripheral nervous system functions; v.2. Central metabolism regulation - eukaryotic transcriptional control; v.3. Positive and negative eukaryotic transcriptional control - mammalian hormones; v.4. Hormones and behavior - muscular contraction; v.5. Muscular contraction and relaxation - sexual reproduction in plants; v.6. Reproductive behavior and mating - X inactivation and the Lyon hypothesis.

Methods of Protein Analysis. Istavan Kerese. Halsted Press, 605 Third Ave., New York, New York 10158. (212) 850-6000. 1984. Deals with electrophoresis, proteins and chromatography.

The Sadtler Standard Gas Chromatography Retention Index Library. Sadtler Research Laboratories, 3316 Spring Garden St., Philadelphia, Pennsylvania 19104. (215) 382-7800. 1986. Annual.

HANDBOOKS AND MANUALS

Advances on Chromatography. Marcel Dekker, Inc., 270 Madison Ave., New York, New York 10016. (212) 696-9000; (800) 228-1160.

Chromatography: A Laboratory Handbook of Chromatographic and Electrophoretic Methods. Van Nostrand Reinhold, 115 Fifth Ave., New York, New York 10003. (212) 254-3232.

CRC Handbook of Chromatography. CRC Press, 2000 Corporate Blvd. N.W., Boca Raton, Florida 33431. (800) 272-7737. Pesticides and related organic chemicals.

Nucleic Acids and Related Compounds. CRC Press, 2000 Corporate Blvd. N.W., Boca Raton, Florida 33431. (800) 272-7737. 1987. Annual. A manual of chromatographic analysis.

Steroids. CRC Press, 2000 Corporate Blvd. N.W., Boca Raton, Florida 33431. (800) 272-7737. 1986. Chromatographic analysis of steroids.

ONLINE DATA BASES

BIOSIS Previews. BIOSIS, 2100 Arch St., Philadelphia, Pennsylvania 19103-1399. (215) 587-4800. Largest and most comprehensive database of research in the life sciences. Contains citations for nearly 9000 primary research journals, monographs, reviews, symposia, preliminary reports, semi-popular journals, selected institutional reports, government reports and research communications.

CAS Source Index–CASSI. Chemical Abstracts Service, 2540 Olentangy River Rd., P.O. Box 3012, Columbus, Ohio 43210. (800) 848-6533 or (614) 421-3600. A listing of bibliographic and library holdings information for scientific and technical primary literature relevant to the chemical sciences.

Computerized Engineering Index–COMPENDEX. Engineering Information Inc., 345 E. 47th St., New York, New York 10017. (212) 705-7600.

Enviro/Energyline Abstracts Plus. R. R. Bowker Co., 121 Chanlon Rd., New Providence, New Jersey 07974. (908) 464-6800.

Environmental Periodicals Bibliography. National Information Services Corp., Ste. 6, Wyman Towers, 3100 St. Paul St., Baltimore, Maryland 21218. (410)243-0797. Online version of abstract of same name.

SCISEARCH. Institute for Scientific Information, University City Science Center, 3501 Market St., Philadelphia, Pennsylvania 19104. (215) 386-0100.

PERIODICALS AND NEWSLETTERS

High-Performance Liquid Chromatography. Academic Press, c/o Harcourt Brace Jovanovich Inc., 6277 Sea Harbor Dr., Orlando, Florida 32887. (800) 346-8648.

Journal of Chromatographic Science. Preston Publications, PO Box 48312, Niles, Illinois 60648. (312) 965-0566. Covers chromatography and electrophoresis.

Journal of Chromatography: Biomedical Applications. Elsevier Science Publishing Co., 655 Avenue of the Americas, New York, New York 10010. (212) 984-5800. Covers chromatography, electrophoresis and biology.

LC GC: Magazine of Liquid and Gas Chromatography. Aster Publishing Co., 859 Willamette St., PO Box 10460, Eugene, Oregon 97440. (503) 343-1200.

RESEARCH CENTERS AND INSTITUTES

Facility for Advanced Instrumentation. University of California Davis, Davis, California 95616. (916) 752-0284.

TRADE ASSOCIATIONS AND PROFESSIONAL SOCIETIES

American Institute of Chemical Engineers. 345 East 47th St., New York, New York 10017. (212) 705-7338.

American Institute of Chemists. 7315 Wisconsin Ave., Bethesda, Maryland 20814. (301) 652-2447.

CHROMIUM
See: METALS AND METALLURGY

CHROMIUM COMPOUNDS
See: METALS AND METALLURGY

CHROMIUM REFINING
See: METALS AND METALLURGY

CHROMIUM RESOURCES
See: METALS AND METALLURGY

CIGARETTE SMOKE
See: AIR POLLUTION

CLARIFICATION
See: WASTEWATER TREATMENT

CLARIFIER
See: WASTEWATER TREATMENT

CLAY

See: SOIL SCIENCE

CLEAN AIR

See: AIR QUALITY

CLEAN WATER

See: WATER QUALITY

CLEARCUTTING

See: FOREST MANAGEMENT

CLIMATE

See also: AGRICULTURE; BIOMES; BIOGEOGRAPHY; HARDINESS; HYDROLOGY; LAND USE; WEATHER

ABSTRACTING AND INDEXING SERVICES

Agrindex. AGRIS Coordinating Center, Via delle Terme di Caracalla, Rome, Italy I-00100. 61 0181-FA01. 1975-.

Air Pollution Titles. Pennsylvania State University, Center for Air Environmental Studies, 226 Fenske Laboratory, University Park, Pennsylvania 16802. (814) 865-1415. 1965. Bibliographic guide to current research literature on air environment, including monitoring and control of air pollution, health effects, effects on agriculture, forests, toxic air contaminants, and global atmospheric pro cases.

Air Pollution Translations. A Bibliography With Abstracts. U.S. Environmental Protection Agency, MD 75, Research Triangle Park, North Carolina 27711. (919) 541-2184. 1969.

Applied Ecology Abstracts Studies in Renewable Natural Resources. Information Retrieval Ltd., 1911 Jefferson Davis Highway, Arlington, Virginia 22202. 1975-. Monthly.

Applied Science and Technology Index. H.W. Wilson Co., 950 University Ave., Bronx, New York 10452. (800) 367-6770. Formerly Industrial Arts Index.

ASFA Aquaculture Abstracts. Cambridge Scientific Abstracts, Inc., 5161 River Rd., Bethesda, Maryland 20816. (301) 961-6750. 1984.

Biological Abstracts. BIOSIS, 2100 Arch St., Philadelphia, Pennsylvania 19103-1399. (215) 587-4800. 1927-.

Biological and Agricultural Index. H.W. Wilson Co., 950 University Ave., Bronx, New York 10452. (800) 367-6770. 1916-. Monthly.

Current Advances in Ecological and Environmental Science. Pergamon Microforms International, Inc., Fairview Park, Elmsford, New York 10523. (914) 592-7720. 1989-. Monthly. Current literature searching service includingjournals, reports, abstracts, etc. This service is available online as part of the CABS database on the hosts BRS and ORBIT search service.

Ecological Abstracts. Geo Abstracts Ltd. Elsevier Applied Science, Crown House, Linton Rd., Barking, England IG 11 8JU. 1974-. Derived from over 600 leading ecological and environmental journals, plus books, conference proceedings, reports and theses.

Environment Abstracts. Bowker A & I Publishing, 121 Chanlon Rd., New Providence, New Jersey 07974. (908) 464-6800. 1974-.

Environment Index. Environment Information Center, Index Research Department, 124 E. 39th St., New York, New York 10016. 1971-. Annual.

Environmental Information Connection–EIC. Planning Information Program, Dept. of Urban and Regional Planning, University of Illinois, 1003 West Nevada, Urbana, Illinois 61801. (217) 333-1369. Also available online.

Environmental Periodicals Bibliography. Environmental Studies Institute, International Academy at Santa Barbara, 800 Garden St., Suite D, Santa Barbara, California 93101. (805) 965-5010. Also available online.

Food Science and Technology Abstracts. International Food Information Service, c/o National Food Laboratory, 6363 Clark Ave., Dublin, California 94568. (800) 336-3782. 1969-.

Forestry Abstracts. C. A. B. International, Wallingford, England OX10 8DE. (0491) 3211. 1939/40-. Monthly. Journal of abstracts of journal articles, conferences, technical reports in the subject areas of: silviculture, forest mensuration and management, physical environment, fire, plant biology, genetics and breeding, mycology and pathology, game and wildlife, fish, protection of forests and other related matter.

General Science Index. H. W. Wilson Co., 950 University Ave., Bronx, New York 10452. 1978-. Monthly, also issued in annual cumulation. Cumulative subject index to English language periodicals in the subject fields of astronomy, botany, chemistry, earth science, environment and conservation, food and nutrition, genetics, mathematics, medicine and health, microbiology, oceanography, physics, physiology and zoology.

Geographical Abstracts. London School of Economics, Dept. of Geography, Regency House, 34 Duke St., London, England 1966-. Continued by Geo Abstracts issued in 6 parts: Pt. A. Landforms and the quaternary; Pt. B. Biogeography and Climatology; Pt. C. Economic geography; Pt. D. Social geography and cartography; Pt. E. Sedimentology; Pt. F. Regional and community planning.

Index to Scientific Book Contents. Institute for Scientific Information, 3501 Market St., Philadelphia, Pennsylvania 19104. (800) 523-1857. 1985-. Annual. Gives contents of science books published.

Multimedia Index to Ecology. National Information Center for Educational Media, University of Southern California, Los Angeles, California 90007.

Science Citation Index. Institute for Scientific Information, 3501 Market St., Philadelphia, Pennsylvania 19104. 1961-.

ALMANACS AND YEARBOOKS

Gale Environmental Almanac. Russ Hoyle. Gale Research Inc., 835 Penobscot Bldg., Detroit, Michigan 48226-4094. (313) 961-2242. 1993. Focuses on the U.S. and Canada, although worldwide and transboundary issues are discussed.

The Weather Almanac. Frank E. Bair, ed. Gale Research Co., 835 Penobscot Bldg., Detroit, Michigan 48226-4094. (313) 961-2242. 1992. Sixth edition. A reference guide to weather, climate, and air quality in the United States and its key cities, compromising statistics, principles, and terminology.

BIBLIOGRAPHIES

Bibliography and Index of Geology. American Geological Institute, 4220 King St., Alexandria, Virginia 22302. Monthly. Includes environmental geology and hydrogeology.

Carbon Dioxide and Climate: A Bibliography. National Technical Information Service, 5285 Port Royal Rd., Springfield, Virginia 22161. (703) 487-4650. 1981.

Current Contents. Agriculture, Biology and Environmental Sciences. Institute for Scientific Information, 3501 Market St., Philadelphia, Pennsylvania 19104. (800) 523-1857. 1973-. Previous title: Current Contents. Agricultural, Food & Veterinary Sciences. Gives the table of contents of periodicals in the fields of agriculture, biology, environmental and related areas.

Directory of Published Proceedings. Interdok Corp., 173 Halstead Ave., Harrison, New York 10528. (914) 835-3506. 1990. Monthly. This is a listing of published proceedings including the series SEMTE (Science/Medicine/Engineering/Technology) and the series SSH (Social Science/Humanities).

EPA Publications Bibliography. U.S. Environmental Protection Agency, Library Systems Branch, 401 M St., SW, Washington, District of Columbia 20460. (202) 260-2090. Quarterly.

Global Change Information Packet. National Agricultural Library, Reference Section, Room 111, 10301 Baltimore Blvd., Beltsville, Maryland 20705-2351. (301) 504-5755. 1991. Books and journal articles on the effects of global climate change.

New Publications of the Geological Survey. U.S. Department of the Interior, Geological Survey, 119 National Center, Reston, Virginia 22092. (703) 648-4460. 1984-. Monthly. Bibliography of geological publications and related government documents published by the Geological Survey.

DIRECTORIES

Canadian Environmental Directory. Canadian Almanac & Directory Publishing Co. Ltd., 134 Adelaide St. E., Ste. 27, Toronto, Ontario, Canada M5C 1K9. (416) 362-4088. 1992. Includes individuals, agencies, firms, and associations.

Directory of Global Climate Change Organizations. Janet Wright. National Agricultural Library, 10301 Baltimore Blvd., Beltsville, Maryland 20705. (301) 504-5755. 1991. Identifies organizations that provide information regarding global climate change issues to the general public.

National Environmental Data Referral Service. National Oceanic and Atmospheric Administration, Department of Commerce, 1825 Connecticut Ave., N.W., Washington, District of Columbia 20235. (202) 673-5548. Also available online.

ENCYCLOPEDIAS AND DICTIONARIES

Cambridge Encyclopedia of Life Sciences. A. E. Friday and David S. Ingram. Cambridge University Press, 40 W 20th St., New York, New York 10011. (212) 924-3900 or (800) 227-0247. 1985. Includes all topics under biology and ecology.

Dictionary of Environmental Science and Technology. Andrew Porteous. John Wiley & Sons, Inc., 605 3rd Ave., New York, New York 10158-0012. (212) 850-6000. 1992.

Dictionary of the Environment. Michael Allaby. New York University Press, 70 Washington Sq. S., New York, New York 10012. (212) 998-2575. 1989.

The Encyclopedia of Atmospheric Sciences and Astrogeology. Rhodes Whitmore Fairbridge. Reinhold Pub. Co., 115 5th Ave., New York, New York 10003. (212) 254-3232. 1967.

The Encyclopedia of Climatology. John E. Oliver and Rhodes W. Fairbridge, eds. Van Nostrand Reinhold, 115 5th Ave., New York, New York 10003. (212) 254-3232. 1987. Belongs in the series Encyclopedia of Earth Sciences, v.11.

Encyclopedia of Environmental Studies. William Ashworth. Facts on File, Inc., 460 Park Ave. S., New York, New York 10016. (212) 683-2244. 1991.

The Encyclopedia of Geochemistry and Environmental Sciences. Rhodes Whitmore Fairbridge. Van Nostrand Reinhold Co., 115 5th Ave., New York, New York 10003. (212) 254-3232. 1972.

Environmental Encyclopedia. William P. Cunningham, Terence Ball, et. al. Gale Research Inc., 835 Penobscot Bldg., Detroit, Michigan 48226-4094. (313) 961-2242. 1993.

Grzimek's Encyclopedia of Ecology. Bernhard Grzimek. Van Nostrand Reinhold, 115 5th Ave., New York, New York 10003. (212) 254-3232. 1976.

McGraw-Hill Encyclopedia of Environmental Science. Sybil P. Parker. McGraw-Hill Science & Engineering Books, 11 W. 19th St., New York, New York 10011. (212) 337-6010. 1980. Covers ecology, man's influence on nature, and environmental protection.

McGraw-Hill Encyclopedia of Science and Technology. McGraw-Hill, 1221 Avenue of the Americas, New York, New York 10020. (212) 512-2000 or (800) 262-4729. 1992. Seventh edition. Issued in multiple volumes including index. Includes all science and technology broad subject areas.

North American Reference Encyclopedia of Ecology and Pollution. William White. North American Pub. Co., 401 N. Broad St., Philadelphia, Pennsylvania 19108. (215) 238-5300. 1972.

Van Nostrand's Scientific Encyclopedia. Glenn D. Considine, ed. Van Nostrand Reinhold, 115 5th Ave., New York, New York 10003. (212) 254-3232. 1983. Sixth edition. Includes all broad subject areas in science.

The Water Encyclopedia. Lewis Publishers, 2000 Corporate Blvd. N.W., Boca Raton, Florida 33431. (800) 272-7737. 1990. 2d ed. Includes groundwater contamination, drinking water, floods, waterborne diseases, global warming, climate change, irrigation, water agencies and organizations, precipitation, oceans and seas, and river, lakes and waterfalls.

GENERAL WORKS

Antarctica and Global Climatic Change. Colin M. Harris. Lewis Publishers, 2000 Corporate Blvd., NW, Boca Raton, Florida 33431. (800) 272-7737. 1991. A guide to recent literature on climatic changes and environmental monitoring.

Carbon Dioxide and Other Greenhouse Gases. Kluwer Academic Publishers, 101 Philip Dr., Assinippi Pk, Norwell, Massachusetts 02061. (617) 871-6600. Looks at environmental aspects of greenhouse effects.

Carbon Dioxide, the Climate and Man. John R. Gribbin. International Institute for Environment and Development, 3 Endsleigh St., London, England CB2 1ER. 1981. Influence on nature of atmospheric carbon dioxide.

Carbon Dioxide, the Greenhouse Effect, and Climate. John R. Justus. U.S. G.P.O., Washington, District of Columbia 20401. (202) 521-0000. 1984.

The Challenge of Global Warming. Dean Edwin Abrahamson, ed. Island Press, 1718 Connecticut Ave. N.W., Suite 300, Washington, District of Columbia 20009. (202) 232-7933. 1989. Focuses on the causes, effects, policy implications, and possible solutions to global warming

The Changing Climate: Responses of the Natural Fauna and Flora. Michael J. Ford. G. Allen and Unwin, 8 Winchester Pl., Winchester, Massachusetts 01890. (617) 729-0830. 1982. Describes the climate changes and the acclimatization of the flora and fauna.

Climate and Man: From the Ice Age to the Global Greenhouse. Fred Pearce. Vision Books in Association with LWT, The Forum 74-80, Camden St., London, England NW1 OEG. 071-388-8811. 1989.

Climate Change and Society: Consequences of Increasing Atmospheric Carbon Dioxide. Westview Press, 5500 Central Ave., Boulder, Colorado 80301. (303) 444-3541. 1982.

Climate Change and U.S. Water Resources. P. E. Waggoner, ed. John Wiley & Sons, Inc., 605 3rd Ave., New York, New York 10158-0012. (212) 850-6000. 1990. Covers latest research in climate changes and subsequent effects on water supply. Topics include future water use, statistics in forecasting, vulnerability of water systems, irrigation, urban water systems, and reallocation by markets and prices.

Climate Change and World Agriculture. Martin Parry. Earthscan Pub. Ltd., 3 Endsleigh St., London, England WC1H ODD. (071)388-2117. 1990. Describes the effects on agriculture, estimating the impacts on plant and animal growth and looking at the geographical limits to different types of farming.

Climate Change–Evaluating the Socio-Economic Impacts. OECD, UNIPUB, 4611-F Assembly Dr., Lanham, Maryland 20706. (301) 459-7666 or (800) 274-4888. 1991. Describes various approaches to better understand the climate change and the socio-economic disruptions associated with it.

Climate Change: The IPCC Response Strategies. World Meteorological Organization/United Nations Env. Program, Intergovernmental Panel on Climate Change. Island Press, 1718 Connecticut Ave. N.W., Suite 300, Washington, District of Columbia 20009. (202) 232-7933. 1991. Identifies and evaluates a wide range of international strategies for limiting or adapting to climate change, and to review available mechanisms for implementing those strategies.

Climates of the States. Gale Research Inc., 835 Penobscot Bldg., Detroit, Michigan 48226-4094. (313) 961-2242. 1986. State-by-state summaries of climate based on first order weather reporting stations for the period 1951-1980.

Climatic Change and Plant Genetic Resources. M. T. Jackson, et al., eds. Belhaven Press, 136 S. Broadway, Irvington, New York 10533. (914) 591-9111. 1990. Cities concerns about the effect of global warming on biological diversity of species is the main thrust of this text. Major portion of the book comes from the second international workshop on plant genetic resources held in 1989.

Climatic Change and Society: Consequences of Increasing Atmospheric Carbon Dioxide. Westview Press, 5500 Central Ave., Boulder, Colorado 80301. (303) 444-3541. 1982. Social aspects of climatic changes.

Direct Effects of Increasing Carbon Dioxide on Vegetation. National Technical Information Service, 5285 Port Royal Rd., Springfield, Virginia 22161. (703) 487-4650. Covers carbon dioxide, vegetation and climate.

Drowning the National Heritage: Climate Change and Coastal Biodiversity in the United States. Walter V. C. Reid and Mark C. Trexler. World Resources Institute, 1709 New York Ave. N.W., Washington, District of Columbia 20006. (800) 822 0504. 1991. Examines erosion, flooding, and salt-water intrusion into groundwater, rivers, bays, and estuaries as well as receding coastlines and altered coastal current and upwelling patterns. Evaluates various policy responses and recommends specific changes to protect the biological wealth of these vital ecosystems.

Earthwatch: The Climate from Space. John E. Harries. E. Horwood, 200 Old Tappan Rd., Old Tappan, New Jersey 07675. (800) 223-2348. 1990. Surveys theories of climate and specifically concentrates on current concerns: ozone holes, the greenhouse effect and El Nino.

Ecotoxicology and Climate. Philippe Bordeaux, et al., eds. John Wiley & Sons, Inc., 605 3rd Ave., New York, New York 10158-0012. (212) 850-6000. 1989. Describes environmental chemistry of toxic pollutants in hot and cold climates. Includes bibliographical references and an index.

Energy and Climate Change. Lewis Publishers, 2000 Corporate Blvd., N.W., Boca Raton, Florida 33431. (407) 994-0555 or (800) 272-7737. 1990. Includes energy scenarios, cost and risk analysis, energy emissions, atmospheric chemistry, and climate effects.

Environmental Change in Iceland: Past and Present. Judith K. Maizels and Chris Caseldine, eds. Kluwer Academic Publishers, 101 Philip Dr., Assinippi Park, Norwell, Massachusetts 02061. (617) 871-6600. 1991. Describes the glacial landforms and paleoclimatology in

Iceland. Volume 7 of the Glaciology and Quaternary Geology Series.

Environmental Viewpoints. Marie Lazzari. Gale Research Inc., 835 Penobscot Bldg., Detroit, Michigan 48226-4094. (313) 961-2242. 1992.

Europhysics Study Conference on Induced Critical Conditions in the Atmosphere. A. Tartaglia. World Scientific, 687 Hartwell St., Teaneck, New Jersey 07666. (800) 227-7562. 1990. Deals with climatology, nuclear winter, ozone layer depletion, and the greenhouse effect.

Global Climate Change: Human and Natural Influences. Paragon House Publishers, 90 5th Ave., New York, New York 10011. (212) 620-2820. Carbon dioxide, methane, chlorofluorocarbons and ozone in the atmosphere; acid rain and water pollution in the hydrosphere; oceanographic and meteorological processes, nuclear war, volcanoes, asteroids, and meteorites.

Global Environmental Issues; a Climatological Approach. David D. Kemp. Routledge, 29 W. 35th St., New York, New York 10001-2291. (212) 244-3336. 1990. A textbook for an introductory college course in geography or environmental studies, but interdisciplinary enough for use in other courses with an environmental approach. Bridges the gulf between technical reports and popular articles on such topics as the greenhouse effect, ozone depletion, nuclear winter, atmospheric turbidity, and drought.

Global Patterns; Climate, Vegetation, and Soils. Wallace E. Akin. University of Oklahoma Press, 1005 Asp Ave., Norman, Oklahoma 73019. (405) 325-5111. 1991. Maps the three systems that dominate and shape life on earth in such a way as to clarify their interaction and combined effect.

An Introduction to Environmental Pattern Analysis. P. J. A. Howard. Parthenon Group Inc., 120 Mill Rd., Park Ridge, New Jersey 07656. (201) 391-6796. 1991. Explains the basic mathematics of the most widely used ordination and cluster analysis methods, types of data to which they are suited and their advantages and disadvantages.

Magill's Survey of Science. Earth Science Series. Frank N. Magill. Salem Press, PO Box 50062, Pasadena, California 91105. 1990-. Five volumes. Includes information on earth's crust, hot spots and volcanic island chains, physical properties of minerals, rock magnetism, physical properties of rocks, and index.

Man-made Carbon Dioxide and Climatic Change. Geo Abstracts Ltd., c/o Elsevier Science Pub., Crown House, Linton Rd., Barking, England IG11 8JU. 1983.

Meteorology of Air Pollution: Implications for the Environment and Its Future. R. S. Scorer. E. Horwood, 66 Wood Lane End, Hemel Hempstead, England HP2 4RG. 1990. Discusses methods of air pollution measurement and future expectations.

The Potential Effects of Global Climate Change on the United States. Joel B. Smith and Dennis A. Tirpak, eds. Hemisphere Publishing Co., 79 Madison Ave., Suite 1110, New York, New York 10016. (212) 725-1999; (800) 821-8312. 1990. Addresses the effects of climate change in vital areas such as water resources, agriculture, sea levels and forests. Also focuses on wetlands, human health, rivers and lakes and analyzes policy options for mitigating the effects of global warming.

Preserving the Global Environment: The Challenge of Shared Leadership. Jessica Tuchman Mathews, ed. World Resources Institute, 1709 New York Ave. N.W., Washington, District of Columbia 20006. (800) 822-0504. 1990. Includes findings on population growth, deforestation and the loss of biological diversity, the ozone layer, energy and climate change, economics, and other critical trends spell out new approaches to international cooperation and regulation in response to the shift from traditional security concerns to a focus on collective global security.

A Primer on Greenhouse Effect Gases. Donald J. Wuebbles and Jae Edmonds. Lewis Publishers, 200 Corporate Blvd. NW, Boca Raton, Florida 33431. (407) 994-0555 or (800)272-7737. 1991. Brings together the most current information available on greenhouse gases. Reveals information critical to developing an understanding of the role of energy and atmospheric chemical and radiative processes in determining atmospheric concentrations of greenhouse gases.

Projecting the Climatic Effects of Increasing Carbon Dioxide. Michael C. MacCracken. National Technical Information Service, 5285 Port Royal Rd., Springfield, Virginia 22161. (703) 487-4650. 1985.

Prospects for Future Climate: A Special US/USSR Report on Climate and Climate Change. Michael C. MacCracken, et al. Lewis Publishers, 2000 Corporate Blvd., N.W., Boca Raton, Florida 33431. (407) 994-0555 or (800) 272-7737. 1990. Describes the effects of the increasing concentration of greenhouse gases and the potential for climate change and impact on agriculture and hydrology. Projections are based on insights from both numerical models and empirical methods.

The Rising Tide: Global Warming and World Sea Levels. Lynne T. Edgerton. Island Press, 1718 Connecticut Ave. N.W., Suite 300, Washington, District of Columbia 20009. (202) 232-7933. 1991. Analysis of global warming and rising world sea level. Outlines state, national and international actions to respond to the effects of global warming on coastal communities and ecosystems.

Soils and the Greenhouse Effect. A. F. Bouwman, ed. John Wiley & Sons, Inc., 605 3rd Ave., New York, New York 10158-0012. (212) 850-6000. 1990. Proceedings of the International Conference on Soils and the Greenhouse Effect, Wageningen, Netherlands, 1989. Covers the present status and future trends concerning the effect of soils and vegetation on the fluxes of greenhouse gases, the surface energy balance, and the water balance. Discusses the role of deforestation and management practices such as mulching, wetlands, agriculture and livestock.

Weather of U.S. Cities. Frank E. Bair. Gale Research Inc., 835 Penobscot Bldg., Detroit, Michigan 48226-4094. (313) 961-2242. 1992. Compilation of U.S. government weather data on 281 cities and weather observation stations.

World Guide to Environmental Issues and Organizations. Peter Brackley. Longman Group Ltd., Longman House, Burnt Mill, Harlow, Essex, England CM20 2J6. (0279) 426721. 1991.

GOVERNMENTAL ORGANIZATIONS

National Environmental Satellite, Data, and Information Service. 1825 Connecticut Ave., N.W., Washington, District of Columbia 20235. (301) 763-7190.

U.S. Environmental Protection Agency: Office of Environmental Processes and Effects Research. 401 M St., S.W., Washington, District of Columbia 20460. (202) 382-5950.

HANDBOOKS AND MANUALS

Environmental Statistics Handbook: Europe. Allan Foster, Oksana Newman. Gale Research Inc., 835 Penobscot Bldg., Detroit, Michigan 48226-4094. (313) 961-2242. 1993.

Policy Options for Stabilizing Global Climate. Daniel A. Lashof and Dennis A. Tirpak. Hemisphere Publishing Co., 79 Madison Ave., Suite 1110, New York, New York 10016. (212) 725-1999. 1990. Covers climatic changes, environmental policy and protection and atmospheric greenhouse effect.

ONLINE DATA BASES

BIOSIS Previews. BIOSIS, 2100 Arch St., Philadelphia, Pennsylvania 19103-1399. (215) 587-4800. Largest and most comprehensive database of research in the life sciences. Contains citations for nearly 9000 primary research journals, monographs, reviews, symposia, preliminary reports, semi-popular journals, selected institutional reports, government reports and research communications.

Cambridge Scientific Abstracts Life Science–CSAL. Cambridge Scientific Abstracts, 5161 River Rd., Bethesda, Maryland 20816. (301) 961-6750. Provides access to the following abstracting services: "Life Sciences Collection," "Aquatic Sciences and Fisheries Abstracts," "Oceanic Abstracts," and "Pollution Abstracts."

Climate Assessment Database. National Weather Service, National Meteorological Center, Climate Analysis Center, Room 808 World Weather Building, Washington, District of Columbia 20233. (301) 763-4670.

Enviro/Energyline Abstracts Plus. R. R. Bowker Co., 121 Chanlon Rd., New Providence, New Jersey 07974. (908) 464-6800.

Environmental Periodicals Bibliography. National Information Services Corp., Ste. 6, Wyman Towers, 3100 St. Paul St., Baltimore, Maryland 21218. (410)243-0797. Online version of abstract of same name.

Global Environmental Change Report. Cutter Information Corp., 37 Broadway, Arlington, Massachusetts 02174-5539. (617) 648-8700. Online access to environmental issues worldwide, including global warming, ozone depletion, deforestation, and acid rain. Online version of periodical of the same name.

Monthly Catalog of United States Government Publications. U.S. G.P.O., Supt. of Docs., PO Box 371954, Pittsburgh, Pennsylvania 15250-7954. (202) 512-0000.

National Technical Information Service. U.S. Department of Commerce, National Technical Information Service, Office of Data Base Services, 5285 Port Royal Rd., Springfield, Virginia 22161. (703) 487-4807. Bibliographic database of government sponsored research and technical reports.

PressNet Environmental Reports. Chemical Information Systems, Inc., 7215 York Rd., Baltimore, Maryland 21212. (301) 321-8440.

SCISEARCH. Institute for Scientific Information, University City Science Center, 3501 Market St., Philadelphia, Pennsylvania 19104. (215) 386-0100.

SIRS Science CD-ROM. Social Issues Resources Series, Inc., PO Box 2348, Boca Raton, Florida 33427-2348. (407) 994-0079. Climatology, ecology, and oceanography.

PERIODICALS AND NEWSLETTERS

AIBC Bulletin. American Institute of Biomedical Climatology, 312 Saint St., Richland, Washington 19115. (509) 375-0873. 1977-. Quarterly. Disseminates articles and news on effects of weather, climate, and the atmosphere on arts and the environment.

Bulletin of American Meteorological Society. American Meteorological Society, 45 Beacon Street, Boston, Massachusetts 02108. (617) 227-2425. Monthly. Bulletin which certifies consulting meteorologists.

Climate Research. Inter-Research, PO Box 1120, W-2124 Amelinghausen, Germany D-2124. 04132. 1990. Three times a year. Presents both basic and applied research as research articles. Reviews and notes concerned with the interactions of climate with organisms, ecosystems and human societies are presented.

Earth Quest. University Corp. for Atmospheric Research, PO Box 3000, Boulder, Colorado 80307. (303) 497-1682. Quarterly. National and international programs addressing global environmental change.

Global Climate Change Digest. Elsevier Science Publishing Co., 655 Avenue of the Americas, New York, New York 10010. (212) 984-5800. Monthly. Topics dealing with ozone depletion and the large-scale climatic changes linked to industrial activity, industrial by-products, and man-made substances.

Global Environmental Change Report. Cutter Information Corp., 37 Broadway, Arlington, Massachusetts 02174-5539. (617) 648-8700. Biweekly. Focus on global warming, ozone depletion, deforestation, and acid rain. Also available online.

Journal of Applied Meteorology. American Meteorological Society, 45 Beacon Street, Boston, Massachusetts 02108. (617) 227-2425. Monthly. Articles on the relationship between weather and environment.

Storm Data. National Environmental Satellite, Data, and Information Service, 2069 Federal Bldg. 4, Washington, District of Columbia 20233. (301) 763-7190. Monthly.

RESEARCH CENTERS AND INSTITUTES

Climate Institute. 316 Pennsylvania Ave., S.E., Suite 403, Washington, District of Columbia 20003. (202) 547-0104.

Mountain Research Station. University of Colorado-Boulder, 818 County Road 116, Nederland, Colorado 80466. (303) 492-8841.

World Resources Institute. 1709 New York Ave., N.W., Washington, District of Columbia 20006. (202) 638-6300.

STATISTICS SOURCES

Comparative Climatic Data for the U.S. U.S. G.P.O, Washington, District of Columbia 20402-9325. (202)

512-0000. Annual. Monthly averages of surface weather data for U.S. and outlying areas.

Marine Fisheries Review. U.S. G.P.O, Washington, District of Columbia 20402-9325. (202) 512-0000. Quarterly. Marine fishery resources, development, and management. Covers fish, shellfish, and marine mammal populations.

National Marine Pollution Program. U.S. G.P.O, Washington, District of Columbia 20402-9325. (202) 512-0000. Annual. Federally funded programs for development, or monitoring activities related to marine pollution.

The State of the Environment. OECD Publications and Information Center, 2001 L St., N.W., Suite 700, Washington, District of Columbia 20036. (202) 785-6323. 1991.

Statistical Record of the Environment. Arsen J. Darnay. Gale Research Inc., 835 Penobscot Bldg., Detroit, Michigan 48226-4094. (313) 961-2242. 1992.

World Resources. World Resources Institute. 1709 New York Ave., N.W., Washington, District of Columbia 20006. (202) 638-6300. Annual. Statistical and textual analysis of world's natural resources and the effects of growth-caused environmental pollution.

TRADE ASSOCIATIONS AND PROFESSIONAL SOCIETIES

American Association of State Climatologists. c/o Dr. Ken Kunkel, Midwest Region Climate Center, 2204 Griffith Dr., Champaign, Illinois 61820. (217) 244-8226.

American Institute of Biomedical Climatology. 1023 Welsh Rd., Philadelphia, Pennsylvania 19115. (215) 673-8368.

American Meteorological Society. 45 Beacon St., Boston, Massachusetts 02108. (617) 227-2425.

CLONING

ABSTRACTING AND INDEXING SERVICES

Biological Abstracts. BIOSIS, 2100 Arch St., Philadelphia, Pennsylvania 19103-1399. (215) 587-4800. 1927-.

Biological and Agricultural Index. H.W. Wilson Co., 950 University Ave., Bronx, New York 10452. (800) 367-6770. 1916-. Monthly.

Biotechnology Research Abstracts. Cambridge Scientific Abstracts, 5161 River Rd., Bethesda, Maryland 20816. (301) 961-6750. Monthly. Includes such broad areas as genetic intervention, biochemical genetics, and microbiological techniques.

Food Science and Technology Abstracts. International Food Information Service, c/o National Food Laboratory, 6363 Clark Ave., Dublin, California 94568. (800) 336-3782. 1969-.

General Science Index. H. W. Wilson Co., 950 University Ave., Bronx, New York 10452. 1978-. Monthly, also issued in annual cumulation. Cumulative subject index to English language periodicals in the subject fields of astronomy, botany, chemistry, earth science, environment and conservation, food and nutrition, genetics,

mathematics, medicine and health, microbiology, oceanography, physics, physiology and zoology.

Genetics Abstracts. Cambridge Scientific Abstracts, 5161 River Rd., Bethesda, Maryland 20816. (301) 961-6750. 1968-. Monthly. Formerly published by Information Retrieval Ltd., London England. Published by Cambridge Scientific Abstracts since 1982.

Science Citation Index. Institute for Scientific Information, 3501 Market St., Philadelphia, Pennsylvania 19104. 1961-.

BIBLIOGRAPHIES

Genetic Engineering, DNA, and Cloning: A Bibliography in the Future of Genetics. Joseph Menditto. Whitston Publishing Co., P.O. Box 958, Troy, New York 12181. (518) 283-4363. 1983.

ENCYCLOPEDIAS AND DICTIONARIES

Cambridge Encyclopedia of Life Sciences. A. E. Friday and David S. Ingram. Cambridge University Press, 40 W 20th St., New York, New York 10011. (212) 924-3900 or (800) 227-0247. 1985. Includes all topics under biology and ecology.

A Dictionary of Genetics. Robert C. King and William A. Stansfield. Oxford University Press, 200 Madison Ave., New York, New York 10016. (212) 679-7300 or (800) 334-4249. 1991. Fourth edition. Includes 7,100 definitions with 250 illustrations. Also includes bibliography of major sources.

Dictionary of Genetics and Cell Biology. Norman Maclean. New York University Press, 70 Washington Sq. S., New York, New York 10012. (212) 998-2575. 1987. Includes the subject areas of cytology and genetics.

Encyclopedic Dictionary of Genetics: With German Term Equivalents and Extensive German/English Index. R. C. King and W. D. Stansfield. VCH Publishers, 303 NW 12th Ave., Deerfield Beach, Florida 33442-1788. (305) 428-5566. 1990. 4th ed. Revised edition of: A Dictionary of Genetics, third edition.

McGraw-Hill Encyclopedia of Science and Technology. McGraw-Hill, 1221 Avenue of the Americas, New York, New York 10020. (212) 512-2000 or (800) 262-4729. 1992. Seventh edition. Issued in multiple volumes including index. Includes all science and technology broad subject areas.

GENERAL WORKS

Basic Cloning Techniques: A Manual of Experimental Procedures. R.H. Pritchard. Blackwell Scientific Publications, PO Box 87, Oxford, England OX2 0DT. 44 0865 791155. 1985.

From Cell to Clone: the Story of Genetic Engineering. Margery Facklam. Harcourt Brace Jovanovich, Inc., 1250 6th Ave., San Diego, California 92101. (800) 346-8648. 1979.

From Clone to Clinic. D.J.A. Crommelin, ed. Kluwer Academic Publishers, 101 Philip Dr., Assinippi Pk., Norwell, Massachusetts 02061. (617) 871-6600. 1990.

Human T Cell Clones: A New Approach to Immune Regulation. Marc Feldmann, ed. Humana Press, P.O.

Box 2148, Clifton, New Jersey 07015. (201) 773-4389. 1984.

Magill's Survey of Science. Life Science Series. Frank N. Magill, ed. Salem Press, PO Box 50062, Pasadena, California 91105. 1991. Six volumes. Contents: v.1. A-Central and peripheral nervous system functions; v.2. Central metabolism regulation - eukaryotic transcriptional control; v.3. Positive and negative eukaryotic transcriptional control - mammalian hormones; v.4. Hormones and behavior - muscular contraction; v.5. Muscular contraction and relaxation - sexual reproduction in plants; v.6. Reproductive behavior and mating - X inactivation and the Lyon hypothesis.

Recombinant DNA Research and Viruses: Cloning and Expression of Viral Genes. Yechiel Becker, ed. Martinus Nijoff/W. Junk, 101 Philips Dr., Norwell, Massachusetts 02061. (617) 871-6600. 1985.

T Cell Clones. Year Book Medical Publishers, Inc., 200 N. LaSalle St., Chicago, Illinois 60601. (800) 622-5410. 1981.

ONLINE DATA BASES

BIOSIS Previews. BIOSIS, 2100 Arch St., Philadelphia, Pennsylvania 19103-1399. (215) 587-4800. Largest and most comprehensive database of research in the life sciences. Contains citations for nearly 9000 primary research journals, monographs, reviews, symposia, preliminary reports, semi-popular journals, selected institutional reports, government reports and research communications.

Cambridge Scientific Abstracts Life Science–CSAL. Cambridge Scientific Abstracts, 5161 River Rd., Bethesda, Maryland 20816. (301) 961-6750. Provides access to the following abstracting services: "Life Sciences Collection," "Aquatic Sciences and Fisheries Abstracts," "Oceanic Abstracts," and "Pollution Abstracts."

PressNet Environmental Reports. Chemical Information Systems, Inc., 7215 York Rd., Baltimore, Maryland 21212. (301) 321-8440.

SCISEARCH. Institute for Scientific Information, University City Science Center, 3501 Market St., Philadelphia, Pennsylvania 19104. (215) 386-0100.

TRADE ASSOCIATIONS AND PROFESSIONAL SOCIETIES

American Institute of Biological Sciences. 730 11th St., N.W., Washington, District of Columbia 20001-4521. (202) 628-1500.

CLOSED ECOLOGICAL SYSTEMS
See: ECOSYSTEMS

CLOUD SEEDING
See: WEATHER

COAGULATION

ABSTRACTING AND INDEXING SERVICES

Biological Abstracts. BIOSIS, 2100 Arch St., Philadelphia, Pennsylvania 19103-1399. (215) 587-4800. 1927-.

Chemical Abstracts. Chemical Abstracts Service, 2540 Olentangy River Rd., PO Box 3012, Columbus, Ohio 43210. (800) 848-6533. 1907-.

Pollution Abstracts. Cambridge Scientific Abstracts, 5161 River Rd., Bethesda, Maryland 20816. (301) 961-6750. Six/year. Indexes worldwide technical literature on environmental pollution. Covers air pollution, marine and freshwater pollution, sewage and wastewater treatment, waste management, toxicology and health, noise pollution, radiation, land pollution, and environmental policies, programs, legislation, and education. Also available online.

Science Citation Index. Institute for Scientific Information, 3501 Market St., Philadelphia, Pennsylvania 19104. 1961-.

ENCYCLOPEDIAS AND DICTIONARIES

Cambridge Encyclopedia of Life Sciences. A. E. Friday and David S. Ingram. Cambridge University Press, 40 W 20th St., New York, New York 10011. (212) 924-3900 or (800) 227-0247. 1985. Includes all topics under biology and ecology.

Encyclopedia of Human Biology. Renato Dulbecco, ed. Academic Press, c/o Harcourt Brace Jovanovich Inc., 6277 Sea Harbor Dr., Orlando, Florida 32887. (800) 346-8648. 1991. Eight volumes.

ONLINE DATA BASES

BIOSIS Previews. BIOSIS, 2100 Arch St., Philadelphia, Pennsylvania 19103-1399. (215) 587-4800. Largest and most comprehensive database of research in the life sciences. Contains citations for nearly 9000 primary research journals, monographs, reviews, symposia, preliminary reports, semi-popular journals, selected institutional reports, government reports and research communications.

Chemical Abstracts-CA. Chemical Abstracts Service, 2540 Olentangy River Rd., P.O. Box 3012, Columbus, Ohio 43210. (800) 848-6533 or (614) 421-3600. Information sources include 9000 journals, patents from 27 countries, two industrial property organizations, new books, conference proceedings, and government research reports.

TRADE ASSOCIATIONS AND PROFESSIONAL SOCIETIES

American Institute of Biological Sciences. 730 11th St., N.W., Washington, District of Columbia 20001-4521. (202) 628-1500.

COAL

ABSTRACTING AND INDEXING SERVICES

Applied Science and Technology Index. H.W. Wilson Co., 950 University Ave., Bronx, New York 10452. (800) 367-6770. Formerly Industrial Arts Index.

Clean Coal Technologies. National Technical Information Service, 5285 Port Royal Road, Springfield, Virginia 22161. (703) 487-4650. Monthly. Desulfurization, coal gasification and liquefaction, flue gas cleanup, and advanced coal combustion.

Energy Information Abstracts Annual 1987 in Retrospect. EIC/Intelligence Inc., 121 Chanlon Rd., New Providence, New Jersey 07974. (908) 464-6800. 1988. Annual. Cumulative edition of the monthly Energy Information Abstracts. Monitors sources in the field of energy including the scientific, technical and business journal literature, conference and symposia proceedings, corporate, government and academic reports.

Engineering Index. The Engineering Index Inc., 345 E. 47th St., New York, New York 10017. 1962-.

ERDA Research Abstracts. U.S. ERDA Technical Information Center, Box 62, Oak Ridge, Tennessee 37830.

Index to Scientific Book Contents. Institute for Scientific Information, 3501 Market St., Philadelphia, Pennsylvania 19104. (800) 523-1857. 1985-. Annual. Gives contents of science books published.

Pollution Abstracts. Cambridge Scientific Abstracts, 5161 River Rd., Bethesda, Maryland 20816. (301) 961-6750. Six/year. Indexes worldwide technical literature on environmental pollution. Covers air pollution, marine and freshwater pollution, sewage and wastewater treatment, waste management, toxicology and health, noise pollution, radiation, land pollution, and environmental policies, programs, legislation, and education. Also available online.

Science Citation Index. Institute for Scientific Information, 3501 Market St., Philadelphia, Pennsylvania 19104. 1961-.

BIBLIOGRAPHIES

Bibliography and Index of Geology. American Geological Institute, 4220 King St., Alexandria, Virginia 22302. Monthly. Includes environmental geology and hydrogeology.

DIRECTORIES

American Coke and Coal Chemicals Institute–Directory and By-Laws. 1255 23rd St., N.W., Washington, District of Columbia 20037. (202) 452-1140. Annual.

Coal Data. National Coal Association, 1130 17th St., N.W., Washington, District of Columbia 20036. (202) 463-2631.

Coal Distribution. U.S. Department of Energy, Energy Information Administration, Coal Division, 1000 Independence Ave. SW, Washington, District of Columbia 20585. (202) 586-5000.

Gale Environmental Sourcebook. Karen Hill. Gale Research Co., 835 Penobscot Bldg., Detroit, Michigan 48226-4094. (313) 961-2242. Contacts, information sources, or general information on environmental topics.

Keystone Coal Industry Manual. Maclean Hunter Publishing Company, 29 N. Wacker Dr., Chicago, Illinois 60606. (312) 726-2802.

ENCYCLOPEDIAS AND DICTIONARIES

Encyclopedia of Chemical Processing and Design. John J. Mcketta and W. A. Cunningham. Marcel Dekker, Inc., 270 Madison Ave., New York, New York 10016. (212) 696-9000; (800) 228-1160. 1992. Thirty-eight volumes.

Encyclopedia of Physical Science and Technology. Robert A. Meyers, ed. Academic Press, c/o Harcourt Brace Jovanovich Inc., 6277 Sea Harbor Dr., Orlando, Florida 32887. (800) 346-8648. Dictionary of engineering, technology and physical sciences.

Glossary of Geology. Robert Latimer Bates and Julia A. Jackson, eds. American Geological Institute, 4220 King St., Alexandria, Virginia 22302-1507. (703) 379-2480 or (800) 336-4764. 1987. Third edition.

Kaiman's Encyclopedia of Energy Topics. Lee Kaiman and J. Masloff. Environmental Design and Research Center, 26799 Elena Rd., Los Altos Hills, California 94022. 1983. Two volumes. Coverage of topics range from natural energy sources that are renewable to nonrenewable, and the application of these energy sources.

Kirk-Othmer Encyclopedia of Chemical Technology. J. I. Kroschwitz, ed. John Wiley & Sons, Inc., 605 3rd Ave., New York, New York 10158-0012. (212) 850-6000. 1992-. All articles in the new edition have been rewritten and updated adding new subjects such as biotechnology, computer topics, analytical techniques and instrumentation, environmental concerns, fuels and energy, inorganic and solid state chemistry; composite materials and material science in general, and pharmaceuticals. Also available online.

McGraw-Hill Encyclopedia of Science and Technology. McGraw-Hill, 1221 Avenue of the Americas, New York, New York 10020. (212) 512-2000 or (800) 262-4729. 1992. Seventh edition. Issued in multiple volumes including index. Includes all science and technology broad subject areas.

McGraw-Hill Encyclopedia of the Geological Sciences. Sybil P. Parker, ed. McGraw-Hill, 1221 Avenue of the Americas, New York, New York 10020. (212) 512-2000 or (800) 262-4729. 1988. Second edition. Published previously in the McGraw-Hill Encyclopedia of Science and Technology.

GENERAL WORKS

Adsorption Studies Evaluating Codisposal of Coal Gasification Ash with PAH-Containing Wastewater Sludges. John William Kilmer. University of Illinois at Urbana-Champaign, Urbana, Illinois 61801. 1986.

Calcium Magnesium Acetate: An Emerging Bulk Chemical for Environmental Applications. D.L. Wise. Elsevier Science Publishing Co., 655 Avenue of the Americas, New York, New York 10010. (212) 989-5800. 1991.

Clean Coal Technology: Programmes and Issues. International Energy Agency. OECD Publications and Information Centre, 2, rue Andre-Pascal, Paris Cedex 16, France F-75775. (1) 4524 8200. 1987. Analyses the number of issues that will affect future coal use. Both economic and environmental points of view are taken into consideration.

Coal Ash Disposal: Solid Waste Impacts. Raymond A. Tripodi and Paul N. Cheremisinoff. Technomic Publishing Co., 851 New Holland Ave., Box 3535, Lancaster, Pennsylvania 17604. (717) 291-5609. 1980.

Comprehensive Report to Congress: Clean Coal Technology Program. U.S. DOE Office of Clean Coal Technology. National Technical Information Service, 5285 Port Royal Rd., Springfield, Virginia 22161. (703) 487-4650. Demonstration of selective catalytic reduction technology for the control of nitrogen oxide emissions from high-sulphur coal- fired boilers.

Environmental Impacts of Coal Mining and Utilization. M. J. Chadwick, et al., eds. Pergamon Microforms International, Inc., Fairview Park, Elmsford, New York 10523. (914) 592-7720. 1987. Presents an up-to-date account of the whole coal fuel cycle and the recent developments to combat and control them.

Magill's Survey of Science. Earth Science Series. Frank N. Magill. Salem Press, PO Box 50062, Pasadena, California 91105. 1990-. Five volumes. Includes information on earth's crust, hot spots and volcanic island chains, physical properties of minerals, rock magnetism, physical properties of rocks, and index.

GOVERNMENTAL ORGANIZATIONS

Environmental Protection Agency: Office of Atmospheric and Indoor Air Programs. Waterside West Building, 401 M St., S.W., Washington, District of Columbia 20460. (202) 382-7404.

HANDBOOKS AND MANUALS

Energy Deskbook. Samuel Glasstone. Van Nostrand Reinhold, 115 5th Ave., New York, New York 10020. (212) 254-3232. 1983. Single volume reference covering all energy resources.

Riegel's Handbook of Industrial Chemistry. James A. Kent, ed. Van Nostrand Reinhold, 115 5th Ave., New York, New York 10020. (212) 254-3232. 1983. Eighth edition. Includes industries such as: wastewater technology, coal technology, phosphate fertilizers, synthetic plastics, man-made textiles, detergents, sugar, animal and vegetable oils, chemical explosives, dyes, nuclear industry, and much more.

ONLINE DATA BASES

CAS Source Index–CASSI. Chemical Abstracts Service, 2540 Olentangy River Rd., P.O. Box 3012, Columbus, Ohio 43210. (800) 848-6533 or (614) 421-3600. A listing of bibliographic and library holdings information for scientific and technical primary literature relevant to the chemical sciences.

Clean-Coal/Synfuels Letter. McGraw-Hill Science & Engineering Books, 11 W. 19th St., New York, New York 10011. (212) 337-6010.

Coal Outlook. Pasha Publications, Inc., 1401 Wilson Blvd., Suite 900, Arlington, Virginia 22209. (800) 424-2908.

Coal Week. McGraw-Hill Science & Engineering Books, 11 W. 19th St., New York, New York 10011. (212) 337-6010.

COALDATA. DECHEMA, Chemische Technik und Biotechnologie e.V., I & D Information Systems and Data Banks, Theodor-Heuss-Allee 25, Postfach 970146, Frankfurt, Germany D-6000. 49 (69) 7564-248.

COALPRO: Coal Research Projects. IEA Coal Research, 14/15 Lower Grosvenor Place, London, England SW 1W OEX. 44 (71) 828-4661.

Computerized Engineering Index–COMPENDEX. Engineering Information Inc., 345 E. 47th St., New York, New York 10017. (212) 705-7600.

Electric Power Industry Abstracts. Utility Data Institute, 1700 K St., N.W., Suite 400, Washington, District of Columbia 20006. (800) 466-3660.

Kirk-Othmer Encyclopedia of Chemical Technology. John Wiley & Sons, Inc., 605 3rd Ave., 5th Floor, New York, New York 10158. (212) 850-6000. Online version of the publication of the same name.

Monthly Catalog of United States Government Publications. U.S. G.P.O., Supt. of Docs., PO Box 371954, Pittsburgh, Pennsylvania 15250-7954. (202) 512-0000.

National Technical Information Service. U.S. Department of Commerce, National Technical Information Service, Office of Data Base Services, 5285 Port Royal Rd., Springfield, Virginia 22161. (703) 487-4807. Bibliographic database of government sponsored research and technical reports.

PERIODICALS AND NEWSLETTERS

Aquatic Toxicology and Risk Assessment. ASTM, 1916 Race St., Philadelphia, Pennsylvania 19103. (215) 299-5400. Annual. Covers aquatic animals, aquatic plants, water pollution, and water quality bioassay.

Ash at Work. American Coal Ash Association, 1000 16th Street, NW, Suite 507, Washington, District of Columbia 20036. (202) 659-2303. Quarterly. Information on fly ash from the combustion of coal.

Environment Week. King Communications Group, Inc., 627 National Press Bldg., Washington, District of Columbia 20045. (202) 638-4260. Weekly. Covers acid rain, solid waste and disposal, clean coal, nuclear and hazardous waste. Also available online.

Journal of American Mining Congress. American Mining Congress, 1920 N Street, NW, Suite 300, Washington, District of Columbia 20036. (202) 861-2800. Monthly. Contains information on the mining industry.

RESEARCH CENTERS AND INSTITUTES

U.S. Forest Service, Sierra Field Station. c/o Center for Environmental Studies, Arizona State University, Temple, Arizona 85287-3211. (602) 965-2975.

STATISTICS SOURCES

Coal Information. International Energy Agency. OECD Publications and Information Center, 2001 L St., N.W., Washington, District of Columbia 20036. (202) 785-6323. 1986-. Annually. Reports on world coal market trends and long-term prospects. Contains analysis on country-specific statistics for OECD member countries and selected non-OECD countries on coal prices, demand, trade, production, and emission standards for coal-fired boilers. Essential facts on coal importing and exporting ports and coal-fired power stations in coal importing regions are also included.

Environmental Data Compendium. OECD Publications and Information Center, 2001 L St., N.W., Suite 700, Washington, District of Columbia 20036. (202) 785-6323. 1989.

Environmental Indicators. OECD Publications and Information Center, 2001 L St., N.W., Suite 700, Washington, District of Columbia 20036. (202) 785-6323. 1991.

Environmental Quality. Council on Environmental Quality. U.S. G.P.O., Washington, District of Columbia 20401. (202) 512-0000. Annual.

The State of the Environment. OECD Publications and Information Center, 2001 L St., N.W., Suite 700, Washington, District of Columbia 20036. (202) 785-6323. 1991.

World Resources. World Resources Institute. 1709 New York Ave., N.W., Washington, District of Columbia 20006. (202) 638-6300. Annual. Statistical and textual analysis of world's natural resources and the effects of growth-caused environmental pollution.

TRADE ASSOCIATIONS AND PROFESSIONAL SOCIETIES

American Chemical Society. 1155 16th St., N.W., Washington, District of Columbia 20036. (202) 872-4600.

American Coal Ash Association. 1913 I St. N.W., Washington, District of Columbia 20006. (202) 659-2303.

American Coke and Coal Chemicals Institute. 1255 23rd St., N.W., Washington, District of Columbia 20037. (202) 452-1140.

American Institute of Chemical Engineers. 345 East 47th St., New York, New York 10017. (212) 705-7338.

American Institute of Chemists. 7315 Wisconsin Ave., Bethesda, Maryland 20814. (301) 652-2447.

American Mining Congress. 1920 N St., N.W., Suite 300, Washington, District of Columbia 20036. (202) 861-2800.

Coal and Slurry Technology Association. 1156 15th St., N.W., Suite 525, Washington, District of Columbia 20005. (202) 296-1133.

Coal Exporters Association of the United States. 1130 17th St., N.W., Washington, District of Columbia 20036. (202) 463-2654.

International Committee for Coal Petrology. Energy and Fuels Res. Center, 517 Deike Bldg., Pennsylvania State University, University Park, Pennsylvania 16802. (814) 865-6544.

National Coal Association. 1130 17th St., N.W., Washington, District of Columbia 20036. (202) 463-2625.

National Independent Coal Operators Association. Box 354, Richland, Virginia 24641. (703) 963-9011.

COAL ANALYSIS
See: COAL

COAL ASH
See: COAL

COAL DESULFURIZATION
See: DESULFURIZATION

COAL GASIFICATION
See: COAL

COAL STORAGE
See: COAL

COAL TARS
See: COAL

COAL TRANSPORT
See: TRANSPORTATION

COASTAL ENGINEERING
See also: COASTAL ZONE MANAGEMENT

ABSTRACTING AND INDEXING SERVICES

Applied Ecology Abstracts Studies in Renewable Natural Resources. Information Retrieval Ltd., 1911 Jefferson Davis Highway, Arlington, Virginia 22202. 1975-. Monthly.

Civil Engineering Hydraulic Abstracts. BHRA Fluid Engineering, Air Science Co., PO Box 143, Corning, New York 14830. (607) 962-5591. Monthly. Abstracts of periodicals that publish in the areas of hydraulic engineering and other related topics.

Environment Abstracts. Bowker A & I Publishing, 121 Chanlon Rd., New Providence, New Jersey 07974. (908) 464-6800. 1974-.

Environment Index. Environment Information Center, Index Research Department, 124 E. 39th St., New York, New York 10016. 1971-. Annual.

Environmental Information Connection–EIC. Planning Information Program, Dept. of Urban and Regional Planning, University of Illinois, 1003 West Nevada, Urbana, Illinois 61801. (217) 333-1369. Also available online.

Environmental Periodicals Bibliography. Environmental Studies Institute, International Academy at Santa Barbara, 800 Garden St., Suite D, Santa Barbara, California 93101. (805) 965-5010. Also available online.

General Science Index. H. W. Wilson Co., 950 University Ave., Bronx, New York 10452. 1978-. Monthly, also issued in annual cumulation. Cumulative subject index to English language periodicals in the subject fields of astronomy, botany, chemistry, earth science, environment and conservation, food and nutrition, genetics, mathematics, medicine and health, microbiology, oceanography, physics, physiology and zoology.

Multimedia Index to Ecology. National Information Center for Educational Media, University of Southern California, Los Angeles, California 90007.

Sea Grant Abstracts. National Sea Grant Depository, Pell Laboratory Bldg., Bay Campus, University of Rhode Island, Narragansett, Rhode Island 02882. (401) 792-6114. 1986-. Quarterly. Published by the National Sea Grant Programs, this collection includes annual reports, serials and newsletters, charts and maps.

BIBLIOGRAPHIES

An Annotated Bibliography of Patents Related to Coastal Engineering. Robert E. Ray. National Technical Information Service, 5285 Port Royal Rd., Springfield, Virginia 22161. (703) 487-4650. 1979.

Bibliography of Publications of the Coastal Engineering Research Center and the Beach Erosion Board. Andre Szuwalski. National Technical Information Service, 5285 Port Royal Rd., Springfield, Virginia 22161. (703) 487-4650. 1981. Covers coastal engineering, oceanography, and ecology.

EPA Publications Bibliography. U.S. Environmental Protection Agency, Library Systems Branch, 401 M St., SW, Washington, District of Columbia 20460. (202) 260-2090. Quarterly.

Sources of Coastal Engineering Information. Yen-hsi Chu. National Technical Information Service, 5285 Port Royal Rd., Springfield, Virginia 22161. (703) 487-4650. 1987.

ENCYCLOPEDIAS AND DICTIONARIES

The Encyclopedia of Beaches and Coastal Environments. Maurice L. Schwartz. Hutchinson Ross Pub. Co., Stroudsburg, Pennsylvania 1982.

The Encyclopedia of Geochemistry and Environmental Sciences. Rhodes Whitmore Fairbridge. Van Nostrand Reinhold Co., 115 5th Ave., New York, New York 10003. (212) 254-3232. 1972.

The Encyclopedia of Oceanography. Rhodes Whitmore Fairbridge. Reinhold Pub. Co., 115 5th Ave., New York, New York 10003. (212) 254-3232. 1966.

McGraw-Hill Encyclopedia of Environmental Science. Sybil P. Parker. McGraw-Hill Science & Engineering Books, 11 W. 19th St., New York, New York 10011.

(212) 337-6010. 1980. Covers ecology, man's influence on nature, and environmental protection.

GENERAL WORKS

Basic Coastal Engineering. R. M. Sorensen. John Wiley & Sons, Inc., 605 3rd Ave., New York, New York 10158-0012. (212) 850-6000. 1978. Covers ocean engineering, hydraulic structures and ocean waves.

HANDBOOKS AND MANUALS

Handbook of Coastal and Ocean Engineering. John B. Herbich. Gulf Publishing Co., Book Division, PO Box 2608, Houston, Texas 77252. (713) 529-4301. 1991. Wave phenomena in coastal structures.

ONLINE DATA BASES

Enviro/Energyline Abstracts Plus. R. R. Bowker Co., 121 Chanlon Rd., New Providence, New Jersey 07974. (908) 464-6800.

Environmental Periodicals Bibliography. National Information Services Corp., Ste. 6, Wyman Towers, 3100 St. Paul St., Baltimore, Maryland 21218. (410)243-0797. Online version of abstract of same name.

Monthly Catalog of United States Government Publications. U.S. G.P.O., Supt. of Docs., PO Box 371954, Pittsburgh, Pennsylvania 15250-7954. (202) 512-0000.

National Technical Information Service. U.S. Department of Commerce, National Technical Information Service, Office of Data Base Services, 5285 Port Royal Rd., Springfield, Virginia 22161. (703) 487-4807. Bibliographic database of government sponsored research and technical reports.

SCISEARCH. Institute for Scientific Information, University City Science Center, 3501 Market St., Philadelphia, Pennsylvania 19104. (215) 386-0100.

PERIODICALS AND NEWSLETTERS

Coastal Engineering. Elsevier, Box 211, Amsterdam, Netherlands 1000 AE. (020) 5803-911. 1977. An international journal for coastal, harbor and offshore engineers, covering hydraulic engineering, ocean waves, coast changes, and shore protection.

COASTAL WATERS

See: COASTS

COASTAL ZONE MANAGEMENT

See also: COASTS

ABSTRACTING AND INDEXING SERVICES

Applied Ecology Abstracts Studies in Renewable Natural Resources. Information Retrieval Ltd., 1911 Jefferson Davis Highway, Arlington, Virginia 22202. 1975-. Monthly.

Civil Engineering Hydraulic Abstracts. BHRA Fluid Engineering, Air Science Co., PO Box 143, Corning, New York 14830. (607) 962-5591. Monthly. Abstracts of periodicals that publish in the areas of hydraulic engineering and other related topics.

Ecology Abstracts. Cambridge Scientific Abstracts, 5161 River Rd., Bethesda, Maryland 20816. (301) 961-6750. Monthly.

Environment Abstracts. Bowker A & I Publishing, 121 Chanlon Rd., New Providence, New Jersey 07974. (908) 464-6800. 1974-.

Environment Index. Environment Information Center, Index Research Department, 124 E. 39th St., New York, New York 10016. 1971-. Annual.

Environmental Information Connection-EIC. Planning Information Program, Dept. of Urban and Regional Planning, University of Illinois, 1003 West Nevada, Urbana, Illinois 61801. (217) 333-1369. Also available online.

Environmental Periodicals Bibliography. Environmental Studies Institute, International Academy at Santa Barbara, 800 Garden St., Suite D, Santa Barbara, California 93101. (805) 965-5010. Also available online.

Multimedia Index to Ecology. National Information Center for Educational Media, University of Southern California, Los Angeles, California 90007.

Oceanic Abstracts. UMI Data Courier, 620 S. 3rd St., Louisville, Kentucky 40202. (800) 626-2823. Formerly: Oceanic Index and Oceanic Citation Journal.

Sea Grant Abstracts. National Sea Grant Depository, Pell Laboratory Bldg., Bay Campus, University of Rhode Island, Narragansett, Rhode Island 02882. (401) 792-6114. 1986-. Quarterly. Published by the National Sea Grant Programs, this collection includes annual reports, serials and newsletters, charts and maps.

BIBLIOGRAPHIES

An Annotated Bibliography of Coastal Zone Management Work Products. Center for Natural Areas, 1983. A compilation of State, Territory, and Federal work products via funding from the Coastal Zone Management Act of 1972, as amended by Center for Natural Areas.

Bibliography and Index of Geology. American Geological Institute, 4220 King St., Alexandria, Virginia 22302. Monthly. Includes environmental geology and hydrogeology.

Coastal Zone Management. Mary A. Vance. Vance Bibliographies, PO Box 229, 112 N. Charter St., Monticello, Illinois 61856. (217) 762-3831. 1985.

EPA Publications Bibliography. U.S. Environmental Protection Agency, Library Systems Branch, 401 M St., SW, Washington, District of Columbia 20460. (202) 260-2090. Quarterly.

ENCYCLOPEDIAS AND DICTIONARIES

The Encyclopedia of Beaches and Coastal Environments. Maurice L. Schwartz. Hutchinson Ross Pub. Co., Stroudsburg, Pennsylvania 1982.

The Encyclopedia of Geochemistry and Environmental Sciences. Rhodes Whitmore Fairbridge. Van Nostrand Reinhold Co., 115 5th Ave., New York, New York 10003. (212) 254-3232. 1972.

The Encyclopedia of Oceanography. Rhodes Whitmore Fairbridge. Reinhold Pub. Co., 115 5th Ave., New York, New York 10003. (212) 254-3232. 1966.

McGraw-Hill Encyclopedia of Science and Technology. McGraw-Hill, 1221 Avenue of the Americas, New York, New York 10020. (212) 512-2000 or (800) 262-4729. 1992. Seventh edition. Issued in multiple volumes including index. Includes all science and technology broad subject areas.

GENERAL WORKS

Coastal Ecosystems: Ecological Considerations for Management of the Coastal Zone. John R. Clark. Conservation Foundation, 1250 24th St. NW, Washington, District of Columbia 20037. (202) 203-4800. 1974.

Environmental Law and the Siting of Facilities: Issues in Land Use and Coastal Zone Management. Michael S. Baram. Ballinger Publishing Co., 10 E. 53rd St., New York, New York 10022. (212) 207-7581. 1976. Law and legislation in the United States relative to coastal zone management.

Magill's Survey of Science. Earth Science Series. Frank N. Magill. Salem Press, PO Box 50062, Pasadena, California 91105. 1990-. Five volumes. Includes information on earth's crust, hot spots and volcanic island chains, physical properties of minerals, rock magnetism, physical properties of rocks, and index.

HANDBOOKS AND MANUALS

Coastal Ecosystem Management. John Ray Clark. John Wiley & Sons, Inc., 605 3rd Ave., New York, New York 10158-0012. (212) 850-6000. 1983. A technical manual for the conservation of coastal resources.

ONLINE DATA BASES

Enviro/Energyline Abstracts Plus. R. R. Bowker Co., 121 Chanlon Rd., New Providence, New Jersey 07974. (908) 464-6800.

Environmental Periodicals Bibliography. National Information Services Corp., Ste. 6, Wyman Towers, 3100 St. Paul St., Baltimore, Maryland 21218. (410)243-0797. Online version of abstract of same name.

Monthly Catalog of United States Government Publications. U.S. G.P.O., Supt. of Docs., PO Box 371954, Pittsburgh, Pennsylvania 15250-7954. (202) 512-0000.

National Technical Information Service. U.S. Department of Commerce, National Technical Information Service, Office of Data Base Services, 5285 Port Royal Rd., Springfield, Virginia 22161. (703) 487-4807. Bibliographic database of government sponsored research and technical reports.

Oceanic Abstracts. Cambridge Scientific Abstracts, 5161 River Rd., Bethesda, Maryland 20816. (301) 961-6750. Online access.

SCISEARCH. Institute for Scientific Information, University City Science Center, 3501 Market St., Philadelphia, Pennsylvania 19104. (215) 386-0100.

PERIODICALS AND NEWSLETTERS

Coastal Management. Taylor & Francis, 1900 Frost Rd., Ste. 101, Bristol, Pennsylvania 19007. (215) 785-5800. 1973-. Quarterly. Journal dealing with environmental resources and law.

RESEARCH CENTERS AND INSTITUTES

Rutgers University, Little Egg Inlet Marine Field Station. Great Bay Blvd., PO Box 278, Tuckerton, New Jersey 08087. (609) 296-5260.

Scripps Institution of Oceanography, Center for Coastal Studies. University of California, San Diego, 9500 Gilman Dr., La Jolla, California 92093. (619) 534-4333.

Sea Grant College Program. University of Delaware, 196 South College Avenue, Newark, Delaware 19716. (302) 451-8182.

Texas A&M University at Galveston Coastal Zone Laboratory. P.O. Box 1675, Galveston, Texas 77553. (409) 740-4465.

University of Maine, Ira C. Darling Center for Research Teaching and Service. Walpole, Maine 04573. (207) 563-3146.

COASTS

See also: COASTAL ENGINEERING; COASTAL ZONE
MANAGEMENT; ESTUARIES

ABSTRACTING AND INDEXING SERVICES

Applied Ecology Abstracts Studies in Renewable Natural Resources. Information Retrieval Ltd., 1911 Jefferson Davis Highway, Arlington, Virginia 22202. 1975-. Monthly.

Applied Science and Technology Index. H.W. Wilson Co., 950 University Ave., Bronx, New York 10452. (800) 367-6770. Formerly Industrial Arts Index.

Biological Abstracts. BIOSIS, 2100 Arch St., Philadelphia, Pennsylvania 19103-1399. (215) 587-4800. 1927-.

Civil Engineering Hydraulic Abstracts. BHRA Fluid Engineering, Air Science Co., PO Box 143, Corning, New York 14830. (607) 962-5591. Monthly. Abstracts of periodicals that publish in the areas of hydraulic engineering and other related topics.

Ecological Abstracts. Geo Abstracts Ltd. Elsevier Applied Science, Crown House, Linton Rd., Barking, England IG 11 8JU. 1974-. Derived from over 600 leading ecological and environmental journals, plus books, conference proceedings, reports and theses.

Ecology Abstracts. Cambridge Scientific Abstracts, 5161 River Rd., Bethesda, Maryland 20816. (301) 961-6750. Monthly.

Environment Abstracts. Bowker A & I Publishing, 121 Chanlon Rd., New Providence, New Jersey 07974. (908) 464-6800. 1974-.

Environment Index. Environment Information Center, Index Research Department, 124 E. 39th St., New York, New York 10016. 1971-. Annual.

Environmental Information Connection–EIC. Planning Information Program, Dept. of Urban and Regional Planning, University of Illinois, 1003 West Nevada, Urbana, Illinois 61801. (217) 333-1369. Also available online.

Environmental Periodicals Bibliography. Environmental Studies Institute, International Academy at Santa Barbara, 800 Garden St., Suite D, Santa Barbara, California 93101. (805) 965-5010. Also available online.

General Science Index. H. W. Wilson Co., 950 University Ave., Bronx, New York 10452. 1978-. Monthly, also issued in annual cumulation. Cumulative subject index to English language periodicals in the subject fields of astronomy, botany, chemistry, earth science, environment and conservation, food and nutrition, genetics, mathematics, medicine and health, microbiology, oceanography, physics, physiology and zoology.

Index to Scientific Book Contents. Institute for Scientific Information, 3501 Market St., Philadelphia, Pennsylvania 19104. (800) 523-1857. 1985-. Annual. Gives contents of science books published.

Multimedia Index to Ecology. National Information Center for Educational Media, University of Southern California, Los Angeles, California 90007.

Oceanic Abstracts. UMI Data Courier, 620 S. 3rd St., Louisville, Kentucky 40202. (800) 626-2823. Formerly: Oceanic Index and Oceanic Citation Journal.

Pollution Abstracts. Cambridge Scientific Abstracts, 5161 River Rd., Bethesda, Maryland 20816. (301) 961-6750. Six/year. Indexes worldwide technical literature on environmental pollution. Covers air pollution, marine and freshwater pollution, sewage and wastewater treatment, waste management, toxicology and health, noise pollution, radiation, land pollution, and environmental policies, programs, legislation, and education. Also available online.

Science Citation Index. Institute for Scientific Information, 3501 Market St., Philadelphia, Pennsylvania 19104. 1961-.

Sea Grant Abstracts. National Sea Grant Depository, Pell Laboratory Bldg., Bay Campus, University of Rhode Island, Narragansett, Rhode Island 02882. (401) 792-6114. 1986-. Quarterly. Published by the National Sea Grant Programs, this collection includes annual reports, serials and newsletters, charts and maps.

ALMANACS AND YEARBOOKS

Ocean Yearbook. The University of Chicago Press, Journals Division, PO Box 37005, Chicago, Illinois 60637. 1978-. Annual. A comprehensive guide to current research and data on living and nonliving resources, marine science and technological environmental, and coastal management.

BIBLIOGRAPHIES

A Bibliography of Numerical Models for Tidal Rivers, Estuaries, and Coastal Waters. University of Rhode Island, International Center for Marine Resource Development, 126 Woodward Hall, Kingston, Rhode Island 20881. (401) 792-2479.

Coastal Land Use. Council of Planning Librarians, 1313 E. 60th St., Chicago, Illinois 60637-2897. (312) 942-2163. Bibliography of shore protection.

Directory of Published Proceedings. Interdok Corp., 173 Halstead Ave., Harrison, New York 10528. (914) 835-3506. 1990. Monthly. This is a listing of published proceedings including the series SEMTE (Science/Medicine/Engineering/Technology) and the series SSH (Social Science/Humanities).

EPA Publications Bibliography. U.S. Environmental Protection Agency, Library Systems Branch, 401 M St., SW, Washington, District of Columbia 20460. (202) 260-2090. Quarterly.

Interactions of Aquaculture, Marine Coastal Ecosystems, and Near-Shore Waters: A Bibliography. Deborah T. Hanfman. National Agricultural Library, 10301 Baltimore Blvd., Beltsville, Maryland 20705-2351. (301) 504-5755. Covers coastal ecology.

DIRECTORIES

Directory of Engineering Societies and Related Organizations. Hemisphere Publishing Co., 79 Madison Ave., Suite 1110, New York, New York 10016. (212) 725-1999 or (800) 821-8312. Irregular.

Directory of Environmental Journals & Media Contacts. Tom Cairns. Council for Environmental Conservation, 80 York Way, London, England N1 9AG. 1985.

Gale Environmental Sourcebook. Karen Hill. Gale Research Co., 835 Penobscot Bldg., Detroit, Michigan 48226-4094. (313) 961-2242. Contacts, information sources, or general information on environmental topics.

ENCYCLOPEDIAS AND DICTIONARIES

The Encyclopedia of Beaches and Coastal Environments. Maurice L. Schwartz. Hutchinson Ross Pub. Co., Stroudsburg, Pennsylvania 1982.

The Encyclopedia of Climatology. John E. Oliver and Rhodes W. Fairbridge, eds. Van Nostrand Reinhold, 115 5th Ave., New York, New York 10003. (212) 254-3232. 1987. Belongs in the series Encyclopedia of Earth Sciences, v.11.

The Encyclopedia of Geochemistry and Environmental Sciences. Rhodes Whitmore Fairbridge. Van Nostrand Reinhold Co., 115 5th Ave., New York, New York 10003. (212) 254-3232. 1972.

The Encyclopedia of Oceanography. Rhodes Whitmore Fairbridge. Reinhold Pub. Co., 115 5th Ave., New York, New York 10003. (212) 254-3232. 1966.

McGraw-Hill Encyclopedia of Environmental Science. Sybil P. Parker. McGraw-Hill Science & Engineering Books, 11 W. 19th St., New York, New York 10011. (212) 337-6010. 1980. Covers ecology, man's influence on nature, and environmental protection.

McGraw-Hill Encyclopedia of Science and Technology. McGraw-Hill, 1221 Avenue of the Americas, New York, New York 10020. (212) 512-2000 or (800) 262-4729. 1992. Seventh edition. Issued in multiple volumes including index. Includes all science and technology broad subject areas.

GENERAL WORKS

And Two if by Sea: Fighting the Attack on America's Coasts. Coast Alliance, Washington, District of Columbia 1986. A citizen's guide to the Coastal Zone Management Act and other coastal laws

Basic Coastal Engineering. R. M. Sorensen. John Wiley & Sons, Inc., 605 3rd Ave., New York, New York 10158-0012. (212) 850-6000. 1978. Covers ocean engineering, hydraulic structures and ocean waves.

Coastal Alert: Ecosystems, Energy, and Offshore Oil Drilling. Dwight Holing. Island Press, 1718 Connecticut Ave. N.W., Suite 300, Washington, District of Columbia 20009. (202) 232-7933. 1990. Describes how offshore drilling affects environment and quality of life, how the government auctions our coast to the oil industry, how the lease sale process works, how energy alternatives can replace offshore drilling; how citizen action works and how to become involved.

Coasts: An Introduction to Coastal Geomorphology. B. Blackwell, 3 Cambridge Ctr., Suite 208, Cambridge, Massachusetts 02142. (617) 225-0401. 1984.

Coasts in Crisis. U.S. Department of the Interior, 1849 C St. NW, Washington, District of Columbia 20240. (202) 208-3171. 1991.

Conservation of Water and Related Land Resources. Peter E. Black. Rowman & Littlefield, Publishers, Inc., 8705 Bollman Pl., Savage, Maryland 20763. (301) 306-0400. 1988. 2d ed. Analysis of the current status of water and land-water resources policy and programming in the United States.

Drowning the National Heritage: Climate Change and Coastal Biodiversity in the United States. Walter V. C. Reid and Mark C. Trexler. World Resources Institute, 1709 New York Ave. N.W., Washington, District of Columbia 20006. (800) 822 0504. 1991. Examines erosion, flooding, and salt-water intrusion into groundwater, rivers, bays, and estuaries as well as receding coastlines and altered coastal current and upwelling patterns. Evaluates various policy responses and recommends specific changes to protect the biological wealth of these vital ecosystems.

Ecology of Sandy Shores. A. C. Brown and A. Mclachlan. Elsevier Science Publishing Co., 655 Avenue of the Americas, New York, New York 10010. (212) 989-5800. 1990. Deals with the biological study of sandy beaches.

Environmental Aspects of Coasts and Islands. BAR, Oxford, England 1981. Maritime anthropology, coastal ecology and environmental ecology.

The Living Ocean. Boyce Thorne-Miller. Island Press, 1718 Connecticut Ave. N.W., Suite 300, Washington, District of Columbia 20009. (202) 232-7933. 1991. Discusses all marine ecosystems, including coastal benthic, shore systems, estuaries, wetlands, and coral reefs, coastal pelagic, deep-sea benthic, hydrothermal vents and others.

Modeling of the Seepage Flux of Ground Water from Coastal Landfills. D. A. Colden. National Technical Information Service, 5285 Port Royal Rd., Springfield, Virginia 22161. (703) 487-4650. 1990. Master's Thesis, Rhode Island University, Kingston.

Physical Oceanography of Coastal Waters. K. F. Bowden. John Wiley & Sons, Inc., 605 3rd Ave., New York, New York 10158-0012. (212) 850-6000. 1984.

The Rising Tide: Global Warming and World Sea Levels. Lynne T. Edgerton. Island Press, 1718 Connecticut Ave. N.W., Suite 300, Washington, District of Columbia 20009. (202) 232-7933. 1991. Analysis of global warming and rising world sea level. Outlines state, national and international actions to respond to the effects of global warming on coastal communities and ecosystems.

Subantarctic Macquarie Island: Environment and Biology. P. M. Selkirk, et al. Cambridge University Press, 40 W. 20th St., New York, New York 10011. (212) 924-3900; (800) 227-0247. 1990. Review of environmental and biologic research on the Macquarie Island. It presents summary of studies done in the last 15 years by Australian scientists. Contains a sequence of 12 chapters that concern the island's discovery and history; situation in the Southern ocean; tectonics and geology; landforms and Quaternary history; vegetation; lakes; birds; mammals; anthropoids; microbiology; near shore environments; and human impact.

GOVERNMENTAL ORGANIZATIONS

Coast Guard. Information Office, 2100 Second St., S.W., Washington, District of Columbia 20593. (202) 267-2229.

HANDBOOKS AND MANUALS

The Economics of Coastal Zone Management: A Manual of Assessment Techniques. Edmund Penning-Rowsell, ed. Belhaven Press, 136 S. Broadway, Irvington, New York 10533. (914) 591-9111. 1991. Manual for assessing and pricing the procedures that protect vulnerable coastlines against flood, storm, high tide and other environmental damage.

The Global Ecology Handbook: What You Can Do about the Environmental Crisis. Walter H. Corson, ed. The Global Tomorrow Coalition, Beacon Pr., 25 Beacon St., Boston, Massachusetts 02108-2800. (617) 742-2110. 1990. Covers environment, energy policy, population growth and other issues. It includes chapters on tropical rain forests, garbage, oceans and coasts, global warming, population growth, agriculture, biological diversity, fresh water, hazardous wastes, and environment and development.

ONLINE DATA BASES

BIOSIS Previews. BIOSIS, 2100 Arch St., Philadelphia, Pennsylvania 19103-1399. (215) 587-4800. Largest and most comprehensive database of research in the life sciences. Contains citations for nearly 9000 primary research journals, monographs, reviews, symposia, preliminary reports, semi-popular journals, selected institutional reports, government reports and research communications.

Civil Engineering Database. American Society of Civil Engineers, 345 E. 47th St., New York, New York 10017. (800) 548-2723.

Enviro/Energyline Abstracts Plus. R. R. Bowker Co., 121 Chanlon Rd., New Providence, New Jersey 07974. (908) 464-6800.

Environmental Periodicals Bibliography. National Information Services Corp., Ste. 6, Wyman Towers, 3100 St. Paul St., Baltimore, Maryland 21218. (410)243-0797. Online version of abstract of same name.

MARINELINE. Informationszentrum Rohstoffgewinnwig Geowissenschaften Wasserwirtschaft, Bundesanstalt fuer Geowissenschaften und Rohstoffe, Postfach 510153, Stilleweg 2, Hanover 51, Germany D-3000. 49 (511) 643-2819.

Monthly Catalog of United States Government Publications. U.S. G.P.O., Supt. of Docs., PO Box 371954, Pittsburgh, Pennsylvania 15250-7954. (202) 512-0000.

National Technical Information Service. U.S. Department of Commerce, National Technical Information Service, Office of Data Base Services, 5285 Port Royal Rd., Springfield, Virginia 22161. (703) 487-4807. Bibliographic database of government sponsored research and technical reports.

Oceanic Abstracts. Cambridge Scientific Abstracts, 5161 River Rd., Bethesda, Maryland 20816. (301) 961-6750. Online access.

PressNet Environmental Reports. Chemical Information Systems, Inc., 7215 York Rd., Baltimore, Maryland 21212. (301) 321-8440.

SCISEARCH. Institute for Scientific Information, University City Science Center, 3501 Market St., Philadelphia, Pennsylvania 19104. (215) 386-0100.

PERIODICALS AND NEWSLETTERS

American Shore and Beach Preservation Association Newsletter. American Shore and Beach Preservation Association, PO Box 279, Middletown, California 95461. (707) 987-2385. 1955-. Quarterly.

Barrier Island Newsletter. National Wildlife Federation, 1400 16th St. N.W., Washington, District of Columbia 20036-2266. (202) 797-6800. 1980-. Quarterly. Newsletter for activists interested in the protection of America's four coasts, through the expansion of the Coastal Barrier Resources system and improvement of the National Flood Insurance Program.

Big Bend Bulletin. Sea Grant Extension Program, 615 Paul Russell Rd., Tallahassee, Florida 32301. (904) 487-3007. Quarterly. Current issues regarding fisheries, coastal processes, and marine education.

The CERCular. U.S. Army Corps. of Engineers, Waterways Experiment Station, PO Box 631, Vicksburg, Mississippi 39180. (601) 634-3774. Quarterly. Army Coastal Engineering Research Center and its work on shore and beach erosion; flood and storm protection; navigation improvements; and the design, construction, operation and maintenance of coastal structures.

Clean Water Report. Business Publishers, Inc., 951 Pershing Dr., Silver Spring, Maryland 20910-4464. (301) 587-6300. 1964-. Biweekly. Key information source for environmental professionals, covering the important issues: groundwater, drinking water, wastewater treatment, drought, wetlands, coastal protection, dioxin, non-point source pollution, agrichemical contamination, cleanup versus prevention issues, and related topics.

Coastal Management. Taylor & Francis, 1900 Frost Rd., Ste. 101, Bristol, Pennsylvania 19007. (215) 785-5800. 1973-. Quarterly. Journal dealing with environmental resources and law.

Coastal Reporter Newsletter. American Littoral Society, Sandy Hook, Highlands, New Jersey 07732. (201) 291-0055. Quarterly. Promotes study and conservation of the coastal zone habitat.

Coastal Research. Geology Dept., Florida State University, Tallahassee, Florida 32306-3026. (904) 644-3208. Three times a year. Sea level, meteorology, coastal and near shore environments, coastal geology, sedimentary research, coastal engineering, and pollution.

Coastal Zone Management. Taylor & Francis, 1900 Frost Road, Suite 101, Bristol, Pennsylvania 19007. (800) 821-8312. Quarterly. Covers social, political, legal, and cultural issues of coastal resources.

Coastlines. New York State Sea Grant Inst., Duchess Hall, SUNY at Stony Brook, Stony Brook, New York 11794-5001. (516) 632-6905. Quarterly. Marine and Great Lakes activities of New York Sea Grant Institute's research and extension programs.

Coastlines. Executive Office of Environmental Affairs, Massachusetts Coastal Zone Management Office, Saltonstall State Office Bldg., Rm. 2006, 100 Cambridge St., Boston, Massachusetts 02202. (617) 727-9530. Nine times a year. Coastal land and water management, port and harbor development, water quality, recreation, public access, and coastal development.

Coastlines. League for Coastal Protection, PO Box 421698, San Francisco, California 94142-1698. Bimonthly. Legislation and planning issues affecting the California coastline.

Coastwatch. Sea Grant College Program, University of North Carolina, PO Box 8605, Raleigh, North Carolina 27695-8605. (919) 737-2454. Monthly. Shellfish contamination, beach erosion, and hurricanes.

Coastwatch. Center for Coastal Studies, 59 Commercial St., PO Box 1036, Provincetown, Massachusetts 02657. (508) 487-3622. Bimonthly. Coastal ecology and biology, whale research, and conservation issues.

Conservation Biology. Blackwell Scientific Publications, 3 Cambridge Ctr., Suite 208, Cambridge, Massachusetts 02142. (617) 225-0401. 1987-. Quarterly. Covers conservation and development, wildlife management the economics, ethics and agroforestry of the extinction crisis.

Conservation Foundation Letter. Conservation Foundation, 1250 24th St. N.W., Washington, District of Columbia 20037. (202) 293-4800. 1966-. Bimonthly. Provides in-depth examinations of environmental issues.

Conserve. Western Pennsylvania Conservancy, 316 4th Ave., Pittsburgh, Pennsylvania 15222. (412) 288-2777. 1971-. Semiannually. Reports on land conservation projects of the western Pennsylvania Conservancy.

Journal of Shoreline Management. Elsevier Science Publishing Co., 655 Avenue of the Americas, New York, New York 10010. (212) 989-5800. Two issues a year. Deals with coastal ecology, coastal zone management, and ocean and shoreline management.

Maine's Coastal Program Newsletter. Maine State Planning Office, Station 38, State House, Augusta, Maine 04333. (207) 289-3261. Quarterly. Gulf of Maine resources.

National Wetlands Newsletter. Environmental Law Institute, 1616 P St., NW, Suite 200, Washington, District of Columbia 20036. (202) 328-5150. Bimonthly. Federal, state, and local laws, policies, and programs concerning wetlands, floodplains, and coastal water resources.

Nature and Resources. Elsevier Science Publishing Co., 655 Avenue of the Americas, New York, New York 10010. (212) 989-5800. 1965-. Quarterly. Provides in-depth reviews of contemporary environmental issues from an international perspective.

Ocean & Shoreline Management. Elsevier Science Publishing Co., 655 Avenue of the Americas, New York, New York 10010. (212) 989-5800. Bimonthly.

Tide. Coastal Conservation Assn., 4801 Woodway, Suite 220 W., Houston, Texas 77056. (713) 626-4222. Bimonthly.

Toxic Substances Journal. Hemisphere Publishing Co., 79 Madison Ave., Suite 1110, New York, New York 10016. (212) 725-1999. Quarterly. Legislation, testing, and guidelines relating to toxic substances.

Underwater Naturalist. American Littoral Society, Sandy Hook, Highlands, New Jersey 07732. (201) 291-0055. Monthly. Covers issues relating to coastal areas.

RESEARCH CENTERS AND INSTITUTES

Center for Remote Sensing. University of Delaware, College of Marine Studies, Newark, Delaware 19711. (302) 451-2336.

South Carolina Sea Grant Consortium. 287 Meeting Street, Charleston, South Carolina 29401. (803) 727-2078.

Texas A&M University, Sea Grant College Program. 1716 Briarcrest Dr., Ste. 702, College Station, Texas 77802. (409) 845-3854.

University of Houston Coastal Center. c/o Office of the Senior Vice President, Houston, Texas 77204-5502. (713) 749-2351.

University of Maine, Maine Sea Grant College Program. 14 Coburn Hall, University of Maine, Orono, Maine 04469-0114. (207) 581-1435.

University of Maryland, Center for Environmental and Estuarine Studies. Center Operations, Horn Point, P.O.Box 775, Cambridge, Maryland 21613. (410) 228-9250.

University of Minnesota, Minnesota Sea Grant College Program. 1518 Cleveland Ave., Ste. 302, St. Paul, Minnesota 55108. (612) 625-9288.

University of New Hampshire, Coastal Marine Laboratory. Department of Zoology, Durham, New Hampshire 03824. (603) 862-2100.

University of New Hampshire, Complex Systems Research Center. Science and Engineering Research Building, Durham, New Hampshire 03824. (603) 862-1792.

University of New Hampshire, Institute of Marine Science and Ocean Engineering. Marine Programs Building, Durham, New Hampshire 03824. (603) 862-2995.

University of Oregon, Oregon Institute of Marine Biology. Charleston, Oregon 97420. (503) 888-2581.

University of Puerto Rico, Sea Grant College Program. Department of Marine Sciences, P.O. Box 5000, Mayaguez, Puerto Rico 00681-5000. (809) 832-3585.

University of Rhode Island, Coastal Resources Center. Narragansett, Rhode Island 02882. (401) 792-6224.

University of Rhode Island, Marine Ecosystems Research Laboratory. Graduate School of Oceanography, Narragansett, Rhode Island 02882. (401) 792-6104.

University of South Carolina at Columbia, Belle W. Baruch Institute for Marine Biology and Coastal Research. Columbia, South Carolina 29208. (803) 777-5288.

University of Southern California, Sea Grant Program. University Park, Los Angeles, California 90089-1231. (213) 740-1961.

University of Texas-Pan American, Coastal Studies Laboratory. P.O. Box 2591, South Padre Island, Texas 78597. (512) 761-2644.

Water and Energy Research Institute of the Western Pacific (*WERI*). University of Guam, UOG Station, Guam 96923. (617) 734-3132.

West Coast Fisheries Development Foundation. 812 S.W. Washington, Suite 900, Portland, Oregon 97205. (503) 222-3518.

Wetlands Institute. Stone Harbor Boulevard, Stone Harbor, New Jersey 08247. (609) 368-1211.

STATISTICS SOURCES

Environmental Data Compendium. OECD Publications and Information Center, 2001 L St., N.W., Suite 700, Washington, District of Columbia 20036. (202) 785-6323. 1989.

Environmental Indicators. OECD Publications and Information Center, 2001 L St., N.W., Suite 700, Washington, District of Columbia 20036. (202) 785-6323. 1991.

Environmental Quality. Council on Environmental Quality. U.S. G.P.O., Washington, District of Columbia 20401. (202) 512-0000. Annual.

The State of the Environment. OECD Publications and Information Center, 2001 L St., N.W., Suite 700, Washington, District of Columbia 20036. (202) 785-6323. 1991.

World Resources. World Resources Institute. 1709 New York Ave., N.W., Washington, District of Columbia 20006. (202) 638-6300. Annual. Statistical and textual analysis of world's natural resources and the effects of growth-caused environmental pollution.

TRADE ASSOCIATIONS AND PROFESSIONAL SOCIETIES

American Littoral Society. Sandy Hook, Highlands, New Jersey 07732. (908) 291-0055.

American Rivers, Inc. 801 Pennsylvania Ave., S.E., Suite 303, Washington, District of Columbia 20003. (202) 547-6900.

American Society of Civil Engineers. 345 East 47th St., New York, New York 10017. (212) 705-7496.

American Society of Naval Engineers. 1452 Duke St., Alexandria, Virginia 22314. (703) 836-6727.

Center for Coastal Studies. 59 Commercial St., P.O. Box 1036, Provincetown, Massachusetts 02657. (508) 487-3622.

Coast Alliance. 235 Pennsylvania Ave., SE, Washington, District of Columbia 20003. (202) 546-9554.

Coastal Conservation Association. 4801 Woodway, Suite 220 W., Houston, Texas 77056. (713) 626-4222.

Coastal Engineering Research Council. Coastal Engineering Research Council, 215 E. Bay St., Suite 302A, Charleston, South Carolina 29401. (803) 723-4864.

The Coastal Society. P.O. Box 2081, Glouster, Massachusetts 01930-2081. (508) 281-9209.

Coastal States Organization. 444 N. Capitol St., N.W., Suite 312, Washington, District of Columbia 20001. (202) 628-9636.

Conservation International. 1015 18th St. N.W., Suite 1002, Washington, District of Columbia 20036. (202) 429-5660. Non-profit organization established in 1987. Provides resources and expertise to private organizations, government agencies and universities of Latin America and Caribbean countries in an effort to develop the capacity and preserve critical habitats.

International Association for the Physical Sciences of the Ocean. P.O. Box 1161, Del Mar, California 92014-1161. (619) 481-0850.

North Atlantic Ports Association. 31 Coventry Dr., Lewes, Delaware 19958. (302) 654-9732.

Save Our Shores. PO Box 103, North Quincy, Massachusetts 02171. (508) 888-4694.

United Citizens Coastal Protection League. P.O. Box 46, Cardiff by the Sea, California 92007. (619) 753-7477.

COBALT

ABSTRACTING AND INDEXING SERVICES

Biological Abstracts. BIOSIS, 2100 Arch St., Philadelphia, Pennsylvania 19103-1399. (215) 587-4800. 1927-.

Chemical Abstracts. Chemical Abstracts Service, 2540 Olentangy River Rd., PO Box 3012, Columbus, Ohio 43210. (800) 848-6533. 1907-.

Cobalt + Cobalt Abstracts. Cobalt Information Center, Columbus, Ohio

ERDA Research Abstracts. U.S. ERDA Technical Information Center, Box 62, Oak Ridge, Tennessee 37830.

General Science Index. H. W. Wilson Co., 950 University Ave., Bronx, New York 10452. 1978-. Monthly, also issued in annual cumulation. Cumulative subject index to English language periodicals in the subject fields of astronomy, botany, chemistry, earth science, environment and conservation, food and nutrition, genetics, mathematics, medicine and health, microbiology, oceanography, physics, physiology and zoology.

Index to Scientific Book Contents. Institute for Scientific Information, 3501 Market St., Philadelphia, Pennsylva-

nia 19104. (800) 523-1857. 1985-. Annual. Gives contents of science books published.

Metals Abstracts. ASM International, 9639 Kinsman, Materials Park, Ohio 44073. (216) 338-5151. 1968-. Published jointly by the Institute of Metals, London and the American Society for Metals. Formed by the Union of Metallurgical Abstracts and Review of Metal Literature.

Physics Briefs. Physikalische Berichte. Physik Verlag, Pappapelallee 3, Postfach 101161, Weinheim, Germany D-6940. 1979-. Semimonthly. In English. Volumes for 1979- issued by the Deutsche Physikalische Gesellschaft and the Fachinformationszentrum Energie Physik, Mathematik in cooperation with the American Institute of Physics.

Science Citation Index. Institute for Scientific Information, 3501 Market St., Philadelphia, Pennsylvania 19104. 1961-.

BIBLIOGRAPHIES

Cobalt and Cobalt Alloys, a Bibliography of Allotropy and Alloy Systems. Facundo Rolf Morral. Cobalt Information Center, Columbus, Ohio 1967.

Cobalt in Agricultural Ecosystems: A Bibliography of the Literature 1950 Through 1971. Robert Lewis Jones. Department of Agronomy, University of Illinois, Urbana, Illinois 61801. 1973.

ENCYCLOPEDIAS AND DICTIONARIES

Encyclopedia of Chemical Processing and Design. John J. Mcketta and W. A. Cunningham. Marcel Dekker, Inc., 270 Madison Ave., New York, New York 10016. (212) 696-9000; (800) 228-1160. 1992. Thirty-eight volumes.

Glossary of Terms in Nuclear Science and Technology. American Nuclear Society, 555 North Kensington Ave., La Grange Park, Illinois 60525. (708) 352-6611. 1986. Prepared by the American Nuclear Society Standards Committee. Subcommittee ANS-9.

Kirk-Othmer Encyclopedia of Chemical Technology. J. I. Kroschwitz, ed. John Wiley & Sons, Inc., 605 3rd Ave., New York, New York 10158-0012. (212) 850-6000. 1992-. All articles in the new edition have been rewritten and updated adding new subjects such as biotechnology, computer topics, analytical techniques and instrumentation, environmental concerns, fuels and energy, inorganic and solid state chemistry; composite materials and material science in general, and pharmaceuticals. Also available online.

McGraw-Hill Encyclopedia of Science and Technology. McGraw-Hill, 1221 Avenue of the Americas, New York, New York 10020. (212) 512-2000 or (800) 262-4729. 1992. Seventh edition. Issued in multiple volumes including index. Includes all science and technology broad subject areas.

Van Nostrand's Scientific Encyclopedia. Glenn D. Considine, ed. Van Nostrand Reinhold, 115 5th Ave., New York, New York 10003. (212) 254-3232. 1983. Sixth edition. Includes all broad subject areas in science.

GENERAL WORKS

BWR Cobalt Source Identification. C.F. Falk. General Electric Co., P.O. Box 861, Gainesville, Florida 32602-

0861. (904) 462-3911. 1982. Safety measures in boiling water reactors.

Cobalt Reduction Guidelines. Electric Power Research Institute, 3412 Hillview Ave., Palo Alto, California 94304. (415) 965-4081. 1990. Deals with nuclear power plants, hard-facing alloys, stress corrosion, and cobalt alloys.

Criteria for Controlling Occupational Exposure to Cobalt. U.S. Department of Health and Human Services, 200 Independence Ave., SW, Room 34AF, Washington, District of Columbia 20201. (202) 472-5543. 1982.

ONLINE DATA BASES

BIOSIS Previews. BIOSIS, 2100 Arch St., Philadelphia, Pennsylvania 19103-1399. (215) 587-4800. Largest and most comprehensive database of research in the life sciences. Contains citations for nearly 9000 primary research journals, monographs, reviews, symposia, preliminary reports, semi-popular journals, selected institutional reports, government reports and research communications.

Chemical Abstracts-CA. Chemical Abstracts Service, 2540 Olentangy River Rd., P.O. Box 3012, Columbus, Ohio 43210. (800) 848-6533 or (614) 421-3600. Information sources include 9000 journals, patents from 27 countries, two industrial property organizations, new books, conference proceedings, and government research reports.

Kirk-Othmer Encyclopedia of Chemical Technology. John Wiley & Sons, Inc., 605 3rd Ave., 5th Floor, New York, New York 10158. (212) 850-6000. Online version of the publication of the same name.

COBALT 60

See: ISOTOPES

COD

See: CHEMICAL OXYGEN DEMAND

COEFFICIENT OF HAZE

See: VISIBILITY

COENZYMES

See: ENZYMES

COKE PETROLEUM

See: PETROLEUM

COLD ENVIRONMENTS
See also: ARCTIC ECOLOGY; POLAR REGIONS

ABSTRACTING AND INDEXING SERVICES

Ecological Abstracts. Geo Abstracts Ltd. Elsevier Applied Science, Crown House, Linton Rd., Barking, England IG 11 8JU. 1974-. Derived from over 600 leading ecological and environmental journals, plus books, conference proceedings, reports and theses.

Engineering Index. The Engineering Index Inc., 345 E. 47th St., New York, New York 10017. 1962-.

Environment Abstracts. Bowker A & I Publishing, 121 Chanlon Rd., New Providence, New Jersey 07974. (908) 464-6800. 1974-.

Environment Index. Environment Information Center, Index Research Department, 124 E. 39th St., New York, New York 10016. 1971-. Annual.

Environmental Information Connection–EIC. Planning Information Program, Dept. of Urban and Regional Planning, University of Illinois, 1003 West Nevada, Urbana, Illinois 61801. (217) 333-1369. Also available online.

Environmental Periodicals Bibliography. Environmental Studies Institute, International Academy at Santa Barbara, 800 Garden St., Suite D, Santa Barbara, California 93101. (805) 965-5010. Also available online.

General Science Index. H. W. Wilson Co., 950 University Ave., Bronx, New York 10452. 1978-. Monthly, also issued in annual cumulation. Cumulative subject index to English language periodicals in the subject fields of astronomy, botany, chemistry, earth science, environment and conservation, food and nutrition, genetics, mathematics, medicine and health, microbiology, oceanography, physics, physiology and zoology.

Science Citation Index. Institute for Scientific Information, 3501 Market St., Philadelphia, Pennsylvania 19104. 1961-.

BIBLIOGRAPHIES

EPA Publications Bibliography. U.S. Environmental Protection Agency, Library Systems Branch, 401 M St., SW, Washington, District of Columbia 20460. (202) 260-2090. Quarterly.

Man in the Cold Environment: A Bibliography with Informative Abstracts. Charles W. Shilling. Undersea and Hyperbaric Medical Society, 9650 Rockville Pike, Bethesda, Maryland 20814. (301) 571-1818. 1981. Bibliography of hypothermia.

ENCYCLOPEDIAS AND DICTIONARIES

The Encyclopedia of Geochemistry and Environmental Sciences. Rhodes Whitmore Fairbridge. Van Nostrand Reinhold Co., 115 5th Ave., New York, New York 10003. (212) 254-3232. 1972.

McGraw-Hill Encyclopedia of Environmental Science. Sybil P. Parker. McGraw-Hill Science & Engineering Books, 11 W. 19th St., New York, New York 10011. (212) 337-6010. 1980. Covers ecology, man's influence on nature, and environmental protection.

GENERAL WORKS

Arctic Environmental Problems. Lassi Heininen. Tampere Peace Research Institute, Tampere, Finland 1990.

Conserving the Polar Regions. Barbara James. Steck-Vaughn Co., PO Box 26015, Austin, Texas 78755. (512) 343-8227. 1991. Focuses on the Arctic and the Antarctic, their uniqueness, relation to world climate, development and conservation.

Ecological Fruit Production in the North. Bart Hall-Beyer, and Jean Richard. B. Hall-Beyer, RR #3, Scotstown, Quebec, Canada JOB 3J0. 1983. Deals with the production of tree fruits and small fruits in North America. Discusses methods of ecological agriculture.

Ecotoxicology and Climate. Philippe Bordeaux, et al., eds. John Wiley & Sons, Inc., 605 3rd Ave., New York, New York 10158-0012. (212) 850-6000. 1989. Describes environmental chemistry of toxic pollutants in hot and cold climates. Includes bibliographical references and an index.

Human Performance in the Cold. Gary A. Laursen. Undersea and Hyperbaric Medical Society, 9650 Rockville Pike, Bethesda, Maryland 20814. (301) 571-1818. 1982.

Hypothermia and Cold Stress. Evan L. Lloyd. Aspen Systems Corp., 1600 Research Blvd., Rockville, Maryland 20850. (301) 251-5554. 1986. Cold therapy, body temperature regulation and adverse effects of cold.

Hypothermia, Causes, Effects, Prevention. Robert S. Pozos. New Win Publishing, Inc., RR 1 Box 384C, Rte. 173 W., Hampton, New Jersey 08827. (201) 735-9701. 1982. Covers physiological effects of cold.

Hypothermia, Frostbite, and Other Cold Injuries: Prevention, Recognition, and Prehospital Treatment. James A. Wilkerson. The Mountaineers, 306 Second Ave. W, Seattle, Washington 98119. (206) 285-2665. 1986. Adverse effects of cold, frostbite and hypothermia.

Hypothermia: Recognition and Prevention. Alice D. Zimmerman. University of Wyoming, P.O. Box 3315, University Station, Laramie, Wyoming 82071. (307) 766-2379. 1983.

Hypothermia: The Facts. Kenneth John Collins. Oxford University Press, Walton St., Oxford, England OX2 6DP. 1983.

The Nature and Treatment of Hypothermia. University of Minnesota Press, 2037 University Ave., SE, Minneapolis, Minnesota 55414. (612) 624-2516. 1983. Therapy relating to hypothermia.

The Permafrost Environment. Stuart A. Harris. Rowman & Littlefield, Publishers, Inc., 8705 Bollman Pl., Savage, Maryland 20763. (301) 306-0400. 1986. Contains the scientific and engineering facets of permafrost.

Polar Lands. Lawrence Williams. Marshall Cavendish Corp., 2415 Jerusalem Ave., North Bellmore, New York 11710. (516) 546-4200. 1990. Living and working in the polar regions without destroying the environment.

ONLINE DATA BASES

Cold. U.S. Army Corps of Engineers, Cold Regions Research and Engineering Laboratory, 22 Lyme Rd., Hanover, New Hampshire 03755-1290. (603) 646-4221.

Cold Regions. Library of Congress, Science & Technology Division, Cold Regions Bibliography Project, Washington, District of Columbia 20540. (202) 707-1181.

Computerized Engineering Index–COMPENDEX. Engineering Information Inc., 345 E. 47th St., New York, New York 10017. (212) 705-7600.

Enviro/Energyline Abstracts Plus. R. R. Bowker Co., 121 Chanlon Rd., New Providence, New Jersey 07974. (908) 464-6800.

Environmental Periodicals Bibliography. National Information Services Corp., Ste. 6, Wyman Towers, 3100 St. Paul St., Baltimore, Maryland 21218. (410)243-0797. Online version of abstract of same name.

Monthly Catalog of United States Government Publications. U.S. G.P.O., Supt. of Docs., PO Box 371954, Pittsburgh, Pennsylvania 15250-7954. (202) 512-0000.

National Technical Information Service. U.S. Department of Commerce, National Technical Information Service, Office of Data Base Services, 5285 Port Royal Rd., Springfield, Virginia 22161. (703) 487-4807. Bibliographic database of government sponsored research and technical reports.

PERIODICALS AND NEWSLETTERS

Cryobiology. Academic Press, c/o Harcourt Brace Jovanovich Inc., 6277 Sea Harbor Dr., Orlando, Florida 32887. (800) 346-8648. Bimonthly.

TRADE ASSOCIATIONS AND PROFESSIONAL SOCIETIES

American Society of Civil Engineers. 345 East 47th St., New York, New York 10017. (212) 705-7496.

COLD INSULATION

See: INSULATION

COLIFORM

See: BACTERIA

COLIFORM BACTERIA

See: BACTERIA

COLIFORM INDEX

See: BACTERIA

COLLECTOR TECHNOLOGY

See: SOLAR ENERGY

COLLOIDS

See: PARTICULATES

COLLUVIUM

See: SOIL SCIENCE

COLORADO ENVIRONMENTAL AGENCIES

GOVERNMENTAL ORGANIZATIONS

Department of Agriculture: Pesticide Registration. Director, Division of Plant Industry, 4th Floor, 1525 Sherman St., Denver, Colorado 80203. (303) 866-2838.

Department of Health: Air Quality. Director, Air Pollution Control Division, 4210 East 11th Ave., Denver, Colorado 80220. (303) 331-8500.

Department of Health: Emergency Preparedness and Community Right-to-Know. Emergency Planning Commission, 4210 East 11th Ave., Denver, Colorado 80220. (303) 331-4858.

Department of Health: Environmental Protection. Director, Air Pollution Control Division, 4210 East 11th Ave., Denver, Colorado 80220. (303) 331-8500.

Department of Health: Water Quality. Director, Water Quality Control Commission, 4210 East 11th Ave., Denver, Colorado 80220. (303) 331-4534.

Department of Natural Resources: Fish and Wildlife. Director, Division of Wildlife, 6060 Broadway, Denver, Colorado 80216. (303) 297-1192.

Department of Natural Resources: Natural Resources. Executive Director, 1313 Sherman St., Room 718, Denver, Colorado 80203. (303) 866-3311.

Hazardous Waste Materials and Waste Management Division: Hazardous Waste Management. Director, 4210 East 11th Ave., Denver, Colorado 80220. (303) 331-4830.

Hazardous Waste Materials and Waste Management Division: Solid Waste Management. Director, 4210 East 11th Ave., Denver, Colorado 80220. (303) 331-4830.

U.S. EPA Region 8: Pollution Prevention. Senior Policy Advisor, 999 18th St., Suite 500, Denver, Colorado 80202-2405. (303) 293-1603.

COLORADO ENVIRONMENTAL LEGISLATION

GENERAL WORKS

Colorado Environmental Law Handbook. Government Institutes, Inc., 4 Research Pl., Ste. 200, Rockville, Maryland 20850. (301) 921-2300. 1991.

COMBINED SEWER OVERFLOWS

See: SEWERS

COMBUSTION

See also: AIR POLLUTION; AIR QUALITY; CARBON DIOXIDE; CARBON MONOXIDE; EMISSIONS; INCINERATION; PARTICULATES

ABSTRACTING AND INDEXING SERVICES

Air Pollution Titles. Pennsylvania State University, Center for Air Environmental Studies, 226 Fenske Laboratory, University Park, Pennsylvania 16802. (814) 865-1415. 1965. Bibliographic guide to current research literature on air environment, including monitoring and control of air pollution, health effects, effects on agriculture, forests, toxic air contaminants, and global atmospheric pro cases.

Air Pollution Translations. A Bibliography With Abstracts. U.S. Environmental Protection Agency, MD 75, Research Triangle Park, North Carolina 27711. (919) 541-2184. 1969.

Bulletin Signaletique: Eau et Assainissement, Pollution Atmospherique, Droit des Pollutions. Centre de Documentation, Centre National de la Recherche Scientifique, 15, quai Anatole France, Paris, France 75700. (1) 45 55 92 25. 1983-. Monthly. Indexes pollution periodicals including water, atmospheric and related pollutions.

Engineering Index. The Engineering Index Inc., 345 E. 47th St., New York, New York 10017. 1962-.

Environment Abstracts. Bowker A & I Publishing, 121 Chanlon Rd., New Providence, New Jersey 07974. (908) 464-6800. 1974-.

Environment Index. Environment Information Center, Index Research Department, 124 E. 39th St., New York, New York 10016. 1971-. Annual.

Environmental Information Connection–EIC. Planning Information Program, Dept. of Urban and Regional Planning, University of Illinois, 1003 West Nevada, Urbana, Illinois 61801. (217) 333-1369. Also available online.

Environmental Periodicals Bibliography. Environmental Studies Institute, International Academy at Santa Barbara, 800 Garden St., Suite D, Santa Barbara, California 93101. (805) 965-5010. Also available online.

ERDA Research Abstracts. U.S. ERDA Technical Information Center, Box 62, Oak Ridge, Tennessee 37830.

Index to Scientific Book Contents. Institute for Scientific Information, 3501 Market St., Philadelphia, Pennsylvania 19104. (800) 523-1857. 1985-. Annual. Gives contents of science books published.

Physics Briefs. Physikalische Berichte. Physik Verlag, Pappapelallee 3, Postfach 101161, Weinheim, Germany D-6940. 1979-. Semimonthly. In English. Volumes for 1979- issued by the Deutsche Physikalische Gesellschaft and the Fachinformationszentrum Energie Physik, Mathematik in cooperation with the American Institute of Physics.

Pollution Abstracts. Cambridge Scientific Abstracts, 5161 River Rd., Bethesda, Maryland 20816. (301) 961-6750. Six/year. Indexes worldwide technical literature on environmental pollution. Covers air pollution, marine and freshwater pollution, sewage and wastewater treatment, waste management, toxicology and health, noise pollu-

tion, radiation, land pollution, and environmental policies, programs, legislation, and education. Also available online.

Science Citation Index. Institute for Scientific Information, 3501 Market St., Philadelphia, Pennsylvania 19104. 1961-.

BIBLIOGRAPHIES

Directory of Published Proceedings. Interdok Corp., 173 Halstead Ave., Harrison, New York 10528. (914) 835-3506. 1990. Monthly. This is a listing of published proceedings including the series SEMTE (Science/Medicine/Engineering/Technology) and the series SSH (Social Science/Humanities).

EPA Publications Bibliography. U.S. Environmental Protection Agency, Library Systems Branch, 401 M St., SW, Washington, District of Columbia 20460. (202) 260-2090. Quarterly.

ENCYCLOPEDIAS AND DICTIONARIES

Encyclopedia of Chemical Processing and Design. John J. Mcketta and W. A. Cunningham. Marcel Dekker, Inc., 270 Madison Ave., New York, New York 10016. (212) 696-9000; (800) 228-1160. 1992. Thirty-eight volumes.

Encyclopedia of Physical Science and Technology. Robert A. Meyers, ed. Academic Press, c/o Harcourt Brace Jovanovich Inc., 6277 Sea Harbor Dr., Orlando, Florida 32887. (800) 346-8648. Dictionary of engineering, technology and physical sciences.

Encyclopedia of Physics. Rita G. Lerner and George L. Trigg. VCH Publishers, 303 NW 12th Ave., Deerfield Beach, Florida 33442-1788. (305) 428-5566. 1991. Second edition.

Kirk-Othmer Encyclopedia of Chemical Technology. J. I. Kroschwitz, ed. John Wiley & Sons, Inc., 605 3rd Ave., New York, New York 10158-0012. (212) 850-6000. 1992-. All articles in the new edition have been rewritten and updated adding new subjects such as biotechnology, computer topics, analytical techniques and instrumentation, environmental concerns, fuels and energy, inorganic and solid state chemistry; composite materials and material science in general, and pharmaceuticals. Also available online.

McGraw-Hill Encyclopedia of Environmental Science. Sybil P. Parker. McGraw-Hill Science & Engineering Books, 11 W. 19th St., New York, New York 10011. (212) 337-6010. 1980. Covers ecology, man's influence on nature, and environmental protection.

GENERAL WORKS

Air Pollution Control. Howard E. Hesketh. Technomic Publishing Co., 851 New Holland Ave., Box 3535, Lancaster, Pennsylvania 17604. (717) 291-5609. 1991. Presents both theory and application data. Provides a background relevant to behavior theories and control techniques for capturing gaseous and particulate air pollutants.

Air Pollution Emission Standards and Guidelines for Municipal Waste Combustors: Economic Analysis of Materials Separation Requirement. B. J. Morton, et al. National Technical Information Service, 5285 Port Royal Rd., Springfield, Virginia 22161. (703) 487-4650.

1990. Final report prepared by the Research Triangle Institute for the Center for Economics Research.

Calcium Magnesium Acetate: An Emerging Bulk Chemical for Environmental Applications. D.L. Wise. Elsevier Science Publishing Co., 655 Avenue of the Americas, New York, New York 10010. (212) 989-5800. 1991.

Combustion Toxicology. Shane C. Gad and Rosalind C. Anderson. CRC Press, 2000 Corporate Blvd., N.W., Boca Raton, Florida 33431. (407) 994-0555; (800) 272-7737. 1990. Evaluates the health hazards of the decomposition products formed when plastics are heated. Coverage includes the basics of inhalation toxicology and heat stress physiology, toxicity of smoke and combustion gases, combustion toxicity testing, regulations, toxicity of polymers by class, flame retardants and other additives, current issues and directions.

Emissions from Combustion Processes–Origin, Measurement, Control. R. E. Clement and R. O. Kagel, eds. Lewis Publishers, 2000 Corporate Blvd., N.W., Boca Raton, Florida 33431. (407) 994-0555 or (800) 272-7737. 1990. Topics discussed include all aspects of combustion from the mechanics, formation, and disposal to emission abatement and risk assessment.

Sources of Ignition: Flammability Characteristics of Chemicals and Products. John Bond. Butterworth-Heinemann, 80 Montvale Ave., Stoneham, Massachusetts 02180. (617) 438-8464; (800) 366-2665. 1991.

HANDBOOKS AND MANUALS

Combustion Efficiency Tables. Harry Taplin. The Association of Energy Engineers, 4025 Pleasantdale Rd, Suite 420, Atlanta, Georgia 30340. (404) 925-9558. 1991. The tables are based on ASME/ANSI Power Test Code 4.1 and are designed to systematically illustrate how different variables impact the combustion process.

ONLINE DATA BASES

Computerized Engineering Index–COMPENDEX. Engineering Information Inc., 345 E. 47th St., New York, New York 10017. (212) 705-7600.

Enviro/Energyline Abstracts Plus. R. R. Bowker Co., 121 Chanlon Rd., New Providence, New Jersey 07974. (908) 464-6800.

Environmental Periodicals Bibliography. National Information Services Corp., Ste. 6, Wyman Towers, 3100 St. Paul St., Baltimore, Maryland 21218. (410)243-0797. Online version of abstract of same name.

Kirk-Othmer Encyclopedia of Chemical Technology. John Wiley & Sons, Inc., 605 3rd Ave., 5th Floor, New York, New York 10158. (212) 850-6000. Online version of the publication of the same name.

PERIODICALS AND NEWSLETTERS

Global Climate Change Digest. Elsevier Science Publishing Co., 655 Avenue of the Americas, New York, New York 10010. (212) 984-5800. Monthly. Topics dealing with ozone depletion and the large-scale climatic changes linked to industrial activity, industrial by-products, and man-made substances.

TRADE ASSOCIATIONS AND PROFESSIONAL SOCIETIES

American Institute of Chemical Engineers. 345 East 47th St., New York, New York 10017. (212) 705-7338.

American Institute of Chemists. 7315 Wisconsin Ave., Bethesda, Maryland 20814. (301) 652-2447.

COMMINUTION

See: WASTE MANAGEMENT

COMMINUTOR

See: WASTE MANAGEMENT

COMMUNITY ECOLOGY

See also: BIOLOGICAL COMMUNITIES; ECOSYSTEMS

ALMANACS AND YEARBOOKS

Gale Environmental Almanac. Russ Hoyle. Gale Research Inc., 835 Penobscot Bldg., Detroit, Michigan 48226-4094. (313) 961-2242. 1993. Focuses on the U.S. and Canada, although worldwide and transboundary issues are discussed.

DIRECTORIES

Canadian Environmental Directory. Canadian Almanac & Directory Publishing Co. Ltd., 134 Adelaide St. E., Ste. 27, Toronto, Ontario, Canada M5C 1K9. (416) 362-4088. 1992. Includes individuals, agencies, firms, and associations.

ENCYCLOPEDIAS AND DICTIONARIES

Dictionary of Environmental Science and Technology. Andrew Porteous. John Wiley & Sons, Inc., 605 3rd Ave., New York, New York 10158-0012. (212) 850-6000. 1992.

Environmental Encyclopedia. William P. Cunningham, Terence Ball, et. al. Gale Research Inc., 835 Penobscot Bldg., Detroit, Michigan 48226-4094. (313) 961-2242. 1993.

GENERAL WORKS

Creating Successful Communities. Michael A. Mantelli, et al. Island Press, 1718 Connecticut Ave. N.W., Suite 300, Washington, District of Columbia 20009. (202) 232-7933. 1990. Compendium of techniques for effective land use and growth management to help communities retain their individuality in the face of rapid growth.

The Environmental Sourcebook. Edith Carol Stein. Lyons & Burford, 31 W. 21st St., New York, New York 10010. (212) 620-9580. 1992. Provides information on 11 specific environmental issues, including population; agriculture; energy; climate and atmosphere; biodiversity; water; oceans; solid waste; hazardous substances and waste; endangered lands; and development.

Environmental Viewpoints. Marie Lazzari. Gale Research Inc., 835 Penobscot Bldg., Detroit, Michigan 48226-4094. (313) 961-2242. 1992.

World Guide to Environmental Issues and Organizations. Peter Brackley. Longman Group Ltd., Longman House, Burnt Mill, Harlow, Essex, England CM20 2J6. (0279) 426721. 1991.

STATISTICS SOURCES

A Community Researcher's Guide to Rural Data. Priscilla Salant. Island Press, 1718 Connecticut Ave. N.W., Suite 300, Washington, District of Columbia 20009. (202) 232-7933. 1990. Comprehensive manual intended for those less familiar with statistical data on rural America. Identifies a wealth of data sources such as the decennial census of population and housing, population reports and surveys, and labor market information.

Statistical Record of the Environment. Arsen J. Darnay. Gale Research Inc., 835 Penobscot Bldg., Detroit, Michigan 48226-4094. (313) 961-2242. 1992.

TRADE ASSOCIATIONS AND PROFESSIONAL SOCIETIES

Institute for Community Design Analysis. 66 Clover Dr., Great Neck, New York 11021. (516) 773-4727.

COMPACTION

See: SOLID WASTE MANAGEMENT

COMPOST

ABSTRACTING AND INDEXING SERVICES

Agrindex. AGRIS Coordinating Center, Via delle Terme di Caracalla, Rome, Italy I-00100. 61 0181-FA01. 1975-.

Applied Ecology Abstracts Studies in Renewable Natural Resources. Information Retrieval Ltd., 1911 Jefferson Davis Highway, Arlington, Virginia 22202. 1975-. Monthly.

Biological and Agricultural Index. H.W. Wilson Co., 950 University Ave., Bronx, New York 10452. (800) 367-6770. 1916-. Monthly.

Environment Abstracts. Bowker A & I Publishing, 121 Chanlon Rd., New Providence, New Jersey 07974. (908) 464-6800. 1974-.

Environment Index. Environment Information Center, Index Research Department, 124 E. 39th St., New York, New York 10016. 1971-. Annual.

Environmental Information Connection–EIC. Planning Information Program, Dept. of Urban and Regional Planning, University of Illinois, 1003 West Nevada, Urbana, Illinois 61801. (217) 333-1369. Also available online.

Environmental Periodicals Bibliography. Environmental Studies Institute, International Academy at Santa Barbara, 800 Garden St., Suite D, Santa Barbara, California 93101. (805) 965-5010. Also available online.

General Science Index. H. W. Wilson Co., 950 University Ave., Bronx, New York 10452. 1978-. Monthly, also

issued in annual cumulation. Cumulative subject index to English language periodicals in the subject fields of astronomy, botany, chemistry, earth science, environment and conservation, food and nutrition, genetics, mathematics, medicine and health, microbiology, oceanography, physics, physiology and zoology.

Multimedia Index to Ecology. National Information Center for Educational Media, University of Southern California, Los Angeles, California 90007.

Pollution Abstracts. Cambridge Scientific Abstracts, 5161 River Rd., Bethesda, Maryland 20816. (301) 961-6750. Six/year. Indexes worldwide technical literature on environmental pollution. Covers air pollution, marine and freshwater pollution, sewage and wastewater treatment, waste management, toxicology and health, noise pollution, radiation, land pollution, and environmental policies, programs, legislation, and education. Also available online.

Science Citation Index. Institute for Scientific Information, 3501 Market St., Philadelphia, Pennsylvania 19104. 1961-.

BIBLIOGRAPHIES

Composts and Composting of Organic Wastes. Jayne T. Maclean. U.S. Department of Agriculture, National Agricultural Library, 10301 Baltimore Blvd., Beltsville, Maryland 20705-2351. (301) 504-5755. 1991.

Current Contents. Agriculture, Biology and Environmental Sciences. Institute for Scientific Information, 3501 Market St., Philadelphia, Pennsylvania 19104. (800) 523-1857. 1973-. Previous title: Current Contents. Agricultural, Food & Veterinary Sciences. Gives the table of contents of periodicals in the fields of agriculture, biology, environmental and related areas.

EPA Publications Bibliography. U.S. Environmental Protection Agency, Library Systems Branch, 401 M St., SW, Washington, District of Columbia 20460. (202) 260-2090. Quarterly.

Vermicomposting, Selected Articles. Flowerfield Enterprises, 10332 Shaver Rd., Kalamazoo, Michigan 49002. (616) 327-0108. 1982.

DIRECTORIES

Municipal Composting: Resources for Local Officials and Communities Organizations. Institute for Local Self-Reliance, 2425 18th St., NW, Washington, District of Columbia 20009. (202) 232-4108. 1980. Deals with refuse and refuse disposal, and compost.

ENCYCLOPEDIAS AND DICTIONARIES

McGraw-Hill Encyclopedia of Environmental Science. Sybil P. Parker. McGraw-Hill Science & Engineering Books, 11 W. 19th St., New York, New York 10011. (212) 337-6010. 1980. Covers ecology, man's influence on nature, and environmental protection.

McGraw-Hill Encyclopedia of Science and Technology. McGraw-Hill, 1221 Avenue of the Americas, New York, New York 10020. (212) 512-2000 or (800) 262-4729. 1992. Seventh edition. Issued in multiple volumes including index. Includes all science and technology broad subject areas.

GENERAL WORKS

Agricultural Ecology. Joy Tivy. John Wiley & Sons, Inc., 605 3rd Ave., New York, New York 10158-0012. (212) 850-6000. 1990. Analyzes the nature of relationships between crops, livestock, and the biophysical environment, and the extent to which man has modified the products and environment to suit his own needs.

Beyond 40 Percent: Record-Setting Recycling and Composting Programs. Brenda Platt, et al. Island Press, 1718 Connecticut Ave. N.W., Suite 300, Washington, District of Columbia 20009. (202) 232-7933. 1991. Produced by the Institute for Local Self-Reliance, this volume documents the operating experience of 17 U.S. communities, from small rural towns to large cities, that are recovering between 32 and 57 percent of their waste.

Biological Reclamation of Solid Wastes. Clarence G. Golueke. Rodale Press, 33 E. Minor St., Emmaus, Pennsylvania 18098. (215) 967-5171. 1977. Compost, refuse, refuse disposal, and biological treatment of sewage.

Compost Toilets: A Guide for Owner-Builders. National Center for Appropriate Technology, PO Box 3838, Butte, Montana 59702. (406) 494-4572. Covers sewage and refuse disposal facilities and toilets.

Composting: the Organic Natural Way. Dick Kitto. Thornsons Publishing Ltd., Wellingborough, Northamptonshire, England NN82RQ. 1988. Covers principles of compost making and its uses.

Composting: Theory and Practice for City, Industry and Farm. JG Press, Box 351, Emmaus, Pennsylvania 18049. (215) 967-4010. 1981. Covers compost science and land utilization.

The Incredible Heap: A Guide to Compost Gardening. Chris Catton. St. Martin's Press, 175 5th Ave., New York, New York 10010. (212) 674-5151. 1984. Covers organic gardening and compost.

Management Strategies for Landscape Waste: Collection, Composting, and Marketing. Illinois Department of Energy and Natural Resources, Office of Solid Waste and Renewable Resources, 325 W. Adams St., Rm. 300, Springfield, Illinois 62706. (217) 785-2800. 1989. Compost, waste, recycling, and refuse collection.

Organic Waste Recycling. Chongrak Polprasert. John Wiley & Sons, Inc., 605 Third Ave., New York, New York 10158. (212) 850-6000. 1989. Covers technologies for treating human waste, animal manure, agricultural residues and wastewater, sludge, algae, aquatic weeds and others.

Save a Landfill: Compost Instead of Bag. Illinois Environmental Protection Agency, 2200 Churchill Rd., PO Box 19276, Springfield, Illinois 62794-9276. (217) 782-2829. 1990. Compost and waste recycling.

Yard Waste Programs: Existing Regulations, Collection, Composting, Compost Characteristics and Land Application. University of Illinois Center for Solid Waste Management and Research, Office of Technology Transfer, School of Public Health, Chicago, Illinois 61801. 1990.

HANDBOOKS AND MANUALS

The Biocycle Guide to Composting Municipal Wastes. JG Press, Box 351, Emmaus, Pennsylvania 18049. (215)

967-4010. 1989. Covers compost, compost plants, refuse, refuse disposal, and the recycling of waste.

Compendium on Solid Waste Management by Vermicomposting. National Technical Information Service, 5285 Port Royal Rd., Springfield, Virginia 22161. (703) 487-4650. 1980. Covers compost, refuse and refuse disposal, and earthworms.

Compost Engineering: Principles and Practice. Robert Tim Haug. Ann Arbor Science, 230 Collingwood, Ann Arbor, Michigan 48106. 1980.

Composting Municipal Sludge: A Technology Evaluation. Noyes Publications, 120 Mill Rd., Park Ridge, New Jersey 07656. (201) 391-8484. 1988. Looks at sewage sludge as fertilizer, compost evaluation and activated sludge process.

A Homeowners Guide to Recycling Yard Wastes: How to Improve the Health and Quality of Your Yard and Garden by Using Grass Clippings, Leaves and Wood Chips. Illinois Cooperative Extension Service, 1715 W. Springfield Ave., Champaign, Illinois 61821. (217) 333-7672. 1989. Compost, waste, recycling and refuse collection.

ONLINE DATA BASES

Current Research Information System–CRIS/USDA. U.S. Department of Agriculture, National Agricultural Library, 10301 Baltimore Blvd., 5th Floor, Beltsville, Maryland 20705-2351. (301) 504-5755. Looks at current research projects in agriculture and allied sciences covering the biological, physical, social and behavioral sciences related to agriculture.

Enviro/Energyline Abstracts Plus. R. R. Bowker Co., 121 Chanlon Rd., New Providence, New Jersey 07974. (908) 464-6800.

Environmental Periodicals Bibliography. National Information Services Corp., Ste. 6, Wyman Towers, 3100 St. Paul St., Baltimore, Maryland 21218. (410)243-0797. Online version of abstract of same name.

Monthly Catalog of United States Government Publications. U.S. G.P.O., Supt. of Docs., PO Box 371954, Pittsburgh, Pennsylvania 15250-7954. (202) 512-0000.

National Technical Information Service. U.S. Department of Commerce, National Technical Information Service, Office of Data Base Services, 5285 Port Royal Rd., Springfield, Virginia 22161. (703) 487-4807. Bibliographic database of government sponsored research and technical reports.

PERIODICALS AND NEWSLETTERS

Compost Science/Land Utilization. JG Press, Box 351, Emmaus, Pennsylvania 18049. (215) 967-4010. Journal of waste recycling.

Journal of Waste Recycling. Chemical Abstracts Service, PO Box 3012, Columbus, Ohio 43210. (614) 421-3600. Bimonthly. Covers compost science, land utilization, waste disposal in the ground and recycling.

TRADE ASSOCIATIONS AND PROFESSIONAL SOCIETIES

American Institute of Biological Sciences. 730 11th St., N.W., Washington, District of Columbia 20001-4521. (202) 628-1500.

American Society of Civil Engineers. 345 East 47th St., New York, New York 10017. (212) 705-7496.

COMPOSTING

See also: AGRICULTURE; BIODEGRADABLE; ORGANIC GARDENING; SOIL SCIENCE; WASTE MANAGEMENT

ABSTRACTING AND INDEXING SERVICES

Agrindex. AGRIS Coordinating Center, Via delle Terme di Caracalla, Rome, Italy I-00100. 61 0181-FA01. 1975-.

Applied Ecology Abstracts Studies in Renewable Natural Resources. Information Retrieval Ltd., 1911 Jefferson Davis Highway, Arlington, Virginia 22202. 1975-. Monthly.

Biological Abstracts. BIOSIS, 2100 Arch St., Philadelphia, Pennsylvania 19103-1399. (215) 587-4800. 1927-.

Biological and Agricultural Index. H.W. Wilson Co., 950 University Ave., Bronx, New York 10452. (800) 367-6770. 1916-. Monthly.

Environment Abstracts. Bowker A & I Publishing, 121 Chanlon Rd., New Providence, New Jersey 07974. (908) 464-6800. 1974-.

Environment Index. Environment Information Center, Index Research Department, 124 E. 39th St., New York, New York 10016. 1971-. Annual.

Environmental Information Connection–EIC. Planning Information Program, Dept. of Urban and Regional Planning, University of Illinois, 1003 West Nevada, Urbana, Illinois 61801. (217) 333-1369. Also available online.

Environmental Periodicals Bibliography. Environmental Studies Institute, International Academy at Santa Barbara, 800 Garden St., Suite D, Santa Barbara, California 93101. (805) 965-5010. Also available online.

General Science Index. H. W. Wilson Co., 950 University Ave., Bronx, New York 10452. 1978-. Monthly, also issued in annual cumulation. Cumulative subject index to English language periodicals in the subject fields of astronomy, botany, chemistry, earth science, environment and conservation, food and nutrition, genetics, mathematics, medicine and health, microbiology, oceanography, physics, physiology and zoology.

Index to Scientific Book Contents. Institute for Scientific Information, 3501 Market St., Philadelphia, Pennsylvania 19104. (800) 523-1857. 1985-. Annual. Gives contents of science books published.

Multimedia Index to Ecology. National Information Center for Educational Media, University of Southern California, Los Angeles, California 90007.

Pollution Abstracts. Cambridge Scientific Abstracts, 5161 River Rd., Bethesda, Maryland 20816. (301) 961-6750. Six/year. Indexes worldwide technical literature on environmental pollution. Covers air pollution, marine and freshwater pollution, sewage and wastewater treatment, waste management, toxicology and health, noise pollution, radiation, land pollution, and environmental policies, programs, legislation, and education. Also available online.

Science Citation Index. Institute for Scientific Information, 3501 Market St., Philadelphia, Pennsylvania 19104. 1961-.

BIBLIOGRAPHIES

Current Contents. Agriculture, Biology and Environmental Sciences. Institute for Scientific Information, 3501 Market St., Philadelphia, Pennsylvania 19104. (800) 523-1857. 1973-. Previous title: Current Contents. Agricultural, Food & Veterinary Sciences. Gives the table of contents of periodicals in the fields of agriculture, biology, environmental and related areas.

Directory of Published Proceedings. Interdok Corp., 173 Halstead Ave., Harrison, New York 10528. (914) 835-3506. 1990. Monthly. This is a listing of published proceedings including the series SEMTE (Science/Medicine/Engineering/Technology) and the series SSH (Social Science/Humanities).

EPA Publications Bibliography. U.S. Environmental Protection Agency, Library Systems Branch, 401 M St., SW, Washington, District of Columbia 20460. (202) 260-2090. Quarterly.

ENCYCLOPEDIAS AND DICTIONARIES

McGraw-Hill Encyclopedia of Environmental Science. Sybil P. Parker. McGraw-Hill Science & Engineering Books, 11 W. 19th St., New York, New York 10011. (212) 337-6010. 1980. Covers ecology, man's influence on nature, and environmental protection.

GENERAL WORKS

The Biocycle Guide to Yard Waste Composting. The Staff of Biocycle, Journal of Waste Recycling. JG Press, Box 351, Emmaus, Pennsylvania 18049. (215)967-4010. 1989. Contains chapters on: planning yard waste utilization programs; collection-evaluation options and methods; cost and economics; composting yard waste with other materials; waste reduction implemented backyard composting; and collection and composting equipment.

Home Composting. Seattle Tilth Association, Dept. NA, 4649 Sunnyside Ave. N., Seattle, Washington 98103. 1990.

Let it Rot! The Home Gardener's Guide to Composting. Stu Campbell. Storey Communications, School House Rd., Pownal, Vermont 05261. (802) 823-5811. 1990.

Wastewater Engineering: Treatment, Disposal, and Reuse. Metcalf & Eddy, Inc. McGraw-Hill Science & Engineering Books, 11 West 19th St., New York, New York 10011. (212) 337-6010. 1991. Reflects the impact of changing federal legislation on environmental quality control and sludge management. Gives a solid overall perspective on wastewater engineering.

HANDBOOKS AND MANUALS

The Art & Science of Composting. BioCycle, 419 State Ave., Emmaus, Pennsylvania 18049. (215) 967-4135. 1988. Composting principles, processes, management, materials, and markets.

ONLINE DATA BASES

BIOSIS Previews. BIOSIS, 2100 Arch St., Philadelphia, Pennsylvania 19103-1399. (215) 587-4800. Largest and most comprehensive database of research in the life sciences. Contains citations for nearly 9000 primary research journals, monographs, reviews, symposia, preliminary reports, semi-popular journals, selected institutional reports, government reports and research communications.

Current Research Information System–CRIS/USDA. U.S. Department of Agriculture, National Agricultural Library, 10301 Baltimore Blvd., 5th Floor, Beltsville, Maryland 20705-2351. (301) 504-5755. Looks at current research projects in agriculture and allied sciences covering the biological, physical, social and behavioral sciences related to agriculture.

Enviro/Energyline Abstracts Plus. R. R. Bowker Co., 121 Chanlon Rd., New Providence, New Jersey 07974. (908) 464-6800.

Environmental Periodicals Bibliography. National Information Services Corp., Ste. 6, Wyman Towers, 3100 St. Paul St., Baltimore, Maryland 21218. (410)243-0797. Online version of abstract of same name.

Monthly Catalog of United States Government Publications. U.S. G.P.O., Supt. of Docs., PO Box 371954, Pittsburgh, Pennsylvania 15250-7954. (202) 512-0000.

National Technical Information Service. U.S. Department of Commerce, National Technical Information Service, Office of Data Base Services, 5285 Port Royal Rd., Springfield, Virginia 22161. (703) 487-4807. Bibliographic database of government sponsored research and technical reports.

SCISEARCH. Institute for Scientific Information, University City Science Center, 3501 Market St., Philadelphia, Pennsylvania 19104. (215) 386-0100.

TRADE ASSOCIATIONS AND PROFESSIONAL SOCIETIES

American Institute of Biological Sciences. 730 11th St., N.W., Washington, District of Columbia 20001-4521. (202) 628-1500.

COMPUTER APPLICATION, ENVIRONMENT

ABSTRACTING AND INDEXING SERVICES

Applied Ecology Abstracts Studies in Renewable Natural Resources. Information Retrieval Ltd., 1911 Jefferson Davis Highway, Arlington, Virginia 22202. 1975-. Monthly.

Applied Science and Technology Index. H.W. Wilson Co., 950 University Ave., Bronx, New York 10452. (800) 367-6770. Formerly Industrial Arts Index.

Biological and Agricultural Index. H.W. Wilson Co., 950 University Ave., Bronx, New York 10452. (800) 367-6770. 1916-. Monthly.

Bulletin Signaletique: Eau et Assainissement, Pollution Atmospherique, Droit des Pollutions. Centre de Documentation, Centre National de la Recherche Scientifique, 15, quai Anatole France, Paris, France 75700. (1) 45 55 92 25. 1983-. Monthly. Indexes pollution periodicals including water, atmospheric and related pollutions.

Engineering Index. The Engineering Index Inc., 345 E. 47th St., New York, New York 10017. 1962-.

Environment Abstracts. Bowker A & I Publishing, 121 Chanlon Rd., New Providence, New Jersey 07974. (908) 464-6800. 1974-.

Environment Index. Environment Information Center, Index Research Department, 124 E. 39th St., New York, New York 10016. 1971-. Annual.

Environmental Information Connection–EIC. Planning Information Program, Dept. of Urban and Regional Planning, University of Illinois, 1003 West Nevada, Urbana, Illinois 61801. (217) 333-1369. Also available online.

Environmental Periodicals Bibliography. Environmental Studies Institute, International Academy at Santa Barbara, 800 Garden St., Suite D, Santa Barbara, California 93101. (805) 965-5010. Also available online.

Index to Scientific Book Contents. Institute for Scientific Information, 3501 Market St., Philadelphia, Pennsylvania 19104. (800) 523-1857. 1985-. Annual. Gives contents of science books published.

Multimedia Index to Ecology. National Information Center for Educational Media, University of Southern California, Los Angeles, California 90007.

BIBLIOGRAPHIES

Current Contents. Agriculture, Biology and Environmental Sciences. Institute for Scientific Information, 3501 Market St., Philadelphia, Pennsylvania 19104. (800) 523-1857. 1973-. Previous title: Current Contents. Agricultural, Food & Veterinary Sciences. Gives the table of contents of periodicals in the fields of agriculture, biology, environmental and related areas.

EPA Publications Bibliography. U.S. Environmental Protection Agency, Library Systems Branch, 401 M St., SW, Washington, District of Columbia 20460. (202) 260-2090. Quarterly.

ENCYCLOPEDIAS AND DICTIONARIES

Encyclopedia of Physical Science and Technology. Robert A. Meyers, ed. Academic Press, c/o Harcourt Brace Jovanovich Inc., 6277 Sea Harbor Dr., Orlando, Florida 32887. (800) 346-8648. Dictionary of engineering, technology and physical sciences.

McGraw-Hill Encyclopedia of Environmental Science. Sybil P. Parker. McGraw-Hill Science & Engineering Books, 11 W. 19th St., New York, New York 10011. (212) 337-6010. 1980. Covers ecology, man's influence on nature, and environmental protection.

ONLINE DATA BASES

Chemical Engineering and Biotechnology Abstracts–CEBA. Orbit Search Service, Maxwell Online Inc., 8000 W. Park Dr., McLean, Virginia 22102. (703) 442-0900 or (800) 456-7248. Monthly. Covers theoretical, practical and commercial material on all aspects of processing safety, and the environment. Also covers process and reaction engineering, measurement and process control, environmental protection and safety, plant design and equipment used in chemical engineering and biotechnology. More than 400 of the world's major primary chemical and process engineering journals are scanned to compile the database. Available from ORBIT.

Computerized Engineering Index–COMPENDEX. Engineering Information Inc., 345 E. 47th St., New York, New York 10017. (212) 705-7600.

Enviro/Energyline Abstracts Plus. R. R. Bowker Co., 121 Chanlon Rd., New Providence, New Jersey 07974. (908) 464-6800.

Environmental Periodicals Bibliography. National Information Services Corp., Ste. 6, Wyman Towers, 3100 St. Paul St., Baltimore, Maryland 21218. (410)243-0797. Online version of abstract of same name.

Monthly Catalog of United States Government Publications. U.S. G.P.O., Supt. of Docs., PO Box 371954, Pittsburgh, Pennsylvania 15250-7954. (202) 512-0000.

National Technical Information Service. U.S. Department of Commerce, National Technical Information Service, Office of Data Base Services, 5285 Port Royal Rd., Springfield, Virginia 22161. (703) 487-4807. Bibliographic database of government sponsored research and technical reports.

RESEARCH CENTERS AND INSTITUTES

Mississippi State University, Research Center. John C. Stennis Space Center, Stennis Space Center, Mississippi 39529-6000. (601) 688-3227.

TRADE ASSOCIATIONS AND PROFESSIONAL SOCIETIES

American Society of Civil Engineers. 345 East 47th St., New York, New York 10017. (212) 705-7496.

CONCRETE

See: CEMENT

CONIFEROUS FORESTS

See: FORESTS

CONIFERS

ABSTRACTING AND INDEXING SERVICES

Applied Ecology Abstracts Studies in Renewable Natural Resources. Information Retrieval Ltd., 1911 Jefferson Davis Highway, Arlington, Virginia 22202. 1975-. Monthly.

Biological and Agricultural Index. H.W. Wilson Co., 950 University Ave., Bronx, New York 10452. (800) 367-6770. 1916-. Monthly.

Ecological Abstracts. Geo Abstracts Ltd. Elsevier Applied Science, Crown House, Linton Rd., Barking, England IG 11 8JU. 1974-. Derived from over 600 leading ecological and environmental journals, plus books, conference proceedings, reports and theses.

Environment Abstracts. Bowker A & I Publishing, 121 Chanlon Rd., New Providence, New Jersey 07974. (908) 464-6800. 1974-.

Environment Index. Environment Information Center, Index Research Department, 124 E. 39th St., New York, New York 10016. 1971-. Annual.

Environmental Information Connection–EIC. Planning Information Program, Dept. of Urban and Regional Planning, University of Illinois, 1003 West Nevada, Urbana, Illinois 61801. (217) 333-1369. Also available online.

Environmental Periodicals Bibliography. Environmental Studies Institute, International Academy at Santa Barbara, 800 Garden St., Suite D, Santa Barbara, California 93101. (805) 965-5010. Also available online.

General Science Index. H. W. Wilson Co., 950 University Ave., Bronx, New York 10452. 1978-. Monthly, also issued in annual cumulation. Cumulative subject index to English language periodicals in the subject fields of astronomy, botany, chemistry, earth science, environment and conservation, food and nutrition, genetics, mathematics, medicine and health, microbiology, oceanography, physics, physiology and zoology.

Multimedia Index to Ecology. National Information Center for Educational Media, University of Southern California, Los Angeles, California 90007.

Science Citation Index. Institute for Scientific Information, 3501 Market St., Philadelphia, Pennsylvania 19104. 1961-.

BIBLIOGRAPHIES

EPA Publications Bibliography. U.S. Environmental Protection Agency, Library Systems Branch, 401 M St., SW, Washington, District of Columbia 20460. (202) 260-2090. Quarterly.

ENCYCLOPEDIAS AND DICTIONARIES

Conifers. Keith Rushforth. Facts on File, Inc., 460 Park Ave. S., New York, New York 10016. (212) 683-2244. 1987. Dictionary of conifers and ornamental conifers.

Encyclopaedia Coniferae. H. N. Moldenke and A. L. Moldenke, Corvallis, Oregon 1986.

McGraw-Hill Encyclopedia of Science and Technology. McGraw-Hill, 1221 Avenue of the Americas, New York, New York 10020. (212) 512-2000 or (800) 262-4729. 1992. Seventh edition. Issued in multiple volumes including index. Includes all science and technology broad subject areas.

GENERAL WORKS

Conifers. D.M. van Gelderen. Timber Press, 9999 SW Wilshire, Portland, Oregon 97225. (800) 327-5680. 1989. Deals with ornamental conifers.

Dwarf Conifers; A Handbook on Low and Slow-Growing Evergreens. Brooklyn Botanic Garden, 1000 Washington Ave., Brooklyn, New York 11225. (718) 622-4433. 1984.

An International Census of the Coniferae, I. John Silba. Moldenke, Plainfield, New Jersey 1984.

Manual of Cultivated Conifers. Gerd Krussmann. Timber Press, 9999 SW Wilshire, Portland, Oregon 97225. (800) 327-5680. 1985.

Northwest Conifers: A Photographic Key. Dale N. Bever. Binford and Mort Publishing, 1202 Northwest 17th Ave., Portland, Oregon 97209. (503) 221-0866. 1981. Identification of Pacific Northwest conifers.

Pinacea: Being a Handbook of the Firs and Pines. Senilis. Bishen Singh Mahendra Pal Singh, 23A Connaught Pl., P.B. 137, Dehra Dun, India 1984.

ONLINE DATA BASES

Cambridge Scientific Abstracts Life Science–CSAL. Cambridge Scientific Abstracts, 5161 River Rd., Bethesda, Maryland 20816. (301) 961-6750. Provides access to the following abstracting services: "Life Sciences Collection," "Aquatic Sciences and Fisheries Abstracts," "Oceanic Abstracts," and "Pollution Abstracts."

Enviro/Energyline Abstracts Plus. R. R. Bowker Co., 121 Chanlon Rd., New Providence, New Jersey 07974. (908) 464-6800.

Environmental Periodicals Bibliography. National Information Services Corp., Ste. 6, Wyman Towers, 3100 St. Paul St., Baltimore, Maryland 21218. (410)243-0797. Online version of abstract of same name.

SCISEARCH. Institute for Scientific Information, University City Science Center, 3501 Market St., Philadelphia, Pennsylvania 19104. (215) 386-0100.

TRADE ASSOCIATIONS AND PROFESSIONAL SOCIETIES

American Institute of Biological Sciences. 730 11th St., N.W., Washington, District of Columbia 20001-4521. (202) 628-1500.

CONNECTICUT ENVIRONMENTAL AGENCIES

GOVERNMENTAL ORGANIZATIONS

Department of Environmental Protection: Hazardous Waste Management. Director, Hazardous Waste Management, State Office Building, 165 Capitol Ave., Hartford, Connecticut 06106. (203) 566-4924.

Department of Labor: Occupational Safety. Director, Occupational Safety and Health, 200 Folly Brook Blvd., Wethersfield, Connecticut 06109. (203) 566-4550.

Emergency Response Commission: Emergency Preparedness and Community Right-to-Know. SARA Title III Coordinator, State Office Building, Room 161, 165 Capitol Ave., Hartford, Connecticut 06106. (203) 566-4856.

Environmental Protection Department: Air Quality. Commissioner, Division of Environmental Quality, 165 Capitol Ave., Hartford, Connecticut 06106. (203) 566-2506.

Environmental Protection Department: Coastal Zone Management. Director, Planning and Coastal Area Management, 18-20 Trinity St., Hartford, Connecticut 06106. (203) 566-7404.

Environmental Protection Department: Environmental Protection. Commissioner, Department of Environmental Quality, 165 Capitol Ave., Room 161, Hartford, Connecticut 06106. (203) 566-2110.

Environmental Protection Department: Fish and Wildlife. Chief, Fish and Wildlife, State Office Building, Room 254, 165 Capitol Ave., Hartford, Connecticut 06106. (203) 566-2287.

Environmental Protection Department: Groundwater Management. Director, Water Compliance Unit, 122 Washington St., Hartford, Connecticut 06106. (203) 566-3245.

Environmental Protection Department: Natural Resources. Commissioner, Division of Environmental Quality, 165 Capitol Ave., Room 161, Hartford, Connecticut 06106. (203) 566-2110.

Environmental Protection Department: Pesticide Registration. Hazardous Materials Management Unit, State Office Building, 165 Capitol Ave., Hartford, Connecticut 06106. (203) 566-4924.

Environmental Protection Department: Solid Waste Department. Director, Solid Waste Management Unit, 122 Washington St., Hartford, Connecticut 06106. (203) 566-5847.

Environmental Protection Department: Underground Storage Tanks. Director, Hazardous Waste Management, State Office Building, 165 Capitol Ave., Hartford, Connecticut 06106. (203) 566-4924.

Environmental Protection Department: Water Quality. Director, Water Compliance Unit, 122 Washington St., Hartford, Connecticut 06106. (203) 566-3245.

Hazardous Waste Management Service: Waste Minimization and Pollution Prevention. Chair, Executive Office, 865 Brook St., Rocky Hill, Connecticut 06067. (203) 244-2007.

CONNECTICUT ENVIRONMENTAL LEGISLATION

GENERAL WORKS

Connecticut Environmental Law Handbook. Government Institutes, Inc., 4 Research Pl., Ste. 200, Rockville, Maryland 20850. (301) 921-2300. 1990.

CONSERVATION OF NATURAL RESOURCES

See also: AGRICULTURAL CONSERVATION; ENERGY CONSERVATION; HUMAN ECOLOGY; NATIONAL PARKS AND RESERVES; PLANT CONSERVATION; RECLAMATION; RECYCLING (WASTE, ETC.); SOIL CONSERVATION; WATER CONSERVATION

ABSTRACTING AND INDEXING SERVICES

Abstracts of Air and Water Conservation Literature. American Petroleum Institute. Central Abstracting and Indexing Service, 275 Madison Avenue, New York, New York 10016. 1972.

Agroforestry Abstracts. C. A. B. International, 845 North Park Ave., Tucson, Arizona 85719. (602) 621-7897 or (800) 528-4841. 1988-. Quarterly. Abstracts journal articles, reports, conferences and books. Focuses on subjects areas such as agroforestry in general; agroforestry systems; trees, animals and crops; conservation; human ecology; social and economic aspects; development, research and methodology.

Applied Ecology Abstracts Studies in Renewable Natural Resources. Information Retrieval Ltd., 1911 Jefferson Davis Highway, Arlington, Virginia 22202. 1975-. Monthly.

Biological Abstracts. BIOSIS, 2100 Arch St., Philadelphia, Pennsylvania 19103-1399. (215) 587-4800. 1927-.

Current Advances in Ecological and Environmental Science. Pergamon Microforms International, Inc., Fairview Park, Elmsford, New York 10523. (914) 592-7720. 1989-. Monthly. Current literature searching service includingjournals, reports, abstracts, etc. This service is available online as part of the CABS database on the hosts BRS and ORBIT search service.

Ecological Abstracts. Geo Abstracts Ltd. Elsevier Applied Science, Crown House, Linton Rd., Barking, England IG 11 8JU. 1974-. Derived from over 600 leading ecological and environmental journals, plus books, conference proceedings, reports and theses.

Ecology Abstracts. Cambridge Scientific Abstracts, 5161 River Rd., Bethesda, Maryland 20816. (301) 961-6750. Monthly.

Environment Abstracts. Bowker A & I Publishing, 121 Chanlon Rd., New Providence, New Jersey 07974. (908) 464-6800. 1974-.

Environment Index. Environment Information Center, Index Research Department, 124 E. 39th St., New York, New York 10016. 1971-. Annual.

Environmental Information Connection–EIC. Planning Information Program, Dept. of Urban and Regional Planning, University of Illinois, 1003 West Nevada, Urbana, Illinois 61801. (217) 333-1369. Also available online.

Environmental Periodicals Bibliography. Environmental Studies Institute, International Academy at Santa Barbara, 800 Garden St., Suite D, Santa Barbara, California 93101. (805) 965-5010. Also available online.

General Science Index. H. W. Wilson Co., 950 University Ave., Bronx, New York 10452. 1978-. Monthly, also issued in annual cumulation. Cumulative subject index to English language periodicals in the subject fields of astronomy, botany, chemistry, earth science, environment and conservation, food and nutrition, genetics, mathematics, medicine and health, microbiology, oceanography, physics, physiology and zoology.

Index to Scientific Book Contents. Institute for Scientific Information, 3501 Market St., Philadelphia, Pennsylvania 19104. (800) 523-1857. 1985-. Annual. Gives contents of science books published.

Multimedia Index to Ecology. National Information Center for Educational Media, University of Southern California, Los Angeles, California 90007.

Pollution Abstracts. Cambridge Scientific Abstracts, 5161 River Rd., Bethesda, Maryland 20816. (301) 961-6750. Six/year. Indexes worldwide technical literature on environmental pollution. Covers air pollution, marine and freshwater pollution, sewage and wastewater treatment, waste management, toxicology and health, noise pollution, radiation, land pollution, and environmental policies, programs, legislation, and education. Also available online.

Science Citation Index. Institute for Scientific Information, 3501 Market St., Philadelphia, Pennsylvania 19104. 1961-.

ALMANACS AND YEARBOOKS

Gale Environmental Almanac. Russ Hoyle. Gale Research Inc., 835 Penobscot Bldg., Detroit, Michigan 48226-4094. (313) 961-2242. 1993. Focuses on the U.S. and Canada, although worldwide and transboundary issues are discussed.

North Country Almanac: Journal of the Adirondack Seasons. Robert F. Hall. Purple Mountain Press, PO Box E-3, Fleischmanns, New York 12430. (914)254-4062. 1990. Essays on the conservation of nature and its resources.

Student Conservation Association Evaluation Report. Student Conservation Assn., Box 550, Charlestown, New Hampshire 03603. (603) 826-4301. Annual.

BIBLIOGRAPHIES

Directory of Country Environmental Studies: An Annotated Bibliography of Environmental and Natural Resources Profiles and Assessments. World Resources Institute, 1709 New York Ave., NW, Washington, District of Columbia 20006. 1990. Concentrates on studies of developing countries. Reports on the condition and trends of the major natural resources of a country and their condition and relationship to economic development.

Directory of Published Proceedings. Interdok Corp., 173 Halstead Ave., Harrison, New York 10528. (914) 835-3506. 1990. Monthly. This is a listing of published proceedings including the series SEMTE (Science/Medicine/Engineering/Technology) and the series SSH (Social Science/Humanities).

EPA Publications Bibliography. U.S. Environmental Protection Agency, Library Systems Branch, 401 M St., SW, Washington, District of Columbia 20460. (202) 260-2090. Quarterly.

DIRECTORIES

Association of Conservation Engineers–Membership Directory. Association of Conservation Engineers, c/o William P. Allinder, Engineering Section, Alabama Department of Conservation and Natural Resources, 64 N. Union St., Montgomery, Alabama 36130. (205) 242-3476.

Canadian Conservation Directory. Canadian Nature Federation, 453 Sussex Dr., Ottawa, Ontario, Canada K1N 6Z4. (613) 238-6154. 1973-. Directory of over 800 natural history, environment and conservation organizations of Canada.

Canadian Environmental Directory. Canadian Almanac & Directory Publishing Co. Ltd., 134 Adelaide St. E., Ste. 27, Toronto, Ontario, Canada M5C 1K9. (416) 362-

4088. 1992. Includes individuals, agencies, firms, and associations.

Conservation and Service Corps Profiles. Human Environment Center, 1001 Connecticut Ave NW, Suite 827, Washington, District of Columbia 20036. (202) 331-8387. Semiannual.

Conservation Directory. National Wildlife Federation, 1400 16th St. N.W., Washington, District of Columbia 20036-2266. (202) 797-6800. 1956-. Annually. Contains information on organizations, agencies, officials, and education programs in the natural resources management field.

Ecological Society of America Bulletin–Directory of Members Issue. Ecological Society of America, c/o Dr. Duncan Patten, Center for Environmental Studies, Arizona State University, Tempe, Arizona 85287. (602) 965-3000.

The United States and the Global Environment: A Guide to American Organizations Concerned with International Environmental Issues. Thaddeus C. Trzyna. California Institute of Public Affairs, PO Box 10, Claremont, California 91711. (714) 624-5212. 1983. A guide to American organizations concerned with international environmental issues.

World Directory of Environmental Organizations. Thaddeus C. Trzyna, ed. California Institute of Public Affairs, PO Box 10, Claremont, California 91711. (714) 624-5212. 1989. 3rd ed. Handbook of organizations and programs concerned with protecting the environment and managing natural resources. It covers national and international organizations, both governmental and nongovernmental, in all parts of the world.

ENCYCLOPEDIAS AND DICTIONARIES

The Agriculture Dictionary. Ray V. Herren and Roy L. Donahue. Delmar Publishers Inc., 2 Computer Dr. W., Albany, New York 12212. (518) 459-1150. 1991. Covers all the agricultural areas including acid rain, acid mine drainage, food additives, agricultural engineering, conservation of the natural resources, microorganisms, triticale and other related topics.

Cambridge Encyclopedia of Life Sciences. A. E. Friday and David S. Ingram. Cambridge University Press, 40 W 20th St., New York, New York 10011. (212) 924-3900 or (800) 227-0247. 1985. Includes all topics under biology and ecology.

Dictionary of Ecology and Environment. P. H. Collin. Collin Pub., 8 The Causeway, Teddington, England TW11 0HE. 1988. Vocabulary of 5,000 words and expressions covering a range of topics relating to ecology, including: climate, vegetation, pollution, waste disposal, and energy conservation.

Dictionary of Environmental Science and Technology. Andrew Porteous. John Wiley & Sons, Inc., 605 3rd Ave., New York, New York 10158-0012. (212) 850-6000. 1992.

Environmental Encyclopedia. William P. Cunningham, Terence Ball, et. al. Gale Research Inc., 835 Penobscot Bldg., Detroit, Michigan 48226-4094. (313) 961-2242. 1993.

Illustrated Encyclopedia of Science and the Future. Mike Biscare, et al., ed. Marshall Cavendish, 58 Old Compton St., London, England 0W1V5 PA. 01-734 6710. 1983. Twenty volumes. Each volume has 5 sections: Frontiers,

Electronics in Action, Medical Science, Military Technology, and Resources.

McGraw-Hill Encyclopedia of Environmental Science. Sybil P. Parker. McGraw-Hill Science & Engineering Books, 11 W. 19th St., New York, New York 10011. (212) 337-6010. 1980. Covers ecology, man's influence on nature, and environmental protection.

McGraw-Hill Encyclopedia of Science and Technology. McGraw-Hill, 1221 Avenue of the Americas, New York, New York 10020. (212) 512-2000 or (800) 262-4729. 1992. Seventh edition. Issued in multiple volumes including index. Includes all science and technology broad subject areas.

Van Nostrand's Scientific Encyclopedia. Glenn D. Considine, ed. Van Nostrand Reinhold, 115 5th Ave., New York, New York 10003. (212) 254-3232. 1983. Sixth edition. Includes all broad subject areas in science.

GENERAL WORKS

50 Simple Things You Can Do to Save the Earth. G.K. Hall & Co., 70 Lincoln St., Boston, Massachusetts 02111. (617) 423-3990. 1991. Citizen participation in environmental protection.

Agriculture and Natural Resources: Planning for Educational Priorities for the Twenty-First Century. Wava G. Haney, ed. Conservation of Natural Resources, 5500 Central Ave., Boulder, Colorado 80301. 1991. A volume in the Social Behavior and Natural Resources Series. Text details the priorities in planning for the 21st century while conserving natural resources and the environment.

America's Downtowns: Growth, Politics, and Preservation. Richard C. Collins. Preservation Press, National Trust for Historic Preservation, 1785 Massachusetts Ave. NW, Washington, District of Columbia 20036. (202) 673-4058. 1991. Examines the efforts of 10 major American cities to integrate preservation values into the local policies that shape downtown growth and development.

Biological Conservation. David W. Ehrenfeld. Holt, Rinehart and Winston, 6277 Sea Harbor Dr., Orlando, Florida 32887. (407) 345-2500. 1970.

Biological Surveys of Estuaries and Coasts. Cambridge University Press, 40 W. 20th St., New York, New York 10011. (212) 924-3900. Coastal ecology, ecological surveys, and estuarine biology.

Breaking New Ground. Gifford Pinchot. Island Press, 1718 Connecticut Ave. N.W., Suite 300, Washington, District of Columbia 20009. (202) 232-7933. 1987. Expounds the views that our precious forests should be managed for maximum yield with minimum long-term negative impact.

Caring for the Earth: A Strategy for Sustainable Living. IUCN. Earthscan, 3 Endsleigh St., London, England 071-388 2117. 1991. Discusses the sustainable living methods to protect the environment.

The Conservation Atlas of Tropical Forests: Asia and the Pacific. N. Mark Collins, Jeffery A. Sayer, and Timothy C. Whitmore. Simon & Schuster, 1230 Avenue of the Americas, New York, New York 10020. (212) 689-7000. 1991. Focuses on closed canopy, and true rain forests. This Asian volume is the first of a set of three–tropical America and Africa being the next. Address such regional subjects as forest wildlife, human impacts on forest lands, and the tropical timber trade; and includes a "Tropical

Forestry Action Plan" to conserve and protect important remaining stands. The second part of the atlas gives a detailed survey of 17 countries plus the island groups of Fiji and the Solomons, but not those of New Caledonia, New Hebrides, or Micronesia.

Conservation of Natural Resources. Gary A. Klee. Prentice-Hall, Rte. 9W, Englewood Cliffs, New Jersey 07632. (201) 592-2000; (800) 634-2863. 1991. Draws together current and useful tools, techniques, and policy strategies for students training to be natural resource managers.

Conserving the World's Biological Diversity. Jeffrey A. McNeely, et al. World Resources Institute, 1709 New York Ave. N.W., Washington, District of Columbia 20006. (800) 822-0504. 1990. Provides a clear concise and well illustrated guide to the meaning and importance of biological diversity. Discusses a broad range of practical approaches to biodiversity preservation, including policy changes, integrated land-use management, species and habitat protection, and pollution control.

Down by the River: The Impact of Federal Water Projects and Policies on Biological Diversity. Constance Elizabeth Hunt with Verne Huser. Island Press, 1718 Connecticut Ave. N.W., Suite 300, Washington, District of Columbia 20009. (202) 232-7933. 1988. Presents case studies of development projects on seven river systems, including the Columbia, the Delaware, the Missouri, and the rivers of Maine ,to illustrate their effect on biological diversity.

Eco-Warriors: Understanding the Radical Environmental Movement. Rik Scarce. Noble Pr., 111 E. Chestnut, Suite 48 A, Chicago, Illinois 60611. (312) 880-0439. 1990. Recounts escapades of pro-ecology sabotage by self styled eco- warriors. Episodes such as the sinking of two whaling ships in Iceland, the botched attempt to hang a banner on Mt. Rushmore, a national tree-sitting week, and raids on research facilities by animal liberation activists.

Economics and Biological Diversity: Developing and Using Economic Incentives to Conserve Biological Resources. Jeffrey A. McNeely. Pinter Pub., 136 S. Broadway, Irvington, New York 10533. (914) 591-9111. 1991. Explains how economic incentives can be applied to conservation while complementing development efforts.

Economics of Protected Areas: A New Look at Benefits and Costs. John A. Dixon and Paul B. Sherman. Island Press, 1718 Connecticut Ave. N.W., Suite 300, Washington, District of Columbia 20009. (202) 232-7933. 1990. Represents a ground-breaking effort to help government examine the costs and benefits of maintaining protected areas. Provides a methodology for assigning monetary values to nature and explains the economic techniques involved.

Environment, Resources, and Conservation. Susan Owens and Peter L. Owens. Cambridge University Press, 40 W 20th St., New York, New York 10011. (212) 924-3900 or (800) 227-0247. 1991. The book studies three cases illuminating problems and policy responses at three levels of geographic scale–international, national, and local. The case of acid rain is used to illustrate a pollution problem with international dimensions; the British coal industry is analyzed as an example of national nonrenewable resource depletion; and renewable wetland ecosystem management illustrates a local concern by analyzing conservation measures.

An Environmental Agenda for the Future. John H. Adams, et al. Island Press, 1718 Connecticut Ave. N.W.,

Washington, District of Columbia 20009. (202) 232-7933. 1985. Contains articles by the CEOs of the 10 largest environmental organizations in the United States.

Environmental Protection Careers Guidebook. U.S. Department of Labor, Employment and Training Administration, 200 Constitution Ave., NW, Washington, District of Columbia 20210. (202) 523-8165. 1980. Includes information on education in environmental protection field.

The Environmental Sourcebook. Edith Carol Stein. Lyons & Burford, 31 W. 21st St., New York, New York 10010. (212) 620-9580. 1992. Provides information on 11 specific environmental issues, including population; agriculture; energy; climate and atmosphere; biodiversity; water; oceans; solid waste; hazardous substances and waste; endangered lands; and development.

Environmental Viewpoints. Marie Lazzari. Gale Research Inc., 835 Penobscot Bldg., Detroit, Michigan 48226-4094. (313) 961-2242. 1992.

Farms of Tomorrow. Trauger Groh. Bio-Dynamic Farming and Gardening Association, PO Box 550, Kimberton, Pennsylvania 19442. (215) 935-7797. 1990. Describes a new approach to farming called community supported agriculture (CSA). It is built upon the solid foundation of organic and biodynamic cultivation, but it focuses on the social and economic conditions that make farming possible.

Great Basin Drama. Darwin Lambert. Roberts Rinehart Pub., PO Box 666, Niwot, Colorado 80544. (303) 652-2921. 1991. Deals with conservation of natural resources and parks.

Green Fields Forever. Charles E. Little. Island Press, 1718 Connecticut Ave. N.W., Suite 300, Washington, District of Columbia 20009. (202) 232-7933. 1987. An objective look at the costs and benefits of conservation tillage, a promising solution to agricultural problems such as decreased yields, soil erosion and reliance on pesticides and herbicides.

Green Warriors. Fred Pearce. Bodley Head, Random Century House, 20 Vauxhall Bridge Rd., London, England SW1V 2SA. 071-973-9730. 1990.

Heaven is Under Our Feet. Don Henley, ed. Longmeadow Press, 201 High Ridge Rd, PO Box 10218, Stamford, Connecticut 06904. (203) 352-2110. 1991. Describes the conservation of natural resources.

How to Save the World: Strategy for World Conservation. Robert Allen. Rowman & Littlefield, Publishers, Inc., 8705 Bollman Pl., Savage, Maryland 20763. (301) 306-0400. 1980. Based on the Global Conservation Strategy prepared in Switzerland in 1980 by the United Nations Environment Program, the World Wildlife Fund and the International Union for Conservation. Presents strategies in four critical areas: food supply, forest, the sea, and endangered species. Sets priorities, identifies obstacles, and recommends cost effective ways of overcoming those obstacles.

Impounded Rivers: Perspectives for Ecological Management. Geoffrey E. Petts. John Wiley & Sons, Inc., 605 3rd Ave., New York, New York 10158. (212) 850-6000. 1984. Environmental aspects of dams, stream ecology and stream conservation.

Inside the Environmental Movement: Meeting the Leadership Challenge. Donald Snow, ed. Island Press, 1718

Connecticut Ave. N.W., Suite 300, Washington, District of Columbia 20009. (202) 232-7933. 1992. Book offers recommendations and concrete solutions which will make it an invaluable resource as the conservation community prepares to meet the formidable challenges that lie ahead.

Keeping Options Alive: The Scientific Basis for Conserving Biodiversity. Walter V. C. Reid and Kenton R. Miller. World Resources Institute, 1709 New York Ave. N.W., Washington, District of Columbia 20006. (800) 822-0504. 1989. Examines the fundamental questions and recommends policies based on the best available scientific information for conserving biodiversity.

Land-Saving Action. Russell L. Brenneman and Sarah M. Bates, eds. Island Press, 1718 Connecticut Ave. N.W., Suite 300, Washington, District of Columbia 20009. (202) 232-7933. 1984. Guide to saving land and an explanation of the conservation tools and techniques developed by individuals and organizations across the country.

Landscape Linkages and Biodiversity. Wendy E. Hudson, ed. Island Press, 1718 Connecticut Ave. N.W., Suite 300, Washington, District of Columbia 20009. (202) 232-7933. 1991. Explains biological diversity conservation, focusing on the need for protecting large areas of the most diverse ecosystems, and connecting these ecosystems with land corridors to allow species to move among them more easily.

The Last Rain Forests: A World Conservation Atlas. Mark Collins, ed. Oxford University Press, 200 Madison Ave., New York, New York 10016. (212) 679-7300; (800) 334-4249. 1990. Containing more than 200 full color photos and maps, this is a guide to the people, flora and fauna of the richest habitats on earth. Maps the world's rain forests, spells out the problems facing these regions, and proposes concrete, realistic strategies for ensuring their survival.

Magill's Survey of Science. Life Science Series. Frank N. Magill, ed. Salem Press, PO Box 50062, Pasadena, California 91105. 1991. Six volumes. Contents: v.1. A-Central and peripheral nervous system functions; v.2. Central metabolism regulation - eukaryotic transcriptional control; v.3. Positive and negative eukaryotic transcriptional control - mammalian hormones; v.4. Hormones and behavior - muscular contraction; v.5. Muscular contraction and relaxation - sexual reproduction in plants; v.6. Reproductive behavior and mating - X inactivation and the Lyon hypothesis.

Monitoring for Conservation and Ecology. Barrie Goldsmith, ed. Chapman & Hall, 29 W 35th St., New York, New York 10001-2291. (212) 244-3336. 1991. Focuses on an audience of those practicing ecology, nature conservation, or other similar land-based sciences. The differences between surveying and monitoring are discussed and emphasis is placed on the nature of monitoring as being purpose- oriented dynamic in philosophy, and often providing a baseline for recording possible changes in the future.

National Leaders of American Conservation. Richard H. Stroud, ed. Smithsonian Institution Press, 470 L'Enfant Plaza, Suite 7100, Washington, District of Columbia 20560. (800) 782-4612. 1985. 2nd ed. Sponsored by the Natural Resources Council of America. The book identifies national conservation leaders in the United States.

Nature Reserves: Island Theory and Conservation Practice. Craig L. Shafer. Smithsonian Institution Press, 470 L'Enfant Plaza, No. 7100, Washington, District of Columbia 20560. (800) 782-4612. 1991. Encompasses ecology, biogeography, evolutionary biology, genetics, paleobiology, as well as legal, social, and economic issues.

Neotropical Wildlife Use and Conservation. John R. Robinson, ed. University of Chicago Press, 5801 Ellis Ave., 4th Fl., Chicago, Illinois 60637. (800) 621-2736. 1991. The importance of wildlife to people, impact of the use of wildlife on population or biological communities.

Paying the Farm Bill: U.S. Agricultural Policy and the Transition to Sustainable Agriculture. Paul Faeth, et al. World Resources Institute, 1709 New York Ave. N.W., Washington, District of Columbia 20006. (800) 822-0504. 1991. Demonstrates that resource conserving agricultural systems are environmentally and economically superior to conventional systems over the long term.

Private Options: Tools and Concepts for Land Conservation. Montana Land Reliance, Land Trust Exchange. Island Press, 1718 Connecticut Ave. N.W., Suite 300, Washington, District of Columbia 20009. (202) 232-7933. 1982. Private land conservation experts offer their expertise on how individuals can help contain urban sprawl, conserve wetlands, and protect wildlife. This book covers estate planning, tax incentives, purchase options, conservation easements and land management.

Protecting Nontidal Wetlands. David G. Burke, et al. American Planning Association, 1776 Massachusetts Ave. N.W., Washington, District of Columbia 20036. (202) 872-0611. 1988. Describes wetlands types and values, looks at the current status of U.S. wetlands, and reviews federal, state, and local regulations to protect nontidal wetlands.

Research Priorities for Conservation Biology. Michael E. Soulfe and Kathryn A. Kohm, eds. Island Press, 1718 Connecticut Ave. N.W., Suite 300, Washington, District of Columbia 20009. (202) 232-7933. 1989. Proposes an urgent research agenda to improve our understanding and preservation of biological diversity.

Saving the Tropical Forests. Judith Gradwohl and Russell Greenberg. Island Press, 1718 Connecticut Ave. N.W., Suite 300, Washington, District of Columbia 20009. (202) 232-7933. 1988. Sourcebook about the causes and effects of tropical deforestation, with case studies, examples of sustainable agriculture and forestry, and a section on the restoration of tropical rain forests.

Species Conservation: A Population Biological Approach. A. Seitz, ed. Birkhauser Verlag, 675 Massachusetts Ave., Cambridge, Massachusetts 02139. (800) 777-4643. 1991.

Taking Stock: The Tropical Forestry Action Plan After Five Years. Robert Winterbottom. World Resources Institute, 1709 New York Ave. N.W., Washington, District of Columbia 20006. (800) 822-0504. 1990. Analyzes Tropical Forestry Action Plan's accomplishments and shortcomings, drawing on the biannual meetings of the TFAP Forestry Advisors' groups, assessments by FAO, various aid agencies, and by such organizations as the World Rainforest Movement, Friends of the Earth, and World Life Fund.

Turning the Tide: Saving the Chesapeake Bay. Tom Horton. Island Press, 1718 Connecticut Ave. N.W., Suite 300, Washington, District of Columbia 20009. (202) 232-7933. 1991. Presents a comprehensive look at two decades of efforts to save the Chesapeake Bay. It outlines which methods have worked, and which have not. Sets a new strategy for the future, calling for greater political coverage, environmental leadership and vision.

World Guide to Environmental Issues and Organizations. Peter Brackley. Longman Group Ltd., Longman House, Burnt Mill, Harlow, Essex, England CM20 2J6. (0279) 426721. 1991.

A Year in the Greenhouse. John Elkington. Gollancz, 14 Henrietta St., Covent Garden, London, England WC2E 8QJ. (071) 836-2006.

GOVERNMENTAL ORGANIZATIONS

Agricultural Research Service. Washington, District of Columbia 20250.

HANDBOOKS AND MANUALS

Environment in Key Words: A Multilingual Handbook of the Environment: English-French-German-Russian. Isaac Paenson. Pergamon Microforms International, Inc., Fairview Park, Elmsford, New York 10523. (914) 592-7720. 1990. Two volumes. Terminology in the areas of ecology, environmental protection, pollution, conservation of natural resources and related areas.

Environmental Statistics Handbook: Europe. Allan Foster, Oksana Newman. Gale Research Inc., 835 Penobscot Bldg., Detroit, Michigan 48226-4094. (313) 961-2242. 1993.

ONLINE DATA BASES

BIOSIS Previews. BIOSIS, 2100 Arch St., Philadelphia, Pennsylvania 19103-1399. (215) 587-4800. Largest and most comprehensive database of research in the life sciences. Contains citations for nearly 9000 primary research journals, monographs, reviews, symposia, preliminary reports, semi-popular journals, selected institutional reports, government reports and research communications.

Cambridge Scientific Abstracts Life Science–CSAL. Cambridge Scientific Abstracts, 5161 River Rd., Bethesda, Maryland 20816. (301) 961-6750. Provides access to the following abstracting services: "Life Sciences Collection," "Aquatic Sciences and Fisheries Abstracts," "Oceanic Abstracts," and "Pollution Abstracts."

Conservation Information Network. The Getty Conservation Institute, 4503 Glencoe Ave., Marina del Rey, California 90292-6537. (213) 822-2287.

CONSO. Canadian Conservation Institute, 1030 Innes Rd., Ottawa, Ontario, Canada K1A OC8. (613) 998-3721.

Current Research Information System–CRIS/USDA. U.S. Department of Agriculture, National Agricultural Library, 10301 Baltimore Blvd., 5th Floor, Beltsville, Maryland 20705-2351. (301) 504-5755. Looks at current research projects in agriculture and allied sciences covering the biological, physical, social and behavioral sciences related to agriculture.

EBIB. Texas A & M University, Sterling C. Evans Library, Reference Division, College Station, Texas 77843. (409) 845-5741.

Energy Conservation News. Business Communications Company, Inc., 25 Van Zant St., Norwalk, Connecticut 06855. (203) 853-4266. Technology and economics of energy conservation at industrial, commercial, and institutional facilities.

Enviro/Energyline Abstracts Plus. R. R. Bowker Co., 121 Chanlon Rd., New Providence, New Jersey 07974. (908) 464-6800.

Environmental Periodicals Bibliography. National Information Services Corp., Ste. 6, Wyman Towers, 3100 St. Paul St., Baltimore, Maryland 21218. (410)243-0797. Online version of abstract of same name.

Monthly Catalog of United States Government Publications. U.S. G.P.O., Supt. of Docs., PO Box 371954, Pittsburgh, Pennsylvania 15250-7954. (202) 512-0000.

National Technical Information Service. U.S. Department of Commerce, National Technical Information Service, Office of Data Base Services, 5285 Port Royal Rd., Springfield, Virginia 22161. (703) 487-4807. Bibliographic database of government sponsored research and technical reports.

PressNet Environmental Reports. Chemical Information Systems, Inc., 7215 York Rd., Baltimore, Maryland 21212. (301) 321-8440.

SCISEARCH. Institute for Scientific Information, University City Science Center, 3501 Market St., Philadelphia, Pennsylvania 19104. (215) 386-0100.

PERIODICALS AND NEWSLETTERS

Alabama Conservation. Alabama Department of Conservation, 64 N. Union St., Montgomery, Alabama 36130. (205) 242-3151. 1929-. Bimonthly. Promotes the wise use of natural resources.

Alabama Department of Conservation Report. Alabama Department of Conservation, 64 N. Union St., Montgomery, Alabama 36130. (205) 242-3151. Annually.

The American Naturalist. Americana Society of Naturalists, Business Sciences, University of Kansas, Lawrence, Kansas 66045. (913) 864-3763. Monthly. Contains information by professionals of the biological sciences.

The Balance Wheel. Association for Conservation Information, c/o Roy Edwards, Virginia Game Department, 4010 W. Broad St., Richmond, Virginia 23230-3916. (804) 367-1000. Quarterly.

Biological Conservation. Applied Science Publishers, 655 Avenue of the Americas, PO Box 5399, New York, New York 10163. (718) 756-6440. Quarterly. Conservation of biological and allied natural resources, plants and animals and their habitats.

Buzzworm: The Environmental Journal. Buzzworm Inc., 2305 Canyon Blvd., No. 206, Boulder, Colorado 80302-5655. (303) 442-1969. 1988-. Quarterly. An independent environmental journal for the reader interested in nature, adventure, travel, the natural environment and the issues of conservation.

Canadian Conservation Institute Technical Bulletin National. Museums of Canada, Quebec, Ontario, Canada K1A 0MB. (613) 776-7000. 1973-. Irregular. Deals with a variety of subjects on conservation of collections.

CAW Waste Watch. Californians Against Waste, Box 289, Sacramento, California 95802. (916) 443-5422.

1978-. Quarterly. Newsletter about natural resources conservation, recycling, anti-litter issues in California and other related topics.

Conservation. National Wildlife Federation, 1400 16th St. N.W., Washington, District of Columbia 20036-2266. (202) 797-6800. 1939-. Biweekly. Covers digest of natural conservation legislation, published when Congress is in session. This newsletter is available to members only.

Conservation Bits and Bytes. National Association of Conservation Districts, 509 Capitol St. NE, Washington, District of Columbia 20002. (202) 547-6223. Quarterly.

Conservation Education Association Newsletter. Conservation Education Association, c/o Conservation Education Center, RR 1, Box 153, Guthrie Center, Iowa 50115. (515) 747-8383. Quarterly. Promotes environmental conservation education.

Conservation News Digest. American Resources Group, 374 Maple Ave., E, Suite 204, Vienna, Virginia 22180. (703) 255-2700. Bimonthly. Non-industrial private forestry and conservation and natural resources.

Conservogram. Soil and Water Conservation Society, 7515 NE Ankeny Rd., Ankeny, Iowa 50021. (515) 289-2331. Bimonthly.

The Earth Care Annual. Russell Wild, ed. Rodale Press, 33 E. Minon St., Emmaus, Pennsylvania 18098. (215) 967-5171; (800) 322-6333. 1990-. Annually. Organized in alphabetical sections such as garbage, greenhouse effect, oceans, ozone, toxic waste, and wildlife, the annual presents environmental problems and offers innovative working solutions.

Earth First! Journal in Defense of Wilderness and Biodiversity. Earth First!, PO Box 5176, Missoula, Montana 59806. Eight/year.

Earth Island Journal. Earth Island Institute, 300 Broadway, #28, San Francisco, California 94133-3312. (415) 788-3666. Quarterly. Local news from around the world on environmental issues.

Earth Work. The Student Conservation Association Inc., PO Box 550, Charlestown, New Hampshire 03603-0550. (603) 826-4301. 1991-. Monthly. Articles focus on the people, agencies, and the nonprofit organizations that protect our parks, refuges, forests and other lands. Carries a special feature entitled JobScan which provides the most comprehensive listing of natural resource and environmental job opportunities anywhere.

Eco-Politics. California League of Conservation Voters, 965 Mission St., # 705, San Francisco, California 94103-2928. (415) 397-7780. Quarterly. News of citizen action on environmental issues.

ECOAlert. CCNB, 180 St. John St., Fredericton, New Brunswick, Canada E3B 4A9. (506) 458-8747. Bimonthly. Conservation news and developments.

ECOL News. Environmental Conservation Library, 300 Nicollet Mall, Minneapolis, Minnesota 55401. (612) 372-6570. Semiannual. Environmental update on the library.

Ecological Applications. Ecological Society of America, Center for Environmental Studies, Arizona State University, Tempe, Arizona 85287. (602) 965-3000. 1991-. Quarterly. Emphasizes the application of basic ecological concepts to a wide range of problems.

Ecological Monographs. Business Office of the Ecological Society of America, Center of Environmental Studies, Arizona State University, Tempe, Arizona 85287-1201. (602) 965-3000. Quarterly. Scientific journal of ecological issues.

Ecological Society of America Bulletin. Ecological Society of America, Center of Environmental Studies, Arizona State University, Tempe, Arizona 85287-1201. (602) 965-3000. Quarterly. Study of living things in relation to their environments.

Ecology. Ecological Society of America, Center of Environmental Studies, Arizona State University, Tempe, Arizona 85287-1201. (602) 965-3000. Bimonthly. Information on the study of living things.

Ecology USA. Business Publishers, Inc., 951 Pershing Dr., Silver Spring, Maryland 20910-4464. (301) 587-6300. 1972-. Biweekly. Contains all the legislation, regulation, and litigation affecting efforts to conserve and protect America's unique environmental and ecological heritage.

Energy Conservation Digest. Editorial Resources, Inc., PO Box 21133, Washington, District of Columbia 20009. (202) 332-2267. Semimonthly. Commercial, residential, and industrial energy conservation issues and policy developments.

Environmental Defense Fund Letter. Environmental Defense Fund, 257 Park Avenue South, New York, New York 10010. (212) 505-2100. 1971-. Bimonthly. Environmental issues of concern.

Environmental Studies & Practice: An Educational Resource and Forum. Yale School of Forestry and Environmental Studies, 205 Prospect St., New Haven, Connecticut 06511. (203) 432-5132. 1991. Bimonthly. Subject matters range widely from air pollution to wildlife biology. Each issue contains a selection of recent publications, from all subject areas of environmental and natural resources management.

Environments. Faculty of Environmental Studies, University of Waterloo, Waterloo, Ontario, Canada N2L 3G1. (519) 885-1211. Three times a year. People in man-made and natural environments.

Florida Conservation News. Florida Department of Natural Resources, 3900 Commonwealth Blvd., Tallahassee, Florida 32303. (904)488-1234. 1965-. Monthly.

Florida Wildlife. Florida Game and Fresh Water Fish Commission, Florida State Game, 620 S. Meridian St., Tallahassee, Florida 32399-1600. (904) 488-5563. 1976-. Bimonthly. State wildlife conservation magazine.

Forest Conservation. Forestry Range Club, Washington State University, Pullman, Washington 99164-3200. 1958-. Annually. None published in 1974. Deals with forest conservation and related topics.

Geojourney. Florida Department of Natural Resources, 3900 Commonwealth Blvd., Tallahassee, Florida 32303. (904) 488-1234. 1980-. Quarterly. Covers activities on resource management, marine resources, parks and recreation, and subjects related to fishing, boating and all uses of Florida's natural resources.

Georgia Conservancy Newsletter. Georgia Conservancy, 3376 Peachtree Rd., NE, Suite 44, Atlanta, Georgia 30326. 1967-. Monthly.

Green Library Journal: Environmental Topics in the Information World. Maria A. Jankowska, ed. Green Library, University of Idaho Library, Moscow, Idaho 83843. (208) 885-6260. Jan 1992-. Scope of the journal would include information sources about: conservation, ecologically balanced regional development, environmental protection, natural resources management, environmental issues in libraries, publishing industries, and information science.

Idaho Wildlife. Idaho Dept. of Fish and Game, P.O. Box 25, 600 S. Walnut, Boise, Idaho 83712. (208) 334-3746. Bimonthly. Covers conservation, wildlife management, fish and game operations and policies.

Illinois Wildlife. Illinois Wildlife Federation, 123 S. Chicago St., Rossville, Illinois 60963. (217) 748-6365. Bimonthly. Deals with outdoor recreational trends.

Iowa Conservationist. Iowa Dept. of Natural Resources, Wallace St. Office Building, Des Moines, Iowa 50319-0034. (515) 281-6159. Monthly. Outdoor recreation opportunities, fish, wildlife, parks and environmental issues.

IUCN Bulletin. World Conservation Union, IUCN Publications Services Unit, 181a Huntingdon Road, Cambridge, England CB3 0DJ. (0223) 277894. Quarterly. News and information from the world's largest and most influential network of governmental and independent conservation interests.

Land Letter. The Conservation Fund, 1800 N. Kent St., Suite 1120, Arlington, Virginia 22209. (703) 522-8008. Thirty four times a year. National land use and conservation policy; legislative, regulatory, and legal developments; use of private and public lands.

League Leader. Izaak Walton League of America, 1401 Wilson Blvd., Level B, Arlington, Virginia 22209. (703) 528-1818. Bimonthly. Soil, forest, water, & other natural resources.

Liaison Conservation Directory. U.S. Office of Endangered Species, Fish & Wildlife Service, Int., Washington, District of Columbia 20240. (703) 235-2407.

Louisiana Conservationist. Louisiana Department of Wildlife & Fisheries, 2000 Quail Dr., Baton Rouge, Louisiana 70808. (504) 765-2916. Bimonthly. Conservation education, outdoor recreation, and commercial utilization of fish and wildlife resources.

Marine Bulletin. National Coalition for Marine Conservation, Box 23298, Savannah, Georgia 31403. (912) 234-8062. Monthly. Marine fisheries, biological research, marine environmental pollution, and the prevention of the over-exploitation of ocean fish.

Marine Conservation News. Center for Marine Conservation, 1725 Desales St., N.W., Suite 500, Washington, District of Columbia 20036. (202) 429-5609. Quarterly. Marine conservation issues: whales, seals, sea turtles, and habitat.

Minnesota Out-of-Doors. Minnesota Conservation Federation, 1036-B Cleveland Ave., S., St. Paul, Minnesota 55116. (612) 690-3077. Monthly. Conservation, natural resources, hunting & fishing.

Minnesota Volunteer. Minnesota Dept. of Natural Resources, 500 Lafayette Rd., St. Paul, Minnesota 55155-4046. (612) 296-3336. Bimonthly. Natural resources & conservation education.

Missouri Wildlife. Conservation Federation of Missouri, 728 W. Main St., Jefferson City, Missouri 65101. (314) 634-2322. Bimonthly. Conservation & environmental news and features.

National Association of Conservation Districts, Tuesday Letter. National Association of Conservation Districts, 509 Capitol Ct., N.E., Washington, District of Columbia 20002. (202) 347-5995. Weekly. Conservation policy at national, state, and local levels.

National Water Line. National Water Resources Association, 3800 North Fairfax Drive, #4, Arlington, Virginia 22203. (703) 524-1544. Monthly. Covers water resource development projects.

Natural Resources Journal. University of New Mexico School of Law, 1117 Stanford, NE, Albuquerque, New Mexico 87131. (505) 277-4820. Quarterly. Study of natural and environmental research.

Nature and Resources. Elsevier Science Publishing Co., 655 Avenue of the Americas, New York, New York 10010. (212) 989-5800. 1965-. Quarterly. Provides in-depth reviews of contemporary environmental issues from an international perspective.

Nature Conservancy Magazine. The Nature Conservancy, 1815 North Lynn St., Arlington, Virginia 22209. (703) 841-5300. 1951-. Bimonthly. Membership magazine covering biotic diversity and related conservation issues.

NCSHPO Newsletter. National Conference of State Historic Preservation Offices, 444 North Capitol Street, NW, Suite 332, Washington, District of Columbia 20001. (202) 624-5465. Monthly. Covers state and federal historic preservation programs.

New Hampshire Conservation News. New Hampshire Association of Conservation Commissions, 54 Portsmouth St., Concord, New Hampshire 03301. (603) 224-7867. 1967-. Quarterly.

Newsletter. Association of Conservation Engineers, c/o William P. Allinder, Alabama Department of Conservation, 64 N. Union St., Montgomery, Alabama 36130. (205) 261-3476. Semiannual.

Northwest Environmental Journal. Institute for Environmental Studies, University of Washington, Seattle, Washington 98195. (206) 543-1812. Biannual. Covers environmental issues in the Northwest states and Canada.

NRDC Newsline. Natural Resources Defense Council, 40 W. 20th St., 11th Fl., New York, New York 10011. (212) 949-0049. Bimonthly. Enforcement news.

NYS Environment. New York State Dept. of Environmental Conservation, 50 Wolf Rd., Albany, New York 12233. (518) 457-2344. Biweekly. Controversial environmental issues in legislation.

Outdoor News Bulletin. Wildlife Management Institute, 1101 14th St., N.W., Suite 725, Washington, District of Columbia 20005. (202) 371-1808. Biweekly. Conservation and wildlife.

Pack & Paddie. Ozark Society, Box 2914, Little Rock, Arkansas 72203. (501) 225-1795. Quarterly. Regional conservation.

Proceedings. Conservation Education Association, c/o Dennis Bryan, Rte. #1, New Franken, Wisconsin 54229. (414) 465-2397.

U. S. Department of the Interior. Conservation Bulletins. Superintendent of Documents, U.S. Government Printing Office, Washington, District of Columbia 20402. Irregular.

Virgin Islands Conservation Society Inc., Newsletter. Virgin Island Conservation Society Inc., Box 226, Cruz Bay, St. John, Virgin Islands 00830. Quarterly.

Washington Report. Interstate Conference on Water Policy, 955 L'Enfant Plaza, 6th Floor, Washington, District of Columbia 20024. (202) 466-7287. Every six weeks. Covers water conservation, development and administration.

Wilderness. The Wilderness Society, 900 17th St. NW, Washington, District of Columbia 20006. (202) 833-2300. Quarterly. Preserving wilderness and wildlife, protecting America's prime forests, parks, rivers, shorelands, and fostering an American land ethic.

Wisconservation. Wisconsin Wildlife Federation, PO Box 231, Reedsburg, Wisconsin 53959.

RESEARCH CENTERS AND INSTITUTES

Center for Marine Conservation. 1725 DeSales St., NW, Suite 500, Washington, District of Columbia 20036. (202) 429-5609.

International Conservation Institute. 45 Elm St., Byfield, Massachusetts 01922. (617) 465-5389.

The Nature Conservancy. 1815 N. Lynn St., Arlington, Virginia 22209. (703) 841-5300.

Project in Conservation Science. University of California, San Diego, Department of Biology C-016, La Jolla, California 92093. (619) 534-2375.

Society for Conservation Biology. Department of Wildlife Ecology, University of Wisconsin, Madison, Wisconsin 53706. (608) 262-2671.

Stanford University, Center for Conservation Biology. Department of Biological Sciences, Sanford, California 94305-5020. (415) 723-5924.

University of Montana, Montana Forest and Conservation Experiment Station. Missoula, Montana 59812. (406) 243-5521.

University of Nevada-Reno, S-S Field Laboratory. Box 10, Wadsworth, Nevada 89442. (702) 575-1057.

University of North Carolina at Chapel Hill, North Carolina Botanical Garden. CB #3375 Totten Center, Chapel Hill, North Carolina 27599. (919) 962-0522.

STATISTICS SOURCES

Agricultural Conservation Program Statistical Summary. U.S. Agricultural Stabilization and Conservation Service, Dept. of Agriculture, Washington, District of Columbia 20013. (202) 512-0000. Annual. Deals with soil erosion control, water conservation, water quality and costs by state and county.

Ecology: Community Profiles. U.S. Fish and Wildlife Service. National Technical Information Service, 5285 Port Royal Road, Springfield, Virginia 22161. (703) 487-4650. Irregular. Data on coastal and inland ecosystems, including wetlands, tidal-flats, near-shore seagrasses, sand dunes, drilling platforms, oyster reefs, estuaries, rivers and streams.

Report to Congress on Automotive Technology Development Program. U.S. Dept. of Energy. Conservation and Renewable Energy Office. National Technical Information Service, 5285 Port Royal Road, Springfield, Virginia 22161. (703) 487-4650. Annual. Programs for improved fuel economy and multi-fuel capability.

Statistical Record of the Environment. Arsen J. Darnay. Gale Research Inc., 835 Penobscot Bldg., Detroit, Michigan 48226-4094. (313) 961-2242. 1992.

TRADE ASSOCIATIONS AND PROFESSIONAL SOCIETIES

African Wildlife Foundation. 1717 Massachusetts Avenue, NW, Washington, District of Columbia 20036. (202) 265-8393.

Alaska Conservation Foundation. 430 West 7th St., Suite 215, Anchorage, Alaska 99501. (907) 276-1917.

American Cave Conservation Association. 131 Main and Cave Sts., P.O. Box 409, Horse Cave, Kentucky 42749. (502) 786-1466.

American Cetacean Society. P.O. Box 2639, San Pedro, California 90731. (213) 548-6279.

American Institute of Biological Sciences. 730 11th St., N.W., Washington, District of Columbia 20001-4521. (202) 628-1500.

American Nature Study Society. 5881 Cold Brook Rd., Homer, New York 13077. (607) 749-3655.

American Society of Civil Engineers. 345 East 47th St., New York, New York 10017. (212) 705-7496.

Association for Conservation. c/o Rod Green, Missouri Dept. of Conservation, 408 S. Polk, Albany, Missouri 64402. (816) 726-3677.

Association for Conservation Information. PO Box 10678, Reno, Nevada 89520. (702) 688-1500.

Association of Conservation Engineers. c/o Terry N. Boyd, Alabama Dept. of Conservation, 64 N. Union St., Montgomery, Alabama 36130. (205) 242-3476.

Basic Foundation. PO Box 47012, St. Petersburg, Florida 33743. (813) 526-9562. Non-profit corporation that was founded to augment efforts at balancing population growth with natural resources.

Bat Conservation International. PO Box 162603, Austin, Texas 78716. (512) 327-9721. Bat Conservation International was established to educate people about the important role that bats play in the environment.

Botanical Society of America. c/o Christopher Haufler, Department of Botany, University of Kansas, Lawrence, Kansas 66045-2106. (913) 864-4301.

California State Parks Foundation. 800 College Ave., P.O. Box 548, Kentfield, California 94914. (415) 258-9975.

Canyon Explorers Club. 1223 Frances Ave., Fullerton, California 92631. Non-profit corporation that was started in 1972 whose purpose is to explore remote areas of the world. Members believe in the preservation of wilderness areas and respect the dignity of native cultures.

Center for Conservation Biology. Department of Biological Sciences, Stanford University, Stanford, California 94305. (415) 723-5924.

Center for International Development and Environment. 1709 New York Ave., N.W., Washington, District of Columbia 20006. (202) 462-0900.

Center for Whale Research. P.O. Box 1577, Friday Harbor, Washington 98250. (206) 378-5835.

Chesapeake Bay Foundation. 162 Prince George St., Annapolis, Maryland 21401. (301) 268-8816.

Children of the Green Earth. P.O. Box 95219, Seattle, Washington 98145. (503) 229-4721.

Community Environmental Council. 930 Miramonte Drive, Santa Barbara, California 93109. (805) 963-0583.

Conservation Foundation. 1250 24th St., N.W., Washington, District of Columbia 20037. (202) 293-4800. The World Wildlife Fund absorbed the Conservation Foundation in 1990.

Conservation International. 1015 18th St. N.W., Suite 1002, Washington, District of Columbia 20036. (202) 429-5660. Non-profit organization established in 1987. Provides resources and expertise to private organizations, government agencies and universities of Latin America and Caribbean countries in an effort to develop the capacity and preserve critical habitats.

Earth First!. PO Box 5176, Missoula, Montana 59806.

Earth Island Institute. 300 Broadway, Suite 28, San Francisco, California 94133. (415) 788-3666.

Ecological Society of America. Arizona State University, Center for Environmental Studies, Tempe, Arizona 85287. (602) 965-3000.

Environmental Defense Fund. 257 Park Ave., S., New York, New York 10010. (212) 505-2100. Non-profit organization that was established more than 20 years ago. Its goals are to protect the earth's environment by providing lasting solutions to global environmental problems.

Friends of the Earth. 218 D St., SE, Washington, District of Columbia 20003. (202) 544-2600.

The Friends of the Everglades. 101 Westward Dr., No. 2, Miami Springs, Florida 33166. (305) 888-1230.

International Marinelife Alliance. 94 Station St., Suite 645, Hingham, Massachusetts 02043. (617) 383-1209.

International Union for the Conservation of Nature, Natural Resources Primate Specialists Group. Dept. of Anatomical Sciences, HSC, State University of New York, Stony Brook, New York 11794. (516) 444-3132.

The Izaak Walton League of America. 1401 Wilson Boulevard, Level B, Arlington, Virginia 22209. (703) 528-1818.

League of Conservation Voters. 1150 Connecticut, N.W., Suite 201, Washington, District of Columbia 20002. (202) 785-8683.

National Audubon Society. 950 Third Ave., New York, New York 10022. (212) 832-3200.

National Coalition for Marine Conservation, Inc. P.O. Box 23298, Savannah, Georgia 31403. (912) 234-8062.

National Geographic Society. 17th and M Streets, NW, Washington, District of Columbia 20036. (202) 857-7000.

National Parks and Conservation Association. 1015 31st St., N.W., Washington, District of Columbia 20007. (202) 944-8530.

National Speleological Society. Cave Ave., Huntsville, Alabama 35810. (205) 852-1300.

National Wildlife Federation. 1400 16th St., N.W., Washington, District of Columbia 20036. (202) 797-6800.

Natural Resources Council of America. 801 Pennsylvania Ave., SE, Suite 410, Washington, District of Columbia 20003. (202) 547-7553.

Natural Resources Defense Council. 40 W. 20th St., New York, New York 10011. (212) 727-2700.

Peninsula Conservation Center. 2448 Watson Ct., Palo Alto, California 94303. (415) 494-9301.

Planning and Conservation League. 909 12th St., Suite 203, Sacramento, California 95814. (916) 444-8726.

Rails-to-Trails Conservancy. 1400 16th St., NW, Washington, District of Columbia 20036. (202) 797-5400.

The Rights Livelihood Awards Foundation. P.O. Box 15072, S-10465, Stockholm, Sweden (08) 702 03 04.

Save the Bay. 434 Smith St., Providence, Rhode Island 02908. (401) 272-3540.

Sea Shepherd Conservation Society. 1314 2nd St., Santa Monica, California 90401. (213) 394-3198.

Student Conservation Association. P.O. Box 550, Charlestown, New Hampshire 03603. (603) 826-4301.

Wilderness Society. 900 17th St., NW, Washington, District of Columbia 20006. (202) 833-2300.

World Nature Association, Inc. PO Box 673, Silver Spring, Maryland 20901. (301) 593-2522.

CONSTRUCTION NOISE
See: NOISE POLLUTION

CONTACT PESTICIDES
See: PESTICIDES

CONTAINMENT
See: CONTAMINATION

CONTAMINATION
See also: BIOLOGICAL CONTAMINATION; CHEMICAL CONTAMINATION

ABSTRACTING AND INDEXING SERVICES

Applied Ecology Abstracts Studies in Renewable Natural Resources. Information Retrieval Ltd., 1911 Jefferson Davis Highway, Arlington, Virginia 22202. 1975-. Monthly.

Biological Abstracts. BIOSIS, 2100 Arch St., Philadelphia, Pennsylvania 19103-1399. (215) 587-4800. 1927-.

Bulletin Signaletique: Eau et Assainissement, Pollution Atmospherique, Droit des Pollutions. Centre de Documentation, Centre National de la Recherche Scientifique, 15, quai Anatole France, Paris, France 75700. (1) 45 55 92 25. 1983-. Monthly. Indexes pollution periodicals including water, atmospheric and related pollutions.

Chemical Abstracts. Chemical Abstracts Service, 2540 Olentangy River Rd., PO Box 3012, Columbus, Ohio 43210. (800) 848-6533. 1907-.

Current Advances in Ecological and Environmental Science. Pergamon Microforms International, Inc., Fairview Park, Elmsford, New York 10523. (914) 592-7720. 1989-. Monthly. Current literature searching service includingjournals, reports, abstracts, etc. This service is available online as part of the CABS database on the hosts BRS and ORBIT search service.

Environment Abstracts. Bowker A & I Publishing, 121 Chanlon Rd., New Providence, New Jersey 07974. (908) 464-6800. 1974-.

Environment Index. Environment Information Center, Index Research Department, 124 E. 39th St., New York, New York 10016. 1971-. Annual.

Environmental Information Connection–EIC. Planning Information Program, Dept. of Urban and Regional Planning, University of Illinois, 1003 West Nevada, Urbana, Illinois 61801. (217) 333-1369. Also available online.

Environmental Periodicals Bibliography. Environmental Studies Institute, International Academy at Santa Barbara, 800 Garden St., Suite D, Santa Barbara, California 93101. (805) 965-5010. Also available online.

Food Science and Technology Abstracts. International Food Information Service, c/o National Food Laboratory, 6363 Clark Ave., Dublin, California 94568. (800) 336-3782. 1969-.

General Science Index. H. W. Wilson Co., 950 University Ave., Bronx, New York 10452. 1978-. Monthly, also issued in annual cumulation. Cumulative subject index to English language periodicals in the subject fields of astronomy, botany, chemistry, earth science, environment and conservation, food and nutrition, genetics, mathematics, medicine and health, microbiology, oceanography, physics, physiology and zoology.

Index to Scientific Book Contents. Institute for Scientific Information, 3501 Market St., Philadelphia, Pennsylvania 19104. (800) 523-1857. 1985-. Annual. Gives contents of science books published.

Multimedia Index to Ecology. National Information Center for Educational Media, University of Southern California, Los Angeles, California 90007.

Pollution Abstracts. Cambridge Scientific Abstracts, 5161 River Rd., Bethesda, Maryland 20816. (301) 961-6750. Six/year. Indexes worldwide technical literature on environmental pollution. Covers air pollution, marine and freshwater pollution, sewage and wastewater treatment, waste management, toxicology and health, noise pollution, radiation, land pollution, and environmental policies, programs, legislation, and education. Also available online.

Science Citation Index. Institute for Scientific Information, 3501 Market St., Philadelphia, Pennsylvania 19104. 1961-.

BIBLIOGRAPHIES

Current Contents. Agriculture, Biology and Environmental Sciences. Institute for Scientific Information, 3501 Market St., Philadelphia, Pennsylvania 19104. (800) 523-1857. 1973-. Previous title: Current Contents. Agricultural, Food & Veterinary Sciences. Gives the table of contents of periodicals in the fields of agriculture, biology, environmental and related areas.

Directory of Published Proceedings. Interdok Corp., 173 Halstead Ave., Harrison, New York 10528. (914) 835-3506. 1990. Monthly. This is a listing of published proceedings including the series SEMTE (Science/Medicine/Engineering/Technology) and the series SSH (Social Science/Humanities).

EPA Publications Bibliography. U.S. Environmental Protection Agency, Library Systems Branch, 401 M St., SW, Washington, District of Columbia 20460. (202) 260-2090. Quarterly.

DIRECTORIES

Gale Environmental Sourcebook. Karen Hill. Gale Research Co., 835 Penobscot Bldg., Detroit, Michigan 48226-4094. (313) 961-2242. Contacts, information sources, or general information on environmental topics.

ENCYCLOPEDIAS AND DICTIONARIES

Grzimek's Encyclopedia of Ecology. Bernhard Grzimek. Van Nostrand Reinhold, 115 5th Ave., New York, New York 10003. (212) 254-3232. 1976.

McGraw-Hill Encyclopedia of Environmental Science. Sybil P. Parker. McGraw-Hill Science & Engineering Books, 11 W. 19th St., New York, New York 10011. (212) 337-6010. 1980. Covers ecology, man's influence on nature, and environmental protection.

McGraw-Hill Encyclopedia of Science and Technology. McGraw-Hill, 1221 Avenue of the Americas, New York, New York 10020. (212) 512-2000 or (800) 262-4729. 1992. Seventh edition. Issued in multiple volumes including index. Includes all science and technology broad subject areas.

North American Reference Encyclopedia of Ecology and Pollution. William White. North American Pub. Co., 401 N. Broad St., Philadelphia, Pennsylvania 19108. (215) 238-5300. 1972.

Van Nostrand's Scientific Encyclopedia. Glenn D. Considine, ed. Van Nostrand Reinhold, 115 5th Ave., New York, New York 10003. (212) 254-3232. 1983. Sixth edition. Includes all broad subject areas in science.

GENERAL WORKS

Biomarkers of Environmental Contamination. John F. McCarthy and Lee R. Shugart. Lewis Publishers, 2000 Corporate Blvd., Boca Raton, Florida 33431. (800) 272-7737. 1990. Reviews the use of biological markers in animals and plants as an innovative approach to evaluating the ecological and physiological effects of environmental contamination.

Contaminant Hydrogeology: A Practical Guide. Chris Palmer and Gettler-Ryan. Lewis Publishers, 2000 Corporate Blvd., N.W., Boca Raton, Florida 33431. (407) 994-0555 or (800) 272-7737. 1991. Contains geologic frameworks for contaminant hydrogeology investigations. Also includes subsurface exploration, sampling and mapping techniques, ground-water monitoring well installation, ground water monitoring and well sampling.

Hydrocarbon Contaminated Soils and Groundwater: Analysis, Fate, Environmental and Public Health Effects, and Remediation. Paul T. Kostecki and Edward J. Calabrese. Lewis Publishers, 2000 Corporate Blvd.,N.W., Boca Raton, Florida 33431. (407) 994-0555 or (800) 272-7737. 1991. Describes perspectives and emerging issues, analytical techniques and site assessments, environmental fate and modeling.

Reviews of Environmental Contamination and Toxicology: v. 120. George W. Ware, ed. Springer-Verlag, 175 5th Ave., New York, New York 10010. (212) 460-1500; (800) 777-4643. 1991. Covers organochlorine pesticides and polychlorinated biphenyls in human adipose tissue, pesticide residues in foods imported into the U.S., and selected trace elements and the use of biomonitors in subtropical and tropical marine ecosystems.

HANDBOOKS AND MANUALS

Contaminated Communities. Michael R. Edelstein. Island Press, 1718 Connecticut Ave., NW, Suite 300, Washington, District of Columbia 20036. (202) 232-7933. 1988. The social and psychological impacts of residential toxic exposure.

ONLINE DATA BASES

BIOSIS Previews. BIOSIS, 2100 Arch St., Philadelphia, Pennsylvania 19103-1399. (215) 587-4800. Largest and most comprehensive database of research in the life sciences. Contains citations for nearly 9000 primary research journals, monographs, reviews, symposia, preliminary reports, semi-popular journals, selected institutional reports, government reports and research communications.

Chemical Abstracts-CA. Chemical Abstracts Service, 2540 Olentangy River Rd., P.O. Box 3012, Columbus, Ohio 43210. (800) 848-6533 or (614) 421-3600. Information sources include 9000 journals, patents from 27 countries, two industrial property organizations, new books, conference proceedings, and government research reports.

Enviro/Energyline Abstracts Plus. R. R. Bowker Co., 121 Chanlon Rd., New Providence, New Jersey 07974. (908) 464-6800.

Enviroline. R. R. Bowker Co., Bowker Electronic Publishing, 121 Chanlon Rd., New Providence, New Jersey 07974. (800) 521-8110.

Environmental Bibliography. Environmental Studies Institute, International Academy at Santa Barbara, 800 Garden St., Ste. D, Santa Barbara, California 93101. (805) 965-5010. International periodical literature dealing with environmental topics such as air pollution, water treatment, energy conservation, noise abatement, soil mechanics, wildlife preservation, and chemical wastes.

Environmental Periodicals Bibliography. National Information Services Corp., Ste. 6, Wyman Towers, 3100 St.

Paul St., Baltimore, Maryland 21218. (410)243-0797. Online version of abstract of same name.

HAZINF. University of Alberta, Department of Chemistry, Edmonton, Alberta, Canada T6G 2G2. (403) 432-3254.

Monthly Catalog of United States Government Publications. U.S. G.P.O., Supt. of Docs., PO Box 371954, Pittsburgh, Pennsylvania 15250-7954. (202) 512-0000.

National Technical Information Service. U.S. Department of Commerce, National Technical Information Service, Office of Data Base Services, 5285 Port Royal Rd., Springfield, Virginia 22161. (703) 487-4807. Bibliographic database of government sponsored research and technical reports.

PressNet Environmental Reports. Chemical Information Systems, Inc., 7215 York Rd., Baltimore, Maryland 21212. (301) 321-8440.

SCISEARCH. Institute for Scientific Information, University City Science Center, 3501 Market St., Philadelphia, Pennsylvania 19104. (215) 386-0100.

PERIODICALS AND NEWSLETTERS

Bulletin of Environmental Contamination and Toxicology. Springer-Verlag, 175 5th Ave., New York, New York 10010. (212) 460-1500; (800) 777-4643. 1966-. Frequency varies. Disseminates advances and discoveries in the areas of soil, air and food contamination and pollution.

STATISTICS SOURCES

Environmental Data Compendium. OECD Publications and Information Center, 2001 L St., N.W., Suite 700, Washington, District of Columbia 20036. (202) 785-6323. 1989.

Environmental Indicators. OECD Publications and Information Center, 2001 L St., N.W., Suite 700, Washington, District of Columbia 20036. (202) 785-6323. 1991.

Environmental Quality. Council on Environmental Quality. U.S. G.P.O., Washington, District of Columbia 20401. (202) 512-0000. Annual.

The State of the Environment. OECD Publications and Information Center, 2001 L St., N.W., Suite 700, Washington, District of Columbia 20036. (202) 785-6323. 1991.

TRADE ASSOCIATIONS AND PROFESSIONAL SOCIETIES

American Institute of Biological Sciences. 730 11th St., N.W., Washington, District of Columbia 20001-4521. (202) 628-1500.

National Fisheries Containment Research Center. Fish and Wildlife Service, U.S. Dept. of the Interior, 4200 New Haven Rd., Columbia, Missouri 65201. (314) 875-5399.

CONTOUR PLOWING AND CONTOUR FURROWING

See: AGRICULTURE

CONTROLLED BURNING

See: AIR POLLUTION

CONTROLLED THERMONUCLEAR REACTORS

See: REACTORS

CONVENTIONS

See: INTERNATIONAL TREATIES

COOLING SYSTEMS (AGRICULTURAL, MUNICIPAL, INDUSTRIAL)

ABSTRACTING AND INDEXING SERVICES

Applied Science and Technology Index. H.W. Wilson Co., 950 University Ave., Bronx, New York 10452. (800) 367-6770. Formerly Industrial Arts Index.

BIBLIOGRAPHIES

Current Contents. Agriculture, Biology and Environmental Sciences. Institute for Scientific Information, 3501 Market St., Philadelphia, Pennsylvania 19104. (800) 523-1857. 1973-. Previous title: Current Contents. Agricultural, Food & Veterinary Sciences. Gives the table of contents of periodicals in the fields of agriculture, biology, environmental and related areas.

ENCYCLOPEDIAS AND DICTIONARIES

Dictionary of Environmental Engineering and Related Sciences: English-Spanish, Spanish-English. Jose T. Villate. Ediciones Universal, 3090 SW 8th St., Miami, Florida 33135. (305) 642-3355. 1979.

Encyclopedia of Chemical Processing and Design. John J. Mcketta and W. A. Cunningham. Marcel Dekker, Inc., 270 Madison Ave., New York, New York 10016. (212) 696-9000; (800) 228-1160. 1992. Thirty-eight volumes.

Encyclopedia of Environmental Science and Engineering. J.R. Pfafflin. Gordon and Breach Science Publishers, Inc., 270 8th Ave., New York, New York 10011. (212) 206-8900. 1992.

Encyclopedia of Physical Science and Technology. Robert A. Meyers, ed. Academic Press, c/o Harcourt Brace Jovanovich Inc., 6277 Sea Harbor Dr., Orlando, Florida 32887. (800) 346-8648. Dictionary of engineering, technology and physical sciences.

Kirk-Othmer Encyclopedia of Chemical Technology. J. I. Kroschwitz, ed. John Wiley & Sons, Inc., 605 3rd Ave., New York, New York 10158-0012. (212) 850-6000. 1992-. All articles in the new edition have been rewritten and updated adding new subjects such as biotechnology, computer topics, analytical techniques and instrumentation, environmental concerns, fuels and energy, inorganic and solid state chemistry; composite materials and material science in general, and pharmaceuticals. Also available online.

GENERAL WORKS

Cooling Tower Technology: Maintenance, Upgrading and Rebuilding. Robert Burger. The Association of Energy Engineers, 4025 Pleasantdale Rd., Suite 420, Atlanta, Georgia 30340. (404) 925-9558. 1990. Second edition. Provides a compendium of successful, readily applicable techniques which can be utilized to improve the performance of any cooling tower.

Ecological Effects of Thermal Discharges. T.E. Langford. Elsevier Science Publishing Co., 655 Avenue of the Americas, New York, New York 10010. (212) 984-5800. 1990. Review of the biological studies which have been carried out in various habitats and in response to a variety of problems related to cooling water usage, particularly on the large scale such as in thermal power stations.

Heating, Cooling, Lighting. John Wiley & Sons, Inc., 605 3rd Ave., New York, New York 10158-0012. (212) 850-6000. 1991.

ONLINE DATA BASES

Kirk-Othmer Encyclopedia of Chemical Technology. John Wiley & Sons, Inc., 605 3rd Ave., 5th Floor, New York, New York 10158. (212) 850-6000. Online version of the publication of the same name.

RESEARCH CENTERS AND INSTITUTES

Cooling Tower Institute. 530 Wells Fargo Dr., Suite 113, Houston, Texas 77273. (713) 583-4087.

TRADE ASSOCIATIONS AND PROFESSIONAL SOCIETIES

American Society of Agricultural Engineers. 2950 Niles Rd., St Joseph, Michigan 49085. (616) 429-0300.

COOLING TOWERS

See: REACTORS

COPPER

See: METALS AND METALLURGY

COPPER SMELTING

See: AIR POLLUTION

COPRECIPITATION

ABSTRACTING AND INDEXING SERVICES

Chemical Abstracts. Chemical Abstracts Service, 2540 Olentangy River Rd., PO Box 3012, Columbus, Ohio 43210. (800) 848-6533. 1907-.

Science Citation Index. Institute for Scientific Information, 3501 Market St., Philadelphia, Pennsylvania 19104. 1961-.

ONLINE DATA BASES

Chemical Abstracts-CA. Chemical Abstracts Service, 2540 Olentangy River Rd., P.O. Box 3012, Columbus, Ohio 43210. (800) 848-6533 or (614) 421-3600. Information sources include 9000 journals, patents from 27 countries, two industrial property organizations, new books, conference proceedings, and government research reports.

CORAL REEF ECOLOGY

See also: BIOLOGICAL DIVERSITY; ECOSYSTEMS

ABSTRACTING AND INDEXING SERVICES

Applied Ecology Abstracts Studies in Renewable Natural Resources. Information Retrieval Ltd., 1911 Jefferson Davis Highway, Arlington, Virginia 22202. 1975-. Monthly.

Biological Abstracts. BIOSIS, 2100 Arch St., Philadelphia, Pennsylvania 19103-1399. (215) 587-4800. 1927-.

Ecological Abstracts. Geo Abstracts Ltd. Elsevier Applied Science, Crown House, Linton Rd., Barking, England IG 11 8JU. 1974-. Derived from over 600 leading ecological and environmental journals, plus books, conference proceedings, reports and theses.

Ecology Abstracts. Cambridge Scientific Abstracts, 5161 River Rd., Bethesda, Maryland 20816. (301) 961-6750. Monthly.

General Science Index. H. W. Wilson Co., 950 University Ave., Bronx, New York 10452. 1978-. Monthly, also issued in annual cumulation. Cumulative subject index to English language periodicals in the subject fields of astronomy, botany, chemistry, earth science, environment and conservation, food and nutrition, genetics, mathematics, medicine and health, microbiology, oceanography, physics, physiology and zoology.

Multimedia Index to Ecology. National Information Center for Educational Media, University of Southern California, Los Angeles, California 90007.

Science Citation Index. Institute for Scientific Information, 3501 Market St., Philadelphia, Pennsylvania 19104. 1961-.

BIBLIOGRAPHIES

Bibliography and Index of Geology. American Geological Institute, 4220 King St., Alexandria, Virginia 22302. Monthly. Includes environmental geology and hydrogeology.

Current Contents. Agriculture, Biology and Environmental Sciences. Institute for Scientific Information, 3501 Market St., Philadelphia, Pennsylvania 19104. (800) 523-1857. 1973-. Previous title: Current Contents. Agricultural, Food & Veterinary Sciences. Gives the table of contents of periodicals in the fields of agriculture, biology, environmental and related areas.

Endangered Coral Reefs of the World. Beth Clewis. Vance Bibliographies, 112 N. Charter St., PO Box 229, Monticello, Illinois 61856. (217) 762-3831. 1990. Coral reef conservation and coral reef ecology.

DIRECTORIES

Coral Reefs of the World. Susan M. Wells. World Conservation Union, IUCN Publications Services Unit, 181a Huntingdon Rd., Cambridge, England CB3 0DJ. (0223) 277894. 1991. Catalogues for the first time the significant coral reefs of the world, their geographical context and ecology, their current condition and status in legislation, and prescriptions for their conservation and sustainable use.

ENCYCLOPEDIAS AND DICTIONARIES

Cambridge Encyclopedia of Life Sciences. A. E. Friday and David S. Ingram. Cambridge University Press, 40 W 20th St., New York, New York 10011. (212) 924-3900 or (800) 227-0247. 1985. Includes all topics under biology and ecology.

The Encyclopedia of Animal Ecology. Peter D. Moore. Facts on File, Inc., 460 Park Ave. S., New York, New York 10016. (212) 683-2244. 1987.

Grzimek's Encyclopedia of Ecology. Bernhard Grzimek. Van Nostrand Reinhold, 115 5th Ave., New York, New York 10003. (212) 254-3232. 1976.

McGraw-Hill Encyclopedia of Environmental Science. Sybil P. Parker. McGraw-Hill Science & Engineering Books, 11 W. 19th St., New York, New York 10011. (212) 337-6010. 1980. Covers ecology, man's influence on nature, and environmental protection.

North American Reference Encyclopedia of Ecology and Pollution. William White. North American Pub. Co., 401 N. Broad St., Philadelphia, Pennsylvania 19108. (215) 238-5300. 1972.

GENERAL WORKS

The Atlantic Barrier Reef Ecosystem at Carrie Bow Cay, Belize, I: Structure and Communities. Klaus Rutzler and Ian G. MacIntyre. Smithsonian Institution Press, 470 L'Enfant Plaza, No. 7100, Washington, District of Columbia 20560. (800) 782-4612. 1982.

Coral Reefs of Florida. Gilbert L. Voss. Pineapple Press, PO Drawer 16008, Sarasota, Florida 34239. (813) 952-1085. 1988.

The Coral Seas. Hans W. Fricke. Putman Berkley Group, 200 Madison Ave., New York, New York 10016. (212) 951-8400. 1976. Wonders and mysteries of underwater life, includes coral reef ecology.

The Ecology of Fishes on Coral Reefs. Peter F. Sale. Academic Press, 1250 Sixth Ave., San Diego, California 92101. (619) 231-0926. 1991.

Magill's Survey of Science. Earth Science Series. Frank N. Magill. Salem Press, PO Box 50062, Pasadena, California 91105. 1990-. Five volumes. Includes information on earth's crust, hot spots and volcanic island chains, physical properties of minerals, rock magnetism, physical properties of rocks, and index.

A Natural History of the Coral Reef. Blandford Press, Villiers House, 41/47 Strand, London, England WC2N 5JE. 071-839 4900. 1983. Coral reef biology and ecology.

ONLINE DATA BASES

BIOSIS Previews. BIOSIS, 2100 Arch St., Philadelphia, Pennsylvania 19103-1399. (215) 587-4800. Largest and most comprehensive database of research in the life sciences. Contains citations for nearly 9000 primary research journals, monographs, reviews, symposia, preliminary reports, semi-popular journals, selected institutional reports, government reports and research communications.

Cambridge Scientific Abstracts Life Science–CSAL. Cambridge Scientific Abstracts, 5161 River Rd., Bethesda, Maryland 20816. (301) 961-6750. Provides access to the following abstracting services: "Life Sciences Collection," "Aquatic Sciences and Fisheries Abstracts," "Oceanic Abstracts," and "Pollution Abstracts."

Monthly Catalog of United States Government Publications. U.S. G.P.O., Supt. of Docs., PO Box 371954, Pittsburgh, Pennsylvania 15250-7954. (202) 512-0000.

National Technical Information Service. U.S. Department of Commerce, National Technical Information Service, Office of Data Base Services, 5285 Port Royal Rd., Springfield, Virginia 22161. (703) 487-4807. Bibliographic database of government sponsored research and technical reports.

SCISEARCH. Institute for Scientific Information, University City Science Center, 3501 Market St., Philadelphia, Pennsylvania 19104. (215) 386-0100.

PERIODICALS AND NEWSLETTERS

Marine Biology. Springer-Verlag, 175 5th Ave., New York, New York 10010. (212) 461-1500; (800) 777-4643. Sixteen/year. Life in oceans and coastal waters.

RESEARCH CENTERS AND INSTITUTES

Newfound Harbor Marine Institute. Route 3, Box 170, Big Pine Key, Florida 33043. (305) 872-2331.

University of Hawaii at Manoa Hawaii Institute of Marine Biology. Coconut Island, P.O. Box 1346, Kaneohe, Hawaii 96744-1346. (808) 236-7401.

University of North Carolina at Wilmington, NOAA National Undersea Research Center. 7205 Wrightsville Avenue, Wilmington, North Carolina 28403. (919) 256-5133.

TRADE ASSOCIATIONS AND PROFESSIONAL SOCIETIES

American Institute of Biological Sciences. 730 11th St., N.W., Washington, District of Columbia 20001-4521. (202) 628-1500.

CORES

See: REACTORS

CORROSION

ABSTRACTING AND INDEXING SERVICES

Applied Science and Technology Index. H.W. Wilson Co., 950 University Ave., Bronx, New York 10452. (800) 367-6770. Formerly Industrial Arts Index.

Chemical Abstracts. Chemical Abstracts Service, 2540 Olentangy River Rd., PO Box 3012, Columbus, Ohio 43210. (800) 848-6533. 1907-.

Energy Information Abstracts Annual 1987 in Retrospect. EIC/Intelligence Inc., 121 Chanlon Rd., New Providence, New Jersey 07974. (908) 464-6800. 1988. Annual. Cumulative edition of the monthly Energy Information Abstracts. Monitors sources in the field of energy including the scientific, technical and business journal literature, conference and symposia proceedings, corporate, government and academic reports.

General Science Index. H. W. Wilson Co., 950 University Ave., Bronx, New York 10452. 1978-. Monthly, also issued in annual cumulation. Cumulative subject index to English language periodicals in the subject fields of astronomy, botany, chemistry, earth science, environment and conservation, food and nutrition, genetics, mathematics, medicine and health, microbiology, oceanography, physics, physiology and zoology.

Metals Abstracts. ASM International, 9639 Kinsman, Materials Park, Ohio 44073. (216) 338-5151. 1968-. Published jointly by the Institute of Metals, London and the American Society for Metals. Formed by the Union of Metallurgical Abstracts and Review of Metal Literature.

Pollution Abstracts. Cambridge Scientific Abstracts, 5161 River Rd., Bethesda, Maryland 20816. (301) 961-6750. Six/year. Indexes worldwide technical literature on environmental pollution. Covers air pollution, marine and freshwater pollution, sewage and wastewater treatment, waste management, toxicology and health, noise pollution, radiation, land pollution, and environmental policies, programs, legislation, and education. Also available online.

Science Citation Index. Institute for Scientific Information, 3501 Market St., Philadelphia, Pennsylvania 19104. 1961-.

DIRECTORIES

McCutcheon's Functional Materials. Manufacturing Confectioner Publishing Co., 175 Rock Rd., Glen Rock, New Jersey 07451. (201) 652-2655. 1985. Annual.

ENCYCLOPEDIAS AND DICTIONARIES

Encyclopedia of Chemical Processing and Design. John J. Mcketta and W. A. Cunningham. Marcel Dekker, Inc., 270 Madison Ave., New York, New York 10016. (212) 696-9000; (800) 228-1160. 1992. Thirty-eight volumes.

Encyclopedia of Industrial Chemical Additives. Michael and Irene Ash. Chemical Publishing Co., 80 Eighth Ave., New York, New York 10011. (212) 255-1950. 1984-87. Four volumes. Comprehensive compilation of tradename products that function as additives in enhancing the properties of various major industrial products.

Encyclopedia of Physical Science and Technology. Robert A. Meyers, ed. Academic Press, c/o Harcourt Brace Jovanovich Inc., 6277 Sea Harbor Dr., Orlando, Florida 32887. (800) 346-8648. Dictionary of engineering, technology and physical sciences.

Encyclopedia of Physics. Rita G. Lerner and George L. Trigg. VCH Publishers, 303 NW 12th Ave., Deerfield Beach, Florida 33442-1788. (305) 428-5566. 1991. Second edition.

Van Nostrand's Scientific Encyclopedia. Glenn D. Considine, ed. Van Nostrand Reinhold, 115 5th Ave., New York, New York 10003. (212) 254-3232. 1983. Sixth edition. Includes all broad subject areas in science.

GENERAL WORKS

Cobalt Reduction Guidelines. Electric Power Research Institute, 3412 Hillview Ave., Palo Alto, California 94304. (415) 965-4081. 1990. Deals with nuclear power plants, hard-facing alloys, stress corrosion, and cobalt alloys.

ONLINE DATA BASES

CAS Source Index–CASSI. Chemical Abstracts Service, 2540 Olentangy River Rd., P.O. Box 3012, Columbus, Ohio 43210. (800) 848-6533 or (614) 421-3600. A listing of bibliographic and library holdings information for scientific and technical primary literature relevant to the chemical sciences.

Chemical Abstracts-CA. Chemical Abstracts Service, 2540 Olentangy River Rd., P.O. Box 3012, Columbus, Ohio 43210. (800) 848-6533 or (614) 421-3600. Information sources include 9000 journals, patents from 27 countries, two industrial property organizations, new books, conference proceedings, and government research reports.

Corrosion. Orbit Search Service, 8000 Westpark Dr., Suite 400, McLean, Virginia 22102. (800) 456-7248.

DOMIS. ECHO Service, BP 2373, Luxembourg L-1023. (352) 488041.

FLUIDEX. STI, a subsidiary of BHR Group Limited, Cranfield, Bedfordshire, England MK43 OAJ. 44 (234) 750422.

Monthly Catalog of United States Government Publications. U.S. G.P.O., Supt. of Docs., PO Box 371954, Pittsburgh, Pennsylvania 15250-7954. (202) 512-0000.

National Technical Information Service. U.S. Department of Commerce, National Technical Information Service, Office of Data Base Services, 5285 Port Royal Rd., Springfield, Virginia 22161. (703) 487-4807. Bibliographic database of government sponsored research and technical reports.

PERIODICALS AND NEWSLETTERS

Appalachian Underground Corrosion Short Course, Proceedings. Comer, Comer Bldg., West Virginia Univ., Morgantown, West Virginia 26506-6070. (304) 293-5695. 1956-. Annually. Provides the practical and theoretical aspects of the causes of corrosion, instrumentation, corrosion surveys, cathodic protection pipe coatings, and miscellaneous methods of corrosion control.

TRADE ASSOCIATIONS AND PROFESSIONAL SOCIETIES

Alkyl Amines Council. 1330 Connecticut Ave., N.W., Washington, District of Columbia 20036. (202) 659-0060.

National Association of Corrosion Engineers. P.O. Box 218340, Houston, Texas 77218. (713) 492-0535.

CORROSION CONTROL

See: CORROSION

CRAYFISH (CRAWFISH)

See also: AQUACULTURE; INTRODUCED SPECIES

ABSTRACTING AND INDEXING SERVICES

Biological Abstracts. BIOSIS, 2100 Arch St., Philadelphia, Pennsylvania 19103-1399. (215) 587-4800. 1927-.

Ecological Abstracts. Geo Abstracts Ltd. Elsevier Applied Science, Crown House, Linton Rd., Barking, England IG 11 8JU. 1974-. Derived from over 600 leading ecological and environmental journals, plus books, conference proceedings, reports and theses.

Index to Scientific Book Contents. Institute for Scientific Information, 3501 Market St., Philadelphia, Pennsylvania 19104. (800) 523-1857. 1985-. Annual. Gives contents of science books published.

Science Citation Index. Institute for Scientific Information, 3501 Market St., Philadelphia, Pennsylvania 19104. 1961-.

BIBLIOGRAPHIES

Current Contents. Agriculture, Biology and Environmental Sciences. Institute for Scientific Information, 3501 Market St., Philadelphia, Pennsylvania 19104. (800) 523-1857. 1973-. Previous title: Current Contents. Agricultural, Food & Veterinary Sciences. Gives the table of contents of periodicals in the fields of agriculture, biology, environmental and related areas.

An Interdisciplinary Bibliography of Freshwater Crayfishes. C. W. Hart, Jr. and Janice Clark. Smithsonian Institution Press, 470 L'Enfant Plaza, No. 7100, Washington, District of Columbia 20560. (800) 782-4612. 1987.

ENCYCLOPEDIAS AND DICTIONARIES

Cambridge Encyclopedia of Life Sciences. A. E. Friday and David S. Ingram. Cambridge University Press, 40 W 20th St., New York, New York 10011. (212) 924-3900 or (800) 227-0247. 1985. Includes all topics under biology and ecology.

McGraw-Hill Encyclopedia of Environmental Science. Sybil P. Parker. McGraw-Hill Science & Engineering Books, 11 W. 19th St., New York, New York 10011. (212) 337-6010. 1980. Covers ecology, man's influence on nature, and environmental protection.

McGraw-Hill Encyclopedia of Science and Technology. McGraw-Hill, 1221 Avenue of the Americas, New York,

New York 10020. (212) 512-2000 or (800) 262-4729. 1992. Seventh edition. Issued in multiple volumes including index. Includes all science and technology broad subject areas.

ONLINE DATA BASES

BIOSIS Previews. BIOSIS, 2100 Arch St., Philadelphia, Pennsylvania 19103-1399. (215) 587-4800. Largest and most comprehensive database of research in the life sciences. Contains citations for nearly 9000 primary research journals, monographs, reviews, symposia, preliminary reports, semi-popular journals, selected institutional reports, government reports and research communications.

Cambridge Scientific Abstracts Life Science–CSAL. Cambridge Scientific Abstracts, 5161 River Rd., Bethesda, Maryland 20816. (301) 961-6750. Provides access to the following abstracting services: "Life Sciences Collection," "Aquatic Sciences and Fisheries Abstracts," "Oceanic Abstracts," and "Pollution Abstracts."

FISHNET. Aquatic Data Center, 1100 Gentry St., North Kansas City, Missouri 64116. (816) 842-5936.

SCISEARCH. Institute for Scientific Information, University City Science Center, 3501 Market St., Philadelphia, Pennsylvania 19104. (215) 386-0100.

RESEARCH CENTERS AND INSTITUTES

University of Southwestern Louisiana, Crawfish Research Center. P.O. Box 44650, Lafayette, Louisiana 70504. (318) 231-5239.

TRADE ASSOCIATIONS AND PROFESSIONAL SOCIETIES

American Institute of Biological Sciences. 730 11th St., N.W., Washington, District of Columbia 20001-4521. (202) 628-1500.

CRIB STRUCTURE
See: SOIL SCIENCE

CROP DAMAGE
See: AGRICULTURE

CROP ROTATION
See: AGRICULTURE

CROPLAND
See: FARMLAND

CROPS

ABSTRACTING AND INDEXING SERVICES

Agricultural Engineering Abstracts. C. A. B. International, 845 North Park Ave., Tucson, Arizona 85719. (602) 621-7897 or (800) 528-4841. 1976-. Monthly. Informs about significant research developments in agricultural engineering and instrumentation. Some of the topics scanned for the abstracts include mechanical power, crop production, crop harvesting and threshing, crop processing and storage, aquaculture, land improvement, protected cultivation, handling and transport, and farm buildings and equipment.

Agrindex. AGRIS Coordinating Center, Via delle Terme di Caracalla, Rome, Italy I-00100. 61 0181-FA01. 1975-.

Agroforestry Abstracts. C. A. B. International, 845 North Park Ave., Tucson, Arizona 85719. (602) 621-7897 or (800) 528-4841. 1988-. Quarterly. Abstracts journal articles, reports, conferences and books. Focuses on subjects areas such as agroforestry in general; agroforestry systems; trees, animals and crops; conservation; human ecology; social and economic aspects; development, research and methodology.

Biological Abstracts. BIOSIS, 2100 Arch St., Philadelphia, Pennsylvania 19103-1399. (215) 587-4800. 1927-.

Biological and Agricultural Index. H.W. Wilson Co., 950 University Ave., Bronx, New York 10452. (800) 367-6770. 1916-. Monthly.

Current Advances in Plant Science. Pergamon Microforms International, Inc., Fairview Park, Elmsford, New York 10523. (914) 592-7720. 1984-. Monthly. Current literature searching service including journals, reports, abstracts, etc. This service is available online as part of the CABS database on the hosts BRS and ORBIT search service.

Ecological Abstracts. Geo Abstracts Ltd. Elsevier Applied Science, Crown House, Linton Rd., Barking, England IG 11 8JU. 1974-. Derived from over 600 leading ecological and environmental journals, plus books, conference proceedings, reports and theses.

Ecology Abstracts. Cambridge Scientific Abstracts, 5161 River Rd., Bethesda, Maryland 20816. (301) 961-6750. Monthly.

Environment Abstracts. Bowker A & I Publishing, 121 Chanlon Rd., New Providence, New Jersey 07974. (908) 464-6800. 1974-.

Environment Index. Environment Information Center, Index Research Department, 124 E. 39th St., New York, New York 10016. 1971-. Annual.

Environmental Information Connection–EIC. Planning Information Program, Dept. of Urban and Regional Planning, University of Illinois, 1003 West Nevada, Urbana, Illinois 61801. (217) 333-1369. Also available online.

Environmental Periodicals Bibliography. Environmental Studies Institute, International Academy at Santa Barbara, 800 Garden St., Suite D, Santa Barbara, California 93101. (805) 965-5010. Also available online.

Field Crop Abstracts. C. A. B. International, 845 North Park Ave., Tucson, Arizona 85719. (602) 621-7897 or (800) 528-4841. 1948-. Monthly. Covers literature on agronomy, field production, crop botany and physiology of all annual field crops, both temperate and tropical.

Food Science and Technology Abstracts. International Food Information Service, c/o National Food Laboratory, 6363 Clark Ave., Dublin, California 94568. (800) 336-3782. 1969-.

General Science Index. H. W. Wilson Co., 950 University Ave., Bronx, New York 10452. 1978-. Monthly, also issued in annual cumulation. Cumulative subject index to English language periodicals in the subject fields of astronomy, botany, chemistry, earth science, environment and conservation, food and nutrition, genetics, mathematics, medicine and health, microbiology, oceanography, physics, physiology and zoology.

Horticultural Abstracts. C. A. B. International, 845 North Park Ave., Tucson, Arizona 85719. (602) 621-7897 or (800) 528-4841. 1931-. Monthly. Covers the literature on fruits, vegetables, ornamental plants, nuts, and plantation crops.

Index to Scientific Book Contents. Institute for Scientific Information, 3501 Market St., Philadelphia, Pennsylvania 19104. (800) 523-1857. 1985-. Annual. Gives contents of science books published.

Pollution Abstracts. Cambridge Scientific Abstracts, 5161 River Rd., Bethesda, Maryland 20816. (301) 961-6750. Six/year. Indexes worldwide technical literature on environmental pollution. Covers air pollution, marine and freshwater pollution, sewage and wastewater treatment, waste management, toxicology and health, noise pollution, radiation, land pollution, and environmental policies, programs, legislation, and education. Also available online.

Science Citation Index. Institute for Scientific Information, 3501 Market St., Philadelphia, Pennsylvania 19104. 1961-.

BIBLIOGRAPHIES

Current Contents. Agriculture, Biology and Environmental Sciences. Institute for Scientific Information, 3501 Market St., Philadelphia, Pennsylvania 19104. (800) 523-1857. 1973-. Previous title: Current Contents. Agricultural, Food & Veterinary Sciences. Gives the table of contents of periodicals in the fields of agriculture, biology, environmental and related areas.

EPA Publications Bibliography. U.S. Environmental Protection Agency, Library Systems Branch, 401 M St., SW, Washington, District of Columbia 20460. (202) 260-2090. Quarterly.

DIRECTORIES

Agricultural Information Resource Centers, a World Directory 1990. Rita C. Fisher. IAALD World Directory Working Group, 716 W. Indiana Ave., Urbana, Illinois 61801-4836. (217) 333-7687. 1990. Includes 3,971 information resource centers that have agriculture related collection and/or information services.

ENCYCLOPEDIAS AND DICTIONARIES

The Agricultural Handbook: A Guide to Terminology. Martin Whitley, et al. BSP Professional Books, 3 Cambridge Center, Suite 208, Cambridge, Massachusetts 02142. 1988. Provides an introductory reference source

of definitions and explanations for agricultural terms. All areas of agriculture are covered including animal and crop production, farm management, policy and institutions.

Elsevier's Dictionary of Horticultural and Agricultural Plant Production in Ten Languages. Elsevier Science Publishing Co., 655 Avenue of Americas, New York, New York 10010. (212) 989-5800. 1990. Language of the text: English, Dutch, French, German, Danish, Swedish, Italian, Spanish, Portuguese and Latin.

Encyclopedia of Human Biology. Renato Dulbecco, ed. Academic Press, c/o Harcourt Brace Jovanovich Inc., 6277 Sea Harbor Dr., Orlando, Florida 32887. (800) 346-8648. 1991. Eight volumes.

The Marshall Cavendish Illustrated Encyclopedia of Plants and Earth Sciences. Marshall Cavendish Corp., 2415 Jerusalem Ave., North Bellmore, New York 11710. (516) 826-4200. 1988.

McGraw-Hill Encyclopedia of Science and Technology. McGraw-Hill, 1221 Avenue of the Americas, New York, New York 10020. (212) 512-2000 or (800) 262-4729. 1992. Seventh edition. Issued in multiple volumes including index. Includes all science and technology broad subject areas.

Van Nostrand's Scientific Encyclopedia. Glenn D. Considine, ed. Van Nostrand Reinhold, 115 5th Ave., New York, New York 10003. (212) 254-3232. 1983. Sixth edition. Includes all broad subject areas in science.

GENERAL WORKS

Air Pollution's Toll on Forests and Crops. James J. MacKenzie and Mohamed T. El-Ashry, eds. Yale University Press, 92 A Yale St., 302 Temple St., New Haven, Connecticut 06520. (203) 432-0960. 1992. Proposes an integrated strategy to reduce pollution levels based on improved energy efficiency, abatement technology, and the use of nonfossil energy technologies. This strategy takes into account other critical problems such as increasing oil imports, failure to attain clean air goals in U.S. cities, and the greenhouse effect.

Climatic Change and Plant Genetic Resources. M. T. Jackson, et al., eds. Belhaven Press, 136 S. Broadway, Irvington, New York 10533. (914) 591-9111. 1990. Cities concerns about the effect of global warming on biological diversity of species is the main thrust of this text. Major portion of the book comes from the second international workshop on plant genetic resources held in 1989.

Crop Residue Management for Conservation. Soil and Water Conservation Society, 7515 Northeast Ankeny Rd., Ankeny, Iowa 50021-9764. (515) 289-2331 or (800) THE-SOIL. 1991. Proceedings of a National Conference sponsored by the Soil and Water Conservation Society, Lexington, KY, August, 1991. State of the art on crop residue management techniques from the experts in the field. It of major consequence for agricultural conservationists and a major component of the conservation compliance provision in the 1985 Food Security Act and the Food, Agriculture, Conservation, and Trade Act of 1990.

Farming in Nature's Image. Judith A. Soule. Island Press, 1718 Connecticut Ave. N.W., Suite 300, Washington, District of Columbia 20009. (202) 232-7933. 1992. Gives a detailed look into the pioneering work of the Land

Institute, the leading educational and research organization for sustainable agriculture.

Farming on the Edge: Saving Family Farms in Marin County, California. John Hart. University of California Press, 2120 Berkeley Way, Berkeley, California 94720. (415) 642-4262; (800) 822-6657. 1991. Case study in successful land-use planning.

Modifying the Root Environment to Reduce Crop Stress. G. F. Arkin and H. M. Taylor, eds. American Society of Agricultural Engineers, 2950 Niles Rd., St. Joseph, Michigan 49085-9659. (616) 429-0300. 1981. Emphasizes the development and understanding of relationship between the plant and its subterranean environment and effect of modification of that environment on plant response.

HANDBOOKS AND MANUALS

The Agricultural Notebook. Primrose McConnell; R. J. Halley, ed. Butterworth-Heinemann, 80 Montvale Ave., Stoneham, Massachusetts 02180. (617) 438-8464 or (800) 366-2665. 1982. Seventeenth edition. Includes data on the business of farming. Topics discussed include soils, drainage, crop physiology, crop nutrition, arable crops, grassland, trees on the farm, weed control, diseases of crops, pests of crops, grain preservation and storage, animal production, farm equipment, farm management, agricultural law, health and safety, and agricultural computers.

Crop Protection Chemical Reference. Chemical and Pharmaceutical Press/Wiley, 605 3rd Ave., New York, New York 10158-0012. (212) 850-6000. 1991. 7th ed. Updated annual edition of a standard reference on label information on crop protection chemicals contains the complete text of some 540 product labels, which provide detailed information concerning what products can be used to treat a certain crop for certain problems, using what quantities of the chemical and under what restrictions and precautions. Appendices provide useful information on such matters as coding required when transporting products, safety practices, calibrations, etc.

Fertile Soil: A Grower's Guide to Organic and Inorganic Fertilizers. Robert Parnes. AgAccess, PO Box 2008, Davis, California 95617. (916) 756-7177. 1990. Comprehensive technical resource on creating fertile soils using a balanced program that does not rely on chemical fertilizers.

ONLINE DATA BASES

BIOSIS Previews. BIOSIS, 2100 Arch St., Philadelphia, Pennsylvania 19103-1399. (215) 587-4800. Largest and most comprehensive database of research in the life sciences. Contains citations for nearly 9000 primary research journals, monographs, reviews, symposia, preliminary reports, semi-popular journals, selected institutional reports, government reports and research communications.

Cambridge Scientific Abstracts Life Science–CSAL. Cambridge Scientific Abstracts, 5161 River Rd., Bethesda, Maryland 20816. (301) 961-6750. Provides access to the following abstracting services: "Life Sciences Collection," "Aquatic Sciences and Fisheries Abstracts," "Oceanic Abstracts," and "Pollution Abstracts."

Current Research Information System–CRIS/USDA. U.S. Department of Agriculture, National Agricultural Library, 10301 Baltimore Blvd., 5th Floor, Beltsville, Maryland 20705-2351. (301) 504-5755. Looks at current research projects in agriculture and allied sciences covering the biological, physical, social and behavioral sciences related to agriculture.

Enviro/Energyline Abstracts Plus. R. R. Bowker Co., 121 Chanlon Rd., New Providence, New Jersey 07974. (908) 464-6800.

Environmental Periodicals Bibliography. National Information Services Corp., Ste. 6, Wyman Towers, 3100 St. Paul St., Baltimore, Maryland 21218. (410)243-0797. Online version of abstract of same name.

SCISEARCH. Institute for Scientific Information, University City Science Center, 3501 Market St., Philadelphia, Pennsylvania 19104. (215) 386-0100.

PERIODICALS AND NEWSLETTERS

Fertilizer Research: An International Journal on Fertilizer Use and Technology. Kluwer Academic Publishers, 101 Philip Dr., Assinippi Park, Norwell, Massachusetts 02061. (617) 871-6600. Monthly. Soils, soil fertility, soil chemistry, crop and animal production and husbandry, crop quality and environment.

RESEARCH CENTERS AND INSTITUTES

University of Nebraska-Lincoln, Center for Microbial Ecology. Lincoln, Nebraska 68588-0343. (402) 472-2253.

TRADE ASSOCIATIONS AND PROFESSIONAL SOCIETIES

American Institute of Biological Sciences. 730 11th St., N.W., Washington, District of Columbia 20001-4521. (202) 628-1500.

American Registry of Certified Professionals in Agronomy, Crops and Soils. c/o American Society of Agronomy, 677 S. Segoe Rd., Madison, Wisconsin 53711. (608) 273-8080.

American Seed Research Foundation. 601 13th N.W., Suite 570 S., Washington, District of Columbia 20005. (202) 638-3128.

Crop Science Society of America. 677 S. Segoe Rd., Madison, Wisconsin 53711. (608) 273-8080.

Native Seeds/Search. 2509 N. Campbell Ave., No. 325, Tucson, Arizona 85719. (602) 327-9123.

Society of Commercial Seed Technologists. c/o Accu-Test Seed Lab., P.O. Box 1712, Brandon, Manitoba, Canada R7A 6S3. (204) 328-5313.

CRUDE-PARAFFIN BASE PETROLEUM

See: PETROLEUM

CRUDE PETROLEUM

See: PETROLEUM

CRYSTALLIZATION

ABSTRACTING AND INDEXING SERVICES

Chemical Abstracts. Chemical Abstracts Service, 2540 Olentangy River Rd., PO Box 3012, Columbus, Ohio 43210. (800) 848-6533. 1907-.

General Science Index. H. W. Wilson Co., 950 University Ave., Bronx, New York 10452. 1978-. Monthly, also issued in annual cumulation. Cumulative subject index to English language periodicals in the subject fields of astronomy, botany, chemistry, earth science, environment and conservation, food and nutrition, genetics, mathematics, medicine and health, microbiology, oceanography, physics, physiology and zoology.

Index to Scientific Book Contents. Institute for Scientific Information, 3501 Market St., Philadelphia, Pennsylvania 19104. (800) 523-1857. 1985-. Annual. Gives contents of science books published.

INIS Atomindex. International Atomic Energy Agency, Wagramerstrasse 5, Vienna, Austria A-1400. 222 23606198. 1988-. Semiannual. Abstracts nuclear energy and nuclear physics topics from journals, conferences, technical reports and other related publications. Issued in 6 parts: Personal Author, Corporate Entry, Subject, Report, Standard Patent, Conference (by place), Conference (by date).

Science Citation Index. Institute for Scientific Information, 3501 Market St., Philadelphia, Pennsylvania 19104. 1961-.

ENCYCLOPEDIAS AND DICTIONARIES

Concise Encyclopedia of Solid State Physics. Rita G. Lerner and George L. Trigg. Addison-Wesley Longman, Rte. 128, Reading, Massachusetts 01867. (617) 944-3700. 1983. "Articles chosen for this volume have been selected from the encyclopedia of physics."

Encyclopedia of Chemical Processing and Design. John J. Mcketta and W. A. Cunningham. Marcel Dekker, Inc., 270 Madison Ave., New York, New York 10016. (212) 696-9000; (800) 228-1160. 1992. Thirty-eight volumes.

Encyclopedia of Physical Science and Technology. Robert A. Meyers, ed. Academic Press, c/o Harcourt Brace Jovanovich Inc., 6277 Sea Harbor Dr., Orlando, Florida 32887. (800) 346-8648. Dictionary of engineering, technology and physical sciences.

Encyclopedia of Physics. Rita G. Lerner and George L. Trigg. VCH Publishers, 303 NW 12th Ave., Deerfield Beach, Florida 33442-1788. (305) 428-5566. 1991. Second edition.

Kirk-Othmer Encyclopedia of Chemical Technology. J. I. Kroschwitz, ed. John Wiley & Sons, Inc., 605 3rd Ave., New York, New York 10158-0012. (212) 850-6000. 1992-. All articles in the new edition have been rewritten and updated adding new subjects such as biotechnology, computer topics, analytical techniques and instrumentation, environmental concerns, fuels and energy, inorganic and solid state chemistry; composite materials and material science in general, and pharmaceuticals. Also available online.

McGraw-Hill Encyclopedia of Science and Technology. McGraw-Hill, 1221 Avenue of the Americas, New York, New York 10020. (212) 512-2000 or (800) 262-4729.

1992. Seventh edition. Issued in multiple volumes including index. Includes all science and technology broad subject areas.

Van Nostrand's Scientific Encyclopedia. Glenn D. Considine, ed. Van Nostrand Reinhold, 115 5th Ave., New York, New York 10003. (212) 254-3232. 1983. Sixth edition. Includes all broad subject areas in science.

ONLINE DATA BASES

Chemical Abstracts-CA. Chemical Abstracts Service, 2540 Olentangy River Rd., P.O. Box 3012, Columbus, Ohio 43210. (800) 848-6533 or (614) 421-3600. Information sources include 9000 journals, patents from 27 countries, two industrial property organizations, new books, conference proceedings, and government research reports.

Chemical Engineering and Biotechnology Abstracts–CEBA. Orbit Search Service, Maxwell Online Inc., 8000 W. Park Dr., McLean, Virginia 22102. (703) 442-0900 or (800) 456-7248. Monthly. Covers theoretical, practical and commercial material on all aspects of processing safety, and the environment. Also covers process and reaction engineering, measurement and process control, environmental protection and safety, plant design and equipment used in chemical engineering and biotechnology. More than 400 of the world's major primary chemical and process engineering journals are scanned to compile the database. Available from ORBIT.

Kirk-Othmer Encyclopedia of Chemical Technology. John Wiley & Sons, Inc., 605 3rd Ave., 5th Floor, New York, New York 10158. (212) 850-6000. Online version of the publication of the same name.

NBS Crystal Data Identification File. National Institute of Standards & Technology, Office of Standard Reference Data, A323 Physics Building, Gaithersburg, Maryland 20899. (301) 975-2208.

CULTIVATION

See: AGRICULTURE

CULTURAL RESOURCES

ABSTRACTING AND INDEXING SERVICES

Applied Ecology Abstracts Studies in Renewable Natural Resources. Information Retrieval Ltd., 1911 Jefferson Davis Highway, Arlington, Virginia 22202. 1975-. Monthly.

General Science Index. H. W. Wilson Co., 950 University Ave., Bronx, New York 10452. 1978-. Monthly, also issued in annual cumulation. Cumulative subject index to English language periodicals in the subject fields of astronomy, botany, chemistry, earth science, environment and conservation, food and nutrition, genetics, mathematics, medicine and health, microbiology, oceanography, physics, physiology and zoology.

Multimedia Index to Ecology. National Information Center for Educational Media, University of Southern California, Los Angeles, California 90007.

GENERAL WORKS

Environment Control for Animals and Plants. Louis D. Albright. American Society of Agricultural Engineers, 2950 Niles Rd., St. Joseph, Michigan 49085-9659. (616) 429-0300. 1990. Deals with the physical aspects of environmental control with some attention to biological factors relevant to successful environment control. Includes 10 executable computer programs that allow the user to explore design options.

RESEARCH CENTERS AND INSTITUTES

Center for Environmental Education and Research. University of Colorado-Boulder, College of Environmental Design, Boulder, Colorado 80309. (303) 492-7711.

TRADE ASSOCIATIONS AND PROFESSIONAL SOCIETIES

Urban Initiatives. 530 W. 25th St., New York, New York 10001. (212) 620-9773.

CUTIE PIE

See: RADIATION INSTRUMENTS

CUTOFF TRENCHES

See: DAMS

CYANIDE

ABSTRACTING AND INDEXING SERVICES

Biological Abstracts. BIOSIS, 2100 Arch St., Philadelphia, Pennsylvania 19103-1399. (215) 587-4800. 1927-.

Chemical Abstracts. Chemical Abstracts Service, 2540 Olentangy River Rd., PO Box 3012, Columbus, Ohio 43210. (800) 848-6533. 1907-.

Pollution Abstracts. Cambridge Scientific Abstracts, 5161 River Rd., Bethesda, Maryland 20816. (301) 961-6750. Six/year. Indexes worldwide technical literature on environmental pollution. Covers air pollution, marine and freshwater pollution, sewage and wastewater treatment, waste management, toxicology and health, noise pollution, radiation, land pollution, and environmental policies, programs, legislation, and education. Also available online.

Science Citation Index. Institute for Scientific Information, 3501 Market St., Philadelphia, Pennsylvania 19104. 1961-.

ENCYCLOPEDIAS AND DICTIONARIES

McGraw-Hill Encyclopedia of Science and Technology. McGraw-Hill, 1221 Avenue of the Americas, New York, New York 10020. (212) 512-2000 or (800) 262-4729. 1992. Seventh edition. Issued in multiple volumes including index. Includes all science and technology broad subject areas.

Van Nostrand's Scientific Encyclopedia. Glenn D. Considine, ed. Van Nostrand Reinhold, 115 5th Ave., New York, New York 10003. (212) 254-3232. 1983. Sixth edition. Includes all broad subject areas in science.

ONLINE DATA BASES

BIOSIS Previews. BIOSIS, 2100 Arch St., Philadelphia, Pennsylvania 19103-1399. (215) 587-4800. Largest and most comprehensive database of research in the life sciences. Contains citations for nearly 9000 primary research journals, monographs, reviews, symposia, preliminary reports, semi-popular journals, selected institutional reports, government reports and research communications.

CERCLIS. Chemical Information Systems, Inc., 7215 York Rd., Baltimore, Maryland 21212. (301) 321-8440. Information on hazardous waste disposal sites that have either been listed by the EPA on the National Priority List (NPL) or nominated for consideration for the NPL.

Chemical Abstracts-CA. Chemical Abstracts Service, 2540 Olentangy River Rd., P.O. Box 3012, Columbus, Ohio 43210. (800) 848-6533 or (614) 421-3600. Information sources include 9000 journals, patents from 27 countries, two industrial property organizations, new books, conference proceedings, and government research reports.

Chemical Abstracts Chemical Name Directory-CHEM-NAME. Chemical Abstracts Service, 2540 Olentangy River Rd., P.O. Box 3012, Columbus, Ohio 43210. (800) 848-6533 or (614) 421-3600. Listing of chemical substances in a dictionary type file. The Chemical Abstracts (CAS) Registry Number, molecular formula, Chemical Abstracts (CA) Substance Index Name, available synonyms, ring data and other chemical substance information is given for each entry.

TRADE ASSOCIATIONS AND PROFESSIONAL SOCIETIES

American Chemical Society. 1155 16th St., N.W., Washington, District of Columbia 20036. (202) 872-4600.

CYCLAMATES

See: FOOD SCIENCE

CYCLODIENE PESTICIDES

See: PESTICIDES

CYCLONE COLLECTOR

See: AIR POLLUTION

CYCLONES

See: WEATHER

CYTOTOXICITY

See: TOXICITY

D

DAM CONSTRUCTION
See: DAMS

DAM SITING
See: DAMS

DAMS
See also: IRRIGATION; POWER GENERATION; RESERVOIRS

ABSTRACTING AND INDEXING SERVICES

Applied Science and Technology Index. H.W. Wilson Co., 950 University Ave., Bronx, New York 10452. (800) 367-6770. Formerly Industrial Arts Index.

Aqualine Abstracts. Water Research Centre. c/o Pergamon Microforms International, Inc., Fairview Park, Elmsford, New York 10523. (914) 592-7720. 1927-. Contains some 8,000 records annually on water and wastewater technology. Covers all aspects of water, wastewater, associated engineering services and the aquatic environment. Over 600 periodicals, as well as books, reports and conference proceedings and other publications from water related institutions worldwide are scanned. Also available online.

ASFA Aquaculture Abstracts. Cambridge Scientific Abstracts, Inc., 5161 River Rd., Bethesda, Maryland 20816. (301) 961-6750. 1984.

Civil Engineering Hydraulic Abstracts. BHRA Fluid Engineering, Air Science Co., PO Box 143, Corning, New York 14830. (607) 962-5591. Monthly. Abstracts of periodicals that publish in the areas of hydraulic engineering and other related topics.

Energy Information Abstracts Annual 1987 in Retrospect. EIC/Intelligence Inc., 121 Chanlon Rd., New Providence, New Jersey 07974. (908) 464-6800. 1988. Annual. Cumulative edition of the monthly Energy Information Abstracts. Monitors sources in the field of energy including the scientific, technical and business journal literature, conference and symposia proceedings, corporate, government and academic reports.

Engineering Index. The Engineering Index Inc., 345 E. 47th St., New York, New York 10017. 1962-.

Environment Abstracts. Bowker A & I Publishing, 121 Chanlon Rd., New Providence, New Jersey 07974. (908) 464-6800. 1974-.

Environment Index. Environment Information Center, Index Research Department, 124 E. 39th St., New York, New York 10016. 1971-. Annual.

Environmental Information Connection–EIC. Planning Information Program, Dept. of Urban and Regional Planning, University of Illinois, 1003 West Nevada, Urbana, Illinois 61801. (217) 333-1369. Also available online.

Environmental Periodicals Bibliography. Environmental Studies Institute, International Academy at Santa Barbara, 800 Garden St., Suite D, Santa Barbara, California 93101. (805) 965-5010. Also available online.

General Science Index. H. W. Wilson Co., 950 University Ave., Bronx, New York 10452. 1978-. Monthly, also issued in annual cumulation. Cumulative subject index to English language periodicals in the subject fields of astronomy, botany, chemistry, earth science, environment and conservation, food and nutrition, genetics, mathematics, medicine and health, microbiology, oceanography, physics, physiology and zoology.

Index to Scientific Book Contents. Institute for Scientific Information, 3501 Market St., Philadelphia, Pennsylvania 19104. (800) 523-1857. 1985-. Annual. Gives contents of science books published.

Pollution Abstracts. Cambridge Scientific Abstracts, 5161 River Rd., Bethesda, Maryland 20816. (301) 961-6750. Six/year. Indexes worldwide technical literature on environmental pollution. Covers air pollution, marine and freshwater pollution, sewage and wastewater treatment, waste management, toxicology and health, noise pollution, radiation, land pollution, and environmental policies, programs, legislation, and education. Also available online.

Science Citation Index. Institute for Scientific Information, 3501 Market St., Philadelphia, Pennsylvania 19104. 1961-.

BIBLIOGRAPHIES

EPA Publications Bibliography. U.S. Environmental Protection Agency, Library Systems Branch, 401 M St., SW, Washington, District of Columbia 20460. (202) 260-2090. Quarterly.

Kepone: A Literature Summary. James Edward Huff. National Technical Information Service, 5285 Port Royal Rd., Springfield, Virginia 22161. (703) 487-4650. 1977.

DIRECTORIES

Roster of State Dam Safety Officials Contacts. Association of State Dam Safety Officials, P.O. Box 55270, Lexington, Kentucky 40555. (606) 257-5140.

ENCYCLOPEDIAS AND DICTIONARIES

Dictionary of Environmental Engineering and Related Sciences: English-Spanish, Spanish-English. Jose T. Villate. Ediciones Universal, 3090 SW 8th St., Miami, Florida 33135. (305) 642-3355. 1979.

Encyclopedia of Environmental Science and Engineering. J.R. Pfafflin. Gordon and Breach Science Publishers, Inc., 270 8th Ave., New York, New York 10011. (212) 206-8900. 1992.

Encyclopedia of Physical Science and Technology. Robert A. Meyers, ed. Academic Press, c/o Harcourt Brace Jovanovich Inc., 6277 Sea Harbor Dr., Orlando, Florida 32887. (800) 346-8648. Dictionary of engineering, technology and physical sciences.

Illustrated Encyclopedia of Science and the Future. Mike Biscare, et al., ed. Marshall Cavendish, 58 Old Compton St., London, England 0W1V5 PA. 01-734 6710. 1983. Twenty volumes. Each volume has 5 sections: Frontiers, Electronics in Action, Medical Science, Military Technology, and Resources.

McGraw-Hill Encyclopedia of Environmental Science. Sybil P. Parker. McGraw-Hill Science & Engineering Books, 11 W. 19th St., New York, New York 10011. (212) 337-6010. 1980. Covers ecology, man's influence on nature, and environmental protection.

McGraw-Hill Encyclopedia of Science and Technology. McGraw-Hill, 1221 Avenue of the Americas, New York, New York 10020. (212) 512-2000 or (800) 262-4729. 1992. Seventh edition. Issued in multiple volumes including index. Includes all science and technology broad subject areas.

The Water Encyclopedia. Lewis Publishers, 2000 Corporate Blvd. N.W., Boca Raton, Florida 33431. (800) 272-7737. 1990. 2d ed. Includes groundwater contamination, drinking water, floods, waterborne diseases, global warming, climate change, irrigation, water agencies and organizations, precipitation, oceans and seas, and river, lakes and waterfalls.

GENERAL WORKS

Application of Environmental Impact Assessment: Highways and Dams. United Nations, 2 United Nations Plaza, Salis Section Rm. DC 2-853, New York, New York 10017. (800) 553-3210. 1987.

An Assessment Methodology for the Environmental Impact of Water Resource Projects. Maurice L. Warner. U.S. G.P.O., Washington, District of Columbia 20401. (202) 512-0000. 1974. Environmental aspects of flood dams and reservoirs.

Construction of Dams and Aircraft Overflights in National Park Units. U.S. Congress. House Committee on Interior and Insular Affairs. U.S. G.P.O., Washington, District of Columbia 20401. Covers national parks and reserves, environmental aspects of dams, airplane noise and air traffic rules.

Dams and the Environment. John A. Dixon. The World Bank, 1818 H. St., N.W., Washington, District of Columbia 20433. 1989.

Great American Bridges and Dams. Preservation Press, 1785 Massachusetts Ave. N.W., Washington, District of Columbia 20036. (202) 673-4058. 1988. A national trust guide to bridges and dams in the United States.

Impounded Rivers: Perspectives for Ecological Management. Geoffrey E. Petts. John Wiley & Sons, Inc., 605 3rd Ave., New York, New York 10158. (212) 850-6000. 1984. Environmental aspects of dams, stream ecology and stream conservation.

Overtapped Oasis: Reform or Revolution for Western Water. Marc Reisner and Sarah Bates. Island Press, 1718 Connecticut Ave. N.W., Suite 300, Washington, District of Columbia 20009. (202) 232-7933. 1990. Comprehensive critique of the cardinal dogma of the American West: that the region is always running out of water and therefore must build more and more dams.

Problems of Hydroelectric Development at Existing Dams. R.J. Taylor. Department of Energy, 5285 Port Royal Rd, Springfield, Virginia 22161. 1979. An analysis of institutional, economic, and environmental restraints.

The Social and Environmental Effects of Large Dams. Edward Goldsmith. Sierra Club Books, 100 Bush St., San Francisco, California 94104. (415) 291-1600. 1986. History of irrigation and the impact of dams on the environment.

HANDBOOKS AND MANUALS

Embankment Dam Instruction Manual. Charles L. Bartholomew. U.S. G.P.O., Washington, District of Columbia 20401. 1987. Measurement of earth dams.

Federal Guidelines for Dam Safety. United States Ad Hoc Interagency Committee on Dam Safety. U.S. G.P.O., Washington, District of Columbia 20401. 1979. Deals with dam safety and dam inspection.

Water Power and Dam Construction Handbook. Richard Taylor, ed. Reed Business Pub., Quadrant House, The Quadrant, Sutton, England SM2 5AS. 1990.

ONLINE DATA BASES

Computerized Engineering Index–COMPENDEX. Engineering Information Inc., 345 E. 47th St., New York, New York 10017. (212) 705-7600.

Enviro/Energyline Abstracts Plus. R. R. Bowker Co., 121 Chanlon Rd., New Providence, New Jersey 07974. (908) 464-6800.

Environmental Periodicals Bibliography. National Information Services Corp., Ste. 6, Wyman Towers, 3100 St. Paul St., Baltimore, Maryland 21218. (410)243-0797. Online version of abstract of same name.

Monthly Catalog of United States Government Publications. U.S. G.P.O., Supt. of Docs., PO Box 371954, Pittsburgh, Pennsylvania 15250-7954. (202) 512-0000.

National Technical Information Service. U.S. Department of Commerce, National Technical Information Service, Office of Data Base Services, 5285 Port Royal Rd., Springfield, Virginia 22161. (703) 487-4807. Bibliographic database of government sponsored research and technical reports.

SCISEARCH. Institute for Scientific Information, University City Science Center, 3501 Market St., Philadelphia, Pennsylvania 19104. (215) 386-0100.

PERIODICALS AND NEWSLETTERS

Civil Engineering ASCE. American Society of Civil Engineers, 345 E 47th St., New York, New York 10017. (212) 705-7288; (800) 548-2723. Monthly. Professional journal that offers a forum for free exchange of ideas relevant to the profession of civil engineering. Covers in regular columns, engineering news, legal trends in engineering, calendar of events, membership news, publications and other items of interest to civil engineers. Formerly, Civil Engineering.

Earthquake Engineering and Structural Dynamics. John Wiley & Sons, Inc., 605 3rd Ave., New York, New York 10158-0012. (212) 850-6000. 1978-. Bimonthly.

Highway and Heavy Construction. Dun Donnelley Pub. Corp., 1350 E. Touhy Ave., Box 5080, Des Plaines, Illinois 60017-8800. (708) 635-8800. 1892-. Fifteen times a year. Features on-site reports of current construction projects nationwide and advises senior personnel on the changing needs and demands of the market.

Hydroelectric Construction. American Society of Civil Engineers, 345 E. 47th St., New York, New York 10017. (212) 705-7288. 1981-. Monthly.

International Water Power and Dam Construction. Reed Business Pub., 205 E. 42d St., New York, New York 10017. 1949-. Monthly. Formerly Water Power and includes practical and theoretical articles and news concerning all aspects of hydro-electric developments and large dam construction throughout the world. Coverage of research into hydraulic machinery, wave and tidal power.

Journal of Engineering Mechanics. American Society of Civil Engineers, 345 E. 47th St., New York, New York 10017. (212) 705-7288; (800) 548-2723. Bimonthly. Covers activity and development in the field of applied mechanics as it relates to civil engineering, research on bioengineering, computational mechanics, computer aided engineering, dynamics of structures, elasticity, experimental analysis and instrumentation, fluid mechanics, flow of granular media, inelastic behavior of solids and structures, probablistic methods, properties of materials, stability of structural elements and systems, and turbulence.

Journal of Geotechnical Engineering. American Society of Civil Engineers, 345 E. 47th St., New York, New York 10017. (212) 705-7288. 1956-. Monthly. Covers the field of soil mechanics and foundations with emphasis on the relationship between the geologic and man-made works.

Journal of Hydraulic Engineering. American Society of Civil Engineers, 345 E. 47th St., New York, New York 10017. (212) 705-7288; (800) 548-2723. 1983-. Monthly. Papers describe the analysis and solutions of problems in hydraulic engineering, hydrology and water resources. Emphasizes concepts, methods, techniques and results that advance knowledge in the hydraulic engineering profession.

Journal of Water Resources Planning and Management. American Society of Civil Engineers, Resource Planning and Management Division, 345 E. 47th St., New York, New York 10017. (212) 705-7288; (800) 548-2723. 1983-. Quarterly. Reports on all phases of planning and management of water resources. Examines social, economic, environmental, and administrative concerns relating to the use and conservation of water.

RESEARCH CENTERS AND INSTITUTES

Murray State University, Center of Excellence for Reservoir Research. College of Science, Murray, Kentucky 42071. (502) 762-2886.

Murray State University, Handcock Biological Station. Murray, Kentucky 42071. (502) 474-2272.

STATISTICS SOURCES

World Resources. World Resources Institute. 1709 New York Ave., N.W., Washington, District of Columbia 20006. (202) 638-6300. Annual. Statistical and textual analysis of world's natural resources and the effects of growth-caused environmental pollution.

TRADE ASSOCIATIONS AND PROFESSIONAL SOCIETIES

American Society of Agricultural Engineers. 2950 Niles Rd., St Joseph, Michigan 49085. (616) 429-0300.

American Society of Civil Engineers. 345 East 47th St., New York, New York 10017. (212) 705-7496.

Slurry Technology Association. 1156 15th St., N.W., Suite 525, Washington, District of Columbia 20005. (202) 296-1133.

United States Committee on Large Dams. P.O. Box 15103, Denver, Colorado 80215. (303) 236-6960.

DDE (DICHLORODIPHENYL-DICHLOROETHYLENE)

See: INSECTICIDES

DDT (DICHLORODIPHENYL-TRICHLOROETHANE)

See: INSECTICIDES

DECIDUOUS

See: FOREST MANAGEMENT

DECIDUOUS FORESTS

See: FORESTS

DECOMPOSERS
See: BACTERIA

DECONTAMINATION
See: RADIOACTIVE DECONTAMINATION

DEEP WELL INJECTION
See: DRILLING

DEFOLIATION

ABSTRACTING AND INDEXING SERVICES

Applied Ecology Abstracts Studies in Renewable Natural Resources. Information Retrieval Ltd., 1911 Jefferson Davis Highway, Arlington, Virginia 22202. 1975-. Monthly.

Biological Abstracts. BIOSIS, 2100 Arch St., Philadelphia, Pennsylvania 19103-1399. (215) 587-4800. 1927-.

Biological and Agricultural Index. H.W. Wilson Co., 950 University Ave., Bronx, New York 10452. (800) 367-6770. 1916-. Monthly.

Ecological Abstracts. Geo Abstracts Ltd. Elsevier Applied Science, Crown House, Linton Rd., Barking, England IG 11 8JU. 1974-. Derived from over 600 leading ecological and environmental journals, plus books, conference proceedings, reports and theses.

Ecology Abstracts. Cambridge Scientific Abstracts, 5161 River Rd., Bethesda, Maryland 20816. (301) 961-6750. Monthly.

Environment Abstracts. Bowker A & I Publishing, 121 Chanlon Rd., New Providence, New Jersey 07974. (908) 464-6800. 1974-.

Environment Index. Environment Information Center, Index Research Department, 124 E. 39th St., New York, New York 10016. 1971-. Annual.

Environmental Information Connection–EIC. Planning Information Program, Dept. of Urban and Regional Planning, University of Illinois, 1003 West Nevada, Urbana, Illinois 61801. (217) 333-1369. Also available online.

Environmental Periodicals Bibliography. Environmental Studies Institute, International Academy at Santa Barbara, 800 Garden St., Suite D, Santa Barbara, California 93101. (805) 965-5010. Also available online.

General Science Index. H. W. Wilson Co., 950 University Ave., Bronx, New York 10452. 1978-. Monthly, also issued in annual cumulation. Cumulative subject index to English language periodicals in the subject fields of astronomy, botany, chemistry, earth science, environment and conservation, food and nutrition, genetics, mathematics, medicine and health, microbiology, oceanography, physics, physiology and zoology.

Index to Scientific Book Contents. Institute for Scientific Information, 3501 Market St., Philadelphia, Pennsylva-

nia 19104. (800) 523-1857. 1985-. Annual. Gives contents of science books published.

Multimedia Index to Ecology. National Information Center for Educational Media, University of Southern California, Los Angeles, California 90007.

Pollution Abstracts. Cambridge Scientific Abstracts, 5161 River Rd., Bethesda, Maryland 20816. (301) 961-6750. Six/year. Indexes worldwide technical literature on environmental pollution. Covers air pollution, marine and freshwater pollution, sewage and wastewater treatment, waste management, toxicology and health, noise pollution, radiation, land pollution, and environmental policies, programs, legislation, and education. Also available online.

Science Citation Index. Institute for Scientific Information, 3501 Market St., Philadelphia, Pennsylvania 19104. 1961-.

BIBLIOGRAPHIES

Current Contents. Agriculture, Biology and Environmental Sciences. Institute for Scientific Information, 3501 Market St., Philadelphia, Pennsylvania 19104. (800) 523-1857. 1973-. Previous title: Current Contents. Agricultural, Food & Veterinary Sciences. Gives the table of contents of periodicals in the fields of agriculture, biology, environmental and related areas.

Directory of Published Proceedings. Interdok Corp., 173 Halstead Ave., Harrison, New York 10528. (914) 835-3506. 1990. Monthly. This is a listing of published proceedings including the series SEMTE (Science/Medicine/Engineering/Technology) and the series SSH (Social Science/Humanities).

EPA Publications Bibliography. U.S. Environmental Protection Agency, Library Systems Branch, 401 M St., SW, Washington, District of Columbia 20460. (202) 260-2090. Quarterly.

ENCYCLOPEDIAS AND DICTIONARIES

Cambridge Encyclopedia of Life Sciences. A. E. Friday and David S. Ingram. Cambridge University Press, 40 W 20th St., New York, New York 10011. (212) 924-3900 or (800) 227-0247. 1985. Includes all topics under biology and ecology.

McGraw-Hill Encyclopedia of Environmental Science. Sybil P. Parker. McGraw-Hill Science & Engineering Books, 11 W. 19th St., New York, New York 10011. (212) 337-6010. 1980. Covers ecology, man's influence on nature, and environmental protection.

McGraw-Hill Encyclopedia of Science and Technology. McGraw-Hill, 1221 Avenue of the Americas, New York, New York 10020. (212) 512-2000 or (800) 262-4729. 1992. Seventh edition. Issued in multiple volumes including index. Includes all science and technology broad subject areas.

Van Nostrand's Scientific Encyclopedia. Glenn D. Considine, ed. Van Nostrand Reinhold, 115 5th Ave., New York, New York 10003. (212) 254-3232. 1983. Sixth edition. Includes all broad subject areas in science.

GENERAL WORKS

How to Identify and Control Noninfectious Diseases of Trees. Forest Service, North Central Forest Exp. Sta. The

Station, 1992 Folwell Ave., St. Paul, Minnesota 55108. (612) 642-5207. 1990. Revised edition. Deals with defoliation of conifers and the diseases and the pests that affect them.

Mapping Insect Defoliation in Eastern Hardwood Forests with Color-IR Aerial Photos. J. D. Ward, et al. U.S. Department of Agriculture, Forest Service, Forest Pest Management, Methods Applications Group, 240 W. Prospect Rd., Fort Collins, Colorado 80526. (303) 224-1100. 1986. An infrared photo interpretation guide of the insect defoliation in the hardwood forests.

Radial Growth of Grand Fir and Douglas Fir Ten Years after Defoliation by the Douglas Fir Tussock Moth in the Blue Mountains Outbreak. Boyd E. Wickman. U.S. Department of Agriculture, Forest Service, Pacific Northwest Research Station, 319 S. W. Pine St., PO Box 3890, Portland, Oregon 97208. (503) 294-5640. 1986.

Rating Forest Stands for Gypsy Moth Defoliation. Owen W. Herrick and David A. Ganser. U.S. Department of Agriculture, Northeastern Forest Experiment Station, 370 Reed Rd., Broomall, Pennsylvania 19008. (215) 461-3104. 1986.

ONLINE DATA BASES

BIOSIS Previews. BIOSIS, 2100 Arch St., Philadelphia, Pennsylvania 19103-1399. (215) 587-4800. Largest and most comprehensive database of research in the life sciences. Contains citations for nearly 9000 primary research journals, monographs, reviews, symposia, preliminary reports, semi-popular journals, selected institutional reports, government reports and research communications.

Cambridge Scientific Abstracts Life Science–CSAL. Cambridge Scientific Abstracts, 5161 River Rd., Bethesda, Maryland 20816. (301) 961-6750. Provides access to the following abstracting services: "Life Sciences Collection," "Aquatic Sciences and Fisheries Abstracts," "Oceanic Abstracts," and "Pollution Abstracts."

Enviro/Energyline Abstracts Plus. R. R. Bowker Co., 121 Chanlon Rd., New Providence, New Jersey 07974. (908) 464-6800.

Environmental Periodicals Bibliography. National Information Services Corp., Ste. 6, Wyman Towers, 3100 St. Paul St., Baltimore, Maryland 21218. (410)243-0797. Online version of abstract of same name.

Monthly Catalog of United States Government Publications. U.S. G.P.O., Supt. of Docs., PO Box 371954, Pittsburgh, Pennsylvania 15250-7954. (202) 512-0000.

National Technical Information Service. U.S. Department of Commerce, National Technical Information Service, Office of Data Base Services, 5285 Port Royal Rd., Springfield, Virginia 22161. (703) 487-4807. Bibliographic database of government sponsored research and technical reports.

SCISEARCH. Institute for Scientific Information, University City Science Center, 3501 Market St., Philadelphia, Pennsylvania 19104. (215) 386-0100.

PERIODICALS AND NEWSLETTERS

Forest Insect and Disease Conditions in Alaska. Alaska, Dept. of Agriculture, Forest Service, Alaska Region, Division of State and Private Forestry, 201 E. 9th St.,

Suite 303, Anchorage, Alaska 99501. (907) 271-2583. 1978-. Annual.

Forest Insect and Disease Conditions in the Intermountain Region. Intermountain Region, Forest Insect and Disease Management, State and Private, USDA Forest Service, 324 25th St., Ogden, Utah 84401. (801) 625-5431. 1979-. Annual.

Forest Insect and Disease Conditions in the Northern Region. U.S. Department of Agriculture, Forest Service, Northern Region, PO Box 8089, Missoula, Montana 59807. (406) 721-5694. 1978-. Annual.

Forest Insect and Disease Conditions in the Pacific Northwest. U.S. Department of Agriculture, Forest Service, Pacific Northwest Region, 319 S. W. Pine St., PO Box 3890, Portland, Oregon 97208. (503) 294-5640. 1978-. Annual.

Forest Insect and Disease Conditions in the United States. U.S. Department of Agriculture, Forest Service, 14th St. and Independence Ave. S.W., Washington, District of Columbia 20250. (202) 447-7454. 1971-. Annual.

Journal of Arboriculture. Society of Arboriculture, 303 W. University Ave., PO Box 908, Urbana, Illinois 61801. (217) 328-2032. 1975-. Monthly.

Newsletter (U.S. Forest Insect and Disease Management, Methods Application Group). The Group, PO Box 2417, Washington, District of Columbia 20013. (703) 235-8065. 1972-. Irregular.

A Summary of Current Forest Insect and Disease Problems for New York State. Society of American Foresters, 5400 Grosvenor Ln., Bethesda, Maryland 20814. (301) 897-8720. 1969/70-.

TRADE ASSOCIATIONS AND PROFESSIONAL SOCIETIES

American Institute of Biological Sciences. 730 11th St., N.W., Washington, District of Columbia 20001-4521. (202) 628-1500.

DEFORESTATION

ABSTRACTING AND INDEXING SERVICES

Applied Ecology Abstracts Studies in Renewable Natural Resources. Information Retrieval Ltd., 1911 Jefferson Davis Highway, Arlington, Virginia 22202. 1975-. Monthly.

Biological Abstracts. BIOSIS, 2100 Arch St., Philadelphia, Pennsylvania 19103-1399. (215) 587-4800. 1927-.

Biological and Agricultural Index. H.W. Wilson Co., 950 University Ave., Bronx, New York 10452. (800) 367-6770. 1916-. Monthly.

Ecological Abstracts. Geo Abstracts Ltd. Elsevier Applied Science, Crown House, Linton Rd., Barking, England IG 11 8JU. 1974-. Derived from over 600 leading ecological and environmental journals, plus books, conference proceedings, reports and theses.

Ecology Abstracts. Cambridge Scientific Abstracts, 5161 River Rd., Bethesda, Maryland 20816. (301) 961-6750. Monthly.

Environment Abstracts. Bowker A & I Publishing, 121 Chanlon Rd., New Providence, New Jersey 07974. (908) 464-6800. 1974-.

Environment Index. Environment Information Center, Index Research Department, 124 E. 39th St., New York, New York 10016. 1971-. Annual.

Environmental Information Connection–EIC. Planning Information Program, Dept. of Urban and Regional Planning, University of Illinois, 1003 West Nevada, Urbana, Illinois 61801. (217) 333-1369. Also available online.

Environmental Periodicals Bibliography. Environmental Studies Institute, International Academy at Santa Barbara, 800 Garden St., Suite D, Santa Barbara, California 93101. (805) 965-5010. Also available online.

General Science Index. H. W. Wilson Co., 950 University Ave., Bronx, New York 10452. 1978-. Monthly, also issued in annual cumulation. Cumulative subject index to English language periodicals in the subject fields of astronomy, botany, chemistry, earth science, environment and conservation, food and nutrition, genetics, mathematics, medicine and health, microbiology, oceanography, physics, physiology and zoology.

Index to Scientific Book Contents. Institute for Scientific Information, 3501 Market St., Philadelphia, Pennsylvania 19104. (800) 523-1857. 1985-. Annual. Gives contents of science books published.

Multimedia Index to Ecology. National Information Center for Educational Media, University of Southern California, Los Angeles, California 90007.

Science Citation Index. Institute for Scientific Information, 3501 Market St., Philadelphia, Pennsylvania 19104. 1961-.

BIBLIOGRAPHIES

Current Contents. Agriculture, Biology and Environmental Sciences. Institute for Scientific Information, 3501 Market St., Philadelphia, Pennsylvania 19104. (800) 523-1857. 1973-. Previous title: Current Contents. Agricultural, Food & Veterinary Sciences. Gives the table of contents of periodicals in the fields of agriculture, biology, environmental and related areas.

Directory of Published Proceedings. Interdok Corp., 173 Halstead Ave., Harrison, New York 10528. (914) 835-3506. 1990. Monthly. This is a listing of published proceedings including the series SEMTE (Science/Medicine/Engineering/Technology) and the series SSH (Social Science/Humanities).

EPA Publications Bibliography. U.S. Environmental Protection Agency, Library Systems Branch, 401 M St., SW, Washington, District of Columbia 20460. (202) 260-2090. Quarterly.

Global Climate Change: Recent Publications. Library of the Department of State. The Library, 2201 C St. N.W., Washington, District of Columbia 20520. 1989.

DIRECTORIES

Gale Environmental Sourcebook. Karen Hill. Gale Research Co., 835 Penobscot Bldg., Detroit, Michigan 48226-4094. (313) 961-2242. Contacts, information sources, or general information on environmental topics.

ENCYCLOPEDIAS AND DICTIONARIES

Cambridge Encyclopedia of Life Sciences. A. E. Friday and David S. Ingram. Cambridge University Press, 40 W 20th St., New York, New York 10011. (212) 924-3900 or (800) 227-0247. 1985. Includes all topics under biology and ecology.

The Encyclopedia of Geochemistry and Environmental Sciences. Rhodes Whitmore Fairbridge. Van Nostrand Reinhold Co., 115 5th Ave., New York, New York 10003. (212) 254-3232. 1972.

McGraw-Hill Encyclopedia of Environmental Science. Sybil P. Parker. McGraw-Hill Science & Engineering Books, 11 W. 19th St., New York, New York 10011. (212) 337-6010. 1980. Covers ecology, man's influence on nature, and environmental protection.

McGraw-Hill Encyclopedia of Science and Technology. McGraw-Hill, 1221 Avenue of the Americas, New York, New York 10020. (212) 512-2000 or (800) 262-4729. 1992. Seventh edition. Issued in multiple volumes including index. Includes all science and technology broad subject areas.

Van Nostrand's Scientific Encyclopedia. Glenn D. Considine, ed. Van Nostrand Reinhold, 115 5th Ave., New York, New York 10003. (212) 254-3232. 1983. Sixth edition. Includes all broad subject areas in science.

GENERAL WORKS

Alternatives to Deforestation: Steps Toward Sustainable Use of the Amazon Rain Forest. Anthony B. Anderson, ed. Columbia University Press, 562 W. 113th St., New York, New York 10025. (212) 316-7100. 1992. Based on papers presented at an international conference in Belem, Brazil, for scientists in several fields, as well as government policy makers and representatives from foundations who are interested in exploring possible sustainable use of the world's largest rain forest, the Amazon, which is now being destroyed on an unprecedented scale.

The Conservation Atlas of Tropical Forests: Asia and the Pacific. N. Mark Collins, Jeffery A. Sayer, and Timothy C. Whitmore. Simon & Schuster, 1230 Avenue of the Americas, New York, New York 10020. (212) 689-7000. 1991. Focuses on closed canopy, and true rain forests. This Asian volume is the first of a set of three–tropical America and Africa being the next. Address such regional subjects as forest wildlife, human impacts on forest lands, and the tropical timber trade; and includes a "Tropical Forestry Action Plan" to conserve and protect important remaining stands. The second part of the atlas gives a detailed survey of 17 countries plus the island groups of Fiji and the Solomons, but not those of New Caledonia, New Hebrides, or Micronesia.

Cutting Our Losses: Policy Reform to Sustain Tropical Forest Resources. Charles V. Barber. World Resources Institute, 1709 New York Ave. N.W., Washington, District of Columbia 20006. (800) 822-0504. 1991. Focuses on the underlying economic social and political forces that drive forest conversation and exploitation.

Ecosystems Experiments. H. A. Mooney, et al., eds. John Wiley & Sons, Inc., 605 3rd Ave., New York, New York 10158-0012. (212) 850-6000. 1991. Explores the potential ecosystem experimentation as a tool for understanding and predicting changes in the biosphere. Areas investigated include deforestation, desertification, El

Nino phenomenon, acid rain, watersheds, wetlands, and aquatic and climatic changes.

Environment in Peril. Anthony B. Wolbarst, ed. Smithsonian Institution Press, 470 L'Enfant Plaza, No. 7100, Washington, District of Columbia 20560. (800) 782-4612. 1991. Brings together in one volume the primary concerns of eleven of the world's leaders in conservation, ecology and public policy. Broad environmental issues covered are: ozone depletion, overpopulation, global warming, thinning forests, extinction of species, spreading deserts, toxic chemicals, and various pollutants.

Global Forests. Roger A. Sedjo and Marion Clawson. Resources for the Future, 1616 P. St. N.W., Rm. 532, Washington, District of Columbia 20036. (202) 328-5086. 1988.

Keeping It Green: Tropical Forestry and the Mitigation of Global Warming. Mark C. Trexler. World Resources Institute, 1709 New York Ave. N.W., Washington, District of Columbia 20006. (800) 822-0504. 1991. Report links knowledge gained from past tropical forestry initiatives with expectations for their future effectiveness in the mitigation of global warming.

Magill's Survey of Science. Life Science Series. Frank N. Magill, ed. Salem Press, PO Box 50062, Pasadena, California 91105. 1991. Six volumes. Contents: v.1. A-Central and peripheral nervous system functions; v.2. Central metabolism regulation - eukaryotic transcriptional control; v.3. Positive and negative eukaryotic transcriptional control - mammalian hormones; v.4. Hormones and behavior - muscular contraction; v.5. Muscular contraction and relaxation - sexual reproduction in plants; v.6. Reproductive behavior and mating - X inactivation and the Lyon hypothesis.

The Next One Hundred Years: Shaping the Fate of Our Living Earth. Jonathan Weiner. Bantam Books, 666 5th Ave., New York, New York 10103. (212) 765-6500; (800) 223-6834. 1991. Explores the following issues: the greenhouse effect, deforestation, the destruction of the ozone layer, the human population explosion and the onset of mass extinctions.

Preserving the Global Environment: The Challenge of Shared Leadership. Jessica Tuchman Mathews, ed. World Resources Institute, 1709 New York Ave. N.W., Washington, District of Columbia 20006. (800) 822-0504. 1990. Includes findings on population growth, deforestation and the loss of biological diversity, the ozone layer, energy and climate change, economics, and other critical trends spell out new approaches to international cooperation and regulation in response to the shift from traditional security concerns to a focus on collective global security.

Public Policies and the Misuse of Forest Resources. Robert Repetto and Malcolm Gillis, eds. Cambridge University Press, 40 W. 20th St., New York, New York 10011. (212) 924-3900; (800) 227-0247. 1988. Case studies of forest policies in developing countries. Also deals with deforestation problems from the environmental point of view.

Saving the Tropical Forests. Judith Gradwohl and Russell Greenberg. Island Press, 1718 Connecticut Ave. N.W., Suite 300, Washington, District of Columbia 20009. (202) 232-7933. 1988. Sourcebook about the causes and effects of tropical deforestation, with case studies, examples of sustainable agriculture and forestry, and a section on the restoration of tropical rain forests.

Taking Stock: The Tropical Forestry Action Plan After Five Years. Robert Winterbottom. World Resources Institute, 1709 New York Ave. N.W., Washington, District of Columbia 20006. (800) 822-0504. 1990. Analyzes Tropical Forestry Action Plan's accomplishments and shortcomings, drawing on the biannual meetings of the TFAP Forestry Advisors' groups, assessments by FAO, various aid agencies, and by such organizations as the World Rainforest Movement, Friends of the Earth, and World Life Fund.

Trees of Life: Saving Tropical Forests and their Biological Wealth. Kenton Miller and Laura Tangley. World Resources Institute, 1709 New York Ave. N.W., Washington, District of Columbia 20006. (800) 822-0504. 1991. Explains what deforestation is doing to the global environment and why rainforest preservation is valid to human welfare around the world.

Tropical Rain Forests and the World Atmosphere. T. Ghillean. Westview Press, 5500 Central Ave., Boulder, Colorado 80301. (303) 444-3541. 1986. Deals with vegetation and climate in the tropics. Also describes the weather patterns in that part of the world.

Tropical Rainforest: A World Survey of Our Most Valuable Endangered Habitat With a Blueprint for its Survival. Arnold Newman. Facts on File, Inc., 460 Park Ave. S., New York, New York 10016. (212) 683-2244; (800) 322-8755. 1990. Considers threats to rain forests, including logging and slash and burn agricultural practices. Presents a variety of measures to preserve our valuable rain forests.

HANDBOOKS AND MANUALS

Forest Regeneration Manual. Mary L. Duryea. Kluwer Academic Publishers, 101 Philip Dr., Assinippi Park, Norwell, Massachusetts 02061. (617) 871-6600. 1991. Volume 36 in the series entitled Forestry Sciences.

ONLINE DATA BASES

BIOSIS Previews. BIOSIS, 2100 Arch St., Philadelphia, Pennsylvania 19103-1399. (215) 587-4800. Largest and most comprehensive database of research in the life sciences. Contains citations for nearly 9000 primary research journals, monographs, reviews, symposia, preliminary reports, semi-popular journals, selected institutional reports, government reports and research communications.

Cambridge Scientific Abstracts Life Science–CSAL. Cambridge Scientific Abstracts, 5161 River Rd., Bethesda, Maryland 20816. (301) 961-6750. Provides access to the following abstracting services: "Life Sciences Collection," "Aquatic Sciences and Fisheries Abstracts," "Oceanic Abstracts," and "Pollution Abstracts."

Enviro/Energyline Abstracts Plus. R. R. Bowker Co., 121 Chanlon Rd., New Providence, New Jersey 07974. (908) 464-6800.

Environmental Periodicals Bibliography. National Information Services Corp., Ste. 6, Wyman Towers, 3100 St. Paul St., Baltimore, Maryland 21218. (410)243-0797. Online version of abstract of same name.

Global Environmental Change Report. Cutter Information Corp., 37 Broadway, Arlington, Massachusetts 02174-5539. (617) 648-8700. Online access to environmental issues worldwide, including global warming, ozone depletion, deforestation, and acid rain. Online version of periodical of the same name.

Monthly Catalog of United States Government Publications. U.S. G.P.O., Supt. of Docs., PO Box 371954, Pittsburgh, Pennsylvania 15250-7954. (202) 512-0000.

National Technical Information Service. U.S. Department of Commerce, National Technical Information Service, Office of Data Base Services, 5285 Port Royal Rd., Springfield, Virginia 22161. (703) 487-4807. Bibliographic database of government sponsored research and technical reports.

SCISEARCH. Institute for Scientific Information, University City Science Center, 3501 Market St., Philadelphia, Pennsylvania 19104. (215) 386-0100.

PERIODICALS AND NEWSLETTERS

Arnoldia. Arnold Arboretum, Harvard University, Jamaica Plain, Massachusetts 02130-2795. (617) 524-1718. 1941-. Quarterly.

The Commonwealth Forestry Review. Commonwealth Forestry Association, c/o Oxford Forestry Institute, South Parks Rd., Oxford, England OX1 3RB. 1921-. Quarterly. Covers forestry practices.

Global Environmental Change Report. Cutter Information Corp., 37 Broadway, Arlington, Massachusetts 02174-5539. (617) 648-8700. Biweekly. Focus on global warming, ozone depletion, deforestation, and acid rain. Also available online.

International Environmental Affairs. University Press of New England, 17 1/2 Lebanon Street, Hanover, New Hampshire 03755. (603) 646-3340. Quarterly. Issues on management of natural resources.

Journal of Arboriculture. Society of Arboriculture, 303 W. University Ave., PO Box 908, Urbana, Illinois 61801. (217) 328-2032. 1975-. Monthly.

Journal of the Royal Society of New Zealand. The Royal Society of New Zealand, Wellington, New Zealand 1971-. Quarterly. Formed by the union of: Transactions of the Royal Society of New Zealand. Earth Sciences; Transactions of the Royal Society of New Zealand. General, and Biological Sciences.

Trees. Springer-Verlag, Heidelberger Platz, Berlin, Germany 030-8207-1. 1987-. Quarterly.

RESEARCH CENTERS AND INSTITUTES

U.S. Forest Service, Institute of Tropical Forestry. Call Box 25000, Rio Piedras, Puerto Rico 00928-2500. (809) 766-5335.

STATISTICS SOURCES

Environmental Data Compendium. OECD Publications and Information Center, 2001 L St., N.W., Suite 700, Washington, District of Columbia 20036. (202) 785-6323. 1989.

Environmental Indicators. OECD Publications and Information Center, 2001 L St., N.W., Suite 700, Washington, District of Columbia 20036. (202) 785-6323. 1991.

Environmental Quality. Council on Environmental Quality. U.S. G.P.O., Washington, District of Columbia 20401. (202) 512-0000. Annual.

The State of the Environment. OECD Publications and Information Center, 2001 L St., N.W., Suite 700, Washington, District of Columbia 20036. (202) 785-6323. 1991.

World Resources. World Resources Institute. 1709 New York Ave., N.W., Washington, District of Columbia 20006. (202) 638-6300. Annual. Statistical and textual analysis of world's natural resources and the effects of growth-caused environmental pollution.

TRADE ASSOCIATIONS AND PROFESSIONAL SOCIETIES

American Institute of Biological Sciences. 730 11th St., N.W., Washington, District of Columbia 20001-4521. (202) 628-1500.

DEGRADATION

See: FLOODS

DEHYDROGENATION

ABSTRACTING AND INDEXING SERVICES

General Science Index. H. W. Wilson Co., 950 University Ave., Bronx, New York 10452. 1978-. Monthly, also issued in annual cumulation. Cumulative subject index to English language periodicals in the subject fields of astronomy, botany, chemistry, earth science, environment and conservation, food and nutrition, genetics, mathematics, medicine and health, microbiology, oceanography, physics, physiology and zoology.

ENCYCLOPEDIAS AND DICTIONARIES

Encyclopedia of Chemical Processing and Design. John J. Mcketta and W. A. Cunningham. Marcel Dekker, Inc., 270 Madison Ave., New York, New York 10016. (212) 696-9000; (800) 228-1160. 1992. Thirty-eight volumes.

Kirk-Othmer Encyclopedia of Chemical Technology. J. I. Kroschwitz, ed. John Wiley & Sons, Inc., 605 3rd Ave., New York, New York 10158-0012. (212) 850-6000. 1992-. All articles in the new edition have been rewritten and updated adding new subjects such as biotechnology, computer topics, analytical techniques and instrumentation, environmental concerns, fuels and energy, inorganic and solid state chemistry; composite materials and material science in general, and pharmaceuticals. Also available online.

ONLINE DATA BASES

Kirk-Othmer Encyclopedia of Chemical Technology. John Wiley & Sons, Inc., 605 3rd Ave., 5th Floor, New York, New York 10158. (212) 850-6000. Online version of the publication of the same name.

DEICING AGENTS

ABSTRACTING AND INDEXING SERVICES

Applied Science and Technology Index. H.W. Wilson Co., 950 University Ave., Bronx, New York 10452. (800) 367-6770. Formerly Industrial Arts Index.

Environment Abstracts. Bowker A & I Publishing, 121 Chanlon Rd., New Providence, New Jersey 07974. (908) 464-6800. 1974-.

Environment Index. Environment Information Center, Index Research Department, 124 E. 39th St., New York, New York 10016. 1971-. Annual.

Environmental Information Connection–EIC. Planning Information Program, Dept. of Urban and Regional Planning, University of Illinois, 1003 West Nevada, Urbana, Illinois 61801. (217) 333-1369. Also available online.

Environmental Periodicals Bibliography. Environmental Studies Institute, International Academy at Santa Barbara, 800 Garden St., Suite D, Santa Barbara, California 93101. (805) 965-5010. Also available online.

General Science Index. H. W. Wilson Co., 950 University Ave., Bronx, New York 10452. 1978-. Monthly, also issued in annual cumulation. Cumulative subject index to English language periodicals in the subject fields of astronomy, botany, chemistry, earth science, environment and conservation, food and nutrition, genetics, mathematics, medicine and health, microbiology, oceanography, physics, physiology and zoology.

BIBLIOGRAPHIES

EPA Publications Bibliography. U.S. Environmental Protection Agency, Library Systems Branch, 401 M St., SW, Washington, District of Columbia 20460. (202) 260-2090. Quarterly.

ENCYCLOPEDIAS AND DICTIONARIES

Encyclopedia of Physical Science and Technology. Robert A. Meyers, ed. Academic Press, c/o Harcourt Brace Jovanovich Inc., 6277 Sea Harbor Dr., Orlando, Florida 32887. (800) 346-8648. Dictionary of engineering, technology and physical sciences.

GENERAL WORKS

Calcium Magnesium Acetate: An Emerging Bulk Chemical for Environmental Applications. D.L. Wise. Elsevier Science Publishing Co., 655 Avenue of the Americas, New York, New York 10010. (212) 989-5800. 1991.

Curtailing Usage of De-icing Agents in Winter Maintenance: Report. OECD Scientific Expert Group. OECD Publications and Information Centre, 2, rue Andre-Pascal, Paris Cedex 16, France F-75775. (1) 4524 8200. 1989. Discusses snow and ice control over the roads using deicing chemicals.

An Economic Analysis of the Environmental Impact of Highway Deicing. Donald M. Murray and Ulrich F. W. Ernst. U.S. Environmental Protection Agency, Office of Research and Development, Municipal Environmental Laboratory, 401 M St., SW, Washington, District of Columbia 20460. (202) 260-2090. 1976.

Environmental Monitoring and Evaluation of Calcium Magnesium Acetate. Richard Ray Horner. Transportation Research Board, National Research Council, 2101 Constitution Ave. NW, Washington, District of Columbia 20418. 1988. Deicing chemicals and snow and ice control of roads.

Survey of Alternatives to the Use of Chlorides for Highway Deicing. Joseph A. Zenewitz. Department of Transportation, Federal Highway Administration, National Technical Information Service, 5285 Port Royal Rd., Springfield, Virginia 22161. (703) 487-4650. 1977.

HANDBOOKS AND MANUALS

Handbook of Highway Engineering. Robert F. Baker, ed. R. E. Krieger Publishing Co., 115 5th Ave., New York, New York 10003. (212) 254-3232. 1982. Provides reference data on the application of technology to highway transportation.

ONLINE DATA BASES

Enviro/Energyline Abstracts Plus. R. R. Bowker Co., 121 Chanlon Rd., New Providence, New Jersey 07974. (908) 464-6800.

Environmental Periodicals Bibliography. National Information Services Corp., Ste. 6, Wyman Towers, 3100 St. Paul St., Baltimore, Maryland 21218. (410)243-0797. Online version of abstract of same name.

PERIODICALS AND NEWSLETTERS

Highways and Transportation: Journal of the Institution of Highways and Transportation & HTTA. The Institution of Highways and Transportation, 3 Lygon Place, Elbury St., London, England SW1 0JS. (01) 730-5245. 1983-. Monthly. Information on roads and traffic for highway and transportation engineers.

Journal of the Transportation Research Forum. Transportation Research Forum, 103 S. Howard St., Box 405, Oxford, Indiana 47971. 1962-. Annual. Continues Transportation Research Forum Proceedings.

DELAWARE ENVIRONMENTAL AGENCIES

GENERAL WORKS

Delaware's Environmental Legacy: Shaping Tomorrow's Environment Today: Report to the Governor and the People of Delaware. Delaware Department of Natural Resources and Environmental Control, Information and Education Section, Office of the Secretary, PO Box 1401, Dover, Delaware 19903. (302) 739-4506. 1988.

GOVERNMENTAL ORGANIZATIONS

Delaware River Basin Commission. 1100 L St., N.W., Room 5113, Washington, District of Columbia 20240. (202) 343-5761.

Department of Agriculture: Pesticide Registration. Pesticide Compliance Supervisor, 2320 South Dupont Highway, Dover, Delaware 19901. (302) 736-4817.

Department of Labor: Occupational Safety. Director, Division of Industrial Affairs, 820 North French St., Wilmington, Delaware 19801. (302) 571-2877.

Department of Natural Resources and Environmental Control: Air Quality. Secretary, 89 Kings Highway, P.O. Box 1401, Dover, Delaware 19903. (302) 739-4764.

Department of Natural Resources and Environmental Control: Coastal Zone Management. Secretary, 89 Kings Highway, Dover, Delaware 19903. (302) 736-4403.

Department of Natural Resources and Environmental Control: Emergency Preparedness and Community Right-to-Know. Chief Program Administrator, Air Resource Section, PO Box 1401, Dover, Delaware 19903. (302) 736-4791.

Department of Natural Resources and Environmental Control: Environmental Protection. Secretary, 89 Kings Highway, Box 1401, Dover, Delaware 19903. (302) 736-4403.

Division of Water Resources: Groundwater Management. Manager, Groundwater Management Section, 89 Kings Highway, Dover, Delaware 19901. (302) 736-5722.

Natural Resources and Environmental Control Department: Fish and Wildlife. Director, Division of Fish and Wildlife, 89 Kings Highway, Box 1401, Dover, Delaware 19903. (302) 739-5295.

Natural Resources and Environmental Control Department: Hazardous Waste Management. Administrator, Waste Management Section, 89 Kings Highway, Box 1401, Dover, Delaware 19903. (302) 736-4781.

Natural Resources and Environmental Control Department: Natural Resources. Secretary, 89 Kings Highway, Box 1401, Dover, Delaware 19903. (302) 736-4403.

Natural Resources and Environmental Control Department: Underground Storage Tanks. Administrator, UST Office, Division of Air and Waste Management, 89 Kings Highway, Dover, Delaware 19903. (302) 736-4764.

Natural Resources and Environmental Control Department: Water Quality. Director, Soil and Water Conservation Division, 89 Kings Highway, Box 1401, Dover, Delaware 19903. (302) 736-4764.

Solid Waste Authority: Solid Waste Management. General Manager, PO Box 455, Dover, Delaware 19903. (302) 736-5361.

U.S. EPA Region 3: Pollution Prevention. Program Manager, 841 Chestnut St., Philadelphia, Pennsylvania 19107. (215) 597-9800.

DEMOGRAPHY

See also: POPULATION

ABSTRACTING AND INDEXING SERVICES

Ecology Abstracts. Cambridge Scientific Abstracts, 5161 River Rd., Bethesda, Maryland 20816. (301) 961-6750. Monthly.

General Science Index. H. W. Wilson Co., 950 University Ave., Bronx, New York 10452. 1978-. Monthly, also issued in annual cumulation. Cumulative subject index to English language periodicals in the subject fields of astronomy, botany, chemistry, earth science, environment and conservation, food and nutrition, genetics, mathematics, medicine and health, microbiology, oceanography, physics, physiology and zoology.

Science Citation Index. Institute for Scientific Information, 3501 Market St., Philadelphia, Pennsylvania 19104. 1961-.

BIBLIOGRAPHIES

A Bibliographic Guide to Population Geography. Wilbur Zelinsky. University of Chicago Press, 5801 Ellis Ave., 4th Fl., Chicago, Illinois 60637. (312) 702-7700; (800) 621-2736. 1976.

Current Contents. Agriculture, Biology and Environmental Sciences. Institute for Scientific Information, 3501 Market St., Philadelphia, Pennsylvania 19104. (800) 523-1857. 1973-. Previous title: Current Contents. Agricultural, Food & Veterinary Sciences. Gives the table of contents of periodicals in the fields of agriculture, biology, environmental and related areas.

Population Education: Sources and Resources. Judith Seltzer and John Robinson. Population Reference Bureau, 777 14th St. N.W., Washington, District of Columbia 20005. (202) 639-8040. 1979.

A Retrospective Bibliography of American Demographic History from Colonial Times to 1983. David R. Gerhan and Robert V. Wells. Greenwood Publishing Group, Inc., 88 Post Rd. W., Box 5007, Westport, Connecticut 06881. (203) 226-3571. 1989.

Teaching Population Geography: An Interdisciplinary Ecological Approach. George Warren Carey. Teachers College Pr., 1234 Amsterdam Ave., New York, New York 10027. (212) 678-3929. 1969. Bibliography on human ecology and demography.

ENCYCLOPEDIAS AND DICTIONARIES

Dictionary of Demography: Terms, Concepts and Institutions. William Petersen and Renee Petersen. Greenwood Publishing Group, Inc., 88 Post Rd. W., PO Box 5007, Westport, Connecticut 06881. (212) 226-3571. 1986. 2 vols.

McGraw-Hill Encyclopedia of Environmental Science. Sybil P. Parker. McGraw-Hill Science & Engineering Books, 11 W. 19th St., New York, New York 10011. (212) 337-6010. 1980. Covers ecology, man's influence on nature, and environmental protection.

McGraw-Hill Encyclopedia of Science and Technology. McGraw-Hill, 1221 Avenue of the Americas, New York, New York 10020. (212) 512-2000 or (800) 262-4729. 1992. Seventh edition. Issued in multiple volumes including index. Includes all science and technology broad subject areas.

GENERAL WORKS

Demography as an Interdiscipline. J. Mayone Stycos, ed. Transaction Pub., Rutgers University, New Brunswick, New Jersey 08903. (201) 932-2280. 1989. Deals with social sciences and the population problem; fertility transition: Europe and the third world compared; migration and social structure; proximate determination of fertility and mortality.

Distributional Aspects of Human Fertility: A Global Comparative Study. Wolfgang Lutz. Academic Press, c/o Harcourt Brace Jovanovich Inc., 6277 Sea Harbor Dr.,

Orlando, Florida 32887. (800) 346-8648. 1989. Studies in population dealing with family characteristics, population growth, birth intervals, fertility and maternal age.

Magill's Survey of Science. Life Science Series. Frank N. Magill, ed. Salem Press, PO Box 50062, Pasadena, California 91105. 1991. Six volumes. Contents: v.1. A-Central and peripheral nervous system functions; v.2. Central metabolism regulation - eukaryotic transcriptional control; v.3. Positive and negative eukaryotic transcriptional control - mammalian hormones; v.4. Hormones and behavior - muscular contraction; v.5. Muscular contraction and relaxation - sexual reproduction in plants; v.6. Reproductive behavior and mating - X inactivation and the Lyon hypothesis.

Stochastic Processes in Demography and Applications. Suddhendu Biswas. John Wiley & Sons, Inc., 605 3rd Ave., New York, New York 10158-0012. (212) 850-6000. 1989. Describes statistical methods applied in demography.

HANDBOOKS AND MANUALS

Demography for Agricultural Planners. D. S. Baldwin. Food and Agriculture Organization of the United Nations, 4611-F, Assembly Dr., Lanham, Maryland 20706-4391. (301) 459-7666; (800) 274-4888. 1975. Deals with the rural population demography and agricultural economics.

Population Growth Estimation: A Handbook of Vital Statistics Measurement. Eli Samplin Marks. Population Council, 1 Dag Hammarskjold Plaza, New York, New York 10017. (212) 644-1300. 1974. Handbook covers population forecasting and other vital statistics.

ONLINE DATA BASES

Monthly Catalog of United States Government Publications. U.S. G.P.O., Supt. of Docs., PO Box 371954, Pittsburgh, Pennsylvania 15250-7954. (202) 512-0000.

National Technical Information Service. U.S. Department of Commerce, National Technical Information Service, Office of Data Base Services, 5285 Port Royal Rd., Springfield, Virginia 22161. (703) 487-4807. Bibliographic database of government sponsored research and technical reports.

SCISEARCH. Institute for Scientific Information, University City Science Center, 3501 Market St., Philadelphia, Pennsylvania 19104. (215) 386-0100.

PERIODICALS AND NEWSLETTERS

European Journal of Population. North-Holland, 655 Avenue of the Americas, New York, New York 10010. (212) 989-5800. 1985-. Quarterly. Published under the auspices of the European Association for Population Studies.

USSR Report. Human Resources. Foreign Broadcast Information Service. National Technical Information Service, 5285 Port Royal Rd., Springfield, Virginia 22161. (703) 487-4650. 1980-. Irregular.

RESEARCH CENTERS AND INSTITUTES

Population Institute. 110 Maryland Ave., N.E., Washington, District of Columbia 20002. (202) 544-3300.

TRADE ASSOCIATIONS AND PROFESSIONAL SOCIETIES

American Institute of Biological Sciences. 730 11th St., N.W., Washington, District of Columbia 20001-4521. (202) 628-1500.

Population-Environment Balance. 1325 G St., N.W., Suite 1003, Washington, District of Columbia 20005. (202) 879-3000.

DENDROCHRONOLOGY

See: TREE RINGS

DENITRIFICATION

ABSTRACTING AND INDEXING SERVICES

ASFA Aquaculture Abstracts. Cambridge Scientific Abstracts, Inc., 5161 River Rd., Bethesda, Maryland 20816. (301) 961-6750. 1984.

Biological Abstracts. BIOSIS, 2100 Arch St., Philadelphia, Pennsylvania 19103-1399. (215) 587-4800. 1927-.

Biological and Agricultural Index. H.W. Wilson Co., 950 University Ave., Bronx, New York 10452. (800) 367-6770. 1916-. Monthly.

Ecological Abstracts. Geo Abstracts Ltd. Elsevier Applied Science, Crown House, Linton Rd., Barking, England IG 11 8JU. 1974-. Derived from over 600 leading ecological and environmental journals, plus books, conference proceedings, reports and theses.

Ecology Abstracts. Cambridge Scientific Abstracts, 5161 River Rd., Bethesda, Maryland 20816. (301) 961-6750. Monthly.

General Science Index. H. W. Wilson Co., 950 University Ave., Bronx, New York 10452. 1978-. Monthly, also issued in annual cumulation. Cumulative subject index to English language periodicals in the subject fields of astronomy, botany, chemistry, earth science, environment and conservation, food and nutrition, genetics, mathematics, medicine and health, microbiology, oceanography, physics, physiology and zoology.

Index to Scientific Book Contents. Institute for Scientific Information, 3501 Market St., Philadelphia, Pennsylvania 19104. (800) 523-1857. 1985-. Annual. Gives contents of science books published.

Pollution Abstracts. Cambridge Scientific Abstracts, 5161 River Rd., Bethesda, Maryland 20816. (301) 961-6750. Six/year. Indexes worldwide technical literature on environmental pollution. Covers air pollution, marine and freshwater pollution, sewage and wastewater treatment, waste management, toxicology and health, noise pollution, radiation, land pollution, and environmental policies, programs, legislation, and education. Also available online.

Science Citation Index. Institute for Scientific Information, 3501 Market St., Philadelphia, Pennsylvania 19104. 1961-.

Soils and Fertilizers. C. A. B. International, 845 North Park Ave., Tucson, Arizona 85719. (602) 621-7897 or (800) 528-4841. 1937-. Monthly. Focuses on soil chemistry, soil physics, soil biology, soil fertility, soil management, soil classification, soil formation, soil conservation, land reclamation, irrigation and damage, fertilizer technology, fertilizer use, plant nutrition, plant water relations, and environmental aspects.

BIBLIOGRAPHIES

Current Contents. Agriculture, Biology and Environmental Sciences. Institute for Scientific Information, 3501 Market St., Philadelphia, Pennsylvania 19104. (800) 523-1857. 1973-. Previous title: Current Contents. Agricultural, Food & Veterinary Sciences. Gives the table of contents of periodicals in the fields of agriculture, biology, environmental and related areas.

ENCYCLOPEDIAS AND DICTIONARIES

Cambridge Dictionary of Biology. Peter M. B. Walker. Cambridge University Press, 40 W. 20th St., New York, New York 10011. (212) 924-3900 or (800) 227-0247. 1989. Includes 10,000 terms in zoology, botany, biochemistry, molecular biology and genetics. Previously published under the title Chambers Biology Dictionary.

A Concise Dictionary of Biology. Elizabeth Martin, ed. Oxford University Press, 200 Madison Ave., New York, New York 10016. (212) 679-7300 or (800) 334-4249. 1990. New edition. Derived from the Concise Science Dictionary, published in 1984.

McGraw-Hill Encyclopedia of Science and Technology. McGraw-Hill, 1221 Avenue of the Americas, New York, New York 10020. (212) 512-2000 or (800) 262-4729. 1992. Seventh edition. Issued in multiple volumes including index. Includes all science and technology broad subject areas.

Van Nostrand's Scientific Encyclopedia. Glenn D. Considine, ed. Van Nostrand Reinhold, 115 5th Ave., New York, New York 10003. (212) 254-3232. 1983. Sixth edition. Includes all broad subject areas in science.

GENERAL WORKS

Dentrification in Soil and Sediment. Niels Peter Revsbech and Jan Sorensen, eds. Plenum Press, 233 Spring St., New York, New York 10013-1578. (212) 620-8000; (800) 221-9369. 1991. The process, its measurement, and its significance are analyzed in 20 papers from a June 1989 symposium in Ahrus, Denmark. Topics included are: biochemistry, genetics, ecophysiology, and the emission of nitrogen-oxygen compounds.

The Impact of Denitrification on In-Stream Dissolved Oxygen Concentration. Ayoub V. Torkian. University of Texas Press, PO Box 7819, Austin, Texas 78713-7819. (512) 471-7233 or (800) 252-3206. 1989. Thesis submitted to University of Texas at Dallas, 1989. Describes water purification by nitrogen removal.

ONLINE DATA BASES

BIOSIS Previews. BIOSIS, 2100 Arch St., Philadelphia, Pennsylvania 19103-1399. (215) 587-4800. Largest and most comprehensive database of research in the life sciences. Contains citations for nearly 9000 primary research journals, monographs, reviews, symposia, preliminary reports, semi-popular journals, selected institutional reports, government reports and research communications.

Monthly Catalog of United States Government Publications. U.S. G.P.O., Supt. of Docs., PO Box 371954, Pittsburgh, Pennsylvania 15250-7954. (202) 512-0000.

National Technical Information Service. U.S. Department of Commerce, National Technical Information Service, Office of Data Base Services, 5285 Port Royal Rd., Springfield, Virginia 22161. (703) 487-4807. Bibliographic database of government sponsored research and technical reports.

SCISEARCH. Institute for Scientific Information, University City Science Center, 3501 Market St., Philadelphia, Pennsylvania 19104. (215) 386-0100.

PERIODICALS AND NEWSLETTERS

Agriculture, Ecosystems & Environment. Elsevier Science Publishing Co., 655 Avenue of the Americas, New York, New York 10010. (212) 989-5800. Eight times a year. This journal is concerned with the interaction of methods of agricultural production, ecosystems and the environment.

Applied Microbiology and Biotechnology. Springer International, 44 Hartz Way, Seacaucus, New Jersey 07094. (201) 348-4033. Six times a year. Covers biotechnology, biochemical engineering, applied genetics and regulation, applied microbial and cell physiology, food biotechnology, and environmental biotechnology.

Biology and Fertility of Soils. Springer International, 44 Hartz Way, Seacaucus, New Jersey 07094. (201) 348-4033. Quarterly. Biological functions, processes and interactions in soils, agriculture, deforestation and industrialization.

Biotechnology and Bioengineering. John Wiley & Sons, Inc., 605 3rd Ave., New York, New York 10158. (212) 850-6000. Monthly. Aerobic and anaerobic processes, systems involving biofilms, algal systems, detoxification and bioremediation and genetic aspects, biosensors, and cellular systems.

Communications in Soil Science and Plant Analysis. M. Dekker, 270 Madison Ave., New York, New York 10016. (212) 696-9000; (800) 228-1160. 1970-.

Environmental Pollution. Applied Science Publications, PO Box 5399, New York, New York 10163. (718) 756-6440. 1987-.

Fertilizer Research: An International Journal on Fertilizer Use and Technology. Kluwer Academic Publishers, 101 Philip Dr., Assinippi Park, Norwell, Massachusetts 02061. (617) 871-6600. Monthly. Soils, soil fertility, soil chemistry, crop and animal production and husbandry, crop quality and environment.

The Great Basin Naturalist. Brigham Young University, 290 Life Science Museum, Provo, Utah 84602. (801) 378-5053.

International Journal of Plant Nutrition, Plant Chemistry, Soil Microbiology and Soil-Bourne Plant Diseases. Kluwer Academic Publishers, 101 Philip Dr., Assinippi Park, Norwell, Massachusetts 02061. (617) 871-6600. 1948-.

The Journal of Applied Bacteriology. Academic Press, c/o Harcourt Brace Jovanovich Inc., 6277 Sea Harbor Dr., Orlando, Florida 32887. (800) 346-8648. Monthly. Deals with agricultural, biological and environmental aspects of bacteriology.

Journal of Environmental Quality. American Society of Agronomy, 677 S. Segoe Rd., Madison, Wisconsin 53711-1086. (608) 273-8080. 1972-. Quarterly. Reports and brief reviews of agricultural ecology, environmental engineering and pollution.

Journal of General Microbiology. Society for General Microbiology, Harvest House, 62 London Rd., Reading, England RG1 5AS.

Limnology and Oceanography. American Society of Limnology and Oceanography, Inc., PO Box 1897, Lawrence, Kansas 66044-8897. (913) 843-1221. Topics in aquatic disciplines.

Research Journal of the Water Pollution Control Federation. Water Pollution Control Federation, 601 Wythe St., Alexandria, Virginia 22314-1994. (800) 556-8700. Bimonthly. Covers area water pollution, sewage and sewage treatment.

Soil Biology and Biochemistry. Pergamon Microforms International, Inc., Fairview Park, Elmsford, New York 10523. (914) 592-7720. Eight times a year. Soil biology, soil biochemistry, nitrogen fixation, nitrogenase activity, sampling microorganisms in soil, soil compaction, and nutrient release in soils.

Water Research. International Association on Water Pollution Research and Control. Pergamon Microforms International, Inc., Fairview Park, Elmsford, New York 10523. (914) 592-7720. 1966-. Monthly. Covers all aspects of the pollution of marine and fresh water and the management of water quality as well as water resources.

DENSITY

See also: POPULATION

ABSTRACTING AND INDEXING SERVICES

Environment Abstracts. Bowker A & I Publishing, 121 Chanlon Rd., New Providence, New Jersey 07974. (908) 464-6800. 1974-.

Environment Index. Environment Information Center, Index Research Department, 124 E. 39th St., New York, New York 10016. 1971-. Annual.

Environmental Information Connection–EIC. Planning Information Program, Dept. of Urban and Regional Planning, University of Illinois, 1003 West Nevada, Urbana, Illinois 61801. (217) 333-1369. Also available online.

Environmental Periodicals Bibliography. Environmental Studies Institute, International Academy at Santa Barbara, 800 Garden St., Suite D, Santa Barbara, California 93101. (805) 965-5010. Also available online.

General Science Index. H. W. Wilson Co., 950 University Ave., Bronx, New York 10452. 1978-. Monthly, also issued in annual cumulation. Cumulative subject index to English language periodicals in the subject fields of astronomy, botany, chemistry, earth science, environment and conservation, food and nutrition, genetics, mathematics, medicine and health, microbiology, oceanography, physics, physiology and zoology.

Science Citation Index. Institute for Scientific Information, 3501 Market St., Philadelphia, Pennsylvania 19104. 1961-.

BIBLIOGRAPHIES

EPA Publications Bibliography. U.S. Environmental Protection Agency, Library Systems Branch, 401 M St., SW, Washington, District of Columbia 20460. (202) 260-2090. Quarterly.

ONLINE DATA BASES

Enviro/Energyline Abstracts Plus. R. R. Bowker Co., 121 Chanlon Rd., New Providence, New Jersey 07974. (908) 464-6800.

Environmental Periodicals Bibliography. National Information Services Corp., Ste. 6, Wyman Towers, 3100 St. Paul St., Baltimore, Maryland 21218. (410)243-0797. Online version of abstract of same name.

SCISEARCH. Institute for Scientific Information, University City Science Center, 3501 Market St., Philadelphia, Pennsylvania 19104. (215) 386-0100.

DEOXYNIVALENOL

ABSTRACTING AND INDEXING SERVICES

Biological Abstracts. BIOSIS, 2100 Arch St., Philadelphia, Pennsylvania 19103-1399. (215) 587-4800. 1927-.

ONLINE DATA BASES

BIOSIS Previews. BIOSIS, 2100 Arch St., Philadelphia, Pennsylvania 19103-1399. (215) 587-4800. Largest and most comprehensive database of research in the life sciences. Contains citations for nearly 9000 primary research journals, monographs, reviews, symposia, preliminary reports, semi-popular journals, selected institutional reports, government reports and research communications.

Chemical Abstracts Chemical Name Directory-CHEMNAME. Chemical Abstracts Service, 2540 Olentangy River Rd., P.O. Box 3012, Columbus, Ohio 43210. (800) 848-6533 or (614) 421-3600. Listing of chemical substances in a dictionary type file. The Chemical Abstracts (CAS) Registry Number, molecular formula, Chemical Abstracts (CA) Substance Index Name, available synonyms, ring data and other chemical substance information is given for each entry.

SCISEARCH. Institute for Scientific Information, University City Science Center, 3501 Market St., Philadelphia, Pennsylvania 19104. (215) 386-0100.

DEPOSIT LAWS
See: RECYCLING (WASTE, ETC.)

DEPOSITION
See: WATER ANALYSIS

DERMAL TOXICITY

GENERAL WORKS

Dermatotoxicology. Francis N. Marzulli and Howard I. Maibach, eds. Hemisphere Publishing Co., 79 Madison Ave., Suite 1110, New York, New York 10016. (212) 725-1999; (800) 821-8312. 1991. 4th ed. Provides information on theoretical aspects and practical test methods, including both in vitro and in vivo approaches. Pays attention to the worldwide movement for the development of suitable alternatives to animals when feasible.

ONLINE DATA BASES

Dermal Absorption. U.S. Environmental Protection Agency, Office of Pesticides and Toxic Substances, 401 M St., SW, Washington, District of Columbia 20460. (202) 260-2090. Toxic effects, absorption, distribution, metabolism, and excretion relation to the dermal absorption of 655 chemicals.

DESALINATION

See also: DIALYSIS; DISTILLATION; OSMOSIS; WATER POLLUTION; WATER RESOURCES

ABSTRACTING AND INDEXING SERVICES

Abstracts of Air and Water Conservation Literature. American Petroleum Institute. Central Abstracting and Indexing Service, 275 Madison Avenue, New York, New York 10016. 1972.

Applied Science and Technology Index. H.W. Wilson Co., 950 University Ave., Bronx, New York 10452. (800) 367-6770. Formerly Industrial Arts Index.

Aqualine Abstracts. Water Research Centre. c/o Pergamon Microforms International, Inc., Fairview Park, Elmsford, New York 10523. (914) 592-7720. 1927-. Contains some 8,000 records annually on water and wastewater technology. Covers all aspects of water, wastewater, associated engineering services and the aquatic environment. Over 600 periodicals, as well as books, reports and conference proceedings and other publications from water related institutions worldwide are scanned. Also available online.

Chemical Abstracts. Chemical Abstracts Service, 2540 Olentangy River Rd., PO Box 3012, Columbus, Ohio 43210. (800) 848-6533. 1907-.

Desalination Abstracts. National Center for Scientific and Technological Information, PO Box 20125, Tel-Aviv, Israel 1966-. Quarterly.

Ecological Abstracts. Geo Abstracts Ltd. Elsevier Applied Science, Crown House, Linton Rd., Barking, England IG 11 8JU. 1974-. Derived from over 600 leading ecological and environmental journals, plus books, conference proceedings, reports and theses.

Engineering Index. The Engineering Index Inc., 345 E. 47th St., New York, New York 10017. 1962-.

Environment Abstracts. Bowker A & I Publishing, 121 Chanlon Rd., New Providence, New Jersey 07974. (908) 464-6800. 1974-.

Environment Index. Environment Information Center, Index Research Department, 124 E. 39th St., New York, New York 10016. 1971-. Annual.

Environmental Information Connection–EIC. Planning Information Program, Dept. of Urban and Regional Planning, University of Illinois, 1003 West Nevada, Urbana, Illinois 61801. (217) 333-1369. Also available online.

Environmental Periodicals Bibliography. Environmental Studies Institute, International Academy at Santa Barbara, 800 Garden St., Suite D, Santa Barbara, California 93101. (805) 965-5010. Also available online.

General Science Index. H. W. Wilson Co., 950 University Ave., Bronx, New York 10452. 1978-. Monthly, also issued in annual cumulation. Cumulative subject index to English language periodicals in the subject fields of astronomy, botany, chemistry, earth science, environment and conservation, food and nutrition, genetics, mathematics, medicine and health, microbiology, oceanography, physics, physiology and zoology.

Index to Scientific Book Contents. Institute for Scientific Information, 3501 Market St., Philadelphia, Pennsylvania 19104. (800) 523-1857. 1985-. Annual. Gives contents of science books published.

Oceanic Abstracts. UMI Data Courier, 620 S. 3rd St., Louisville, Kentucky 40202. (800) 626-2823. Formerly: Oceanic Index and Oceanic Citation Journal.

Pollution Abstracts. Cambridge Scientific Abstracts, 5161 River Rd., Bethesda, Maryland 20816. (301) 961-6750. Six/year. Indexes worldwide technical literature on environmental pollution. Covers air pollution, marine and freshwater pollution, sewage and wastewater treatment, waste management, toxicology and health, noise pollution, radiation, land pollution, and environmental policies, programs, legislation, and education. Also available online.

Science Citation Index. Institute for Scientific Information, 3501 Market St., Philadelphia, Pennsylvania 19104. 1961-.

BIBLIOGRAPHIES

Current Contents. Agriculture, Biology and Environmental Sciences. Institute for Scientific Information, 3501 Market St., Philadelphia, Pennsylvania 19104. (800) 523-1857. 1973-. Previous title: Current Contents. Agricultural, Food & Veterinary Sciences. Gives the table of contents of periodicals in the fields of agriculture, biology, environmental and related areas.

Desalination Technology. Vance Bibliographies, PO Box 229, 112 N. Charter St., Monticello, Illinois 61856. (217) 762-3831. 1981.

Directory of Published Proceedings. Interdok Corp., 173 Halstead Ave., Harrison, New York 10528. (914) 835-3506. 1990. Monthly. This is a listing of published proceedings including the series SEMTE (Science/Medicine/Engineering/Technology) and the series SSH (Social Science/Humanities).

EPA Publications Bibliography. U.S. Environmental Protection Agency, Library Systems Branch, 401 M St., SW,

Washington, District of Columbia 20460. (202) 260-2090. Quarterly.

Salt, Evaporites, and Brines: An Annotated Bibliography. Vivian S. Hall and Mary R. Spencer. Oryx Press, 4041 N. Central Ave., #700, Phoenix, Arizona 85012. (602) 265-2651; (800) 279-6799. 1984.

DIRECTORIES

Desalination Directory: Desalination and Water Purification. Elsevier Science Publishing Co., 655 Avenue of the Americas, New York, New York 10010. (212) 989-5800. 1981-.

ENCYCLOPEDIAS AND DICTIONARIES

Dictionary of Environmental Engineering and Related Sciences: English-Spanish, Spanish-English. Jose T. Villate. Ediciones Universal, 3090 SW 8th St., Miami, Florida 33135. (305) 642-3355. 1979.

Encyclopedia of Chemical Processing and Design. John J. Mcketta and W. A. Cunningham. Marcel Dekker, Inc., 270 Madison Ave., New York, New York 10016. (212) 696-9000; (800) 228-1160. 1992. Thirty-eight volumes.

Encyclopedia of Environmental Science and Engineering. J.R. Pfafflin. Gordon and Breach Science Publishers, Inc., 270 8th Ave., New York, New York 10011. (212) 206-8900. 1992.

The Encyclopedia of Geochemistry and Environmental Sciences. Rhodes Whitmore Fairbridge. Van Nostrand Reinhold Co., 115 5th Ave., New York, New York 10003. (212) 254-3232. 1972.

Encyclopedia of Physical Science and Technology. Robert A. Meyers, ed. Academic Press, c/o Harcourt Brace Jovanovich Inc., 6277 Sea Harbor Dr., Orlando, Florida 32887. (800) 346-8648. Dictionary of engineering, technology and physical sciences.

English-Russian Dictionary of Environmental Protection: About 14,000 Terms. E.L. Milovanov. Pergamon Microforms International, Inc., Fairview Park, Elmsford, New York 10523. (914) 592-7720. 1981.

Kirk-Othmer Encyclopedia of Chemical Technology. J. I. Kroschwitz, ed. John Wiley & Sons, Inc., 605 3rd Ave., New York, New York 10158-0012. (212) 850-6000. 1992-. All articles in the new edition have been rewritten and updated adding new subjects such as biotechnology, computer topics, analytical techniques and instrumentation, environmental concerns, fuels and energy, inorganic and solid state chemistry; composite materials and material science in general, and pharmaceuticals. Also available online.

McGraw-Hill Encyclopedia of Science and Technology. McGraw-Hill, 1221 Avenue of the Americas, New York, New York 10020. (212) 512-2000 or (800) 262-4729. 1992. Seventh edition. Issued in multiple volumes including index. Includes all science and technology broad subject areas.

Van Nostrand's Scientific Encyclopedia. Glenn D. Considine, ed. Van Nostrand Reinhold, 115 5th Ave., New York, New York 10003. (212) 254-3232. 1983. Sixth edition. Includes all broad subject areas in science.

The Water Encyclopedia. Lewis Publishers, 2000 Corporate Blvd. N.W., Boca Raton, Florida 33431. (800) 272-7737. 1990. 2d ed. Includes groundwater contamination, drinking water, floods, waterborne diseases, global warming, climate change, irrigation, water agencies and organizations, precipitation, oceans and seas, and river, lakes and waterfalls.

GENERAL WORKS

Biological Effects of Effluent From a Desalination Plant at Key West, Florida. William D. Clarke, et al. Federal Water Quality Administration, U.S. Dept. of the Interior, 1849 C St. NW, Washington, District of Columbia 20240. (202) 208-3171. 1970.

Desalination and Water Re-Use. Miriam Balaban, ed. Institution of Chemical Engineers, c/o Hemisphere Pub., 1900 Frost Rd., Suite 101, Bristol, Pennsylvania 19007-1598. (215) 785-5800. 1991. Four volumes. Includes the papers presented at a four-day symposium organized by the Institution of Chemical Engineers (UK) on behalf of the European Federation of Chemical Engineers Working Parties on Desalination and Water Technology and the Membrane Society.

Desalination Materials Manual. Dow Chemical Company. Office of Water Research and Technology, U.S. Dept. of the Interior, Washington, District of Columbia 20240. 1975.

Disposal of Brines Produced in Renovation of Municipal Wastewater. Burns and Roe. Federal Water Quality Administration, U.S. Dept. of the Interior, 1849 C St. NW, Washington, District of Columbia 20240. (202) 208-3171. 1970.

Saline Water Processing: Desalination and Treatment of Seawater, Brackish Water, and Industrial Waste Water. Hans-Gunter Heitmann, ed. VCH Publishers, 303 NW 12th Ave., Deerfield Beach, Florida 33442-1788. (305) 428-5566. 1990. Desalination and treatment of seawater, brackish water, and industrial waste water.

HANDBOOKS AND MANUALS

Desalination Processes and Multistage Flash Distillation Practice. Arshad Hassan Khan. Elsevier Science Publishing Co., 655 Avenue of the Americas, New York, New York 10010. (212) 984-5800. 1986. Saline water conservation through flash distillation process.

Desalting Handbook for Planners. Catalytic Inc. U.S. Department of the Interior, Office of Water Research and Technology, Washington, District of Columbia 20240. 1979. 2d ed.

Water Desalination. Headquarters, Dept. of the Army, Washington, District of Columbia 20310. (202) 695-6153. 1986-.

ONLINE DATA BASES

Chemical Abstracts-CA. Chemical Abstracts Service, 2540 Olentangy River Rd., P.O. Box 3012, Columbus, Ohio 43210. (800) 848-6533 or (614) 421-3600. Information sources include 9000 journals, patents from 27 countries, two industrial property organizations, new books, conference proceedings, and government research reports.

Chemical Engineering and Biotechnology Abstracts–CEBA. Orbit Search Service, Maxwell Online Inc., 8000 W. Park Dr., McLean, Virginia 22102. (703) 442-0900 or (800) 456-7248. Monthly. Covers theoretical, practical and commercial material on all aspects of processing safety, and the environment. Also covers process and reaction engineering, measurement and process control, environmental protection and safety, plant design and equipment used in chemical engineering and biotechnology. More than 400 of the world's major primary chemical and process engineering journals are scanned to compile the database. Available from ORBIT.

Computerized Engineering Index–COMPENDEX. Engineering Information Inc., 345 E. 47th St., New York, New York 10017. (212) 705-7600.

Enviro/Energyline Abstracts Plus. R. R. Bowker Co., 121 Chanlon Rd., New Providence, New Jersey 07974. (908) 464-6800.

Environmental Periodicals Bibliography. National Information Services Corp., Ste. 6, Wyman Towers, 3100 St. Paul St., Baltimore, Maryland 21218. (410)243-0797. Online version of abstract of same name.

Kirk-Othmer Encyclopedia of Chemical Technology. John Wiley & Sons, Inc., 605 3rd Ave., 5th Floor, New York, New York 10158. (212) 850-6000. Online version of the publication of the same name.

Monthly Catalog of United States Government Publications. U.S. G.P.O., Supt. of Docs., PO Box 371954, Pittsburgh, Pennsylvania 15250-7954. (202) 512-0000.

National Technical Information Service. U.S. Department of Commerce, National Technical Information Service, Office of Data Base Services, 5285 Port Royal Rd., Springfield, Virginia 22161. (703) 487-4807. Bibliographic database of government sponsored research and technical reports.

Oceanic Abstracts. Cambridge Scientific Abstracts, 5161 River Rd., Bethesda, Maryland 20816. (301) 961-6750. Online access.

PressNet Environmental Reports. Chemical Information Systems, Inc., 7215 York Rd., Baltimore, Maryland 21212. (301) 321-8440.

SCISEARCH. Institute for Scientific Information, University City Science Center, 3501 Market St., Philadelphia, Pennsylvania 19104. (215) 386-0100.

PERIODICALS AND NEWSLETTERS

Applied Solar Energy. Allerton Press Inc., 150 5th Ave., New York, New York 10011. (212) 924-3950. 1965-. Six times a year.

Desalination. Elsevier, Box 211, Amsterdam, Netherlands 1000 AE. 020-5803-911. 1966-. Forty-two times a year. The international journal on the science and technology of desalting and water purification. Formed by the merger of the Journal of Membrane Science and Desalination.

Desalination and Water Re-Use Technologies in Japan. Annual Report. Water Re-Use Promotion Center, Landix Akasaka Bldg, 2-3-4, Akasaka, Minato-ku, Tokyo, Japan 1981-. Annual.

Marine Technology. Society of Naval Architects and Marine Engineers, 601 Pavonia Ave., Jersey City, New Jersey 07306. (201) 498-4800. 1964-1987.

Pure Water from the Sea. International Desalination Association, Box 328, Englewood, New Jersey 07631. (201) 567-0188. Bimonthly.

TRADE ASSOCIATIONS AND PROFESSIONAL SOCIETIES

American Institute of Chemical Engineers. 345 East 47th St., New York, New York 10017. (212) 705-7338.

American Institute of Chemists. 7315 Wisconsin Ave., Bethesda, Maryland 20814. (301) 652-2447.

American Society of Civil Engineers. 345 East 47th St., New York, New York 10017. (212) 705-7496.

International Desalination Association. P.O. Box 387, Topsfield, Massachusetts 01983. (508) 356-2727.

DESERT ECOSYSTEMS
See: ECOSYSTEMS

DESERT PLANTS
See: DESERTS

DESERTIFICATION
See: DESERTS

DESERTS
See also: ARID ZONES

ABSTRACTING AND INDEXING SERVICES

Biological Abstracts. BIOSIS, 2100 Arch St., Philadelphia, Pennsylvania 19103-1399. (215) 587-4800. 1927-.

Biological and Agricultural Index. H.W. Wilson Co., 950 University Ave., Bronx, New York 10452. (800) 367-6770. 1916-. Monthly.

Ecological Abstracts. Geo Abstracts Ltd. Elsevier Applied Science, Crown House, Linton Rd., Barking, England IG 11 8JU. 1974-. Derived from over 600 leading ecological and environmental journals, plus books, conference proceedings, reports and theses.

Ecology Abstracts. Cambridge Scientific Abstracts, 5161 River Rd., Bethesda, Maryland 20816. (301) 961-6750. Monthly.

General Science Index. H. W. Wilson Co., 950 University Ave., Bronx, New York 10452. 1978-. Monthly, also issued in annual cumulation. Cumulative subject index to English language periodicals in the subject fields of astronomy, botany, chemistry, earth science, environment and conservation, food and nutrition, genetics, mathematics, medicine and health, microbiology, oceanography, physics, physiology and zoology.

Geographical Abstracts. London School of Economics, Dept. of Geography, Regency House, 34 Duke St., London, England 1966-. Continued by Geo Abstracts issued in 6 parts: Pt. A. Landforms and the quaternary; Pt. B. Biogeography and Climatology; Pt. C. Economic geography; Pt. D. Social geography and cartography; Pt. E. Sedimentology; Pt. F. Regional and community planning.

Index to Scientific Book Contents. Institute for Scientific Information, 3501 Market St., Philadelphia, Pennsylvania 19104. (800) 523-1857. 1985-. Annual. Gives contents of science books published.

Science Citation Index. Institute for Scientific Information, 3501 Market St., Philadelphia, Pennsylvania 19104. 1961-.

BIBLIOGRAPHIES

Bibliography and Index of Geology. American Geological Institute, 4220 King St., Alexandria, Virginia 22302. Monthly. Includes environmental geology and hydrogeology.

Current Contents. Agriculture, Biology and Environmental Sciences. Institute for Scientific Information, 3501 Market St., Philadelphia, Pennsylvania 19104. (800) 523-1857. 1973-. Previous title: Current Contents. Agricultural, Food & Veterinary Sciences. Gives the table of contents of periodicals in the fields of agriculture, biology, environmental and related areas.

World Desertification: Cause and Effect, A Literature Review and Annotated Bibliography. Wade C. Sherbrooke. University of Arizona, Office of Arid Land Studies, 1230 N. Park, # 102, Tucson, Arizona 85719. (602) 621-1441. 1973.

ENCYCLOPEDIAS AND DICTIONARIES

Cambridge Encyclopedia of Life Sciences. A. E. Friday and David S. Ingram. Cambridge University Press, 40 W 20th St., New York, New York 10011. (212) 924-3900 or (800) 227-0247. 1985. Includes all topics under biology and ecology.

The Encyclopedia of Climatology. John E. Oliver and Rhodes W. Fairbridge, eds. Van Nostrand Reinhold, 115 5th Ave., New York, New York 10003. (212) 254-3232. 1987. Belongs in the series Encyclopedia of Earth Sciences, v.11.

Grzimek's Encyclopedia of Ecology. Bernhard Grzimek. Van Nostrand Reinhold, 115 5th Ave., New York, New York 10003. (212) 254-3232. 1976.

McGraw-Hill Encyclopedia of Science and Technology. McGraw-Hill, 1221 Avenue of the Americas, New York, New York 10020. (212) 512-2000 or (800) 262-4729. 1992. Seventh edition. Issued in multiple volumes including index. Includes all science and technology broad subject areas.

North American Reference Encyclopedia of Ecology and Pollution. William White. North American Pub. Co., 401 N. Broad St., Philadelphia, Pennsylvania 19108. (215) 238-5300. 1972.

Van Nostrand's Scientific Encyclopedia. Glenn D. Considine, ed. Van Nostrand Reinhold, 115 5th Ave., New York, New York 10003. (212) 254-3232. 1983. Sixth edition. Includes all broad subject areas in science.

GENERAL WORKS

The Ecology of Desert Communities. Gary A. Polis, ed. University of Arizona Press, 1230 N. Park, No. 102, Tucson, Arizona 85719. (602) 621-1441. 1991. Presents the relatively new ideas and syntheses of this beta generation of desert biologists. Focuses on the structure of desert communities since the early 1970s. Synthesizes new ideas on desert communities.

Ecosystems Experiments. H. A. Mooney, et al., eds. John Wiley & Sons, Inc., 605 3rd Ave., New York, New York 10158-0012. (212) 850-6000. 1991. Explores the potential ecosystem experimentation as a tool for understanding and predicting changes in the biosphere. Areas investigated include deforestation, desertification, El Nino phenomenon, acid rain, watersheds, wetlands, and aquatic and climatic changes.

Effects of Aerosols and Surface Shadowing on Bidirectional Reflectance Measurements of Deserts Microform. David E. Bowker. National Aeronautics and Space Administration, Scientific and Technical Information Office, 5285 Port Royal Rd., Springfield, Virginia 22161. (703) 487-4805. 1987. NASA technical paper; #2756.

Environment in Peril. Anthony B. Wolbarst, ed. Smithsonian Institution Press, 470 L'Enfant Plaza, No. 7100, Washington, District of Columbia 20560. (800) 782-4612. 1991. Brings together in one volume the primary concerns of eleven of the world's leaders in conservation, ecology and public policy. Broad environmental issues covered are: ozone depletion, overpopulation, global warming, thinning forests, extinction of species, spreading deserts, toxic chemicals, and various pollutants.

Magill's Survey of Science. Earth Science Series. Frank N. Magill. Salem Press, PO Box 50062, Pasadena, California 91105. 1990-. Five volumes. Includes information on earth's crust, hot spots and volcanic island chains, physical properties of minerals, rock magnetism, physical properties of rocks, and index.

Magill's Survey of Science. Life Science Series. Frank N. Magill, ed. Salem Press, PO Box 50062, Pasadena, California 91105. 1991. Six volumes. Contents: v.1. A-Central and peripheral nervous system functions; v.2. Central metabolism regulation - eukaryotic transcriptional control; v.3. Positive and negative eukaryotic transcriptional control - mammalian hormones; v.4. Hormones and behavior - muscular contraction; v.5. Muscular contraction and relaxation - sexual reproduction in plants; v.6. Reproductive behavior and mating - X inactivation and the Lyon hypothesis.

Paleoenvironments in the Namib Desert: The Lower Tumas Basin in the Late Cenozoic. Justin Wilkinson. University of Chicago Press, Committee on Geographical Studies, 5801 Ellis Ave., 4th Floor, Chicago, Illinois 60637. (800) 621-2736. 1990. Focuses on the great coastal desert of Southwestern Africa the Namib, and explores the complex changes in depositional environments throughout the Cenzoic.

United States Sources of Information in the Area of Decertification. United States. U.S. Environmental Protection Agency, Assistant Administrator for Planning and Management, Office of Administration, Washington, District of Columbia 1977.

GOVERNMENTAL ORGANIZATIONS

Office of Environmental Affairs: Bureau of Reclamation. 18th and C St., N.W., Washington, District of Columbia 20240. (202) 343-4662.

ONLINE DATA BASES

BIOSIS Previews. BIOSIS, 2100 Arch St., Philadelphia, Pennsylvania 19103-1399. (215) 587-4800. Largest and most comprehensive database of research in the life sciences. Contains citations for nearly 9000 primary research journals, monographs, reviews, symposia, preliminary reports, semi-popular journals, selected institutional reports, government reports and research communications.

Cambridge Scientific Abstracts Life Science–CSAL. Cambridge Scientific Abstracts, 5161 River Rd., Bethesda, Maryland 20816. (301) 961-6750. Provides access to the following abstracting services: "Life Sciences Collection," "Aquatic Sciences and Fisheries Abstracts," "Oceanic Abstracts," and "Pollution Abstracts."

Monthly Catalog of United States Government Publications. U.S. G.P.O., Supt. of Docs., PO Box 371954, Pittsburgh, Pennsylvania 15250-7954. (202) 512-0000.

National Technical Information Service. U.S. Department of Commerce, National Technical Information Service, Office of Data Base Services, 5285 Port Royal Rd., Springfield, Virginia 22161. (703) 487-4807. Bibliographic database of government sponsored research and technical reports.

SCISEARCH. Institute for Scientific Information, University City Science Center, 3501 Market St., Philadelphia, Pennsylvania 19104. (215) 386-0100.

PERIODICALS AND NEWSLETTERS

Arid Soil Research and Rehabilitation. Taylor & Francis, 1900 Frost Rd., Ste. 101, Bristol, Pennsylvania 19007. (215) 785-5800. Quarterly. Scientific studies on desert, arid, and semi-arid soil research and recovery.

Chihuahuan Desert Newsbriefs. Chihuahuan Desert Research Institute, Box 1334, Alpine, Texas 79831. 1983-. Semiannually.

El Paisano. Desert Protective Council, Inc., PO Box 4294, Palm Springs, California 92263. (619) 670-7127. Quarterly. Environmental study of the desert.

Problems of Desert Development. Allerton Press, Inc., 150 Fifth Ave., New York, New York 10011. (212) 924-3950. Bimonthly.

RESEARCH CENTERS AND INSTITUTES

Aridland Watershed Management Research Unit. 2000 East Allen Road, Tucson, Arizona 85719. (602) 629-6381.

Arizona-Sonora Desert Museum. 2021 N. Kinney Road, Tucson, Arizona 85743. (602) 883-1380.

Chihuahuan Desert Research Institute. P.O. Box 1334, Alpine, Texas 79831. (915) 837-8370.

Desert Turfgrass Research Facility. University of Arizona, Forbes Building, Tucson, Arizona 85721. (602) 621-1851.

Herbarium. University of California, Los Angeles, 405 Hilgard Avenue, Los Angeles, California 90024. (213) 825-3620.

National Center for Intermedia Transport Research. University of California, Los Angeles, 5531 Boelter,

Department of Chemical Engineering, Los Angeles, California 90024-1592. (213) 825-9741.

University of Nevada-Reno, Desert Research Institute, Biological Sciences Center. P.O. Box 60220, Reno, Nevada 89506. (702) 673-7321.

University of Nevada-Reno, Desert Research Institute, Energy and Environmental Engineering Center. P.O. Box 60220, Reno, Nevada 89506. (702) 677-3107.

University of New Mexico, Institute of Southwestern Biology. Biology Building, Albuquerque, New Mexico 87131. (505) 277-5340.

TRADE ASSOCIATIONS AND PROFESSIONAL SOCIETIES

American Institute of Biological Sciences. 730 11th St., N.W., Washington, District of Columbia 20001-4521. (202) 628-1500.

American Society of Naturalists. Department of Ecology and Evolation, State University of New York, Stony Brook, New York 11794. (516) 632-8589.

Association for Arid Land Studies. c/o International Center for Arid and Semi-Arid Land Studies, Texas Tech. University, P.O. Box 41036, Lubbock, Texas 79409-1036. (806) 742-2218.

Desert Botanical Garden. 1201 N. Galvin Pkwy., Phoenix, Arizona 85008. (602) 941-1225.

Desert Protective Council. P.O. Box 4294, Palm Springs, California 92263. (619) 397-4264.

DESICCANTS

ABSTRACTING AND INDEXING SERVICES

Ecological Abstracts. Geo Abstracts Ltd. Elsevier Applied Science, Crown House, Linton Rd., Barking, England IG 11 8JU. 1974-. Derived from over 600 leading ecological and environmental journals, plus books, conference proceedings, reports and theses.

Ecology Abstracts. Cambridge Scientific Abstracts, 5161 River Rd., Bethesda, Maryland 20816. (301) 961-6750. Monthly.

Food Science and Technology Abstracts. International Food Information Service, c/o National Food Laboratory, 6363 Clark Ave., Dublin, California 94568. (800) 336-3782. 1969-.

General Science Index. H. W. Wilson Co., 950 University Ave., Bronx, New York 10452. 1978-. Monthly, also issued in annual cumulation. Cumulative subject index to English language periodicals in the subject fields of astronomy, botany, chemistry, earth science, environment and conservation, food and nutrition, genetics, mathematics, medicine and health, microbiology, oceanography, physics, physiology and zoology.

Science Citation Index. Institute for Scientific Information, 3501 Market St., Philadelphia, Pennsylvania 19104. 1961-.

BIBLIOGRAPHIES

Comprehensive Bibliography of Drying References: Covering Bulletins, Booklets, Books, Chapters, Bibliographies.

Carl W. Hall. American Society of Agricultural Engineers, 2950 Niles Rd., St. Joseph, Michigan 49085-9659. (616) 429-0300. 1980.

ENCYCLOPEDIAS AND DICTIONARIES

Cambridge Dictionary of Biology. Peter M. B. Walker. Cambridge University Press, 40 W. 20th St., New York, New York 10011. (212) 924-3900 or (800) 227-0247. 1989. Includes 10,000 terms in zoology, botany, biochemistry, molecular biology and genetics. Previously published under the title Chambers Biology Dictionary.

A Concise Dictionary of Biology. Elizabeth Martin, ed. Oxford University Press, 200 Madison Ave., New York, New York 10016. (212) 679-7300 or (800) 334-4249. 1990. New edition. Derived from the Concise Science Dictionary, published in 1984.

Dictionary of Drying. Carl W. Hall. Marcel Dekker Inc., 270 Madison Ave., New York, New York 10016. (212) 696-9000 or (800) 228-1160. 1979.

GENERAL WORKS

Advanced Desiccant Materials Assessment. Gas Research Institute, 8600 W. Bryn Mawr Ave., Chicago, Illinois 60631. (312) 399-8100. 1988. Deals with air conditioning and gas appliances.

Desiccants and Humectants. Ronald W. James. Noyes Publications, 120 Mill Rd., Park Ridge, New Jersey 07656. (201) 391-8484. 1973. Patents relative to humectants and drying agents.

Process Drying Practice. Edward M. Cook and Harman D. Dumont. McGraw-Hill, 1221 Avenue of the Americas, New York, New York 10020. (212) 512-2000 or (800) 262-4729. 1991.

Simulations and Economic Analyses of Desiccant Cooling Systems. Benjamin Shelpuk, et al. Solar Energy Research Institute, available from National Technical Information Services, 5285 Port Royal Rd., Springfield, Virginia 22161. (703) 487-4650. 1979.

HANDBOOKS AND MANUALS

Military Standard: Activated Desiccants. U.S. Department of Defense, The Pentagon, Washington, District of Columbia 20301-1155. (703) 545-6700. Looseleaf; standards for drying agents in the United States.

Operator's Organizational, DS, GS, and Depot Maintenance Manual. U.S. G.P.O, Washington, District of Columbia 20401. (202) 512-0000. 1988. Covers repair parts and special tools list for dehumidifier, desiccant, electric and air distribution manifolds.

DESULFURIZATION

ABSTRACTING AND INDEXING SERVICES

Applied Science and Technology Index. H.W. Wilson Co., 950 University Ave., Bronx, New York 10452. (800) 367-6770. Formerly Industrial Arts Index.

Chemical Abstracts. Chemical Abstracts Service, 2540 Olentangy River Rd., PO Box 3012, Columbus, Ohio 43210. (800) 848-6533. 1907-.

Clean Coal Technologies. National Technical Information Service, 5285 Port Royal Road, Springfield, Virginia 22161. (703) 487-4650. Monthly. Desulfurization, coal gasification and liquefaction, flue gas cleanup, and advanced coal combustion.

Ecological Abstracts. Geo Abstracts Ltd. Elsevier Applied Science, Crown House, Linton Rd., Barking, England IG 11 8JU. 1974-. Derived from over 600 leading ecological and environmental journals, plus books, conference proceedings, reports and theses.

General Science Index. H. W. Wilson Co., 950 University Ave., Bronx, New York 10452. 1978-. Monthly, also issued in annual cumulation. Cumulative subject index to English language periodicals in the subject fields of astronomy, botany, chemistry, earth science, environment and conservation, food and nutrition, genetics, mathematics, medicine and health, microbiology, oceanography, physics, physiology and zoology.

Metals Abstracts. ASM International, 9639 Kinsman, Materials Park, Ohio 44073. (216) 338-5151. 1968-. Published jointly by the Institute of Metals, London and the American Society for Metals. Formed by the Union of Metallurgical Abstracts and Review of Metal Literature.

Pollution Abstracts. Cambridge Scientific Abstracts, 5161 River Rd., Bethesda, Maryland 20816. (301) 961-6750. Six/year. Indexes worldwide technical literature on environmental pollution. Covers air pollution, marine and freshwater pollution, sewage and wastewater treatment, waste management, toxicology and health, noise pollution, radiation, land pollution, and environmental policies, programs, legislation, and education. Also available online.

Science Citation Index. Institute for Scientific Information, 3501 Market St., Philadelphia, Pennsylvania 19104. 1961-.

BIBLIOGRAPHIES

Coal Desulfurization: A Bibliography. M. Catherine Grissom, ed. United States Department of Energy, Technical Information Center, 1000 Independence Ave. SW, Oak Ridge, Tennessee 20585. (202) 586-5000. 1983.

ENCYCLOPEDIAS AND DICTIONARIES

Encyclopedia of Chemical Processing and Design. John J. Mcketta and W. A. Cunningham. Marcel Dekker, Inc., 270 Madison Ave., New York, New York 10016. (212) 696-9000; (800) 228-1160. 1992. Thirty-eight volumes.

Kirk-Othmer Encyclopedia of Chemical Technology. J. I. Kroschwitz, ed. John Wiley & Sons, Inc., 605 3rd Ave., New York, New York 10158-0012. (212) 850-6000. 1992-. All articles in the new edition have been rewritten and updated adding new subjects such as biotechnology, computer topics, analytical techniques and instrumentation, environmental concerns, fuels and energy, inorganic and solid state chemistry; composite materials and material science in general, and pharmaceuticals. Also available online.

McGraw-Hill Encyclopedia of Science and Technology. McGraw-Hill, 1221 Avenue of the Americas, New York, New York 10020. (212) 512-2000 or (800) 262-4729. 1992. Seventh edition. Issued in multiple volumes in-

cluding index. Includes all science and technology broad subject areas.

Ullmanns Encyclopedia of Industrial Chemistry. Hans Jurgen Arpe and Wolfgang Gerhartz, eds. VCH Publishers, 303 NW 12th Ave., Deerfield Beach, Florida 33442-1788. (305) 428-5566. 1990. Designed to keep up with the broad spectrum of chemical technology. Thirty-six volumes of the encyclopedia have been divided into two sets: the 28 A volumes contain alphabetically arranged articles on chemicals, product groups, processes and technological concepts; and the 8 B volumes are compendia of basic knowledge in industrial chemistry.

Van Nostrand's Scientific Encyclopedia. Glenn D. Considine, ed. Van Nostrand Reinhold, 115 5th Ave., New York, New York 10003. (212) 254-3232. 1983. Sixth edition. Includes all broad subject areas in science.

GENERAL WORKS

Desulphurisation 2: Technologies and Strategies for Reducing Sulphur Emissions. Hemisphere Publishing Co., 79 Madison Ave., Suite 1110, New York, New York 10016. (212) 725-1999. 1991. Proceedings of a Symposium held in Sheffield, March 1991.

Desulphurization in Coal Combustion Systems. Hemisphere Publishing Co., 79 Madison Ave., Suite 1110, New York, New York 10016. (212) 725-1999. 1989.

Disposal of Flue Gas Cleaning Water. R.B. Fling. National Technical Information Service, 5285 Port Royal Rd., Springfield, Virginia 22161. (703) 487-4650. Annual.

Disposal of Flue Gas Desulfurization Wastes. P.R. Hurt. U.S. Environmental Protection Agency, 401 M St. SW, Washington, District of Columbia 20460. (202) 260-2090. 1981.

The Problem of Sulphur. Butterworth-Heinemann, 80 Montvale Ave., Stoneham, Massachusetts 02180. (617) 438-8464. 1989.

ONLINE DATA BASES

CERCLIS. Chemical Information Systems, Inc., 7215 York Rd., Baltimore, Maryland 21212. (301) 321-8440. Information on hazardous waste disposal sites that have either been listed by the EPA on the National Priority List (NPL) or nominated for consideration for the NPL.

Chemical Abstracts-CA. Chemical Abstracts Service, 2540 Olentangy River Rd., P.O. Box 3012, Columbus, Ohio 43210. (800) 848-6533 or (614) 421-3600. Information sources include 9000 journals, patents from 27 countries, two industrial property organizations, new books, conference proceedings, and government research reports.

Chemical Engineering and Biotechnology Abstracts–CEBA. Orbit Search Service, Maxwell Online Inc., 8000 W. Park Dr., McLean, Virginia 22102. (703) 442-0900 or (800) 456-7248. Monthly. Covers theoretical, practical and commercial material on all aspects of processing safety, and the environment. Also covers process and reaction engineering, measurement and process control, environmental protection and safety, plant design and equipment used in chemical engineering and biotechnology. More than 400 of the world's major primary chemical and process engineering journals are scanned to compile the database. Available from ORBIT.

Kirk-Othmer Encyclopedia of Chemical Technology. John Wiley & Sons, Inc., 605 3rd Ave., 5th Floor, New York, New York 10158. (212) 850-6000. Online version of the publication of the same name.

Monthly Catalog of United States Government Publications. U.S. G.P.O., Supt. of Docs., PO Box 371954, Pittsburgh, Pennsylvania 15250-7954. (202) 512-0000.

National Technical Information Service. U.S. Department of Commerce, National Technical Information Service, Office of Data Base Services, 5285 Port Royal Rd., Springfield, Virginia 22161. (703) 487-4807. Bibliographic database of government sponsored research and technical reports.

PERIODICALS AND NEWSLETTERS

Clean Coal Today. U.S. Department of Energy, 1000 Independence Ave., S.W., Washington, District of Columbia 20585. (202) 252-1760. 1990-. Quarterly.

FGD Newsletter. McIlvaine Co., 2970 Maria Ave., Northbrook, Illinois 60062. (708) 272-0010. Monthly. Desulphurization and flue gases, purification of fluidized-bed furnaces, and coal-fired power plants.

FGD Quarterly Report. The Laboratory, Highway 54 and Alexander Dr., Research Triangle Park, North Carolina 27711. (919) 541-2821. Quarterly.

DETENTION DAMS

See: DAMS

DETERGENTS AND SOAPS

ABSTRACTING AND INDEXING SERVICES

Ecology Abstracts. Cambridge Scientific Abstracts, 5161 River Rd., Bethesda, Maryland 20816. (301) 961-6750. Monthly.

Pollution Abstracts. Cambridge Scientific Abstracts, 5161 River Rd., Bethesda, Maryland 20816. (301) 961-6750. Six/year. Indexes worldwide technical literature on environmental pollution. Covers air pollution, marine and freshwater pollution, sewage and wastewater treatment, waste management, toxicology and health, noise pollution, radiation, land pollution, and environmental policies, programs, legislation, and education. Also available online.

Science Citation Index. Institute for Scientific Information, 3501 Market St., Philadelphia, Pennsylvania 19104. 1961-.

DIRECTORIES

Blue Book and Catalog Edition of Soap and Chemical Specialties. McNairr-Dorland Co., 101 W. 31st, New York, New York 10001. 1955-. Annually.

Emulsifiers & Detergents–International Edition. McCutcheon's Publications, 175 Rock Rd., Glen Rock, New Jersey 07452. (201) 652-2655.

ENCYCLOPEDIAS AND DICTIONARIES

Encyclopedia of Chemical Processing and Design. John J. Mcketta and W. A. Cunningham. Marcel Dekker, Inc., 270 Madison Ave., New York, New York 10016. (212) 696-9000; (800) 228-1160. 1992. Thirty-eight volumes.

Kirk-Othmer Encyclopedia of Chemical Technology. J. I. Kroschwitz, ed. John Wiley & Sons, Inc., 605 3rd Ave., New York, New York 10158-0012. (212) 850-6000. 1992-. All articles in the new edition have been rewritten and updated adding new subjects such as biotechnology, computer topics, analytical techniques and instrumentation, environmental concerns, fuels and energy, inorganic and solid state chemistry; composite materials and material science in general, and pharmaceuticals. Also available online.

GENERAL WORKS

The Manufacture of Soaps and other Detergents, and Glycerine. Halsted Press, 605 3rd Ave., New York, New York 10158. (212) 850-6000. 1985. Ellis Horwood series in applied science and industrial technology.

HANDBOOKS AND MANUALS

Riegel's Handbook of Industrial Chemistry. James A. Kent, ed. Van Nostrand Reinhold, 115 5th Ave., New York, New York 10020. (212) 254-3232. 1983. Eighth edition. Includes industries such as: wastewater technology, coal technology, phosphate fertilizers, synthetic plastics, man-made textiles, detergents, sugar, animal and vegetable oils, chemical explosives, dyes, nuclear industry, and much more.

ONLINE DATA BASES

The Cleaning Products Competitive Intelligence Database. Strategic Intelligence Systems, Inc., 404 Park Ave., South, New York, New York 10016. (212) 725-5954.

Kirk-Othmer Encyclopedia of Chemical Technology. John Wiley & Sons, Inc., 605 3rd Ave., 5th Floor, New York, New York 10158. (212) 850-6000. Online version of the publication of the same name.

PERIODICALS AND NEWSLETTERS

Soap, Cosmetics, Chemical Specialties. MacNair-Dorland Co., 101 W. 31st, New York, New York 10001. 1925-. Monthly. Formerly entitled Soap and Chemical Specialties

SPC Soap Perfumery & Cosmetics. United Trade Press Ltd., UTP House, 33-35 Bowling Green Ln., London, England EC1R 0DA. (01) 837 1212. 1928-. Monthly.

STATISTICS SOURCES

Cosmetics/Household Products Advertising Trends. FIND/SVP, 625 Avenue of the Americas, New York, New York 10011. (212) 645-4500. 1991. Media expenditures by the personal care industry, highlighting product areas which are experiencing extremes in the level of competitive activity and the scope of each company's efforts.

Detergent Chemicals. FIND/SVP, 625 Avenue of the Americas, New York, New York 10011. (212) 645-4500. 1990.

The Heavy-Duty Detergent Market. FIND/SVP, 625 Avenue of the Americas, New York, New York 10011. (800) 346-3787. 1992. Technological developments, total sales in retail dollars, local and state regulations, sales projections to 1996, and market composition.

Household Cleaners. FIND/SVP, 625 Avenue of the Americas, New York, New York 10011. (212) 645-4500. 1991. Covers all-purpose cleaners, bathroom cleaners, scouring powders and liquids, and disinfectants.

Household Specialty Cleaners. FIND/SVP, 625 Avenue of the Americas, New York, New York 10011. (212) 645-4500. 1992. Analyzes the household specialty cleaners market including toilet-bowl cleaners, window/glass cleaners, oven cleaners, and drain cleaners.

The Room Deodorizer Market. FIND/SVP, 625 Avenue of the Americas, New York, New York 10011. (212) 645-4500. 1991. Retail market for room deodorizers, primarily air fresheners and carpet deodorizers, but also toilet bowl deodorizers.

Specialty Household Chemicals. FIND/SVP, 625 Avenue of the Americas, New York, New York 10011. (212) 645-4500. 1991.

The Toilet Soap Market. FIND/SVP, 625 Avenue of the Americas, New York, New York 10011. (212) 645-4500. 1992. Market for toilet soaps, including: deodorant, antibacterial, medicated, beauty, liquid, moisturizing, specialty, multipurpose and "pure".

Zeolites: Detergents Dominate Demand; Opportunities in Chemicals. FIND/SVP, 625 Avenue of the Americas, New York, New York 10011. (800) 346-3787. 1991. Examines the U.S. market for zeolites, microcrystalline solids containing cavities and channels of molecular dimensions.

TRADE ASSOCIATIONS AND PROFESSIONAL SOCIETIES

Soap and Detergent Association. 475 Park Ave., S., New York, New York 10016. (212) 725-1262.

DETOXIFICATION

See: TOXICITY

DETRITUS

See: ORGANIC WASTE

DEWATERING

See: WASTEWATER TREATMENT

DIALYSIS

See also: DESALINATION; SALT; WATER RESOURCES

ABSTRACTING AND INDEXING SERVICES

Applied Science and Technology Index. H.W. Wilson Co., 950 University Ave., Bronx, New York 10452. (800) 367-6770. Formerly Industrial Arts Index.

Chemical Abstracts. Chemical Abstracts Service, 2540 Olentangy River Rd., PO Box 3012, Columbus, Ohio 43210. (800) 848-6533. 1907-.

Ecological Abstracts. Geo Abstracts Ltd. Elsevier Applied Science, Crown House, Linton Rd., Barking, England IG 11 8JU. 1974-. Derived from over 600 leading ecological and environmental journals, plus books, conference proceedings, reports and theses.

Environment Abstracts. Bowker A & I Publishing, 121 Chanlon Rd., New Providence, New Jersey 07974. (908) 464-6800. 1974-.

Environment Index. Environment Information Center, Index Research Department, 124 E. 39th St., New York, New York 10016. 1971-. Annual.

Environmental Information Connection–EIC. Planning Information Program, Dept. of Urban and Regional Planning, University of Illinois, 1003 West Nevada, Urbana, Illinois 61801. (217) 333-1369. Also available online.

Environmental Periodicals Bibliography. Environmental Studies Institute, International Academy at Santa Barbara, 800 Garden St., Suite D, Santa Barbara, California 93101. (805) 965-5010. Also available online.

General Science Index. H. W. Wilson Co., 950 University Ave., Bronx, New York 10452. 1978-. Monthly, also issued in annual cumulation. Cumulative subject index to English language periodicals in the subject fields of astronomy, botany, chemistry, earth science, environment and conservation, food and nutrition, genetics, mathematics, medicine and health, microbiology, oceanography, physics, physiology and zoology.

Index to Scientific Book Contents. Institute for Scientific Information, 3501 Market St., Philadelphia, Pennsylvania 19104. (800) 523-1857. 1985-. Annual. Gives contents of science books published.

Pollution Abstracts. Cambridge Scientific Abstracts, 5161 River Rd., Bethesda, Maryland 20816. (301) 961-6750. Six/year. Indexes worldwide technical literature on environmental pollution. Covers air pollution, marine and freshwater pollution, sewage and wastewater treatment, waste management, toxicology and health, noise pollution, radiation, land pollution, and environmental policies, programs, legislation, and education. Also available online.

Science Citation Index. Institute for Scientific Information, 3501 Market St., Philadelphia, Pennsylvania 19104. 1961-.

BIBLIOGRAPHIES

EPA Publications Bibliography. U.S. Environmental Protection Agency, Library Systems Branch, 401 M St., SW, Washington, District of Columbia 20460. (202) 260-2090. Quarterly.

ENCYCLOPEDIAS AND DICTIONARIES

Cambridge Dictionary of Biology. Peter M. B. Walker. Cambridge University Press, 40 W. 20th St., New York,

New York 10011. (212) 924-3900 or (800) 227-0247. 1989. Includes 10,000 terms in zoology, botany, biochemistry, molecular biology and genetics. Previously published under the title Chambers Biology Dictionary.

A Concise Dictionary of Biology. Elizabeth Martin, ed. Oxford University Press, 200 Madison Ave., New York, New York 10016. (212) 679-7300 or (800) 334-4249. 1990. New edition. Derived from the Concise Science Dictionary, published in 1984.

Encyclopedia of Chemical Processing and Design. John J. Mcketta and W. A. Cunningham. Marcel Dekker, Inc., 270 Madison Ave., New York, New York 10016. (212) 696-9000; (800) 228-1160. 1992. Thirty-eight volumes.

Encyclopedia of Human Biology. Renato Dulbecco, ed. Academic Press, c/o Harcourt Brace Jovanovich Inc., 6277 Sea Harbor Dr., Orlando, Florida 32887. (800) 346-8648. 1991. Eight volumes.

Kirk-Othmer Encyclopedia of Chemical Technology. J. I. Kroschwitz, ed. John Wiley & Sons, Inc., 605 3rd Ave., New York, New York 10158-0012. (212) 850-6000. 1992-. All articles in the new edition have been rewritten and updated adding new subjects such as biotechnology, computer topics, analytical techniques and instrumentation, environmental concerns, fuels and energy, inorganic and solid state chemistry; composite materials and material science in general, and pharmaceuticals. Also available online.

McGraw-Hill Encyclopedia of Science and Technology. McGraw-Hill, 1221 Avenue of the Americas, New York, New York 10020. (212) 512-2000 or (800) 262-4729. 1992. Seventh edition. Issued in multiple volumes including index. Includes all science and technology broad subject areas.

The New York Times Encyclopedic Dictionary of the Environment. Paul Sarnoff. Quadrangle Books, New York, New York 1971. Focuses on state-of-the-art methods of pollution control, abatement, prevention and removal.

Van Nostrand's Scientific Encyclopedia. Glenn D. Considine, ed. Van Nostrand Reinhold, 115 5th Ave., New York, New York 10003. (212) 254-3232. 1983. Sixth edition. Includes all broad subject areas in science.

GENERAL WORKS

Hazards in Reuse of Disposable Dialysis Devices. Committee on Aging, United States Senate. U.S. G.P.O., Washington, District of Columbia 20401. (202) 512-0000. 1986.

ONLINE DATA BASES

Chemical Abstracts-CA. Chemical Abstracts Service, 2540 Olentangy River Rd., P.O. Box 3012, Columbus, Ohio 43210. (800) 848-6533 or (614) 421-3600. Information sources include 9000 journals, patents from 27 countries, two industrial property organizations, new books, conference proceedings, and government research reports.

Enviro/Energyline Abstracts Plus. R. R. Bowker Co., 121 Chanlon Rd., New Providence, New Jersey 07974. (908) 464-6800.

Environmental Periodicals Bibliography. National Information Services Corp., Ste. 6, Wyman Towers, 3100 St.

Paul St., Baltimore, Maryland 21218. (410)243-0797. Online version of abstract of same name.

Kirk-Othmer Encyclopedia of Chemical Technology. John Wiley & Sons, Inc., 605 3rd Ave., 5th Floor, New York, New York 10158. (212) 850-6000. Online version of the publication of the same name.

Monthly Catalog of United States Government Publications. U.S. G.P.O., Supt. of Docs., PO Box 371954, Pittsburgh, Pennsylvania 15250-7954. (202) 512-0000.

National Technical Information Service. U.S. Department of Commerce, National Technical Information Service, Office of Data Base Services, 5285 Port Royal Rd., Springfield, Virginia 22161. (703) 487-4807. Bibliographic database of government sponsored research and technical reports.

SCISEARCH. Institute for Scientific Information, University City Science Center, 3501 Market St., Philadelphia, Pennsylvania 19104. (215) 386-0100.

TRADE ASSOCIATIONS AND PROFESSIONAL SOCIETIES

American Institute of Chemical Engineers. 345 East 47th St., New York, New York 10017. (212) 705-7338.

American Institute of Chemists. 7315 Wisconsin Ave., Bethesda, Maryland 20814. (301) 652-2447.

DIAZINON
See: INSECTICIDES

DIBENZOFURANS

ABSTRACTING AND INDEXING SERVICES

Biological Abstracts. BIOSIS, 2100 Arch St., Philadelphia, Pennsylvania 19103-1399. (215) 587-4800. 1927-.

Chemical Abstracts. Chemical Abstracts Service, 2540 Olentangy River Rd., PO Box 3012, Columbus, Ohio 43210. (800) 848-6533. 1907-.

Ecological Abstracts. Geo Abstracts Ltd. Elsevier Applied Science, Crown House, Linton Rd., Barking, England IG 11 8JU. 1974-. Derived from over 600 leading ecological and environmental journals, plus books, conference proceedings, reports and theses.

Environment Abstracts. Bowker A & I Publishing, 121 Chanlon Rd., New Providence, New Jersey 07974. (908) 464-6800. 1974-.

Environment Index. Environment Information Center, Index Research Department, 124 E. 39th St., New York, New York 10016. 1971-. Annual.

Environmental Information Connection–EIC. Planning Information Program, Dept. of Urban and Regional Planning, University of Illinois, 1003 West Nevada, Urbana, Illinois 61801. (217) 333-1369. Also available online.

Environmental Periodicals Bibliography. Environmental Studies Institute, International Academy at Santa Barbara, 800 Garden St., Suite D, Santa Barbara, California 93101. (805) 965-5010. Also available online.

Science Citation Index. Institute for Scientific Information, 3501 Market St., Philadelphia, Pennsylvania 19104. 1961-.

Selected Water Abstracts on Dioxins and Dibenzofurans in Carcinogenesis, 1980-1986. Anthony J. Girardi. National Cancer Institute, U. S. Dept. of Health and Human Services, Public Health Service, National Institutes of Health, Washington, District of Columbia 20402-9325. (202) 783-3238. 1987.

BIBLIOGRAPHIES

EPA Publications Bibliography. U.S. Environmental Protection Agency, Library Systems Branch, 401 M St., SW, Washington, District of Columbia 20460. (202) 260-2090. Quarterly.

ENCYCLOPEDIAS AND DICTIONARIES

McGraw-Hill Encyclopedia of Environmental Science. Sybil P. Parker. McGraw-Hill Science & Engineering Books, 11 W. 19th St., New York, New York 10011. (212) 337-6010. 1980. Covers ecology, man's influence on nature, and environmental protection.

McGraw-Hill Encyclopedia of Science and Technology. McGraw-Hill, 1221 Avenue of the Americas, New York, New York 10020. (212) 512-2000 or (800) 262-4729. 1992. Seventh edition. Issued in multiple volumes including index. Includes all science and technology broad subject areas.

Van Nostrand's Scientific Encyclopedia. Glenn D. Considine, ed. Van Nostrand Reinhold, 115 5th Ave., New York, New York 10003. (212) 254-3232. 1983. Sixth edition. Includes all broad subject areas in science.

GENERAL WORKS

Chlorinated Dioxins and Dibenzofurans in Perspective. Christoffer Rappe, et al. Lewis Publishers, 2000 Corporate Blvd., N.W., Boca Raton, Florida 33431. (407) 994-0555 or (800) 272-7737. 1986. Gives the latest human exposure data and the most advanced analytical techniques developed in the continuing effort against contamination by chlorinated dioxins and dibenzofurans.

Chlorinated Dioxins and Dibenzofurans in the Total Environment. Gangadhar Chordhary, Lawrence H. Keith, and Christoffer Rappe. Butterworth-Heinemann, 80 Montvale Ave., Stoneham, Massachusetts 02180. (617) 438-8464. 1985. Environmental aspects and toxicology of tetrachlorodibenzodioxin and dibenzofurans.

Interim Procedures for Estimating Risks Associated with Exposures to Mixtures of Chlorinated Dibenzo-RHO-Dioxins-and- Dibenzofurans. Judith S. Bellin. U.S. Environmental Protection Agency, 401 M St., SW, Washington, District of Columbia 20460. (202) 260-2090.

Performance of RCRA Method 8280 for the Analysis of Dibenzo-P- Dioxins and Dibenzofurans in Hazardous Waste Samples. J.M. Ballard. U.S. Environmental Protection Agency, Environmental Monitoring Systems Laboratory, 944 E. Harmon, Las Vegas, Nevada 89119. (702) 798-2100. 1986.

ONLINE DATA BASES

BIOSIS Previews. BIOSIS, 2100 Arch St., Philadelphia, Pennsylvania 19103-1399. (215) 587-4800. Largest and

most comprehensive database of research in the life sciences. Contains citations for nearly 9000 primary research journals, monographs, reviews, symposia, preliminary reports, semi-popular journals, selected institutional reports, government reports and research communications.

Chemical Abstracts-CA. Chemical Abstracts Service, 2540 Olentangy River Rd., P.O. Box 3012, Columbus, Ohio 43210. (800) 848-6533 or (614) 421-3600. Information sources include 9000 journals, patents from 27 countries, two industrial property organizations, new books, conference proceedings, and government research reports.

Chemical Abstracts Chemical Name Directory-CHEMNAME. Chemical Abstracts Service, 2540 Olentangy River Rd., P.O. Box 3012, Columbus, Ohio 43210. (800) 848-6533 or (614) 421-3600. Listing of chemical substances in a dictionary type file. The Chemical Abstracts (CAS) Registry Number, molecular formula, Chemical Abstracts (CA) Substance Index Name, available synonyms, ring data and other chemical substance information is given for each entry.

Chemical Carcinogenesis Research Information System-CCRIS. National Library of Medicine, 8600 Rockville Pike, Bethesda, Maryland 20894. (800) 638-8480. Individual assay results and test conditions for 1,451 chemicals in the areas of carcinogenicity, mutagenicity, tumor promotion, and cocarcinogenicity.

Chemical Collection System/Request Tracking-CCS/RTS. U.S. Environmental Protection Agency, Office of Pesticides and Toxic Substances, 401 M St., SW, Washington, District of Columbia 20460. (202) 260-2090. Contains information on various properties of a number of chemicals including environmental effects, test and analysis methods, and health effects. Available from EPA.

Chemical Dictionary Online-CHEMLINE. Chemical Abstracts Service, 2540 Olentangy River Rd., Columbus, Ohio 43210. (614) 421-3600 or (800) 848-6533. Part of MEDLINE of the National Library of Medicine (NLM). File of 900,000 names for chemical substances, representing 450,000 unique compounds. It contains such information as Chemical Abstracts (CA) Service Registry Numbers, molecular formulas, preferred chemical nomenclature, and generic and ring structure information. Available on NLM's ELHILL system.

Chemical Engineering and Biotechnology Abstracts-CEBA. Orbit Search Service, Maxwell Online Inc., 8000 W. Park Dr., McLean, Virginia 22102. (703) 442-0900 or (800) 456-7248. Monthly. Covers theoretical, practical and commercial material on all aspects of processing safety, and the environment. Also covers process and reaction engineering, measurement and process control, environmental protection and safety, plant design and equipment used in chemical engineering and biotechnology. More than 400 of the world's major primary chemical and process engineering journals are scanned to compile the database. Available from ORBIT.

Chemical Exposure. Science Applications International Corp., Health & Environmental Information, P.O. Box 2501, Oak Ridge, Tennessee 37831. (615) 482-9031. Database of chemicals that have been identified in both human tissues and body fluids and in feral and food animals. Contains reference to journal articles, conferences, and reports. Covers the whole fields of information related to human and animal exposure to food, air,

and water contaminants and pharmaceuticals. Its records include information on chemical properties, formulas, tissues measured, analytical method used, demographics and more. Available on DIALOG.

Enviro/Energyline Abstracts Plus. R. R. Bowker Co., 121 Chanlon Rd., New Providence, New Jersey 07974. (908) 464-6800.

Environmental Periodicals Bibliography. National Information Services Corp., Ste. 6, Wyman Towers, 3100 St. Paul St., Baltimore, Maryland 21218. (410)243-0797. Online version of abstract of same name.

Monthly Catalog of United States Government Publications. U.S. G.P.O., Supt. of Docs., PO Box 371954, Pittsburgh, Pennsylvania 15250-7954. (202) 512-0000.

National Technical Information Service. U.S. Department of Commerce, National Technical Information Service, Office of Data Base Services, 5285 Port Royal Rd., Springfield, Virginia 22161. (703) 487-4807. Bibliographic database of government sponsored research and technical reports.

TRADE ASSOCIATIONS AND PROFESSIONAL SOCIETIES

American Chemical Society. 1155 16th St., N.W., Washington, District of Columbia 20036. (202) 872-4600.

DICAMBA

ABSTRACTING AND INDEXING SERVICES

Applied Ecology Abstracts Studies in Renewable Natural Resources. Information Retrieval Ltd., 1911 Jefferson Davis Highway, Arlington, Virginia 22202. 1975-. Monthly.

Biological Abstracts. BIOSIS, 2100 Arch St., Philadelphia, Pennsylvania 19103-1399. (215) 587-4800. 1927-.

Biological and Agricultural Index. H.W. Wilson Co., 950 University Ave., Bronx, New York 10452. (800) 367-6770. 1916-. Monthly.

Chemical Abstracts. Chemical Abstracts Service, 2540 Olentangy River Rd., PO Box 3012, Columbus, Ohio 43210. (800) 848-6533. 1907-.

Ecology Abstracts. Cambridge Scientific Abstracts, 5161 River Rd., Bethesda, Maryland 20816. (301) 961-6750. Monthly.

Multimedia Index to Ecology. National Information Center for Educational Media, University of Southern California, Los Angeles, California 90007.

Science Citation Index. Institute for Scientific Information, 3501 Market St., Philadelphia, Pennsylvania 19104. 1961-.

ENCYCLOPEDIAS AND DICTIONARIES

Encyclopedia of Trademarks and Synonyms. H. Bennett, ed. Chemical Publishing Co., 80 Eighth Ave., New York, New York 10011. (212) 255-1950. 1981. Three volumes. Includes chemical compounds, compositions consisting of one or more chemicals and other products. Also included are abbreviated names and WHO free names.

McGraw-Hill Encyclopedia of Environmental Science. Sybil P. Parker. McGraw-Hill Science & Engineering Books, 11 W. 19th St., New York, New York 10011. (212) 337-6010. 1980. Covers ecology, man's influence on nature, and environmental protection.

McGraw-Hill Encyclopedia of Science and Technology. McGraw-Hill, 1221 Avenue of the Americas, New York, New York 10020. (212) 512-2000 or (800) 262-4729. 1992. Seventh edition. Issued in multiple volumes including index. Includes all science and technology broad subject areas.

Van Nostrand's Scientific Encyclopedia. Glenn D. Considine, ed. Van Nostrand Reinhold, 115 5th Ave., New York, New York 10003. (212) 254-3232. 1983. Sixth edition. Includes all broad subject areas in science.

ONLINE DATA BASES

BIOSIS Previews. BIOSIS, 2100 Arch St., Philadelphia, Pennsylvania 19103-1399. (215) 587-4800. Largest and most comprehensive database of research in the life sciences. Contains citations for nearly 9000 primary research journals, monographs, reviews, symposia, preliminary reports, semi-popular journals, selected institutional reports, government reports and research communications.

Chemical Abstracts-CA. Chemical Abstracts Service, 2540 Olentangy River Rd., P.O. Box 3012, Columbus, Ohio 43210. (800) 848-6533 or (614) 421-3600. Information sources include 9000 journals, patents from 27 countries, two industrial property organizations, new books, conference proceedings, and government research reports.

Chemical Carcinogenesis Research Information System–CCRIS. National Library of Medicine, 8600 Rockville Pike, Bethesda, Maryland 20894. (800) 638-8480. Individual assay results and test conditions for 1,451 chemicals in the areas of carcinogenicity, mutagenicity, tumor promotion, and cocarcinogenicity.

Monthly Catalog of United States Government Publications. U.S. G.P.O., Supt. of Docs., PO Box 371954, Pittsburgh, Pennsylvania 15250-7954. (202) 512-0000.

National Technical Information Service. U.S. Department of Commerce, National Technical Information Service, Office of Data Base Services, 5285 Port Royal Rd., Springfield, Virginia 22161. (703) 487-4807. Bibliographic database of government sponsored research and technical reports.

DICHLOROPHENOL

ABSTRACTING AND INDEXING SERVICES

Biological Abstracts. BIOSIS, 2100 Arch St., Philadelphia, Pennsylvania 19103-1399. (215) 587-4800. 1927-.

Chemical Abstracts. Chemical Abstracts Service, 2540 Olentangy River Rd., PO Box 3012, Columbus, Ohio 43210. (800) 848-6533. 1907-.

ENCYCLOPEDIAS AND DICTIONARIES

McGraw-Hill Encyclopedia of Environmental Science. Sybil P. Parker. McGraw-Hill Science & Engineering Books, 11 W. 19th St., New York, New York 10011.

(212) 337-6010. 1980. Covers ecology, man's influence on nature, and environmental protection.

Van Nostrand's Scientific Encyclopedia. Glenn D. Considine, ed. Van Nostrand Reinhold, 115 5th Ave., New York, New York 10003. (212) 254-3232. 1983. Sixth edition. Includes all broad subject areas in science.

GENERAL WORKS

Ambient Water Quality Criteria for 2, 4-Dichlorophenol. U. S. Environmental Protection Agency. National Technical Information Service, 5285 Port Royal Rd., Springfield, Virginia 22161. (703) 487-4650. 1980. Describes the regulations and standards criteria set by the EPA.

ONLINE DATA BASES

BIOSIS Previews. BIOSIS, 2100 Arch St., Philadelphia, Pennsylvania 19103-1399. (215) 587-4800. Largest and most comprehensive database of research in the life sciences. Contains citations for nearly 9000 primary research journals, monographs, reviews, symposia, preliminary reports, semi-popular journals, selected institutional reports, government reports and research communications.

Chemical Abstracts-CA. Chemical Abstracts Service, 2540 Olentangy River Rd., P.O. Box 3012, Columbus, Ohio 43210. (800) 848-6533 or (614) 421-3600. Information sources include 9000 journals, patents from 27 countries, two industrial property organizations, new books, conference proceedings, and government research reports.

Chemical Abstracts Chemical Name Directory-CHEM-NAME. Chemical Abstracts Service, 2540 Olentangy River Rd., P.O. Box 3012, Columbus, Ohio 43210. (800) 848-6533 or (614) 421-3600. Listing of chemical substances in a dictionary type file. The Chemical Abstracts (CAS) Registry Number, molecular formula, Chemical Abstracts (CA) Substance Index Name, available synonyms, ring data and other chemical substance information is given for each entry.

Chemical Carcinogenesis Research Information System–CCRIS. National Library of Medicine, 8600 Rockville Pike, Bethesda, Maryland 20894. (800) 638-8480. Individual assay results and test conditions for 1,451 chemicals in the areas of carcinogenicity, mutagenicity, tumor promotion, and cocarcinogenicity.

Chemical Collection System/Request Tracking–CCS/RTS. U.S. Environmental Protection Agency, Office of Pesticides and Toxic Substances, 401 M St., SW, Washington, District of Columbia 20460. (202) 260-2090. Contains information on various properties of a number of chemicals including environmental effects, test and analysis methods, and health effects. Available from EPA.

Chemical Dictionary Online–CHEMLINE. Chemical Abstracts Service, 2540 Olentangy River Rd., Columbus, Ohio 43210. (614) 421-3600 or (800) 848-6533. Part of MEDLINE of the National Library of Medicine (NLM). File of 900,000 names for chemical substances, representing 450,000 unique compounds. It contains such information as Chemical Abstracts (CA) Service Registry Numbers, molecular formulas, preferred chemical nomenclature, and generic and ring structure information. Available on NLM's ELHILL system.

Chemical Exposure. Science Applications International Corp., Health & Environmental Information, P.O. Box 2501, Oak Ridge, Tennessee 37831. (615) 482-9031. Database of chemicals that have been identified in both human tissues and body fluids and in feral and food animals. Contains reference to journal articles, conferences, and reports. Covers the whole fields of information related to human and animal exposure to food, air, and water contaminants and pharmaceuticals. Its records include information on chemical properties, formulas, tissues measured, analytical method used, demographics and more. Available on DIALOG.

TRADE ASSOCIATIONS AND PROFESSIONAL SOCIETIES

American Chemical Society. 1155 16th St., N.W., Washington, District of Columbia 20036. (202) 872-4600.

DIELDRIN

See: INSECTICIDES

DIESEL FUEL

ABSTRACTING AND INDEXING SERVICES

Applied Science and Technology Index. H.W. Wilson Co., 950 University Ave., Bronx, New York 10452. (800) 367-6770. Formerly Industrial Arts Index.

Engineering Index. The Engineering Index Inc., 345 E. 47th St., New York, New York 10017. 1962-.

ERDA Research Abstracts. U.S. ERDA Technical Information Center, Box 62, Oak Ridge, Tennessee 37830.

Science Citation Index. Institute for Scientific Information, 3501 Market St., Philadelphia, Pennsylvania 19104. 1961-.

DIRECTORIES

Diesel & Gas Turbine Catalog. 13555 Bishop's Court, Brookfield, Wisconsin 53005. (414) 784-9177. Annual.

Diesel Fuel–Wholesale. 5711 S. 86th Circle, Omaha, Nebraska 68127. (402) 593-4600. Annual.

ENCYCLOPEDIAS AND DICTIONARIES

Dictionary of Environmental Engineering and Related Sciences: English-Spanish, Spanish-English. Jose T. Villate. Ediciones Universal, 3090 SW 8th St., Miami, Florida 33135. (305) 642-3355. 1979.

Encyclopedia of Environmental Science and Engineering. J.R. Pfafflin. Gordon and Breach Science Publishers, Inc., 270 8th Ave., New York, New York 10011. (212) 206-8900. 1992.

Encyclopedia of Physical Science and Technology. Robert A. Meyers, ed. Academic Press, c/o Harcourt Brace

Jovanovich Inc., 6277 Sea Harbor Dr., Orlando, Florida 32887. (800) 346-8648. Dictionary of engineering, technology and physical sciences.

McGraw-Hill Encyclopedia of Science and Technology. McGraw-Hill, 1221 Avenue of the Americas, New York, New York 10020. (212) 512-2000 or (800) 262-4729. 1992. Seventh edition. Issued in multiple volumes including index. Includes all science and technology broad subject areas.

Van Nostrand's Scientific Encyclopedia. Glenn D. Considine, ed. Van Nostrand Reinhold, 115 5th Ave., New York, New York 10003. (212) 254-3232. 1983. Sixth edition. Includes all broad subject areas in science.

GENERAL WORKS

A Matrix Approach to Biological Investigation of Synthetic Fuels. U.S. Environmental Protection Agency, Health Effects Research Laboratory, Office of Research and Development, MD 75, Research Triangle Park, North Carolina (919) 541-2184. Covers toxicology of shale oils, diesel fuels, jet planes, and synthetic fuels.

ONLINE DATA BASES

Computerized Engineering Index–COMPENDEX. Engineering Information Inc., 345 E. 47th St., New York, New York 10017. (212) 705-7600.

DIET

See: NUTRITION

DIFFUSED AIR

See: AIR QUALITY

DIFFUSION, ATMOSPHERIC

See: ATMOSPHERE

DIGESTER

ABSTRACTING AND INDEXING SERVICES

Applied Science and Technology Index. H.W. Wilson Co., 950 University Ave., Bronx, New York 10452. (800) 367-6770. Formerly Industrial Arts Index.

Biological Abstracts. BIOSIS, 2100 Arch St., Philadelphia, Pennsylvania 19103-1399. (215) 587-4800. 1927-.

Biological and Agricultural Index. H.W. Wilson Co., 950 University Ave., Bronx, New York 10452. (800) 367-6770. 1916-. Monthly.

Ecological Abstracts. Geo Abstracts Ltd. Elsevier Applied Science, Crown House, Linton Rd., Barking, England IG 11 8JU. 1974-. Derived from over 600 leading ecological and environmental journals, plus books, conference proceedings, reports and theses.

Environment Abstracts. Bowker A & I Publishing, 121 Chanlon Rd., New Providence, New Jersey 07974. (908) 464-6800. 1974-.

Environment Index. Environment Information Center, Index Research Department, 124 E. 39th St., New York, New York 10016. 1971-. Annual.

Environmental Information Connection–EIC. Planning Information Program, Dept. of Urban and Regional Planning, University of Illinois, 1003 West Nevada, Urbana, Illinois 61801. (217) 333-1369. Also available online.

Environmental Periodicals Bibliography. Environmental Studies Institute, International Academy at Santa Barbara, 800 Garden St., Suite D, Santa Barbara, California 93101. (805) 965-5010. Also available online.

General Science Index. H. W. Wilson Co., 950 University Ave., Bronx, New York 10452. 1978-. Monthly, also issued in annual cumulation. Cumulative subject index to English language periodicals in the subject fields of astronomy, botany, chemistry, earth science, environment and conservation, food and nutrition, genetics, mathematics, medicine and health, microbiology, oceanography, physics, physiology and zoology.

Geographical Abstracts. London School of Economics, Dept. of Geography, Regency House, 34 Duke St., London, England 1966-. Continued by Geo Abstracts issued in 6 parts: Pt. A. Landforms and the quaternary; Pt. B. Biogeography and Climatology; Pt. C. Economic geography; Pt. D. Social geography and cartography; Pt. E. Sedimentology; Pt. F. Regional and community planning.

Pollution Abstracts. Cambridge Scientific Abstracts, 5161 River Rd., Bethesda, Maryland 20816. (301) 961-6750. Six/year. Indexes worldwide technical literature on environmental pollution. Covers air pollution, marine and freshwater pollution, sewage and wastewater treatment, waste management, toxicology and health, noise pollution, radiation, land pollution, and environmental policies, programs, legislation, and education. Also available online.

Science Citation Index. Institute for Scientific Information, 3501 Market St., Philadelphia, Pennsylvania 19104. 1961-.

BIBLIOGRAPHIES

EPA Publications Bibliography. U.S. Environmental Protection Agency, Library Systems Branch, 401 M St., SW, Washington, District of Columbia 20460. (202) 260-2090. Quarterly.

ENCYCLOPEDIAS AND DICTIONARIES

McGraw-Hill Encyclopedia of Environmental Science. Sybil P. Parker. McGraw-Hill Science & Engineering Books, 11 W. 19th St., New York, New York 10011. (212) 337-6010. 1980. Covers ecology, man's influence on nature, and environmental protection.

McGraw-Hill Encyclopedia of Science and Technology. McGraw-Hill, 1221 Avenue of the Americas, New York, New York 10020. (212) 512-2000 or (800) 262-4729. 1992. Seventh edition. Issued in multiple volumes including index. Includes all science and technology broad subject areas.

The New York Times Encyclopedic Dictionary of the Environment. Paul Sarnoff. Quadrangle Books, New York, New York 1971. Focuses on state-of-the-art methods of pollution control, abatement, prevention and removal.

Van Nostrand's Scientific Encyclopedia. Glenn D. Considine, ed. Van Nostrand Reinhold, 115 5th Ave., New York, New York 10003. (212) 254-3232. 1983. Sixth edition. Includes all broad subject areas in science.

GENERAL WORKS

Biodegradation of PCBs Sorbed to Sewage Sludge Lagoon Sediments in an Aerobic Digester. William Amdor Chantry. University of Wisconsin Press, 114 N. Murray St., Madison, Wisconsin 53715. (608) 262-8782. 1989.

Report on the Design and Operation of a Full-Scale Anaerobic Dairy Manure Digester: Final Report. Elizabeth Coppinger, et al. U.S. Department of Energy, Solar Energy Research Institute, 5285 Port Royal Rd., Springfield, Virginia 22161. (703) 487-4650. 1979.

ONLINE DATA BASES

BIOSIS Previews. BIOSIS, 2100 Arch St., Philadelphia, Pennsylvania 19103-1399. (215) 587-4800. Largest and most comprehensive database of research in the life sciences. Contains citations for nearly 9000 primary research journals, monographs, reviews, symposia, preliminary reports, semi-popular journals, selected institutional reports, government reports and research communications.

Cambridge Scientific Abstracts Life Science–CSAL. Cambridge Scientific Abstracts, 5161 River Rd., Bethesda, Maryland 20816. (301) 961-6750. Provides access to the following abstracting services: "Life Sciences Collection," "Aquatic Sciences and Fisheries Abstracts," "Oceanic Abstracts," and "Pollution Abstracts."

Enviro/Energyline Abstracts Plus. R. R. Bowker Co., 121 Chanlon Rd., New Providence, New Jersey 07974. (908) 464-6800.

Environmental Periodicals Bibliography. National Information Services Corp., Ste. 6, Wyman Towers, 3100 St. Paul St., Baltimore, Maryland 21218. (410)243-0797. Online version of abstract of same name.

Monthly Catalog of United States Government Publications. U.S. G.P.O., Supt. of Docs., PO Box 371954, Pittsburgh, Pennsylvania 15250-7954. (202) 512-0000.

National Technical Information Service. U.S. Department of Commerce, National Technical Information Service, Office of Data Base Services, 5285 Port Royal Rd., Springfield, Virginia 22161. (703) 487-4807. Bibliographic database of government sponsored research and technical reports.

SCISEARCH. Institute for Scientific Information, University City Science Center, 3501 Market St., Philadelphia, Pennsylvania 19104. (215) 386-0100.

PERIODICALS AND NEWSLETTERS

Agriculture, Ecosystems & Environment. Elsevier Science Publishing Co., 655 Avenue of the Americas, New York, New York 10010. (212) 989-5800. Eight times a year. This journal is concerned with the interaction of methods of agricultural production, ecosystems and the environment.

Environmental Science and Technology. American Chemical Society, 1155 16th St. N.W., Washington, District of Columbia 20036. (800) 227-5558. 1967-. Monthly. Contains research articles on various aspects of environmental chemistry, interpretative articles by invited experts and commentary on the scientific aspects of environmental management.

The Journal of Biological Chemistry. American Society of Biological Chemists, 428 E. Preston St., Baltimore, Maryland 21202. Three times a month. Biological, agricultural, and energy aspects of the environment.

Journal of Environmental Engineering. American Society for Civil Engineers, 345 East 47th Street, New York, New York 10017. (212) 705-7496. Bimonthly. Covers problems in the environment and sanitation.

TAPPI Journal. Technical Association of the Pulp and Paper Industry, Box 105113, Atlanta, Georgia 30348-5113. (404) 446-1400. Monthly. Covers new technology and advancements in the pulp and paper industry.

Water Engineering & Management. Scranton Gillette Communications, Inc., 380 E. Northwest Hwy., Des Plaines, Illinois 60016-2282. (708) 298-6622. 1986-. Monthly. A professional trade publication which includes latest legislative news in the area of water quality, EPA criteria for drinking water, pesticides, and related standards. Includes articles of interest by water professionals and has regular news features such as forthcoming conferences, products at work, surveys, company profiles, etc.

TRADE ASSOCIATIONS AND PROFESSIONAL SOCIETIES

American Institute of Biological Sciences. 730 11th St., N.W., Washington, District of Columbia 20001-4521. (202) 628-1500.

American Institute of Chemical Engineers. 345 East 47th St., New York, New York 10017. (212) 705-7338.

American Institute of Chemists. 7315 Wisconsin Ave., Bethesda, Maryland 20814. (301) 652-2447.

DIISOCYANATES

ABSTRACTING AND INDEXING SERVICES

Applied Science and Technology Index. H.W. Wilson Co., 950 University Ave., Bronx, New York 10452. (800) 367-6770. Formerly Industrial Arts Index.

Chemical Abstracts. Chemical Abstracts Service, 2540 Olentangy River Rd., PO Box 3012, Columbus, Ohio 43210. (800) 848-6533. 1907-.

Science Citation Index. Institute for Scientific Information, 3501 Market St., Philadelphia, Pennsylvania 19104. 1961-.

GENERAL WORKS

Occupational Exposures to Diisocyanates. National Institute for Occupational Safety and Health. Department of Health and Human Services, Public Health Service, Center for Disease Control, National Institute for Occu-

pational Safety and Health, 200 Independence Ave. SW, Cincinnati, Ohio 20201. (202) 619-1296. 1978. Discusses toxicology of isocyanates and safety measures that are in practice.

ONLINE DATA BASES

CERCLIS. Chemical Information Systems, Inc., 7215 York Rd., Baltimore, Maryland 21212. (301) 321-8440. Information on hazardous waste disposal sites that have either been listed by the EPA on the National Priority List (NPL) or nominated for consideration for the NPL.

Chemical Abstracts-CA. Chemical Abstracts Service, 2540 Olentangy River Rd., P.O. Box 3012, Columbus, Ohio 43210. (800) 848-6533 or (614) 421-3600. Information sources include 9000 journals, patents from 27 countries, two industrial property organizations, new books, conference proceedings, and government research reports.

Chemical Abstracts Chemical Name Directory-CHEM-NAME. Chemical Abstracts Service, 2540 Olentangy River Rd., P.O. Box 3012, Columbus, Ohio 43210. (800) 848-6533 or (614) 421-3600. Listing of chemical substances in a dictionary type file. The Chemical Abstracts (CAS) Registry Number, molecular formula, Chemical Abstracts (CA) Substance Index Name, available synonyms, ring data and other chemical substance information is given for each entry.

Chemical Carcinogenesis Research Information System–CCRIS. National Library of Medicine, 8600 Rockville Pike, Bethesda, Maryland 20894. (800) 638-8480. Individual assay results and test conditions for 1,451 chemicals in the areas of carcinogenicity, mutagenicity, tumor promotion, and cocarcinogenicity.

DIKE EMBANKMENT
See: DAMS

DIMETHOATE

ABSTRACTING AND INDEXING SERVICES

Science Citation Index. Institute for Scientific Information, 3501 Market St., Philadelphia, Pennsylvania 19104. 1961-.

ONLINE DATA BASES

Chemical Abstracts Chemical Name Directory-CHEM-NAME. Chemical Abstracts Service, 2540 Olentangy River Rd., P.O. Box 3012, Columbus, Ohio 43210. (800) 848-6533 or (614) 421-3600. Listing of chemical substances in a dictionary type file. The Chemical Abstracts (CAS) Registry Number, molecular formula, Chemical Abstracts (CA) Substance Index Name, available synonyms, ring data and other chemical substance information is given for each entry.

Chemical Carcinogenesis Research Information System–CCRIS. National Library of Medicine, 8600 Rockville Pike, Bethesda, Maryland 20894. (800) 638-8480. Individual assay results and test conditions for 1,451 chemicals in the areas of carcinogenicity, mutagenicity, tumor promotion, and cocarcinogenicity.

Chemical Collection System/Request Tracking–CCS/ RTS. U.S. Environmental Protection Agency, Office of Pesticides and Toxic Substances, 401 M St., SW, Washington, District of Columbia 20460. (202) 260-2090. Contains information on various properties of a number of chemicals including environmental effects, test and analysis methods, and health effects. Available from EPA.

Chemical Dictionary Online–CHEMLINE. Chemical Abstracts Service, 2540 Olentangy River Rd., Columbus, Ohio 43210. (614) 421-3600 or (800) 848-6533. Part of MEDLINE of the National Library of Medicine (NLM). File of 900,000 names for chemical substances, representing 450,000 unique compounds. It contains such information as Chemical Abstracts (CA) Service Registry Numbers, molecular formulas, preferred chemical nomenclature, and generic and ring structure information. Available on NLM's ELHILL system.

Chemical Exposure. Science Applications International Corp., Health & Environmental Information, P.O. Box 2501, Oak Ridge, Tennessee 37831. (615) 482-9031. Database of chemicals that have been identified in both human tissues and body fluids and in feral and food animals. Contains reference to journal articles, conferences, and reports. Covers the whole fields of information related to human and animal exposure to food, air, and water contaminants and pharmaceuticals. Its records include information on chemical properties, formulas, tissues measured, analytical method used, demographics and more. Available on DIALOG.

TRADE ASSOCIATIONS AND PROFESSIONAL SOCIETIES

American Chemical Society. 1155 16th St., N.W., Washington, District of Columbia 20036. (202) 872-4600.

DIMICTIC LAKES

See: LAKES

DIOXINS

See also: AGENT ORANGE; DEFOLIATION; HEXACHLOROPHENE; HERBICIDES; PESTICIDES

ABSTRACTING AND INDEXING SERVICES

Applied Ecology Abstracts Studies in Renewable Natural Resources. Information Retrieval Ltd., 1911 Jefferson Davis Highway, Arlington, Virginia 22202. 1975-. Monthly.

Biological Abstracts. BIOSIS, 2100 Arch St., Philadelphia, Pennsylvania 19103-1399. (215) 587-4800. 1927-.

Biological and Agricultural Index. H.W. Wilson Co., 950 University Ave., Bronx, New York 10452. (800) 367-6770. 1916-. Monthly.

Chemical Abstracts. Chemical Abstracts Service, 2540 Olentangy River Rd., PO Box 3012, Columbus, Ohio 43210. (800) 848-6533. 1907-.

Ecological Abstracts. Geo Abstracts Ltd. Elsevier Applied Science, Crown House, Linton Rd., Barking, England IG 11 8JU. 1974-. Derived from over 600 leading ecological

and environmental journals, plus books, conference proceedings, reports and theses.

General Science Index. H. W. Wilson Co., 950 University Ave., Bronx, New York 10452. 1978-. Monthly, also issued in annual cumulation. Cumulative subject index to English language periodicals in the subject fields of astronomy, botany, chemistry, earth science, environment and conservation, food and nutrition, genetics, mathematics, medicine and health, microbiology, oceanography, physics, physiology and zoology.

Index to Scientific Book Contents. Institute for Scientific Information, 3501 Market St., Philadelphia, Pennsylvania 19104. (800) 523-1857. 1985-. Annual. Gives contents of science books published.

Multimedia Index to Ecology. National Information Center for Educational Media, University of Southern California, Los Angeles, California 90007.

Pesticides Abstracts. U.S. Environmental Protection Agency, Office of Pesticides Programs, 345 Curtland, Atlanta, Georgia 30365. (404) 347-2864. 1981. Monthly. Formerly: Health Aspects of Pesticides Abstracts Bulletin.

Science Citation Index. Institute for Scientific Information, 3501 Market St., Philadelphia, Pennsylvania 19104. 1961-.

Selected Water Abstracts on Dioxins and Dibenzofurans in Carcinogenesis, 1980-1986. Anthony J. Girardi. National Cancer Institute, U. S. Dept. of Health and Human Services, Public Health Service, National Institutes of Health, Washington, District of Columbia 20402-9325. (202) 783-3238. 1987.

BIBLIOGRAPHIES

Current Contents. Agriculture, Biology and Environmental Sciences. Institute for Scientific Information, 3501 Market St., Philadelphia, Pennsylvania 19104. (800) 523-1857. 1973-. Previous title: Current Contents. Agricultural, Food & Veterinary Sciences. Gives the table of contents of periodicals in the fields of agriculture, biology, environmental and related areas.

Dioxin Bibliography. Kay Flowers. TCT Engineers, 1908 Inner Belt Business Center Dr., St. Louis, Missouri 63114-5700. (314) 426-0880. 1984.

Review of Literature on Herbicides. U.S. Veterans Health Services and Research Administration. U.S. G.P.O., Washington, District of Columbia 20401. (202) 512-0000. Annual. Health effects of agent orange, phenoxy herbicides and other dioxins.

ENCYCLOPEDIAS AND DICTIONARIES

Cambridge Encyclopedia of Life Sciences. A. E. Friday and David S. Ingram. Cambridge University Press, 40 W 20th St., New York, New York 10011. (212) 924-3900 or (800) 227-0247. 1985. Includes all topics under biology and ecology.

Grzimek's Encyclopedia of Ecology. Bernhard Grzimek. Van Nostrand Reinhold, 115 5th Ave., New York, New York 10003. (212) 254-3232. 1976.

McGraw-Hill Encyclopedia of Environmental Science. Sybil P. Parker. McGraw-Hill Science & Engineering Books, 11 W. 19th St., New York, New York 10011.

(212) 337-6010. 1980. Covers ecology, man's influence on nature, and environmental protection.

McGraw-Hill Encyclopedia of Science and Technology. McGraw-Hill, 1221 Avenue of the Americas, New York, New York 10020. (212) 512-2000 or (800) 262-4729. 1992. Seventh edition. Issued in multiple volumes including index. Includes all science and technology broad subject areas.

North American Reference Encyclopedia of Ecology and Pollution. William White. North American Pub. Co., 401 N. Broad St., Philadelphia, Pennsylvania 19108. (215) 238-5300. 1972.

Van Nostrand's Scientific Encyclopedia. Glenn D. Considine, ed. Van Nostrand Reinhold, 115 5th Ave., New York, New York 10003. (212) 254-3232. 1983. Sixth edition. Includes all broad subject areas in science.

GENERAL WORKS

CDC Interference in Dioxin Water Standards. Committee on Government Operations. U.S. G.P.O., Washington, District of Columbia 20401. (202) 512-0000. 1991. Hearing before the Human Resources and Intergovernmental Relations Subcommittee of the Committee on Government Operations, House of Representatives, 101st Congress, 2d session, July 26, 1991. Provides the basic standards for dioxin content in water.

Chlorinated Dioxins and Dibenzofurans in Perspective. Christoffer Rappe, et al. Lewis Publishers, 2000 Corporate Blvd., N.W., Boca Raton, Florida 33431. (407) 994-0555 or (800) 272-7737. 1986. Gives the latest human exposure data and the most advanced analytical techniques developed in the continuing effort against contamination by chlorinated dioxins and dibenzofurans.

Chlorinated Dioxins and Dibenzofurans in the Total Environment. Gangadhar Chordhary, Lawrence H. Keith, and Christoffer Rappe. Butterworth-Heinemann, 80 Montvale Ave., Stoneham, Massachusetts 02180. (617) 438-8464. 1985. Environmental aspects and toxicology of tetrachlorodibenzodioxin and dibenzofurans.

Dioxin Contamination of Milk. Committee on Energy and Commerce. Subcommittee on Health and Environment. U.S. G.P.O., Washington, District of Columbia 20401. (202) 512-0000. 1990. Hearing before the subcommittee on Health and the Environment of the Committee on Energy and Commerce, House of Representatives, 101st Congress, 1st session, September 8, 1989. Contains facts about dioxin contamination of milk and the health effects on the environment.

Environmental Issues: An Anthology of 1989. Thomas W. Joyce, ed. TAPPI Press, Technology Park/Atlanta, PO Box 105113, Atlanta, Georgia 30348. (404) 446-1400. 1990. Contains 39 papers on environmental, safety and occupational health concerns from 11 TAPPI, CPPA and AIChE meetings held during 1989. Also included is a literature review of over 200 papers published in 1989.

Interim Procedures for Estimating Risks Associated with Exposures to Mixtures of Chlorinated Dibenzo-RHO-Dioxins-and- Dibenzofurans. Judith S. Bellin. U.S. Environmental Protection Agency, 401 M St., SW, Washington, District of Columbia 20460. (202) 260-2090.

TAPPI Environmental Conference Proceedings, Seattle, WA, April 9-11, 1990. TAPPI Press, Technology Park/Atlanta, PO Box 105113, Atlanta, Georgia 30348. (404)

446-1400. 1990. Contains 11 papers presented at the conference covering industrial pollution and its remedies.

ONLINE DATA BASES

BIOSIS Previews. BIOSIS, 2100 Arch St., Philadelphia, Pennsylvania 19103-1399. (215) 587-4800. Largest and most comprehensive database of research in the life sciences. Contains citations for nearly 9000 primary research journals, monographs, reviews, symposia, preliminary reports, semi-popular journals, selected institutional reports, government reports and research communications.

CERCLIS. Chemical Information Systems, Inc., 7215 York Rd., Baltimore, Maryland 21212. (301) 321-8440. Information on hazardous waste disposal sites that have either been listed by the EPA on the National Priority List (NPL) or nominated for consideration for the NPL.

Chemical Abstracts-CA. Chemical Abstracts Service, 2540 Olentangy River Rd., P.O. Box 3012, Columbus, Ohio 43210. (800) 848-6533 or (614) 421-3600. Information sources include 9000 journals, patents from 27 countries, two industrial property organizations, new books, conference proceedings, and government research reports.

Chemical Abstracts Chemical Name Directory-CHEMNAME. Chemical Abstracts Service, 2540 Olentangy River Rd., P.O. Box 3012, Columbus, Ohio 43210. (800) 848-6533 or (614) 421-3600. Listing of chemical substances in a dictionary type file. The Chemical Abstracts (CAS) Registry Number, molecular formula, Chemical Abstracts (CA) Substance Index Name, available synonyms, ring data and other chemical substance information is given for each entry.

Chemical Carcinogenesis Research Information System–CCRIS. National Library of Medicine, 8600 Rockville Pike, Bethesda, Maryland 20894. (800) 638-8480. Individual assay results and test conditions for 1,451 chemicals in the areas of carcinogenicity, mutagenicity, tumor promotion, and cocarcinogenicity.

Chemical Collection System/Request Tracking–CCS/RTS. U.S. Environmental Protection Agency, Office of Pesticides and Toxic Substances, 401 M St., SW, Washington, District of Columbia 20460. (202) 260-2090. Contains information on various properties of a number of chemicals including environmental effects, test and analysis methods, and health effects. Available from EPA.

Chemical Dictionary Online–CHEMLINE. Chemical Abstracts Service, 2540 Olentangy River Rd., Columbus, Ohio 43210. (614) 421-3600 or (800) 848-6533. Part of MEDLINE of the National Library of Medicine (NLM). File of 900,000 names for chemical substances, representing 450,000 unique compounds. It contains such information as Chemical Abstracts (CA) Service Registry Numbers, molecular formulas, preferred chemical nomenclature, and generic and ring structure information. Available on NLM's ELHILL system.

Chemical Exposure. Science Applications International Corp., Health & Environmental Information, P.O. Box 2501, Oak Ridge, Tennessee 37831. (615) 482-9031. Database of chemicals that have been identified in both human tissues and body fluids and in feral and food animals. Contains reference to journal articles, conferences, and reports. Covers the whole fields of informa-

tion related to human and animal exposure to food, air, and water contaminants and pharmaceuticals. Its records include information on chemical properties, formulas, tissues measured, analytical method used, demographics and more. Available on DIALOG.

Monthly Catalog of United States Government Publications. U.S. G.P.O., Supt. of Docs., PO Box 371954, Pittsburgh, Pennsylvania 15250-7954. (202) 512-0000.

National Technical Information Service. U.S. Department of Commerce, National Technical Information Service, Office of Data Base Services, 5285 Port Royal Rd., Springfield, Virginia 22161. (703) 487-4807. Bibliographic database of government sponsored research and technical reports.

SCISEARCH. Institute for Scientific Information, University City Science Center, 3501 Market St., Philadelphia, Pennsylvania 19104. (215) 386-0100.

PERIODICALS AND NEWSLETTERS

Clean Water Report. Business Publishers, Inc., 951 Pershing Dr., Silver Spring, Maryland 20910-4464. (301) 587-6300. 1964-. Biweekly. Key information source for environmental professionals, covering the important issues: groundwater, drinking water, wastewater treatment, drought, wetlands, coastal protection, dioxin, non-point source pollution, agrichemical contamination, cleanup versus prevention issues, and related topics.

DIQUAT

ABSTRACTING AND INDEXING SERVICES

Biological Abstracts. BIOSIS, 2100 Arch St., Philadelphia, Pennsylvania 19103-1399. (215) 587-4800. 1927-.

Chemical Abstracts. Chemical Abstracts Service, 2540 Olentangy River Rd., PO Box 3012, Columbus, Ohio 43210. (800) 848-6533. 1907-.

Pollution Abstracts. Cambridge Scientific Abstracts, 5161 River Rd., Bethesda, Maryland 20816. (301) 961-6750. Six/year. Indexes worldwide technical literature on environmental pollution. Covers air pollution, marine and freshwater pollution, sewage and wastewater treatment, waste management, toxicology and health, noise pollution, radiation, land pollution, and environmental policies, programs, legislation, and education. Also available online.

Science Citation Index. Institute for Scientific Information, 3501 Market St., Philadelphia, Pennsylvania 19104. 1961-.

ENCYCLOPEDIAS AND DICTIONARIES

Encyclopedia of Trademarks and Synonyms. H. Bennett, ed. Chemical Publishing Co., 80 Eighth Ave., New York, New York 10011. (212) 255-1950. 1981. Three volumes. Includes chemical compounds, compositions consisting of one or more chemicals and other products. Also included are abbreviated names and WHO free names.

McGraw-Hill Encyclopedia of Science and Technology. McGraw-Hill, 1221 Avenue of the Americas, New York, New York 10020. (212) 512-2000 or (800) 262-4729. 1992. Seventh edition. Issued in multiple volumes in-

cluding index. Includes all science and technology broad subject areas.

ONLINE DATA BASES

BIOSIS Previews. BIOSIS, 2100 Arch St., Philadelphia, Pennsylvania 19103-1399. (215) 587-4800. Largest and most comprehensive database of research in the life sciences. Contains citations for nearly 9000 primary research journals, monographs, reviews, symposia, preliminary reports, semi-popular journals, selected institutional reports, government reports and research communications.

Chemical Abstracts-CA. Chemical Abstracts Service, 2540 Olentangy River Rd., P.O. Box 3012, Columbus, Ohio 43210. (800) 848-6533 or (614) 421-3600. Information sources include 9000 journals, patents from 27 countries, two industrial property organizations, new books, conference proceedings, and government research reports.

Chemical Abstracts Chemical Name Directory-CHEMNAME. Chemical Abstracts Service, 2540 Olentangy River Rd., P.O. Box 3012, Columbus, Ohio 43210. (800) 848-6533 or (614) 421-3600. Listing of chemical substances in a dictionary type file. The Chemical Abstracts (CAS) Registry Number, molecular formula, Chemical Abstracts (CA) Substance Index Name, available synonyms, ring data and other chemical substance information is given for each entry.

Chemical Carcinogenesis Research Information System-CCRIS. National Library of Medicine, 8600 Rockville Pike, Bethesda, Maryland 20894. (800) 638-8480. Individual assay results and test conditions for 1,451 chemicals in the areas of carcinogenicity, mutagenicity, tumor promotion, and cocarcinogenicity.

DISASTERS (NATURAL, HUMAN-RELATED)

ABSTRACTING AND INDEXING SERVICES

Current Advances in Ecological and Environmental Science. Pergamon Microforms International, Inc., Fairview Park, Elmsford, New York 10523. (914) 592-7720. 1989-. Monthly. Current literature searching service including journals, reports, abstracts, etc. This service is available online as part of the CABS database on the hosts BRS and ORBIT search service.

General Science Index. H. W. Wilson Co., 950 University Ave., Bronx, New York 10452. 1978-. Monthly, also issued in annual cumulation. Cumulative subject index to English language periodicals in the subject fields of astronomy, botany, chemistry, earth science, environment and conservation, food and nutrition, genetics, mathematics, medicine and health, microbiology, oceanography, physics, physiology and zoology.

Pollution Abstracts. Cambridge Scientific Abstracts, 5161 River Rd., Bethesda, Maryland 20816. (301) 961-6750. Six/year. Indexes worldwide technical literature on environmental pollution. Covers air pollution, marine and freshwater pollution, sewage and wastewater treatment, waste management, toxicology and health, noise pollution, radiation, land pollution, and environmental poli-

cies, programs, legislation, and education. Also available online.

Science Citation Index. Institute for Scientific Information, 3501 Market St., Philadelphia, Pennsylvania 19104. 1961-.

BIBLIOGRAPHIES

A Selected Annotated Bibliography of 1989 Hazards Publications. Dave Morton. Natural Hazards Center, Campus Box 482, University of Colorado, Boulder, Colorado 80309-0482. (303) 492-6819. 1990. Contains 292 entries in 12 categories: earthquakes and tsunamis; floods, hurricanes, cyclones, tornados and severe storms, volcanoes; technological hazards; health and medical hazards; miscellaneous hazards; coastal zone management and planning; landslides and other mass earth movements; water resources and wetland management and climate and drought.

ENCYCLOPEDIAS AND DICTIONARIES

Hazardous Materials Dictionary. Ronny J. Coleman and Kara Hewson Williams. Technomic Publishing Co., 851 New Holland Ave., Box 3535, Lancaster, Pennsylvania 17604. (717) 291-5609. 1988. Defines more than 2600 specialized words which are critical for communication, especially under the stressful circumstances of an emergency. Identifies many of the unique terms that apply to the handling of hazardous materials emergencies.

McGraw-Hill Encyclopedia of Environmental Science. Sybil P. Parker. McGraw-Hill Science & Engineering Books, 11 W. 19th St., New York, New York 10011. (212) 337-6010. 1980. Covers ecology, man's influence on nature, and environmental protection.

McGraw-Hill Encyclopedia of Science and Technology. McGraw-Hill, 1221 Avenue of the Americas, New York, New York 10020. (212) 512-2000 or (800) 262-4729. 1992. Seventh edition. Issued in multiple volumes including index. Includes all science and technology broad subject areas.

GENERAL WORKS

Community Right-to-Know and Small Business. U.S. Environmental Protection Agency, Office of Solid Waste and Emergency Response, 401 M St., S.W., Washington, District of Columbia 20460. (202) 260-2090. 1988. Interprets the community Right-to-Know Act of 1986, especially Sections 311 and 312.

Environmental Hazards of War: Releasing Dangerous Forces in an Industrialized World. Arthur H. Westing. SAGE Pub., 2111 W. Hillcrest Dr., Newbury Park, California 91320. (805) 499-0721. 1990. Population living downstream from hydrologic facilities, and near or adjacent to chemical and nuclear plants, greatly increases the potential risk to civilians from collateral damage by war. This book examines such a situation.

Fire in the Rain. Peter Gould. Carolina Biological Supply Company, 2700 York Rd., Burlington, North Carolina 27215. (919) 584-0381. 1990. Describes the Chernobyl accident.

Hazardous Materials Transportation Accidents. National Fire Protection Association, 1 Battery Park, Quincy, Massachusetts 02269. (617) 770-3000; (800) 344-3555. 1978. Compilation of articles from Fire Journal and Fire

Command. Deals with transportation of hazardous substances, their combustibility during accidents and preventive measures.

Hidden Dangers: Environmental Consequences of Preparing for War. Anne H. Ehrlich and John W. Birks, eds. Sierra Club Books, 100 Bush St., San Francisco, California 94104. (415) 291-1600. 1991. Considers a number of questions concerning the dangers–health-related, environmental, psychological, economic, etc.–that have been and are still being engendered by the U.S. and other nations, since the 1940s, to manufacture, store, and dispose of nuclear, chemical, and biological weapons.

In the Wake of the Exxon Valdez: Devastating Impact of Alaska's Oil Spill. Art Davidson. Sierra Club Books, 100 Bush St., San Francisco, California 94104. (415) 291-1600. 1990. Story of environmental risk and the consequences that arise.

National Transportation Safety Board Marine Accident Report: Prince William Sound, Alaska, March 24, 1989 Grounding of the U.S. Tankship Exxon Valdez. National Transportation Safety Board, 800 Independence Avenue, SW, Washington, District of Columbia 20544. (202) 382-6600. 1990.

Natural Disaster Studies. National Academy Press, 2101 Constitution Ave. N.W., PO Box 285, Washington, District of Columbia 20418. (202) 334-3313. 1991. An investigative series of the Committee on Natural Disasters issued by the National Research Council, Committee on Natural Disasters.

Out of the Channel: The Exxon Valdez Oil Spill in Prince William Sound. John Keeble. Harper & Row, 10 E. 53rd St., New York, New York 10022. (212) 207-7000. 1991. Presents a detailed account of the disaster, its implications and ramifications.

Reactor Accidents: Nuclear Safety and the Role of Institutional Failure. David Mosey. Nuclear Engineering International Special Publications, c/o Butterworth-Heinemann, 80 Montvale Ave., Stoneham, Massachusetts 02180. (617) 438-8464; (800) 366-2665. 1990.

Safe Handling of Chemical Carcinogens, Mutagens, and Highly Toxic Substances. Douglas B. Walters, ed. Ann Arbor Science, 230 Collingwood, Ann Arbor, Michigan 48106. 1980-. Prevention and control of occupational accidents.

Sharing Environmental Risks: How to Control Governments' Losses in Natural Disasters. Raymond J. Burby, et al. Westview Press, 5500 Central Ave., Boulder, Colorado 80301. (303) 444-3541. 1991. Deals with ways and means to control costs in the aftermath of a disaster. Explains risk insurance and how it can help.

Sunken Nuclear Submarines: A Threat to the Environment?. Viking Oliver Eriksen. Norwegian Univ. Pr., Oxford Univ. Pr., 200 Madison Ave., New York, New York 10016. (212) 679-7300; (800) 334-4249. 1990. Part 1 is a survey of existing submarines, based upon surmise and extrapolation from public knowledge of civilian terrestrial and nautical reactors. Part 2 describes potential accident scenarios and their potential for nuclide release, and Part 3 briefly sketches the oceanographic factors governing dispersion of radioactive nuclides.

The Truth About Chernobyl. Evelyn Rossiter. Basic Books, 10 E. 53rd St., New York, New York 10022. (212) 207-7057. 1991. Describes how bureaucratic mistakes caused the disaster.

GOVERNMENTAL ORGANIZATIONS

Office of Public Affairs. 1717 H St., N.W., Washington, District of Columbia 20555. (301) 492-7715.

HANDBOOKS AND MANUALS

A Guide to the Safe Handling of Hazardous Materials Accidents. ASTM, 1916 Race St., Philadelphia, Pennsylvania 19103-1187. (215) 299-5400. 1990. 2d ed. Planning and training document to assure the safest, most effective handling of a hazardous material accident.

Handbook of Emergency Management: Programs and Policies Dealing With Major Hazards and Disasters. William L. Waugh, Jr., and Ronald John Hy, eds. Greenwood Publishing Group, Inc., 88 Post Rd. W., Box 5007, Westport, Connecticut 06881. (203) 226-3571. 1990.

How to Respond to Hazardous Chemical Spills. W. Unterberg, et al. Noyes Publications, 120 Mill Rd., Park Ridge, New Jersey 07656. (201) 391-8484. 1988. Reference manual of countermeasures is designed to assist responders to spills of hazardous substances.

Spill Reporting Procedures Guide. Robert E. Abbott. Bureau of National Affairs, 1231 25th St. N.W., Washington, District of Columbia 20037. (202) 452-4200. 1990. This aid to fulfilling the requisite federal, state, and local reporting requirements contains the verbal and written reporting requirements for oil, hazardous substances, hazardous wastes, hazardous materials, excess air emissions, wastewater excursions, underground tank leaks, and SARA Title III.

ONLINE DATA BASES

Cambridge Scientific Abstracts Life Science–CSAL. Cambridge Scientific Abstracts, 5161 River Rd., Bethesda, Maryland 20816. (301) 961-6750. Provides access to the following abstracting services: "Life Sciences Collection," "Aquatic Sciences and Fisheries Abstracts," "Oceanic Abstracts," and "Pollution Abstracts."

Monthly Catalog of United States Government Publications. U.S. G.P.O., Supt. of Docs., PO Box 371954, Pittsburgh, Pennsylvania 15250-7954. (202) 512-0000.

National Technical Information Service. U.S. Department of Commerce, National Technical Information Service, Office of Data Base Services, 5285 Port Royal Rd., Springfield, Virginia 22161. (703) 487-4807. Bibliographic database of government sponsored research and technical reports.

PressNet Environmental Reports. Chemical Information Systems, Inc., 7215 York Rd., Baltimore, Maryland 21212. (301) 321-8440.

PERIODICALS AND NEWSLETTERS

Community and Worker Right-to-Know News. Thompson Publishing Group, 1725 K St. NW, Washington, District of Columbia 20006. (800) 424-2959. Bimonthly. Reports on chemical disclosure requirements and industrial liability.

Emergency Preparedness News. Business Publishers, Inc., 951 Pershing Drive, Silver Spring, Maryland 20910. (301) 587-6300. Biweekly. Emergency management techniques and technologies.

Hazard Monthly. Research Alternatives, Inc., 1401 Rockville Pike, Rockville, Maryland 20852. (301) 424-2803. Monthly. Covers natural disasters and hazardous substances.

National Emergency Training Guide. Emergency Response Institute, 4537 Foxhall Drive, NW, Olympia, Washington 98506. (206) 491-7785. Annual. Covers topics of emergency search and rescue.

Natural Hazards Observer. University of Colorado, Hazards Res. & Apl. Info. Ctr., Campus Box 482, Boulder, Colorado 80309. (303) 492-6818. Bimonthly. Hazards-legislation at federal, state, and local levels.

Nature and Resources. Elsevier Science Publishing Co., 655 Avenue of the Americas, New York, New York 10010. (212) 989-5800. 1965-. Quarterly. Provides indepth reviews of contemporary environmental issues from an international perspective.

STATISTICS SOURCES

Public Health Consequences of Disasters. U.S. G.P.O., Washington, District of Columbia 20401. (202) 512-0000. 1989. Natural and human-generated disasters impact on public health.

TRADE ASSOCIATIONS AND PROFESSIONAL SOCIETIES

Natural Hazards Research and Applications Information Center. Campus Box 482, University of Colorado, Boulder, Colorado 80309. (303) 492-6818.

DISCLIMAX

See: ECOSYSTEMS

DISPENSERS

ABSTRACTING AND INDEXING SERVICES

Science Citation Index. Institute for Scientific Information, 3501 Market St., Philadelphia, Pennsylvania 19104. 1961-.

ONLINE DATA BASES

PressNet Environmental Reports. Chemical Information Systems, Inc., 7215 York Rd., Baltimore, Maryland 21212. (301) 321-8440.

DISPERSION MODEL

See: AIR POLLUTION

DISPOSAL METHODS

See: HAZARDOUS WASTES

DISPOSAL SITES
See: HAZARDOUS WASTES

DISPOSAL SYSTEMS
See: HAZARDOUS WASTES

DISSOLVED OXYGEN

ABSTRACTING AND INDEXING SERVICES

Abstracts of Air and Water Conservation Literature. American Petroleum Institute. Central Abstracting and Indexing Service, 275 Madison Avenue, New York, New York 10016. 1972.

Applied Science and Technology Index. H.W. Wilson Co., 950 University Ave., Bronx, New York 10452. (800) 367-6770. Formerly Industrial Arts Index.

Aqualine Abstracts. Water Research Centre. c/o Pergamon Microforms International, Inc., Fairview Park, Elmsford, New York 10523. (914) 592-7720. 1927-. Contains some 8,000 records annually on water and wastewater technology. Covers all aspects of water, wastewater, associated engineering services and the aquatic environment. Over 600 periodicals, as well as books, reports and conference proceedings and other publications from water related institutions worldwide are scanned. Also available online.

ASFA Aquaculture Abstracts. Cambridge Scientific Abstracts, Inc., 5161 River Rd., Bethesda, Maryland 20816. (301) 961-6750. 1984.

Chemical Abstracts. Chemical Abstracts Service, 2540 Olentangy River Rd., PO Box 3012, Columbus, Ohio 43210. (800) 848-6533. 1907-.

Environment Abstracts. Bowker A & I Publishing, 121 Chanlon Rd., New Providence, New Jersey 07974. (908) 464-6800. 1974-.

Environment Index. Environment Information Center, Index Research Department, 124 E. 39th St., New York, New York 10016. 1971-. Annual.

Environmental Information Connection–EIC. Planning Information Program, Dept. of Urban and Regional Planning, University of Illinois, 1003 West Nevada, Urbana, Illinois 61801. (217) 333-1369. Also available online.

Environmental Periodicals Bibliography. Environmental Studies Institute, International Academy at Santa Barbara, 800 Garden St., Suite D, Santa Barbara, California 93101. (805) 965-5010. Also available online.

Index to Scientific Book Contents. Institute for Scientific Information, 3501 Market St., Philadelphia, Pennsylvania 19104. (800) 523-1857. 1985-. Annual. Gives contents of science books published.

Science Citation Index. Institute for Scientific Information, 3501 Market St., Philadelphia, Pennsylvania 19104. 1961-.

BIBLIOGRAPHIES

EPA Publications Bibliography. U.S. Environmental Protection Agency, Library Systems Branch, 401 M St., SW, Washington, District of Columbia 20460. (202) 260-2090. Quarterly.

ONLINE DATA BASES

CAS Source Index–CASSI. Chemical Abstracts Service, 2540 Olentangy River Rd., P.O. Box 3012, Columbus, Ohio 43210. (800) 848-6533 or (614) 421-3600. A listing of bibliographic and library holdings information for scientific and technical primary literature relevant to the chemical sciences.

Chemical Abstracts-CA. Chemical Abstracts Service, 2540 Olentangy River Rd., P.O. Box 3012, Columbus, Ohio 43210. (800) 848-6533 or (614) 421-3600. Information sources include 9000 journals, patents from 27 countries, two industrial property organizations, new books, conference proceedings, and government research reports.

Enviro/Energyline Abstracts Plus. R. R. Bowker Co., 121 Chanlon Rd., New Providence, New Jersey 07974. (908) 464-6800.

Environmental Periodicals Bibliography. National Information Services Corp., Ste. 6, Wyman Towers, 3100 St. Paul St., Baltimore, Maryland 21218. (410)243-0797. Online version of abstract of same name.

TRADE ASSOCIATIONS AND PROFESSIONAL SOCIETIES

American Institute of Chemical Engineers. 345 East 47th St., New York, New York 10017. (212) 705-7338.

American Institute of Chemists. 7315 Wisconsin Ave., Bethesda, Maryland 20814. (301) 652-2447.

DISSOLVED SOLIDS

ABSTRACTING AND INDEXING SERVICES

Abstracts of Air and Water Conservation Literature. American Petroleum Institute. Central Abstracting and Indexing Service, 275 Madison Avenue, New York, New York 10016. 1972.

Applied Science and Technology Index. H.W. Wilson Co., 950 University Ave., Bronx, New York 10452. (800) 367-6770. Formerly Industrial Arts Index.

Aqualine Abstracts. Water Research Centre. c/o Pergamon Microforms International, Inc., Fairview Park, Elmsford, New York 10523. (914) 592-7720. 1927-. Contains some 8,000 records annually on water and wastewater technology. Covers all aspects of water, wastewater, associated engineering services and the aquatic environment. Over 600 periodicals, as well as books, reports and conference proceedings and other publications from water related institutions worldwide are scanned. Also available online.

Chemical Abstracts. Chemical Abstracts Service, 2540 Olentangy River Rd., PO Box 3012, Columbus, Ohio 43210. (800) 848-6533. 1907-.

Environment Abstracts. Bowker A & I Publishing, 121 Chanlon Rd., New Providence, New Jersey 07974. (908) 464-6800. 1974-.

Environment Index. Environment Information Center, Index Research Department, 124 E. 39th St., New York, New York 10016. 1971-. Annual.

Environmental Information Connection–EIC. Planning Information Program, Dept. of Urban and Regional Planning, University of Illinois, 1003 West Nevada, Urbana, Illinois 61801. (217) 333-1369. Also available online.

Environmental Periodicals Bibliography. Environmental Studies Institute, International Academy at Santa Barbara, 800 Garden St., Suite D, Santa Barbara, California 93101. (805) 965-5010. Also available online.

Index to Scientific Book Contents. Institute for Scientific Information, 3501 Market St., Philadelphia, Pennsylvania 19104. (800) 523-1857. 1985-. Annual. Gives contents of science books published.

BIBLIOGRAPHIES

EPA Publications Bibliography. U.S. Environmental Protection Agency, Library Systems Branch, 401 M St., SW, Washington, District of Columbia 20460. (202) 260-2090. Quarterly.

GENERAL WORKS

Sources of Concentrations of Dissolved Solids and Selenium in the San Joaquin River and its Tributaries, California, October 1985 to March 1987. Daphne G. Clifton and Robert J. Gilliom. Department of the Interior, U.S. Geological Survey, 119 National Center, Reston, Virginia 22092. (703) 648-4460. 1989. Report describes sediment transportation in rivers and tributaries.

ONLINE DATA BASES

CAS Source Index–CASSI. Chemical Abstracts Service, 2540 Olentangy River Rd., P.O. Box 3012, Columbus, Ohio 43210. (800) 848-6533 or (614) 421-3600. A listing of bibliographic and library holdings information for scientific and technical primary literature relevant to the chemical sciences.

Chemest. Technical Database Services, Inc., 10 Columbus Circle, New York, New York 10019. (212) 245-0044. Covers methods of estimating 11 important properties: water solubility, soil adsorption coefficient, bioconcentration factor, acid dissociation constant, activity coefficient, boiling point, vapor pressure, water volatilization rate, Henry's Law Constant, melting point, and liquid viscosity.

Chemical Abstracts-CA. Chemical Abstracts Service, 2540 Olentangy River Rd., P.O. Box 3012, Columbus, Ohio 43210. (800) 848-6533 or (614) 421-3600. Information sources include 9000 journals, patents from 27 countries, two industrial property organizations, new books, conference proceedings, and government research reports.

Enviro/Energyline Abstracts Plus. R. R. Bowker Co., 121 Chanlon Rd., New Providence, New Jersey 07974. (908) 464-6800.

Environmental Periodicals Bibliography. National Information Services Corp., Ste. 6, Wyman Towers, 3100 St.

Paul St., Baltimore, Maryland 21218. (410)243-0797. Online version of abstract of same name.

Monthly Catalog of United States Government Publications. U.S. G.P.O., Supt. of Docs., PO Box 371954, Pittsburgh, Pennsylvania 15250-7954. (202) 512-0000.

National Technical Information Service. U.S. Department of Commerce, National Technical Information Service, Office of Data Base Services, 5285 Port Royal Rd., Springfield, Virginia 22161. (703) 487-4807. Bibliographic database of government sponsored research and technical reports.

TRADE ASSOCIATIONS AND PROFESSIONAL SOCIETIES

American Institute of Chemical Engineers. 345 East 47th St., New York, New York 10017. (212) 705-7338.

American Institute of Chemists. 7315 Wisconsin Ave., Bethesda, Maryland 20814. (301) 652-2447.

DISTILLATION

ABSTRACTING AND INDEXING SERVICES

Abstracts of Air and Water Conservation Literature. American Petroleum Institute. Central Abstracting and Indexing Service, 275 Madison Avenue, New York, New York 10016. 1972.

Applied Science and Technology Index. H.W. Wilson Co., 950 University Ave., Bronx, New York 10452. (800) 367-6770. Formerly Industrial Arts Index.

Chemical Abstracts. Chemical Abstracts Service, 2540 Olentangy River Rd., PO Box 3012, Columbus, Ohio 43210. (800) 848-6533. 1907-.

Environment Abstracts. Bowker A & I Publishing, 121 Chanlon Rd., New Providence, New Jersey 07974. (908) 464-6800. 1974-.

Environment Index. Environment Information Center, Index Research Department, 124 E. 39th St., New York, New York 10016. 1971-. Annual.

Environmental Information Connection–EIC. Planning Information Program, Dept. of Urban and Regional Planning, University of Illinois, 1003 West Nevada, Urbana, Illinois 61801. (217) 333-1369. Also available online.

Environmental Periodicals Bibliography. Environmental Studies Institute, International Academy at Santa Barbara, 800 Garden St., Suite D, Santa Barbara, California 93101. (805) 965-5010. Also available online.

General Science Index. H. W. Wilson Co., 950 University Ave., Bronx, New York 10452. 1978-. Monthly, also issued in annual cumulation. Cumulative subject index to English language periodicals in the subject fields of astronomy, botany, chemistry, earth science, environment and conservation, food and nutrition, genetics, mathematics, medicine and health, microbiology, oceanography, physics, physiology and zoology.

Index to Scientific Book Contents. Institute for Scientific Information, 3501 Market St., Philadelphia, Pennsylvania 19104. (800) 523-1857. 1985-. Annual. Gives contents of science books published.

Physics Briefs. Physikalische Berichte. Physik Verlag, Pappapelallee 3, Postfach 101161, Weinheim, Germany D-6940. 1979-. Semimonthly. In English. Volumes for 1979- issued by the Deutsche Physikalische Gesellschaft and the Fachinformationszentrum Energie Physik, Mathematik in cooperation with the American Institute of Physics.

Pollution Abstracts. Cambridge Scientific Abstracts, 5161 River Rd., Bethesda, Maryland 20816. (301) 961-6750. Six/year. Indexes worldwide technical literature on environmental pollution. Covers air pollution, marine and freshwater pollution, sewage and wastewater treatment, waste management, toxicology and health, noise pollution, radiation, land pollution, and environmental policies, programs, legislation, and education. Also available online.

Science Citation Index. Institute for Scientific Information, 3501 Market St., Philadelphia, Pennsylvania 19104. 1961-.

BIBLIOGRAPHIES

Distillation Bibliography. Dr. Frank C. Vibrandt. Newman Library, Rm. 6030, Virginia Polytechnic Institute, Blacksburg, Virginia 24061. (703) 961-5593.

EPA Publications Bibliography. U.S. Environmental Protection Agency, Library Systems Branch, 401 M St., SW, Washington, District of Columbia 20460. (202) 260-2090. Quarterly.

ENCYCLOPEDIAS AND DICTIONARIES

Encyclopedia of Chemical Processing and Design. John J. Mcketta and W. A. Cunningham. Marcel Dekker, Inc., 270 Madison Ave., New York, New York 10016. (212) 696-9000; (800) 228-1160. 1992. Thirty-eight volumes.

Encyclopedia of Physical Science and Technology. Robert A. Meyers, ed. Academic Press, c/o Harcourt Brace Jovanovich Inc., 6277 Sea Harbor Dr., Orlando, Florida 32887. (800) 346-8648. Dictionary of engineering, technology and physical sciences.

European Federation of Chemical Engineering. Working Party on Distillation. Six-Language Vocabulary of Distillation Terms. Institution of Chemical Engineers for the European Federation of Chemical Engineering, London, England Text in English, French, Spanish, Russian, Italian, and German.

Kirk-Othmer Encyclopedia of Chemical Technology. J. I. Kroschwitz, ed. John Wiley & Sons, Inc., 605 3rd Ave., New York, New York 10158-0012. (212) 850-6000. 1992-. All articles in the new edition have been rewritten and updated adding new subjects such as biotechnology, computer topics, analytical techniques and instrumentation, environmental concerns, fuels and energy, inorganic and solid state chemistry; composite materials and material science in general, and pharmaceuticals. Also available online.

McGraw-Hill Encyclopedia of Science and Technology. McGraw-Hill, 1221 Avenue of the Americas, New York, New York 10020. (212) 512-2000 or (800) 262-4729. 1992. Seventh edition. Issued in multiple volumes including index. Includes all science and technology broad subject areas.

Van Nostrand's Scientific Encyclopedia. Glenn D. Considine, ed. Van Nostrand Reinhold, 115 5th Ave., New York, New York 10003. (212) 254-3232. 1983. Sixth edition. Includes all broad subject areas in science.

GENERAL WORKS

Distillation Operations. Henry Z. Kister. McGraw-Hill, 1221 Avenue of the Americas, New York, New York 10020. (212) 512-2000 or (800) 262-4729.

Treatment Technologies. Environment Protection Agency. Government Institutes, Inc., 4 Research Pl., Ste. 200, Rockville, Maryland 20850. (301)921-2300. 1991. 2nd ed. Provides a clear explanation of 24 treatment technologies and evaluates the effectiveness of the design and operations of each type of treatment. This new edition has more supporting numerical data, examples for a better understanding of the technology and an updated reference for specific industrial wastes.

HANDBOOKS AND MANUALS

Handbook of Laboratory Distillation. Erich Kreel. 655 Avenue of the Americas, New York, New York 10010. (212) 989-5800. An introduction into the pilot plant distillation.

ONLINE DATA BASES

CAS Source Index–CASSI. Chemical Abstracts Service, 2540 Olentangy River Rd., P.O. Box 3012, Columbus, Ohio 43210. (800) 848-6533 or (614) 421-3600. A listing of bibliographic and library holdings information for scientific and technical primary literature relevant to the chemical sciences.

Chemical Abstracts-CA. Chemical Abstracts Service, 2540 Olentangy River Rd., P.O. Box 3012, Columbus, Ohio 43210. (800) 848-6533 or (614) 421-3600. Information sources include 9000 journals, patents from 27 countries, two industrial property organizations, new books, conference proceedings, and government research reports.

Chemical Engineering and Biotechnology Abstracts–CEBA. Orbit Search Service, Maxwell Online Inc., 8000 W. Park Dr., McLean, Virginia 22102. (703) 442-0900 or (800) 456-7248. Monthly. Covers theoretical, practical and commercial material on all aspects of processing safety, and the environment. Also covers process and reaction engineering, measurement and process control, environmental protection and safety, plant design and equipment used in chemical engineering and biotechnology. More than 400 of the world's major primary chemical and process engineering journals are scanned to compile the database. Available from ORBIT.

Enviro/Energyline Abstracts Plus. R. R. Bowker Co., 121 Chanlon Rd., New Providence, New Jersey 07974. (908) 464-6800.

Environmental Periodicals Bibliography. National Information Services Corp., Ste. 6, Wyman Towers, 3100 St. Paul St., Baltimore, Maryland 21218. (410)243-0797. Online version of abstract of same name.

Kirk-Othmer Encyclopedia of Chemical Technology. John Wiley & Sons, Inc., 605 3rd Ave., 5th Floor, New York, New York 10158. (212) 850-6000. Online version of the publication of the same name.

Monthly Catalog of United States Government Publications. U.S. G.P.O., Supt. of Docs., PO Box 371954, Pittsburgh, Pennsylvania 15250-7954. (202) 512-0000.

National Technical Information Service. U.S. Department of Commerce, National Technical Information Service, Office of Data Base Services, 5285 Port Royal Rd., Springfield, Virginia 22161. (703) 487-4807. Bibliographic database of government sponsored research and technical reports.

PERIODICALS AND NEWSLETTERS

Analytical Biochemistry. Academic Press, 111 Fifth Ave., New York, New York 10003. (800) 346-8648. Covers biological and chemical topics relating to the environment.

TRADE ASSOCIATIONS AND PROFESSIONAL SOCIETIES

American Institute of Chemical Engineers. 345 East 47th St., New York, New York 10017. (212) 705-7338.

American Institute of Chemists. 7315 Wisconsin Ave., Bethesda, Maryland 20814. (301) 652-2447.

DISTRIBUTION LINES
See also: ELECTRIC POWER LINES–ENVIRONMENTAL ASPECTS

ABSTRACTING AND INDEXING SERVICES

Applied Science and Technology Index. H.W. Wilson Co., 950 University Ave., Bronx, New York 10452. (800) 367-6770. Formerly Industrial Arts Index.

Environment Abstracts. Bowker A & I Publishing, 121 Chanlon Rd., New Providence, New Jersey 07974. (908) 464-6800. 1974-.

Environment Index. Environment Information Center, Index Research Department, 124 E. 39th St., New York, New York 10016. 1971-. Annual.

Environmental Information Connection–EIC. Planning Information Program, Dept. of Urban and Regional Planning, University of Illinois, 1003 West Nevada, Urbana, Illinois 61801. (217) 333-1369. Also available online.

Environmental Periodicals Bibliography. Environmental Studies Institute, International Academy at Santa Barbara, 800 Garden St., Suite D, Santa Barbara, California 93101. (805) 965-5010. Also available online.

General Science Index. H. W. Wilson Co., 950 University Ave., Bronx, New York 10452. 1978-. Monthly, also issued in annual cumulation. Cumulative subject index to English language periodicals in the subject fields of astronomy, botany, chemistry, earth science, environment and conservation, food and nutrition, genetics, mathematics, medicine and health, microbiology, oceanography, physics, physiology and zoology.

Index to Scientific Book Contents. Institute for Scientific Information, 3501 Market St., Philadelphia, Pennsylvania 19104. (800) 523-1857. 1985-. Annual. Gives contents of science books published.

BIBLIOGRAPHIES

EPA Publications Bibliography. U.S. Environmental Protection Agency, Library Systems Branch, 401 M St., SW, Washington, District of Columbia 20460. (202) 260-2090. Quarterly.

ENCYCLOPEDIAS AND DICTIONARIES

Encyclopedia of Physical Science and Technology. Robert A. Meyers, ed. Academic Press, c/o Harcourt Brace Jovanovich Inc., 6277 Sea Harbor Dr., Orlando, Florida 32887. (800) 346-8648. Dictionary of engineering, technology and physical sciences.

McGraw-Hill Encyclopedia of Science and Technology. McGraw-Hill, 1221 Avenue of the Americas, New York, New York 10020. (212) 512-2000 or (800) 262-4729. 1992. Seventh edition. Issued in multiple volumes including index. Includes all science and technology broad subject areas.

Van Nostrand's Scientific Encyclopedia. Glenn D. Considine, ed. Van Nostrand Reinhold, 115 5th Ave., New York, New York 10003. (212) 254-3232. 1983. Sixth edition. Includes all broad subject areas in science.

GENERAL WORKS

Stray Voltage. Robert J. Gustafson. Energy Research and Development Division, Energy and Environmental Policy Department, National Rural Electric Cooperative Association, 1800 Massachusetts Ave., NW, Washington, District of Columbia 20036. (202) 857-9500. 1988. Seasonal variations in grounding and primary neutral-to-earth voltages.

Stray Voltages in Agriculture: Workshop. American Society of Agricultural Engineers, 2950 Niles Rd., St. Joseph, Michigan 49085-9659. (616) 429-0300. 1983. Includes the effects of stray voltage on animals, source of stray voltage, diagnostic procedures for detection and measurement and treatments or corrective procedure for stray voltage problem. The workshop was sponsored by the National Rural Electric Cooperative Association in Minneapolis, MN.

HANDBOOKS AND MANUALS

Transmission Line Design Manual. Holland H. Farr. Water and Power Resources Service, Engineering and Research Center, P.O. Box 25007, Denver Federal Center, Denver, Colorado 80225. 1980.

ONLINE DATA BASES

Enviro/Energyline Abstracts Plus. R. R. Bowker Co., 121 Chanlon Rd., New Providence, New Jersey 07974. (908) 464-6800.

Environmental Periodicals Bibliography. National Information Services Corp., Ste. 6, Wyman Towers, 3100 St. Paul St., Baltimore, Maryland 21218. (410)243-0797. Online version of abstract of same name.

Monthly Catalog of United States Government Publications. U.S. G.P.O., Supt. of Docs., PO Box 371954, Pittsburgh, Pennsylvania 15250-7954. (202) 512-0000.

National Technical Information Service. U.S. Department of Commerce, National Technical Information Service, Office of Data Base Services, 5285 Port Royal

Rd., Springfield, Virginia 22161. (703) 487-4807. Bibliographic database of government sponsored research and technical reports.

DISTRIBUTION OF ORGANISMS

See also: BIOGEOGRAPHY; BIOMES

ABSTRACTING AND INDEXING SERVICES

Environment Abstracts. Bowker A & I Publishing, 121 Chanlon Rd., New Providence, New Jersey 07974. (908) 464-6800. 1974-.

Environment Index. Environment Information Center, Index Research Department, 124 E. 39th St., New York, New York 10016. 1971-. Annual.

Environmental Information Connection–EIC. Planning Information Program, Dept. of Urban and Regional Planning, University of Illinois, 1003 West Nevada, Urbana, Illinois 61801. (217) 333-1369. Also available online.

Environmental Periodicals Bibliography. Environmental Studies Institute, International Academy at Santa Barbara, 800 Garden St., Suite D, Santa Barbara, California 93101. (805) 965-5010. Also available online.

General Science Index. H. W. Wilson Co., 950 University Ave., Bronx, New York 10452. 1978-. Monthly, also issued in annual cumulation. Cumulative subject index to English language periodicals in the subject fields of astronomy, botany, chemistry, earth science, environment and conservation, food and nutrition, genetics, mathematics, medicine and health, microbiology, oceanography, physics, physiology and zoology.

Index to Scientific Book Contents. Institute for Scientific Information, 3501 Market St., Philadelphia, Pennsylvania 19104. (800) 523-1857. 1985-. Annual. Gives contents of science books published.

BIBLIOGRAPHIES

EPA Publications Bibliography. U.S. Environmental Protection Agency, Library Systems Branch, 401 M St., SW, Washington, District of Columbia 20460. (202) 260-2090. Quarterly.

ENCYCLOPEDIAS AND DICTIONARIES

McGraw-Hill Encyclopedia of Environmental Science. Sybil P. Parker. McGraw-Hill Science & Engineering Books, 11 W. 19th St., New York, New York 10011. (212) 337-6010. 1980. Covers ecology, man's influence on nature, and environmental protection.

ONLINE DATA BASES

Enviro/Energyline Abstracts Plus. R. R. Bowker Co., 121 Chanlon Rd., New Providence, New Jersey 07974. (908) 464-6800.

Environmental Periodicals Bibliography. National Information Services Corp., Ste. 6, Wyman Towers, 3100 St. Paul St., Baltimore, Maryland 21218. (410)243-0797. Online version of abstract of same name.

Monthly Catalog of United States Government Publications. U.S. G.P.O., Supt. of Docs., PO Box 371954, Pittsburgh, Pennsylvania 15250-7954. (202) 512-0000.

National Technical Information Service. U.S. Department of Commerce, National Technical Information Service, Office of Data Base Services, 5285 Port Royal Rd., Springfield, Virginia 22161. (703) 487-4807. Bibliographic database of government sponsored research and technical reports.

TRADE ASSOCIATIONS AND PROFESSIONAL SOCIETIES

American Institute of Biological Sciences. 730 11th St., N.W., Washington, District of Columbia 20001-4521. (202) 628-1500.

DISTRICT OF COLUMBIA ENVIRONMENTAL AGENCIES

GOVERNMENTAL ORGANIZATIONS

Consumer and Regulatory Affairs Department: Groundwater Management. Administrator, Housing and Environmental Regulations, 614 H St., N.W., Washington, District of Columbia 20001. (202) 727-7395.

Department of Consumer and Regulatory Affairs: Air Quality. Administrator, Housing and Environmental Regulations, 614 H St., N.W., Washington, District of Columbia 20001. (202) 727-7395.

Department of Consumer and Regulatory Affairs: Environmental Protection. Administrator, Housing and Environmental Regulations, 614 H St., N.W., Washington, District of Columbia 20001. (202) 727-7395.

Department of Consumer and Regulatory Affairs: Fish and Wildlife. Administrator, Housing and Environmental Regulations, 614 H St., N.W., Washington, District of Columbia 20001. (202) 727-7395.

Department of Consumer and Regulatory Affairs: Hazardous Waste Management. Administrator, Housing and Environmental Regulations, 614 H St., N.W., Washington, District of Columbia 20001. (202) 727-7395.

Department of Consumer and Regulatory Affairs: Natural Resources. Administrator, Housing and Environmental Regulations, 614 H St., N.W., Washington, District of Columbia 20001. (202) 727-7395.

Department of Consumer and Regulatory Affairs: Pesticide Registration. Branch Chief, Pesticides and Hazardous Waste Management Branch, Environmental Control Division, Suite 114, 5010 Overlook Ave., S.W., Washington, District of Columbia 20032-5397. (202) 783-3194.

Department of Consumer and Regulatory Affairs: Underground Storage Tanks. Pesticides and Hazardous Waste Management Branch, 5010 Overlook Ave., S.W., Room 114, Washington, District of Columbia 20032. (202) 783-3190.

Department of Consumer and Regulatory Affairs: Water Quality. Administrator, Housing and Environmental Regulations, 614 H St., N.W., Washington, District of Columbia 20001. (202) 727-7395.

Department of Employment Services: Occupational Safety. Associate Director, Occupational Safety and Health

Office, 950 Upshur St., N.W., Washington, District of Columbia 20011. (202) 576-6651.

Department of Public Works: Solid Waste Management. Administrator, Public Space Maintenance Administration, 4701 Shephard Pkwy., S.W., Washington, District of Columbia 20032. (202) 767-8512.

Office of Emergency Preparedness: Emergency Preparedness and Community Right-to-Know. Chair, Emergency Response Commission for Title III, 2000 14th St., N.W., Frank Reeves Center for Municipal Affairs, Washington, District of Columbia 20009. (202) 727-6161.

U.S. EPA Region 3: Pollution Prevention. Program Manager, 841 Chestnut St., Philadelphia, Pennsylvania 19107. (215) 597-9800.

DIURNAL CHANGES

ABSTRACTING AND INDEXING SERVICES

Index to Scientific Book Contents. Institute for Scientific Information, 3501 Market St., Philadelphia, Pennsylvania 19104. (800) 523-1857. 1985-. Annual. Gives contents of science books published.

Science Citation Index. Institute for Scientific Information, 3501 Market St., Philadelphia, Pennsylvania 19104. 1961-.

ENCYCLOPEDIAS AND DICTIONARIES

McGraw-Hill Encyclopedia of Science and Technology. McGraw-Hill, 1221 Avenue of the Americas, New York, New York 10020. (212) 512-2000 or (800) 262-4729. 1992. Seventh edition. Issued in multiple volumes including index. Includes all science and technology broad subject areas.

TRADE ASSOCIATIONS AND PROFESSIONAL SOCIETIES

American Institute of Biomedical Climatology. 1023 Welsh Rd., Philadelphia, Pennsylvania 19115. (215) 673-8368.

DNA

ABSTRACTING AND INDEXING SERVICES

Applied Ecology Abstracts Studies in Renewable Natural Resources. Information Retrieval Ltd., 1911 Jefferson Davis Highway, Arlington, Virginia 22202. 1975-. Monthly.

Biological Abstracts. BIOSIS, 2100 Arch St., Philadelphia, Pennsylvania 19103-1399. (215) 587-4800. 1927-.

Biotechnology Research Abstracts. Cambridge Scientific Abstracts, 5161 River Rd., Bethesda, Maryland 20816. (301) 961-6750. Monthly. Includes such broad areas as genetic intervention, biochemical genetics, and microbiological techniques.

Cancergram. U.S. Department of Health and Human Services, 200 Independence Ave. SW, Washington, District of Columbia 20201. (202) 619-0257. 1988. Monthly. International Cancer Research Data Bank relating to molecular biology and DNA.

Current Advances in Plant Science. Pergamon Microforms International, Inc., Fairview Park, Elmsford, New York 10523. (914) 592-7720. 1984-. Monthly. Current literature searching service including journals, reports, abstracts, etc. This service is available online as part of the CABS database on the hosts BRS and ORBIT search service.

Current Cancer Research on Molecular Biology of DNA Tumor Viruses: Replication and Genetics. National Cancer Institute. U.S. Department of Health and Human Services, Public Health Service, National Institutes of Health, 9000 Rockville Pike, Bethesda, Maryland 20892. (301) 496-4000. 1980. Annual.

Ecology Abstracts. Cambridge Scientific Abstracts, 5161 River Rd., Bethesda, Maryland 20816. (301) 961-6750. Monthly.

Environment Abstracts. Bowker A & I Publishing, 121 Chanlon Rd., New Providence, New Jersey 07974. (908) 464-6800. 1974-.

Environment Index. Environment Information Center, Index Research Department, 124 E. 39th St., New York, New York 10016. 1971-. Annual.

Environmental Information Connection–EIC. Planning Information Program, Dept. of Urban and Regional Planning, University of Illinois, 1003 West Nevada, Urbana, Illinois 61801. (217) 333-1369. Also available online.

Environmental Periodicals Bibliography. Environmental Studies Institute, International Academy at Santa Barbara, 800 Garden St., Suite D, Santa Barbara, California 93101. (805) 965-5010. Also available online.

General Science Index. H. W. Wilson Co., 950 University Ave., Bronx, New York 10452. 1978-. Monthly, also issued in annual cumulation. Cumulative subject index to English language periodicals in the subject fields of astronomy, botany, chemistry, earth science, environment and conservation, food and nutrition, genetics, mathematics, medicine and health, microbiology, oceanography, physics, physiology and zoology.

Genetics Abstracts. Cambridge Scientific Abstracts, 5161 River Rd., Bethesda, Maryland 20816. (301) 961-6750. 1968-. Monthly. Formerly published by Information Retrieval Ltd., London England. Published by Cambridge Scientific Abstracts since 1982.

Index to Scientific Book Contents. Institute for Scientific Information, 3501 Market St., Philadelphia, Pennsylvania 19104. (800) 523-1857. 1985-. Annual. Gives contents of science books published.

Multimedia Index to Ecology. National Information Center for Educational Media, University of Southern California, Los Angeles, California 90007.

Science Citation Index. Institute for Scientific Information, 3501 Market St., Philadelphia, Pennsylvania 19104. 1961-.

Selected Abstracts on DNA Viral Transforming Proteins. International Cancer Research Data Bank. U.S. Department of Health and Human Services, Public Health Service, National Institutes of Health, 9000 Rockville Pike, Bethesda, Maryland 20892. (301) 496-4000.

Selected Abstracts on Rearrangements of DNA Sequences as They Occur in Nature. William C. Summers. U.S. Department of Health and Human Services, Public

Health Service, National Institutes of Health, 9000 Rockville Pike, Bethesda, Maryland 20892. (301) 496-4000. 1983. Potential models for differentiation and tumorigenesis.

ALMANACS AND YEARBOOKS

Nucleic Acids and Molecular Biology. Fritz Eckstein. Springer-Verlag, 175 5th Ave., New York, New York 10010. (212) 460-1500 or (800) 777-4643. 1987. Annual.

BIBLIOGRAPHIES

EPA Publications Bibliography. U.S. Environmental Protection Agency, Library Systems Branch, 401 M St., SW, Washington, District of Columbia 20460. (202) 260-2090. Quarterly.

DIRECTORIES

Gale Environmental Sourcebook. Karen Hill. Gale Research Co., 835 Penobscot Bldg., Detroit, Michigan 48226-4094. (313) 961-2242. Contacts, information sources, or general information on environmental topics.

ENCYCLOPEDIAS AND DICTIONARIES

Cambridge Encyclopedia of Life Sciences. A. E. Friday and David S. Ingram. Cambridge University Press, 40 W 20th St., New York, New York 10011. (212) 924-3900 or (800) 227-0247. 1985. Includes all topics under biology and ecology.

A Dictionary of Genetics. Robert C. King and William A. Stansfield. Oxford University Press, 200 Madison Ave., New York, New York 10016. (212) 679-7300 or (800) 334-4249. 1991. Fourth edition. Includes 7,100 definitions with 250 illustrations. Also includes bibliography of major sources.

Dictionary of Genetics and Cell Biology. Norman Maclean. New York University Press, 70 Washington Sq. S., New York, New York 10012. (212) 998-2575. 1987. Includes the subject areas of cytology and genetics.

Dictionary of Microbiology and Molecular Biology. Paul Singleton and Diana Sainsbury. John Wiley & Sons, Inc., 605 3rd Ave., New York, New York 10158-0012. (212) 850-6000. 1987. Second edition. Comprehensive dictionary with "classical descriptive aspects of microbiology to current developments in related areas of bioenergetics, biochemistry and molecular biology." Entries give synonyms, cross references, and references to pertinent works. Miscellaneous appendixes. Bibliography.

Encyclopedia of Human Biology. Renato Dulbecco, ed. Academic Press, c/o Harcourt Brace Jovanovich Inc., 6277 Sea Harbor Dr., Orlando, Florida 32887. (800) 346-8648. 1991. Eight volumes.

Encyclopedic Dictionary of Genetics: With German Term Equivalents and Extensive German/English Index. R. C. King and W. D. Stansfield. VCH Publishers, 303 NW 12th Ave., Deerfield Beach, Florida 33442-1788. (305) 428-5566. 1990. 4th ed. Revised edition of: A Dictionary of Genetics, third edition.

Gnomic: A Dictionary of Genetic Codes. Edward N. Trifonov. Balaban, 220 E. 23rd St., Suite 909, New York, New York 10010-4606. (212) 683-8333 or (800) 422-8824. 1986. Deals with DNA and nucleotide sequence.

Life Sciences on File. Diagram Group. Facts on File, Inc., 460 Park Ave. S., New York, New York 10016. (212) 683-2244. 1986. Encyclopedia of pictorial collection in life sciences. Deals with all major topics in life sciences including ecology.

Macmillan Dictionary of Toxicology. Ernest Hodgson, et al. Van Nostrand Reinhold, 115 5th Ave., New York, New York 10003. (212) 254-3232. 1988. Intended as a "starting point" to the literature of toxicology. American spelling is used with cross references to British version of words. Contains a list of references. Signed entries give explanatory definitions and cross references.

McGraw-Hill Encyclopedia of Science and Technology. McGraw-Hill, 1221 Avenue of the Americas, New York, New York 10020. (212) 512-2000 or (800) 262-4729. 1992. Seventh edition. Issued in multiple volumes including index. Includes all science and technology broad subject areas.

The Nutrition and Health Encyclopedia. David F. Tver and Percy Russell. Van Nostrand Reinhold, 115 5th Ave., New York, New York 10003. (212) 254-3232. 1989.

Van Nostrand's Scientific Encyclopedia. Glenn D. Considine, ed. Van Nostrand Reinhold, 115 5th Ave., New York, New York 10003. (212) 254-3232. 1983. Sixth edition. Includes all broad subject areas in science.

GENERAL WORKS

Magill's Survey of Science. Life Science Series. Frank N. Magill, ed. Salem Press, PO Box 50062, Pasadena, California 91105. 1991. Six volumes. Contents: v.1. A-Central and peripheral nervous system functions; v.2. Central metabolism regulation - eukaryotic transcriptional control; v.3. Positive and negative eukaryotic transcriptional control - mammalian hormones; v.4. Hormones and behavior - muscular contraction; v.5. Muscular contraction and relaxation - sexual reproduction in plants; v.6. Reproductive behavior and mating - X inactivation and the Lyon hypothesis.

ONLINE DATA BASES

BIOSIS Previews. BIOSIS, 2100 Arch St., Philadelphia, Pennsylvania 19103-1399. (215) 587-4800. Largest and most comprehensive database of research in the life sciences. Contains citations for nearly 9000 primary research journals, monographs, reviews, symposia, preliminary reports, semi-popular journals, selected institutional reports, government reports and research communications.

Cambridge Scientific Abstracts Life Science–CSAL. Cambridge Scientific Abstracts, 5161 River Rd., Bethesda, Maryland 20816. (301) 961-6750. Provides access to the following abstracting services: "Life Sciences Collection," "Aquatic Sciences and Fisheries Abstracts," "Oceanic Abstracts," and "Pollution Abstracts."

Enviro/Energyline Abstracts Plus. R. R. Bowker Co., 121 Chanlon Rd., New Providence, New Jersey 07974. (908) 464-6800.

Environmental Periodicals Bibliography. National Information Services Corp., Ste. 6, Wyman Towers, 3100 St. Paul St., Baltimore, Maryland 21218. (410)243-0797. Online version of abstract of same name.

Monthly Catalog of United States Government Publications. U.S. G.P.O., Supt. of Docs., PO Box 371954, Pittsburgh, Pennsylvania 15250-7954. (202) 512-0000.

National Technical Information Service. U.S. Department of Commerce, National Technical Information Service, Office of Data Base Services, 5285 Port Royal Rd., Springfield, Virginia 22161. (703) 487-4807. Bibliographic database of government sponsored research and technical reports.

PERIODICALS AND NEWSLETTERS

DNA and Cell Biology. Mary Ann Liebert, Inc., 1651 3rd Ave., New York, New York 10128. (212) 289-2300. 1981-. Ten times a year. Covers eukaryotic or prokaryotic gene structure, organization, expression and evolution. Papers, short communications, reviews, and editorials. Includes studies of genetics at RNA or protein levels.

DNA and Protein Engineering Techniques. Alan R. Liss, 41 E. 11th St., New York, New York 10003. (212) 475-7700. 1988-. Six times a year. Covers recombinant DNA, Genetic intervention methods, proteins, and recombinant proteins.

RESEARCH CENTERS AND INSTITUTES

American Type Culture Collection. 12301 Parklawn Drive, Rockville, Maryland 20852. (301) 881-2600.

Center for Molecular Biology. Wayne State University, 5047 Gullen Mall, Detroit, Michigan 48202. (313) 577-0616.

Massachusetts Institute of Technology, Comprehensive NMR Center for Biomedical Research. Francis Bitter National Magnet Laboratory, NW 14-5121, 170 Albany Street, Cambridge, Massachusetts 02139. (617) 253-5592.

Rockefeller University, Laboratory of Molecular Cell Biology. 1230 York Ave., New York, New York 10021-6399. (212) 570-8791.

Sheldon Biotechnology Centre. McGill University, 3773 University St., Montreal, Quebec, Canada H3A 2B4. (514) 398-3998.

University of Wisconsin-Madison, Zoological Museum. Lowell Noland Building, 225 North Mills, Madison, Wisconsin 53706. (608) 262-3766.

STATISTICS SOURCES

Biomaterials. FIND/SVP, 625 Avenue of the Americas, New York, New York 10011. (212) 645-4500. 1991. Examines the U.S. and worldwide markets for the following biomaterials segments–recombinant DNA pharmaceuticals; hyaluronic acid; collagen; biosensors; human skin and organ replacement; knee prosthetic devices; and new-drug delivery systems.

Environmental Data Compendium. OECD Publications and Information Center, 2001 L St., N.W., Suite 700, Washington, District of Columbia 20036. (202) 785-6323. 1989.

Environmental Indicators. OECD Publications and Information Center, 2001 L St., N.W., Suite 700, Washington, District of Columbia 20036. (202) 785-6323. 1991.

Environmental Quality. Council on Environmental Quality. U.S. G.P.O., Washington, District of Columbia 20401. (202) 512-0000. Annual.

The State of the Environment. OECD Publications and Information Center, 2001 L St., N.W., Suite 700, Washington, District of Columbia 20036. (202) 785-6323. 1991.

TRADE ASSOCIATIONS AND PROFESSIONAL SOCIETIES

American Institute of Biological Sciences. 730 11th St., N.W., Washington, District of Columbia 20001-4521. (202) 628-1500.

DOLOMITE

ABSTRACTING AND INDEXING SERVICES

Biological Abstracts. BIOSIS, 2100 Arch St., Philadelphia, Pennsylvania 19103-1399. (215) 587-4800. 1927-.

General Science Index. H. W. Wilson Co., 950 University Ave., Bronx, New York 10452. 1978-. Monthly, also issued in annual cumulation. Cumulative subject index to English language periodicals in the subject fields of astronomy, botany, chemistry, earth science, environment and conservation, food and nutrition, genetics, mathematics, medicine and health, microbiology, oceanography, physics, physiology and zoology.

Index to Scientific Book Contents. Institute for Scientific Information, 3501 Market St., Philadelphia, Pennsylvania 19104. (800) 523-1857. 1985-. Annual. Gives contents of science books published.

Science Citation Index. Institute for Scientific Information, 3501 Market St., Philadelphia, Pennsylvania 19104. 1961-.

BIBLIOGRAPHIES

Bibliography and Index of Geology. American Geological Institute, 4220 King St., Alexandria, Virginia 22302. Monthly. Includes environmental geology and hydrogeology.

ENCYCLOPEDIAS AND DICTIONARIES

McGraw-Hill Encyclopedia of Science and Technology. McGraw-Hill, 1221 Avenue of the Americas, New York, New York 10020. (212) 512-2000 or (800) 262-4729. 1992. Seventh edition. Issued in multiple volumes including index. Includes all science and technology broad subject areas.

Van Nostrand's Scientific Encyclopedia. Glenn D. Considine, ed. Van Nostrand Reinhold, 115 5th Ave., New York, New York 10003. (212) 254-3232. 1983. Sixth edition. Includes all broad subject areas in science.

GENERAL WORKS

Magill's Survey of Science. Earth Science Series. Frank N. Magill. Salem Press, PO Box 50062, Pasadena, California 91105. 1990-. Five volumes. Includes information on earth's crust, hot spots and volcanic island chains, physical properties of minerals, rock magnetism, physical properties of rocks, and index.

Sedimentology and Geochemistry of Dolostones. Vijai Shukla. The Society of Economic Paleontologists and Mineralogists, P.O. Box 4756, Tulsa, Oklahoma 74159-0756. (918) 743-9765. 1988.

HANDBOOKS AND MANUALS

Handbook for Flue Gas Desulfurization Scrubbing with Limestone. D.S. Henzel. Noyes Publications, 120 Mill Rd., Park Ridge, New Jersey 07656. (201) 391-8484. 1982. Chemical technology of scrubbers.

ONLINE DATA BASES

BIOSIS Previews. BIOSIS, 2100 Arch St., Philadelphia, Pennsylvania 19103-1399. (215) 587-4800. Largest and most comprehensive database of research in the life sciences. Contains citations for nearly 9000 primary research journals, monographs, reviews, symposia, preliminary reports, semi-popular journals, selected institutional reports, government reports and research communications.

DOLPHINS

See also: FISH AND FISHERIES; PORPOISES; MARINE MAMMALS

ABSTRACTING AND INDEXING SERVICES

Biological and Agricultural Index. H.W. Wilson Co., 950 University Ave., Bronx, New York 10452. (800) 367-6770. 1916-. Monthly.

ALMANACS AND YEARBOOKS

Dolphins, Porpoises and Whales of the World: The IUCN Red Data Book. M. Klinowska. The World Conservation Union, IUCN Publications Services Unit, 181a Huntingdon Road, Cambridge, England CB3 0DJ. (0223) 277894. 1991. Reviews the status of all cetacean species. Detailed accounts are provided for each species, describing their distribution, population, threats, and the conservation measures required to ensure their survival.

PERIODICALS AND NEWSLETTERS

Dolphin Log. Cousteau Society Inc., 8440 Santa Monica Blvd., Los Angeles, California 90069. (804) 627-1144. Six issues a year. Covers marine animals, the oceans, science, natural history, and the arts as they relate to global water system. Magazine is for ages 7-15.

RESEARCH CENTERS AND INSTITUTES

Project Circle. Marine World Africa USA, Marine World Parkway, Vallejo, California 94589. (707) 644-4000.

TRADE ASSOCIATIONS AND PROFESSIONAL SOCIETIES

Cousteau Society. Cousteau Society Membership Center, 930 W 21st St., Norfolk, Virginia 23517. In addition to carrying on the many research projects and explorations made famous by Jacques-Yves Cousteau, the Society publishes educational materials and numerous Technical publications as well as Calypso Log (monthly) and Dolphin Log (bimonthly children's publication).

DOMESTIC ANIMALS

ABSTRACTING AND INDEXING SERVICES

Agroforestry Abstracts. C. A. B. International, 845 North Park Ave., Tucson, Arizona 85719. (602) 621-7897 or (800) 528-4841. 1988-. Quarterly. Abstracts journal articles, reports, conferences and books. Focuses on subjects areas such as agroforestry in general; agroforestry systems; trees, animals and crops; conservation; human ecology; social and economic aspects; development, research and methodology.

Animal Breeding Abstracts. C. A. B. International, 845 North Park Ave., Tucson, Arizona 85719. (602) 621-7897 or (800) 528-4841. 1933-. Monthly. Abstracts covers the literature on animal breeding, genetics, reproduction and production. Includes areas of biological research such as immunogenetics, genetic engineering and fertility improvement.

Applied Ecology Abstracts Studies in Renewable Natural Resources. Information Retrieval Ltd., 1911 Jefferson Davis Highway, Arlington, Virginia 22202. 1975-. Monthly.

Biological and Agricultural Index. H.W. Wilson Co., 950 University Ave., Bronx, New York 10452. (800) 367-6770. 1916-. Monthly.

Biotechnology Research Abstracts. Cambridge Scientific Abstracts, 5161 River Rd., Bethesda, Maryland 20816. (301) 961-6750. Monthly. Includes such broad areas as genetic intervention, biochemical genetics, and microbiological techniques.

Environment Abstracts. Bowker A & I Publishing, 121 Chanlon Rd., New Providence, New Jersey 07974. (908) 464-6800. 1974-.

Environment Index. Environment Information Center, Index Research Department, 124 E. 39th St., New York, New York 10016. 1971-. Annual.

Environmental Information Connection–EIC. Planning Information Program, Dept. of Urban and Regional Planning, University of Illinois, 1003 West Nevada, Urbana, Illinois 61801. (217) 333-1369. Also available online.

Environmental Periodicals Bibliography. Environmental Studies Institute, International Academy at Santa Barbara, 800 Garden St., Suite D, Santa Barbara, California 93101. (805) 965-5010. Also available online.

Food Science and Technology Abstracts. International Food Information Service, c/o National Food Laboratory, 6363 Clark Ave., Dublin, California 94568. (800) 336-3782. 1969-.

General Science Index. H. W. Wilson Co., 950 University Ave., Bronx, New York 10452. 1978-. Monthly, also issued in annual cumulation. Cumulative subject index to English language periodicals in the subject fields of astronomy, botany, chemistry, earth science, environment and conservation, food and nutrition, genetics, mathematics, medicine and health, microbiology, oceanography, physics, physiology and zoology.

Index to Scientific Book Contents. Institute for Scientific Information, 3501 Market St., Philadelphia, Pennsylvania 19104. (800) 523-1857. 1985-. Annual. Gives contents of science books published.

Multimedia Index to Ecology. National Information Center for Educational Media, University of Southern California, Los Angeles, California 90007.

BIBLIOGRAPHIES

EPA Publications Bibliography. U.S. Environmental Protection Agency, Library Systems Branch, 401 M St., SW, Washington, District of Columbia 20460. (202) 260-2090. Quarterly.

DIRECTORIES

Agricultural Information Resource Centers, a World Directory 1990. Rita C. Fisher. IAALD World Directory Working Group, 716 W. Indiana Ave., Urbana, Illinois 61801-4836. (217) 333-7687. 1990. Includes 3,971 information resource centers that have agriculture related collection and/or information services.

Animal Organizations and Services Directory. Kathleen A. Reece. Animal Stories Pub., 16787 Beach Blvd., Huntington Beach, California 92647. 1990-91. Fourth edition. Devoted to animals, pets and wildlife.

ENCYCLOPEDIAS AND DICTIONARIES

The Complete Encyclopedia of the Animal World. David M.Burn, ed. Octopus Books, 59 Grosvenor St., London, England W1. 1980. Consists of 6 parts in one volume includes: the distribution of animals, animal names and classification, the animal kingdom, the way of animals, the conservation of animals, and where to see animals.

The Completely Illustrated Atlas of Reptiles and Amphibians for the Terrarium. Jerry G. Walls, ed. TFH Publications, One TFH Plaza, Union and 3rd Pl., Neptune City, New Jersey 07753. (908) 988-8400. 1988. Includes care and feeding, breeding and natural history of snakes, lizards, turtles, frogs, toads, salamanders, newts, and all other terrarium animals. Also includes additional references and a list of common names.

Dictionary of Animals. Michael Chinery, ed. Arco Pub. Inc., 215 Park Ave. S., New York, New York 10003. 1984.

The Encyclopedia of Animal Ecology. Peter D. Moore. Facts on File, Inc., 460 Park Ave. S., New York, New York 10016. (212) 683-2244. 1987.

Encyclopedia of Human Biology. Renato Dulbecco, ed. Academic Press, c/o Harcourt Brace Jovanovich Inc., 6277 Sea Harbor Dr., Orlando, Florida 32887. (800) 346-8648. 1991. Eight volumes.

The Encyclopedia of North American Wildlife. Stanley Klein. Facts on File, Inc., 460 Park Ave. S., New York, New York 10016. (212) 683-2244. 1983. Includes mammals, birds, reptiles, amphibians, and fish. Appendices include information on wildlife conservation organizations, a bibliographical list of endangered species and an index of Latin names.

Grzimek's Animal Life Encyclopedia. Van Nostrand Reinhold, 115 5th Ave., New York, New York 10003. (212) 254-3232. 1975. Thirteen volumes. Includes lower animals, insects, mollusks, fishes, amphibians, reptiles, birds, and mammals.

Life Sciences on File. Diagram Group. Facts on File, Inc., 460 Park Ave. S., New York, New York 10016. (212) 683-2244. 1986. Encyclopedia of pictorial collection in life sciences. Deals with all major topics in life sciences including ecology.

Macmillan Illustrated Animal Encyclopedia. Philip Whitfield, ed. Macmillan Publishing Co., 866 3rd Ave., New York, New York 10022. (212) 702-2000. 1984. Provides a comprehensive catalog of the staggering range of animal types within the vertebrate group. Also the IUCN endangered species are noted and includes common names, range and habitat. Includes mammals, birds, reptiles, amphibians, and fish.

Nature in America Your A-Z Guide to Our Country's Animals, Plants, Landforms and Other Natural Features. Readers Digest Association, 260 Madison Ave., New York, New York 10016. 1991. Reference guide of nature in North America. Explores plants, animals, weather, land forms, and wildlife habitats. Includes over 1000 photographs and illustrations for some 1200 entries.

Remarkable Animals: A Unique Encyclopedia of Wildlife Wonders. Guinness Books, 33 London Rd., Enfield, England EN2 6DJ. 1987. Includes mammals, birds, fishes, amphibians, reptiles, insects, and arachnids.

Van Nostrand's Scientific Encyclopedia. Glenn D. Considine, ed. Van Nostrand Reinhold, 115 5th Ave., New York, New York 10003. (212) 254-3232. 1983. Sixth edition. Includes all broad subject areas in science.

HANDBOOKS AND MANUALS

Walker's Mammals of the World. Ronald M. Nowak. Johns Hopkins University Press, 701 W. 40th St., Ste. 275, Baltimore, Maryland 21211-2190. (410) 516-6900. 1991. Fifth edition 2 vols. Describes: monotremata; massupialia; insectivora; macroscelida; dermoptra; chiroptra; scandentia; primates; xenarthra; pholidota; langomorpha; rodentia; cetacea; carnivora; pemipedia; tubulidentata; proboscidea; hyracoidia; sirenia; perissodactyla; and artiodactyla. Includes a bibliography of literature cited.

ONLINE DATA BASES

Current Research Information System–CRIS/USDA. U.S. Department of Agriculture, National Agricultural Library, 10301 Baltimore Blvd., 5th Floor, Beltsville, Maryland 20705-2351. (301) 504-5755. Looks at current research projects in agriculture and allied sciences covering the biological, physical, social and behavioral sciences related to agriculture.

Enviro/Energyline Abstracts Plus. R. R. Bowker Co., 121 Chanlon Rd., New Providence, New Jersey 07974. (908) 464-6800.

Environmental Periodicals Bibliography. National Information Services Corp., Ste. 6, Wyman Towers, 3100 St. Paul St., Baltimore, Maryland 21218. (410)243-0797. Online version of abstract of same name.

Monthly Catalog of United States Government Publications. U.S. G.P.O., Supt. of Docs., PO Box 371954, Pittsburgh, Pennsylvania 15250-7954. (202) 512-0000.

National Technical Information Service. U.S. Department of Commerce, National Technical Information Service, Office of Data Base Services, 5285 Port Royal Rd., Springfield, Virginia 22161. (703) 487-4807. Bibliographic database of government sponsored research and technical reports.

RESEARCH CENTERS AND INSTITUTES

U.S. Forest Service, Shrub Sciences Laboratory. 735 N. 500 E., Provo, Utah 84606. (801) 377-5717.

DOMESTIC CHEMICALS

ABSTRACTING AND INDEXING SERVICES

Applied Ecology Abstracts Studies in Renewable Natural Resources. Information Retrieval Ltd., 1911 Jefferson Davis Highway, Arlington, Virginia 22202. 1975-. Monthly.

Biological and Agricultural Index. H.W. Wilson Co., 950 University Ave., Bronx, New York 10452. (800) 367-6770. 1916-. Monthly.

Environment Abstracts. Bowker A & I Publishing, 121 Chanlon Rd., New Providence, New Jersey 07974. (908) 464-6800. 1974-.

Environment Index. Environment Information Center, Index Research Department, 124 E. 39th St., New York, New York 10016. 1971-. Annual.

Environmental Information Connection–EIC. Planning Information Program, Dept. of Urban and Regional Planning, University of Illinois, 1003 West Nevada, Urbana, Illinois 61801. (217) 333-1369. Also available online.

Environmental Periodicals Bibliography. Environmental Studies Institute, International Academy at Santa Barbara, 800 Garden St., Suite D, Santa Barbara, California 93101. (805) 965-5010. Also available online.

General Science Index. H. W. Wilson Co., 950 University Ave., Bronx, New York 10452. 1978-. Monthly, also issued in annual cumulation. Cumulative subject index to English language periodicals in the subject fields of astronomy, botany, chemistry, earth science, environment and conservation, food and nutrition, genetics, mathematics, medicine and health, microbiology, oceanography, physics, physiology and zoology.

Index to Scientific Book Contents. Institute for Scientific Information, 3501 Market St., Philadelphia, Pennsylvania 19104. (800) 523-1857. 1985-. Annual. Gives contents of science books published.

Multimedia Index to Ecology. National Information Center for Educational Media, University of Southern California, Los Angeles, California 90007.

BIBLIOGRAPHIES

EPA Publications Bibliography. U.S. Environmental Protection Agency, Library Systems Branch, 401 M St., SW, Washington, District of Columbia 20460. (202) 260-2090. Quarterly.

ENCYCLOPEDIAS AND DICTIONARIES

Ullmanns Encyclopedia of Industrial Chemistry. Hans Jurgen Arpe and Wolfgang Gerhartz, eds. VCH Publishers, 303 NW 12th Ave., Deerfield Beach, Florida 33442-1788. (305) 428-5566. 1990. Designed to keep up with the broad spectrum of chemical technology. Thirty-six volumes of the encyclopedia have been divided into two sets: the 28 A volumes contain alphabetically arranged articles on chemicals, product groups, processes and technological concepts; and the 8 B volumes are compendia of basic knowledge in industrial chemistry.

Van Nostrand's Scientific Encyclopedia. Glenn D. Considine, ed. Van Nostrand Reinhold, 115 5th Ave., New York, New York 10003. (212) 254-3232. 1983. Sixth edition. Includes all broad subject areas in science.

HANDBOOKS AND MANUALS

Household Hazards: a Guide to Detoxifying Your Home. League of Women Voters of Albany County, 119 Washington Ave., Albany, New York 12207. 1988. Covers household supplies and appliances safety measures.

ONLINE DATA BASES

Enviro/Energyline Abstracts Plus. R. R. Bowker Co., 121 Chanlon Rd., New Providence, New Jersey 07974. (908) 464-6800.

Environmental Periodicals Bibliography. National Information Services Corp., Ste. 6, Wyman Towers, 3100 St. Paul St., Baltimore, Maryland 21218. (410)243-0797. Online version of abstract of same name.

Monthly Catalog of United States Government Publications. U.S. G.P.O., Supt. of Docs., PO Box 371954, Pittsburgh, Pennsylvania 15250-7954. (202) 512-0000.

National Technical Information Service. U.S. Department of Commerce, National Technical Information Service, Office of Data Base Services, 5285 Port Royal Rd., Springfield, Virginia 22161. (703) 487-4807. Bibliographic database of government sponsored research and technical reports.

PERIODICALS AND NEWSLETTERS

Chemicals Quarterly Industry Report. United States. Business and Defense Services Administration. U.S. Deptartment of Commerce, Washington, District of Columbia 20230. (202)377-2000. Covers chemicals, rubber, and Allied products.

DOMESTIC COOLING SYSTEMS
See: COOLING SYSTEMS

DOMESTIC HEATING SYSTEMS
See: HEATING SYSTEMS

DOMESTIC NOISE
See: NOISE POLLUTION

DOMESTIC REFUSE
See: WASTE DISPOSAL

DOMINANCE (ECOLOGICAL)

ABSTRACTING AND INDEXING SERVICES

Applied Ecology Abstracts Studies in Renewable Natural Resources. Information Retrieval Ltd., 1911 Jefferson Davis Highway, Arlington, Virginia 22202. 1975-. Monthly.

Biological Abstracts. BIOSIS, 2100 Arch St., Philadelphia, Pennsylvania 19103-1399. (215) 587-4800. 1927-.

Biological and Agricultural Index. H.W. Wilson Co., 950 University Ave., Bronx, New York 10452. (800) 367-6770. 1916-. Monthly.

Current Advances in Ecological and Environmental Science. Pergamon Microforms International, Inc., Fairview Park, Elmsford, New York 10523. (914) 592-7720. 1989-. Monthly. Current literature searching service includingjournals, reports, abstracts, etc. This service is available online as part of the CABS database on the hosts BRS and ORBIT search service.

Ecological Abstracts. Geo Abstracts Ltd. Elsevier Applied Science, Crown House, Linton Rd., Barking, England IG 11 8JU. 1974-. Derived from over 600 leading ecological and environmental journals, plus books, conference proceedings, reports and theses.

Ecology Abstracts. Cambridge Scientific Abstracts, 5161 River Rd., Bethesda, Maryland 20816. (301) 961-6750. Monthly.

Environment Abstracts. Bowker A & I Publishing, 121 Chanlon Rd., New Providence, New Jersey 07974. (908) 464-6800. 1974-.

Environment Index. Environment Information Center, Index Research Department, 124 E. 39th St., New York, New York 10016. 1971-. Annual.

Environmental Information Connection–EIC. Planning Information Program, Dept. of Urban and Regional Planning, University of Illinois, 1003 West Nevada, Urbana, Illinois 61801. (217) 333-1369. Also available online.

Environmental Periodicals Bibliography. Environmental Studies Institute, International Academy at Santa Barbara, 800 Garden St., Suite D, Santa Barbara, California 93101. (805) 965-5010. Also available online.

General Science Index. H. W. Wilson Co., 950 University Ave., Bronx, New York 10452. 1978-. Monthly, also issued in annual cumulation. Cumulative subject index to English language periodicals in the subject fields of astronomy, botany, chemistry, earth science, environment and conservation, food and nutrition, genetics, mathematics, medicine and health, microbiology, oceanography, physics, physiology and zoology.

Index to Scientific Book Contents. Institute for Scientific Information, 3501 Market St., Philadelphia, Pennsylvania 19104. (800) 523-1857. 1985-. Annual. Gives contents of science books published.

Multimedia Index to Ecology. National Information Center for Educational Media, University of Southern California, Los Angeles, California 90007.

Science Citation Index. Institute for Scientific Information, 3501 Market St., Philadelphia, Pennsylvania 19104. 1961-.

BIBLIOGRAPHIES

Current Contents. Agriculture, Biology and Environmental Sciences. Institute for Scientific Information, 3501 Market St., Philadelphia, Pennsylvania 19104. (800) 523-1857. 1973-. Previous title: Current Contents. Agricultural, Food & Veterinary Sciences. Gives the table of contents of periodicals in the fields of agriculture, biology, environmental and related areas.

Directory of Published Proceedings. Interdok Corp., 173 Halstead Ave., Harrison, New York 10528. (914) 835-3506. 1990. Monthly. This is a listing of published proceedings including the series SEMTE (Science/Medicine/Engineering/Technology) and the series SSH (Social Science/Humanities).

EPA Publications Bibliography. U.S. Environmental Protection Agency, Library Systems Branch, 401 M St., SW, Washington, District of Columbia 20460. (202) 260-2090. Quarterly.

ENCYCLOPEDIAS AND DICTIONARIES

Cambridge Encyclopedia of Life Sciences. A. E. Friday and David S. Ingram. Cambridge University Press, 40 W 20th St., New York, New York 10011. (212) 924-3900 or (800) 227-0247. 1985. Includes all topics under biology and ecology.

McGraw-Hill Encyclopedia of Science and Technology. McGraw-Hill, 1221 Avenue of the Americas, New York, New York 10020. (212) 512-2000 or (800) 262-4729. 1992. Seventh edition. Issued in multiple volumes including index. Includes all science and technology broad subject areas.

Van Nostrand's Scientific Encyclopedia. Glenn D. Considine, ed. Van Nostrand Reinhold, 115 5th Ave., New York, New York 10003. (212) 254-3232. 1983. Sixth edition. Includes all broad subject areas in science.

ONLINE DATA BASES

BIOSIS Previews. BIOSIS, 2100 Arch St., Philadelphia, Pennsylvania 19103-1399. (215) 587-4800. Largest and most comprehensive database of research in the life sciences. Contains citations for nearly 9000 primary research journals, monographs, reviews, symposia, preliminary reports, semi-popular journals, selected institutional reports, government reports and research communications.

Cambridge Scientific Abstracts Life Science–CSAL. Cambridge Scientific Abstracts, 5161 River Rd., Bethesda, Maryland 20816. (301) 961-6750. Provides access to the following abstracting services: "Life Sciences Collection," "Aquatic Sciences and Fisheries Abstracts," "Oceanic Abstracts," and "Pollution Abstracts."

Current Research Information System–CRIS/USDA. U.S. Department of Agriculture, National Agricultural Library, 10301 Baltimore Blvd., 5th Floor, Beltsville, Maryland 20705-2351. (301) 504-5755. Looks at current research projects in agriculture and allied sciences covering the biological, physical, social and behavioral sciences related to agriculture.

Enviro/Energyline Abstracts Plus. R. R. Bowker Co., 121 Chanlon Rd., New Providence, New Jersey 07974. (908) 464-6800.

Environmental Periodicals Bibliography. National Information Services Corp., Ste. 6, Wyman Towers, 3100 St. Paul St., Baltimore, Maryland 21218. (410)243-0797. Online version of abstract of same name.

Monthly Catalog of United States Government Publications. U.S. G.P.O., Supt. of Docs., PO Box 371954, Pittsburgh, Pennsylvania 15250-7954. (202) 512-0000.

National Technical Information Service. U.S. Department of Commerce, National Technical Information Service, Office of Data Base Services, 5285 Port Royal Rd., Springfield, Virginia 22161. (703) 487-4807. Bibliographic database of government sponsored research and technical reports.

SCISEARCH. Institute for Scientific Information, University City Science Center, 3501 Market St., Philadelphia, Pennsylvania 19104. (215) 386-0100.

TRADE ASSOCIATIONS AND PROFESSIONAL SOCIETIES

American Institute of Biological Sciences. 730 11th St., N.W., Washington, District of Columbia 20001-4521. (202) 628-1500.

DOSE ESTIMATION

See: RISK ANALYSIS

DOSE RESPONSE PROFILES

See: RISK ANALYSIS

DOSIMETRY

See also: RADIATION EXPOSURE

ABSTRACTING AND INDEXING SERVICES

Environment Abstracts. Bowker A & I Publishing, 121 Chanlon Rd., New Providence, New Jersey 07974. (908) 464-6800. 1974-.

Environment Index. Environment Information Center, Index Research Department, 124 E. 39th St., New York, New York 10016. 1971-. Annual.

Environmental Information Connection–EIC. Planning Information Program, Dept. of Urban and Regional Planning, University of Illinois, 1003 West Nevada, Urbana, Illinois 61801. (217) 333-1369. Also available online.

Environmental Periodicals Bibliography. Environmental Studies Institute, International Academy at Santa Barbara, 800 Garden St., Suite D, Santa Barbara, California 93101. (805) 965-5010. Also available online.

Physics Briefs. Physikalische Berichte. Physik Verlag, Pappapelallee 3, Postfach 101161, Weinheim, Germany D-6940. 1979-. Semimonthly. In English. Volumes for 1979- issued by the Deutsche Physikalische Gesellschaft and the Fachinformationszentrum Energie Physik, Mathematik in cooperation with the American Institute of Physics.

Science Citation Index. Institute for Scientific Information, 3501 Market St., Philadelphia, Pennsylvania 19104. 1961-.

BIBLIOGRAPHIES

EPA Publications Bibliography. U.S. Environmental Protection Agency, Library Systems Branch, 401 M St., SW, Washington, District of Columbia 20460. (202) 260-2090. Quarterly.

ENCYCLOPEDIAS AND DICTIONARIES

Encyclopedia of Physical Science and Technology. Robert A. Meyers, ed. Academic Press, c/o Harcourt Brace Jovanovich Inc., 6277 Sea Harbor Dr., Orlando, Florida 32887. (800) 346-8648. Dictionary of engineering, technology and physical sciences.

Encyclopedia of Physics. Rita G. Lerner and George L. Trigg. VCH Publishers, 303 NW 12th Ave., Deerfield Beach, Florida 33442-1788. (305) 428-5566. 1991. Second edition.

Van Nostrand's Scientific Encyclopedia. Glenn D. Considine, ed. Van Nostrand Reinhold, 115 5th Ave., New York, New York 10003. (212) 254-3232. 1983. Sixth edition. Includes all broad subject areas in science.

GENERAL WORKS

Comparative Dosimetry of Radon in Mines and Homes. Commission on Life Science, National Research Council. National Academy Press, 2101 Constitution Ave. N.W., PO Box 285, Washington, District of Columbia 20418. (202) 334-3313. 1991.

MILDOS–a Computer Program for Calculating Environmental Radiation Doses from Uranium Recovery Operations. D. L. Strenge. National Technical Information Service, 5285 Port Royal Rd., Springfield, Virginia 22161. (703) 487-4650. 1981.

ONLINE DATA BASES

Enviro/Energyline Abstracts Plus. R. R. Bowker Co., 121 Chanlon Rd., New Providence, New Jersey 07974. (908) 464-6800.

Environmental Periodicals Bibliography. National Information Services Corp., Ste. 6, Wyman Towers, 3100 St. Paul St., Baltimore, Maryland 21218. (410)243-0797. Online version of abstract of same name.

DOUGLAS FIRS

See: FORESTS

DRAINAGE

See: SOIL SCIENCE

DREDGE SPOIL

See: DREDGING

DREDGE SPOIL DISPOSAL
See: DREDGING

DREDGE SPOIL TREATMENT
See: DREDGING

DREDGING
See also: MARINE BIOLOGY

ABSTRACTING AND INDEXING SERVICES

Applied Science and Technology Index. H.W. Wilson Co., 950 University Ave., Bronx, New York 10452. (800) 367-6770. Formerly Industrial Arts Index.

Aqualine Abstracts. Water Research Centre. c/o Pergamon Microforms International, Inc., Fairview Park, Elmsford, New York 10523. (914) 592-7720. 1927-. Contains some 8,000 records annually on water and wastewater technology. Covers all aspects of water, wastewater, associated engineering services and the aquatic environment. Over 600 periodicals, as well as books, reports and conference proceedings and other publications from water related institutions worldwide are scanned. Also available online.

Environment Abstracts. Bowker A & I Publishing, 121 Chanlon Rd., New Providence, New Jersey 07974. (908) 464-6800. 1974-.

Environment Index. Environment Information Center, Index Research Department, 124 E. 39th St., New York, New York 10016. 1971-. Annual.

Environmental Information Connection–EIC. Planning Information Program, Dept. of Urban and Regional Planning, University of Illinois, 1003 West Nevada, Urbana, Illinois 61801. (217) 333-1369. Also available online.

Environmental Periodicals Bibliography. Environmental Studies Institute, International Academy at Santa Barbara, 800 Garden St., Suite D, Santa Barbara, California 93101. (805) 965-5010. Also available online.

General Science Index. H. W. Wilson Co., 950 University Ave., Bronx, New York 10452. 1978-. Monthly, also issued in annual cumulation. Cumulative subject index to English language periodicals in the subject fields of astronomy, botany, chemistry, earth science, environment and conservation, food and nutrition, genetics, mathematics, medicine and health, microbiology, oceanography, physics, physiology and zoology.

Index to Scientific Book Contents. Institute for Scientific Information, 3501 Market St., Philadelphia, Pennsylvania 19104. (800) 523-1857. 1985-. Annual. Gives contents of science books published.

Pollution Abstracts. Cambridge Scientific Abstracts, 5161 River Rd., Bethesda, Maryland 20816. (301) 961-6750. Six/year. Indexes worldwide technical literature on environmental pollution. Covers air pollution, marine and freshwater pollution, sewage and wastewater treatment, waste management, toxicology and health, noise pollution, radiation, land pollution, and environmental poli-

cies, programs, legislation, and education. Also available online.

Science Citation Index. Institute for Scientific Information, 3501 Market St., Philadelphia, Pennsylvania 19104. 1961-.

BIBLIOGRAPHIES

EPA Publications Bibliography. U.S. Environmental Protection Agency, Library Systems Branch, 401 M St., SW, Washington, District of Columbia 20460. (202) 260-2090. Quarterly.

ENCYCLOPEDIAS AND DICTIONARIES

Dictionary of Environmental Engineering and Related Sciences: English-Spanish, Spanish-English. Jose T. Villate. Ediciones Universal, 3090 SW 8th St., Miami, Florida 33135. (305) 642-3355. 1979.

Encyclopedia of Environmental Science and Engineering. J.R. Pfafflin. Gordon and Breach Science Publishers, Inc., 270 8th Ave., New York, New York 10011. (212) 206-8900. 1992.

McGraw-Hill Encyclopedia of Science and Technology. McGraw-Hill, 1221 Avenue of the Americas, New York, New York 10020. (212) 512-2000 or (800) 262-4729. 1992. Seventh edition. Issued in multiple volumes including index. Includes all science and technology broad subject areas.

Van Nostrand's Scientific Encyclopedia. Glenn D. Considine, ed. Van Nostrand Reinhold, 115 5th Ave., New York, New York 10003. (212) 254-3232. 1983. Sixth edition. Includes all broad subject areas in science.

ONLINE DATA BASES

Enviro/Energyline Abstracts Plus. R. R. Bowker Co., 121 Chanlon Rd., New Providence, New Jersey 07974. (908) 464-6800.

Environmental Periodicals Bibliography. National Information Services Corp., Ste. 6, Wyman Towers, 3100 St. Paul St., Baltimore, Maryland 21218. (410)243-0797. Online version of abstract of same name.

Monthly Catalog of United States Government Publications. U.S. G.P.O., Supt. of Docs., PO Box 371954, Pittsburgh, Pennsylvania 15250-7954. (202) 512-0000.

National Technical Information Service. U.S. Department of Commerce, National Technical Information Service, Office of Data Base Services, 5285 Port Royal Rd., Springfield, Virginia 22161. (703) 487-4807. Bibliographic database of government sponsored research and technical reports.

PERIODICALS AND NEWSLETTERS

Environmental Effects of Dredging. U.S. Army Corps of Engineers, Waterways Experiment Station, PO Box 631, Vicksburg, Mississippi 39180. (601) 634-3774. Quarterly. Effects of dredging and dredged material disposal operations and the development of technically, environmentally, and economically feasible dredging and disposal alternatives.

DRILLING

ABSTRACTING AND INDEXING SERVICES

Applied Science and Technology Index. H.W. Wilson Co., 950 University Ave., Bronx, New York 10452. (800) 367-6770. Formerly Industrial Arts Index.

Energy Information Abstracts Annual 1987 in Retrospect. EIC/Intelligence Inc., 121 Chanlon Rd., New Providence, New Jersey 07974. (908) 464-6800. 1988. Annual. Cumulative edition of the monthly Energy Information Abstracts. Monitors sources in the field of energy including the scientific, technical and business journal literature, conference and symposia proceedings, corporate, government and academic reports.

Environment Abstracts. Bowker A & I Publishing, 121 Chanlon Rd., New Providence, New Jersey 07974. (908) 464-6800. 1974-.

Environment Index. Environment Information Center, Index Research Department, 124 E. 39th St., New York, New York 10016. 1971-. Annual.

Environmental Information Connection–EIC. Planning Information Program, Dept. of Urban and Regional Planning, University of Illinois, 1003 West Nevada, Urbana, Illinois 61801. (217) 333-1369. Also available online.

Environmental Periodicals Bibliography. Environmental Studies Institute, International Academy at Santa Barbara, 800 Garden St., Suite D, Santa Barbara, California 93101. (805) 965-5010. Also available online.

Index to Scientific Book Contents. Institute for Scientific Information, 3501 Market St., Philadelphia, Pennsylvania 19104. (800) 523-1857. 1985-. Annual. Gives contents of science books published.

Science Citation Index. Institute for Scientific Information, 3501 Market St., Philadelphia, Pennsylvania 19104. 1961-.

BIBLIOGRAPHIES

Bibliography and Index of Geology. American Geological Institute, 4220 King St., Alexandria, Virginia 22302. Monthly. Includes environmental geology and hydrogeology.

EPA Publications Bibliography. U.S. Environmental Protection Agency, Library Systems Branch, 401 M St., SW, Washington, District of Columbia 20460. (202) 260-2090. Quarterly.

DIRECTORIES

Offshore Contractors and Equipment Worldwide Directory. PennWell Books, Box 1260, Tulsa, Oklahoma 74101. (918) 831-3161. 1984.

Offshore Rig Owners Personnel Directory. Offshore Data Services, Inc., Box 19909, Houston, Texas 77224. (713) 781-2713.

Offshore Services and Equipment Directory. Greene Dot, Inc., Box 28663, San Diego, California 92128. (619) 485-7237.

Oil and Gas Exploration and Development. American Business Directories, Inc., 5711 S. 86th Circle, Omaha, Nebraska 68127. (402) 593-4600.

Solid Waste & Power–Waste-to-Energy Industry Directory Issue. HCI Publications, 410 Archibald St., Kansas City, Missouri 64111. (816) 931-1311.

ENCYCLOPEDIAS AND DICTIONARIES

An A-Z of Offshore Oil and Gas: An Illustrated International Glossary and Reference Guide to the Offshore Oil & Gas Industries and their Technology. Harry Whitehead. Gulf Publishing Co., Book Division, PO Box 2608, Houston, Texas 77252. (713) 529-4301. Second edition. Defines and explains some 4000 specialized terms in current use in the oil and gas industries. Second edition includes 900 new entries in the key areas of new terminology, components, rig construction, new technologies, new discoveries, drilling technology, drilling fluid and med technology and key offshore locations.

Dictionary of Environmental Engineering and Related Sciences: English-Spanish, Spanish-English. Jose T. Villate. Ediciones Universal, 3090 SW 8th St., Miami, Florida 33135. (305) 642-3355. 1979.

Encyclopedia of Environmental Science and Engineering. J.R. Pfafflin. Gordon and Breach Science Publishers, Inc., 270 8th Ave., New York, New York 10011. (212) 206-8900. 1992.

Encyclopedia of Physical Science and Technology. Robert A. Meyers, ed. Academic Press, c/o Harcourt Brace Jovanovich Inc., 6277 Sea Harbor Dr., Orlando, Florida 32887. (800) 346-8648. Dictionary of engineering, technology and physical sciences.

McGraw-Hill Encyclopedia of Science and Technology. McGraw-Hill, 1221 Avenue of the Americas, New York, New York 10020. (212) 512-2000 or (800) 262-4729. 1992. Seventh edition. Issued in multiple volumes including index. Includes all science and technology broad subject areas.

Van Nostrand's Scientific Encyclopedia. Glenn D. Considine, ed. Van Nostrand Reinhold, 115 5th Ave., New York, New York 10003. (212) 254-3232. 1983. Sixth edition. Includes all broad subject areas in science.

GENERAL WORKS

Coastal Alert: Ecosystems, Energy, and Offshore Oil Drilling. Dwight Holing. Island Press, 1718 Connecticut Ave. N.W., Suite 300, Washington, District of Columbia 20009. (202) 232-7933. 1990. Describes how offshore drilling affects environment and quality of life, how the government auctions our coast to the oil industry, how the lease sale process works, how energy alternatives can replace offshore drilling; how citizen action works and how to become involved.

Magill's Survey of Science. Earth Science Series. Frank N. Magill. Salem Press, PO Box 50062, Pasadena, California 91105. 1990-. Five volumes. Includes information on earth's crust, hot spots and volcanic island chains, physical properties of minerals, rock magnetism, physical properties of rocks, and index.

ONLINE DATA BASES

Enviro/Energyline Abstracts Plus. R. R. Bowker Co., 121 Chanlon Rd., New Providence, New Jersey 07974. (908) 464-6800.

Environmental Periodicals Bibliography. National Information Services Corp., Ste. 6, Wyman Towers, 3100 St. Paul St., Baltimore, Maryland 21218. (410)243-0797. Online version of abstract of same name.

International Petroleum Abstracts. John Wiley & Sons, Ltd., Baffers Lane, Chichester, Sussex, England PO1 91UD. 44 (243) 770215.

International Petroleum Annual. U.S. Department of Energy, Integrated Technical Information System, P.O. Box 62, Oak Ridge, Tennessee 37831. (615) 576-1222.

Monthly Catalog of United States Government Publications. U.S. G.P.O., Supt. of Docs., PO Box 371954, Pittsburgh, Pennsylvania 15250-7954. (202) 512-0000.

National Technical Information Service. U.S. Department of Commerce, National Technical Information Service, Office of Data Base Services, 5285 Port Royal Rd., Springfield, Virginia 22161. (703) 487-4807. Bibliographic database of government sponsored research and technical reports.

RESEARCH CENTERS AND INSTITUTES

Massachusetts Institute of Technology, MIT Sea Grant College Program. E38-300, 292 Main St., Cambridge, Massachusetts 02139. (617) 253-7041.

STATISTICS SOURCES

Offshore: Incorporating the Oilman. Offshore, P.O. Box 2895, Tulsa, Oklahoma 74101. Monthly. Offshore oil and gas exploration, production, transportation, and finance.

TRADE ASSOCIATIONS AND PROFESSIONAL SOCIETIES

Get Oil Out. P.O. Box 1513, Santa Barbara, California 93102. (805) 965-1519.

National Drilling Contractors Association. 3008 Millwood Ave., Columbia, South Carolina 29205. (803) 252-5646.

DRILLING RIGS, OFFSHORE

See: DRILLING

DRINKING WATER

See: WATER QUALITY

DRIP IRRIGATION

See: IRRIGATION

DROUGHT

ABSTRACTING AND INDEXING SERVICES

Applied Ecology Abstracts Studies in Renewable Natural Resources. Information Retrieval Ltd., 1911 Jefferson Davis Highway, Arlington, Virginia 22202. 1975-. Monthly.

Biological and Agricultural Index. H.W. Wilson Co., 950 University Ave., Bronx, New York 10452. (800) 367-6770. 1916-. Monthly.

Biotechnology Research Abstracts. Cambridge Scientific Abstracts, 5161 River Rd., Bethesda, Maryland 20816. (301) 961-6750. Monthly. Includes such broad areas as genetic intervention, biochemical genetics, and microbiological techniques.

Ecological Abstracts. Geo Abstracts Ltd. Elsevier Applied Science, Crown House, Linton Rd., Barking, England IG 11 8JU. 1974-. Derived from over 600 leading ecological and environmental journals, plus books, conference proceedings, reports and theses.

Index to Scientific Book Contents. Institute for Scientific Information, 3501 Market St., Philadelphia, Pennsylvania 19104. (800) 523-1857. 1985-. Annual. Gives contents of science books published.

Multimedia Index to Ecology. National Information Center for Educational Media, University of Southern California, Los Angeles, California 90007.

Science Citation Index. Institute for Scientific Information, 3501 Market St., Philadelphia, Pennsylvania 19104. 1961-.

BIBLIOGRAPHIES

Current Contents. Agriculture, Biology and Environmental Sciences. Institute for Scientific Information, 3501 Market St., Philadelphia, Pennsylvania 19104. (800) 523-1857. 1973-. Previous title: Current Contents. Agricultural, Food & Veterinary Sciences. Gives the table of contents of periodicals in the fields of agriculture, biology, environmental and related areas.

ENCYCLOPEDIAS AND DICTIONARIES

McGraw-Hill Encyclopedia of Science and Technology. McGraw-Hill, 1221 Avenue of the Americas, New York, New York 10020. (212) 512-2000 or (800) 262-4729. 1992. Seventh edition. Issued in multiple volumes including index. Includes all science and technology broad subject areas.

Van Nostrand's Scientific Encyclopedia. Glenn D. Considine, ed. Van Nostrand Reinhold, 115 5th Ave., New York, New York 10003. (212) 254-3232. 1983. Sixth edition. Includes all broad subject areas in science.

ONLINE DATA BASES

Monthly Catalog of United States Government Publications. U.S. G.P.O., Supt. of Docs., PO Box 371954, Pittsburgh, Pennsylvania 15250-7954. (202) 512-0000.

National Technical Information Service. U.S. Department of Commerce, National Technical Information Service, Office of Data Base Services, 5285 Port Royal Rd., Springfield, Virginia 22161. (703) 487-4807. Biblio-

graphic database of government sponsored research and technical reports.

PressNet Environmental Reports. Chemical Information Systems, Inc., 7215 York Rd., Baltimore, Maryland 21212. (301) 321-8440.

SCISEARCH. Institute for Scientific Information, University City Science Center, 3501 Market St., Philadelphia, Pennsylvania 19104. (215) 386-0100.

RESEARCH CENTERS AND INSTITUTES

Water Resources Association of the Delaware River Basin. Box 867, Davis Road, Valley Forge, Pennsylvania 19481. (215) 783-0634.

STATISTICS SOURCES

Compendium on Water Supply, Drought, and Conservation. National Regulatory Research Institute. U.S. G.P.O, Washington, District of Columbia 20402-9325. (202) 512-0000. 1989. Water supply and demand, drought, conservation, utility ratemaking and regulatory issues.

TRADE ASSOCIATIONS AND PROFESSIONAL SOCIETIES

American Institute of Biological Sciences. 730 11th St., N.W., Washington, District of Columbia 20001-4521. (202) 628-1500.

DRYLAND FARMING

See also: AGRICULTURE

ABSTRACTING AND INDEXING SERVICES

Agrindex. AGRIS Coordinating Center, Via delle Terme di Caracalla, Rome, Italy I-00100. 61 0181-FA01. 1975-.

Applied Ecology Abstracts Studies in Renewable Natural Resources. Information Retrieval Ltd., 1911 Jefferson Davis Highway, Arlington, Virginia 22202. 1975-. Monthly.

Applied Science and Technology Index. H.W. Wilson Co., 950 University Ave., Bronx, New York 10452. (800) 367-6770. Formerly Industrial Arts Index.

Biological and Agricultural Index. H.W. Wilson Co., 950 University Ave., Bronx, New York 10452. (800) 367-6770. 1916-. Monthly.

Environment Abstracts. Bowker A & I Publishing, 121 Chanlon Rd., New Providence, New Jersey 07974. (908) 464-6800. 1974-.

Environment Index. Environment Information Center, Index Research Department, 124 E. 39th St., New York, New York 10016. 1971-. Annual.

Environmental Information Connection-EIC. Planning Information Program, Dept. of Urban and Regional Planning, University of Illinois, 1003 West Nevada, Urbana, Illinois 61801. (217) 333-1369. Also available online.

Environmental Periodicals Bibliography. Environmental Studies Institute, International Academy at Santa Barbara, 800 Garden St., Suite D, Santa Barbara, California 93101. (805) 965-5010. Also available online.

General Science Index. H. W. Wilson Co., 950 University Ave., Bronx, New York 10452. 1978-. Monthly, also issued in annual cumulation. Cumulative subject index to English language periodicals in the subject fields of astronomy, botany, chemistry, earth science, environment and conservation, food and nutrition, genetics, mathematics, medicine and health, microbiology, oceanography, physics, physiology and zoology.

Index to Scientific Book Contents. Institute for Scientific Information, 3501 Market St., Philadelphia, Pennsylvania 19104. (800) 523-1857. 1985-. Annual. Gives contents of science books published.

Multimedia Index to Ecology. National Information Center for Educational Media, University of Southern California, Los Angeles, California 90007.

BIBLIOGRAPHIES

Bibliography of Dryland Agriculture. S. Reihl. Dryland Agricultural Technical Committee, Administration Bldg. A 422, Corvallis, Oregon 97331. (503) 737-2513. 1980. Covers arid regions agriculture.

Comprehensive Bibliography of Drying References: Covering Bulletins, Booklets, Books, Chapters, Bibliographies. Carl W. Hall. American Society of Agricultural Engineers, 2950 Niles Rd., St. Joseph, Michigan 49085-9659. (616) 429-0300. 1980.

Current Contents. Agriculture, Biology and Environmental Sciences. Institute for Scientific Information, 3501 Market St., Philadelphia, Pennsylvania 19104. (800) 523-1857. 1973-. Previous title: Current Contents. Agricultural, Food & Veterinary Sciences. Gives the table of contents of periodicals in the fields of agriculture, biology, environmental and related areas.

Directory of Published Proceedings. Interdok Corp., 173 Halstead Ave., Harrison, New York 10528. (914) 835-3506. 1990. Monthly. This is a listing of published proceedings including the series SEMTE (Science/Medicine/Engineering/Technology) and the series SSH (Social Science/Humanities).

Dryland Farming. Henry Gilbert. U.S. Department of Agriculture, 10301 Baltimore Blvd., Beltsville, Maryland 20705-2351. (301) 504-5755. 1987.

EPA Publications Bibliography. U.S. Environmental Protection Agency, Library Systems Branch, 401 M St., SW, Washington, District of Columbia 20460. (202) 260-2090. Quarterly.

ENCYCLOPEDIAS AND DICTIONARIES

Dictionary of Drying. Carl W. Hall. Marcel Dekker Inc., 270 Madison Ave., New York, New York 10016. (212) 696-9000 or (800) 228-1160. 1979.

Dictionary of Environmental Engineering and Related Sciences: English-Spanish, Spanish-English. Jose T. Villate. Ediciones Universal, 3090 SW 8th St., Miami, Florida 33135. (305) 642-3355. 1979.

Encyclopedia of Environmental Science and Engineering. J.R. Pfafflin. Gordon and Breach Science Publishers, Inc., 270 8th Ave., New York, New York 10011. (212) 206-8900. 1992.

The Encyclopedia of Geochemistry and Environmental Sciences. Rhodes Whitmore Fairbridge. Van Nostrand Reinhold Co., 115 5th Ave., New York, New York 10003. (212) 254-3232. 1972.

Van Nostrand's Scientific Encyclopedia. Glenn D. Considine, ed. Van Nostrand Reinhold, 115 5th Ave., New York, New York 10003. (212) 254-3232. 1983. Sixth edition. Includes all broad subject areas in science.

GENERAL WORKS

Analysis and Development of a Solar Energy Regenerated Desiccant Crop Drying Facility: Phase I, Final Report. S. M. Ko, et al. Lockheed Missiles and Space Co., available from National Technical Information Service, 5285 Port Royal Rd, Springfield, Virginia 22161. (703) 487-4650. 1977.

Analysis and Development of Regenerated Desiccant Systems for Industrial and Agricultural Drying. D. V. Merrifield and J. W. Fletcher. National Technical Information Center, 5285 Port Royal Rd., Springfield, Virginia 22161. (703) 487-4650. 1977. Prepared by Lockheed Missiles and Space Company Inc., Huntsville Research Engineering Center, Huntsville, AL, under subcontract 7296, LMSC-HREC TR D568133, for Oak Ridge National Laboratory, Oak Ridge, TN.

Development of a Solar Desiccant Dehumidifier: Second Technical Progress Report. M. E. Gunderson, et al. National Technical Information Services, 5285 Port Royal Rd., Springfield, Virginia 22161. (703) 487-4650. 1980.

Drying '89. Arun S. Mujumdar and Michel Roques. Hemisphere Publishing Co., 79 Madison Ave., Suite 1110, New York, New York 10016. (212) 725-1999. 1990. Papers from the 10th International Drying Symposium held at Versailles, France, Sept. 5-8, 1988.

Dryland Agriculture. H.E. Dregne. American Society of Agronomy, 677 S. Segoe Rd., Madison, Wisconsin 53711-1086. (608) 273-8080. 1983.

Paddy Drying Manual. N. C. Teter. Food and Agriculture Organization of the United Nations, 4611-F Assembly Dr., Lanham, Maryland 20706-4391. (301) 459-7666 or (800) 274-4888. 1987.

Process Drying Practice. Edward M. Cook and Harman D. Dumont. McGraw-Hill, 1221 Avenue of the Americas, New York, New York 10020. (212) 512-2000 or (800) 262-4729. 1991.

Production Response of Illinois Farmers to Premiums for Low- Temperature Dried Corn. Lowell D. Hill, et al. Dept. of Agricultural Economics, Agricultural Experiment Station, University of Illinois at Urbana-Champaign, Urbana, Illinois 61801. 1987. Describes the procedure for drying of corn and its prices.

HANDBOOKS AND MANUALS

Dehumidification Handbook. Cargocaire Engineering Corp., PO Box 640, Amesbury, Massachusetts 01913. 1982.

Handbook of Dehumidification Technology. G. W. Brundrett. Butterworth-Heinemann, 80 Montvale Ave., Stoneham, Massachusetts 02180. (617) 438-8464 or (800) 366-2665. 1987.

Handbook of Industrial Drying. Arun S. Majumdar, ed. Marcel Dekker Inc., 270 Madison Ave., New York, New York 10016. (212) 696-9000 or (800) 228-1160. 1987.

ONLINE DATA BASES

Enviro/Energyline Abstracts Plus. R. R. Bowker Co., 121 Chanlon Rd., New Providence, New Jersey 07974. (908) 464-6800.

Environmental Periodicals Bibliography. National Information Services Corp., Ste. 6, Wyman Towers, 3100 St. Paul St., Baltimore, Maryland 21218. (410)243-0797. Online version of abstract of same name.

Monthly Catalog of United States Government Publications. U.S. G.P.O., Supt. of Docs., PO Box 371954, Pittsburgh, Pennsylvania 15250-7954. (202) 512-0000.

National Technical Information Service. U.S. Department of Commerce, National Technical Information Service, Office of Data Base Services, 5285 Port Royal Rd., Springfield, Virginia 22161. (703) 487-4807. Bibliographic database of government sponsored research and technical reports.

SCISEARCH. Institute for Scientific Information, University City Science Center, 3501 Market St., Philadelphia, Pennsylvania 19104. (215) 386-0100.

DUMPS

See: WASTE STORAGE

DUNE EROSION

ABSTRACTING AND INDEXING SERVICES

Applied Ecology Abstracts Studies in Renewable Natural Resources. Information Retrieval Ltd., 1911 Jefferson Davis Highway, Arlington, Virginia 22202. 1975-. Monthly.

Applied Science and Technology Index. H.W. Wilson Co., 950 University Ave., Bronx, New York 10452. (800) 367-6770. Formerly Industrial Arts Index.

Biological Abstracts. BIOSIS, 2100 Arch St., Philadelphia, Pennsylvania 19103-1399. (215) 587-4800. 1927-.

Ecological Abstracts. Geo Abstracts Ltd. Elsevier Applied Science, Crown House, Linton Rd., Barking, England IG 11 8JU. 1974-. Derived from over 600 leading ecological and environmental journals, plus books, conference proceedings, reports and theses.

Ecology Abstracts. Cambridge Scientific Abstracts, 5161 River Rd., Bethesda, Maryland 20816. (301) 961-6750. Monthly.

Environment Abstracts. Bowker A & I Publishing, 121 Chanlon Rd., New Providence, New Jersey 07974. (908) 464-6800. 1974-.

Environment Index. Environment Information Center, Index Research Department, 124 E. 39th St., New York, New York 10016. 1971-. Annual.

Environmental Information Connection-EIC. Planning Information Program, Dept. of Urban and Regional Planning, University of Illinois, 1003 West Nevada,

Urbana, Illinois 61801. (217) 333-1369. Also available online.

Environmental Periodicals Bibliography. Environmental Studies Institute, International Academy at Santa Barbara, 800 Garden St., Suite D, Santa Barbara, California 93101. (805) 965-5010. Also available online.

Multimedia Index to Ecology. National Information Center for Educational Media, University of Southern California, Los Angeles, California 90007.

BIBLIOGRAPHIES

Bibliography and Index of Geology. American Geological Institute, 4220 King St., Alexandria, Virginia 22302. Monthly. Includes environmental geology and hydrogeology.

EPA Publications Bibliography. U.S. Environmental Protection Agency, Library Systems Branch, 401 M St., SW, Washington, District of Columbia 20460. (202) 260-2090. Quarterly.

GENERAL WORKS

Magill's Survey of Science. Earth Science Series. Frank N. Magill. Salem Press, PO Box 50062, Pasadena, California 91105. 1990-. Five volumes. Includes information on earth's crust, hot spots and volcanic island chains, physical properties of minerals, rock magnetism, physical properties of rocks, and index.

ONLINE DATA BASES

BIOSIS Previews. BIOSIS, 2100 Arch St., Philadelphia, Pennsylvania 19103-1399. (215) 587-4800. Largest and most comprehensive database of research in the life sciences. Contains citations for nearly 9000 primary research journals, monographs, reviews, symposia, preliminary reports, semi-popular journals, selected institutional reports, government reports and research communications.

Enviro/Energyline Abstracts Plus. R. R. Bowker Co., 121 Chanlon Rd., New Providence, New Jersey 07974. (908) 464-6800.

Environmental Periodicals Bibliography. National Information Services Corp., Ste. 6, Wyman Towers, 3100 St. Paul St., Baltimore, Maryland 21218. (410)243-0797. Online version of abstract of same name.

STATISTICS SOURCES

Ecology: Community Profiles. U.S. Fish and Wildlife Service. National Technical Information Service, 5285 Port Royal Road, Springfield, Virginia 22161. (703) 487-4650. Irregular. Data on coastal and inland ecosystems, including wetlands, tidal-flats, near-shore seagrasses, sand dunes, drilling platforms, oyster reefs, estuaries, rivers and streams.

TRADE ASSOCIATIONS AND PROFESSIONAL SOCIETIES

Save the Dunes Council. PO Box 114, Beverly Shores, Indiana 46301. (219) 879-3937.

DUST

See also: SOIL SCIENCE

ABSTRACTING AND INDEXING SERVICES

Environment Abstracts. Bowker A & I Publishing, 121 Chanlon Rd., New Providence, New Jersey 07974. (908) 464-6800. 1974-.

Environment Index. Environment Information Center, Index Research Department, 124 E. 39th St., New York, New York 10016. 1971-. Annual.

Environmental Information Connection–EIC. Planning Information Program, Dept. of Urban and Regional Planning, University of Illinois, 1003 West Nevada, Urbana, Illinois 61801. (217) 333-1369. Also available online.

Environmental Periodicals Bibliography. Environmental Studies Institute, International Academy at Santa Barbara, 800 Garden St., Suite D, Santa Barbara, California 93101. (805) 965-5010. Also available online.

Index to Scientific Book Contents. Institute for Scientific Information, 3501 Market St., Philadelphia, Pennsylvania 19104. (800) 523-1857. 1985-. Annual. Gives contents of science books published.

Science Citation Index. Institute for Scientific Information, 3501 Market St., Philadelphia, Pennsylvania 19104. 1961-.

BIBLIOGRAPHIES

Bibliography and Index of Geology. American Geological Institute, 4220 King St., Alexandria, Virginia 22302. Monthly. Includes environmental geology and hydrogeology.

Current Contents. Agriculture, Biology and Environmental Sciences. Institute for Scientific Information, 3501 Market St., Philadelphia, Pennsylvania 19104. (800) 523-1857. 1973-. Previous title: Current Contents. Agricultural, Food & Veterinary Sciences. Gives the table of contents of periodicals in the fields of agriculture, biology, environmental and related areas.

EPA Publications Bibliography. U.S. Environmental Protection Agency, Library Systems Branch, 401 M St., SW, Washington, District of Columbia 20460. (202) 260-2090. Quarterly.

ENCYCLOPEDIAS AND DICTIONARIES

Encyclopedia of Chemical Processing and Design. John J. Mcketta and W. A. Cunningham. Marcel Dekker, Inc., 270 Madison Ave., New York, New York 10016. (212) 696-9000; (800) 228-1160. 1992. Thirty-eight volumes.

Kirk-Othmer Encyclopedia of Chemical Technology. J. I. Kroschwitz, ed. John Wiley & Sons, Inc., 605 3rd Ave., New York, New York 10158-0012. (212) 850-6000. 1992-. All articles in the new edition have been rewritten and updated adding new subjects such as biotechnology, computer topics, analytical techniques and instrumentation, environmental concerns, fuels and energy, inorganic and solid state chemistry; composite materials and material science in general, and pharmaceuticals. Also available online.

GENERAL WORKS

Magill's Survey of Science. Earth Science Series. Frank N. Magill. Salem Press, PO Box 50062, Pasadena, California 91105. 1990-. Five volumes. Includes information on earth's crust, hot spots and volcanic island chains, physical properties of minerals, rock magnetism, physical properties of rocks, and index.

ONLINE DATA BASES

Enviro/Energyline Abstracts Plus. R. R. Bowker Co., 121 Chanlon Rd., New Providence, New Jersey 07974. (908) 464-6800.

Environmental Periodicals Bibliography. National Information Services Corp., Ste. 6, Wyman Towers, 3100 St. Paul St., Baltimore, Maryland 21218. (410)243-0797. Online version of abstract of same name.

Kirk-Othmer Encyclopedia of Chemical Technology. John Wiley & Sons, Inc., 605 3rd Ave., 5th Floor, New York, New York 10158. (212) 850-6000. Online version of the publication of the same name.

Monthly Catalog of United States Government Publications. U.S. G.P.O., Supt. of Docs., PO Box 371954, Pittsburgh, Pennsylvania 15250-7954. (202) 512-0000.

National Technical Information Service. U.S. Department of Commerce, National Technical Information Service, Office of Data Base Services, 5285 Port Royal Rd., Springfield, Virginia 22161. (703) 487-4807. Bibliographic database of government sponsored research and technical reports.

DUST COLLECTORS

ABSTRACTING AND INDEXING SERVICES

Applied Science and Technology Index. H.W. Wilson Co., 950 University Ave., Bronx, New York 10452. (800) 367-6770. Formerly Industrial Arts Index.

Environment Abstracts. Bowker A & I Publishing, 121 Chanlon Rd., New Providence, New Jersey 07974. (908) 464-6800. 1974-.

Environment Index. Environment Information Center, Index Research Department, 124 E. 39th St., New York, New York 10016. 1971-. Annual.

Environmental Information Connection–EIC. Planning Information Program, Dept. of Urban and Regional Planning, University of Illinois, 1003 West Nevada, Urbana, Illinois 61801. (217) 333-1369. Also available online.

Environmental Periodicals Bibliography. Environmental Studies Institute, International Academy at Santa Barbara, 800 Garden St., Suite D, Santa Barbara, California 93101. (805) 965-5010. Also available online.

Pollution Abstracts. Cambridge Scientific Abstracts, 5161 River Rd., Bethesda, Maryland 20816. (301) 961-6750. Six/year. Indexes worldwide technical literature on environmental pollution. Covers air pollution, marine and freshwater pollution, sewage and wastewater treatment, waste management, toxicology and health, noise pollution, radiation, land pollution, and environmental policies, programs, legislation, and education. Also available online.

BIBLIOGRAPHIES

EPA Publications Bibliography. U.S. Environmental Protection Agency, Library Systems Branch, 401 M St., SW, Washington, District of Columbia 20460. (202) 260-2090. Quarterly.

ENCYCLOPEDIAS AND DICTIONARIES

Van Nostrand's Scientific Encyclopedia. Glenn D. Considine, ed. Van Nostrand Reinhold, 115 5th Ave., New York, New York 10003. (212) 254-3232. 1983. Sixth edition. Includes all broad subject areas in science.

ONLINE DATA BASES

Enviro/Energyline Abstracts Plus. R. R. Bowker Co., 121 Chanlon Rd., New Providence, New Jersey 07974. (908) 464-6800.

Environmental Periodicals Bibliography. National Information Services Corp., Ste. 6, Wyman Towers, 3100 St. Paul St., Baltimore, Maryland 21218. (410)243-0797. Online version of abstract of same name.

DUSTFALL JARS
See: AIR POLLUTION

DYES

ABSTRACTING AND INDEXING SERVICES

Biological Abstracts. BIOSIS, 2100 Arch St., Philadelphia, Pennsylvania 19103-1399. (215) 587-4800. 1927-.

Biotechnology Research Abstracts. Cambridge Scientific Abstracts, 5161 River Rd., Bethesda, Maryland 20816. (301) 961-6750. Monthly. Includes such broad areas as genetic intervention, biochemical genetics, and microbiological techniques.

Chemical Abstracts. Chemical Abstracts Service, 2540 Olentangy River Rd., PO Box 3012, Columbus, Ohio 43210. (800) 848-6533. 1907-.

Ecology Abstracts. Cambridge Scientific Abstracts, 5161 River Rd., Bethesda, Maryland 20816. (301) 961-6750. Monthly.

Environment Abstracts. Bowker A & I Publishing, 121 Chanlon Rd., New Providence, New Jersey 07974. (908) 464-6800. 1974-.

Environment Index. Environment Information Center, Index Research Department, 124 E. 39th St., New York, New York 10016. 1971-. Annual.

Environmental Information Connection–EIC. Planning Information Program, Dept. of Urban and Regional Planning, University of Illinois, 1003 West Nevada, Urbana, Illinois 61801. (217) 333-1369. Also available online.

Environmental Periodicals Bibliography. Environmental Studies Institute, International Academy at Santa Barbara, 800 Garden St., Suite D, Santa Barbara, California 93101. (805) 965-5010. Also available online.

General Science Index. H. W. Wilson Co., 950 University Ave., Bronx, New York 10452. 1978-. Monthly, also issued in annual cumulation. Cumulative subject index to English language periodicals in the subject fields of astronomy, botany, chemistry, earth science, environment and conservation, food and nutrition, genetics, mathematics, medicine and health, microbiology, oceanography, physics, physiology and zoology.

Index to Scientific Book Contents. Institute for Scientific Information, 3501 Market St., Philadelphia, Pennsylvania 19104. (800) 523-1857. 1985-. Annual. Gives contents of science books published.

Pollution Abstracts. Cambridge Scientific Abstracts, 5161 River Rd., Bethesda, Maryland 20816. (301) 961-6750. Six/year. Indexes worldwide technical literature on environmental pollution. Covers air pollution, marine and freshwater pollution, sewage and wastewater treatment, waste management, toxicology and health, noise pollution, radiation, land pollution, and environmental policies, programs, legislation, and education. Also available online.

Science Citation Index. Institute for Scientific Information, 3501 Market St., Philadelphia, Pennsylvania 19104. 1961-.

BIBLIOGRAPHIES

EPA Publications Bibliography. U.S. Environmental Protection Agency, Library Systems Branch, 401 M St., SW, Washington, District of Columbia 20460. (202) 260-2090. Quarterly.

DIRECTORIES

American Association of Textile Chemists and Colorists–Membership Directory. Box 12215, Research Triangle Park, North Carolina 27709. (919) 549-8141. Annual.

American Dyestuff Reporter–Process Controls Buyers' Guide Issue. Harmon Cove Towers, Promenade A, Suite 2, Secaucus, New Jersey 07094. (201) 867-4200. Annual.

American Glass Review–Glass Factory Directory Issue. 1115 Clifton Ave., Clifton, New Jersey 07013. (201) 779-1600. Annual.

Textile Chemist and Colorist–Buyer's Guide Issue. American Association of Textile Chemists and Colorists, Box 12215, Research Triangle Park, North Carolina 27709. (919) 549-8141.

ENCYCLOPEDIAS AND DICTIONARIES

Chem Address Book. F. W. Derz, ed. Walter De Gruyter, New York, New York 1974. Includes over 180000 names (synonyms) in alphabetical order for chemical compounds and chemicals, radioactive labelled compounds, isotopes, dyes, polymers, etc. and their molecular formulas.

A Dictionary of Dyes and Dying. K. G. Ponting. Bell & Hyman Ltd., Denmark House, 37-39 Queen Elizabeth St., London, England SE1 2QB. 1981.

Encyclopedia of Industrial Chemical Additives. Michael and Irene Ash. Chemical Publishing Co., 80 Eighth Ave., New York, New York 10011. (212) 255-1950. 1984-87. Four volumes. Comprehensive compilation of tradename products that function as additives in enhancing the properties of various major industrial products.

McGraw-Hill Encyclopedia of Science and Technology. McGraw-Hill, 1221 Avenue of the Americas, New York, New York 10020. (212) 512-2000 or (800) 262-4729. 1992. Seventh edition. Issued in multiple volumes including index. Includes all science and technology broad subject areas.

Van Nostrand's Scientific Encyclopedia. Glenn D. Considine, ed. Van Nostrand Reinhold, 115 5th Ave., New York, New York 10003. (212) 254-3232. 1983. Sixth edition. Includes all broad subject areas in science.

HANDBOOKS AND MANUALS

The Sigma-Aldrich Handbook of Stains, Dyes and Indicators. Floyd J. Green. Aldrich Chemical Co., 1001 W. St. Paul Ave., Milwaukee, Wisconsin 53233. (414) 273-3850 or (800) 558-9160. 1990.

ONLINE DATA BASES

BIOSIS Previews. BIOSIS, 2100 Arch St., Philadelphia, Pennsylvania 19103-1399. (215) 587-4800. Largest and most comprehensive database of research in the life sciences. Contains citations for nearly 9000 primary research journals, monographs, reviews, symposia, preliminary reports, semi-popular journals, selected institutional reports, government reports and research communications.

Chemical Abstracts-CA. Chemical Abstracts Service, 2540 Olentangy River Rd., P.O. Box 3012, Columbus, Ohio 43210. (800) 848-6533 or (614) 421-3600. Information sources include 9000 journals, patents from 27 countries, two industrial property organizations, new books, conference proceedings, and government research reports.

Enviro/Energyline Abstracts Plus. R. R. Bowker Co., 121 Chanlon Rd., New Providence, New Jersey 07974. (908) 464-6800.

Environmental Periodicals Bibliography. National Information Services Corp., Ste. 6, Wyman Towers, 3100 St. Paul St., Baltimore, Maryland 21218. (410)243-0797. Online version of abstract of same name.

STATISTICS SOURCES

Advances in Coating Materials, Techniques & Equipment. FIND/SVP, 625 Avenue of the Americas, New York, New York 10011. (212) 645-4500. 1991. Development of sophisticated materials, operating systems and surface modification techniques in areas as diverse as aerospace, lawn-mower components and microelectrics.

Dyes & Organic Pigments to 1994. FIND/SVP, 625 Avenue of the Americas, New York, New York 10011. (212) 645-4500. 1990.

Powder Coatings. FIND/SVP, 625 Avenue of the Americas, New York, New York 10011. (212) 645-4500. 1991. Comprehensive of the U.S. market for powder coatings by material type.

TRADE ASSOCIATIONS AND PROFESSIONAL SOCIETIES

Color Association of the United States. 343 Lexington Ave., New York, New York 10016. (212) 683-9531.

Dry Color Manufacturers Association. P.O. Box 20839, Alexandria, Virginia 22320. (703) 684-4044.

United States Operating Committee on ETAD. 1330
Connecticut Ave., N.W., Suite 300, Washington, District
of Columbia 20036-1702. (202) 659-0060.

DYSPHOTIC

See: HYDRAULICS

DYSTROPHIC LAKES

See: LAKES

E

E COLI (ESCHERICHIA COLI)

ABSTRACTING AND INDEXING SERVICES

Biological and Agricultural Index. H.W. Wilson Co., 950 University Ave., Bronx, New York 10452. (800) 367-6770. 1916-. Monthly.

Biology Digest. Data Courier, Plexus Pub Inc., 143 Old Marlton Pike, Medford, New Jersey 08055. 1974-. Monthly. Abstracts biology periodicals.

Biotechnology Research Abstracts. Cambridge Scientific Abstracts, 5161 River Rd., Bethesda, Maryland 20816. (301) 961-6750. Monthly. Includes such broad areas as genetic intervention, biochemical genetics, and microbiological techniques.

Current Advances in Ecological and Environmental Science. Pergamon Microforms International, Inc., Fairview Park, Elmsford, New York 10523. (914) 592-7720. 1989-. Monthly. Current literature searching service includingjournals, reports, abstracts, etc. This service is available online as part of the CABS database on the hosts BRS and ORBIT search service.

Ecological Abstracts. Geo Abstracts Ltd. Elsevier Applied Science, Crown House, Linton Rd., Barking, England IG 11 8JU. 1974-. Derived from over 600 leading ecological and environmental journals, plus books, conference proceedings, reports and theses.

Ecology Abstracts. Cambridge Scientific Abstracts, 5161 River Rd., Bethesda, Maryland 20816. (301) 961-6750. Monthly.

Food Science and Technology Abstracts. International Food Information Service, c/o National Food Laboratory, 6363 Clark Ave., Dublin, California 94568. (800) 336-3782. 1969-.

General Science Index. H. W. Wilson Co., 950 University Ave., Bronx, New York 10452. 1978-. Monthly, also issued in annual cumulation. Cumulative subject index to English language periodicals in the subject fields of astronomy, botany, chemistry, earth science, environment and conservation, food and nutrition, genetics, mathematics, medicine and health, microbiology, oceanography, physics, physiology and zoology.

Genetics Abstracts. Cambridge Scientific Abstracts, 5161 River Rd., Bethesda, Maryland 20816. (301) 961-6750. 1968-. Monthly. Formerly published by Information Retrieval Ltd., London England. Published by Cambridge Scientific Abstracts since 1982.

Index to Scientific Book Contents. Institute for Scientific Information, 3501 Market St., Philadelphia, Pennsylvania 19104. (800) 523-1857. 1985-. Annual. Gives contents of science books published.

Science Citation Index. Institute for Scientific Information, 3501 Market St., Philadelphia, Pennsylvania 19104. 1961-.

BIBLIOGRAPHIES

Current Contents. Agriculture, Biology and Environmental Sciences. Institute for Scientific Information, 3501 Market St., Philadelphia, Pennsylvania 19104. (800) 523-1857. 1973-. Previous title: Current Contents. Agricultural, Food & Veterinary Sciences. Gives the table of contents of periodicals in the fields of agriculture, biology, environmental and related areas.

ENCYCLOPEDIAS AND DICTIONARIES

Cambridge Encyclopedia of Life Sciences. A. E. Friday and David S. Ingram. Cambridge University Press, 40 W 20th St., New York, New York 10011. (212) 924-3900 or (800) 227-0247. 1985. Includes all topics under biology and ecology.

Dictionary of Genetics and Cell Biology. Norman Maclean. New York University Press, 70 Washington Sq. S., New York, New York 10012. (212) 998-2575. 1987. Includes the subject areas of cytology and genetics.

Dictionary of Microbiology and Molecular Biology. Paul Singleton and Diana Sainsbury. John Wiley & Sons, Inc., 605 3rd Ave., New York, New York 10158-0012. (212) 850-6000. 1987. Second edition. Comprehensive dictionary with "classical descriptive aspects of microbiology to current developments in related areas of bioenergetics, biochemistry and molecular biology." Entries give synonyms, cross references, and references to pertinent works. Miscellaneous appendixes. Bibliography.

Encyclopedia of Human Biology. Renato Dulbecco, ed. Academic Press, c/o Harcourt Brace Jovanovich Inc., 6277 Sea Harbor Dr., Orlando, Florida 32887. (800) 346-8648. 1991. Eight volumes.

McGraw-Hill Encyclopedia of Science and Technology. McGraw-Hill, 1221 Avenue of the Americas, New York, New York 10020. (212) 512-2000 or (800) 262-4729. 1992. Seventh edition. Issued in multiple volumes including index. Includes all science and technology broad subject areas.

The Nutrition and Health Encyclopedia. David F. Tver and Percy Russell. Van Nostrand Reinhold, 115 5th Ave., New York, New York 10003. (212) 254-3232. 1989.

Van Nostrand's Scientific Encyclopedia. Glenn D. Considine, ed. Van Nostrand Reinhold, 115 5th Ave., New York, New York 10003. (212) 254-3232. 1983. Sixth edition. Includes all broad subject areas in science.

GENERAL WORKS

Escheria Coli and Salmonella Typherium: Cellular and Molecular Biology. Frederick C. Neidhardt. American Society for Microbiology, 1325 Massachusetts Ave., N.W., Washington, District of Columbia 20005. (202) 737-3600. 1987.

Magill's Survey of Science. Life Science Series. Frank N. Magill, ed. Salem Press, PO Box 50062, Pasadena, California 91105. 1991. Six volumes. Contents: v.1. A-Central and peripheral nervous system functions; v.2. Central metabolism regulation - eukaryotic transcriptional control; v.3. Positive and negative eukaryotic transcriptional control - mammalian hormones; v.4. Hormones and behavior - muscular contraction; v.5. Muscular contraction and relaxation - sexual reproduction in plants; v.6. Reproductive behavior and mating - X inactivation and the Lyon hypothesis.

Protein Refolding. George Georgiou and Eliana De Barnardez-Clark, eds. American Chemical Society, 1155 16th St. N.W., Washington, District of Columbia 20036. (202) 872-4600; (800) 227-5558. 1991. Studies protein recovery, aggregation, formation, structure, and other features.

HANDBOOKS AND MANUALS

Handbook of Toxicology. W. Thomas Shier and Dietrich Mebs. Marcel Dekker, Inc., 270 Madison Ave., New York, New York 10016. (212) 696-9000; (800) 228-1160. 1990. Covers most toxins for which sufficient research has been done to clearly establish the identity and characteristics of the toxin.

ONLINE DATA BASES

Cambridge Scientific Abstracts Life Science–CSAL. Cambridge Scientific Abstracts, 5161 River Rd., Bethesda, Maryland 20816. (301) 961-6750. Provides access to the following abstracting services: "Life Sciences Collection," "Aquatic Sciences and Fisheries Abstracts," "Oceanic Abstracts," and "Pollution Abstracts."

Monthly Catalog of United States Government Publications. U.S. G.P.O., Supt. of Docs., PO Box 371954, Pittsburgh, Pennsylvania 15250-7954. (202) 512-0000.

National Technical Information Service. U.S. Department of Commerce, National Technical Information Service, Office of Data Base Services, 5285 Port Royal Rd., Springfield, Virginia 22161. (703) 487-4807. Bibliographic database of government sponsored research and technical reports.

SCISEARCH. Institute for Scientific Information, University City Science Center, 3501 Market St., Philadelphia, Pennsylvania 19104. (215) 386-0100.

EARTH

ABSTRACTING AND INDEXING SERVICES

Applied Science and Technology Index. H.W. Wilson Co., 950 University Ave., Bronx, New York 10452. (800) 367-6770. Formerly Industrial Arts Index.

Ecological Abstracts. Geo Abstracts Ltd. Elsevier Applied Science, Crown House, Linton Rd., Barking, England IG 11 8JU. 1974-. Derived from over 600 leading ecological and environmental journals, plus books, conference proceedings, reports and theses.

Engineering Index. The Engineering Index Inc., 345 E. 47th St., New York, New York 10017. 1962-.

Environment Abstracts. Bowker A & I Publishing, 121 Chanlon Rd., New Providence, New Jersey 07974. (908) 464-6800. 1974-.

Environment Index. Environment Information Center, Index Research Department, 124 E. 39th St., New York, New York 10016. 1971-. Annual.

Environmental Information Connection–EIC. Planning Information Program, Dept. of Urban and Regional Planning, University of Illinois, 1003 West Nevada, Urbana, Illinois 61801. (217) 333-1369. Also available online.

Environmental Periodicals Bibliography. Environmental Studies Institute, International Academy at Santa Barbara, 800 Garden St., Suite D, Santa Barbara, California 93101. (805) 965-5010. Also available online.

General Science Index. H. W. Wilson Co., 950 University Ave., Bronx, New York 10452. 1978-. Monthly, also issued in annual cumulation. Cumulative subject index to English language periodicals in the subject fields of astronomy, botany, chemistry, earth science, environment and conservation, food and nutrition, genetics, mathematics, medicine and health, microbiology, oceanography, physics, physiology and zoology.

Geo Abstracts, Social Geography and Cartography. Geo Abstracts Ltd., c/o Elsevier Science Pub., Crown House, Linton Rd., Barking, England 1611 8JU.

Geographical Abstracts. London School of Economics, Dept. of Geography, Regency House, 34 Duke St., London, England 1966-. Continued by Geo Abstracts issued in 6 parts: Pt. A. Landforms and the quaternary; Pt. B. Biogeography and Climatology; Pt. C. Economic geography; Pt. D. Social geography and cartography; Pt. E. Sedimentology; Pt. F. Regional and community planning.

Index to Scientific Book Contents. Institute for Scientific Information, 3501 Market St., Philadelphia, Pennsylvania 19104. (800) 523-1857. 1985-. Annual. Gives contents of science books published.

Science Citation Index. Institute for Scientific Information, 3501 Market St., Philadelphia, Pennsylvania 19104. 1961-.

BIBLIOGRAPHIES

Bibliography and Index of Geology. American Geological Institute, 4220 King St., Alexandria, Virginia 22302. Monthly. Includes environmental geology and hydrogeology.

EPA Publications Bibliography. U.S. Environmental Protection Agency, Library Systems Branch, 401 M St., SW, Washington, District of Columbia 20460. (202) 260-2090. Quarterly.

New Publications of the Geological Survey. U.S. Department of the Interior, Geological Survey, 119 National Center, Reston, Virginia 22092. (703) 648-4460. 1984-. Monthly. Bibliography of geological publications and related government documents published by the Geological Survey.

DIRECTORIES

Environmental Telephone Directory. Government Institutes, Inc., 4 Research Pl., Ste. 200, Rockville, Maryland 20850. (301) 921-2300.

ENCYCLOPEDIAS AND DICTIONARIES

The Encyclopedia of Climatology. John E. Oliver and Rhodes W. Fairbridge, eds. Van Nostrand Reinhold, 115 5th Ave., New York, New York 10003. (212) 254-3232. 1987. Belongs in the series Encyclopedia of Earth Sciences, v.11.

The Encyclopedia of Geochemistry and Environmental Sciences. Rhodes Whitmore Fairbridge. Van Nostrand Reinhold Co., 115 5th Ave., New York, New York 10003. (212) 254-3232. 1972.

Glossary of Geology. Robert Latimer Bates and Julia A. Jackson, eds. American Geological Institute, 4220 King St., Alexandria, Virginia 22302-1507. (703) 379-2480 or (800) 336-4764. 1987. Third edition.

McGraw-Hill Encyclopedia of Science and Technology. McGraw-Hill, 1221 Avenue of the Americas, New York, New York 10020. (212) 512-2000 or (800) 262-4729. 1992. Seventh edition. Issued in multiple volumes including index. Includes all science and technology broad subject areas.

McGraw-Hill Encyclopedia of the Geological Sciences. Sybil P. Parker, ed. McGraw-Hill, 1221 Avenue of the Americas, New York, New York 10020. (212) 512-2000 or (800) 262-4729. 1988. Second edition. Published previously in the McGraw-Hill Encyclopedia of Science and Technology.

Van Nostrand's Scientific Encyclopedia. Glenn D. Considine, ed. Van Nostrand Reinhold, 115 5th Ave., New York, New York 10003. (212) 254-3232. 1983. Sixth edition. Includes all broad subject areas in science.

GENERAL WORKS

Earthright. H. Patricia Hynes. St. Martin's Press, 175 5th Ave., New York, New York 10010. (212) 674-5151. 1990. Guide to practical ways to resolve problems with pesticides, water pollution, garbage disposal, the ozone layer and global warming.

The Essential Whole Earth Catalog. The Point Foundation. Doubleday, 666 5th Ave., New York, New York 10103. (212) 765-6500; (800) 223-6834. 1986.

Geotechnical and Environmental Geophysics. Stanley H. Ward. Society of Exploration Geophysicists, PO Box 702740, Tulsa, Oklahoma 74170-2740. (918) 493-3516. 1990.

Magill's Survey of Science. Earth Science Series. Frank N. Magill. Salem Press, PO Box 50062, Pasadena, California 91105. 1990-. Five volumes. Includes information on earth's crust, hot spots and volcanic island chains, physical properties of minerals, rock magnetism, physical properties of rocks, and index.

ONLINE DATA BASES

Computerized Engineering Index–COMPENDEX. Engineering Information Inc., 345 E. 47th St., New York, New York 10017. (212) 705-7600.

Enviro/Energyline Abstracts Plus. R. R. Bowker Co., 121 Chanlon Rd., New Providence, New Jersey 07974. (908) 464-6800.

Environmental Periodicals Bibliography. National Information Services Corp., Ste. 6, Wyman Towers, 3100 St. Paul St., Baltimore, Maryland 21218. (410)243-0797. Online version of abstract of same name.

Monthly Catalog of United States Government Publications. U.S. G.P.O., Supt. of Docs., PO Box 371954, Pittsburgh, Pennsylvania 15250-7954. (202) 512-0000.

National Technical Information Service. U.S. Department of Commerce, National Technical Information Service, Office of Data Base Services, 5285 Port Royal Rd., Springfield, Virginia 22161. (703) 487-4807. Bibliographic database of government sponsored research and technical reports.

NOAA Earth Systems Data Directory. National Oceanic and Atmospheric Administration, National Environmental Data Referral Service, 1825 Connecticut Ave., N.W., Washington, District of Columbia 20235. (202) 673-5548.

Whole Earth Lectronic Link. The Well, 25 Gate Five Rd., Sausalito, California 94965. (415) 332-1716.

PERIODICALS AND NEWSLETTERS

Earth First! Journal in Defense of Wilderness and Biodiversity. Earth First!, PO Box 5176, Missoula, Montana 59806. Eight/year.

Earth Science. American Geological Institute, 4220 King Street, Alexandria, Virginia 22302. (703) 379-2480. Quarterly. Covers geological issues.

Earthwatch Magazine. Earthwatch Expeditions, 680 Mt. Auburn St., Box 403, Watertown, Massachusetts 02272. (617) 926-8200. Bimonthly. Worldwide research expeditions, endangered species, cultures, and world health.

Not Man Apart. Friends of the Earth, 218 D St. SE, Washington, District of Columbia 20003. (202) 544-2600. Bimonthly.

Planet Earth. Planetary Citizens, Box 1509, Mt. Shasta, California 96067. (415) 325-2939.

RESEARCH CENTERS AND INSTITUTES

Pennsylvania State University, Environmental Resources Research Institute. 100 Land and Water Resource Building, University Park, Pennsylvania 16802. (814) 863-0291.

Society for Conservation Biology. Department of Wildlife Ecology, University of Wisconsin, Madison, Wisconsin 53706. (608) 262-2671.

TRADE ASSOCIATIONS AND PROFESSIONAL SOCIETIES

American Institute of Biological Sciences. 730 11th St., N.W., Washington, District of Columbia 20001-4521. (202) 628-1500.

Earth First!. PO Box 5176, Missoula, Montana 59806.

Earth Regeneration Society. 1442A Walnut St., #57, Berkeley, California 94709. (415) 525-7723.

Earthcare Network. c/o Michael McCloskey, 408 C St., N.E., Washington, District of Columbia 20002. (202) 547-1141.

Earthwatch. 680 Mt. Auburn St., P.O. Box 403, Watertown, Massachusetts 02272. (617) 926-8200.

Eco-Justice Project and Network. Cornell University, Anabel Taylor Hall, Ithaca, New York 14850. 1990.

Friends of the Earth. 218 D St., SE, Washington, District of Columbia 20003. (202) 544-2600.

International Association for the Advancement of Earth & Environmental Sciences. Northeastern Illinois University, Geography & Environmental Studies, 5500 N. St. Louis Ave., Chicago, Illinois 60625. (312) 794-2628.

Kids for a Clean Environment. P.O. Box 158254, Nashville, Tennessee 37215. (615) 331-0708.

Seismological Society of America. El Cerrito Professional Bldg., Suite 201, El Cerrito, California 94530. (415) 525-5474.

Windstar Foundation. 2317 Snowmass Creek Rd., Snowmass, Colorado 81654. (303) 927-4777. Foundation begun by John Denver offering information on a wide range of personal-action issues.

EARTHQUAKES

ABSTRACTING AND INDEXING SERVICES

Applied Science and Technology Index. H.W. Wilson Co., 950 University Ave., Bronx, New York 10452. (800) 367-6770. Formerly Industrial Arts Index.

Civil Engineering Hydraulic Abstracts. BHRA Fluid Engineering, Air Science Co., PO Box 143, Corning, New York 14830. (607) 962-5591. Monthly. Abstracts of periodicals that publish in the areas of hydraulic engineering and other related topics.

Environment Abstracts. Bowker A & I Publishing, 121 Chanlon Rd., New Providence, New Jersey 07974. (908) 464-6800. 1974-.

Environment Index. Environment Information Center, Index Research Department, 124 E. 39th St., New York, New York 10016. 1971-. Annual.

Environmental Information Connection–EIC. Planning Information Program, Dept. of Urban and Regional Planning, University of Illinois, 1003 West Nevada, Urbana, Illinois 61801. (217) 333-1369. Also available online.

Environmental Periodicals Bibliography. Environmental Studies Institute, International Academy at Santa Barbara, 800 Garden St., Suite D, Santa Barbara, California 93101. (805) 965-5010. Also available online.

General Science Index. H. W. Wilson Co., 950 University Ave., Bronx, New York 10452. 1978-. Monthly, also issued in annual cumulation. Cumulative subject index to English language periodicals in the subject fields of astronomy, botany, chemistry, earth science, environment and conservation, food and nutrition, genetics, mathematics, medicine and health, microbiology, oceanography, physics, physiology and zoology.

Geo Abstracts, Social Geography and Cartography. Geo Abstracts Ltd., c/o Elsevier Science Pub., Crown House, Linton Rd., Barking, England 1611 8JU.

Geographical Abstracts. London School of Economics, Dept. of Geography, Regency House, 34 Duke St., London, England 1966-. Continued by Geo Abstracts issued in 6 parts: Pt. A. Landforms and the quaternary; Pt. B. Biogeography and Climatology; Pt. C. Economic geography; Pt. D. Social geography and cartography; Pt. E. Sedimentology; Pt. F. Regional and community planning.

Index to Scientific Book Contents. Institute for Scientific Information, 3501 Market St., Philadelphia, Pennsylvania 19104. (800) 523-1857. 1985-. Annual. Gives contents of science books published.

Physics Briefs. Physikalische Berichte. Physik Verlag, Pappapelallee 3, Postfach 101161, Weinheim, Germany D-6940. 1979-. Semimonthly. In English. Volumes for 1979- issued by the Deutsche Physikalische Gesellschaft and the Fachinformationszentrum Energie Physik, Mathematik in cooperation with the American Institute of Physics.

Science Citation Index. Institute for Scientific Information, 3501 Market St., Philadelphia, Pennsylvania 19104. 1961-.

BIBLIOGRAPHIES

Bibliography and Index of Geology. American Geological Institute, 4220 King St., Alexandria, Virginia 22302. Monthly. Includes environmental geology and hydrogeology.

Earthquake Prediction. David A. Tyckoson. Oryx Press, 4041 N. Central at Indian School Rd., Ste. 700, Phoenix, Arizona 85012-3397. (602) 265-2651. 1986.

EPA Publications Bibliography. U.S. Environmental Protection Agency, Library Systems Branch, 401 M St., SW, Washington, District of Columbia 20460. (202) 260-2090. Quarterly.

New Publications of the Geological Survey. U.S. Department of the Interior, Geological Survey, 119 National Center, Reston, Virginia 22092. (703) 648-4460. 1984-. Monthly. Bibliography of geological publications and related government documents published by the Geological Survey.

ENCYCLOPEDIAS AND DICTIONARIES

Dictionary of Civil Engineering. John S. Scott. Halsted Press, Division of J. Wiley, 605 3rd Ave., New York, New York 10158. (212) 850-6000. 1981. Third edition.

The Encyclopedia of Climatology. John E. Oliver and Rhodes W. Fairbridge, eds. Van Nostrand Reinhold, 115 5th Ave., New York, New York 10003. (212) 254-3232. 1987. Belongs in the series Encyclopedia of Earth Sciences, v.11.

Encyclopedia of Physical Science and Technology. Robert A. Meyers, ed. Academic Press, c/o Harcourt Brace Jovanovich Inc., 6277 Sea Harbor Dr., Orlando, Florida 32887. (800) 346-8648. Dictionary of engineering, technology and physical sciences.

Glossary of Geology. Robert Latimer Bates and Julia A. Jackson, eds. American Geological Institute, 4220 King St., Alexandria, Virginia 22302-1507. (703) 379-2480 or (800) 336-4764. 1987. Third edition.

The Marshall Cavendish Illustrated Encyclopedia of Plants and Earth Sciences. Marshall Cavendish Corp., 2415 Jerusalem Ave., North Bellmore, New York 11710. (516) 826-4200. 1988.

McGraw-Hill Encyclopedia of Science and Technology. McGraw-Hill, 1221 Avenue of the Americas, New York, New York 10020. (212) 512-2000 or (800) 262-4729. 1992. Seventh edition. Issued in multiple volumes including index. Includes all science and technology broad subject areas.

McGraw-Hill Encyclopedia of the Geological Sciences. Sybil P. Parker, ed. McGraw-Hill, 1221 Avenue of the Americas, New York, New York 10020. (212) 512-2000 or (800) 262-4729. 1988. Second edition. Published previously in the McGraw-Hill Encyclopedia of Science and Technology.

Van Nostrand's Scientific Encyclopedia. Glenn D. Considine, ed. Van Nostrand Reinhold, 115 5th Ave., New York, New York 10003. (212) 254-3232. 1983. Sixth edition. Includes all broad subject areas in science.

GENERAL WORKS

Magill's Survey of Science. Earth Science Series. Frank N. Magill. Salem Press, PO Box 50062, Pasadena, California 91105. 1990-. Five volumes. Includes information on earth's crust, hot spots and volcanic island chains, physical properties of minerals, rock magnetism, physical properties of rocks, and index.

ONLINE DATA BASES

Civil Engineering Database. American Society of Civil Engineers, 345 E. 47th St., New York, New York 10017. (800) 548-2723.

Enviro/Energyline Abstracts Plus. R. R. Bowker Co., 121 Chanlon Rd., New Providence, New Jersey 07974. (908) 464-6800.

Environmental Periodicals Bibliography. National Information Services Corp., Ste. 6, Wyman Towers, 3100 St. Paul St., Baltimore, Maryland 21218. (410)243-0797. Online version of abstract of same name.

GeoRef. American Geological Institute, 4220 King St., Alexandria, Virginia 22302. (703) 379-2480.

Monthly Catalog of United States Government Publications. U.S. G.P.O., Supt. of Docs., PO Box 371954, Pittsburgh, Pennsylvania 15250-7954. (202) 512-0000.

National Technical Information Service. U.S. Department of Commerce, National Technical Information Service, Office of Data Base Services, 5285 Port Royal Rd., Springfield, Virginia 22161. (703) 487-4807. Bibliographic database of government sponsored research and technical reports.

PERIODICALS AND NEWSLETTERS

Earth Science. American Geological Institute, 4220 King Street, Alexandria, Virginia 22302. (703) 379-2480. Quarterly. Covers geological issues.

Earthquake Engineering and Structural Dynamics. John Wiley & Sons, Inc., 605 3rd Ave., New York, New York 10158-0012. (212) 850-6000. 1978-. Bimonthly.

Earthquakes & Volcanos. Geological Survey. U.S. Geological Survey, 12201 Sunrise Valley Dr., Reston, Virginia 22092. (703) 648-4460. Bimonthly. Earthquake information bulletin.

TRADE ASSOCIATIONS AND PROFESSIONAL SOCIETIES

American Society of Civil Engineers. 345 East 47th St., New York, New York 10017. (212) 705-7496.

Earthquake Engineering Research Institute. 6431 Fairmont, Suite 7, El Cerrito, California 94530. (415) 525-3668.

National Information Service for Earthquake Engineering. Earthquake Engineering Research Center, 1301 S. 46th St., University of California, Richmond, California 94804. (415) 231-9554.

Seismological Society of America. El Cerrito Professional Bldg., Suite 201, El Cerrito, California 94530. (415) 525-5474.

ECOLOGICAL BALANCE

See: ECOLOGY

ECOLOGICAL IMBALANCE

See: ECOLOGY

ECOLOGICAL RESERVES

ABSTRACTING AND INDEXING SERVICES

Applied Ecology Abstracts Studies in Renewable Natural Resources. Information Retrieval Ltd., 1911 Jefferson Davis Highway, Arlington, Virginia 22202. 1975-. Monthly.

Biological and Agricultural Index. H.W. Wilson Co., 950 University Ave., Bronx, New York 10452. (800) 367-6770. 1916-. Monthly.

Current Advances in Ecological and Environmental Science. Pergamon Microforms International, Inc., Fairview Park, Elmsford, New York 10523. (914) 592-7720. 1989-. Monthly. Current literature searching service includingjournals, reports, abstracts, etc. This service is available online as part of the CABS database on the hosts BRS and ORBIT search service.

Ecological Abstracts. Geo Abstracts Ltd. Elsevier Applied Science, Crown House, Linton Rd., Barking, England IG 11 8JU. 1974-. Derived from over 600 leading ecological and environmental journals, plus books, conference proceedings, reports and theses.

Environment Abstracts. Bowker A & I Publishing, 121 Chanlon Rd., New Providence, New Jersey 07974. (908) 464-6800. 1974-.

Environment Index. Environment Information Center, Index Research Department, 124 E. 39th St., New York, New York 10016. 1971-. Annual.

Environmental Information Connection–EIC. Planning Information Program, Dept. of Urban and Regional Planning, University of Illinois, 1003 West Nevada, Urbana, Illinois 61801. (217) 333-1369. Also available online.

Environmental Periodicals Bibliography. Environmental Studies Institute, International Academy at Santa Barbara, 800 Garden St., Suite D, Santa Barbara, California 93101. (805) 965-5010. Also available online.

Multimedia Index to Ecology. National Information Center for Educational Media, University of Southern California, Los Angeles, California 90007.

BIBLIOGRAPHIES

Bibliography on the International Network of Biosphere Reserves. U.S. MAB Coordinating Committee for Biosphere Reserves. United States Man and the Biosphere Program, Available from National Technical Information Service, 5285 Port Royal Rd., Springfield, Virginia 22161. (703) 487-4650. 1990.

EPA Publications Bibliography. U.S. Environmental Protection Agency, Library Systems Branch, 401 M St., SW, Washington, District of Columbia 20460. (202) 260-2090. Quarterly.

DIRECTORIES

United Nations List of National Parks and Protected Areas. World Conservation Monitoring Centre. World Conservation Union, IUCN Publications Services Unit, 181a Huntingdon Road, Cambridge, England CB3 0DJ. (0223) 277894. 1990. Standard list of national parks and other protected areas. Includes lists of world heritage sites, biosphere reserves and wetlands of international importance.

United States Man and the Biosphere Program: Directory of Biosphere Reserves in the United States. National Technical Information Service, 5285 Port Royal Rd., Springfield, Virginia 22161. (703) 487-4650. 1991. Research on biosphere, natural areas, and national parks and reserves.

ENCYCLOPEDIAS AND DICTIONARIES

Grzimek's Encyclopedia of Ecology. Bernhard Grzimek. Van Nostrand Reinhold, 115 5th Ave., New York, New York 10003. (212) 254-3232. 1976.

The Marshall Cavendish Illustrated Encyclopedia of Plants and Earth Sciences. Marshall Cavendish Corp., 2415 Jerusalem Ave., North Bellmore, New York 11710. (516) 826-4200. 1988.

North American Reference Encyclopedia of Ecology and Pollution. William White. North American Pub. Co., 401 N. Broad St., Philadelphia, Pennsylvania 19108. (215) 238-5300. 1972.

GENERAL WORKS

Experimental Ecological Reserves. U.S. G.P.O, Washington, District of Columbia 20401. (202) 512-0000. 1977. Ecological research on natural areas.

Wildlife Reserves and Corridors in the Urban Environment. Lowell W. Adams. National Institute for Urban Wildlife, 10921 Trotting Ridge Way, Columbia, Maryland 21044. (301) 596-3311. 1989. Reviews the knowledge base on wildlife habitat reserves and corridors in urban and urbanizing areas. Provides guidelines and approaches to ecological landscape planning and wildlife conservation in these regions.

ONLINE DATA BASES

Enviro/Energyline Abstracts Plus. R. R. Bowker Co., 121 Chanlon Rd., New Providence, New Jersey 07974. (908) 464-6800.

Environmental Periodicals Bibliography. National Information Services Corp., Ste. 6, Wyman Towers, 3100 St. Paul St., Baltimore, Maryland 21218. (410)243-0797. Online version of abstract of same name.

ECOLOGICAL SUCCESSION

See: ECOLOGY

ECOLOGY

See also: CONSERVATION OF NATURAL RESOURCES; ENVIRONMENTAL CHEMISTRY; HABITAT (ECOLOGY)

ABSTRACTING AND INDEXING SERVICES

Abstracts of Air and Water Conservation Literature. American Petroleum Institute. Central Abstracting and Indexing Service, 275 Madison Avenue, New York, New York 10016. 1972.

Applied Ecology Abstracts Studies in Renewable Natural Resources. Information Retrieval Ltd., 1911 Jefferson Davis Highway, Arlington, Virginia 22202. 1975-. Monthly.

Applied Science and Technology Index. H.W. Wilson Co., 950 University Ave., Bronx, New York 10452. (800) 367-6770. Formerly Industrial Arts Index.

ASFA Aquaculture Abstracts. Cambridge Scientific Abstracts, Inc., 5161 River Rd., Bethesda, Maryland 20816. (301) 961-6750. 1984.

Biological Abstracts. BIOSIS, 2100 Arch St., Philadelphia, Pennsylvania 19103-1399. (215) 587-4800. 1927-.

Biological and Agricultural Index. H.W. Wilson Co., 950 University Ave., Bronx, New York 10452. (800) 367-6770. 1916-. Monthly.

Biology Digest. Data Courier, Plexus Pub Inc., 143 Old Marlton Pike, Medford, New Jersey 08055. 1974-. Monthly. Abstracts biology periodicals.

Civil Engineering Hydraulic Abstracts. BHRA Fluid Engineering, Air Science Co., PO Box 143, Corning, New York 14830. (607) 962-5591. Monthly. Abstracts of periodicals that publish in the areas of hydraulic engineering and other related topics.

Current Advances in Ecological and Environmental Science. Pergamon Microforms International, Inc., Fairview Park, Elmsford, New York 10523. (914) 592-7720. 1989-. Monthly. Current literature searching service includingjournals, reports, abstracts, etc. This service is available online as part of the CABS database on the hosts BRS and ORBIT search service.

Ecological Abstracts. Geo Abstracts Ltd. Elsevier Applied Science, Crown House, Linton Rd., Barking, England IG 11 8JU. 1974-. Derived from over 600 leading ecological and environmental journals, plus books, conference proceedings, reports and theses.

Ecology Abstracts. Cambridge Scientific Abstracts, 5161 River Rd., Bethesda, Maryland 20816. (301) 961-6750. Monthly.

Engineering Index. The Engineering Index Inc., 345 E. 47th St., New York, New York 10017. 1962-.

Environment Abstracts. Bowker A & I Publishing, 121 Chanlon Rd., New Providence, New Jersey 07974. (908) 464-6800. 1974-.

Environment Index. Environment Information Center, Index Research Department, 124 E. 39th St., New York, New York 10016. 1971-. Annual.

Environmental Information Connection–EIC. Planning Information Program, Dept. of Urban and Regional Planning, University of Illinois, 1003 West Nevada, Urbana, Illinois 61801. (217) 333-1369. Also available online.

Environmental Periodicals Bibliography. Environmental Studies Institute, International Academy at Santa Barbara, 800 Garden St., Suite D, Santa Barbara, California 93101. (805) 965-5010. Also available online.

General Science Index. H. W. Wilson Co., 950 University Ave., Bronx, New York 10452. 1978-. Monthly, also issued in annual cumulation. Cumulative subject index to English language periodicals in the subject fields of astronomy, botany, chemistry, earth science, environment and conservation, food and nutrition, genetics, mathematics, medicine and health, microbiology, oceanography, physics, physiology and zoology.

Geo Abstracts, Social Geography and Cartography. Geo Abstracts Ltd., c/o Elsevier Science Pub., Crown House, Linton Rd., Barking, England 1611 8JU.

Geographical Abstracts. London School of Economics, Dept. of Geography, Regency House, 34 Duke St., London, England 1966-. Continued by Geo Abstracts issued in 6 parts: Pt. A. Landforms and the quaternary; Pt. B. Biogeography and Climatology; Pt. C. Economic geography; Pt. D. Social geography and cartography; Pt. E. Sedimentology; Pt. F. Regional and community planning.

Index to Scientific Book Contents. Institute for Scientific Information, 3501 Market St., Philadelphia, Pennsylvania 19104. (800) 523-1857. 1985-. Annual. Gives contents of science books published.

Mineralogical Abstracts. Mineralogical Society, 41 Queen's Gate, London, England SW7 5HR. 71 5847916. Quarterly. Abstracts of journal articles, conferences, technical reports and specialized books in the areas of minerals, clay minerals, economic minerals, ore deposits,

environmental studies, experimental mineralogy, gemstones, geochemistry, petrology, lunar and planetary studies and other related areas in mineralogy.

Multimedia Index to Ecology. National Information Center for Educational Media, University of Southern California, Los Angeles, California 90007.

Pollution Abstracts. Cambridge Scientific Abstracts, 5161 River Rd., Bethesda, Maryland 20816. (301) 961-6750. Six/year. Indexes worldwide technical literature on environmental pollution. Covers air pollution, marine and freshwater pollution, sewage and wastewater treatment, waste management, toxicology and health, noise pollution, radiation, land pollution, and environmental policies, programs, legislation, and education. Also available online.

Science Citation Index. Institute for Scientific Information, 3501 Market St., Philadelphia, Pennsylvania 19104. 1961-.

ALMANACS AND YEARBOOKS

Advances in Ecological Research. Academic Press, c/o Harcourt Brace Jovanovich Inc., 6277 Sea Harbor Dr., Orlando, Florida 32887. (800) 346-8648.

Gale Environmental Almanac. Russ Hoyle. Gale Research Inc., 835 Penobscot Bldg., Detroit, Michigan 48226-4094. (313) 961-2242. 1993. Focuses on the U.S. and Canada, although worldwide and transboundary issues are discussed.

BIBLIOGRAPHIES

Accessions List. Environmental Science Information Center. Library and Information Services Division. National Oceanic and Atmospheric Administration, U.S. Department of Commerce, Washington, District of Columbia 20230. (202) 377-2985. Monthly.

Bibliography and Index of Geology. American Geological Institute, 4220 King St., Alexandria, Virginia 22302. Monthly. Includes environmental geology and hydrogeology.

Deep Ecology and Environmental Ethics: A Selected and Annotated Bibliography of Materials Published Since 1980. Teresa DeGroh. Council of Planning Librarians, 1313 E. 60th St., Chicago, Illinois 60637-2897. (312) 942-2163. 1987. Covers human ecology and environmental protection.

Ecological Restoration of Prince William Sound and the Gulf of Alaska: An Annotated Bibliography of Relevant Literature: Preliminary Draft. Restoration Planning Work Group, Oregon State University, Corvallis, Oregon 97311. 1990.

Environment-Employment-New Industrial Societies. Maryse Gaudier. International Labour Organization, H4, rue des Morillons, Geneva 22, Switzerland CH-1211. 1991. Situates environmental issues within the context of industrial societies at the threshold of the 21st century; critically evaluates the harmonization of ecology, modern technology and human resources.

EPA Publications Bibliography. U.S. Environmental Protection Agency, Library Systems Branch, 401 M St., SW, Washington, District of Columbia 20460. (202) 260-2090. Quarterly.

Teaching Population Geography: An Interdisciplinary Ecological Approach. George Warren Carey. Teachers College Pr., 1234 Amsterdam Ave., New York, New York 10027. (212) 678-3929. 1969. Bibliography on human ecology and demography.

DIRECTORIES

Canadian Conservation Directory. Canadian Nature Federation, 453 Sussex Dr., Ottawa, Ontario, Canada K1N 6Z4. (613) 238-6154. 1973-. Directory of over 800 natural history, environment and conservation organizations of Canada.

Canadian Environmental Directory. Canadian Almanac & Directory Publishing Co. Ltd., 134 Adelaide St. E., Ste. 27, Toronto, Ontario, Canada M5C 1K9. (416) 362-4088. 1992. Includes individuals, agencies, firms, and associations.

Directory of Computer Software Applications. Environmental Pollution and Control. National Technical Information Service, 5285 Port Royal Rd., Springfield, Virginia 22161. (703) 487-4650. 1977-1980.

Directory of Environmental Organizations. Educational Communications, Box 35473, Los Angeles, California 90035. (213) 559-9160. Semiannual. Environmental organizations names, addresses, & phone numbers.

Ecological Society of America Bulletin–Directory of Members Issue. Ecological Society of America, c/o Dr. Duncan Patten, Center for Environmental Studies, Arizona State University, Tempe, Arizona 85287. (602) 965-3000.

The Environmental Address Book: How to Reach the Environment's Greatest Champions and Worst Offenders. Michael Levine. Perigee Books, 200 Madison Ave., New York, New York 10016. (800) 631-8571. 1991. Names and addresses of organizations, agencies, celebrities, political figures, and businesses (local, state, national, and international level) concerned with the state of the world's environment.

Environmental & Ecological Services. American Business Directories, Inc., 5711 S. 86th Circle, Omaha, Nebraska 68127. (402) 593-4600.

Environmental Telephone Directory. Government Institutes, Inc., 4 Research Pl., Ste. 200, Rockville, Maryland 20850. (301) 921-2300.

The Green Encyclopedia. Irene Franck, David Brownstone. Prentice-Hall, Rte. 9W, Englewood Cliffs, New York 07632. (201) 592-2000. 1992. Covers environmental organizations.

Macrocosm U.S.A. Sandra L. Brockway. Macrocosm U.S.A., Box 969, Cambria, California 93428-0969. (805) 927-8030. Annual. Covers organizations, businesses, publishers, and publications concerned with various global and humanitarian issues including ecology.

National Directory of Citizen Volunteer Environmental Monitoring Programs. Virginia Lee and Eleanor Lee. Rhode Island Sea Grant College Program, Narragansett Bay Campus, Narragansett, Rhode Island 02882. (401) 792-6842. 1990.

Save L.A.: An Environmental Resource Directory: The Thinking and Caring Person's Directory of Environmental Products, Services, and Resources for the Los Angeles Area. Tricia R. Hoffman and Nan Kathryn Fuchs. Chronicle Books, 275 5th St., San Francisco, California

94103. (415) 777-7240; (800) 722-6657. 1990. This comprehensive guidebook opens with a brief overview of the most pressing ecological issues peculiar to the Los Angeles area and then goes on to provide a list of some 1000 resources targeted for the environmental challenges the city Angelenos faces.

ENCYCLOPEDIAS AND DICTIONARIES

Cambridge Dictionary of Biology. Peter M. B. Walker. Cambridge University Press, 40 W. 20th St., New York, New York 10011. (212) 924-3900 or (800) 227-0247. 1989. Includes 10,000 terms in zoology, botany, biochemistry, molecular biology and genetics. Previously published under the title Chambers Biology Dictionary.

Cambridge Encyclopedia of Life Sciences. A. E. Friday and David S. Ingram. Cambridge University Press, 40 W 20th St., New York, New York 10011. (212) 924-3900 or (800) 227-0247. 1985. Includes all topics under biology and ecology.

A Concise Dictionary of Biology. Elizabeth Martin, ed. Oxford University Press, 200 Madison Ave., New York, New York 10016. (212) 679-7300 or (800) 334-4249. 1990. New edition. Derived from the Concise Science Dictionary, published in 1984.

Dictionary of Dangerous Pollutants, Ecology, and Environment. David F. Tver. Industrial Press, 200 Madison Ave., New York, New York 10016. (212) 889-6330. 1981.

Dictionary of Ecology and Environment. P. H. Collin. Collin Pub., 8 The Causeway, Teddington, England TW11 0HE. 1988. Vocabulary of 5,000 words and expressions covering a range of topics relating to ecology, including: climate, vegetation, pollution, waste disposal, and energy conservation.

A Dictionary of Ecology, Evolution and Systematics. R. J. Lincoln, G. A. Boxshall and P. F. Clark. Cambridge University Press, 40 W 20th St., New York, New York 10011. (212) 924-3900; (800) 227-0247. 1984.

Dictionary of Environment and Development. Earthscan, 3 Endsleigh St., London, England 071-388 2117. 1991.

Dictionary of Environmental Terms. Alan Gilpin. Routledge, 29 W 35th St., New York, New York 10001-2291. (212) 244-3336. 1978. Covers human ecology and includes a bibliography.

The Encyclopedia of Animal Ecology. Peter D. Moore. Facts on File, Inc., 460 Park Ave. S., New York, New York 10016. (212) 683-2244. 1987.

Encyclopedia of Environmental Studies. William Ashworth. Facts on File, Inc., 460 Park Ave. S., New York, New York 10016. (212) 683-2244. 1991.

Encyclopedia of Human Biology. Renato Dulbecco, ed. Academic Press, c/o Harcourt Brace Jovanovich Inc., 6277 Sea Harbor Dr., Orlando, Florida 32887. (800) 346-8648. 1991. Eight volumes.

The Environmental Dictionary. James J. King. PennWell Books, PO Box 21288, Tulsa, Oklahoma 74121. (918) 831-9421; (800) 752-9764. 1989. Gives more than 5,000 definitions of terms used and applied by the EPA.

Environmental Encyclopedia. William P. Cunningham, Terence Ball, et. al. Gale Research Inc., 835 Penobscot

Bldg., Detroit, Michigan 48226-4094. (313) 961-2242. 1993.

Environmental Regulatory Glossary. G. William Frick and Thomas P. Sullivan. Government Institutes, Inc., 4 Research Pl., Rockville, Maryland 20850. (301) 921-2300. 1990. Over 4,000 entries. Definitions were gathered from the Code of Federal Regulations, EPA documents, and Federal Environmental Statutes.

The Facts on File Dictionary of Environmental Science. L. Harold Stevenson and Bruce Wyman. Facts on File, Inc., 460 Park Ave. S., New York, New York 10016. (212) 683-2244. 1991.

Grzimek's Encyclopedia of Ecology. Bernhard Grzimek. Van Nostrand Reinhold, 115 5th Ave., New York, New York 10003. (212) 254-3232. 1976.

Illustrated Encyclopedia of Science and the Future. Mike Biscare, et al., ed. Marshall Cavendish, 58 Old Compton St., London, England 0W1V5 PA. 01-734 6710. 1983. Twenty volumes. Each volume has 5 sections: Frontiers, Electronics in Action, Medical Science, Military Technology, and Resources.

The Life of Prairies and Plains. Durward Leon Allen. McGraw-Hill Science & Engineering Books, 11 W. 19th St., New York, New York 10011. (212) 337-6010. 1967.

The Marshall Cavendish Illustrated Encyclopedia of Plants and Earth Sciences. Marshall Cavendish Corp., 2415 Jerusalem Ave., North Bellmore, New York 11710. (516) 826-4200. 1988.

McGraw-Hill Encyclopedia of Science and Technology. McGraw-Hill, 1221 Avenue of the Americas, New York, New York 10020. (212) 512-2000 or (800) 262-4729. 1992. Seventh edition. Issued in multiple volumes including index. Includes all science and technology broad subject areas.

North American Reference Encyclopedia of Ecology and Pollution. William White. North American Pub. Co., 401 N. Broad St., Philadelphia, Pennsylvania 19108. (215) 238-5300. 1972.

Van Nostrand's Scientific Encyclopedia. Glenn D. Considine, ed. Van Nostrand Reinhold, 115 5th Ave., New York, New York 10003. (212) 254-3232. 1983. Sixth edition. Includes all broad subject areas in science.

GENERAL WORKS

50 Simple Things You Can Do to Save the Earth. G.K. Hall & Co., 70 Lincoln St., Boston, Massachusetts 02111. (617) 423-3990. 1991. Citizen participation in environmental protection.

Acid Precipitation. Springer-Verlag, 175 5th Ave., New York, New York 10010. (212) 460-1500; (800) 777-4643. 1989-. 5 volume set. Deals with various aspects of acidic precipitations such as: biological and ecological effects; sources, deposition and canopy interactions; soils aquatic processes and lake acidification. Also includes case studies and an international overview and assessment.

Agroecology and Small Farm Development. Miguel A. Altieri. CRC Press, 2000 Corporate Blvd. N.W., Boca Raton, Florida 33431. (800) 272-7737. 1989. Reviews physical and social context of small farm agriculture, small farm development approaches, production systems, the dynamics of traditional agriculture, and research methodologies.

Agroecology: Researching the Ecological Basis for Sustainable Agriculture. Stephen R. Gliessman, ed. Springer-Verlag, 175 5th Ave., New York, New York 10010. (212) 460-1500; (800) 777-4643. 1990. Demonstrates in a series of international case studies how to combine the more production-oriented focus of the agronomist with the more systems-oriented viewpoint of the ecologist. Methodology for evaluating and quantifying agroecosystem is presented.

And Two if by Sea: Fighting the Attack on America's Coasts. Coast Alliance, Washington, District of Columbia 1986. A citizen's guide to the Coastal Zone Management Act and other coastal laws

Antarctic Ecosystems: Ecological Change and Conservation. K.R. Kerry, ed. Springer-Verlag, 175 5th Ave., New York, New York 10010. (212) 460-1500 or (800) 777-4643. 1990. Papers from a Symposium held in the University of Tasmania, Hobart, Australia, August-September 1988. Deals with conservation of nature in the antarctic.

Assessing Ecological Risks of Biotechnology. Lev R. Ginzburg. Butterworth-Heinemann, 80 Montvale Ave., Stoneham, Massachusetts 02180. (617) 438-8464; (800) 366-2665. 1991. Presents an analysis of the ecological risk associated with genetically engineered microorganisms, organisms that, through gene splicing, have obtained additional genetic information.

Atlas of the Environment. Geoffrey Lean, et al. Prentice Hall, Rte. 9W, Englewood Cliffs, New York 07632. (201) 592-2000. 1990. Guide to the major environmental issues around the world that makes good use of numerous maps and diagrams to present the increasing amount of information available in this field. Covers related subjects such as indigenous people and refugees, the education gap, natural and human induced disasters, wildlife trade, and migration routes.

The Background of Ecology. Robert P. McIntosh. Carolina Biological Supply Company, 2700 York Road, Burlington, North Carolina 27215. (919) 584-0381. 1985.

Biogeochemistry: An Analysis of Global Change. William H. Schlesinger. Academic Press, c/o Harcourt Brace Jovanovich Inc., 6277 Sea Harbor Dr., Orlando, Florida 32887. (800) 346-8648. 1991. Examines global changes that have occurred and are occurring in our water, air, and on land, relates them to the global cycles of water, carbon, nitrogen, phosphorous, and sulfur.

Biological Surveys of Estuaries and Coasts. Cambridge University Press, 40 W. 20th St., New York, New York 10011. (212) 924-3900. Coastal ecology, ecological surveys, and estuarine biology.

Changing Landscapes: An Ecological Perspective. Isaak Samuel Zonneveld and Richard T. T. Forman. Springer-Verlag, 175 5th Ave, New York, New York 10010. (212) 460-1500 or (800) 777-4643. 1990. Ecology and landscape protection.

The Colorado Front Range: A Century of Ecological Change. University of Utah Press, 401 Kendall D. Graff Building, Salt Lake City, Utah 84112. (801) 581-7274. 1991.

Comparative Analysis of Ecosystems Patterns, Mechanisms, and Theories. Jonathan Cole, ed. Springer-Verlag, 175 5th Ave., New York, New York 10010. (212) 460-1500; (800) 777-4643. 1991. Includes papers from a conference held in Milbrook, New York, 1989.

Comparative Ecology of Microorganisms and Macroorganisms. John H. Andrews. Springer-Verlag, 175 5th Ave., New York, New York 10010. (212) 460-1500. 1991. Constructs a format in which to compare the ecologies of large and small plant and animal organisms. Examines the differences between the sizes, and explores what similarities or parallels can be identified, and where they don't seem to exist. The ideas are illustrated by applying evolutionary principles to the individual organism.

Constructed Wetlands for Wastewater Treatment. Donald A. Hammer. Lewis Publishers, 200 Corporate Blvd. NW, Boca Raton, Florida 33431. (407) 994-0555 or (800)272-7737. 1989. Presents general principles of wetland ecology, hydrology, soil chemistry, vegetation, microbiology, and wildlife dependence on wetlands. It provides management guidelines, beginning with policies and regulations, and including siting and construction and operations and monitoring of constructed wetland systems.

The Control of Nature. John A. McPhee. Noonday Pr., 19 Union Sq. W, New York, New York 10003. (212) 741-6900. 1990. Describes the strategies and tactics through which people attempt to control nature.

A Critique for Ecology. Robert Henry Peters. Cambridge University Press, 40 W. 20th St., New York, New York 10011. (212) 924-3900. Offers examples of scientific criticism of contemporary ecology.

Deep Ecology. Bill Devall and George Sessions. G. M. Smith, PO Box 667, Layton, Utah 84041. (801) 554-9800; (800) 421-8714. 1985. Explores the philosophical, psychological and sociological roots of today's environmental movement and offers specific direct action suggestions for individuals to practice.

Defending the Earth. South End Press, 116 St. Botolph St., Boston, Massachusetts 02115. (800) 533-8478. 1991.

Design for a Livable Planet: How You Can Help Clean Up the Environment. Jon Naar. Perennial Library, 10 E. 53d St., New York, New York 10022. (212) 207-7000; (800) 242-7737. 1990. Explains the dangers we present to our environment and what we can do about it. Also available from Carolina Biological Supply Co., 2700 York Rd., Burlington, NC.

Domestication: The Decline of Environmental Appreciation. Helmut Hemmer. Cambridge University Press, 40 W. 20th St., New York, New York 10011. (212) 924-3900; (800) 227-0247. 1990. The books proposes the thesis that domestication must lead to reduced environmental appreciation. The origins of domesticated mammals, their scientific nomenclature, the relationships between feral mammals and their wild progenitors, and modern attempts at domestication are also covered.

The Dream of the Earth. Thomas Berry. Sierra Club Books, 100 Bush St., San Francisco, California 94104. (415) 291-1600. 1988. Describes the ecological fate from a species perspective.

Earth Education: A New Beginning. Steve Van Matre. Institute for Earth Education, PO Box 288, Warrenville, Illinois 60555. (708) 393-3096. 1990. Describes environmental education which adopts an alternative foundation for improving awareness about the environment through changes in attitudes and life styles.

Eco-Warriors: Understanding the Radical Environmental Movement. Rik Scarce. Noble Pr., 111 E. Chestnut, Suite 48 A, Chicago, Illinois 60611. (312) 880-0439. 1990.

Recounts escapades of pro-ecology sabotage by self styled eco-warriors. Episodes such as the sinking of two whaling ships in Iceland, the botched attempt to hang a banner on Mt. Rushmore, a national tree-sitting week, and raids on research facilities by animal liberation activists.

Ecological Engineering: An Introduction to Ecotechnology. William J. Mitsch and Sven Erik Jorgensen, eds. John Wiley & Sons, Inc., 605 3rd Ave., New York, New York 10158-0012. (212) 850-6000. 1989. Presents 12 international case studies of ecological engineering. The case studies survey problems and existing methodologies indicate where methods are ecologically sound, and illustrate examples of the use of ecological engineering.

Ecological Genetics and Air Pollution. George E. Taylor, Jr., ed. Springer-Verlag, 175 5th Ave., New York, New York 10010. (212) 460-1500; (800) 777-4643. 1991. Describes role of air pollution in governing the genetic structure and evolution of plant species.

Ecological Heterogeneity. Jurek Kolasa, et al., eds. Springer-Verlag, 175 5th Ave., New York, New York 10010. (212) 460-1500. 1991. Examines the meaning of heterogeneity in a particular environment and its consequences for individuals, populations, and communities of plants and animals. Among the topics of the 14 papers are the causes of heterogeneity, system and observer dependence, dimension and scale, ecosystem organization, temporal and spatial changes, new models of competition and landscape patterns, and applications in desert, temperate, and marine areas.

Ecological Implications of Contemporary Agriculture. H. Eijsackers and A. Quispel, eds. Munksgaard International, PO Box 2148, Copenhagen K, Denmark DK-1016. 1988. Proceedings of the 4th European Symposium, September 7-12, 1986, Wageningen. Ecological bulletins are published in cooperation with ecological journals; holarctic ecology and Oikos. They consist of monographs, reports, and symposium proceedings on topics of international interest.

Ecological Processes and Cumulative Impacts Illustrated by Bottomland Harwood Wetland Ecosystems. James G. Gosselink, et al. Lewis Publishers, 2000 Corporate Blvd., N.W., Boca Raton, Florida 33431. (407) 994-0555 or (800) 272-7737. 1990. Covers the ecological processes in bottomland hardwood forests and relates these processes to human activities.

The Ecological Self. Freya Mathews. Rowman & Littlefield, Publishers, Inc., 8705 Bollman Pl., Savage, Maryland 20763. (301) 306-0400. 1991. Considers the metaphysical foundations of ecological ethics.

Ecologue: The Environmental Catalogue and Consumer's Guide for a Safe Earth. Bruce N. Anderson, ed. Prentice Hall, Rte. 9W, Englewood Cliffs, New York 07632. (201) 592-2000. 1990. Compares and evaluates the cost, performance, energy efficiency and effect on the environment of a wide range of products used in everyday settings. The book is arranged according to the products used: groceries, household cleaners, clothing, personal care items, baby care, appliances and transportation.

Ecology and Land Management in Amazonia. Michael J. Eden. Belhaven Press, 136 S. Broadway, Irvington, New York 10533. (914) 591-9111. 1990. Deals with three major areas: the rain forest as a global resource and its role in sustaining life on the planet as a whole; needs of the countries with large tracts of tropical rain forest (including the factors that relate to how one can utilize land, the climate, geomorphology, hydrology, soils and ecology); and how the Amazonia rain forest can be conserved, including the role of national parks and management at the regional level.

The Ecology and Management of Aquatic Terrestrial Ecotones. R. J. Naiman and H. Decamps, eds. Parthenon Pub., Casterton Hall, Carnforth, England LA6 2LA. 1990.

Ecology and Management of Food Industry Pests. J. Richard Gorham. AOAC International, 2200 Wilson Blvd., Suite 400, Arlington, Virginia 22201-3301. (703) 522-3032.

Ecology: Balance and Imbalance in Nature. Shirley Fung. Longman Cheshire, 95 Coventry St., South Melbourne, VIC, Australia 3205. 1991.

Ecology, Community, and Lifestyle: Outline of an Ecosophy. David Rothenberg. Cambridge University Press, 40 W. 20th St., New York, New York 10011. (212) 924-3900. 1989. Handbook on strategy and tactics for environmentalists.

Ecology, Economics, Ethics: The Broken Circle. Herbert R. Bormann and Stephen R. Kellert, eds. Yale University Press, 302 Temple St., New Haven, Connecticut 06520. (203) 432-0960. 1991. Addresses a wide range of concerns and offers practical remedies including: economic incentives for conservation, technical adaptations to use resources effectively; better accounting procedures for measuring the environmental system that better explains our responsibility to the environment.

Ecology for Beginners. Stephen Croall. Pantheon Books, 201 E 50th St., New York, New York 10022. (212) 751-2600. 1981. The story of man's struggle with the environment.

The Ecology of a Garden: The First Fifteen Years. Jennifer Owen. Cambridge University Press, 40 W. 20th St., New York, New York 10011. (212) 924-3900; (800) 227-0247. 1991.

Ecology of Biological Invasions of North America and Hawaii. H. G. Baker, et al. Springer-Verlag, 175 5th Ave., New York, New York 10010. (212) 460-1500; (800) 777-4643. 1986.

Ecology of Photosynthesis in Sun and Shade. J. R. Evans, et al. CSIRO, PO Box 89, East Melbourne, VIC, Australia 3002. 1988. The popular topic of function analysis of the photosynthetic apparatus in response to irradiance, and problems of acclimation and photoinhibition are also discussed.

Ecology of Sandy Shores. A. C. Brown and A. Mclachlan. Elsevier Science Publishing Co., 655 Avenue of the Americas, New York, New York 10010. (212) 989-5800. 1990. Deals with the biological study of sandy beaches.

The Ecology of the Ancient Greek World. Robert Sallares. Cornell University Press, 124 Roberts Place, Ithaca, New York 14850. 1991. Synthesis of ancient history and biological or physical anthropology. Includes chapters on demography and on agriculture in ancient Greece and Egypt. Also includes extensive notes and bibliographies.

The Ecology of Urban Habitats. O.L. Gilbert. Chapman & Hall, 29 W. 35th St., New York, New York 10001-2291. (212) 244-3336. 1989.

Economics and Biological Diversity: Developing and Using Economic Incentives to Conserve Biological Resources. Jeffrey A. McNeely. Pinter Pub., 136 S. Broadway, Irvington, New York 10533. (914) 591-9111. 1991. Explains how economic incentives can be applied to conservation while complementing development efforts.

Ecosystems Experiments. H. A. Mooney, et al., eds. John Wiley & Sons, Inc., 605 3rd Ave., New York, New York 10158-0012. (212) 850-6000. 1991. Explores the potential ecosystem experimentation as a tool for understanding and predicting changes in the biosphere. Areas investigated include deforestation, desertification, El Nino phenomenon, acid rain, watersheds, wetlands, and aquatic and climatic changes.

Ecotoxicology and Climate. Philippe Bordeaux, et al., eds. John Wiley & Sons, Inc., 605 3rd Ave., New York, New York 10158-0012. (212) 850-6000. 1989. Describes environmental chemistry of toxic pollutants in hot and cold climates. Includes bibliographical references and an index.

Elton's Ecologists: A History of the Bureau of Animal Population. Peter Crowcroft. University of Chicago Press, 5801 Ellis Ave., 4th Fl., Chicago, Illinois 60637. (312) 702-7700. 1991. The story of a smallish university department chronicles an enterprise that appreciably shaped the history of ecology during the mid-decades of the 20th century.

Emergence: The New Science of Becoming. Lindisfarne Press, RR4, Box 94A-1, Hudson, New York 12534. (518) 851-9155. Covers ecology and philosophy of biology.

The End of Nature. Bill McKibben. Anchor Books, 666 5th Ave., New York, New York 10103. (212) 765-6500; (800) 223-6834. 1990.

Environment-Employment–New Industrial Societies: A Bibliographic Map. International Labor Organization, 4, rue des Morillons, Geneva 22, Switzerland CH-1211. 1991.

Environment, Resources, and Conservation. Susan Owens and Peter L. Owens. Cambridge University Press, 40 W 20th St., New York, New York 10011. (212) 924-3900 or (800) 227-0247. 1991. The book studies three cases illuminating problems and policy responses at three levels of geographic scale–international, national, and local. The case of acid rain is used to illustrate a pollution problem with international dimensions; the British coal industry is analyzed as an example of national nonrenewable resource depletion; and renewable wetland ecosystem management illustrates a local concern by analyzing conservation measures.

Environmental Aspects of Applied Biology. Association of Applied Biologists, Institute of Horticultural Research, Littlehampton, England BN17 6LP. 1988. Volume 1 contains environmental impacts of crop protection and practices within the agricultural ecosystem (crop protection topics). Volume 2 includes environmental aspects of post-harvest practices, the plant response to the combined stresses of pollution, climate and soil conditions, and the straw problem. Includes bibliographies.

Environmental Aspects of Coasts and Islands. BAR, Oxford, England 1981. Maritime anthropology, coastal ecology and environmental ecology.

Environmental Biology. E. J. W. Barrington. John Wiley & Sons, Inc., 605 3rd Ave., New York, New York 10158-

0012. (212) 850-6000. 1980. Resource and Environmental Series.

Environmental Data Bases: Design, Implementation, and Maintenance. Gene Y. Michael. Lewis Publishers, 2000 Corporate Blvd., N.W., Boca Raton, Florida 33431. (407) 994-0555 or (800) 272-7737. 1991. Describes how the data bases for environmental information came into existence. Includes data requirements, design, software, hardware configurations, PC system management, and other related matters.

The Environmental Gardener: The Solution to Pollution for Lawns and Gardens. Laurence Sombke. MasterMedia, 17 E. 89th St., New York, New York 10128. (212) 348-2020. 1991.

Environmental Impacts of Agricultural Production Activities. Larry W. Canter. Lewis Publishers, 200 Corporate Blvd. NW, Boca Raton, Florida 33431. (407) 994-0555 or (800)272-7737. Volume in general deals with agricultural production technologies and its environmental impacts. It includes case studies and has chapters that separately deal with water and soil impacts; air quality impacts; noise and solid waste impacts. Most importantly it evaluates emerging agricultural technologies and includes a bibliography on the subject.

Environmental Restoration: Science and Strategies for Restoring the Earth. John J. Berger. Island Press, 1718 Connecticut Ave. N.W., Suite 300, Washington, District of Columbia 20009. (202) 232-7933. 1990. Overview techniques of restoration.

The Environmental Sourcebook. Edith Carol Stein. Lyons & Burford, 31 W. 21st St., New York, New York 10010. (212) 620-9580. 1992. Provides information on 11 specific environmental issues, including population; agriculture; energy; climate and atmosphere; biodiversity; water; oceans; solid waste; hazardous substances and waste; endangered lands; and development.

Environmental Viewpoints. Marie Lazzari. Gale Research Inc., 835 Penobscot Bldg., Detroit, Michigan 48226-4094. (313) 961-2242. 1992.

Every Day is Earth Day: Simple Practical Things You Can Do to Help Clean Up the Planet. Peggy Taylor and Laura Danylin Duprez. New Age Journal, 342 Western Ave., Brighton, Massachusetts 02135. 1990.

Expert Systems for Environmental Applications. Judith M. Hushon, ed. American Chemical Society, 1155 16th St. N.W., Washington, District of Columbia 20036. (202) 872-4600; (800) 227-5558. 1990. Overview of environmental expert systems and its future applications for environmental protection.

For Earth's Sake: The Life and Times of David Brower. David R. Brower. Gibbs Smith, PO Box 667, Layton, Utah 84041. (801) 554-9800; (800) 421-8714. 1990. Personal reflections that catalog events and commentary and provides explanatory insight into several events of America's contemporary environmental history.

Forest Stand Dynamics. Chadwick Dearing Oliver and Bruce C. Larson. McGraw-Hill Science & Engineering Books, 11 W. 19th St., New York, New York 10011. (212) 337-6010. 1990. Offers a unique synthesis of information from the fields of silviculture, ecology, and physiology that shows how different types of forest develop and outlines appropriate forest management techniques for each type.

Foundations of Ecology. Leslie A. Real. University of Chicago Press, 5801 Ellis Ave., 4th Fl., Chicago, Illinois 60637. (312) 568-1550 or (800) 621-2736. Forty classic papers that have laid the foundation of modern ecology and are ideal for graduate courses that deal with the development of ecological ideas.

The Fragile Environment. Laurie Friday and Ronald Laskey, eds. Cambridge University Press, 40 W. 20th St., New York, New York 10011. (212) 924-3900; (800) 227-0247. 1989. The fragile environment brings together a team of distinguished authors to consider areas of urgent environmental concern.

From the Land. Nancy P. Pittman, ed. Island Press, 1718 Connecticut Ave. N.W., Suite 300, Washington, District of Columbia 20009. (202) 232-7933. 1988. Anthology comes from 13 years of the Land–a journal of conservation writings from the '40s and '50s. Through fiction, essay, poetry, and philosophy we learn how our small farms have given way to today's agribusiness.

GAIA, an Atlas of Planet Management. Norman Myers. Anchor Pr./Doubleday, 666 5th Ave., New York, New York 10103. (212) 765-6500; (800) 223-6834. Resource atlas including a wealth of data on the environment with text by authoritative environmentalists.

GAIA Connections: An Introduction to Ecology, Ecoethics and Economics. Alan S. Miller. Rowman & Littlefield, Publishers, Inc., 8705 Bollman Pl., Savage, Maryland 20763. (301) 306-0400. 1991. Synthesis of humanity's ethical and economic options in coping with the global environmental crisis.

Global Climate Change: Human and Natural Influences. Paragon House Publishers, 90 5th Ave., New York, New York 10011. (212) 620-2820. Carbon dioxide, methane, chlorofluorocarbons and ozone in the atmosphere; acid rain and water pollution in the hydrosphere; oceanographic and meteorological processes, nuclear war, volcanoes, asteroids, and meteorites.

Global Ecology. Colin Tudge. Oxford University Press, 200 Madison Ave., New York, New York 10016. (212) 679-7300 or (800) 334-4249. Overview of ecological science including climate and habitats of our planet while emphasizing the global unity of earth's ecosystem.

The Greater Yellowstone Ecosystem. Robert B. Keiter and Mark S. Boyce, eds. Yale University Press, 302 Temple St., New Haven, Connecticut 06520. (203) 432-0960. 1991. Discusses key resource management issues in the greater Yellowstone ecosystem, using them as starting points to debate the manner in which humans should interact with the environment of this area.

The Green Machine: Ecology and the Balance of Nature. Wallace Arthur. B. Blackwell, 3 Cambridge Ctr., Suite 208, Cambridge, Massachusetts 02142. (617) 225-0401. 1990. Provides an overview of most topics routinely included in ecology courses. Includes trophic dynamics, predator-prey theory, competition coevolution, and species diversity. Evolutionary topics such as plate tectonics, geologic time, speciation, extinction, and natural selection are also included.

Hands-On Ecology. Children's Press, 5440 N. Cumberland Ave., Chicago, Illinois 60656. (312) 693-0800. 1991. Practical ways of conserving the environment.

Helping Nature Heal: An Introduction to Environmental Restoration. Richard Nilsen, ed. Ten Speed Press, P.O.

Box 7123, Berkeley, California 94707. (800) 841-2665. 1991.

Holistic Resource Management. Allan Savory. Island Press, 1718 Connecticut Ave. N.W., Suite 300, Washington, District of Columbia 20009. (202) 232-7933. 1988. Presents a comprehensive planning model that treats people and their environment as a whole. Discusses the scientific and management principles of the model, followed by detailed descriptions of each tool and guideline.

Holistic Resource Management Work Book. Sam Bingham and Allan Savory. Island Press, 1718 Connecticut Ave. N.W., Suite 300, Washington, District of Columbia 20009. (202) 232-7933. 1989. Provides practical instruction in financial, biological, and land planning segments necessary to apply the holistic management model.

Home Ecology. Karen Christensen. Fulcrum Publishing, 350 Indiana St., Ste. 350, Golden, Colorado 80401. (303) 277-1623. 1990. Simple and practical ways to green homes.

How to Save the World: Strategy for World Conservation. Robert Allen. Rowman & Littlefield, Publishers, Inc., 8705 Bollman Pl., Savage, Maryland 20763. (301) 306-0400. 1980. Based on the Global Conservation Strategy prepared in Switzerland in 1980 by the United Nations Environment Program, the World Wildlife Fund and the International Union for Conservation. Presents strategies in four critical areas: food supply, forest, the sea, and endangered species. Sets priorities, identifies obstacles, and recommends cost effective ways of overcoming those obstacles.

The Human Impact on the Natural Environment. Andrew Goudie. MIT Press, 55 Hayward St., Cambridge, Massachusetts 02142. (617) 253-2884. 1986. Discusses man's influence on nature.

Human Performance Physiology and Environmental Medicine Atterrestrial Extremes. Kent B. Pandolf, et al., eds. WCB Brown and Benchmark Pr., 2460 Kerper Blvd., Dubuque, Iowa 52001. (800) 338-5578. 1988. Includes the most current information available on the physiological and medical responses to heat, cold, altitude, poor air quality and hyperbaric conditions.

Impounded Rivers: Perspectives for Ecological Management. Geoffrey E. Petts. John Wiley & Sons, Inc., 605 3rd Ave., New York, New York 10158. (212) 850-6000. 1984. Environmental aspects of dams, stream ecology and stream conservation.

In Search of Environmental Excellence: Moving Beyond Blame. Bruce Piasecki and Peter Asmus. Simon and Schuster, 1230 Avenue of the Americas, New York, New York 10020. (212) 689-7000. 1990. Analyses of the roles and motivations of government, business/industry, and the general public in solving environmental problems.

Into Harmony with the Planet: The Delicate Balance Between Industry and the Environment. Michael Allaby. Bloomsbury Pub., 2 Soho Sq., London, England W1V 5DE. 1990. Describes the ecosystem and its delicate balance. Also discusses the effect industry and its pollutants on the environment.

An Introduction to Environmental Pattern Analysis. P. J. A. Howard. Parthenon Group Inc., 120 Mill Rd., Park Ridge, New Jersey 07656. (201) 391-6796. 1991. Explains the basic mathematics of the most widely used ordination and cluster analysis methods, types of data to

which they are suited and their advantages and disadvantages.

Laboratory Manual of General Ecology. George W. Cox. Carolina Biological Supply Company, 2700 York Rd., Burlington, North Carolina 27215. (919) 584-0381. 1989. 6th ed. Provides a good section on activities, exercises and references in the field of ecology as a whole.

Last Stand of the Red Spruce. Robert A. Mello. Island Press, 1718 Connecticut Ave. N.W., Suite 300, Washington, District of Columbia 20009. (202) 232-7933. 1987. Hypothesizes that acid rain is the most likely culprit that is killing the trees.

Life, Space, and Time: A Course in Environmental Biology. Howard Barraclough Fell. Harper & Row, 10 E. 53rd St., New York, New York 10022. (212) 207-7000; (800) 242-7737. 1974. Deals with natural history and ecological matters.

Linking the Natural Environment and the Economy: Essays the Eco-Eco Group. Carl Folke, ed. Kluwer Academic Publishers, 101 Philip Dr., Assinippi Park, Norwell, Massachusetts 02061. (617) 871-6600. 1991. Volume 1 of the series entitled Ecology, Economy and Environment.

Long-Term Ecological Research: An International Perspective. Paul G. Risser, ed. John Wiley & Sons, Inc., 605 3rd Ave., New York, New York 10158-0012. (212) 850-6000. 1991. Describes and analyzes research programs in various ecosystems such as temperate forests, arid steppes, deserts, temperate and tropical grasslands, aquatic systems from countries including Scotland, Kenya, USA, Australia, Canada, Germany, and France.

Magill's Survey of Science. Earth Science Series. Frank N. Magill. Salem Press, PO Box 50062, Pasadena, California 91105. 1990-. Five volumes. Includes information on earth's crust, hot spots and volcanic island chains, physical properties of minerals, rock magnetism, physical properties of rocks, and index.

Making the Switch. Sacramento League of Women Voters. Golden Empire Health Planning Center, P.O. Box 649, Sacramento, California 98120. (916) 448-1198. 1988. Alternatives to using toxic chemicals in the home.

Mind and Nature: A Necessary Unit. Gregory Bateson. Bantam Books, 666 5th Ave., New York, New York 10103. (212) 765-6500; (800) 223-6834. 1988. Reveals the pattern which connects man and nature.

Monitoring for Conservation and Ecology. Barrie Goldsmith, ed. Chapman & Hall, 29 W 35th St., New York, New York 10001-2291. (212) 244-3336. 1991. Focuses on an audience of those practicing ecology, nature conservation, or other similar land-based sciences. The differences between surveying and monitoring are discussed and emphasis is placed on the nature of monitoring as being purpose- oriented dynamic in philosophy, and often providing a baseline for recording possible changes in the future.

Natural Microbial Communities: Ecological and Physiological Features. Tomomichi Yanagita. Springer-Verlag, 175 5th Ave., New York, New York 10010. (212) 460-1500; (800) 777-4643. 1990. Translation of a work which originally appeared in Japanese entitled Microbial Ecology.

Nature Reserves: Island Theory and Conservation Practice. Craig L. Shafer. Smithsonian Institution Press, 470

L'Enfant Plaza, No. 7100, Washington, District of Columbia 20560. (800) 782-4612. 1991. Encompasses ecology, biogeography, evolutionary biology, genetics, paleobiology, as well as legal, social, and economic issues.

The New Organic Grower. Eliot Coleman. Chelsea Green Publishing, PO Box 130, Post Mills, Vermont 05058-0130. (802) 333-9073. 1989. Covers crop rotation, green manures, tillage, seeding, transplanting, cultivation, and garden pests.

New World New Mind: Moving toward Conscious Evolution. Robert E. Ornstein. Simon & Schuster, 1230 Avenue of the Americas, New York, New York 10020. (212) 698-7000; (800) 223-2348. 1990. Proposes revolutionary new ways to close the dangerous gap between our current mind set and the high-tech world of today.

New World Parrots in Crisis. Steven R. Beissinger and Noel F. R. Snyder, eds. Smithsonian Institution Press, 470 L'Enfant Plaza, No. 7100, Washington, District of Columbia 20560. (800) 782-4612. 1991. Provides an overview of the hazards facing neotropical parrots one of the world's most threatened group of birds, as well as a detailed discussion of a range of possible conservation solutions.

The Next One Hundred Years: Shaping the Fate of Our Living Earth. Jonathan Weiner. Bantam Books, 666 5th Ave., New York, New York 10103. (212) 765-6500; (800) 223-6834. 1991. Explores the following issues: the greenhouse effect, deforestation, the destruction of the ozone layer, the human population explosion and the onset of mass extinctions.

The Northwest Greenbook. Jonathan King. Sasquatch Books, 1931 2nd Ave., Seattle, Washington 98101. (206) 441-5555. 1991.

Nutrient Cycling in Terrestrial Ecosystems Field Methods. A. F. Harrison, et al. Elsevier Science Publishing Co., 655 Avenue of the Americas, New York, New York 10010. (212) 984-5800. 1990. Describes a wide range of methods for the estimation of nutrient fluxes. The book is divided into sections dealing with inputs, turnover, losses and plant uptake processes.

The Ocean in Human Affairs. S. Fred Singer, ed. Paragon House Publishers, 90 5th Ave., New York, New York 10011. (212) 620-2820. 1990. Describes the role of the oceans on climate, its resources, energy and water projects in the eastern Mediterranean and other related essays on marine topics.

Our Common Future. World Commission on Environment and Development. Oxford University Press, 200 Madison Ave., New York, New York 10016. (212) 679-7300; (800) 334-4249. 1987. Cautions that it is time that economy and ecology worked hand in hand, so that governments and their people can take responsibility not just for environmental damage, but for the policies that cause the damage.

Paleoenvironments in the Namib Desert: The Lower Tumas Basin in the Late Cenozoic. Justin Wilkinson. University of Chicago Press, Committee on Geographical Studies, 5801 Ellis Ave., 4th Floor, Chicago, Illinois 60637. (800) 621-2736. 1990. Focuses on the great coastal desert of Southwestern Africa the Namib, and explores the complex changes in depositional environments throughout the Cenozoic.

Parameter Estimation in Ecology. O. Richter and D. Sondgerath. VCH Publishers, 303 NW 12th Ave., Deer-

field Beach, Florida 33442-1788. (305) 428-5566. 1990. Brings together the different aspects of biological modelling, in particular ecological modelling using both stochastic and deterministic models.

Physiological Plant Ecology. O. L. Lange, et al., eds. Springer-Verlag, 175 5th Ave., New York, New York 10010. (212) 460-1500; (800) 777-4643. 1981-1983. Contents: Volume 1 - Responses to the physical environment; Volume 2 - Water relations and carbon assimilation; Volume 3 - Responses to the chemical and biological environment; Volume 4 - Ecosystem processes (mineral cycling, productivity, and man's influence).

Planet under Stress: The Challenge of Global Change. Constance Mungall and Digby J. McLaren, eds. Oxford University Press, 200 Madison Ave., New York, New York 10016. (212) 679-7300; (800) 334-4249. 1991.

Plant-Animal Interactions; Evolutionary Ecology in Tropical and Temperate Regions. Peter W. Price, et al. John Wiley & Sons, Inc., 605 3rd Ave., New York, New York 10158-0012. (212) 850-6000. 1991. Comprises a comparative analysis of the existing ecological systems of temperate and tropical regions.

Plant Demography in Vegetation Succession. Krystyna Falinska. Kluwer Academic Publishers, 101 Philip Dr., Assinippi Park, Norwell, Massachusetts 02061. (617) 871-6600. 1991.

Pocket Flora of the Redwood Forest. Rudolf Willem Becking. Island Press, 1718 Connecticut Ave. N.W., Suite 300, Washington, District of Columbia 20009. (202) 232-7933. 1982. Guide to 212 of the most frequently seen plants in the Redwood Forest of the Pacific Coast. It is interspersed with accurate drawing color photographs and systematic keys to plant identification.

Principles and Measurements in Environmental Biology. F. I. Woodward and J. E. Sheehy. Butterworth-Heinemann, 80 Montvale Ave., Stoneham, Massachusetts 02180. (617) 438-8464. 1983.

Private Options: Tools and Concepts for Land Conservation. Montana Land Reliance, Land Trust Exchange. Island Press, 1718 Connecticut Ave. N.W., Suite 300, Washington, District of Columbia 20009. (202) 232-7933. 1982. Private land conservation experts offer their expertise on how individuals can help contain urban sprawl, conserve wetlands, and protect wildlife. This book covers estate planning, tax incentives, purchase options, conservation easements and land management.

Redevelopment of Degraded Ecosystems. H. Regier, et al., eds. Parthenon Pub., Casterton Hall, Carnforth, England LA6 2LA. 1991. Volume 8 in the "Man and the Biosphere" series published jointly with UNESCO.

Responses of Plants to Environmental Stresses. J. Levitt. Academic Press, c/o Harcourt Brace Jovanovich Inc., 6277 Sea Harbor Dr., Orlando, Florida 32887. (800) 346-8648. 1980. 2nd ed. Volume 1 covers chilling, freezing and high temperature. Volume 2 contains water, radiation, salt, and other stresses.

Risk Assessment in Genetic Engineering; Environmental Release of Organisms. Morris A. Levin and Harlee Strauss. McGraw-Hill, 1221 Avenue of the Americas, New York, New York 10020. (212) 512-2000; (800) 262-4729. 1991. Investigates issues such as the transport of microorganisms via air, water, and soil; the persistence and establishment of viruses, bacteria, and plants; and the genetic transfer via viruses.

Save Our Planet: 750 Everyday Ways You Can Help Clean Up the Earth. Diane MacEachern. Dell Pub., 666 5th Ave., New York, New York 10103. (212) 765-6500; (800) 255-4133. 1990. Practical guide to ways in which everyone can help clean up the earth.

Saving America's Wildlife. Thomas R. Dunlap. Princeton University Press, 41 Williams St., Princeton, New Jersey 08540. (609) 258-4900. 1988. Explores how we have deepened our commitment to and broadened the scope of animal conservation through the 1980s.

Saving the Mediterranean: The Politics of International Environmental Cooperation. Peter M. Haas. Columbia University Press, 562 W. 113th St., New York, New York 10025. (212) 316-7100. 1990. Focuses on the international pollution management of the Mediterranean. Ninety scientists and international officials were interviewed to ascertain how the international community responded to this particular threat.

Seabirds of the Farallon Islands: Ecology, Dynamics, and Structure of an Upwelling-System Community. David G. Ainley and Robert J. Boekelheide, eds. Stanford University, Stanford, California 94305-2235. (415) 723-9434. 1990. History of seabird populations at the Farallons, a general discussion of patterns in the marine environment, and the general feeding ecology of Farallon seabirds.

Signs of Hope: Working towards Our Common Future. Linda Starke. Oxford University Press, Walton St., Oxford, England 1990. Sequel to the report of the World Commission on Environment and Development Commissioned by the Centre For Our Common Future. Records the progress made in the implementation of the recommendations of Our Common Future and looks at initiatives being taken by governments, industry, scientists, non-governmental organizations and the media.

Silent Spring. Rachel Carson. Carolina Biological Supply Company, 2700 York Rd., Burlington, North Carolina 27215. (919) 584-0381. 1987.

Soil Organisms as Components of Ecosystems. U. Lohm. Swedish Natural Science Research Council, P.O. Box 6711, Stockholm, Sweden S-113 85. 08-15-1580. 1977. Covers soil ecology and soil fauna.

Strengthening Environmental Cooperation with Developing Countries. OECD Publications and Information Center, 2001 L St. N.W., Ste. 700, Washington, District of Columbia 20036. (202) 785-OECD. 1989. Report from an OECD seminar involving developing countries, aid and environmental agencies, multinational financing institutions, and non-governmental organizations concludes that early environmental assessment of development assistance projects and programs can play a key role in improving international cooperation for sustainable development.

Subantarctic Macquarie Island: Environment and Biology. P. M. Selkirk, et al. Cambridge University Press, 40 W. 20th St., New York, New York 10011. (212) 924-3900; (800) 227-0247. 1990. Review of environmental and biologic research on the Macquarie Island. It presents summary of studies done in the last 15 years by Australian scientists. Contains a sequence of 12 chapters that concern the island's discovery and history; situation in the Southern ocean; tectonics and geology; landforms and Quaternary history; vegetation; lakes; birds; mammals; anthropoids; microbiology; near shore environments; and human impact.

The Temperate Forest Ecosystem. Yang Hanxi. Institute of Terrestrial Ecology, Merlewood Research Station, Grange-over-Sands, England LA11 6JU. 1987. Topics in forest ecology.

Terrestrial and Aquatic Ecosystems: Perturbation and Recovery. Oscar Ravera, ed. E. Horwood, 1230 Avenue of the Americas, New York, New York 10020. (800) 223-2348. 1991. Presented at the 5th European Ecological Symposium held at Siena, Italy in 1989. Some of the topics included: biological responses to the changing ecosystem; anthropogenic perturbations of the community and ecosystem; restoration of degraded ecosystems; environmental management and strategies.

Tropical Rainforest: A World Survey of Our Most Valuable Endangered Habitat With a Blueprint for its Survival. Arnold Newman. Facts on File, Inc., 460 Park Ave. S., New York, New York 10016. (212) 683-2244; (800) 322-8755. 1990. Considers threats to rain forests, including logging and slash and burn agricultural practices. Presents a variety of measures to preserve our valuable rain forests.

The Uses of Ecology: Lake Washington and Beyond. W. T. Edmondson. University of Washington Press, PO Box 50096, Seattle, Washington 98145-5096. (206) 543-4050; (800) 441-4115. 1991. Author delivered most of the contents of this book as a Danz lecture at the University of Washington. Gives an account of the pollution and recovery of Lake Washington and describes how communities worked and applied lessons learned from Lake Washington cleanup. Includes extensive documentation and bibliographies.

Vertebrate Ecology in Northern Neotropics. John F. Esenberg, ed. Smithsonian Institution Press, 470 L'Enfant Plaza, No. 7100, Washington, District of Columbia 20560. (800) 782-4612. 1979. Comparison of faunas found in tropical forests covering several mammalian species, including the red howler monkey, crab-eating fox, cebus monkey, and the didelphid marsupials.

The Violence of Green Revolution. Vandana Shiva. Humanities Pr. Intl., 171 1st Ave., Atlantic Highlands, New Jersey 07716-1289. (201) 872-1441; (800) 221-3845. 1991.

Wetlands: A Threatened Landscape. Michael Williams. B. Blackwell, 3 Cambridge Ctr., Suite 208, Cambridge, Massachusetts 02142. (617) 225-0401. 1990. Explores the evolution and composition of wetlands and their physical and biological dynamics, considers the impact of agriculture, industry, urbanization, and recreation upon them, and examines what steps we are taking and what steps should be considered to manage and preserve wetlands.

Whole Earth Ecolog: The Best of Environmental Tools and Ideas. J. Baldwin, ed. Harmony Books, 201 E. 50th St., New York, New York 10022. (212) 572-6120. 1990. Provides in-depth reviews of materials that have been meticulously reviewed by the staff of Whole Earth Access. Lists hundreds of materials that have the potential for making things a little easier on the planet.

Wildlife of the Florida Keys: A Natural History. James D. Lazell, Jr. Island Press, 1718 Connecticut Ave. N.W., Suite 300, Washington, District of Columbia 20009. (202) 232-7933. 1989. Identifies habits, behaviors, and histories of most of the species indigenous to the Keys.

Wildlife Reserves and Corridors in the Urban Environment. Lowell W. Adams. National Institute for Urban

Wildlife, 10921 Trotting Ridge Way, Columbia, Maryland 21044. (301) 596-3311. 1989. Reviews the knowledge base on wildlife habitat reserves and corridors in urban and urbanizing areas. Provides guidelines and approaches to ecological landscape planning and wildlife conservation in these regions.

World Guide to Environmental Issues and Organizations. Peter Brackley. Longman Group Ltd., Longman House, Burnt Mill, Harlow, Essex, England CM20 2J6. (0279) 426721. 1991.

GOVERNMENTAL ORGANIZATIONS

Department of Ecology: Environmental Protection. Director, Mail Stop PV-11, Olympia, Washington 98504. (206) 459-6168.

National Science Foundation. 1800 G St., N.W., Washington, District of Columbia 20550. (202) 357-9498.

Office of Public Affairs: Fish and Wildlife Service. 18th and C St., N.W., Washington, District of Columbia 20240. (202) 343-5634.

U.S. Environmental Protection Agency: Office of Environmental Processes and Effects Research. 401 M St., S.W., Washington, District of Columbia 20460. (202) 382-5950.

HANDBOOKS AND MANUALS

The Earth Report. Edward Goldsmith. Price Stern Sloan, Inc., 360 N. La Cienega Blvd., Los Angeles, California 90048. (213) 657-6100. 1988.

Environment in Key Words: A Multilingual Handbook of the Environment: English-French-German-Russian. Isaac Paenson. Pergamon Microforms International, Inc., Fairview Park, Elmsford, New York 10523. (914) 592-7720. 1990. Two volumes. Terminology in the areas of ecology, environmental protection, pollution, conservation of natural resources and related areas.

Environmental Career Guide: Job Opportunities with the Earth in Mind. Nicholas Basta. John Wiley & Sons, Inc., 605 3rd Ave., New York, New York 10158-0012. (212) 850-6000. 1991. Complete guide to the many career options in the growing environmental field. Shows how to find employers engaged in environmental activity, and how to get the job. Lists key environmental businesses–manufacturing, government agencies, engineering consulting firms, waste handling firms, and others. Lists key professional careers in environmental conservation and maps career strategies.

Environmental Statistics Handbook: Europe. Allan Foster, Oksana Newman. Gale Research Inc., 835 Penobscot Bldg., Detroit, Michigan 48226-4094. (313) 961-2242. 1993.

The Global Ecology Handbook: What You Can Do about the Environmental Crisis. Walter H. Corson, ed. The Global Tomorrow Coalition, Beacon Pr., 25 Beacon St., Boston, Massachusetts 02108-2800. (617) 742-2110. 1990. Covers environment, energy policy, population growth and other issues. It includes chapters on tropical rain forests, garbage, oceans and coasts, global warming, population growth, agriculture, biological diversity, fresh water, hazardous wastes, and environment and development.

Pira's International Environmental Information Sources. Pira, Randalls Rd., Leatherhead, England KT22 7RU. 0372 376161. 1990. Sourcebook includes over 2,000 entries from more than 20 countries, including Australia, Finland, Germany, the United Kingdom, and the United States. Entries are from organizations, research centers, legislative and regulatory bodies, directories, online databases and periodicals. Subject areas covered are: air, noise, water and land pollution, waste control and disposal, recycling, energy recovery and nature conservation.

Your Resource Guide to Environmental Organizations. John Seredich, ed. Smiling Dolphins Press, 4 Segura, Irvine, California 92715. 1991. Includes the purposes, programs, accomplishments, volunteer opportunities, publications and membership benefits of 150 environmental organizations.

ONLINE DATA BASES

AGRICOLA. U.S. Department of Agriculture, Office of Public Affairs, 14 Independence Ave., S.W., Washington, District of Columbia 20250. (202) 447-7454.

BIOSIS Previews. BIOSIS, 2100 Arch St., Philadelphia, Pennsylvania 19103-1399. (215) 587-4800. Largest and most comprehensive database of research in the life sciences. Contains citations for nearly 9000 primary research journals, monographs, reviews, symposia, preliminary reports, semi-popular journals, selected institutional reports, government reports and research communications.

Cambridge Scientific Abstracts Life Science–CSAL. Cambridge Scientific Abstracts, 5161 River Rd., Bethesda, Maryland 20816. (301) 961-6750. Provides access to the following abstracting services: "Life Sciences Collection," "Aquatic Sciences and Fisheries Abstracts," "Oceanic Abstracts," and "Pollution Abstracts."

Computerized Engineering Index–COMPENDEX. Engineering Information Inc., 345 E. 47th St., New York, New York 10017. (212) 705-7600.

Enviro/Energyline Abstracts Plus. R. R. Bowker Co., 121 Chanlon Rd., New Providence, New Jersey 07974. (908) 464-6800.

Environment Reporter. Bureau of National Affairs, 1231 25th St., N.W., Rm. 215, Washington, District of Columbia 20037. (800) 372-1033. Online version of periodical of the same name.

Environmental Business Journal. EnviroQuest, PO Box 371769, San Diego, California 92137. (619) 295-7685. Online access.

Environmental Periodicals Bibliography. National Information Services Corp., Ste. 6, Wyman Towers, 3100 St. Paul St., Baltimore, Maryland 21218. (410)243-0797. Online version of abstract of same name.

Monthly Catalog of United States Government Publications. U.S. G.P.O., Supt. of Docs., PO Box 371954, Pittsburgh, Pennsylvania 15250-7954. (202) 512-0000.

National Technical Information Service. U.S. Department of Commerce, National Technical Information Service, Office of Data Base Services, 5285 Port Royal Rd., Springfield, Virginia 22161. (703) 487-4807. Bibliographic database of government sponsored research and technical reports.

PHYTOMED. Biologische Bundesanstalt fuer Land-und Forstwirtschaft, Dokumentationsstelle fuer Phytomedizin, Koenign-Luise-Strasse 19, Berlin, Germany D-1000. 49 (30) 83041.

PressNet Environmental Reports. Chemical Information Systems, Inc., 7215 York Rd., Baltimore, Maryland 21212. (301) 321-8440.

SCISEARCH. Institute for Scientific Information, University City Science Center, 3501 Market St., Philadelphia, Pennsylvania 19104. (215) 386-0100.

SIRS Science CD-ROM. Social Issues Resources Series, Inc., PO Box 2348, Boca Raton, Florida 33427-2348. (407) 994-0079. Climatology, ecology, and oceanography.

PERIODICALS AND NEWSLETTERS

Agriculture, Ecosystems & Environment. Elsevier Science Publishing Co., 655 Avenue of the Americas, New York, New York 10010. (212) 989-5800. Eight times a year. This journal is concerned with the interaction of methods of agricultural production, ecosystems and the environment.

Agro-Ecosystems. Elsevier Science Publishing Co., 655 Avenue of the Americas, New York, New York 10010. (212) 989-5800. 1982-. Quarterly. Journal of International Association for Ecology featuring ecological interactions between agricultural and managed forest systems.

Alabama Conservation. Alabama Department of Conservation, 64 N. Union St., Montgomery, Alabama 36130. (205) 242-3151. 1929-. Bimonthly. Promotes the wise use of natural resources.

Alabama Department of Conservation Report. Alabama Department of Conservation, 64 N. Union St., Montgomery, Alabama 36130. (205) 242-3151. Annually.

Alaska Center for the Environment Center News. Alaska Center for the Environment, 700 H St., #4, Anchorage, Alaska 99501. (907) 274-3621. 1972-. Bimonthly. Topics deal with environmental education and Alaskan issues, land use, hazardous waste, etc.

Alberta Naturalist. Federation of Alberta Naturalists, Box 1472, Edmonton, Ontario, Canada 1971-. Quarterly.

Alert. Missouri Coalition for the Environment Foundation, 6267 Delmar Blvd., St. Louis, Missouri 63130. (314) 727-0600. 1969-. Quarterly. Published for the statewide environmental citizen activist organization.

Alternatives. University of Waterloo, Environmental Studies, ES1, Rm. 325, Waterloo, Ontario, Canada N2L 3G1. (519) 746-2031. 1971-. Quarterly. Perspectives on society, technology, and the environment. Professional and academic level information and theory.

Ambio: A Journal of the Human Environment. Royal Swedish Academy of Sciences. Pergamon Microforms International, Inc., Fairview Park, Elmsford, New York 10523. (914) 592-7720. 1971-. Monthly. Publishes recent work in the interrelated fields of environmental management, technology and the natural sciences.

American Environmental Laboratory. American Laboratory Postcard Deck, 30 Controls Dr., Box 870, Shelton, Connecticut 06484-0870. (203) 926-9310. 1989-. Bimonthly. Articles dealing with the collection and analysis of environmental samples, the development of instruments and the laboratories that use them.

The American Naturalist. Americana Society of Naturalists, Business Sciences, University of Kansas, Lawrence, Kansas 66045. (913) 864-3763. Monthly. Contains information by professionals of the biological sciences.

AMUSE-News. Amuse, Pearringron Post, Pittsboro, North Carolina 27312-8548. (919) 732-7306. 1982-. Quarterly. Medium for current information on arts and the environment.

Annual Editions: Environment. Dushkin Publishing Group, Sluice Dock, Guilford, Connecticut 06437. (203) 453-4351. 9th ed. This volume consists of articles compiled from the public press relating to the specific subject area.

Annual Review of Ecology and Systematics. Annual Reviews Inc., 4139 El Camino Way, Palo Alto, California 94303-0897. (800) 523-8635. 1970-. Annual. Original articles critically assessing the significant research literature in ecology and systematics.

Applied and Environmental Microbiology Journal. American Society for Microbiology, 1325 Massachusetts Avenue N.W., Washington, District of Columbia 20005. (202) 737-3600. Monthly. Articles on industrial and food microbiology and ecological studies.

Aquasphere. New England Aquarium, Central Wharf, Boston, Massachusetts 02110. (617) 742-8830. 1963. Articles on any subject related to the world of water. Emphasis on ecology, environment, and aquatic animals.

Archives of Clinical Ecology Journal. Clinical Ecology Publications, 3069 South Detroit Way, Denver, Colorado 80210. (303) 756-7880. Quarterly. Effects of the environment on human health.

Areas of Concern. Areas of Concern, Box 47, Bryn Mawr, Pennsylvania 19010. (215) 525-1129. 1971-. Monthly. Consumer, environmental and public affairs.

Audubon Society of Rhode Island Report. Audubon Society of Rhode Island, 12 Sanderson Rd., Smithfield, Rhode Island 02917. (401) 231-6444. 1966. Bimonthly. Covers current and historical natural history and ecology topics.

Baseline. W. S. Dept. of Ecology, Mail stop PV-11, Olympia, Washington 98504. (206) 459-6145. 1982-. Monthly. General information about ecology programs.

Biomedical and Environmental Sciences. Academic Press, 1250 6th Ave., San Diego, California 92101. (619) 699-6742. 1988-. Quarterly. International Journal with special emphasis on scientific data and information from China.

Bulletin of Society of Vector Ecologists. Society of Vector Ecologists, Box 87, Santa Ana, California 92702. (714) 971-2421. Twice a year. Covers disease prevention and control measures.

Bulletin of the Ecological Society of America. Arizona State University, Center for Environmental Studies, Tempe, Arizona 85287. (602) 965-3000.

Buzzworm: The Environmental Journal. Buzzworm Inc., 2305 Canyon Blvd., No. 206, Boulder, Colorado 80302-5655. (303) 442-1969. 1988-. Quarterly. An independent environmental journal for the reader interested in nature, adventure, travel, the natural environment and the issues of conservation.

C. E. C. Member's Report. Community Environmental Council, 930 Miramonte Dr., Santa Barbara, California 93109. Monthly. Newsletter about the community, its problems with environmental matters, etc.

Catalyst: Economics for the Living Earth. Catalyst Investing in Social Change, 64 Main St., Montpelier, Vermont 05602. (802) 223-7943. 1983-. Quarterly. Discusses grassroots enterprises working for social change and a humane economy. Focuses on ecological balance, articles on forest destruction, energy issues, native peoples issues and community- based economics.

CBE Environmental Review. Citizens for Better Environment, 407 S. Dearborn, Ste. 1775, Chicago, Illinois 60605. (312) 939-1530. 1975-. Quarterly. Documentation of environmental matters.

CENYC Environmental Bulletin. CENYC, 51 Cahmbers St., New York, New York 10007. (212) 566-0990. 1971-. Bimonthly. Environmental briefs of interest in New York City area residents.

CERP. Dana Silk, ed. UNESCO, 7, place de Fontenoy, Paris, France F-75700. (331) 45 68 40 67. Discusses forest and agroforestry ecosystems, urban development and planning.

ChemEcology. Chemical Manufacturers Association, 2501 M St. NW, Washington, District of Columbia 20037. (202) 887-1100. Monthly. Articles on how the chemical industry deals with environmental issues.

Chemosphere: Chemistry, Biology and Toxicology as Related to Environmental Problems. Pergamon Microforms International, Inc., Fairview Park, Elmsford, New York 10523. (914) 592-7720. 1970-. Offers maximum dissemination of investigations related to the health and safety of every aspect of life. Environmental protection encompasses a very wide field and relies on scientific research in chemistry, biology, physics, toxicology and inter-related disciplines.

Children's Environment Quarterly. Center for Human Environments, 33 W. 42nd St., New York, New York 10036. (212) 790-4550. 1974-. Quarterly.

The Compendium Newsletter. Educational Communications, Box 351419, Los Angeles, California 90035. (310) 559-9160. 1972-. Bimonthly. Comprehensive summary of environmental issues and activities. National emphasis lists radio and TV shows produced by Educational Communications.

Down to Earth. Montana Environmental Information Center, Box 1184, Helena, Montana 59624. (406) 443-2520. Quarterly. Montana environmental news & concerns.

Duckological. Ducks Unlimited, 1 Waterfowl Way, Long Grove, Illinois 60047. (708) 438-4300. Bimonthly. Protection of ducks.

E Magazine. Earth Action Network, 28 Knight St., Norwalk, Connecticut 06851. (203) 854-5559. Bimonthly. News, information, and commentary on environmental issues.

EARR: Environment and Natural Resources. Academic Publishers, Box 786, Cooper Station, New York, New York 10276. (212) 206-8900. Monthly. All aspects of environmental and natural resources.

The Earth Care Annual. Russell Wild, ed. Rodale Press, 33 E. Minon St., Emmaus, Pennsylvania 18098. (215) 967-5171; (800) 322-6333. 1990-. Annually. Organized in alphabetical sections such as garbage, greenhouse effect, oceans, ozone, toxic waste, and wildlife, the annual presents environmental problems and offers innovative working solutions.

Earth First! Journal in Defense of Wilderness and Biodiversity. Earth First!, PO Box 5176, Missoula, Montana 59806. Eight/year.

Earth Island Journal. Earth Island Institute, 300 Broadway, #28, San Francisco, California 94133-3312. (415) 788-3666. Quarterly. Local news from around the world on environmental issues.

Earth Work. The Student Conservation Association Inc., PO Box 550, Charlestown, New Hampshire 03603-0550. (603) 826-4301. 1991-. Monthly. Articles focus on the people, agencies, and the nonprofit organizations that protect our parks, refuges, forests and other lands. Carries a special feature entitled JobScan which provides the most comprehensive listing of natural resource and environmental job opportunities anywhere.

Earthstewards Network News. Holyearth Foundation, Box 10697, Winslow, Washington 98110. (206) 842-7986. Bimonthly.

Earthwatch Magazine. Earthwatch Expeditions, 680 Mt. Auburn St., Box 403, Watertown, Massachusetts 02272. (617) 926-8200. Bimonthly. Worldwide research expeditions, endangered species, cultures, and world health.

Eco-Humane Letter. International Ecology Society, 1471 Barcly St., St. Paul, Minnesota 55106-1405. (612) 774-4971. Irregular. Issues concerning animals, wildlife, and the environment.

Eco-News. Environmental Action Coalition, 625 Broadway, 2nd Fl., New York, New York 10012. (212) 677-1601. Monthly. Children's environmental newsletter on pollution, nature, and ecology.

Eco Newsletter. Antarctica Project, 218 D St., SE, Washington, District of Columbia 20003. (202) 544-2600. Quarterly. Conservation news.

Ecolert. Orba Information Ltd., 265 Cray St. W., Montreal, Quebec, Canada 1971-. Weekly.

Ecological Applications. Ecological Society of America, Center for Environmental Studies, Arizona State University, Tempe, Arizona 85287. (602) 965-3000. 1991-. Quarterly. Emphasizes the application of basic ecological concepts to a wide range of problems.

Ecological Engineering. The Journal of Ecotechnology. Elsevier Science Publishing Co., 655 Avenue of the Americas, New York, New York 10010. (212) 984-5800. 1992. Quarterly. Specific areas of coverage will include habitat reconstruction, rehabilitation, biomanipulation, restoration and conservation.

Ecological Modeling. Elsevier Science Publishing Co., Inc., Journal Information Ctr., 655 Ave. of the Americas, New York, New York 10010. Computer models used in environmentalist issues.

Ecological Monographs. Business Office of the Ecological Society of America, Center of Environmental Studies, Arizona State University, Tempe, Arizona 85287-1201. (602) 965-3000. Quarterly. Scientific journal of ecological issues.

Ecological Society of America Bulletin. Ecological Society of America, Center of Environmental Studies, Arizona State University, Tempe, Arizona 85287-1201. (602) 965-3000. Quarterly. Study of living things in relation to their environments.

Ecological Studies; Analysis and Synthesis. Springer-Verlag, 175 5th Ave., New York, New York 10010. (212) 460-1500. Quarterly.

Ecologie. Les Editions Humus, Inc., 4545 Pierre-de-Coubertin, Montreal, Quebec, Canada H1V 3R2. (514) 252-3148. Bimonthly. Environmental scientific and international information.

Ecologist. Tycooly Publishing International, Box C-166, Riverton, New Jersey 08077. Bimonthly. Magazine for environment and development.

Ecologist. MIT Press, 55 Hayward St., Cambridge, Massachusetts 02142. (617) 253-2889. Bimonthly. Man's impact on the biosphere and social, economic and political barriers.

Ecology. Ecological Society of America, Center of Environmental Studies, Arizona State University, Tempe, Arizona 85287-1201. (602) 965-3000. Bimonthly. Information on the study of living things.

Ecology Center Newsletter. Ecology Center, 2530 San Pablo Ave., Berkeley, California 94702. (510) 548-2220. Monthly. Politics and philosophy of the environment.

Ecology Digest. Ecology Digest, Box 60961, Sacramento, California 95860. (916) 961-2942. Quarterly. Articles on environmental and political issues.

Ecology International. INTECOL–International Association for Ecology, c/o Institute of Ecology, University of Georgia, Athens, Georgia 30602. (404) 542-2968. Semi-annual.

Ecology Reports. Ecology Center of Ann Arbor, 417 Detroit St., Ann Arbor, Michigan 48104. (313) 461-3186. Ten times a year. Environmental awareness through local and state research and education.

Ecology USA. Business Publishers, Inc., 951 Pershing Dr., Silver Spring, Maryland 20910-4464. (301) 587-6300. 1972-. Biweekly. Contains all the legislation, regulation, and litigation affecting efforts to conserve and protect America's unique environmental and ecological heritage.

Ecolution: The Eco Home Newsletter. Eco Home Network, 4344 Russell Ave., Los Angeles, California 90027. (213) 662-5207. Bimonthly. News of pollution and abatement.

Ecomod. ISEM–North America Chapter, Water Quality Division, South Florida Water Management District, P.O. Box 24608, West Palm Beach, Florida 33416. (407) 686-8800. Monthly. Current events in ecological and environmental modeling.

Econews. Northcoast Environmental Center, 879 Ninth St., Arcata, California 95521. (707) 822-6918. Eleven times a year. Environmental news focusing on northwestern California.

Economic News Notes. National Association of Home Builders, 15th & M St., N.W., Washington, District of Columbia 20005. (202) 822-0434. Monthly.

Ecosphere. Forum International, 91 Gregory Ln., Ste. 21, Pleasant Hill, California 94523. (510) 671-2900. Bi-

monthly. Eco-development, ecology, ecosystems, interface between culture-environment-tourism.

Ecotoxicology and Environmental Safety. Academic Press, c/o Harcourt Brace Jovanovich Inc., 6277 Sea Harbor Dr., Orlando, Florida 32887. (800) 346-8648. 1977-. Bimonthly.

The Eleventh Commandment: Toward an Ethic of Ecology. Eleventh Commandment Fellowship, PO Box 14667, San Francisco, California 94114. (415) 626-6064. Semi-annual.

Emergency Preparedness News. Business Publishers, Inc., 951 Pershing Drive, Silver Spring, Maryland 20910. (301) 587-6300. Biweekly. Emergency management techniques and technologies.

ENFO. 1251-B Miller Ave., Winter Park, Florida 32789-4827. (407) 644-5377. Bimonthly. Water resources, parks, wildlife air quality, growth management, government and private actions.

Environ: A Magazine for Ecological Living & Health Wary. Canary Press, Box 2204, Ft. Collins, Colorado 80522. (303) 224-0083. Quarterly. Consumer alternatives for ecologically sound lifestyles.

Environews. New York State Dept. of Law Environmental Protection Bureau, 2 World Trade Center, Rm. 4772, New York, New York 10048. (212) 341-2246. Bimonthly. News of environmental issues.

Environment. Scientists Institute for Public Information, 560 Trinity Ave., St. Louis, Missouri 63130. 1958-. Monthly. Formerly Scientist and Citizen.

Environment Careers. PH Publishing, Inc., 760 Whalers Way, STE. 100-A, Fort Collins, Colorado 80525. (303) 229-0029. Monthly. Career opportunities in the field.

Environment Report. Trends Publishing, Inc., 1079 National Press Bldg., Washington, District of Columbia 20045. (202) 393-0031. Semimonthly. Developments in environment, ecology and pollution abatement, with emphasis on policy, research, and development.

Environment Reporter. Bureau of National Affairs, 1231 25th St. NW, Washington, District of Columbia 20037. (800) 372-1033. Weekly. Issues of pollution control and environmental activity. Also available online.

Environmental Business Journal. EnviroQuest, PO Box 371769, San Diego, California 92137. (619) 295-7685. Monthly. Products relating to environmental protection.

Environmental Communicator. North American Association for Environmental Education, P.O. Box 400, Troy, Ohio 45373. (513) 339-6835. Bimonthly. Information on environmental topics and teaching methods.

Environmental Defense Fund Letter. Environmental Defense Fund, 257 Park Avenue South, New York, New York 10010. (212) 505-2100. 1971-. Bimonthly. Environmental issues of concern.

Environmental Entomology. Entomological Society of America, 9301 Annapolis Road, Lanham, Maryland 20706. (301) 731-4538. Bimonthly. Covers ecology and population dynamics.

Environmental History Newsletter. American Society for Environmental History, 6727 College Station, Duke University, History Dept., Durham, North Carolina 27708. (303) 871-2347. Quarterly.

Environmental Hotline. Devel Associated, Inc., 7208 Jefferson St., N.E., Albuquerque, New Mexico 87109. (505) 345-8732. Monthly. Regulations and analysis of key environmental issues.

Environmental Professional. National Association of Environmental Professionals, P.O. Box 15210, Alexandria, Virginia 22309-0210. (703) 660-2364. Quarterly. Covers effective impact assessment, regulation, and environmental protection.

Environmental Progress. American Institute of Chemical Engineers, 345 E. 47th St., New York, New York 10017. (212) 705-7338. Quarterly. Deals with environmental policies, protection and management-especially relating to chemicals.

Environmental Review. American Society for Environmental History, Department of History, University of Oregon, Corvallis, Oregon 97331. Quarterly. Covers human ecology as seen through history and the humanities.

Environmental Studies & Practice: An Educational Resource and Forum. Yale School of Forestry and Environmental Studies, 205 Prospect St., New Haven, Connecticut 06511. (203) 432-5132. 1991. Bimonthly. Subject matters range widely from air pollution to wildlife biology. Each issue contains a selection of recent publications, from all subject areas of environmental and natural resources management.

Environments. Faculty of Environmental Studies, University of Waterloo, Waterloo, Ontario, Canada N2L 3G1. (519) 885-1211. Three times a year. People in manmade and natural environments.

EPA Bulletin. U.S. Environmental Protection Agency, 401 M St., S.W., A-107, Washington, District of Columbia 20460. (202) 755-0890. Monthly. News of conservation and legislation.

EPA Journal. U.S. Environmental Protection Agency, 401 M St., S.W., A-107, Washington, District of Columbia 20460. (202) 382-4393. Bimonthly. Air and water pollution, pesticides, noise, solid waste.

EPA Publications Bibliography Quarterly. 5285 Port Royal Rd., Springfield, Virginia 22161. (703) 487-4650. Quarterly. Literary reviews of books and articles.

Everyone's Back Yard. Citizen's Clearinghouse for Hazardous Wastes, P.O. Box 926, Arlington, Virginia 22216. (703) 276-7070. Bimonthly. Contains news, views, and resources for grassroots environmental activists.

FPIRG Citizen Agenda. Florida Public Interest Research Group, 1441 E Fletcher Ave., Ste. 2200-3, Tampa, Florida 33612. (813) 971-7564. Citizen actions for environmental protection.

Global Ecology and Biogeography Letter. Blackwell Scientific Publications, 3 Cambridge Ctr., Suite 208, Cambridge, Massachusetts 02142. (617) 225-0401. 1991. Bimonthly. Global Ecology and Biogeography Letters is a sister publication of Journal of Biogeography and is only available with a subscription to the Journal. Provides a fast-track outlet for short research papers, news items, editorials, and book reviews. Topics related to the major scientific concerns of our present era, such as global warming, world sea-level rises, environmental acidification, development and conservation, biodiversity, and important new theories and themes in biogeography and ecology.

The Great Basin Naturalist. Brigham Young University, 290 Life Science Museum, Provo, Utah 84602. (801) 378-5053.

Green Letter. Green Letter, Box 9242, Berkeley, California 94709. Bimonthly. Information about the worldwide green movement.

Green Library Journal: Environmental Topics in the Information World. Maria A. Jankowska, ed. Green Library, University of Idaho Library, Moscow, Idaho 83843. (208) 885-6260. Jan 1992-. Scope of the journal would include information sources about: conservation, ecologically balanced regional development, environmental protection, natural resources management, environmental issues in libraries, publishing industries, and information science.

Green Light News. Green Light News, Box 12, Liberty Sq., Ellenville, New York 12428. (914) 647-3300. Monthly. Ecology news.

Green Party News. Green Party of B.C., 831 Commercial Dr., Vancouver, British Columbia, Canada V5L. (604) 254-8165. Quarterly. Covers environmental politics in British Columbia.

Greenletter. Woodstock Resort, Woodstock Inn, Woodstock, Vermont 05091-1298. (802) 457-1100. Quarterly. Ecological and environmental topics.

The Hudson Valley Green Times. Hudson Valley Grass Roots Energy and Environment Network, 30 E. Market St., P.O. Box 208, Red Hook, New York 12571. (914) 758-4484. Bimonthly. Energy and environment news with emphasis on Hudson Valley.

Journal of Biogeography. Blackwell Scientific Publications Inc., 3 Cambridge Ctr., Suite 208, Cambridge, Massachusetts 02142. (617) 225-0401.

Journal of Chemical Ecology. Plenum Press, 233 Spring St., New York, New York 10013-1578. (212) 620-8000. Monthly. Articles on the origin, function, and significance of natural chemicals.

Journal of Environmental Quality. American Society of Agronomy, 677 S. Segoe Rd., Madison, Wisconsin 53711-1086. (608) 273-8080. 1972-. Quarterly. Reports and brief reviews of agricultural ecology, environmental engineering and pollution.

Journal of Environmental Science and Health. Marcel Dekker, Inc., 270 Madison Ave., New York, New York 10016. (212) 696-9000. Bimonthly. Concerns pesticides, food contaminants, chemical carcinogens, and agricultural wastes.

Journal of Environmental Sciences. Institute of Environmental Sciences, 940 East Northwest Highway, Mt. Prospect, Illinois 60656. (312) 255-1561. Bimonthly. Covers research, controlling and teaching of environmental sciences.

The Journal of Social Ecology. Institute for Social Ecology, P.O. Box 89, Plainfield, Vermont 05667. 1983-. Issues relating to human ecology.

The Journal of Wildlife Management. The Wildlife Society, 5410 Grosvenor Ln., Bethesda, Maryland 20814. (301) 897-9770. Quarterly. Covers wildlife management and research.

Maine Environment. Natural Resource Council of Maine, 20 Willow St., Augusta, Maine 04330. 1974-. Monthly. Environmental activities and problems in Maine.

Maine Environment Systems. A.S.M.E.R., PO Box 57, Orangeburg, New York 10962. (914) 634-8221. Bimonthly. Synergy between behavioral researchers and the design profession.

Man-Environment Systems. Association for the Study of Man-Environment Relations, PO Box 57, Orangeburg, New York 10962. (914) 634-8221. Bimonthly.

Mazingira: The World Forum for Environment and Development. UNIPUB, 4611-F Assembly Dr., Lanham, Maryland 20706-4391. (301) 459-7666 or (800) 274-4888. Quarterly. Impact of economic growth on environment.

MoPIRG Reports. Missouri Public Interest Research Group, Box 8276, St. Louis, Missouri 63156. (314) 534-7474. Quarterly. Consumer/environmental citizen advocacy.

Nature and Resources. Elsevier Science Publishing Co., 655 Avenue of the Americas, New York, New York 10010. (212) 989-5800. 1965-. Quarterly. Provides indepth reviews of contemporary environmental issues from an international perspective.

Network News. World Environment Center, 419 Park Avenue South, Suite 1403, New York, New York 10016. (212) 683-4700. Quarterly. Covers international environmental issues.

The New Cubicle: A Magazine about Man and his Environment. De Young Press, Rte. 1, Box 76, Stark, Kansas 66775. (316) 754-3203. Monthly. Environmental magazine covering political, sociological, and legal issues.

New England Environmental Network News. Lincoln Filene Center for Citizenship, Civic Education Foundation/Tufts, Medford, Massachusetts 02155. (617) 381-3451. Quarterly. State environmental news.

News Net. UN-NGLS, 2 UN Plaza, #DC2-1103, New York, New York 10017. (212) 963-3125. Environment & development issues.

NJPIRG. New Jersey Public Interest Research Group, 99 Bayard St., New Brunswick, New Jersey 08901-2120. Semiannual. Consumer & environmental advocacy actions.

North Carolina Environmental Bulletin. North Carolina Office of Intergovernmental Relations, 116 W. Jones St., Raleigh, North Carolina 27603. Monthly. State environmental news.

Northeastern Environmental Science. Northeastern Science Foundation, Box 746, Troy, New York 12181. (518) 273-3247. Semiannual. Environmental research & policies.

NRDC Newsline. Natural Resources Defense Council, 40 W. 20th St., 11th Fl., New York, New York 10011. (212) 949-0049. Bimonthly. Enforcement news.

NYS Environment. New York State Dept. of Environmental Conservation, 50 Wolf Rd., Albany, New York 12233. (518) 457-2344. Biweekly. Controversial environmental issues in legislation.

Oecologia. Springer-Verlag, 175 5th Ave., New York, New York 10010. (212) 460-1500. Monthly. Devoted to aquatic ecology.

Ohio Environmental Report. Ohio Environmental Council, 22 E. Gay St., # 300, Columbus, Ohio 43215. (614) 224-4900. Monthly. News on environmental issues and projects in Ohio.

One World. Trans-Species Unlimited, Box 1553, Williamsport, Pennsylvania 17703. (717) 322-3252. Irregular. Vegetarianism and animal rights.

Outdoors Unlittered Pitch-In News. Outdoors Unlittered, 200-1676 Martin Dr., White Rock, British Columbia, Canada V4A 6E7. (403) 429-0517. Semiannually. Solid waste and litter problems

Pollution Control Newsletter. Arizona State Dept. of Health Services, Bureau of Air Quality Control, 1740 W. Adams St., Phoenix, Arizona 85007. (602) 542-1000. Eight times a year.

Protection Ecology. Elsevier Science Publishing Co., Journal Information Center, 655 Avenue of the Americas, New York, New York 10010. (212) 989-5800. Livestock and agricultural ecology and pest control.

Sierra Club Bulletin. Sierra Club Books, 100 Bush St., San Francisco, California 94104. (415) 291-1600. 1893-. Ten times a year.

Sierra Magazine. Sierra Club Books, 100 Bush St., San Francisco, California 94104. (415) 291-1600. Bimonthly. Covers the environment and ecological systems.

Sunrise. International Ecology Society, 1471 Barclay St., St. Paul, Minnesota 55106-1405. (612) 774-4971. Monthly.

Tennessee Environmental Council Newsletter. Tennessee Environmental Council, 1725 Church St., Nashville, Tennessee 37203-2921. (615) 321-5075.

Utah Environmental News. Utah State Division of Health, 44 Medical Drive, Salt Lake City, Utah 84113.

World Resource Review. SUPCON International, PO Box 5275, 1 Heritage Plaza, Woodridge, Illinois 60517. (708) 910-1551. 1981-. Quarterly. Covers all phases of policy discussions and their developments, including such topics as global change, energy production and use, ecosystem impacts of development activities, environmental law, solution of transnational environmental problems, global flow of strategic industrial materials, regional, national, and local resource management, natural resources, food, agriculture and forestry.

RESEARCH CENTERS AND INSTITUTES

Alaska Cooperative Fishery and Wildlife Research Unit. 138 Arctic Health Research Unit, University of Alaska-Fairbanks, Fairbanks, Alaska 99775-0110. (907) 474-7661.

Albion College, Whitehouse Nature Center. Albion, Michigan 49224. (517) 629-2030.

Archie Carr Center for Sea Turtle Research. University of Florida, Department of Zoology, Gainesville, Florida 32611. (904) 392-5194.

Atlantic Center for the Environment. 39 S. Main St., Ipswich, Massachusetts 01938. (508) 356-0038.

Botanical Herbarium. University of Cincinnati, Department of Biological Sciences, Cincinnati, Ohio 45221-0006. (513) 556-9761.

California Institute of Public Affairs. P.O. Box 10, Claremont, California 91711. (714) 624-5212.

Comparative Behavior Laboratory. University of Florida, Florida Museum of Natural History, Gainesville, Florida 32611. (904) 392-6570.

Coolidge Center for Environmental Leadership. 1675 Massachusetts Ave., Suite 4, Cambridge, Massachusetts 02138. (617) 864-5085.

Ecology Action Educational Institute. Box 3895, Modesto, California 95352. (209) 576-0739.

Ecology Center. 2530 San Pablo Ave., Berkeley, California 94702. (510) 548-2220.

Long-Term Ecological Research Project. University of Colorado-Boulder, CB 450, Boulder, Colorado 80309. (303) 492-6198.

Marine Cooperative Fish and Wildlife Research Unit. U.S. Fish and Wildlife Service, 240 Nutting Hall, University of Maine, Orono, Maine 04469. (207) 581-2870.

Marsh Botanical Garden. Yale University, PO Box 6666, Biology Department, New Haven, Connecticut 06511-8112. (203) 432-3906.

Michigan State University, W.K. Kellogg Biological Station. 3700 East Gull Lake Drive, Hickory Corners, Michigan 49060. (616) 671-5117.

Mississippi State University, Mississippi Remote Sensing Center. P.O. Box FR, Mississippi State, Mississippi 39762. (601) 325-3279.

Mount Evans Field Station. University of Denver, 16 Colorado Highway 5, Idaho Springs, Colorado 80452. (303) 871-3540.

Mountain Research Station. University of Colorado-Boulder, 818 County Road 116, Nederland, Colorado 80466. (303) 492-8841.

Mt. Desert Island Biological Laboratory. Salsbury Cove, Maine 04672. (207) 288-3605.

National Park Service Cooperative Unit. Institute of Ecology, University of Georgia, Athens, Georgia 30602. (404) 542-8301.

New York University, Laboratory of Microbial Ecology. 735 Brown Building, New York, New York 10003. (212) 998-8268.

Ohio Biological Survey. Biological Sciences Building, Ohio State University, 1315 Kinnear Rd., Columbus, Ohio 43212-1192. (614) 292-9645.

Ohio State University, Acarology Laboratory. 484 West 12th Avenue, Columbus, Ohio 43210. (614) 292-7180.

Ohio State University, Franz Theodore Stone Laboratory. 1541 Research Center, 1314 Kinnear Road, Columbus, Ohio 43212. (614) 292-8949.

Ohio State University, Ohio Cooperative Fish and Wildlife Research Unit. 1735 Neil Avenue, Columbus, Ohio 43210. (614) 292-6112.

Pennsylvania State University, Center for Statistical Ecology and Environmental Statistics. Department of Statistics, 303 Pond Laboratory, University Park, Pennsylvania 16802. (814) 865-9442.

Philip L. Boyd Deep Canyon Desert Research Center. University of California, Riverside, PO Box 1738, Palm Desert, California 92261. (619) 341-3655.

Rockefeller University, Field Research Center for Ecology and Ethology. Tyrrel Road, Millbrook, New York 12545. (212) 570-8628.

San Diego State University, Systems Ecology Research Group. San Diego, California 92182. (619) 594-5976.

Shippensburg University, Vertebrate Museum. Franklin Science Center, Shippensburg, Pennsylvania 17257. (714) 532-1407.

Southwestern Research Station. American Museum of Natural History, Portal, Arizona 85632. (602) 558-2396.

St. Catherine's Island Research Program. Office of Grants and Fellowships, American Museum of Natural History, Central Park West at 79th Street, New York, New York 10024. (212) 873-1300.

State Univerity of New York College of Environmental Science and Forestry. Adirondak Ecological Center, Huntington Forest, Newcomb, New York 12852. (518) 582-4551.

State University of New York at Oneonta, Biological Field Station. RD 2, Box 1066, Cooperstown, New York 13326. (607) 547-8778.

State University of New York at Stony Brook, Ecology Laboratory. Stony Brook, New York 11797-5245. (516) 623-8600.

Stroud Water Research Center. 512 Spencer Road, Avondale, Pennsylvania 19311. (215) 268-2153.

Tall Timbers Research Station. R.R. 1, Box 678, Tallahassee, Florida 32312. (904) 893-4153.

Texas Tech University, Brush Control Research Center. Goddard Range and Wildlife Building, Lubbock, Texas 79409. (806) 742-2841.

U.S. Forest Service, Forestry Sciences Laboratory. I-26 Agricultural Building, University of Missouri- Columbia, Columbia, Missouri 65211. (314) 875-5341.

U.S. Forest Service, Forestry Sciences Laboratory. 1221 South Main Street, Moscow, Idaho 83843. (208) 882-3557.

U.S. Forest Service, Institute of Northern Forestry. 308 Tanana Drive, University of Alaska, Fairbanks, Alaska 99775-5500. (907) 474-8163.

U.S. Forest Service, San Joaquin Experimental Range. 24075 Highway 41, Coarsegold, California 93614. (209) 868-3349.

University of Alabama, Arboretum. Box 870344, Tuscaloosa, Alabama 35487-0344. (205) 553-3278.

University of Georgia, Institute of Ecology. 103 Ecology Building, Athens, Georgia 30602. (404) 542-2968.

University of Georgia, Savanna River Ecology Laboratory. P.O. Box Drawer E, Aiken, South Carolina 29801. (803) 725-2472.

University of Guam. Marine Laboratory, UOG Station, Guam 96923. (671) 734-2421.

University of Hawaii at Manoa, Environmental Center. 2550 Campus Road, Honolulu, Hawaii 96822. (808) 956-7361.

University of Houston Coastal Center. c/o Office of the Senior Vice President, Houston, Texas 77204-5502. (713) 749-2351.

University of Iowa, Iowa Lakeside Laboratory. R.R. 2, Box 305, Milford, Iowa 51351. (712) 337-3669.

University of Kansas, Fitch Natural History Reservation. Lawrence, Kansas 66044. (913) 843-3612.

University of Kansas, Kansas Biological Survey. 2041 Constant Avenue-Foley Hall, Lawrence, Kansas 66047-2906. (913) 864-7725.

University of Kansas, Kansas Ecological Reserves. Lawrence, Kansas 66045. (913) 864-3236.

University of Kansas, McGregor Herbarium. Joseph S. Bridwell Botanical Research Laboratory, 2045 Constant Ave., Campus West, Lawrence, Kansas 66047. (913) 864-4493.

University of Kansas, Museum of Natural History. Dyche Hall, Lawrence, Kansas 66045. (913) 864-4541.

University of Michigan, Biological Station. Pellston, Michigan 49769. (616) 539-8406.

University of Michigan, Matthaei Botanical Gardens. 1800 North Dixboro Road, Ann Arbor, Michigan 48105. (313) 763-7060.

University of Michigan, Nichols Arboretum. Ann Arbor, Michigan 48109-1115. (313) 763-9315.

University of Minnesota, Bell Museum of Natural History. 10 Church St., S.E., Minneapolis, Minnesota 55455. (612) 624-4112.

University of Minnesota, Cedar Creek Natural History Area. 2660 Fawn Lake Drive NE, Bethel, Minnesota 55005. (612) 434-5131.

University of Minnesota, Cloquet Forestry Center. 175 University Road, Cloquet, Minnesota 55720. (218) 879-0850.

University of Minnesota, Lake Itasca Forestry and Biological Station. Post Office, Lake Itasca, Minnesota 56460. (218) 266-3345.

University of Missouri-Columbia, Clair L. Kucera Research Station At Tucker Prairie. Columbia, Missouri 65211. (314) 882-7541.

University of North Dakota, Institute for Ecological Studies. Box 8278, University Station, Grand Forks, North Dakota 58202. (701) 777-2851.

University of Oklahoma, Biological Station. Star Route B, Kingston, Oklahoma 73439. (405) 564-2463.

University of Oregon, Herbarium. Department of Biology, Eugene, Oregon 97403. (503) 346-3033.

University of Texas at Arlington, Center for Corbicula Research. Department of Biology, P.O.Box 19498, Arlington, Texas 76019. (817) 273-2412.

University of Texas at Austin, Brackenridge Field Laboratory. Lake Austin Boulevard, Austin, Texas 78712. (512) 471-7131.

University of Texas at Austin, Texas Natural History Laboratory. Texas Memorial Museum, 2400 Trinity, Austin, Texas 78705. (512) 471-5302.

University of Wisconsin-Madison, Center for Biotic Systems. 1042 WARF Office Building, 610 Walnut Street, Madison, Wisconsin 53705. (608) 262-9937.

University of Wisconsin-Madison, Center for Human Systems. 1042 WARF Building, 610 North Walnut Street, Madison, Wisconsin 53705. (608) 262-9937.

University of Wisconsin-Madison, Center for Restoration Ecology. Arboretum, 1207 Seminole Highway, Madison, Wisconsin 53711. (608) 263-7889.

University of Wisconsin-Madison, Marine Studies Centers. Department of Botany, 132 Birge Hall, Madison, Wisconsin 53706. (608) 262-1057.

University of Wisconsin-Milwaukee, Field Station. 3095 Blue Goose Road, Saukville, Wisconsin 53080. (414) 675-6844.

USDA Biological Control of Insects Research Laboratory. P.O. Box 7629, Columbia, Missouri 65205. (314) 875-5361.

Utah State University, Ecology Center. Logan, Utah 84322-5200. (801) 750-2555.

STATISTICS SOURCES

Ecology: Community Profiles. U.S. Fish and Wildlife Service. National Technical Information Service, 5285 Port Royal Road, Springfield, Virginia 22161. (703) 487-4650. Irregular. Data on coastal and inland ecosystems, including wetlands, tidal-flats, near-shore seagrasses, sand dunes, drilling platforms, oyster reefs, estuaries, rivers and streams.

Statistical Record of the Environment. Arsen J. Darnay. Gale Research Inc., 835 Penobscot Bldg., Detroit, Michigan 48226-4094. (313) 961-2242. 1992.

TRADE ASSOCIATIONS AND PROFESSIONAL SOCIETIES

American Institute of Biological Sciences. 730 11th St., N.W., Washington, District of Columbia 20001-4521. (202) 628-1500.

American Nature Study Society. 5881 Cold Brook Rd., Homer, New York 13077. (607) 749-3655.

American Society for Environmental History. Center for Technical Studies, New Jersey Institute of Technology, Newark, New Jersey 07102. (201) 596-3270.

American Society of Civil Engineers. 345 East 47th St., New York, New York 10017. (212) 705-7496.

American Society of Naturalists. Department of Ecology and Evolation, State University of New York, Stony Brook, New York 11794. (516) 632-8589.

Americans for the Environment. 1400 16th St. N.W., Washington, District of Columbia 20036. (202) 797-6665.

Association for the Study of Man-Environment Relations. Box 57, Orangeburg, New York 10962. (914) 634-8221.

Bat Conservation International. PO Box 162603, Austin, Texas 78716. (512) 327-9721. Bat Conservation International was established to educate people about the important role that bats play in the environment.

Center for Religion, Ethics and Social Policy. Anabel Taylor Hall, Cornell University, Ithaca, New York 14853. (607) 255-6486.

Chemical Manufacturers Association. 2501 M St., N.W., Washington, District of Columbia 20037. (202) 887-1100.

Cosanti Foundation. HC 74, Box 4136, Mayer, Arizona 86333. (602) 632-7135.

Ducks Unlimited. 1 Waterfowl Way, Long Grove, Illinois 60047. (708) 438-4300.

Earth Ecology Foundation. 612 N. 2nd St., Fresno, California 93702. (209) 442-3034.

Earth First!. PO Box 5176, Missoula, Montana 59806.

Earth Island Institute. 300 Broadway, Suite 28, San Francisco, California 94133. (415) 788-3666.

Earth Society Foundation. 585 Fifth Ave., New York, New York 10017. (718) 574-3059.

Earthwatch. 680 Mt. Auburn St., P.O. Box 403, Watertown, Massachusetts 02272. (617) 926-8200.

Ecological Society of America. Arizona State University, Center for Environmental Studies, Tempe, Arizona 85287. (602) 965-3000.

Eleventh Commandment Fellowship. P.O. Box 14667, San Francisco, California 94114. (415) 626-6064.

Environic Foundation International. 916 St. Vincent St., South Bend, Indiana 46617. (219) 259-9976.

Environmental & Energy Study Institute. 122 C St., N.W., Suite 700, Washington, District of Columbia 20001. (202) 628-1400.

Environmental Defense Fund. 257 Park Ave., S., New York, New York 10010. (212) 505-2100. Non-profit organization that was established more than 20 years ago. Its goals are to protect the earth's environment by providing lasting solutions to global environmental problems.

Federation of Western Outdoor Clubs. 365 K St. N.W., Ste. 400, Seattle, Washington 98102. (206) 322-3050.

Global Tomorrow Coalition. 1325 G St., N.W., Suite 915, Washington, District of Columbia 20005-3103. (202) 628-4016.

Green Committees of Correspondence. P.O. Box 30208, Kansas City, Missouri 64112. (816) 931-9366.

Greenpeace. 1436 U St., NW, Washington, District of Columbia 20009. (202) 462-1177.

The Human Ecology Action League, Inc. P.O. Box 49126, Atlanta, Georgia 30359-1126. (404) 248-1898.

Human Environment Center. 1001 Connecticut Ave., N.W., Ste. 827, Washington, District of Columbia 20003. (202) 331-8387.

Institute for Community Economic and Ecological Development. 1807 2nd St., Santa Fe, New Mexico 87501. (505) 986-1401.

INTECOL–International Association for Ecology. Drawer E, Aiken, South Carolina 29802. (803) 725-2472.

International Association for Ecology. Institute of Ecology, University of Georgia, Athens, Georgia 30606. (404) 542-2968.

International Association for the Advancement of Earth & Environmental Sciences. Northeastern Illinois University, Geography & Environmental Studies, 5500 N. St. Louis Ave., Chicago, Illinois 60625. (312) 794-2628.

International Commission on Human Ecology and Ethnology. Box 3495, Grand Central Station, New York, New York 10163.

International Ecology Society. 1471 Barclay St., St. Paul, Minnesota 55106. (612) 774-4971.

International Society for Ecological Modeling/North American Chapter. Water Quality Division, South Florida Water Management District, PO Box 24680, West Palm Beach, Florida 33416. (407) 686-8800.

International Society of Chemical Ecology. University of South Florida, Dept. of Biology, Tampa, Florida 33620. (813) 974-2336.

John Muir Institute for Environmental Studies. 743 Wilson St., Napa, California 94559. (707) 252-8333.

League for Ecological Democracy. P.O. Box 1858, San Pedro, California 90733. (213) 833-2633.

National Audubon Society. 950 Third Ave., New York, New York 10022. (212) 832-3200.

Organization of Biological Field Stations. Box 351, Eureka, Missouri 63025. (314) 938-5346.

Outdoor Ethics Guild. c/o Bruce Bandurski, General Delivery, Bucks Harbor, Maine 04618.

Outdoor Writers Association of America. 2017 Cato Ave., Suite 101, State College, Pennsylvania 16801. (814) 234-1011.

Planet Drum. Box 31251, San Francisco, California 94131. (415) 285-6556.

The Prairie Club. 940 Lee St., Suite 204, Des Plaines, Illinois 60016. (708) 299-8402.

Safari Club International. 4800 W. Gates Pass Rd., Tucson, Arizona 85745. (602) 620-1220.

Sierra Club. 100 Bush St., San Francisco, California 94104. (415) 291-1600.

Smithsonian Institution. National Museum of Natural History, NHB-106, Washington, District of Columbia 20560. (202) 786-2821.

Society for Ecological Restoration. 1207 Seminole Hwy., Madison, Wisconsin 53711. (608) 262-9547.

Society of Vector Ecologists. Box 87, Santa Anna, California 92702. (714) 971-2421.

Thorne Ecological Institute. 5398 Manhattan Circle, Boulder, Colorado 80303. (303) 499-3647.

Threshold, International Center for Environmental Renewal. Drawer CU, Bisbee, Arizona 85603. (602) 432-7353.

United Nations Information Centre. 1889 F St. N.W., Ground Floor, Washington, District of Columbia 20006. (202) 289-8670.

United States Operating Committee on ETAD. 1330 Connecticut Ave., N.W., Suite 300, Washington, District of Columbia 20036-1702. (202) 659-0060.

United States Public Interest Research Group. 215 Pennsylvania Ave., SE, Washington, District of Columbia 20003. (202) 546-9707.

World Future Society. 4916 St. Elmo Ave., Bethesda, Maryland 20814. (301) 656-8274.

ECOLOGY, TROPICAL

See: TROPICAL ECOLOGY

ECONOMICS, ENVIRONMENTAL

ABSTRACTING AND INDEXING SERVICES

Applied Ecology Abstracts Studies in Renewable Natural Resources. Information Retrieval Ltd., 1911 Jefferson Davis Highway, Arlington, Virginia 22202. 1975-. Monthly.

Applied Science and Technology Index. H.W. Wilson Co., 950 University Ave., Bronx, New York 10452. (800) 367-6770. Formerly Industrial Arts Index.

Current Advances in Ecological and Environmental Science. Pergamon Microforms International, Inc., Fairview Park, Elmsford, New York 10523. (914) 592-7720. 1989-. Monthly. Current literature searching service includingj-ournals, reports, abstracts, etc. This service is available online as part of the CABS database on the hosts BRS and ORBIT search service.

Environment Abstracts. Bowker A & I Publishing, 121 Chanlon Rd., New Providence, New Jersey 07974. (908) 464-6800. 1974-.

Environment Index. Environment Information Center, Index Research Department, 124 E. 39th St., New York, New York 10016. 1971-. Annual.

Environmental Information Connection–EIC. Planning Information Program, Dept. of Urban and Regional Planning, University of Illinois, 1003 West Nevada, Urbana, Illinois 61801. (217) 333-1369. Also available online.

Environmental Periodicals Bibliography. Environmental Studies Institute, International Academy at Santa Barbara, 800 Garden St., Suite D, Santa Barbara, California 93101. (805) 965-5010. Also available online.

General Science Index. H. W. Wilson Co., 950 University Ave., Bronx, New York 10452. 1978-. Monthly, also issued in annual cumulation. Cumulative subject index to English language periodicals in the subject fields of astronomy, botany, chemistry, earth science, environment and conservation, food and nutrition, genetics, mathematics, medicine and health, microbiology, oceanography, physics, physiology and zoology.

Geographical Abstracts. London School of Economics, Dept. of Geography, Regency House, 34 Duke St., London, England 1966-. Continued by Geo Abstracts issued in 6 parts: Pt. A. Landforms and the quaternary; Pt. B. Biogeography and Climatology; Pt. C. Economic geography; Pt. D. Social geography and cartography; Pt. E. Sedimentology; Pt. F. Regional and community planning.

Index to Scientific Book Contents. Institute for Scientific Information, 3501 Market St., Philadelphia, Pennsylvania 19104. (800) 523-1857. 1985-. Annual. Gives contents of science books published.

Mineralogical Abstracts. Mineralogical Society, 41 Queen's Gate, London, England SW7 5HR. 71 5847916. Quarterly. Abstracts of journal articles, conferences, technical reports and specialized books in the areas of minerals, clay minerals, economic minerals, ore deposits, environmental studies, experimental mineralogy, gemstones, geochemistry, petrology, lunar and planetary studies and other related areas in mineralogy.

Multimedia Index to Ecology. National Information Center for Educational Media, University of Southern California, Los Angeles, California 90007.

Sea Grant Abstracts. National Sea Grant Depository, Pell Laboratory Bldg., Bay Campus, University of Rhode Island, Narragansett, Rhode Island 02882. (401) 792-6114. 1986-. Quarterly. Published by the National Sea Grant Programs, this collection includes annual reports, serials and newsletters, charts and maps.

BIBLIOGRAPHIES

EPA Publications Bibliography. U.S. Environmental Protection Agency, Library Systems Branch, 401 M St., SW, Washington, District of Columbia 20460. (202) 260-2090. Quarterly.

DIRECTORIES

Directory of Environmental Investing. Michael Silverstein. Environmental Economics, 1026 Irving st., Philadelphia, Pennsylvania 19107. (215) 925-7168. Annual. Publicly-traded companies, plus Fortune 500 firms involved in environmental services.

Environmental Grantmaking Foundations. Environmental Data Research Institute, 797 Elmwood Avenue, Rochester, New York 14620-2946. (800) 724-0968. 1992. Fund raising for regional, state, and local organizations that work on environmental issues.

Environmental Industries Marketplace. Karen Napoleone Meech. Gale Research Inc., 835 Penobscot Bldg., Detroit, 48226-4904. (313) 961-2242. 1992.

Green Earth Resource Guide: A Comprehensive Guide About Environmentally Friendly Services and Products Books, Clean Air... Cheryl Gorder. Blue Bird Pub., 1713 East Broadway #306, Tempe, Arizona 85282. (602) 968-4088; (800) 654-1993. 1991. Book emphasizes positive steps we can take to help planets. Consists of two parts. Part one profiles people or businesses that are environmentally-friendly and are actively involved with projects and products; part two has resources listings of things concerned with environmental problems. Includes a company index with addresses and phone numbers.

ENCYCLOPEDIAS AND DICTIONARIES

The Life of Prairies and Plains. Durward Leon Allen. McGraw-Hill Science & Engineering Books, 11 W. 19th St., New York, New York 10011. (212) 337-6010. 1967.

Van Nostrand's Scientific Encyclopedia. Glenn D. Considine, ed. Van Nostrand Reinhold, 115 5th Ave., New

York, New York 10003. (212) 254-3232. 1983. Sixth edition. Includes all broad subject areas in science.

GENERAL WORKS

Air Pollution Emission Standards and Guidelines for Municipal Waste Combustors: Economic Analysis of Materials Separation Requirement. B. J. Morton, et al. National Technical Information Service, 5285 Port Royal Rd., Springfield, Virginia 22161. (703) 487-4650. 1990. Final report prepared by the Research Triangle Institute for the Center for Economics Research.

Analysis of Army Hazardous Waste Disposal Cost Data. B. J. Kim, et al. Construction Engineering Research Lab (Army), c/o National Technical Information Service, 5185 Port Royal Rd., Springfield, Virginia 22161. 1991. Order number: AD-A236 654/0LDM.

A Comparison of Disposable and Reusable Diapers. Kristin Rahenkamp. National Conference of State Legislatures, 1050 17th St., Suite 2100, Denver, Colorado 80265-2101. (303) 623-7800. 1990. Economics, environmental impacts and legislative options relating to diapers.

Costing the Earth. Frances Cairncross. The Economist Books, PO Box 87, Osney Mead, Oxford, England OX2 0DT. (44) 865 791155/794376.

Ecological Economics. Robert Costanza. Columbia University Press, 562 W. 113th Street, New York, New York 10025. (212) 316-7100. 1991. The science and management of sustainability.

Ecology, Economics, Ethics: The Broken Circle. Herbert R. Bormann and Stephen R. Kellert, eds. Yale University Press, 302 Temple St., New Haven, Connecticut 06520. (203) 432-0960. 1991. Addresses a wide range of concerns and offers practical remedies including: economic incentives for conservation, technical adaptations to use resources effectively; better accounting procedures for measuring the environmental system that better explains our responsibility to the environment.

Economics and Biological Diversity: Developing and Using Economic Incentives to Conserve Biological Resources. Jeffrey A. McNeely. Pinter Pub., 136 S. Broadway, Irvington, New York 10533. (914) 591-9111. 1991. Explains how economic incentives can be applied to conservation while complementing development efforts.

Economics of Natural Resources and the Environment. David W. Pearce. Johns Hopkins University Press, 701 W. 40th St., Suite 275, Baltimore, Maryland 21211. (410) 516-6900. 1990.

The Ecopolitics of Development in the Third World: Politics and Environment in Brazil. Roberto Pereira Guimaraes. L. Rienner Publishers, 1800 30th St, Suite 314, Boulder, Colorado 80301. (303) 444-6684. 1991. History of environmental policy in Brazil.

Ecopreneuring: The Complete Guide to Small Business Opportunities from the Environmental Revolution. Steven J. Bennett. John Wiley & Sons, Inc., 605 3rd Ave., New York, New York 10158-0012. (212) 850-6000. 1991. Covers opportunities in recycling, energy conservation, personal care products, safe foods, and investment services. Offers practical information, including market size, growth potential, and capital requirement. Provides a directory of resources.

Environmental Costs of Electricity. Richard L. Ottinger, et al. Oceana Publications Inc., 75 Main St., Dobbs Ferry, New York 10522. (914) 693-8100. 1990. Report reviews and analyzes the studies that have been made to quantify the external costs of environmental damages caused by electric supply and demand-reduction technologies. It reviews ways to incorporate these costs in electric utility planning, bid evaluation and resource selection procedures.

Environmental Investments: The Costs of a Clean Government. Island Press, 1718 Connecticut Ave. N.W., Suite 300, Washington, District of Columbia 20009. (202) 232-7933. 1991. Report tells industry what to expect in direct expenses for implementing pollution control measures and undertaking compliance activities for environmental laws.

Estimating Costs of Air Pollution Control. William M. Vatavuk. Lewis Publishers, 2000 Corporate Blvd., N.W., Boca Raton, Florida 33431. (407) 994-0555 or (800) 272-7737. 1990. Deals with information to select, size, and estimate budget/study level capital and annual costs for a variety of air pollution control equipment.

GAIA Connections: An Introduction to Ecology, Ecoethics and Economics. Alan S. Miller. Rowman & Littlefield, Publishers, Inc., 8705 Bollman Pl., Savage, Maryland 20763. (301) 306-0400. 1991. Synthesis of humanity's ethical and economic options in coping with the global environmental crisis.

The Green Consumer Supermarket Guide. Joel Makower, et al. Penguin Books, 375 Hudson St., New York, New York 10014. (212) 366-2000; (800) 253-2304. 1991. A buying guide to products that don't cost the earth.

Human Investment and Resource Use: A New Research Orientation at the Environment/Economics Interface. Michael Young and Natarajan Ishwaran, eds. UNESCO, 7, place de Fontenoy, Paris, France F-75700. (331) 45 68 40 67. 1989. Explores the issue of the environment/economics interface, parcularly the effect of the level and nature of human investments in determining the manner in which natural resources are utilized.

In the U.S. Interest: Resources, Growth, and Security in the Developing World. Janet Welsh Brown, ed. World Resources Institute, 1709 New York Ave. N.W., Washington, District of Columbia 20006. (800) 822-0504. 1990.

Linking the Natural Environment and the Economy: Essays the Eco-Eco Group. Carl Folke, ed. Kluwer Academic Publishers, 101 Philip Dr., Assinippi Park, Norwell, Massachusetts 02061. (617) 871-6600. 1991. Volume 1 of the series entitled Ecology, Economy and Environment.

Maintaining a Satisfactory Environment: At What Price?. N. Akerman, ed. Westview Press, 5500 Central Ave., Boulder, Colorado 80301. (303) 444-3541. 1990.

Nontoxic, Natural and Earthwise: How to Protect Yourself and Your Family from Harmful Products and Live in Harmony with the Earth. Debra Lynn Dadd. Jeremy P. Tarcher, 5858 Wilshire Blvd., Ste. 200, Los Angeles, California 90036. (213) 935-9980. 1990. Evaluation of household products and recommendations as to natural and homemade alternatives.

Out of the Channel: The Exxon Valdez Oil Spill in Prince William Sound. John Keeble. Harper & Row, 10 E. 53rd St., New York, New York 10022. (212) 207-7000. 1991.

Presents a detailed account of the disaster, its implications and ramifications.

Promoting Environmentally Sound Economic Progress: What the North Can Do. Robert Repetto. World Resources Institute, 1709 New York Ave. N.W., Washington, District of Columbia 20006. (800) 822-0504. 1990. Spells out actions that must be taken if the world economy is going to continue to develop and yet avoid the environmental degradation that threatens to undermine living standards.

Resource Accounting in Costa Rica. Wilfrido Cruz and Robert Repetto. World Resources Institute, 1709 New York Ave. N.W., Washington, District of Columbia 20006. (800) 822-0504. 1991.

The Solution to Pollution in the Workplace. Laurence Sombke, et al. MasterMedia, 17 E. 89th St., New York, New York 10028. (212) 348-2020. 1991. Non-technical guidebook for cost-effective, practical tips and actions to help businesses, big and small, take a proactive role in solving pollution problems.

Steady-State Economics. Herman E. Daly. Island Press, 1718 Connecticut Ave. N.W., Suite 300, Washington, District of Columbia 20009. (202) 232-7933. 1991.

The Temperate Forest Ecosystem. Yang Hanxi. Institute of Terrestrial Ecology, Merlewood Research Station, Grange-over-Sands, England LA11 6JU. 1987. Topics in forest ecology.

Transforming Technology: An Agenda for Environmentally Sustainable Growth in the Twenty-First Century. George Heaton, et al. World Resources Institute, 1709 New York Ave. N.W., Washington, District of Columbia 20006. (800) 822-0504. 1991. Explores the extraordinarily rich potential of new technologies to resolve environmental and economic problems.

Values for the Environment–A Guide to the Economic Appraisal. HMSO, UNIPUB, 4611 - F Assembly Dr., Lanham, Maryland 20706. (301) 459-7666 or (800) 274-4888. 1991. Practical guide to the economic treatment of the environment in project appraisal using cost benefit analysis as the decision framework.

Valuing Wildlife: Economic and Social Perspectives. Daniel J. Decker and Gary R. Goff, eds. Westview Press, 5500 Central Ave., Boulder, Colorado 80301. (303) 444-3541. 1987. State of the art guide to determining the value of wildlife, the application for environmental impact assessment, and strategies in wildlife planning and policy.

Wasting Assets: Natural Resources in the National Income Accounts. Robert Repetto and William B. Magrath. World Resources Institute, 1709 New York Ave. N.W., Washington, District of Columbia 20006. (800) 822-0504. 1989. Using Indonesia's timber, petroleum and soils as examples, this report tests and applies a new methodology for integrating natural resource depletion into a revised national accounting system that can more accurately reflect economic reality.

Wetlands: A Threatened Landscape. Michael Williams. B. Blackwell, 3 Cambridge Ctr., Suite 208, Cambridge, Massachusetts 02142. (617) 225-0401. 1990. Explores the evolution and composition of wetlands and their physical and biological dynamics, considers the impact of agriculture, industry, urbanization, and recreation upon them, and examines what steps we are taking and what steps should be considered to manage and preserve wetlands.

The World Bank and the Environment: A Progress Report, Fiscal 1991. World Bank, UNIPUB, 4611-F Assembly Dr., Lanham, Maryland 20706. (301) 459-7666 or (800) 274-4888. 1991. Describes specific environmental strategies and environmental lending in the Bank's four operational regions: Asia, Europe, the Middle East and North Africa, and Latin America and the Caribbean.

GOVERNMENTAL ORGANIZATIONS

Bureau of Economic Analysis: Environmental Economics Division. 1404 K St., N.W., Washington, District of Columbia 20230. (202) 523-0687.

HANDBOOKS AND MANUALS

Chemical Economics Handbook. SRI International, 333 Ravenswood Ave., Menlo Park, California 14025-3493. (415) 859-4771. 1983-. 33 vols. Provides an in-depth evaluation of the present and future economic status of major chemical substances

The Green Consumer. John Elkington, Julia Hailes, and Joel Makower. Penguin Books, 375 Hudson St., New York, New York 10014. (212) 366-2000. 1990. Shoppers guide to purchasing ecological products and services.

ONLINE DATA BASES

BioBusiness. Dialog Information Services, Inc., Marketing Dept., 3460 Hillview Avenue, Palo Alto, California 94304. (800) 334-2564 or (415) 858-3810. Provides information based on evaluations of the economic and business aspects of biological and biomedical research.

Business and the Environment. Cutter Information Corp., 37 Broadway, Arlington, Massachusetts 02174-4439. (617) 648-8700. Online version of periodical of the same name.

Enviro/Energyline Abstracts Plus. R. R. Bowker Co., 121 Chanlon Rd., New Providence, New Jersey 07974. (908) 464-6800.

Environmental Business Journal. EnviroQuest, PO Box 371769, San Diego, California 92137. (619) 295-7685. Online access.

Environmental Periodicals Bibliography. National Information Services Corp., Ste. 6, Wyman Towers, 3100 St. Paul St., Baltimore, Maryland 21218. (410)243-0797. Online version of abstract of same name.

GeoRef. American Geological Institute, 4220 King St., Alexandria, Virginia 22302. (703) 379-2480.

Green Marketing Report. Business Publishers, Inc., 951 Pershing Dr., Silver Spring, Maryland 20910. (301) 587-6300. Online version of periodical of the same name.

Green Markets. McGraw-Hill Science & Engineering Books, 11 W. 19th St., New York, New York 10011. (212) 337-6010.

Monthly Catalog of United States Government Publications. U.S. G.P.O., Supt. of Docs., PO Box 371954, Pittsburgh, Pennsylvania 15250-7954. (202) 512-0000.

National Technical Information Service. U.S. Department of Commerce, National Technical Information Service, Office of Data Base Services, 5285 Port Royal Rd., Springfield, Virginia 22161. (703) 487-4807. Biblio-

graphic database of government sponsored research and technical reports.

SCISEARCH. Institute for Scientific Information, University City Science Center, 3501 Market St., Philadelphia, Pennsylvania 19104. (215) 386-0100.

PERIODICALS AND NEWSLETTERS

Ash at Work. American Coal Ash Association, 1000 16th Street, NW, Suite 507, Washington, District of Columbia 20036. (202) 659-2303. Quarterly. Information on fly ash from the combustion of coal.

Association of Environmental and Resource Economists Newsletter. Association of Environmental and Resource Economists, 1616 P St. NW, Washington, District of Columbia 20036. (202) 328-5000. Semiannual.

Business and the Environment. Cutter Information Corp., 37 Broadway, Arlington, Massachusetts 02174. (617) 648-8700. Semimonthly. Global news and analysis on environmental trends. Also available online.

Environmental Business Journal. EnviroQuest, PO Box 371769, San Diego, California 92137. (619) 295-7685. Monthly. Products relating to environmental protection.

Forum for Applied Research and Public Policy. University of Tennessee, Energy, Environment and Resources Center, Knoxville, Tennessee 37996-0710. (919) 966-3561. 1986-. Quarterly. Presents a discussion of options by academic, government and corporate experts in energy, environment and economic development.

International Permaculture Solutions Journal. Yankee Permaculture, P.O. Box 16683, Wichita, Kansas 67216. Irregular. Tools for sustainable lifestyles, extensive green pages, and resources directory.

Intersections. Center for Urban Environment Studies, Rensselaer Polytechnic Institute, Troy, New York 12180-3590. Annual. Urban and environmental studies.

Investor's Environmental Report. Investor Responsibility Research Center, 1755 Massachusetts Ave., NW, Suite 600, Washington, District of Columbia 20036. (202) 234-7500. Quarterly. Environmental topics of particular relevance to the investment and corporate communities.

Journal of Environmental Economics and Management. Academic Press, c/o Harcourt Brace Jovanovich Inc., 6277 Sea Harbor Dr., Orlando, Florida 32887. (800) 346-8648. Quarterly. Linkages between economic & environmental systems.

Nature and Resources. Elsevier Science Publishing Co., 655 Avenue of the Americas, New York, New York 10010. (212) 989-5800. 1965-. Quarterly. Provides in-depth reviews of contemporary environmental issues from an international perspective.

TRADE ASSOCIATIONS AND PROFESSIONAL SOCIETIES

Association of Environmental and Resource Economists. 1616 P St., N.W., Washington, District of Columbia 20036. (202) 328-5000.

Coalition for Environmentally Responsible Economics. 711 Atlantic Ave., Boston, Massachusetts 02111. (617) 451-0927.

Council on Economic Priorities. 30 Irving Place, New York, New York 10003. (212) 420-1133.

National Council for Environmental Balance. 4169 Westport Rd., P.O. Box 7732, Louisville, Kentucky 40207. (502) 896-8731.

National Environmental Development Association. 1440 New York Ave., N.W., Suite 300, Washington, District of Columbia 20005. (202) 638-1230.

ECOSPHERES

See: ECOSYSTEMS

ECOSYSTEMS

See also: BIOLOGICAL DIVERSITY; CORAL REEF ECOLOGY

ABSTRACTING AND INDEXING SERVICES

Abstracts of Air and Water Conservation Literature. American Petroleum Institute. Central Abstracting and Indexing Service, 275 Madison Avenue, New York, New York 10016. 1972.

Applied Ecology Abstracts Studies in Renewable Natural Resources. Information Retrieval Ltd., 1911 Jefferson Davis Highway, Arlington, Virginia 22202. 1975-. Monthly.

Applied Science and Technology Index. H.W. Wilson Co., 950 University Ave., Bronx, New York 10452. (800) 367-6770. Formerly Industrial Arts Index.

Aqualine Abstracts. Water Research Centre. c/o Pergamon Microforms International, Inc., Fairview Park, Elmsford, New York 10523. (914) 592-7720. 1927-. Contains some 8,000 records annually on water and wastewater technology. Covers all aspects of water, wastewater, associated engineering services and the aquatic environment. Over 600 periodicals, as well as books, reports and conference proceedings and other publications from water related institutions worldwide are scanned. Also available online.

ASFA Aquaculture Abstracts. Cambridge Scientific Abstracts, Inc., 5161 River Rd., Bethesda, Maryland 20816. (301) 961-6750. 1984.

Biological Abstracts. BIOSIS, 2100 Arch St., Philadelphia, Pennsylvania 19103-1399. (215) 587-4800. 1927-.

Biological and Agricultural Index. H.W. Wilson Co., 950 University Ave., Bronx, New York 10452. (800) 367-6770. 1916-. Monthly.

Current Advances in Ecological and Environmental Science. Pergamon Microforms International, Inc., Fairview Park, Elmsford, New York 10523. (914) 592-7720. 1989-. Monthly. Current literature searching service including journals, reports, abstracts, etc. This service is available online as part of the CABS database on the hosts BRS and ORBIT search service.

Ecological Abstracts. Geo Abstracts Ltd. Elsevier Applied Science, Crown House, Linton Rd., Barking, England IG 11 8JU. 1974-. Derived from over 600 leading ecological and environmental journals, plus books, conference proceedings, reports and theses.

Ecology Abstracts. Cambridge Scientific Abstracts, 5161 River Rd., Bethesda, Maryland 20816. (301) 961-6750. Monthly.

Engineering Index. The Engineering Index Inc., 345 E. 47th St., New York, New York 10017. 1962-.

Environment Abstracts. Bowker A & I Publishing, 121 Chanlon Rd., New Providence, New Jersey 07974. (908) 464-6800. 1974-.

Environment Index. Environment Information Center, Index Research Department, 124 E. 39th St., New York, New York 10016. 1971-. Annual.

Environmental Information Connection-EIC. Planning Information Program, Dept. of Urban and Regional Planning, University of Illinois, 1003 West Nevada, Urbana, Illinois 61801. (217) 333-1369. Also available online.

Environmental Periodicals Bibliography. Environmental Studies Institute, International Academy at Santa Barbara, 800 Garden St., Suite D, Santa Barbara, California 93101. (805) 965-5010. Also available online.

General Science Index. H. W. Wilson Co., 950 University Ave., Bronx, New York 10452. 1978-. Monthly, also issued in annual cumulation. Cumulative subject index to English language periodicals in the subject fields of astronomy, botany, chemistry, earth science, environment and conservation, food and nutrition, genetics, mathematics, medicine and health, microbiology, oceanography, physics, physiology and zoology.

Geo Abstracts, Social Geography and Cartography. Geo Abstracts Ltd., c/o Elsevier Science Pub., Crown House, Linton Rd., Barking, England 1611 8JU.

Geographical Abstracts. London School of Economics, Dept. of Geography, Regency House, 34 Duke St., London, England 1966-. Continued by Geo Abstracts issued in 6 parts: Pt. A. Landforms and the quaternary; Pt. B. Biogeography and Climatology; Pt. C. Economic geography; Pt. D. Social geography and cartography; Pt. E. Sedimentology; Pt. F. Regional and community planning.

Index to Scientific Book Contents. Institute for Scientific Information, 3501 Market St., Philadelphia, Pennsylvania 19104. (800) 523-1857. 1985-. Annual. Gives contents of science books published.

Mineralogical Abstracts. Mineralogical Society, 41 Queen's Gate, London, England SW7 5HR. 71 5847916. Quarterly. Abstracts of journal articles, conferences, technical reports and specialized books in the areas of minerals, clay minerals, economic minerals, ore deposits, environmental studies, experimental mineralogy, gemstones, geochemistry, petrology, lunar and planetary studies and other related areas in mineralogy.

Multimedia Index to Ecology. National Information Center for Educational Media, University of Southern California, Los Angeles, California 90007.

Pollution Abstracts. Cambridge Scientific Abstracts, 5161 River Rd., Bethesda, Maryland 20816. (301) 961-6750. Six/year. Indexes worldwide technical literature on environmental pollution. Covers air pollution, marine and freshwater pollution, sewage and wastewater treatment, waste management, toxicology and health, noise pollution, radiation, land pollution, and environmental poli-

cies, programs, legislation, and education. Also available online.

Science Citation Index. Institute for Scientific Information, 3501 Market St., Philadelphia, Pennsylvania 19104. 1961-.

Sea Grant Abstracts. National Sea Grant Depository, Pell Laboratory Bldg., Bay Campus, University of Rhode Island, Narragansett, Rhode Island 02882. (401) 792-6114. 1986-. Quarterly. Published by the National Sea Grant Programs, this collection includes annual reports, serials and newsletters, charts and maps.

ALMANACS AND YEARBOOKS

Advances in Ecological Research. Academic Press, c/o Harcourt Brace Jovanovich Inc., 6277 Sea Harbor Dr., Orlando, Florida 32887. (800) 346-8648.

Gale Environmental Almanac. Russ Hoyle. Gale Research Inc., 835 Penobscot Bldg., Detroit, Michigan 48226-4094. (313) 961-2242. 1993. Focuses on the U.S. and Canada, although worldwide and transboundary issues are discussed.

BIBLIOGRAPHIES

Bibliography and Index of Geology. American Geological Institute, 4220 King St., Alexandria, Virginia 22302. Monthly. Includes environmental geology and hydrogeology.

Directory of Published Proceedings. Interdok Corp., 173 Halstead Ave., Harrison, New York 10528. (914) 835-3506. 1990. Monthly. This is a listing of published proceedings including the series SEMTE (Science/Medicine/Engineering/Technology) and the series SSH (Social Science/Humanities).

EPA Publications Bibliography. U.S. Environmental Protection Agency, Library Systems Branch, 401 M St., SW, Washington, District of Columbia 20460. (202) 260-2090. Quarterly.

DIRECTORIES

Canadian Environmental Directory. Canadian Almanac & Directory Publishing Co. Ltd., 134 Adelaide St. E., Ste. 27, Toronto, Ontario, Canada M5C 1K9. (416) 362-4088. 1992. Includes individuals, agencies, firms, and associations.

Coral Reefs of the World. Susan M. Wells. World Conservation Union, IUCN Publications Services Unit, 181a Huntingdon Rd., Cambridge, England CB3 0DJ. (0223) 277894. 1991. Catalogues for the first time the significant coral reefs of the world, their geographical context and ecology, their current condition and status in legislation, and prescriptions for their conservation and sustainable use.

Ecological Society of America Bulletin-Directory of Members Issue. Ecological Society of America, c/o Dr. Duncan Patten, Center for Environmental Studies, Arizona State University, Tempe, Arizona 85287. (602) 965-3000.

Environmental Telephone Directory. Government Institutes, Inc., 4 Research Pl., Ste. 200, Rockville, Maryland 20850. (301) 921-2300.

Gale Environmental Sourcebook. Karen Hill. Gale Research Co., 835 Penobscot Bldg., Detroit, Michigan

48226-4094. (313) 961-2242. Contacts, information sources, or general information on environmental topics.

The Green Encyclopedia. Irene Franck, David Brownstone. Prentice-Hall, Rte. 9W, Englewood Cliffs, New York 07632. (201) 592-2000. 1992. Covers environmental organizations.

ENCYCLOPEDIAS AND DICTIONARIES

Cambridge Encyclopedia of Life Sciences. A. E. Friday and David S. Ingram. Cambridge University Press, 40 W 20th St., New York, New York 10011. (212) 924-3900 or (800) 227-0247. 1985. Includes all topics under biology and ecology.

Dictionary of Environmental Engineering and Related Sciences: English-Spanish, Spanish-English. Jose T. Villate. Ediciones Universal, 3090 SW 8th St., Miami, Florida 33135. (305) 642-3355. 1979.

Dictionary of the Environment. Michael Allaby. New York University Press, 70 Washington Sq. S., New York, New York 10012. (212) 998-2575. 1989.

The Encyclopedia of Animal Ecology. Peter D. Moore. Facts on File, Inc., 460 Park Ave. S., New York, New York 10016. (212) 683-2244. 1987.

Encyclopedia of Community Planning and Environmental Management. Marilyn Spigel Schultz. Facts on File, Inc., 460 Park Ave. S., New York, New York 10016. (212) 683-2244. 1984.

Encyclopedia of Environmental Science and Engineering. J.R. Pfafflin. Gordon and Breach Science Publishers, Inc., 270 8th Ave., New York, New York 10011. (212) 206-8900. 1992.

Encyclopedia of Human Biology. Renato Dulbecco, ed. Academic Press, c/o Harcourt Brace Jovanovich Inc., 6277 Sea Harbor Dr., Orlando, Florida 32887. (800) 346-8648. 1991. Eight volumes.

The Environmental Dictionary. James J. King. PennWell Books, PO Box 21288, Tulsa, Oklahoma 74121. (918) 831-9421; (800) 752-9764. 1989. Gives more than 5,000 definitions of terms used and applied by the EPA.

Environmental Encyclopedia. William P. Cunningham, Terence Ball, et. al. Gale Research Inc., 835 Penobscot Bldg., Detroit, Michigan 48226-4094. (313) 961-2242. 1993.

Grzimek's Encyclopedia of Ecology. Bernhard Grzimek. Van Nostrand Reinhold, 115 5th Ave., New York, New York 10003. (212) 254-3232. 1976.

McGraw-Hill Encyclopedia of Science and Technology. McGraw-Hill, 1221 Avenue of the Americas, New York, New York 10020. (212) 512-2000 or (800) 262-4729. 1992. Seventh edition. Issued in multiple volumes including index. Includes all science and technology broad subject areas.

North American Reference Encyclopedia of Ecology and Pollution. William White. North American Pub. Co., 401 N. Broad St., Philadelphia, Pennsylvania 19108. (215) 238-5300. 1972.

Van Nostrand's Scientific Encyclopedia. Glenn D. Considine, ed. Van Nostrand Reinhold, 115 5th Ave., New York, New York 10003. (212) 254-3232. 1983. Sixth edition. Includes all broad subject areas in science.

GENERAL WORKS

Acid Precipitation. Springer-Verlag, 175 5th Ave., New York, New York 10010. (212) 460-1500; (800) 777-4643. 1989-. 5 volume set. Deals with various aspects of acidic precipitations such as: biological and ecological effects; sources, deposition and canopy interactions; soils aquatic processes and lake acidification. Also includes case studies and an international overview and assessment.

Agricultural Ecology. Joy Tivy. John Wiley & Sons, Inc., 605 3rd Ave., New York, New York 10158-0012. (212) 850-6000. 1990. Analyzes the nature of relationships between crops, livestock, and the biophysical environment, and the extent to which man has modified the products and environment to suit his own needs.

Agroecology and Small Farm Development. Miguel A. Altieri. CRC Press, 2000 Corporate Blvd. N.W., Boca Raton, Florida 33431. (800) 272-7737. 1989. Reviews physical and social context of small farm agriculture, small farm development approaches, production systems, the dynamics of traditional agriculture, and research methodologies.

Agroecology: Researching the Ecological Basis for Sustainable Agriculture. Stephen R. Gliessman, ed. Springer-Verlag, 175 5th Ave., New York, New York 10010. (212) 460-1500; (800) 777-4643. 1990. Demonstrates in a series of international case studies how to combine the more production-oriented focus of the agronomist with the more systems-oriented viewpoint of the ecologist. Methodology for evaluating and quantifying agroecosystem is presented.

America's Downtowns: Growth, Politics, and Preservation. Richard C. Collins. Preservation Press, National Trust for Historic Preservation, 1785 Massachusetts Ave. NW, Washington, District of Columbia 20036. (202) 673-4058. 1991. Examines the efforts of 10 major American cities to integrate preservation values into the local policies that shape downtown growth and development.

Ancient Forests of the Pacific Northwest. Elliot A. Norse. Island Press, 1718 Connecticut Ave. N.W., Suite 300, Washington, District of Columbia 20009. (202) 232-7933. 1990. Comprehensive assessment of the biological value of the ancient forests, information about how logging and atmospheric changes threaten the forests, and convincing arguments that replicated ecosystems are too weak to support biodiversity.

Antarctic Ecosystems: Ecological Change and Conservation. K.R. Kerry, ed. Springer-Verlag, 175 5th Ave., New York, New York 10010. (212) 460-1500 or (800) 777-4643. 1990. Papers from a Symposium held in the University of Tasmania, Hobart, Australia, August-September 1988. Deals with conservation of nature in the antarctic.

The Atlantic Barrier Reef Ecosystem at Carrie Bow Cay, Belize, I: Structure and Communities. Klaus Rutzler and Ian G. MacIntyre. Smithsonian Institution Press, 470 L'Enfant Plaza, No. 7100, Washington, District of Columbia 20560. (800) 782-4612. 1982.

The Background of Ecology. Robert P. McIntosh. Carolina Biological Supply Company, 2700 York Road, Burlington, North Carolina 27215. (919) 584-0381. 1985.

Barriers to a Better Environment: What Stops Us Solving Environmental Problems?. Stephen Trudgill. Belhaven Press, 136 S. Broadway, Irvington, New York 10533. (914) 591-9111. 1990. Postulates several types of barriers that one may come across while dealing with environmental problems: technological, and economic, social, and political barriers. Suggests the importance of holistic framework for the successful development and implementation of environmental solutions.

Biogeochemistry: An Analysis of Global Change. William H. Schlesinger. Academic Press, c/o Harcourt Brace Jovanovich Inc., 6277 Sea Harbor Dr., Orlando, Florida 32887. (800) 346-8648. 1991. Examines global changes that have occurred and are occurring in our water, air, and on land, relates them to the global cycles of water, carbon, nitrogen, phosphorous, and sulfur.

Carbon Dioxide, the Climate and Man. John R. Gribbin. International Institute for Environment and Development, 3 Endsleigh St., London, England CB2 1ER. 1981. Influence on nature of atmospheric carbon dioxide.

Chemical Evolution. Stephen Finney Mason. Oxford University Press, 200 Madison Ave., New York, New York 10016. (212) 679-7300; (800) 334-4249. 1991. Describes the history of ideas in the study of chemistry and the development of modern theories on chemical evolution. Relates the history of chemicals.

Climate and Man: From the Ice Age to the Global Greenhouse. Fred Pearce. Vision Books in Association with LWT, The Forum 74-80, Camden St., London, England NW1 OEG. 071-388-8811. 1989.

Coastal Alert: Ecosystems, Energy, and Offshore Oil Drilling. Dwight Holing. Island Press, 1718 Connecticut Ave. N.W., Suite 300, Washington, District of Columbia 20009. (202) 232-7933. 1990. Describes how offshore drilling affects environment and quality of life, how the government auctions our coast to the oil industry, how the lease sale process works, how energy alternatives can replace offshore drilling; how citizen action works and how to become involved.

Comparative Analysis of Ecosystems Patterns, Mechanisms, and Theories. Jonathan Cole, ed. Springer-Verlag, 175 5th Ave., New York, New York 10010. (212) 460-1500; (800) 777-4643. 1991. Includes papers from a conference held in Milbrook, New York, 1989.

Conserving the World's Biological Diversity. Jeffrey A. McNeely, et al. World Resources Institute, 1709 New York Ave. N.W., Washington, District of Columbia 20006. (800) 822-0504. 1990. Provides a clear concise and well illustrated guide to the meaning and importance of biological diversity. Discusses a broad range of practical approaches to biodiversity preservation, including policy changes, integrated land-use management, species and habitat protection, and pollution control.

Constructed Wetlands for Wastewater Treatment. Donald A. Hammer. Lewis Publishers, 200 Corporate Blvd. NW, Boca Raton, Florida 33431. (407) 994-0555 or (800)272-7737. 1989. Presents general principles of wetland ecology, hydrology, soil chemistry, vegetation, microbiology, and wildlife dependence on wetlands. It provides management guidelines, beginning with policies and regulations, and including siting and construction and operations and monitoring of constructed wetland systems.

The Control of Nature. John A. McPhee. Noonday Pr., 19 Union Sq. W, New York, New York 10003. (212) 741-6900. 1990. Describes the strategies and tactics through which people attempt to control nature.

A Critique for Ecology. Robert Henry Peters. Cambridge University Press, 40 W. 20th St., New York, New York

10011. (212) 924-3900. Offers examples of scientific criticism of contemporary ecology.

Defending the Earth. South End Press, 116 St. Botolph St., Boston, Massachusetts 02115. (800) 533-8478. 1991.

Domestication: The Decline of Environmental Appreciation. Helmut Hemmer. Cambridge University Press, 40 W. 20th St., New York, New York 10011. (212) 924-3900; (800) 227-0247. 1990. The books proposes the thesis that domestication must lead to reduced environmental appreciation. The origins of domesticated mammals, their scientific nomenclature, the relationships between feral mammals and their wild progenitors, and modern attempts at domestication are also covered.

Down by the River: The Impact of Federal Water Projects and Policies on Biological Diversity. Constance Elizabeth Hunt with Verne Huser. Island Press, 1718 Connecticut Ave. N.W., Suite 300, Washington, District of Columbia 20009. (202) 232-7933. 1988. Presents case studies of development projects on seven river systems, including the Columbia, the Delaware, the Missouri, and the rivers of Maine ,to illustrate their effect on biological diversity.

The Dream of the Earth. Thomas Berry. Sierra Club Books, 100 Bush St., San Francisco, California 94104. (415) 291-1600. 1988. Describes the ecological fate from a species perspective.

Earth Education: A New Beginning. Steve Van Matre. Institute for Earth Education, PO Box 288, Warrenville, Illinois 60555. (708) 393-3096. 1990. Describes environmental education which adopts an alternative foundation for improving awareness about the environment through changes in attitudes and life styles.

Eco-Warriors: Understanding the Radical Environmental Movement. Rik Scarce. Noble Pr., 111 E. Chestnut, Suite 48 A, Chicago, Illinois 60611. (312) 880-0439. 1990. Recounts escapades of pro-ecology sabotage by self styled eco- warriors. Episodes such as the sinking of two whaling ships in Iceland, the botched attempt to hang a banner on Mt. Rushmore, a national tree-sitting week, and raids on research facilities by animal liberation activists.

Ecological Genetics and Air Pollution. George E. Taylor, Jr., ed. Springer-Verlag, 175 5th Ave., New York, New York 10010. (212) 460-1500; (800) 777-4643. 1991. Describes role of air pollution in governing the genetic structure and evolution of plant species.

Ecological Heterogeneity. Jurek Kolasa, et al., eds. Springer-Verlag, 175 5th Ave., New York, New York 10010. (212) 460-1500. 1991. Examines the meaning of heterogeneity in a particular environment and its consequences for individuals, populations, and communities of plants and animals. Among the topics of the 14 papers are the causes of heterogeneity, system and observer dependence, dimension and scale, ecosystem organization, temporal and spatial changes, new models of competition and landscape patterns, and applications in desert, temperate, and marine areas.

Ecological Processes and Cumulative Impacts Illustrated by Bottomland Harwood Wetland Ecosystems. James G. Gosselink, et al. Lewis Publishers, 2000 Corporate Blvd., N.W., Boca Raton, Florida 33431. (407) 994-0555 or (800) 272-7737. 1990. Covers the ecological processes in bottomland hardwood forests and relates these processes to human activities.

The Ecological Self. Freya Mathews. Rowman & Littlefield, Publishers, Inc., 8705 Bollman Pl., Savage, Maryland 20763. (301) 306-0400. 1991. Considers the metaphysical foundations of ecological ethics.

Ecology, Community, and Lifestyle: Outline of an Ecosophy. David Rothenberg. Cambridge University Press, 40 W. 20th St., New York, New York 10011. (212) 924-3900. 1989. Handbook on strategy and tactics for environmentalists.

Ecology for Beginners. Stephen Croall. Pantheon Books, 201 E 50th St., New York, New York 10022. (212) 751-2600. 1981. The story of man's struggle with the environment.

The Ecology of a Garden: The First Fifteen Years. Jennifer Owen. Cambridge University Press, 40 W. 20th St., New York, New York 10011. (212) 924-3900; (800) 227-0247. 1991.

Ecology of Sandy Shores. A. C. Brown and A. Mclachlan. Elsevier Science Publishing Co., 655 Avenue of the Americas, New York, New York 10010. (212) 989-5800. 1990. Deals with the biological study of sandy beaches.

The Ecology of the Ancient Greek World. Robert Sallares. Cornell University Press, 124 Roberts Place, Ithaca, New York 14850. 1991. Synthesis of ancient history and biological or physical anthropology. Includes chapters on demography and on agriculture in ancient Greece and Egypt. Also includes extensive notes and bibliographies.

The Ecology of Urban Habitats. O.L. Gilbert. Chapman & Hall, 29 W. 35th St., New York, New York 10001-2291. (212) 244-3336. 1989.

Ecosystems Experiments. H. A. Mooney, et al., eds. John Wiley & Sons, Inc., 605 3rd Ave., New York, New York 10158-0012. (212) 850-6000. 1991. Explores the potential ecosystem experimentation as a tool for understanding and predicting changes in the biosphere. Areas investigated include deforestation, desertification, El Nino phenomenon, acid rain, watersheds, wetlands, and aquatic and climatic changes.

Ecosystems of Florida. Ronald L. Myers and John J. Ewel, eds. Central Florida University, Dist. by Univ. Presses of Florida, 15 N.W. 15th St., Gainesville, Florida 32603. (904) 392-1351. 1990. Presents an ecosystem setting with geology, geography and soils, climate, and 13 ecosystems in a broad human context of historical biogeography and current human influences. Also presents community vulnerability and management techniques and issues in conservation.

Elton's Ecologists: A History of the Bureau of Animal Population. Peter Crowcroft. University of Chicago Press, 5801 Ellis Ave., 4th Fl., Chicago, Illinois 60637. (312) 702-7700. 1991. The story of a smallish university department chronicles an enterprise that appreciably shaped the history of ecology during the mid-decades of the 20th century.

Emergence: The New Science of Becoming. Lindisfarne Press, RR4, Box 94A-1, Hudson, New York 12534. (518) 851-9155. Covers ecology and philosophy of biology.

Environmental Biotechnology. A. Balaozej and V. Prnivarovna, eds. Elsevier Science Publishing Co., 655 Avenue of the Americas, New York, New York 10010. (212) 989-5800. 1991. Proceedings of the International Symposium on Biotechnology, Bratislava, Czechoslovakia, June 27-29, 1990.

The Environmental Gardener: The Solution to Pollution for Lawns and Gardens. Laurence Sombke. MasterMedia, 17 E. 89th St., New York, New York 10128. (212) 348-2020. 1991.

Environmental Policies for Cities in the 1990s. OECD Publications and Information Center, 2001 L St. N.W., Suite 700, Washington, District of Columbia 20036. (202) 785-OECD. 1991. Examines existing urban environmental improvement policies and suggests practical solutions to urban renewal, urban transportation and urban energy management.

The Environmental Sourcebook. Edith Carol Stein. Lyons & Burford, 31 W. 21st St., New York, New York 10010. (212) 620-9580. 1992. Provides information on 11 specific environmental issues, including population; agriculture; energy; climate and atmosphere; biodiversity; water; oceans; solid waste; hazardous substances and waste; endangered lands; and development.

Environmental Viewpoints. Marie Lazzari. Gale Research Inc., 835 Penobscot Bldg., Detroit, Michigan 48226-4094. (313) 961-2242. 1992.

Foundations of Ecology. Leslie A. Real. University of Chicago Press, 5801 Ellis Ave., 4th Fl., Chicago, Illinois 60637. (312) 568-1550 or (800) 621-2736. Forty classic papers that have laid the foundation of modern ecology and are ideal for graduate courses that deal with the development of ecological ideas.

The Fragile Environment. Laurie Friday and Ronald Laskey, eds. Cambridge University Press, 40 W. 20th St., New York, New York 10011. (212) 924-3900; (800) 227-0247. 1989. The fragile environment brings together a team of distinguished authors to consider areas of urgent environmental concern.

The Fragile South Pacific: An Ecological Odyssey. Andrew Mitchell. University of Texas Press, PO Box 7819, Austin, Texas 78713-7819. (512) 471-7233 or (800) 252-3206. 1991. Narrative of the ecology and natural history of the major South Pacific islands, the story of their human inhabitants, how they got there, and human impacts on those islands.

From the Land. Nancy P. Pittman, ed. Island Press, 1718 Connecticut Ave. N.W., Suite 300, Washington, District of Columbia 20009. (202) 232-7933. 1988. Anthology comes from 13 years of the Land–a journal of conservation writings from the '40s and '50s. Through fiction, essay, poetry, and philosophy we learn how our small farms have given way to today's agribusiness.

Global Climate Change: Human and Natural Influences. Paragon House Publishers, 90 5th Ave., New York, New York 10011. (212) 620-2820. Carbon dioxide, methane, chlorofluorocarbons and ozone in the atmosphere; acid rain and water pollution in the hydrosphere; oceanographic and meteorological processes, nuclear war, volcanoes, asteroids, and meteorites.

Global Ecology. Colin Tudge. Oxford University Press, 200 Madison Ave., New York, New York 10016. (212) 679-7300 or (800) 334-4249. Overview of ecological science including climate and habitats of our planet while emphasizing the global unity of earth's ecosystem.

The Green Machine: Ecology and the Balance of Nature. Wallace Arthur. B. Blackwell, 3 Cambridge Ctr., Suite 208, Cambridge, Massachusetts 02142. (617) 225-0401. 1990. Provides an overview of most topics routinely included in ecology courses. Includes trophic dynamics, predator-prey theory, competition coevolution, and species diversity. Evolutionary topics such as plate tectonics, geologic time, speciation, extinction, and natural selection are also included.

Helping Nature Heal: An Introduction to Environmental Restoration. Richard Nilsen, ed. Ten Speed Press, P.O. Box 7123, Berkeley, California 94707. (800) 841-2665. 1991.

The Human Impact on the Natural Environment. Andrew Goudie. MIT Press, 55 Hayward St., Cambridge, Massachusetts 02142. (617) 253-2884. 1986. Discusses man's influence on nature.

Imperiled Planet: Restoring Our Endangered Ecosystems. Edward Goldsmith, et al. MIT Press, 55 Hayward St., Cambridge, Massachusetts 02142. (617) 253-2884; (800) 356-0343. 1990. Presentation of a wide range of ecosystems, showing how they work, the traditional forms of human use, threats and losses, causes of destruction, and preservation attempts.

Impounded Rivers: Perspectives for Ecological Management. Geoffrey E. Petts. John Wiley & Sons, Inc., 605 3rd Ave., New York, New York 10158. (212) 850-6000. 1984. Environmental aspects of dams, stream ecology and stream conservation.

In Search of Environmental Excellence: Moving Beyond Blame. Bruce Piasecki and Peter Asmus. Simon and Schuster, 1230 Avenue of the Americas, New York, New York 10020. (212) 689-7000. 1990. Analyses of the roles and motivations of government, business/industry, and the general public in solving environmental problems.

Into Harmony with the Planet: The Delicate Balance Between Industry and the Environment. Michael Allaby. Bloomsbury Pub., 2 Soho Sq., London, England W1V 5DE. 1990. Describes the ecosystem and its delicate balance. Also discusses the effect industry and its pollutants on the environment.

Laboratory Manual of General Ecology. George W. Cox. Carolina Biological Supply Company, 2700 York Rd., Burlington, North Carolina 27215. (919) 584-0381. 1989. 6th ed. Provides a good section on activities, exercises and references in the field of ecology as a whole.

Land Degradation: Development and Breakdown of Terrestrial Environments. C. J. Barrow. Cambridge University Press, 40 W. 20th St., New York, New York 10011. (212) 924-3900; (800) 227-0247. 1991.

Landscape Linkages and Biodiversity. Wendy E. Hudson, ed. Island Press, 1718 Connecticut Ave. N.W., Suite 300, Washington, District of Columbia 20009. (202) 232-7933. 1991. Explains biological diversity conservation, focusing on the need for protecting large areas of the most diverse ecosystems, and connecting these ecosystems with land corridors to allow species to move among them more easily.

Large Marine Ecosystems: Patterns, Processes, and Yields. Kenneth Sherman, et al., eds. American Association for the Advancement of Science, 1333 H St. N.W., 8th Flr., Washington, District of Columbia 20005. (202) 326-6400. 1990. Deals with the conservation and management of vitally important components of the ecosphere.

Magill's Survey of Science. Earth Science Series. Frank N. Magill. Salem Press, PO Box 50062, Pasadena, California 91105. 1990-. Five volumes. Includes information on earth's crust, hot spots and volcanic island chains, physical properties of minerals, rock magnetism, physical properties of rocks, and index.

Magill's Survey of Science. Life Science Series. Frank N. Magill, ed. Salem Press, PO Box 50062, Pasadena, California 91105. 1991. Six volumes. Contents: v.1. A-Central and peripheral nervous system functions; v.2. Central metabolism regulation - eukaryotic transcriptional control; v.3. Positive and negative eukaryotic transcriptional control - mammalian hormones; v.4. Hormones and behavior - muscular contraction; v.5. Muscular contraction and relaxation - sexual reproduction in plants; v.6. Reproductive behavior and mating - X inactivation and the Lyon hypothesis.

Making Peace with the Planet. Barry Commoner. Pantheon Books, 201 E. 50th St., New York, New York 10220. (212) 751-2000. 1990. Reviews the vast efforts made in the public and private sphere to address and control damage to the environment.

Management and Restoration of Human-Impacted Resources: Approaches to Ecosystem Rehabilitation. Kathrin Schreckenberg, et al, eds. UNESCO, 7, place de Fontenoy, Paris, France F-75700. (331) 45 68 40 67. 1990. MAB Digest 5.

Managing Marine Environments. Richard A. Kenchington. Taylor & Francis, 1900 Frost Rd., Ste. 101, Bristol, Pennsylvania 19007. (215) 785-5800. 1990. Contemporary issues of multiple-use planning and management of marine environments and natural resources.

Mind and Nature: A Necessary Unit. Gregory Bateson. Bantam Books, 666 5th Ave., New York, New York 10103. (212) 765-6500; (800) 223-6834. 1988. Reveals the pattern which connects man and nature.

Monitoring for Conservation and Ecology. Barrie Goldsmith, ed. Chapman & Hall, 29 W 35th St., New York, New York 10001-2291. (212) 244-3336. 1991. Focuses on an audience of those practicing ecology, nature conservation, or other similar land-based sciences. The differences between surveying and monitoring are discussed and emphasis is placed on the nature of monitoring as being purpose- oriented dynamic in philosophy, and often providing a baseline for recording possible changes in the future.

Nature Reserves: Island Theory and Conservation Practice. Craig L. Shafer. Smithsonian Institution Press, 470 L'Enfant Plaza, No. 7100, Washington, District of Columbia 20560. (800) 782-4612. 1991. Encompasses ecology, biogeography, evolutionary biology, genetics, paleobiology, as well as legal, social, and economic issues.

New World New Mind: Moving toward Conscious Evolution. Robert E. Ornstein. Simon & Schuster, 1230 Avenue of the Americas, New York, New York 10020. (212) 698-7000; (800) 223-2348. 1990. Proposes revolutionary new ways to close the dangerous gap between our current mind set and the high-tech world of today.

New World Parrots in Crisis. Steven R. Beissinger and Noel F. R. Snyder, eds. Smithsonian Institution Press, 470 L'Enfant Plaza, No. 7100, Washington, District of Columbia 20560. (800) 782-4612. 1991. Provides an overview of the hazards facing neotropical parrots one of the world's most threatened group of birds, as well as a detailed discussion of a range of possible conservation solutions.

The Next One Hundred Years: Shaping the Fate of Our Living Earth. Jonathan Weiner. Bantam Books, 666 5th Ave., New York, New York 10103. (212) 765-6500; (800) 223-6834. 1991. Explores the following issues: the greenhouse effect, deforestation, the destruction of the ozone layer, the human population explosion and the onset of mass extinctions.

The Northwest Greenbook. Jonathan King. Sasquatch Books, 1931 2nd Ave., Seattle, Washington 98101. (206) 441-5555. 1991.

Nutrient Cycling in Terrestrial Ecosystems Field Methods. A. F. Harrison, et al. Elsevier Science Publishing Co., 655 Avenue of the Americas, New York, New York 10010. (212) 984-5800. 1990. Describes a wide range of methods for the estimation of nutrient fluxes. The book is divided into sections dealing with inputs, turnover, losses and plant uptake processes.

Our Common Future. World Commission on Environment and Development. Oxford University Press, 200 Madison Ave., New York, New York 10016. (212) 679-7300; (800) 334-4249. 1987. Cautions that it is time that economy and ecology worked hand in hand, so that governments and their people can take responsibility not just for environmental damage, but for the policies that cause the damage.

Paleoenvironments in the Namib Desert: The Lower Tumas Basin in the Late Cenozoic. Justin Wilkinson. University of Chicago Press, Committee on Geographical Studies, 5801 Ellis Ave., 4th Floor, Chicago, Illinois 60637. (800) 621-2736. 1990. Focuses on the great coastal desert of Southwestern Africa the Namib, and explores the complex changes in depositional environments throughout the Cenozoic.

Pastures: Their Ecology and Management. R. H. M. Langer, ed. Oxford University Press, 200 Madison Ave., New York, New York 10016. (212) 679-7300; (800) 334-4249. 1990. Covers such areas as the grasslands of New Zealand, pasture plants, pasture as an ecosystem, pasture establishment, soil fertility, management, assessment, livestock production, animal disorders, high country pastures, hay or silage, seed production, weeds, pests, and plant diseases.

Physiological Plant Ecology. O. L. Lange, et al., eds. Springer-Verlag, 175 5th Ave., New York, New York 10010. (212) 460-1500; (800) 777-4643. 1981-1983. Contents: Volume 1 - Responses to the physical environment; Volume 2 - Water relations and carbon assimilation; Volume 3 - Responses to the chemical and biological environment; Volume 4 - Ecosystem processes (mineral cycling, productivity, and man's influence).

Plant-Animal Interactions; Evolutionary Ecology in Tropical and Temperate Regions. Peter W. Price, et al. John Wiley & Sons, Inc., 605 3rd Ave., New York, New York 10158-0012. (212) 850-6000. 1991. Comprises a comparative analysis of the existing ecological systems of temperate and tropical regions.

Plant Demography in Vegetation Succession. Krystyna Falinska. Kluwer Academic Publishers, 101 Philip Dr., Assinippi Park, Norwell, Massachusetts 02061. (617) 871-6600. 1991.

Preserving the Global Environment: The Challenge of Shared Leadership. Jessica Tuchman Mathews, ed. World Resources Institute, 1709 New York Ave. N.W., Washington, District of Columbia 20006. (800) 822-

0504. 1990. Includes findings on population growth, deforestation and the loss of biological diversity, the ozone layer, energy and climate change, economics, and other critical trends spell out new approaches to international cooperation and regulation in response to the shift from traditional security concerns to a focus on collective global security.

Redevelopment of Degraded Ecosystems. H. Regier, et al., eds. Parthenon Pub., Casterton Hall, Carnforth, England LA6 2LA. 1991. Volume 8 in the "Man and the Biosphere" series published jointly with UNESCO.

Research Priorities for Conservation Biology. Michael E. Soulfe and Kathryn A. Kohm, eds. Island Press, 1718 Connecticut Ave. N.W., Suite 300, Washington, District of Columbia 20009. (202) 232-7933. 1989. Proposes an urgent research agenda to improve our understanding and preservation of biological diversity.

Responses of Plants to Environmental Stresses. J. Levitt. Academic Press, c/o Harcourt Brace Jovanovich Inc., 6277 Sea Harbor Dr., Orlando, Florida 32887. (800) 346-8648. 1980. 2nd ed. Volume 1 covers chilling, freezing and high temperature. Volume 2 contains water, radiation, salt, and other stresses.

The Rising Tide: Global Warming and World Sea Levels. Lynne T. Edgerton. Island Press, 1718 Connecticut Ave. N.W., Suite 300, Washington, District of Columbia 20009. (202) 232-7933. 1991. Analysis of global warming and rising world sea level. Outlines state, national and international actions to respond to the effects of global warming on coastal communities and ecosystems.

Seabirds of the Farallon Islands: Ecology, Dynamics, and Structure of an Upwelling-System Community. David G. Ainley and Robert J. Boekelheide, eds. Stanford University, Stanford, California 94305-2235. (415) 723-9434. 1990. History of seabird populations at the Farallons, a general discussion of patterns in the marine environment, and the general feeding ecology of Farallon seabirds.

Silent Spring. Rachel Carson. Carolina Biological Supply Company, 2700 York Rd., Burlington, North Carolina 27215. (919) 584-0381. 1987.

Southern Exposure: Deciding Antarctica's Future. Lee A. Kimball. World Resources Institute, 1709 New York Ave. N.W., Washington, District of Columbia 20006. (800) 822-0504. 1990. Reviews Antarctica's importance from a global perspective.

Subantarctic Macquarie Island: Environment and Biology. P. M. Selkirk, et al. Cambridge University Press, 40 W. 20th St., New York, New York 10011. (212) 924-3900; (800) 227-0247. 1990. Review of environmental and biologic research on the Macquarie Island. It presents summary of studies done in the last 15 years by Australian scientists. Contains a sequence of 12 chapters that concern the island's discovery and history; situation in the Southern ocean; tectonics and geology; landforms and Quaternary history; vegetation; lakes; birds; mammals; anthropoids; microbiology; near shore environments; and human impact.

Success and Dominance in Ecosystems. Edward O. Wilson. Ecology Institute, Nordbunte 23, Oldendorf/Luhe, Germany 1990. Proposes that the success of a species is measured by its evolutionary longevity and its dominance by its ability to dominate or control the appropriation of biomass and energy in ecosystems. Explores how and why social insects, representing only 2 percent of insect species but accounting for one-half of insect biomass, became the ecological center of terrestrial ecosystems. Much of the social insects success is attributed to their ability to function as highly structured superorganisms.

Terrestrial and Aquatic Ecosystems: Perturbation and Recovery. Oscar Ravera, ed. E. Horwood, 1230 Avenue of the Americas, New York, New York 10020. (800) 223-2348. 1991. Presented at the 5th European Ecological Symposium held at Siena, Italy in 1989. Some of the topics included: biological responses to the changing ecosystem; anthropogenic perturbations of the community and ecosystem; restoration of degraded ecosystems; environmental management and strategies.

Towards a Green Scotland: Contributions to the Debate. Karen Allan and Nick Radcliffe, eds. Scottish Green Party, 11 Forth St., Edinburgh, Scotland 1990.

Tropical Rainforest: A World Survey of Our Most Valuable Endangered Habitat With a Blueprint for its Survival. Arnold Newman. Facts on File, Inc., 460 Park Ave. S., New York, New York 10016. (212) 683-2244; (800) 322-8755. 1990. Considers threats to rain forests, including logging and slash and burn agricultural practices. Presents a variety of measures to preserve our valuable rain forests.

The Uses of Ecology: Lake Washington and Beyond. W. T. Edmondson. University of Washington Press, PO Box 50096, Seattle, Washington 98145-5096. (206) 543-4050; (800) 441-4115. 1991. Author delivered most of the contents of this book as a Danz lecture at the University of Washington. Gives an account of the pollution and recovery of Lake Washington and describes how communities worked and applied lessons learned from Lake Washington cleanup. Includes extensive documentation and bibliographies.

Valuing Wildlife: Economic and Social Perspectives. Daniel J. Decker and Gary R. Goff, eds. Westview Press, 5500 Central Ave., Boulder, Colorado 80301. (303) 444-3541. 1987. State of the art guide to determining the value of wildlife, the application for environmental impact assessment, and strategies in wildlife planning and policy.

Where Have All the Birds Gone?. John Terborgh. Princeton University Press, 41 Williams St., Princeton, New Jersey 08540. (609) 258-4900. 1989. Includes topics such as: population monitoring, ecological consequences of fragmentation, evolution of migration, social and territorial behaviors of wintering songbirds.

Wildlife Extinction. Charles L. Cadieux. Stone Wall Pr., 1241 30th St. N.W., Washington, District of Columbia 20007. (202) 333-1860. 1991. Presents a worldwide picture of animals in danger of extinction and addresses controversial issues such as exploding human population, the role of zoos and wildlife parks, hunting and poaching.

Wildlife Reserves and Corridors in the Urban Environment. Lowell W. Adams. National Institute for Urban Wildlife, 10921 Trotting Ridge Way, Columbia, Maryland 21044. (301) 596-3311. 1989. Reviews the knowledge base on wildlife habitat reserves and corridors in urban and urbanizing areas. Provides guidelines and approaches to ecological landscape planning and wildlife conservation in these regions.

World Guide to Environmental Issues and Organizations. Peter Brackley. Longman Group Ltd., Longman House, Burnt Mill, Harlow, Essex, England CM20 2J6. (0279) 426721. 1991.

GOVERNMENTAL ORGANIZATIONS

U.S. Environmental Protection Agency: Office of Environmental Processes and Effects Research. 401 M St., S.W., Washington, District of Columbia 20460. (202) 382-5950.

HANDBOOKS AND MANUALS

Environmental Statistics Handbook: Europe. Allan Foster, Oksana Newman. Gale Research Inc., 835 Penobscot Bldg., Detroit, Michigan 48226-4094. (313) 961-2242. 1993.

Mediterranean-Type Ecosystems: A Data Source Book. Kluwer Academic Publishers, 101 Philip Dr., Assinippi Park, Norwell, Massachusetts 02061. (617) 871-6600. 1988. Covers ecology and bioclimatology.

Permaculture: A Practical Guide for a Sustainable Future. B. C. Mollison. Island Press, 1718 Connecticut Ave. N.W., Suite 300, Washington, District of Columbia 20009. (202) 232-7933. 1990.

Your Resource Guide to Environmental Organizations. John Seredich, ed. Smiling Dolphins Press, 4 Segura, Irvine, California 92715. 1991. Includes the purposes, programs, accomplishments, volunteer opportunities, publications and membership benefits of 150 environmental organizations.

ONLINE DATA BASES

BIOSIS Previews. BIOSIS, 2100 Arch St., Philadelphia, Pennsylvania 19103-1399. (215) 587-4800. Largest and most comprehensive database of research in the life sciences. Contains citations for nearly 9000 primary research journals, monographs, reviews, symposia, preliminary reports, semi-popular journals, selected institutional reports, government reports and research communications.

Cambridge Scientific Abstracts Life Science–CSAL. Cambridge Scientific Abstracts, 5161 River Rd., Bethesda, Maryland 20816. (301) 961-6750. Provides access to the following abstracting services: "Life Sciences Collection," "Aquatic Sciences and Fisheries Abstracts," "Oceanic Abstracts," and "Pollution Abstracts."

Computerized Engineering Index–COMPENDEX. Engineering Information Inc., 345 E. 47th St., New York, New York 10017. (212) 705-7600.

Enviro/Energyline Abstracts Plus. R. R. Bowker Co., 121 Chanlon Rd., New Providence, New Jersey 07974. (908) 464-6800.

Environmental Business Journal. EnviroQuest, PO Box 371769, San Diego, California 92137. (619) 295-7685. Online access.

Environmental Fate Databases. Syracuse Research Cooperation, Merrill Lane, Syracuse, New York 13210. (312) 426-3200. Environmental fate of chemicals.

Environmental Periodicals Bibliography. National Information Services Corp., Ste. 6, Wyman Towers, 3100 St.

Paul St., Baltimore, Maryland 21218. (410)243-0797. Online version of abstract of same name.

Monthly Catalog of United States Government Publications. U.S. G.P.O., Supt. of Docs., PO Box 371954, Pittsburgh, Pennsylvania 15250-7954. (202) 512-0000.

National Technical Information Service. U.S. Department of Commerce, National Technical Information Service, Office of Data Base Services, 5285 Port Royal Rd., Springfield, Virginia 22161. (703) 487-4807. Bibliographic database of government sponsored research and technical reports.

PressNet Environmental Reports. Chemical Information Systems, Inc., 7215 York Rd., Baltimore, Maryland 21212. (301) 321-8440.

PERIODICALS AND NEWSLETTERS

Agriculture, Ecosystems & Environment. Elsevier Science Publishing Co., 655 Avenue of the Americas, New York, New York 10010. (212) 989-5800. Eight times a year. This journal is concerned with the interaction of methods of agricultural production, ecosystems and the environment.

Agro-Ecosystems. Elsevier Science Publishing Co., 655 Avenue of the Americas, New York, New York 10010. (212) 989-5800. 1982-. Quarterly. Journal of International Association for Ecology featuring ecological interactions between agricultural and managed forest systems.

Ambio: A Journal of the Human Environment. Royal Swedish Academy of Sciences. Pergamon Microforms International, Inc., Fairview Park, Elmsford, New York 10523. (914) 592-7720. 1971-. Monthly. Publishes recent work in the interrelated fields of environmental management, technology and the natural sciences.

The American Naturalist. Americana Society of Naturalists, Business Sciences, University of Kansas, Lawrence, Kansas 66045. (913) 864-3763. Monthly. Contains information by professionals of the biological sciences.

Annual Review of Ecology and Systematics. Annual Reviews Inc., 4139 El Camino Way, Palo Alto, California 94303-0897. (800) 523-8635. 1970-. Annual. Original articles critically assessing the significant research literature in ecology and systematics.

Applied and Environmental Microbiology Journal. American Society for Microbiology, 1325 Massachusetts Avenue N.W., Washington, District of Columbia 20005. (202) 737-3600. Monthly. Articles on industrial and food microbiology and ecological studies.

Aquasphere. New England Aquarium, Central Wharf, Boston, Massachusetts 02110. (617) 742-8830. 1963. Articles on any subject related to the world of water. Emphasis on ecology, environment, and aquatic animals.

Audubon. National Audubon Society, 950 3rd Ave., New York, New York 10022. (212) 832-3200. 1899-. Bimonthly.

Audubon Activist. National Audubon Society, 950 3rd Ave., New York, New York 10022. (212) 832-3200. 1986-. Bimonthly. Provide the latest information on important environmental issues throughout the country.

Audubon Society of Rhode Island Report. Audubon Society of Rhode Island, 12 Sanderson Rd., Smithfield, Rhode Island 02917. (401) 231-6444. 1966. Bimonthly.

Covers current and historical natural history and ecology topics.

Balance Report. Population Environment Balance, 1325 6th St. N.W., #1003, Washington, District of Columbia 20005. (202) 879-3000. Quarterly.

Baseline. W. S. Dept. of Ecology, Mail stop PV-11, Olympia, Washington 98504. (206) 459-6145. 1982-. Monthly. General information about ecology programs.

Bulletin of the Ecological Society of America. Arizona State University, Center for Environmental Studies, Tempe, Arizona 85287. (602) 965-3000.

Catalyst: Economics for the Living Earth. Catalyst Investing in Social Change, 64 Main St., Montpelier, Vermont 05602. (802) 223-7943. 1983-. Quarterly. Discusses grassroots enterprises working for social change and a humane economy. Focuses on ecological balance, articles on forest destruction, energy issues, native peoples issues and community- based economics.

Chemosphere: Chemistry, Biology and Toxicology as Related to Environmental Problems. Pergamon Microforms International, Inc., Fairview Park, Elmsford, New York 10523. (914) 592-7720. 1970-. Offers maximum dissemination of investigations related to the health and safety of every aspect of life. Environmental protection encompasses a very wide field and relies on scientific research in chemistry, biology, physics, toxicology and inter-related disciplines.

Coastal Reporter Newsletter. American Littoral Society, Sandy Hook, Highlands, New Jersey 07732. (201) 291-0055. Quarterly. Promotes study and conservation of the coastal zone habitat.

Down to Earth. Montana Environmental Information Center, Box 1184, Helena, Montana 59624. (406) 443-2520. Quarterly. Montana environmental news & concerns.

EARR: Environment and Natural Resources. Academic Publishers, Box 786, Cooper Station, New York, New York 10276. (212) 206-8900. Monthly. All aspects of environmental and natural resources.

Earth Science. American Geological Institute, 4220 King Street, Alexandria, Virginia 22302. (703) 379-2480. Quarterly. Covers geological issues.

Earth Work. The Student Conservation Association Inc., PO Box 550, Charlestown, New Hampshire 03603-0550. (603) 826-4301. 1991-. Monthly. Articles focus on the people, agencies, and the nonprofit organizations that protect our parks, refuges, forests and other lands. Carries a special feature entitled JobScan which provides the most comprehensive listing of natural resource and environmental job opportunities anywhere.

Earthstewards Network News. Holyearth Foundation, Box 10697, Winslow, Washington 98110. (206) 842-7986. Bimonthly.

Eco-Log. California Conservation Council, Box 5572, Pasadena, California 91107.

Eco-News. Environmental Action Coalition, 625 Broadway, 2nd Fl., New York, New York 10012. (212) 677-1601. Monthly. Children's environmental newsletter on pollution, nature, and ecology.

Ecological Applications. Ecological Society of America, Center for Environmental Studies, Arizona State University, Tempe, Arizona 85287. (602) 965-3000. 1991-. Quarterly. Emphasizes the application of basic ecological concepts to a wide range of problems.

Ecological Monographs. Business Office of the Ecological Society of America, Center of Environmental Studies, Arizona State University, Tempe, Arizona 85287-1201. (602) 965-3000. Quarterly. Scientific journal of ecological issues.

Ecological Society of America Bulletin. Ecological Society of America, Center of Environmental Studies, Arizona State University, Tempe, Arizona 85287-1201. (602) 965-3000. Quarterly. Study of living things in relation to their environments.

Ecologie. Les Editions Humus, Inc., 4545 Pierre-de-Coubertin, Montreal, Quebec, Canada H1V 3R2. (514) 252-3148. Bimonthly. Environmental scientific and international information.

Ecologist. Tycooly Publishing International, Box C-166, Riverton, New Jersey 08077. Bimonthly. Magazine for environment and development.

Ecologist. MIT Press, 55 Hayward St., Cambridge, Massachusetts 02142. (617) 253-2889. Bimonthly. Man's impact on the biosphere and social, economic and political barriers.

Ecology. Ecological Society of America, Center of Environmental Studies, Arizona State University, Tempe, Arizona 85287-1201. (602) 965-3000. Bimonthly. Information on the study of living things.

Ecology Center Newsletter. Ecology Center, 2530 San Pablo Ave., Berkeley, California 94702. (510) 548-2220. Monthly. Politics and philosophy of the environment.

Ecology USA. Business Publishers, Inc., 951 Pershing Dr., Silver Spring, Maryland 20910-4464. (301) 587-6300. 1972-. Biweekly. Contains all the legislation, regulation, and litigation affecting efforts to conserve and protect America's unique environmental and ecological heritage.

Ecolution: The Eco Home Newsletter. Eco Home Network, 4344 Russell Ave., Los Angeles, California 90027. (213) 662-5207. Bimonthly. News of pollution and abatement.

Ecomod. ISEM–North America Chapter, Water Quality Division, South Florida Water Management District, P.O. Box 24608, West Palm Beach, Florida 33416. (407) 686-8800. Monthly. Current events in ecological and environmental modeling.

Econews. Northcoast Environmental Center, 879 Ninth St., Arcata, California 95521. (707) 822-6918. Eleven times a year. Environmental news focusing on northwestern California.

Economic News Notes. National Association of Home Builders, 15th & M St., N.W., Washington, District of Columbia 20005. (202) 822-0434. Monthly.

Ecosphere. Forum International, 91 Gregory Ln., Ste. 21, Pleasant Hill, California 94523. (510) 671-2900. Bimonthly. Eco-development, ecology, ecosystems, interface between culture-environment-tourism.

Ecotoxicology and Environmental Safety. Academic Press, c/o Harcourt Brace Jovanovich Inc., 6277 Sea Harbor Dr., Orlando, Florida 32887. (800) 346-8648. 1977-. Bimonthly.

Emergency Preparedness News. Business Publishers, Inc., 951 Pershing Drive, Silver Spring, Maryland 20910. (301) 587-6300. Biweekly. Emergency management techniques and technologies.

Environ: A Magazine for Ecological Living & Health Wary. Canary Press, Box 2204, Ft. Collins, Colorado 80522. (303) 224-0083. Quarterly. Consumer alternatives for ecologically sound lifestyles.

Environment Careers. PH Publishing, Inc., 760 Whalers Way, STE. 100-A, Fort Collins, Colorado 80525. (303) 229-0029. Monthly. Career opportunities in the field.

Environmental Business Journal. EnviroQuest, PO Box 371769, San Diego, California 92137. (619) 295-7685. Monthly. Products relating to environmental protection.

Environmental Hotline. Devel Associated, Inc., 7208 Jefferson St., N.E., Albuquerque, New Mexico 87109. (505) 345-8732. Monthly. Regulations and analysis of key environmental issues.

Environmental Professional. National Association of Environmental Professionals, P.O. Box 15210, Alexandria, Virginia 22309-0210. (703) 660-2364. Quarterly. Covers effective impact assessment, regulation, and environmental protection.

Environmental Progress. American Institute of Chemical Engineers, 345 E. 47th St., New York, New York 10017. (212) 705-7338. Quarterly. Deals with environmental policies, protection and management-especially relating to chemicals.

Environmental Review. American Society for Environmental History, Department of History, University of Oregon, Corvallis, Oregon 97331. Quarterly. Covers human ecology as seen through history and the humanities.

Environmental Studies & Practice: An Educational Resource and Forum. Yale School of Forestry and Environmental Studies, 205 Prospect St., New Haven, Connecticut 06511. (203) 432-5132. 1991. Bimonthly. Subject matters range widely from air pollution to wildlife biology. Each issue contains a selection of recent publications, from all subject areas of environmental and natural resources management.

Environmental Technology and Economics. Technomic Publishing Co., 750 Summer St., Stamford, Connecticut 06902. (717) 291-5609. 1966-. Semimonthly.

Environments. Faculty of Environmental Studies, University of Waterloo, Waterloo, Ontario, Canada N2L 3G1. (519) 885-1211. Three times a year. People in manmade and natural environments.

EPA Bulletin. U.S. Environmental Protection Agency, 401 M St., S.W., A-107, Washington, District of Columbia 20460. (202) 755-0890. Monthly. News of conservation and legislation.

Estuaries. Chesapeake Biological Laboratory, 1 William St., Solomons, Maryland 20688-0038. (410) 326-4281. Quarterly. Journal of the Estuarine Research Federation dealing with estuaries and estuarine biology.

The Everglades Reporter. Friends of the Everglades, 202 Park St., #4, Miami, Florida 33166. (305) 888-1230. Five times a year. Ecology and nature conservation of the Florida Everglades.

Everyone's Back Yard. Citizen's Clearinghouse for Hazardous Wastes, P.O. Box 926, Arlington, Virginia 22216. (703) 276-7070. Bimonthly. Contains news, views, and resources for grassroots environmental activists.

Global Ecology and Biogeography Letter. Blackwell Scientific Publications, 3 Cambridge Ctr., Suite 208, Cambridge, Massachusetts 02142. (617) 225-0401. 1991. Bimonthly. Global Ecology and Biogeography Letters is a sister publication of Journal of Biogeography and is only available with a subscription to the Journal. Provides a fast-track outlet for short research papers, news items, editorials, and book reviews. Topics related to the major scientific concerns of our present era, such as global warming, world sea-level rises, environmental acidification, development and conservation, biodiversity, and important new theories and themes in biogeography and ecology.

The Great Basin Naturalist. Brigham Young University, 290 Life Science Museum, Provo, Utah 84602. (801) 378-5053.

Green Letter. Green Letter, Box 9242, Berkeley, California 94709. Bimonthly. Information about the worldwide green movement.

Green Library Journal: Environmental Topics in the Information World. Maria A. Jankowska, ed. Green Library, University of Idaho Library, Moscow, Idaho 83843. (208) 885-6260. Jan 1992-. Scope of the journal would include information sources about: conservation, ecologically balanced regional development, environmental protection, natural resources management, environmental issues in libraries, publishing industries, and information science.

Green Light News. Green Light News, Box 12, Liberty Sq., Ellenville, New York 12428. (914) 647-3300. Monthly. Ecology news.

Green Party News. Green Party of B.C., 831 Commercial Dr., Vancouver, British Columbia, Canada V5L. (604) 254-8165. Quarterly. Covers environmental politics in British Columbia.

Greenletter. Woodstock Resort, Woodstock Inn, Woodstock, Vermont 05091-1298. (802) 457-1100. Quarterly. Ecological and environmental topics.

Greenpeace Magazine. Greenpeace, 1436 U St., NW, Washington, District of Columbia 20009. (202) 462-1177. Bimonthly. Deals with nature and wildlife conservation, and environmental protection.

Housatonic Current. Housatonic Valley Assn., Box 28, Cornwall Bridge, Connecticut 06754. (203) 672-6678. Quarterly. Environmental programs and land planning throughout the Housatonic River Watershed.

Human Ecology Forum. New York State College of Human Ecology, Cornell University, Martha Van Rensselaer Hall, Ithaca, New York 14853. Quarterly.

Human Factors. Human Factors Society, Publications Division, Box 1369, Santa Monica, California 90406-1369. (310) 394-1811. Bimonthly. Deals with human engineering and human factors.

Journal of Biogeography. Blackwell Scientific Publications Inc., 3 Cambridge Ctr., Suite 208, Cambridge, Massachusetts 02142. (617) 225-0401.

Journal of Environmental Sciences. Institute of Environmental Sciences, 940 East Northwest Highway, Mt.

Prospect, Illinois 60656. (312) 255-1561. Bimonthly. Covers research, controlling and teaching of environmental sciences.

MoPIRG Reports. Missouri Public Interest Research Group, Box 8276, St. Louis, Missouri 63156. (314) 534-7474. Quarterly. Consumer/environmental citizen advocacy.

Nature and Resources. Elsevier Science Publishing Co., 655 Avenue of the Americas, New York, New York 10010. (212) 989-5800. 1965-. Quarterly. Provides indepth reviews of contemporary environmental issues from an international perspective.

NJPIRG. New Jersey Public Interest Research Group, 99 Bayard St., New Brunswick, New Jersey 08901-2120. Semiannual. Consumer & environmental advocacy actions.

Northeastern Environmental Science. Northeastern Science Foundation, Box 746, Troy, New York 12181. (518) 273-3247. Semiannual. Environmental research & policies.

Northern Line. Northern Alaska Environmental Center, 218 Driveway, Fairbanks, Alaska 99701. (907) 452-5021. Quarterly. State environmental news.

On the Edge. Wildlife Preservation Trust International, 34th St. & Girard Ave., Philadelphia, Pennsylvania 19104. (215) 222-2191. Semiannual. Animal conservation, endangered species and captive breeding.

One World. Trans-Species Unlimited, Box 1553, Williamsport, Pennsylvania 17703. (717) 322-3252. Irregular. Vegetarianism and animal rights.

Outdoors Unlimited. Outdoor Writers Association of America, 4141 West Bradley Rd., Milwaukee, Wisconsin 53209. 1940-. Monthly.

Pennsylvania Econotes. Pennsylvania Department on Environmental Resources, Box 1467, Harrisburg, Pennsylvania 17120. 1972-. Monthly.

Pollution Control Newsletter. Arizona State Dept. of Health Services, Bureau of Air Quality Control, 1740 W. Adams St., Phoenix, Arizona 85007. (602) 542-1000. Eight times a year.

Probe Post. Pollution Probe Foundation, 12 Madison Ave., Toronto, Ontario, Canada M5R 2S1. (416) 926-1647. Quarterly. Acid rain, toxic waste, renewable energy, deep ecology, land use, and greenhouse effect.

Protection Ecology. Elsevier Science Publishing Co., Journal Information Center, 655 Avenue of the Americas, New York, New York 10010. (212) 989-5800. Livestock and agricultural ecology and pest control.

Sierra Club Bulletin. Sierra Club Books, 100 Bush St., San Francisco, California 94104. (415) 291-1600. 1893-. Ten times a year.

World Resource Review. SUPCON International, PO Box 5275, 1 Heritage Plaza, Woodridge, Illinois 60517. (708) 910-1551. 1981-. Quarterly. Covers all phases of policy discussions and their developments, including such topics as global change, energy production and use, ecosystem impacts of development activities, environmental law, solution of transnational environmental problems, global flow of strategic industrial materials, regional, national, and local resource management, natural resources, food, agriculture and forestry.

RESEARCH CENTERS AND INSTITUTES

Antioch University, Environmental Studies Center. Yellow Springs, Ohio 45387. (513) 767-7331.

Center for Strategic Wildland Management Studies. University of Michigan, School of Natural Resources, Ann Arbor, Michigan 48109. (313) 763-2200.

Institute of Ecology. University of California, Davis, Davis, California 95616. (916) 752-3026.

Manomet Bird Observatory. P.O. Box 1770, Manomet, Massachusetts 02345. (508) 224-6521.

University of Alaska Anchorage, Arctic Environmental Information and Data Center. 707 A Street, Anchorage, Alaska 99501. (907) 257-2733.

University of Alaska Fairbanks, Institute of Arctic Biology. Fairbanks, Alaska 99775. (907) 474-7648.

University of Georgia, Institute of Ecology. 103 Ecology Building, Athens, Georgia 30602. (404) 542-2968.

University of Idaho, Wilderness Research Center. Moscow, Idaho 83843. (208) 885-7911.

University of Kansas, John H. Nelson Environmental Study Area. Division of Biological Sciences, Lawrence, Kansas 66045. (913) 864-3236.

University of Michigan, Wetland Ecosystem Research Group. Department of Chemical Engineering, 3094 Dow Building, Ann Arbor, Michigan 48109. (313) 764-3362.

University of Mississippi, Biological Field Station. Department of Biology, University, Mississippi 38677. (601) 232-5479.

University of Nebraska-Lincoln, Center for Microbial Ecology. Lincoln, Nebraska 68588-0343. (402) 472-2253.

University of North Dakota, Institute for Ecological Studies. Box 8278, University Station, Grand Forks, North Dakota 58202. (701) 777-2851.

University of Wisconsin-Madison, Center for Restoration Ecology. Arboretum, 1207 Seminole Highway, Madison, Wisconsin 53711. (608) 263-7889.

Urban Vegetation Laboratory. Morton Arboretum, Route 53, Lisle, Illinois 60532. (708) 968-0074.

STATISTICS SOURCES

Ecology: Community Profiles. U.S. Fish and Wildlife Service. National Technical Information Service, 5285 Port Royal Road, Springfield, Virginia 22161. (703) 487-4650. Irregular. Data on coastal and inland ecosystems, including wetlands, tidal-flats, near-shore seagrasses, sand dunes, drilling platforms, oyster reefs, estuaries, rivers and streams.

Environmental Data Compendium. OECD Publications and Information Center, 2001 L St., N.W., Suite 700, Washington, District of Columbia 20036. (202) 785-6323. 1989.

Environmental Indicators. OECD Publications and Information Center, 2001 L St., N.W., Suite 700, Washington, District of Columbia 20036. (202) 785-6323. 1991.

Environmental Quality. Council on Environmental Quality. U.S. G.P.O., Washington, District of Columbia 20401. (202) 512-0000. Annual.

The State of the Environment. OECD Publications and Information Center, 2001 L St., N.W., Suite 700, Washington, District of Columbia 20036. (202) 785-6323. 1991.

Statistical Record of the Environment. Arsen J. Darnay. Gale Research Inc., 835 Penobscot Bldg., Detroit, Michigan 48226-4094. (313) 961-2242. 1992.

World Resources. World Resources Institute. 1709 New York Ave., N.W., Washington, District of Columbia 20006. (202) 638-6300. Annual. Statistical and textual analysis of world's natural resources and the effects of growth-caused environmental pollution.

TRADE ASSOCIATIONS AND PROFESSIONAL SOCIETIES

American Institute of Biological Sciences. 730 11th St., N.W., Washington, District of Columbia 20001-4521. (202) 628-1500.

American Nature Study Society. 5881 Cold Brook Rd., Homer, New York 13077. (607) 749-3655.

American Ornithologists' Union. Smithsonian Institution, National Museum of Natural History, Washington, District of Columbia 20560. (202) 357-1970.

American Society of Civil Engineers. 345 East 47th St., New York, New York 10017. (212) 705-7496.

American Society of Naturalists. Department of Ecology and Evolation, State University of New York, Stony Brook, New York 11794. (516) 632-8589.

Association for the Study of Man-Environment Relations. Box 57, Orangeburg, New York 10962. (914) 634-8221.

Association of Ecosystem Research Centers. Ecology Center, Logan, Utah 84322-5205. (801) 750-2555.

Ecological Society of America. Arizona State University, Center for Environmental Studies, Tempe, Arizona 85287. (602) 965-3000.

Goldman Environmental Foundation. 1160 Battery St., Suite 400, San Francisco, California 94111. (415) 788-1090.

Green Committees of Correspondence. P.O. Box 30208, Kansas City, Missouri 64112. (816) 931-9366.

Greenpeace. 1436 U St., NW, Washington, District of Columbia 20009. (202) 462-1177.

Inland Bird Banding Association. RD 2, Box 26, Wisner, Nebraska 68791. (402) 529-6679.

Institute of Ecosystem Studies. Box AB, Millbrook, New York 12545-0129. (914) 677-5976.

International Ecology Society. 1471 Barclay St., St. Paul, Minnesota 55106. (612) 774-4971.

John Muir Institute for Environmental Studies. 743 Wilson St., Napa, California 94559. (707) 252-8333.

National Center for Urban Environmental Studies. 516 N. Charles St., Suite 501, Baltimore, Maryland 21201. (301) 727-6212.

Natural Resources Defense Council. 40 W. 20th St., New York, New York 10011. (212) 727-2700.

Organization of Biological Field Stations. Box 351, Eureka, Missouri 63025. (314) 938-5346.

Planet Drum. Box 31251, San Francisco, California 94131. (415) 285-6556.

Safari Club International. 4800 W. Gates Pass Rd., Tucson, Arizona 85745. (602) 620-1220.

Sierra Club. 100 Bush St., San Francisco, California 94104. (415) 291-1600.

Smithsonian Institution. National Museum of Natural History, NHB-106, Washington, District of Columbia 20560. (202) 786-2821.

United Nations Information Centre. 1889 F St. N.W., Ground Floor, Washington, District of Columbia 20006. (202) 289-8670.

United New Conservationists. P.O. Box 362, Campbell, California 95009. (408) 241-5769.

United States Operating Committee on ETAD. 1330 Connecticut Ave., N.W., Suite 300, Washington, District of Columbia 20036-1702. (202) 659-0060.

Urban Land Institute. 625 Indiana Ave., N.W., Washington, District of Columbia 20004. (202) 624-7000.

EDAPHIC

See: ENVIRONMENT CONDITION

EDIBLE OILS

See: NUTRITION

EDUCATION, ENVIRONMENTAL

ABSTRACTING AND INDEXING SERVICES

Engineering Index. The Engineering Index Inc., 345 E. 47th St., New York, New York 10017. 1962-.

Geographical Abstracts. London School of Economics, Dept. of Geography, Regency House, 34 Duke St., London, England 1966-. Continued by Geo Abstracts issued in 6 parts: Pt. A. Landforms and the quaternary; Pt. B. Biogeography and Climatology; Pt. C. Economic geography; Pt. D. Social geography and cartography; Pt. E. Sedimentology; Pt. F. Regional and community planning.

Index to Scientific Book Contents. Institute for Scientific Information, 3501 Market St., Philadelphia, Pennsylvania 19104. (800) 523-1857. 1985-. Annual. Gives contents of science books published.

ALMANACS AND YEARBOOKS

Gale Environmental Almanac. Russ Hoyle. Gale Research Inc., 835 Penobscot Bldg., Detroit, Michigan 48226-4094. (313) 961-2242. 1993. Focuses on the U.S. and Canada, although worldwide and transboundary issues are discussed.

BIBLIOGRAPHIES

Environmental Education: A Guide to Information Sources. William B. Stapp. Gale Research Co., 835

Penobscot Bldg., Detroit, Michigan 48226-4094. (313) 961-2242. 1975. Man and the Environment Information Guide Series; v.1.

DIRECTORIES

Canadian Environmental Directory. Canadian Almanac & Directory Publishing Co. Ltd., 134 Adelaide St. E., Ste. 27, Toronto, Ontario, Canada M5C 1K9. (416) 362-4088. 1992. Includes individuals, agencies, firms, and associations.

The Green Encyclopedia. Irene Franck, David Brownstone. Prentice-Hall, Rte. 9W, Englewood Cliffs, New York 07632. (201) 592-2000. 1992. Covers environmental organizations.

New Careers: A Directory of Jobs and Internship in Technology and Society. R. Hefland, ed. Student Pugeash USA, 1638 R St. NW, Suite 32, Washington, District of Columbia 20009. (202) 328-6555. 1990-. Third edition. Includes organizations from 15 major cities nationwide including Washington, DC, Boston, New York, San Francisco, and Chicago. An index to organizations is provided.

Solid Waste Education Recycling Directory. Teresa Jones, et al. Lewis Publishers, 200 Corporate Blvd. NW, Boca Raton, Florida 33431. (407) 994-0555 or (800)272-7737. 1990. Summarizes recycling education curricula for each state covering all levels, K-12. Provides names, addresses, phone numbers, information about the availability of materials, how you collect them, and how much they cost.

ENCYCLOPEDIAS AND DICTIONARIES

Encyclopedia of Environmental Studies. William Ashworth. Facts on File, Inc., 460 Park Ave. S., New York, New York 10016. (212) 683-2244. 1991.

Environmental Encyclopedia. William P. Cunningham, Terence Ball, et. al. Gale Research Inc., 835 Penobscot Bldg., Detroit, Michigan 48226-4094. (313) 961-2242. 1993.

GENERAL WORKS

The Complete Guide to Environmental Careers. CEIP Fund. Island Press, 1718 Connecticut Ave. N.W., Suite 300, Washington, District of Columbia 20009. (202) 232-7933. 1989. Presents information needed to plan any career search. Case studies discuss how environmental organizations, government, and industry are working to manage and protect natural resources.

Earth Education: A New Beginning. Steve Van Matre. Institute for Earth Education, PO Box 288, Warrenville, Illinois 60555. (708) 393-3096. 1990. Describes environmental education which adopts an alternative foundation for improving awareness about the environment through changes in attitudes and life styles.

Environmental Pollution. Inderscience Enterprises Ltd., World Trade Center Bldg., 110 Avenue Louis Casai, Case Postale 306, Geneva-Airport, Switzerland CH-1215. (44) 908-314248. 1991. Special issue of the International Journal of Environment and Pollution. Proceedings of the 1st International Conference on Environmental Pollution held at the Congress Centre, Lisbon, April 15-19, 1991.

Environmental Viewpoints. Marie Lazzari. Gale Research Inc., 835 Penobscot Bldg., Detroit, Michigan 48226-4094. (313) 961-2242. 1992.

How Green Are You?. David Bellamy. Clarkson N. Potter, Inc., 225 Park Ave., S., New York, New York 10003. (212) 254-1600. 1991. Information and projects about ecology and environmental concerns that teach how to conserve energy, protect wildlife, and reduce pollution.

Into Adolescence. Caring for Our Planet and Our Health: A Curriculum for Grades 5-8. Lisa K. Hunter. Network Publications, PO Box 1830, Santa Cruz, California 95061-1830. (408) 438-4060. 1991.

GOVERNMENTAL ORGANIZATIONS

New England Interstate Water Pollution Control Commission. 85 Merrimac St., Boston, Massachusetts 02114. (617) 367-8522.

HANDBOOKS AND MANUALS

Entering Adulthood. Creating a Healthy Environment: A Curriculum for Grades 9-12. Donna Lloyd-Kolkin. Network Publications, PO Box 1830, Santa Cruz, California 95061-1830. (408) 438-4060. 1990.

Environmental Career Guide: Job Opportunities with the Earth in Mind. Nicholas Basta. John Wiley & Sons, Inc., 605 3rd Ave., New York, New York 10158-0012. (212) 850-6000. 1991. Complete guide to the many career options in the growing environmental field. Shows how to find employers engaged in environmental activity, and how to get the job. Lists key environmental businesses--manufacturing, government agencies, engineering consulting firms, waste handling firms, and others. Lists key professional careers in environmental conservation and maps career strategies.

Environmental Statistics Handbook: Europe. Allan Foster, Oksana Newman. Gale Research Inc., 835 Penobscot Bldg., Detroit, Michigan 48226-4094. (313) 961-2242. 1993.

ONLINE DATA BASES

Computerized Engineering Index–COMPENDEX. Engineering Information Inc., 345 E. 47th St., New York, New York 10017. (212) 705-7600.

Instructional Resources Information System. Ohio State University, Environmental Quality Instructional Resources Center, 1200 Chambers Rd., Room 310, Columbus, Ohio 43212. (614) 292-6717. Training materials in the area of water resources, water quality, solid wastes, hazardous wastes, and toxic materials.

Monthly Catalog of United States Government Publications. U.S. G.P.O., Supt. of Docs., PO Box 371954, Pittsburgh, Pennsylvania 15250-7954. (202) 512-0000.

National Technical Information Service. U.S. Department of Commerce, National Technical Information Service, Office of Data Base Services, 5285 Port Royal Rd., Springfield, Virginia 22161. (703) 487-4807. Bibliographic database of government sponsored research and technical reports.

SCISEARCH. Institute for Scientific Information, University City Science Center, 3501 Market St., Philadelphia, Pennsylvania 19104. (215) 386-0100.

PERIODICALS AND NEWSLETTERS

Alliance Exchange. Alliance for Environmental Education Inc., Box 1040, 3421 M. St., N.W., Washington, District of Columbia 20007. (202) 797-4530. Quarterly. Publishes material relating to environmental education. Reports on national conferences held and acts as an information base to help efforts of self-supporting education and teacher training centers for environmental education.

Clearing Magazine. Environmental Education Project, 19600 S. Molalla Ave., Oregon City, Oregon 97045. (503) 656-0155. Five times a year. Resource materials, teaching ideas, and information for those interested in providing environmental education.

Conservation Education Association Newsletter. Conservation Education Association, c/o Conservation Education Center, RR 1, Box 153, Guthrie Center, Iowa 50115. (515) 747-8383. Quarterly. Promotes environmental conservation education.

Environmental Communicator. North American Association for Environmental Education, P.O. Box 400, Troy, Ohio 45373. (513) 339-6835. Bimonthly. Information on environmental topics and teaching methods.

Environmental Outlook. Institute for Environmental Studies, University of Washington, FM-12, Seattle, Washington 98105. (206) 543-1812. Monthly. Regional and local environmental education.

Feather in the Wind. Last Chance Forever, 506 Ave. A, San Antonio, Texas 78215. (512) 224-7228. Semiannual. Birds of prey and their relation to the environment.

GEM Notes: an Update of the Groundwater Education in Michigan Program. Groundwater Education in Michigan, Institute of Water Research, Michigan State University, 25 Manly Miles Bldg., 1405 S. Harrison Rd., East Lansing, Michigan 48824. (517) 355-9543. 1988-. Irregular.

Green Library Journal: Environmental Topics in the Information World. Maria A. Jankowska, ed. Green Library, University of Idaho Library, Moscow, Idaho 83843. (208) 885-6260. Jan 1992-. Scope of the journal would include information sources about: conservation, ecologically balanced regional development, environmental protection, natural resources management, environmental issues in libraries, publishing industries, and information science.

INFORM Reports. INFORM Inc., 381 Park Ave., So., New York, New York 10016. (212) 689-4040. Quarterly. INFORM is a nonprofit environmental research & education organization for the preservation and conservation of natural resources and public health.

The Journal of Environmental Education. Heldref Publications, 4000 Albemarle Street, NW, Washington, District of Columbia 20016. (202) 362-6445. Quarterly. Teaching methods, case studies, and evaluations of new research.

N.A.E.E. Newsletter. National Association for Environmental Education, Box 1295, Miami, Florida 33143. 1972-. Monthly.

National Environmental Training Association Newsletter. National Environmental Training Association, 2930 E. Camelback Rd., Phoenix, Arizona 85016. (602) 956-

6099. Bimonthly. Covers environmental training programs and training materials.

North American Association for Environmental Education Magazine. North American Association for Environmental Education, Box 400, Troy, Ohio 45373. (513) 339-6835. Bimonthly.

Priorities For Long Life and Good Health. American Council on Health and Science, 1995 Broadway, 16th Floor, New York, New York 10023. (212) 362-7044. Quarterly. Covers evaluations of food, chemicals, and health.

Talking Leaves. Institute for Earth Education, PO Box 288, Warrenville, Illinois 60555. (708) 393-3096. Quarterly. Programs and events dealing with earth and ecology education.

RESEARCH CENTERS AND INSTITUTES

Center for Environmental Education and Research. University of Colorado-Boulder, College of Environmental Design, Boulder, Colorado 80309. (303) 492-7711.

Queens College of City University of New York, Center for Environmental Teaching and Research. Queens College of City University of New York, Center for Environmental Teaching and Research, Caumsett State Park, 31 Lloyd Harper Rd., Huntington, New York 11743. (516) 421-3526.

Renew America. 17 16th Street, N. W., Suite 710, Washington, District of Columbia 20036. (202) 232-2252.

Rocky Mountain Institute. 1739 Snowmass Creek Rd, Snowmass, Colorado 81654. (303) 927-3128.

World Environment Center. 419 Park Avenue, Suite 1403, New York, New York 10016. (212) 683-4700.

TRADE ASSOCIATIONS AND PROFESSIONAL SOCIETIES

Alliance for Environmental Education, Inc. 10751 Ambassador Dr., No. 201, Manassas, Virginia 22110. (703) 335-1025. A coalition of organizations that works at the regional, state, and national level to promote environmental education.

American Nature Study Society. 5881 Cold Brook Rd., Homer, New York 13077. (607) 749-3655.

American Society for Environmental Education. 1592 Union St., Suite 210, San Francisco, California 94123. (415) 931-7000.

American Society for Environmental History. Center for Technical Studies, New Jersey Institute of Technology, Newark, New Jersey 07102. (201) 596-3270.

Citizens for a Better Environment. 33 E. Congress, Suite 523, Chicago, Illinois 60605. (312) 939-1530.

Earth Communications Office. 1925 Century Park East, Suite 2300, Los Angeles, California 90067. (213) 277-1665.

Environmental Action Coalition. 625 Broadway, 2nd Fl., New York, New York 10012. (212) 677-1601.

Environmental Action Foundation. 6930 Carroll Ave., 6th Fl., Takoma Park, Maryland 20912. (202) 745-4870.

Environmental Action, Inc. 1525 New Hampshire Ave., NW, Washington, District of Columbia 20036. (202) 745-4870.

Environmental Quality Industrial Resources Center. The Ohio State University, 1200 Chambers Rd., Room 310, Columbus, Ohio 43212. (614) 292-6717.

Environmental Studies Institute. 800 Garden St., Suite D, Santa Barbara, California 93101. (805) 965-5010.

ERIC Clearinghouse for Science, Mathematics, and Environmental Education. Ohio State University, 1200 Chambers Rd., 3rd Floor, Columbus, Ohio 43212. (614) 292-6717.

Government Institutes, Inc. 966 Hungerford Dr., #24, Rockville, Maryland 20850. (301) 251-9250.

INFORM. 381 Park Avenue S., New York, New York 10016. (212) 689-4040.

Institute for Earth Education. PO Box 288, Warrenville, Illinois 60555. (708) 393-3096.

Institute for the Human Environment. c/o Institute of International Education, 41 Sutter No. 510, San Francisco, California 94104. (415) 362-6520.

Kids for a Clean Environment. P.O. Box 158254, Nashville, Tennessee 37215. (615) 331-0708.

Learning Alliance. 494 Broadway, New York, New York 10012. (212) 226-7171.

Meadowcreek Project, Inc. Fox, Alaska 72051. (501) 363-4500.

National Audubon Society. 950 Third Ave., New York, New York 10022. (212) 832-3200.

National Environmental Health Association. South Tower, 720 S. Colorado Blvd., #970, Denver, Colorado 80222. (303) 756-9090.

National Environmental Training Association. 2930 E. Camelback Rd., Phoenix, Arizona 85016. (602) 956-6099.

National Geographic Society. 17th and M Streets, NW, Washington, District of Columbia 20036. (202) 857-7000.

National Wildlife Federation. 1400 16th St., N.W., Washington, District of Columbia 20036. (202) 797-6800.

North American Association for Environmental Education. 1255 23rd St., N.W., Suite 400, Washington, District of Columbia 20037. (202) 862-1991.

Point Foundation. 27 Gate Five Rd., Sausalito, California 94965. (415) 332-1716.

Sierra Club. 100 Bush St., San Francisco, California 94104. (415) 291-1600.

TreePeople. 12601 Mulholland Dr., Beverly Hills, California 90210. (818) 753-4600.

Western Regional Environmental Education Council. c/o Idaho Dept. of Fish & Game, 600 S. Walnut, Box 25, Boise, Idaho 83707. (208) 334-3747.

Windstar Foundation. 2317 Snowmass Creek Rd., Snowmass, Colorado 81654. (303) 927-4777. Foundation begun by John Denver offering information on a wide range of personal-action issues.

World Peace University. P.O. Box 10869, Eugene, Oregon 97440. (503) 741-1794.

EFFLUENT CONTROL PROGRAMS

See also: EMISSION

ABSTRACTING AND INDEXING SERVICES

Applied Science and Technology Index. H.W. Wilson Co., 950 University Ave., Bronx, New York 10452. (800) 367-6770. Formerly Industrial Arts Index.

Environment Abstracts. Bowker A & I Publishing, 121 Chanlon Rd., New Providence, New Jersey 07974. (908) 464-6800. 1974-.

Environment Index. Environment Information Center, Index Research Department, 124 E. 39th St., New York, New York 10016. 1971-. Annual.

Environmental Information Connection–EIC. Planning Information Program, Dept. of Urban and Regional Planning, University of Illinois, 1003 West Nevada, Urbana, Illinois 61801. (217) 333-1369. Also available online.

Environmental Periodicals Bibliography. Environmental Studies Institute, International Academy at Santa Barbara, 800 Garden St., Suite D, Santa Barbara, California 93101. (805) 965-5010. Also available online.

BIBLIOGRAPHIES

EPA Publications Bibliography. U.S. Environmental Protection Agency, Library Systems Branch, 401 M St., SW, Washington, District of Columbia 20460. (202) 260-2090. Quarterly.

ONLINE DATA BASES

Enviro/Energyline Abstracts Plus. R. R. Bowker Co., 121 Chanlon Rd., New Providence, New Jersey 07974. (908) 464-6800.

Environmental Fate Databases. Syracuse Research Cooperation, Merrill Lane, Syracuse, New York 13210. (312) 426-3200. Environmental fate of chemicals.

Environmental Periodicals Bibliography. National Information Services Corp., Ste. 6, Wyman Towers, 3100 St. Paul St., Baltimore, Maryland 21218. (410)243-0797. Online version of abstract of same name.

Monthly Catalog of United States Government Publications. U.S. G.P.O., Supt. of Docs., PO Box 371954, Pittsburgh, Pennsylvania 15250-7954. (202) 512-0000.

National Technical Information Service. U.S. Department of Commerce, National Technical Information Service, Office of Data Base Services, 5285 Port Royal Rd., Springfield, Virginia 22161. (703) 487-4807. Bibliographic database of government sponsored research and technical reports.

EFFLUENT STANDARDS

See also: EMISSION

ABSTRACTING AND INDEXING SERVICES

Environment Abstracts. Bowker A & I Publishing, 121 Chanlon Rd., New Providence, New Jersey 07974. (908) 464-6800. 1974-.

Environment Index. Environment Information Center, Index Research Department, 124 E. 39th St., New York, New York 10016. 1971-. Annual.

Environmental Information Connection–EIC. Planning Information Program, Dept. of Urban and Regional Planning, University of Illinois, 1003 West Nevada, Urbana, Illinois 61801. (217) 333-1369. Also available online.

Environmental Periodicals Bibliography. Environmental Studies Institute, International Academy at Santa Barbara, 800 Garden St., Suite D, Santa Barbara, California 93101. (805) 965-5010. Also available online.

BIBLIOGRAPHIES

EPA Publications Bibliography. U.S. Environmental Protection Agency, Library Systems Branch, 401 M St., SW, Washington, District of Columbia 20460. (202) 260-2090. Quarterly.

GENERAL WORKS

Aquaculture Techniques: Water Use and Discharge Quality. George W. Klontz. Idaho Water Research Institute, University of Idaho, Moscow, Idaho 83843. Covers aquaculture techniques, fish culture, and effluent quality.

Developing Document for Effluent Limitations Guidelines, New Source Performance Standards and Pretreatment Standards for the Metal Molding and Casting Point Source Category. Industrial Technology Division, Office of Water Regulations and Standards, U.S. Environmental Protection Agency., 401 M St. SW, Washington, District of Columbia 20460. (202) 260-5400. 1986. Environmental aspects of metal work, effluent quality and water use.

ONLINE DATA BASES

Enviro/Energyline Abstracts Plus. R. R. Bowker Co., 121 Chanlon Rd., New Providence, New Jersey 07974. (908) 464-6800.

Environmental Fate Databases. Syracuse Research Cooperation, Merrill Lane, Syracuse, New York 13210. (312) 426-3200. Environmental fate of chemicals.

Environmental Periodicals Bibliography. National Information Services Corp., Ste. 6, Wyman Towers, 3100 St. Paul St., Baltimore, Maryland 21218. (410)243-0797. Online version of abstract of same name.

SCISEARCH. Institute for Scientific Information, University City Science Center, 3501 Market St., Philadelphia, Pennsylvania 19104. (215) 386-0100.

EFFLUENT TREATMENT

See also: EMISSION; WASTEWATER TREATMENT

ABSTRACTING AND INDEXING SERVICES

Applied Science and Technology Index. H.W. Wilson Co., 950 University Ave., Bronx, New York 10452. (800) 367-6770. Formerly Industrial Arts Index.

Chemical Abstracts. Chemical Abstracts Service, 2540 Olentangy River Rd., PO Box 3012, Columbus, Ohio 43210. (800) 848-6533. 1907-.

Engineering Index. The Engineering Index Inc., 345 E. 47th St., New York, New York 10017. 1962-.

BIBLIOGRAPHIES

Directory of Published Proceedings. Interdok Corp., 173 Halstead Ave., Harrison, New York 10528. (914) 835-3506. 1990. Monthly. This is a listing of published proceedings including the series SEMTE (Science/Medicine/Engineering/Technology) and the series SSH (Social Science/Humanities).

ENCYCLOPEDIAS AND DICTIONARIES

Dictionary of Biotechnology. J. Coombs. Elsevier Science Publishing Co., 655 Avenue of the Americas, New York, New York 10010. (212) 984-5800. 1986. Areas covered in this dictionary include: fermentation; brewing; vaccines; plant tissue; culture; antibiotic production; production and use of enzymes; biomass; byproduct recovery and effluent treatment; equipment; processes; micro-organisms and biochemicals.

Encyclopedia of Physical Science and Technology. Robert A. Meyers, ed. Academic Press, c/o Harcourt Brace Jovanovich Inc., 6277 Sea Harbor Dr., Orlando, Florida 32887. (800) 346-8648. Dictionary of engineering, technology and physical sciences.

The New York Times Encyclopedic Dictionary of the Environment. Paul Sarnoff. Quadrangle Books, New York, New York 1971. Focuses on state-of-the-art methods of pollution control, abatement, prevention and removal.

GENERAL WORKS

Effluent Treatment and Waste Disposal. Institution of Chemical Engineers. Hemisphere Publishing Corp., 79 Madison Ave., Suite 1110, New York, New York 10016. (212) 725-1999. 1990. Provides a detailed analysis of the strides which industry has taken to address the pollution of waterways.

Effluents from Livestock. J. K. R. Gasser, et al., eds. Applied Science Publications, PO Box 5399, New York, New York 10163. (718) 756-6440. 1980. Proceedings of a seminar to discuss work carried out within the EEC under the programme Effluents from Intensive Livestock, organized by Prof. H. Vetter and held at Bad Zwischenahn, 2-5 October, 1979.

ONLINE DATA BASES

Chemical Abstracts-CA. Chemical Abstracts Service, 2540 Olentangy River Rd., P.O. Box 3012, Columbus, Ohio 43210. (800) 848-6533 or (614) 421-3600. Information sources include 9000 journals, patents from 27 countries, two industrial property organizations, new books, conference proceedings, and government research reports.

Computerized Engineering Index–COMPENDEX. Engineering Information Inc., 345 E. 47th St., New York, New York 10017. (212) 705-7600.

Environmental Fate Databases. Syracuse Research Cooperation, Merrill Lane, Syracuse, New York 13210. (312) 426-3200. Environmental fate of chemicals.

Monthly Catalog of United States Government Publications. U.S. G.P.O., Supt. of Docs., PO Box 371954, Pittsburgh, Pennsylvania 15250-7954. (202) 512-0000.

National Technical Information Service. U.S. Department of Commerce, National Technical Information Service, Office of Data Base Services, 5285 Port Royal Rd., Springfield, Virginia 22161. (703) 487-4807. Bibliographic database of government sponsored research and technical reports.

SCISEARCH. Institute for Scientific Information, University City Science Center, 3501 Market St., Philadelphia, Pennsylvania 19104. (215) 386-0100.

TRADE ASSOCIATIONS AND PROFESSIONAL SOCIETIES

American Institute of Biological Sciences. 730 11th St., N.W., Washington, District of Columbia 20001-4521. (202) 628-1500.

EFFLUENTS

See also: EMISSIONS

ABSTRACTING AND INDEXING SERVICES

Abstracts of Air and Water Conservation Literature. American Petroleum Institute. Central Abstracting and Indexing Service, 275 Madison Avenue, New York, New York 10016. 1972.

Applied Science and Technology Index. H.W. Wilson Co., 950 University Ave., Bronx, New York 10452. (800) 367-6770. Formerly Industrial Arts Index.

Aqualine Abstracts. Water Research Centre. c/o Pergamon Microforms International, Inc., Fairview Park, Elmsford, New York 10523. (914) 592-7720. 1927-. Contains some 8,000 records annually on water and wastewater technology. Covers all aspects of water, wastewater, associated engineering services and the aquatic environment. Over 600 periodicals, as well as books, reports and conference proceedings and other publications from water related institutions worldwide are scanned. Also available online.

Biological Abstracts. BIOSIS, 2100 Arch St., Philadelphia, Pennsylvania 19103-1399. (215) 587-4800. 1927-.

Chemical Abstracts. Chemical Abstracts Service, 2540 Olentangy River Rd., PO Box 3012, Columbus, Ohio 43210. (800) 848-6533. 1907-.

Civil Engineering Hydraulic Abstracts. BHRA Fluid Engineering, Air Science Co., PO Box 143, Corning, New York 14830. (607) 962-5591. Monthly. Abstracts of periodicals that publish in the areas of hydraulic engineering and other related topics.

Ecological Abstracts. Geo Abstracts Ltd. Elsevier Applied Science, Crown House, Linton Rd., Barking, England IG 11 8JU. 1974-. Derived from over 600 leading ecological

and environmental journals, plus books, conference proceedings, reports and theses.

Environment Abstracts. Bowker A & I Publishing, 121 Chanlon Rd., New Providence, New Jersey 07974. (908) 464-6800. 1974-.

Environment Index. Environment Information Center, Index Research Department, 124 E. 39th St., New York, New York 10016. 1971-. Annual.

Environmental Information Connection–EIC. Planning Information Program, Dept. of Urban and Regional Planning, University of Illinois, 1003 West Nevada, Urbana, Illinois 61801. (217) 333-1369. Also available online.

Environmental Periodicals Bibliography. Environmental Studies Institute, International Academy at Santa Barbara, 800 Garden St., Suite D, Santa Barbara, California 93101. (805) 965-5010. Also available online.

General Science Index. H. W. Wilson Co., 950 University Ave., Bronx, New York 10452. 1978-. Monthly, also issued in annual cumulation. Cumulative subject index to English language periodicals in the subject fields of astronomy, botany, chemistry, earth science, environment and conservation, food and nutrition, genetics, mathematics, medicine and health, microbiology, oceanography, physics, physiology and zoology.

Geographical Abstracts. London School of Economics, Dept. of Geography, Regency House, 34 Duke St., London, England 1966-. Continued by Geo Abstracts issued in 6 parts: Pt. A. Landforms and the quaternary; Pt. B. Biogeography and Climatology; Pt. C. Economic geography; Pt. D. Social geography and cartography; Pt. E. Sedimentology; Pt. F. Regional and community planning.

Index to Scientific Book Contents. Institute for Scientific Information, 3501 Market St., Philadelphia, Pennsylvania 19104. (800) 523-1857. 1985-. Annual. Gives contents of science books published.

Pollution Abstracts. Cambridge Scientific Abstracts, 5161 River Rd., Bethesda, Maryland 20816. (301) 961-6750. Six/year. Indexes worldwide technical literature on environmental pollution. Covers air pollution, marine and freshwater pollution, sewage and wastewater treatment, waste management, toxicology and health, noise pollution, radiation, land pollution, and environmental policies, programs, legislation, and education. Also available online.

Science Citation Index. Institute for Scientific Information, 3501 Market St., Philadelphia, Pennsylvania 19104. 1961-.

BIBLIOGRAPHIES

Directory of Published Proceedings. Interdok Corp., 173 Halstead Ave., Harrison, New York 10528. (914) 835-3506. 1990. Monthly. This is a listing of published proceedings including the series SEMTE (Science/Medicine/Engineering/Technology) and the series SSH (Social Science/Humanities).

EPA Publications Bibliography. U.S. Environmental Protection Agency, Library Systems Branch, 401 M St., SW, Washington, District of Columbia 20460. (202) 260-2090. Quarterly.

ENCYCLOPEDIAS AND DICTIONARIES

Encyclopedia of Physical Science and Technology. Robert A. Meyers, ed. Academic Press, c/o Harcourt Brace Jovanovich Inc., 6277 Sea Harbor Dr., Orlando, Florida 32887. (800) 346-8648. Dictionary of engineering, technology and physical sciences.

McGraw-Hill Encyclopedia of Environmental Science. Sybil P. Parker. McGraw-Hill Science & Engineering Books, 11 W. 19th St., New York, New York 10011. (212) 337-6010. 1980. Covers ecology, man's influence on nature, and environmental protection.

McGraw-Hill Encyclopedia of Science and Technology. McGraw-Hill, 1221 Avenue of the Americas, New York, New York 10020. (212) 512-2000 or (800) 262-4729. 1992. Seventh edition. Issued in multiple volumes including index. Includes all science and technology broad subject areas.

Van Nostrand's Scientific Encyclopedia. Glenn D. Considine, ed. Van Nostrand Reinhold, 115 5th Ave., New York, New York 10003. (212) 254-3232. 1983. Sixth edition. Includes all broad subject areas in science.

GENERAL WORKS

Acute Lethality Data for Ontario's Petroleum Refinery Effluents Covering the Period from December 1988 to May 1989. Ontario Ministry of Environment, c/o National Technical Information Service, 5285 Port Royal Rd., Springfield, Virginia 22161. (703) 487-4650. 1990. Order number MIC-91-02537 LDM.

Acute Lethality Data for Ontario's Petroleum Refinery Effluents covering the Period June 1989 to November 1989. J. T. Lee. Ontario Ministry of the Environment, c/o National Technical Information Service, 5285 Port Royal Rd., Springfield, Virginia 22161. (703) 487-4650. 1989. Order number MIC-91-02523 LDM.

Aquaculture Techniques: Water Use and Discharge Quality. George W. Klontz. Idaho Water Research Institute, University of Idaho, Moscow, Idaho 83843. Covers aquaculture techniques, fish culture, and effluent quality.

Development Document for the Effluent Monitoring Regulation for the Metal Casting Sector. Ontario Ministry of the Environment, Toronto. National Technical Information Service, 5285 Port Royal Rd., Springfield, Virginia 22161. (703) 487-4650. 1990.

Economic Instruments for Environmental Protection. OECD Publications and Information Center, 2001 L St. N.W., Suite 700, Washington, District of Columbia 20036. (202) 785-OECD. 1989. Reviews the current role of economic instruments and assesses their effectiveness and future potential. Discusses charges and taxes on effluents, user and product charges, tax relief and subsidies for anti-pollution investments, and trading of pollution rights. Problems of enforcement, and implications for the polluter pays principle are also covered.

Some Economic Impacts of Freshwater Stream Effluent Discharge Limits on Selected Small Communities in Mississippi. Leo R. Cheatham. Water Resources Research Institute, Mississippi State University, Mississippi State, Mississippi 39762. Water supply, water pollution and drinking water contamination.

TAPPI Environmental Conference Proceedings, Seattle, WA, April 9-11, 1990. TAPPI Press, Technology Park/Atlanta, PO Box 105113, Atlanta, Georgia 30348. (404)

446-1400. 1990. Contains 11 papers presented at the conference covering industrial pollution and its remedies.

Toxicity Reduction in Industrial Effluents. Perry W. Lanford, et al. Van Nostrand Reinhold, 115 5th Ave., New York, New York 10003. (212) 254-3232. 1990. Overview of aquatic toxicology and toxicity reduction. Specific treatment technologies that can be used to reduce toxicity, such as aerobic and anaerobic biological treatment, air and steam stripping of volatile organics, granulated carbon absorption, powdered activated carbon treatment and chemical oxidation, are discussed in detail.

Treatability Studies for the Inorganic Chemicals Manufacturing Point Source Category. United States Environmental Protection Agency. Environmental Protection Agency, Effluent Guidelines Division, 401 M. St., SW, Washington, District of Columbia 20460. (202) 260-2090. 1980. Topics in sewage purification.

Use of Soil for Treatment and Final Disposal of Effluents and Sludge. P. R. C. Oliveira and S. A. S. Almeida, eds. Pergamon Microforms International, Inc., Fairview Park, Elmsford, New York 10523. (914) 592-7720. 1988. Proceedings of an IAWPRC Seminar held in Salvador, Bahia, Brazil, August 13-15, 1986. Contains a broad scope of topics regarding the treatment and final disposal of effluents and sludge on land.

HANDBOOKS AND MANUALS

Economic Analysis of Proposed Revised Effluent Guidelines and Standards for the Inorganic Chemicals Industry. National Technical Information Service, 5285 Port Royal Rd., Springfield, Virginia 22161. (703) 487-4650. 1980. Covers effluent quality and sewage purification technology.

ONLINE DATA BASES

BIOSIS Previews. BIOSIS, 2100 Arch St., Philadelphia, Pennsylvania 19103-1399. (215) 587-4800. Largest and most comprehensive database of research in the life sciences. Contains citations for nearly 9000 primary research journals, monographs, reviews, symposia, preliminary reports, semi-popular journals, selected institutional reports, government reports and research communications.

Chemical Abstracts-CA. Chemical Abstracts Service, 2540 Olentangy River Rd., P.O. Box 3012, Columbus, Ohio 43210. (800) 848-6533 or (614) 421-3600. Information sources include 9000 journals, patents from 27 countries, two industrial property organizations, new books, conference proceedings, and government research reports.

Enviro/Energyline Abstracts Plus. R. R. Bowker Co., 121 Chanlon Rd., New Providence, New Jersey 07974. (908) 464-6800.

Environmental Fate Databases. Syracuse Research Cooperation, Merrill Lane, Syracuse, New York 13210. (312) 426-3200. Environmental fate of chemicals.

Environmental Periodicals Bibliography. National Information Services Corp., Ste. 6, Wyman Towers, 3100 St. Paul St., Baltimore, Maryland 21218. (410)243-0797. Online version of abstract of same name.

Monthly Catalog of United States Government Publications. U.S. G.P.O., Supt. of Docs., PO Box 371954, Pittsburgh, Pennsylvania 15250-7954. (202) 512-0000.

National Technical Information Service. U.S. Department of Commerce, National Technical Information Service, Office of Data Base Services, 5285 Port Royal Rd., Springfield, Virginia 22161. (703) 487-4807. Bibliographic database of government sponsored research and technical reports.

SCISEARCH. Institute for Scientific Information, University City Science Center, 3501 Market St., Philadelphia, Pennsylvania 19104. (215) 386-0100.

PERIODICALS AND NEWSLETTERS

Atmospheric Environment. Pergamon Microforms International, Inc., Fairview Park, Elmsford, New York 10523. (914) 592-7720. 1966-. Publishes papers on all aspects of man's interactions with his atmospheric environment, including the administrative, economic and political aspects of these interactions. Air pollution research and its applications are covered, taking into account changes in the atmospheric flow patterns, temperature distributions and chemical constitution caused by natural and artificial variations in the earth's surface.

Eco/Log Week. Southam Business Information, 1450 Don Mills Rd., Don Mills, Ontario, Canada M3D 2X7. (416) 445-6641. Weekly. Effluent treatment, emission controls, waste disposal, and land use and reclamation.

TRADE ASSOCIATIONS AND PROFESSIONAL SOCIETIES

American Pulpwood Association. 1025 Vermont Ave., N.W., Suite 1020, Washington, District of Columbia 20005. (202) 347-2900.

National Council of the Paper Industry for Air and Stream Improvements. 260 Madison Ave., New York, New York 10016. (212) 532-9000.

Pulp Chemicals Association. P.O. Box 105113, Atlanta, Georgia 30348. (404) 446-1290.

EIS

See: ENVIRONMENTAL IMPACT STATEMENT

ELECTRIC AUTOMOBILES

See: TRANSPORTATION

ELECTRIC POWER LINES–ENVIRONMENTAL ASPECTS

See also: DISTRIBUTION LINES; ELECTROMAGNETIC RADIATION

ABSTRACTING AND INDEXING SERVICES

Applied Science and Technology Index. H.W. Wilson Co., 950 University Ave., Bronx, New York 10452. (800) 367-6770. Formerly Industrial Arts Index.

Engineering Index. The Engineering Index Inc., 345 E. 47th St., New York, New York 10017. 1962-.

General Science Index. H. W. Wilson Co., 950 University Ave., Bronx, New York 10452. 1978-. Monthly, also issued in annual cumulation. Cumulative subject index to English language periodicals in the subject fields of astronomy, botany, chemistry, earth science, environment and conservation, food and nutrition, genetics, mathematics, medicine and health, microbiology, oceanography, physics, physiology and zoology.

Index to Scientific Book Contents. Institute for Scientific Information, 3501 Market St., Philadelphia, Pennsylvania 19104. (800) 523-1857. 1985-. Annual. Gives contents of science books published.

BIBLIOGRAPHIES

Birds and Power Lines: A Bibliography. Charles A. Goulty. Council of Planning Librarians, 1313 E. 60th St., Chicago, Illinois 60637-2897. (312) 942-2163. 1988. Bird mortality due to electric lines.

Current Contents. Agriculture, Biology and Environmental Sciences. Institute for Scientific Information, 3501 Market St., Philadelphia, Pennsylvania 19104. (800) 523-1857. 1973-. Previous title: Current Contents. Agricultural, Food & Veterinary Sciences. Gives the table of contents of periodicals in the fields of agriculture, biology, environmental and related areas.

Directory of Published Proceedings. Interdok Corp., 173 Halstead Ave., Harrison, New York 10528. (914) 835-3506. 1990. Monthly. This is a listing of published proceedings including the series SEMTE (Science/Medicine/Engineering/Technology) and the series SSH (Social Science/Humanities).

Siting of Power Lines and Communication Towers. Lynne De Merritt. Council of Planning Librarians, 1313 E. 60th St., Chicago, Illinois 60637-2897. (312) 942-2163. 1990. A bibliography on the potential health effects of electric and magnetic fields.

DIRECTORIES

Power Transmission Equipment–Wholesale. American Business Directories, Inc., 5711 S. 86th Circle, Omaha, Nebraska 68127. (402) 593-4600.

ENCYCLOPEDIAS AND DICTIONARIES

Dictionary of Environmental Engineering and Related Sciences: English-Spanish, Spanish-English. Jose T. Villate. Ediciones Universal, 3090 SW 8th St., Miami, Florida 33135. (305) 642-3355. 1979.

Encyclopedia of Environmental Science and Engineering. J.R. Pfafflin. Gordon and Breach Science Publishers, Inc., 270 8th Ave., New York, New York 10011. (212) 206-8900. 1992.

Encyclopedia of Physical Science and Technology. Robert A. Meyers, ed. Academic Press, c/o Harcourt Brace Jovanovich Inc., 6277 Sea Harbor Dr., Orlando, Florida 32887. (800) 346-8648. Dictionary of engineering, technology and physical sciences.

McGraw-Hill Encyclopedia of Environmental Science. Sybil P. Parker. McGraw-Hill Science & Engineering Books, 11 W. 19th St., New York, New York 10011.

(212) 337-6010. 1980. Covers ecology, man's influence on nature, and environmental protection.

Van Nostrand's Scientific Encyclopedia. Glenn D. Considine, ed. Van Nostrand Reinhold, 115 5th Ave., New York, New York 10003. (212) 254-3232. 1983. Sixth edition. Includes all broad subject areas in science.

GENERAL WORKS

Stray Voltage. American Society of Agricultural Engineers, 2950 Niles Rd., St. Joseph, Michigan 49085-9659. (616) 429-0300. 1985. Proceedings of the National Stray Voltage Symposium, October 10-12, 1984, New York. Includes animal sensitivity, electrical system characteristics and source identification and mitigation and protection.

Stray Voltage. Robert J. Gustafson. Energy Research and Development Division, Energy and Environmental Policy Department, National Rural Electric Cooperative Association, 1800 Massachusetts Ave., NW, Washington, District of Columbia 20036. (202) 857-9500. 1988. Seasonal variations in grounding and primary neutral-to-earth voltages.

Stray Voltages in Agriculture: Workshop. American Society of Agricultural Engineers, 2950 Niles Rd., St. Joseph, Michigan 49085-9659. (616) 429-0300. 1983. Includes the effects of stray voltage on animals, source of stray voltage, diagnostic procedures for detection and measurement and treatments or corrective procedure for stray voltage problem. The workshop was sponsored by the National Rural Electric Cooperative Association in Minneapolis, MN.

Visual Amenity Aspects of High Voltage Transmission. George A. Goulty. John Wiley & Sons, Inc., 605 3rd Ave., New York, New York (212) 850-6000. 1990. High tension electric power distribution, overhead electric lines, and location of poles and towers.

HANDBOOKS AND MANUALS

Transmission Line Design Manual. Holland H. Farr. Water and Power Resources Service, Engineering and Research Center, P.O. Box 25007, Denver Federal Center, Denver, Colorado 80225. 1980.

ONLINE DATA BASES

Computerized Engineering Index–COMPENDEX. Engineering Information Inc., 345 E. 47th St., New York, New York 10017. (212) 705-7600.

EBIB. Texas A & M University, Sterling C. Evans Library, Reference Division, College Station, Texas 77843. (409) 845-5741.

Electric Power Industry Abstracts. Utility Data Institute, 1700 K St., N.W., Suite 400, Washington, District of Columbia 20006. (800) 466-3660.

Monthly Catalog of United States Government Publications. U.S. G.P.O., Supt. of Docs., PO Box 371954, Pittsburgh, Pennsylvania 15250-7954. (202) 512-0000.

National Technical Information Service. U.S. Department of Commerce, National Technical Information Service, Office of Data Base Services, 5285 Port Royal Rd., Springfield, Virginia 22161. (703) 487-4807. Bibliographic database of government sponsored research and technical reports.

PERIODICALS AND NEWSLETTERS

Power Line. Utility Action Foundation, 724 Dupont Circle Bldg., Washington, District of Columbia 20036. 1977-. Monthly.

TRADE ASSOCIATIONS AND PROFESSIONAL SOCIETIES

American Water Resources Association. 5410 Grosvenor Lane, Suite 220, Bethesda, Maryland 20814. (301) 493-8600.

ELECTRIC UTILITIES

See also: POWER RESOURCES

ABSTRACTING AND INDEXING SERVICES

Applied Science and Technology Index. H.W. Wilson Co., 950 University Ave., Bronx, New York 10452. (800) 367-6770. Formerly Industrial Arts Index.

Electric Energy Systems. National Technical Information Service, 5285 Port Royal Rd., Springfield, Virginia 22161. (703) 487-4650. Monthly. Fossil and hydroelectric power generation, transmission, environmental control technology, and policy.

Engineering Index. The Engineering Index Inc., 345 E. 47th St., New York, New York 10017. 1962-.

Environment Abstracts. Bowker A & I Publishing, 121 Chanlon Rd., New Providence, New Jersey 07974. (908) 464-6800. 1974-.

Environment Index. Environment Information Center, Index Research Department, 124 E. 39th St., New York, New York 10016. 1971-. Annual.

Environmental Information Connection–EIC. Planning Information Program, Dept. of Urban and Regional Planning, University of Illinois, 1003 West Nevada, Urbana, Illinois 61801. (217) 333-1369. Also available online.

Environmental Periodicals Bibliography. Environmental Studies Institute, International Academy at Santa Barbara, 800 Garden St., Suite D, Santa Barbara, California 93101. (805) 965-5010. Also available online.

ERDA Research Abstracts. U.S. ERDA Technical Information Center, Box 62, Oak Ridge, Tennessee 37830.

General Science Index. H. W. Wilson Co., 950 University Ave., Bronx, New York 10452. 1978-. Monthly, also issued in annual cumulation. Cumulative subject index to English language periodicals in the subject fields of astronomy, botany, chemistry, earth science, environment and conservation, food and nutrition, genetics, mathematics, medicine and health, microbiology, oceanography, physics, physiology and zoology.

Geographical Abstracts. London School of Economics, Dept. of Geography, Regency House, 34 Duke St., London, England 1966-. Continued by Geo Abstracts issued in 6 parts: Pt. A. Landforms and the quaternary; Pt. B. Biogeography and Climatology; Pt. C. Economic geography; Pt. D. Social geography and cartography; Pt. E. Sedimentology; Pt. F. Regional and community planning.

Index to Scientific Book Contents. Institute for Scientific Information, 3501 Market St., Philadelphia, Pennsylvania 19104. (800) 523-1857. 1985-. Annual. Gives contents of science books published.

BIBLIOGRAPHIES

EPA Publications Bibliography. U.S. Environmental Protection Agency, Library Systems Branch, 401 M St., SW, Washington, District of Columbia 20460. (202) 260-2090. Quarterly.

DIRECTORIES

Directory of Selected U.S. Cogeneration, Small Power, and Industrial Power Plants. Utility Data Institute, 1700 K St., N.W., Suite 400, Washington, District of Columbia 20006. (202) 466-3660.

Directory of U.S. Cogeneration, Small Power & Industrial Power Plants. FIND/SVP, 625 Avenue of the Americas, New York, New York 10011. (212) 645-4500. Semiannual. More than 4800 cogeneration, small power and industrial power projects, refuse-to-energy plants, gas turbine and combined-cycle facilities, geothermal units, coal and wood-fired plants, wind and solar installations and a variety of other plant types.

Historical Plant Cost and Annual Production Expenses for Selected Electric Plants. Department of Energy, 1000 Independence Ave., N.W., Washington, District of Columbia 20585. (202) 586-8800. Annual.

Inventory of Power Plants in the United States. Department of Energy, 1000 Independence Ave., N.W., Washington, District of Columbia 20585. (202) 586-8800. Annual. Inventory of individual electric power plants operating, added, and retired and planned for operation. Includes information on ownership, capacity, and energy source.

ENCYCLOPEDIAS AND DICTIONARIES

Dictionary of Environmental Engineering and Related Sciences: English-Spanish, Spanish-English. Jose T. Villate. Ediciones Universal, 3090 SW 8th St., Miami, Florida 33135. (305) 642-3355. 1979.

Encyclopedia of Environmental Science and Engineering. J.R. Pfafflin. Gordon and Breach Science Publishers, Inc., 270 8th Ave., New York, New York 10011. (212) 206-8900. 1992.

Encyclopedia of Physical Science and Technology. Robert A. Meyers, ed. Academic Press, c/o Harcourt Brace Jovanovich Inc., 6277 Sea Harbor Dr., Orlando, Florida 32887. (800) 346-8648. Dictionary of engineering, technology and physical sciences.

McGraw-Hill Encyclopedia of Science and Technology. McGraw-Hill, 1221 Avenue of the Americas, New York, New York 10020. (212) 512-2000 or (800) 262-4729. 1992. Seventh edition. Issued in multiple volumes including index. Includes all science and technology broad subject areas.

Van Nostrand's Scientific Encyclopedia. Glenn D. Considine, ed. Van Nostrand Reinhold, 115 5th Ave., New York, New York 10003. (212) 254-3232. 1983. Sixth edition. Includes all broad subject areas in science.

GENERAL WORKS

Environmental Costs of Electricity. Richard L. Ottinger, et al. Oceana Publications Inc., 75 Main St., Dobbs Ferry, New York 10522. (914) 693-8100. 1990. Report reviews and analyzes the studies that have been made to quantify the external costs of environmental damages caused by electric supply and demand-reduction technologies. It reviews ways to incorporate these costs in electric utility planning, bid evaluation and resource selection procedures.

ONLINE DATA BASES

Computerized Engineering Index–COMPENDEX. Engineering Information Inc., 345 E. 47th St., New York, New York 10017. (212) 705-7600.

EBIB. Texas A & M University, Sterling C. Evans Library, Reference Division, College Station, Texas 77843. (409) 845-5741.

Electric Power Industry Abstracts. Utility Data Institute, 1700 K St., N.W., Suite 400, Washington, District of Columbia 20006. (800) 466-3660.

Enviro/Energyline Abstracts Plus. R. R. Bowker Co., 121 Chanlon Rd., New Providence, New Jersey 07974. (908) 464-6800.

Environmental Periodicals Bibliography. National Information Services Corp., Ste. 6, Wyman Towers, 3100 St. Paul St., Baltimore, Maryland 21218. (410)243-0797. Online version of abstract of same name.

Monthly Catalog of United States Government Publications. U.S. G.P.O., Supt. of Docs., PO Box 371954, Pittsburgh, Pennsylvania 15250-7954. (202) 512-0000.

National Technical Information Service. U.S. Department of Commerce, National Technical Information Service, Office of Data Base Services, 5285 Port Royal Rd., Springfield, Virginia 22161. (703) 487-4807. Bibliographic database of government sponsored research and technical reports.

RESEARCH CENTERS AND INSTITUTES

Electric Power Research Institute. 3412 Hillview Ave., Palo Alto, California 94304. (415) 855-2000.

STATISTICS SOURCES

Commercial Nuclear Power. U.S. G.P.O, Washington, District of Columbia 20402-9325. (202) 512-0000. Annual. Current status, and future development of commercial nuclear power plants.

Electric Perspectives. Edison Electric Institute, 1111 19th St., NW, Washington, District of Columbia 20036-3691. Bimonthly. Business, regulatory, and technological developments concerning electric utilities.

Electric Utility Power Disturbances in the U.S. by Geographic Region. FIND/SVP, 625 Avenue of the Americas, New York, New York 10011. (212) 645-4500. Voltage spikes, surges, sustained over voltages, EMI and RFI noise, glitches, sags, brownouts, outages, harmonic distortion, and frequency drifts.

Electricity Supply and Demand. North American Electric Reliability Council, 101 College Rd., E., Princeton, New Jersey 08540-6601. Annual. Forecasts of electricity supply and demand by region and subregion.

Statistical Yearbook. Edison Electric Institute, 1111 19th St., NW, Washington, District of Columbia 20036-3691. Annual. Electric utility industry financial and operating data.

TRADE ASSOCIATIONS AND PROFESSIONAL SOCIETIES

American Water Resources Association. 5410 Grosvenor Lane, Suite 220, Bethesda, Maryland 20814. (301) 493-8600.

Edison Electric Institute. 701 Pennsylvania Ave., N.W., Washington, District of Columbia 20004-2696. (202) 508-5000.

National Association of Power Engineers. 2350 E. Devon Ave., Suite 115, Des Plaines, Illinois 60018. (718) 298-0600.

National Electrical Manufacturers Association. 2101 L St., N.W., Washington, District of Columbia 20037. (202) 457-8400.

ELECTRICAL HEATING

ABSTRACTING AND INDEXING SERVICES

Applied Science and Technology Index. H.W. Wilson Co., 950 University Ave., Bronx, New York 10452. (800) 367-6770. Formerly Industrial Arts Index.

Engineering Index. The Engineering Index Inc., 345 E. 47th St., New York, New York 10017. 1962-.

Environment Abstracts. Bowker A & I Publishing, 121 Chanlon Rd., New Providence, New Jersey 07974. (908) 464-6800. 1974-.

Environment Index. Environment Information Center, Index Research Department, 124 E. 39th St., New York, New York 10016. 1971-. Annual.

Environmental Information Connection–EIC. Planning Information Program, Dept. of Urban and Regional Planning, University of Illinois, 1003 West Nevada, Urbana, Illinois 61801. (217) 333-1369. Also available online.

Environmental Periodicals Bibliography. Environmental Studies Institute, International Academy at Santa Barbara, 800 Garden St., Suite D, Santa Barbara, California 93101. (805) 965-5010. Also available online.

ERDA Research Abstracts. U.S. ERDA Technical Information Center, Box 62, Oak Ridge, Tennessee 37830.

General Science Index. H. W. Wilson Co., 950 University Ave., Bronx, New York 10452. 1978-. Monthly, also issued in annual cumulation. Cumulative subject index to English language periodicals in the subject fields of astronomy, botany, chemistry, earth science, environment and conservation, food and nutrition, genetics, mathematics, medicine and health, microbiology, oceanography, physics, physiology and zoology.

Geographical Abstracts. London School of Economics, Dept. of Geography, Regency House, 34 Duke St., London, England 1966-. Continued by Geo Abstracts issued in 6 parts: Pt. A. Landforms and the quaternary;

Pt. B. Biogeography and Climatology; Pt. C. Economic geography; Pt. D. Social geography and cartography; Pt. E. Sedimentology; Pt. F. Regional and community planning.

Index to Scientific Book Contents. Institute for Scientific Information, 3501 Market St., Philadelphia, Pennsylvania 19104. (800) 523-1857. 1985-. Annual. Gives contents of science books published.

BIBLIOGRAPHIES

EPA Publications Bibliography. U.S. Environmental Protection Agency, Library Systems Branch, 401 M St., SW, Washington, District of Columbia 20460. (202) 260-2090. Quarterly.

ENCYCLOPEDIAS AND DICTIONARIES

Dictionary of Environmental Engineering and Related Sciences: English-Spanish, Spanish-English. Jose T. Villate. Ediciones Universal, 3090 SW 8th St., Miami, Florida 33135. (305) 642-3355. 1979.

Encyclopedia of Environmental Science and Engineering. J.R. Pfafflin. Gordon and Breach Science Publishers, Inc., 270 8th Ave., New York, New York 10011. (212) 206-8900. 1992.

Encyclopedia of Physical Science and Technology. Robert A. Meyers, ed. Academic Press, c/o Harcourt Brace Jovanovich Inc., 6277 Sea Harbor Dr., Orlando, Florida 32887. (800) 346-8648. Dictionary of engineering, technology and physical sciences.

Van Nostrand's Scientific Encyclopedia. Glenn D. Considine, ed. Van Nostrand Reinhold, 115 5th Ave., New York, New York 10003. (212) 254-3232. 1983. Sixth edition. Includes all broad subject areas in science.

ONLINE DATA BASES

Computerized Engineering Index–COMPENDEX. Engineering Information Inc., 345 E. 47th St., New York, New York 10017. (212) 705-7600.

EBIB. Texas A & M University, Sterling C. Evans Library, Reference Division, College Station, Texas 77843. (409) 845-5741.

Electric Power Industry Abstracts. Utility Data Institute, 1700 K St., N.W., Suite 400, Washington, District of Columbia 20006. (800) 466-3660.

Enviro/Energyline Abstracts Plus. R. R. Bowker Co., 121 Chanlon Rd., New Providence, New Jersey 07974. (908) 464-6800.

Environmental Periodicals Bibliography. National Information Services Corp., Ste. 6, Wyman Towers, 3100 St. Paul St., Baltimore, Maryland 21218. (410)243-0797. Online version of abstract of same name.

Monthly Catalog of United States Government Publications. U.S. G.P.O., Supt. of Docs., PO Box 371954, Pittsburgh, Pennsylvania 15250-7954. (202) 512-0000.

National Technical Information Service. U.S. Department of Commerce, National Technical Information Service, Office of Data Base Services, 5285 Port Royal Rd., Springfield, Virginia 22161. (703) 487-4807. Bibliographic database of government sponsored research and technical reports.

ELECTRICITY BLACKOUTS
See: POWER OUTAGE

ELECTRICITY CONSERVATION

ABSTRACTING AND INDEXING SERVICES

Applied Science and Technology Index. H.W. Wilson Co., 950 University Ave., Bronx, New York 10452. (800) 367-6770. Formerly Industrial Arts Index.

Ecological Abstracts. Geo Abstracts Ltd. Elsevier Applied Science, Crown House, Linton Rd., Barking, England IG 11 8JU. 1974-. Derived from over 600 leading ecological and environmental journals, plus books, conference proceedings, reports and theses.

Engineering Index. The Engineering Index Inc., 345 E. 47th St., New York, New York 10017. 1962-.

Environment Abstracts. Bowker A & I Publishing, 121 Chanlon Rd., New Providence, New Jersey 07974. (908) 464-6800. 1974-.

Environment Index. Environment Information Center, Index Research Department, 124 E. 39th St., New York, New York 10016. 1971-. Annual.

Environmental Information Connection–EIC. Planning Information Program, Dept. of Urban and Regional Planning, University of Illinois, 1003 West Nevada, Urbana, Illinois 61801. (217) 333-1369. Also available online.

Environmental Periodicals Bibliography. Environmental Studies Institute, International Academy at Santa Barbara, 800 Garden St., Suite D, Santa Barbara, California 93101. (805) 965-5010. Also available online.

ERDA Research Abstracts. U.S. ERDA Technical Information Center, Box 62, Oak Ridge, Tennessee 37830.

General Science Index. H. W. Wilson Co., 950 University Ave., Bronx, New York 10452. 1978-. Monthly, also issued in annual cumulation. Cumulative subject index to English language periodicals in the subject fields of astronomy, botany, chemistry, earth science, environment and conservation, food and nutrition, genetics, mathematics, medicine and health, microbiology, oceanography, physics, physiology and zoology.

Geographical Abstracts. London School of Economics, Dept. of Geography, Regency House, 34 Duke St., London, England 1966-. Continued by Geo Abstracts issued in 6 parts: Pt. A. Landforms and the quaternary; Pt. B. Biogeography and Climatology; Pt. C. Economic geography; Pt. D. Social geography and cartography; Pt. E. Sedimentology; Pt. F. Regional and community planning.

Index to Scientific Book Contents. Institute for Scientific Information, 3501 Market St., Philadelphia, Pennsylvania 19104. (800) 523-1857. 1985-. Annual. Gives contents of science books published.

BIBLIOGRAPHIES

Directory of Published Proceedings. Interdok Corp., 173 Halstead Ave., Harrison, New York 10528. (914) 835-3506. 1990. Monthly. This is a listing of published proceedings including the series SEMTE (Science/Medicine/Engineering/Technology) and the series SSH (Social Science/Humanities).

EPA Publications Bibliography. U.S. Environmental Protection Agency, Library Systems Branch, 401 M St., SW, Washington, District of Columbia 20460. (202) 260-2090. Quarterly.

ENCYCLOPEDIAS AND DICTIONARIES

Dictionary of Environmental Engineering and Related Sciences: English-Spanish, Spanish-English. Jose T. Villate. Ediciones Universal, 3090 SW 8th St., Miami, Florida 33135. (305) 642-3355. 1979.

Encyclopedia of Environmental Science and Engineering. J.R. Pfafflin. Gordon and Breach Science Publishers, Inc., 270 8th Ave., New York, New York 10011. (212) 206-8900. 1992.

Encyclopedia of Physical Science and Technology. Robert A. Meyers, ed. Academic Press, c/o Harcourt Brace Jovanovich Inc., 6277 Sea Harbor Dr., Orlando, Florida 32887. (800) 346-8648. Dictionary of engineering, technology and physical sciences.

Encyclopedia of Physics. Rita G. Lerner and George L. Trigg. VCH Publishers, 303 NW 12th Ave., Deerfield Beach, Florida 33442-1788. (305) 428-5566. 1991. Second edition.

McGraw-Hill Encyclopedia of Environmental Science. Sybil P. Parker. McGraw-Hill Science & Engineering Books, 11 W. 19th St., New York, New York 10011. (212) 337-6010. 1980. Covers ecology, man's influence on nature, and environmental protection.

Van Nostrand's Scientific Encyclopedia. Glenn D. Considine, ed. Van Nostrand Reinhold, 115 5th Ave., New York, New York 10003. (212) 254-3232. 1983. Sixth edition. Includes all broad subject areas in science.

GENERAL WORKS

Electricity and the Environment. International Atomic Energy Agency, Wagramerstrasse 5, Vienna, Austria Discusses the health environmental factors, and the economic factors involved in supplying electrical services.

Electricity End-Use Efficiency. OECD Publications and Information Centre, 2, rue Andre-Pascal, Paris Cedex 16, France F-75775. 1989. Government policy on electric utilities, electric power conservation, household appliances and energy consumption in industry.

ONLINE DATA BASES

Computerized Engineering Index–COMPENDEX. Engineering Information Inc., 345 E. 47th St., New York, New York 10017. (212) 705-7600.

EBIB. Texas A & M University, Sterling C. Evans Library, Reference Division, College Station, Texas 77843. (409) 845-5741.

Electric Power Industry Abstracts. Utility Data Institute, 1700 K St., N.W., Suite 400, Washington, District of Columbia 20006. (800) 466-3660.

Enviro/Energyline Abstracts Plus. R. R. Bowker Co., 121 Chanlon Rd., New Providence, New Jersey 07974. (908) 464-6800.

Environmental Periodicals Bibliography. National Information Services Corp., Ste. 6, Wyman Towers, 3100 St. Paul St., Baltimore, Maryland 21218. (410)243-0797. Online version of abstract of same name.

Monthly Catalog of United States Government Publications. U.S. G.P.O., Supt. of Docs., PO Box 371954, Pittsburgh, Pennsylvania 15250-7954. (202) 512-0000.

National Technical Information Service. U.S. Department of Commerce, National Technical Information Service, Office of Data Base Services, 5285 Port Royal Rd., Springfield, Virginia 22161. (703) 487-4807. Bibliographic database of government sponsored research and technical reports.

PressNet Environmental Reports. Chemical Information Systems, Inc., 7215 York Rd., Baltimore, Maryland 21212. (301) 321-8440.

STATISTICS SOURCES

World Resources. World Resources Institute. 1709 New York Ave., N.W., Washington, District of Columbia 20006. (202) 638-6300. Annual. Statistical and textual analysis of world's natural resources and the effects of growth-caused environmental pollution.

ELECTRICITY IN AGRICULTURE–SAFETY MEASURES

See also: DISTRIBUTION LINES; ELECTRIC POWER LINES; LIVESTOCK HOUSING

ABSTRACTING AND INDEXING SERVICES

Applied Science and Technology Index. H.W. Wilson Co., 950 University Ave., Bronx, New York 10452. (800) 367-6770. Formerly Industrial Arts Index.

Engineering Index. The Engineering Index Inc., 345 E. 47th St., New York, New York 10017. 1962-.

Environment Abstracts. Bowker A & I Publishing, 121 Chanlon Rd., New Providence, New Jersey 07974. (908) 464-6800. 1974-.

Environment Index. Environment Information Center, Index Research Department, 124 E. 39th St., New York, New York 10016. 1971-. Annual.

Environmental Information Connection–EIC. Planning Information Program, Dept. of Urban and Regional Planning, University of Illinois, 1003 West Nevada, Urbana, Illinois 61801. (217) 333-1369. Also available online.

Environmental Periodicals Bibliography. Environmental Studies Institute, International Academy at Santa Barbara, 800 Garden St., Suite D, Santa Barbara, California 93101. (805) 965-5010. Also available online.

ERDA Research Abstracts. U.S. ERDA Technical Information Center, Box 62, Oak Ridge, Tennessee 37830.

General Science Index. H. W. Wilson Co., 950 University Ave., Bronx, New York 10452. 1978-. Monthly, also

issued in annual cumulation. Cumulative subject index to English language periodicals in the subject fields of astronomy, botany, chemistry, earth science, environment and conservation, food and nutrition, genetics, mathematics, medicine and health, microbiology, oceanography, physics, physiology and zoology.

Geographical Abstracts. London School of Economics, Dept. of Geography, Regency House, 34 Duke St., London, England 1966-. Continued by Geo Abstracts issued in 6 parts: Pt. A. Landforms and the quaternary; Pt. B. Biogeography and Climatology; Pt. C. Economic geography; Pt. D. Social geography and cartography; Pt. E. Sedimentology; Pt. F. Regional and community planning.

Index to Scientific Book Contents. Institute for Scientific Information, 3501 Market St., Philadelphia, Pennsylvania 19104. (800) 523-1857. 1985-. Annual. Gives contents of science books published.

BIBLIOGRAPHIES

Current Contents. Agriculture, Biology and Environmental Sciences. Institute for Scientific Information, 3501 Market St., Philadelphia, Pennsylvania 19104. (800) 523-1857. 1973-. Previous title: Current Contents. Agricultural, Food & Veterinary Sciences. Gives the table of contents of periodicals in the fields of agriculture, biology, environmental and related areas.

Directory of Published Proceedings. Interdok Corp., 173 Halstead Ave., Harrison, New York 10528. (914) 835-3506. 1990. Monthly. This is a listing of published proceedings including the series SEMTE (Science/Medicine/Engineering/Technology) and the series SSH (Social Science/Humanities).

EPA Publications Bibliography. U.S. Environmental Protection Agency, Library Systems Branch, 401 M St., SW, Washington, District of Columbia 20460. (202) 260-2090. Quarterly.

ENCYCLOPEDIAS AND DICTIONARIES

Dictionary of Environmental Engineering and Related Sciences: English-Spanish, Spanish-English. Jose T. Villate. Ediciones Universal, 3090 SW 8th St., Miami, Florida 33135. (305) 642-3355. 1979.

Encyclopedia of Environmental Science and Engineering. J.R. Pfafflin. Gordon and Breach Science Publishers, Inc., 270 8th Ave., New York, New York 10011. (212) 206-8900. 1992.

Encyclopedia of Physical Science and Technology. Robert A. Meyers, ed. Academic Press, c/o Harcourt Brace Jovanovich Inc., 6277 Sea Harbor Dr., Orlando, Florida 32887. (800) 346-8648. Dictionary of engineering, technology and physical sciences.

Van Nostrand's Scientific Encyclopedia. Glenn D. Considine, ed. Van Nostrand Reinhold, 115 5th Ave., New York, New York 10003. (212) 254-3232. 1983. Sixth edition. Includes all broad subject areas in science.

GENERAL WORKS

Electrical Energy in Agriculture. Kenneth L. McFate. Elsevier Science Publishing Co., 655 Avenue of the Americas, New York, New York 10010. (212) 984-5800. 1989.

Stray Voltage. American Society of Agricultural Engineers, 2950 Niles Rd., St. Joseph, Michigan 49085-9659. (616) 429-0300. 1985. Proceedings of the National Stray Voltage Symposium, October 10-12, 1984, New York. Includes animal sensitivity, electrical system characteristics and source identification and mitigation and protection.

Stray Voltage. Robert J. Gustafson. Energy Research and Development Division, Energy and Environmental Policy Department, National Rural Electric Cooperative Association, 1800 Massachusetts Ave., NW, Washington, District of Columbia 20036. (202) 857-9500. 1988. Seasonal variations in grounding and primary neutral-to-earth voltages.

Stray Voltages in Agriculture: Workshop. American Society of Agricultural Engineers, 2950 Niles Rd., St. Joseph, Michigan 49085-9659. (616) 429-0300. 1983. Includes the effects of stray voltage on animals, source of stray voltage, diagnostic procedures for detection and measurement and treatments or corrective procedure for stray voltage problem. The workshop was sponsored by the National Rural Electric Cooperative Association in Minneapolis, MN.

ONLINE DATA BASES

Computerized Engineering Index–COMPENDEX. Engineering Information Inc., 345 E. 47th St., New York, New York 10017. (212) 705-7600.

EBIB. Texas A & M University, Sterling C. Evans Library, Reference Division, College Station, Texas 77843. (409) 845-5741.

Electric Power Industry Abstracts. Utility Data Institute, 1700 K St., N.W., Suite 400, Washington, District of Columbia 20006. (800) 466-3660.

Enviro/Energyline Abstracts Plus. R. R. Bowker Co., 121 Chanlon Rd., New Providence, New Jersey 07974. (908) 464-6800.

Environmental Periodicals Bibliography. National Information Services Corp., Ste. 6, Wyman Towers, 3100 St. Paul St., Baltimore, Maryland 21218. (410)243-0797. Online version of abstract of same name.

Monthly Catalog of United States Government Publications. U.S. G.P.O., Supt. of Docs., PO Box 371954, Pittsburgh, Pennsylvania 15250-7954. (202) 512-0000.

National Technical Information Service. U.S. Department of Commerce, National Technical Information Service, Office of Data Base Services, 5285 Port Royal Rd., Springfield, Virginia 22161. (703) 487-4807. Bibliographic database of government sponsored research and technical reports.

SCISEARCH. Institute for Scientific Information, University City Science Center, 3501 Market St., Philadelphia, Pennsylvania 19104. (215) 386-0100.

TRADE ASSOCIATIONS AND PROFESSIONAL SOCIETIES

American Institute of Biological Sciences. 730 11th St., N.W., Washington, District of Columbia 20001-4521. (202) 628-1500.

National Rural Electric Cooperative Association. 1800 Massachusetts Ave., N.W., Washington, District of Columbia 20036. (202) 857-9500.

ELECTRICITY USAGE, INDUSTRIAL

ABSTRACTING AND INDEXING SERVICES

Applied Science and Technology Index. H.W. Wilson Co., 950 University Ave., Bronx, New York 10452. (800) 367-6770. Formerly Industrial Arts Index.

Engineering Index. The Engineering Index Inc., 345 E. 47th St., New York, New York 10017. 1962-.

Environment Abstracts. Bowker A & I Publishing, 121 Chanlon Rd., New Providence, New Jersey 07974. (908) 464-6800. 1974-.

Environment Index. Environment Information Center, Index Research Department, 124 E. 39th St., New York, New York 10016. 1971-. Annual.

Environmental Information Connection–EIC. Planning Information Program, Dept. of Urban and Regional Planning, University of Illinois, 1003 West Nevada, Urbana, Illinois 61801. (217) 333-1369. Also available online.

Environmental Periodicals Bibliography. Environmental Studies Institute, International Academy at Santa Barbara, 800 Garden St., Suite D, Santa Barbara, California 93101. (805) 965-5010. Also available online.

ERDA Research Abstracts. U.S. ERDA Technical Information Center, Box 62, Oak Ridge, Tennessee 37830.

General Science Index. H. W. Wilson Co., 950 University Ave., Bronx, New York 10452. 1978-. Monthly, also issued in annual cumulation. Cumulative subject index to English language periodicals in the subject fields of astronomy, botany, chemistry, earth science, environment and conservation, food and nutrition, genetics, mathematics, medicine and health, microbiology, oceanography, physics, physiology and zoology.

Geographical Abstracts. London School of Economics, Dept. of Geography, Regency House, 34 Duke St., London, England 1966-. Continued by Geo Abstracts issued in 6 parts: Pt. A. Landforms and the quaternary; Pt. B. Biogeography and Climatology; Pt. C. Economic geography; Pt. D. Social geography and cartography; Pt. E. Sedimentology; Pt. F. Regional and community planning.

Index to Scientific Book Contents. Institute for Scientific Information, 3501 Market St., Philadelphia, Pennsylvania 19104. (800) 523-1857. 1985-. Annual. Gives contents of science books published.

BIBLIOGRAPHIES

EPA Publications Bibliography. U.S. Environmental Protection Agency, Library Systems Branch, 401 M St., SW, Washington, District of Columbia 20460. (202) 260-2090. Quarterly.

ENCYCLOPEDIAS AND DICTIONARIES

Dictionary of Environmental Engineering and Related Sciences: English-Spanish, Spanish-English. Jose T. Villate. Ediciones Universal, 3090 SW 8th St., Miami, Florida 33135. (305) 642-3355. 1979.

Encyclopedia of Environmental Science and Engineering. J.R. Pfafflin. Gordon and Breach Science Publishers, Inc., 270 8th Ave., New York, New York 10011. (212) 206-8900. 1992.

Encyclopedia of Physical Science and Technology. Robert A. Meyers, ed. Academic Press, c/o Harcourt Brace Jovanovich Inc., 6277 Sea Harbor Dr., Orlando, Florida 32887. (800) 346-8648. Dictionary of engineering, technology and physical sciences.

Van Nostrand's Scientific Encyclopedia. Glenn D. Considine, ed. Van Nostrand Reinhold, 115 5th Ave., New York, New York 10003. (212) 254-3232. 1983. Sixth edition. Includes all broad subject areas in science.

ONLINE DATA BASES

Computerized Engineering Index–COMPENDEX. Engineering Information Inc., 345 E. 47th St., New York, New York 10017. (212) 705-7600.

Electric Power Industry Abstracts. Utility Data Institute, 1700 K St., N.W., Suite 400, Washington, District of Columbia 20006. (800) 466-3660.

Enviro/Energyline Abstracts Plus. R. R. Bowker Co., 121 Chanlon Rd., New Providence, New Jersey 07974. (908) 464-6800.

Environmental Periodicals Bibliography. National Information Services Corp., Ste. 6, Wyman Towers, 3100 St. Paul St., Baltimore, Maryland 21218. (410)243-0797. Online version of abstract of same name.

Monthly Catalog of United States Government Publications. U.S. G.P.O., Supt. of Docs., PO Box 371954, Pittsburgh, Pennsylvania 15250-7954. (202) 512-0000.

National Technical Information Service. U.S. Department of Commerce, National Technical Information Service, Office of Data Base Services, 5285 Port Royal Rd., Springfield, Virginia 22161. (703) 487-4807. Bibliographic database of government sponsored research and technical reports.

TRADE ASSOCIATIONS AND PROFESSIONAL SOCIETIES

National Rural Electric Cooperative Association. 1800 Massachusetts Ave., N.W., Washington, District of Columbia 20036. (202) 857-9500.

ELECTRODIALYSIS

ABSTRACTING AND INDEXING SERVICES

Applied Science and Technology Index. H.W. Wilson Co., 950 University Ave., Bronx, New York 10452. (800) 367-6770. Formerly Industrial Arts Index.

Chemical Abstracts. Chemical Abstracts Service, 2540 Olentangy River Rd., PO Box 3012, Columbus, Ohio 43210. (800) 848-6533. 1907-.

Engineering Index. The Engineering Index Inc., 345 E. 47th St., New York, New York 10017. 1962-.

Environment Abstracts. Bowker A & I Publishing, 121 Chanlon Rd., New Providence, New Jersey 07974. (908) 464-6800. 1974-.

Environment Index. Environment Information Center, Index Research Department, 124 E. 39th St., New York, New York 10016. 1971-. Annual.

Environmental Information Connection–EIC. Planning Information Program, Dept. of Urban and Regional Planning, University of Illinois, 1003 West Nevada, Urbana, Illinois 61801. (217) 333-1369. Also available online.

Environmental Periodicals Bibliography. Environmental Studies Institute, International Academy at Santa Barbara, 800 Garden St., Suite D, Santa Barbara, California 93101. (805) 965-5010. Also available online.

General Science Index. H. W. Wilson Co., 950 University Ave., Bronx, New York 10452. 1978-. Monthly, also issued in annual cumulation. Cumulative subject index to English language periodicals in the subject fields of astronomy, botany, chemistry, earth science, environment and conservation, food and nutrition, genetics, mathematics, medicine and health, microbiology, oceanography, physics, physiology and zoology.

Index to Scientific Book Contents. Institute for Scientific Information, 3501 Market St., Philadelphia, Pennsylvania 19104. (800) 523-1857. 1985-. Annual. Gives contents of science books published.

Pollution Abstracts. Cambridge Scientific Abstracts, 5161 River Rd., Bethesda, Maryland 20816. (301) 961-6750. Six/year. Indexes worldwide technical literature on environmental pollution. Covers air pollution, marine and freshwater pollution, sewage and wastewater treatment, waste management, toxicology and health, noise pollution, radiation, land pollution, and environmental policies, programs, legislation, and education. Also available online.

BIBLIOGRAPHIES

Bibliography and Index of Geology. American Geological Institute, 4220 King St., Alexandria, Virginia 22302. Monthly. Includes environmental geology and hydrogeology.

EPA Publications Bibliography. U.S. Environmental Protection Agency, Library Systems Branch, 401 M St., SW, Washington, District of Columbia 20460. (202) 260-2090. Quarterly.

ENCYCLOPEDIAS AND DICTIONARIES

McGraw-Hill Encyclopedia of Science and Technology. McGraw-Hill, 1221 Avenue of the Americas, New York, New York 10020. (212) 512-2000 or (800) 262-4729. 1992. Seventh edition. Issued in multiple volumes including index. Includes all science and technology broad subject areas.

Van Nostrand's Scientific Encyclopedia. Glenn D. Considine, ed. Van Nostrand Reinhold, 115 5th Ave., New York, New York 10003. (212) 254-3232. 1983. Sixth edition. Includes all broad subject areas in science.

GENERAL WORKS

Magill's Survey of Science. Earth Science Series. Frank N. Magill. Salem Press, PO Box 50062, Pasadena, California 91105. 1990-. Five volumes. Includes information on earth's crust, hot spots and volcanic island chains, physical properties of minerals, rock magnetism, physical properties of rocks, and index.

ONLINE DATA BASES

CAS Source Index–CASSI. Chemical Abstracts Service, 2540 Olentangy River Rd., P.O. Box 3012, Columbus, Ohio 43210. (800) 848-6533 or (614) 421-3600. A listing of bibliographic and library holdings information for scientific and technical primary literature relevant to the chemical sciences.

Chemical Abstracts-CA. Chemical Abstracts Service, 2540 Olentangy River Rd., P.O. Box 3012, Columbus, Ohio 43210. (800) 848-6533 or (614) 421-3600. Information sources include 9000 journals, patents from 27 countries, two industrial property organizations, new books, conference proceedings, and government research reports.

Computerized Engineering Index–COMPENDEX. Engineering Information Inc., 345 E. 47th St., New York, New York 10017. (212) 705-7600.

Enviro/Energyline Abstracts Plus. R. R. Bowker Co., 121 Chanlon Rd., New Providence, New Jersey 07974. (908) 464-6800.

Environmental Periodicals Bibliography. National Information Services Corp., Ste. 6, Wyman Towers, 3100 St. Paul St., Baltimore, Maryland 21218. (410)243-0797. Online version of abstract of same name.

Monthly Catalog of United States Government Publications. U.S. G.P.O., Supt. of Docs., PO Box 371954, Pittsburgh, Pennsylvania 15250-7954. (202) 512-0000.

National Technical Information Service. U.S. Department of Commerce, National Technical Information Service, Office of Data Base Services, 5285 Port Royal Rd., Springfield, Virginia 22161. (703) 487-4807. Bibliographic database of government sponsored research and technical reports.

ELECTROLYSIS

ABSTRACTING AND INDEXING SERVICES

Applied Science and Technology Index. H.W. Wilson Co., 950 University Ave., Bronx, New York 10452. (800) 367-6770. Formerly Industrial Arts Index.

Chemical Abstracts. Chemical Abstracts Service, 2540 Olentangy River Rd., PO Box 3012, Columbus, Ohio 43210. (800) 848-6533. 1907-.

Engineering Index. The Engineering Index Inc., 345 E. 47th St., New York, New York 10017. 1962-.

Environment Abstracts. Bowker A & I Publishing, 121 Chanlon Rd., New Providence, New Jersey 07974. (908) 464-6800. 1974-.

Environment Index. Environment Information Center, Index Research Department, 124 E. 39th St., New York, New York 10016. 1971-. Annual.

Environmental Information Connection–EIC. Planning Information Program, Dept. of Urban and Regional Planning, University of Illinois, 1003 West Nevada, Urbana, Illinois 61801. (217) 333-1369. Also available online.

Environmental Periodicals Bibliography. Environmental Studies Institute, International Academy at Santa Barba-

ra, 800 Garden St., Suite D, Santa Barbara, California 93101. (805) 965-5010. Also available online.

General Science Index. H. W. Wilson Co., 950 University Ave., Bronx, New York 10452. 1978-. Monthly, also issued in annual cumulation. Cumulative subject index to English language periodicals in the subject fields of astronomy, botany, chemistry, earth science, environment and conservation, food and nutrition, genetics, mathematics, medicine and health, microbiology, oceanography, physics, physiology and zoology.

Index to Scientific Book Contents. Institute for Scientific Information, 3501 Market St., Philadelphia, Pennsylvania 19104. (800) 523-1857. 1985-. Annual. Gives contents of science books published.

Physics Briefs. Physikalische Berichte. Physik Verlag, Pappapelallee 3, Postfach 101161, Weinheim, Germany D-6940. 1979-. Semimonthly. In English. Volumes for 1979- issued by the Deutsche Physikalische Gesellschaft and the Fachinformationszentrum Energie Physik, Mathematik in cooperation with the American Institute of Physics.

Pollution Abstracts. Cambridge Scientific Abstracts, 5161 River Rd., Bethesda, Maryland 20816. (301) 961-6750. Six/year. Indexes worldwide technical literature on environmental pollution. Covers air pollution, marine and freshwater pollution, sewage and wastewater treatment, waste management, toxicology and health, noise pollution, radiation, land pollution, and environmental policies, programs, legislation, and education. Also available online.

Science Citation Index. Institute for Scientific Information, 3501 Market St., Philadelphia, Pennsylvania 19104. 1961-.

BIBLIOGRAPHIES

Bibliography and Index of Geology. American Geological Institute, 4220 King St., Alexandria, Virginia 22302. Monthly. Includes environmental geology and hydrogeology.

EPA Publications Bibliography. U.S. Environmental Protection Agency, Library Systems Branch, 401 M St., SW, Washington, District of Columbia 20460. (202) 260-2090. Quarterly.

ENCYCLOPEDIAS AND DICTIONARIES

Dictionary of Environmental Engineering and Related Sciences: English-Spanish, Spanish-English. Jose T. Villate. Ediciones Universal, 3090 SW 8th St., Miami, Florida 33135. (305) 642-3355. 1979.

Encyclopedia of Environmental Science and Engineering. J.R. Pfafflin. Gordon and Breach Science Publishers, Inc., 270 8th Ave., New York, New York 10011. (212) 206-8900. 1992.

Encyclopedia of Physical Science and Technology. Robert A. Meyers, ed. Academic Press, c/o Harcourt Brace Jovanovich Inc., 6277 Sea Harbor Dr., Orlando, Florida 32887. (800) 346-8648. Dictionary of engineering, technology and physical sciences.

Encyclopedia of Physics. Rita G. Lerner and George L. Trigg. VCH Publishers, 303 NW 12th Ave., Deerfield Beach, Florida 33442-1788. (305) 428-5566. 1991. Second edition.

McGraw-Hill Encyclopedia of Science and Technology. McGraw-Hill, 1221 Avenue of the Americas, New York, New York 10020. (212) 512-2000 or (800) 262-4729. 1992. Seventh edition. Issued in multiple volumes including index. Includes all science and technology broad subject areas.

Van Nostrand's Scientific Encyclopedia. Glenn D. Considine, ed. Van Nostrand Reinhold, 115 5th Ave., New York, New York 10003. (212) 254-3232. 1983. Sixth edition. Includes all broad subject areas in science.

GENERAL WORKS

Magill's Survey of Science. Earth Science Series. Frank N. Magill. Salem Press, PO Box 50062, Pasadena, California 91105. 1990-. Five volumes. Includes information on earth's crust, hot spots and volcanic island chains, physical properties of minerals, rock magnetism, physical properties of rocks, and index.

ONLINE DATA BASES

Chemical Abstracts-CA. Chemical Abstracts Service, 2540 Olentangy River Rd., P.O. Box 3012, Columbus, Ohio 43210. (800) 848-6533 or (614) 421-3600. Information sources include 9000 journals, patents from 27 countries, two industrial property organizations, new books, conference proceedings, and government research reports.

Chemical Engineering and Biotechnology Abstracts–CEBA. Orbit Search Service, Maxwell Online Inc., 8000 W. Park Dr., McLean, Virginia 22102. (703) 442-0900 or (800) 456-7248. Monthly. Covers theoretical, practical and commercial material on all aspects of processing safety, and the environment. Also covers process and reaction engineering, measurement and process control, environmental protection and safety, plant design and equipment used in chemical engineering and biotechnology. More than 400 of the world's major primary chemical and process engineering journals are scanned to compile the database. Available from ORBIT.

Computerized Engineering Index–COMPENDEX. Engineering Information Inc., 345 E. 47th St., New York, New York 10017. (212) 705-7600.

Enviro/Energyline Abstracts Plus. R. R. Bowker Co., 121 Chanlon Rd., New Providence, New Jersey 07974. (908) 464-6800.

Environmental Periodicals Bibliography. National Information Services Corp., Ste. 6, Wyman Towers, 3100 St. Paul St., Baltimore, Maryland 21218. (410)243-0797. Online version of abstract of same name.

Monthly Catalog of United States Government Publications. U.S. G.P.O., Supt. of Docs., PO Box 371954, Pittsburgh, Pennsylvania 15250-7954. (202) 512-0000.

National Technical Information Service. U.S. Department of Commerce, National Technical Information Service, Office of Data Base Services, 5285 Port Royal Rd., Springfield, Virginia 22161. (703) 487-4807. Bibliographic database of government sponsored research and technical reports.

TRADE ASSOCIATIONS AND PROFESSIONAL SOCIETIES

American Institute of Chemical Engineers. 345 East 47th St., New York, New York 10017. (212) 705-7338.

American Institute of Chemists. 7315 Wisconsin Ave., Bethesda, Maryland 20814. (301) 652-2447.

ELECTROMAGNETIC NOISE

See also: NOISE POLLUTION

ABSTRACTING AND INDEXING SERVICES

Applied Science and Technology Index. H.W. Wilson Co., 950 University Ave., Bronx, New York 10452. (800) 367-6770. Formerly Industrial Arts Index.

Engineering Index. The Engineering Index Inc., 345 E. 47th St., New York, New York 10017. 1962-.

Environment Abstracts. Bowker A & I Publishing, 121 Chanlon Rd., New Providence, New Jersey 07974. (908) 464-6800. 1974-.

Environment Index. Environment Information Center, Index Research Department, 124 E. 39th St., New York, New York 10016. 1971-. Annual.

Environmental Information Connection–EIC. Planning Information Program, Dept. of Urban and Regional Planning, University of Illinois, 1003 West Nevada, Urbana, Illinois 61801. (217) 333-1369. Also available online.

Environmental Periodicals Bibliography. Environmental Studies Institute, International Academy at Santa Barbara, 800 Garden St., Suite D, Santa Barbara, California 93101. (805) 965-5010. Also available online.

General Science Index. H. W. Wilson Co., 950 University Ave., Bronx, New York 10452. 1978-. Monthly, also issued in annual cumulation. Cumulative subject index to English language periodicals in the subject fields of astronomy, botany, chemistry, earth science, environment and conservation, food and nutrition, genetics, mathematics, medicine and health, microbiology, oceanography, physics, physiology and zoology.

Index to Scientific Book Contents. Institute for Scientific Information, 3501 Market St., Philadelphia, Pennsylvania 19104. (800) 523-1857. 1985-. Annual. Gives contents of science books published.

Physics Briefs. Physikalische Berichte. Physik Verlag, Pappapelallee 3, Postfach 101161, Weinheim, Germany D-6940. 1979-. Semimonthly. In English. Volumes for 1979- issued by the Deutsche Physikalische Gesellschaft and the Fachinformationszentrum Energie Physik, Mathematik in cooperation with the American Institute of Physics.

BIBLIOGRAPHIES

EPA Publications Bibliography. U.S. Environmental Protection Agency, Library Systems Branch, 401 M St., SW, Washington, District of Columbia 20460. (202) 260-2090. Quarterly.

ENCYCLOPEDIAS AND DICTIONARIES

Encyclopedia of Physical Science and Technology. Robert A. Meyers, ed. Academic Press, c/o Harcourt Brace Jovanovich Inc., 6277 Sea Harbor Dr., Orlando, Florida

32887. (800) 346-8648. Dictionary of engineering, technology and physical sciences.

Van Nostrand's Scientific Encyclopedia. Glenn D. Considine, ed. Van Nostrand Reinhold, 115 5th Ave., New York, New York 10003. (212) 254-3232. 1983. Sixth edition. Includes all broad subject areas in science.

GENERAL WORKS

Electronic System Design: Interference and Noise Control Techniques. John R. Barnes. Prentice Hall, Rte. 9W, Englewood Cliffs, New Jersey 07632. (201) 592-2000. 1987. Deals with electronic circuit design and electromagnetic noise.

ONLINE DATA BASES

Computerized Engineering Index–COMPENDEX. Engineering Information Inc., 345 E. 47th St., New York, New York 10017. (212) 705-7600.

Enviro/Energyline Abstracts Plus. R. R. Bowker Co., 121 Chanlon Rd., New Providence, New Jersey 07974. (908) 464-6800.

Environmental Periodicals Bibliography. National Information Services Corp., Ste. 6, Wyman Towers, 3100 St. Paul St., Baltimore, Maryland 21218. (410)243-0797. Online version of abstract of same name.

Monthly Catalog of United States Government Publications. U.S. G.P.O., Supt. of Docs., PO Box 371954, Pittsburgh, Pennsylvania 15250-7954. (202) 512-0000.

National Technical Information Service. U.S. Department of Commerce, National Technical Information Service, Office of Data Base Services, 5285 Port Royal Rd., Springfield, Virginia 22161. (703) 487-4807. Bibliographic database of government sponsored research and technical reports.

ELECTROMAGNETIC RADIATION

See also: ELECTRIC POWER LINES–ENVIRONMENTAL ASPECTS

ABSTRACTING AND INDEXING SERVICES

Applied Science and Technology Index. H.W. Wilson Co., 950 University Ave., Bronx, New York 10452. (800) 367-6770. Formerly Industrial Arts Index.

Engineering Index. The Engineering Index Inc., 345 E. 47th St., New York, New York 10017. 1962-.

Environment Abstracts. Bowker A & I Publishing, 121 Chanlon Rd., New Providence, New Jersey 07974. (908) 464-6800. 1974-.

Environment Index. Environment Information Center, Index Research Department, 124 E. 39th St., New York, New York 10016. 1971-. Annual.

Environmental Information Connection–EIC. Planning Information Program, Dept. of Urban and Regional Planning, University of Illinois, 1003 West Nevada, Urbana, Illinois 61801. (217) 333-1369. Also available online.

Environmental Periodicals Bibliography. Environmental Studies Institute, International Academy at Santa Barbara, 800 Garden St., Suite D, Santa Barbara, California 93101. (805) 965-5010. Also available online.

General Science Index. H. W. Wilson Co., 950 University Ave., Bronx, New York 10452. 1978-. Monthly, also issued in annual cumulation. Cumulative subject index to English language periodicals in the subject fields of astronomy, botany, chemistry, earth science, environment and conservation, food and nutrition, genetics, mathematics, medicine and health, microbiology, oceanography, physics, physiology and zoology.

Index to Scientific Book Contents. Institute for Scientific Information, 3501 Market St., Philadelphia, Pennsylvania 19104. (800) 523-1857. 1985-. Annual. Gives contents of science books published.

Physics Briefs. Physikalische Berichte. Physik Verlag, Pappapelallee 3, Postfach 101161, Weinheim, Germany D-6940. 1979-. Semimonthly. In English. Volumes for 1979- issued by the Deutsche Physikalische Gesellschaft and the Fachinformationszentrum Energie Physik, Mathematik in cooperation with the American Institute of Physics.

Science Citation Index. Institute for Scientific Information, 3501 Market St., Philadelphia, Pennsylvania 19104. 1961-.

BIBLIOGRAPHIES

Bibliography and Index of Geology. American Geological Institute, 4220 King St., Alexandria, Virginia 22302. Monthly. Includes environmental geology and hydrogeology.

EPA Publications Bibliography. U.S. Environmental Protection Agency, Library Systems Branch, 401 M St., SW, Washington, District of Columbia 20460. (202) 260-2090. Quarterly.

ENCYCLOPEDIAS AND DICTIONARIES

Dictionary of Environmental Engineering and Related Sciences: English-Spanish, Spanish-English. Jose T. Villate. Ediciones Universal, 3090 SW 8th St., Miami, Florida 33135. (305) 642-3355. 1979.

Encyclopedia of Environmental Science and Engineering. J.R. Pfafflin. Gordon and Breach Science Publishers, Inc., 270 8th Ave., New York, New York 10011. (212) 206-8900. 1992.

Encyclopedia of Human Biology. Renato Dulbecco, ed. Academic Press, c/o Harcourt Brace Jovanovich Inc., 6277 Sea Harbor Dr., Orlando, Florida 32887. (800) 346-8648. 1991. Eight volumes.

Encyclopedia of Physical Science and Technology. Robert A. Meyers, ed. Academic Press, c/o Harcourt Brace Jovanovich Inc., 6277 Sea Harbor Dr., Orlando, Florida 32887. (800) 346-8648. Dictionary of engineering, technology and physical sciences.

McGraw-Hill Encyclopedia of Science and Technology. McGraw-Hill, 1221 Avenue of the Americas, New York, New York 10020. (212) 512-2000 or (800) 262-4729. 1992. Seventh edition. Issued in multiple volumes including index. Includes all science and technology broad subject areas.

Van Nostrand's Scientific Encyclopedia. Glenn D. Considine, ed. Van Nostrand Reinhold, 115 5th Ave., New York, New York 10003. (212) 254-3232. 1983. Sixth edition. Includes all broad subject areas in science.

GENERAL WORKS

Atoms and Light: Interactions. John N. Dodd. Plenum Press, 233 Spring St., New York, New York 10013-1578. (212) 620-8000. 1991. Deals with electromagnetic radiation, electromagnetic interactions, light and atoms.

Magill's Survey of Science. Earth Science Series. Frank N. Magill. Salem Press, PO Box 50062, Pasadena, California 91105. 1990-. Five volumes. Includes information on earth's crust, hot spots and volcanic island chains, physical properties of minerals, rock magnetism, physical properties of rocks, and index.

HANDBOOKS AND MANUALS

CRC Handbook of Biological Effects of Electromagnetic Fields. Charles Polk. CRC Press, 2000 Corporate Blvd. N.W., Boca Raton, Florida 33431. (800) 272-7737. 1986. Presents current knowledge about the effects of electromagnetic fields on living matter.

Tables of Physical and Chemical Constants and Some Mathematical Functions. G. W. C. Kaye, et al. Longman Group Ltd., Longman House, Burnt Mill, Harlow, England CM20 2J6. 0279 426721. 1988. Fifteenth edition. Includes tables on mechanical properties, density, elasticity, viscosity, surface tension, temperature and heat. Also covers radiation, optics, chemistry, electrochemistry, astrophysics, and chemical thermodynamics.

ONLINE DATA BASES

Computerized Engineering Index–COMPENDEX. Engineering Information Inc., 345 E. 47th St., New York, New York 10017. (212) 705-7600.

Enviro/Energyline Abstracts Plus. R. R. Bowker Co., 121 Chanlon Rd., New Providence, New Jersey 07974. (908) 464-6800.

Environmental Periodicals Bibliography. National Information Services Corp., Ste. 6, Wyman Towers, 3100 St. Paul St., Baltimore, Maryland 21218. (410)243-0797. Online version of abstract of same name.

Monthly Catalog of United States Government Publications. U.S. G.P.O., Supt. of Docs., PO Box 371954, Pittsburgh, Pennsylvania 15250-7954. (202) 512-0000.

National Technical Information Service. U.S. Department of Commerce, National Technical Information Service, Office of Data Base Services, 5285 Port Royal Rd., Springfield, Virginia 22161. (703) 487-4807. Bibliographic database of government sponsored research and technical reports.

TRADE ASSOCIATIONS AND PROFESSIONAL SOCIETIES

International Bio-Environmental Foundation. 15300 Ventura Blvd., Suite 405, Sherman Oaks, California 91403. (818) 907-5483.

ELECTROPLATING

ABSTRACTING AND INDEXING SERVICES

Applied Science and Technology Index. H.W. Wilson Co., 950 University Ave., Bronx, New York 10452. (800) 367-6770. Formerly Industrial Arts Index.

Chemical Abstracts. Chemical Abstracts Service, 2540 Olentangy River Rd., PO Box 3012, Columbus, Ohio 43210. (800) 848-6533. 1907-.

Electroplating & Metal Finishing. Wheatland Journals Ltd., Penn House, Penn Place, Rickmansworth, England WD3 1FN.

Engineering Index. The Engineering Index Inc., 345 E. 47th St., New York, New York 10017. 1962-.

Environment Abstracts. Bowker A & I Publishing, 121 Chanlon Rd., New Providence, New Jersey 07974. (908) 464-6800. 1974-.

Environment Index. Environment Information Center, Index Research Department, 124 E. 39th St., New York, New York 10016. 1971-. Annual.

Environmental Information Connection–EIC. Planning Information Program, Dept. of Urban and Regional Planning, University of Illinois, 1003 West Nevada, Urbana, Illinois 61801. (217) 333-1369. Also available online.

Environmental Periodicals Bibliography. Environmental Studies Institute, International Academy at Santa Barbara, 800 Garden St., Suite D, Santa Barbara, California 93101. (805) 965-5010. Also available online.

General Science Index. H. W. Wilson Co., 950 University Ave., Bronx, New York 10452. 1978-. Monthly, also issued in annual cumulation. Cumulative subject index to English language periodicals in the subject fields of astronomy, botany, chemistry, earth science, environment and conservation, food and nutrition, genetics, mathematics, medicine and health, microbiology, oceanography, physics, physiology and zoology.

Geographical Abstracts. London School of Economics, Dept. of Geography, Regency House, 34 Duke St., London, England 1966-. Continued by Geo Abstracts issued in 6 parts: Pt. A. Landforms and the quaternary; Pt. B. Biogeography and Climatology; Pt. C. Economic geography; Pt. D. Social geography and cartography; Pt. E. Sedimentology; Pt. F. Regional and community planning.

Index to Scientific Book Contents. Institute for Scientific Information, 3501 Market St., Philadelphia, Pennsylvania 19104. (800) 523-1857. 1985-. Annual. Gives contents of science books published.

Physics Briefs. Physikalische Berichte. Physik Verlag, Pappapelallee 3, Postfach 101161, Weinheim, Germany D-6940. 1979-. Semimonthly. In English. Volumes for 1979- issued by the Deutsche Physikalische Gesellschaft and the Fachinformationszentrum Energie Physik, Mathematik in cooperation with the American Institute of Physics.

BIBLIOGRAPHIES

EPA Publications Bibliography. U.S. Environmental Protection Agency, Library Systems Branch, 401 M St., SW, Washington, District of Columbia 20460. (202) 260-2090. Quarterly.

DIRECTORIES

Metal Finishing Guidebook Directory. Metals and Plastics Publications, Inc., 3 University Plaza, Hackensack, New Jersey 07601. (201) 487-3700. Annual. Covers electroplating and metal finishing.

Plating. American Business Directories, Inc., 5711 S. 86th Circle, Omaha, Nebraska 68127. (402) 593-4600.

Plating and Surface Finishing-American Electroplaters' and Surface Finishers Society Branch Directory. American Electroplaters' and Surface Finishers Society, 12644 Research Parkway, Orlando, Florida 32826. (407) 281-6441.

Plating and Surface Finishing–Directory of American Electroplaters' and Surface Finishers Society of Boards and Committees Issue. American Electroplaters' and Surface Finishers Society, 12644 Research Parkway, Orlando, Florida 32826. (407) 281-6441.

ENCYCLOPEDIAS AND DICTIONARIES

Dictionary of Environmental Engineering and Related Sciences: English-Spanish, Spanish-English. Jose T. Villate. Ediciones Universal, 3090 SW 8th St., Miami, Florida 33135. (305) 642-3355. 1979.

Encyclopedia of Chemical Processing and Design. John J. Mcketta and W. A. Cunningham. Marcel Dekker, Inc., 270 Madison Ave., New York, New York 10016. (212) 696-9000; (800) 228-1160. 1992. Thirty-eight volumes.

Encyclopedia of Environmental Science and Engineering. J.R. Pfafflin. Gordon and Breach Science Publishers, Inc., 270 8th Ave., New York, New York 10011. (212) 206-8900. 1992.

Encyclopedia of Physical Science and Technology. Robert A. Meyers, ed. Academic Press, c/o Harcourt Brace Jovanovich Inc., 6277 Sea Harbor Dr., Orlando, Florida 32887. (800) 346-8648. Dictionary of engineering, technology and physical sciences.

Kirk-Othmer Encyclopedia of Chemical Technology. J. I. Kroschwitz, ed. John Wiley & Sons, Inc., 605 3rd Ave., New York, New York 10158-0012. (212) 850-6000. 1992-. All articles in the new edition have been rewritten and updated adding new subjects such as biotechnology, computer topics, analytical techniques and instrumentation, environmental concerns, fuels and energy, inorganic and solid state chemistry; composite materials and material science in general, and pharmaceuticals. Also available online.

McGraw-Hill Encyclopedia of Science and Technology. McGraw-Hill, 1221 Avenue of the Americas, New York, New York 10020. (212) 512-2000 or (800) 262-4729. 1992. Seventh edition. Issued in multiple volumes including index. Includes all science and technology broad subject areas.

Van Nostrand's Scientific Encyclopedia. Glenn D. Considine, ed. Van Nostrand Reinhold, 115 5th Ave., New York, New York 10003. (212) 254-3232. 1983. Sixth edition. Includes all broad subject areas in science.

HANDBOOKS AND MANUALS

Electroplating Wastewater Pollution Control Technology. George C. Cushnie. Noyes Publications, 120 Mill Rd., Park Ridge, New Jersey 07656. (201) 391-8484. 1985. Environmental aspects of electroplating waste disposal and sewage purification.

Guidance Manual for Electroplating and Metal Finishing Pretreatment Standards. U.S. Environmental Protection Agency, 401 M St., SW, Washington, District of Columbia 20460. (202) 260-2090. 1984. Environmental aspects of electroplating and metal finishing.

ONLINE DATA BASES

CAS Source Index–CASSI. Chemical Abstracts Service, 2540 Olentangy River Rd., P.O. Box 3012, Columbus, Ohio 43210. (800) 848-6533 or (614) 421-3600. A listing of bibliographic and library holdings information for scientific and technical primary literature relevant to the chemical sciences.

Chemical Abstracts-CA. Chemical Abstracts Service, 2540 Olentangy River Rd., P.O. Box 3012, Columbus, Ohio 43210. (800) 848-6533 or (614) 421-3600. Information sources include 9000 journals, patents from 27 countries, two industrial property organizations, new books, conference proceedings, and government research reports.

Chemical Engineering and Biotechnology Abstracts–CEBA. Orbit Search Service, Maxwell Online Inc., 8000 W. Park Dr., McLean, Virginia 22102. (703) 442-0900 or (800) 456-7248. Monthly. Covers theoretical, practical and commercial material on all aspects of processing safety, and the environment. Also covers process and reaction engineering, measurement and process control, environmental protection and safety, plant design and equipment used in chemical engineering and biotechnology. More than 400 of the world's major primary chemical and process engineering journals are scanned to compile the database. Available from ORBIT.

Computerized Engineering Index–COMPENDEX. Engineering Information Inc., 345 E. 47th St., New York, New York 10017. (212) 705-7600.

Enviro/Energyline Abstracts Plus. R. R. Bowker Co., 121 Chanlon Rd., New Providence, New Jersey 07974. (908) 464-6800.

Environmental Periodicals Bibliography. National Information Services Corp., Ste. 6, Wyman Towers, 3100 St. Paul St., Baltimore, Maryland 21218. (410)243-0797. Online version of abstract of same name.

Kirk-Othmer Encyclopedia of Chemical Technology. John Wiley & Sons, Inc., 605 3rd Ave., 5th Floor, New York, New York 10158. (212) 850-6000. Online version of the publication of the same name.

Monthly Catalog of United States Government Publications. U.S. G.P.O., Supt. of Docs., PO Box 371954, Pittsburgh, Pennsylvania 15250-7954. (202) 512-0000.

National Technical Information Service. U.S. Department of Commerce, National Technical Information Service, Office of Data Base Services, 5285 Port Royal Rd., Springfield, Virginia 22161. (703) 487-4807. Bibliographic database of government sponsored research and technical reports.

PERIODICALS AND NEWSLETTERS

Plating. American Electroplaters and Surface Finishers Society, 12644 Research Pkwy., Orlando, Florida 32826. (407) 281-6441. Monthly.

TRADE ASSOCIATIONS AND PROFESSIONAL SOCIETIES

American Institute of Chemical Engineers. 345 East 47th St., New York, New York 10017. (212) 705-7338.

American Institute of Chemists. 7315 Wisconsin Ave., Bethesda, Maryland 20814. (301) 652-2447.

ELECTROSTATIC PRECIPITATION

ABSTRACTING AND INDEXING SERVICES

Applied Science and Technology Index. H.W. Wilson Co., 950 University Ave., Bronx, New York 10452. (800) 367-6770. Formerly Industrial Arts Index.

Chemical Abstracts. Chemical Abstracts Service, 2540 Olentangy River Rd., PO Box 3012, Columbus, Ohio 43210. (800) 848-6533. 1907-.

Engineering Index. The Engineering Index Inc., 345 E. 47th St., New York, New York 10017. 1962-.

Environment Abstracts. Bowker A & I Publishing, 121 Chanlon Rd., New Providence, New Jersey 07974. (908) 464-6800. 1974-.

Environment Index. Environment Information Center, Index Research Department, 124 E. 39th St., New York, New York 10016. 1971-. Annual.

Environmental Information Connection–EIC. Planning Information Program, Dept. of Urban and Regional Planning, University of Illinois, 1003 West Nevada, Urbana, Illinois 61801. (217) 333-1369. Also available online.

Environmental Periodicals Bibliography. Environmental Studies Institute, International Academy at Santa Barbara, 800 Garden St., Suite D, Santa Barbara, California 93101. (805) 965-5010. Also available online.

General Science Index. H. W. Wilson Co., 950 University Ave., Bronx, New York 10452. 1978-. Monthly, also issued in annual cumulation. Cumulative subject index to English language periodicals in the subject fields of astronomy, botany, chemistry, earth science, environment and conservation, food and nutrition, genetics, mathematics, medicine and health, microbiology, oceanography, physics, physiology and zoology.

Index to Scientific Book Contents. Institute for Scientific Information, 3501 Market St., Philadelphia, Pennsylvania 19104. (800) 523-1857. 1985-. Annual. Gives contents of science books published.

Physics Briefs. Physikalische Berichte. Physik Verlag, Pappapelallee 3, Postfach 101161, Weinheim, Germany D-6940. 1979-. Semimonthly. In English. Volumes for 1979- issued by the Deutsche Physikalische Gesellschaft and the Fachinformationszentrum Energie Physik, Mathematik in cooperation with the American Institute of Physics.

Pollution Abstracts. Cambridge Scientific Abstracts, 5161 River Rd., Bethesda, Maryland 20816. (301) 961-6750.

Six/year. Indexes worldwide technical literature on environmental pollution. Covers air pollution, marine and freshwater pollution, sewage and wastewater treatment, waste management, toxicology and health, noise pollution, radiation, land pollution, and environmental policies, programs, legislation, and education. Also available online.

BIBLIOGRAPHIES

EPA Publications Bibliography. U.S. Environmental Protection Agency, Library Systems Branch, 401 M St., SW, Washington, District of Columbia 20460. (202) 260-2090. Quarterly.

ENCYCLOPEDIAS AND DICTIONARIES

Encyclopedia of Chemical Processing and Design. John J. Mcketta and W. A. Cunningham. Marcel Dekker, Inc., 270 Madison Ave., New York, New York 10016. (212) 696-9000; (800) 228-1160. 1992. Thirty-eight volumes.

Encyclopedia of Physical Science and Technology. Robert A. Meyers, ed. Academic Press, c/o Harcourt Brace Jovanovich Inc., 6277 Sea Harbor Dr., Orlando, Florida 32887. (800) 346-8648. Dictionary of engineering, technology and physical sciences.

Kirk-Othmer Encyclopedia of Chemical Technology. J. I. Kroschwitz, ed. John Wiley & Sons, Inc., 605 3rd Ave., New York, New York 10158-0012. (212) 850-6000. 1992-. All articles in the new edition have been rewritten and updated adding new subjects such as biotechnology, computer topics, analytical techniques and instrumentation, environmental concerns, fuels and energy, inorganic and solid state chemistry; composite materials and material science in general, and pharmaceuticals. Also available online.

McGraw-Hill Encyclopedia of Science and Technology. McGraw-Hill, 1221 Avenue of the Americas, New York, New York 10020. (212) 512-2000 or (800) 262-4729. 1992. Seventh edition. Issued in multiple volumes including index. Includes all science and technology broad subject areas.

The New York Times Encyclopedic Dictionary of the Environment. Paul Sarnoff. Quadrangle Books, New York, New York 1971. Focuses on state-of-the-art methods of pollution control, abatement, prevention and removal.

Van Nostrand's Scientific Encyclopedia. Glenn D. Considine, ed. Van Nostrand Reinhold, 115 5th Ave., New York, New York 10003. (212) 254-3232. 1983. Sixth edition. Includes all broad subject areas in science.

GENERAL WORKS

Air Pollution Control. Howard E. Hesketh. Technomic Publishing Co., 851 New Holland Ave., Box 3535, Lancaster, Pennsylvania 17604. (717) 291-5609. 1991. Presents both theory and application data. Provides a background relevant to behavior theories and control techniques for capturing gaseous and particulate air pollutants.

ONLINE DATA BASES

CAS Source Index–CASSI. Chemical Abstracts Service, 2540 Olentangy River Rd., P.O. Box 3012, Columbus,

Ohio 43210. (800) 848-6533 or (614) 421-3600. A listing of bibliographic and library holdings information for scientific and technical primary literature relevant to the chemical sciences.

Chemical Abstracts-CA. Chemical Abstracts Service, 2540 Olentangy River Rd., P.O. Box 3012, Columbus, Ohio 43210. (800) 848-6533 or (614) 421-3600. Information sources include 9000 journals, patents from 27 countries, two industrial property organizations, new books, conference proceedings, and government research reports.

Computerized Engineering Index–COMPENDEX. Engineering Information Inc., 345 E. 47th St., New York, New York 10017. (212) 705-7600.

Enviro/Energyline Abstracts Plus. R. R. Bowker Co., 121 Chanlon Rd., New Providence, New Jersey 07974. (908) 464-6800.

Environmental Periodicals Bibliography. National Information Services Corp., Ste. 6, Wyman Towers, 3100 St. Paul St., Baltimore, Maryland 21218. (410)243-0797. Online version of abstract of same name.

Kirk-Othmer Encyclopedia of Chemical Technology. John Wiley & Sons, Inc., 605 3rd Ave., 5th Floor, New York, New York 10158. (212) 850-6000. Online version of the publication of the same name.

Monthly Catalog of United States Government Publications. U.S. G.P.O., Supt. of Docs., PO Box 371954, Pittsburgh, Pennsylvania 15250-7954. (202) 512-0000.

National Technical Information Service. U.S. Department of Commerce, National Technical Information Service, Office of Data Base Services, 5285 Port Royal Rd., Springfield, Virginia 22161. (703) 487-4807. Bibliographic database of government sponsored research and technical reports.

RESEARCH CENTERS AND INSTITUTES

Texas A & M University, Separation and Ingredient Sciences Laboratory. Food Protein Research and Development Center, College Station, Texas 77843-2476. (409) 845-2741.

ELEMENTS

ABSTRACTING AND INDEXING SERVICES

Applied Science and Technology Index. H.W. Wilson Co., 950 University Ave., Bronx, New York 10452. (800) 367-6770. Formerly Industrial Arts Index.

Chemical Abstracts. Chemical Abstracts Service, 2540 Olentangy River Rd., PO Box 3012, Columbus, Ohio 43210. (800) 848-6533. 1907-.

Ecology Abstracts. Cambridge Scientific Abstracts, 5161 River Rd., Bethesda, Maryland 20816. (301) 961-6750. Monthly.

Energy Information Abstracts Annual 1987 in Retrospect. EIC/Intelligence Inc., 121 Chanlon Rd., New Providence, New Jersey 07974. (908) 464-6800. 1988. Annual. Cumulative edition of the monthly Energy Information Abstracts. Monitors sources in the field of energy including the scientific, technical and business journal literature, conference and symposia proceedings, corporate, government and academic reports.

Environment Abstracts. Bowker A & I Publishing, 121 Chanlon Rd., New Providence, New Jersey 07974. (908) 464-6800. 1974-.

Environment Index. Environment Information Center, Index Research Department, 124 E. 39th St., New York, New York 10016. 1971-. Annual.

Environmental Information Connection–EIC. Planning Information Program, Dept. of Urban and Regional Planning, University of Illinois, 1003 West Nevada, Urbana, Illinois 61801. (217) 333-1369. Also available online.

Environmental Periodicals Bibliography. Environmental Studies Institute, International Academy at Santa Barbara, 800 Garden St., Suite D, Santa Barbara, California 93101. (805) 965-5010. Also available online.

ERDA Research Abstracts. U.S. ERDA Technical Information Center, Box 62, Oak Ridge, Tennessee 37830.

General Science Index. H. W. Wilson Co., 950 University Ave., Bronx, New York 10452. 1978-. Monthly, also issued in annual cumulation. Cumulative subject index to English language periodicals in the subject fields of astronomy, botany, chemistry, earth science, environment and conservation, food and nutrition, genetics, mathematics, medicine and health, microbiology, oceanography, physics, physiology and zoology.

Index to Scientific Book Contents. Institute for Scientific Information, 3501 Market St., Philadelphia, Pennsylvania 19104. (800) 523-1857. 1985-. Annual. Gives contents of science books published.

INIS Atomindex. International Atomic Energy Agency, Wagramerstrasse 5, Vienna, Austria A-1400. 222 23606198. 1988-. Semiannual. Abstracts nuclear energy and nuclear physics topics from journals, conferences, technical reports and other related publications. Issued in 6 parts: Personal Author, Corporate Entry, Subject, Report, Standard Patent, Conference (by place), Conference (by date).

Physics Briefs. Physikalische Berichte. Physik Verlag, Pappapelallee 3, Postfach 101161, Weinheim, Germany D-6940. 1979-. Semimonthly. In English. Volumes for 1979- issued by the Deutsche Physikalische Gesellschaft and the Fachinformationszentrum Energie Physik, Mathematik in cooperation with the American Institute of Physics.

Science Citation Index. Institute for Scientific Information, 3501 Market St., Philadelphia, Pennsylvania 19104. 1961-.

BIBLIOGRAPHIES

EPA Publications Bibliography. U.S. Environmental Protection Agency, Library Systems Branch, 401 M St., SW, Washington, District of Columbia 20460. (202) 260-2090. Quarterly.

ENCYCLOPEDIAS AND DICTIONARIES

Encyclopedia of Electrochemistry of Elements. A. J. Bard. Marcel Dekker, Inc., 270 Madison Ave., New York, New York 10016. (212) 696-9000 or (800) 228-1160. Encyclopedic treatment of the subject area of electrochemistry and related subjects.

Encyclopedia of Human Biology. Renato Dulbecco, ed. Academic Press, c/o Harcourt Brace Jovanovich Inc., 6277 Sea Harbor Dr., Orlando, Florida 32887. (800) 346-8648. 1991. Eight volumes.

Encyclopedia of Physical Science and Technology. Robert A. Meyers, ed. Academic Press, c/o Harcourt Brace Jovanovich Inc., 6277 Sea Harbor Dr., Orlando, Florida 32887. (800) 346-8648. Dictionary of engineering, technology and physical sciences.

Encyclopedia of Physics. Rita G. Lerner and George L. Trigg. VCH Publishers, 303 NW 12th Ave., Deerfield Beach, Florida 33442-1788. (305) 428-5566. 1991. Second edition.

The Encyclopedia of the Chemical Elements. Clifford A. Hampel. Reinhold Pub. Co., 115 5th Ave., New York, New York 10003. (212)254-3232. 1968.

McGraw-Hill Encyclopedia of Science and Technology. McGraw-Hill, 1221 Avenue of the Americas, New York, New York 10020. (212) 512-2000 or (800) 262-4729. 1992. Seventh edition. Issued in multiple volumes including index. Includes all science and technology broad subject areas.

Van Nostrand's Scientific Encyclopedia. Glenn D. Considine, ed. Van Nostrand Reinhold, 115 5th Ave., New York, New York 10003. (212) 254-3232. 1983. Sixth edition. Includes all broad subject areas in science.

GENERAL WORKS

Alkali Metals: An Update. F.S. Messiha. ANKHO International, Syracuse, New York (315) 463-0182. 1984.

The Biological Alkylation of Heavy Elements. P. J. Craig and F. Glockling. Royal Society of Chemistry, Thomas Graham House Science Park, Milton Rd., Cambridge, England CB4 4WF. 1988. Covers alkylation, heavy elements, and organic compounds.

The Chemistry of Lithium, Sodium, Potassium, Rubidium, Cesium and Francium. William A. Hart. Pergamon Microforms International, Inc., Fairview Park, Elmsford, New York 10523. (914) 592-7720. 1973.

The Elements: Their Origin, Abundance, and Distribution. P.A. Cox. Oxford University Press, 200 Madison Ave., New York, New York 10016. (212) 679-7300. 1989.

Health and Environmental Effects Document for Boron and Boron Compounds. National Technical Information Service, 5285 Port Royal Rd., Springfield, Virginia 22161. (703) 487-4650. 1991.

Sensitive Biochemical and Behavioral Indicators of Trace Substance Exposure. Edward J. Massaro. Center for Environmental Research Information, U.S. Environmental Protection Agency, 26 W. Martin Luther King Dr., Cincinnati, Ohio 45268. (518) 569-7931. 1981.

HANDBOOKS AND MANUALS

Handbook of the Elements. Samuel Ruben. Open Court Pub. Co., 407 S. Dearborn, #1300, Chicago, Illinois 60605. (312) 939-1500. 1990. Third edition. Provides essential information on the 108 known chemical elements.

Nuclear Reactions in Heavy Elements: A Data Handbook. V.M. Gorbachev. Pergamon Microforms International,

Inc., Fairview Park, Elmsford, New York 10523. (914) 592-7720. 1979. Covers nuclear reactions, nuclear fission and heavy elements.

Tables of Physical and Chemical Constants and Some Mathematical Functions. G. W. C. Kaye, et al. Longman Group Ltd., Longman House, Burnt Mill, Harlow, England CM20 2J6. 0279 426721. 1988. Fifteenth edition. Includes tables on mechanical properties, density, elasticity, viscosity, surface tension, temperature and heat. Also covers radiation, optics, chemistry, electrochemistry, astrophysics, and chemical thermodynamics.

ONLINE DATA BASES

Chemical Abstracts-CA. Chemical Abstracts Service, 2540 Olentangy River Rd., P.O. Box 3012, Columbus, Ohio 43210. (800) 848-6533 or (614) 421-3600. Information sources include 9000 journals, patents from 27 countries, two industrial property organizations, new books, conference proceedings, and government research reports.

Enviro/Energyline Abstracts Plus. R. R. Bowker Co., 121 Chanlon Rd., New Providence, New Jersey 07974. (908) 464-6800.

Environmental Periodicals Bibliography. National Information Services Corp., Ste. 6, Wyman Towers, 3100 St. Paul St., Baltimore, Maryland 21218. (410)243-0797. Online version of abstract of same name.

Monthly Catalog of United States Government Publications. U.S. G.P.O., Supt. of Docs., PO Box 371954, Pittsburgh, Pennsylvania 15250-7954. (202) 512-0000.

National Technical Information Service. U.S. Department of Commerce, National Technical Information Service, Office of Data Base Services, 5285 Port Royal Rd., Springfield, Virginia 22161. (703) 487-4807. Bibliographic database of government sponsored research and technical reports.

EMBRYOLOGY

ABSTRACTING AND INDEXING SERVICES

ASFA Aquaculture Abstracts. Cambridge Scientific Abstracts, Inc., 5161 River Rd., Bethesda, Maryland 20816. (301) 961-6750. 1984.

Biological Abstracts. BIOSIS, 2100 Arch St., Philadelphia, Pennsylvania 19103-1399. (215) 587-4800. 1927-.

Biological and Agricultural Index. H.W. Wilson Co., 950 University Ave., Bronx, New York 10452. (800) 367-6770. 1916-. Monthly.

Biology Digest. Data Courier, Plexus Pub Inc., 143 Old Marlton Pike, Medford, New Jersey 08055. 1974-. Monthly. Abstracts biology periodicals.

Ecological Abstracts. Geo Abstracts Ltd. Elsevier Applied Science, Crown House, Linton Rd., Barking, England IG 11 8JU. 1974-. Derived from over 600 leading ecological and environmental journals, plus books, conference proceedings, reports and theses.

General Science Index. H. W. Wilson Co., 950 University Ave., Bronx, New York 10452. 1978-. Monthly, also issued in annual cumulation. Cumulative subject index to English language periodicals in the subject fields of

astronomy, botany, chemistry, earth science, environment and conservation, food and nutrition, genetics, mathematics, medicine and health, microbiology, oceanography, physics, physiology and zoology.

Index to Scientific Book Contents. Institute for Scientific Information, 3501 Market St., Philadelphia, Pennsylvania 19104. (800) 523-1857. 1985-. Annual. Gives contents of science books published.

Pollution Abstracts. Cambridge Scientific Abstracts, 5161 River Rd., Bethesda, Maryland 20816. (301) 961-6750. Six/year. Indexes worldwide technical literature on environmental pollution. Covers air pollution, marine and freshwater pollution, sewage and wastewater treatment, waste management, toxicology and health, noise pollution, radiation, land pollution, and environmental policies, programs, legislation, and education. Also available online.

BIBLIOGRAPHIES

Current Contents. Agriculture, Biology and Environmental Sciences. Institute for Scientific Information, 3501 Market St., Philadelphia, Pennsylvania 19104. (800) 523-1857. 1973-. Previous title: Current Contents. Agricultural, Food & Veterinary Sciences. Gives the table of contents of periodicals in the fields of agriculture, biology, environmental and related areas.

ENCYCLOPEDIAS AND DICTIONARIES

Cambridge Encyclopedia of Life Sciences. A. E. Friday and David S. Ingram. Cambridge University Press, 40 W 20th St., New York, New York 10011. (212) 924-3900 or (800) 227-0247. 1985. Includes all topics under biology and ecology.

A Dictionary of Genetics. Robert C. King and William A. Stansfield. Oxford University Press, 200 Madison Ave., New York, New York 10016. (212) 679-7300 or (800) 334-4249. 1991. Fourth edition. Includes 7,100 definitions with 250 illustrations. Also includes bibliography of major sources.

Dictionary of Genetics and Cell Biology. Norman Maclean. New York University Press, 70 Washington Sq. S., New York, New York 10012. (212) 998-2575. 1987. Includes the subject areas of cytology and genetics.

Encyclopedic Dictionary of Genetics: With German Term Equivalents and Extensive German/English Index. R. C. King and W. D. Stansfield. VCH Publishers, 303 NW 12th Ave., Deerfield Beach, Florida 33442-1788. (305) 428-5566. 1990. 4th ed. Revised edition of: A Dictionary of Genetics, third edition.

McGraw-Hill Encyclopedia of Science and Technology. McGraw-Hill, 1221 Avenue of the Americas, New York, New York 10020. (212) 512-2000 or (800) 262-4729. 1992. Seventh edition. Issued in multiple volumes including index. Includes all science and technology broad subject areas.

Van Nostrand's Scientific Encyclopedia. Glenn D. Considine, ed. Van Nostrand Reinhold, 115 5th Ave., New York, New York 10003. (212) 254-3232. 1983. Sixth edition. Includes all broad subject areas in science.

ONLINE DATA BASES

BIOSIS Previews. BIOSIS, 2100 Arch St., Philadelphia, Pennsylvania 19103-1399. (215) 587-4800. Largest and most comprehensive database of research in the life sciences. Contains citations for nearly 9000 primary research journals, monographs, reviews, symposia, preliminary reports, semi-popular journals, selected institutional reports, government reports and research communications.

Monthly Catalog of United States Government Publications. U.S. G.P.O., Supt. of Docs., PO Box 371954, Pittsburgh, Pennsylvania 15250-7954. (202) 512-0000.

National Technical Information Service. U.S. Department of Commerce, National Technical Information Service, Office of Data Base Services, 5285 Port Royal Rd., Springfield, Virginia 22161. (703) 487-4807. Bibliographic database of government sponsored research and technical reports.

SCISEARCH. Institute for Scientific Information, University City Science Center, 3501 Market St., Philadelphia, Pennsylvania 19104. (215) 386-0100.

TRADE ASSOCIATIONS AND PROFESSIONAL SOCIETIES

American Institute of Biological Sciences. 730 11th St., N.W., Washington, District of Columbia 20001-4521. (202) 628-1500.

American Society of Naturalists. Department of Ecology and Evolation, State University of New York, Stony Brook, New York 11794. (516) 632-8589.

EMERGENCY CORE COOLING SYSTEMS

See: COOLING SYSTEMS

EMERGENCY RESPONSE PLANNING

DIRECTORIES

Emergency Response Directory for Hazardous Materials Accidents. Pamela Lawrence. Odin Press, PO Box 536, Lenox Hill Sta., New York, New York 10021. (212) 744-2538. Biennial. Governmental agencies, chemical manufacturers and transporters, hotlines and strike teams, burn care centers, civil defense and disaster centers concerned with the containment and cleanup of chemical spills and other hazardous material accidents.

GENERAL WORKS

Emergency Planning and Community Right to Know. Sarith Guerra. Management Information Service, 777 N. Capitol St., NE, Ste. 500, Washington, District of Columbia 20002-420. (800) 745-8780. 1991. Covers the reporting of health risks from hazardous substances.

Emergency Response Planning Guidelines Set 5. American Industrial Hygiene Association, 345 White Pond Dr., Akron, Ohio 44320. (216) 873-2442. 1991. Includes guidelines for acrylic acid, 1,3-butadiene, epichlorohydrin, tetrafluoroethylene, and vinyl acetate.

When All Else Fails!: Enforcement of The Emergency Planning and Community Right-To-Know Act; A Self

Help Manual for Local Emergency Planning Committees. U.S. Environmental Protection Agency, Office of Solid Waste and Emergency Response, 401 M St. SW, Washington, District of Columbia 20460. (202) 260-2090. 1990.

GOVERNMENTAL ORGANIZATIONS

Emergency Management Agency: Emergency Preparedness and Community Right-to-Know. Emergency Response Commission, PO Box 4501, Fondren Station, Jackson, Mississippi 39296-4501. (601) 960-9973.

Emergency Management Agency: Emergency Preparedness and Community Right-to-Know. Emergency Response Commission, Comprehensive Emergency Management, 5500 Bishop Blvd., Cheyenne, Wyoming 82009. (307) 777-7566.

Emergency Preparedness and Community Right-to-Know. Director, 290 Bigelow Bldg., 450 North Syndicate, St Paul, Minnesota 55104. (612) 643-3000.

Emergency Response Commission: Emergency Preparedness and Community Right-to-Know. Chair, PO Box O, Juneau, Alaska 99811. (907) 465-2600.

Emergency Response Commission: Emergency Preparedness and Community Right-to-Know. Division of Emergency Services, Building 341, 5036 East McDowell Rd., Phoenix, Arizona 85008. (602) 231-6326.

Emergency Response Commission: Emergency Preparedness and Community Right-to-Know. SARA Title III Coordinator, State Office Building, Room 161, 165 Capitol Ave., Hartford, Connecticut 06106. (203) 566-4856.

Emergency Response Commission: Emergency Preparedness and Community Right-to-Know. Chair, 205 Butler St., S.E., Floyd Towers East, 11th Floor, Suite 1166, Atlanta, Georgia 30334. (404) 656-6905.

Emergency Response Commission: Emergency Preparedness and Community Right-to-Know. Chair, State House, Boise, Idaho 83720. (208) 334-5888.

Emergency Response Commission: Emergency Preparedness and Community Right-to-Know. Director, 5500 West Bradbury Ave., Indianapolis, Indiana 46241. (317) 243-5176.

Emergency Response Commission: Emergency Preparedness and Community Right-to-Know. Chairman, Statehouse Station #11, 157 Capitol Street, Augusta, Maine 04333. (207) 289-4080.

Emergency Response Commission: Emergency Preparedness and Community Right-to-Know. Department of Environmental Protection, Division of Environmental Quality, Bureau of Hazardous Substances Information, Trenton, New Jersey 08625. (609) 292-6714.

Emergency Response Commission: Emergency Preparedness and Community Right-to-Know. Director, c/o State Fire Marshal, 3000 Market Street Plaza, Suite 534, Salem, Oregon 97310. (503) 378-2885.

Emergency Response Commission: Emergency Preparedness and Community Right-to-Know. Chair, 3041 Sidco, Nashville, Tennessee 37204. (615) 252-3300.

Emergency Response Commission: Emergency Preparedness and Community Right-to-Know. Director, Office of Emergency Services, State Capitol Bldg. 1, Room EB-80, Charlestown, West Virginia 25305. (304) 348-5380.

ONLINE DATA BASES

Chemical Hazard Response Information System–CHRIS. U.S. Coast Guard. Office of Research and Development, 2100 2d St., NW., Rm. 5410 C, Washington, District of Columbia 20593. (202) 783-3238. Contains information needed to respond to emergencies that occur during the transport of hazardous chemicals, as well as information that can help prevent emergency situations. Each of the approximately 1,300 records include information on physical and chemical properties, health and fire hazards, labeling, chemical reactivity, hazard classification and water pollution. Available on CIS and on Microdex's TOMES Plus series.

Hazardline. Occupational Health Services, Inc., 450 7th Ave., Ste. 2407, New York, New York 10123. (212) 967-1100. More than 3600 dangerous materials, including physical and chemical descriptions, standards and regulations, and safety precautions for handling.

MHIDAS. U.K. Atomic Energy Authority, Safety and Reliability Directorate, Wiashaw Lane, Culcheta, Warrington, England WA3 4NE. 44 (925) 31244.

Monthly Catalog of United States Government Publications. U.S. G.P.O., Supt. of Docs., PO Box 371954, Pittsburgh, Pennsylvania 15250-7954. (202) 512-0000.

National Technical Information Service. U.S. Department of Commerce, National Technical Information Service, Office of Data Base Services, 5285 Port Royal Rd., Springfield, Virginia 22161. (703) 487-4807. Bibliographic database of government sponsored research and technical reports.

PERIODICALS AND NEWSLETTERS

Emergency Preparedness News. Business Publishers, Inc., 951 Pershing Drive, Silver Spring, Maryland 20910. (301) 587-6300. Biweekly. Emergency management techniques and technologies.

STATISTICS SOURCES

Hazmat Emergency Response Contracting. FIND/SVP, 625 Avenue of the Americas, New York, New York 10011. (800) 346-3787. 1991. Challenges facing existing contractors and the business strategies required for continued success in the market.

EMISSION CONTROL TECHNOLOGY

See: AIR POLLUTION

EMISSIONS

See also: AIR QUALITY

ABSTRACTING AND INDEXING SERVICES

Applied Science and Technology Index. H.W. Wilson Co., 950 University Ave., Bronx, New York 10452. (800) 367-6770. Formerly Industrial Arts Index.

Biological Abstracts. BIOSIS, 2100 Arch St., Philadelphia, Pennsylvania 19103-1399. (215) 587-4800. 1927-.

Chemical Abstracts. Chemical Abstracts Service, 2540 Olentangy River Rd., PO Box 3012, Columbus, Ohio 43210. (800) 848-6533. 1907-.

Environment Abstracts. Bowker A & I Publishing, 121 Chanlon Rd., New Providence, New Jersey 07974. (908) 464-6800. 1974-.

Environment Index. Environment Information Center, Index Research Department, 124 E. 39th St., New York, New York 10016. 1971-. Annual.

Environmental Information Connection–EIC. Planning Information Program, Dept. of Urban and Regional Planning, University of Illinois, 1003 West Nevada, Urbana, Illinois 61801. (217) 333-1369. Also available online.

Environmental Periodicals Bibliography. Environmental Studies Institute, International Academy at Santa Barbara, 800 Garden St., Suite D, Santa Barbara, California 93101. (805) 965-5010. Also available online.

Geographical Abstracts. London School of Economics, Dept. of Geography, Regency House, 34 Duke St., London, England 1966-. Continued by Geo Abstracts issued in 6 parts: Pt. A. Landforms and the quaternary; Pt. B. Biogeography and Climatology; Pt. C. Economic geography; Pt. D. Social geography and cartography; Pt. E. Sedimentology; Pt. F. Regional and community planning.

ALMANACS AND YEARBOOKS

Environmental Almanac. World Resources Institute. Houghton Mifflin, 1 Beacon St., Boston, Massachusetts 02108. (617) 725-5000; (800) 225-3362. 1991. Covers consumer products, energy, endangered species, food safety, global warming, solid wastes, toxics, wetlands and other related areas. Also included are the names and addresses of the chief environmental executives for all 50 states.

BIBLIOGRAPHIES

EPA Publications Bibliography. U.S. Environmental Protection Agency, Library Systems Branch, 401 M St., SW, Washington, District of Columbia 20460. (202) 260-2090. Quarterly.

Health Effects of Diesel Engine Emissions. Silas Jackson. U.S. Department of Health and Human Services, Public Health Services, National Institutes of Health, 9000 Rockville Pike, Bethesda, Maryland 20892. (301) 496-4000. 1984.

List of Publications Sent to Government Depository Libraries. U.S. National Commission on Air Quality, Washington, District of Columbia 1980.

DIRECTORIES

Criteria Pollutant Point Source Directory. North American Water Office, Box 174, Lake Elmo, Minnesota 55042. (612) 770-3861. Biennial. Utilities, smelters, refineries, and other facilities that emit more than 1000 tons of particulates, sulfur oxides, nitrogen oxides, volatile organic compounds, or carbon monoxide.

Gale Environmental Sourcebook. Karen Hill. Gale Research Co., 835 Penobscot Bldg., Detroit, Michigan 48226-4094. (313) 961-2242. Contacts, information sources, or general information on environmental topics.

ENCYCLOPEDIAS AND DICTIONARIES

A Dictionary of Air Pollution Terms. Air & Waste Management Association, P.O. Box 2861, Pittsburgh, Pennsylvania 15230. (412) 233-3444. 1989.

Encyclopedia of Physical Science and Technology. Robert A. Meyers, ed. Academic Press, c/o Harcourt Brace Jovanovich Inc., 6277 Sea Harbor Dr., Orlando, Florida 32887. (800) 346-8648. Dictionary of engineering, technology and physical sciences.

McGraw-Hill Encyclopedia of Environmental Science. Sybil P. Parker. McGraw-Hill Science & Engineering Books, 11 W. 19th St., New York, New York 10011. (212) 337-6010. 1980. Covers ecology, man's influence on nature, and environmental protection.

McGraw-Hill Encyclopedia of Science and Technology. McGraw-Hill, 1221 Avenue of the Americas, New York, New York 10020. (212) 512-2000 or (800) 262-4729. 1992. Seventh edition. Issued in multiple volumes including index. Includes all science and technology broad subject areas.

Van Nostrand's Scientific Encyclopedia. Glenn D. Considine, ed. Van Nostrand Reinhold, 115 5th Ave., New York, New York 10003. (212) 254-3232. 1983. Sixth edition. Includes all broad subject areas in science.

GENERAL WORKS

Acid Rain and Emissions Trading: Implementing a Market Approach to Pollution Control. Roger K. Raufer and Stephen L. Feldman. Rowman & Littlefield, Publishers, Inc., 8705 Bollman Pl., Savage, Maryland 20763. (301) 306-0400. 1987. Methodological approach to the acid rain issue whereby emissions trading could be performed through a controlled leasing policy instead of outright trades. A comprehensive examination of the concerns surrounding the implementation of the market approach for dealing with acid rain.

Acute Lethality Data for Ontario's Petroleum Refinery Effluents Covering the Period from December 1988 to May 1989. Ontario Ministry of Environment, c/o National Technical Information Service, 5285 Port Royal Rd., Springfield, Virginia 22161. (703) 487-4650. 1990. Order number MIC-91-02537 LDM.

Acute Lethality Data for Ontario's Petroleum Refinery Effluents covering the Period June 1989 to November 1989. J. T. Lee. Ontario Ministry of the Environment, c/o National Technical Information Service, 5285 Port Royal Rd., Springfield, Virginia 22161. (703) 487-4650. 1989. Order number MIC-91-02523 LDM.

Air Emissions from Municipal Solid Waste Landfills. Environmental Protection Agency. National Technical Information Service, 5285 Port Royal Rd., Springfield, Virginia 22161. (703) 487-4650. 1991. Background information for proposed standards and guidelines. Order number PB91-197061LDM.

Air Monitoring for Toxic Exposure. Shirley A. Ness. Van Nostrand Reinhold, 115 5th Ave., New York, New York 10003. (212) 354-3232. 1991. Explains the procedures for evaluating potentially harmful exposure to people from

hazardous materials including chemicals, radon and bioaerosols. Presents practical information on how to perform air sampling, collect biological and bulk samples, evaluate dermal exposures, and determine the advantages and limitations of a given method.

Air Pollution Control. Howard E. Hesketh. Technomic Publishing Co., 851 New Holland Ave., Box 3535, Lancaster, Pennsylvania 17604. (717) 291-5609. 1991. Presents both theory and application data. Provides a background relevant to behavior theories and control techniques for capturing gaseous and particulate air pollutants.

Air Pollution Emission Standards and Guidelines for Municipal Waste Combustors: Economic Analysis of Materials Separation Requirement. B. J. Morton, et al. National Technical Information Service, 5285 Port Royal Rd., Springfield, Virginia 22161. (703) 487-4650. 1990. Final report prepared by the Research Triangle Institute for the Center for Economics Research.

Air/Superfund National Technical Guidance Study Series. Database of Emission Rate Measurement Projects. B. Eklund, et al. U.S. Environmental Protection Agency, 401 M St. SW, Washington, District of Columbia 20460. (202) 260-2090. 1991. Emission rate measurements of polluted air conducted at different projects and compiled into a database.

Car Trouble. James J. MacKenzie, et al. World Resources Institute, 1709 New York Ave., N.W., Washington, District of Columbia 20006. 1992. Reviews the technical options for air purification, cleaner fuels, more flexible transportation systems, and more intelligent city planning, among others.

Comprehensive Report to Congress: Clean Coal Technology Program. U.S. DOE Office of Clean Coal Technology. National Technical Information Service, 5285 Port Royal Rd., Springfield, Virginia 22161. (703) 487-4650. Demonstration of selective catalytic reduction technology for the control of nitrogen oxide emissions from high-sulphur coal- fired boilers.

Control of Fugitive and Hazardous Dusts. C. Cowherd, et al. Noyes Publications, 120 Mill Rd., Park Ridge, New Jersey 07656. (201) 391-8484. 1990. Coverage is of source identification, magnitude estimation, selection and evaluation of control measures, and control plan formulation. Among the sources discussed: paved and unpaved roads, open waste piles and staging areas, dry surface impoundments, landfills, land treatment, and waste stabilization.

Control Strategies for Photochemical Oxidants Across Europe. OECD Publications and Information Center, 2001 L St. N.W., Suite 700, Washington, District of Columbia 20036. (202) 785-OECD. 1990. Describes the emissions causing high photochemical oxidant levels, analyzes possible emission control technologies and their costs, evaluates the impact of economically feasible control scenarios.

Emissions from Combustion Processes–Origin, Measurement, Control. R. E. Clement and R. O. Kagel, eds. Lewis Publishers, 2000 Corporate Blvd., N.W., Boca Raton, Florida 33431. (407) 994-0555 or (800) 272-7737. 1990. Topics discussed include all aspects of combustion from the mechanics, formation, and disposal to emission abatement and risk assessment.

Emissions: Misfueling, Catalytic Deactivation and Alternative Catalyst. Society of Automotive Engineers, 400 Commonwealth Dr., Warrendale, Pennsylvania 15096. (412) 776-4841. 1985. Automobile catalytic converters, internal combustion engines, spark ignition, and alternative fuels.

Energy Technologies for Reducing Emissions of Greenhouse Gases. OECD Publications and Information Center, 2001 L St. N.W., Suite 700, Washington, District of Columbia 20036. (202) 785-OECD. 1989. Gives suggestions for dealing with the emissions of gases that can produce a change in the global climate.

Industrial Waste Gases: Utilization and Minimization. RCG/Hagler Bailly Inc. Technomic Publishing Co., 851 New Holland Ave., Box 3535, Lancaster, Pennsylvania 17604. (717) 291-5609. 1990. Also released under title Industrial Waste Gas Management. Deals with factory and trade waste and the effluents that are released into the atmosphere.

Minding the Carbon Store: Weighing U.S. Forestry Strategies to Slow Global Warming. Mark C. Trexler. World Resources Institute, 1709 New York Ave. N.W., Washington, District of Columbia 20006. (800) 833 0504. 1991. Assesses the strengths and weaknesses of each of the major domestic forestry options, including their costs and carbon benefits.

The Statehouse Effect: State Policies to Cool the Greenhouse. Daniel A. Lashof and Eric L. Washburn. Natural Resources Defense Council, 40 W. 20th St., New York, New York 10011. (212) 727-2700. 1990. Discusses the need for states to take the initiative in controlling CO_2 emissions. Details the sources of greenhouse gases and explains how greenhouse emissions can be reduced through energy efficiency, renewable energy strategies, recycling, and taxation and reforms in transportation, agriculture and forests.

Techniques for Measuring Indoor Air. John Y. Yocom and Sharon M. McCarthy. John Wiley & Sons, Inc., 605 3rd Ave., New York, New York 10158-0012. (212) 850-6000. 1991. Addresses the recent, rapid expansion of interest in indoor air quality and its contribution to total human exposure to air pollutants by presenting past and present developments and also the directions that the field seems to be taking.

Transport Policy and the Environment. OECD Publications and Information Center, 2001 L St., N.W., Suite 700, Washington, District of Columbia 20036. (202) 785-OECD. 1990. Describes how the government is addressing the adverse environmental effects of transport and the challenges that lie ahead.

GOVERNMENTAL ORGANIZATIONS

U.S. Environmental Protection Agency: Air Emission Factor Clearinghouse. Research Triangle Park, North Carolina 27711. (919) 541-0888.

U.S. Environmental Protection Agency: National Enforcement Investigations Center. Building 53, Box 25227, Denver, Colorado 80225. (303) 236-5100.

U.S. Environmental Protection Agency: Office of Mobile Services. 401 M St., S.W., Washington, District of Columbia 20460. (202) 382-7645.

HANDBOOKS AND MANUALS

Managing Indoor Air Quality. Shirely J. Hansen. The Association of Energy Engineers, 4025 Pleasantdale Rd., Suite 420, Atlanta, Georgia 30340. (404) 925-9558. 1991. Includes readily applicable air quality control measures and preventive strategies that can head off the economic and legal problems.

Motor Emission Control Manual. Michael J. Kromida. Hearst Books, 105 Madison Ave., New York, New York 10016. (212) 889-3050. 1989. Ninth edition. Revised edition of Motor's Emission Control Manual. Describes the effects of emission from automobile exhausts and the consequent problems.

ONLINE DATA BASES

Air Toxics Report. Business Publishers, Inc., 951 Pershing Dr., Silver Spring, Maryland 20910. (301) 587-6300. Online version of periodical of the same name.

BIOSIS Previews. BIOSIS, 2100 Arch St., Philadelphia, Pennsylvania 19103-1399. (215) 587-4800. Largest and most comprehensive database of research in the life sciences. Contains citations for nearly 9000 primary research journals, monographs, reviews, symposia, preliminary reports, semi-popular journals, selected institutional reports, government reports and research communications.

Chemical Abstracts-CA. Chemical Abstracts Service, 2540 Olentangy River Rd., P.O. Box 3012, Columbus, Ohio 43210. (800) 848-6533 or (614) 421-3600. Information sources include 9000 journals, patents from 27 countries, two industrial property organizations, new books, conference proceedings, and government research reports.

Enviro/Energyline Abstracts Plus. R. R. Bowker Co., 121 Chanlon Rd., New Providence, New Jersey 07974. (908) 464-6800.

Environmental Periodicals Bibliography. National Information Services Corp., Ste. 6, Wyman Towers, 3100 St. Paul St., Baltimore, Maryland 21218. (410)243-0797. Online version of abstract of same name.

Global Environmental Change Report. Cutter Information Corp., 37 Broadway, Arlington, Massachusetts 02174-5539. (617) 648-8700. Online access to environmental issues worldwide, including global warming, ozone depletion, deforestation, and acid rain. Online version of periodical of the same name.

Monthly Catalog of United States Government Publications. U.S. G.P.O., Supt. of Docs., PO Box 371954, Pittsburgh, Pennsylvania 15250-7954. (202) 512-0000.

National Emissions Data System. U.S. Environmental Protection Agency, Office of Air Quality Planning and Standards, National Air Data Branch, 401 M St. SW, Washington, District of Columbia 20460. (202) 260-2090. Pollutant emissions and 10,000 sources in 3,300 areas across the United States and territories.

National Technical Information Service. U.S. Department of Commerce, National Technical Information Service, Office of Data Base Services, 5285 Port Royal Rd., Springfield, Virginia 22161. (703) 487-4807. Bibliographic database of government sponsored research and technical reports.

SCISEARCH. Institute for Scientific Information, University City Science Center, 3501 Market St., Philadelphia, Pennsylvania 19104. (215) 386-0100.

PERIODICALS AND NEWSLETTERS

Air Toxics Report. Business Publishers, Inc., 951 Pershing Dr., Silver Spring, Maryland 20910-4464. (301) 587-6300. 1988-. Monthly. Directed towards organizations and facilities that are or may be affected by regulations under the Clean Air Act and National Emission Standards for Hazardous Air Pollutants, with articles on government regulation, studies, compliance, violations and legal actions. Also available online.

Automotive Air Pollution. U.S. Department of Health and Human Services, 200 Independence Ave. SW, Washington, District of Columbia 20201. (202) 619-0257. 1965-. Concerns automotive air pollution.

Eco/Log Week. Southam Business Information, 1450 Don Mills Rd., Don Mills, Ontario, Canada M3D 2X7. (416) 445-6641. Weekly. Effluent treatment, emission controls, waste disposal, and land use and reclamation.

Global Environmental Change Report. Cutter Information Corp., 37 Broadway, Arlington, Massachusetts 02174-5539. (617) 648-8700. Biweekly. Focus on global warming, ozone depletion, deforestation, and acid rain. Also available online.

Indoor Environment. S. Karger Publishing, Inc., 26 West Avon Rd., PO Box 529, Farmington, Connecticut 06085. Bimonthly. The quality of the indoor environment at home and in the workplace, building design, materials, ventilation and air conditioning, and chemistry.

Journal of Environmental Health. National Environmental Health Association, 720 South Colorado Boulevard, Suite 970, Denver, Colorado 80222. (303) 756-9090. Bimonthly. Covers phases in environmental health.

National Air Toxics Information Clearinghouse Newsletter. National Air Toxic Information Clearinghouse, P.O. Box 13000, Research Triangle Park, North Carolina 27709. (919) 541-9100. Bimonthly. Covers noncriteria pollutant emissions.

STATISTICS SOURCES

Automotive Fluids & Chemicals. FIND/SVP, 625 Avenue of the Americas, New York, New York 10011. (212) 645-4500. 1990.

Environmental Data Compendium. OECD Publications and Information Center, 2001 L St., N.W., Suite 700, Washington, District of Columbia 20036. (202) 785-6323. 1989.

Environmental Indicators. OECD Publications and Information Center, 2001 L St., N.W., Suite 700, Washington, District of Columbia 20036. (202) 785-6323. 1991.

Environmental Quality. Council on Environmental Quality. U.S. G.P.O., Washington, District of Columbia 20401. (202) 512-0000. Annual.

The State of the Environment. OECD Publications and Information Center, 2001 L St., N.W., Suite 700, Washington, District of Columbia 20036. (202) 785-6323. 1991.

World Resources. World Resources Institute. 1709 New York Ave., N.W., Washington, District of Columbia

20006. (202) 638-6300. Annual. Statistical and textual analysis of world's natural resources and the effects of growth-caused environmental pollution.

TRADE ASSOCIATIONS AND PROFESSIONAL SOCIETIES

Association of Local Air Pollution Control Officials. 444 North Capitol St., N.W., Washington, District of Columbia 20001 (202) 624-7864.

Automotive Chemical Manufacturers Council. 300 Sylvan Ave., P.O. Box 1638, Englewood Cliffs, New Jersey 07632-0638. (201) 569-8500.

Automotive Exhaust Systems Manufacturers Council. 300 Sylvan Ave., Englewood Cliffs, New Jersey 07632. (201) 569-8500.

Automotive Products Emissions Committee. 300 Sylvan Ave., Englewood Cliffs, New Jersey 07632. (201) 569-8500.

Engine Manufacturers Association. 111 E. Wacker Dr., Chicago, Illinois 60601. (312) 644-6610.

Industrial Chemical Research Association. 1811 Monroe St., Dearborn, Michigan 48124. (313) 563-0360.

Industrial Gas Clearing Institute. 1707 L St., N.W., Suite 570, Washington, District of Columbia 20036. (202) 457-0911.

Manufacturers of Emission Controls Association. 1707 L St., N.W., Suite 570, Washington, District of Columbia 20036. (202) 296-4797.

National Automotive Muffler Association. P.O. Box 1857, West Covina, California 91793. (213) 338-2417.

Society of Automotive Engineers. 400 Commonwealth Dr., Warrendale, Pennsylvania 15096. (412) 776-4841.

ENDANGERED SPECIES (ANIMALS, PLANTS)

ABSTRACTING AND INDEXING SERVICES

ASFA Aquaculture Abstracts. Cambridge Scientific Abstracts, Inc., 5161 River Rd., Bethesda, Maryland 20816. (301) 961-6750. 1984.

Biological Abstracts. BIOSIS, 2100 Arch St., Philadelphia, Pennsylvania 19103-1399. (215) 587-4800. 1927-.

Biological and Agricultural Index. H.W. Wilson Co., 950 University Ave., Bronx, New York 10452. (800) 367-6770. 1916-. Monthly.

Biology Digest. Data Courier, Plexus Pub Inc., 143 Old Marlton Pike, Medford, New Jersey 08055. 1974-. Monthly. Abstracts biology periodicals.

Current Advances in Ecological and Environmental Science. Pergamon Microforms International, Inc., Fairview Park, Elmsford, New York 10523. (914) 592-7720. 1989-. Monthly. Current literature searching service including journals, reports, abstracts, etc. This service is available online as part of the CABS database on the hosts BRS and ORBIT search service.

Ecological Abstracts. Geo Abstracts Ltd. Elsevier Applied Science, Crown House, Linton Rd., Barking, England IG 11 8JU. 1974-. Derived from over 600 leading ecological

and environmental journals, plus books, conference proceedings, reports and theses.

Ecology Abstracts. Cambridge Scientific Abstracts, 5161 River Rd., Bethesda, Maryland 20816. (301) 961-6750. Monthly.

Environment Abstracts. Bowker A & I Publishing, 121 Chanlon Rd., New Providence, New Jersey 07974. (908) 464-6800. 1974-.

Environment Index. Environment Information Center, Index Research Department, 124 E. 39th St., New York, New York 10016. 1971-. Annual.

Environmental Information Connection–EIC. Planning Information Program, Dept. of Urban and Regional Planning, University of Illinois, 1003 West Nevada, Urbana, Illinois 61801. (217) 333-1369. Also available online.

Environmental Periodicals Bibliography. Environmental Studies Institute, International Academy at Santa Barbara, 800 Garden St., Suite D, Santa Barbara, California 93101. (805) 965-5010. Also available online.

General Science Index. H. W. Wilson Co., 950 University Ave., Bronx, New York 10452. 1978-. Monthly, also issued in annual cumulation. Cumulative subject index to English language periodicals in the subject fields of astronomy, botany, chemistry, earth science, environment and conservation, food and nutrition, genetics, mathematics, medicine and health, microbiology, oceanography, physics, physiology and zoology.

Index to Scientific Book Contents. Institute for Scientific Information, 3501 Market St., Philadelphia, Pennsylvania 19104. (800) 523-1857. 1985-. Annual. Gives contents of science books published.

Pollution Abstracts. Cambridge Scientific Abstracts, 5161 River Rd., Bethesda, Maryland 20816. (301) 961-6750. Six/year. Indexes worldwide technical literature on environmental pollution. Covers air pollution, marine and freshwater pollution, sewage and wastewater treatment, waste management, toxicology and health, noise pollution, radiation, land pollution, and environmental policies, programs, legislation, and education. Also available online.

Science Citation Index. Institute for Scientific Information, 3501 Market St., Philadelphia, Pennsylvania 19104. 1961-.

ALMANACS AND YEARBOOKS

Bird Conservation. University of Wisconsin Press, 114 N. Murray St., Madison, Wisconsin 53715. (608) 262-8782. Annual. Topics relating to the protection of birds of the United States, including endangered species.

Convention on International Trade in Endangered Species of Wild Fauna and Flora. Federal Wildlife Permit Office, Washington, District of Columbia Annual. Covers endangered species and wild animal trade.

Endangered Species Report. Defenders of Wildlife, 1244 19th St. NW, Washington, District of Columbia 20036. (202) 659-9510. Annual.

Environmental Almanac. World Resources Institute. Houghton Mifflin, 1 Beacon St., Boston, Massachusetts 02108. (617) 725-5000; (800) 225-3362. 1991. Covers consumer products, energy, endangered species, food

safety, global warming, solid wastes, toxics, wetlands and other related areas. Also included are the names and addresses of the chief environmental executives for all 50 states.

Threatened Primates of Africa: The IUCN Red Data Book. Phyllis C. Lee. World Conservation Union, IUCN Publications Services Unit, 181a Huntingdon Road, Cambridge, England CB3 0DJ. (0223) 277894. 1988. Comprehensive review of the conservation status of African primates.

BIBLIOGRAPHIES

Endangered Plant Species of the World and Their Endangered Habitats: A Compilation of the Literature. Meryl A. Miasek. New York Botanical Garden Library, 200th St. & Southern Blvd., Bronx, New York 10458. (718)817-8705. 1985. Bibliography of plant conservation and endangered species.

Endangered Vertebrates: a Selected Annotated Bibliography, 1981-1988. Sylva Baker. Garland Publishing, Inc., 1000A Sherman Ave., Hamden, Connecticut 06514. (203) 281-4487. 1990. Covers scientific literature, legislative activity, organizations active in the field, and periodicals devoted to the subject.

EPA Publications Bibliography. U.S. Environmental Protection Agency, Library Systems Branch, 401 M St., SW, Washington, District of Columbia 20460. (202) 260-2090. Quarterly.

DIRECTORIES

Breeders Directory. American Minor Breeds Conservancy, PO Box 477, Pittsboro, North Carolina 27312. (919) 542-5704. Member breeders of endangered and uncommon livestock varieties.

Gale Environmental Sourcebook. Karen Hill. Gale Research Co., 835 Penobscot Bldg., Detroit, Michigan 48226-4094. (313) 961-2242. Contacts, information sources, or general information on environmental topics.

IUCN Amphibia-Reptilia Red Data Book. B. Groombridge. World Conservation Union, IUCN Publications Services Unit, 181a Huntingdon Road, Cambridge, England CB3 0DJ. (0223) 277894. 1982.

IUCN Invertebrate Red Data Book. S.M. Wells. World Conservation Union, IUCN Publications Services Unit, 181a Huntingdon Road, Cambridge, England CB3 0DJ. (0223) 277894. 1983.

IUCN Mammal Red Data Book: The Americas and Australasia. J. Thornback. World Conservation Union, IUCN Publications Services Unit, 181a Huntingdon Road, Cambridge, England CB3 0DJ. (0223) 277894. 1982.

IUCN Plant Red Data Book. G. Lucas. World Conservation Union, IUCN Publications Services Unit, 181a Huntingdon Road, Cambridge, England CB3 0DJ. (0223) 277894. 1978.

IUCN Red List of Threatened Animals. World Conservation Monitoring Centre. World Conservation Union, IUCN Publications Services Unit, 181a Huntingdon Road, Cambridge, England CB3 0DJ. (0223) 277894. 1990. Aims to focus attention of the plight of the earth's vanishing wildlife.

Threatened Birds of Africa and Related Islands. N. Collar. World Conservation Union, IUCN Publications Services Unit, 181a Huntingdon Road, Cambridge, England CB3 0DJ. (0223) 277894. 1985.

Threatened Swallowtail Butterflies of the World. N. Mark Collins. World Conservation Union, IUCN Publications Services Unit, 181a Huntingdon Road, Cambridge, England CB3 0DJ. (0223) 277894. 1988.

ENCYCLOPEDIAS AND DICTIONARIES

Cambridge Encyclopedia of Life Sciences. A. E. Friday and David S. Ingram. Cambridge University Press, 40 W 20th St., New York, New York 10011. (212) 924-3900 or (800) 227-0247. 1985. Includes all topics under biology and ecology.

The Encyclopedia of Animal Ecology. Peter D. Moore. Facts on File, Inc., 460 Park Ave. S., New York, New York 10016. (212) 683-2244. 1987.

Grzimek's Encyclopedia of Ecology. Bernhard Grzimek. Van Nostrand Reinhold, 115 5th Ave., New York, New York 10003. (212) 254-3232. 1976.

McGraw-Hill Encyclopedia of Environmental Science. Sybil P. Parker. McGraw-Hill Science & Engineering Books, 11 W. 19th St., New York, New York 10011. (212) 337-6010. 1980. Covers ecology, man's influence on nature, and environmental protection.

McGraw-Hill Encyclopedia of Science and Technology. McGraw-Hill, 1221 Avenue of the Americas, New York, New York 10020. (212) 512-2000 or (800) 262-4729. 1992. Seventh edition. Issued in multiple volumes including index. Includes all science and technology broad subject areas.

North American Reference Encyclopedia of Ecology and Pollution. William White. North American Pub. Co., 401 N. Broad St., Philadelphia, Pennsylvania 19108. (215) 238-5300. 1972.

Van Nostrand's Scientific Encyclopedia. Glenn D. Considine, ed. Van Nostrand Reinhold, 115 5th Ave., New York, New York 10003. (212) 254-3232. 1983. Sixth edition. Includes all broad subject areas in science.

GENERAL WORKS

Balancing on the Brink of Extinction: The Endangered Species Act and Lessons for the Future. Kathryn A. Kohm, ed. Island Press, 1718 Connecticut Ave. N.W., Suite 300, Washington, District of Columbia 20009. (202) 232-7933. 1991. Twenty essays providing an overview of the law's conception and history and its potential for protecting the remaining endangered species.

A Conservation Strategy for the Northern Spotted Owl. Jack Ward Thomas. U.S. Interagency Scientific Committee, Portland, Oregon 1990. Includes topics in endangered species and wildlife management.

Decline of the Sea Turtles: Causes and Prevention. National Research Council, Committee on Sea Turtle Conservation. National Academy Press, 2101 Constitution Ave., NW, PO Box 285, Washington, District of Columbia 20055. (202) 334-3313. 1990. Conservation of endangered species, especially sea turtles.

The Endangered Kingdom: The Struggle to Save America's Wildlife. Roger L. DiSilvestro. John Wiley & Sons, Inc., 605 3rd Ave., New York, New York 10158-0012.

(212) 850-6000. 1989. Describes the historical perspective and overview of present-day wildlife conservation. Included are game animals, endangered species, and nongame species.

Environment in Peril. Anthony B. Wolbarst, ed. Smithsonian Institution Press, 470 L'Enfant Plaza, No. 7100, Washington, District of Columbia 20560. (800) 782-4612. 1991. Brings together in one volume the primary concerns of eleven of the world's leaders in conservation, ecology and public policy. Broad environmental issues covered are: ozone depletion, overpopulation, global warming, thinning forests, extinction of species, spreading deserts, toxic chemicals, and various pollutants.

Environmental Fact Sheet: EPA's Endangered Species Protection Program. U.S. Environmental Protection Agency, Office of Pesticides and Toxic Substances, 401 M St. SW, Washington, District of Columbia 20460. (202) 260-2090. 1990.

Game Wars: The Undercover Pursuit of Wildlife Poachers. Marc Reisner. Academic Marketing, Penguin USA, 375 Hudson St., New York, New York 10014. (212) 366-2000; (800) 253-2304. 1991. Provides a first hand account of the life and dangers encountered by federal wildlife agents working for U.S. Fish and Wildlife Service: the elaborate covers they devise; the meticulous preparation necessary to pull off a successful sting; the weeks, months, even years they spend putting together their traps and cases; and the dangers they face as they impersonate big game hunters, ivory trades; and professional smugglers.

Imperiled Planet: Restoring Our Endangered Ecosystems. Edward Goldsmith, et al. MIT Press, 55 Hayward St., Cambridge, Massachusetts 02142. (617) 253-2884; (800) 356-0343. 1990. Presentation of a wide range of ecosystems, showing how they work, the traditional forms of human use, threats and losses, causes of destruction, and preservation attempts.

International Trade in Endangered Species of Wild Fauna and Flora: Amendment to the Convention of March 3, 1973, Done at Bonn June 22, 1979. United States Dept. of State. U.S. G.P.O., Washington, District of Columbia 20401. (202) 512-0000. 1991. Law and legislation relating to endangered species and wild animal trade.

Saving America's Wildlife. Thomas R. Dunlap. Princeton University Press, 41 Williams St., Princeton, New Jersey 08540. (609) 258-4900. 1988. Explores how we have deepened our commitment to and broadened the scope of animal conservation through the 1980s.

A Stillness in the Pines: The Ecology of the Red-Cockaded Woodpecker. Robert W. McFarlane. Norton, 500 5th Ave., New York, New York 10110. (800) 223-2584 or (212) 354-5500. 1992. Tells the story of the decline of the red-cockaded woodpecker, a specialized inhabitant of mature Southeastern pine forests.

Tropical Deforestation and Species Extinction. T.C. Whitmore. World Conservation Union, IUCN Publications Services Unit, 181a Huntingdon Road, Cambridge, England CB3 0DJ. (0223) 277894. 1992. Conservationist's perception of how fast tropical forests are being lost and what the consequences are for biological diversity.

Wildlife Extinction. Charles L. Cadieux. Stone Wall Pr., 1241 30th St. N.W., Washington, District of Columbia 20007. (202) 333-1860. 1991. Presents a worldwide picture of animals in danger of extinction and addresses controversial issues such as exploding human population, the role of zoos and wildlife parks, hunting and poaching.

HANDBOOKS AND MANUALS

The Atlas of Endangered Species. John A. Burton. Macmillan Publishing Co., 866 Third Ave., New York, New York 10022. (212) 702-2000. 1991. Animal and plant survival and the steps to save their extinction.

Collins Guide to the Rare Mammals of the World. John A. Burton and Vivian G. Burton. Collins, 77/85 Fulham Palace Rd., London, England W6 8JB. 071-493 7070. 1988. Includes all the mammal species which might be considered threatened.

Endangered Species Listing Handbook. U.S. Department of the Interior, U.S. Fish and Wildlife Service, Washington, District of Columbia 20240. (202) 343-5634. 1989. Looseleaf format.

Idaho and Wyoming: Endangered and Sensitive Plant Field Guide. U.S. Department of Agriculture, Forest Service, Intermountain Region, 324 25th St., Ogden, Utah 84401. 1990. Manual for identification of rare plants in Idaho and Wyoming as well as endangered species. Also covers plant conservation.

IUCN Red List of Threatened Animals. IUCN Conservation Monitoring Centre. World Conservation Union, Ave. du Mont-Blanc, CH-1196, Gland, Sweden 022-647181. 1988. Details on rare animals and endangered species.

The Official World Wildlife Fund Guide to Endangered Species of North America. David W. Lowe, ed. Beacham Publishing, Inc., 2100 S. St. NW, Washington, District of Columbia 20008. (202) 234-0877. 1990. Two volumes. Guide to endangered plants and animals. Describes 540 endangered or threatened species including their habitat, behavior, and recovery. Includes: directories of the Offices of the U.S. Fish and Wildlife Service, Offices of the National Marine Fisheries Service, State Heritage Programs, Bureau of Land Management Offices, National Forest Service Offices, National Wildlife Refuges, Canadian agencies, and state offices.

ONLINE DATA BASES

BIOSIS Previews. BIOSIS, 2100 Arch St., Philadelphia, Pennsylvania 19103-1399. (215) 587-4800. Largest and most comprehensive database of research in the life sciences. Contains citations for nearly 9000 primary research journals, monographs, reviews, symposia, preliminary reports, semi-popular journals, selected institutional reports, government reports and research communications.

Cold Regions. Library of Congress, Science & Technology Division, Cold Regions Bibliography Project, Washington, District of Columbia 20540. (202) 707-1181.

Enviro/Energyline Abstracts Plus. R. R. Bowker Co., 121 Chanlon Rd., New Providence, New Jersey 07974. (908) 464-6800.

Environmental Periodicals Bibliography. National Information Services Corp., Ste. 6, Wyman Towers, 3100 St. Paul St., Baltimore, Maryland 21218. (410)243-0797. Online version of abstract of same name.

Monthly Catalog of United States Government Publications. U.S. G.P.O., Supt. of Docs., PO Box 371954, Pittsburgh, Pennsylvania 15250-7954. (202) 512-0000.

National Technical Information Service. U.S. Department of Commerce, National Technical Information Service, Office of Data Base Services, 5285 Port Royal Rd., Springfield, Virginia 22161. (703) 487-4807. Bibliographic database of government sponsored research and technical reports.

PressNet Environmental Reports. Chemical Information Systems, Inc., 7215 York Rd., Baltimore, Maryland 21212. (301) 321-8440.

SCISEARCH. Institute for Scientific Information, University City Science Center, 3501 Market St., Philadelphia, Pennsylvania 19104. (215) 386-0100.

PERIODICALS AND NEWSLETTERS

City Sierran. Sierra Club-NYC Group, 625 Broadway, 2nd Fl., New York, New York 10012. (212) 473-7841. 1984-. Quarterly. Reports environmental news to Sierra Club members in New York City. Writers are activists and experts on acid rain, pollution, toxic wastes, recycling, endangered species, etc.

Earthwatch Magazine. Earthwatch Expeditions, 680 Mt. Auburn St., Box 403, Watertown, Massachusetts 02272. (617) 926-8200. Bimonthly. Worldwide research expeditions, endangered species, cultures, and world health.

Ecotoxicology and Environmental Safety. Academic Press, c/o Harcourt Brace Jovanovich Inc., 6277 Sea Harbor Dr., Orlando, Florida 32887. (800) 346-8648. 1977-. Bimonthly.

RESEARCH CENTERS AND INSTITUTES

Hudsonia LTD. Bard College Field Station, Annadale, New York 12504. (914) 758-1881.

Last Chance Forever. 506 Avenue A, San Antonio, Texas 78215. (512) 224-7228.

The Nature Conservancy. 1815 N. Lynn St., Arlington, Virginia 22209. (703) 841-5300.

Project in Conservation Science. University of California, San Diego, Department of Biology C-016, La Jolla, California 92093. (619) 534-2375.

Southeast California Research Station. 2140 Eastman Avenue, Suite 100, Ventura, California 93003. (805) 644-1766.

Texas A & M University, Schubot Exotic Bird Health Center. 119 VMS Building, College Station, Texas 77843-4467. (409) 845-5941.

Tri-State Bird Rescue and Research, Inc. 110 Possum Hollow Road, Wilmington, Delaware 19711. (302) 737-9543.

U.S. Forest Service, Forestry Sciences Laboratory. Arizona State University, Temple, Arizona 85287. (602) 379-4365.

University of Alabama, Arboretum. Box 870344, Tuscaloosa, Alabama 35487-0344. (205) 553-3278.

University of Oklahoma, Oklahoma Biological Survey. Sutton Hall, Room 303, 625 Elm Avenue, Norman, Oklahoma 73019. (405) 325-4034.

Vermont Institute of Natural Science. Church Hill, Woodstock, Vermont 05091. (802) 457-2779.

STATISTICS SOURCES

Ecology: Community Profiles. U.S. Fish and Wildlife Service. National Technical Information Service, 5285 Port Royal Road, Springfield, Virginia 22161. (703) 487-4650. Irregular. Data on coastal and inland ecosystems, including wetlands, tidal-flats, near-shore seagrasses, sand dunes, drilling platforms, oyster reefs, estuaries, rivers and streams.

Environmental Data Compendium. OECD Publications and Information Center, 2001 L St., N.W., Suite 700, Washington, District of Columbia 20036. (202) 785-6323. 1989.

Environmental Indicators. OECD Publications and Information Center, 2001 L St., N.W., Suite 700, Washington, District of Columbia 20036. (202) 785-6323. 1991.

Environmental Quality. Council on Environmental Quality. U.S. G.P.O., Washington, District of Columbia 20401. (202) 512-0000. Annual.

The State of the Environment. OECD Publications and Information Center, 2001 L St., N.W., Suite 700, Washington, District of Columbia 20036. (202) 785-6323. 1991.

World Resources. World Resources Institute. 1709 New York Ave., N.W., Washington, District of Columbia 20006. (202) 638-6300. Annual. Statistical and textual analysis of world's natural resources and the effects of growth-caused environmental pollution.

TRADE ASSOCIATIONS AND PROFESSIONAL SOCIETIES

American Institute of Biological Sciences. 730 11th St., N.W., Washington, District of Columbia 20001-4521. (202) 628-1500.

American Society of Naturalists. Department of Ecology and Evolation, State University of New York, Stony Brook, New York 11794. (516) 632-8589.

Cycad Society. c/o David S. Mayo, 1161 Phyllis Ct., Mountain View, California 94040. (415) 964-7898.

The Eagle Foundation Inc. 300 E. Hickory St., Apple River, Illinois 61001. (815) 594-2259.

Endangered Species Act Reauthorization Coordinating Committee. 900 17th St. N.W., Washington, District of Columbia 20006-2596. (202) 833-2300.

Greenpeace. 1436 U St., NW, Washington, District of Columbia 20009. (202) 462-1177.

International Bird Research Center. 699 Potter St., Berkeley, California 94710. (415) 841-9086.

International Snow Leopard Trust. 16463 S.E. 35th St., Bellevue, Washington 98008.

Monitor Consortium. 1506 19th St., N.W., Washington, District of Columbia 20036. (202) 234-6576.

National Audubon Society. 950 Third Ave., New York, New York 10022. (212) 832-3200.

National Trappers Association. P.O. Box 3667, Bloomington, Illinois 61702. (309) 829-2422.

North American Falconers Association. 820 Jay Pl., Berthoud, Colorado 80513.

Rainforest Action Network. 301 Broadway, Suite 28, San Francisco, California 94133. (415) 398-4404.

Rare and Endangered Native Plant Exchange. Biology Dept., County College of Morris, Rt. 10 and Center Grove Rd., Randolph, New Jersey 07869. (201) 361-5000.

RARE Center for Tropical Bird Conservation. 15290 Walnut St., Philadelphia, Pennsylvania 19102. (215) 568-0420.

Rare, Inc. 1601 Connecticut Ave., N.W., Washington, District of Columbia 20009.

Whooping Crane Conservation Association, Inc. 1007 Carmel Ave., Lafayette, Louisiana 70501. (318) 234-6339.

Wilson Ornithological Society. Dept. of Internal Medicine, Gastroenterology Division, University of Texas, Medical Branch, Galveston, Texas 77550.

The Xerces Society. 10 SW Ash St., Portland, Oregon 97204. (503) 222-2788.

ENDOSULFAN

See also: PESTICIDES; TOXICITY

ABSTRACTING AND INDEXING SERVICES

Applied Science and Technology Index. H.W. Wilson Co., 950 University Ave., Bronx, New York 10452. (800) 367-6770. Formerly Industrial Arts Index.

Biological Abstracts. BIOSIS, 2100 Arch St., Philadelphia, Pennsylvania 19103-1399. (215) 587-4800. 1927-.

Chemical Abstracts. Chemical Abstracts Service, 2540 Olentangy River Rd., PO Box 3012, Columbus, Ohio 43210. (800) 848-6533. 1907-.

Pollution Abstracts. Cambridge Scientific Abstracts, 5161 River Rd., Bethesda, Maryland 20816. (301) 961-6750. Six/year. Indexes worldwide technical literature on environmental pollution. Covers air pollution, marine and freshwater pollution, sewage and wastewater treatment, waste management, toxicology and health, noise pollution, radiation, land pollution, and environmental policies, programs, legislation, and education. Also available online.

Science Citation Index. Institute for Scientific Information, 3501 Market St., Philadelphia, Pennsylvania 19104. 1961-.

HANDBOOKS AND MANUALS

Dangerous Properties of Industrial Materials. Irving Newton Sax. Van Nostrand Reinhold, 115 5th Ave., New York, New York 10003. (212) 254-3232. 1989. 7th ed. Deals with hazardous substances and chemically induced occupational diseases.

Handbook of Environmental Data on Organic Chemicals. Karel Verschueren. Van Nostrand Reinhold, 115 5th Ave., New York, New York 10003. (212) 254-3232. 1983. Covers individual substances as well as mixtures and preparations. The profiles include: properties, air pollution factors, water pollution factors, and biological effects.

ONLINE DATA BASES

BIOSIS Previews. BIOSIS, 2100 Arch St., Philadelphia, Pennsylvania 19103-1399. (215) 587-4800. Largest and most comprehensive database of research in the life sciences. Contains citations for nearly 9000 primary research journals, monographs, reviews, symposia, preliminary reports, semi-popular journals, selected institutional reports, government reports and research communications.

Chemical Abstracts-CA. Chemical Abstracts Service, 2540 Olentangy River Rd., P.O. Box 3012, Columbus, Ohio 43210. (800) 848-6533 or (614) 421-3600. Information sources include 9000 journals, patents from 27 countries, two industrial property organizations, new books, conference proceedings, and government research reports.

Chemical Abstracts Chemical Name Directory-CHEM-NAME. Chemical Abstracts Service, 2540 Olentangy River Rd., P.O. Box 3012, Columbus, Ohio 43210. (800) 848-6533 or (614) 421-3600. Listing of chemical substances in a dictionary type file. The Chemical Abstracts (CAS) Registry Number, molecular formula, Chemical Abstracts (CA) Substance Index Name, available synonyms, ring data and other chemical substance information is given for each entry.

Chemical Carcinogenesis Research Information System-CCRIS. National Library of Medicine, 8600 Rockville Pike, Bethesda, Maryland 20894. (800) 638-8480. Individual assay results and test conditions for 1,451 chemicals in the areas of carcinogenicity, mutagenicity, tumor promotion, and cocarcinogenicity.

ENDOTHERMS

ABSTRACTING AND INDEXING SERVICES

Applied Science and Technology Index. H.W. Wilson Co., 950 University Ave., Bronx, New York 10452. (800) 367-6770. Formerly Industrial Arts Index.

General Science Index. H. W. Wilson Co., 950 University Ave., Bronx, New York 10452. 1978-. Monthly, also issued in annual cumulation. Cumulative subject index to English language periodicals in the subject fields of astronomy, botany, chemistry, earth science, environment and conservation, food and nutrition, genetics, mathematics, medicine and health, microbiology, oceanography, physics, physiology and zoology.

Index to Scientific Book Contents. Institute for Scientific Information, 3501 Market St., Philadelphia, Pennsylvania 19104. (800) 523-1857. 1985-. Annual. Gives contents of science books published.

Science Citation Index. Institute for Scientific Information, 3501 Market St., Philadelphia, Pennsylvania 19104. 1961-.

ENCYCLOPEDIAS AND DICTIONARIES

Van Nostrand's Scientific Encyclopedia. Glenn D. Considine, ed. Van Nostrand Reinhold, 115 5th Ave., New

York, New York 10003. (212) 254-3232. 1983. Sixth edition. Includes all broad subject areas in science.

HANDBOOKS AND MANUALS

Practical Electroplating Handbook. N.V. Parthasaradhy. Prentice Hall, Rte. 9W, Englewood Cliffs, New Jersey 07632. (201) 592-2000. 1989.

ENDRIN

See also: DIELDRIN; PESTICIDES

ABSTRACTING AND INDEXING SERVICES

Biological Abstracts. BIOSIS, 2100 Arch St., Philadelphia, Pennsylvania 19103-1399. (215) 587-4800. 1927-.

Chemical Abstracts. Chemical Abstracts Service, 2540 Olentangy River Rd., PO Box 3012, Columbus, Ohio 43210. (800) 848-6533. 1907-.

General Science Index. H. W. Wilson Co., 950 University Ave., Bronx, New York 10452. 1978-. Monthly, also issued in annual cumulation. Cumulative subject index to English language periodicals in the subject fields of astronomy, botany, chemistry, earth science, environment and conservation, food and nutrition, genetics, mathematics, medicine and health, microbiology, oceanography, physics, physiology and zoology.

Index to Scientific Book Contents. Institute for Scientific Information, 3501 Market St., Philadelphia, Pennsylvania 19104. (800) 523-1857. 1985-. Annual. Gives contents of science books published.

Pollution Abstracts. Cambridge Scientific Abstracts, 5161 River Rd., Bethesda, Maryland 20816. (301) 961-6750. Six/year. Indexes worldwide technical literature on environmental pollution. Covers air pollution, marine and freshwater pollution, sewage and wastewater treatment, waste management, toxicology and health, noise pollution, radiation, land pollution, and environmental policies, programs, legislation, and education. Also available online.

ALMANACS AND YEARBOOKS

Hazardous Chemicals Information Annual. Van Nostrand Reinhold, Information Services, 115 5th Ave., New York, New York 10003. (212) 254-3232. 1987. Annual.

BIBLIOGRAPHIES

Aldrin and Endrin in Water: A Bibliography. National Technical Information Service, 5285 Port Royal Rd., Springfield, Virginia 22161. (703) 487-4650. 1972. Water Resources Scientific Information Center Bibliography series, WRSIC 72-203.

GENERAL WORKS

Ambient Water Quality Criteria for Endrin. U.S. Environmental Protection Agency. National Technical Information Service, 5285 Port Royal Rd., Springfield, Virginia 22161. (703) 487-4650. 1980.

Bioassay of Endrin for Possible Carcinogenicity. National Cancer Institute, Div. of Cancer Cause and Prevention,

Carcinogenesis Testing Program, NIH Bldg. 31, Room 10A 24, 9030 Old Georgetown Rd., Bethesda, Maryland 20892. (301) 496-7403. 1978.

HANDBOOKS AND MANUALS

Clean Air Handbook. Government Institutes, Inc., 4 Research Pl., Ste. 200, Rockville, Maryland 20850. (301) 921-2300. Analyzes the requirements of the Clean Air Act and its 1990 amendments, as well as what can be expected in terms of new regulation.

Documentation of the Threshold Limit Values. American Conference of Governmental Industrial Hygienists, 6500 Glenway, Building D-5, Cincinnati, Ohio 45211. 1991. Provides threshold limit value documentation for any physical phenomenon in the environment, including chemical substances and physical agents.

NIOSH Pocket Guide to Chemical Hazards. National Institute for Occupational Safety and Health, 1600 Clifton Rd. NE, Atlanta, Georgia 30333. (404) 639-3286. 1990. Presents sources of general industrial hygiene and medical surveillance information for workers, employees and others. Presents key information and data in an abbreviated format for 398 individual chemicals or chemical types.

The Pesticide Handbook: Profiles for Action. International Organization of Consumers Unions, Emmastraat 9, The Hague, Netherlands 2595 EG. 1989.

Treatability Manual. U.S. Environmental Protection Agency, Office of Research and Development, 401 M St., SW, Washington, District of Columbia 20460. (202) 260-2090. 1983-. V.1 Treatability data. v.2 Change 2. Industrial Descriptions. v.3 Change 2. Technology for Control/removal of pollutants. v.4. Cost estimating. v.5. Change 2 summary.

ONLINE DATA BASES

BIOSIS Previews. BIOSIS, 2100 Arch St., Philadelphia, Pennsylvania 19103-1399. (215) 587-4800. Largest and most comprehensive database of research in the life sciences. Contains citations for nearly 9000 primary research journals, monographs, reviews, symposia, preliminary reports, semi-popular journals, selected institutional reports, government reports and research communications.

CERCLIS. Chemical Information Systems, Inc., 7215 York Rd., Baltimore, Maryland 21212. (301) 321-8440. Information on hazardous waste disposal sites that have either been listed by the EPA on the National Priority List (NPL) or nominated for consideration for the NPL.

Chemical Abstracts-CA. Chemical Abstracts Service, 2540 Olentangy River Rd., P.O. Box 3012, Columbus, Ohio 43210. (800) 848-6533 or (614) 421-3600. Information sources include 9000 journals, patents from 27 countries, two industrial property organizations, new books, conference proceedings, and government research reports.

Chemical Abstracts Chemical Name Directory-CHEMNAME. Chemical Abstracts Service, 2540 Olentangy River Rd., P.O. Box 3012, Columbus, Ohio 43210. (800) 848-6533 or (614) 421-3600. Listing of chemical substances in a dictionary type file. The Chemical Abstracts (CAS) Registry Number, molecular formula, Chemical Abstracts (CA) Substance Index Name, available syn-

onyms, ring data and other chemical substance information is given for each entry.

Chemical Carcinogenesis Research Information System-CCRIS. National Library of Medicine, 8600 Rockville Pike, Bethesda, Maryland 20894. (800) 638-8480. Individual assay results and test conditions for 1,451 chemicals in the areas of carcinogenicity, mutagenicity, tumor promotion, and cocarcinogenicity.

PERIODICALS AND NEWSLETTERS

Aquatic Toxicology. Elsevier Science Publishing Co., 655 Avenue of the Americas, New York, New York 10010. (212) 989-5800. 1981-. 6/year.

Environmental Science and Technology. American Chemical Society, 1155 16th St. N.W., Washington, District of Columbia 20036. (800) 227-5558. 1967-. Monthly. Contains research articles on various aspects of environmental chemistry, interpretative articles by invited experts and commentary on the scientific aspects of environmental management.

Environmental Science & Technology. American Chemical Society, 1155 16th St. N.W., Washington, District of Columbia 20036. (800) 227-5558. Covers pollution, sanitary chemistry and environmental engineering.

Water Research. International Association on Water Pollution Research and Control. Pergamon Microforms International, Inc., Fairview Park, Elmsford, New York 10523. (914) 592-7720. 1966-. Monthly. Covers all aspects of the pollution of marine and fresh water and the management of water quality as well as water resources.

ENERGY

ABSTRACTING AND INDEXING SERVICES

Agricultural Engineering Abstracts. C. A. B. International, 845 North Park Ave., Tucson, Arizona 85719. (602) 621-7897 or (800) 528-4841. 1976-. Monthly. Informs about significant research developments in agricultural engineering and instrumentation. Some of the topics scanned for the abstracts include mechanical power, crop production, crop harvesting and threshing, crop processing and storage, aquaculture, land improvement, protected cultivation, handling and transport, and farm buildings and equipment.

Applied Science and Technology Index. H.W. Wilson Co., 950 University Ave., Bronx, New York 10452. (800) 367-6770. Formerly Industrial Arts Index.

Buildings Energy Technology. National Technical Information Service, 5285 Port Royal Rd., Springfield, Virginia 22161. (703) 487-4650. Monthly. Technology required for energy conservation in buildings and communities.

Civil Engineering Hydraulic Abstracts. BHRA Fluid Engineering, Air Science Co., PO Box 143, Corning, New York 14830. (607) 962-5591. Monthly. Abstracts of periodicals that publish in the areas of hydraulic engineering and other related topics.

Ecology Abstracts. Cambridge Scientific Abstracts, 5161 River Rd., Bethesda, Maryland 20816. (301) 961-6750. Monthly.

EIS: Digests of Environmental Impact Statements. Cambridge Scientific Abstracts, 5161 River Rd., Bethesda, Maryland 20816. (301) 951-1400. 1970-. Bimonthly. Provides detailed abstracts of all the environmental impact statements issued by the federal government each year and indexes them. Also extracts the key issues from the complex government released environmental impact statements. Contents include areas such as: air transportation, defense programs, energy, hazardous substances, land use, manufacturing, parks, refuges, forests, research and development, roads and railroads, urban and social programs, wastes, and water.

Engineering Index. The Engineering Index Inc., 345 E. 47th St., New York, New York 10017. 1962-.

ERDA Research Abstracts. U.S. ERDA Technical Information Center, Box 62, Oak Ridge, Tennessee 37830.

General Science Index. H. W. Wilson Co., 950 University Ave., Bronx, New York 10452. 1978-. Monthly, also issued in annual cumulation. Cumulative subject index to English language periodicals in the subject fields of astronomy, botany, chemistry, earth science, environment and conservation, food and nutrition, genetics, mathematics, medicine and health, microbiology, oceanography, physics, physiology and zoology.

Geographical Abstracts. London School of Economics, Dept. of Geography, Regency House, 34 Duke St., London, England 1966-. Continued by Geo Abstracts issued in 6 parts: Pt. A. Landforms and the quaternary; Pt. B. Biogeography and Climatology; Pt. C. Economic geography; Pt. D. Social geography and cartography; Pt. E. Sedimentology; Pt. F. Regional and community planning.

Green Engineering: A Current Awareness Bulletin. Institution of Mechanical Engineers, 1 Birdcage Walk, Westminster, London, England SW1H 9JJ. 71973 1266/7. 1991. Monthly. Covers acid rain, aerosol technology, biotechnology chlorofluorocarbons, chemical and process engineering, environmental protection, energy conservation, energy generation, greenhouse effect, materials, pollution, recycling, waste disposal, and other environmental topics.

Highway Research Abstracts. Transportation Research Board, National Research Council, 2101 Constitution Ave. NW., Washington, District of Columbia 20418. 1931-. Monthly. Provides information about highway and nonrail mass transit. It also deals with related environmental issues such as energy and environment, environmental design, climate, safety, human factors, and soils.

Index to Scientific Book Contents. Institute for Scientific Information, 3501 Market St., Philadelphia, Pennsylvania 19104. (800) 523-1857. 1985-. Annual. Gives contents of science books published.

Mineralogical Abstracts. Mineralogical Society, 41 Queen's Gate, London, England SW7 5HR. 71 5847916. Quarterly. Abstracts of journal articles, conferences, technical reports and specialized books in the areas of minerals, clay minerals, economic minerals, ore deposits, environmental studies, experimental mineralogy, gemstones, geochemistry, petrology, lunar and planetary studies and other related areas in mineralogy.

Physics Briefs. Physikalische Berichte. Physik Verlag, Pappapelallee 3, Postfach 101161, Weinheim, Germany D-6940. 1979-. Semimonthly. In English. Volumes for 1979- issued by the Deutsche Physikalische Gesellschaft and the Fachinformationszentrum Energie Physik, Mathematik in cooperation with the American Institute of Physics.

Science Citation Index. Institute for Scientific Information, 3501 Market St., Philadelphia, Pennsylvania 19104. 1961-.

ALMANACS AND YEARBOOKS

Annual Review of Energy. Annual Reviews Inc., 4139 El Camino Way, Palo Alto, California 94303-0897. (800) 523-8635. Annual.

Environmental Almanac. World Resources Institute. Houghton Mifflin, 1 Beacon St., Boston, Massachusetts 02108. (617) 725-5000; (800) 225-3362. 1991. Covers consumer products, energy, endangered species, food safety, global warming, solid wastes, toxics, wetlands and other related areas. Also included are the names and addresses of the chief environmental executives for all 50 states.

Gale Environmental Almanac. Russ Hoyle. Gale Research Inc., 835 Penobscot Bldg., Detroit, Michigan 48226-4094. (313) 961-2242. 1993. Focuses on the U.S. and Canada, although worldwide and transboundary issues are discussed.

BIBLIOGRAPHIES

Alternative Sources of Energy. Barbara K. Harrah. Scarecrow Press, 52 Liberty St., Metuchen, New Jersey 08840. (908) 548-8600. 1975. A bibliography of solar, geothermal, wind, and tidal energy, and environmental architecture.

Consumer Energy Research: An Annotated Bibliography. C. Dennis Anderson and Gordon H. G. McDougall. Consumer Research and Evaluation Branch, Consumer and Corporate Affairs, Ottawa, Ontario, Canada 1984. Two volumes, revised. Prefatory material in English and French. Bibliography dealing with energy consumed in the residential sector and for most part is limited to annotations of empirical studies.

Directory of Country Environmental Studies: An Annotated Bibliography of Environmental and Natural Resources Profiles and Assessments. World Resources Institute, 1709 New York Ave., NW, Washington, District of Columbia 20006. 1990. Concentrates on studies of developing countries. Reports on the condition and trends of the major natural resources of a country and their condition and relationship to economic development.

Energy and the Social Sciences: A Bibliographic Guide to the Literature. E. J. Yanarella and Ann-Marie Yanarella. Westview Press, 5500 Central Ave., Boulder, Colorado 80301. (303) 444-3541. 1983. Focuses on the needs of social scientists entering the "miasma of energy policy studies."

Energy Guide: A Directory of Information Resources. Virginia Bemis, et al. Garland Publishers, 136 Madison Ave., New York, New York 10016. (212) 686-7492 or (800) 627-6273. 1977.

Energy Information Guide. R. David Weber. ABC-CLIO, PO Box 1911, Santa Barbara, California 93116-1911. (805) 963-4221. 1982. Three volumes. Includes more than 2000 reference works on energy and energy related topics. Volume 1: General and Alternative Energy Sources; volume 2: Nuclear and Electric Power: volume 3: Fossil Fuels.

Energy Update: A Guide to Current Literature. R. David Weber. Energy Information Press, 1100 Industrial Suite 9, San Carlos, California 94070. (415) 594-0743. 1991. Some 1000 reference works are fully identified as well as 75 databases available for purchase or use on an online system. All forms of conventional and alternate energy sources are covered with consideration given to conservation and environmental impact.

DIRECTORIES

The AEE Directory of Energy Professionals. Fairmont Press, 700 Indian Trail, Lilburn, Georgia 30247. (404) 925-9388. 1980-. Annual. Lists members of the Association of Energy Engineers and their specialties. The membership consists of individuals who represent all facets of energy engineering/management. Also includes geographic listing and government references.

Canadian Environmental Directory. Canadian Almanac & Directory Publishing Co. Ltd., 134 Adelaide St. E., Ste. 27, Toronto, Ontario, Canada M5C 1K9. (416) 362-4088. 1992. Includes individuals, agencies, firms, and associations.

The Directory of Consultants in Energy Technologies. Research Publications, 12 Lunar Drive, Woodbridge, Connecticut 06525. (203) 397-2600. 1985. Scientists and engineers in the fields of air, land and water projects; environmental and agricultural analysis.

Energy Conservation and Management Consultants. American Business Directories, Inc., 5711 S. 86th Circle, Omaha, Nebraska 68127. (402) 593-4600.

Energy Information Centers Directory. U.S. Council for Energy Awareness, 1776 I St., N.W., Suite 400, Washington, District of Columbia 20006-2495. (202) 293-0770.

Energy Resource Institute–Directory of Energy Alternatives. Energy Research Institute, 6850 Rattlesnake Hammock Rd., Hwy. 951, Naples, Florida 33962. (813) 793-1922.

Energy User News–Directory of Energy Consultants Issue. Fairchild Publications/Capitol Cities Media, Inc., 7 E. 12th St., New York, New York 10003. (212) 741-4428.

Guide to Energy Specialists. Porter B. Bennett, ed. Center for International Environment Information, 300 E 42d St., New York, New York 10017. (212) 697-3232. 1979. Lists energy specialists who are willing to answer questions in the area of their expertise.

International Directory of New and Renewable Energy: Information Sources and Research Centres. UNESCO, 7 place de Fontenoy, 75700 Paris, France F-75700. 1986. Second edition. Contains a total of 3,956 entries representing 156 countries. Profiles of the organizations associated with new and renewable energy areas are included.

International Who's Who in Energy and Nuclear Sciences. Longman Editorial Team. Longman, c/o Gale Research Inc., 835 Penobscot Bldg., Detroit, Michigan 48226-4094. (313) 961-2242. 1983. Deals with the subject areas of energy and nuclear science. Gives professional biographical profiles of over 3800 individuals arranged by surname from A to Z. Also includes a country and topic list of the same people.

National Directory of Safe Energy Organizations. Public Citizen's Critical Mass Energy Project, 215 Pennsylvania Ave., S.E., Washington, District of Columbia 20003. (202) 546-4996.

U. S. Energy and Environmental Interest Groups: Institutional Profiles. Lettie McSpadden Wenner. Greenwood Publishing Group, Inc., 88 Post Rd. W., PO Box 5007, Westport, Connecticut 06881. (212) 226-3571. 1990. Included are organizations that lobby in the energy and environmental policy areas including business corporations and trade associations, not-for-profit public interest groups, and professional research groups, and governmental organizations.

World Directory of Energy Information. Facts on File, Inc., 460 Park Ave. S., New York, New York 10016. (212) 683-2244. 1982-84. Three volumes. Contents: v.1. Western Europe. v.2. Middle East, Africa and Asia/ Pacific. v.3. The Americas including the Caribbean.

ENCYCLOPEDIAS AND DICTIONARIES

Dictionary of Energy. Malcolm Slesser. Nichols Pub., PO Box 96, New York, New York 10024. 1988. Provides information on concepts, ideas, definitions and explanations in areas of interdisciplinary nature connected with energy.

A Dictionary of Environmental Quotations. Barbara K. Rodes and Rice Odell. Simon and Schuster, 15 Columbus Circle, New York, New York 10023. (212) 373-7342. 1992. Collection of nearly 3000 quotations arranged by topic, such as air, noise, energy, nature, pollution, forests, oceans, and other subjects on the environment.

Encyclopedia of Human Biology. Renato Dulbecco, ed. Academic Press, c/o Harcourt Brace Jovanovich Inc., 6277 Sea Harbor Dr., Orlando, Florida 32887. (800) 346-8648. 1991. Eight volumes.

Encyclopedia of Physical Science and Technology. Robert A. Meyers, ed. Academic Press, c/o Harcourt Brace Jovanovich Inc., 6277 Sea Harbor Dr., Orlando, Florida 32887. (800) 346-8648. Dictionary of engineering, technology and physical sciences.

Encyclopedia of Physics. Rita G. Lerner and George L. Trigg. VCH Publishers, 303 NW 12th Ave., Deerfield Beach, Florida 33442-1788. (305) 428-5566. 1991. Second edition.

Energy Dictionary. V. Daniel Hunt. Van Nostrand Reinhold, 115 5th Ave., New York, New York 10003. (212) 254-3232. 1979. Covers the broad field of energy including fossil, nuclear, solar, geothermal, ocean, and wind energy.

Energy Terminology: A Multilingual Glossary. Pergamon Microforms International, Inc., Fairview Park, Elmsford, New York 10523. (914) 592-7720. 1986. Second edition. Contains 1500 defined terms and concepts related to the field of energy together with an index of several thousand undefined keywords used in the definitions of these terms and concepts. Contents appear in four languages: English, French, German and Spanish.

Environmental Encyclopedia. William P. Cunningham, Terence Ball, et. al. Gale Research Inc., 835 Penobscot Bldg., Detroit, Michigan 48226-4094. (313) 961-2242. 1993.

Illustrated Encyclopedia of Science and the Future. Mike Biscare, et al., ed. Marshall Cavendish, 58 Old Compton

St., London, England 0W1V5 PA. 01-734 6710. 1983. Twenty volumes. Each volume has 5 sections: Frontiers, Electronics in Action, Medical Science, Military Technology, and Resources.

Life Sciences on File. Diagram Group. Facts on File, Inc., 460 Park Ave. S., New York, New York 10016. (212) 683-2244. 1986. Encyclopedia of pictorial collection in life sciences. Deals with all major topics in life sciences including ecology.

McGraw-Hill Encyclopedia of Science and Technology. McGraw-Hill, 1221 Avenue of the Americas, New York, New York 10020. (212) 512-2000 or (800) 262-4729. 1992. Seventh edition. Issued in multiple volumes including index. Includes all science and technology broad subject areas.

The Nutrition and Health Encyclopedia. David F. Tver and Percy Russell. Van Nostrand Reinhold, 115 5th Ave., New York, New York 10003. (212) 254-3232. 1989.

Van Nostrand's Scientific Encyclopedia. Glenn D. Considine, ed. Van Nostrand Reinhold, 115 5th Ave., New York, New York 10003. (212) 254-3232. 1983. Sixth edition. Includes all broad subject areas in science.

GENERAL WORKS

Air Pollution's Toll on Forests and Crops. James J. MacKenzie and Mohamed T. El-Ashry, eds. Yale University Press, 92 A Yale St., 302 Temple St., New Haven, Connecticut 06520. (203) 432-0960. 1992. Proposes an integrated strategy to reduce pollution levels based on improved energy efficiency, abatement technology, and the use of nonfossil energy technologies. This strategy takes into account other critical problems such as increasing oil imports, failure to attain clean air goals in U.S. cities, and the greenhouse effect.

Bioenergy and the Environment. Janos Pasztor and Lars A. Kristoferson, eds. Westview Press, 5500 Central Ave., Boulder, Colorado 80301. (303) 444-3541. 1990. Includes 14 contributions which addresses issues such as the demand for biomass fuels including wood, charcoal, agricultural residues, and alcohol.

The Consumer Guide to Home Energy Savings. The American Council for an Energy Efficient Economy, 1001 Connecticut Ave., N.W., #535, Washington, District of Columbia 20036. (202) 429-8873. 1991.

Cool Energy: The Renewable Solution to Global Warming. Michael Brower. Union of Concerned Scientists, 26 Church St., Cambridge, Massachusetts 02238. (617) 547-5552. 1990. Describes how fossil fuel and renewable energy sources could be used to avoid global warming and air pollution.

Direct Energy Conversion. Stanley W. Angrist. Allyn and Bacon, 160 Gould St., Needham Heights, Massachusetts 02194. (617) 455-1250; (800) 852-8024. 1982. Techniques in mechanical engineering and applied mechanics.

Direct Solar Energy. T. Nejat Veziroglu, ed. Nova Science Publishers. Inc, 283 Commack Rd., Suite 300, Commack, New York 11725-3104. (516) 499-3103; (516) 499-3106. 1991. Examines direct solar energy aspects such as solar radiation, greenhouses, water heaters, heat pumps, distillation/potable water and energy storage.

Driving Forces: Motor Vehicle Trends and Their Implications for Global Warming, Energy Strategies, and Trans-

portation. James J. MacKenzie and Michael P. Walsh. World Resources Institute, 1709 New York Ave., Washington, District of Columbia 20006. (800) 822-0504. 1990. Overview of new-vehicle fuel efficiency, reductions in air pollution emissions, and overall improvements in transportation and land-use as they relate to global warming planning. Also available through State University of New York Press.

Energy and Architecture. Christopher Flavin. Worldwatch Institute, 1776 Massachusetts Ave. NW, Washington, District of Columbia 20036. 1980. Solar energy and conservation potential.

Energy and Climate Change. Lewis Publishers, 2000 Corporate Blvd., N.W., Boca Raton, Florida 33431. (407) 994-0555 or (800) 272-7737. 1990. Includes energy scenarios, cost and risk analysis, energy emissions, atmospheric chemistry, and climate effects.

Energy and Environmental Strategies for the 1990's. Mary Jo Winer and Marilyn Jackson, eds. Fairmont Pr., 700 Indian Trail, Lilburn, Georgia 30247. (404) 925-9388. 1991. Papers from the 13th World Energy Engineering Congress and the World Environmental Engineering Congress organized by the Association of Energy Engineers and sponsored by the U.S. Department of Energy, Office of Institutional Programs.

Energy and the Environment. J. Dunderdale, ed. Royal Society of Chemistry, c/o CRC Press, 2000 Corporate Blvd. N.W., Boca Raton, Florida 33431-9868. (800) 272-7737. 1990. Compares the environmental impact of the various energy producing and using processes. The book covers the types and quantities of pollutants produced by these processes, looks at the interaction of these pollutants with the atmosphere, and reviews the use of renewable sources as possible alternatives.

Energy and the Environment in the 21st Century. Jefferson W. Tester, et al., eds. MIT Press, 55 Hayward St., Cambridge, Massachusetts 02142. (617) 253-2884; (800) 356-0343. 1991. Proceedings of the conference held at the Massachusetts Institute of Technology, Cambridge, MA, March 26-28, 1990. Compendium of more than 80 original contributions, providing the basis for an international agenda of energy and environmental technology policy.

Energy, Resources and Environment. John Blunden and Alan Reddish, eds. Hodder & Stoughton, PO Box 257, North Pomfret, Vermont 05053. (802) 457-1911. 1991.

Energy Technologies and the Environment. U.S. Department of Energy, 1000 Independence Avenue, SW, Washington, District of Columbia 20585. (202) 586-5000. 1988.

Energy, the Environment, and Public Policy: Issues for the 1990s. David L. McKee, ed. Praeger Publishers, 1 Madison Ave., New York, New York 10010-3603. (212) 685-5300. 1991. Addresses the extent and gravity of our environmental situation, from industrial waste to acid rain, from the Alaskan oil spill to the destruction of the rain forests.

Environment and Energy. T. Nejat Veziroglu, ed. Nova Science Publishers, Inc., 283 Commack Rd., Ste. 300, Commack, New York 11725. (516) 499-3103. 1991. Based on a conference and a volume in the series Energy and Environmental Progress–I, Vol F. Deals mostly with environmental pollution engineering and the energy technology involved in the process.

Environmental Consequences of and Control Processes for Energy Technologies. Argonne National Laboratory. Noyes Publications, 120 Mill Rd., Park Ridge, New Jersey 07656. (201) 391-8484. 1990. Describes energy technologies which will be in use in the United States during the next 20 years.

Environmental Viewpoints. Marie Lazzari. Gale Research Inc., 835 Penobscot Bldg., Detroit, Michigan 48226-4094. (313) 961-2242. 1992.

Global Energy Futures and the Carbon Dioxide Problem. Council on Environmental Quality, Old Executive Office Bldg., Rm. 154, Washington, District of Columbia 20500. (202) 395-5080. 1981. Fossil fuels and energy policy.

Groundwater Residue Sampling Design. Ralph G. Nash and Anne R. Leslie, eds. American Chemical Society, 1155 16th St. N.W., Washington, District of Columbia 20036. (202) 872-4600; (800) 227-5558. 1991. Gives an overview of the approach taken by government agencies and discusses in great detail the various techniques in sampling and analysis of groundwater.

Replacing Gasoline: Alternative Fuels for Light-Duty Vehicles. Congress of the U.S., c/o U.S. Government Printing Office, Office of Technology Assesment, N. Capitol & H Sts. NW, Washington, District of Columbia 20401. (202) 512-0000. 1990. Gives information on alternatives to standard gasoline. Some of the alternatives are: electricity, hydrogen, compressed natural gas, liquified natural gas, liquid propane gas, methanol, ethanol, and reformulated gasoline.

Societal Issues and Economics of Energy and the Environment. T. Nejat Veziroglu, ed. Nova Science Publishers Inc., 283 Commack Rd., Suite 300, Commack, New York 11725-3401. (516) 499-3103; (516) 499-3106. 1990. Deals with important societal issues and the economics of energy and the environment. Focuses on why the environment, as a resource, must be protected at all cost.

Solar Hydrogen: Moving Beyond Fossil Fuels. Joan M. Ogden and Robert H. Williams. World Resources Institute, 1709 New York Ave. N.W., Washington, District of Columbia 20006. (800) 822-0504. 1989. Traces the technical breakthroughs associated with solar hydrogen. Assesses the new fuel's potential as a replacement for oil, compares its costs and uses with those of both traditional and synthetic fuels, and charts a path for developing solar hydrogen markets.

State of the Art of Energy-Efficiency: Future Directions. Edward Vine and Drury Crawley, eds. University-Wide Energy Research Group, University of California, 2120 Berkeley Way, Berkeley, California 94720. (415) 642-4262; (800) 822-6657. 1991. Practical compilation of energy-efficient technologies and programs, resource planning, and data collection and analysis for buildings, which account for more than half of all U.S. energy.

World Guide to Environmental Issues and Organizations. Peter Brackley. Longman Group Ltd., Longman House, Burnt Mill, Harlow, Essex, England CM20 2J6. (0279) 426721. 1991.

GOVERNMENTAL ORGANIZATIONS

Energy Information Administration. James Forrestal Building, 1000 Independence Ave., S.W., Washington, District of Columbia 20585. (202) 586-5830.

Energy Research Office. James Forrestal Building, 1000 Independence Ave., S.W., Washington, District of Columbia 20585. (202) 586-5430.

Information and Communications: Extension Service. 14th and Independence Ave., S.W., Washington, District of Columbia 20250. (202) 447-3029.

Office of Public Information: Federal Energy Regulatory Commission. 825 North Capitol St., N.E., Washington, District of Columbia 20426. (202) 357-8055.

Public Affairs Office. James Forrestal Building, 1000 Independence Ave., S.W., Washington, District of Columbia 20585. (202) 586-6250.

HANDBOOKS AND MANUALS

Energy Handbook. Robert L. Loftness. Van Nostrand Reinhold, 115 5th Ave., New York, New York 10003. (212) 254-3232. 1984. Second edition. Resource book on energy with current data taking into consideration the environmental control technologies. Includes an appendix with an energy conversion factor, a glossary and a general index.

Environmental Statistics Handbook: Europe. Allan Foster, Oksana Newman. Gale Research Inc., 835 Penobscot Bldg., Detroit, Michigan 48226-4094. (313) 961-2242. 1993.

The Global Ecology Handbook: What You Can Do about the Environmental Crisis. Walter H. Corson, ed. The Global Tomorrow Coalition, Beacon Pr., 25 Beacon St., Boston, Massachusetts 02108-2800. (617) 742-2110. 1990. Covers environment, energy policy, population growth and other issues. It includes chapters on tropical rain forests, garbage, oceans and coasts, global warming, population growth, agriculture, biological diversity, fresh water, hazardous wastes, and environment and development.

ONLINE DATA BASES

Alternative Energy Digests. International Academy at Santa Barbara, 800 Garden St., Suite D, Santa Barbara, California 93101. (805) 965-5010.

Computerized Engineering Index–COMPENDEX. Engineering Information Inc., 345 E. 47th St., New York, New York 10017. (212) 705-7600.

EBIB. Texas A & M University, Sterling C. Evans Library, Reference Division, College Station, Texas 77843. (409) 845-5741.

Energy Conservation News. Business Communications Company, Inc., 25 Van Zant St., Norwalk, Connecticut 06855. (203) 853-4266. Technology and economics of energy conservation at industrial, commercial, and institutional facilities.

IBSEDEX. Building Services Research & Information Association, Old Bracknell Lane West, Bracknell, Berkshire, England RG12 4AH. 44 (344) 426511.

Life Sciences from NTIS. National Technical Information Center for the Utilization of Federal Technology, 5285 Port Royal Rd., Springfield, Virginia 22161. (703) 487-4650.

Monthly Catalog of United States Government Publications. U.S. G.P.O., Supt. of Docs., PO Box 371954, Pittsburgh, Pennsylvania 15250-7954. (202) 512-0000.

National Technical Information Service. U.S. Department of Commerce, National Technical Information Service, Office of Data Base Services, 5285 Port Royal Rd., Springfield, Virginia 22161. (703) 487-4807. Bibliographic database of government sponsored research and technical reports.

POWER. U.S. Department of Energy, Energy Library, MA-232.2, Washington, District of Columbia 20585. (202) 586-9534. Monographs, proceedings, and other materials related to the energy field, including conservation and environmental aspects.

PERIODICALS AND NEWSLETTERS

Alliance for Clean Energy Newsletter. Alliance for Clean Energy, 1901 N. Ft. Myer Dr., 12th Fl., Roslyn, Virginia 22209. (703) 841-0626. Weekly.

Catalyst for Environment/Energy. Catalyst for Environment/Energy, New York, New York 1970-. Irregular. Dedicated to efficient energy and environmental management.

Energy & Environment. Multi-Science Publishing Co. Ltd., 107 High St., Brentwood, Essex, England CM14 4RX. 0277-224632. Quarterly.

Energy & Environment Alert. National Council for Environmental Balance, Inc., 4169 Westport Rd., Box 7732, Louisville, Kentucky 40207. (502) 896-8731. Quarterly. Energy environment, agriculture, chemistry, entomology, and mineral resources.

Energy and Housing Report. Business Publishers, Inc., 951 Pershing Dr., Silver Spring, Maryland 20910. (301) 587-6300. Monthly. Energy conservation problems; developments in home energy products.

Energy Conservation Digest. Editorial Resources, Inc., PO Box 21133, Washington, District of Columbia 20009. (202) 332-2267. Semimonthly. Commercial, residential, and industrial energy conservation issues and policy developments.

Energy Today. Trends Publishing, Inc., 1079 National Press Bldg., Washington, District of Columbia 20045. (202) 393-0031. 1973-. Semimonthly.

Environmental Action. Environmental Action Foundation, 6930 Carroll Ave., Ste. 600, Takoma Park, Maryland 20912. (301) 891-1100. Bimonthly. Impact of humans and industry on the environment.

Forum for Applied Research and Public Policy. University of Tennessee, Energy, Environment and Resources Center, Knoxville, Tennessee 37996-0710. (919) 966-3561. 1986-. Quarterly. Presents a discussion of options by academic, government and corporate experts in energy, environment and economic development.

Home Energy. Energy Auditor & Retrofitter, Inc., 2124 Kittredge St., Suite 95, Berkeley, California 94704. Bimonthly. Deals with building retrofits to save on energy consumption.

The Hudson Valley Green Times. Hudson Valley Grass Roots Energy and Environment Network, 30 E. Market St., P.O. Box 208, Red Hook, New York 12571. (914) 758-4484. Bimonthly. Energy and environment news with emphasis on Hudson Valley.

International Journal of Energy, Environment, Economics. Nova Science Publishers, Inc., 283 Commack Rd.,

Ste. 300, Commack, New York 11725. (516) 499-3103. 1991-. Quarterly. Aims to provide a vehicle for the multidisciplinary field of energy-environment economics between research scientists, engineers and economists. The areas covered would be technological, environmental, economic and social feasibility.

The International Journal of Global Energy Issues. Inderscience Enterprises Ltd., World Trade Center Building, 110 Avenue Louis Casai, Case Postale 306, Geneva-Airport, Switzerland (44) 908-314248. 1989-. Quarterly. Provides a forum and an authoritative source of information in the field of energy issues and related topics.

Journal of Energy, Natural Resources & Environmental Law. College of Law, University of Utah, Salt Lake City, Utah 84112. Semiannual. Legal aspects of energy development, natural resources, and environment.

Maine Audubon News. Maine Audubon Society, Old Route 1, Falmouth, Maine 04105. (207) 781-2330. Monthly. Wild life conservation, energy conservation, and alternative sources of energy.

Newsletter. Americans for Energy Independence, 1629 K St., NW, Washington, District of Columbia 20006. (202) 466-2105. Quarterly. Developments in energy policy; legislative, educational, and media strategies.

Northern Sun News. Northern Sun Alliance, 1519 E. Franklin Ave., Minneapolis, Minnesota 55404. (612) 874-1540. Ten times a year. Alternatives in energy.

People, Food. People Food, 35751 Oak Springs Dr., Tollhouse, California 93667. (209) 855-3710. Annual.

Plant Energy Management. Walker-Davis Pub. Inc., 2500 Office Center, Willow Grove, Pennsylvania 19090. Quarterly.

Power Energy Ecology. Taylor & Francis, 1900 Frost Rd., Suite 101, Bristol, Pennsylvania 19007. (215) 785-5800. Quarterly. Energy conservation, power efficiency, renewable energy development, and global environment protection.

Power Line. Environmental Action Foundation, 6930 Carroll Ave., Ste. 600, Takoma Park, Maryland 20912. (301) 891-1100. Biannual.

Renewable Energy: An International Journal. Pergamon Microforms International, Inc., Fairview Park, Elmsford, New York 10523. (914) 592-7720. 1991-. Six issues a year. Topics include environmental protection and renewable sources of energy.

Strategic Planning for Energy and the Environment Journal. Energy Engineering, 700 Indian Trail, Lilburn, Georgia 30247. 1990-. Quarterly. Concentrates on the background, new developments and policy issues which impact corporate planning for energy and environmental issues.

Utility Reporter. Merton Allen Associates, PO Box 15640, Plantation, Florida 33318-5640. (305)473-9560. Monthly. Covers current activities in power generation and energy conservation.

RESEARCH CENTERS AND INSTITUTES

Center for Energy Policy and Research. c/o New York Institute of Technology, Old Westbury, New York 11568. (516) 686-7578.

International Institute for Energy Conservation. 420 C St., N.E., Washington, District of Columbia 20002. (202) 546-3388.

Lawrence Berkeley Laboratory, Chemical Biodynamics Division. One Cyclotron Road, Berkeley, California 94720. (415) 486-4355.

University of Tennessee at Knoxville, Energy Environment and Resource Center. 327 South Stadium Hall, Knoxville, Tennessee 37996. (615) 974-4251.

World Resources Institute. 1709 New York Ave., N.W., Washington, District of Columbia 20006. (202) 638-6300.

STATISTICS SOURCES

OECD Environmental Data Compendium 1989. OECD Publications and Information Center, 2001 L St. N.W., Suite 700, Washington, District of Columbia 20036. (202) 785-OECD. 1989. Provides statistical data for OECD countries on air pollution, water pollution, the marine environment, land use, forests, wildlife, solid waste, noise and radioactivity. Also provides data on the underlying pressures on the environment such as energy use, transportation, industrial activity and agriculture.

Statistical Record of the Environment. Arsen J. Darnay. Gale Research Inc., 835 Penobscot Bldg., Detroit, Michigan 48226-4094. (313) 961-2242. 1992.

World Energy Statistics and Balances. International Energy Agency. OECD Publications and Information Center, Suite 700, 2001 L St. N.W., Ste. 700, Washington, District of Columbia 20036. (202) 785-6323. 1989-. A compilation of energy production and consumption statistics for 85 non-OECD countries and regions, including developing countries, Central and Eastern European countries, and the Soviet Union.

World Resources. World Resources Institute. 1709 New York Ave., N.W., Washington, District of Columbia 20006. (202) 638-6300. Annual. Statistical and textual analysis of world's natural resources and the effects of growth-caused environmental pollution.

TRADE ASSOCIATIONS AND PROFESSIONAL SOCIETIES

Alliance for Clean Energy. 1901 N. Ft. Myer Dr., 12th Fl., Roslyn, Virginia 22209. (703) 841-0626.

The Alliance to Save Energy. 1725 K St., N.W., Suite 914, Washington, District of Columbia 20006. (202) 857-0666.

Alternative Sources of Energy. 620 Central Ave. N., Milaca, Minnesota 56353. (612) 983-6892. An association.

American Council for an Energy Efficient Economy. 1001 Connecticut Ave., N.W., Suite 535, Washington, District of Columbia 20036. (202) 429-8873.

American Wind Energy Association. 777 North Capitol, NE, Suite 805, Washington, District of Columbia 20002. (202) 408-8988.

Cogeneration and Independent Power Coalition of America. 1025 Thomas Jefferson St., N.W., Box 1, Washington, District of Columbia 20007. (202) 965-1134.

CONCERN, Inc. 1794 Columbia Rd, NW, Washington, District of Columbia 20009. (202) 328-8160.

Energy Research Institute. 6850 Rattlesnake Hammock Rd., Hwy. 951, Naples, Florida 33962. (813) 793-1922.

Environmental and Energy Study Institute. 122 C St., N.W., Suite 700, Washington, District of Columbia 20001. (202) 628-1400.

Friends of the Earth. 218 D St., SE, Washington, District of Columbia 20003. (202) 544-2600.

Greenpeace. 1436 U St., NW, Washington, District of Columbia 20009. (202) 462-1177.

Institute of Environmental Sciences. 940 E. Northwest Hwy., Mount Prospect, Illinois 60056. (708) 255-1561.

Institute of Food Technologists. 221 N. LaSalle St., Chicago, Illinois 60601. (312) 782-8424.

National Association of Energy Service Companies. 1440 New York Ave. N.W., Washington, District of Columbia 20005. (202) 371-7000.

National Council for Environmental Balance. 4169 Westport Rd., P.O. Box 7732, Louisville, Kentucky 40207. (502) 896-8731.

National Wood Energy Association. 777 N. Capitol St. N.W., Suite 805, Washington, District of Columbia 20002. (202) 408-0664.

Natural POWWER. 5420 Mayfield Rd., Cleveland, Ohio 44124. (216) 442-5600.

Railway Fuel & Operating Officers Association. Box 8496, Springfield, Illinois 62791. (217) 544-7834.

Safe Energy Communication Council. 1717 Massachusetts Ave., N.W., LL215, Washington, District of Columbia 20036. (202) 483-8491.

Society of Exploration Geo-Physicists. P.O. Box 702740, Tulsa, Oklahoma 74170. (918) 493-3516.

Solid Fuel Advisory Council of America. Star Rt. 104, Bristol, New Hampshire 03222. (603) 744-8627.

U.S. Council for Energy Awareness. 1776 I St., N.W., Suite 400, Washington, District of Columbia 20006. (202) 293-0770.

Union of Concerned Scientists. 26 Church St., Cambridge, Massachusetts 02238. (617) 547-5552.

United States Energy Association. 1620 I St., N.W., Suite 615, Washington, District of Columbia 20006. (202) 331-0415.

Windstar Foundation. 2317 Snowmass Creek Rd., Snowmass, Colorado 81654. (303) 927-4777. Foundation begun by John Denver offering information on a wide range of personal-action issues.

ENERGY CONSERVATION

See also: ARCHITECTURE AND ENERGY CONSERVATION; CONSERVATION OF NATURAL RESOURCES; ENERGY POLICY; RECYCLING (WASTE, ETC.)

ABSTRACTING AND INDEXING SERVICES

Applied Ecology Abstracts Studies in Renewable Natural Resources. Information Retrieval Ltd., 1911 Jefferson Davis Highway, Arlington, Virginia 22202. 1975-. Monthly.

Biological and Agricultural Index. H.W. Wilson Co., 950 University Ave., Bronx, New York 10452. (800) 367-6770. 1916-. Monthly.

Ecological Abstracts. Geo Abstracts Ltd. Elsevier Applied Science, Crown House, Linton Rd., Barking, England IG 11 8JU. 1974-. Derived from over 600 leading ecological and environmental journals, plus books, conference proceedings, reports and theses.

Ecology Abstracts. Cambridge Scientific Abstracts, 5161 River Rd., Bethesda, Maryland 20816. (301) 961-6750. Monthly.

Energy Information Abstracts Annual 1987 in Retrospect. EIC/Intelligence Inc., 121 Chanlon Rd., New Providence, New Jersey 07974. (908) 464-6800. 1988. Annual. Cumulative edition of the monthly Energy Information Abstracts. Monitors sources in the field of energy including the scientific, technical and business journal literature, conference and symposia proceedings, corporate, government and academic reports.

Environment Abstracts. Bowker A & I Publishing, 121 Chanlon Rd., New Providence, New Jersey 07974. (908) 464-6800. 1974-.

Environment Index. Environment Information Center, Index Research Department, 124 E. 39th St., New York, New York 10016. 1971-. Annual.

Environmental Information Connection-EIC. Planning Information Program, Dept. of Urban and Regional Planning, University of Illinois, 1003 West Nevada, Urbana, Illinois 61801. (217) 333-1369. Also available online.

Environmental Periodicals Bibliography. Environmental Studies Institute, International Academy at Santa Barbara, 800 Garden St., Suite D, Santa Barbara, California 93101. (805) 965-5010. Also available online.

ERDA Research Abstracts. U.S. ERDA Technical Information Center, Box 62, Oak Ridge, Tennessee 37830.

General Science Index. H. W. Wilson Co., 950 University Ave., Bronx, New York 10452. 1978-. Monthly, also issued in annual cumulation. Cumulative subject index to English language periodicals in the subject fields of astronomy, botany, chemistry, earth science, environment and conservation, food and nutrition, genetics, mathematics, medicine and health, microbiology, oceanography, physics, physiology and zoology.

Geographical Abstracts. London School of Economics, Dept. of Geography, Regency House, 34 Duke St., London, England 1966-. Continued by Geo Abstracts issued in 6 parts: Pt. A. Landforms and the quaternary; Pt. B. Biogeography and Climatology; Pt. C. Economic geography; Pt. D. Social geography and cartography; Pt. E. Sedimentology; Pt. F. Regional and community planning.

Index to Scientific Book Contents. Institute for Scientific Information, 3501 Market St., Philadelphia, Pennsylvania 19104. (800) 523-1857. 1985-. Annual. Gives contents of science books published.

Multimedia Index to Ecology. National Information Center for Educational Media, University of Southern California, Los Angeles, California 90007.

Physics Briefs. Physikalische Berichte. Physik Verlag, Pappapelallee 3, Postfach 101161, Weinheim, Germany D-6940. 1979-. Semimonthly. In English. Volumes for 1979- issued by the Deutsche Physikalische Gesellschaft and the Fachinformationszentrum Energie Physik, Mathematik in cooperation with the American Institute of Physics.

ALMANACS AND YEARBOOKS

Gale Environmental Almanac. Russ Hoyle. Gale Research Inc., 835 Penobscot Bldg., Detroit, Michigan 48226-4094. (313) 961-2242. 1993. Focuses on the U.S. and Canada, although worldwide and transboundary issues are discussed.

BIBLIOGRAPHIES

Current Contents. Agriculture, Biology and Environmental Sciences. Institute for Scientific Information, 3501 Market St., Philadelphia, Pennsylvania 19104. (800) 523-1857. 1973-. Previous title: Current Contents. Agricultural, Food & Veterinary Sciences. Gives the table of contents of periodicals in the fields of agriculture, biology, environmental and related areas.

Directory of Published Proceedings. Interdok Corp., 173 Halstead Ave., Harrison, New York 10528. (914) 835-3506. 1990. Monthly. This is a listing of published proceedings including the series SEMTE (Science/Medicine/Engineering/Technology) and the series SSH (Social Science/Humanities).

EPA Publications Bibliography. U.S. Environmental Protection Agency, Library Systems Branch, 401 M St., SW, Washington, District of Columbia 20460. (202) 260-2090. Quarterly.

DIRECTORIES

Canadian Environmental Directory. Canadian Almanac & Directory Publishing Co. Ltd., 134 Adelaide St. E., Ste. 27, Toronto, Ontario, Canada M5C 1K9. (416) 362-4088. 1992. Includes individuals, agencies, firms, and associations.

Energy Conservation and Management Consultants. American Business Directories, Inc., 5711 S. 86th Circle, Omaha, Nebraska 68127. (402) 593-4600.

Energy Conservation Products Retail Directory. American Business Directories, Inc., 5711 S. 86th Circle, Omaha, Nebraska 68127. (402) 593-4600. Annual.

The Green Encyclopedia. Irene Franck, David Brownstone. Prentice-Hall, Rte. 9W, Englewood Cliffs, New York 07632. (201) 592-2000. 1992. Covers environmental organizations.

ENCYCLOPEDIAS AND DICTIONARIES

Encyclopedia of Chemical Processing and Design. John J. Mcketta and W. A. Cunningham. Marcel Dekker, Inc., 270 Madison Ave., New York, New York 10016. (212) 696-9000; (800) 228-1160. 1992. Thirty-eight volumes.

Encyclopedia of Environmental Studies. William Ashworth. Facts on File, Inc., 460 Park Ave. S., New York, New York 10016. (212) 683-2244. 1991.

Encyclopedia of Physical Science and Technology. Robert A. Meyers, ed. Academic Press, c/o Harcourt Brace Jovanovich Inc., 6277 Sea Harbor Dr., Orlando, Florida 32887. (800) 346-8648. Dictionary of engineering, technology and physical sciences.

Energy Statistics: Definitions, Units of Measure, and Conversion Factors. Department of International Economic and Social Affairs, Statistical Office. United Nations, 2 United Nations Plz., Salis Section, Rm. DC 2-853, New York, New York 10017. (800) 553-3210. 1987. Terminology of statistical methods in power resources.

Environmental Encyclopedia. William P. Cunningham, Terence Ball, et. al. Gale Research Inc., 835 Penobscot Bldg., Detroit, Michigan 48226-4094. (313) 961-2242. 1993.

McGraw Hill Encyclopedia of Energy. Sybil P. Parker. McGraw-Hill Science & Engineering Books, 1221 Avenue of Americas, New York, New York 10020. (212) 512-2000 or (800) 262-4729. 1981. Second edition. Major issues in energy are discussed in six feature articles. The second section has 300 alphabetically arranged entries relating to energy.

McGraw-Hill Encyclopedia of Environmental Science. Sybil P. Parker. McGraw-Hill Science & Engineering Books, 11 W. 19th St., New York, New York 10011. (212) 337-6010. 1980. Covers ecology, man's influence on nature, and environmental protection.

McGraw-Hill Encyclopedia of Science and Technology. McGraw-Hill, 1221 Avenue of the Americas, New York, New York 10020. (212) 512-2000 or (800) 262-4729. 1992. Seventh edition. Issued in multiple volumes including index. Includes all science and technology broad subject areas.

Van Nostrand's Scientific Encyclopedia. Glenn D. Considine, ed. Van Nostrand Reinhold, 115 5th Ave., New York, New York 10003. (212) 254-3232. 1983. Sixth edition. Includes all broad subject areas in science.

GENERAL WORKS

Air Pollution's Toll on Forests and Crops. James J. MacKenzie and Mohamed T. El-Ashry, eds. Yale University Press, 92 A Yale St., 302 Temple St., New Haven, Connecticut 06520. (203) 432-0960. 1992. Proposes an integrated strategy to reduce pollution levels based on improved energy efficiency, abatement technology, and the use of nonfossil energy technologies. This strategy takes into account other critical problems such as increasing oil imports, failure to attain clean air goals in U.S. cities, and the greenhouse effect.

Conservation and Heat Transfer. Nejat T. Veziroglu, ed. Nova Science Publishers Inc., 283 Commack Rd., Suite 300, Commack, New York 11725-3104. (516) 499-3103; (516) 499-3106. 1991. Describes methods of conservation and heat transfer.

Direct Energy Conversion. Stanley W. Angrist. Allyn and Bacon, 160 Gould St., Needham Heights, Massachusetts 02194. (617) 455-1250; (800) 852-8024. 1982. Techniques in mechanical engineering and applied mechanics.

Energy Conversion Systems. Harry A. Sorensen. John Wiley & Sons, Inc., 605 3rd Ave., New York, New York

10158-0012. (212) 850-6000. 1983. Includes power and power plants.

World Guide to Environmental Issues and Organizations. Peter Brackley. Longman Group Ltd., Longman House, Burnt Mill, Harlow, Essex, England CM20 2J6. (0279) 426721. 1991.

HANDBOOKS AND MANUALS

Energy Conservation in Existing Buildings. Albert Thumann. The Association of Energy Engineers, 4025 Pleasantdale Rd., Suite 420, Atlanta, Georgia 30340. (404) 925-9558. 1991. Step-by-step guide to implement a comprehensive energy conservation program in existing buildings. Includes figures to calculate energy efficient opportunities.

Environmental Statistics Handbook: Europe. Allan Foster, Oksana Newman. Gale Research Inc., 835 Penobscot Bldg., Detroit, Michigan 48226-4094. (313) 961-2242. 1993.

Plant Engineers and Managers Guide to Energy Conservation. Albert Thumann. The Association of Energy Engineers, 4025 Pleasantdale Rd., Suite 420, Atlanta, Georgia 30340. (404) 925-9558. 1991. Fifth edition. Covers both management and technical strategies which can be utilized to conserve energy.

Power Generation, Energy Management and Environmental Sourcebook. Marilyn Jackson. The Association of Energy Engineers, 4025 Pleasantdale Rd., Suite 420, Atlanta, Georgia 30340. (404) 925-9558. 1992. Includes practical solutions to energy and environmental problems.

ONLINE DATA BASES

Energy Conservation News. Business Communications Company, Inc., 25 Van Zant St., Norwalk, Connecticut 06855. (203) 853-4266. Technology and economics of energy conservation at industrial, commercial, and institutional facilities.

Enviro/Energyline Abstracts Plus. R. R. Bowker Co., 121 Chanlon Rd., New Providence, New Jersey 07974. (908) 464-6800.

Environmental Periodicals Bibliography. National Information Services Corp., Ste. 6, Wyman Towers, 3100 St. Paul St., Baltimore, Maryland 21218. (410)243-0797. Online version of abstract of same name.

Monthly Catalog of United States Government Publications. U.S. G.P.O., Supt. of Docs., PO Box 371954, Pittsburgh, Pennsylvania 15250-7954. (202) 512-0000.

National Technical Information Service. U.S. Department of Commerce, National Technical Information Service, Office of Data Base Services, 5285 Port Royal Rd., Springfield, Virginia 22161. (703) 487-4807. Bibliographic database of government sponsored research and technical reports.

PressNet Environmental Reports. Chemical Information Systems, Inc., 7215 York Rd., Baltimore, Maryland 21212. (301) 321-8440.

SCISEARCH. Institute for Scientific Information, University City Science Center, 3501 Market St., Philadelphia, Pennsylvania 19104. (215) 386-0100.

PERIODICALS AND NEWSLETTERS

Energy Conservation Digest. Editorial Resources, Inc., PO Box 21133, Washington, District of Columbia 20009. (202) 332-2267. Semimonthly. Commercial, residential, and industrial energy conservation issues and policy developments.

Energy Conversion and Management. Pergamon Microforms International, Inc., Fairview Park, Elmsford, New York 10523. (914) 592-7720. 1980. Quarterly. Topics in direct energy conversion and thermoelectricity.

IEEE Transactions on Energy Conversion. Institute of Electrical and Electronics Engineers, 345 E. 47th St., New York, New York 10017. (212) 705-7900. Quarterly. Deals with power apparatus and systems.

International Journal of Energy, Environment, Economics. Nova Science Publishers, Inc., 283 Commack Rd., Ste. 300, Commack, New York 11725. (516) 499-3103. 1991-. Quarterly. Aims to provide a vehicle for the multidisciplinary field of energy-environment economics between research scientists, engineers and economists. The areas covered would be technological, environmental, economic and social feasibility.

STATISTICS SOURCES

Statistical Record of the Environment. Arsen J. Darnay. Gale Research Inc., 835 Penobscot Bldg., Detroit, Michigan 48226-4094. (313) 961-2242. 1992.

Transportation Energy Data Book. Stacy C. Davis and Patricia S. Hu. Oak Ridge National Laboratory, Transportation Energy Group, PO Box 2008, Oak Ridge, Tennessee 37831-6050. (615) 576-1746. 1991. Eleventh edition. Data book represents an assembly and display of statistics that characterize transportation activity and presents data on other factors that influence transportation energy use.

ENERGY CONVERSION

ABSTRACTING AND INDEXING SERVICES

Biological and Agricultural Index. H.W. Wilson Co., 950 University Ave., Bronx, New York 10452. (800) 367-6770. 1916-. Monthly.

Civil Engineering Hydraulic Abstracts. BHRA Fluid Engineering, Air Science Co., PO Box 143, Corning, New York 14830. (607) 962-5591. Monthly. Abstracts of periodicals that publish in the areas of hydraulic engineering and other related topics.

ERDA Research Abstracts. U.S. ERDA Technical Information Center, Box 62, Oak Ridge, Tennessee 37830.

General Science Index. H. W. Wilson Co., 950 University Ave., Bronx, New York 10452. 1978-. Monthly, also issued in annual cumulation. Cumulative subject index to English language periodicals in the subject fields of astronomy, botany, chemistry, earth science, environment and conservation, food and nutrition, genetics, mathematics, medicine and health, microbiology, oceanography, physics, physiology and zoology.

Geographical Abstracts. London School of Economics, Dept. of Geography, Regency House, 34 Duke St., London, England 1966-. Continued by Geo Abstracts

issued in 6 parts: Pt. A. Landforms and the quaternary; Pt. B. Biogeography and Climatology; Pt. C. Economic geography; Pt. D. Social geography and cartography; Pt. E. Sedimentology; Pt. F. Regional and community planning.

Index to Scientific Book Contents. Institute for Scientific Information, 3501 Market St., Philadelphia, Pennsylvania 19104. (800) 523-1857. 1985-. Annual. Gives contents of science books published.

INIS Atomindex. International Atomic Energy Agency, Wagramerstrasse 5, Vienna, Austria A-1400. 222 23606198. 1988-. Semiannual. Abstracts nuclear energy and nuclear physics topics from journals, conferences, technical reports and other related publications. Issued in 6 parts: Personal Author, Corporate Entry, Subject, Report, Standard Patent, Conference (by place), Conference (by date).

BIBLIOGRAPHIES

Directory of Published Proceedings. Interdok Corp., 173 Halstead Ave., Harrison, New York 10528. (914) 835-3506. 1990. Monthly. This is a listing of published proceedings including the series SEMTE (Science/Medicine/Engineering/Technology) and the series SSH (Social Science/Humanities).

ENCYCLOPEDIAS AND DICTIONARIES

Encyclopedia of Physical Science and Technology. Robert A. Meyers, ed. Academic Press, c/o Harcourt Brace Jovanovich Inc., 6277 Sea Harbor Dr., Orlando, Florida 32887. (800) 346-8648. Dictionary of engineering, technology and physical sciences.

Van Nostrand's Scientific Encyclopedia. Glenn D. Considine, ed. Van Nostrand Reinhold, 115 5th Ave., New York, New York 10003. (212) 254-3232. 1983. Sixth edition. Includes all broad subject areas in science.

GENERAL WORKS

Direct Energy Conversion. Stanley W. Angrist. Allyn and Bacon, 160 Gould St., Needham Heights, Massachusetts 02194. (617) 455-1250; (800) 852-8024. 1982. Techniques in mechanical engineering and applied mechanics.

ONLINE DATA BASES

Monthly Catalog of United States Government Publications. U.S. G.P.O., Supt. of Docs., PO Box 371954, Pittsburgh, Pennsylvania 15250-7954. (202) 512-0000.

National Technical Information Service. U.S. Department of Commerce, National Technical Information Service, Office of Data Base Services, 5285 Port Royal Rd., Springfield, Virginia 22161. (703) 487-4807. Bibliographic database of government sponsored research and technical reports.

ENERGY ECONOMICS

ABSTRACTING AND INDEXING SERVICES

ERDA Research Abstracts. U.S. ERDA Technical Information Center, Box 62, Oak Ridge, Tennessee 37830.

General Science Index. H. W. Wilson Co., 950 University Ave., Bronx, New York 10452. 1978-. Monthly, also issued in annual cumulation. Cumulative subject index to English language periodicals in the subject fields of astronomy, botany, chemistry, earth science, environment and conservation, food and nutrition, genetics, mathematics, medicine and health, microbiology, oceanography, physics, physiology and zoology.

BIBLIOGRAPHIES

Directory of Published Proceedings. Interdok Corp., 173 Halstead Ave., Harrison, New York 10528. (914) 835-3506. 1990. Monthly. This is a listing of published proceedings including the series SEMTE (Science/Medicine/Engineering/Technology) and the series SSH (Social Science/Humanities).

DIRECTORIES

Environmental Industries Marketplace. Karen Napoleone Meech. Gale Research Inc., 835 Penobscot Bldg., Detroit, 48226-4904. (313) 961-2242. 1992.

ENCYCLOPEDIAS AND DICTIONARIES

Encyclopedia of Physical Science and Technology. Robert A. Meyers, ed. Academic Press, c/o Harcourt Brace Jovanovich Inc., 6277 Sea Harbor Dr., Orlando, Florida 32887. (800) 346-8648. Dictionary of engineering, technology and physical sciences.

McGraw Hill Encyclopedia of Energy. Sybil P. Parker. McGraw-Hill Science & Engineering Books, 1221 Avenue of Americas, New York, New York 10020. (212) 512-2000 or (800) 262-4729. 1981. Second edition. Major issues in energy are discussed in six feature articles. The second section has 300 alphabetically arranged entries relating to energy.

Van Nostrand's Scientific Encyclopedia. Glenn D. Considine, ed. Van Nostrand Reinhold, 115 5th Ave., New York, New York 10003. (212) 254-3232. 1983. Sixth edition. Includes all broad subject areas in science.

ONLINE DATA BASES

Monthly Catalog of United States Government Publications. U.S. G.P.O., Supt. of Docs., PO Box 371954, Pittsburgh, Pennsylvania 15250-7954. (202) 512-0000.

National Technical Information Service. U.S. Department of Commerce, National Technical Information Service, Office of Data Base Services, 5285 Port Royal Rd., Springfield, Virginia 22161. (703) 487-4807. Bibliographic database of government sponsored research and technical reports.

ENERGY POLICY

ABSTRACTING AND INDEXING SERVICES

ERDA Research Abstracts. U.S. ERDA Technical Information Center, Box 62, Oak Ridge, Tennessee 37830.

ALMANACS AND YEARBOOKS

Gale Environmental Almanac. Russ Hoyle. Gale Research Inc., 835 Penobscot Bldg., Detroit, Michigan

48226-4094. (313) 961-2242. 1993. Focuses on the U.S. and Canada, although worldwide and transboundary issues are discussed.

BIBLIOGRAPHIES

Energy and the Social Sciences: A Bibliographic Guide to the Literature. E. J. Yanarella and Ann-Marie Yanarella. Westview Press, 5500 Central Ave., Boulder, Colorado 80301. (303) 444-3541. 1983. Focuses on the needs of social scientists entering the "miasma of energy policy studies."

Energy Guide: A Directory of Information Resources. Virginia Bemis, et al. Garland Publishers, 136 Madison Ave., New York, New York 10016. (212) 686-7492 or (800) 627-6273. 1977.

DIRECTORIES

Canadian Environmental Directory. Canadian Almanac & Directory Publishing Co. Ltd., 134 Adelaide St. E., Ste. 27, Toronto, Ontario, Canada M5C 1K9. (416) 362-4088. 1992. Includes individuals, agencies, firms, and associations.

Environmental Industries Marketplace. Karen Napoleone Meech. Gale Research Inc., 835 Penobscot Bldg., Detroit, 48226-4904. (313) 961-2242. 1992.

The Green Encyclopedia. Irene Franck, David Brownstone. Prentice-Hall, Rte. 9W, Englewood Cliffs, New York 07632. (201) 592-2000. 1992. Covers environmental organizations.

ENCYCLOPEDIAS AND DICTIONARIES

Dictionary of the Environment. Michael Allaby. New York University Press, 70 Washington Sq. S., New York, New York 10012. (212) 998-2575. 1989.

Environmental Encyclopedia. William P. Cunningham, Terence Ball, et. al. Gale Research Inc., 835 Penobscot Bldg., Detroit, Michigan 48226-4094. (313) 961-2242. 1993.

McGraw-Hill Encyclopedia of Environmental Science. Sybil P. Parker. McGraw-Hill Science & Engineering Books, 11 W. 19th St., New York, New York 10011. (212) 337-6010. 1980. Covers ecology, man's influence on nature, and environmental protection.

Van Nostrand's Scientific Encyclopedia. Glenn D. Considine, ed. Van Nostrand Reinhold, 115 5th Ave., New York, New York 10003. (212) 254-3232. 1983. Sixth edition. Includes all broad subject areas in science.

GENERAL WORKS

Energy for a Habitable World: A Call for Action. Pierre Elliott Trudeau. Crane Russak & Co., 1900 Frost Rd., Suite 101, Bristol, Pennsylvania 19007-1598. (215) 785-5800. 1991. Summary of the report of the InterAction Council, a group of some 30 former heads of state founded in 1983. Discusses the need for cogent energy policies to deal with the world crisis.

The Environmental Sourcebook. Edith Carol Stein. Lyons & Burford, 31 W. 21st St., New York, New York 10010. (212) 620-9580. 1992. Provides information on 11 specific environmental issues, including population; agriculture; energy; climate and atmosphere; biodiversity; water;

oceans; solid waste; hazardous substances and waste; endangered lands; and development.

Environmental Viewpoints. Marie Lazzari. Gale Research Inc., 835 Penobscot Bldg., Detroit, Michigan 48226-4094. (313) 961-2242. 1992.

World Guide to Environmental Issues and Organizations. Peter Brackley. Longman Group Ltd., Longman House, Burnt Mill, Harlow, Essex, England CM20 2J6. (0279) 426721. 1991.

HANDBOOKS AND MANUALS

Environmental Statistics Handbook: Europe. Allan Foster, Oksana Newman. Gale Research Inc., 835 Penobscot Bldg., Detroit, Michigan 48226-4094. (313) 961-2242. 1993.

ONLINE DATA BASES

Monthly Catalog of United States Government Publications. U.S. G.P.O., Supt. of Docs., PO Box 371954, Pittsburgh, Pennsylvania 15250-7954. (202) 512-0000.

National Technical Information Service. U.S. Department of Commerce, National Technical Information Service, Office of Data Base Services, 5285 Port Royal Rd., Springfield, Virginia 22161. (703) 487-4807. Bibliographic database of government sponsored research and technical reports.

STATISTICS SOURCES

Statistical Record of the Environment. Arsen J. Darnay. Gale Research Inc., 835 Penobscot Bldg., Detroit, Michigan 48226-4094. (313) 961-2242. 1992.

ENERGY RESOURCES

See also: BIOMASS; ENERGY CONSERVATION; ENERGY CONVERSION; ENERGY POLICY; FUELS; NUCLEAR POWER; RENEWABLE ENERGY RESOURCES; SOLAR ENERGY

ABSTRACTING AND INDEXING SERVICES

Applied Science and Technology Index. H.W. Wilson Co., 950 University Ave., Bronx, New York 10452. (800) 367-6770. Formerly Industrial Arts Index.

Biological and Agricultural Index. H.W. Wilson Co., 950 University Ave., Bronx, New York 10452. (800) 367-6770. 1916-. Monthly.

Current Advances in Ecological and Environmental Science. Pergamon Microforms International, Inc., Fairview Park, Elmsford, New York 10523. (914) 592-7720. 1989-. Monthly. Current literature searching service includingjournals, reports, abstracts, etc. This service is available online as part of the CABS database on the hosts BRS and ORBIT search service.

Energy: An Abstract Newsletter. National Technical Information Service, 5285 Port Royal Rd., Springfield, Virginia 22161. (703) 487-4650. Weekly. Energy use, supply, and demand; power and heat generation; energy conservation, transmission, and storage; fuel conversion processes; energy policies, regulations, engines, and fuels.

Energy Storage Systems. National Technical Information Service, 5285 Port Royal Rd., Springfield, Virginia 22161. (703) 487-4650. Bimonthly.

Engineering Index. The Engineering Index Inc., 345 E. 47th St., New York, New York 10017. 1962-.

ERDA Research Abstracts. U.S. ERDA Technical Information Center, Box 62, Oak Ridge, Tennessee 37830.

General Science Index. H. W. Wilson Co., 950 University Ave., Bronx, New York 10452. 1978-. Monthly, also issued in annual cumulation. Cumulative subject index to English language periodicals in the subject fields of astronomy, botany, chemistry, earth science, environment and conservation, food and nutrition, genetics, mathematics, medicine and health, microbiology, oceanography, physics, physiology and zoology.

Geographical Abstracts. London School of Economics, Dept. of Geography, Regency House, 34 Duke St., London, England 1966-. Continued by Geo Abstracts issued in 6 parts: Pt. A. Landforms and the quaternary; Pt. B. Biogeography and Climatology; Pt. C. Economic geography; Pt. D. Social geography and cartography; Pt. E. Sedimentology; Pt. F. Regional and community planning.

Index to Scientific Book Contents. Institute for Scientific Information, 3501 Market St., Philadelphia, Pennsylvania 19104. (800) 523-1857. 1985-. Annual. Gives contents of science books published.

Ocean Wave and Tidal Energy. National Technical Information Service, 5285 Port Royal Rd., Springfield, Virginia 22161. (703) 487-4650. 1988. Bimonthly. Ocean thermal energy conversion systems; salinity gradient power systems.

Physics Briefs. Physikalische Berichte. Physik Verlag, Pappapelallee 3, Postfach 101161, Weinheim, Germany D-6940. 1979-. Semimonthly. In English. Volumes for 1979- issued by the Deutsche Physikalische Gesellschaft and the Fachinformationszentrum Energie Physik, Mathematik in cooperation with the American Institute of Physics.

Pollution Abstracts. Cambridge Scientific Abstracts, 5161 River Rd., Bethesda, Maryland 20816. (301) 961-6750. Six/year. Indexes worldwide technical literature on environmental pollution. Covers air pollution, marine and freshwater pollution, sewage and wastewater treatment, waste management, toxicology and health, noise pollution, radiation, land pollution, and environmental policies, programs, legislation, and education. Also available online.

Science Citation Index. Institute for Scientific Information, 3501 Market St., Philadelphia, Pennsylvania 19104. 1961-.

Sea Grant Abstracts. National Sea Grant Depository, Pell Laboratory Bldg., Bay Campus, University of Rhode Island, Narragansett, Rhode Island 02882. (401) 792-6114. 1986-. Quarterly. Published by the National Sea Grant Programs, this collection includes annual reports, serials and newsletters, charts and maps.

Wind Energy Technology. National Technical Information Service, 5285 Port Royal Rd., Springfield, Virginia 22161. (703) 487-4650. 1988. Bimonthly. Information on all aspects of energy from the wind.

ALMANACS AND YEARBOOKS

Gale Environmental Almanac. Russ Hoyle. Gale Research Inc., 835 Penobscot Bldg., Detroit, Michigan 48226-4094. (313) 961-2242. 1993. Focuses on the U.S. and Canada, although worldwide and transboundary issues are discussed.

BIBLIOGRAPHIES

Current Contents. Agriculture, Biology and Environmental Sciences. Institute for Scientific Information, 3501 Market St., Philadelphia, Pennsylvania 19104. (800) 523-1857. 1973-. Previous title: Current Contents. Agricultural, Food & Veterinary Sciences. Gives the table of contents of periodicals in the fields of agriculture, biology, environmental and related areas.

DIRECTORIES

Canadian Environmental Directory. Canadian Almanac & Directory Publishing Co. Ltd., 134 Adelaide St. E., Ste. 27, Toronto, Ontario, Canada M5C 1K9. (416) 362-4088. 1992. Includes individuals, agencies, firms, and associations.

Environmental Industries Marketplace. Karen Napoleone Meech. Gale Research Inc., 835 Penobscot Bldg., Detroit, 48226-4904. (313) 961-2242. 1992.

ENCYCLOPEDIAS AND DICTIONARIES

Encyclopedia of Environmental Studies. William Ashworth. Facts on File, Inc., 460 Park Ave. S., New York, New York 10016. (212) 683-2244. 1991.

Encyclopedia of Physical Science and Technology. Robert A. Meyers, ed. Academic Press, c/o Harcourt Brace Jovanovich Inc., 6277 Sea Harbor Dr., Orlando, Florida 32887. (800) 346-8648. Dictionary of engineering, technology and physical sciences.

Environmental Encyclopedia. William P. Cunningham, Terence Ball, et. al. Gale Research Inc., 835 Penobscot Bldg., Detroit, Michigan 48226-4094. (313) 961-2242. 1993.

McGraw-Hill Encyclopedia of Environmental Science. Sybil P. Parker. McGraw-Hill Science & Engineering Books, 11 W. 19th St., New York, New York 10011. (212) 337-6010. 1980. Covers ecology, man's influence on nature, and environmental protection.

Van Nostrand's Scientific Encyclopedia. Glenn D. Considine, ed. Van Nostrand Reinhold, 115 5th Ave., New York, New York 10003. (212) 254-3232. 1983. Sixth edition. Includes all broad subject areas in science.

GENERAL WORKS

Air Pollution's Toll on Forests and Crops. James J. MacKenzie and Mohamed T. El-Ashry, eds. Yale University Press, 92 A Yale St., 302 Temple St., New Haven, Connecticut 06520. (203) 432-0960. 1992. Proposes an integrated strategy to reduce pollution levels based on improved energy efficiency, abatement technology, and the use of nonfossil energy technologies. This strategy takes into account other critical problems such as increasing oil imports, failure to attain clean air goals in U.S. cities, and the greenhouse effect.

Driving Forces: Motor Vehicle Trends and Their Implications for Global Warming, Energy Strategies, and Transportation. James J. MacKenzie and Michael P. Walsh. World Resources Institute, 1709 New York Ave., Washington, District of Columbia 20006. (800) 822-0504. 1990. Overview of new-vehicle fuel efficiency, reductions in air pollution emissions, and overall improvements in transportation and land-use as they relate to global warming planning. Also available through State University of New York Press.

Energy and Climate Change. Lewis Publishers, 2000 Corporate Blvd., N.W., Boca Raton, Florida 33431. (407) 994-0555 or (800) 272-7737. 1990. Includes energy scenarios, cost and risk analysis, energy emissions, atmospheric chemistry, and climate effects.

Energy-Environment-Quality of Life. Inderscience Enterprises Ltd., World Trade Center Bldg., 110 Avenue Louis Casai, Case Postale 306, Geneva-Airport, Switzerland CH1215. (44) 908-314248. 1991. A special publication of the International Journal of Global Energy. Contains the proceedings of the 13th annual International Scientific Forum on Energy (ISFE) held at the UNESCO building, Paris, France, December 4-7, 1989. Focuses on important energy issues facing the planet, their likely impact on the environment and their effects on the quality of life.

Environmental Consequences of and Control Processes for Energy Technologies. Argonne National Laboratory. Noyes Publications, 120 Mill Rd., Park Ridge, New Jersey 07656. (201) 391-8484. 1990. Describes energy technologies which will be in use in the United States during the next 20 years.

Environmental Viewpoints. Marie Lazzari. Gale Research Inc., 835 Penobscot Bldg., Detroit, Michigan 48226-4094. (313) 961-2242. 1992.

Greenhouse Gas Emissions–The Energy Dimension. OECD Publications and Information Center, 2001 L St., N.W., Suite 700, Washington, District of Columbia 20036. (202) 785-OECD. Source for a comprehensive discussion on the relationship between energy use and greenhouse emissions as they relate to the energy used by geographical and regional sectors.

Report on Renewable Energy and Utility Regulation. National Association of Regulatory Utility Commissioners, 1102 ICC Bldg., PO Box 684, Washington, District of Columbia 20044-0684. (202) 898-2200. 1990. Recently released NARUC report that addresses some key questions and makes some basic conclusions about potential of renewable energy resources.

Solar Hydrogen: Moving Beyond Fossil Fuels. Joan M. Ogden and Robert H. Williams. World Resources Institute, 1709 New York Ave. N.W., Washington, District of Columbia 20006. (800) 822-0504. 1989. Traces the technical breakthroughs associated with solar hydrogen. Assesses the new fuel's potential as a replacement for oil, compares its costs and uses with those of both traditional and synthetic fuels, and charts a path for developing solar hydrogen markets.

The World Bank and the Environment: A Progress Report, Fiscal 1991. World Bank, UNIPUB, 4611-F Assembly Dr., Lanham, Maryland 20706. (301) 459-7666 or (800) 274-4888. 1991. Describes specific environmental strategies and environmental lending in the Bank's four operational regions: Asia, Europe, the Middle East and North Africa, and Latin America and the Caribbean.

World Guide to Environmental Issues and Organizations. Peter Brackley. Longman Group Ltd., Longman House, Burnt Mill, Harlow, Essex, England CM20 2J6. (0279) 426721. 1991.

GOVERNMENTAL ORGANIZATIONS

Energy Information Administration. James Forrestal Building, 1000 Independence Ave., S.W., Washington, District of Columbia 20585. (202) 586-5830.

Energy Research Office. James Forrestal Building, 1000 Independence Ave., S.W., Washington, District of Columbia 20585. (202) 586-5430.

Office of Public Information: Federal Energy Regulatory Commission. 825 North Capitol St., N.E., Washington, District of Columbia 20426. (202) 357-8055.

Public Affairs Office. James Forrestal Building, 1000 Independence Ave., S.W., Washington, District of Columbia 20585. (202) 586-6250.

Public Affairs Office: U.S. Geological Survey. 119 National Center, 12201 Sunrise Valley Dr., Reston, Virginia 22092. (703) 648-4460.

HANDBOOKS AND MANUALS

Environmental Statistics Handbook: Europe. Allan Foster, Oksana Newman. Gale Research Inc., 835 Penobscot Bldg., Detroit, Michigan 48226-4094. (313) 961-2242. 1993.

ONLINE DATA BASES

Computerized Engineering Index–COMPENDEX. Engineering Information Inc., 345 E. 47th St., New York, New York 10017. (212) 705-7600.

EBIB. Texas A & M University, Sterling C. Evans Library, Reference Division, College Station, Texas 77843. (409) 845-5741.

Greenwire. American Political Network, 282 North Washington St., Falls Church, Virginia 22046. (703) 237-5130. 1991. Daily. Daily electronic 12-page summary of the last 24 hours of news coverage of environmental issues worldwide. Monday through Friday at 10 am EST, it can be accessed by a PC, modem and an 800 number contains issues on environmental protection, energy/natural resources, business science, 50-state news, worldwide headlines, TV monitor, daily calendar, marketplace battles, Capitol Hill, spotlight story, global issues, environment and the law, solid waste and focus interviews.

Monthly Catalog of United States Government Publications. U.S. G.P.O., Supt. of Docs., PO Box 371954, Pittsburgh, Pennsylvania 15250-7954. (202) 512-0000.

National Technical Information Service. U.S. Department of Commerce, National Technical Information Service, Office of Data Base Services, 5285 Port Royal Rd., Springfield, Virginia 22161. (703) 487-4807. Bibliographic database of government sponsored research and technical reports.

NODC Data Inventory Data Base. U.S. National Environmental Satellite, Data, and Information Service, National Oceanographic Data Center, 1825 Connecticut Ave., N.W., Suite 406, Washington, District of Columbia 20235. (202) 673-5594. Information on National Oceanographic Data Center holdings.

POWER. U.S. Department of Energy, Energy Library, MA-232.2, Washington, District of Columbia 20585. (202) 586-9534. Monographs, proceedings, and other materials related to the energy field, including conservation and environmental aspects.

PressNet Environmental Reports. Chemical Information Systems, Inc., 7215 York Rd., Baltimore, Maryland 21212. (301) 321-8440.

PERIODICALS AND NEWSLETTERS

The Amicus Journal. Natural Resources Defense Council, 40 West 20th Street, New York, New York 10011. (212) 727-2700. Quarterly. Articles on environmental affairs.

Analytical Chemistry. American Chemical Society, 1155 16th St. N.W., Washington, District of Columbia 20036. (800) 227-5558. 1929-. Bimonthly. Articles for chemists, life scientists and engineers.

Energy & Environment Alert. National Council for Environmental Balance, Inc., 4169 Westport Rd., Box 7732, Louisville, Kentucky 40207. (502) 896-8731. Quarterly. Energy environment, agriculture, chemistry, entomology, and mineral resources.

Forum for Applied Research and Public Policy. University of Tennessee, Energy, Environment and Resources Center, Knoxville, Tennessee 37996-0710. (919) 966-3561. 1986-. Quarterly. Presents a discussion of options by academic, government and corporate experts in energy, environment and economic development.

International Journal of Energy, Environment, Economics. Nova Science Publishers, Inc., 283 Commack Rd., Ste. 300, Commack, New York 11725. (516) 499-3103. 1991-. Quarterly. Aims to provide a vehicle for the multidisciplinary field of energy-environment economics between research scientists, engineers and economists. The areas covered would be technological, environmental, economic and social feasibility.

The International Journal of Global Energy Issues. Inderscience Enterprises Ltd., World Trade Center Building, 110 Avenue Louis Casai, Case Postale 306, Geneva-Airport, Switzerland (44) 908-314248. 1989-. Quarterly. Provides a forum and an authoritative source of information in the field of energy issues and related topics.

Journal of Energy, Natural Resources & Environmental Law. College of Law, University of Utah, Salt Lake City, Utah 84112. Semiannual. Legal aspects of energy development, natural resources, and environment.

Renewable Energy: An International Journal. Pergamon Microforms International, Inc., Fairview Park, Elmsford, New York 10523. (914) 592-7720. 1991-. Six issues a year. Topics include environmental protection and renewable sources of energy.

Strategic Planning for Energy and the Environment Journal. Energy Engineering, 700 Indian Trail, Lilburn, Georgia 30247. 1990-. Quarterly. Concentrates on the background, new developments and policy issues which impact corporate planning for energy and environmental issues.

World Resource Review. SUPCON International, PO Box 5275, 1 Heritage Plaza, Woodridge, Illinois 60517. (708) 910-1551. 1981-. Quarterly. Covers all phases of policy discussions and their developments, including such topics as global change, energy production and use, ecosystem impacts of development activities, environmental law, solution of transnational environmental problems, global flow of strategic industrial materials, regional, national, and local resource management, natural resources, food, agriculture and forestry.

RESEARCH CENTERS AND INSTITUTES

Lawrence Berkeley Laboratory, Chemical Biodynamics Division. One Cyclotron Road, Berkeley, California 94720. (415) 486-4355.

Resources for the Future, Inc. Energy and Natural Resources Division. 1616 P Street, N.W., Washington, District of Columbia 20036. (202) 328-5000.

Water and Energy Research Institute of the Western Pacific (*WERI*). University of Guam, UOG Station, Guam 96923. (617) 734-3132.

STATISTICS SOURCES

Statistical Record of the Environment. Arsen J. Darnay. Gale Research Inc., 835 Penobscot Bldg., Detroit, Michigan 48226-4094. (313) 961-2242. 1992.

TRADE ASSOCIATIONS AND PROFESSIONAL SOCIETIES

Environmental and Energy Study Institute. 122 C St., N.W., Suite 700, Washington, District of Columbia 20001. (202) 628-1400.

Illinois Hazardous Waste Research and Information Center. One East Hazelwood Dr., Champaign, Illinois 61820. (217) 333-8940.

National Council for Environmental Balance. 4169 Westport Rd., P.O. Box 7732, Louisville, Kentucky 40207. (502) 896-8731.

National Wood Energy Association. 777 N. Capitol St. N.W., Suite 805, Washington, District of Columbia 20002. (202) 408-0664.

U.S. Council for Energy Awareness. 1776 I St., N.W., Suite 400, Washington, District of Columbia 20006. (202) 293-0770.

ENTRAINMENT

See: AIR POLLUTION

ENTROPY

ABSTRACTING AND INDEXING SERVICES

Applied Science and Technology Index. H.W. Wilson Co., 950 University Ave., Bronx, New York 10452. (800) 367-6770. Formerly Industrial Arts Index.

Chemical Abstracts. Chemical Abstracts Service, 2540 Olentangy River Rd., PO Box 3012, Columbus, Ohio 43210. (800) 848-6533. 1907-.

General Science Index. H. W. Wilson Co., 950 University Ave., Bronx, New York 10452. 1978-. Monthly, also issued in annual cumulation. Cumulative subject index to English language periodicals in the subject fields of astronomy, botany, chemistry, earth science, environment and conservation, food and nutrition, genetics,

mathematics, medicine and health, microbiology, oceanography, physics, physiology and zoology.

Geographical Abstracts. London School of Economics, Dept. of Geography, Regency House, 34 Duke St., London, England 1966-. Continued by Geo Abstracts issued in 6 parts: Pt. A. Landforms and the quaternary; Pt. B. Biogeography and Climatology; Pt. C. Economic geography; Pt. D. Social geography and cartography; Pt. E. Sedimentology; Pt. F. Regional and community planning.

Physics Briefs. Physikalische Berichte. Physik Verlag, Pappapelallee 3, Postfach 101161, Weinheim, Germany D-6940. 1979-. Semimonthly. In English. Volumes for 1979- issued by the Deutsche Physikalische Gesellschaft and the Fachinformationszentrum Energie Physik, Mathematik in cooperation with the American Institute of Physics.

ENCYCLOPEDIAS AND DICTIONARIES

Cambridge Dictionary of Biology. Peter M. B. Walker. Cambridge University Press, 40 W. 20th St., New York, New York 10011. (212) 924-3900 or (800) 227-0247. 1989. Includes 10,000 terms in zoology, botany, biochemistry, molecular biology and genetics. Previously published under the title Chambers Biology Dictionary.

A Concise Dictionary of Biology. Elizabeth Martin, ed. Oxford University Press, 200 Madison Ave., New York, New York 10016. (212) 679-7300 or (800) 334-4249. 1990. New edition. Derived from the Concise Science Dictionary, published in 1984.

Encyclopedia of Physical Science and Technology. Robert A. Meyers, ed. Academic Press, c/o Harcourt Brace Jovanovich Inc., 6277 Sea Harbor Dr., Orlando, Florida 32887. (800) 346-8648. Dictionary of engineering, technology and physical sciences.

Encyclopedia of Physics. Rita G. Lerner and George L. Trigg. VCH Publishers, 303 NW 12th Ave., Deerfield Beach, Florida 33442-1788. (305) 428-5566. 1991. Second edition.

Van Nostrand's Scientific Encyclopedia. Glenn D. Considine, ed. Van Nostrand Reinhold, 115 5th Ave., New York, New York 10003. (212) 254-3232. 1983. Sixth edition. Includes all broad subject areas in science.

GENERAL WORKS

Entropy: Into the Greenhouse World. Jeremy Rifkin. Bantam Books, 666 Fifth Ave., New York, New York 10103. (212) 765-6500. 1989.

ONLINE DATA BASES

Chemical Abstracts-CA. Chemical Abstracts Service, 2540 Olentangy River Rd., P.O. Box 3012, Columbus, Ohio 43210. (800) 848-6533 or (614) 421-3600. Information sources include 9000 journals, patents from 27 countries, two industrial property organizations, new books, conference proceedings, and government research reports.

NBSFLUIDS. National Institute of Standards & Technology, Office of Standard Reference Data, A323 Physics Building, Gaithersburg, Maryland 20899. (301) 975-2208.

ENVIRONMENT CONDITION

ABSTRACTING AND INDEXING SERVICES

Agroforestry Abstracts. C. A. B. International, 845 North Park Ave., Tucson, Arizona 85719. (602) 621-7897 or (800) 528-4841. 1988-. Quarterly. Abstracts journal articles, reports, conferences and books. Focuses on subjects areas such as agroforestry in general; agroforestry systems; trees, animals and crops; conservation; human ecology; social and economic aspects; development, research and methodology.

Applied Ecology Abstracts Studies in Renewable Natural Resources. Information Retrieval Ltd., 1911 Jefferson Davis Highway, Arlington, Virginia 22202. 1975-. Monthly.

ASFA Aquaculture Abstracts. Cambridge Scientific Abstracts, Inc., 5161 River Rd., Bethesda, Maryland 20816. (301) 961-6750. 1984.

Biological Abstracts. BIOSIS, 2100 Arch St., Philadelphia, Pennsylvania 19103-1399. (215) 587-4800. 1927-.

Biological and Agricultural Index. H.W. Wilson Co., 950 University Ave., Bronx, New York 10452. (800) 367-6770. 1916-. Monthly.

Biotechnology Research Abstracts. Cambridge Scientific Abstracts, 5161 River Rd., Bethesda, Maryland 20816. (301) 961-6750. Monthly. Includes such broad areas as genetic intervention, biochemical genetics, and microbiological techniques.

Bulletin Signaletique: Eau et Assainissement, Pollution Atmospherique, Droit des Pollutions. Centre de Documentation, Centre National de la Recherche Scientifique, 15, quai Anatole France, Paris, France 75700. (1) 45 55 92 25. 1983-. Monthly. Indexes pollution periodicals including water, atmospheric and related pollutions.

Chemical Abstracts. Chemical Abstracts Service, 2540 Olentangy River Rd., PO Box 3012, Columbus, Ohio 43210. (800) 848-6533. 1907-.

Civil Engineering Hydraulic Abstracts. BHRA Fluid Engineering, Air Science Co., PO Box 143, Corning, New York 14830. (607) 962-5591. Monthly. Abstracts of periodicals that publish in the areas of hydraulic engineering and other related topics.

Current Advances in Ecological and Environmental Science. Pergamon Microforms International, Inc., Fairview Park, Elmsford, New York 10523. (914) 592-7720. 1989-. Monthly. Current literature searching service includingjournals, reports, abstracts, etc. This service is available online as part of the CABS database on the hosts BRS and ORBIT search service.

Ecological Abstracts. Geo Abstracts Ltd. Elsevier Applied Science, Crown House, Linton Rd., Barking, England IG 11 8JU. 1974-. Derived from over 600 leading ecological and environmental journals, plus books, conference proceedings, reports and theses.

Ecology Abstracts. Cambridge Scientific Abstracts, 5161 River Rd., Bethesda, Maryland 20816. (301) 961-6750. Monthly.

Engineering Index. The Engineering Index Inc., 345 E. 47th St., New York, New York 10017. 1962-.

General Science Index. H. W. Wilson Co., 950 University Ave., Bronx, New York 10452. 1978-. Monthly, also issued in annual cumulation. Cumulative subject index to English language periodicals in the subject fields of astronomy, botany, chemistry, earth science, environment and conservation, food and nutrition, genetics, mathematics, medicine and health, microbiology, oceanography, physics, physiology and zoology.

Geographical Abstracts. London School of Economics, Dept. of Geography, Regency House, 34 Duke St., London, England 1966-. Continued by Geo Abstracts issued in 6 parts: Pt. A. Landforms and the quaternary; Pt. B. Biogeography and Climatology; Pt. C. Economic geography; Pt. D. Social geography and cartography; Pt. E. Sedimentology; Pt. F. Regional and community planning.

Highway Research Abstracts. Transportation Research Board, National Research Council, 2101 Constitution Ave. NW., Washington, District of Columbia 20418. 1931-. Monthly. Provides information about highway and nonrail mass transit. It also deals with related environmental issues such as energy and environment, environmental design, climate, safety, human factors, and soils.

Index to Scientific Book Contents. Institute for Scientific Information, 3501 Market St., Philadelphia, Pennsylvania 19104. (800) 523-1857. 1985-. Annual. Gives contents of science books published.

Multimedia Index to Ecology. National Information Center for Educational Media, University of Southern California, Los Angeles, California 90007.

Pesticides Abstracts. U.S. Environmental Protection Agency, Office of Pesticides Programs, 345 Curtland, Atlanta, Georgia 30365. (404) 347-2864. 1981. Monthly. Formerly: Health Aspects of Pesticides Abstracts Bulletin.

Pollution Abstracts. Cambridge Scientific Abstracts, 5161 River Rd., Bethesda, Maryland 20816. (301) 961-6750. Six/year. Indexes worldwide technical literature on environmental pollution. Covers air pollution, marine and freshwater pollution, sewage and wastewater treatment, waste management, toxicology and health, noise pollution, radiation, land pollution, and environmental policies, programs, legislation, and education. Also available online.

Priority Issue Reporting Service-PIRS. Information for Public Affairs, Inc., Client Services Dept., 1900 14th St., Sacramento, California 95814.

Science Citation Index. Institute for Scientific Information, 3501 Market St., Philadelphia, Pennsylvania 19104. 1961-.

Soils and Fertilizers. C. A. B. International, 845 North Park Ave., Tucson, Arizona 85719. (602) 621-7897 or (800) 528-4841. 1937-. Monthly. Focuses on soil chemistry, soil physics, soil biology, soil fertility, soil management, soil classification, soil formation, soil conservation, land reclamation, irrigation and damage, fertilizer technology, fertilizer use, plant nutrition, plant water relations, and environmental aspects.

ALMANACS AND YEARBOOKS

Environmental Almanac. World Resources Institute. Houghton Mifflin, 1 Beacon St., Boston, Massachusetts

02108. (617) 725-5000; (800) 225-3362. 1991. Covers consumer products, energy, endangered species, food safety, global warming, solid wastes, toxics, wetlands and other related areas. Also included are the names and addresses of the chief environmental executives for all 50 states.

BIBLIOGRAPHIES

Current Contents. Agriculture, Biology and Environmental Sciences. Institute for Scientific Information, 3501 Market St., Philadelphia, Pennsylvania 19104. (800) 523-1857. 1973-. Previous title: Current Contents. Agricultural, Food & Veterinary Sciences. Gives the table of contents of periodicals in the fields of agriculture, biology, environmental and related areas.

Directory of Country Environmental Studies: An Annotated Bibliography of Environmental and Natural Resources Profiles and Assessments. World Resources Institute, 1709 New York Ave., NW, Washington, District of Columbia 20006. 1990. Concentrates on studies of developing countries. Reports on the condition and trends of the major natural resources of a country and their condition and relationship to economic development.

Directory of Published Proceedings. Interdok Corp., 173 Halstead Ave., Harrison, New York 10528. (914) 835-3506. 1990. Monthly. This is a listing of published proceedings including the series SEMTE (Science/Medicine/Engineering/Technology) and the series SSH (Social Science/Humanities).

DIRECTORIES

Directory of Environmental Organizations. Educational Communications, Box 35473, Los Angeles, California 90035. (213) 559-9160. Semiannual. Environmental organizations names, addresses, & phone numbers.

Ecological Society of America Bulletin–Directory of Members Issue. Ecological Society of America, c/o Dr. Duncan Patten, Center for Environmental Studies, Arizona State University, Tempe, Arizona 85287. (602) 965-3000.

Environmental Telephone Directory. Government Institutes, Inc., 4 Research Pl., Ste. 200, Rockville, Maryland 20850. (301) 921-2300.

ERMD Directory. Special Libraries Association, Environmental Resources Management Division, Forest Resources Lib., AQ-15, Seattle, Washington 98195. Irregular. Listing of membership, services, contact persons, and consultants in environmental areas.

The Green Index: Directory of Environmental Organisations in Britain and Ireland. Cassell PLC, Publishers Distribution Center, PO Box C831, Rutherford, New Jersey 07070. (201) 939-6064; (201) 939-6065. 1990.

New Jersey Environmental Directory. Youth Environmental Society, Box 441, Cranbury, New Jersey 08512. (609) 655-8030. Annual. Annotated listings of organizations which affect environmental issues.

ENCYCLOPEDIAS AND DICTIONARIES

Cambridge Encyclopedia of Life Sciences. A. E. Friday and David S. Ingram. Cambridge University Press, 40 W 20th St., New York, New York 10011. (212) 924-3900 or (800) 227-0247. 1985. Includes all topics under biology and ecology.

Dictionary of Environment and Development. Earthscan, 3 Endsleigh St., London, England 071-388 2117. 1991.

A Dictionary of Environmental Quotations. Barbara K. Rodes and Rice Odell. Simon and Schuster, 15 Columbus Circle, New York, New York 10023. (212) 373-7342. 1992. Collection of nearly 3000 quotations arranged by topic, such as air, noise, energy, nature, pollution, forests, oceans, and other subjects on the environment.

The Encyclopedia of Geochemistry and Environmental Sciences. Rhodes Whitmore Fairbridge. Van Nostrand Reinhold Co., 115 5th Ave., New York, New York 10003. (212) 254-3232. 1972.

Encyclopedia of Human Biology. Renato Dulbecco, ed. Academic Press, c/o Harcourt Brace Jovanovich Inc., 6277 Sea Harbor Dr., Orlando, Florida 32887. (800) 346-8648. 1991. Eight volumes.

English-Russian Dictionary of Environmental Protection: About 14,000 Terms. E.L. Milovanov. Pergamon Microforms International, Inc., Fairview Park, Elmsford, New York 10523. (914) 592-7720. 1981.

Environmental Regulatory Glossary. G. William Frick and Thomas P. Sullivan. Government Institutes, Inc., 4 Research Pl., Rockville, Maryland 20850. (301) 921-2300. 1990. Over 4,000 entries. Definitions were gathered from the Code of Federal Regulations, EPA documents, and Federal Environmental Statutes.

The Facts on File Dictionary of Environmental Science. L. Harold Stevenson and Bruce Wyman. Facts on File, Inc., 460 Park Ave. S., New York, New York 10016. (212) 683-2244. 1991.

Glossary of Geology. Robert Latimer Bates and Julia A. Jackson, eds. American Geological Institute, 4220 King St., Alexandria, Virginia 22302-1507. (703) 379-2480 or (800) 336-4764. 1987. Third edition.

Grzimek's Encyclopedia of Ecology. Bernhard Grzimek. Van Nostrand Reinhold, 115 5th Ave., New York, New York 10003. (212) 254-3232. 1976.

McGraw-Hill Encyclopedia of Environmental Science. Sybil P. Parker. McGraw-Hill Science & Engineering Books, 11 W. 19th St., New York, New York 10011. (212) 337-6010. 1980. Covers ecology, man's influence on nature, and environmental protection.

McGraw-Hill Encyclopedia of the Geological Sciences. Sybil P. Parker, ed. McGraw-Hill, 1221 Avenue of the Americas, New York, New York 10020. (212) 512-2000 or (800) 262-4729. 1988. Second edition. Published previously in the McGraw-Hill Encyclopedia of Science and Technology.

North American Reference Encyclopedia of Ecology and Pollution. William White. North American Pub. Co., 401 N. Broad St., Philadelphia, Pennsylvania 19108. (215) 238-5300. 1972.

Role of Environment Factors. R. P. Pharis, et al. Springer-Verlag, 175 5th Ave., New York, New York 10010. (212) 460-1500 or (800) 777-4643. 1985. Encyclopedia of plant physiology.

Van Nostrand's Scientific Encyclopedia. Glenn D. Considine, ed. Van Nostrand Reinhold, 115 5th Ave., New

York, New York 10003. (212) 254-3232. 1983. Sixth edition. Includes all broad subject areas in science.

GENERAL WORKS

Applied Isotope Hydrogeology: A Case Study in Northern Switzerland. F. J. Pearson, Jr., et al. Elsevier Science Publishing Co., Inc, 655 Avenue of the Americas, New York, New York 10010. (212) 989-5800. 1991. This is a case study in northern Switzerland about radioactive waste disposal in the ground. Includes bibliographical references and an index.

Atlas of the Environment. Geoffrey Lean, et al. Prentice Hall, Rte. 9W, Englewood Cliffs, New York 07632. (201) 592-2000. 1990. Guide to the major environmental issues around the world that makes good use of numerous maps and diagrams to present the increasing amount of information available in this field. Covers related subjects such as indigenous people and refugees, the education gap, natural and human induced disasters, wildlife trade, and migration routes.

Barriers to a Better Environment: What Stops Us Solving Environmental Problems?. Stephen Trudgill. Belhaven Press, 136 S. Broadway, Irvington, New York 10533. (914) 591-9111. 1990. Postulates several types of barriers that one may come across while dealing with environmental problems: technological, and economic, social, and political barriers. Suggests the importance of holistic framework for the successful development and implementation of environmental solutions.

Biogeochemistry: An Analysis of Global Change. William H. Schlesinger. Academic Press, c/o Harcourt Brace Jovanovich Inc., 6277 Sea Harbor Dr., Orlando, Florida 32887. (800) 346-8648. 1991. Examines global changes that have occurred and are occurring in our water, air, and on land, relates them to the global cycles of water, carbon, nitrogen, phosphorous, and sulfur.

Blueprint for a Green Planet: Your Practical Guide to Restoring the World's Environment. John Seymour and Herbert Giraardet. Prentice Hall, Rte. 9W, Englewood Cliffs, New Jersey 07632. (201) 592-2000; (800) 634-2863. 1987. Background information and analysis of the root causes of pollution and waste in contemporary society.

Blueprint for the Environment: A Plan for Federal Action. T. Alan, ed. Howe Brothers, Box 6394, Salt Lake City, Utah 84106. (801) 485-7409. 1989.

Chemistry, Agriculture and the Environment. Mervyn L. Richardson. Royal Society of Chemistry, Thomas Graham House, Science Park, Milton Rd., Cambridge, England CB4 4WF. 44(0)223420066. 1991. Provides an overview of the chemical pollution of the environment caused by modern agricultural practices worldwide, and describes the effects of agrochemicals used in intensive animal and crop production on the air, water, soil, plants, and animals including humans. Also available through CRC Press.

Development without Destruction: Evolving Environmental Perceptions. M. Tolba. Cassell PLC, Publishers Distribution Center, PO Box C831, Rutherford, New Jersey 07070. (201) 939-6064/5. 1982.

Domestication: The Decline of Environmental Appreciation. Helmut Hemmer. Cambridge University Press, 40 W. 20th St., New York, New York 10011. (212) 924-3900; (800) 227-0247. 1990. The books proposes the thesis that domestication must lead to reduced environmental appreciation. The origins of domesticated mammals, their scientific nomenclature, the relationships between feral mammals and their wild progenitors, and modern attempts at domestication are also covered.

Driving Forces: Motor Vehicle Trends and Their Implications for Global Warming, Energy Strategies, and Transportation. James J. MacKenzie and Michael P. Walsh. World Resources Institute, 1709 New York Ave., Washington, District of Columbia 20006. (800) 822-0504. 1990. Overview of new-vehicle fuel efficiency, reductions in air pollution emissions, and overall improvements in transportation and land-use as they relate to global warming planning. Also available through State University of New York Press.

Ecological Engineering: An Introduction to Ecotechnology. William J. Mitsch and Sven Erik Jorgensen, eds. John Wiley & Sons, Inc., 605 3rd Ave., New York, New York 10158-0012. (212) 850-6000. 1989. Presents 12 international case studies of ecological engineering. The case studies survey problems and existing methodologies indicate where methods are ecologically sound, and illustrate examples of the use of ecological engineering.

Ecotoxicology and Climate. Philippe Bordeaux, et al., eds. John Wiley & Sons, Inc., 605 3rd Ave., New York, New York 10158-0012. (212) 850-6000. 1989. Describes environmental chemistry of toxic pollutants in hot and cold climates. Includes bibliographical references and an index.

Energy and Climate Change. Lewis Publishers, 2000 Corporate Blvd., N.W., Boca Raton, Florida 33431. (407) 994-0555 or (800) 272-7737. 1990. Includes energy scenarios, cost and risk analysis, energy emissions, atmospheric chemistry, and climate effects.

Energy and the Environment. J. Dunderdale, ed. Royal Society of Chemistry, c/o CRC Press, 2000 Corporate Blvd. N.W., Boca Raton, Florida 33431-9868. (800) 272-7737. 1990. Compares the environmental impact of the various energy producing and using processes. The book covers the types and quantities of pollutants produced by these processes, looks at the interaction of these pollutants with the atmosphere, and reviews the use of renewable sources as possible alternatives.

Enhanced Biodegradation of Pesticides in the Environment. Kenneth D. Racke and Joel R. Coats, eds. American Chemical Society, 1155 16th St. N.W., Washington, District of Columbia 20036. (202) 872-4600; (800) 227-5558. 1990. Discusses pesticides in the soil, microbial ecosystems, and the effects of long term application of herbicides on the soil.

Environmental Biology. E. J. W. Barrington. John Wiley & Sons, Inc., 605 3rd Ave., New York, New York 10158-0012. (212) 850-6000. 1980. Resource and Environmental Series.

Environmental Change in Iceland: Past and Present. Judith K. Maizels and Chris Caseldine, eds. Kluwer Academic Publishers, 101 Philip Dr., Assinippi Park, Norwell, Massachusetts 02061. (617) 871-6600. 1991. Describes the glacial landforms and paleoclimatology in Iceland. Volume 7 of the Glaciology and Quaternary Geology Series.

Environmental Consequences of and Control Processes for Energy Technologies. Argonne National Laboratory. Noyes Publications, 120 Mill Rd., Park Ridge, New

Jersey 07656. (201) 391-8484. 1990. Describes energy technologies which will be in use in the United States during the next 20 years.

Environmental Degradation and Crisis in India. S. S. Negi. Indus Pub. Co. (South Asia Books), Box 502, Columbia, Missouri 65205. (314) 474-0116. 1991. Discusses environmental planning and management in the conservation of natural resources.

Environmental Hazards of War: Releasing Dangerous Forces in an Industrialized World. Arthur H. Westing. SAGE Pub., 2111 W. Hillcrest Dr., Newbury Park, California 91320. (805) 499-0721. 1990. Population living downstream from hydrologic facilities, and near or adjacent to chemical and nuclear plants, greatly increases the potential risk to civilians from collateral damage by war. This book examines such a situation.

Environmental Impacts of Coal Mining and Utilization. M. J. Chadwick, et al., eds. Pergamon Microforms International, Inc., Fairview Park, Elmsford, New York 10523. (914) 592-7720. 1987. Presents an up-to-date account of the whole coal fuel cycle and the recent developments to combat and control them.

Environmental Risk: Evaluation and Finance in Real Estate. Albert R. Wilson. Lewis Publishers, 2000 Corporate Blvd., N.W., Boca Raton, Florida 33431. (407) 994-0555 or (800) 272-7737. 1991. Deals with the ownership of hazardous materials effected property, types of environmental audits, property evaluation, and legal implications.

Envirosoft 86. P. Zanetti, ed. Computational Mechanics Inc., 25 Bridge St., Billerica, Massachusetts 01821. 1986. Environmental software part of the proceedings of the International Conference on Development and Applications of Computer Techniques to Environmental Studies, Los Angeles, 1986.

Envirosoft 88: Computer Techniques in Environmental Studies. P. Zannetti, ed. Computational Mechanics Inc., 25 Bridge St., Billerica, Massachusetts 01821. (508) 667-5841. 1988. Proceedings of the 2nd International Conference, Envirosoft 88, covering the development and application of computer techniques to environmental problems.

The Feasibility of Using Computer Graphics in Environmental Evaluations. Daniel D. McGeehan. National Technical Information Service, 5285 Port Royal Rd., Springfield, Virginia 22161. (703) 487-4650. 1981.

Federal Lands: A Guide to Planning, Management, and State Revenues. Sally K. Fairfax. Island Press, 1718 Connecticut Ave. N.W., Suite 300, Washington, District of Columbia 20009. (202) 232-7933. 1987. Comprehensive reference on the management and allocation of revenues from public lands.

Feeding Tomorrow's World. Albert Sasson. Centre for Agriculture and Rural Cooperation and UNESCO, 7 Place de Fontenoy, Paris, France 1990. Analyzes Green Revolution and biotechnological revolution and tries to answer other pressing questions through a pluridisciplinary approach to human nutrition and food production. Synthesizes the scientific, economic, socioeconomic and environmental aspects of nutrition throughout the world.

Food Contamination from Environmental Sources. J. O. Nriagu and M. S. Simmons, eds. John Wiley & Sons, Inc., 605 3rd Ave., New York, New York 10158-0012. (212)

850-6000. 1990. Discusses the accumulation and transfer of contaminants through the food chain to the consumer.

The Fragile Environment. Laurie Friday and Ronald Laskey, eds. Cambridge University Press, 40 W. 20th St., New York, New York 10011. (212) 924-3900; (800) 227-0247. 1989. The fragile environment brings together a team of distinguished authors to consider areas of urgent environmental concern.

Immunochemical Methods for Environmental Analysis. Jeanette M. Van Emon and Ralph O. Mumma, eds. American Chemical Society, 1155 16th St. N.W., Washington, District of Columbia 20036. (202) 872-4600; (800) 227-5558. 1990. Describes antibodies used as analytical tools to study environmentally important compounds. Discusses various applications in food industry, environmental analysis, and applications in agriculture.

Imperiled Planet: Restoring Our Endangered Ecosystems. Edward Goldsmith, et al. MIT Press, 55 Hayward St., Cambridge, Massachusetts 02142. (617) 253-2884; (800) 356-0343. 1990. Presentation of a wide range of ecosystems, showing how they work, the traditional forms of human use, threats and losses, causes of destruction, and preservation attempts.

Institute of Environmental Sciences' National Conference and Workshop, Environmental Stress Screening of Electronic Hardware Proceedings. The Institute of Environmental Sciences, 940 E. Northwest Highway, Mt. Prospect, Illinois 60056. (708) 255-1561. Environmental testing and environmental stress screening of electronic hardware.

Instrumental Analysis of Pollutants. C. N. Hewitt, ed. Elsevier Science Publishing Co., 655 Avenue of the Americas, New York, New York 10010. (212) 989-5800. 1991.

An Introduction to Environmental Pattern Analysis. P. J. A. Howard. Parthenon Group Inc., 120 Mill Rd., Park Ridge, New Jersey 07656. (201) 391-6796. 1991. Explains the basic mathematics of the most widely used ordination and cluster analysis methods, types of data to which they are suited and their advantages and disadvantages.

Lessons Learned in Global Environmental Governance. Peter H. Sand. World Resources Institute, 1709 New York Ave. N.W., Washington, District of Columbia 20006. (800) 822-0504. 1990. Takes stock of significant international environmental initiatives to date and highlights innovative features of transnational regimes for setting and implementing standards.

Magill's Survey of Science. Life Science Series. Frank N. Magill, ed. Salem Press, PO Box 50062, Pasadena, California 91105. 1991. Six volumes. Contents: v.1. A-Central and peripheral nervous system functions; v.2. Central metabolism regulation - eukaryotic transcriptional control; v.3. Positive and negative eukaryotic transcriptional control - mammalian hormones; v.4. Hormones and behavior - muscular contraction; v.5. Muscular contraction and relaxation - sexual reproduction in plants; v.6. Reproductive behavior and mating - X inactivation and the Lyon hypothesis.

Nature Tourism: Managing for the Environment. Tensie Whelan. Island Press, 1718 Connecticut Ave. N.W., Suite 300, Washington, District of Columbia 20009. (202) 232-7933. 1991. Provides practical advice and models for planning and developing a nature tourism industry, evaluating economic benefits and marketing nature tourism.

Pesticide Residues in Food. Food and Agriculture Organization of the United Nations, 4611-F Assembly Dr., Lanham, Maryland 20706-4391. (800) 274-4888. 1990.

Policies For Maximizing Nature Tourism's Contribution to Sustainable Development. Kreg Lindberg. World Resources Institute, 1709 New York Ave. N.W., Washington, District of Columbia 20006. (800) 822-0504. 1991. Examines how better economic management of nature tourism can promote development and conservation without degrading the natural resources on which development depends.

Promoting Environmentally Sound Economic Progress: What the North Can Do. Robert Repetto. World Resources Institute, 1709 New York Ave. N.W., Washington, District of Columbia 20006. (800) 822-0504. 1990. Spells out actions that must be taken if the world economy is going to continue to develop and yet avoid the environmental degradation that threatens to undermine living standards.

Real Estate Transactions and Environmental Risks: A Practical Guide. Donald C. Nanney. PennWell Books, PO Box 21288, Tulsa, Oklahoma 74121. (918) 831-9421; (800) 752-9764. 1990. Presents general principles used when approaching environmental issues from a real estate agent's point of view.

Signs of Hope: Working towards Our Common Future. Linda Starke. Oxford University Press, Walton St., Oxford, England 1990. Sequel to the report of the World Commission on Environment and Development Commissioned by the Centre For Our Common Future. Records the progress made in the implementation of the recommendations of Our Common Future and looks at initiatives being taken by governments, industry, scientists, non-governmental organizations and the media.

Societal Issues and Economics of Energy and the Environment. T. Nejat Veziroglu, ed. Nova Science Publishers Inc., 283 Commack Rd., Suite 300, Commack, New York 11725-3401. (516) 499-3103; (516) 499-3106. 1990. Deals with important societal issues and the economics of energy and the environment. Focuses on why the environment, as a resource, must be protected at all cost.

Solar Hydrogen: Moving Beyond Fossil Fuels. Joan M. Ogden and Robert H. Williams. World Resources Institute, 1709 New York Ave. N.W., Washington, District of Columbia 20006. (800) 822-0504. 1989. Traces the technical breakthroughs associated with solar hydrogen. Assesses the new fuel's potential as a replacement for oil, compares its costs and uses with those of both traditional and synthetic fuels, and charts a path for developing solar hydrogen markets.

The State of the Earth Atlas. Joni Seger, ed. Touchstone/Simon and Schuster, Rockefeller Center, 1230 Avenue of the Americas, New York, New York 10020. 1990. Deals with environmental issues such as air quality, urban sprawl, toxic waste, tropical forests and tourism from a socioeconomic perspective.

State of the Environment and Supplement: Environmental Indicators. UNIPUB, 4611-F Assembly Dr., Lanham, Maryland 20706. (301) 459-7666 or (800) 274-4888. 1991. Reviews the recent progress of OECD countries regarding environmental objectives by analyzing world

ecological and economic independence and the need for sustainable development.

The State of the Environment with Supplement: Environmental Indicators. A. Preliminary Set. Organization for Economic Co-Operation and Development. OECD Publications and Information Centre, 2001 L. St. NW, Suite 700, Washington, District of Columbia 20036-4095. (202) 785-6323. 1991. Provides a review of the environment today for the purpose of assessing the "progress achieved over the past two decades...the lifetime of environmental policies and institutions in most member countries."

Steady-State Economics. Herman E. Daly. Island Press, 1718 Connecticut Ave. N.W., Suite 300, Washington, District of Columbia 20009. (202) 232-7933. 1991.

Sunken Nuclear Submarines: A Threat to the Environment?. Viking Oliver Eriksen. Norwegian Univ. Pr., Oxford Univ. Pr., 200 Madison Ave., New York, New York 10016. (212) 679-7300; (800) 334-4249. 1990. Part 1 is a survey of existing submarines, based upon surmise and extrapolation from public knowledge of civilian terrestrial and nautical reactors. Part 2 describes potential accident scenarios and their potential for nuclide release, and Part 3 briefly sketches the oceanographic factors governing dispersion of radioactive nuclides.

A Technical Framework for Life-Cycle Assessment. Society of Environmental Toxicology and Chemistry and the SETAC Foundation for Environmental Education, 1101 14th St, NW, Washington, District of Columbia 20005. (202) 371-1275. 1991. Evaluates the environmental burdens associated with a product, process or activity.

Temperature and Environmental Effects on the Testis. Plenum Press, 233 Spring St., New York, New York 10013-1578. (212) 620-8000; (800) 221-9369. 1991. Role of intrinsic and extrinsic temperature alterations in testis physiology and male fertility.

Tourism Planning: An Integrated and Sustainable Development Approach. Van Nostrand Reinhold, 115 5th Ave., New York, New York 10003. (212) 254-3232. 1991. Provides guidelines and approaches for developing tourism that take environmental, socioeconomic and institutional issues into account.

Transforming Technology: An Agenda for Environmentally Sustainable Growth in the Twenty-First Century. George Heaton, et al. World Resources Institute, 1709 New York Ave. N.W., Washington, District of Columbia 20006. (800) 822-0504. 1991. Explores the extraordinarily rich potential of new technologies to resolve environmental and economic problems.

Transport and the Environment. OECD Publications and Information Center, 2001 L St., N.W., Suite 700, Washington, District of Columbia 20036. (202) 785-OECD. 1988. Comprehensive overview of the impact on the environment of road transport. Assesses the efficacy of technical changes to motor vehicles to reduce air pollution and noise and evaluates innovations in the management of the transport systems of ten large cities in OECD countries.

Transport Policy and the Environment. OECD Publications and Information Center, 2001 L St., N.W., Suite 700, Washington, District of Columbia 20036. (202) 785-OECD. 1990. Describes how the government is addressing the adverse environmental effects of transport and the challenges that lie ahead.

Troubled Skies, Troubled Waters: The Story of Acid Rain. Jon R. Loma. Viking, 375 Hudson St., New York, New York 10014. (212) 366-2000 or (800) 631-3577. 1984.

Wildlife Toxicology. Tony J. Peterle. Van Nostrand Reinhold, 115 5th Ave., New York, New York 10003. (212) 354-3232. 1991. Presents an historical overview of the toxicology problem and summarizes the principal laws, testing protocols, and roles of leading U.S. federal agencies, especially EPA. Examines state and local issues, monitoring programs, and contains an unique section on the regulation of toxic substances overseas.

Yellowstone Vegetation, Consequences of Environment and History in a Natural Setting. Don G. Despain. Roberts Rinhart Pub., PO Box 666, Niwot, Colorado 80544. (303) 652-2921. 1990. Explores Yellowstone's vegetation types in their habitats and communities, in their origins and distribution, and in their succession after devastation by fire, wind, and insects.

GOVERNMENTAL ORGANIZATIONS

Agricultural Research Service. Washington, District of Columbia 20250.

Bureau of Economic Analysis: Environmental Economics Division. 1404 K St., N.W., Washington, District of Columbia 20230. (202) 523-0687.

Federal Highway Administration: Right-of-Way and Environment. 400 7th St., S.W., Washington, District of Columbia 20590. (202) 366-0342.

Office of Public Affairs: National Oceanic and Atmospheric Administration. 14th and Constitution Avenues, N.W., Washington, District of Columbia 20230. (202) 377-2985.

Office of Public Information: Federal Energy Regulatory Commission. 825 North Capitol St., N.E., Washington, District of Columbia 20426. (202) 357-8055.

Public Affairs Office: Environmental Research Laboratories. 3100 Marine St., Boulder, Colorado 80303. (303) 497-6286.

U.S. Environmental Protection Agency: Assistant Administrator for Policy, Planning and Evaluation. 401 M St., S.W., Washington, District of Columbia 20460. (202) 382-4332.

U.S. Environmental Protection Agency: Assistant Administrator for Solid Waste and Emergency Response. 401 M St., S.W., Washington, District of Columbia 20460. (202) 382-4610.

U.S. Environmental Protection Agency: Office of Exploratory Research. 401 M St., S.W., Washington, District of Columbia 20460. (202) 382-5750.

U.S. Environmental Protection Agency: Office of Toxic Substances. 401 M St., S.W., Washington, District of Columbia 20460. (202) 382-3813.

HANDBOOKS AND MANUALS

Biotechnology and the Environment. J. Gibbs, et al. Stockton Press, 257 Park Ave. S, New York, New York 10010. (212) 673-4400 or (800) 221-2123. 1987. Overview of the regulatory legislation in biotechnology.

California: An Environmental Atlas and Guide. Bern Kreissman and Barbara Lekisch. Bear Klaw Press, 1100 Industrial Rd. #9, San Carlos, California 94071. (916) 753-7788. 1991. Devoted primarily to "natural features such as rivers, faultlines, habitat, and sanctuaries." An ensuing second volume will show man-made elements such as "power transmission lines, energy-generating plants, and toxic dump sites."

Environment in Key Words: A Multilingual Handbook of the Environment: English-French-German-Russian. Isaac Paenson. Pergamon Microforms International, Inc., Fairview Park, Elmsford, New York 10523. (914) 592-7720. 1990. Two volumes. Terminology in the areas of ecology, environmental protection, pollution, conservation of natural resources and related areas.

Environmental Career Guide: Job Opportunities with the Earth in Mind. Nicholas Basta. John Wiley & Sons, Inc., 605 3rd Ave., New York, New York 10158-0012. (212) 850-6000. 1991. Complete guide to the many career options in the growing environmental field. Shows how to find employers engaged in environmental activity, and how to get the job. Lists key environmental businesses–manufacturing, government agencies, engineering consulting firms, waste handling firms, and others. Lists key professional careers in environmental conservation and maps career strategies.

Guidance for the Reregistration of Pesticide Products Containing Lindane as the Active Ingredient. U.S. Environmental Protection Agency, Office of the Pesticides and Toxic Substances, 401 M St., SW, Washington, District of Columbia 20460. (202) 260-2090. 1985. The Federal Insecticide, Fungicide, Rodenticide Act directs EPA to reregister all pesticides as expeditiously as possible. The guide helps the user to carry out this task and to participate in the EPA's registration standard program. Includes extensive tabular data to the pesticides and an extensive bibliography.

Handbook of Chemical Property Estimation Methods. Warren J. Lyman, et al. McGraw-Hill Science & Engineering Books, 11 W. 19th St., New York, New York 10011. (212) 337-6010. 1982.

Handbook of Environmental Data on Organic Chemicals. Karel Verschueren. Van Nostrand Reinhold, 115 5th Ave., New York, New York 10003. (212) 254-3232. 1983. Covers individual substances as well as mixtures and preparations. The profiles include: properties, air pollution factors, water pollution factors, and biological effects.

Permaculture: A Practical Guide for a Sustainable Future. B. C. Mollison. Island Press, 1718 Connecticut Ave. N.W., Suite 300, Washington, District of Columbia 20009. (202) 232-7933. 1990.

Pesticide Handbook. Peter Hurst. Journeyman Press, 955 Massachusetts Ave., Cambridge, Massachusetts 02139. (617) 868-3305. 1990.

Pira's International Environmental Information Sources. Pira, Randalls Rd., Leatherhead, England KT22 7RU. 0372 376161. 1990. Sourcebook includes over 2,000 entries from more than 20 countries, including Australia, Finland, Germany, the United Kingdom, and the United States. Entries are from organizations, research centers, legislative and regulatory bodies, directories, online databases and periodicals. Subject areas covered are: air, noise, water and land pollution, waste control and disposal, recycling, energy recovery and nature conservation.

Your Resource Guide to Environmental Organizations. John Seredich, ed. Smiling Dolphins Press, 4 Segura, Irvine, California 92715. 1991. Includes the purposes, programs, accomplishments, volunteer opportunities, publications and membership benefits of 150 environmental organizations.

ONLINE DATA BASES

BIOSIS Previews. BIOSIS, 2100 Arch St., Philadelphia, Pennsylvania 19103-1399. (215) 587-4800. Largest and most comprehensive database of research in the life sciences. Contains citations for nearly 9000 primary research journals, monographs, reviews, symposia, preliminary reports, semi-popular journals, selected institutional reports, government reports and research communications.

Cambridge Scientific Abstracts Life Science–CSAL. Cambridge Scientific Abstracts, 5161 River Rd., Bethesda, Maryland 20816. (301) 961-6750. Provides access to the following abstracting services: "Life Sciences Collection," "Aquatic Sciences and Fisheries Abstracts," "Oceanic Abstracts," and "Pollution Abstracts."

Chemical Abstracts-CA. Chemical Abstracts Service, 2540 Olentangy River Rd., P.O. Box 3012, Columbus, Ohio 43210. (800) 848-6533 or (614) 421-3600. Information sources include 9000 journals, patents from 27 countries, two industrial property organizations, new books, conference proceedings, and government research reports.

Computerized Engineering Index–COMPENDEX. Engineering Information Inc., 345 E. 47th St., New York, New York 10017. (212) 705-7600.

Environmental Business Journal. EnviroQuest, PO Box 371769, San Diego, California 92137. (619) 295-7685. Online access.

GeoRef. American Geological Institute, 4220 King St., Alexandria, Virginia 22302. (703) 379-2480.

Monthly Catalog of United States Government Publications. U.S. G.P.O., Supt. of Docs., PO Box 371954, Pittsburgh, Pennsylvania 15250-7954. (202) 512-0000.

Multispectral Scanner and Photographic Imagery. U.S. Environmental Protection Agency, Office of Modeling and Monitoring Systems and Quality Assurance, 401 M St., S.W., Washington, District of Columbia 20460. (202) 260-2090. An index for various data tapes containing multispectral imagery from aircraft and satellites relating to sources of pollution.

National Technical Information Service. U.S. Department of Commerce, National Technical Information Service, Office of Data Base Services, 5285 Port Royal Rd., Springfield, Virginia 22161. (703) 487-4807. Bibliographic database of government sponsored research and technical reports.

SCISEARCH. Institute for Scientific Information, University City Science Center, 3501 Market St., Philadelphia, Pennsylvania 19104. (215) 386-0100.

PERIODICALS AND NEWSLETTERS

Advances in Environment, Behavior, and Design. Plenum Press, 233 Spring St., New York, New York 10013. (212) 620-8000; (800) 221-9369.

Advisor. Great Lakes Commission, 2200 North Bonisteel Blvd., Ann Arbor, Michigan 48109. (313) 665-9135. 1956-. Monthly. Concerns current developments relating to activities of the Great Lakes Commission and its eight member states. Includes environment, economy, and Great Lakes related issues.

Alaska Center for the Environment Center News. Alaska Center for the Environment, 700 H St., #4, Anchorage, Alaska 99501. (907) 274-3621. 1972-. Bimonthly. Topics deal with environmental education and Alaskan issues, land use, hazardous waste, etc.

Alternatives. University of Waterloo, Environmental Studies, ES1, Rm. 325, Waterloo, Ontario, Canada N2L 3G1. (519) 746-2031. 1971-. Quarterly. Perspectives on society, technology, and the environment. Professional and academic level information and theory.

American Environmental Laboratory. American Laboratory Postcard Deck, 30 Controls Dr., Box 870, Shelton, Connecticut 06484-0870. (203) 926-9310. 1989-. Bimonthly. Articles dealing with the collection and analysis of environmental samples, the development of instruments and the laboratories that use them.

The Amicus Journal. Natural Resources Defense Council, 40 West 20th Street, New York, New York 10011. (212) 727-2700. Quarterly. Articles on environmental affairs.

ANJEC Report. Association of New Jersey Environmental Commissions, Box 157, Mendham, New Jersey 07945. (201) 539-7547. 1969-. Quarterly. Informs environmental commissioners and interested citizens about environmental issues, laws and regulations, particularly those that effect New Jersey.

Archives of Environmental Contamination. Springer-Verlag, 175 5th Ave., New York, New York 10010. (212) 460-1500. 1972-. Bimonthly.

Areas of Concern. Areas of Concern, Box 47, Bryn Mawr, Pennsylvania 19010. (215) 525-1129. 1971-. Monthly. Consumer, environmental and public affairs.

Bulletin of Environmental Contamination and Toxicology. Springer-Verlag, 175 5th Ave., New York, New York 10010. (212) 460-1500; (800) 777-4643. 1966-. Frequency varies. Disseminates advances and discoveries in the areas of soil, air and food contamination and pollution.

CA Selects: Environment Pollution. Chemical Abstracts Services, 2540 Olentangy River Rd., Box 3012, Columbus, Ohio 43210. (800) 848-6533. 1978-. Biweekly. Abstracts on pollution of the environment by gaseous, liquid, solid and radioactive wastes.

Canadian Environmental Mediation Newsletter. Conflict Management Resources, Osgoode Law School, York Univ., 4700 Keely St., Downsview, Ontario, Canada M3J 2R5. 1986-. Quarterly. Deals with environmental resources development dispute resolution.

Chemical Engineering Progress Magazine. American Institute of Chemical Engineers, 345 E. 47th St., New York, New York 10017. (212) 705-7338. Monthly. Articles covering environmental controls for chemical and petrochemical industrial plants.

The Compendium Newsletter. Educational Communications, Box 351419, Los Angeles, California 90035. (310) 559-9160. 1972-. Bimonthly. Comprehensive summary of environmental issues and activities. National emphasis lists radio and TV shows produced by Educational Communications.

Conservationist. New York State Dept. of Environmental Conservation, 50 Wolf Rd., Albany, New York 12233. (518) 457-6668. 1946-. Bimonthly. Covers all aspects of conservation and outdoor recreation, scientific information, art and history of New York State.

Critical Reviews in Environmental Control. CRC Press, 2000 Corporate Blvd. N.W., Boca Raton, Florida 33431. (800) 272-7737. Four times a year. Articles on environment and environmental control.

Earth Science. American Geological Institute, 4220 King Street, Alexandria, Virginia 22302. (703) 379-2480. Quarterly. Covers geological issues.

Earth Words. Friends of the Earth, 701-251 Laurier Ave., W., Ottawa, Ontario, Canada K1P 5J6. (613) 230-3352. Quarterly. Informs citizens and decision makers about environmental issues.

Earthwatch Oregon. Oregon Environmental Council, 2637 S. W. Water Ave., Portland, Oregon 97201. 1969-. Monthly.

Ecological Engineering. The Journal of Ecotechnology. Elsevier Science Publishing Co., 655 Avenue of the Americas, New York, New York 10010. (212) 984-5800. 1992. Quarterly. Specific areas of coverage will include habitat reconstruction, rehabilitation, biomanipulation, restoration and conservation.

Ecological Society of America Bulletin. Ecological Society of America, Center of Environmental Studies, Arizona State University, Tempe, Arizona 85287-1201. (602) 965-3000. Quarterly. Study of living things in relation to their environments.

Ecology Center Newsletter. Ecology Center, 2530 San Pablo Ave., Berkeley, California 94702. (510) 548-2220. Monthly. Politics and philosophy of the environment.

Ecology Reports. Ecology Center of Ann Arbor, 417 Detroit St., Ann Arbor, Michigan 48104. (313) 461-3186. Ten times a year. Environmental awareness through local and state research and education.

Environment. Heldref Publications, 4000 Albemarle Street, NW, Washington, District of Columbia 20016. (202) 362-6445. Ten a year. Covers science and science policy.

Environment Research. Academic Press, c/o Harcourt Brace Jovanovich Inc., 6277 Sea Harbor Dr., Orlando, Florida 32887. (800) 346-8648. Bimonthly. Journal of environmental medicine and sciences.

Environmental Action. Environmental Action Foundation, 6930 Carroll Ave., Ste. 600, Takoma Park, Maryland 20912. (301) 891-1100. Bimonthly. Impact of humans and industry on the environment.

Environmental Affairs. Boston College Law School, 885 Centre St., Newton Center, Massachusetts 02159. Quarterly. Legal issues regarding the environment.

Environmental Business Journal. EnviroQuest, PO Box 371769, San Diego, California 92137. (619) 295-7685. Monthly. Products relating to environmental protection.

Environmental Communicator. North American Association for Environmental Education, P.O. Box 400, Troy, Ohio 45373. (513) 339-6835. Bimonthly. Information on environmental topics and teaching methods.

Environmental Defense Fund Letter. Environmental Defense Fund, 257 Park Avenue South, New York, New York 10010. (212) 505-2100. 1971-. Bimonthly. Environmental issues of concern.

Environmental Education Report and Newsletter. American Society for Environmental Education, P.O. Box 800, White River, New Hampshire 03755. (603) 448-6697. Quarterly. Contemporary environmental issues.

Environmental Professional. National Association of Environmental Professionals, P.O. Box 15210, Alexandria, Virginia 22309-0210. (703) 660-2364. Quarterly. Covers effective impact assessment, regulation, and environmental protection.

Environmental Protection Agency Journal. U.S. Environmental Protection Agency MC A-107, 401 M St. SW, Washington, District of Columbia 20460. (202) 260-2090. Bimonthly. Addresses environmental matters of interest.

Environmental Protection Agency Regulatory Agenda. U.S. Environmental Protection Agency, 401 M St. SW, Washington, District of Columbia 20460. (202) 260-2090. Twice a year. Information on the status of proposed regulations.

Environmental Review. American Society for Environmental History, Department of History, University of Oregon, Corvallis, Oregon 97331. Quarterly. Covers human ecology as seen through history and the humanities.

Environmental Science and Technology. American Chemical Society, 1155 16th St. N.W., Washington, District of Columbia 20036. (800) 227-5558. 1967-. Monthly. Contains research articles on various aspects of environmental chemistry, interpretative articles by invited experts and commentary on the scientific aspects of environmental management.

Environmental Spectrum. New Jersey Cooperative Extension Service, Cook College, Rutgers University, P.O. Box 231, New Brunswick, New Jersey 08903. 1968-. Bimonthly. Emphasis on air/noise pollution, energy, water and other environmental topics.

Environmental Studies & Practice: An Educational Resource and Forum. Yale School of Forestry and Environmental Studies, 205 Prospect St., New Haven, Connecticut 06511. (203) 432-5132. 1991. Bimonthly. Subject matters range widely from air pollution to wildlife biology. Each issue contains a selection of recent publications, from all subject areas of environmental and natural resources management.

Environments. Faculty of Environmental Studies, University of Waterloo, Waterloo, Ontario, Canada N2L 3G1. (519) 885-1211. Three times a year. People in man-made and natural environments.

Forum for Applied Research and Public Policy. University of Tennessee, Energy, Environment and Resources Center, Knoxville, Tennessee 37996-0710. (919) 966-3561. 1986-. Quarterly. Presents a discussion of options by academic, government and corporate experts in energy, environment and economic development.

Friend O'Wildlife. North Carolina Wildlife Federation,Inc., Box 10626, Raleigh, North Carolina 27605. (919) 833-1923. 1959-. Bimonthly. Covers North Carolina wildlife conservation and related hunting, fishing and boating activities and other environmental issues.

Green Marketing Report. Business Publishers, Inc., 951 Pershing Dr., Silver Spring, Maryland 20910-4464. (301) 587-6300. 1990-. Monthly. Looks at the steps taken by product manufacturers and advertisers to address consumers' environmental concerns as well as government examination of (and challenges to) some companies' environmental claims. Also available online.

The Highlands Voice. West Virginia Highlands, 1205 Quarrier St. Lower Level, Charleston, West Virginia 25301. Monthly. Covers environmental topics in the Appalachian area of West Virginia.

Housatonic Current. Housatonic Valley Assn., Box 28, Cornwall Bridge, Connecticut 06754. (203) 672-6678. Quarterly. Environmental programs and land planning throughout the Housatonic River Watershed.

The Hudson Valley Green Times. Hudson Valley Grass Roots Energy and Environment Network, 30 E. Market St., P.O. Box 208, Red Hook, New York 12571. (914) 758-4484. Bimonthly. Energy and environment news with emphasis on Hudson Valley.

INFORM Reports. INFORM Inc., 381 Park Ave., So., New York, New York 10016. (212) 689-4040. Quarterly. INFORM is a nonprofit environmental research & education organization for the preservation and conservation of natural resources and public health.

International Journal of Energy, Environment, Economics. Nova Science Publishers, Inc., 283 Commack Rd., Ste. 300, Commack, New York 11725. (516) 499-3103. 1991-. Quarterly. Aims to provide a vehicle for the multidisciplinary field of energy-environment economics between research scientists, engineers and economists. The areas covered would be technological, environmental, economic and social feasibility.

The International Journal of Global Energy Issues. Inderscience Enterprises Ltd., World Trade Center Building, 110 Avenue Louis Casai, Case Postale 306, Geneva-Airport, Switzerland (44) 908-314248. 1989-. Quarterly. Provides a forum and an authoritative source of information in the field of energy issues and related topics.

Journal of Applied Meteorology. American Meteorological Society, 45 Beacon Street, Boston, Massachusetts 02108. (617) 227-2425. Monthly. Articles on the relationship between weather and environment.

Journal of Applied Physiology. American Physiology Society, 9650 Rockville Pike, Bethesda, Maryland 20814-3991. Monthly. Covers physiological aspects of exercise, adaption, respiration, and exertion.

The Journal of Environmental Education. Heldref Publications, 4000 Albemarle Street, NW, Washington, District of Columbia 20016. (202) 362-6445. Quarterly. Teaching methods, case studies, and evaluations of new research.

Journal of Environmental Sciences. Institute of Environmental Sciences, 940 East Northwest Highway, Mt. Prospect, Illinois 60656. (312) 255-1561. Bimonthly. Covers research, controlling and teaching of environmental sciences.

Journal of Environmental Systems. Baywood Pub. Co., Inc., 26 Austin Ave., Box 337, Amityville, New York 11701. (516) 691-1270. Quarterly. Analysis, design, and management of our environment.

Keep Tahoe Blue. League to Save Lake Tahoe, 2197 Lake Tahoe Rd., Box 10110, S. Lake Tahoe, California 95731. (916) 541-5388. Quarterly. Environmental balance, recreational opportunities, and scenic beauty of Tahoe Basin.

Montana Outdoors. Montana Dept. of Fish, Wildlife, and Parks, 930 Custer Ave., W., Helena, Montana 59620. (406) 444-2474. Bimonthly. Wildlife and fisheries management.

NAEP Newsletter. National Association of Environmental Professionals, P.O. Box 15210, Alexandria, Virginia 22309-0210. (703) 660-2364. Monthly. Covers environmental planning, management, review and research.

Nation's Business. Chamber of Commerce of the United States, 1615 H Street , NW, Washington, District of Columbia 20062. (202) 659-6000. Monthly.

Natural Resources Journal. University of New Mexico School of Law, 1117 Stanford, NE, Albuquerque, New Mexico 87131. (505) 277-4820. Quarterly. Study of natural and environmental research.

Nature and Resources. Elsevier Science Publishing Co., 655 Avenue of the Americas, New York, New York 10010. (212) 989-5800. 1965-. Quarterly. Provides in-depth reviews of contemporary environmental issues from an international perspective.

Network News. World Environment Center, 419 Park Avenue South, Suite 1403, New York, New York 10016. (212) 683-4700. Quarterly. Covers international environmental issues.

New Environmental Bulletin. New Environment Association, 270 Fenway Dr., Syracuse, New York 13224. (315) 446-8009. Monthly. New pattern of living.

Northwest Environmental Journal. Institute for Environmental Studies, University of Washington, Seattle, Washington 98195. (206) 543-1812. Biannual. Covers environmental issues in the Northwest states and Canada.

Pollution Engineering. Cahners Publishing Co., 249 W. 17th St., New York, New York 10011. (212) 645-0067. 1969-. Monthly.

Rodale's Environmental Action Bulletin. Rodale Press, 33 E. Minor St., Emmaus, Pennsylvania 18098. (215) 967-5171. 1970-. Semimonthly.

RESEARCH CENTERS AND INSTITUTES

Center for Advanced Decision Support for Water and Environmental Systems. University of Colorado-Boulder, 2945 Center Green Court, Suite B, Boulder, Colorado 80301. (303) 492-3972.

Center for Environmental Sciences. University of Colorado-Denver, P.O. Box 173364, Denver, Colorado 80217-3364. (303) 5556-4277.

Center for Technology, Environment, and Development. Clark University, 16 Claremont St., Worcester, Massachusetts 01610. (508) 751-4606.

Coolidge Center for Environmental Leadership. 1675 Massachusetts Ave., Suite 4, Cambridge, Massachusetts 02138. (617) 864-5085.

Institute for Environmental Management. Western Illinois University, College of Arts and Sciences, Macomb, Illinois 61455. (309) 298-1266.

National Coastal Resources Research and Development Institute. Hatfield Marine Science Center, 2030 South Marine Science Dr., Newport, Oregon 97365. (503) 867-0131.

Pennsylvania State University, Environmental Resources Research Institute. 100 Land and Water Resource Building, University Park, Pennsylvania 16802. (814) 863-0291.

Precambrian Paleobiology Research Group. Geology Building, Center for the Study of Evolution and Origin of Life, University of California, Los Angeles, Los Angeles, California 90024. (213) 825-1170.

Rutgers University, Center for Agricultural Molecular Biology. Cook College, P.O. Box 231, New Brunswick, New Jersey 08903. (908) 932-8165.

Saskatchewan Fisheries Laboratory. Saskatchewan Parks and Renewable Resources, 112 Research Drive, Saskatoon, Saskatchewan, Canada S7K 2H6. (306) 933-5776.

School for Field Studies. 16 Broadway, Box S, Beverly, Massachusetts 01915. (508) 927-7777.

Southwest Research and Information Center. P.O. Box 4524, Albuquerque, New Mexico 87106. (505) 262-1862.

State University of New York at Plattsburg, Center for Earth and Environmental Science. Plattsburg, New York 12901. (518) 564-2028.

Tufts University. Curtis Hall, 474 Boston Avenue, Medford, Massachusetts 02155. (617) 381-3486.

University of Georgia, Institute of Ecology. 103 Ecology Building, Athens, Georgia 30602. (404) 542-2968.

University of Maine, Environmental Studies Center. Coburn Hall #11, Orono, Maine 04469. (207) 581-1490.

University of Maryland, Center for Environmental and Estuarine Studies. Center Operations, Horn Point, P.O.Box 775, Cambridge, Maryland 21613. (410) 228-9250.

University of Massachusetts, Environmental Institute. Blaisdell House, Amherst, Massachusetts 01003-0040. (413) 545-2842.

University of Missouri-Rolla, Environmental Research Center. Rolla, Missouri 65401. (314) 341-4485.

University of Nevada-Las Vegas, Environmental Research Center. 4505 S. Maryland Parkway, Las Vegas, Nevada 89154-4009. (702) 739-3382.

University of Nevada-Las Vegas, Marjorie Barrick Museum of Natural History. Las Vegas, Nevada 89154. (702) 739-3381.

University of Texas at El Paso, Laboratory for Environmental Biology. Department of Biology, EL Paso, Texas 79968. (915) 747-5164.

University of Washington, Institute for Environmental Studies. Engineering Annex FM-12, Seattle, Washington 98195. (206) 543-1812.

University of Wisconsin-Madison, Biotron. 2115 Observatory Drive, Madison, Wisconsin 53706. (608) 262-4900.

University of Wisconsin-Madison, Environmental Remote Sensing Center. 1225 West Dayton Street, Madison, Wisconsin 53706. (608) 263-3251.

University of Wisconsin-Madison, Institute for Environmental Studies. 1017 WARF Office Building, 610 Walnut Street, Madison, Wisconsin 53705. (608) 262-5957.

Wisconsin Department of Natural Resources, Bureau of Research. Box 7921, Madison, Wisconsin 53707. (608) 266-8170.

World Resources Institute. 1709 New York Ave., N.W., Washington, District of Columbia 20006. (202) 638-6300.

STATISTICS SOURCES

The State of the Environment. OECD Publications and Information Center, 2001 L St., N.W., Suite 700, Washington, District of Columbia 20036. (202) 785-6323. 1991.

TRADE ASSOCIATIONS AND PROFESSIONAL SOCIETIES

American Society of Civil Engineers. 345 East 47th St., New York, New York 10017. (212) 705-7496.

Association of New Jersey Environmental Commissions. PO Box 157, 300 Mendham Rd., Mendham, New Jersey 07945. (201) 539-7547.

Better World Society. 1100 17th St., NW, Suite 502, Washington, District of Columbia 20036. (202) 331-3770. International non-profit membership organization that attempts to increase individual awareness of global issues related to the sustainability of life on earth.

Center for Environmental Information, Inc. 99 Court St., Rochester, New York 14604. (716) 546-3796.

Conservation Foundation. 1250 24th St., N.W., Washington, District of Columbia 20037. (202) 293-4800. The World Wildlife Fund absorbed the Conservation Foundation in 1990.

Ecological Society of America. Arizona State University, Center for Environmental Studies, Tempe, Arizona 85287. (602) 965-3000.

Environmental Defense Fund. 257 Park Ave., S., New York, New York 10010. (212) 505-2100. Non-profit organization that was established more than 20 years ago. Its goals are to protect the earth's environment by providing lasting solutions to global environmental problems.

Environmental Industry Council. 1825 K St., N.W., Suite 210, Washington, District of Columbia 20006. (202) 331-7706.

Environmental Media Association. 10536 Culver Blvd., Culver City, California 90232. (213) 559-9334.

Environmental Mutagen Society. 1600 Wilson Blvd., Suite 905, Arlington, Virginia 22209. (703) 525-1191.

Environmental Task Force. 6930 Carroll Ave., 6th Floor, Takoma Park, Maryland 20912. (202) 745-4870.

Human Environment Center. 1001 Connecticut Ave., N.W., Ste. 827, Washington, District of Columbia 20003. (202) 331-8387.

INFORM. 381 Park Avenue S., New York, New York 10016. (212) 689-4040.

Institute for Environmental Auditing. PO Box 23686, L'Enfant Plaza Station, Washington, District of Columbia 20026-3686. (703) 818-1000.

Institute of Environmental Sciences. 940 E. Northwest Hwy., Mount Prospect, Illinois 60056. (708) 255-1561.

National Association of Environmental Professionals. PO Box 15210, Alexandria, Virginia 22309-0210. (703) 660-2364.

National Environmental Development Association. 1440 New York Ave., N.W., Suite 300, Washington, District of Columbia 20005. (202) 638-1230.

The Public Environment Center. 1 Milligan Pl., New York, New York 10011. (212) 691-4877.

Public Interest Research Group. 215 Pennsylvania Ave. S.E., Washington, District of Columbia 20003. (202) 546-9707.

Rene Dubos Center for Human Environments. 100 E. 85th St., New York, New York 10028. (212) 249-7745.

Safari Club International. 4800 W. Gates Pass Rd., Tucson, Arizona 85745. (602) 620-1220.

Scientists' Institute for Public Information. 355 Lexington Ave., New York, New York 10017. (212) 661-9110.

Threshold, International Center for Environmental Renewal. Drawer CU, Bisbee, Arizona 85603. (602) 432-7353.

United Nations Environment Programme. DC2-0803 United Nations, New York, New York 10017. (212) 963-8093.

ENVIRONMENTAL AUDIT

ABSTRACTING AND INDEXING SERVICES

Applied Science and Technology Index. H.W. Wilson Co., 950 University Ave., Bronx, New York 10452. (800) 367-6770. Formerly Industrial Arts Index.

Environment Abstracts. Bowker A & I Publishing, 121 Chanlon Rd., New Providence, New Jersey 07974. (908) 464-6800. 1974-.

Environment Index. Environment Information Center, Index Research Department, 124 E. 39th St., New York, New York 10016. 1971-. Annual.

Environmental Information Connection–EIC. Planning Information Program, Dept. of Urban and Regional Planning, University of Illinois, 1003 West Nevada, Urbana, Illinois 61801. (217) 333-1369. Also available online.

Environmental Periodicals Bibliography. Environmental Studies Institute, International Academy at Santa Barbara, 800 Garden St., Suite D, Santa Barbara, California 93101. (805) 965-5010. Also available online.

Index to Scientific Book Contents. Institute for Scientific Information, 3501 Market St., Philadelphia, Pennsylvania 19104. (800) 523-1857. 1985-. Annual. Gives contents of science books published.

BIBLIOGRAPHIES

EPA Publications Bibliography. U.S. Environmental Protection Agency, Library Systems Branch, 401 M St., SW, Washington, District of Columbia 20460. (202) 260-2090. Quarterly.

ENCYCLOPEDIAS AND DICTIONARIES

McGraw-Hill Encyclopedia of Environmental Science. Sybil P. Parker. McGraw-Hill Science & Engineering Books, 11 W. 19th St., New York, New York 10011. (212) 337-6010. 1980. Covers ecology, man's influence on nature, and environmental protection.

Van Nostrand's Scientific Encyclopedia. Glenn D. Considine, ed. Van Nostrand Reinhold, 115 5th Ave., New York, New York 10003. (212) 254-3232. 1983. Sixth edition. Includes all broad subject areas in science.

GENERAL WORKS

Air Pollution Control. Howard E. Hesketh. Technomic Publishing Co., 851 New Holland Ave., Box 3535, Lancaster, Pennsylvania 17604. (717) 291-5609. 1991. Presents both theory and application data. Provides a background relevant to behavior theories and control techniques for capturing gaseous and particulate air pollutants.

Environmental Audits. Government Institutes Inc., 4 Research Place, #200, Rockville, Maryland 20850. (301) 921-2300. 6th edition. Contains guidance for conducting and managing environmental audit.

ONLINE DATA BASES

Enviro/Energyline Abstracts Plus. R. R. Bowker Co., 121 Chanlon Rd., New Providence, New Jersey 07974. (908) 464-6800.

Environmental Periodicals Bibliography. National Information Services Corp., Ste. 6, Wyman Towers, 3100 St. Paul St., Baltimore, Maryland 21218. (410)243-0797. Online version of abstract of same name.

Monthly Catalog of United States Government Publications. U.S. G.P.O., Supt. of Docs., PO Box 371954, Pittsburgh, Pennsylvania 15250-7954. (202) 512-0000.

National Technical Information Service. U.S. Department of Commerce, National Technical Information Service, Office of Data Base Services, 5285 Port Royal Rd., Springfield, Virginia 22161. (703) 487-4807. Bibliographic database of government sponsored research and technical reports.

PERIODICALS AND NEWSLETTERS

Association of Environmental and Resource Economists Newsletter. Association of Environmental and Resource Economists, 1616 P St. NW, Washington, District of Columbia 20036. (202) 328-5000. Semiannual.

Environmental Auditor: Compliance-Risk Assessment-Resource Management. Springer-Verlag, 175 5th Ave., New York, New York 10010. (212) 460-1500. Quarterly.

TRADE ASSOCIATIONS AND PROFESSIONAL SOCIETIES

Association of Environmental and Resource Economists. 1616 P St., N.W., Washington, District of Columbia 20036. (202) 328-5000.

ENVIRONMENTAL CHEMISTRY

ABSTRACTING AND INDEXING SERVICES

Applied Science and Technology Index. H.W. Wilson Co., 950 University Ave., Bronx, New York 10452. (800) 367-6770. Formerly Industrial Arts Index.

Biological and Agricultural Index. H.W. Wilson Co., 950 University Ave., Bronx, New York 10452. (800) 367-6770. 1916-. Monthly.

Biology Digest. Data Courier, Plexus Pub Inc., 143 Old Marlton Pike, Medford, New Jersey 08055. 1974-. Monthly. Abstracts biology periodicals.

Bulletin Signaletique: Eau et Assainissement, Pollution Atmospherique, Droit des Pollutions. Centre de Documentation, Centre National de la Recherche Scientifique, 15, quai Anatole France, Paris, France 75700. (1) 45 55 92 25. 1983-. Monthly. Indexes pollution periodicals including water, atmospheric and related pollutions.

Chemical Abstracts. Chemical Abstracts Service, 2540 Olentangy River Rd., PO Box 3012, Columbus, Ohio 43210. (800) 848-6533. 1907-.

Current Advances in Ecological and Environmental Science. Pergamon Microforms International, Inc., Fairview Park, Elmsford, New York 10523. (914) 592-7720. 1989-. Monthly. Current literature searching service including journals, reports, abstracts, etc. This service is available online as part of the CABS database on the hosts BRS and ORBIT search service.

Ecological Abstracts. Geo Abstracts Ltd. Elsevier Applied Science, Crown House, Linton Rd., Barking, England IG 11 8JU. 1974-. Derived from over 600 leading ecological and environmental journals, plus books, conference proceedings, reports and theses.

ERDA Research Abstracts. U.S. ERDA Technical Information Center, Box 62, Oak Ridge, Tennessee 37830.

General Science Index. H. W. Wilson Co., 950 University Ave., Bronx, New York 10452. 1978-. Monthly, also issued in annual cumulation. Cumulative subject index to English language periodicals in the subject fields of astronomy, botany, chemistry, earth science, environment and conservation, food and nutrition, genetics, mathematics, medicine and health, microbiology, oceanography, physics, physiology and zoology.

Geographical Abstracts. London School of Economics, Dept. of Geography, Regency House, 34 Duke St., London, England 1966-. Continued by Geo Abstracts issued in 6 parts: Pt. A. Landforms and the quaternary; Pt. B. Biogeography and Climatology; Pt. C. Economic geography; Pt. D. Social geography and cartography; Pt. E. Sedimentology; Pt. F. Regional and community planning.

Index to Scientific Book Contents. Institute for Scientific Information, 3501 Market St., Philadelphia, Pennsylvania 19104. (800) 523-1857. 1985-. Annual. Gives contents of science books published.

Mineralogical Abstracts. Mineralogical Society, 41 Queen's Gate, London, England SW7 5HR. 71 5847916. Quarterly. Abstracts of journal articles, conferences, technical reports and specialized books in the areas of minerals, clay minerals, economic minerals, ore deposits, environmental studies, experimental mineralogy, gemstones, geochemistry, petrology, lunar and planetary studies and other related areas in mineralogy.

ALMANACS AND YEARBOOKS

Environmental Chemistry. Royal Society of Chemistry, Burlington House, Piccadilly, London, England W1V 0BN. 71 4378656. Biennial. A review of recent literature concerning the organic chemistry of environments.

BIBLIOGRAPHIES

Chemical Spills: A Bibliography. Vance Bibliographies, PO Box 229, 112 N. Charter St., Monticello, Illinois 61856. (217) 762-3831. Looks at hazardous substances and environmental chemistry.

Current Contents. Agriculture, Biology and Environmental Sciences. Institute for Scientific Information, 3501 Market St., Philadelphia, Pennsylvania 19104. (800) 523-1857. 1973-. Previous title: Current Contents. Agricultural, Food & Veterinary Sciences. Gives the table of contents of periodicals in the fields of agriculture, biology, environmental and related areas.

Directory of Published Proceedings. Interdok Corp., 173 Halstead Ave., Harrison, New York 10528. (914) 835-3506. 1990. Monthly. This is a listing of published proceedings including the series SEMTE (Science/Medicine/Engineering/Technology) and the series SSH (Social Science/Humanities).

DIRECTORIES

Chem Sources–International. Directories Publishing Co., Box 1824, Clemson, South Carolina 29633. (803) 646-7840.

Chemcyclopedia. American Chemical Society, 1155 16th St. N.W., Washington, District of Columbia 20036. (800) 227-5558.

Chemical Guide to the United States. Noyes Publications, 120 Mill Rd., Park Ridge, New Jersey 07656. (201) 391-8484.

Chemical Week–Financial Survey of the 300 Largest Companies in the U.S. Chemical Process Industries Issue. 816 7th Ave., New York, New York 10019. (212) 586-3430. Annual.

Chemical Wholesalers Directory. American Business Directories, Inc., 5711 S. 86th Circle, Omaha, Nebraska 68127. (402) 593-4600.

Chemicals Directory. Kevin R. Fitzgerald. Cahners Publishing Co., 249 W. 17th St., New York, New York 10011. (212) 645-0067. 1991. Covers manufacturers and suppliers of chemicals and raw materials, containers and packaging, transportation services and storage facilities, and environmental services companies.

ENCYCLOPEDIAS AND DICTIONARIES

Chem Sources–USA. Chemical Sources International Inc., PO Box 1884, Ormond Beach, Florida 32175-1884.

Annual. Includes chemical nomenclature of some 130,000 chemicals of all classifications, trade name index, classified/trade name, company directory, and company index. Also includes paid advertising.

The Encyclopedia of Geochemistry and Environmental Sciences. Rhodes Whitmore Fairbridge. Van Nostrand Reinhold Co., 115 5th Ave., New York, New York 10003. (212) 254-3232. 1972.

Encyclopedia of Physical Science and Technology. Robert A. Meyers, ed. Academic Press, c/o Harcourt Brace Jovanovich Inc., 6277 Sea Harbor Dr., Orlando, Florida 32887. (800) 346-8648. Dictionary of engineering, technology and physical sciences.

Glossary of Geology. Robert Latimer Bates and Julia A. Jackson, eds. American Geological Institute, 4220 King St., Alexandria, Virginia 22302-1507. (703) 379-2480 or (800) 336-4764. 1987. Third edition.

Grzimek's Encyclopedia of Ecology. Bernhard Grzimek. Van Nostrand Reinhold, 115 5th Ave., New York, New York 10003. (212) 254-3232. 1976.

Kirk-Othmer Encyclopedia of Chemical Technology. J. I. Kroschwitz, ed. John Wiley & Sons, Inc., 605 3rd Ave., New York, New York 10158-0012. (212) 850-6000. 1992-. All articles in the new edition have been rewritten and updated adding new subjects such as biotechnology, computer topics, analytical techniques and instrumentation, environmental concerns, fuels and energy, inorganic and solid state chemistry; composite materials and material science in general, and pharmaceuticals. Also available online.

McGraw-Hill Encyclopedia of Environmental Science. Sybil P. Parker. McGraw-Hill Science & Engineering Books, 11 W. 19th St., New York, New York 10011. (212) 337-6010. 1980. Covers ecology, man's influence on nature, and environmental protection.

McGraw-Hill Encyclopedia of Science and Technology. McGraw-Hill, 1221 Avenue of the Americas, New York, New York 10020. (212) 512-2000 or (800) 262-4729. 1992. Seventh edition. Issued in multiple volumes including index. Includes all science and technology broad subject areas.

McGraw-Hill Encyclopedia of the Geological Sciences. Sybil P. Parker, ed. McGraw-Hill, 1221 Avenue of the Americas, New York, New York 10020. (212) 512-2000 or (800) 262-4729. 1988. Second edition. Published previously in the McGraw-Hill Encyclopedia of Science and Technology.

North American Reference Encyclopedia of Ecology and Pollution. William White. North American Pub. Co., 401 N. Broad St., Philadelphia, Pennsylvania 19108. (215) 238-5300. 1972.

Ullmanns Encyclopedia of Industrial Chemistry. Hans Jurgen Arpe and Wolfgang Gerhartz, eds. VCH Publishers, 303 NW 12th Ave., Deerfield Beach, Florida 33442-1788. (305) 428-5566. 1990. Designed to keep up with the broad spectrum of chemical technology. Thirty-six volumes of the encyclopedia have been divided into two sets: the 28 A volumes contain alphabetically arranged articles on chemicals, product groups, processes and technological concepts; and the 8 B volumes are compendia of basic knowledge in industrial chemistry.

Van Nostrand's Scientific Encyclopedia. Glenn D. Considine, ed. Van Nostrand Reinhold, 115 5th Ave., New York, New York 10003. (212) 254-3232. 1983. Sixth edition. Includes all broad subject areas in science.

GENERAL WORKS

Biogeochemistry: An Analysis of Global Change. William H. Schlesinger. Academic Press, c/o Harcourt Brace Jovanovich Inc., 6277 Sea Harbor Dr., Orlando, Florida 32887. (800) 346-8648. 1991. Examines global changes that have occurred and are occurring in our water, air, and on land, relates them to the global cycles of water, carbon, nitrogen, phosphorous, and sulfur.

Black Carbon in the Environment. John Wiley and Sons, 605 Third Ave., New York, New York 10158-0012. (212) 850-6000. Environmental chemistry and environmental aspects of soot.

Compilation of EPA's Sampling and Analysis Methods. William Mueller, et al. Lewis Publishers, 2000 Corporate Blvd., N.W., Boca Raton, Florida 33431. (407) 994-0555 or (800) 272-7737. 1991. Aids with rapid searching of sampling and analytical method summaries. More than 650 method/analytical summaries from the database are included in this volume.

Diversity of Environmental Biogeochemistry. J. Berthelin, ed. Elsevier Science Publishing Co., 655 Avenue of the Americas, New York, New York 10010. (212) 989-5800. 1991.

Ecological Physical Chemistry. C. Rossi, ed. Elsevier Science Publishing Co., 655 Avenue of the Americas, New York, New York 10010. (212) 989-5800. 1991. Proceedings of a workshop held in Sienna, Italy, November 1990. Papers deal mostly with physical and environmental chemistry.

Environmental Chemistry. Stanley E. Manahan. Lewis Publishers, 2000 Corporate Blvd., N.W., Boca Raton, Florida 33431. (407) 994-0555 or (800) 272-7737. 1991. Fifth edition. Deals with environmental chemistry and chemical hazards.

Environmental Chemistry and Toxicology of Aluminum. Timothy E. Lewis. Lewis Publishers, 2000 Corporate Blvd., N.W., Boca Raton, Florida 33431. (407) 994-0555 or (800) 272-7737. 1989. Examines the sources, fate, transport, and health effects of aluminum in aquatic and terrestrial environments. Also includes the latest advances in the study of aluminum in the environment; toxicity research–aquatic and terrestrial biota; neurotoxicity and possible links to Alzheimer's disease; different forms of aluminum in soils and soil water; coordination chemistry; specification and analytical methods.

Environmental Chemistry of Herbicides. Raj Grover and Alan J. Cessna. CRC Press, 2000 Corporate Blvd. N.W., Boca Raton, Florida 33431. (800) 272-7737. 1990. Vol. 1: Adsorption and bioavailability. Mass flow and dispersion, herbicides in surface waters. Evaporation from soils and crops. Dissipation from soil. Transformations in soil. Vol. 2: Dissipation of transformations in water and sediment. Nature, transport, and fate of airborne residues, absorption and transport in plants. Transformations in biosphere. Bioaccumulation and food chain accumulation. Photochemical transformations. Bound residues. Predictability and environmental chemistry.

Environmental Inorganic Chemistry. Pergamon Microforms International, Inc., Fairview Park, Elmsford, New York 10523. (914) 592-7720. Environmentally important physiochemical properties of inorganic chemicals.

Environmental Problem Solving Using Gas and Liquid Chromatography. Elsevier Science Publishing Co., 655 Avenue of the Americas, New York, New York 10010. (212) 984-5800. Covers environmental chemistry and chromatographic analysis.

Facets of Modern Biogeochemistry. V. Ittekkott, et al. Springer-Verlag, 175 5th Ave., New York, New York 10010. (212) 460-1500; (800) 777-4643. 1990. Deals with the geochemistry of marine sediments and related areas.

Introductory Chemistry for the Environmental Sciences. S. J. de Mora, et al. Cambridge University Press, 40 W. 20th St., New York, New York 10011. (212) 924-3900; (800) 227-0247. 1991.

Multimedia Environmental Models: The Fugacity Approach. Donald Mackay. Lewis Publishers, 2000 Corporate Blvd., N.W., Boca Raton, Florida 33431. (407) 994-0555 or (800) 272-7737. 1991. Discusses basic concepts, environmental chemicals and their properties, and the nature of the environmental media.

Reviews of Environmental Contamination and Toxicology: v. 120. George W. Ware, ed. Springer-Verlag, 175 5th Ave., New York, New York 10010. (212) 460-1500; (800) 777-4643. 1991. Covers organochlorine pesticides and polychlorinated biphenyls in human adipose tissue, pesticide residues in foods imported into the U.S., and selected trace elements and the use of biomonitors in subtropical and tropical marine ecosystems.

HANDBOOKS AND MANUALS

CRC Handbook of Radiation Chemistry. Yoneho Tabata, ed. CRC Press, 2000 Corporate Blvd. N.W., Boca Raton, Florida 33431. (800) 272-7737. 1991. Covers broad fields from basic to applied in radiation chemistry and its related fields.

The Environmental Chemistry of Aluminum. Garrison Sposito. CRC Press, 2000 Corporate Blvd. N.W., Boca Raton, Florida 33431. (800) 272-7737. 1989. Environmental aspects of aluminum content in water, soil and acid deposition.

Handbook of Air Pollution Analysis. Roy M. Harrison. Chapman & Hall, 29 W. 35th St., New York, New York 10001-2291. (212) 244-3336. 1986. Topics in environmental chemistry and measurement of air pollution.

The Handbook of Environmental Chemistry. O. Hutzinger. Springer-Verlag, 175 5th Ave., New York, New York 10010. (212) 460-1500. Irregular. Distribution and equilibria between environmental compartments, pathways, thermodynamics and kinetics.

Reactions and Processes. P.B. Barraclough. Springer-Verlag, 175 5th Ave., New York, New York 10010. (212) 460-1500. 1988. Covers natural environment and the biological cycles, reaction and processes, anthropogenic compounds, air and water pollution.

Synthetic Organic Chemicals. U.S. G.P.O., Washington, District of Columbia 20401. (202) 512-0000. 1967. An annual publication on production and sales in the U.S. for all synthetic organic chemicals produced commercially. About 800 chemicals and 800 manufacturers are included in the USITC surveys, but because of confidentiality requirements only parts of the data are published. U.S. Tariff Commission acts under the provisions of Section 332 of the Tariff Act of 1930, as amended.

Tables of Physical and Chemical Constants and Some Mathematical Functions. G. W. C. Kaye, et al. Longman Group Ltd., Longman House, Burnt Mill, Harlow, England CM20 2J6. 0279 426721. 1988. Fifteenth edition. Includes tables on mechanical properties, density, elasticity, viscosity, surface tension, temperature and heat. Also covers radiation, optics, chemistry, electrochemistry, astrophysics, and chemical thermodynamics.

ONLINE DATA BASES

Beilstein Online. Beilstein Institute, Varrentrappstrasse 40-42, 6000 Frankfurt am Main 90, Germany 49 (69) 79171.

Chemical Abstracts-CA. Chemical Abstracts Service, 2540 Olentangy River Rd., P.O. Box 3012, Columbus, Ohio 43210. (800) 848-6533 or (614) 421-3600. Information sources include 9000 journals, patents from 27 countries, two industrial property organizations, new books, conference proceedings, and government research reports.

Chemical Exposure. Science Applications International Corp., Health & Environmental Information, P.O. Box 2501, Oak Ridge, Tennessee 37831. (615) 482-9031. Database of chemicals that have been identified in both human tissues and body fluids and in feral and food animals. Contains reference to journal articles, conferences, and reports. Covers the whole fields of information related to human and animal exposure to food, air, and water contaminants and pharmaceuticals. Its records include information on chemical properties, formulas, tissues measured, analytical method used, demographics and more. Available on DIALOG.

Chemical Hazard Response Information System–CHRIS. U.S. Coast Guard. Office of Research and Development, 2100 2d St., NW., Rm. 5410 C, Washington, District of Columbia 20593. (202) 783-3238. Contains information needed to respond to emergencies that occur during the transport of hazardous chemicals, as well as information that can help prevent emergency situations. Each of the approximately 1,300 records include information on physical and chemical properties, health and fire hazards, labeling, chemical reactivity, hazard classification and water pollution. Available on CIS and on Microdex's TOMES Plus series.

Chemical Week. Chemical Week Associates, 816 7th Ave., New York, New York 10019. (212) 586-3430. Online version of periodical of the same name.

CHEMLINE. National Library of Medicine, Toxicology Information Program, 8600 Rockville Pike, Bethesda, Maryland 20894. (800) 638-8480.

CHEMTRAN. ChemShare Corporation, P.O. Box 1885, Houston, Texas 77251. (713) 627-8945.

CJACS: Chemical Journals of the American Chemical Society. American Chemical Society, 1155 16th St. N.W., Washington, District of Columbia 20036. (800) 227-5558.

CJAOAC: Chemical Journals of the Association of Official Analytical Chemists. Association of Official Analytical Chemists, 2200 Wilson Blvd., Suite 400-P, Arlington, Virginia 22201-3301. (703) 522-3032.

CJELSEVIER. Elsevier Science Publishing Co., Excerpta Medica, Molemverf 1, 1014 AG Amsterdam, Netherlands 31 (20) 5803507.

CRDS. Orbit Search Service, 8000 Westpark Dr., Suite 400, McLean, Virginia 22102. (800) 456-7248.

Current Contents Search. Institute for Scientific Information, 3501 Market St., Philadelphia, Pennsylvania 19104. (800) 523-1857.

Environmental Bibliography. Environmental Studies Institute, International Academy at Santa Barbara, 800 Garden St., Ste. D, Santa Barbara, California 93101. (805) 965-5010. International periodical literature dealing with environmental topics such as air pollution, water treatment, energy conservation, noise abatement, soil mechanics, wildlife preservation, and chemical wastes.

Environmental Fate Databases. Syracuse Research Cooperation, Merrill Lane, Syracuse, New York 13210. (312) 426-3200. Environmental fate of chemicals.

Fine Chemical Database. Chemron, Inc., 3038 Orchard Hill, San Antonio, Texas 78230-3057. (512) 493-2247.

GeoRef. American Geological Institute, 4220 King St., Alexandria, Virginia 22302. (703) 379-2480.

Gmelin Formula Index. Gmelin Institut fuer Anorganische Chemie der Max-Planck- Gellschaft zur Foerderung der Wissenschaften, Varrentrappstrasse 40-42, Frankfurt, Germany D-6000. 49 (69) 7917-577.

HODOC: Handbook of Data on Organic Compounds. CRC Press, 2000 Corporate Blvd. N.W., Boca Raton, Florida 33431. (800) 727-7737.

KEMI-INFO. Danish National Institute of Occupational Health, Produktregestret, Lerso Parkalle 105, Copenhagen 0, Denmark 45 (31) 299711.

Kirk-Othmer Encyclopedia of Chemical Technology. John Wiley & Sons, Inc., 605 3rd Ave., 5th Floor, New York, New York 10158. (212) 850-6000. Online version of the publication of the same name.

Monthly Catalog of United States Government Publications. U.S. G.P.O., Supt. of Docs., PO Box 371954, Pittsburgh, Pennsylvania 15250-7954. (202) 512-0000.

National Technical Information Service. U.S. Department of Commerce, National Technical Information Service, Office of Data Base Services, 5285 Port Royal Rd., Springfield, Virginia 22161. (703) 487-4807. Bibliographic database of government sponsored research and technical reports.

POLYMAT. Deutsches Kunststoff-Institut, Schlossgartenstrasse 6, D-6100 Darmstadt, Germany 49 (6151) 162106.

REPRORISK System. Micromedex, Inc., 600 Grant St., Denver, Colorado 80203. (800) 525-9083 or (303) 831-1400. Reproductive risks to females and males caused by drugs, chemicals, and physical and environmental agents. Includes the Teratogen Information System (TERIS), which deals with the teratogenicity of over 700 drugs and environmental agents that affect a fetus. One of the additional modules under development is the REPRO-TEXT database, containing a ranking system for reproductive hazards and the general toxicity of over 600 chemicals, emphasizing chronic occupational exposures.

SCISEARCH. Institute for Scientific Information, University City Science Center, 3501 Market St., Philadelphia, Pennsylvania 19104. (215) 386-0100.

PERIODICALS AND NEWSLETTERS

Analytical Biochemistry. Academic Press, 111 Fifth Ave., New York, New York 10003. (800) 346-8648. Covers biological and chemical topics relating to the environment.

Chemical Week. Chemical Week Associates, 816 7th Ave., New York, New York 10019. (212) 586-3430. Online version of the periodical of the same name.

Chemoecology. Thieme Medical Publishers, 381 Park Ave. S., New York, New York 10016. (212) 683-5088. Quarterly. Topics in environmental chemistry.

Environmental Geochemistry and Health. Society for Environmental Geochemistry and Health, c/o Willard R. Chappell, University of Colorado, Denver, Center for Environmental Sciences, Campus Box 136, Denver, Colorado 80204. (303) 556-3460. Quarterly.

Environmental Toxicology and Chemistry. Society of Environmental Toxicology and Chemistry. Pergamon Microforms International, Inc., Fairview Park, Elmsford, New York 10523. (914) 592-7720. 1981-. Monthly. Contains information on environmental toxicology, and chemistry, including the application of science to hazard assessment.

Journal of Chemical Ecology. Plenum Press, 233 Spring St., New York, New York 10013-1578. (212) 620-8000. Monthly. Articles on the origin, function, and significance of natural chemicals.

Synthetic Organic Chemical Manufacturers Association Newsletter. Synthetic Organic Chemical Manufacturers Association, 1330 Connecticut Avenue, NW, Washington, District of Columbia 20036. (202) 659-0060. Biweekly. Covers trade, environmental and safety issues.

Toxicological and Environmental Chemistry. Gordon and Breach Science Publishers, Inc., 270 8th Ave., New York, New York 10011. (212) 206-8900. Quarterly.

RESEARCH CENTERS AND INSTITUTES

University of New Haven, Institute of Analytical and Environmental Chemistry. 300 Orange Avenue, West Haven, Connecticut 06516. (203) 932-7171.

TRADE ASSOCIATIONS AND PROFESSIONAL SOCIETIES

The Acrylonitrile Group. c/o Joseph E. Hadley Jr., 1815 H St., N.W., Suite 1000, Washington, District of Columbia 20006. (202) 296-6300.

Center for Chemical Process Safety. c/o American Institute of Chemical Engineers, 345 E. 47th St., 12th Floor, New York, New York 10017. (212) 705-7319.

Chemical Communications Association. c/o Fleishman-Hilliard, Inc., 40 W. 57th St., New York, New York 10019. (212) 265-9150.

Chemical Manufacturers Association. 2501 M St., N.W., Washington, District of Columbia 20037. (202) 887-1100.

Chemical Referral Center. c/o Chemical Manufacturers Association, 2501 M St., N.W., Washington, District of Columbia 20037. (202) 887-1100.

Chemical Specialties Manufacturers Association. 1913 I St., N.W., Washington, District of Columbia 20006. (202) 872-8110.

Council of Chemical Association Executives. c/o CMA, 2501 M St., N.W., Washington, District of Columbia 20037. (202) 887-1265.

Industrial Chemical Research Association. 1811 Monroe St., Dearborn, Michigan 48124. (313) 563-0360.

Industrial Specialty Chemical Association. c/o Sigmund Domanski, 1520 Locust St., 5th Floor, Philadelphia, Pennsylvania 19102. (215) 546-9608.

National Institute for Chemical Studies. 2300 MacCorkle Ave., S.E., Charleston, West Virginia 25304. (304) 346-6264.

Society for Environmental Geochemistry and Health. c/o Wilard R. Chappell, University of Colorado, Denver Center for Environmental Sciences, P.O. Box 136, Denver, Colorado 80217-3364. (303) 556-3460.

Synthetic Organic Chemical Manufacturers Association. 1330 Connecticut Ave., N.W., Suite 300, Washington, District of Columbia 20036. (202) 659-0060.

ENVIRONMENTAL COST

ABSTRACTING AND INDEXING SERVICES

Applied Science and Technology Index. H.W. Wilson Co., 950 University Ave., Bronx, New York 10452. (800) 367-6770. Formerly Industrial Arts Index.

Biological Abstracts. BIOSIS, 2100 Arch St., Philadelphia, Pennsylvania 19103-1399. (215) 587-4800. 1927-.

Environment Abstracts. Bowker A & I Publishing, 121 Chanlon Rd., New Providence, New Jersey 07974. (908) 464-6800. 1974-.

Environment Index. Environment Information Center, Index Research Department, 124 E. 39th St., New York, New York 10016. 1971-. Annual.

Environmental Information Connection–EIC. Planning Information Program, Dept. of Urban and Regional Planning, University of Illinois, 1003 West Nevada, Urbana, Illinois 61801. (217) 333-1369. Also available online.

Environmental Periodicals Bibliography. Environmental Studies Institute, International Academy at Santa Barbara, 800 Garden St., Suite D, Santa Barbara, California 93101. (805) 965-5010. Also available online.

General Science Index. H. W. Wilson Co., 950 University Ave., Bronx, New York 10452. 1978-. Monthly, also issued in annual cumulation. Cumulative subject index to English language periodicals in the subject fields of astronomy, botany, chemistry, earth science, environment and conservation, food and nutrition, genetics, mathematics, medicine and health, microbiology, oceanography, physics, physiology and zoology.

Index to Scientific Book Contents. Institute for Scientific Information, 3501 Market St., Philadelphia, Pennsylvania 19104. (800) 523-1857. 1985-. Annual. Gives contents of science books published.

Science Citation Index. Institute for Scientific Information, 3501 Market St., Philadelphia, Pennsylvania 19104. 1961-.

BIBLIOGRAPHIES

EPA Publications Bibliography. U.S. Environmental Protection Agency, Library Systems Branch, 401 M St., SW, Washington, District of Columbia 20460. (202) 260-2090. Quarterly.

ENCYCLOPEDIAS AND DICTIONARIES

Compendium of Hazardous Chemicals in Schools and Colleges. Forum for Scientific Excellence. J. B. Lippincott, 227 E. Washington Sq., Philadelphia, Pennsylvania 19105. (215) 238-4200; (800) 982-4377. 1990. Encyclopedia of more than 950 hazardous chemicals found in academic institutions. Contains all the data necessary for identifying these chemicals and their hazardous effects.

McGraw-Hill Encyclopedia of Environmental Science. Sybil P. Parker. McGraw-Hill Science & Engineering Books, 11 W. 19th St., New York, New York 10011. (212) 337-6010. 1980. Covers ecology, man's influence on nature, and environmental protection.

GENERAL WORKS

Chemical Ecotoxicology. Jaakko Paasivirta. Lewis Publishers, 200 Corporate Blvd. NW, Boca Raton, Florida 33431. (407) 994-0555 or (800)272-7737. 1991. Presents an in-depth discussion of risk assessment, chemical cycles, structure-activity relationships, organohalogens, oil residues, mercury, sampling and analysis of trace chemicals, and emissions from the forest industry. Outlines the chemical basis for applied research in environmental protection and provides important data regarding the fate and effects of various chemicals on wildlife.

Chemicals in the Environment. Selper, 33 Westville Grange, Westbury Road, Ealing, London, England W5 2LJ. Cites environmental chemistry and chemical and technical aspects of environmental pollutants.

Ecotoxicology and Climate. Philippe Bordeaux, et al., eds. John Wiley & Sons, Inc., 605 3rd Ave., New York, New York 10158-0012. (212) 850-6000. 1989. Describes environmental chemistry of toxic pollutants in hot and cold climates. Includes bibliographical references and an index.

Environmental Chemistry. Stanley E. Manahan. Lewis Publishers, 2000 Corporate Blvd., N.W., Boca Raton, Florida 33431. (407) 994-0555 or (800) 272-7737. 1991. Fifth edition. Deals with environmental chemistry and chemical hazards.

Environmental Chemistry: Australian Perspective. Greg Laidler. Longman Cheshire, South Melbourne, Australia 1991.

Hazard Assessment of Chemicals. Academic Press, c/o Harcourt Brace Jovanovich Inc., 6277 Sea Harbor Dr., Orlando, Florida 32887. (800) 346-8648. 1981-. Annually. Presents comprehensive authoritative reviews of new and significant developments in the area of hazard assessment of chemicals or chemical classes.

Human Investment and Resource Use: A New Research Orientation at the Environment/Economics Interface. Michael Young and Natarajan Ishwaran, eds. UNESCO, 7, place de Fontenoy, Paris, France F-75700. (331) 45 68 40 67. 1989. Explores the issue of the environment/economics interface, parcularly the effect of the level and nature of human investments in determining the manner in which natural resources are utilized.

Liquid Chromatography/Mass Spectrometry: Applications in Agricultural, Pharmaceutical and Environmental Chemistry. Mark A. Brown, ed. American Chemical Society, 1155 16th St. N.W., Washington, District of Columbia 20036. (202) 872-4600; (800) 227-5558. 1990. Review of the development of LC/MS techniques for enhancing structural information for high-performance LC/MS.

The Tradeoff Between Cost and Risk in Hazardous Waste Management. Kenneth S. Sewall. Garland Publishers, 136 Madison Ave., New York, New York 10016. (212) 686-7492 or (800) 627-6273. 1990. Management and risk assessment of hazardous waste sites.

HANDBOOKS AND MANUALS

Concise Manual of Chemical and Environmental Safety in Schools and Colleges. Forum for Scientific Excellence. J. B. Lippincott, 227 E. Washington Sq., Philadelphia, Pennsylvania 19105. (215) 238-4200; (800) 982-4377. 1991.

Guidance for the Reregistration of Pesticide Products Containing Lindane as the Active Ingredient. U.S. Environmental Protection Agency, Office of the Pesticides and Toxic Substances, 401 M St., SW, Washington, District of Columbia 20460. (202) 260-2090. 1985. The Federal Insecticide, Fungicide, Rodenticide Act directs EPA to reregister all pesticides as expeditiously as possible. The guide helps the user to carry out this task and to participate in the EPA's registration standard program. Includes extensive tabular data to the pesticides and an extensive bibliography.

Handbook of Chemical Property Estimation Methods. Warren J. Lyman, et al. McGraw-Hill Science & Engineering Books, 11 W. 19th St., New York, New York 10011. (212) 337-6010. 1982.

Pira's International Environmental Information Sources. Pira, Randalls Rd., Leatherhead, England KT22 7RU. 0372 376161. 1990. Sourcebook includes over 2,000 entries from more than 20 countries, including Australia, Finland, Germany, the United Kingdom, and the United States. Entries are from organizations, research centers, legislative and regulatory bodies, directories, online databases and periodicals. Subject areas covered are: air, noise, water and land pollution, waste control and disposal, recycling, energy recovery and nature conservation.

ONLINE DATA BASES

BIOSIS Previews. BIOSIS, 2100 Arch St., Philadelphia, Pennsylvania 19103-1399. (215) 587-4800. Largest and most comprehensive database of research in the life sciences. Contains citations for nearly 9000 primary research journals, monographs, reviews, symposia, preliminary reports, semi-popular journals, selected institutional reports, government reports and research communications.

Enviro/Energyline Abstracts Plus. R. R. Bowker Co., 121 Chanlon Rd., New Providence, New Jersey 07974. (908) 464-6800.

Environmental Periodicals Bibliography. National Information Services Corp., Ste. 6, Wyman Towers, 3100 St. Paul St., Baltimore, Maryland 21218. (410)243-0797. Online version of abstract of same name.

Monthly Catalog of United States Government Publications. U.S. G.P.O., Supt. of Docs., PO Box 371954, Pittsburgh, Pennsylvania 15250-7954. (202) 512-0000.

National Technical Information Service. U.S. Department of Commerce, National Technical Information Service, Office of Data Base Services, 5285 Port Royal Rd., Springfield, Virginia 22161. (703) 487-4807. Bibliographic database of government sponsored research and technical reports.

ENVIRONMENTAL EDUCATION

See: EDUCATION, ENVIRONMENTAL

ENVIRONMENTAL ENGINEERING

See also: ENVIRONMENTAL IMPACT ASSESSMENT; ENVIRONMENTAL POLICY; ENVIRONMENTAL PROTECTION; HEALTH, ENVIRONMENTAL; POLLUTION

ABSTRACTING AND INDEXING SERVICES

Applied Science and Technology Index. H.W. Wilson Co., 950 University Ave., Bronx, New York 10452. (800) 367-6770. Formerly Industrial Arts Index.

Aqualine Abstracts. Water Research Centre. c/o Pergamon Microforms International, Inc., Fairview Park, Elmsford, New York 10523. (914) 592-7720. 1927-. Contains some 8,000 records annually on water and wastewater technology. Covers all aspects of water, wastewater, associated engineering services and the aquatic environment. Over 600 periodicals, as well as books, reports and conference proceedings and other publications from water related institutions worldwide are scanned. Also available online.

Ecological Abstracts. Geo Abstracts Ltd. Elsevier Applied Science, Crown House, Linton Rd., Barking, England IG 11 8JU. 1974-. Derived from over 600 leading ecological and environmental journals, plus books, conference proceedings, reports and theses.

Ecology Abstracts. Cambridge Scientific Abstracts, 5161 River Rd., Bethesda, Maryland 20816. (301) 961-6750. Monthly.

Engineering Index. The Engineering Index Inc., 345 E. 47th St., New York, New York 10017. 1962-.

ERDA Research Abstracts. U.S. ERDA Technical Information Center, Box 62, Oak Ridge, Tennessee 37830.

Index to Scientific Book Contents. Institute for Scientific Information, 3501 Market St., Philadelphia, Pennsylvania 19104. (800) 523-1857. 1985-. Annual. Gives contents of science books published.

Mineralogical Abstracts. Mineralogical Society, 41 Queen's Gate, London, England SW7 5HR. 71 5847916. Quarterly. Abstracts of journal articles, conferences, technical reports and specialized books in the areas of minerals, clay minerals, economic minerals, ore deposits, environmental studies, experimental mineralogy, gemstones, geochemistry, petrology, lunar and planetary studies and other related areas in mineralogy.

Physics Briefs. Physikalische Berichte. Physik Verlag, Pappapelallee 3, Postfach 101161, Weinheim, Germany

D-6940. 1979-. Semimonthly. In English. Volumes for 1979- issued by the Deutsche Physikalische Gesellschaft and the Fachinformationszentrum Energie Physik, Mathematik in cooperation with the American Institute of Physics.

ALMANACS AND YEARBOOKS

Environmental Almanac. World Resources Institute. Houghton Mifflin, 1 Beacon St., Boston, Massachusetts 02108. (617) 725-5000; (800) 225-3362. 1991. Covers consumer products, energy, endangered species, food safety, global warming, solid wastes, toxics, wetlands and other related areas. Also included are the names and addresses of the chief environmental executives for all 50 states.

BIBLIOGRAPHIES

Bibliography of the Computer in Environmental Design. Kaiman Lee. Environmental Design and Research Center, 26799 Elena Rd., Los Altos Hills, California 94022. 1973.

Current Contents. Agriculture, Biology and Environmental Sciences. Institute for Scientific Information, 3501 Market St., Philadelphia, Pennsylvania 19104. (800) 523-1857. 1973-. Previous title: Current Contents. Agricultural, Food & Veterinary Sciences. Gives the table of contents of periodicals in the fields of agriculture, biology, environmental and related areas.

Directory of Published Proceedings. Interdok Corp., 173 Halstead Ave., Harrison, New York 10528. (914) 835-3506. 1990. Monthly. This is a listing of published proceedings including the series SEMTE (Science/Medicine/Engineering/Technology) and the series SSH (Social Science/Humanities).

Environmental Engineering. Mary A. Vance. Vance Bibliographies, PO Box 229, 112 N. Charter St., Monticello, Illinois 61856. (217) 762-3831. 1983.

Environmental Planning: A Guide to Information Sources. Michael J. Meshenberg. Gale Research Co., 835 Penobscot Bldg., Detroit, Michigan 48226-4094. (313) 961-2242. 1976. Focuses on environmental engineering and planning. Part of the series Man and the Environment Information Guide Series, v.3.

List of Publications of the U.S. Army Engineer Waterways Experiment Station. U.S. Army Corps of Engineers, Waterways Experiment Station, PO Box 631, Vicksburg, Mississippi 39180. (601) 634-3774. Annual. Covers hydraulic and environmental engineering, coastal engineering, soil mechanics, concrete, and pavements.

Publications. Argonne National Laboratory. Energy and Environmental Systems Division. National Technical Information Service, 5285 Port Royal Rd., Springfield, Virginia 22161. (703) 487-4650. Annual. Covers topics in environmental engineering.

DIRECTORIES

Consultant Directory. American Academy of Environmental Engineers, 132 Holiday Ct., #100, Annapolis, Maryland 21401. (301) 266-3311. 1985-. Annually.

Directory of Behavior and Environmental Design. Research and Design Institute, Providence, Rhode Island

Includes experts in human ecology and environmental engineering.

Environmental Industries Marketplace. Karen Napoleone Meech. Gale Research Inc., 835 Penobscot Bldg., Detroit, 48226-4904. (313) 961-2242. 1992.

Green Earth Resource Guide: A Comprehensive Guide About Environmentally Friendly Services and Products Books, Clean Air... Cheryl Gorder. Blue Bird Pub., 1713 East Broadway #306, Tempe, Arizona 85282. (602) 968-4088; (800) 654-1993. 1991. Book emphasizes positive steps we can take to help planets. Consists of two parts. Part one profiles people or businesses that are environmentally-friendly and are actively involved with projects and products; part two has resources listings of things concerned with environmental problems. Includes a company index with addresses and phone numbers.

Register of Environmental Engineering Graduate Programs. W. R. Knocke and G. L. Amy. Association of Environmental Engineering Professors, c/o Prof. Bruce Rittman, University of Illinois, 3221 Newmark CE Laboratory, 208 N. Romine, Urbana, Illinois 61801. (217) 333-6964. 1989. Two volumes. Catalog of environmental engineering graduate programs in the United States and Canada. Includes a brief description of the program, university, tuition and fees, support mechanisms, and geographical location.

Who's Who in Environmental Engineering. American Academy of Environmental Engineers, 132 Holiday Court, Suite 206, Annapolis, Maryland 21401. (301) 266-3311. 1980. Annual. Directory of environmental engineers who are certified by the academy.

World Directory of Environmental Organizations. Thaddeus C. Trzyna, ed. California Institute of Public Affairs, PO Box 10, Claremont, California 91711. (714) 624-5212. 1989. 3rd ed. Handbook of organizations and programs concerned with protecting the environment and managing natural resources. It covers national and international organizations, both governmental and nongovernmental, in all parts of the world.

World Environment Directory. Business Publishers, Inc., PO Box 1067, Silver Spring, Maryland 20910. (301) 587-6300. 1974-. Annually. Gives vital information on developing environmental legislation, regulations and business opportunities.

ENCYCLOPEDIAS AND DICTIONARIES

Dictionary of Environmental Engineering and Related Sciences: English-Spanish, Spanish-English. Jose T. Villate. Ediciones Universal, 3090 SW 8th St., Miami, Florida 33135. (305) 642-3355. 1979.

Dictionary of Environmental Protection Technology: In Four Languages, English, German, French, Russian. Egon Seidel. Elsevier Science Publishing Co., 655 Avenue of the Americas, New York, New York 10010. (212) 984-5800. 1988.

Dictionary of Environmental Science and Technology. Andrew Porteous. John Wiley & Sons, Inc., 605 3rd Ave., New York, New York 10158-0012. (212) 850-6000. 1992.

Encyclopedia of Environmental Control Technology. Paul N. Cheremisinoff, ed. Gulf Publishing Co., Book Division, PO Box 2608, Houston, Texas 77252. (713) 529-4301 or (800) 231-6275. 1992. Volume 1: Thermal

Treatment of Hazardous Wastes; volume 2: Air Pollution Control; volume 3: Wastewater Treatment Technology; volume 4: Hazardous Waste Containment and Treatment; volumes 5 through 8 in progress. Provides in-depth coverage of specialized topics related to environmental and industrial pollution control problems and state-of-the-art information on technology and research as well as projections of future trends in the field.

Encyclopedia of Environmental Science and Engineering. J.R. Pfafflin. Gordon and Breach Science Publishers, Inc., 270 8th Ave., New York, New York 10011. (212) 206-8900. 1992.

Encyclopedia of Physical Science and Technology. Robert A. Meyers, ed. Academic Press, c/o Harcourt Brace Jovanovich Inc., 6277 Sea Harbor Dr., Orlando, Florida 32887. (800) 346-8648. Dictionary of engineering, technology and physical sciences.

Encyclopedia of Physics. Rita G. Lerner and George L. Trigg. VCH Publishers, 303 NW 12th Ave., Deerfield Beach, Florida 33442-1788. (305) 428-5566. 1991. Second edition.

English-Russian Dictionary of Environmental Protection: About 14,000 Terms. E.L. Milovanov. Pergamon Microforms International, Inc., Fairview Park, Elmsford, New York 10523. (914) 592-7720. 1981.

Environmental Engineering Dictionary. C. C. Lee. Government Institutes, Inc., 4 Research Pl., Ste. 200, Rockville, Maryland 20850. (301) 921-2300. 1989. Defines over 6000 engineering terms relating to pollutioncontrol technologies, monitoring, risk assessment, sampling andanalysis, quality control, permitting, and environmentally-regulated engineering and science. Includes bibliographical references (p. 612-627).

The Facts on File Dictionary of Environmental Science. L. Harold Stevenson and Bruce Wyman. Facts on File, Inc., 460 Park Ave. S., New York, New York 10016. (212) 683-2244. 1991.

Glossary of Geology. Robert Latimer Bates and Julia A. Jackson, eds. American Geological Institute, 4220 King St., Alexandria, Virginia 22302-1507. (703) 379-2480 or (800) 336-4764. 1987. Third edition.

McGraw-Hill Encyclopedia of Environmental Science. Sybil P. Parker. McGraw-Hill Science & Engineering Books, 11 W. 19th St., New York, New York 10011. (212) 337-6010. 1980. Covers ecology, man's influence on nature, and environmental protection.

McGraw-Hill Encyclopedia of the Geological Sciences. Sybil P. Parker, ed. McGraw-Hill, 1221 Avenue of the Americas, New York, New York 10020. (212) 512-2000 or (800) 262-4729. 1988. Second edition. Published previously in the McGraw-Hill Encyclopedia of Science and Technology.

Van Nostrand's Scientific Encyclopedia. Glenn D. Considine, ed. Van Nostrand Reinhold, 115 5th Ave., New York, New York 10003. (212) 254-3232. 1983. Sixth edition. Includes all broad subject areas in science.

GENERAL WORKS

Aboveground Storage Tank Management: A Practical Guide. Joyce A. Rizzo and Albert D. Young. Government Institutes, Inc., 4 Research Pl., Suite 200, Rockville, Maryland 20850. (301) 921-2300. 1990. Describes how to design, build, manage, and operate above ground storage tanks in compliance with federal and state regulations.

Agricultural Engineering Conference 1990. EA Books/ Accents Pubs., 1990. Conference sponsored by the Institute of Engineers, Australia and co-sponsored by the American Society of Agricultural Engineers, held in Toowoomba, Australia, November 1990. Topics cover a wide range of agricultural engineering topics, including soil and water, processing of biological materials, structures and environment, power and machinery, systems and modeling, instrumentation and measurement, education, and international perspectives.

Chemical Processes in Wastewater Treatment. W. J. Eilbeck and G. Mattock. John Wiley & Sons, Inc., 605 3rd Ave., New York, New York 10185-0012. (212) 850-6000. 1984.

Computer Aided Systems for Environmental Engineering Decision Making. Jehng-Jung Kao. University of Illinois at Urbana-Champaign, Urbana, Illinois 61801. 1990.

Computer Graphics and Environmental Planning. Prentice-Hall, Rte. 9 W, Englewood Cliffs, New Jersey 07632. (201) 592-2000. 1983.

Ecological Engineering: An Introduction to Ecotechnology. William J. Mitsch and Sven Erik Jorgensen, eds. John Wiley & Sons, Inc., 605 3rd Ave., New York, New York 10158-0012. (212) 850-6000. 1989. Presents 12 international case studies of ecological engineering. The case studies survey problems and existing methodologies indicate where methods are ecologically sound, and illustrate examples of the use of ecological engineering.

Energy and Environmental Strategies for the 1990's. Mary Jo Winer and Marilyn Jackson, eds. Fairmont Pr., 700 Indian Trail, Lilburn, Georgia 30247. (404) 925-9388. 1991. Papers from the 13th World Energy Engineering Congress and the World Environmental Engineering Congress organized by the Association of Energy Engineers and sponsored by the U.S. Department of Energy, Office of Institutional Programs.

Environment and Energy. T. Nejat Veziroglu, ed. Nova Science Publishers, Inc., 283 Commack Rd., Ste. 300, Commack, New York 11725. (516) 499-3103. 1991. Based on a conference and a volume in the series Energy and Environmental Progress–I, Vol F. Deals mostly with environmental pollution engineering and the energy technology involved in the process.

Environment, Resources, and Conservation. Susan Owens and Peter L. Owens. Cambridge University Press, 40 W 20th St., New York, New York 10011. (212) 924-3900 or (800) 227-0247. 1991. The book studies three cases illuminating problems and policy responses at three levels of geographic scale–international, national, and local. The case of acid rain is used to illustrate a pollution problem with international dimensions; the British coal industry is analyzed as an example of national nonrenewable resource depletion; and renewable wetland ecosystem management illustrates a local concern by analyzing conservation measures.

Environmental Biogeochemistry. R. Hallberg. Publishing House/FRN, P.O. Box 6711, Stockholm, Sweden S-113 85. 08-15-1580. 1983. Biogeochemistry and environmental engineering.

Environmental Biology for Engineers. George Camougis. McGraw-Hill Science & Engineering Books, 11 West 19th St., New York, New York 10011. (212) 337-6010.

1981. Deals with environmental impact analysis, ecology, environmental engineering and environmental legislation.

Environmental Engineering and Sanitation. Joseph A. Salvato. John Wiley & Sons, Inc., 605 3rd Ave., New York, New York 10158-0012. (212) 850-6000. 1992. 3d ed. Applies principles of sanitary science and engineering to sanitation and environmental health. It includes design, construction, maintenance, and operations of sanitation plants and structures. Provides state-of-the-art information on environmental factors associated with chronic and non-infectious diseases; environmental engineering planning and impact analysis; waste management and control; food sanitation; administration of health and sanitation programs; acid rain; noise control; campground sanitation, etc.

Environmental Policies for Cities in the 1990s. OECD Publications and Information Center, 2001 L St. N.W., Suite 700, Washington, District of Columbia 20036. (202) 785-OECD. 1991. Examines existing urban environmental improvement policies and suggests practical solutions to urban renewal, urban transportation and urban energy management.

Environmental Pollution and Control. P. Aarne Vesiling, et al. Butterworth-Heinemann, 80 Montvale Ave., Stoneham, Massachusetts 02180. (617) 438-8468; (800) 366-2665. 1990. Describes the more important aspects of environmental engineering science and technology.

Envirosoft 86. P. Zanetti, ed. Computational Mechanics Inc., 25 Bridge St., Billerica, Massachusetts 01821. 1986. Environmental software part of the proceedings of the International Conference on Development and Applications of Computer Techniques to Environmental Studies, Los Angeles, 1986.

Geotechnical and Environmental Geophysics. Stanley H. Ward. Society of Exploration Geophysicists, PO Box 702740, Tulsa, Oklahoma 74170-2740. (918) 493-3516. 1990.

Groundwater Contamination. J. H. Guswa, et al. Noyes Publications, 120 Mill Rd., Park Ridge, New Jersey 07656. (201) 391-8484. 1984. A technology review of equipment, methods, and field techniques; an overview of groundwater hydrology and a methodology for estimating groundwater contamination under emergency response conditions.

Hazardous Waste Management Engineering. Edward J. Martin and James H. Johnson. PennWell Books, PO Box 21288, Tulsa, Oklahoma 74121. (918) 831-9421; (800) 752-9764. 1986. Covers the basic principles and applications of the most current hazardous waste technologies. Provides a wealth of data and techniques that can be immediately applied to analyzing, designing and developing effective hazardous waste management solutions.

Impact Models to Assess Regional Acidification. Juha Kamari. Kluwer Academic Publishers, 101 Philip Dr., Assinippi Park, Norwell, Massachusetts 02061. (617) 871-6600. 1990. Contains a description of the development and use of the Regional Acidification Information and Simulation (RAINS) model, an integrated assessment model of developing and determining control strategies to reduce regional acidification in Europe.

In the U.S. Interest: Resources, Growth, and Security in the Developing World. Janet Welsh Brown, ed. World Resources Institute, 1709 New York Ave. N.W., Washington, District of Columbia 20006. (800) 822-0504. 1990.

Institute of Environmental Sciences' National Conference and Workshop, Environmental Stress Screening of Electronic Hardware Proceedings. The Institute of Environmental Sciences, 940 E. Northwest Highway, Mt. Prospect, Illinois 60056. (708) 255-1561. Environmental testing and environmental stress screening of electronic hardware.

Introduction to Environmental Engineering and Science. Gilbert M. Masters. Prentice-Hall, Rte. 9W, Englewood Cliffs, New Jersey 07632. (201) 592-2000; (800) 639-2863. 1991. An introduction to the fundamental principles common to most environmental problems is followed by major sections on water pollution, hazardous waste and risk assessment, waste treatment technologies, air pollution, global climate change, hazardous substances, and risk analysis, includes problems.

Underground Storage Tank Management: A Practical Guide. Hart Environmental Management Corp. Government Institutes Inc., 4 Research Place, Suite 200, Rockville, Maryland 20850. (301) 921-2300. 1991. 3rd ed. Presents the latest in the state-of-the-art tank design, how to predict tank leaks, test tank integrity, avoid costly tank replacement through low-cost retrofit and maintenance techniques, and how to respond to leaks.

GOVERNMENTAL ORGANIZATIONS

Energy Information Administration. James Forrestal Building, 1000 Independence Ave., S.W., Washington, District of Columbia 20585. (202) 586-5830.

Energy Research Office. James Forrestal Building, 1000 Independence Ave., S.W., Washington, District of Columbia 20585. (202) 586-5430.

National Science Foundation. 1800 G St., N.W., Washington, District of Columbia 20550. (202) 357-9498.

U.S. Environmental Protection Agency: Office of Exploratory Research. 401 M St., S.W., Washington, District of Columbia 20460. (202) 382-5750.

U.S. Environmental Protection Agency: Office of Technology Transfer and Regulatory Support. 401 M St., S.W., Washington, District of Columbia 20460.

HANDBOOKS AND MANUALS

Handbook of Engineering Control Methods for Occupational Radiation Protection. Michael K. Orn. Prentice Hall, Rte 9W, Englewood Cliffs, New Jersey 07632. (201) 592-2000 or (800) 922-0579. 1992. Deals with radiological safety in the workplace.

Handbook of Environmental Health and Safety, Principles and Practices. Herman Koren. Lewis Publishers, 2000 Corporate Blvd., N.W., Boca Raton, Florida 33431. (800) 272-7737. 1991. Two volumes. Current issues and regulations are presented. The broad spectrum of topics is presented outlining the relationship of the environment to humans and also environmental health emergencies and how to deal with them.

Handbook of Highway Engineering. Robert F. Baker, ed. R. E. Krieger Publishing Co., 115 5th Ave., New York, New York 10003. (212) 254-3232. 1982. Provides reference data on the application of technology to highway transportation.

Industrial and Hazardous Waste Treatment. Nelson Leonard Nemerow and Avijit Dasgupta. Van Nostrand Reinhold, 115 5th Ave., New York, New York 10003. (212) 254-3232. 1991. Factory and trade waste, and hazardous waste purification.

Pira's International Environmental Information Sources. Pira, Randalls Rd., Leatherhead, England KT22 7RU. 0372 376161. 1990. Sourcebook includes over 2,000 entries from more than 20 countries, including Australia, Finland, Germany, the United Kingdom, and the United States. Entries are from organizations, research centers, legislative and regulatory bodies, directories, online databases and periodicals. Subject areas covered are: air, noise, water and land pollution, waste control and disposal, recycling, energy recovery and nature conservation.

Standard Handbook of Environmental Engineering. Robert A. Corbitt. McGraw-Hill, 1221 Ave. of the Americas, New York, New York 10020. (212) 512-2000 or (800) 262-4729. 1990. Hands-on reference to understand environmental engineering technology. Covers air quality control, water supply, wastewater disposal, waste management, stormwater and hazardous wastes.

Treatability Manual. U.S. Environmental Protection Agency, Office of Research and Development, 401 M St., SW, Washington, District of Columbia 20460. (202) 260-2090. 1983-. V.1 Treatability data. v.2 Change 2. Industrial Descriptions. v.3 Change 2. Technology for Control/removal of pollutants. v.4. Cost estimating. v.5. Change 2 summary.

ONLINE DATA BASES

Chemical Engineering. McGraw-Hill Science & Engineering Books, 11 W. 19th St., New York, New York 10011. (212) 337-6010. Online version of periodical of the same name.

Chemical Engineering and Biotechnology Abstracts–CEBA. Orbit Search Service, Maxwell Online Inc., 8000 W. Park Dr., McLean, Virginia 22102. (703) 442-0900 or (800) 456-7248. Monthly. Covers theoretical, practical and commercial material on all aspects of processing safety, and the environment. Also covers process and reaction engineering, measurement and process control, environmental protection and safety, plant design and equipment used in chemical engineering and biotechnology. More than 400 of the world's major primary chemical and process engineering journals are scanned to compile the database. Available from ORBIT.

Civil Engineering Database. American Society of Civil Engineers, 345 E. 47th St., New York, New York 10017. (800) 548-2723.

Computerized Engineering Index–COMPENDEX. Engineering Information Inc., 345 E. 47th St., New York, New York 10017. (212) 705-7600.

DECHEMA Environmental Technology Equipment Data–DETEQ. STN International, c/o Chemical Abstracts Service, 2540 Olentangy River Road, P.O. Box 3012, Columbus, Ohio 43210. Information on the manufacturers of apparatus and technical equipment in the field of environmental engineering. Corresponds to the "ACHEMA Handbook Pollution Control."

GeoRef. American Geological Institute, 4220 King St., Alexandria, Virginia 22302. (703) 379-2480.

IBSEDEX. Building Services Research & Information Association, Old Bracknell Lane West, Bracknell, Berkshire, England RG12 4AH. 44 (344) 426511.

Life Sciences from NTIS. National Technical Information Center for the Utilization of Federal Technology, 5285 Port Royal Rd., Springfield, Virginia 22161. (703) 487-4650.

Monthly Catalog of United States Government Publications. U.S. G.P.O., Supt. of Docs., PO Box 371954, Pittsburgh, Pennsylvania 15250-7954. (202) 512-0000.

National Technical Information Service. U.S. Department of Commerce, National Technical Information Service, Office of Data Base Services, 5285 Port Royal Rd., Springfield, Virginia 22161. (703) 487-4807. Bibliographic database of government sponsored research and technical reports.

SCISEARCH. Institute for Scientific Information, University City Science Center, 3501 Market St., Philadelphia, Pennsylvania 19104. (215) 386-0100.

PERIODICALS AND NEWSLETTERS

Advances in Environment, Behavior, and Design. Plenum Press, 233 Spring St., New York, New York 10013. (212) 620-8000; (800) 221-9369.

Agricultural Engineering Magazine. American Society of Agricultural Engineers, 2950 Niles Road, St Joseph, Michigan 49085. (616) 429-0300. Bimonthly. Irrigation and other large scale projects with environmental significance.

AIChE Journal. American Institute of Chemical Engineers, 345 East 47th Street, New York, New York 10017. (212) 705-7338. Monthly. Papers on all areas of chemical engineering.

Analytical Chemistry. American Chemical Society, 1155 16th St. N.W., Washington, District of Columbia 20036. (800) 227-5558. 1929-. Bimonthly. Articles for chemists, life scientists and engineers.

Annual Meeting Proceedings. Institute of Environmental Sciences, 940 E. Northwest Highway, Mt. Prospect, Illinois 60056. (708) 255-1561. Annual. Environmental simulation and environmental contamination control.

Association of Environmental Engineering Professors Newsletter. Association of Environmental Engineering Professors, c/o Prof. Bruce Rittmann, University of Illinois, 3221 Newmark CE Laboratory, 208 N. Romine, Urbana, Illinois 61801. (217) 333-6964. Three/year.

Chemical & Engineering News. American Chemical Society, 1155 16th St. N.W., Washington, District of Columbia 20036. (800) 227-5558. Weekly. Cites technical and business developments in the chemical process industry.

Chemical Engineering. McGraw-Hill Science & Engineering Books, 11 W. 19th St., New York, New York 10011. (212) 337-6010. Monthly. Articles on new engineering techniques and equipment. Also available online.

Chemical Engineering Progress Magazine. American Institute of Chemical Engineers, 345 E. 47th St., New York, New York 10017. (212) 705-7338. Monthly. Articles covering environmental controls for chemical and petrochemical industrial plants.

Civil Engineering ASCE. American Society of Civil Engineers, 345 E 47th St., New York, New York 10017.

(212) 705-7288; (800) 548-2723. Monthly. Professional journal that offers a forum for free exchange of ideas relevant to the profession of civil engineering. Covers in regular columns, engineering news, legal trends in engineering, calendar of events, membership news, publications and other items of interest to civil engineers. Formerly, Civil Engineering.

The Diplomate. American Academy of Environmental Engineers, 130 Holiday Court, Ste. 100, Annapolis, Maryland 21401. (301) 266-3311. Quarterly. Issues and happenings in the environmental field.

Ecological Engineering. The Journal of Ecotechnology. Elsevier Science Publishing Co., 655 Avenue of the Americas, New York, New York 10010. (212) 984-5800. 1992. Quarterly. Specific areas of coverage will include habitat reconstruction, rehabilitation, biomanipulation, restoration and conservation.

Ecomod. ISEM–North America Chapter, Water Quality Division, South Florida Water Management District, P.O. Box 24608, West Palm Beach, Florida 33416. (407) 686-8800. Monthly. Current events in ecological and environmental modeling.

Environment Report. Trends Publishing, Inc., 1079 National Press Bldg., Washington, District of Columbia 20045. (202) 393-0031. Semimonthly. Developments in environment, ecology and pollution abatement, with emphasis on policy, research, and development.

Environmental Defense Fund Letter. Environmental Defense Fund, 257 Park Avenue South, New York, New York 10010. (212) 505-2100. 1971-. Bimonthly. Environmental issues of concern.

Environmental Engineering News. Purdue University, School of Civil Engineering, Lafayette, Indiana 47907. (317) 494-2194. Monthly. Trends in environmental engineering.

Environmental Engineering Selection Guide. American Academy of Environmental Engineers, 132 Holiday Ct., # 206, Annapolis, Maryland 21401. (301) 266-3311. Annual. Certified environmental engineers in consulting, education, and manufacturing.

Environmental Science and Engineering. Davcom Communications Inc., 10 Petch Circle, Aurora, Ontario, Canada L4G 5N7. (416) 727-4666. Bimonthly. Water, sewage, and pollution control.

Environmental Science and Technology. American Chemical Society, 1155 16th St. N.W., Washington, District of Columbia 20036. (800) 227-5558. 1967-. Monthly. Contains research articles on various aspects of environmental chemistry, interpretative articles by invited experts and commentary on the scientific aspects of environmental management.

Environmental Science & Technology. American Chemical Society, 1155 16th St. N.W., Washington, District of Columbia 20036. (800) 227-5558. Covers pollution, sanitary chemistry and environmental engineering.

Environmental Technology. Park Publishing Co., 333 Hudson St., New York, New York 10013. (212) 255-1500. Semimonthly. Research on pollution abatement.

ESE Notes. UNC Dept. of Environmental Science & Engineering School of Public Health, CB# 7400, Chapel Hill, North Carolina 27599-7400. (919) 966-1171. Quarterly. Research and training activities of the EPA.

Federal Facilities Environmental Journal. Executive Enterprises Publications Co., Inc., 22 W. 21st St., New York, New York 10010-6990. (212) 645-7880. Quarterly. Environmental issues at federal facilities.

Impact Assessment Bulletin. Center for Technology Assessment and Policy Studies, Rose Hulman Institute of Technology, Georgia Institute of Technology, Terra Haute, Indiana 47803-3999. (812) 877-1511. Quarterly. Covers the assessment of environmental and technical impact.

Industrial Safety and Hygiene News. Chilton Book Co., 201 King of Prussia Rd., Radnor, Pennsylvania 19089. (215) 964-4000. Monthly. Covers fire protection, security, and emergency first aid equipment.

Journal of Engineering Mechanics. American Society of Civil Engineers, 345 E. 47th St., New York, New York 10017. (212) 705-7288; (800) 548-2723. Bimonthly. Covers activity and development in the field of applied mechanics as it relates to civil engineering, research on bioengineering, computational mechanics, computer aided engineering, dynamics of structures, elasticity, experimental analysis and instrumentation, fluid mechanics, flow of granular media, inelastic behavior of solids and structures, probablistic methods, properties of materials, stability of structural elements and systems, and turbulence.

Journal of Environmental Engineering. American Society for Civil Engineers, 345 East 47th Street, New York, New York 10017. (212) 705-7496. Bimonthly. Covers problems in the environment and sanitation.

Journal of Environmental Quality. American Society of Agronomy, 677 S. Segoe Rd., Madison, Wisconsin 53711-1086. (608) 273-8080. 1972-. Quarterly. Reports and brief reviews of agricultural ecology, environmental engineering and pollution.

Journal of Environmental Science and Health. Marcel Dekker, Inc., 270 Madison Ave., New York, New York 10016. (212) 696-9000. Bimonthly. Concerns pesticides, food contaminants, chemical carcinogens, and agricultural wastes.

Journal of Environmental Sciences. Institute of Environmental Sciences, 940 East Northwest Highway, Mt. Prospect, Illinois 60656. (312) 255-1561. Bimonthly. Covers research, controlling and teaching of environmental sciences.

Journal of Geotechnical Engineering. American Society of Civil Engineers, 345 E. 47th St., New York, New York 10017. (212) 705-7288. 1956-. Monthly. Covers the field of soil mechanics and foundations with emphasis on the relationship between the geologic and man-made works.

Journal of the Association of Environmental Scientists and Engineers. Association of Environmental Scientists and Engineers, 2718 S.W. Kelly, # C-190, Portland, Oregon 97201. (503) 635-5129. Quarterly. Technical aspects of environmental management.

Northwest Environmental Journal. Institute for Environmental Studies, University of Washington, Seattle, Washington 98195. (206) 543-1812. Biannual. Covers environmental issues in the Northwest states and Canada.

Plant Engineering. Cahners Publishing Co., 249 W. 17th St., New York, New York 10011. (212) 645-0067. Twenty-one times a year. Covers operating and maintaining industrial plant systems.

Pollution Engineering. Cahners Publishing Co., 249 W. 17th St., New York, New York 10011. (212) 645-0067. 1969-. Monthly.

Process Safety & Environmental Protection. Taylor & Francis, 1900 Frost Rd., Ste. 101, Bristol, Pennsylvania 19007. (215) 785-5800. Quarterly.

RESEARCH CENTERS AND INSTITUTES

Center for Advanced Decision Support for Water and Environmental Systems. University of Colorado-Boulder, 2945 Center Green Court, Suite B, Boulder, Colorado 80301. (303) 492-3972.

Environmental Engineering and Sciences Department. Virginia Polytech Institute and State University, 330 Norris Hall, Department of Civil Engineering, Blacksburg, Virginia 24061. (703) 961-6635.

Environmental Engineering Science Research Laboratory. University of Florida, College of Engineering, 217 Black Hall, Gainesville, Florida 32611. (904) 392-0841.

Environmental Systems Engineering Institute. University of Central Florida, Department of Civil Engineering and Environmental Science, PO Box 25000, Orlando, Florida 32816. (305) 275-2785.

U.S. Forest Service, Forest Engineering Research Project. George W. Andrews Forestry Sciences Laboratory, Auburn University, Devall Street, Auburn, Alabama 36849. (205) 826-8700.

University of Arizona, Environmental Engineering Laboratory. Civil Engineering Department, Room 206, Tucson, Arizona 85721. (602) 621-6586.

University of Illinois, Institute for Environmental Studies. 408 South Goodwin Avenue, Urbana, Illinois 61801. (217) 333-4178.

University of Nevada-Reno, Desert Research Institute, Energy and Environmental Engineering Center. P.O. Box 60220, Reno, Nevada 89506. (702) 677-3107.

University of Oklahoma, Bureau of Water and Environmental Resources Research. P.O. Box 2850, Norman, Oklahoma 73070. (405) 325-2960.

STATISTICS SOURCES

Statistical Methods for the Environmental Sciences. A.H. El-Shaarwi, ed. Kluwer Academic Publishers, 101 Philip Dr., Assinippi Pk., Norwell, Massachusetts 02061. (617) 871-6600. 1991.

TRADE ASSOCIATIONS AND PROFESSIONAL SOCIETIES

American Academy of Environmental Engineers. 130 Holiday Court, #100, Annapolis, Maryland 21404. (301) 266-3311.

American Institute of Chemical Engineers. 345 East 47th St., New York, New York 10017. (212) 705-7338.

American Institute of Chemists. 7315 Wisconsin Ave., Bethesda, Maryland 20814. (301) 652-2447.

American Society for Engineering Education. 11 Dupont Circle, Suite 200, Washington, District of Columbia 20036. (202) 293-7080.

American Society for Engineering Management. P.O. Box 820, Rolla, Missouri 65401. (314) 341-2101.

American Society of Civil Engineers. 345 East 47th St., New York, New York 10017. (212) 705-7496.

Association of Environmental Engineering Professors. Department of Civil Engineering, Virginia Polytechnic Institute and State University, Blacksburg, Virginia 24061. (703) 231-6021.

Association of New Jersey Environmental Commissions. PO Box 157, 300 Mendham Rd., Mendham, New Jersey 07945. (201) 539-7547.

Center for Environmental Information, Inc. 99 Court St., Rochester, New York 14604. (716) 546-3796.

Environmental Defense Fund. 257 Park Ave., S., New York, New York 10010. (212) 505-2100. Non-profit organization that was established more than 20 years ago. Its goals are to protect the earth's environment by providing lasting solutions to global environmental problems.

Environmental Industry Council. 1825 K St., N.W., Suite 210, Washington, District of Columbia 20006. (202) 331-7706.

Environmental Task Force. 6930 Carroll Ave., 6th Floor, Takoma Park, Maryland 20912. (202) 745-4870.

Federation of Environmental Technologists. P.O. Box 185, Milwaukee, Wisconsin 53201. (414) 251-8163.

Institute of Environmental Sciences. 940 E. Northwest Hwy., Mount Prospect, Illinois 60056. (708) 255-1561.

Institute of Noise Control Engineering. Box 3206, Arlington Branch, Poughkeepsie, New York 12603. (914) 462-4006.

International Clearinghouse for Environmental Technologies. 12600 West Colfax Ave., Suite C-310, Lakewood, Colorado 80215. (303) 233-1248.

International Federation of Professional & Technical Engineers. 8701 Georgia Ave., Suite 701, Silver Spring, Maryland 20910. (301) 565-9016.

National Association of Environmental Professionals. PO Box 15210, Alexandria, Virginia 22309-0210. (703) 660-2364.

National Environmental Development Association. 1440 New York Ave., N.W., Suite 300, Washington, District of Columbia 20005. (202) 638-1230.

National Society of Professional Engineers. 1420 King St., Alexandria, Virginia 22314. (703) 684-2800.

New England Association of Environmental Biologists. 25 Nashua Rd., Bedford, New Hampshire 03102. (603) 472-5191.

Professional Engineers in Private Practice. 1420 King St., Alexandria, Virginia 22314. (703) 684-2862.

Reliability Engineering and Management Institute. 7340 N. La Oesta Ave., Tucson, Arizona 85704. (602) 297-2679.

Society of Manufacturing Engineers. 1 SME Dr., Box 930, Dearborn, Michigan 48121. (313) 271-1500.

Society of Women Engineers. 345 E. 47th St., Rm. 305, New York, New York 10017. (212) 705-7855.

ENVIRONMENTAL ETHICS

ABSTRACTING AND INDEXING SERVICES

Applied Science and Technology Index. H.W. Wilson Co., 950 University Ave., Bronx, New York 10452. (800) 367-6770. Formerly Industrial Arts Index.

Biological Abstracts. BIOSIS, 2100 Arch St., Philadelphia, Pennsylvania 19103-1399. (215) 587-4800. 1927-.

Current Advances in Ecological and Environmental Science. Pergamon Microforms International, Inc., Fairview Park, Elmsford, New York 10523. (914) 592-7720. 1989-. Monthly. Current literature searching service including journals, reports, abstracts, etc. This service is available online as part of the CABS database on the hosts BRS and ORBIT search service.

Ecological Abstracts. Geo Abstracts Ltd. Elsevier Applied Science, Crown House, Linton Rd., Barking, England IG 11 8JU. 1974-. Derived from over 600 leading ecological and environmental journals, plus books, conference proceedings, reports and theses.

Geographical Abstracts. London School of Economics, Dept. of Geography, Regency House, 34 Duke St., London, England 1966-. Continued by Geo Abstracts issued in 6 parts: Pt. A. Landforms and the quaternary; Pt. B. Biogeography and Climatology; Pt. C. Economic geography; Pt. D. Social geography and cartography; Pt. E. Sedimentology; Pt. F. Regional and community planning.

Index to Scientific Book Contents. Institute for Scientific Information, 3501 Market St., Philadelphia, Pennsylvania 19104. (800) 523-1857. 1985-. Annual. Gives contents of science books published.

Priority Issue Reporting Service–PIRS. Information for Public Affairs, Inc., Client Services Dept., 1900 14th St., Sacramento, California 95814.

ALMANACS AND YEARBOOKS

Gale Environmental Almanac. Russ Hoyle. Gale Research Inc., 835 Penobscot Bldg., Detroit, Michigan 48226-4094. (313) 961-2242. 1993. Focuses on the U.S. and Canada, although worldwide and transboundary issues are discussed.

BIBLIOGRAPHIES

Agent Orange and Vietnam: An Annotated Bibliography. Scarecrow Press, 52 Liberty St., Metuchen, New Jersey 08840. (908) 548-8600. Ethical and political aspects of man's relationship to the environment.

Current Contents. Agriculture, Biology and Environmental Sciences. Institute for Scientific Information, 3501 Market St., Philadelphia, Pennsylvania 19104. (800) 523-1857. 1973-. Previous title: Current Contents. Agricultural, Food & Veterinary Sciences. Gives the table of contents of periodicals in the fields of agriculture, biology, environmental and related areas.

Deep Ecology and Environmental Ethics: A Selected and Annotated Bibliography of Materials Published Since 1980. Teresa DeGroh. Council of Planning Librarians, 1313 E. 60th St., Chicago, Illinois 60637-2897. (312) 942-2163. 1987. Covers human ecology and environmental protection.

Ecophilosophy: A Field Guide to the Literature. Donald Edward Davis. R. & E. Miles Publishers, International Sales, PO Box 1916, San Pedro, California 90733. 1989.

Environmental Ethics: A Selected Bibliography for the Environmental Professional. Deborah A. Simmons. Council of Planning Librarians, 1313 E. 60th St., Chicago, Illinois 60637-2897. (312) 942-2163. 1988. Moral and ethical aspects of human ecology.

DIRECTORIES

Canadian Environmental Directory. Canadian Almanac & Directory Publishing Co. Ltd., 134 Adelaide St. E., Ste. 27, Toronto, Ontario, Canada M5C 1K9. (416) 362-4088. 1992. Includes individuals, agencies, firms, and associations.

The Green Encyclopedia. Irene Franck, David Brownstone. Prentice-Hall, Rte. 9W, Englewood Cliffs, New York 07632. (201) 592-2000. 1992. Covers environmental organizations.

ENCYCLOPEDIAS AND DICTIONARIES

Dictionary of Environmental Engineering and Related Sciences: English-Spanish, Spanish-English. Jose T. Villate. Ediciones Universal, 3090 SW 8th St., Miami, Florida 33135. (305) 642-3355. 1979.

Dictionary of Environmental Science and Technology. Andrew Porteous. John Wiley & Sons, Inc., 605 3rd Ave., New York, New York 10158-0012. (212) 850-6000. 1992.

Encyclopedia of Bioethics. Warren T. Reich, ed. Free Press, 866 3rd Ave., New York, New York 10022. (212) 702-2004 or (800) 257-5755. 1978. Four volumes. Includes review articles in the field of bioethics by 330 reviewers representing fields such as: surgery, Islamic studies, pediatrics, philosophy, environmental sciences, theology, psychiatry, etc.

Encyclopedia of Environmental Science and Engineering. J.R. Pfafflin. Gordon and Breach Science Publishers, Inc., 270 8th Ave., New York, New York 10011. (212) 206-8900. 1992.

Encyclopedia of Environmental Studies. William Ashworth. Facts on File, Inc., 460 Park Ave. S., New York, New York 10016. (212) 683-2244. 1991.

Environmental Encyclopedia. William P. Cunningham, Terence Ball, et. al. Gale Research Inc., 835 Penobscot Bldg., Detroit, Michigan 48226-4094. (313) 961-2242. 1993.

The Facts on File Dictionary of Environmental Science. L. Harold Stevenson and Bruce Wyman. Facts on File, Inc., 460 Park Ave. S., New York, New York 10016. (212) 683-2244. 1991.

McGraw-Hill Encyclopedia of Environmental Science. Sybil P. Parker. McGraw-Hill Science & Engineering Books, 11 W. 19th St., New York, New York 10011. (212) 337-6010. 1980. Covers ecology, man's influence on nature, and environmental protection.

GENERAL WORKS

Ecology, Economics, Ethics: The Broken Circle. Herbert R. Bormann and Stephen R. Kellert, eds. Yale University Press, 302 Temple St., New Haven, Connecticut 06520.

(203) 432-0960. 1991. Addresses a wide range of concerns and offers practical remedies including: economic incentives for conservation, technical adaptations to use resources effectively; better accounting procedures for measuring the environmental system that better explains our responsibility to the environment.

Environment Ideology and Policy. Frances Sandbach. Rowman & Littlefield, Publishers, Inc., 8705 Bollman Pl., Savage, Maryland 20763. (301) 306-0400. 1980. Describes the environmental movement, behavioral assessments, alternative technologies, environmental evaluation, economic analysis, environmental policies and other environment related areas.

Environmental Ethics. Holmes Tolston. Temple University Press, 1601 N. Broad St., USB 306, Philadelphia, Pennsylvania 19122. (215) 787-8787. 1988.

Environmental Ethics for Engineers. Alistairs Gunn and P. Aarne Veslind. Lewis Publishers, 2000 Corporate Blvd.,N.W., Boca Raton, Florida 33431. (407) 994-0555 or (800) 272-7737. 1986. Consists of two parts. The first part is a primer on professional ethics as applied to the environment. The second part is comprised of various articles. Some are written to foster a development ofenvironmental ethics, while others deal with controversial issues and professional approaches to ethics.

Environmental Viewpoints. Marie Lazzari. Gale Research Inc., 835 Penobscot Bldg., Detroit, Michigan 48226-4094. (313) 961-2242. 1992.

Shopping for a Better World. The Council for Economic Priorities. Ballantine Books, 201 E. 50th St., New York, New York 10022. (212) 572-2620; (800) 733-3000. 1991. Rev. ed. Investigates 206 companies and over 2,015 products.

To Heal the Earth: The Case for an Earth Ethic. Robert F. Harrington. Hancock House, 1431 Harrison Ave., Blaine, Washington 98230. 1990. Moral and ethical aspects of human ecology and environmental protection.

Upstream/Downstream: Issues in Environmental Ethics. Donald Scherer, ed. Temple University, Broad & Oxford Sts., University Services Bldg., Room 305, Philadelphia, Pennsylvania 19122. (215) 787-8787. 1991. Assesses effects of pollution and global warming. Predicts environmental damage scientifically. Provides property owners with information on modifications to satisfy environmental requirements and cost-benefit analysis.

World Guide to Environmental Issues and Organizations. Peter Brackley. Longman Group Ltd., Longman House, Burnt Mill, Harlow, Essex, England CM20 2J6. (0279) 426721. 1991.

GOVERNMENTAL ORGANIZATIONS

Coast Guard. Information Office, 2100 Second St., S.W., Washington, District of Columbia 20593. (202) 267-2229.

Office of Public Information: Federal Energy Regulatory Commission. 825 North Capitol St., N.E., Washington, District of Columbia 20426. (202) 357-8055.

HANDBOOKS AND MANUALS

Environmental Career Guide: Job Opportunities with the Earth in Mind. Nicholas Basta. John Wiley & Sons, Inc., 605 3rd Ave., New York, New York 10158-0012. (212)

850-6000. 1991. Complete guide to the many career options in the growing environmental field. Shows how to find employers engaged in environmental activity, and how to get the job. Lists key environmental businesses–manufacturing, government agencies, engineering consulting firms, waste handling firms, and others. Lists key professional careers in environmental conservation and maps career strategies.

Environmental Statistics Handbook: Europe. Allan Foster, Oksana Newman. Gale Research Inc., 835 Penobscot Bldg., Detroit, Michigan 48226-4094. (313) 961-2242. 1993.

Pira's International Environmental Information Sources. Pira, Randalls Rd., Leatherhead, England KT22 7RU. 0372 376161. 1990. Sourcebook includes over 2,000 entries from more than 20 countries, including Australia, Finland, Germany, the United Kingdom, and the United States. Entries are from organizations, research centers, legislative and regulatory bodies, directories, online databases and periodicals. Subject areas covered are: air, noise, water and land pollution, waste control and disposal, recycling, energy recovery and nature conservation.

ONLINE DATA BASES

BIOSIS Previews. BIOSIS, 2100 Arch St., Philadelphia, Pennsylvania 19103-1399. (215) 587-4800. Largest and most comprehensive database of research in the life sciences. Contains citations for nearly 9000 primary research journals, monographs, reviews, symposia, preliminary reports, semi-popular journals, selected institutional reports, government reports and research communications.

Environmental Business Journal. EnviroQuest, PO Box 371769, San Diego, California 92137. (619) 295-7685. Online access.

Monthly Catalog of United States Government Publications. U.S. G.P.O., Supt. of Docs., PO Box 371954, Pittsburgh, Pennsylvania 15250-7954. (202) 512-0000.

National Technical Information Service. U.S. Department of Commerce, National Technical Information Service, Office of Data Base Services, 5285 Port Royal Rd., Springfield, Virginia 22161. (703) 487-4807. Bibliographic database of government sponsored research and technical reports.

SCISEARCH. Institute for Scientific Information, University City Science Center, 3501 Market St., Philadelphia, Pennsylvania 19104. (215) 386-0100.

PERIODICALS AND NEWSLETTERS

Environmental Action. Environmental Action Foundation, 6930 Carroll Ave., Ste. 600, Takoma Park, Maryland 20912. (301) 891-1100. Bimonthly. Impact of humans and industry on the environment.

Environmental Business Journal. EnviroQuest, PO Box 371769, San Diego, California 92137. (619) 295-7685. Monthly. Products relating to environmental protection.

Environmental Defense Fund Letter. Environmental Defense Fund, 257 Park Avenue South, New York, New York 10010. (212) 505-2100. 1971-. Bimonthly. Environmental issues of concern.

Environmental Education Report and Newsletter. American Society for Environmental Education, P.O. Box 800, White River, New Hampshire 03755. (603) 448-6697. Quarterly. Contemporary environmental issues.

Environmental Ethics. Environmental Ethics, Department of Philosophy, University of North Texas, P.O. Box 13496, Denton, Texas 76203-3496. (817) 565-2727. Quarterly. Covers philosophical aspects of environmental problems.

FPIRG Citizen Agenda. Florida Public Interest Research Group, 1441 E Fletcher Ave., Ste. 2200-3, Tampa, Florida 33612. (813) 971-7564. Citizen actions for environmental protection.

Green Marketing Report. Business Publishers, Inc., 951 Pershing Dr., Silver Spring, Maryland 20910-4464. (301) 587-6300. 1990-. Monthly. Looks at the steps taken by product manufacturers and advertisers to address consumers' environmental concerns as well as government examination of (and challenges to) some companies' environmental claims. Also available online.

Minding the Earth. Latham Foundation, Latham Plaza Bldg., Clement & Shiller Sts., Alameda, California 94501. (206) 463-9773. Quarterly. Environmental ethics.

RESEARCH CENTERS AND INSTITUTES

Ecology Center. 2530 San Pablo Ave., Berkeley, California 94702. (510) 548-2220.

The Keystone Center. P.O. Box 8606, Keystone, Colorado 80435. (303) 468-5822.

State University of New York College of Environmental Science and Forestry. Institute for Environmental Policy and Planning, Bray Hall, Room 320, Syracuse, New York 13210. (315) 470-6636.

University of North Carolina at Chapel Hill, Institute for Environmental Studies. CB #7410, 311 Pittsboro Street, Chapel Hill, North Carolina 27599-7410. (919) 966-2358.

University of Wisconsin-Madison, Institute for Environmental Studies. 1017 WARF Office Building, 610 Walnut Street, Madison, Wisconsin 53705. (608) 262-5957.

STATISTICS SOURCES

Statistical Record of the Environment. Arsen J. Darnay. Gale Research Inc., 835 Penobscot Bldg., Detroit, Michigan 48226-4094. (313) 961-2242. 1992.

TRADE ASSOCIATIONS AND PROFESSIONAL SOCIETIES

American Society of Civil Engineers. 345 East 47th St., New York, New York 10017. (212) 705-7496.

Americans for the Environment. 1400 16th St. N.W., Washington, District of Columbia 20036. (202) 797-6665.

Center for Environmental Information, Inc. 99 Court St., Rochester, New York 14604. (716) 546-3796.

Center for Religion, Ethics and Social Policy. Anabel Taylor Hall, Cornell University, Ithaca, New York 14853. (607) 255-6486.

Conservation Law Foundation of New England, Inc. 3 Joy St., Boston, Massachusetts 02108. (617) 742-2540.

Council on Economic Priorities. 30 Irving Place, New York, New York 10003. (212) 420-1133.

Environmental Defense Fund. 257 Park Ave., S., New York, New York 10010. (212) 505-2100. Non-profit organization that was established more than 20 years ago. Its goals are to protect the earth's environment by providing lasting solutions to global environmental problems.

Institute of Environmental Sciences. 940 E. Northwest Hwy., Mount Prospect, Illinois 60056. (708) 255-1561.

ENVIRONMENTAL FATE

ABSTRACTING AND INDEXING SERVICES

Applied Ecology Abstracts Studies in Renewable Natural Resources. Information Retrieval Ltd., 1911 Jefferson Davis Highway, Arlington, Virginia 22202. 1975-. Monthly.

Bulletin Signaletique: Eau et Assainissement, Pollution Atmospherique, Droit des Pollutions. Centre de Documentation, Centre National de la Recherche Scientifique, 15, quai Anatole France, Paris, France 75700. (1) 45 55 92 25. 1983-. Monthly. Indexes pollution periodicals including water, atmospheric and related pollutions.

Current Advances in Ecological and Environmental Science. Pergamon Microforms International, Inc., Fairview Park, Elmsford, New York 10523. (914) 592-7720. 1989-. Monthly. Current literature searching service including journals, reports, abstracts, etc. This service is available online as part of the CABS database on the hosts BRS and ORBIT search service.

Ecological Abstracts. Geo Abstracts Ltd. Elsevier Applied Science, Crown House, Linton Rd., Barking, England IG 11 8JU. 1974-. Derived from over 600 leading ecological and environmental journals, plus books, conference proceedings, reports and theses.

Ecology Abstracts. Cambridge Scientific Abstracts, 5161 River Rd., Bethesda, Maryland 20816. (301) 961-6750. Monthly.

Index to Scientific Book Contents. Institute for Scientific Information, 3501 Market St., Philadelphia, Pennsylvania 19104. (800) 523-1857. 1985-. Annual. Gives contents of science books published.

Multimedia Index to Ecology. National Information Center for Educational Media, University of Southern California, Los Angeles, California 90007.

ALMANACS AND YEARBOOKS

Gale Environmental Almanac. Russ Hoyle. Gale Research Inc., 835 Penobscot Bldg., Detroit, Michigan 48226-4094. (313) 961-2242. 1993. Focuses on the U.S. and Canada, although worldwide and transboundary issues are discussed.

BIBLIOGRAPHIES

Current Contents. Agriculture, Biology and Environmental Sciences. Institute for Scientific Information, 3501 Market St., Philadelphia, Pennsylvania 19104. (800) 523-1857. 1973-. Previous title: Current Contents. Agricultural, Food & Veterinary Sciences. Gives the table of

contents of periodicals in the fields of agriculture, biology, environmental and related areas.

DIRECTORIES

Canadian Environmental Directory. Canadian Almanac & Directory Publishing Co. Ltd., 134 Adelaide St. E., Ste. 27, Toronto, Ontario, Canada M5C 1K9. (416) 362-4088. 1992. Includes individuals, agencies, firms, and associations.

The Green Encyclopedia. Irene Franck, David Brownstone. Prentice-Hall, Rte. 9W, Englewood Cliffs, New York 07632. (201) 592-2000. 1992. Covers environmental organizations.

ENCYCLOPEDIAS AND DICTIONARIES

Encyclopedia of Environmental Studies. William Ashworth. Facts on File, Inc., 460 Park Ave. S., New York, New York 10016. (212) 683-2244. 1991.

Environmental Encyclopedia. William P. Cunningham, Terence Ball, et. al. Gale Research Inc., 835 Penobscot Bldg., Detroit, Michigan 48226-4094. (313) 961-2242. 1993.

The Facts on File Dictionary of Environmental Science. L. Harold Stevenson and Bruce Wyman. Facts on File, Inc., 460 Park Ave. S., New York, New York 10016. (212) 683-2244. 1991.

McGraw-Hill Encyclopedia of Environmental Science. Sybil P. Parker. McGraw-Hill Science & Engineering Books, 11 W. 19th St., New York, New York 10011. (212) 337-6010. 1980. Covers ecology, man's influence on nature, and environmental protection.

GENERAL WORKS

Environmental Viewpoints. Marie Lazzari. Gale Research Inc., 835 Penobscot Bldg., Detroit, Michigan 48226-4094. (313) 961-2242. 1992.

Modeling the Environmental Fate of Microorganisms. Criston J. Hurst. American Society for Microbiology, 1325 Massachusetts Ave. NW, Washington, District of Columbia 20005. (202) 737-3600. 1991. Mathematical models of microbial ecology.

Petroleum Contaminated Soils: Remediation Techniques, Environmental Fate and Risk Assessment. Paul T. Kostecki and Edward J. Calabrese. Lewis Publishers, 200 Corporate Blvd. NW, Boca Raton, Florida 33431. (407) 994-0555 or (800)272-7737. 1991. Three volumes. Provides valuable information to determine feasible solutions to petroleum contaminated soils.

World Guide to Environmental Issues and Organizations. Peter Brackley. Longman Group Ltd., Longman House, Burnt Mill, Harlow, Essex, England CM20 2J6. (0279) 426721. 1991.

HANDBOOKS AND MANUALS

Environmental Statistics Handbook: Europe. Allan Foster, Oksana Newman. Gale Research Inc., 835 Penobscot Bldg., Detroit, Michigan 48226-4094. (313) 961-2242. 1993.

ONLINE DATA BASES

Environmental Fate Databases. Syracuse Research Cooperation, Merrill Lane, Syracuse, New York 13210. (312) 426-3200. Environmental fate of chemicals.

Monthly Catalog of United States Government Publications. U.S. G.P.O., Supt. of Docs., PO Box 371954, Pittsburgh, Pennsylvania 15250-7954. (202) 512-0000.

National Technical Information Service. U.S. Department of Commerce, National Technical Information Service, Office of Data Base Services, 5285 Port Royal Rd., Springfield, Virginia 22161. (703) 487-4807. Bibliographic database of government sponsored research and technical reports.

STATISTICS SOURCES

Statistical Record of the Environment. Arsen J. Darnay. Gale Research Inc., 835 Penobscot Bldg., Detroit, Michigan 48226-4094. (313) 961-2242. 1992.

ENVIRONMENTAL HEALTH
See: HEALTH, ENVIRONMENTAL

ENVIRONMENTAL IMPACT ASSESSMENT

ABSTRACTING AND INDEXING SERVICES

Applied Science and Technology Index. H.W. Wilson Co., 950 University Ave., Bronx, New York 10452. (800) 367-6770. Formerly Industrial Arts Index.

ASFA Aquaculture Abstracts. Cambridge Scientific Abstracts, Inc., 5161 River Rd., Bethesda, Maryland 20816. (301) 961-6750. 1984.

Biological Abstracts. BIOSIS, 2100 Arch St., Philadelphia, Pennsylvania 19103-1399. (215) 587-4800. 1927-.

Biotechnology Research Abstracts. Cambridge Scientific Abstracts, 5161 River Rd., Bethesda, Maryland 20816. (301) 961-6750. Monthly. Includes such broad areas as genetic intervention, biochemical genetics, and microbiological techniques.

Ecological Abstracts. Geo Abstracts Ltd. Elsevier Applied Science, Crown House, Linton Rd., Barking, England IG 11 8JU. 1974-. Derived from over 600 leading ecological and environmental journals, plus books, conference proceedings, reports and theses.

Ecology Abstracts. Cambridge Scientific Abstracts, 5161 River Rd., Bethesda, Maryland 20816. (301) 961-6750. Monthly.

Energy Information Abstracts Annual 1987 in Retrospect. EIC/Intelligence Inc., 121 Chanlon Rd., New Providence, New Jersey 07974. (908) 464-6800. 1988. Annual. Cumulative edition of the monthly Energy Information Abstracts. Monitors sources in the field of energy including the scientific, technical and business journal literature, conference and symposia proceedings, corporate, government and academic reports.

Engineering Index. The Engineering Index Inc., 345 E. 47th St., New York, New York 10017. 1962-.

ERDA Research Abstracts. U.S. ERDA Technical Information Center, Box 62, Oak Ridge, Tennessee 37830.

Geographical Abstracts. London School of Economics, Dept. of Geography, Regency House, 34 Duke St., London, England 1966-. Continued by Geo Abstracts issued in 6 parts: Pt. A. Landforms and the quaternary; Pt. B. Biogeography and Climatology; Pt. C. Economic geography; Pt. D. Social geography and cartography; Pt. E. Sedimentology; Pt. F. Regional and community planning.

Index to Scientific Book Contents. Institute for Scientific Information, 3501 Market St., Philadelphia, Pennsylvania 19104. (800) 523-1857. 1985-. Annual. Gives contents of science books published.

Mineralogical Abstracts. Mineralogical Society, 41 Queen's Gate, London, England SW7 5HR. 71 5847916. Quarterly. Abstracts of journal articles, conferences, technical reports and specialized books in the areas of minerals, clay minerals, economic minerals, ore deposits, environmental studies, experimental mineralogy, gemstones, geochemistry, petrology, lunar and planetary studies and other related areas in mineralogy.

Pollution Abstracts. Cambridge Scientific Abstracts, 5161 River Rd., Bethesda, Maryland 20816. (301) 961-6750. Six/year. Indexes worldwide technical literature on environmental pollution. Covers air pollution, marine and freshwater pollution, sewage and wastewater treatment, waste management, toxicology and health, noise pollution, radiation, land pollution, and environmental policies, programs, legislation, and education. Also available online.

Science Citation Index. Institute for Scientific Information, 3501 Market St., Philadelphia, Pennsylvania 19104. 1961-.

ALMANACS AND YEARBOOKS

Environmental Almanac. World Resources Institute. Houghton Mifflin, 1 Beacon St., Boston, Massachusetts 02108. (617) 725-5000; (800) 225-3362. 1991. Covers consumer products, energy, endangered species, food safety, global warming, solid wastes, toxics, wetlands and other related areas. Also included are the names and addresses of the chief environmental executives for all 50 states.

BIBLIOGRAPHIES

Current Contents. Agriculture, Biology and Environmental Sciences. Institute for Scientific Information, 3501 Market St., Philadelphia, Pennsylvania 19104. (800) 523-1857. 1973-. Previous title: Current Contents. Agricultural, Food & Veterinary Sciences. Gives the table of contents of periodicals in the fields of agriculture, biology, environmental and related areas.

Environmental Impact Assessment: A Bibliography with Abstracts. B. Clark, et al. Cassell PLC, Publishers Distribution Center, PO Box C831, Rutherford, New Jersey 07070. (201) 939-6064/5. 1980.

ENCYCLOPEDIAS AND DICTIONARIES

Dictionary of Environmental Engineering and Related Sciences: English-Spanish, Spanish-English. Jose T. Villate. Ediciones Universal, 3090 SW 8th St., Miami, Florida 33135. (305) 642-3355. 1979.

Encyclopedia of Chemical Processing and Design. John J. Mcketta and W. A. Cunningham. Marcel Dekker, Inc., 270 Madison Ave., New York, New York 10016. (212) 696-9000; (800) 228-1160. 1992. Thirty-eight volumes.

Encyclopedia of Environmental Science and Engineering. J.R. Pfafflin. Gordon and Breach Science Publishers, Inc., 270 8th Ave., New York, New York 10011. (212) 206-8900. 1992.

The Facts on File Dictionary of Environmental Science. L. Harold Stevenson and Bruce Wyman. Facts on File, Inc., 460 Park Ave. S., New York, New York 10016. (212) 683-2244. 1991.

Glossary of Geology. Robert Latimer Bates and Julia A. Jackson, eds. American Geological Institute, 4220 King St., Alexandria, Virginia 22302-1507. (703) 379-2480 or (800) 336-4764. 1987. Third edition.

Kirk-Othmer Encyclopedia of Chemical Technology. J. I. Kroschwitz, ed. John Wiley & Sons, Inc., 605 3rd Ave., New York, New York 10158-0012. (212) 850-6000. 1992-. All articles in the new edition have been rewritten and updated adding new subjects such as biotechnology, computer topics, analytical techniques and instrumentation, environmental concerns, fuels and energy, inorganic and solid state chemistry; composite materials and material science in general, and pharmaceuticals. Also available online.

McGraw-Hill Encyclopedia of Environmental Science. Sybil P. Parker. McGraw-Hill Science & Engineering Books, 11 W. 19th St., New York, New York 10011. (212) 337-6010. 1980. Covers ecology, man's influence on nature, and environmental protection.

McGraw-Hill Encyclopedia of the Geological Sciences. Sybil P. Parker, ed. McGraw-Hill, 1221 Avenue of the Americas, New York, New York 10020. (212) 512-2000 or (800) 262-4729. 1988. Second edition. Published previously in the McGraw-Hill Encyclopedia of Science and Technology.

GENERAL WORKS

Application of Environmental Impact Assessment: Highways and Dams. United Nations, 2 United Nations Plaza, Salis Section Rm. DC 2-853, New York, New York 10017. (800) 553-3210. 1987.

Development Concept Plan Environmental Assessment: Gulf Coast, Everglades National Park, Florida. U.S. National Park Service, Department of the Interior, PO Box 37127, Washington, District of Columbia 20013. (202) 208-6843. 1990. Land use concepts in the Everglades National Park.

Development without Destruction: Evolving Environmental Perceptions. M. Tolba. Cassell PLC, Publishers Distribution Center, PO Box C831, Rutherford, New Jersey 07070. (201) 939-6064/5. 1982.

Environmental Biology for Engineers. George Camougis. McGraw-Hill Science & Engineering Books, 11 West 19th St., New York, New York 10011. (212) 337-6010. 1981. Deals with environmental impact analysis, ecology, environmental engineering and environmental legislation.

Environmental Engineering and Sanitation. Joseph A. Salvato. John Wiley & Sons, Inc., 605 3rd Ave., New York, New York 10158-0012. (212) 850-6000. 1992. 3d ed. Applies principles of sanitary science and engineering to sanitation and environmental health. It includes design, construction, maintenance, and operations of sanitation plants and structures. Provides state-of-the-art information on environmental factors associated with chronic and non-infectious diseases; environmental engineering planning and impact analysis; waste management and control; food sanitation; administration of health and sanitation programs; acid rain; noise control; campground sanitation, etc.

Environmental Hazard Assessment of Effluents. Pergamon Microforms International, Inc., Fairview Park, Elmsford, New York 10523. (914) 592-7720. Concepts of effluent testing, biomonitoring, hazard assessment, and disposal.

Environmental Impact Assessment for Developing Countries. A. K. Biswas and Q. Geping, eds. Cassell PLC, Publishers Distribution Center, PO Box C831, Rutherford, New Jersey 07070. (201) 939-6064; (201) 939-6065. 1987.

Environmental Impacts of Hazardous Waste Treatment, Storage and Disposal Facilities. Rodolfo N. Salcedo, et al. Technomic Publishing Co., 851 New Holland Ave., Box 3535, Lancaster, Pennsylvania 17604. (717) 291-5609. 1989. Provides guidance in dealing with the many obstacles and preliminary requirements in siting TSD facilities.

Evaluation of Environmental Data for Regulatory and Impact Assessment. S. Ramamoorthy and E. Baddaloo. Elsevier Science Publishing Co., 655 Avenue of the Americas, New York, New York 10010. (212) 984-5800. 1991.

Hazard Assessment of Chemicals. Academic Press, c/o Harcourt Brace Jovanovich Inc., 6277 Sea Harbor Dr., Orlando, Florida 32887. (800) 346-8648. 1981-. Annually. Presents comprehensive authoritative reviews of new and significant developments in the area of hazard assessment of chemicals or chemical classes.

Policies and Systems of Environmental Impact Assessment. UNIPUB, 4611-F Assembly Dr., Lanham, Maryland 20706. (301) 459-7666 or (800) 274-4888. 1991. Describes current trends and experience gained regarding policies and systems of environmental impact assessment (EIA) in the ECE region.

Recycling and Incineration: Evaluating Choices. Richard A. Denison and John Ruston. Island Press, 1718 Connecticut Ave. N.W., Suite 300, Washington, District of Columbia 20009. (202) 232-7933. 1990. Presents the technology, economics, environmental concerns, and legal intricacies behind these two approaches. Includes basics of waste reduction, recycling, and incineration; cost comparisons of the two approaches; an evaluation of the health and environmental impacts.

Report on Renewable Energy and Utility Regulation. National Association of Regulatory Utility Commissioners, 1102 ICC Bldg., PO Box 684, Washington, District of Columbia 20044-0684. (202) 898-2200. 1990. Recently released NARUC report that addresses some key questions and makes some basic conclusions about potential of renewable energy resources.

The Role of Environmental Impact Assessment in the Planning Process. M. Clark and J. Herington, eds. Cassell PLC, Publishers Distribution Center, PO Box C831, Rutherford, New Jersey 07070. (201) 939-6064; (201) 939-6065. 1988.

Strengthening Environmental Cooperation with Developing Countries. OECD Publications and Information Center, 2001 L St. N.W., Ste. 700, Washington, District of Columbia 20036. (202) 785-OECD. 1989. Report from an OECD seminar involving developing countries, aid and environmental agencies, multinational financing institutions, and non-governmental organizations concludes that early environmental assessment of development assistance projects and programs can play a key role in improving international cooperation for sustainable development.

A Technical Framework for Life-Cycle Assessment. Society of Environmental Toxicology and Chemistry and the SETAC Foundation for Environmental Education, 1101 14th St, NW, Washington, District of Columbia 20005. (202) 371-1275. 1991. Evaluates the environmental burdens associated with a product, process or activity.

Use of the Environmental Impact Computer System. Thomas M. Whiteside. Department of Urban and Regional Planning, University of Illinois at Urbana-Champaign, Urbana, Illinois 61801. 1988.

Valuing Wildlife: Economic and Social Perspectives. Daniel J. Decker and Gary R. Goff, eds. Westview Press, 5500 Central Ave., Boulder, Colorado 80301. (303) 444-3541. 1987. State of the art guide to determining the value of wildlife, the application for environmental impact assessment, and strategies in wildlife planning and policy.

GOVERNMENTAL ORGANIZATIONS

Assistant Attorney General: Environment and Resources Division, Department of Justice. Room 2143, 10th St. and Constitution Ave., N.W., Washington, District of Columbia 20530. (202) 514-2701.

Environment, Safety and Health Office: Department of Energy. James Forrestal Building, 1000 Independence Ave., S.W., Washington, District of Columbia 20585. (202) 586-6151.

Federal Highway Administration: Right-of-Way and Environment. 400 7th St., S.W., Washington, District of Columbia 20590. (202) 366-0342.

Office of Public Affairs: Fish and Wildlife Service. 18th and C St., N.W., Washington, District of Columbia 20240. (202) 343-5634.

Public Information Office: Federal Highway Administration. 400 7th St., S.W., Washington, District of Columbia 20590. (202) 366-0660.

U.S. Environmental Protection Agency: Air Risk Information Support Center. Research Triangle Park, North Carolina 27711. (919) 541-0888.

U.S. Environmental Protection Agency: Office of Environmental Engineering and Technology. 401 M St., S.W., Washington, District of Columbia 20460. (202) 382-2600.

U.S. Environmental Protection Agency: Office of Federal Activities. 401 M St., S.W., Washington, District of Columbia 20460. (202) 382-5053.

HANDBOOKS AND MANUALS

Environmental Career Guide: Job Opportunities with the Earth in Mind. Nicholas Basta. John Wiley & Sons, Inc., 605 3rd Ave., New York, New York 10158-0012. (212) 850-6000. 1991. Complete guide to the many career options in the growing environmental field. Shows how to find employers engaged in environmental activity, and how to get the job. Lists key environmental businesses–manufacturing, government agencies, engineering consulting firms, waste handling firms, and others. Lists key professional careers in environmental conservation and maps career strategies.

Handbook of Environmental Data on Organic Chemicals. Karel Verschueren. Van Nostrand Reinhold, 115 5th Ave., New York, New York 10003. (212) 254-3232. 1983. Covers individual substances as well as mixtures and preparations. The profiles include: properties, air pollution factors, water pollution factors, and biological effects.

Handbook of Highway Engineering. Robert F. Baker, ed. R. E. Krieger Publishing Co., 115 5th Ave., New York, New York 10003. (212) 254-3232. 1982. Provides reference data on the application of technology to highway transportation.

Pira's International Environmental Information Sources. Pira, Randalls Rd., Leatherhead, England KT22 7RU. 0372 376161. 1990. Sourcebook includes over 2,000 entries from more than 20 countries, including Australia, Finland, Germany, the United Kingdom, and the United States. Entries are from organizations, research centers, legislative and regulatory bodies, directories, online databases and periodicals. Subject areas covered are: air, noise, water and land pollution, waste control and disposal, recycling, energy recovery and nature conservation.

The Solid Waste Handbook: A Practical Guide. William D. Robinson, ed. John Wiley & Sons, Inc., 605 3rd Ave., New York, New York 10158-0012. (212) 850-6000. 1986. Covers the field of solid waste management, including legislation, regulation, planning, finance, technologies, operations, economics administration, and future trends.

Standard Handbook of Environmental Engineering. Robert A. Corbitt. McGraw-Hill, 1221 Ave. of the Americas, New York, New York 10020. (212) 512-2000 or (800) 262-4729. 1990. Hands-on reference to understand environmental engineering technology. Covers air quality control, water supply, wastewater disposal, waste management, stormwater and hazardous wastes.

ONLINE DATA BASES

BIOSIS Previews. BIOSIS, 2100 Arch St., Philadelphia, Pennsylvania 19103-1399. (215) 587-4800. Largest and most comprehensive database of research in the life sciences. Contains citations for nearly 9000 primary research journals, monographs, reviews, symposia, pre-liminary reports, semi-popular journals, selected institutional reports, government reports and research communications.

Computerized Engineering Index–COMPENDEX. Engineering Information Inc., 345 E. 47th St., New York, New York 10017. (212) 705-7600.

Digests of Environmental Impact Statements. Cambridge Scientific Abstracts, 5161 River Rd., Bethesda, Maryland 20816. (301) 961-6750. Abstracts and indexes of approximately 500 environmental impact studies.

Environmental Technical Information System. U.S. Army Corps of Engineers, Construction Engineering Research Laboratory, ETIS Support Program, 1003 W. Nevada St., Urbana, Illinois 61801. (217) 333-1369. The environmental effects of activities by the U.S. Department of Defense activities and other major governmental programs.

Kirk-Othmer Encyclopedia of Chemical Technology. John Wiley & Sons, Inc., 605 3rd Ave., 5th Floor, New York, New York 10158. (212) 850-6000. Online version of the publication of the same name.

Monthly Catalog of United States Government Publications. U.S. G.P.O., Supt. of Docs., PO Box 371954, Pittsburgh, Pennsylvania 15250-7954. (202) 512-0000.

National Technical Information Service. U.S. Department of Commerce, National Technical Information Service, Office of Data Base Services, 5285 Port Royal Rd., Springfield, Virginia 22161. (703) 487-4807. Bibliographic database of government sponsored research and technical reports.

PressNet Environmental Reports. Chemical Information Systems, Inc., 7215 York Rd., Baltimore, Maryland 21212. (301) 321-8440.

SCISEARCH. Institute for Scientific Information, University City Science Center, 3501 Market St., Philadelphia, Pennsylvania 19104. (215) 386-0100.

PERIODICALS AND NEWSLETTERS

Ecologist. MIT Press, 55 Hayward St., Cambridge, Massachusetts 02142. (617) 253-2889. Bimonthly. Man's impact on the biosphere and social, economic and political barriers.

Environment Research. Academic Press, c/o Harcourt Brace Jovanovich Inc., 6277 Sea Harbor Dr., Orlando, Florida 32887. (800) 346-8648. Bimonthly. Journal of environmental medicine and sciences.

Environmental Impact Assessment Review. Elsevier Science Publishing Co., 655 Avenue of the Americas, New York, New York 10010. (212) 989-5800. Quarterly.

Environmental Impact of Soft Drink Delivery System. National Association for Plastic Container Recovery, 4828 Pkwy. Plaza Blvd., Suite 260, Charlotte, North Carolina 28217. (704) 357-3250. Irregular.

Fundamentals & Applied Toxicology. Academic Press, c/o Marcourt Brace, PO Box 6250, 6277 Sea Harbor Dr., Orlando, Florida 32887. (218) 723-9828. 8/year. Covers risk assessment and safety studies of toxic agents.

Impact Assessment Bulletin. Center for Technology Assessment and Policy Studies, Rose Hulman Institute of Technology, Georgia Institute of Technology, Terra Haute, Indiana 47803-3999. (812) 877-1511. Quarterly.

Covers the assessment of environmental and technical impact.

RESEARCH CENTERS AND INSTITUTES

Academy of Natural Sciences of Philadelphia, Division of Environmental Research. 19th Street and the Parkway, Philadelphia, Pennsylvania 19103. (215) 299-1081.

Baylor University, Institute of Environmental Studies. B.U. Box 7266, Waco, Texas 76798-7266. (817) 755-3406.

Tufts University. Curtis Hall, 474 Boston Avenue, Medford, Massachusetts 02155. (617) 381-3486.

U.S. Forest Service, Aquatic Ecosystem Analysis Laboratory. 105 Page, Brigham Young University, Provo, Utah 84602. (801) 378-4928.

University of Nevada-Las Vegas, Marjorie Barrick Museum of Natural History. Las Vegas, Nevada 89154. (702) 739-3381.

University of Oklahoma, Oklahoma Biological Survey. Sutton Hall, Room 303, 625 Elm Avenue, Norman, Oklahoma 73019. (405) 325-4034.

University of Tennessee at Knoxville, Biology Consortium. M303 Walters Life Sciences Building, Knoxville, Tennessee 37996. (615) 974-6841.

University of Wisconsin-Madison, Institute for Environmental Studies. 1017 WARF Office Building, 610 Walnut Street, Madison, Wisconsin 53705. (608) 262-5957.

TRADE ASSOCIATIONS AND PROFESSIONAL SOCIETIES

American Society of Civil Engineers. 345 East 47th St., New York, New York 10017. (212) 705-7496.

Americans for the Environment. 1400 16th St. N.W., Washington, District of Columbia 20036. (202) 797-6665.

Association of New Jersey Environmental Commissions. PO Box 157, 300 Mendham Rd., Mendham, New Jersey 07945. (201) 539-7547.

CEIP Fund. 68 Harrison Ave., 5th Fl., Boston, Massachusetts 02111. (617) 426-4375.

Center for Environmental Information, Inc. 99 Court St., Rochester, New York 14604. (716) 546-3796.

Institute of Environmental Sciences. 940 E. Northwest Hwy., Mount Prospect, Illinois 60056. (708) 255-1561.

John Muir Institute for Environmental Studies. 743 Wilson St., Napa, California 94559. (707) 252-8333.

National Environmental Development Association. 1440 New York Ave., N.W., Suite 300, Washington, District of Columbia 20005. (202) 638-1230.

ENVIRONMENTAL IMPACT STATEMENT

ABSTRACTING AND INDEXING SERVICES

Applied Science and Technology Index. H.W. Wilson Co., 950 University Ave., Bronx, New York 10452. (800) 367-6770. Formerly Industrial Arts Index.

Biological Abstracts. BIOSIS, 2100 Arch St., Philadelphia, Pennsylvania 19103-1399. (215) 587-4800. 1927-.

Ecology Abstracts. Cambridge Scientific Abstracts, 5161 River Rd., Bethesda, Maryland 20816. (301) 961-6750. Monthly.

EIS: Digests of Environmental Impact Statements. Cambridge Scientific Abstracts, 5161 River Rd., Bethesda, Maryland 20816. (301) 951-1400. 1970-. Bimonthly. Provides detailed abstracts of all the environmental impact statements issued by the federal government each year and indexes them. Also extracts the key issues from the complex government released environmental impact statements. Contents include areas such as: air transportation, defense programs, energy, hazardous substances, land use, manufacturing, parks, refuges, forests, research and development, roads and railroads, urban and social programs, wastes, and water.

EIS, Key to Environmental Impact Statements. Information Resources Press, 2100 M St., NW, Suite 316, Washington, District of Columbia 20037.

Engineering Index. The Engineering Index Inc., 345 E. 47th St., New York, New York 10017. 1962-.

Environment Abstracts. Bowker A & I Publishing, 121 Chanlon Rd., New Providence, New Jersey 07974. (908) 464-6800. 1974-.

Environment Index. Environment Information Center, Index Research Department, 124 E. 39th St., New York, New York 10016. 1971-. Annual.

Environmental Information Connection-EIC. Planning Information Program, Dept. of Urban and Regional Planning, University of Illinois, 1003 West Nevada, Urbana, Illinois 61801. (217) 333-1369. Also available online.

Environmental Periodicals Bibliography. Environmental Studies Institute, International Academy at Santa Barbara, 800 Garden St., Suite D, Santa Barbara, California 93101. (805) 965-5010. Also available online.

ERDA Research Abstracts. U.S. ERDA Technical Information Center, Box 62, Oak Ridge, Tennessee 37830.

Geographical Abstracts. London School of Economics, Dept. of Geography, Regency House, 34 Duke St., London, England 1966-. Continued by Geo Abstracts issued in 6 parts: Pt. A. Landforms and the quaternary; Pt. B. Biogeography and Climatology; Pt. C. Economic geography; Pt. D. Social geography and cartography; Pt. E. Sedimentology; Pt. F. Regional and community planning.

Index to Scientific Book Contents. Institute for Scientific Information, 3501 Market St., Philadelphia, Pennsylvania 19104. (800) 523-1857. 1985-. Annual. Gives contents of science books published.

Mineralogical Abstracts. Mineralogical Society, 41 Queen's Gate, London, England SW7 5HR. 71 5847916. Quarterly. Abstracts of journal articles, conferences, technical reports and specialized books in the areas of minerals, clay minerals, economic minerals, ore deposits, environmental studies, experimental mineralogy, gemstones, geochemistry, petrology, lunar and planetary studies and other related areas in mineralogy.

Pollution Abstracts. Cambridge Scientific Abstracts, 5161 River Rd., Bethesda, Maryland 20816. (301) 961-6750. Six/year. Indexes worldwide technical literature on envi-

ronmental pollution. Covers air pollution, marine and freshwater pollution, sewage and wastewater treatment, waste management, toxicology and health, noise pollution, radiation, land pollution, and environmental policies, programs, legislation, and education. Also available online.

Science Citation Index. Institute for Scientific Information, 3501 Market St., Philadelphia, Pennsylvania 19104. 1961-.

ALMANACS AND YEARBOOKS

Environmental Almanac. World Resources Institute. Houghton Mifflin, 1 Beacon St., Boston, Massachusetts 02108. (617) 725-5000; (800) 225-3362. 1991. Covers consumer products, energy, endangered species, food safety, global warming, solid wastes, toxics, wetlands and other related areas. Also included are the names and addresses of the chief environmental executives for all 50 states.

BIBLIOGRAPHIES

Bibliography and Index of Geology. American Geological Institute, 4220 King St., Alexandria, Virginia 22302. Monthly. Includes environmental geology and hydrogeology.

Current Contents. Agriculture, Biology and Environmental Sciences. Institute for Scientific Information, 3501 Market St., Philadelphia, Pennsylvania 19104. (800) 523-1857. 1973-. Previous title: Current Contents. Agricultural, Food & Veterinary Sciences. Gives the table of contents of periodicals in the fields of agriculture, biology, environmental and related areas.

EPA Publications Bibliography. U.S. Environmental Protection Agency, Library Systems Branch, 401 M St., SW, Washington, District of Columbia 20460. (202) 260-2090. Quarterly.

DIRECTORIES

Environmental Impact Statement Directory: The National Network of EIS- Related Agencies and Organizations. Marc Landy, ed. IFI/Plenum, 233 Spring Street, New York, New York 10013. (800) 221-9369. 1981. Environmental impact statements classified as general, physical and cultural. Includes general directories, physical directories and cultural directories. Not available online.

ENCYCLOPEDIAS AND DICTIONARIES

Dictionary of Environmental Engineering and Related Sciences: English-Spanish, Spanish-English. Jose T. Villate. Ediciones Universal, 3090 SW 8th St., Miami, Florida 33135. (305) 642-3355. 1979.

Encyclopedia of Environmental Science and Engineering. J.R. Pfafflin. Gordon and Breach Science Publishers, Inc., 270 8th Ave., New York, New York 10011. (212) 206-8900. 1992.

Glossary of Geology. Robert Latimer Bates and Julia A. Jackson, eds. American Geological Institute, 4220 King St., Alexandria, Virginia 22302-1507. (703) 379-2480 or (800) 336-4764. 1987. Third edition.

McGraw-Hill Encyclopedia of Environmental Science. Sybil P. Parker. McGraw-Hill Science & Engineering Books, 11 W. 19th St., New York, New York 10011.

(212) 337-6010. 1980. Covers ecology, man's influence on nature, and environmental protection.

McGraw-Hill Encyclopedia of the Geological Sciences. Sybil P. Parker, ed. McGraw-Hill, 1221 Avenue of the Americas, New York, New York 10020. (212) 512-2000 or (800) 262-4729. 1988. Second edition. Published previously in the McGraw-Hill Encyclopedia of Science and Technology.

GENERAL WORKS

Environmental Impacts of Hazardous Waste Treatment, Storage and Disposal Facilities. Rodolfo N. Salcedo, et al. Technomic Publishing Co., 851 New Holland Ave., Box 3535, Lancaster, Pennsylvania 17604. (717) 291-5609. 1989. Provides guidance in dealing with the many obstacles and preliminary requirements in siting TSD facilities.

Evaluation of Environmental Data for Regulatory and Impact Assessment. S. Ramamoorthy and E. Baddaloo. Elsevier Science Publishing Co., 655 Avenue of the Americas, New York, New York 10010. (212) 984-5800. 1991.

Magill's Survey of Science. Earth Science Series. Frank N. Magill. Salem Press, PO Box 50062, Pasadena, California 91105. 1990-. Five volumes. Includes information on earth's crust, hot spots and volcanic island chains, physical properties of minerals, rock magnetism, physical properties of rocks, and index.

Report on Renewable Energy and Utility Regulation. National Association of Regulatory Utility Commissioners, 1102 ICC Bldg., PO Box 684, Washington, District of Columbia 20044-0684. (202) 898-2200. 1990. Recently released NARUC report that addresses some key questions and makes some basic conclusions about potential of renewable energy resources.

Use of the Environmental Impact Computer System. Thomas M. Whiteside. Department of Urban and Regional Planning, University of Illinois at Urbana-Champaign, Urbana, Illinois 61801. 1988.

GOVERNMENTAL ORGANIZATIONS

Federal Highway Administration: Right-of-Way and Environment. 400 7th St., S.W., Washington, District of Columbia 20590. (202) 366-0342.

Office of Environmental Affairs: Bureau of Reclamation. 18th and C St., N.W., Washington, District of Columbia 20240. (202) 343-4662.

Public Information Office: Federal Highway Administration. 400 7th St., S.W., Washington, District of Columbia 20590. (202) 366-0660.

U.S. Environmental Protection Agency: Office of Environmental Engineering and Technology. 401 M St., S.W., Washington, District of Columbia 20460. (202) 382-2600.

U.S. Environmental Protection Agency: Office of Federal Activities. 401 M St., S.W., Washington, District of Columbia 20460. (202) 382-5053.

HANDBOOKS AND MANUALS

Environmental Career Guide: Job Opportunities with the Earth in Mind. Nicholas Basta. John Wiley & Sons, Inc.,

605 3rd Ave., New York, New York 10158-0012. (212) 850-6000. 1991. Complete guide to the many career options in the growing environmental field. Shows how to find employers engaged in environmental activity, and how to get the job. Lists key environmental businesses–manufacturing, government agencies, engineering consulting firms, waste handling firms, and others. Lists key professional careers in environmental conservation and maps career strategies.

Pira's International Environmental Information Sources. Pira, Randalls Rd., Leatherhead, England KT22 7RU. 0372 376161. 1990. Sourcebook includes over 2,000 entries from more than 20 countries, including Australia, Finland, Germany, the United Kingdom, and the United States. Entries are from organizations, research centers, legislative and regulatory bodies, directories, online databases and periodicals. Subject areas covered are: air, noise, water and land pollution, waste control and disposal, recycling, energy recovery and nature conservation.

ONLINE DATA BASES

BIOSIS Previews. BIOSIS, 2100 Arch St., Philadelphia, Pennsylvania 19103-1399. (215) 587-4800. Largest and most comprehensive database of research in the life sciences. Contains citations for nearly 9000 primary research journals, monographs, reviews, symposia, preliminary reports, semi-popular journals, selected institutional reports, government reports and research communications.

Computerized Engineering Index–COMPENDEX. Engineering Information Inc., 345 E. 47th St., New York, New York 10017. (212) 705-7600.

Digests of Environmental Impact Statements. Cambridge Scientific Abstracts, 5161 River Rd., Bethesda, Maryland 20816. (301) 961-6750. Abstracts and indexes of approximately 500 environmental impact studies.

Enviro/Energyline Abstracts Plus. R. R. Bowker Co., 121 Chanlon Rd., New Providence, New Jersey 07974. (908) 464-6800.

Environmental Periodicals Bibliography. National Information Services Corp., Ste. 6, Wyman Towers, 3100 St. Paul St., Baltimore, Maryland 21218. (410)243-0797. Online version of abstract of same name.

Monthly Catalog of United States Government Publications. U.S. G.P.O., Supt. of Docs., PO Box 371954, Pittsburgh, Pennsylvania 15250-7954. (202) 512-0000.

National Technical Information Service. U.S. Department of Commerce, National Technical Information Service, Office of Data Base Services, 5285 Port Royal Rd., Springfield, Virginia 22161. (703) 487-4807. Bibliographic database of government sponsored research and technical reports.

PressNet Environmental Reports. Chemical Information Systems, Inc., 7215 York Rd., Baltimore, Maryland 21212. (301) 321-8440.

SCISEARCH. Institute for Scientific Information, University City Science Center, 3501 Market St., Philadelphia, Pennsylvania 19104. (215) 386-0100.

PERIODICALS AND NEWSLETTERS

Ecologist. MIT Press, 55 Hayward St., Cambridge, Massachusetts 02142. (617) 253-2889. Bimonthly. Man's impact on the biosphere and social, economic and political barriers.

Environment Research. Academic Press, c/o Harcourt Brace Jovanovich Inc., 6277 Sea Harbor Dr., Orlando, Florida 32887. (800) 346-8648. Bimonthly. Journal of environmental medicine and sciences.

Environmental Geology & Water Sciences. Springer-Verlag, 175 Fifth Avenue, New York, New York 10010. (212) 460-1500. Bimonthly. Covers interactions between humanity and Earth.

Fundamentals & Applied Toxicology. Academic Press, c/o Marcourt Brace, PO Box 6250, 6277 Sea Harbor Dr., Orlando, Florida 32887. (218) 723-9828. 8/year. Covers risk assessment and safety studies of toxic agents.

Impact Assessment Bulletin. Center for Technology Assessment and Policy Studies, Rose Hulman Institute of Technology, Georgia Institute of Technology, Terra Haute, Indiana 47803-3999. (812) 877-1511. Quarterly. Covers the assessment of environmental and technical impact.

Inventory of Reports. National Technical Information Service, 5285 Port Royal Rd., Washington, District of Columbia 22161. (703) 487-4650. Annual. Environmental impact analysis.

Waste Recovery Report. ICON, Inc., 211 S. 45th St., Philadelphia, Pennsylvania 19104. (215) 349-6500. Monthly. Recycling, waste-to-energy, and other resource recovery fields.

RESEARCH CENTERS AND INSTITUTES

Academy of Natural Sciences of Philadelphia, Division of Environmental Research. 19th Street and the Parkway, Philadelphia, Pennsylvania 19103. (215) 299-1081.

Bemidji State University, Center for Environmental Studies. Bemidji, Minnesota 56601. (218) 755-2910.

National Research Council. 2101 Constitution Ave., N.W., Washington, District of Columbia 20418. (202) 334-2000.

University of Hawaii at Manoa, Environmental Center. 2550 Campus Road, Honolulu, Hawaii 96822. (808) 956-7361.

University of Illinois, Institute for Environmental Studies. 408 South Goodwin Avenue, Urbana, Illinois 61801. (217) 333-4178.

University of Tennessee at Knoxville, Biology Consortium. M303 Walters Life Sciences Building, Knoxville, Tennessee 37996. (615) 974-6841.

University of Wisconsin-Madison, Institute for Environmental Studies. 1017 WARF Office Building, 610 Walnut Street, Madison, Wisconsin 53705. (608) 262-5957.

TRADE ASSOCIATIONS AND PROFESSIONAL SOCIETIES

American Society of Civil Engineers. 345 East 47th St., New York, New York 10017. (212) 705-7496.

Americans for the Environment. 1400 16th St. N.W., Washington, District of Columbia 20036. (202) 797-6665.

Association of New Jersey Environmental Commissions. PO Box 157, 300 Mendham Rd., Mendham, New Jersey 07945. (201) 539-7547.

Center for Environmental Information, Inc. 99 Court St., Rochester, New York 14604. (716) 546-3796.

Environmental Task Force. 6930 Carroll Ave., 6th Floor, Takoma Park, Maryland 20912. (202) 745-4870.

Institute of Environmental Sciences. 940 E. Northwest Hwy., Mount Prospect, Illinois 60056. (708) 255-1561.

National Environmental Development Association. 1440 New York Ave., N.W., Suite 300, Washington, District of Columbia 20005. (202) 638-1230.

ENVIRONMENTAL LEGISLATION

See also: SPECIFIC STATES, E.G. ALABAMA ENVIRONMENTAL LEGISLATION, ETC.

ABSTRACTING AND INDEXING SERVICES

Applied Science and Technology Index. H.W. Wilson Co., 950 University Ave., Bronx, New York 10452. (800) 367-6770. Formerly Industrial Arts Index.

Aqualine Abstracts. Water Research Centre. c/o Pergamon Microforms International, Inc., Fairview Park, Elmsford, New York 10523. (914) 592-7720. 1927-. Contains some 8,000 records annually on water and wastewater technology. Covers all aspects of water, wastewater, associated engineering services and the aquatic environment. Over 600 periodicals, as well as books, reports and conference proceedings and other publications from water related institutions worldwide are scanned. Also available online.

Engineering Index. The Engineering Index Inc., 345 E. 47th St., New York, New York 10017. 1962-.

Environment. Newsbank, Inc., 58 Pine St., New Canaan, Connecticut 06840. (203)966-1100. Monthly.

The Environmental Law Digest. Environmental Law Institute, 1616 P St., NW, Suite 200, Washington, District of Columbia 20036. (202) 328-5150. 1984. Monthly.

Foods ADLIBRA. K & M Pub. Inc., 2000 Frankfort Ave., Louisville, Kentucky 40206. Semimonthly. Contains abstracts of current literature concerning the food industry. Topics covered include: food technology, food packaging, new food products, world food economics, nutrition, patents, and marketing.

Geographical Abstracts. London School of Economics, Dept. of Geography, Regency House, 34 Duke St., London, England 1966-. Continued by Geo Abstracts issued in 6 parts: Pt. A. Landforms and the quaternary; Pt. B. Biogeography and Climatology; Pt. C. Economic geography; Pt. D. Social geography and cartography; Pt. E. Sedimentology; Pt. F. Regional and community planning.

Index to Scientific Book Contents. Institute for Scientific Information, 3501 Market St., Philadelphia, Pennsylvania 19104. (800) 523-1857. 1985-. Annual. Gives contents of science books published.

Priority Issue Reporting Service–PIRS. Information for Public Affairs, Inc., Client Services Dept., 1900 14th St., Sacramento, California 95814.

ALMANACS AND YEARBOOKS

Gale Environmental Almanac. Russ Hoyle. Gale Research Inc., 835 Penobscot Bldg., Detroit, Michigan 48226-4094. (313) 961-2242. 1993. Focuses on the U.S. and Canada, although worldwide and transboundary issues are discussed.

BIBLIOGRAPHIES

Current Contents. Agriculture, Biology and Environmental Sciences. Institute for Scientific Information, 3501 Market St., Philadelphia, Pennsylvania 19104. (800) 523-1857. 1973-. Previous title: Current Contents. Agricultural, Food & Veterinary Sciences. Gives the table of contents of periodicals in the fields of agriculture, biology, environmental and related areas.

Environmental Law: A Guide to Information Sources. Mortimer D. Schwartz. Gale Research Co., 835 Penobscot Bldg., Detroit, Michigan 48226-4094. (313) 961-2242. 1977. Man and the Environment Information Guide Series, v.6.

International Environmental Law. Robert J. Munro. Oceana Publications Inc., 75 Main St., Dobbs Ferry, New York 10522. (914) 693-8100. 1990. This international law bibliography extends beyond the usual legal sources, and includes a diverse array of law-related and non- law publications that discuss the topic of the world's environment and international law.

World Environment Law Bibliography. Virginia Evans Templeton. Fred B. Rothman & Co., 10368 W. Centennial Rd., Littleton, Colorado 80127. (303) 979-5657. 1987. Non-periodical literature in law and the social sciences publishing since 1970 in various languages with selected reviews and annotations from periodicals.

DIRECTORIES

Canadian Environmental Directory. Canadian Almanac & Directory Publishing Co. Ltd., 134 Adelaide St. E., Ste. 27, Toronto, Ontario, Canada M5C 1K9. (416) 362-4088. 1992. Includes individuals, agencies, firms, and associations.

Directory of State Environmental Agencies. Kathryn Hubler and Timothy R. Henderson, eds. Environmental Law Institute in cooperation with the Natural Resources Committee of the American Bar Association General Practice Section, 1616 P St. N.W. #200, Washington, District of Columbia 20036. (202) 328-5150. 1985.

ENCYCLOPEDIAS AND DICTIONARIES

Dictionary of Environmental Science and Technology. Andrew Porteous. John Wiley & Sons, Inc., 605 3rd Ave., New York, New York 10158-0012. (212) 850-6000. 1992.

Encyclopedia of Chemical Processing and Design. John J. Mcketta and W. A. Cunningham. Marcel Dekker, Inc., 270 Madison Ave., New York, New York 10016. (212) 696-9000; (800) 228-1160. 1992. Thirty-eight volumes.

Encyclopedia of Environmental Studies. William Ashworth. Facts on File, Inc., 460 Park Ave. S., New York, New York 10016. (212) 683-2244. 1991.

Environmental Encyclopedia. William P. Cunningham, Terence Ball, et. al. Gale Research Inc., 835 Penobscot Bldg., Detroit, Michigan 48226-4094. (313) 961-2242. 1993.

Environmental Regulatory Glossary. G. William Frick and Thomas P. Sullivan. Government Institutes, Inc., 4 Research Pl., Rockville, Maryland 20850. (301) 921-2300. 1990. Over 4,000 entries. Definitions were gathered from the Code of Federal Regulations, EPA documents, and Federal Environmental Statutes.

The Facts on File Dictionary of Environmental Science. L. Harold Stevenson and Bruce Wyman. Facts on File, Inc., 460 Park Ave. S., New York, New York 10016. (212) 683-2244. 1991.

Kirk-Othmer Encyclopedia of Chemical Technology. J. I. Kroschwitz, ed. John Wiley & Sons, Inc., 605 3rd Ave., New York, New York 10158-0012. (212) 850-6000. 1992-. All articles in the new edition have been rewritten and updated adding new subjects such as biotechnology, computer topics, analytical techniques and instrumentation, environmental concerns, fuels and energy, inorganic and solid state chemistry; composite materials and material science in general, and pharmaceuticals. Also available online.

Modern Plastics Encyclopedia. Modern Plastics Encyclopedia, PO Box 602, Highstown, New Jersey 08520-9955. 1992. Contains information on a broad range of topics from resin manufacture to semi finished materials. Includes environmental and safety regulations, on manufacture, use, and recycling and related matter.

Pollution Control Guide. Commerce Clearing House, 4205 W Peterson Ave., Chicago, Illinois 60646. (312) 583-8500. 1973-1985. National environmental policy: Water standards, effluent limitations, permit programs, solid-waste-radiation, noise, pesticides, toxic substances, air standards-emission limitations, and state implementation plans.

GENERAL WORKS

And Two if by Sea: Fighting the Attack on America's Coasts. Coast Alliance, Washington, District of Columbia 1986. A citizen's guide to the Coastal Zone Management Act and other coastal laws

Balancing on the Brink of Extinction: The Endangered Species Act and Lessons for the Future. Kathryn A. Kohm, ed. Island Press, 1718 Connecticut Ave. N.W., Suite 300, Washington, District of Columbia 20009. (202) 232-7933. 1991. Twenty essays providing an overview of the law's conception and history and its potential for protecting the remaining endangered species.

Chemical Hazards in the Workplace. Ronald M. Scott. Lewis Publishers, 200 Corporate Blvd. NW, Boca Raton, Florida 33431. (407) 994-0555 or (800)272-7737. 1989. Presents basics of toxicology. Reports a sampling of the accumulated knowledge of the hazards of specific compounds in the workplace. Also discusses the federal regulatory agencies charged with worker protection and the specific practices involved in maintaining safety and regulatory compliance.

Clean Air Act 1990 Amendments: Law and Practice. J. M. Stensvaag. John Wiley & Sons, Inc., 605 3rd Ave., New York, New York 10158-0012. (212) 850-6000. 1991. In-depth practical analysis of the 1990 Amendments to the Clean Air Act that includes compliance requirements, the new operating permit system, the enhanced enforcement provisions and criminal penalties, potential for citizen enforcement, and the increased reporting requirements.

Community Right-to-Know and Small Business. U.S. Environmental Protection Agency, Office of Solid Waste and Emergency Response, 401 M St., S.W., Washington, District of Columbia 20460. (202) 260-2090. 1988. Interprets the community Right-to-Know Act of 1986, especially Sections 311 and 312.

Compact School and College Administrator's Guide for Compliance with Federal and State Right-to-Know Regulations. Forum for Scientific Excellence. J. B. Lippincott, 227 E. Washington Sq., Philadelphia, Pennsylvania 19105. (215) 238-4200; (800) 982-4377. 1989. Presents the legal and technical language of current hazardous chemical regulations in meaningful, easily understandable terms. Provides a simplified, step-by-step program for compliance.

The Conservation Easement in California. Thomas S. Barrett & Putnam Livermore for the Trust for Public Land. Island Press, 1718 Connecticut Ave. N.W., Suite 300, Washington, District of Columbia 20009. (202) 232-7933. 1983. Conservation lawyers discuss techniques, tax implications and solutions to potential problems.

Construction and Environmental Insurance Case Digests. Wiley Law Publications Editorial Staff. John Wiley & Sons, Inc., 605 3rd Ave., New York, New York 10158-0012. (212) 850-6000. 1991. Quick reference to help construction industry practitioners and environmental practitioners determine the prevailing legal interpretation in the field of construction and environmental insurance coverage.

Construction of Dams and Aircraft Overflights in National Park Units. U.S. Congress. House Committee on Interior and Insular Affairs. U.S. G.P.O., Washington, District of Columbia 20401. Covers national parks and reserves, environmental aspects of dams, airplane noise and air traffic rules.

Environmental Biology for Engineers. George Camougis. McGraw-Hill Science & Engineering Books, 11 West 19th St., New York, New York 10011. (212) 337-6010. 1981. Deals with environmental impact analysis, ecology, environmental engineering and environmental legislation.

Environmental Disputes: Community Involvement in Conflict Resolution. James E. Crowfoot and Julia M. Wondolleck, eds. Island Press, 1718 Connecticut Ave. N.W., Suite 300, Washington, District of Columbia 20009. (202) 232-7933. 1990. Set of procedures for settling disputes over environmental policies without litigation.

Environmental Fact Sheet: Pesticide Reregistration. U.S. Environmental Protection Agency, Office of Pesticides and Toxic Substances, 401 M St. SW, Washington, District of Columbia 20460. (202) 260-2090. 1990.

Environmental Fact Sheet: Risk/Benefit Balancing Under the Federal Insecticide, Fungicide, and Rodenticide Act. U.S. Environmental Protection Agency, Office of Pesticides and Toxic Substances, 401 M St. SW, Washington, District of Columbia 20460. (202) 260-2090. 1990.

Environmental Impacts of Hazardous Waste Treatment, Storage and Disposal Facilities. Rodolfo N. Salcedo, et al. Technomic Publishing Co., 851 New Holland Ave., Box 3535, Lancaster, Pennsylvania 17604. (717) 291-5609. 1989. Provides guidance in dealing with the many obstacles and preliminary requirements in siting TSD facilities.

Environmental Lender Liability. O. T. Smith. John Wiley & Sons, Inc., 605 3rd Ave., New York, New York 10158-0012. (212) 850-6000. 1991. Covers the leaders' aspects of environmental law. Focuses on the liability of lenders for hazardous waste cleanup. Also discusses other provisions of federal environmental law statutes and the impact of bankruptcy on environmental obligations. Analyzes the newly proposed EPA guidelines on lender liability and includes relevant forms, checklists, and working documents.

Environmental Liability and Real Property Transactions. Joel S. Moskowitz. John Wiley & Sons, Inc., 605 3rd Ave., New York, New York 10158-0012. (212) 850-6000. 1989. Examines the growing body of environmental laws and regulations, and outlines ways to avoid liability. Appendix contains numerous sample forms which can be used for negotiating the purchase or sale of contaminated property.

Environmental Viewpoints. Marie Lazzari. Gale Research Inc., 835 Penobscot Bldg., Detroit, Michigan 48226-4094. (313) 961-2242. 1992.

EPA's RCRA/Superfund & EPCRA Hotlines: Questions and Answers. Government Institutes, Inc., 4 Research Pl., Suite 200, Rockville, Maryland 20850. (301) 921-2300. 1991. Actual test of the Significant Questions and Resolved Issues internal EPA reports released each month by the RCRA/Superfund Industrial assistance Hotline, and the Emergency Planning and Community Right-to-Know Industrial Hotline covering 1989 and 1990.

Federal Regulation of Hazardous Wastes: A Guide to RCRA. John Quarles. Environmental Law Institute, 1616 P St., NW, Suite 200, Washington, District of Columbia 20036. (202) 328-5150. 1982. Law and legislation in connection with hazardous wastes.

Fundamentals of Environmental Compliance Inspections. Government Institutes Inc., 4 Research Place, #200, Rockville, Maryland 20850. (301) 921-2300. Developed by EPA for their inspector training course. Gives technical and procedural insight into compliance inspections.

Harnessing Science for Environmental Regulation. John D. Graham. Praeger Publishers, 1 Madison Ave., New York, New York 10010-3603. (212) 685-5300. 1991. Environmental law in the United States relating to hazardous substances.

Hazardous Materials Transportation. Department of California Highway Patrol, PO Box 94298, Sacramento, California 94298-0001. (916) 445-1865. 1985. Hazardous substances transportation law and legislation in California.

Hazardous Waste Laws, Regulations, and Taxes for the U.S. Petroleum Refining Industry: An Overview. David E. Fenster. PennWell Books, PO Box 21288, Tulsa, Oklahoma 74121. (918) 831-9421; (800) 752-9764. 1990. Describes the impact of hazardous waste legislation on the petroleum refining industry.

Hazardous Waste Management: Recent Changes and Policy Alternatives. Daniel Carol. Congress of the United States, Congressional Budget Office, c/o U.S. Government Printing Office, N. Capitol & H Sts. NW, Washington, District of Columbia 20401. (202) 512-0000. 1985. Describes the economic aspects of hazardous wastes. Also includes the law and legislation in the United States regarding hazardous wastes aa well as government policy.

Hazardous Waste Management: Reducing the Risk. Council on Economic Priorities. Island Press, 1718 Connecticut Ave. N.W., Suite 300, Washington, District of Columbia 20009. (202) 232-7933. 1986. Includes information for regulatory agencies, waste generators, host communities, and public officials. Topics include compliance, liabilities, technologies, corporate and public relations, groundwater monitoring, key laws and recommendations.

Hazardous Waste Regulatory Guide: State Waste Management Programs. J. J. Keller & Associates, Inc., 3003 W. Breezewood, PO Box 368, Neenah, Wisconsin 54957-0368. (414) 722-2848. 1992. State by state guide to laws relating to hazardous wastes.

The Hazardous Waste System. U.S. Environmental Protection Agency, Office of Solid Waste and Emergency Response, 401 M St., SW April 9, 1992, Washington, District of Columbia 20460. (202) 382-4610. 1987. Hazardous wastes law and legislation in the United States.

How the Environmental Legal & Regulatory System Works: A Business Primer. Government Institutes, Inc., 4 Research Pl., Ste. 200, Rockville, Maryland 20850. (301) 921-2300. Explains where environmental laws originates; conflicts between federal, state, and local laws; how laws and regulations are made; how the regulated community can affect the development of regulations; the environmental regulatory agencies; how the laws are enforced; and what regulations apply to what business activities.

Identifying and Regulating Carcinogens. M. Dekker, 270 Madison Ave., New York, New York 10016. (212) 696-9000. 1989. Health risk assessment and testing.

Index of Hazardous Contents of Commercial Products in Schools and Colleges. The Forum for Scientific Excellence. J. B. Lippincott, 227 E. Washington Sq., Philadelphia, Pennsylvania 19105. (215) 238-4200; (800) 982-4377. 1990. Lists the hazardous components found in thousands of commercial products used in educational institutions.

Islands under Siege: National Parks and the Politics of External Threats. John C. Freemuth. University Press of Kansas, 329 Carruth, Lawrence, Kansas 66045. (913) 864-4154. 1991. Outlines a diverse set of political strategies, evaluating each in terms of environmental effectiveness and political feasibility.

Legal Responses to Indoor Air Pollution. Frank B. Cross. Quorum Books, Div. of Greenwood Publishing Group, Inc., 88 Post Rd. W., Box 5007, Westport, Connecticut 06881. (203) 226-3571. 1990. Examines the under-recognized risks of indoor air pollution and the shortcomings of regulatory and judicial responses to these risks.

Legal Risk Mitigation for the Environmental Professional. Jack V. Matson. Lewis Publishers, 2000 Corporate Blvd., N.W., Boca Raton, Florida 33431. (407) 994-0555 or

(800) 272-7737. 1991. Describes environmental statutes concerning civil and criminal provisions. Differentiates civil and criminal activities, professional practice, mitigating professional risks, and case studies.

Lessons Learned in Global Environmental Governance. Peter H. Sand. World Resources Institute, 1709 New York Ave. N.W., Washington, District of Columbia 20006. (800) 822-0504. 1990. Takes stock of significant international environmental initiatives to date and highlights innovative features of transnational regimes for setting and implementing standards.

List of Lists of Worldwide Hazardous Chemicals and Pollutants. The Forum of Scientific Excellence. J. B. Lippincott, 227 E. Washington Sq., Philadelphia, Pennsylvania 19105. (215) 238-4200; (800) 982-4377. 1990. Extensive compilation of regulated hazardous chemicals and environmental pollutants in existence. Includes separate lists of substances that are regulated by more than 40 states, as well as federal and international agencies. A master list of the regulated material is also included in both alphabetical and CAS number sequence.

Nature Reserves: Island Theory and Conservation Practice. Craig L. Shafer. Smithsonian Institution Press, 470 L'Enfant Plaza, No. 7100, Washington, District of Columbia 20560. (800) 782-4612. 1991. Encompasses ecology, biogeography, evolutionary biology, genetics, paleobiology, as well as legal, social, and economic issues.

Oil and Gas Law: The North Sea Exploration. Kenneth R. Simmonds. Oceana Publications Inc., 75 Main St., Dobbs Ferry, New York 10522. (914) 693-8100. 1988. Surveys the legal framework within which operators have to carry out the exploration and exploitation of North Sea oil and gas resources.

Our Common Lands: Defending the National Parks. David J. Simon, ed. Island Press, 1718 Connecticut Ave. N.W., Suite 300, Washington, District of Columbia 20009. (202) 232-7933. 1988. Explains the complexities of key environmental laws and how they can be used to protect our national parks. Includes discussion of successful and unsuccessful attempts to use the laws and how the courts interpret them.

Overtapped Oasis: Reform or Revolution for Western Water. Marc Reisner and Sarah Bates. Island Press, 1718 Connecticut Ave. N.W., Suite 300, Washington, District of Columbia 20009. (202) 232-7933. 1990. Comprehensive critique of the cardinal dogma of the American West: that the region is always running out of water and therefore must build more and more dams.

PCB Compliance Guide for Electrical Equipment. John W. Coryell. Bureau of National Affairs, 1231 25th St. N.W., Washington, District of Columbia 20037. (202) 452-4200. 1991.

Petroleum Contaminated Soils, Volume 2. Edward J. Calabrese and Paul T. Kostecki. Lewis Publishers, 200 Corporate Blvd. NW, Boca Raton, Florida 33431. (407) 994-0555 or (800)272-7737. 1989. Proceedings of the Third National Conference on Petroleum Contaminated Soils held at the University of Massachusetts-Amherst, September 19-21, 1988.

Plastics: America's Packaging Dilemma. Nancy A. Wolf and Ellen D. Feldman. Island Press, 1718 Connecticut Ave. N.W., Ste. 300, Washington, District of Columbia 20009. (202) 232-7933. 1991. Source books on plastics deal with packaging, building materials, consumer goods, electrical products, transportation, industrial machinery, adhesives, legislative and regulatory issues. Also covers the controversies over plastics incineration, degradability, and recyclability.

Popping the Plastics Question: Plastics Recycling and Bans on Plastics - Contacts, Resources and Legislation. Joan Mullany. National League of Cities, 1301 Pennsylvania Ave. N.W., Washington, District of Columbia 20004. (202) 626-3150. 1990.

Proof of Causation and Damages in Toxic Chemical, Hazardous Waste, and Drug Cases. Sheila L. Birnbaum. Practicing Law Institute, 810 7th Ave., New York, New York 10019. (212) 765-5700. 1987.

Public Policy for Chemicals: National and International Issues. Conservation Foundation, 1250 24th St., NW, Washington, District of Columbia 20037. (202) 293-4800. 1980. Legal aspects of chemicals and hazardous substances.

RCRA Compliance Implementation Guide. Mary P. Bauer and Elizabeth J. Kellar. Government Institutes, Inc., 4 Research Pl., Suite 200, Rockville, Maryland 20850. (301) 921-2300. 1990. Interprets how a particular situation fits into the whole compliance process. Step-by-step directions are given to satisfy the compliance program. Also included are copies of EPA reports, manifests and forms.

Real Estate Transactions and Environmental Risks: A Practical Guide. Donald C. Nanney. PennWell Books, PO Box 21288, Tulsa, Oklahoma 74121. (918) 831-9421; (800) 752-9764. 1990. Presents general principles used when approaching environmental issues from a real estate agent's point of view.

Regulating the Environment: An Overview of Federal Environmental Laws. Neil Stoloff. Oceana Publications Inc., 75 Main St., Dobbs Ferry, New York 10522. (914) 693-8100. 1991. An overview of federal environmental laws.

Regulation of Agrochemicals: A Driving Force in Their Evolution. Gino J. Marco, et al., eds. American Chemical Society, 1155 16th St. N.W., Washington, District of Columbia 20036. (800) 227-5558. 1991. Agrochemicals and the regulatory process before 1970, subsequent regulations and their impact on pesticide chemistry.

Regulatory Management: A Guide to Conducting Environmental Affairs and Minimizing Liability. James T. Egan. Lewis Publishers, 2000 Corporate Blvd., Boca Raton, Florida 33431. (800) 272-7737. 1991.

Reserved Water Rights Settlement Manual. Peter W. Sly. Island Press, 1718 Connecticut Ave. N.W., Suite 300, Washington, District of Columbia 20009. (202) 232-7933. 1988. Manual provides a negotiating process for settling water disputes between states and/or reservations.

Restoration of Petroleum-Contaminated Aquifers. Stephen M. Testa and Duane L. Winegardner. Lewis Publishers, 200 Corporate Blvd. NW, Boca Raton, Florida 33431. (407) 994-0555 or (800)272-7737. 1991. Presents information on restoring aquifers contaminated by petroleum products and derivatives. Discusses the regulatory environment and framework within which environmental issues are addressed and explains the geochemistry of petroleum.

SARA Title III: Intent and Implementation of Hazardous Materials Regulations. Frank L. Fire and Nancy K. Grant. PennWell Books, PO Box 21288, Tulsa, Oklahoma 74121. (918) 831-9421; (800) 752-9764. 1990. Addresses what is required for implementation of hazardous materials regulations.

Sources for the Future. Wallace Oates. Resources for the Future, 1616 P St., NW, Washington, District of Columbia 20036. (202) 328-5086. Examines emissions taxes, abatement subsides, and transferable emission permits in a national, regional, and global context.

State and Local Government Solid Waste Management. James T. O'Reilly. Clark Boardman Callaghan, 155 Pfingsten Rd., Deerfield, Illinois 60015. (800) 221-9428. 1991. To be revised annually. Focuses on municipal solid waste issues.

State Environmental Law Special Report. Government Institutes, Inc., 4 Research Pl., Ste. 200, Rockville, Maryland 20850. (301) 921-2300. 1991. Provides a nationwide perspective of state environmental trends from 43 states. Highlights are included from recent and forthcoming major events in hazardous and solid waste control, underground storage tanks, state superfunds, special land use regulations, etc.

Staying Out of Trouble: What You Should Know about the New Hazardous Waste Law. National Association of Manufacturers, 1331 Pennsylvania Ave., NW, Suite 1500 N., Washington, District of Columbia 20004. (202) 637-3000. 1985. Hazardous waste laws and legislation in the United States. Also covers refuse and disposal.

Supplier Notification Requirements. U.S. Environmental Protection Agency, Office of Pesticides and Toxic Substances, 401 M St., SW, Washington, District of Columbia 20460. (202) 260-2090. 1990. Legal aspects of reporting on chemicals and hazardous wastes.

Tort Liability In Emergency Planning. John C. Pine. U.S. Environmental Protection Agency, 401 M St. SW, Washington, District of Columbia 20460. (202) 260-2090. 1988.

Transforming Technology: An Agenda for Environmentally Sustainable Growth in the Twenty-First Century. George Heaton, et al. World Resources Institute, 1709 New York Ave. N.W., Washington, District of Columbia 20006. (800) 822-0504. 1991. Explores the extraordinarily rich potential of new technologies to resolve environmental and economic problems.

Transportation of Hazardous Materials: A Management Guide for Generators and Manufactuerers. William E. Kenworthy. Government Institutes, Inc., 4 Research Pl., Suite 200, Rockville, Maryland 20850. (301) 921-2300. 1989. A management guide for generators of hazardous waste. Covers of hazardous materials regulation, alternative shipping methods for generators, and useful approaches for achieving compliance.

Underground Storage Tanks: A Primer on the New Federal Regulatory Program. American Bar Association, 750 N. Lake Shore Dr., Chicago, Illinois 60611. (312) 988-5000. 1989. Environmental law relative to hazardous waste sites, waste disposal sites and underground storage.

Wastewater Engineering: Treatment, Disposal, and Reuse. Metcalf & Eddy, Inc. McGraw-Hill Science & Engineering Books, 11 West 19th St., New York, New York 10011. (212) 337-6010. 1991. Reflects the impact of changing federal legislation on environmental quality control and sludge management. Gives a solid overall perspective on wastewater engineering.

Water Law. William Goldfarb. Lewis Publishers, 200 Corporate Blvd. NW, Boca Raton, Florida 33431. (407) 994-0555 or (800)272-7737. 1988. Explains all legal terms and covers all aspects of water laws, including water pollution law.

Water Resources Planning. Andrew A. Dzurik. Rowman & Littlefield, Publishers, Inc., 8705 Bollman Pl., Savage, Maryland 20763. (301) 306-0400. 1990. Offers a comprehensive survey of all aspects of water resources planning and management.

Wetlands: Mitigating and Regulating Development Impacts. David Salvesen. The Urban Land Institute, 1090 Vermont Ave. N.W., Washington, District of Columbia 20005. (202) 289-8500; (800) 237-9196. 1990. Presents the latest examination of the conflicts surrounding development of wetlands. Explains both federal and state wetland regulations. Included is an up-to-date review of important wetlands case law and a detailed look at six of the toughest state programs.

Wetlands Protection: The Role of Economics. Paul F. Scodari. Environmental Law Institute, 1616 P St. N.W., Suite 200, Washington, District of Columbia 20036. (202) 328-5150. 1990. Discussion of market economics as applied to wetland functions and values. Key features include the science of wetland valuation, principles and methods of wetland valuation, principles and methods for valuing wetland goods, the implementation of wetland valuation, and the natural resource damage assessment.

Wildlife and Habitat Law. Jack W. Grosse. Oceana Publications Inc., 75 Main St., Dobbs Ferry, New York 10522. (914) 693-8100. 1991. Covers questions of overall management, control and protection of wildlife and habitat. Issues of shared and conflicting power with the states are covered.

World Guide to Environmental Issues and Organizations. Peter Brackley. Longman Group Ltd., Longman House, Burnt Mill, Harlow, Essex, England CM20 2J6. (0279) 426721. 1991.

Written Hazard Communication Program for Schools and Colleges. Forum for Scientific Excellence. J. B. Lippincott, 227 E. Washington Sq., Philadelphia, Pennsylvania 19105. (215) 238-4200; (800) 982-4377. 1989. Identifies all the requirements an educational institution must meet to ensure that its hazardous chemical compliance program is appropriate and adequate. Specific examples of written program requirements, MSDS format, hazard assessment criteria and communication vehicles and formats are included.

GOVERNMENTAL ORGANIZATIONS

Office of Public Information: Federal Energy Regulatory Commission. 825 North Capitol St., N.E., Washington, District of Columbia 20426. (202) 357-8055.

Public Affairs Office. James Forrestal Building, 1000 Independence Ave., S.W., Washington, District of Columbia 20585. (202) 586-6250.

U.S. Environmental Protection Agency: Assistant Administrator for Solid Waste and Emergency Response.

401 M St., S.W., Washington, District of Columbia 20460. (202) 382-4610.

U.S. Environmental Protection Agency: Assistant Administrator for Water. 401 M St., S.W., Washington, District of Columbia 20460. (202) 382-5700.

U.S. Environmental Protection Agency: CERCLA Enforcement Division. 401 M St., S.W., Washington, District of Columbia 20460. (202) 382-4812.

U.S. Environmental Protection Agency: Office of Compliance Monitoring. 401 M St., S.W., Washington, District of Columbia 20460. (202) 382-3807.

U.S. Environmental Protection Agency: Office of Criminal Enforcement. 401 M St., S.W., Washington, District of Columbia 20460. (202) 475-9660.

U.S. Environmental Protection Agency: Office of Municipal Pollution Control. 401 M St., S.W., Washington, District of Columbia 20460. (202) 382-5850.

U.S. Environmental Protection Agency: Office of Policy Analysis. 401 M St., S.W., Washington, District of Columbia 20460. (202) 382-4034.

U.S. Environmental Protection Agency: Office of Water Regulations and Standards. 401 M St., S.W., Washington, District of Columbia 20460. (202) 382-5400.

U.S. Environmental Protection Agency: RCRA Enforcement Division. 401 M St., S.W., Washington, District of Columbia 20460. (202) 382-4808.

U.S. Environmental Protection Agency: RCRA/Superfund Hotline. 401 M St., S.W., Washington, District of Columbia 20460. (202) 382-9346.

HANDBOOKS AND MANUALS

Clean Air Handbook. Government Institutes, Inc., 4 Research Pl., Ste. 200, Rockville, Maryland 20850. (301) 921-2300. Analyzes the requirements of the Clean Air Act and its 1990 amendments, as well as what can be expected in terms of new regulation.

Clean Water Handbook. Government Institutes, Inc., 4 Research Pl., Ste. 200, Rockville, Maryland 20850. (301) 921-2300. 1990. Offers straightforward explanation on enforcement, toxics, water quality standards, efficient limitations, NPDES, stormwater and nonpoint discharge control.

The Complete Guide to Hazardous Waste Regulations. Travis P. Wagner. Global Professional Publications, 2805 McGraw Ave., PO Box 19539, Irvine, California 92713-9539. (800) 854-7179. A comprehensive, step-by-step guide to the regulation of hazardous wastes under RCRA, TSCA, HMTA, and Superfund.

Environmental Career Guide: Job Opportunities with the Earth in Mind. Nicholas Basta. John Wiley & Sons, Inc., 605 3rd Ave., New York, New York 10158-0012. (212) 850-6000. 1991. Complete guide to the many career options in the growing environmental field. Shows how to find employers engaged in environmental activity, and how to get the job. Lists key environmental businesses–manufacturing, government agencies, engineering consulting firms, waste handling firms, and others. Lists key professional careers in environmental conservation and maps career strategies.

Environmental Dispute Handbook: Liability and Claims. Robert E. Carpenter, et al. John Wiley & Sons, Inc., 605

3rd Ave., New York, New York 10158-0012. (212) 850-6000. 1991. Two volumes. Explains as clearly as possible the claims and liabilities arising from environmental litigation. Covers environmental liability; parties potentially liable for environmental damage, such as property owners, insurers, transporters, etc.; remedies; and procedural considerations.

The Environmental Handbook for Property Transfer and Financing. Michael K. Prescott. Lewis Publishers, 200 Corporate Blvd. NW, Boca Raton, Florida 33431. (407) 994-0555 or (800)272-7737. 1990. Covers liability for environmental damages in the United States.

Environmental Hazards: Radioactive Materials and Wastes: A Reference Handbook. E. Willard Miller and Ruby M. Miller. ABC-Clio, 130 Cremona Dr., PO Box 1911, Santa Barbara, California 93116-1911. (805) 968-1911; (800) 422-2546. 1990. Information source on radioactive materials and wastes. Introductory chapters describe the nature and characteristics of both natural and manufactured radioactive materials. Also provides information on laws, regulations, and treaties about waste materials. Including a directory of private, governmental, and international organizations that deal with radioactive wastes.

Environmental Law Handbook. Government Institutes, Inc., 4 Research Pl., Ste. 200, Rockville, Maryland 20850. (301) 921-2300. Current compliance information on Environmental Law Fundamentals; Enforcement and Liabilities; RCRA; UST; SARA Title III; CERCLA; Water; Air; TSCA; OSHA/Noise; SDWA; NEPA; Pesticides; and Asbestos.

The Environmental Liability Handbook for Property Transfer and Financing. Michael K. Prescott and Douglas S. Brossman. Lewis Publishers, 2000 Corporate Blvd., N.W., Boca Raton, Florida 33431. (407) 994-0555 or (800) 272-7737. 1990. Provides an analysis of existing environmental legislation and trends that demonstrate the importance of the environmental site assessment in today's transactional market.

Environmental Statistics Handbook: Europe. Allan Foster, Oksana Newman. Gale Research Inc., 835 Penobscot Bldg., Detroit, Michigan 48226-4094. (313) 961-2242. 1993.

Guide to the Management of Hazardous Waste: A Handbook for the Businessman and the Concerned Citizen. J. William Haun. Fulcrum Publishing, 350 Indiana St., Ste. 350, Golden, Colorado 80401. (303) 277-1623. 1991. Fact book on hazardous waste management, including factory and trade waste, and hazardous waste law and legislation in the United States.

Handbook of Chemical and Environmental Safety in Schools and Colleges. Forum for Scientific Excellence, Inc. J. B. Lippincott, 227 E. Washington Sq., Philadelphia, Pennsylvania 19105. (215) 238-4200. 1990. Hazardous substances safety measures and school plant management. A single resource book containing all of the information outlined in a 5 volume training manual.

Handbook on Marine Pollution. Edgar Gold. Assuranceforeningen Gard, Postboks 1563 Myrene, Arendal, Norway N-4801. 1985. Law and legislation relative to marine pollution.

Handbook on Procedures for Implementing the National Environmental Policy Act. U.S. Office of Surface Mining Reclamation and Enforcement. Office of Surface Mining

Reclamation and Enforcement, Washington, District of Columbia Environmental law in the United States.

Hazard Communication Guide: Federal & State Right-to-Know Standards. J. J. Keller & Associates, Inc., 3003 W. Breezewood, PO Box 368, Neenah, Wisconsin 54957-0368. (414) 722-2848. 1985. Deals with legal aspects of industrial hygiene, hazardous substances, and industrial safety.

Hazard Communication Standard Inspection Manual. Government Institutes, Inc., 4 Research Pl., Ste. 200, Rockville, Maryland 20850. (301) 921-2300. 1991. Includes detailed inspection procedures. Covers hazard communication program, hazard determination procedures, new enforcement guidance on the construction industry, employee information and training, labeling, trade secrets, MSDS completeness, and the instances in which OSHA inspectors are instructed to issue citations.

Hazardous Materials Guide: Shipping, Materials Handling, and Transportation. J. J. Keller & Associates, Inc., 3003 W. Breezewood, PO Box 368, Neenah, Wisconsin 54957-0368. (414) 722-2848. Laws and procedures relating to the packing and transportation of hazardous substances.

Hazardous Waste Audit Program: A Regulatory & Safety Compliance System: Evaluation Guidelines, Monitoring Procedures, Checklists, Forms. J. J. Keller & Associates, Inc., 3003 W. Breezewood, PO Box 368, Neenah, Wisconsin 54957-0368. (414) 722-2848. 1986.

Hazardous Waste Management Guide. California Safety Council, Sacramento, California 1988. Covers California law and legislation relating to hazardous wastes.

Laboratory Chemical Standards: The Complete OSHA Compliance Manual. Bureau of National Affairs, 1231 25th St. N.W., Washington, District of Columbia 20037. (800) 372-1033. 1990. OSHA's new lab standard applies to laboratories that use hazardous chemicals and requires a written plan that satisfies federal guidelines.

The Law of Hazardous Waste. Susan M. Cooke. Matthew Bender, DM Dept., 1275 Broadway, Albany, New York 12204. (800) 833-3630. 1992. Management, cleanup, liability, and litigation.

Multi-Media Compliance Inspection Manual, 4th edition. Government Institutes, Inc., 4 Research Pl., Ste. 200, Rockville, Maryland 20850. (301) 921-2300. Multimedia compliance audit inspection of facilities that result in effluents, emissions, wastes or materials regulated under several laws such as Clean Water Act, Clean Air Act, RCRA and TSCA.

National Environmental Policy Act Handbook. U.S. Bureau of Reclamation. U.S. Department of the Interior, Bureau of Reclamation, Washington, District of Columbia 20240. (202) 208-4662. 1990. Covers environmental law and environmental impact statements.

NPDES Permit Handbook. Government Institutes, Inc., 4 Research Pl., Ste. 200, Rockville, Maryland 20850. (301) 921-2300. 1989. Gives details on what a permit is, who needs one, how to apply and renew, establishing efficient limits, compliance deadlines and schedules, special provisions, permitting procedures, and enforcement.

Our National Wetland Heritage. Jon A. Kusler. Environmental Law Institute, 1616 P St., NW, Suite 200, Washington, District of Columbia 20036. (202) 328-5150. 1983. Discusses practical ways to preserve and protect wetlands and their benefits, which include recreation, wildlife habitat, pollution and flood control, scientific research and groundwater recharge.

PCB Regulation Manual. Glenn Kuntz. PennWell Books, PO Box 21288, Tulsa, Oklahoma 74121. (918) 831-9421; (800) 752-9764. 1990. 3rd ed. Provides the corporate environmental manager or plant engineer with a practical guide to compliance with PCB regulations.

Pira's International Environmental Information Sources. Pira, Randalls Rd., Leatherhead, England KT22 7RU. 0372 376161. 1990. Sourcebook includes over 2,000 entries from more than 20 countries, including Australia, Finland, Germany, the United Kingdom, and the United States. Entries are from organizations, research centers, legislative and regulatory bodies, directories, online databases and periodicals. Subject areas covered are: air, noise, water and land pollution, waste control and disposal, recycling, energy recovery and nature conservation.

The Poisoned Well: New Strategies for Groundwater Protection. Eric P. Jorgensen, ed. Island Press, 1718 Connecticut Ave. N.W., Suite 300, Washington, District of Columbia 20009. (202) 232-7933. 1989. Explains how individuals can work with agencies and the courts to enforce water laws, how the major federal water laws, work what remedies exist for each type of groundwater contamination, and what state and local programs may be helpful.

Practical Handbook of Ground Water Monitoring. David M. Nielsen. Lewis Publishers, 2000 Corporate Blvd., N.W., Boca Raton, Florida 33431. (407) 994-0555 or (800) 272-7737. 1991. Covers the complete spectrum of state-of-the-science technology applied to investigations of ground water quality. Emphasis is placed on the practical application of current technology, and minimum theory is discussed.

Preparing for Emergency Planning. National Association of Manufacturers, 1331 Pennsylvania Ave., NW, Suite 1500 N., Washington, District of Columbia 20004. (202) 637-3000. 1987. Explains the Emergency Planning and Community Right-to-Know Act under the Superfund Law.

RCRA Hazardous Wastes Handbook. Crowell & Moring. Government Institutes, Inc., 4 Research Place, Suite 200, Rockville, Maryland 20850. (301) 921-2300. 1989. 8th ed. Analyzes the impact of the Resource Conservation and Recovery Act on the business, while incorporating the most recent regulatory changes to the RCRA. These include the final 1988 underground storage tank rules, the medical waste regulations, permit modification regulations, amendments regarding corrective action and closures, the exemption for "treatability tests," waste export rules, etc. Includes the complete test of the RCRA statute as currently amended.

RCRA Inspection Manual. Environment Protection Agency. Government Institutes, Inc., 4 Research Pl., Suite 200, Rockville, Maryland 20850. (301) 921-2300. 1989. 2nd ed. Developed by EPA to support its inspectors in conducting complex field inspections. It covers the key topics that will help eliminate deficiencies, satisfy inspections and avoid civil and criminal penalties.

Resource Conservation and Recovery Act Handbook. ERT, Marketing Dept., 696 Virginia Road, Concord, Massachusetts 01742. Law relating to hazardous wastes and waste sites.

Resource Conservation and Recovery Act Inspection Manual. U.S. Environmental Protection Agency. Government Institutes, Inc., 4 Research Pl., Ste. 200, Rockville, Maryland 20850. (301) 921-2300. 1989.

The Solid Waste Handbook: A Practical Guide. William D. Robinson, ed. John Wiley & Sons, Inc., 605 3rd Ave., New York, New York 10158-0012. (212) 850-6000. 1986. Covers the field of solid waste management, including legislation, regulation, planning, finance, technologies, operations, economics administration, and future trends.

Standard Handbook of Hazardous Waste Treatment and Disposal. Harry M. Freeman, ed. McGraw-Hill Science & Engineering Books, 11 West 19th St., New York, New York 10011. (212) 337-6010. 1989. A reference of alternatives and innovative technologies for managing hazardous waste and cleaning up abandoned disposal sites.

Storm Water: Guidance Manual for the Preparation of NPDES Permit Applications for Storm Water Discharges Associated with Industrial Activity. Government Institutes, Inc., 4 Research Pl., Ste. 200, Rockville, Maryland 20850. (301) 921-2300. 1991. Provides an overview of the new EPA regulations; contains an overview of the permitting process and information regarding the permit application requirements.

Superfund Handbook. Sidley & Austin, 696 Virginia Road, Concord, Massachusetts 01742. 1987. Law and legislation relating to refuse, refuse disposal, and its environmental aspects.

Superfund Manual: Legal and Management Strategies. Crowell & Moring. Government Institutes, Inc., 4 Research Pl., Suite 200, Rockville, Maryland 20850. (301) 921-2300. 1990. 4th ed. Industrial liability for hazardous waste and pollution damage at hazardous waste sites are explained. Explains the latest developments in the Superfund program. Includes the interrelationships between Superfund and RCRA; new regulations to implement Emergency Planning and the Community Right-to-Know Act; revisions to the National Contingency Plan; new EPA guidance documents relating to cleanup standards, site studies, and settlement procedures; court decisions and the special problems.

TSCA Handbook. Government Institutes, Inc., 4 Research Pl., Ste. 200, Rockville, Maryland 20850. (301) 921-2300. 1989. 2nd edition. Details existing chemical regulation under TSCA; EPA's program for evaluating and regulating new chemical substances; PMN preparations and follow through; civil and criminal liability; inspections and audits; required testing of chemical substances and mixtures and exemptions from PMN requirements.

ONLINE DATA BASES

Air Toxics Report. Business Publishers, Inc., 951 Pershing Dr., Silver Spring, Maryland 20910. (301) 587-6300. Online version of periodical of the same name.

Business and the Environment. Cutter Information Corp., 37 Broadway, Arlington, Massachusetts 02174-4439. (617) 648-8700. Online version of periodical of the same name.

Chemical Regulation Reporter. Bureau of National Affairs, BNA PLUS, 1231 25th St., N.W., Room 215, Washington, District of Columbia 20037. (800) 452-7773. Online version of periodicals of the same name.

Chemical Regulations and Guidelines System–CRGS. Network Management, 11242 Waples Mill Rd., Fairfax, Virginia 22030. (703) 359-9400. Maintains bibliographical information on the state of regulatory material, October 1982 to the present, on control of selected chemical substances or classes. It contains U.S. Statutes, promulgated regulations, available government standards and guidelines, and support documents. CRGS follows the regulatory cycle and includes a reference to each document including main documents and revisions in the Federal Register. Available on DIALOG.

Chemical Substance Control. Bureau of National Affairs, BNA PLUS, 1231 25th ST., N.W., Rm. 215, Washington, District of Columbia 20037. (800) 452-7773. Online version of periodical of the same name.

Computer-Aided Environmental Legislative Data Systems–CELDS. U.S. Army Corps of Engineers, Planning Information Programs (PIP), Dept. of Urban and Regional Planning, University of Illinois, 1003 West Nevada, Urbana, Illinois 61801. (217) 333-1369. Federal and state environmental regulations and standards.

Computerized Engineering Index–COMPENDEX. Engineering Information Inc., 345 E. 47th St., New York, New York 10017. (212) 705-7600.

Enflex Info. ERM Computer Services, Inc., 855 Springdale Dr., Exton, Pennsylvania 19341. (215) 524-3600. Text of all U.S. federal and state environmental regulations, including those covering hazardous materials, the transportation of hazardous materials, health and safety.

Environment Reporter. Bureau of National Affairs, 1231 25th St., N.W., Rm. 215, Washington, District of Columbia 20037. (800) 372-1033. Online version of periodical of the same name.

Environment Week. NewsNet, Inc., 945 Haverford Rd., Bryn Mawr, Pennsylvania 19010. (800) 345-1301. Online version of periodical of same name.

Environmental Compliance Update. High Tech Publishing Co., Ridge, New York

Environmental Health News. Occupational Health Services, Inc., 450 7th Ave., New York, New York 10123. (212) 967-1100. Online access to court decisions, regulatory changes, and medical and scientific news related to hazardous substances.

Environmental Law Reporter. Environmental Law Institute, 1616 P St., N.W., Suite 200, Washington, District of Columbia 20036. (202) 328-5150. News, analysis, commentary, primary documents, and other materials dealing with environmental law, including statutes and regulations, pending litigation, and Superfund cases.

Environmental Manager's Compliance Advisor. Business & Legal Reports, Inc., 64 Wall St., Madison, Connecticut 06443. (203) 245-7448. Online version of periodical of same name.

Federal Register Search System. Chemical Information Systems, Inc., 7215 York Rd., Baltimore, Maryland 21212. (301) 321-8440. Regulations, rules, standards, and guidelines involving chemical substances and cross-referencing to other citations on related substances.

Food, Cosmetics & Drug Packaging. Elsevier Advanced Technology Publications, Mayfield House, 256 Banbury Rd., Oxford, England OX2 7DH. 44 (865) 512242.

Foods ADLIBRA. General Mills, Inc., Foods Adlibra Publications, 9000 Plymouth Ave., North, Minneapolis, Minnesota 55427. (612) 540-3463. Online version of periodical of same name.

Greenwire. American Political Network, 282 North Washington St., Falls Church, Virginia 22046. (703) 237-5130. 1991. Daily. Daily electronic 12-page summary of the last 24 hours of news coverage of environmental issues worldwide. Monday through Friday at 10 am EST, it can be accessed by a PC, modem and an 800 number contains issues on environmental protection, energy/natural resources, business science, 50-state news, worldwide headlines, TV monitor, daily calendar, marketplace battles, Capitol Hill, spotlight story, global issues, environment and the law, solid waste and focus interviews.

Ground Water Federal Register Notices. National Ground Water Information Center, National Water Well Association, 6375 Riverside Dr., Dublin, Ohio 43017. (614) 761-1711.

Ground Water Industry Standards. National Ground Water Information Center, National Water Well Association, 6375 Riverside Dr., Dublin, Ohio 43017. (614) 761-1711.

Ground Water Job Mart. National Ground Water Information Center, National Water Well Association, 6375 Riverside Dr., Dublin, Ohio 43017. (614) 761-1711.

Ground Water Monitor. Business Publishers, Inc., 951 Pershing Dr., Silver Spring, Maryland 20910. (301) 587-6300. Online version of periodical of the same name.

Ground Water On-Line. National Water Well Association, National Ground Water Information Center, 6375 Riverside Dr., Dublin, Ohio 43017. (614) 761-1711. Technical literature covering all aspects of groundwater and well technology.

Ground Water Regulations. National Ground Water Information Center, National Water Well Association, 6375 Riverside Dr., Dublin, Ohio 43017. (614) 761-1711.

Hydrowire. HCI Publications, 410 Archibald St., Kansas City, Missouri 64111. (816) 931-1311.

Kirk-Othmer Encyclopedia of Chemical Technology. John Wiley & Sons, Inc., 605 3rd Ave., 5th Floor, New York, New York 10158. (212) 850-6000. Online version of the publication of the same name.

LEXIS Environmental Library. Mead Data Central, Inc., P.O. Box 933, Dayton, Ohio 45401. (800) 227-4908.

Monthly Catalog of United States Government Publications. U.S. G.P.O., Supt. of Docs., PO Box 371954, Pittsburgh, Pennsylvania 15250-7954. (202) 512-0000.

National Technical Information Service. U.S. Department of Commerce, National Technical Information Service, Office of Data Base Services, 5285 Port Royal Rd., Springfield, Virginia 22161. (703) 487-4807. Bibliographic database of government sponsored research and technical reports.

OPTS Regulation Tracking System. U.S. Environmental Protection Agency, Office of Pesticides and Toxic Substances, 401 M St., S.W., Washington, District of Colum-

bia 20460. (202) 260-2090. Histories of various regulations, as well as compliance.

PressNet Environmental Reports. Chemical Information Systems, Inc., 7215 York Rd., Baltimore, Maryland 21212. (301) 321-8440.

SCISEARCH. Institute for Scientific Information, University City Science Center, 3501 Market St., Philadelphia, Pennsylvania 19104. (215) 386-0100.

State Environmental Report. NewsNet, Inc., 945 Haverford Rd., Bryn Mawr, Pennsylvania 19010. (800) 345-1301.

State Regulation Report: Toxics. NewsNet, Inc., 945 Haverford Rd., Bryn Mawr, Pennsylvania 19010. (215) 527-8030. Toxic substances control and hazardous waste management at the state level.

WESTLAW Environmental Law Library. West Publishing Company, 50 W. Kellogg Blvd., PO Box 64526, St. Paul, Minnesota 55164-0526. (612) 228-2500. Text of U.S. federal court decisions, statutes and regulations, administrative law publications, specialized files, and texts and periodicals dealing with the environmental law.

PERIODICALS AND NEWSLETTERS

Air Toxics Report. Business Publishers, Inc., 951 Pershing Dr., Silver Spring, Maryland 20910-4464. (301) 587-6300. 1988-. Monthly. Directed towards organizations and facilities that are or may be affected by regulations under the Clean Air Act and National Emission Standards for Hazardous Air Pollutants, with articles on government regulation, studies, compliance, violations and legal actions. Also available online.

Air/Water Pollution Report. Business Publishers, Inc., 951 Pershing Dr., Silver Spring, Maryland 20910-4464. (301) 587-6300. 1963-. Weekly. Reports on the hard news and in-depth features for practical use by environmental managers. It keeps readers informed on the latest news from government and industry. Also available online.

Alert. Missouri Coalition for the Environment Foundation, 6267 Delmar Blvd., St. Louis, Missouri 63130. (314) 727-0600. 1969-. Quarterly. Published for the statewide environmental citizen activist organization.

American Industrial Hygiene Council Quarterly. American Industrial Health Council, 1330 Connecticut Avenue, NW, Suite 300, Washington, District of Columbia 20036. (202) 659-0060. Quarterly. Scientific issues related to proposed standards for regulating products.

The Amicus Journal. Natural Resources Defense Council, 40 West 20th Street, New York, New York 10011. (212) 727-2700. Quarterly. Articles on environmental affairs.

ANJEC Report. Association of New Jersey Environmental Commissions, Box 157, Mendham, New Jersey 07945. (201) 539-7547. 1969-. Quarterly. Informs environmental commissioners and interested citizens about environmental issues, laws and regulations, particularly those that effect New Jersey.

Asbestos Control Report. Business Publishers, Inc., 951 Pershing Drive, Silver Spring, Maryland 20910-4464. (301) 587-6300. Biweekly. Information on asbestos control techniques, research, and regulations. Also available online.

Balance. National Environmental Development Association, 1440 New York Avenue, NW, Suite 300, Washington, District of Columbia 20005. (202) 638-1230. Quarterly. Impact of environmental legislation on business and industry.

BNA's National Environmental Watch. Bureau of National Affairs, BNA Plus, 1231 25th St, NW, Washington, District of Columbia 20037. (202) 452-4200. Weekly. News, technological reviews, and regulatory information regarding industry's impact on the environment.

Boston College Environmental Affairs Law Review. Boston College Law School, 885 Centre Street, Newton Centre, Massachusetts 02159. (617) 552-8000. Quarterly. Forum for diversity of environmental issues.

Briefing. National Association of Manufacturers, 1331 Pennsylvania Avenue, NW, Suite 1500 North, Washington, District of Columbia 20004. (202) 637-3000. Weekly. Environmental issues as they relate to manufacturing.

Business and the Environment. Cutter Information Corp., 37 Broadway, Arlington, Massachusetts 02174. (617) 648-8700. Semimonthly. Global news and analysis on environmental trends. Also available online.

California Today. 909 12th St., #203, Sacramento, California 95814-2931. (916) 448-8726. 1965-. Bimonthly. Review of California environmental legislation and activities of PCL.

Campaign California Report. Campaign California, 926 J. St. #300, Sacramento, California 95814. (213) 393-3701. 1978-. Quarterly. Focuses on progressive politics in California, emphasis on reform of environmental laws.

Chemical & Radiation Waste Litigation Reporter. Chemical & Radiation Waste Litigation Reporter, Inc., 1980-. Monthly.

Chemical Regulation Reporter. Bureau of National Affairs, 1231 25th St. NW, Washington, District of Columbia 20037. (202) 452-4200. Weekly. Periodical covering legislative, regulatory, and industry action affecting controls on pesticides. Also available online.

Chemical Substances Control. Bureau of National Affairs, 1231 25th St. NW, Washington, District of Columbia 20037. (202) 452-4200. Biweekly. Periodical covering regulatory compliance and management of chemicals. Also available online.

Chemical Times & Trends. Chemical Specialties Manufacturers Association, 1913 Eye Street, NW, Washington, District of Columbia 20006. (202) 872-8110. Quarterly. Discusses trends in manufacturing/selling of industrial, household, and personal care products.

Coastal Zone Management. Taylor & Francis, 1900 Frost Road, Suite 101, Bristol, Pennsylvania 19007. (800) 821-8312. Quarterly. Covers social, political, legal, and cultural issues of coastal resources.

Community and Worker Right-to-Know News. Thompson Publishing Group, 1725 K St. NW, Washington, District of Columbia 20006. (800) 424-2959. Bimonthly. Reports on chemical disclosure requirements and industrial liability.

Ecology Law Quarterly. School of Law of the University of California, Berkeley, Boalt Hall, Rm. 20, Berkeley, California 94720. (510)642-0457. Quarterly. Environmental law in the United States.

Ecology USA. Business Publishers, Inc., 951 Pershing Dr., Silver Spring, Maryland 20910-4464. (301) 587-6300. 1972-. Biweekly. Contains all the legislation, regulation, and litigation affecting efforts to conserve and protect America's unique environmental and ecological heritage.

ECON; Environmental Contractor. Duane Enterprises, 319 West St., Braintree, Massachusetts 02184. (914) 737-2676. Monthly. Information in the asbestos industry.

Environment Daily. Pasha Publications Inc., 1401 Wilson Blvd., Suite 900, Arlington, Virginia 22209-9970. (703) 528-1244. 1991-. Daily. Reports brief wrap-up of the previous day's highlights from: Committee agendas and reports; Congressional Record; Federal Register; Agency Audits; CBD business opportunities; GAO, CBO, and OTA studies; Budget documents; court decisions; advocacy groups.

Environment Reporter. Bureau of National Affairs, 1231 25th St. NW, Washington, District of Columbia 20037. (800) 372-1033. Weekly. Issues of pollution control and environmental activity. Also available online.

Environmental Action. Environmental Action Foundation, 6930 Carroll Ave., Ste. 600, Takoma Park, Maryland 20912. (301) 891-1100. Bimonthly. Impact of humans and industry on the environment.

Environmental Bulletin. New Jersey Conservation Foundation, 300 Mendham Rd., Morristown, New Jersey 07960. (201) 539-7540. Monthly. State environmental legislation bulletin.

Environmental Compliance in your State. Business and Legal Reports, 64 Wall St., Madison, Connecticut 06443. (203) 245-7448. Monthly. Environmental law at the national and state levels.

Environmental Compliance Letter. Ste. 850, 2350 Lakeside Blvd., Richardson, Texas 75085. (214) 644-8971. Regulatory issues on environment.

Environmental Control News. E.F. Williams, 3637 Park Ave. #224, Memphis, Tennessee 38111. (901) 458-4696. Monthly. Regulatory, legislative, environmental, and technical developments.

Environmental Defense Fund Letter. Environmental Defense Fund, 257 Park Avenue South, New York, New York 10010. (212) 505-2100. 1971-. Bimonthly. Environmental issues of concern.

Environmental Forum. Environmental Law Institute, 1616 P St., N.W., # 200, Washington, District of Columbia 20036. (202) 328-5150. Bimonthly. Policy on environmental protection.

Environmental Health News. University of Washington, School of Public Health, Dept. of Environmental Health, Seattle, Washington 98195. (206) 543-3222. Quarterly. Occupational health, air pollution and safety.

Environmental Law in New York. Berle, Kass & Case, 45 Rockefeller Plaza, New York, New York 10111. (212) 765-1800. Bimonthly. Covers environmental law decisions by state and federal courts .

Environmental Liability Monitor. Business Publishers, Inc., 951 Pershing Dr., Silver Spring, Maryland 20910-4464. (301) 587-6300. 1990-. Monthly. Reports about environmental liability in all areas.

Environmental Litigation News. Environmental Compliance Inst., Aetna Bldg., Suite 850, 2350 Lakeside Blvd., Richardson, Texas 75082-4342. (214) 644-8971. Monthly. Environmental compliance legislation.

Environmental Manager's Compliance Advisor. Business & Legal Reports, Inc., 64 Wall St., Madison, Connecticut 06443-1513. (203) 245-7448. Biweekly. Integrated environmental compliance system. Also available online.

Environmental Monitoring & Assessment. Kluwer Academic Publishers, 101 Philip Dr., Assinippi Pk., Norwell, Massachusetts 02061. (617) 871-6600. Monthly. Legislation, enforcement, and technology.

Environmental Notice Bulletin. New York State Dept. of Environmental Conservation, 50 Wolf Rd., Albany, New York 12233. (518) 457-6668. Weekly. Information on state environmental quality review actions.

Environmental Policy Alert. Inside Washington Publishers, P.O. Box 7167, Ben Franklin Station, Washington, District of Columbia 20044. Biweekly. Deals with environmental policy news.

Environmental Protection News. Stevens Publishing Co., PO Box 2604, Waco, Texas 76706. (817) 776-9000. 1990-. Weekly. Covers topics such as: The EPA looking at the Endangered Species Act; The Indoor Air Bill debate intensifies in Congress; Capitol Hill considers new Hazmat Trade Laws; The EPA turns to the media to help prosecute polluters; The Superfund fiasco is not the fault of contractors?; and other environmental topics.

Environmental Regulation From the State Capital: Waste Disposal and Pollution Control. Wakeman/Walworth, 300 N. Washington St., Alexandria, Virginia 22314. (703) 549-8606. Legislative action concerning pollution control.

Environmental Statutes. Government Institutes, Inc., 4 Research Pl., Ste. 200, Rockville, Maryland 20850. (301) 921-2300. Annual. Complete text of twelve major environmental statutes.

Environs. King Hall School of Law, University of California, Environmental Law Society, King Hall, University of California, Davis, California 95616. (916) 752-6703. Environmental law and natural resource management in the western United States.

European Environment Review. European Environment Review, 23, Ave. Gen. Eisenhower, B-1030, Brussels, Belgium Quarterly. Environmental policy and law in the European Economic Community countries.

Everyone's Back Yard. Citizen's Clearinghouse for Hazardous Wastes, P.O. Box 926, Arlington, Virginia 22216. (703) 276-7070. Bimonthly. Contains news, views, and resources for grassroots environmental activists.

Federal Facilities Environmental Journal. Executive Enterprises Publications Co., Inc., 22 W. 21st St., New York, New York 10010-6990. (212) 645-7880. Quarterly. Environmental issues at federal facilities.

Flashpoint. National Association of Solvent Recyclers, 1333 New Hampshire Ave., N.W., No. 1100, Washington, District of Columbia 20036. (202) 463-6956. Biweekly. Overview of recycling hazardous waste fuel blending & related industries.

Georgia Environmental Law Letter. Georgia Law Letter Pub., 10 Park Place South, PO Box 1597, Atlanta, Georgia 30301-1597. 1989-. Monthly.

Ground Water Newsletter. Water Information Center, Inc., 125 East Bethpage Road, Plainview, New York 11803. (516) 249-7634. Biweekly. Covers ground water exploration, development, and management.

Ground Water Pollution News. Buraff Publications, 1350 Connecticut Ave., NW, Washington, District of Columbia 20036. (202) 862-0990. Biweekly. Legislation, regulation and litigation concerning ground water pollution.

Harvard Environmental Law Review. Environmental Law Review, c/o Publication Center, Harvard Law School, 202 Austin Hall, Cambridge, Massachusetts 02138. (617) 495-3110. Semiannual. Law reviews of cases involving the environment.

The Harvard Environmental Law Review: HELR. Harvard Environmental Law Review, 202 Austin Hall, Harvard Law Review, Cambridge, Massachusetts 02138. (617) 495-3110. Semiannual.

Hazardous Substances Advisor. J. J. Keller & Associates, Inc., 3003 W. Breezewood, PO Box 368, Neenah, Washington 54957-0368. (414) 722-2848. Monthly. Report on Congressional and regulatory activity to control or eliminate situations created by hazardous and toxic substances.

Hazardous Waste and Toxic Torts. Leader Publications, 111 Eighth Ave., New York, New York 10011. (212) 463-5709. Monthly.

Hazardous Waste Consultant. McCoy & Associates, 13701 West Jewell Avenue, Suite 202, Lakewood, Colorado 80228. (303) 987-0333. Bimonthly. Information on hazardous and toxic waste issues.

Hazardous Waste Litigation Reporter. Andrews Communications, Inc., 1646 Westchester Pike, Westtown, Pennsylvania 19395. (215) 399-6600. Biweekly.

International Environment Reporter. Bureau of National Affairs, 1231 25th St. N.W., Washington, District of Columbia 20037. (202) 452-4200. Monthly. International environment law and policy in the major industrial nations.

International Environmental Affairs. University Press of New England, 17 1/2 Lebanon Street, Hanover, New Hampshire 03755. (603) 646-3340. Quarterly. Issues on management of natural resources.

International Environmental Law and Regulation. Butterworth Legal Publishers, 289 E. 5th St., St. Paul, Minnesota 55101. (612) 227-4200. Covers issues in environmental law. Looseleaf format.

International Journal of Environment and Pollution. Inderscience Enterprises Ltd., World Trade Center Bldg., 110 Avenue Louis Casai, Case Postale 306, Geneva-Airport, Switzerland CH-1215. (44) 908-314248. 1991-. Publishes original state-of-the-art articles, book reviews, and technical papers in the areas of: Environmental policies, protection, institutional aspects of pollution, risk assessments of all forms of pollution, protection of soil and ground water, waste disposal strategies, ecological impact of pollutants and other related topics.

Journal of Energy, Natural Resources & Environmental Law. College of Law, University of Utah, Salt Lake City, Utah 84112. Semiannual. Legal aspects of energy development, natural resources, and environment.

Land Management & Environmental Report. John Wiley & Sons, Inc., Box 1239, Brooklandville, Maryland 21022. Legal aspects of land use.

Law Digest. Association of Metropolitan Sewerage Agencies, 1000 Connecticut Avenue, NW, Suite 1006, Washington, District of Columbia 20036. (202) 833-2672. Monthly. Legal issues on environmental and regulatory matters.

Multinational Environmental Outlook. Business Publishers, Inc., 951 Pershing Dr., Silver Spring, Maryland 20910-4464. (301) 587-6300. 1974-. Biweekly. Covers developments in world environmental problems such as acid rain, deforestation, soil erosion, overfishing, threats to health, animal extinction, population growth, diminishing water supply and other related matters. Also available online.

National Environmental Enforcement Journal. National Association of Attorneys General, 444 N. Capitol, N.W., Suite 403, Washington, District of Columbia 20001. Monthly. Litigation and inventive settlements in cases of waste dumping and pollution.

NCAMP's Technical Report. National Coalition Against the Misuse of Pesticides, 530 7th St., S.E., Washington, District of Columbia 20003. (202) 543-5450. Monthly. Actions on state & federal levels, legislation & litigation.

Noise Regulation Report. Business Publishers, Inc., 951 Pershing Dr., Silver Spring, Maryland 20910-4464. (301) 587-6300. 1974-. Biweekly. Focuses exclusively on noise abatement and control. Covers developments in this field, news from the federal government including regulatory activities at key federal agencies such as FAA and OSHA. Also covers hard to find information on which state and local governments are doing to enforce noise abatement laws.

North Carolina Environmental Law Letter. M. Lee Smith Pub. & Printers, 162 4th Ave., N., Box 2678, Arcade Sta., Nashville, Tennessee 37219. (615) 242-7395. Monthly. Environmental law developments that affect North Carolina companies.

Nuclear Waste News. Business Publishers, Inc., 951 Pershing Dr., Silver Spring, Maryland 20910-4464. (301) 587-6300. 1981-. Weekly. Covers up-to-the-minute information on radioactive wastes management. Includes facts on all aspects of radioactive wastes such as generation, packaging, transportation, processing, storage and disposal.

NYS Environment. New York State Dept. of Environmental Conservation, 50 Wolf Rd., Albany, New York 12233. (518) 457-2344. Biweekly. Controversial environmental issues in legislation.

Pennsylvania Environmental Law Letter. Andrews Communications, Inc., 1646 Westchester Pike, Westtown, Pennsylvania 19395. (215) 399-6600. Monthly.

Stanford Environmental Law Journal. Stanford Environmental Law Society, Stanford Law School, Stanford, California 94305. (415)723-4421. Annual.

Texas Pollution Report. Report Publications, P.O. Box 12368, Austin, Texas 78711. (512) 478-5663. Weekly. Covers regulatory activity, court decisions and legislation.

Utility Reporter. Merton Allen Associates, PO Box 15640, Plantation, Florida 33318-5640. (305)473-9560.

Monthly. Covers current activities in power generation and energy conservation.

Washington Environmental Protection Report. Callahan Publication, P.O. Box 3751, Washington, District of Columbia 20007. (703) 356-1925. Biweekly.

World Resource Review. SUPCON International, PO Box 5275, 1 Heritage Plaza, Woodridge, Illinois 60517. (708) 910-1551. 1981-. Quarterly. Covers all phases of policy discussions and their developments, including such topics as global change, energy production and use, ecosystem impacts of development activities, environmental law, solution of transnational environmental problems, global flow of strategic industrial materials, regional, national, and local resource management, natural resources, food, agriculture and forestry.

RESEARCH CENTERS AND INSTITUTES

Center for Law in the Public Interest. 5750 Wilshire Blvd., Suite 561, Los Angeles, California 90036. (213) 470-3000.

Environmental Law Institute. 1616 P St., N.W., Suite 200, Washington, District of Columbia 20036. (202) 328-5150.

National Research Council. 2101 Constitution Ave., N.W., Washington, District of Columbia 20418. (202) 334-2000.

State University of New York College of Environmental Science and Forestry. Institute for Environmental Policy and Planning, Bray Hall, Room 320, Syracuse, New York 13210. (315) 470-6636.

University of Houston, Environmental Liability Law Program. Law Center, 4800 Calhoun, Houston, Texas 77204-6381. (208) 749-1393.

University of Tennessee at Knoxville, Waste Management Research and Education Institute. 327 South Stadium Hall, Knoxville, Tennessee 37996-0710. (615) 974-4251.

University of Wisconsin-Madison, Institute for Environmental Studies. 1017 WARF Office Building, 610 Walnut Street, Madison, Wisconsin 53705. (608) 262-5957.

STATISTICS SOURCES

Statistical Record of the Environment. Arsen J. Darnay. Gale Research Inc., 835 Penobscot Bldg., Detroit, Michigan 48226-4094. (313) 961-2242. 1992.

TRADE ASSOCIATIONS AND PROFESSIONAL SOCIETIES

American Society of Civil Engineers. 345 East 47th St., New York, New York 10017. (212) 705-7496.

Association of New Jersey Environmental Commissions. PO Box 157, 300 Mendham Rd., Mendham, New Jersey 07945. (201) 539-7547.

Center for Environmental Information, Inc. 99 Court St., Rochester, New York 14604. (716) 546-3796.

Clean Water Action Project. c/o David Zwick, 1320 18th St. N.W., Washington, District of Columbia 20003. (202) 457-1286.

Council on Ocean Law. 1709 New York Ave., NW, Suite 700, Washington, District of Columbia 20006. (202) 347-3766.

Environmental and Energy Study Institute. 122 C St., N.W., Suite 700, Washington, District of Columbia 20001. (202) 628-1400.

Environmental Compliance Institute. Aetna Bldg., Suite 850, 2350 Lakeside Blvd., Richardson, Texas 75082-4342. (214) 644-8971.

Environmental Defense Fund. 257 Park Ave., S., New York, New York 10010. (212) 505-2100. Non-profit organization that was established more than 20 years ago. Its goals are to protect the earth's environment by providing lasting solutions to global environmental problems.

Environmental Industry Council. 1825 K St., N.W., Suite 210, Washington, District of Columbia 20006. (202) 331-7706.

Environmental Safety. 1700 N. More St., Suite 1920, Arlington, Virginia 22209. (703) 527-8300.

Government Institutes, Inc. 966 Hungerford Dr., #24, Rockville, Maryland 20850. (301) 251-9250.

Harvard Environmental Law Society. 202 Austin Hall, Harvard Law School, Cambridge, Massachusetts 02138. (617) 495-3125.

National Association of Environmental Professionals. PO Box 15210, Alexandria, Virginia 22309-0210. (703) 660-2364.

National Environmental Development Association. 1440 New York Ave., N.W., Suite 300, Washington, District of Columbia 20005. (202) 638-1230.

National Governors Association. Hall of the States, Suite 250, 444 N. Capitol St., N.W., Washington, District of Columbia 20001-1572. (202) 624-5300.

Northeast Conservation Law Enforcement Chiefs' Association. Dept. of Natural Resources, 1800 Washington St., S.E., Charleston, West Virginia 25305. (304) 348-2784.

Planning and Conservation League. 909 12th St., Suite 203, Sacramento, California 95814. (916) 444-8726.

Public Citizen. PO Box 19404, Washington, District of Columbia 20036. (202) 293-9142.

Sierra Club. 100 Bush St., San Francisco, California 94104. (415) 291-1600.

Sierra Club Legal Defense Fund. 180 Montgomery St., Ste. 1400, San Francisco, California 94104. (415) 627-6700.

Society for Animal Protective Legislation. PO Box 3719, Georgetown Station, Washington, District of Columbia 20007. (202) 337-2334.

ENVIRONMENTAL MANAGEMENT

ABSTRACTING AND INDEXING SERVICES

Applied Ecology Abstracts Studies in Renewable Natural Resources. Information Retrieval Ltd., 1911 Jefferson Davis Highway, Arlington, Virginia 22202. 1975-. Monthly.

Applied Science and Technology Index. H.W. Wilson Co., 950 University Ave., Bronx, New York 10452. (800) 367-6770. Formerly Industrial Arts Index.

ASFA Aquaculture Abstracts. Cambridge Scientific Abstracts, Inc., 5161 River Rd., Bethesda, Maryland 20816. (301) 961-6750. 1984.

Biological Abstracts. BIOSIS, 2100 Arch St., Philadelphia, Pennsylvania 19103-1399. (215) 587-4800. 1927-.

Bulletin Signaletique: Eau et Assainissement, Pollution Atmospherique, Droit des Pollutions. Centre de Documentation, Centre National de la Recherche Scientifique, 15, quai Anatole France, Paris, France 75700. (1) 45 55 92 25. 1983-. Monthly. Indexes pollution periodicals including water, atmospheric and related pollutions.

Ecological Abstracts. Geo Abstracts Ltd. Elsevier Applied Science, Crown House, Linton Rd., Barking, England IG 11 8JU. 1974-. Derived from over 600 leading ecological and environmental journals, plus books, conference proceedings, reports and theses.

Ecology Abstracts. Cambridge Scientific Abstracts, 5161 River Rd., Bethesda, Maryland 20816. (301) 961-6750. Monthly.

Engineering Index. The Engineering Index Inc., 345 E. 47th St., New York, New York 10017. 1962-.

Geographical Abstracts. London School of Economics, Dept. of Geography, Regency House, 34 Duke St., London, England 1966-. Continued by Geo Abstracts issued in 6 parts: Pt. A. Landforms and the quaternary; Pt. B. Biogeography and Climatology; Pt. C. Economic geography; Pt. D. Social geography and cartography; Pt. E. Sedimentology; Pt. F. Regional and community planning.

Index to Scientific Book Contents. Institute for Scientific Information, 3501 Market St., Philadelphia, Pennsylvania 19104. (800) 523-1857. 1985-. Annual. Gives contents of science books published.

Multimedia Index to Ecology. National Information Center for Educational Media, University of Southern California, Los Angeles, California 90007.

Pollution Abstracts. Cambridge Scientific Abstracts, 5161 River Rd., Bethesda, Maryland 20816. (301) 961-6750. Six/year. Indexes worldwide technical literature on environmental pollution. Covers air pollution, marine and freshwater pollution, sewage and wastewater treatment, waste management, toxicology and health, noise pollution, radiation, land pollution, and environmental policies, programs, legislation, and education. Also available online.

BIBLIOGRAPHIES

Chemical Engineering Bibliography. Martyn S. Ray. Noyes Publications, 120 Mill Rd., Park Ridge, New Jersey 07656. (201) 391-8484. Contains 20,000 references from 40 journals published over the period 1967-1988. Some of the topics covered include: energy conservation, environmental management, biotechnology, plant operations, absorption and cooling towers, membrane separation and other chemical engineering areas.

Current Contents. Agriculture, Biology and Environmental Sciences. Institute for Scientific Information, 3501 Market St., Philadelphia, Pennsylvania 19104. (800) 523-1857. 1973-. Previous title: Current Contents. Agricultural, Food & Veterinary Sciences. Gives the table of contents of periodicals in the fields of agriculture, biology, environmental and related areas.

DIRECTORIES

Environmental Organization Computer Readable Directory. Environmental Research Information, Inc., 575 8th Ave., New York, New York 10018-3011. (212) 465-1060. Also available online.

Environmental Studies to Natural Resources Management: An Annotated Guide to University and Government Training Programs in the United States. Sierra Club. International Earthcare Center, 802 2nd Ave., New York, New York 10017. 1980.

The Green Activity Book. Meryl Doney. Lion Publishing Corp., 1705 Hubbard Ave., Batavia, Illinois 60510. (708) 879-0707. 1991. Environmental problems and relevant activities and projects.

The Green Index: Directory of Environmental Organisations in Britain and Ireland. Cassell PLC, Publishers Distribution Center, PO Box C831, Rutherford, New Jersey 07070. (201) 939-6064; (201) 939-6065. 1990.

Guide to State Environmental Programs. Bureau of National Affairs, 1231 25th St., NW, Washington, District of Columbia 20037. (800) 372-1033. 1990.

ENCYCLOPEDIAS AND DICTIONARIES

Dictionary of Environmental Engineering and Related Sciences: English-Spanish, Spanish-English. Jose T. Villate. Ediciones Universal, 3090 SW 8th St., Miami, Florida 33135. (305) 642-3355. 1979.

Encyclopedia of Environmental Science and Engineering. J.R. Pfafflin. Gordon and Breach Science Publishers, Inc., 270 8th Ave., New York, New York 10011. (212) 206-8900. 1992.

Encyclopedia of Physical Science and Technology. Robert A. Meyers, ed. Academic Press, c/o Harcourt Brace Jovanovich Inc., 6277 Sea Harbor Dr., Orlando, Florida 32887. (800) 346-8648. Dictionary of engineering, technology and physical sciences.

The Environmental Dictionary. James J. King. PennWell Books, PO Box 21288, Tulsa, Oklahoma 74121. (918) 831-9421; (800) 752-9764. 1989. Gives more than 5,000 definitions of terms used and applied by the EPA.

The Facts on File Dictionary of Environmental Science. L. Harold Stevenson and Bruce Wyman. Facts on File, Inc., 460 Park Ave. S., New York, New York 10016. (212) 683-2244. 1991.

McGraw-Hill Encyclopedia of Environmental Science. Sybil P. Parker. McGraw-Hill Science & Engineering Books, 11 W. 19th St., New York, New York 10011. (212) 337-6010. 1980. Covers ecology, man's influence on nature, and environmental protection.

GENERAL WORKS

Advances in Water Treatment and Environmental Management. George Thomas. Elsevier Science Publishing Co., 655 Avenue of the Americas, New York, New York 10010. (212) 984-5800. 1991. Measurement and control of groundwater quality, rivers, river management, estuaries, and beaches.

Caring for the Earth: A Strategy for Sustainable Living. IUCN. Earthscan, 3 Endsleigh St., London, England 071-388 2117. 1991. Discusses the sustainable living methods to protect the environment.

Environmental Indicators. OECD Publication and Information Center, 2001 L St. N.W., Suite 700, Washington, District of Columbia 20036. (202) 785-OECD. 1991. Comprehensive assessments of environmental issues in industrialized countries. Charts the progress achieved over the past 20 years, and points to problems still remaining and sets an agenda of environmental issues to be dealt with in the 1990s.

Environmental Management in Developing Countries. OECD, UNIPUB, 4611-F Assembly Dr., Lanham, Maryland 20706. (301) 459-7666 or (800) 274-4888. 1991. Comprised of papers from a conference which looks at environmental management in a developmental context.

Environmental Modelling for Developing Countries. Asit K. Biswas, et al., eds. Cassell PLC, Publishers Distribution Center, PO Box C831, Rutherford, New Jersey 07070. (201) 939-6064/5. 1990. Explores how mathematical models can be effectively used in developing countries to improve environmental planning and management processes, with emphasis on modelling applications rather than knowledge accumulation.

An Environmental Odyssey: People, Pollution and Politics in the Life of a Practical Scientist. Merril Eisenbud. University of Washington Press, PO Box 50096, Seattle, Washington 98145-5096. (206) 543-4050 or (800) 441-4115. 1990. A professional biography where Eisenbud writes about a number of environmental challenges. He concludes with a 54-year perspective on the development of his field, on current environmental hazards, on the political pitfalls confronting environmentalists, and on the harmful effects of technology on human health.

Federal Lands: A Guide to Planning, Management, and State Revenues. Sally K. Fairfax. Island Press, 1718 Connecticut Ave. N.W., Suite 300, Washington, District of Columbia 20009. (202) 232-7933. 1987. Comprehensive reference on the management and allocation of revenues from public lands.

Food Chain Yields, Models, and Management of Large Marine Ecosystems. Kenneth Sherman, et al., eds. Westview Press, 5500 Central Ave., Boulder, Colorado 80301. (303) 444-3541. 1991. Describes marine ecology, its productive resources and its management.

Hazardous Waste Measurements. Milagros S. Simmons, ed. Lewis Publishers, 200 Corporate Blvd. NW, Boca Raton, Florida 33431. (407) 994-0555 or (800)272-7737. 1991. Focuses on recent developments in field testing methods and quality assurance.

Integrated Environmental Management. John Cairns, Jr. and Todd V. Crawford. Lewis Publishers, 2000 Corporate Blvd., N.W., Boca Raton, Florida 33431. (407) 994-0555 or (800) 272-7737. 1991. Discusses the need for integrated environmental systems management, managing environmental risks, applied ecology, a strategy for the long-term management of the Savannah River site lands, and the role of the endangered species act in the conservation of biological diversity.

Integrated Physical, Socio-Economic and Environmental Planning. Y. Ahmad and F. Muller, eds. Cassell PLC, Publishers Distribution Center, PO Box C831, Rutherford, New Jersey 07070. (201) 939-6064; (201) 939-6065. 1983.

Integrating Environment into Business: A Guide to Policy Making and Implementation. Environment Council. Environment Council and 3M United Kingdom PLC, 80 York Way, London, England N1 9AG. 071 278 4736. 1990. Outcome of the Environmental Policy Workshop which was held in February 1990. Addresses the issues to help businesses and other organizations to implement environmental legislations and other behavioral changes that might affect their operations.

Introduction to Environmental Management. Elsevier Science Publishing Co., 655 Avenue of the Americas, New York, New York 10010. (212) 984-5800. 1991. Environmental protection and environmental aspects of agriculture.

Large Marine Ecosystems: Patterns, Processes, and Yields. Kenneth Sherman, et al., eds. American Association for the Advancement of Science, 1333 H St. N.W., 8th Flr., Washington, District of Columbia 20005. (202) 326-6400. 1990. Deals with the conservation and management of vitally important components of the ecosphere.

Lessons Learned in Global Environmental Governance. Peter H. Sand. World Resources Institute, 1709 New York Ave. N.W., Washington, District of Columbia 20006. (800) 822-0504. 1990. Takes stock of significant international environmental initiatives to date and highlights innovative features of transnational regimes for setting and implementing standards.

Nature Tourism: Managing for the Environment. Tensie Whelan. Island Press, 1718 Connecticut Ave. N.W., Suite 300, Washington, District of Columbia 20009. (202) 232-7933. 1991. Provides practical advice and models for planning and developing a nature tourism industry, evaluating economic benefits and marketing nature tourism.

Saving the Mediterranean: The Politics of International Environmental Cooperation. Peter M. Haas. Columbia University Press, 562 W. 113th St., New York, New York 10025. (212) 316-7100. 1990. Focuses on the international pollution management of the Mediterranean. Ninety scientists and international officials were interviewed to ascertain how the international community responded to this particular threat.

Sustainable Development and Environmental Management of Small Islands. W. Beller, et al., eds. Parthenon Pub., Casterton Hall, Carnforth, England LA6 2LA. 1990. Volume 5 in the Man and the Biosphere series published jointly with UNESCO.

Technological Responses to the Greenhouse Effect. George Thurlow, ed. Elsevier Science Publishing Co., 655 Avenue of the Americas, New York, New York 10010. (212) 989-5800. 1990. Watt Committee on Energy (London) working with 23 British experts has reported on various greenhouse gases, their sources and sinks, followed by an analysis of the release of these gases in "energy conversion" primarily in electric power production.

Written Hazard Communication Program for Schools and Colleges. Forum for Scientific Excellence. J. B. Lippincott, 227 E. Washington Sq., Philadelphia, Pennsylvania

19105. (215) 238-4200; (800) 982-4377. 1989. Identifies all the requirements an educational institution must meet to ensure that its hazardous chemical compliance program is appropriate and adequate. Specific examples of written program requirements, MSDS format, hazard assessment criteria and communication vehicles and formats are included.

GOVERNMENTAL ORGANIZATIONS

Environment, Safety and Health Office: Department of Energy. James Forrestal Building, 1000 Independence Ave., S.W., Washington, District of Columbia 20585. (202) 586-6151.

Minerals Management Service. Room 1442, M5612, 18th and C St., N.W., Washington, District of Columbia 20240. (202) 208-3500.

Office of Public Affairs: Bureau of Land Management. 18th and C St., N.W., Washington, District of Columbia 20240. (202) 208-3435.

U.S. Environmental Protection Agency: Office of Regulatory Management and Evaluation. 401 M St., S.W., Washington, District of Columbia 20460. (202) 382-4028.

U.S. Environmental Protection Agency: Office of Research Program Management. 401 M St., S.W., Washington, District of Columbia 20460. (202) 382-7500.

HANDBOOKS AND MANUALS

Environmental Career Guide: Job Opportunities with the Earth in Mind. Nicholas Basta. John Wiley & Sons, Inc., 605 3rd Ave., New York, New York 10158-0012. (212) 850-6000. 1991. Complete guide to the many career options in the growing environmental field. Shows how to find employers engaged in environmental activity, and how to get the job. Lists key environmental businesses–manufacturing, government agencies, engineering consulting firms, waste handling firms, and others. Lists key professional careers in environmental conservation and maps career strategies.

Environmental Health and Safety Manager's Handbook, 2nd edition. Government Institutes, Inc., 4 Research Pl., Ste. 200, Rockville, Maryland 20850. (301) 921-2300. Organization and management of environmental programs, criteria for developing a program, human resources, communication; information management; government inspections and enforcement.

Environmental Management Handbook: Toxic Chemical Materials and Waste. Leopold C. Kokoszka. Marcel Dekker, Inc., 270 Madison Ave., New York, New York 10016. (212) 696-9000; (800) 228-1160. 1989.

Pira's International Environmental Information Sources. Pira, Randalls Rd., Leatherhead, England KT22 7RU. 0372 376161. 1990. Sourcebook includes over 2,000 entries from more than 20 countries, including Australia, Finland, Germany, the United Kingdom, and the United States. Entries are from organizations, research centers, legislative and regulatory bodies, directories, online databases and periodicals. Subject areas covered are: air, noise, water and land pollution, waste control and disposal, recycling, energy recovery and nature conservation.

Power Generation, Energy Management and Environmental Sourcebook. Marilyn Jackson. The Association of

Energy Engineers, 4025 Pleasantdale Rd., Suite 420, Atlanta, Georgia 30340. (404) 925-9558. 1992. Includes practical solutions to energy and environmental problems.

Your Resource Guide to Environmental Organizations. John Seredich, ed. Smiling Dolphins Press, 4 Segura, Irvine, California 92715. 1991. Includes the purposes, programs, accomplishments, volunteer opportunities, publications and membership benefits of 150 environmental organizations.

ONLINE DATA BASES

Asbestos Information System–AIS. U.S. Environmental Protection Agency, Office of Pesticides and Toxic Substances, 401 M St., SW, Washington, District of Columbia 20460. (202) 260-2090. Information on asbestos including chemical use, exposure, manufacturing, the human population, and environmental releases.

BIOSIS Previews. BIOSIS, 2100 Arch St., Philadelphia, Pennsylvania 19103-1399. (215) 587-4800. Largest and most comprehensive database of research in the life sciences. Contains citations for nearly 9000 primary research journals, monographs, reviews, symposia, preliminary reports, semi-popular journals, selected institutional reports, government reports and research communications.

Chemical Engineering and Biotechnology Abstracts–CEBA. Orbit Search Service, Maxwell Online Inc., 8000 W. Park Dr., McLean, Virginia 22102. (703) 442-0900 or (800) 456-7248. Monthly. Covers theoretical, practical and commercial material on all aspects of processing safety, and the environment. Also covers process and reaction engineering, measurement and process control, environmental protection and safety, plant design and equipment used in chemical engineering and biotechnology. More than 400 of the world's major primary chemical and process engineering journals are scanned to compile the database. Available from ORBIT.

Computer-Aided Environmental Legislative Data Systems–CELDS. U.S. Army Corps of Engineers, Planning Information Programs (PIP), Dept. of Urban and Regional Planning, University of Illinois, 1003 West Nevada, Urbana, Illinois 61801. (217) 333-1369. Federal and state environmental regulations and standards.

Computerized Engineering Index–COMPENDEX. Engineering Information Inc., 345 E. 47th St., New York, New York 10017. (212) 705-7600.

Environmental Manager's Compliance Advisor. Business & Legal Reports, Inc., 64 Wall St., Madison, Connecticut 06443. (203) 245-7448. Online version of periodical of same name.

Environmental Organization Computer Readable Directory Database. Environmental Research Information, Inc., 575 8th Ave., New York, New York 10018-3011. (212) 465-1060. Federal, state, and local agencies, legislative committees, public and private organizations, and individuals concerned with environmental issues. Online version of directory of same name.

Monthly Catalog of United States Government Publications. U.S. G.P.O., Supt. of Docs., PO Box 371954, Pittsburgh, Pennsylvania 15250-7954. (202) 512-0000.

National Technical Information Service. U.S. Department of Commerce, National Technical Information Service, Office of Data Base Services, 5285 Port Royal Rd., Springfield, Virginia 22161. (703) 487-4807. Bibliographic database of government sponsored research and technical reports.

PressNet Environmental Reports. Chemical Information Systems, Inc., 7215 York Rd., Baltimore, Maryland 21212. (301) 321-8440.

SCISEARCH. Institute for Scientific Information, University City Science Center, 3501 Market St., Philadelphia, Pennsylvania 19104. (215) 386-0100.

State Environmental Report. NewsNet, Inc., 945 Haverford Rd., Bryn Mawr, Pennsylvania 19010. (800) 345-1301.

PERIODICALS AND NEWSLETTERS

Air/Water Pollution Report. Business Publishers, Inc., 951 Pershing Dr., Silver Spring, Maryland 20910-4464. (301) 587-6300. 1963-. Weekly. Reports on the hard news and in-depth features for practical use by environmental managers. It keeps readers informed on the latest news from government and industry. Also available online.

Ambio: A Journal of the Human Environment. Royal Swedish Academy of Sciences. Pergamon Microforms International, Inc., Fairview Park, Elmsford, New York 10523. (914) 592-7720. 1971-. Monthly. Publishes recent work in the interrelated fields of environmental management, technology and the natural sciences.

Balance. National Environmental Development Association, 1440 New York Avenue, NW, Suite 300, Washington, District of Columbia 20005. (202) 638-1230. Quarterly. Impact of environmental legislation on business and industry.

The Balance Wheel. Association for Conservation Information, c/o Roy Edwards, Virginia Game Department, 4010 W. Broad St., Richmond, Virginia 23230-3916. (804) 367-1000. Quarterly.

Biomass and Bioenergy. Pergamon Microforms International, Inc., Fairview Park, Elmsford, New York 10523. (914) 592-7720. 1991-. Monthly. Key areas covered by this journal are: Biomass-sources, energy, crop production processes, genetic improvements, composition; biological residues: wastes from agricultural production and forestry, processing industries, and municipal sources; bioenergy processes: fermentations, thermochemical conversions, liquid and gaseous fuels, and petrochemical substitutes; bioenergy utilization: direct combustion gasification, electricity production, chemical processes, and by-product remediation. Also includes environmental management and economic aspects of biomass and bioenergy.

Catalyst for Environment/Energy. Catalyst for Environment/Energy, New York, New York 1970-. Irregular. Dedicated to efficient energy and environmental management.

CEM Report. Center for Environmental Management, U.S. Environmental Protection Agency, 26 W. Martin Luther King Dr., Cincinnati, Ohio 45268. (617) 381-3486. Quarterly. Articles on the activities of CEM.

The Diplomate. American Academy of Environmental Engineers, 130 Holiday Court, Ste. 100, Annapolis, Maryland 21401. (301) 266-3311. Quarterly. Issues and happenings in the environmental field.

E Magazine. Earth Action Network, 28 Knight St., Norwalk, Connecticut 06851. (203) 854-5559. Bimonthly. News, information, and commentary on environmental issues.

Earth Work. The Student Conservation Association Inc., PO Box 550, Charlestown, New Hampshire 03603-0550. (603) 826-4301. 1991-. Monthly. Articles focus on the people, agencies, and the nonprofit organizations that protect our parks, refuges, forests and other lands. Carries a special feature entitled JobScan which provides the most comprehensive listing of natural resource and environmental job opportunities anywhere.

Ecological Applications. Ecological Society of America, Center for Environmental Studies, Arizona State University, Tempe, Arizona 85287. (602) 965-3000. 1991-. Quarterly. Emphasizes the application of basic ecological concepts to a wide range of problems.

Ecomod. ISEM–North America Chapter, Water Quality Division, South Florida Water Management District, P.O. Box 24608, West Palm Beach, Florida 33416. (407) 686-8800. Monthly. Current events in ecological and environmental modeling.

Environment. Heldref Publications, 4000 Albemarle Street, NW, Washington, District of Columbia 20016. (202) 362-6445. Ten a year. Covers science and science policy.

Environment Research. Academic Press, c/o Harcourt Brace Jovanovich Inc., 6277 Sea Harbor Dr., Orlando, Florida 32887. (800) 346-8648. Bimonthly. Journal of environmental medicine and sciences.

Environmental Action. Environmental Action Foundation, 6930 Carroll Ave., Ste. 600, Takoma Park, Maryland 20912. (301) 891-1100. Bimonthly. Impact of humans and industry on the environment.

Environmental Lab. Mediacom, Inc., 760 Whalers Way, Suite 100, Bldg. A, Fort Collins, Colorado 80525. (303) 229-0029. Monthly.

Environmental Liability Monitor. Business Publishers, Inc., 951 Pershing Dr., Silver Spring, Maryland 20910-4464. (301) 587-6300. 1990-. Monthly. Reports about environmental liability in all areas.

Environmental Management. Springer-Verlag, 175 5th Ave., New York, New York 10010. (212) 460-1500. Six times a year.

Environmental Management: Journal of Industrial Sanitation and Facilities Management. Environmental Management Assn., 255 Detroit St., Suite 200, Denver, Colorado 80206. (303) 320-7855. Quarterly.

Environmental Management News. Stevens Publishing Co., PO Box 1604, Waco, Texas 76710. (817) 776-9000. Semimonthly. Legal issues, technological advances and trends in the environmental arena.

Environmental Management Review. Government Institutes, Inc., 4 Research Pl., Ste. 200, Rockville, Maryland 20850. (301) 921-2300. Quarterly. Environmental risk assessment, enforcement priorities, regulatory requirements, and organizing and managing compliance programs.

Environmental Manager. Executive Enterprises Publications Co., Inc., 22 W. 21st St., 10th Fl., New York, New York 10010-6990. (212) 645-7880. Monthly. Toxic waste cleanups, waste minimization, and underground storage tank leaks.

Environmental Manager's Compliance Advisor. Business & Legal Reports, Inc., 64 Wall St., Madison, Connecticut 06443-1513. (203) 245-7448. Biweekly. Integrated environmental compliance system. Also available online.

Environmental Protection. Carol Mouche, ed. Stevens Publishing Co., PO Box 2604, Waco, Texas 76706. (817) 776-9000. Nine times a year. Trade journal devoted to the areas of waste water; hazardous materials; risk assessment; environmental audits.

Environmental Science and Technology. American Chemical Society, 1155 16th St. N.W., Washington, District of Columbia 20036. (800) 227-5558. 1967-. Monthly. Contains research articles on various aspects of environmental chemistry, interpretative articles by invited experts and commentary on the scientific aspects of environmental management.

Environmental Science & Technology. American Chemical Society, 1155 16th St. N.W., Washington, District of Columbia 20036. (800) 227-5558. Covers pollution, sanitary chemistry and environmental engineering.

Everyone's Back Yard. Citizen's Clearinghouse for Hazardous Wastes, P.O. Box 926, Arlington, Virginia 22216. (703) 276-7070. Bimonthly. Contains news, views, and resources for grassroots environmental activists.

Green Marketing Report. Business Publishers, Inc., 951 Pershing Dr., Silver Spring, Maryland 20910-4464. (301) 587-6300. 1990-. Monthly. Looks at the steps taken by product manufacturers and advertisers to address consumers' environmental concerns as well as government examination of (and challenges to) some companies' environmental claims. Also available online.

International Environmental Affairs. University Press of New England, 17 1/2 Lebanon Street, Hanover, New Hampshire 03755. (603) 646-3340. Quarterly. Issues on management of natural resources.

Journal of Environmental Planning and Management. Carfax Publishing Company, P.O. Box 2025, Dunnellon, Florida 32630. Biannual. Covers issues of environmental policy, planning, management, land-use, impact assessment, valuation, audits, regulatory aspects of natural resources, environmental protection, conservation and human-environment interactions.

Maine Times/Maine Environmental Weekly. Maine Times, Maine Environmental Weekly, 41 Main St., Topsham, Maine 04086. 1968-. Weekly.

Michigan Waste Report. Michigan Waste Report, Inc., 400 Ann, SW, Suite 204, Grand Rapids, Michigan 49504. (616) 363-3262. Biweekly. Covers information about waste management.

NAEP Newsletter. National Association of Environmental Professionals, P.O. Box 15210, Alexandria, Virginia 22309-0210. (703) 660-2364. Monthly. Covers environmental planning, management, review and research.

Nature and Resources. Elsevier Science Publishing Co., 655 Avenue of the Americas, New York, New York 10010. (212) 989-5800. 1965-. Quarterly. Provides in-depth reviews of contemporary environmental issues from an international perspective.

RESEARCH CENTERS AND INSTITUTES

Clark University, Program for International Development and Social Change. 950 Main St., Worcester, Massachusetts 01610.

Ecology Center. 2530 San Pablo Ave., Berkeley, California 94702. (510) 548-2220.

Environmental Law Institute. 1616 P St., N.W., Suite 200, Washington, District of Columbia 20036. (202) 328-5150.

National Research Council. 2101 Constitution Ave., N.W., Washington, District of Columbia 20418. (202) 334-2000.

World Environment Center. 419 Park Avenue, Suite 1403, New York, New York 10016. (212) 683-4700.

World Resources Institute. 1709 New York Ave., N.W., Washington, District of Columbia 20006. (202) 638-6300.

TRADE ASSOCIATIONS AND PROFESSIONAL SOCIETIES

American Society of Civil Engineers. 345 East 47th St., New York, New York 10017. (212) 705-7496.

Association of New Jersey Environmental Commissions. PO Box 157, 300 Mendham Rd., Mendham, New Jersey 07945. (201) 539-7547.

Center for Environmental Information, Inc. 99 Court St., Rochester, New York 14604. (716) 546-3796.

Center for Environmental Management. Tufts University, Curtis Hall, 474 Boston Ave., Medford, Massachusetts 02155. (617) 381-3486.

Environmental Design Research Association. P.O. Box 24083, Oklahoma City, Oklahoma 73124. (405) 843-4863.

Environmental Management Association. 255 Detroit St., Suite 200, Denver, Colorado 80206. (303) 320-7855.

Environmental Mediation International. 1775 Pennsylvania Ave., N.W., Suite 1000, Washington, District of Columbia 20036. (202) 457-0457.

Institute for Environmental Auditing. PO Box 23686, L'Enfant Plaza Station, Washington, District of Columbia 20026-3686. (703) 818-1000.

Institute of Environmental Sciences. 940 E. Northwest Hwy., Mount Prospect, Illinois 60056. (708) 255-1561.

International Environmental Bureau. 61, route de Chene, CH-1208, Geneva, Switzerland (412) 2786-5111.

National Association of Environmental Professionals. PO Box 15210, Alexandria, Virginia 22309-0210. (703) 660-2364.

Sierra Club. 100 Bush St., San Francisco, California 94104. (415) 291-1600.

ENVIRONMENTAL POLICY

See also: CONSERVATION OF NATURAL RESOURCES; ENVIRONMENTAL LEGISLATION; ENVIRONMENTAL PROTECTION; HEALTH, ENVIRONMENTAL; HUMAN ECOLOGY; NATURAL RESOURCES; POLLUTION

ABSTRACTING AND INDEXING SERVICES

Applied Science and Technology Index. H.W. Wilson Co., 950 University Ave., Bronx, New York 10452. (800) 367-6770. Formerly Industrial Arts Index.

Bulletin Signaletique: Eau et Assainissement, Pollution Atmospherique, Droit des Pollutions. Centre de Documentation, Centre National de la Recherche Scientifique, 15, quai Anatole France, Paris, France 75700. (1) 45 55 92 25. 1983-. Monthly. Indexes pollution periodicals including water, atmospheric and related pollutions.

Engineering Index. The Engineering Index Inc., 345 E. 47th St., New York, New York 10017. 1962-.

Geographical Abstracts. London School of Economics, Dept. of Geography, Regency House, 34 Duke St., London, England 1966-. Continued by Geo Abstracts issued in 6 parts: Pt. A. Landforms and the quaternary; Pt. B. Biogeography and Climatology; Pt. C. Economic geography; Pt. D. Social geography and cartography; Pt. E. Sedimentology; Pt. F. Regional and community planning.

Index to Scientific Book Contents. Institute for Scientific Information, 3501 Market St., Philadelphia, Pennsylvania 19104. (800) 523-1857. 1985-. Annual. Gives contents of science books published.

Pollution Abstracts. Cambridge Scientific Abstracts, 5161 River Rd., Bethesda, Maryland 20816. (301) 961-6750. Six/year. Indexes worldwide technical literature on environmental pollution. Covers air pollution, marine and freshwater pollution, sewage and wastewater treatment, waste management, toxicology and health, noise pollution, radiation, land pollution, and environmental policies, programs, legislation, and education. Also available online.

Priority Issue Reporting Service–PIRS. Information for Public Affairs, Inc., Client Services Dept., 1900 14th St., Sacramento, California 95814.

ALMANACS AND YEARBOOKS

European Environmental Yearbook, 1991. Doctor Institute of Environmental Studies. BNA Books, 1250 23rd St. NW, Washington, District of Columbia 20037. (202) 452-4276. 1991. The yearbook has been prepared with the cooperation of and financial assistance from the Commission of the European Communities/Brussels. It is a comprehensive guide to the environmental policies, laws, and regulations of the European Economic Community. Compares countries' responses to air and water pollution, nuclear safety, toxic and hazardous waste, land reclamation and other issues.

Gale Environmental Almanac. Russ Hoyle. Gale Research Inc., 835 Penobscot Bldg., Detroit, Michigan 48226-4094. (313) 961-2242. 1993. Focuses on the U.S. and Canada, although worldwide and transboundary issues are discussed.

BIBLIOGRAPHIES

Current Contents. Agriculture, Biology and Environmental Sciences. Institute for Scientific Information, 3501 Market St., Philadelphia, Pennsylvania 19104. (800) 523-1857. 1973-. Previous title: Current Contents. Agricultural, Food & Veterinary Sciences. Gives the table of contents of periodicals in the fields of agriculture, biology, environmental and related areas.

Deep Ecology and Environmental Ethics: A Selected and Annotated Bibliography of Materials Published Since 1980. Teresa DeGroh. Council of Planning Librarians, 1313 E. 60th St., Chicago, Illinois 60637-2897. (312) 942-2163. 1987. Covers human ecology and environmental protection.

Environmental Economics: A Guide to Information Sources. Barry C. Field and Cleve E. Willis. Gale Research Co., 835 Penobscot Bldg., Detroit, Michigan 48226-4094. (313) 961-2242. 1979. Man and the Environment Information Guide Series; v.8

Environmental Issues in the Third World: A Bibliography. Joan Nordquist. Reference and Research Services, 511 Lincoln St., Santa Cruz, California 95060. (408) 426-4479. 1991.

DIRECTORIES

Canadian Environmental Directory. Canadian Almanac & Directory Publishing Co. Ltd., 134 Adelaide St. E., Ste. 27, Toronto, Ontario, Canada M5C 1K9. (416) 362-4088. 1992. Includes individuals, agencies, firms, and associations.

Directory of Federal Contacts on Environmental Protection. Naval Energy and Environmental Support Activity/Department of Navy, Code 112, Port Hueneme, California 93043. (805) 982-5667.

Directory of State Environmental Agencies. Kathyrn Hubler and Timothy R. Henderson, eds. Environmental Law Institute in cooperation with the Natural Resources Committee of the American Bar Association General Practice Section, 1616 P St. N.W. #200, Washington, District of Columbia 20036. (202) 328-5150. 1985.

Directory of State Environmental Planning Agencies. United States Air Force Directorate of Engineering and Services. The Directorate, 1616 P St. N.W., No. 200, Washington, District of Columbia 20036. 1977. On microfiche.

Environmental Organization Computer Readable Directory. Environmental Research Information, Inc., 575 8th Ave., New York, New York 10018-3011. (212) 465-1060. Also available online.

Environmental Politics and Policy. Congressional Quarterly, Inc., 1414 22nd St., N.W., Washington, District of Columbia 20037. (202) 887-8500.

Environmental Telephone Directory. Government Institutes, Inc., 4 Research Pl., Ste. 200, Rockville, Maryland 20850. (301) 921-2300.

EPA Headquarters Telephone Directory. Government Institutes, Inc., 4 Research Pl., Ste. 200, Rockville, Maryland 20850. (301) 921-2300. Key to converting the Federal Telecommunications System phone numbers to outside commercial numbers.

Guide to State Environmental Programs. Bureau of National Affairs, 1231 25th St., NW, Washington, District of Columbia 20037. (800) 372-1033. 1990.

The Harbinger File: A Directory of Citizen Groups, Government Agencies and Environmental Education Programs Concerned with California Environmental Issues. Harbinger Communications, 50 Rustic Lane, Santa Cruz, California 95060. (415) 429-8727. 1990/91.

INFOTERRA–World Directory of Environmental Expertise. United States National Focal Point for UNEP/INFOTERRA, Environmental Protection Agency, 401 M St., S.W., Rm 2903, Washington, District of Columbia 20460. (202) 382-5917.

International Directory for Sources of Environmental Information. United States National Focal Point for UNEP/INFOTERRA, Environmental Protection Agency, 401 M St., S.W., Rm 2903, Washington, District of Columbia 20460. (202) 382-5917.

U. S. Energy and Environmental Interest Groups: Institutional Profiles. Lettie McSpadden Wenner. Greenwood Publishing Group, Inc., 88 Post Rd. W., PO Box 5007, Westport, Connecticut 06881. (212) 226-3571. 1990. Included are organizations that lobby in the energy and environmental policy areas including business corporations and trade associations, not-for-profit public interest groups, and professional research groups, and governmental organizations.

World Directory of Environmental Organizations. Thaddeus C. Trzyna, ed. California Institute of Public Affairs, PO Box 10, Claremont, California 91711. (714) 624-5212. 1989. 3rd ed. Handbook of organizations and programs concerned with protecting the environment and managing natural resources. It covers national and international organizations, both governmental and nongovernmental, in all parts of the world.

World Directory of Environmental Research Centers. William K. Wilson. Oryx Press, 4041 N. Central Ave., #700, Phoenix, Arizona 85012. (602) 265-2651; (800) 279-6799. 1974.

ENCYCLOPEDIAS AND DICTIONARIES

Dictionary of Ecology and Environment. P. H. Collin. Collin Pub., 8 The Causeway, Teddington, England TW11 0HE. 1988. Vocabulary of 5,000 words and expressions covering a range of topics relating to ecology, including: climate, vegetation, pollution, waste disposal, and energy conservation.

Dictionary of Environmental Engineering and Related Sciences: English-Spanish, Spanish-English. Jose T. Villate. Ediciones Universal, 3090 SW 8th St., Miami, Florida 33135. (305) 642-3355. 1979.

Encyclopedia of Environmental Science and Engineering. J.R. Pfafflin. Gordon and Breach Science Publishers, Inc., 270 8th Ave., New York, New York 10011. (212) 206-8900. 1992.

Encyclopedia of Environmental Studies. William Ashworth. Facts on File, Inc., 460 Park Ave. S., New York, New York 10016. (212) 683-2244. 1991.

Environmental Encyclopedia. William P. Cunningham, Terence Ball, et. al. Gale Research Inc., 835 Penobscot Bldg., Detroit, Michigan 48226-4094. (313) 961-2242. 1993.

Environmental Regulatory Glossary. G. William Frick and Thomas P. Sullivan. Government Institutes, Inc., 4 Research Pl., Rockville, Maryland 20850. (301) 921-2300. 1990. Over 4,000 entries. Definitions were gathered from the Code of Federal Regulations, EPA documents, and Federal Environmental Statutes.

The Facts on File Dictionary of Environmental Science. L. Harold Stevenson and Bruce Wyman. Facts on File, Inc.,

460 Park Ave. S., New York, New York 10016. (212) 683-2244. 1991.

McGraw-Hill Encyclopedia of Environmental Science. Sybil P. Parker. McGraw-Hill Science & Engineering Books, 11 W. 19th St., New York, New York 10011. (212) 337-6010. 1980. Covers ecology, man's influence on nature, and environmental protection.

GENERAL WORKS

Agricultural and Environmental Policies: Opportunities for Integration. OECD Publications and Information Center, 2001 L St. N.W., Suite 700, Washington, District of Columbia 20036. (202) 785-OECD. 1989. Describes a broad range of approaches by OECD countries to integrating environmental and agricultural policies and argues that eventual cuts in economic support for agriculture and withdrawal of land from production could produce important benefits for the environment.

Atlas of the Environment. Geoffrey Lean, et al. Prentice Hall, Rte. 9W, Englewood Cliffs, New York 07632. (201) 592-2000. 1990. Guide to the major environmental issues around the world that makes good use of numerous maps and diagrams to present the increasing amount of information available in this field. Covers related subjects such as indigenous people and refugees, the education gap, natural and human induced disasters, wildlife trade, and migration routes.

Atlas of the United States Environmental Issues. Robert J. Mason. Maxwell Macmillan International, 866 3rd Ave., New York, New York 10022. (212) 702-2000. Describes the texture of our environmental health using maps, photographs, charts, graphs, and diagrams.

Between Two Worlds: Science, the Environmental Movement, and Policy Choice. Lynton Keith Caldwell. Cambridge University Press, 40 W. 20th St., New York, New York 10011. (212) 924-3900; (800) 227-0247. 1990. Focuses on international and political communication regarding the environment.

Computer Models in Environmental Planning. Steven I. Gordon. Van Nostrand Reinhold, 115 5th Ave., New York, New York 10003. (212) 254-3232. 1985.

Deep Ecology. Bill Devall and George Sessions. G. M. Smith, PO Box 667, Layton, Utah 84041. (801) 554-9800; (800) 421-8714. 1985. Explores the philosophical, psychological and sociological roots of today's environmental movement and offers specific direct action suggestions for individuals to practice.

Defending the Earth. South End Press, 116 St. Botolph St., Boston, Massachusetts 02115. (800) 533-8478. 1991.

Ecology, Economics, Ethics: The Broken Circle. Herbert R. Bormann and Stephen R. Kellert, eds. Yale University Press, 302 Temple St., New Haven, Connecticut 06520. (203) 432-0960. 1991. Addresses a wide range of concerns and offers practical remedies including: economic incentives for conservation, technical adaptations to use resources effectively; better accounting procedures for measuring the environmental system that better explains our responsibility to the environment.

Economic Instruments for Environmental Protection. OECD Publications and Information Center, 2001 L St. N.W., Suite 700, Washington, District of Columbia 20036. (202) 785-OECD. 1989. Reviews the current role of economic instruments and assesses their effectiveness

and future potential. Discusses charges and taxes on effluents, user and product charges, tax relief and subsidies for anti-pollution investments, and trading of pollution rights. Problems of enforcement, and implications for the polluter pays principle are also covered.

Economics and the Environment: A Reconciliation. Walter Block. Fraser Institute, 626 Bute St., Vancouver, British Columbia, Canada V6E3M1. (604) 688-0221. 1990. Environmental policy and how it impacts on the national economy.

The Ecopolitics of Development in the Third World: Politics and Environment in Brazil. Roberto Pereira Guimaraes. L. Rienner Publishers, 1800 30th St, Suite 314, Boulder, Colorado 80301. (303) 444-6684. 1991. History of environmental policy in Brazil.

Energy and the Environment in the 21st Century. Jefferson W. Tester, et al., eds. MIT Press, 55 Hayward St., Cambridge, Massachusetts 02142. (617) 253-2884; (800) 356-0343. 1991. Proceedings of the conference held at the Massachusetts Institute of Technology, Cambridge, MA, March 26-28, 1990. Compendium of more than 80 original contributions, providing the basis for an international agenda of energy and environmental technology policy.

Energy and the Environment Policy Overview. OECD Publications and Information Center, 2001 L St. N.W., Suite 700, Washington, District of Columbia 20036. (202) 785-OECD. 1990. Analyzes the way energy policies can be adapted to environmental concerns.

Energy, the Environment, and Public Policy: Issues for the 1990s. David L. McKee, ed. Praeger Publishers, 1 Madison Ave., New York, New York 10010-3603. (212) 685-5300. 1991. Addresses the extent and gravity of our environmental situation, from industrial waste to acid rain, from the Alaskan oil spill to the destruction of the rain forests.

Environment Ideology and Policy. Frances Sandbach. Rowman & Littlefield, Publishers, Inc., 8705 Bollman Pl., Savage, Maryland 20763. (301) 306-0400. 1980. Describes the environmental movement, behavioral assessments, alternative technologies, environmental evaluation, economic analysis, environmental policies and other environment related areas.

Environmental Disputes: Community Involvement in Conflict Resolution. James E. Crowfoot and Julia M. Wondolleck, eds. Island Press, 1718 Connecticut Ave. N.W., Suite 300, Washington, District of Columbia 20009. (202) 232-7933. 1990. Set of procedures for settling disputes over environmental policies without litigation.

Environmental Indicators. OECD Publication and Information Center, 2001 L St. N.W., Suite 700, Washington, District of Columbia 20036. (202) 785-OECD. 1991. Comprehensive assessments of environmental issues in industrialized countries. Charts the progress achieved over the past 20 years, and points to problems still remaining and sets an agenda of environmental issues to be dealt with in the 1990s.

Environmental Investments: The Costs of a Clean Government. Island Press, 1718 Connecticut Ave. N.W., Suite 300, Washington, District of Columbia 20009. (202) 232-7933. 1991. Report tells industry what to expect in direct expenses for implementing pollution control measures and undertaking compliance activities for environmental laws.

Environmental Policies for Cities in the 1990s. OECD Publications and Information Center, 2001 L St. N.W., Suite 700, Washington, District of Columbia 20036. (202) 785-OECD. 1991. Examines existing urban environmental improvement policies and suggests practical solutions to urban renewal, urban transportation and urban energy management.

Environmental Policy Benefits: Monetary Valuation. OECD Publications and Information Center, 2001 L St., N.W., Suite 700, Washington, District of Columbia 20036. (202) 785-OECD. 1989. Report explores monetary evaluations for benefits in the environmental policies decision making process.

Environmental Reporting and Recordkeeping Requirements. Government Institutes, Inc., 4 Research Pl., Ste. 200, Rockville, Maryland 20850. (301) 921-2300. Reporting and recordkeeping under Clean Air, Clean Water, RCRA, CERCLA, SARA, TSCA, and OSHA.

Environmental Viewpoints. Marie Lazzari. Gale Research Inc., 835 Penobscot Bldg., Detroit, Michigan 48226-4094. (313) 961-2242. 1992.

Federal Lands: A Guide to Planning, Management, and State Revenues. Sally K. Fairfax. Island Press, 1718 Connecticut Ave. N.W., Suite 300, Washington, District of Columbia 20009. (202) 232-7933. 1987. Comprehensive reference on the management and allocation of revenues from public lands.

Fighting Toxics. Gary Cohen and John O'Connor, eds. Island Press, 1718 Connecticut Ave. N.W., Suite 300, Washington, District of Columbia 20009. (202) 232-7933. 1990. Investigates the toxic hazards in the community, determining the health risks they pose, and launching an effective campaign to eliminate them.

The Forest and the Trees: A Guide to Excellent Forestry. Gordon Robinson. Island Press, 1718 Connecticut Ave. N.W., Suite 300, Washington, District of Columbia 20009. (202) 232-7933. 1988. Gives concerned citizens who are not foresters the technical information they need to compete with the experts when commenting on how our national forests should be managed.

Forests and Forestry in China. S. D. Richardson. Island Press, 1718 Connecticut Ave. N.W., Suite 300, Washington, District of Columbia 20009. (202) 232-7933. 1990. In-depth look at current forest practice in China, including how China manages forest resources.

Free Market Environmentalism. Terry L. Anderson and Donald R. Leal. Westview Press, 5500 Central Ave., Boulder, Colorado 80301. (303) 444-3541. 1991. Examines the prospects and pitfalls of improving natural resource allocation and environmental quality through market processes.

GAIA, an Atlas of Planet Management. Norman Myers. Anchor Pr./Doubleday, 666 5th Ave., New York, New York 10103. (212) 765-6500; (800) 223-6834. Resource atlas including a wealth of data on the environment with text by authoritative environmentalists.

GAIA Connections: An Introduction to Ecology, Ecoethics and Economics. Alan S. Miller. Rowman & Littlefield, Publishers, Inc., 8705 Bollman Pl., Savage, Maryland 20763. (301) 306-0400. 1991. Synthesis of humanity's ethical and economic options in coping with the global environmental crisis.

Global Warming: The Greenpeace Report. Jeremy Leggett. Oxford University Press, 200 Madison Ave., New York, New York 10016. (800) 334-4249. 1990. Climate change and consequences of global warming, and means for abating and even halting global warming.

In Search of Environmental Excellence: Moving Beyond Blame. Bruce Piasecki and Peter Asmus. Simon and Schuster, 1230 Avenue of the Americas, New York, New York 10020. (212) 689-7000. 1990. Analyses of the roles and motivations of government, business/industry, and the general public in solving environmental problems.

Integrating Environment into Business: A Guide to Policy Making and Implementation. Environment Council. Environment Council and 3M United Kingdom PLC, 80 York Way, London, England N1 9AG. 071 278 4736. 1990. Outcome of the Environmental Policy Workshop which was held in February 1990. Addresses the issues to help businesses and other organizations to implement environmental legislations and other behavioral changes that might affect their operations.

Islands under Siege: National Parks and the Politics of External Threats. John C. Freemuth. University Press of Kansas, 329 Carruth, Lawrence, Kansas 66045. (913) 864-4154. 1991. Outlines a diverse set of political strategies, evaluating each in terms of environmental effectiveness and political feasibility.

Magill's Survey of Science. Life Science Series. Frank N. Magill, ed. Salem Press, PO Box 50062, Pasadena, California 91105. 1991. Six volumes. Contents: v.1. A-Central and peripheral nervous system functions; v.2. Central metabolism regulation - eukaryotic transcriptional control; v.3. Positive and negative eukaryotic transcriptional control - mammalian hormones; v.4. Hormones and behavior - muscular contraction; v.5. Muscular contraction and relaxation - sexual reproduction in plants; v.6. Reproductive behavior and mating - X inactivation and the Lyon hypothesis.

Making Things Happen: How to Be an Effective Volunteer. Joan Wolfe. Island Press, 1718 Connecticut Ave. N.W., Suite 300, Washington, District of Columbia 20009. (202) 232-7933. 1991. Environmental movement is nurtured by volunteers. This book teaches volunteers the basic skills they need to make a stronger impact.

Natural Resource Conservation: An Ecological Approach. Oliver S. Owen. Macmillan Publishing Co., 866 3rd Ave., New York, New York 10022. (212) 702-2000. 1990. Covers environmental protection, conservation of natural resources and ecology.

Natural Resources for the 21st Century. R. Neil Sampson and Dwight Hair, eds. Island Press, 1718 Connecticut Ave. N.W., Suite 300, Washington, District of Columbia 20009. (202) 232-7933. 1990. Looks at lost or diminished resources, as well as those that appear to be rebounding. It offers a reliable status report on water, croplands, soil, forests, wetlands, rangelands, fisheries, wildlife, and wilderness.

New World New Mind: Moving toward Conscious Evolution. Robert E. Ornstein. Simon & Schuster, 1230 Avenue of the Americas, New York, New York 10020. (212) 698-7000; (800) 223-2348. 1990. Proposes revolutionary new ways to close the dangerous gap between our current mind set and the high-tech world of today.

The New York Environment Book. Eric A. Goldstein. Island Press, 1718 Connecticut Ave. N.W., Suite 300, Washington, District of Columbia 20009. (202) 232-7933. 1990. Provides an in-depth analysis of New York City's environment. The five areas surveyed are: solid waste disposal, hazardous substances, water pollution, air quality, and drinking water quality. Discusses past clean-up efforts, and offers an agenda for the future. Describes and analyzes the general environment of urban areas, and offers solutions for their special environmental problems.

Our Common Future. World Commission on Environment and Development. Oxford University Press, 200 Madison Ave., New York, New York 10016. (212) 679-7300; (800) 334-4249. 1987. Cautions that it is time that economy and ecology worked hand in hand, so that governments and their people can take responsibility not just for environmental damage, but for the policies that cause the damage.

The Philosophy and Practice of Wildlife Management. Frederick F. Gilbert and Donald G. Dodds. Krieger Publishing Co., Inc., PO Box 9542, Melbourne, Florida 32902-9542. (407) 724-9542. 1992. Shows the mechanisms and historical foundations of wildlife management and traces the evolution of increasingly sophisticated approaches to the management of our natural fauna.

Policy Implication of Greenhouse Warming. National Academy Press, 2101 Constitution Ave. N.W., PO Box 285, Washington, District of Columbia 20418. (202) 334-3313. 1991. Identifies what could be done to counter potential greenhouse warming. It has a helpful section on question and answers about greenhouse warming.

Prosperity without Pollution. Joel S. Hirschhorn and Kirsten U. Oldenburg. Van Nostrand Reinhold, 115 5th Ave., New York, New York 10003. (212) 254-3232. 1991. Explains how to decrease pollution without making a sacrifice in our standard of living.

Refinery System Safety for Contractors: A Six Volume Set. Fluke & Associates, Inc. PennWell Books, PO Box 21288, Tulsa, Oklahoma 74121. (918) 831-9421; (800) 752-9764. 1991. Employee-training and documentation manuals that comply with the safety regulations of OSHA and insurance carriers.

Reforming the Forest Service. Randal O'Toole. Island Press, 1718 Connecticut Ave. N.W., Suite 300, Washington, District of Columbia 20009. (202) 232-7933. 1988. Investigates possible economic inefficiencies and environmental consequences of the agency and proposes sweeping reforms to make the forest service more environmentally sensitive and efficient.

Reopening the Western Frontier. Ed Marston, ed. Island Press, 1718 Connecticut Ave. N.W., Suite 300, Washington, District of Columbia 20009. (202) 232-7933. 1989. Documents the changes and challenges that lie ahead as the West's natural resource economies–oil and gas, uranium, mining, and ranching–decline.

Restoration of Petroleum-Contaminated Aquifers. Stephen M. Testa and Duane L. Winegardner. Lewis Publishers, 200 Corporate Blvd. NW, Boca Raton, Florida 33431. (407) 994-0555 or (800)272-7737. 1991. Presents information on restoring aquifers contaminated by petroleum products and derivatives. Discusses the regulatory environment and framework within which environmental issues are addressed and explains the geochemistry of petroleum.

The Rising Tide: Global Warming and World Sea Levels. Lynne T. Edgerton. Island Press, 1718 Connecticut Ave. N.W., Suite 300, Washington, District of Columbia 20009. (202) 232-7933. 1991. Analysis of global warming and rising world sea level. Outlines state, national and international actions to respond to the effects of global warming on coastal communities and ecosystems.

Rural Environment Planning for Sustainable Communities. Frederic O. Sargent, et al. Island Press, 1718 Connecticut Ave. N.W., Ste. 300, Washington, District of Columbia 20009. (202) 232-7933. 1991.

Shattering: Food, Politics, and the Loss of Genetic Diversity. Cary Fowler. University of Arizona Press, 1230 N. Park, No. 102, Tucson, Arizona 85719. (602) 621-1441. 1990. Reviews the development of genetic diversity over 10,000 years of human agriculture and its loss in our lifetimes.

Signs of Hope: Working towards Our Common Future. Linda Starke. Oxford University Press, Walton St., Oxford, England 1990. Sequel to the report of the World Commission on Environment and Development Commissioned by the Centre For Our Common Future. Records the progress made in the implementation of the recommendations of Our Common Future and looks at initiatives being taken by governments, industry, scientists, non-governmental organizations and the media.

Soil Management for Sustainability. R. Lal and F. J. Pierce, eds. Soil and Water Conservation Society, 7515 NE Ankeny Rd., Ankeny, Iowa 50021-9764. (515) 289-2331. 1991. Topics discussed in the book include: soil structure, soil compaction, and predicting soil erosion and its effects on crop productivity. Also covered are the basic processes, management options, and policy issues and priorities. Published in cooperation with the World Association of Soil and Water Conservation and the Soil Science Society of America

Sources for the Future. Wallace Oates. Resources for the Future, 1616 P St., NW, Washington, District of Columbia 20036. (202) 328-5086. Examines emissions taxes, abatement subsides, and transferable emission permits in a national, regional, and global context.

The Statehouse Effect: State Policies to Cool the Greenhouse. Daniel A. Lashof and Eric L. Washburn. Natural Resources Defense Council, 40 W. 20th St., New York, New York 10011. (212) 727-2700. 1990. Discusses the need for states to take the initiative in controlling CO_2 emissions. Details the sources of greenhouse gases and explains how greenhouse emissions can be reduced through energy efficiency, renewable energy strategies, recycling, and taxation and reforms in transportation, agriculture and forests.

Stones in a Glass House: CFCs and Ozone Depletion. Douglas G. Cogan. Investor Responsibility Research Center, 1755 Massachusetts Ave., NW, Suite 600, Washington, District of Columbia 20036. (202) 234-7500. 1988. Environmental aspects of air pollution.

The Student Environmental Action Guide. The Student Environmental Action Coalition. Earthworks Press, 1400 Shattuck Ave., No. 25, Berkeley, California 94709. (510) 652-8533. 1991. The coalition in collaboration with Earth Works has made adaptations to student lifestyles.

Tree Talk: The People and Politics of Timber. Ray Raphael. Island Press, 1718 Connecticut Ave. N.W., Suite 300, Washington, District of Columbia 20009.

(202) 232-7933. Looks at the forest industry from the perspective of environmentalists, loggers, old-time woodsmen and young pioneers.

Turning the Tide: Saving the Chesapeake Bay. Tom Horton. Island Press, 1718 Connecticut Ave. N.W., Suite 300, Washington, District of Columbia 20009. (202) 232-7933. 1991. Presents a comprehensive look at two decades of efforts to save the Chesapeake Bay. It outlines which methods have worked, and which have not. Sets a new strategy for the future, calling for greater political coverage, environmental leadership and vision.

Wildlife, Forests, and Forestry. Malcolm L. Hunter, Jr. Prentice Hall, Rte 9W, Englewood Cliffs, New Jersey 07632. (201) 592-2000. 1990. Presents new ideas that will form the basis of forest wildlife management in years to come. It looks at the costs of managing wildlife, as well as national policies on forest wildlife management and quantitative techniques for measuring diversity.

World Guide to Environmental Issues and Organizations. Peter Brackley. Longman Group Ltd., Longman House, Burnt Mill, Harlow, Essex, England CM20 2J6. (0279) 426721. 1991.

GOVERNMENTAL ORGANIZATIONS

Bureau of Oceans and International Environmental and Scientific Affairs. 2201 C St., N.W., Washington, District of Columbia 20520. (202) 647-1554.

Occupational Safety and Health Administration: Directorate for Policy. 200 Constitution Ave., N.W., Washington, District of Columbia 20210. (202) 523-8021.

Office of Public Affairs: Bureau of Land Management. 18th and C St., N.W., Washington, District of Columbia 20240. (202) 208-3435.

Office of Public Information: Federal Energy Regulatory Commission. 825 North Capitol St., N.E., Washington, District of Columbia 20426. (202) 357-8055.

U.S. Environmental Protection Agency: Office of Policy Analysis. 401 M St., S.W., Washington, District of Columbia 20460. (202) 382-4034.

U.S. Environmental Protection Agency: Office of Regulatory Management and Evaluation. 401 M St., S.W., Washington, District of Columbia 20460. (202) 382-4028.

U.S. Environmental Protection Agency: Office of Technology Transfer and Regulatory Support. 401 M St., S.W., Washington, District of Columbia 20460.

HANDBOOKS AND MANUALS

Atlas of Environmental Issues. Nick Middleton. Facts on File, Inc., 460 Park Ave. S., New York, New York 10016. (212) 683-2244. 1989. Includes soil erosion, deforestation, mechanized agriculture, oil pollution of the oceans, acid rain, overfishing, and nuclear power.

Environmental Career Guide: Job Opportunities with the Earth in Mind. Nicholas Basta. John Wiley & Sons, Inc., 605 3rd Ave., New York, New York 10158-0012. (212) 850-6000. 1991. Complete guide to the many career options in the growing environmental field. Shows how to find employers engaged in environmental activity, and how to get the job. Lists key environmental businesses–manufacturing, government agencies, engineering consulting firms, waste handling firms, and others. Lists

key professional careers in environmental conservation and maps career strategies.

Environmental Communication and Public Relations Handbook. Government Institutes, Inc., 4 Research Pl., Ste. 200, Rockville, Maryland 20850. (301) 921-2300. Managing the environmental disclosure requirements of OSHA and SARA.

Environmental Statistics Handbook: Europe. Allan Foster, Oksana Newman. Gale Research Inc., 835 Penobscot Bldg., Detroit, Michigan 48226-4094. (313) 961-2242. 1993.

EPA Organization and Functions Manual. Government Institutes, Inc., 4 Research Pl., Ste. 200, Rockville, Maryland 20850. (301) 921-2300. Detailed descriptions of exactly which office, division or support staff lab, within the EPA is responsible for various functions; includes a comprehensive organization chart for each office.

NPDES Compliance Inspection Manual. Government Institutes, Inc., 4 Research Pl., Ste. 200, Rockville, Maryland 20850. (301) 921-2300. 1988. Provides basic guidance on inspection procedures, and gives a wealth of specific technical information for accurate compliance.

Pira's International Environmental Information Sources. Pira, Randalls Rd., Leatherhead, England KT22 7RU. 0372 376161. 1990. Sourcebook includes over 2,000 entries from more than 20 countries, including Australia, Finland, Germany, the United Kingdom, and the United States. Entries are from organizations, research centers, legislative and regulatory bodies, directories, online databases and periodicals. Subject areas covered are: air, noise, water and land pollution, waste control and disposal, recycling, energy recovery and nature conservation.

ONLINE DATA BASES

BNA Environment Daily. Bureau of National Affairs, BNA PLUS, 1231 25th St., N.W., Rm. 215, Washington, District of Columbia 20037. (800) 452-7773.

BNA International Environment Report. Bureau of National Affairs, BNA PLUS, 1231 25th St., N.W., Rm. 215, Washington, District of Columbia 20037. (800) 452-7773.

Business and the Environment. Cutter Information Corp., 37 Broadway, Arlington, Massachusetts 02174-4439. (617) 648-8700. Online version of periodical of the same name.

Computerized Engineering Index–COMPENDEX. Engineering Information Inc., 345 E. 47th St., New York, New York 10017. (212) 705-7600.

ENREP. Commission of the European Communities, Database Distribution Service, 200 Rue de le Loi, Brussels, Belgium 1049. 32 (2) 2350001.

Environmental Organization Computer Readable Directory Database. Environmental Research Information, Inc., 575 8th Ave., New York, New York 10018-3011. (212) 465-1060. Federal, state, and local agencies, legislative committees, public and private organizations, and individuals concerned with environmental issues. Online version of directory of same name.

Monthly Catalog of United States Government Publications. U.S. G.P.O., Supt. of Docs., PO Box 371954, Pittsburgh, Pennsylvania 15250-7954. (202) 512-0000.

National Technical Information Service. U.S. Department of Commerce, National Technical Information Service, Office of Data Base Services, 5285 Port Royal Rd., Springfield, Virginia 22161. (703) 487-4807. Bibliographic database of government sponsored research and technical reports.

PressNet Environmental Reports. Chemical Information Systems, Inc., 7215 York Rd., Baltimore, Maryland 21212. (301) 321-8440.

SCISEARCH. Institute for Scientific Information, University City Science Center, 3501 Market St., Philadelphia, Pennsylvania 19104. (215) 386-0100.

State Environmental Report. NewsNet, Inc., 945 Haverford Rd., Bryn Mawr, Pennsylvania 19010. (800) 345-1301.

PERIODICALS AND NEWSLETTERS

The Amicus Journal. Natural Resources Defense Council, 40 West 20th Street, New York, New York 10011. (212) 727-2700. Quarterly. Articles on environmental affairs.

ANJEC Report. Association of New Jersey Environmental Commissions, Box 157, Mendham, New Jersey 07945. (201) 539-7547. 1969-. Quarterly. Informs environmental commissioners and interested citizens about environmental issues, laws and regulations, particularly those that effect New Jersey.

Briefing. National Association of Manufacturers, 1331 Pennsylvania Avenue, NW, Suite 1500 North, Washington, District of Columbia 20004. (202) 637-3000. Weekly. Environmental issues as they relate to manufacturing.

California Environmental Directory. California Institute of Public Affairs, Box 189040, Sacramento, California 95818. (916) 442-2472. 1973-. Irregular. Directory of public, private and academic organizations located in California that are concerned with environmental protection.

Citizen Alert Newsletter. Citizen Alert, Box 5391, Reno, Nevada 89513. (702) 827-4200. 1975-. Quarterly. Raises awareness and about nuclear, military and environmental issues facing Nevada.

Earthwatch Oregon. Oregon Environmental Council, 2637 S. W. Water Ave., Portland, Oregon 97201. 1969-. Monthly.

Eco-Politics. California League of Conservation Voters, 965 Mission St., # 705, San Francisco, California 94103-2928. (415) 397-7780. Quarterly. News of citizen action on environmental issues.

Ecological Applications. Ecological Society of America, Center for Environmental Studies, Arizona State University, Tempe, Arizona 85287. (602) 965-3000. 1991-. Quarterly. Emphasizes the application of basic ecological concepts to a wide range of problems.

Ecology Digest. Ecology Digest, Box 60961, Sacramento, California 95860. (916) 961-2942. Quarterly. Articles on environmental and political issues.

Environment. Heldref Publications, 4000 Albemarle Street, NW, Washington, District of Columbia 20016.

(202) 362-6445. Ten a year. Covers science and science policy.

Environment Report. Trends Publishing, Inc., 1079 National Press Bldg., Washington, District of Columbia 20045. (202) 393-0031. Semimonthly. Developments in environment, ecology and pollution abatement, with emphasis on policy, research, and development.

Environment Today. Enterprise Communications Inc., 1483 Chain Bridge Rd., Suite 202, McLean, Virginia 22101-4599. (703) 448-0322. Nine times a year. Magazine for environmental professionals, including corporate waste generators, municipal utilities managers, and governmental decision makers.

Environment Week. King Communications Group, Inc., 627 National Press Bldg., Washington, District of Columbia 20045. (202) 638-4260. Weekly. Covers acid rain, solid waste and disposal, clean coal, nuclear and hazardous waste. Also available online.

Environmental Action. Environmental Action Foundation, 6930 Carroll Ave., Ste. 600, Takoma Park, Maryland 20912. (301) 891-1100. Bimonthly. Impact of humans and industry on the environment.

Environmental and Urban Issues. FAU/FIU Joint Center for Environmental and Urban Problems, Florida Atlantic University, Fort Lauderdale, Florida 33301. Quarterly. Environmental policy and regional planning in Florida.

Environmental Defense Fund Letter. Environmental Defense Fund, 257 Park Avenue South, New York, New York 10010. (212) 505-2100. 1971-. Bimonthly. Environmental issues of concern.

Environmental Education Report and Newsletter. American Society for Environmental Education, P.O. Box 800, White River, New Hampshire 03755. (603) 448-6697. Quarterly. Contemporary environmental issues.

Environmental Forum. Environmental Law Institute, 1616 P St., N.W., # 200, Washington, District of Columbia 20036. (202) 328-5150. Bimonthly. Policy on environmental protection.

Environmental Management. Springer-Verlag, 175 5th Ave., New York, New York 10010. (212) 460-1500. Six times a year.

Environmental News. Environmental Studies Unit, University of Waikato, Hamilton, New Zealand 1980-. Deals with a comprehensive treatment of environmental issues such as protection, policy research and related areas.

Environmental Policy Alert. Inside Washington Publishers, P.O. Box 7167, Ben Franklin Station, Washington, District of Columbia 20044. Biweekly. Deals with environmental policy news.

Environmental Review. Citizens for a Better Environment, 407 S. Dearborn, Ste. 1775, Chicago, Illinois 60605. (312) 939-1530. Quarterly. Environmental policy and environmental protection issues in the Midwest.

EPA Policy Alert. Inside Washington Publishers, 1235 Jefferson Davis Hwy., #1206, Arlington, Virginia 22202. (703) 892-8500. Biweekly. News of legislation and enforcement.

European Environment Review. European Environment Review, 23, Ave. Gen. Eisenhower, B-1030, Brussels, Belgium Quarterly. Environmental policy and law in the European Economic Community countries.

Forum for Applied Research and Public Policy. University of Tennessee, Energy, Environment and Resources Center, Knoxville, Tennessee 37996-0710. (919) 966-3561. 1986-. Quarterly. Presents a discussion of options by academic, government and corporate experts in energy, environment and economic development.

Green Marketing Report. Business Publishers, Inc., 951 Pershing Dr., Silver Spring, Maryland 20910-4464. (301) 587-6300. 1990-. Monthly. Looks at the steps taken by product manufacturers and advertisers to address consumers' environmental concerns as well as government examination of (and challenges to) some companies' environmental claims. Also available online.

High Country News. High Country Foundation, 124 Grand Ave., Box 1090, Paonia, Colorado 81428-1090. (303) 527-4898. Biweekly. Environmental and public-lands issues in the Rocky Mountain region.

Inside E.P.A. Weekly Report. Inside Washington Publishers, P.O. Box 7167, Ban Franklin Station, Washington, District of Columbia 20044. Weekly. Environmental policy trends.

International Environment Reporter. Bureau of National Affairs, 1231 25th St. N.W., Washington, District of Columbia 20037. (202) 452-4200. Monthly. International environment law and policy in the major industrial nations.

International Environmental Affairs. University Press of New England, 17 1/2 Lebanon Street, Hanover, New Hampshire 03755. (603) 646-3340. Quarterly. Issues on management of natural resources.

International Journal of Environment and Pollution. Inderscience Enterprises Ltd., World Trade Center Bldg., 110 Avenue Louis Casai, Case Postale 306, Geneva-Airport, Switzerland CH-1215. (44) 908-314248. 1991-. Publishes original state-of-the-art articles, book reviews, and technical papers in the areas of: Environmental policies, protection, institutional aspects of pollution, risk assessments of all forms of pollution, protection of soil and ground water, waste disposal strategies, ecological impact of pollutants and other related topics.

International Journal of Environmental Studies. Gordon and Breach Science Publishers, Inc., 270 8th Ave., New York, New York 10011. (212) 206-8900. Irregular. Science, technology and policy relating to the environment.

International Permaculture Solutions Journal. Yankee Permaculture, P.O. Box 16683, Wichita, Kansas 67216. Irregular. Tools for sustainable lifestyles, extensive green pages, and resources directory.

Intersections. Center for Urban Environment Studies, Rensselaer Polytechnic Institute, Troy, New York 12180-3590. Annual. Urban and environmental studies.

The Journal of Environmental Education. Heldref Publications, 4000 Albemarle Street, NW, Washington, District of Columbia 20016. (202) 362-6445. Quarterly. Teaching methods, case studies, and evaluations of new research.

Land Letter. The Conservation Fund, 1800 N. Kent St., Suite 1120, Arlington, Virginia 22209. (703) 522-8008. Thirty four times a year. National land use and conservation policy; legislative, regulatory, and legal developments; use of private and public lands.

NAEP Newsletter. National Association of Environmental Professionals, P.O. Box 15210, Alexandria, Virginia 22309-0210. (703) 660-2364. Monthly. Covers environmental planning, management, review and research.

National News Report. Sierra Club Books, 100 Bush St., San Francisco, California 94104. (415) 291-1600. 1969-. Weekly.

Nature and Resources. Elsevier Science Publishing Co., 655 Avenue of the Americas, New York, New York 10010. (212) 989-5800. 1965-. Quarterly. Provides in-depth reviews of contemporary environmental issues from an international perspective.

World Resource Review. SUPCON International, PO Box 5275, 1 Heritage Plaza, Woodridge, Illinois 60517. (708) 910-1551. 1981-. Quarterly. Covers all phases of policy discussions and their developments, including such topics as global change, energy production and use, ecosystem impacts of development activities, environmental law, solution of transnational environmental problems, global flow of strategic industrial materials, regional, national, and local resource management, natural resources, food, agriculture and forestry.

RESEARCH CENTERS AND INSTITUTES

Coolidge Center for Environmental Leadership. 1675 Massachusetts Ave., Suite 4, Cambridge, Massachusetts 02138. (617) 864-5085.

Ecology Center. 2530 San Pablo Ave., Berkeley, California 94702. (510) 548-2220.

Environmental Law Institute. 1616 P St., N.W., Suite 200, Washington, District of Columbia 20036. (202) 328-5150.

Environmental Policy Institute. 218 D St., S.E., Washington, District of Columbia 20003. (202) 544-2600.

World Environment Center. 419 Park Avenue, Suite 1403, New York, New York 10016. (212) 683-4700.

World Resources Institute. 1709 New York Ave., N.W., Washington, District of Columbia 20006. (202) 638-6300.

STATISTICS SOURCES

Statistical Record of the Environment. Arsen J. Darnay. Gale Research Inc., 835 Penobscot Bldg., Detroit, Michigan 48226-4094. (313) 961-2242. 1992.

TRADE ASSOCIATIONS AND PROFESSIONAL SOCIETIES

American Association for the Advancement of Science. 1333 H St., N.W., Washington, District of Columbia 20005. (202) 326-6400.

American Society of Civil Engineers. 345 East 47th St., New York, New York 10017. (212) 705-7496.

Americans for the Environment. 1400 16th St. N.W., Washington, District of Columbia 20036. (202) 797-6665.

Association of New Jersey Environmental Commissions. PO Box 157, 300 Mendham Rd., Mendham, New Jersey 07945. (201) 539-7547.

Cause for Concern. R.D. 1, Box 570, Stewartsville, New Jersey 08886. (201) 479-4110.

Center for Environmental Information, Inc. 99 Court St., Rochester, New York 14604. (716) 546-3796.

Chamber of Commerce of the United States. 1615 H St., N.W., Washington, District of Columbia 20062. (202) 659-6000.

Environmental Action Foundation. 6930 Carroll Ave., 6th Fl., Takoma Park, Maryland 20912. (202) 745-4870.

Environmental Defense Fund. 257 Park Ave., S., New York, New York 10010. (212) 505-2100. Non-profit organization that was established more than 20 years ago. Its goals are to protect the earth's environment by providing lasting solutions to global environmental problems.

Forest Trust. PO Box 519, Santa Fe, New Mexico 87504-0519. (505) 983-8992.

Friends of the Earth. 218 D St., SE, Washington, District of Columbia 20003. (202) 544-2600.

League of Conservation Voters. 1150 Connecticut, N.W., Suite 201, Washington, District of Columbia 20002. (202) 785-8683.

National Governors Association. Hall of the States, Suite 250, 444 N. Capitol St., N.W., Washington, District of Columbia 20001-1572. (202) 624-5300.

Public Citizen. PO Box 19404, Washington, District of Columbia 20036. (202) 293-9142.

Public Interest Research Group. 215 Pennsylvania Ave. S.E., Washington, District of Columbia 20003. (202) 546-9707.

Rene Dubos Center for Human Environments. 100 E. 85th St., New York, New York 10028. (212) 249-7745.

Scientists' Institute for Public Information. 355 Lexington Ave., New York, New York 10017. (212) 661-9110.

Sierra Club. 100 Bush St., San Francisco, California 94104. (415) 291-1600.

United Nations Environment Programme. DC2-0803 United Nations, New York, New York 10017. (212) 963-8093.

United States Public Interest Research Group. 215 Pennsylvania Ave., SE, Washington, District of Columbia 20003. (202) 546-9707.

ENVIRONMENTAL PROTECTION

See also: AGRICULTURAL CONSERVATION; CONSERVATION OF NATURAL RESOURCES; ENVIRONMENTAL ENGINEERING; ENVIRONMENTAL LEGISLATION; ENVIRONMENTAL IMPACT ASSESSMENT; ENVIRONMENTAL POLICY

ABSTRACTING AND INDEXING SERVICES

Abstracts of Air and Water Conservation Literature. American Petroleum Institute. Central Abstracting and Indexing Service, 275 Madison Avenue, New York, New York 10016. 1972.

Applied Ecology Abstracts Studies in Renewable Natural Resources. Information Retrieval Ltd., 1911 Jefferson Davis Highway, Arlington, Virginia 22202. 1975-. Monthly.

Applied Science and Technology Index. H.W. Wilson Co., 950 University Ave., Bronx, New York 10452. (800) 367-6770. Formerly Industrial Arts Index.

Biological Abstracts. BIOSIS, 2100 Arch St., Philadelphia, Pennsylvania 19103-1399. (215) 587-4800. 1927-.

Biological and Agricultural Index. H.W. Wilson Co., 950 University Ave., Bronx, New York 10452. (800) 367-6770. 1916-. Monthly.

Biology Digest. Data Courier, Plexus Pub Inc., 143 Old Marlton Pike, Medford, New Jersey 08055. 1974-. Monthly. Abstracts biology periodicals.

Biotechnology Research Abstracts. Cambridge Scientific Abstracts, 5161 River Rd., Bethesda, Maryland 20816. (301) 961-6750. Monthly. Includes such broad areas as genetic intervention, biochemical genetics, and microbiological techniques.

Bulletin Signaletique: Eau et Assainissement, Pollution Atmospherique, Droit des Pollutions. Centre de Documentation, Centre National de la Recherche Scientifique, 15, quai Anatole France, Paris, France 75700. (1) 45 55 92 25. 1983-. Monthly. Indexes pollution periodicals including water, atmospheric and related pollutions.

Current Advances in Ecological and Environmental Science. Pergamon Microforms International, Inc., Fairview Park, Elmsford, New York 10523. (914) 592-7720. 1989-. Monthly. Current literature searching service includingjournals, reports, abstracts, etc. This service is available online as part of the CABS database on the hosts BRS and ORBIT search service.

Ecological Abstracts. Geo Abstracts Ltd. Elsevier Applied Science, Crown House, Linton Rd., Barking, England IG 11 8JU. 1974-. Derived from over 600 leading ecological and environmental journals, plus books, conference proceedings, reports and theses.

Ecology Abstracts. Cambridge Scientific Abstracts, 5161 River Rd., Bethesda, Maryland 20816. (301) 961-6750. Monthly.

Engineering Index. The Engineering Index Inc., 345 E. 47th St., New York, New York 10017. 1962-.

Environmental Information Connection–EIC. Planning Information Program, Dept. of Urban and Regional Planning, University of Illinois, 1003 West Nevada, Urbana, Illinois 61801. (217) 333-1369. Also available online.

Environmental Research Laboratories Publication Abstracts. National Oceanic and Atmospheric Administration. Environmental Research Laboratories, 325 Broadway, Boulder, Colorado 80303. 1990. Annual. Sixth annual bibliography of NOAA Environmental Research Laboratories staff publications, FY 89. Covers journal articles, official ERL reports, conference papers, and publications released in cooperation with universities and by ERL funded contractors.

EPA Index: A Key to U.S. Environmental Protection Agency Reports and Superintendent of Documents and NTIS Numbers. Cynthia E. Bower and Mary L. Rhoads, eds. Oryx Press, 4041 N. Central at Indian School Rd., Ste. 700, Phoenix, Arizona 85012-3397. (602) 265-2651. 1983. Identifies and locates certain numbered EPA reports published prior to 1982. The list is not comprehensive. Arranged by report number and by title.

Geographical Abstracts. London School of Economics, Dept. of Geography, Regency House, 34 Duke St., London, England 1966-. Continued by Geo Abstracts issued in 6 parts: Pt. A. Landforms and the quaternary; Pt. B. Biogeography and Climatology; Pt. C. Economic geography; Pt. D. Social geography and cartography; Pt. E. Sedimentology; Pt. F. Regional and community planning.

Green Engineering: A Current Awareness Bulletin. Institution of Mechanical Engineers, 1 Birdcage Walk, Westminster, London, England SW1H 9JJ. 71973 1266/7. 1991. Monthly. Covers acid rain, aerosol technology, biotechnology chlorofluorocarbons, chemical and process engineering, environmental protection, energy conservation, energy generation, greenhouse effect, materials, pollution, recycling, waste disposal, and other environmental topics.

Index to Scientific Book Contents. Institute for Scientific Information, 3501 Market St., Philadelphia, Pennsylvania 19104. (800) 523-1857. 1985-. Annual. Gives contents of science books published.

Multimedia Index to Ecology. National Information Center for Educational Media, University of Southern California, Los Angeles, California 90007.

Pesticides Abstracts. U.S. Environmental Protection Agency, Office of Pesticides Programs, 345 Curtland, Atlanta, Georgia 30365. (404) 347-2864. 1981. Monthly. Formerly: Health Aspects of Pesticides Abstracts Bulletin.

Pollution Abstracts. Cambridge Scientific Abstracts, 5161 River Rd., Bethesda, Maryland 20816. (301) 961-6750. Six/year. Indexes worldwide technical literature on environmental pollution. Covers air pollution, marine and freshwater pollution, sewage and wastewater treatment, waste management, toxicology and health, noise pollution, radiation, land pollution, and environmental policies, programs, legislation, and education. Also available online.

Priority Issue Reporting Service–PIRS. Information for Public Affairs, Inc., Client Services Dept., 1900 14th St., Sacramento, California 95814.

Summaries of Foreign Government Environmental Reports. U.S. Environmental Protection Agency, 401 M St., S.W., Washington, District of Columbia 20460. (202) 260-2090.

ALMANACS AND YEARBOOKS

European Environmental Yearbook, 1991. Doctor Institute of Environmental Studies. BNA Books, 1250 23rd St. NW, Washington, District of Columbia 20037. (202) 452-4276. 1991. The yearbook has been prepared with the cooperation of and financial assistance from the Commission of the European Communities/Brussels. It is a comprehensive guide to the environmental policies, laws, and regulations of the European Economic Community. Compares countries' responses to air and water pollution, nuclear safety, toxic and hazardous waste, land reclamation and other issues.

Gale Environmental Almanac. Russ Hoyle. Gale Research Inc., 835 Penobscot Bldg., Detroit, Michigan 48226-4094. (313) 961-2242. 1993. Focuses on the U.S. and Canada, although worldwide and transboundary issues are discussed.

Handbook for State/EPA Agreements. U.S. Environmental Protection Agency. U.S. Environmental Protection Agency, 401 M St. SW, Washington, District of Columbia 20460. (202) 260-2090. Annual. Environmental protection and policy in the United States.

BIBLIOGRAPHIES

Bibliography and Index of Geology. American Geological Institute, 4220 King St., Alexandria, Virginia 22302. Monthly. Includes environmental geology and hydrogeology.

A Bibliography of Documents Issued by the GAO on Matters Related to Environmental Protection. U.S. General Accounting Office, 441 G St., NW, Washington, District of Columbia 20548. 1985.

Coastal Land Use. Council of Planning Librarians, 1313 E. 60th St., Chicago, Illinois 60637-2897. (312) 942-2163. Bibliography of shore protection.

Current Contents. Agriculture, Biology and Environmental Sciences. Institute for Scientific Information, 3501 Market St., Philadelphia, Pennsylvania 19104. (800) 523-1857. 1973-. Previous title: Current Contents. Agricultural, Food & Veterinary Sciences. Gives the table of contents of periodicals in the fields of agriculture, biology, environmental and related areas.

Deep Ecology and Environmental Ethics: A Selected and Annotated Bibliography of Materials Published Since 1980. Teresa DeGroh. Council of Planning Librarians, 1313 E. 60th St., Chicago, Illinois 60637-2897. (312) 942-2163. 1987. Covers human ecology and environmental protection.

Directory of Published Proceedings. Interdok Corp., 173 Halstead Ave., Harrison, New York 10528. (914) 835-3506. 1990. Monthly. This is a listing of published proceedings including the series SEMTE (Science/Medicine/Engineering/Technology) and the series SSH (Social Science/Humanities).

Environment-Employment-New Industrial Societies. Maryse Gaudier. International Labour Organization, H4, rue des Morillons, Geneva 22, Switzerland CH-1211. 1991. Situates environmental issues within the context of industrial societies at the threshold of the 21st century; critically evaluates the harmonization of ecology, modern technology and human resources.

Environmental Protection. U.S. General Accounting Office, Resources, Community, and Economic Development Division, 441 G St., NW, Washington, District of Columbia 20548. (202) 275-5067. 1990. Bibliography of GAO documents of environmental protection.

U.S. Environmental Protection Agency Library System Book Catalog. U.S. Environmental Protection Agency, Library Systems Branch. U.S. G.P.O., Washington, District of Columbia 20401. (202) 512-0000. Annual. Includes the monographic collection of the 28 libraries comprising the library system of the Environmental Protection Agency.

DIRECTORIES

Access EPA. Environmental Protection Agency. Office of Information Resources Management, National Technical Information Service, 5285 Port Royal Rd., Springfield, Virginia 22161. (703) 487-4650. 1991. This is a series of directories that provides contact information and descriptions of services offered by EPA's libraries, databases, information centers, clearinghouses, hotlines, dockets, record management programs and related information sources. At the present time there are seven directories in the series and one consolidated volume entitled ACCESS EPA. PB91–151563. The seven directories are Public Information Tools (PB91-151571); Major EPA Dockets (PB91-151589); Clearinghouses and Hotlines (PB91-151597); Records Management Programs (PB91-151605); Major Environmental Databases (PB91-151613); Libraries and Information Services (PB91-151621); State Environmental Libraries (PB91-151639). Note there is a contact for each state even though there is not an "environmental Library" in each state.

Canadian Environmental Directory. Canadian Almanac & Directory Publishing Co. Ltd., 134 Adelaide St. E., Ste. 27, Toronto, Ontario, Canada M5C 1K9. (416) 362-4088. 1992. Includes individuals, agencies, firms, and associations.

Directory of Environmental Information Sources. Thomas F. P. Sullivan, ed. Government Institutes, Inc., 4 Research Pl., Ste. 200, Rockville, Maryland 20850. (301) 921-2300. 1992. 3d ed.

Directory of Environmental Journals & Media Contacts. Tom Cairns. Council for Environmental Conservation, 80 York Way, London, England N1 9AG. 1985.

Directory of Environmental Scientists in Agriculture. Roland D. Hauck. Council for Agricultural Science and Technology, Memorial Union, Iowa State University, Ames, Iowa 50011. 1979. Second edition. Special publication no.6. Pt.1 is organized by environmental topics which the scientists included in this directory are qualified to discuss. pt.2. lists administrators and liaison officers of state and federal research, extension, and regulatory organizations. pt.3. alphabetical listing of the scientists with address and telephone numbers.

Directory of Federal Environmental Research and Development Programs. William G. Margetts, et al., eds. Government R & D Report, MIT Branch, PO Box 85, Cambridge, Massachusetts 02139. (617) 356-2424. 1978. Provides information on environmental programs supported by various agencies/departments of the federal government. Budget data are also provided.

Directory of State Environmental Libraries. U.S. Environmental Protection Agency, Office of Information Resources Management, 401 M St., SW, Washington, District of Columbia 20460. (202) 260-2090. 1988-. Annually.

The Environmental Address Book: How to Reach the Environment's Greatest Champions and Worst Offenders. Michael Levine. Perigee Books, 200 Madison Ave., New York, New York 10016. (800) 631-8571. 1991. Names and addresses of organizations, agencies, celebrities, political figures, and businesses (local, state, national, and international level) concerned with the state of the world's environment.

Environmental Hotline. U.S. Environmental Protection Agency, Region V, Office of Public Information, 230 S. Dearborn St., Chicago, Illinois 60604. Annual.

Environmental Software Directory. Donley Technology, PO Box 335, Garrisonville, Virginia 22463. (703) 659-1954. 1989-. Annually. Provides descriptive access to commercial and government databases, software and online systems related to hazardous materials manage-

ment, water and wastewater, groundwater, soils, mapping, air pollution and ecology.

Environmental Telephone Directory. Government Institutes, Inc., 4 Research Pl., Ste. 200, Rockville, Maryland 20850. (301) 921-2300. 1990-1991. Complete addresses and phone numbers for Senators and Representatives with their Environmental Aides, full information on Senate and House Committees and Subcommittees and Federal and Executive agencies dealing with environmental issues, and detailed information on state environmental agencies.

Green Earth Resource Guide: A Comprehensive Guide About Environmentally Friendly Services and Products Books, Clean Air... Cheryl Gorder. Blue Bird Pub., 1713 East Broadway #306, Tempe, Arizona 85282. (602) 968-4088; (800) 654-1993. 1991. Book emphasizes positive steps we can take to help planets. Consists of two parts. Part one profiles people or businesses that are environmentally-friendly and are actively involved with projects and products; part two has resources listings of things concerned with environmental problems. Includes a company index with addresses and phone numbers.

The Green Encyclopedia. Irene Franck, David Brownstone. Prentice-Hall, Rte. 9W, Englewood Cliffs, New York 07632. (201) 592-2000. 1992. Covers environmental organizations.

Guide to EPA Hotlines, Clearinghouses, Libraries, and Dockets. United States Environmental Protection Agency. U.S. G.P.O., Washington, District of Columbia 20401. (202) 512-0000. 1990.

National Directory of Farmland Protection Organizations. Nancy Bushwick. NASDA Research Foundation, Farmland Project, 14 Independence Ave. SW, Washington, District of Columbia 20250. (202)720-8732. 1983. Organizations which deal with soil conservation and rural land use.

The United States and the Global Environment: A Guide to American Organizations Concerned with International Environmental Issues. Thaddeus C. Trzyna. California Institute of Public Affairs, PO Box 10, Claremont, California 91711. (714) 624-5212. 1983. A guide to American organizations concerned with international environmental issues.

World Directory of Environmental Organizations. Thaddeus C. Trzyna, ed. California Institute of Public Affairs, PO Box 10, Claremont, California 91711. (714) 624-5212. 1989. 3rd ed. Handbook of organizations and programs concerned with protecting the environment and managing natural resources. It covers national and international organizations, both governmental and nongovernmental, in all parts of the world.

World Environment Directory. Business Publishers, Inc., PO Box 1067, Silver Spring, Maryland 20910. (301) 587-6300. 1974-. Annually. Gives vital information on developing environmental legislation, regulations and business opportunities.

The World Environment Handbook. Mark Baker. World Environment Center, 605 3rd Ave., Suite 1704, New York, New York 10158. 1985. Directory of natural resource management agencies and non-governmental environmental organizations in 145 countries.

ENCYCLOPEDIAS AND DICTIONARIES

Cambridge Encyclopedia of Life Sciences. A. E. Friday and David S. Ingram. Cambridge University Press, 40 W 20th St., New York, New York 10011. (212) 924-3900 or (800) 227-0247. 1985. Includes all topics under biology and ecology.

Dictionary of Environmental Engineering and Related Sciences: English-Spanish, Spanish-English. Jose T. Villate. Ediciones Universal, 3090 SW 8th St., Miami, Florida 33135. (305) 642-3355. 1979.

Dictionary of Environmental Protection. Otto E. Tutzauer. Fred B. Rothman, 10368 W. Centennial Rd., Littleton, California 80127. (303) 979-5657. 1979.

Dictionary of Environmental Protection Technology: In Four Languages, English, German, French, Russian. Egon Seidel. Elsevier Science Publishing Co., 655 Avenue of the Americas, New York, New York 10010. (212) 984-5800. 1988.

Dictionary of Environmental Science and Technology. Andrew Porteous. John Wiley & Sons, Inc., 605 3rd Ave., New York, New York 10158-0012. (212) 850-6000. 1992.

Dictionary of the Environment. Michael Allaby. New York University Press, 70 Washington Sq. S., New York, New York 10012. (212) 998-2575. 1989.

Encyclopedia of Community Planning and Environmental Management. Marilyn Spigel Schultz. Facts on File, Inc., 460 Park Ave. S., New York, New York 10016. (212) 683-2244. 1984.

Encyclopedia of Environmental Science and Engineering. J.R. Pfafflin. Gordon and Breach Science Publishers, Inc., 270 8th Ave., New York, New York 10011. (212) 206-8900. 1992.

Encyclopedia of Physics. Rita G. Lerner and George L. Trigg. VCH Publishers, 303 NW 12th Ave., Deerfield Beach, Florida 33442-1788. (305) 428-5566. 1991. Second edition.

English-Russian Dictionary of Environmental Protection: About 14,000 Terms. E.L. Milovanov. Pergamon Microforms International, Inc., Fairview Park, Elmsford, New York 10523. (914) 592-7720. 1981.

Environmental Encyclopedia. William P. Cunningham, Terence Ball, et. al. Gale Research Inc., 835 Penobscot Bldg., Detroit, Michigan 48226-4094. (313) 961-2242. 1993.

Environmental Engineering Dictionary. C. C. Lee. Government Institutes, Inc., 4 Research Pl., Ste. 200, Rockville, Maryland 20850. (301) 921-2300. 1989. Defines over 6000 engineering terms relating to pollutioncontrol technologies, monitoring, risk assessment, sampling andanalysis, quality control, permitting, and environmentally-regulated engineering and science. Includes bibliographical references (p. 612-627).

Environmental Regulatory Glossary. G. William Frick and Thomas P. Sullivan. Government Institutes, Inc., 4 Research Pl., Rockville, Maryland 20850. (301) 921-2300. 1990. Over 4,000 entries. Definitions were gathered from the Code of Federal Regulations, EPA documents, and Federal Environmental Statutes.

EPB Online Vocabulary Aid. Environmental Studies Institute, International Academy at Santa Barbara, 800 Garden St., Ste. D, Dept. ADWL-R, Santa Barbara, California 93101. (805) 965-5010. Annual. Deals with human ecology and environmental protection terminology.

The Facts on File Dictionary of Environmental Science. L. Harold Stevenson and Bruce Wyman. Facts on File, Inc., 460 Park Ave. S., New York, New York 10016. (212) 683-2244. 1991.

Grzimek's Encyclopedia of Ecology. Bernhard Grzimek. Van Nostrand Reinhold, 115 5th Ave., New York, New York 10003. (212) 254-3232. 1976.

McGraw Hill Encyclopedia of Energy. Sybil P. Parker. McGraw-Hill Science & Engineering Books, 1221 Avenue of Americas, New York, New York 10020. (212) 512-2000 or (800) 262-4729. 1981. Second edition. Major issues in energy are discussed in six feature articles. The second section has 300 alphabetically arranged entries relating to energy.

McGraw-Hill Encyclopedia of Environmental Science. Sybil P. Parker. McGraw-Hill Science & Engineering Books, 11 W. 19th St., New York, New York 10011. (212) 337-6010. 1980. Covers ecology, man's influence on nature, and environmental protection.

McGraw-Hill Encyclopedia of Science and Technology. McGraw-Hill, 1221 Avenue of the Americas, New York, New York 10020. (212) 512-2000 or (800) 262-4729. 1992. Seventh edition. Issued in multiple volumes including index. Includes all science and technology broad subject areas.

North American Reference Encyclopedia of Ecology and Pollution. William White. North American Pub. Co., 401 N. Broad St., Philadelphia, Pennsylvania 19108. (215) 238-5300. 1972.

NSCA Environmental Glossary. J. Dunmore. National Society for Clean Air, 136 North Street, Brighton, England BN1 1RG. 1905. Covers air pollution, noise, water pollution, wastes and radiation.

Ullmanns Encyclopedia of Industrial Chemistry. Hans Jurgen Arpe and Wolfgang Gerhartz, eds. VCH Publishers, 303 NW 12th Ave., Deerfield Beach, Florida 33442-1788. (305) 428-5566. 1990. Designed to keep up with the broad spectrum of chemical technology. Thirty-six volumes of the encyclopedia have been divided into two sets: the 28 A volumes contain alphabetically arranged articles on chemicals, product groups, processes and technological concepts; and the 8 B volumes are compendia of basic knowledge in industrial chemistry.

Van Nostrand's Scientific Encyclopedia. Glenn D. Considine, ed. Van Nostrand Reinhold, 115 5th Ave., New York, New York 10003. (212) 254-3232. 1983. Sixth edition. Includes all broad subject areas in science.

GENERAL WORKS

50 Simple Things You Can Do to Save the Earth. G.K. Hall & Co., 70 Lincoln St., Boston, Massachusetts 02111. (617) 423-3990. 1991. Citizen participation in environmental protection.

Biologic Environmental Protection by Design. David Wann. Johnson Books, PO Box 990, Boulder, Colorado 80306. (800) 662-2665. 1990. Provides a compendium of ideas and strategies for various environmental problems.

Blueprint for a Green Planet: Your Practical Guide to Restoring the World's Environment. John Seymour and Herbert Giraardet. Prentice Hall, Rte. 9W, Englewood Cliffs, New Jersey 07632. (201) 592-2000; (800) 634-2863. 1987. Background information and analysis of the root causes of pollution and waste in contemporary society.

Borrowed Earth, Borrowed Time: Healing America's Chemical Wounds. Glenn E. Schweitzer. Plenum Press, 233 Spring St., New York, New York 10013-1578. (212) 620-8000; (800) 221-9369. 1991. Deals with chemical contamination and the problem of industrial dumping.

Building Sustainable Communities: An Environmental Guide for Local Governments. The Global Cities Project. Center for the Study of Law and Politics, 2962 Filmore St., San Francisco, California 94123. (415) 775-0791. 1991. Series of handbooks provide local government with a variety of cost-effective options for developing strategies and programs addressing local environmental problems. The first four reports in this series are: 1. Water: Conservation and Reclamation. 2. Solid Waste: Reduction, Reuse and Recycling. 3. Toxics: Management and Reduction. 4. Transportation: Efficiency and Alternatives. Additional titles to be released in 1991 and 1992 will include: Energy and Alternatives, Urban Forestry, Air Quality, Pollution Prevention and Mitigation, Greenhouse Gases: Reduction and Ozone Protection, Land Use: Stewardship and the Planning Process, Open Space: Preservation and Acquisition, Water Quality: Pollution Prevention and Mitigation, and Environmental Management: Making Your Policies Stick.

Caring for the Earth: A Strategy for Sustainable Living. IUCN. Earthscan, 3 Endsleigh St., London, England 071-388 2117. 1991. Discusses the sustainable living methods to protect the environment.

Chemical Concepts in Pollutant Behavior. Ian J. Tinsley. John Wiley & Sons, Inc., 605 3rd Ave., New York, New York 10158-0012. (212) 850-6000. 1979.

The Complete Guide to Environmental Careers. CEIP Fund. Island Press, 1718 Connecticut Ave. N.W., Suite 300, Washington, District of Columbia 20009. (202) 232-7933. 1989. Presents information needed to plan any career search. Case studies discuss how environmental organizations, government, and industry are working to manage and protect natural resources.

The Control of Nature. John A. McPhee. Noonday Pr., 19 Union Sq. W, New York, New York 10003. (212) 741-6900. 1990. Describes the strategies and tactics through which people attempt to control nature.

Crossroads: Environmental Priorities for the Future. Peter Borrelli, ed. Island Press, 1718 Connecticut Ave. N.W., Suite 300, Washington, District of Columbia 20009. (202) 232-7933. 1988. An assessment of the environmental movement written by some of the country's top environmental leaders, activists and authors.

Deep Ecology. Bill Devall and George Sessions. G. M. Smith, PO Box 667, Layton, Utah 84041. (801) 554-9800; (800) 421-8714. 1985. Explores the philosophical, psychological and sociological roots of today's environmental movement and offers specific direct action suggestions for individuals to practice.

Demanding Clean Food and Water. Plenum Press, 233 Spring St., New York, New York 10013. (212) 620-8000. Details specific chemicals to avoid in foods and discusses

approaches for eradicating pests without polluting the environment.

Design for a Livable Planet: How You Can Help Clean Up the Environment. Jon Naar. Perennial Library, 10 E. 53d St., New York, New York 10022. (212) 207-7000; (800) 242-7737. 1990. Explains the dangers we present to our environment and what we can do about it. Also available from Carolina Biological Supply Co., 2700 York Rd., Burlington, NC.

DOE Model Conference on Waste Management and Environmental Restoration: Proceedings. National Technical Information Service, 5285 Port Royal Rd., Springfield, Virginia 22161. (703) 487-4650. 1990.

Earthright. H. Patricia Hynes. St. Martin's Press, 175 5th Ave., New York, New York 10010. (212) 674-5151. 1990. Guide to practical ways to resolve problems with pesticides, water pollution, garbage disposal, the ozone layer and global warming.

Ecology, Community, and Lifestyle: Outline of an Ecosophy. David Rothenberg. Cambridge University Press, 40 W. 20th St., New York, New York 10011. (212) 924-3900. 1989. Handbook on strategy and tactics for environmentalists.

Economic Instruments for Environmental Protection. OECD Publications and Information Center, 2001 L St. N.W., Suite 700, Washington, District of Columbia 20036. (202) 785-OECD. 1989. Reviews the current role of economic instruments and assesses their effectiveness and future potential. Discusses charges and taxes on effluents, user and product charges, tax relief and subsidies for anti-pollution investments, and trading of pollution rights. Problems of enforcement, and implications for the polluter pays principle are also covered.

The End of Nature. Bill McKibben. Anchor Books, 666 5th Ave., New York, New York 10103. (212) 765-6500; (800) 223-6834. 1990.

Energy-Environment-Quality of Life. Inderscience Enterprises Ltd., World Trade Center Bldg., 110 Avenue Louis Casai, Case Postale 306, Geneva-Airport, Switzerland CH1215. (44) 908-314248. 1991. A special publication of the International Journal of Global Energy. Contains the proceedings of the 13th annual International Scientific Forum on Energy (ISFE) held at the UNESCO building, Paris, France, December 4-7, 1989. Focuses on important energy issues facing the planet, their likely impact on the environment and their effects on the quality of life.

Environment-Employment–New Industrial Societies: A Bibliographic Map. International Labor Organization, 4, rue des Morillons, Geneva 22, Switzerland CH-1211. 1991.

The Environment: Problems and Solutions. Stuart Bruchey, ed. Garland Publishing, Inc., 1000A Sherman Ave., Hamden, Connecticut 06514. (203) 281-4487. 1991. Topics covered: forested wetlands and agriculture, the political economy of smog in southern California, environmental limits to growth in world agriculture, the tradeoff between cost and risk in hazardous waste management, and the protection of groundwater from agricultural pollution.

An Environmental Agenda for the Future. John H. Adams, et al. Island Press, 1718 Connecticut Ave. N.W., Washington, District of Columbia 20009. (202) 232-7933. 1985. Contains articles by the CEOs of the 10 largest environmental organizations in the United States.

Environmental America. D.J. Herda. Millbrook Press, 2 Old New Milford Rd., PO Box 335, Brookfield, Connecticut 06804-0335. (203) 740-2220. 1991. Focuses on environmental issues, concerns and steps being taken to counteract damage.

Environmental Disputes: Community Involvement in Conflict Resolution. James E. Crowfoot and Julia M. Wondolleck, eds. Island Press, 1718 Connecticut Ave. N.W., Suite 300, Washington, District of Columbia 20009. (202) 232-7933. 1990. Set of procedures for settling disputes over environmental policies without litigation.

Environmental Indicators. OECD Publication and Information Center, 2001 L St. N.W., Suite 700, Washington, District of Columbia 20036. (202) 785-OECD. 1991. Comprehensive assessments of environmental issues in industrialized countries. Charts the progress achieved over the past 20 years, and points to problems still remaining and sets an agenda of environmental issues to be dealt with in the 1990s.

Environmental Investments: The Costs of a Clean Government. Island Press, 1718 Connecticut Ave. N.W., Suite 300, Washington, District of Columbia 20009. (202) 232-7933. 1991. Report tells industry what to expect in direct expenses for implementing pollution control measures and undertaking compliance activities for environmental laws.

Environmental Issues: An Anthology of 1989. Thomas W. Joyce, ed. TAPPI Press, Technology Park/Atlanta, PO Box 105113, Atlanta, Georgia 30348. (404) 446-1400. 1990. Contains 39 papers on environmental, safety and occupational health concerns from 11 TAPPI, CPPA and AIChE meetings held during 1989. Also included is a literature review of over 200 papers published in 1989.

An Environmental Odyssey: People, Pollution and Politics in the Life of a Practical Scientist. Merril Eisenbud. University of Washington Press, PO Box 50096, Seattle, Washington 98145-5096. (206) 543-4050 or (800) 441-4115. 1990. A professional biography where Eisenbud writes about a number of environmental challenges. He concludes with a 54-year perspective on the development of his field, on current environmental hazards, on the political pitfalls confronting environmentalists, and on the harmful effects of technology on human health.

Environmental Problems: Nature, Economy and State. R. J. Johnston. Belhaven Press, 136 S. Broadway, Irvington, New York 10533. (914) 591-9111. 1990. Argues that environmental studies should be regarded as a unified social and natural science, central to the survival of the human species.

Environmental Protection and Biological Forms of Control of Pest Organisms. B. Lundholm. Swedish National Science Research Council, Editorial Service, P.O. Box 6711, Stockholm, Sweden S-113 85. 08-15-1580. 1980. Environmental aspects of pests and natural pesticides.

Environmental Protection Careers Guidebook. U.S. Department of Labor, Employment and Training Administration, 200 Constitution Ave., NW, Washington, District of Columbia 20210. (202) 523-8165. 1980. Includes information on education in environmental protection field.

Environmental Protection: Meeting Public Expectations with Limited Resources. U.S. General Accounting Office,

441 G St., NW, Washington, District of Columbia 20548. (202) 275-5067. 1991. Monthly.

Environmental Reporting and Recordkeeping Requirements. Government Institutes, Inc., 4 Research Pl., Ste. 200, Rockville, Maryland 20850. (301) 921-2300. Reporting and recordkeeping under Clean Air, Clean Water, RCRA, CERCLA, SARA, TSCA, and OSHA.

Environmental Viewpoints. Marie Lazzari. Gale Research Inc., 835 Penobscot Bldg., Detroit, Michigan 48226-4094. (313) 961-2242. 1992.

Future Risk: Research Strategies for the 1990's. The Science Advisory Board, U.S. Environmental Protection Agency, 401 M St. SW, Washington, District of Columbia 20460. (202) 260-2090. 1988. Strategies for sources, transport and fate research, strategies for exposure assessment research, and ecological effects research.

The Green Consumer Supermarket Guide. Joel Makower, et al. Penguin Books, 375 Hudson St., New York, New York 10014. (212) 366-2000; (800) 253-2304. 1991. A buying guide to products that don't cost the earth.

Green Warriors. Fred Pearce. Bodley Head, Random Century House, 20 Vauxhall Bridge Rd., London, England SW1V 2SA. 071-973-9730. 1990.

Hazardous Waste Management: New Regulation and New Technology. Brian Price. Financial Times Bus. Info. Ltd., 50-64 Broadway, 7th Fl., London, England 071-799 2002. 1990.

Impact Models to Assess Regional Acidification. Juha Kamari. Kluwer Academic Publishers, 101 Philip Dr., Assinippi Park, Norwell, Massachusetts 02061. (617) 871-6600. 1990. Contains a description of the development and use of the Regional Acidification Information and Simulation (RAINS) model, an integrated assessment model of developing and determining control strategies to reduce regional acidification in Europe.

Index of Hazardous Contents of Commercial Products in Schools and Colleges. The Forum for Scientific Excellence. J. B. Lippincott, 227 E. Washington Sq., Philadelphia, Pennsylvania 19105. (215) 238-4200; (800) 982-4377. 1990. Lists the hazardous components found in thousands of commercial products used in educational institutions.

Industrial and Federal Environmental Markets Report. Government Institutes, Inc., 4 Research Pl., Ste. 200, Rockville, Maryland 20850. (301) 921-2300. Environmental industry developments and environmental laws and policies.

Inside the Environmental Movement: Meeting the Leadership Challenge. Donald Snow, ed. Island Press, 1718 Connecticut Ave. N.W., Suite 300, Washington, District of Columbia 20009. (202) 232-7933. 1992. Book offers recommendations and concrete solutions which will make it an invaluable resource as the conservation community prepares to meet the formidable challenges that lie ahead.

Insurance Claims for Environmental Damages. Lynne M. Miller, ed. PennWell Books, PO Box 21288, Tulsa, Oklahoma 74121. (918) 831-9421; (800) 752-9764. 1989. Case management and technical strategies are presented for effectively handling environmental claims.

International Protection of the Environment. Bernard Ruster and Bruno Simma. Oceana Publications Inc., 75

Main St., Dobbs Ferry, New York 10522. (914) 693-8100. 1990. The 31 volume set is now in a loose-leaf format that will bring and keep the document up-to-date. Contains the documents of environmental law in the world.

International Regulation of Whaling. Patricia Birnie. Oceana Publications Inc., 75 Main St., Dobbs Ferry, New York 10522. (914) 693-8100. 1985. A chronological account of the development of international law pertaining to the regulation of whaling. Traces the growing relationship of the regulation of whaling to the development of other relevant laws and institutions for the conservation of migratory species.

The Legal Regime of the Protection of the Mediterranean against Pollution from Land-Based Sources. S. Kuwabara. Cassell PLC, Publishers Distribution Center, PO Box C831, Rutherford, New Jersey 07070. (201) 939-6064; (201) 939-6065. 1984.

Lessons Learned in Global Environmental Governance. Peter H. Sand. World Resources Institute, 1709 New York Ave. N.W., Washington, District of Columbia 20006. (800) 822-0504. 1990. Takes stock of significant international environmental initiatives to date and highlights innovative features of transnational regimes for setting and implementing standards.

Magill's Survey of Science. Earth Science Series. Frank N. Magill. Salem Press, PO Box 50062, Pasadena, California 91105. 1990-. Five volumes. Includes information on earth's crust, hot spots and volcanic island chains, physical properties of minerals, rock magnetism, physical properties of rocks, and index.

Maintaining a Satisfactory Environment: At What Price?. N. Akerman, ed. Westview Press, 5500 Central Ave., Boulder, Colorado 80301. (303) 444-3541. 1990.

Making Peace with the Planet. Barry Commoner. Pantheon Books, 201 E. 50th St., New York, New York 10220. (212) 751-2000. 1990. Reviews the vast efforts made in the public and private sphere to address and control damage to the environment.

Making Things Happen: How to Be an Effective Volunteer. Joan Wolfe. Island Press, 1718 Connecticut Ave. N.W., Suite 300, Washington, District of Columbia 20009. (202) 232-7933. 1991. Environmental movement is nurtured by volunteers. This book teaches volunteers the basic skills they need to make a stronger impact.

Marine and Estuarine Protection: Programs and Activities. U.S. Environmental Protection Agency, Office of Water, 401 M St. SW, Washington, District of Columbia 20460. (202) 260-2090. 1989.

Media and the Environment. Craig L. LaMay and Everette E. Dennis. Island Press, 1718 Connecticut Ave. N.W., Suite 300, Washington, District of Columbia 20009. (202) 232-7933. 1992. Explores environmental reporting.

Meeting Environmental Work Force Needs. Information Dynamics, 111 Claybrook Dr., Silver Spring, Maryland 20902. 1985. Proceedings of the Second National Conference on Meeting Environmental Workforce Needs, April 1-3, 1985: Education and Training to Assure a Qualified Work Force.

The New York Environment Book. Eric A. Goldstein. Island Press, 1718 Connecticut Ave. N.W., Suite 300, Washington, District of Columbia 20009. (202) 232-

7933. 1990. Provides an in-depth analysis of New York City's environment. The five areas surveyed are: solid waste disposal, hazardous substances, water pollution, air quality, and drinking water quality. Discusses past clean-up efforts, and offers an agenda for the future. Describes and analyzes the general environment of urban areas, and offers solutions for their special environmental problems.

The Northwest Greenbook. Jonathan King. Sasquatch Books, 1931 2nd Ave., Seattle, Washington 98101. (206) 441-5555. 1991.

Our Earth, Ourselves: The Action-Oriented Guide to Help You Protect and Preserve Our Planet. Ruth Caplan and the Staff of Environmental Action. Bantam Books, 666 5th Ave., New York, New York 10103. (212) 765-6500; (800) 223-6834. 1990. Provides practical advice on what we can do to reverse the damage already done to our air, water, and land.

Pollution and Its Containment. Institution of Civil Engineers Infrastructure Policy Group. Telford, 1 Heron Quay, London, England E14 9XF. (071) 987-6999. 1990.

Preventing Pollution Through Technical Assistance: One State's Experience. Mark H. Dorfman, et al. INFORM Inc., 381 Park Ave. S., New York, New York 10016. (212) 689-4040. 1990. Examines the state of North Carolina's voluntary program aimed at assisting the industry in pollution prevention. It also includes a glossary, a bibliography of information sources and helpful statistical tables of data collected.

Private Options: Tools and Concepts for Land Conservation. Montana Land Reliance, Land Trust Exchange. Island Press, 1718 Connecticut Ave. N.W., Suite 300, Washington, District of Columbia 20009. (202) 232-7933. 1982. Private land conservation experts offer their expertise on how individuals can help contain urban sprawl, conserve wetlands, and protect wildlife. This book covers estate planning, tax incentives, purchase options, conservation easements and land management.

Prosperity without Pollution. Joel S. Hirschhorn and Kirsten U. Oldenburg. Van Nostrand Reinhold, 115 5th Ave., New York, New York 10003. (212) 254-3232. 1991. Explains how to decrease pollution without making a sacrifice in our standard of living.

The Protection and Management of Our Natural Resources, Wildlife and Habitat. W. Jack Grosse. Oceana Publications Inc., 75 Main St., Dobbs Ferry, New York 10522. (914) 693-8100. 1992. Covers question of overall management, control and protection of wildlife and habitat. Additionally, as the federal government has recently created numerous acts which serve to control wildlife and habitat, many questions have emerged over shared and conflicting power with the states.

Real Estate Transactions and Environmental Risks: A Practical Guide. Donald C. Nanney. PennWell Books, PO Box 21288, Tulsa, Oklahoma 74121. (918) 831-9421; (800) 752-9764. 1990. Presents general principles used when approaching environmental issues from a real estate agent's point of view.

Refinery System Safety for Contractors: A Six Volume Set. Fluke & Associates, Inc. PennWell Books, PO Box 21288, Tulsa, Oklahoma 74121. (918) 831-9421; (800) 752-9764. 1991. Employee-training and documentation manuals that comply with the safety regulations of OSHA and insurance carriers.

Saving the Earth: A Citizen's Guide to Environmental Action. Will Steger. Knopf, 201 E. 50th St., New York, New York 10022. (301) 848-1900; (800) 733-3000. 1990. Describes the causes and effects of the major environmental threats, and offers practical solutions. A complete resource guide, providing specific information to aid individuals and organizations wanting to take action.

The Shaping of Environmentalism in America. Victor B. Scheffer. University of Washington Press, PO Box 50096, Seattle, Washington 98145-5096. (206) 543-4050; (800) 441-4115. 1991. History of environmental policy and protection in the United States.

The Solution to Pollution in the Workplace. Laurence Sombke, et al. MasterMedia, 17 E. 89th St., New York, New York 10028. (212) 348-2020. 1991. Non-technical guidebook for cost-effective, practical tips and actions to help businesses, big and small, take a proactive role in solving pollution problems.

The Student Environmental Action Guide. The Student Environmental Action Coalition. Earthworks Press, 1400 Shattuck Ave., No. 25, Berkeley, California 94709. (510) 652-8533. 1991. The coalition in collaboration with Earth Works has made adaptations to student lifestyles.

Sunken Nuclear Submarines: A Threat to the Environment?. Viking Oliver Eriksen. Norwegian Univ. Pr., Oxford Univ. Pr., 200 Madison Ave., New York, New York 10016. (212) 679-7300; (800) 334-4249. 1990. Part 1 is a survey of existing submarines, based upon surmise and extrapolation from public knowledge of civilian terrestrial and nautical reactors. Part 2 describes potential accident scenarios and their potential for nuclide release, and Part 3 briefly sketches the oceanographic factors governing dispersion of radioactive nuclides.

Technology of Environmental Pollution Control. Esber I. Shaheen. PennWell Books, PO Box 21288, Tulsa, Oklahoma 74121. (918) 831-9421; (800) 752-9764. 1992. 2d ed. Covers the environmental spectrum in an attempt to update the reader on new technologies and topics regarding pollution control.

Whole Earth Ecolog: The Best of Environmental Tools and Ideas. J. Baldwin, ed. Harmony Books, 201 E. 50th St., New York, New York 10022. (212) 572-6120. 1990. Provides in-depth reviews of materials that have been meticulously reviewed by the staff of Whole Earth Access. Lists hundreds of materials that have the potential for making things a little easier on the planet.

World Guide to Environmental Issues and Organizations. Peter Brackley. Longman Group Ltd., Longman House, Burnt Mill, Harlow, Essex, England CM20 2J6. (0279) 426721. 1991.

The World Watch Reader on Global Environmental Issues. W. W. Norton & Co., Inc., 500 5th Ave., New York, New York 10110. (800) 223-4830. 1991.

A Year in the Greenhouse. John Elkington. Gollancz, 14 Henrietta St., Covent Garden, London, England WC2E 8QJ. (071) 836-2006.

GOVERNMENTAL ORGANIZATIONS

Coast Guard. Information Office, 2100 Second St., S.W., Washington, District of Columbia 20593. (202) 267-2229.

Delaware River Basin Commission. 1100 L St., N.W., Room 5113, Washington, District of Columbia 20240. (202) 343-5761.

Department of Ecology: Environmental Protection. Director, Mail Stop PV-11, Olympia, Washington 98504. (206) 459-6168.

Department of Environmental Quality: Environmental Protection. Director, Herschler Building, 4W, Cheyenne, Wyoming 82002. (307) 777-7938.

Susquehanna River Basin Commission. Department of Interior Building, 1100 L St., N.W., Room 5113, Washington, District of Columbia 20240. (202) 343-4091.

U.S. Environmental Protection Agency: Office of Criminal Enforcement. 401 M St., S.W., Washington, District of Columbia 20460. (202) 475-9660.

HANDBOOKS AND MANUALS

Concise Manual of Chemical and Environmental Safety in Schools and Colleges. Forum for Scientific Excellence. J. B. Lippincott, 227 E. Washington Sq., Philadelphia, Pennsylvania 19105. (215) 238-4200; (800) 982-4377. 1991.

Cross-Reference Index of Hazardous Chemicals, Synonyms, and CAS Registry Numbers. The Forum for Scientific Excellence. J. B. Lippincott, 227 E. Washington Sq., Philadelphia, Pennsylvania 19105. (215) 238-4200; (800) 982-4377. 1990. Contains more than 50,000 synonyms for the hazardous chemicals and environmental pollutants identified. Comprehensive resource title available for properly identifying common names, chemical names and product names associated with these chemicals.

Environment in Key Words: A Multilingual Handbook of the Environment: English-French-German-Russian. Isaac Paenson. Pergamon Microforms International, Inc., Fairview Park, Elmsford, New York 10523. (914) 592-7720. 1990. Two volumes. Terminology in the areas of ecology, environmental protection, pollution, conservation of natural resources and related areas.

Environmental Career Guide: Job Opportunities with the Earth in Mind. Nicholas Basta. John Wiley & Sons, Inc., 605 3rd Ave., New York, New York 10158-0012. (212) 850-6000. 1991. Complete guide to the many career options in the growing environmental field. Shows how to find employers engaged in environmental activity, and how to get the job. Lists key environmental businesses–manufacturing, government agencies, engineering consulting firms, waste handling firms, and others. Lists key professional careers in environmental conservation and maps career strategies.

Environmental Statistics Handbook: Europe. Allan Foster, Oksana Newman. Gale Research Inc., 835 Penobscot Bldg., Detroit, Michigan 48226-4094. (313) 961-2242. 1993.

The Global Ecology Handbook: What You Can Do about the Environmental Crisis. Walter H. Corson, ed. The Global Tomorrow Coalition, Beacon Pr., 25 Beacon St., Boston, Massachusetts 02108-2800. (617) 742-2110. 1990. Covers environment, energy policy, population growth and other issues. It includes chapters on tropical rain forests, garbage, oceans and coasts, global warming, population growth, agriculture, biological diversity, fresh water, hazardous wastes, and environment and development.

The Green Consumer. John Elkington, Julia Hailes, and Joel Makower. Penguin Books, 375 Hudson St., New York, New York 10014. (212) 366-2000. 1990. Shoppers guide to purchasing ecological products and services.

Household Hazards: a Guide to Detoxifying Your Home. League of Women Voters of Albany County, 119 Washington Ave., Albany, New York 12207. 1988. Covers household supplies and appliances safety measures.

Pira's International Environmental Information Sources. Pira, Randalls Rd., Leatherhead, England KT22 7RU. 0372 376161. 1990. Sourcebook includes over 2,000 entries from more than 20 countries, including Australia, Finland, Germany, the United Kingdom, and the United States. Entries are from organizations, research centers, legislative and regulatory bodies, directories, online databases and periodicals. Subject areas covered are: air, noise, water and land pollution, waste control and disposal, recycling, energy recovery and nature conservation.

RCRA Inspection Manual. Environment Protection Agency. Government Institutes, Inc., 4 Research Pl., Suite 200, Rockville, Maryland 20850. (301) 921-2300. 1989. 2nd ed. Developed by EPA to support its inspectors in conducting complex field inspections. It covers the key topics that will help eliminate deficiencies, satisfy inspections and avoid civil and criminal penalties.

Your Resource Guide to Environmental Organizations. John Seredich, ed. Smiling Dolphins Press, 4 Segura, Irvine, California 92715. 1991. Includes the purposes, programs, accomplishments, volunteer opportunities, publications and membership benefits of 150 environmental organizations.

ONLINE DATA BASES

BIOSIS Previews. BIOSIS, 2100 Arch St., Philadelphia, Pennsylvania 19103-1399. (215) 587-4800. Largest and most comprehensive database of research in the life sciences. Contains citations for nearly 9000 primary research journals, monographs, reviews, symposia, preliminary reports, semi-popular journals, selected institutional reports, government reports and research communications.

BNA Environment Daily. Bureau of National Affairs, BNA PLUS, 1231 25th St., N.W., Rm. 215, Washington, District of Columbia 20037. (800) 452-7773.

BNA International Environment Report. Bureau of National Affairs, BNA PLUS, 1231 25th St., N.W., Rm. 215, Washington, District of Columbia 20037. (800) 452-7773.

Chemical Engineering and Biotechnology Abstracts–CEBA. Orbit Search Service, Maxwell Online Inc., 8000 W. Park Dr., McLean, Virginia 22102. (703) 442-0900 or (800) 456-7248. Monthly. Covers theoretical, practical and commercial material on all aspects of processing safety, and the environment. Also covers process and reaction engineering, measurement and process control, environmental protection and safety, plant design and equipment used in chemical engineering and biotechnology. More than 400 of the world's major primary chemical and process engineering journals are scanned to compile the database. Available from ORBIT.

Computerized Engineering Index–COMPENDEX. Engineering Information Inc., 345 E. 47th St., New York, New York 10017. (212) 705-7600.

Current Research Information System–CRIS/USDA. U.S. Department of Agriculture, National Agricultural Library, 10301 Baltimore Blvd., 5th Floor, Beltsville, Maryland 20705-2351. (301) 504-5755. Looks at current research projects in agriculture and allied sciences covering the biological, physical, social and behavioral sciences related to agriculture.

ENREP. Commission of the European Communities, Database Distribution Service, 200 Rue de le Loi, Brussels, Belgium 1049. 32 (2) 2350001.

Enviroline. R. R. Bowker Co., Bowker Electronic Publishing, 121 Chanlon Rd., New Providence, New Jersey 07974. (800) 521-8110.

Environment Library. OCLC Online Computer Library Center, Inc., 6565 Frantz Rd., Dublin, Ohio 43017. (614) 764-6000. Bibliographic and cataloging information for English and foreign-language materials on the topic of environmental issues.

Environment Reporter. Bureau of National Affairs, 1231 25th St., N.W., Rm. 215, Washington, District of Columbia 20037. (800) 372-1033. Online version of periodical of the same name.

Environment Week. NewsNet, Inc., 945 Haverford Rd., Bryn Mawr, Pennsylvania 19010. (800) 345-1301. Online version of periodical of same name.

Environmental Bibliography. Environmental Studies Institute, International Academy at Santa Barbara, 800 Garden St., Ste. D, Santa Barbara, California 93101. (805) 965-5010. International periodical literature dealing with environmental topics such as air pollution, water treatment, energy conservation, noise abatement, soil mechanics, wildlife preservation, and chemical wastes.

Greenwire. American Political Network, 282 North Washington St., Falls Church, Virginia 22046. (703) 237-5130. 1991. Daily. Daily electronic 12-page summary of the last 24 hours of news coverage of environmental issues worldwide. Monday through Friday at 10 am EST, it can be accessed by a PC, modem and an 800 number contains issues on environmental protection, energy/natural resources, business science, 50-state news, worldwide headlines, TV monitor, daily calendar, marketplace battles, Capitol Hill, spotlight story, global issues, environment and the law, solid waste and focus interviews.

Monthly Catalog of United States Government Publications. U.S. G.P.O., Supt. of Docs., PO Box 371954, Pittsburgh, Pennsylvania 15250-7954. (202) 512-0000.

Multinational Environmental Outlook. Business Publishers, Inc., 951 Pershing Dr., Silver Spring, Maryland 20910-4464. (301) 587-6300. Environmental problems and solutions in countries outside the United States and their impact on the United States.

National Environmental Data Referral Service Database. National Oceanic & Atmospheric Administration, Department of Commerce, 1825 Connecticut Ave., N.W., Washington, District of Columbia 20235. (202) 673-5548. Data files, published data sources, documentation references, and organizations that make environmental data available.

National Technical Information Service. U.S. Department of Commerce, National Technical Information Service, Office of Data Base Services, 5285 Port Royal Rd., Springfield, Virginia 22161. (703) 487-4807. Bibliographic database of government sponsored research and technical reports.

PressNet Environmental Reports. Chemical Information Systems, Inc., 7215 York Rd., Baltimore, Maryland 21212. (301) 321-8440.

SCISEARCH. Institute for Scientific Information, University City Science Center, 3501 Market St., Philadelphia, Pennsylvania 19104. (215) 386-0100.

State Environmental Report. NewsNet, Inc., 945 Haverford Rd., Bryn Mawr, Pennsylvania 19010. (800) 345-1301.

PERIODICALS AND NEWSLETTERS

Advances in Environmental Science and Engineering. Gordon and Breach Science Publishers, Inc., 270 8th Ave., New York, New York 10011. (212) 206-8900. Annual.

Air/Water Pollution Report. Business Publishers, Inc., 951 Pershing Dr., Silver Spring, Maryland 20910-4464. (301) 587-6300. 1963-. Weekly. Reports on the hard news and in-depth features for practical use by environmental managers. It keeps readers informed on the latest news from government and industry. Also available online.

ANJEC Report. Association of New Jersey Environmental Commissions, Box 157, Mendham, New Jersey 07945. (201) 539-7547. 1969-. Quarterly. Informs environmental commissioners and interested citizens about environmental issues, laws and regulations, particularly those that effect New Jersey.

Better Times. America the Beautiful Fund, 219 Shoreham Bldg., Washington, District of Columbia 20005. (202) 638-1649. Semiannual. Local volunteer environmental action projects involving environmental design, land preservation, green plantings, and historical and cultural preservation.

Between the Issues. Ecology Action Center, 1657 Barrington St., #520, Halifax, Nova Scotia, Canada B3J 2A1. (506) 422-4311. 1975-. Bimonthly. Newsletter that deals with environmental protection, uranium mining, waste, energy, agriculture, forestry, pesticides, and urban planning.

BNA's National Environmental Watch. Bureau of National Affairs, BNA Plus, 1231 25th St, NW, Washington, District of Columbia 20037. (202) 452-4200. Weekly. News, technological reviews, and regulatory information regarding industry's impact on the environment.

British Columbia Ministry of Environment, Annual Report. British Columbia, Ministry of Environment, 810 Blanchard, 1st Fl., Victoria, British Columbia, Canada (604) 387-9418. 1976-. Annually. Review of work carried out during the year by the Ministry of the Environment, including fish, wildlife, water management, and parks.

Buzzworm: The Environmental Journal. Buzzworm Inc., 2305 Canyon Blvd., No. 206, Boulder, Colorado 80302-5655. (303) 442-1969. 1988-. Quarterly. An independent environmental journal for the reader interested in nature, adventure, travel, the natural environment and the issues of conservation.

California Environmental Directory. California Institute of Public Affairs, Box 189040, Sacramento, California 95818. (916) 442-2472. 1973-. Irregular. Directory of public, private and academic organizations located in California that are concerned with environmental protection.

California Tomorrow. California Tomorrow, Ft. Mason Ctr., Building B, #315, San Francisco, California 94123. (415) 441-7631. 1965-. Quarterly. Illustrates need for system of comprehensive state/regional planning to protect and improve the Californian environment.

Canadian Environmental Control Newsletter. 6 Garamond Ct., Don Mills, Ontario, Canada M3C 1Z5. (416) 441-2992. 1945-. Covers the general topic of pollution and the environmental control measures designed to fight it.

Chemosphere: Chemistry, Biology and Toxicology as Related to Environmental Problems. Pergamon Microforms International, Inc., Fairview Park, Elmsford, New York 10523. (914) 592-7720. 1970-. Offers maximum dissemination of investigations related to the health and safety of every aspect of life. Environmental protection encompasses a very wide field and relies on scientific research in chemistry, biology, physics, toxicology and inter-related disciplines.

Citizen's Bulletin. Connecticut Dept. of Environmental Protection, 165 Capitol Ave., Hartford, Connecticut 06106. (203) 566-3489. Monthly. Information on departmental programs and environmental issues.

COPIRG Outlook. Colorado Public Interest Research Group, 1724 Gilpin St., Denver, Colorado 80218. (303) 355-1861. Quarterly. Covers consumer rights, environmental protection, and citizen action organization.

The Earth Care Annual. Russell Wild, ed. Rodale Press, 33 E. Minon St., Emmaus, Pennsylvania 18098. (215) 967-5171; (800) 322-6333. 1990-. Annually. Organized in alphabetical sections such as garbage, greenhouse effect, oceans, ozone, toxic waste, and wildlife, the annual presents environmental problems and offers innovative working solutions.

Earth First! Journal in Defense of Wilderness and Biodiversity. Earth First!, PO Box 5176, Missoula, Montana 59806. Eight/year.

Earthwatch Magazine. Earthwatch Expeditions, 680 Mt. Auburn St., Box 403, Watertown, Massachusetts 02272. (617) 926-8200. Bimonthly. Worldwide research expeditions, endangered species, cultures, and world health.

Ecotoxicology and Environmental Safety. Academic Press, c/o Harcourt Brace Jovanovich Inc., 6277 Sea Harbor Dr., Orlando, Florida 32887. (800) 346-8648. 1977-. Bimonthly.

The Egg-An Eco-Justice Quarterly. Eco-Justice Project and Network, Cornell University, Anabel Taylor Hall, Ithaca, New York 14850. Quarterly.

Environment. Heldref Publications, 4000 Albemarle Street, NW, Washington, District of Columbia 20016. (202) 362-6445. Ten a year. Covers science and science policy.

Environment International: A Journal of Science, Technology, Health, Monitoring and Policy. Pergamon Microforms International, Inc., Fairview Park, Elmsford, New York 10523. (914) 592-7720. 1974-. Bimonthly. Includes vital data, causes of pollution, and methods for protection, covering the entire field of environmental protection.

Environment Reporter. Bureau of National Affairs, 1231 25th St. NW, Washington, District of Columbia 20037. (800) 372-1033. Weekly. Issues of pollution control and environmental activity. Also available online.

Environmental Claims Journal. Executive Enterprises Publications Co., Inc., 22 W. 21st St., New York, New York 10010-6990. (212) 645-7880. Quarterly. News of environmental professionals, risk managers, and insurance executives.

Environmental Defense Fund Letter. Environmental Defense Fund, 257 Park Avenue South, New York, New York 10010. (212) 505-2100. 1971-. Bimonthly. Environmental issues of concern.

Environmental Management. Springer-Verlag, 175 5th Ave., New York, New York 10010. (212) 460-1500. Six times a year.

Environmental News. Environmental Studies Unit, University of Waikato, Hamilton, New Zealand 1980-. Deals with a comprehensive treatment of environmental issues such as protection, policy research and related areas.

Environmental News. N.J. Department of Environmental Protection, 401 E. State St., CN 402, Trenton, New Jersey 08625. (609) 984-6773. Bimonthly. News of state programs relating to cleaner air, water, land management, conservation and preservation of natural resources.

Environmental Pollution. Applied Science Publications, PO Box 5399, New York, New York 10163. (718) 756-6440. 1987-.

Environmental Professional. National Association of Environmental Professionals, P.O. Box 15210, Alexandria, Virginia 22309-0210. (703) 660-2364. Quarterly. Covers effective impact assessment, regulation, and environmental protection.

Environmental Progress. American Institute of Chemical Engineers, 345 E. 47th St., New York, New York 10017. (212) 705-7338. Quarterly. Deals with environmental policies, protection and management-especially relating to chemicals.

Environmental Protection Agency Journal. U.S. Environmental Protection Agency MC A-107, 401 M St. SW, Washington, District of Columbia 20460. (202) 260-2090. Bimonthly. Addresses environmental matters of interest.

Environmental Protection Agency Regulatory Agenda. U.S. Environmental Protection Agency, 401 M St. SW, Washington, District of Columbia 20460. (202) 260-2090. Twice a year. Information on the status of proposed regulations.

Environmental Protection News. Stevens Publishing Co., PO Box 2604, Waco, Texas 76706. (817) 776-9000. 1990-. Weekly. Covers topics such as: The EPA looking at the Endangered Species Act; The Indoor Air Bill debate intensifies in Congress; Capitol Hill considers new Hazmat Trade Laws; The EPA turns to the media to help prosecute polluters; The Superfund fiasco is not the fault of contractors?; and other environmental topics.

Environmental Quality. U.S. Joint Publication Research Service, 1000 N. Glebe Rd., Arlington, Virginia 22201.

(703) 557-4630. Semimonthly. Policy issues relating to environmental protection.

Environmental Review. Citizens for a Better Environment, 407 S. Dearborn, Ste. 1775, Chicago, Illinois 60605. (312) 939-1530. Quarterly. Environmental policy and environmental protection issues in the Midwest.

Environmental Scene. Arizona Dept. of Environmental Quality, 2005 N. Central, Phoenix, Arizona 85004. (602) 257-6940. Quarterly. State programs in areas of air quality, water quality and waste programs.

Environmental Spectrum. New Jersey Cooperative Extension Service, Cook College, Rutgers University, P.O. Box 231, New Brunswick, New Jersey 08903. 1968-. Bimonthly. Emphasis on air/noise pollution, energy, water and other environmental topics.

Environmental Studies & Practice: An Educational Resource and Forum. Yale School of Forestry and Environmental Studies, 205 Prospect St., New Haven, Connecticut 06511. (203) 432-5132. 1991. Bimonthly. Subject matters range widely from air pollution to wildlife biology. Each issue contains a selection of recent publications, from all subject areas of environmental and natural resources management.

Environmental Technology. Park Publishing Co., 333 Hudson St., New York, New York 10013. (212) 255-1500. Semimonthly. Research on pollution abatement.

Environmental Toxicology and Chemistry. Society of Environmental Toxicology and Chemistry. Pergamon Microforms International, Inc., Fairview Park, Elmsford, New York 10523. (914) 592-7720. 1981-. Monthly. Contains information on environmental toxicology, and chemistry, including the application of science to hazard assessment.

Garbage: The Practical Journal for the Environment. Old House Journal Corp., 2 Main St., Gloucester, Massachusetts 01930. (508) 283-4629. Bimonthly. Issues in municipal wastes.

Global Environmental Change: Human and Policy Dimensions. James K. Mitchell, ed. Department of Geography, Lucy Stone Hall, Kilmer Campus, New Brunswick, New Jersey 08903. (201) 932-4103. 1991. Five issues a year. Produced in cooperation with the United Nations University, including its International Human Dimensions of Global Change Programme. Addresses the human, ecological and public policy aspects of environmental processes that might affect the sustainability of life on Earth.

Green Alternative Information for Action. Earth Island Inst., 300 Broadway, Suite 28, San Francisco, California 94133. (415) 788-3666. Monthly.

Green Letter. Green Letter, Box 9242, Berkeley, California 94709. Bimonthly. Information about the worldwide green movement.

Green Library Journal: Environmental Topics in the Information World. Maria A. Jankowska, ed. Green Library, University of Idaho Library, Moscow, Idaho 83843. (208) 885-6260. Jan 1992-. Scope of the journal would include information sources about: conservation, ecologically balanced regional development, environmental protection, natural resources management, environmental issues in libraries, publishing industries, and information science.

Green Light News. Green Light News, Box 12, Liberty Sq., Ellenville, New York 12428. (914) 647-3300. Monthly. Ecology news.

Greenletter. Woodstock Resort, Woodstock Inn, Woodstock, Vermont 05091-1298. (802) 457-1100. Quarterly. Ecological and environmental topics.

Greenpeace Magazine. Greenpeace, 1436 U St., NW, Washington, District of Columbia 20009. (202) 462-1177. Bimonthly. Deals with nature and wildlife conservation, and environmental protection.

The Holocene: An Interdisciplinary Journal Focusing on Recent Environmental Change. Edward Arnold, c/o Cambridge University Press, 40 W. 20th St., New York, New York 10011-4211. (212) 924-3900. Three times a year.

Hotline. Ohio Environmental Council, 22 E. Gay St., #300, Columbus, Ohio 43215. (614) 486-4055. Ten times a year. Breaking news relating to environmental protection.

Housatonic Current. Housatonic Valley Assn., Box 28, Cornwall Bridge, Connecticut 06754. (203) 672-6678. Quarterly. Environmental programs and land planning throughout the Housatonic River Watershed.

Human Factors Society Bulletin. Human Factors Society, PO Box 1369, Santa Monica, California 90406-1369. (310) 394-1811. Monthly.

Inside E.P.A. Weekly Report. Inside Washington Publishers, P.O. Box 7167, Ban Franklin Station, Washington, District of Columbia 20044. Weekly. Environmental policy trends.

It's Time to Go Wild. American Wildlands, 7600 E. Arapahoe Rd., Suite 114, Englewood, Colorado 80112. (303) 771-0380. Quarterly. Protection and proper use of wilderness lands and rivers.

Journal of Environmental Quality. American Society of Agronomy, 677 S. Segoe Rd., Madison, Wisconsin 53711-1086. (608) 273-8080. 1972-. Quarterly. Reports and brief reviews of agricultural ecology, environmental engineering and pollution.

Journal of Environmental Science and Health. Marcel Dekker, Inc., 270 Madison Ave., New York, New York 10016. (212) 696-9000. Bimonthly. Concerns pesticides, food contaminants, chemical carcinogens, and agricultural wastes.

Maine Environment. Natural Resource Council of Maine, 20 Willow St., Augusta, Maine 04330. 1974-. Monthly. Environmental activities and problems in Maine.

Marine Bulletin. National Coalition for Marine Conservation, Box 23298, Savannah, Georgia 31403. (912) 234-8062. Monthly. Marine fisheries, biological research, marine environmental pollution, and the prevention of the over-exploitation of ocean fish.

Mecca News. Minnesota Environmental Control Citizens Association, PO Box 80089, St. Paul, Minnesota 55108. Monthly.

Mountain Research and Development. University of California Press, 2120 Berkeley Way, Berkeley, California 94720. (415) 642-7485; (800) 822-6657. Quarterly. Environmental & land use problems.

Muir & Friends. John Muir Institute of Environmental Studies, 2118 C. Vine St., Berkeley, California 94709. 1970-. Monthly.

NAEP Newsletter. National Association of Environmental Professionals, P.O. Box 15210, Alexandria, Virginia 22309-0210. (703) 660-2364. Monthly. Covers environmental planning, management, review and research.

National Geographic. National Geographic Society, 17th & M Sts. NW, Washington, District of Columbia 20036. (202) 857-7000. Monthly. Articles on geography, culture, natural history, and the environment.

National News Report. Sierra Club Books, 100 Bush St., San Francisco, California 94104. (415) 291-1600. 1969-. Weekly.

Nature and Resources. Elsevier Science Publishing Co., 655 Avenue of the Americas, New York, New York 10010. (212) 989-5800. 1965-. Quarterly. Provides in-depth reviews of contemporary environmental issues from an international perspective.

New York City Environmental Bulletin. Council on the Environment of New York City, 51 Chambers St., New York, New York 10007. (212) 566-0990. Bimonthly. Environmental briefs of interest to city residents.

North Carolina Environmental Bulletin. North Carolina Office of Intergovernmental Relations, 116 W. Jones St., Raleigh, North Carolina 27603. Monthly. State environmental news.

Not Man Apart. Friends of the Earth, 218 D St. SE, Washington, District of Columbia 20003. (202) 544-2600. Bimonthly.

Ohio Environmental Report. Ohio Environmental Council, 22 E. Gay St., # 300, Columbus, Ohio 43215. (614) 224-4900. Monthly. News on environmental issues and projects in Ohio.

OSPIRG Citizen Agenda. Oregon State Public Interest Research Group, 027 SW Arthur St., Portland, Oregon 97201. (503) 222-9641. Quarterly. Consumer rights, environmental protection, & citizen action.

PIRGIM Citizen Connection. Public Interest Research Group on Michigan, 212 S. 4th Ave. #207, Ann Arbor, Michigan 48104. (313) 662-6597. Quarterly. Environmental and consumer protection.

Pollution Prevention. Executive Enterprises Publications Co., Inc., 22 W. 21st St., New York, New York 10010-6990. (212) 645-7880 or (800) 332-8804. 1991. Quarterly. Includes practical approaches to reducing waste, case studies of successful waste reduction programs and the saving they provide, analyses of new technologies and their efficacy in reducing waste, and updates of federal and state legislative initiatives and their impacts on industries.

Protect. Tennessee Environmental Council, 1725 Church St., Nashville, Tennessee 37203-2921. (615) 321-5075. Bimonthly.

Protection Ecology. Elsevier Science Publishing Co., Journal Information Center, 655 Avenue of the Americas, New York, New York 10010. (212) 989-5800. Livestock and agricultural ecology and pest control.

The UNESCO Courier. UNESCO, 7 place de Fontenoy, Paris, France F-75700. 1948-. Monthly. Each issue deals with a theme of universal interest including regular features on the environment, world heritage and UNESCO activities.

Utility Reporter. Merton Allen Associates, PO Box 15640, Plantation, Florida 33318-5640. (305)473-9560. Monthly. Covers current activities in power generation and energy conservation.

Washington Environmental Protection Report. Callahan Publication, P.O. Box 3751, Washington, District of Columbia 20007. (703) 356-1925. Biweekly.

World Resource Review. SUPCON International, PO Box 5275, 1 Heritage Plaza, Woodridge, Illinois 60517. (708) 910-1551. 1981-. Quarterly. Covers all phases of policy discussions and their developments, including such topics as global change, energy production and use, ecosystem impacts of development activities, environmental law, solution of transnational environmental problems, global flow of strategic industrial materials, regional, national, and local resource management, natural resources, food, agriculture and forestry.

RESEARCH CENTERS AND INSTITUTES

Ecology Center. 2530 San Pablo Ave., Berkeley, California 94702. (510) 548-2220.

Legacy. 1100 Revere Dr., Olonomowoc, Wisconsin 53066. (414) 567-3454.

National Research Council. 2101 Constitution Ave., N.W., Washington, District of Columbia 20418. (202) 334-2000.

Renew America. 17 16th Street, N. W., Suite 710, Washington, District of Columbia 20036. (202) 232-2252.

World Environment Center. 419 Park Avenue, Suite 1403, New York, New York 10016. (212) 683-4700.

World Resources Institute. 1709 New York Ave., N.W., Washington, District of Columbia 20006. (202) 638-6300.

STATISTICS SOURCES

Statistical Record of the Environment. Arsen J. Darnay. Gale Research Inc., 835 Penobscot Bldg., Detroit, Michigan 48226-4094. (313) 961-2242. 1992.

TRADE ASSOCIATIONS AND PROFESSIONAL SOCIETIES

American Society of Naturalists. Department of Ecology and Evolation, State University of New York, Stony Brook, New York 11794. (516) 632-8589.

Association for the Study of Man-Environment Relations. Box 57, Orangeburg, New York 10962. (914) 634-8221.

Association of Environmental Engineering Professors. Department of Civil Engineering, Virginia Polytechnic Institute and State University, Blacksburg, Virginia 24061. (703) 231-6021.

Association of New Jersey Environmental Commissions. PO Box 157, 300 Mendham Rd., Mendham, New Jersey 07945. (201) 539-7547.

CEIP Fund. 68 Harrison Ave., 5th Fl., Boston, Massachusetts 02111. (617) 426-4375.

Center for Environmental Information, Inc. 99 Court St., Rochester, New York 14604. (716) 546-3796.

Earth First!. PO Box 5176, Missoula, Montana 59806.

Earthwatch. 680 Mt. Auburn St., P.O. Box 403, Watertown, Massachusetts 02272. (617) 926-8200.

Environmental Action, Inc. 1525 New Hampshire Ave., NW, Washington, District of Columbia 20036. (202) 745-4870.

Environmental Defense Fund. 257 Park Ave., S., New York, New York 10010. (212) 505-2100. Non-profit organization that was established more than 20 years ago. Its goals are to protect the earth's environment by providing lasting solutions to global environmental problems.

Friends of Africa in America. 330 S. Broadway, Tarrytown, New York 10591. (914) 631-5168.

Global Tomorrow Coalition. 1325 G St., N.W., Suite 915, Washington, District of Columbia 20005-3103. (202) 628-4016.

Goldman Environmental Foundation. 1160 Battery St., Suite 400, San Francisco, California 94111. (415) 788-1090.

Institute for 21st Century Studies. 1611 N. Kent St., Suite 610, Arlington, Virginia 22209. (703) 841-0048.

Institute of Environmental Sciences. 940 E. Northwest Hwy., Mount Prospect, Illinois 60056. (708) 255-1561.

Legal Environmental Assistance Foundation. 1115 N. Gadsden St., Tallahassee, Florida 32303. (904) 681-2591.

National Association of Environmental Professionals. PO Box 15210, Alexandria, Virginia 22309-0210. (703) 660-2364.

National Council of the Paper Industry for Air and Stream Improvements. 260 Madison Ave., New York, New York 10016. (212) 532-9000.

National Oil Recyclers Association. 805 15th St., N.W., Suite 900, Washington, District of Columbia 20005. (202) 962-3020.

Scientists' Institute for Public Information. 355 Lexington Ave., New York, New York 10017. (212) 661-9110.

Sierra Club. 100 Bush St., San Francisco, California 94104. (415) 291-1600.

United Nations Environment Programme. DC2-0803 United Nations, New York, New York 10017. (212) 963-8093.

ENVIRONMENTAL PROTECTION AGENCIES. GENERAL OFFICES

GOVERNMENTAL ORGANIZATIONS

Environmental Protection Agency: Public Information Center. 401 M St., S.W., Washington, District of Columbia 20460. (202) 382-2080.

Environmental Protection Agency: Small Business Ombudsman Office. 401 M St., S.W., 1A49C-1108, Washington, District of Columbia 20460. (202) 557-7777.

U.S. Environmental Protection Agency: Communications and Public Affairs Office. 401 M St., S.W., Washington, District of Columbia 20460. (202) 382-4361.

U.S. Environmental Protection Agency: Cooperative Environmental Management Office. Room 605, 499 South Capitol St., S.W., Washington, District of Columbia 20460. (202) 475-9741.

U.S. Environmental Protection Agency: Dockets. 401 M St., S.W., Washington, District of Columbia 20460. (202) 382-5926.

U.S. Environmental Protection Agency: Freedom of Information Office. 401 M St., S.W., Washington, District of Columbia 20460. (202) 382-4048.

U.S. Environmental Protection Agency: Library, Room 2404. 401 M St., S.W., Washington, District of Columbia 20460. (202) 382-5921.

U.S. Environmental Protection Agency, PM-233: EPA Regulatory Agenda. 401 M St., S.W., Washington, District of Columbia 20460. (202) 382-5480.

ENVIRONMENTAL PROTECTION AGENCIES. REGIONAL OFFICES

GOVERNMENTAL ORGANIZATIONS

EPA RCRA/OUST Superfund Hotline. EPA: Office of Solid Waste (OS305), 401 M St. SW, WA, District of Columbia 20460. (800) 424-9346; (800) 346-5009.

Region 8 Office. One Denver Place, 999 18th St., Suite 500, Denver, Colorado 80202. (303) 293-1603.

U.S. EPA Region 1: Pollution Prevention. Program Manager, JFK Federal Building, Boston, Massachusetts 02203. (617) 565-3715.

U.S. EPA Region 10: Pollution Prevention. Chief, Hazardous Waste Policy Office, 1200 Sixth Ave., Seattle, Washington 98101. (206) 442-5810.

U.S. EPA Region 2: Pollution Prevention. Regional Contact, 26 Federal Plaza, New York, New York 10278. (212) 264-2525.

U.S. EPA Region 3: Pollution Prevention. Program Manager, 841 Chestnut St., Philadelphia, Pennsylvania 19107. (215) 597-9800.

U.S. EPA Region 4: Pollution Prevention. Program Manager, 345 Courtland St., N.E., Atlanta, Georgia 30365. (404) 347-7109.

U.S. EPA Region 5: Pollution Prevention. 230 South Dearborn St., Chicago, Illinois 60604. (312) 353-2000.

U.S. EPA Region 6: Pollution Prevention. Coordinator, 1445 Ross Ave., Suite 1200, Dallas, Texas 75202-2733. (214) 655-6444.

U.S. EPA Region 7: Pollution Prevention. Section Chief, State Programs Section, 726 Minnesota Ave., Kansas City, Missouri 66101. (913) 551-7006.

U.S. EPA Region 8: Pollution Prevention. Senior Policy Advisor, 999 18th St., Suite 500, Denver, Colorado 80202-2405. (303) 293-1603.

U.S. EPA Region 9: Pollution Prevention. Deputy Director, Hazardous Waste, 215 Fremont St., San Francisco, California 94105. (415) 556-6322.

ENVIRONMENTAL QUALITY

ABSTRACTING AND INDEXING SERVICES

Air Pollution Titles. Pennsylvania State University, Center for Air Environmental Studies, 226 Fenske Laboratory, University Park, Pennsylvania 16802. (814) 865-1415. 1965. Bibliographic guide to current research literature on air environment, including monitoring and control of air pollution, health effects, effects on agriculture, forests, toxic air contaminants, and global atmospheric pro cases.

Air Pollution Translations. A Bibliography With Abstracts. U.S. Environmental Protection Agency, MD 75, Research Triangle Park, North Carolina 27711. (919) 541-2184. 1969.

Applied Ecology Abstracts Studies in Renewable Natural Resources. Information Retrieval Ltd., 1911 Jefferson Davis Highway, Arlington, Virginia 22202. 1975-. Monthly.

Biological Abstracts. BIOSIS, 2100 Arch St., Philadelphia, Pennsylvania 19103-1399. (215) 587-4800. 1927-.

Biological and Agricultural Index. H.W. Wilson Co., 950 University Ave., Bronx, New York 10452. (800) 367-6770. 1916-. Monthly.

Bulletin Signaletique: Eau et Assainissement, Pollution Atmospherique, Droit des Pollutions. Centre de Documentation, Centre National de la Recherche Scientifique, 15, quai Anatole France, Paris, France 75700. (1) 45 55 92 25. 1983-. Monthly. Indexes pollution periodicals including water, atmospheric and related pollutions.

Current Advances in Ecological and Environmental Science. Pergamon Microforms International, Inc., Fairview Park, Elmsford, New York 10523. (914) 592-7720. 1989-. Monthly. Current literature searching service includingjournals, reports, abstracts, etc. This service is available online as part of the CABS database on the hosts BRS and ORBIT search service.

Ecology Abstracts. Cambridge Scientific Abstracts, 5161 River Rd., Bethesda, Maryland 20816. (301) 961-6750. Monthly.

Index to Scientific Book Contents. Institute for Scientific Information, 3501 Market St., Philadelphia, Pennsylvania 19104. (800) 523-1857. 1985-. Annual. Gives contents of science books published.

Multimedia Index to Ecology. National Information Center for Educational Media, University of Southern California, Los Angeles, California 90007.

Pollution Abstracts. Cambridge Scientific Abstracts, 5161 River Rd., Bethesda, Maryland 20816. (301) 961-6750. Six/year. Indexes worldwide technical literature on environmental pollution. Covers air pollution, marine and freshwater pollution, sewage and wastewater treatment, waste management, toxicology and health, noise pollution, radiation, land pollution, and environmental policies, programs, legislation, and education. Also available online.

Priority Issue Reporting Service–PIRS. Information for Public Affairs, Inc., Client Services Dept., 1900 14th St., Sacramento, California 95814.

Selected References on Environmental Quality as It Relates to Health. National Library of Medicine, 8600

Rockville Pike, Bethesda, Maryland 20894. (800) 638-8480. 1977.

ALMANACS AND YEARBOOKS

Gale Environmental Almanac. Russ Hoyle. Gale Research Inc., 835 Penobscot Bldg., Detroit, Michigan 48226-4094. (313) 961-2242. 1993. Focuses on the U.S. and Canada, although worldwide and transboundary issues are discussed.

BIBLIOGRAPHIES

Current Contents. Agriculture, Biology and Environmental Sciences. Institute for Scientific Information, 3501 Market St., Philadelphia, Pennsylvania 19104. (800) 523-1857. 1973-. Previous title: Current Contents. Agricultural, Food & Veterinary Sciences. Gives the table of contents of periodicals in the fields of agriculture, biology, environmental and related areas.

DIRECTORIES

Canadian Environmental Directory. Canadian Almanac & Directory Publishing Co. Ltd., 134 Adelaide St. E., Ste. 27, Toronto, Ontario, Canada M5C 1K9. (416) 362-4088. 1992. Includes individuals, agencies, firms, and associations.

ENCYCLOPEDIAS AND DICTIONARIES

Dictionary of Environmental Engineering and Related Sciences: English-Spanish, Spanish-English. Jose T. Villate. Ediciones Universal, 3090 SW 8th St., Miami, Florida 33135. (305) 642-3355. 1979.

Dictionary of Environmental Science and Technology. Andrew Porteous. John Wiley & Sons, Inc., 605 3rd Ave., New York, New York 10158-0012. (212) 850-6000. 1992.

Encyclopedia of Environmental Science and Engineering. J.R. Pfafflin. Gordon and Breach Science Publishers, Inc., 270 8th Ave., New York, New York 10011. (212) 206-8900. 1992.

Encyclopedia of Environmental Studies. William Ashworth. Facts on File, Inc., 460 Park Ave. S., New York, New York 10016. (212) 683-2244. 1991.

The Encyclopedia of Geochemistry and Environmental Sciences. Rhodes Whitmore Fairbridge. Van Nostrand Reinhold Co., 115 5th Ave., New York, New York 10003. (212) 254-3232. 1972.

Encyclopedia of Physical Science and Technology. Robert A. Meyers, ed. Academic Press, c/o Harcourt Brace Jovanovich Inc., 6277 Sea Harbor Dr., Orlando, Florida 32887. (800) 346-8648. Dictionary of engineering, technology and physical sciences.

Encyclopedia of Physics. Rita G. Lerner and George L. Trigg. VCH Publishers, 303 NW 12th Ave., Deerfield Beach, Florida 33442-1788. (305) 428-5566. 1991. Second edition.

English-Russian Dictionary of Environmental Protection: About 14,000 Terms. E.L. Milovanov. Pergamon Microforms International, Inc., Fairview Park, Elmsford, New York 10523. (914) 592-7720. 1981.

Environmental Encyclopedia. William P. Cunningham, Terence Ball, et. al. Gale Research Inc., 835 Penobscot

Bldg., Detroit, Michigan 48226-4094. (313) 961-2242. 1993.

The Facts on File Dictionary of Environmental Science. L. Harold Stevenson and Bruce Wyman. Facts on File, Inc., 460 Park Ave. S., New York, New York 10016. (212) 683-2244. 1991.

Grzimek's Encyclopedia of Ecology. Bernhard Grzimek. Van Nostrand Reinhold, 115 5th Ave., New York, New York 10003. (212) 254-3232. 1976.

McGraw-Hill Encyclopedia of Environmental Science. Sybil P. Parker. McGraw-Hill Science & Engineering Books, 11 W. 19th St., New York, New York 10011. (212) 337-6010. 1980. Covers ecology, man's influence on nature, and environmental protection.

North American Reference Encyclopedia of Ecology and Pollution. William White. North American Pub. Co., 401 N. Broad St., Philadelphia, Pennsylvania 19108. (215) 238-5300. 1972.

Ullmanns Encyclopedia of Industrial Chemistry. Hans Jurgen Arpe and Wolfgang Gerhartz, eds. VCH Publishers, 303 NW 12th Ave., Deerfield Beach, Florida 33442-1788. (305) 428-5566. 1990. Designed to keep up with the broad spectrum of chemical technology. Thirty-six volumes of the encyclopedia have been divided into two sets: the 28 A volumes contain alphabetically arranged articles on chemicals, product groups, processes and technological concepts; and the 8 B volumes are compendia of basic knowledge in industrial chemistry.

GENERAL WORKS

Atlas of the Environment. Geoffrey Lean, et al. Prentice Hall, Rte. 9W, Englewood Cliffs, New York 07632. (201) 592-2000. 1990. Guide to the major environmental issues around the world that makes good use of numerous maps and diagrams to present the increasing amount of information available in this field. Covers related subjects such as indigenous people and refugees, the education gap, natural and human induced disasters, wildlife trade, and migration routes.

Biomarkers of Environmental Contamination. John F. McCarthy and Lee R. Shugart. Lewis Publishers, 2000 Corporate Blvd., Boca Raton, Florida 33431. (800) 272-7737. 1990. Reviews the use of biological markers in animals and plants as an innovative approach to evaluating the ecological and physiological effects of environmental contamination.

Compilation of EPA's Sampling and Analysis Methods. William Mueller, et al. Lewis Publishers, 2000 Corporate Blvd., N.W., Boca Raton, Florida 33431. (407) 994-0555 or (800) 272-7737. 1991. Aids with rapid searching of sampling and analytical method summaries. More than 650 method/analytical summaries from the database are included in this volume.

Emergency Planning and Community Right to Know. Sarith Guerra. Management Information Service, 777 N. Capitol St., NE, Ste. 500, Washington, District of Columbia 20002-420. (800) 745-8780. 1991. Covers the reporting of health risks from hazardous substances.

Energy-Environment-Quality of Life. Inderscience Enterprises Ltd., World Trade Center Bldg., 110 Avenue Louis Casai, Case Postale 306, Geneva-Airport, Switzerland CH1215. (44) 908-314248. 1991. A special publication of the International Journal of Global Energy. Contains the proceedings of the 13th annual International Scientific Forum on Energy (ISFE) held at the UNESCO building, Paris, France, December 4-7, 1989. Focuses on important energy issues facing the planet, their likely impact on the environment and their effects on the quality of life.

Environment and Quality of Life. OECD Publications and Information Center, 2001 L St., N.W., Suite 700, Washington, District of Columbia 20036. (202) 785-OECD. International comparisons of environmental data and environmental indicators, as well as more specific studies on water policy, energy policy, noise reduction and transportation in 24 member countries.

Environment, Resources, and Conservation. Susan Owens and Peter L. Owens. Cambridge University Press, 40 W 20th St., New York, New York 10011. (212) 924-3900 or (800) 227-0247. 1991. The book studies three cases illuminating problems and policy responses at three levels of geographic scale–international, national, and local. The case of acid rain is used to illustrate a pollution problem with international dimensions; the British coal industry is analyzed as an example of national nonrenewable resource depletion; and renewable wetland ecosystem management illustrates a local concern by analyzing conservation measures.

Environmental Modelling for Developing Countries. Asit K. Biswas, et al., eds. Cassell PLC, Publishers Distribution Center, PO Box C831, Rutherford, New Jersey 07070. (201) 939-6064/5. 1990. Explores how mathematical models can be effectively used in developing countries to improve environmental planning and management processes, with emphasis on modelling applications rather than knowledge accumulation.

Environmental Pollution. Inderscience Enterprises Ltd., World Trade Center Bldg., 110 Avenue Louis Casai, Case Postale 306, Geneva-Airport, Switzerland CH-1215. (44) 908-314248. 1991. Special issue of the International Journal of Environment and Pollution. Proceedings of the 1st International Conference on Environmental Pollution held at the Congress Centre, Lisbon, April 15-19, 1991.

Environmental Risk: Evaluation and Finance in Real Estate. Albert R. Wilson. Lewis Publishers, 2000 Corporate Blvd., N.W., Boca Raton, Florida 33431. (407) 994-0555 or (800) 272-7737. 1991. Deals with the ownership of hazardous materials effected property, types of environmental audits, property evaluation, and legal implications.

Environmental Sampling and Analysis. Lawrence H. Keith. Lewis Publishers, 2000 Corporate Blvd., N.W., Boca Raton, Florida 33431. (407) 994-0555 or (800) 272-7737. 1991. Provides a basis for understanding the principles that affect the choices made in environmental sampling and analysis.

The Environmental Sourcebook. Edith Carol Stein. Lyons & Burford, 31 W. 21st St., New York, New York 10010. (212) 620-9580. 1992. Provides information on 11 specific environmental issues, including population; agriculture; energy; climate and atmosphere; biodiversity; water; oceans; solid waste; hazardous substances and waste; endangered lands; and development.

Environmental Viewpoints. Marie Lazzari. Gale Research Inc., 835 Penobscot Bldg., Detroit, Michigan 48226-4094. (313) 961-2242. 1992.

Feasibility of Environmental Monitoring and Exposure Assessment for a Municipal Waste Combustor. C. Sonich-Mullin. U.S. Environmental Protection Agency, 401 M St., SW, Washington, District of Columbia 20460. (202) 260-2090. 1991.

Global Energy Futures and the Carbon Dioxide Problem. Council on Environmental Quality, Old Executive Office Bldg., Rm. 154, Washington, District of Columbia 20500. (202) 395-5080. 1981. Fossil fuels and energy policy.

Hazardous Waste Measurements. Milagros S. Simmons, ed. Lewis Publishers, 200 Corporate Blvd. NW, Boca Raton, Florida 33431. (407) 994-0555 or (800)272-7737. 1991. Focuses on recent developments in field testing methods and quality assurance.

Institute of Environmental Sciences' National Conference and Workshop, Environmental Stress Screening of Electronic Hardware Proceedings. The Institute of Environmental Sciences, 940 E. Northwest Highway, Mt. Prospect, Illinois 60056. (708) 255-1561. Environmental testing and environmental stress screening of electronic hardware.

An Introduction to Environmental Pattern Analysis. P. J. A. Howard. Parthenon Group Inc., 120 Mill Rd., Park Ridge, New Jersey 07656. (201) 391-6796. 1991. Explains the basic mathematics of the most widely used ordination and cluster analysis methods, types of data to which they are suited and their advantages and disadvantages.

Lessons Learned in Global Environmental Governance. Peter H. Sand. World Resources Institute, 1709 New York Ave. N.W., Washington, District of Columbia 20006. (800) 822-0504. 1990. Takes stock of significant international environmental initiatives to date and highlights innovative features of transnational regimes for setting and implementing standards.

Principles of Environmental Sampling. Lawrence H. Keith, ed. American Chemical Society, 1155 16th St. N.W., Washington, District of Columbia 20036. (202) 872-4600; (800) 227-5558. 1988. Overview of the sampling process and its various applications.

Promoting Environmentally Sound Economic Progress: What the North Can Do. Robert Repetto. World Resources Institute, 1709 New York Ave. N.W., Washington, District of Columbia 20006. (800) 822-0504. 1990. Spells out actions that must be taken if the world economy is going to continue to develop and yet avoid the environmental degradation that threatens to undermine living standards.

Rules and Regulations, Department of Environmental Quality, Land Quality Division, State of Wyoming. Dept. of Environmental Quality, 122 W. 25th St., Hersler Bldg., 3rd Fl., Cheyenne, Wyoming 82002. (307) 777-7756. 1989.

Wastewater Engineering: Treatment, Disposal, and Reuse. Metcalf & Eddy, Inc. McGraw-Hill Science & Engineering Books, 11 West 19th St., New York, New York 10011. (212) 337-6010. 1991. Reflects the impact of changing federal legislation on environmental quality control and sludge management. Gives a solid overall perspective on wastewater engineering.

World Guide to Environmental Issues and Organizations. Peter Brackley. Longman Group Ltd., Longman House,

Burnt Mill, Harlow, Essex, England CM20 2J6. (0279) 426721. 1991.

GOVERNMENTAL ORGANIZATIONS

Department of Environmental Quality: Air Quality. Administrator, Air Quality Division, Herschler Building, Cheyenne, Wyoming (307) 777-7391.

Department of Environmental Quality: Environmental Protection. Director, Herschler Building, 4W, Cheyenne, Wyoming 82002. (307) 777-7938.

Department of Environmental Quality: Solid Waste Management. Supervisor, Solid Waste Program, Herschler Building, Cheyenne, Wyoming 82002. (307) 777-7090.

Department of Environmental Quality: Underground Storage Tanks. Engineering Supervisor, Water Quality Division, Herschler Building, Cheyenne, Wyoming 82002. (307) 777-7090.

Department of Environmental Quality: Waste Minimization and Pollution Prevention. Program Manager, Solid Waste Management Program, Herschler Building, 4th Floor, West Wing, 122 West 25th St., Cheyenne, Wyoming 82002. (307) 777-7752.

Department of Environmental Quality: Water Quality. Administrator, Water Quality Division, Herschler Building, Cheyenne, Wyoming 82002. (307) 777-7781.

Emergency Management Agency: Emergency Preparedness and Community Right-to-Know. Emergency Response Commission, PO Box 4501, Fondren Station, Jackson, Mississippi 39296-4501. (601) 960-9973.

Emergency Management Agency: Emergency Preparedness and Community Right-to-Know. Emergency Response Commission, Comprehensive Emergency Management, 5500 Bishop Blvd., Cheyenne, Wyoming 82009. (307) 777-7566.

Emergency Preparedness and Community Right-to-Know. Director, 290 Bigelow Bldg., 450 North Syndicate, St Paul, Minnesota 55104. (612) 643-3000.

Emergency Response Commission: Emergency Preparedness and Community Right-to-Know. Chair, PO Box O, Juneau, Alaska 99811. (907) 465-2600.

Emergency Response Commission: Emergency Preparedness and Community Right-to-Know. Division of Emergency Services, Building 341, 5036 East McDowell Rd., Phoenix, Arizona 85008. (602) 231-6326.

Emergency Response Commission: Emergency Preparedness and Community Right-to-Know. SARA Title III Coordinator, State Office Building, Room 161, 165 Capitol Ave., Hartford, Connecticut 06106. (203) 566-4856.

Emergency Response Commission: Emergency Preparedness and Community Right-to-Know. Chair, 205 Butler St., S.E., Floyd Towers East, 11th Floor, Suite 1166, Atlanta, Georgia 30334. (404) 656-6905.

Emergency Response Commission: Emergency Preparedness and Community Right-to-Know. Chair, State House, Boise, Idaho 83720. (208) 334-5888.

Emergency Response Commission: Emergency Preparedness and Community Right-to-Know. Director, 5500

West Bradbury Ave., Indianapolis, Indiana 46241. (317) 243-5176.

Emergency Response Commission: Emergency Preparedness and Community Right-to-Know. Chairman, Statehouse Station #11, 157 Capitol Street, Augusta, Maine 04333. (207) 289-4080.

Emergency Response Commission: Emergency Preparedness and Community Right-to-Know. Department of Environmental Protection, Division of Environmental Quality, Bureau of Hazardous Substances Information, Trenton, New Jersey 08625. (609) 292-6714.

Emergency Response Commission: Emergency Preparedness and Community Right-to-Know. Director, c/o State Fire Marshal, 3000 Market Street Plaza, Suite 534, Salem, Oregon 97310. (503) 378-2885.

Emergency Response Commission: Emergency Preparedness and Community Right-to-Know. Chair, 3041 Sidco, Nashville, Tennessee 37204. (615) 252-3300.

Emergency Response Commission: Emergency Preparedness and Community Right-to-Know. Director, Office of Emergency Services, State Capitol Bldg. 1, Room EB-80, Charlestown, West Virginia 25305. (304) 348-5380.

National Environmental Satellite, Data, and Information Service. 1825 Connecticut Ave., N.W., Washington, District of Columbia 20235. (301) 763-7190.

Occupational Safety and Health Administration: Directorate of Safety Standards Programs. 200 Constitution Ave., N.W., Washington, District of Columbia 20210. (202) 523-8063.

Office of Public Affairs. 1717 H St., N.W., Washington, District of Columbia 20555. (301) 492-7715.

U.S. Environmental Protection Agency: Office of Modeling and Monitoring Systems and Quality Assurance. 401 M St., S.W., Washington, District of Columbia 20460. (202) 382-5767.

HANDBOOKS AND MANUALS

Environmental Statistics Handbook: Europe. Allan Foster, Oksana Newman. Gale Research Inc., 835 Penobscot Bldg., Detroit, Michigan 48226-4094. (313) 961-2242. 1993.

Pira's International Environmental Information Sources. Pira, Randalls Rd., Leatherhead, England KT22 7RU. 0372 376161. 1990. Sourcebook includes over 2,000 entries from more than 20 countries, including Australia, Finland, Germany, the United Kingdom, and the United States. Entries are from organizations, research centers, legislative and regulatory bodies, directories, online databases and periodicals. Subject areas covered are: air, noise, water and land pollution, waste control and disposal, recycling, energy recovery and nature conservation.

ONLINE DATA BASES

BIOSIS Previews. BIOSIS, 2100 Arch St., Philadelphia, Pennsylvania 19103-1399. (215) 587-4800. Largest and most comprehensive database of research in the life sciences. Contains citations for nearly 9000 primary research journals, monographs, reviews, symposia, preliminary reports, semi-popular journals, selected institutional reports, government reports and research communications.

Computer-Aided Environmental Legislative Data Systems–CELDS. U.S. Army Corps of Engineers, Planning Information Programs (PIP), Dept. of Urban and Regional Planning, University of Illinois, 1003 West Nevada, Urbana, Illinois 61801. (217) 333-1369. Federal and state environmental regulations and standards.

Current Research Information System–CRIS/USDA. U.S. Department of Agriculture, National Agricultural Library, 10301 Baltimore Blvd., 5th Floor, Beltsville, Maryland 20705-2351. (301) 504-5755. Looks at current research projects in agriculture and allied sciences covering the biological, physical, social and behavioral sciences related to agriculture.

EPA's Sampling and Analysis Methods Database. William Mueller, et al. Lewis Publishers, 2000 Corporate Blvd., N.W., Boca Raton, Florida 33431. (407) 994-0555 or (800) 272-7737. 1990. Three volumes, five diskettes. Compiled by EPA chemists. Permits rapid searches of sampling and analytical method summaries: v.1. Industrial chemicals; v.2. Pesticides, Herbicides, Dioxins, and PCBs; v.3. Elements and Water Quality Parameters.

Monthly Catalog of United States Government Publications. U.S. G.P.O., Supt. of Docs., PO Box 371954, Pittsburgh, Pennsylvania 15250-7954. (202) 512-0000.

National Technical Information Service. U.S. Department of Commerce, National Technical Information Service, Office of Data Base Services, 5285 Port Royal Rd., Springfield, Virginia 22161. (703) 487-4807. Bibliographic database of government sponsored research and technical reports.

SCISEARCH. Institute for Scientific Information, University City Science Center, 3501 Market St., Philadelphia, Pennsylvania 19104. (215) 386-0100.

PERIODICALS AND NEWSLETTERS

Beyond Waste. Oregon Department of Environmental Quality, 811 S.W. 6th Ave., Portland, Oregon 97204. (503) 229-6044. Monthly.

Catalyst for Environmental Quality. Catalyst for Environmental/Energy, New York, New York

Ecomod. ISEM–North America Chapter, Water Quality Division, South Florida Water Management District, P.O. Box 24608, West Palm Beach, Florida 33416. (407) 686-8800. Monthly. Current events in ecological and environmental modeling.

EDF Letter. Environmental Defense Fund, 257 Park Ave. S., 16th Fl., New York, New York 10010-7304. (212) 505-2100. Bimonthly. Reports environmental quality & public health.

Emergency Preparedness News. Business Publishers, Inc., 951 Pershing Drive, Silver Spring, Maryland 20910. (301) 587-6300. Biweekly. Emergency management techniques and technologies.

Environment. Heldref Publications, 4000 Albemarle Street, NW, Washington, District of Columbia 20016. (202) 362-6445. Ten a year. Covers science and science policy.

Environment Research. Academic Press, c/o Harcourt Brace Jovanovich Inc., 6277 Sea Harbor Dr., Orlando, Florida 32887. (800) 346-8648. Bimonthly. Journal of environmental medicine and sciences.

Environmental Defense Fund Letter. Environmental Defense Fund, 257 Park Avenue South, New York, New York 10010. (212) 505-2100. 1971-. Bimonthly. Environmental issues of concern.

Environmental Geology & Water Sciences. Springer-Verlag, 175 Fifth Avenue, New York, New York 10010. (212) 460-1500. Bimonthly. Covers interactions between humanity and Earth.

Environmental Notice Bulletin. New York State Dept. of Environmental Conservation, 50 Wolf Rd., Albany, New York 12233. (518) 457-6668. Weekly. Information on state environmental quality review actions.

Environmental Review. American Society for Environmental History, Department of History, University of Oregon, Corvallis, Oregon 97331. Quarterly. Covers human ecology as seen through history and the humanities.

Environmental Science and Technology. American Chemical Society, 1155 16th St. N.W., Washington, District of Columbia 20036. (800) 227-5558. 1967-. Monthly. Contains research articles on various aspects of environmental chemistry, interpretative articles by invited experts and commentary on the scientific aspects of environmental management.

Environmental Spectrum. New Jersey Cooperative Extension Service, Cook College, Rutgers University, P.O. Box 231, New Brunswick, New Jersey 08903. 1968-. Bimonthly. Emphasis on air/noise pollution, energy, water and other environmental topics.

Environmental Toxicology and Chemistry. Society of Environmental Toxicology and Chemistry. Pergamon Microforms International, Inc., Fairview Park, Elmsford, New York 10523. (914) 592-7720. 1981-. Monthly. Contains information on environmental toxicology, and chemistry, including the application of science to hazard assessment.

Journal of Environmental Quality. American Society of Agronomy, 677 S. Segoe Rd., Madison, Wisconsin 53711-1086. (608) 273-8080. 1972-. Quarterly. Reports and brief reviews of agricultural ecology, environmental engineering and pollution.

Journal of Environmental Sciences. Institute of Environmental Sciences, 940 East Northwest Highway, Mt. Prospect, Illinois 60656. (312) 255-1561. Bimonthly. Covers research, controlling and teaching of environmental sciences.

NAEP Newsletter. National Association of Environmental Professionals, P.O. Box 15210, Alexandria, Virginia 22309-0210. (703) 660-2364. Monthly. Covers environmental planning, management, review and research.

RESEARCH CENTERS AND INSTITUTES

Baylor University, Institute of Environmental Studies. B.U. Box 7266, Waco, Texas 76798-7266. (817) 755-3406.

Boston University, Center for Energy and Environmental Studies. 675 Commonwealth Avenue, Boston, Massachusetts 02215. (617) 353-3083.

Oregon State University, Environmental Remote Sensing Applications Laboratory. Peavy Hall 108, College of Forestry, Corvallis, Oregon 97331. (503) 737-3056.

Pennsylvania State University, Environmental Resources Research Institute. 100 Land and Water Resource Building, University Park, Pennsylvania 16802. (814) 863-0291.

Queens College of City University of New York, Center for the Biology of Natural Systems. Flushing, New York 11367. (718) 670-4180.

Resources for the Future, Inc., Quality of the Environment Division. 1616 P Street, N.W., Washington, District of Columbia 20036. (202) 328-5000.

State University of New York at Stony Brook, Ecology Laboratory. Stony Brook, New York 11797-5245. (516) 623-8600.

Tufts University. Curtis Hall, 474 Boston Avenue, Medford, Massachusetts 02155. (617) 381-3486.

University of Hawaii at Manoa, Environmental Center. 2550 Campus Road, Honolulu, Hawaii 96822. (808) 956-7361.

University of Illinois, Institute for Environmental Studies. 408 South Goodwin Avenue, Urbana, Illinois 61801. (217) 333-4178.

University of Maryland, Center for Environmental and Estuarine Studies. Center Operations, Horn Point, P.O.Box 775, Cambridge, Maryland 21613. (410) 228-9250.

University of Massachusetts, Environmental Institute. Blaisdell House, Amherst, Massachusetts 01003-0040. (413) 545-2842.

University of Minnesota, All University Council on Environmental Quality. 330 Humphrey Center, 301 19th Avenue South, Minneapolis, Minnesota 55455. (612) 625-1551.

University of Minnesota, Duluth, Center for Water and The Environment. Natural Resources Research Institute, 5103 Miller Trunk Highway, Duluth, Minnesota 55811. (218) 720-4270.

University of Missouri, Environmental Trace Substances Research Center. 5450 South Sinclair Road, Columbia, Missouri 65203. (314) 882-2151.

University of Missouri-Rolla, Environmental Research Center. Rolla, Missouri 65401. (314) 341-4485.

University of Oklahoma, Environmental & Ground Water Institute. 200 Felgar Street, Room 127, Norman, Oklahoma 73019-0470. (405) 325-5202.

University of Oregon, Environmental Studies Center. Room 104, Condon Hall, Eugene, Oregon 97403. (503) 686-5006.

University of Washington, Institute for Environmental Studies. Engineering Annex FM-12, Seattle, Washington 98195. (206) 543-1812.

University of Wisconsin-Madison, Institute for Environmental Studies. 1017 WARF Office Building, 610 Walnut Street, Madison, Wisconsin 53705. (608) 262-5957.

STATISTICS SOURCES

Environmental Quality Index. National Wildlife Federation, 1400 16th St. NW, Washington, District of Columbia 20036-2266. (202) 797-6800. Annual.

Statistical Record of the Environment. Arsen J. Darnay. Gale Research Inc., 835 Penobscot Bldg., Detroit, Michigan 48226-4094. (313) 961-2242. 1992.

TRADE ASSOCIATIONS AND PROFESSIONAL SOCIETIES

Alliance for Environmental Education, Inc. 10751 Ambassador Dr., No. 201, Manassas, Virginia 22110. (703) 335-1025. A coalition of organizations that works at the regional, state, and national level to promote environmental education.

America The Beautiful Fund. 219 Shoreham Bldg., N.W., Washington, District of Columbia 20005. (202) 638-1649.

American Council on the Environment. 1301 20th St., N.W., Suite 113, Washington, District of Columbia 20036. (202) 659-1900.

American Society of Civil Engineers. 345 East 47th St., New York, New York 10017. (212) 705-7496.

Association of New Jersey Environmental Commissions. PO Box 157, 300 Mendham Rd., Mendham, New Jersey 07945. (201) 539-7547.

Center for Environmental Information, Inc. 99 Court St., Rochester, New York 14604. (716) 546-3796.

Environmental Defense Fund. 257 Park Ave., S., New York, New York 10010. (212) 505-2100. Non-profit organization that was established more than 20 years ago. Its goals are to protect the earth's environment by providing lasting solutions to global environmental problems.

Environmental Quality Industrial Resources Center. The Ohio State University, 1200 Chambers Rd., Room 310, Columbus, Ohio 43212. (614) 292-6717.

Environmental Task Force. 6930 Carroll Ave., 6th Floor, Takoma Park, Maryland 20912. (202) 745-4870.

International Association of Environmental Testing Laboratories. 1911 Ft. Myer Dr., Arlington, Virginia 22209. (703) 524-2427.

National Association of Counties, Committee on Environment, Energy and Land Use. Solid and Hazardous Waste Subcommittee, 440 First St., N.W., Washington, District of Columbia 20001. (202) 393-6226.

ENZYMES

See also: FOOD SCIENCE

ABSTRACTING AND INDEXING SERVICES

ASFA Aquaculture Abstracts. Cambridge Scientific Abstracts, Inc., 5161 River Rd., Bethesda, Maryland 20816. (301) 961-6750. 1984.

Biological and Agricultural Index. H.W. Wilson Co., 950 University Ave., Bronx, New York 10452. (800) 367-6770. 1916-. Monthly.

Biotechnology Research Abstracts. Cambridge Scientific Abstracts, 5161 River Rd., Bethesda, Maryland 20816. (301) 961-6750. Monthly. Includes such broad areas as genetic intervention, biochemical genetics, and microbiological techniques.

Crop Physiology Abstracts. C. A. B. International, 845 North Park Ave., Tucson, Arizona 85719. (602) 621-7897 or (800) 528-4841. 1975-. Monthly. Abstracts focus on the physiology of all higher plants of economic importance. Aspects include germination, reproductive development, nitrogen fixation, metabolic inhibitors, salinity, radiobiology, enzymes, membranes and other related areas.

Current Advances in Plant Science. Pergamon Microforms International, Inc., Fairview Park, Elmsford, New York 10523. (914) 592-7720. 1984-. Monthly. Current literature searching service including journals, reports, abstracts, etc. This service is available online as part of the CABS database on the hosts BRS and ORBIT search service.

Ecology Abstracts. Cambridge Scientific Abstracts, 5161 River Rd., Bethesda, Maryland 20816. (301) 961-6750. Monthly.

Environment Abstracts. Bowker A & I Publishing, 121 Chanlon Rd., New Providence, New Jersey 07974. (908) 464-6800. 1974-.

Environment Index. Environment Information Center, Index Research Department, 124 E. 39th St., New York, New York 10016. 1971-. Annual.

Environmental Information Connection–EIC. Planning Information Program, Dept. of Urban and Regional Planning, University of Illinois, 1003 West Nevada, Urbana, Illinois 61801. (217) 333-1369. Also available online.

Environmental Periodicals Bibliography. Environmental Studies Institute, International Academy at Santa Barbara, 800 Garden St., Suite D, Santa Barbara, California 93101. (805) 965-5010. Also available online.

Food Science and Technology Abstracts. International Food Information Service, c/o National Food Laboratory, 6363 Clark Ave., Dublin, California 94568. (800) 336-3782. 1969-.

Genetics Abstracts. Cambridge Scientific Abstracts, 5161 River Rd., Bethesda, Maryland 20816. (301) 961-6750. 1968-. Monthly. Formerly published by Information Retrieval Ltd., London England. Published by Cambridge Scientific Abstracts since 1982.

Index to Scientific Book Contents. Institute for Scientific Information, 3501 Market St., Philadelphia, Pennsylvania 19104. (800) 523-1857. 1985-. Annual. Gives contents of science books published.

Microbiology Abstracts. Section A. Industrial and Applied Microbiology. Cambridge Scientific Abstracts, 5161 River Rd., Bethesda, Maryland 20816. (301) 961-6750. 1972-.

Pollution Abstracts. Cambridge Scientific Abstracts, 5161 River Rd., Bethesda, Maryland 20816. (301) 961-6750. Six/year. Indexes worldwide technical literature on environmental pollution. Covers air pollution, marine and freshwater pollution, sewage and wastewater treatment, waste management, toxicology and health, noise pollution, radiation, land pollution, and environmental policies, programs, legislation, and education. Also available online.

Science Citation Index. Institute for Scientific Information, 3501 Market St., Philadelphia, Pennsylvania 19104. 1961-.

BIBLIOGRAPHIES

Current Contents. Agriculture, Biology and Environmental Sciences. Institute for Scientific Information, 3501 Market St., Philadelphia, Pennsylvania 19104. (800) 523-1857. 1973-. Previous title: Current Contents. Agricultural, Food & Veterinary Sciences. Gives the table of contents of periodicals in the fields of agriculture, biology, environmental and related areas.

EPA Publications Bibliography. U.S. Environmental Protection Agency, Library Systems Branch, 401 M St., SW, Washington, District of Columbia 20460. (202) 260-2090. Quarterly.

DIRECTORIES

McCutcheon's Functional Materials. Manufacturing Confectioner Publishing Co., 175 Rock Rd., Glen Rock, New Jersey 07451. (201) 652-2655. 1985. Annual.

ENCYCLOPEDIAS AND DICTIONARIES

Cambridge Dictionary of Biology. Peter M. B. Walker. Cambridge University Press, 40 W. 20th St., New York, New York 10011. (212) 924-3900 or (800) 227-0247. 1989. Includes 10,000 terms in zoology, botany, biochemistry, molecular biology and genetics. Previously published under the title Chambers Biology Dictionary.

A Concise Dictionary of Biology. Elizabeth Martin, ed. Oxford University Press, 200 Madison Ave., New York, New York 10016. (212) 679-7300 or (800) 334-4249. 1990. New edition. Derived from the Concise Science Dictionary, published in 1984.

Dictionary of Biotechnology. J. Coombs. Elsevier Science Publishing Co., 655 Avenue of the Americas, New York, New York 10010. (212) 984-5800. 1986. Areas covered in this dictionary include: fermentation; brewing; vaccines; plant tissue; culture; antibiotic production; production and use of enzymes; biomass; byproduct recovery and effluent treatment; equipment; processes; micro-organisms and biochemicals.

A Dictionary of Genetics. Robert C. King and William A. Stansfield. Oxford University Press, 200 Madison Ave., New York, New York 10016. (212) 679-7300 or (800) 334-4249. 1991. Fourth edition. Includes 7,100 definitions with 250 illustrations. Also includes bibliography of major sources.

Dictionary of Genetics and Cell Biology. Norman Maclean. New York University Press, 70 Washington Sq. S., New York, New York 10012. (212) 998-2575. 1987. Includes the subject areas of cytology and genetics.

Encyclopedia of Chemical Processing and Design. John J. Mcketta and W. A. Cunningham. Marcel Dekker, Inc., 270 Madison Ave., New York, New York 10016. (212) 696-9000; (800) 228-1160. 1992. Thirty-eight volumes.

Encyclopedia of Human Biology. Renato Dulbecco, ed. Academic Press, c/o Harcourt Brace Jovanovich Inc., 6277 Sea Harbor Dr., Orlando, Florida 32887. (800) 346-8648. 1991. Eight volumes.

Encyclopedia of Industrial Chemical Additives. Michael and Irene Ash. Chemical Publishing Co., 80 Eighth Ave., New York, New York 10011. (212) 255-1950. 1984-87. Four volumes. Comprehensive compilation of tradename products that function as additives in enhancing the properties of various major industrial products.

Encyclopedic Dictionary of Genetics: With German Term Equivalents and Extensive German/English Index. R. C. King and W. D. Stansfield. VCH Publishers, 303 NW 12th Ave., Deerfield Beach, Florida 33442-1788. (305) 428-5566. 1990. 4th ed. Revised edition of: A Dictionary of Genetics, third edition.

Enzyme Nomenclature 1984. Edwin C. Webb. Academic Press, c/o Harcourt Brace Jovanovich Inc., 6277 Sea Harbor Dr., Orlando, Florida 32887. (800) 346-8648. 1992. Fifth edition. "This edition is a revision of the Recommendations (1978) of the Nomenclature Committee of IUB, and has been approved for publication by the Executive Committee of the International Union of Biochemistry." Includes 2728 enzymes. It considers classification and nomenclature, their units of activity and standard methods of assay, together with symbols used in the description of enzyme kinetics.

Kirk-Othmer Encyclopedia of Chemical Technology. J. I. Kroschwitz, ed. John Wiley & Sons, Inc., 605 3rd Ave., New York, New York 10158-0012. (212) 850-6000. 1992-. All articles in the new edition have been rewritten and updated adding new subjects such as biotechnology, computer topics, analytical techniques and instrumentation, environmental concerns, fuels and energy, inorganic and solid state chemistry; composite materials and material science in general, and pharmaceuticals. Also available online.

Life Sciences on File. Diagram Group. Facts on File, Inc., 460 Park Ave. S., New York, New York 10016. (212) 683-2244. 1986. Encyclopedia of pictorial collection in life sciences. Deals with all major topics in life sciences including ecology.

Ullmanns Encyclopedia of Industrial Chemistry. Hans Jurgen Arpe and Wolfgang Gerhartz, eds. VCH Publishers, 303 NW 12th Ave., Deerfield Beach, Florida 33442-1788. (305) 428-5566. 1990. Designed to keep up with the broad spectrum of chemical technology. Thirty-six volumes of the encyclopedia have been divided into two sets: the 28 A volumes contain alphabetically arranged articles on chemicals, product groups, processes and technological concepts; and the 8 B volumes are compendia of basic knowledge in industrial chemistry.

Van Nostrand's Scientific Encyclopedia. Glenn D. Considine, ed. Van Nostrand Reinhold, 115 5th Ave., New York, New York 10003. (212) 254-3232. 1983. Sixth edition. Includes all broad subject areas in science.

GENERAL WORKS

Biocatalysis; Fundamentals of Enzyme Deactivation Kinetics. Ajit Sadana. Prentice Hall, Rte. 9 W., Englewood Cliffs, New Jersey 07632. (201) 592-2000; (800) 634-2863. 1991. Focuses on the chemical kinetics of enzymes in bioreactions as used in the biotechnology and chemical industries.

Biocatalysts for Industry. Jonathan S. Dordick, ed. Plenum Press, 233 Spring St., New York, New York 10013-1578. (212) 620-8000; (800) 221-9369. 1991. Contributed papers address the applications of enzymes or whole cells to carry out selective transformations of commercial importance, as biocatalysts in the food, pharmaceutical, and chemical industries. Includes general uses of biocatalysts, biocatalysts without chemical competition, emerging biocatalysts for conventional chemical processing, and future directions of biocatalysts.

Magill's Survey of Science. Life Science Series. Frank N. Magill, ed. Salem Press, PO Box 50062, Pasadena, California 91105. 1991. Six volumes. Contents: v.1. A-Central and peripheral nervous system functions; v.2. Central metabolism regulation - eukaryotic transcriptional control; v.3. Positive and negative eukaryotic transcriptional control - mammalian hormones; v.4. Hormones and behavior - muscular contraction; v.5. Muscular contraction and relaxation - sexual reproduction in plants; v.6. Reproductive behavior and mating - X inactivation and the Lyon hypothesis.

Microbial Enzymes in Aquatic Environments. Ryszard J. Chrost. Springer-Varlag, 175 5th Ave., New York, New York 10010. (212) 460-1500. 1991. Brings together studies on enzymatic degradation processes from disciplines as diverse as water and sediment research, bacterial and algal aquatic ecophysiology, eutrophication, nutrient cycling, and biogeochemistry, in both freshwater and marine ecosystem.

A Study of Enzymes. Stephen Kuby, ed. CRC Press, 2000 Corporate Blvd. N.W., Boca Raton, Florida 33431. (407) 994-0555; (800) 272-7737. 1991. 2 vols. Deals in detail with selected topics in enzyme mechanisms.

HANDBOOKS AND MANUALS

Enzyme Handbook. D. Schomburg and M. Salzmann, eds. Springer-Verlag, 175 5th Ave., New York, New York 10010. (212) 460-1500; (800) 777-4643. 1990. The enzymes are arranged in accord with the 1984 Enzyme Commission list of enzymes and follow-up supplements. Information contained for each enzyme is organized in seven basic sections.

ONLINE DATA BASES

Current Research Information System–CRIS/USDA. U.S. Department of Agriculture, National Agricultural Library, 10301 Baltimore Blvd., 5th Floor, Beltsville, Maryland 20705-2351. (301) 504-5755. Looks at current research projects in agriculture and allied sciences covering the biological, physical, social and behavioral sciences related to agriculture.

Enviro/Energyline Abstracts Plus. R. R. Bowker Co., 121 Chanlon Rd., New Providence, New Jersey 07974. (908) 464-6800.

Environmental Periodicals Bibliography. National Information Services Corp., Ste. 6, Wyman Towers, 3100 St. Paul St., Baltimore, Maryland 21218. (410)243-0797. Online version of abstract of same name.

Kirk-Othmer Encyclopedia of Chemical Technology. John Wiley & Sons, Inc., 605 3rd Ave., 5th Floor, New York, New York 10158. (212) 850-6000. Online version of the publication of the same name.

Monthly Catalog of United States Government Publications. U.S. G.P.O., Supt. of Docs., PO Box 371954, Pittsburgh, Pennsylvania 15250-7954. (202) 512-0000.

National Technical Information Service. U.S. Department of Commerce, National Technical Information Service, Office of Data Base Services, 5285 Port Royal Rd., Springfield, Virginia 22161. (703) 487-4807. Bibliographic database of government sponsored research and technical reports.

SCISEARCH. Institute for Scientific Information, University City Science Center, 3501 Market St., Philadelphia, Pennsylvania 19104. (215) 386-0100.

PERIODICALS AND NEWSLETTERS

Biogenic Amines. Pergamon Microforms International, Inc., Fairview Park, Elmsford, New York 10523. (914) 592-7720. 1984-. Bimonthly. Journal including of all aspects of research on biogenic amines and amino acid transmitters, their relating compounds and their interaction phenomena.

Methods in Enzymology. Sidney P. Colowick and Nathan O. Kaplan, eds. Academic Press, c/o Harcourt Brace Jovanovich Inc., 6277 Sea Harbor Dr., Orlando, Florida 32887. (800) 346-8648. 1955-. Series of volumes in enzymology. Each volume has a distinct title.

RESEARCH CENTERS AND INSTITUTES

Institute of Biological Chemistry. Washington State University, Clark Hall, Pullman, Washington 99164. (509) 335-3412.

Laboratory of Chemical Biodynamics. University of California, Berkeley, Berkeley, California 64720. (415) 486-4311.

University of Minnesota, Industry/University Cooperative Research Center for Biocatalytic Processing. 240 Gortner Laboratory, 1479 Gortner Avenue, St. Paul, Minnesota 55108. (612) 624-6774.

University of Oregon, Institute of Molecular Biology. Eugene, Oregon 97403. (503) 686-5151.

University of Wisconsin-Madison, Institute for Enzyme Research. 1710 University Avenue, Madison, Wisconsin 53705. (608) 262-2140.

TRADE ASSOCIATIONS AND PROFESSIONAL SOCIETIES

American Institute of Chemical Engineers. 345 East 47th St., New York, New York 10017. (212) 705-7338.

American Institute of Chemists. 7315 Wisconsin Ave., Bethesda, Maryland 20814. (301) 652-2447.

EPICENTERS

See: EARTHQUAKES

EPIDEMICS AND EPIDEMIOLOGY

ABSTRACTING AND INDEXING SERVICES

Biotechnology Research Abstracts. Cambridge Scientific Abstracts, 5161 River Rd., Bethesda, Maryland 20816. (301) 961-6750. Monthly. Includes such broad areas as genetic intervention, biochemical genetics, and microbiological techniques.

Helminthological Abstracts. C. A. B. International, 845 North Park Ave., Tucson, Arizona 85719. (602) 621-7897 or (800) 528-4841. 1969. Monthly. Continues Helminthological Abstracts and Series A: Animal and Human Helminthology. Covers the literature on parasitic helminths such as gastrointestinal nematodes, liver flukes, hydatid, trichinella, and other related areas.

Pollution Abstracts. Cambridge Scientific Abstracts, 5161 River Rd., Bethesda, Maryland 20816. (301) 961-6750. Six/year. Indexes worldwide technical literature on environmental pollution. Covers air pollution, marine and freshwater pollution, sewage and wastewater treatment, waste management, toxicology and health, noise pollution, radiation, land pollution, and environmental policies, programs, legislation, and education. Also available online.

ENCYCLOPEDIAS AND DICTIONARIES

McGraw-Hill Encyclopedia of Science and Technology. McGraw-Hill, 1221 Avenue of the Americas, New York, New York 10020. (212) 512-2000 or (800) 262-4729. 1992. Seventh edition. Issued in multiple volumes including index. Includes all science and technology broad subject areas.

GENERAL WORKS

Exposure Assessment for Epidemiology and Hazard Control. Lewis Publishers, 2000 Corporate Blvd., N.W., Boca Raton, Florida 33431. (407) 994-0555 or (800) 272-7737. 1991. Examines the various approaches to answering questions on the topic. Includes measurement of current exposures, the application of toxicological relationships including biological markers and sample models; an epidemiological evaluation of exposure-effect relationships, including new methods for evaluation and models for population exposure estimates, and strategies for exposure assessments.

A Science of Impurity: Water Analysis in Nineteenth Century Britain. Christopher Hamlin. University of California Press, Berkeley, California 94720. (510) 642-4247. 1990. Presents a series of biographies of scientists and government officials responsible for London's water quality during a period of pressing need and sparse scientific knowledge. Also presents some chemical information, placing chemical and epidemiological concepts in perspective, which is needed to grasp the inconsistencies of water analysis in 19th-century Britain.

GOVERNMENTAL ORGANIZATIONS

National Center for Health Statistics: Public Health Service. 6525 Belcrest Rd., Hyattsville, Maryland 20782. (301) 436-7016.

ONLINE DATA BASES

Enviroline. R. R. Bowker Co., Bowker Electronic Publishing, 121 Chanlon Rd., New Providence, New Jersey 07974. (800) 521-8110.

Monthly Catalog of United States Government Publications. U.S. G.P.O., Supt. of Docs., PO Box 371954, Pittsburgh, Pennsylvania 15250-7954. (202) 512-0000.

National Technical Information Service. U.S. Department of Commerce, National Technical Information Service, Office of Data Base Services, 5285 Port Royal Rd., Springfield, Virginia 22161. (703) 487-4807. Bibliographic database of government sponsored research and technical reports.

NIOSHTIC. U.S. Department of Health and Human Services, Centers for Disease Control, National Institute for Occupational Safety and Health, 4676 Columbia Parkway, Cincinnati, Ohio 45226. (513) 533-8317.

PERIODICALS AND NEWSLETTERS

American Journal of Epidemiology. Society for Epidemiologic Research, 20007 E. Monument Street, Baltimore, Maryland 21205. (301) 955-3441. Biweekly. Reporting of epidemiologic studies in the U.S.

Archives of Environmental Health: An International Journal. Heldref Publications, Helen Dwight Reid Educational Foundation, 4000 Albemarle St., NW, Washington, District of Columbia 20016-1851. Bimonthly. Documentation on the effects of environmental agents on human health.

Ecological Applications. Ecological Society of America, Center for Environmental Studies, Arizona State University, Tempe, Arizona 85287. (602) 965-3000. 1991-. Quarterly. Emphasizes the application of basic ecological concepts to a wide range of problems.

Ecological Monographs. Business Office of the Ecological Society of America, Center of Environmental Studies, Arizona State University, Tempe, Arizona 85287-1201. (602) 965-3000. Quarterly. Scientific journal of ecological issues.

Journal of Wild Culture. Society for the Preservation of Wild Culture, 158 Crawford St., Toronto, Ontario, Canada M6J 2V4. (416) 588-8266. Quarterly. Deals with wildlife preservation.

RESEARCH CENTERS AND INSTITUTES

U.S. Forest Service, Forestry Sciences Laboratory. 222 South 22nd Street, Laramie, Wyoming 82070. (307) 742-6621.

STATISTICS SOURCES

World Resources. World Resources Institute. 1709 New York Ave., N.W., Washington, District of Columbia 20006. (202) 638-6300. Annual. Statistical and textual analysis of world's natural resources and the effects of growth-caused environmental pollution.

TRADE ASSOCIATIONS AND PROFESSIONAL SOCIETIES

American Epidemiological Society. Emory University School of Medicine, Division of Public Health, 1599 Clifton Rd., N.E., Atlanta, Georgia 30329. (404) 727-0199.

Association for Conservation Information. PO Box 10678, Reno, Nevada 89520. (702) 688-1500.

Society for Epidemiologic Research. Colorada State University, Department of Health, Microbiology Bldg., Room B107, Ft. Collins, Colorado 80523. (303) 491-6156.

EPIFAUNA

See: BENTHOS

EPILIMNION

See: LAKES

EROSION

See also: AGRICULTURE; FLOODS; WATER POLLUTION; WETLANDS

ABSTRACTING AND INDEXING SERVICES

Abstracts of Air and Water Conservation Literature. American Petroleum Institute. Central Abstracting and Indexing Service, 275 Madison Avenue, New York, New York 10016. 1972.

Applied Ecology Abstracts Studies in Renewable Natural Resources. Information Retrieval Ltd., 1911 Jefferson Davis Highway, Arlington, Virginia 22202. 1975-. Monthly.

Applied Science and Technology Index. H.W. Wilson Co., 950 University Ave., Bronx, New York 10452. (800) 367-6770. Formerly Industrial Arts Index.

Biological Abstracts. BIOSIS, 2100 Arch St., Philadelphia, Pennsylvania 19103-1399. (215) 587-4800. 1927-.

Biological and Agricultural Index. H.W. Wilson Co., 950 University Ave., Bronx, New York 10452. (800) 367-6770. 1916-. Monthly.

Civil Engineering Hydraulic Abstracts. BHRA Fluid Engineering, Air Science Co., PO Box 143, Corning, New York 14830. (607) 962-5591. Monthly. Abstracts of periodicals that publish in the areas of hydraulic engineering and other related topics.

Ecology Abstracts. Cambridge Scientific Abstracts, 5161 River Rd., Bethesda, Maryland 20816. (301) 961-6750. Monthly.

Environment Abstracts. Bowker A & I Publishing, 121 Chanlon Rd., New Providence, New Jersey 07974. (908) 464-6800. 1974-.

Environment Index. Environment Information Center, Index Research Department, 124 E. 39th St., New York, New York 10016. 1971-. Annual.

Environmental Information Connection–EIC. Planning Information Program, Dept. of Urban and Regional Planning, University of Illinois, 1003 West Nevada, Urbana, Illinois 61801. (217) 333-1369. Also available online.

Environmental Periodicals Bibliography. Environmental Studies Institute, International Academy at Santa Barbara, 800 Garden St., Suite D, Santa Barbara, California 93101. (805) 965-5010. Also available online.

General Science Index. H. W. Wilson Co., 950 University Ave., Bronx, New York 10452. 1978-. Monthly, also issued in annual cumulation. Cumulative subject index to English language periodicals in the subject fields of astronomy, botany, chemistry, earth science, environment and conservation, food and nutrition, genetics, mathematics, medicine and health, microbiology, oceanography, physics, physiology and zoology.

Index to Scientific Book Contents. Institute for Scientific Information, 3501 Market St., Philadelphia, Pennsylva-

nia 19104. (800) 523-1857. 1985-. Annual. Gives contents of science books published.

Multimedia Index to Ecology. National Information Center for Educational Media, University of Southern California, Los Angeles, California 90007.

Pollution Abstracts. Cambridge Scientific Abstracts, 5161 River Rd., Bethesda, Maryland 20816. (301) 961-6750. Six/year. Indexes worldwide technical literature on environmental pollution. Covers air pollution, marine and freshwater pollution, sewage and wastewater treatment, waste management, toxicology and health, noise pollution, radiation, land pollution, and environmental policies, programs, legislation, and education. Also available online.

Science Citation Index. Institute for Scientific Information, 3501 Market St., Philadelphia, Pennsylvania 19104. 1961-.

BIBLIOGRAPHIES

A Bibliography of Forest and Rangeland as Nonpoint Sources of Pollution. John M. Fowler. New Mexico State University, Cooperative Extension Service, PO Box 30001, Las Cruces, New Mexico 88003. 1980. Covers erosion, water pollution, sedimentation, deposition, and forest and range management.

Current Contents. Agriculture, Biology and Environmental Sciences. Institute for Scientific Information, 3501 Market St., Philadelphia, Pennsylvania 19104. (800) 523-1857. 1973-. Previous title: Current Contents. Agricultural, Food & Veterinary Sciences. Gives the table of contents of periodicals in the fields of agriculture, biology, environmental and related areas.

Directory of Published Proceedings. Interdok Corp., 173 Halstead Ave., Harrison, New York 10528. (914) 835-3506. 1990. Monthly. This is a listing of published proceedings including the series SEMTE (Science/Medicine/Engineering/Technology) and the series SSH (Social Science/Humanities).

Effects of Bank Stabilization on the Physical and Chemical Characteristics of Streams and Small Rivers: An Annotated Bibliography. Daniel H. Stern. U.S. G.P.O., Washington, District of Columbia 20401. (202) 512-0000. 1980. Covers stream channelization, rivers, streambank planting, erosion and turbidity.

EPA Publications Bibliography. U.S. Environmental Protection Agency, Library Systems Branch, 401 M St., SW, Washington, District of Columbia 20460. (202) 260-2090. Quarterly.

DIRECTORIES

Certified Professional Erosion and Sediment Control Specialists– Directory. Office of the Registry/Certified Professional Erosion and Sediment Control Specialists, 677 S. Segoe Rd., Madison, Wisconsin 53711. (503) 326-2826.

Gale Environmental Sourcebook. Karen Hill. Gale Research Co., 835 Penobscot Bldg., Detroit, Michigan 48226-4094. (313) 961-2242. Contacts, information sources, or general information on environmental topics.

ENCYCLOPEDIAS AND DICTIONARIES

The Encyclopedia of Geochemistry and Environmental Sciences. Rhodes Whitmore Fairbridge. Van Nostrand Reinhold Co., 115 5th Ave., New York, New York 10003. (212) 254-3232. 1972.

Glossary of Geology. Robert Latimer Bates and Julia A. Jackson, eds. American Geological Institute, 4220 King St., Alexandria, Virginia 22302-1507. (703) 379-2480 or (800) 336-4764. 1987. Third edition.

McGraw-Hill Encyclopedia of Science and Technology. McGraw-Hill, 1221 Avenue of the Americas, New York, New York 10020. (212) 512-2000 or (800) 262-4729. 1992. Seventh edition. Issued in multiple volumes including index. Includes all science and technology broad subject areas.

McGraw-Hill Encyclopedia of the Geological Sciences. Sybil P. Parker, ed. McGraw-Hill, 1221 Avenue of the Americas, New York, New York 10020. (212) 512-2000 or (800) 262-4729. 1988. Second edition. Published previously in the McGraw-Hill Encyclopedia of Science and Technology.

Van Nostrand's Scientific Encyclopedia. Glenn D. Considine, ed. Van Nostrand Reinhold, 115 5th Ave., New York, New York 10003. (212) 254-3232. 1983. Sixth edition. Includes all broad subject areas in science.

GENERAL WORKS

Cover Crops for Clean Water. W. L. Hargrove, ed. Soil and Water Conservation Society, 7515 Northeast Ankeny Rd., Ankeny, Iowa 50021-9764. (515) 289-2331; (800) THE-SOIL. 1991. Includes the latest information on the role of cover crops in water quality management, including means of reducing water runoff, soil erosion, agrichemical loss in runoff, and nitrate leaching to groundwater.

Drowning the National Heritage: Climate Change and Coastal Biodiversity in the United States. Walter V. C. Reid and Mark C. Trexler. World Resources Institute, 1709 New York Ave. N.W., Washington, District of Columbia 20006. (800) 822 0504. 1991. Examines erosion, flooding, and salt-water intrusion into groundwater, rivers, bays, and estuaries as well as receding coastlines and altered coastal current and upwelling patterns. Evaluates various policy responses and recommends specific changes to protect the biological wealth of these vital ecosystems.

Environmental Restoration: Science and Strategies for Restoring the Earth. John J. Berger. Island Press, 1718 Connecticut Ave. N.W., Suite 300, Washington, District of Columbia 20009. (202) 232-7933. 1990. Overview techniques of restoration.

Green Fields Forever. Charles E. Little. Island Press, 1718 Connecticut Ave. N.W., Suite 300, Washington, District of Columbia 20009. (202) 232-7933. 1987. An objective look at the costs and benefits of conservation tillage, a promising solution to agricultural problems such as decreased yields, soil erosion and reliance on pesticides and herbicides.

Nutrient Cycling in Terrestrial Ecosystems Field Methods. A. F. Harrison, et al. Elsevier Science Publishing Co., 655 Avenue of the Americas, New York, New York 10010. (212) 984-5800. 1990. Describes a wide range of methods for the estimation of nutrient fluxes. The book is divided into sections dealing with inputs, turnover, losses and plant uptake processes.

Soil Erosion by Water as Related to Management of Tillage and Surface Residues, Terracing, and Contouring in Eastern Oregon. R. R. Allmaras. U.S. Department of Agriculture, Science and Education Administration, Agricultural Research, 800 Buchanan St., Albany, California 94710. (510) 559-6082. 1980. Covers soil erosion and soil management and tillage.

Soil Erosion: Quiet Crisis in the World Economy. Lester R. Brown, Edward C. Wolf. Worldwatch Institute, 1776 Massachusetts Ave., N.W., Washington, District of Columbia 20036-1904. 1984.

Soil Management for Sustainability. R. Lal and F. J. Pierce, eds. Soil and Water Conservation Society, 7515 NE Ankeny Rd., Ankeny, Iowa 50021-9764. (515) 289-2331. 1991. Topics discussed in the book include: soil structure, soil compaction, and predicting soil erosion and its effects on crop productivity. Also covered are the basic processes, management options, and policy issues and priorities. Published in cooperation with the World Association of Soil and Water Conservation and the Soil Science Society of America

GOVERNMENTAL ORGANIZATIONS

Office of Environmental Affairs: Bureau of Reclamation. 18th and C St., N.W., Washington, District of Columbia 20240. (202) 343-4662.

HANDBOOKS AND MANUALS

National Engineering Handbook. Section 3, Sedimentation. U.S. Department of Agriculture, Soil Conservation Service, 14 Independence Ave., SW, Washington, District of Columbia 20250. (202) 447-7454. 1983. Deals with sedimentation, deposition, and erosion in the United States.

ONLINE DATA BASES

BIOSIS Previews. BIOSIS, 2100 Arch St., Philadelphia, Pennsylvania 19103-1399. (215) 587-4800. Largest and most comprehensive database of research in the life sciences. Contains citations for nearly 9000 primary research journals, monographs, reviews, symposia, preliminary reports, semi-popular journals, selected institutional reports, government reports and research communications.

Current Research Information System–CRIS/USDA. U.S. Department of Agriculture, National Agricultural Library, 10301 Baltimore Blvd., 5th Floor, Beltsville, Maryland 20705-2351. (301) 504-5755. Looks at current research projects in agriculture and allied sciences covering the biological, physical, social and behavioral sciences related to agriculture.

Enviro/Energyline Abstracts Plus. R. R. Bowker Co., 121 Chanlon Rd., New Providence, New Jersey 07974. (908) 464-6800.

Environmental Periodicals Bibliography. National Information Services Corp., Ste. 6, Wyman Towers, 3100 St. Paul St., Baltimore, Maryland 21218. (410)243-0797. Online version of abstract of same name.

Monthly Catalog of United States Government Publications. U.S. G.P.O., Supt. of Docs., PO Box 371954, Pittsburgh, Pennsylvania 15250-7954. (202) 512-0000.

National Technical Information Service. U.S. Department of Commerce, National Technical Information Service, Office of Data Base Services, 5285 Port Royal Rd., Springfield, Virginia 22161. (703) 487-4807. Bibliographic database of government sponsored research and technical reports.

SCISEARCH. Institute for Scientific Information, University City Science Center, 3501 Market St., Philadelphia, Pennsylvania 19104. (215) 386-0100.

PERIODICALS AND NEWSLETTERS

IECA Report. International Erosion Control Association, P.O. Box 195, Pinole, California 94564. (415) 223-2134. Bimonthly. Covers urban erosion and sediment control.

RESEARCH CENTERS AND INSTITUTES

Purdue University, Great Lakes Coastal Research Laboratory. School of Civil Engineering, West Lafayette, Indiana 47907. (317) 494-3713.

U.S. Forest Service, Forestry Sciences Laboratory. 860 North 1200 East, Logan, Utah 84321. (801) 752-1311.

University of Wisconsin-Madison, Sea Grant Advisory Services. Walkway Mall, 522 Bayshore Drive, Sister Bay, Wisconsin 54234. (414) 854-5329.

USDA National Sedimentation Laboratory. P.O.Box 1157, Oxford, Missouri 38655. (601) 232-2900.

USDA Wind Erosion Research Unit. Room 105-B, East Waters Hall, Kansas State University, Manhattan, Kansas 66506. (913) 532-6807.

Virginia Water Resources Research Center. Virginia Polytech Institute and State University, 617 North Main Street, Blacksburg, Virginia 24060. (703) 231-5624.

STATISTICS SOURCES

Agricultural Conservation Program Statistical Summary. U.S. Agricultural Stabilization and Conservation Service, Dept. of Agriculture, Washington, District of Columbia 20013. (202) 512-0000. Annual. Deals with soil erosion control, water conservation, water quality and costs by state and county.

Environmental Data Compendium. OECD Publications and Information Center, 2001 L St., N.W., Suite 700, Washington, District of Columbia 20036. (202) 785-6323. 1989.

Environmental Indicators. OECD Publications and Information Center, 2001 L St., N.W., Suite 700, Washington, District of Columbia 20036. (202) 785-6323. 1991.

Environmental Quality. Council on Environmental Quality. U.S. G.P.O., Washington, District of Columbia 20401. (202) 512-0000. Annual.

The State of the Environment. OECD Publications and Information Center, 2001 L St., N.W., Suite 700, Washington, District of Columbia 20036. (202) 785-6323. 1991.

TRADE ASSOCIATIONS AND PROFESSIONAL SOCIETIES

Association of Soil & Foundation Engineers. 8811 Colesville Rd., Suite G106, Silver Spring, Maryland 20910. (301) 563-2733.

International Center for the Solution of Environmental Problems. 535 Lovett Blvd., Houston, Texas 77006. (713) 527-8711.

International Erosion Control Association. Box 4904, Steamboat Springs, Colorado 80477. (303) 879-3010.

National Association of State Land Reclamationists. 459 B Carlisle Dr., Herndon, Virginia 22070. (703) 709-8654.

EROSION CONTROL

See: EROSION

ESCARPMENT

See: EROSION

ESTUARIES

See also: BAYS; MARINE POLLUTION; WATER POLLUTION; WETLANDS

ABSTRACTING AND INDEXING SERVICES

Abstracts of Air and Water Conservation Literature. American Petroleum Institute. Central Abstracting and Indexing Service, 275 Madison Avenue, New York, New York 10016. 1972.

Applied Ecology Abstracts Studies in Renewable Natural Resources. Information Retrieval Ltd., 1911 Jefferson Davis Highway, Arlington, Virginia 22202. 1975-. Monthly.

Applied Science and Technology Index. H.W. Wilson Co., 950 University Ave., Bronx, New York 10452. (800) 367-6770. Formerly Industrial Arts Index.

ASFA Aquaculture Abstracts. Cambridge Scientific Abstracts, Inc., 5161 River Rd., Bethesda, Maryland 20816. (301) 961-6750. 1984.

Biological Abstracts. BIOSIS, 2100 Arch St., Philadelphia, Pennsylvania 19103-1399. (215) 587-4800. 1927-.

Biological and Agricultural Index. H.W. Wilson Co., 950 University Ave., Bronx, New York 10452. (800) 367-6770. 1916-. Monthly.

Biology Digest. Data Courier, Plexus Pub Inc., 143 Old Marlton Pike, Medford, New Jersey 08055. 1974-. Monthly. Abstracts biology periodicals.

Civil Engineering Hydraulic Abstracts. BHRA Fluid Engineering, Air Science Co., PO Box 143, Corning, New York 14830. (607) 962-5591. Monthly. Abstracts of periodicals that publish in the areas of hydraulic engineering and other related topics.

Current Advances in Ecological and Environmental Science. Pergamon Microforms International, Inc., Fairview Park, Elmsford, New York 10523. (914) 592-7720. 1989-.

Monthly. Current literature searching service including journals, reports, abstracts, etc. This service is available online as part of the CABS database on the hosts BRS and ORBIT search service.

Ecological Abstracts. Geo Abstracts Ltd. Elsevier Applied Science, Crown House, Linton Rd., Barking, England IG 11 8JU. 1974-. Derived from over 600 leading ecological and environmental journals, plus books, conference proceedings, reports and theses.

Ecology Abstracts. Cambridge Scientific Abstracts, 5161 River Rd., Bethesda, Maryland 20816. (301) 961-6750. Monthly.

Environment Abstracts. Bowker A & I Publishing, 121 Chanlon Rd., New Providence, New Jersey 07974. (908) 464-6800. 1974-.

Environment Index. Environment Information Center, Index Research Department, 124 E. 39th St., New York, New York 10016. 1971-. Annual.

Environmental Information Connection–EIC. Planning Information Program, Dept. of Urban and Regional Planning, University of Illinois, 1003 West Nevada, Urbana, Illinois 61801. (217) 333-1369. Also available online.

Environmental Periodicals Bibliography. Environmental Studies Institute, International Academy at Santa Barbara, 800 Garden St., Suite D, Santa Barbara, California 93101. (805) 965-5010. Also available online.

General Science Index. H. W. Wilson Co., 950 University Ave., Bronx, New York 10452. 1978-. Monthly, also issued in annual cumulation. Cumulative subject index to English language periodicals in the subject fields of astronomy, botany, chemistry, earth science, environment and conservation, food and nutrition, genetics, mathematics, medicine and health, microbiology, oceanography, physics, physiology and zoology.

Index to Scientific Book Contents. Institute for Scientific Information, 3501 Market St., Philadelphia, Pennsylvania 19104. (800) 523-1857. 1985-. Annual. Gives contents of science books published.

Multimedia Index to Ecology. National Information Center for Educational Media, University of Southern California, Los Angeles, California 90007.

Pollution Abstracts. Cambridge Scientific Abstracts, 5161 River Rd., Bethesda, Maryland 20816. (301) 961-6750. Six/year. Indexes worldwide technical literature on environmental pollution. Covers air pollution, marine and freshwater pollution, sewage and wastewater treatment, waste management, toxicology and health, noise pollution, radiation, land pollution, and environmental policies, programs, legislation, and education. Also available online.

Science Citation Index. Institute for Scientific Information, 3501 Market St., Philadelphia, Pennsylvania 19104. 1961-.

BIBLIOGRAPHIES

A Bibliography of Numerical Models for Tidal Rivers, Estuaries, and Coastal Waters. University of Rhode Island, International Center for Marine Resource Development, 126 Woodward Hall, Kingston, Rhode Island 20881. (401) 792-2479.

Directory of Published Proceedings. Interdok Corp., 173 Halstead Ave., Harrison, New York 10528. (914) 835-3506. 1990. Monthly. This is a listing of published proceedings including the series SEMTE (Science/Medicine/Engineering/Technology) and the series SSH (Social Science/Humanities).

EPA Publications Bibliography. U.S. Environmental Protection Agency, Library Systems Branch, 401 M St., SW, Washington, District of Columbia 20460. (202) 260-2090. Quarterly.

Estuarine Pollution, a Bibliography. Water Resources Scientific Information Center. National Technical Information Service, 5285 Port Royal Rd., Springfield, Virginia 22161. (703) 487-4650. 1976.

DIRECTORIES

Gale Environmental Sourcebook. Karen Hill. Gale Research Co., 835 Penobscot Bldg., Detroit, Michigan 48226-4094. (313) 961-2242. Contacts, information sources, or general information on environmental topics.

ENCYCLOPEDIAS AND DICTIONARIES

Cambridge Encyclopedia of Life Sciences. A. E. Friday and David S. Ingram. Cambridge University Press, 40 W 20th St., New York, New York 10011. (212) 924-3900 or (800) 227-0247. 1985. Includes all topics under biology and ecology.

Dictionary of Environmental Engineering and Related Sciences: English-Spanish, Spanish-English. Jose T. Villate. Ediciones Universal, 3090 SW 8th St., Miami, Florida 33135. (305) 642-3355. 1979.

Encyclopedia of Environmental Science and Engineering. J.R. Pfafflin. Gordon and Breach Science Publishers, Inc., 270 8th Ave., New York, New York 10011. (212) 206-8900. 1992.

The Encyclopedia of Geochemistry and Environmental Sciences. Rhodes Whitmore Fairbridge. Van Nostrand Reinhold Co., 115 5th Ave., New York, New York 10003. (212) 254-3232. 1972.

Grzimek's Encyclopedia of Ecology. Bernhard Grzimek. Van Nostrand Reinhold, 115 5th Ave., New York, New York 10003. (212) 254-3232. 1976.

McGraw-Hill Encyclopedia of Environmental Science. Sybil P. Parker. McGraw-Hill Science & Engineering Books, 11 W. 19th St., New York, New York 10011. (212) 337-6010. 1980. Covers ecology, man's influence on nature, and environmental protection.

North American Reference Encyclopedia of Ecology and Pollution. William White. North American Pub. Co., 401 N. Broad St., Philadelphia, Pennsylvania 19108. (215) 238-5300. 1972.

Van Nostrand's Scientific Encyclopedia. Glenn D. Considine, ed. Van Nostrand Reinhold, 115 5th Ave., New York, New York 10003. (212) 254-3232. 1983. Sixth edition. Includes all broad subject areas in science.

GENERAL WORKS

Biological Surveys of Estuaries and Coasts. Cambridge University Press, 40 W. 20th St., New York, New York 10011. (212) 924-3900. Coastal ecology, ecological surveys, and estuarine biology.

Drowning the National Heritage: Climate Change and Coastal Biodiversity in the United States. Walter V. C. Reid and Mark C. Trexler. World Resources Institute, 1709 New York Ave. N.W., Washington, District of Columbia 20006. (800) 822 0504. 1991. Examines erosion, flooding, and salt-water intrusion into groundwater, rivers, bays, and estuaries as well as receding coastlines and altered coastal current and upwelling patterns. Evaluates various policy responses and recommends specific changes to protect the biological wealth of these vital ecosystems.

Ecology of Estuaries: Anthropogenic Effects. CRC Press, 2000 Corporate Blvd. N.W., Boca Raton, Florida 33431. (800) 272-7737. 1992. Covers estuarine ecology and environmental aspects of estuarine pollution.

Estuaries and Tidal Marshes. National Institute for Urban Wildlife, 10921 Trotting Ridge Way, Columbia, Maryland 21044. (301) 596-3311. 1986. Topics in estuarine and tidemarsh ecology.

The Living Ocean. Boyce Thorne-Miller. Island Press, 1718 Connecticut Ave. N.W., Suite 300, Washington, District of Columbia 20009. (202) 232-7933. 1991. Discusses all marine ecosystems, including coastal benthic, shore systems, estuaries, wetlands, and coral reefs, coastal pelagic, deep-sea benthic, hydrothermal vents and others.

Marine and Estuarine Protection: Programs and Activities. U.S. Environmental Protection Agency, Office of Water, 401 M St. SW, Washington, District of Columbia 20460. (202) 260-2090. 1989.

Protection of River Basins, Lakes, and Estuaries. Robert C. Ryans. American Fisheries Society, 5410 Grosvenor Lane, Bethesda, Maryland 20814. (301) 897-8616. 1988. Fifteen years of cooperation toward solving environmental problems in the USSR and USA.

Stream, Lake, Estuary, and Ocean Pollution. Nelson Leonard Nemerow. Van Nostrand Reinhold, 115 5th Ave., New York, New York 10003. (800) 926-2665. 1991.

Turning the Tide: Saving the Chesapeake Bay. Tom Horton. Island Press, 1718 Connecticut Ave. N.W., Suite 300, Washington, District of Columbia 20009. (202) 232-7933. 1991. Presents a comprehensive look at two decades of efforts to save the Chesapeake Bay. It outlines which methods have worked, and which have not. Sets a new strategy for the future, calling for greater political coverage, environmental leadership and vision.

GOVERNMENTAL ORGANIZATIONS

U.S. Environmental Protection Agency: Office of Marine and Estuarine Protection. 401 M St., S.W., Washington, District of Columbia 20460. (202) 382-8580.

ONLINE DATA BASES

BIOSIS Previews. BIOSIS, 2100 Arch St., Philadelphia, Pennsylvania 19103-1399. (215) 587-4800. Largest and most comprehensive database of research in the life sciences. Contains citations for nearly 9000 primary research journals, monographs, reviews, symposia, preliminary reports, semi-popular journals, selected institutional reports, government reports and research communications.

Cambridge Scientific Abstracts Life Science–CSAL. Cambridge Scientific Abstracts, 5161 River Rd., Bethesda, Maryland 20816. (301) 961-6750. Provides access to the following abstracting services: "Life Sciences Collection," "Aquatic Sciences and Fisheries Abstracts," "Oceanic Abstracts," and "Pollution Abstracts."

Current Research Information System–CRIS/USDA. U.S. Department of Agriculture, National Agricultural Library, 10301 Baltimore Blvd., 5th Floor, Beltsville, Maryland 20705-2351. (301) 504-5755. Looks at current research projects in agriculture and allied sciences covering the biological, physical, social and behavioral sciences related to agriculture.

Enviro/Energyline Abstracts Plus. R. R. Bowker Co., 121 Chanlon Rd., New Providence, New Jersey 07974. (908) 464-6800.

Enviroline. R. R. Bowker Co., Bowker Electronic Publishing, 121 Chanlon Rd., New Providence, New Jersey 07974. (800) 521-8110.

Environmental Bibliography. Environmental Studies Institute, International Academy at Santa Barbara, 800 Garden St., Ste. D, Santa Barbara, California 93101. (805) 965-5010. International periodical literature dealing with environmental topics such as air pollution, water treatment, energy conservation, noise abatement, soil mechanics, wildlife preservation, and chemical wastes.

Environmental Periodicals Bibliography. National Information Services Corp., Ste. 6, Wyman Towers, 3100 St. Paul St., Baltimore, Maryland 21218. (410)243-0797. Online version of abstract of same name.

Monthly Catalog of United States Government Publications. U.S. G.P.O., Supt. of Docs., PO Box 371954, Pittsburgh, Pennsylvania 15250-7954. (202) 512-0000.

National Technical Information Service. U.S. Department of Commerce, National Technical Information Service, Office of Data Base Services, 5285 Port Royal Rd., Springfield, Virginia 22161. (703) 487-4807. Bibliographic database of government sponsored research and technical reports.

SCISEARCH. Institute for Scientific Information, University City Science Center, 3501 Market St., Philadelphia, Pennsylvania 19104. (215) 386-0100.

PERIODICALS AND NEWSLETTERS

Estuaries. Chesapeake Biological Laboratory, 1 William St., Solomons, Maryland 20688-0038. (410) 326-4281. Quarterly. Journal of the Estuarine Research Federation dealing with estuaries and estuarine biology.

RESEARCH CENTERS AND INSTITUTES

Academy of Natural Sciences of Philadelphia, Division of Environmental Research. 19th Street and the Parkway, Philadelphia, Pennsylvania 19103. (215) 299-1081.

Florida Sea Grant College Program. University of Florida, Building 803, Room 4, Gainesville, Florida 32611-0341. (904) 392-5870.

Hudsonia LTD. Bard College Field Station, Annadale, New York 12504. (914) 758-1881.

Louisiana Universities Marine Consortium. Chauvin, Louisiana 70344. (504) 851-2800.

Maritime Center. 10 North Water Street, South Norwalk, Connecticut 06854. (203) 852-0700.

Mote Marine Laboratory. 1600 Thompson Park, Sarasota, Florida 34236. (813) 388-4441.

Shannon Point Marine Center. Western Washington University, 1900 Shannon Point Rd., Anacortes, Washington 98221. (206) 293-2188.

University of Maryland, Center for Environmental and Estuarine Studies. Center Operations, Horn Point, P.O.Box 775, Cambridge, Maryland 21613. (410) 228-9250.

University of New Hampshire, Jackson Estuarine Laboratory. 85 Adams Point Road, Durham, New Hampshire 03824-3406. (603) 862-2175.

University of New Hampshire, New Hampshire Sea Grant College Program. Marine Programs Building, Durham, New Hampshire 03824-3512. (603) 749-1565.

University of Oregon, Oregon Institute of Marine Biology. Charleston, Oregon 97420. (503) 888-2581.

University of Rhode Island, Marine Ecosystems Research Laboratory. Graduate School of Oceanography, Narragansett, Rhode Island 02882. (401) 792-6104.

STATISTICS SOURCES

Ecology: Community Profiles. U.S. Fish and Wildlife Service. National Technical Information Service, 5285 Port Royal Road, Springfield, Virginia 22161. (703) 487-4650. Irregular. Data on coastal and inland ecosystems, including wetlands, tidal-flats, near-shore seagrasses, sand dunes, drilling platforms, oyster reefs, estuaries, rivers and streams.

Environmental Data Compendium. OECD Publications and Information Center, 2001 L St., N.W., Suite 700, Washington, District of Columbia 20036. (202) 785-6323. 1989.

Environmental Indicators. OECD Publications and Information Center, 2001 L St., N.W., Suite 700, Washington, District of Columbia 20036. (202) 785-6323. 1991.

Environmental Quality. Council on Environmental Quality. U.S. G.P.O., Washington, District of Columbia 20401. (202) 512-0000. Annual.

Estuaries of the United States: Vital Statistics of a National Resource Base. U.S. Ocean Assessments Division, Coastal and Estuaries Assessment Branch, Rockville, Maryland 1990. Data on nation's estuaries, coasts, and marine resources conservation.

The State of the Environment. OECD Publications and Information Center, 2001 L St., N.W., Suite 700, Washington, District of Columbia 20036. (202) 785-6323. 1991.

TRADE ASSOCIATIONS AND PROFESSIONAL SOCIETIES

American Institute of Biological Sciences. 730 11th St., N.W., Washington, District of Columbia 20001-4521. (202) 628-1500.

American Society of Naturalists. Department of Ecology and Evolation, State University of New York, Stony Brook, New York 11794. (516) 632-8589.

Atlantic Estuarine Research Society. c/o Michael Ewing, Old Dominion University, Applied Marine Research Lab, Norfolk, Virginia 23529-0456. (804) 683-4195.

Estuarine Research Federation. P.O. Box 544, Crownsville, Maryland 21032-0544. (301) 266-5489.

ETHANE

ABSTRACTING AND INDEXING SERVICES

Applied Science and Technology Index. H.W. Wilson Co., 950 University Ave., Bronx, New York 10452. (800) 367-6770. Formerly Industrial Arts Index.

Biological Abstracts. BIOSIS, 2100 Arch St., Philadelphia, Pennsylvania 19103-1399. (215) 587-4800. 1927-.

Chemical Abstracts. Chemical Abstracts Service, 2540 Olentangy River Rd., PO Box 3012, Columbus, Ohio 43210. (800) 848-6533. 1907-.

Environment Abstracts. Bowker A & I Publishing, 121 Chanlon Rd., New Providence, New Jersey 07974. (908) 464-6800. 1974-.

Environment Index. Environment Information Center, Index Research Department, 124 E. 39th St., New York, New York 10016. 1971-. Annual.

Environmental Information Connection–EIC. Planning Information Program, Dept. of Urban and Regional Planning, University of Illinois, 1003 West Nevada, Urbana, Illinois 61801. (217) 333-1369. Also available online.

Environmental Periodicals Bibliography. Environmental Studies Institute, International Academy at Santa Barbara, 800 Garden St., Suite D, Santa Barbara, California 93101. (805) 965-5010. Also available online.

ERDA Research Abstracts. U.S. ERDA Technical Information Center, Box 62, Oak Ridge, Tennessee 37830.

General Science Index. H. W. Wilson Co., 950 University Ave., Bronx, New York 10452. 1978-. Monthly, also issued in annual cumulation. Cumulative subject index to English language periodicals in the subject fields of astronomy, botany, chemistry, earth science, environment and conservation, food and nutrition, genetics, mathematics, medicine and health, microbiology, oceanography, physics, physiology and zoology.

Science Citation Index. Institute for Scientific Information, 3501 Market St., Philadelphia, Pennsylvania 19104. 1961-.

BIBLIOGRAPHIES

EPA Publications Bibliography. U.S. Environmental Protection Agency, Library Systems Branch, 401 M St., SW, Washington, District of Columbia 20460. (202) 260-2090. Quarterly.

ENCYCLOPEDIAS AND DICTIONARIES

Van Nostrand's Scientific Encyclopedia. Glenn D. Considine, ed. Van Nostrand Reinhold, 115 5th Ave., New York, New York 10003. (212) 254-3232. 1983. Sixth edition. Includes all broad subject areas in science.

GENERAL WORKS

Teratologic Assessment of Butylene Oxide, Styrene Oxide and Methyl Bromide. Melvin R. Sikov. U.S. G.P.O., Washington, District of Columbia 20401. (202) 512-0000. 1981. Toxicology aspects of the following: butene, styrene, bromomethane, teratogenic agents, hydrocarbons, and ethers.

ONLINE DATA BASES

BIOSIS Previews. BIOSIS, 2100 Arch St., Philadelphia, Pennsylvania 19103-1399. (215) 587-4800. Largest and most comprehensive database of research in the life sciences. Contains citations for nearly 9000 primary research journals, monographs, reviews, symposia, preliminary reports, semi-popular journals, selected institutional reports, government reports and research communications.

Chemical Abstracts-CA. Chemical Abstracts Service, 2540 Olentangy River Rd., P.O. Box 3012, Columbus, Ohio 43210. (800) 848-6533 or (614) 421-3600. Information sources include 9000 journals, patents from 27 countries, two industrial property organizations, new books, conference proceedings, and government research reports.

Enviro/Energyline Abstracts Plus. R. R. Bowker Co., 121 Chanlon Rd., New Providence, New Jersey 07974. (908) 464-6800.

Environmental Periodicals Bibliography. National Information Services Corp., Ste. 6, Wyman Towers, 3100 St. Paul St., Baltimore, Maryland 21218. (410)243-0797. Online version of abstract of same name.

Monthly Catalog of United States Government Publications. U.S. G.P.O., Supt. of Docs., PO Box 371954, Pittsburgh, Pennsylvania 15250-7954. (202) 512-0000.

National Technical Information Service. U.S. Department of Commerce, National Technical Information Service, Office of Data Base Services, 5285 Port Royal Rd., Springfield, Virginia 22161. (703) 487-4807. Bibliographic database of government sponsored research and technical reports.

NBSFLUIDS. National Institute of Standards & Technology, Office of Standard Reference Data, A323 Physics Building, Gaithersburg, Maryland 20899. (301) 975-2208.

RESEARCH CENTERS AND INSTITUTES

Wetlands Institute. Stone Harbor Boulevard, Stone Harbor, New Jersey 08247. (609) 368-1211.

TRADE ASSOCIATIONS AND PROFESSIONAL SOCIETIES

American Chemical Society. 1155 16th St., N.W., Washington, District of Columbia 20036. (202) 872-4600.

American Institute of Biological Sciences. 730 11th St., N.W., Washington, District of Columbia 20001-4521. (202) 628-1500.

ETHANOL

ABSTRACTING AND INDEXING SERVICES

Applied Science and Technology Index. H.W. Wilson Co., 950 University Ave., Bronx, New York 10452. (800) 367-6770. Formerly Industrial Arts Index.

Biological Abstracts. BIOSIS, 2100 Arch St., Philadelphia, Pennsylvania 19103-1399. (215) 587-4800. 1927-.

Chemical Abstracts. Chemical Abstracts Service, 2540 Olentangy River Rd., PO Box 3012, Columbus, Ohio 43210. (800) 848-6533. 1907-.

Environment Abstracts. Bowker A & I Publishing, 121 Chanlon Rd., New Providence, New Jersey 07974. (908) 464-6800. 1974-.

Environment Index. Environment Information Center, Index Research Department, 124 E. 39th St., New York, New York 10016. 1971-. Annual.

Environmental Information Connection–EIC. Planning Information Program, Dept. of Urban and Regional Planning, University of Illinois, 1003 West Nevada, Urbana, Illinois 61801. (217) 333-1369. Also available online.

Environmental Periodicals Bibliography. Environmental Studies Institute, International Academy at Santa Barbara, 800 Garden St., Suite D, Santa Barbara, California 93101. (805) 965-5010. Also available online.

ERDA Research Abstracts. U.S. ERDA Technical Information Center, Box 62, Oak Ridge, Tennessee 37830.

Food Science and Technology Abstracts. International Food Information Service, c/o National Food Laboratory, 6363 Clark Ave., Dublin, California 94568. (800) 336-3782. 1969-.

General Science Index. H. W. Wilson Co., 950 University Ave., Bronx, New York 10452. 1978-. Monthly, also issued in annual cumulation. Cumulative subject index to English language periodicals in the subject fields of astronomy, botany, chemistry, earth science, environment and conservation, food and nutrition, genetics, mathematics, medicine and health, microbiology, oceanography, physics, physiology and zoology.

Science Citation Index. Institute for Scientific Information, 3501 Market St., Philadelphia, Pennsylvania 19104. 1961-.

BIBLIOGRAPHIES

EPA Publications Bibliography. U.S. Environmental Protection Agency, Library Systems Branch, 401 M St., SW, Washington, District of Columbia 20460. (202) 260-2090. Quarterly.

Gasohol Sourcebook: Literature Survey and Abstracts. N. P. Cheremisinoff and P. N. Cheremisinoff. Ann Arbor Science, 230 Collingwood, PO Box 1425, Ann Arbor, Michigan 48106. 1981. Volume includes: biotechnology and bioconversion; ethanol and methanol production; automotive and other fuels; production of chemical feedstocks; and economics of alcohol production.

ENCYCLOPEDIAS AND DICTIONARIES

Encyclopedia of Chemical Processing and Design. John J. Mcketta and W. A. Cunningham. Marcel Dekker, Inc., 270 Madison Ave., New York, New York 10016. (212) 696-9000; (800) 228-1160. 1992. Thirty-eight volumes.

Kirk-Othmer Encyclopedia of Chemical Technology. J. I. Kroschwitz, ed. John Wiley & Sons, Inc., 605 3rd Ave., New York, New York 10158-0012. (212) 850-6000. 1992-. All articles in the new edition have been rewritten and updated adding new subjects such as biotechnology, computer topics, analytical techniques and instrumentation, environmental concerns, fuels and energy, inorganic and solid state chemistry; composite materials and material science in general, and pharmaceuticals. Also available online.

McGraw-Hill Encyclopedia of Science and Technology. McGraw-Hill, 1221 Avenue of the Americas, New York, New York 10020. (212) 512-2000 or (800) 262-4729. 1992. Seventh edition. Issued in multiple volumes including index. Includes all science and technology broad subject areas.

The Nutrition and Health Encyclopedia. David F. Tver and Percy Russell. Van Nostrand Reinhold, 115 5th Ave., New York, New York 10003. (212) 254-3232. 1989.

Van Nostrand's Scientific Encyclopedia. Glenn D. Considine, ed. Van Nostrand Reinhold, 115 5th Ave., New York, New York 10003. (212) 254-3232. 1983. Sixth edition. Includes all broad subject areas in science.

GENERAL WORKS

Replacing Gasoline: Alternative Fuels for Light-Duty Vehicles. Congress of the U.S., c/o U.S. Government Printing Office, Office of Technology Assesment, N. Capitol & H Sts. NW, Washington, District of Columbia 20401. (202) 512-0000. 1990. Gives information on alternatives to standard gasoline. Some of the alternatives are: electricity, hydrogen, compressed natural gas, liquified natural gas, liquid propane gas, methanol, ethanol, and reformulated gasoline.

ONLINE DATA BASES

BIOSIS Previews. BIOSIS, 2100 Arch St., Philadelphia, Pennsylvania 19103-1399. (215) 587-4800. Largest and most comprehensive database of research in the life sciences. Contains citations for nearly 9000 primary research journals, monographs, reviews, symposia, preliminary reports, semi-popular journals, selected institutional reports, government reports and research communications.

Chemical Abstracts-CA. Chemical Abstracts Service, 2540 Olentangy River Rd., P.O. Box 3012, Columbus, Ohio 43210. (800) 848-6533 or (614) 421-3600. Information sources include 9000 journals, patents from 27 countries, two industrial property organizations, new books, conference proceedings, and government research reports.

Enviro/Energyline Abstracts Plus. R. R. Bowker Co., 121 Chanlon Rd., New Providence, New Jersey 07974. (908) 464-6800.

Environmental Periodicals Bibliography. National Information Services Corp., Ste. 6, Wyman Towers, 3100 St.

Paul St., Baltimore, Maryland 21218. (410)243-0797. Online version of abstract of same name.

Kirk-Othmer Encyclopedia of Chemical Technology. John Wiley & Sons, Inc., 605 3rd Ave., 5th Floor, New York, New York 10158. (212) 850-6000. Online version of the publication of the same name.

Monthly Catalog of United States Government Publications. U.S. G.P.O., Supt. of Docs., PO Box 371954, Pittsburgh, Pennsylvania 15250-7954. (202) 512-0000.

National Technical Information Service. U.S. Department of Commerce, National Technical Information Service, Office of Data Base Services, 5285 Port Royal Rd., Springfield, Virginia 22161. (703) 487-4807. Bibliographic database of government sponsored research and technical reports.

TRADE ASSOCIATIONS AND PROFESSIONAL SOCIETIES

American Chemical Society. 1155 16th St., N.W., Washington, District of Columbia 20036. (202) 872-4600.

American Institute of Biological Sciences. 730 11th St., N.W., Washington, District of Columbia 20001-4521. (202) 628-1500.

ETHERS

ABSTRACTING AND INDEXING SERVICES

Applied Science and Technology Index. H.W. Wilson Co., 950 University Ave., Bronx, New York 10452. (800) 367-6770. Formerly Industrial Arts Index.

Chemical Abstracts. Chemical Abstracts Service, 2540 Olentangy River Rd., PO Box 3012, Columbus, Ohio 43210. (800) 848-6533. 1907-.

Environment Abstracts. Bowker A & I Publishing, 121 Chanlon Rd., New Providence, New Jersey 07974. (908) 464-6800. 1974-.

Environment Index. Environment Information Center, Index Research Department, 124 E. 39th St., New York, New York 10016. 1971-. Annual.

Environmental Information Connection–EIC. Planning Information Program, Dept. of Urban and Regional Planning, University of Illinois, 1003 West Nevada, Urbana, Illinois 61801. (217) 333-1369. Also available online.

Environmental Periodicals Bibliography. Environmental Studies Institute, International Academy at Santa Barbara, 800 Garden St., Suite D, Santa Barbara, California 93101. (805) 965-5010. Also available online.

General Science Index. H. W. Wilson Co., 950 University Ave., Bronx, New York 10452. 1978-. Monthly, also issued in annual cumulation. Cumulative subject index to English language periodicals in the subject fields of astronomy, botany, chemistry, earth science, environment and conservation, food and nutrition, genetics, mathematics, medicine and health, microbiology, oceanography, physics, physiology and zoology.

Pollution Abstracts. Cambridge Scientific Abstracts, 5161 River Rd., Bethesda, Maryland 20816. (301) 961-6750. Six/year. Indexes worldwide technical literature on environmental pollution. Covers air pollution, marine and freshwater pollution, sewage and wastewater treatment, waste management, toxicology and health, noise pollution, radiation, land pollution, and environmental policies, programs, legislation, and education. Also available online.

Science Citation Index. Institute for Scientific Information, 3501 Market St., Philadelphia, Pennsylvania 19104. 1961-.

BIBLIOGRAPHIES

EPA Publications Bibliography. U.S. Environmental Protection Agency, Library Systems Branch, 401 M St., SW, Washington, District of Columbia 20460. (202) 260-2090. Quarterly.

ENCYCLOPEDIAS AND DICTIONARIES

The Concise Russian-English Chemical Glossary: Acids, Esters, Ethers, and Salts. James F. Shipp. Wychwood Press, PO Box 10, College Park, Maryland 20740. 1983. Lists four of the basic substances commonly occurring in chemical and environmental literature: acids, esters, ethers and salts.

Van Nostrand's Scientific Encyclopedia. Glenn D. Considine, ed. Van Nostrand Reinhold, 115 5th Ave., New York, New York 10003. (212) 254-3232. 1983. Sixth edition. Includes all broad subject areas in science.

GENERAL WORKS

Research Priorities for Conservation Biology. Michael E. Soulfe and Kathryn A. Kohm, eds. Island Press, 1718 Connecticut Ave. N.W., Suite 300, Washington, District of Columbia 20009. (202) 232-7933. 1989. Proposes an urgent research agenda to improve our understanding and preservation of biological diversity.

ONLINE DATA BASES

Chemical Abstracts-CA. Chemical Abstracts Service, 2540 Olentangy River Rd., P.O. Box 3012, Columbus, Ohio 43210. (800) 848-6533 or (614) 421-3600. Information sources include 9000 journals, patents from 27 countries, two industrial property organizations, new books, conference proceedings, and government research reports.

Enviro/Energyline Abstracts Plus. R. R. Bowker Co., 121 Chanlon Rd., New Providence, New Jersey 07974. (908) 464-6800.

Environmental Periodicals Bibliography. National Information Services Corp., Ste. 6, Wyman Towers, 3100 St. Paul St., Baltimore, Maryland 21218. (410)243-0797. Online version of abstract of same name.

STATISTICS SOURCES

Solvents & the Environment. FIND/SVP, 625 Avenue of the Americas, New York, New York 10011. (212) 645-4500. 1991. Demand forecasts on hydrocarbons for 1995 and 2000; chlorinated, ketones, alcohols and alcohol esters, ethers, glycols and other esters, and recycled solvents.

TRADE ASSOCIATIONS AND PROFESSIONAL SOCIETIES

American Chemical Society. 1155 16th St., N.W., Washington, District of Columbia 20036. (202) 872-4600.

ETHOLOGY

ABSTRACTING AND INDEXING SERVICES

Applied Ecology Abstracts Studies in Renewable Natural Resources. Information Retrieval Ltd., 1911 Jefferson Davis Highway, Arlington, Virginia 22202. 1975-. Monthly.

Biological Abstracts. BIOSIS, 2100 Arch St., Philadelphia, Pennsylvania 19103-1399. (215) 587-4800. 1927-.

Biological and Agricultural Index. H.W. Wilson Co., 950 University Ave., Bronx, New York 10452. (800) 367-6770. 1916-. Monthly.

Current Advances in Ecological and Environmental Science. Pergamon Microforms International, Inc., Fairview Park, Elmsford, New York 10523. (914) 592-7720. 1989-. Monthly. Current literature searching service includingjournals, reports, abstracts, etc. This service is available online as part of the CABS database on the hosts BRS and ORBIT search service.

Ecological Abstracts. Geo Abstracts Ltd. Elsevier Applied Science, Crown House, Linton Rd., Barking, England IG 11 8JU. 1974-. Derived from over 600 leading ecological and environmental journals, plus books, conference proceedings, reports and theses.

Ecology Abstracts. Cambridge Scientific Abstracts, 5161 River Rd., Bethesda, Maryland 20816. (301) 961-6750. Monthly.

Environment Abstracts. Bowker A & I Publishing, 121 Chanlon Rd., New Providence, New Jersey 07974. (908) 464-6800. 1974-.

Environment Index. Environment Information Center, Index Research Department, 124 E. 39th St., New York, New York 10016. 1971-. Annual.

Environmental Information Connection–EIC. Planning Information Program, Dept. of Urban and Regional Planning, University of Illinois, 1003 West Nevada, Urbana, Illinois 61801. (217) 333-1369. Also available online.

Environmental Periodicals Bibliography. Environmental Studies Institute, International Academy at Santa Barbara, 800 Garden St., Suite D, Santa Barbara, California 93101. (805) 965-5010. Also available online.

General Science Index. H. W. Wilson Co., 950 University Ave., Bronx, New York 10452. 1978-. Monthly, also issued in annual cumulation. Cumulative subject index to English language periodicals in the subject fields of astronomy, botany, chemistry, earth science, environment and conservation, food and nutrition, genetics, mathematics, medicine and health, microbiology, oceanography, physics, physiology and zoology.

Multimedia Index to Ecology. National Information Center for Educational Media, University of Southern California, Los Angeles, California 90007.

Science Citation Index. Institute for Scientific Information, 3501 Market St., Philadelphia, Pennsylvania 19104. 1961-.

BIBLIOGRAPHIES

EPA Publications Bibliography. U.S. Environmental Protection Agency, Library Systems Branch, 401 M St., SW, Washington, District of Columbia 20460. (202) 260-2090. Quarterly.

ENCYCLOPEDIAS AND DICTIONARIES

Cambridge Encyclopedia of Life Sciences. A. E. Friday and David S. Ingram. Cambridge University Press, 40 W 20th St., New York, New York 10011. (212) 924-3900 or (800) 227-0247. 1985. Includes all topics under biology and ecology.

A Dictionary of Ethology. Colin Beer. Harvard University Press, 79 Garden St., Cambridge, Massachusetts 02138. (617) 495-2600. 1992. Dictionary of animal behavior and related terms.

The Dictionary of Ethology and Animal Learning. Romano Harre and Roger Lamb. Blackwell Scientific Publications, PO Box 87, Oxford, England OX2 0DT. 44 0865 791155. 1986. The biological study of animal behavior dictionary.

Encyclopedia of Human Biology. Renato Dulbecco, ed. Academic Press, c/o Harcourt Brace Jovanovich Inc., 6277 Sea Harbor Dr., Orlando, Florida 32887. (800) 346-8648. 1991. Eight volumes.

Grzimek's Encyclopedia of Ethology. Bernard Grzimek. Van Nostrand Reinhold, 115 5th Ave., New York, New York 10003. (212) 254-3232. 1977. Comprehensive detailed coverage on animal behavior.

McGraw-Hill Encyclopedia of Environmental Science. Sybil P. Parker. McGraw-Hill Science & Engineering Books, 11 W. 19th St., New York, New York 10011. (212) 337-6010. 1980. Covers ecology, man's influence on nature, and environmental protection.

Van Nostrand's Scientific Encyclopedia. Glenn D. Considine, ed. Van Nostrand Reinhold, 115 5th Ave., New York, New York 10003. (212) 254-3232. 1983. Sixth edition. Includes all broad subject areas in science.

GENERAL WORKS

Animal Remains in Archaeology. Rosemary-Margaret Luff. Shire Publications, Cromwell House, Church St., Princes Risborough, Aylesbury, England HP17 9AJ. 1984. Methodology of archaeology relating to animal remains.

Current Paleoethnobotany: Analytical Methods and Cultural Interpretations of Archaeological Plant Remains. Christine A. Hastorf and Virginia S. Popper. University of Chicago Press, 5801 Ellis Ave., 4th Floor, Chicago, Illinois 60637. (800) 621-2736. 1988. Prehistoric archeology and ecology.

Magill's Survey of Science. Life Science Series. Frank N. Magill, ed. Salem Press, PO Box 50062, Pasadena, California 91105. 1991. Six volumes. Contents: v.1. A-Central and peripheral nervous system functions; v.2. Central metabolism regulation - eukaryotic transcriptional control; v.3. Positive and negative eukaryotic transcriptional control - mammalian hormones; v.4. Hor-

mones and behavior - muscular contraction; v.5. Muscular contraction and relaxation - sexual reproduction in plants; v.6. Reproductive behavior and mating - X inactivation and the Lyon hypothesis.

Primate Responses to Environmental Change. Hillary O. Box, ed. Chapman & Hall, 29 W. 35th St., New York, New York 10001-2291. (212) 244-3336. 1991. Contributions of 24 authors grouped around the subject area of behavioral and physiological responses by primates to environmental change.

Valuing Wildlife: Economic and Social Perspectives. Daniel J. Decker and Gary R. Goff, eds. Westview Press, 5500 Central Ave., Boulder, Colorado 80301. (303) 444-3541. 1987. State of the art guide to determining the value of wildlife, the application for environmental impact assessment, and strategies in wildlife planning and policy.

HANDBOOKS AND MANUALS

An Ethnobiology Source Book. Richard I. Ford. Garland Publishers, 136 Madison Ave., New York, New York 10016. (212) 686-7492 or (800) 627-6273. 1986. The uses of plants and animals by, and the food habits of, American Indians.

ONLINE DATA BASES

BIOSIS Previews. BIOSIS, 2100 Arch St., Philadelphia, Pennsylvania 19103-1399. (215) 587-4800. Largest and most comprehensive database of research in the life sciences. Contains citations for nearly 9000 primary research journals, monographs, reviews, symposia, preliminary reports, semi-popular journals, selected institutional reports, government reports and research communications.

Cambridge Scientific Abstracts Life Science–CSAL. Cambridge Scientific Abstracts, 5161 River Rd., Bethesda, Maryland 20816. (301) 961-6750. Provides access to the following abstracting services: "Life Sciences Collection," "Aquatic Sciences and Fisheries Abstracts," "Oceanic Abstracts," and "Pollution Abstracts."

Enviro/Energyline Abstracts Plus. R. R. Bowker Co., 121 Chanlon Rd., New Providence, New Jersey 07974. (908) 464-6800.

Environmental Periodicals Bibliography. National Information Services Corp., Ste. 6, Wyman Towers, 3100 St. Paul St., Baltimore, Maryland 21218. (410)243-0797. Online version of abstract of same name.

Monthly Catalog of United States Government Publications. U.S. G.P.O., Supt. of Docs., PO Box 371954, Pittsburgh, Pennsylvania 15250-7954. (202) 512-0000.

National Technical Information Service. U.S. Department of Commerce, National Technical Information Service, Office of Data Base Services, 5285 Port Royal Rd., Springfield, Virginia 22161. (703) 487-4807. Bibliographic database of government sponsored research and technical reports.

SCISEARCH. Institute for Scientific Information, University City Science Center, 3501 Market St., Philadelphia, Pennsylvania 19104. (215) 386-0100.

PERIODICALS AND NEWSLETTERS

Behavioral Ecology and Sociobiology. Springer-Verlag, 175 5th Ave., New York, New York 10010. (212) 460-1500. 1976-. Eight times a year. Environmental studies.

International Journal of Biosocial and Medical Research. Life Sciences Press, P.O. Box 1174, Takoma, Washington 98401-1174. (206) 922-0442. Semiannual. Deals with psychological and psychobiological aspects of environments.

Journal of Ethnobiology. Center for Western Studies, Flagstaff, Arizona Semiannual. Covers archaeology and ethnozoology of plant and animal remains.

Journal of Insect Behavior. Plenum Press, 233 Spring St., New York, New York 0013-1578. (212) 620-8000. Quarterly. Agricultural and biological aspects of insect behavior.

TRADE ASSOCIATIONS AND PROFESSIONAL SOCIETIES

American Institute of Biological Sciences. 730 11th St., N.W., Washington, District of Columbia 20001-4521. (202) 628-1500.

American Society of Naturalists. Department of Ecology and Evolation, State University of New York, Stony Brook, New York 11794. (516) 632-8589.

ETHYLENE

ABSTRACTING AND INDEXING SERVICES

Chemical Abstracts. Chemical Abstracts Service, 2540 Olentangy River Rd., PO Box 3012, Columbus, Ohio 43210. (800) 848-6533. 1907-.

General Science Index. H. W. Wilson Co., 950 University Ave., Bronx, New York 10452. 1978-. Monthly, also issued in annual cumulation. Cumulative subject index to English language periodicals in the subject fields of astronomy, botany, chemistry, earth science, environment and conservation, food and nutrition, genetics, mathematics, medicine and health, microbiology, oceanography, physics, physiology and zoology.

BIBLIOGRAPHIES

Ethylene Dibromide Toxicology. U.S. Department of Health and Human Services, Public Health Services, National Institutes of Health, 9000 Rockville Pike, Bethesda, Maryland 20892. (301) 496-4000. 1984.

ENCYCLOPEDIAS AND DICTIONARIES

Encyclopedia of Chemical Processing and Design. John J. Mcketta and W. A. Cunningham. Marcel Dekker, Inc., 270 Madison Ave., New York, New York 10016. (212) 696-9000; (800) 228-1160. 1992. Thirty-eight volumes.

Kirk-Othmer Encyclopedia of Chemical Technology. J. I. Kroschwitz, ed. John Wiley & Sons, Inc., 605 3rd Ave., New York, New York 10158-0012. (212) 850-6000. 1992-. All articles in the new edition have been rewritten and updated adding new subjects such as biotechnology, computer topics, analytical techniques and instrumentation, environmental concerns, fuels and energy, inorganic and solid state chemistry; composite materials and material science in general, and pharmaceuticals. Also available online.

Van Nostrand's Scientific Encyclopedia. Glenn D. Considine, ed. Van Nostrand Reinhold, 115 5th Ave., New York, New York 10003. (212) 254-3232. 1983. Sixth edition. Includes all broad subject areas in science.

GENERAL WORKS

The River of the Mother of God and Other Essays. Aldo Leopold. University of Wisconsin Press, 114 N. Murray St., Madison, Wisconsin 53715. (608) 262-8782. 1991. Brings together 60 of Leopold's previously unpublished or illusive essays.

ONLINE DATA BASES

Chemical Abstracts-CA. Chemical Abstracts Service, 2540 Olentangy River Rd., P.O. Box 3012, Columbus, Ohio 43210. (800) 848-6533 or (614) 421-3600. Information sources include 9000 journals, patents from 27 countries, two industrial property organizations, new books, conference proceedings, and government research reports.

Dewitt Petrochemical Newsletter. DeWitt and Company, 16800 Greenspoint Park, North Atrium Suite 120, Houston, Texas 77060. (713) 875-5525.

Kirk-Othmer Encyclopedia of Chemical Technology. John Wiley & Sons, Inc., 605 3rd Ave., 5th Floor, New York, New York 10158. (212) 850-6000. Online version of the publication of the same name.

PERIODICALS AND NEWSLETTERS

Housatonic Current. Housatonic Valley Assn., Box 28, Cornwall Bridge, Connecticut 06754. (203) 672-6678. Quarterly. Environmental programs and land planning throughout the Housatonic River Watershed.

STATISTICS SOURCES

Chemical Retorts. FIND/SVP, 625 Avenue of the Americas, New York, New York 10011. (212) 645-4500. 1991. Profiles the collapse of selected commodity petrochemical margins including, VCM, PVC, ethylene, polyethylene and chlorine.

TRADE ASSOCIATIONS AND PROFESSIONAL SOCIETIES

American Institute of Biological Sciences. 730 11th St., N.W., Washington, District of Columbia 20001-4521. (202) 628-1500.

EULITHORAL
See: LAKES

EURPHAGNUS
See: NUTRITION

EURYHALINE
See: SALT

EUTROPHIC LAKES
See: LAKES

EUTROPHICATION

ABSTRACTING AND INDEXING SERVICES

Abstracts of Air and Water Conservation Literature. American Petroleum Institute. Central Abstracting and Indexing Service, 275 Madison Avenue, New York, New York 10016. 1972.

Algae Abstracts: A Guide to the Literature. IFI/Plenum, 233 Spring St., New York, New York 10013. (800) 221-9369. Covers algology, water pollution and eutrophication.

Applied Science and Technology Index. H.W. Wilson Co., 950 University Ave., Bronx, New York 10452. (800) 367-6770. Formerly Industrial Arts Index.

Aqualine Abstracts. Water Research Centre. c/o Pergamon Microforms International, Inc., Fairview Park, Elmsford, New York 10523. (914) 592-7720. 1927-. Contains some 8,000 records annually on water and wastewater technology. Covers all aspects of water, wastewater, associated engineering services and the aquatic environment. Over 600 periodicals, as well as books, reports and conference proceedings and other publications from water related institutions worldwide are scanned. Also available online.

ASFA Aquaculture Abstracts. Cambridge Scientific Abstracts, Inc., 5161 River Rd., Bethesda, Maryland 20816. (301) 961-6750. 1984.

Biological Abstracts. BIOSIS, 2100 Arch St., Philadelphia, Pennsylvania 19103-1399. (215) 587-4800. 1927-.

Biological and Agricultural Index. H.W. Wilson Co., 950 University Ave., Bronx, New York 10452. (800) 367-6770. 1916-. Monthly.

Chemical Abstracts. Chemical Abstracts Service, 2540 Olentangy River Rd., PO Box 3012, Columbus, Ohio 43210. (800) 848-6533. 1907-.

Civil Engineering Hydraulic Abstracts. BHRA Fluid Engineering, Air Science Co., PO Box 143, Corning, New York 14830. (607) 962-5591. Monthly. Abstracts of periodicals that publish in the areas of hydraulic engineering and other related topics.

Current Advances in Ecological and Environmental Science. Pergamon Microforms International, Inc., Fairview Park, Elmsford, New York 10523. (914) 592-7720. 1989-. Monthly. Current literature searching service including journals, reports, abstracts, etc. This service is available online as part of the CABS database on the hosts BRS and ORBIT search service.

Ecological Abstracts. Geo Abstracts Ltd. Elsevier Applied Science, Crown House, Linton Rd., Barking, England IG 11 8JU. 1974-. Derived from over 600 leading ecological

and environmental journals, plus books, conference proceedings, reports and theses.

Ecology Abstracts. Cambridge Scientific Abstracts, 5161 River Rd., Bethesda, Maryland 20816. (301) 961-6750. Monthly.

Eutrophication: A Bimonthly Summary of Current Literature. University of Wisconsin-Madison, Water Resources Information Program, 1513 University Ave., Madison, Wisconsin 53706.

General Science Index. H. W. Wilson Co., 950 University Ave., Bronx, New York 10452. 1978-. Monthly, also issued in annual cumulation. Cumulative subject index to English language periodicals in the subject fields of astronomy, botany, chemistry, earth science, environment and conservation, food and nutrition, genetics, mathematics, medicine and health, microbiology, oceanography, physics, physiology and zoology.

Geographical Abstracts. London School of Economics, Dept. of Geography, Regency House, 34 Duke St., London, England 1966-. Continued by Geo Abstracts issued in 6 parts: Pt. A. Landforms and the quaternary; Pt. B. Biogeography and Climatology; Pt. C. Economic geography; Pt. D. Social geography and cartography; Pt. E. Sedimentology; Pt. F. Regional and community planning.

Pollution Abstracts. Cambridge Scientific Abstracts, 5161 River Rd., Bethesda, Maryland 20816. (301) 961-6750. Six/year. Indexes worldwide technical literature on environmental pollution. Covers air pollution, marine and freshwater pollution, sewage and wastewater treatment, waste management, toxicology and health, noise pollution, radiation, land pollution, and environmental policies, programs, legislation, and education. Also available online.

BIBLIOGRAPHIES

Current Contents. Agriculture, Biology and Environmental Sciences. Institute for Scientific Information, 3501 Market St., Philadelphia, Pennsylvania 19104. (800) 523-1857. 1973-. Previous title: Current Contents. Agricultural, Food & Veterinary Sciences. Gives the table of contents of periodicals in the fields of agriculture, biology, environmental and related areas.

ENCYCLOPEDIAS AND DICTIONARIES

Cambridge Encyclopedia of Life Sciences. A. E. Friday and David S. Ingram. Cambridge University Press, 40 W 20th St., New York, New York 10011. (212) 924-3900 or (800) 227-0247. 1985. Includes all topics under biology and ecology.

Macmillan Dictionary of Toxicology. Ernest Hodgson, et al. Van Nostrand Reinhold, 115 5th Ave., New York, New York 10003. (212) 254-3232. 1988. Intended as a "starting point" to the literature of toxicology. American spelling is used with cross references to British version of words. Contains a list of references. Signed entries give explanatory definitions and cross references.

McGraw-Hill Encyclopedia of Environmental Science. Sybil P. Parker. McGraw-Hill Science & Engineering Books, 11 W. 19th St., New York, New York 10011. (212) 337-6010. 1980. Covers ecology, man's influence on nature, and environmental protection.

Van Nostrand's Scientific Encyclopedia. Glenn D. Considine, ed. Van Nostrand Reinhold, 115 5th Ave., New York, New York 10003. (212) 254-3232. 1983. Sixth edition. Includes all broad subject areas in science.

GENERAL WORKS

The Control of Eutrophication of Lakes and Reservoirs. S. O. Ryding and W. Rast, eds. Parthenon Pub., Casterton Hall, Carnforth, England LA6 2LA. 1990. Volume 1 of the Man and the Biosphere series published jointly with UNESCO.

Eutrophication Management Framework for the Policy-Maker. Walter Rast, et al. UNESCO, 7, place de Fontenoy, Paris, France F-75700. (331) 45 68 40 67. 1989. MAB Digest 1.

Eutrophication of Fresh Waters. David Harper. Chapman & Hall, 29 West 35th St., New York, New York 10001-2291. (212) 244-3336. 1992. Principles, problems, and restoration of marine ecosystems.

Lake and Reservoir Restoration. Butterworth-Heinemann, 80 Montvale Ave., Stoneham, Massachusetts 02180. (617) 438-8464. 1986. Covers lake renewal, reservoirs, water quality management and eutrophication.

Microbial Enzymes in Aquatic Environments. Ryszard J. Chrost. Springer-Varlag, 175 5th Ave., New York, New York 10010. (212) 460-1500. 1991. Brings together studies on enzymatic degradation processes from disciplines as diverse as water and sediment research, bacterial and algal aquatic ecophysiology, eutrophication, nutrient cycling, and biogeochemistry, in both freshwater and marine ecosystem.

ONLINE DATA BASES

BIOSIS Previews. BIOSIS, 2100 Arch St., Philadelphia, Pennsylvania 19103-1399. (215) 587-4800. Largest and most comprehensive database of research in the life sciences. Contains citations for nearly 9000 primary research journals, monographs, reviews, symposia, preliminary reports, semi-popular journals, selected institutional reports, government reports and research communications.

Cambridge Scientific Abstracts Life Science–CSAL. Cambridge Scientific Abstracts, 5161 River Rd., Bethesda, Maryland 20816. (301) 961-6750. Provides access to the following abstracting services: "Life Sciences Collection," "Aquatic Sciences and Fisheries Abstracts," "Oceanic Abstracts," and "Pollution Abstracts."

Chemical Abstracts-CA. Chemical Abstracts Service, 2540 Olentangy River Rd., P.O. Box 3012, Columbus, Ohio 43210. (800) 848-6533 or (614) 421-3600. Information sources include 9000 journals, patents from 27 countries, two industrial property organizations, new books, conference proceedings, and government research reports.

Current Research Information System–CRIS/USDA. U.S. Department of Agriculture, National Agricultural Library, 10301 Baltimore Blvd., 5th Floor, Beltsville, Maryland 20705-2351. (301) 504-5755. Looks at current research projects in agriculture and allied sciences covering the biological, physical, social and behavioral sciences related to agriculture.

National Eutrophication Study Data Base. U.S. Environmental Protection Agency, Environmental Monitoring Systems Laboratory, Las Vegas, 401 M St. SW, Washington, District of Columbia 20460. (202) 260-2090. Water quality data collected over a one-year period for each of some 800 lakes and their tributaries in 48 states.

SCISEARCH. Institute for Scientific Information, University City Science Center, 3501 Market St., Philadelphia, Pennsylvania 19104. (215) 386-0100.

RESEARCH CENTERS AND INSTITUTES

University of Wisconsin-Madison, Water Resources Center. 1975 Willow Drive, Madison, Wisconsin 53706. (608) 262-3577.

STATISTICS SOURCES

World Resources. World Resources Institute. 1709 New York Ave., N.W., Washington, District of Columbia 20006. (202) 638-6300. Annual. Statistical and textual analysis of world's natural resources and the effects of growth-caused environmental pollution.

TRADE ASSOCIATIONS AND PROFESSIONAL SOCIETIES

American Institute of Biological Sciences. 730 11th St., N.W., Washington, District of Columbia 20001-4521. (202) 628-1500.

American Society of Naturalists. Department of Ecology and Evolation, State University of New York, Stony Brook, New York 11794. (516) 632-8589.

EUTROPHICATION, PHOSPHATE

See: EUTROPHICATION

EVAPORATION

ABSTRACTING AND INDEXING SERVICES

Applied Science and Technology Index. H.W. Wilson Co., 950 University Ave., Bronx, New York 10452. (800) 367-6770. Formerly Industrial Arts Index.

Biological Abstracts. BIOSIS, 2100 Arch St., Philadelphia, Pennsylvania 19103-1399. (215) 587-4800. 1927-.

Chemical Abstracts. Chemical Abstracts Service, 2540 Olentangy River Rd., PO Box 3012, Columbus, Ohio 43210. (800) 848-6533. 1907-.

Environment Abstracts. Bowker A & I Publishing, 121 Chanlon Rd., New Providence, New Jersey 07974. (908) 464-6800. 1974-.

Environment Index. Environment Information Center, Index Research Department, 124 E. 39th St., New York, New York 10016. 1971-. Annual.

Environmental Information Connection–EIC. Planning Information Program, Dept. of Urban and Regional Planning, University of Illinois, 1003 West Nevada, Urbana, Illinois 61801. (217) 333-1369. Also available online.

Environmental Periodicals Bibliography. Environmental Studies Institute, International Academy at Santa Barbara, 800 Garden St., Suite D, Santa Barbara, California 93101. (805) 965-5010. Also available online.

General Science Index. H. W. Wilson Co., 950 University Ave., Bronx, New York 10452. 1978-. Monthly, also issued in annual cumulation. Cumulative subject index to English language periodicals in the subject fields of astronomy, botany, chemistry, earth science, environment and conservation, food and nutrition, genetics, mathematics, medicine and health, microbiology, oceanography, physics, physiology and zoology.

Irrigation and Drainage Abstracts. C. A. B. International, 845 North Park Ave., Tucson, Arizona 85719. (602) 621-7897 or (800) 258-4841. 1975-. Quarterly. Subject areas scanned are: water management, irrigation of crop plants, drainage, soil water relations, plant water relations, salinity and toxicity problems, soil condition, evaporotranspiration, evaporation, land use, streams, water quality, and other related areas.

Physics Briefs. Physikalische Berichte. Physik Verlag, Pappapelallee 3, Postfach 101161, Weinheim, Germany D-6940. 1979-. Semimonthly. In English. Volumes for 1979- issued by the Deutsche Physikalische Gesellschaft and the Fachinformationszentrum Energie Physik, Mathematik in cooperation with the American Institute of Physics.

Pollution Abstracts. Cambridge Scientific Abstracts, 5161 River Rd., Bethesda, Maryland 20816. (301) 961-6750. Six/year. Indexes worldwide technical literature on environmental pollution. Covers air pollution, marine and freshwater pollution, sewage and wastewater treatment, waste management, toxicology and health, noise pollution, radiation, land pollution, and environmental policies, programs, legislation, and education. Also available online.

Science Citation Index. Institute for Scientific Information, 3501 Market St., Philadelphia, Pennsylvania 19104. 1961-.

BIBLIOGRAPHIES

Bibliography and Index of Geology. American Geological Institute, 4220 King St., Alexandria, Virginia 22302. Monthly. Includes environmental geology and hydrogeology.

EPA Publications Bibliography. U.S. Environmental Protection Agency, Library Systems Branch, 401 M St., SW, Washington, District of Columbia 20460. (202) 260-2090. Quarterly.

ENCYCLOPEDIAS AND DICTIONARIES

Encyclopedia of Physics. Rita G. Lerner and George L. Trigg. VCH Publishers, 303 NW 12th Ave., Deerfield Beach, Florida 33442-1788. (305) 428-5566. 1991. Second edition.

The Encyclopedia of Soil Science. Rhodes W. Fairbridge. Academic Press, c/o Harcourt Brace Jovanovich Inc., 6277 Sea Harbor Dr., Orlando, Florida 32887. (800) 346-8648. 1979-. Includes soil physics, soil chemistry, soil biology, soil fertility and plant nutrition, soil genesis, classification and cartography.

McGraw-Hill Encyclopedia of Environmental Science. Sybil P. Parker. McGraw-Hill Science & Engineering

Books, 11 W. 19th St., New York, New York 10011. (212) 337-6010. 1980. Covers ecology, man's influence on nature, and environmental protection.

Ullmanns Encyclopedia of Industrial Chemistry. Hans Jurgen Arpe and Wolfgang Gerhartz, eds. VCH Publishers, 303 NW 12th Ave., Deerfield Beach, Florida 33442-1788. (305) 428-5566. 1990. Designed to keep up with the broad spectrum of chemical technology. Thirty-six volumes of the encyclopedia have been divided into two sets: the 28 A volumes contain alphabetically arranged articles on chemicals, product groups, processes and technological concepts; and the 8 B volumes are compendia of basic knowledge in industrial chemistry.

Van Nostrand's Scientific Encyclopedia. Glenn D. Considine, ed. Van Nostrand Reinhold, 115 5th Ave., New York, New York 10003. (212) 254-3232. 1983. Sixth edition. Includes all broad subject areas in science.

GENERAL WORKS

Magill's Survey of Science. Earth Science Series. Frank N. Magill. Salem Press, PO Box 50062, Pasadena, California 91105. 1990-. Five volumes. Includes information on earth's crust, hot spots and volcanic island chains, physical properties of minerals, rock magnetism, physical properties of rocks, and index.

HANDBOOKS AND MANUALS

Handbook of Evaporation Technology. Paul E. Minton. Noyes Publications, 120 Mill Rd., Park Ridge, New Jersey 07656. (201) 391-8484. 1986.

ONLINE DATA BASES

BIOSIS Previews. BIOSIS, 2100 Arch St., Philadelphia, Pennsylvania 19103-1399. (215) 587-4800. Largest and most comprehensive database of research in the life sciences. Contains citations for nearly 9000 primary research journals, monographs, reviews, symposia, preliminary reports, semi-popular journals, selected institutional reports, government reports and research communications.

Chemical Abstracts-CA. Chemical Abstracts Service, 2540 Olentangy River Rd., P.O. Box 3012, Columbus, Ohio 43210. (800) 848-6533 or (614) 421-3600. Information sources include 9000 journals, patents from 27 countries, two industrial property organizations, new books, conference proceedings, and government research reports.

Enviro/Energyline Abstracts Plus. R. R. Bowker Co., 121 Chanlon Rd., New Providence, New Jersey 07974. (908) 464-6800.

Environmental Periodicals Bibliography. National Information Services Corp., Ste. 6, Wyman Towers, 3100 St. Paul St., Baltimore, Maryland 21218. (410)243-0797. Online version of abstract of same name.

Monthly Catalog of United States Government Publications. U.S. G.P.O., Supt. of Docs., PO Box 371954, Pittsburgh, Pennsylvania 15250-7954. (202) 512-0000.

National Technical Information Service. U.S. Department of Commerce, National Technical Information Service, Office of Data Base Services, 5285 Port Royal Rd., Springfield, Virginia 22161. (703) 487-4807. Biblio-

graphic database of government sponsored research and technical reports.

SCISEARCH. Institute for Scientific Information, University City Science Center, 3501 Market St., Philadelphia, Pennsylvania 19104. (215) 386-0100.

TRADE ASSOCIATIONS AND PROFESSIONAL SOCIETIES

American Institute of Chemical Engineers. 345 East 47th St., New York, New York 10017. (212) 705-7338.

American Institute of Chemists. 7315 Wisconsin Ave., Bethesda, Maryland 20814. (301) 652-2447.

EVAPOTRANSPIRATION

See: SOIL SCIENCE

EVERGLADES

See also: MARSHES

ABSTRACTING AND INDEXING SERVICES

Abstracts of Air and Water Conservation Literature. American Petroleum Institute. Central Abstracting and Indexing Service, 275 Madison Avenue, New York, New York 10016. 1972.

Applied Ecology Abstracts Studies in Renewable Natural Resources. Information Retrieval Ltd., 1911 Jefferson Davis Highway, Arlington, Virginia 22202. 1975-. Monthly.

Biological Abstracts. BIOSIS, 2100 Arch St., Philadelphia, Pennsylvania 19103-1399. (215) 587-4800. 1927-.

Biological and Agricultural Index. H.W. Wilson Co., 950 University Ave., Bronx, New York 10452. (800) 367-6770. 1916-. Monthly.

Ecological Abstracts. Geo Abstracts Ltd. Elsevier Applied Science, Crown House, Linton Rd., Barking, England IG 11 8JU. 1974-. Derived from over 600 leading ecological and environmental journals, plus books, conference proceedings, reports and theses.

Environment Abstracts. Bowker A & I Publishing, 121 Chanlon Rd., New Providence, New Jersey 07974. (908) 464-6800. 1974-.

Environment Index. Environment Information Center, Index Research Department, 124 E. 39th St., New York, New York 10016. 1971-. Annual.

Environmental Information Connection–EIC. Planning Information Program, Dept. of Urban and Regional Planning, University of Illinois, 1003 West Nevada, Urbana, Illinois 61801. (217) 333-1369. Also available online.

Environmental Periodicals Bibliography. Environmental Studies Institute, International Academy at Santa Barbara, 800 Garden St., Suite D, Santa Barbara, California 93101. (805) 965-5010. Also available online.

General Science Index. H. W. Wilson Co., 950 University Ave., Bronx, New York 10452. 1978-. Monthly, also issued in annual cumulation. Cumulative subject index

to English language periodicals in the subject fields of astronomy, botany, chemistry, earth science, environment and conservation, food and nutrition, genetics, mathematics, medicine and health, microbiology, oceanography, physics, physiology and zoology.

Index to Scientific Book Contents. Institute for Scientific Information, 3501 Market St., Philadelphia, Pennsylvania 19104. (800) 523-1857. 1985-. Annual. Gives contents of science books published.

Multimedia Index to Ecology. National Information Center for Educational Media, University of Southern California, Los Angeles, California 90007.

Science Citation Index. Institute for Scientific Information, 3501 Market St., Philadelphia, Pennsylvania 19104. 1961-.

BIBLIOGRAPHIES

EPA Publications Bibliography. U.S. Environmental Protection Agency, Library Systems Branch, 401 M St., SW, Washington, District of Columbia 20460. (202) 260-2090. Quarterly.

DIRECTORIES

Gale Environmental Sourcebook. Karen Hill. Gale Research Co., 835 Penobscot Bldg., Detroit, Michigan 48226-4094. (313) 961-2242. Contacts, information sources, or general information on environmental topics.

ENCYCLOPEDIAS AND DICTIONARIES

Van Nostrand's Scientific Encyclopedia. Glenn D. Considine, ed. Van Nostrand Reinhold, 115 5th Ave., New York, New York 10003. (212) 254-3232. 1983. Sixth edition. Includes all broad subject areas in science.

GENERAL WORKS

Development Concept Plan Environmental Assessment: Gulf Coast, Everglades National Park, Florida. U.S. National Park Service, Department of the Interior, PO Box 37127, Washington, District of Columbia 20013. (202) 208-6843. 1990. Land use concepts in the Everglades National Park.

Everglades National Park Protection and Expansion Act of 1989. U.S. House Committee on Interior and Insular Affairs. U.S. G.P.O., Washington, District of Columbia 20401. (202) 512-0000. 1991. Law and legislation relating to national parks and reserves and the conservation of natural resources with special reference to Everglades National Park.

ONLINE DATA BASES

BIOSIS Previews. BIOSIS, 2100 Arch St., Philadelphia, Pennsylvania 19103-1399. (215) 587-4800. Largest and most comprehensive database of research in the life sciences. Contains citations for nearly 9000 primary research journals, monographs, reviews, symposia, preliminary reports, semi-popular journals, selected institutional reports, government reports and research communications.

Cambridge Scientific Abstracts Life Science–CSAL. Cambridge Scientific Abstracts, 5161 River Rd., Bethesda, Maryland 20816. (301) 961-6750. Provides access to the

following abstracting services: "Life Sciences Collection," "Aquatic Sciences and Fisheries Abstracts," "Oceanic Abstracts," and "Pollution Abstracts."

Enviro/Energyline Abstracts Plus. R. R. Bowker Co., 121 Chanlon Rd., New Providence, New Jersey 07974. (908) 464-6800.

Environmental Periodicals Bibliography. National Information Services Corp., Ste. 6, Wyman Towers, 3100 St. Paul St., Baltimore, Maryland 21218. (410)243-0797. Online version of abstract of same name.

Monthly Catalog of United States Government Publications. U.S. G.P.O., Supt. of Docs., PO Box 371954, Pittsburgh, Pennsylvania 15250-7954. (202) 512-0000.

National Technical Information Service. U.S. Department of Commerce, National Technical Information Service, Office of Data Base Services, 5285 Port Royal Rd., Springfield, Virginia 22161. (703) 487-4807. Bibliographic database of government sponsored research and technical reports.

SCISEARCH. Institute for Scientific Information, University City Science Center, 3501 Market St., Philadelphia, Pennsylvania 19104. (215) 386-0100.

STATISTICS SOURCES

Environmental Data Compendium. OECD Publications and Information Center, 2001 L St., N.W., Suite 700, Washington, District of Columbia 20036. (202) 785-6323. 1989.

Environmental Indicators. OECD Publications and Information Center, 2001 L St., N.W., Suite 700, Washington, District of Columbia 20036. (202) 785-6323. 1991.

Environmental Quality. Council on Environmental Quality. U.S. G.P.O., Washington, District of Columbia 20401. (202) 512-0000. Annual.

The State of the Environment. OECD Publications and Information Center, 2001 L St., N.W., Suite 700, Washington, District of Columbia 20036. (202) 785-6323. 1991.

TRADE ASSOCIATIONS AND PROFESSIONAL SOCIETIES

American Society of Naturalists. Department of Ecology and Evolation, State University of New York, Stony Brook, New York 11794. (516) 632-8589.

The Friends of the Everglades. 101 Westward Dr., No. 2, Miami Springs, Florida 33166. (305) 888-1230.

EXCRETION
See: SLUDGE

EXOTIC SPECIES
See: ENDANGERED SPECIES

EXPLOSIVES

ABSTRACTING AND INDEXING SERVICES

Environment Abstracts. Bowker A & I Publishing, 121 Chanlon Rd., New Providence, New Jersey 07974. (908) 464-6800. 1974-.

Environment Index. Environment Information Center, Index Research Department, 124 E. 39th St., New York, New York 10016. 1971-. Annual.

Environmental Information Connection–EIC. Planning Information Program, Dept. of Urban and Regional Planning, University of Illinois, 1003 West Nevada, Urbana, Illinois 61801. (217) 333-1369. Also available online.

Environmental Periodicals Bibliography. Environmental Studies Institute, International Academy at Santa Barbara, 800 Garden St., Suite D, Santa Barbara, California 93101. (805) 965-5010. Also available online.

General Science Index. H. W. Wilson Co., 950 University Ave., Bronx, New York 10452. 1978-. Monthly, also issued in annual cumulation. Cumulative subject index to English language periodicals in the subject fields of astronomy, botany, chemistry, earth science, environment and conservation, food and nutrition, genetics, mathematics, medicine and health, microbiology, oceanography, physics, physiology and zoology.

Pollution Abstracts. Cambridge Scientific Abstracts, 5161 River Rd., Bethesda, Maryland 20816. (301) 961-6750. Six/year. Indexes worldwide technical literature on environmental pollution. Covers air pollution, marine and freshwater pollution, sewage and wastewater treatment, waste management, toxicology and health, noise pollution, radiation, land pollution, and environmental policies, programs, legislation, and education. Also available online.

Science Citation Index. Institute for Scientific Information, 3501 Market St., Philadelphia, Pennsylvania 19104. 1961-.

BIBLIOGRAPHIES

EPA Publications Bibliography. U.S. Environmental Protection Agency, Library Systems Branch, 401 M St., SW, Washington, District of Columbia 20460. (202) 260-2090. Quarterly.

Explosives Detection. National Technical Information Service, 5285 Port Royal Rd., Springfield, Virginia 22161. (703) 487-4650. 1986. Bibliography of explosives taken from COMPENDEX.

ENCYCLOPEDIAS AND DICTIONARIES

Dictionary of Blasting Technology. Barbara Student-Bilharz. VCH Publishers, 303 NW 12th Ave., Deerfield Beach, Florida 33442-1788. (305) 428-5566. 1988. Polyglot dictionary in German, French and English covering explosives and blasting.

Encyclopedia of Explosives and Related Items. Seymour M. Kaye. National Technical Information Service, 5285 Port Royal Rd., Springfield, Virginia 22161. (703) 487-4650. 1978.

Explosives. Rudolf Meyer. VCH Publishers, 303 NW 12th Ave., Deerfield Beach, Florida 33442-1788. (305) 428-5566. 1992.

Van Nostrand's Scientific Encyclopedia. Glenn D. Considine, ed. Van Nostrand Reinhold, 115 5th Ave., New York, New York 10003. (212) 254-3232. 1983. Sixth edition. Includes all broad subject areas in science.

GENERAL WORKS

Census of manufacturers. Preliminary report. Industry Series. Explosives. U.S. G.P.O., Washington, District of Columbia 20401. (202) 512-0000. 1987. Quinquennial. Industrial data published as part of current Industrial Reports Series.

A Technical Assessment of Portable Explosives Vapor Detection Devices. Marc R. Nyden. U.S. Department of Justice, Office of Justice Programs, National Institute of Justice, Constitution Ave. & 10th St. NW, Washington, District of Columbia 20530. (202) 514-2000. 1990. Evaluation of technology relating to explosives detectors.

Toxicity and Metabolism of Explosives. Jehuda Yinon. CRC Press, 2000 Corporate Blvd. N.W., Boca Raton, Florida 33431. (800) 272-7737. 1990. Safety measures relating to military explosives.

HANDBOOKS AND MANUALS

Ammo Operations in the Desert. Headquarters, Dept. of the Army, Washington, District of Columbia 20310. (202) 695-6153. 1990. Safety measures in the military relating to ammunition and explosives.

Deadly Brew: Advanced Improvised Explosives. Seymour Lecker. Paladin Press, 2523 Broadway, Boulder, Colorado 80304. (303) 443-7250. 1987.

Explosives Usage Policy. United States. Bureau of Alcohol, Tobacco, and Firearms. Department of Treasury, Bureau of Alcohol, Tobacco, and Firearms, 650 Massachusetts Ave. NW, Washington, District of Columbia 20226. (202) 927-8500. Transportation and safety measures relating to explosives.

Handbook of Dangerous Materials. N. Irving Sax. Reinhold Pub. Co., 115 5th Ave., New York, New York 10003. (212)254-3232. 1951. Covers medical mycology and safety measures relating to chemicals, explosives, and radioactivity.

Military Explosives. Headquarters, Dept. of the Army, Washington, District of Columbia 20310. (202) 695-6153. 1990. Army manual dealing with handling explosives.

Society Meeting (194th, 1987). American Chemical Society, 1155 16th St. N.W., Washington, District of Columbia 20036. (800) 227-5558.

ONLINE DATA BASES

Chemical Age Project File. MBC Information Services Ltd., Paulton House, 8 Shepherdess Walk, London, England N1 7LB. 44 (71) 490-0049.

Enviro/Energyline Abstracts Plus. R. R. Bowker Co., 121 Chanlon Rd., New Providence, New Jersey 07974. (908) 464-6800.

Environmental Periodicals Bibliography. National Information Services Corp., Ste. 6, Wyman Towers, 3100 St. Paul St., Baltimore, Maryland 21218. (410)243-0797. Online version of abstract of same name.

Monthly Catalog of United States Government Publications. U.S. G.P.O., Supt. of Docs., PO Box 371954, Pittsburgh, Pennsylvania 15250-7954. (202) 512-0000.

National Technical Information Service. U.S. Department of Commerce, National Technical Information Service, Office of Data Base Services, 5285 Port Royal Rd., Springfield, Virginia 22161. (703) 487-4807. Bibliographic database of government sponsored research and technical reports.

PERIODICALS AND NEWSLETTERS

The Explosives Engineer. Hercules Inc., Hercules Plaza, 313 N. Market St., Wilmington, Delaware 19894-0001. (302) 594-5000. Bimonthly. Articles dealing with design, manufacturers and safety measures involving explosives and blasting.

STATISTICS SOURCES

Explosives Incidents Report. Bureau of Alcohol, Tobacco, and Firearms, 650 Massachusetts Ave. NW, Washington, District of Columbia 20226. (202) 927-8500. Annual. Data on offenses against property.

Industrial Explosives Markets. FIND/SVP, 625 Avenue of the Americas, New York, New York 10011. (212) 645-4500. 1990.

EXPOSURE, RADIATION

See: RADIATION EXPOSURE

EXTINCT SPECIES

See also: ENDANGERED SPECIES

ABSTRACTING AND INDEXING SERVICES

Applied Ecology Abstracts Studies in Renewable Natural Resources. Information Retrieval Ltd., 1911 Jefferson Davis Highway, Arlington, Virginia 22202. 1975-. Monthly.

Biological Abstracts. BIOSIS, 2100 Arch St., Philadelphia, Pennsylvania 19103-1399. (215) 587-4800. 1927-.

Biological and Agricultural Index. H.W. Wilson Co., 950 University Ave., Bronx, New York 10452. (800) 367-6770. 1916-. Monthly.

Biology Digest. Data Courier, Plexus Pub Inc., 143 Old Marlton Pike, Medford, New Jersey 08055. 1974-. Monthly. Abstracts biology periodicals.

Ecological Abstracts. Geo Abstracts Ltd. Elsevier Applied Science, Crown House, Linton Rd., Barking, England IG 11 8JU. 1974-. Derived from over 600 leading ecological and environmental journals, plus books, conference proceedings, reports and theses.

Ecology Abstracts. Cambridge Scientific Abstracts, 5161 River Rd., Bethesda, Maryland 20816. (301) 961-6750. Monthly.

Environment Abstracts. Bowker A & I Publishing, 121 Chanlon Rd., New Providence, New Jersey 07974. (908) 464-6800. 1974-.

Environment Index. Environment Information Center, Index Research Department, 124 E. 39th St., New York, New York 10016. 1971-. Annual.

Environmental Information Connection–EIC. Planning Information Program, Dept. of Urban and Regional Planning, University of Illinois, 1003 West Nevada, Urbana, Illinois 61801. (217) 333-1369. Also available online.

Environmental Periodicals Bibliography. Environmental Studies Institute, International Academy at Santa Barbara, 800 Garden St., Suite D, Santa Barbara, California 93101. (805) 965-5010. Also available online.

General Science Index. H. W. Wilson Co., 950 University Ave., Bronx, New York 10452. 1978-. Monthly, also issued in annual cumulation. Cumulative subject index to English language periodicals in the subject fields of astronomy, botany, chemistry, earth science, environment and conservation, food and nutrition, genetics, mathematics, medicine and health, microbiology, oceanography, physics, physiology and zoology.

Index to Scientific Book Contents. Institute for Scientific Information, 3501 Market St., Philadelphia, Pennsylvania 19104. (800) 523-1857. 1985-. Annual. Gives contents of science books published.

Multimedia Index to Ecology. National Information Center for Educational Media, University of Southern California, Los Angeles, California 90007.

Pollution Abstracts. Cambridge Scientific Abstracts, 5161 River Rd., Bethesda, Maryland 20816. (301) 961-6750. Six/year. Indexes worldwide technical literature on environmental pollution. Covers air pollution, marine and freshwater pollution, sewage and wastewater treatment, waste management, toxicology and health, noise pollution, radiation, land pollution, and environmental policies, programs, legislation, and education. Also available online.

Science Citation Index. Institute for Scientific Information, 3501 Market St., Philadelphia, Pennsylvania 19104. 1961-.

BIBLIOGRAPHIES

Current Contents. Agriculture, Biology and Environmental Sciences. Institute for Scientific Information, 3501 Market St., Philadelphia, Pennsylvania 19104. (800) 523-1857. 1973-. Previous title: Current Contents. Agricultural, Food & Veterinary Sciences. Gives the table of contents of periodicals in the fields of agriculture, biology, environmental and related areas.

EPA Publications Bibliography. U.S. Environmental Protection Agency, Library Systems Branch, 401 M St., SW, Washington, District of Columbia 20460. (202) 260-2090. Quarterly.

DIRECTORIES

Gale Environmental Sourcebook. Karen Hill. Gale Research Co., 835 Penobscot Bldg., Detroit, Michigan

48226-4094. (313) 961-2242. Contacts, information sources, or general information on environmental topics.

ENCYCLOPEDIAS AND DICTIONARIES

The Encyclopedia of Animal Ecology. Peter D. Moore. Facts on File, Inc., 460 Park Ave. S., New York, New York 10016. (212) 683-2244. 1987.

Grzimek's Encyclopedia of Ecology. Bernhard Grzimek. Van Nostrand Reinhold, 115 5th Ave., New York, New York 10003. (212) 254-3232. 1976.

McGraw-Hill Encyclopedia of Environmental Science. Sybil P. Parker. McGraw-Hill Science & Engineering Books, 11 W. 19th St., New York, New York 10011. (212) 337-6010. 1980. Covers ecology, man's influence on nature, and environmental protection.

McGraw-Hill Encyclopedia of Science and Technology. McGraw-Hill, 1221 Avenue of the Americas, New York, New York 10020. (212) 512-2000 or (800) 262-4729. 1992. Seventh edition. Issued in multiple volumes including index. Includes all science and technology broad subject areas.

North American Reference Encyclopedia of Ecology and Pollution. William White. North American Pub. Co., 401 N. Broad St., Philadelphia, Pennsylvania 19108. (215) 238-5300. 1972.

Van Nostrand's Scientific Encyclopedia. Glenn D. Considine, ed. Van Nostrand Reinhold, 115 5th Ave., New York, New York 10003. (212) 254-3232. 1983. Sixth edition. Includes all broad subject areas in science.

GENERAL WORKS

Dying Planet; The Extinction of Species. Jon Erickson. Tab Books, PO Box 40, Blue Ridge Summit, Pennsylvania 17294-0850. (717) 794-2191. 1991.

Global Catastrophes in Earth History. Virgil L. Sharpton and Peter Douglas Ward. Geological Society of America, 3300 Penrose Pl., PO Box 9140, Boulder, Colorado 80301. (303) 447-2020. 1990. Covers Extinction (Biology), Cretaceous/Tertiary boundary and Volcanism.

The Great Dying. Kenneth J. Hsu. Harcourt Brace Jovanovich, Inc., 1250 6th Ave., San Diego, California 92101. (800) 346-8648. 1986. Deals with paleontology, extinction, and periodicity in geology.

Magill's Survey of Science. Life Science Series. Frank N. Magill, ed. Salem Press, PO Box 50062, Pasadena, California 91105. 1991. Six volumes. Contents: v.1. A-Central and peripheral nervous system functions; v.2. Central metabolism regulation - eukaryotic transcriptional control; v.3. Positive and negative eukaryotic transcriptional control - mammalian hormones; v.4. Hormones and behavior - muscular contraction; v.5. Muscular contraction and relaxation - sexual reproduction in plants; v.6. Reproductive behavior and mating - X inactivation and the Lyon hypothesis.

Nemesis: The Death-Star and Other Theories of Mass Extinction. Donald Goldsmith. Walker & Co., New York, New York 1985.

On Methuselah's Trail: Living Fossils and the Great Extinctions. Peter Douglas Ward. W. H. Freeman, 41 Madison Ave., New York, New York 10010. (212) 576-9400. 1992. Biological aspects of extinction.

A Stillness in the Pines: The Ecology of the Red-Cockaded Woodpecker. Robert W. McFarlane. Norton, 500 5th Ave., New York, New York 10110. (800) 223-2584 or (212) 354-5500. 1992. Tells the story of the decline of the red-cockaded woodpecker, a specialized inhabitant of mature Southeastern pine forests.

HANDBOOKS AND MANUALS

Collins Guide to the Rare Mammals of the World. John A. Burton and Vivian G. Burton. Collins, 77/85 Fulham Palace Rd., London, England W6 8JB. 071-493 7070. 1988. Includes all the mammal species which might be considered threatened.

Extinct Species of the World. Jean Christophe Balouet. Barron's, 200 Liberty St., New York, New York 10281. (212) 416-2700. 1990. Deals with extinction and nature conservation.

The Official World Wildlife Fund Guide to Endangered Species of North America. David W. Lowe, ed. Beacham Publishing, Inc., 2100 S. St. NW, Washington, District of Columbia 20008. (202) 234-0877. 1990. Two volumes. Guide to endangered plants and animals. Describes 540 endangered or threatened species including their habitat, behavior and, recovery. Includes: directories of the Offices of the U.S. Fish and Wildlife Service, Offices ofthe National Marine Fisheries Service, State Heritage Programs, Bureau of Land Management Offices, National Forest Service Offices, National Wildlife Refuges, Canadian agencies, and state offices.

ONLINE DATA BASES

BIOSIS Previews. BIOSIS, 2100 Arch St., Philadelphia, Pennsylvania 19103-1399. (215) 587-4800. Largest and most comprehensive database of research in the life sciences. Contains citations for nearly 9000 primary research journals, monographs, reviews, symposia, preliminary reports, semi-popular journals, selected institutional reports, government reports and research communications.

Cambridge Scientific Abstracts Life Science–CSAL. Cambridge Scientific Abstracts, 5161 River Rd., Bethesda, Maryland 20816. (301) 961-6750. Provides access to the following abstracting services: "Life Sciences Collection," "Aquatic Sciences and Fisheries Abstracts," "Oceanic Abstracts," and "Pollution Abstracts."

Current Research Information System–CRIS/USDA. U.S. Department of Agriculture, National Agricultural Library, 10301 Baltimore Blvd., 5th Floor, Beltsville, Maryland 20705-2351. (301) 504-5755. Looks at current research projects in agriculture and allied sciences covering the biological, physical, social and behavioral sciences related to agriculture.

Enviro/Energyline Abstracts Plus. R. R. Bowker Co., 121 Chanlon Rd., New Providence, New Jersey 07974. (908) 464-6800.

Environmental Periodicals Bibliography. National Information Services Corp., Ste. 6, Wyman Towers, 3100 St. Paul St., Baltimore, Maryland 21218. (410)243-0797. Online version of abstract of same name.

Monthly Catalog of United States Government Publications. U.S. G.P.O., Supt. of Docs., PO Box 371954, Pittsburgh, Pennsylvania 15250-7954. (202) 512-0000.

National Technical Information Service. U.S. Department of Commerce, National Technical Information Service, Office of Data Base Services, 5285 Port Royal Rd., Springfield, Virginia 22161. (703) 487-4807. Bibliographic database of government sponsored research and technical reports.

PressNet Environmental Reports. Chemical Information Systems, Inc., 7215 York Rd., Baltimore, Maryland 21212. (301) 321-8440.

SCISEARCH. Institute for Scientific Information, University City Science Center, 3501 Market St., Philadelphia, Pennsylvania 19104. (215) 386-0100.

STATISTICS SOURCES

Environmental Data Compendium. OECD Publications and Information Center, 2001 L St., N.W., Suite 700, Washington, District of Columbia 20036. (202) 785-6323. 1989.

Environmental Indicators. OECD Publications and Information Center, 2001 L St., N.W., Suite 700, Washington, District of Columbia 20036. (202) 785-6323. 1991.

Environmental Quality. Council on Environmental Quality. U.S. G.P.O., Washington, District of Columbia 20401. (202) 512-0000. Annual.

The State of the Environment. OECD Publications and Information Center, 2001 L St., N.W., Suite 700, Washington, District of Columbia 20036. (202) 785-6323. 1991.

TRADE ASSOCIATIONS AND PROFESSIONAL SOCIETIES

American Institute of Biological Sciences. 730 11th St., N.W., Washington, District of Columbia 20001-4521. (202) 628-1500.

EXTIRPATED SPECIES

See: ENDANGERED SPECIES

EXTRA HIGH VOLTAGE TRANSMISSION

See also: DISTRIBUTION LINES

ABSTRACTING AND INDEXING SERVICES

Environment Abstracts. Bowker A & I Publishing, 121 Chanlon Rd., New Providence, New Jersey 07974. (908) 464-6800. 1974-.

Environment Index. Environment Information Center, Index Research Department, 124 E. 39th St., New York, New York 10016. 1971-. Annual.

Environmental Information Connection–EIC. Planning Information Program, Dept. of Urban and Regional Planning, University of Illinois, 1003 West Nevada, Urbana, Illinois 61801. (217) 333-1369. Also available online.

Environmental Periodicals Bibliography. Environmental Studies Institute, International Academy at Santa Barbara, 800 Garden St., Suite D, Santa Barbara, California 93101. (805) 965-5010. Also available online.

Index to Scientific Book Contents. Institute for Scientific Information, 3501 Market St., Philadelphia, Pennsylvania 19104. (800) 523-1857. 1985-. Annual. Gives contents of science books published.

BIBLIOGRAPHIES

Directory of Published Proceedings. Interdok Corp., 173 Halstead Ave., Harrison, New York 10528. (914) 835-3506. 1990. Monthly. This is a listing of published proceedings including the series SEMTE (Science/Medicine/Engineering/Technology) and the series SSH (Social Science/Humanities).

EPA Publications Bibliography. U.S. Environmental Protection Agency, Library Systems Branch, 401 M St., SW, Washington, District of Columbia 20460. (202) 260-2090. Quarterly.

ENCYCLOPEDIAS AND DICTIONARIES

Encyclopedia of Physical Science and Technology. Robert A. Meyers, ed. Academic Press, c/o Harcourt Brace Jovanovich Inc., 6277 Sea Harbor Dr., Orlando, Florida 32887. (800) 346-8648. Dictionary of engineering, technology and physical sciences.

GENERAL WORKS

Extra High Voltage A.C. Transmission Engineering. John Wiley & Sons, Inc., 605 3rd Ave., New York, New York (212) 850-6000. 1986. High tension electric power distribution.

Visual Amenity Aspects of High Voltage Transmission. George A. Goulty. John Wiley & Sons, Inc., 605 3rd Ave., New York, New York (212) 850-6000. 1990. High tension electric power distribution, overhead electric lines, and location of poles and towers.

ONLINE DATA BASES

Enviro/Energyline Abstracts Plus. R. R. Bowker Co., 121 Chanlon Rd., New Providence, New Jersey 07974. (908) 464-6800.

Environmental Periodicals Bibliography. National Information Services Corp., Ste. 6, Wyman Towers, 3100 St. Paul St., Baltimore, Maryland 21218. (410)243-0797. Online version of abstract of same name.

Monthly Catalog of United States Government Publications. U.S. G.P.O., Supt. of Docs., PO Box 371954, Pittsburgh, Pennsylvania 15250-7954. (202) 512-0000.

National Technical Information Service. U.S. Department of Commerce, National Technical Information Service, Office of Data Base Services, 5285 Port Royal Rd., Springfield, Virginia 22161. (703) 487-4807. Bibliographic database of government sponsored research and technical reports.

EXTRATERRESTRIAL DISPOSAL

ABSTRACTING AND INDEXING SERVICES

Environment Abstracts. Bowker A & I Publishing, 121 Chanlon Rd., New Providence, New Jersey 07974. (908) 464-6800. 1974-.

Environment Index. Environment Information Center, Index Research Department, 124 E. 39th St., New York, New York 10016. 1971-. Annual.

Environmental Information Connection–EIC. Planning Information Program, Dept. of Urban and Regional Planning, University of Illinois, 1003 West Nevada, Urbana, Illinois 61801. (217) 333-1369. Also available online.

Environmental Periodicals Bibliography. Environmental Studies Institute, International Academy at Santa Barbara, 800 Garden St., Suite D, Santa Barbara, California 93101. (805) 965-5010. Also available online.

General Science Index. H. W. Wilson Co., 950 University Ave., Bronx, New York 10452. 1978-. Monthly, also issued in annual cumulation. Cumulative subject index to English language periodicals in the subject fields of astronomy, botany, chemistry, earth science, environment and conservation, food and nutrition, genetics, mathematics, medicine and health, microbiology, oceanography, physics, physiology and zoology.

Index to Scientific Book Contents. Institute for Scientific Information, 3501 Market St., Philadelphia, Pennsylvania 19104. (800) 523-1857. 1985-. Annual. Gives contents of science books published.

BIBLIOGRAPHIES

Directory of Published Proceedings. Interdok Corp., 173 Halstead Ave., Harrison, New York 10528. (914) 835-3506. 1990. Monthly. This is a listing of published proceedings including the series SEMTE (Science/Medicine/Engineering/Technology) and the series SSH (Social Science/Humanities).

EPA Publications Bibliography. U.S. Environmental Protection Agency, Library Systems Branch, 401 M St., SW, Washington, District of Columbia 20460. (202) 260-2090. Quarterly.

ENCYCLOPEDIAS AND DICTIONARIES

McGraw-Hill Encyclopedia of Environmental Science. Sybil P. Parker. McGraw-Hill Science & Engineering Books, 11 W. 19th St., New York, New York 10011.

(212) 337-6010. 1980. Covers ecology, man's influence on nature, and environmental protection.

Van Nostrand's Scientific Encyclopedia. Glenn D. Considine, ed. Van Nostrand Reinhold, 115 5th Ave., New York, New York 10003. (212) 254-3232. 1983. Sixth edition. Includes all broad subject areas in science.

HANDBOOKS AND MANUALS

Handbook of Geophysics and the Space Environment. Adolph S. Jursa, ed. Air Force Geophysics Laboratory, Air Force Systems Command, United States Air Force, c/o National Technical Information Service, 5285 Port Royal Rd., Springfield, Virginia 22161. (703) 487-4650. 1985. Two volumes. Broad subject areas covered are space, atmosphere, and terrestrial environment. Includes topics such as solar radiation, sunspots, solar wind, geomagnetic fields, radiation belts, cosmic radiation, atmospheric gases, etc.

ONLINE DATA BASES

Enviro/Energyline Abstracts Plus. R. R. Bowker Co., 121 Chanlon Rd., New Providence, New Jersey 07974. (908) 464-6800.

Environmental Periodicals Bibliography. National Information Services Corp., Ste. 6, Wyman Towers, 3100 St. Paul St., Baltimore, Maryland 21218. (410)243-0797. Online version of abstract of same name.

Monthly Catalog of United States Government Publications. U.S. G.P.O., Supt. of Docs., PO Box 371954, Pittsburgh, Pennsylvania 15250-7954. (202) 512-0000.

National Technical Information Service. U.S. Department of Commerce, National Technical Information Service, Office of Data Base Services, 5285 Port Royal Rd., Springfield, Virginia 22161. (703) 487-4807. Bibliographic database of government sponsored research and technical reports.

EXUVIA

See: WATER POLLUTION

F

FABRIC DUST COLLECTORS

See: DUST COLLECTORS

FABRIC FILTERS

See: DUST COLLECTORS

FACIATION

See: ECOSYSTEMS

FACTORY AND TRADE WASTES

See also: HAZARDOUS WASTES

ABSTRACTING AND INDEXING SERVICES

Applied Science and Technology Index. H.W. Wilson Co., 950 University Ave., Bronx, New York 10452. (800) 367-6770. Formerly Industrial Arts Index.

Aqualine Abstracts. Water Research Centre. c/o Pergamon Microforms International, Inc., Fairview Park, Elmsford, New York 10523. (914) 592-7720. 1927-. Contains some 8,000 records annually on water and wastewater technology. Covers all aspects of water, wastewater, associated engineering services and the aquatic environment. Over 600 periodicals, as well as books, reports and conference proceedings and other publications from water related institutions worldwide are scanned. Also available online.

Biological and Agricultural Index. H.W. Wilson Co., 950 University Ave., Bronx, New York 10452. (800) 367-6770. 1916-. Monthly.

Engineering Index. The Engineering Index Inc., 345 E. 47th St., New York, New York 10017. 1962-.

Environment Abstracts. Bowker A & I Publishing, 121 Chanlon Rd., New Providence, New Jersey 07974. (908) 464-6800. 1974-.

Environment Index. Environment Information Center, Index Research Department, 124 E. 39th St., New York, New York 10016. 1971-. Annual.

Environmental Information Connection–EIC. Planning Information Program, Dept. of Urban and Regional Planning, University of Illinois, 1003 West Nevada,

Urbana, Illinois 61801. (217) 333-1369. Also available online.

Environmental Periodicals Bibliography. Environmental Studies Institute, International Academy at Santa Barbara, 800 Garden St., Suite D, Santa Barbara, California 93101. (805) 965-5010. Also available online.

Index to Scientific Book Contents. Institute for Scientific Information, 3501 Market St., Philadelphia, Pennsylvania 19104. (800) 523-1857. 1985-. Annual. Gives contents of science books published.

BIBLIOGRAPHIES

Current Contents. Agriculture, Biology and Environmental Sciences. Institute for Scientific Information, 3501 Market St., Philadelphia, Pennsylvania 19104. (800) 523-1857. 1973-. Previous title: Current Contents. Agricultural, Food & Veterinary Sciences. Gives the table of contents of periodicals in the fields of agriculture, biology, environmental and related areas.

Directory of Published Proceedings. Interdok Corp., 173 Halstead Ave., Harrison, New York 10528. (914) 835-3506. 1990. Monthly. This is a listing of published proceedings including the series SEMTE (Science/Medicine/Engineering/Technology) and the series SSH (Social Science/Humanities).

EPA Publications Bibliography. U.S. Environmental Protection Agency, Library Systems Branch, 401 M St., SW, Washington, District of Columbia 20460. (202) 260-2090. Quarterly.

ENCYCLOPEDIAS AND DICTIONARIES

Dictionary of Dangerous Pollutants, Ecology, and Environment. David F. Tver. Industrial Press, 200 Madison Ave., New York, New York 10016. (212) 889-6330. 1981.

Dictionary of Environmental Engineering and Related Sciences: English-Spanish, Spanish-English. Jose T. Villate. Ediciones Universal, 3090 SW 8th St., Miami, Florida 33135. (305) 642-3355. 1979.

Encyclopedia of Environmental Control Technology. Paul N. Cheremisinoff, ed. Gulf Publishing Co., Book Division, PO Box 2608, Houston, Texas 77252. (713) 529-4301 or (800) 231-6275. 1992. Volume 1: Thermal Treatment of Hazardous Wastes; volume 2: Air Pollution Control; volume 3: Wastewater Treatment Technology; volume 4: Hazardous Waste Containment and Treatment; volumes 5 through 8 in progress. Provides in-depth coverage of specialized topics related to environmental and industrial pollution control problems and state-of-the-art information on technology and research as well as projections of future trends in the field.

Encyclopedia of Environmental Science and Engineering. J.R. Pfafflin. Gordon and Breach Science Publishers, Inc., 270 8th Ave., New York, New York 10011. (212) 206-8900. 1992.

McGraw-Hill Encyclopedia of Environmental Science. Sybil P. Parker. McGraw-Hill Science & Engineering Books, 11 W. 19th St., New York, New York 10011. (212) 337-6010. 1980. Covers ecology, man's influence on nature, and environmental protection.

McGraw-Hill Encyclopedia of Science and Technology. McGraw-Hill, 1221 Avenue of the Americas, New York, New York 10020. (212) 512-2000 or (800) 262-4729. 1992. Seventh edition. Issued in multiple volumes including index. Includes all science and technology broad subject areas.

GENERAL WORKS

A Citizen's Guide to Promoting Toxic Waste Reduction. Lauren Kenworthy and Eric Schaeffer. INFORM, 381 Park Ave. S., New York, New York 10016. (212) 689-4040. 1990. The how-to manual describes source reduction and its benefits, five strategies plants can use to reduce their hazardous wastes at the source, a step-by-step process for gathering background facts, and interviewing company representatives and analyzing data.

Hazardous and Industrial Wastes, 1990. Joseph P. Martin, et al., eds. Technomic Publishing Co., 851 Holland Ave., Box 3535, Lancaster, Pennsylvania 17604. (717) 291-5609. 1990. Proceedings of the 22nd Mid-Atlantic Industrial Waste Conference, June 24-27, 1990, Drexel University, Philadelphia, PA. Fifty-one new reports on developments in industrial and hazardous waste management, technology and regulation were presented.

Hazardous Waste from Small Quantity Generators. Seymour I. Schwartz, et al. Island Press, 1718 Connecticut Ave. N.W., Suite 300, Washington, District of Columbia 20009. (202) 232-7933. 1990. Examines the role small businesses play in degrading the environment. Includes information on the extent and seriousness of the problem, regulations; and liability issues; national, state, and local programs for SQ Gas in California, analysis of methods for managing SQG waste; policy options for promoting legal methods; and discouraging illegal methods.

Hazardous Waste Minimization Audit Studies on the Paint Manufacturing Industry. Jacobs Engineering Group, Inc., S. Lake Ave., Pasadena, California 91171. (818)449-2171. 1987. Factory and trade wastes and disposal in the paint industry.

Industrial Waste Gases: Utilization and Minimization. RCG/Hagler Bailly Inc. Technomic Publishing Co., 851 New Holland Ave., Box 3535, Lancaster, Pennsylvania 17604. (717) 291-5609. 1990. Also released under title Industrial Waste Gas Management. Deals with factory and trade waste and the effluents that are released into the atmosphere.

Madison Conference of Applied Research & Practice on Municipal & Industrial Waste. Dept. of Engineering Professional Development, University of Wisconsin-Madison, Madison, Wisconsin 53706. 1990. Annual. Sewage disposal, factory and trade waste, soil liners, ground water clean up, landfill leachate treatment,

groundwater monitary systems, evaluation of groundwater and soil gas remedial action; leachate generation estimates and landfills.

Preventing Pollution Through Technical Assistance: One State's Experience. Mark H. Dorfman, et al. INFORM Inc., 381 Park Ave. S., New York, New York 10016. (212) 689-4040. 1990. Examines the state of North Carolina's voluntary program aimed at assisting the industry in pollution prevention. It also includes a glossary, a bibliography of information sources and helpful statistical tables of data collected.

Principles of Water Quality Management. William Wesley Eckenfelder. CBI, Boston, Massachusetts 1980.

Saline Water Processing: Desalination and Treatment of Seawater, Brackish Water, and Industrial Waste Water. Hans-Gunter Heitmann, ed. VCH Publishers, 303 NW 12th Ave., Deerfield Beach, Florida 33442-1788. (305) 428-5566. 1990. Desalination and treatment of seawater, brackish water, and industrial waste water.

Serious Reduction of Hazardous Waste: Summary. Congress of the U.S., c/o U.S. Government Printing Office, Office of Technology Assessment, N. Capitol & H Sts. NW, Washington, District of Columbia 20401. (202) 512-0000. 1986. Deals with waste reduction from factories and air pollution control.

HANDBOOKS AND MANUALS

Guide to the Management of Hazardous Waste: A Handbook for the Businessman and the Concerned Citizen. J. William Haun. Fulcrum Publishing, 350 Indiana St., Ste. 350, Golden, Colorado 80401. (303) 277-1623. 1991. Fact book on hazardous waste management, including factory and trade waste, and hazardous waste law and legislation in the United States.

Industrial and Hazardous Waste Treatment. Nelson Leonard Nemerow and Avijit Dasgupta. Van Nostrand Reinhold, 115 5th Ave., New York, New York 10003. (212) 254-3232. 1991. Factory and trade waste, and hazardous waste purification.

Methods for Toxicity Tests of Single Substances and Liquid Complex Wastes With Marine Unicellular Algae. Gerald E. Walsh. Environmental Protection Agency, U.S. Environmental Research Laboratory, 401 M St. SW, Washington, District of Columbia 20460. (202) 260-2090. 1988. Deals with the impact of factory and trade waste on the marine environment, especially on algae and other biological forms.

Treatability Manual. U.S. Environmental Protection Agency, Office of Research and Development, 401 M St., SW, Washington, District of Columbia 20460. (202) 260-2090. 1983-. V.1 Treatability data. v.2 Change 2. Industrial Descriptions. v.3 Change 2. Technology for Control/removal of pollutants. v.4. Cost estimating. v.5. Change 2 summary.

ONLINE DATA BASES

Computerized Engineering Index–COMPENDEX. Engineering Information Inc., 345 E. 47th St., New York, New York 10017. (212) 705-7600.

Enviro/Energyline Abstracts Plus. R. R. Bowker Co., 121 Chanlon Rd., New Providence, New Jersey 07974. (908) 464-6800.

Environmental Periodicals Bibliography. National Information Services Corp., Ste. 6, Wyman Towers, 3100 St. Paul St., Baltimore, Maryland 21218. (410)243-0797. Online version of abstract of same name.

Monthly Catalog of United States Government Publications. U.S. G.P.O., Supt. of Docs., PO Box 371954, Pittsburgh, Pennsylvania 15250-7954. (202) 512-0000.

National Technical Information Service. U.S. Department of Commerce, National Technical Information Service, Office of Data Base Services, 5285 Port Royal Rd., Springfield, Virginia 22161. (703) 487-4807. Bibliographic database of government sponsored research and technical reports.

SCISEARCH. Institute for Scientific Information, University City Science Center, 3501 Market St., Philadelphia, Pennsylvania 19104. (215) 386-0100.

STATISTICS SOURCES

Tracking Toxic Substances at Industrial Facilities: Engineering Mass Balance Versus Materials Accounting. National Research Council–Committee to Evaluate Mass Balance Information for Facilities Handling Toxic Substances. National Academy Press, 2101 Constitution Ave., NW, Washington, District of Columbia 20418. (202) 334-3343. 1990. Covers measurement of factory and trade waste and hazardous substances.

World Resources. World Resources Institute. 1709 New York Ave., N.W., Washington, District of Columbia 20006. (202) 638-6300. Annual. Statistical and textual analysis of world's natural resources and the effects of growth-caused environmental pollution.

FALLOW

See: AGRICULTURE

FAMINE

See: DISASTERS

FARM BUILDING–SAFETY MEASURES

See also: LIVESTOCK HOUSING

ABSTRACTING AND INDEXING SERVICES

Agricultural Engineering Abstracts. C. A. B. International, 845 North Park Ave., Tucson, Arizona 85719. (602) 621-7897 or (800) 528-4841. 1976-. Monthly. Informs about significant research developments in agricultural engineering and instrumentation. Some of the topics scanned for the abstracts include mechanical power, crop production, crop harvesting and threshing, crop processing and storage, aquaculture, land improvement, protected cultivation, handling and transport, and farm buildings and equipment.

Agrindex. AGRIS Coordinating Center, Via delle Terme di Caracalla, Rome, Italy I-00100. 61 0181-FA01. 1975-.

Applied Ecology Abstracts Studies in Renewable Natural Resources. Information Retrieval Ltd., 1911 Jefferson Davis Highway, Arlington, Virginia 22202. 1975-. Monthly.

Applied Science and Technology Index. H.W. Wilson Co., 950 University Ave., Bronx, New York 10452. (800) 367-6770. Formerly Industrial Arts Index.

Biological and Agricultural Index. H.W. Wilson Co., 950 University Ave., Bronx, New York 10452. (800) 367-6770. 1916-. Monthly.

Environment Abstracts. Bowker A & I Publishing, 121 Chanlon Rd., New Providence, New Jersey 07974. (908) 464-6800. 1974-.

Environment Index. Environment Information Center, Index Research Department, 124 E. 39th St., New York, New York 10016. 1971-. Annual.

Environmental Information Connection–EIC. Planning Information Program, Dept. of Urban and Regional Planning, University of Illinois, 1003 West Nevada, Urbana, Illinois 61801. (217) 333-1369. Also available online.

Environmental Periodicals Bibliography. Environmental Studies Institute, International Academy at Santa Barbara, 800 Garden St., Suite D, Santa Barbara, California 93101. (805) 965-5010. Also available online.

General Science Index. H. W. Wilson Co., 950 University Ave., Bronx, New York 10452. 1978-. Monthly, also issued in annual cumulation. Cumulative subject index to English language periodicals in the subject fields of astronomy, botany, chemistry, earth science, environment and conservation, food and nutrition, genetics, mathematics, medicine and health, microbiology, oceanography, physics, physiology and zoology.

Index to Scientific Book Contents. Institute for Scientific Information, 3501 Market St., Philadelphia, Pennsylvania 19104. (800) 523-1857. 1985-. Annual. Gives contents of science books published.

Multimedia Index to Ecology. National Information Center for Educational Media, University of Southern California, Los Angeles, California 90007.

BIBLIOGRAPHIES

Current Contents. Agriculture, Biology and Environmental Sciences. Institute for Scientific Information, 3501 Market St., Philadelphia, Pennsylvania 19104. (800) 523-1857. 1973-. Previous title: Current Contents. Agricultural, Food & Veterinary Sciences. Gives the table of contents of periodicals in the fields of agriculture, biology, environmental and related areas.

EPA Publications Bibliography. U.S. Environmental Protection Agency, Library Systems Branch, 401 M St., SW, Washington, District of Columbia 20460. (202) 260-2090. Quarterly.

ENCYCLOPEDIAS AND DICTIONARIES

Dictionary of Environmental Engineering and Related Sciences: English-Spanish, Spanish-English. Jose T. Villate. Ediciones Universal, 3090 SW 8th St., Miami, Florida 33135. (305) 642-3355. 1979.

Encyclopedia of Environmental Science and Engineering. J.R. Pfafflin. Gordon and Breach Science Publishers, Inc., 270 8th Ave., New York, New York 10011. (212) 206-8900. 1992.

GENERAL WORKS

Environmental and Functional Engineering of Agricultural Buildings. Henry J. Barre. Van Nostrand Reinhold, 115 5th Ave., New York, New York 10003. (212) 254-3232. 1988.

Environmental Control for Agricultural Buildings. Merle L. Esmay. AVI Pub. Co., 250 Post Rd. E., PO Box 831, Westport, Connecticut 06881. 1986.

Farm Building Series Circular. Michigan State University, Cooperative Extension Service, East Lansing, Michigan 48824. Irregular.

ONLINE DATA BASES

Current Research Information System–CRIS/USDA. U.S. Department of Agriculture, National Agricultural Library, 10301 Baltimore Blvd., 5th Floor, Beltsville, Maryland 20705-2351. (301) 504-5755. Looks at current research projects in agriculture and allied sciences covering the biological, physical, social and behavioral sciences related to agriculture.

Enviro/Energyline Abstracts Plus. R. R. Bowker Co., 121 Chanlon Rd., New Providence, New Jersey 07974. (908) 464-6800.

Environmental Periodicals Bibliography. National Information Services Corp., Ste. 6, Wyman Towers, 3100 St. Paul St., Baltimore, Maryland 21218. (410)243-0797. Online version of abstract of same name.

Monthly Catalog of United States Government Publications. U.S. G.P.O., Supt. of Docs., PO Box 371954, Pittsburgh, Pennsylvania 15250-7954. (202) 512-0000.

National Technical Information Service. U.S. Department of Commerce, National Technical Information Service, Office of Data Base Services, 5285 Port Royal Rd., Springfield, Virginia 22161. (703) 487-4807. Bibliographic database of government sponsored research and technical reports.

PressNet Environmental Reports. Chemical Information Systems, Inc., 7215 York Rd., Baltimore, Maryland 21212. (301) 321-8440.

SCISEARCH. Institute for Scientific Information, University City Science Center, 3501 Market St., Philadelphia, Pennsylvania 19104. (215) 386-0100.

PERIODICALS AND NEWSLETTERS

Plan Sheet M. University of Minnesota, Agricultural Extension Service, 1444 Cleveland Ave. N., St. Paul, Minnesota 55108. Irregular.

TRADE ASSOCIATIONS AND PROFESSIONAL SOCIETIES

American Institute of Biological Sciences. 730 11th St., N.W., Washington, District of Columbia 20001-4521. (202) 628-1500.

American Society of Agricultural Engineers. 2950 Niles Rd., St Joseph, Michigan 49085. (616) 429-0300.

FARM MANURE

See: FERTILIZERS

FARMING

See also: AGRICULTURE; CROPS; ORGANIC GARDENING AND FARMING

GENERAL WORKS

Farming in Nature's Image. Judith A. Soule. Island Press, 1718 Connecticut Ave. N.W., Suite 300, Washington, District of Columbia 20009. (202) 232-7933. 1992. Gives a detailed look into the pioneering work of the Land Institute, the leading educational and research organization for sustainable agriculture.

Plowman's Folly. Edward H. Faulkner. Island Press, 1718 Connecticut Ave. N.W., Suite 300, Washington, District of Columbia 20009. (202) 232-7933. 1987.

The Violence of Green Revolution. Vandana Shiva. Humanities Pr. Intl., 171 1st Ave., Atlantic Highlands, New Jersey 07716-1289. (201) 872-1441; (800) 221-3845. 1991.

FARMLAND

ABSTRACTING AND INDEXING SERVICES

Agrindex. AGRIS Coordinating Center, Via delle Terme di Caracalla, Rome, Italy I-00100. 61 0181-FA01. 1975-.

Biological and Agricultural Index. H.W. Wilson Co., 950 University Ave., Bronx, New York 10452. (800) 367-6770. 1916-. Monthly.

Environment Abstracts. Bowker A & I Publishing, 121 Chanlon Rd., New Providence, New Jersey 07974. (908) 464-6800. 1974-.

Environment Index. Environment Information Center, Index Research Department, 124 E. 39th St., New York, New York 10016. 1971-. Annual.

Environmental Information Connection–EIC. Planning Information Program, Dept. of Urban and Regional Planning, University of Illinois, 1003 West Nevada, Urbana, Illinois 61801. (217) 333-1369. Also available online.

Environmental Periodicals Bibliography. Environmental Studies Institute, International Academy at Santa Barbara, 800 Garden St., Suite D, Santa Barbara, California 93101. (805) 965-5010. Also available online.

Field Crop Abstracts. C. A. B. International, 845 North Park Ave., Tucson, Arizona 85719. (602) 621-7897 or (800) 528-4841. 1948-. Monthly. Covers literature on agronomy, field production, crop botany and physiology of all annual field crops, both temperate and tropical.

General Science Index. H. W. Wilson Co., 950 University Ave., Bronx, New York 10452. 1978-. Monthly, also issued in annual cumulation. Cumulative subject index to English language periodicals in the subject fields of astronomy, botany, chemistry, earth science, environment and conservation, food and nutrition, genetics, mathematics, medicine and health, microbiology, oceanography, physics, physiology and zoology.

Geographical Abstracts. London School of Economics, Dept. of Geography, Regency House, 34 Duke St., London, England 1966-. Continued by Geo Abstracts issued in 6 parts: Pt. A. Landforms and the quaternary; Pt. B. Biogeography and Climatology; Pt. C. Economic geography; Pt. D. Social geography and cartography; Pt. E. Sedimentology; Pt. F. Regional and community planning.

Science Citation Index. Institute for Scientific Information, 3501 Market St., Philadelphia, Pennsylvania 19104. 1961-.

BIBLIOGRAPHIES

Current Contents. Agriculture, Biology and Environmental Sciences. Institute for Scientific Information, 3501 Market St., Philadelphia, Pennsylvania 19104. (800) 523-1857. 1973-. Previous title: Current Contents. Agricultural, Food & Veterinary Sciences. Gives the table of contents of periodicals in the fields of agriculture, biology, environmental and related areas.

EPA Publications Bibliography. U.S. Environmental Protection Agency, Library Systems Branch, 401 M St., SW, Washington, District of Columbia 20460. (202) 260-2090. Quarterly.

ENCYCLOPEDIAS AND DICTIONARIES

The Agricultural Handbook: A Guide to Terminology. Martin Whitley, et al. BSP Professional Books, 3 Cambridge Center, Suite 208, Cambridge, Massachusetts 02142. 1988. Provides an introductory reference source of definitions and explanations for agricultural terms. All areas of agriculture are covered including animal and crop production, farm management, policy and institutions.

McGraw-Hill Encyclopedia of Science and Technology. McGraw-Hill, 1221 Avenue of the Americas, New York, New York 10020. (212) 512-2000 or (800) 262-4729. 1992. Seventh edition. Issued in multiple volumes including index. Includes all science and technology broad subject areas.

Van Nostrand's Scientific Encyclopedia. Glenn D. Considine, ed. Van Nostrand Reinhold, 115 5th Ave., New York, New York 10003. (212) 254-3232. 1983. Sixth edition. Includes all broad subject areas in science.

GENERAL WORKS

Farming on the Edge: Saving Family Farms in Marin County, California. John Hart. University of California Press, 2120 Berkeley Way, Berkeley, California 94720. (415) 642-4262; (800) 822-6657. 1991. Case study in successful land-use planning.

Farms of Tomorrow. Trauger Groh. Bio-Dynamic Farming and Gardening Association, PO Box 550, Kimberton, Pennsylvania 19442. (215) 935-7797. 1990. Describes a new approach to farming called community supported agriculture (CSA). It is built upon the solid foundation of organic and biodynamic cultivation, but it focuses on the social and economic conditions that make farming possible.

Grass Productivity. A. Voisin. Island Press, 1718 Connecticut Ave. N.W., Suite 300, Washington, District of Columbia 20009. (202) 232-7933. 1988. Textbook of scientific information concerning every aspect of management "where the cow and the grass meet." Voisin's "rational grazing" method maximizes productivity in both grass and cattle operations.

Plowman's Folly. Edward H. Faulkner. Island Press, 1718 Connecticut Ave. N.W., Suite 300, Washington, District of Columbia 20009. (202) 232-7933. 1987.

UK Pesticides for Farmers and Growers. H. Kidd and D. Hartley, eds. Royal Society of Chemistry, c/o CRC Press, 2000 Corporate Blvd. N.W., Boca Raton, Florida 33431-9868. (800) 272-7737. 1987. Practical guide to pesticides designed specifically to meet the needs of farmers and growers.

The Violence of Green Revolution. Vandana Shiva. Humanities Pr. Intl., 171 1st Ave., Atlantic Highlands, New Jersey 07716-1289. (201) 872-1441; (800) 221-3845. 1991.

HANDBOOKS AND MANUALS

The Agricultural Notebook. Primrose McConnell; R. J. Halley, ed. Butterworth-Heinemann, 80 Montvale Ave., Stoneham, Massachusetts 02180. (617) 438-8464 or (800) 366-2665. 1982. Seventeenth edition. Includes data on the business of farming. Topics discussed include soils, drainage, crop physiology, crop nutrition, arable crops, grassland, trees on the farm, weed control, diseases of crops, pests of crops, grain preservation and storage, animal production, farm equipment, farm management, agricultural law, health and safety, and agricultural computers.

ONLINE DATA BASES

Cambridge Scientific Abstracts Life Science–CSAL. Cambridge Scientific Abstracts, 5161 River Rd., Bethesda, Maryland 20816. (301) 961-6750. Provides access to the following abstracting services: "Life Sciences Collection," "Aquatic Sciences and Fisheries Abstracts," "Oceanic Abstracts," and "Pollution Abstracts."

Current Research Information System–CRIS/USDA. U.S. Department of Agriculture, National Agricultural Library, 10301 Baltimore Blvd., 5th Floor, Beltsville, Maryland 20705-2351. (301) 504-5755. Looks at current research projects in agriculture and allied sciences covering the biological, physical, social and behavioral sciences related to agriculture.

Enviro/Energyline Abstracts Plus. R. R. Bowker Co., 121 Chanlon Rd., New Providence, New Jersey 07974. (908) 464-6800.

Environmental Periodicals Bibliography. National Information Services Corp., Ste. 6, Wyman Towers, 3100 St. Paul St., Baltimore, Maryland 21218. (410)243-0797. Online version of abstract of same name.

SCISEARCH. Institute for Scientific Information, University City Science Center, 3501 Market St., Philadelphia, Pennsylvania 19104. (215) 386-0100.

PERIODICALS AND NEWSLETTERS

Farmland. American Farmland Trust, 1920 N St., NW, Suite 400, Washington, District of Columbia 20036. (202) 659-5170. Quarterly. Voluntary land protection programs to protect farmland from conversion pressures, soil erosion, and other environmental impacts.

STATISTICS SOURCES

World Resources. World Resources Institute. 1709 New York Ave., N.W., Washington, District of Columbia

20006. (202) 638-6300. Annual. Statistical and textual analysis of world's natural resources and the effects of growth-caused environmental pollution.

TRADE ASSOCIATIONS AND PROFESSIONAL SOCIETIES

American Farmland Trust. 1920 N St., N.W., Suite 400, Washington, District of Columbia 20036. (202) 659-5170.

American Institute of Biological Sciences. 730 11th St., N.W., Washington, District of Columbia 20001-4521. (202) 628-1500.

Farmland Industries. 3315 N. Oak Trafficway, P.O. Box 7305, Kansas City, Missouri 64116. (816) 459-6000.

FAST BREEDER REACTORS

See: REACTORS

FATE

See: ENVIRONMENTAL FATE

FATTY ACIDS

ABSTRACTING AND INDEXING SERVICES

Biological Abstracts. BIOSIS, 2100 Arch St., Philadelphia, Pennsylvania 19103-1399. (215) 587-4800. 1927-.

Biotechnology Research Abstracts. Cambridge Scientific Abstracts, 5161 River Rd., Bethesda, Maryland 20816. (301) 961-6750. Monthly. Includes such broad areas as genetic intervention, biochemical genetics, and microbiological techniques.

Chemical Abstracts. Chemical Abstracts Service, 2540 Olentangy River Rd., PO Box 3012, Columbus, Ohio 43210. (800) 848-6533. 1907-.

Food Science and Technology Abstracts. International Food Information Service, c/o National Food Laboratory, 6363 Clark Ave., Dublin, California 94568. (800) 336-3782. 1969-.

General Science Index. H. W. Wilson Co., 950 University Ave., Bronx, New York 10452. 1978-. Monthly, also issued in annual cumulation. Cumulative subject index to English language periodicals in the subject fields of astronomy, botany, chemistry, earth science, environment and conservation, food and nutrition, genetics, mathematics, medicine and health, microbiology, oceanography, physics, physiology and zoology.

Microbiology Abstracts. Section A. Industrial and Applied Microbiology. Cambridge Scientific Abstracts, 5161 River Rd., Bethesda, Maryland 20816. (301) 961-6750. 1972-.

Pollution Abstracts. Cambridge Scientific Abstracts, 5161 River Rd., Bethesda, Maryland 20816. (301) 961-6750. Six/year. Indexes worldwide technical literature on environmental pollution. Covers air pollution, marine and freshwater pollution, sewage and wastewater treatment, waste management, toxicology and health, noise pollution, radiation, land pollution, and environmental poli-

cies, programs, legislation, and education. Also available online.

Science Citation Index. Institute for Scientific Information, 3501 Market St., Philadelphia, Pennsylvania 19104. 1961-.

BIBLIOGRAPHIES

Fish Oil: Role of Omega-3S in Health and Nutrition: January 1979-December 1990. Deborah Hanfman. National Agricultural Library, 10301 Baltimore Blvd., Beltsville, Maryland 20705-2351. (301) 504-5755. 1991. Health aspects of fish oils in human nutrition.

Fish Oils: January 1989 through July 1990: 653 Citations. Jacqueline Van De Kamp. U.S. Department of Health and Human Services, 200 Independence Ave. SW, Washington, District of Columbia 20201. (202) 619-0257. 1990. Therapeutic use of fatty acids and fish oils.

ENCYCLOPEDIAS AND DICTIONARIES

Encyclopedia of Chemical Processing and Design. John J. Mcketta and W. A. Cunningham. Marcel Dekker, Inc., 270 Madison Ave., New York, New York 10016. (212) 696-9000; (800) 228-1160. 1992. Thirty-eight volumes.

Encyclopedia of Human Biology. Renato Dulbecco, ed. Academic Press, c/o Harcourt Brace Jovanovich Inc., 6277 Sea Harbor Dr., Orlando, Florida 32887. (800) 346-8648. 1991. Eight volumes.

Kirk-Othmer Encyclopedia of Chemical Technology. J. I. Kroschwitz, ed. John Wiley & Sons, Inc., 605 3rd Ave., New York, New York 10158-0012. (212) 850-6000. 1992-. All articles in the new edition have been rewritten and updated adding new subjects such as biotechnology, computer topics, analytical techniques and instrumentation, environmental concerns, fuels and energy, inorganic and solid state chemistry; composite materials and material science in general, and pharmaceuticals. Also available online.

McGraw-Hill Encyclopedia of Science and Technology. McGraw-Hill, 1221 Avenue of the Americas, New York, New York 10020. (212) 512-2000 or (800) 262-4729. 1992. Seventh edition. Issued in multiple volumes including index. Includes all science and technology broad subject areas.

The Nutrition and Health Encyclopedia. David F. Tver and Percy Russell. Van Nostrand Reinhold, 115 5th Ave., New York, New York 10003. (212) 254-3232. 1989.

Van Nostrand's Scientific Encyclopedia. Glenn D. Considine, ed. Van Nostrand Reinhold, 115 5th Ave., New York, New York 10003. (212) 254-3232. 1983. Sixth edition. Includes all broad subject areas in science.

GENERAL WORKS

Magill's Survey of Science. Life Science Series. Frank N. Magill, ed. Salem Press, PO Box 50062, Pasadena, California 91105. 1991. Six volumes. Contents: v.1. A-Central and peripheral nervous system functions; v.2. Central metabolism regulation - eukaryotic transcriptional control; v.3. Positive and negative eukaryotic transcriptional control - mammalian hormones; v.4. Hormones and behavior - muscular contraction; v.5. Muscular contraction and relaxation - sexual reproduction in plants; v.6. Reproductive behavior and mating - X inactivation and the Lyon hypothesis.

HANDBOOKS AND MANUALS

FDA Food Additives Analytical Manual. C. Warner, et al., eds. Association of Official Analytical Chemists, 2200 Wilson Blvd., Suite 400-P, Arlington, Virginia 22201-3301. (703) 522-3032. 1983-1987. 2 vols. Provides methodology for determining compliance with food additive regulations. Contains analytical methods that have been evaluated by the FDA or found to operate satisfactorily in at least two laboratories.

Handbook of Toxicology. W. Thomas Shier and Dietrich Mebs. Marcel Dekker, Inc., 270 Madison Ave., New York, New York 10016. (212) 696-9000; (800) 228-1160. 1990. Covers most toxins for which sufficient research has been done to clearly establish the identity and characteristics of the toxin.

ONLINE DATA BASES

BIOSIS Previews. BIOSIS, 2100 Arch St., Philadelphia, Pennsylvania 19103-1399. (215) 587-4800. Largest and most comprehensive database of research in the life sciences. Contains citations for nearly 9000 primary research journals, monographs, reviews, symposia, preliminary reports, semi-popular journals, selected institutional reports, government reports and research communications.

Chemical Abstracts-CA. Chemical Abstracts Service, 2540 Olentangy River Rd., P.O. Box 3012, Columbus, Ohio 43210. (800) 848-6533 or (614) 421-3600. Information sources include 9000 journals, patents from 27 countries, two industrial property organizations, new books, conference proceedings, and government research reports.

Kirk-Othmer Encyclopedia of Chemical Technology. John Wiley & Sons, Inc., 605 3rd Ave., 5th Floor, New York, New York 10158. (212) 850-6000. Online version of the publication of the same name.

TRADE ASSOCIATIONS AND PROFESSIONAL SOCIETIES

American Chemical Society. 1155 16th St., N.W., Washington, District of Columbia 20036. (202) 872-4600.

American Institute of Biological Sciences. 730 11th St., N.W., Washington, District of Columbia 20001-4521. (202) 628-1500.

FECAL COLIFORM BACTERIA

See: BACTERIA

FECUNDITY

ABSTRACTING AND INDEXING SERVICES

Applied Ecology Abstracts Studies in Renewable Natural Resources. Information Retrieval Ltd., 1911 Jefferson Davis Highway, Arlington, Virginia 22202. 1975-. Monthly.

ASFA Aquaculture Abstracts. Cambridge Scientific Abstracts, Inc., 5161 River Rd., Bethesda, Maryland 20816. (301) 961-6750. 1984.

Biological Abstracts. BIOSIS, 2100 Arch St., Philadelphia, Pennsylvania 19103-1399. (215) 587-4800. 1927-.

Biological and Agricultural Index. H.W. Wilson Co., 950 University Ave., Bronx, New York 10452. (800) 367-6770. 1916-. Monthly.

Ecology Abstracts. Cambridge Scientific Abstracts, 5161 River Rd., Bethesda, Maryland 20816. (301) 961-6750. Monthly.

General Science Index. H. W. Wilson Co., 950 University Ave., Bronx, New York 10452. 1978-. Monthly, also issued in annual cumulation. Cumulative subject index to English language periodicals in the subject fields of astronomy, botany, chemistry, earth science, environment and conservation, food and nutrition, genetics, mathematics, medicine and health, microbiology, oceanography, physics, physiology and zoology.

Geographical Abstracts. London School of Economics, Dept. of Geography, Regency House, 34 Duke St., London, England 1966-. Continued by Geo Abstracts issued in 6 parts: Pt. A. Landforms and the quaternary; Pt. B. Biogeography and Climatology; Pt. C. Economic geography; Pt. D. Social geography and cartography; Pt. E. Sedimentology; Pt. F. Regional and community planning.

Index to Scientific Book Contents. Institute for Scientific Information, 3501 Market St., Philadelphia, Pennsylvania 19104. (800) 523-1857. 1985-. Annual. Gives contents of science books published.

Medical Gynaecology and Fertility Abstracts. Family Centre Ltd., London, England Monthly.

Multimedia Index to Ecology. National Information Center for Educational Media, University of Southern California, Los Angeles, California 90007.

Science Citation Index. Institute for Scientific Information, 3501 Market St., Philadelphia, Pennsylvania 19104. 1961-.

ENCYCLOPEDIAS AND DICTIONARIES

Cambridge Dictionary of Biology. Peter M. B. Walker. Cambridge University Press, 40 W. 20th St., New York, New York 10011. (212) 924-3900 or (800) 227-0247. 1989. Includes 10,000 terms in zoology, botany, biochemistry, molecular biology and genetics. Previously published under the title Chambers Biology Dictionary.

Cambridge Encyclopedia of Life Sciences. A. E. Friday and David S. Ingram. Cambridge University Press, 40 W 20th St., New York, New York 10011. (212) 924-3900 or (800) 227-0247. 1985. Includes all topics under biology and ecology.

A Concise Dictionary of Biology. Elizabeth Martin, ed. Oxford University Press, 200 Madison Ave., New York, New York 10016. (212) 679-7300 or (800) 334-4249. 1990. New edition. Derived from the Concise Science Dictionary, published in 1984.

Van Nostrand's Scientific Encyclopedia. Glenn D. Considine, ed. Van Nostrand Reinhold, 115 5th Ave., New York, New York 10003. (212) 254-3232. 1983. Sixth edition. Includes all broad subject areas in science.

ONLINE DATA BASES

BIOSIS Previews. BIOSIS, 2100 Arch St., Philadelphia, Pennsylvania 19103-1399. (215) 587-4800. Largest and most comprehensive database of research in the life sciences. Contains citations for nearly 9000 primary research journals, monographs, reviews, symposia, preliminary reports, semi-popular journals, selected institutional reports, government reports and research communications.

SCISEARCH. Institute for Scientific Information, University City Science Center, 3501 Market St., Philadelphia, Pennsylvania 19104. (215) 386-0100.

PERIODICALS AND NEWSLETTERS

Fertility and Sterility. American Fertility Society, 2140 11th Ave. S., Birmingham, Alabama 35205-2800. (205) 933-8494. Monthly.

Journal of Reproduction and Fertility. Abstract Series. Journals of Reproduction and Fertility, Ltd., Cambridge, England Monthly.

STATISTICS SOURCES

Fertility of American Women. U.S. Bureau of the Census, Department of Commerce, Washington, District of Columbia 20233. (301) 763-4040. Annual. Data on fertility, childbirth and birth rate.

TRADE ASSOCIATIONS AND PROFESSIONAL SOCIETIES

American Institute of Biological Sciences. 730 11th St., N.W., Washington, District of Columbia 20001-4521. (202) 628-1500.

FEED CROPS

See: AGRICULTURE

FEEDLOT RUNOFF

See: WASTE DISPOSAL

FENS

See also: BOGS; WETLANDS

ABSTRACTING AND INDEXING SERVICES

Biological Abstracts. BIOSIS, 2100 Arch St., Philadelphia, Pennsylvania 19103-1399. (215) 587-4800. 1927-.

Biological and Agricultural Index. H.W. Wilson Co., 950 University Ave., Bronx, New York 10452. (800) 367-6770. 1916-. Monthly.

Science Citation Index. Institute for Scientific Information, 3501 Market St., Philadelphia, Pennsylvania 19104. 1961-.

ENCYCLOPEDIAS AND DICTIONARIES

Van Nostrand's Scientific Encyclopedia. Glenn D. Considine, ed. Van Nostrand Reinhold, 115 5th Ave., New York, New York 10003. (212) 254-3232. 1983. Sixth edition. Includes all broad subject areas in science.

ONLINE DATA BASES

BIOSIS Previews. BIOSIS, 2100 Arch St., Philadelphia, Pennsylvania 19103-1399. (215) 587-4800. Largest and most comprehensive database of research in the life sciences. Contains citations for nearly 9000 primary research journals, monographs, reviews, symposia, preliminary reports, semi-popular journals, selected institutional reports, government reports and research communications.

SCISEARCH. Institute for Scientific Information, University City Science Center, 3501 Market St., Philadelphia, Pennsylvania 19104. (215) 386-0100.

TRADE ASSOCIATIONS AND PROFESSIONAL SOCIETIES

American Institute of Biological Sciences. 730 11th St., N.W., Washington, District of Columbia 20001-4521. (202) 628-1500.

FENTHION

ABSTRACTING AND INDEXING SERVICES

Biological Abstracts. BIOSIS, 2100 Arch St., Philadelphia, Pennsylvania 19103-1399. (215) 587-4800. 1927-.

Chemical Abstracts. Chemical Abstracts Service, 2540 Olentangy River Rd., PO Box 3012, Columbus, Ohio 43210. (800) 848-6533. 1907-.

Index to Scientific Book Contents. Institute for Scientific Information, 3501 Market St., Philadelphia, Pennsylvania 19104. (800) 523-1857. 1985-. Annual. Gives contents of science books published.

Science Citation Index. Institute for Scientific Information, 3501 Market St., Philadelphia, Pennsylvania 19104. 1961-.

ENCYCLOPEDIAS AND DICTIONARIES

Encyclopedia of Trademarks and Synonyms. H. Bennett, ed. Chemical Publishing Co., 80 Eighth Ave., New York, New York 10011. (212) 255-1950. 1981. Three volumes. Includes chemical compounds, compositions consisting of one or more chemicals and other products. Also included are abbreviated names and WHO free names.

Van Nostrand's Scientific Encyclopedia. Glenn D. Considine, ed. Van Nostrand Reinhold, 115 5th Ave., New York, New York 10003. (212) 254-3232. 1983. Sixth edition. Includes all broad subject areas in science.

GENERAL WORKS

Bioassay of Fenthion for Possible Carcinogenicity. Department of Health and Human Services, 200 Independence Ave. SW, Washington, District of Columbia 20201. (202) 619-0257. 1979. Covers carcinogens and organophosphorus compounds and toxicology of insecticides.

ONLINE DATA BASES

BIOSIS Previews. BIOSIS, 2100 Arch St., Philadelphia, Pennsylvania 19103-1399. (215) 587-4800. Largest and most comprehensive database of research in the life sciences. Contains citations for nearly 9000 primary research journals, monographs, reviews, symposia, preliminary reports, semi-popular journals, selected institutional reports, government reports and research communications.

CERCLIS. Chemical Information Systems, Inc., 7215 York Rd., Baltimore, Maryland 21212. (301) 321-8440. Information on hazardous waste disposal sites that have either been listed by the EPA on the National Priority List (NPL) or nominated for consideration for the NPL.

Chemical Abstracts-CA. Chemical Abstracts Service, 2540 Olentangy River Rd., P.O. Box 3012, Columbus, Ohio 43210. (800) 848-6533 or (614) 421-3600. Information sources include 9000 journals, patents from 27 countries, two industrial property organizations, new books, conference proceedings, and government research reports.

Chemical Abstracts Chemical Name Directory-CHEM-NAME. Chemical Abstracts Service, 2540 Olentangy River Rd., P.O. Box 3012, Columbus, Ohio 43210. (800) 848-6533 or (614) 421-3600. Listing of chemical substances in a dictionary type file. The Chemical Abstracts (CAS) Registry Number, molecular formula, Chemical Abstracts (CA) Substance Index Name, available synonyms, ring data and other chemical substance information is given for each entry.

Chemical Carcinogenesis Research Information System–CCRIS. National Library of Medicine, 8600 Rockville Pike, Bethesda, Maryland 20894. (800) 638-8480. Individual assay results and test conditions for 1,451 chemicals in the areas of carcinogenicity, mutagenicity, tumor promotion, and cocarcinogenicity.

TRADE ASSOCIATIONS AND PROFESSIONAL SOCIETIES

American Institute of Biological Sciences. 730 11th St., N.W., Washington, District of Columbia 20001-4521. (202) 628-1500.

FENVALERATE

ABSTRACTING AND INDEXING SERVICES

Biological Abstracts. BIOSIS, 2100 Arch St., Philadelphia, Pennsylvania 19103-1399. (215) 587-4800. 1927-.

Index to Scientific Book Contents. Institute for Scientific Information, 3501 Market St., Philadelphia, Pennsylvania 19104. (800) 523-1857. 1985-. Annual. Gives contents of science books published.

Science Citation Index. Institute for Scientific Information, 3501 Market St., Philadelphia, Pennsylvania 19104. 1961-.

ENCYCLOPEDIAS AND DICTIONARIES

Van Nostrand's Scientific Encyclopedia. Glenn D. Considine, ed. Van Nostrand Reinhold, 115 5th Ave., New York, New York 10003. (212) 254-3232. 1983. Sixth edition. Includes all broad subject areas in science.

ONLINE DATA BASES

BIOSIS Previews. BIOSIS, 2100 Arch St., Philadelphia, Pennsylvania 19103-1399. (215) 587-4800. Largest and most comprehensive database of research in the life sciences. Contains citations for nearly 9000 primary research journals, monographs, reviews, symposia, preliminary reports, semi-popular journals, selected institutional reports, government reports and research communications.

FERAL

See: WILDLIFE

FERMENTATION

See also: FOOD SCIENCE; RESPIRATION

RESEARCH CENTERS AND INSTITUTES

Bioanalytical Center. Washington State University, Troy Hall, Pullman, Washington 99164. (509) 335-5126.

Biomass Research Center. University of Arkansas, Fayetteville, Arkansas 72701. (501) 575-6299.

University of Iowa, University Large Scale Fermentation Facility. Department of Microbiology, Iowa City, Iowa 52242. (319) 335-7780.

FERTILIZER RUNOFF

See: WASTE DISPOSAL

FERTILIZERS

ABSTRACTING AND INDEXING SERVICES

Agricultural Engineering Abstracts. C. A. B. International, 845 North Park Ave., Tucson, Arizona 85719. (602) 621-7897 or (800) 528-4841. 1976-. Monthly. Informs about significant research developments in agricultural engineering and instrumentation. Some of the topics scanned for the abstracts include mechanical power, crop production, crop harvesting and threshing, crop processing and storage, aquaculture, land improvement, protected cultivation, handling and transport, and farm buildings and equipment.

Agrindex. AGRIS Coordinating Center, Via delle Terme di Caracalla, Rome, Italy I-00100. 61 0181-FA01. 1975-.

Applied Science and Technology Index. H.W. Wilson Co., 950 University Ave., Bronx, New York 10452. (800) 367-6770. Formerly Industrial Arts Index.

ASFA Aquaculture Abstracts. Cambridge Scientific Abstracts, Inc., 5161 River Rd., Bethesda, Maryland 20816. (301) 961-6750. 1984.

Biological Abstracts. BIOSIS, 2100 Arch St., Philadelphia, Pennsylvania 19103-1399. (215) 587-4800. 1927-.

Biological and Agricultural Index. H.W. Wilson Co., 950 University Ave., Bronx, New York 10452. (800) 367-6770. 1916-. Monthly.

Chemical Abstracts. Chemical Abstracts Service, 2540 Olentangy River Rd., PO Box 3012, Columbus, Ohio 43210. (800) 848-6533. 1907-.

Ecological Abstracts. Geo Abstracts Ltd. Elsevier Applied Science, Crown House, Linton Rd., Barking, England IG 11 8JU. 1974-. Derived from over 600 leading ecological and environmental journals, plus books, conference proceedings, reports and theses.

Fertilizer Abstracts. National Fertilizer Development Center, Muscle Shoals, Alabama 35660. Contains information on fertilizers technology, marketing use, and related research.

Field Crop Abstracts. C. A. B. International, 845 North Park Ave., Tucson, Arizona 85719. (602) 621-7897 or (800) 528-4841. 1948-. Monthly. Covers literature on agronomy, field production, crop botany and physiology of all annual field crops, both temperate and tropical.

General Science Index. H. W. Wilson Co., 950 University Ave., Bronx, New York 10452. 1978-. Monthly, also issued in annual cumulation. Cumulative subject index to English language periodicals in the subject fields of astronomy, botany, chemistry, earth science, environment and conservation, food and nutrition, genetics, mathematics, medicine and health, microbiology, oceanography, physics, physiology and zoology.

Geographical Abstracts. London School of Economics, Dept. of Geography, Regency House, 34 Duke St., London, England 1966-. Continued by Geo Abstracts issued in 6 parts: Pt. A. Landforms and the quaternary; Pt. B. Biogeography and Climatology; Pt. C. Economic geography; Pt. D. Social geography and cartography; Pt. E. Sedimentology; Pt. F. Regional and community planning.

Index to Scientific Book Contents. Institute for Scientific Information, 3501 Market St., Philadelphia, Pennsylvania 19104. (800) 523-1857. 1985-. Annual. Gives contents of science books published.

Pollution Abstracts. Cambridge Scientific Abstracts, 5161 River Rd., Bethesda, Maryland 20816. (301) 961-6750. Six/year. Indexes worldwide technical literature on environmental pollution. Covers air pollution, marine and freshwater pollution, sewage and wastewater treatment, waste management, toxicology and health, noise pollution, radiation, land pollution, and environmental policies, programs, legislation, and education. Also available online.

Science Citation Index. Institute for Scientific Information, 3501 Market St., Philadelphia, Pennsylvania 19104. 1961-.

Soils and Fertilizers. C. A. B. International, 845 North Park Ave., Tucson, Arizona 85719. (602) 621-7897 or (800) 528-4841. 1937-. Monthly. Focuses on soil chemistry, soil physics, soil biology, soil fertility, soil management, soil classification, soil formation, soil conservation, land reclamation, irrigation and damage, fertilizer technology, fertilizer use, plant nutrition, plant water relations, and environmental aspects.

BIBLIOGRAPHIES

Bibliography and Index of Geology. American Geological Institute, 4220 King St., Alexandria, Virginia 22302. Monthly. Includes environmental geology and hydrogeology.

Bibliography of Livestock Waste Management. U.S. Government Printing Office, Washington, District of Columbia 20402-9325. (202) 783-3238. 1972. Covers agricultural and animal waste, manure handling, and feedlots.

Climate, Fertilizers, and Soil Fertility: January 1981 - February 1991. Susan Whitmore. National Agricultural Library, 10301 Baltimore Blvd., Beltsville, Maryland 20705-2351. (301) 504-5755. 1991.

Manure: Uses, Costs and Benefits, January 1984-May 1990. Jayne T. Maclean. National Agricultural Library, 10301 Baltimore Blvd., Beltsville, Maryland 20705-2351. (301) 504-5755. 1990. Topics in manures, fertilizers and organic wastes as fertilizers.

DIRECTORIES

Directory, Fertilizer Research in the U.S. Victor L. Sheldon. National Fertilizer Development Center, Muscle Shoals, Alabama 35660. 1981.

ENCYCLOPEDIAS AND DICTIONARIES

Encyclopedia of Chemical Processing and Design. John J. Mcketta and W. A. Cunningham. Marcel Dekker, Inc., 270 Madison Ave., New York, New York 10016. (212) 696-9000; (800) 228-1160. 1992. Thirty-eight volumes.

The Encyclopedia of Soil Science. Rhodes W. Fairbridge. Academic Press, c/o Harcourt Brace Jovanovich Inc., 6277 Sea Harbor Dr., Orlando, Florida 32887. (800) 346-8648. 1979-. Includes soil physics, soil chemistry, soil biology, soil fertility and plant nutrition, soil genesis, classification and cartography.

Kirk-Othmer Encyclopedia of Chemical Technology. J. I. Kroschwitz, ed. John Wiley & Sons, Inc., 605 3rd Ave., New York, New York 10158-0012. (212) 850-6000. 1992-. All articles in the new edition have been rewritten and updated adding new subjects such as biotechnology, computer topics, analytical techniques and instrumentation, environmental concerns, fuels and energy, inorganic and solid state chemistry; composite materials and material science in general, and pharmaceuticals. Also available online.

McGraw-Hill Encyclopedia of Environmental Science. Sybil P. Parker. McGraw-Hill Science & Engineering Books, 11 W. 19th St., New York, New York 10011. (212) 337-6010. 1980. Covers ecology, man's influence on nature, and environmental protection.

Van Nostrand's Scientific Encyclopedia. Glenn D. Considine, ed. Van Nostrand Reinhold, 115 5th Ave., New York, New York 10003. (212) 254-3232. 1983. Sixth edition. Includes all broad subject areas in science.

GENERAL WORKS

Agricultural Waste Utilization and Management. American Society of Agricultural Engineers, 2950 Niles Rd., St. Joseph, Michigan 49085-9659. (616) 429-0300. 1985. Proceedings of the Fifth International Symposium on Agricultural Wastes, December 16-17, 1985, Chicago, IL. Covers topics such as liquid manure storage and transportation, energy recovery from wastes, digester types and design, recycling for feed, fuel and fertilizer, land applications and odor control.

Chemistry, Agriculture and the Environment. Mervyn L. Richardson. Royal Society of Chemistry, Thomas Graham House, Science Park, Milton Rd., Cambridge, England CB4 4WF. 44(0)223420066. 1991. Provides an overview of the chemical pollution of the environment caused by modern agricultural practices worldwide, and describes the effects of agrochemicals used in intensive animal and crop production on the air, water, soil, plants, and animals including humans. Also available through CRC Press.

Effluents from Livestock. J. K. R. Gasser, et al., eds. Applied Science Publications, PO Box 5399, New York, New York 10163. (718) 756-6440. 1980. Proceedings of a seminar to discuss work carried out within the EEC under the programme Effluents from Intensive Livestock, organized by Prof. H. Vetter and held at Bad Zwischenahn, 2-5 October, 1979.

Livestock Waste, a Renewable Resource. American Society of Agricultural Engineers, 2950 Niles Rd., St. Joseph, Michigan 49085-9659. (616) 429-0300. 1981. Papers presented at the 4th International Symposium on Livestock Wastes, Amarillo, TX, 1980. Topics covered include: processing manure for feed, methane production, land application, lagoons, runoff, odors, economics, stabilization, treatment, collection and transport, storage and solid-liquid separation.

Magill's Survey of Science. Earth Science Series. Frank N. Magill. Salem Press, PO Box 50062, Pasadena, California 91105. 1990-. Five volumes. Includes information on earth's crust, hot spots and volcanic island chains, physical properties of minerals, rock magnetism, physical properties of rocks, and index.

Nutrient Cycling in Terrestrial Ecosystems Field Methods. A. F. Harrison, et al. Elsevier Science Publishing Co., 655 Avenue of the Americas, New York, New York 10010. (212) 984-5800. 1990. Describes a wide range of methods for the estimation of nutrient fluxes. The book is divided into sections dealing with inputs, turnover, losses and plant uptake processes.

GOVERNMENTAL ORGANIZATIONS

TVA Public Information Office. 400 West Summit Hill Dr., Knoxville, Tennessee 37902. (615) 632-8000.

HANDBOOKS AND MANUALS

Farm Chemical Handbook. Meister Publishing Co., 37733 Euclid Ave., Willoughby, Ohio 44094. (216) 942-2000. Annual. Covers fertilizers and manures.

Fertile Soil: A Grower's Guide to Organic and Inorganic Fertilizers. Robert Parnes. AgAccess, PO Box 2008, Davis, California 95617. (916) 756-7177. 1990. Comprehensive technical resource on creating fertile soils using a balanced program that does not rely on chemical fertilizers.

Handbook on Environmental Aspects of Fertilizer Use. Martinus Nijhoff/W. Junk, 101 Philips Dr., Boston, Massachusetts 02061. (617) 871-6600. 1983.

Livestock Waste Facilities Handbook. Midwest Plan Service, Ames, Iowa 1985. Deals with agricultural waste management and manure handling in livestock waste facilities.

Western Fertilizer Handbook. California Fertilizer Association, Soil Improvement Committee. Interstate Publishers, 510 Vermillion St., PO Box 50, Danville, Illinois 61834-0050. (217) 446-0500. 1990. Covers soil management and crops nutrition.

ONLINE DATA BASES

BIOSIS Previews. BIOSIS, 2100 Arch St., Philadelphia, Pennsylvania 19103-1399. (215) 587-4800. Largest and most comprehensive database of research in the life sciences. Contains citations for nearly 9000 primary research journals, monographs, reviews, symposia, preliminary reports, semi-popular journals, selected institutional reports, government reports and research communications.

Cambridge Scientific Abstracts Life Science–CSAL. Cambridge Scientific Abstracts, 5161 River Rd., Bethesda, Maryland 20816. (301) 961-6750. Provides access to the following abstracting services: "Life Sciences Collection," "Aquatic Sciences and Fisheries Abstracts," "Oceanic Abstracts," and "Pollution Abstracts."

CERCLIS. Chemical Information Systems, Inc., 7215 York Rd., Baltimore, Maryland 21212. (301) 321-8440. Information on hazardous waste disposal sites that have either been listed by the EPA on the National Priority List (NPL) or nominated for consideration for the NPL.

CHEM-INTELL–Chemical Trade and Production Statistics Database. Chemical Intelligence Services, 39A Bowling Green Lane, London, England EC1R. OBJ 44 (71) 833-3812.

Chemical Abstracts-CA. Chemical Abstracts Service, 2540 Olentangy River Rd., P.O. Box 3012, Columbus, Ohio 43210. (800) 848-6533 or (614) 421-3600. Information sources include 9000 journals, patents from 27 countries, two industrial property organizations, new books, conference proceedings, and government research reports.

Chemical Age Project File. MBC Information Services Ltd., Paulton House, 8 Shepherdess Walk, London, England N1 7LB. 44 (71) 490-0049.

Chemical Carcinogenesis Research Information System–CCRIS. National Library of Medicine, 8600 Rockville Pike, Bethesda, Maryland 20894. (800) 638-8480. Individual assay results and test conditions for 1,451 chemicals in the areas of carcinogenicity, mutagenicity, tumor promotion, and cocarcinogenicity.

Chemical Collection System/Request Tracking–CCS/RTS. U.S. Environmental Protection Agency, Office of Pesticides and Toxic Substances, 401 M St., SW, Washington, District of Columbia 20460. (202) 260-2090. Contains information on various properties of a number of chemicals including environmental effects, test and analysis methods, and health effects. Available from EPA.

Chemical Dictionary Online–CHEMLINE. Chemical Abstracts Service, 2540 Olentangy River Rd., Columbus, Ohio 43210. (614) 421-3600 or (800) 848-6533. Part of MEDLINE of the National Library of Medicine (NLM). File of 900,000 names for chemical substances, representing 450,000 unique compounds. It contains such information as Chemical Abstracts (CA) Service Registry

Numbers, molecular formulas, preferred chemical no- menclature, and generic and ring structure information. Available on NLM's ELHILL system.

Chemical Exposure. Science Applications International Corp., Health & Environmental Information, P.O. Box 2501, Oak Ridge, Tennessee 37831. (615) 482-9031. Database of chemicals that have been identified in both human tissues and body fluids and in feral and food animals. Contains reference to journal articles, confer- ences, and reports. Covers the whole fields of informa- tion related to human and animal exposure to food, air, and water contaminants and pharmaceuticals. Its records include information on chemical properties, formulas, tissues measured, analytical method used, demographics and more. Available on DIALOG.

Chemical Plant Database. Chemical Intelligence Ser- vices, 39A Bowling Green Lane, London, England EC 1R OBJ. 44 (71) 833-3812.

Inorganic & Fertilizer Chemical Forecast Database. Probe Economics, Inc., 241 Lexington Ave., Mt. Kisco, New York 10549. (914) 241-0744.

Inorganic & Fertilizer Chemicals. Sage Data, Inc., 104 Carnegie Ctr., Princeton, New Jersey 08540. (609) 924- 3000.

Kirk-Othmer Encyclopedia of Chemical Technology. John Wiley & Sons, Inc., 605 3rd Ave., 5th Floor, New York, New York 10158. (212) 850-6000. Online version of the publication of the same name.

Monthly Catalog of United States Government Publica- tions. U.S. G.P.O., Supt. of Docs., PO Box 371954, Pittsburgh, Pennsylvania 15250-7954. (202) 512-0000.

National Technical Information Service. U.S. Depart- ment of Commerce, National Technical Information Service, Office of Data Base Services, 5285 Port Royal Rd., Springfield, Virginia 22161. (703) 487-4807. Biblio- graphic database of government sponsored research and technical reports.

SCISEARCH. Institute for Scientific Information, Uni- versity City Science Center, 3501 Market St., Philadel- phia, Pennsylvania 19104. (215) 386-0100.

PERIODICALS AND NEWSLETTERS

Agrichemical Age Magazine. HBJ Farm Publications, 731 Market Street, San Francisco, California 94103-2011. (415) 495-3340. Eleven times a year. Use and application of agricultural chemicals.

American Fertilizer. Ware Bros., Philadelphia, Pennsyl- vania Biweekly.

Farm Chemicals Magazine. Meister Publishing Co., 37733 Euclid Avenue, Willoughby, Ohio 44094. (216) 942-2000. Monthly. Covers the production, marketing and application of fertilizers and crop protection chemi- cals.

Fertilizer Progress. Clear Window, Inc., 15444 Clayton Road, #314, St. Louis, Missouri 63011. (202) 861-4900. Bimonthly. Covers business and management of fertiliz- ers and farm chemicals.

Fertilizer Research: An International Journal on Fertilizer Use and Technology. Kluwer Academic Publishers, 101 Philip Dr., Assinippi Park, Norwell, Massachusetts 02061. (617) 871-6600. Monthly. Soils, soil fertility, soil

chemistry, crop and animal production and husbandry, crop quality and environment.

Journal of Pesticide Science. Elsevier Science Publishing Co., Journal Information Center, 655 Avenue of the Americas, New York, New York 10010. (212) 989-5800. Quarterly. Pesticide science in general, agrochemistry and chemistry of biologically active natural products.

Plant Food Review. The Fertilizer Institute, 501 2nd Ave. NE, Washington, District of Columbia (202)675-8250. Quarterly.

STATISTICS SOURCES

Commercial Fertilizers. Tennessee Valley Authority. U.S. G.P.O., Washington, District of Columbia 20401. (202) 512-0000. Annual. Deals with commercial fertilizer con- sumption by state and type of nutrient.

Fertilizer Trade Statistics, 1970-88. Harry Vroomen. U.S. Deptartment of Agriculture, Economic Research Service, 14 Independence Ave., SW, Washington, District of Columbia 20250. (202) 447-7454. 1989.

The Market for Agricultural Chemicals. FIND/SVP, 625 Avenue of the Americas, New York, New York 10011. (212) 645-4500. 1990. Covers the markets for three types of agricultural chemicals: fertilizers, pesticide and natural and biotechnology products.

TRADE ASSOCIATIONS AND PROFESSIONAL SOCIETIES

American Institute of Biological Sciences. 730 11th St., N.W., Washington, District of Columbia 20001-4521. (202) 628-1500.

American Society of Agricultural Engineers. 2950 Niles Rd., St Joseph, Michigan 49085. (616) 429-0300.

Fertilizer Institute. 501 2nd Ave., N.E., Washington, District of Columbia 20002. (202) 675-8250.

National Agricultural Chemicals Association. 1155 15th St., N.W., Madison Building, Suite 900, Washington, District of Columbia 20005. (202) 296-1585.

National Fertilizer Solutions Association. 339 Consort Dr., Manchester, Missouri 63011. (314) 256-4900.

FIBERGLASS

ABSTRACTING AND INDEXING SERVICES

Applied Science and Technology Index. H.W. Wilson Co., 950 University Ave., Bronx, New York 10452. (800) 367- 6770. Formerly Industrial Arts Index.

Chemical Abstracts. Chemical Abstracts Service, 2540 Olentangy River Rd., PO Box 3012, Columbus, Ohio 43210. (800) 848-6533. 1907-.

Engineering Index. The Engineering Index Inc., 345 E. 47th St., New York, New York 10017. 1962-.

Environment Abstracts. Bowker A & I Publishing, 121 Chanlon Rd., New Providence, New Jersey 07974. (908) 464-6800. 1974-.

Environment Index. Environment Information Center, Index Research Department, 124 E. 39th St., New York, New York 10016. 1971-. Annual.

Environmental Information Connection–EIC. Planning Information Program, Dept. of Urban and Regional Planning, University of Illinois, 1003 West Nevada, Urbana, Illinois 61801. (217) 333-1369. Also available online.

Environmental Periodicals Bibliography. Environmental Studies Institute, International Academy at Santa Barbara, 800 Garden St., Suite D, Santa Barbara, California 93101. (805) 965-5010. Also available online.

General Science Index. H. W. Wilson Co., 950 University Ave., Bronx, New York 10452. 1978-. Monthly, also issued in annual cumulation. Cumulative subject index to English language periodicals in the subject fields of astronomy, botany, chemistry, earth science, environment and conservation, food and nutrition, genetics, mathematics, medicine and health, microbiology, oceanography, physics, physiology and zoology.

Index to Scientific Book Contents. Institute for Scientific Information, 3501 Market St., Philadelphia, Pennsylvania 19104. (800) 523-1857. 1985-. Annual. Gives contents of science books published.

Physics Briefs. Physikalische Berichte. Physik Verlag, Pappapelallee 3, Postfach 101161, Weinheim, Germany D-6940. 1979-. Semimonthly. In English. Volumes for 1979- issued by the Deutsche Physikalische Gesellschaft and the Fachinformationszentrum Energie Physik, Mathematik in cooperation with the American Institute of Physics.

Pollution Abstracts. Cambridge Scientific Abstracts, 5161 River Rd., Bethesda, Maryland 20816. (301) 961-6750. Six/year. Indexes worldwide technical literature on environmental pollution. Covers air pollution, marine and freshwater pollution, sewage and wastewater treatment, waste management, toxicology and health, noise pollution, radiation, land pollution, and environmental policies, programs, legislation, and education. Also available online.

Science Citation Index. Institute for Scientific Information, 3501 Market St., Philadelphia, Pennsylvania 19104. 1961-.

BIBLIOGRAPHIES

EPA Publications Bibliography. U.S. Environmental Protection Agency, Library Systems Branch, 401 M St., SW, Washington, District of Columbia 20460. (202) 260-2090. Quarterly.

ENCYCLOPEDIAS AND DICTIONARIES

Encyclopedia of Chemical Processing and Design. John J. Mcketta and W. A. Cunningham. Marcel Dekker, Inc., 270 Madison Ave., New York, New York 10016. (212) 696-9000; (800) 228-1160. 1992. Thirty-eight volumes.

Kirk-Othmer Encyclopedia of Chemical Technology. J. I. Kroschwitz, ed. John Wiley & Sons, Inc., 605 3rd Ave., New York, New York 10158-0012. (212) 850-6000. 1992-. All articles in the new edition have been rewritten and updated adding new subjects such as biotechnology, computer topics, analytical techniques and instrumentation, environmental concerns, fuels and energy, inorganic and solid state chemistry; composite materials and material science in general, and pharmaceuticals. Also available online.

McGraw-Hill Encyclopedia of Science and Technology. McGraw-Hill, 1221 Avenue of the Americas, New York, New York 10020. (212) 512-2000 or (800) 262-4729. 1992. Seventh edition. Issued in multiple volumes including index. Includes all science and technology broad subject areas.

Van Nostrand's Scientific Encyclopedia. Glenn D. Considine, ed. Van Nostrand Reinhold, 115 5th Ave., New York, New York 10003. (212) 254-3232. 1983. Sixth edition. Includes all broad subject areas in science.

HANDBOOKS AND MANUALS

Handbook of Fiberglass and Advanced Plastics Composites. George Lubin. Van Nostrand Reinhold, 115 5th Ave., New York, New York 10003. (212) 254-3232. 1969. Deals with reinforced plastics, fibrous composites, and glass fibers.

ONLINE DATA BASES

Chemical Abstracts-CA. Chemical Abstracts Service, 2540 Olentangy River Rd., P.O. Box 3012, Columbus, Ohio 43210. (800) 848-6533 or (614) 421-3600. Information sources include 9000 journals, patents from 27 countries, two industrial property organizations, new books, conference proceedings, and government research reports.

Computerized Engineering Index–COMPENDEX. Engineering Information Inc., 345 E. 47th St., New York, New York 10017. (212) 705-7600.

Enviro/Energyline Abstracts Plus. R. R. Bowker Co., 121 Chanlon Rd., New Providence, New Jersey 07974. (908) 464-6800.

Environmental Periodicals Bibliography. National Information Services Corp., Ste. 6, Wyman Towers, 3100 St. Paul St., Baltimore, Maryland 21218. (410)243-0797. Online version of abstract of same name.

Kirk-Othmer Encyclopedia of Chemical Technology. John Wiley & Sons, Inc., 605 3rd Ave., 5th Floor, New York, New York 10158. (212) 850-6000. Online version of the publication of the same name.

Monthly Catalog of United States Government Publications. U.S. G.P.O., Supt. of Docs., PO Box 371954, Pittsburgh, Pennsylvania 15250-7954. (202) 512-0000.

National Technical Information Service. U.S. Department of Commerce, National Technical Information Service, Office of Data Base Services, 5285 Port Royal Rd., Springfield, Virginia 22161. (703) 487-4807. Bibliographic database of government sponsored research and technical reports.

SCISEARCH. Institute for Scientific Information, University City Science Center, 3501 Market St., Philadelphia, Pennsylvania 19104. (215) 386-0100.

TRADE ASSOCIATIONS AND PROFESSIONAL SOCIETIES

Fibre Box Association. 2850 Golf Rd., Rolling Meadows, Illinois 60008. (708) 364-9600.

FILTRATION

ABSTRACTING AND INDEXING SERVICES

Applied Science and Technology Index. H.W. Wilson Co., 950 University Ave., Bronx, New York 10452. (800) 367-6770. Formerly Industrial Arts Index.

Biological Abstracts. BIOSIS, 2100 Arch St., Philadelphia, Pennsylvania 19103-1399. (215) 587-4800. 1927-.

Environment Abstracts. Bowker A & I Publishing, 121 Chanlon Rd., New Providence, New Jersey 07974. (908) 464-6800. 1974-.

Environment Index. Environment Information Center, Index Research Department, 124 E. 39th St., New York, New York 10016. 1971-. Annual.

Environmental Information Connection–EIC. Planning Information Program, Dept. of Urban and Regional Planning, University of Illinois, 1003 West Nevada, Urbana, Illinois 61801. (217) 333-1369. Also available online.

Environmental Periodicals Bibliography. Environmental Studies Institute, International Academy at Santa Barbara, 800 Garden St., Suite D, Santa Barbara, California 93101. (805) 965-5010. Also available online.

Food Science and Technology Abstracts. International Food Information Service, c/o National Food Laboratory, 6363 Clark Ave., Dublin, California 94568. (800) 336-3782. 1969-.

General Science Index. H. W. Wilson Co., 950 University Ave., Bronx, New York 10452. 1978-. Monthly, also issued in annual cumulation. Cumulative subject index to English language periodicals in the subject fields of astronomy, botany, chemistry, earth science, environment and conservation, food and nutrition, genetics, mathematics, medicine and health, microbiology, oceanography, physics, physiology and zoology.

Index to Scientific Book Contents. Institute for Scientific Information, 3501 Market St., Philadelphia, Pennsylvania 19104. (800) 523-1857. 1985-. Annual. Gives contents of science books published.

Pollution Abstracts. Cambridge Scientific Abstracts, 5161 River Rd., Bethesda, Maryland 20816. (301) 961-6750. Six/year. Indexes worldwide technical literature on environmental pollution. Covers air pollution, marine and freshwater pollution, sewage and wastewater treatment, waste management, toxicology and health, noise pollution, radiation, land pollution, and environmental policies, programs, legislation, and education. Also available online.

Science Citation Index. Institute for Scientific Information, 3501 Market St., Philadelphia, Pennsylvania 19104. 1961-.

BIBLIOGRAPHIES

EPA Publications Bibliography. U.S. Environmental Protection Agency, Library Systems Branch, 401 M St., SW, Washington, District of Columbia 20460. (202) 260-2090. Quarterly.

DIRECTORIES

Filters–Air & Gas-Retail. 5711 S. 86th Circle, Omaha, Nebraska 68127. (402) 593-4600. Annual.

ENCYCLOPEDIAS AND DICTIONARIES

Encyclopedia of Chemical Processing and Design. John J. Mcketta and W. A. Cunningham. Marcel Dekker, Inc., 270 Madison Ave., New York, New York 10016. (212) 696-9000; (800) 228-1160. 1992. Thirty-eight volumes.

Encyclopedia of Physics. Rita G. Lerner and George L. Trigg. VCH Publishers, 303 NW 12th Ave., Deerfield Beach, Florida 33442-1788. (305) 428-5566. 1991. Second edition.

The Encyclopedia of Soil Science. Rhodes W. Fairbridge. Academic Press, c/o Harcourt Brace Jovanovich Inc., 6277 Sea Harbor Dr., Orlando, Florida 32887. (800) 346-8648. 1979-. Includes soil physics, soil chemistry, soil biology, soil fertility and plant nutrition, soil genesis, classification and cartography.

Kirk-Othmer Encyclopedia of Chemical Technology. J. I. Kroschwitz, ed. John Wiley & Sons, Inc., 605 3rd Ave., New York, New York 10158-0012. (212) 850-6000. 1992-. All articles in the new edition have been rewritten and updated adding new subjects such as biotechnology, computer topics, analytical techniques and instrumentation, environmental concerns, fuels and energy, inorganic and solid state chemistry; composite materials and material science in general, and pharmaceuticals. Also available online.

Ullmanns Encyclopedia of Industrial Chemistry. Hans Jurgen Arpe and Wolfgang Gerhartz, eds. VCH Publishers, 303 NW 12th Ave., Deerfield Beach, Florida 33442-1788. (305) 428-5566. 1990. Designed to keep up with the broad spectrum of chemical technology. Thirty-six volumes of the encyclopedia have been divided into two sets: the 28 A volumes contain alphabetically arranged articles on chemicals, product groups, processes and technological concepts; and the 8 B volumes are compendia of basic knowledge in industrial chemistry.

Van Nostrand's Scientific Encyclopedia. Glenn D. Considine, ed. Van Nostrand Reinhold, 115 5th Ave., New York, New York 10003. (212) 254-3232. 1983. Sixth edition. Includes all broad subject areas in science.

GENERAL WORKS

Affinity Membranes. Elias Klein. John Wiley & Sons, Inc., 605 3rd Ave., New York, New York (212) 850-6000. 1991. The chemistry and performance of affinity membranes in absorptive separation processes.

Removal of Soluble Manganese from Water by Oxide-Coated Filter Media. William R. Knocke. AWWA Research Foundation, 6666 W. Quincy Ave., Denver, Colorado 80235. (303) 794-7711. 1990. Covers water purification and manganese removal.

Treatment Technologies. Environment Protection Agency. Government Institutes, Inc., 4 Research Pl., Ste. 200, Rockville, Maryland 20850. (301)921-2300. 1991. 2nd ed. Provides a clear explanation of 24 treatment technologies and evaluates the effectiveness of the design and operations of each type of treatment. This new edition has more supporting numerical data, examples for a better understanding of the technology and an updated reference for specific industrial wastes.

HANDBOOKS AND MANUALS

Filters and Filtration Handbook. R.H. Warring. Gulf Publishing Co., Book Division, PO Box 2608, Houston, Texas 77252. (713) 529-4301. 1981.

Screening Equipment Handbook: For Industrial and Municipal Water and Wastewater Treatment. Tom M. Pankratz. Technomic Publishing Co., Lancaster, Pennsylvania 1988. Covers the water purification equipment industry, fish screens, and filters and filtration.

Ultrafiltration Handbook. Munir Cheryan. Technomic Publishing Co., 851 New Holland Ave., Box 3535, Lancaster, Pennsylvania 17604. (717) 291-5609. 1986. Covers filters and filtration, and membranes technology.

Water Treatment Handbook. Degremont s.a., 184, ave. du 18-Juin-1940, Rueil-Malmaison, France F-92500. 1991. Sixth edition. Part 1 is a general survey of water and its action on the materials with which it comes into contact, and theoretical principles of separation and correction processes used in water treatment. Part 2 describes the process and the treatment plant beginning with the separation process.

ONLINE DATA BASES

BIOSIS Previews. BIOSIS, 2100 Arch St., Philadelphia, Pennsylvania 19103-1399. (215) 587-4800. Largest and most comprehensive database of research in the life sciences. Contains citations for nearly 9000 primary research journals, monographs, reviews, symposia, preliminary reports, semi-popular journals, selected institutional reports, government reports and research communications.

Enviro/Energyline Abstracts Plus. R. R. Bowker Co., 121 Chanlon Rd., New Providence, New Jersey 07974. (908) 464-6800.

Environmental Periodicals Bibliography. National Information Services Corp., Ste. 6, Wyman Towers, 3100 St. Paul St., Baltimore, Maryland 21218. (410)243-0797. Online version of abstract of same name.

Kirk-Othmer Encyclopedia of Chemical Technology. John Wiley & Sons, Inc., 605 3rd Ave., 5th Floor, New York, New York 10158. (212) 850-6000. Online version of the publication of the same name.

Monthly Catalog of United States Government Publications. U.S. G.P.O., Supt. of Docs., PO Box 371954, Pittsburgh, Pennsylvania 15250-7954. (202) 512-0000.

National Technical Information Service. U.S. Department of Commerce, National Technical Information Service, Office of Data Base Services, 5285 Port Royal Rd., Springfield, Virginia 22161. (703) 487-4807. Bibliographic database of government sponsored research and technical reports.

SCISEARCH. Institute for Scientific Information, University City Science Center, 3501 Market St., Philadelphia, Pennsylvania 19104. (215) 386-0100.

PERIODICALS AND NEWSLETTERS

Filtration and Separation. Elsevier Science Publishing Co., 655 Avenue of the Americas, New York, New York 10010. (212) 984-5800. Bimonthly. Filtration, separation dust control, air filtration or gas cleaning equipment; manufacturers of such equipment and designers.

Filtration News. Eagle Publication, Inc., 42400 Nine Mile Road, Suite B, Novi, Michigan 48375. (313) 347-3486. Bimonthly. Information on equipment and components used for particulate removal.

Liquid Filtration Newsletter. McIlvanine Co., 2970 Maria Ave., Northbrook, Illinois 60062. (708) 272-0010. Monthly. Industry information and product comparisons.

STATISTICS SOURCES

Portable Electric Air Cleaners/Purifiers. FIND/SVP, 625 Avenue of the Americas, New York, New York 10011. (212) 645-4500. 1991. Projects ownership incidence and the market size of portable electric oil cleaners/purifiers, delineated brand shares, prices paid, types of filtration, types of outlet.

TRADE ASSOCIATIONS AND PROFESSIONAL SOCIETIES

American Institute of Biological Sciences. 730 11th St., N.W., Washington, District of Columbia 20001-4521. (202) 628-1500.

FIRE

ABSTRACTING AND INDEXING SERVICES

Forestry Abstracts. C. A. B. International, Wallingford, England OX10 8DE. (0491) 3211. 1939/40-. Monthly. Journal of abstracts of journal articles, conferences, technical reports in the subject areas of: silviculture, forest mensuration and management, physical environment, fire, plant biology, genetics and breeding, mycology and pathology, game and wildlife, fish, protection of forests and other related matter.

BIBLIOGRAPHIES

The Effects of Fire and Other Disturbances on Small Mammals and Their Predators. Catherine H. Ream. U.S. Department of Agriculture, Forest Service, 324 25th St., Ogden, Utah 84401. 1981. Includes mammal populations, predatory animals, fire ecology, and animal ecology.

Fire in North America Wetland Ecosystems and Fire-Wildlife Relations: An Annotated Bibliography. Ronald E. Kirby. Fish and Wildlife Service, Department of the Interior, 18th & C Sts., N.W., Washington, District of Columbia 20240. (202) 653-8750. 1988.

The Role of Fire in the Ecosystems of Forests and Grasslands. Glenna Dunning. Vance Bibliographies, PO Box 229, 112 N. Charter St., Monticello, Illinois 61856. (217) 762-3831. 1990.

ENCYCLOPEDIAS AND DICTIONARIES

FIREDOC Vocabulary List. Nora H. Jason. National Institute of Standards and Technology, Rte. I-270 & Quince Orchard Rd., Gaithersburg, Maryland 20899. (301) 975-2000. 1985. Terminology of FIREDOC computer program.

Grzimek's Encyclopedia of Ecology. Bernhard Grzimek. Van Nostrand Reinhold, 115 5th Ave., New York, New York 10003. (212) 254-3232. 1976.

North American Reference Encyclopedia of Ecology and Pollution. William White. North American Pub. Co., 401 N. Broad St., Philadelphia, Pennsylvania 19108. (215) 238-5300. 1972.

GENERAL WORKS

Fire Ecology, United States and Southern Canada. Henry A. Wright. John Wiley & Sons, Inc., 605 3rd Ave., New York, New York 10158-0012. (212) 850-6000. 1982. Procedures in prescribed burning.

Fire in the Tropical Biota: Ecosystem Processes and Global Challenges. J.G. Goldammer. Springer-Verlag, 175 5th Ave., New York, New York 10010. (212) 460-1500. 1990. Covers fire ecology, wildfires, botany, tropical fires, and biotic communities.

Natural Fire: Its Ecology in Forests. Laurence Pringle. William Morrow & Co., 1350 Avenue of the Americas, New York, New York 10019. (212) 261-6500. 1979. Explains the beneficial effects of periodic fires to forests and their wildlife.

HANDBOOKS AND MANUALS

Firefighter's Hazardous Materials Reference Book. Daniel J. Davis and Grant T. Christianson. Van Nostrand Reinhold, 115 5th Ave., New York, New York 10003. (212) 254-3232. 1991. List of hazardous materials. For quick reference, each hazardous material is given its own page with material's name in bold at the top.

FIREWOOD

See: FORESTS

FISH

ABSTRACTING AND INDEXING SERVICES

Aquatic Sciences and Fisheries Abstracts. Cambridge Scientific Abstracts, 5161 River Rd., Bethesda, Maryland 20816. (301) 961-6750. Monthly. Compiled by the United Nations Dept. of Economic and Social Affairs, the Food and Agriculture Organization of the United Nations and the Intergovernmental Oceanographic Commission with the collaboration of other agencies. Includes the broad subject areas of ecology, fisheries, marine biology, public policy, aquatic biology, and aquatic ecology.

ASFA Aquaculture Abstracts. Cambridge Scientific Abstracts, Inc., 5161 River Rd., Bethesda, Maryland 20816. (301) 961-6750. 1984.

Biological Abstracts. BIOSIS, 2100 Arch St., Philadelphia, Pennsylvania 19103-1399. (215) 587-4800. 1927-.

Biological and Agricultural Index. H.W. Wilson Co., 950 University Ave., Bronx, New York 10452. (800) 367-6770. 1916-. Monthly.

Civil Engineering Hydraulic Abstracts. BHRA Fluid Engineering, Air Science Co., PO Box 143, Corning, New York 14830. (607) 962-5591. Monthly. Abstracts of periodicals that publish in the areas of hydraulic engineering and other related topics.

Environment Abstracts. Bowker A & I Publishing, 121 Chanlon Rd., New Providence, New Jersey 07974. (908) 464-6800. 1974-.

Environment Index. Environment Information Center, Index Research Department, 124 E. 39th St., New York, New York 10016. 1971-. Annual.

Environmental Information Connection–EIC. Planning Information Program, Dept. of Urban and Regional Planning, University of Illinois, 1003 West Nevada, Urbana, Illinois 61801. (217) 333-1369. Also available online.

Environmental Periodicals Bibliography. Environmental Studies Institute, International Academy at Santa Barbara, 800 Garden St., Suite D, Santa Barbara, California 93101. (805) 965-5010. Also available online.

Fisheries Review. U.S. Fish and Wildlife Service. U.S. G.P.O., Washington, District of Columbia 20401. (202) 512-0000. Quarterly. Abstracting service dealing with fisheries and ichthyology.

Food Science and Technology Abstracts. International Food Information Service, c/o National Food Laboratory, 6363 Clark Ave., Dublin, California 94568. (800) 336-3782. 1969-.

Forestry Abstracts. C. A. B. International, Wallingford, England OX10 8DE. (0491) 3211. 1939/40-. Monthly. Journal of abstracts of journal articles, conferences, technical reports in the subject areas of: silviculture, forest mensuration and management, physical environment, fire, plant biology, genetics and breeding, mycology and pathology, game and wildlife, fish, protection of forests and other related matter.

General Science Index. H. W. Wilson Co., 950 University Ave., Bronx, New York 10452. 1978-. Monthly, also issued in annual cumulation. Cumulative subject index to English language periodicals in the subject fields of astronomy, botany, chemistry, earth science, environment and conservation, food and nutrition, genetics, mathematics, medicine and health, microbiology, oceanography, physics, physiology and zoology.

Index to Scientific Book Contents. Institute for Scientific Information, 3501 Market St., Philadelphia, Pennsylvania 19104. (800) 523-1857. 1985-. Annual. Gives contents of science books published.

Index Veterinarius. C. A. B. International, 845 North Park Ave., Tucson, Arizona 85719. (602) 621-7897 or (800) 528-4841. 1933-. Monthly. A monthly subject and author index to the world's veterinary literature. References are given to abstracts published in Veterinary Bulletin. Animals included in the index are: cattle, horses, sheep, goats, pigs, poultry, cats, dogs, rabbits, cagebirds, laboratory animals, wildlife, zoo animals, fish and other domestic animals.

INIS Atomindex. International Atomic Energy Agency, Wagramerstrasse 5, Vienna, Austria A-1400. 222 23606198. 1988-. Semiannual. Abstracts nuclear energy and nuclear physics topics from journals, conferences, technical reports and other related publications. Issued in 6 parts: Personal Author, Corporate Entry, Subject, Report, Standard Patent, Conference (by place), Conference (by date).

Pollution Abstracts. Cambridge Scientific Abstracts, 5161 River Rd., Bethesda, Maryland 20816. (301) 961-6750. Six/year. Indexes worldwide technical literature on envi-

ronmental pollution. Covers air pollution, marine and freshwater pollution, sewage and wastewater treatment, waste management, toxicology and health, noise pollution, radiation, land pollution, and environmental policies, programs, legislation, and education. Also available online.

Science Citation Index. Institute for Scientific Information, 3501 Market St., Philadelphia, Pennsylvania 19104. 1961-.

ALMANACS AND YEARBOOKS

Association of Midwest Fish and Wildlife Agencies Proceedings. Michigan Department of Natural Resources, Box 30028, Lansing, Michigan 48909. (517) 373-1263. Annual.

BIBLIOGRAPHIES

Current Contents. Agriculture, Biology and Environmental Sciences. Institute for Scientific Information, 3501 Market St., Philadelphia, Pennsylvania 19104. (800) 523-1857. 1973-. Previous title: Current Contents. Agricultural, Food & Veterinary Sciences. Gives the table of contents of periodicals in the fields of agriculture, biology, environmental and related areas.

Directory of Published Proceedings. Interdok Corp., 173 Halstead Ave., Harrison, New York 10528. (914) 835-3506. 1990. Monthly. This is a listing of published proceedings including the series SEMTE (Science/Medicine/Engineering/Technology) and the series SSH (Social Science/Humanities).

EPA Publications Bibliography. U.S. Environmental Protection Agency, Library Systems Branch, 401 M St., SW, Washington, District of Columbia 20460. (202) 260-2090. Quarterly.

ENCYCLOPEDIAS AND DICTIONARIES

Dictionary of Evolutionary Fish Osteology. Alfonso L. Rojo. CRC Press, 2000 Corporate Blvd. NW, Boca Raton, Florida 33431. (407) 994-0555 or (800) 272-7737. 1991. Describes the preparation of fish skeletons and gives the translation of each term in five languages (French, German, Latin, Russian, and Spanish). Offers a rationale for the understanding of nomenclature of all fish skeletal structures.

Dr. Axelrod's Atlas of Freshwater Aquarium Fishes. H. R. Axelrod, ed. TFH Publications, 1 TFH Plaza, Neptune City, New Jersey 07753. (908) 988-8400. 1989. Third edition. Identifies fish, their common names, scientific name, range, habitat, water condition, size and food requirement. Includes colored illustrations and 4500 photos in full color.

Dr. Burgess's Atlas of Marine Aquarium Fishes. W. E. Burgess, et al. TFH Publications, 1 TFH Plaza, Neptune City, New Jersey 07753. (908) 988-8400. 1988. Pictorial aid for identification of marine fishes. More than 400 photos in full color are included. Also includes scientific name and common name, food habits, size and habitat.

The Encyclopedia of North American Wildlife. Stanley Klein. Facts on File, Inc., 460 Park Ave. S., New York, New York 10016. (212) 683-2244. 1983. Includes mammals, birds, reptiles, amphibians, and fish. Appendices include information on wildlife conservation organiza-

tions, a bibliographical list of endangered species and an index of Latin names.

Fish: Five Language Dictionary of Fish, Crustaceans, and Mollusks. Willibad Krane. Behr's Verlag, c/o Van Nostrand Reinhold, 115 5th Ave., New York, New York 10003. 1986.

Grzimek's Animal Life Encyclopedia. Van Nostrand Reinhold, 115 5th Ave., New York, New York 10003. (212) 254-3232. 1975. Thirteen volumes. Includes lower animals, insects, mollusks, fishes, amphibians, reptiles, birds, and mammals.

Macmillan Illustrated Animal Encyclopedia. Philip Whitfield, ed. Macmillan Publishing Co., 866 3rd Ave., New York, New York 10022. (212) 702-2000. 1984. Provides a comprehensive catalog of the staggering range of animal types within the vertebrate group. Also the IUCN endangered species are noted and includes common names, range and habitat. Includes mammals, birds, reptiles, amphibians, and fish.

The Nutrition and Health Encyclopedia. David F. Tver and Percy Russell. Van Nostrand Reinhold, 115 5th Ave., New York, New York 10003. (212) 254-3232. 1989.

Remarkable Animals: A Unique Encyclopedia of Wildlife Wonders. Guinness Books, 33 London Rd., Enfield, England EN2 6DJ. 1987. Includes mammals, birds, fishes, amphibians, reptiles, insects, and arachnids.

Van Nostrand's Scientific Encyclopedia. Glenn D. Considine, ed. Van Nostrand Reinhold, 115 5th Ave., New York, New York 10003. (212) 254-3232. 1983. Sixth edition. Includes all broad subject areas in science.

GENERAL WORKS

Fish Quality Control by Computer Vision. L. F. Pau and R. Olafsson, eds. Marcel Dekker, Inc., 270 Madison Ave., New York, New York 10016. (212) 696-9000; (800) 228-1160. 1991. Explores how computer vision and image processing can be applied to such aspects of the fishing industry as the quality inspection of fish and fish products for defects; the measurement and sorting by length, weight, species, shape, orientation, etc. in the processes of packaging, handling, selection, registration and pricing.

The Snake River: Window to the West. Tim Palmer. Island Press, 1718 Connecticut Ave. N.W., Suite 300, Washington, District of Columbia 20009. (202) 232-7933. 1991. Offers information about instream flows for fish and wildlife; groundwater management and quality; water conservation and efficiency; pollution of streams from agriculture and logging; small hydroelectric development; and reclamation of riparian habitat.

ONLINE DATA BASES

BIOSIS Previews. BIOSIS, 2100 Arch St., Philadelphia, Pennsylvania 19103-1399. (215) 587-4800. Largest and most comprehensive database of research in the life sciences. Contains citations for nearly 9000 primary research journals, monographs, reviews, symposia, preliminary reports, semi-popular journals, selected institutional reports, government reports and research communications.

Enviro/Energyline Abstracts Plus. R. R. Bowker Co., 121 Chanlon Rd., New Providence, New Jersey 07974. (908) 464-6800.

Environmental Periodicals Bibliography. National Information Services Corp., Ste. 6, Wyman Towers, 3100 St. Paul St., Baltimore, Maryland 21218. (410)243-0797. Online version of abstract of same name.

FISHNET. Aquatic Data Center, 1100 Gentry St., North Kansas City, Missouri 64116. (816) 842-5936.

Monthly Catalog of United States Government Publications. U.S. G.P.O., Supt. of Docs., PO Box 371954, Pittsburgh, Pennsylvania 15250-7954. (202) 512-0000.

National Technical Information Service. U.S. Department of Commerce, National Technical Information Service, Office of Data Base Services, 5285 Port Royal Rd., Springfield, Virginia 22161. (703) 487-4807. Bibliographic database of government sponsored research and technical reports.

SCISEARCH. Institute for Scientific Information, University City Science Center, 3501 Market St., Philadelphia, Pennsylvania 19104. (215) 386-0100.

PERIODICALS AND NEWSLETTERS

Alaska Fishery and Fur. U.S. Department of the Interior, 1849 C St. NW, Washington, District of Columbia 20240. (202) 208-3171. Annually.

Atlantic Salmon Journal. Atlantic Salmon Federation, 1435 St. Alexandre, Rm. 1030, Montreal, Quebec, Canada (514) 842-8059. 1951-. Quarterly.

Environmental Biology of Fishes. Dr. W. Junk Publishers, Postbus 163, Dordrecht, Netherlands 3300 AD. 1976-.

Journal of Fish Biology. Academic Press, c/o Harcourt Brace Jovanovich Inc., 6277 Sea Harbor Dr., Orlando, Florida 32887. (800) 346-8648. Quarterly.

Marine Bulletin. National Coalition for Marine Conservation, Box 23298, Savannah, Georgia 31403. (912) 234-8062. Monthly. Marine fisheries, biological research, marine environmental pollution, and the prevention of the over-exploitation of ocean fish.

RESEARCH CENTERS AND INSTITUTES

Jamie Whitten Delta States Research Center. PO Box 225, Stoneville, Mississippi 3877-0225. (601) 686-5231.

Montana State University, Montana Cooperative Fishery Research Unit. Biology Department, Bozeman, Montana 59715. (406) 994-3491.

University of Maryland, Sea Grant College. 1123 Taliaferro Hall, College Park, Maryland 20742. (301) 405-6371.

University of Massachusetts, Marine Station. P.O. Box 7125, Lanesville Station, 932 Washington Street, Gloucester, Massachusetts 01930. (508) 281-1930.

University of Mississippi, Biological Field Station. Department of Biology, University, Mississippi 38677. (601) 232-5479.

University of Mississippi, Biological Museum. Department of Biology, University, Mississippi 38677. (601) 232-7204.

University of New Hampshire, Anadromous Fish and Aquatic Invertebrate Research Facility. Marine Institute, Department of Zoology, Durham, New Hampshire 03824. (603) 862-2103.

University of North Carolina at Wilmington, NOAA National Undersea Research Center. 7205 Wrightsville Avenue, Wilmington, North Carolina 28403. (919) 256-5133.

University of Wisconsin-Madison, Center for Biotic Systems. 1042 WARF Office Building, 610 Walnut Street, Madison, Wisconsin 53705. (608) 262-9937.

University of Wyoming, Red Buttes Environmental Biology Laboratory. Box 3166, University Station, Laramie, Wyoming 82071. (307) 745-8504.

STATISTICS SOURCES

Ecology: Community Profiles. U.S. Fish and Wildlife Service. National Technical Information Service, 5285 Port Royal Road, Springfield, Virginia 22161. (703) 487-4650. Irregular. Data on coastal and inland ecosystems, including wetlands, tidal-flats, near-shore seagrasses, sand dunes, drilling platforms, oyster reefs, estuaries, rivers and streams.

Report on the Nation's Renewable Resources. U.S. Forest Service. U.S. G.P.O., Washington, District of Columbia 20401. (202) 512-0000. Quinquennial. Projections of resource use and supply from 1920 to 2040, covering wilderness, wildlife, fish, range, timber, water and minerals.

Statistical Summary of Fish and Wildlife Restoration. U.S. Fish and Wildlife Service. U.S. G.P.O., Washington, District of Columbia 20401. (202) 512-0000. Annual. Data on hunting, fishing activities, and restoration.

TRADE ASSOCIATIONS AND PROFESSIONAL SOCIETIES

American Institute of Biological Sciences. 730 11th St., N.W., Washington, District of Columbia 20001-4521. (202) 628-1500.

American Society of Naturalists. Department of Ecology and Evolation, State University of New York, Stony Brook, New York 11794. (516) 632-8589.

Association of Midwest Fish and Wildlife Agencies. c/o John Urbain, Michigan Dept. of Natural Resources, Box 30028, Lansing, Michigan 48909. (517) 373-1263.

Atlantic Salmon Federation. P.O. Box 429, St. Andrews, New Brunswick, Canada E0G 2X0. (506) 529-4581.

Columbia Basin Fish & Wildlife Authority. 2000 SW First Ave., Suite 170, Portland, Oregon 97201. (503) 294-7031.

Future Fisherman Foundation. 1250 Grove Ave., Ste. 300, Barrington, Illinois 60010. (708) 381-4061.

National Fish & Wildlife Federation. 18th & C Streets, N.W., Rm 2626, Washington, District of Columbia 20240. (202) 343-1040.

North American Native Fishers Association. 123 W. Mt. Airy Ave., Philadelphia, Pennsylvania 19119. (215) 247-0384.

Southeastern Fishes Council. 1300 Blue Spruce Dr., Ft. Collins, Colorado 80524. (303) 493-4855.

Sport Fishing Institute. 1010 Massachusetts Ave., N.W., Washington, District of Columbia 20001. (202) 898-0770.

Trout Unlimited. 800 Folin Ln., S.E., Ste. 250, Vienna, Virginia 22180. (703) 281-1100.

FISH AND FISHERIES

See also: INTERNATIONAL TREATIES

ABSTRACTING AND INDEXING SERVICES

Aquatic Sciences and Fisheries Abstracts. Cambridge Scientific Abstracts, 5161 River Rd., Bethesda, Maryland 20816. (301) 961-6750. Monthly. Compiled by the United Nations Dept. of Economic and Social Affairs, the Food and Agriculture Organization of the United Nations and the Intergovernmental Oceanographic Commission with the collaboration of other agencies. Includes the broad subject areas of ecology, fisheries, marine biology, public policy, aquatic biology, and aquatic ecology.

ASFA Aquaculture Abstracts. Cambridge Scientific Abstracts, Inc., 5161 River Rd., Bethesda, Maryland 20816. (301) 961-6750. 1984.

Biological Abstracts. BIOSIS, 2100 Arch St., Philadelphia, Pennsylvania 19103-1399. (215) 587-4800. 1927-.

Biology Digest. Data Courier, Plexus Pub Inc., 143 Old Marlton Pike, Medford, New Jersey 08055. 1974-. Monthly. Abstracts biology periodicals.

Current Advances in Ecological and Environmental Science. Pergamon Microforms International, Inc., Fairview Park, Elmsford, New York 10523. (914) 592-7720. 1989-. Monthly. Current literature searching service includingjournals, reports, abstracts, etc. This service is available online as part of the CABS database on the hosts BRS and ORBIT search service.

Ecological Abstracts. Geo Abstracts Ltd. Elsevier Applied Science, Crown House, Linton Rd., Barking, England IG 11 8JU. 1974-. Derived from over 600 leading ecological and environmental journals, plus books, conference proceedings, reports and theses.

Ecology Abstracts. Cambridge Scientific Abstracts, 5161 River Rd., Bethesda, Maryland 20816. (301) 961-6750. Monthly.

Environment Abstracts. Bowker A & I Publishing, 121 Chanlon Rd., New Providence, New Jersey 07974. (908) 464-6800. 1974-.

Environment Index. Environment Information Center, Index Research Department, 124 E. 39th St., New York, New York 10016. 1971-. Annual.

Environmental Information Connection–EIC. Planning Information Program, Dept. of Urban and Regional Planning, University of Illinois, 1003 West Nevada, Urbana, Illinois 61801. (217) 333-1369. Also available online.

Environmental Periodicals Bibliography. Environmental Studies Institute, International Academy at Santa Barbara, 800 Garden St., Suite D, Santa Barbara, California 93101. (805) 965-5010. Also available online.

Fisheries Review. U.S. Fish and Wildlife Service. U.S. G.P.O., Washington, District of Columbia 20401. (202) 512-0000. Quarterly. Abstracting service dealing with fisheries and ichthyology.

General Science Index. H. W. Wilson Co., 950 University Ave., Bronx, New York 10452. 1978-. Monthly, also issued in annual cumulation. Cumulative subject index to English language periodicals in the subject fields of astronomy, botany, chemistry, earth science, environment and conservation, food and nutrition, genetics, mathematics, medicine and health, microbiology, oceanography, physics, physiology and zoology.

Geographical Abstracts. London School of Economics, Dept. of Geography, Regency House, 34 Duke St., London, England 1966-. Continued by Geo Abstracts issued in 6 parts: Pt. A. Landforms and the quaternary; Pt. B. Biogeography and Climatology; Pt. C. Economic geography; Pt. D. Social geography and cartography; Pt. E. Sedimentology; Pt. F. Regional and community planning.

Index to Scientific Book Contents. Institute for Scientific Information, 3501 Market St., Philadelphia, Pennsylvania 19104. (800) 523-1857. 1985-. Annual. Gives contents of science books published.

INIS Atomindex. International Atomic Energy Agency, Wagramerstrasse 5, Vienna, Austria A-1400. 222 23606198. 1988-. Semiannual. Abstracts nuclear energy and nuclear physics topics from journals, conferences, technical reports and other related publications. Issued in 6 parts: Personal Author, Corporate Entry, Subject, Report, Standard Patent, Conference (by place), Conference (by date).

Oceanic Abstracts. UMI Data Courier, 620 S. 3rd St., Louisville, Kentucky 40202. (800) 626-2823. Formerly: Oceanic Index and Oceanic Citation Journal.

Pollution Abstracts. Cambridge Scientific Abstracts, 5161 River Rd., Bethesda, Maryland 20816. (301) 961-6750. Six/year. Indexes worldwide technical literature on environmental pollution. Covers air pollution, marine and freshwater pollution, sewage and wastewater treatment, waste management, toxicology and health, noise pollution, radiation, land pollution, and environmental policies, programs, legislation, and education. Also available online.

Science Citation Index. Institute for Scientific Information, 3501 Market St., Philadelphia, Pennsylvania 19104. 1961-.

Sea Grant Abstracts. National Sea Grant Depository, Pell Laboratory Bldg., Bay Campus, University of Rhode Island, Narragansett, Rhode Island 02882. (401) 792-6114. 1986-. Quarterly. Published by the National Sea Grant Programs, this collection includes annual reports, serials and newsletters, charts and maps.

BIBLIOGRAPHIES

Current Contents. Agriculture, Biology and Environmental Sciences. Institute for Scientific Information, 3501 Market St., Philadelphia, Pennsylvania 19104. (800) 523-1857. 1973-. Previous title: Current Contents. Agricultural, Food & Veterinary Sciences. Gives the table of contents of periodicals in the fields of agriculture, biology, environmental and related areas.

EPA Publications Bibliography. U.S. Environmental Protection Agency, Library Systems Branch, 401 M St., SW, Washington, District of Columbia 20460. (202) 260-2090. Quarterly.

DIRECTORIES

Fisheries Socio-Economic Data Locator. Office of Fisheries Management/National Marine Fisheries Service, 1335 East-West Highway, Silver Spring, Maryland 20910. (202) 634-7218.

Gale Environmental Sourcebook. Karen Hill. Gale Research Co., 835 Penobscot Bldg., Detroit, Michigan 48226-4094. (313) 961-2242. Contacts, information sources, or general information on environmental topics.

National Listing of Fisheries Offices. Fish and Wildlife Service, Department of the Interior, 18th & C Sts., N.W., Washington, District of Columbia 20240. (202) 653-8750.

ENCYCLOPEDIAS AND DICTIONARIES

Dr. Axelrod's Atlas of Freshwater Aquarium Fishes. H. R. Axelrod, ed. TFH Publications, 1 TFH Plaza, Neptune City, New Jersey 07753. (908) 988-8400. 1989. Third edition. Identifies fish, their common names, scientific name, range, habitat, water condition, size and food requirement. Includes colored illustrations and 4500 photos in full color.

Dr. Burgess's Atlas of Marine Aquarium Fishes. W. E. Burgess, et al. TFH Publications, 1 TFH Plaza, Neptune City, New Jersey 07753. (908) 988-8400. 1988. Pictorial aid for identification of marine fishes. More than 400 photos in full color are included. Also includes scientific name and common name, food habits, size and habitat.

Illustrated Encyclopedia of Science and the Future. Mike Biscare, et al., ed. Marshall Cavendish, 58 Old Compton St., London, England 0W1V5 PA. 01-734 6710. 1983. Twenty volumes. Each volume has 5 sections: Frontiers, Electronics in Action, Medical Science, Military Technology, and Resources.

GENERAL WORKS

Fishing Vessel Safety: Blueprint for a National Program. National Research Council. Committee on Fishing Vessel Safety. National Academy Press, 2101 Constitution Ave. NW, PO Box 285, Washington, District of Columbia 20055. (202) 334-3313. 1991. Comprehensive assessment of vessel and personnel safety in the U.S. commercial fishing fleet. Includes a chronology of safety efforts and summarizes various parameters of commercial fishing industry.

Free Market Environmentalism. Terry L. Anderson and Donald R. Leal. Westview Press, 5500 Central Ave., Boulder, Colorado 80301. (303) 444-3541. 1991. Examines the prospects and pitfalls of improving natural resource allocation and environmental quality through market processes.

GOVERNMENTAL ORGANIZATIONS

Bureau of Oceans and International Environmental and Scientific Affairs. 2201 C St., N.W., Washington, District of Columbia 20520. (202) 647-1554.

TVA Public Information Office. 400 West Summit Hill Dr., Knoxville, Tennessee 37902. (615) 632-8000.

ONLINE DATA BASES

Aquaculture. National Oceanic and Atmospheric Administration, National Environmental Data Referral Service, 1825 Connecticut Ave., N.W., Washington, District of Columbia 20235. (202) 673-5548.

Aqualine. Water Research Center, Medmenham Laboratory, Marlow, Buckinghamshire, England SL7 2HD. Literature on water and wastewater technology.

AQUAREF. Environment Canada, WATDOC, Inland Waters Directorate, Ottawa, Ontario, Canada K1A OH3. (819) 997-2324.

BIOSIS Previews. BIOSIS, 2100 Arch St., Philadelphia, Pennsylvania 19103-1399. (215) 587-4800. Largest and most comprehensive database of research in the life sciences. Contains citations for nearly 9000 primary research journals, monographs, reviews, symposia, preliminary reports, semi-popular journals, selected institutional reports, government reports and research communications.

Enviro/Energyline Abstracts Plus. R. R. Bowker Co., 121 Chanlon Rd., New Providence, New Jersey 07974. (908) 464-6800.

Environmental Periodicals Bibliography. National Information Services Corp., Ste. 6, Wyman Towers, 3100 St. Paul St., Baltimore, Maryland 21218. (410)243-0797. Online version of abstract of same name.

FISHNET. Aquatic Data Center, 1100 Gentry St., North Kansas City, Missouri 64116. (816) 842-5936.

Monthly Catalog of United States Government Publications. U.S. G.P.O., Supt. of Docs., PO Box 371954, Pittsburgh, Pennsylvania 15250-7954. (202) 512-0000.

National Technical Information Service. U.S. Department of Commerce, National Technical Information Service, Office of Data Base Services, 5285 Port Royal Rd., Springfield, Virginia 22161. (703) 487-4807. Bibliographic database of government sponsored research and technical reports.

Oceanic Abstracts. Cambridge Scientific Abstracts, 5161 River Rd., Bethesda, Maryland 20816. (301) 961-6750. Online access.

PERIODICALS AND NEWSLETTERS

Alaska Fishery and Fur. U.S. Department of the Interior, 1849 C St. NW, Washington, District of Columbia 20240. (202) 208-3171. Annually.

Geojourney. Florida Department of Natural Resources, 3900 Commonwealth Blvd., Tallahassee, Florida 32303. (904) 488-1234. 1980-. Quarterly. Covers activities on resource management, marine resources, parks and recreation, and subjects related to fishing, boating and all uses of Florida's natural resources.

Missouri Conservationist. Missouri Deptartment of Conservation, Box 180, Jefferson City, Missouri 65102. (314) 751-4115. Monthly. Game, fish, and forestry management and hunting and fishing techniques.

RESEARCH CENTERS AND INSTITUTES

Alaska Cooperative Fishery and Wildlife Research Unit. 138 Arctic Health Research Unit, University of Alaska-Fairbanks, Fairbanks, Alaska 99775-0110. (907) 474-7661.

Alaska Fisheries Science Center. 7600 Sand Point Way NE, BIN C15700, Seattle, Washington 98115. (206) 526-4000.

Aquatic Research Institute. 2242 Davis Court, Hayward, California 94545. (415) 782-4058.

Auburn University, International Center for Aquaculture. Auburn, Alabama 36849-5124. (205) 826-4786.

Florida Sea Grant College Program. University of Florida, Building 803, Room 4, Gainesville, Florida 32611-0341. (904) 392-5870.

Maine Department of Inland Fisheries and Wildlife, Fishery Research Management Division. Fisheries Laboratory, P.O. Box 1298, Bangor, Maine 04401. (207) 941-4461.

Mansfield University, Fisheries Program. Grant Science Center, Mansfield, Pennsylvania 16933. (717) 662-4539.

Marine/Freshwater Biomedical Center. Oregon State University, Department of Food Science, Corvallis, Oregon 97331. (503) 737-4193.

Marine Resources Research Institute. South Carolina Wildlife and Marine Resources Dept., Charleston, South Carolina 29412. (803) 795-6350.

Maritime Center. 10 North Water Street, South Norwalk, Connecticut 06854. (203) 852-0700.

Minnesota Transgenic Fish Group. University of Minnesota, Department of Animal Science, 1988 Fitch Ave., St. Paul, Minnesota 55108. (612) 624-4277.

Montana State University, Montana Cooperative Fishery Research Unit. Biology Department, Bozeman, Montana 59715. (406) 994-3491.

National Fisheries Education & Research Foundation, Inc. 1525 Wilson Blvd., Ste. 500, Arlington, Virginia 22209. (703) 524-9216.

North Carolina Aquarium/Roanoke Island. P.O. Box 967, Airport Road, Manteo, North Carolina 27954. (919) 473-3493.

Northwest Fisheries Science Center. 2725 Montlake Boulevard East, Seattle, Washington 98112. (206) 553-1872.

Oklahoma Fishery Research Laboratory. 500 East Constellation, Norman, Oklahoma 73072. (405) 325-7288.

Oregon State University, Oregon Cooperative Fishery Research Unit. 104 Nash Hall, Corvallis, Oregon 97331. (503) 737-4531.

Oregon State University, Oregon Sea Grant College Program. Administrative Services Building-A 500, Corvallis, Oregon 97331. (503) 737-2714.

Rhode Island Sea Grant Marine Advisory Service. Narragansett Bay Campus, University of Rhode Island, Narragansett, Rhode Island 02882. (401) 792-6211.

Rutgers University, Fisheries and Aquaculture Technology Extension Center. P.O. Box 231, New Brunswick, New Jersey 08903. (908) 932-8959.

Rutgers University, Rutgers Shellfish Research Laboratory. P.O. Box 06230, Port North Norris, New Jersey 08349. (609) 785-0074.

Southern Illinois University at Carbondale, Cooperative Fisheries Research Laboratory. Carbondale, Illinois 62901. (618) 536-7761.

Tennessee Technological University, Tennessee Cooperative Fishery Research Unit. TTU Box 5114, Cookeville, Tennessee 38505. (615) 372-3094.

University of Georgia, Marine Extension Service. P.O. Box 13687, Savannah, Georgia 31416. (912) 356-2496.

University of Hawaii at Manoa Hawaii Cooperative Fishery Research Unit. 2538 The Mall, Honolulu, Hawaii 96822. (808) 956-8350.

University of Hawaii at Manoa Hawaii Institute of Marine Biology. Coconut Island, P.O. Box 1346, Kaneohe, Hawaii 96744-1346. (808) 236-7401.

University of Hawaii at Manoa Hawaii Undersea Research Laboratory. 1000 Pope Road, MSB 303, Honolulu, Hawaii 96822. (808) 956-6335.

University of Maine, Center for Marine Studies. 14 Coburn Hall, Orono, Maine 04469. (207) 581-1435.

University of Maine, Maine Sea Grant College Program. 14 Coburn Hall, University of Maine, Orono, Maine 04469-0114. (207) 581-1435.

University of Maine, Migratory Fish Research Institute. Department of Zoology, Orono, Maine 04469. (207) 581-2548.

University of Maryland, Sea Grant College. 1123 Taliaferro Hall, College Park, Maryland 20742. (301) 405-6371.

University of Massachusetts, Cooperative Marine Research Program. The Environmental Institute, Blaisdell House, Amherst, Massachusetts 01003-0040. (413) 545-2842.

University of New Hampshire, Anadromous Fish and Aquatic Invertebrate Research Facility. Marine Institute, Department of Zoology, Durham, New Hampshire 03824. (603) 862-2103.

University of New Hampshire, Coastal Marine Laboratory. Department of Zoology, Durham, New Hampshire 03824. (603) 862-2100.

University of New Hampshire, New Hampshire Sea Grant College Program. Marine Programs Building, Durham, New Hampshire 03824-3512. (603) 749-1565.

University of Oklahoma, Aquatic Ecology and Fisheries Research Center. 730 Van Vleet Oval, Room 314, Richards Hall, Norman, Oklahoma 73019. (405) 325-4821.

University of Rhode Island, International Center for Marine Resource Development (*ICMRD*). 126 Woodward Hall, Kingston, Rhode Island 02881. (401) 792-2479.

University of Rhode Island, Sea Grant College Program. Graduate School of Oceanography, Narragansett, Rhode Island 02882-1197. (401) 792-6800.

University of Southern California, Fish Harbor Marine Research Laboratory. 820 South Seaside Avenue, Terminal Island, California 90731. (310) 830-4570.

University of Washington, Fisheries Research Institute. School of Fisheries, WH-10, Seattle, Washington 98195. (206) 543-4650.

University of Wisconsin-Stevens Point, Wisconsin Cooperative Fishery Research Unit. College of Natural Resources, Stevens Point, Wisconsin 54481. (715) 346-2178.

Utah State University, Bear Lake Biological Laboratory. c/o Department of Fisheries and Wildlife, Logan, Utah 84322-5210. (801) 753-2459.

Utah State University, Utah Cooperative Fish and Wildlife Research Unit. Logan, Utah 84322. (801) 750-2509.

Vancouver Aquarium Research Department. Van Dusen Aquatic Science Centre, P.O.Box 3232, Vancouver, British Columbia, Canada V6B 3X8. (604) 685-3364.

Virginia Cooperative Fish and Wildlife Research Unit. Virginia Polytech Institute and State University, 106 Cheatham Hall, Blacksburg, Virginia 24061. (703) 231-5927.

Washington Cooperative Fishery and Wildlife Research Unit. University of Washington, School of Fisheries, WH-10, Seattle, Washington 98195. (206) 543-6475.

Water Resources Institute. Grand Valley State University, Allendale, Michigan 49401. (616) 895-3749.

West Coast Fisheries Development Foundation. 812 S.W. Washington, Suite 900, Portland, Oregon 97205. (503) 222-3518.

Wyoming Cooperative Fishery and Wildlife Research Unit. University of Wyoming, Box 3166, University Station, Laramie, Wyoming 82071. (307) 766-5415.

STATISTICS SOURCES

Current Fisheries Statistics. U.S. G.P.O., Washington, District of Columbia 20401. (202) 512-0000. Annual. Production and trade of fish products, including fresh, frozen, canned, cured, and nonedible products.

Environmental Data Compendium. OECD Publications and Information Center, 2001 L St., N.W., Suite 700, Washington, District of Columbia 20036. (202) 785-6323. 1989.

Environmental Indicators. OECD Publications and Information Center, 2001 L St., N.W., Suite 700, Washington, District of Columbia 20036. (202) 785-6323. 1991.

Environmental Quality. Council on Environmental Quality. U.S. G.P.O., Washington, District of Columbia 20401. (202) 512-0000. Annual.

Fish and Fish Egg Distribution Report. U.S. Fish and Wildlife Service. U.S. G.P.O., Washington, District of Columbia 20401. (202) 512-0000. Annual. Propagation and distribution activities of the National Fish Hatchery System.

Fisheries of the U.S. U.S. G.P.O., Washington, District of Columbia 20401. (202) 512-0000. Annual. Fish landings, fish trade, prices, consumption, production of fishery products, and industry employment.

Marine Fisheries Review. U.S. G.P.O, Washington, District of Columbia 20402-9325. (202) 512-0000. Quarterly. Marine fishery resources, development, and management. Covers fish, shellfish, and marine mammal populations.

Species Profiles: Life Histories and Environmental Requirements of Coastal Fishes and Invertebrates. U.S. G.P.O, Washington, District of Columbia 20402-9325. (202) 512-0000. Annual. Life cycle and environmental requirements of selected fish and shellfish species, by coastal region.

The State of the Environment. OECD Publications and Information Center, 2001 L St., N.W., Suite 700, Washington, District of Columbia 20036. (202) 785-6323. 1991.

Status of the Fishery Resources Off the Northeastern U.S. U.S. National Marine Fisheries Service. National Technical Information Service, Springfield, Virginia 22161. (703) 487-4650. Annual. Covers Atlantic ocean finfish and shellfish landings.

World Resources. World Resources Institute. 1709 New York Ave., N.W., Washington, District of Columbia 20006. (202) 638-6300. Annual. Statistical and textual analysis of world's natural resources and the effects of growth-caused environmental pollution.

TRADE ASSOCIATIONS AND PROFESSIONAL SOCIETIES

American Fisheries Society. 5410 Grosvenor Ln., Suite 110, Bethesda, Maryland 20814. (301) 897-8616.

American Institute of Biological Sciences. 730 11th St., N.W., Washington, District of Columbia 20001-4521. (202) 628-1500.

Association of University Fisheries and Wildlife Program Administrators. Department of Wildlife and Fisheries Sciences, Texas A & M University, College Station, Texas 77843-2258. (409) 845-1261.

Bigelow Laboratory for Ocean Sciences, Division of Northeast Research Foundation, Inc. Mckown Point, West Boothbay Harbor, Maine 04575. (207) 633-2173.

FishAmerica Foundation. c/o Sport Fishing Institute, 1010 Massachusetts Ave., N.W., Suite 320, Washington, District of Columbia 20001. (202) 898-0869.

Gulf & Caribbean Fisheries Institute. Sea Grant Consortium, 287 Meeting St., Charleston, South Carolina 29401. (803) 727-2078.

Inland Commercial Fisheries Association. c/o Green Island Fishing Co., Inc., 11 Ogden St., Marinette, Wisconsin 54143. (715) 732-1313.

National Fish & Wildlife Federation. 18th & C Streets, N.W., Rm 2626, Washington, District of Columbia 20240. (202) 343-1040.

National Fisheries Containment Research Center. Fish and Wildlife Service, U.S. Dept. of the Interior, 4200 New Haven Rd., Columbia, Missouri 65201. (314) 875-5399.

National Fisheries Institute. 1525 Wilson Blvd., Suite 500, Arlington, Virginia 22209. (703) 524-8880.

Southeastern Fishes Council. 1300 Blue Spruce Dr., Ft. Collins, Colorado 80524. (303) 493-4855.

Sport Fishing Institute. 1010 Massachusetts Ave., N.W., Washington, District of Columbia 20001. (202) 898-0770.

FISH AND WILDLIFE MANAGEMENT

See also: HYDROELECTRIC POWER; RESERVOIRS

ABSTRACTING AND INDEXING SERVICES

Applied Ecology Abstracts Studies in Renewable Natural Resources. Information Retrieval Ltd., 1911 Jefferson Davis Highway, Arlington, Virginia 22202. 1975-. Monthly.

Aquatic Sciences and Fisheries Abstracts. Cambridge Scientific Abstracts, 5161 River Rd., Bethesda, Maryland 20816. (301) 961-6750. Monthly. Compiled by the United Nations Dept. of Economic and Social Affairs, the Food and Agriculture Organization of the United Nations and the Intergovernmental Oceanographic Commission with the collaboration of other agencies. Includes the broad subject areas of ecology, fisheries, marine biology, public policy, aquatic biology, and aquatic ecology.

ASFA Aquaculture Abstracts. Cambridge Scientific Abstracts, Inc., 5161 River Rd., Bethesda, Maryland 20816. (301) 961-6750. 1984.

Biological Abstracts. BIOSIS, 2100 Arch St., Philadelphia, Pennsylvania 19103-1399. (215) 587-4800. 1927-.

Current Advances in Ecological and Environmental Science. Pergamon Microforms International, Inc., Fairview Park, Elmsford, New York 10523. (914) 592-7720. 1989-. Monthly. Current literature searching service includingjournals, reports, abstracts, etc. This service is available online as part of the CABS database on the hosts BRS and ORBIT search service.

Ecological Abstracts. Geo Abstracts Ltd. Elsevier Applied Science, Crown House, Linton Rd., Barking, England IG 11 8JU. 1974-. Derived from over 600 leading ecological and environmental journals, plus books, conference proceedings, reports and theses.

Ecology Abstracts. Cambridge Scientific Abstracts, 5161 River Rd., Bethesda, Maryland 20816. (301) 961-6750. Monthly.

Environment Abstracts. Bowker A & I Publishing, 121 Chanlon Rd., New Providence, New Jersey 07974. (908) 464-6800. 1974-.

Environment Index. Environment Information Center, Index Research Department, 124 E. 39th St., New York, New York 10016. 1971-. Annual.

Environmental Information Connection–EIC. Planning Information Program, Dept. of Urban and Regional Planning, University of Illinois, 1003 West Nevada, Urbana, Illinois 61801. (217) 333-1369. Also available online.

Environmental Periodicals Bibliography. Environmental Studies Institute, International Academy at Santa Barbara, 800 Garden St., Suite D, Santa Barbara, California 93101. (805) 965-5010. Also available online.

Fisheries Review. U.S. Fish and Wildlife Service. U.S. G.P.O., Washington, District of Columbia 20401. (202) 512-0000. Quarterly. Abstracting service dealing with fisheries and ichthyology.

Forestry Abstracts. C. A. B. International, Wallingford, England OX10 8DE. (0491) 3211. 1939/40-. Monthly. Journal of abstracts of journal articles, conferences, technical reports in the subject areas of: silviculture, forest mensuration and management, physical environment, fire, plant biology, genetics and breeding, mycology and pathology, game and wildlife, fish, protection of forests and other related matter.

General Science Index. H. W. Wilson Co., 950 University Ave., Bronx, New York 10452. 1978-. Monthly, also issued in annual cumulation. Cumulative subject index to English language periodicals in the subject fields of astronomy, botany, chemistry, earth science, environment and conservation, food and nutrition, genetics, mathematics, medicine and health, microbiology, oceanography, physics, physiology and zoology.

Geographical Abstracts. London School of Economics, Dept. of Geography, Regency House, 34 Duke St., London, England 1966-. Continued by Geo Abstracts issued in 6 parts: Pt. A. Landforms and the quaternary; Pt. B. Biogeography and Climatology; Pt. C. Economic geography; Pt. D. Social geography and cartography; Pt. E. Sedimentology; Pt. F. Regional and community planning.

Index to Scientific Book Contents. Institute for Scientific Information, 3501 Market St., Philadelphia, Pennsylvania 19104. (800) 523-1857. 1985-. Annual. Gives contents of science books published.

Multimedia Index to Ecology. National Information Center for Educational Media, University of Southern California, Los Angeles, California 90007.

Pollution Abstracts. Cambridge Scientific Abstracts, 5161 River Rd., Bethesda, Maryland 20816. (301) 961-6750. Six/year. Indexes worldwide technical literature on environmental pollution. Covers air pollution, marine and freshwater pollution, sewage and wastewater treatment, waste management, toxicology and health, noise pollution, radiation, land pollution, and environmental policies, programs, legislation, and education. Also available online.

Science Citation Index. Institute for Scientific Information, 3501 Market St., Philadelphia, Pennsylvania 19104. 1961-.

Sea Grant Abstracts. National Sea Grant Depository, Pell Laboratory Bldg., Bay Campus, University of Rhode Island, Narragansett, Rhode Island 02882. (401) 792-6114. 1986-. Quarterly. Published by the National Sea Grant Programs, this collection includes annual reports, serials and newsletters, charts and maps.

BIBLIOGRAPHIES

EPA Publications Bibliography. U.S. Environmental Protection Agency, Library Systems Branch, 401 M St., SW, Washington, District of Columbia 20460. (202) 260-2090. Quarterly.

ENCYCLOPEDIAS AND DICTIONARIES

Cambridge Encyclopedia of Life Sciences. A. E. Friday and David S. Ingram. Cambridge University Press, 40 W 20th St., New York, New York 10011. (212) 924-3900 or

(800) 227-0247. 1985. Includes all topics under biology and ecology.

The Encyclopedia of Animal Ecology. Peter D. Moore. Facts on File, Inc., 460 Park Ave. S., New York, New York 10016. (212) 683-2244. 1987.

McGraw-Hill Encyclopedia of Environmental Science. Sybil P. Parker. McGraw-Hill Science & Engineering Books, 11 W. 19th St., New York, New York 10011. (212) 337-6010. 1980. Covers ecology, man's influence on nature, and environmental protection.

McGraw-Hill Encyclopedia of Science and Technology. McGraw-Hill, 1221 Avenue of the Americas, New York, New York 10020. (212) 512-2000 or (800) 262-4729. 1992. Seventh edition. Issued in multiple volumes including index. Includes all science and technology broad subject areas.

Van Nostrand's Scientific Encyclopedia. Glenn D. Considine, ed. Van Nostrand Reinhold, 115 5th Ave., New York, New York 10003. (212) 254-3232. 1983. Sixth edition. Includes all broad subject areas in science.

GENERAL WORKS

Game Wars: The Undercover Pursuit of Wildlife Poachers. Marc Reisner. Academic Marketing, Penguin USA, 375 Hudson St., New York, New York 10014. (212) 366-2000; (800) 253-2304. 1991. Provides a first hand account of the life and dangers encountered by federal wildlife agents working for U.S. Fish and Wildlife Service: the elaborate covers they devise; the meticulous preparation necessary to pull off a successful sting; the weeks, months, even years they spend putting together their traps and cases; and the dangers they face as they impersonate big game hunters, ivory trades; and professional smugglers.

Managing our Wildlife Resources. Stanley H. Anderson. Prentice-Hall, Rte. 9W, Englewood Cliffs, New Jersey 07632. (201) 592-2000; (800) 634-2863. 1991. Reviews wildlife management, history, population characteristic, and habitat intervention; emphasizes planning, developing programs, and the impact of pollutants.

GOVERNMENTAL ORGANIZATIONS

Game and Fish Commission: Fish and Wildlife. Director, #2 Natural Resources Dr., Little Rock, Arkansas 72205. (501) 223-6305.

Game and Fish Commission: Fish and Wildlife. Director, 5400 Bishop Blvd., Cheyenne, Wyoming 82002. (307) 777-7632.

Game and Fish Department: Fish and Wildlife. Director, 2221 W. Greenway Rd., Phoenix, Arizona 85023. (602) 942-3000.

Game and Fish Department: Fish and Wildlife. Director, Villagra Building, Santa Fe, New Mexico 87503. (505) 827-7899.

Game and Fish Department: Fish and Wildlife. Commissioner, 100 North Bismark Expressway, Bismark, North Dakota 58501. (701) 221-6300.

Game and Fresh Water Fish Commission: Fish and Wildlife. Executive Director, 620 South Meridan St., Tallahassee, Florida 32399-1600. (904) 488-2975.

Game and Inland Fisheries Department: Fish and Wildlife. Executive Director, Fresh Water, 4010 W. Broad St., Richmond, Virginia 23230. (804) 367-9231.

Game and Park Commission: Fish and Wildlife. Director, 2200 North 33rd St., PO Box 30370, Lincoln, Nebraska 68503-0370. (402) 464-0641.

Office of Public Affairs: Fish and Wildlife Service. 18th and C St., N.W., Washington, District of Columbia 20240. (202) 343-5634.

U.S. Environmental Protection Agency: Office of Pesticide Programs. 401 M St., S.W., Washington, District of Columbia 20460. (202) 557-7090.

ONLINE DATA BASES

Enviro/Energyline Abstracts Plus. R. R. Bowker Co., 121 Chanlon Rd., New Providence, New Jersey 07974. (908) 464-6800.

Environmental Periodicals Bibliography. National Information Services Corp., Ste. 6, Wyman Towers, 3100 St. Paul St., Baltimore, Maryland 21218. (410)243-0797. Online version of abstract of same name.

Fish and Wildlife Reference Service Database. U.S. Fish and Wildlife Service, The Maxima Corporation, 5430 Grosvenor Lane, Suite 110, Bethesda, Maryland 20814. (301) 492-6403. State fish and game agency technical reports covering American fish and wildlife.

FISHNET. Aquatic Data Center, 1100 Gentry St., North Kansas City, Missouri 64116. (816) 842-5936.

SCISEARCH. Institute for Scientific Information, University City Science Center, 3501 Market St., Philadelphia, Pennsylvania 19104. (215) 386-0100.

PERIODICALS AND NEWSLETTERS

British Columbia Ministry of Environment, Annual Report. British Columbia, Ministry of Environment, 810 Blanchard, 1st Fl., Victoria, British Columbia, Canada (604) 387-9418. 1976-. Annually. Review of work carried out during the year by the Ministry of the Environment, including fish, wildlife, water management, and parks.

Ecological Applications. Ecological Society of America, Center for Environmental Studies, Arizona State University, Tempe, Arizona 85287. (602) 965-3000. 1991-. Quarterly. Emphasizes the application of basic ecological concepts to a wide range of problems.

Fish and Wildlife Reference Service Newsletter. U.S. Fish and Wildlife Reference Service, 5430 Grosvenor Lane, Suite 110, Bethesda, Maryland 20814. (800) 582-3421. Quarterly. Federal Aid in Fish and Wildlife Program.

Florida Fish & Wildlife News. Florida Wildlife Federation, Box 6870, Tallahassee, Florida 32314-6870. (904) 656-7113. Monthly. Conservation news concerning fish & wildlife.

Friend O'Wildlife. North Carolina Wildlife Federation,Inc., Box 10626, Raleigh, North Carolina 27605. (919) 833-1923. 1959-. Bimonthly. Covers North Carolina wildlife conservation and related hunting, fishing and boating activities and other environmental issues.

IAFWA Newsletter. International Association of Fish and Wildlife Agencies, 444 N. Capitol St., NW, #534, Washington, District of Columbia 20001. (202) 624-7890.

Bimonthly. Fish & wildlife conservation, fishing, wildlife management.

Idaho Wildlife. Idaho Dept. of Fish and Game, P.O. Box 25, 600 S. Walnut, Boise, Idaho 83712. (208) 334-3746. Bimonthly. Covers conservation, wildlife management, fish and game operations and policies.

Illinois Wildlife. Illinois Wildlife Federation, 123 S. Chicago St., Rossville, Illinois 60963. (217) 748-6365. Bimonthly. Deals with outdoor recreational trends.

Liaison Conservation Directory. U.S. Office of Endangered Species, Fish & Wildlife Service, Int., Washington, District of Columbia 20240. (703) 235-2407.

Maine Fish. Maine Fish, 284 State St., Sta. 41, Augusta, Maine 04333. (207) 289-2871. Quarterly. Fish & wildlife research & management.

Minnesota Division of Game & Fish, Technical Bulletin. Minnesota Dept. of Conservation, 90 W. Plato Blvd., St. Paul, Minnesota 55107. Irregular.

Minnesota Out-of-Doors. Minnesota Conservation Federation, 1036-B Cleveland Ave., S., St. Paul, Minnesota 55116. (612) 690-3077. Monthly. Conservation, natural resources, hunting & fishing.

Missouri Conservationist. Missouri Deptartment of Conservation, Box 180, Jefferson City, Missouri 65102. (314) 751-4115. Monthly. Game, fish, and forestry management and hunting and fishing techniques.

New York Fish and Game Journal. Dept. of Fish and Wildlife, Environmental Conservation, Albany, New York 12233-4750. Semiannual. Fish and game management studies in New York.

Ohio Fish and Wildlife Reports. Ohio Dept. of Natural Resources, Division of Wildlife, 1500 Dublin Rd., Columbus, Ohio 43215. (614) 265-7036. Irregular. Administration of fish and wildlife conservation.

Proceedings of WAFWA. Western Association of Fish, 1416 9th St., Sacramento, California 95814. (916) 445-9880. Annual. Research and management of fish and wildlife.

RESEARCH CENTERS AND INSTITUTES

Albion College, Whitehouse Nature Center. Albion, Michigan 49224. (517) 629-2030.

Auburn University, Alabama Cooperative Fish and Wildlife Research Unit. 331 Funchess Hall, Auburn, Alabama 36849. (205) 844-4796.

Maine Department of Inland Fisheries and Wildlife, Fishery Research Management Division. Fisheries Laboratory, P.O. Box 1298, Bangor, Maine 04401. (207) 941-4461.

Marine Cooperative Fish and Wildlife Research Unit. U.S. Fish and Wildlife Service, 240 Nutting Hall, University of Maine, Orono, Maine 04469. (207) 581-2870.

Michigan State University, Department of Fisheries and Wildlife. East Lansing, Michigan 48824. (517) 353-0647.

Mississippi Cooperative Fish & Wildlife Research Unit. Mississippi State University, P.O. Box BX, Mississippi State, Mississippi 39762. (601) 325-2643.

Missouri Cooperative Fish and Wildlife Research Unit. University of Missouri, 112 Stephens Hall, Columbia, Missouri 65211. (314) 882-3524.

Museum of Comparative Zoology. Harvard University, 26 Oxford Street, Cambridge, Massachusetts 02138. (617) 495-2460.

North Carolina Cooperative Fish and Wildlife Unit. North Carolina State University, Raleigh, North Carolina 27695-7617. (919) 737-2631.

Ohio State University, Ohio Cooperative Fish and Wildlife Research Unit. 1735 Neil Avenue, Columbus, Ohio 43210. (614) 292-6112.

Oklahoma State University, Oklahoma Cooperative Fish and Wildlife Research Unit. 404 Life Sciences Building, Stillwater, Oklahoma 74078. (405) 744-6342.

Oregon Department of Fish and Wildlife Research & Development Section. 850 S.W. 15th Street, Oregon State University, Corvallis, Oregon 97333. (503) 737-3241.

Pennsylvania State University, Pennsylvania Cooperative Fish and Wildlife Research Unit. Ferguson Building, University Park, Pennsylvania 16802. (814) 865-6592.

South Dakota State University, South Dakota Cooperative Fish and Wildlife Research Unit. P.O. Box 2206, Brookings, South Dakota 57007. (605) 688-6121.

U.S. Forest Service, Aquatic Ecosystem Analysis Laboratory. 105 Page, Brigham Young University, Provo, Utah 84602. (801) 378-4928.

University of Idaho Forest, Wildlife and Range Experiment Station. Moscow, Idaho 83843. (208) 885-6441.

University of Idaho, Idaho Cooperative Fish and Wildlife Research Unit. College of Forestry, Wildlife and Range Sciences, Moscow, Idaho 83843. (208) 885-6336.

University of Massachusetts, Massachusetts Cooperative Fish and Wildlife Unit. Holdworth Hall, Amherst, Massachusetts 01003. (413) 545-0398.

University of Washington, Center for Quantitative Science in Forestry, Fisheries and Wildlife. 3737 Fifteenth Avenue N.E., HR-20, Seattle, Washington 98195. (206) 543-1191.

Utah State University, Utah Cooperative Fish and Wildlife Research Unit. Logan, Utah 84322. (801) 750-2509.

Washington Department of Wildlife, Fisheries Management Division. 600 Capitol Way North, Olympia, Washington 98504-1091. (206) 753-5713.

TRADE ASSOCIATIONS AND PROFESSIONAL SOCIETIES

American Association of Zoo Keepers. Topeka Zoo, 635 Gage Blvd., Topeka, Kansas 66606. (913) 272-5821.

American Institute of Biological Sciences. 730 11th St., N.W., Washington, District of Columbia 20001-4521. (202) 628-1500.

Association of University Fisheries and Wildlife Program Administrators. Department of Wildlife and Fisheries Sciences, Texas A & M University, College Station, Texas 77843-2258. (409) 845-1261.

Columbia Basin Fish & Wildlife Authority. 2000 SW First Ave., Suite 170, Portland, Oregon 97201. (503) 294-7031.

International Association of Fish & Wildlife Agencies. 444 N. Capitol St., N.W., Suite 534, Washington, District of Columbia 20001. (202) 624-7890.

National Fish & Wildlife Federation. 18th & C Streets, N.W., Rm 2626, Washington, District of Columbia 20240. (202) 343-1040.

National Military Fish & Wildlife Association. c/o Slader G. Buck, P.O. Box 230128, Encinitas, California 92023. (619) 725-4540.

Northeast Association of Fish & Wildlife Resource Agencies. Division of Fish & Wildlife, Dept. of Environmental Conservation, 50 Wolf Rd., Albany, New York 12233. (518) 457-5691.

Southeastern Association of Fish & Wildlife Agencies. c/o Joe L. Herring, 102 Rodney Dr., Baton Rouge, Louisiana 70808. (504) 766-0519.

Southeastern Cooperative Wildlife & Fisheries Statistics Project. Institute of Statistics, North Carolina State University, Box 8203, Raleigh, North Carolina 27695. (919) 737-2531.

Western Association of Fish & Wildlife Agencies. Dept. of Fish & Game, 1416 Ninth St., Sacramento, California 95814. (916) 323-7319.

FISH FARMS

See: AQUACULTURE

FISH GENETICS

See: GENETICS

FISH HATCHERIES

See: AQUACULTURE

FISHERIES

See: FISH AND FISHERIES

FISSION, ATOMIC

See: NUCLEAR POWER

FLAME RETARDANTS

ABSTRACTING AND INDEXING SERVICES

Applied Science and Technology Index. H.W. Wilson Co., 950 University Ave., Bronx, New York 10452. (800) 367-6770. Formerly Industrial Arts Index.

ENCYCLOPEDIAS AND DICTIONARIES

Encyclopedia of Industrial Chemical Additives. Michael and Irene Ash. Chemical Publishing Co., 80 Eighth Ave., New York, New York 10011. (212) 255-1950. 1984-87. Four volumes. Comprehensive compilation of tradename products that function as additives in enhancing the properties of various major industrial products.

FLAVORS

See: FOOD SCIENCE

FLOC

See: SEWAGE

FLOCCULATION

See: WASTEWATER TREATMENT

FLOOD CONTROL

See: FLOODS

FLOODS

See also: AQUATIC ECOSYSTEMS; EROSION; LAND USE; WETLANDS

ABSTRACTING AND INDEXING SERVICES

Applied Science and Technology Index. H.W. Wilson Co., 950 University Ave., Bronx, New York 10452. (800) 367-6770. Formerly Industrial Arts Index.

Aqualine Abstracts. Water Research Centre. c/o Pergamon Microforms International, Inc., Fairview Park, Elmsford, New York 10523. (914) 592-7720. 1927-. Contains some 8,000 records annually on water and wastewater technology. Covers all aspects of water, wastewater, associated engineering services and the aquatic environment. Over 600 periodicals, as well as books, reports and conference proceedings and other publications from water related institutions worldwide are scanned. Also available online.

Biological and Agricultural Index. H.W. Wilson Co., 950 University Ave., Bronx, New York 10452. (800) 367-6770. 1916-. Monthly.

Civil Engineering Hydraulic Abstracts. BHRA Fluid Engineering, Air Science Co., PO Box 143, Corning, New York 14830. (607) 962-5591. Monthly. Abstracts of periodicals that publish in the areas of hydraulic engineering and other related topics.

Ecological Abstracts. Geo Abstracts Ltd. Elsevier Applied Science, Crown House, Linton Rd., Barking, England IG 11 8JU. 1974-. Derived from over 600 leading ecological and environmental journals, plus books, conference proceedings, reports and theses.

Ecology Abstracts. Cambridge Scientific Abstracts, 5161 River Rd., Bethesda, Maryland 20816. (301) 961-6750. Monthly.

Engineering Index. The Engineering Index Inc., 345 E. 47th St., New York, New York 10017. 1962-.

Environment Abstracts. Bowker A & I Publishing, 121 Chanlon Rd., New Providence, New Jersey 07974. (908) 464-6800. 1974-.

Environment Index. Environment Information Center, Index Research Department, 124 E. 39th St., New York, New York 10016. 1971-. Annual.

Environmental Information Connection–EIC. Planning Information Program, Dept. of Urban and Regional Planning, University of Illinois, 1003 West Nevada, Urbana, Illinois 61801. (217) 333-1369. Also available online.

Environmental Periodicals Bibliography. Environmental Studies Institute, International Academy at Santa Barbara, 800 Garden St., Suite D, Santa Barbara, California 93101. (805) 965-5010. Also available online.

General Science Index. H. W. Wilson Co., 950 University Ave., Bronx, New York 10452. 1978-. Monthly, also issued in annual cumulation. Cumulative subject index to English language periodicals in the subject fields of astronomy, botany, chemistry, earth science, environment and conservation, food and nutrition, genetics, mathematics, medicine and health, microbiology, oceanography, physics, physiology and zoology.

Geographical Abstracts. London School of Economics, Dept. of Geography, Regency House, 34 Duke St., London, England 1966-. Continued by Geo Abstracts issued in 6 parts: Pt. A. Landforms and the quaternary; Pt. B. Biogeography and Climatology; Pt. C. Economic geography; Pt. D. Social geography and cartography; Pt. E. Sedimentology; Pt. F. Regional and community planning.

Index to Scientific Book Contents. Institute for Scientific Information, 3501 Market St., Philadelphia, Pennsylvania 19104. (800) 523-1857. 1985-. Annual. Gives contents of science books published.

Science Citation Index. Institute for Scientific Information, 3501 Market St., Philadelphia, Pennsylvania 19104. 1961-.

BIBLIOGRAPHIES

Bibliography and Index of Geology. American Geological Institute, 4220 King St., Alexandria, Virginia 22302. Monthly. Includes environmental geology and hydrogeology.

Directory of Published Proceedings. Interdok Corp., 173 Halstead Ave., Harrison, New York 10528. (914) 835-3506. 1990. Monthly. This is a listing of published proceedings including the series SEMTE (Science/Medicine/Engineering/Technology) and the series SSH (Social Science/Humanities).

EPA Publications Bibliography. U.S. Environmental Protection Agency, Library Systems Branch, 401 M St., SW, Washington, District of Columbia 20460. (202) 260-2090. Quarterly.

Review and Evaluation of Urban Flood Flow Frequency. U.S. Department of the Interior, 1849 C St. NW,

Washington, District of Columbia 20240. (202) 208-3171. 1980. Covers flood forecasting, flood routing and urban runoff.

DIRECTORIES

National Directory of Floodplain Managers. Association of State Floodplain Managers, Box 2051, Madison, Wisconsin 53701-2051. (608) 266-1926.

ENCYCLOPEDIAS AND DICTIONARIES

McGraw-Hill Encyclopedia of Science and Technology. McGraw-Hill, 1221 Avenue of the Americas, New York, New York 10020. (212) 512-2000 or (800) 262-4729. 1992. Seventh edition. Issued in multiple volumes including index. Includes all science and technology broad subject areas.

Van Nostrand's Scientific Encyclopedia. Glenn D. Considine, ed. Van Nostrand Reinhold, 115 5th Ave., New York, New York 10003. (212) 254-3232. 1983. Sixth edition. Includes all broad subject areas in science.

The Water Encyclopedia. Lewis Publishers, 2000 Corporate Blvd. N.W., Boca Raton, Florida 33431. (800) 272-7737. 1990. 2d ed. Includes groundwater contamination, drinking water, floods, waterborne diseases, global warming, climate change, irrigation, water agencies and organizations, precipitation, oceans and seas, and river, lakes and waterfalls.

GENERAL WORKS

Drowning the National Heritage: Climate Change and Coastal Biodiversity in the United States. Walter V. C. Reid and Mark C. Trexler. World Resources Institute, 1709 New York Ave. N.W., Washington, District of Columbia 20006. (800) 822 0504. 1991. Examines erosion, flooding, and salt-water intrusion into groundwater, rivers, bays, and estuaries as well as receding coastlines and altered coastal current and upwelling patterns. Evaluates various policy responses and recommends specific changes to protect the biological wealth of these vital ecosystems.

Magill's Survey of Science. Earth Science Series. Frank N. Magill. Salem Press, PO Box 50062, Pasadena, California 91105. 1990-. Five volumes. Includes information on earth's crust, hot spots and volcanic island chains, physical properties of minerals, rock magnetism, physical properties of rocks, and index.

GOVERNMENTAL ORGANIZATIONS

National Weather Service. 8060 13th St., Silver Spring, Maryland 20910. (301) 443-8910.

TVA Public Information Office. 400 West Summit Hill Dr., Knoxville, Tennessee 37902. (615) 632-8000.

HANDBOOKS AND MANUALS

Our National Wetland Heritage. Jon A. Kusler. Environmental Law Institute, 1616 P St., NW, Suite 200, Washington, District of Columbia 20036. (202) 328-5150. 1983. Discusses practical ways to preserve and protect wetlands and their benefits, which include recreation, wildlife habitat, pollution and flood control, scientific research and groundwater recharge.

ONLINE DATA BASES

Computerized Engineering Index–COMPENDEX. Engineering Information Inc., 345 E. 47th St., New York, New York 10017. (212) 705-7600.

Enviro/Energyline Abstracts Plus. R. R. Bowker Co., 121 Chanlon Rd., New Providence, New Jersey 07974. (908) 464-6800.

Environmental Periodicals Bibliography. National Information Services Corp., Ste. 6, Wyman Towers, 3100 St. Paul St., Baltimore, Maryland 21218. (410)243-0797. Online version of abstract of same name.

FLUIDEX. STI, a subsidiary of BHR Group Limited, Cranfield, Bedfordshire, England MK43 OAJ. 44 (234) 750422.

Monthly Catalog of United States Government Publications. U.S. G.P.O., Supt. of Docs., PO Box 371954, Pittsburgh, Pennsylvania 15250-7954. (202) 512-0000.

National Technical Information Service. U.S. Department of Commerce, National Technical Information Service, Office of Data Base Services, 5285 Port Royal Rd., Springfield, Virginia 22161. (703) 487-4807. Bibliographic database of government sponsored research and technical reports.

SCISEARCH. Institute for Scientific Information, University City Science Center, 3501 Market St., Philadelphia, Pennsylvania 19104. (215) 386-0100.

RESEARCH CENTERS AND INSTITUTES

University of Nevada-Reno, S-S Field Laboratory. Box 10, Wadsworth, Nevada 89442. (702) 575-1057.

TRADE ASSOCIATIONS AND PROFESSIONAL SOCIETIES

American Institute of Biological Sciences. 730 11th St., N.W., Washington, District of Columbia 20001-4521. (202) 628-1500.

American Society of Civil Engineers. 345 East 47th St., New York, New York 10017. (212) 705-7496.

Association of State Floodplain Managers. P.O. Box 2051, Madison, Wisconsin 53701-2051. (608) 266-1926.

International Center for the Solution of Environmental Problems. 535 Lovett Blvd., Houston, Texas 77006. (713) 527-8711.

FLORA

See also: BOTANICAL ECOLOGY

ABSTRACTING AND INDEXING SERVICES

Biological Abstracts. BIOSIS, 2100 Arch St., Philadelphia, Pennsylvania 19103-1399. (215) 587-4800. 1927-.

Pollution Abstracts. Cambridge Scientific Abstracts, 5161 River Rd., Bethesda, Maryland 20816. (301) 961-6750. Six/year. Indexes worldwide technical literature on environmental pollution. Covers air pollution, marine and freshwater pollution, sewage and wastewater treatment, waste management, toxicology and health, noise pollution, radiation, land pollution, and environmental poli-

cies, programs, legislation, and education. Also available online.

Science Citation Index. Institute for Scientific Information, 3501 Market St., Philadelphia, Pennsylvania 19104. 1961-.

GENERAL WORKS

Pocket Flora of the Redwood Forest. Rudolf Willem Becking. Island Press, 1718 Connecticut Ave. N.W., Suite 300, Washington, District of Columbia 20009. (202) 232-7933. 1982. Guide to 212 of the most frequently seen plants in the Redwood Forest of the Pacific Coast. It is interspersed with accurate drawing color photographs and systematic keys to plant identification.

ONLINE DATA BASES

BIOSIS Previews. BIOSIS, 2100 Arch St., Philadelphia, Pennsylvania 19103-1399. (215) 587-4800. Largest and most comprehensive database of research in the life sciences. Contains citations for nearly 9000 primary research journals, monographs, reviews, symposia, preliminary reports, semi-popular journals, selected institutional reports, government reports and research communications.

SCISEARCH. Institute for Scientific Information, University City Science Center, 3501 Market St., Philadelphia, Pennsylvania 19104. (215) 386-0100.

RESEARCH CENTERS AND INSTITUTES

Herbarium. William Jewell College, Liberty, Missouri 64068. (816) 781-7700.

North Carolina State University, Herbarium. Box 7612, Raleigh, North Carolina 27695. (919) 515-2700.

Ohio Biological Survey. Biological Sciences Building, Ohio State University, 1315 Kinnear Rd., Columbus, Ohio 43212-1192. (614) 292-9645.

Organization for Flora Neotropica. New York Botanical Garden, Kazimirov Boulevard and 200th Street, Bronx, New York 10458. (212) 220-8742.

Sul Ross State University Herbarium. Alpine, Texas 79830. (915) 837-8112.

University of Idaho Herbarium. Department of Biological Sciences, Moscow, Idaho 83843. (208) 885-6798.

University of Kentucky, Herbarium. School of Biological Science, Room 216 Funkhouser, Morgan 101, Lexington, Kentucky 40506. (606) 257-3240.

University of North Carolina at Chapel Hill, Herbarium. 401 Coker Hall 010A, CB 3280, Chapel Hill, North Carolina 27599-3280. (919) 962-6931.

University of Oregon, Herbarium. Department of Biology, Eugene, Oregon 97403. (503) 346-3033.

University of South Dakota, South Dakota Herbarium. Biology Department, Vermillion, South Dakota 57069. (605) 677-6176.

University of Tennessee at Knoxville, Tennessee State Herbarium. Knoxville, Tennessee 37916. (615) 974-6212.

University of Wisconsin-Madison, Herbarium. Birge Hall, Madison, Wisconsin 53706. (608) 262-2792.

University of Wyoming, Rocky Mountain Herbarium. Aven Nelson Building, 3165 University Station, Laramie, Wyoming 82071. (307) 766-2236.

TRADE ASSOCIATIONS AND PROFESSIONAL SOCIETIES

American Institute of Biological Sciences. 730 11th St., N.W., Washington, District of Columbia 20001-4521. (202) 628-1500.

FLORIDA ENVIRONMENTAL AGENCIES

GOVERNMENTAL ORGANIZATIONS

Department of Agriculture and Consumer Affairs: Pesticide Registration. Director, Division of Inspection, 3125 Conner Blvd., Tallahassee, Florida 32399-1650. (904) 488-3731.

Department of Community Affairs: Emergency Preparedness and Community Right-to-Know. Chair, Emergency Response Commission, 2740 Centerview Dr., Tallahassee, Florida 32399-2149. (904) 488-1472.

Department of Natural Resources: Natural Resources. Executive Director, 3900 Commonwealth Blvd., Tallahassee, Florida 32399-3000. (904) 488-1554.

Environmental Regulation Department: Air Quality. Division Director, Division of Air Resources Management, 2600 Blairstone Rd., Tallahassee, Florida 32399-2400. (904) 488-1344.

Environmental Regulation Department: Coastal Zone Management. Environmental Administrator, Coastal Zone Management, 2600 Blairstone Rd., Tallahassee, Florida 32399-2400. (904) 488-6221.

Environmental Regulation Department: Environmental Protection. Secretary, Twin Towers, 2600 Blairstone Rd., Tallahassee, Florida 32399-2400. (904) 488-4805.

Environmental Regulation Department: Groundwater Management. Chief, Bureau of Groundwater Management, 2600 Blairstone Rd., Tallahassee, Florida 32399-2400. (904) 488-3601.

Environmental Regulation Department: Hazardous Waste Management. Chief, Bureau of Groundwater Protection, 2600 Blairstone Rd., Tallahassee, Florida 32399-2400. (904) 488-3601.

Environmental Regulation Department: Solid Waste Management. Director, 2600 Blairstone Rd., Tallahassee, Florida 32399-2400. (904) 488-0190.

Environmental Regulation Department: Underground Storage Tanks. Division Director, Environmental Operations Division, 2600 Blairstone Rd., Tallahassee, Florida 32399-2400. (904) 487-3299.

Environmental Regulation Department: Water Quality. Chief, Surface Water Management, 2600 Blairstone Rd., Tallahassee, Florida 32399-2400. (904) 488-6221.

Game and Fresh Water Fish Commission: Fish and Wildlife. Executive Director, 620 South Meridan St., Tallahassee, Florida 32399-1600. (904) 488-2975.

U.S. EPA Region 3: Pollution Prevention. Program Manager, 841 Chestnut St., Philadelphia, Pennsylvania 19107. (215) 597-9800.

FLUE GAS

ABSTRACTING AND INDEXING SERVICES

Air Pollution Technical Publications of the United States Environmental Protection Agency. U.S. Environmental Protection Agency, Mail Drop 75, Research Triangle Park, North Carolina 27711. (919) 541-2184. 1976. Quarterly.

Applied Science and Technology Index. H.W. Wilson Co., 950 University Ave., Bronx, New York 10452. (800) 367-6770. Formerly Industrial Arts Index.

Clean Coal Technologies. National Technical Information Service, 5285 Port Royal Road, Springfield, Virginia 22161. (703) 487-4650. Monthly. Desulfurization, coal gasification and liquefaction, flue gas cleanup, and advanced coal combustion.

Engineering Index. The Engineering Index Inc., 345 E. 47th St., New York, New York 10017. 1962-.

Environment Abstracts. Bowker A & I Publishing, 121 Chanlon Rd., New Providence, New Jersey 07974. (908) 464-6800. 1974-.

Environment Index. Environment Information Center, Index Research Department, 124 E. 39th St., New York, New York 10016. 1971-. Annual.

Environmental Information Connection–EIC. Planning Information Program, Dept. of Urban and Regional Planning, University of Illinois, 1003 West Nevada, Urbana, Illinois 61801. (217) 333-1369. Also available online.

Environmental Periodicals Bibliography. Environmental Studies Institute, International Academy at Santa Barbara, 800 Garden St., Suite D, Santa Barbara, California 93101. (805) 965-5010. Also available online.

Geographical Abstracts. London School of Economics, Dept. of Geography, Regency House, 34 Duke St., London, England 1966-. Continued by Geo Abstracts issued in 6 parts: Pt. A. Landforms and the quaternary; Pt. B. Biogeography and Climatology; Pt. C. Economic geography; Pt. D. Social geography and cartography; Pt. E. Sedimentology; Pt. F. Regional and community planning.

Pollution Abstracts. Cambridge Scientific Abstracts, 5161 River Rd., Bethesda, Maryland 20816. (301) 961-6750. Six/year. Indexes worldwide technical literature on environmental pollution. Covers air pollution, marine and freshwater pollution, sewage and wastewater treatment, waste management, toxicology and health, noise pollution, radiation, land pollution, and environmental policies, programs, legislation, and education. Also available online.

Science Citation Index. Institute for Scientific Information, 3501 Market St., Philadelphia, Pennsylvania 19104. 1961-.

BIBLIOGRAPHIES

Annotated Bibliography of Literature on Flue Gas Conditioning. U.S. Environmental Protection Agency, Division of Stationary Source Enforcement. U.S. Environmental Protection Agency, 401 M St., SW, Washington, District of Columbia (202) 260-2090. 1981. Covers flue gases and fly ash.

EPA Publications Bibliography. U.S. Environmental Protection Agency, Library Systems Branch, 401 M St., SW, Washington, District of Columbia 20460. (202) 260-2090. Quarterly.

ENCYCLOPEDIAS AND DICTIONARIES

McGraw-Hill Encyclopedia of Science and Technology. McGraw-Hill, 1221 Avenue of the Americas, New York, New York 10020. (212) 512-2000 or (800) 262-4729. 1992. Seventh edition. Issued in multiple volumes including index. Includes all science and technology broad subject areas.

GENERAL WORKS

Disposal of Flue Gas Cleaning Water. R.B. Fling. National Technical Information Service, 5285 Port Royal Rd., Springfield, Virginia 22161. (703) 487-4650. Annual.

Disposal of Flue Gas Desulfurization Wastes. P.R. Hurt. U.S. Environmental Protection Agency, 401 M St. SW, Washington, District of Columbia 20460. (202) 260-2090. 1981.

Environmental Assessment of a Reciprocating Engine Retrofitted with Selective Catalytic Reduction. C. Castaldini. National Technical Information Service, 5285 Port Royal Rd., Springfield, Virginia 22161. (703) 487-4650. Measurement of flue gases and environmental aspects of internal combustion engines.

Impact of NOx Selective Catalytic Reduction Process on Flue Gas Cleaning Systems. G.D. Jones. Industrial Environmental Research Laboratory, Environmental Protection Agency, Raleigh, North Carolina 27604. (919) 834-4015. 1982. Covers catalytic cracking, efficiency of boilers, purification of flue gases and pollution control equipment.

ONLINE DATA BASES

Computerized Engineering Index–COMPENDEX. Engineering Information Inc., 345 E. 47th St., New York, New York 10017. (212) 705-7600.

Enviro/Energyline Abstracts Plus. R. R. Bowker Co., 121 Chanlon Rd., New Providence, New Jersey 07974. (908) 464-6800.

Environmental Periodicals Bibliography. National Information Services Corp., Ste. 6, Wyman Towers, 3100 St. Paul St., Baltimore, Maryland 21218. (410)243-0797. Online version of abstract of same name.

Monthly Catalog of United States Government Publications. U.S. G.P.O., Supt. of Docs., PO Box 371954, Pittsburgh, Pennsylvania 15250-7954. (202) 512-0000.

National Technical Information Service. U.S. Department of Commerce, National Technical Information Service, Office of Data Base Services, 5285 Port Royal Rd., Springfield, Virginia 22161. (703) 487-4807. Biblio-

graphic database of government sponsored research and technical reports.

PERIODICALS AND NEWSLETTERS

Atmospheric Environment. Pergamon Microforms International, Inc., Fairview Park, Elmsford, New York 10523. (914) 592-7720. 1966-. Publishes papers on all aspects of man's interactions with his atmospheric environment, including the administrative, economic and political aspects of these interactions. Air pollution research and its applications are covered, taking into account changes in the atmospheric flow patterns, temperature distributions and chemical constitution caused by natural and artificial variations in the earth's surface.

FGD Newsletter. McIlvaine Co., 2970 Maria Ave., Northbrook, Illinois 60062. (708) 272-0010. Monthly. Desulphurization and flue gases, purification of fluidized-bed furnaces, and coal-fired power plants.

FGD Quarterly Report. The Laboratory, Highway 54 and Alexander Dr., Research Triangle Park, North Carolina 27711. (919) 541-2821. Quarterly.

FLUIDIZED BED COMBUSTION

See also: COMBUSTION; COAL; SULPHUR DIOXIDE

ABSTRACTING AND INDEXING SERVICES

Environment Abstracts. Bowker A & I Publishing, 121 Chanlon Rd., New Providence, New Jersey 07974. (908) 464-6800. 1974-.

Environment Index. Environment Information Center, Index Research Department, 124 E. 39th St., New York, New York 10016. 1971-. Annual.

Environmental Information Connection–EIC. Planning Information Program, Dept. of Urban and Regional Planning, University of Illinois, 1003 West Nevada, Urbana, Illinois 61801. (217) 333-1369. Also available online.

Environmental Periodicals Bibliography. Environmental Studies Institute, International Academy at Santa Barbara, 800 Garden St., Suite D, Santa Barbara, California 93101. (805) 965-5010. Also available online.

General Science Index. H. W. Wilson Co., 950 University Ave., Bronx, New York 10452. 1978-. Monthly, also issued in annual cumulation. Cumulative subject index to English language periodicals in the subject fields of astronomy, botany, chemistry, earth science, environment and conservation, food and nutrition, genetics, mathematics, medicine and health, microbiology, oceanography, physics, physiology and zoology.

Index to Scientific Book Contents. Institute for Scientific Information, 3501 Market St., Philadelphia, Pennsylvania 19104. (800) 523-1857. 1985-. Annual. Gives contents of science books published.

Pollution Abstracts. Cambridge Scientific Abstracts, 5161 River Rd., Bethesda, Maryland 20816. (301) 961-6750. Six/year. Indexes worldwide technical literature on environmental pollution. Covers air pollution, marine and freshwater pollution, sewage and wastewater treatment, waste management, toxicology and health, noise pollu-

tion, radiation, land pollution, and environmental policies, programs, legislation, and education. Also available online.

Science Citation Index. Institute for Scientific Information, 3501 Market St., Philadelphia, Pennsylvania 19104. 1961-.

BIBLIOGRAPHIES

EPA Publications Bibliography. U.S. Environmental Protection Agency, Library Systems Branch, 401 M St., SW, Washington, District of Columbia 20460. (202) 260-2090. Quarterly.

ENCYCLOPEDIAS AND DICTIONARIES

Dictionary of Environmental Engineering and Related Sciences: English-Spanish, Spanish-English. Jose T. Villate. Ediciones Universal, 3090 SW 8th St., Miami, Florida 33135. (305) 642-3355. 1979.

Encyclopedia of Environmental Science and Engineering. J.R. Pfafflin. Gordon and Breach Science Publishers, Inc., 270 8th Ave., New York, New York 10011. (212) 206-8900. 1992.

McGraw-Hill Encyclopedia of Environmental Science. Sybil P. Parker. McGraw-Hill Science & Engineering Books, 11 W. 19th St., New York, New York 10011. (212) 337-6010. 1980. Covers ecology, man's influence on nature, and environmental protection.

Van Nostrand's Scientific Encyclopedia. Glenn D. Considine, ed. Van Nostrand Reinhold, 115 5th Ave., New York, New York 10003. (212) 254-3232. 1983. Sixth edition. Includes all broad subject areas in science.

GENERAL WORKS

The Current State of Atmospheric Fluidized-Bed Combustion Technology. Electric Power Research Institute. The World Bank, Washington, District of Columbia 1989.

Fluidized Bed Combustion and Applied Technology. Hemisphere Publishing Co., 79 Madison Ave., Suite 1110, New York, New York 10016. (212) 725-1999. 1984.

ONLINE DATA BASES

Enviro/Energyline Abstracts Plus. R. R. Bowker Co., 121 Chanlon Rd., New Providence, New Jersey 07974. (908) 464-6800.

Environmental Periodicals Bibliography. National Information Services Corp., Ste. 6, Wyman Towers, 3100 St. Paul St., Baltimore, Maryland 21218. (410)243-0797. Online version of abstract of same name.

FLUME

ABSTRACTING AND INDEXING SERVICES

Environment Abstracts. Bowker A & I Publishing, 121 Chanlon Rd., New Providence, New Jersey 07974. (908) 464-6800. 1974-.

Environment Index. Environment Information Center, Index Research Department, 124 E. 39th St., New York, New York 10016. 1971-. Annual.

Environmental Information Connection–EIC. Planning Information Program, Dept. of Urban and Regional Planning, University of Illinois, 1003 West Nevada, Urbana, Illinois 61801. (217) 333-1369. Also available online.

Environmental Periodicals Bibliography. Environmental Studies Institute, International Academy at Santa Barbara, 800 Garden St., Suite D, Santa Barbara, California 93101. (805) 965-5010. Also available online.

General Science Index. H. W. Wilson Co., 950 University Ave., Bronx, New York 10452. 1978-. Monthly, also issued in annual cumulation. Cumulative subject index to English language periodicals in the subject fields of astronomy, botany, chemistry, earth science, environment and conservation, food and nutrition, genetics, mathematics, medicine and health, microbiology, oceanography, physics, physiology and zoology.

Index to Scientific Book Contents. Institute for Scientific Information, 3501 Market St., Philadelphia, Pennsylvania 19104. (800) 523-1857. 1985-. Annual. Gives contents of science books published.

Science Citation Index. Institute for Scientific Information, 3501 Market St., Philadelphia, Pennsylvania 19104. 1961-.

BIBLIOGRAPHIES

EPA Publications Bibliography. U.S. Environmental Protection Agency, Library Systems Branch, 401 M St., SW, Washington, District of Columbia 20460. (202) 260-2090. Quarterly.

ENCYCLOPEDIAS AND DICTIONARIES

Van Nostrand's Scientific Encyclopedia. Glenn D. Considine, ed. Van Nostrand Reinhold, 115 5th Ave., New York, New York 10003. (212) 254-3232. 1983. Sixth edition. Includes all broad subject areas in science.

GENERAL WORKS

Hydraulic Data for Shallow Open-Channel Flow in a High- Gradient Flume with Large Bed Material. Fred J. Watts. Deptartment of the Interior, U.S. Geological Survey, 119 National Center, Reston, Virginia 22092. (703) 648-4460. 1989. Hydraulic engineering channels and flumes.

ONLINE DATA BASES

Enviro/Energyline Abstracts Plus. R. R. Bowker Co., 121 Chanlon Rd., New Providence, New Jersey 07974. (908) 464-6800.

Environmental Periodicals Bibliography. National Information Services Corp., Ste. 6, Wyman Towers, 3100 St. Paul St., Baltimore, Maryland 21218. (410)243-0797. Online version of abstract of same name.

FLUORESCENCE

ABSTRACTING AND INDEXING SERVICES

Biological Abstracts. BIOSIS, 2100 Arch St., Philadelphia, Pennsylvania 19103-1399. (215) 587-4800. 1927-.

Biological and Agricultural Index. H.W. Wilson Co., 950 University Ave., Bronx, New York 10452. (800) 367-6770. 1916-. Monthly.

Chemical Abstracts. Chemical Abstracts Service, 2540 Olentangy River Rd., PO Box 3012, Columbus, Ohio 43210. (800) 848-6533. 1907-.

Environment Abstracts. Bowker A & I Publishing, 121 Chanlon Rd., New Providence, New Jersey 07974. (908) 464-6800. 1974-.

Environment Index. Environment Information Center, Index Research Department, 124 E. 39th St., New York, New York 10016. 1971-. Annual.

Environmental Information Connection–EIC. Planning Information Program, Dept. of Urban and Regional Planning, University of Illinois, 1003 West Nevada, Urbana, Illinois 61801. (217) 333-1369. Also available online.

Environmental Periodicals Bibliography. Environmental Studies Institute, International Academy at Santa Barbara, 800 Garden St., Suite D, Santa Barbara, California 93101. (805) 965-5010. Also available online.

Food Science and Technology Abstracts. International Food Information Service, c/o National Food Laboratory, 6363 Clark Ave., Dublin, California 94568. (800) 336-3782. 1969-.

General Science Index. H. W. Wilson Co., 950 University Ave., Bronx, New York 10452. 1978-. Monthly, also issued in annual cumulation. Cumulative subject index to English language periodicals in the subject fields of astronomy, botany, chemistry, earth science, environment and conservation, food and nutrition, genetics, mathematics, medicine and health, microbiology, oceanography, physics, physiology and zoology.

Index to Scientific Book Contents. Institute for Scientific Information, 3501 Market St., Philadelphia, Pennsylvania 19104. (800) 523-1857. 1985-. Annual. Gives contents of science books published.

Physics Briefs. Physikalische Berichte. Physik Verlag, Pappapelallee 3, Postfach 101161, Weinheim, Germany D-6940. 1979-. Semimonthly. In English. Volumes for 1979- issued by the Deutsche Physikalische Gesellschaft and the Fachinformationszentrum Energie Physik, Mathematik in cooperation with the American Institute of Physics.

Pollution Abstracts. Cambridge Scientific Abstracts, 5161 River Rd., Bethesda, Maryland 20816. (301) 961-6750. Six/year. Indexes worldwide technical literature on environmental pollution. Covers air pollution, marine and freshwater pollution, sewage and wastewater treatment, waste management, toxicology and health, noise pollution, radiation, land pollution, and environmental policies, programs, legislation, and education. Also available online.

Science Citation Index. Institute for Scientific Information, 3501 Market St., Philadelphia, Pennsylvania 19104. 1961-.

BIBLIOGRAPHIES

EPA Publications Bibliography. U.S. Environmental Protection Agency, Library Systems Branch, 401 M St., SW, Washington, District of Columbia 20460. (202) 260-2090. Quarterly.

ENCYCLOPEDIAS AND DICTIONARIES

A Dictionary of Genetics. Robert C. King and William A. Stansfield. Oxford University Press, 200 Madison Ave., New York, New York 10016. (212) 679-7300 or (800) 334-4249. 1991. Fourth edition. Includes 7,100 definitions with 250 illustrations. Also includes bibliography of major sources.

Dictionary of Genetics and Cell Biology. Norman Maclean. New York University Press, 70 Washington Sq. S., New York, New York 10012. (212) 998-2575. 1987. Includes the subject areas of cytology and genetics.

Encyclopedia of Human Biology. Renato Dulbecco, ed. Academic Press, c/o Harcourt Brace Jovanovich Inc., 6277 Sea Harbor Dr., Orlando, Florida 32887. (800) 346-8648. 1991. Eight volumes.

Encyclopedia of Physics. Rita G. Lerner and George L. Trigg. VCH Publishers, 303 NW 12th Ave., Deerfield Beach, Florida 33442-1788. (305) 428-5566. 1991. Second edition.

Encyclopedic Dictionary of Genetics: With German Term Equivalents and Extensive German/English Index. R. C. King and W. D. Stansfield. VCH Publishers, 303 NW 12th Ave., Deerfield Beach, Florida 33442-1788. (305) 428-5566. 1990. 4th ed. Revised edition of: A Dictionary of Genetics, third edition.

Van Nostrand's Scientific Encyclopedia. Glenn D. Considine, ed. Van Nostrand Reinhold, 115 5th Ave., New York, New York 10003. (212) 254-3232. 1983. Sixth edition. Includes all broad subject areas in science.

GENERAL WORKS

Biophysical and Biochemical Aspects of Fluorescence Spectroscopy. Plenum Press, 233 Spring St., New York, New York 10013-1578. (212) 620-8000. 1991. Topics in biochemistry and molecular biology.

HANDBOOKS AND MANUALS

A Fluorescence Standard Reference Material, Quinine Sulfate Dihydrate. R.A. Velapoldi. National Bureau of Standards, Gaithersburg, Maryland 20899. (301)975-2000. 1980. Standards for fluorescence, quinine sulfate optical properties, and materials.

Handbook of Photon Interaction Coefficients in Radioisotope- Excited X-Ray Fluorescence Analysis. O.S. Marenkov. Nova Science Publishers, Inc., 283 Commack Rd., Ste. 300, Commack, New York 11725. (516) 499-3103. 1991.

ONLINE DATA BASES

BIOSIS Previews. BIOSIS, 2100 Arch St., Philadelphia, Pennsylvania 19103-1399. (215) 587-4800. Largest and most comprehensive database of research in the life sciences. Contains citations for nearly 9000 primary research journals, monographs, reviews, symposia, preliminary reports, semi-popular journals, selected institu-

tional reports, government reports and research communications.

Chemical Abstracts-CA. Chemical Abstracts Service, 2540 Olentangy River Rd., P.O. Box 3012, Columbus, Ohio 43210. (800) 848-6533 or (614) 421-3600. Information sources include 9000 journals, patents from 27 countries, two industrial property organizations, new books, conference proceedings, and government research reports.

Enviro/Energyline Abstracts Plus. R. R. Bowker Co., 121 Chanlon Rd., New Providence, New Jersey 07974. (908) 464-6800.

Environmental Periodicals Bibliography. National Information Services Corp., Ste. 6, Wyman Towers, 3100 St. Paul St., Baltimore, Maryland 21218. (410)243-0797. Online version of abstract of same name.

FLUORIDATION

ABSTRACTING AND INDEXING SERVICES

Abstracts of Air and Water Conservation Literature. American Petroleum Institute. Central Abstracting and Indexing Service, 275 Madison Avenue, New York, New York 10016. 1972.

Biological Abstracts. BIOSIS, 2100 Arch St., Philadelphia, Pennsylvania 19103-1399. (215) 587-4800. 1927-.

Biological and Agricultural Index. H.W. Wilson Co., 950 University Ave., Bronx, New York 10452. (800) 367-6770. 1916-. Monthly.

Environment Abstracts. Bowker A & I Publishing, 121 Chanlon Rd., New Providence, New Jersey 07974. (908) 464-6800. 1974-.

Environment Index. Environment Information Center, Index Research Department, 124 E. 39th St., New York, New York 10016. 1971-. Annual.

Environmental Information Connection–EIC. Planning Information Program, Dept. of Urban and Regional Planning, University of Illinois, 1003 West Nevada, Urbana, Illinois 61801. (217) 333-1369. Also available online.

Environmental Periodicals Bibliography. Environmental Studies Institute, International Academy at Santa Barbara, 800 Garden St., Suite D, Santa Barbara, California 93101. (805) 965-5010. Also available online.

General Science Index. H. W. Wilson Co., 950 University Ave., Bronx, New York 10452. 1978-. Monthly, also issued in annual cumulation. Cumulative subject index to English language periodicals in the subject fields of astronomy, botany, chemistry, earth science, environment and conservation, food and nutrition, genetics, mathematics, medicine and health, microbiology, oceanography, physics, physiology and zoology.

Index to Scientific Book Contents. Institute for Scientific Information, 3501 Market St., Philadelphia, Pennsylvania 19104. (800) 523-1857. 1985-. Annual. Gives contents of science books published.

Science Citation Index. Institute for Scientific Information, 3501 Market St., Philadelphia, Pennsylvania 19104. 1961-.

BIBLIOGRAPHIES

EPA Publications Bibliography. U.S. Environmental Protection Agency, Library Systems Branch, 401 M St., SW, Washington, District of Columbia 20460. (202) 260-2090. Quarterly.

ENCYCLOPEDIAS AND DICTIONARIES

Encyclopedia of Physics. Rita G. Lerner and George L. Trigg. VCH Publishers, 303 NW 12th Ave., Deerfield Beach, Florida 33442-1788. (305) 428-5566. 1991. Second edition.

Van Nostrand's Scientific Encyclopedia. Glenn D. Considine, ed. Van Nostrand Reinhold, 115 5th Ave., New York, New York 10003. (212) 254-3232. 1983. Sixth edition. Includes all broad subject areas in science.

ONLINE DATA BASES

BIOSIS Previews. BIOSIS, 2100 Arch St., Philadelphia, Pennsylvania 19103-1399. (215) 587-4800. Largest and most comprehensive database of research in the life sciences. Contains citations for nearly 9000 primary research journals, monographs, reviews, symposia, preliminary reports, semi-popular journals, selected institutional reports, government reports and research communications.

CAS Source Index–CASSI. Chemical Abstracts Service, 2540 Olentangy River Rd., P.O. Box 3012, Columbus, Ohio 43210. (800) 848-6533 or (614) 421-3600. A listing of bibliographic and library holdings information for scientific and technical primary literature relevant to the chemical sciences.

Enviro/Energyline Abstracts Plus. R. R. Bowker Co., 121 Chanlon Rd., New Providence, New Jersey 07974. (908) 464-6800.

Environmental Periodicals Bibliography. National Information Services Corp., Ste. 6, Wyman Towers, 3100 St. Paul St., Baltimore, Maryland 21218. (410)243-0797. Online version of abstract of same name.

TRADE ASSOCIATIONS AND PROFESSIONAL SOCIETIES

American Chemical Society. 1155 16th St., N.W., Washington, District of Columbia 20036. (202) 872-4600.

Americans United to Combat Fluoridation. 915 Stone Rd., Laurel Springs, New Jersey 08021. (609) 783-0013.

Center for Health Action. P.O. Box 270, Forest Park Station, Springfield, Massachusetts 01108. (413) 782-2115.

International Society for Fluoride Research. P.O. Box 692, Warren, Michigan 48090. (313) 375-5544.

Safe Water Coalition. 150 Woodland Ave., San Anselmo, California 94960. (415) 453-0158.

FLUORIDES

ABSTRACTING AND INDEXING SERVICES

Biological Abstracts. BIOSIS, 2100 Arch St., Philadelphia, Pennsylvania 19103-1399. (215) 587-4800. 1927-.

Chemical Abstracts. Chemical Abstracts Service, 2540 Olentangy River Rd., PO Box 3012, Columbus, Ohio 43210. (800) 848-6533. 1907-.

Environment Abstracts. Bowker A & I Publishing, 121 Chanlon Rd., New Providence, New Jersey 07974. (908) 464-6800. 1974-.

Environment Index. Environment Information Center, Index Research Department, 124 E. 39th St., New York, New York 10016. 1971-. Annual.

Environmental Information Connection–EIC. Planning Information Program, Dept. of Urban and Regional Planning, University of Illinois, 1003 West Nevada, Urbana, Illinois 61801. (217) 333-1369. Also available online.

Environmental Periodicals Bibliography. Environmental Studies Institute, International Academy at Santa Barbara, 800 Garden St., Suite D, Santa Barbara, California 93101. (805) 965-5010. Also available online.

General Science Index. H. W. Wilson Co., 950 University Ave., Bronx, New York 10452. 1978-. Monthly, also issued in annual cumulation. Cumulative subject index to English language periodicals in the subject fields of astronomy, botany, chemistry, earth science, environment and conservation, food and nutrition, genetics, mathematics, medicine and health, microbiology, oceanography, physics, physiology and zoology.

Index to Scientific Book Contents. Institute for Scientific Information, 3501 Market St., Philadelphia, Pennsylvania 19104. (800) 523-1857. 1985-. Annual. Gives contents of science books published.

INIS Atomindex. International Atomic Energy Agency, Wagramerstrasse 5, Vienna, Austria A-1400. 222 23606198. 1988-. Semiannual. Abstracts nuclear energy and nuclear physics topics from journals, conferences, technical reports and other related publications. Issued in 6 parts: Personal Author, Corporate Entry, Subject, Report, Standard Patent, Conference (by place), Conference (by date).

Science Citation Index. Institute for Scientific Information, 3501 Market St., Philadelphia, Pennsylvania 19104. 1961-.

BIBLIOGRAPHIES

EPA Publications Bibliography. U.S. Environmental Protection Agency, Library Systems Branch, 401 M St., SW, Washington, District of Columbia 20460. (202) 260-2090. Quarterly.

ENCYCLOPEDIAS AND DICTIONARIES

Encyclopedia of Physics. Rita G. Lerner and George L. Trigg. VCH Publishers, 303 NW 12th Ave., Deerfield Beach, Florida 33442-1788. (305) 428-5566. 1991. Second edition.

Ullmanns Encyclopedia of Industrial Chemistry. Hans Jurgen Arpe and Wolfgang Gerhartz, eds. VCH Publishers, 303 NW 12th Ave., Deerfield Beach, Florida 33442-1788. (305) 428-5566. 1990. Designed to keep up with the broad spectrum of chemical technology. Thirty-six volumes of the encyclopedia have been divided into two sets: the 28 A volumes contain alphabetically arranged articles on chemicals, product groups, processes and technological concepts; and the 8 B volumes are compendia of basic knowledge in industrial chemistry.

Van Nostrand's Scientific Encyclopedia. Glenn D. Considine, ed. Van Nostrand Reinhold, 115 5th Ave., New York, New York 10003. (212) 254-3232. 1983. Sixth edition. Includes all broad subject areas in science.

GENERAL WORKS

The Metabolism and Toxicity of Fluoride. Gary M. Whitford. Karger, 26 W. Avon Rd., Box 529, Farmington, Connecticut 06085. (203) 675-7834. 1989.

HANDBOOKS AND MANUALS

Complete Guide to Vitamins, Minerals and Supplements. H. Winter Griffith. Fisher Books, 3499 N. Campbell Ave., Suite 909, Tucson, Arizona 85712. (602) 325-5263. 1988. Includes name, brand name, reasons to use, who should use, recommended daily allowance, and other related data in the form of a chart.

Graphite Fluorides and Carbon-Fluorine Compounds. Tsuyoshi Nakajima. CRC Press, 2000 Corporate Blvd. N.W., Boca Raton, Florida 33431. (800) 272-7737. 1991.

ONLINE DATA BASES

BIOSIS Previews. BIOSIS, 2100 Arch St., Philadelphia, Pennsylvania 19103-1399. (215) 587-4800. Largest and most comprehensive database of research in the life sciences. Contains citations for nearly 9000 primary research journals, monographs, reviews, symposia, preliminary reports, semi-popular journals, selected institutional reports, government reports and research communications.

CAS Source Index–CASSI. Chemical Abstracts Service, 2540 Olentangy River Rd., P.O. Box 3012, Columbus, Ohio 43210. (800) 848-6533 or (614) 421-3600. A listing of bibliographic and library holdings information for scientific and technical primary literature relevant to the chemical sciences.

Chemical Abstracts-CA. Chemical Abstracts Service, 2540 Olentangy River Rd., P.O. Box 3012, Columbus, Ohio 43210. (800) 848-6533 or (614) 421-3600. Information sources include 9000 journals, patents from 27 countries, two industrial property organizations, new books, conference proceedings, and government research reports.

Enviro/Energyline Abstracts Plus. R. R. Bowker Co., 121 Chanlon Rd., New Providence, New Jersey 07974. (908) 464-6800.

Environmental Periodicals Bibliography. National Information Services Corp., Ste. 6, Wyman Towers, 3100 St. Paul St., Baltimore, Maryland 21218. (410)243-0797. Online version of abstract of same name.

TRADE ASSOCIATIONS AND PROFESSIONAL SOCIETIES

International Society for Fluoride Research. P.O. Box 692, Warren, Michigan 48090. (313) 375-5544.

FLUORINATED HYDROCARBONS

See also: CHLOROFLUOROCARBONS

ABSTRACTING AND INDEXING SERVICES

Chemical Abstracts. Chemical Abstracts Service, 2540 Olentangy River Rd., PO Box 3012, Columbus, Ohio 43210. (800) 848-6533. 1907-.

Environment Abstracts. Bowker A & I Publishing, 121 Chanlon Rd., New Providence, New Jersey 07974. (908) 464-6800. 1974-.

Environment Index. Environment Information Center, Index Research Department, 124 E. 39th St., New York, New York 10016. 1971-. Annual.

Environmental Information Connection–EIC. Planning Information Program, Dept. of Urban and Regional Planning, University of Illinois, 1003 West Nevada, Urbana, Illinois 61801. (217) 333-1369. Also available online.

Environmental Periodicals Bibliography. Environmental Studies Institute, International Academy at Santa Barbara, 800 Garden St., Suite D, Santa Barbara, California 93101. (805) 965-5010. Also available online.

General Science Index. H. W. Wilson Co., 950 University Ave., Bronx, New York 10452. 1978-. Monthly, also issued in annual cumulation. Cumulative subject index to English language periodicals in the subject fields of astronomy, botany, chemistry, earth science, environment and conservation, food and nutrition, genetics, mathematics, medicine and health, microbiology, oceanography, physics, physiology and zoology.

Index to Scientific Book Contents. Institute for Scientific Information, 3501 Market St., Philadelphia, Pennsylvania 19104. (800) 523-1857. 1985-. Annual. Gives contents of science books published.

Science Citation Index. Institute for Scientific Information, 3501 Market St., Philadelphia, Pennsylvania 19104. 1961-.

BIBLIOGRAPHIES

EPA Publications Bibliography. U.S. Environmental Protection Agency, Library Systems Branch, 401 M St., SW, Washington, District of Columbia 20460. (202) 260-2090. Quarterly.

Synthesis of Fluorinated Hydrocarbons: A Compilation. U.S. National Aeronautics and Space Administration, Technology Utilization Division. Technology Utilization Division, Office of Technology Utilization, NASA, Washington, District of Columbia 1968.

ENCYCLOPEDIAS AND DICTIONARIES

McGraw-Hill Encyclopedia of Environmental Science. Sybil P. Parker. McGraw-Hill Science & Engineering Books, 11 W. 19th St., New York, New York 10011. (212) 337-6010. 1980. Covers ecology, man's influence on nature, and environmental protection.

Ullmanns Encyclopedia of Industrial Chemistry. Hans Jurgen Arpe and Wolfgang Gerhartz, eds. VCH Publishers, 303 NW 12th Ave., Deerfield Beach, Florida 33442-1788. (305) 428-5566. 1990. Designed to keep up with the broad spectrum of chemical technology. Thirty-six volumes of the encyclopedia have been divided into two sets: the 28 A volumes contain alphabetically arranged articles on chemicals, product groups, processes and

technological concepts; and the 8 B volumes are compendia of basic knowledge in industrial chemistry.

Van Nostrand's Scientific Encyclopedia. Glenn D. Considine, ed. Van Nostrand Reinhold, 115 5th Ave., New York, New York 10003. (212) 254-3232. 1983. Sixth edition. Includes all broad subject areas in science.

ONLINE DATA BASES

CAS Source Index–CASSI. Chemical Abstracts Service, 2540 Olentangy River Rd., P.O. Box 3012, Columbus, Ohio 43210. (800) 848-6533 or (614) 421-3600. A listing of bibliographic and library holdings information for scientific and technical primary literature relevant to the chemical sciences.

Chemical Abstracts-CA. Chemical Abstracts Service, 2540 Olentangy River Rd., P.O. Box 3012, Columbus, Ohio 43210. (800) 848-6533 or (614) 421-3600. Information sources include 9000 journals, patents from 27 countries, two industrial property organizations, new books, conference proceedings, and government research reports.

Chemical Carcinogenesis Research Information System–CCRIS. National Library of Medicine, 8600 Rockville Pike, Bethesda, Maryland 20894. (800) 638-8480. Individual assay results and test conditions for 1,451 chemicals in the areas of carcinogenicity, mutagenicity, tumor promotion, and cocarcinogenicity.

Enviro/Energyline Abstracts Plus. R. R. Bowker Co., 121 Chanlon Rd., New Providence, New Jersey 07974. (908) 464-6800.

Environmental Periodicals Bibliography. National Information Services Corp., Ste. 6, Wyman Towers, 3100 St. Paul St., Baltimore, Maryland 21218. (410)243-0797. Online version of abstract of same name.

Monthly Catalog of United States Government Publications. U.S. G.P.O., Supt. of Docs., PO Box 371954, Pittsburgh, Pennsylvania 15250-7954. (202) 512-0000.

National Technical Information Service. U.S. Department of Commerce, National Technical Information Service, Office of Data Base Services, 5285 Port Royal Rd., Springfield, Virginia 22161. (703) 487-4807. Bibliographic database of government sponsored research and technical reports.

FLUORINE

ABSTRACTING AND INDEXING SERVICES

Biological Abstracts. BIOSIS, 2100 Arch St., Philadelphia, Pennsylvania 19103-1399. (215) 587-4800. 1927-.

Chemical Abstracts. Chemical Abstracts Service, 2540 Olentangy River Rd., PO Box 3012, Columbus, Ohio 43210. (800) 848-6533. 1907-.

Environment Abstracts. Bowker A & I Publishing, 121 Chanlon Rd., New Providence, New Jersey 07974. (908) 464-6800. 1974-.

Environment Index. Environment Information Center, Index Research Department, 124 E. 39th St., New York, New York 10016. 1971-. Annual.

Environmental Information Connection–EIC. Planning Information Program, Dept. of Urban and Regional Planning, University of Illinois, 1003 West Nevada, Urbana, Illinois 61801. (217) 333-1369. Also available online.

Environmental Periodicals Bibliography. Environmental Studies Institute, International Academy at Santa Barbara, 800 Garden St., Suite D, Santa Barbara, California 93101. (805) 965-5010. Also available online.

General Science Index. H. W. Wilson Co., 950 University Ave., Bronx, New York 10452. 1978-. Monthly, also issued in annual cumulation. Cumulative subject index to English language periodicals in the subject fields of astronomy, botany, chemistry, earth science, environment and conservation, food and nutrition, genetics, mathematics, medicine and health, microbiology, oceanography, physics, physiology and zoology.

Index to Scientific Book Contents. Institute for Scientific Information, 3501 Market St., Philadelphia, Pennsylvania 19104. (800) 523-1857. 1985-. Annual. Gives contents of science books published.

Pollution Abstracts. Cambridge Scientific Abstracts, 5161 River Rd., Bethesda, Maryland 20816. (301) 961-6750. Six/year. Indexes worldwide technical literature on environmental pollution. Covers air pollution, marine and freshwater pollution, sewage and wastewater treatment, waste management, toxicology and health, noise pollution, radiation, land pollution, and environmental policies, programs, legislation, and education. Also available online.

Science Citation Index. Institute for Scientific Information, 3501 Market St., Philadelphia, Pennsylvania 19104. 1961-.

BIBLIOGRAPHIES

EPA Publications Bibliography. U.S. Environmental Protection Agency, Library Systems Branch, 401 M St., SW, Washington, District of Columbia 20460. (202) 260-2090. Quarterly.

Fluorine, Its Compounds, and Air Pollution: A Bibliography with Abstracts. U.S. Environmental Protection Agency, Office of Air Quality Planning Standards, MD 75, Research Triangle Park, North Carolina 27711. 1976.

ENCYCLOPEDIAS AND DICTIONARIES

Encyclopedia of Chemical Processing and Design. John J. Mcketta and W. A. Cunningham. Marcel Dekker, Inc., 270 Madison Ave., New York, New York 10016. (212) 696-9000; (800) 228-1160. 1992. Thirty-eight volumes.

Encyclopedia of Physics. Rita G. Lerner and George L. Trigg. VCH Publishers, 303 NW 12th Ave., Deerfield Beach, Florida 33442-1788. (305) 428-5566. 1991. Second edition.

Kirk-Othmer Encyclopedia of Chemical Technology. J. I. Kroschwitz, ed. John Wiley & Sons, Inc., 605 3rd Ave., New York, New York 10158-0012. (212) 850-6000. 1992-. All articles in the new edition have been rewritten and updated adding new subjects such as biotechnology, computer topics, analytical techniques and instrumentation, environmental concerns, fuels and energy, inorganic and solid state chemistry; composite materials and material science in general, and pharmaceuticals. Also available online.

Ullmanns Encyclopedia of Industrial Chemistry. Hans Jurgen Arpe and Wolfgang Gerhartz, eds. VCH Publishers, 303 NW 12th Ave., Deerfield Beach, Florida 33442-1788. (305) 428-5566. 1990. Designed to keep up with the broad spectrum of chemical technology. Thirty-six volumes of the encyclopedia have been divided into two sets: the 28 A volumes contain alphabetically arranged articles on chemicals, product groups, processes and technological concepts; and the 8 B volumes are compendia of basic knowledge in industrial chemistry.

Van Nostrand's Scientific Encyclopedia. Glenn D. Considine, ed. Van Nostrand Reinhold, 115 5th Ave., New York, New York 10003. (212) 254-3232. 1983. Sixth edition. Includes all broad subject areas in science.

HANDBOOKS AND MANUALS

Catalog Handbook of Fine Chemicals. Aldrich Chemical Co., 1001 W. St. Paul Ave., Milwaukee, Wisconsin 53233. (414) 273-3850 or (800) 558-9160. 1990/1991. Contains more than 27,000 products of which over 4,000 are new. Includes: chemicals, equipment, glassware, books, software, research products, bulk quantities, new products, custom synthesis and rare chemicals.

Documentation of the Threshold Limit Values. American Conference of Governmental Industrial Hygienists, 6500 Glenway, Building D-5, Cincinnati, Ohio 45211. 1991. Provides threshold limit value documentation for any physical phenomenon in the environment, including chemical substances and physical agents.

Handbook of Environmental Data on Organic Chemicals. Karel Verschueren. Van Nostrand Reinhold, 115 5th Ave., New York, New York 10003. (212) 254-3232. 1983. Covers individual substances as well as mixtures and preparations. The profiles include: properties, air pollution factors, water pollution factors, and biological effects.

Identification of Pure Organic Compounds. Ernest Hamlin Huntress. John Wiley & Sons, Inc., 605 Third Ave., New York, New York 10158-0012. (212) 850-6000. 1941. Tables of data on selected compounds of order I (compounds of carbon with hydrogen or with hydrogen and oxygen).

NIOSH Pocket Guide to Chemical Hazards. National Institute for Occupational Safety and Health, 1600 Clifton Rd. NE, Atlanta, Georgia 30333. (404) 639-3286. 1990. Presents sources of general industrial hygiene and medical surveillance information for workers, employees and others. Presents key information and data in an abbreviated format for 398 individual chemicals or chemical types.

ONLINE DATA BASES

BIOSIS Previews. BIOSIS, 2100 Arch St., Philadelphia, Pennsylvania 19103-1399. (215) 587-4800. Largest and most comprehensive database of research in the life sciences. Contains citations for nearly 9000 primary research journals, monographs, reviews, symposia, preliminary reports, semi-popular journals, selected institutional reports, government reports and research communications.

CAS Source Index–CASSI. Chemical Abstracts Service, 2540 Olentangy River Rd., P.O. Box 3012, Columbus, Ohio 43210. (800) 848-6533 or (614) 421-3600. A listing of bibliographic and library holdings information for

scientific and technical primary literature relevant to the chemical sciences.

Chemical Abstracts-CA. Chemical Abstracts Service, 2540 Olentangy River Rd., P.O. Box 3012, Columbus, Ohio 43210. (800) 848-6533 or (614) 421-3600. Information sources include 9000 journals, patents from 27 countries, two industrial property organizations, new books, conference proceedings, and government research reports.

Enviro/Energyline Abstracts Plus. R. R. Bowker Co., 121 Chanlon Rd., New Providence, New Jersey 07974. (908) 464-6800.

Environmental Periodicals Bibliography. National Information Services Corp., Ste. 6, Wyman Towers, 3100 St. Paul St., Baltimore, Maryland 21218. (410)243-0797. Online version of abstract of same name.

Kirk-Othmer Encyclopedia of Chemical Technology. John Wiley & Sons, Inc., 605 3rd Ave., 5th Floor, New York, New York 10158. (212) 850-6000. Online version of the publication of the same name.

Monthly Catalog of United States Government Publications. U.S. G.P.O., Supt. of Docs., PO Box 371954, Pittsburgh, Pennsylvania 15250-7954. (202) 512-0000.

National Technical Information Service. U.S. Department of Commerce, National Technical Information Service, Office of Data Base Services, 5285 Port Royal Rd., Springfield, Virginia 22161. (703) 487-4807. Bibliographic database of government sponsored research and technical reports.

PERIODICALS AND NEWSLETTERS

Analytical Chemistry. American Chemical Society, 1155 16th St. N.W., Washington, District of Columbia 20036. (800) 227-5558. 1929-. Bimonthly. Articles for chemists, life scientists and engineers.

Journal of Chemical and Engineering Data. American Chemical Society, 1155 16th St. N.W., Washington, District of Columbia 20036. (202) 872-4600; (800) 227-5558. 1959-. Quarterly.

Journal of Fluorine Chemistry. Elsevier Science Publishing Co., 655 Avenue of the Americas, New York, New York 10010. (212) 984-5800. Quarterly.

Journal of the Water Pollution Control Federation. Water Pollution Control Federation, 801 Wythe St., Alexandria, Virginia 22314-1994. (703) 684-2400. Monthly. Deals with sewage and pollution.

FLYASH

ABSTRACTING AND INDEXING SERVICES

Biological Abstracts. BIOSIS, 2100 Arch St., Philadelphia, Pennsylvania 19103-1399. (215) 587-4800. 1927-.

Chemical Abstracts. Chemical Abstracts Service, 2540 Olentangy River Rd., PO Box 3012, Columbus, Ohio 43210. (800) 848-6533. 1907-.

Environment Abstracts. Bowker A & I Publishing, 121 Chanlon Rd., New Providence, New Jersey 07974. (908) 464-6800. 1974-.

Environment Index. Environment Information Center, Index Research Department, 124 E. 39th St., New York, New York 10016. 1971-. Annual.

Environmental Information Connection-EIC. Planning Information Program, Dept. of Urban and Regional Planning, University of Illinois, 1003 West Nevada, Urbana, Illinois 61801. (217) 333-1369. Also available online.

Environmental Periodicals Bibliography. Environmental Studies Institute, International Academy at Santa Barbara, 800 Garden St., Suite D, Santa Barbara, California 93101. (805) 965-5010. Also available online.

General Science Index. H. W. Wilson Co., 950 University Ave., Bronx, New York 10452. 1978-. Monthly, also issued in annual cumulation. Cumulative subject index to English language periodicals in the subject fields of astronomy, botany, chemistry, earth science, environment and conservation, food and nutrition, genetics, mathematics, medicine and health, microbiology, oceanography, physics, physiology and zoology.

Geographical Abstracts. London School of Economics, Dept. of Geography, Regency House, 34 Duke St., London, England 1966-. Continued by Geo Abstracts issued in 6 parts: Pt. A. Landforms and the quaternary; Pt. B. Biogeography and Climatology; Pt. C. Economic geography; Pt. D. Social geography and cartography; Pt. E. Sedimentology; Pt. F. Regional and community planning.

Index to Scientific Book Contents. Institute for Scientific Information, 3501 Market St., Philadelphia, Pennsylvania 19104. (800) 523-1857. 1985-. Annual. Gives contents of science books published.

Pollution Abstracts. Cambridge Scientific Abstracts, 5161 River Rd., Bethesda, Maryland 20816. (301) 961-6750. Six/year. Indexes worldwide technical literature on environmental pollution. Covers air pollution, marine and freshwater pollution, sewage and wastewater treatment, waste management, toxicology and health, noise pollution, radiation, land pollution, and environmental policies, programs, legislation, and education. Also available online.

Science Citation Index. Institute for Scientific Information, 3501 Market St., Philadelphia, Pennsylvania 19104. 1961-.

BIBLIOGRAPHIES

Annotated Bibliography of Literature on Flue Gas Conditioning. U.S. Environmental Protection Agency, Division of Stationary Source Enforcement. U.S. Environmental Protection Agency, 401 M St., SW, Washington, District of Columbia (202) 260-2090. 1981. Covers flue gases and fly ash.

EPA Publications Bibliography. U.S. Environmental Protection Agency, Library Systems Branch, 401 M St., SW, Washington, District of Columbia 20460. (202) 260-2090. Quarterly.

Toxic Residues in Foods, 1979-March 1987. Charles N. Bebee. National Agricultural Library, 10301 Baltimore Blvd., Beltsville, Maryland 20705-2351. (301) 504-5755. 1987. Quick bibliography series: NAL-BIBL. QB 87-70

ENCYCLOPEDIAS AND DICTIONARIES

McGraw-Hill Encyclopedia of Science and Technology. McGraw-Hill, 1221 Avenue of the Americas, New York, New York 10020. (212) 512-2000 or (800) 262-4729. 1992. Seventh edition. Issued in multiple volumes including index. Includes all science and technology broad subject areas.

Van Nostrand's Scientific Encyclopedia. Glenn D. Considine, ed. Van Nostrand Reinhold, 115 5th Ave., New York, New York 10003. (212) 254-3232. 1983. Sixth edition. Includes all broad subject areas in science.

GENERAL WORKS

Fly Ash Utilization in Soil-Bentonite Slurry Trench Cutoff Walls. University Microfilms International, 300 N. Zeeb Rd., Ann Arbor, Michigan 48106. (313) 761-4700. 1990.

Municipal Solid Waste Incinerator Ash Management and Disposal Data Entries. The Institute, 2425 18th St., N.W., Washington, District of Columbia 20009. (202) 232-4108. Database on solid waste resources recovery and economic development, including municipal solid waste ash.

Treatment and Conditioning of Radioactive Incinerator Ashes. L. Crecille, ed. Elsevier Science Publishing Co., 655 Avenue of the Americas, New York, New York 10010. (212) 989-5800. 1991. Incineration of radioactive wastes and purification of fly ash.

ONLINE DATA BASES

BIOSIS Previews. BIOSIS, 2100 Arch St., Philadelphia, Pennsylvania 19103-1399. (215) 587-4800. Largest and most comprehensive database of research in the life sciences. Contains citations for nearly 9000 primary research journals, monographs, reviews, symposia, preliminary reports, semi-popular journals, selected institutional reports, government reports and research communications.

Chemical Abstracts-CA. Chemical Abstracts Service, 2540 Olentangy River Rd., P.O. Box 3012, Columbus, Ohio 43210. (800) 848-6533 or (614) 421-3600. Information sources include 9000 journals, patents from 27 countries, two industrial property organizations, new books, conference proceedings, and government research reports.

Enviro/Energyline Abstracts Plus. R. R. Bowker Co., 121 Chanlon Rd., New Providence, New Jersey 07974. (908) 464-6800.

Environmental Periodicals Bibliography. National Information Services Corp., Ste. 6, Wyman Towers, 3100 St. Paul St., Baltimore, Maryland 21218. (410)243-0797. Online version of abstract of same name.

Monthly Catalog of United States Government Publications. U.S. G.P.O., Supt. of Docs., PO Box 371954, Pittsburgh, Pennsylvania 15250-7954. (202) 512-0000.

National Technical Information Service. U.S. Department of Commerce, National Technical Information Service, Office of Data Base Services, 5285 Port Royal Rd., Springfield, Virginia 22161. (703) 487-4807. Bibliographic database of government sponsored research and technical reports.

RESEARCH CENTERS AND INSTITUTES

Center for Research and Technology Development. 1825 K Street, N.W., Washington, District of Columbia 20006-1202. (202) 785-3756.

FLYWAY
See: MIGRATION

FOG

ABSTRACTING AND INDEXING SERVICES

Index to Scientific Book Contents. Institute for Scientific Information, 3501 Market St., Philadelphia, Pennsylvania 19104. (800) 523-1857. 1985-. Annual. Gives contents of science books published.

Pollution Abstracts. Cambridge Scientific Abstracts, 5161 River Rd., Bethesda, Maryland 20816. (301) 961-6750. Six/year. Indexes worldwide technical literature on environmental pollution. Covers air pollution, marine and freshwater pollution, sewage and wastewater treatment, waste management, toxicology and health, noise pollution, radiation, land pollution, and environmental policies, programs, legislation, and education. Also available online.

Science Citation Index. Institute for Scientific Information, 3501 Market St., Philadelphia, Pennsylvania 19104. 1961-.

ENCYCLOPEDIAS AND DICTIONARIES

The Encyclopedia of Climatology. John E. Oliver and Rhodes W. Fairbridge, eds. Van Nostrand Reinhold, 115 5th Ave., New York, New York 10003. (212) 254-3232. 1987. Belongs in the series Encyclopedia of Earth Sciences, v.11.

GENERAL WORKS

Atmospheric Temperature, Density and Pressure. Allen E. Cole. Meteorology Division, Air Force Geophysics Laboratory, Hanscom Air Force Base, Massachusetts 01731. (617) 377-3237. 1983. Includes atmospheric density, atmospheric pressure, and atmospheric temperature.

Sea Fog. Pin-hau Wang. Springer-Verlag, 175 5th Ave., New York, New York 10010. (212) 460-1500. 1985. Deals with meteorology.

Water Vapor, Precipitation, Clouds and Fog. D. D. Grantham. Meteorology Division, Air Force Geophysics Laboratory, Hanscom Air Force Base, Massachusetts 01731. (617) 377-3237. 1983. Covers precipitation, atmospheric water vapor, fog and clouds.

HANDBOOKS AND MANUALS

U.S. Air Force Geophysics Laboratory. Adolph S. Jursa. Phillips Laboratory, 29 Randolph Rd., Hanscom Air Force Base, Bedford, Massachusetts 01731-3010. (617) 377-5191. 1985.

FOLPET

See: FUNGICIDES

FOOD ADDITIVES

See: FOOD SCIENCE

FOOD CONTAMINATION

See also: FOOD SCIENCE

ABSTRACTING AND INDEXING SERVICES

Agrindex. AGRIS Coordinating Center, Via delle Terme di Caracalla, Rome, Italy I-00100. 61 0181-FA01. 1975-.

Applied Science and Technology Index. H.W. Wilson Co., 950 University Ave., Bronx, New York 10452. (800) 367-6770. Formerly Industrial Arts Index.

Biological Abstracts. BIOSIS, 2100 Arch St., Philadelphia, Pennsylvania 19103-1399. (215) 587-4800. 1927-.

Biotechnology Research Abstracts. Cambridge Scientific Abstracts, 5161 River Rd., Bethesda, Maryland 20816. (301) 961-6750. Monthly. Includes such broad areas as genetic intervention, biochemical genetics, and microbiological techniques.

Chemical Abstracts. Chemical Abstracts Service, 2540 Olentangy River Rd., PO Box 3012, Columbus, Ohio 43210. (800) 848-6533. 1907-.

Current Advances in Ecological and Environmental Science. Pergamon Microforms International, Inc., Fairview Park, Elmsford, New York 10523. (914) 592-7720. 1989-. Monthly. Current literature searching service including journals, reports, abstracts, etc. This service is available online as part of the CABS database on the hosts BRS and ORBIT search service.

Ecological Abstracts. Geo Abstracts Ltd. Elsevier Applied Science, Crown House, Linton Rd., Barking, England IG 11 8JU. 1974-. Derived from over 600 leading ecological and environmental journals, plus books, conference proceedings, reports and theses.

Environment Abstracts. Bowker A & I Publishing, 121 Chanlon Rd., New Providence, New Jersey 07974. (908) 464-6800. 1974-.

Environment Index. Environment Information Center, Index Research Department, 124 E. 39th St., New York, New York 10016. 1971-. Annual.

Environmental Information Connection–EIC. Planning Information Program, Dept. of Urban and Regional Planning, University of Illinois, 1003 West Nevada, Urbana, Illinois 61801. (217) 333-1369. Also available online.

Environmental Periodicals Bibliography. Environmental Studies Institute, International Academy at Santa Barbara, 800 Garden St., Suite D, Santa Barbara, California 93101. (805) 965-5010. Also available online.

Food Science and Technology Abstracts. International Food Information Service, c/o National Food Laborato-

ry, 6363 Clark Ave., Dublin, California 94568. (800) 336-3782. 1969-.

Foods ADLIBRA. K & M Pub. Inc., 2000 Frankfort Ave., Louisville, Kentucky 40206. Semimonthly. Contains abstracts of current literature concerning the food industry. Topics covered include: food technology, food packaging, new food products, world food economics, nutrition, patents, and marketing.

General Science Index. H. W. Wilson Co., 950 University Ave., Bronx, New York 10452. 1978-. Monthly, also issued in annual cumulation. Cumulative subject index to English language periodicals in the subject fields of astronomy, botany, chemistry, earth science, environment and conservation, food and nutrition, genetics, mathematics, medicine and health, microbiology, oceanography, physics, physiology and zoology.

Index to Scientific Book Contents. Institute for Scientific Information, 3501 Market St., Philadelphia, Pennsylvania 19104. (800) 523-1857. 1985-. Annual. Gives contents of science books published.

Science Citation Index. Institute for Scientific Information, 3501 Market St., Philadelphia, Pennsylvania 19104. 1961-.

ALMANACS AND YEARBOOKS

Environmental Almanac. World Resources Institute. Houghton Mifflin, 1 Beacon St., Boston, Massachusetts 02108. (617) 725-5000; (800) 225-3362. 1991. Covers consumer products, energy, endangered species, food safety, global warming, solid wastes, toxics, wetlands and other related areas. Also included are the names and addresses of the chief environmental executives for all 50 states.

BIBLIOGRAPHIES

EPA Publications Bibliography. U.S. Environmental Protection Agency, Library Systems Branch, 401 M St., SW, Washington, District of Columbia 20460. (202) 260-2090. Quarterly.

Food Pollution: A Bibliography. Joan Nordquist. Reference and Research Services, 511 Lincoln St., Santa Cruz, California 95060. (408) 426-4479. 1990. Bibliography of food adulteration and inspection, food additives and toxicology.

Food Safety, 1990: An Annotated Bibliography of the Literature. Dorothy C. Gosting, et al. Butterworth-Heinemann, 80 Montvale Ave., Stoneham, Massachusetts 02180. (617) 438-8464 or (800) 366-2665. 1991. Deals with the areas of environmental health and toxicology in relation to food safety and preservation. The bibliography is divided into three major parts headed "Diet and Health," "Safety of Food Components," and "Foodborne Microbial Illness." The appendix is titled "Food-and-Water-Associated Viruses."

ENCYCLOPEDIAS AND DICTIONARIES

Encyclopedia of Food Science. Y. H. Hui, ed. John Wiley & Sons, Inc., 605 3rd Ave., New York, New York 10158-0012. (212) 850-6000. 1991. Deals with the properties, analysis and processing of foods including: grains and bakery products, beans, nuts, seeds, fruits and vegetables, dairy products, meat products, poultry and fish products, and alcoholic beverages. Emphasis is placed on issues associated with food additives and food spoilage.

Encyclopedia of Food Science. M. S. Peterson and A. H. Johnson. The AVI Pub. Co., 250 Post Rd. E., PO Box 831, Westport, Connecticut 06881. 1978. Consists of short individually authored articles in an alphabetical arrangement, each with a brief bibliography. A section entitled "Food Science Around the World" includes information on food science and the food industries in various countries.

Encyclopedia of Physics. Rita G. Lerner and George L. Trigg. VCH Publishers, 303 NW 12th Ave., Deerfield Beach, Florida 33442-1788. (305) 428-5566. 1991. Second edition.

McGraw-Hill Encyclopedia of Environmental Science. Sybil P. Parker. McGraw-Hill Science & Engineering Books, 11 W. 19th St., New York, New York 10011. (212) 337-6010. 1980. Covers ecology, man's influence on nature, and environmental protection.

The Nutrition and Health Encyclopedia. David F. Tver and Percy Russell. Van Nostrand Reinhold, 115 5th Ave., New York, New York 10003. (212) 254-3232. 1989.

GENERAL WORKS

Aluminum in Food and the Environment. Robert C. Massey. Royal Society of Chemistry, c/o CRC Press, 2000 Corporate Blvd. N.W., Boca Raton, Florida 33431-9868. (800)272-7737. 1990. Looks at the adverse health effects associated with aluminum. The evidence of aluminum's involvement in both dialysis dementia and Alzheimer's disease is reviewed and biochemical mechanisms by which aluminum may exert its detrimental effects on brain tissue are discussed.

The Chemical Analysis of Foods: A Practical Treatise on the Examination of Foodstuffs and the Detection of Adulterants. Henry Edward Cox. J. & A. Churchill, Rover Stevenson House, 1-3 Banter's Place, Leith Walk, Edinburgh, England EH1 3AF. (031) 556-2424. 1977.

Chemical & Radionuclide Food Contamination. MSS Information Corp., Edison, New Jersey 1973. Covers radioactive contamination of food.

Chemicals in the Human Food Chain. Carl K. Winter, et al. Van Nostrand Reinhold, 115 5th Ave., New York, New York 10003. (212) 254-3232. 1990. Deals with prevention of food contamination by pesticides and other toxic chemicals.

Demanding Clean Food and Water. Plenum Press, 233 Spring St., New York, New York 10013. (212) 620-8000. Details specific chemicals to avoid in foods and discusses approaches for eradicating pests without polluting the environment.

Dioxin Contamination of Milk. Committee on Energy and Commerce. Subcommittee on Health and Environment. U.S. G.P.O., Washington, District of Columbia 20401. (202) 512-0000. 1990. Hearing before the subcommittee on Health and the Environment of the Committee on Energy and Commerce, House of Representatives, 101st Congress, 1st session, September 8, 1989. Contains facts about dioxin contamination of milk and the health effects on the environment.

Food Contamination from Environmental Sources. J. O. Nriagu and M. S. Simmons, eds. John Wiley & Sons, Inc.,

605 3rd Ave., New York, New York 10158-0012. (212) 850-6000. 1990. Discusses the accumulation and transfer of contaminants through the food chain to the consumer.

Immunoassays for Trace Chemical Analysis; Monitoring Toxic Chemicals in Humans, Food, and the Environment. Martin Vandelaan, et al. American Chemical Society, 1155 16th St., N.W., Washington, District of Columbia 20036. (202) 872-4600; (800) 227-5558. Deals with the use of immunoassays as alternative methods for conducting sampling for chemical residues in food and the environment, for natural toxins, and for monitoring human exposure to toxic chemicals.

Immunochemical Methods for Environmental Analysis. Jeanette M. Van Emon and Ralph O. Mumma, eds. American Chemical Society, 1155 16th St. N.W., Washington, District of Columbia 20036. (202) 872-4600; (800) 227-5558. 1990. Describes antibodies used as analytical tools to study environmentally important compounds. Discusses various applications in food industry, environmental analysis, and applications in agriculture.

Metal Contamination of Food. Conor Reilly. Elsevier Science Publishing Co., 655 Avenue of the Americas, New York, New York 10010. (212) 984-5800. 1991. Analysis of testing of metals in food.

Methods for Assessing Exposure of Human and Non-Human Biota. R. G. Tardiff and B. D. Goldstein, eds. John Wiley & Sons, Inc., 605 3rd Ave., New York, New York 10158-0012. (212) 850-6000. 1991. Provides a critical and collective evaluation of approaches to chemical exposure assessment.

Microbial Toxins in Focus and Feeds. Albert E. Pohland, et al., eds. Plenum Press, 233 Spring St., New York, New York 10013. (212) 620-8000; (800) 221-9369. 1990. Proceedings of a Symposium on Cellular and Molecular Mode of Action of Selected Microbial Toxins in Foods and Feeds, Oct. 31- Nov. 2, 1988, Chevy Chase, MD.

Pesticide Residues and Food Safety: A Harvest of Viewpoints. B. G. Tweedy, et al., eds. American Chemical Society, 1155 16th St. N.W., Washington, District of Columbia 20036. (202) 872-4600; (800) 227-5558. 1991. Discusses all the issues raised in connection with the use of pesticides in the United States. Some of the issues are the economic and social aspects, impact assessment programs, food safety, consumer attitude, pesticide free fruit crops, integrated pest management, EPA's program for validation of pesticides, and other related matters.

Pesticide Residues in Food. Food and Agriculture Organization of the United Nations, 4611-F Assembly Dr., Lanham, Maryland 20706-4391. (800) 274-4888. 1990.

HANDBOOKS AND MANUALS

CRC Handbook of Naturally Occurring Food Toxicants. Miloslav Rechcigal, Jr. CRC Press, 2000 Corporate Blvd. N.W., Boca Raton, Florida 33431. (800) 272-7737. 1983. Covers food contamination and poisoning and their adverse effects.

Guidelines for Evaluation of Potential Product Contamination and Procedures for Withdrawal and/or Recall of Food Products. American Meat Institute, PO Box 3556 Washington, District of Columbia 20007. (703) 841-2400. 1981. Food contamination, product recall and food handling.

Handbook of Toxic Fungal Metabolites. Richard J. Cole and Richard H. Cox. Academic Press, c/o Harcourt Brace Jovanovich Inc., 6277 Sea Harbor Dr., Orlando, Florida 32887. (800) 346-8648. Oriented toward fungal metabolites that elicit a toxic response in vertebrate animals. Also includes metabolites that show little or no known acute toxicity.

Handbook on International Food Regulatory Toxicology. SP Medical & Scientific Books, New York, New York 1980-. Toxicity of food additives and pesticide residues, as well as food-contamination prevention and control.

Safe Food Handling. Michael Jacob. World Health Organization, Ave. Appia, Geneva, Switzerland CH-1211. 1989. A training guide for managers of food service establishments.

ONLINE DATA BASES

BIOSIS Previews. BIOSIS, 2100 Arch St., Philadelphia, Pennsylvania 19103-1399. (215) 587-4800. Largest and most comprehensive database of research in the life sciences. Contains citations for nearly 9000 primary research journals, monographs, reviews, symposia, preliminary reports, semi-popular journals, selected institutional reports, government reports and research communications.

Chemical Abstracts-CA. Chemical Abstracts Service, 2540 Olentangy River Rd., P.O. Box 3012, Columbus, Ohio 43210. (800) 848-6533 or (614) 421-3600. Information sources include 9000 journals, patents from 27 countries, two industrial property organizations, new books, conference proceedings, and government research reports.

Current Research Information System–CRIS/USDA. U.S. Department of Agriculture, National Agricultural Library, 10301 Baltimore Blvd., 5th Floor, Beltsville, Maryland 20705-2351. (301) 504-5755. Looks at current research projects in agriculture and allied sciences covering the biological, physical, social and behavioral sciences related to agriculture.

Enviro/Energyline Abstracts Plus. R. R. Bowker Co., 121 Chanlon Rd., New Providence, New Jersey 07974. (908) 464-6800.

Environmental Periodicals Bibliography. National Information Services Corp., Ste. 6, Wyman Towers, 3100 St. Paul St., Baltimore, Maryland 21218. (410)243-0797. Online version of abstract of same name.

Epidemiology Information System. Oak Ridge National Laboratory, Toxicology Information Response Center, Building 2001, P.O. Box 2008, Oak Ridge, Tennessee 37831-6050. (615) 576-1746.

Foods ADLIBRA. General Mills, Inc., Foods Adlibra Publications, 9000 Plymouth Ave., North, Minneapolis, Minnesota 55427. (612) 540-3463. Online version of periodical of same name.

Monthly Catalog of United States Government Publications. U.S. G.P.O., Supt. of Docs., PO Box 371954, Pittsburgh, Pennsylvania 15250-7954. (202) 512-0000.

National Technical Information Service. U.S. Department of Commerce, National Technical Information Service, Office of Data Base Services, 5285 Port Royal Rd., Springfield, Virginia 22161. (703) 487-4807. Bibliographic database of government sponsored research and technical reports.

PressNet Environmental Reports. Chemical Information Systems, Inc., 7215 York Rd., Baltimore, Maryland 21212. (301) 321-8440.

SCISEARCH. Institute for Scientific Information, University City Science Center, 3501 Market St., Philadelphia, Pennsylvania 19104. (215) 386-0100.

PERIODICALS AND NEWSLETTERS

Analytical Biochemistry. Academic Press, 111 Fifth Ave., New York, New York 10003. (800) 346-8648. Covers biological and chemical topics relating to the environment.

Bulletin of Environmental Contamination and Toxicology. Springer-Verlag, 175 5th Ave., New York, New York 10010. (212) 460-1500; (800) 777-4643. 1966-. Frequency varies. Disseminates advances and discoveries in the areas of soil, air and food contamination and pollution.

Environ: A Magazine for Ecological Living & Health Wary. Canary Press, Box 2204, Ft. Collins, Colorado 80522. (303) 224-0083. Quarterly. Consumer alternatives for ecologically sound lifestyles.

Food Additives and Contaminants. Taylor & Francis, 1900 Frost Rd., Suite 101, Bristol, Pennsylvania 19007. (215) 785-5580. Bimonthly.

Food and Chemical Toxicology. Pergamon Microforms International Inc., Fairview Park, Elmsford, New York 10523. (914) 592-7720. Monthly. Information and risks of food and chemicals.

Journal of Agricultural and Food Chemistry. American Chemical Society, 1155 16th St. N.W., Washington, District of Columbia 20036. (202) 872-4600; (800) 227-5558. 1953-. Monthly. Contains documentation of significant advances in the science of agriculture and food chemistry.

The Journal of Biological Chemistry. American Society of Biological Chemists, 428 E. Preston St., Baltimore, Maryland 21202. Three times a month. Biological, agricultural, and energy aspects of the environment.

Journal of Environmental Science and Health. Marcel Dekker, Inc., 270 Madison Ave., New York, New York 10016. (212) 696-9000. Bimonthly. Concerns pesticides, food contaminants, chemical carcinogens, and agricultural wastes.

Priorities For Long Life and Good Health. American Council on Health and Science, 1995 Broadway, 16th Floor, New York, New York 10023. (212) 362-7044. Quarterly. Covers evaluations of food, chemicals, and health.

TRADE ASSOCIATIONS AND PROFESSIONAL SOCIETIES

American Institute of Biological Sciences. 730 11th St., N.W., Washington, District of Columbia 20001-4521. (202) 628-1500.

FOOD INSPECTION

ABSTRACTING AND INDEXING SERVICES

Agrindex. AGRIS Coordinating Center, Via delle Terme di Caracalla, Rome, Italy I-00100. 61 0181-FA01. 1975-.

Applied Science and Technology Index. H.W. Wilson Co., 950 University Ave., Bronx, New York 10452. (800) 367-6770. Formerly Industrial Arts Index.

Biological and Agricultural Index. H.W. Wilson Co., 950 University Ave., Bronx, New York 10452. (800) 367-6770. 1916-. Monthly.

Environment Abstracts. Bowker A & I Publishing, 121 Chanlon Rd., New Providence, New Jersey 07974. (908) 464-6800. 1974-.

Environment Index. Environment Information Center, Index Research Department, 124 E. 39th St., New York, New York 10016. 1971-. Annual.

Environmental Information Connection–EIC. Planning Information Program, Dept. of Urban and Regional Planning, University of Illinois, 1003 West Nevada, Urbana, Illinois 61801. (217) 333-1369. Also available online.

Environmental Periodicals Bibliography. Environmental Studies Institute, International Academy at Santa Barbara, 800 Garden St., Suite D, Santa Barbara, California 93101. (805) 965-5010. Also available online.

Food Science and Technology Abstracts. International Food Information Service, c/o National Food Laboratory, 6363 Clark Ave., Dublin, California 94568. (800) 336-3782. 1969-.

Foods ADLIBRA. K & M Pub. Inc., 2000 Frankfort Ave., Louisville, Kentucky 40206. Semimonthly. Contains abstracts of current literature concerning the food industry. Topics covered include: food technology, food packaging, new food products, world food economics, nutrition, patents, and marketing.

General Science Index. H. W. Wilson Co., 950 University Ave., Bronx, New York 10452. 1978-. Monthly, also issued in annual cumulation. Cumulative subject index to English language periodicals in the subject fields of astronomy, botany, chemistry, earth science, environment and conservation, food and nutrition, genetics, mathematics, medicine and health, microbiology, oceanography, physics, physiology and zoology.

Index to Scientific Book Contents. Institute for Scientific Information, 3501 Market St., Philadelphia, Pennsylvania 19104. (800) 523-1857. 1985-. Annual. Gives contents of science books published.

Science Citation Index. Institute for Scientific Information, 3501 Market St., Philadelphia, Pennsylvania 19104. 1961-.

ALMANACS AND YEARBOOKS

Environmental Almanac. World Resources Institute. Houghton Mifflin, 1 Beacon St., Boston, Massachusetts 02108. (617) 725-5000; (800) 225-3362. 1991. Covers consumer products, energy, endangered species, food safety, global warming, solid wastes, toxics, wetlands and other related areas. Also included are the names and addresses of the chief environmental executives for all 50 states.

List of Chemical Compounds, Authorized for Use and Under USDA Inspection and Grading Programs. U.S. Dept. of Agriculture, Food Safety and Quality Service. U.S. G.P.O., Washington, District of Columbia 20401. (202) 512-0000. Annual. Covers food adulteration and

inspection, egg products industry, equipment and supplies, and meat industry trade.

List of Proprietary Substances and Nonfood Compounds Authorized for Use Under USDA Inspection and Grading Programs: microform. U.S. Dept. of Agriculture, Food Safety and Inspection Service. U.S. G.P.O., Washington, District of Columbia 20401. (202) 512-0000. Annual. Food adulteration and inspection, meat industry and trade, and egg products industry.

BIBLIOGRAPHIES

EPA Publications Bibliography. U.S. Environmental Protection Agency, Library Systems Branch, 401 M St., SW, Washington, District of Columbia 20460. (202) 260-2090. Quarterly.

Food Safety, 1990: An Annotated Bibliography of the Literature. Dorothy C. Gosting, et al. Butterworth-Heinemann, 80 Montvale Ave., Stoneham, Massachusetts 02180. (617) 438-8464 or (800) 366-2665. 1991. Deals with the areas of environmental health and toxicology in relation to food safety and preservation. The bibliography is divided into three major parts headed "Diet and Health," "Safety of Food Components," and "Food-borne Microbial Illness." The appendix is titled "Food-and-Water-Associated Viruses."

ENCYCLOPEDIAS AND DICTIONARIES

McGraw-Hill Encyclopedia of Environmental Science. Sybil P. Parker. McGraw-Hill Science & Engineering Books, 11 W. 19th St., New York, New York 10011. (212) 337-6010. 1980. Covers ecology, man's influence on nature, and environmental protection.

HANDBOOKS AND MANUALS

FDA Inspection Operation Manual. U.S. Dept. of Health and Human Services, Public Health Service, Food and Drug Administration. U.S. G.P.O., Washington, District of Columbia 20401. (202) 512-0000. Food and drug adulteration and inspection. Looseleaf format.

Inspecting Incoming Food Materials. U.S. Dept. of Health and Human Services, Public Health Service, Food and Drug Administration. U.S. G.P.O., Washington, District of Columbia 20401. (202) 512-0000. 1990. Covers food adulteration and inspection procedures.

Inspection System Guide (ISG). U.S. Deptartment of Agriculture, Food Safety and Inspection Service, 14 Independence Ave., SW, Washington, District of Columbia 20250. (202) 447-7454. Food adulteration and inspection as well as standards for food safety measures. Looseleaf format.

Manuals of Food Quality Control. Food and Agriculture Organization of the United Nations. Food and Agriculture Organization of the United Nations, Via delle Terme di Caracalla, Rome, Italy 00100. 61 0181-FA01. 1986. Food and nutrition, and adulteration and inspection guidelines.

PMS Blue Book. Department of Health and Human Services, Food and Drug Administration, Public Health Service, 5600 Fishers Ln., Rockville, Maryland 20857. (301) 443-1544. Annual.

ONLINE DATA BASES

Current Research Information System–CRIS/USDA. U.S. Department of Agriculture, National Agricultural Library, 10301 Baltimore Blvd., 5th Floor, Beltsville, Maryland 20705-2351. (301) 504-5755. Looks at current research projects in agriculture and allied sciences covering the biological, physical, social and behavioral sciences related to agriculture.

Enviro/Energyline Abstracts Plus. R. R. Bowker Co., 121 Chanlon Rd., New Providence, New Jersey 07974. (908) 464-6800.

Environmental Periodicals Bibliography. National Information Services Corp., Ste. 6, Wyman Towers, 3100 St. Paul St., Baltimore, Maryland 21218. (410)243-0797. Online version of abstract of same name.

Foods ADLIBRA. General Mills, Inc., Foods Adlibra Publications, 9000 Plymouth Ave., North, Minneapolis, Minnesota 55427. (612) 540-3463. Online version of periodical of same name.

Monthly Catalog of United States Government Publications. U.S. G.P.O., Supt. of Docs., PO Box 371954, Pittsburgh, Pennsylvania 15250-7954. (202) 512-0000.

National Technical Information Service. U.S. Department of Commerce, National Technical Information Service, Office of Data Base Services, 5285 Port Royal Rd., Springfield, Virginia 22161. (703) 487-4807. Bibliographic database of government sponsored research and technical reports.

PressNet Environmental Reports. Chemical Information Systems, Inc., 7215 York Rd., Baltimore, Maryland 21212. (301) 321-8440.

PERIODICALS AND NEWSLETTERS

AMS Food Purchases. Weekly Summary. U.S. Deptartment of Agriculture, Agricultural Marketing Service, 14 Independence Ave., SW, Washington, District of Columbia 20250. (202) 447-7454. Weekly. Food industry trade, quality control and food adulteration and inspection.

FDA Enforcement Report. Food and Drug Administration, 5600 Fishers Ln., Rockville, Maryland 20857. (301)443-1544. Weekly. Legal actions covering food adulteration and inspection.

Food News for Consumers. U.S. Deptartment of Agriculture, Food Safety and Quality Service, 14 Independence Ave., SW, Washington, District of Columbia 20250. (202) 447-7454. Quarterly. Consumer protection in the area of food adulteration.

Journal of Food Protection. International Association of Milk, Food, and Environmental Sanitarians, 502 E. Lincoln Way, Ames, Iowa 50010-6666. (515) 232-6699. Covers milk hygiene and food adulteration and inspection procedures.

FOOD IRRADIATION

See: FOOD PROCESSING AND TREATMENT

FOOD OILS

See: NUTRITION

FOOD POISONING

See also: BACTERIA; CONTAMINATION; TOXICOLOGY

ABSTRACTING AND INDEXING SERVICES

Agrindex. AGRIS Coordinating Center, Via delle Terme di Caracalla, Rome, Italy I-00100. 61 0181-FA01. 1975-.

Biological Abstracts. BIOSIS, 2100 Arch St., Philadelphia, Pennsylvania 19103-1399. (215) 587-4800. 1927-.

Biological and Agricultural Index. H.W. Wilson Co., 950 University Ave., Bronx, New York 10452. (800) 367-6770. 1916-. Monthly.

Chemical Abstracts. Chemical Abstracts Service, 2540 Olentangy River Rd., PO Box 3012, Columbus, Ohio 43210. (800) 848-6533. 1907-.

Ecological Abstracts. Geo Abstracts Ltd. Elsevier Applied Science, Crown House, Linton Rd., Barking, England IG 11 8JU. 1974-. Derived from over 600 leading ecological and environmental journals, plus books, conference proceedings, reports and theses.

Environment Abstracts. Bowker A & I Publishing, 121 Chanlon Rd., New Providence, New Jersey 07974. (908) 464-6800. 1974-.

Environment Index. Environment Information Center, Index Research Department, 124 E. 39th St., New York, New York 10016. 1971-. Annual.

Environmental Information Connection–EIC. Planning Information Program, Dept. of Urban and Regional Planning, University of Illinois, 1003 West Nevada, Urbana, Illinois 61801. (217) 333-1369. Also available online.

Environmental Periodicals Bibliography. Environmental Studies Institute, International Academy at Santa Barbara, 800 Garden St., Suite D, Santa Barbara, California 93101. (805) 965-5010. Also available online.

Food Science and Technology Abstracts. International Food Information Service, c/o National Food Laboratory, 6363 Clark Ave., Dublin, California 94568. (800) 336-3782. 1969-.

Foods ADLIBRA. K & M Pub. Inc., 2000 Frankfort Ave., Louisville, Kentucky 40206. Semimonthly. Contains abstracts of current literature concerning the food industry. Topics covered include: food technology, food packaging, new food products, world food economics, nutrition, patents, and marketing.

General Science Index. H. W. Wilson Co., 950 University Ave., Bronx, New York 10452. 1978-. Monthly, also issued in annual cumulation. Cumulative subject index to English language periodicals in the subject fields of astronomy, botany, chemistry, earth science, environment and conservation, food and nutrition, genetics, mathematics, medicine and health, microbiology, oceanography, physics, physiology and zoology.

Index to Scientific Book Contents. Institute for Scientific Information, 3501 Market St., Philadelphia, Pennsylvania 19104. (800) 523-1857. 1985-. Annual. Gives contents of science books published.

Science Citation Index. Institute for Scientific Information, 3501 Market St., Philadelphia, Pennsylvania 19104. 1961-.

ALMANACS AND YEARBOOKS

Environmental Almanac. World Resources Institute. Houghton Mifflin, 1 Beacon St., Boston, Massachusetts 02108. (617) 725-5000; (800) 225-3362. 1991. Covers consumer products, energy, endangered species, food safety, global warming, solid wastes, toxics, wetlands and other related areas. Also included are the names and addresses of the chief environmental executives for all 50 states.

BIBLIOGRAPHIES

Current Contents. Agriculture, Biology and Environmental Sciences. Institute for Scientific Information, 3501 Market St., Philadelphia, Pennsylvania 19104. (800) 523-1857. 1973-. Previous title: Current Contents. Agricultural, Food & Veterinary Sciences. Gives the table of contents of periodicals in the fields of agriculture, biology, environmental and related areas.

Directory of Published Proceedings. Interdok Corp., 173 Halstead Ave., Harrison, New York 10528. (914) 835-3506. 1990. Monthly. This is a listing of published proceedings including the series SEMTE (Science/Medicine/Engineering/Technology) and the series SSH (Social Science/Humanities).

EPA Publications Bibliography. U.S. Environmental Protection Agency, Library Systems Branch, 401 M St., SW, Washington, District of Columbia 20460. (202) 260-2090. Quarterly.

Food Pollution: A Bibliography. Joan Nordquist. Reference and Research Services, 511 Lincoln St., Santa Cruz, California 95060. (408) 426-4479. 1990. Bibliography of food adulteration and inspection, food additives and toxicology.

ENCYCLOPEDIAS AND DICTIONARIES

Encyclopedia of Human Biology. Renato Dulbecco, ed. Academic Press, c/o Harcourt Brace Jovanovich Inc., 6277 Sea Harbor Dr., Orlando, Florida 32887. (800) 346-8648. 1991. Eight volumes.

McGraw-Hill Encyclopedia of Environmental Science. Sybil P. Parker. McGraw-Hill Science & Engineering Books, 11 W. 19th St., New York, New York 10011. (212) 337-6010. 1980. Covers ecology, man's influence on nature, and environmental protection.

The Nutrition and Health Encyclopedia. David F. Tver and Percy Russell. Van Nostrand Reinhold, 115 5th Ave., New York, New York 10003. (212) 254-3232. 1989.

ONLINE DATA BASES

BIOSIS Previews. BIOSIS, 2100 Arch St., Philadelphia, Pennsylvania 19103-1399. (215) 587-4800. Largest and most comprehensive database of research in the life sciences. Contains citations for nearly 9000 primary research journals, monographs, reviews, symposia, preliminary reports, semi-popular journals, selected institutional reports, government reports and research communications.

Chemical Abstracts-CA. Chemical Abstracts Service, 2540 Olentangy River Rd., P.O. Box 3012, Columbus, Ohio 43210. (800) 848-6533 or (614) 421-3600. Information sources include 9000 journals, patents from 27 countries, two industrial property organizations, new books, conference proceedings, and government research reports.

Current Research Information System–CRIS/USDA. U.S. Department of Agriculture, National Agricultural Library, 10301 Baltimore Blvd., 5th Floor, Beltsville, Maryland 20705-2351. (301) 504-5755. Looks at current research projects in agriculture and allied sciences covering the biological, physical, social and behavioral sciences related to agriculture.

Enviro/Energyline Abstracts Plus. R. R. Bowker Co., 121 Chanlon Rd., New Providence, New Jersey 07974. (908) 464-6800.

Environmental Periodicals Bibliography. National Information Services Corp., Ste. 6, Wyman Towers, 3100 St. Paul St., Baltimore, Maryland 21218. (410)243-0797. Online version of abstract of same name.

Foods ADLIBRA. General Mills, Inc., Foods Adlibra Publications, 9000 Plymouth Ave., North, Minneapolis, Minnesota 55427. (612) 540-3463. Online version of periodical of same name.

Monthly Catalog of United States Government Publications. U.S. G.P.O., Supt. of Docs., PO Box 371954, Pittsburgh, Pennsylvania 15250-7954. (202) 512-0000.

National Technical Information Service. U.S. Department of Commerce, National Technical Information Service, Office of Data Base Services, 5285 Port Royal Rd., Springfield, Virginia 22161. (703) 487-4807. Bibliographic database of government sponsored research and technical reports.

PressNet Environmental Reports. Chemical Information Systems, Inc., 7215 York Rd., Baltimore, Maryland 21212. (301) 321-8440.

PERIODICALS AND NEWSLETTERS

Bulletin of Environmental Contamination and Toxicology. Springer-Verlag, 175 5th Ave., New York, New York 10010. (212) 460-1500; (800) 777-4643. 1966-. Frequency varies. Disseminates advances and discoveries in the areas of soil, air and food contamination and pollution.

The Journal of Biological Chemistry. American Society of Biological Chemists, 428 E. Preston St., Baltimore, Maryland 21202. Three times a month. Biological, agricultural, and energy aspects of the environment.

TRADE ASSOCIATIONS AND PROFESSIONAL SOCIETIES

American Institute of Biological Sciences. 730 11th St., N.W., Washington, District of Columbia 20001-4521. (202) 628-1500.

FOOD PRESERVATION

See: FOOD PROCESSING AND TREATMENT

FOOD PROCESSING AND TREATMENT

See also: FOOD SCIENCE

ABSTRACTING AND INDEXING SERVICES

Agrindex. AGRIS Coordinating Center, Via delle Terme di Caracalla, Rome, Italy I-00100. 61 0181-FA01. 1975-.

Biological Abstracts. BIOSIS, 2100 Arch St., Philadelphia, Pennsylvania 19103-1399. (215) 587-4800. 1927-.

Biological and Agricultural Index. H.W. Wilson Co., 950 University Ave., Bronx, New York 10452. (800) 367-6770. 1916-. Monthly.

Biotechnology Research Abstracts. Cambridge Scientific Abstracts, 5161 River Rd., Bethesda, Maryland 20816. (301) 961-6750. Monthly. Includes such broad areas as genetic intervention, biochemical genetics, and microbiological techniques.

Chemical Abstracts. Chemical Abstracts Service, 2540 Olentangy River Rd., PO Box 3012, Columbus, Ohio 43210. (800) 848-6533. 1907-.

Current Advances in Ecological and Environmental Science. Pergamon Microforms International, Inc., Fairview Park, Elmsford, New York 10523. (914) 592-7720. 1989-. Monthly. Current literature searching scrvice includingjournals, reports, abstracts, etc. This service is available online as part of the CABS database on the hosts BRS and ORBIT search service.

Ecology Abstracts. Cambridge Scientific Abstracts, 5161 River Rd., Bethesda, Maryland 20816. (301) 961-6750. Monthly.

Engineering Index. The Engineering Index Inc., 345 E. 47th St., New York, New York 10017. 1962-.

Environment Abstracts. Bowker A & I Publishing, 121 Chanlon Rd., New Providence, New Jersey 07974. (908) 464-6800. 1974-.

Environment Index. Environment Information Center, Index Research Department, 124 E. 39th St., New York, New York 10016. 1971-. Annual.

Environmental Information Connection–EIC. Planning Information Program, Dept. of Urban and Regional Planning, University of Illinois, 1003 West Nevada, Urbana, Illinois 61801. (217) 333-1369. Also available online.

Environmental Periodicals Bibliography. Environmental Studies Institute, International Academy at Santa Barbara, 800 Garden St., Suite D, Santa Barbara, California 93101. (805) 965-5010. Also available online.

Food Science and Technology Abstracts. International Food Information Service, c/o National Food Laboratory, 6363 Clark Ave., Dublin, California 94568. (800) 336-3782. 1969-.

Foods ADLIBRA. K & M Pub. Inc., 2000 Frankfort Ave., Louisville, Kentucky 40206. Semimonthly. Contains abstracts of current literature concerning the food industry. Topics covered include: food technology, food packaging, new food products, world food economics, nutrition, patents, and marketing.

General Science Index. H. W. Wilson Co., 950 University Ave., Bronx, New York 10452. 1978-. Monthly, also issued in annual cumulation. Cumulative subject index to English language periodicals in the subject fields of astronomy, botany, chemistry, earth science, environment and conservation, food and nutrition, genetics, mathematics, medicine and health, microbiology, oceanography, physics, physiology and zoology.

Index to Scientific Book Contents. Institute for Scientific Information, 3501 Market St., Philadelphia, Pennsylvania 19104. (800) 523-1857. 1985-. Annual. Gives contents of science books published.

INIS Atomindex. International Atomic Energy Agency, Wagramerstrasse 5, Vienna, Austria A-1400. 222 23606198. 1988-. Semiannual. Abstracts nuclear energy and nuclear physics topics from journals, conferences, technical reports and other related publications. Issued in 6 parts: Personal Author, Corporate Entry, Subject, Report, Standard Patent, Conference (by place), Conference (by date).

Pollution Abstracts. Cambridge Scientific Abstracts, 5161 River Rd., Bethesda, Maryland 20816. (301) 961-6750. Six/year. Indexes worldwide technical literature on environmental pollution. Covers air pollution, marine and freshwater pollution, sewage and wastewater treatment, waste management, toxicology and health, noise pollution, radiation, land pollution, and environmental policies, programs, legislation, and education. Also available online.

ALMANACS AND YEARBOOKS

Environmental Almanac. World Resources Institute. Houghton Mifflin, 1 Beacon St., Boston, Massachusetts 02108. (617) 725-5000; (800) 225-3362. 1991. Covers consumer products, energy, endangered species, food safety, global warming, solid wastes, toxics, wetlands and other related areas. Also included are the names and addresses of the chief environmental executives for all 50 states.

BIBLIOGRAPHIES

Butylated Hydroxanisole of Butylates Hydroxytoluene. Philip Wcxler. U.S. Department of Health and Human Services, Public Health Services, National Institutes of Health, 9000 Rockville Pike, Bethesda, Maryland 20892. (301) 496-4000. 1984.

Current Contents. Agriculture, Biology and Environmental Sciences. Institute for Scientific Information, 3501 Market St., Philadelphia, Pennsylvania 19104. (800) 523-1857. 1973-. Previous title: Current Contents. Agricultural, Food & Veterinary Sciences. Gives the table of contents of periodicals in the fields of agriculture, biology, environmental and related areas.

Directory of Published Proceedings. Interdok Corp., 173 Halstead Ave., Harrison, New York 10528. (914) 835-3506. 1990. Monthly. This is a listing of published proceedings including the series SEMTE (Science/Medicine/Engineering/Technology) and the series SSH (Social Science/Humanities).

EPA Publications Bibliography. U.S. Environmental Protection Agency, Library Systems Branch, 401 M St., SW, Washington, District of Columbia 20460. (202) 260-2090. Quarterly.

Food Safety, 1990: An Annotated Bibliography of the Literature. Dorothy C. Gosting, et al. Butterworth-Heinemann, 80 Montvale Ave., Stoneham, Massachusetts 02180. (617) 438-8464 or (800) 366-2665. 1991. Deals with the areas of environmental health and toxicology in relation to food safety and preservation. The bibliography is divided into three major parts headed "Diet and Health," "Safety of Food Components," and "Food-borne Microbial Illness." The appendix is titled "Food-and-Water-Associated Viruses."

DIRECTORIES

Food Production Management–Advertisers Buyers Guide Issue. 2619 Maryland Ave., Baltimore, Maryland 21218. (301) 467-3338. Annual.

ENCYCLOPEDIAS AND DICTIONARIES

Dictionary of Microbiology and Molecular Biology. Paul Singleton and Diana Sainsbury. John Wiley & Sons, Inc., 605 3rd Ave., New York, New York 10158-0012. (212) 850-6000. 1987. Second edition. Comprehensive dictionary with "classical descriptive aspects of microbiology to current developments in related areas of bioenergetics, biochemistry and molecular biology." Entries give synonyms, cross references, and references to pertinent works. Miscellaneous appendixes. Bibliography.

Dictionary of Nutrition and Food Technology. Arnold E. Bender. Butterworth-Heinemann, 80 Montvale Ave., Stoneham, Massachusetts 02180. (617) 438-8464. Equipment and techniques, abbreviations, proper names, and the composition of common foods; covers agriculture, engineering, microbiology, biochemistry, and aspects of medicine.

Encyclopedia of Chemical Processing and Design. John J. Mcketta and W. A. Cunningham. Marcel Dekker, Inc., 270 Madison Ave., New York, New York 10016. (212) 696-9000; (800) 228-1160. 1992. Thirty-eight volumes.

Encyclopedia of Food Engineering. C. W. Hall, et al. AVI Pub. Co., 250 Post Rd. E., PO Box 831, Westport, Connecticut 06881. 1986. Presents technical data on the application of modern engineering to the food processing industry. Entries are alphabetically arranged and include equipment, facilities, machinery, processes, relevant engineering concepts, and physical properties of selected foods.

Encyclopedia of Food Science. Y. H. Hui, ed. John Wiley & Sons, Inc., 605 3rd Ave., New York, New York 10158-0012. (212) 850-6000. 1991. Deals with the properties, analysis and processing of foods including: grains and bakery products, beans, nuts, seeds, fruits and vegetables, dairy products, meat products, poultry and fish products, and alcoholic beverages. Emphasis is placed on issues associated with food additives and food spoilage.

Encyclopedia of Food Science. M. S. Peterson and A. H. Johnson. The AVI Pub. Co., 250 Post Rd. E., PO Box 831, Westport, Connecticut 06881. 1978. Consists of short individually authored articles in an alphabetical arrangement, each with a brief bibliography. A section entitled "Food Science Around the World" includes information on food science and the food industries in various countries.

Encyclopedia of Human Biology. Renato Dulbecco, ed. Academic Press, c/o Harcourt Brace Jovanovich Inc., 6277 Sea Harbor Dr., Orlando, Florida 32887. (800) 346-8648. 1991. Eight volumes.

Foods and Food Production Encyclopedia. D. M. Considine and G. D. Considine, eds. Van Nostrand Reinhold, 115 5th Ave., New York, New York 10020. (212) 254-3232. 1982. Three fundamental stages of food production

are discussed: the start or initiation; the nurture; and the processing.

Kirk-Othmer Encyclopedia of Chemical Technology. J. I. Kroschwitz, ed. John Wiley & Sons, Inc., 605 3rd Ave., New York, New York 10158-0012. (212) 850-6000. 1992-. All articles in the new edition have been rewritten and updated adding new subjects such as biotechnology, computer topics, analytical techniques and instrumentation, environmental concerns, fuels and energy, inorganic and solid state chemistry; composite materials and material science in general, and pharmaceuticals. Also available online.

McGraw-Hill Encyclopedia of Environmental Science. Sybil P. Parker. McGraw-Hill Science & Engineering Books, 11 W. 19th St., New York, New York 10011. (212) 337-6010. 1980. Covers ecology, man's influence on nature, and environmental protection.

McGraw-Hill Encyclopedia of Science and Technology. McGraw-Hill, 1221 Avenue of the Americas, New York, New York 10020. (212) 512-2000 or (800) 262-4729. 1992. Seventh edition. Issued in multiple volumes including index. Includes all science and technology broad subject areas.

The Nutrition and Health Encyclopedia. David F. Tver and Percy Russell. Van Nostrand Reinhold, 115 5th Ave., New York, New York 10003. (212) 254-3232. 1989.

Ullmanns Encyclopedia of Industrial Chemistry. Hans Jurgen Arpe and Wolfgang Gerhartz, eds. VCH Publishers, 303 NW 12th Ave., Deerfield Beach, Florida 33442-1788. (305) 428-5566. 1990. Designed to keep up with the broad spectrum of chemical technology. Thirty-six volumes of the encyclopedia have been divided into two sets: the 28 A volumes contain alphabetically arranged articles on chemicals, product groups, processes and technological concepts; and the 8 B volumes are compendia of basic knowledge in industrial chemistry.

Van Nostrand's Scientific Encyclopedia. Glenn D. Considine, ed. Van Nostrand Reinhold, 115 5th Ave., New York, New York 10003. (212) 254-3232. 1983. Sixth edition. Includes all broad subject areas in science.

GENERAL WORKS

Biotechnological Innovations in Food Processing. Butterworth-Heinemann, 80 Montvale Ave., Stoneham, Massachusetts 02180. (617) 438-8464. 1991.

Ecology and Management of Food Industry Pests. J. Richard Gorham. AOAC International, 2200 Wilson Blvd., Suite 400, Arlington, Virginia 22201-3301. (703) 522-3032.

Food Contamination from Environmental Sources. J. O. Nriagu and M. S. Simmons, eds. John Wiley & Sons, Inc., 605 3rd Ave., New York, New York 10158-0012. (212) 850-6000. 1990. Discusses the accumulation and transfer of contaminants through the food chain to the consumer.

Food Protection Technology. Charles W. Felix. Lewis Publishers, 2000 Corporate Blvd., N.W., Boca Raton, Florida 33431. (407) 994-0555 or (800) 272-7737. 1987. Updates the new and proven techniques and methods in food protection technology.

Instrumental Methods for Quality Assurance in Foods. Daniel Y. C. Fung and Richard F. Matthews. Marcell

Dekker Inc., 270 Madison Ave., New York, New York 10016. (212) 696-9000; (800) 228-1160. 1991.

Physical, Chemical and Biological Changes in Food Caused by Thermal Processing. Tore Hoyem. Applied Science Publishers, Crown House, Linton Rd., Barking, England IG 11 8JU. 1977.

Taking Stock: The Tropical Forestry Action Plan After Five Years. Robert Winterbottom. World Resources Institute, 1709 New York Ave. N.W., Washington, District of Columbia 20006. (800) 822-0504. 1990. Analyzes Tropical Forestry Action Plan's accomplishments and shortcomings, drawing on the biannual meetings of the TFAP Forestry Advisors' groups, assessments by FAO, various aid agencies, and by such organizations as the World Rainforest Movement, Friends of the Earth, and World Life Fund.

ONLINE DATA BASES

BIOSIS Previews. BIOSIS, 2100 Arch St., Philadelphia, Pennsylvania 19103-1399. (215) 587-4800. Largest and most comprehensive database of research in the life sciences. Contains citations for nearly 9000 primary research journals, monographs, reviews, symposia, preliminary reports, semi-popular journals, selected institutional reports, government reports and research communications.

Cambridge Scientific Abstracts Life Science–CSAL. Cambridge Scientific Abstracts, 5161 River Rd., Bethesda, Maryland 20816. (301) 961-6750. Provides access to the following abstracting services: "Life Sciences Collection," "Aquatic Sciences and Fisheries Abstracts," "Oceanic Abstracts," and "Pollution Abstracts."

Chemical Abstracts–CA. Chemical Abstracts Service, 2540 Olentangy River Rd., P.O. Box 3012, Columbus, Ohio 43210. (800) 848-6533 or (614) 421-3600. Information sources include 9000 journals, patents from 27 countries, two industrial property organizations, new books, conference proceedings, and government research reports.

Chemical Age Project File. MBC Information Services Ltd., Paulton House, 8 Shepherdess Walk, London, England N1 7LB. 44 (71) 490-0049.

Chemical Business Newsbase. Royal Society of Chemistry, Thomas Graham House, Science Park, Milton Rd., Cambridge, England CB4 4WF. 44 (223) 420066.

Chemical Engineering and Biotechnology Abstracts–CEBA. Orbit Search Service, Maxwell Online Inc., 8000 W. Park Dr., McLean, Virginia 22102. (703) 442-0900 or (800) 456-7248. Monthly. Covers theoretical, practical and commercial material on all aspects of processing safety, and the environment. Also covers process and reaction engineering, measurement and process control, environmental protection and safety, plant design and equipment used in chemical engineering and biotechnology. More than 400 of the world's major primary chemical and process engineering journals are scanned to compile the database. Available from ORBIT.

Computerized Engineering Index–COMPENDEX. Engineering Information Inc., 345 E. 47th St., New York, New York 10017. (212) 705-7600.

Current Research Information System–CRIS/USDA. U.S. Department of Agriculture, National Agricultural Library, 10301 Baltimore Blvd., 5th Floor, Beltsville, Maryland 20705-2351. (301) 504-5755. Looks at current research projects in agriculture and allied sciences covering the biological, physical, social and behavioral sciences related to agriculture.

Enviro/Energyline Abstracts Plus. R. R. Bowker Co., 121 Chanlon Rd., New Providence, New Jersey 07974. (908) 464-6800.

Environmental Periodicals Bibliography. National Information Services Corp., Ste. 6, Wyman Towers, 3100 St. Paul St., Baltimore, Maryland 21218. (410)243-0797. Online version of abstract of same name.

Foods ADLIBRA. General Mills, Inc., Foods Adlibra Publications, 9000 Plymouth Ave., North, Minneapolis, Minnesota 55427. (612) 540-3463. Online version of periodical of same name.

FROSTI: Food RA Online Scientific and Technical Information. Leatherhead Food Research Association, Randalls Rd., Leatherhead, Surrey, England KT22 7RY. 44 (372) 376761.

FSTA: Food Science and Technology Abstracts. International Food Information Service, Melibocusstrasse 52, 6000 Frankfurt, Germany 49 (69) 669007-8.

Kirk-Othmer Encyclopedia of Chemical Technology. John Wiley & Sons, Inc., 605 3rd Ave., 5th Floor, New York, New York 10158. (212) 850-6000. Online version of the publication of the same name.

Monthly Catalog of United States Government Publications. U.S. G.P.O., Supt. of Docs., PO Box 371954, Pittsburgh, Pennsylvania 15250-7954. (202) 512-0000.

National Technical Information Service. U.S. Department of Commerce, National Technical Information Service, Office of Data Base Services, 5285 Port Royal Rd., Springfield, Virginia 22161. (703) 487-4807. Bibliographic database of government sponsored research and technical reports.

SCISEARCH. Institute for Scientific Information, University City Science Center, 3501 Market St., Philadelphia, Pennsylvania 19104. (215) 386-0100.

PERIODICALS AND NEWSLETTERS

Applied and Environmental Microbiology Journal. American Society for Microbiology, 1325 Massachusetts Avenue N.W., Washington, District of Columbia 20005. (202) 737-3600. Monthly. Articles on industrial and food microbiology and ecological studies.

Food Flavourings, Ingredients, Processing, Packaging. United Trade Press Ltd, London, England Monthly.

Food Processing. Techpress (FPI) Ltd., Bromley, England Quarterly.

The Journal of Biological Chemistry. American Society of Biological Chemists, 428 E. Preston St., Baltimore, Maryland 21202. Three times a month. Biological, agricultural, and energy aspects of the environment.

Journal of Food Processing and Preservation. Food and Nutrition Press, 2 Corporation Dr., PO Box 374, Trumbull, Connecticut 06611. (203) 261-8587. Quarterly.

Trends in Food Science and Technology. Elsevier Science Publishing Co., 655 Avenue of the Americas, New York, New York 10010. (212) 984-5800. Monthly. A news and reviews journal that discusses recent developments in all areas of the food science and technology field. It includes feature articles, view points, book reviews, conference calendar and job trends.

RESEARCH CENTERS AND INSTITUTES

State University of New York at Albany, Center for Biological Macromolecules. Chemistry Department, 1400 Washington Avenue, Albany, New York 12222. (518) 422-4454.

TRADE ASSOCIATIONS AND PROFESSIONAL SOCIETIES

American Council on Science and Health. 1995 Broadway, 16th Floor, New York, New York 10023. (212) 362-7044.

American Institute of Biological Sciences. 730 11th St., N.W., Washington, District of Columbia 20001-4521. (202) 628-1500.

American Institute of Chemical Engineers. 345 East 47th St., New York, New York 10017. (212) 705-7338.

American Institute of Chemists. 7315 Wisconsin Ave., Bethesda, Maryland 20814. (301) 652-2447.

Food & Drug Law Institute. 1000 Vermont Ave., N.W., Suite 1200, Washington, District of Columbia 20036. (202) 371-1420.

Food & Water, Inc. 225 Lafayette St., Suite 612, New York, New York 10012. (212) 941-9340.

National Coalition to Stop Food and Water Irradiation. 225 Lafayette St., Ste. 613, New York, New York 10012. (212) 941-9340.

FOOD SCIENCE

ABSTRACTING AND INDEXING SERVICES

Agrindex. AGRIS Coordinating Center, Via delle Terme di Caracalla, Rome, Italy I-00100. 61 0181-FA01. 1975-.

Applied Science and Technology Index. H.W. Wilson Co., 950 University Ave., Bronx, New York 10452. (800) 367-6770. Formerly Industrial Arts Index.

Biodeterioration Abstracts. Farnham Royal, Slough, England SL2 3BN. Quarterly.

Biological Abstracts. BIOSIS, 2100 Arch St., Philadelphia, Pennsylvania 19103-1399. (215) 587-4800. 1927-.

Biological and Agricultural Index. H.W. Wilson Co., 950 University Ave., Bronx, New York 10452. (800) 367-6770. 1916-. Monthly.

Biotechnology Research Abstracts. Cambridge Scientific Abstracts, 5161 River Rd., Bethesda, Maryland 20816. (301) 961-6750. Monthly. Includes such broad areas as genetic intervention, biochemical genetics, and microbiological techniques.

Chemical Abstracts. Chemical Abstracts Service, 2540 Olentangy River Rd., PO Box 3012, Columbus, Ohio 43210. (800) 848-6533. 1907-.

Current Advances in Ecological and Environmental Science. Pergamon Microforms International, Inc., Fairview Park, Elmsford, New York 10523. (914) 592-7720. 1989-. Monthly. Current literature searching service including journals, reports, abstracts, etc. This service is available online as part of the CABS database on the hosts BRS and ORBIT search service.

Ecological Abstracts. Geo Abstracts Ltd. Elsevier Applied Science, Crown House, Linton Rd., Barking, England IG 11 8JU. 1974-. Derived from over 600 leading ecological and environmental journals, plus books, conference proceedings, reports and theses.

Ecology Abstracts. Cambridge Scientific Abstracts, 5161 River Rd., Bethesda, Maryland 20816. (301) 961-6750. Monthly.

Environment Abstracts. Bowker A & I Publishing, 121 Chanlon Rd., New Providence, New Jersey 07974. (908) 464-6800. 1974-.

Environment Index. Environment Information Center, Index Research Department, 124 E. 39th St., New York, New York 10016. 1971-. Annual.

Environmental Information Connection–EIC. Planning Information Program, Dept. of Urban and Regional Planning, University of Illinois, 1003 West Nevada, Urbana, Illinois 61801. (217) 333-1369. Also available online.

Environmental Periodicals Bibliography. Environmental Studies Institute, International Academy at Santa Barbara, 800 Garden St., Suite D, Santa Barbara, California 93101. (805) 965-5010. Also available online.

Food and Nutrition Quarterly Index. Oryx Press, 4041 N. Central at Indian School Rd., Ste. 700, Phoenix, Arizona 85012-3397. (602) 265-2651. 1985-. Quarterly. Abstracting service succeeds the Food and Nutrition Bibliography which was issued from 1980-1984 and covered the literature from 1978-1980, and was a continuation of the FNIC catalog and its supplements.

Food Science and Technology Abstracts. International Food Information Service, c/o National Food Laboratory, 6363 Clark Ave., Dublin, California 94568. (800) 336-3782. 1969-.

Foods ADLIBRA. K & M Pub. Inc., 2000 Frankfort Ave., Louisville, Kentucky 40206. Semimonthly. Contains abstracts of current literature concerning the food industry. Topics covered include: food technology, food packaging, new food products, world food economics, nutrition, patents, and marketing.

General Science Index. H. W. Wilson Co., 950 University Ave., Bronx, New York 10452. 1978-. Monthly, also issued in annual cumulation. Cumulative subject index to English language periodicals in the subject fields of astronomy, botany, chemistry, earth science, environment and conservation, food and nutrition, genetics, mathematics, medicine and health, microbiology, oceanography, physics, physiology and zoology.

Index to Scientific Book Contents. Institute for Scientific Information, 3501 Market St., Philadelphia, Pennsylvania 19104. (800) 523-1857. 1985-. Annual. Gives contents of science books published.

INIS Atomindex. International Atomic Energy Agency, Wagramerstrasse 5, Vienna, Austria A-1400. 222 23606198. 1988-. Semiannual. Abstracts nuclear energy and nuclear physics topics from journals, conferences, technical reports and other related publications. Issued in 6 parts: Personal Author, Corporate Entry, Subject,

Report, Standard Patent, Conference (by place), Conference (by date).

Pollution Abstracts. Cambridge Scientific Abstracts, 5161 River Rd., Bethesda, Maryland 20816. (301) 961-6750. Six/year. Indexes worldwide technical literature on environmental pollution. Covers air pollution, marine and freshwater pollution, sewage and wastewater treatment, waste management, toxicology and health, noise pollution, radiation, land pollution, and environmental policies, programs, legislation, and education. Also available online.

Science Citation Index. Institute for Scientific Information, 3501 Market St., Philadelphia, Pennsylvania 19104. 1961-.

ALMANACS AND YEARBOOKS

CRC Critical Reviews of Food Science and Nutrition. Chemical Rubber Company. CRC Press, 2000 Corporate Blvd. N.W., Boca Raton, Florida 33431. (800) 272-7737. 1979. Food, nutrition, and food-processing industry.

Environmental Almanac. World Resources Institute. Houghton Mifflin, 1 Beacon St., Boston, Massachusetts 02108. (617) 725-5000; (800) 225-3362. 1991. Covers consumer products, energy, endangered species, food safety, global warming, solid wastes, toxics, wetlands and other related areas. Also included are the names and addresses of the chief environmental executives for all 50 states.

BIBLIOGRAPHIES

Cholesterol in Foods and Its Effects on Animals and Humans. National Technical Information Service, 5285 Port Royal Rd., Springfield, Virginia 22161. (703) 487-4650.

Current Contents. Agriculture, Biology and Environmental Sciences. Institute for Scientific Information, 3501 Market St., Philadelphia, Pennsylvania 19104. (800) 523-1857. 1973-. Previous title: Current Contents. Agricultural, Food & Veterinary Sciences. Gives the table of contents of periodicals in the fields of agriculture, biology, environmental and related areas.

Dietary Cholesterol: Health Concerns and the Food Industry. National Technical Information Service, 5285 Port Royal Rd., Springfield, Virginia 22161. (703) 487-4650. 1989.

Directory of Published Proceedings. Interdok Corp., 173 Halstead Ave., Harrison, New York 10528. (914) 835-3506. 1990. Monthly. This is a listing of published proceedings including the series SEMTE (Science/Medicine/Engineering/Technology) and the series SSH (Social Science/Humanities).

EPA Publications Bibliography. U.S. Environmental Protection Agency, Library Systems Branch, 401 M St., SW, Washington, District of Columbia 20460. (202) 260-2090. Quarterly.

Food Additives and Their Impact on Health. Oryx Press, 4041 N. Central at Indian School Rd., Ste. 700, Phoenix, Arizona 85012-3397. (602) 265-2651. 1988. Bibliography of health aspects and toxicology of food additives.

Food and Nutrition Information Guide. Paula Szilard. Libraries Unlimited, Inc., PO Box 6633, Englewood, Colorado 80155-6633. (303) 770-1220. 1987. Focuses on

reference materials on human nutrition dietetics, food science and technology, and related subjects such as food service. It covers chiefly English-language materials published in the last ten years.

Food Science. Helen Charley. John Wiley & Sons, Inc., 605 3rd Ave., New York, New York 10158-0012. (212) 850-6000. 1982. Second edition.

Food, Science, and Technology: A Bibliography of Recommended Materials. Richard E. Wallace. National Agricultural Library, 10301 Baltimore Blvd., Beltsville, Maryland 20705-2351. (301) 504-5755. 1978.

Information Sources in Agriculture and Food Science. G. P. Lilley. Butterworth-Heinemann, 80 Montvale Ave., Stoneham, Massachusetts 02180. (617) 438-8464. 1981.

DIRECTORIES

Agricultural Information Resource Centers, a World Directory 1990. Rita C. Fisher. IAALD World Directory Working Group, 716 W. Indiana Ave., Urbana, Illinois 61801-4836. (217) 333-7687. 1990. Includes 3,971 information resource centers that have agriculture related collection and/or information services.

Directory of Food and Nutrition Information Services and Resources. Robyn C. Frank, ed. Oryx Press, 4041 N. Central at Indian School Rd., Ste. 700, Phoenix, Arizona 85012-3397. (602) 265-2651. 1984. Focuses on nutrition education, food science, food service management, and related aspects of applied nutrition.

ENCYCLOPEDIAS AND DICTIONARIES

The Agriculture Dictionary. Ray V. Herren and Roy L. Donahue. Delmar Publishers Inc., 2 Computer Dr. W., Albany, New York 12212. (518) 459-1150. 1991. Covers all the agricultural areas including acid rain, acid mine drainage, food additives, agricultural engineering, conservation of the natural resources, microorganisms, triticale and other related topics.

Dictionary of Agricultural and Food Engineering. Arthur W. Farrall. Interstate Publishers, 510 N. Vermillion St., PO Box 50, Danville, Illinois 61834-0050. (217) 446-0500. 1979.

Dictionary of Biotechnology. J. Coombs. Elsevier Science Publishing Co., 655 Avenue of the Americas, New York, New York 10010. (212) 984-5800. 1986. Areas covered in this dictionary include: fermentation; brewing; vaccines; plant tissue; culture; antibiotic production; production and use of enzymes; biomass; byproduct recovery and effluent treatment; equipment; processes; micro-organisms and biochemicals.

The Dictionary of Sodium, Fats, and Cholesterol. Barbara Kraus. Putnam Berkley Group, 200 Madison Ave., New York, New York 10016. (212) 951-8400. 1990. Food composition, fat, cholesterol, and sodium.

Encyclopedia of Chemical Processing and Design. John J. Mcketta and W. A. Cunningham. Marcel Dekker, Inc., 270 Madison Ave., New York, New York 10016. (212) 696-9000; (800) 228-1160. 1992. Thirty-eight volumes.

Encyclopedia of Common Natural Ingredients Used in Foods, Drugs, and Cosmetics. John Wiley & Sons, Inc., 605 3rd Ave., New York, New York 10158-0012. (212) 850-6000. 1980. Includes 300 natural ingredients used in food, cosmetics and drugs. Each entry lists genus and species, synonyms, general description, chemical composition, pharmacologic and biological activity, uses, commercial preparation, regulatory status and references.

Encyclopedia of Food Science. Y. H. Hui, ed. John Wiley & Sons, Inc., 605 3rd Ave., New York, New York 10158-0012. (212) 850-6000. 1991. Deals with the properties, analysis and processing of foods including: grains and bakery products, beans, nuts, seeds, fruits and vegetables, dairy products, meat products, poultry and fish products, and alcoholic beverages. Emphasis is placed on issues associated with food additives and food spoilage.

Encyclopedia of Food Science. M. S. Peterson and A. H. Johnson. The AVI Pub. Co., 250 Post Rd. E., PO Box 831, Westport, Connecticut 06881. 1978. Consists of short individually authored articles in an alphabetical arrangement, each with a brief bibliography. A section entitled "Food Science Around the World" includes information on food science and the food industries in various countries.

Encyclopedia of Human Biology. Renato Dulbecco, ed. Academic Press, c/o Harcourt Brace Jovanovich Inc., 6277 Sea Harbor Dr., Orlando, Florida 32887. (800) 346-8648. 1991. Eight volumes.

Encyclopedia of Industrial Chemical Additives. Michael and Irene Ash. Chemical Publishing Co., 80 Eighth Ave., New York, New York 10011. (212) 255-1950. 1984-87. Four volumes. Comprehensive compilation of tradename products that function as additives in enhancing the properties of various major industrial products.

Encyclopedia of Physics. Rita G. Lerner and George L. Trigg. VCH Publishers, 303 NW 12th Ave., Deerfield Beach, Florida 33442-1788. (305) 428-5566. 1991. Second edition.

Food and Nutrition Encyclopedia. A. H. Ensminger, et al. Pegus Press, 648 W. Sierra Ave, Clovis, California 93612. 1983. Two volumes. Covers commodities, nutrients, concepts, nutrition disorders and simple nutritional biochemistry with both brief and extensive entries.

Illustrated Encyclopedia of Science and the Future. Mike Biscare, et al., ed. Marshall Cavendish, 58 Old Compton St., London, England 0W1V5 PA. 01-734 6710. 1983. Twenty volumes. Each volume has 5 sections: Frontiers, Electronics in Action, Medical Science, Military Technology, and Resources.

Kirk-Othmer Encyclopedia of Chemical Technology. J. I. Kroschwitz, ed. John Wiley & Sons, Inc., 605 3rd Ave., New York, New York 10158-0012. (212) 850-6000. 1992-. All articles in the new edition have been rewritten and updated adding new subjects such as biotechnology, computer topics, analytical techniques and instrumentation, environmental concerns, fuels and energy, inorganic and solid state chemistry; composite materials and material science in general, and pharmaceuticals. Also available online.

Life Sciences on File. Diagram Group. Facts on File, Inc., 460 Park Ave. S., New York, New York 10016. (212) 683-2244. 1986. Encyclopedia of pictorial collection in life sciences. Deals with all major topics in life sciences including ecology.

Longman Illustrated Dictionary of Food Science. Nicholas Light. Longman, Burnt Hill, Harlow, England CM20 2J6. (0279) 26721. 1989. Food, its components, nutrition, preparation and preservation.

Macmillan Dictionary of Toxicology. Ernest Hodgson, et al. Van Nostrand Reinhold, 115 5th Ave., New York, New York 10003. (212) 254-3232. 1988. Intended as a "starting point" to the literature of toxicology. American spelling is used with cross references to British version of words. Contains a list of references. Signed entries give explanatory definitions and cross references.

McGraw-Hill Encyclopedia of Environmental Science. Sybil P. Parker. McGraw-Hill Science & Engineering Books, 11 W. 19th St., New York, New York 10011. (212) 337-6010. 1980. Covers ecology, man's influence on nature, and environmental protection.

McGraw-Hill Encyclopedia of Science and Technology. McGraw-Hill, 1221 Avenue of the Americas, New York, New York 10020. (212) 512-2000 or (800) 262-4729. 1992. Seventh edition. Issued in multiple volumes including index. Includes all science and technology broad subject areas.

The Nutrition and Health Encyclopedia. David F. Tver and Percy Russell. Van Nostrand Reinhold, 115 5th Ave., New York, New York 10003. (212) 254-3232. 1989.

Van Nostrand's Scientific Encyclopedia. Glenn D. Considine, ed. Van Nostrand Reinhold, 115 5th Ave., New York, New York 10003. (212) 254-3232. 1983. Sixth edition. Includes all broad subject areas in science.

The World Encyclopedia of Food. L. Patrick Coyle. Facts on File, Inc., 460 Park Ave. S., New York, New York 10016. (212) 683-2244. 1982. Arranged alphabetically. Includes 4000 foods and beverages from all over the world. Contains illustrations and brief information on ethnic and foreign foods.

GENERAL WORKS

Biocatalysts for Industry. Jonathan S. Dordick, ed. Plenum Press, 233 Spring St., New York, New York 10013-1578. (212) 620-8000; (800) 221-9369. 1991. Contributed papers address the applications of enzymes or whole cells to carry out selective transformations of commercial importance, as biocatalysts in the food, pharmaceutical, and chemical industries. Includes general uses of biocatalysts, biocatalysts without chemical competition, emerging biocatalysts for conventional chemical processing, and future directions of biocatalysts.

The Chemical Analysis of Foods: A Practical Treatise on the Examination of Foodstuffs and the Detection of Adulterants. Henry Edward Cox. J. & A. Churchill, Rover Stevenson House, 1-3 Banter's Place, Leith Walk, Edinburgh, England EH1 3AF. (031) 556-2424. 1977.

Chemicals in the Human Food Chain. Carl K. Winter, et al. Van Nostrand Reinhold, 115 5th Ave., New York, New York 10003. (212) 254-3232. 1990. Deals with prevention of food contamination by pesticides and other toxic chemicals.

Cholesterol Metabolism, LDL, and the LDL Receptor. N.B. Myant. Academic Press, c/o Harcourt Brace Jovanovich Inc., 6277 Sea Harbor Dr., Orlando, Florida 32887. (800) 346-8648. 1990.

Food Contamination from Environmental Sources. J. O. Nriagu and M. S. Simmons, eds. John Wiley & Sons, Inc., 605 3rd Ave., New York, New York 10158-0012. (212) 850-6000. 1990. Discusses the accumulation and transfer of contaminants through the food chain to the consumer.

Food Science. Gordon Gerard Birch. Pergamon Microforms International, Inc., Fairview Park, Elmsford, New York 10523. (914) 592-7720. 1977. Science, technology, engineering of food.

Food Science and Nutrition: Current Issues and Answers. Fergus Clydesdale. Prentice-Hall, Rte. 9W, Englewood Cliffs, New Jersey 07632. (201) 592-2000. 1979. Food additives and food-processing industry.

Grocery Shopping Guide: A Consumer's Manual for Selecting Foods Lower in Dietary Saturated Fat and Cholesterol. Nelda Mercer. University of Michigan Medical Center, 1500 E. Medical Center Dr., Ann Arbor, Michigan 48109. (313) 936-4000. 1989. Fat content, sodium content, and cholesterol content of food.

Instrumental Methods for Quality Assurance in Foods. Daniel Y. C. Fung and Richard F. Matthews. Marcell Dekker Inc., 270 Madison Ave., New York, New York 10016. (212) 696-9000; (800) 228-1160. 1991.

Microbial Toxins in Focus and Feeds. Albert E. Pohland, et al., eds. Plenum Press, 233 Spring St., New York, New York 10013. (212) 620-8000; (800) 221-9369. 1990. Proceedings of a Symposium on Cellular and Molecular Mode of Action of Selected Microbial Toxins in Foods and Feeds, Oct. 31- Nov. 2, 1988, Chevy Chase, MD.

The Science of Food. P. Gaman. Pergamon Microforms International, Inc., Fairview Park, Elmsford, New York 10523. (914) 592-7720. 1977. An introduction to food science, nutrition, and microbiology.

The Science of Food. Marion Bennion. John Wiley & Sons, Inc., 605 3rd Ave., New York, New York 10158-0012. (800) 225-5945. 1980.

HANDBOOKS AND MANUALS

FDA Food Additives Analytical Manual. C. Warner, et al., eds. Association of Official Analytical Chemists, 2200 Wilson Blvd., Suite 400-P, Arlington, Virginia 22201-3301. (703) 522-3032. 1983-1987. 2 vols. Provides methodology for determining compliance with food additive regulations. Contains analytical methods that have been evaluated by the FDA or found to operate satisfactorily in at least two laboratories.

Food Additives Handbook. Van Nostrand Reinhold, 115 Fifth Ave., New York, New York 10003. (212) 254-3232. 1989. Toxicology of food additives.

Food Additives Tables. Food Law Research Centre, Univ. of Brussels. Elsevier Science Publishing Co., 655 Avenue of the Americas, New York, New York 10010. (212) 984-5800. 1988. Three volumes. Data on the regulatory status of food additives used in specific foods from 19 countries is included. Arrangement is by class of food.

Handbook of Food Additives. T. E. Furia, ed. CRC Press, 2000 Corporate Blvd. N.W., Boca Raton, Florida 33431. (800) 272-7737. 1972-1980. Second edition. Two volumes. Additives are discussed by broad categories and a table indicates the regulatory status of food additives, giving pertinent FEMA numbers and FDA regulation numbers. Volume 2 updates volume 1.

ONLINE DATA BASES

AGRICOLA. U.S. Department of Agriculture, Office of Public Affairs, 14 Independence Ave., S.W., Washington, District of Columbia 20250. (202) 447-7454.

AGRIS. Food and Agriculture Organization of the United Nations, Via delle Terme di Caracalla, Rome, Italy 00100. 61 0181-FA01.

BioPatents. BIOSIS, 2100 Arch St., Philadelphia, Pennsylvania 19103. (800) 523-4806.

Bioprocessing Technology. Mead Data Central, Inc., P.O. Box 933, Dayton, Ohio 45401. (800) 227-4908.

BIOSIS Previews. BIOSIS, 2100 Arch St., Philadelphia, Pennsylvania 19103-1399. (215) 587-4800. Largest and most comprehensive database of research in the life sciences. Contains citations for nearly 9000 primary research journals, monographs, reviews, symposia, preliminary reports, semi-popular journals, selected institutional reports, government reports and research communications.

Biotechnology Abstracts. Derwent Publications Ltd., 6845 Elm St., McLean, Virginia 22101. (703) 790-0400. Includes material on genetic manipulation, biochemical engineering, fermentation, biocatalysis, cell hybridization, in vitro plant propagation and industrial waste management.

Cambridge Scientific Abstracts Life Science–CSAL. Cambridge Scientific Abstracts, 5161 River Rd., Bethesda, Maryland 20816. (301) 961-6750. Provides access to the following abstracting services: "Life Sciences Collection," "Aquatic Sciences and Fisheries Abstracts," "Oceanic Abstracts," and "Pollution Abstracts."

Chemical Abstracts-CA. Chemical Abstracts Service, 2540 Olentangy River Rd., P.O. Box 3012, Columbus, Ohio 43210. (800) 848-6533 or (614) 421-3600. Information sources include 9000 journals, patents from 27 countries, two industrial property organizations, new books, conference proceedings, and government research reports.

Current Research Information System–CRIS/USDA. U.S. Department of Agriculture, National Agricultural Library, 10301 Baltimore Blvd., 5th Floor, Beltsville, Maryland 20705-2351. (301) 504-5755. Looks at current research projects in agriculture and allied sciences covering the biological, physical, social and behavioral sciences related to agriculture.

Enviro/Energyline Abstracts Plus. R. R. Bowker Co., 121 Chanlon Rd., New Providence, New Jersey 07974. (908) 464-6800.

Environmental Fate Databases. Syracuse Research Cooperation, Merrill Lane, Syracuse, New York 13210. (312) 426-3200. Environmental fate of chemicals.

Environmental Periodicals Bibliography. National Information Services Corp., Ste. 6, Wyman Towers, 3100 St. Paul St., Baltimore, Maryland 21218. (410)243-0797. Online version of abstract of same name.

Foods ADLIBRA. General Mills, Inc., Foods Adlibra Publications, 9000 Plymouth Ave., North, Minneapolis, Minnesota 55427. (612) 540-3463. Online version of periodical of same name.

FROSTI: Food RA Online Scientific and Technical Information. Leatherhead Food Research Association, Randalls Rd., Leatherhead, Surrey, England KT22 7RY. 44 (372) 376761.

The Frozen Foods Industry Competitive Intelligence Database. Strategic Intelligence Systems, Inc., 404 Park Ave.,

South, Suite 1301, New York, New York 10016. (212) 725-5954.

FSTA: Food Science and Technology Abstracts. International Food Information Service, Melibocusstrasse 52, 6000 Frankfurt, Germany 49 (69) 669007-8.

Kirk-Othmer Encyclopedia of Chemical Technology. John Wiley & Sons, Inc., 605 3rd Ave., 5th Floor, New York, New York 10158. (212) 850-6000. Online version of the publication of the same name.

Life Sciences from NTIS. National Technical Information Center for the Utilization of Federal Technology, 5285 Port Royal Rd., Springfield, Virginia 22161. (703) 487-4650.

Monthly Catalog of United States Government Publications. U.S. G.P.O., Supt. of Docs., PO Box 371954, Pittsburgh, Pennsylvania 15250-7954. (202) 512-0000.

National Technical Information Service. U.S. Department of Commerce, National Technical Information Service, Office of Data Base Services, 5285 Port Royal Rd., Springfield, Virginia 22161. (703) 487-4807. Bibliographic database of government sponsored research and technical reports.

SCISEARCH. Institute for Scientific Information, University City Science Center, 3501 Market St., Philadelphia, Pennsylvania 19104. (215) 386-0100.

PERIODICALS AND NEWSLETTERS

Analytical Biochemistry. Academic Press, 111 Fifth Ave., New York, New York 10003. (800) 346-8648. Covers biological and chemical topics relating to the environment.

Applied and Environmental Microbiology Journal. American Society for Microbiology, 1325 Massachusetts Avenue N.W., Washington, District of Columbia 20005. (202) 737-3600. Monthly. Articles on industrial and food microbiology and ecological studies.

Ecology of Food and Nutrition. Gordon & Breach Science Publishers, Inc., 270 8th Ave., New York, New York 10011. (212) 206-8900. Quarterly.

Food Additives and Contaminants. Taylor & Francis, 1900 Frost Rd., Suite 101, Bristol, Pennsylvania 19007. (215) 785-5580. Bimonthly.

Food and Chemical Toxicology. Pergamon Microforms International Inc., Fairview Park, Elmsford, New York 10523. (914) 592-7720. Monthly. Information and risks of food and chemicals.

International Journal of Food Science & Technology. Blackwell Scientific Publications, PO Box 87, Oxford, England OX2 0DT. 44 0865 79115. Quarterly.

Journal of Agricultural and Food Chemistry. American Chemical Society, 1155 16th St. N.W., Washington, District of Columbia 20036. (202) 872-4600; (800) 227-5558. 1953-. Monthly. Contains documentation of significant advances in the science of agriculture and food chemistry.

The Journal of Biological Chemistry. American Society of Biological Chemists, 428 E. Preston St., Baltimore, Maryland 21202. Three times a month. Biological, agricultural, and energy aspects of the environment.

Trends in Food Science and Technology. Elsevier Science Publishing Co., 655 Avenue of the Americas, New York, New York 10010. (212) 984-5800. Monthly. A news and reviews journal that discusses recent developments in all areas of the food science and technology field. It includes feature articles, view points, book reviews, conference calendar and job trends.

TRADE ASSOCIATIONS AND PROFESSIONAL SOCIETIES

American Chemical Society. 1155 16th St., N.W., Washington, District of Columbia 20036. (202) 872-4600.

American Council on Science and Health. 1995 Broadway, 16th Floor, New York, New York 10023. (212) 362-7044.

American Institute of Biological Sciences. 730 11th St., N.W., Washington, District of Columbia 20001-4521. (202) 628-1500.

Association of Food Industries. 177 Main St., P.O. Box 776, Matawan, New Jersey 07747. (201) 583-8188.

Canned Food Information Council. 500 N. Michigan Ave., Suite 300, Chicago, Illinois 60611. (312) 836-7279.

Flavor and Extract Manufacturers Association of the United States. 1620 I St., N.W., Suite 925, Washington, District of Columbia 20006. (202) 293-5800.

Food & Drug Law Institute. 1000 Vermont Ave., N.W., Suite 1200, Washington, District of Columbia 20036. (202) 371-1420.

The Glutamate Association–U.S. 5775 Peachtree-Dunwoody Rd., Suite 500-D, Atlanta, Georgia 30342. (404) 252-3663.

Institute of Food Technologists. 221 N. LaSalle St., Chicago, Illinois 60601. (312) 782-8424.

International Association of Milk, Food, & Environmental Sanitarians. 502 E. Lincoln Way, Ames, Iowa 50010. (515) 232-6699.

International Food Additives Council. 5775 Peachtree-Dunwoody Rd., Suite 500-D, Atlanta, Georgia 30342. (404) 252-3663.

International Food Information Council. 1100 Connecticut Ave., N.W., Suite 430, Washington, District of Columbia 20036. (202) 296-6540.

National Association of Fruits, Flavors and Syrups. P.O. Box 776, 177 Main St., Matawan, New Jersey 07747. (201) 583-8272.

National Food & Energy Council. 409 VanDiver West, Suite 202, Columbia, Missouri 65202. (314) 875-7155.

National Food Processors Association. 1401 New York Ave., N.W., 4th Floor, Washington, District of Columbia 20005. (202) 639-5900.

Society of Flavor Chemists. c/o Denise McCafferty, McCormick and Co., 204 Wright Ave., Hunt Valley, Maryland 21031. (301) 771-7491.

FOOD SUPPLEMENTS

See: NUTRITION

FOOD WASTES

See also: MUNICIPAL WASTES

ABSTRACTING AND INDEXING SERVICES

Agrindex. AGRIS Coordinating Center, Via delle Terme di Caracalla, Rome, Italy I-00100. 61 0181-FA01. 1975-.

Applied Science and Technology Index. H.W. Wilson Co., 950 University Ave., Bronx, New York 10452. (800) 367-6770. Formerly Industrial Arts Index.

Biological Abstracts. BIOSIS, 2100 Arch St., Philadelphia, Pennsylvania 19103-1399. (215) 587-4800. 1927-.

Biological and Agricultural Index. H.W. Wilson Co., 950 University Ave., Bronx, New York 10452. (800) 367-6770. 1916-. Monthly.

Ecological Abstracts. Geo Abstracts Ltd. Elsevier Applied Science, Crown House, Linton Rd., Barking, England IG 11 8JU. 1974-. Derived from over 600 leading ecological and environmental journals, plus books, conference proceedings, reports and theses.

Environment Abstracts. Bowker A & I Publishing, 121 Chanlon Rd., New Providence, New Jersey 07974. (908) 464-6800. 1974-.

Environment Index. Environment Information Center, Index Research Department, 124 E. 39th St., New York, New York 10016. 1971-. Annual.

Environmental Information Connection–EIC. Planning Information Program, Dept. of Urban and Regional Planning, University of Illinois, 1003 West Nevada, Urbana, Illinois 61801. (217) 333-1369. Also available online.

Environmental Periodicals Bibliography. Environmental Studies Institute, International Academy at Santa Barbara, 800 Garden St., Suite D, Santa Barbara, California 93101. (805) 965-5010. Also available online.

Food Science and Technology Abstracts. International Food Information Service, c/o National Food Laboratory, 6363 Clark Ave., Dublin, California 94568. (800) 336-3782. 1969-.

General Science Index. H. W. Wilson Co., 950 University Ave., Bronx, New York 10452. 1978-. Monthly, also issued in annual cumulation. Cumulative subject index to English language periodicals in the subject fields of astronomy, botany, chemistry, earth science, environment and conservation, food and nutrition, genetics, mathematics, medicine and health, microbiology, oceanography, physics, physiology and zoology.

Index to Scientific Book Contents. Institute for Scientific Information, 3501 Market St., Philadelphia, Pennsylvania 19104. (800) 523-1857. 1985-. Annual. Gives contents of science books published.

Science Citation Index. Institute for Scientific Information, 3501 Market St., Philadelphia, Pennsylvania 19104. 1961-.

BIBLIOGRAPHIES

Current Contents. Agriculture, Biology and Environmental Sciences. Institute for Scientific Information, 3501 Market St., Philadelphia, Pennsylvania 19104. (800) 523-1857. 1973-. Previous title: Current Contents. Agricultural, Food & Veterinary Sciences. Gives the table of contents of periodicals in the fields of agriculture, biology, environmental and related areas.

EPA Publications Bibliography. U.S. Environmental Protection Agency, Library Systems Branch, 401 M St., SW, Washington, District of Columbia 20460. (202) 260-2090. Quarterly.

ENCYCLOPEDIAS AND DICTIONARIES

McGraw-Hill Encyclopedia of Environmental Science. Sybil P. Parker. McGraw-Hill Science & Engineering Books, 11 W. 19th St., New York, New York 10011. (212) 337-6010. 1980. Covers ecology, man's influence on nature, and environmental protection.

GENERAL WORKS

Food Industry Wastes: Disposal and Recovery. A. Herzka. Applied Science Publishers, Crown House, Linton Rd., Barking, England IG 11 8JU. 1981.

ONLINE DATA BASES

BIOSIS Previews. BIOSIS, 2100 Arch St., Philadelphia, Pennsylvania 19103-1399. (215) 587-4800. Largest and most comprehensive database of research in the life sciences. Contains citations for nearly 9000 primary research journals, monographs, reviews, symposia, preliminary reports, semi-popular journals, selected institutional reports, government reports and research communications.

Cambridge Scientific Abstracts Life Science–CSAL. Cambridge Scientific Abstracts, 5161 River Rd., Bethesda, Maryland 20816. (301) 961-6750. Provides access to the following abstracting services: "Life Sciences Collection," "Aquatic Sciences and Fisheries Abstracts," "Oceanic Abstracts," and "Pollution Abstracts."

Current Research Information System–CRIS/USDA. U.S. Department of Agriculture, National Agricultural Library, 10301 Baltimore Blvd., 5th Floor, Beltsville, Maryland 20705-2351. (301) 504-5755. Looks at current research projects in agriculture and allied sciences covering the biological, physical, social and behavioral sciences related to agriculture.

Enviro/Energyline Abstracts Plus. R. R. Bowker Co., 121 Chanlon Rd., New Providence, New Jersey 07974. (908) 464-6800.

Environmental Periodicals Bibliography. National Information Services Corp., Ste. 6, Wyman Towers, 3100 St. Paul St., Baltimore, Maryland 21218. (410)243-0797. Online version of abstract of same name.

Monthly Catalog of United States Government Publications. U.S. G.P.O., Supt. of Docs., PO Box 371954, Pittsburgh, Pennsylvania 15250-7954. (202) 512-0000.

National Technical Information Service. U.S. Department of Commerce, National Technical Information Service, Office of Data Base Services, 5285 Port Royal Rd., Springfield, Virginia 22161. (703) 487-4807. Bibliographic database of government sponsored research and technical reports.

PressNet Environmental Reports. Chemical Information Systems, Inc., 7215 York Rd., Baltimore, Maryland 21212. (301) 321-8440.

SCISEARCH. Institute for Scientific Information, University City Science Center, 3501 Market St., Philadelphia, Pennsylvania 19104. (215) 386-0100.

STATISTICS SOURCES

How Solid Waste Issues Are Affecting Consumer Behavior. Food Marketing Institute, Research Department, 1750 K St., NW, Washington, District of Columbia 20006. 1990. Consumer attitudes and practices regarding solid waste disposal.

Solid Waste Management in the Food Distribution Industry. Food Marketing Institute, Research Department, 1750 K St., NW, Washington, District of Columbia 20006. 1990.

TRADE ASSOCIATIONS AND PROFESSIONAL SOCIETIES

American Institute of Biological Sciences. 730 11th St., N.W., Washington, District of Columbia 20001-4521. (202) 628-1500.

FOREST ECOSYSTEMS

See also: BIOMES; FORESTS

ABSTRACTING AND INDEXING SERVICES

Biological Abstracts. BIOSIS, 2100 Arch St., Philadelphia, Pennsylvania 19103-1399. (215) 587-4800. 1927-.

Biological and Agricultural Index. H.W. Wilson Co., 950 University Ave., Bronx, New York 10452. (800) 367-6770. 1916-. Monthly.

Science Citation Index. Institute for Scientific Information, 3501 Market St., Philadelphia, Pennsylvania 19104. 1961-.

ALMANACS AND YEARBOOKS

Environmental Almanac. World Resources Institute. Houghton Mifflin, 1 Beacon St., Boston, Massachusetts 02108. (617) 725-5000; (800) 225-3362. 1991. Covers consumer products, energy, endangered species, food safety, global warming, solid wastes, toxics, wetlands and other related areas. Also included are the names and addresses of the chief environmental executives for all 50 states.

ENCYCLOPEDIAS AND DICTIONARIES

Dictionary of Forest Structural Terminology. C.J. Geldenhuys, ed. Foundation for Research Development, Pretoria, Republic of #South Africa 1988.

GENERAL WORKS

Taking Stock: The Tropical Forestry Action Plan After Five Years. Robert Winterbottom. World Resources Institute, 1709 New York Ave. N.W., Washington, District of Columbia 20006. (800) 822-0504. 1990. Analyzes Tropical Forestry Action Plan's accomplishments and shortcomings, drawing on the biannual meetings of the TFAP Forestry Advisors' groups, assessments by FAO, various aid agencies, and by such organizations

as the World Rainforest Movement, Friends of the Earth, and World Life Fund.

ONLINE DATA BASES

Current Research Information System–CRIS/USDA. U.S. Department of Agriculture, National Agricultural Library, 10301 Baltimore Blvd., 5th Floor, Beltsville, Maryland 20705-2351. (301) 504-5755. Looks at current research projects in agriculture and allied sciences covering the biological, physical, social and behavioral sciences related to agriculture.

SCISEARCH. Institute for Scientific Information, University City Science Center, 3501 Market St., Philadelphia, Pennsylvania 19104. (215) 386-0100.

PERIODICALS AND NEWSLETTERS

Journal of Arboriculture. Society of Arboriculture, 303 W. University Ave., PO Box 908, Urbana, Illinois 61801. (217) 328-2032. 1975-. Monthly.

RESEARCH CENTERS AND INSTITUTES

Department of Forest Resources. University of Arkansas at Monticello, Monticello, Arkansas 71655. (501) 460-1052.

Michigan Technological University, Center for Intensive Forestry in Northern Regions. School of Forestry and Wood Products, Houghton, Michigan 49931. (906) 487-2897.

University of Maine, Dwight D. Demeritt Forest. College of Forest Resources, 206 Nutting Hall, Orono, Maine 04469. (207) 827-7804.

TRADE ASSOCIATIONS AND PROFESSIONAL SOCIETIES

American Institute of Biological Sciences. 730 11th St., N.W., Washington, District of Columbia 20001-4521. (202) 628-1500.

FOREST FIRES

ABSTRACTING AND INDEXING SERVICES

Index to Scientific Book Contents. Institute for Scientific Information, 3501 Market St., Philadelphia, Pennsylvania 19104. (800) 523-1857. 1985-. Annual. Gives contents of science books published.

BIBLIOGRAPHIES

Current Contents. Agriculture, Biology and Environmental Sciences. Institute for Scientific Information, 3501 Market St., Philadelphia, Pennsylvania 19104. (800) 523-1857. 1973-. Previous title: Current Contents. Agricultural, Food & Veterinary Sciences. Gives the table of contents of periodicals in the fields of agriculture, biology, environmental and related areas.

FOREST MANAGEMENT

ABSTRACTING AND INDEXING SERVICES

Applied Ecology Abstracts Studies in Renewable Natural Resources. Information Retrieval Ltd., 1911 Jefferson Davis Highway, Arlington, Virginia 22202. 1975-. Monthly.

Biological Abstracts. BIOSIS, 2100 Arch St., Philadelphia, Pennsylvania 19103-1399. (215) 587-4800. 1927-.

Biological and Agricultural Index. H.W. Wilson Co., 950 University Ave., Bronx, New York 10452. (800) 367-6770. 1916-. Monthly.

Current Advances in Ecological and Environmental Science. Pergamon Microforms International, Inc., Fairview Park, Elmsford, New York 10523. (914) 592-7720. 1989-. Monthly. Current literature searching service includingjournals, reports, abstracts, etc. This service is available online as part of the CABS database on the hosts BRS and ORBIT search service.

Ecological Abstracts. Geo Abstracts Ltd. Elsevier Applied Science, Crown House, Linton Rd., Barking, England IG 11 8JU. 1974-. Derived from over 600 leading ecological and environmental journals, plus books, conference proceedings, reports and theses.

Ecology Abstracts. Cambridge Scientific Abstracts, 5161 River Rd., Bethesda, Maryland 20816. (301) 961-6750. Monthly.

Environment Abstracts. Bowker A & I Publishing, 121 Chanlon Rd., New Providence, New Jersey 07974. (908) 464-6800. 1974-.

Environment Index. Environment Information Center, Index Research Department, 124 E. 39th St., New York, New York 10016. 1971-. Annual.

Environmental Information Connection–EIC. Planning Information Program, Dept. of Urban and Regional Planning, University of Illinois, 1003 West Nevada, Urbana, Illinois 61801. (217) 333-1369. Also available online.

Environmental Periodicals Bibliography. Environmental Studies Institute, International Academy at Santa Barbara, 800 Garden St., Suite D, Santa Barbara, California 93101. (805) 965-5010. Also available online.

Forest Products Abstracts. C. A. B. International, 845 North Park Ave., Tucson, Arizona 85719. (602) 621-7897 or (800) 528-4841. Bimonthly. Contains abstracts in the area of forest product industry; wood properties; timber extraction; conversion and measurement; damage to timber and timber production; utilization of wood; pulp industries and the chemical utilization of wood and other related areas.

Forestry Abstracts. C. A. B. International, Wallingford, England OX10 8DE. (0491) 3211. 1939/40-. Monthly. Journal of abstracts of journal articles, conferences, technical reports in the subject areas of: silviculture, forest mensuration and management, physical environment, fire, plant biology, genetics and breeding, mycology and pathology, game and wildlife, fish, protection of forests and other related matter.

General Science Index. H. W. Wilson Co., 950 University Ave., Bronx, New York 10452. 1978-. Monthly, also issued in annual cumulation. Cumulative subject index to English language periodicals in the subject fields of astronomy, botany, chemistry, earth science, environment and conservation, food and nutrition, genetics, mathematics, medicine and health, microbiology, oceanography, physics, physiology and zoology.

Geographical Abstracts. London School of Economics, Dept. of Geography, Regency House, 34 Duke St., London, England 1966-. Continued by Geo Abstracts issued in 6 parts: Pt. A. Landforms and the quaternary; Pt. B. Biogeography and Climatology; Pt. C. Economic geography; Pt. D. Social geography and cartography; Pt. E. Sedimentology; Pt. F. Regional and community planning.

Index to Scientific Book Contents. Institute for Scientific Information, 3501 Market St., Philadelphia, Pennsylvania 19104. (800) 523-1857. 1985-. Annual. Gives contents of science books published.

Multimedia Index to Ecology. National Information Center for Educational Media, University of Southern California, Los Angeles, California 90007.

Science Citation Index. Institute for Scientific Information, 3501 Market St., Philadelphia, Pennsylvania 19104. 1961-.

ALMANACS AND YEARBOOKS

Forest Management Chemicals. Forest Pest Management, Forest Service, U.S. Department of Agriculture. U.S. G.P.O., Washington, District of Columbia 20401. (202) 512-0000. Annual. Use of pesticides and insect control.

BIBLIOGRAPHIES

Current Contents. Agriculture, Biology and Environmental Sciences. Institute for Scientific Information, 3501 Market St., Philadelphia, Pennsylvania 19104. (800) 523-1857. 1973-. Previous title: Current Contents. Agricultural, Food & Veterinary Sciences. Gives the table of contents of periodicals in the fields of agriculture, biology, environmental and related areas.

EPA Publications Bibliography. U.S. Environmental Protection Agency, Library Systems Branch, 401 M St., SW, Washington, District of Columbia 20460. (202) 260-2090. Quarterly.

ENCYCLOPEDIAS AND DICTIONARIES

Dictionary of Forest Structural Terminology. C.J. Geldenhuys, ed. Foundation for Research Development, Pretoria, Republic of #South Africa 1988.

Dictionary of Forestry in Five Languages. Johannes Weck, et al. Elsevier Science Publishing Co., 655 Avenue of the Americas, New York, New York 10010. (212) 989-5800. 1966. Contains definitions in German, English, French, Spanish, and Russian.

McGraw-Hill Encyclopedia of Environmental Science. Sybil P. Parker. McGraw-Hill Science & Engineering Books, 11 W. 19th St., New York, New York 10011. (212) 337-6010. 1980. Covers ecology, man's influence on nature, and environmental protection.

Van Nostrand's Scientific Encyclopedia. Glenn D. Considine, ed. Van Nostrand Reinhold, 115 5th Ave., New York, New York 10003. (212) 254-3232. 1983. Sixth edition. Includes all broad subject areas in science.

GENERAL WORKS

Alternatives to Deforestation: Steps Toward Sustainable Use of the Amazon Rain Forest. Anthony B. Anderson, ed. Columbia University Press, 562 W. 113th St., New York, New York 10025. (212) 316-7100. 1992. Based on papers presented at an international conference in Belem, Brazil, for scientists in several fields, as well as government policy makers and representatives from foundations who are interested in exploring possible sustainable use of the world's largest rain forest, the Amazon, which is now being destroyed on an unprecedented scale.

Ancient Forests of the Pacific Northwest. Elliot A. Norse. Island Press, 1718 Connecticut Ave. N.W., Suite 300, Washington, District of Columbia 20009. (202) 232-7933. 1990. Comprehensive assessment of the biological value of the ancient forests, information about how logging and atmospheric changes threaten the forests, and convincing arguments that replicated ecosystems are too weak to support biodiversity.

Breaking New Ground. Gifford Pinchot. Island Press, 1718 Connecticut Ave. N.W., Suite 300, Washington, District of Columbia 20009. (202) 232-7933. 1987. Expounds the views that our precious forests should be managed for maximum yield with minimum long-term negative impact.

Burning and Empire, the Story of American Forest Fires. Stewart Hall Holbrook. Macmillan Publishing Co., 866 3rd Ave., New York, New York 10022. (212) 702-2000. 1943.

Cutting Our Losses: Policy Reform to Sustain Tropical Forest Resources. Charles V. Barber. World Resources Institute, 1709 New York Ave. N.W., Washington, District of Columbia 20006. (800) 822-0504. 1991. Focuses on the underlying economic social and political forces that drive forest conversation and exploitation.

The Disappearing Russian Forest: A Dilemma in Soviet Resource Management. Brenton M. Barr and Kathleen Braden. Rowman & Littlefield, Publishers, Inc., 8705 Bollman Pl., Savage, Maryland 20763. (301) 306-0400. 1988. Focuses on the crisis in the Soviet forest industry caused by the resource depletion and regional imbalance in the supply and demand for commercial timber. It emphasizes how Soviet decision-makers actually deal with management and day-to-day operations in utilization of that country's timber stocks.

Economic and Ecological Sustainability of Tropical Rain Forest Management. Kathrin Schreckenberg and Malcolm Hadley, eds. UNESCO, 7, place de Fontenoy, Paris, France F-75700. (331) 45 68 40 67. 1991.

Environmental Aspects of Plantation Forestry in Wales. J. E. G. Good, ed. Institute of Terrestrial Ecology, Merlewood Research Station, Grange-Over-Sands, England LA11 6JU. 1987. Proceedings of a symposium held at the Snowdonia National Park Study Centre, Plas Tan-Y-Bwlch, Maentwrog, Gwynedd, North Wales, 20-21 November 1986.

Envirosoft 86. P. Zanetti, ed. Computational Mechanics Inc., 25 Bridge St., Billerica, Massachusetts 01821. 1986. Environmental software part of the proceedings of the International Conference on Development and Applications of Computer Techniques to Environmental Studies, Los Angeles, 1986.

Envirosoft 88: Computer Techniques in Environmental Studies. P. Zannetti, ed. Computational Mechanics Inc., 25 Bridge St., Billerica, Massachusetts 01821. (508) 667-5841. 1988. Proceedings of the 2nd International Conference, Envirosoft 88, covering the development and application of computer techniques to environmental problems.

The Forest and the Trees: A Guide to Excellent Forestry. Gordon Robinson. Island Press, 1718 Connecticut Ave. N.W., Suite 300, Washington, District of Columbia 20009. (202) 232-7933. 1988. Gives concerned citizens who are not foresters the technical information they need to compete with the experts when commenting on how our national forests should be managed.

Forest Industry Wastewaters Biological Treatment. A. A. O. Luonsi and P. K. Rantala, eds. Pergamon Microforms International, Inc., Fairview Park, Elmsford, New York 10523. (914) 592-7720. 1988. First volume of the proceedings of an IAWPRC Symposium held at the University of Technology, Finland, June 9-12, 1987. Includes a wide range of research and practical results in the field of biological treatment of various pulp and paper mill effluents and sludges. Includes reports from various parts of the world including discussions on the choice of internal and external measures in pollution control.

Forest Stand Dynamics. Chadwick Dearing Oliver and Bruce C. Larson. McGraw-Hill Science & Engineering Books, 11 W. 19th St., New York, New York 10011. (212) 337-6010. 1990. Offers a unique synthesis of information from the fields of silviculture, ecology, and physiology that shows how different types of forest develop and outlines appropriate forest management techniques for each type.

Forestry Research: A Mandate for Change. National Research Council (U.S.) Board on Biology. National Academy Press, 2101 Constitution Ave. N.W., PO Box 285, Washington, District of Columbia 20418. (202) 334-3313. 1990. Begins with a general look at societal needs and concerns for the forest; it then explores the gap between society's requirements and the status of forestry research. Specific research needs by field are then addressed and conclusions and recommendations are supplied.

Forests and Forestry in China. S. D. Richardson. Island Press, 1718 Connecticut Ave. N.W., Suite 300, Washington, District of Columbia 20009. (202) 232-7933. 1990. In-depth look at current forest practice in China, including how China manages forest resources.

Global Forests. Roger A. Sedjo and Marion Clawson. Resources for the Future, 1616 P. St. N.W., Rm. 532, Washington, District of Columbia 20036. (202) 328-5086. 1988.

How to Predict the Spread and Intensity of Forest and Range Fires. Richard C. Rothermel. U.S. Department of Agriculture, Forest Service, Intermountain Forest and Range Experiment Station, 324 25th St., Ogden, Utah 84401. 1983. Detection, prevention, and control of forest fires.

Keeping It Green: Tropical Forestry and the Mitigation of Global Warming. Mark C. Trexler. World Resources Institute, 1709 New York Ave. N.W., Washington, District of Columbia 20006. (800) 822-0504. 1991. Report links knowledge gained from past tropical forestry initiatives with expectations for their future effectiveness in the mitigation of global warming.

Last Stand of the Red Spruce. Robert A. Mello. Island Press, 1718 Connecticut Ave. N.W., Suite 300, Washington, District of Columbia 20009. (202) 232-7933. 1987. Hypothesizes that acid rain is the most likely culprit that is killing the trees.

Magill's Survey of Science. Life Science Series. Frank N. Magill, ed. Salem Press, PO Box 50062, Pasadena, California 91105. 1991. Six volumes. Contents: v.1. A-Central and peripheral nervous system functions; v.2. Central metabolism regulation - eukaryotic transcriptional control; v.3. Positive and negative eukaryotic transcriptional control - mammalian hormones; v.4. Hormones and behavior - muscular contraction; v.5. Muscular contraction and relaxation - sexual reproduction in plants; v.6. Reproductive behavior and mating - X inactivation and the Lyon hypothesis.

The Mighty Rain Forest. John Nicol. Sterling Pub. Co. Inc., 387 Park Ave. S., New York, New York 10016. (212) 532-7160; (800) 367-9692. 1990. Focuses on the emotive debate on the environment regarding rainforests and the paper manufacturers. Includes a bibliography and a list of organizations working in rainforest conservation.

Public Policies and the Misuse of Forest Resources. Robert Repetto and Malcolm Gillis, eds. Cambridge University Press, 40 W. 20th St., New York, New York 10011. (212) 924-3900; (800) 227-0247. 1988. Case studies of forest policies in developing countries. Also deals with deforestation problems from the environmental point of view.

Rain Forest Regeneration and Management. G. Pompa, et al., eds. Parthenon Group Inc., 120 Mill Rd., Park Ridge, New Jersey 07656. (201) 391-6796. 1991. Explores the management implications of present scientific knowledge on rain forest generation. Providing case studies.

Reforming the Forest Service. Randal O'Toole. Island Press, 1718 Connecticut Ave. N.W., Suite 300, Washington, District of Columbia 20009. (202) 232-7933. 1988. Investigates possible economic inefficiencies and environmental consequences of the agency and proposes sweeping reforms to make the forest service more environmentally sensitive and efficient.

Saving the Tropical Forests. Judith Gradwohl and Russell Greenberg. Island Press, 1718 Connecticut Ave. N.W., Suite 300, Washington, District of Columbia 20009. (202) 232-7933. 1988. Sourcebook about the causes and effects of tropical deforestation, with case studies, examples of sustainable agriculture and forestry, and a section on the restoration of tropical rain forests.

Shading Our Cities. Gary Moll and Sara Ebenreck, eds. Island Press, 1718 Connecticut Ave. N.W., Suite 300, Washington, District of Columbia 20009. (202)232-7933. 1989. Handbook to help neighborhood groups, local officials, and planners develop urban forestry projects, not only to beautify their cities, but also to help reduce energy demand, improve air quality, protect water supplies, and contribute to healthier living conditions.

The Simple Act of Planting a Tree: A Citizen Forester's Guide to Healing Your Neighborhood, Your City, and Your World. Andy Lipkis. Jeremy P. Tarcher, 5858 Wilshire Blvd., Ste. 200, Los Angeles, California 90036. (213) 935-9980. 1990. Covers tree planting and urban forestry.

Three Men and a Forester. Ian S. Mahood. Harbour Pub., PO Box 219, Madeira Park, British Columbia, Canada V0N 2H0. 1990. Describes forest management in British Columbia and the forest products industry.

Tree Talk: The People and Politics of Timber. Ray Raphael. Island Press, 1718 Connecticut Ave. N.W., Suite 300, Washington, District of Columbia 20009. (202) 232-7933. Looks at the forest industry from the perspective of environmentalists, loggers, old-time woodsmen and young pioneers.

Trees of Life: Saving Tropical Forests and their Biological Wealth. Kenton Miller and Laura Tangley. World Resources Institute, 1709 New York Ave. N.W., Washington, District of Columbia 20006. (800) 822-0504. 1991. Explains what deforestation is doing to the global environment and why rainforest preservation is valid to human welfare around the world.

Wildlife, Forests, and Forestry. Malcolm L. Hunter, Jr. Prentice Hall, Rte 9W, Englewood Cliffs, New Jersey 07632. (201) 592-2000. 1990. Presents new ideas that will form the basis of forest wildlife management in years to come. It looks at the costs of managing wildlife, as well as national policies on forest wildlife management and quantitative techniques for measuring diversity.

The World Bank and the Environment: A Progress Report, Fiscal 1991. World Bank, UNIPUB, 4611-F Assembly Dr., Lanham, Maryland 20706. (301) 459-7666 or (800) 274-4888. 1991. Describes specific environmental strategies and environmental lending in the Bank's four operational regions: Asia, Europe, the Middle East and North Africa, and Latin America and the Caribbean.

GOVERNMENTAL ORGANIZATIONS

Information Office: Forest Service. PO Box 2417, Washington, District of Columbia 20013. (202) 447-3760.

HANDBOOKS AND MANUALS

The Forest Farmer's Handbook. Orville Camp. Sky River Press, 2466 Virginia St., #205, Berkeley, California 94709. (510) 841-1368. 1984. A guide to natural selection forest management and tree crops.

Forest Regeneration Manual. Mary L. Duryea. Kluwer Academic Publishers, 101 Philip Dr., Assinippi Park, Norwell, Massachusetts 02061. (617) 871-6600. 1991. Volume 36 in the series entitled Forestry Sciences.

State and Private Forestry Learning System: Quick Reference Guide. U.S. Department of Agriculture, Forest Service, 14 Independence Ave., SW, Washington, District of Columbia 20250. 1983. Forestry schools and education in the United States.

Timber Sale Administration Handbook. U.S. Department of Agriculture, Forest Service, 324 25th St., Ogden, Utah 84401. 1984. Economic aspects of forest management.

ONLINE DATA BASES

BIOSIS Previews. BIOSIS, 2100 Arch St., Philadelphia, Pennsylvania 19103-1399. (215) 587-4800. Largest and most comprehensive database of research in the life sciences. Contains citations for nearly 9000 primary research journals, monographs, reviews, symposia, preliminary reports, semi-popular journals, selected institu-

tional reports, government reports and research communications.

Cambridge Scientific Abstracts Life Science–CSAL. Cambridge Scientific Abstracts, 5161 River Rd., Bethesda, Maryland 20816. (301) 961-6750. Provides access to the following abstracting services: "Life Sciences Collection," "Aquatic Sciences and Fisheries Abstracts," "Oceanic Abstracts," and "Pollution Abstracts."

Current Research Information System–CRIS/USDA. U.S. Department of Agriculture, National Agricultural Library, 10301 Baltimore Blvd., 5th Floor, Beltsville, Maryland 20705-2351. (301) 504-5755. Looks at current research projects in agriculture and allied sciences covering the biological, physical, social and behavioral sciences related to agriculture.

Enviro/Energyline Abstracts Plus. R. R. Bowker Co., 121 Chanlon Rd., New Providence, New Jersey 07974. (908) 464-6800.

Environmental Periodicals Bibliography. National Information Services Corp., Ste. 6, Wyman Towers, 3100 St. Paul St., Baltimore, Maryland 21218. (410)243-0797. Online version of abstract of same name.

FOREST. Forest Products Research Society, 2801 Marshall Court, Madison, Wisconsin 53705. (608) 231-1361.

Monthly Catalog of United States Government Publications. U.S. G.P.O., Supt. of Docs., PO Box 371954, Pittsburgh, Pennsylvania 15250-7954. (202) 512-0000.

National Technical Information Service. U.S. Department of Commerce, National Technical Information Service, Office of Data Base Services, 5285 Port Royal Rd., Springfield, Virginia 22161. (703) 487-4807. Bibliographic database of government sponsored research and technical reports.

SCISEARCH. Institute for Scientific Information, University City Science Center, 3501 Market St., Philadelphia, Pennsylvania 19104. (215) 386-0100.

PERIODICALS AND NEWSLETTERS

Action Society for the Protection of New Hampshire Forests. The Forest Society, 54 Portsmouth St., Concord, New Hampshire 03301. (603) 224-9945. 1971-. Quarterly. Contains current news on New Hampshire environmental/conservation issues.

Agro-Ecosystems. Elsevier Science Publishing Co., 655 Avenue of the Americas, New York, New York 10010. (212) 989-5800. 1982-. Quarterly. Journal of International Association for Ecology featuring ecological interactions between agricultural and managed forest systems.

American Forests: The Magazine of Trees & Forests. American Forestry Association, 1516 P St. N.W., Washington, District of Columbia 20005. (202) 667-3300. Bimonthly.

CERP. Dana Silk, ed. UNESCO, 7, place de Fontenoy, Paris, France F-75700. (331) 45 68 40 67. Discusses forest and agroforestry ecosystems, urban development and planning.

Ecological Applications. Ecological Society of America, Center for Environmental Studies, Arizona State University, Tempe, Arizona 85287. (602) 965-3000. 1991-. Quarterly. Emphasizes the application of basic ecological concepts to a wide range of problems.

Ecological Monographs. Business Office of the Ecological Society of America, Center of Environmental Studies, Arizona State University, Tempe, Arizona 85287-1201. (602) 965-3000. Quarterly. Scientific journal of ecological issues.

Forest Conservation. Forestry Range Club, Washington State University, Pullman, Washington 99164-3200. 1958-. Annually. None published in 1974. Deals with forest conservation and related topics.

Missouri Conservationist. Missouri Deptartment of Conservation, Box 180, Jefferson City, Missouri 65102. (314) 751-4115. Monthly. Game, fish, and forestry management and hunting and fishing techniques.

Natural Resources & Earth Sciences. NTIS, 5285 Port Royal Rd., Springfield, Virginia 22161. (703) 487-4650. Weekly. Mineral industry, natural resources management, hydrology, limnology, soil conservation, watershed management, forestry, soil sciences, & geology.

Public Land News. Resources Publishing Co., 1010 Vermont Avenue, NW, Suite 708, Washington, District of Columbia 20005. (202) 638-7529. Biweekly. Covers land use and land development.

A Summary of Current Forest Insect and Disease Problems for New York State. Society of American Foresters, 5400 Grosvenor Ln., Bethesda, Maryland 20814. (301) 897-8720. 1969/70-.

RESEARCH CENTERS AND INSTITUTES

Blodgett Forest Research Station. University of California, Berkeley, 4531 Blodgett Forest Road, Georgetown, California 95634. (916) 333-4475.

Coolidge Center for Environmental Leadership. 1675 Massachusetts Ave., Suite 4, Cambridge, Massachusetts 02138. (617) 864-5085.

Forest Products Laboratory. University of California, Berkeley, 1301 South 46th Street, Richmond, California 94804. (510) 231-9452.

Forest Products Research Society. 2801 Marshall Ct., Madison, Wisconsin 53705. (608) 231-1361.

Michigan State University, Dunbar Forest Experiment Station. Route 1, Box 179, Sault Ste. Marie, Michigan 49783. (906) 632-3932.

Michigan State University, Fred Russ Research Forest. 20673 Marcellis Highway, Decatur, Michigan 49045. (616) 782-5652.

Michigan Technological University, Ford Forestry Center. Route 2, Box 7361, Lansing, Michigan 49946. (906) 487-2454.

Mississippi Forest Products Utilization Laboratory. Mississippi State University, P.O. Drawer FP, Mississippi State, Mississippi 39762. (601) 325-2116.

National Park Service Cooperative Park Studies Unit. University of Washington, College of Forest Resources AR-10, Seattle, Washington 98195. (206) 543-1587.

North Carolina State University Cooperative Tree Improvement Programs. P.O. Box 8002, Raleigh, North Carolina 27695. (919) 515-3168.

Oregon State University, Forest Research Laboratory. College of Forestry, Corvallis, Oregon 97331. (503) 737-2221.

State University of New York College of Environmental Science and Forestry. Syracuse Forest Experiment Station, 452 Lafayette Rd., Syracuse, New York 13205. (315) 469-3053.

Texas Forest Products Laboratory. Texas A&M University, P.O. Box 310, Lafkin, Texas 75901. (409) 639-8180.

Tropical Resources Institute. Yale University, School of Forestry and Environmental Studies, 205 Prospect St., New Haven, Connecticut 06511. (203) 432-5109.

U.S. Forest Service, Forest Tree Seed Laboratory. P.O. Box 906, Starkville, Mississippi 39759. (601) 323-8160.

U.S. Forest Service, Forestry Sciences Laboratory. Montana State University, Bozeman, Montana 59717. (406) 994-4852.

U.S. Forest Service, Forestry Sciences Laboratory. South Dakota School of Mines and Technology, Rapid City, South Dakota 57701. (605) 394-1960.

U.S. Forest Service, Intermountain Fire Sciences. P.O. Box 8089, Missoula, Montana 59807. (406) 329-3495.

U.S. Forest Service, Pacific Southwest Forest and Range Experiment Station. P.O. Box 245, 1960 Addison Street, Berkeley, California 94701. (415) 486-3292.

U.S. Forest Service, Rocky Mountain Forest and Range Experiment Station. 240 West Prospect Road, Fort Collins, Colorado 80526-2098. (303) 498-1126.

U.S. Forest Service, Timber Management Research Project. George W. Andrews Forestry Sciences Laboratory, DeVall Drive, Auburn University, Alabama 36849. (205) 826-8700.

University Forest. West Virginia University, Morgantown, West Virginia 26506. (304) 293-2941.

University of Missouri-Columbia, University Forest. 1-30 Agriculture Building, Columbia, Missouri 65211. (314) 222-8373.

Utah State University, Institute for Land Rehabilitation. College of Natural Resources, Logan, Utah 84322-5230. (801) 750-2547.

Wildland Resources Center. University of California, 145 Walter Mulford Hall, Berkeley, California 94720. (415) 642-0263.

STATISTICS SOURCES

Forest Industries. Forest Industries, 500 Howard St., San Francisco, California 94105. Monthly. Concerned with logging, pulpwood and forest management, and the manufacture oflumber, plywood, board, and pulp.

TRADE ASSOCIATIONS AND PROFESSIONAL SOCIETIES

American Forestry Association. PO Box 2000, Washington, District of Columbia 20013. (202) 667-3300. A citizen conservation organization, that was founded in 1875, to foster the protection, wise management, and enjoyment of forest resources in America and throughout the world.

American Institute of Biological Sciences. 730 11th St., N.W., Washington, District of Columbia 20001-4521. (202) 628-1500.

American Society of Naturalists. Department of Ecology and Evolation, State University of New York, Stony Brook, New York 11794. (516) 632-8589.

Association of Consulting Foresters. 5410 Grosvenor Ln., Suite 205, Bethesda, Maryland 20814. (301) 530-6795.

Children of the Green Earth. P.O. Box 95219, Seattle, Washington 98145. (503) 229-4721.

Forest Conservation Communications Association. Hall of the States, 444 N. Capitol St., N.W., Washington, District of Columbia 20001.

Forest Farmers Association. 4 Executive Park, Box 95385, Atlanta, Georgia 30347. (404) 325-2954.

Forest Industries Council. 1250 Connecticut Ave., N.W., Suite 320, Washington, District of Columbia 20036. (202) 833-1596.

National Association of Conservation Districts. 509 Capitol Court, N.E., Washington, District of Columbia 20002. (202) 547-6223.

National Association of State Foresters. 444 Capitol St., N.W., Hall of the States, Washington, District of Columbia 20001. (202) 624-5415.

National Forest Recreation Association. Rt. 3, Box 210, Hwy. 89 N., Flagstaff, Arizona 86004. (602) 526-4330.

National Hardwood Lumber Association. Box 34518, Memphis, Tennessee 38184. (901) 377-1818.

National Institute on Park & Grounds Management. Box 1936, Appleton, Wisconsin 54913. (414) 733-2301.

New England Forestry Foundation, Inc. 85 Newbury St., Boston, Massachusetts 02116. (617) 437-1441.

Northeastern Lumber Manufacturers Association. 272 Tuttle Rd., P.O. Box 87 A, Cumberland Center, Maine 04021. (207) 829-6901.

Save the Redwoods League. 114 Sansome St., Rm. 605, San Francisco, California 94104. (415) 362-2352.

Society for Range Management. 1839 York St., Denver, Colorado 80206. (303) 355-7070.

Society of American Foresters. 5400 Grosvenor Lane, Bethesda, Maryland 20814. (301) 897-8720.

Southern Forest Products Association. Box 52468, New Orleans, Louisiana 70152. (504) 443-4464.

Timber Products Manufacturers. 951 E. Third Ave., Spokane, Washington 99202. (509) 535-4646.

Western Forestry & Conservation Association. 4033 SW Canyon Rd., Portland, Oregon 97221. (503) 226-4562.

FORESTS

See also: NATIONAL PARKS AND RESERVES

ABSTRACTING AND INDEXING SERVICES

Applied Ecology Abstracts Studies in Renewable Natural Resources. Information Retrieval Ltd., 1911 Jefferson Davis Highway, Arlington, Virginia 22202. 1975-. Monthly.

Biological Abstracts. BIOSIS, 2100 Arch St., Philadelphia, Pennsylvania 19103-1399. (215) 587-4800. 1927-.

Biological and Agricultural Index. H.W. Wilson Co., 950 University Ave., Bronx, New York 10452. (800) 367-6770. 1916-. Monthly.

Current Advances in Ecological and Environmental Science. Pergamon Microforms International, Inc., Fairview Park, Elmsford, New York 10523. (914) 592-7720. 1989-. Monthly. Current literature searching service including journals, reports, abstracts, etc. This service is available online as part of the CABS database on the hosts BRS and ORBIT search service.

Ecological Abstracts. Geo Abstracts Ltd. Elsevier Applied Science, Crown House, Linton Rd., Barking, England IG 11 8JU. 1974-. Derived from over 600 leading ecological and environmental journals, plus books, conference proceedings, reports and theses.

Environment Abstracts. Bowker A & I Publishing, 121 Chanlon Rd., New Providence, New Jersey 07974. (908) 464-6800. 1974-.

Environment Index. Environment Information Center, Index Research Department, 124 E. 39th St., New York, New York 10016. 1971-. Annual.

Environmental Information Connection–EIC. Planning Information Program, Dept. of Urban and Regional Planning, University of Illinois, 1003 West Nevada, Urbana, Illinois 61801. (217) 333-1369. Also available online.

Environmental Periodicals Bibliography. Environmental Studies Institute, International Academy at Santa Barbara, 800 Garden St., Suite D, Santa Barbara, California 93101. (805) 965-5010. Also available online.

Forest Products Abstracts. C. A. B. International, 845 North Park Ave., Tucson, Arizona 85719. (602) 621-7897 or (800) 528-4841. Bimonthly. Contains abstracts in the area of forest product industry; wood properties; timber extraction; conversion and measurement; damage to timber and timber production; utilization of wood; pulp industries and the chemical utilization of wood and other related areas.

Forestry Abstracts. C. A. B. International, Wallingford, England OX10 8DE. (0491) 3211. 1939/40-. Monthly. Journal of abstracts of journal articles, conferences, technical reports in the subject areas of: silviculture, forest mensuration and management, physical environment, fire, plant biology, genetics and breeding, mycology and pathology, game and wildlife, fish, protection of forests and other related matter.

General Science Index. H. W. Wilson Co., 950 University Ave., Bronx, New York 10452. 1978-. Monthly, also issued in annual cumulation. Cumulative subject index to English language periodicals in the subject fields of astronomy, botany, chemistry, earth science, environment and conservation, food and nutrition, genetics, mathematics, medicine and health, microbiology, oceanography, physics, physiology and zoology.

Index to Scientific Book Contents. Institute for Scientific Information, 3501 Market St., Philadelphia, Pennsylvania 19104. (800) 523-1857. 1985-. Annual. Gives contents of science books published.

Multimedia Index to Ecology. National Information Center for Educational Media, University of Southern California, Los Angeles, California 90007.

Science Citation Index. Institute for Scientific Information, 3501 Market St., Philadelphia, Pennsylvania 19104. 1961-.

Weed Abstracts. C. A. B. International, 845 North Park Ave., Tucson, Arizona 85719. (602) 621-7897 or (800) 528-4841. 1954-. Monthly. Abstracts the world literature on weeds, weed control and allied subjects.

BIBLIOGRAPHIES

Current Contents. Agriculture, Biology and Environmental Sciences. Institute for Scientific Information, 3501 Market St., Philadelphia, Pennsylvania 19104. (800) 523-1857. 1973-. Previous title: Current Contents. Agricultural, Food & Veterinary Sciences. Gives the table of contents of periodicals in the fields of agriculture, biology, environmental and related areas.

Directory of Published Proceedings. Interdok Corp., 173 Halstead Ave., Harrison, New York 10528. (914) 835-3506. 1990. Monthly. This is a listing of published proceedings including the series SEMTE (Science/Medicine/Engineering/Technology) and the series SSH (Social Science/Humanities).

EPA Publications Bibliography. U.S. Environmental Protection Agency, Library Systems Branch, 401 M St., SW, Washington, District of Columbia 20460. (202) 260-2090. Quarterly.

Forest Environmental Resource Planning: A Selective Bibliography. Lizbeth Ann Jones. Council of Planning Librarians, 1313 E. 60th St., Chicago, Illinois 60637-2897. (312) 942-2163. 1977.

Land Planning in National Parks and Forests: A Selective Bibliography. Julia Johnson. Council of Planning Librarians, 1313 E. 60th St., Chicago, Illinois 60637-2897. (312) 942-2163. 1977. Covers forest reserves, rural land use, and national parks reserves.

Law, Policy, Planning, and Administration in Forestry. Judith L. Schwab. Vance Bibliographies, PO Box 229, 112 N. Charter St., Monticello, Illinois 61856. (217) 762-3831. 1982.

List of Periodicals and Serials in the Forestry Library. Commonwealth Forestry Association, c/o Oxford Forestry Institute, Oxford, England OX1 3RB. 1968. Covers agriculture and forests and forestry.

Nonindustrial Private Forest Ownership Studies: A Bibliography. William B. Kurtz. CPL Bibliographies, 1313 E. 60th St., Chicago, Illinois 60637-2897. (312) 942-2163. 1981.

Urban Forests: A Selected Bibliography. Anthony G. White. Council of Planning Librarians, 1313 E. 60th St., Chicago, Illinois 60637-2897. (312) 942-2163. 1977. Covers trees in cities.

Water Quality and Forestry. Jodee Kuske. National Agricultural Library, 10301 Baltimore Blvd., Beltsville, Maryland 20705-2351. (301) 504-5755. 1991.

DIRECTORIES

Agricultural Information Resource Centers, a World Directory 1990. Rita C. Fisher. IAALD World Directory Working Group, 716 W. Indiana Ave., Urbana, Illinois 61801-4836. (217) 333-7687. 1990. Includes 3,971 information resource centers that have agriculture related collection and/or information services.

Association of Consulting Foresters–Membership Specialization Directory. Association of Consulting Foresters, 5410 Grosvenor Lane, Suite 205, Bethesda, Maryland 20814. (301) 530-6795.

Crow's Buyers and Sellers Guide of the Forest Products Industries. C. C. Crow Publications, Inc., Box 25749, Portland, Oregon 97225. (503) 646-8075.

Directory of the Forest Products Industry. Miller Freeman Publications, Inc., 500 Howard St., San Francisco, California 94105. (415) 397-1881.

Directory of Urban Forestry Professionals. Urban Forestry Professionals, PO Box 2000, Washington, District of Columbia 20013.

Forest Industries–Equipment Catalog & Buyers Guide Issue. Miller Freeman Publications, Inc., 500 Howard St., San Francisco, California 94105. (415) 397-1881.

Friends of the Trees...Yearbook. Friends of the Trees, PO Box 1466, Chelan, Washington 98816. 1986-. Annually. Devoted to the care of trees and citizen participation in such activities.

Gale Environmental Sourcebook. Karen Hill. Gale Research Co., 835 Penobscot Bldg., Detroit, Michigan 48226-4094. (313) 961-2242. Contacts, information sources, or general information on environmental topics.

Guide to Experts in Forestry and Natural Resources. Northeastern Forest Experimentation Service/Forest Service/U.S. Department of Agriculture, 5 Radnor Corporate Center, Suite 200, Radnor, Pennsylvania 19087. (215) 975-4229.

Lumbermens Red Book. Lumbermens Credit Association, 111 W. Jackson Blvd., 10th Fl., Chicago, Illinois 60604. (312) 427-0733.

ENCYCLOPEDIAS AND DICTIONARIES

Cambridge Encyclopedia of Life Sciences. A. E. Friday and David S. Ingram. Cambridge University Press, 40 W 20th St., New York, New York 10011. (212) 924-3900 or (800) 227-0247. 1985. Includes all topics under biology and ecology.

A Dictionary of Environmental Quotations. Barbara K. Rodes and Rice Odell. Simon and Schuster, 15 Columbus Circle, New York, New York 10023. (212) 373-7342. 1992. Collection of nearly 3000 quotations arranged by topic, such as air, noise, energy, nature, pollution, forests, oceans, and other subjects on the environment.

Dictionary of Forest Structural Terminology. C.J. Geldenhuys, ed. Foundation for Research Development, Pretoria, Republic of #South Africa 1988.

Dictionary of Forest Terminology. Society of American Foresters, 5400 Grosvenor Ln., Bethesda, Maryland 20814. (301) 897-8720. 1987.

Dictionary of Forestry in Five Languages. Johannes Weck, et al. Elsevier Science Publishing Co., 655 Avenue of the Americas, New York, New York 10010. (212) 989-5800. 1966. Contains definitions in German, English, French, Spanish, and Russian.

Encyclopedia of Chemical Processing and Design. John J. Mcketta and W. A. Cunningham. Marcel Dekker, Inc., 270 Madison Ave., New York, New York 10016. (212) 696-9000; (800) 228-1160. 1992. Thirty-eight volumes.

Illustrated Encyclopedia of Science and the Future. Mike Biscare, et al., ed. Marshall Cavendish, 58 Old Compton St., London, England 0W1V5 PA. 01-734 6710. 1983. Twenty volumes. Each volume has 5 sections: Frontiers, Electronics in Action, Medical Science, Military Technology, and Resources.

Kirk-Othmer Encyclopedia of Chemical Technology. J. I. Kroschwitz, ed. John Wiley & Sons, Inc., 605 3rd Ave., New York, New York 10158-0012. (212) 850-6000. 1992-. All articles in the new edition have been rewritten and updated adding new subjects such as biotechnology, computer topics, analytical techniques and instrumentation, environmental concerns, fuels and energy, inorganic and solid state chemistry; composite materials and material science in general, and pharmaceuticals. Also available online.

McGraw-Hill Encyclopedia of Environmental Science. Sybil P. Parker. McGraw-Hill Science & Engineering Books, 11 W. 19th St., New York, New York 10011. (212) 337-6010. 1980. Covers ecology, man's influence on nature, and environmental protection.

McGraw-Hill Encyclopedia of Science and Technology. McGraw-Hill, 1221 Avenue of the Americas, New York, New York 10020. (212) 512-2000 or (800) 262-4729. 1992. Seventh edition. Issued in multiple volumes including index. Includes all science and technology broad subject areas.

Van Nostrand's Scientific Encyclopedia. Glenn D. Considine, ed. Van Nostrand Reinhold, 115 5th Ave., New York, New York 10003. (212) 254-3232. 1983. Sixth edition. Includes all broad subject areas in science.

GENERAL WORKS

Acidic Deposition and Forest Soils. Dan Binkley. Springer-Verlag, 175 Fifth Ave., New York, New York 10010. (212) 460-1500 or (800) 777-4643. 1990. Environmental aspects of acid deposition, forest soils and soil acidity.

Air Pollution's Toll on Forests and Crops. James J. MacKenzie and Mohamed T. El-Ashry, eds. Yale University Press, 92 A Yale St., 302 Temple St., New Haven, Connecticut 06520. (203) 432-0960. 1992. Proposes an integrated strategy to reduce pollution levels based on improved energy efficiency, abatement technology, and the use of nonfossil energy technologies. This strategy takes into account other critical problems such as increasing oil imports, failure to attain clean air goals in U.S. cities, and the greenhouse effect.

Ancient Forests of the Pacific Northwest. Elliot A. Norse. Island Press, 1718 Connecticut Ave. N.W., Suite 300, Washington, District of Columbia 20009. (202) 232-7933. 1990. Comprehensive assessment of the biological value of the ancient forests, information about how logging and atmospheric changes threaten the forests, and convincing arguments that replicated ecosystems are too weak to support biodiversity.

Breaking New Ground. Gifford Pinchot. Island Press, 1718 Connecticut Ave. N.W., Suite 300, Washington, District of Columbia 20009. (202) 232-7933. 1987. Expounds the views that our precious forests should be managed for maximum yield with minimum long-term negative impact.

Cutting Our Losses: Policy Reform to Sustain Tropical Forest Resources. Charles V. Barber. World Resources Institute, 1709 New York Ave. N.W., Washington, District of Columbia 20006. (800) 822-0504. 1991. Focuses on the underlying economic social and political forces that drive forest conversation and exploitation.

The Disappearing Russian Forest: A Dilemma in Soviet Resource Management. Brenton M. Barr and Kathleen Braden. Rowman & Littlefield, Publishers, Inc., 8705 Bollman Pl., Savage, Maryland 20763. (301) 306-0400. 1988. Focuses on the crisis in the Soviet forest industry caused by the resource depletion and regional imbalance in the supply and demand for commercial timber. It emphasizes how Soviet decision-makers actually deal with management and day-to-day operations in utilization of that country's timber stocks.

Draft Report: Fossil Ridge Wilderness Study Area: Grand Mesa, Uncompahgre and Gunnison National Forests, Taylor River Ranger District, Gunnison County, Colorado. U.S. Department of Agriculture, Forest Service, PO Box 25127, Lakewood, Colorado 80225. 1982.

The Ecology of a Tropical Forest. Egbert J. Leigh, Jr., et al., eds. Smithsonian Institution Press, 470 L'Enfant Plaza, No. 7100, Washington, District of Columbia 20560. (800) 782-4612. 1983. Describes the rhythm of plant reproduction through the seasons and how it affects animal population.

The Effects of Air Pollution and Acid Rain on Fish, Wildlife, and Their Habitats: Forests. Louis Borghi. Fish and Wildlife Service, Department of the Interior, Washington, District of Columbia 20240. (202) 653-8750. 1982. Effect of acid precipitation on plants and forest ecology.

Environmental Aspects of Plantation Forestry in Wales. J. E. G. Good, ed. Institute of Terrestrial Ecology, Merlewood Research Station, Grange-Over-Sands, England LA11 6JU. 1987. Proceedings of a symposium held at the Snowdonia National Park Study Centre, Plas Tan-Y-Bwlch, Maentwrog, Gwynedd, North Wales, 20-21 November 1986.

The Forest and the Trees: A Guide to Excellent Forestry. Gordon Robinson. Island Press, 1718 Connecticut Ave. N.W., Suite 300, Washington, District of Columbia 20009. (202) 232-7933. 1988. Gives concerned citizens who are not foresters the technical information they need to compete with the experts when commenting on how our national forests should be managed.

Forest Nature Conservation Guidelines. HMSO, UNIPUB, 4611-F Assembly Dr., Lanham, Maryland 20706. (301) 459-7666 or (800) 274-4888. 1991. Contains practical conservation advice to those involved in forestry.

Forest Stand Dynamics. Chadwick Dearing Oliver and Bruce C. Larson. McGraw-Hill Science & Engineering Books, 11 W. 19th St., New York, New York 10011. (212) 337-6010. 1990. Offers a unique synthesis of information from the fields of silviculture, ecology, and physiology that shows how different types of forest

develop and outlines appropriate forest management techniques for each type.

Forestry Research: A Mandate for Change. National Research Council (U.S.) Board on Biology. National Academy Press, 2101 Constitution Ave. N.W., PO Box 285, Washington, District of Columbia 20418. (202) 334-3313. 1990. Begins with a general look at societal needs and concerns for the forest; it then explores the gap between society's requirements and the status of forestry research. Specific research needs by field are then addressed and conclusions and recommendations are supplied.

Forests and Forestry in China. S. D. Richardson. Island Press, 1718 Connecticut Ave. N.W., Suite 300, Washington, District of Columbia 20009. (202) 232-7933. 1990. In-depth look at current forest practice in China, including how China manages forest resources.

Forests for Whom and for What?. Marion Clawson. Johns Hopkins University Press, 701 W. 40th St., Ste. 275, Baltimore, Maryland 21211. (410) 516-6900. 1975. Policy relative to forests and forestry.

Global Forest Resources. Alexander S. Mather. Timber Press, 9999 S.W. Wilshire, Portland, Oregon 97225. (503) 292-0745; (800) 327-5680. 1990. Covers all major aspects, from the extent and distribution of the resource base to the control, management, and use of forests. Historical, environmental, and sociological features are blended into the coverage. Numerous maps, figures, and tables are supplied.

Global Forests. Roger A. Sedjo and Marion Clawson. Resources for the Future, 1616 P. St. N.W., Rm. 532, Washington, District of Columbia 20036. (202) 328-5086. 1988.

International Environmental Information Sources. Pira, Randalls Rd., Leatherhead, England KT22 7RU. 0372 376161. 1990. Contains valuable business and technical contacts for environmental information sources worldwide. Information sources cover the following subjects: Air, noise, water and land pollution; waste control and disposal; recycling; energy recovery; nature conservation. Informational sources include associations, research organizations, legislative/regulatory agencies, directories, statistics, on-line databases, magazines and news letters in 24 countries.

Islands under Siege: National Parks and the Politics of External Threats. John C. Freemuth. University Press of Kansas, 329 Carruth, Lawrence, Kansas 66045. (913) 864-4154. 1991. Outlines a diverse set of political strategies, evaluating each in terms of environmental effectiveness and political feasibility.

The Lands Nobody Wanted: Policy for National Forests in the Eastern United States. William E. Shands. Conservation Foundation, 1250 24th St. NW, Washington, District of Columbia 20037. (202) 293-4800. 1977. Forest conservation, forest reserves, and forest policy.

Last Stand of the Red Spruce. Robert A. Mello. Island Press, 1718 Connecticut Ave. N.W., Suite 300, Washington, District of Columbia 20009. (202) 232-7933. 1987. Hypothesizes that acid rain is the most likely culprit that is killing the trees.

Long-Term Ecological Research: An International Perspective. Paul G. Risser, ed. John Wiley & Sons, Inc., 605 3rd Ave., New York, New York 10158-0012. (212) 850-6000. 1991. Describes and analyzes research programs in various ecosystems such as temperate forests, arid steppes, deserts, temperate and tropical grasslands, aquatic systems from countries including Scotland, Kenya, USA, Australia, Canada, Germany, and France.

Mining in National Forests. U.S. Department of Agriculture, Forest Service, 14 Independence Ave., S.W., Washington, District of Columbia 20250. (202) 447-7454. 1974. Forest reserves, mines and minerals in the U.S.

Our Common Lands: Defending the National Parks. David J. Simon, ed. Island Press, 1718 Connecticut Ave. N.W., Suite 300, Washington, District of Columbia 20009. (202) 232-7933. 1988. Explains the complexities of key environmental laws and how they can be used to protect our national parks. Includes discussion of successful and unsuccessful attempts to use the laws and how the courts interpret them.

Plant Demography in Vegetation Succession. Krystyna Falinska. Kluwer Academic Publishers, 101 Philip Dr., Assinippi Park, Norwell, Massachusetts 02061. (617) 871-6600. 1991.

Pocket Flora of the Redwood Forest. Rudolf Willem Becking. Island Press, 1718 Connecticut Ave. N.W., Suite 300, Washington, District of Columbia 20009. (202) 232-7933. 1982. Guide to 212 of the most frequently seen plants in the Redwood Forest of the Pacific Coast. It is interspersed with accurate drawing color photographs and systematic keys to plant identification.

Public Policies and the Misuse of Forest Resources. Robert Repetto and Malcolm Gillis, eds. Cambridge University Press, 40 W. 20th St., New York, New York 10011. (212) 924-3900; (800) 227-0247. 1988. Case studies of forest policies in developing countries. Also deals with deforestation problems from the environmental point of view.

Reforesting the Earth. Sandra Postel, Lori Heise. Worldwatch Institute, 1776 Massachusetts Ave., N.W., Washington, District of Columbia 20036-1904. 1988.

Reforming the Forest Service. Randal O'Toole. Island Press, 1718 Connecticut Ave. N.W., Suite 300, Washington, District of Columbia 20009. (202) 232-7933. 1988. Investigates possible economic inefficiencies and environmental consequences of the agency and proposes sweeping reforms to make the forest service more environmentally sensitive and efficient.

Saving the Tropical Forests. Judith Gradwohl and Russell Greenberg. Island Press, 1718 Connecticut Ave. N.W., Suite 300, Washington, District of Columbia 20009. (202) 232-7933. 1988. Sourcebook about the causes and effects of tropical deforestation, with case studies, examples of sustainable agriculture and forestry, and a section on the restoration of tropical rain forests.

Shading Our Cities. Gary Moll and Sara Ebenreck, eds. Island Press, 1718 Connecticut Ave. N.W., Suite 300, Washington, District of Columbia 20009. (202)232-7933. 1989. Handbook to help neighborhood groups, local officials, and planners develop urban forestry projects, not only to beautify their cities, but also to help reduce energy demand, improve air quality, protect water supplies, and contribute to healthier living conditions.

The Simple Act of Planting a Tree: A Citizen Forester's Guide to Healing Your Neighborhood, Your City, and Your World. Andy Lipkis. Jeremy P. Tarcher, 5858 Wilshire Blvd., Ste. 200, Los Angeles, California 90036.

(213) 935-9980. 1990. Covers tree planting and urban forestry.

Taking Stock: The Tropical Forestry Action Plan After Five Years. Robert Winterbottom. World Resources Institute, 1709 New York Ave. N.W., Washington, District of Columbia 20006. (800) 822-0504. 1990. Analyzes Tropical Forestry Action Plan's accomplishments and shortcomings, drawing on the biannual meetings of the TFAP Forestry Advisors' groups, assessments by FAO, various aid agencies, and by such organizations as the World Rainforest Movement, Friends of the Earth, and World Life Fund.

The Temperate Forest Ecosystem. Yang Hanxi. Institute of Terrestrial Ecology, Merlewood Research Station, Grange-over-Sands, England LA11 6JU. 1987. Topics in forest ecology.

Three Men and a Forester. Ian S. Mahood. Harbour Pub., PO Box 219, Madeira Park, British Columbia, Canada V0N 2H0. 1990. Describes forest management in British Columbia and the forest products industry.

Tree Crops: A Permanent Agriculture. J. Russell Smith. Island Press, 1718 Connecticut Ave. N.W., Suite 300, Washington, District of Columbia 20009. (202) 232-7933. 1987. Most complete reference for growing high yield fruit and nut bearing trees. First published in 1929, this guide to the development of successful tree crops illustrates that vast, untapped food sources can be harvested from common species of trees.

Tree Talk: The People and Politics of Timber. Ray Raphael. Island Press, 1718 Connecticut Ave. N.W., Suite 300, Washington, District of Columbia 20009. (202) 232-7933. Looks at the forest industry from the perspective of environmentalists, loggers, old-time woodsmen and young pioneers.

Trees of Life: Saving Tropical Forests and their Biological Wealth. Kenton Miller and Laura Tangley. World Resources Institute, 1709 New York Ave. N.W., Washington, District of Columbia 20006. (800) 822-0504. 1991. Explains what deforestation is doing to the global environment and why rainforest preservation is valid to human welfare around the world.

Tropical Rain Forests and the World Atmosphere. T. Ghillean. Westview Press, 5500 Central Ave., Boulder, Colorado 80301. (303) 444-3541. 1986. Deals with vegetation and climate in the tropics. Also describes the weather patterns in that part of the world.

Tropical Rainforest: A World Survey of Our Most Valuable Endangered Habitat With a Blueprint for its Survival. Arnold Newman. Facts on File, Inc., 460 Park Ave. S., New York, New York 10016. (212) 683-2244; (800) 322-8755. 1990. Considers threats to rain forests, including logging and slash and burn agricultural practices. Presents a variety of measures to preserve our valuable rain forests.

Tropical Resources: Ecology and Development. Jose I. Furtado, et al., eds. Harwood Academic Publishers, PO Box 786, Cooper Sta., New York, New York 10276. (212) 206-8900. 1990. Overview of global tropical resources, both terrestrial and aquatic. Subjects discussed include forest resources, wildlife resources, general land use, pasture resources, economic development, fisheries, marine resources, and aquaculture.

Wildlife, Forests, and Forestry. Malcolm L. Hunter, Jr. Prentice Hall, Rte 9W, Englewood Cliffs, New Jersey

07632. (201) 592-2000. 1990. Presents new ideas that will form the basis of forest wildlife management in years to come. It looks at the costs of managing wildlife, as well as national policies on forest wildlife management and quantitative techniques for measuring diversity.

GOVERNMENTAL ORGANIZATIONS

Information Office: Forest Service. PO Box 2417, Washington, District of Columbia 20013. (202) 447-3760.

National Agricultural Library. Route 1, Beltsville, Maryland 20705. (301) 344-4348.

TVA Public Information Office. 400 West Summit Hill Dr., Knoxville, Tennessee 37902. (615) 632-8000.

HANDBOOKS AND MANUALS

Chainsaws in Tropical Forests: A Manual. Food and Agriculture Organization of the United Nations, Via delle Terme di Caracalla, Rome, Italy 00100. 61 0181-FA01. 1980. Tree felling-equipment and supplies and logging machinery.

Forest Regeneration Manual. Mary L. Duryea. Kluwer Academic Publishers, 101 Philip Dr., Assinippi Park, Norwell, Massachusetts 02061. (617) 871-6600. 1991. Volume 36 in the series entitled Forestry Sciences.

The Global Ecology Handbook: What You Can Do about the Environmental Crisis. Walter H. Corson, ed. The Global Tomorrow Coalition, Beacon Pr., 25 Beacon St., Boston, Massachusetts 02108-2800. (617) 742-2110. 1990. Covers environment, energy policy, population growth and other issues. It includes chapters on tropical rain forests, garbage, oceans and coasts, global warming, population growth, agriculture, biological diversity, fresh water, hazardous wastes, and environment and development.

ONLINE DATA BASES

BioBusiness. Dialog Information Services, Inc., Marketing Dept., 3460 Hillview Avenue, Palo Alto, California 94304. (800) 334-2564 or (415) 858-3810. Provides information based on evaluations of the economic and business aspects of biological and biomedical research.

BIOSIS Previews. BIOSIS, 2100 Arch St., Philadelphia, Pennsylvania 19103-1399. (215) 587-4800. Largest and most comprehensive database of research in the life sciences. Contains citations for nearly 9000 primary research journals, monographs, reviews, symposia, preliminary reports, semi-popular journals, selected institutional reports, government reports and research communications.

Cambridge Scientific Abstracts Life Science–CSAL. Cambridge Scientific Abstracts, 5161 River Rd., Bethesda, Maryland 20816. (301) 961-6750. Provides access to the following abstracting services: "Life Sciences Collection," "Aquatic Sciences and Fisheries Abstracts," "Oceanic Abstracts," and "Pollution Abstracts."

Current Research Information System–CRIS/USDA. U.S. Department of Agriculture, National Agricultural Library, 10301 Baltimore Blvd., 5th Floor, Beltsville, Maryland 20705-2351. (301) 504-5755. Looks at current research projects in agriculture and allied sciences covering the biological, physical, social and behavioral sciences related to agriculture.

Enviro/Energyline Abstracts Plus. R. R. Bowker Co., 121 Chanlon Rd., New Providence, New Jersey 07974. (908) 464-6800.

Environmental Periodicals Bibliography. National Information Services Corp., Ste. 6, Wyman Towers, 3100 St. Paul St., Baltimore, Maryland 21218. (410)243-0797. Online version of abstract of same name.

FOREST. Forest Products Research Society, 2801 Marshall Court, Madison, Wisconsin 53705. (608) 231-1361.

Kirk-Othmer Encyclopedia of Chemical Technology. John Wiley & Sons, Inc., 605 3rd Ave., 5th Floor, New York, New York 10158. (212) 850-6000. Online version of the publication of the same name.

Monthly Catalog of United States Government Publications. U.S. G.P.O., Supt. of Docs., PO Box 371954, Pittsburgh, Pennsylvania 15250-7954. (202) 512-0000.

National Technical Information Service. U.S. Department of Commerce, National Technical Information Service, Office of Data Base Services, 5285 Port Royal Rd., Springfield, Virginia 22161. (703) 487-4807. Bibliographic database of government sponsored research and technical reports.

Oil and Hazardous Materials Technical Assistance Data System. U.S. Environmental Protection Agency, Office of Solid Waste and Emergency Response, 401 M St., S.W., Washington, District of Columbia 20460. (202) 260-2090. Hazardous substances and their deleterious effects on water quality and other environmental media.

RISI Forest Products. Resource Information Systems, 110 Great Rd., Bedford, Massachusetts 01730. (617) 271-0030.

SCISEARCH. Institute for Scientific Information, University City Science Center, 3501 Market St., Philadelphia, Pennsylvania 19104. (215) 386-0100.

PERIODICALS AND NEWSLETTERS

Action Society for the Protection of New Hampshire Forests. The Forest Society, 54 Portsmouth St., Concord, New Hampshire 03301. (603) 224-9945. 1971-. Quarterly. Contains current news on New Hampshire environmental/conservation issues.

American Forests: The Magazine of Trees & Forests. American Forestry Association, 1516 P St. N.W., Washington, District of Columbia 20005. (202) 667-3300. Bimonthly.

Between the Issues. Ecology Action Center, 1657 Barrington St., #520, Halifax, Nova Scotia, Canada B3J 2A1. (506) 422-4311. 1975-. Bimonthly. Newsletter that deals with environmental protection, uranium mining, waste, energy, agriculture, forestry, pesticides, and urban planning.

Ecological Applications. Ecological Society of America, Center for Environmental Studies, Arizona State University, Tempe, Arizona 85287. (602) 965-3000. 1991-. Quarterly. Emphasizes the application of basic ecological concepts to a wide range of problems.

Ecological Monographs. Business Office of the Ecological Society of America, Center of Environmental Studies, Arizona State University, Tempe, Arizona 85287-1201. (602) 965-3000. Quarterly. Scientific journal of ecological issues.

Forest and Conservation History. Forest History Society, 701 Vickers Ave., Durham, North Carolina 27701. (919) 682-9319. Quarterly.

Forest Conservation. Forestry Range Club, Washington State University, Pullman, Washington 99164-3200. 1958-. Annually. None published in 1974. Deals with forest conservation and related topics.

Forest Notes. Society for the Protection of New Hampshire Forests, 54 Portsmouth St., Concord, New Hampshire 03301. (603) 224-9945. 1937-. Quarterly. Devoted to forestry, land protection and other issues affecting New Hampshire natural resources.

Forest Science. Society of American Foresters, 5400 Grosvenor Ln., Bethesda, Maryland 20814-2198. (301) 897-8720. Quarterly. Silviculture, soils, biometry, diseases, recreation, photosynthesis, tree physiology, management, harvesting, and policy analysis.

Forest Watch: The Citizen's Forestry Magazine. Cascade Holistic Economic Consultants, 14417 SE Laurie Ave., Oak Grove, Oregon 97207. (503) 652-7049. Eleven times a year.

Forest World. World Forestry Center, 4033 SW Canyon Rd., Portland, Oregon 97221. (503) 228-1367. Quarterly. Forest and natural resource issues.

Forests and People. Louisiana Forestry Assn., PO Drawer 5067, Alexandria, Louisiana 71307-5067. (318) 443-2558. Quarterly.

Journal of Arboriculture. Society of Arboriculture, 303 W. University Ave., PO Box 908, Urbana, Illinois 61801. (217) 328-2032. 1975-. Monthly.

The Journal of World Forest Management. A B Academic Publishers, Herts, England Quarterly.

League Leader. Izaak Walton League of America, 1401 Wilson Blvd., Level B, Arlington, Virginia 22209. (703) 528-1818. Bimonthly. Soil, forest, water, & other natural resources.

Nature and Resources. Elsevier Science Publishing Co., 655 Avenue of the Americas, New York, New York 10010. (212) 989-5800. 1965-. Quarterly. Provides in-depth reviews of contemporary environmental issues from an international perspective.

New Forests. Martinus Nijhoff Publishers, 101 Philips Dr., Boston, Massachusetts 02061. (617) 871-6600. Quarterly. Topics in biology, biotechnology, and management of afforestation and reforestation.

Public Land News. Resources Publishing Co., 1010 Vermont Avenue, NW, Suite 708, Washington, District of Columbia 20005. (202) 638-7529. Biweekly. Covers land use and land development.

A Summary of Current Forest Insect and Disease Problems for New York State. Society of American Foresters, 5400 Grosvenor Ln., Bethesda, Maryland 20814. (301) 897-8720. 1969/70-.

Wilderness. The Wilderness Society, 900 17th St. NW, Washington, District of Columbia 20006. (202) 833-2300. Quarterly. Preserving wilderness and wildlife, protecting America's prime forests, parks, rivers, shorelands, and fostering an American land ethic.

World Wood. Miller Freeman Publications, Inc., 500 Harrison St., San Francisco, California 94105. (415) 397-

1881. Forest products industry, lumbering, and forest management.

RESEARCH CENTERS AND INSTITUTES

Bartlett Arboretum. University of Connecticut, 151 Brookdale Rd., Stamford, Connecticut 06903. (203) 322-6971.

Coolidge Center for Environmental Leadership. 1675 Massachusetts Ave., Suite 4, Cambridge, Massachusetts 02138. (617) 864-5085.

Cooperative National Park Resources Studies Unit. University of California, Davis, Institute of Ecology, Davis, California 95616. (916) 752-7119.

Core Arboretum. West Virginia University, PO Box 6057, Morgantown, West Virginia 26506-6057. (304) 293-5201.

Department of Forest Resources. University of Arkansas at Monticello, Monticello, Arkansas 71655. (501) 460-1052.

Earth Sciences Centre. University of Toronto, 33 Willcocks St., Toronto, Ontario, Canada M5S 3B3. (416) 978-3248.

Forest Products Laboratory. University of California, Berkeley, 1301 South 46th Street, Richmond, California 94804. (510) 231-9452.

Forest Products Research Society. 2801 Marshall Ct., Madison, Wisconsin 53705. (608) 231-1361.

Michigan Technological University, Great Lakes Area Resource Studies Unit. Department of Biological Sciences, Houghton, Michigan 49931. (906) 487-2478.

National Park Service Cooperative Park Studies Unit. University of Washington, College of Forest Resources AR-10, Seattle, Washington 98195. (206) 543-1587.

National Park Service Cooperative Unit. Institute of Ecology, University of Georgia, Athens, Georgia 30602. (404) 542-8301.

North Carolina State University, Pulp and Paper Laboratory. College of Forest Resources, Box 8005, Raleigh, North Carolina 247695. (919) 737-2888.

Oregon Cooperative Park Studies Unit. College of Forestry, Oregon State University, Corvallis, Oregon 97331. (503) 737-2056.

Reynolds Homestead Agricultural Experiment Station. Virginia Polytech Institute and State University, PO Box 70, Critz, Virginia 24082. (703) 694-4135.

Texas A&M University, Forest Genetics Laboratory. College Station, Texas 77843. (409) 845-1325.

Tropical Resources Institute. Yale University, School of Forestry and Environmental Studies, 205 Prospect St., New Haven, Connecticut 06511. (203) 432-5109.

U.S. Forest Service, Forest Engineering Research Project. George W. Andrews Forestry Sciences Laboratory, Auburn University, Devall Street, Auburn, Alabama 36849. (205) 826-8700.

U.S. Forest Service, Forest Hydrology Laboratory. Southern Forest Experiment Station, P.O. Box 947, Oxford, Mississippi 38655. (601) 234-2744.

U.S. Forest Service, Forest Products Laboratory. One Gifford Pinchot Drive, Madison, Wisconsin 53705-2398. (608) 231-9200.

U.S. Forest Service, Forest Tree Seed Laboratory. P.O. Box 906, Starkville, Mississippi 39759. (601) 323-8160.

U.S. Forest Service, Forestry Sciences Laboratory. Carlton Street, Athens, Georgia 30602. (404) 546-2441.

U.S. Forest Service, Forestry Sciences Laboratory. Montana State University, Bozeman, Montana 59717. (406) 994-4852.

U.S. Forest Service, Forestry Sciences Laboratory. Southern Illinois University at Carbondale, Carbondale, Illinois 62901-4630. (618) 453-2318.

U.S. Forest Service, Forestry Sciences Laboratory. I-26 Agricultural Building, University of Missouri- Columbia, Columbia, Missouri 65211. (314) 875-5341.

U.S. Forest Service, Forestry Sciences Laboratory. Forest Hill Road, Houghton, Michigan 49931. (906) 482-6303.

U.S. Forest Service, Forestry Sciences Laboratory. 222 South 22nd Street, Laramie, Wyoming 82070. (307) 742-6621.

U.S. Forest Service, Forestry Sciences Laboratory. 1221 South Main Street, Moscow, Idaho 83843. (208) 882-3557.

U.S. Forest Service, Forestry Sciences Laboratory. South Dakota School of Mines and Technology, Rapid City, South Dakota 57701. (605) 394-1960.

U.S. Forest Service, Institute of Forest Genetics. 2480 Carson Road, Placerville, California 95667. (916) 622-1225.

U.S. Forest Service, Institute of Northern Forestry. 308 Tanana Drive, University of Alaska, Fairbanks, Alaska 99775-5500. (907) 474-8163.

U.S. Forest Service, Institute of Tropical Forestry. Call Box 25000, Rio Piedras, Puerto Rico 00928-2500. (809) 766-5335.

U.S. Forest Service, Intermountain Research Station. 324 25th Street, Ogden, Utah 84401. (801) 625-5431.

U.S. Forest Service, North Central Forest Experiment Station. 1407 South Harrison Road, Suite 220, East Lansing, Michigan 48823. (517) 355-7740.

U.S. Forest Service, Northeastern Forest Experiment Station. 5 Godfrey Dr., Orono, Maine 04473. (207) 866-4140.

U.S. Forest Service, Redwood Science Laboratory. 1700 Bayview Dr., Arcata, California 95521. (707) 822-3691.

U.S. Forest Service, Timber Management Research Project. George W. Andrews Forestry Sciences Laboratory, DeVall Drive, Auburn University, Alabama 36849. (205) 826-8700.

University of Alaska Fairbanks, Forestry Soils Laboratory. Fairbanks, Alaska 99775. (907) 474-7114.

University of Arizona, Boyce Thompson Arboretum. P.O. Box AB, Superior, Arizona 85723. (602) 689-2811.

University of Arizona, Laboratory of Tree-Ring Research. Tucson, Arizona 85721. (602) 621-2191.

University of Georgia, Institute of Ecology. 103 Ecology Building, Athens, Georgia 30602. (404) 542-2968.

University of Idaho Cooperative Park Studies Unit. College of Forestry, Wildlife and Range Sciences, Moscow, Idaho 83843. (208) 885-7990.

University of Idaho Forest, Wildlife and Range Experiment Station. Moscow, Idaho 83843. (208) 885-6441.

University of Maine, Cooperative Forestry Research Unit. College of Forest Resources, Orono, Maine 04469. (207) 581-2893.

University of Maine, Dwight D. Demeritt Forest. College of Forest Resources, 206 Nutting Hall, Orono, Maine 04469. (207) 827-7804.

University of Minnesota, Center for Natural Resource Policy and Management. 110 Green Hall, 1530 North Cleveland Avenue, St. Paul, Minnesota 55108. (612) 624-9796.

University of Minnesota, Cloquet Forestry Center. 175 University Road, Cloquet, Minnesota 55720. (218) 879-0850.

University of Minnesota, Lake Itasca Forestry and Biological Station. Post Office, Lake Itasca, Minnesota 56460. (218) 266-3345.

University of Missouri-Columbia, Schnabel Woods. 1-30 Agricultural Building, Columbia, Missouri 65211. (314) 882-6446.

University of Montana, Montana Forest and Conservation Experiment Station. Missoula, Montana 59812. (406) 243-5521.

University of Tennessee at Knoxville, Forestry Experiment Stations and Arboretum. 901 Kerr Hollow Road, Oak Ridge, Tennessee 37830. (615) 483-3571.

University of Washington, Center for Quantitative Science in Forestry, Fisheries and Wildlife. 3737 Fifteenth Avenue N.E., HR-20, Seattle, Washington 98195. (206) 543-1191.

University of Washington, Institute of Forest Resources. 216 Anderson Hall, College of Forest Resources, Seattle, Washington 98195. (206) 685-1928.

University of Wyoming, National Park Service Research Center. Box 3166, University Station, Laramie, Wyoming 82071. (307) 766-4227.

Utah State University, Watershed Science Unit. Range Science Department, Logan, Utah 84322-5250. (801) 750-2759.

Willowwood Arboretum. PO Box 1295, Morristown, New Jersey 07962-1295. (201) 326-7600.

World Forestry Center. 4033 S.W. Canyon Rd., Portland, Oregon 97221. (503) 228-1367.

World Resources Institute. 1709 New York Ave., N.W., Washington, District of Columbia 20006. (202) 638-6300.

STATISTICS SOURCES

Environmental Data Compendium. OECD Publications and Information Center, 2001 L St., N.W., Suite 700, Washington, District of Columbia 20036. (202) 785-6323. 1989.

Environmental Indicators. OECD Publications and Information Center, 2001 L St., N.W., Suite 700, Washington, District of Columbia 20036. (202) 785-6323. 1991.

Environmental Quality. Council on Environmental Quality. U.S. G.P.O., Washington, District of Columbia 20401. (202) 512-0000. Annual.

Evaluation of the Role of Ozone, Acid Deposition, and Other Airborne Pollutants in the Forests of Eastern North America. J.H.B. Garner. U.S. G.P.O., Washington, District of Columbia 20401. (202) 512-0000. 1989. Effects of air pollution on forests in the eastern U.S. and Canada, based on a review of field studies conducted primarily during 1960-1989. Pollutants studied include sulfur dioxide (SO_2), nitrogen oxides, ozone and other photochemical oxidants, and acid precipitation components.

Land Areas of the National Forest System. U.S. Forest Service. U.S. G.P.O., Washington, District of Columbia 20401. (202) 512-0000. Annual. Data on wilderness, scenic-research, monument and recreation areas, and game refuges.

Local Climatological Data. National Environmental Satellite, Data, and Information Service, 2069 Federal Bldg. 4, Washington, District of Columbia 20233. (301) 763-7190. Monthly.

National Forests Fire Report. U.S. Department of Agriculture, Forest Service, 14 Independence Ave., S.W., Washington, District of Columbia 20250. (202) 447-7454. Annual.

New Perspectives on Silvicultural Management of Northern Hardwoods. U.S. G.P.O, Washington, District of Columbia 20402-9325. (202) 512-0000. 1989. Timber stand condition and other factors involved in selecting management strategies for northern U.S. and Canada hardwood forests.

OECD Environmental Data Compendium 1989. OECD Publications and Information Center, 2001 L St. N.W., Suite 700, Washington, District of Columbia 20036. (202) 785-OECD. 1989. Provides statistical data for OECD countries on air pollution, water pollution, the marine environment, land use, forests, wildlife, solid waste, noise and radioactivity. Also provides data on the underlying pressures on the environment such as energy use, transportation, industrial activity and agriculture.

The State of the Environment. OECD Publications and Information Center, 2001 L St., N.W., Suite 700, Washington, District of Columbia 20036. (202) 785-6323. 1991.

Statistical Roundup. National Forest Products Association, 1250 Connecticut Ave., NW, Suite 200, Washington, District of Columbia 20036. 1980-. Monthly. Production and shipments, orders, consumption, foreign trade, and employment.

U.S. Forest Planting Report. U.S. Department of Agriculture, Forest Service, 14 Independence Ave. SW, Washington, District of Columbia 20250. (202) 447-7454. Annual. Covers afforestation, strip mining and reclamation of land in the United States.

World Resources. World Resources Institute. 1709 New York Ave., N.W., Washington, District of Columbia 20006. (202) 638-6300. Annual. Statistical and textual analysis of world's natural resources and the effects of growth-caused environmental pollution.

TRADE ASSOCIATIONS AND PROFESSIONAL SOCIETIES

American Forage and Grassland Council. P.O. Box 891, Georgetown, Texas 78627.

American Forest Council. 1250 Connecticut Ave., N.W., Suite 320, Washington, District of Columbia 20036. (202) 463-2455.

American Forestry Association. PO Box 2000, Washington, District of Columbia 20013. (202) 667-3300. A citizen conservation organization, that was founded in 1875, to foster the protection, wise management, and enjoyment of forest resources in America and throughout the world.

American Institute of Biological Sciences. 730 11th St., N.W., Washington, District of Columbia 20001-4521. (202) 628-1500.

American Society of Consulting Arborists. 3895 Upham, No. 12, Wheatridge, Colorado 80033. (303) 420-9554.

American Society of Naturalists. Department of Ecology and Evolation, State University of New York, Stony Brook, New York 11794. (516) 632-8589.

Association for Conservation Information. PO Box 10678, Reno, Nevada 89520. (702) 688-1500.

Association of Consulting Foresters. 5410 Grosvenor Ln., Suite 205, Bethesda, Maryland 20814. (301) 530-6795.

Cascade Holistic Economic Consultants. 14417 S.E. Laurie Ave., Oak Grove, Oregon 97207. (503) 652-7049.

Children of the Green Earth. P.O. Box 95219, Seattle, Washington 98145. (503) 229-4721.

Food and Agriculture Organization. Liaison Office for North America, 1001 22nd St., N.W., Washington, District of Columbia 20437. (202) 653-2402.

Forest Conservation Communications Association. Hall of the States, 444 N. Capitol St., N.W., Washington, District of Columbia 20001.

Forest Farmers Association. 4 Executive Park, Box 95385, Atlanta, Georgia 30347. (404) 325-2954.

Forest History Society, Inc. 701 Vickers Ave., Durham, North Carolina 27701. (919) 682-9319.

Forest Industries Council. 1250 Connecticut Ave., N.W., Suite 320, Washington, District of Columbia 20036. (202) 833-1596.

Forest Trust. PO Box 519, Santa Fe, New Mexico 87504-0519. (505) 983-8992.

Forestry, Conservation Communications Association. c/o Donald W. Pfohl, P.O. Box 1466, Mesa, Arizona 85211-1466. (602) 644-3166.

Friends of the U.S. National Arboretum. 3501 New York Ave., N.E., Washington, District of Columbia 20002. (202) 544-8733.

International Society of Arboriculture. P.O. Box 908, 303 W. University Ave., Urbana, Illinois 61801. (217) 328-2032.

International Tree Crops Institute U.S.A. P.O. Box 4460, Davis, California 95617. (916) 753-4535.

National Association of State Foresters. 444 Capitol St., N.W., Hall of the States, Washington, District of Columbia 20001. (202) 624-5415.

National Council of Forestry Association. c/o Northeastern Loggers Assn., Rt. 28, Box 69, Old Forge, New York 13420. (315) 369-3078.

National Forest Association. 1250 Connecticut Ave.,N.W., Suite 200, Washington, District of Columbia 20036. (202) 463-2700.

National Hardwood Lumber Association. Box 34518, Memphis, Tennessee 38184. (901) 377-1818.

National Parks and Conservation Association. 1015 31st St., N.W., Washington, District of Columbia 20007. (202) 944-8530.

National Recreation & Park Association. 3101 Park Center Dr., Alexandria, Virginia 22302. (703) 820-4940.

National Trails Council. Box 493, Brookings, South Dakota 57006.

National Woodland Owners Association. 374 Maple Ave., E., Suite 210, Vienna, Virginia 22180. (703) 255-2300.

Natural Resources Defense Council. 40 W. 20th St., New York, New York 10011. (212) 727-2700.

New England Forestry Foundation, Inc. 85 Newbury St., Boston, Massachusetts 02116. (617) 437-1441.

New Forests Project. 731 8th St., SE, Washington, District of Columbia 20003. (202) 547-3800.

North American Family Campers Association. 16 Evergreen Terr., North Reading, Massachusetts 01864. (508) 664-4294.

Northeastern Lumber Manufacturers Association. 272 Tuttle Rd., P.O. Box 87 A, Cumberland Center, Maine 04021. (207) 829-6901.

Northwest Forestry Association. 1500 S.W. First Ave., Suite 770, Portland, Oregon 97201. (503) 222-9505.

Pacific Logging Congress. 4494 River Rd., N., Salem, Oregon 97303. (503) 393-6754.

Save the Redwoods League. 114 Sansome St., Rm. 605, San Francisco, California 94104. (415) 362-2352.

Silent Running Society. P.O. Box 529, Howell, New Jersey 07731. (201) 364-0539.

Society for Range Management. 1839 York St., Denver, Colorado 80206. (303) 355-7070.

Society of American Foresters. 5400 Grosvenor Lane, Bethesda, Maryland 20814. (301) 897-8720.

Society of Nematologists. c/o R.N. Huehel, Ph.D., USDA, ARS, Nematology Laboratory, Bldg. 011A BARC-W, Beetsville, Maryland 20705. (301) 344-3081.

Southern Forest Products Association. Box 52468, New Orleans, Louisiana 70152. (504) 443-4464.

Timber Products Manufacturers. 951 E. Third Ave., Spokane, Washington 99202. (509) 535-4646.

TreePeople. 12601 Mulholland Dr., Beverly Hills, California 90210. (818) 753-4600.

Trees for Tomorrow. 611 Sheridan St., P.O. Box 609, Eagle River, Wisconsin 54521. (715) 479-6456.

Western Forestry & Conservation Association. 4033 SW Canyon Rd., Portland, Oregon 97221. (503) 226-4562.

Wilderness Society. 900 17th St., NW, Washington, District of Columbia 20006. (202) 833-2300.

FORMALDEHYDE

ABSTRACTING AND INDEXING SERVICES

Biological Abstracts. BIOSIS, 2100 Arch St., Philadelphia, Pennsylvania 19103-1399. (215) 587-4800. 1927-.

Biotechnology Research Abstracts. Cambridge Scientific Abstracts, 5161 River Rd., Bethesda, Maryland 20816. (301) 961-6750. Monthly. Includes such broad areas as genetic intervention, biochemical genetics, and microbiological techniques.

Chemical Abstracts. Chemical Abstracts Service, 2540 Olentangy River Rd., PO Box 3012, Columbus, Ohio 43210. (800) 848-6533. 1907-.

Environment Abstracts. Bowker A & I Publishing, 121 Chanlon Rd., New Providence, New Jersey 07974. (908) 464-6800. 1974-.

Environment Index. Environment Information Center, Index Research Department, 124 E. 39th St., New York, New York 10016. 1971-. Annual.

Environmental Information Connection–EIC. Planning Information Program, Dept. of Urban and Regional Planning, University of Illinois, 1003 West Nevada, Urbana, Illinois 61801. (217) 333-1369. Also available online.

Environmental Periodicals Bibliography. Environmental Studies Institute, International Academy at Santa Barbara, 800 Garden St., Suite D, Santa Barbara, California 93101. (805) 965-5010. Also available online.

Science Citation Index. Institute for Scientific Information, 3501 Market St., Philadelphia, Pennsylvania 19104. 1961-.

BIBLIOGRAPHIES

EPA Publications Bibliography. U.S. Environmental Protection Agency, Library Systems Branch, 401 M St., SW, Washington, District of Columbia 20460. (202) 260-2090. Quarterly.

Formaldehyde Toxicology. Siles Jackson. National Institutes of Health, Bethesda, Maryland 1982. Adverse effects of formaldehyde.

Health Aspects of Urea-formaldehyde Compounds: A Selected Bibliography with Abstracts. Federation of American Societies for Experimental Biology, 9650 Rockville Pike, Bethesda, Maryland 20814. (301) 530-7000. 1980. Covers urea-formaldehyde resins and insulating materials.

ENCYCLOPEDIAS AND DICTIONARIES

Encyclopedia of Chemical Processing and Design. John J. Mcketta and W. A. Cunningham. Marcel Dekker, Inc., 270 Madison Ave., New York, New York 10016. (212) 696-9000; (800) 228-1160. 1992. Thirty-eight volumes.

Kirk-Othmer Encyclopedia of Chemical Technology. J. I. Kroschwitz, ed. John Wiley & Sons, Inc., 605 3rd Ave., New York, New York 10158-0012. (212) 850-6000. 1992-. All articles in the new edition have been rewritten and updated adding new subjects such as biotechnology, computer topics, analytical techniques and instrumentation, environmental concerns, fuels and energy, inorganic and solid state chemistry; composite materials and material science in general, and pharmaceuticals. Also available online.

GENERAL WORKS

Environmental Issues: An Anthology of 1989. Thomas W. Joyce, ed. TAPPI Press, Technology Park/Atlanta, PO Box 105113, Atlanta, Georgia 30348. (404) 446-1400. 1990. Contains 39 papers on environmental, safety and occupational health concerns from 11 TAPPI, CPPA and AIChE meetings held during 1989. Also included is a literature review of over 200 papers published in 1989.

An Evaluation of Formaldehyde Problems in Residential Mobile Homes. Geomet Inc. U.S. Department of Housing and Urban Development, Office of Policy Development and Research, 451 7th St. SW, Washington, District of Columbia 20410. (202) 708-1422. 1981. Environmental safety measures relating to formaldehyde in mobile homes.

Formaldehyde. World Health Organization, Ave. Appia, Geneva, Switzerland CH-1211. 1989. Physiological effects and toxicology of formaldehyde.

Formaldehyde: Environmental and Technical Information for Problem Spills. Technical Services Branch, Environment Protection Programs Directorate, Environmental Protection Service, 425 St. Joseph Blvd., 3rd Fl., Hull, Quebec, Canada K1A 0H3. (613) 953-5921. 1985.

Formaldehyde: Evidence of Carcinogenicity. U.S. Department of Health and Human Services, Public Health Service, 200 Independence Ave. SW, Washington, District of Columbia 20201. (202) 619-1296. 1981.

Formaldehyde Sensitivity and Toxicity. Susan E. Feinman. CRC Press, 2000 Corporate Blvd. N.W., Boca Raton, Florida 33431. (800) 272-7737. 1988. Covers allergy, contact dermatitis, and allergenicity.

Indoor Air Quality Control Techniques: Radon, Formaldehyde, Combustion Products. W.J. Fisk. Noyes Publications, 120 Mill Rd., Park Ridge, New Jersey 07656. (201) 391-8484. 1987. Air quality in the United States.

Release of Formaldehyde from Various Consumer Products. John A. Pickrell. Inhalation Toxicology Research Institute, Lovelace Biomedical and Environmental Research Institute, PO Box 5890, Albuquerque, New Mexico 87185. (505) 845-1183. 1982. Environmental aspects of formaldehyde.

An Update on Formaldehyde. U.S. Consumer Product Safety Commission, 5401 Westbard Ave., Bethesda, Maryland 20207. (301) 492-6580. 1990.

HANDBOOKS AND MANUALS

Formaldehyde: Analytical Chemistry and Toxicology. Victor Turoski. American Chemical Society, 1155 16th St. N.W., Washington, District of Columbia 20036. (800) 227-5558. 1985.

ONLINE DATA BASES

BIOSIS Previews. BIOSIS, 2100 Arch St., Philadelphia, Pennsylvania 19103-1399. (215) 587-4800. Largest and most comprehensive database of research in the life sciences. Contains citations for nearly 9000 primary research journals, monographs, reviews, symposia, preliminary reports, semi-popular journals, selected institutional reports, government reports and research communications.

Chemical Abstracts-CA. Chemical Abstracts Service, 2540 Olentangy River Rd., P.O. Box 3012, Columbus, Ohio 43210. (800) 848-6533 or (614) 421-3600. Information sources include 9000 journals, patents from 27 countries, two industrial property organizations, new books, conference proceedings, and government research reports.

Enviro/Energyline Abstracts Plus. R. R. Bowker Co., 121 Chanlon Rd., New Providence, New Jersey 07974. (908) 464-6800.

Environmental Periodicals Bibliography. National Information Services Corp., Ste. 6, Wyman Towers, 3100 St. Paul St., Baltimore, Maryland 21218. (410)243-0797. Online version of abstract of same name.

Kirk-Othmer Encyclopedia of Chemical Technology. John Wiley & Sons, Inc., 605 3rd Ave., 5th Floor, New York, New York 10158. (212) 850-6000. Online version of the publication of the same name.

PERIODICALS AND NEWSLETTERS

Indoor Pollution News. Buraff Publications, 1350 Connecticut Ave., NW, Suite 100, Washington, District of Columbia 20036. (202) 862-0990. Biweekly. Air quality in buildings (including radon, formaldehyde, solvents and asbestos) or other air pollutions, such as lead in pipes.

TRADE ASSOCIATIONS AND PROFESSIONAL SOCIETIES

American Chemical Society. 1155 16th St., N.W., Washington, District of Columbia 20036. (202) 872-4600.

Cure Formaldehyde Poisoning Association. 9255 Lynnwood Rd., Waconia, Minnesota 55387. (612) 442-4665.

Formaldehyde Institute. 1330 Connecticut Ave., N.W., Suite 300, Washington, District of Columbia 20036. (202) 659-0060.

FOSSIL FUELS

See also: FUELS

ABSTRACTING AND INDEXING SERVICES

Advanced Fossil Energy Technologies. National Technical Information Service, 5285 Port Royal Road, Springfield, Virginia 22161. (703) 487-4650. Bimonthly. Department of Energy-sponsored reports in the field of fossil energy technology.

Aqualine Abstracts. Water Research Centre. c/o Pergamon Microforms International, Inc., Fairview Park, Elmsford, New York 10523. (914) 592-7720. 1927-. Contains some 8,000 records annually on water and wastewater technology. Covers all aspects of water, wastewater, associated engineering services and the aquatic environment. Over 600 periodicals, as well as books, reports and conference proceedings and other publications from water related institutions worldwide are scanned. Also available online.

Biological Abstracts. BIOSIS, 2100 Arch St., Philadelphia, Pennsylvania 19103-1399. (215) 587-4800. 1927-.

Ecological Abstracts. Geo Abstracts Ltd. Elsevier Applied Science, Crown House, Linton Rd., Barking, England IG 11 8JU. 1974-. Derived from over 600 leading ecological and environmental journals, plus books, conference proceedings, reports and theses.

Science Citation Index. Institute for Scientific Information, 3501 Market St., Philadelphia, Pennsylvania 19104. 1961-.

GENERAL WORKS

Cool Energy: The Renewable Solution to Global Warming. Michael Brower. Union of Concerned Scientists, 26 Church St., Cambridge, Massachusetts 02238. (617) 547-5552. 1990. Describes how fossil fuel and renewable energy sources could be used to avoid global warming and air pollution.

CPSC Warns of Carbon Monoxide Hazard with Oil/ Wood Combination Furnaces. U.S. Consumer Product Safety Commission, 5401 Westbard Ave., Bethesda, Maryland 20207. (301) 492-6580. 1984. Safety measures relating to carbon monoxide and product safety of furnaces.

Emission Control in Electricity Generation and Industry. OECD Publications and Information Center, 2001 L St., N.W., Suite 700, Washington, District of Columbia 20036. (202) 785-OECD. 1989. Describes progress in IEA countries in reducing the impact of fossil fuel burning on the environment; systems in place for SO2 and NOx control; economic and energy security implications of the various emissions control strategies; of more rational use of energy; the development of combined heat and power and district heating.

Global Energy Futures and the Carbon Dioxide Problem. Council on Environmental Quality, Old Executive Office Bldg., Rm. 154, Washington, District of Columbia 20500. (202) 395-5080. 1981. Fossil fuels and energy policy.

The Homeowner's Guide to Coalburning Stoves and Furnaces. James Warner Morrison. Arco Pub. Inc., 215 Park Ave. S., New York, New York 10003. 1981.

Minding the Carbon Store: Weighing U.S. Forestry Strategies to Slow Global Warming. Mark C. Trexler. World Resources Institute, 1709 New York Ave. N.W., Washington, District of Columbia 20006. (800) 833 0504. 1991. Assesses the strengths and weaknesses of each of the major domestic forestry options, including their costs and carbon benefits.

Power Generation and the Environment. P. S. Liss and P. A. H. Saunders. Oxford University Press, 200 Madison Ave., New York, New York 10016. (212) 679-7300; (800) 334-4249. 1990. Analyses the problems and possibilities inherent in producing electricity on a large scale.

ONLINE DATA BASES

BIOSIS Previews. BIOSIS, 2100 Arch St., Philadelphia, Pennsylvania 19103-1399. (215) 587-4800. Largest and most comprehensive database of research in the life sciences. Contains citations for nearly 9000 primary research journals, monographs, reviews, symposia, preliminary reports, semi-popular journals, selected institutional reports, government reports and research communications.

EBIB. Texas A & M University, Sterling C. Evans Library, Reference Division, College Station, Texas 77843. (409) 845-5741.

TRADE ASSOCIATIONS AND PROFESSIONAL SOCIETIES

American Institute of Biological Sciences. 730 11th St., N.W., Washington, District of Columbia 20001-4521. (202) 628-1500.

FRACTIONAL DISTILLATION

See: DISTILLATION

FREEZING

See: FOOD PROCESSING AND TREATMENT

FREIGHT TRANSPORTATION

See: TRANSPORTATION

FREON

See also: OZONE LAYER

ABSTRACTING AND INDEXING SERVICES

Applied Science and Technology Index. H.W. Wilson Co., 950 University Ave., Bronx, New York 10452. (800) 367-6770. Formerly Industrial Arts Index.

Biological Abstracts. BIOSIS, 2100 Arch St., Philadelphia, Pennsylvania 19103-1399. (215) 587-4800. 1927-.

Biological and Agricultural Index. H.W. Wilson Co., 950 University Ave., Bronx, New York 10452. (800) 367-6770. 1916-. Monthly.

Chemical Abstracts. Chemical Abstracts Service, 2540 Olentangy River Rd., PO Box 3012, Columbus, Ohio 43210. (800) 848-6533. 1907-.

Science Citation Index. Institute for Scientific Information, 3501 Market St., Philadelphia, Pennsylvania 19104. 1961-.

ENCYCLOPEDIAS AND DICTIONARIES

Van Nostrand's Scientific Encyclopedia. Glenn D. Considine, ed. Van Nostrand Reinhold, 115 5th Ave., New York, New York 10003. (212) 254-3232. 1983. Sixth edition. Includes all broad subject areas in science.

ONLINE DATA BASES

BIOSIS Previews. BIOSIS, 2100 Arch St., Philadelphia, Pennsylvania 19103-1399. (215) 587-4800. Largest and most comprehensive database of research in the life sciences. Contains citations for nearly 9000 primary research journals, monographs, reviews, symposia, preliminary reports, semi-popular journals, selected institutional reports, government reports and research communications.

Chemical Abstracts-CA. Chemical Abstracts Service, 2540 Olentangy River Rd., P.O. Box 3012, Columbus, Ohio 43210. (800) 848-6533 or (614) 421-3600. Information sources include 9000 journals, patents from 27 countries, two industrial property organizations, new books, conference proceedings, and government research reports.

SCISEARCH. Institute for Scientific Information, University City Science Center, 3501 Market St., Philadelphia, Pennsylvania 19104. (215) 386-0100.

TRADE ASSOCIATIONS AND PROFESSIONAL SOCIETIES

American Chemical Society. 1155 16th St., N.W., Washington, District of Columbia 20036. (202) 872-4600.

FRESHWATER ECOSYSTEMS

See also: AQUATIC BIOMES; AQUATIC ECOSYSTEMS

ABSTRACTING AND INDEXING SERVICES

Applied Ecology Abstracts Studies in Renewable Natural Resources. Information Retrieval Ltd., 1911 Jefferson Davis Highway, Arlington, Virginia 22202. 1975-. Monthly.

Aqualine Abstracts. Water Research Centre. c/o Pergamon Microforms International, Inc., Fairview Park, Elmsford, New York 10523. (914) 592-7720. 1927-. Contains some 8,000 records annually on water and wastewater technology. Covers all aspects of water, wastewater, associated engineering services and the aquatic environment. Over 600 periodicals, as well as books, reports and conference proceedings and other publications from water related institutions worldwide are scanned. Also available online.

Biological Abstracts. BIOSIS, 2100 Arch St., Philadelphia, Pennsylvania 19103-1399. (215) 587-4800. 1927-.

Biological and Agricultural Index. H.W. Wilson Co., 950 University Ave., Bronx, New York 10452. (800) 367-6770. 1916-. Monthly.

Chemical Abstracts. Chemical Abstracts Service, 2540 Olentangy River Rd., PO Box 3012, Columbus, Ohio 43210. (800) 848-6533. 1907-.

Current Advances in Ecological and Environmental Science. Pergamon Microforms International, Inc., Fairview Park, Elmsford, New York 10523. (914) 592-7720. 1989-. Monthly. Current literature searching service including journals, reports, abstracts, etc. This service is available online as part of the CABS database on the hosts BRS and ORBIT search service.

Ecological Abstracts. Geo Abstracts Ltd. Elsevier Applied Science, Crown House, Linton Rd., Barking, England IG 11 8JU. 1974-. Derived from over 600 leading ecological and environmental journals, plus books, conference proceedings, reports and theses.

Ecology Abstracts. Cambridge Scientific Abstracts, 5161 River Rd., Bethesda, Maryland 20816. (301) 961-6750. Monthly.

Environment Abstracts. Bowker A & I Publishing, 121 Chanlon Rd., New Providence, New Jersey 07974. (908) 464-6800. 1974-.

Environment Index. Environment Information Center, Index Research Department, 124 E. 39th St., New York, New York 10016. 1971-. Annual.

Environmental Information Connection–EIC. Planning Information Program, Dept. of Urban and Regional Planning, University of Illinois, 1003 West Nevada, Urbana, Illinois 61801. (217) 333-1369. Also available online.

Environmental Periodicals Bibliography. Environmental Studies Institute, International Academy at Santa Barbara, 800 Garden St., Suite D, Santa Barbara, California 93101. (805) 965-5010. Also available online.

General Science Index. H. W. Wilson Co., 950 University Ave., Bronx, New York 10452. 1978-. Monthly, also issued in annual cumulation. Cumulative subject index to English language periodicals in the subject fields of astronomy, botany, chemistry, earth science, environment and conservation, food and nutrition, genetics, mathematics, medicine and health, microbiology, oceanography, physics, physiology and zoology.

Geographical Abstracts. London School of Economics, Dept. of Geography, Regency House, 34 Duke St., London, England 1966-. Continued by Geo Abstracts issued in 6 parts: Pt. A. Landforms and the quaternary; Pt. B. Biogeography and Climatology; Pt. C. Economic geography; Pt. D. Social geography and cartography; Pt. E. Sedimentology; Pt. F. Regional and community planning.

Index to Scientific Book Contents. Institute for Scientific Information, 3501 Market St., Philadelphia, Pennsylvania 19104. (800) 523-1857. 1985-. Annual. Gives contents of science books published.

Multimedia Index to Ecology. National Information Center for Educational Media, University of Southern California, Los Angeles, California 90007.

Pollution Abstracts. Cambridge Scientific Abstracts, 5161 River Rd., Bethesda, Maryland 20816. (301) 961-6750. Six/year. Indexes worldwide technical literature on environmental pollution. Covers air pollution, marine and freshwater pollution, sewage and wastewater treatment, waste management, toxicology and health, noise pollution, radiation, land pollution, and environmental policies, programs, legislation, and education. Also available online.

Science Citation Index. Institute for Scientific Information, 3501 Market St., Philadelphia, Pennsylvania 19104. 1961-.

BIBLIOGRAPHIES

Current Contents. Agriculture, Biology and Environmental Sciences. Institute for Scientific Information, 3501 Market St., Philadelphia, Pennsylvania 19104. (800) 523-1857. 1973-. Previous title: Current Contents. Agricultural, Food & Veterinary Sciences. Gives the table of contents of periodicals in the fields of agriculture, biology, environmental and related areas.

Directory of Published Proceedings. Interdok Corp., 173 Halstead Ave., Harrison, New York 10528. (914) 835-3506. 1990. Monthly. This is a listing of published proceedings including the series SEMTE (Science/Medicine/Engineering/Technology) and the series SSH (Social Science/Humanities).

EPA Publications Bibliography. U.S. Environmental Protection Agency, Library Systems Branch, 401 M St., SW, Washington, District of Columbia 20460. (202) 260-2090. Quarterly.

ENCYCLOPEDIAS AND DICTIONARIES

Cambridge Encyclopedia of Life Sciences. A. E. Friday and David S. Ingram. Cambridge University Press, 40 W 20th St., New York, New York 10011. (212) 924-3900 or (800) 227-0247. 1985. Includes all topics under biology and ecology.

The Encyclopedia of Animal Ecology. Peter D. Moore. Facts on File, Inc., 460 Park Ave. S., New York, New York 10016. (212) 683-2244. 1987.

McGraw-Hill Encyclopedia of Environmental Science. Sybil P. Parker. McGraw-Hill Science & Engineering Books, 11 W. 19th St., New York, New York 10011. (212) 337-6010. 1980. Covers ecology, man's influence on nature, and environmental protection.

McGraw-Hill Encyclopedia of Science and Technology. McGraw-Hill, 1221 Avenue of the Americas, New York, New York 10020. (212) 512-2000 or (800) 262-4729. 1992. Seventh edition. Issued in multiple volumes including index. Includes all science and technology broad subject areas.

GENERAL WORKS

Alternatives in Regulated River Management. J. A. Gore and G. E. Petts, eds. CRC Press, 2000 Corporate Blvd. N.W., Boca Raton, Florida 33431. (800) 272-7737. 1989. Provides an alternative to the emphasis on ecological effects of river regulation and is a source of alternatives for managerial decision making.

Better Trout Habitat. Christopher J. Hunter. Island Press, 1718 Connecticut Ave. N.W., Suite 300, Washington, District of Columbia 20009. (202) 232-7933. 1991. Explains the physical, chemical and biological needs of trout, and shows how climate, geology, vegetation, and flowing water all help to create trout habitats. Book includes 14 detailed case studies of successful trout stream restoration projects.

Biogeochemistry of Major World Rivers. Egon T. Degens, et al. John Wiley & Sons, Inc., 605 3rd Ave., New York, New York 10158-0012. (212) 850-6000. 1991.

Cache la Poudre: The Natural History of Rocky Mountain River. Howard Ensign Evans and Mary Alice Evans. University Press of Colorado, PO Box 849, Niwot, Colorado 80544. (303) 530-5337. 1991. Includes a summary of the ecological and cultural values of the river corridor. Describes the corridor's flora, fauna, geology, insects, people and history.

Flagellates in Freshwater Ecosystems. R. I. Jones. Kluwer Academic Publishers, 101 Philip Dr., Assinippi Park,

Norwell, Massachusetts 02061. (617) 871-6600. 1988. Developments in hydrobiology and freshwater invertebrates.

Freshwater Ecology: Principles and Applications. Michael Jeffries and Derek Mills. Belhaven Press, 136 S. Broadway, Irvington, New York 10533. (914) 591-9111. 1991. Explains and illustrates the principles of freshwater ecology and their application to the management and conservation of plant and animal life, and the impact of human actions on lakes, rivers and streams.

Life History and Ecology of the Slider Turtle. J. Whitfield Gibbons. Smithsonian Institution Press, 470 L'Enfant Plaza #7100, Washington, District of Columbia 20560. (800) 782-4612. 1990. Deals with all that is known about a species, its taxonomic status and genetics, reproduction and growth, population structure and demography, population ecology, and bioenergetics.

Regulatory Protection of Critical Transitional Areas Within Freshwater Wetlands Ecosystems. Curtis R. LaPierre. University of Illinois, Urbana-Champaign, Illinois 61801. 1990. Law and legislation relating to watershed management.

River Pollution: An Ecological Perspective. S. M. Haslam. Belhaven Press, 136 S. Broadway, Irvington, New York 10533. (914) 591-9111. 1990. Describes the impact of natural and man-made pollution in the ecosystem of freshwater streams, stressing understanding of processes and techniques of measurement.

Turtles of the World. Carl H. Ernst and Roger W. Barbour. Smithsonian Institution Press, 470 L'Enfant Plaza #7100, Washington, District of Columbia 20560. (800) 782-4612. 1989. Comprehensive coverage of the world's 257 turtle species.

The Uses of Ecology: Lake Washington and Beyond. W. T. Edmondson. University of Washington Press, PO Box 50096, Seattle, Washington 98145-5096. (206) 543-4050; (800) 441-4115. 1991. Author delivered most of the contents of this book as a Danz lecture at the University of Washington. Gives an account of the pollution and recovery of Lake Washington and describes how communities worked and applied lessons learned from Lake Washington cleanup. Includes extensive documentation and bibliographies.

Water. Hans Silvester. Thomasson-Grant, 1 Morton Dr., Suite 500, Charlottesville, Virginia 22901. (804) 977-1780. 1990. Details the dangers posed by the industrial society to the flow of clean water

HANDBOOKS AND MANUALS

Biota of Freshwater Ecosystems Identification Manual. U.S. Environmental Protection Agency, 401 M St., SW, Washington, District of Columbia 20460. (202) 260-2090. 1972. Water pollution control research relating to fresh-water fauna.

The Functioning of Freshwater Ecosystems. E. D. Le Cren and R. H. Lowe-McConnell. Cambridge University Press, 40 W. 20th St., New York, New York 10011. (212) 924-3900. 1979. Freshwater ecology and freshwater productivity.

ONLINE DATA BASES

BIOSIS Previews. BIOSIS, 2100 Arch St., Philadelphia, Pennsylvania 19103-1399. (215) 587-4800. Largest and

most comprehensive database of research in the life sciences. Contains citations for nearly 9000 primary research journals, monographs, reviews, symposia, preliminary reports, semi-popular journals, selected institutional reports, government reports and research communications.

Chemical Abstracts-CA. Chemical Abstracts Service, 2540 Olentangy River Rd., P.O. Box 3012, Columbus, Ohio 43210. (800) 848-6533 or (614) 421-3600. Information sources include 9000 journals, patents from 27 countries, two industrial property organizations, new books, conference proceedings, and government research reports.

Current Research Information System–CRIS/USDA. U.S. Department of Agriculture, National Agricultural Library, 10301 Baltimore Blvd., 5th Floor, Beltsville, Maryland 20705-2351. (301) 504-5755. Looks at current research projects in agriculture and allied sciences covering the biological, physical, social and behavioral sciences related to agriculture.

Enviro/Energyline Abstracts Plus. R. R. Bowker Co., 121 Chanlon Rd., New Providence, New Jersey 07974. (908) 464-6800.

Environmental Periodicals Bibliography. National Information Services Corp., Ste. 6, Wyman Towers, 3100 St. Paul St., Baltimore, Maryland 21218. (410)243-0797. Online version of abstract of same name.

Monthly Catalog of United States Government Publications. U.S. G.P.O., Supt. of Docs., PO Box 371954, Pittsburgh, Pennsylvania 15250-7954. (202) 512-0000.

National Stream Quality Accounting Network. National Water Data Exchange, U.S. Geological Survey, 421 National Center, Reston, Virginia 22092. (703) 648-4000. 150 hydrologic measurements collected at daily, monthly and quarterly intervals from more than 500 monitoring stations in the U.S.

National Technical Information Service. U.S. Department of Commerce, National Technical Information Service, Office of Data Base Services, 5285 Port Royal Rd., Springfield, Virginia 22161. (703) 487-4807. Bibliographic database of government sponsored research and technical reports.

PERIODICALS AND NEWSLETTERS

Applied and Environmental Microbiology Journal. American Society for Microbiology, 1325 Massachusetts Avenue N.W., Washington, District of Columbia 20005. (202) 737-3600. Monthly. Articles on industrial and food microbiology and ecological studies.

Facets of Freshwater. Freshwater Biological Research Foundation, 2500 Shadywood Rd., Box 90, Navarre, Minnesota 55392. (612) 471-8407. 1970-. Quarterly. Topics in freshwater biological research.

Florida Environments. Florida Environments Pub., 215 N. Main St., PO Box 1617, High Springs, Florida 32643. (904) 454-2007. Monthly. Florida's hazardous materials/wastes, wildlife, regulation, drinking/ground/surface waters, air, and solid waste.

The Journal of Freshwater. Freshwater Biological Research Foundation, 2500 Shadywood Rd., Box 90, Navarre, Minnesota 55392. (612) 471-8407. 1977-. Quarterly.

Journal of Groundwater. Association of Ground Water Scientists and Engineers, Division of National Water Well Association, 6375 Riverside Dr., Dublin, Ohio 43017. (614) 761-1711. 1963-. Bimonthly. Serial dealing with all forms of ground water and its quality.

RESEARCH CENTERS AND INSTITUTES

Academy of Natural Sciences of Philadelphia, Division of Environmental Research. 19th Street and the Parkway, Philadelphia, Pennsylvania 19103. (215) 299-1081.

Center for Limnology. University of Colorado-Boulder, Department of EPO Biology, Boulder, Colorado 80309-0334. (303) 492-6379.

Rensselaer Polytechnic Institute, Rensselaer Fresh Water Institute. MRC 203, Troy, New York 12181-3590. (518) 276-6757.

University of Georgia, Institute of Ecology. 103 Ecology Building, Athens, Georgia 30602. (404) 542-2968.

University of Hawaii at Manoa Hawaii Cooperative Fishery Research Unit. 2538 The Mall, Honolulu, Hawaii 96822. (808) 956-8350.

University of Kansas, Kansas Biological Survey. 2041 Constant Avenue-Foley Hall, Lawrence, Kansas 66047-2906. (913) 864-7725.

University of Maryland, Center for Environmental and Estuarine Studies. Center Operations, Horn Point, P.O.Box 775, Cambridge, Maryland 21613. (410) 228-9250.

University of Minnesota, Gray Freshwater Biological Institute. P.O. Box 100, Navarre, Minnesota 55392. (612) 471-8476.

University of Mississippi, Biological Museum. Department of Biology, University, Mississippi 38677. (601) 232-7204.

University of Pittsburgh, Pymatuning Laboratory of Ecology. R.R. #1, Box 7, Linesville, Pennsylvania 16424. (814) 683-5813.

University of Texas at Arlington, Center for Corbicula Research. Department of Biology, P.O.Box 19498, Arlington, Texas 76019. (817) 273-2412.

University of Texas at Austin, Culture Collection of Algae. Department of Botany, Austin, Texas 78713. (512) 471-4019.

University of Washington, Laboratory of Radiation Ecology. Fisheries Research Center, College of Fisheries, Seattle, Washington 98195. (206) 543-4259.

University of Wisconsin-Madison, Center for Biotic Systems. 1042 WARF Office Building, 610 Walnut Street, Madison, Wisconsin 53705. (608) 262-9937.

Water and Energy Research Institute of the Western Pacific (*WERI*). University of Guam, UOG Station, Guam 96923. (617) 734-3132.

World Resources Institute. 1709 New York Ave., N.W., Washington, District of Columbia 20006. (202) 638-6300.

TRADE ASSOCIATIONS AND PROFESSIONAL SOCIETIES

American Institute of Biological Sciences. 730 11th St., N.W., Washington, District of Columbia 20001-4521. (202) 628-1500.

American Society of Naturalists. Department of Ecology and Evolation, State University of New York, Stony Brook, New York 11794. (516) 632-8589.

Association of Ground Water Scientists and Engineers. PO Box 1248, Hardwick, Vermont 05843. (803) 472-6956.

Freshwater Foundation. spring Hill Center, 728 County Rd. 6, Wayzata, New Mexico 55391. (612) 449-0092.

FRESHWATER FISH

See: FISH

FUEL ADDITIVES

ABSTRACTING AND INDEXING SERVICES

Applied Science and Technology Index. H.W. Wilson Co., 950 University Ave., Bronx, New York 10452. (800) 367-6770. Formerly Industrial Arts Index.

Chemical Abstracts. Chemical Abstracts Service, 2540 Olentangy River Rd., PO Box 3012, Columbus, Ohio 43210. (800) 848-6533. 1907-.

Engineering Index. The Engineering Index Inc., 345 E. 47th St., New York, New York 10017. 1962-.

Environment Abstracts. Bowker A & I Publishing, 121 Chanlon Rd., New Providence, New Jersey 07974. (908) 464-6800. 1974-.

Environment Index. Environment Information Center, Index Research Department, 124 E. 39th St., New York, New York 10016. 1971-. Annual.

Environmental Information Connection–EIC. Planning Information Program, Dept. of Urban and Regional Planning, University of Illinois, 1003 West Nevada, Urbana, Illinois 61801. (217) 333-1369. Also available online.

Environmental Periodicals Bibliography. Environmental Studies Institute, International Academy at Santa Barbara, 800 Garden St., Suite D, Santa Barbara, California 93101. (805) 965-5010. Also available online.

ERDA Research Abstracts. U.S. ERDA Technical Information Center, Box 62, Oak Ridge, Tennessee 37830.

General Science Index. H. W. Wilson Co., 950 University Ave., Bronx, New York 10452. 1978-. Monthly, also issued in annual cumulation. Cumulative subject index to English language periodicals in the subject fields of astronomy, botany, chemistry, earth science, environment and conservation, food and nutrition, genetics, mathematics, medicine and health, microbiology, oceanography, physics, physiology and zoology.

Index to Scientific Book Contents. Institute for Scientific Information, 3501 Market St., Philadelphia, Pennsylvania 19104. (800) 523-1857. 1985-. Annual. Gives contents of science books published.

Physics Briefs. Physikalische Berichte. Physik Verlag, Pappapelallee 3, Postfach 101161, Weinheim, Germany D-6940. 1979-. Semimonthly. In English. Volumes for 1979- issued by the Deutsche Physikalische Gesellschaft and the Fachinformationszentrum Energie Physik, Mathematik in cooperation with the American Institute of Physics.

Pollution Abstracts. Cambridge Scientific Abstracts, 5161 River Rd., Bethesda, Maryland 20816. (301) 961-6750. Six/year. Indexes worldwide technical literature on environmental pollution. Covers air pollution, marine and freshwater pollution, sewage and wastewater treatment, waste management, toxicology and health, noise pollution, radiation, land pollution, and environmental policies, programs, legislation, and education. Also available online.

Science Citation Index. Institute for Scientific Information, 3501 Market St., Philadelphia, Pennsylvania 19104. 1961-.

BIBLIOGRAPHIES

EPA Publications Bibliography. U.S. Environmental Protection Agency, Library Systems Branch, 401 M St., SW, Washington, District of Columbia 20460. (202) 260-2090. Quarterly.

ENCYCLOPEDIAS AND DICTIONARIES

Encyclopedia of Physical Science and Technology. Robert A. Meyers, ed. Academic Press, c/o Harcourt Brace Jovanovich Inc., 6277 Sea Harbor Dr., Orlando, Florida 32887. (800) 346-8648. Dictionary of engineering, technology and physical sciences.

Encyclopedia of Physics. Rita G. Lerner and George L. Trigg. VCH Publishers, 303 NW 12th Ave., Deerfield Beach, Florida 33442-1788. (305) 428-5566. 1991. Second edition.

GENERAL WORKS

Effects of Fuel Additives on Air Pollutant Emissions from Distillated-Oil-Fired Furnaces. G. B. Martin. U.S. Environmental Protection Agency, Office of Air Programs, MD 75, Research Triangle Park, North Carolina 27711. 1971. Air pollution caused by oil burners and petroleum additives.

Fuels and Fuel Additives for Highway Vehicles and Their Combustion Products. National Research Council, Committee on Toxicology. National Academy of Sciences, 2101 Constitution Ave., NW, Washington, District of Columbia 20418. (202) 334-2000. 1976. Evaluation of the potential effects of fuels and fuel additives on health.

Gasoline and Diesel Fuel Additives. K. Owen. John Wiley & Sons Inc., 605 3rd Ave., New York, New York 10158-0012. (212) 850-6000. 1989. Environmental effects of motor fuels-additives and diesel fuels- additives.

HANDBOOKS AND MANUALS

Clean Air Handbook. Government Institutes, Inc., 4 Research Pl., Ste. 200, Rockville, Maryland 20850. (301) 921-2300. Analyzes the requirements of the Clean Air Act and its 1990 amendments, as well as what can be expected in terms of new regulation.

ONLINE DATA BASES

Chemical Abstracts-CA. Chemical Abstracts Service, 2540 Olentangy River Rd., P.O. Box 3012, Columbus, Ohio 43210. (800) 848-6533 or (614) 421-3600. Information sources include 9000 journals, patents from 27 countries, two industrial property organizations, new books, conference proceedings, and government research reports.

Computerized Engineering Index–COMPENDEX. Engineering Information Inc., 345 E. 47th St., New York, New York 10017. (212) 705-7600.

Enviro/Energyline Abstracts Plus. R. R. Bowker Co., 121 Chanlon Rd., New Providence, New Jersey 07974. (908) 464-6800.

Environmental Periodicals Bibliography. National Information Services Corp., Ste. 6, Wyman Towers, 3100 St. Paul St., Baltimore, Maryland 21218. (410)243-0797. Online version of abstract of same name.

PressNet Environmental Reports. Chemical Information Systems, Inc., 7215 York Rd., Baltimore, Maryland 21212. (301) 321-8440.

TRADE ASSOCIATIONS AND PROFESSIONAL SOCIETIES

Diethylenetriamine Producers Importers Alliance. 1330 Connecticut Ave., N.W., Washington, District of Columbia 20036. (202) 659-0060.

Ethylene Oxide Industry Council. 2501 M St., N.W., Suite 330, Washington, District of Columbia 20037. (202) 887-1100.

FUEL GAS DESULFURIZATION
See: DESULFURIZATION

FUEL STORAGE ACCIDENTS

ABSTRACTING AND INDEXING SERVICES

Applied Science and Technology Index. H.W. Wilson Co., 950 University Ave., Bronx, New York 10452. (800) 367-6770. Formerly Industrial Arts Index.

Engineering Index. The Engineering Index Inc., 345 E. 47th St., New York, New York 10017. 1962-.

Environment Abstracts. Bowker A & I Publishing, 121 Chanlon Rd., New Providence, New Jersey 07974. (908) 464-6800. 1974-.

Environment Index. Environment Information Center, Index Research Department, 124 E. 39th St., New York, New York 10016. 1971-. Annual.

Environmental Information Connection–EIC. Planning Information Program, Dept. of Urban and Regional Planning, University of Illinois, 1003 West Nevada, Urbana, Illinois 61801. (217) 333-1369. Also available online.

Environmental Periodicals Bibliography. Environmental Studies Institute, International Academy at Santa Barbara, 800 Garden St., Suite D, Santa Barbara, California 93101. (805) 965-5010. Also available online.

ERDA Research Abstracts. U.S. ERDA Technical Information Center, Box 62, Oak Ridge, Tennessee 37830.

General Science Index. H. W. Wilson Co., 950 University Ave., Bronx, New York 10452. 1978-. Monthly, also issued in annual cumulation. Cumulative subject index to English language periodicals in the subject fields of astronomy, botany, chemistry, earth science, environment and conservation, food and nutrition, genetics, mathematics, medicine and health, microbiology, oceanography, physics, physiology and zoology.

BIBLIOGRAPHIES

EPA Publications Bibliography. U.S. Environmental Protection Agency, Library Systems Branch, 401 M St., SW, Washington, District of Columbia 20460. (202) 260-2090. Quarterly.

ENCYCLOPEDIAS AND DICTIONARIES

Dictionary of Environmental Engineering and Related Sciences: English-Spanish, Spanish-English. Jose T. Villate. Ediciones Universal, 3090 SW 8th St., Miami, Florida 33135. (305) 642-3355. 1979.

Encyclopedia of Environmental Science and Engineering. J.R. Pfafflin. Gordon and Breach Science Publishers, Inc., 270 8th Ave., New York, New York 10011. (212) 206-8900. 1992.

Encyclopedia of Physical Science and Technology. Robert A. Meyers, ed. Academic Press, c/o Harcourt Brace Jovanovich Inc., 6277 Sea Harbor Dr., Orlando, Florida 32887. (800) 346-8648. Dictionary of engineering, technology and physical sciences.

McGraw-Hill Encyclopedia of Environmental Science. Sybil P. Parker. McGraw-Hill Science & Engineering Books, 11 W. 19th St., New York, New York 10011. (212) 337-6010. 1980. Covers ecology, man's influence on nature, and environmental protection.

ONLINE DATA BASES

Computerized Engineering Index–COMPENDEX. Engineering Information Inc., 345 E. 47th St., New York, New York 10017. (212) 705-7600.

Enviro/Energyline Abstracts Plus. R. R. Bowker Co., 121 Chanlon Rd., New Providence, New Jersey 07974. (908) 464-6800.

Environmental Periodicals Bibliography. National Information Services Corp., Ste. 6, Wyman Towers, 3100 St. Paul St., Baltimore, Maryland 21218. (410)243-0797. Online version of abstract of same name.

Monthly Catalog of United States Government Publications. U.S. G.P.O., Supt. of Docs., PO Box 371954, Pittsburgh, Pennsylvania 15250-7954. (202) 512-0000.

National Technical Information Service. U.S. Department of Commerce, National Technical Information Service, Office of Data Base Services, 5285 Port Royal Rd., Springfield, Virginia 22161. (703) 487-4807. Bibliographic database of government sponsored research and technical reports.

PressNet Environmental Reports. Chemical Information Systems, Inc., 7215 York Rd., Baltimore, Maryland 21212. (301) 321-8440.

FUEL STORAGE TANKS

ABSTRACTING AND INDEXING SERVICES

Applied Science and Technology Index. H.W. Wilson Co., 950 University Ave., Bronx, New York 10452. (800) 367-6770. Formerly Industrial Arts Index.

Engineering Index. The Engineering Index Inc., 345 E. 47th St., New York, New York 10017. 1962-.

Environment Abstracts. Bowker A & I Publishing, 121 Chanlon Rd., New Providence, New Jersey 07974. (908) 464-6800. 1974-.

Environment Index. Environment Information Center, Index Research Department, 124 E. 39th St., New York, New York 10016. 1971-. Annual.

Environmental Information Connection–EIC. Planning Information Program, Dept. of Urban and Regional Planning, University of Illinois, 1003 West Nevada, Urbana, Illinois 61801. (217) 333-1369. Also available online.

Environmental Periodicals Bibliography. Environmental Studies Institute, International Academy at Santa Barbara, 800 Garden St., Suite D, Santa Barbara, California 93101. (805) 965-5010. Also available online.

ERDA Research Abstracts. U.S. ERDA Technical Information Center, Box 62, Oak Ridge, Tennessee 37830.

General Science Index. H. W. Wilson Co., 950 University Ave., Bronx, New York 10452. 1978-. Monthly, also issued in annual cumulation. Cumulative subject index to English language periodicals in the subject fields of astronomy, botany, chemistry, earth science, environment and conservation, food and nutrition, genetics, mathematics, medicine and health, microbiology, oceanography, physics, physiology and zoology.

BIBLIOGRAPHIES

EPA Publications Bibliography. U.S. Environmental Protection Agency, Library Systems Branch, 401 M St., SW, Washington, District of Columbia 20460. (202) 260-2090. Quarterly.

Spent Fuel Storage. National Technical Information Service, 5285 Port Royal Rd., Springfield, Virginia 22161. (703) 487-4650. 1984. Bibliography of spent reactor fuel storage and reactor fuel reprocessing.

ENCYCLOPEDIAS AND DICTIONARIES

Dictionary of Environmental Engineering and Related Sciences: English-Spanish, Spanish-English. Jose T. Villate. Ediciones Universal, 3090 SW 8th St., Miami, Florida 33135. (305) 642-3355. 1979.

Encyclopedia of Environmental Science and Engineering. J.R. Pfafflin. Gordon and Breach Science Publishers, Inc., 270 8th Ave., New York, New York 10011. (212) 206-8900. 1992.

Encyclopedia of Physical Science and Technology. Robert A. Meyers, ed. Academic Press, c/o Harcourt Brace Jovanovich Inc., 6277 Sea Harbor Dr., Orlando, Florida 32887. (800) 346-8648. Dictionary of engineering, technology and physical sciences.

McGraw-Hill Encyclopedia of Environmental Science. Sybil P. Parker. McGraw-Hill Science & Engineering Books, 11 W. 19th St., New York, New York 10011. (212) 337-6010. 1980. Covers ecology, man's influence on nature, and environmental protection.

GENERAL WORKS

Aboveground Storage Tank Management: A Practical Guide. Joyce A. Rizzo and Albert D. Young. Government Institutes, Inc., 4 Research Pl., Suite 200, Rockville, Maryland 20850. (301) 921-2300. 1990. Describes how to design, build, manage, and operate above ground storage tanks in compliance with federal and state regulations.

American National Standard, Criticality Safety Criteria for the Handling, Storage and Transportation of LWR Fuel Outside Reactors. American Nuclear Society. American Nuclear Society, 555 N. Kensington Ave., La Grange Park, Illinois 60525. (708) 352-6611. 1984. Safety measures and standards relating to nuclear fuels.

American National Standard Guidelines for Establishing Site- Related Parameters for Site Selection and Design of an Independent Spent Fuel Storage Installation. American National Standards Institute. American Nuclear Society, 555 N. Kensington Ave., La Grange Park, Illinois 60525. (708) 352-6611. 1981.

Design Bases for Facilities for LMFBR Spent Fuel Storage in Liquid Metal Outside the Primary Coolant Boundary. American National Standards Institute. American Nuclear Society, 555 N. Kensington Ave., La Grange Park, Illinois 60525. (708) 352-6611. 1985. Spent reactor fuel storage standards.

Distillate Fuel. Howard L. Chesneau. ASTM, 1916 Race St., Philadelphia, Pennsylvania 19103-1187. (215) 299-5400. 1988. Contamination, storage, and handling.

Improved Fire Protection for Underground Fuel Storage and Fuel Transfer Areas. William H. Pomroy. U.S. Department of the Interior, Bureau of Mines, Pittsburgh, Pennsylvania 1985. Prevention and control of mine fires and underground storage of petroleum products.

Storage of Water Reactor Spent Fuel in Water Pools: Survey of World Experience. International Atomic Energy and the Nuclear Energy Agency. UNIPUB, 4611-F Assembly Dr., Lanham Seabrook, Maryland 20706-4391. (301) 459-7666. 1982. Nuclear fuels storage techniques.

Underground Storage Tank Management: A Practical Guide. Hart Environmental Management Corp. Government Institutes Inc., 4 Research Place, Suite 200, Rockville, Maryland 20850. (301) 921-2300. 1991. 3rd ed. Presents the latest in the state-of-the-art tank design, how to predict tank leaks, test tank integrity, avoid costly tank replacement through low-cost retrofit and maintenance techniques, and how to respond to leaks.

HANDBOOKS AND MANUALS

Fuel Handling and Storage Systems in Nuclear Power Plants: A Safety Guide. International Atomic Energy Agency. UNIPUB, 1984. Safety measures relating to nuclear fuels and atomic power plants.

Guidebook on Spent Fuel Storage. International Atomic Energy Agency, Wagramerstrasse 5, Vienna, Austria A-1400. 222 23606198. 1991. Radioactive waste disposal.

ONLINE DATA BASES

Computerized Engineering Index–COMPENDEX. Engineering Information Inc., 345 E. 47th St., New York, New York 10017. (212) 705-7600.

Enviro/Energyline Abstracts Plus. R. R. Bowker Co., 121 Chanlon Rd., New Providence, New Jersey 07974. (908) 464-6800.

Environmental Periodicals Bibliography. National Information Services Corp., Ste. 6, Wyman Towers, 3100 St. Paul St., Baltimore, Maryland 21218. (410)243-0797. Online version of abstract of same name.

Monthly Catalog of United States Government Publications. U.S. G.P.O., Supt. of Docs., PO Box 371954, Pittsburgh, Pennsylvania 15250-7954. (202) 512-0000.

National Technical Information Service. U.S. Department of Commerce, National Technical Information Service, Office of Data Base Services, 5285 Port Royal Rd., Springfield, Virginia 22161. (703) 487-4807. Bibliographic database of government sponsored research and technical reports.

PressNet Environmental Reports. Chemical Information Systems, Inc., 7215 York Rd., Baltimore, Maryland 21212. (301) 321-8440.

STATISTICS SOURCES

Spent Nuclear Fuel Discharges from U.S. Reactors. U.S. G.P.O., Washington, District of Columbia 20402-9325. (202) 512-0000. 1991. Commercial nuclear power plant spent fuel discharges, shipments, storage capacity, and inventory.

FUEL SUBSTITUTION

ABSTRACTING AND INDEXING SERVICES

Applied Science and Technology Index. H.W. Wilson Co., 950 University Ave., Bronx, New York 10452. (800) 367-6770. Formerly Industrial Arts Index.

Chemical Abstracts. Chemical Abstracts Service, 2540 Olentangy River Rd., PO Box 3012, Columbus, Ohio 43210. (800) 848-6533. 1907-.

Engineering Index. The Engineering Index Inc., 345 E. 47th St., New York, New York 10017. 1962-.

Environment Abstracts. Bowker A & I Publishing, 121 Chanlon Rd., New Providence, New Jersey 07974. (908) 464-6800. 1974-.

Environment Index. Environment Information Center, Index Research Department, 124 E. 39th St., New York, New York 10016. 1971-. Annual.

Environmental Information Connection–EIC. Planning Information Program, Dept. of Urban and Regional Planning, University of Illinois, 1003 West Nevada, Urbana, Illinois 61801. (217) 333-1369. Also available online.

Environmental Periodicals Bibliography. Environmental Studies Institute, International Academy at Santa Barbara, 800 Garden St., Suite D, Santa Barbara, California 93101. (805) 965-5010. Also available online.

General Science Index. H. W. Wilson Co., 950 University Ave., Bronx, New York 10452. 1978-. Monthly, also issued in annual cumulation. Cumulative subject index to English language periodicals in the subject fields of astronomy, botany, chemistry, earth science, environment and conservation, food and nutrition, genetics, mathematics, medicine and health, microbiology, oceanography, physics, physiology and zoology.

Geographical Abstracts. London School of Economics, Dept. of Geography, Regency House, 34 Duke St., London, England 1966-. Continued by Geo Abstracts issued in 6 parts: Pt. A. Landforms and the quaternary; Pt. B. Biogeography and Climatology; Pt. C. Economic geography; Pt. D. Social geography and cartography; Pt. E. Sedimentology; Pt. F. Regional and community planning.

Physics Briefs. Physikalische Berichte. Physik Verlag, Pappapelallee 3, Postfach 101161, Weinheim, Germany D-6940. 1979-. Semimonthly. In English. Volumes for 1979- issued by the Deutsche Physikalische Gesellschaft and the Fachinformationszentrum Energie Physik, Mathematik in cooperation with the American Institute of Physics.

BIBLIOGRAPHIES

EPA Publications Bibliography. U.S. Environmental Protection Agency, Library Systems Branch, 401 M St., SW, Washington, District of Columbia 20460. (202) 260-2090. Quarterly.

DIRECTORIES

Directory of Energy Alternatives. Energy Research Inst., 6850 Rattlesnake Hammock Rd., Naples, Florida 33962. (813) 793-1922. Semimonthly. Individuals and companies interested in development of alternative energy sources, including alcohol, wind, methane, solar, biomass, waste, and hydrogen.

Energy Resource Institute–Directory of Energy Alternatives. Energy Research Institute, 6850 Rattlesnake Hammock Rd., Hwy. 951, Naples, Florida 33962. (813) 793-1922.

Generating Energy Alternatives. Investor Responsibility Research Center, 1755 Massachusetts Ave., N.W., Suite 600, Washington, District of Columbia 20036. (202) 939-7500.

Independent Energy–Industry Directory Issue. Alternative Sources of Energy, Inc., 107 S. Central Ave., Milaca, Minnesota 56353. (612) 983-6892.

Manufacturers List. Synerjy, Box 1854, Cathedral Station, New York, New York 10025. (212) 865-9595.

ENCYCLOPEDIAS AND DICTIONARIES

Dictionary of Environmental Engineering and Related Sciences: English-Spanish, Spanish-English. Jose T. Villate. Ediciones Universal, 3090 SW 8th St., Miami, Florida 33135. (305) 642-3355. 1979.

Encyclopedia of Environmental Science and Engineering. J.R. Pfafflin. Gordon and Breach Science Publishers, Inc., 270 8th Ave., New York, New York 10011. (212) 206-8900. 1992.

Encyclopedia of Physical Science and Technology. Robert A. Meyers, ed. Academic Press, c/o Harcourt Brace

Jovanovich Inc., 6277 Sea Harbor Dr., Orlando, Florida 32887. (800) 346-8648. Dictionary of engineering, technology and physical sciences.

McGraw-Hill Encyclopedia of Environmental Science. Sybil P. Parker. McGraw-Hill Science & Engineering Books, 11 W. 19th St., New York, New York 10011. (212) 337-6010. 1980. Covers ecology, man's influence on nature, and environmental protection.

GENERAL WORKS

Driving Forces: Motor Vehicle Trends and Their Implications for Global Warming, Energy Strategies, and Transportation. James J. MacKenzie and Michael P. Walsh. World Resources Institute, 1709 New York Ave., Washington, District of Columbia 20006. (800) 822-0504. 1990. Overview of new-vehicle fuel efficiency, reductions in air pollution emissions, and overall improvements in transportation and land-use as they relate to global warming planning. Also available through State University of New York Press.

Replacing Gasoline: Alternative Fuels for Light-Duty Vehicles. Congress of the U.S., c/o U.S. Government Printing Office, Office of Technology Assesment, N. Capitol & H Sts. NW, Washington, District of Columbia 20401. (202) 512-0000. 1990. Gives information on alternatives to standard gasoline. Some of the alternatives are: electricity, hydrogen, compressed natural gas, liquified natural gas, liquid propane gas, methanol, ethanol, and reformulated gasoline.

Steering a New Course: Transportation, Energy and the Environment. Deborah Gordon. Island Press, 1718 Connecticut Ave. N.W., Suite 300, Washington, District of Columbia 20009. (202) 232-7933. 1991. Includes a history of modern American transportation, an overview of the U.S. transportation sector, and an in-depth discussion of the strategies that hold the most promise for the future. Also has information on alternative fuels, advances in mass transit, ultra fuel efficient vehicles, high-occupancy vehicle facilities and telecommuting and alternative work schedules.

ONLINE DATA BASES

Chemical Abstracts-CA. Chemical Abstracts Service, 2540 Olentangy River Rd., P.O. Box 3012, Columbus, Ohio 43210. (800) 848-6533 or (614) 421-3600. Information sources include 9000 journals, patents from 27 countries, two industrial property organizations, new books, conference proceedings, and government research reports.

Clean-Coal/Synfuels Letter. McGraw-Hill Science & Engineering Books, 11 W. 19th St., New York, New York 10011. (212) 337-6010.

Computerized Engineering Index–COMPENDEX. Engineering Information Inc., 345 E. 47th St., New York, New York 10017. (212) 705-7600.

Enviro/Energyline Abstracts Plus. R. R. Bowker Co., 121 Chanlon Rd., New Providence, New Jersey 07974. (908) 464-6800.

Environmental Periodicals Bibliography. National Information Services Corp., Ste. 6, Wyman Towers, 3100 St. Paul St., Baltimore, Maryland 21218. (410)243-0797. Online version of abstract of same name.

Monthly Catalog of United States Government Publications. U.S. G.P.O., Supt. of Docs., PO Box 371954, Pittsburgh, Pennsylvania 15250-7954. (202) 512-0000.

National Technical Information Service. U.S. Department of Commerce, National Technical Information Service, Office of Data Base Services, 5285 Port Royal Rd., Springfield, Virginia 22161. (703) 487-4807. Bibliographic database of government sponsored research and technical reports.

PressNet Environmental Reports. Chemical Information Systems, Inc., 7215 York Rd., Baltimore, Maryland 21212. (301) 321-8440.

PERIODICALS AND NEWSLETTERS

Alternate Energy Transportation. Campbell Publishing, EV Consultants, Inc., PO Box 20041, New York, New York 10025. (212) 222-0160. Monthly. Vehicles powered by natural gas, methanol, hydrogen, or direct energy from the sun.

Alternative Energy. AE Publications, 205 S. Beverly Dr., Suite 208, Beverly Hills, California 90212. (310) 273-3486. Monthly. Biomass, solar photovoltaic, solar thermal, hydrogen fuel, nuclear fusion, battery systems, and cogeneration.

TRADE ASSOCIATIONS AND PROFESSIONAL SOCIETIES

Alternative Energy Resources Organization. 44 N. Last Chance Gulch, Helena, Montana 59601. (406) 443-7272.

FUEL TRANSPORT ACCIDENTS

ABSTRACTING AND INDEXING SERVICES

Applied Science and Technology Index. H.W. Wilson Co., 950 University Ave., Bronx, New York 10452. (800) 367-6770. Formerly Industrial Arts Index.

Engineering Index. The Engineering Index Inc., 345 E. 47th St., New York, New York 10017. 1962-.

Environment Abstracts. Bowker A & I Publishing, 121 Chanlon Rd., New Providence, New Jersey 07974. (908) 464-6800. 1974-.

Environment Index. Environment Information Center, Index Research Department, 124 E. 39th St., New York, New York 10016. 1971-. Annual.

Environmental Information Connection–EIC. Planning Information Program, Dept. of Urban and Regional Planning, University of Illinois, 1003 West Nevada, Urbana, Illinois 61801. (217) 333-1369. Also available online.

Environmental Periodicals Bibliography. Environmental Studies Institute, International Academy at Santa Barbara, 800 Garden St., Suite D, Santa Barbara, California 93101. (805) 965-5010. Also available online.

ERDA Research Abstracts. U.S. ERDA Technical Information Center, Box 62, Oak Ridge, Tennessee 37830.

General Science Index. H. W. Wilson Co., 950 University Ave., Bronx, New York 10452. 1978-. Monthly, also issued in annual cumulation. Cumulative subject index to English language periodicals in the subject fields of astronomy, botany, chemistry, earth science, environ-

ment and conservation, food and nutrition, genetics, mathematics, medicine and health, microbiology, oceanography, physics, physiology and zoology.

BIBLIOGRAPHIES

Directory of Published Proceedings. Interdok Corp., 173 Halstead Ave., Harrison, New York 10528. (914) 835-3506. 1990. Monthly. This is a listing of published proceedings including the series SEMTE (Science/Medicine/Engineering/Technology) and the series SSH (Social Science/Humanities).

EPA Publications Bibliography. U.S. Environmental Protection Agency, Library Systems Branch, 401 M St., SW, Washington, District of Columbia 20460. (202) 260-2090. Quarterly.

ENCYCLOPEDIAS AND DICTIONARIES

Dictionary of Environmental Engineering and Related Sciences: English-Spanish, Spanish-English. Jose T. Villate. Ediciones Universal, 3090 SW 8th St., Miami, Florida 33135. (305) 642-3355. 1979.

Encyclopedia of Environmental Science and Engineering. J.R. Pfafflin. Gordon and Breach Science Publishers, Inc., 270 8th Ave., New York, New York 10011. (212) 206-8900. 1992.

Encyclopedia of Physical Science and Technology. Robert A. Meyers, ed. Academic Press, c/o Harcourt Brace Jovanovich Inc., 6277 Sea Harbor Dr., Orlando, Florida 32887. (800) 346-8648. Dictionary of engineering, technology and physical sciences.

McGraw-Hill Encyclopedia of Environmental Science. Sybil P. Parker. McGraw-Hill Science & Engineering Books, 11 W. 19th St., New York, New York 10011. (212) 337-6010. 1980. Covers ecology, man's influence on nature, and environmental protection.

ONLINE DATA BASES

Computerized Engineering Index–COMPENDEX. Engineering Information Inc., 345 E. 47th St., New York, New York 10017. (212) 705-7600.

Enviro/Energyline Abstracts Plus. R. R. Bowker Co., 121 Chanlon Rd., New Providence, New Jersey 07974. (908) 464-6800.

Environmental Periodicals Bibliography. National Information Services Corp., Ste. 6, Wyman Towers, 3100 St. Paul St., Baltimore, Maryland 21218. (410)243-0797. Online version of abstract of same name.

Monthly Catalog of United States Government Publications. U.S. G.P.O., Supt. of Docs., PO Box 371954, Pittsburgh, Pennsylvania 15250-7954. (202) 512-0000.

National Technical Information Service. U.S. Department of Commerce, National Technical Information Service, Office of Data Base Services, 5285 Port Royal Rd., Springfield, Virginia 22161. (703) 487-4807. Bibliographic database of government sponsored research and technical reports.

PressNet Environmental Reports. Chemical Information Systems, Inc., 7215 York Rd., Baltimore, Maryland 21212. (301) 321-8440.

FUELS

ABSTRACTING AND INDEXING SERVICES

Applied Science and Technology Index. H.W. Wilson Co., 950 University Ave., Bronx, New York 10452. (800) 367-6770. Formerly Industrial Arts Index.

Chemical Abstracts. Chemical Abstracts Service, 2540 Olentangy River Rd., PO Box 3012, Columbus, Ohio 43210. (800) 848-6533. 1907-.

Energy Information Abstracts Annual 1987 in Retrospect. EIC/Intelligence Inc., 121 Chanlon Rd., New Providence, New Jersey 07974. (908) 464-6800. 1988. Annual. Cumulative edition of the monthly Energy Information Abstracts. Monitors sources in the field of energy including the scientific, technical and business journal literature, conference and symposia proceedings, corporate, government and academic reports.

Engineering Index. The Engineering Index Inc., 345 E. 47th St., New York, New York 10017. 1962-.

Environment Abstracts. Bowker A & I Publishing, 121 Chanlon Rd., New Providence, New Jersey 07974. (908) 464-6800. 1974-.

Environment Index. Environment Information Center, Index Research Department, 124 E. 39th St., New York, New York 10016. 1971-. Annual.

Environmental Information Connection–EIC. Planning Information Program, Dept. of Urban and Regional Planning, University of Illinois, 1003 West Nevada, Urbana, Illinois 61801. (217) 333-1369. Also available online.

Environmental Periodicals Bibliography. Environmental Studies Institute, International Academy at Santa Barbara, 800 Garden St., Suite D, Santa Barbara, California 93101. (805) 965-5010. Also available online.

General Science Index. H. W. Wilson Co., 950 University Ave., Bronx, New York 10452. 1978-. Monthly, also issued in annual cumulation. Cumulative subject index to English language periodicals in the subject fields of astronomy, botany, chemistry, earth science, environment and conservation, food and nutrition, genetics, mathematics, medicine and health, microbiology, oceanography, physics, physiology and zoology.

Geographical Abstracts. London School of Economics, Dept. of Geography, Regency House, 34 Duke St., London, England 1966-. Continued by Geo Abstracts issued in 6 parts: Pt. A. Landforms and the quaternary; Pt. B. Biogeography and Climatology; Pt. C. Economic geography; Pt. D. Social geography and cartography; Pt. E. Sedimentology; Pt. F. Regional and community planning.

Index to Scientific Book Contents. Institute for Scientific Information, 3501 Market St., Philadelphia, Pennsylvania 19104. (800) 523-1857. 1985-. Annual. Gives contents of science books published.

Physics Briefs. Physikalische Berichte. Physik Verlag, Pappapelallee 3, Postfach 101161, Weinheim, Germany D-6940. 1979-. Semimonthly. In English. Volumes for 1979- issued by the Deutsche Physikalische Gesellschaft and the Fachinformationszentrum Energie Physik, Mathematik in cooperation with the American Institute of Physics.

Pollution Abstracts. Cambridge Scientific Abstracts, 5161 River Rd., Bethesda, Maryland 20816. (301) 961-6750. Six/year. Indexes worldwide technical literature on environmental pollution. Covers air pollution, marine and freshwater pollution, sewage and wastewater treatment, waste management, toxicology and health, noise pollution, radiation, land pollution, and environmental policies, programs, legislation, and education. Also available online.

Science Citation Index. Institute for Scientific Information, 3501 Market St., Philadelphia, Pennsylvania 19104. 1961-.

BIBLIOGRAPHIES

Bibliography and Index of Geology. American Geological Institute, 4220 King St., Alexandria, Virginia 22302. Monthly. Includes environmental geology and hydrogeology.

Directory of Published Proceedings. Interdok Corp., 173 Halstead Ave., Harrison, New York 10528. (914) 835-3506. 1990. Monthly. This is a listing of published proceedings including the series SEMTE (Science/Medicine/Engineering/Technology) and the series SSH (Social Science/Humanities).

EPA Publications Bibliography. U.S. Environmental Protection Agency, Library Systems Branch, 401 M St., SW, Washington, District of Columbia 20460. (202) 260-2090. Quarterly.

DIRECTORIES

Fuel Oil News–Source Book Issue. Hunter Publishing Company, Inc., 950 Lee St., Des Plaines, Illinois 60016. (708) 296-0770.

Wood Heating Alliance–Membership Directory. Wood Heating Alliance, 1101 Connecticut Ave., N.W., Suite 700, Washington, District of Columbia 20036. (202) 857-1181.

ENCYCLOPEDIAS AND DICTIONARIES

Dictionary of Energy. Malcolm Slesser. Nichols Pub., PO Box 96, New York, New York 10024. 1988. Provides information on concepts, ideas, definitions and explanations in areas of interdisciplinary nature connected with energy.

Encyclopedia of Physical Science and Technology. Robert A. Meyers, ed. Academic Press, c/o Harcourt Brace Jovanovich Inc., 6277 Sea Harbor Dr., Orlando, Florida 32887. (800) 346-8648. Dictionary of engineering, technology and physical sciences.

Energy Dictionary. V. Daniel Hunt. Van Nostrand Reinhold, 115 5th Ave., New York, New York 10003. (212) 254-3232. 1979. Covers the broad field of energy including fossil, nuclear, solar, geothermal, ocean, and wind energy.

McGraw-Hill Encyclopedia of Environmental Science. Sybil P. Parker. McGraw-Hill Science & Engineering Books, 11 W. 19th St., New York, New York 10011. (212) 337-6010. 1980. Covers ecology, man's influence on nature, and environmental protection.

McGraw-Hill Encyclopedia of Science and Technology. McGraw-Hill, 1221 Avenue of the Americas, New York, New York 10020. (212) 512-2000 or (800) 262-4729.

1992. Seventh edition. Issued in multiple volumes including index. Includes all science and technology broad subject areas.

Van Nostrand's Scientific Encyclopedia. Glenn D. Considine, ed. Van Nostrand Reinhold, 115 5th Ave., New York, New York 10003. (212) 254-3232. 1983. Sixth edition. Includes all broad subject areas in science.

GENERAL WORKS

Biomass, Catalysts and Liquid Fuels. Technomic Publishing Co., 851 New Holland Ave., Box 3535, Lancaster, Pennsylvania 17604. (717) 291-5609.

Car Trouble. James J. MacKenzie, et al. World Resources Institute, 1709 New York Ave., N.W., Washington, District of Columbia 20006. 1992. Reviews the technical options for air purification, cleaner fuels, more flexible transportation systems, and more intelligent city planning, among others.

Drive for Clean Air: Natural Gas and Methane Vehicles. James Spencer Cannon. INFORM, 381 Park Ave. S., New York, New York 10016. (212) 689-4040. 1989.

Driving Forces: Motor Vehicle Trends and Their Implications for Global Warming, Energy Strategies, and Transportation. James J. MacKenzie and Michael P. Walsh. World Resources Institute, 1709 New York Ave., Washington, District of Columbia 20006. (800) 822-0504. 1990. Overview of new-vehicle fuel efficiency, reductions in air pollution emissions, and overall improvements in transportation and land-use as they relate to global warming planning. Also available through State University of New York Press.

Magill's Survey of Science. Earth Science Series. Frank N. Magill. Salem Press, PO Box 50062, Pasadena, California 91105. 1990-. Five volumes. Includes information on earth's crust, hot spots and volcanic island chains, physical properties of minerals, rock magnetism, physical properties of rocks, and index.

Replacing Gasoline: Alternative Fuels for Light-Duty Vehicles. Congress of the U.S., c/o U.S. Government Printing Office, Office of Technology Assesment, N. Capitol & H Sts. NW, Washington, District of Columbia 20401. (202) 512-0000. 1990. Gives information on alternatives to standard gasoline. Some of the alternatives are: electricity, hydrogen, compressed natural gas, liquified natural gas, liquid propane gas, methanol, ethanol, and reformulated gasoline.

Solar Hydrogen: Moving Beyond Fossil Fuels. Joan M. Ogden and Robert H. Williams. World Resources Institute, 1709 New York Ave. N.W., Washington, District of Columbia 20006. (800) 822-0504. 1989. Traces the technical breakthroughs associated with solar hydrogen. Assesses the new fuel's potential as a replacement for oil, compares its costs and uses with those of both traditional and synthetic fuels, and charts a path for developing solar hydrogen markets.

Steering a New Course: Transportation, Energy and the Environment. Deborah Gordon. Island Press, 1718 Connecticut Ave. N.W., Suite 300, Washington, District of Columbia 20009. (202) 232-7933. 1991. Includes a history of modern American transportation, an overview of the U.S. transportation sector, and an in-depth discussion of the strategies that hold the most promise for the future. Also has information on alternative fuels, advances in mass transit, ultra fuel efficient vehicles, high-occupancy vehicle facilities and telecommuting and alternative work schedules.

Substitute Fuels for Road Transport: A Technology Assessment. OECD Publications and Information Center, 2001 L. St., N.W., Suite 700, Washington, District of Columbia 20036. (202) 785-OECD. 1990. Report analyzes the availability, economics, technical problems and effects on the environment from the use of substitute fuels.

GOVERNMENTAL ORGANIZATIONS

U.S. Environmental Protection Agency: Office of Mobile Services. 401 M St., S.W., Washington, District of Columbia 20460. (202) 382-7645.

ONLINE DATA BASES

Alternative Energy Digests. International Academy at Santa Barbara, 800 Garden St., Suite D, Santa Barbara, California 93101. (805) 965-5010.

Chemical Abstracts-CA. Chemical Abstracts Service, 2540 Olentangy River Rd., P.O. Box 3012, Columbus, Ohio 43210. (800) 848-6533 or (614) 421-3600. Information sources include 9000 journals, patents from 27 countries, two industrial property organizations, new books, conference proceedings, and government research reports.

Computerized Engineering Index–COMPENDEX. Engineering Information Inc., 345 E. 47th St., New York, New York 10017. (212) 705-7600.

EBIB. Texas A & M University, Sterling C. Evans Library, Reference Division, College Station, Texas 77843. (409) 845-5741.

Enviro/Energyline Abstracts Plus. R. R. Bowker Co., 121 Chanlon Rd., New Providence, New Jersey 07974. (908) 464-6800.

Environmental Periodicals Bibliography. National Information Services Corp., Ste. 6, Wyman Towers, 3100 St. Paul St., Baltimore, Maryland 21218. (410)243-0797. Online version of abstract of same name.

Monthly Catalog of United States Government Publications. U.S. G.P.O., Supt. of Docs., PO Box 371954, Pittsburgh, Pennsylvania 15250-7954. (202) 512-0000.

National Technical Information Service. U.S. Department of Commerce, National Technical Information Service, Office of Data Base Services, 5285 Port Royal Rd., Springfield, Virginia 22161. (703) 487-4807. Bibliographic database of government sponsored research and technical reports.

PERIODICALS AND NEWSLETTERS

Biomass and Bioenergy. Pergamon Microforms International, Inc., Fairview Park, Elmsford, New York 10523. (914) 592-7720. 1991-. Monthly. Key areas covered by this journal are: Biomass-sources, energy, crop production processes, genetic improvements, composition; biological residues: wastes from agricultural production and forestry, processing industries, and municipal sources; bioenergy processes: fermentations, thermochemical conversions, liquid and gaseous fuels, and petrochemical substitutes; bioenergy utilization: direct combustion gasification, electricity production, chemical processes, and by-product remediation. Also includes environmental

management and economic aspects of biomass and bioenergy.

The Clean Fuels Report. J. E. Sinor Consultants, Inc., 6964 North 79th Street, Suite 1, PO Box 649, Niwot, Colorado 80544. (303) 652-2632. Deals with new fuel choices, costs, and regulations.

RESEARCH CENTERS AND INSTITUTES

Bemidji State University, Center for Environmental Studies. Bemidji, Minnesota 56601. (218) 755-2910.

STATISTICS SOURCES

New Directions in Transportation Fuels. FIND/SVP, 625 Avenue of the Americas, New York, New York 10011. (212) 645-4500. 1991. Covers the following modes of transport: cars, buses, trucks, jet aircraft and railroads.

World Resources. World Resources Institute. 1709 New York Ave., N.W., Washington, District of Columbia 20006. (202) 638-6300. Annual. Statistical and textual analysis of world's natural resources and the effects of growth-caused environmental pollution.

TRADE ASSOCIATIONS AND PROFESSIONAL SOCIETIES

Clean Fuels Development Coalition. 1129 20th St., N.W., Suite 500, Washington, District of Columbia 20036. (202) 822-1715.

Council on Alternate Fuels. 1225 Eye St., Suite 320, Washington, District of Columbia 20005. (202) 898-0711.

Institute of Gas Technology. 1225 I. St., N.W., Suite 320, Washington, District of Columbia 20005. (202) 898-0711.

Wood Heating Alliance. 1101 Connecticut Ave., N.W., Suite 700, Washington, District of Columbia 20036. (202) 857-1181.

FUMIGANTS

See also: PESTICIDES

ABSTRACTING AND INDEXING SERVICES

Applied Science and Technology Index. H.W. Wilson Co., 950 University Ave., Bronx, New York 10452. (800) 367-6770. Formerly Industrial Arts Index.

Biological Abstracts. BIOSIS, 2100 Arch St., Philadelphia, Pennsylvania 19103-1399. (215) 587-4800. 1927-.

Biological and Agricultural Index. H.W. Wilson Co., 950 University Ave., Bronx, New York 10452. (800) 367-6770. 1916-. Monthly.

Chemical Abstracts. Chemical Abstracts Service, 2540 Olentangy River Rd., PO Box 3012, Columbus, Ohio 43210. (800) 848-6533. 1907-.

Ecology Abstracts. Cambridge Scientific Abstracts, 5161 River Rd., Bethesda, Maryland 20816. (301) 961-6750. Monthly.

Environment Abstracts. Bowker A & I Publishing, 121 Chanlon Rd., New Providence, New Jersey 07974. (908) 464-6800. 1974-.

Environment Index. Environment Information Center, Index Research Department, 124 E. 39th St., New York, New York 10016. 1971-. Annual.

Environmental Information Connection–EIC. Planning Information Program, Dept. of Urban and Regional Planning, University of Illinois, 1003 West Nevada, Urbana, Illinois 61801. (217) 333-1369. Also available online.

Environmental Periodicals Bibliography. Environmental Studies Institute, International Academy at Santa Barbara, 800 Garden St., Suite D, Santa Barbara, California 93101. (805) 965-5010. Also available online.

General Science Index. H. W. Wilson Co., 950 University Ave., Bronx, New York 10452. 1978-. Monthly, also issued in annual cumulation. Cumulative subject index to English language periodicals in the subject fields of astronomy, botany, chemistry, earth science, environment and conservation, food and nutrition, genetics, mathematics, medicine and health, microbiology, oceanography, physics, physiology and zoology.

Index to Scientific Book Contents. Institute for Scientific Information, 3501 Market St., Philadelphia, Pennsylvania 19104. (800) 523-1857. 1985-. Annual. Gives contents of science books published.

Pesticides Abstracts. U.S. Environmental Protection Agency, Office of Pesticides Programs, 345 Curtland, Atlanta, Georgia 30365. (404) 347-2864. 1981. Monthly. Formerly: Health Aspects of Pesticides Abstracts Bulletin.

Pollution Abstracts. Cambridge Scientific Abstracts, 5161 River Rd., Bethesda, Maryland 20816. (301) 961-6750. Six/year. Indexes worldwide technical literature on environmental pollution. Covers air pollution, marine and freshwater pollution, sewage and wastewater treatment, waste management, toxicology and health, noise pollution, radiation, land pollution, and environmental policies, programs, legislation, and education. Also available online.

Science Citation Index. Institute for Scientific Information, 3501 Market St., Philadelphia, Pennsylvania 19104. 1961-.

BIBLIOGRAPHIES

EPA Publications Bibliography. U.S. Environmental Protection Agency, Library Systems Branch, 401 M St., SW, Washington, District of Columbia 20460. (202) 260-2090. Quarterly.

ENCYCLOPEDIAS AND DICTIONARIES

McGraw-Hill Encyclopedia of Environmental Science. Sybil P. Parker. McGraw-Hill Science & Engineering Books, 11 W. 19th St., New York, New York 10011. (212) 337-6010. 1980. Covers ecology, man's influence on nature, and environmental protection.

Van Nostrand's Scientific Encyclopedia. Glenn D. Considine, ed. Van Nostrand Reinhold, 115 5th Ave., New York, New York 10003. (212) 254-3232. 1983. Sixth edition. Includes all broad subject areas in science.

HANDBOOKS AND MANUALS

Agricultural Chemicals. William Thomas Thomson. Thomson Publications, Box 9335, Fresno, California 93791. (209) 435-2163. 1991. Book 1: Insecticides and acaricides. Book 2: Herbicides. Book 3: Fumigants, growth regulators, repellents and rodenticides. Book 4: Fungicides.

Pesticide Background Statements. Volume II, Fungicides and Fumigants. J.F. Sassaman. Forest Service, U.S. Department of Agriculture, PO Box 96090, Washington, District of Columbia 20090. (202) 720-3760. 1986.

ONLINE DATA BASES

BIOSIS Previews. BIOSIS, 2100 Arch St., Philadelphia, Pennsylvania 19103-1399. (215) 587-4800. Largest and most comprehensive database of research in the life sciences. Contains citations for nearly 9000 primary research journals, monographs, reviews, symposia, preliminary reports, semi-popular journals, selected institutional reports, government reports and research communications.

CERCLIS. Chemical Information Systems, Inc., 7215 York Rd., Baltimore, Maryland 21212. (301) 321-8440. Information on hazardous waste disposal sites that have either been listed by the EPA on the National Priority List (NPL) or nominated for consideration for the NPL.

Chemical Abstracts-CA. Chemical Abstracts Service, 2540 Olentangy River Rd., P.O. Box 3012, Columbus, Ohio 43210. (800) 848-6533 or (614) 421-3600. Information sources include 9000 journals, patents from 27 countries, two industrial property organizations, new books, conference proceedings, and government research reports.

Chemical Carcinogenesis Research Information System–CCRIS. National Library of Medicine, 8600 Rockville Pike, Bethesda, Maryland 20894. (800) 638-8480. Individual assay results and test conditions for 1,451 chemicals in the areas of carcinogenicity, mutagenicity, tumor promotion, and cocarcinogenicity.

Chemical Collection System/Request Tracking–CCS/RTS. U.S. Environmental Protection Agency, Office of Pesticides and Toxic Substances, 401 M St., SW, Washington, District of Columbia 20460. (202) 260-2090. Contains information on various properties of a number of chemicals including environmental effects, test and analysis methods, and health effects. Available from EPA.

Chemical Dictionary Online–CHEMLINE. Chemical Abstracts Service, 2540 Olentangy River Rd., Columbus, Ohio 43210. (614) 421-3600 or (800) 848-6533. Part of MEDLINE of the National Library of Medicine (NLM). File of 900,000 names for chemical substances, representing 450,000 unique compounds. It contains such information as Chemical Abstracts (CA) Service Registry Numbers, molecular formulas, preferred chemical nomenclature, and generic and ring structure information. Available on NLM's ELHILL system.

Chemical Exposure. Science Applications International Corp., Health & Environmental Information, P.O. Box 2501, Oak Ridge, Tennessee 37831. (615) 482-9031. Database of chemicals that have been identified in both human tissues and body fluids and in feral and food animals. Contains reference to journal articles, conferences, and reports. Covers the whole fields of informa-

tion related to human and animal exposure to food, air, and water contaminants and pharmaceuticals. Its records include information on chemical properties, formulas, tissues measured, analytical method used, demographics and more. Available on DIALOG.

Enviro/Energyline Abstracts Plus. R. R. Bowker Co., 121 Chanlon Rd., New Providence, New Jersey 07974. (908) 464-6800.

Environmental Periodicals Bibliography. National Information Services Corp., Ste. 6, Wyman Towers, 3100 St. Paul St., Baltimore, Maryland 21218. (410)243-0797. Online version of abstract of same name.

Monthly Catalog of United States Government Publications. U.S. G.P.O., Supt. of Docs., PO Box 371954, Pittsburgh, Pennsylvania 15250-7954. (202) 512-0000.

National Technical Information Service. U.S. Department of Commerce, National Technical Information Service, Office of Data Base Services, 5285 Port Royal Rd., Springfield, Virginia 22161. (703) 487-4807. Bibliographic database of government sponsored research and technical reports.

SCISEARCH. Institute for Scientific Information, University City Science Center, 3501 Market St., Philadelphia, Pennsylvania 19104. (215) 386-0100.

FUMIGATION

See also: PESTICIDES

ABSTRACTING AND INDEXING SERVICES

Applied Science and Technology Index. H.W. Wilson Co., 950 University Ave., Bronx, New York 10452. (800) 367-6770. Formerly Industrial Arts Index.

Biological Abstracts. BIOSIS, 2100 Arch St., Philadelphia, Pennsylvania 19103-1399. (215) 587-4800. 1927-.

Biological and Agricultural Index. H.W. Wilson Co., 950 University Ave., Bronx, New York 10452. (800) 367-6770. 1916-. Monthly.

Chemical Abstracts. Chemical Abstracts Service, 2540 Olentangy River Rd., PO Box 3012, Columbus, Ohio 43210. (800) 848-6533. 1907-.

Ecology Abstracts. Cambridge Scientific Abstracts, 5161 River Rd., Bethesda, Maryland 20816. (301) 961-6750. Monthly.

Environment Abstracts. Bowker A & I Publishing, 121 Chanlon Rd., New Providence, New Jersey 07974. (908) 464-6800. 1974-.

Environment Index. Environment Information Center, Index Research Department, 124 E. 39th St., New York, New York 10016. 1971-. Annual.

Environmental Information Connection–EIC. Planning Information Program, Dept. of Urban and Regional Planning, University of Illinois, 1003 West Nevada, Urbana, Illinois 61801. (217) 333-1369. Also available online.

Environmental Periodicals Bibliography. Environmental Studies Institute, International Academy at Santa Barba-

ra, 800 Garden St., Suite D, Santa Barbara, California 93101. (805) 965-5010. Also available online.

Pesticides Abstracts. U.S. Environmental Protection Agency, Office of Pesticides Programs, 345 Curtland, Atlanta, Georgia 30365. (404) 347-2864. 1981. Monthly. Formerly: Health Aspects of Pesticides Abstracts Bulletin.

Pollution Abstracts. Cambridge Scientific Abstracts, 5161 River Rd., Bethesda, Maryland 20816. (301) 961-6750. Six/year. Indexes worldwide technical literature on environmental pollution. Covers air pollution, marine and freshwater pollution, sewage and wastewater treatment, waste management, toxicology and health, noise pollution, radiation, land pollution, and environmental policies, programs, legislation, and education. Also available online.

Science Citation Index. Institute for Scientific Information, 3501 Market St., Philadelphia, Pennsylvania 19104. 1961-.

BIBLIOGRAPHIES

EPA Publications Bibliography. U.S. Environmental Protection Agency, Library Systems Branch, 401 M St., SW, Washington, District of Columbia 20460. (202) 260-2090. Quarterly.

ENCYCLOPEDIAS AND DICTIONARIES

McGraw-Hill Encyclopedia of Environmental Science. Sybil P. Parker. McGraw-Hill Science & Engineering Books, 11 W. 19th St., New York, New York 10011. (212) 337-6010. 1980. Covers ecology, man's influence on nature, and environmental protection.

Van Nostrand's Scientific Encyclopedia. Glenn D. Considine, ed. Van Nostrand Reinhold, 115 5th Ave., New York, New York 10003. (212) 254-3232. 1983. Sixth edition. Includes all broad subject areas in science.

GENERAL WORKS

Soil Fumigation: How and Why It Works. Harry S. Fenwick. University of Idaho, College of Agriculture, Moscow, Idaho 83843. 1971.

HANDBOOKS AND MANUALS

Manual of Fumigation for Insect Control. E. J. Bond. Food and Agriculture Organization of the United Nations, Via delle Terme di Caracalla, Rome, Italy 00100. 61 0181-FA01. 1984.

ONLINE DATA BASES

BIOSIS Previews. BIOSIS, 2100 Arch St., Philadelphia, Pennsylvania 19103-1399. (215) 587-4800. Largest and most comprehensive database of research in the life sciences. Contains citations for nearly 9000 primary research journals, monographs, reviews, symposia, preliminary reports, semi-popular journals, selected institutional reports, government reports and research communications.

CERCLIS. Chemical Information Systems, Inc., 7215 York Rd., Baltimore, Maryland 21212. (301) 321-8440. Information on hazardous waste disposal sites that have either been listed by the EPA on the National Priority List (NPL) or nominated for consideration for the NPL.

Chemical Abstracts-CA. Chemical Abstracts Service, 2540 Olentangy River Rd., P.O. Box 3012, Columbus, Ohio 43210. (800) 848-6533 or (614) 421-3600. Information sources include 9000 journals, patents from 27 countries, two industrial property organizations, new books, conference proceedings, and government research reports.

Enviro/Energyline Abstracts Plus. R. R. Bowker Co., 121 Chanlon Rd., New Providence, New Jersey 07974. (908) 464-6800.

Environmental Periodicals Bibliography. National Information Services Corp., Ste. 6, Wyman Towers, 3100 St. Paul St., Baltimore, Maryland 21218. (410)243-0797. Online version of abstract of same name.

Monthly Catalog of United States Government Publications. U.S. G.P.O., Supt. of Docs., PO Box 371954, Pittsburgh, Pennsylvania 15250-7954. (202) 512-0000.

National Technical Information Service. U.S. Department of Commerce, National Technical Information Service, Office of Data Base Services, 5285 Port Royal Rd., Springfield, Virginia 22161. (703) 487-4807. Bibliographic database of government sponsored research and technical reports.

SCISEARCH. Institute for Scientific Information, University City Science Center, 3501 Market St., Philadelphia, Pennsylvania 19104. (215) 386-0100.

FUNGI

See also: AGRICULTURE; ECOSYSTEMS; FOOD SCIENCE; NUTRITION

ABSTRACTING AND INDEXING SERVICES

Applied Ecology Abstracts Studies in Renewable Natural Resources. Information Retrieval Ltd., 1911 Jefferson Davis Highway, Arlington, Virginia 22202. 1975-. Monthly.

Biological Abstracts. BIOSIS, 2100 Arch St., Philadelphia, Pennsylvania 19103-1399. (215) 587-4800. 1927-.

Biological and Agricultural Index. H.W. Wilson Co., 950 University Ave., Bronx, New York 10452. (800) 367-6770. 1916-. Monthly.

Biotechnology Research Abstracts. Cambridge Scientific Abstracts, 5161 River Rd., Bethesda, Maryland 20816. (301) 961-6750. Monthly. Includes such broad areas as genetic intervention, biochemical genetics, and microbiological techniques.

Ecological Abstracts. Geo Abstracts Ltd. Elsevier Applied Science, Crown House, Linton Rd., Barking, England IG 11 8JU. 1974-. Derived from over 600 leading ecological and environmental journals, plus books, conference proceedings, reports and theses.

Ecology Abstracts. Cambridge Scientific Abstracts, 5161 River Rd., Bethesda, Maryland 20816. (301) 961-6750. Monthly.

Environment Abstracts. Bowker A & I Publishing, 121 Chanlon Rd., New Providence, New Jersey 07974. (908) 464-6800. 1974-.

Environment Index. Environment Information Center, Index Research Department, 124 E. 39th St., New York, New York 10016. 1971-. Annual.

Environmental Information Connection–EIC. Planning Information Program, Dept. of Urban and Regional Planning, University of Illinois, 1003 West Nevada, Urbana, Illinois 61801. (217) 333-1369. Also available online.

Environmental Periodicals Bibliography. Environmental Studies Institute, International Academy at Santa Barbara, 800 Garden St., Suite D, Santa Barbara, California 93101. (805) 965-5010. Also available online.

Food Science and Technology Abstracts. International Food Information Service, c/o National Food Laboratory, 6363 Clark Ave., Dublin, California 94568. (800) 336-3782. 1969-.

Forestry Abstracts. C. A. B. International, Wallingford, England OX10 8DE. (0491) 3211. 1939/40-. Monthly. Journal of abstracts of journal articles, conferences, technical reports in the subject areas of: silviculture, forest mensuration and management, physical environment, fire, plant biology, genetics and breeding, mycology and pathology, game and wildlife, fish, protection of forests and other related matter.

General Science Index. H. W. Wilson Co., 950 University Ave., Bronx, New York 10452. 1978-. Monthly, also issued in annual cumulation. Cumulative subject index to English language periodicals in the subject fields of astronomy, botany, chemistry, earth science, environment and conservation, food and nutrition, genetics, mathematics, medicine and health, microbiology, oceanography, physics, physiology and zoology.

Index of Fungi. C. A. B. International, 845 North Park Ave., Tucson, Arizona 85719. (602) 621-7897 or (800) 528-4841. 1947-. Semiannual. A list of names of new genera, species and intraspeific taxa, new names of fungi and lichens.

Index to Scientific Book Contents. Institute for Scientific Information, 3501 Market St., Philadelphia, Pennsylvania 19104. (800) 523-1857. 1985-. Annual. Gives contents of science books published.

Multimedia Index to Ecology. National Information Center for Educational Media, University of Southern California, Los Angeles, California 90007.

Pollution Abstracts. Cambridge Scientific Abstracts, 5161 River Rd., Bethesda, Maryland 20816. (301) 961-6750. Six/year. Indexes worldwide technical literature on environmental pollution. Covers air pollution, marine and freshwater pollution, sewage and wastewater treatment, waste management, toxicology and health, noise pollution, radiation, land pollution, and environmental policies, programs, legislation, and education. Also available online.

Science Citation Index. Institute for Scientific Information, 3501 Market St., Philadelphia, Pennsylvania 19104. 1961-.

ALMANACS AND YEARBOOKS

Review of Applied Mycology. Commonwealth Mycological Institute, Ferry Ln., Kew, Richmond, England TW9 3AF. 1969. Covers plant diseases and pathology, specifically phytopathogenic fungi.

BIBLIOGRAPHIES

Directory of Published Proceedings. Interdok Corp., 173 Halstead Ave., Harrison, New York 10528. (914) 835-3506. 1990. Monthly. This is a listing of published proceedings including the series SEMTE (Science/Medicine/Engineering/Technology) and the series SSH (Social Science/Humanities).

EPA Publications Bibliography. U.S. Environmental Protection Agency, Library Systems Branch, 401 M St., SW, Washington, District of Columbia 20460. (202) 260-2090. Quarterly.

ENCYCLOPEDIAS AND DICTIONARIES

Cambridge Dictionary of Biology. Peter M. B. Walker. Cambridge University Press, 40 W. 20th St., New York, New York 10011. (212) 924-3900 or (800) 227-0247. 1989. Includes 10,000 terms in zoology, botany, biochemistry, molecular biology and genetics. Previously published under the title Chambers Biology Dictionary.

Cambridge Encyclopedia of Life Sciences. A. E. Friday and David S. Ingram. Cambridge University Press, 40 W 20th St., New York, New York 10011. (212) 924-3900 or (800) 227-0247. 1985. Includes all topics under biology and ecology.

A Concise Dictionary of Biology. Elizabeth Martin, ed. Oxford University Press, 200 Madison Ave., New York, New York 10016. (212) 679-7300 or (800) 334-4249. 1990. New edition. Derived from the Concise Science Dictionary, published in 1984.

Dictionary of Microbiology and Molecular Biology. Paul Singleton and Diana Sainsbury. John Wiley & Sons, Inc., 605 3rd Ave., New York, New York 10158-0012. (212) 850-6000. 1987. Second edition. Comprehensive dictionary with "classical descriptive aspects of microbiology to current developments in related areas of bioenergetics, biochemistry and molecular biology." Entries give synonyms, cross references, and references to pertinent works. Miscellaneous appendixes. Bibliography.

Encyclopedia of Human Biology. Renato Dulbecco, ed. Academic Press, c/o Harcourt Brace Jovanovich Inc., 6277 Sea Harbor Dr., Orlando, Florida 32887. (800) 346-8648. 1991. Eight volumes.

The Encyclopedia of Mushrooms. Colin Dickinson and John Lucas, eds. Putnam Berkley Group, 200 Madison Ave., New York, New York 10016. (212) 951-8400. 1979. First American edition. Traces many different common kinds of fungi. Emphasis is placed on larger fungi.

McGraw-Hill Encyclopedia of Environmental Science. Sybil P. Parker. McGraw-Hill Science & Engineering Books, 11 W. 19th St., New York, New York 10011. (212) 337-6010. 1980. Covers ecology, man's influence on nature, and environmental protection.

Mycotoxic Fungi, Mycotoxins, Mycotoxicoses: An Encyclopedic Handbook. Thomas D. Wyllie and Lawrence G. Morehouse. Marcel Dekker, Inc., 270 Madison Ave., New York, New York 10016. (212) 696-9000; (800) 228-1160. 1977. Covers mycotoxic fungi and chemistry of mycotoxins, mycotoxicoses of domestic and laboratory animals, and mycotoxicoses of man and plants.

The Nutrition and Health Encyclopedia. David F. Tver and Percy Russell. Van Nostrand Reinhold, 115 5th Ave., New York, New York 10003. (212) 254-3232. 1989.

Van Nostrand's Scientific Encyclopedia. Glenn D. Considine, ed. Van Nostrand Reinhold, 115 5th Ave., New York, New York 10003. (212) 254-3232. 1983. Sixth edition. Includes all broad subject areas in science.

GENERAL WORKS

Magill's Survey of Science. Life Science Series. Frank N. Magill, ed. Salem Press, PO Box 50062, Pasadena, California 91105. 1991. Six volumes. Contents: v.1. A-Central and peripheral nervous system functions; v.2. Central metabolism regulation - eukaryotic transcriptional control; v.3. Positive and negative eukaryotic transcriptional control - mammalian hormones; v.4. Hormones and behavior - muscular contraction; v.5. Muscular contraction and relaxation - sexual reproduction in plants; v.6. Reproductive behavior and mating - X inactivation and the Lyon hypothesis.

Microbes and Microbial Products as Herbicides. Robert E. Hoagland, ed. American Chemical Society, 1155 16th St. N.W., Washington, District of Columbia 20036. (202) 872-4600; (800) 227-5558. 1990. Discusses the suitability of host specific phytotoxins, synthetic derivatives of abcisic acid, phytoalexins, pathogens, soilborne fungi, its biochemistry and other potential microbial product herbicides.

Molecular Industrial Mycology; Systems and Applications for Filamentous Fungi. Marcel Dekker, Inc., 270 Madison Ave., New York, New York 10016. (212) 696-9000; (800) 228-1160. Genetics and molecular biology of fungus species that are economically significant in industry.

Molecular Strategies of Pathogens and Host Plants. Suresh S. Patil, et al., eds. Springer-Verlag, 175 5th Ave, New York, New York 10010. (212) 460-1500. 1991. Papers from an April seminar in Honolulu discusses the molecular interactions between plant pathogens and their hosts, considering the strategies of various bacteria and fungi, the plant's response, and an approach to breeding disease-resistant plants.

HANDBOOKS AND MANUALS

A Colour Atlas of Poisonous Fungi: A Handbook for Pharmacists, Doctors, and Biologists. Andreas Bresinsky. Wolfe Publishing Ltd., Brook House, 2-16 Torrington Pl., London, England WC1E 7LT. 1990.

Fungi Without Gills. Martin B. Ellis. Chapman & Hall, 29 W. 35th St., New York, New York 10001-2291. (212) 244-3336. 1990. Identification of gastromycetes and hymenomycetes.

IMI Descriptions of Fungi and Bacteria. International Mycological Institute, Kew, England Four sets a year. Identification of pathogenic bacteria and pathogenic fungi.

Mushrooms and Toadstools: A Color Field Guide. U. Nonis. Hippocrene Books, 171 Madison Ave., New York,

New York 10016. (212) 685-4371. 1982. Includes 168 species of fungi reproduced and described that were selected from 1500 which were studied. The specimens were actually tested for edibility, toxicity, and are guaranteed.

Mushrooms Demystified: A Comprehensive Guide to the Fleshy Fungi of the Central California Coast. David Arora. Ten Speed Press, P.O. Box 7123, Berkeley, California 94707. (800) 841-2665. 1979. Second edition. Covers covers the United States and Canada. Generously illustrated and includes lots of information on geography, climate and other related details for the growth of mushrooms.

New Generation Guide to the Fungi of Britain and Europe. Stefan Buczacki, ed. University of Texas Press, PO Box 7819, Austin, Texas 78713-7819. (512) 471-7233 or (800) 252-3206. 1989. This directory includes over 1,350 species of fungi, representative of all major groups.

Pictorial Handbook of Medically Important Fungi and Aerobic Actinomycetes. Michael R. McGinnis. Praeger Publishers, 1 Madison Ave., New York, New York 10010-3603. (212) 685-5300. 1982.

ONLINE DATA BASES

BIOSIS Previews. BIOSIS, 2100 Arch St., Philadelphia, Pennsylvania 19103-1399. (215) 587-4800. Largest and most comprehensive database of research in the life sciences. Contains citations for nearly 9000 primary research journals, monographs, reviews, symposia, preliminary reports, semi-popular journals, selected institutional reports, government reports and research communications.

Biotechnology Abstracts. Derwent Publications Ltd., 6845 Elm St., McLean, Virginia 22101. (703) 790-0400. Includes material on genetic manipulation, biochemical engineering, fermentation, biocatalysis, cell hybridization, in vitro plant propagation and industrial waste management.

Cambridge Scientific Abstracts Life Science–CSAL. Cambridge Scientific Abstracts, 5161 River Rd., Bethesda, Maryland 20816. (301) 961-6750. Provides access to the following abstracting services: "Life Sciences Collection," "Aquatic Sciences and Fisheries Abstracts," "Oceanic Abstracts," and "Pollution Abstracts."

Enviro/Energyline Abstracts Plus. R. R. Bowker Co., 121 Chanlon Rd., New Providence, New Jersey 07974. (908) 464-6800.

Environmental Periodicals Bibliography. National Information Services Corp., Ste. 6, Wyman Towers, 3100 St. Paul St., Baltimore, Maryland 21218. (410)243-0797. Online version of abstract of same name.

Monthly Catalog of United States Government Publications. U.S. G.P.O., Supt. of Docs., PO Box 371954, Pittsburgh, Pennsylvania 15250-7954. (202) 512-0000.

National Technical Information Service. U.S. Department of Commerce, National Technical Information Service, Office of Data Base Services, 5285 Port Royal Rd., Springfield, Virginia 22161. (703) 487-4807. Bibliographic database of government sponsored research and technical reports.

SCISEARCH. Institute for Scientific Information, University City Science Center, 3501 Market St., Philadelphia, Pennsylvania 19104. (215) 386-0100.

PERIODICALS AND NEWSLETTERS

Applied and Environmental Microbiology Journal. American Society for Microbiology, 1325 Massachusetts Avenue N.W., Washington, District of Columbia 20005. (202) 737-3600. Monthly. Articles on industrial and food microbiology and ecological studies.

CMI Descriptions of Pathogenic Fungi and Bacteria. Commonwealth Mycological Institute, Ferry Lane, Kew, Richmond, England TW9 3AF. 1964-. Four sets a year.

The Mycologist. C.U.P., Cambridge, Massachusetts Quarterly. Bulletin of the British Mycological Society.

RESEARCH CENTERS AND INSTITUTES

Fungal Genetics Stock Center. Department of Microbiology, University of Kansas Medical Center, Kansas City, Kansas 66103. (913) 588-7044.

Louisiana State University, Mycological Herbarium. Department of Botany, Room 305, Life Sciences Building, Baton Rouge, Louisiana 70803. (504) 388-8487.

Michigan State University, Microbial Ecology Center. 540 Plant and Soil Sciences Building, East Lansing, Michigan 48824-1325. (517) 353-9021.

Pennsylvania State University, Mushroom Research Center. Department of Plant Pathology, 211 Buckhorn, University Park, Pennsylvania 16802. (814) 863-2168.

Purdue University, Arthur Herbarium. Department of Botany and Plant Pathology, 115 S. Lilly Hall, Rm. 1-423, West Lafayette, Indiana 47907. (317) 494-4623.

University of Wyoming, Wilhelm G. Solheim Mycological Herbarium. 3165 University Station, Laramie, Wyoming 82071. (307) 766-2236.

TRADE ASSOCIATIONS AND PROFESSIONAL SOCIETIES

American Institute of Biological Sciences. 730 11th St., N.W., Washington, District of Columbia 20001-4521. (202) 628-1500.

FUNGICIDES

ABSTRACTING AND INDEXING SERVICES

Applied Ecology Abstracts Studies in Renewable Natural Resources. Information Retrieval Ltd., 1911 Jefferson Davis Highway, Arlington, Virginia 22202. 1975-. Monthly.

ASFA Aquaculture Abstracts. Cambridge Scientific Abstracts, Inc., 5161 River Rd., Bethesda, Maryland 20816. (301) 961-6750. 1984.

Biological and Agricultural Index. H.W. Wilson Co., 950 University Ave., Bronx, New York 10452. (800) 367-6770. 1916-. Monthly.

Biotechnology Research Abstracts. Cambridge Scientific Abstracts, 5161 River Rd., Bethesda, Maryland 20816. (301) 961-6750. Monthly. Includes such broad areas as genetic intervention, biochemical genetics, and microbiological techniques.

Ecological Abstracts. Geo Abstracts Ltd. Elsevier Applied Science, Crown House, Linton Rd., Barking, England IG

11 8JU. 1974-. Derived from over 600 leading ecological and environmental journals, plus books, conference proceedings, reports and theses.

Ecology Abstracts. Cambridge Scientific Abstracts, 5161 River Rd., Bethesda, Maryland 20816. (301) 961-6750. Monthly.

Environment Abstracts. Bowker A & I Publishing, 121 Chanlon Rd., New Providence, New Jersey 07974. (908) 464-6800. 1974-.

Environment Index. Environment Information Center, Index Research Department, 124 E. 39th St., New York, New York 10016. 1971-. Annual.

Environmental Information Connection–EIC. Planning Information Program, Dept. of Urban and Regional Planning, University of Illinois, 1003 West Nevada, Urbana, Illinois 61801. (217) 333-1369. Also available online.

Environmental Periodicals Bibliography. Environmental Studies Institute, International Academy at Santa Barbara, 800 Garden St., Suite D, Santa Barbara, California 93101. (805) 965-5010. Also available online.

General Science Index. H. W. Wilson Co., 950 University Ave., Bronx, New York 10452. 1978-. Monthly, also issued in annual cumulation. Cumulative subject index to English language periodicals in the subject fields of astronomy, botany, chemistry, earth science, environment and conservation, food and nutrition, genetics, mathematics, medicine and health, microbiology, oceanography, physics, physiology and zoology.

Index to Scientific Book Contents. Institute for Scientific Information, 3501 Market St., Philadelphia, Pennsylvania 19104. (800) 523-1857. 1985-. Annual. Gives contents of science books published.

Microbiology Abstracts. Section A. Industrial and Applied Microbiology. Cambridge Scientific Abstracts, 5161 River Rd., Bethesda, Maryland 20816. (301) 961-6750. 1972-.

Multimedia Index to Ecology. National Information Center for Educational Media, University of Southern California, Los Angeles, California 90007.

Pesticides Abstracts. U.S. Environmental Protection Agency, Office of Pesticides Programs, 345 Curtland, Atlanta, Georgia 30365. (404) 347-2864. 1981. Monthly. Formerly: Health Aspects of Pesticides Abstracts Bulletin.

Pollution Abstracts. Cambridge Scientific Abstracts, 5161 River Rd., Bethesda, Maryland 20816. (301) 961-6750. Six/year. Indexes worldwide technical literature on environmental pollution. Covers air pollution, marine and freshwater pollution, sewage and wastewater treatment, waste management, toxicology and health, noise pollution, radiation, land pollution, and environmental policies, programs, legislation, and education. Also available online.

Science Citation Index. Institute for Scientific Information, 3501 Market St., Philadelphia, Pennsylvania 19104. 1961-.

BIBLIOGRAPHIES

Directory of Published Proceedings. Interdok Corp., 173 Halstead Ave., Harrison, New York 10528. (914) 835-3506. 1990. Monthly. This is a listing of published proceedings including the series SEMTE (Science/Medicine/Engineering/Technology) and the series SSH (Social Science/Humanities).

EPA Publications Bibliography. U.S. Environmental Protection Agency, Library Systems Branch, 401 M St., SW, Washington, District of Columbia 20460. (202) 260-2090. Quarterly.

Pesticide Applicator Training Materials: A Bibliography. Barbara O. Stommel. National Agricultural Library, 10301 Baltimore Blvd, Beltsville, Maryland 20705-2351. (301) 504-5755. 1991.

DIRECTORIES

European Directory of Agrochemical Products. H. Kidd and D. James, eds. Royal Society of Chemistry, c/o CRC Press, 2000 Corporate Blvd. N.W., Boca Raton, Florida 33431-9868. (800) 272-7737. 1990. Provides comprehensive information on over 26,000 agrochemical products currently manufactured, marketed or used in 25 European countries.

ENCYCLOPEDIAS AND DICTIONARIES

Cambridge Encyclopedia of Life Sciences. A. E. Friday and David S. Ingram. Cambridge University Press, 40 W 20th St., New York, New York 10011. (212) 924-3900 or (800) 227-0247. 1985. Includes all topics under biology and ecology.

McGraw-Hill Encyclopedia of Environmental Science. Sybil P. Parker. McGraw-Hill Science & Engineering Books, 11 W. 19th St., New York, New York 10011. (212) 337-6010. 1980. Covers ecology, man's influence on nature, and environmental protection.

McGraw-Hill Encyclopedia of Science and Technology. McGraw-Hill, 1221 Avenue of the Americas, New York, New York 10020. (212) 512-2000 or (800) 262-4729. 1992. Seventh edition. Issued in multiple volumes including index. Includes all science and technology broad subject areas.

Van Nostrand's Scientific Encyclopedia. Glenn D. Considine, ed. Van Nostrand Reinhold, 115 5th Ave., New York, New York 10003. (212) 254-3232. 1983. Sixth edition. Includes all broad subject areas in science.

GENERAL WORKS

Environmental Fact Sheet: Risk/Benefit Balancing Under the Federal Insecticide, Fungicide, and Rodenticide Act. U.S. Environmental Protection Agency, Office of Pesticides and Toxic Substances, 401 M St. SW, Washington, District of Columbia 20460. (202) 260-2090. 1990.

Managing Resistance to Agrochemicals: From Fundamental Research to Practical Strategies. Maurice B. Green, et al., eds. American Chemical Society, 1155 16th St. N.W., Washington, District of Columbia 20036. (800) 227-5558. 1990. A compilation of chapters written by some of the foremost scientists in pesticide and pest management research today.

Microbes and Microbial Products as Herbicides. Robert E. Hoagland, ed. American Chemical Society, 1155 16th St. N.W., Washington, District of Columbia 20036. (202) 872-4600; (800) 227-5558. 1990. Discusses the suitability of host specific phytotoxins, synthetic derivatives of abcisic acid, phytoalexins, pathogens, soilborne fungi, its biochemistry and other potential microbial product herbicides.

Modern Selective Fungicides. H. Lyr. John Wiley & Sons, Inc., 605 3rd Ave., New York, New York 10158-0012. (212) 850-6000. 1987. Properties, applications, mechanisms of action.

Naturally Occurring Pest Bioregulators. Paul A. Hedin. American Chemical Society, 1155 16th St. NW, Washington, District of Columbia 20036. (202) 872-4600; (800) 227-5558. 1991. Symposium papers on naturally occurring biologically active chemicals grouped in five general sections: bioregulation of insect behavior and development; allelochemicals for control of insects and other animals; phytoalexins and phototoxins in plant pest control; mechanisms of plant resistance to insects; and allelochemicals as plant disease control agents.

HANDBOOKS AND MANUALS

Agricultural Chemicals. William Thomas Thomson. Thomson Publications, Box 9335, Fresno, California 93791. (209) 435-2163. 1991. Book 1: Insecticides and acaricides. Book 2: Herbicides. Book 3: Fumigants, growth regulators, repellents and rodenticides. Book 4: Fungicides.

The Agrochemicals Handbook. H. Kidd and D. Hartlet, eds. Royal Society of Chemistry, c/o CRC Press, 2000 Corporate Blvd., N.W., Boca Raton, Florida 33431-9868. (800) 272-7737. 1991. 3rd ed. Contains comprehensive worldwide information and data on substances which are active components of agriculture chemical products currently used in crop protection and pest control.

European Directory of Agrochemical Products. Royal Society of Chemistry, Thomas Graham House, Science Park, Milton Rd., Cambridge, England CB4 4WF. 1990. 4th ed. Volume 1: Fungicides. Volume 2: Herbicides. Volume 3: Insecticides. Volume 4: Growth regulators including rodenticides; molluscicides; nematicides; repellents and synerists.

The Insecticide, Herbicide, Fungicide Quick Guide and Data Book. B. G. Page and N. T. Thomson. Thomson Publications, PO Box 9335, Fresno, California 93791. (209) 435-2163. 1984. Annually.

Soil Fungicides. A. P. Sinha. CRC Press, 2000 Corporate Blvd. N.W., Boca Raton, Florida 33431. (800) 272-7737. 1988.

ONLINE DATA BASES

Biotechnology Abstracts. Derwent Publications Ltd., 6845 Elm St., McLean, Virginia 22101. (703) 790-0400. Includes material on genetic manipulation, biochemical engineering, fermentation, biocatalysis, cell hybridization, in vitro plant propagation and industrial waste management.

Chemical Carcinogenesis Research Information System–CCRIS. National Library of Medicine, 8600 Rockville Pike, Bethesda, Maryland 20894. (800) 638-8480. Individual assay results and test conditions for 1,451 chemicals in the areas of carcinogenicity, mutagenicity, tumor promotion, and cocarcinogenicity.

Chemical Collection System/Request Tracking–CCS/RTS. U.S. Environmental Protection Agency, Office of Pesticides and Toxic Substances, 401 M St., SW, Wash-

ington, District of Columbia 20460. (202) 260-2090. Contains information on various properties of a number of chemicals including environmental effects, test and analysis methods, and health effects. Available from EPA.

Chemical Dictionary Online–CHEMLINE. Chemical Abstracts Service, 2540 Olentangy River Rd., Columbus, Ohio 43210. (614) 421-3600 or (800) 848-6533. Part of MEDLINE of the National Library of Medicine (NLM). File of 900,000 names for chemical substances, representing 450,000 unique compounds. It contains such information as Chemical Abstracts (CA) Service Registry Numbers, molecular formulas, preferred chemical nomenclature, and generic and ring structure information. Available on NLM's ELHILL system.

Chemical Exposure. Science Applications International Corp., Health & Environmental Information, P.O. Box 2501, Oak Ridge, Tennessee 37831. (615) 482-9031. Database of chemicals that have been identified in both human tissues and body fluids and in feral and food animals. Contains reference to journal articles, conferences, and reports. Covers the whole fields of information related to human and animal exposure to food, air, and water contaminants and pharmaceuticals. Its records include information on chemical properties, formulas, tissues measured, analytical method used, demographics and more. Available on DIALOG.

Enviro/Energyline Abstracts Plus. R. R. Bowker Co., 121 Chanlon Rd., New Providence, New Jersey 07974. (908) 464-6800.

Environmental Periodicals Bibliography. National Information Services Corp., Ste. 6, Wyman Towers, 3100 St. Paul St., Baltimore, Maryland 21218. (410)243-0797. Online version of abstract of same name.

Monthly Catalog of United States Government Publications. U.S. G.P.O., Supt. of Docs., PO Box 371954, Pittsburgh, Pennsylvania 15250-7954. (202) 512-0000.

National Technical Information Service. U.S. Department of Commerce, National Technical Information Service, Office of Data Base Services, 5285 Port Royal Rd., Springfield, Virginia 22161. (703) 487-4807. Bibliographic database of government sponsored research and technical reports.

SCISEARCH. Institute for Scientific Information, University City Science Center, 3501 Market St., Philadelphia, Pennsylvania 19104. (215) 386-0100.

PERIODICALS AND NEWSLETTERS

Pesticide & Toxic Chemical News. Food Chemical News, Inc., 1101 Pennsylvania Avenue, SE, Washington, District of Columbia 20003. (202) 544-1980. Weekly. Covers government regulations of chemical pollution, transportation, disposal and occupational health. Also available online.

RESEARCH CENTERS AND INSTITUTES

University of Illinois, Laboratory of Plant Pigment Biochemistry and Photobiology. 1302 West Pennsylvania, Urbana, Illinois 61801. (217) 333-1968.

STATISTICS SOURCES

Fungicides, Insecticides & Nematicides Used of Sugar Beet. FIND/SVP, 625 Avenue of the Americas, New York, New York 10011. (800) 346-3787. 1991. Focuses on the diseases and pests that attack the sugar-beet crop in Western developed countries.

TRADE ASSOCIATIONS AND PROFESSIONAL SOCIETIES

American Chemical Society. 1155 16th St., N.W., Washington, District of Columbia 20036. (202) 872-4600.

American Institute of Biological Sciences. 730 11th St., N.W., Washington, District of Columbia 20001-4521. (202) 628-1500.

FUR INDUSTRY

See also: ENDANGERED SPECIES

ABSTRACTING AND INDEXING SERVICES

Applied Ecology Abstracts Studies in Renewable Natural Resources. Information Retrieval Ltd., 1911 Jefferson Davis Highway, Arlington, Virginia 22202. 1975-. Monthly.

Biological and Agricultural Index. H.W. Wilson Co., 950 University Ave., Bronx, New York 10452. (800) 367-6770. 1916-. Monthly.

Environment Abstracts. Bowker A & I Publishing, 121 Chanlon Rd., New Providence, New Jersey 07974. (908) 464-6800. 1974-.

Environment Index. Environment Information Center, Index Research Department, 124 E. 39th St., New York, New York 10016. 1971-. Annual.

Environmental Information Connection–EIC. Planning Information Program, Dept. of Urban and Regional Planning, University of Illinois, 1003 West Nevada, Urbana, Illinois 61801. (217) 333-1369. Also available online.

Environmental Periodicals Bibliography. Environmental Studies Institute, International Academy at Santa Barbara, 800 Garden St., Suite D, Santa Barbara, California 93101. (805) 965-5010. Also available online.

Multimedia Index to Ecology. National Information Center for Educational Media, University of Southern California, Los Angeles, California 90007.

BIBLIOGRAPHIES

EPA Publications Bibliography. U.S. Environmental Protection Agency, Library Systems Branch, 401 M St., SW, Washington, District of Columbia 20460. (202) 260-2090. Quarterly.

GENERAL WORKS

The Mode in Furs. Ruth Turner Wilcox. Scribner Educational Publishers, 866 3rd Ave., New York, New York 10022. (212) 702-2000. 1951. The history of furred costume of the world from the earliest times to the present.

HANDBOOKS AND MANUALS

Identification Manual. Peter Drollinger. Convention on International Trade in Endangered Species of Wild Fauna and Flora, Lausanne, Switzerland 1987. Identification of rare animals, endangered species and fur.

ONLINE DATA BASES

Enviro/Energyline Abstracts Plus. R. R. Bowker Co., 121 Chanlon Rd., New Providence, New Jersey 07974. (908) 464-6800.

Environmental Periodicals Bibliography. National Information Services Corp., Ste. 6, Wyman Towers, 3100 St. Paul St., Baltimore, Maryland 21218. (410)243-0797. Online version of abstract of same name.

PressNet Environmental Reports. Chemical Information Systems, Inc., 7215 York Rd., Baltimore, Maryland 21212. (301) 321-8440.

FUR TRADE

See also: ENDANGERED SPECIES

ABSTRACTING AND INDEXING SERVICES

Applied Ecology Abstracts Studies in Renewable Natural Resources. Information Retrieval Ltd., 1911 Jefferson Davis Highway, Arlington, Virginia 22202. 1975-. Monthly.

Environment Abstracts. Bowker A & I Publishing, 121 Chanlon Rd., New Providence, New Jersey 07974. (908) 464-6800. 1974-.

Environment Index. Environment Information Center, Index Research Department, 124 E. 39th St., New York, New York 10016. 1971-. Annual.

Environmental Information Connection–EIC. Planning Information Program, Dept. of Urban and Regional Planning, University of Illinois, 1003 West Nevada, Urbana, Illinois 61801. (217) 333-1369. Also available online.

Environmental Periodicals Bibliography. Environmental Studies Institute, International Academy at Santa Barbara, 800 Garden St., Suite D, Santa Barbara, California 93101. (805) 965-5010. Also available online.

Multimedia Index to Ecology. National Information Center for Educational Media, University of Southern California, Los Angeles, California 90007.

BIBLIOGRAPHIES

EPA Publications Bibliography. U.S. Environmental Protection Agency, Library Systems Branch, 401 M St., SW, Washington, District of Columbia 20460. (202) 260-2090. Quarterly.

ONLINE DATA BASES

Enviro/Energyline Abstracts Plus. R. R. Bowker Co., 121 Chanlon Rd., New Providence, New Jersey 07974. (908) 464-6800.

Environmental Periodicals Bibliography. National Information Services Corp., Ste. 6, Wyman Towers, 3100 St.

Paul St., Baltimore, Maryland 21218. (410)243-0797. Online version of abstract of same name.

PressNet Environmental Reports. Chemical Information Systems, Inc., 7215 York Rd., Baltimore, Maryland 21212. (301) 321-8440.

FURNACES

ABSTRACTING AND INDEXING SERVICES

Applied Science and Technology Index. H.W. Wilson Co., 950 University Ave., Bronx, New York 10452. (800) 367-6770. Formerly Industrial Arts Index.

Engineering Index. The Engineering Index Inc., 345 E. 47th St., New York, New York 10017. 1962-.

Environment Abstracts. Bowker A & I Publishing, 121 Chanlon Rd., New Providence, New Jersey 07974. (908) 464-6800. 1974-.

Environment Index. Environment Information Center, Index Research Department, 124 E. 39th St., New York, New York 10016. 1971-. Annual.

Environmental Information Connection–EIC. Planning Information Program, Dept. of Urban and Regional Planning, University of Illinois, 1003 West Nevada, Urbana, Illinois 61801. (217) 333-1369. Also available online.

Environmental Periodicals Bibliography. Environmental Studies Institute, International Academy at Santa Barbara, 800 Garden St., Suite D, Santa Barbara, California 93101. (805) 965-5010. Also available online.

General Science Index. H. W. Wilson Co., 950 University Ave., Bronx, New York 10452. 1978-. Monthly, also issued in annual cumulation. Cumulative subject index to English language periodicals in the subject fields of astronomy, botany, chemistry, earth science, environment and conservation, food and nutrition, genetics, mathematics, medicine and health, microbiology, oceanography, physics, physiology and zoology.

Index to Scientific Book Contents. Institute for Scientific Information, 3501 Market St., Philadelphia, Pennsylvania 19104. (800) 523-1857. 1985-. Annual. Gives contents of science books published.

Pollution Abstracts. Cambridge Scientific Abstracts, 5161 River Rd., Bethesda, Maryland 20816. (301) 961-6750.

Six/year. Indexes worldwide technical literature on environmental pollution. Covers air pollution, marine and freshwater pollution, sewage and wastewater treatment, waste management, toxicology and health, noise pollution, radiation, land pollution, and environmental policies, programs, legislation, and education. Also available online.

Science Citation Index. Institute for Scientific Information, 3501 Market St., Philadelphia, Pennsylvania 19104. 1961-.

BIBLIOGRAPHIES

EPA Publications Bibliography. U.S. Environmental Protection Agency, Library Systems Branch, 401 M St., SW, Washington, District of Columbia 20460. (202) 260-2090. Quarterly.

ENCYCLOPEDIAS AND DICTIONARIES

McGraw-Hill Encyclopedia of Environmental Science. Sybil P. Parker. McGraw-Hill Science & Engineering Books, 11 W. 19th St., New York, New York 10011. (212) 337-6010. 1980. Covers ecology, man's influence on nature, and environmental protection.

Van Nostrand's Scientific Encyclopedia. Glenn D. Considine, ed. Van Nostrand Reinhold, 115 5th Ave., New York, New York 10003. (212) 254-3232. 1983. Sixth edition. Includes all broad subject areas in science.

ONLINE DATA BASES

Computerized Engineering Index–COMPENDEX. Engineering Information Inc., 345 E. 47th St., New York, New York 10017. (212) 705-7600.

Enviro/Energyline Abstracts Plus. R. R. Bowker Co., 121 Chanlon Rd., New Providence, New Jersey 07974. (908) 464-6800.

Environmental Periodicals Bibliography. National Information Services Corp., Ste. 6, Wyman Towers, 3100 St. Paul St., Baltimore, Maryland 21218. (410)243-0797. Online version of abstract of same name.

FUSION R & D
See: NUCLEAR POWER

G

GABION

See: EROSION

GALLIUM

ABSTRACTING AND INDEXING SERVICES

Chemical Abstracts. Chemical Abstracts Service, 2540 Olentangy River Rd., PO Box 3012, Columbus, Ohio 43210. (800) 848-6533. 1907-.

General Science Index. H. W. Wilson Co., 950 University Ave., Bronx, New York 10452. 1978-. Monthly, also issued in annual cumulation. Cumulative subject index to English language periodicals in the subject fields of astronomy, botany, chemistry, earth science, environment and conservation, food and nutrition, genetics, mathematics, medicine and health, microbiology, oceanography, physics, physiology and zoology.

Physics Briefs. Physikalische Berichte. Physik Verlag, Pappapelallee 3, Postfach 101161, Weinheim, Germany D-6940. 1979-. Semimonthly. In English. Volumes for 1979- issued by the Deutsche Physikalische Gesellschaft and the Fachinformationszentrum Energie Physik, Mathematik in cooperation with the American Institute of Physics.

Pollution Abstracts. Cambridge Scientific Abstracts, 5161 River Rd., Bethesda, Maryland 20816. (301) 961-6750. Six/year. Indexes worldwide technical literature on environmental pollution. Covers air pollution, marine and freshwater pollution, sewage and wastewater treatment, waste management, toxicology and health, noise pollution, radiation, land pollution, and environmental policies, programs, legislation, and education. Also available online.

Science Citation Index. Institute for Scientific Information, 3501 Market St., Philadelphia, Pennsylvania 19104. 1961-.

BIBLIOGRAPHIES

Gallium Bibliography. M. W. Brennecke. ALCOA-Aluminum Company of America, Alcoa Bldg., Pittsburgh, Pennsylvania 15219. (412) 553-4545. 1959.

ENCYCLOPEDIAS AND DICTIONARIES

Encyclopedia of Chemical Processing and Design. John J. Mcketta and W. A. Cunningham. Marcel Dekker, Inc., 270 Madison Ave., New York, New York 10016. (212) 696-9000; (800) 228-1160. 1992. Thirty-eight volumes.

Kirk-Othmer Encyclopedia of Chemical Technology. J. I. Kroschwitz, ed. John Wiley & Sons, Inc., 605 3rd Ave., New York, New York 10158-0012. (212) 850-6000. 1992-. All articles in the new edition have been rewritten and updated adding new subjects such as biotechnology, computer topics, analytical techniques and instrumentation, environmental concerns, fuels and energy, inorganic and solid state chemistry; composite materials and material science in general, and pharmaceuticals. Also available online.

Van Nostrand's Scientific Encyclopedia. Glenn D. Considine, ed. Van Nostrand Reinhold, 115 5th Ave., New York, New York 10003. (212) 254-3232. 1983. Sixth edition. Includes all broad subject areas in science.

GENERAL WORKS

The Chemistry of Gallium. Ivan Arsenevich Sheka. Elsevier Science Publishing Co., 655 Avenue of the Americas, New York, New York 10010. (212) 984-5800. 1966.

HANDBOOKS AND MANUALS

The Chemistry of Aluminium, Gallium, Indium and Thallium. Kenneth Wade. Pergamon Press, Headington Hill Hall, Oxford, England OX3 0BW. 1975.

ONLINE DATA BASES

Chemical Abstracts-CA. Chemical Abstracts Service, 2540 Olentangy River Rd., P.O. Box 3012, Columbus, Ohio 43210. (800) 848-6533 or (614) 421-3600. Information sources include 9000 journals, patents from 27 countries, two industrial property organizations, new books, conference proceedings, and government research reports.

Kirk-Othmer Encyclopedia of Chemical Technology. John Wiley & Sons, Inc., 605 3rd Ave., 5th Floor, New York, New York 10158. (212) 850-6000. Online version of the publication of the same name.

STATISTICS SOURCES

Minerals Yearbook: Gallium. U.S. Department of the Interior, Bureau of Mines, 810 7th St. NW, Washington, District of Columbia 20241. (202) 501-9649. Annual.

A Survey of the Market, Supply, and Availability of Gallium. Fred D. Rosi. National Technical Information Service, 5285 Port Royal Rd., Springfield, Virginia 22161. (703) 487-4650. 1980.

GAME FISH

See: WATER QUALITY

GAME PRESERVES

ABSTRACTING AND INDEXING SERVICES

Applied Ecology Abstracts Studies in Renewable Natural Resources. Information Retrieval Ltd., 1911 Jefferson Davis Highway, Arlington, Virginia 22202. 1975-. Monthly.

Biological and Agricultural Index. H.W. Wilson Co., 950 University Ave., Bronx, New York 10452. (800) 367-6770. 1916-. Monthly.

Current Advances in Ecological and Environmental Science. Pergamon Microforms International, Inc., Fairview Park, Elmsford, New York 10523. (914) 592-7720. 1989-. Monthly. Current literature searching service includingjournals, reports, abstracts, etc. This service is available online as part of the CABS database on the hosts BRS and ORBIT search service.

Ecological Abstracts. Geo Abstracts Ltd. Elsevier Applied Science, Crown House, Linton Rd., Barking, England IG 11 8JU. 1974-. Derived from over 600 leading ecological and environmental journals, plus books, conference proceedings, reports and theses.

Ecology Abstracts. Cambridge Scientific Abstracts, 5161 River Rd., Bethesda, Maryland 20816. (301) 961-6750. Monthly.

Environment Abstracts. Bowker A & I Publishing, 121 Chanlon Rd., New Providence, New Jersey 07974. (908) 464-6800. 1974-.

Environment Index. Environment Information Center, Index Research Department, 124 E. 39th St., New York, New York 10016. 1971-. Annual.

Environmental Information Connection–EIC. Planning Information Program, Dept. of Urban and Regional Planning, University of Illinois, 1003 West Nevada, Urbana, Illinois 61801. (217) 333-1369. Also available online.

Environmental Periodicals Bibliography. Environmental Studies Institute, International Academy at Santa Barbara, 800 Garden St., Suite D, Santa Barbara, California 93101. (805) 965-5010. Also available online.

General Science Index. H. W. Wilson Co., 950 University Ave., Bronx, New York 10452. 1978-. Monthly, also issued in annual cumulation. Cumulative subject index to English language periodicals in the subject fields of astronomy, botany, chemistry, earth science, environment and conservation, food and nutrition, genetics, mathematics, medicine and health, microbiology, oceanography, physics, physiology and zoology.

Multimedia Index to Ecology. National Information Center for Educational Media, University of Southern California, Los Angeles, California 90007.

BIBLIOGRAPHIES

EPA Publications Bibliography. U.S. Environmental Protection Agency, Library Systems Branch, 401 M St., SW,

Washington, District of Columbia 20460. (202) 260-2090. Quarterly.

ENCYCLOPEDIAS AND DICTIONARIES

The Encyclopedia of Animal Ecology. Peter D. Moore. Facts on File, Inc., 460 Park Ave. S., New York, New York 10016. (212) 683-2244. 1987.

McGraw-Hill Encyclopedia of Environmental Science. Sybil P. Parker. McGraw-Hill Science & Engineering Books, 11 W. 19th St., New York, New York 10011. (212) 337-6010. 1980. Covers ecology, man's influence on nature, and environmental protection.

McGraw-Hill Encyclopedia of Science and Technology. McGraw-Hill, 1221 Avenue of the Americas, New York, New York 10020. (212) 512-2000 or (800) 262-4729. 1992. Seventh edition. Issued in multiple volumes including index. Includes all science and technology broad subject areas.

ONLINE DATA BASES

Cambridge Scientific Abstracts Life Science–CSAL. Cambridge Scientific Abstracts, 5161 River Rd., Bethesda, Maryland 20816. (301) 961-6750. Provides access to the following abstracting services: "Life Sciences Collection," "Aquatic Sciences and Fisheries Abstracts," "Oceanic Abstracts," and "Pollution Abstracts."

Enviro/Energyline Abstracts Plus. R. R. Bowker Co., 121 Chanlon Rd., New Providence, New Jersey 07974. (908) 464-6800.

Environmental Periodicals Bibliography. National Information Services Corp., Ste. 6, Wyman Towers, 3100 St. Paul St., Baltimore, Maryland 21218. (410)243-0797. Online version of abstract of same name.

SCISEARCH. Institute for Scientific Information, University City Science Center, 3501 Market St., Philadelphia, Pennsylvania 19104. (215) 386-0100.

TRADE ASSOCIATIONS AND PROFESSIONAL SOCIETIES

American Society of Naturalists. Department of Ecology and Evolation, State University of New York, Stony Brook, New York 11794. (516) 632-8589.

Game Conservation International. P.O. Box 17444, San Antonio, Texas 78217. (512) 824-7509.

North American Gamebird Association. Box 2105, Cayce-West Columbia, South Carolina 29171. (803) 796-8163.

GAMMA RAY IRRADIATION

See: RADIATION EXPOSURE

GARBAGE

See also: SOLID WASTES

ABSTRACTING AND INDEXING SERVICES

Biological and Agricultural Index. H.W. Wilson Co., 950 University Ave., Bronx, New York 10452. (800) 367-6770. 1916-. Monthly.

Engineering Index. The Engineering Index Inc., 345 E. 47th St., New York, New York 10017. 1962-.

Environment Abstracts. Bowker A & I Publishing, 121 Chanlon Rd., New Providence, New Jersey 07974. (908) 464-6800. 1974-.

Environment Index. Environment Information Center, Index Research Department, 124 E. 39th St., New York, New York 10016. 1971-. Annual.

Environmental Information Connection–EIC. Planning Information Program, Dept. of Urban and Regional Planning, University of Illinois, 1003 West Nevada, Urbana, Illinois 61801. (217) 333-1369. Also available online.

Environmental Periodicals Bibliography. Environmental Studies Institute, International Academy at Santa Barbara, 800 Garden St., Suite D, Santa Barbara, California 93101. (805) 965-5010. Also available online.

General Science Index. H. W. Wilson Co., 950 University Ave., Bronx, New York 10452. 1978-. Monthly, also issued in annual cumulation. Cumulative subject index to English language periodicals in the subject fields of astronomy, botany, chemistry, earth science, environment and conservation, food and nutrition, genetics, mathematics, medicine and health, microbiology, oceanography, physics, physiology and zoology.

Index to Scientific Book Contents. Institute for Scientific Information, 3501 Market St., Philadelphia, Pennsylvania 19104. (800) 523-1857. 1985-. Annual. Gives contents of science books published.

Pollution Abstracts. Cambridge Scientific Abstracts, 5161 River Rd., Bethesda, Maryland 20816. (301) 961-6750. Six/year. Indexes worldwide technical literature on environmental pollution. Covers air pollution, marine and freshwater pollution, sewage and wastewater treatment, waste management, toxicology and health, noise pollution, radiation, land pollution, and environmental policies, programs, legislation, and education. Also available online.

Science Citation Index. Institute for Scientific Information, 3501 Market St., Philadelphia, Pennsylvania 19104. 1961-.

BIBLIOGRAPHIES

EPA Publications Bibliography. U.S. Environmental Protection Agency, Library Systems Branch, 401 M St., SW, Washington, District of Columbia 20460. (202) 260-2090. Quarterly.

Waste Disposal and Treatment in the Food Processing Industry: Citations for the BioBusiness Database. National Technical Information Service, 5285 Port Royal Rd., Springfield, Virginia 22161. (703) 487-4650. 1989.

DIRECTORIES

Trash & Garbage Removal Directory. American Business Directories, Inc., 5711 S. 86th Circle, Omaha, Nebraska 68127. (402) 593-4600.

ENCYCLOPEDIAS AND DICTIONARIES

The New York Times Encyclopedic Dictionary of the Environment. Paul Sarnoff. Quadrangle Books, New York, New York 1971. Focuses on state-of-the-art methods of pollution control, abatement, prevention and removal.

GENERAL WORKS

Cartons, Cans, and Orange Peels–Where Does Your Garbage Go?. Joanna Foster. Clarion Books, 215 Park Avenue, S, New York, New York 10003. (212) 420-5800. 1991. Discusses composition of garbage and trash, methods of disposal, and recycling.

Garbage and Recycling. Judith Woodburn. Gareth Stevens, Inc., 7317 W. Green Tree Rd., Milwaukee, Wisconsin 53223. (414) 466-7550. 1991. Solid waste crisis, landfill crowding, and recycling.

Garbage and Recycling. Kathlyn Gay. Enslow Publishers, Bloy St. & Ramsey Ave., PO Box 777, Hillside, New Jersey 07205. (908) 964-4116. 1991. Garbage accumulation and different recycling solutions which may prevent the situation from getting worse.

The Garbage Dilemma: A Community Guide to Solid Waste Management. Marilyn Rosenzweig. League of Women Voters of Illinois Education Fund, 332 S. Michigan Ave., Chicago, Illinois 60604. (312) 939-5935. 1990. Refuse and refuse disposal, hazardous wastes and recycling of waste.

Garbage in the Cities: Refuse, Reform, and the Environment, 1880-1980. Martin V. Melosi. Texas A & M University Press, College Station, Texas 77843. 1981. Environmental history of refuse and refuse disposal in the United States.

Garbage: The History and Future of Garbage in America. Katie Kelly. Saturday Review Press, 201 Park Ave. S., Rm. 1305, New York, New York 10017. 1973. Refuse and refuse disposal in the United States.

Public Attitudes Toward Garbage Disposal. National Solid Wastes Management Association, 1730 Rhode Island Ave., NW, Ste. 1000, Washington, District of Columbia 20036. (202) 659-4613. 1990.

Rush to Burn: Solving America's Garbage Crisis?. Island Press, 1718 Connecticut Ave. N.W., Suite 300, Washington, District of Columbia 20009. (202) 232-7933. 1989. Describes incineration, refuse and refuse disposal.

Solid Waste Management and the Environment: The Mounting Garbage and Trash Crisis. Homer A. Neal. Prentice-Hall, Rte. 9W, Englewood Cliffs, New Jersey 07632. (201) 592-2000. 1987. Environmental aspects of refuse and refuse disposal.

War on Waste: Can America Win its Battle With Garbage?. Louis Blumberg and Robert Gottlieb. Island Press, 1718 Connecticut Ave. N.W., Suite 300, Washington, District of Columbia 20009. (202) 232-7933. 1989. In-depth analysis of the waste disposal crisis.

HANDBOOKS AND MANUALS

The Global Ecology Handbook: What You Can Do about the Environmental Crisis. Walter H. Corson, ed. The Global Tomorrow Coalition, Beacon Pr., 25 Beacon St., Boston, Massachusetts 02108-2800. (617) 742-2110.

1990. Covers environment, energy policy, population growth and other issues. It includes chapters on tropical rain forests, garbage, oceans and coasts, global warming, population growth, agriculture, biological diversity, fresh water, hazardous wastes, and environment and development.

Waste Management Control Handbook for Dairy Food Plants. W. J. Harper. U.S. Environmental Protection Agency, Office of Research and Development, 26 W. Martin Luther King Dr., Cincinnati, Ohio 45268. (513) 569-7931. 1984. Waste disposal in the food processing plants.

ONLINE DATA BASES

Computerized Engineering Index–COMPENDEX. Engineering Information Inc., 345 E. 47th St., New York, New York 10017. (212) 705-7600.

Enviro/Energyline Abstracts Plus. R. R. Bowker Co., 121 Chanlon Rd., New Providence, New Jersey 07974. (908) 464-6800.

Environmental Periodicals Bibliography. National Information Services Corp., Ste. 6, Wyman Towers, 3100 St. Paul St., Baltimore, Maryland 21218. (410)243-0797. Online version of abstract of same name.

Monthly Catalog of United States Government Publications. U.S. G.P.O., Supt. of Docs., PO Box 371954, Pittsburgh, Pennsylvania 15250-7954. (202) 512-0000.

National Technical Information Service. U.S. Department of Commerce, National Technical Information Service, Office of Data Base Services, 5285 Port Royal Rd., Springfield, Virginia 22161. (703) 487-4807. Bibliographic database of government sponsored research and technical reports.

SCISEARCH. Institute for Scientific Information, University City Science Center, 3501 Market St., Philadelphia, Pennsylvania 19104. (215) 386-0100.

PERIODICALS AND NEWSLETTERS

Everyone's Back Yard. Citizen's Clearinghouse for Hazardous Wastes, P.O. Box 926, Arlington, Virginia 22216. (703) 276-7070. Bimonthly. Contains news, views, and resources for grassroots environmental activists.

Garbage: The Practical Journal for the Environment. Old House Journal Corp., 2 Main St., Gloucester, Massachusetts 01930. (508) 283-4629. Bimonthly. Issues in municipal wastes.

Outdoors Unlittered Pitch-In News. Outdoors Unlittered, 200-1676 Martin Dr., White Rock, British Columbia, Canada V4A 6E7. (403) 429-0517. Semiannually. Solid waste and litter problems

GARBAGE GRINDING

See: SOLID WASTE TREATMENT

GAS CHROMATOGRAPHY

See: CHROMATOGRAPHY

GAS DISPOSAL, LAND

ABSTRACTING AND INDEXING SERVICES

Environment Abstracts. Bowker A & I Publishing, 121 Chanlon Rd., New Providence, New Jersey 07974. (908) 464-6800. 1974-.

Environment Index. Environment Information Center, Index Research Department, 124 E. 39th St., New York, New York 10016. 1971-. Annual.

Environmental Information Connection–EIC. Planning Information Program, Dept. of Urban and Regional Planning, University of Illinois, 1003 West Nevada, Urbana, Illinois 61801. (217) 333-1369. Also available online.

Environmental Periodicals Bibliography. Environmental Studies Institute, International Academy at Santa Barbara, 800 Garden St., Suite D, Santa Barbara, California 93101. (805) 965-5010. Also available online.

General Science Index. H. W. Wilson Co., 950 University Ave., Bronx, New York 10452. 1978-. Monthly, also issued in annual cumulation. Cumulative subject index to English language periodicals in the subject fields of astronomy, botany, chemistry, earth science, environment and conservation, food and nutrition, genetics, mathematics, medicine and health, microbiology, oceanography, physics, physiology and zoology.

BIBLIOGRAPHIES

EPA Publications Bibliography. U.S. Environmental Protection Agency, Library Systems Branch, 401 M St., SW, Washington, District of Columbia 20460. (202) 260-2090. Quarterly.

Land Disposal of Municipal and Industrial Wastes. Robert W. Lockerby. Vance Bibliographies, PO Box 229, 112 N. Charter St., Monticello, Illinois 61856. (217) 762-3831. 1982. Bibliography of sewage irrigation.

GENERAL WORKS

An Environmental Assessment of Potential Gas and Leachate Problems at Land Disposal Sites. U.S. Environmental Protection Agency, 401 M St. SW, Washington, District of Columbia 20460. (202) 260-2090. 1975.

Land Disposal of Hazardous Waste: Engineering and Environmental Issues. J.R. Gronow. John Wiley & Sons, Inc., 605 3rd Ave., New York, New York 10158-0012. (212) 850-6000. 1988. Waste disposal and teaching at hazardous waste sites.

Land Disposal of Hexachlorobenzene Wastes: Controlling Vapor Movement in Soil. Walter J. Farmer. National Technical Information Service, 5285 Port Royal Rd., Springfield, Virginia 22161. (703) 487-4650. 1980. Hazardous substances and soil chemistry.

Leaking Underground Gasoline Storage Tanks. Better Government Association, 230 N. Michigan Ave., Chicago, Illinois 60601. (312) 641-1181. 1988. Water, pollution, and environmental aspects of gasoline storage.

HANDBOOKS AND MANUALS

Flue Gas Cleaning Wastes Disposal and Utilization. D. Khoury. Noyes Publications, 120 Mill Rd., Park Ridge,

New Jersey 07656. (201) 391-8484. 1981. Pollution technology relating to flue gases, purification, and waste disposal.

ONLINE DATA BASES

Enviro/Energyline Abstracts Plus. R. R. Bowker Co., 121 Chanlon Rd., New Providence, New Jersey 07974. (908) 464-6800.

Environmental Periodicals Bibliography. National Information Services Corp., Ste. 6, Wyman Towers, 3100 St. Paul St., Baltimore, Maryland 21218. (410)243-0797. Online version of abstract of same name.

Monthly Catalog of United States Government Publications. U.S. G.P.O., Supt. of Docs., PO Box 371954, Pittsburgh, Pennsylvania 15250-7954. (202) 512-0000.

National Technical Information Service. U.S. Department of Commerce, National Technical Information Service, Office of Data Base Services, 5285 Port Royal Rd., Springfield, Virginia 22161. (703) 487-4807. Bibliographic database of government sponsored research and technical reports.

TRADE ASSOCIATIONS AND PROFESSIONAL SOCIETIES

American Public Gas Association. 11094-D Lee Hwy., Ste. 102, Fairfax, Virginia 22030. (703) 352-3890.

Gas Appliance Manufacturers Association. 1901 N. Moore St., Ste. 1100, Arlington, Virginia 22209. (703) 525-9565.

Gas Processors Association. 6526 E. 60th St., Tulsa, Oklahoma 74145. (918) 493-3872.

GAS LEAKS

ABSTRACTING AND INDEXING SERVICES

Engineering Index. The Engineering Index Inc., 345 E. 47th St., New York, New York 10017. 1962-.

Environment Abstracts. Bowker A & I Publishing, 121 Chanlon Rd., New Providence, New Jersey 07974. (908) 464-6800. 1974-.

Environment Index. Environment Information Center, Index Research Department, 124 E. 39th St., New York, New York 10016. 1971-. Annual.

Environmental Information Connection–EIC. Planning Information Program, Dept. of Urban and Regional Planning, University of Illinois, 1003 West Nevada, Urbana, Illinois 61801. (217) 333-1369. Also available online.

Environmental Periodicals Bibliography. Environmental Studies Institute, International Academy at Santa Barbara, 800 Garden St., Suite D, Santa Barbara, California 93101. (805) 965-5010. Also available online.

General Science Index. H. W. Wilson Co., 950 University Ave., Bronx, New York 10452. 1978-. Monthly, also issued in annual cumulation. Cumulative subject index to English language periodicals in the subject fields of astronomy, botany, chemistry, earth science, environment and conservation, food and nutrition, genetics, mathematics, medicine and health, microbiology, oceanography, physics, physiology and zoology.

BIBLIOGRAPHIES

EPA Publications Bibliography. U.S. Environmental Protection Agency, Library Systems Branch, 401 M St., SW, Washington, District of Columbia 20460. (202) 260-2090. Quarterly.

ONLINE DATA BASES

Computerized Engineering Index–COMPENDEX. Engineering Information Inc., 345 E. 47th St., New York, New York 10017. (212) 705-7600.

Enviro/Energyline Abstracts Plus. R. R. Bowker Co., 121 Chanlon Rd., New Providence, New Jersey 07974. (908) 464-6800.

Environmental Periodicals Bibliography. National Information Services Corp., Ste. 6, Wyman Towers, 3100 St. Paul St., Baltimore, Maryland 21218. (410)243-0797. Online version of abstract of same name.

TRADE ASSOCIATIONS AND PROFESSIONAL SOCIETIES

American Public Gas Association. 11094-D Lee Hwy., Ste. 102, Fairfax, Virginia 22030. (703) 352-3890.

Compressed Air & Gas Institute. c/o John H. Addington, Thomas Associates, Inc., 1300 Sumner Ave., Cleveland, Ohio 44115. (216) 241-7333.

Compressed Gas Association. Crystal Gateway #1, Suite 501, 1235 Jefferson Davis Hwy., Arlington, Virginia 22202. (703) 979-0900.

Gas Appliance Manufacturers Association. 1901 N. Moore St., Ste. 1100, Arlington, Virginia 22209. (703) 525-9565.

Gas Processors Association. 6526 E. 60th St., Tulsa, Oklahoma 74145. (918) 493-3872.

Industrial Biotechnology Association. 1625 K St., N.W., Suite 1100, Washington, District of Columbia 20006-1604. (202) 857-0244.

GAS TURBINES

ABSTRACTING AND INDEXING SERVICES

Environment Abstracts. Bowker A & I Publishing, 121 Chanlon Rd., New Providence, New Jersey 07974. (908) 464-6800. 1974-.

Environment Index. Environment Information Center, Index Research Department, 124 E. 39th St., New York, New York 10016. 1971-. Annual.

Environmental Information Connection–EIC. Planning Information Program, Dept. of Urban and Regional Planning, University of Illinois, 1003 West Nevada, Urbana, Illinois 61801. (217) 333-1369. Also available online.

Environmental Periodicals Bibliography. Environmental Studies Institute, International Academy at Santa Barbara, 800 Garden St., Suite D, Santa Barbara, California 93101. (805) 965-5010. Also available online.

General Science Index. H. W. Wilson Co., 950 University Ave., Bronx, New York 10452. 1978-. Monthly, also issued in annual cumulation. Cumulative subject index

GAS TURBINES   *Encyclopedia of Environmental Information Sources*

to English language periodicals in the subject fields of astronomy, botany, chemistry, earth science, environment and conservation, food and nutrition, genetics, mathematics, medicine and health, microbiology, oceanography, physics, physiology and zoology.

Pollution Abstracts. Cambridge Scientific Abstracts, 5161 River Rd., Bethesda, Maryland 20816. (301) 961-6750. Six/year. Indexes worldwide technical literature on environmental pollution. Covers air pollution, marine and freshwater pollution, sewage and wastewater treatment, waste management, toxicology and health, noise pollution, radiation, land pollution, and environmental policies, programs, legislation, and education. Also available online.

BIBLIOGRAPHIES

EPA Publications Bibliography. U.S. Environmental Protection Agency, Library Systems Branch, 401 M St., SW, Washington, District of Columbia 20460. (202) 260-2090. Quarterly.

ENCYCLOPEDIAS AND DICTIONARIES

Encyclopedia of Chemical Processing and Design. John J. Mcketta and W. A. Cunningham. Marcel Dekker, Inc., 270 Madison Ave., New York, New York 10016. (212) 696-9000; (800) 228-1160. 1992. Thirty-eight volumes.

Kirk-Othmer Encyclopedia of Chemical Technology. J. I. Kroschwitz, ed. John Wiley & Sons, Inc., 605 3rd Ave., New York, New York 10158-0012. (212) 850-6000. 1992-. All articles in the new edition have been rewritten and updated adding new subjects such as biotechnology, computer topics, analytical techniques and instrumentation, environmental concerns, fuels and energy, inorganic and solid state chemistry; composite materials and material science in general, and pharmaceuticals. Also available online.

GENERAL WORKS

Baseline Data on Utilization of Low-Grade Fuels in Gas Turbine Applications. Electric Power Research Institute, 3412 Hillview Ave., Palo Alto, California 94304. (415) 965-4081. 1981. Economic comparisons, hot component corrosion, and emissions evaluation.

Combustion Modification Controls for Stationary Gas Turbine. R. Larkin. U.S. Environmental Protection Agency, Industrial Environmental Research Laboratory, MD 75, Research Triangle Park, North Carolina 27711. 1982. Environmental monitoring of gas turbines.

ONLINE DATA BASES

Enviro/Energyline Abstracts Plus. R. R. Bowker Co., 121 Chanlon Rd., New Providence, New Jersey 07974. (908) 464-6800.

Environmental Periodicals Bibliography. National Information Services Corp., Ste. 6, Wyman Towers, 3100 St. Paul St., Baltimore, Maryland 21218. (410)243-0797. Online version of abstract of same name.

Kirk-Othmer Encyclopedia of Chemical Technology. John Wiley & Sons, Inc., 605 3rd Ave., 5th Floor, New York, New York 10158. (212) 850-6000. Online version of the publication of the same name.

Monthly Catalog of United States Government Publications. U.S. G.P.O., Supt. of Docs., PO Box 371954, Pittsburgh, Pennsylvania 15250-7954. (202) 512-0000.

National Technical Information Service. U.S. Department of Commerce, National Technical Information Service, Office of Data Base Services, 5285 Port Royal Rd., Springfield, Virginia 22161. (703) 487-4807. Bibliographic database of government sponsored research and technical reports.

GASOLINE

ABSTRACTING AND INDEXING SERVICES

Applied Science and Technology Index. H.W. Wilson Co., 950 University Ave., Bronx, New York 10452. (800) 367-6770. Formerly Industrial Arts Index.

Engineering Index. The Engineering Index Inc., 345 E. 47th St., New York, New York 10017. 1962-.

Environment Abstracts. Bowker A & I Publishing, 121 Chanlon Rd., New Providence, New Jersey 07974. (908) 464-6800. 1974-.

Environment Index. Environment Information Center, Index Research Department, 124 E. 39th St., New York, New York 10016. 1971-. Annual.

Environmental Information Connection–EIC. Planning Information Program, Dept. of Urban and Regional Planning, University of Illinois, 1003 West Nevada, Urbana, Illinois 61801. (217) 333-1369. Also available online.

Environmental Periodicals Bibliography. Environmental Studies Institute, International Academy at Santa Barbara, 800 Garden St., Suite D, Santa Barbara, California 93101. (805) 965-5010. Also available online.

ERDA Research Abstracts. U.S. ERDA Technical Information Center, Box 62, Oak Ridge, Tennessee 37830.

General Science Index. H. W. Wilson Co., 950 University Ave., Bronx, New York 10452. 1978-. Monthly, also issued in annual cumulation. Cumulative subject index to English language periodicals in the subject fields of astronomy, botany, chemistry, earth science, environment and conservation, food and nutrition, genetics, mathematics, medicine and health, microbiology, oceanography, physics, physiology and zoology.

Geographical Abstracts. London School of Economics, Dept. of Geography, Regency House, 34 Duke St., London, England 1966-. Continued by Geo Abstracts issued in 6 parts: Pt. A. Landforms and the quaternary; Pt. B. Biogeography and Climatology; Pt. C. Economic geography; Pt. D. Social geography and cartography; Pt. E. Sedimentology; Pt. F. Regional and community planning.

Index to Scientific Book Contents. Institute for Scientific Information, 3501 Market St., Philadelphia, Pennsylvania 19104. (800) 523-1857. 1985-. Annual. Gives contents of science books published.

Pollution Abstracts. Cambridge Scientific Abstracts, 5161 River Rd., Bethesda, Maryland 20816. (301) 961-6750. Six/year. Indexes worldwide technical literature on environmental pollution. Covers air pollution, marine and freshwater pollution, sewage and wastewater treatment,

678

waste management, toxicology and health, noise pollution, radiation, land pollution, and environmental policies, programs, legislation, and education. Also available online.

BIBLIOGRAPHIES

EPA Publications Bibliography. U.S. Environmental Protection Agency, Library Systems Branch, 401 M St., SW, Washington, District of Columbia 20460. (202) 260-2090. Quarterly.

ENCYCLOPEDIAS AND DICTIONARIES

Encyclopedia of Physical Science and Technology. Robert A. Meyers, ed. Academic Press, c/o Harcourt Brace Jovanovich Inc., 6277 Sea Harbor Dr., Orlando, Florida 32887. (800) 346-8648. Dictionary of engineering, technology and physical sciences.

Energy Terminology: A Multilingual Glossary. Pergamon Microforms International, Inc., Fairview Park, Elmsford, New York 10523. (914) 592-7720. 1986. Second edition. Contains 1500 defined terms and concepts related to the field of energy together with an index of several thousand undefined keywords used in the definitions of these terms and concepts. Contents appear in four languages: English, French, German and Spanish.

Van Nostrand's Scientific Encyclopedia. Glenn D. Considine, ed. Van Nostrand Reinhold, 115 5th Ave., New York, New York 10003. (212) 254-3232. 1983. Sixth edition. Includes all broad subject areas in science.

GENERAL WORKS

Air Pollution: EPA's Strategy to Control Emissions of Benzene and Gasoline Vapor. U.S. General Accounting Office. Washington, District of Columbia 1985. Environmental aspects of benzene.

Demonstrations of Vapor Control Technology for Gasoline Loading of Barges. S. S. Gross. U.S. Environmental Protection Agency, Industrial Environmental Research Laboratory, MD 75, Research Triangle Park, North Carolina 27711. 1984. Air pollution in the United States caused by gasoline.

Hydrocarbon Control Strategies for Gasoline Marketing Operations. R. L. Norton. U.S. Environmental Protection Agency, Office of Air and Waste Management, MD 75, Research Triangle Park, North Carolina 27711. 1978. Pollution control of motor vehicle exhaust.

The Motor Gasoline Industry: Past, Present, and the Future. Energy Information Administration. U.S. G.P.O., Washington, District of Columbia 20401. (202) 512-0000. 1991. Includes a great deal of historical and current statistical information. The book is grouped under topics such as history, chemistry (and combustion), supply constraints, distribution, pricing, alternative fuels, and future outlook.

Report to the President and Congress on the Need for Leaded Gasoline on the Farm. U.S. Environmental Protection Agency, 401 M St., SW, Washington, District of Columbia 20460. (202) 260-2090. 1988. Environmental aspects of gasoline used in farm equipment.

ONLINE DATA BASES

Computerized Engineering Index–COMPENDEX. Engineering Information Inc., 345 E. 47th St., New York, New York 10017. (212) 705-7600.

Enviro/Energyline Abstracts Plus. R. R. Bowker Co., 121 Chanlon Rd., New Providence, New Jersey 07974. (908) 464-6800.

Environmental Periodicals Bibliography. National Information Services Corp., Ste. 6, Wyman Towers, 3100 St. Paul St., Baltimore, Maryland 21218. (410)243-0797. Online version of abstract of same name.

Monthly Catalog of United States Government Publications. U.S. G.P.O., Supt. of Docs., PO Box 371954, Pittsburgh, Pennsylvania 15250-7954. (202) 512-0000.

National Technical Information Service. U.S. Department of Commerce, National Technical Information Service, Office of Data Base Services, 5285 Port Royal Rd., Springfield, Virginia 22161. (703) 487-4807. Bibliographic database of government sponsored research and technical reports.

TRADE ASSOCIATIONS AND PROFESSIONAL SOCIETIES

American Petroleum Institute. 1220 L St., N.W., Washington, District of Columbia 20005. (202) 682-8000.

Industrial Biotechnology Association. 1625 K St., N.W., Suite 1100, Washington, District of Columbia 20006-1604. (202) 857-0244.

GASTROPODS

ABSTRACTING AND INDEXING SERVICES

Biological Abstracts. BIOSIS, 2100 Arch St., Philadelphia, Pennsylvania 19103-1399. (215) 587-4800. 1927-.

Biological and Agricultural Index. H.W. Wilson Co., 950 University Ave., Bronx, New York 10452. (800) 367-6770. 1916-. Monthly.

Environment Abstracts. Bowker A & I Publishing, 121 Chanlon Rd., New Providence, New Jersey 07974. (908) 464-6800. 1974-.

Environment Index. Environment Information Center, Index Research Department, 124 E. 39th St., New York, New York 10016. 1971-. Annual.

Environmental Information Connection–EIC. Planning Information Program, Dept. of Urban and Regional Planning, University of Illinois, 1003 West Nevada, Urbana, Illinois 61801. (217) 333-1369. Also available online.

Environmental Periodicals Bibliography. Environmental Studies Institute, International Academy at Santa Barbara, 800 Garden St., Suite D, Santa Barbara, California 93101. (805) 965-5010. Also available online.

General Science Index. H. W. Wilson Co., 950 University Ave., Bronx, New York 10452. 1978-. Monthly, also issued in annual cumulation. Cumulative subject index to English language periodicals in the subject fields of astronomy, botany, chemistry, earth science, environment and conservation, food and nutrition, genetics,

mathematics, medicine and health, microbiology, oceanography, physics, physiology and zoology.

Index to Scientific Book Contents. Institute for Scientific Information, 3501 Market St., Philadelphia, Pennsylvania 19104. (800) 523-1857. 1985-. Annual. Gives contents of science books published.

Pollution Abstracts. Cambridge Scientific Abstracts, 5161 River Rd., Bethesda, Maryland 20816. (301) 961-6750. Six/year. Indexes worldwide technical literature on environmental pollution. Covers air pollution, marine and freshwater pollution, sewage and wastewater treatment, waste management, toxicology and health, noise pollution, radiation, land pollution, and environmental policies, programs, legislation, and education. Also available online.

BIBLIOGRAPHIES

EPA Publications Bibliography. U.S. Environmental Protection Agency, Library Systems Branch, 401 M St., SW, Washington, District of Columbia 20460. (202) 260-2090. Quarterly.

ENCYCLOPEDIAS AND DICTIONARIES

Cambridge Dictionary of Biology. Peter M. B. Walker. Cambridge University Press, 40 W. 20th St., New York, New York 10011. (212) 924-3900 or (800) 227-0247. 1989. Includes 10,000 terms in zoology, botany, biochemistry, molecular biology and genetics. Previously published under the title Chambers Biology Dictionary.

Cambridge Encyclopedia of Life Sciences. A. E. Friday and David S. Ingram. Cambridge University Press, 40 W 20th St., New York, New York 10011. (212) 924-3900 or (800) 227-0247. 1985. Includes all topics under biology and ecology.

A Concise Dictionary of Biology. Elizabeth Martin, ed. Oxford University Press, 200 Madison Ave., New York, New York 10016. (212) 679-7300 or (800) 334-4249. 1990. New edition. Derived from the Concise Science Dictionary, published in 1984.

Van Nostrand's Scientific Encyclopedia. Glenn D. Considine, ed. Van Nostrand Reinhold, 115 5th Ave., New York, New York 10003. (212) 254-3232. 1983. Sixth edition. Includes all broad subject areas in science.

GENERAL WORKS

A Functional Biology of Marine Gastropods. Roger N. Hughes. Johns Hopkins University Press, 701 W. 40th St., Ste. 275, Baltimore, Maryland 21211. (410) 516-6900. 1986. Covers marine invertebrates.

Sea-Slug Gastropods. Wesley M. Farmer. W.M. Farmer Enterprises, Tempe, Arizona 1980. Gastropods and mollusks in the Pacific coast.

ONLINE DATA BASES

BIOSIS Previews. BIOSIS, 2100 Arch St., Philadelphia, Pennsylvania 19103-1399. (215) 587-4800. Largest and most comprehensive database of research in the life sciences. Contains citations for nearly 9000 primary research journals, monographs, reviews, symposia, preliminary reports, semi-popular journals, selected institutional reports, government reports and research communications.

Enviro/Energyline Abstracts Plus. R. R. Bowker Co., 121 Chanlon Rd., New Providence, New Jersey 07974. (908) 464-6800.

Environmental Periodicals Bibliography. National Information Services Corp., Ste. 6, Wyman Towers, 3100 St. Paul St., Baltimore, Maryland 21218. (410)243-0797. Online version of abstract of same name.

SCISEARCH. Institute for Scientific Information, University City Science Center, 3501 Market St., Philadelphia, Pennsylvania 19104. (215) 386-0100.

GEMS
See: GLOBAL ENVIRONMENT MONITORING SYSTEMS

GENE SPLICING
See: BIOTECHNOLOGY

GENE TRANSPLANT
See: BIOTECHNOLOGY

GENERATORS
ABSTRACTING AND INDEXING SERVICES

Applied Science and Technology Index. H.W. Wilson Co., 950 University Ave., Bronx, New York 10452. (800) 367-6770. Formerly Industrial Arts Index.

Engineering Index. The Engineering Index Inc., 345 E. 47th St., New York, New York 10017. 1962-.

Environment Abstracts. Bowker A & I Publishing, 121 Chanlon Rd., New Providence, New Jersey 07974. (908) 464-6800. 1974-.

Environment Index. Environment Information Center, Index Research Department, 124 E. 39th St., New York, New York 10016. 1971-. Annual.

Environmental Information Connection–EIC. Planning Information Program, Dept. of Urban and Regional Planning, University of Illinois, 1003 West Nevada, Urbana, Illinois 61801. (217) 333-1369. Also available online.

Environmental Periodicals Bibliography. Environmental Studies Institute, International Academy at Santa Barbara, 800 Garden St., Suite D, Santa Barbara, California 93101. (805) 965-5010. Also available online.

General Science Index. H. W. Wilson Co., 950 University Ave., Bronx, New York 10452. 1978-. Monthly, also issued in annual cumulation. Cumulative subject index to English language periodicals in the subject fields of astronomy, botany, chemistry, earth science, environment and conservation, food and nutrition, genetics, mathematics, medicine and health, microbiology, oceanography, physics, physiology and zoology.

Pollution Abstracts. Cambridge Scientific Abstracts, 5161 River Rd., Bethesda, Maryland 20816. (301) 961-6750. Six/year. Indexes worldwide technical literature on envi-

ronmental pollution. Covers air pollution, marine and freshwater pollution, sewage and wastewater treatment, waste management, toxicology and health, noise pollution, radiation, land pollution, and environmental policies, programs, legislation, and education. Also available online.

BIBLIOGRAPHIES

EPA Publications Bibliography. U.S. Environmental Protection Agency, Library Systems Branch, 401 M St., SW, Washington, District of Columbia 20460. (202) 260-2090. Quarterly.

ENCYCLOPEDIAS AND DICTIONARIES

Encyclopedia of Physical Science and Technology. Robert A. Meyers, ed. Academic Press, c/o Harcourt Brace Jovanovich Inc., 6277 Sea Harbor Dr., Orlando, Florida 32887. (800) 346-8648. Dictionary of engineering, technology and physical sciences.

Van Nostrand's Scientific Encyclopedia. Glenn D. Considine, ed. Van Nostrand Reinhold, 115 5th Ave., New York, New York 10003. (212) 254-3232. 1983. Sixth edition. Includes all broad subject areas in science.

HANDBOOKS AND MANUALS

EPA Hazardous Waste Numbers for Waste Streams Commonly Generated by Small Quantity Generators. U.S. Environmental Protection Agency, 401 M St., SW, Washington, District of Columbia 20460. (202) 260-2090. 1986. Identification of hazardous wastes.

ONLINE DATA BASES

Computerized Engineering Index–COMPENDEX. Engineering Information Inc., 345 E. 47th St., New York, New York 10017. (212) 705-7600.

Enviro/Energyline Abstracts Plus. R. R. Bowker Co., 121 Chanlon Rd., New Providence, New Jersey 07974. (908) 464-6800.

Environmental Periodicals Bibliography. National Information Services Corp., Ste. 6, Wyman Towers, 3100 St. Paul St., Baltimore, Maryland 21218. (410)243-0797. Online version of abstract of same name.

GENETIC RESISTANCE

See also: INTEGRATED PEST MANAGEMENT (IPM); NATURAL SELECTION; PESTICIDES

ABSTRACTING AND INDEXING SERVICES

Applied Ecology Abstracts Studies in Renewable Natural Resources. Information Retrieval Ltd., 1911 Jefferson Davis Highway, Arlington, Virginia 22202. 1975-. Monthly.

ASFA Aquaculture Abstracts. Cambridge Scientific Abstracts, Inc., 5161 River Rd., Bethesda, Maryland 20816. (301) 961-6750. 1984.

Biological Abstracts. BIOSIS, 2100 Arch St., Philadelphia, Pennsylvania 19103-1399. (215) 587-4800. 1927-.

Biological and Agricultural Index. H.W. Wilson Co., 950 University Ave., Bronx, New York 10452. (800) 367-6770. 1916-. Monthly.

Biology Digest. Data Courier, Plexus Pub Inc., 143 Old Marlton Pike, Medford, New Jersey 08055. 1974-. Monthly. Abstracts biology periodicals.

Biotechnology Research Abstracts. Cambridge Scientific Abstracts, 5161 River Rd., Bethesda, Maryland 20816. (301) 961-6750. Monthly. Includes such broad areas as genetic intervention, biochemical genetics, and microbiological techniques.

Current Advances in Ecological and Environmental Science. Pergamon Microforms International, Inc., Fairview Park, Elmsford, New York 10523. (914) 592-7720. 1989-. Monthly. Current literature searching service including journals, reports, abstracts, etc. This service is available online as part of the CABS database on the hosts BRS and ORBIT search service.

Ecology Abstracts. Cambridge Scientific Abstracts, 5161 River Rd., Bethesda, Maryland 20816. (301) 961-6750. Monthly.

Environment Abstracts. Bowker A & I Publishing, 121 Chanlon Rd., New Providence, New Jersey 07974. (908) 464-6800. 1974-.

Environment Index. Environment Information Center, Index Research Department, 124 E. 39th St., New York, New York 10016. 1971-. Annual.

Environmental Information Connection–EIC. Planning Information Program, Dept. of Urban and Regional Planning, University of Illinois, 1003 West Nevada, Urbana, Illinois 61801. (217) 333-1369. Also available online.

Environmental Periodicals Bibliography. Environmental Studies Institute, International Academy at Santa Barbara, 800 Garden St., Suite D, Santa Barbara, California 93101. (805) 965-5010. Also available online.

General Science Index. H. W. Wilson Co., 950 University Ave., Bronx, New York 10452. 1978-. Monthly, also issued in annual cumulation. Cumulative subject index to English language periodicals in the subject fields of astronomy, botany, chemistry, earth science, environment and conservation, food and nutrition, genetics, mathematics, medicine and health, microbiology, oceanography, physics, physiology and zoology.

Genetics Abstracts. Cambridge Scientific Abstracts, 5161 River Rd., Bethesda, Maryland 20816. (301) 961-6750. 1968-. Monthly. Formerly published by Information Retrieval Ltd., London England. Published by Cambridge Scientific Abstracts since 1982.

Index to Scientific Book Contents. Institute for Scientific Information, 3501 Market St., Philadelphia, Pennsylvania 19104. (800) 523-1857. 1985-. Annual. Gives contents of science books published.

Multimedia Index to Ecology. National Information Center for Educational Media, University of Southern California, Los Angeles, California 90007.

Science Citation Index. Institute for Scientific Information, 3501 Market St., Philadelphia, Pennsylvania 19104. 1961-.

BIBLIOGRAPHIES

Effect of Air Pollution on Pinus Strobus L. and Genetic Resistance. Henry D. Gerhold. U.S. Corvallis Environmental Research Laboratory, 200 SW 35th St., Corvallis, Oregon 97333. (503) 754-4600. 1977. Effect of air pollution on white pine.

EPA Publications Bibliography. U.S. Environmental Protection Agency, Library Systems Branch, 401 M St., SW, Washington, District of Columbia 20460. (202) 260-2090. Quarterly.

Integrated Pest Management. Jayne T. Maclean. National Agricultural Library, 10301 Baltimore Blvd., Beltsville, Maryland 20705-2351. (301) 504-5755. 1985.

ENCYCLOPEDIAS AND DICTIONARIES

Cambridge Encyclopedia of Life Sciences. A. E. Friday and David S. Ingram. Cambridge University Press, 40 W 20th St., New York, New York 10011. (212) 924-3900 or (800) 227-0247. 1985. Includes all topics under biology and ecology.

A Dictionary of Genetics. Robert C. King and William A. Stansfield. Oxford University Press, 200 Madison Ave., New York, New York 10016. (212) 679-7300 or (800) 334-4249. 1991. Fourth edition. Includes 7,100 definitions with 250 illustrations. Also includes bibliography of major sources.

Dictionary of Genetics and Cell Biology. Norman Maclean. New York University Press, 70 Washington Sq. S., New York, New York 10012. (212) 998-2575. 1987. Includes the subject areas of cytology and genetics.

Encyclopedia of Human Biology. Renato Dulbecco, ed. Academic Press, c/o Harcourt Brace Jovanovich Inc., 6277 Sea Harbor Dr., Orlando, Florida 32887. (800) 346-8648. 1991. Eight volumes.

Encyclopedic Dictionary of Genetics: With German Term Equivalents and Extensive German/English Index. R. C. King and W. D. Stansfield. VCH Publishers, 303 NW 12th Ave., Deerfield Beach, Florida 33442-1788. (305) 428-5566. 1990. 4th ed. Revised edition of: A Dictionary of Genetics, third edition.

McGraw-Hill Encyclopedia of Environmental Science. Sybil P. Parker. McGraw-Hill Science & Engineering Books, 11 W. 19th St., New York, New York 10011. (212) 337-6010. 1980. Covers ecology, man's influence on nature, and environmental protection.

McGraw-Hill Encyclopedia of Science and Technology. McGraw-Hill, 1221 Avenue of the Americas, New York, New York 10020. (212) 512-2000 or (800) 262-4729. 1992. Seventh edition. Issued in multiple volumes including index. Includes all science and technology broad subject areas.

Van Nostrand's Scientific Encyclopedia. Glenn D. Considine, ed. Van Nostrand Reinhold, 115 5th Ave., New York, New York 10003. (212) 254-3232. 1983. Sixth edition. Includes all broad subject areas in science.

GENERAL WORKS

Genetic Resistance to Pesticides. Biological Sciences Curriculum Study, Pleasantville, New York Study and teaching of biology and genetics.

HANDBOOKS AND MANUALS

Integrated Pest Management. ANR Publications, University of California, 6701 San Pablo Ave., Oakland, California 94608-1239. (510) 642-2431. 1990-. Irregular. Provides and orderly, scientifically based system for diagnosing, recording, evaluating, preventing, and treating pest problems in a variety of crops.

ONLINE DATA BASES

BIOSIS Previews. BIOSIS, 2100 Arch St., Philadelphia, Pennsylvania 19103-1399. (215) 587-4800. Largest and most comprehensive database of research in the life sciences. Contains citations for nearly 9000 primary research journals, monographs, reviews, symposia, preliminary reports, semi-popular journals, selected institutional reports, government reports and research communications.

Biotechnology Abstracts. Derwent Publications Ltd., 6845 Elm St., McLean, Virginia 22101. (703) 790-0400. Includes material on genetic manipulation, biochemical engineering, fermentation, biocatalysis, cell hybridization, in vitro plant propagation and industrial waste management.

Cambridge Scientific Abstracts Life Science–CSAL. Cambridge Scientific Abstracts, 5161 River Rd., Bethesda, Maryland 20816. (301) 961-6750. Provides access to the following abstracting services: "Life Sciences Collection," "Aquatic Sciences and Fisheries Abstracts," "Oceanic Abstracts," and "Pollution Abstracts."

Chemical Engineering and Biotechnology Abstracts–CEBA. Orbit Search Service, Maxwell Online Inc., 8000 W. Park Dr., McLean, Virginia 22102. (703) 442-0900 or (800) 456-7248. Monthly. Covers theoretical, practical and commercial material on all aspects of processing safety, and the environment. Also covers process and reaction engineering, measurement and process control, environmental protection and safety, plant design and equipment used in chemical engineering and biotechnology. More than 400 of the world's major primary chemical and process engineering journals are scanned to compile the database. Available from ORBIT.

Enviro/Energyline Abstracts Plus. R. R. Bowker Co., 121 Chanlon Rd., New Providence, New Jersey 07974. (908) 464-6800.

Environmental Periodicals Bibliography. National Information Services Corp., Ste. 6, Wyman Towers, 3100 St. Paul St., Baltimore, Maryland 21218. (410)243-0797. Online version of abstract of same name.

Monthly Catalog of United States Government Publications. U.S. G.P.O., Supt. of Docs., PO Box 371954, Pittsburgh, Pennsylvania 15250-7954. (202) 512-0000.

National Technical Information Service. U.S. Department of Commerce, National Technical Information Service, Office of Data Base Services, 5285 Port Royal Rd., Springfield, Virginia 22161. (703) 487-4807. Bibliographic database of government sponsored research and technical reports.

SCISEARCH. Institute for Scientific Information, University City Science Center, 3501 Market St., Philadelphia, Pennsylvania 19104. (215) 386-0100.

TRADE ASSOCIATIONS AND PROFESSIONAL SOCIETIES

American Institute of Biological Sciences. 730 11th St., N.W., Washington, District of Columbia 20001-4521. (202) 628-1500.

GENETICS

ABSTRACTING AND INDEXING SERVICES

AgBiotech News and Information. C. A. B. International, 845 North Park Ave., Tucson, Arizona 85719. (602) 621-7897 or (800) 528-4841. 1989-. Bimonthly. Includes news items on topics such as research, companies, products, patents, books, education, diary, people, equipment, and legal issues. Also reviews articles and conference reports. Abstracts journal articles, reports, conferences, and books. Also includes biological control, bioenvironmental interactions and stress resistance and genetics.

Animal Breeding Abstracts. C. A. B. International, 845 North Park Ave., Tucson, Arizona 85719. (602) 621-7897 or (800) 528-4841. 1933-. Monthly. Abstracts covers the literature on animal breeding, genetics, reproduction and production. Includes areas of biological research such as immunogenetics, genetic engineering and fertility improvement.

ASFA Aquaculture Abstracts. Cambridge Scientific Abstracts, Inc., 5161 River Rd., Bethesda, Maryland 20816. (301) 961-6750. 1984.

Biological Abstracts. BIOSIS, 2100 Arch St., Philadelphia, Pennsylvania 19103-1399. (215) 587-4800. 1927-.

Biological and Agricultural Index. H.W. Wilson Co., 950 University Ave., Bronx, New York 10452. (800) 367-6770. 1916-. Monthly.

Biology Digest. Data Courier, Plexus Pub Inc., 143 Old Marlton Pike, Medford, New Jersey 08055. 1974-. Monthly. Abstracts biology periodicals.

Biotechnology Research Abstracts. Cambridge Scientific Abstracts, 5161 River Rd., Bethesda, Maryland 20816. (301) 961-6750. Monthly. Includes such broad areas as genetic intervention, biochemical genetics, and microbiological techniques.

Current Advances in Plant Science. Pergamon Microforms International, Inc., Fairview Park, Elmsford, New York 10523. (914) 592-7720. 1984-. Monthly. Current literature searching service including journals, reports, abstracts, etc. This service is available online as part of the CABS database on the hosts BRS and ORBIT search service.

Ecology Abstracts. Cambridge Scientific Abstracts, 5161 River Rd., Bethesda, Maryland 20816. (301) 961-6750. Monthly.

Environment Abstracts. Bowker A & I Publishing, 121 Chanlon Rd., New Providence, New Jersey 07974. (908) 464-6800. 1974-.

Environment Index. Environment Information Center, Index Research Department, 124 E. 39th St., New York, New York 10016. 1971-. Annual.

Environmental Information Connection–EIC. Planning Information Program, Dept. of Urban and Regional Planning, University of Illinois, 1003 West Nevada, Urbana, Illinois 61801. (217) 333-1369. Also available online.

Environmental Periodicals Bibliography. Environmental Studies Institute, International Academy at Santa Barbara, 800 Garden St., Suite D, Santa Barbara, California 93101. (805) 965-5010. Also available online.

General Science Index. H. W. Wilson Co., 950 University Ave., Bronx, New York 10452. 1978-. Monthly, also issued in annual cumulation. Cumulative subject index to English language periodicals in the subject fields of astronomy, botany, chemistry, earth science, environment and conservation, food and nutrition, genetics, mathematics, medicine and health, microbiology, oceanography, physics, physiology and zoology.

Genetics Abstracts. Cambridge Scientific Abstracts, 5161 River Rd., Bethesda, Maryland 20816. (301) 961-6750. 1968-. Monthly. Formerly published by Information Retrieval Ltd., London England. Published by Cambridge Scientific Abstracts since 1982.

Geographical Abstracts. London School of Economics, Dept. of Geography, Regency House, 34 Duke St., London, England 1966-. Continued by Geo Abstracts issued in 6 parts: Pt. A. Landforms and the quaternary; Pt. B. Biogeography and Climatology; Pt. C. Economic geography; Pt. D. Social geography and cartography; Pt. E. Sedimentology; Pt. F. Regional and community planning.

Index to Scientific Book Contents. Institute for Scientific Information, 3501 Market St., Philadelphia, Pennsylvania 19104. (800) 523-1857. 1985-. Annual. Gives contents of science books published.

Pollution Abstracts. Cambridge Scientific Abstracts, 5161 River Rd., Bethesda, Maryland 20816. (301) 961-6750. Six/year. Indexes worldwide technical literature on environmental pollution. Covers air pollution, marine and freshwater pollution, sewage and wastewater treatment, waste management, toxicology and health, noise pollution, radiation, land pollution, and environmental policies, programs, legislation, and education. Also available online.

Science Citation Index. Institute for Scientific Information, 3501 Market St., Philadelphia, Pennsylvania 19104. 1961-.

Telegen Reporter Annual. Bowker A & I Publishing. 245 W 17th St., New York, New York 10011. 1989. Provides up-to-date reviews of the pharmaceutical, agricultural, industrial and energy applications of the products, processes, and markets of genetic engineering and biotechnology. Also addresses economic, social, regulatory, patent, and public policy issues. This annual cumulation abstracts and indexes information from scientific, technical, and business journals, conference and symposium proceedings, and academic government,and corporate reports.

BIBLIOGRAPHIES

EPA Publications Bibliography. U.S. Environmental Protection Agency, Library Systems Branch, 401 M St., SW, Washington, District of Columbia 20460. (202) 260-2090. Quarterly.

Genetic Engineering, DNA, and Cloning: A Bibliography in the Future of Genetics. Joseph Menditto. Whitston

Publishing Co., P.O. Box 958, Troy, New York 12181. (518) 283-4363. 1983.

DIRECTORIES

Gale Environmental Sourcebook. Karen Hill. Gale Research Co., 835 Penobscot Bldg., Detroit, Michigan 48226-4094. (313) 961-2242. Contacts, information sources, or general information on environmental topics.

ENCYCLOPEDIAS AND DICTIONARIES

Cambridge Encyclopedia of Life Sciences. A. E. Friday and David S. Ingram. Cambridge University Press, 40 W 20th St., New York, New York 10011. (212) 924-3900 or (800) 227-0247. 1985. Includes all topics under biology and ecology.

A Dictionary of Genetics. Robert C. King and William A. Stansfield. Oxford University Press, 200 Madison Ave., New York, New York 10016. (212) 679-7300 or (800) 334-4249. 1991. Fourth edition. Includes 7,100 definitions with 250 illustrations. Also includes bibliography of major sources.

Dictionary of Genetics and Cell Biology. Norman Maclean. New York University Press, 70 Washington Sq. S., New York, New York 10012. (212) 998-2575. 1987. Includes the subject areas of cytology and genetics.

Encyclopedia of Bioethics. Warren T. Reich, ed. Free Press, 866 3rd Ave., New York, New York 10022. (212) 702-2004 or (800) 257-5755. 1978. Four volumes. Includes review articles in the field of bioethics by 330 reviewers representing fields such as: surgery, Islamic studies, pediatrics, philosophy, environmental sciences, theology, psychiatry, etc.

Encyclopedia of Human Biology. Renato Dulbecco, ed. Academic Press, c/o Harcourt Brace Jovanovich Inc., 6277 Sea Harbor Dr., Orlando, Florida 32887. (800) 346-8648. 1991. Eight volumes.

Encyclopedic Dictionary of Genetics: With German Term Equivalents and Extensive German/English Index. R. C. King and W. D. Stansfield. VCH Publishers, 303 NW 12th Ave., Deerfield Beach, Florida 33442-1788. (305) 428-5566. 1990. 4th ed. Revised edition of: A Dictionary of Genetics, third edition.

McGraw-Hill Encyclopedia of Science and Technology. McGraw-Hill, 1221 Avenue of the Americas, New York, New York 10020. (212) 512-2000 or (800) 262-4729. 1992. Seventh edition. Issued in multiple volumes including index. Includes all science and technology broad subject areas.

Van Nostrand's Scientific Encyclopedia. Glenn D. Considine, ed. Van Nostrand Reinhold, 115 5th Ave., New York, New York 10003. (212) 254-3232. 1983. Sixth edition. Includes all broad subject areas in science.

GENERAL WORKS

Aging, Genetics and the Environment. Dept. of Health, Education, and Welfare, Public Health Service, National Institutes of Health, 9000 Rockville Pike, Bethesda, Maryland 20892. (301) 496-4000. 1979. Covers metals in the body.

Assessing Ecological Risks of Biotechnology. Lev R. Ginzburg. Butterworth-Heinemann, 80 Montvale Ave., Stoneham, Massachusetts 02180. (617) 438-8464; (800) 366-2665. 1991. Presents an analysis of the ecological risk associated with genetically engineered microorganisms, organisms that, through gene splicing, have obtained additional genetic information.

Bacterial Genetic Systems. Jeffrey H. Miller, ed. Academic Press, c/o Harcourt Brace Jovanovich Inc., 6277 Sea Harbor Dr., Orlando, Florida 32887. (800) 346-8648. 1991. A volume in the Methods in Enzymology series, no. 204.

Ecological Genetics and Air Pollution. George E. Taylor, Jr., ed. Springer-Verlag, 175 5th Ave., New York, New York 10010. (212) 460-1500; (800) 777-4643. 1991. Describes role of air pollution in governing the genetic structure and evolution of plant species.

Evolutionary Genetics and Environmental Stress. Ary A. Hoffmann. Oxford University Press, 200 Madison Ave., New York, New York 10016. (212) 679-7300 or (800) 334-4249. 1991. Outlines the results of numerous laboratory experiments and field studies from such diverse disciplines as agriculture, biochemistry, developmental biology, ecology, molecular biology, and genetics.

From Cell to Clone: the Story of Genetic Engineering. Margery Facklam. Harcourt Brace Jovanovich, Inc., 1250 6th Ave., San Diego, California 92101. (800) 346-8648. 1979.

From Clone to Clinic. D.J.A. Crommelin, ed. Kluwer Academic Publishers, 101 Philip Dr., Assinippi Pk., Norwell, Massachusetts 02061. (617) 871-6600. 1990.

Genetic Aspects of Plant Mineral Nutrition. N. El Bassam, et al., eds. Kluwer Academic Publishers, 101 Philip Dr., Assinippi Park, Norwell, Massachusetts 02061. (617) 871-6600. 1990. Proceedings of the 3rd International Symposium on Genetic Aspects of Plant Mineral Nutritions, Braunschweig, 1988. Papers discuss the fact that many nutritional characteristics are independently inherited and could be selected for a breeding program. Discusses development of plant breeding techniques. Special features include papers on genetic variation in symbiotic systems and a timely section on the creation of genotypes with increased efficiency of ion absorption under conditions of low input agriculture.

Genetic Engineering of Plants: An Agricultural Perspective. Isune Kosuge. Plenum Press, 233 Spring St., New York, New York 10013-1578. (212) 620-8000. 1983. Plant breeding techniques and plant genetic engineering.

Genetic Resistance to Pesticides. Biological Sciences Curriculum Study, Pleasantville, New York Study and teaching of biology and genetics.

Genetically Altered Viruses and the Environment. Bernard Fields. Cold Spring Harbor Laboratory Press, PO Box 100, Cold Spring Harbor, New York 11724. (800) 843-4388. 1985. Covers virology, viral genetics, environmental microbiology, and genetic engineering.

Magill's Survey of Science. Life Science Series. Frank N. Magill, ed. Salem Press, PO Box 50062, Pasadena, California 91105. 1991. Six volumes. Contents: v.1. A-Central and peripheral nervous system functions; v.2. Central metabolism regulation - eukaryotic transcriptional control; v.3. Positive and negative eukaryotic transcriptional control - mammalian hormones; v.4. Hormones and behavior - muscular contraction; v.5. Muscular contraction and relaxation - sexual reproduction in plants; v.6. Reproductive behavior and mating - X inactivation and the Lyon hypothesis.

Nature Reserves: Island Theory and Conservation Practice. Craig L. Shafer. Smithsonian Institution Press, 470 L'Enfant Plaza, No. 7100, Washington, District of Columbia 20560. (800) 782-4612. 1991. Encompasses ecology, biogeography, evolutionary biology, genetics, paleobiology, as well as legal, social, and economic issues.

Risk Assessment in Genetic Engineering; Environmental Release of Organisms. Morris A. Levin and Harlee Strauss. McGraw-Hill, 1221 Avenue of the Americas, New York, New York 10020. (212) 512-2000; (800) 262-4729. 1991. Investigates issues such as the transport of microorganisms via air, water, and soil; the persistence and establishment of viruses, bacteria, and plants; and the genetic transfer via viruses.

Secondary Metabolism in Microorganisms, Plants and Animals. Martin Luckner. Springer-Verlag, 175 5th Ave., New York, New York 10010. (212) 460-1500. 1990. Includes reviews of the latest results on the biosynthesis for age and degradation of secondary metabolites and characteristics of compounds of specialized cells from all groups of organisms. Has new chapters on: the transport of secondary compounds with the producer organism; the significance of colored and toxic secondary products; and on the improvement of secondary product biosynthesis by genetical means.

Shattering: Food, Politics, and the Loss of Genetic Diversity. Cary Fowler. University of Arizona Press, 1230 N. Park, No. 102, Tucson, Arizona 85719. (602) 621-1441. 1990. Reviews the development of genetic diversity over 10,000 years of human agriculture and its loss in our lifetimes.

HANDBOOKS AND MANUALS

Genetics and Conservation: A Reference for Managing Wild Animal and Plant Populations. Christine M. Schonewald-Cox. Benjamin/Cummings Publishing Co., 390 Bridge Pkwy., Redwood City, California 94065. (415) 594-4400. 1983. Germplasm resources and population genetics.

ONLINE DATA BASES

Applied Genetics News. NewsNet, Inc., 945 Haverford Rd., Bryn Mawr, Pennsylvania 19010. (800) 345-1301.

BIOSIS Previews. BIOSIS, 2100 Arch St., Philadelphia, Pennsylvania 19103-1399. (215) 587-4800. Largest and most comprehensive database of research in the life sciences. Contains citations for nearly 9000 primary research journals, monographs, reviews, symposia, preliminary reports, semi-popular journals, selected institutional reports, government reports and research communications.

Biotechnology Abstracts. Derwent Publications Ltd., 6845 Elm St., McLean, Virginia 22101. (703) 790-0400. Includes material on genetic manipulation, biochemical engineering, fermentation, biocatalysis, cell hybridization, in vitro plant propagation and industrial waste management.

Cambridge Scientific Abstracts Life Science–CSAL. Cambridge Scientific Abstracts, 5161 River Rd., Bethesda, Maryland 20816. (301) 961-6750. Provides access to the following abstracting services: "Life Sciences Collection," "Aquatic Sciences and Fisheries Abstracts," "Oceanic Abstracts," and "Pollution Abstracts."

Chemical Engineering and Biotechnology Abstracts–CEBA. Orbit Search Service, Maxwell Online Inc., 8000 W. Park Dr., McLean, Virginia 22102. (703) 442-0900 or (800) 456-7248. Monthly. Covers theoretical, practical and commercial material on all aspects of processing safety, and the environment. Also covers process and reaction engineering, measurement and process control, environmental protection and safety, plant design and equipment used in chemical engineering and biotechnology. More than 400 of the world's major primary chemical and process engineering journals are scanned to compile the database. Available from ORBIT.

Enviro/Energyline Abstracts Plus. R. R. Bowker Co., 121 Chanlon Rd., New Providence, New Jersey 07974. (908) 464-6800.

Environmental Periodicals Bibliography. National Information Services Corp., Ste. 6, Wyman Towers, 3100 St. Paul St., Baltimore, Maryland 21218. (410)243-0797. Online version of abstract of same name.

Genetic Toxicity. U.S. Environmental Protection Agency, Office of Pesticides and Toxic Substances, 401 M St. SW, Washington, District of Columbia 20460. (202) 260-2090. Mutagenicity information on more than 2600 chemicals tested on 38 biological systems.

Monthly Catalog of United States Government Publications. U.S. G.P.O., Supt. of Docs., PO Box 371954, Pittsburgh, Pennsylvania 15250-7954. (202) 512-0000.

National Technical Information Service. U.S. Department of Commerce, National Technical Information Service, Office of Data Base Services, 5285 Port Royal Rd., Springfield, Virginia 22161. (703) 487-4807. Bibliographic database of government sponsored research and technical reports.

PHYTOMED. Biologische Bundesanstalt fuer Land-und Forstwirtschaft, Dokumentationstelle fuer Phytomedizin, Koenign-Luise-Strasse 19, Berlin, Germany D-1000. 49 (30) 83041.

SCISEARCH. Institute for Scientific Information, University City Science Center, 3501 Market St., Philadelphia, Pennsylvania 19104. (215) 386-0100.

PERIODICALS AND NEWSLETTERS

Environmental and Molecular Mutagenesis. Wiley-Liss, 605 3rd Ave., New York, New York 10158-0012. (212) 850-6000. 1974-. Eight issues per year. Provides an international forum for research on basic mechanisms of mutation, the detection of mutagens, and the implications of environmental mutagens for human health.

Genetic Engineering Letter. Environews, Inc., 952 National Press Bldg., Washington, District of Columbia 20045. (202) 662-7299. Twice a month. Covers developments in the field of biotechnology.

RESEARCH CENTERS AND INSTITUTES

American Type Culture Collection. 12301 Parklawn Drive, Rockville, Maryland 20852. (301) 881-2600.

Center for Molecular Genetics. University of California, San Diego, 9500 Gilman Dr., La Jolla, California 92093. (619) 534-0396.

Committee on Evolutionary Biology. University of Chicago, 915 East 57th Street, Chicago, Illinois 60637. (312) 702-8940.

Developmental Biology Center. University of California, Irvine, Irvine, California 92717. (714) 856-5957.

Fungal Genetics Stock Center. Department of Microbiology, University of Kansas Medical Center, Kansas City, Kansas 66103. (913) 588-7044.

Genetic Stock Center for Cockroaches. Virginia Polytech Institute and State University, Blacksburg, Virginia 24061. (703) 961-5844.

Genetics and Developmental Biology Program. West Virginia University, Division of Plant and Soil Science, College of Agriculture, Morgantown, West Virginia 26506. (304) 293-6256.

Jamie Whitten Delta States Research Center. PO Box 225, Stoneville, Mississippi 3877-0225. (601) 686-5231.

Joseph M. Long Marine Laboratory. University of California, Santa Cruz, 100 Shaffer, Santa Cruz, California 95060. (408) 459-2464.

Massachusetts Institute of Technology Biotechnology Process Engineering Center. Room 20A-207, Cambridge, Massachusetts 02139. (617) 253-0805.

Molecular Biology Institute. University of California, Los Angeles, 405 Hilgard Avenue, Los Angeles, California 90024. (213) 825-1018.

National Drosophila Species Resource Center. Department of Biological Sciences, Bowling Green State University, Bowling Green, Ohio 43403-0212. (419) 372-2096.

Ohio University, Edison Animal Biotechnology Center. West Green, Athens, Ohio 45701. (614) 593-4713.

Rockefeller University, Laboratory of Genetics. 1230 York Avenue, New York, New York 10021-6399. (212) 570-8644.

Rutgers University, Waksman Institute. P.O. Box 759, Piscataway, New Jersey 08855. (908) 932-4257.

State University of New York at Albany, Center for Biological Macromolecules. Chemistry Department, 1400 Washington Avenue, Albany, New York 12222. (518) 422-4454.

State University of New York at Plattsburg, Biochemistry/Biophysics Program. Plattsburg, New York 12901. (518) 564-3159.

Texas A&M University, Faculty of Genetics. College Station, Texas 77843. (409) 845-8877.

Texas A&M University, Forest Genetics Laboratory. College Station, Texas 77843. (409) 845-1325.

U.S. Forest Service, Forestry Sciences Laboratory. Southern Illinois University at Carbondale, Carbondale, Illinois 62901-4630. (618) 453-2318.

U.S. Forest Service, Institute of Forest Genetics. 2480 Carson Road, Placerville, California 95667. (916) 622-1225.

University of Maine, Migratory Fish Research Institute. Department of Zoology, Orono, Maine 04469. (207) 581-2548.

University of Michigan, Museum of Zoology. 1082 University Museums, Ann Arbor, Michigan 48109. (313) 764-0476.

University of Minnesota, Institute for Advanced Studies In Biological Process Technology. 240 Gortner Laboratory, 1479 Gortner Avenue, St. Paul, Minnesota 55108. (612) 624-6774.

University of Notre Dame, Vector Biology Laboratory. Notre Dame, Indiana 46556. (219) 239-7366.

University of Tennessee at Knoxville, Biology Consortium. M303 Walters Life Sciences Building, Knoxville, Tennessee 37996. (615) 974-6841.

University of Texas at Austin, Genetics Institute. Department of Zoology, 528 Patterson Laboratories, Austin, Texas 78712. (512) 471-6268.

University of Washington, Institute for Environmental Studies. Engineering Annex FM-12, Seattle, Washington 98195. (206) 543-1812.

University of Wisconsin-Stevens Point, Wisconsin Cooperative Fishery Research Unit. College of Natural Resources, Stevens Point, Wisconsin 54481. (715) 346-2178.

USDA Plant Gene Expression Center. 800 Buchanan Street, Albany, California 94710. (510) 559-5900.

World Resources Institute. 1709 New York Ave., N.W., Washington, District of Columbia 20006. (202) 638-6300.

STATISTICS SOURCES

Environmental Data Compendium. OECD Publications and Information Center, 2001 L St., N.W., Suite 700, Washington, District of Columbia 20036. (202) 785-6323. 1989.

Environmental Indicators. OECD Publications and Information Center, 2001 L St., N.W., Suite 700, Washington, District of Columbia 20036. (202) 785-6323. 1991.

Environmental Quality. Council on Environmental Quality. U.S. G.P.O., Washington, District of Columbia 20401. (202) 512-0000. Annual.

The State of the Environment. OECD Publications and Information Center, 2001 L St., N.W., Suite 700, Washington, District of Columbia 20036. (202) 785-6323. 1991.

TRADE ASSOCIATIONS AND PROFESSIONAL SOCIETIES

American Genetic Association. P.O. Box 39, Buckeystown, Maryland 21717. (301) 695-9292.

American Institute of Biological Sciences. 730 11th St., N.W., Washington, District of Columbia 20001-4521. (202) 628-1500.

American Society of Naturalists. Department of Ecology and Evolation, State University of New York, Stony Brook, New York 11794. (516) 632-8589.

Genetic Toxicology Association. c/o Kerry Dearfield, USEPA, 401 M St., S.W., Washington, District of Columbia 20460. (703) 557-9780.

Genetics Society of America. 9650 Rockville Pike, Bethesda, Maryland 20814. (301) 571-1825.

Industrial Biotechnology Association. 1625 K St., N.W., Suite 1100, Washington, District of Columbia 20006-1604. (202) 857-0244.

International Genetics Federation. c/o Prof. Peter R. Day, Center for Agricultural Molecular Biology, Cook College, P.O. Box 231, Rutgers University, New Brunswick, New Jersey 08903. (908) 932-8165.

GEOGRAPHY, ENVIRONMENTAL

See also: ATMOSPHERE

ABSTRACTING AND INDEXING SERVICES

Biological and Agricultural Index. H.W. Wilson Co., 950 University Ave., Bronx, New York 10452. (800) 367-6770. 1916-. Monthly.

Current Advances in Ecological and Environmental Science. Pergamon Microforms International, Inc., Fairview Park, Elmsford, New York 10523. (914) 592-7720. 1989-. Monthly. Current literature searching service includingjournals, reports, abstracts, etc. This service is available online as part of the CABS database on the hosts BRS and ORBIT search service.

Ecology Abstracts. Cambridge Scientific Abstracts, 5161 River Rd., Bethesda, Maryland 20816. (301) 961-6750. Monthly.

Environment Abstracts. Bowker A & I Publishing, 121 Chanlon Rd., New Providence, New Jersey 07974. (908) 464-6800. 1974-.

Environment Index. Environment Information Center, Index Research Department, 124 E. 39th St., New York, New York 10016. 1971-. Annual.

Environmental Information Connection–EIC. Planning Information Program, Dept. of Urban and Regional Planning, University of Illinois, 1003 West Nevada, Urbana, Illinois 61801. (217) 333-1369. Also available online.

Environmental Periodicals Bibliography. Environmental Studies Institute, International Academy at Santa Barbara, 800 Garden St., Suite D, Santa Barbara, California 93101. (805) 965-5010. Also available online.

General Science Index. H. W. Wilson Co., 950 University Ave., Bronx, New York 10452. 1978-. Monthly, also issued in annual cumulation. Cumulative subject index to English language periodicals in the subject fields of astronomy, botany, chemistry, earth science, environment and conservation, food and nutrition, genetics, mathematics, medicine and health, microbiology, oceanography, physics, physiology and zoology.

Geo Abstracts, Social Geography and Cartography. Geo Abstracts Ltd., c/o Elsevier Science Pub., Crown House, Linton Rd., Barking, England 1611 8JU.

Index to Scientific Book Contents. Institute for Scientific Information, 3501 Market St., Philadelphia, Pennsylvania 19104. (800) 523-1857. 1985-. Annual. Gives contents of science books published.

Mineralogical Abstracts. Mineralogical Society, 41 Queen's Gate, London, England SW7 5HR. 71 5847916. Quarterly. Abstracts of journal articles, conferences, technical reports and specialized books in the areas of minerals, clay minerals, economic minerals, ore deposits, environmental studies, experimental mineralogy, gem-stones, geochemistry, petrology, lunar and planetary studies and other related areas in mineralogy.

BIBLIOGRAPHIES

Bibliography and Index of Geology. American Geological Institute, 4220 King St., Alexandria, Virginia 22302. Monthly. Includes environmental geology and hydrogeology.

EPA Publications Bibliography. U.S. Environmental Protection Agency, Library Systems Branch, 401 M St., SW, Washington, District of Columbia 20460. (202) 260-2090. Quarterly.

New Publications of the Geological Survey. U.S. Department of the Interior, Geological Survey, 119 National Center, Reston, Virginia 22092. (703) 648-4460. 1984-. Monthly. Bibliography of geological publications and related government documents published by the Geological Survey.

ENCYCLOPEDIAS AND DICTIONARIES

Cambridge Encyclopedia of Life Sciences. A. E. Friday and David S. Ingram. Cambridge University Press, 40 W 20th St., New York, New York 10011. (212) 924-3900 or (800) 227-0247. 1985. Includes all topics under biology and ecology.

Dictionary of Environmental Protection Technology: In Four Languages, English, German, French, Russian. Egon Seidel. Elsevier Science Publishing Co., 655 Avenue of the Americas, New York, New York 10010. (212) 984-5800. 1988.

The Encyclopedia of Geochemistry and Environmental Sciences. Rhodes Whitmore Fairbridge. Van Nostrand Reinhold Co., 115 5th Ave., New York, New York 10003. (212) 254-3232. 1972.

English-Russian Dictionary of Environmental Protection: About 14,000 Terms. E.L. Milovanov. Pergamon Microforms International, Inc., Fairview Park, Elmsford, New York 10523. (914) 592-7720. 1981.

Environmental Engineering Dictionary. C. C. Lee. Government Institutes, Inc., 4 Research Pl., Ste. 200, Rockville, Maryland 20850. (301) 921-2300. 1989. Defines over 6000 engineering terms relating to pollutioncontrol technologies, monitoring, risk assessment, sampling andanalysis, quality control, permitting, and environmentally-regulated engineering and science. Includes bibliographical references (p. 612-627).

Glossary of Geology. Robert Latimer Bates and Julia A. Jackson, eds. American Geological Institute, 4220 King St., Alexandria, Virginia 22302-1507. (703) 379-2480 or (800) 336-4764. 1987. Third edition.

Grzimek's Encyclopedia of Ecology. Bernhard Grzimek. Van Nostrand Reinhold, 115 5th Ave., New York, New York 10003. (212) 254-3232. 1976.

McGraw-Hill Encyclopedia of Environmental Science. Sybil P. Parker. McGraw-Hill Science & Engineering Books, 11 W. 19th St., New York, New York 10011. (212) 337-6010. 1980. Covers ecology, man's influence on nature, and environmental protection.

McGraw-Hill Encyclopedia of the Geological Sciences. Sybil P. Parker, ed. McGraw-Hill, 1221 Avenue of the Americas, New York, New York 10020. (212) 512-2000 or (800) 262-4729. 1988. Second edition. Published previously in the McGraw-Hill Encyclopedia of Science and Technology.

North American Reference Encyclopedia of Ecology and Pollution. William White. North American Pub. Co., 401 N. Broad St., Philadelphia, Pennsylvania 19108. (215) 238-5300. 1972.

GENERAL WORKS

Environmental Determinism in Twentieth Century American Geography: Reflection in the Professional Journals. Joanna Eunice Beck. University of California Press, 2120 Berkeley Way, Berkeley, California 94720. (510) 642-4262; (800) 822-6657. 1985. Covers human ecology and man's influence on the environment.

Magill's Survey of Science. Earth Science Series. Frank N. Magill. Salem Press, PO Box 50062, Pasadena, California 91105. 1990-. Five volumes. Includes information on earth's crust, hot spots and volcanic island chains, physical properties of minerals, rock magnetism, physical properties of rocks, and index.

HANDBOOKS AND MANUALS

Environmental Geography: A Handbook for Teachers. Keith Wheeler. Hart-Davis Educational, St. Albans, England 1976. Study and teaching of human ecology.

ONLINE DATA BASES

Enviro/Energyline Abstracts Plus. R. R. Bowker Co., 121 Chanlon Rd., New Providence, New Jersey 07974. (908) 464-6800.

Environmental Periodicals Bibliography. National Information Services Corp., Ste. 6, Wyman Towers, 3100 St. Paul St., Baltimore, Maryland 21218. (410)243-0797. Online version of abstract of same name.

GeoRef. American Geological Institute, 4220 King St., Alexandria, Virginia 22302. (703) 379-2480.

SCISEARCH. Institute for Scientific Information, University City Science Center, 3501 Market St., Philadelphia, Pennsylvania 19104. (215) 386-0100.

TRADE ASSOCIATIONS AND PROFESSIONAL SOCIETIES

American Geographical Society. 156 5th Ave., Suite 600, New York, New York 10010-7002. (212) 242-0214.

Association of American Geographers. 1710 16th St., N.W., Washington, District of Columbia 20009-3198. (202) 234-1450.

National Geographic Society. 17th and M Streets, NW, Washington, District of Columbia 20036. (202) 857-7000.

GEOLOGY, ENVIRONMENTAL

ABSTRACTING AND INDEXING SERVICES

General Science Index. H. W. Wilson Co., 950 University Ave., Bronx, New York 10452. 1978-. Monthly, also issued in annual cumulation. Cumulative subject index to English language periodicals in the subject fields of astronomy, botany, chemistry, earth science, environ-

ment and conservation, food and nutrition, genetics, mathematics, medicine and health, microbiology, oceanography, physics, physiology and zoology.

Geographical Abstracts. London School of Economics, Dept. of Geography, Regency House, 34 Duke St., London, England 1966-. Continued by Geo Abstracts issued in 6 parts: Pt. A. Landforms and the quaternary; Pt. B. Biogeography and Climatology; Pt. C. Economic geography; Pt. D. Social geography and cartography; Pt. E. Sedimentology; Pt. F. Regional and community planning.

Index to Scientific Book Contents. Institute for Scientific Information, 3501 Market St., Philadelphia, Pennsylvania 19104. (800) 523-1857. 1985-. Annual. Gives contents of science books published.

Meteorological and Geoastrophysical Abstracts. American Meteorological Society, 45 Beacon St., Boston, Massachusetts 02108. (617) 227-2425.

Mineralogical Abstracts. Mineralogical Society, 41 Queen's Gate, London, England SW7 5HR. 71 5847916. Quarterly. Abstracts of journal articles, conferences, technical reports and specialized books in the areas of minerals, clay minerals, economic minerals, ore deposits, environmental studies, experimental mineralogy, gemstones, geochemistry, petrology, lunar and planetary studies and other related areas in mineralogy.

BIBLIOGRAPHIES

A Bibliographic Guide to Recent Research in Environmental Geology and Natural Hazards. Mark E. Richner. Vance Bibliographies, PO Box 229, 112 N. Charter St., Monticello, Illinois 61856. (217) 762-3831. 1981. Covers natural disasters, land use planning, and water resource development.

Bibliography and Index of Geology. American Geological Institute, 4220 King St., Alexandria, Virginia 22302. Monthly. Includes environmental geology and hydrogeology.

New Publications of the Geological Survey. U.S. Department of the Interior, Geological Survey, 119 National Center, Reston, Virginia 22092. (703) 648-4460. 1984-. Monthly. Bibliography of geological publications and related government documents published by the Geological Survey.

DIRECTORIES

Directory of Certified Petroleum Geologists. American Association of Petroleum Geologists, Box 979, Tulsa, Oklahoma 74101. (918) 584-2555.

The Geophysical Directory Regional and Worldwide Coverage. Geophysical Directory Inc., 2200 Welch Ave., PO Box 130508, Houston, Texas 77219. (713) 529-8789. 1988. Annual. Forty-third edition. Gives addresses and company profiles classified by their function. Also includes a list of U.S. Government agencies utilizing geophysics.

ENCYCLOPEDIAS AND DICTIONARIES

Dictionary of Environmental Protection Technology: In Four Languages, English, German, French, Russian. Egon Seidel. Elsevier Science Publishing Co., 655 Avenue of the Americas, New York, New York 10010. (212) 984-5800. 1988.

A Dictionary of Landscape: A Dictionary of Terms Used in the Description of the World's Land Surface. George A. Goulty. Avebury Technical, c/o Gower, Gower House, Croft Rd., Aldershot, England GU11 3HR. (0252) 331551. 1991. Earth sciences dictionary. Covers architecture, building construction, horticulture, and town planning.

The Encyclopedia of Geochemistry and Environmental Sciences. Rhodes Whitmore Fairbridge. Van Nostrand Reinhold Co., 115 5th Ave., New York, New York 10003. (212) 254-3232. 1972.

English-Russian Dictionary of Environmental Protection: About 14,000 Terms. E.L. Milovanov. Pergamon Microforms International, Inc., Fairview Park, Elmsford, New York 10523. (914) 592-7720. 1981.

Environmental Engineering Dictionary. C. C. Lee. Government Institutes, Inc., 4 Research Pl., Ste. 200, Rockville, Maryland 20850. (301) 921-2300. 1989. Defines over 6000 engineering terms relating to pollutioncontrol technologies, monitoring, risk assessment, sampling andanalysis, quality control, permitting, and environmentally-regulated engineering and science. Includes bibliographical references (p. 612-627).

Grzimek's Encyclopedia of Ecology. Bernhard Grzimek. Van Nostrand Reinhold, 115 5th Ave., New York, New York 10003. (212) 254-3232. 1976.

McGraw-Hill Encyclopedia of Environmental Science. Sybil P. Parker. McGraw-Hill Science & Engineering Books, 11 W. 19th St., New York, New York 10011. (212) 337-6010. 1980. Covers ecology, man's influence on nature, and environmental protection.

North American Reference Encyclopedia of Ecology and Pollution. William White. North American Pub. Co., 401 N. Broad St., Philadelphia, Pennsylvania 19108. (215) 238-5300. 1972.

GENERAL WORKS

Environmental Geology. Ronald W. Tank. Oxford University Press, 200 Madison Ave., New York, New York 10016. (212) 679-7300. 1983. Mines, mineral resources, natural disasters and conservation of natural resources.

Magill's Survey of Science. Earth Science Series. Frank N. Magill. Salem Press, PO Box 50062, Pasadena, California 91105. 1990-. Five volumes. Includes information on earth's crust, hot spots and volcanic island chains, physical properties of minerals, rock magnetism, physical properties of rocks, and index.

HANDBOOKS AND MANUALS

Handbook of Geophysics and the Space Environment. Adolph S. Jursa, ed. Air Force Geophysics Laboratory, Air Force Systems Command, United States Air Force, c/o National Technical Information Serveice, 5285 Port Royal Rd., Springfield, Virginia 22161. (703) 487-4650. 1985. Two volumes. Broad subject areas covered are space, atmosphere, and terrestrial environment. Includes topics such as solar radiation, sunspots, solar wind, geomagnetic fields, radiation belts, cosmic radiation, atmospheric gases, etc.

ONLINE DATA BASES

GEOBASE. Elsevier/GEO Abstracts, Regency House, 34 Duke St., Norwich, England NR3 3AP. 44 (603) 626327.

GEOLINE. Informationszentrum Rohstoffgewinnung, Geowissenschaften Wasserwirtschaft, Bundesanstalt fuer Geowissenschaften und Rohstoffe (BGR), Postfach 510153, Stilleweg 2, Hannover 51, Germany D-3000. 49 (511) 643-2819.

Geomechanics Abstracts. Rockmechanics Information Service, Imperial College of Science, Technology and Medicine, Department of Mineral Resources Engineering, Royal School of Mines, Prince Consort Rd., London, England SW7 2BP. 44 (71) 589-5111, x6436.

GeoRef. American Geological Institute, 4220 King St., Alexandria, Virginia 22302. (703) 379-2480.

PERIODICALS AND NEWSLETTERS

Environmental Geology & Water Sciences. Springer-Verlag, 175 Fifth Avenue, New York, New York 10010. (212) 460-1500. Bimonthly. Covers interactions between humanity and Earth.

Progress in Physical Geography. Cambridge University Press, 40 W. 20th St., New York, New York 10011. (212) 924-3900. Quarterly. Studies on animate and inanimate aspects of the earth, ocean, and atmosphere with interest in man-environment interaction .

TRADE ASSOCIATIONS AND PROFESSIONAL SOCIETIES

American Geological Institute. 4220 King St., Alexandria, Virginia 22302. (703) 379-2480.

American Institute of Professional Geologists. 7828 Vance Dr., Suite 103, Arvada, Colorado 80003. (303) 431-0831.

Association of Engineering Geologists. 323 Boston Post Rd., Suite 2D, Sudbury, Massachusetts 01776. (508) 443-4639.

Geological Society of America. P.O. Box 9140, 3300 Penrose Pl., Boulder, Colorado 80301. (303) 447-2020.

GEORGIA ENVIRONMENTAL AGENCIES

GOVERNMENTAL ORGANIZATIONS

Department of Agriculture: Pesticide Registration. Assistant Commissioner, Entomology and Pesticide Division, 19 Martin Luther King Pkwy., S.W., Atlanta, Georgia 30334. (404) 656-4958.

Department of Labor: Occupational Safety. Assistant Commissioner, Field Services, 254 Washington St., S.W., Atlanta, Georgia 30334. (404) 656-3014.

Department of Natural Resources: Air Quality. Air Protection Branch Chief, Environmental Protection Division, Floyd Towers East, Room 1162, 205 Butler St., S.E., Atlanta, Georgia 30334. (404) 656-6900.

Department of Natural Resources: Coastal Zone Management. Director, Coastal Resources Division, 1200 Glynn Ave., Brunswick, Georgia 31523-9990. (912) 264-7221.

Department of Natural Resources: Environmental Protection. Commissioner, 205 Butler St., S.E., Floyd Towers, Suite 1252, Atlanta, Georgia 30334. (404) 656-4713.

Department of Natural Resources: Fish and Wildlife. Director, Game and Fish Division, 205 Butler St., S.E., Floyd Towers East, Suite 1362, Atlanta, Georgia 30334. (404) 656-3523.

Department of Natural Resources: Groundwater Management. Manager, State Groundwater Program, 205 Butler St., S.E., Atlanta, Georgia 30334. (404) 656-5660.

Department of Natural Resources: Natural Resources. Commissioner, 205 Butler St., S.E., Floyd Towers, Suite 1252, Atlanta, Georgia 30334. (404) 656-3500.

Department of Natural Resources: Underground Storage Tanks. Assistant Director, Environmental Protection Division, 205 Butler St., S.W., Floyd Towers East, Suite 1152, Atlanta, Georgia 30334. (404) 656-3500.

Department of Natural Resources: Water Quality. Branch Chief, 205 Butler St., S.E., Floyd Towers East, Suite 1252, Atlanta, Georgia 30334. (404) 656-4708.

Emergency Response Commission: Emergency Preparedness and Community Right-to-Know. Chair, 205 Butler St., S.E., Floyd Towers East, 11th Floor, Suite 1166, Atlanta, Georgia 30334. (404) 656-6905.

Environmental Health and Safety Division: Waste Minimization and Pollution Prevention. Director, Hazardous Waste Treatment Assistance Program, Georgia Institute of Technology, O'Keefe Building, Room 037, Atlanta, Georgia 30332. (404) 894-3806.

Environmental Protection Division: Hazardous Waste Management. Land Protection Branch Chief, Industrial and Hazardous Waste Program, 205 Butler St., S.W., Floyd Towers East, Suite 1252, Atlanta, Georgia 30334. (404) 656-2833.

Environmental Protection Division: Solid Waste Management. Land Protection Branch Chief, Industrial and Hazardous Waste Program, 205 Butler St., S.E., Floyd Towers East, Atlanta, Georgia 30334. (404) 656-2833.

GEORGIA ENVIRONMENTAL LEGISLATION

GENERAL WORKS

Encyclopedia of Georgia Law. Harrison Co., 3110 Crossing Park, Norcross, Georgia 30071. (404) 447-9150.

Georgia Environmental Law Handbook. Government Institutes, Inc., 4 Research Pl., Ste. 200, Rockville, Maryland 20850. (301) 921-2300. 1990.

GEOTHERMAL DRILLING

See: DRILLING

GEOTHERMAL ENERGY

ABSTRACTING AND INDEXING SERVICES

Applied Science and Technology Index. H.W. Wilson Co., 950 University Ave., Bronx, New York 10452. (800) 367-6770. Formerly Industrial Arts Index.

Engineering Index. The Engineering Index Inc., 345 E. 47th St., New York, New York 10017. 1962-.

Environment Abstracts. Bowker A & I Publishing, 121 Chanlon Rd., New Providence, New Jersey 07974. (908) 464-6800. 1974-.

Environment Index. Environment Information Center, Index Research Department, 124 E. 39th St., New York, New York 10016. 1971-. Annual.

Environmental Information Connection–EIC. Planning Information Program, Dept. of Urban and Regional Planning, University of Illinois, 1003 West Nevada, Urbana, Illinois 61801. (217) 333-1369. Also available online.

Environmental Periodicals Bibliography. Environmental Studies Institute, International Academy at Santa Barbara, 800 Garden St., Suite D, Santa Barbara, California 93101. (805) 965-5010. Also available online.

ERDA Research Abstracts. U.S. ERDA Technical Information Center, Box 62, Oak Ridge, Tennessee 37830.

General Science Index. H. W. Wilson Co., 950 University Ave., Bronx, New York 10452. 1978-. Monthly, also issued in annual cumulation. Cumulative subject index to English language periodicals in the subject fields of astronomy, botany, chemistry, earth science, environment and conservation, food and nutrition, genetics, mathematics, medicine and health, microbiology, oceanography, physics, physiology and zoology.

Geothermal Energy. National Technical Information Service, 5285 Port Royal Rd., Springfield, Virginia 22161. (703) 487-4650. Bimonthly. Technology required for economic recovery of geothermal energy and its use.

BIBLIOGRAPHIES

EPA Publications Bibliography. U.S. Environmental Protection Agency, Library Systems Branch, 401 M St., SW, Washington, District of Columbia 20460. (202) 260-2090. Quarterly.

Geothermal Energy. Diana Niskern. Library of Congress, Science and Technology Division, Reference Section, Washington, District of Columbia 20540. (202) 207-1181. 1983.

Geothermal Resources Exploration and Exploitation. U.S. Energy Research and Development Administration, Technical Information Center, PO Box 2001, Oak Ridge, Tennessee 37831. (615) 576-4444. 1976.

ENCYCLOPEDIAS AND DICTIONARIES

The Encyclopedia of Geochemistry and Environmental Sciences. Rhodes Whitmore Fairbridge. Van Nostrand Reinhold Co., 115 5th Ave., New York, New York 10003. (212) 254-3232. 1972.

Encyclopedia of Physical Science and Technology. Robert A. Meyers, ed. Academic Press, c/o Harcourt Brace

Jovanovich Inc., 6277 Sea Harbor Dr., Orlando, Florida 32887. (800) 346-8648. Dictionary of engineering, technology and physical sciences.

Encyclopedia of Physics. Rita G. Lerner and George L. Trigg. VCH Publishers, 303 NW 12th Ave., Deerfield Beach, Florida 33442-1788. (305) 428-5566. 1991. Second edition.

Energy Terminology: A Multilingual Glossary. Pergamon Microforms International, Inc., Fairview Park, Elmsford, New York 10523. (914) 592-7720. 1986. Second edition. Contains 1500 defined terms and concepts related to the field of energy together with an index of several thousand undefined keywords used in the definitions of these terms and concepts. Contents appear in four languages: English, French, German and Spanish.

McGraw-Hill Encyclopedia of Environmental Science. Sybil P. Parker. McGraw-Hill Science & Engineering Books, 11 W. 19th St., New York, New York 10011. (212) 337-6010. 1980. Covers ecology, man's influence on nature, and environmental protection.

McGraw-Hill Encyclopedia of Science and Technology. McGraw-Hill, 1221 Avenue of the Americas, New York, New York 10020. (212) 512-2000 or (800) 262-4729. 1992. Seventh edition. Issued in multiple volumes including index. Includes all science and technology broad subject areas.

Van Nostrand's Scientific Encyclopedia. Glenn D. Considine, ed. Van Nostrand Reinhold, 115 5th Ave., New York, New York 10003. (212) 254-3232. 1983. Sixth edition. Includes all broad subject areas in science.

GENERAL WORKS

Indirect Solar, Geothermal, and Nuclear Energy. T. Nejat Veziroglu, ed. Nova Science Publishers Inc., 283 Commack Rd., Suite 300, Commack, New York 11725-3401. (516) 499-3103; (516) 499-3106. 1991. Presents several focussed sectors of the energy spectrum: wind energy, ocean energy, gravitational energy, I.C. engines, and fluidized beds and looks at nuclear energy.

HANDBOOKS AND MANUALS

Geothermal Heating: A Handbook of Engineering Economics. R. Harrison. Pergamon Microforms International, Inc., Fairview Park, Elmsford, New York 10523. (914) 592-7720. 1990.

Handbook of Geothermal Energy. L.M. Edwards. Gulf Publishing Co., Book Division, PO Box 2608, Houston, Texas 77252. (713) 529-4301. 1982. Methods relating to use of geothermal resources.

ONLINE DATA BASES

Computerized Engineering Index–COMPENDEX. Engineering Information Inc., 345 E. 47th St., New York, New York 10017. (212) 705-7600.

EBIB. Texas A & M University, Sterling C. Evans Library, Reference Division, College Station, Texas 77843. (409) 845-5741.

Electric Power Industry Abstracts. Utility Data Institute, 1700 K St., N.W., Suite 400, Washington, District of Columbia 20006. (800) 466-3660.

Enviro/Energyline Abstracts Plus. R. R. Bowker Co., 121 Chanlon Rd., New Providence, New Jersey 07974. (908) 464-6800.

Environmental Periodicals Bibliography. National Information Services Corp., Ste. 6, Wyman Towers, 3100 St. Paul St., Baltimore, Maryland 21218. (410)243-0797. Online version of abstract of same name.

PERIODICALS AND NEWSLETTERS

Geothermal Progress Monitor Report. National Technical Information Service, 5285 Port Royal Rd., Springfield, Virginia 22161. (703) 487-4650. Annual. Statistics on the development of geothermal resources.

The Solar Thermal Report. Solar Liaison, Chicago, Illinois Quarterly. Covers solar energy and geothermal resources.

STATISTICS SOURCES

World Resources. World Resources Institute. 1709 New York Ave., N.W., Washington, District of Columbia 20006. (202) 638-6300. Annual. Statistical and textual analysis of world's natural resources and the effects of growth-caused environmental pollution.

TRADE ASSOCIATIONS AND PROFESSIONAL SOCIETIES

Geothermal Resources Council. P.O. Box 1350, Davis, California 95617. (916) 758-2360.

GERMICIDES

See: PESTICIDES

GLACIAL FLOUR

See: STREAMS

GLASS

See also: RECYCLING

ABSTRACTING AND INDEXING SERVICES

Engineering Index. The Engineering Index Inc., 345 E. 47th St., New York, New York 10017. 1962-.

Environment Abstracts. Bowker A & I Publishing, 121 Chanlon Rd., New Providence, New Jersey 07974. (908) 464-6800. 1974-.

Environment Index. Environment Information Center, Index Research Department, 124 E. 39th St., New York, New York 10016. 1971-. Annual.

Environmental Information Connection–EIC. Planning Information Program, Dept. of Urban and Regional Planning, University of Illinois, 1003 West Nevada, Urbana, Illinois 61801. (217) 333-1369. Also available online.

Environmental Periodicals Bibliography. Environmental Studies Institute, International Academy at Santa Barba-

ra, 800 Garden St., Suite D, Santa Barbara, California 93101. (805) 965-5010. Also available online.

General Science Index. H. W. Wilson Co., 950 University Ave., Bronx, New York 10452. 1978-. Monthly, also issued in annual cumulation. Cumulative subject index to English language periodicals in the subject fields of astronomy, botany, chemistry, earth science, environment and conservation, food and nutrition, genetics, mathematics, medicine and health, microbiology, oceanography, physics, physiology and zoology.

Pollution Abstracts. Cambridge Scientific Abstracts, 5161 River Rd., Bethesda, Maryland 20816. (301) 961-6750. Six/year. Indexes worldwide technical literature on environmental pollution. Covers air pollution, marine and freshwater pollution, sewage and wastewater treatment, waste management, toxicology and health, noise pollution, radiation, land pollution, and environmental policies, programs, legislation, and education. Also available online.

Science Citation Index. Institute for Scientific Information, 3501 Market St., Philadelphia, Pennsylvania 19104. 1961-.

BIBLIOGRAPHIES

EPA Publications Bibliography. U.S. Environmental Protection Agency, Library Systems Branch, 401 M St., SW, Washington, District of Columbia 20460. (202) 260-2090. Quarterly.

DIRECTORIES

Glass Factory Directory. National Glass Budget, Box 7138, Pittsburgh, Pennsylvania 15213. (412) 682-5136. Annual.

Glass Magazine–Directory of Suppliers Section. 8200 Greensboro Dr., Suite 302, McLean, Virginia 22102. (703) 442-4890. Monthly.

ENCYCLOPEDIAS AND DICTIONARIES

Van Nostrand's Scientific Encyclopedia. Glenn D. Considine, ed. Van Nostrand Reinhold, 115 5th Ave., New York, New York 10003. (212) 254-3232. 1983. Sixth edition. Includes all broad subject areas in science.

GENERAL WORKS

Glass, Science and Technology. Academic Press, c/o Harcourt Brace Jovanovich Inc., 6277 Sea Harbor Dr., Orlando, Florida 32887. (800) 346-8648. Annual. Structure, microstructure, and properties of glass.

How on Earth Do We Recycle Glass?. Joanna Randolph Rott. Millbrook Press, 2 Old New Milford Rd., PO Box 335, Brookfield, Connecticut 06804-0335. (203) 740-2220. 1992. Making of glass and the problems causes by glass waste; ways of using discarded glass.

ONLINE DATA BASES

Computerized Engineering Index–COMPENDEX. Engineering Information Inc., 345 E. 47th St., New York, New York 10017. (212) 705-7600.

DOMIS. ECHO Service, BP 2373, Luxembourg L-1023. (352) 488041.

Enviro/Energyline Abstracts Plus. R. R. Bowker Co., 121 Chanlon Rd., New Providence, New Jersey 07974. (908) 464-6800.

Environmental Periodicals Bibliography. National Information Services Corp., Ste. 6, Wyman Towers, 3100 St. Paul St., Baltimore, Maryland 21218. (410)243-0797. Online version of abstract of same name.

STATISTICS SOURCES

Facing America's Trash: What Next for Municipal Solid Waste?. U.S. Office of Technology Assessment. Van Nostrand Reinhold, Washington, District of Columbia 20401. (202) 512-0000. 1991. Generation, composition and cost of recycling municipal solid waste.

Glass Materials & Chemicals. FIND/SVP, 625 Avenue of the Americas, New York, New York 10011. (212) 645-4500. 1991.

TRADE ASSOCIATIONS AND PROFESSIONAL SOCIETIES

American Natural Soda Ash Corporation. Eight Wright St., Westport, Connecticut 06880. (203) 226-9056.

Glass Packaging Institute. 1801 K St., N.W., Suite 1105L, Washington, District of Columbia 20006. (202) 887-4850.

Glass, Pottery, Plastics, & Allied Workers International Union. 608 E. Baltimore Pike, Box 607, Media, Pennsylvania 19063. (215) 565-5051.

Glass Technical Institute. 12653 Portada Pl., San Diego, California 92130. (619) 481-1277.

GLIADIN

ABSTRACTING AND INDEXING SERVICES

Biological Abstracts. BIOSIS, 2100 Arch St., Philadelphia, Pennsylvania 19103-1399. (215) 587-4800. 1927-.

Environment Abstracts. Bowker A & I Publishing, 121 Chanlon Rd., New Providence, New Jersey 07974. (908) 464-6800. 1974-.

Environment Index. Environment Information Center, Index Research Department, 124 E. 39th St., New York, New York 10016. 1971-. Annual.

Environmental Information Connection–EIC. Planning Information Program, Dept. of Urban and Regional Planning, University of Illinois, 1003 West Nevada, Urbana, Illinois 61801. (217) 333-1369. Also available online.

Environmental Periodicals Bibliography. Environmental Studies Institute, International Academy at Santa Barbara, 800 Garden St., Suite D, Santa Barbara, California 93101. (805) 965-5010. Also available online.

General Science Index. H. W. Wilson Co., 950 University Ave., Bronx, New York 10452. 1978-. Monthly, also issued in annual cumulation. Cumulative subject index to English language periodicals in the subject fields of astronomy, botany, chemistry, earth science, environment and conservation, food and nutrition, genetics, mathematics, medicine and health, microbiology, oceanography, physics, physiology and zoology.

Science Citation Index. Institute for Scientific Information, 3501 Market St., Philadelphia, Pennsylvania 19104. 1961-.

BIBLIOGRAPHIES

EPA Publications Bibliography. U.S. Environmental Protection Agency, Library Systems Branch, 401 M St., SW, Washington, District of Columbia 20460. (202) 260-2090. Quarterly.

ENCYCLOPEDIAS AND DICTIONARIES

Van Nostrand's Scientific Encyclopedia. Glenn D. Considine, ed. Van Nostrand Reinhold, 115 5th Ave., New York, New York 10003. (212) 254-3232. 1983. Sixth edition. Includes all broad subject areas in science.

ONLINE DATA BASES

BIOSIS Previews. BIOSIS, 2100 Arch St., Philadelphia, Pennsylvania 19103-1399. (215) 587-4800. Largest and most comprehensive database of research in the life sciences. Contains citations for nearly 9000 primary research journals, monographs, reviews, symposia, preliminary reports, semi-popular journals, selected institutional reports, government reports and research communications.

Enviro/Energyline Abstracts Plus. R. R. Bowker Co., 121 Chanlon Rd., New Providence, New Jersey 07974. (908) 464-6800.

Environmental Periodicals Bibliography. National Information Services Corp., Ste. 6, Wyman Towers, 3100 St. Paul St., Baltimore, Maryland 21218. (410)243-0797. Online version of abstract of same name.

GLOBAL ENVIRONMENT MONITORING SYSTEMS

ABSTRACTING AND INDEXING SERVICES

Engineering Index. The Engineering Index Inc., 345 E. 47th St., New York, New York 10017. 1962-.

Environment Abstracts. Bowker A & I Publishing, 121 Chanlon Rd., New Providence, New Jersey 07974. (908) 464-6800. 1974-.

Environment Index. Environment Information Center, Index Research Department, 124 E. 39th St., New York, New York 10016. 1971-. Annual.

Environmental Information Connection–EIC. Planning Information Program, Dept. of Urban and Regional Planning, University of Illinois, 1003 West Nevada, Urbana, Illinois 61801. (217) 333-1369. Also available online.

Environmental Periodicals Bibliography. Environmental Studies Institute, International Academy at Santa Barbara, 800 Garden St., Suite D, Santa Barbara, California 93101. (805) 965-5010. Also available online.

Geographical Abstracts. London School of Economics, Dept. of Geography, Regency House, 34 Duke St., London, England 1966-. Continued by Geo Abstracts issued in 6 parts: Pt. A. Landforms and the quaternary; Pt. B. Biogeography and Climatology; Pt. C. Economic geography; Pt. D. Social geography and cartography; Pt. E. Sedimentology; Pt. F. Regional and community planning.

BIBLIOGRAPHIES

EPA Publications Bibliography. U.S. Environmental Protection Agency, Library Systems Branch, 401 M St., SW, Washington, District of Columbia 20460. (202) 260-2090. Quarterly.

DIRECTORIES

Gale Environmental Sourcebook. Karen Hill. Gale Research Co., 835 Penobscot Bldg., Detroit, Michigan 48226-4094. (313) 961-2242. Contacts, information sources, or general information on environmental topics.

GENERAL WORKS

Escaping the Heat Trap. Irving Mintzer and William R. Moomaw. World Resources Institute, 1709 New York Ave. N.W., Washington, District of Columbia 20006. (800) 822-0504. 1991. Report is based on a series of scenarios developed using WRI's Model of Warming Commitment. Investigates the potential of societies to dramatically limit the rate of future greenhouse gas buildup and reduce to zero annual commitment to global warming.

Global Environment Issues. E. El-Hinnawi and M. Hashmi, eds. Cassell PLC, Publishers Distribution Center, Rutherford, New Jersey 07070. (201) 939-6064; (201) 939-6065. 1982.

Global Environmental Issues; a Climatological Approach. David D. Kemp. Routledge, 29 W. 35th St., New York, New York 10001-2291. (212) 244-3336. 1990. A textbook for an introductory college course in geography or environmental studies, but interdisciplinary enough for use in other courses with an environmental approach. Bridges the gulf between technical reports and popular articles on such topics as the greenhouse effect, ozone depletion, nuclear winter, atmospheric turbidity, and drought.

Global Pollution and Health: Results of Health-Related Environmental Monitoring. World Health Organization, Ave. Appia, Geneva, Switzerland CH-1211. 1987. International cooperation in environmental monitoring.

Hazardous Waste Management Engineering. Edward J. Martin and James H. Johnson. PennWell Books, PO Box 21288, Tulsa, Oklahoma 74121. (918) 831-9421; (800) 752-9764. 1986. Covers the basic principles and applications of the most current hazardous waste technologies. Provides a wealth of data and techniques that can be immediately applied to analyzing, designing and developing effective hazardous waste management solutions.

Trees of Life: Saving Tropical Forests and their Biological Wealth. Kenton Miller and Laura Tangley. World Resources Institute, 1709 New York Ave. N.W., Washington, District of Columbia 20006. (800) 822-0504. 1991. Explains what deforestation is doing to the global environment and why rainforest preservation is valid to human welfare around the world.

ONLINE DATA BASES

Computerized Engineering Index–COMPENDEX. Engineering Information Inc., 345 E. 47th St., New York, New York 10017. (212) 705-7600.

Enviro/Energyline Abstracts Plus. R. R. Bowker Co., 121 Chanlon Rd., New Providence, New Jersey 07974. (908) 464-6800.

Environmental Periodicals Bibliography. National Information Services Corp., Ste. 6, Wyman Towers, 3100 St. Paul St., Baltimore, Maryland 21218. (410)243-0797. Online version of abstract of same name.

Global Environmental Change Report. Cutter Information Corp., 37 Broadway, Arlington, Massachusetts 02174-5539. (617) 648-8700. Online access to environmental issues worldwide, including global warming, ozone depletion, deforestation, and acid rain. Online version of periodical of the same name.

Monthly Catalog of United States Government Publications. U.S. G.P.O., Supt. of Docs., PO Box 371954, Pittsburgh, Pennsylvania 15250-7954. (202) 512-0000.

National Technical Information Service. U.S. Department of Commerce, National Technical Information Service, Office of Data Base Services, 5285 Port Royal Rd., Springfield, Virginia 22161. (703) 487-4807. Bibliographic database of government sponsored research and technical reports.

SCISEARCH. Institute for Scientific Information, University City Science Center, 3501 Market St., Philadelphia, Pennsylvania 19104. (215) 386-0100.

PERIODICALS AND NEWSLETTERS

Earth Quest. University Corp. for Atmospheric Research, PO Box 3000, Boulder, Colorado 80307. (303) 497-1682. Quarterly. National and international programs addressing global environmental change.

Earth Science. American Geological Institute, 4220 King Street, Alexandria, Virginia 22302. (703) 379-2480. Quarterly. Covers geological issues.

Global Climate Change Digest. Elsevier Science Publishing Co., 655 Avenue of the Americas, New York, New York 10010. (212) 984-5800. Monthly. Topics dealing with ozone depletion and the large-scale climatic changes linked to industrial activity, industrial by-products, and man-made substances.

Global Environmental Change: Human and Policy Dimensions. James K. Mitchell, ed. Department of Geography, Lucy Stone Hall, Kilmer Campus, New Brunswick, New Jersey 08903. (201) 932-4103. 1991. Five issues a year. Produced in cooperation with the United Nations University, including its International Human Dimensions of Global Change Programme. Addresses the human, ecological and public policy aspects of environmental processes that might affect the sustainability of life on Earth.

Global Environmental Change Report. Cutter Information Corp., 37 Broadway, Arlington, Massachusetts 02174-5539. (617) 648-8700. Biweekly. Focus on global warming, ozone depletion, deforestation, and acid rain. Also available online.

World Resource Review. SUPCON International, PO Box 5275, 1 Heritage Plaza, Woodridge, Illinois 60517. (708)

910-1551. 1981-. Quarterly. Covers all phases of policy discussions and their developments, including such topics as global change, energy production and use, ecosystem impacts of development activities, environmental law, solution of transnational environmental problems, global flow of strategic industrial materials, regional, national, and local resource management, natural resources, food, agriculture and forestry.

RESEARCH CENTERS AND INSTITUTES

Center for Technology, Environment, and Development. Clark University, 16 Claremont St., Worcester, Massachusetts 01610. (508) 751-4606.

Pacific Institute for Studies in Development, Environment, and Security. 1681 Shattuck Ave., Suite H, Berkeley, California 94709. (415) 843-9550.

Worldwatch Institute. 1776 Massachusetts Ave., N.W., Washington, District of Columbia 20036. (202) 452-1999.

STATISTICS SOURCES

Environmental Data Compendium. OECD Publications and Information Center, 2001 L St., N.W., Suite 700, Washington, District of Columbia 20036. (202) 785-6323. 1989.

Environmental Indicators. OECD Publications and Information Center, 2001 L St., N.W., Suite 700, Washington, District of Columbia 20036. (202) 785-6323. 1991.

Environmental Quality. Council on Environmental Quality. U.S. G.P.O., Washington, District of Columbia 20401. (202) 512-0000. Annual.

The State of the Environment. OECD Publications and Information Center, 2001 L St., N.W., Suite 700, Washington, District of Columbia 20036. (202) 785-6323. 1991.

Trends '90: A Compendium of Data on Global Change. Thomas A. Boden, et al. Carbon Dioxide Information Analysis Center, Environmental Sciences Division, Oak Ridge National Laboratory, Oak Ridge, Tennessee 37831-6335. 1990. Source of frequently used global change data. Includes estimates of global and national CO_2 emissions from the burning of fossil fuels and from the production of cement and other pollutants.

World Resources. World Resources Institute. 1709 New York Ave., N.W., Washington, District of Columbia 20006. (202) 638-6300. Annual. Statistical and textual analysis of world's natural resources and the effects of growth-caused environmental pollution.

TRADE ASSOCIATIONS AND PROFESSIONAL SOCIETIES

Global Tomorrow Coalition. 1325 G St., N.W., Suite 915, Washington, District of Columbia 20005-3103. (202) 628-4016.

GLOBAL WARMING

See also: GREENHOUSE EFFECT

ABSTRACTING AND INDEXING SERVICES

Abstracts of Air and Water Conservation Literature. American Petroleum Institute. Central Abstracting and Indexing Service, 275 Madison Avenue, New York, New York 10016. 1972.

Air Pollution Technical Publications of the United States Environmental Protection Agency. U.S. Environmental Protection Agency, Mail Drop 75, Research Triangle Park, North Carolina 27711. (919) 541-2184. 1976. Quarterly.

Air Pollution Titles. Pennsylvania State University, Center for Air Environmental Studies, 226 Fenske Laboratory, University Park, Pennsylvania 16802. (814) 865-1415. 1965. Bibliographic guide to current research literature on air environment, including monitoring and control of air pollution, health effects, effects on agriculture, forests, toxic air contaminants, and global atmospheric pro cases.

Air Pollution Translations. A Bibliography With Abstracts. U.S. Environmental Protection Agency, MD 75, Research Triangle Park, North Carolina 27711. (919) 541-2184. 1969.

Applied Ecology Abstracts Studies in Renewable Natural Resources. Information Retrieval Ltd., 1911 Jefferson Davis Highway, Arlington, Virginia 22202. 1975-. Monthly.

Applied Science and Technology Index. H.W. Wilson Co., 950 University Ave., Bronx, New York 10452. (800) 367-6770. Formerly Industrial Arts Index.

Biological Abstracts. BIOSIS, 2100 Arch St., Philadelphia, Pennsylvania 19103-1399. (215) 587-4800. 1927-.

Biological and Agricultural Index. H.W. Wilson Co., 950 University Ave., Bronx, New York 10452. (800) 367-6770. 1916-. Monthly.

Bulletin Signaletique: Eau et Assainissement, Pollution Atmospherique, Droit des Pollutions. Centre de Documentation, Centre National de la Recherche Scientifique, 15, quai Anatole France, Paris, France 75700. (1) 45 55 92 25. 1983-. Monthly. Indexes pollution periodicals including water, atmospheric and related pollutions.

Current Advances in Ecological and Environmental Science. Pergamon Microforms International, Inc., Fairview Park, Elmsford, New York 10523. (914) 592-7720. 1989-. Monthly. Current literature searching service includingjournals, reports, abstracts, etc. This service is available online as part of the CABS database on the hosts BRS and ORBIT search service.

Ecological Abstracts. Geo Abstracts Ltd. Elsevier Applied Science, Crown House, Linton Rd., Barking, England IG 11 8JU. 1974-. Derived from over 600 leading ecological and environmental journals, plus books, conference proceedings, reports and theses.

Engineering Index. The Engineering Index Inc., 345 E. 47th St., New York, New York 10017. 1962-.

Environment Abstracts. Bowker A & I Publishing, 121 Chanlon Rd., New Providence, New Jersey 07974. (908) 464-6800. 1974-.

Environment Index. Environment Information Center, Index Research Department, 124 E. 39th St., New York, New York 10016. 1971-. Annual.

Environmental Information Connection–EIC. Planning Information Program, Dept. of Urban and Regional Planning, University of Illinois, 1003 West Nevada, Urbana, Illinois 61801. (217) 333-1369. Also available online.

Environmental Periodicals Bibliography. Environmental Studies Institute, International Academy at Santa Barbara, 800 Garden St., Suite D, Santa Barbara, California 93101. (805) 965-5010. Also available online.

ERDA Research Abstracts. U.S. ERDA Technical Information Center, Box 62, Oak Ridge, Tennessee 37830.

General Science Index. H. W. Wilson Co., 950 University Ave., Bronx, New York 10452. 1978-. Monthly, also issued in annual cumulation. Cumulative subject index to English language periodicals in the subject fields of astronomy, botany, chemistry, earth science, environment and conservation, food and nutrition, genetics, mathematics, medicine and health, microbiology, oceanography, physics, physiology and zoology.

Geo Abstracts, Social Geography and Cartography. Geo Abstracts Ltd., c/o Elsevier Science Pub., Crown House, Linton Rd., Barking, England 1611 8JU.

Geographical Abstracts. London School of Economics, Dept. of Geography, Regency House, 34 Duke St., London, England 1966-. Continued by Geo Abstracts issued in 6 parts: Pt. A. Landforms and the quaternary; Pt. B. Biogeography and Climatology; Pt. C. Economic geography; Pt. D. Social geography and cartography; Pt. E. Sedimentology; Pt. F. Regional and community planning.

Index to Scientific Book Contents. Institute for Scientific Information, 3501 Market St., Philadelphia, Pennsylvania 19104. (800) 523-1857. 1985-. Annual. Gives contents of science books published.

Multimedia Index to Ecology. National Information Center for Educational Media, University of Southern California, Los Angeles, California 90007.

Pollution Abstracts. Cambridge Scientific Abstracts, 5161 River Rd., Bethesda, Maryland 20816. (301) 961-6750. Six/year. Indexes worldwide technical literature on environmental pollution. Covers air pollution, marine and freshwater pollution, sewage and wastewater treatment, waste management, toxicology and health, noise pollution, radiation, land pollution, and environmental policies, programs, legislation, and education. Also available online.

Science Citation Index. Institute for Scientific Information, 3501 Market St., Philadelphia, Pennsylvania 19104. 1961-.

ALMANACS AND YEARBOOKS

Environmental Almanac. World Resources Institute. Houghton Mifflin, 1 Beacon St., Boston, Massachusetts 02108. (617) 725-5000; (800) 225-3362. 1991. Covers consumer products, energy, endangered species, food safety, global warming, solid wastes, toxics, wetlands and other related areas. Also included are the names and addresses of the chief environmental executives for all 50 states.

BIBLIOGRAPHIES

Current Contents. Agriculture, Biology and Environmental Sciences. Institute for Scientific Information, 3501 Market St., Philadelphia, Pennsylvania 19104. (800) 523-1857. 1973-. Previous title: Current Contents. Agricultural, Food & Veterinary Sciences. Gives the table of contents of periodicals in the fields of agriculture, biology, environmental and related areas.

EPA Publications Bibliography. U.S. Environmental Protection Agency, Library Systems Branch, 401 M St., SW, Washington, District of Columbia 20460. (202) 260-2090. Quarterly.

Global Change Information Packet. National Agricultural Library, Reference Section, Room 111, 10301 Baltimore Blvd., Beltsville, Maryland 20705-2351. (301) 504-5755. 1991. Books and journal articles on the effects of global climate change.

Global Climate Change: Recent Publications. Library of the Department of State. The Library, 2201 C St. N.W., Washington, District of Columbia 20520. 1989.

DIRECTORIES

Directory of Global Climate Change Organizations. Janet Wright. National Agricultural Library, 10301 Baltimore Blvd., Beltsville, Maryland 20705. (301) 504-5755. 1991. Identifies organizations that provide information regarding global climate change issues to the general public.

Gale Environmental Sourcebook. Karen Hill. Gale Research Co., 835 Penobscot Bldg., Detroit, Michigan 48226-4094. (313) 961-2242. Contacts, information sources, or general information on environmental topics.

ENCYCLOPEDIAS AND DICTIONARIES

Cambridge Encyclopedia of Life Sciences. A. E. Friday and David S. Ingram. Cambridge University Press, 40 W 20th St., New York, New York 10011. (212) 924-3900 or (800) 227-0247. 1985. Includes all topics under biology and ecology.

The Encyclopedia of Climatology. John E. Oliver and Rhodes W. Fairbridge, eds. Van Nostrand Reinhold, 115 5th Ave., New York, New York 10003. (212) 254-3232. 1987. Belongs in the series Encyclopedia of Earth Sciences, v.11.

Encyclopedia of Environmental Science and Engineering. J.R. Pfafflin. Gordon and Breach Science Publishers, Inc., 270 8th Ave., New York, New York 10011. (212) 206-8900. 1992.

The Encyclopedia of Geochemistry and Environmental Sciences. Rhodes Whitmore Fairbridge. Van Nostrand Reinhold Co., 115 5th Ave., New York, New York 10003. (212) 254-3232. 1972.

Encyclopedia of Physical Science and Technology. Robert A. Meyers, ed. Academic Press, c/o Harcourt Brace Jovanovich Inc., 6277 Sea Harbor Dr., Orlando, Florida 32887. (800) 346-8648. Dictionary of engineering, technology and physical sciences.

McGraw-Hill Encyclopedia of Environmental Science. Sybil P. Parker. McGraw-Hill Science & Engineering Books, 11 W. 19th St., New York, New York 10011. (212) 337-6010. 1980. Covers ecology, man's influence on nature, and environmental protection.

Van Nostrand's Scientific Encyclopedia. Glenn D. Considine, ed. Van Nostrand Reinhold, 115 5th Ave., New York, New York 10003. (212) 254-3232. 1983. Sixth edition. Includes all broad subject areas in science.

GENERAL WORKS

Air Pollution's Toll on Forests and Crops. James J. MacKenzie and Mohamed T. El-Ashry, eds. Yale University Press, 92 A Yale St., 302 Temple St., New Haven, Connecticut 06520. (203) 432-0960. 1992. Proposes an integrated strategy to reduce pollution levels based on improved energy efficiency, abatement technology, and the use of nonfossil energy technologies. This strategy takes into account other critical problems such as increasing oil imports, failure to attain clean air goals in U.S. cities, and the greenhouse effect.

Air Quality. Lewis Publishers, 200 Corporate Blvd. NW, Boca Raton, Florida 33431. (407) 994-0555 or (800)272-7737. 2nd edition. Air pollution and control, stratosphere O3 depletion, global warming, and indoor air pollution.

Antarctica and Global Climatic Change. Colin M. Harris. Lewis Publishers, 2000 Corporate Blvd., NW, Boca Raton, Florida 33431. (800) 272-7737. 1991. A guide to recent literature on climatic changes and environmental monitoring.

Biogeochemistry: An Analysis of Global Change. William H. Schlesinger. Academic Press, c/o Harcourt Brace Jovanovich Inc., 6277 Sea Harbor Dr., Orlando, Florida 32887. (800) 346-8648. 1991. Examines global changes that have occurred and are occurring in our water, air, and on land, relates them to the global cycles of water, carbon, nitrogen, phosphorous, and sulfur.

Can We Delay a Greenhouse Warming?. U.S. G.P.O., Washington, District of Columbia 20401. (202) 512-0000. The effectiveness and feasibility of options to slow a build-up of carbon dioxide in the atmosphere.

Carbon Dioxide and Global Change: Earth in Transition. Sherwood B. Idso. IBR Press, 631 E. Laguna Dr., Tempe, Arizona 85282. (602) 966-8693. 1989. Discusses environmental aspects of greenhouse effect.

The Challenge of Global Warming. Dean Edwin Abrahamson, ed. Island Press, 1718 Connecticut Ave. N.W., Suite 300, Washington, District of Columbia 20009. (202) 232-7933. 1989. Focuses on the causes, effects, policy implications, and possible solutions to global warming

The Changing Atmosphere: A Global Challenge. John Firor. Yale University Press, 302 Temple St., 92 A Yale Sta., New Haven, Connecticut 06520. (203) 432-0960. 1990. Examines three atmospheric problems: Acid rain, ozone depletion, and climate heating.

Climatic Change and Plant Genetic Resources. M. T. Jackson, et al., eds. Belhaven Press, 136 S. Broadway, Irvington, New York 10533. (914) 591-9111. 1990. Cities concerns about the effect of global warming on biological diversity of species is the main thrust of this text. Major portion of the book comes from the second international workshop on plant genetic resources held in 1989.

Cool Energy: The Renewable Solution to Global Warming. Michael Brower. Union of Concerned Scientists, 26 Church St., Cambridge, Massachusetts 02238. (617) 547-5552. 1990. Describes how fossil fuel and renewable energy sources could be used to avoid global warming and air pollution.

Dead Heat. M. Oppenheimer and R. Boyle. IB Tauris, 110 Gloucester Ave., London, England NW1 8JA. 071 483 2681. 1990. Guide to global warming and some possible solutions.

Environment in Peril. Anthony B. Wolbarst, ed. Smithsonian Institution Press, 470 L'Enfant Plaza, No. 7100, Washington, District of Columbia 20560. (800) 782-4612. 1991. Brings together in one volume the primary concerns of eleven of the world's leaders in conservation, ecology and public policy. Broad environmental issues covered are: ozone depletion, overpopulation, global warming, thinning forests, extinction of species, spreading deserts, toxic chemicals, and various pollutants.

The Environment: Problems and Solutions. Stuart Bruchey, ed. Garland Publishing, Inc., 1000A Sherman Ave., Hamden, Connecticut 06514. (203) 281-4487. 1991. Topics covered: forested wetlands and agriculture, the political economy of smog in southern California, environmental limits to growth in world agriculture, the tradeoff between cost and risk in hazardous waste management, and the protection of groundwater from agricultural pollution.

Escaping the Heat Trap. Irving Mintzer and William R. Moomaw. World Resources Institute, 1709 New York Ave. N.W., Washington, District of Columbia 20006. (800) 822-0504. 1991. Report is based on a series of scenarios developed using WRI's Model of Warming Commitment. Investigates the potential of societies to dramatically limit the rate of future greenhouse gas buildup and reduce to zero annual commitment to global warming.

Global Air Pollution: Problems for the 1990s. Howard Bridgman. Belhaven Press, 136 S. Broadway, Irvington, New York 10533. (914) 591-9111. 1990. Addresses the environmental problems caused by human activities resulting in change and deterioration of the earth's atmosphere.

Global Warming. Stephen Henry Schneider. Sierra Club Books, 100 Bush St., San Francisco, California 94104. (415) 291-1600. 1989. Climatic changes due to the greenhouse effect.

Global Warming: Do We Know Enough to Act?. S. Fred Singer. Center for the Study of American Business, Washington University, Campus Box 1208, One Brookings Dr., St. Louis, Missouri 63130-4899. (314) 935-5630. 1991.

Global Warming: The Greenpeace Report. Jeremy Leggett. Oxford University Press, 200 Madison Ave., New York, New York 10016. (800) 334-4249. 1990. Climate change and consequences of global warming, and means for abating and even halting global warming.

Greenhouse Effect: Life on a Warmer Planet. Rebecca Johnson. Carolina Biological Supply Company, 2700 York Rd., Burlington, North Carolina 27215. (919) 584-0381. 1990. Discusses the effects of what may be the most serious environmental problem ever. Suggests steps everyone can take to reduce the impact of global warming.

Greenhouse Effect, Sea Level Rise, and Coastal Wetlands. U.S. Environmental Protection Agency, 401 M St., S.W., Washington, District of Columbia 20460. (202) 260-

2090. 1988. Deals with wetland conservation and atmospheric greenhouse effect.

Greenhouse Gas Emissions–The Energy Dimension. OECD Publications and Information Center, 2001 L St., N.W., Suite 700, Washington, District of Columbia 20036. (202) 785-OECD. Source for a comprehensive discussion on the relationship between energy use and greenhouse emissions as they relate to the energy used by geographical and regional sectors.

The Greenhouse Trap: What We're Doing to the Atmosphere and How We Can Slow Global Warming. Francesca Lyman and James J. MacKenzie. World Resources Institute, 1709 New York Ave. N.W., Washington, District of Columbia 20006. (800) 822-0504. 1990. Traces the history of the greenhouse effect and show how the current crisis has come about. Possible future consequences, based on the most credible scientific research available, are described and assessed.

Greenhouse Warming: Negotiating a Global Regime. Jessica Tuchman Mathews, ed. World Resources Institute, 1709 New York Ave. N.W., Washington, District of Columbia 20006. (800) 822-0504. 1991. Offers specific suggestions for formulating, implementing, and enforcing a global regime to combat greenhouse warming.

The Hole in the Sky: Man's Threat to the Ozone Layer. John R. Gribbin. Bantam Books, 666 5th Ave., New York, New York 10103. (212) 765-6500; (800) 223-6834. 1988. Scientific revelations about the ozone layer and global warming.

Keeping It Green: Tropical Forestry and the Mitigation of Global Warming. Mark C. Trexler. World Resources Institute, 1709 New York Ave. N.W., Washington, District of Columbia 20006. (800) 822-0504. 1991. Report links knowledge gained from past tropical forestry initiatives with expectations for their future effectiveness in the mitigation of global warming.

Long-Term Ecological Research: An International Perspective. Paul G. Risser, ed. John Wiley & Sons, Inc., 605 3rd Ave., New York, New York 10158-0012. (212) 850-6000. 1991. Describes and analyzes research programs in various ecosystems such as temperate forests, arid steppes, deserts, temperate and tropical grasslands, aquatic systems from countries including Scotland, Kenya, USA, Australia, Canada, Germany, and France.

Minding the Carbon Store: Weighing U.S. Forestry Strategies to Slow Global Warming. Mark C. Trexler. World Resources Institute, 1709 New York Ave. N.W., Washington, District of Columbia 20006. (800) 833 0504. 1991. Assesses the strengths and weaknesses of each of the major domestic forestry options, including their costs and carbon benefits.

Ozone Crisis: The 15-Year Evolution of a Sudden Global Emergency. Sharon L. Roan. John Wiley & Sons, Inc., 605 3rd Ave., New York, New York 10158-0012. (212) 850-6000. 1989. Chronicles the experiences of F. Sherwood Rowland and Mario Molina, the scientists who first made the ozone depletion discovery.

Ozone Depletion: Health and Environmental Consequences. John Wiley & Sons, Inc., 605 3rd Ave., New York, New York 10158-0012. (212) 850-6000. 1989.

Policy Implication of Greenhouse Warming. National Academy Press, 2101 Constitution Ave. N.W., PO Box 285, Washington, District of Columbia 20418. (202) 334-3313. 1991. Identifies what could be done to counter potential greenhouse warming. It has a helpful section on question and answers about greenhouse warming.

The Potential Effects of Global Climate Change on the United States. Joel B. Smith and Dennis A. Tirpak, eds. Hemisphere Publishing Co., 79 Madison Ave., Suite 1110, New York, New York 10016. (212) 725-1999; (800) 821-8312. 1990. Addresses the effects of climate change in vital areas such as water resources, agriculture, sea levels and forests. Also focuses on wetlands, human health, rivers and lakes and analyzes policy options for mitigating the effects of global warming.

A Primer on Greenhouse Effect Gases. Donald J. Wuebbles and Jae Edmonds. Lewis Publishers, 200 Corporate Blvd. NW, Boca Raton, Florida 33431. (407) 994-0555 or (800)272-7737. 1991. Brings together the most current information available on greenhouse gases. Reveals information critical to developing an understanding of the role of energy and atmospheric chemical and radiative processes in determining atmospheric concentrations of greenhouse gases.

Prospects for Future Climate: A Special US/USSR Report on Climate and Climate Change. Michael C. MacCracken, et al. Lewis Publishers, 2000 Corporate Blvd., N.W., Boca Raton, Florida 33431. (407) 994-0555 or (800) 272-7737. 1990. Describes the effects of the increasing concentration of greenhouse gases and the potential for climate change and impact on agriculture and hydrology. Projections are based on insights from both numerical models and empirical methods.

The Rising Tide: Global Warming and World Sea Levels. Lynne T. Edgerton. Island Press, 1718 Connecticut Ave. N.W., Suite 300, Washington, District of Columbia 20009. (202) 232-7933. 1991. Analysis of global warming and rising world sea level. Outlines state, national and international actions to respond to the effects of global warming on coastal communities and ecosystems.

Slowing Global Warming: A Worldwide Strategy. Christopher Flavin. Worldwatch Institute, 1776 Massachusetts Ave. N.W., Washington, District of Columbia 20036. How to cope with environmental warming as an environmental threat.

Soils and the Greenhouse Effect. A. F. Bouwman, ed. John Wiley & Sons, Inc., 605 3rd Ave., New York, New York 10158-0012. (212) 850-6000. 1990. Proceedings of the International Conference on Soils and the Greenhouse Effect, Wageningen, Netherlands, 1989. Covers the present status and future trends concerning the effect of soils and vegetation on the fluxes of greenhouse gases, the surface energy balance, and the water balance. Discusses the role of deforestation and management practices such as mulching, wetlands, agriculture and livestock.

HANDBOOKS AND MANUALS

The Global Ecology Handbook: What You Can Do about the Environmental Crisis. Walter H. Corson, ed. The Global Tomorrow Coalition, Beacon Pr., 25 Beacon St., Boston, Massachusetts 02108-2800. (617) 742-2110. 1990. Covers environment, energy policy, population growth and other issues. It includes chapters on tropical rain forests, garbage, oceans and coasts, global warming, population growth, agriculture, biological diversity, fresh water, hazardous wastes, and environment and development.

ONLINE DATA BASES

BIOSIS Previews. BIOSIS, 2100 Arch St., Philadelphia, Pennsylvania 19103-1399. (215) 587-4800. Largest and most comprehensive database of research in the life sciences. Contains citations for nearly 9000 primary research journals, monographs, reviews, symposia, preliminary reports, semi-popular journals, selected institutional reports, government reports and research communications.

Computerized Engineering Index–COMPENDEX. Engineering Information Inc., 345 E. 47th St., New York, New York 10017. (212) 705-7600.

Enviro/Energyline Abstracts Plus. R. R. Bowker Co., 121 Chanlon Rd., New Providence, New Jersey 07974. (908) 464-6800.

Environmental Periodicals Bibliography. National Information Services Corp., Ste. 6, Wyman Towers, 3100 St. Paul St., Baltimore, Maryland 21218. (410)243-0797. Online version of abstract of same name.

Global Environmental Change Report. Cutter Information Corp., 37 Broadway, Arlington, Massachusetts 02174-5539. (617) 648-8700. Online access to environmental issues worldwide, including global warming, ozone depletion, deforestation, and acid rain. Online version of periodical of the same name.

Greenhouse Effect Report. Business Publishers, Inc., 951 Pershing Dr., Silver Spring, Maryland 20910-4464. (301) 587-6300. Access to regulatory, legislative, business, and technological news and developments. Online version of periodical of same name.

SCISEARCH. Institute for Scientific Information, University City Science Center, 3501 Market St., Philadelphia, Pennsylvania 19104. (215) 386-0100.

PERIODICALS AND NEWSLETTERS

Atmospheric Environment. Pergamon Microforms International, Inc., Fairview Park, Elmsford, New York 10523. (914) 592-7720. 1966-. Publishes papers on all aspects of man's interactions with his atmospheric environment, including the administrative, economic and political aspects of these interactions. Air pollution research and its applications are covered, taking into account changes in the atmospheric flow patterns, temperature distributions and chemical constitution caused by natural and artificial variations in the earth's surface.

Earth Quest. University Corp. for Atmospheric Research, PO Box 3000, Boulder, Colorado 80307. (303) 497-1682. Quarterly. National and international programs addressing global environmental change.

Earth Science. American Geological Institute, 4220 King Street, Alexandria, Virginia 22302. (703) 379-2480. Quarterly. Covers geological issues.

Global Climate Change Digest. Elsevier Science Publishing Co., 655 Avenue of the Americas, New York, New York 10010. (212) 984-5800. Monthly. Topics dealing with ozone depletion and the large-scale climatic changes linked to industrial activity, industrial by-products, and man-made substances.

Global Ecology and Biogeography Letter. Blackwell Scientific Publications, 3 Cambridge Ctr., Suite 208, Cambridge, Massachusetts 02142. (617) 225-0401. 1991. Bimonthly. Global Ecology and Biogeography Letters is a sister publication of Journal of Biogeography and is only available with a subscription to the Journal. Provides a fast-track outlet for short research papers, news items, editorials, and book reviews. Topics related to the major scientific concerns of our present era, such as global warming, world sea-level rises, environmental acidification, development and conservation, biodiversity, and important new theories and themes in biogeography and ecology.

Global Environmental Change: Human and Policy Dimensions. James K. Mitchell, ed. Department of Geography, Lucy Stone Hall, Kilmer Campus, New Brunswick, New Jersey 08903. (201) 932-4103. 1991. Five issues a year. Produced in cooperation with the United Nations University, including its International Human Dimensions of Global Change Programme. Addresses the human, ecological and public policy aspects of environmental processes that might affect the sustainability of life on Earth.

Global Environmental Change Report. Cutter Information Corp., 37 Broadway, Arlington, Massachusetts 02174-5539. (617) 648-8700. Biweekly. Focus on global warming, ozone depletion, deforestation, and acid rain. Also available online.

Greenhouse Effect Report. Business Publishers, Inc., 951 Pershing Dr., Silver Spring, Maryland 20910-4464. (301)587-6300. 1988-. Biweekly. This is a newsletter on international, governmental, regulatory, business and technological actions on global warming and the greenhouse effect. Also available online.

International Environmental Affairs. University Press of New England, 17 1/2 Lebanon Street, Hanover, New Hampshire 03755. (603) 646-3340. Quarterly. Issues on management of natural resources.

Journal of Biogeography. Blackwell Scientific Publications Inc., 3 Cambridge Ctr., Suite 208, Cambridge, Massachusetts 02142. (617) 225-0401.

Nature and Resources. Elsevier Science Publishing Co., 655 Avenue of the Americas, New York, New York 10010. (212) 989-5800. 1965-. Quarterly. Provides indepth reviews of contemporary environmental issues from an international perspective.

RESEARCH CENTERS AND INSTITUTES

Worldwatch Institute. 1776 Massachusetts Ave., N.W., Washington, District of Columbia 20036. (202) 452-1999.

STATISTICS SOURCES

Energy Policy Implications of Global Warming. U.S. G.P.O., Washington, District of Columbia 20401. (202) 512-0000. 1989. Energy policy implications of the global warming trend and other climatic changes resulting from atmospheric concentrations of heat-retaining gases.

Environmental Data Compendium. OECD Publications and Information Center, 2001 L St., N.W., Suite 700, Washington, District of Columbia 20036. (202) 785-6323. 1989.

Environmental Indicators. OECD Publications and Information Center, 2001 L St., N.W., Suite 700, Washington, District of Columbia 20036. (202) 785-6323. 1991.

Environmental Quality. Council on Environmental Quality. U.S. G.P.O., Washington, District of Columbia 20401. (202) 512-0000. Annual.

The State of the Environment. OECD Publications and Information Center, 2001 L St., N.W., Suite 700, Washington, District of Columbia 20036. (202) 785-6323. 1991.

Trends '90: A Compendium of Data on Global Change. Thomas A. Boden, et al. Carbon Dioxide Information Analysis Center, Environmental Sciences Division, Oak Ridge National Laboratory, Oak Ridge, Tennessee 37831-6335. 1990. Source of frequently used global change data. Includes estimates of global and national CO_2 emissions from the burning of fossil fuels and from the production of cement and other pollutants.

World Resources. World Resources Institute. 1709 New York Ave., N.W., Washington, District of Columbia 20006. (202) 638-6300. Annual. Statistical and textual analysis of world's natural resources and the effects of growth-caused environmental pollution.

TRADE ASSOCIATIONS AND PROFESSIONAL SOCIETIES

Air Resources Information Clearinghouse. 99 Court St., Rochester, New York 14604. (716) 546-3796.

American Institute of Biological Sciences. 730 11th St., N.W., Washington, District of Columbia 20001-4521. (202) 628-1500.

Better World Society. 1100 17th St., NW, Suite 502, Washington, District of Columbia 20036. (202) 331-3770. International non-profit membership organization that attempts to increase individual awareness of global issues related to the sustainability of life on earth.

Earth Island Institute. 300 Broadway, Suite 28, San Francisco, California 94133. (415) 788-3666.

EarthSave. 706 Frederick St., Santa Cruz, California 95062. (408) 423-4069.

Friends of the United Nations Environment Programme. 2013 Q St., N.W., Washington, District of Columbia 20009. (202) 234-3600.

Global Tomorrow Coalition. 1325 G St., N.W., Suite 915, Washington, District of Columbia 20005-3103. (202) 628-4016.

Greenhouse Crisis Foundation. 1130 17th St., NW, Suite 630, Washington, District of Columbia 20036. (202) 466-2823.

Union of Concerned Scientists. 26 Church St., Cambridge, Massachusetts 02238. (617) 547-5552.

GLUFOSINATE

ABSTRACTING AND INDEXING SERVICES

Biological Abstracts. BIOSIS, 2100 Arch St., Philadelphia, Pennsylvania 19103-1399. (215) 587-4800. 1927-.

Chemical Abstracts. Chemical Abstracts Service, 2540 Olentangy River Rd., PO Box 3012, Columbus, Ohio 43210. (800) 848-6533. 1907-.

General Science Index. H. W. Wilson Co., 950 University Ave., Bronx, New York 10452. 1978-. Monthly, also

issued in annual cumulation. Cumulative subject index to English language periodicals in the subject fields of astronomy, botany, chemistry, earth science, environment and conservation, food and nutrition, genetics, mathematics, medicine and health, microbiology, oceanography, physics, physiology and zoology.

Science Citation Index. Institute for Scientific Information, 3501 Market St., Philadelphia, Pennsylvania 19104. 1961-.

ENCYCLOPEDIAS AND DICTIONARIES

Encyclopedia of Trademarks and Synonyms. H. Bennett, ed. Chemical Publishing Co., 80 Eighth Ave., New York, New York 10011. (212) 255-1950. 1981. Three volumes. Includes chemical compounds, compositions consisting of one or more chemicals and other products. Also included are abbreviated names and WHO free names.

Van Nostrand's Scientific Encyclopedia. Glenn D. Considine, ed. Van Nostrand Reinhold, 115 5th Ave., New York, New York 10003. (212) 254-3232. 1983. Sixth edition. Includes all broad subject areas in science.

ONLINE DATA BASES

BIOSIS Previews. BIOSIS, 2100 Arch St., Philadelphia, Pennsylvania 19103-1399. (215) 587-4800. Largest and most comprehensive database of research in the life sciences. Contains citations for nearly 9000 primary research journals, monographs, reviews, symposia, preliminary reports, semi-popular journals, selected institutional reports, government reports and research communications.

Chemical Abstracts-CA. Chemical Abstracts Service, 2540 Olentangy River Rd., P.O. Box 3012, Columbus, Ohio 43210. (800) 848-6533 or (614) 421-3600. Information sources include 9000 journals, patents from 27 countries, two industrial property organizations, new books, conference proceedings, and government research reports.

Chemical Abstracts Chemical Name Directory-CHEMNAME. Chemical Abstracts Service, 2540 Olentangy River Rd., P.O. Box 3012, Columbus, Ohio 43210. (800) 848-6533 or (614) 421-3600. Listing of chemical substances in a dictionary type file. The Chemical Abstracts (CAS) Registry Number, molecular formula, Chemical Abstracts (CA) Substance Index Name, available synonyms, ring data and other chemical substance information is given for each entry.

Chemical Carcinogenesis Research Information System-CCRIS. National Library of Medicine, 8600 Rockville Pike, Bethesda, Maryland 20894. (800) 638-8480. Individual assay results and test conditions for 1,451 chemicals in the areas of carcinogenicity, mutagenicity, tumor promotion, and cocarcinogenicity.

Chemical Collection System/Request Tracking-CCS/ RTS. U.S. Environmental Protection Agency, Office of Pesticides and Toxic Substances, 401 M St., SW, Washington, District of Columbia 20460. (202) 260-2090. Contains information on various properties of a number of chemicals including environmental effects, test and analysis methods, and health effects. Available from EPA.

Chemical Dictionary Online-CHEMLINE. Chemical Abstracts Service, 2540 Olentangy River Rd., Columbus,

Ohio 43210. (614) 421-3600 or (800) 848-6533. Part of MEDLINE of the National Library of Medicine (NLM). File of 900,000 names for chemical substances, representing 450,000 unique compounds. It contains such information as Chemical Abstracts (CA) Service Registry Numbers, molecular formulas, preferred chemical nomenclature, and generic and ring structure information. Available on NLM's ELHILL system.

Chemical Exposure. Science Applications International Corp., Health & Environmental Information, P.O. Box 2501, Oak Ridge, Tennessee 37831. (615) 482-9031. Database of chemicals that have been identified in both human tissues and body fluids and in feral and food animals. Contains reference to journal articles, conferences, and reports. Covers the whole fields of information related to human and animal exposure to food, air, and water contaminants and pharmaceuticals. Its records include information on chemical properties, formulas, tissues measured, analytical method used, demographics and more. Available on DIALOG.

GLUTATHIONE

ABSTRACTING AND INDEXING SERVICES

Biological Abstracts. BIOSIS, 2100 Arch St., Philadelphia, Pennsylvania 19103-1399. (215) 587-4800. 1927-.

Chemical Abstracts. Chemical Abstracts Service, 2540 Olentangy River Rd., PO Box 3012, Columbus, Ohio 43210. (800) 848-6533. 1907-.

General Science Index. H. W. Wilson Co., 950 University Ave., Bronx, New York 10452. 1978-. Monthly, also issued in annual cumulation. Cumulative subject index to English language periodicals in the subject fields of astronomy, botany, chemistry, earth science, environment and conservation, food and nutrition, genetics, mathematics, medicine and health, microbiology, oceanography, physics, physiology and zoology.

Science Citation Index. Institute for Scientific Information, 3501 Market St., Philadelphia, Pennsylvania 19104. 1961-.

ENCYCLOPEDIAS AND DICTIONARIES

Encyclopedia of Trademarks and Synonyms. H. Bennett, ed. Chemical Publishing Co., 80 Eighth Ave., New York, New York 10011. (212) 255-1950. 1981. Three volumes. Includes chemical compounds, compositions consisting of one or more chemicals and other products. Also included are abbreviated names and WHO free names.

Van Nostrand's Scientific Encyclopedia. Glenn D. Considine, ed. Van Nostrand Reinhold, 115 5th Ave., New York, New York 10003. (212) 254-3232. 1983. Sixth edition. Includes all broad subject areas in science.

GENERAL WORKS

Function of Glutathione. Agne Larsson. Raven Press, 1185 Avenue of the Americas, New York, New York 10036. (212) 930-9500. 1983. Biochemical, physiological, toxicological, and clinical aspects.

Glutathione: Chemical, Biochemical, and Medical Aspects. David Dolphin. John Wiley & Sons, Inc., 605 3rd Ave., New York, New York 10158-0012. (212) 850-6000.

1989. Covers derivatives, metabolism, and physiological effect of glutathione.

Glutathione Conjugation. Helmut Sies. Academic Press, 1250 Sixth Ave., San Diego, California 92101. (619) 231-0926. 1988. Glutathione transferases and their mechanisms and biological significance.

Glutathione: Metabolism and Physiological Functions. Jose Vina. CRC Press, 2000 Corporate Blvd. N.W., Boca Raton, Florida 33431. (800) 272-7737. 1990. Metabolism and physiological effects of glutathione.

ONLINE DATA BASES

BIOSIS Previews. BIOSIS, 2100 Arch St., Philadelphia, Pennsylvania 19103-1399. (215) 587-4800. Largest and most comprehensive database of research in the life sciences. Contains citations for nearly 9000 primary research journals, monographs, reviews, symposia, preliminary reports, semi-popular journals, selected institutional reports, government reports and research communications.

CERCLIS. Chemical Information Systems, Inc., 7215 York Rd., Baltimore, Maryland 21212. (301) 321-8440. Information on hazardous waste disposal sites that have either been listed by the EPA on the National Priority List (NPL) or nominated for consideration for the NPL.

Chemical Abstracts-CA. Chemical Abstracts Service, 2540 Olentangy River Rd., P.O. Box 3012, Columbus, Ohio 43210. (800) 848-6533 or (614) 421-3600. Information sources include 9000 journals, patents from 27 countries, two industrial property organizations, new books, conference proceedings, and government research reports.

Chemical Abstracts Chemical Name Directory-CHEMNAME. Chemical Abstracts Service, 2540 Olentangy River Rd., P.O. Box 3012, Columbus, Ohio 43210. (800) 848-6533 or (614) 421-3600. Listing of chemical substances in a dictionary type file. The Chemical Abstracts (CAS) Registry Number, molecular formula, Chemical Abstracts (CA) Substance Index Name, available synonyms, ring data and other chemical substance information is given for each entry.

Chemical Carcinogenesis Research Information System-CCRIS. National Library of Medicine, 8600 Rockville Pike, Bethesda, Maryland 20894. (800) 638-8480. Individual assay results and test conditions for 1,451 chemicals in the areas of carcinogenicity, mutagenicity, tumor promotion, and cocarcinogenicity.

Chemical Collection System/Request Tracking-CCS/RTS. U.S. Environmental Protection Agency, Office of Pesticides and Toxic Substances, 401 M St., SW, Washington, District of Columbia 20460. (202) 260-2090. Contains information on various properties of a number of chemicals including environmental effects, test and analysis methods, and health effects. Available from EPA.

Chemical Dictionary Online-CHEMLINE. Chemical Abstracts Service, 2540 Olentangy River Rd., Columbus, Ohio 43210. (614) 421-3600 or (800) 848-6533. Part of MEDLINE of the National Library of Medicine (NLM). File of 900,000 names for chemical substances, representing 450,000 unique compounds. It contains such information as Chemical Abstracts (CA) Service Registry Numbers, molecular formulas, preferred chemical no-

menclature, and generic and ring structure information. Available on NLM's ELHILL system.

Chemical Exposure. Science Applications International Corp., Health & Environmental Information, P.O. Box 2501, Oak Ridge, Tennessee 37831. (615) 482-9031. Database of chemicals that have been identified in both human tissues and body fluids and in feral and food animals. Contains reference to journal articles, conferences, and reports. Covers the whole fields of information related to human and animal exposure to food, air, and water contaminants and pharmaceuticals. Its records include information on chemical properties, formulas, tissues measured, analytical method used, demographics and more. Available on DIALOG.

GRAIN DUST

ABSTRACTING AND INDEXING SERVICES

Agrindex. AGRIS Coordinating Center, Via delle Terme di Caracalla, Rome, Italy I-00100. 61 0181-FA01. 1975-.

Biological Abstracts. BIOSIS, 2100 Arch St., Philadelphia, Pennsylvania 19103-1399. (215) 587-4800. 1927-.

Biological and Agricultural Index. H.W. Wilson Co., 950 University Ave., Bronx, New York 10452. (800) 367-6770. 1916-. Monthly.

Ecological Abstracts. Geo Abstracts Ltd. Elsevier Applied Science, Crown House, Linton Rd., Barking, England IG 11 8JU. 1974-. Derived from over 600 leading ecological and environmental journals, plus books, conference proceedings, reports and theses.

Environment Abstracts. Bowker A & I Publishing, 121 Chanlon Rd., New Providence, New Jersey 07974. (908) 464-6800. 1974-.

Environment Index. Environment Information Center, Index Research Department, 124 E. 39th St., New York, New York 10016. 1971-. Annual.

Environmental Information Connection-EIC. Planning Information Program, Dept. of Urban and Regional Planning, University of Illinois, 1003 West Nevada, Urbana, Illinois 61801. (217) 333-1369. Also available online.

Environmental Periodicals Bibliography. Environmental Studies Institute, International Academy at Santa Barbara, 800 Garden St., Suite D, Santa Barbara, California 93101. (805) 965-5010. Also available online.

General Science Index. H. W. Wilson Co., 950 University Ave., Bronx, New York 10452. 1978-. Monthly, also issued in annual cumulation. Cumulative subject index to English language periodicals in the subject fields of astronomy, botany, chemistry, earth science, environment and conservation, food and nutrition, genetics, mathematics, medicine and health, microbiology, oceanography, physics, physiology and zoology.

Grain Dust Abstracts. Fang S. Lai. U.S. Dept. of Agriculture, Science and Education Administration, 14 Independence Ave., SW, Washington, District of Columbia 20250. (202) 447-7454. 1981. Topics in grain dust explosions.

Science Citation Index. Institute for Scientific Information, 3501 Market St., Philadelphia, Pennsylvania 19104. 1961-.

BIBLIOGRAPHIES

Current Contents. Agriculture, Biology and Environmental Sciences. Institute for Scientific Information, 3501 Market St., Philadelphia, Pennsylvania 19104. (800) 523-1857. 1973-. Previous title: Current Contents. Agricultural, Food & Veterinary Sciences. Gives the table of contents of periodicals in the fields of agriculture, biology, environmental and related areas.

EPA Publications Bibliography. U.S. Environmental Protection Agency, Library Systems Branch, 401 M St., SW, Washington, District of Columbia 20460. (202) 260-2090. Quarterly.

GENERAL WORKS

Grain Dust, Problems and Utilization. L. D. Schnake. U.S. Department of Agriculture, 14 Independence Ave., S.W., Washington, District of Columbia 20250. (202) 447-7454. 1981. Safety measures relating to grain elevators.

Grain Industry Dust Explosions and Fires. Occupational Safety and Health Branch, Labour Canada, Phase 2 Place du Porpage, 165 Hotel de Ville, Ottawa, Ontario, Canada K1AOJ2. (613) 997-3520. 1984.

Review of Literature Related to Engineering Aspects of Grain Dust Explosions. David F. Aldis. U.S. Department of Agriculture, Science and Education Administration, 14 Independence Ave., S.W., Washington, District of Columbia 20250. (202) 447-7454. 1979. Fires and fire prevention in grain elevators.

ONLINE DATA BASES

BIOSIS Previews. BIOSIS, 2100 Arch St., Philadelphia, Pennsylvania 19103-1399. (215) 587-4800. Largest and most comprehensive database of research in the life sciences. Contains citations for nearly 9000 primary research journals, monographs, reviews, symposia, preliminary reports, semi-popular journals, selected institutional reports, government reports and research communications.

Cambridge Scientific Abstracts Life Science–CSAL. Cambridge Scientific Abstracts, 5161 River Rd., Bethesda, Maryland 20816. (301) 961-6750. Provides access to the following abstracting services: "Life Sciences Collection," "Aquatic Sciences and Fisheries Abstracts," "Oceanic Abstracts," and "Pollution Abstracts."

Enviro/Energyline Abstracts Plus. R. R. Bowker Co., 121 Chanlon Rd., New Providence, New Jersey 07974. (908) 464-6800.

Environmental Periodicals Bibliography. National Information Services Corp., Ste. 6, Wyman Towers, 3100 St. Paul St., Baltimore, Maryland 21218. (410)243-0797. Online version of abstract of same name.

SCISEARCH. Institute for Scientific Information, University City Science Center, 3501 Market St., Philadelphia, Pennsylvania 19104. (215) 386-0100.

GRASSES

ABSTRACTING AND INDEXING SERVICES

Agrindex. AGRIS Coordinating Center, Via delle Terme di Caracalla, Rome, Italy I-00100. 61 0181-FA01. 1975-.

Biological Abstracts. BIOSIS, 2100 Arch St., Philadelphia, Pennsylvania 19103-1399. (215) 587-4800. 1927-.

Biological and Agricultural Index. H.W. Wilson Co., 950 University Ave., Bronx, New York 10452. (800) 367-6770. 1916-. Monthly.

Ecological Abstracts. Geo Abstracts Ltd. Elsevier Applied Science, Crown House, Linton Rd., Barking, England IG 11 8JU. 1974-. Derived from over 600 leading ecological and environmental journals, plus books, conference proceedings, reports and theses.

Environment Abstracts. Bowker A & I Publishing, 121 Chanlon Rd., New Providence, New Jersey 07974. (908) 464-6800. 1974-.

Environment Index. Environment Information Center, Index Research Department, 124 E. 39th St., New York, New York 10016. 1971-. Annual.

Environmental Information Connection–EIC. Planning Information Program, Dept. of Urban and Regional Planning, University of Illinois, 1003 West Nevada, Urbana, Illinois 61801. (217) 333-1369. Also available online.

Environmental Periodicals Bibliography. Environmental Studies Institute, International Academy at Santa Barbara, 800 Garden St., Suite D, Santa Barbara, California 93101. (805) 965-5010. Also available online.

General Science Index. H. W. Wilson Co., 950 University Ave., Bronx, New York 10452. 1978-. Monthly, also issued in annual cumulation. Cumulative subject index to English language periodicals in the subject fields of astronomy, botany, chemistry, earth science, environment and conservation, food and nutrition, genetics, mathematics, medicine and health, microbiology, oceanography, physics, physiology and zoology.

Geographical Abstracts. London School of Economics, Dept. of Geography, Regency House, 34 Duke St., London, England 1966-. Continued by Geo Abstracts issued in 6 parts: Pt. A. Landforms and the quaternary; Pt. B. Biogeography and Climatology; Pt. C. Economic geography; Pt. D. Social geography and cartography; Pt. E. Sedimentology; Pt. F. Regional and community planning.

Pollution Abstracts. Cambridge Scientific Abstracts, 5161 River Rd., Bethesda, Maryland 20816. (301) 961-6750. Six/year. Indexes worldwide technical literature on environmental pollution. Covers air pollution, marine and freshwater pollution, sewage and wastewater treatment, waste management, toxicology and health, noise pollution, radiation, land pollution, and environmental policies, programs, legislation, and education. Also available online.

Science Citation Index. Institute for Scientific Information, 3501 Market St., Philadelphia, Pennsylvania 19104. 1961-.

BIBLIOGRAPHIES

Current Contents. Agriculture, Biology and Environmental Sciences. Institute for Scientific Information, 3501 Market St., Philadelphia, Pennsylvania 19104. (800) 523-1857. 1973-. Previous title: Current Contents. Agricultural, Food & Veterinary Sciences. Gives the table of contents of periodicals in the fields of agriculture, biology, environmental and related areas.

EPA Publications Bibliography. U.S. Environmental Protection Agency, Library Systems Branch, 401 M St., SW, Washington, District of Columbia 20460. (202) 260-2090. Quarterly.

The Protection of Lawn and Turf Grasses, 1979-April 1991. Charles N. Bebee. National Agricultural Library, 10301 Baltimore Blvd., Beltsville, Maryland 20705-2351. (301) 504-5755. 1991. Citations from AGRICOLA concerning diseases and other environmental considerations. Volume 107 of Bibliographies and literature of Agriculture.

ENCYCLOPEDIAS AND DICTIONARIES

Van Nostrand's Scientific Encyclopedia. Glenn D. Considine, ed. Van Nostrand Reinhold, 115 5th Ave., New York, New York 10003. (212) 254-3232. 1983. Sixth edition. Includes all broad subject areas in science.

GENERAL WORKS

Grass Productivity. A. Voisin. Island Press, 1718 Connecticut Ave. N.W., Suite 300, Washington, District of Columbia 20009. (202) 232-7933. 1988. Textbook of scientific information concerning every aspect of management "where the cow and the grass meet." Voisin's "rational grazing" method maximizes productivity in both grass and cattle operations.

ONLINE DATA BASES

BIOSIS Previews. BIOSIS, 2100 Arch St., Philadelphia, Pennsylvania 19103-1399. (215) 587-4800. Largest and most comprehensive database of research in the life sciences. Contains citations for nearly 9000 primary research journals, monographs, reviews, symposia, preliminary reports, semi-popular journals, selected institutional reports, government reports and research communications.

Cambridge Scientific Abstracts Life Science–CSAL. Cambridge Scientific Abstracts, 5161 River Rd., Bethesda, Maryland 20816. (301) 961-6750. Provides access to the following abstracting services: "Life Sciences Collection," "Aquatic Sciences and Fisheries Abstracts," "Oceanic Abstracts," and "Pollution Abstracts."

Enviro/Energyline Abstracts Plus. R. R. Bowker Co., 121 Chanlon Rd., New Providence, New Jersey 07974. (908) 464-6800.

Environmental Periodicals Bibliography. National Information Services Corp., Ste. 6, Wyman Towers, 3100 St. Paul St., Baltimore, Maryland 21218. (410)243-0797. Online version of abstract of same name.

SCISEARCH. Institute for Scientific Information, University City Science Center, 3501 Market St., Philadelphia, Pennsylvania 19104. (215) 386-0100.

TRADE ASSOCIATIONS AND PROFESSIONAL SOCIETIES

American Forage and Grassland Council. P.O. Box 891, Georgetown, Texas 78627.

American Institute of Biological Sciences. 730 11th St., N.W., Washington, District of Columbia 20001-4521. (202) 628-1500.

Grassland Heritage Foundation. P.O. Box 344, Shawnee Mission, Kansas 66201-0394. (913) 677-3326.

Save the Tall Grass Prairie, Inc. PO Box 557, Topeka, Kansas 66601. (913) 357-4681.

Tallgrass Prairie Alliance. 4101 W. 54th Terrance, Shawnee Mission, Kansas 66205.

GRASSLAND BIOMES

See also: AGRICULTURE; BIOMES; ECOSYSTEMS

ABSTRACTING AND INDEXING SERVICES

Agrindex. AGRIS Coordinating Center, Via delle Terme di Caracalla, Rome, Italy I-00100. 61 0181-FA01. 1975-.

Applied Ecology Abstracts Studies in Renewable Natural Resources. Information Retrieval Ltd., 1911 Jefferson Davis Highway, Arlington, Virginia 22202. 1975-. Monthly.

Biological Abstracts. BIOSIS, 2100 Arch St., Philadelphia, Pennsylvania 19103-1399. (215) 587-4800. 1927-.

Biological and Agricultural Index. H.W. Wilson Co., 950 University Ave., Bronx, New York 10452. (800) 367-6770. 1916-. Monthly.

Ecology Abstracts. Cambridge Scientific Abstracts, 5161 River Rd., Bethesda, Maryland 20816. (301) 961-6750. Monthly.

Environment Abstracts. Bowker A & I Publishing, 121 Chanlon Rd., New Providence, New Jersey 07974. (908) 464-6800. 1974-.

Environment Index. Environment Information Center, Index Research Department, 124 E. 39th St., New York, New York 10016. 1971-. Annual.

Environmental Information Connection–EIC. Planning Information Program, Dept. of Urban and Regional Planning, University of Illinois, 1003 West Nevada, Urbana, Illinois 61801. (217) 333-1369. Also available online.

Environmental Periodicals Bibliography. Environmental Studies Institute, International Academy at Santa Barbara, 800 Garden St., Suite D, Santa Barbara, California 93101. (805) 965-5010. Also available online.

General Science Index. H. W. Wilson Co., 950 University Ave., Bronx, New York 10452. 1978-. Monthly, also issued in annual cumulation. Cumulative subject index to English language periodicals in the subject fields of astronomy, botany, chemistry, earth science, environment and conservation, food and nutrition, genetics, mathematics, medicine and health, microbiology, oceanography, physics, physiology and zoology.

Geographical Abstracts. London School of Economics, Dept. of Geography, Regency House, 34 Duke St.,

London, England 1966-. Continued by Geo Abstracts issued in 6 parts: Pt. A. Landforms and the quaternary; Pt. B. Biogeography and Climatology; Pt. C. Economic geography; Pt. D. Social geography and cartography; Pt. E. Sedimentology; Pt. F. Regional and community planning.

Herbage Abstracts. C. A. B. International, 845 North Park Ave., Tucson, Arizona 85719. (602) 621-7897 or (800) 528-4841. 1931-. Monthly. Covers management, productivity and economics of grasslands, rangelands and fodder crops, grassland ecology, seed production, toxic plants, land use and farming systems, weed control, agricultural meteorology, and other related areas.

Multimedia Index to Ecology. National Information Center for Educational Media, University of Southern California, Los Angeles, California 90007.

Science Citation Index. Institute for Scientific Information, 3501 Market St., Philadelphia, Pennsylvania 19104. 1961-.

Weed Abstracts. C. A. B. International, 845 North Park Ave., Tucson, Arizona 85719. (602) 621-7897 or (800) 528-4841. 1954-. Monthly. Abstracts the world literature on weeds, weed control and allied subjects.

BIBLIOGRAPHIES

Current Contents. Agriculture, Biology and Environmental Sciences. Institute for Scientific Information, 3501 Market St., Philadelphia, Pennsylvania 19104. (800) 523-1857. 1973-. Previous title: Current Contents. Agricultural, Food & Veterinary Sciences. Gives the table of contents of periodicals in the fields of agriculture, biology, environmental and related areas.

EPA Publications Bibliography. U.S. Environmental Protection Agency, Library Systems Branch, 401 M St., SW, Washington, District of Columbia 20460. (202) 260-2090. Quarterly.

ENCYCLOPEDIAS AND DICTIONARIES

The Life of the African Plains. Leslie Brown. McGraw-Hill Science & Engineering Books, 11 W. 19th St., New York, New York 10011. (212) 337-6010. 1972.

McGraw-Hill Encyclopedia of Environmental Science. Sybil P. Parker. McGraw-Hill Science & Engineering Books, 11 W. 19th St., New York, New York 10011. (212) 337-6010. 1980. Covers ecology, man's influence on nature, and environmental protection.

Van Nostrand's Scientific Encyclopedia. Glenn D. Considine, ed. Van Nostrand Reinhold, 115 5th Ave., New York, New York 10003. (212) 254-3232. 1983. Sixth edition. Includes all broad subject areas in science.

GENERAL WORKS

The Effects of Air Pollution and Acid Rain on Fish, Wildlife, and Their Habitats: Grasslands. M.A. Peterson. U.S. G.P.O, Washington, District of Columbia 20401. (202) 512-0000. 1982. Effects of acid precipitation on plants and grassland ecology.

Grass Productivity. A. Voisin. Island Press, 1718 Connecticut Ave. N.W., Suite 300, Washington, District of Columbia 20009. (202) 232-7933. 1988. Textbook of scientific information concerning every aspect of management "where the cow and the grass meet." Voisin's

"rational grazing" method maximizes productivity in both grass and cattle operations.

Pastures: Their Ecology and Management. R. H. M. Langer, ed. Oxford University Press, 200 Madison Ave., New York, New York 10016. (212) 679-7300; (800) 334-4249. 1990. Covers such areas as the grasslands of New Zealand, pasture plants, pasture as an ecosystem, pasture establishment, soil fertility, management, assessment, livestock production, animal disorders, high country pastures, hay or silage, seed production, weeds, pests, and plant diseases.

Perspectives in Grassland Ecology: Results and Applications of the US/IBP Grassland Biome Study. Norman R. French. Springer-Verlag, 175 5th Ave., New York, New York 10010. (212) 460-1500. 1979. Covers range management and grassland ecology.

HANDBOOKS AND MANUALS

The Agricultural Notebook. Primrose McConnell; R. J. Halley, ed. Butterworth-Heinemann, 80 Montvale Ave., Stoneham, Massachusetts 02180. (617) 438-8464 or (800) 366-2665. 1982. Seventeenth edition. Includes data on the business of farming. Topics discussed include soils, drainage, crop physiology, crop nutrition, arable crops, grassland, trees on the farm, weed control, diseases of crops, pests of crops, grain preservation and storage, animal production, farm equipment, farm management, agricultural law, health and safety, and agricultural computers.

ONLINE DATA BASES

BIOSIS Previews. BIOSIS, 2100 Arch St., Philadelphia, Pennsylvania 19103-1399. (215) 587-4800. Largest and most comprehensive database of research in the life sciences. Contains citations for nearly 9000 primary research journals, monographs, reviews, symposia, preliminary reports, semi-popular journals, selected institutional reports, government reports and research communications.

Cambridge Scientific Abstracts Life Science–CSAL. Cambridge Scientific Abstracts, 5161 River Rd., Bethesda, Maryland 20816. (301) 961-6750. Provides access to the following abstracting services: "Life Sciences Collection," "Aquatic Sciences and Fisheries Abstracts," "Oceanic Abstracts," and "Pollution Abstracts."

Enviro/Energyline Abstracts Plus. R. R. Bowker Co., 121 Chanlon Rd., New Providence, New Jersey 07974. (908) 464-6800.

Environmental Periodicals Bibliography. National Information Services Corp., Ste. 6, Wyman Towers, 3100 St. Paul St., Baltimore, Maryland 21218. (410)243-0797. Online version of abstract of same name.

Monthly Catalog of United States Government Publications. U.S. G.P.O., Supt. of Docs., PO Box 371954, Pittsburgh, Pennsylvania 15250-7954. (202) 512-0000.

National Technical Information Service. U.S. Department of Commerce, National Technical Information Service, Office of Data Base Services, 5285 Port Royal Rd., Springfield, Virginia 22161. (703) 487-4807. Bibliographic database of government sponsored research and technical reports.

SCISEARCH. Institute for Scientific Information, University City Science Center, 3501 Market St., Philadelphia, Pennsylvania 19104. (215) 386-0100.

RESEARCH CENTERS AND INSTITUTES

U.S. Forest Service, Sierra Field Station. c/o Center for Environmental Studies, Arizona State University, Temple, Arizona 85287-3211. (602) 965-2975.

TRADE ASSOCIATIONS AND PROFESSIONAL SOCIETIES

American Institute of Biological Sciences. 730 11th St., N.W., Washington, District of Columbia 20001-4521. (202) 628-1500.

Grassland Heritage Foundation. P.O. Box 344, Shawnee Mission, Kansas 66201-0394. (913) 677-3326.

Save the Tall Grass Prairie, Inc. PO Box 557, Topeka, Kansas 66601. (913) 357-4681.

GREASES

See also: LUBRICATING OILS

ABSTRACTING AND INDEXING SERVICES

Environment Abstracts. Bowker A & I Publishing, 121 Chanlon Rd., New Providence, New Jersey 07974. (908) 464-6800. 1974-.

Environment Index. Environment Information Center, Index Research Department, 124 E. 39th St., New York, New York 10016. 1971-. Annual.

Environmental Information Connection–EIC. Planning Information Program, Dept. of Urban and Regional Planning, University of Illinois, 1003 West Nevada, Urbana, Illinois 61801. (217) 333-1369. Also available online.

Environmental Periodicals Bibliography. Environmental Studies Institute, International Academy at Santa Barbara, 800 Garden St., Suite D, Santa Barbara, California 93101. (805) 965-5010. Also available online.

General Science Index. H. W. Wilson Co., 950 University Ave., Bronx, New York 10452. 1978-. Monthly, also issued in annual cumulation. Cumulative subject index to English language periodicals in the subject fields of astronomy, botany, chemistry, earth science, environment and conservation, food and nutrition, genetics, mathematics, medicine and health, microbiology, oceanography, physics, physiology and zoology.

Science Citation Index. Institute for Scientific Information, 3501 Market St., Philadelphia, Pennsylvania 19104. 1961-.

BIBLIOGRAPHIES

EPA Publications Bibliography. U.S. Environmental Protection Agency, Library Systems Branch, 401 M St., SW, Washington, District of Columbia 20460. (202) 260-2090. Quarterly.

ENCYCLOPEDIAS AND DICTIONARIES

Van Nostrand's Scientific Encyclopedia. Glenn D. Considine, ed. Van Nostrand Reinhold, 115 5th Ave., New York, New York 10003. (212) 254-3232. 1983. Sixth edition. Includes all broad subject areas in science.

ONLINE DATA BASES

Enviro/Energyline Abstracts Plus. R. R. Bowker Co., 121 Chanlon Rd., New Providence, New Jersey 07974. (908) 464-6800.

Environmental Periodicals Bibliography. National Information Services Corp., Ste. 6, Wyman Towers, 3100 St. Paul St., Baltimore, Maryland 21218. (410)243-0797. Online version of abstract of same name.

GREAT DISMAL SWAMPS

ABSTRACTING AND INDEXING SERVICES

Ecological Abstracts. Geo Abstracts Ltd. Elsevier Applied Science, Crown House, Linton Rd., Barking, England IG 11 8JU. 1974-. Derived from over 600 leading ecological and environmental journals, plus books, conference proceedings, reports and theses.

Environment Abstracts. Bowker A & I Publishing, 121 Chanlon Rd., New Providence, New Jersey 07974. (908) 464-6800. 1974-.

Environment Index. Environment Information Center, Index Research Department, 124 E. 39th St., New York, New York 10016. 1971-. Annual.

Environmental Information Connection–EIC. Planning Information Program, Dept. of Urban and Regional Planning, University of Illinois, 1003 West Nevada, Urbana, Illinois 61801. (217) 333-1369. Also available online.

Environmental Periodicals Bibliography. Environmental Studies Institute, International Academy at Santa Barbara, 800 Garden St., Suite D, Santa Barbara, California 93101. (805) 965-5010. Also available online.

BIBLIOGRAPHIES

EPA Publications Bibliography. U.S. Environmental Protection Agency, Library Systems Branch, 401 M St., SW, Washington, District of Columbia 20460. (202) 260-2090. Quarterly.

ONLINE DATA BASES

Enviro/Energyline Abstracts Plus. R. R. Bowker Co., 121 Chanlon Rd., New Providence, New Jersey 07974. (908) 464-6800.

Environmental Periodicals Bibliography. National Information Services Corp., Ste. 6, Wyman Towers, 3100 St. Paul St., Baltimore, Maryland 21218. (410)243-0797. Online version of abstract of same name.

SCISEARCH. Institute for Scientific Information, University City Science Center, 3501 Market St., Philadelphia, Pennsylvania 19104. (215) 386-0100.

TRADE ASSOCIATIONS AND PROFESSIONAL SOCIETIES

American Institute of Biological Sciences. 730 11th St., N.W., Washington, District of Columbia 20001-4521. (202) 628-1500.

GREAT LAKES

See: LAKES

GREEN BELTS

See: PRESERVES, ECOLOGICAL

GREEN HOUSES

ABSTRACTING AND INDEXING SERVICES

Agricultural Engineering Abstracts. C. A. B. International, 845 North Park Ave., Tucson, Arizona 85719. (602) 621-7897 or (800) 528-4841. 1976-. Monthly. Informs about significant research developments in agricultural engineering and instrumentation. Some of the topics scanned for the abstracts include mechanical power, crop production, crop harvesting and threshing, crop processing and storage, aquaculture, land improvement, protected cultivation, handling and transport, and farm buildings and equipment.

Biological and Agricultural Index. H.W. Wilson Co., 950 University Ave., Bronx, New York 10452. (800) 367-6770. 1916-. Monthly.

Energy Information Abstracts Annual 1987 in Retrospect. EIC/Intelligence Inc., 121 Chanlon Rd., New Providence, New Jersey 07974. (908) 464-6800. 1988. Annual. Cumulative edition of the monthly Energy Information Abstracts. Monitors sources in the field of energy including the scientific, technical and business journal literature, conference and symposia proceedings, corporate, government and academic reports.

Environment Abstracts. Bowker A & I Publishing, 121 Chanlon Rd., New Providence, New Jersey 07974. (908) 464-6800. 1974-.

Environment Index. Environment Information Center, Index Research Department, 124 E. 39th St., New York, New York 10016. 1971-. Annual.

Environmental Information Connection-EIC. Planning Information Program, Dept. of Urban and Regional Planning, University of Illinois, 1003 West Nevada, Urbana, Illinois 61801. (217) 333-1369. Also available online.

Environmental Periodicals Bibliography. Environmental Studies Institute, International Academy at Santa Barbara, 800 Garden St., Suite D, Santa Barbara, California 93101. (805) 965-5010. Also available online.

Science Citation Index. Institute for Scientific Information, 3501 Market St., Philadelphia, Pennsylvania 19104. 1961-.

BIBLIOGRAPHIES

Current Contents. Agriculture, Biology and Environmental Sciences. Institute for Scientific Information, 3501 Market St., Philadelphia, Pennsylvania 19104. (800) 523-1857. 1973-. Previous title: Current Contents. Agricultural, Food & Veterinary Sciences. Gives the table of contents of periodicals in the fields of agriculture, biology, environmental and related areas.

EPA Publications Bibliography. U.S. Environmental Protection Agency, Library Systems Branch, 401 M St., SW, Washington, District of Columbia 20460. (202) 260-2090. Quarterly.

DIRECTORIES

Gale Environmental Sourcebook. Karen Hill. Gale Research Co., 835 Penobscot Bldg., Detroit, Michigan 48226-4094. (313) 961-2242. Contacts, information sources, or general information on environmental topics.

ONLINE DATA BASES

Enviro/Energyline Abstracts Plus. R. R. Bowker Co., 121 Chanlon Rd., New Providence, New Jersey 07974. (908) 464-6800.

Environmental Periodicals Bibliography. National Information Services Corp., Ste. 6, Wyman Towers, 3100 St. Paul St., Baltimore, Maryland 21218. (410)243-0797. Online version of abstract of same name.

SCISEARCH. Institute for Scientific Information, University City Science Center, 3501 Market St., Philadelphia, Pennsylvania 19104. (215) 386-0100.

STATISTICS SOURCES

Environmental Data Compendium. OECD Publications and Information Center, 2001 L St., N.W., Suite 700, Washington, District of Columbia 20036. (202) 785-6323. 1989.

Environmental Indicators. OECD Publications and Information Center, 2001 L St., N.W., Suite 700, Washington, District of Columbia 20036. (202) 785-6323. 1991.

Environmental Quality. Council on Environmental Quality. U.S. G.P.O., Washington, District of Columbia 20401. (202) 512-0000. Annual.

The State of the Environment. OECD Publications and Information Center, 2001 L St., N.W., Suite 700, Washington, District of Columbia 20036. (202) 785-6323. 1991.

TRADE ASSOCIATIONS AND PROFESSIONAL SOCIETIES

American Institute of Biological Sciences. 730 11th St., N.W., Washington, District of Columbia 20001-4521. (202) 628-1500.

New Alchemy Institute. 237 Hatchville Rd., East Falmouth, Massachusetts 02536. (508) 564-6301.

GREEN MANURE

See: FERTILIZERS

GREEN POWER

See: PETROLEUM

ONLINE DATA BASES

Green Markets. McGraw-Hill Science & Engineering Books, 11 W. 19th St., New York, New York 10011. (212) 337-6010.

GREEN PRODUCTS

ABSTRACTING AND INDEXING SERVICES

Applied Ecology Abstracts Studies in Renewable Natural Resources. Information Retrieval Ltd., 1911 Jefferson Davis Highway, Arlington, Virginia 22202. 1975-. Monthly.

Ecological Abstracts. Geo Abstracts Ltd. Elsevier Applied Science, Crown House, Linton Rd., Barking, England IG 11 8JU. 1974-. Derived from over 600 leading ecological and environmental journals, plus books, conference proceedings, reports and theses.

Index to Scientific Book Contents. Institute for Scientific Information, 3501 Market St., Philadelphia, Pennsylvania 19104. (800) 523-1857. 1985-. Annual. Gives contents of science books published.

Multimedia Index to Ecology. National Information Center for Educational Media, University of Southern California, Los Angeles, California 90007.

Priority Issue Reporting Service–PIRS. Information for Public Affairs, Inc., Client Services Dept., 1900 14th St., Sacramento, California 95814.

BIBLIOGRAPHIES

The Economics of "Green Consumerism": A Bibliography. Leslie Anderson Morales. Public Affairs Information Service, 521 W. 43rd St., New York, New York 10036. (212) 736-6629. 1991. Economic impact of environmentally safe products and services from the perspectives of the consumer, wholesaler, and provider.

DIRECTORIES

Co-Op America's Business and Organizational Member Directory. Co-Op America, 2100 M St. NW, No. 403, Washington, District of Columbia 20063. (202) 872-5307. Annual. Small businesses, co-operatives, and non-profit organizations that produce environmentally benign products such as nontoxic household products, plant based paints, organic foods, and energy saving devices.

Environmental & Ecological Services. American Business Directories, Inc., 5711 S. 86th Circle, Omaha, Nebraska 68127. (402) 593-4600.

Green Earth Resource Guide: A Comprehensive Guide About Environmentally Friendly Services and Products Books, Clean Air... Cheryl Gorder. Blue Bird Pub., 1713 East Broadway #306, Tempe, Arizona 85282. (602) 968-4088; (800) 654-1993. 1991. Book emphasizes positive steps we can take to help planets. Consists of two parts. Part one profiles people or businesses that are environmentally-friendly and are actively involved with projects

and products; part two has resources listings of things concerned with environmental problems. Includes a company index with addresses and phone numbers.

The Green Pages: Your Everyday Shopping Guide to Environmentally Safe Products. Random House, Inc., 201 E. 50th St., New York, New York 10022. (212) 751-2600. 1990.

Save L.A.: An Environmental Resource Directory: The Thinking and Caring Person's Directory of Environmental Products, Services, and Resources for the Los Angeles Area. Tricia R. Hoffman and Nan Kathryn Fuchs. Chronicle Books, 275 5th St., San Francisco, California 94103. (415) 777-7240; (800) 722-6657. 1990. This comprehensive guidebook opens with a brief overview of the most pressing ecological issues peculiar to the Los Angeles area and then goes on to provide a list of some 1000 resources targeted for the environmental challenges the city Angelenos faces.

Shopping for a Better Environment. Laurence Tasaday. Meadowbrook Press, Inc., 18318 Minnetonka Blvd., Deephaven, Minnesota 55391. (612) 473-5400. 1991. A brand name guide to environmentally responsible shopping.

GENERAL WORKS

Ecologue: The Environmental Catalogue and Consumer's Guide for a Safe Earth. Bruce N. Anderson, ed. Prentice Hall, Rte. 9W, Englewood Cliffs, New York 07632. (201) 592-2000. 1990. Compares and evaluates the cost, performance, energy efficiency and effect on the environment of a wide range of products used in everyday settings. The book is arranged according to the products used: groceries, household cleaners, clothing, personal care items, baby care, appliances and transportation.

Environmental Labelling in OECD Countries. OECD, UNIPUB, 4611-F Assembly Dr., Lanham, Maryland 20706. (301) 459-7666 or (800) 274-4888. 1991. Describes the origin and aims of the existing government sponsored labelling programs in the OECD countries.

The Green Consumer Supermarket Guide. Joel Makower, et al. Penguin Books, 375 Hudson St., New York, New York 10014. (212) 366-2000; (800) 253-2304. 1991. A buying guide to products that don't cost the earth.

The Green Shopping Revolution. Food Marketing Institute, Research Department, 1750 K St., NW, Washington, District of Columbia 20006. 1990. How solid wastes are affecting consumer behavior and citizen participation in packaging and waste minimization.

Shopping for a Better World. The Council for Economic Priorities. Ballantine Books, 201 E. 50th St., New York, New York 10022. (212) 572-2620; (800) 733-3000. 1991. Rev. ed. Investigates 206 companies and over 2,015 products.

HANDBOOKS AND MANUALS

The Green Consumer. John Elkington, Julia Hailes, and Joel Makower. Penguin Books, 375 Hudson St., New York, New York 10014. (212) 366-2000. 1990. Shoppers guide to purchasing ecological products and services.

The Green Lifestyle Handbook. Jeremy Rifkin. Henry Holt & Co., 115 W. 18th St., 6th Fl., New York, New York 10011. (212) 886-9200. 1990. Citizen participation in environmental protection.

ONLINE DATA BASES

Business and the Environment. Cutter Information Corp., 37 Broadway, Arlington, Massachusetts 02174-4439. (617) 648-8700. Online version of periodical of the same name.

Green Marketing Report. Business Publishers, Inc., 951 Pershing Dr., Silver Spring, Maryland 20910. (301) 587-6300. Online version of periodical of the same name.

Monthly Catalog of United States Government Publications. U.S. G.P.O., Supt. of Docs., PO Box 371954, Pittsburgh, Pennsylvania 15250-7954. (202) 512-0000.

National Technical Information Service. U.S. Department of Commerce, National Technical Information Service, Office of Data Base Services, 5285 Port Royal Rd., Springfield, Virginia 22161. (703) 487-4807. Bibliographic database of government sponsored research and technical reports.

PERIODICALS AND NEWSLETTERS

Business and the Environment. Cutter Information Corp., 37 Broadway, Arlington, Massachusetts 02174. (617) 648-8700. Semimonthly. Global news and analysis on environmental trends. Also available online.

EPI Environmental Products Index. Duane Enterprises, 319 West St., Braintree, Massachusetts 02184. (617) 848-6150. Product and technology for testing, monitoring, transportation.

Green Marketing Report. Business Publishers, Inc., 951 Pershing Dr., Silver Spring, Maryland 20910-4464. (301) 587-6300. 1990-. Monthly. Looks at the steps taken by product manufacturers and advertisers to address consumers' environmental concerns as well as government examination of (and challenges to) some companies' environmental claims. Also available online.

International Permaculture Solutions Journal. Yankee Permaculture, P.O. Box 16683, Wichita, Kansas 67216. Irregular. Tools for sustainable lifestyles, extensive green pages, and resources directory.

STATISTICS SOURCES

The Impact of Green Consumerism on Food & Beverage Industries. FIND/SVP, 625 Avenue of the Americas, New York, New York 10011. (212) 645-4500. 1991/92.

TRADE ASSOCIATIONS AND PROFESSIONAL SOCIETIES

Co-Op America. 2100 M St., NW, Suite 403, Washington, District of Columbia 20063. (202) 872-5307.

GREEN REVOLUTION

See also: AGRICULTURE

ABSTRACTING AND INDEXING SERVICES

Applied Ecology Abstracts Studies in Renewable Natural Resources. Information Retrieval Ltd., 1911 Jefferson Davis Highway, Arlington, Virginia 22202. 1975-. Monthly.

Biological and Agricultural Index. H.W. Wilson Co., 950 University Ave., Bronx, New York 10452. (800) 367-6770. 1916-. Monthly.

Ecological Abstracts. Geo Abstracts Ltd. Elsevier Applied Science, Crown House, Linton Rd., Barking, England IG 11 8JU. 1974-. Derived from over 600 leading ecological and environmental journals, plus books, conference proceedings, reports and theses.

Index to Scientific Book Contents. Institute for Scientific Information, 3501 Market St., Philadelphia, Pennsylvania 19104. (800) 523-1857. 1985-. Annual. Gives contents of science books published.

Multimedia Index to Ecology. National Information Center for Educational Media, University of Southern California, Los Angeles, California 90007.

BIBLIOGRAPHIES

Current Contents. Agriculture, Biology and Environmental Sciences. Institute for Scientific Information, 3501 Market St., Philadelphia, Pennsylvania 19104. (800) 523-1857. 1973-. Previous title: Current Contents. Agricultural, Food & Veterinary Sciences. Gives the table of contents of periodicals in the fields of agriculture, biology, environmental and related areas.

The Green Revolution. T. R. Liao. Library of Congress, Science and Technology Division, Reference Sectiion, Washington, District of Columbia 20540. (202) 707-1181. 1980. Agricultural innovations in developing countries.

The Green Revolution: An International Bibliography. M. Bazlui Karim. Greenwood Publishing Group, Inc., 88 Post Rd. W., PO Box 5007, New York, New York 06881. (212) 226-3571. 1986. Covers economic aspects of agriculture, food supply, green revolution, and agricultural innovations.

ENCYCLOPEDIAS AND DICTIONARIES

The New York Times Encyclopedic Dictionary of the Environment. Paul Sarnoff. Quadrangle Books, New York, New York 1971. Focuses on state-of-the-art methods of pollution control, abatement, prevention and removal.

GENERAL WORKS

Beyond the Green Revolution. Kenneth A. Dahlberg. Plenum Press, 233 Spring St., New York, New York 10013-1578. (212) 620-8000; (800) 221-9369. 1979. The ecology and politics of global agricultural development.

Environment, Energy, and Society. Craig R. Humphrey. Wadsworth Pub. Co., 10 Davis Dr., Belmont, California 94002. (415) 595-2350. 1982. Social aspects of environmental and population policy and the green revolution.

Feeding Tomorrow's World. Albert Sasson. Centre for Agriculture and Rural Cooperation and UNESCO, 7 Place de Fontenoy, Paris, France 1990. Analyzes Green Revolution and biotechnological revolution and tries to answer other pressing questions through a pluridisciplinary approach to human nutrition and food production. Synthesizes the scientific, economic, socioeconomic and environmental aspects of nutrition throughout the world.

The Green Revolution Revisited: Critique and Alternatives. Bernhard Glaeser. Unwin Hyman, c/o Routledge

Chapman & Hall Inc., 29 W. 35th St., New York, New York 10001. (212) 244-6412. 1987. Economic aspects of agricultural innovations in developing countries.

ONLINE DATA BASES

Monthly Catalog of United States Government Publications. U.S. G.P.O., Supt. of Docs., PO Box 371954, Pittsburgh, Pennsylvania 15250-7954. (202) 512-0000.

National Technical Information Service. U.S. Department of Commerce, National Technical Information Service, Office of Data Base Services, 5285 Port Royal Rd., Springfield, Virginia 22161. (703) 487-4807. Bibliographic database of government sponsored research and technical reports.

SCISEARCH. Institute for Scientific Information, University City Science Center, 3501 Market St., Philadelphia, Pennsylvania 19104. (215) 386-0100.

PERIODICALS AND NEWSLETTERS

Green Perspectives. Green Perspectives, Box 111, Vermont, Vermont 05402. Monthly. News and information on the Green Program Project.

TRADE ASSOCIATIONS AND PROFESSIONAL SOCIETIES

American Institute of Biological Sciences. 730 11th St., N.W., Washington, District of Columbia 20001-4521. (202) 628-1500.

GREENHOUSE EFFECT

See also: AIR POLLUTION; ATMOSPHERE; COMBUSTION; GLOBAL WARMING; OZONE LAYER

ABSTRACTING AND INDEXING SERVICES

Abstracts of Air and Water Conservation Literature. American Petroleum Institute. Central Abstracting and Indexing Service, 275 Madison Avenue, New York, New York 10016. 1972.

Air Pollution Technical Publications of the United States Environmental Protection Agency. U.S. Environmental Protection Agency, Mail Drop 75, Research Triangle Park, North Carolina 27711. (919) 541-2184. 1976. Quarterly.

Air Pollution Titles. Pennsylvania State University, Center for Air Environmental Studies, 226 Fenske Laboratory, University Park, Pennsylvania 16802. (814) 865-1415. 1965. Bibliographic guide to current research literature on air environment, including monitoring and control of air pollution, health effects, effects on agriculture, forests, toxic air contaminants, and global atmospheric pro cases.

Air Pollution Translations. A Bibliography With Abstracts. U.S. Environmental Protection Agency, MD 75, Research Triangle Park, North Carolina 27711. (919) 541-2184. 1969.

Applied Ecology Abstracts Studies in Renewable Natural Resources. Information Retrieval Ltd., 1911 Jefferson Davis Highway, Arlington, Virginia 22202. 1975-. Monthly.

ASFA Aquaculture Abstracts. Cambridge Scientific Abstracts, Inc., 5161 River Rd., Bethesda, Maryland 20816. (301) 961-6750. 1984.

Biological Abstracts. BIOSIS, 2100 Arch St., Philadelphia, Pennsylvania 19103-1399. (215) 587-4800. 1927-.

Biological and Agricultural Index. H.W. Wilson Co., 950 University Ave., Bronx, New York 10452. (800) 367-6770. 1916-. Monthly.

Bulletin Signaletique: Eau et Assainissement, Pollution Atmospherique, Droit des Pollutions. Centre de Documentation, Centre National de la Recherche Scientifique, 15, quai Anatole France, Paris, France 75700. (1) 45 55 92 25. 1983-. Monthly. Indexes pollution periodicals including water, atmospheric and related pollutions.

Current Advances in Ecological and Environmental Science. Pergamon Microforms International, Inc., Fairview Park, Elmsford, New York 10523. (914) 592-7720. 1989-. Monthly. Current literature searching service including journals, reports, abstracts, etc. This service is available online as part of the CABS database on the hosts BRS and ORBIT search service.

Ecological Abstracts. Geo Abstracts Ltd. Elsevier Applied Science, Crown House, Linton Rd., Barking, England IG 11 8JU. 1974-. Derived from over 600 leading ecological and environmental journals, plus books, conference proceedings, reports and theses.

Ecology Abstracts. Cambridge Scientific Abstracts, 5161 River Rd., Bethesda, Maryland 20816. (301) 961-6750. Monthly.

Engineering Index. The Engineering Index Inc., 345 E. 47th St., New York, New York 10017. 1962-.

Environment Abstracts. Bowker A & I Publishing, 121 Chanlon Rd., New Providence, New Jersey 07974. (908) 464-6800. 1974-.

Environment Index. Environment Information Center, Index Research Department, 124 E. 39th St., New York, New York 10016. 1971-. Annual.

Environmental Information Connection–EIC. Planning Information Program, Dept. of Urban and Regional Planning, University of Illinois, 1003 West Nevada, Urbana, Illinois 61801. (217) 333-1369. Also available online.

Environmental Periodicals Bibliography. Environmental Studies Institute, International Academy at Santa Barbara, 800 Garden St., Suite D, Santa Barbara, California 93101. (805) 965-5010. Also available online.

ERDA Research Abstracts. U.S. ERDA Technical Information Center, Box 62, Oak Ridge, Tennessee 37830.

General Science Index. H. W. Wilson Co., 950 University Ave., Bronx, New York 10452. 1978-. Monthly, also issued in annual cumulation. Cumulative subject index to English language periodicals in the subject fields of astronomy, botany, chemistry, earth science, environment and conservation, food and nutrition, genetics, mathematics, medicine and health, microbiology, oceanography, physics, physiology and zoology.

Geographical Abstracts. London School of Economics, Dept. of Geography, Regency House, 34 Duke St., London, England 1966-. Continued by Geo Abstracts issued in 6 parts: Pt. A. Landforms and the quaternary; Pt. B. Biogeography and Climatology; Pt. C. Economic geography; Pt. D. Social geography and cartography; Pt. E. Sedimentology; Pt. F. Regional and community planning.

Green Engineering: A Current Awareness Bulletin. Institution of Mechanical Engineers, 1 Birdcage Walk, Westminster, London, England SW1H 9JJ. 71973 1266/7. 1991. Monthly. Covers acid rain, aerosol technology, biotechnology chlorofluorocarbons, chemical and process engineering, environmental protection, energy conservation, energy generation, greenhouse effect, materials, pollution, recycling, waste disposal, and other environmental topics.

Index to Scientific Book Contents. Institute for Scientific Information, 3501 Market St., Philadelphia, Pennsylvania 19104. (800) 523-1857. 1985-. Annual. Gives contents of science books published.

Multimedia Index to Ecology. National Information Center for Educational Media, University of Southern California, Los Angeles, California 90007.

Pollution Abstracts. Cambridge Scientific Abstracts, 5161 River Rd., Bethesda, Maryland 20816. (301) 961-6750. Six/year. Indexes worldwide technical literature on environmental pollution. Covers air pollution, marine and freshwater pollution, sewage and wastewater treatment, waste management, toxicology and health, noise pollution, radiation, land pollution, and environmental policies, programs, legislation, and education. Also available online.

Priority Issue Reporting Service–PIRS. Information for Public Affairs, Inc., Client Services Dept., 1900 14th St., Sacramento, California 95814.

Science Citation Index. Institute for Scientific Information, 3501 Market St., Philadelphia, Pennsylvania 19104. 1961-.

BIBLIOGRAPHIES

Current Contents. Agriculture, Biology and Environmental Sciences. Institute for Scientific Information, 3501 Market St., Philadelphia, Pennsylvania 19104. (800) 523-1857. 1973-. Previous title: Current Contents. Agricultural, Food & Veterinary Sciences. Gives the table of contents of periodicals in the fields of agriculture, biology, environmental and related areas.

EPA Publications Bibliography. U.S. Environmental Protection Agency, Library Systems Branch, 401 M St., SW, Washington, District of Columbia 20460. (202) 260-2090. Quarterly.

Global Climate Change: Recent Publications. Library of the Department of State. The Library, 2201 C St. N.W., Washington, District of Columbia 20520. 1989.

DIRECTORIES

Directory of Global Climate Change Organizations. Janet Wright. National Agricultural Library, 10301 Baltimore Blvd., Beltsville, Maryland 20705. (301) 504-5755. 1991. Identifies organizations that provide information regarding global climate change issues to the general public.

ENCYCLOPEDIAS AND DICTIONARIES

Cambridge Encyclopedia of Life Sciences. A. E. Friday and David S. Ingram. Cambridge University Press, 40 W 20th St., New York, New York 10011. (212) 924-3900 or

(800) 227-0247. 1985. Includes all topics under biology and ecology.

The Encyclopedia of Climatology. John E. Oliver and Rhodes W. Fairbridge, eds. Van Nostrand Reinhold, 115 5th Ave., New York, New York 10003. (212) 254-3232. 1987. Belongs in the series Encyclopedia of Earth Sciences, v.11.

Encyclopedia of Environmental Science and Engineering. J.R. Pfafflin. Gordon and Breach Science Publishers, Inc., 270 8th Ave., New York, New York 10011. (212) 206-8900. 1992.

The Encyclopedia of Geochemistry and Environmental Sciences. Rhodes Whitmore Fairbridge. Van Nostrand Reinhold Co., 115 5th Ave., New York, New York 10003. (212) 254-3232. 1972.

Encyclopedia of Physical Science and Technology. Robert A. Meyers, ed. Academic Press, c/o Harcourt Brace Jovanovich Inc., 6277 Sea Harbor Dr., Orlando, Florida 32887. (800) 346-8648. Dictionary of engineering, technology and physical sciences.

Grzimek's Encyclopedia of Ecology. Bernhard Grzimek. Van Nostrand Reinhold, 115 5th Ave., New York, New York 10003. (212) 254-3232. 1976.

Illustrated Encyclopedia of Science and the Future. Mike Biscare, et al., ed. Marshall Cavendish, 58 Old Compton St., London, England 0W1V5 PA. 01-734 6710. 1983. Twenty volumes. Each volume has 5 sections: Frontiers, Electronics in Action, Medical Science, Military Technology, and Resources.

McGraw-Hill Encyclopedia of Environmental Science. Sybil P. Parker. McGraw-Hill Science & Engineering Books, 11 W. 19th St., New York, New York 10011. (212) 337-6010. 1980. Covers ecology, man's influence on nature, and environmental protection.

McGraw-Hill Encyclopedia of Science and Technology. McGraw-Hill, 1221 Avenue of the Americas, New York, New York 10020. (212) 512-2000 or (800) 262-4729. 1992. Seventh edition. Issued in multiple volumes including index. Includes all science and technology broad subject areas.

North American Reference Encyclopedia of Ecology and Pollution. William White. North American Pub. Co., 401 N. Broad St., Philadelphia, Pennsylvania 19108. (215) 238-5300. 1972.

Van Nostrand's Scientific Encyclopedia. Glenn D. Considine, ed. Van Nostrand Reinhold, 115 5th Ave., New York, New York 10003. (212) 254-3232. 1983. Sixth edition. Includes all broad subject areas in science.

GENERAL WORKS

Air Pollution's Toll on Forests and Crops. James J. MacKenzie and Mohamed T. El-Ashry, eds. Yale University Press, 92 A Yale St., 302 Temple St., New Haven, Connecticut 06520. (203) 432-0960. 1992. Proposes an integrated strategy to reduce pollution levels based on improved energy efficiency, abatement technology, and the use of nonfossil energy technologies. This strategy takes into account other critical problems such as increasing oil imports, failure to attain clean air goals in U.S. cities, and the greenhouse effect.

Can We Delay a Greenhouse Warming?. U.S. G.P.O., Washington, District of Columbia 20401. (202) 512-

0000. The effectiveness and feasibility of options to slow a build-up of carbon dioxide in the atmosphere.

Carbon Dioxide and Global Change: Earth in Transition. Sherwood B. Idso. IBR Press, 631 E. Laguna Dr., Tempe, Arizona 85282. (602) 966-8693. 1989. Discusses environmental aspects of greenhouse effect.

Carbon Dioxide and Other Greenhouse Gases. Kluwer Academic Publishers, 101 Philip Dr., Assinippi Pk, Norwell, Massachusetts 02061. (617) 871-6600. Looks at environmental aspects of greenhouse effects.

Carbon Dioxide, the Climate and Man. John R. Gribbin. International Institute for Environment and Development, 3 Endsleigh St., London, England CB2 1ER. 1981. Influence on nature of atmospheric carbon dioxide.

The Challenge of Global Warming. Dean Edwin Abrahamson, ed. Island Press, 1718 Connecticut Ave. N.W., Suite 300, Washington, District of Columbia 20009. (202) 232-7933. 1989. Focuses on the causes, effects, policy implications, and possible solutions to global warming

The Changing Atmosphere: A Global Challenge. John Firor. Yale University Press, 302 Temple St., 92 A Yale Sta., New Haven, Connecticut 06520. (203) 432-0960. 1990. Examines three atmospheric problems: Acid rain, ozone depletion, and climate heating.

Climate and Man: From the Ice Age to the Global Greenhouse. Fred Pearce. Vision Books in Association with LWT, The Forum 74-80, Camden St., London, England NW1 OEG. 071-388-8811. 1989.

Climatic Change and Plant Genetic Resources. M. T. Jackson, et al., eds. Belhaven Press, 136 S. Broadway, Irvington, New York 10533. (914) 591-9111. 1990. Cities concerns about the effect of global warming on biological diversity of species is the main thrust of this text. Major portion of the book comes from the second international workshop on plant genetic resources held in 1989.

Dead Heat. M. Oppenheimer and R. Boyle. IB Tauris, 110 Gloucester Ave., London, England NW1 8JA. 071 483 2681. 1990. Guide to global warming and some possible solutions.

The End of Nature. Bill McKibben. Anchor Books, 666 5th Ave., New York, New York 10103. (212) 765-6500; (800) 223-6834. 1990.

Energy Technologies for Reducing Emissions of Greenhouse Gases. OECD Publications and Information Center, 2001 L St. N.W., Suite 700, Washington, District of Columbia 20036. (202) 785-OECD. 1989. Gives suggestions for dealing with the emissions of gases that can produce a change in the global climate.

Environment in Peril. Anthony B. Wolbarst, ed. Smithsonian Institution Press, 470 L'Enfant Plaza, No. 7100, Washington, District of Columbia 20560. (800) 782-4612. 1991. Brings together in one volume the primary concerns of eleven of the world's leaders in conservation, ecology and public policy. Broad environmental issues covered are: ozone depletion, overpopulation, global warming, thinning forests, extinction of species, spreading deserts, toxic chemicals, and various pollutants.

Escaping the Heat Trap. Irving Mintzer and William R. Moomaw. World Resources Institute, 1709 New York Ave. N.W., Washington, District of Columbia 20006. (800) 822-0504. 1991. Report is based on a series of

scenarios developed using WRI's Model of Warming Commitment. Investigates the potential of societies to dramatically limit the rate of future greenhouse gas buildup and reduce to zero annual commitment to global warming.

Europhysics Study Conference on Induced Critical Conditions in the Atmosphere. A. Tartaglia. World Scientific, 687 Hartwell St., Teaneck, New Jersey 07666. (800) 227-7562. 1990. Deals with climatology, nuclear winter, ozone layer depletion, and the greenhouse effect.

Global Climate Change: Human and Natural Influences. Paragon House Publishers, 90 5th Ave., New York, New York 10011. (212) 620-2820. Carbon dioxide, methane, chlorofluorocarbons and ozone in the atmosphere; acid rain and water pollution in the hydrosphere; oceanographic and meteorological processes, nuclear war, volcanoes, asteroids, and meteorites.

Global Energy Futures and the Carbon Dioxide Problem. Council on Environmental Quality, Old Executive Office Bldg., Rm. 154, Washington, District of Columbia 20500. (202) 395-5080. 1981. Fossil fuels and energy policy.

Global Warming. Stephen Henry Schneider. Sierra Club Books, 100 Bush St., San Francisco, California 94104. (415) 291-1600. 1989. Climatic changes due to the greenhouse effect.

Global Warming: Do We Know Enough to Act?. S. Fred Singer. Center for the Study of American Business, Washington University, Campus Box 1208, One Brookings Dr., St. Louis, Missouri 63130-4899. (314) 935-5630. 1991.

Global Warming: The Greenpeace Report. Jeremy Leggett. Oxford University Press, 200 Madison Ave., New York, New York 10016. (800) 334-4249. 1990. Climate change and consequences of global warming, and means for abating and even halting global warming.

The Greenhouse Effect and Ozone Layer. Philip Neal. Dryad, 15 Sherman Ave., Takoma Park, Maryland 20912. (301) 891-3729. 1989. Covers atmospheric carbon dioxide and effects of carbon dioxide on climate.

Greenhouse Effect: Life on a Warmer Planet. Rebecca Johnson. Carolina Biological Supply Company, 2700 York Rd., Burlington, North Carolina 27215. (919) 584-0381. 1990. Discusses the effects of what may be the most serious environmental problem ever. Suggests steps everyone can take to reduce the impact of global warming.

Greenhouse Effect, Sea Level Rise, and Coastal Wetlands. U.S. Environmental Protection Agency, 401 M St., S.W., Washington, District of Columbia 20460. (202) 260-2090. 1988. Deals with wetland conservation and atmospheric greenhouse effect.

Greenhouse Gas Emissions–The Energy Dimension. OECD Publications and Information Center, 2001 L St., N.W., Suite 700, Washington, District of Columbia 20036. (202) 785-OECD. Source for a comprehensive discussion on the relationship between energy use and greenhouse emissions as they relate to the energy used by geographical and regional sectors.

The Greenhouse Trap: What We're Doing to the Atmosphere and How We Can Slow Global Warming. Francesca Lyman and James J. MacKenzie. World Resources Institute, 1709 New York Ave. N.W., Washington,

District of Columbia 20006. (800) 822-0504. 1990. Traces the history of the greenhouse effect and show how the current crisis has come about. Possible future consequences, based on the most credible scientific research available, are described and assessed.

Greenhouse Warming: Negotiating a Global Regime. Jessica Tuchman Mathews, ed. World Resources Institute, 1709 New York Ave. N.W., Washington, District of Columbia 20006. (800) 822-0504. 1991. Offers specific suggestions for formulating, implementing, and enforcing a global regime to combat greenhouse warming.

IMAGE, An Integrated Model to Assess the Greenhouse Effect. Jan Rotmans. Kluwer Academic Publishers, 101 Philip Dr., Assinippi Park, Norwell, Massachusetts 02061. (617) 871-6600. 1990. Explains how the computer simulation model IMAGE is constructed, the fundamental assumptions on which it is based, the ways in which it has been verified, and how to use it.

Keeping It Green: Tropical Forestry and the Mitigation of Global Warming. Mark C. Trexler. World Resources Institute, 1709 New York Ave. N.W., Washington, District of Columbia 20006. (800) 822-0504. 1991. Report links knowledge gained from past tropical forestry initiatives with expectations for their future effectiveness in the mitigation of global warming.

Long-Term Ecological Research: An International Perspective. Paul G. Risser, ed. John Wiley & Sons, Inc., 605 3rd Ave., New York, New York 10158-0012. (212) 850-6000. 1991. Describes and analyzes research programs in various ecosystems such as temperate forests, arid steppes, deserts, temperate and tropical grasslands, aquatic systems from countries including Scotland, Kenya, USA, Australia, Canada, Germany, and France.

Magill's Survey of Science. Life Science Series. Frank N. Magill, ed. Salem Press, PO Box 50062, Pasadena, California 91105. 1991. Six volumes. Contents: v.1. A-Central and peripheral nervous system functions; v.2. Central metabolism regulation - eukaryotic transcriptional control; v.3. Positive and negative eukaryotic transcriptional control - mammalian hormones; v.4. Hormones and behavior - muscular contraction; v.5. Muscular contraction and relaxation - sexual reproduction in plants; v.6. Reproductive behavior and mating - X inactivation and the Lyon hypothesis.

The Next One Hundred Years: Shaping the Fate of Our Living Earth. Jonathan Weiner. Bantam Books, 666 5th Ave., New York, New York 10103. (212) 765-6500; (800) 223-6834. 1991. Explores the following issues: the greenhouse effect, deforestation, the destruction of the ozone layer, the human population explosion and the onset of mass extinctions.

Ozone Depletion: Health and Environmental Consequences. John Wiley & Sons, Inc., 605 3rd Ave., New York, New York 10158-0012. (212) 850-6000. 1989.

Policy Implication of Greenhouse Warming. National Academy Press, 2101 Constitution Ave. N.W., PO Box 285, Washington, District of Columbia 20418. (202) 334-3313. 1991. Identifies what could be done to counter potential greenhouse warming. It has a helpful section on question and answers about greenhouse warming.

Potential Effects of Climate Change in the United Kingdom. HMSO, UNIPUB, 4611-F Assembly Dr., Lanham, Maryland 20706. (301) 459-7666 or (800) 274-4888. 1991. Considers the potential impacts of climate change in the UK in a wide variety of environmental and socioeconomic areas.

The Potential Effects of Global Climate Change on the United States. Joel B. Smith and Dennis A. Tirpak, eds. Hemisphere Publishing Co., 79 Madison Ave., Suite 1110, New York, New York 10016. (212) 725-1999; (800) 821-8312. 1990. Addresses the effects of climate change in vital areas such as water resources, agriculture, sea levels and forests. Also focuses on wetlands, human health, rivers and lakes and analyzes policy options for mitigating the effects of global warming.

A Primer on Greenhouse Effect Gases. Donald J. Wuebbles and Jae Edmonds. Lewis Publishers, 200 Corporate Blvd. NW, Boca Raton, Florida 33431. (407) 994-0555 or (800)272-7737. 1991. Brings together the most current information available on greenhouse gases. Reveals information critical to developing an understanding of the role of energy and atmospheric chemical and radiative processes in determining atmospheric concentrations of greenhouse gases.

Prospects for Future Climate: A Special US/USSR Report on Climate and Climate Change. Michael C. MacCracken, et al. Lewis Publishers, 2000 Corporate Blvd., N.W., Boca Raton, Florida 33431. (407) 994-0555 or (800) 272-7737. 1990. Describes the effects of the increasing concentration of greenhouse gases and the potential for climate change and impact on agriculture and hydrology. Projections are based on insights from both numerical models and empirical methods.

The Rising Tide: Global Warming and World Sea Levels. Lynne T. Edgerton. Island Press, 1718 Connecticut Ave. N.W., Suite 300, Washington, District of Columbia 20009. (202) 232-7933. 1991. Analysis of global warming and rising world sea level. Outlines state, national and international actions to respond to the effects of global warming on coastal communities and ecosystems.

Slowing Global Warming: A Worldwide Strategy. Christopher Flavin. Worldwatch Institute, 1776 Massachusetts Ave. N.W., Washington, District of Columbia 20036. How to cope with environmental warming as an environmental threat.

Soils and the Greenhouse Effect. A. F. Bouwman, ed. John Wiley & Sons, Inc., 605 3rd Ave., New York, New York 10158-0012. (212) 850-6000. 1990. Proceedings of the International Conference on Soils and the Greenhouse Effect, Wageningen, Netherlands, 1989. Covers the present status and future trends concerning the effect of soils and vegetation on the fluxes of greenhouse gases, the surface energy balance, and the water balance. Discusses the role of deforestation and management practices such as mulching, wetlands, agriculture and livestock.

Sources for the Future. Wallace Oates. Resources for the Future, 1616 P St., NW, Washington, District of Columbia 20036. (202) 328-5086. Examines emissions taxes, abatement subsides, and transferable emission permits in a national, regional, and global context.

The Statehouse Effect: State Policies to Cool the Greenhouse. Daniel A. Lashof and Eric L. Washburn. Natural Resources Defense Council, 40 W. 20th St., New York, New York 10011. (212) 727-2700. 1990. Discusses the need for states to take the initiative in controlling CO2 emissions. Details the sources of greenhouse gases and explains how greenhouse emissions can be reduced through energy efficiency, renewable energy strategies, recycling, and taxation and reforms in transportation, agriculture and forests.

Technological Responses to the Greenhouse Effect. George Thurlow, ed. Elsevier Science Publishing Co., 655 Avenue of the Americas, New York, New York 10010. (212) 989-5800. 1990. Watt Committee on Energy (London) working with 23 British experts has reported on various greenhouse gases, their sources and sinks, followed by an analysis of the release of these gases in "energy conversion" primarily in electric power production.

World on Fire: Saving the Endangered Earth. George J. Mitchell. Scribner Educational Publishers, 866 3d Ave., New York, New York 10022. (212) 702-2000; (800) 257-5755. 1991. Discusses the problems entailed with the issues of greenhouse effect, acid rain, the rift in the stratosphere ozone layer, and the destruction of tropical rain forests.

HANDBOOKS AND MANUALS

The Global Ecology Handbook: What You Can Do about the Environmental Crisis. Walter H. Corson, ed. The Global Tomorrow Coalition, Beacon Pr., 25 Beacon St., Boston, Massachusetts 02108-2800. (617) 742-2110. 1990. Covers environment, energy policy, population growth and other issues. It includes chapters on tropical rain forests, garbage, oceans and coasts, global warming, population growth, agriculture, biological diversity, fresh water, hazardous wastes, and environment and development.

ONLINE DATA BASES

BIOSIS Previews. BIOSIS, 2100 Arch St., Philadelphia, Pennsylvania 19103-1399. (215) 587-4800. Largest and most comprehensive database of research in the life sciences. Contains citations for nearly 9000 primary research journals, monographs, reviews, symposia, preliminary reports, semi-popular journals, selected institutional reports, government reports and research communications.

Cambridge Scientific Abstracts Life Science–CSAL. Cambridge Scientific Abstracts, 5161 River Rd., Bethesda, Maryland 20816. (301) 961-6750. Provides access to the following abstracting services: "Life Sciences Collection," "Aquatic Sciences and Fisheries Abstracts," "Oceanic Abstracts," and "Pollution Abstracts."

Computerized Engineering Index–COMPENDEX. Engineering Information Inc., 345 E. 47th St., New York, New York 10017. (212) 705-7600.

Enviro/Energyline Abstracts Plus. R. R. Bowker Co., 121 Chanlon Rd., New Providence, New Jersey 07974. (908) 464-6800.

Environment Week. NewsNet, Inc., 945 Haverford Rd., Bryn Mawr, Pennsylvania 19010. (800) 345-1301. Online version of periodical of same name.

Environmental Periodicals Bibliography. National Information Services Corp., Ste. 6, Wyman Towers, 3100 St. Paul St., Baltimore, Maryland 21218. (410)243-0797. Online version of abstract of same name.

Global Environmental Change Report. Cutter Information Corp., 37 Broadway, Arlington, Massachusetts 02174-5539. (617) 648-8700. Online access to environmental issues worldwide, including global warming,

ozone depletion, deforestation, and acid rain. Online version of periodical of the same name.

Greenhouse Effect Report. Business Publishers, Inc., 951 Pershing Dr., Silver Spring, Maryland 20910-4464. (301) 587-6300. Access to regulatory, legislative, business, and technological news and developments. Online version of periodical of same name.

Monthly Catalog of United States Government Publications. U.S. G.P.O., Supt. of Docs., PO Box 371954, Pittsburgh, Pennsylvania 15250-7954. (202) 512-0000.

National Technical Information Service. U.S. Department of Commerce, National Technical Information Service, Office of Data Base Services, 5285 Port Royal Rd., Springfield, Virginia 22161. (703) 487-4807. Bibliographic database of government sponsored research and technical reports.

PressNet Environmental Reports. Chemical Information Systems, Inc., 7215 York Rd., Baltimore, Maryland 21212. (301) 321-8440.

SCISEARCH. Institute for Scientific Information, University City Science Center, 3501 Market St., Philadelphia, Pennsylvania 19104. (215) 386-0100.

PERIODICALS AND NEWSLETTERS

Atmospheric Environment. Pergamon Microforms International, Inc., Fairview Park, Elmsford, New York 10523. (914) 592-7720. 1966-. Publishes papers on all aspects of man's interactions with his atmospheric environment, including the administrative, economic and political aspects of these interactions. Air pollution research and its applications are covered, taking into account changes in the atmospheric flow patterns, temperature distributions and chemical constitution caused by natural and artificial variations in the earth's surface.

Global Climate Change Digest. Elsevier Science Publishing Co., 655 Avenue of the Americas, New York, New York 10010. (212) 984-5800. Monthly. Topics dealing with ozone depletion and the large-scale climatic changes linked to industrial activity, industrial by-products, and man-made substances.

Global Ecology and Biogeography Letter. Blackwell Scientific Publications, 3 Cambridge Ctr., Suite 208, Cambridge, Massachusetts 02142. (617) 225-0401. 1991. Bimonthly. Global Ecology and Biogeography Letters is a sister publication of Journal of Biogeography and is only available with a subscription to the Journal. Provides a fast-track outlet for short research papers, news items, editorials, and book reviews. Topics related to the major scientific concerns of our present era, such as global warming, world sea-level rises, environmental acidification, development and conservation, biodiversity, and important new theories and themes in biogeography and ecology.

Global Environmental Change Report. Cutter Information Corp., 37 Broadway, Arlington, Massachusetts 02174-5539. (617) 648-8700. Biweekly. Focus on global warming, ozone depletion, deforestation, and acid rain. Also available online.

Greenhouse Effect Report. Business Publishers, Inc., 951 Pershing Dr., Silver Spring, Maryland 20910-4464. (301)587-6300. 1988-. Biweekly. This is a newsletter on international, governmental, regulatory, business and technological actions on global warming and the greenhouse effect. Also available online.

International Environmental Affairs. University Press of New England, 17 1/2 Lebanon Street, Hanover, New Hampshire 03755. (603) 646-3340. Quarterly. Issues on management of natural resources.

International Journal of Energy, Environment, Economics. Nova Science Publishers, Inc., 283 Commack Rd., Ste. 300, Commack, New York 11725. (516) 499-3103. 1991-. Quarterly. Aims to provide a vehicle for the multidisciplinary field of energy-environment economics between research scientists, engineers and economists. The areas covered would be technological, environmental, economic and social feasibility.

Journal of Biogeography. Blackwell Scientific Publications Inc., 3 Cambridge Ctr., Suite 208, Cambridge, Massachusetts 02142. (617) 225-0401.

Nature and Resources. Elsevier Science Publishing Co., 655 Avenue of the Americas, New York, New York 10010. (212) 989-5800. 1965-. Quarterly. Provides indepth reviews of contemporary environmental issues from an international perspective.

Probe Post. Pollution Probe Foundation, 12 Madison Ave., Toronto, Ontario, Canada M5R 2S1. (416) 926-1647. Quarterly. Acid rain, toxic waste, renewable energy, deep ecology, land use, and greenhouse effect.

RESEARCH CENTERS AND INSTITUTES

Worldwatch Institute. 1776 Massachusetts Ave., N.W., Washington, District of Columbia 20036. (202) 452-1999.

STATISTICS SOURCES

Trends '90: A Compendium of Data on Global Change. Thomas A. Boden, et al. Carbon Dioxide Information Analysis Center, Environmental Sciences Division, Oak Ridge National Laboratory, Oak Ridge, Tennessee 37831-6335. 1990. Source of frequently used global change data. Includes estimates of global and national CO_2 emissions from the burning of fossil fuels and from the production of cement and other pollutants.

World Resources. World Resources Institute. 1709 New York Ave., N.W., Washington, District of Columbia 20006. (202) 638-6300. Annual. Statistical and textual analysis of world's natural resources and the effects of growth-caused environmental pollution.

TRADE ASSOCIATIONS AND PROFESSIONAL SOCIETIES

Air Resources Information Clearinghouse. 99 Court St., Rochester, New York 14604. (716) 546-3796.

American Institute of Biological Sciences. 730 11th St., N.W., Washington, District of Columbia 20001-4521. (202) 628-1500.

GREENPEACE

ABSTRACTING AND INDEXING SERVICES

Applied Ecology Abstracts Studies in Renewable Natural Resources. Information Retrieval Ltd., 1911 Jefferson

Davis Highway, Arlington, Virginia 22202. 1975-. Monthly.

Environment Abstracts. Bowker A & I Publishing, 121 Chanlon Rd., New Providence, New Jersey 07974. (908) 464-6800. 1974-.

Environment Index. Environment Information Center, Index Research Department, 124 E. 39th St., New York, New York 10016. 1971-. Annual.

Environmental Information Connection–EIC. Planning Information Program, Dept. of Urban and Regional Planning, University of Illinois, 1003 West Nevada, Urbana, Illinois 61801. (217) 333-1369. Also available online.

Environmental Periodicals Bibliography. Environmental Studies Institute, International Academy at Santa Barbara, 800 Garden St., Suite D, Santa Barbara, California 93101. (805) 965-5010. Also available online.

Multimedia Index to Ecology. National Information Center for Educational Media, University of Southern California, Los Angeles, California 90007.

BIBLIOGRAPHIES

EPA Publications Bibliography. U.S. Environmental Protection Agency, Library Systems Branch, 401 M St., SW, Washington, District of Columbia 20460. (202) 260-2090. Quarterly.

ENCYCLOPEDIAS AND DICTIONARIES

Grzimek's Encyclopedia of Ecology. Bernhard Grzimek. Van Nostrand Reinhold, 115 5th Ave., New York, New York 10003. (212) 254-3232. 1976.

North American Reference Encyclopedia of Ecology and Pollution. William White. North American Pub. Co., 401 N. Broad St., Philadelphia, Pennsylvania 19108. (215) 238-5300. 1972.

Van Nostrand's Scientific Encyclopedia. Glenn D. Considine, ed. Van Nostrand Reinhold, 115 5th Ave., New York, New York 10003. (212) 254-3232. 1983. Sixth edition. Includes all broad subject areas in science.

GENERAL WORKS

The Greenpeace Guide to Paper. Greenpeace, 1436 U St., NW, Washington, District of Columbia 20009. (202) 462-1177. 1990. Waste paper recycling and environmental aspects of paper industry.

The Greenpeace Story. Michael Brown. Prentice-Hall, 1870 Birchmount Rd., Scarborough, Ontario, Canada M1P 2J7. (416) 293-3621. 1989. History of Greenpeace Foundation and its work towards nature and conservation.

Warriors of the Rainbow. Robert Hunter. Holt, Rinehart and Winston, 6277 Sea Harbor Dr., Orlando, Florida 32887. (407) 345-2500. 1979. Chronicles the Greenpeace movement.

ONLINE DATA BASES

Enviro/Energyline Abstracts Plus. R. R. Bowker Co., 121 Chanlon Rd., New Providence, New Jersey 07974. (908) 464-6800.

Environmental Periodicals Bibliography. National Information Services Corp., Ste. 6, Wyman Towers, 3100 St. Paul St., Baltimore, Maryland 21218. (410)243-0797. Online version of abstract of same name.

PressNet Environmental Reports. Chemical Information Systems, Inc., 7215 York Rd., Baltimore, Maryland 21212. (301) 321-8440.

SCISEARCH. Institute for Scientific Information, University City Science Center, 3501 Market St., Philadelphia, Pennsylvania 19104. (215) 386-0100.

PERIODICALS AND NEWSLETTERS

Greenpeace Magazine. Greenpeace, 1436 U St., NW, Washington, District of Columbia 20009. (202) 462-1177. Bimonthly. Deals with nature and wildlife conservation, and environmental protection.

TRADE ASSOCIATIONS AND PROFESSIONAL SOCIETIES

Greenpeace. 1436 U St., NW, Washington, District of Columbia 20009. (202) 462-1177.

GROSS ALPHA + BETA

See: RADIATION POLLUTION

GROUND COVER

See: EROSION

GROUNDWATER

See also: HYDROLOGY

ABSTRACTING AND INDEXING SERVICES

Aqualine Abstracts. Water Research Centre. c/o Pergamon Microforms International, Inc., Fairview Park, Elmsford, New York 10523. (914) 592-7720. 1927-. Contains some 8,000 records annually on water and wastewater technology. Covers all aspects of water, wastewater, associated engineering services and the aquatic environment. Over 600 periodicals, as well as books, reports and conference proceedings and other publications from water related institutions worldwide are scanned. Also available online.

ASFA Aquaculture Abstracts. Cambridge Scientific Abstracts, Inc., 5161 River Rd., Bethesda, Maryland 20816. (301) 961-6750. 1984.

Biological Abstracts. BIOSIS, 2100 Arch St., Philadelphia, Pennsylvania 19103-1399. (215) 587-4800. 1927-.

Biological and Agricultural Index. H.W. Wilson Co., 950 University Ave., Bronx, New York 10452. (800) 367-6770. 1916-. Monthly.

Ecology Abstracts. Cambridge Scientific Abstracts, 5161 River Rd., Bethesda, Maryland 20816. (301) 961-6750. Monthly.

General Science Index. H. W. Wilson Co., 950 University Ave., Bronx, New York 10452. 1978-. Monthly, also issued in annual cumulation. Cumulative subject index to English language periodicals in the subject fields of astronomy, botany, chemistry, earth science, environment and conservation, food and nutrition, genetics, mathematics, medicine and health, microbiology, oceanography, physics, physiology and zoology.

Geographical Abstracts. London School of Economics, Dept. of Geography, Regency House, 34 Duke St., London, England 1966-. Continued by Geo Abstracts issued in 6 parts: Pt. A. Landforms and the quaternary; Pt. B. Biogeography and Climatology; Pt. C. Economic geography; Pt. D. Social geography and cartography; Pt. E. Sedimentology; Pt. F. Regional and community planning.

Index to Scientific Book Contents. Institute for Scientific Information, 3501 Market St., Philadelphia, Pennsylvania 19104. (800) 523-1857. 1985-. Annual. Gives contents of science books published.

Pollution Abstracts. Cambridge Scientific Abstracts, 5161 River Rd., Bethesda, Maryland 20816. (301) 961-6750. Six/year. Indexes worldwide technical literature on environmental pollution. Covers air pollution, marine and freshwater pollution, sewage and wastewater treatment, waste management, toxicology and health, noise pollution, radiation, land pollution, and environmental policies, programs, legislation, and education. Also available online.

BIBLIOGRAPHIES

Bibliography and Index of Geology. American Geological Institute, 4220 King St., Alexandria, Virginia 22302. Monthly. Includes environmental geology and hydrogeology.

Current Contents. Agriculture, Biology and Environmental Sciences. Institute for Scientific Information, 3501 Market St., Philadelphia, Pennsylvania 19104. (800) 523-1857. 1973-. Previous title: Current Contents. Agricultural, Food & Veterinary Sciences. Gives the table of contents of periodicals in the fields of agriculture, biology, environmental and related areas.

New Publications of the Geological Survey. U.S. Department of the Interior, Geological Survey, 119 National Center, Reston, Virginia 22092. (703) 648-4460. 1984-. Monthly. Bibliography of geological publications and related government documents published by the Geological Survey.

DIRECTORIES

Ground Water Age–Directory of Manufacturers. National Trade Publications, Inc., 13 Century Hill, Latham, New York 12110. (518) 783-1281.

Ground Water Monitoring Review–Buyers Guide Issue. Water Well Journal Publishing Company/National Water Well Association, 6375 Riverside Dr., Dublin, Ohio 43017. (614) 761-3222.

Ground Water Monitoring Review–Consultant and Contractor Directory Issue. Water Well Journal Publishing Co., National Water Well Association, 6375 Riverside Dr., Dublin, Ohio 43017. (614) 761-3222.

ENCYCLOPEDIAS AND DICTIONARIES

Cambridge Encyclopedia of Life Sciences. A. E. Friday and David S. Ingram. Cambridge University Press, 40 W 20th St., New York, New York 10011. (212) 924-3900 or (800) 227-0247. 1985. Includes all topics under biology and ecology.

Dictionary of Civil Engineering. John S. Scott. Halsted Press, Division of J. Wiley, 605 3rd Ave., New York, New York 10158. (212) 850-6000. 1981. Third edition.

Dictionary of Environmental Engineering and Related Sciences: English-Spanish, Spanish-English. Jose T. Villate. Ediciones Universal, 3090 SW 8th St., Miami, Florida 33135. (305) 642-3355. 1979.

Elsevier's Dictionary of Horticultural and Agricultural Plant Production in Ten Languages. Elsevier Science Publishing Co., 655 Avenue of Americas, New York, New York 10010. (212) 989-5800. 1990. Language of the text: English, Dutch, French, German, Danish, Swedish, Italian, Spanish, Portuguese and Latin.

Encyclopedia of Environmental Science and Engineering. J.R. Pfafflin. Gordon and Breach Science Publishers, Inc., 270 8th Ave., New York, New York 10011. (212) 206-8900. 1992.

Encyclopedia of Physical Science and Technology. Robert A. Meyers, ed. Academic Press, c/o Harcourt Brace Jovanovich Inc., 6277 Sea Harbor Dr., Orlando, Florida 32887. (800) 346-8648. Dictionary of engineering, technology and physical sciences.

Grzimek's Encyclopedia of Ecology. Bernhard Grzimek. Van Nostrand Reinhold, 115 5th Ave., New York, New York 10003. (212) 254-3232. 1976.

McGraw-Hill Encyclopedia of Environmental Science. Sybil P. Parker. McGraw-Hill Science & Engineering Books, 11 W. 19th St., New York, New York 10011. (212) 337-6010. 1980. Covers ecology, man's influence on nature, and environmental protection.

North American Reference Encyclopedia of Ecology and Pollution. William White. North American Pub. Co., 401 N. Broad St., Philadelphia, Pennsylvania 19108. (215) 238-5300. 1972.

GENERAL WORKS

Applied Isotope Hydrogeology: A Case Study in Northern Switzerland. F. J. Pearson, Jr., et al. Elsevier Science Publishing Co., Inc, 655 Avenue of the Americas, New York, New York 10010. (212) 989-5800. 1991. This is a case study in northern Switzerland about radioactive waste disposal in the ground. Includes bibliographical references and an index.

Beneath the Bottom Line: Agricultural Approaches to Reduce Agrichemical Contamination of Groundwater. Office of Technology Assessment, U.S. Congress, Washington, District of Columbia 20510-8025. (202) 224-8996. 1991. Identifies ways to minimize contamination of ground water by agricultural chemicals.

Ground Water. H. M. Raghunath. John Wiley & Sons, Inc., 605 3rd Ave., New York, New York 10158-0012.

(212) 850-6000. 1987. Hydrogeology, ground water survey and pumping tests, rural water supply and irrigation systems.

Ground Water and Toxicological Risk. Jenifer S. Heath. Lewis Publishers, 2000 Corporate Blvd., N.W., Boca Raton, Florida 33431. (407) 994-0555 or (800) 272-7737. 1991. Discusses the nature of ground water, the nature of toxicology, risk assessment, basics of risk perception and two case studies of reaction.

Ground Water and Vadose Zone Monitoring. David M. Nielsen and A. Ivan Johnson, eds. PennWell Books, PO Box 21288, Tulsa, Oklahoma 74121. (918) 831-9421; (800) 752-9764. 1988. Contains 22 papers presented at the symposium on standards and development for ground water and Vadose Zone monitoring investigations.

Groundwater and Soil Contamination Remediation. Water Science and Technology Board. National Academy Press, Washington, District of Columbia (202) 334-3343. 1990. Science, policy and public perception.

Groundwater Contamination. J. H. Guswa, et al. Noyes Publications, 120 Mill Rd., Park Ridge, New Jersey 07656. (201) 391-8484. 1984. A technology review of equipment, methods, and field techniques; an overview of groundwater hydrology and a methodology for estimating groundwater contamination under emergency response conditions.

Groundwater Protection: Local Success Stories. Milou Carolan. Internal City Management Association, 777 N. Capital St., NE, Suite 500, Washington, District of Columbia 20002-4201. (800) 745-8780. 1990. Case studies from local governments that have created effective programs for protecting the local water supply by evaluating contamination sources and developing community support.

Groundwater Remediation and Petroleum: A Guide for Underground Storage Tanks. David C. Noonan and James T. Curtis. PennWell Books, PO Box 21288, Tulsa, Oklahoma 74121. (918) 831-9421; (800) 752-9764. 1990. Guide for personnel charged with the responsibility of addressing contamination caused by leaking underground storage tanks.

Groundwater Residue Sampling Design. Ralph G. Nash and Anne R. Leslie, eds. American Chemical Society, 1155 16th St. N.W., Washington, District of Columbia 20036. (202) 872-4600; (800) 227-5558. 1991. Gives an overview of the approach taken by government agencies and discusses in great detail the various techniques in sampling and analysis of groundwater.

Magill's Survey of Science. Earth Science Series. Frank N. Magill. Salem Press, PO Box 50062, Pasadena, California 91105. 1990-. Five volumes. Includes information on earth's crust, hot spots and volcanic island chains, physical properties of minerals, rock magnetism, physical properties of rocks, and index.

HANDBOOKS AND MANUALS

Ground Water Age–Handbook Issue. National Trade Publications, Inc., 13 Century Hill, Latham, New York 12110. (518) 783-1281.

Ground Water Handbook. Government Institutes, Inc., 4 Research Pl., Ste 200, Rockville, Maryland 20850. (301) 921-2300. 1989. Includes highlights of chapters on ground water contamination, use of models in managing ground water protection programs, ground water restoration, ground water quality investigations, basic hydrogeology, monitoring well design and construction, ground water sampling, ground water tracers and basic geology.

Ground Water Manual: A Guide for the Investigation, Development, and Management of Ground Water Resources. U.S. G.P.O., Washington, District of Columbia 20401. (202) 512-0000. 1981. Underground water resources in the water states.

Groundwater Chemicals Desk Reference. John H. Montgomery. Lewis Publishers, 2000 Corporate Blvd. NW, Boca Raton, Florida 33431. (407) 994-0555 or (800)272-7737. 1990. Protection and remediation of the groundwater environment. Includes profiles of chemical compounds promulgated by the EPA under the Clean Water Act of 1977.

Groundwater Chemicals Desk Reference, Volume II. John Montgomery. Lewis Publishers, 2000 Corporate Blvd., N.W., Boca Raton, Florida 33431. (407) 994-0555 or (800) 272-7737. 1991. Contains abbreviations, symbols, chemicals, conversion factors, CAS index, RTECS number index empirical formula, and synonym index.

ONLINE DATA BASES

BIOSIS Previews. BIOSIS, 2100 Arch St., Philadelphia, Pennsylvania 19103-1399. (215) 587-4800. Largest and most comprehensive database of research in the life sciences. Contains citations for nearly 9000 primary research journals, monographs, reviews, symposia, preliminary reports, semi-popular journals, selected institutional reports, government reports and research communications.

Ground Water Federal Register Notices. National Ground Water Information Center, National Water Well Association, 6375 Riverside Dr., Dublin, Ohio 43017. (614) 761-1711.

Ground Water Industry Standards. National Ground Water Information Center, National Water Well Association, 6375 Riverside Dr., Dublin, Ohio 43017. (614) 761-1711.

Ground Water Job Mart. National Ground Water Information Center, National Water Well Association, 6375 Riverside Dr., Dublin, Ohio 43017. (614) 761-1711.

Ground Water Monitor. Business Publishers, Inc., 951 Pershing Dr., Silver Spring, Maryland 20910. (301) 587-6300. Online version of periodical of the same name.

Ground Water On-Line. National Water Well Association, National Ground Water Information Center, 6375 Riverside Dr., Dublin, Ohio 43017. (614) 761-1711. Technical literature covering all aspects of groundwater and well technology.

Ground Water Regulations. National Ground Water Information Center, National Water Well Association, 6375 Riverside Dr., Dublin, Ohio 43017. (614) 761-1711.

Ground Water Sampling Devices. National Ground Water Information Center, National Well Water Association, 6375 Riverside Dr., Dublin, Ohio 43017. (614) 761-1711.

SCISEARCH. Institute for Scientific Information, University City Science Center, 3501 Market St., Philadelphia, Pennsylvania 19104. (215) 386-0100.

PERIODICALS AND NEWSLETTERS

Ground Water. Water Well Journal Publishing Co., 6375 Riverside Dr., Dublin, Ohio 43017. (614) 761-3222. Bimonthly. Contains technical papers for NWWA.

Ground Water Age. National Trade Publications, Inc., 13 Century Hill, Latham, New York 12110. (518) 783-1281. Monthly. Covers product and literature developments and industry news.

Ground Water Monitor. Business Publishers, Inc., 951 Pershing Dr., Silver Spring, Maryland 20910-4464. (301) 587-6300. Biweekly. Legislation, litigation, regulations and quality problems on ground water. Also available online.

Ground Water Monitoring Review. Water Well Journal Publishing Co. National Water Well Association, 6375 Riverside Drive, Dublin, Ohio 43017. (614) 761-3222. Quarterly. Covers protection and restoration of ground water.

Ground Water Newsletter. Water Information Center, Inc., 125 East Bethpage Road, Plainview, New York 11803. (516) 249-7634. Biweekly. Covers ground water exploration, development, and management.

Ground Water Pollution News. Buraff Publications, 1350 Connecticut Ave., NW, Washington, District of Columbia 20036. (202) 862-0990. Biweekly. Legislation, regulation and litigation concerning ground water pollution.

The Groundwater Newsletter. Water Information Center, Inc., 125 E. Bethpage Rd., Plainview, New York 11803. (516) 249-7634. Semimonthly.

RESEARCH CENTERS AND INSTITUTES

Groundwater Research Center. University of Cincinnati, College of Engineering, Mail Location 18, Cincinnati, Ohio 45221-0018. (513) 475-2933.

National Center for Ground Water Research. University of Oklahoma, 200 Telgar St., Rm. 127, Norman, Oklahoma 73019-0470. (405) 325-5202.

TRADE ASSOCIATIONS AND PROFESSIONAL SOCIETIES

Ground Water Institute. P.O. Box 580981, Minneapolis, Minnesota 55458-0981. (612) 636-3204.

Groundwater Management Caucus. Box 637, White Deer, Texas 79097. (806) 883-2501.

Groundwater Management Districts Association. 1125 Maize Rd., Colby, Kansas 67701. (913) 462-3915.

GROUNDWATER RUNOFF

See: HYDROLOGY

GROWTH INHIBITION

See: MICROORGANISMS

GYPSUM

ABSTRACTING AND INDEXING SERVICES

Biological Abstracts. BIOSIS, 2100 Arch St., Philadelphia, Pennsylvania 19103-1399. (215) 587-4800. 1927-.

Environment Abstracts. Bowker A & I Publishing, 121 Chanlon Rd., New Providence, New Jersey 07974. (908) 464-6800. 1974-.

Environment Index. Environment Information Center, Index Research Department, 124 E. 39th St., New York, New York 10016. 1971-. Annual.

Environmental Information Connection–EIC. Planning Information Program, Dept. of Urban and Regional Planning, University of Illinois, 1003 West Nevada, Urbana, Illinois 61801. (217) 333-1369. Also available online.

Environmental Periodicals Bibliography. Environmental Studies Institute, International Academy at Santa Barbara, 800 Garden St., Suite D, Santa Barbara, California 93101. (805) 965-5010. Also available online.

Pollution Abstracts. Cambridge Scientific Abstracts, 5161 River Rd., Bethesda, Maryland 20816. (301) 961-6750. Six/year. Indexes worldwide technical literature on environmental pollution. Covers air pollution, marine and freshwater pollution, sewage and wastewater treatment, waste management, toxicology and health, noise pollution, radiation, land pollution, and environmental policies, programs, legislation, and education. Also available online.

BIBLIOGRAPHIES

EPA Publications Bibliography. U.S. Environmental Protection Agency, Library Systems Branch, 401 M St., SW, Washington, District of Columbia 20460. (202) 260-2090. Quarterly.

ENCYCLOPEDIAS AND DICTIONARIES

Encyclopedia of Chemical Processing and Design. John J. Mcketta and W. A. Cunningham. Marcel Dekker, Inc., 270 Madison Ave., New York, New York 10016. (212) 696-9000; (800) 228-1160. 1992. Thirty-eight volumes.

Kirk-Othmer Encyclopedia of Chemical Technology. J. I. Kroschwitz, ed. John Wiley & Sons, Inc., 605 3rd Ave., New York, New York 10158-0012. (212) 850-6000. 1992-. All articles in the new edition have been rewritten and updated adding new subjects such as biotechnology, computer topics, analytical techniques and instrumentation, environmental concerns, fuels and energy, inorganic and solid state chemistry; composite materials and material science in general, and pharmaceuticals. Also available online.

Van Nostrand's Scientific Encyclopedia. Glenn D. Considine, ed. Van Nostrand Reinhold, 115 5th Ave., New York, New York 10003. (212) 254-3232. 1983. Sixth edition. Includes all broad subject areas in science.

GENERAL WORKS

The Chemistry and Technology of Gypsum. Richard A. Kuntze. American Society for Testing and Materials, 1916 S. Race St., Philadelphia, Pennsylvania 19103. (215) 299-5585. 1984.

Occurrence, Characteristics, and Genesis of Carbonate, Gypsum, and Silica Accumulations in Soils. W. D. Nettleton. Soil Science Society of America, 677 S. Segoe Rd., Madison, Wisconsin 53611. (608) 273-8080. 1991.

The Roles of Gypsum in Agriculture. Adolph Mehlich. United States Gypsum, Chemicals Division, 101 S. Wacker Dr., Chicago, Illinois 60606. (312) 606-4000. 1974. Effect of gypsum, fertilizers and manures on plants.

ONLINE DATA BASES

BIOSIS Previews. BIOSIS, 2100 Arch St., Philadelphia, Pennsylvania 19103-1399. (215) 587-4800. Largest and most comprehensive database of research in the life sciences. Contains citations for nearly 9000 primary research journals, monographs, reviews, symposia, preliminary reports, semi-popular journals, selected institutional reports, government reports and research communications.

Enviro/Energyline Abstracts Plus. R. R. Bowker Co., 121 Chanlon Rd., New Providence, New Jersey 07974. (908) 464-6800.

Environmental Periodicals Bibliography. National Information Services Corp., Ste. 6, Wyman Towers, 3100 St. Paul St., Baltimore, Maryland 21218. (410)243-0797. Online version of abstract of same name.

Kirk-Othmer Encyclopedia of Chemical Technology. John Wiley & Sons, Inc., 605 3rd Ave., 5th Floor, New York, New York 10158. (212) 850-6000. Online version of the publication of the same name.

PERIODICALS AND NEWSLETTERS

Gypsum. U.S. Department of the Interior, Bureau of Mines, 810 7th St., NW, Washington, District of Columbia 20241. (202) 501-9649. Monthly. Statistics on the gypsum industry.

TRADE ASSOCIATIONS AND PROFESSIONAL SOCIETIES

Gypsum Association. 801 First St. N.W., No. 510, Washington, District of Columbia 20002. (202) 289-5440.

H

HABITAT (ECOLOGY)

ABSTRACTING AND INDEXING SERVICES

Applied Ecology Abstracts Studies in Renewable Natural Resources. Information Retrieval Ltd., 1911 Jefferson Davis Highway, Arlington, Virginia 22202. 1975-. Monthly.

ASFA Aquaculture Abstracts. Cambridge Scientific Abstracts, Inc., 5161 River Rd., Bethesda, Maryland 20816. (301) 961-6750. 1984.

Biological and Agricultural Index. H.W. Wilson Co., 950 University Ave., Bronx, New York 10452. (800) 367-6770. 1916-. Monthly.

Current Advances in Ecological and Environmental Science. Pergamon Microforms International, Inc., Fairview Park, Elmsford, New York 10523. (914) 592-7720. 1989-. Monthly. Current literature searching service includingjournals, reports, abstracts, etc. This service is available online as part of the CABS database on the hosts BRS and ORBIT search service.

Ecological Abstracts. Geo Abstracts Ltd. Elsevier Applied Science, Crown House, Linton Rd., Barking, England IG 11 8JU. 1974-. Derived from over 600 leading ecological and environmental journals, plus books, conference proceedings, reports and theses.

Ecology Abstracts. Cambridge Scientific Abstracts, 5161 River Rd., Bethesda, Maryland 20816. (301) 961-6750. Monthly.

General Science Index. H. W. Wilson Co., 950 University Ave., Bronx, New York 10452. 1978-. Monthly, also issued in annual cumulation. Cumulative subject index to English language periodicals in the subject fields of astronomy, botany, chemistry, earth science, environment and conservation, food and nutrition, genetics, mathematics, medicine and health, microbiology, oceanography, physics, physiology and zoology.

Geographical Abstracts. London School of Economics, Dept. of Geography, Regency House, 34 Duke St., London, England 1966-. Continued by Geo Abstracts issued in 6 parts: Pt. A. Landforms and the quaternary; Pt. B. Biogeography and Climatology; Pt. C. Economic geography; Pt. D. Social geography and cartography; Pt. E. Sedimentology; Pt. F. Regional and community planning.

Index to Scientific Book Contents. Institute for Scientific Information, 3501 Market St., Philadelphia, Pennsylvania 19104. (800) 523-1857. 1985-. Annual. Gives contents of science books published.

Multimedia Index to Ecology. National Information Center for Educational Media, University of Southern California, Los Angeles, California 90007.

Pollution Abstracts. Cambridge Scientific Abstracts, 5161 River Rd., Bethesda, Maryland 20816. (301) 961-6750. Six/year. Indexes worldwide technical literature on environmental pollution. Covers air pollution, marine and freshwater pollution, sewage and wastewater treatment, waste management, toxicology and health, noise pollution, radiation, land pollution, and environmental policies, programs, legislation, and education. Also available online.

BIBLIOGRAPHIES

Current Contents. Agriculture, Biology and Environmental Sciences. Institute for Scientific Information, 3501 Market St., Philadelphia, Pennsylvania 19104. (800) 523-1857. 1973-. Previous title: Current Contents. Agricultural, Food & Veterinary Sciences. Gives the table of contents of periodicals in the fields of agriculture, biology, environmental and related areas.

ENCYCLOPEDIAS AND DICTIONARIES

Cambridge Dictionary of Biology. Peter M. B. Walker. Cambridge University Press, 40 W. 20th St., New York, New York 10011. (212) 924-3900 or (800) 227-0247. 1989. Includes 10,000 terms in zoology, botany, biochemistry, molecular biology and genetics. Previously published under the title Chambers Biology Dictionary.

Cambridge Encyclopedia of Life Sciences. A. E. Friday and David S. Ingram. Cambridge University Press, 40 W 20th St., New York, New York 10011. (212) 924-3900 or (800) 227-0247. 1985. Includes all topics under biology and ecology.

A Concise Dictionary of Biology. Elizabeth Martin, ed. Oxford University Press, 200 Madison Ave., New York, New York 10016. (212) 679-7300 or (800) 334-4249. 1990. New edition. Derived from the Concise Science Dictionary, published in 1984.

Elsevier's Dictionary of Horticultural and Agricultural Plant Production in Ten Languages. Elsevier Science Publishing Co., 655 Avenue of Americas, New York, New York 10010. (212) 989-5800. 1990. Language of the text: English, Dutch, French, German, Danish, Swedish, Italian, Spanish, Portuguese and Latin.

The Encyclopedia of Animal Ecology. Peter D. Moore. Facts on File, Inc., 460 Park Ave. S., New York, New York 10016. (212) 683-2244. 1987.

Grzimek's Encyclopedia of Ecology. Bernhard Grzimek. Van Nostrand Reinhold, 115 5th Ave., New York, New York 10003. (212) 254-3232. 1976.

McGraw-Hill Encyclopedia of Environmental Science. Sybil P. Parker. McGraw-Hill Science & Engineering Books, 11 W. 19th St., New York, New York 10011. (212) 337-6010. 1980. Covers ecology, man's influence on nature, and environmental protection.

McGraw-Hill Encyclopedia of Science and Technology. McGraw-Hill, 1221 Avenue of the Americas, New York, New York 10020. (212) 512-2000 or (800) 262-4729. 1992. Seventh edition. Issued in multiple volumes including index. Includes all science and technology broad subject areas.

North American Reference Encyclopedia of Ecology and Pollution. William White. North American Pub. Co., 401 N. Broad St., Philadelphia, Pennsylvania 19108. (215) 238-5300. 1972.

Van Nostrand's Scientific Encyclopedia. Glenn D. Considine, ed. Van Nostrand Reinhold, 115 5th Ave., New York, New York 10003. (212) 254-3232. 1983. Sixth edition. Includes all broad subject areas in science.

GENERAL WORKS

Earth-Sheltered Habitat. Gideon Golany. Van Nostrand Reinhold, 115 5th Ave., New York, New York 10003. (212) 254-3232. 1983. History, architecture, urban design, and underground architecture.

Ecological Effects of Thermal Discharges. T.E. Langford. Elsevier Science Publishing Co., 655 Avenue of the Americas, New York, New York 10010. (212) 984-5800. 1990. Review of the biological studies which have been carried out in various habitats and in response to a variety of problems related to cooling water usage, particularly on the large scale such as in thermal power stations.

The Ecology of Urban Habitats. O.L. Gilbert. Chapman & Hall, 29 W. 35th St., New York, New York 10001-2291. (212) 244-3336. 1989.

Habitat Destruction. Tony Hare. Gloucester Press, 95 Madison Ave., New York, New York 10016. (212) 447-7788. 1991. Factors threatening animal and plant habitats, such as pollution and depletion of our natural resources.

Magill's Survey of Science. Life Science Series. Frank N. Magill, ed. Salem Press, PO Box 50062, Pasadena, California 91105. 1991. Six volumes. Contents: v.1. A-Central and peripheral nervous system functions; v.2. Central metabolism regulation - eukaryotic transcriptional control; v.3. Positive and negative eukaryotic transcriptional control - mammalian hormones; v.4. Hormones and behavior - muscular contraction; v.5. Muscular contraction and relaxation - sexual reproduction in plants; v.6. Reproductive behavior and mating - X inactivation and the Lyon hypothesis.

The Protection and Management of Our Natural Resources, Wildlife and Habitat. W. Jack Grosse. Oceana Publications Inc., 75 Main St., Dobbs Ferry, New York 10522. (914) 693-8100. 1992. Covers question of overall management, control and protection of wildlife and habitat. Additionally, as the federal government has recently created numerous acts which serve to control wildlife and habitat, many questions have emerged over shared and conflicting power with the states.

The State of the Earth Atlas. Joni Seger, ed. Touchstone/Simon and Schuster, Rockefeller Center, 1230 Avenue of the Americas, New York, New York 10020. 1990. Deals with environmental issues such as air quality, urban sprawl, toxic waste, tropical forests and tourism from a socioeconomic perspective.

Strategies for Human Settlements: Habitat and Environment. Gwen Bell. University of Hawaii Press, 840 Kolowalu St., Honolulu, Hawaii 96822. (808) 956-8257. 1076. Community development and environmental policy.

HANDBOOKS AND MANUALS

Fish Habitat Improvement Handbook. Monte E. Seehorn. U.S. Department of Agriculture, Forest Service, Southern Region, 1720 Peachtree Rd., NW, Atlanta, Georgia 30367. 1985.

Wildlife and Fisheries Habitat Improvement Handbook. Neil F. Payne. Wildlife and Fisheries, Department of the Interior, 18th and C Sts. NW, Washington, District of Columbia 20240. (202) 653-8750. 1990.

ONLINE DATA BASES

Monthly Catalog of United States Government Publications. U.S. G.P.O., Supt. of Docs., PO Box 371954, Pittsburgh, Pennsylvania 15250-7954. (202) 512-0000.

National Technical Information Service. U.S. Department of Commerce, National Technical Information Service, Office of Data Base Services, 5285 Port Royal Rd., Springfield, Virginia 22161. (703) 487-4807. Bibliographic database of government sponsored research and technical reports.

Natural Resources Metabase. National Information Services Corporation, Ste. 6, Wyman Towers, 3100 St. Paul St., Baltimore, Maryland 21218. (301) 243-0797. Published and unpublished reports and other materials dealing with natural resources and environmental issues released by U.S. and Canadian government agencies and organizations.

SCISEARCH. Institute for Scientific Information, University City Science Center, 3501 Market St., Philadelphia, Pennsylvania 19104. (215) 386-0100.

PERIODICALS AND NEWSLETTERS

Defenders. Defenders of Wildlife, 1244 19th St. NW, Washington, District of Columbia 20036. (202) 659-9510. Bimonthly. Wildlife and conservation.

Habitat. Pergamon Microforms International, Inc., Fairview Park, Elmsford, New York 10523. (914) 592-7720. Quarterly. An international multidisciplinary journal concerning all aspects of human settlements, both urban and rural.

STATISTICS SOURCES

World Resources. World Resources Institute. 1709 New York Ave., N.W., Washington, District of Columbia 20006. (202) 638-6300. Annual. Statistical and textual analysis of world's natural resources and the effects of growth-caused environmental pollution.

TRADE ASSOCIATIONS AND PROFESSIONAL SOCIETIES

Defenders of Wildlife. 1244 19th St., NW, Washington, District of Columbia 20036. (202) 659-9510.

Wildlife Habitat Enhancement Council. 1010 Wayne Ave., Suite 1240, Silver Spring, Maryland 20910. (301) 588-8994.

HALOCARBONS

ABSTRACTING AND INDEXING SERVICES

Chemical Abstracts. Chemical Abstracts Service, 2540 Olentangy River Rd., PO Box 3012, Columbus, Ohio 43210. (800) 848-6533. 1907-.

General Science Index. H. W. Wilson Co., 950 University Ave., Bronx, New York 10452. 1978-. Monthly, also issued in annual cumulation. Cumulative subject index to English language periodicals in the subject fields of astronomy, botany, chemistry, earth science, environment and conservation, food and nutrition, genetics, mathematics, medicine and health, microbiology, oceanography, physics, physiology and zoology.

Physics Briefs. Physikalische Berichte. Physik Verlag, Pappapelallee 3, Postfach 101161, Weinheim, Germany D-6940. 1979-. Semimonthly. In English. Volumes for 1979- issued by the Deutsche Physikalische Gesellschaft and the Fachinformationszentrum Energie Physik, Mathematik in cooperation with the American Institute of Physics.

Pollution Abstracts. Cambridge Scientific Abstracts, 5161 River Rd., Bethesda, Maryland 20816. (301) 961-6750. Six/year. Indexes worldwide technical literature on environmental pollution. Covers air pollution, marine and freshwater pollution, sewage and wastewater treatment, waste management, toxicology and health, noise pollution, radiation, land pollution, and environmental policies, programs, legislation, and education. Also available online.

BIBLIOGRAPHIES

Halocarbons and the Stratospheric Ozone Layer. George D. Havas. Science Reference Section, Science and Technology Division, Library of Congress, 101 Independence Ave. SE, Washington, District of Columbia 20540. (202)707-5000. 1989.

ENCYCLOPEDIAS AND DICTIONARIES

Glossary of Geology. Robert Latimer Bates and Julia A. Jackson, eds. American Geological Institute, 4220 King St., Alexandria, Virginia 22302-1507. (703) 379-2480 or (800) 336-4764. 1987. Third edition.

McGraw-Hill Encyclopedia of Science and Technology. McGraw-Hill, 1221 Avenue of the Americas, New York, New York 10020. (212) 512-2000 or (800) 262-4729. 1992. Seventh edition. Issued in multiple volumes including index. Includes all science and technology broad subject areas.

McGraw-Hill Encyclopedia of the Geological Sciences. Sybil P. Parker, ed. McGraw-Hill, 1221 Avenue of the Americas, New York, New York 10020. (212) 512-2000 or (800) 262-4729. 1988. Second edition. Published previously in the McGraw-Hill Encyclopedia of Science and Technology.

Van Nostrand's Scientific Encyclopedia. Glenn D. Considine, ed. Van Nostrand Reinhold, 115 5th Ave., New York, New York 10003. (212) 254-3232. 1983. Sixth edition. Includes all broad subject areas in science.

GENERAL WORKS

Halocarbons: Environmental Effects of Chlorofluoromethane Release. National Research Council. Committee on Impacts of Stratospheric Change. National Academy of Sciences, 2101 Constitution Ave., NW, Washington, District of Columbia 20418. (202) 334-2000. 1976.

Halogenated Biphenyls, Terphenyls, Naphthalenes, Dibenzodioxins, and Related Products. Elsevier Science Publishing Co., 655 Avenue of the Americas, New York, New York 10010. (212) 984-5800. 1989. Toxicology and environmental aspects of halocarbons.

Regulating Chlorofluorocarbon Emissions. Kathleen A. Wolf. RAND, 1700 Main St., Santa Monica, California 90401. (310) 393-0411. 1980. Effects on chemical production.

Toxicology of Halogenated Hydrocarbons. M. A. Q. Khan. Pergamon Microforms International, Inc., Fairview Park, Elmsford, New York 10523. (914) 592-7720. 1981. Environmental health and ecological effects.

ONLINE DATA BASES

CAS Source Index–CASSI. Chemical Abstracts Service, 2540 Olentangy River Rd., P.O. Box 3012, Columbus, Ohio 43210. (800) 848-6533 or (614) 421-3600. A listing of bibliographic and library holdings information for scientific and technical primary literature relevant to the chemical sciences.

Chemical Abstracts-CA. Chemical Abstracts Service, 2540 Olentangy River Rd., P.O. Box 3012, Columbus, Ohio 43210. (800) 848-6533 or (614) 421-3600. Information sources include 9000 journals, patents from 27 countries, two industrial property organizations, new books, conference proceedings, and government research reports.

Chemical Carcinogenesis Research Information System–CCRIS. National Library of Medicine, 8600 Rockville Pike, Bethesda, Maryland 20894. (800) 638-8480. Individual assay results and test conditions for 1,451 chemicals in the areas of carcinogenicity, mutagenicity, tumor promotion, and cocarcinogenicity.

Chemical Collection System/Request Tracking–CCS/RTS. U.S. Environmental Protection Agency, Office of Pesticides and Toxic Substances, 401 M St., SW, Washington, District of Columbia 20460. (202) 260-2090. Contains information on various properties of a number of chemicals including environmental effects, test and analysis methods, and health effects. Available from EPA.

Chemical Dictionary Online–CHEMLINE. Chemical Abstracts Service, 2540 Olentangy River Rd., Columbus, Ohio 43210. (614) 421-3600 or (800) 848-6533. Part of MEDLINE of the National Library of Medicine (NLM). File of 900,000 names for chemical substances, representing 450,000 unique compounds. It contains such information as Chemical Abstracts (CA) Service Registry Numbers, molecular formulas, preferred chemical no-

menclature, and generic and ring structure information. Available on NLM's ELHILL system.

Chemical Exposure. Science Applications International Corp., Health & Environmental Information, P.O. Box 2501, Oak Ridge, Tennessee 37831. (615) 482-9031. Database of chemicals that have been identified in both human tissues and body fluids and in feral and food animals. Contains reference to journal articles, conferences, and reports. Covers the whole fields of information related to human and animal exposure to food, air, and water contaminants and pharmaceuticals. Its records include information on chemical properties, formulas, tissues measured, analytical method used, demographics and more. Available on DIALOG.

PERIODICALS AND NEWSLETTERS

Halogenated Solvent Industry Alliance Newsletter. Halogenated Solvent Industry Alliance, 1225 19th Street, NW, Suite 300, Washington, District of Columbia 20036. (202) 223-5890. Bimonthly. Covers legislative and regulatory problems involving halogenated solvents.

Solvents Update. Halogenated Solvents Industry Alliance, 1225 19th Street, NW, Suite 300, Washington, District of Columbia 20036. (202) 223-5890. Monthly. Regulations and standards of state and national agencies.

TRADE ASSOCIATIONS AND PROFESSIONAL SOCIETIES

Halogenated Solvents Industry Alliance. 1225 19th St., N.W., Suite 300, Washington, District of Columbia 20036. (202) 223-5890.

HAMMERMILL

See: SOLID WASTE TREATMENT

HARBORS

See also: COASTS

ABSTRACTING AND INDEXING SERVICES

Abstracts of Air and Water Conservation Literature. American Petroleum Institute. Central Abstracting and Indexing Service, 275 Madison Avenue, New York, New York 10016. 1972.

Civil Engineering Hydraulic Abstracts. BHRA Fluid Engineering, Air Science Co., PO Box 143, Corning, New York 14830. (607) 962-5591. Monthly. Abstracts of periodicals that publish in the areas of hydraulic engineering and other related topics.

Environment Abstracts. Bowker A & I Publishing, 121 Chanlon Rd., New Providence, New Jersey 07974. (908) 464-6800. 1974-.

Environment Index. Environment Information Center, Index Research Department, 124 E. 39th St., New York, New York 10016. 1971-. Annual.

Environmental Information Connection-EIC. Planning Information Program, Dept. of Urban and Regional Planning, University of Illinois, 1003 West Nevada,

Urbana, Illinois 61801. (217) 333-1369. Also available online.

Environmental Periodicals Bibliography. Environmental Studies Institute, International Academy at Santa Barbara, 800 Garden St., Suite D, Santa Barbara, California 93101. (805) 965-5010. Also available online.

General Science Index. H. W. Wilson Co., 950 University Ave., Bronx, New York 10452. 1978-. Monthly, also issued in annual cumulation. Cumulative subject index to English language periodicals in the subject fields of astronomy, botany, chemistry, earth science, environment and conservation, food and nutrition, genetics, mathematics, medicine and health, microbiology, oceanography, physics, physiology and zoology.

Pollution Abstracts. Cambridge Scientific Abstracts, 5161 River Rd., Bethesda, Maryland 20816. (301) 961-6750. Six/year. Indexes worldwide technical literature on environmental pollution. Covers air pollution, marine and freshwater pollution, sewage and wastewater treatment, waste management, toxicology and health, noise pollution, radiation, land pollution, and environmental policies, programs, legislation, and education. Also available online.

Science Citation Index. Institute for Scientific Information, 3501 Market St., Philadelphia, Pennsylvania 19104. 1961-.

Sea Grant Abstracts. National Sea Grant Depository, Pell Laboratory Bldg., Bay Campus, University of Rhode Island, Narragansett, Rhode Island 02882. (401) 792-6114. 1986-. Quarterly. Published by the National Sea Grant Programs, this collection includes annual reports, serials and newsletters, charts and maps.

BIBLIOGRAPHIES

EPA Publications Bibliography. U.S. Environmental Protection Agency, Library Systems Branch, 401 M St., SW, Washington, District of Columbia 20460. (202) 260-2090. Quarterly.

Port Planning. Paul D. Marr. Council of Planning Librarians, 1313 E. 60th St., Chicago, Illinois 60637-2897. (312) 942-2163. 1987.

DIRECTORIES

World Port Index. U.S. Navy Hydrographic Office, Washington, District of Columbia 1976. Annual.

ENCYCLOPEDIAS AND DICTIONARIES

Van Nostrand's Scientific Encyclopedia. Glenn D. Considine, ed. Van Nostrand Reinhold, 115 5th Ave., New York, New York 10003. (212) 254-3232. 1983. Sixth edition. Includes all broad subject areas in science.

ONLINE DATA BASES

Enviro/Energyline Abstracts Plus. R. R. Bowker Co., 121 Chanlon Rd., New Providence, New Jersey 07974. (908) 464-6800.

Environmental Periodicals Bibliography. National Information Services Corp., Ste. 6, Wyman Towers, 3100 St. Paul St., Baltimore, Maryland 21218. (410)243-0797. Online version of abstract of same name.

RESEARCH CENTERS AND INSTITUTES

University of Massachusetts At Boston, Urban Harbors Institute. Harbor Campus, Boston, Massachusetts 02125. (617) 287-5570.

TRADE ASSOCIATIONS AND PROFESSIONAL SOCIETIES

North Atlantic Ports Association. 31 Coventry Dr., Lewes, Delaware 19958. (302) 654-9732.

HARD WATER

See: WASTE DISPOSAL

HARDINESS

See also: ACCLIMATIZATION

ABSTRACTING AND INDEXING SERVICES

Biological Abstracts. BIOSIS, 2100 Arch St., Philadelphia, Pennsylvania 19103-1399. (215) 587-4800. 1927-.

Current Advances in Ecological and Environmental Science. Pergamon Microforms International, Inc., Fairview Park, Elmsford, New York 10523. (914) 592-7720. 1989-. Monthly. Current literature searching service includingjournals, reports, abstracts, etc. This service is available online as part of the CABS database on the hosts BRS and ORBIT search service.

Environment Abstracts. Bowker A & I Publishing, 121 Chanlon Rd., New Providence, New Jersey 07974. (908) 464-6800. 1974-.

Environment Index. Environment Information Center, Index Research Department, 124 E. 39th St., New York, New York 10016. 1971-. Annual.

Environmental Information Connection–EIC. Planning Information Program, Dept. of Urban and Regional Planning, University of Illinois, 1003 West Nevada, Urbana, Illinois 61801. (217) 333-1369. Also available online.

Environmental Periodicals Bibliography. Environmental Studies Institute, International Academy at Santa Barbara, 800 Garden St., Suite D, Santa Barbara, California 93101. (805) 965-5010. Also available online.

General Science Index. H. W. Wilson Co., 950 University Ave., Bronx, New York 10452. 1978-. Monthly, also issued in annual cumulation. Cumulative subject index to English language periodicals in the subject fields of astronomy, botany, chemistry, earth science, environment and conservation, food and nutrition, genetics, mathematics, medicine and health, microbiology, oceanography, physics, physiology and zoology.

Science Citation Index. Institute for Scientific Information, 3501 Market St., Philadelphia, Pennsylvania 19104. 1961-.

BIBLIOGRAPHIES

EPA Publications Bibliography. U.S. Environmental Protection Agency, Library Systems Branch, 401 M St., SW, Washington, District of Columbia 20460. (202) 260-2090. Quarterly.

ENCYCLOPEDIAS AND DICTIONARIES

Van Nostrand's Scientific Encyclopedia. Glenn D. Considine, ed. Van Nostrand Reinhold, 115 5th Ave., New York, New York 10003. (212) 254-3232. 1983. Sixth edition. Includes all broad subject areas in science.

GENERAL WORKS

Breeding Plants for Less Favorable Environments. M. N. Christiansen. R.E. Krieger, 605 3rd Ave., New York, New York 10158-0012. (212) 850-6000. 1990. Effects of stress on plants.

Responses of Plants to Environmental Stresses. J. Levitt. Academic Press, c/o Harcourt Brace Jovanovich Inc., 6277 Sea Harbor Dr., Orlando, Florida 32887. (800) 346-8648. 1980. 2nd ed. Volume 1 covers chilling, freezing and high temperature. Volume 2 contains water, radiation, salt, and other stresses.

ONLINE DATA BASES

BIOSIS Previews. BIOSIS, 2100 Arch St., Philadelphia, Pennsylvania 19103-1399. (215) 587-4800. Largest and most comprehensive database of research in the life sciences. Contains citations for nearly 9000 primary research journals, monographs, reviews, symposia, preliminary reports, semi-popular journals, selected institutional reports, government reports and research communications.

Enviro/Energyline Abstracts Plus. R. R. Bowker Co., 121 Chanlon Rd., New Providence, New Jersey 07974. (908) 464-6800.

Environmental Periodicals Bibliography. National Information Services Corp., Ste. 6, Wyman Towers, 3100 St. Paul St., Baltimore, Maryland 21218. (410)243-0797. Online version of abstract of same name.

HARDWOOD, FOREST COVER

See: FORESTS

HARVEST WASTES

See: WASTE DISPOSAL

HARVESTING TECHNIQUES

See: AGRICULTURE

HAWAII ENVIRONMENTAL AGENCIES

GOVERNMENTAL ORGANIZATIONS

Board of Land and Natural Resources: Natural Resources. Chairman, 1151 Punchbowl St., Honolulu, Hawaii 96813. (808) 548-6550.

Department of Agriculture: Pesticide Registration. Administrator, Plant Industry Division, 1428 South King St., Honolulu, Hawaii 96814. (808) 548-7119.

Department of Health: Air Quality. Deputy Director, Environmental Protection and Health Services Division, 1250 Punchbowl St., PO Box 3378, Honolulu, Hawaii 96813. (808) 548-4139.

Department of Health: Emergency Preparedness and Community Right-to-Know. Chair, State Emergency Response Commission, PO Box 3378, Honolulu, Hawaii 96801-9904. (808) 548-6505.

Department of Health: Environmental Protection. Deputy Director, Environmental Protection and Health Services, 1250 Punchbowl St., Honolulu, Hawaii 96813. (808) 548-4139.

Department of Health: Hazardous Waste Management. Deputy Director, Environmental Protection and Health Services, 1250 Punchbowl St., Honolulu, Hawaii 96813. (808) 548-4139.

Department of Health: Solid Waste Management. Deputy Director, Environmental Protection and Health Services Division, 1250 Punchbowl St., Honolulu, Hawaii 96813. (808) 548-4139.

Department of Health: Water Quality. Deputy Director, Environmental Protection and Health Services Division, 1250 Punchbowl St., Honolulu, Hawaii 96813. (808) 548-4139.

Department of Land and Natural Resources: Groundwater Management. Deputy Director, Water and Land Development Division, 1151 Punchbowl St., Honolulu, Hawaii 96813. (808) 548-7533.

Labor and Industrial Relations Department: Occupational Safety. Administrator, Occupational Safety and Health Division, 830 Punchbowl St., Room 423, Honolulu, Hawaii 96813. (808) 548-4155.

Land and Natural Resources Department: Fish and Wildlife. Acting Administrator, Division of Forestry and Wildlife, 1151 Punchbowl St., Honolulu, Hawaii 96813. (808) 548-8850.

Office of State Planning: Coastal Zone Management. Chief, State Capitol, PO Box 2359, Honolulu, Hawaii 96813. (808) 548-3026.

U.S. EPA Region 9: Pollution Prevention. Deputy Director, Hazardous Waste, 215 Fremont St., San Francisco, California 94105. (415) 556-6322.

HAWAII ENVIRONMENTAL LEGISLATION

GENERAL WORKS

Environment Hawaii. Environment Hawaii Pub., Honolulu, Hawaii

Hawaii Environmental Resources 1990 Directory. Office of Environmental Control, State of Hawaii, 220 S King St., 4th Fl., Honolulu, Hawaii 96813. (808) 586-4185. 1990.

HAZARD ASSESSMENT
See: RISK ANALYSIS

HAZARDOUS AIR POLLUTANTS
See: AIR POLLUTION

HAZARDOUS MATERIALS
See also: HAZARDOUS WASTES; TRANSPORTATION OF HAZARDOUS MATERIALS

ABSTRACTING AND INDEXING SERVICES

Applied Science and Technology Index. H.W. Wilson Co., 950 University Ave., Bronx, New York 10452. (800) 367-6770. Formerly Industrial Arts Index.

Biological Abstracts. BIOSIS, 2100 Arch St., Philadelphia, Pennsylvania 19103-1399. (215) 587-4800. 1927-.

Biological and Agricultural Index. H.W. Wilson Co., 950 University Ave., Bronx, New York 10452. (800) 367-6770. 1916-. Monthly.

Chemical Abstracts. Chemical Abstracts Service, 2540 Olentangy River Rd., PO Box 3012, Columbus, Ohio 43210. (800) 848-6533. 1907-.

EIS: Digests of Environmental Impact Statements. Cambridge Scientific Abstracts, 5161 River Rd., Bethesda, Maryland 20816. (301) 951-1400. 1970-. Bimonthly. Provides detailed abstracts of all the environmental impact statements issued by the federal government each year and indexes them. Also extracts the key issues from the complex government released environmental impact statements. Contents include areas such as: air transportation, defense programs, energy, hazardous substances, land use, manufacturing, parks, refuges, forests, research and development, roads and railroads, urban and social programs, wastes, and water.

Environment Abstracts. Bowker A & I Publishing, 121 Chanlon Rd., New Providence, New Jersey 07974. (908) 464-6800. 1974-.

Environment Index. Environment Information Center, Index Research Department, 124 E. 39th St., New York, New York 10016. 1971-. Annual.

Environmental Information Connection–EIC. Planning Information Program, Dept. of Urban and Regional Planning, University of Illinois, 1003 West Nevada, Urbana, Illinois 61801. (217) 333-1369. Also available online.

Environmental Periodicals Bibliography. Environmental Studies Institute, International Academy at Santa Barbara, 800 Garden St., Suite D, Santa Barbara, California 93101. (805) 965-5010. Also available online.

General Science Index. H. W. Wilson Co., 950 University Ave., Bronx, New York 10452. 1978-. Monthly, also issued in annual cumulation. Cumulative subject index to English language periodicals in the subject fields of astronomy, botany, chemistry, earth science, environment and conservation, food and nutrition, genetics,

mathematics, medicine and health, microbiology, oceanography, physics, physiology and zoology.

Geographical Abstracts. London School of Economics, Dept. of Geography, Regency House, 34 Duke St., London, England 1966-. Continued by Geo Abstracts issued in 6 parts: Pt. A. Landforms and the quaternary; Pt. B. Biogeography and Climatology; Pt. C. Economic geography; Pt. D. Social geography and cartography; Pt. E. Sedimentology; Pt. F. Regional and community planning.

Pollution Abstracts. Cambridge Scientific Abstracts, 5161 River Rd., Bethesda, Maryland 20816. (301) 961-6750. Six/year. Indexes worldwide technical literature on environmental pollution. Covers air pollution, marine and freshwater pollution, sewage and wastewater treatment, waste management, toxicology and health, noise pollution, radiation, land pollution, and environmental policies, programs, legislation, and education. Also available online.

Science Citation Index. Institute for Scientific Information, 3501 Market St., Philadelphia, Pennsylvania 19104. 1961-.

ALMANACS AND YEARBOOKS

Consolidated List of Products Whose Consumption and/ or Sale Have Been Banned, Withdrawn, Severely Restricted or Not Approved by Governments. United Nations, 2 United Nations Plaza, Salis Section Rm. DC 2-853, New York, New York 10017. (800) 553-3210. Biennial. International legislation against hazardous substances.

Hazardous Chemicals Information Annual. Van Nostrand Reinhold, Information Services, 115 5th Ave., New York, New York 10003. (212) 254-3232. 1987. Annual.

BIBLIOGRAPHIES

Chemical Spills: A Bibliography. Vance Bibliographies, PO Box 229, 112 N. Charter St., Monticello, Illinois 61856. (217) 762-3831. Looks at hazardous substances and environmental chemistry.

Current Contents. Agriculture, Biology and Environmental Sciences. Institute for Scientific Information, 3501 Market St., Philadelphia, Pennsylvania 19104. (800) 523-1857. 1973-. Previous title: Current Contents. Agricultural, Food & Veterinary Sciences. Gives the table of contents of periodicals in the fields of agriculture, biology, environmental and related areas.

EPA Publications Bibliography. U.S. Environmental Protection Agency, Library Systems Branch, 401 M St., SW, Washington, District of Columbia 20460. (202) 260-2090. Quarterly.

Hazardous Materials: Sources of Information on Their Transportation. Nigel Lees. British Library Science Reference and Information Service, London, England 1990.

Toxic and Hazardous Materials: A Sourcebook and Guide to Information Sources. James K. Webster. Greenwood Publishing Group, Inc., 88 Post Rd. W., PO Box 5007, New York, New York 06881. (212) 226-3571. 1987.

DIRECTORIES

Directory of Chemical Waste Transporters. Chemical Waste Transport Institute. National Solid Waste Management Association, 1730 Rhode Island Ave. N.W.,

Suite 1000, Washington, District of Columbia 20036. (202) 659-4613. 1989.

Hazardous Location Equipment Directory [UL label]. 333 Pfingsten Rd., Northbrook, Illinois 60062-2096. (708) 272-8800. Annual.

Hazardous Materials Advisory Council–Directory. Hazardous Materials Advisory Council, 1110 Vermont Ave., N.W., Suite 250, Washington, District of Columbia 20005. (202) 728-1460.

Hazardous Materials Control Directory. Hazardous Materials Control Research Institute, 9300 Columbia Blvd., Silver Spring, Maryland 20910. (301) 587-9390.

ENCYCLOPEDIAS AND DICTIONARIES

Compendium of Hazardous Chemicals in Schools and Colleges. Forum for Scientific Excellence. J. B. Lippincott, 227 E. Washington Sq., Philadelphia, Pennsylvania 19105. (215) 238-4200; (800) 982-4377. 1990. Encyclopedia of more than 950 hazardous chemicals found in academic institutions. Contains all the data necessary for identifying these chemicals and their hazardous effects.

Encyclopedia of Chemical Processing and Design. John J. Mcketta and W. A. Cunningham. Marcel Dekker, Inc., 270 Madison Ave., New York, New York 10016. (212) 696-9000; (800) 228-1160. 1992. Thirty-eight volumes.

Handbook of Hazardous Chemicals and Carcinogens. Marshall Sittig. Noyes Publications, 120 Mill Rd., Park Ridge, New Jersey 07656. (201) 391-8484. 1985.

Hazardous Chemicals Desk Reference. Richard J. Lewis. Van Nostrand Reinhold, 115 Fifth Ave., New York, New York 10003. (212) 254-3232. 1991. Information on the hazardous properties of some 5500 chemicals commonly cncountered in industry, laboratories, environment, and the workplace.

Hazardous Materials Dictionary. Ronny J. Coleman and Kara Hewson Williams. Technomic Publishing Co., 851 New Holland Ave., Box 3535, Lancaster, Pennsylvania 17604. (717) 291-5609. 1988. Defines more than 2600 specialized words which are critical for communication, especially under the stressful circumstances of an emergency. Identifies many of the unique terms that apply to the handling of hazardous materials emergencies.

Hazardous Substances. Melvin Berger. Enslow Publishers, Bloy St. & Ramsey Ave., PO Box 777, Hillside, New Jersey 07205. (908) 964-4116. 1986.

Kirk-Othmer Encyclopedia of Chemical Technology. J. I. Kroschwitz, ed. John Wiley & Sons, Inc., 605 3rd Ave., New York, New York 10158-0012. (212) 850-6000. 1992-. All articles in the new edition have been rewritten and updated adding new subjects such as biotechnology, computer topics, analytical techniques and instrumentation, environmental concerns, fuels and energy, inorganic and solid state chemistry; composite materials and material science in general, and pharmaceuticals. Also available online.

McGraw-Hill Encyclopedia of Environmental Science. Sybil P. Parker. McGraw-Hill Science & Engineering Books, 11 W. 19th St., New York, New York 10011. (212) 337-6010. 1980. Covers ecology, man's influence on nature, and environmental protection.

McGraw-Hill Encyclopedia of Science and Technology. McGraw-Hill, 1221 Avenue of the Americas, New York,

New York 10020. (212) 512-2000 or (800) 262-4729. 1992. Seventh edition. Issued in multiple volumes including index. Includes all science and technology broad subject areas.

Van Nostrand's Scientific Encyclopedia. Glenn D. Considine, ed. Van Nostrand Reinhold, 115 5th Ave., New York, New York 10003. (212) 254-3232. 1983. Sixth edition. Includes all broad subject areas in science.

GENERAL WORKS

Book of Lists for Regulated Hazardous Substances. Government Institutes, Inc., 4 Research Pl., Ste. 200, Rockville, Maryland 20850. (301) 921-2300. 1991. Convenient source of the most frequently referenced lists for environmental compliance and regulatory information.

Chemical Hazards in the Workplace. Ronald M. Scott. Lewis Publishers, 200 Corporate Blvd. NW, Boca Raton, Florida 33431. (407) 994-0555 or (800)272-7737. 1989. Presents basics of toxicology. Reports a sampling of the accumulated knowledge of the hazards of specific compounds in the workplace. Also discusses the federal regulatory agencies charged with worker protection and the specific practices involved in maintaining safety and regulatory compliance.

A Citizen's Guide to Promoting Toxic Waste Reduction. Lauren Kenworthy and Eric Schaeffer. INFORM, 381 Park Ave. S., New York, New York 10016. (212) 689-4040. 1990. The how-to manual describes source reduction and its benefits, five strategies plants can use to reduce their hazardous wastes at the source, a step-by-step process for gathering background facts, and interviewing company representatives and analyzing data.

Classification of Floating CHRIS Chemicals for the Development of a Spill Response Manual. A. T. Szhula. National Technical Information Service, 5285 Port Royal Rd, Springfield, Virginia 22161. (703) 487-4650. Covers classification of chemical spills.

Compact School and College Administrator's Guide for Compliance with Federal and State Right-to-Know Regulations. Forum for Scientific Excellence. J. B. Lippincott, 227 E. Washington Sq., Philadelphia, Pennsylvania 19105. (215) 238-4200; (800) 982-4377. 1989. Presents the legal and technical language of current hazardous chemical regulations in meaningful, easily understandable terms. Provides a simplified, step-by-step program for compliance.

Controlling Chemical Hazards: Fundamentals of the Management of Toxic Chemicals. Raymond P. Cote and Peter G. Wells, eds. Unwin Hyman, 77/85 Fulham Palace Rd., London, England W6 8JB. 081 741 7070. 1991. Gives an overview of the properties, fate of, and dilemmas involving hazardous chemicals.

Countermeasures to Airborne Hazardous Chemicals. J. M. Holmes and C. H. Byers. Noyes Publications, 120 Mill Rd., Park Ridge, New Jersey 07656. (201) 391-8484. 1990. Presents a study of major incidents involving the release of hazardous chemicals and reviews the entire spectrum of activities, recommends appropriate action and gives technical guidance.

Design of Warning Labels and Instructions. Joseph P. Ryan. Global Professional Publications, 2805 McGraw Ave., PO Box 19539, Irvine, California 92713-9539. (800) 854-7179. 1990. Describes the techniques for design and writing crucial cautionary, safety, hazard and other kinds of labels.

Environmental Impacts of Hazardous Waste Treatment, Storage and Disposal Facilities. Rodolfo N. Salcedo, et al. Technomic Publishing Co., 851 New Holland Ave., Box 3535, Lancaster, Pennsylvania 17604. (717) 291-5609. 1989. Provides guidance in dealing with the many obstacles and preliminary requirements in siting TSD facilities.

Extremely Hazardous Substances: Superfund Chemical Profiles. U. S. Environment Protection Agency. Noyes Publications, 120 Mill Rd., Park Ridge, New Jersey 07656. (201) 391-8484. 1988. Contains chemical profiles for each of the 366 chemicals listed as extremely hazardous substances by the USEPA in 1988. The EPA developed this set of documents for use in dealing with Section 302 of Title III of the Superfund Amendments and Reauthorization Act (SARA). Each profile contains a summary of documented information which has been reviewed for accuracy and completeness.

Fire Protection Management for Hazardous Materials. Byron L. Briese, ed. Government Institutes, Inc., 4 Research Pl., Suite 200, Rockville, Maryland 20850. (301) 921-2300. 1991. Designed as a guide to the industry, this manual gives standard fire and building codes and a framework needed to manage the federal, state and local requirements and the specific technical needs of the individual facility.

Fundamentals of Hazardous Materials Incidents. Reginald L. Campbell and Roland E. Langford. Lewis Publishers, 2000 Corporate Blvd., N.W., Boca Raton, Florida 33431. (407) 994-0555 or (800) 272-7737. 1990. Gives basic introduction to anatomy and physiology, toxicology. Discusses hazardous materials and workers protection, environmental protection, hazard communication and medical surveillance, factors affecting personnel, personal protection equipment and other related topics.

Fundamentals of Laboratory Safety: Physical Hazards in the Academic Laboratory. William J. Mahn. Van Nostrand Reinhold, 115 5th Ave., New York, New York 10003. (212) 254-3232. 1991. Discusses safety methods in chemical laboratories, accident prevention and the various hazardous materials in use in the labs.

Hazard Assessment of Chemicals. Academic Press, c/o Harcourt Brace Jovanovich Inc., 6277 Sea Harbor Dr., Orlando, Florida 32887. (800) 346-8648. 1981-. Annually. Presents comprehensive authoritative reviews of new and significant developments in the area of hazard assessment of chemicals or chemical classes.

Hazardous Laboratory Chemicals; Disposal Guide. M. A. Armour. CRC Press, 2000 Corporate Blvd., N.W., Suite 700, Boca Raton, Florida 33431. (407) 994-0555; (800) 272-7737. 1991. Chemical disposal procedures are designed to enable chemicals to be recycled or disposed of inhouse, eliminating the need to incinerate them or take them to a landfill. Disposal methods for heavy metals, salts, explosive chemicals such as picric acid, and toxic organic materials are included.

Hazardous Materials Exposure; Emergency Response and Patient Care. Jonathan Borak, et al. Prentice-Hall, Rte. 9W, Englewood Cliffs, New Jersey 07632. (201) 592-2000; (800) 634-2863. 1991. Focuses on the emergency medical service sector and hazardous materials releases. Provides EMS personnel and other first responders with an education and training program for improving medical knowledge and performance skills.

Hazardous Materials Transportation Accidents. National Fire Protection Association, 1 Battery Park, Quincy, Massachusetts 02269. (617) 770-3000; (800) 344-3555. 1978. Compilation of articles from Fire Journal and Fire Command. Deals with transportation of hazardous substances, their combustibility during accidents and preventive measures.

Hazardous Substances Resource Guide. Richard Pohanish, Stanley Greene. Gale Research Inc., 835 Penobscot Bldg., Detroit, Michigan 48226-4094. (313) 961-2242. 1993.

Hazardous Waste Chemistry, Toxicology and Treatment. Stanley E. Manahan. Lewis Publishers, 2000 Corporate Blvd., N.W., Boca Raton, Florida 33431. (407) 994-0555 or (800) 272-7737. 1990. Reviews hazardous wastes, their chemistry and toxicology. Gives a basic coverage of chemistry and biochemistry, environmental chemical processes, and toxicology.

Hazardous Waste Management. S. Maltezou, et al., eds. Cassell PLC, Publishers Distribution Center, PO Box C831, Rutherford, New Jersey 07070. (201) 939-6064; (201) 939-6065. 1989.

Hazardous Wastes and Hazardous Materials. Hazardous Materials Control Research Institute, 9300 Columbia Blvd., Silver Spring, Maryland 20910. (301) 587-9390. 1987.

Hazards in the Chemical Laboratory. L. Bretherick, ed. Royal Society of Chemistry, c/o CRC Press, 2000 Corporate Blvd. N.W., Boca Raton, Florida 33431-9868. (800) 272-7737. 1986. 4th ed. Handbook of safety practices, measures and toxic effects for laboratories handling dangerous chemicals.

Index of Hazardous Contents of Commercial Products in Schools and Colleges. The Forum for Scientific Excellence. J. B. Lippincott, 227 E. Washington Sq., Philadelphia, Pennsylvania 19105. (215) 238-4200; (800) 982-4377. 1990. Lists the hazardous components found in thousands of commercial products used in educational institutions.

List of Lists of Worldwide Hazardous Chemicals and Pollutants. The Forum of Scientific Excellence. J. B. Lippincott, 227 E. Washington Sq., Philadelphia, Pennsylvania 19105. (215) 238-4200; (800) 982-4377. 1990. Extensive compilation of regulated hazardous chemicals and environmental pollutants in existence. Includes separate lists of substances that are regulated by more than 40 states, as well as federal and international agencies. A master list of the regulated material is also included in both alphabetical and CAS number sequence.

Meeting Environmental Work Force Needs. Information Dynamics, 111 Claybrook Dr., Silver Spring, Maryland 20902. 1985. Proceedings of the Second National Conference on Meeting Environmental Workforce Needs, April 1-3, 1985: Education and Training to Assure a Qualified Work Force.

The New York Environment Book. Eric A. Goldstein. Island Press, 1718 Connecticut Ave. N.W., Suite 300, Washington, District of Columbia 20009. (202) 232-7933. 1990. Provides an in-depth analysis of New York City's environment. The five areas surveyed are: solid waste disposal, hazardous substances, water pollution, air quality, and drinking water quality. Discusses past clean-

up efforts, and offers an agenda for the future. Describes and analyzes the general environment of urban areas, and offers solutions for their special environmental problems.

PCB Compliance Guide for Electrical Equipment. John W. Coryell. Bureau of National Affairs, 1231 25th St. N.W., Washington, District of Columbia 20037. (202) 452-4200. 1991.

Proceedings of the 44th Industrial Waste Conference May 1989, Purdue University. John W. Bell, ed. Lewis Publishers, 2000 Corporate Blvd., N.W., Boca Raton, Florida 33431. (407) 994-0555 or (800) 272-7737. 1990. Includes new research, case histories and operating data, on every conceivable facet of today's big problem with unparalleled appropriate, usable information and data for current industrial waste problems.

Proctor and Hughes' Chemical Hazards of the Workplace. G. J. Hathaway, et al. Global Professional Publications, 2805 McGraw Ave., PO Box 19539, Irvine, California 92713-9539. (800) 854-7179. 1991. Third edition. Includes 100 new chemicals and the new 1991 Threshold Limit Values. Gives a practical easy-to-use introduction to toxicology and hazards of over 600 chemicals most likely to be encountered in the workplace.

Public Policy for Chemicals: National and International Issues. Conservation Foundation, 1250 24th St., NW, Washington, District of Columbia 20037. (202) 293-4800. 1980. Legal aspects of chemicals and hazardous substances.

Response Manual for Combatting Spills of Floating Hazardous CHRIS Chemicals. National Technical Information Service, 5285 Port Royal Rd., Springfield, Virginia 22161. (703) 487-4650. Covers chemical spills, hazardous substance accidents, and marine pollution.

Risk Assessment for Hazardous Installations. J. C. Chicken. Pergamon Microforms International, Inc., Fairview Park, Elmsford, New York 10523. (914) 592-7720. 1986.

Risk Assessment of Groundwater Pollution Control. William F. McTernan and Edward Kaplan, eds. American Society of Civil Engineers, 345 E. 47th St., New York, New York 10017. (212) 705-7288; (800) 548-2723. 1990.

SARA Title III: Intent and Implementation of Hazardous Materials Regulations. Frank L. Fire and Nancy K. Grant. PennWell Books, PO Box 21288, Tulsa, Oklahoma 74121. (918) 831-9421; (800) 752-9764. 1990. Addresses what is required for implementation of hazardous materials regulations.

Skin Penetration; Hazardous Chemicals at Work. Philippe Grandjean. Taylor & Francis, 79 Madison Ave., New York, New York 10016. (212) 725-1999 or (800) 821-8312. 1990. Mechanisms of percutaneous absorption and methods of evaluating its significance. Reviews different classes of chemicals, emphasizing those considered major skin hazards.

Survey of Chemicals Tested for Carcinogenicity. Science Resource Center, Kensington, Maryland 1976. Entries from scientific literature from approximately 1913 to 1973, reporting on groups of animals treated with any chemical compounds and subsequently examined for tumors.

Toxic Hazard Assessment of Chemicals. M. L. Richardson. Royal Society of Chemistry, c/o CRC Press, 2000 Corporate Blvd. N.W., Boca Raton, Florida 33431-9868. (800) 272-7737. 1989. Provides basic guidance on means of retrieving, validating, and interpreting data in order to make a toxicological hazard assessment upon a chemical.

Toxicological Chemistry: A Guide to Toxic Substances in Chemistry. Stanley E. Manahan. Lewis Publishers, 200 Corporate Blvd. NW, Boca Raton, Florida 33431. (407) 994-0555 or (800)272-7737. 1989. Defines toxicological chemistry and gives information on its origin and use. Emphasizes the chemical formulas, structures, and reactions of toxic substances.

Transportation of Hazardous Materials: A Management Guide for Generators and Manufactuerers. William E. Kenworthy. Government Institutes, Inc., 4 Research Pl., Suite 200, Rockville, Maryland 20850. (301) 921-2300. 1989. A management guide for generators of hazardous waste. Covers of hazardous materials regulation, alternative shipping methods for generators, and useful approaches for achieving compliance.

Treatment Potential for 56 EPA Listed Hazardous Chemicals in Soil. Ronald C. Sims, et al. Robert S. Kerr Environmental Research Laboratory, U.S. Environmental Protection Agency, PO Box 1198, Ada, Oklahoma 74820. (405) 332-8800. 1988.

GOVERNMENTAL ORGANIZATIONS

Centers for Disease Control: National Institute for Occupational Safety and Health. D-36, 1600 Clifton Rd. N.E., Atlanta, Georgia 30333. (404) 639-3771.

Division of the Environment: Solid Waste Management. Chief, Bureau of Hazardous Materials, 450 West State St., Boise, Idaho 83720. (208) 334-5879.

U.S. Environmental Protection Agency: Office of Emergency and Remedial Response. Emergency Response Division, 401 M St., S.W., Washington, District of Columbia 20460. (202) 382-2180.

U.S. Environmental Protection Agency: Office of Waste Programs Enforcement. 401 M St., S.W., Washington, District of Columbia 20460. (202) 382-4814.

HANDBOOKS AND MANUALS

Bretherick's Handbook of Reactive Chemical Hazards. L. Bretherick. Butterworth-Heinemann, 80 Montvale Ave., Stoneham, Massachusetts 02180. (617) 438-8464; (800) 366-2665. 1990. Lists compounds or elements in order by Hill chemical formula: to aid verification, the International Union of Pure and Applied Chemistry systematic name and the Chemical Abstracts Service Registry Number are recorded. Also lists chemicals that react in some violent fashion with the main chemical cited. A brief description of the type of reaction and citations to the literature in which the reaction was reported are included.

The Comprehensive Handbook of Hazardous Materials: Regulations, Handling, Monitoring, and Safety. Hildegarde L. A. Sacarello. Lewis Publishers, 2000 Corporate Blvd., N.W., Boca Raton, Florida 33431. (407) 994-0555 or (800) 272-7737. 1991. Includes major governmental environmental and training regulations, chemical properties of hazardous materials toxicology, medical program and record keeping, safety planning and principles,personal protective equipment, respiratory protection and fit testing, and other related areas.

Concise Manual of Chemical and Environmental Safety in Schools and Colleges. Forum for Scientific Excellence.

J. B. Lippincott, 227 E. Washington Sq., Philadelphia, Pennsylvania 19105. (215) 238-4200; (800) 982-4377. 1991.

CRC Handbook of Incineration of Hazardous Wastes. William S. Rickman, ed. CRC Press, 2000 Corporate Blvd. N.W., Boca Raton, Florida 33431. (800) 272-7737. 1991.

Cross-Reference Index of Hazardous Chemicals, Synonyms, and CAS Registry Numbers. The Forum for Scientific Excellence. J. B. Lippincott, 227 E. Washington Sq., Philadelphia, Pennsylvania 19105. (215) 238-4200; (800) 982-4377. 1990. Contains more than 50,000 synonyms for the hazardous chemicals and environmental pollutants identified. Comprehensive resource title available for properly identifying common names, chemical names and product names associated with these chemicals.

Dangerous Properties of Industrial Materials. Irving Newton Sax. Van Nostrand Reinhold, 115 5th Ave., New York, New York 10003. (212) 254-3232. 1989. 7th ed. Deals with hazardous substances and chemically induced occupational diseases.

Environmental Hazards: Radioactive Materials and Wastes: A Reference Handbook. E. Willard Miller and Ruby M. Miller. ABC-Clio, 130 Cremona Dr., PO Box 1911, Santa Barbara, California 93116-1911. (805) 968-1911; (800) 422-2546. 1990. Information source on radioactive materials and wastes. Introductory chapters describe the nature and characteristics of both natural and manufactured radioactive materials. Also provides information on laws, regulations, and treaties about waste materials. Including a directory of private, governmental, and international organizations that deal with radioactive wastes.

Environmental Management Handbook: Toxic Chemical Materials and Waste. Leopold C. Kokoszka. Marcel Dekker, Inc., 270 Madison Ave., New York, New York 10016. (212) 696-9000; (800) 228-1160. 1989.

Exposure Factors Handbook. U.S. Environmental Protection Agency, Office of Health and Environmental Assessment, Exposure Assessment Group, 401 M St. SW, Washington, District of Columbia 20460. (202) 382-5480. 1989. Assessing human exposure including drinking water consumption, consumption rates of broad classes of food including fruits, vegetables, beef, dairy products, and fish; soil ingestion; inhalation rate; skin area; activity patterns and body weight.

Final Covers on Hazardous Waste Landfills and Surface Impoundments. Office of Solid Waste and Emergency Response, U.S. Environment Protection Agency, U.S. G.P.O., Washington, District of Columbia 20402-9325. (202) 783-3238. 1989. Technical Guidance Document series EPA/530-SW-89-047. Shipping list no. 89-483-P.

Firefighter's Hazardous Materials Reference Book. Daniel J. Davis and Grant T. Christianson. Van Nostrand Reinhold, 115 5th Ave., New York, New York 10003. (212) 254-3232. 1991. List of hazardous materials. For quick reference, each hazardous material is given its own page with material's name in bold at the top.

The Generator's Guide to Hazardous Materials/Waste Management. Leo H. Traverse. Van Nostrand Reinhold, 115 5th Ave., New York, New York 10003. (212) 254-3232. 1991. Comprehensive information source for hazardous waste and hazardous materials management.

Handbook of Chemical and Environmental Safety in Schools and Colleges. Forum for Scientific Excellence, Inc. J. B. Lippincott, 227 E. Washington Sq., Philadelphia, Pennsylvania 19105. (215) 238-4200. 1990. Hazardous substances safety measures and school plant management. A single resource book containing all of the information outlined in a 5 volume training manual.

Hazard Communication Guide: Federal & State Right-to-Know Standards. J. J. Keller & Associates, Inc., 3003 W. Breezewood, PO Box 368, Neenah, Wisconsin 54957-0368. (414) 722-2848. 1985. Deals with legal aspects of industrial hygiene, hazardous substances, and industrial safety.

Hazard Communication Standard Inspection Manual. Government Institutes, Inc., 4 Research Pl., Ste. 200, Rockville, Maryland 20850. (301) 921-2300. 1991. Includes detailed inspection procedures. Covers hazard communication program, hazard determination procedures, new enforcement guidance on the construction industry, employee information and training, labeling, trade secrets, MSDS completeness, and the instances in which OSHA inspectors are instructed to issue citations.

Hazardous Chemicals Data Book. G. Weiss, ed. Noyes Publications, 120 Mill Rd., Park Ridge, New Jersey 07656. (201) 391-8484. 1986. 2d ed. Supplies instant information on 1015 hazardous chemicals. The data will provide rapid assistance to personnel involved with handling of hazardous chemical materials and related accidents.

The Hazardous Chemicals on File Collection. Craig T. Norback. Facts on File, Inc., 460 Park Ave. S., New York, New York 10016. (212) 683-2244. A guide for the general public seeking up-to-date, authoritative information on the characteristics of, and protection against, hazardous materials in the workplace

Hazardous Materials Guide: Shipping, Materials Handling, and Transportation. J. J. Keller & Associates, Inc., 3003 W. Breezewood, PO Box 368, Neenah, Wisconsin 54957-0368. (414) 722-2848. Laws and procedures relating to the packing and transportation of hazardous substances.

Hazardous Waste Minimization Handbook. Thomas E. Higgins, et al. Lewis Publishers, 2000 Corporate Blvd., Boca Raton, Florida 33431. (407) 994-0555 or (800) 272-7737. 1989. Describes how to make changes in waste handling, manufacturing, and purchasing to reduce costs and liabilities of waste disposal.

How to Respond to Hazardous Chemical Spills. W. Unterberg, et al. Noyes Publications, 120 Mill Rd., Park Ridge, New Jersey 07656. (201) 391-8484. 1988. Reference manual of countermeasures is designed to assist responders to spills of hazardous substances.

Manual for Preventing Spills of Hazardous Substances at Fixed Facilities. Hemisphere Publishing Co., 79 Madison Ave., Suite 1110, New York, New York 10016. (212) 725-1999. Environmental monitoring of chemical spills and hazardous substances.

NIOSH Pocket Guide to Chemical Hazards. National Institute for Occupational Safety and Health, 1600 Clifton Rd. NE, Atlanta, Georgia 30333. (404) 639-3286. 1990. Presents sources of general industrial hygiene and medical surveillance information for workers, employees and others. Presents key information and data in an abbreviated format for 398 individual chemicals or chemical types.

Recommendations of the Transport of Dangerous Goods: Test and Criteria. United Nations Publications, Sales Section, Room DC2-0853, Department 733, New York, New York 10017. (800) 253-9646. Companion to the ORANGE BOOK which provides technical guidelines on the transport of dangerous explosive substances and organic peroxides.

Synthetic Organic Chemicals. U.S. G.P.O., Washington, District of Columbia 20401. (202) 512-0000. 1967. An annual publication on production and sales in the U.S. for all synthetic organic chemicals produced commercially. About 800 chemicals and 800 manufacturers are included in the USITC surveys, but because of confidentiality requirements only parts of the data are published. U.S. Tariff Commission acts under the provisions of Section 332 of the Tariff Act of 1930, as amended.

TSCA Handbook. Government Institutes, Inc., 4 Research Pl., Ste. 200, Rockville, Maryland 20850. (301) 921-2300. 1989. 2nd edition. Details existing chemical regulation under TSCA; EPA's program for evaluating and regulating new chemical substances; PMN preparations and follow through; civil and criminal liability; inspections and audits; required testing of chemical substances and mixtures and exemptions from PMN requirements.

ONLINE DATA BASES

BIOSIS Previews. BIOSIS, 2100 Arch St., Philadelphia, Pennsylvania 19103-1399. (215) 587-4800. Largest and most comprehensive database of research in the life sciences. Contains citations for nearly 9000 primary research journals, monographs, reviews, symposia, preliminary reports, semi-popular journals, selected institutional reports, government reports and research communications.

CERCLIS. Chemical Information Systems, Inc., 7215 York Rd., Baltimore, Maryland 21212. (301) 321-8440. Information on hazardous waste disposal sites that have either been listed by the EPA on the National Priority List (NPL) or nominated for consideration for the NPL.

Chem-Bank. SilverPlatter Information, Inc., 37 Walnut St., Wellesley Hills, Massachusetts 02181. 617-239-0306. Registry of Toxic Effects of Chemical Substances; Oil and Hazardous Materials Technical Assistance Data System; Chemical Hazard Response Information System; and the Toxic Substances Control Act Initial Inventory.

Chemical Abstracts-CA. Chemical Abstracts Service, 2540 Olentangy River Rd., P.O. Box 3012, Columbus, Ohio 43210. (800) 848-6533 or (614) 421-3600. Information sources include 9000 journals, patents from 27 countries, two industrial property organizations, new books, conference proceedings, and government research reports.

Chemical Hazard Response Information System–CHRIS. U.S. Coast Guard. Office of Research and Development, 2100 2d St., NW., Rm. 5410 C, Washington, District of Columbia 20593. (202) 783-3238. Contains information needed to respond to emergencies that occur during the transport of hazardous chemicals, as well as information that can help prevent emergency situations. Each of the approximately 1,300 records include information on physical and chemical properties, health and fire hazards, labeling, chemical reactivity, hazard classification and water pollution. Available on CIS and on Microdex's TOMES Plus series.

Chemical Safety Newsbase. Royal Society of Chemistry, Thomas Graham House, Science Park, Milton Rd., Cambridge, England CB4 4WF. 44 (223) 420066.

Chemical Substance Control. Bureau of National Affairs, BNA PLUS, 1231 25th ST., N.W., Rm. 215, Washington, District of Columbia 20037. (800) 452-7773. Online version of periodical of the same name.

Engineered Materials Abstracts. The Institute of Metals, Materials Information, 1 Carlton House Terrace, London, England SW1 Y5DB. 44 (71) 839-4071.

Enviro/Energyline Abstracts Plus. R. R. Bowker Co., 121 Chanlon Rd., New Providence, New Jersey 07974. (908) 464-6800.

Environmental Periodicals Bibliography. National Information Services Corp., Ste. 6, Wyman Towers, 3100 St. Paul St., Baltimore, Maryland 21218. (410)243-0797. Online version of abstract of same name.

Global Indexing System. U.S. Environmental Protection Agency, 401 M St., S.W., Washington, District of Columbia 20460. (202) 260-2090. International information on various qualities of chemicals.

Hazardline. Occupational Health Services, Inc., 450 7th Ave., Ste. 2407, New York, New York 10123. (212) 967-1100. More than 3600 dangerous materials, including physical and chemical descriptions, standards and regulations, and safety precautions for handling.

Hazardous Materials Intelligence Report. World Information Systems, PO Box 535, Cambridge, Massachusetts 02238. (617) 491-5100. Online access to federal, state, and local legislation, regulations, and programs related to hazardous waste and hazardous material management. Online version of the periodical of the same name.

Industrial Health & Hazards Update. Merton Allen Associates, P.O. Box 15640, Plantation, Florida 33318-5640. (305) 473-9560.

Kirk-Othmer Encyclopedia of Chemical Technology. John Wiley & Sons, Inc., 605 3rd Ave., 5th Floor, New York, New York 10158. (212) 850-6000. Online version of the publication of the same name.

MHIDAS. U.K. Atomic Energy Authority, Safety and Reliability Directorate, Wiashaw Lane, Culcheta, Warrington, England WA3 4NE. 44 (925) 31244.

Monthly Catalog of United States Government Publications. U.S. G.P.O., Supt. of Docs., PO Box 371954, Pittsburgh, Pennsylvania 15250-7954. (202) 512-0000.

National Technical Information Service. U.S. Department of Commerce, National Technical Information Service, Office of Data Base Services, 5285 Port Royal Rd., Springfield, Virginia 22161. (703) 487-4807. Bibliographic database of government sponsored research and technical reports.

SCISEARCH. Institute for Scientific Information, University City Science Center, 3501 Market St., Philadelphia, Pennsylvania 19104. (215) 386-0100.

Suspect Chemicals Sourcebook. Roytech Publications, Inc., 7910 Woodmont Ave., Ste. 902, Bethesda, Maryland 20814. (301) 654-4281. References to U.S. federal regulations and precautionary data pertaining to the manufacture, sale, storage, use, and transportation of

more than 5,000 industrial chemical substances. Online version of handbook of the same name.

Toxic Materials News. Business Publishers, Inc., 951 Pershing Dr., Silver Spring, Maryland 20910-4464. (301) 587-6300. Legislation, regulations, and litigation concerning toxic substances. Online version of periodical of the same name.

PERIODICALS AND NEWSLETTERS

Air Pollution Control. Bureau of National Affairs, 1231 25th St. NW, Washington, District of Columbia 20037. (202) 452-4200. Biweekly. A reference and advisory service on the control of air pollution, designed to meet the information needs of individuals responsible for complying with EPA and state air pollution control regulations.

Annual Report of the Inhalation Toxicology Research Institute. Inhalation Toxicology Research Institute. Lovelace Biomedical and Environmental Research Institute, 5285 Port Royal Rd., Springfield, Virginia 22161. (703) 487-4650. 1972/73-. Annual. Deals with aerosols, poisonous gases and radioactive substances. Describes the impact on inhalation of these hazardous substances.

Chemical Substances Control. Bureau of National Affairs, 1231 25th St. NW, Washington, District of Columbia 20037. (202) 452-4200. Biweekly. Periodical covering regulatory compliance and management of chemicals. Also available online.

Dangerous Properties of Industrial Materials Report. Van Nostrand Reinhold, 115 5th Avenue, New York, New York 10003. (212) 254-3232. Bimonthly. Chemical and environmental review of hazardous industrial materials.

Environmental Protection Magazine. Stevens Publishing Co., 225 New Road, PO Box 2604, Waco, Texas 76702-2573. (817) 776-9000. Air and water pollution, wastewater and hazardous materials.

Florida Environments. Florida Environments Pub., 215 N. Main St., PO Box 1617, High Springs, Florida 32643. (904) 454-2007. Monthly. Florida's hazardous materials/wastes, wildlife, regulation, drinking/ground/surface waters, air, and solid waste.

Focus. Hazardous Materials Control Research Institute, 9300 Columbia Blvd, Silver Spring, Maryland 20910-1702. (301) 587-9390. Monthly. Covers hazardous materials technology and legislation.

Harvard Environmental Law Review. Environmental Law Review, c/o Publication Center, Harvard Law School, 202 Austin Hall, Cambridge, Massachusetts 02138. (617) 495-3110. Semiannual. Law reviews of cases involving the environment.

Hazard Monthly. Research Alternatives, Inc., 1401 Rockville Pike, Rockville, Maryland 20852. (301) 424-2803. Monthly. Covers natural disasters and hazardous substances.

Hazardous Materials Control. Hazardous Materials Control Research Institute, 9300 Columbia Blvd., Silver Spring, Maryland 20910-1702. (301) 587-9390. Bimonthly. Information, innovations and articles in the hazardous materials field.

Hazardous Materials Intelligence Report. World Information Systems, P.O. Box 535, Harvard Square Station, Cambridge, Massachusetts 02238. (617) 491-5100.

Weekly. Timely information on hazardous substances rules and procedures.

Hazardous Materials Management. Canadian Hazardous Materials Mgmt., 12 Salem Ave., Toronto, Ontario, Canada M6H 3C2. (416) 536-5974. Biweekly. All aspects of pollution control, including air quality, water treatment, and solid waste.

Hazardous Materials Transportation. Bureau of National Affairs, 1231 25th St. NW, Washington, District of Columbia 20037. (202) 452-4200. Monthly. Covers rules and regulations governing the shipment of hazardous materials in the U.S.

Hazardous Materials World. HazMat World, Circulation Dept., P.O. Box 3021, Wheaton, Illinois 60137. (708) 858-1888. Monthly. Covers biobusiness, hazardous wastes management, and hazardous substance safety measures.

Hazardous Substances and Public Health: A Publication of the Agency for Toxic Substances and Disease Registry. Agency for Toxic Substances and Disease Registry, Department of Health and Human Services, 1600 Clifton Rd. NE, M/S E33, Atlanta, Georgia 30333. (404) 639-0727. Quarterly.

Hazardous Waste and Toxic Torts. Leader Publications, 111 Eighth Ave., New York, New York 10011. (212) 463-5709. Monthly.

Hazardous Waste Consultant. McCoy & Associates, 13701 West Jewell Avenue, Suite 202, Lakewood, Colorado 80228. (303) 987-0333. Bimonthly. Information on hazardous and toxic waste issues.

Hazardous Waste News. Business Publishers, Inc., 951 Pershing Drive, Silver Spring, Maryland 20910-4464. (301) 587-6300. Weekly. Covers legislative, regulatory and judicial decisions on hazardous waste. Also available online.

Hazmat News: The Authoritative News Resource for Hazardous Control and Waste Management. Stevens Publishing Co., PO Box 2604, Waco, Texas 76702-2604. (817) 776-9000. Semimonthly. Hazardous materials transportation, storage, and disposal.

Hazmat World. Tower-Borner Publishing, Inc., Bldg. C, Suite 206, 800 Roosevelt Rd., Glen Ellyn, Illinois 60137. (708) 858-1888. Monthly. Covers hazardous management issues and technology.

HazTech News. Business Publishers, Inc., 951 Pershing Drive, Silver Spring, Maryland 20910. (301) 587-6300. Biweekly. Covers developments and discoveries in waste management.

Journal of Analytical Toxicology. Preston Publications, PO Box 48312, 7800 Merrimac, Niles, Illinois 60648. (708) 965-0566. Bimonthly. Articles on industrial toxicology, environmental pollution and pharmaceuticals.

Management of World Wastes. Communication Channels, 6255 Barfield Road, Atlanta, Georgia 30328. (404) 256-9800. Monthly. Covers public and private waste operations.

Pollution Engineering. Cahners Publishing Co., 249 W. 17th St., New York, New York 10011. (212) 645-0067. 1969-. Monthly.

State Environment Report: Toxic Substances & Hazardous Wastes. Business Publishers, Inc., 951 Pershing Drive, Silver Spring, Maryland 20910. (301) 587-6300. Weekly. Covers state legislative and regulatory initiatives.

Synthetic Organic Chemical Manufacturers Association Newsletter. Synthetic Organic Chemical Manufacturers Association, 1330 Connecticut Avenue, NW, Washington, District of Columbia 20036. (202) 659-0060. Biweekly. Covers trade, environmental and safety issues.

Toxic Materials News. Business Publishers, Inc., 951 Pershing Dr., Silver Spring, Maryland 20910-4464. (301) 587-6300. 1974-. Weekly. Informs on regulations governing the manufacture, handling, transport, distribution and disposal of toxic chemicals and pesticides. Also available online.

Toxic Materials Transport. Business Publishers, Inc., 951 Pershing Dr., Silver Spring, Maryland 20910. (301) 587-6300. Biweekly. Covers new laws and regulations at federal, state and local levels.

STATISTICS SOURCES

Hazmat Emergency Response Contracting. FIND/SVP, 625 Avenue of the Americas, New York, New York 10011. (800) 346-3787. 1991. Challenges facing existing contractors and the business strategies required for continued success in the market.

OSHA Regulated Hazardous Substances: Health, Toxicity, Economic, and Technological Data. U.S. Occupational Safety and Health Administration. Noyes Publications, 120 Mill Rd., Park Ridge, New Jersey 07656. (201) 391-8484. 1990. Provides industrial exposure data and control technologies for more than 650 substances currently regulated, or candidates for regulation, by the Occupational Safety and Health Administration.

Tracking Toxic Substances at Industrial Facilities: Engineering Mass Balance Versus Materials Accounting. National Research Council–Committee to Evaluate Mass Balance Information for Facilities Handling Toxic Substances. National Academy Press, 2101 Constitution Ave., NW, Washington, District of Columbia 20418. (202) 334-3343. 1990. Covers measurement of factory and trade waste and hazardous substances.

TRADE ASSOCIATIONS AND PROFESSIONAL SOCIETIES

Alaska Conservation Foundation. 430 West 7th St., Suite 215, Anchorage, Alaska 99501. (907) 276-1917.

CEIP Fund. 68 Harrison Ave., 5th Fl., Boston, Massachusetts 02111. (617) 426-4375.

Center for Hazardous Materials Research. 320 William Pitt Way, University of Pittsburgh Applied Research Center, Pittsburgh, Pennsylvania 15238. (412) 826-5320.

Environmental Quality Industrial Resources Center. The Ohio State University, 1200 Chambers Rd., Room 310, Columbus, Ohio 43212. (614) 292-6717.

Hazardous Materials Advisory Council. 1110 Vermont Ave. N.W., Ste. 250, Washington, District of Columbia 20005. (202) 728-1460.

Hazardous Materials Control Research Institute. 7237 Hanover Pkwy., Greenbelt, Maryland 20770. (301) 982-9500.

Hazardous Waste Treatment Council. 1440 New York Ave., Suite 310, Washington, District of Columbia 20005. (202) 783-0870.

National Environmental Training Association. 2930 E. Camelback Rd., Phoenix, Arizona 85016. (602) 956-6099.

Synthetic Organic Chemical Manufacturers Association. 1330 Connecticut Ave., N.W., Suite 300, Washington, District of Columbia 20036. (202) 659-0060.

HAZARDOUS WASTE DISPOSAL

ABSTRACTING AND INDEXING SERVICES

Applied Science and Technology Index. H.W. Wilson Co., 950 University Ave., Bronx, New York 10452. (800) 367-6770. Formerly Industrial Arts Index.

Biological Abstracts. BIOSIS, 2100 Arch St., Philadelphia, Pennsylvania 19103-1399. (215) 587-4800. 1927-.

Biological and Agricultural Index. H.W. Wilson Co., 950 University Ave., Bronx, New York 10452. (800) 367-6770. 1916-. Monthly.

Bulletin Signaletique: Eau et Assainissement, Pollution Atmospherique, Droit des Pollutions. Centre de Documentation, Centre National de la Recherche Scientifique, 15, quai Anatole France, Paris, France 75700. (1) 45 55 92 25. 1983-. Monthly. Indexes pollution periodicals including water, atmospheric and related pollutions.

Chemical Abstracts. Chemical Abstracts Service, 2540 Olentangy River Rd., PO Box 3012, Columbus, Ohio 43210. (800) 848-6533. 1907-.

Current Advances in Ecological and Environmental Science. Pergamon Microforms International, Inc., Fairview Park, Elmsford, New York 10523. (914) 592-7720. 1989-. Monthly. Current literature searching service includingjournals, reports, abstracts, etc. This service is available online as part of the CABS database on the hosts BRS and ORBIT search service.

Ecological Abstracts. Geo Abstracts Ltd. Elsevier Applied Science, Crown House, Linton Rd., Barking, England IG 11 8JU. 1974-. Derived from over 600 leading ecological and environmental journals, plus books, conference proceedings, reports and theses.

Environment Abstracts. Bowker A & I Publishing, 121 Chanlon Rd., New Providence, New Jersey 07974. (908) 464-6800. 1974-.

Environment Index. Environment Information Center, Index Research Department, 124 E. 39th St., New York, New York 10016. 1971-. Annual.

Environmental Information Connection–EIC. Planning Information Program, Dept. of Urban and Regional Planning, University of Illinois, 1003 West Nevada, Urbana, Illinois 61801. (217) 333-1369. Also available online.

Environmental Periodicals Bibliography. Environmental Studies Institute, International Academy at Santa Barbara, 800 Garden St., Suite D, Santa Barbara, California 93101. (805) 965-5010. Also available online.

General Science Index. H. W. Wilson Co., 950 University Ave., Bronx, New York 10452. 1978-. Monthly, also issued in annual cumulation. Cumulative subject index to English language periodicals in the subject fields of astronomy, botany, chemistry, earth science, environment and conservation, food and nutrition, genetics, mathematics, medicine and health, microbiology, oceanography, physics, physiology and zoology.

Geographical Abstracts. London School of Economics, Dept. of Geography, Regency House, 34 Duke St., London, England 1966-. Continued by Geo Abstracts issued in 6 parts: Pt. A. Landforms and the quaternary; Pt. B. Biogeography and Climatology; Pt. C. Economic geography; Pt. D. Social geography and cartography; Pt. E. Sedimentology; Pt. F. Regional and community planning.

Index to Scientific Book Contents. Institute for Scientific Information, 3501 Market St., Philadelphia, Pennsylvania 19104. (800) 523-1857. 1985-. Annual. Gives contents of science books published.

Pollution Abstracts. Cambridge Scientific Abstracts, 5161 River Rd., Bethesda, Maryland 20816. (301) 961-6750. Six/year. Indexes worldwide technical literature on environmental pollution. Covers air pollution, marine and freshwater pollution, sewage and wastewater treatment, waste management, toxicology and health, noise pollution, radiation, land pollution, and environmental policies, programs, legislation, and education. Also available online.

Science Citation Index. Institute for Scientific Information, 3501 Market St., Philadelphia, Pennsylvania 19104. 1961-.

BIBLIOGRAPHIES

Current Contents. Agriculture, Biology and Environmental Sciences. Institute for Scientific Information, 3501 Market St., Philadelphia, Pennsylvania 19104. (800) 523-1857. 1973-. Previous title: Current Contents. Agricultural, Food & Veterinary Sciences. Gives the table of contents of periodicals in the fields of agriculture, biology, environmental and related areas.

EPA Publications Bibliography. U.S. Environmental Protection Agency, Library Systems Branch, 401 M St., SW, Washington, District of Columbia 20460. (202) 260-2090. Quarterly.

Nuclear Facility Decommissioning and Site Remedial Actions: A Selected Bibliography. National Technical Information Service, 5285 Port Royal Rd., Springfield, Virginia 22161. (703) 487-4650. Annual. Nuclear facility decommissioning, uranium mill tailings management, and radioactive waste site remedial actions.

DIRECTORIES

California Hazardous Waste Directory 1991-1992: A Comprehensive Guide to the Environmental Services Marketplace. In Media Res, 848 California St., San Francisco, California 94108. (415) 772-8949 or (800) 675-1945. 1991. An alphabetical list of companies dealing with hazardous wastes.

Hazardous Waste Management Facilities Directory: Treatment, Storage, Disposal and Recycling. U. S. Environmental Protection Agency. Noyes Publications, 120 Mill Rd., Park Ridge, New Jersey 07656. (201) 391-8484. 1990. Provides geographical listings of 1045 commercial hazardous waste management facilities, along with information on the types of commercial services offered and types of wastes managed. It is a compilation of recent data from EPA data bases and includes the facility name, address, contact person, and phone number.

Hazardous Waste Practitioners Directory. Hazardous Waste Action Coalition, c/o American Consulting Engineers Council, 1015 15th St. NW, No. 802, Washington, District of Columbia 20005. (202) 347-7474. Annual. Engineering firms responsible for designing cleanup solutions for hazardous waste sites.

Hazardous Waste Services Directory: Transporters, Disposal Sites, Laboratories, Consultants, and Specialized Services. George McDowell. J. J. Keller & Associates, Inc., 3003 W. Breezewood, PO Box 368, Neenah, Wisconsin 54957-0368. (414) 722-2848. Semiannual. Guide to various services available in the field of hazardous waste.

Who's Who in Environmental Engineering. American Academy of Environmental Engineers, 132 Holiday Court, Suite 206, Annapolis, Maryland 21401. (301) 266-3311. 1980. Annual. Directory of environmental engineers who are certified by the academy.

ENCYCLOPEDIAS AND DICTIONARIES

Encyclopedia of Environmental Control Technology. Paul N. Cheremisinoff, ed. Gulf Publishing Co., Book Division, PO Box 2608, Houston, Texas 77252. (713) 529-4301 or (800) 231-6275. 1992. Volume 1: Thermal Treatment of Hazardous Wastes; volume 2: Air Pollution Control; volume 3: Wastewater Treatment Technology; volume 4: Hazardous Waste Containment and Treatment; volumes 5 through 8 in progress. Provides in-depth coverage of specialized topics related to environmental and industrial pollution control problems and state-of-the-art information on technology and research as well as projections of future trends in the field.

McGraw-Hill Encyclopedia of Environmental Science. Sybil P. Parker. McGraw-Hill Science & Engineering Books, 11 W. 19th St., New York, New York 10011. (212) 337-6010. 1980. Covers ecology, man's influence on nature, and environmental protection.

Van Nostrand's Scientific Encyclopedia. Glenn D. Considine, ed. Van Nostrand Reinhold, 115 5th Ave., New York, New York 10003. (212) 254-3232. 1983. Sixth edition. Includes all broad subject areas in science.

GENERAL WORKS

Analyses of Hazardous Substances in Air. A. Kettrup, ed. VCH Publishers, 303 NW 12th Ave., Deerfield Beach, Florida 33442-1788. (305) 428-5566. 1991. Proceedings from the Commission for the Investigation of Health Hazards of Chemical Compounds in the Work Area. Included are 16 analytical methods for determining organic compounds and heavy metals in the air of work areas by high pressure liquid chromatography, gas chromatography, infrared spectroscopy and atomic absorption spectrometry.

Analysis of Army Hazardous Waste Disposal Cost Data. B. J. Kim, et al. Construction Engineering Research Lab (Army), c/o National Technical Information Service, 5185 Port Royal Rd., Springfield, Virginia 22161. 1991. Order number: AD-A236 654/0LDM.

Applied Isotope Hydrogeology: A Case Study in Northern Switzerland. F. J. Pearson, Jr., et al. Elsevier Science Publishing Co., Inc, 655 Avenue of the Americas, New York, New York 10010. (212) 989-5800. 1991. This is a case study in northern Switzerland about radioactive waste disposal in the ground. Includes bibliographical references and an index.

Characterization of Hazardous Waste Generation and Disposal in Yukon. Moneco Consultants Ltd., Calgary (Alberta). National Technical Information Service, 5285 Port Royal Rd., Springfield, Virginia 22161. (703) 487-4650. 1990.

Chemical, Physical, and Biological Properties of Compounds Present at Hazardous Waste Sites: Final Report. U.S. Environmental Protection Agency. Clement Associates Inc., Arlington, Virginia 1985.

A Citizen's Guide to Promoting Toxic Waste Reduction. Lauren Kenworthy and Eric Schaeffer. INFORM, 381 Park Ave. S., New York, New York 10016. (212) 689-4040. 1990. The how-to manual describes source reduction and its benefits, five strategies plants can use to reduce their hazardous wastes at the source, a step-by-step process for gathering background facts, and interviewing company representatives and analyzing data.

Desulphurisation 2: Technologies and Strategies for Reducing Sulphur Emissions. Hemisphere Publishing Co., 79 Madison Ave., Suite 1110, New York, New York 10016. (212) 725-1999. 1991. Proceedings of a Symposium held in Sheffield, March 1991.

Detection of Subsurface Hazardous Waste Containers by Nondestructive Techniques. Arthur E. Lord and Robert M. Koerner. Noyes Publications, 120 Mill Rd., Park Ridge, New Jersey 07656. (201) 391-8484. 1990. Describes a study undertaken to identify and assess the best possible NDT techniques for detecting and delineating hazardous waste, particularly in steel and plastic containers buried beneath soil or water.

Emerging Technologies in Hazardous Waste Management. D. William Tedder and Frederick G. Pohland, eds. American Chemical Society, 1155 16th St. N.W., Washington, District of Columbia 20036. (202) 872-4600; (800) 227-5558. 1990. Hazardous waste management technology.

Emerging Technologies in Hazardous Waste Management II. D. William Tedder and Frederick G. Pohland, eds. American Chemical Society, 1155 16th St. N.W., Washington, District of Columbia 20036. (202) 872-4600; (800) 227-5558. 1991. Developed from a symposium sponsored by the Division of Industrial and Engineering Chemistry, Inc. of the American Chemical Society at the Industrial and Engineering Chemistry Special Symposium, Atlantic City, NJ, June 4-7, 1990.

The Environmental Challenge of the 1990's. U.S. Environmental Protection Agency, 401 M St. SW, Washington, District of Columbia 20460. (202) 260-2090. 1991. Provides an overview of past and present projects for pollution prevention, focusing on the promotion of clean technologies and clean products in both the public and private sectors. Covers new prevention ideas relating to solid and hazardous wastes, pesticides, drinking water, wastewater and toxic substances.

Environmental Impacts of Hazardous Waste Treatment, Storage and Disposal Facilities. Rodolfo N. Salcedo, et al. Technomic Publishing Co., 851 New Holland Ave., Box

3535, Lancaster, Pennsylvania 17604. (717) 291-5609. 1989. Provides guidance in dealing with the many obstacles and preliminary requirements in siting TSD facilities.

Environmental Lender Liability. O. T. Smith. John Wiley & Sons, Inc., 605 3rd Ave., New York, New York 10158-0012. (212) 850-6000. 1991. Covers the leaders' aspects of environmental law. Focuses on the liability of lenders for hazardous waste cleanup. Also discusses other provisions of federal environmental law statutes and the impact of bankruptcy on environmental obligations. Analyzes the newly proposed EPA guidelines on lender liability and includes relevant forms, checklists, and working documents.

Hazardous and Industrial Wastes, 1991. Technomic Publishing Co., 851 New Holland Ave., Box 3535, Lancaster, Pennsylvania 17604. (717) 291-5609. 1991. Proceedings of the 23rd Mid-Atlantic Industrial Waste Conference held at Drexel University, 1991.

Hazardous Laboratory Chemicals; Disposal Guide. M. A. Armour. CRC Press, 2000 Corporate Blvd., N.W., Suite 700, Boca Raton, Florida 33431. (407) 994-0555; (800) 272-7737. 1991. Chemical disposal procedures are designed to enable chemicals to be recycled or disposed of inhouse, eliminating the need to incinerate them or take them to a landfill. Disposal methods for heavy metals, salts, explosive chemicals such as picric acid, and toxic organic materials are included.

Hazardous Waste Chemistry, Toxicology and Treatment. Stanley E. Manahan. Lewis Publishers, 2000 Corporate Blvd., N.W., Boca Raton, Florida 33431. (407) 994-0555 or (800) 272-7737. 1990. Reviews hazardous wastes, their chemistry and toxicology. Gives a basic coverage of chemistry and biochemistry, environmental chemical processes, and toxicology.

Hazardous Waste from Small Quantity Generators. Seymour I. Schwartz, et al. Island Press, 1718 Connecticut Ave. N.W., Suite 300, Washington, District of Columbia 20009. (202) 232-7933. 1990. Examines the role small businesses play in degrading the environment. Includes information on the extent and seriousness of the problem, regulations; and liability issues; national, state, and local programs for SQ Gas in California, analysis of methods for managing SQG waste; policy options for promoting legal methods; and discouraging illegal methods.

Hazardous Waste Management: New Regulation and New Technology. Brian Price. Financial Times Bus. Info. Ltd., 50-64 Broadway, 7th Fl., London, England 071-799 2002. 1990.

Hazardous Waste Management: Reducing the Risk. Council on Economic Priorities. Island Press, 1718 Connecticut Ave. N.W., Suite 300, Washington, District of Columbia 20009. (202) 232-7933. 1986. Includes information for regulatory agencies, waste generators, host communities, and public officials. Topics include compliance, liabilities, technologies, corporate and public relations, groundwater monitoring, key laws and recommendations.

Hazardous Waste Management: The Basics, the Issues and the Controversy: Proceedings of the Commission on the Arizona Environment's Summer Conference. Commission on the Arizona Environment, Phoenix, Arizona

How to Select Hazardous Waste Treatment Technologies for Soil and Sludges: Alternative, Innovative and Emerging Technologies. Tim Holden, et al. Noyes Publications, 120 Mill Rd., Park Ridge, New Jersey 07656. (201) 391-8484. 1989. Guide for screening feasible alternative, innovative and emerging treatment technologies for contaminated soils and sludges at CERCLA (Superfund) sites. The technology data were selected from individual treatment technology vendors.

In Situ Vitrification of Transuranic Wastes. K. H. Oma, et al. Pacific Northwest Laboratory, National Technical Information Service, 5285 Port Royal Rd., Springfield, Virginia 22161. (703) 487-4650. 1983. Prepared for the U.S. Department of Energy under contract by Pacific Northwest Laboratory, Richland, WA.

Incineration for Site Cleanup and Destruction of Hazardous Wastes. Howard E. Hesketh. Technomic Publishing Co., 851 New Holland Ave., Box 3535, Lancaster, Pennsylvania 17604. (717) 291-5609; (800) 233-9936. 1990.

Infectious Waste Management. Frank L. Cross. Technomic Publishing Co., 851 New Holland Ave., Box 3535, Lancaster, Pennsylvania 17604. (717) 291-5609; (800) 233-9936. 1990.

The Management of Radioactive Waste. Uranium Institute, 12th Floor, Bowater House, 68 Knightsbridge, London, England SW1X 7LT. 071-225 0303. 1991. Discusses methods of disposal of radioactive wastes and the hazards involved.

Management of Radioactive Waste: The Issues for Local Authorities. Stuart Kemp, ed. Telford, Telford House, 1 Heron Quay, London, England E14 9XF. (071) 987-6999. 1991. Proceedings of the conference organized by the National Steering Committee, Nuclear Free Local Authorities, and held in Manchester on February 12, 1991.

Managing Environmental Risks. Air & Waste Management Association, PO Box 2861, Pittsburgh, Pennsylvania 15230. (412) 232-3444. 1990. Papers presented at the Air & Waste Management Association International Specialty Conference, held in October 1989 in Quebec City, contains topics such as risks related to hazardous waste sites, chemical contaminants, and biotechnology.

Pollution: Causes, Effects and Control. Roy Michael Harrison. Royal Society of Chemistry, c/o CRC Press, 2000 Corporate Blvd. N.W., Boca Raton, Florida 33431. (800) 272-7737. 1990. 2nd ed. Deals with environmental pollution and its associated problems and legal ramifications.

Preventing Pollution Through Technical Assistance: One State's Experience. Mark H. Dorfman, et al. INFORM Inc., 381 Park Ave. S., New York, New York 10016. (212) 689-4040. 1990. Examines the state of North Carolina's voluntary program aimed at assisting the industry in pollution prevention. It also includes a glossary, a bibliography of information sources and helpful statistical tables of data collected.

Proceedings of the 44th Industrial Waste Conference May 1989, Purdue University. John W. Bell, ed. Lewis Publishers, 2000 Corporate Blvd., N.W., Boca Raton, Florida 33431. (407) 994-0555 or (800) 272-7737. 1990. Includes new research, case histories and operating data, on every conceivable facet of today's big problem with unparalleled appropriate, usable information and data for current industrial waste problems.

Proceedings of the 45th Industrial Waste Conference, May 1990 at Purdue University. Ross A. Duckworth. Lewis Publishers, 2000 Corporate Blvd., N.W., Boca Raton, Florida 33431. (407) 994-0555 or (800) 272-7737. 1991. Subject areas included in the conference were: site remediation, hazardous waste minimization and treatment, biological systems, aerobic processes, anaerobic processes, sludge treatment, respirometry, new processes, equipment, and applications.

RCRA Compliance Implementation Guide. Mary P. Bauer and Elizabeth J. Kellar. Government Institutes, Inc., 4 Research Pl., Suite 200, Rockville, Maryland 20850. (301) 921-2300. 1990. Interprets how a particular situation fits into the whole compliance process. Step-by-step directions are given to satisfy the compliance program. Also included are copies of EPA reports, manifests and forms.

Safe Disposal of Hazardous Wastes. Roger Batstone, ed. The World Bank, 1818 H. St. N.W., Washington, District of Columbia 20433. 1990. Describes the special needs and problem of the management of hazardous wastes in developing countries.

Safety in the Use of Asbestos. International Labour Office, 49 Sheridan Ave., Albany, New York 12210. (518) 436-9686. 1990. An ILO code of practice. The first part of the code includes monitoring in the work place, preventive measures, the protection and supervision of the workers' health, and the packaging, handling, transport and disposal of asbestos waste. More detailed guidance on the limitation of exposure to asbestos in specific activities is given in the second part of the code, which includes sections on mining and milling, asbestos cement, textiles, friction materials, and the removal of asbestos-containing materials.

Treatability Studies for Hazardous Waste Sites. Hazardous Waste Action Coalition, 1015 15th St. N.W., Suite 802, Washington, District of Columbia 20005. (202) 347-7474. 1990. Assesses the use of treatability studies for evaluating the effectiveness and cost of treatment technologies performed at hazardous waste sites.

Waste Management: Towards A Sustainable Society. Om Prakash Kharbanda and E. A. Stallworthy. Auburn House, 14 Dedham St., Dover, Massachusetts 02030-0658. (505) 785-2220; (800) 223-2665. 1990. Describes the generation of various types of hazardous and nonhazardous wastes, with a whole chapter devoted to acid rain.

GOVERNMENTAL ORGANIZATIONS

U.S. Environmental Protection Agency: Assistant Administrator for Solid Waste and Emergency Response. 401 M St., S.W., Washington, District of Columbia 20460. (202) 382-4610.

U.S. Environmental Protection Agency: Office of Waste Programs Enforcement. 401 M St., S.W., Washington, District of Columbia 20460. (202) 382-4814.

HANDBOOKS AND MANUALS

Environmental Hazards: Radioactive Materials and Wastes: A Reference Handbook. E. Willard Miller and Ruby M. Miller. ABC-Clio, 130 Cremona Dr., PO Box 1911, Santa Barbara, California 93116-1911. (805) 968-1911; (800) 422-2546. 1990. Information source on radioactive materials and wastes. Introductory chapters describe the nature and characteristics of both natural and manufactured radioactive materials. Also provides information on laws, regulations, and treaties about waste materials. Including a directory of private, governmental, and international organizations that deal with radioactive wastes.

The Generator's Guide to Hazardous Materials/Waste Management. Leo H. Traverse. Van Nostrand Reinhold, 115 5th Ave., New York, New York 10003. (212) 254-3232. 1991. Comprehensive information source for hazardous waste and hazardous materials management.

Guide to the Management of Hazardous Waste: A Handbook for the Businessman and the Concerned Citizen. J. William Haun. Fulcrum Publishing, 350 Indiana St., Ste. 350, Golden, Colorado 80401. (303) 277-1623. 1991. Fact book on hazardous waste management, including factory and trade waste, and hazardous waste law and legislation in the United States.

Handbook of Hazardous Waste Management for Small Quantity Generators. Russell W. Phifer and William R. McTigue, Jr. Lewis Publishers, 2000 Corporate Blvd., N.W., Boca Raton, Florida 33431. (407) 994-0555 or (800) 272-7737. 1988. Includes practical "how to" instructions, state/federal regulations, overview, lab waste management, interpretations of regulation, enforcement, generator checklist, etc.

Handbook: Responding to Discharges of Sinking Hazardous Substances. K. R. Boyer. National Technical Information Service, 5285 Port Royal Rd., Springfield, Virginia 22161. (703) 487-4650. 1987.

Hazardous Waste Management Strategies for Health Care Facilities. Nelson S. Slavik. American Hospital Association, 840 North Lake Shore Dr., Chicago, Illinois 60611. 1987. Contains helpful information for health care facilities in the management of their chemical, cytotoxic, infectious, and radiological wastes.

Industrial and Hazardous Waste Treatment. Nelson Leonard Nemerow and Avijit Dasgupta. Van Nostrand Reinhold, 115 5th Ave., New York, New York 10003. (212) 254-3232. 1991. Factory and trade waste, and hazardous waste purification.

Managing Industrial Hazardous Waste–Practical Handbook. Gary F. Lindgren. Lewis Publishers, 2000 Corporate Blvd., N.W., Boca Raton, Florida 33431. (407) 994-0555 or (800) 272-7737. 1989. Explains the regulations regarding identification and listing of hazardous wastes.

RCRA Hazardous Wastes Handbook. Crowell & Moring. Government Institutes, Inc., 4 Research Place, Suite 200, Rockville, Maryland 20850. (301) 921-2300. 1989. 8th ed. Analyzes the impact of the Resource Conservation and Recovery Act on the business, while incorporating the most recent regulatory changes to the RCRA. These include the final 1988 underground storage tank rules, the medical waste regulations, permit modification regulations, amendments regarding corrective action and closures, the exemption for "treatability tests," waste export rules, etc. Includes the complete test of the RCRA statute as currently amended.

Siting Hazardous Waste Treatment Facilities; the Nimby Syndrome. Kent E. Portney. Auburn House, 14 Dedham St., Dover, Massachusetts 02030-0658. (800) 223-2665.

1991. Advice to producers of hazardous waste on how to overcome people's reluctance to have it shipped into their neighborhood.

Standard Handbook of Hazardous Waste Treatment and Disposal. Harry M. Freeman, ed. McGraw-Hill Science & Engineering Books, 11 West 19th St., New York, New York 10011. (212) 337-6010. 1989. A reference of alternatives and innovative technologies for managing hazardous waste and cleaning up abandoned disposal sites.

Storage, Shipment, Handling, and Disposal of Chemical Agents and Hazardous Chemicals. Department of the Army, The Pentagon, Washington, District of Columbia 20310. (202) 545-6700. 1989. Safety measures and transportation of chemicals.

Superfund Manual: Legal and Management Strategies. Crowell & Moring. Government Institutes, Inc., 4 Research Pl., Suite 200, Rockville, Maryland 20850. (301) 921-2300. 1990. 4th ed. Industrial liability for hazardous waste and pollution damage at hazardous waste sites are explained. Explains the latest developments in the Superfund program. Includes the interrelationships between Superfund and RCRA; new regulations to implement Emergency Planning and the Community Right-to-Know Act; revisions to the National Contingency Plan; new EPA guidance documents relating to cleanup standards, site studies, and settlement procedures; court decisions and the special problems.

ONLINE DATA BASES

BIOSIS Previews. BIOSIS, 2100 Arch St., Philadelphia, Pennsylvania 19103-1399. (215) 587-4800. Largest and most comprehensive database of research in the life sciences. Contains citations for nearly 9000 primary research journals, monographs, reviews, symposia, preliminary reports, semi-popular journals, selected institutional reports, government reports and research communications.

CERCLIS. Chemical Information Systems, Inc., 7215 York Rd., Baltimore, Maryland 21212. (301) 321-8440. Information on hazardous waste disposal sites that have either been listed by the EPA on the National Priority List (NPL) or nominated for consideration for the NPL.

Chemical Abstracts-CA. Chemical Abstracts Service, 2540 Olentangy River Rd., P.O. Box 3012, Columbus, Ohio 43210. (800) 848-6533 or (614) 421-3600. Information sources include 9000 journals, patents from 27 countries, two industrial property organizations, new books, conference proceedings, and government research reports.

Enviro/Energyline Abstracts Plus. R. R. Bowker Co., 121 Chanlon Rd., New Providence, New Jersey 07974. (908) 464-6800.

Environmental Periodicals Bibliography. National Information Services Corp., Ste. 6, Wyman Towers, 3100 St. Paul St., Baltimore, Maryland 21218. (410)243-0797. Online version of abstract of same name.

Hazardline. Occupational Health Services, Inc., 450 7th Ave., Ste. 2407, New York, New York 10123. (212) 967-1100. More than 3600 dangerous materials, including physical and chemical descriptions, standards and regulations, and safety precautions for handling.

Hazardous Materials Intelligence Report. World Information Systems, PO Box 535, Cambridge, Massachusetts 02238. (617) 491-5100. Online access to federal, state, and local legislation, regulations, and programs related to hazardous waste and hazardous material management. Online version of the periodical of the same name.

Hazardous Waste Database. U.S. Environmental Protection Agency, Office of Administration and Resources Management, 401 M St., S.W., Washington, District of Columbia 20460. (202) 260-2090. Hazardous waste directives, treatment and disposal of hazardous waste, and its storage.

Hazardous Waste News. Business Publishers, Inc., 951 Pershing Dr., Silver Spring, Maryland 20910-4464. (301) 587-6300. Online access to legislative, regulatory, and judicial decisions at the federal and state levels relating to the field of hazardous waste management. Online version of the periodical of the same name.

PressNet Environmental Reports. Chemical Information Systems, Inc., 7215 York Rd., Baltimore, Maryland 21212. (301) 321-8440.

Report on Defense Plant Wastes. Business Publishers, Inc., 951 Pershing Dr., Silver Spring, Maryland 20910-4464. (301) 587-6300. Laws, regulations, cleanup actions, contracts, and court actions affecting U.S. defense, weapons production, government hospitals and laboratories, and other government institutions. Online version of periodical of the same name.

SCISEARCH. Institute for Scientific Information, University City Science Center, 3501 Market St., Philadelphia, Pennsylvania 19104. (215) 386-0100.

Toxic Materials News. Business Publishers, Inc., 951 Pershing Dr., Silver Spring, Maryland 20910-4464. (301) 587-6300. Legislation, regulations, and litigation concerning toxic substances. Online version of periodical of the same name.

PERIODICALS AND NEWSLETTERS

Annual Report of Abandoned or Uncontrolled Hazardous Waste Disposal Sites and Hazardous Waste Remedial Fund, 1990 Appendix. Iowa Dept. of Natural Resources. National Technical Information Service, 5285 Port Royal Rd., Springfield, Virginia 22161. (703) 487-4650. 1991. Annual.

Annual Report on Abandonment or Uncontrolled Hazardous Waste Disposal Sites and Hazardous Waste Remedial Fund. Iowa Dept. of Natural Resources. National Technical Information Service, 5285 Port Royal Rd., Springfield, Virginia 22161. (703) 487-4650. Annual.

Asbestos Control Report. Business Publishers, Inc., 951 Pershing Drive, Silver Spring, Maryland 20910-4464. (301) 587-6300. Biweekly. Information on asbestos control techniques, research, and regulations. Also available online.

Community and Worker Right-to-Know News. Thompson Publishing Group, 1725 K St. NW, Washington, District of Columbia 20006. (800) 424-2959. Bimonthly. Reports on chemical disclosure requirements and industrial liability.

Hazardous Materials Intelligence Report. World Information Systems, P.O. Box 535, Harvard Square Station, Cambridge, Massachusetts 02238. (617) 491-5100.

Weekly. Timely information on hazardous substances rules and procedures.

Hazardous Waste and Hazardous Materials. Mary Ann Liebert, Inc., 1651 3rd Avenue, New York, New York 10128. (212) 289-2300. Quarterly. Industrial waste technology.

Hazardous Waste and Toxic Torts. Leader Publications, 111 Eighth Ave., New York, New York 10011. (212) 463-5709. Monthly.

Hazardous Waste Consultant. McCoy & Associates, 13701 West Jewell Avenue, Suite 202, Lakewood, Colorado 80228. (303) 987-0333. Bimonthly. Information on hazardous and toxic waste issues.

Hazardous Waste News. Business Publishers, Inc., 951 Pershing Drive, Silver Spring, Maryland 20910-4464. (301) 587-6300. Weekly. Covers legislative, regulatory and judicial decisions on hazardous waste. Also available online.

Hazmat News: The Authoritative News Resource for Hazardous Control and Waste Management. Stevens Publishing Co., PO Box 2604, Waco, Texas 76702-2604. (817) 776-9000. Semimonthly. Hazardous materials transportation, storage, and disposal.

Hazmat World. Tower-Borner Publishing, Inc., Bldg. C, Suite 206, 800 Roosevelt Rd., Glen Ellyn, Illinois 60137. (708) 858-1888. Monthly. Covers hazardous management issues and technology.

HazTech News. Business Publishers, Inc., 951 Pershing Drive, Silver Spring, Maryland 20910. (301) 587-6300. Biweekly. Covers developments and discoveries in waste management.

INFORM Reports. INFORM Inc., 381 Park Ave., So., New York, New York 10016. (212) 689-4040. Quarterly. INFORM is a nonprofit environmental research & education organization for the preservation and conservation of natural resources and public health.

Inside the EPA'S Superfund Report. Inside Washington Publishers, PO Box 7167, Ben Franklin Station, Washington, District of Columbia 20044. Biweekly. Liability for hazardous substances pollution and damages.

Management of World Wastes. Communication Channels, 6255 Barfield Road, Atlanta, Georgia 30328. (404) 256-9800. Monthly. Covers public and private waste operations.

Nuclear Waste News. Business Publishers, Inc., 951 Pershing Dr., Silver Spring, Maryland 20910-4464. (301) 587-6300. 1981-. Weekly. Covers up-to-the-minute information on radioactive wastes management. Includes facts on all aspects of radioactive wastes such as generation, packaging, transportation, processing, storage and disposal.

Pollution Equipment News. Rimbach Publishing, Inc., 8650 Babcock Boulevard, Pittsburgh, Pennsylvania 15237. (412) 364-5366. Bimonthly. Covers new products, techniques, and literature.

Report on Defense Plant Wastes. Business Publishers, Inc., 951 Pershing Dr., Silver Spring, Maryland 20910-4464. (301) 587-6300. 1989-. Biweekly. Reports on environmental laws, regulations, cleanups, contracts and court actions affecting U.S. defense weapons production, government hospitals and other government institutions. Also available online.

Sludge Newsletter. Business Publishers, Inc., 951 Pershing Dr., Silver Spring, Maryland 20910-4464. (301) 587-6300. 1976-. Biweekly. Reports on continuing changes at EPA, plus an array of new hazardous waste management and industrial pretreatment requirements that will affect municipal sludge.

State Environment Report: Toxic Substances & Hazardous Wastes. Business Publishers, Inc., 951 Pershing Drive, Silver Spring, Maryland 20910. (301) 587-6300. Weekly. Covers state legislative and regulatory initiatives.

Toxic Materials News. Business Publishers, Inc., 951 Pershing Dr., Silver Spring, Maryland 20910-4464. (301) 587-6300. 1974-. Weekly. Informs on regulations governing the manufacture, handling, transport, distribution and disposal of toxic chemicals and pesticides. Also available online.

Toxic Materials Transport. Business Publishers, Inc., 951 Pershing Dr., Silver Spring, Maryland 20910. (301) 587-6300. Biweekly. Covers new laws and regulations at federal, state and local levels.

RESEARCH CENTERS AND INSTITUTES

Boston University, Center for Energy and Environmental Studies. 675 Commonwealth Avenue, Boston, Massachusetts 02215. (617) 353-3083.

Environmental Research Institute for Hazardous Materials and Wastes. University of Connecticut, Rt. 44, Langley Bldg., Box U210, Storrs, Connecticut 06269-3210. (203) 486-4015.

New York State Center for Hazardous Waste Management. State University of New York at Buffalo, Jarvis Hall 207, Buffalo, New York 14260. (716) 636-3446.

Pennsylvania State University, Office of Hazardous and Toxic Waste Management. Environmental Resources Research Institute, University Park, Pennsylvania 16802. (814) 863-0291.

University of Michigan, Radiation Safety Service. North University Building, Room 1101, Ann Arbor, Michigan 48109-1057. (313) 764-4420.

University of Nevada-Las Vegas, Environmental Research Center. 4505 S. Maryland Parkway, Las Vegas, Nevada 89154-4009. (702) 739-3382.

STATISTICS SOURCES

Hazardous Waste. U.S. General Accounting Office. U.S. G.P.O., Washington, District of Columbia 20401. (202) 512-0000. 1989. Expenditures on and enforcement actions relating to clean-up.

Radioactive Material Released from Nuclear Power Plants. U.S. Nuclear Regulatory Commission. U.S. G.P.O., Washington, District of Columbia 20401. (202) 512-0000. Annual. Data on radioactive content of airborne and liquid effluents and solid wastes from nuclear power plants.

Report on Low-Level Radioactive Waste Management Progress. U.S. Dept. of Energy. Nuclear Energy Office. National Technical Information Service, 5285 Port Royal Road, Springfield, Virginia 22161. (703) 487-4650. Annual. Disposal of waste generated by nuclear power plants and non-utility sources by states.

TRADE ASSOCIATIONS AND PROFESSIONAL SOCIETIES

Air and Waste Management Association. Box 2861, Pittsburgh, Pennsylvania 15230. (412) 232-3444.

American Chemical Society. 1155 16th St., N.W., Washington, District of Columbia 20036. (202) 872-4600.

American College of Toxicology. 9650 Rockville Pike, Bethesda, Maryland 20814. (301) 571-1840.

American Institute of Biological Sciences. 730 11th St., N.W., Washington, District of Columbia 20001-4521. (202) 628-1500.

Association of State and Territorial Solid Waste Management Officials. 444 North Capitol St., N.W., Suite 388, Washington, District of Columbia 20001. (202) 624-5828.

Hazardous Waste Treatment Council. 1440 New York Ave., Suite 310, Washington, District of Columbia 20005. (202) 783-0870.

Illinois Hazardous Waste Research and Information Center. One East Hazelwood Dr., Champaign, Illinois 61820. (217) 333-8940.

INFORM. 381 Park Avenue S., New York, New York 10016. (212) 689-4040.

International Clearinghouse for Environmental Technologies. 12600 West Colfax Ave., Suite C-310, Lakewood, Colorado 80215. (303) 233-1248.

National Environmental Training Association. 2930 E. Camelback Rd., Phoenix, Arizona 85016. (602) 956-6099.

Nuclear Waste Project. 218 D St., S.E., Washington, District of Columbia 20003. (202) 544-2600.

Waste Systems Institute of Michigan, Inc. 400 Ann, N.W., Suite 204, Grand Rapids, Michigan 49504. (616) 363-3262.

HAZARDOUS WASTE SITES

See also: LANDFILLS; SANITARY LANDFILL; TRANSPORTATION OF HAZARDOUS MATERIALS

ABSTRACTING AND INDEXING SERVICES

Applied Science and Technology Index. H.W. Wilson Co., 950 University Ave., Bronx, New York 10452. (800) 367-6770. Formerly Industrial Arts Index.

Biological and Agricultural Index. H.W. Wilson Co., 950 University Ave., Bronx, New York 10452. (800) 367-6770. 1916-. Monthly.

Ecological Abstracts. Geo Abstracts Ltd. Elsevier Applied Science, Crown House, Linton Rd., Barking, England IG 11 8JU. 1974-. Derived from over 600 leading ecological and environmental journals, plus books, conference proceedings, reports and theses.

Environment Abstracts. Bowker A & I Publishing, 121 Chanlon Rd., New Providence, New Jersey 07974. (908) 464-6800. 1974-.

Environment Index. Environment Information Center, Index Research Department, 124 E. 39th St., New York, New York 10016. 1971-. Annual.

Environmental Information Connection–EIC. Planning Information Program, Dept. of Urban and Regional Planning, University of Illinois, 1003 West Nevada, Urbana, Illinois 61801. (217) 333-1369. Also available online.

Environmental Periodicals Bibliography. Environmental Studies Institute, International Academy at Santa Barbara, 800 Garden St., Suite D, Santa Barbara, California 93101. (805) 965-5010. Also available online.

BIBLIOGRAPHIES

EPA Publications Bibliography. U.S. Environmental Protection Agency, Library Systems Branch, 401 M St., SW, Washington, District of Columbia 20460. (202) 260-2090. Quarterly.

DIRECTORIES

Hazardous Waste Sites: Descriptions of Sites on Current National Priorities List. Office of Emergency and Remedial Response, U.S. Environmental Protection Agency, 401 M St., S.W., Washington, District of Columbia 20460. (202) 382-2090.

GENERAL WORKS

Characterization of Municipal Waste Combustor Ashes and Leachates from Municipal Solid Waste Landfills, Monofills, and Codisposal Sites. U.S. Environmental Protection Agency, Office of Solid Waste, 401 M St., S.W., Washington, District of Columbia 20460. (202) 260-2090. 1987.

Clean Sites Annual Report. Clean Sites, Inc., 1199 N. Fairfax St., Alexandria, Virginia 22314. (703) 683-8522.

Environmental Impacts of Hazardous Waste Treatment, Storage and Disposal Facilities. Rodolfo N. Salcedo, et al. Technomic Publishing Co., 851 New Holland Ave., Box 3535, Lancaster, Pennsylvania 17604. (717) 291-5609. 1989. Provides guidance in dealing with the many obstacles and preliminary requirements in siting TSD facilities.

Health Effects from Hazardous Waste Sites. Julian B. Andelman and Dwight W. Underhill. Lewis Publishers, 2000 Corporate Blvd., N.W., Boca Raton, Florida 33431. (407) 994-0555 or (800) 272-7737. 1987.

International Technologies for Hazardous Waste Site Cleanup. Thomas Nunno, et al. Noyes Publications, 120 Mill Rd., Park Ridge, New Jersey 07656. (201) 391-8484. 1990. Identifies 95 international technologies that could be utilized for hazardous waste site remediation within the United States.

HANDBOOKS AND MANUALS

Hazardous Waste Containment and Treatment. Paul N. Cheremisinoff. Gulf Publishing Co., Book Division, PO Box 2608, Houston, Texas 77252. (713) 529-4301. 1990. Environmental control technology relating to hazardous wastes and hazardous waste sites.

Resource Conservation and Recovery Act Handbook. ERT, Marketing Dept., 696 Virginia Road, Concord, Massachusetts 01742. Law relating to hazardous wastes and waste sites.

Resource Conservation and Recovery Act Inspection Manual. U.S. Environmental Protection Agency. Government Institutes, Inc., 4 Research Pl., Ste. 200, Rockville, Maryland 20850. (301) 921-2300. 1989.

Siting Hazardous Waste Treatment Facilities; the Nimby Syndrome. Kent E. Portney. Auburn House, 14 Dedham St., Dover, Massachusetts 02030-0658. (800) 223-2665. 1991. Advice to producers of hazardous waste on how to overcome people's reluctance to have it shipped into their neighborhood.

ONLINE DATA BASES

CERCLIS. Chemical Information Systems, Inc., 7215 York Rd., Baltimore, Maryland 21212. (301) 321-8440. Information on hazardous waste disposal sites that have either been listed by the EPA on the National Priority List (NPL) or nominated for consideration for the NPL.

Enviro/Energyline Abstracts Plus. R. R. Bowker Co., 121 Chanlon Rd., New Providence, New Jersey 07974. (908) 464-6800.

Environmental Periodicals Bibliography. National Information Services Corp., Ste. 6, Wyman Towers, 3100 St. Paul St., Baltimore, Maryland 21218. (410)243-0797. Online version of abstract of same name.

Hazardous Waste Site Data Base. U.S. Environmental Protection Agency, Environmental Monitoring Systems Lab, PO Box 93478, Las Vegas, Nevada 89193-3478. (702) 798-2525. Identifies a total of 944 chemical constituents for more than 5000 wells at over 350 hazardous waste sites nationwide.

Monthly Catalog of United States Government Publications. U.S. G.P.O., Supt. of Docs., PO Box 371954, Pittsburgh, Pennsylvania 15250-7954. (202) 512-0000.

National Technical Information Service. U.S. Department of Commerce, National Technical Information Service, Office of Data Base Services, 5285 Port Royal Rd., Springfield, Virginia 22161. (703) 487-4807. Bibliographic database of government sponsored research and technical reports.

PressNet Environmental Reports. Chemical Information Systems, Inc., 7215 York Rd., Baltimore, Maryland 21212. (301) 321-8440.

SCISEARCH. Institute for Scientific Information, University City Science Center, 3501 Market St., Philadelphia, Pennsylvania 19104. (215) 386-0100.

STATISTICS SOURCES

The Market for Hazardous Waste Site Remediation Services. FIND/SVP, 625 Avenue of the Americas, New York, New York 10011. (212) 645-4500. 1991/92. Market for hazardous waste site remediation equipment and services. These include biological, thermal, and physical techniques as well as solidification/vitrification.

TRADE ASSOCIATIONS AND PROFESSIONAL SOCIETIES

Clean Sites, Inc. 1199 N. Fairfax St., Alexandria, Virginia 22314. (703) 683-8522.

Concerned Neighbor in Action. P.O. Box 3847, Riverside, California 92519.

HAZARDOUS WASTES
See also: RADIOACTIVE WASTES

ABSTRACTING AND INDEXING SERVICES

Applied Science and Technology Index. H.W. Wilson Co., 950 University Ave., Bronx, New York 10452. (800) 367-6770. Formerly Industrial Arts Index.

Biological Abstracts. BIOSIS, 2100 Arch St., Philadelphia, Pennsylvania 19103-1399. (215) 587-4800. 1927-.

Biological and Agricultural Index. H.W. Wilson Co., 950 University Ave., Bronx, New York 10452. (800) 367-6770. 1916-. Monthly.

Bulletin Signaletique: Eau et Assainissement, Pollution Atmospherique, Droit des Pollutions. Centre de Documentation, Centre National de la Recherche Scientifique, 15, quai Anatole France, Paris, France 75700. (1) 45 55 92 25. 1983-. Monthly. Indexes pollution periodicals including water, atmospheric and related pollutions.

Chemical Abstracts. Chemical Abstracts Service, 2540 Olentangy River Rd., PO Box 3012, Columbus, Ohio 43210. (800) 848-6533. 1907-.

Environment Abstracts. Bowker A & I Publishing, 121 Chanlon Rd., New Providence, New Jersey 07974. (908) 464-6800. 1974-.

Environment Index. Environment Information Center, Index Research Department, 124 E. 39th St., New York, New York 10016. 1971-. Annual.

Environmental Information Connection–EIC. Planning Information Program, Dept. of Urban and Regional Planning, University of Illinois, 1003 West Nevada, Urbana, Illinois 61801. (217) 333-1369. Also available online.

Environmental Periodicals Bibliography. Environmental Studies Institute, International Academy at Santa Barbara, 800 Garden St., Suite D, Santa Barbara, California 93101. (805) 965-5010. Also available online.

General Science Index. H. W. Wilson Co., 950 University Ave., Bronx, New York 10452. 1978-. Monthly, also issued in annual cumulation. Cumulative subject index to English language periodicals in the subject fields of astronomy, botany, chemistry, earth science, environment and conservation, food and nutrition, genetics, mathematics, medicine and health, microbiology, oceanography, physics, physiology and zoology.

Geographical Abstracts. London School of Economics, Dept. of Geography, Regency House, 34 Duke St., London, England 1966-. Continued by Geo Abstracts issued in 6 parts: Pt. A. Landforms and the quaternary; Pt. B. Biogeography and Climatology; Pt. C. Economic geography; Pt. D. Social geography and cartography; Pt. E. Sedimentology; Pt. F. Regional and community planning.

Index to Scientific Book Contents. Institute for Scientific Information, 3501 Market St., Philadelphia, Pennsylvania 19104. (800) 523-1857. 1985-. Annual. Gives contents of science books published.

Pollution Abstracts. Cambridge Scientific Abstracts, 5161 River Rd., Bethesda, Maryland 20816. (301) 961-6750. Six/year. Indexes worldwide technical literature on envi-

ronmental pollution. Covers air pollution, marine and freshwater pollution, sewage and wastewater treatment, waste management, toxicology and health, noise pollution, radiation, land pollution, and environmental policies, programs, legislation, and education. Also available online.

Science Citation Index. Institute for Scientific Information, 3501 Market St., Philadelphia, Pennsylvania 19104. 1961-.

ALMANACS AND YEARBOOKS

Environmental Almanac. World Resources Institute. Houghton Mifflin, 1 Beacon St., Boston, Massachusetts 02108. (617) 725-5000; (800) 225-3362. 1991. Covers consumer products, energy, endangered species, food safety, global warming, solid wastes, toxics, wetlands and other related areas. Also included are the names and addresses of the chief environmental executives for all 50 states.

BIBLIOGRAPHIES

Biodegradation of Toxic Wastes: Citations from the Energy Database. National Technical Information Service, 5285 Port Royal Road, Springfield, Virginia 22161. (703) 487-4650. 1990.

A Catalog of Hazardous and Solid Waste Publications. U.S. Environmental Protection Agency, 401 M St., S.W., Washington, District of Columbia 20460. (202) 260-2090. 1990. Covers hazardous wastes, refuse, and refuse disposal.

Chemical Plant Wastes: A Bibliography. Vance Bibliographies, PO Box 229, 112 N. Charter St., Monticello, Illinois 61856. (217) 762-3831.

EPA Publications Bibliography. U.S. Environmental Protection Agency, Library Systems Branch, 401 M St., SW, Washington, District of Columbia 20460. (202) 260-2090. Quarterly.

Hazardous Waste Bibliography. National Institute for Occupational Safety and Health, Washington, District of Columbia 1989.

Hazardous Waste Minimization Bibliography. Waste Programs Planning Section, Office of Waste Programs, Arizona Dept. of Environmental Quality, 3033 N. Central, Phoenix, Arizona 85012. (602) 207-2381. 1990.

Radioactive Waste as a Social and Political Issue: A Bibliography. Frederick Frankena. AMS Press, 56 E. 13th St., New York, New York 10003. (212) 777-4700. 1991.

DIRECTORIES

Directory of Chemical Waste Transporters. Chemical Waste Transport Institute. National Solid Waste Management Association, 1730 Rhode Island Ave. N.W., Suite 1000, Washington, District of Columbia 20036. (202) 659-4613. 1989.

Environmental Politics and Policy. Congressional Quarterly, Inc., 1414 22nd St., N.W., Washington, District of Columbia 20037. (202) 887-8500.

Gale Environmental Sourcebook. Karen Hill. Gale Research Co., 835 Penobscot Bldg., Detroit, Michigan 48226-4094. (313) 961-2242. Contacts, information sources, or general information on environmental topics.

Hazardous Materials Advisory Council–Directory. Hazardous Materials Advisory Council, 1110 Vermont Ave., N.W., Suite 250, Washington, District of Columbia 20005. (202) 728-1460.

Hazardous Materials Control Directory. Hazardous Materials Control Research Institute, 9300 Columbia Blvd., Silver Spring, Maryland 20910. (301) 587-9390.

Hazardous Waste Consultant–Directory of Commercial Hazardous Waste Management Facilities Issue. McCoy and Associates, Inc., 13701 W. Jewel Ave., No. 252, Lakewood, Colorado 80228. (303) 987-0333.

Hazardous Waste Services Directory: Transporters, Disposal Sites, Laboratories, Consultants, and Specialized Services. George McDowell. J. J. Keller & Associates, Inc., 3003 W. Breezewood, PO Box 368, Neenah, Wisconsin 54957-0368. (414) 722-2848. Semiannual. Guide to various services available in the field of hazardous waste.

ENCYCLOPEDIAS AND DICTIONARIES

Encyclopedia of Environmental Control Technology. Paul N. Cheremisinoff, ed. Gulf Publishing Co., Book Division, PO Box 2608, Houston, Texas 77252. (713) 529-4301 or (800) 231-6275. 1992. Volume 1: Thermal Treatment of Hazardous Wastes; volume 2: Air Pollution Control; volume 3: Wastewater Treatment Technology; volume 4: Hazardous Waste Containment and Treatment; volumes 5 through 8 in progress. Provides in-depth coverage of specialized topics related to environmental and industrial pollution control problems and state-of-the-art information on technology and research as well as projections of future trends in the field.

Hazardous Chemicals Desk Reference. Richard J. Lewis. Van Nostrand Reinhold, 115 Fifth Ave., New York, New York 10003. (212) 254-3232. 1991. Information on the hazardous properties of some 5500 chemicals commonly encountered in industry, laboratories, environment, and the workplace.

McGraw-Hill Encyclopedia of Environmental Science. Sybil P. Parker. McGraw-Hill Science & Engineering Books, 11 W. 19th St., New York, New York 10011. (212) 337-6010. 1980. Covers ecology, man's influence on nature, and environmental protection.

Van Nostrand's Scientific Encyclopedia. Glenn D. Considine, ed. Van Nostrand Reinhold, 115 5th Ave., New York, New York 10003. (212) 254-3232. 1983. Sixth edition. Includes all broad subject areas in science.

GENERAL WORKS

Analyses of Hazardous Substances in Air. A. Kettrup, ed. VCH Publishers, 303 NW 12th Ave., Deerfield Beach, Florida 33442-1788. (305) 428-5566. 1991. Proceedings from the Commission for the Investigation of Health Hazards of Chemical Compounds in the Work Area. Included are 16 analytical methods for determining organic compounds and heavy metals in the air of work areas by high pressure liquid chromatography, gas chromatography, infrared spectroscopy and atomic absorption spectrometry.

Analyses of Hazardous Substances in Biological Materials. J. Angere, ed. VCH Publishers, 303 NW 12th Ave., Deerfield Beach, Florida 33442-1788. (305) 428-5566.

1991. Discusses industrial hygiene and the various toxic substances involved.

Biotechnology Application in Hazardous Waste Treatment. Gordon Lewandowski. Engineering Foundation, 345 E. 47th St., New York, New York 10017. (212) 705-7835. 1989. Trends in hazardous waste treatment using biotechnological methods.

Chemical Contamination and Its Victims: Medical Remedies, Legal Redress, and Public Policy. David W. Schnare, ed. Greenwood Publishing Group, Inc., 88 Post Rd., W., Box 5007, Westport, Connecticut 06881. (203) 226-3571. 1989. Covers toxicology, hazardous waste, and liability for hazardous substances pollution damages.

Chemical, Physical, and Biological Properties of Compounds Present at Hazardous Waste Sites: Final Report. U.S. Environmental Protection Agency. Clement Associates Inc., Arlington, Virginia 1985.

Cutting Chemical Wastes. David J. Sarokin, et al. INFORM, 381 Park Ave. S., New York, New York 10016. (212) 689-4040. 1985. Describes the activities of 29 organic chemical plants that are trying to reduce hazardous chemical wastes.

Detection of Subsurface Hazardous Waste Containers by Nondestructive Techniques. Arthur E. Lord and Robert M. Koerner. Noyes Publications, 120 Mill Rd., Park Ridge, New Jersey 07656. (201) 391-8484. 1990. Describes a study undertaken to identify and assess the best possible NDT techniques for detecting and delineating hazardous waste, particularly in steel and plastic containers buried beneath soil or water.

Drinking Water Hazards: How to Know If There Are Toxic Chemicals in Your Water and What to Do If There Are. John Cary Stewart. Envirographics, PO Box 334, Hiram, Ohio 44234. (216) 527-5207. 1990. Documents the increase of cancer and other diseases that may be environmentally induced. Discusses the increases in the use of synthetic organic chemicals, and covers each group of drinking water contaminants in some detail: inorganic chemicals, heavy metals, bacteria and viruses, radionuclides, nitrates, and organic chemicals, including pesticides.

Emerging Technologies in Hazardous Waste Management. D. William Tedder and Frederick G. Pohland, eds. American Chemical Society, 1155 16th St. N.W., Washington, District of Columbia 20036. (202) 872-4600; (800) 227-5558. 1990. Hazardous waste management technology.

Emerging Technologies in Hazardous Waste Management II. D. William Tedder and Frederick G. Pohland, eds. American Chemical Society, 1155 16th St. N.W., Washington, District of Columbia 20036. (202) 872-4600; (800) 227-5558. 1991. Developed from a symposium sponsored by the Division of Industrial and Engineering Chemistry, Inc. of the American Chemical Society at the Industrial and Engineering Chemistry Special Symposium, Atlantic City, NJ, June 4-7, 1990.

The Environment: Problems and Solutions. Stuart Bruchey, ed. Garland Publishing, Inc., 1000A Sherman Ave., Hamden, Connecticut 06514. (203) 281-4487. 1991. Topics covered: forested wetlands and agriculture, the political economy of smog in southern California, environmental limits to growth in world agriculture, the tradeoff between cost and risk in hazardous waste

management, and the protection of groundwater from agricultural pollution.

Environmental Impacts of Hazardous Waste Treatment, Storage and Disposal Facilities. Rodolfo N. Salcedo, et al. Technomic Publishing Co., 851 New Holland Ave., Box 3535, Lancaster, Pennsylvania 17604. (717) 291-5609. 1989. Provides guidance in dealing with the many obstacles and preliminary requirements in siting TSD facilities.

Environmentally Acceptable Incineration of Chlorinated Chemical Waste. Martin A. de Zeeuw. Coronet Books, 311 Bainbridge St., Philadelphia, Pennsylvania 19147. (215) 925-2762. 1987.

Federal Regulation of Hazardous Wastes: A Guide to RCRA. John Quarles. Environmental Law Institute, 1616 P St., NW, Suite 200, Washington, District of Columbia 20036. (202) 328-5150. 1982. Law and legislation in connection with hazardous wastes.

Hazardous and Industrial Wastes, 1990. Joseph P. Martin, et al., eds. Technomic Publishing Co., 851 Holland Ave., Box 3535, Lancaster, Pennsylvania 17604. (717) 291-5609. 1990. Proceedings of the 22nd Mid-Atlantic Industrial Waste Conference, June 24-27, 1990, Drexel University, Philadelphia, PA. Fifty-one new reports on developments in industrial and hazardouswaste management, technology and regulation were presented.

Hazardous and Industrial Wastes, 1991. Technomic Publishing Co., 851 New Holland Ave., Box 3535, Lancaster, Pennsylvania 17604. (717) 291-5609. 1991. Proceedings of the 23rd Mid-Atlantic Industrial Waste Conference held at Drexel University, 1991.

Hazardous Substances Resource Guide. Richard Pohanish, Stanley Greene. Gale Research Inc., 835 Penobscot Bldg., Detroit, Michigan 48226-4094. (313) 961-2242. 1993.

Hazardous Waste: Efforts to Address Problems at Federal Prisons. U.S. General Accounting Office, 441 G St., NW, Washington, District of Columbia 20548. (202) 275-5067. 1990.

Hazardous Waste Land Treatment. Municipal Environmental Research Laboratory, Office of Research and Development, U.S. Environmental Protection Agency, 26 W. Martin Luther King Dr., Cincinnati, Ohio 45268. (513) 569-7931. 1983. Covers hazardous wastes, sanitary landfills and waste disposal in the ground.

Hazardous Waste Law and Practice. John-Mark Stensvaag. John Wiley & Sons, Inc., 605 3rd Ave., New York, New York 10158-0012. (212) 850-6000. 1986-1989. 2 vols. Discusses the intricacies of defining hazardous wastes and shows potentially regulated entities how to make that determination. Guides the user through the listed hazardous wastes under the EPA's Subtitle C, discussing commercial chemical products, specific and nonspecific source wastes, derivative wastes, delisted wastes, and exclusions.

Hazardous Waste Laws, Regulations, and Taxes for the U.S. Petroleum Refining Industry: An Overview. David E. Fenster. PennWell Books, PO Box 21288, Tulsa, Oklahoma 74121. (918) 831-9421; (800) 752-9764. 1990. Describes the impact of hazardous waste legislation on the petroleum refining industry.

Hazardous Waste Management. S. Maltezou, et al., eds. Cassell PLC, Publishers Distribution Center, PO Box

C831, Rutherford, New Jersey 07070. (201) 939-6064; (201) 939-6065. 1989.

Hazardous Waste Management Engineering. Edward J. Martin and James H. Johnson. PennWell Books, PO Box 21288, Tulsa, Oklahoma 74121. (918) 831-9421; (800) 752-9764. 1986. Covers the basic principles and applications of the most current hazardous waste technologies. Provides a wealth of data and techniques that can be immediately applied to analyzing, designing and developing effective hazardous waste management solutions.

Hazardous Waste Management: New Regulation and New Technology. Brian Price. Financial Times Bus. Info. Ltd., 50-64 Broadway, 7th Fl., London, England 071-799 2002. 1990.

Hazardous Waste Management: Recent Changes and Policy Alternatives. Daniel Carol. Congress of the United States, Congressional Budget Office, c/o U.S. Government Printing Office, N. Capitol & H Sts. NW, Washington, District of Columbia 20401. (202) 512-0000. 1985. Describes the economic aspects of hazardous wastes. Also includes the law and legislation in the United States regarding hazardous wastes aa well as government policy.

Hazardous Waste Management: Reducing the Risk. Council on Economic Priorities. Island Press, 1718 Connecticut Ave. N.W., Suite 300, Washington, District of Columbia 20009. (202) 232-7933. 1986. Includes information for regulatory agencies, waste generators, host communities, and public officials. Topics include compliance, liabilities, technologies, corporate and public relations, groundwater monitoring, key laws and recommendations.

Hazardous Waste Measurements. Milagros S. Simmons, ed. Lewis Publishers, 200 Corporate Blvd. NW, Boca Raton, Florida 33431. (407) 994-0555 or (800)272-7737. 1991. Focuses on recent developments in field testing methods and quality assurance.

Hazardous Waste Minimization Assessment, Fort Carson, CO. Seshasayi Dharmavaram, et al. National Technical Information Service, 5285 Port Royal Rd., Springfield, Virginia 22161. (703) 487-4650. 1991.

Hazardous Waste Minimization Assessment, Fort Meade, MD. Seshasayi Dharmavaram and Bernard A. Donahue. National Technical Information Service, 5285 Port Royal Rd., Springfield, Virginia 22161. (703) 487-4650. 1991.

Hazardous Waste Minimization Audit Studies on the Paint Manufacturing Industry. Jacobs Engineering Group, Inc., S. Lake Ave., Pasadena, California 91171. (818)449-2171. 1987. Factory and trade wastes and disposal in the paint industry.

Hazardous Waste Regulatory Guide: State Waste Management Programs. J. J. Keller & Associates, Inc., 3003 W. Breezewood, PO Box 368, Neenah, Wisconsin 54957-0368. (414) 722-2848. 1992. State by state guide to laws relating to hazardous wastes.

The Hazardous Waste System. U.S. Environmental Protection Agency, Office of Solid Waste and Emergency Response, 401 M St., SW April 9, 1992, Washington, District of Columbia 20460. (202) 382-4610. 1987. Hazardous wastes law and legislation in the United States.

Hazardous Wastes and Hazardous Materials. Hazardous Materials Control Research Institute, 9300 Columbia

Blvd., Silver Spring, Maryland 20910. (301) 587-9390. 1987.

High Level Radioactive Waste Management. American Society of Civil Engineers, 345 E. 47th St., New York, New York 10017. (212) 705-7288; (800) 548-2723. 1991. Proceedings of International Topical Meeting hosted by the University of Nevada Las Vegas, April 8-12, 1990.

High Level Radioactive Waste Management. American Society of Civil Engineers, 345 E. 47th St., New York, New York 10017. (212) 705-7288; (800) 548-2723. 1992. Proceedings of the 2nd Annual International Conference, Las Vegas, Nevada, April 28-May 3, 1991.

How to Meet Requirements for Hazardous Waste Landfill Design, Construction and Closure. U. S. Environmental Protection Agency. Noyes Publications, 120 Mill Rd., Park Ridge, New Jersey 07656. (201) 391-8484. 1990. Outlines in detail the provisions of the minimum technology guidance regulations, and offers practical and detailed technology transfer information on the construction of hazardous waste facilities that comply with these requirements.

Incinerating Hazardous Wastes. Harry M. Freeman, ed. Technomic Publishing Co., 851 New Holland Ave., Box 3535, Lancaster, Pennsylvania 17604. (717) 291-5609. 1988. Book provides the essence of the thermal destruction research program at the EPA Lab in Cincinnati, Ohio. Highlights papers that have represented significant contributions to the field of incineration research. Provides a general overview of the role of incineration in the United States today.

Incineration for Site Cleanup and Destruction of Hazardous Wastes. Howard E. Hesketh. Technomic Publishing Co., 851 New Holland Ave., Box 3535, Lancaster, Pennsylvania 17604. (717) 291-5609; (800) 233-9936. 1990.

Infectious Waste Management. Frank L. Cross. Technomic Publishing Co., 851 New Holland Ave., Box 3535, Lancaster, Pennsylvania 17604. (717) 291-5609; (800) 233-9936. 1990.

Inside the Poison Trade. Coronet/MTI Film & Video, 108 Wilmot Rd., Deerfield, Illinois 60015. 1990. This video shows what the Greenpeace organization is doing to stop chemical waste export to Africa, as well as the efforts of other organizations.

Managing Environmental Risks. Air & Waste Management Association, PO Box 2861, Pittsburgh, Pennsylvania 15230. (412) 232-3444. 1990. Papers presented at the Air & Waste Management Association International Specialty Conference, held in October 1989 in Quebec City, contains topics such as risks related to hazardous waste sites, chemical contaminants, and biotechnology.

Managing Health Care Hazards. Linda F. Chaff. Labelmaster, 574 N. Pulaski Rd., Chicago, Illinois 60646. (312) 478-0900. 1988.

Municipal Solid Waste Incinerator Ash Management and Disposal Data Entries. The Institute, 2425 18th St., N.W., Washington, District of Columbia 20009. (202) 232-4108. Database on solid waste resources recovery and economic development, including municipal solid waste ash.

Physicochemical and Biological Detoxification of Hazardous Wastes. Yeun C. Wu, ed. Technomic Publishing Co., 851 New Holland Ave., Box 3535, Lancaster, Pennsylvania 17604. (717) 291-5609. 1989. 2 volume set. Proceedings of the International Conference of Physicochemical and Biological Detoxification of Hazardous Wastes, May 3-5, 1988, Atlantic City, NJ. Provides new information on a variety of established, new and in-development methods for treating a wide range of industrial and municipal hazardous wastes.

Preventing Pollution Through Technical Assistance: One State's Experience. Mark H. Dorfman, et al. INFORM Inc., 381 Park Ave. S., New York, New York 10016. (212) 689-4040. 1990. Examines the state of North Carolina's voluntary program aimed at assisting the industry in pollution prevention. It also includes a glossary, a bibliography of information sources and helpful statistical tables of data collected.

RCRA Compliance Implementation Guide. Mary P. Bauer and Elizabeth J. Kellar. Government Institutes, Inc., 4 Research Pl., Suite 200, Rockville, Maryland 20850. (301) 921-2300. 1990. Interprets how a particular situation fits into the whole compliance process. Step-by-step directions are given to satisfy the compliance program. Also included are copies of EPA reports, manifests and forms.

Risk Assessment of Groundwater Pollution Control. William F. McTernan and Edward Kaplan, eds. American Society of Civil Engineers, 345 E. 47th St., New York, New York 10017. (212) 705-7288; (800) 548-2723. 1990.

Scientific Basis for Nuclear Waste Management XII. Werner Lutze, ed. Materials Research Society, 9800 McKnight Rd., Pittsburgh, Pennsylvania 15237. (412) 367-3003. 1989. Symposium held in Berlin Germany October 1988. Volume 127 of the Materials Research society Symposium Proceedings.

Serious Reduction of Hazardous Waste: Summary. Congress of the U.S., c/o U.S. Government Printing Office, Office of Technology Assessment, N. Capitol & H Sts. NW, Washington, District of Columbia 20401. (202) 512-0000. 1986. Deals with waste reduction from factories and air pollution control.

Staying Out of Trouble: What You Should Know about the New Hazardous Waste Law. National Association of Manufacturers, 1331 Pennsylvania Ave., NW, Suite 1500 N., Washington, District of Columbia 20004. (202) 637-3000. 1985. Hazardous waste laws and legislation in the United States. Also covers refuse and disposal.

Supplier Notification Requirements. U.S. Environmental Protection Agency, Office of Pesticides and Toxic Substances, 401 M St., SW, Washington, District of Columbia 20460. (202) 260-2090. 1990. Legal aspects of reporting on chemicals and hazardous wastes.

Techniques for Hazardous Chemical and Waste Spill Control. L. Albert Weaver. L.A. Weaver, 308 E. Jones St., Raleigh, North Carolina 27601. 1983.

Transportation of Hazardous Materials: A Management Guide for Generators and Manufactuerers. William E. Kenworthy. Government Institutes, Inc., 4 Research Pl., Suite 200, Rockville, Maryland 20850. (301) 921-2300. 1989. A management guide for generators of hazardous waste. Covers of hazardous materials regulation, alternative shipping methods for generators, and useful approaches for achieving compliance.

Waste Minimization: Manufacturer's Strategies for Success. National Association of Manufacturers, 1331 Penn-

sylvania Ave., NW, Suite 1500 N., Washington, District of Columbia 20004. (202) 637-3000. 1989.

Waste Reduction: Policy and Practice. Waste Management Inc. and Piper & Marbury. Executive Enterprises Publications Co., Inc., 22 W. 21st St., New York, New York 10010-6990. (212) 645-7880. 1990. Examines waste reduction on a national level. Gives an overview of the makeup of hazardous waste and municipal solid waste streams and different means of reducing the generation of those streams. Case studies of waste reduction in industry are described.

Written Hazard Communication Program for Schools and Colleges. Forum for Scientific Excellence. J. B. Lippincott, 227 E. Washington Sq., Philadelphia, Pennsylvania 19105. (215) 238-4200; (800) 982-4377. 1989. Identifies all the requirements an educational institution must meet to ensure that its hazardous chemical compliance program is appropriate and adequate. Specific examples of written program requirements, MSDS format, hazard assessment criteria and communication vehicles and formats are included.

GOVERNMENTAL ORGANIZATIONS

U.S. Environmental Protection Agency: Assistant Administrator for Solid Waste and Emergency Response. 401 M St., S.W., Washington, District of Columbia 20460. (202) 382-4610.

U.S. Environmental Protection Agency: Office of Civil Enforcement. 401 M St., S.W., Washington, District of Columbia 20460. (202) 382-4544.

U.S. Environmental Protection Agency: Office of Environmental Engineering and Technology. 401 M St., S.W., Washington, District of Columbia 20460. (202) 382-2600.

U.S. Environmental Protection Agency: Office of Toxic Substances. 401 M St., S.W., Washington, District of Columbia 20460. (202) 382-3813.

HANDBOOKS AND MANUALS

The Complete Guide to Hazardous Waste Regulations. Travis P. Wagner. Global Professional Publications, 2805 McGraw Ave., PO Box 19539, Irvine, California 92713-9539. (800) 854-7179. A comprehensive, step-by-step guide to the regulation of hazardous wastes under RCRA, TSCA, HMTA, and Superfund.

Dangerous Properties of Industrial Materials. Irving Newton Sax. Van Nostrand Reinhold, 115 5th Ave., New York, New York 10003. (212) 254-3232. 1989. 7th ed. Deals with hazardous substances and chemically induced occupational diseases.

Environmental Management Handbook: Toxic Chemical Materials and Waste. Leopold C. Kokoszka. Marcel Dekker, Inc., 270 Madison Ave., New York, New York 10016. (212) 696-9000; (800) 228-1160. 1989.

EPA's Handbook Responding to Sinking Hazardous Substances. Pudvan Publishing Co., Inc., 1935 Shermer Rd., Northbrook, Illinois 60062. (312) 498-9840. 1988. Prepared by the U.S. Environmental Protection Agency and the United States Coast Guard.

Final Covers on Hazardous Waste Landfills and Surface Impoundments. Office of Solid Waste and Emergency Response, U.S. Environment Protection Agency, U.S.

G.P.O., Washington, District of Columbia 20402-9325. (202) 783-3238. 1989. Technical Guidance Document series EPA/530-SW-89-047. Shipping list no. 89-483-P.

The Generator's Guide to Hazardous Materials/Waste Management. Leo H. Traverse. Van Nostrand Reinhold, 115 5th Ave., New York, New York 10003. (212) 254-3232. 1991. Comprehensive information source for hazardous waste and hazardous materials management.

The Global Ecology Handbook: What You Can Do about the Environmental Crisis. Walter H. Corson, ed. The Global Tomorrow Coalition, Beacon Pr., 25 Beacon St., Boston, Massachusetts 02108-2800. (617) 742-2110. 1990. Covers environment, energy policy, population growth and other issues. It includes chapters on tropical rain forests, garbage, oceans and coasts, global warming, population growth, agriculture, biological diversity, fresh water, hazardous wastes, and environment and development.

Guide to Hazardous Products Around the Home: A Personal Action Manual for Protecting Your Health and Environment. Household Hazardous Waste Project, 901 S. National Ave., Box 87, Springfield, Missouri 65804. 1989. Covers hazardous substances, safety measures, home accidents, and prevention.

Guide to the Management of Hazardous Waste: A Handbook for the Businessman and the Concerned Citizen. J. William Haun. Fulcrum Publishing, 350 Indiana St., Ste. 350, Golden, Colorado 80401. (303) 277-1623. 1991. Fact book on hazardous waste management, including factory and trade waste, and hazardous waste law and legislation in the United States.

A Guide to the Safe Handling of Hazardous Materials Accidents. ASTM, 1916 Race St., Philadelphia, Pennsylvania 19103-1187. (215) 299-5400. 1990. 2d ed. Planning and training document to assure the safest, most effective handling of a hazardous material accident.

Handbook: Responding to Discharges of Sinking Hazardous Substances. K. R. Boyer. National Technical Information Service, 5285 Port Royal Rd., Springfield, Virginia 22161. (703) 487-4650. 1987.

Hazardous Waste Audit Program: A Regulatory & Safety Compliance System: Evaluation Guidelines, Monitoring Procedures, Checklists, Forms. J. J. Keller & Associates, Inc., 3003 W. Breezewood, PO Box 368, Neenah, Wisconsin 54957-0368. (414) 722-2848. 1986.

Hazardous Waste Containment and Treatment. Paul N. Cheremisnoff. Gulf Publishing Co., Book Division, PO Box 2608, Houston, Texas 77252. (713) 529-4301. 1990. Environmental control technology relating to hazardous wastes and hazardous waste sites.

Hazardous Waste Identification and Classification Manual. Travis P. Wagner. Global Professional Publications, 2805 McGraw Ave., PO Box 19539, Irvine, California 92713-9539. (800) 854-7179.

Hazardous Waste Incineration Calculations. Joseph P. Reynolds. John Wiley & Sons, Inc., 605 3rd Ave., New York, New York 10158-0012. (212) 850-6000. 1991.

Hazardous Waste Management. H. M. Freeman. Global Professional Publications, 2805 McGraw Ave., PO Box 19539, Irvine, California 92713-9539. (800) 854-7179.

Hazardous Waste Management Guide. California Safety Council, Sacramento, California 1988. Covers California law and legislation relating to hazardous wastes.

Hazardous Waste Minimization Handbook. Thomas E. Higgins, et al. Lewis Publishers, 2000 Corporate Blvd., Boca Raton, Florida 33431. (407) 994-0555 or (800) 272-7737. 1989. Describes how to make changes in waste handling, manufacturing, and purchasing to reduce costs and liabilities of waste disposal.

Hazardous Waste Minimization Manual for Small Quantity Generators. Center for Hazardous Materials Research, University of Pittsburgh, 320 William Pitt Way, Pittsburgh, Pennsylvania 15238. (412) 826-5320. 1989. Recycling of hazardous waste and its legal aspects.

Industrial and Hazardous Waste Treatment. Nelson Leonard Nemerow and Avijit Dasgupta. Van Nostrand Reinhold, 115 5th Ave., New York, New York 10003. (212) 254-3232. 1991. Factory and trade waste, and hazardous waste purification.

Managing Industrial Hazardous Waste–Practical Handbook. Gary F. Lindgren. Lewis Publishers, 2000 Corporate Blvd., N.W., Boca Raton, Florida 33431. (407) 994-0555 or (800) 272-7737. 1989. Explains the regulations regarding identification and listing of hazardous wastes.

Medical Waste Incineration Handbook. C. C. Lee. Government Institutes, Inc., 4 Research Pl., Suite 200, Rockville, Maryland 20850. (301) 921-2300. 1990. Covers incineration, equipment, measurement techniques, potential emissions, maintenance, safety guidance, operational problems and solutions, and the federal and state regulatory framework. Includes a list of addresses and phone numbers of manufacturers of medical waste incinerators and manufacturers of air pollution control equipment.

Preparing for Emergency Planning. National Association of Manufacturers, 1331 Pennsylvania Ave., NW, Suite 1500 N., Washington, District of Columbia 20004. (202) 637-3000. 1987. Explains the Emergency Planning and Community Right-to-Know Act under the Superfund Law.

RCRA Hazardous Wastes Handbook. Crowell & Moring. Government Institutes, Inc., 4 Research Place, Suite 200, Rockville, Maryland 20850. (301) 921-2300. 1989. 8th ed. Analyzes the impact of the Resource Conservation and Recovery Act on the business, while incorporating the most recent regulatory changes to the RCRA. These include the final 1988 underground storage tank rules, the medical waste regulations, permit modification regulations, amendments regarding corrective action and closures, the exemption for "treatability tests," waste export rules, etc. Includes the complete test of the RCRA statute as currently amended.

Resource Conservation and Recovery Act Handbook. ERT, Marketing Dept., 696 Virginia Road, Concord, Massachusetts 01742. Law relating to hazardous wastes and waste sites.

Resource Conservation and Recovery Act Inspection Manual. U.S. Environmental Protection Agency. Government Institutes, Inc., 4 Research Pl., Ste. 200, Rockville, Maryland 20850. (301) 921-2300. 1989.

Siting Hazardous Waste Treatment Facilities; the Nimby Syndrome. Kent E. Portney. Auburn House, 14 Dedham St., Dover, Massachusetts 02030-0658. (800) 223-2665. 1991. Advice to producers of hazardous waste on how to overcome people's reluctance to have it shipped into their neighborhood.

Standard Handbook of Environmental Engineering. Robert A. Corbitt. McGraw-Hill, 1221 Ave. of the Americas, New York, New York 10020. (212) 512-2000 or (800) 262-4729. 1990. Hands-on reference to understand environmental engineering technology. Covers air quality control, water supply, wastewater disposal, waste management, stormwater and hazardous wastes.

Standard Handbook of Hazardous Waste Treatment and Disposal. Harry M. Freeman, ed. McGraw-Hill Science & Engineering Books, 11 West 19th St., New York, New York 10011. (212) 337-6010. 1989. A reference of alternatives and innovative technologies for managing hazardous waste and cleaning up abandoned disposal sites.

Superfund Manual: Legal and Management Strategies. Crowell & Moring. Government Institutes, Inc., 4 Research Pl., Suite 200, Rockville, Maryland 20850. (301) 921-2300. 1990. 4th ed. Industrial liability for hazardous waste and pollution damage at hazardous waste sites are explained. Explains the latest developments in the Superfund program. Includes the interrelationships between Superfund and RCRA; new regulations to implement Emergency Planning and the Community Right-to-Know Act; revisions to the National Contingency Plan; new EPA guidance documents relating to cleanup standards, site studies, and settlement procedures; court decisions and the special problems.

Waste Minimization Opportunity Assessment Manual. Government Institutes, Inc., 4 Research Pl., Ste. 200, Rockville, Maryland 20850. (301) 921-2300. 1988. Deals with managing hazardous waste and its minimization.

ONLINE DATA BASES

Air/Water Pollution Report. NewsNet, Inc., 945 Haverford Rd., Bryn Mawr, Pennsylvania 19010. (800) 345-1301. Online version of periodical of same name.

ANEUPLOIDY. Oak Ridge National Laboratory, Environmental Mutagen Information Center, Building 2001, P.O. Box 2008, Oak Ridge, Tennessee 37831-6050. (615) 574-7871.

BIOSIS Previews. BIOSIS, 2100 Arch St., Philadelphia, Pennsylvania 19103-1399. (215) 587-4800. Largest and most comprehensive database of research in the life sciences. Contains citations for nearly 9000 primary research journals, monographs, reviews, symposia, preliminary reports, semi-popular journals, selected institutional reports, government reports and research communications.

BNA Toxics Law Daily. Bureau of National Affairs, BNA PLUS, 1231 25th St., N.W., Rm. 215, Washington, District of Columbia 20037. (800) 454-7773.

CERCLIS. Chemical Information Systems, Inc., 7215 York Rd., Baltimore, Maryland 21212. (301) 321-8440. Information on hazardous waste disposal sites that have either been listed by the EPA on the National Priority List (NPL) or nominated for consideration for the NPL.

Chemical Abstracts-CA. Chemical Abstracts Service, 2540 Olentangy River Rd., P.O. Box 3012, Columbus, Ohio 43210. (800) 848-6533 or (614) 421-3600. Information sources include 9000 journals, patents from 27 countries, two industrial property organizations, new

books, conference proceedings, and government research reports.

Enviro/Energyline Abstracts Plus. R. R. Bowker Co., 121 Chanlon Rd., New Providence, New Jersey 07974. (908) 464-6800.

Environmental Periodicals Bibliography. National Information Services Corp., Ste. 6, Wyman Towers, 3100 St. Paul St., Baltimore, Maryland 21218. (410)243-0797. Online version of abstract of same name.

ETICBACK: Environmental Teratology Information Center Backfile. Oak Ridge National Laboratory, Environmental Teratology Information Center, Building 2001, P.O. Box 2008, Oak Ridge, Tennessee 37831-6050. (615) 574-7871.

HADB. National Library of Medicine, Toxicology Information Program, 8600 Rockville Pike, Bethesda, Maryland 20894. (800) 638-8480.

Hazardous Waste Database. U.S. Environmental Protection Agency, Office of Administration and Resources Management, 401 M St., S.W., Washington, District of Columbia 20460. (202) 260-2090. Hazardous waste directives, treatment and disposal of hazardous waste, and its storage.

Hazardous Waste News. Business Publishers, Inc., 951 Pershing Dr., Silver Spring, Maryland 20910-4464. (301) 587-6300. Online access to legislative, regulatory, and judicial decisions at the federal and state levels relating to the field of hazardous waste management. Online version of the periodical of the same name.

HAZINF. University of Alberta, Department of Chemistry, Edmonton, Alberta, Canada T6G 2G2. (403) 432-3254.

Monthly Catalog of United States Government Publications. U.S. G.P.O., Supt. of Docs., PO Box 371954, Pittsburgh, Pennsylvania 15250-7954. (202) 512-0000.

National Technical Information Service. U.S. Department of Commerce, National Technical Information Service, Office of Data Base Services, 5285 Port Royal Rd., Springfield, Virginia 22161. (703) 487-4807. Bibliographic database of government sponsored research and technical reports.

Nuclear Waste News–Online. Business Publishers, Inc., 951 Pershing Dr., Silver Spring, Maryland 20910-4464. (301) 587-6300. Federal and legislation regulation and research and development activities concerning the generation, packaging, transportation, processing, and disposal of nuclear wastes.

OHM-TADS (Oil and Hazardous Materials-Technical Assistance Data System). U.S. Environmental Protection Agency, Emergency Response Division, 410 M St., S.W., Washington, District of Columbia 20460. (800) 479-2449.

PressNet Environmental Reports. Chemical Information Systems, Inc., 7215 York Rd., Baltimore, Maryland 21212. (301) 321-8440.

Report on Defense Plant Wastes. Business Publishers, Inc., 951 Pershing Dr., Silver Spring, Maryland 20910-4464. (301) 587-6300. Laws, regulations, cleanup actions, contracts, and court actions affecting U.S. defense, weapons production, government hospitals and laboratories, and other government institutions. Online version of periodical of the same name.

SCISEARCH. Institute for Scientific Information, University City Science Center, 3501 Market St., Philadelphia, Pennsylvania 19104. (215) 386-0100.

TOXALL. National Library of Medicine, Specialized Information Services Division, 8600 Rockville Pike, Bethesda, Maryland 20894. (301) 496-6531.

Toxic Materials News. Business Publishers, Inc., 951 Pershing Dr., Silver Spring, Maryland 20910-4464. (301) 587-6300. Legislation, regulations, and litigation concerning toxic substances. Online version of periodical of the same name.

TOXLIT. National Library of Medicine, Toxicology Information Program, 8600 Rockville Pike, Bethesda, Maryland 20894. (800) 638-8480.

TSCA Chemical Substances Inventory. U.S. Environmental Protection Agency, Office of Pesticides and Toxic Substances, 401 M St., S.W., Washington, District of Columbia 20460. (202) 260-2090.

TSCATS. U.S. Environmental Protection Agency, Office of Pesticides and Toxic Substances, 401 M St., S.W., Washington, District of Columbia 20460. (202) 382-3524.

PERIODICALS AND NEWSLETTERS

Action Bulletin. Citizen's Clearing House for Hazardous Wastes, Box 926, Arlington, Virginia 22216. (703) 276-7070. 1982-. Quarterly. Environmental hazards and neighborhood organizations faced with toxic problems.

Annual Report of Abandoned or Uncontrolled Hazardous Waste Disposal Sites and Hazardous Waste Remedial Fund, 1990 Appendix. Iowa Dept. of Natural Resources. National Technical Information Service, 5285 Port Royal Rd., Springfield, Virginia 22161. (703) 487-4650. 1991. Annual.

Annual Report on Abandonment or Uncontrolled Hazardous Waste Disposal Sites and Hazardous Waste Remedial Fund. Iowa Dept. of Natural Resources. National Technical Information Service, 5285 Port Royal Rd., Springfield, Virginia 22161. (703) 487-4650. Annual.

Asbestos Control Report. Business Publishers, Inc., 951 Pershing Drive, Silver Spring, Maryland 20910-4464. (301) 587-6300. Biweekly. Information on asbestos control techniques, research, and regulations. Also available online.

Chemical & Radiation Waste Litigation Reporter. Chemical & Radiation Waste Litigation Reporter, Inc., 1980-. Monthly.

Dangerous Properties of Industrial Materials Report. Van Nostrand Reinhold, 115 5th Avenue, New York, New York 10003. (212) 254-3232. Bimonthly. Chemical and environmental review of hazardous industrial materials.

Environment Week. King Communications Group, Inc., 627 National Press Bldg., Washington, District of Columbia 20045. (202) 638-4260. Weekly. Covers acid rain, solid waste and disposal, clean coal, nuclear and hazardous waste. Also available online.

Environmental Action. Environmental Action Foundation, 6930 Carroll Ave., Ste. 600, Takoma Park, Maryland 20912. (301) 891-1100. Bimonthly. Impact of humans and industry on the environment.

Environmental Liability Monitor. Business Publishers, Inc., 951 Pershing Dr., Silver Spring, Maryland 20910-4464. (301) 587-6300. 1990-. Monthly. Reports about environmental liability in all areas.

Flashpoint. National Association of Solvent Recyclers, 1333 New Hampshire Ave., N.W., No. 1100, Washington, District of Columbia 20036. (202) 463-6956. Biweekly. Overview of recycling hazardous waste fuel blending & related industries.

Focus. Hazardous Materials Control Research Institute, 9300 Columbia Blvd, Silver Spring, Maryland 20910-1702. (301) 587-9390. Monthly. Covers hazardous materials technology and legislation.

Harvard Environmental Law Review. Environmental Law Review, c/o Publication Center, Harvard Law School, 202 Austin Hall, Cambridge, Massachusetts 02138. (617) 495-3110. Semiannual. Law reviews of cases involving the environment.

Hazardous Materials Control. Hazardous Materials Control Research Institute, 9300 Columbia Blvd., Silver Spring, Maryland 20910-1702. (301) 587-9390. Bimonthly. Information, innovations and articles in the hazardous materials field.

Hazardous Materials Transportation. Bureau of National Affairs, 1231 25th St. NW, Washington, District of Columbia 20037. (202) 452-4200. Monthly. Covers rules and regulations governing the shipment of hazardous materials in the U.S.

Hazardous Materials World. HazMat World, Circulation Dept., P.O. Box 3021, Wheaton, Illinois 60137. (708) 858-1888. Monthly. Covers biobusiness, hazardous wastes management, and hazardous substance safety measures.

Hazardous Substances Advisor. J. J. Keller & Associates, Inc., 3003 W. Breezewood, PO Box 368, Neenah, Washington 54957-0368. (414) 722-2848. Monthly. Report on Congressional and regulatory activity to control or eliminate situations created by hazardous and toxic substances.

Hazardous Waste and Toxic Torts. Leader Publications, 111 Eighth Ave., New York, New York 10011. (212) 463-5709. Monthly.

Hazardous Waste Consultant. McCoy & Associates, 13701 West Jewell Avenue, Suite 202, Lakewood, Colorado 80228. (303) 987-0333. Bimonthly. Information on hazardous and toxic waste issues.

Hazardous Waste Litigation Reporter. Andrews Communications, Inc., 1646 Westchester Pike, Westtown, Pennsylvania 19395. (215) 399-6600. Biweekly.

Hazardous Waste News. Business Publishers, Inc., 951 Pershing Drive, Silver Spring, Maryland 20910-4464. (301) 587-6300. Weekly. Covers legislative, regulatory and judicial decisions on hazardous waste. Also available online.

Hazmat News: The Authoritative News Resource for Hazardous Control and Waste Management. Stevens Publishing Co., PO Box 2604, Waco, Texas 76702-2604. (817) 776-9000. Semimonthly. Hazardous materials transportation, storage, and disposal.

Hazmat World. Tower-Borner Publishing, Inc., Bldg. C, Suite 206, 800 Roosevelt Rd., Glen Ellyn, Illinois 60137.

(708) 858-1888. Monthly. Covers hazardous management issues and technology.

HazTech News. Business Publishers, Inc., 951 Pershing Drive, Silver Spring, Maryland 20910. (301) 587-6300. Biweekly. Covers developments and discoveries in waste management.

Inside the EPA'S Superfund Report. Inside Washington Publishers, PO Box 7167, Ben Franklin Station, Washington, District of Columbia 20044. Biweekly. Liability for hazardous substances pollution and damages.

Journal of Air and Waste Management Association. Air and Waste Management Association, P.O. Box 2861, Pittsburgh, Pennsylvania 15230. (412) 232-3444. Monthly. Current events in air pollution control and hazardous wastes.

Journal of Analytical Toxicology. Preston Publications, PO Box 48312, 7800 Merrimac, Niles, Illinois 60648. (708) 965-0566. Bimonthly. Articles on industrial toxicology, environmental pollution and pharmaceuticals.

Journal of Environmental Science and Health. Marcel Dekker, Inc., 270 Madison Ave., New York, New York 10016. (212) 696-9000. Bimonthly. Concerns pesticides, food contaminants, chemical carcinogens, and agricultural wastes.

Journal of Toxicology: Clinical Toxicology. Marcel Dekker, Inc., 270 Madison Ave., New York, New York 10016. (212) 696-9000. Bimonthly. Covers all facets of medical toxicology.

Journal of Toxicology: Cutaneous and Ocular Toxicology. Marcel Dekker, Inc., 270 Madison Ave., New York, New York 10016. (212) 696-9000. Quarterly. Covers dermatological, toxicological, and ophthalmological studies.

Journal of Toxicology: Toxin Reviews. Marcel Dekker, Inc., 270 Madison Ave., New York, New York 10016. (212) 696-9000. Three times a year. Covers new underutilized substances.

The Minimizer. Center for Hazardous Materials Research, University of Pittsburgh Applied Research Center, 320 William Pitt Way, Pittsburgh, Pennsylvania 15238. (412) 826-5320. Quarterly. Environmental and regulatory information regarding solid and hazardous waste.

Multinational Environmental Outlook. Business Publishers, Inc., 951 Pershing Dr., Silver Spring, Maryland 20910-4464. (301) 587-6300. 1974-. Biweekly. Covers developments in world environmental problems such as acid rain, deforestation, soil erosion, overfishing, threats to health, animal extinction, population growth, diminishing water supply and other related matters. Also available online.

Nuclear Waste News. Business Publishers, Inc., 951 Pershing Dr., Silver Spring, Maryland 20910-4464. (301) 587-6300. 1981-. Weekly. Covers up-to-the-minute information on radioactive wastes management. Includes facts on all aspects of radioactive wastes such as generation, packaging, transportation, processing, storage and disposal.

Pollution Equipment News. Rimbach Publishing, Inc., 8650 Babcock Boulevard, Pittsburgh, Pennsylvania 15237. (412) 364-5366. Bimonthly. Covers new products, techniques, and literature.

Probe Post. Pollution Probe Foundation, 12 Madison Ave., Toronto, Ontario, Canada M5R 2S1. (416) 926-1647. Quarterly. Acid rain, toxic waste, renewable energy, deep ecology, land use, and greenhouse effect.

Rachel's Hazardous Waste News. Environmental Research Foundation, PO Box 3541, Princeton, New Jersey 08543-3541. (609) 683-0707. Weekly. Topics include landfills, toxins, incinerators, health and the environment, grassroots lobbying, and community energy conservation.

Report on Defense Plant Wastes. Business Publishers, Inc., 951 Pershing Dr., Silver Spring, Maryland 20910-4464. (301) 587-6300. 1989-. Biweekly. Reports on environmental laws, regulations, cleanups, contracts and court actions affecting U.S. defense weapons production, government hospitals and other government institutions. Also available online.

State Environment Report: Toxic Substances & Hazardous Wastes. Business Publishers, Inc., 951 Pershing Drive, Silver Spring, Maryland 20910. (301) 587-6300. Weekly. Covers state legislative and regulatory initiatives.

Texas Pollution Report. Report Publications, P.O. Box 12368, Austin, Texas 78711. (512) 478-5663. Weekly. Covers regulatory activity, court decisions and legislation.

Toxic Materials News. Business Publishers, Inc., 951 Pershing Dr., Silver Spring, Maryland 20910-4464. (301) 587-6300. 1974-. Weekly. Informs on regulations governing the manufacture, handling, transport, distribution and disposal of toxic chemicals and pesticides. Also available online.

Toxicology & Applied Pharmacology. Academic Press, P.O. Box 6250, c/o Harcourt Brace, 6277 Sea Harbor Dr., Orlando, Florida 32887. (218) 723-9828. Fifteen times a year. Covers the effects of chemicals on living organisms.

Toxics Law Reporter. Bureau of National Affairs, 1231 25th St. NW, Washington, District of Columbia 20037. (202) 452-4200. Weekly. Covers legal developments of toxic tort.

RESEARCH CENTERS AND INSTITUTES

Engineering Research Center for Hazardous Substances Control. University of California, Los Angeles, 6722 Boelter Hall, Los Angeles, California 90024. (213) 206-3071.

Environmental Research Center. Washington State University, 305 Troy Hall, Pullman, Washington 99164-4430. (509) 335-8536.

Environmental Research Foundation. PO Box 3541, Princeton, New Jersey 08543-3541. (609) 683-0707.

Environmental Research Institute for Hazardous Materials and Wastes. University of Connecticut, Rt. 44, Langley Bldg., Box U210, Storrs, Connecticut 06269-3210. (203) 486-4015.

Michigan State University, Center for Environmental Toxicology. C 231 Holden Hall, East Lansing, Michigan 48824. (517) 353-6469.

New York State Center for Hazardous Waste Management. State University of New York at Buffalo, Jarvis Hall 207, Buffalo, New York 14260. (716) 636-3446.

Pacific Basin Consortium for Hazardous Waste Research. Environmental and Policy Institute, 1777 East-West Rd., Honolulu, Hawaii 96848. (808) 944-7555.

Resources for the Future, Inc., Quality of the Environment Division. 1616 P Street, N.W., Washington, District of Columbia 20036. (202) 328-5000.

State University of New York at Oswego, Research Center. King Hall, Oswego, New York 13126. (315) 341-3639.

University Center for Environmental and Hazardous Materials Studies. Virginia Polytech Institute and State University, 1020 Derring Hall, Blacksburg, Virginia 24061. (703) 951-5538.

University of Alabama, Alabama Waste Exchange. P.O. Box 870203, Tuscaloosa, Alabama 35487. (205) 348-5889.

University of Alabama, Environmental Institute for Waste Management Studies. P.O. Box 870203, Tuscaloosa, Alabama 35487-0203. (205) 348-8401.

University of Alabama, Hazardous Materials Management Resource Recovery. Department of Chemical Engineering, P.O. Box 870203, Tuscaloosa, Alabama 35487-0203. (205) 348-8401.

University of Alabama, Project Rose. P.O. Box 870203, Tuscaloosa, Alabama 35487-0203. (205) 348-4878.

University of North Carolina at Chapel Hill, Institute for Environmental Studies. CB #7410, 311 Pittsboro Street, Chapel Hill, North Carolina 27599-7410. (919) 966-2358.

University of Tennessee at Knoxville, Center for Environmental Biotechnology. 10515 Research Drive, Knoxville, Tennessee 37932. (615) 675-9450.

University of Wisconsin-Madison, Water Chemistry Program. 660 North Park Street, Madison, Wisconsin 53706. (608) 262-2470.

Wisconsin Applied Water Pollution Research Consortium. University of Wisconsin-Madison, 3204 Engineering Building, 1415 Johnson Dr., Madison, Wisconsin 53706. (608) 262-7248.

STATISTICS SOURCES

Environmental Data Compendium. OECD Publications and Information Center, 2001 L St., N.W., Suite 700, Washington, District of Columbia 20036. (202) 785-6323. 1989.

Environmental Indicators. OECD Publications and Information Center, 2001 L St., N.W., Suite 700, Washington, District of Columbia 20036. (202) 785-6323. 1991.

Environmental Quality. Council on Environmental Quality. U.S. G.P.O., Washington, District of Columbia 20401. (202) 512-0000. Annual.

The State of the Environment. OECD Publications and Information Center, 2001 L St., N.W., Suite 700, Washington, District of Columbia 20036. (202) 785-6323. 1991.

TRADE ASSOCIATIONS AND PROFESSIONAL SOCIETIES

Air and Waste Management Association. Box 2861, Pittsburgh, Pennsylvania 15230. (412) 232-3444.

American Chemical Society. 1155 16th St., N.W., Washington, District of Columbia 20036. (202) 872-4600.

American College of Toxicology. 9650 Rockville Pike, Bethesda, Maryland 20814. (301) 571-1840.

Association of State and Territorial Solid Waste Management Officials. 444 North Capitol St., N.W., Suite 388, Washington, District of Columbia 20001. (202) 624-5828.

Chemical Waste Transportation Council. 1730 Rhode Island Ave., N.W., Suite 1000, Washington, District of Columbia 20036. (202) 659-4613.

Citizen's Clearinghouse for Hazardous Wastes, Inc. P.O. Box 6806, Falls Church, Virginia 22040. (703) 237-2249.

Citizens for a Better Environment. 33 E. Congress, Suite 523, Chicago, Illinois 60605. (312) 939-1530.

Clean Sites, Inc. 1199 N. Fairfax St., Alexandria, Virginia 22314. (703) 683-8522.

ECRI. 5200 Butler Pike, Plymouth Meeting, Pennsylvania 19462. (215) 825-6000.

Environmental Quality Industrial Resources Center. The Ohio State University, 1200 Chambers Rd., Room 310, Columbus, Ohio 43212. (614) 292-6717.

Hardwood Research Council. Box 34518, Memphis, Tennessee 38184. (901) 377-1824.

Hazardous Materials Advisory Council. 1110 Vermont Ave. N.W., Ste. 250, Washington, District of Columbia 20005. (202) 728-1460.

Hazardous Materials Control Research Institute. 7237 Hanover Pkwy., Greenbelt, Maryland 20770. (301) 982-9500.

Hazardous Waste Treatment Council. 1440 New York Ave., Suite 310, Washington, District of Columbia 20005. (202) 783-0870.

Hazardous Water Federation. Div. 3314, P.O. Box 5800, Albuquerque, New Mexico 87185. (505) 846-2655.

Illinois Hazardous Waste Research and Information Center. One East Hazelwood Dr., Champaign, Illinois 61820. (217) 333-8940.

Institute of Chemical Waste Management. 1730 Rhode Island Ave., N.W., Suite 1000, Washington, District of Columbia 20036. (202) 659-4613.

International Society of Chemical Ecology. University of South Florida, Dept. of Biology, Tampa, Florida 33620. (813) 974-2336.

National Association of Local Governments on Hazardous Wastes.

National Environmental Health Association. South Tower, 720 S. Colorado Blvd., #970, Denver, Colorado 80222. (303) 756-9090.

National Environmental Training Association. 2930 E. Camelback Rd., Phoenix, Arizona 85016. (602) 956-6099.

Pulp Chemicals Association. P.O. Box 105113, Atlanta, Georgia 30348. (404) 446-1290.

HEALTH, ENVIRONMENTAL

See also: INDUSTRIAL HYGIENE

ABSTRACTING AND INDEXING SERVICES

Abstracts of Air and Water Conservation Literature. American Petroleum Institute. Central Abstracting and Indexing Service, 275 Madison Avenue, New York, New York 10016. 1972.

Abstracts on Health Effects of Environmental Pollutants. BIOSIS, 2100 Arch St., Philadelphia, Pennsylvania 19103. (215) 587-4800; (800) 523-4806.

Applied Science and Technology Index. H.W. Wilson Co., 950 University Ave., Bronx, New York 10452. (800) 367-6770. Formerly Industrial Arts Index.

Biological and Agricultural Index. H.W. Wilson Co., 950 University Ave., Bronx, New York 10452. (800) 367-6770. 1916-. Monthly.

Chemical Abstracts. Chemical Abstracts Service, 2540 Olentangy River Rd., PO Box 3012, Columbus, Ohio 43210. (800) 848-6533. 1907-.

Current Advances in Ecological and Environmental Science. Pergamon Microforms International, Inc., Fairview Park, Elmsford, New York 10523. (914) 592-7720. 1989-. Monthly. Current literature searching service including journals, reports, abstracts, etc. This service is available online as part of the CABS database on the hosts BRS and ORBIT search service.

Ecological Abstracts. Geo Abstracts Ltd. Elsevier Applied Science, Crown House, Linton Rd., Barking, England IG 11 8JU. 1974-. Derived from over 600 leading ecological and environmental journals, plus books, conference proceedings, reports and theses.

Engineering Index. The Engineering Index Inc., 345 E. 47th St., New York, New York 10017. 1962-.

Environment Abstracts. Bowker A & I Publishing, 121 Chanlon Rd., New Providence, New Jersey 07974. (908) 464-6800. 1974-.

Environment Index. Environment Information Center, Index Research Department, 124 E. 39th St., New York, New York 10016. 1971-. Annual.

Environmental Information Connection–EIC. Planning Information Program, Dept. of Urban and Regional Planning, University of Illinois, 1003 West Nevada, Urbana, Illinois 61801. (217) 333-1369. Also available online.

Environmental Periodicals Bibliography. Environmental Studies Institute, International Academy at Santa Barbara, 800 Garden St., Suite D, Santa Barbara, California 93101. (805) 965-5010. Also available online.

General Science Index. H. W. Wilson Co., 950 University Ave., Bronx, New York 10452. 1978-. Monthly, also issued in annual cumulation. Cumulative subject index to English language periodicals in the subject fields of astronomy, botany, chemistry, earth science, environment and conservation, food and nutrition, genetics, mathematics, medicine and health, microbiology, oceanography, physics, physiology and zoology.

Geographical Abstracts. London School of Economics, Dept. of Geography, Regency House, 34 Duke St.,

London, England 1966-. Continued by Geo Abstracts issued in 6 parts: Pt. A. Landforms and the quaternary; Pt. B. Biogeography and Climatology; Pt. C. Economic geography; Pt. D. Social geography and cartography; Pt. E. Sedimentology; Pt. F. Regional and community planning.

Index to Scientific Book Contents. Institute for Scientific Information, 3501 Market St., Philadelphia, Pennsylvania 19104. (800) 523-1857. 1985-. Annual. Gives contents of science books published.

Pollution Abstracts. Cambridge Scientific Abstracts, 5161 River Rd., Bethesda, Maryland 20816. (301) 961-6750. Six/year. Indexes worldwide technical literature on environmental pollution. Covers air pollution, marine and freshwater pollution, sewage and wastewater treatment, waste management, toxicology and health, noise pollution, radiation, land pollution, and environmental policies, programs, legislation, and education. Also available online.

Public Health Engineering Abstracts. U.S. G.P.O., Washington, District of Columbia 20401. (202) 512-0000. Monthly.

Science Citation Index. Institute for Scientific Information, 3501 Market St., Philadelphia, Pennsylvania 19104. 1961-.

Selected References on Environmental Quality as It Relates to Health. National Library of Medicine, 8600 Rockville Pike, Bethesda, Maryland 20894. (800) 638-8480. 1977.

ALMANACS AND YEARBOOKS

Environmental Almanac. World Resources Institute. Houghton Mifflin, 1 Beacon St., Boston, Massachusetts 02108. (617) 725-5000; (800) 225-3362. 1991. Covers consumer products, energy, endangered species, food safety, global warming, solid wastes, toxics, wetlands and other related areas. Also included are the names and addresses of the chief environmental executives for all 50 states.

Gale Environmental Almanac. Russ Hoyle. Gale Research Inc., 835 Penobscot Bldg., Detroit, Michigan 48226-4094. (313) 961-2242. 1993. Focuses on the U.S. and Canada, although worldwide and transboundary issues are discussed.

BIBLIOGRAPHIES

Current Contents. Agriculture, Biology and Environmental Sciences. Institute for Scientific Information, 3501 Market St., Philadelphia, Pennsylvania 19104. (800) 523-1857. 1973-. Previous title: Current Contents. Agricultural, Food & Veterinary Sciences. Gives the table of contents of periodicals in the fields of agriculture, biology, environmental and related areas.

Environmental Health and Toxicology. Centers for Disease Control, Center for Environmental Health and Injury Control, Chamblee 27 F-29, Atlanta, Georgia 30333. (404) 488-4588. 1991. A selected bibliography of printed information sources.

EPA Publications Bibliography. U.S. Environmental Protection Agency, Library Systems Branch, 401 M St., SW, Washington, District of Columbia 20460. (202) 260-2090. Quarterly.

Food Safety, 1990: An Annotated Bibliography of the Literature. Dorothy C. Gosting, et al. Butterworth-Heinemann, 80 Montvale Ave., Stoneham, Massachusetts 02180. (617) 438-8464 or (800) 366-2665. 1991. Deals with the areas of environmental health and toxicology in relation to food safety and preservation. The bibliography is divided into three major parts headed "Diet and Health," "Safety of Food Components," and "Foodborne Microbial Illness." The appendix is titled "Food-and-Water-Associated Viruses."

Some Publicly Available Sources of Computerized Information on Environmental Health and Toxicology. Kathy Deck. Centers for Disease Control, 1600 Clifton Rd., N.E., Atlanta, Georgia 30333. (404) 488-4588. 1991.

Toxicological / Environmental Health Information Source Update. Centers for Disease Control, 1600 Clifton Rd. NE, Atlanta, Georgia 30333. (404) 488-4588. Lists recent online bibliographic databases relating to environmental health and toxicology.

DIRECTORIES

Canadian Environmental Directory. Canadian Almanac & Directory Publishing Co. Ltd., 134 Adelaide St. E., Ste. 27, Toronto, Ontario, Canada M5C 1K9. (416) 362-4088. 1992. Includes individuals, agencies, firms, and associations.

Directory of Environmental/Health Protection Professionals. National Environmental Health Association, 720 S. Colorado Blvd., Suite 970, Denver, Colorado 80222. (303) 756-9090.

Directory of Medical Specialists. Marquis Who's Who/Macmillan Directory Division, 3002 Glenview Rd., Wilmette, Illinois 60091. (312) 441-2387.

The Green Encyclopedia. Irene Franck, David Brownstone. Prentice-Hall, Rte. 9W, Englewood Cliffs, New York 07632. (201) 592-2000. 1992. Covers environmental organizations.

Linscott's Directory of Immunological & Biological Reagents. William D. Linscott, 40 Glen Dr., Mill Valley, California 94941. (415) 383-2666.

New England Network of Light Directory. Sirius Community, Box 388, Amherst, Massachusetts 01004. (413) 256-8015. Annual. New age communities, holistic health centers, and ashrams.

Physicians' Desk Reference. Medical Economics Company, 680 Kinderkamack Rd., Oradell, New Jersey 07649. (201) 262-3030. 1974-.

ENCYCLOPEDIAS AND DICTIONARIES

Cambridge Encyclopedia of Life Sciences. A. E. Friday and David S. Ingram. Cambridge University Press, 40 W 20th St., New York, New York 10011. (212) 924-3900 or (800) 227-0247. 1985. Includes all topics under biology and ecology.

Dictionary of Environmental Science and Technology. Andrew Porteous. John Wiley & Sons, Inc., 605 3rd Ave., New York, New York 10158-0012. (212) 850-6000. 1992.

Encyclopedia of Allergy and Environmental Illness: A Self-Help Approach. Ellen Rothera. Sterling Pub. Co., 387 Park Ave, South, New York, New York 10016-8810. (212) 532-7160 or (800) 367-9692. 1991. Presents the problem of multiple environmental allergies and deals with allergic reactions to such things as foods, food additives, household cleaners, molds, cooking gas, and air pollution.

Encyclopedia of Environmental Science and Engineering. J.R. Pfafflin. Gordon and Breach Science Publishers, Inc., 270 8th Ave., New York, New York 10011. (212) 206-8900. 1992.

Encyclopedia of Environmental Studies. William Ashworth. Facts on File, Inc., 460 Park Ave. S., New York, New York 10016. (212) 683-2244. 1991.

Encyclopedia of Occupational Health and Safety. Luigi Parmeggiani. International Labour Office, 49 Sheridan Ave., Albany, New York 12210. (518) 436-9686. 1983. Reference work concerned with workers' safety and health, information for those with no specialized medical or with technical knowledge.

Environmental Encyclopedia. William P. Cunningham, Terence Ball, et. al. Gale Research Inc., 835 Penobscot Bldg., Detroit, Michigan 48226-4094. (313) 961-2242. 1993.

McGraw-Hill Encyclopedia of Environmental Science. Sybil P. Parker. McGraw-Hill Science & Engineering Books, 11 W. 19th St., New York, New York 10011. (212) 337-6010. 1980. Covers ecology, man's influence on nature, and environmental protection.

McGraw-Hill Encyclopedia of Science and Technology. McGraw-Hill, 1221 Avenue of the Americas, New York, New York 10020. (212) 512-2000 or (800) 262-4729. 1992. Seventh edition. Issued in multiple volumes including index. Includes all science and technology broad subject areas.

Ullmanns Encyclopedia of Industrial Chemistry. Hans Jurgen Arpe and Wolfgang Gerhartz, eds. VCH Publishers, 303 NW 12th Ave., Deerfield Beach, Florida 33442-1788. (305) 428-5566. 1990. Designed to keep up with the broad spectrum of chemical technology. Thirty-six volumes of the encyclopedia have been divided into two sets: the 28 A volumes contain alphabetically arranged articles on chemicals, product groups, processes and technological concepts; and the 8 B volumes are compendia of basic knowledge in industrial chemistry.

Van Nostrand's Scientific Encyclopedia. Glenn D. Considine, ed. Van Nostrand Reinhold, 115 5th Ave., New York, New York 10003. (212) 254-3232. 1983. Sixth edition. Includes all broad subject areas in science.

The Water Encyclopedia. Lewis Publishers, 2000 Corporate Blvd. N.W., Boca Raton, Florida 33431. (800) 272-7737. 1990. 2d ed. Includes groundwater contamination, drinking water, floods, waterborne diseases, global warming, climate change, irrigation, water agencies and organizations, precipitation, oceans and seas, and river, lakes and waterfalls.

GENERAL WORKS

Advances in Neurobehavioral Toxicology: Applications in Environmental and Occupational Health. Barry L. Johnson, et al. Lewis Publishers, 2000 Corporate Blvd., N.W., Boca Raton, Florida 33431. (407) 994-0555 or (800) 272-7737. 1991. Focuses on neurobehavioral methods and their development and application in environmental and occupational health. Includes new methods to assess human neurotoxicity; human exposure to, and health effects of, neurotoxic substances; and animal methods that model human toxicity.

Air Toxics and Risk Assessment. Edward J. Calabrese and Elaina M. Kenyon. Lewis Publishers, 200 Corporate Blvd. NW, Boca Raton, Florida 33431. (407) 994-0555 or (800)272-7737. 1991. Does risk assessments for more than 110 chemicals that are confirmed or probable air toxics. All chemicals are analyzed with a scientifically sound methodology to assess public health risks.

Analyses of Hazardous Substances in Biological Materials. J. Angere, ed. VCH Publishers, 303 NW 12th Ave., Deerfield Beach, Florida 33442-1788. (305) 428-5566. 1991. Discusses industrial hygiene and the various toxic substances involved.

Applied Isotope Hydrogeology: A Case Study in Northern Switzerland. F. J. Pearson, Jr., et al. Elsevier Science Publishing Co., Inc, 655 Avenue of the Americas, New York, New York 10010. (212) 989-5800. 1991. This is a case study in northern Switzerland about radioactive waste disposal in the ground. Includes bibliographical references and an index.

Carcinogens and Mutagens in the Environment. Hans F. Stich, ed. CRC Press, 2000 Corporate Blvd. N.W., Boca Raton, Florida 33431. (800) 272-7737. 1982-. Naturally occurring compounds, endogenous modulation.

Carcinogens in Industry and the Environment. James M. Sontag, ed. M. Dekker, 270 Madison Ave., New York, New York 10016. (212) 696-9000. 1981. Environmentally induced diseases and industrial hygiene.

Chemical Contamination in the Human Environment. Morton Lippmann. Oxford University Press, 200 Madison Ave., New York, New York 10016. (212) 679-7300. 1979. Deals with pollution and environmental health.

Chemical Hazards of the Work Place. Nick H. Proctor and edited by Gloria J. Hathaway, et al. Van Nostrand Reinhold, 115 5th Ave., New York, New York 10003. (212) 254-3232. 1991. 3d ed.

Chromatography of Environmental Hazards. Elsevier Science Publishing Co., 655 Avenue of the Americas, New York, New York 10010. (212) 984-5800. Covers carcinogens, mutagens, and teratogens, metals, gaseous and industrial pollutants, pesticides, and drugs of abuse.

Common Sense Pest Control. William Olkowski, et al. Tauton Pr., 63 South Main St., Box 5506, Newton, Connecticut 06740-5506. 1991. Discusses ways to manage other living organisms that are regarded as pests.

Criteria for a Recommended Standard, Occupational Exposure to Malathion. U.S. Department of Health and Human Services, Public Health Service, National Institute for Occupational Safety and Health, Robert A. Taft Lab, 4676 Columbia Pkwy., Cincinnati, Ohio 45226. (513) 684-8465. 1976.

Dermatotoxicology. Francis N. Marzulli and Howard I. Maibach, eds. Hemisphere Publishing Co., 79 Madison Ave., Suite 1110, New York, New York 10016. (212) 725-1999; (800) 821-8312. 1991. 4th ed. Provides information on theoretical aspects and practical test methods, including both in vitro and in vivo approaches. Pays attention to the worldwide movement for the development of suitable alternatives to animals when feasible.

Design for a Livable Planet: How You Can Help Clean Up the Environment. Jon Naar. Perennial Library, 10 E. 53d

St., New York, New York 10022. (212) 207-7000; (800) 242-7737. 1990. Explains the dangers we present to our environment and what we can do about it. Also available from Carolina Biological Supply Co., 2700 York Rd., Burlington, NC.

Environment and Health: Themes in Medical Geography. Rais Akhtar, ed. Ashish Pub. House, Box 502, Columbia, Missouri 65205. (314) 474-0116. 1991. Discusses environmental health.

The Environmental Sourcebook. Edith Carol Stein. Lyons & Burford, 31 W. 21st St., New York, New York 10010. (212) 620-9580. 1992. Provides information on 11 specific environmental issues, including population; agriculture; energy; climate and atmosphere; biodiversity; water; oceans; solid waste; hazardous substances and waste; endangered lands; and development.

Environmental Viewpoints. Marie Lazzari. Gale Research Inc., 835 Penobscot Bldg., Detroit, Michigan 48226-4094. (313) 961-2242. 1992.

Fate of Pesticides and Chemicals in the Environment. Jerald L. Schnoor, ed. John Wiley & Sons, Inc., 605 3rd Ave., New York, New York 10158-0012. (212) 850-6000. 1992. Focuses on the necessity to improve our deteriorating standards of public health, environmental science and technology with a total systems approach through the pooled talents of scientists and engineers.

Fighting Toxics. Gary Cohen and John O'Connor, eds. Island Press, 1718 Connecticut Ave. N.W., Suite 300, Washington, District of Columbia 20009. (202) 232-7933. 1990. Investigates the toxic hazards in the community, determining the health risks they pose, and launching an effective campaign to eliminate them.

Guidelines for the Radiation Protection of Workers in Industry, Ionising Radiations. International Labour Office, 49 Sheridan Ave., Albany, New York 12210. (518) 436-9686. 1989. Provides technical information on protection against radiation in specific installations and for specific equipment. Designed to be used in conjunction with the ILO code of practice Radiation Protection of Workers (ionising rations), they describe the requirements of workers engaged in radiation work with external sources and unsealed sources.

Hazardous Wastes and Hazardous Materials. Hazardous Materials Control Research Institute, 9300 Columbia Blvd., Silver Spring, Maryland 20910. (301) 587-9390. 1987.

Health and the Global Environment. Ross Hume Hall. B. Blackwell, 3 Cambridge Ctr., Suite 208, Cambridge, Massachusetts 02142. (617) 225-0401. 1990.

Health Effects of Airborne Particles. Harvard University, 79 John F. Kennedy St., Cambridge, Massachusetts 02130.

Health Effects of Drinking Water Treatment Technologies. Lewis Publishers, 200 Corporate Blvd. NW, Boca Raton, Florida 33431. (407) 994-0555 or (800)272-7737. 1989. Evaluates the public health impact from the most widespread drinking water treatment technologies, with particular emphasis on disinfection. Focuses solely on the most common treatment technologies and practices used today.

Healthy Homes, Healthy Kids. Joyce M. Schoemaker and Charity Y. Vitale. Island Press, 1718 Connecticut Ave. N.W., Suite 300, Washington, District of Columbia

20009. (202) 232-7933. 1991. Identifies many hazards that parents tend to overlook. It translates technical, scientific information into an accessible how-to guide to help parents protect children from even the most toxic substances.

Hidden Dangers: Environmental Consequences of Preparing for War. Anne H. Ehrlich and John W. Birks, eds. Sierra Club Books, 100 Bush St., San Francisco, California 94104. (415) 291-1600. 1991. Considers a number of questions concerning the dangers–health-related, environmental, psychological, economic, etc.–that have been and are still being engendered by the U.S. and other nations, since the 1940s, to manufacture, store, and dispose of nuclear, chemical, and biological weapons.

How to Live with Low-Level Radiation: A Nutritional Protection Plan. Leon Chaitow. Healing Arts Pr., 1 Park St., Rochester, Vermont 05767. (802) 767-3174. 1988. Discusses the problem of low-level radiation in depth and offers safe, nutritional measures to counteract this invisible hazard.

Hydrocarbon Contaminated Soils and Groundwater: Analysis, Fate, Environmental and Public Health Effects, and Remediation. Paul T. Kostecki and Edward J. Calabrese. Lewis Publishers, 2000 Corporate Blvd.,N.W., Boca Raton, Florida 33431. (407) 994-0555 or (800) 272-7737. 1991. Describes perspectives and emerging issues, analytical techniques and site assessments, environmental fate and modeling.

Immunochemical Methods for Environmental Analysis. Jeanette M. Van Emon and Ralph O. Mumma, eds. American Chemical Society, 1155 16th St. N.W., Washington, District of Columbia 20036. (202) 872-4600; (800) 227-5558. 1990. Describes antibodies used as analytical tools to study environmentally important compounds. Discusses various applications in food industry, environmental analysis, and applications in agriculture.

Index of Hazardous Contents of Commercial Products in Schools and Colleges. The Forum for Scientific Excellence. J. B. Lippincott, 227 E. Washington Sq., Philadelphia, Pennsylvania 19105. (215) 238-4200; (800) 982-4377. 1990. Lists the hazardous components found in thousands of commercial products used in educational institutions.

Media and the Environment. Craig L. LaMay and Everette E. Dennis. Island Press, 1718 Connecticut Ave. N.W., Suite 300, Washington, District of Columbia 20009. (202) 232-7933. 1992. Explores environmental reporting.

Nontoxic, Natural and Earthwise: How to Protect Yourself and Your Family from Harmful Products and Live in Harmony with the Earth. Debra Lynn Dadd. Jeremy P. Tarcher, 5858 Wilshire Blvd., Ste. 200, Los Angeles, California 90036. (213) 935-9980. 1990. Evaluation of household products and recommendations as to natural and homemade alternatives.

Pentachlorophenol Health and Safety Guide. World Health Organization, Ave. Appia, Geneva, Switzerland CH-1221. (518) 436-9686. 1989.

Petroleum Contaminated Soils: Remediation Techniques, Environmental Fate and Risk Assessment. Paul T. Kostecki and Edward J. Calabrese. Lewis Publishers, 200 Corporate Blvd. NW, Boca Raton, Florida 33431. (407) 994-0555 or (800)272-7737. 1991. Three volumes. Pro-

vides valuable information to determine feasible solutions to petroleum contaminated soils.

Principles of Environmental Health Science. K. H. Mancy and Robert Gray. Lewis Publishers, 2000 Corporate Blvd., N.W., Boca Raton, Florida 33431. (407) 994-0555 or (800) 272-7737. 1991. Discusses global environmental changes and the related issues and controversies, environmental contaminants, food and water, community air and indoor pollution, radiological health and solid waste, and nimby syndrome.

Radiation Exposure and Occupational Risks. G. Keller, et al. Springer-Verlag, 175 5th Ave., New York, New York 10010. (212) 460-1500; (800) 777-4643. 1990. Discusses radiation exposure injuries in the workplace and prevention.

Radioactive Aerosols. A. C. Chamberlin. Cambridge University Press, 40 W 20th St., New York, New York 10011. (212) 924-3900; (800) 227-0247. 1991. Describes radioactive gases and particles which are dispersed in the environment, either from natural causes or following nuclear test and accidental emissions.

Safety and Health for Engineers. Roger L. Brauer. Global Professional Publications, 2805 McGraw Ave., PO Box 19539, Irvine, California 92713-9539. (800) 854-7179. 1990. Discusses the ethical, technical, legal, social and economic considerations involving safety and health in engineering planning and practice.

Safety in the Use of Asbestos. International Labour Office, 49 Sheridan Ave., Albany, New York 12210. (518) 436-9686. 1990. An ILO code of practice. The first part of the code includes monitoring in the work place, preventive measures, the protection and supervision of the workers' health, and the packaging, handling, transport and disposal of asbestos waste. More detailed guidance on the limitation of exposure to asbestos in specific activities is given in the second part of the code, which includes sections on mining and milling, asbestos cement, textiles, friction materials, and the removal of asbestos-containing materials.

Safety in the Use of Mineral and Synthetic Fibers. International Labour Office, 49 Sheridan Ave., Albany, New York 12210. (518) 436-9686. 1990. Working document for, and report of, a meeting of experts set up by the ILO to study the questions contained in this book, including discussions of man-made fibers, natural mineral fibers other than asbestos, and synthetic organic fibers. The meeting defined certain preventive measures based on adopting safe working methods, controlling the working environment and the exposure of workers to mineral and synthetic fibers, and monitoring the health of the workers.

Silent Spring Revisited. Gino J. Marco, et al., eds. American Chemical Society, 1155 16th St. N.W., Washington, District of Columbia 20036. (202) 872-4600; (800) 227-5558. 1987. Discusses Rachel Carson's vision and legacy. Traces the evolution of government regulations and the current pesticide registration criteria. Critically appraises the existing conditions and evaluates hazards.

Technology, Law, and the Working Environment. Nicholas A. Ashford and Charles C. Caldart. Global Professional Publications, 2805 McGraw Ave., PO Box 19539, Irvine, California 92713-9539. (800) 854-7179. 1991. Discusses how to improve safety and health conditions through creative uses of workplace technology and application of relevant health and safety laws.

Toxicological Evaluations. Volume 1: Potential Health Hazards of Existing Chemicals. B. G. Chemie, ed. Springer-Verlag, 115 5th Ave., New York, New York 10010. (212) 460-1500; (800) 777-4643. 1990. Identifies thousands of compounds which might possibly be toxic and to date several hundreds that have been investigated. Contains results of the first 57 reviews of the literature.

Trace Elements in Health and Disease. A. Aitio, et al., eds. Royal Society of Chemistry, c/o CRC Press, 2000 Corporate Blvd. N.W., Boca Raton, Florida 33431-9868. (800) 272-7737. 1991. Reviews the newest data available on both nutritional and toxicological aspects of trace elements. Assesses the current state of knowledge on the relationship between trace elements and human health and disease.

World Guide to Environmental Issues and Organizations. Peter Brackley. Longman Group Ltd., Longman House, Burnt Mill, Harlow, Essex, England CM20 2J6. (0279) 426721. 1991.

Written Hazard Communication Program for Schools and Colleges. Forum for Scientific Excellence. J. B. Lippincott, 227 E. Washington Sq., Philadelphia, Pennsylvania 19105. (215) 238-4200; (800) 982-4377. 1989. Identifies all the requirements an educational institution must meet to ensure that its hazardous chemical compliance program is appropriate and adequate. Specific examples of written program requirements, MSDS format, hazard assessment criteria and communication vehicles and formats are included.

GOVERNMENTAL ORGANIZATIONS

Energy Research Office. James Forrestal Building, 1000 Independence Ave., S.W., Washington, District of Columbia 20585. (202) 586-5430.

Environment, Safety and Health Office: Department of Energy. James Forrestal Building, 1000 Independence Ave., S.W., Washington, District of Columbia 20585. (202) 586-6151.

National Center for Health Statistics: Public Health Service. 6525 Belcrest Rd., Hyattsville, Maryland 20782. (301) 436-7016.

National Institute of Environmental Health Science. PO Box 12233, Research Triangle Park, North Carolina 27709. (919) 541-3345.

Occupational Safety and Health Administration: Assistant Secretary for Occupational Safety and Health. 200 Constitution Ave., N.W., Washington, District of Columbia 20210. (202) 523-7162.

Occupational Safety and Health Administration: Directorate of Administrative Programs. 200 Constitution Ave., N.W., Washington, District of Columbia 20210. (202) 523-8576.

Occupational Safety and Health Administration: Directorate of Compliance Programs. 200 Constitution Ave., N.W., Washington, District of Columbia 20210. (202) 523-9308.

Occupational Safety and Health Administration: Directorate of Federal- State Operations. 200 Constitution Ave., N.W., Washington, District of Columbia 20210. (202) 523-7251.

Occupational Safety and Health Administration: Directorate of Health Standards Programs. 200 Constitution Ave., N.W., Washington, District of Columbia 20210. (202) 523-7075.

Occupational Safety and Health Administration: Publications Office. 200 Constitution Ave., N.W., Room N3101, Washington, District of Columbia 20210. (202) 523-9668.

U.S. Department of Labor: Mine Safety and Health Administration. 4015 Wilson Blvd., Arlington, Virginia 22203. (703) 235-1452.

U.S. Environmental Protection Agency: Office of Health and Environmental Assessment. 401 M St., S.W., Washington, District of Columbia 20460. (202) 382-7317.

U.S. Environmental Protection Agency: Office of Health Research. 401 M St., S.W., Washington, District of Columbia 20460. (202) 382-5900.

U.S. Environmental Protection Agency: Office of Pesticide Programs. 401 M St., S.W., Washington, District of Columbia 20460. (202) 557-7090.

HANDBOOKS AND MANUALS

Chemical Information Manual. Government Institutes, Inc., 4 Research Pl., Ste. 200, Rockville, Maryland 20850. (301) 921-2300. 1991. Handbook presenting a variety of useful data on each chemical substances, including proper identification, OSHA exposure limits, description and physical properties, carcinogenic status, health effects and toxicology, sampling and analysis.

Environmental Health and Safety Manager's Handbook, 2nd edition. Government Institutes, Inc., 4 Research Pl., Ste. 200, Rockville, Maryland 20850. (301) 921-2300. Organization and management of environmental programs, criteria for developing a program, human resources, communication; information management; government inspections and enforcement.

Environmental Statistics Handbook: Europe. Allan Foster, Oksana Newman. Gale Research Inc., 835 Penobscot Bldg., Detroit, Michigan 48226-4094. (313) 961-2242. 1993.

Green Index: A State-by-State Guide to the Nation's Environmental Health. Island Press, 1718 Connecticut Ave. N.W., Suite 300, Washington, District of Columbia 20009. (202) 232-7933. 1991-. Biennially. Compares state by state more than 250 environmental categories. Includes an overall environmental quality score for each state.

Handbook of Environmental Health and Safety, Principles and Practices. Herman Koren. Lewis Publishers, 2000 Corporate Blvd., N.W., Boca Raton, Florida 33431. (800) 272-7737. 1991. Two volumes. Current issues and regulations are presented. The broad spectrum of topics is presented outlining the relationship of the environment to humans and also environmental health emergencies and how to deal with them.

Health & Medical Aspects of Chemical Industries. ABBE Publishers Association of Washington DC, 4111 Gallows Rd., Annandale, Virginia 22003-1862. 1984. Health aspects of chemical industries, industrial waste, and chemically enforced occupational diseases.

Hygiene Guide Series. American Industrial Hygiene Association, 345 White Pond Dr., Akron, Ohio 44320. (216) 873-2442. 1955-. 1 v. (loose-leaf).

RCRA Hazardous Wastes Handbook. Crowell & Moring. Government Institutes, Inc., 4 Research Place, Suite 200, Rockville, Maryland 20850. (301) 921-2300. 1989. 8th ed. Analyzes the impact of the Resource Conservation and Recovery Act on the business, while incorporating the most recent regulatory changes to the RCRA. These include the final 1988 underground storage tank rules, the medical waste regulations, permit modification regulations, amendments regarding corrective action and closures, the exemption for "treatability tests," waste export rules, etc. Includes the complete test of the RCRA statute as currently amended.

Synthetic Organic Chemicals. U.S. G.P.O., Washington, District of Columbia 20401. (202) 512-0000. 1967. An annual publication on production and sales in the U.S. for all synthetic organic chemicals produced commercially. About 800 chemicals and 800 manufacturers are included in the USITC surveys, but because of confidentiality requirements only parts of the data are published. U.S. Tariff Commission acts under the provisions of Section 332 of the Tariff Act of 1930, as amended.

ONLINE DATA BASES

BAKER. St. Baker Inc., 222 Red School Lane, Phillipsburg, New Jersey 08865. (201) 859-2151.

Biomedical Materials. Elsevier Advanced Technology Publications, Mayfield House, 256 Banbury Rd., Oxford, England OX2 1OH. 44 (865) 512242.

Cancerlit. U.S. National Institutes of Health, National Eye Institute, Building 31, Rm. 6A32, Bethesda, Maryland 20892. (301) 496-5248.

Cancerquest Online. CDC AIDS Weekly/NCI Cancer Weekly, 206 Roger St, N.E., Suite 104, Atlanta, Georgia 30317. (404) 377-8895.

CERCLIS. Chemical Information Systems, Inc., 7215 York Rd., Baltimore, Maryland 21212. (301) 321-8440. Information on hazardous waste disposal sites that have either been listed by the EPA on the National Priority List (NPL) or nominated for consideration for the NPL.

Chemical Abstracts-CA. Chemical Abstracts Service, 2540 Olentangy River Rd., P.O. Box 3012, Columbus, Ohio 43210. (800) 848-6533 or (614) 421-3600. Information sources include 9000 journals, patents from 27 countries, two industrial property organizations, new books, conference proceedings, and government research reports.

Chemical Carcinogenesis Research Information System–CCRIS. National Library of Medicine, 8600 Rockville Pike, Bethesda, Maryland 20894. (800) 638-8480. Individual assay results and test conditions for 1,451 chemicals in the areas of carcinogenicity, mutagenicity, tumor promotion, and cocarcinogenicity.

Chemical Collection System/Request Tracking–CCS/RTS. U.S. Environmental Protection Agency, Office of Pesticides and Toxic Substances, 401 M St., SW, Washington, District of Columbia 20460. (202) 260-2090. Contains information on various properties of a number of chemicals including environmental effects, test and analysis methods, and health effects. Available from EPA.

Chemical Dictionary Online–CHEMLINE. Chemical Abstracts Service, 2540 Olentangy River Rd., Columbus, Ohio 43210. (614) 421-3600 or (800) 848-6533. Part of MEDLINE of the National Library of Medicine (NLM). File of 900,000 names for chemical substances, representing 450,000 unique compounds. It contains such information as Chemical Abstracts (CA) Service Registry Numbers, molecular formulas, preferred chemical nomenclature, and generic and ring structure information. Available on NLM's ELHILL system.

Chemical Evaluation Search and Retrieval System. Michigan State Department of Natural Resources, Surface Water Quality Division, Great Lakes and Environmental Assessment Section, Knapp's Office Center, PO Box 30028, Lansing, Michigan 48909. (517) 373-2190. Covers toxicology information on compounds of environmental concern, providing acute and chronic toxicity data for aquatic and terrestrial life as well as information on carcinogenicity, mutagenicity, and reproductive and developmental effects, bioconcentration, and environmental fate.

Chemical Exposure. Science Applications International Corp., Health & Environmental Information, P.O. Box 2501, Oak Ridge, Tennessee 37831. (615) 482-9031. Database of chemicals that have been identified in both human tissues and body fluids and in feral and food animals. Contains reference to journal articles, conferences, and reports. Covers the whole fields of information related to human and animal exposure to food, air, and water contaminants and pharmaceuticals. Its records include information on chemical properties, formulas, tissues measured, analytical method used, demographics and more. Available on DIALOG.

Chemical Hazard Response Information System–CHRIS. U.S. Coast Guard. Office of Research and Development, 2100 2d St., NW., Rm. 5410 C, Washington, District of Columbia 20593. (202) 783-3238. Contains information needed to respond to emergencies that occur during the transport of hazardous chemicals, as well as information that can help prevent emergency situations. Each of the approximately 1,300 records include information on physical and chemical properties, health and fire hazards, labeling, chemical reactivity, hazard classification and water pollution. Available on CIS and on Microdex's TOMES Plus series.

CHEMINFO. Canadian Centre for Occupational Health & Safety, 250 Main St., East, Hamilton, Ontario, Canada L8N 1H6. (800) 263-8276.

CISDOC. International Occupational Safety & Health Information Centre, International Labour Office, Geneva 22, Switzerland CH-1211. 41 (22) 996740.

Clinical Abstracts. Medical Information Systems, Reference & Index Services, Inc., 3845 N. Meridian St., Indianapolis, Indiana 46208. (317) 923-1575.

Computerized Engineering Index–COMPENDEX. Engineering Information Inc., 345 E. 47th St., New York, New York 10017. (212) 705-7600.

Consumer Drug Information. American Society of Hospital Pharmacists, Database Services Division, 4630 Montgomery Ave., Bethesda, Maryland 20814. (301) 657-3000.

CRDS. Orbit Search Service, 8000 Westpark Dr., Suite 400, McLean, Virginia 22102. (800) 456-7248.

Dermal Absorption. U.S. Environmental Protection Agency, Office of Pesticides and Toxic Substances, 401 M St., SW, Washington, District of Columbia 20460. (202) 260-2090. Toxic effects, absorption, distribution, metabolism, and excretion relation to the dermal absorption of 655 chemicals.

Diagnosis. George Thieme Verlag, Ruedigerstrasse 14, Stuttgart 30, Germany D-7000.

EMBASE Drug Information. Elsevier Science Publishing Co., Excerpta Medica, Molenwerf 1, 1014 AG Amsterdam, Netherlands 31 (20) 5803507.

EMCANCER. Elsevier Science Publishing Co., Excerpta Medica, Molenwerf 1, 1014 AG Amsterdam, Netherlands 31 (20) 5803507.

EMDRUGS. Elsevier Science Publishing Co., Excerpta Medica, Molenwerf 1, 1014 AG Amsterdam, Netherlands 31 (20) 5803507.

EMFORENSIC. Elsevier Science Publishing Co., Excerpta Medica, Molenwerf 1, 1014 AG Amsterdam, Netherlands 31 (20) 5803507.

Enviro/Energyline Abstracts Plus. R. R. Bowker Co., 121 Chanlon Rd., New Providence, New Jersey 07974. (908) 464-6800.

Environmental Health News. Occupational Health Services, Inc., 450 7th Ave., New York, New York 10123. (212) 967-1100. Online access to court decisions, regulatory changes, and medical and scientific news related to hazardous substances.

Environmental Periodicals Bibliography. National Information Services Corp., Ste. 6, Wyman Towers, 3100 St. Paul St., Baltimore, Maryland 21218. (410)243-0797. Online version of abstract of same name.

ETICBACK: Environmental Teratology Information Center Backfile. Oak Ridge National Laboratory, Environmental Teratology Information Center, Building 2001, P.O. Box 2008, Oak Ridge, Tennessee 37831-6050. (615) 574-7871.

Forensic Science Database. Home Office Forensic Science Service, Central Research and Support Establishment, Aldermaston, Reading, Berkshire, England RG7 4PN. 44 (734) 814100.

Global Indexing System. U.S. Environmental Protection Agency, 401 M St., S.W., Washington, District of Columbia 20460. (202) 260-2090. International information on various qualities of chemicals.

HADB. National Library of Medicine, Toxicology Information Program, 8600 Rockville Pike, Bethesda, Maryland 20894. (800) 638-8480.

Hazard Communication Compliance Manual Database. Bureau of National Affairs, BNA PLUS, 1231 25th St., N.W., Rm. 215, Washington, District of Columbia 20037. (800) 452-7773.

Hazardline. Occupational Health Services, Inc., 450 7th Ave., Ste. 2407, New York, New York 10123. (212) 967-1100. More than 3600 dangerous materials, including physical and chemical descriptions, standards and regulations, and safety precautions for handling.

Hazardous Materials Intelligence Report. World Information Systems, PO Box 535, Cambridge, Massachusetts 02238. (617) 491-5100. Online access to federal, state, and local legislation, regulations, and programs related to

hazardous waste and hazardous material management. Online version of the periodical of the same name.

Hazardous Waste News. Business Publishers, Inc., 951 Pershing Dr., Silver Spring, Maryland 20910-4464. (301) 587-6300. Online access to legislative, regulatory, and judicial decisions at the federal and state levels relating to the field of hazardous waste management. Online version of the periodical of the same name.

Health Periodicals Database. Information Access Company, 362 Lakeside Dr., Foster City, California 94404. (800) 227-8431.

HealthNet. HealthNet, Ltd., 716 E. Carlisle, Milwaukee, Wisconsin 53217. (414) 963-8829.

Industrial Health & Hazards Update. Merton Allen Associates, P.O. Box 15640, Plantation, Florida 33318-5640. (305) 473-9560.

Life Sciences from NTIS. National Technical Information Center for the Utilization of Federal Technology, 5285 Port Royal Rd., Springfield, Virginia 22161. (703) 487-4650.

Medical Toxicology and Environmental Health. Department of Health and Social Security, Medical Toxiclology & Environmental Health Division, Hannibal House, Rm. 719, Elephant and Castle, London, England SE1 6TE. 44 (71) 972-2162.

Medical Waste News. Business Publishers, Inc., 951 Pershing Dr., Silver Spring, Maryland 20910-4464. (301) 587-6300. Online access to regulation, legislation, and technological news and developments related to medical waste management and disposal. Online version of the periodical of the same name.

MEDIS. Mead Data Central, Inc., P.O. Box 933, Dayton, Ohio 45401. (800) 227-4908.

Monthly Catalog of United States Government Publications. U.S. G.P.O., Supt. of Docs., PO Box 371954, Pittsburgh, Pennsylvania 15250-7954. (202) 512-0000.

National Technical Information Service. U.S. Department of Commerce, National Technical Information Service, Office of Data Base Services, 5285 Port Royal Rd., Springfield, Virginia 22161. (703) 487-4807. Bibliographic database of government sponsored research and technical reports.

Pharmaceutical and Healthcare Industries News Database. PJB Publications Ltd., 18-20 Hill Rise, Richmond, Surrey, England TW10 6UA. 44 (81) 948-0751.

PHTM. Bureau of Hygiene and Tropical Diseases, Keppel St., London, England WC1E 7HT. 44 (71) 636-8636.

PNI. UMI Data Courier, 620 S. 3rd St., Louisville, Kentucky 40202-2475. (502) 583-4111; 800 626-2823.

PressNet Environmental Reports. Chemical Information Systems, Inc., 7215 York Rd., Baltimore, Maryland 21212. (301) 321-8440.

REPRORISK System. Micromedex, Inc., 600 Grant St., Denver, Colorado 80203. (800) 525-9083 or (303) 831-1400. Reproductive risks to females and males caused by drugs, chemicals, and physical and environmental agents. Includes the Teratogen Information System (TERIS), which deals with the teratogenicity of over 700 drugs and environmental agents that affect a fetus. One of the additional modules under development is the REPRO-TEXT database, containing a ranking system for reproductive hazards and the general toxicity of over 600 chemicals, emphasizing chronic occupational exposures.

REPROTOX. Columbia Hospital for Women, Reproductive Toxicology Center, 2440 M St., N.W., Suite 217, Washington, District of Columbia 20037-1404. (202) 293-5137. Industrial and environmental chemicals and their effects on human fertility, pregnancy, and fetal development.

SCISEARCH. Institute for Scientific Information, University City Science Center, 3501 Market St., Philadelphia, Pennsylvania 19104. (215) 386-0100.

PERIODICALS AND NEWSLETTERS

American Academy of Environmental Medicine Newsletter. American Academy of Environmental Medicine, Box 16106, Denver, Colorado 80216. (303) 622-9755. Quarterly.

American Industrial Hygiene Association Journal. American Industrial Hygiene Association, 345 White Pond Drive, Akron, Ohio 44320. (216) 873-2442. Monthly. Reports relating to occupational and environmental health hazards.

American Journal of Public Health. American Public Health Association, 1015 15th St., NW, Washington, District of Columbia 20005. (202) 789-5600. Monthly. Current news and events of the public health field.

Analytical Chemistry. American Chemical Society, 1155 16th St. N.W., Washington, District of Columbia 20036. (800) 227-5558. 1929-. Bimonthly. Articles for chemists, life scientists and engineers.

Archives of Clinical Ecology Journal. Clinical Ecology Publications, 3069 South Detroit Way, Denver, Colorado 80210. (303) 756-7880. Quarterly. Effects of the environment on human health.

Archives of Environmental Health: An International Journal. Heldref Publications, Helen Dwight Reid Educational Foundation, 4000 Albemarle St., NW, Washington, District of Columbia 20016-1851. Bimonthly. Documentation on the effects of environmental agents on human health.

Asbestos Control Report. Business Publishers, Inc., 951 Pershing Drive, Silver Spring, Maryland 20910-4464. (301) 587-6300. Biweekly. Information on asbestos control techniques, research, and regulations. Also available online.

Asbestos Information Association of North American Newsletter. Asbestos Information Association/North America, 1745 Jefferson Davis Highway, Suite 509, Arlington, Virginia 22202. (703) 979-1150. Monthly. Issues pertaining to asbestos and health.

Bulletin of Environmental Contamination and Toxicology. Springer-Verlag, 175 5th Ave., New York, New York 10010. (212) 460-1500; (800) 777-4643. 1966-. Frequency varies. Disseminates advances and discoveries in the areas of soil, air and food contamination and pollution.

Common Sense Pest Control Quarterly. Bio-Integral Resource Center, PO Box 7414, Berkeley, California 94707. (415) 524-2567. Four times a year. Least-toxic management of pests on indoor plants, pests that damage paper, controlling fleas and ticks on pets, and garden pests.

The Delicate Balance. National Center for Environmental Health Strategies, 1100 Rural Ave., Voorhers, New Jersey 08043. (609) 429-5358. 1990. Quarterly.

Earthwatch Magazine. Earthwatch Expeditions, 680 Mt. Auburn St., Box 403, Watertown, Massachusetts 02272. (617) 926-8200. Bimonthly. Worldwide research expeditions, endangered species, cultures, and world health.

EHP, Environmental Health Perspectives. National Institute of Environmental Health Sciences, National Institutes of Health, Dept. of Health Education and Welfare, Box 12233, Bldg. 101, Rm. A 259, Research Triangle Park, North Carolina 27709. (919) 541-3406. 1972-. Bimonthly.

Environ: A Magazine for Ecological Living & Health Wary. Canary Press, Box 2204, Ft. Collins, Colorado 80522. (303) 224-0083. Quarterly. Consumer alternatives for ecologically sound lifestyles.

Environmental Action. Environmental Action Foundation, 6930 Carroll Ave., Ste. 600, Takoma Park, Maryland 20912. (301) 891-1100. Bimonthly. Impact of humans and industry on the environment.

Environmental and Molecular Mutagenesis. Wiley-Liss, 605 3rd Ave., New York, New York 10158-0012. (212) 850-6000. 1974-. Eight issues per year. Provides an international forum for research on basic mechanisms of mutation, the detection of mutagens, and the implications of environmental mutagens for human health.

Environmental Defense Fund Letter. Environmental Defense Fund, 257 Park Avenue South, New York, New York 10010. (212) 505-2100. 1971-. Bimonthly. Environmental issues of concern.

Environmental Health Letter. Business Publishers, Inc., 951 Pershing Dr., Silver Spring, Maryland 20910-4464. (301) 587-6300. 1961-. Biweekly. Covers areas such as: indoor air, asbestos health effects, toxic substances testing, health problems at wastewater plants, risk-based sludge rules, medical waste, developmental toxicity risk assessment, animal carcinogen tests, pesticide risk, air toxics, aerospace chemicals, lead, radionuclide emissions, state right-to-know statutes, and incinerator emissions.

Environmental Health News. University of Washington, School of Public Health, Dept. of Environmental Health, Seattle, Washington 98195. (206) 543-3222. Quarterly. Occupational health, air pollution and safety.

Environmental Health Perspectives. National Institute of Environmental Health Sciences, P.O. Box 12233, Research Triangle Park, North Carolina 27709. (919) 541-3406. Bimonthly. Proceedings from science conferences and issues on target organisms.

Environmental Health Report. S.D. Gregory, Box 7955, Dallas, Texas 75209. (214) 725-6492. Monthly. Physicians, environmental scientists, and public health practitioners concerned with environmental health.

Environmental Health Trends Report. National Environmental Health Assn., South Tower, 720 S. Colorado Blvd., Ste. 970, Denver, Colorado 80222. (303) 756-9090. Quarterly.

Environmental Mutagen Society Newsletter. Dr. Virginia Houk. U.S. Environmental Protection Agency, M/D-68, Research Triangle Park, North Carolina 27711. (919) 541-2815. Twice a year. Studies of mutagens.

Environmental Pollution & Control. National Technical Information Service, 5285 Port Royal Rd., Springfield, Virginia 22161. (703) 487-4650. Weekly. Covers air, noise, solid waste, water pollution, radiation, environmental health and safety, pesticide pollution and control.

Environmental Review. Citizens for a Better Environment, 407 S. Dearborn, Ste. 1775, Chicago, Illinois 60605. (312) 939-1530. Quarterly. Environmental policy and environmental protection issues in the Midwest.

Environmental Science and Technology. American Chemical Society, 1155 16th St. N.W., Washington, District of Columbia 20036. (800) 227-5558. 1967-. Monthly. Contains research articles on various aspects of environmental chemistry, interpretative articles by invited experts and commentary on the scientific aspects of environmental management.

Hazardous Materials Intelligence Report. World Information Systems, P.O. Box 535, Harvard Square Station, Cambridge, Massachusetts 02238. (617) 491-5100. Weekly. Timely information on hazardous substances rules and procedures.

Hazardous Substances and Public Health: A Publication of the Agency for Toxic Substances and Disease Registry. Agency for Toxic Substances and Disease Registry, Department of Health and Human Services, 1600 Clifton Rd. NE, M/S E33, Atlanta, Georgia 30333. (404) 639-0727. Quarterly.

HazTech News. Business Publishers, Inc., 951 Pershing Drive, Silver Spring, Maryland 20910. (301) 587-6300. Biweekly. Covers developments and discoveries in waste management.

Health & Environment Digest. Freshwater Biological Research Foundation, 2500 Shadywood Road, Box 90, Navarre, Minnesota 55392. (612) 471-8407. Monthly. Public health effects of environmental contaminants of water, air, and soil.

INFORM Reports. INFORM Inc., 381 Park Ave., So., New York, New York 10016. (212) 689-4040. Quarterly. INFORM is a nonprofit environmental research & education organization for the preservation and conservation of natural resources and public health.

International Journal of Biosocial and Medical Research. Life Sciences Press, P.O. Box 1174, Takoma, Washington 98401-1174. (206) 922-0442. Semiannual. Deals with psychological and psychobiological aspects of environments.

Job Safety and Health. Bureau of National Affairs, 1231 25th St. NW, Washington, District of Columbia 20037. (202) 452-4200. Biweekly. Covers job safety and health laws.

Journal of Environmental Health. National Environmental Health Association, 720 South Colorado Boulevard, Suite 970, Denver, Colorado 80222. (303) 756-9090. Bimonthly. Covers phases in environmental health.

Journal of Environmental Science and Health. Marcel Dekker, Inc., 270 Madison Ave., New York, New York 10016. (212) 696-9000. Bimonthly. Concerns pesticides, food contaminants, chemical carcinogens, and agricultural wastes.

Journal of Occupational Medicine. Williams & Wilkins, P.O. Box 64380, Baltimore, Maryland 21264. (301) 528-4105. Monthly. Issues on the maintenance and improvement of the health of workers.

Journal of Toxicology and Environmental Health. Taylor & Francis, 1900 Frost Road, Suite 101, Bristol, Pennsylvania 19007. (800) 821-8312. Monthly. Covers toxilogical effects of environmental pollution.

Medical Waste News. Business Publishers, Inc., 951 Pershing Dr., Silver Spring, Maryland 20910-4464. (301) 587-6300. 1989-. Biweekly. Covers EPA regulations and actions, state and nationwide changes in the laws, which management firms are landing big contracts, and also reports on technology such as: incineration, autoclaving, microwaves, etc. Also available online.

NCLEHA Newsletter. National Conference of Local Environmental Health Administrators, Allegheny County Health Department, Bureau of Environmental Health, 33333 Forbes Avenue, Pittsburgh, Pennsylvania 15213. (412) 578-8030. Twice a year. Covers local environmental health programs.

New York State Environment. New York State Journal for Health Physical Education, Dutchess Community College, Poughkeepsie, New York 12601. Semimonthly. State environmental news.

Occupational Hazards. Penton Publishing Co., 1100 Superior Ave., Cleveland, Ohio 44114. (216) 696-7000. Monthly. Covers safety management and plant protection.

Occupational Health and Safety. Stevens Publishing Co., P.O. Box 2604, Waco, Texas 76714. (817) 776-9000. Monthly. Covers occupational health and safety.

Occupational Safety and Health Reporter. Bureau of National Affairs, 1231 25th St. NW, Washington, District of Columbia 20037. (202) 452-4200. Weekly. Covers federal safety and health standards, regulations, and policies. Also available online.

Pest Control Technology. Gei, Inc., 4012 Bridge Ave., Cleveland, Ohio 44113. (316) 961-4130. Monthly. Articles on pests and pesticides.

Priorities For Long Life and Good Health. American Council on Health and Science, 1995 Broadway, 16th Floor, New York, New York 10023. (212) 362-7044. Quarterly. Covers evaluations of food, chemicals, and health.

Public Health Engineer. Institution of Public Health Engineers, Municipal Publications, 32 Eccleston Square, London, England SW1V IP3. 1895-. Monthly.

Synthetic Organic Chemical Manufacturers Association Newsletter. Synthetic Organic Chemical Manufacturers Association, 1330 Connecticut Avenue, NW, Washington, District of Columbia 20036. (202) 659-0060. Biweekly. Covers trade, environmental and safety issues.

RESEARCH CENTERS AND INSTITUTES

Advanced Sciences Research and Development Corporation. P.O. Box 127, Lakemont, Georgia 30552. (404) 782-2092.

Boston University, Center for Energy and Environmental Studies. 675 Commonwealth Avenue, Boston, Massachusetts 02215. (617) 353-3083.

Ecology Center. 2530 San Pablo Ave., Berkeley, California 94702. (510) 548-2220.

Sanitary Engineering and Environmental Health Research Laboratory. University of California, Berkeley, 1301 South 46th, Building 112, Richmond, California 94804. (415) 231-9449.

University of South Carolina at Columbia, International Center for Public Health Research. Wedge Plantation, P.O. Box 699, McClellanville, South Carolina 29458. (803) 527-1371.

STATISTICS SOURCES

Occupational Safety Equipment. FIND/SVP, 625 Avenue of the Americas, New York, New York 10011. (212) 645-4500.

Statistical Record of the Environment. Arsen J. Darnay. Gale Research Inc., 835 Penobscot Bldg., Detroit, Michigan 48226-4094. (313) 961-2242. 1992.

World Resources. World Resources Institute. 1709 New York Ave., N.W., Washington, District of Columbia 20006. (202) 638-6300. Annual. Statistical and textual analysis of world's natural resources and the effects of growth-caused environmental pollution.

TRADE ASSOCIATIONS AND PROFESSIONAL SOCIETIES

Alliance for Environmental Education, Inc. 10751 Ambassador Dr., No. 201, Manassas, Virginia 22110. (703) 335-1025. A coalition of organizations that works at the regional, state, and national level to promote environmental education.

American Academy of Environmental Medicine. Box 16106, Denver, Colorado 80216. (313) 622-9755.

American Council on Science and Health. 1995 Broadway, 16th Floor, New York, New York 10023. (212) 362-7044.

American Industrial Health Council. 1330 Connecticut Ave., N.W., Suite 300, Washington, District of Columbia 20036. (202) 659-0060.

American Industrial Hygiene Association. 345 White Pond Dr., PO Box 8390, Akron, Ohio 44320. (216) 873-2442.

American Institute of Biological Sciences. 730 11th St., N.W., Washington, District of Columbia 20001-4521. (202) 628-1500.

American Institute of Biomedical Climatology. 1023 Welsh Rd., Philadelphia, Pennsylvania 19115. (215) 673-8368.

American Medical Association. 515 N. State St., Chicago, Illinois 60610. (312) 645-4818.

American Public Health Association. 1015 15th St., N.W., Washington, District of Columbia 20005. (202) 789-5600.

Americans for the Environment. 1400 16th St. N.W., Washington, District of Columbia 20036. (202) 797-6665.

Asbestos Information Association of North America. 1745 Jefferson Davis Highway, Suite 509, Arlington, Virginia 22202. (703) 979-1150.

Association of Environmental Engineering Professors. Department of Civil Engineering, Virginia Polytechnic Institute and State University, Blacksburg, Virginia 24061. (703) 231-6021.

Association of Federal Safety and Health Professionals. 7549 Wilhelm Dr., Lanham, Maryland 20706-3737. (301) 552-2104.

Association of University Environmental Health. Institute of Environmental Medicine, NYU Medical Center, 550 First Ave., New York, New York 10016. (212) 340-5280.

Biomedical Engineering Society. P.O. Box 2399, Culver City, California 90231. (213) 206-6443.

CEIP Fund. 68 Harrison Ave., 5th Fl., Boston, Massachusetts 02111. (617) 426-4375.

Center for Environmental Information, Inc. 99 Court St., Rochester, New York 14604. (716) 546-3796.

Citizen's Clearinghouse for Hazardous Wastes, Inc. P.O. Box 6806, Falls Church, Virginia 22040. (703) 237-2249.

Conference of Local Environmental Health Administrators. 1395 Blue Tent Ct., Cool, California 95614-2120. (916) 823-1736.

Conference of State Health and Environmental Managers. c/o David Cochran, 3909 Cresthill Dr., Austin, Texas 78731. (512) 453-6723.

Conservation Law Foundation of New England, Inc. 3 Joy St., Boston, Massachusetts 02108. (617) 742-2540.

ECRI. 5200 Butler Pike, Plymouth Meeting, Pennsylvania 19462. (215) 825-6000.

Environmental Defense Fund. 257 Park Ave., S., New York, New York 10010. (212) 505-2100. Non-profit organization that was established more than 20 years ago. Its goals are to protect the earth's environment by providing lasting solutions to global environmental problems.

Environmental Mutagen Society. 1600 Wilson Blvd., Suite 905, Arlington, Virginia 22209. (703) 525-1191.

Environmental Quality Industrial Resources Center. The Ohio State University, 1200 Chambers Rd., Room 310, Columbus, Ohio 43212. (614) 292-6717.

Friends of the Earth. 218 D St., SE, Washington, District of Columbia 20003. (202) 544-2600.

Health and Energy Institute. 615 Kenevec, Takoma Park, Maryland 20912. (301) 585-5541.

Health Physics Society. 8000 Westpark Dr., Suite 400, McLean, Virginia 22102. (703) 790-1745.

IEEE Engineering in Medicine and Biology Society. c/o Inst. of Electrical and Electronics Engineers, 345 E. 47th St., New York, New York 10017. (212) 705-7867.

Industrial Health Foundation. 34 Penn Cir. W., Pittsburgh, Pennsylvania 15206. (412) 363-6600.

Industrial Safety Equipment Association. 1901 N. Moore St., Arlington, Virginia 22209. (703) 525-1695.

Infectious Disease Society of America. c/o Vincent T. Andriole, M.D., 333 Cedar St., 201-202 LCI, New Haven, Connecticut 06510. (203) 785-8782.

INFORM. 381 Park Avenue S., New York, New York 10016. (212) 689-4040.

Institute of Environmental Sciences. 940 E. Northwest Hwy., Mount Prospect, Illinois 60056. (708) 255-1561.

International Association of Milk, Food, & Environmental Sanitarians. 502 E. Lincoln Way, Ames, Iowa 50010. (515) 232-6699.

International Board of Environmental Medicine. 2114 Martingale Dr., Norman, Oklahoma 73072. (405) 329-8437.

National Association of Manufacturers. 1331 Pennsylvania Ave., N.W., Suite 1500 North, Washington, District of Columbia 20004. (202) 637-3000.

National Center for Environmental Health Strategies. 1100 Rural Ave., Voorhees, New Jersey 08043. (609) 429-5358.

National Conference of Local Environmental Health Administrators. 1395 Blue Tent Ct., Cool, California 95614-2120. (916) 823-1736.

National Environmental Health Association. South Tower, 720 S. Colorado Blvd., #970, Denver, Colorado 80222. (303) 756-9090.

National Health Council. 1730 M St. N.W., Ste. 500, Washington, District of Columbia 20036. (202) 785-3913.

Nuclear Information and Records Management. 210 Fifth Ave., New York, New York 10010. (212) 683-9221.

Public Citizen Health Research Group. 2000 P St., N.W., Suite 700, Washington, District of Columbia 20036. (202) 872-0320.

The Public Environment Center. 1 Milligan Pl., New York, New York 10011. (212) 691-4877.

Society for Environmental Geochemistry and Health. c/o Wilard R. Chappell, University of Colorado, Denver Center for Environmental Sciences, P.O. Box 136, Denver, Colorado 80217-3364. (303) 556-3460.

Society for Industrial Microbiology. Box 12534, Arlington, Virginia 22209. (703) 941-5373.

Society for Occupational & Environmental Health. 6728 Old McLeen Village Dr., McLean, Virginia 22101. (703) 556-9222.

Society for Vector Ecology. Box 87, Santa Ana, California 92702. (714) 971-2421.

Synthetic Organic Chemical Manufacturers Association. 1330 Connecticut Ave., N.W., Suite 300, Washington, District of Columbia 20036. (202) 659-0060.

Textile Processors, Service Trades, Health Care, Professional & Technical Employees International Union. 303 E. Wacker Dr., Suite 1109, Chicago, Illinois 60601. (312) 946-0450.

United States Committee for UNICEF. 333 E. 38th St., New York, New York 10016. (212) 686-5522.

United States Operating Committee on ETAD. 1330 Connecticut Ave., N.W., Suite 300, Washington, District of Columbia 20036-1702. (202) 659-0060.

HEARING LOSS

See: NOISE POLLUTION

HEAT EXCHANGERS

ABSTRACTING AND INDEXING SERVICES

Applied Science and Technology Index. H.W. Wilson Co., 950 University Ave., Bronx, New York 10452. (800) 367-6770. Formerly Industrial Arts Index.

Engineering Index. The Engineering Index Inc., 345 E. 47th St., New York, New York 10017. 1962-.

Environment Abstracts. Bowker A & I Publishing, 121 Chanlon Rd., New Providence, New Jersey 07974. (908) 464-6800. 1974-.

Environment Index. Environment Information Center, Index Research Department, 124 E. 39th St., New York, New York 10016. 1971-. Annual.

Environmental Information Connection–EIC. Planning Information Program, Dept. of Urban and Regional Planning, University of Illinois, 1003 West Nevada, Urbana, Illinois 61801. (217) 333-1369. Also available online.

Environmental Periodicals Bibliography. Environmental Studies Institute, International Academy at Santa Barbara, 800 Garden St., Suite D, Santa Barbara, California 93101. (805) 965-5010. Also available online.

ERDA Research Abstracts. U.S. ERDA Technical Information Center, Box 62, Oak Ridge, Tennessee 37830.

General Science Index. H. W. Wilson Co., 950 University Ave., Bronx, New York 10452. 1978-. Monthly, also issued in annual cumulation. Cumulative subject index to English language periodicals in the subject fields of astronomy, botany, chemistry, earth science, environment and conservation, food and nutrition, genetics, mathematics, medicine and health, microbiology, oceanography, physics, physiology and zoology.

Index to Scientific Book Contents. Institute for Scientific Information, 3501 Market St., Philadelphia, Pennsylvania 19104. (800) 523-1857. 1985-. Annual. Gives contents of science books published.

Pollution Abstracts. Cambridge Scientific Abstracts, 5161 River Rd., Bethesda, Maryland 20816. (301) 961-6750. Six/year. Indexes worldwide technical literature on environmental pollution. Covers air pollution, marine and freshwater pollution, sewage and wastewater treatment, waste management, toxicology and health, noise pollution, radiation, land pollution, and environmental policies, programs, legislation, and education. Also available online.

Science Citation Index. Institute for Scientific Information, 3501 Market St., Philadelphia, Pennsylvania 19104. 1961-.

BIBLIOGRAPHIES

EPA Publications Bibliography. U.S. Environmental Protection Agency, Library Systems Branch, 401 M St., SW, Washington, District of Columbia 20460. (202) 260-2090. Quarterly.

DIRECTORIES

Air-to-Air Heat Exchangers: Directory and Buyers' Guide. 1100 Massachusetts Ave., Arlington, Massachusetts 02174. (617) 648-8700. Irregular.

ENCYCLOPEDIAS AND DICTIONARIES

Dictionary of Environmental Engineering and Related Sciences: English-Spanish, Spanish-English. Jose T. Villate. Ediciones Universal, 3090 SW 8th St., Miami, Florida 33135. (305) 642-3355. 1979.

Encyclopedia of Environmental Science and Engineering. J.R. Pfafflin. Gordon and Breach Science Publishers, Inc., 270 8th Ave., New York, New York 10011. (212) 206-8900. 1992.

Encyclopedia of Physical Science and Technology. Robert A. Meyers, ed. Academic Press, c/o Harcourt Brace Jovanovich Inc., 6277 Sea Harbor Dr., Orlando, Florida 32887. (800) 346-8648. Dictionary of engineering, technology and physical sciences.

Encyclopedia of Physics. Rita G. Lerner and George L. Trigg. VCH Publishers, 303 NW 12th Ave., Deerfield Beach, Florida 33442-1788. (305) 428-5566. 1991. Second edition.

Kirk-Othmer Encyclopedia of Chemical Technology. J. I. Kroschwitz, ed. John Wiley & Sons, Inc., 605 3rd Ave., New York, New York 10158-0012. (212) 850-6000. 1992-. All articles in the new edition have been rewritten and updated adding new subjects such as biotechnology, computer topics, analytical techniques and instrumentation, environmental concerns, fuels and energy, inorganic and solid state chemistry; composite materials and material science in general, and pharmaceuticals. Also available online.

Van Nostrand's Scientific Encyclopedia. Glenn D. Considine, ed. Van Nostrand Reinhold, 115 5th Ave., New York, New York 10003. (212) 254-3232. 1983. Sixth edition. Includes all broad subject areas in science.

GENERAL WORKS

Compact Heat Exchangers. R. K. Shah. American Society of Mechanical Engineers, 345 E. 47th St., New York, New York 10017. (212) 705-7722. 1992. History, technological advancement, and mechanical design problems.

Conservation and Heat Transfer. Nejat T. Veziroglu, ed. Nova Science Publishers Inc., 283 Commack Rd., Suite 300, Commack, New York 11725-3104. (516) 499-3103; (516) 499-3106. 1991. Describes methods of conservation and heat transfer.

Heat Exchangers. S. Kakac. Hemisphere Publishing Co., 79 Madison Ave., Suite 1110, New York, New York 10016. (212) 725-1999. 1981. Thermal-hydraulic fundamentals and design.

Heat Exchangers–Theory and Practice. J. Taborek. McGraw-Hill Science & Engineering Books, 11 W. 19th St., New York, New York 10011. (212) 337-6010. 1983.

Industrial Heat Exchangers. Graham Walker. Hemisphere Publishing Co., 79 Madison Ave., Suite 1110, New York, New York 10016. (212) 725-1999. 1982.

HANDBOOKS AND MANUALS

Heat Exchangers: Design and Theory Sourcebook. Naim Afgan. Scripta Book Co., Washington, District of Columbia 1974.

ONLINE DATA BASES

Computerized Engineering Index–COMPENDEX. Engineering Information Inc., 345 E. 47th St., New York, New York 10017. (212) 705-7600.

Enviro/Energyline Abstracts Plus. R. R. Bowker Co., 121 Chanlon Rd., New Providence, New Jersey 07974. (908) 464-6800.

Environmental Periodicals Bibliography. National Information Services Corp., Ste. 6, Wyman Towers, 3100 St. Paul St., Baltimore, Maryland 21218. (410)243-0797. Online version of abstract of same name.

Kirk-Othmer Encyclopedia of Chemical Technology. John Wiley & Sons, Inc., 605 3rd Ave., 5th Floor, New York, New York 10158. (212) 850-6000. Online version of the publication of the same name.

HEATING SYSTEMS

ABSTRACTING AND INDEXING SERVICES

Applied Science and Technology Index. H.W. Wilson Co., 950 University Ave., Bronx, New York 10452. (800) 367-6770. Formerly Industrial Arts Index.

Engineering Index. The Engineering Index Inc., 345 E. 47th St., New York, New York 10017. 1962-.

Environment Abstracts. Bowker A & I Publishing, 121 Chanlon Rd., New Providence, New Jersey 07974. (908) 464-6800. 1974-.

Environment Index. Environment Information Center, Index Research Department, 124 E. 39th St., New York, New York 10016. 1971-. Annual.

Environmental Information Connection–EIC. Planning Information Program, Dept. of Urban and Regional Planning, University of Illinois, 1003 West Nevada, Urbana, Illinois 61801. (217) 333-1369. Also available online.

Environmental Periodicals Bibliography. Environmental Studies Institute, International Academy at Santa Barbara, 800 Garden St., Suite D, Santa Barbara, California 93101. (805) 965-5010. Also available online.

General Science Index. H. W. Wilson Co., 950 University Ave., Bronx, New York 10452. 1978-. Monthly, also issued in annual cumulation. Cumulative subject index to English language periodicals in the subject fields of astronomy, botany, chemistry, earth science, environment and conservation, food and nutrition, genetics, mathematics, medicine and health, microbiology, oceanography, physics, physiology and zoology.

Index to Scientific Book Contents. Institute for Scientific Information, 3501 Market St., Philadelphia, Pennsylvania 19104. (800) 523-1857. 1985-. Annual. Gives contents of science books published.

Pollution Abstracts. Cambridge Scientific Abstracts, 5161 River Rd., Bethesda, Maryland 20816. (301) 961-6750. Six/year. Indexes worldwide technical literature on environmental pollution. Covers air pollution, marine and freshwater pollution, sewage and wastewater treatment, waste management, toxicology and health, noise pollution, radiation, land pollution, and environmental poli-

cies, programs, legislation, and education. Also available online.

BIBLIOGRAPHIES

EPA Publications Bibliography. U.S. Environmental Protection Agency, Library Systems Branch, 401 M St., SW, Washington, District of Columbia 20460. (202) 260-2090. Quarterly.

DIRECTORIES

Heating Equipment Dealers & Contractors Directory. 5711 S. 86th Circle, Omaha, Nebraska 68127. (402) 593-4600. Annual.

Heating-Plumbing Air Conditioning–Buyers' Guide Issue. 1450 Don Mills Rd., Don Mills, Ontario, Canada M3B 2X7. (416) 445-6641. Annual.

Heating, Ventilating, Refrigeration & Air Conditioning Year Book and Daily Buyers' Guide. 34 Palace Court, ESCA House, Bayswater, England W2 4JG. (71) 292488. Annual.

Who's Who in the Plumbing-Heating-Cooling Industry. National Association of Plumbing-Heating-Cooling Contractors, 180 S. Washington St., P.O. Box 6808, Falls Church, Virginia 22046. (703) 237-8100.

Wood Heating Alliance–Membership Directory. Wood Heating Alliance, 1101 Connecticut Ave., N.W., Suite 700, Washington, District of Columbia 20036. (202) 857-1181.

ENCYCLOPEDIAS AND DICTIONARIES

Dictionary of Environmental Engineering and Related Sciences: English-Spanish, Spanish-English. Jose T. Villate. Ediciones Universal, 3090 SW 8th St., Miami, Florida 33135. (305) 642-3355. 1979.

Encyclopedia of Chemical Processing and Design. John J. Mcketta and W. A. Cunningham. Marcel Dekker, Inc., 270 Madison Ave., New York, New York 10016. (212) 696-9000; (800) 228-1160. 1992. Thirty-eight volumes.

Encyclopedia of Environmental Science and Engineering. J.R. Pfafflin. Gordon and Breach Science Publishers, Inc., 270 8th Ave., New York, New York 10011. (212) 206-8900. 1992.

Encyclopedia of Physical Science and Technology. Robert A. Meyers, ed. Academic Press, c/o Harcourt Brace Jovanovich Inc., 6277 Sea Harbor Dr., Orlando, Florida 32887. (800) 346-8648. Dictionary of engineering, technology and physical sciences.

Encyclopedia of Physics. Rita G. Lerner and George L. Trigg. VCH Publishers, 303 NW 12th Ave., Deerfield Beach, Florida 33442-1788. (305) 428-5566. 1991. Second edition.

Kirk-Othmer Encyclopedia of Chemical Technology. J. I. Kroschwitz, ed. John Wiley & Sons, Inc., 605 3rd Ave., New York, New York 10158-0012. (212) 850-6000. 1992-. All articles in the new edition have been rewritten and updated adding new subjects such as biotechnology, computer topics, analytical techniques and instrumentation, environmental concerns, fuels and energy, inorganic and solid state chemistry; composite materials and material science in general, and pharmaceuticals. Also available online.

Van Nostrand's Scientific Encyclopedia. Glenn D. Considine, ed. Van Nostrand Reinhold, 115 5th Ave., New York, New York 10003. (212) 254-3232. 1983. Sixth edition. Includes all broad subject areas in science.

GENERAL WORKS

Heating, Cooling, Lighting. John Wiley & Sons, Inc., 605 3rd Ave., New York, New York 10158-0012. (212) 850-6000. 1991.

HANDBOOKS AND MANUALS

Heating, Ventilation, and Air-Conditioning Systems Estimating Manual. A. M. Khashab. McGraw-Hill Science & Engineering Books, 11 W. 19th St., New York, New York 10011. (212) 337-6010. 1984.

The Master Handbook of All Home Heating Systems. Billy L. Price. Tab Books, PO Box 40, Blue Ridge Summit, Pennsylvania 17294-2191. (717) 794-2191. 1979. Tune up, repair, installation, and maintenance as well as heating equipment and supplies.

ONLINE DATA BASES

Computerized Engineering Index–COMPENDEX. Engineering Information Inc., 345 E. 47th St., New York, New York 10017. (212) 705-7600.

Enviro/Energyline Abstracts Plus. R. R. Bowker Co., 121 Chanlon Rd., New Providence, New Jersey 07974. (908) 464-6800.

Environmental Periodicals Bibliography. National Information Services Corp., Ste. 6, Wyman Towers, 3100 St. Paul St., Baltimore, Maryland 21218. (410)243-0797. Online version of abstract of same name.

IBSEDEX. Building Services Research & Information Association, Old Bracknell Lane West, Bracknell, Berkshire, England RG12 4AH. 44 (344) 426511.

Kirk-Othmer Encyclopedia of Chemical Technology. John Wiley & Sons, Inc., 605 3rd Ave., 5th Floor, New York, New York 10158. (212) 850-6000. Online version of the publication of the same name.

PERIODICALS AND NEWSLETTERS

Energy and Housing Report. Business Publishers, Inc., 951 Pershing Dr., Silver Spring, Maryland 20910. (301) 587-6300. Monthly. Energy conservation problems; developments in home energy products.

TRADE ASSOCIATIONS AND PROFESSIONAL SOCIETIES

American Society of Heating, Refrigerating and Air-Conditioning Engineers. 1791 Tullie Circle, N.E., Atlanta, Georgia 30329. (404) 636-8400.

Heat Exchange Institute. c/o Christine M. Devor, Thomas Associates, Inc., 1230 Keith Bldg., Cleveland, Ohio 44115. (216) 241-7333.

Home Ventilating Institute Division of the Air Movement Control Association. 30 W. University Drive, Arlington Heights, Illinois 60004. (312) 394-0150.

Industrial Heating Equipment Association. 1901 N. Moore St., Arlington, Virginia 22209. (703) 525-2513.

National Environmental Balancing Bureau. 8224 Old Courthouse Rd., Vienna, Virginia 19103. (215) 564-3484.

Wood Heating Alliance. 1101 Connecticut Ave., N.W., Suite 700, Washington, District of Columbia 20036. (202) 857-1181.

HEAVY METALS

ABSTRACTING AND INDEXING SERVICES

Applied Science and Technology Index. H.W. Wilson Co., 950 University Ave., Bronx, New York 10452. (800) 367-6770. Formerly Industrial Arts Index.

ASFA Aquaculture Abstracts. Cambridge Scientific Abstracts, Inc., 5161 River Rd., Bethesda, Maryland 20816. (301) 961-6750. 1984.

Biotechnology Research Abstracts. Cambridge Scientific Abstracts, 5161 River Rd., Bethesda, Maryland 20816. (301) 961-6750. Monthly. Includes such broad areas as genetic intervention, biochemical genetics, and microbiological techniques.

Bulletin Signaletique: Eau et Assainissement, Pollution Atmospherique, Droit des Pollutions. Centre de Documentation, Centre National de la Recherche Scientifique, 15, quai Anatole France, Paris, France 75700. (1) 45 55 92 25. 1983-. Monthly. Indexes pollution periodicals including water, atmospheric and related pollutions.

Chemical Abstracts. Chemical Abstracts Service, 2540 Olentangy River Rd., PO Box 3012, Columbus, Ohio 43210. (800) 848-6533. 1907-.

Ecological Abstracts. Geo Abstracts Ltd. Elsevier Applied Science, Crown House, Linton Rd., Barking, England IG 11 8JU. 1974-. Derived from over 600 leading ecological and environmental journals, plus books, conference proceedings, reports and theses.

Ecology Abstracts. Cambridge Scientific Abstracts, 5161 River Rd., Bethesda, Maryland 20816. (301) 961-6750. Monthly.

Engineering Index. The Engineering Index Inc., 345 E. 47th St., New York, New York 10017. 1962-.

Environment Abstracts. Bowker A & I Publishing, 121 Chanlon Rd., New Providence, New Jersey 07974. (908) 464-6800. 1974-.

Environment Index. Environment Information Center, Index Research Department, 124 E. 39th St., New York, New York 10016. 1971-. Annual.

Environmental Information Connection–EIC. Planning Information Program, Dept. of Urban and Regional Planning, University of Illinois, 1003 West Nevada, Urbana, Illinois 61801. (217) 333-1369. Also available online.

Environmental Periodicals Bibliography. Environmental Studies Institute, International Academy at Santa Barbara, 800 Garden St., Suite D, Santa Barbara, California 93101. (805) 965-5010. Also available online.

ERDA Research Abstracts. U.S. ERDA Technical Information Center, Box 62, Oak Ridge, Tennessee 37830.

General Science Index. H. W. Wilson Co., 950 University Ave., Bronx, New York 10452. 1978-. Monthly, also issued in annual cumulation. Cumulative subject index to English language periodicals in the subject fields of astronomy, botany, chemistry, earth science, environment and conservation, food and nutrition, genetics, mathematics, medicine and health, microbiology, oceanography, physics, physiology and zoology.

Geographical Abstracts. London School of Economics, Dept. of Geography, Regency House, 34 Duke St., London, England 1966-. Continued by Geo Abstracts issued in 6 parts: Pt. A. Landforms and the quaternary; Pt. B. Biogeography and Climatology; Pt. C. Economic geography; Pt. D. Social geography and cartography; Pt. E. Sedimentology; Pt. F. Regional and community planning.

Index to Scientific Book Contents. Institute for Scientific Information, 3501 Market St., Philadelphia, Pennsylvania 19104. (800) 523-1857. 1985-. Annual. Gives contents of science books published.

Mineralogical Abstracts. Mineralogical Society, 41 Queen's Gate, London, England SW7 5HR. 71 5847916. Quarterly. Abstracts of journal articles, conferences, technical reports and specialized books in the areas of minerals, clay minerals, economic minerals, ore deposits, environmental studies, experimental mineralogy, gemstones, geochemistry, petrology, lunar and planetary studies and other related areas in mineralogy.

Physics Briefs. Physikalische Berichte. Physik Verlag, Pappapelallee 3, Postfach 101161, Weinheim, Germany D-6940. 1979-. Semimonthly. In English. Volumes for 1979- issued by the Deutsche Physikalische Gesellschaft and the Fachinformationszentrum Energie Physik, Mathematik in cooperation with the American Institute of Physics.

Pollution Abstracts. Cambridge Scientific Abstracts, 5161 River Rd., Bethesda, Maryland 20816. (301) 961-6750. Six/year. Indexes worldwide technical literature on environmental pollution. Covers air pollution, marine and freshwater pollution, sewage and wastewater treatment, waste management, toxicology and health, noise pollution, radiation, land pollution, and environmental policies, programs, legislation, and education. Also available online.

Science Citation Index. Institute for Scientific Information, 3501 Market St., Philadelphia, Pennsylvania 19104. 1961-.

BIBLIOGRAPHIES

Bibliography and Index of Geology. American Geological Institute, 4220 King St., Alexandria, Virginia 22302. Monthly. Includes environmental geology and hydrogeology.

EPA Publications Bibliography. U.S. Environmental Protection Agency, Library Systems Branch, 401 M St., SW, Washington, District of Columbia 20460. (202) 260-2090. Quarterly.

Heavy Metals in Water: A Bibliography. Water Resources Scientific Information Center, Office of Water Research and Technology, Washington, District of Columbia 1977.

ENCYCLOPEDIAS AND DICTIONARIES

Dictionary of Environmental Engineering and Related Sciences: English-Spanish, Spanish-English. Jose T. Villate. Ediciones Universal, 3090 SW 8th St., Miami, Florida 33135. (305) 642-3355. 1979.

Encyclopedia of Environmental Science and Engineering. J.R. Pfafflin. Gordon and Breach Science Publishers, Inc., 270 8th Ave., New York, New York 10011. (212) 206-8900. 1992.

Encyclopedia of Physical Science and Technology. Robert A. Meyers, ed. Academic Press, c/o Harcourt Brace Jovanovich Inc., 6277 Sea Harbor Dr., Orlando, Florida 32887. (800) 346-8648. Dictionary of engineering, technology and physical sciences.

Encyclopedia of Physics. Rita G. Lerner and George L. Trigg. VCH Publishers, 303 NW 12th Ave., Deerfield Beach, Florida 33442-1788. (305) 428-5566. 1991. Second edition.

McGraw-Hill Encyclopedia of Science and Technology. McGraw-Hill, 1221 Avenue of the Americas, New York, New York 10020. (212) 512-2000 or (800) 262-4729. 1992. Seventh edition. Issued in multiple volumes including index. Includes all science and technology broad subject areas.

Van Nostrand's Scientific Encyclopedia. Glenn D. Considine, ed. Van Nostrand Reinhold, 115 5th Ave., New York, New York 10003. (212) 254-3232. 1983. Sixth edition. Includes all broad subject areas in science.

GENERAL WORKS

Analytical Aspects of Mercury and Other Heavy Metals in the Environment. R. W. Frei. Gordon and Breach Science Publishers, Inc., 270 8th Ave., New York, New York 10011. (212) 206-8900. 1975. Heavy metals and pollution measurement.

Biological Effects of Heavy Metals. E. C. Foulkes. CRC Press, 2000 Corporate Blvd. N.W., Boca Raton, Florida 33431. (800) 272-7737. 1990. Two volumes. Reviews general mechanisms of metal carcinogenesis. It illustrates this effect by detailed reference to some specific metals, including Cd, Co and Ni. The material illustrates the common threads running through the field of metal carcinogenesis.

Biosorption of Heavy Metals. Bohumil Volesky. CRC Press, 2000 Corporate Blvd., N.W., Boca Raton, Florida 33431. (407) 994-0555; (800) 272-7737. 1990. Comprehensive multidisciplinary review of the phenomenon of biosorption and of the state of development of biosorbent materials.

Contamination of Animal Feedstuffs: Chemicals, Mycotoxins, Heavy Metals. U.S. Department of Health and Human Services, Public Health Services, National Institutes of Health, 9000 Rockville Pike, Bethesda, Maryland 20892. (301) 496-4000. 1981.

Environmental Contamination of Lead and Other Heavy Metals. G. L. Rolfe. Institute for Environmental Studies, University of Illinois at Urbana- Champaign, Urbana-Champaign, Illinois 61801. 1977. Environmental aspects of lead pollution.

The Heavy Elements: Chemistry, Environmental Impact and Health Effects. Jack E. Fergusson. Pergamon Microforms International, Inc., Fairview Park, Elmsford, New York 10523. (914) 592-7720. 1990. Provides a broad survey of the heavy elements, their relevant chemistry, environmental impacts and health effects.

Heavy Metals in Natural Waters. James W. Moore. Springer-Verlag, 175 5th Ave., New York, New York 10010. (212) 460-1500. 1984. Applied monitoring and impact assessment.

Heavy Metals in the Environment: International Conference. J. P. Vernet. CEP Consultants, 26 Albany St., Edinburgh, Scotland EH1 3QH. 1989.

Heavy Metals in the Marine Environment. Robert W. Furness and Philip S. Rainbow. CRC Press, 2000 Corporate Blvd. N.W., Boca Raton, Florida 33431. (800) 272-7737. 1990. Includes heavy metals in the marine environment, trace metals in sea water, metals in the marine atmosphere, processes affecting metal concentration in estuarine and coastal marine sediments, heavy metal levels in marine invertebrates, use of microalgae and invertebrates to monitor metal levels in estuaries and coastal waters, toxic effects of metals, and the incidence of metal pollution in marine ecosystems.

In Situ Immobilization of Heavy-Metal-Contaminated Soils. G. Czupyrna, et al. Noyes Publications, 120 Mill Rd., Park Ridge, New Jersey 07656. (201) 391-8484. 1989. Reports on an evaluation of various treatment chemicals for the in situ immobilization of heavy-metal-contaminated soils.

Magill's Survey of Science. Earth Science Series. Frank N. Magill. Salem Press, PO Box 50062, Pasadena, California 91105. 1990-. Five volumes. Includes information on earth's crust, hot spots and volcanic island chains, physical properties of minerals, rock magnetism, physical properties of rocks, and index.

Managing the Heavy Metals on the Land. Geoffrey Winthrop Leeper. Marcel Dekker, Inc., 270 Madison Ave., New York, New York 10016. (212) 696-9000; (800) 228-1160. 1978. Effect of heavy metals on plants, sewage irrigation, and soil pollution.

Optoelectronics for Environmental Science. S. Martellucci and A. N. Chester, eds. Plenum Press, 233 Spring St., New York, New York 10013-1578. (212) 620-8000; (800) 221-9369. 1991. Contribution of lasers and the optical sciences to specific problems, in situ measurements, atmospheric ozone, lidar detection, wind velocity, oceanographic measurements, heavy metal detection, toxic metals, and trace analysis. Proceedings of the 14th course of the International School of Quantum Electronics on Optoelectronics for Environmental Sciences, held September 3-12, 1989, in Erice, Italy.

Removal of Heavy Metals from Groundwaters. Robert W. Peters. Lewis Publishers, 2000 Corporate Blvd., N.W., Boca Raton, Florida 33431. (407) 994-0555 or (800) 272-7737. 1991. Describes the sources of heavy metal contamination, classification of metals by industry, extent of the contamination problem, toxicity associated with various heavy metals, effects of heavy metals in biological wastewater treatment operations, leaching of heavy metals from sludges, modeling of heavy metals in the saturated and unsaturated zones, and other related areas.

Removal of Heavy Metals from Wastewaters. Stephen Beszedits. B and L Information Services, PO Box 458, Station L, Toronto, Ontario, Canada M6E 2W4. (416) 657-1197. 1980. Covers wastewater treatment, electrodialysis, heavy metals, ultrafication, ozonization, foam separation, and ion exchange process.

Toxicity of Heavy Metals in the Environment. Frederick W. Oehme. Marcel Dekker, Inc., 270 Madison Ave., New York, New York 10016. (212) 696-9000; (800) 228-1160. 1978. Toxicology and environmental aspects of heavy metals.

ONLINE DATA BASES

Chemical Abstracts-CA. Chemical Abstracts Service, 2540 Olentangy River Rd., P.O. Box 3012, Columbus, Ohio 43210. (800) 848-6533 or (614) 421-3600. Information sources include 9000 journals, patents from 27 countries, two industrial property organizations, new books, conference proceedings, and government research reports.

Computerized Engineering Index–COMPENDEX. Engineering Information Inc., 345 E. 47th St., New York, New York 10017. (212) 705-7600.

Enviro/Energyline Abstracts Plus. R. R. Bowker Co., 121 Chanlon Rd., New Providence, New Jersey 07974. (908) 464-6800.

Environmental Periodicals Bibliography. National Information Services Corp., Ste. 6, Wyman Towers, 3100 St. Paul St., Baltimore, Maryland 21218. (410)243-0797. Online version of abstract of same name.

RESEARCH CENTERS AND INSTITUTES

Northeast Louisiana University, Soil-Plant Analysis Laboratory. Room 117, Chemistry and Natural Sciences Building, Monroe, Louisiana 71209-0505. (318) 342-1948.

University of San Francisco, Institute of Chemical Biology. Ignarian Heights, Room H342, San Francisco, California 94117-1080. (415) 666-6415.

HELICOPTERS

See: TRANSPORTATION

HEPATOTOXICITY

See: TOXICITY

HEPTACHLOR

ABSTRACTING AND INDEXING SERVICES

Biological Abstracts. BIOSIS, 2100 Arch St., Philadelphia, Pennsylvania 19103-1399. (215) 587-4800. 1927-.

Biological and Agricultural Index. H.W. Wilson Co., 950 University Ave., Bronx, New York 10452. (800) 367-6770. 1916-. Monthly.

Chemical Abstracts. Chemical Abstracts Service, 2540 Olentangy River Rd., PO Box 3012, Columbus, Ohio 43210. (800) 848-6533. 1907-.

Pollution Abstracts. Cambridge Scientific Abstracts, 5161 River Rd., Bethesda, Maryland 20816. (301) 961-6750.

Six/year. Indexes worldwide technical literature on environmental pollution. Covers air pollution, marine and freshwater pollution, sewage and wastewater treatment, waste management, toxicology and health, noise pollution, radiation, land pollution, and environmental policies, programs, legislation, and education. Also available online.

Science Citation Index. Institute for Scientific Information, 3501 Market St., Philadelphia, Pennsylvania 19104. 1961-.

ENCYCLOPEDIAS AND DICTIONARIES

Encyclopedia of Chemical Technology. Raymond E. Kirk. John Wiley & Sons, Inc., 605 3rd Ave., New York, New York 10158-0012. (212) 850-6000. 1991-. 4th ed. Also known as Kirk Othmer Encyclopedia of Chemical Technology; consists of 26 volumes.

Encyclopedia of Trademarks and Synonyms. H. Bennett, ed. Chemical Publishing Co., 80 Eighth Ave., New York, New York 10011. (212) 255-1950. 1981. Three volumes. Includes chemical compounds, compositions consisting of one or more chemicals and other products. Also included are abbreviated names and WHO free names.

The New York Times Encyclopedic Dictionary of the Environment. Paul Sarnoff. Quadrangle Books, New York, New York 1971. Focuses on state-of-the-art methods of pollution control, abatement, prevention and removal.

Van Nostrand's Scientific Encyclopedia. Glenn D. Considine, ed. Van Nostrand Reinhold, 115 5th Ave., New York, New York 10003. (212) 254-3232. 1983. Sixth edition. Includes all broad subject areas in science.

GENERAL WORKS

Carcinogenicity Assessment of Chlordane and Heptachlor/Heptachlor Epoxide. Carcinogen Assessment Group, Office of Health and Environmental Assessment, U.S. Environmental Protection Agency, 401 Elm St. SW, Washington, District of Columbia 20460. (202) 260-7317. 1986.

Chemical, Physical, and Biological Properties of Compounds Present at Hazardous Waste Sites: Final Report. U.S. Environmental Protection Agency. Clement Associates Inc., Arlington, Virginia 1985.

Heptachlor. World Health Organization, Q Corp., 49 Sheridan Ave., Albany, New York 12221. (518) 436-9686. 1984. Toxicity and environmental physiological effects.

Heptachlor Contamination. Jerry Rafats. National Agricultural Library, 10301 Baltimore Blvd., Beltsville, Maryland 20705-2351. (301) 504-5755. 1986. Environmental aspects of pesticides.

Heptachlor Health and Safety Guide. World Health Organization, Ave. Appia, Geneva, Switzerland CH-1211. 1988. Toxicology and safety measures relative to heptachlor.

Silent Spring Revisited. Gino J. Marco, et al., eds. American Chemical Society, 1155 16th St. N.W., Washington, District of Columbia 20036. (202) 872-4600; (800) 227-5558. 1987. Discusses Rachel Carson's vision and legacy. Traces the evolution of government regulations and the current pesticide registration criteria.

Critically appraises the existing conditions and evaluates hazards.

Toxicological Profile for Heptachlor/Heptachlor Epoxide. Dynamac Corporation. Oak Ridge National Laboratory, PO Box 2008, Oak Ridge, Tennessee 37831-6050. (615) 576-1746. 1989. Adverse effects and toxicity of heptachlor.

Treatment Potential for 56 EPA Listed Hazardous Chemicals in Soil. Ronald C. Sims, et al. Robert S. Kerr Environmental Research Laboratory, U.S. Environmental Protection Agency, PO Box 1198, Ada, Oklahoma 74820. (405) 332-8800. 1988.

HANDBOOKS AND MANUALS

Documentation of the Threshold Limit Values. American Conference of Governmental Industrial Hygienists, 6500 Glenway, Building D-5, Cincinnati, Ohio 45211. 1991. Provides threshold limit value documentation for any physical phenomenon in the environment, including chemical substances and physical agents.

Handbook of Chemistry and Physics. CRC Press, 2000 Corporate Blvd. N.W., Boca Raton, Florida 33431. (800) 272-7737. Annually.

Hazardous Chemicals Data Book. G. Weiss, ed. Noyes Publications, 120 Mill Rd., Park Ridge, New Jersey 07656. (201) 391-8484. 1986. 2d ed. Supplies instant information on 1015 hazardous chemicals. The data will provide rapid assistance to personnel involved with handling of hazardous chemical materials and related accidents.

NIOSH Pocket Guide to Chemical Hazards. National Institute for Occupational Safety and Health, 1600 Clifton Rd. NE, Atlanta, Georgia 30333. (404) 639-3286. 1990. Presents sources of general industrial hygiene and medical surveillance information for workers, employees and others. Presents key information and data in an abbreviated format for 398 individual chemicals or chemical types.

Treatability Manual. U.S. Environmental Protection Agency, Office of Research and Development, 401 M St., SW, Washington, District of Columbia 20460. (202) 260-2090. 1983-. V.1 Treatability data. v.2 Change 2. Industrial Descriptions. v.3 Change 2. Technology for Control/removal of pollutants. v.4. Cost estimating. v.5. Change 2 summary.

ONLINE DATA BASES

BIOSIS Previews. BIOSIS, 2100 Arch St., Philadelphia, Pennsylvania 19103-1399. (215) 587-4800. Largest and most comprehensive database of research in the life sciences. Contains citations for nearly 9000 primary research journals, monographs, reviews, symposia, preliminary reports, semi-popular journals, selected institutional reports, government reports and research communications.

Chemical Abstracts-CA. Chemical Abstracts Service, 2540 Olentangy River Rd., P.O. Box 3012, Columbus, Ohio 43210. (800) 848-6533 or (614) 421-3600. Information sources include 9000 journals, patents from 27 countries, two industrial property organizations, new books, conference proceedings, and government research reports.

Chemical Abstracts Chemical Name Directory-CHEMNAME. Chemical Abstracts Service, 2540 Olentangy River Rd., P.O. Box 3012, Columbus, Ohio 43210. (800) 848-6533 or (614) 421-3600. Listing of chemical substances in a dictionary type file. The Chemical Abstracts (CAS) Registry Number, molecular formula, Chemical Abstracts (CA) Substance Index Name, available synonyms, ring data and other chemical substance information is given for each entry.

Chemical Carcinogenesis Research Information System-CCRIS. National Library of Medicine, 8600 Rockville Pike, Bethesda, Maryland 20894. (800) 638-8480. Individual assay results and test conditions for 1,451 chemicals in the areas of carcinogenicity, mutagenicity, tumor promotion, and cocarcinogenicity.

Chemical Collection System/Request Tracking-CCS/RTS. U.S. Environmental Protection Agency, Office of Pesticides and Toxic Substances, 401 M St., SW, Washington, District of Columbia 20460. (202) 260-2090. Contains information on various properties of a number of chemicals including environmental effects, test and analysis methods, and health effects. Available from EPA.

Chemical Dictionary Online-CHEMLINE. Chemical Abstracts Service, 2540 Olentangy River Rd., Columbus, Ohio 43210. (614) 421-3600 or (800) 848-6533. Part of MEDLINE of the National Library of Medicine (NLM). File of 900,000 names for chemical substances, representing 450,000 unique compounds. It contains such information as Chemical Abstracts (CA) Service Registry Numbers, molecular formulas, preferred chemical nomenclature, and generic and ring structure information. Available on NLM's ELHILL system.

Chemical Exposure. Science Applications International Corp., Health & Environmental Information, P.O. Box 2501, Oak Ridge, Tennessee 37831. (615) 482-9031. Database of chemicals that have been identified in both human tissues and body fluids and in feral and food animals. Contains reference to journal articles, conferences, and reports. Covers the whole fields of information related to human and animal exposure to food, air, and water contaminants and pharmaceuticals. Its records include information on chemical properties, formulas, tissues measured, analytical method used, demographics and more. Available on DIALOG.

PERIODICALS AND NEWSLETTERS

Aquatic Toxicology. Elsevier Science Publishing Co., 655 Avenue of the Americas, New York, New York 10010. (212) 989-5800. 1981-. 6/year.

Environmental Science and Technology. American Chemical Society, 1155 16th St. N.W., Washington, District of Columbia 20036. (800) 227-5558. 1967-. Monthly. Contains research articles on various aspects of environmental chemistry, interpretative articles by invited experts and commentary on the scientific aspects of environmental management.

IARC Monographs on the Evaluation of the Carcinogenic Risk of Chemicals to Man. International Agency for Research on Cancer, Q Corp., 49 Sheridan Ave., Albany, New York 12221. (518) 436-9686. 1972-. Irregular.

Technical Paper-Agricultural Experiment Station. University of California Press, 2120 Berkeley Way, Berkeley, California 94720. (510) 642-4247. 1924-. Monthly (irregularly).

TRADE ASSOCIATIONS AND PROFESSIONAL SOCIETIES

American Chemical Society. 1155 16th St., N.W., Washington, District of Columbia 20036. (202) 872-4600.

HERBICIDES

See also: PESTICIDES

ABSTRACTING AND INDEXING SERVICES

Applied Science and Technology Index. H.W. Wilson Co., 950 University Ave., Bronx, New York 10452. (800) 367-6770. Formerly Industrial Arts Index.

Biological Abstracts. BIOSIS, 2100 Arch St., Philadelphia, Pennsylvania 19103-1399. (215) 587-4800. 1927-.

Biological and Agricultural Index. H.W. Wilson Co., 950 University Ave., Bronx, New York 10452. (800) 367-6770. 1916-. Monthly.

Chemical Abstracts. Chemical Abstracts Service, 2540 Olentangy River Rd., PO Box 3012, Columbus, Ohio 43210. (800) 848-6533. 1907-.

Ecological Abstracts. Geo Abstracts Ltd. Elsevier Applied Science, Crown House, Linton Rd., Barking, England IG 11 8JU. 1974-. Derived from over 600 leading ecological and environmental journals, plus books, conference proceedings, reports and theses.

Ecology Abstracts. Cambridge Scientific Abstracts, 5161 River Rd., Bethesda, Maryland 20816. (301) 961-6750. Monthly.

Field Crop Abstracts. C. A. B. International, 845 North Park Ave., Tucson, Arizona 85719. (602) 621-7897 or (800) 528-4841. 1948-. Monthly. Covers literature on agronomy, field production, crop botany and physiology of all annual field crops, both temperate and tropical.

General Science Index. H. W. Wilson Co., 950 University Ave., Bronx, New York 10452. 1978-. Monthly, also issued in annual cumulation. Cumulative subject index to English language periodicals in the subject fields of astronomy, botany, chemistry, earth science, environment and conservation, food and nutrition, genetics, mathematics, medicine and health, microbiology, oceanography, physics, physiology and zoology.

Herbage Abstracts. C. A. B. International, 845 North Park Ave., Tucson, Arizona 85719. (602) 621-7897 or (800) 528-4841. 1931-. Monthly. Covers management, productivity and economics of grasslands, rangelands and fodder crops, grassland ecology, seed production, toxic plants, land use and farming systems, weed control, agricultural meteorology, and other related areas.

Pesticides Abstracts. U.S. Environmental Protection Agency, Office of Pesticides Programs, 345 Curtland, Atlanta, Georgia 30365. (404) 347-2864. 1981. Monthly. Formerly: Health Aspects of Pesticides Abstracts Bulletin.

Pollution Abstracts. Cambridge Scientific Abstracts, 5161 River Rd., Bethesda, Maryland 20816. (301) 961-6750. Six/year. Indexes worldwide technical literature on environmental pollution. Covers air pollution, marine and freshwater pollution, sewage and wastewater treatment, waste management, toxicology and health, noise pollution, radiation, land pollution, and environmental poli-

cies, programs, legislation, and education. Also available online.

Weed Abstracts. C. A. B. International, 845 North Park Ave., Tucson, Arizona 85719. (602) 621-7897 or (800) 528-4841. 1954-. Monthly. Abstracts the world literature on weeds, weed control and allied subjects.

BIBLIOGRAPHIES

Herbicides, Ecological Effects, 1982-1987. Jayne T. Maclean. National Agricultural Library, 10301 Baltimore Blvd., Beltsville, Maryland 20705-2351. (301) 504-5755. 1988.

Review of Literature on Herbicides. U.S. Veterans Health Services and Research Administration. U.S. G.P.O., Washington, District of Columbia 20401. (202) 512-0000. Annual. Health effects of agent orange, phenoxy herbicides and other dioxins.

DIRECTORIES

European Directory of Agrochemical Products. H. Kidd and D. James, eds. Royal Society of Chemistry, c/o CRC Press, 2000 Corporate Blvd. N.W., Boca Raton, Florida 33431-9868. (800) 272-7737. 1990. Provides comprehensive information on over 26,000 agrochemical products currently manufactured, marketed or used in 25 European countries.

ENCYCLOPEDIAS AND DICTIONARIES

Encyclopedia of Chemical Processing and Design. John J. Mcketta and W. A. Cunningham. Marcel Dekker, Inc., 270 Madison Ave., New York, New York 10016. (212) 696-9000; (800) 228-1160. 1992. Thirty-eight volumes.

Kirk-Othmer Encyclopedia of Chemical Technology. J. I. Kroschwitz, ed. John Wiley & Sons, Inc., 605 3rd Ave., New York, New York 10158-0012. (212) 850-6000. 1992-. All articles in the new edition have been rewritten and updated adding new subjects such as biotechnology, computer topics, analytical techniques and instrumentation, environmental concerns, fuels and energy, inorganic and solid state chemistry; composite materials and material science in general, and pharmaceuticals. Also available online.

McGraw-Hill Encyclopedia of Environmental Science. Sybil P. Parker. McGraw-Hill Science & Engineering Books, 11 W. 19th St., New York, New York 10011. (212) 337-6010. 1980. Covers ecology, man's influence on nature, and environmental protection.

GENERAL WORKS

Biologically Active Natural Products: Potential Use in Agriculture. Horace G. Culter and Richard B. Russell, eds. American Chemical Society, 1155 16th St. N.W., Washington, District of Columbia 20036. (202) 872-4600; (800) 227-5558. 1988. Describes natural products and their potential use in agriculture.

Enhanced Biodegradation of Pesticides in the Environment. Kenneth D. Racke and Joel R. Coats, eds. American Chemical Society, 1155 16th St. N.W., Washington, District of Columbia 20036. (202) 872-4600; (800) 227-5558. 1990. Discusses pesticides in the soil, microbial ecosystems, and the effects of long term application of herbicides on the soil.

Environmental Chemistry of Herbicides. Raj Grover and Alan J. Cessna. CRC Press, 2000 Corporate Blvd. N.W., Boca Raton, Florida 33431. (800) 272-7737. 1990. Vol. 1: Adsorption and bioavailability. Mass flow and dispersion, herbicides in surface waters. Evaporation from soils and crops. Dissipation from soil. Transformations in soil. Vol. 2: Dissipation of transformations in water and sediment. Nature, transport, and fate of airborne residues, absorption and transport in plants. Transformations in biosphere. Bioaccumulation and food chain accumulation. Photochemical transformations. Bound residues. Predictability and environmental chemistry.

Green Fields Forever. Charles E. Little. Island Press, 1718 Connecticut Ave. N.W., Suite 300, Washington, District of Columbia 20009. (202) 232-7933. 1987. An objective look at the costs and benefits of conservation tillage, a promising solution to agricultural problems such as decreased yields, soil erosion and reliance on pesticides and herbicides.

Herbicides: Chemistry, Degradation, and Mode of Action. P. C. Kearney and D. D. Kaufman, eds. Marcel Dekker, Inc., 270 Madison Ave., New York, New York 10016. (212) 696-9000; (800) 228-1160. 1988. 2d ed.

Imidazolinone Herbicides. Dale L. Shaner, ed. CRC Press, 2000 Corporate Blvd. N.W., Boca Raton, Florida 33431. (407) 994-0555 or (800) 272-7737. 1991.

Influence of Environmental Factors on the Control of Grape, Pests, Diseases and Weeds. R. Cavalloro. A. A. Balkema, Old Post Rd., Brookfield, Vermont 05036. (802) 276-3162. 1989. Influence of environmental factors on cultivation of vines, and impact of insects, mites, diseases and weeds and pesticides.

Microbes and Microbial Products as Herbicides. Robert E. Hoagland, ed. American Chemical Society, 1155 16th St. N.W., Washington, District of Columbia 20036. (202) 872-4600; (800) 227-5558. 1990. Discusses the suitability of host specific phytotoxins, synthetic derivatives of abcisic acid, phytoalexins, pathogens, soilborne fungi, its biochemistry and other potential microbial product herbicides.

Microbial Control of Weeds. David O. TeBeest, ed. Chapman & Hall, 29 W. 35th St., New York, New York 10001-2291. (212) 244-3336. 1991. Summarizes the progress that has been made over the last 20 years in the biological control of weeds.

Naturally Occurring Pest Bioregulators. Paul A. Hedin. American Chemical Society, 1155 16th St. NW, Washington, District of Columbia 20036. (202) 872-4600; (800) 227-5558. 1991. Symposium papers on naturally occurring biologically active chemicals grouped in five general sections: bioregulation of insect behavior and development; allelochemicals for control of insects and other animals; phytoalexins and phototoxins in plant pest control; mechanisms of plant resistance to insects; and allelochemicals as plant disease control agents.

North Central Weed Science Society. Research Report. Michael Barrett, ed. North Central Weed Science Society, 309 W. Clark St., Champaign, Illinois 61820. (217) 356-3182. 1990.

Principles of Weed Control in California. Thomson Publications, PO Box 9335, Fresno, California 93791. (209) 435-2163. 1989. 2d ed. Describes irrigated or California-type agricultural weed control methods. Also

includes growers, chemical company reps, pest control advisors, extension people, etc.

Proceedings, North Central Weed Science Society Conference. North Central Weed Science Society, 309 W. Clark St., Champaign, Illinois 61820. (217) 356-3182. 1989. Forty-Fourth North Central Weed Science Society Conference held December 5-7, 1989 in Lexington, Kentucky. Topics included are: cereals and oilseeds; computers; maize and sorghum; edaphic factors; environmental and health; equipment and application methods; extension; forage and range weed control; forests, rights- of- ways and industrial weed control; herbicide physiology; horticulture and aquatics; resident eduction; soybeans and annual legumes and; weed ecology and biology.

HANDBOOKS AND MANUALS

Agricultural Chemicals. William Thomas Thomson. Thomson Publications, Box 9335, Fresno, California 93791. (209) 435-2163. 1991. Book 1: Insecticides and acaricides. Book 2: Herbicides. Book 3: Fumigants, growth regulators, repellents and rodenticides. Book 4: Fungicides.

The Agrochemicals Handbook. H. Kidd and D. Hartlet, eds. Royal Society of Chemistry, c/o CRC Press, 2000 Corporate Blvd., N.W., Boca Raton, Florida 33431-9868. (800) 272-7737. 1991. 3rd ed. Contains comprehensive worldwide information and data on substances which are active components of agriculture chemical products currently used in crop protection and pest control.

Aquatic Plant Identification and Herbicide Use Guide: Aquatic Plants and Susceptibility to Herbicides. Howard E. Westerdahl. National Technical Information Service, 5285 Port Royal Rd., Springfield, Virginia 22161. (703) 487-4650. 1988.

European Directory of Agrochemical Products. Royal Society of Chemistry, Thomas Graham House, Science Park, Milton Rd., Cambridge, England CB4 4WF. 1990. 4th ed. Volume 1: Fungicides. Volume 2: Herbicides. Volume 3: Insecticides. Volume 4: Growth regulators including rodenticides; molluscicides; nematicides; repellents and synerists.

Herbicide Manual. Gary W. Hansen. U.S. G.P.O., Washington, District of Columbia 20401. (202) 512-0000. 1984. A guide to supervise pest management and to train personnel.

A Manual on Ground Applications of Forestry Herbicides. James H. Miller. U.S. Department of Agriculture, Forest Service, 1720 Peachtree Rd. NW, Atlanta, Georgia 30367. 1990.

ONLINE DATA BASES

BIOSIS Previews. BIOSIS, 2100 Arch St., Philadelphia, Pennsylvania 19103-1399. (215) 587-4800. Largest and most comprehensive database of research in the life sciences. Contains citations for nearly 9000 primary research journals, monographs, reviews, symposia, preliminary reports, semi-popular journals, selected institutional reports, government reports and research communications.

Cambridge Scientific Abstracts Life Science–CSAL. Cambridge Scientific Abstracts, 5161 River Rd., Bethesda, Maryland 20816. (301) 961-6750. Provides access to the following abstracting services: "Life Sciences Collec-

tion," "Aquatic Sciences and Fisheries Abstracts," "Oceanic Abstracts," and "Pollution Abstracts."

CERCLIS. Chemical Information Systems, Inc., 7215 York Rd., Baltimore, Maryland 21212. (301) 321-8440. Information on hazardous waste disposal sites that have either been listed by the EPA on the National Priority List (NPL) or nominated for consideration for the NPL.

Chemical Abstracts-CA. Chemical Abstracts Service, 2540 Olentangy River Rd., P.O. Box 3012, Columbus, Ohio 43210. (800) 848-6533 or (614) 421-3600. Information sources include 9000 journals, patents from 27 countries, two industrial property organizations, new books, conference proceedings, and government research reports.

Chemical Collection System/Request Tracking–CCS/RTS. U.S. Environmental Protection Agency, Office of Pesticides and Toxic Substances, 401 M St., SW, Washington, District of Columbia 20460. (202) 260-2090. Contains information on various properties of a number of chemicals including environmental effects, test and analysis methods, and health effects. Available from EPA.

Chemical Dictionary Online–CHEMLINE. Chemical Abstracts Service, 2540 Olentangy River Rd., Columbus, Ohio 43210. (614) 421-3600 or (800) 848-6533. Part of MEDLINE of the National Library of Medicine (NLM). File of 900,000 names for chemical substances, representing 450,000 unique compounds. It contains such information as Chemical Abstracts (CA) Service Registry Numbers, molecular formulas, preferred chemical nomenclature, and generic and ring structure information. Available on NLM's ELHILL system.

Chemical Exposure. Science Applications International Corp., Health & Environmental Information, P.O. Box 2501, Oak Ridge, Tennessee 37831. (615) 482-9031. Database of chemicals that have been identified in both human tissues and body fluids and in feral and food animals. Contains reference to journal articles, conferences, and reports. Covers the whole fields of information related to human and animal exposure to food, air, and water contaminants and pharmaceuticals. Its records include information on chemical properties, formulas, tissues measured, analytical method used, demographics and more. Available on DIALOG.

Kirk-Othmer Encyclopedia of Chemical Technology. John Wiley & Sons, Inc., 605 3rd Ave., 5th Floor, New York, New York 10158. (212) 850-6000. Online version of the publication of the same name.

PERIODICALS AND NEWSLETTERS

Weed Research. Blackwell Scientific Publications, 3 Cambridge Ctr., Suite 208, Cambridge, Massachusetts 02142. (617) 225-0401. 1974-. Six times a year.

Weed Technology. Weed Science Society of America, 309 W. Clark St., Champaign, Illinois 61820. (217) 356-3182. Quarterly. Weed control and herbicides.

RESEARCH CENTERS AND INSTITUTES

University of the Virgin Islands, Environmental Research Center. St. Thomas, Virgin Islands 00802. (809) 776-9200.

TRADE ASSOCIATIONS AND PROFESSIONAL SOCIETIES

American Chemical Society. 1155 16th St., N.W., Washington, District of Columbia 20036. (202) 872-4600.

American Institute of Biological Sciences. 730 11th St., N.W., Washington, District of Columbia 20001-4521. (202) 628-1500.

International Center for the Solution of Environmental Problems. 535 Lovett Blvd., Houston, Texas 77006. (713) 527-8711.

Weed Science Society of America. 309 W. Clark St., Champaign, Illinois 61820. (217) 356-3182.

HERBIVORE

ABSTRACTING AND INDEXING SERVICES

Biological Abstracts. BIOSIS, 2100 Arch St., Philadelphia, Pennsylvania 19103-1399. (215) 587-4800. 1927-.

Ecology Abstracts. Cambridge Scientific Abstracts, 5161 River Rd., Bethesda, Maryland 20816. (301) 961-6750. Monthly.

Science Citation Index. Institute for Scientific Information, 3501 Market St., Philadelphia, Pennsylvania 19104. 1961-.

ENCYCLOPEDIAS AND DICTIONARIES

Cambridge Dictionary of Biology. Peter M. B. Walker. Cambridge University Press, 40 W. 20th St., New York, New York 10011. (212) 924-3900 or (800) 227-0247. 1989. Includes 10,000 terms in zoology, botany, biochemistry, molecular biology and genetics. Previously published under the title Chambers Biology Dictionary.

A Concise Dictionary of Biology. Elizabeth Martin, ed. Oxford University Press, 200 Madison Ave., New York, New York 10016. (212) 679-7300 or (800) 334-4249. 1990. New edition. Derived from the Concise Science Dictionary, published in 1984.

Van Nostrand's Scientific Encyclopedia. Glenn D. Considine, ed. Van Nostrand Reinhold, 115 5th Ave., New York, New York 10003. (212) 254-3232. 1983. Sixth edition. Includes all broad subject areas in science.

GENERAL WORKS

Bioenergetics of Wild Herbivores. Robert J. Hudson. CRC Press, 2000 Corporate Blvd. N.W., Boca Raton, Florida 33431. (800) 272-7737. 1985. Includes ungulata, bioenergetics, and mammals.

Herbivory, the Dynamics of Animal-Plant Interactions. Michael J. Crawley. University of California Press, 2120 Berkeley Way, Berkeley, California 94720. (415) 642-4247; (800) 822-6657. 1983. The dynamics of animal-plant interactions.

Megaherbivores. R. Norman Owen-Smith. Cambridge University Press, 40 W. 20th St., New York, New York 10011. (212) 924-3900. 1988. The influence of very large body size on ecology; cover ungulata and mammals.

HANDBOOKS AND MANUALS

Managing Industrial Hazardous Waste–Practical Handbook. Gary F. Lindgren. Lewis Publishers, 2000 Corporate Blvd., N.W., Boca Raton, Florida 33431. (407) 994-0555 or (800) 272-7737. 1989. Explains the regulations regarding identification and listing of hazardous wastes.

ONLINE DATA BASES

BIOSIS Previews. BIOSIS, 2100 Arch St., Philadelphia, Pennsylvania 19103-1399. (215) 587-4800. Largest and most comprehensive database of research in the life sciences. Contains citations for nearly 9000 primary research journals, monographs, reviews, symposia, preliminary reports, semi-popular journals, selected institutional reports, government reports and research communications.

HEXACHLOROBENZENE

ABSTRACTING AND INDEXING SERVICES

Biological and Agricultural Index. H.W. Wilson Co., 950 University Ave., Bronx, New York 10452. (800) 367-6770. 1916-. Monthly.

Chemical Abstracts. Chemical Abstracts Service, 2540 Olentangy River Rd., PO Box 3012, Columbus, Ohio 43210. (800) 848-6533. 1907-.

Pollution Abstracts. Cambridge Scientific Abstracts, 5161 River Rd., Bethesda, Maryland 20816. (301) 961-6750. Six/year. Indexes worldwide technical literature on environmental pollution. Covers air pollution, marine and freshwater pollution, sewage and wastewater treatment, waste management, toxicology and health, noise pollution, radiation, land pollution, and environmental policies, programs, legislation, and education. Also available online.

Science Citation Index. Institute for Scientific Information, 3501 Market St., Philadelphia, Pennsylvania 19104. 1961-.

ENCYCLOPEDIAS AND DICTIONARIES

The Condensed Chemical Dictionary. Gessner G. Hawley. Van Nostrand Reinhold, 115 5th Ave., New York, New York 10003. (212) 254-3232. 1981. 10th ed.

Encyclopedia of Chemical Technology. Raymond E. Kirk. John Wiley & Sons, Inc., 605 3rd Ave., New York, New York 10158-0012. (212) 850-6000. 1991-. 4th ed. Also known as Kirk Othmer Encyclopedia of Chemical Technology; consists of 26 volumes.

Ullmanns Encyclopedia of Industrial Chemistry. Hans Jurgen Arpe and Wolfgang Gerhartz, eds. VCH Publishers, 303 NW 12th Ave., Deerfield Beach, Florida 33442-1788. (305) 428-5566. 1990. Designed to keep up with the broad spectrum of chemical technology. Thirty-six volumes of the encyclopedia have been divided into two sets: the 28 A volumes contain alphabetically arranged articles on chemicals, product groups, processes and technological concepts; and the 8 B volumes are compendia of basic knowledge in industrial chemistry.

GENERAL WORKS

Environment Impact of Nonpoint Source Pollution. Michael R. Overcash and James M. Davidson, eds. Ann Arbor Science, 230 Collingwood, Ann Arbor, Michigan 48106. 1980.

Hexachlorobenzene Distribution in Domestic Animals. Dennis Wayne Wilson. University of Illinois at Urbana-Champaign, Urbana-Champaign, Illinois 61801. 1979.

Identification of Selected Federal Activities Directed to Chemicals Near- Term Concern. U.S. Environmental Protection Agency, Office of Toxic Substances, 401 M St., S.W., Washington, District of Columbia 20460. (202) 260-2090. 1976.

Status Assessment of Toxic Chemicals: Hexachlorobenzene. T. R. Blackwood. National Technical Information Service, 5285 Port Royal Rd., Springfield, Virginia 22161. (703) 487-4650. 1980.

HANDBOOKS AND MANUALS

Catalog Handbook of Fine Chemicals. Aldrich Chemical Co., 1001 W. St. Paul Ave., Milwaukee, Wisconsin 53233. (414) 273-3850 or (800) 558-9160. 1990/1991. Contains more than 27,000 products of which over 4,000 are new. Includes: chemicals, equipment, glassware, books, software, research products, bulk quantities, new products, custom synthesis and rare chemicals.

CRC Handbook of Chemistry and Physics. CRC Press, 2000 Corporate Blvd. N.W., Boca Raton, Florida 33431. (407) 994-0555; (800) 272-7737. 1988. 67th ed.

Treatability Manual. U.S. Environmental Protection Agency, Office of Research and Development, 401 M St., SW, Washington, District of Columbia 20460. (202) 260-2090. 1983-. V.1 Treatability data. v.2 Change 2. Industrial Descriptions. v.3 Change 2. Technology for Control/removal of pollutants. v.4. Cost estimating. v.5. Change 2 summary.

ONLINE DATA BASES

Chemical Abstracts-CA. Chemical Abstracts Service, 2540 Olentangy River Rd., P.O. Box 3012, Columbus, Ohio 43210. (800) 848-6533 or (614) 421-3600. Information sources include 9000 journals, patents from 27 countries, two industrial property organizations, new books, conference proceedings, and government research reports.

Chemical Abstracts Chemical Name Directory-CHEMNAME. Chemical Abstracts Service, 2540 Olentangy River Rd., P.O. Box 3012, Columbus, Ohio 43210. (800) 848-6533 or (614) 421-3600. Listing of chemical substances in a dictionary type file. The Chemical Abstracts (CAS) Registry Number, molecular formula, Chemical Abstracts (CA) Substance Index Name, available synonyms, ring data and other chemical substance information is given for each entry.

Chemical Carcinogenesis Research Information System–CCRIS. National Library of Medicine, 8600 Rockville Pike, Bethesda, Maryland 20894. (800) 638-8480. Individual assay results and test conditions for 1,451 chemicals in the areas of carcinogenicity, mutagenicity, tumor promotion, and cocarcinogenicity.

Chemical Collection System/Request Tracking–CCS/RTS. U.S. Environmental Protection Agency, Office of

Pesticides and Toxic Substances, 401 M St., SW, Washington, District of Columbia 20460. (202) 260-2090. Contains information on various properties of a number of chemicals including environmental effects, test and analysis methods, and health effects. Available from EPA.

Chemical Dictionary Online–CHEMLINE. Chemical Abstracts Service, 2540 Olentangy River Rd., Columbus, Ohio 43210. (614) 421-3600 or (800) 848-6533. Part of MEDLINE of the National Library of Medicine (NLM). File of 900,000 names for chemical substances, representing 450,000 unique compounds. It contains such information as Chemical Abstracts (CA) Service Registry Numbers, molecular formulas, preferred chemical nomenclature, and generic and ring structure information. Available on NLM's ELHILL system.

Chemical Exposure. Science Applications International Corp., Health & Environmental Information, P.O. Box 2501, Oak Ridge, Tennessee 37831. (615) 482-9031. Database of chemicals that have been identified in both human tissues and body fluids and in feral and food animals. Contains reference to journal articles, conferences, and reports. Covers the whole fields of information related to human and animal exposure to food, air, and water contaminants and pharmaceuticals. Its records include information on chemical properties, formulas, tissues measured, analytical method used, demographics and more. Available on DIALOG.

PERIODICALS AND NEWSLETTERS

Analytical Chemistry. American Chemical Society, 1155 16th St. N.W., Washington, District of Columbia 20036. (800) 227-5558. 1929-. Bimonthly. Articles for chemists, life scientists and engineers.

Ecotoxicology and Environmental Safety. Academic Press, c/o Harcourt Brace Jovanovich Inc., 6277 Sea Harbor Dr., Orlando, Florida 32887. (800) 346-8648. 1977-. Bimonthly.

Environmental Science and Technology. American Chemical Society, 1155 16th St. N.W., Washington, District of Columbia 20036. (800) 227-5558. 1967-. Monthly. Contains research articles on various aspects of environmental chemistry, interpretative articles by invited experts and commentary on the scientific aspects of environmental management.

TRADE ASSOCIATIONS AND PROFESSIONAL SOCIETIES

American Chemical Society. 1155 16th St., N.W., Washington, District of Columbia 20036. (202) 872-4600.

HEXACHLOROPHENE

ABSTRACTING AND INDEXING SERVICES

Biological and Agricultural Index. H.W. Wilson Co., 950 University Ave., Bronx, New York 10452. (800) 367-6770. 1916-. Monthly.

Chemical Abstracts. Chemical Abstracts Service, 2540 Olentangy River Rd., PO Box 3012, Columbus, Ohio 43210. (800) 848-6533. 1907-.

Pollution Abstracts. Cambridge Scientific Abstracts, 5161 River Rd., Bethesda, Maryland 20816. (301) 961-6750.

Six/year. Indexes worldwide technical literature on environmental pollution. Covers air pollution, marine and freshwater pollution, sewage and wastewater treatment, waste management, toxicology and health, noise pollution, radiation, land pollution, and environmental policies, programs, legislation, and education. Also available online.

Science Citation Index. Institute for Scientific Information, 3501 Market St., Philadelphia, Pennsylvania 19104. 1961-.

BIBLIOGRAPHIES

Hexachlorophene: January 1969 through March 1972. Geraldine D. Nowak. National Institutes of Health, Department of Health and Human Services, Bethesda, Maryland 1972.

ENCYCLOPEDIAS AND DICTIONARIES

Ullmanns Encyclopedia of Industrial Chemistry. Hans Jurgen Arpe and Wolfgang Gerhartz, eds. VCH Publishers, 303 NW 12th Ave., Deerfield Beach, Florida 33442-1788. (305) 428-5566. 1990. Designed to keep up with the broad spectrum of chemical technology. Thirty-six volumes of the encyclopedia have been divided into two sets: the 28 A volumes contain alphabetically arranged articles on chemicals, product groups, processes and technological concepts; and the 8 B volumes are compendia of basic knowledge in industrial chemistry.

GENERAL WORKS

Bioassay of Hexachlorophene for Possible Carcinogenicity. National Cancer Institute, Cancer Cause and Prevention Division, 9030 Old Georgetown Rd., Bethesda, Maryland 20892. (301) 496-7403. 1978.

ONLINE DATA BASES

Chemical Abstracts-CA. Chemical Abstracts Service, 2540 Olentangy River Rd., P.O. Box 3012, Columbus, Ohio 43210. (800) 848-6533 or (614) 421-3600. Information sources include 9000 journals, patents from 27 countries, two industrial property organizations, new books, conference proceedings, and government research reports.

Chemical Abstracts Chemical Name Directory-CHEM-NAME. Chemical Abstracts Service, 2540 Olentangy River Rd., P.O. Box 3012, Columbus, Ohio 43210. (800) 848-6533 or (614) 421-3600. Listing of chemical substances in a dictionary type file. The Chemical Abstracts (CAS) Registry Number, molecular formula, Chemical Abstracts (CA) Substance Index Name, available synonyms, ring data and other chemical substance information is given for each entry.

Chemical Carcinogenesis Research Information System–CCRIS. National Library of Medicine, 8600 Rockville Pike, Bethesda, Maryland 20894. (800) 638-8480. Individual assay results and test conditions for 1,451 chemicals in the areas of carcinogenicity, mutagenicity, tumor promotion, and cocarcinogenicity.

Chemical Collection System/Request Tracking–CCS/RTS. U.S. Environmental Protection Agency, Office of Pesticides and Toxic Substances, 401 M St., SW, Washington, District of Columbia 20460. (202) 260-2090. Contains information on various properties of a number of chemicals including environmental effects, test and analysis methods, and health effects. Available from EPA.

Chemical Dictionary Online–CHEMLINE. Chemical Abstracts Service, 2540 Olentangy River Rd., Columbus, Ohio 43210. (614) 421-3600 or (800) 848-6533. Part of MEDLINE of the National Library of Medicine (NLM). File of 900,000 names for chemical substances, representing 450,000 unique compounds. It contains such information as Chemical Abstracts (CA) Service Registry Numbers, molecular formulas, preferred chemical nomenclature, and generic and ring structure information. Available on NLM's ELHILL system.

Chemical Exposure. Science Applications International Corp., Health & Environmental Information, P.O. Box 2501, Oak Ridge, Tennessee 37831. (615) 482-9031. Database of chemicals that have been identified in both human tissues and body fluids and in feral and food animals. Contains reference to journal articles, conferences, and reports. Covers the whole fields of information related to human and animal exposure to food, air, and water contaminants and pharmaceuticals. Its records include information on chemical properties, formulas, tissues measured, analytical method used, demographics and more. Available on DIALOG.

TRADE ASSOCIATIONS AND PROFESSIONAL SOCIETIES

American Chemical Society. 1155 16th St., N.W., Washington, District of Columbia 20036. (202) 872-4600.

HIBERNATION

See also: ACCLIMATIZATION

ABSTRACTING AND INDEXING SERVICES

Biological Abstracts. BIOSIS, 2100 Arch St., Philadelphia, Pennsylvania 19103-1399. (215) 587-4800. 1927-.

Biological and Agricultural Index. H.W. Wilson Co., 950 University Ave., Bronx, New York 10452. (800) 367-6770. 1916-. Monthly.

Ecology Abstracts. Cambridge Scientific Abstracts, 5161 River Rd., Bethesda, Maryland 20816. (301) 961-6750. Monthly.

Science Citation Index. Institute for Scientific Information, 3501 Market St., Philadelphia, Pennsylvania 19104. 1961-.

ENCYCLOPEDIAS AND DICTIONARIES

Cambridge Dictionary of Biology. Peter M. B. Walker. Cambridge University Press, 40 W. 20th St., New York, New York 10011. (212) 924-3900 or (800) 227-0247. 1989. Includes 10,000 terms in zoology, botany, biochemistry, molecular biology and genetics. Previously published under the title Chambers Biology Dictionary.

A Concise Dictionary of Biology. Elizabeth Martin, ed. Oxford University Press, 200 Madison Ave., New York, New York 10016. (212) 679-7300 or (800) 334-4249. 1990. New edition. Derived from the Concise Science Dictionary, published in 1984.

McGraw-Hill Encyclopedia of Environmental Science. Sybil P. Parker. McGraw-Hill Science & Engineering Books, 11 W. 19th St., New York, New York 10011. (212) 337-6010. 1980. Covers ecology, man's influence on nature, and environmental protection.

Van Nostrand's Scientific Encyclopedia. Glenn D. Considine, ed. Van Nostrand Reinhold, 115 5th Ave., New York, New York 10003. (212) 254-3232. 1983. Sixth edition. Includes all broad subject areas in science.

ONLINE DATA BASES

BIOSIS Previews. BIOSIS, 2100 Arch St., Philadelphia, Pennsylvania 19103-1399. (215) 587-4800. Largest and most comprehensive database of research in the life sciences. Contains citations for nearly 9000 primary research journals, monographs, reviews, symposia, preliminary reports, semi-popular journals, selected institutional reports, government reports and research communications.

TRADE ASSOCIATIONS AND PROFESSIONAL SOCIETIES

American Institute of Biological Sciences. 730 11th St., N.W., Washington, District of Columbia 20001-4521. (202) 628-1500.

HIGH SULFUR COAL

See: COAL

HIGHWAYS

See also: AUTOMOBILES; LAND USE; TRANSPORTATION; URBAN DESIGN AND PLANNING

ABSTRACTING AND INDEXING SERVICES

Applied Science and Technology Index. H.W. Wilson Co., 950 University Ave., Bronx, New York 10452. (800) 367-6770. Formerly Industrial Arts Index.

Engineering Index. The Engineering Index Inc., 345 E. 47th St., New York, New York 10017. 1962-.

Environment Abstracts. Bowker A & I Publishing, 121 Chanlon Rd., New Providence, New Jersey 07974. (908) 464-6800. 1974-.

Environment Index. Environment Information Center, Index Research Department, 124 E. 39th St., New York, New York 10016. 1971-. Annual.

Environmental Information Connection–EIC. Planning Information Program, Dept. of Urban and Regional Planning, University of Illinois, 1003 West Nevada, Urbana, Illinois 61801. (217) 333-1369. Also available online.

Environmental Periodicals Bibliography. Environmental Studies Institute, International Academy at Santa Barbara, 800 Garden St., Suite D, Santa Barbara, California 93101. (805) 965-5010. Also available online.

Highway Research Abstracts. Transportation Research Board, National Research Council, 2101 Constitution Ave. NW., Washington, District of Columbia 20418. 1931-. Monthly. Provides information about highway and nonrail mass transit. It also deals with related environmental issues such as energy and environment, environmental design, climate, safety, human factors, and soils.

Index to Scientific Book Contents. Institute for Scientific Information, 3501 Market St., Philadelphia, Pennsylvania 19104. (800) 523-1857. 1985-. Annual. Gives contents of science books published.

Pollution Abstracts. Cambridge Scientific Abstracts, 5161 River Rd., Bethesda, Maryland 20816. (301) 961-6750. Six/year. Indexes worldwide technical literature on environmental pollution. Covers air pollution, marine and freshwater pollution, sewage and wastewater treatment, waste management, toxicology and health, noise pollution, radiation, land pollution, and environmental policies, programs, legislation, and education. Also available online.

Transportation Research News. National Academy of Science, Transportation Research Board, Box 289, Washington, District of Columbia 20055. (202) 334-3213. 1982. Monthly.

BIBLIOGRAPHIES

EPA Publications Bibliography. U.S. Environmental Protection Agency, Library Systems Branch, 401 M St., SW, Washington, District of Columbia 20460. (202) 260-2090. Quarterly.

Highways and the Environment. D. J. Coleman. Council of Planning Librarians, 1313 E. 60th St., Chicago, Illinois 60637-2897. (312) 942-2163. 1973. Features the effects of highways on the physical, biological, recreational and aesthetic environments and of techniques for the analysis of these effects.

Highways and Wetlands: Annotated Bibliography. Paul A. Erickson. Federal Highway Administration, Office of Development, 400 7th St. SW, Washington, District of Columbia 20590. (202) 366-0630. 1980.

ENCYCLOPEDIAS AND DICTIONARIES

McGraw-Hill Encyclopedia of Environmental Science. Sybil P. Parker. McGraw-Hill Science & Engineering Books, 11 W. 19th St., New York, New York 10011. (212) 337-6010. 1980. Covers ecology, man's influence on nature, and environmental protection.

GENERAL WORKS

Application of Environmental Impact Assessment: Highways and Dams. United Nations, 2 United Nations Plaza, Salis Section Rm. DC 2-853, New York, New York 10017. (800) 553-3210. 1987.

Effects of Highways on Wildlife. National Technical Information Service, 5285 Port Royal Rd., Springfield, Virginia 22161. (703) 487-4650. 1982. Wildlife conservation and environmental aspects of roads and highways.

Highway-Wildlife Relationships. Urban Wildlife Research Center, Inc. National Technical Information Service, 5285 Port Royal Rd., Springfield, Virginia 22161. (703) 487-4650. 1975. Design and construction and environmental aspects of roads and wildlife conservation.

Watershed Management Field Manual. Food and Agriculture Organization of the United Nations, 46110F

Assembly Dr., Lanham, Maryland 20706-4391. (800) 274-4888. 1986.

GOVERNMENTAL ORGANIZATIONS

Public Information Office: Federal Highway Administration. 400 7th St., S.W., Washington, District of Columbia 20590. (202) 366-0660.

HANDBOOKS AND MANUALS

Guidelines for the Management of Highway Runoff on Wetlands. N. P. Kobriger. Transportation Research Board, National Research Council, 2101 Constitution Ave. NW, Washington, District of Columbia 20418. 1983. Wetland conversion and environmental aspects of road and runoffs.

ONLINE DATA BASES

Computerized Engineering Index–COMPENDEX. Engineering Information Inc., 345 E. 47th St., New York, New York 10017. (212) 705-7600.

Enviro/Energyline Abstracts Plus. R. R. Bowker Co., 121 Chanlon Rd., New Providence, New Jersey 07974. (908) 464-6800.

Environmental Periodicals Bibliography. National Information Services Corp., Ste. 6, Wyman Towers, 3100 St. Paul St., Baltimore, Maryland 21218. (410)243-0797. Online version of abstract of same name.

Transportation Research Information Service–TRIS. Transportation Research Board, Box 289, Washington, District of Columbia 20055. (202) 334-3213.

PERIODICALS AND NEWSLETTERS

Highway and Heavy Construction. Dun Donnelley Pub. Corp., 1350 E. Touhy Ave., Box 5080, Des Plaines, Illinois 60017-8800. (708) 635-8800. 1892-. Fifteen times a year. Features on-site reports of current construction projects nationwide and advises senior personnel on the changing needs and demands of the market.

TRADE ASSOCIATIONS AND PROFESSIONAL SOCIETIES

American Public Works Association. 106 W. 11th St., Ste. 1800, Kansas City, Missouri 64105-1806. (816) 472-6100.

American Society of Civil Engineers. 345 East 47th St., New York, New York 10017. (212) 705-7496.

Transportation Research Board. Box 289, Washington, District of Columbia 20055. (202) 334-3213.

HORMONES

ABSTRACTING AND INDEXING SERVICES

Biological Abstracts. BIOSIS, 2100 Arch St., Philadelphia, Pennsylvania 19103-1399. (215) 587-4800. 1927-.

Biological and Agricultural Index. H.W. Wilson Co., 950 University Ave., Bronx, New York 10452. (800) 367-6770. 1916-. Monthly.

Biotechnology Research Abstracts. Cambridge Scientific Abstracts, 5161 River Rd., Bethesda, Maryland 20816. (301) 961-6750. Monthly. Includes such broad areas as genetic intervention, biochemical genetics, and microbiological techniques.

Environment Abstracts. Bowker A & I Publishing, 121 Chanlon Rd., New Providence, New Jersey 07974. (908) 464-6800. 1974-.

Environment Index. Environment Information Center, Index Research Department, 124 E. 39th St., New York, New York 10016. 1971-. Annual.

Environmental Information Connection–EIC. Planning Information Program, Dept. of Urban and Regional Planning, University of Illinois, 1003 West Nevada, Urbana, Illinois 61801. (217) 333-1369. Also available online.

Environmental Periodicals Bibliography. Environmental Studies Institute, International Academy at Santa Barbara, 800 Garden St., Suite D, Santa Barbara, California 93101. (805) 965-5010. Also available online.

Food Science and Technology Abstracts. International Food Information Service, c/o National Food Laboratory, 6363 Clark Ave., Dublin, California 94568. (800) 336-3782. 1969-.

Pollution Abstracts. Cambridge Scientific Abstracts, 5161 River Rd., Bethesda, Maryland 20816. (301) 961-6750. Six/year. Indexes worldwide technical literature on environmental pollution. Covers air pollution, marine and freshwater pollution, sewage and wastewater treatment, waste management, toxicology and health, noise pollution, radiation, land pollution, and environmental policies, programs, legislation, and education. Also available online.

Science Citation Index. Institute for Scientific Information, 3501 Market St., Philadelphia, Pennsylvania 19104. 1961-.

ALMANACS AND YEARBOOKS

Hormones, Drugs, and Aggression. Eden Medical Research, St. Albans, Vermont 05481. Annual.

Progress in Hormone Biochemistry and Pharmacology. Eden Medical Research, St. Albans, Vermont Annual.

BIBLIOGRAPHIES

EPA Publications Bibliography. U.S. Environmental Protection Agency, Library Systems Branch, 401 M St., SW, Washington, District of Columbia 20460. (202) 260-2090. Quarterly.

ENCYCLOPEDIAS AND DICTIONARIES

Cambridge Dictionary of Biology. Peter M. B. Walker. Cambridge University Press, 40 W. 20th St., New York, New York 10011. (212) 924-3900 or (800) 227-0247. 1989. Includes 10,000 terms in zoology, botany, biochemistry, molecular biology and genetics. Previously published under the title Chambers Biology Dictionary.

A Concise Dictionary of Biology. Elizabeth Martin, ed. Oxford University Press, 200 Madison Ave., New York, New York 10016. (212) 679-7300 or (800) 334-4249. 1990. New edition. Derived from the Concise Science Dictionary, published in 1984.

Encyclopedia of Human Biology. Renato Dulbecco, ed. Academic Press, c/o Harcourt Brace Jovanovich Inc., 6277 Sea Harbor Dr., Orlando, Florida 32887. (800) 346-8648. 1991. Eight volumes.

The Nutrition and Health Encyclopedia. David F. Tver and Percy Russell. Van Nostrand Reinhold, 115 5th Ave., New York, New York 10003. (212) 254-3232. 1989.

Role of Environment Factors. R. P. Pharis, et al. Springer-Verlag, 175 5th Ave., New York, New York 10010. (212) 460-1500 or (800) 777-4643. 1985. Encyclopedia of plant physiology.

Van Nostrand's Scientific Encyclopedia. Glenn D. Considine, ed. Van Nostrand Reinhold, 115 5th Ave., New York, New York 10003. (212) 254-3232. 1983. Sixth edition. Includes all broad subject areas in science.

GENERAL WORKS

Current Cancer Research on Role of Hormones in Carcinogenesis and Related Studies of Hormone Receptors. National Technical Information Service, 5285 Port Royal Rd., Springfield, Virginia 22161. (703) 487-4650. 1980.

Magill's Survey of Science. Life Science Series. Frank N. Magill, ed. Salem Press, PO Box 50062, Pasadena, California 91105. 1991. Six volumes. Contents: v.1. A-Central and peripheral nervous system functions; v.2. Central metabolism regulation - eukaryotic transcriptional control; v.3. Positive and negative eukaryotic transcriptional control - mammalian hormones; v.4. Hormones and behavior - muscular contraction; v.5. Muscular contraction and relaxation - sexual reproduction in plants; v.6. Reproductive behavior and mating - X inactivation and the Lyon hypothesis.

HANDBOOKS AND MANUALS

CRC Handbook of Endocrinology. George H. Gass. CRC Press, 2000 Corporate Blvd. N.W., Boca Raton, Florida 33431. (800) 272-7737. 1987. Endocrine glands and hormones.

CRC Handbook of Hormones, Vitamins, and Radiopaques. Matthew Verderame. CRC Press, 2000 Corporate Blvd. N.W., Boca Raton, Florida 33431. (800) 272-7737. 1986. Covers contrast media, hormones, and vitamins.

Handbook of Vitamins, Minerals, and Hormones. Roman J. Kutsky. Van Nostrand Reinhold, 115 5th Ave., New York, New York 10003. (212) 254-3232. 1981. Covers vitamins, hormones and minerals in the body.

Steroids. CRC Press, 2000 Corporate Blvd. N.W., Boca Raton, Florida 33431. (800) 272-7737. 1986. Chromatographic analysis of steroids.

ONLINE DATA BASES

BIOSIS Previews. BIOSIS, 2100 Arch St., Philadelphia, Pennsylvania 19103-1399. (215) 587-4800. Largest and most comprehensive database of research in the life sciences. Contains citations for nearly 9000 primary research journals, monographs, reviews, symposia, preliminary reports, semi-popular journals, selected institutional reports, government reports and research communications.

Cambridge Scientific Abstracts Life Science–CSAL. Cambridge Scientific Abstracts, 5161 River Rd., Bethesda, Maryland 20816. (301) 961-6750. Provides access to the following abstracting services: "Life Sciences Collection," "Aquatic Sciences and Fisheries Abstracts," "Oceanic Abstracts," and "Pollution Abstracts."

Enviro/Energyline Abstracts Plus. R. R. Bowker Co., 121 Chanlon Rd., New Providence, New Jersey 07974. (908) 464-6800.

Environmental Periodicals Bibliography. National Information Services Corp., Ste. 6, Wyman Towers, 3100 St. Paul St., Baltimore, Maryland 21218. (410)243-0797. Online version of abstract of same name.

SCISEARCH. Institute for Scientific Information, University City Science Center, 3501 Market St., Philadelphia, Pennsylvania 19104. (215) 386-0100.

PERIODICALS AND NEWSLETTERS

Molecular and Cellular Endocrinology. North-Holland, Shannon, Ireland Monthly.

TRADE ASSOCIATIONS AND PROFESSIONAL SOCIETIES

American Institute of Biological Sciences. 730 11th St., N.W., Washington, District of Columbia 20001-4521. (202) 628-1500.

HOUSEHOLD WASTES

See: MUNICIPAL WASTES

HUMAN ECOLOGY

See also: CONSERVATION OF NATURAL RESOURCES; ENVIRONMENTAL POLICY; POPULATION

ABSTRACTING AND INDEXING SERVICES

Agroforestry Abstracts. C. A. B. International, 845 North Park Ave., Tucson, Arizona 85719. (602) 621-7897 or (800) 528-4841. 1988-. Quarterly. Abstracts journal articles, reports, conferences and books. Focuses on subjects areas such as agroforestry in general; agroforestry systems; trees, animals and crops; conservation; human ecology; social and economic aspects; development, research and methodology.

Biological and Agricultural Index. H.W. Wilson Co., 950 University Ave., Bronx, New York 10452. (800) 367-6770. 1916-. Monthly.

Current Advances in Ecological and Environmental Science. Pergamon Microforms International, Inc., Fairview Park, Elmsford, New York 10523. (914) 592-7720. 1989-. Monthly. Current literature searching service includingjournals, reports, abstracts, etc. This service is available online as part of the CABS database on the hosts BRS and ORBIT search service.

Ecology Abstracts. Cambridge Scientific Abstracts, 5161 River Rd., Bethesda, Maryland 20816. (301) 961-6750. Monthly.

Environment Abstracts. Bowker A & I Publishing, 121 Chanlon Rd., New Providence, New Jersey 07974. (908) 464-6800. 1974-.

Environment Index. Environment Information Center, Index Research Department, 124 E. 39th St., New York, New York 10016. 1971-. Annual.

Environmental Information Connection–EIC. Planning Information Program, Dept. of Urban and Regional Planning, University of Illinois, 1003 West Nevada, Urbana, Illinois 61801. (217) 333-1369. Also available online.

Environmental Periodicals Bibliography. Environmental Studies Institute, International Academy at Santa Barbara, 800 Garden St., Suite D, Santa Barbara, California 93101. (805) 965-5010. Also available online.

General Science Index. H. W. Wilson Co., 950 University Ave., Bronx, New York 10452. 1978-. Monthly, also issued in annual cumulation. Cumulative subject index to English language periodicals in the subject fields of astronomy, botany, chemistry, earth science, environment and conservation, food and nutrition, genetics, mathematics, medicine and health, microbiology, oceanography, physics, physiology and zoology.

Geo Abstracts, Social Geography and Cartography. Geo Abstracts Ltd., c/o Elsevier Science Pub., Crown House, Linton Rd., Barking, England 1611 8JU.

Geographical Abstracts. London School of Economics, Dept. of Geography, Regency House, 34 Duke St., London, England 1966-. Continued by Geo Abstracts issued in 6 parts: Pt. A. Landforms and the quaternary; Pt. B. Biogeography and Climatology; Pt. C. Economic geography; Pt. D. Social geography and cartography; Pt. E. Sedimentology; Pt. F. Regional and community planning.

Index to Scientific Book Contents. Institute for Scientific Information, 3501 Market St., Philadelphia, Pennsylvania 19104. (800) 523-1857. 1985-. Annual. Gives contents of science books published.

BIBLIOGRAPHIES

Current Contents. Agriculture, Biology and Environmental Sciences. Institute for Scientific Information, 3501 Market St., Philadelphia, Pennsylvania 19104. (800) 523-1857. 1973-. Previous title: Current Contents. Agricultural, Food & Veterinary Sciences. Gives the table of contents of periodicals in the fields of agriculture, biology, environmental and related areas.

Environmental Education: A Guide to Information Sources. William B. Stapp. Gale Research Co., 835 Penobscot Bldg., Detroit, Michigan 48226-4094. (313) 961-2242. 1975. Man and the Environment Information Guide Series; v.1.

Environmental Values, 1860-1972: A Guide to Information Sources. Loren C. Owings. Gale Research Co., 835 Penobscot Bldg., Detroit, Michigan 48226-4094. (313) 961-2242. 1976. This bibliography includes the broad areas of human ecology, nature and outdoor life. It belongs in the series entitled Man and the Environment Information Guide Series, v.4.

EPA Publications Bibliography. U.S. Environmental Protection Agency, Library Systems Branch, 401 M St., SW, Washington, District of Columbia 20460. (202) 260-2090. Quarterly.

Human Ecology: A Guide to Information Sources. Frederick Sargent. Gale Research Co., 835 Penobscot Bldg., Detroit, Michigan 48226-4094. (313) 961-2242 or (800) 877-4253. 1983.

Human Ecology: Monographs Published in the 1980's. Mary A. Vance. Vance Bibliographies, PO Box 229, 112 N. Charter St., Monticello, Illinois 61856. (217) 762-3831. 1987.

Social Ecology: Monographs. Mary A. Vance. Vance Bibliographies, PO Box 229, 112 N. Charter St., Monticello, Illinois 61856. (217) 762-3831. 1987.

DIRECTORIES

International Directory of Human Ecologists. Richard J. Borden. Society for Human Ecology, College of the Atlantic, Bar Harbor, Massachusetts 04609. (207) 288-5015. 1989.

ENCYCLOPEDIAS AND DICTIONARIES

Cambridge Encyclopedia of Life Sciences. A. E. Friday and David S. Ingram. Cambridge University Press, 40 W 20th St., New York, New York 10011. (212) 924-3900 or (800) 227-0247. 1985. Includes all topics under biology and ecology.

McGraw-Hill Encyclopedia of Science and Technology. McGraw-Hill, 1221 Avenue of the Americas, New York, New York 10020. (212) 512-2000 or (800) 262-4729. 1992. Seventh edition. Issued in multiple volumes including index. Includes all science and technology broad subject areas.

The New York Times Encyclopedic Dictionary of the Environment. Paul Sarnoff. Quadrangle Books, New York, New York 1971. Focuses on state-of-the-art methods of pollution control, abatement, prevention and removal.

Van Nostrand's Scientific Encyclopedia. Glenn D. Considine, ed. Van Nostrand Reinhold, 115 5th Ave., New York, New York 10003. (212) 254-3232. 1983. Sixth edition. Includes all broad subject areas in science.

GENERAL WORKS

Biosphere Politics: A New Consciousness for a New Century. Jeremy Rifkin. Crown Publishing Group, 201 E. 50th St., New York, New York 10022. (212) 751-2600. 1991. Covers human ecology, nonrenewable natural resources and environmental policy.

GAIA Connections: An Introduction to Ecology, Ecoethics and Economics. Alan S. Miller. Rowman & Littlefield, Publishers, Inc., 8705 Bollman Pl., Savage, Maryland 20763. (301) 306-0400. 1991. Synthesis of humanity's ethical and economic options in coping with the global environmental crisis.

Urban Patterns: Studies in Human Ecology. George A. Theodorson. Pennsylvania State University Press, Barbara Bldg., Ste. C, University Park, Pennsylvania 16802. (814) 865-1372. 1982.

HANDBOOKS AND MANUALS

Call to Action: Handbook for Ecology, Peace, and Justice. Sierra Club Books, 100 Bush St., San Francisco, California 94104. (415) 291-1600. 1990. Covers environmental policy and international relations.

ONLINE DATA BASES

Enviro/Energyline Abstracts Plus. R. R. Bowker Co., 121 Chanlon Rd., New Providence, New Jersey 07974. (908) 464-6800.

Environmental Periodicals Bibliography. National Information Services Corp., Ste. 6, Wyman Towers, 3100 St. Paul St., Baltimore, Maryland 21218. (410)243-0797. Online version of abstract of same name.

Monthly Catalog of United States Government Publications. U.S. G.P.O., Supt. of Docs., PO Box 371954, Pittsburgh, Pennsylvania 15250-7954. (202) 512-0000.

National Technical Information Service. U.S. Department of Commerce, National Technical Information Service, Office of Data Base Services, 5285 Port Royal Rd., Springfield, Virginia 22161. (703) 487-4807. Bibliographic database of government sponsored research and technical reports.

SCISEARCH. Institute for Scientific Information, University City Science Center, 3501 Market St., Philadelphia, Pennsylvania 19104. (215) 386-0100.

PERIODICALS AND NEWSLETTERS

Human Ecology Forum. New York State College of Human Ecology, Cornell University, Martha Van Rensselaer Hall, Ithaca, New York 14853. Quarterly.

Urban Ecology. Elsevier, Box 211, Amsterdam, Netherlands 1000 AE. (020) 5803-911. Quarterly.

TRADE ASSOCIATIONS AND PROFESSIONAL SOCIETIES

The Human Ecology Action League, Inc. P.O. Box 49126, Atlanta, Georgia 30359-1126. (404) 248-1898.

HUMAN GENETICS

See: GENETICS

HUMAN-MACHINE INTERFACES

ABSTRACTING AND INDEXING SERVICES

Agricultural Engineering Abstracts. C. A. B. International, 845 North Park Ave., Tucson, Arizona 85719. (602) 621-7897 or (800) 528-4841. 1976-. Monthly. Informs about significant research developments in agricultural engineering and instrumentation. Some of the topics scanned for the abstracts include mechanical power, crop production, crop harvesting and threshing, crop processing and storage, aquaculture, land improvement, protected cultivation, handling and transport, and farm buildings and equipment.

Ergonomics Abstracts. Taylor & Francis, 4 John St., London, England WC1N 2ET. 1990-. Bimonthly. Provides details on recent additions to the international literature on human factors in human-machine systems and physical environmental influences.

General Science Index. H. W. Wilson Co., 950 University Ave., Bronx, New York 10452. 1978-. Monthly, also issued in annual cumulation. Cumulative subject index to English language periodicals in the subject fields of astronomy, botany, chemistry, earth science, environment and conservation, food and nutrition, genetics, mathematics, medicine and health, microbiology, oceanography, physics, physiology and zoology.

BIBLIOGRAPHIES

Environment-Employment-New Industrial Societies. Maryse Gaudier. International Labour Organization, H4, rue des Morillons, Geneva 22, Switzerland CH-1211. 1991. Situates environmental issues within the context of industrial societies at the threshold of the 21st century; critically evaluates the harmonization of ecology, modern technology and human resources.

GENERAL WORKS

Environment-Employment–New Industrial Societies: A Bibliographic Map. International Labor Organization, 4, rue des Morillons, Geneva 22, Switzerland CH-1211. 1991.

HANDBOOKS AND MANUALS

Human Factors Design Handbook: Information and Guidelines for the Design of Systems, Facilities, Equipment, and Products for Human Use. Wesley E. Woodson, et al. McGraw-Hill, 1221 Avenue of Americas, New York, New York 10020. (212) 512-2000 or (800) 262-4729. 1992. Second edition. Provides a general reference to key human factors questions and human-product interface design suggestions in a form that engineers and designers can utilize with a minimum of searching or study. Includes a selective bibliography.

HUMAN POPULATION

See also: POPULATION

ABSTRACTING AND INDEXING SERVICES

Biological Abstracts. BIOSIS, 2100 Arch St., Philadelphia, Pennsylvania 19103-1399. (215) 587-4800. 1927-.

Biological and Agricultural Index. H.W. Wilson Co., 950 University Ave., Bronx, New York 10452. (800) 367-6770. 1916-. Monthly.

Current Advances in Ecological and Environmental Science. Pergamon Microforms International, Inc., Fairview Park, Elmsford, New York 10523. (914) 592-7720. 1989-. Monthly. Current literature searching service includingjournals, reports, abstracts, etc. This service is available online as part of the CABS database on the hosts BRS and ORBIT search service.

Ecological Abstracts. Geo Abstracts Ltd. Elsevier Applied Science, Crown House, Linton Rd., Barking, England IG 11 8JU. 1974-. Derived from over 600 leading ecological and environmental journals, plus books, conference proceedings, reports and theses.

Environment Abstracts. Bowker A & I Publishing, 121 Chanlon Rd., New Providence, New Jersey 07974. (908) 464-6800. 1974-.

Environment Index. Environment Information Center, Index Research Department, 124 E. 39th St., New York, New York 10016. 1971-. Annual.

Environmental Information Connection–EIC. Planning Information Program, Dept. of Urban and Regional Planning, University of Illinois, 1003 West Nevada, Urbana, Illinois 61801. (217) 333-1369. Also available online.

Environmental Periodicals Bibliography. Environmental Studies Institute, International Academy at Santa Barbara, 800 Garden St., Suite D, Santa Barbara, California 93101. (805) 965-5010. Also available online.

General Science Index. H. W. Wilson Co., 950 University Ave., Bronx, New York 10452. 1978-. Monthly, also issued in annual cumulation. Cumulative subject index to English language periodicals in the subject fields of astronomy, botany, chemistry, earth science, environment and conservation, food and nutrition, genetics, mathematics, medicine and health, microbiology, oceanography, physics, physiology and zoology.

Pollution Abstracts. Cambridge Scientific Abstracts, 5161 River Rd., Bethesda, Maryland 20816. (301) 961-6750. Six/year. Indexes worldwide technical literature on environmental pollution. Covers air pollution, marine and freshwater pollution, sewage and wastewater treatment, waste management, toxicology and health, noise pollution, radiation, land pollution, and environmental policies, programs, legislation, and education. Also available online.

Science Citation Index. Institute for Scientific Information, 3501 Market St., Philadelphia, Pennsylvania 19104. 1961-.

BIBLIOGRAPHIES

Current Contents. Agriculture, Biology and Environmental Sciences. Institute for Scientific Information, 3501 Market St., Philadelphia, Pennsylvania 19104. (800) 523-1857. 1973-. Previous title: Current Contents. Agricultural, Food & Veterinary Sciences. Gives the table of contents of periodicals in the fields of agriculture, biology, environmental and related areas.

EPA Publications Bibliography. U.S. Environmental Protection Agency, Library Systems Branch, 401 M St., SW, Washington, District of Columbia 20460. (202) 260-2090. Quarterly.

ENCYCLOPEDIAS AND DICTIONARIES

McGraw-Hill Encyclopedia of Environmental Science. Sybil P. Parker. McGraw-Hill Science & Engineering Books, 11 W. 19th St., New York, New York 10011. (212) 337-6010. 1980. Covers ecology, man's influence on nature, and environmental protection.

ONLINE DATA BASES

BIOSIS Previews. BIOSIS, 2100 Arch St., Philadelphia, Pennsylvania 19103-1399. (215) 587-4800. Largest and most comprehensive database of research in the life sciences. Contains citations for nearly 9000 primary research journals, monographs, reviews, symposia, preliminary reports, semi-popular journals, selected institutional reports, government reports and research communications.

Cambridge Scientific Abstracts Life Science–CSAL. Cambridge Scientific Abstracts, 5161 River Rd., Bethesda, Maryland 20816. (301) 961-6750. Provides access to the following abstracting services: "Life Sciences Collection," "Aquatic Sciences and Fisheries Abstracts," "Oceanic Abstracts," and "Pollution Abstracts."

Enviro/Energyline Abstracts Plus. R. R. Bowker Co., 121 Chanlon Rd., New Providence, New Jersey 07974. (908) 464-6800.

Environmental Periodicals Bibliography. National Information Services Corp., Ste. 6, Wyman Towers, 3100 St. Paul St., Baltimore, Maryland 21218. (410)243-0797. Online version of abstract of same name.

Monthly Catalog of United States Government Publications. U.S. G.P.O., Supt. of Docs., PO Box 371954, Pittsburgh, Pennsylvania 15250-7954. (202) 512-0000.

National Technical Information Service. U.S. Department of Commerce, National Technical Information Service, Office of Data Base Services, 5285 Port Royal Rd., Springfield, Virginia 22161. (703) 487-4807. Bibliographic database of government sponsored research and technical reports.

SCISEARCH. Institute for Scientific Information, University City Science Center, 3501 Market St., Philadelphia, Pennsylvania 19104. (215) 386-0100.

PERIODICALS AND NEWSLETTERS

USSR Report. Human Resources. Foreign Broadcast Information Service. National Technical Information Service, 5285 Port Royal Rd., Springfield, Virginia 22161. (703) 487-4650. 1980-. Irregular.

RESEARCH CENTERS AND INSTITUTES

University of Wisconsin-Madison, Center for Human Systems. 1042 WARF Building, 610 North Walnut Street, Madison, Wisconsin 53705. (608) 262-9937.

TRADE ASSOCIATIONS AND PROFESSIONAL SOCIETIES

American Institute of Biological Sciences. 730 11th St., N.W., Washington, District of Columbia 20001-4521. (202) 628-1500.

American Society of Naturalists. Department of Ecology and Evolation, State University of New York, Stony Brook, New York 11794. (516) 632-8589.

HUMIC ACID

ABSTRACTING AND INDEXING SERVICES

Biological Abstracts. BIOSIS, 2100 Arch St., Philadelphia, Pennsylvania 19103-1399. (215) 587-4800. 1927-.

Environment Abstracts. Bowker A & I Publishing, 121 Chanlon Rd., New Providence, New Jersey 07974. (908) 464-6800. 1974-.

Environment Index. Environment Information Center, Index Research Department, 124 E. 39th St., New York, New York 10016. 1971-. Annual.

Environmental Information Connection–EIC. Planning Information Program, Dept. of Urban and Regional Planning, University of Illinois, 1003 West Nevada, Urbana, Illinois 61801. (217) 333-1369. Also available online.

Environmental Periodicals Bibliography. Environmental Studies Institute, International Academy at Santa Barbara, 800 Garden St., Suite D, Santa Barbara, California 93101. (805) 965-5010. Also available online.

General Science Index. H. W. Wilson Co., 950 University Ave., Bronx, New York 10452. 1978-. Monthly, also issued in annual cumulation. Cumulative subject index to English language periodicals in the subject fields of astronomy, botany, chemistry, earth science, environment and conservation, food and nutrition, genetics, mathematics, medicine and health, microbiology, oceanography, physics, physiology and zoology.

Pollution Abstracts. Cambridge Scientific Abstracts, 5161 River Rd., Bethesda, Maryland 20816. (301) 961-6750. Six/year. Indexes worldwide technical literature on environmental pollution. Covers air pollution, marine and freshwater pollution, sewage and wastewater treatment, waste management, toxicology and health, noise pollution, radiation, land pollution, and environmental policies, programs, legislation, and education. Also available online.

Science Citation Index. Institute for Scientific Information, 3501 Market St., Philadelphia, Pennsylvania 19104. 1961-.

BIBLIOGRAPHIES

Bibliography and Index of Geology. American Geological Institute, 4220 King St., Alexandria, Virginia 22302. Monthly. Includes environmental geology and hydrogeology.

EPA Publications Bibliography. U.S. Environmental Protection Agency, Library Systems Branch, 401 M St., SW, Washington, District of Columbia 20460. (202) 260-2090. Quarterly.

ENCYCLOPEDIAS AND DICTIONARIES

McGraw-Hill Encyclopedia of Environmental Science. Sybil P. Parker. McGraw-Hill Science & Engineering Books, 11 W. 19th St., New York, New York 10011. (212) 337-6010. 1980. Covers ecology, man's influence on nature, and environmental protection.

Van Nostrand's Scientific Encyclopedia. Glenn D. Considine, ed. Van Nostrand Reinhold, 115 5th Ave., New York, New York 10003. (212) 254-3232. 1983. Sixth edition. Includes all broad subject areas in science.

GENERAL WORKS

Aquatic Humic Substances. I. H. Suffet. American Chemical Society, 1155 16th St. N.W., Washington, District of Columbia 20036. (800) 227-5558. 1989. Influence on fate and treatment of pollutants.

Geochemistry of Marine Humic Compounds. Mohammed A. Rashid. Springer-Verlag, 175 5th Ave., New York, New York 10010. (212) 460-1500. 1985.

Humus Acids of Soils. Dmitrii Sergeevich Orlov. National Technical Information Service, 5285 Port Royal Rd., Springfield, Virginia 22161. (703) 487-4650. 1985. Topics in soil chemistry.

Humus Chemistry: Genesis, Composition, Reactions. F. J. Stevenson. John Wiley & Sons, Inc., 605 3rd Ave., New York, New York 10158-0012. (212) 850-6000. 1982. Covers soil biochemistry.

Magill's Survey of Science. Earth Science Series. Frank N. Magill. Salem Press, PO Box 50062, Pasadena, California 91105. 1990-. Five volumes. Includes information on earth's crust, hot spots and volcanic island chains, physical properties of minerals, rock magnetism, physical properties of rocks, and index.

ONLINE DATA BASES

BIOSIS Previews. BIOSIS, 2100 Arch St., Philadelphia, Pennsylvania 19103-1399. (215) 587-4800. Largest and most comprehensive database of research in the life sciences. Contains citations for nearly 9000 primary research journals, monographs, reviews, symposia, preliminary reports, semi-popular journals, selected institutional reports, government reports and research communications.

Enviro/Energyline Abstracts Plus. R. R. Bowker Co., 121 Chanlon Rd., New Providence, New Jersey 07974. (908) 464-6800.

Environmental Periodicals Bibliography. National Information Services Corp., Ste. 6, Wyman Towers, 3100 St. Paul St., Baltimore, Maryland 21218. (410)243-0797. Online version of abstract of same name.

SCISEARCH. Institute for Scientific Information, University City Science Center, 3501 Market St., Philadelphia, Pennsylvania 19104. (215) 386-0100.

HUMUS

ABSTRACTING AND INDEXING SERVICES

Biological Abstracts. BIOSIS, 2100 Arch St., Philadelphia, Pennsylvania 19103-1399. (215) 587-4800. 1927-.

Biological and Agricultural Index. H.W. Wilson Co., 950 University Ave., Bronx, New York 10452. (800) 367-6770. 1916-. Monthly.

Ecological Abstracts. Geo Abstracts Ltd. Elsevier Applied Science, Crown House, Linton Rd., Barking, England IG 11 8JU. 1974-. Derived from over 600 leading ecological and environmental journals, plus books, conference proceedings, reports and theses.

Environment Abstracts. Bowker A & I Publishing, 121 Chanlon Rd., New Providence, New Jersey 07974. (908) 464-6800. 1974-.

Environment Index. Environment Information Center, Index Research Department, 124 E. 39th St., New York, New York 10016. 1971-. Annual.

Environmental Information Connection–EIC. Planning Information Program, Dept. of Urban and Regional Planning, University of Illinois, 1003 West Nevada, Urbana, Illinois 61801. (217) 333-1369. Also available online.

Environmental Periodicals Bibliography. Environmental Studies Institute, International Academy at Santa Barbara, 800 Garden St., Suite D, Santa Barbara, California 93101. (805) 965-5010. Also available online.

General Science Index. H. W. Wilson Co., 950 University Ave., Bronx, New York 10452. 1978-. Monthly, also issued in annual cumulation. Cumulative subject index to English language periodicals in the subject fields of astronomy, botany, chemistry, earth science, environment and conservation, food and nutrition, genetics, mathematics, medicine and health, microbiology, oceanography, physics, physiology and zoology.

Index to Scientific Book Contents. Institute for Scientific Information, 3501 Market St., Philadelphia, Pennsylvania 19104. (800) 523-1857. 1985-. Annual. Gives contents of science books published.

Science Citation Index. Institute for Scientific Information, 3501 Market St., Philadelphia, Pennsylvania 19104. 1961-.

BIBLIOGRAPHIES

Current Contents. Agriculture, Biology and Environmental Sciences. Institute for Scientific Information, 3501 Market St., Philadelphia, Pennsylvania 19104. (800) 523-1857. 1973-. Previous title: Current Contents. Agricultural, Food & Veterinary Sciences. Gives the table of contents of periodicals in the fields of agriculture, biology, environmental and related areas.

EPA Publications Bibliography. U.S. Environmental Protection Agency, Library Systems Branch, 401 M St., SW, Washington, District of Columbia 20460. (202) 260-2090. Quarterly.

ENCYCLOPEDIAS AND DICTIONARIES

Cambridge Dictionary of Biology. Peter M. B. Walker. Cambridge University Press, 40 W. 20th St., New York, New York 10011. (212) 924-3900 or (800) 227-0247. 1989. Includes 10,000 terms in zoology, botany, biochemistry, molecular biology and genetics. Previously published under the title Chambers Biology Dictionary.

Cambridge Encyclopedia of Life Sciences. A. E. Friday and David S. Ingram. Cambridge University Press, 40 W 20th St., New York, New York 10011. (212) 924-3900 or (800) 227-0247. 1985. Includes all topics under biology and ecology.

A Concise Dictionary of Biology. Elizabeth Martin, ed. Oxford University Press, 200 Madison Ave., New York, New York 10016. (212) 679-7300 or (800) 334-4249. 1990. New edition. Derived from the Concise Science Dictionary, published in 1984.

Elsevier's Dictionary of Horticultural and Agricultural Plant Production in Ten Languages. Elsevier Science Publishing Co., 655 Avenue of Americas, New York, New York 10010. (212) 989-5800. 1990. Language of the text: English, Dutch, French, German, Danish, Swedish, Italian, Spanish, Portuguese and Latin.

The Encyclopedia of Soil Science. Rhodes W. Fairbridge. Academic Press, c/o Harcourt Brace Jovanovich Inc., 6277 Sea Harbor Dr., Orlando, Florida 32887. (800) 346-8648. 1979-. Includes soil physics, soil chemistry, soil biology, soil fertility and plant nutrition, soil genesis, classification and cartography.

Glossary of Geology. Robert Latimer Bates and Julia A. Jackson, eds. American Geological Institute, 4220 King St., Alexandria, Virginia 22302-1507. (703) 379-2480 or (800) 336-4764. 1987. Third edition.

McGraw-Hill Encyclopedia of Environmental Science. Sybil P. Parker. McGraw-Hill Science & Engineering Books, 11 W. 19th St., New York, New York 10011. (212) 337-6010. 1980. Covers ecology, man's influence on nature, and environmental protection.

McGraw-Hill Encyclopedia of Science and Technology. McGraw-Hill, 1221 Avenue of the Americas, New York, New York 10020. (212) 512-2000 or (800) 262-4729. 1992. Seventh edition. Issued in multiple volumes including index. Includes all science and technology broad subject areas.

McGraw-Hill Encyclopedia of the Geological Sciences. Sybil P. Parker, ed. McGraw-Hill, 1221 Avenue of the Americas, New York, New York 10020. (212) 512-2000 or (800) 262-4729. 1988. Second edition. Published previously in the McGraw-Hill Encyclopedia of Science and Technology.

The New York Times Encyclopedic Dictionary of the Environment. Paul Sarnoff. Quadrangle Books, New York, New York 1971. Focuses on state-of-the-art methods of pollution control, abatement, prevention and removal.

Van Nostrand's Scientific Encyclopedia. Glenn D. Considine, ed. Van Nostrand Reinhold, 115 5th Ave., New York, New York 10003. (212) 254-3232. 1983. Sixth edition. Includes all broad subject areas in science.

ONLINE DATA BASES

BIOSIS Previews. BIOSIS, 2100 Arch St., Philadelphia, Pennsylvania 19103-1399. (215) 587-4800. Largest and most comprehensive database of research in the life sciences. Contains citations for nearly 9000 primary research journals, monographs, reviews, symposia, preliminary reports, semi-popular journals, selected institutional reports, government reports and research communications.

Enviro/Energyline Abstracts Plus. R. R. Bowker Co., 121 Chanlon Rd., New Providence, New Jersey 07974. (908) 464-6800.

Environmental Periodicals Bibliography. National Information Services Corp., Ste. 6, Wyman Towers, 3100 St. Paul St., Baltimore, Maryland 21218. (410)243-0797. Online version of abstract of same name.

SCISEARCH. Institute for Scientific Information, University City Science Center, 3501 Market St., Philadelphia, Pennsylvania 19104. (215) 386-0100.

HURRICANES

See: WEATHER

HYDRAULIC ENGINEERING

ABSTRACTING AND INDEXING SERVICES

Environment Abstracts. Bowker A & I Publishing, 121 Chanlon Rd., New Providence, New Jersey 07974. (908) 464-6800. 1974-.

Environment Index. Environment Information Center, Index Research Department, 124 E. 39th St., New York, New York 10016. 1971-. Annual.

Environmental Information Connection–EIC. Planning Information Program, Dept. of Urban and Regional Planning, University of Illinois, 1003 West Nevada, Urbana, Illinois 61801. (217) 333-1369. Also available online.

Environmental Periodicals Bibliography. Environmental Studies Institute, International Academy at Santa Barbara, 800 Garden St., Suite D, Santa Barbara, California 93101. (805) 965-5010. Also available online.

General Science Index. H. W. Wilson Co., 950 University Ave., Bronx, New York 10452. 1978-. Monthly, also issued in annual cumulation. Cumulative subject index to English language periodicals in the subject fields of astronomy, botany, chemistry, earth science, environment and conservation, food and nutrition, genetics, mathematics, medicine and health, microbiology, oceanography, physics, physiology and zoology.

BIBLIOGRAPHIES

EPA Publications Bibliography. U.S. Environmental Protection Agency, Library Systems Branch, 401 M St., SW, Washington, District of Columbia 20460. (202) 260-2090. Quarterly.

DIRECTORIES

Environmental Industries Marketplace. Karen Napoleone Meech. Gale Research Inc., 835 Penobscot Bldg., Detroit, 48226-4904. (313) 961-2242. 1992.

ENCYCLOPEDIAS AND DICTIONARIES

McGraw-Hill Encyclopedia of Environmental Science. Sybil P. Parker. McGraw-Hill Science & Engineering Books, 11 W. 19th St., New York, New York 10011. (212) 337-6010. 1980. Covers ecology, man's influence on nature, and environmental protection.

HANDBOOKS AND MANUALS

Engineering Field Manual. U.S. Soil Conservation Service, PO Box 2890, Washington, District of Columbia 20013. (202) 205-0027. 1984. Procedures recommended for water and soil conservation.

Handbook of Suggested Practices for the Design and Installation of Ground-Water Monitoring Wells. Linda Aller. Environmental Monitoring Systems Laboratory, PO Box 15027, Las Vegas, Nevada 89104. (702) 798-2000. 1991.

Hydropower Engineering Handbook. John S. Gulliver. McGraw-Hill Science & Engineering Books, 11 W. 19th St., New York, New York 10011. (212) 337-6010. 1991. Hydroelectric power plants and hydraulic engineering.

ONLINE DATA BASES

Enviro/Energyline Abstracts Plus. R. R. Bowker Co., 121 Chanlon Rd., New Providence, New Jersey 07974. (908) 464-6800.

Environmental Periodicals Bibliography. National Information Services Corp., Ste. 6, Wyman Towers, 3100 St. Paul St., Baltimore, Maryland 21218. (410)243-0797. Online version of abstract of same name.

PERIODICALS AND NEWSLETTERS

Journal of Hydraulic Engineering. American Society of Civil Engineers, 345 E. 47th St., New York, New York 10017. (212) 705-7288; (800) 548-2723. 1983-. Monthly. Papers describe the analysis and solutions of problems in hydraulic engineering, hydrology and water resources. Emphasizes concepts, methods, techniques and results that advance knowledge in the hydraulic engineering profession.

HYDRAULICS

ABSTRACTING AND INDEXING SERVICES

Applied Science and Technology Index. H.W. Wilson Co., 950 University Ave., Bronx, New York 10452. (800) 367-6770. Formerly Industrial Arts Index.

Biological and Agricultural Index. H.W. Wilson Co., 950 University Ave., Bronx, New York 10452. (800) 367-6770. 1916-. Monthly.

Engineering Index. The Engineering Index Inc., 345 E. 47th St., New York, New York 10017. 1962-.

Environment Abstracts. Bowker A & I Publishing, 121 Chanlon Rd., New Providence, New Jersey 07974. (908) 464-6800. 1974-.

Environment Index. Environment Information Center, Index Research Department, 124 E. 39th St., New York, New York 10016. 1971-. Annual.

Environmental Information Connection–EIC. Planning Information Program, Dept. of Urban and Regional Planning, University of Illinois, 1003 West Nevada, Urbana, Illinois 61801. (217) 333-1369. Also available online.

Environmental Periodicals Bibliography. Environmental Studies Institute, International Academy at Santa Barbara, 800 Garden St., Suite D, Santa Barbara, California 93101. (805) 965-5010. Also available online.

General Science Index. H. W. Wilson Co., 950 University Ave., Bronx, New York 10452. 1978-. Monthly, also issued in annual cumulation. Cumulative subject index to English language periodicals in the subject fields of astronomy, botany, chemistry, earth science, environment and conservation, food and nutrition, genetics, mathematics, medicine and health, microbiology, oceanography, physics, physiology and zoology.

Index to Scientific Book Contents. Institute for Scientific Information, 3501 Market St., Philadelphia, Pennsylvania 19104. (800) 523-1857. 1985-. Annual. Gives contents of science books published.

Pollution Abstracts. Cambridge Scientific Abstracts, 5161 River Rd., Bethesda, Maryland 20816. (301) 961-6750. Six/year. Indexes worldwide technical literature on environmental pollution. Covers air pollution, marine and freshwater pollution, sewage and wastewater treatment, waste management, toxicology and health, noise pollution, radiation, land pollution, and environmental policies, programs, legislation, and education. Also available online.

Science Citation Index. Institute for Scientific Information, 3501 Market St., Philadelphia, Pennsylvania 19104. 1961-.

BIBLIOGRAPHIES

EPA Publications Bibliography. U.S. Environmental Protection Agency, Library Systems Branch, 401 M St., SW, Washington, District of Columbia 20460. (202) 260-2090. Quarterly.

Leakage and Loss in Fluid Systems. Scientific and Technical Information Ltd., 4 Kings Meadow, Ferry Hinksey Rd., Oxford, England OX2 0DU. (0865) 798898. 1990. A bibliography of leak detection, monitoring, control and modelling in pipelines, dams, reservoirs, and associated pumping systems.

DIRECTORIES

National Fluid Power Association–Membership Directory. 3333 N. Mayfair Rd., Suite 311, Milwaukee, Wisconsin 53222. (414) 259-0990. Annual.

ENCYCLOPEDIAS AND DICTIONARIES

Dictionary of Civil Engineering. John S. Scott. Halsted Press, Division of J. Wiley, 605 3rd Ave., New York, New York 10158. (212) 850-6000. 1981. Third edition.

McGraw-Hill Encyclopedia of Environmental Science. Sybil P. Parker. McGraw-Hill Science & Engineering Books, 11 W. 19th St., New York, New York 10011. (212) 337-6010. 1980. Covers ecology, man's influence on nature, and environmental protection.

McGraw-Hill Encyclopedia of Science and Technology. McGraw-Hill, 1221 Avenue of the Americas, New York, New York 10020. (212) 512-2000 or (800) 262-4729. 1992. Seventh edition. Issued in multiple volumes including index. Includes all science and technology broad subject areas.

Van Nostrand's Scientific Encyclopedia. Glenn D. Considine, ed. Van Nostrand Reinhold, 115 5th Ave., New York, New York 10003. (212) 254-3232. 1983. Sixth edition. Includes all broad subject areas in science.

GENERAL WORKS

Water Engineering and Landscape: Water Control and Landscape Transformation in the Modern Period. D. Cosgrove and G. Petts, eds. Belhaven Press, 136 S. Broadway, Irvington, New York 10533. (914) 591-9111. 1990. Examines the role played by water management in the environment.

HANDBOOKS AND MANUALS

Engineer Construction Equipment Repairer. U.S. Army Training Support Center, Reserve Schools Division, Fort Eustis, Virginia 23604. (804) 878-5251. 1987.

Highway Drainage Guidelines. Federal Highway Administration, 400 7th St. SW, Washington, District of Columbia 20590. (202) 366-0630. 1987. Hydraulic considerations in highway planning and location, highway construction, and hydraulic design of culverts.

ONLINE DATA BASES

Computerized Engineering Index–COMPENDEX. Engineering Information Inc., 345 E. 47th St., New York, New York 10017. (212) 705-7600.

Enviro/Energyline Abstracts Plus. R. R. Bowker Co., 121 Chanlon Rd., New Providence, New Jersey 07974. (908) 464-6800.

Environmental Periodicals Bibliography. National Information Services Corp., Ste. 6, Wyman Towers, 3100 St. Paul St., Baltimore, Maryland 21218. (410)243-0797. Online version of abstract of same name.

PERIODICALS AND NEWSLETTERS

Hydrosoft. Computational Mechanics Publications Inc., 400 W. Cummings Park, Suite 6200, Woburn, Massachusetts 01801. Quarterly. Covers software for hydraulics, hydrology and hydrodynamics.

Stochastic Hydrology and Hydraulics. Springer-Verlag, 175 5th Ave., New York, New York 10010. (212) 460-1500. Four times a year. Statistical methods in hydraulics.

HYDROCARBONS

See also: AIR QUALITY; COMBUSTION; EMISSIONS

ABSTRACTING AND INDEXING SERVICES

Biological and Agricultural Index. H.W. Wilson Co., 950 University Ave., Bronx, New York 10452. (800) 367-6770. 1916-. Monthly.

Chemical Abstracts. Chemical Abstracts Service, 2540 Olentangy River Rd., PO Box 3012, Columbus, Ohio 43210. (800) 848-6533. 1907-.

Environment Abstracts. Bowker A & I Publishing, 121 Chanlon Rd., New Providence, New Jersey 07974. (908) 464-6800. 1974-.

Environment Index. Environment Information Center, Index Research Department, 124 E. 39th St., New York, New York 10016. 1971-. Annual.

Environmental Information Connection–EIC. Planning Information Program, Dept. of Urban and Regional Planning, University of Illinois, 1003 West Nevada, Urbana, Illinois 61801. (217) 333-1369. Also available online.

Environmental Periodicals Bibliography. Environmental Studies Institute, International Academy at Santa Barbara, 800 Garden St., Suite D, Santa Barbara, California 93101. (805) 965-5010. Also available online.

General Science Index. H. W. Wilson Co., 950 University Ave., Bronx, New York 10452. 1978-. Monthly, also issued in annual cumulation. Cumulative subject index to English language periodicals in the subject fields of astronomy, botany, chemistry, earth science, environment and conservation, food and nutrition, genetics, mathematics, medicine and health, microbiology, oceanography, physics, physiology and zoology.

Geographical Abstracts. London School of Economics, Dept. of Geography, Regency House, 34 Duke St., London, England 1966-. Continued by Geo Abstracts issued in 6 parts: Pt. A. Landforms and the quaternary; Pt. B. Biogeography and Climatology; Pt. C. Economic geography; Pt. D. Social geography and cartography; Pt. E. Sedimentology; Pt. F. Regional and community planning.

Index to Scientific Book Contents. Institute for Scientific Information, 3501 Market St., Philadelphia, Pennsylvania 19104. (800) 523-1857. 1985-. Annual. Gives contents of science books published.

Pollution Abstracts. Cambridge Scientific Abstracts, 5161 River Rd., Bethesda, Maryland 20816. (301) 961-6750. Six/year. Indexes worldwide technical literature on environmental pollution. Covers air pollution, marine and freshwater pollution, sewage and wastewater treatment, waste management, toxicology and health, noise pollution, radiation, land pollution, and environmental policies, programs, legislation, and education. Also available online.

Science Citation Index. Institute for Scientific Information, 3501 Market St., Philadelphia, Pennsylvania 19104. 1961-.

BIBLIOGRAPHIES

Bibliography and Index of Geology. American Geological Institute, 4220 King St., Alexandria, Virginia 22302. Monthly. Includes environmental geology and hydrogeology.

EPA Publications Bibliography. U.S. Environmental Protection Agency, Library Systems Branch, 401 M St., SW, Washington, District of Columbia 20460. (202) 260-2090. Quarterly.

ENCYCLOPEDIAS AND DICTIONARIES

Encyclopedia of Chemical Processing and Design. John J. Mcketta and W. A. Cunningham. Marcel Dekker, Inc., 270 Madison Ave., New York, New York 10016. (212) 696-9000; (800) 228-1160. 1992. Thirty-eight volumes.

Encyclopedia of Electrochemistry of Elements. A. J. Bard. Marcel Dekker, Inc., 270 Madison Ave., New York, New York 10016. (212) 696-9000 or (800) 228-1160. Encyclopedic treatment of the subject area of electrochemistry and related subjects.

Encyclopedia of Human Biology. Renato Dulbecco, ed. Academic Press, c/o Harcourt Brace Jovanovich Inc., 6277 Sea Harbor Dr., Orlando, Florida 32887. (800) 346-8648. 1991. Eight volumes.

Encyclopedia of Physics. Rita G. Lerner and George L. Trigg. VCH Publishers, 303 NW 12th Ave., Deerfield Beach, Florida 33442-1788. (305) 428-5566. 1991. Second edition.

Kirk-Othmer Encyclopedia of Chemical Technology. J. I. Kroschwitz, ed. John Wiley & Sons, Inc., 605 3rd Ave., New York, New York 10158-0012. (212) 850-6000. 1992-. All articles in the new edition have been rewritten and updated adding new subjects such as biotechnology, computer topics, analytical techniques and instrumentation, environmental concerns, fuels and energy, inorganic and solid state chemistry; composite materials and material science in general, and pharmaceuticals. Also available online.

McGraw-Hill Encyclopedia of Environmental Science. Sybil P. Parker. McGraw-Hill Science & Engineering Books, 11 W. 19th St., New York, New York 10011. (212) 337-6010. 1980. Covers ecology, man's influence on nature, and environmental protection.

McGraw-Hill Encyclopedia of Science and Technology. McGraw-Hill, 1221 Avenue of the Americas, New York,

New York 10020. (212) 512-2000 or (800) 262-4729. 1992. Seventh edition. Issued in multiple volumes including index. Includes all science and technology broad subject areas.

Ullmanns Encyclopedia of Industrial Chemistry. Hans Jurgen Arpe and Wolfgang Gerhartz, eds. VCH Publishers, 303 NW 12th Ave., Deerfield Beach, Florida 33442-1788. (305) 428-5566. 1990. Designed to keep up with the broad spectrum of chemical technology. Thirty-six volumes of the encyclopedia have been divided into two sets: the 28 A volumes contain alphabetically arranged articles on chemicals, product groups, processes and technological concepts; and the 8 B volumes are compendia of basic knowledge in industrial chemistry.

Van Nostrand's Scientific Encyclopedia. Glenn D. Considine, ed. Van Nostrand Reinhold, 115 5th Ave., New York, New York 10003. (212) 254-3232. 1983. Sixth edition. Includes all broad subject areas in science.

GENERAL WORKS

Fates and Biological Effects of Polycyclic Aromatic Hydrocarbons in Aquatic Systems. John P. Giesy. U.S. Environmental Protection Agency, Center for Environmental Research Information, 26 W. Martin Luther King Dr., Cincinnati, Ohio 45268. (513) 569-7931. 1983. Aquatic biology, water pollution, and environmental aspects of hydrocarbons.

Groundwater Remediation and Petroleum: A Guide for Underground Storage Tanks. David C. Noonan and James T. Curtis. PennWell Books, PO Box 21288, Tulsa, Oklahoma 74121. (918) 831-9421; (800) 752-9764. 1990. Guide for personnel charged with the responsibility of addressing contamination caused by leaking underground storage tanks.

Health and Ecological Assessment of Polynuclear Aromatic Hydrocarbons. Si Duk Lee and Lester Grant, eds. Chem-Orbital, PO Box 134, Park Forest, Illinois 60466. (708) 748-0440. 1981.

Hydrocarbon Contaminated Soils and Groundwater: Analysis, Fate, Environmental and Public Health Effects, and Remediation. Paul T. Kostecki and Edward J. Calabrese. Lewis Publishers, 2000 Corporate Blvd.,N.W., Boca Raton, Florida 33431. (407) 994-0555 or (800) 272-7737. 1991. Describes perspectives and emerging issues, analytical techniques and site assessments, environmental fate and modeling.

Hydrocarbon Control Strategies for Gasoline Marketing Operations. R. L. Norton. U.S. Environmental Protection Agency, Office of Air and Waste Management, MD 75, Research Triangle Park, North Carolina 27711. 1978. Pollution control of motor vehicle exhaust.

Investigating Hydrocarbon Spills. James M. Davidson. Lewis Publishers, 2000 Corporate Blvd., N.W., Boca Raton, Florida 33431. (407) 994-0555 or (800) 272-7737. 1991. Includes regulatory reviews, scope of investigations, identification of a problem, phased approach and preparation for remediation.

Magill's Survey of Science. Earth Science Series. Frank N. Magill. Salem Press, PO Box 50062, Pasadena, California 91105. 1990-. Five volumes. Includes information on earth's crust, hot spots and volcanic island chains, physical properties of minerals, rock magnetism, physical properties of rocks, and index.

Microbial Hydrocarbon Degradation in Sediments Impacted by the Exxon Valdez Oil Spill; Final Report. Water Research Center, University of Alaska, Fairbanks, 460 Duckering Bldg., Fairbanks, Alaska 99775. (907) 474-7350. 1990.

Response of Marine Animals to Petroleum and Specific Petroleum Hydrocarbons. Jerry M. Neff. John Wiley & Sons, Inc., 605 3rd Ave., New York, New York 10158-0012. (212) 850-6000. 1981. Effect of water and oil pollution on marine fauna.

Soil Vapor Extraction Technology. Tom A. Pedersen. Noyes Publications, 120 Mill Rd., Park Ridge, New Jersey 07656. (201) 391-8484. 1991. Environmental aspects of hydrocarbons.

Toxicological Profile for Carbon Tetrachloride. Agency for Toxic Substances and Disease Registry, U.S. Public Health Service, 1600 Clifton Rd. NE, Atlanta, Georgia 30333. (404) 452-4111. 1989.

HANDBOOKS AND MANUALS

Database for Hydrocarbon-Contaminated Site Remediation: Software and Manual. C.E. Spear. Electric Power Research Institute, 3412 Hillview Ave., Palo Alto, California 94304. (415) 965-4081. 1990. Waste disposal, gas manufacture and works, and hazardous waste sites.

Energy Deskbook. Samuel Glasstone. Van Nostrand Reinhold, 115 5th Ave., New York, New York 10020. (212) 254-3232. 1983. Single volume reference covering all energy resources.

Handbook of Vapor Pressures and Heats of Vaporization of Hydrocarbons and Related Compounds. Randolph C. Wilhoit. Thermodynamics Research Center, Dept. of Chemistry, Texas A & M Univ., Drawer C, Lewis St., University Campus, College Station, Texas 77843. (409) 845-1436. 1971. Covers data on vapor liquid equilibrium tables and hydrocarbon tables.

ONLINE DATA BASES

CAS Source Index–CASSI. Chemical Abstracts Service, 2540 Olentangy River Rd., P.O. Box 3012, Columbus, Ohio 43210. (800) 848-6533 or (614) 421-3600. A listing of bibliographic and library holdings information for scientific and technical primary literature relevant to the chemical sciences.

Chemical Abstracts-CA. Chemical Abstracts Service, 2540 Olentangy River Rd., P.O. Box 3012, Columbus, Ohio 43210. (800) 848-6533 or (614) 421-3600. Information sources include 9000 journals, patents from 27 countries, two industrial property organizations, new books, conference proceedings, and government research reports.

Chemical Collection System/Request Tracking–CCS/RTS. U.S. Environmental Protection Agency, Office of Pesticides and Toxic Substances, 401 M St., SW, Washington, District of Columbia 20460. (202) 260-2090. Contains information on various properties of a number of chemicals including environmental effects, test and analysis methods, and health effects. Available from EPA.

Chemical Dictionary Online–CHEMLINE. Chemical Abstracts Service, 2540 Olentangy River Rd., Columbus, Ohio 43210. (614) 421-3600 or (800) 848-6533. Part of MEDLINE of the National Library of Medicine (NLM).

File of 900,000 names for chemical substances, representing 450,000 unique compounds. It contains such information as Chemical Abstracts (CA) Service Registry Numbers, molecular formulas, preferred chemical nomenclature, and generic and ring structure information. Available on NLM's ELHILL system.

Chemical Exposure. Science Applications International Corp., Health & Environmental Information, P.O. Box 2501, Oak Ridge, Tennessee 37831. (615) 482-9031. Database of chemicals that have been identified in both human tissues and body fluids and in feral and food animals. Contains reference to journal articles, conferences, and reports. Covers the whole fields of information related to human and animal exposure to food, air, and water contaminants and pharmaceuticals. Its records include information on chemical properties, formulas, tissues measured, analytical method used, demographics and more. Available on DIALOG.

Dewitt Petrochemical Newsletter. DeWitt and Company, 16800 Greenspoint Park, North Atrium Suite 120, Houston, Texas 77060. (713) 875-5525.

Enviro/Energyline Abstracts Plus. R. R. Bowker Co., 121 Chanlon Rd., New Providence, New Jersey 07974. (908) 464-6800.

Environmental Periodicals Bibliography. National Information Services Corp., Ste. 6, Wyman Towers, 3100 St. Paul St., Baltimore, Maryland 21218. (410)243-0797. Online version of abstract of same name.

Kirk-Othmer Encyclopedia of Chemical Technology. John Wiley & Sons, Inc., 605 3rd Ave., 5th Floor, New York, New York 10158. (212) 850-6000. Online version of the publication of the same name.

SCISEARCH. Institute for Scientific Information, University City Science Center, 3501 Market St., Philadelphia, Pennsylvania 19104. (215) 386-0100.

STATISTICS SOURCES

Solvents & the Environment. FIND/SVP, 625 Avenue of the Americas, New York, New York 10011. (212) 645-4500. 1991. Demand forecasts on hydrocarbons for 1995 and 2000; chlorinated, ketones, alcohols and alcohol esters, ethers, glycols and other esters, and recycled solvents.

TRADE ASSOCIATIONS AND PROFESSIONAL SOCIETIES

American Institute of Chemical Engineers. 345 East 47th St., New York, New York 10017. (212) 705-7338.

American Institute of Chemists. 7315 Wisconsin Ave., Bethesda, Maryland 20814. (301) 652-2447.

HYDROCHLORIC ACID

ABSTRACTING AND INDEXING SERVICES

Applied Science and Technology Index. H.W. Wilson Co., 950 University Ave., Bronx, New York 10452. (800) 367-6770. Formerly Industrial Arts Index.

Chemical Abstracts. Chemical Abstracts Service, 2540 Olentangy River Rd., PO Box 3012, Columbus, Ohio 43210. (800) 848-6533. 1907-.

Environment Abstracts. Bowker A & I Publishing, 121 Chanlon Rd., New Providence, New Jersey 07974. (908) 464-6800. 1974-.

Environment Index. Environment Information Center, Index Research Department, 124 E. 39th St., New York, New York 10016. 1971-. Annual.

Environmental Information Connection–EIC. Planning Information Program, Dept. of Urban and Regional Planning, University of Illinois, 1003 West Nevada, Urbana, Illinois 61801. (217) 333-1369. Also available online.

Environmental Periodicals Bibliography. Environmental Studies Institute, International Academy at Santa Barbara, 800 Garden St., Suite D, Santa Barbara, California 93101. (805) 965-5010. Also available online.

General Science Index. H. W. Wilson Co., 950 University Ave., Bronx, New York 10452. 1978-. Monthly, also issued in annual cumulation. Cumulative subject index to English language periodicals in the subject fields of astronomy, botany, chemistry, earth science, environment and conservation, food and nutrition, genetics, mathematics, medicine and health, microbiology, oceanography, physics, physiology and zoology.

Physics Briefs. Physikalische Berichte. Physik Verlag, Pappapelallee 3, Postfach 101161, Weinheim, Germany D-6940. 1979-. Semimonthly. In English. Volumes for 1979- issued by the Deutsche Physikalische Gesellschaft and the Fachinformationszentrum Energie Physik, Mathematik in cooperation with the American Institute of Physics.

Pollution Abstracts. Cambridge Scientific Abstracts, 5161 River Rd., Bethesda, Maryland 20816. (301) 961-6750. Six/year. Indexes worldwide technical literature on environmental pollution. Covers air pollution, marine and freshwater pollution, sewage and wastewater treatment, waste management, toxicology and health, noise pollution, radiation, land pollution, and environmental policies, programs, legislation, and education. Also available online.

Science Citation Index. Institute for Scientific Information, 3501 Market St., Philadelphia, Pennsylvania 19104. 1961-.

BIBLIOGRAPHIES

EPA Publications Bibliography. U.S. Environmental Protection Agency, Library Systems Branch, 401 M St., SW, Washington, District of Columbia 20460. (202) 260-2090. Quarterly.

ENCYCLOPEDIAS AND DICTIONARIES

Encyclopedia of Physics. Rita G. Lerner and George L. Trigg. VCH Publishers, 303 NW 12th Ave., Deerfield Beach, Florida 33442-1788. (305) 428-5566. 1991. Second edition.

Ullmanns Encyclopedia of Industrial Chemistry. Hans Jurgen Arpe and Wolfgang Gerhartz, eds. VCH Publishers, 303 NW 12th Ave., Deerfield Beach, Florida 33442-1788. (305) 428-5566. 1990. Designed to keep up with the broad spectrum of chemical technology. Thirty-six volumes of the encyclopedia have been divided into two sets: the 28 A volumes contain alphabetically arranged articles on chemicals, product groups, processes and technological concepts; and the 8 B volumes are compendia of basic knowledge in industrial chemistry.

Van Nostrand's Scientific Encyclopedia. Glenn D. Considine, ed. Van Nostrand Reinhold, 115 5th Ave., New York, New York 10003. (212) 254-3232. 1983. Sixth edition. Includes all broad subject areas in science.

GENERAL WORKS

Chlorine and Hydrogen Chloride. National Academy of Sciences, 2101 Constitution Ave., NW, Washington, District of Columbia 20418. (202) 334-2000. 1976. Medical and biologic effects of environmental pollutants.

ONLINE DATA BASES

CAS Source Index–CASSI. Chemical Abstracts Service, 2540 Olentangy River Rd., P.O. Box 3012, Columbus, Ohio 43210. (800) 848-6533 or (614) 421-3600. A listing of bibliographic and library holdings information for scientific and technical primary literature relevant to the chemical sciences.

Chemical Abstracts-CA. Chemical Abstracts Service, 2540 Olentangy River Rd., P.O. Box 3012, Columbus, Ohio 43210. (800) 848-6533 or (614) 421-3600. Information sources include 9000 journals, patents from 27 countries, two industrial property organizations, new books, conference proceedings, and government research reports.

Chemical Collection System/Request Tracking–CCS/RTS. U.S. Environmental Protection Agency, Office of Pesticides and Toxic Substances, 401 M St., SW, Washington, District of Columbia 20460. (202) 260-2090. Contains information on various properties of a number of chemicals including environmental effects, test and analysis methods, and health effects. Available from EPA.

Chemical Dictionary Online–CHEMLINE. Chemical Abstracts Service, 2540 Olentangy River Rd., Columbus, Ohio 43210. (614) 421-3600 or (800) 848-6533. Part of MEDLINE of the National Library of Medicine (NLM). File of 900,000 names for chemical substances, representing 450,000 unique compounds. It contains such information as Chemical Abstracts (CA) Service Registry Numbers, molecular formulas, preferred chemical nomenclature, and generic and ring structure information. Available on NLM's ELHILL system.

Chemical Exposure. Science Applications International Corp., Health & Environmental Information, P.O. Box 2501, Oak Ridge, Tennessee 37831. (615) 482-9031. Database of chemicals that have been identified in both human tissues and body fluids and in feral and food animals. Contains reference to journal articles, conferences, and reports. Covers the whole fields of information related to human and animal exposure to food, air, and water contaminants and pharmaceuticals. Its records include information on chemical properties, formulas, tissues measured, analytical method used, demographics and more. Available on DIALOG.

Enviro/Energyline Abstracts Plus. R. R. Bowker Co., 121 Chanlon Rd., New Providence, New Jersey 07974. (908) 464-6800.

Environmental Periodicals Bibliography. National Information Services Corp., Ste. 6, Wyman Towers, 3100 St.

Paul St., Baltimore, Maryland 21218. (410)243-0797. Online version of abstract of same name.

TRADE ASSOCIATIONS AND PROFESSIONAL SOCIETIES

American Institute of Chemists. 7315 Wisconsin Ave., Bethesda, Maryland 20814. (301) 652-2447.

HYDROELECTRIC POWER (HYDROPOWER)

See also: DAMS; FISH AND WILDLIFE MANAGEMENT; POWER GENERATION; WATER MANAGEMENT

ABSTRACTING AND INDEXING SERVICES

Applied Science and Technology Index. H.W. Wilson Co., 950 University Ave., Bronx, New York 10452. (800) 367-6770. Formerly Industrial Arts Index.

Biological and Agricultural Index. H.W. Wilson Co., 950 University Ave., Bronx, New York 10452. (800) 367-6770. 1916-. Monthly.

Civil Engineering Hydraulic Abstracts. BHRA Fluid Engineering, Air Science Co., PO Box 143, Corning, New York 14830. (607) 962-5591. Monthly. Abstracts of periodicals that publish in the areas of hydraulic engineering and other related topics.

Energy Information Abstracts Annual 1987 in Retrospect. EIC/Intelligence Inc., 121 Chanlon Rd., New Providence, New Jersey 07974. (908) 464-6800. 1988. Annual. Cumulative edition of the monthly Energy Information Abstracts. Monitors sources in the field of energy including the scientific, technical and business journal literature, conference and symposia proceedings, corporate, government and academic reports.

Engineering Index. The Engineering Index Inc., 345 E. 47th St., New York, New York 10017. 1962-.

Environment Abstracts. Bowker A & I Publishing, 121 Chanlon Rd., New Providence, New Jersey 07974. (908) 464-6800. 1974-.

Environment Index. Environment Information Center, Index Research Department, 124 E. 39th St., New York, New York 10016. 1971-. Annual.

Environmental Information Connection–EIC. Planning Information Program, Dept. of Urban and Regional Planning, University of Illinois, 1003 West Nevada, Urbana, Illinois 61801. (217) 333-1369. Also available online.

Environmental Periodicals Bibliography. Environmental Studies Institute, International Academy at Santa Barbara, 800 Garden St., Suite D, Santa Barbara, California 93101. (805) 965-5010. Also available online.

ERDA Research Abstracts. U.S. ERDA Technical Information Center, Box 62, Oak Ridge, Tennessee 37830.

General Science Index. H. W. Wilson Co., 950 University Ave., Bronx, New York 10452. 1978-. Monthly, also issued in annual cumulation. Cumulative subject index to English language periodicals in the subject fields of astronomy, botany, chemistry, earth science, environment and conservation, food and nutrition, genetics,

mathematics, medicine and health, microbiology, oceanography, physics, physiology and zoology.

Index to Scientific Book Contents. Institute for Scientific Information, 3501 Market St., Philadelphia, Pennsylvania 19104. (800) 523-1857. 1985-. Annual. Gives contents of science books published.

Pollution Abstracts. Cambridge Scientific Abstracts, 5161 River Rd., Bethesda, Maryland 20816. (301) 961-6750. Six/year. Indexes worldwide technical literature on environmental pollution. Covers air pollution, marine and freshwater pollution, sewage and wastewater treatment, waste management, toxicology and health, noise pollution, radiation, land pollution, and environmental policies, programs, legislation, and education. Also available online.

Science Citation Index. Institute for Scientific Information, 3501 Market St., Philadelphia, Pennsylvania 19104. 1961-.

ALMANACS AND YEARBOOKS

Hydroelectric Power Resources of the United States, Developed and Underdeveloped. Federal Energy Regulatory Commission, 825 N. Capital St. NE, Washington, District of Columbia 20426. (202) 208-0200. 1980.

BIBLIOGRAPHIES

EPA Publications Bibliography. U.S. Environmental Protection Agency, Library Systems Branch, 401 M St., SW, Washington, District of Columbia 20460. (202) 260-2090. Quarterly.

ENCYCLOPEDIAS AND DICTIONARIES

Dictionary of Civil Engineering. John S. Scott. Halsted Press, Division of J. Wiley, 605 3rd Ave., New York, New York 10158. (212) 850-6000. 1981. Third edition.

Dictionary of Environmental Engineering and Related Sciences: English-Spanish, Spanish-English. Jose T. Villate. Ediciones Universal, 3090 SW 8th St., Miami, Florida 33135. (305) 642-3355. 1979.

Dictionary of Environmental Protection Technology: In Four Languages, English, German, French, Russian. Egon Seidel. Elsevier Science Publishing Co., 655 Avenue of the Americas, New York, New York 10010. (212) 984-5800. 1988.

Encyclopedia of Environmental Science and Engineering. J.R. Pfafflin. Gordon and Breach Science Publishers, Inc., 270 8th Ave., New York, New York 10011. (212) 206-8900. 1992.

Encyclopedia of Physical Science and Technology. Robert A. Meyers, ed. Academic Press, c/o Harcourt Brace Jovanovich Inc., 6277 Sea Harbor Dr., Orlando, Florida 32887. (800) 346-8648. Dictionary of engineering, technology and physical sciences.

Energy Terminology: A Multilingual Glossary. Pergamon Microforms International, Inc., Fairview Park, Elmsford, New York 10523. (914) 592-7720. 1986. Second edition. Contains 1500 defined terms and concepts related to the field of energy together with an index of several thousand undefined keywords used in the definitions of these terms and concepts. Contents appear in four languages: English, French, German and Spanish.

English-Russian Dictionary of Environmental Protection: About 14,000 Terms. E.L. Milovanov. Pergamon Microforms International, Inc., Fairview Park, Elmsford, New York 10523. (914) 592-7720. 1981.

Environmental Engineering Dictionary. C. C. Lee. Government Institutes, Inc., 4 Research Pl., Ste. 200, Rockville, Maryland 20850. (301) 921-2300. 1989. Defines over 6000 engineering terms relating to pollutioncontrol technologies, monitoring, risk assessment, sampling andanalysis, quality control, permitting, and environmentally-regulated engineering and science. Includes bibliographical references (p. 612-627).

Kaiman's Encyclopedia of Energy Topics. Lee Kaiman and J. Masloff. Environmental Design and Research Center, 26799 Elena Rd., Los Altos Hills, California 94022. 1983. Two volumes. Coverage of topics range from natural energy sources that are renewable to nonrenewable, and the application of these energy sources.

McGraw-Hill Encyclopedia of Environmental Science. Sybil P. Parker. McGraw-Hill Science & Engineering Books, 11 W. 19th St., New York, New York 10011. (212) 337-6010. 1980. Covers ecology, man's influence on nature, and environmental protection.

McGraw-Hill Encyclopedia of Science and Technology. McGraw-Hill, 1221 Avenue of the Americas, New York, New York 10020. (212) 512-2000 or (800) 262-4729. 1992. Seventh edition. Issued in multiple volumes including index. Includes all science and technology broad subject areas.

Van Nostrand's Scientific Encyclopedia. Glenn D. Considine, ed. Van Nostrand Reinhold, 115 5th Ave., New York, New York 10003. (212) 254-3232. 1983. Sixth edition. Includes all broad subject areas in science.

GENERAL WORKS

Energy Regulation: Hydropower Impacts on Fish Should be Adequately Considered. U.S. General Accounting Office, 441 G St., NW, Washington, District of Columbia (202) 275-5067. 1986.

Physical Impacts of Small-Scale Hydroelectric Facilities and their Effects on Fish and Wildlife. Haydon Rochester. Fish and Wildlife Service, Department of the Interior, 18th and C Sts., NW, Washington, District of Columbia 20240. (202) 653-8750. 1984.

Power Plants: Effects on Fish and Shellfish Behavior. Charles H. Hocutt. Academic Press, c/o Harcourt Brace Jovanovich Inc., 6277 Sea Harbor Dr., Orlando, Florida 32887. (800) 346-8648. 1980.

Problems of Hydroelectric Development at Existing Dams. R.J. Taylor. Department of Energy, 5285 Port Royal Rd, Springfield, Virginia 22161. 1979. An analysis of institutional, economic, and environmental restraints.

Rivers at Risk: The Concerned Citizen's Guide to Hydropower. John D. Echeverria. Island Press, 1718 Connecticut Ave., NW, Suite 300, Washington, District of Columbia 20009. (202) 232-7933. 1989. Offers practical understanding of how to influence government decisions about hydropower development on the nation's rivers.

Simulating the Environmental Impact of a Large Hydroelectric Project. Normand Therien. Society for Computer Simulation, 4838 Ronson Ct., San Diego, California 92111. (619) 277-3888. 1981. Environmental aspects of hydroelectric power plants.

GOVERNMENTAL ORGANIZATIONS

Office of Environmental Affairs: Bureau of Reclamation. 18th and C St., N.W., Washington, District of Columbia 20240. (202) 343-4662.

Office of Public Information: Federal Energy Regulatory Commission. 825 North Capitol St., N.E., Washington, District of Columbia 20426. (202) 357-8055.

ONLINE DATA BASES

Computerized Engineering Index–COMPENDEX. Engineering Information Inc., 345 E. 47th St., New York, New York 10017. (212) 705-7600.

EBIB. Texas A & M University, Sterling C. Evans Library, Reference Division, College Station, Texas 77843. (409) 845-5741.

Electric Power Industry Abstracts. Utility Data Institute, 1700 K St., N.W., Suite 400, Washington, District of Columbia 20006. (800) 466-3660.

Enviro/Energyline Abstracts Plus. R. R. Bowker Co., 121 Chanlon Rd., New Providence, New Jersey 07974. (908) 464-6800.

Environmental Periodicals Bibliography. National Information Services Corp., Ste. 6, Wyman Towers, 3100 St. Paul St., Baltimore, Maryland 21218. (410)243-0797. Online version of abstract of same name.

Hydrowire. HCI Publications, 410 Archibald St., Kansas City, Missouri 64111. (816) 931-1311.

Monthly Catalog of United States Government Publications. U.S. G.P.O., Supt. of Docs., PO Box 371954, Pittsburgh, Pennsylvania 15250-7954. (202) 512-0000.

National Technical Information Service. U.S. Department of Commerce, National Technical Information Service, Office of Data Base Services, 5285 Port Royal Rd., Springfield, Virginia 22161. (703) 487-4807. Bibliographic database of government sponsored research and technical reports.

TRADE ASSOCIATIONS AND PROFESSIONAL SOCIETIES

National Hydropower Association. 555 13th St., N.W., Suite 900 E., Washington, District of Columbia 20004. (202) 637-8115.

HYDROGEN AS FUEL

ABSTRACTING AND INDEXING SERVICES

Applied Science and Technology Index. H.W. Wilson Co., 950 University Ave., Bronx, New York 10452. (800) 367-6770. Formerly Industrial Arts Index.

Biological Abstracts. BIOSIS, 2100 Arch St., Philadelphia, Pennsylvania 19103-1399. (215) 587-4800. 1927-.

Biological and Agricultural Index. H.W. Wilson Co., 950 University Ave., Bronx, New York 10452. (800) 367-6770. 1916-. Monthly.

Chemical Abstracts. Chemical Abstracts Service, 2540 Olentangy River Rd., PO Box 3012, Columbus, Ohio 43210. (800) 848-6533. 1907-.

Energy Information Abstracts Annual 1987 in Retrospect. EIC/Intelligence Inc., 121 Chanlon Rd., New Providence, New Jersey 07974. (908) 464-6800. 1988. Annual. Cumulative edition of the monthly Energy Information Abstracts. Monitors sources in the field of energy including the scientific, technical and business journal literature, conference and symposia proceedings, corporate, government and academic reports.

Environment Abstracts. Bowker A & I Publishing, 121 Chanlon Rd., New Providence, New Jersey 07974. (908) 464-6800. 1974-.

Environment Index. Environment Information Center, Index Research Department, 124 E. 39th St., New York, New York 10016. 1971-. Annual.

Environmental Information Connection–EIC. Planning Information Program, Dept. of Urban and Regional Planning, University of Illinois, 1003 West Nevada, Urbana, Illinois 61801. (217) 333-1369. Also available online.

Environmental Periodicals Bibliography. Environmental Studies Institute, International Academy at Santa Barbara, 800 Garden St., Suite D, Santa Barbara, California 93101. (805) 965-5010. Also available online.

ERDA Research Abstracts. U.S. ERDA Technical Information Center, Box 62, Oak Ridge, Tennessee 37830.

General Science Index. H. W. Wilson Co., 950 University Ave., Bronx, New York 10452. 1978-. Monthly, also issued in annual cumulation. Cumulative subject index to English language periodicals in the subject fields of astronomy, botany, chemistry, earth science, environment and conservation, food and nutrition, genetics, mathematics, medicine and health, microbiology, oceanography, physics, physiology and zoology.

Index to Scientific Book Contents. Institute for Scientific Information, 3501 Market St., Philadelphia, Pennsylvania 19104. (800) 523-1857. 1985-. Annual. Gives contents of science books published.

Physics Briefs. Physikalische Berichte. Physik Verlag, Pappapelallee 3, Postfach 101161, Weinheim, Germany D-6940. 1979-. Semimonthly. In English. Volumes for 1979- issued by the Deutsche Physikalische Gesellschaft and the Fachinformationszentrum Energie Physik, Mathematik in cooperation with the American Institute of Physics.

Pollution Abstracts. Cambridge Scientific Abstracts, 5161 River Rd., Bethesda, Maryland 20816. (301) 961-6750. Six/year. Indexes worldwide technical literature on environmental pollution. Covers air pollution, marine and freshwater pollution, sewage and wastewater treatment, waste management, toxicology and health, noise pollution, radiation, land pollution, and environmental policies, programs, legislation, and education. Also available online.

Science Citation Index. Institute for Scientific Information, 3501 Market St., Philadelphia, Pennsylvania 19104. 1961-.

BIBLIOGRAPHIES

EPA Publications Bibliography. U.S. Environmental Protection Agency, Library Systems Branch, 401 M St., SW, Washington, District of Columbia 20460. (202) 260-2090. Quarterly.

Hydrogen as a Fuel: A Bibliography. Vance Bibliographies, PO Box 229, 112 N. Charter St., Monticello, Illinois 61856. (217) 762-3831. 1988.

Hydrogen Energy: A Bibliography with Abstracts. University of New Mexico, Albuquerque, New Mexico 87131. Annual.

Hydrogen Fuels: A Bibliography. National Technical Information Service, 5285 Port Royal Rd., Springfield, Virginia 22161. (703) 487-4650.

DIRECTORIES

Directory of Hydrogen Energy Products and Services. Pergamon Microforms International Inc., Fairview Park, Elmsford, New York 10523. (914) 592-7720. 1980.

Hydrogen Energy Coordinating Committee Annual Report: Summary of Department of Energy Hydrogen Programs. Department of Energy, 1000 Independence Ave., S.W., Washington, District of Columbia 20585. (202) 586-5000.

Summaries of DOE Hydrogen Programs. Hydrogen Energy Coordinating Committee/Office of Conservation and Renewable Energy, Department of Energy, 1000 Independence Ave., S.W., Washington, District of Columbia 20585. (202) 586-6104.

ENCYCLOPEDIAS AND DICTIONARIES

Dictionary of Energy. Malcolm Slesser. Nichols Pub., PO Box 96, New York, New York 10024. 1988. Provides information on concepts, ideas, definitions and explanations in areas of interdisciplinary nature connected with energy.

Encyclopedia of Chemical Processing and Design. John J. Mcketta and W. A. Cunningham. Marcel Dekker, Inc., 270 Madison Ave., New York, New York 10016. (212) 696-9000; (800) 228-1160. 1992. Thirty-eight volumes.

Encyclopedia of Physical Science and Technology. Robert A. Meyers, ed. Academic Press, c/o Harcourt Brace Jovanovich Inc., 6277 Sea Harbor Dr., Orlando, Florida 32887. (800) 346-8648. Dictionary of engineering, technology and physical sciences.

Encyclopedia of Physics. Rita G. Lerner and George L. Trigg. VCH Publishers, 303 NW 12th Ave., Deerfield Beach, Florida 33442-1788. (305) 428-5566. 1991. Second edition.

Illustrated Encyclopedia of Science and the Future. Mike Biscare, et al., ed. Marshall Cavendish, 58 Old Compton St., London, England 0W1V5 PA. 01-734 6710. 1983. Twenty volumes. Each volume has 5 sections: Frontiers, Electronics in Action, Medical Science, Military Technology, and Resources.

Kirk-Othmer Encyclopedia of Chemical Technology. J. I. Kroschwitz, ed. John Wiley & Sons, Inc., 605 3rd Ave., New York, New York 10158-0012. (212) 850-6000. 1992-. All articles in the new edition have been rewritten and updated adding new subjects such as biotechnology, computer topics, analytical techniques and instrumentation, environmental concerns, fuels and energy, inorganic and solid state chemistry; composite materials and material science in general, and pharmaceuticals. Also available online.

McGraw-Hill Encyclopedia of Environmental Science. Sybil P. Parker. McGraw-Hill Science & Engineering Books, 11 W. 19th St., New York, New York 10011. (212) 337-6010. 1980. Covers ecology, man's influence on nature, and environmental protection.

McGraw-Hill Encyclopedia of Science and Technology. McGraw-Hill, 1221 Avenue of the Americas, New York, New York 10020. (212) 512-2000 or (800) 262-4729. 1992. Seventh edition. Issued in multiple volumes including index. Includes all science and technology broad subject areas.

GENERAL WORKS

Driving Forces: Motor Vehicle Trends and Their Implications for Global Warming, Energy Strategies, and Transportation. James J. MacKenzie and Michael P. Walsh. World Resources Institute, 1709 New York Ave., Washington, District of Columbia 20006. (800) 822-0504. 1990. Overview of new-vehicle fuel efficiency, reductions in air pollution emissions, and overall improvements in transportation and land-use as they relate to global warming planning. Also available through State University of New York Press.

Energy Options. John Bockris. John Wiley & Sons, Inc., 605 3rd Ave., New York, New York 10158-0012. (212) 850-6000. 1980.

The Forever Fuel: The Story of Hydrogen. Peter Hoffman. Westview Press, 5500 Central Ave., Boulder, Colorado 80301. (303) 444-3541. 1981.

Hydrogen Energy and Power Generation. T. Nejat Veziroglu, ed. Nova Science Publishers Inc., 283 Commack Rd., Suite 300, Commack, New York 11725-3104. (516) 499-3103; (516) 499-3106. 1991. Deals with clean energy and with other new and increasingly significant forms of energy generation, i.e. cogeneration, waste energy. Defines the role of hydrogen energy in the upcoming decade.

Hydrogen, Its Technology and Implications. Kenneth Cox. CRC Press, 2000 Corporate Blvd. N.W., Boca Raton, Florida 33431. (800) 272-7737. 1979. Production technology, transmissions, and storage.

Progress in Hydrogen Energy. Kluwer Academic Publishers, 101 Philip Dr., Assinippi Park, Norwell, Massachusetts 02061. (617) 871-6600. 1987.

Solar-Hydrogen Energy Systems. Tokio Ohta. Pergamon Microforms International, Inc., Fairview Park, Elmsford, New York 10523. (914) 592-7720. 1979.

Solar Hydrogen: Moving Beyond Fossil Fuels. Joan M. Ogden and Robert H. Williams. World Resources Institute, 1709 New York Ave. N.W., Washington, District of Columbia 20006. (800) 822-0504. 1989. Traces the technical breakthroughs associated with solar hydrogen. Assesses the new fuel's potential as a replacement for oil, compares its costs and uses with those of both traditional and synthetic fuels, and charts a path for developing solar hydrogen markets.

HANDBOOKS AND MANUALS

Energy Deskbook. Samuel Glasstone. Van Nostrand Reinhold, 115 5th Ave., New York, New York 10020. (212) 254-3232. 1983. Single volume reference covering all energy resources.

ONLINE DATA BASES

BIOSIS Previews. BIOSIS, 2100 Arch St., Philadelphia, Pennsylvania 19103-1399. (215) 587-4800. Largest and most comprehensive database of research in the life sciences. Contains citations for nearly 9000 primary research journals, monographs, reviews, symposia, preliminary reports, semi-popular journals, selected institutional reports, government reports and research communications.

CAS Source Index–CASSI. Chemical Abstracts Service, 2540 Olentangy River Rd., P.O. Box 3012, Columbus, Ohio 43210. (800) 848-6533 or (614) 421-3600. A listing of bibliographic and library holdings information for scientific and technical primary literature relevant to the chemical sciences.

Chemical Abstracts-CA. Chemical Abstracts Service, 2540 Olentangy River Rd., P.O. Box 3012, Columbus, Ohio 43210. (800) 848-6533 or (614) 421-3600. Information sources include 9000 journals, patents from 27 countries, two industrial property organizations, new books, conference proceedings, and government research reports.

EBIB. Texas A & M University, Sterling C. Evans Library, Reference Division, College Station, Texas 77843. (409) 845-5741.

Enviro/Energyline Abstracts Plus. R. R. Bowker Co., 121 Chanlon Rd., New Providence, New Jersey 07974. (908) 464-6800.

Environmental Periodicals Bibliography. National Information Services Corp., Ste. 6, Wyman Towers, 3100 St. Paul St., Baltimore, Maryland 21218. (410)243-0797. Online version of abstract of same name.

Kirk-Othmer Encyclopedia of Chemical Technology. John Wiley & Sons, Inc., 605 3rd Ave., 5th Floor, New York, New York 10158. (212) 850-6000. Online version of the publication of the same name.

Monthly Catalog of United States Government Publications. U.S. G.P.O., Supt. of Docs., PO Box 371954, Pittsburgh, Pennsylvania 15250-7954. (202) 512-0000.

National Technical Information Service. U.S. Department of Commerce, National Technical Information Service, Office of Data Base Services, 5285 Port Royal Rd., Springfield, Virginia 22161. (703) 487-4807. Bibliographic database of government sponsored research and technical reports.

NBSFLUIDS. National Institute of Standards & Technology, Office of Standard Reference Data, A323 Physics Building, Gaithersburg, Maryland 20899. (301) 975-2208.

PressNet Environmental Reports. Chemical Information Systems, Inc., 7215 York Rd., Baltimore, Maryland 21212. (301) 321-8440.

PERIODICALS AND NEWSLETTERS

International Journal of Hydrogen Energy. Pergamon Microforms International, Inc., Fairview Park, Elmsford, New York 10523. (914) 592-7720. Monthly.

TRADE ASSOCIATIONS AND PROFESSIONAL SOCIETIES

American Chemical Society. 1155 16th St., N.W., Washington, District of Columbia 20036. (202) 872-4600.

American Institute of Chemical Engineers. 345 East 47th St., New York, New York 10017. (212) 705-7338.

American Institute of Chemists. 7315 Wisconsin Ave., Bethesda, Maryland 20814. (301) 652-2447.

HYDROGEN CHLORIDE

ABSTRACTING AND INDEXING SERVICES

Applied Science and Technology Index. H.W. Wilson Co., 950 University Ave., Bronx, New York 10452. (800) 367-6770. Formerly Industrial Arts Index.

Biological Abstracts. BIOSIS, 2100 Arch St., Philadelphia, Pennsylvania 19103-1399. (215) 587-4800. 1927-.

Chemical Abstracts. Chemical Abstracts Service, 2540 Olentangy River Rd., PO Box 3012, Columbus, Ohio 43210. (800) 848-6533. 1907-.

Environment Abstracts. Bowker A & I Publishing, 121 Chanlon Rd., New Providence, New Jersey 07974. (908) 464-6800. 1974-.

Environment Index. Environment Information Center, Index Research Department, 124 E. 39th St., New York, New York 10016. 1971-. Annual.

Environmental Information Connection–EIC. Planning Information Program, Dept. of Urban and Regional Planning, University of Illinois, 1003 West Nevada, Urbana, Illinois 61801. (217) 333-1369. Also available online.

Environmental Periodicals Bibliography. Environmental Studies Institute, International Academy at Santa Barbara, 800 Garden St., Suite D, Santa Barbara, California 93101. (805) 965-5010. Also available online.

General Science Index. H. W. Wilson Co., 950 University Ave., Bronx, New York 10452. 1978-. Monthly, also issued in annual cumulation. Cumulative subject index to English language periodicals in the subject fields of astronomy, botany, chemistry, earth science, environment and conservation, food and nutrition, genetics, mathematics, medicine and health, microbiology, oceanography, physics, physiology and zoology.

Physics Briefs. Physikalische Berichte. Physik Verlag, Pappapelallee 3, Postfach 101161, Weinheim, Germany D-6940. 1979-. Semimonthly. In English. Volumes for 1979- issued by the Deutsche Physikalische Gesellschaft and the Fachinformationszentrum Energie Physik, Mathematik in cooperation with the American Institute of Physics.

Pollution Abstracts. Cambridge Scientific Abstracts, 5161 River Rd., Bethesda, Maryland 20816. (301) 961-6750. Six/year. Indexes worldwide technical literature on environmental pollution. Covers air pollution, marine and freshwater pollution, sewage and wastewater treatment, waste management, toxicology and health, noise pollution, radiation, land pollution, and environmental policies, programs, legislation, and education. Also available online.

Science Citation Index. Institute for Scientific Information, 3501 Market St., Philadelphia, Pennsylvania 19104. 1961-.

BIBLIOGRAPHIES

EPA Publications Bibliography. U.S. Environmental Protection Agency, Library Systems Branch, 401 M St., SW, Washington, District of Columbia 20460. (202) 260-2090. Quarterly.

ENCYCLOPEDIAS AND DICTIONARIES

Ullmanns Encyclopedia of Industrial Chemistry. Hans Jurgen Arpe and Wolfgang Gerhartz, eds. VCH Publishers, 303 NW 12th Ave., Deerfield Beach, Florida 33442-1788. (305) 428-5566. 1990. Designed to keep up with the broad spectrum of chemical technology. Thirty-six volumes of the encyclopedia have been divided into two sets: the 28 A volumes contain alphabetically arranged articles on chemicals, product groups, processes and technological concepts; and the 8 B volumes are compendia of basic knowledge in industrial chemistry.

Van Nostrand's Scientific Encyclopedia. Glenn D. Considine, ed. Van Nostrand Reinhold, 115 5th Ave., New York, New York 10003. (212) 254-3232. 1983. Sixth edition. Includes all broad subject areas in science.

GENERAL WORKS

Chlorine and Hydrogen Chloride. National Academy of Sciences, 2101 Constitution Ave., NW, Washington, District of Columbia 20418. (202) 334-2000. 1976. Medical and biologic effects of environmental pollutants.

Reference Method for Source Testing. Environment Canada, WATDOC, Inland Waters Directorate, Ottawa, Ontario, Canada K1A 0H3. (819) 997-2324. 1991.

ONLINE DATA BASES

BIOSIS Previews. BIOSIS, 2100 Arch St., Philadelphia, Pennsylvania 19103-1399. (215) 587-4800. Largest and most comprehensive database of research in the life sciences. Contains citations for nearly 9000 primary research journals, monographs, reviews, symposia, preliminary reports, semi-popular journals, selected institutional reports, government reports and research communications.

CAS Source Index–CASSI. Chemical Abstracts Service, 2540 Olentangy River Rd., P.O. Box 3012, Columbus, Ohio 43210. (800) 848-6533 or (614) 421-3600. A listing of bibliographic and library holdings information for scientific and technical primary literature relevant to the chemical sciences.

Chemical Abstracts-CA. Chemical Abstracts Service, 2540 Olentangy River Rd., P.O. Box 3012, Columbus, Ohio 43210. (800) 848-6533 or (614) 421-3600. Information sources include 9000 journals, patents from 27 countries, two industrial property organizations, new books, conference proceedings, and government research reports.

Enviro/Energyline Abstracts Plus. R. R. Bowker Co., 121 Chanlon Rd., New Providence, New Jersey 07974. (908) 464-6800.

Environmental Periodicals Bibliography. National Information Services Corp., Ste. 6, Wyman Towers, 3100 St. Paul St., Baltimore, Maryland 21218. (410)243-0797. Online version of abstract of same name.

TRADE ASSOCIATIONS AND PROFESSIONAL SOCIETIES

American Chemical Society. 1155 16th St., N.W., Washington, District of Columbia 20036. (202) 872-4600.

American Institute of Chemical Engineers. 345 East 47th St., New York, New York 10017. (212) 705-7338.

American Institute of Chemists. 7315 Wisconsin Ave., Bethesda, Maryland 20814. (301) 652-2447.

HYDROGEN FLUORIDE

ABSTRACTING AND INDEXING SERVICES

Applied Science and Technology Index. H.W. Wilson Co., 950 University Ave., Bronx, New York 10452. (800) 367-6770. Formerly Industrial Arts Index.

Chemical Abstracts. Chemical Abstracts Service, 2540 Olentangy River Rd., PO Box 3012, Columbus, Ohio 43210. (800) 848-6533. 1907-.

Environment Abstracts. Bowker A & I Publishing, 121 Chanlon Rd., New Providence, New Jersey 07974. (908) 464-6800. 1974-.

Environment Index. Environment Information Center, Index Research Department, 124 E. 39th St., New York, New York 10016. 1971-. Annual.

Environmental Information Connection–EIC. Planning Information Program, Dept. of Urban and Regional Planning, University of Illinois, 1003 West Nevada, Urbana, Illinois 61801. (217) 333-1369. Also available online.

Environmental Periodicals Bibliography. Environmental Studies Institute, International Academy at Santa Barbara, 800 Garden St., Suite D, Santa Barbara, California 93101. (805) 965-5010. Also available online.

General Science Index. H. W. Wilson Co., 950 University Ave., Bronx, New York 10452. 1978-. Monthly, also issued in annual cumulation. Cumulative subject index to English language periodicals in the subject fields of astronomy, botany, chemistry, earth science, environment and conservation, food and nutrition, genetics, mathematics, medicine and health, microbiology, oceanography, physics, physiology and zoology.

Physics Briefs. Physikalische Berichte. Physik Verlag, Pappapelallee 3, Postfach 101161, Weinheim, Germany D-6940. 1979-. Semimonthly. In English. Volumes for 1979- issued by the Deutsche Physikalische Gesellschaft and the Fachinformationszentrum Energie Physik, Mathematik in cooperation with the American Institute of Physics.

Pollution Abstracts. Cambridge Scientific Abstracts, 5161 River Rd., Bethesda, Maryland 20816. (301) 961-6750. Six/year. Indexes worldwide technical literature on environmental pollution. Covers air pollution, marine and freshwater pollution, sewage and wastewater treatment, waste management, toxicology and health, noise pollution, radiation, land pollution, and environmental policies, programs, legislation, and education. Also available online.

Science Citation Index. Institute for Scientific Information, 3501 Market St., Philadelphia, Pennsylvania 19104. 1961-.

BIBLIOGRAPHIES

EPA Publications Bibliography. U.S. Environmental Protection Agency, Library Systems Branch, 401 M St., SW, Washington, District of Columbia 20460. (202) 260-2090. Quarterly.

ENCYCLOPEDIAS AND DICTIONARIES

Ullmanns Encyclopedia of Industrial Chemistry. Hans Jurgen Arpe and Wolfgang Gerhartz, eds. VCH Publishers, 303 NW 12th Ave., Deerfield Beach, Florida 33442-1788. (305) 428-5566. 1990. Designed to keep up with the broad spectrum of chemical technology. Thirty-six volumes of the encyclopedia have been divided into two sets: the 28 A volumes contain alphabetically arranged articles on chemicals, product groups, processes and technological concepts; and the 8 B volumes are compendia of basic knowledge in industrial chemistry.

Van Nostrand's Scientific Encyclopedia. Glenn D. Considine, ed. Van Nostrand Reinhold, 115 5th Ave., New York, New York 10003. (212) 254-3232. 1983. Sixth edition. Includes all broad subject areas in science.

GENERAL WORKS

Criteria for a Recommended Standard: Occupational Exposure to Hydrogen Flouride. U.S. G.P.O., Washington, District of Columbia 20401. (202) 512-0000. 1976.

Hydrogen Chloride and Hydrogen Flouride Emission Factors for the NAPAP Emission Inventory. U.S. Environmental Protection Agency, MD 75, Research Triangle Park, North Carolina 27711. 1986. Environmental aspects of chlorides, acid disposition and hydrogen flouride.

Summary Review of Health Effects Associated with Hydrogen Flouride. U.S. Environmental Protection Agency, MD 75, Research Triangle Park, North Carolina 27711. 1989.

ONLINE DATA BASES

CAS Source Index–CASSI. Chemical Abstracts Service, 2540 Olentangy River Rd., P.O. Box 3012, Columbus, Ohio 43210. (800) 848-6533 or (614) 421-3600. A listing of bibliographic and library holdings information for scientific and technical primary literature relevant to the chemical sciences.

Chemical Abstracts-CA. Chemical Abstracts Service, 2540 Olentangy River Rd., P.O. Box 3012, Columbus, Ohio 43210. (800) 848-6533 or (614) 421-3600. Information sources include 9000 journals, patents from 27 countries, two industrial property organizations, new books, conference proceedings, and government research reports.

Enviro/Energyline Abstracts Plus. R. R. Bowker Co., 121 Chanlon Rd., New Providence, New Jersey 07974. (908) 464-6800.

Environmental Periodicals Bibliography. National Information Services Corp., Ste. 6, Wyman Towers, 3100 St. Paul St., Baltimore, Maryland 21218. (410)243-0797. Online version of abstract of same name.

TRADE ASSOCIATIONS AND PROFESSIONAL SOCIETIES

American Chemical Society. 1155 16th St., N.W., Washington, District of Columbia 20036. (202) 872-4600.

HYDROGEN PEROXIDE

ABSTRACTING AND INDEXING SERVICES

Applied Science and Technology Index. H.W. Wilson Co., 950 University Ave., Bronx, New York 10452. (800) 367-6770. Formerly Industrial Arts Index.

Chemical Abstracts. Chemical Abstracts Service, 2540 Olentangy River Rd., PO Box 3012, Columbus, Ohio 43210. (800) 848-6533. 1907-.

Environment Abstracts. Bowker A & I Publishing, 121 Chanlon Rd., New Providence, New Jersey 07974. (908) 464-6800. 1974-.

Environment Index. Environment Information Center, Index Research Department, 124 E. 39th St., New York, New York 10016. 1971-. Annual.

Environmental Information Connection–EIC. Planning Information Program, Dept. of Urban and Regional Planning, University of Illinois, 1003 West Nevada, Urbana, Illinois 61801. (217) 333-1369. Also available online.

Environmental Periodicals Bibliography. Environmental Studies Institute, International Academy at Santa Barbara, 800 Garden St., Suite D, Santa Barbara, California 93101. (805) 965-5010. Also available online.

General Science Index. H. W. Wilson Co., 950 University Ave., Bronx, New York 10452. 1978-. Monthly, also issued in annual cumulation. Cumulative subject index to English language periodicals in the subject fields of astronomy, botany, chemistry, earth science, environment and conservation, food and nutrition, genetics, mathematics, medicine and health, microbiology, oceanography, physics, physiology and zoology.

Physics Briefs. Physikalische Berichte. Physik Verlag, Pappapelallee 3, Postfach 101161, Weinheim, Germany D-6940. 1979-. Semimonthly. In English. Volumes for 1979- issued by the Deutsche Physikalische Gesellschaft and the Fachinformationszentrum Energie Physik, Mathematik in cooperation with the American Institute of Physics.

Pollution Abstracts. Cambridge Scientific Abstracts, 5161 River Rd., Bethesda, Maryland 20816. (301) 961-6750. Six/year. Indexes worldwide technical literature on environmental pollution. Covers air pollution, marine and freshwater pollution, sewage and wastewater treatment, waste management, toxicology and health, noise pollution, radiation, land pollution, and environmental policies, programs, legislation, and education. Also available online.

Science Citation Index. Institute for Scientific Information, 3501 Market St., Philadelphia, Pennsylvania 19104. 1961-.

BIBLIOGRAPHIES

EPA Publications Bibliography. U.S. Environmental Protection Agency, Library Systems Branch, 401 M St., SW,

Washington, District of Columbia 20460. (202) 260-2090. Quarterly.

ENCYCLOPEDIAS AND DICTIONARIES

Encyclopedia of Chemical Processing and Design. John J. Mcketta and W. A. Cunningham. Marcel Dekker, Inc., 270 Madison Ave., New York, New York 10016. (212) 696-9000; (800) 228-1160. 1992. Thirty-eight volumes.

Kirk-Othmer Encyclopedia of Chemical Technology. J. I. Kroschwitz, ed. John Wiley & Sons, Inc., 605 3rd Ave., New York, New York 10158-0012. (212) 850-6000. 1992-. All articles in the new edition have been rewritten and updated adding new subjects such as biotechnology, computer topics, analytical techniques and instrumentation, environmental concerns, fuels and energy, inorganic and solid state chemistry; composite materials and material science in general, and pharmaceuticals. Also available online.

Ullmanns Encyclopedia of Industrial Chemistry. Hans Jurgen Arpe and Wolfgang Gerhartz, eds. VCH Publishers, 303 NW 12th Ave., Deerfield Beach, Florida 33442-1788. (305) 428-5566. 1990. Designed to keep up with the broad spectrum of chemical technology. Thirty-six volumes of the encyclopedia have been divided into two sets: the 28 A volumes contain alphabetically arranged articles on chemicals, product groups, processes and technological concepts; and the 8 B volumes are compendia of basic knowledge in industrial chemistry.

Van Nostrand's Scientific Encyclopedia. Glenn D. Considine, ed. Van Nostrand Reinhold, 115 5th Ave., New York, New York 10003. (212) 254-3232. 1983. Sixth edition. Includes all broad subject areas in science.

GENERAL WORKS

Hydrogen Peroxide in Organic Chemistry. Jean-Pierre Schirmann. Edition et Documentation Industrielle, 5 rue Jules Lefelvre, Paris, France 75009. 1979.

Hydrogen Peroxide-Use or Abuse?. The Academy, Chicago, Illinois 1988.

HANDBOOKS AND MANUALS

FDA Food Additives Analytical Manual. C. Warner, et al., eds. Association of Official Analytical Chemists, 2200 Wilson Blvd., Suite 400-P, Arlington, Virginia 22201-3301. (703) 522-3032. 1983-1987. 2 vols. Provides methodology for determining compliance with food additive regulations. Contains analytical methods that have been evaluated by the FDA or found to operate satisfactorily in at least two laboratories.

ONLINE DATA BASES

CAS Source Index–CASSI. Chemical Abstracts Service, 2540 Olentangy River Rd., P.O. Box 3012, Columbus, Ohio 43210. (800) 848-6533 or (614) 421-3600. A listing of bibliographic and library holdings information for scientific and technical primary literature relevant to the chemical sciences.

Chemical Abstracts-CA. Chemical Abstracts Service, 2540 Olentangy River Rd., P.O. Box 3012, Columbus, Ohio 43210. (800) 848-6533 or (614) 421-3600. Information sources include 9000 journals, patents from 27 countries, two industrial property organizations, new

books, conference proceedings, and government research reports.

Enviro/Energyline Abstracts Plus. R. R. Bowker Co., 121 Chanlon Rd., New Providence, New Jersey 07974. (908) 464-6800.

Environmental Periodicals Bibliography. National Information Services Corp., Ste. 6, Wyman Towers, 3100 St. Paul St., Baltimore, Maryland 21218. (410)243-0797. Online version of abstract of same name.

Kirk-Othmer Encyclopedia of Chemical Technology. John Wiley & Sons, Inc., 605 3rd Ave., 5th Floor, New York, New York 10158. (212) 850-6000. Online version of the publication of the same name.

TRADE ASSOCIATIONS AND PROFESSIONAL SOCIETIES

American Chemical Society. 1155 16th St., N.W., Washington, District of Columbia 20036. (202) 872-4600.

American Institute of Chemical Engineers. 345 East 47th St., New York, New York 10017. (212) 705-7338.

American Institute of Chemists. 7315 Wisconsin Ave., Bethesda, Maryland 20814. (301) 652-2447.

HYDROGEN SULFIDE

ABSTRACTING AND INDEXING SERVICES

Applied Science and Technology Index. H.W. Wilson Co., 950 University Ave., Bronx, New York 10452. (800) 367-6770. Formerly Industrial Arts Index.

Chemical Abstracts. Chemical Abstracts Service, 2540 Olentangy River Rd., PO Box 3012, Columbus, Ohio 43210. (800) 848-6533. 1907-.

Environment Abstracts. Bowker A & I Publishing, 121 Chanlon Rd., New Providence, New Jersey 07974. (908) 464-6800. 1974-.

Environment Index. Environment Information Center, Index Research Department, 124 E. 39th St., New York, New York 10016. 1971-. Annual.

Environmental Information Connection–EIC. Planning Information Program, Dept. of Urban and Regional Planning, University of Illinois, 1003 West Nevada, Urbana, Illinois 61801. (217) 333-1369. Also available online.

Environmental Periodicals Bibliography. Environmental Studies Institute, International Academy at Santa Barbara, 800 Garden St., Suite D, Santa Barbara, California 93101. (805) 965-5010. Also available online.

General Science Index. H. W. Wilson Co., 950 University Ave., Bronx, New York 10452. 1978-. Monthly, also issued in annual cumulation. Cumulative subject index to English language periodicals in the subject fields of astronomy, botany, chemistry, earth science, environment and conservation, food and nutrition, genetics, mathematics, medicine and health, microbiology, oceanography, physics, physiology and zoology.

Geographical Abstracts. London School of Economics, Dept. of Geography, Regency House, 34 Duke St., London, England 1966-. Continued by Geo Abstracts issued in 6 parts: Pt. A. Landforms and the quaternary;

Pt. B. Biogeography and Climatology; Pt. C. Economic geography; Pt. D. Social geography and cartography; Pt. E. Sedimentology; Pt. F. Regional and community planning.

Physics Briefs. Physikalische Berichte. Physik Verlag, Pappapelallee 3, Postfach 101161, Weinheim, Germany D-6940. 1979-. Semimonthly. In English. Volumes for 1979- issued by the Deutsche Physikalische Gesellschaft and the Fachinformationszentrum Energie Physik, Mathematik in cooperation with the American Institute of Physics.

Pollution Abstracts. Cambridge Scientific Abstracts, 5161 River Rd., Bethesda, Maryland 20816. (301) 961-6750. Six/year. Indexes worldwide technical literature on environmental pollution. Covers air pollution, marine and freshwater pollution, sewage and wastewater treatment, waste management, toxicology and health, noise pollution, radiation, land pollution, and environmental policies, programs, legislation, and education. Also available online.

Science Citation Index. Institute for Scientific Information, 3501 Market St., Philadelphia, Pennsylvania 19104. 1961-.

BIBLIOGRAPHIES

EPA Publications Bibliography. U.S. Environmental Protection Agency, Library Systems Branch, 401 M St., SW, Washington, District of Columbia 20460. (202) 260-2090. Quarterly.

ENCYCLOPEDIAS AND DICTIONARIES

Dictionary of Energy. Malcolm Slesser. Nichols Pub., PO Box 96, New York, New York 10024. 1988. Provides information on concepts, ideas, definitions and explanations in areas of interdisciplinary nature connected with energy.

Ullmanns Encyclopedia of Industrial Chemistry. Hans Jurgen Arpe and Wolfgang Gerhartz, eds. VCH Publishers, 303 NW 12th Ave., Deerfield Beach, Florida 33442-1788. (305) 428-5566. 1990. Designed to keep up with the broad spectrum of chemical technology. Thirty-six volumes of the encyclopedia have been divided into two sets: the 28 A volumes contain alphabetically arranged articles on chemicals, product groups, processes and technological concepts; and the 8 B volumes are compendia of basic knowledge in industrial chemistry.

Van Nostrand's Scientific Encyclopedia. Glenn D. Considine, ed. Van Nostrand Reinhold, 115 5th Ave., New York, New York 10003. (212) 254-3232. 1983. Sixth edition. Includes all broad subject areas in science.

GENERAL WORKS

Effect of Hydrogen Sulfide on Fish and Invertebrates. National Technical Information Service, 5285 Port Royal Rd., Springfield, Virginia 22161. (703) 487-4650. 1976. Effect of water pollution on fish and freshwater invertebrates.

Hydrogen Sulfide. World Health Organization, Ave. Appia, Geneva, Switzerland CH-1211. 1988. Environmental health criteria relating to hydrogen sulfide.

Occupational Exposure to Hydrogen Sulfide. National Institute for Occupational Safety and Health. U.S.

G.P.O., Washington, District of Columbia 20401. (202) 512-0000. 1976.

Standard Reference Method for Ambient Testing. Environmental Protection Service, 425 St. Joseph Blvd., 3rd Fl., Hull, Quebec, Canada K1A 0H3. (613) 953-5921. 1984.

HANDBOOKS AND MANUALS

Process Design Manual for Sulfide Control in Sanitary Sewerage Systems. Richard D. Pomeroy. U.S. Environmental Protection Agency, 401 M St., SW, Washington, District of Columbia 20460. (202) 260-2090. 1974.

ONLINE DATA BASES

CAS Source Index–CASSI. Chemical Abstracts Service, 2540 Olentangy River Rd., P.O. Box 3012, Columbus, Ohio 43210. (800) 848-6533 or (614) 421-3600. A listing of bibliographic and library holdings information for scientific and technical primary literature relevant to the chemical sciences.

Chemical Abstracts-CA. Chemical Abstracts Service, 2540 Olentangy River Rd., P.O. Box 3012, Columbus, Ohio 43210. (800) 848-6533 or (614) 421-3600. Information sources include 9000 journals, patents from 27 countries, two industrial property organizations, new books, conference proceedings, and government research reports.

Enviro/Energyline Abstracts Plus. R. R. Bowker Co., 121 Chanlon Rd., New Providence, New Jersey 07974. (908) 464-6800.

Environmental Periodicals Bibliography. National Information Services Corp., Ste. 6, Wyman Towers, 3100 St. Paul St., Baltimore, Maryland 21218. (410)243-0797. Online version of abstract of same name.

TRADE ASSOCIATIONS AND PROFESSIONAL SOCIETIES

American Chemical Society. 1155 16th St., N.W., Washington, District of Columbia 20036. (202) 872-4600.

American Institute of Chemical Engineers. 345 East 47th St., New York, New York 10017. (212) 705-7338.

American Institute of Chemists. 7315 Wisconsin Ave., Bethesda, Maryland 20814. (301) 652-2447.

HYDROLOGIC CYCLE (WATER CYCLE)

See: HYDROLOGY

HYDROLOGY

See also: WATER WELLS

ABSTRACTING AND INDEXING SERVICES

Abstracts of Air and Water Conservation Literature. American Petroleum Institute. Central Abstracting and Indexing Service, 275 Madison Avenue, New York, New York 10016. 1972.

Agrindex. AGRIS Coordinating Center, Via delle Terme di Caracalla, Rome, Italy I-00100. 61 0181-FA01. 1975-.

Applied Science and Technology Index. H.W. Wilson Co., 950 University Ave., Bronx, New York 10452. (800) 367-6770. Formerly Industrial Arts Index.

Aqualine Abstracts. Water Research Centre. c/o Pergamon Microforms International, Inc., Fairview Park, Elmsford, New York 10523. (914) 592-7720. 1927-. Contains some 8,000 records annually on water and wastewater technology. Covers all aspects of water, wastewater, associated engineering services and the aquatic environment. Over 600 periodicals, as well as books, reports and conference proceedings and other publications from water related institutions worldwide are scanned. Also available online.

ASFA Aquaculture Abstracts. Cambridge Scientific Abstracts, Inc., 5161 River Rd., Bethesda, Maryland 20816. (301) 961-6750. 1984.

Environment Abstracts. Bowker A & I Publishing, 121 Chanlon Rd., New Providence, New Jersey 07974. (908) 464-6800. 1974-.

Environment Index. Environment Information Center, Index Research Department, 124 E. 39th St., New York, New York 10016. 1971-. Annual.

Environmental Information Connection–EIC. Planning Information Program, Dept. of Urban and Regional Planning, University of Illinois, 1003 West Nevada, Urbana, Illinois 61801. (217) 333-1369. Also available online.

Environmental Periodicals Bibliography. Environmental Studies Institute, International Academy at Santa Barbara, 800 Garden St., Suite D, Santa Barbara, California 93101. (805) 965-5010. Also available online.

General Science Index. H. W. Wilson Co., 950 University Ave., Bronx, New York 10452. 1978-. Monthly, also issued in annual cumulation. Cumulative subject index to English language periodicals in the subject fields of astronomy, botany, chemistry, earth science, environment and conservation, food and nutrition, genetics, mathematics, medicine and health, microbiology, oceanography, physics, physiology and zoology.

Highway Research Abstracts. Transportation Research Board, National Research Council, 2101 Constitution Ave. NW., Washington, District of Columbia 20418. 1931-. Monthly. Provides information about highway and nonrail mass transit. It also deals with related environmental issues such as energy and environment, environmental design, climate, safety, human factors, and soils.

Meteorological and Geoastrophysical Abstracts. American Meteorological Society, 45 Beacon St., Boston, Massachusetts 02108. (617) 227-2425.

Pollution Abstracts. Cambridge Scientific Abstracts, 5161 River Rd., Bethesda, Maryland 20816. (301) 961-6750. Six/year. Indexes worldwide technical literature on environmental pollution. Covers air pollution, marine and freshwater pollution, sewage and wastewater treatment, waste management, toxicology and health, noise pollution, radiation, land pollution, and environmental policies, programs, legislation, and education. Also available online.

Science Citation Index. Institute for Scientific Information, 3501 Market St., Philadelphia, Pennsylvania 19104. 1961-.

BIBLIOGRAPHIES

Bibliography on Regulation of Development for Stormwater Management. Bruce K. Ferguson. Vance Bibliographies, PO Box 229, 112 N. Charter St., Monticello, Illinois 61856. (217) 762-3831. 1978. Covers storm sewers, runoff, and drainage.

Current Contents. Agriculture, Biology and Environmental Sciences. Institute for Scientific Information, 3501 Market St., Philadelphia, Pennsylvania 19104. (800) 523-1857. 1973-. Previous title: Current Contents. Agricultural, Food & Veterinary Sciences. Gives the table of contents of periodicals in the fields of agriculture, biology, environmental and related areas.

EPA Publications Bibliography. U.S. Environmental Protection Agency, Library Systems Branch, 401 M St., SW, Washington, District of Columbia 20460. (202) 260-2090. Quarterly.

Geraghty & Miller's Groundwater Bibliography. Frits Van Der Leeden. Lewis Publishers, 200 Corporate Blvd. NW, Boca Raton, Florida 33431. (407) 994-0555 or (800)272-7737. 1991. 5th ed. Since the last edition, this essential research aid reflects increased interest in areas such as ground water contamination, modeling, and legal issues. Contains a listing of general bibliographies, periodicals, and books, followed by a subject section covering 3 specific aspects of hydrogeology.

Infiltration and Recharge of Stormwater. Bruce K. Ferguson. Vance Bibliographies, 112 N. Charters St., PO Box 229, Monticello, Illinois 61856. (217) 762-3831. 1984. A resource conserving alternative for the urban infrastructure.

Marine Science Newsletters–1977: An Annotated Bibliography. Charlotte M. Ashby. National Oceanic and Atmospheric Administration, National Environmental Data Referral Service, Washington, District of Columbia 1977. NOAA Technical Memorandum EDS NODC; 5.

New Publications of the Geological Survey. U.S. Department of the Interior, Geological Survey, 119 National Center, Reston, Virginia 22092. (703) 648-4460. 1984-. Monthly. Bibliography of geological publications and related government documents published by the Geological Survey.

Storm Sewers: Monographs. Mary A. Vance. Vance Bibliographies, 112 N. Charter St., PO Box 229, Monticello, Illinois 61856. (217) 762-3831. 1984.

DIRECTORIES

Gale Environmental Sourcebook. Karen Hill. Gale Research Co., 835 Penobscot Bldg., Detroit, Michigan 48226-4094. (313) 961-2242. Contacts, information sources, or general information on environmental topics.

Ground Water Age–Directory of Manufacturers. National Trade Publications, Inc., 13 Century Hill, Latham, New York 12110. (518) 783-1281.

Ground Water Monitoring Review–Buyers Guide Issue. Water Well Journal Publishing Company/National Water Well Association, 6375 Riverside Dr., Dublin, Ohio 43017. (614) 761-3222.

Ground Water Monitoring Review–Consultant and Contractor Directory Issue. Water Well Journal Publishing Co., National Water Well Association, 6375 Riverside Dr., Dublin, Ohio 43017. (614) 761-3222.

Who's Who in Environmental Engineering. American Academy of Environmental Engineers, 132 Holiday Court, Suite 206, Annapolis, Maryland 21401. (301) 266-3311. 1980. Annual. Directory of environmental engineers who are certified by the academy.

ENCYCLOPEDIAS AND DICTIONARIES

Elsevier's Dictionary of Hydrology and Water Quality Management. J. D. Van der Tuin. Elsevier Science Publishing Co., 655 Avenue of the Americas, New York, New York 10010. (212) 989-5800. 1991. The languages are English, French, Spanish, Dutch, and German. Freshwater environment constitutes the main subject of this dictionary. Defines more than 37,000 terms.

Elsevier's Dictionary of Water and Hydraulic Engineering. J. D. Van Der Tuin. Elsevier Science Publishing Co., 655 Avenue of the Americas, New York, New York 10010. (212) 989-5800. 1987. The text is in English, Spanish, French, Dutch and German.

Glossary of Geology. Robert Latimer Bates and Julia A. Jackson, eds. American Geological Institute, 4220 King St., Alexandria, Virginia 22302-1507. (703) 379-2480 or (800) 336-4764. 1987. Third edition.

McGraw-Hill Encyclopedia of the Geological Sciences. Sybil P. Parker, ed. McGraw-Hill, 1221 Avenue of the Americas, New York, New York 10020. (212) 512-2000 or (800) 262-4729. 1988. Second edition. Published previously in the McGraw-Hill Encyclopedia of Science and Technology.

Van Nostrand's Scientific Encyclopedia. Glenn D. Considine, ed. Van Nostrand Reinhold, 115 5th Ave., New York, New York 10003. (212) 254-3232. 1983. Sixth edition. Includes all broad subject areas in science.

The Water Encyclopedia. Lewis Publishers, 2000 Corporate Blvd. N.W., Boca Raton, Florida 33431. (800) 272-7737. 1990. 2d ed. Includes groundwater contamination, drinking water, floods, waterborne diseases, global warming, climate change, irrigation, water agencies and organizations, precipitation, oceans and seas, and river, lakes and waterfalls.

GENERAL WORKS

Advances in Water Treatment and Environmental Management. George Thomas. Elsevier Science Publishing Co., 655 Avenue of the Americas, New York, New York 10010. (212) 984-5800. 1991. Measurement and control of groundwater quality, rivers, river management, estuaries, and beaches.

Applied Isotope Hydrogeology: A Case Study in Northern Switzerland. F. J. Pearson, Jr., et al. Elsevier Science Publishing Co., Inc, 655 Avenue of the Americas, New York, New York 10010. (212) 989-5800. 1991. This is a case study in northern Switzerland about radioactive waste disposal in the ground. Includes bibliographical references and an index.

Beneath the Bottom Line: Agricultural Approaches to Reduce Agrichemical Contamination of Groundwater. Office of Technology Assessment, U.S. Congress, Washington, District of Columbia 20510-8025. (202) 224-8996. 1991. Identifies ways to minimize contamination of ground water by agricultural chemicals.

Contaminant Hydrogeology: A Practical Guide. Chris Palmer and Gettler-Ryan. Lewis Publishers, 2000 Corporate Blvd., N.W., Boca Raton, Florida 33431. (407) 994-0555 or (800) 272-7737. 1991. Contains geologic frameworks for contaminant hydrogeology investigations. Also includes subsurface exploration, sampling and mapping techniques, ground-water monitoring well installation, ground water monitoring and well sampling.

Contaminant Transport in Groundwater. H.E. Kobus and W. Kinzelbach. A. A. Balkema, Old Post Rd., Brookfield, Vermont 05036. (802) 276-3162. 1989. Describes physical and chemical processes, model building and application as well as remedial action.

Contamination of Ground Water Prevention, Assessment, Restoration. Michael Barcelona, et al. Noyes Publications, 120 Mill Rd., Park Ridge, New Jersey 07656. (201) 391-8484. 1990. Provides regulatory agencies and industry a convenient source of technical information on the management of contaminated ground water.

Design of Water Quality Monitoring Systems. Robert C. Ward. Van Nostrand Reinhold, 115 5th Ave., New York, New York 10003. (212) 254-3232. 1990. Describes the essential tools to design a system that gets consistently valid results. Features the latest methods of sampling and lab analysis, data handling and analysis, reporting, and information utilization, and includes case studies of system design projects.

Dream–Analytical Ground Water Flow Programs. Bernadine A. Bonn and Stewart A. Rounds. Lewis Publishers, 2000 Corporate Blvd., N.W., Boca Raton, Florida 33431. (407) 994-0555 or (800) 272-7737. 1990. Software for basic field work, including the first-cut evaluation of remediation design.

Drinking Water and Groundwater Remediation Cost Evaluation: Air Stripping. Robert M. Clark and Jeffrey Q. Adams. Lewis Publishers, 2000 Corporate Blvd. N.W., Boca Raton, Florida 33431. (800) 272-7737. 1991. The new software program shows air stripping costs and performance of the remediation of hazardous waste sites or drinking water treatment. The program helps do cost comparisons of the technology against other available technologies.

Drinking Water and Groundwater Remediation Cost Evaluation: Granular Activated Carbon. Robert M. Clark and Jeffrey Q. Adams. Lewis Publishers, 2000 Corporate Blvd. N.W., Boca Raton, Florida 33431. (800) 272-7737. 1991. Shows GAC costs and performance for the remediation of hazardous waste sites or drinking water treatment. Compares the cost of the technology against other available technologies.

Econometric and Dynamic Modelling–Exemplified by Caesium in Lakes after Chernobyl. Lars Hakanson. Springer-Verlag, 175 5th Ave., New York, New York 10010. (212) 460-1500 or (800) 777-4643. 1991. Details methods to establish representative and compatible lake data models and load after the Chernobyl accident. Deals with ecotoxicology and hydrogeology.

The Environment: Problems and Solutions. Stuart Bruchey, ed. Garland Publishing, Inc., 1000A Sherman Ave., Hamden, Connecticut 06514. (203) 281-4487. 1991. Topics covered: forested wetlands and agriculture, the political economy of smog in southern California, environmental limits to growth in world agriculture, the tradeoff between cost and risk in hazardous waste management, and the protection of groundwater from agricultural pollution.

Evaluation of Longitudinal Dispersivity from Tracer Test Data. Claire Welty and Lynn W. Gelhar. Ralph M. Parsons Laboratory for Water Resources and Hydrodynamics, Massachusetts Institute of Technology, Cambridge, Massachusetts 02139. 1989. Groundwater flow, tracers, and diffusion in hydrology.

Field Comparison of Ground-Water Sampling Methods. Ronald Paul Blegen. National Technical Information Service, 5285 Port Royal, Springfield, Virginia 22161. (703) 487-4650. 1988. Thesis (M.S.)–Geoscience, University of Nevada, Las Vegas, 1988.

Geochemical Modeling of Ground Water. William J. Deutsch and Stanley R. Peterson. Lewis Publishers, 2000 Corporate Blvd., N.W., Boca Raton, Florida 33431. (407) 994-0555 or (800) 272-7737. 1991. Explains the natural chemical system, geochemical processes, development of, conceptual model, computer codes and geochemical models.

Geotechnical and Environmental Geophysics. Stanley H. Ward. Society of Exploration Geophysicists, PO Box 702740, Tulsa, Oklahoma 74170-2740. (918) 493-3516. 1990.

Ground Water. H. M. Raghunath. John Wiley & Sons, Inc., 605 3rd Ave., New York, New York 10158-0012. (212) 850-6000. 1987. Hydrogeology, ground water survey and pumping tests, rural water supply and irrigation systems.

Ground Water and Toxicological Risk. Jenifer S. Heath. Lewis Publishers, 2000 Corporate Blvd., N.W., Boca Raton, Florida 33431. (407) 994-0555 or (800) 272-7737. 1991. Discusses the nature of ground water, the nature of toxicology, risk assessment, basics of risk perception and two case studies of reaction.

Ground Water and Vadose Zone Monitoring. David M. Nielsen and A. Ivan Johnson, eds. PennWell Books, PO Box 21288, Tulsa, Oklahoma 74121. (918) 831-9421; (800) 752-9764. 1988. Contains 22 papers presented at the symposium on standards and development for ground water and Vadose Zone monitoring investigations.

Groundwater Contamination. J. H. Guswa, et al. Noyes Publications, 120 Mill Rd., Park Ridge, New Jersey 07656. (201) 391-8484. 1984. A technology review of equipment, methods, and field techniques; an overview of groundwater hydrology and a methodology for estimating groundwater contamination under emergency response conditions.

Groundwater Contamination: Sources, Control, and Preventive Measures. Chester D. Rail. Technomic Publishing Co., 851 New Holland Ave., Box 3535, Lancaster, Pennsylvania 17604. (717) 291-5609. 1989. Reviews the presently known sources of groundwater contamination and its many complex interactions, including managerial and political implications.

Groundwater Protection: Local Success Stories. Milou Carolan. Internal City Management Association, 777 N. Capital St., NE, Suite 500, Washington, District of Columbia 20002-4201. (800) 745-8780. 1990. Case studies from local governments that have created effective programs for protecting the local water supply by evaluat-

ing contamination sources and developing community support.

Groundwater Remediation and Petroleum: A Guide for Underground Storage Tanks. David C. Noonan and James T. Curtis. PennWell Books, PO Box 21288, Tulsa, Oklahoma 74121. (918) 831-9421; (800) 752-9764. 1990. Guide for personnel charged with the responsibility of addressing contamination caused by leaking underground storage tanks.

Groundwater Residue Sampling Design. Ralph G. Nash and Anne R. Leslie, eds. American Chemical Society, 1155 16th St. N.W., Washington, District of Columbia 20036. (202) 872-4600; (800) 227-5558. 1991. Gives an overview of the approach taken by government agencies and discusses in great detail the various techniques in sampling and analysis of groundwater.

Hydrodynamic Forces. Eduard Naudascher. A. A. Balkema, Old Post Rd., Brookfield, Vermont 05036. (802) 276-3162. 1991. Covers fluctuating and mean hydrodynamic forces, hydrodynamic forces on high-head gates, and hydrodynamic forces on low-head gates and other related information.

Hydrogeological Assessment of the Closed Coboconk Landfill. Gartner Lee Ltd. Toronto (Ontario). National Technical Information Service, 5285 Port Royal Rd., Springfield, Virginia 22161. (703) 487-4650. 1989.

Hydrological Application of Weather Radar. I. D. Cluckie and C. G. Collier, eds. E. Horwood, 66 Wood Lane End, Hemel Hempstead, England HP2 4RG. 1991.

Hydrological Problems of Surface Mining. Peter Wood. IEA Coal Research, 14/15 Lower Grosvenor Place, London, England SW 1W OEX. 44 (71) 828-4661. 1981.

Metals in Groundwater. Herbert E. Allen. Lewis Publishers, 2000 Corporate Blvd., N.W., Boca Raton, Florida 33431. (407) 994-0555 or (800) 272-7737. 1991. Discusses in depth the state of the knowledge of metal sorption by aquifer materials. The status of chemical partitioning, hydrologic transport models is also considered. Includes agricultural, wastewater, and mining field-site examples.

Microcomputers in Environmental Biology. J. N. R. Jeffers, ed. Parthenon Pub., Casterton Hall, Carnforth, England LA6 2LA. Lancs. 1991. Contains extensive lists of programs written specially to show the ways in which microcomputers can be most usefully employed in the analysis of experiments and surveys, the analysis of multivariate data, radio tagging and the analysis of animal movement, and in modeling complex systems.

Modeling of the Seepage Flux of Ground Water from Coastal Landfills. D. A. Colden. National Technical Information Service, 5285 Port Royal Rd., Springfield, Virginia 22161. (703) 487-4650. 1990. Master's Thesis, Rhode Island University, Kingston.

New Technologies in Urban Drainage. C. Maksimovic. Elsevier Science Publishing Co., 655 Avenue of the Americas, New York, New York 10010. (212) 984-5800. 1991. Advances in rainfall-runoff modelling, hydrodynamics and quality modelling of receiving waters, and urban drainage in specific climates.

Point-of-Use/Entry Treatment of Drinking Water. Noyes Publications, 120 Mill Rd., Park Ridge, New Jersey 07656. (201) 391-8484. 1990. Covers the administrative and technical aspects of utilizing POU/POE systems to solve individual and small community drinking water problems.

Promotion of Women's Participation in Water Resources Development. UNIPUB, 4611-F Assembly Dr., Lanham, Maryland 20706-4391. (301) 459-7666; (800) 274-4888. 1990.

Protecting Ground Water: The Hidden Resource. U.S. Environmental Protection Agency, Office of Public Affairs, 401 M St. SW, Washington, District of Columbia 20460. (202) 260-2090. 1984.

Protecting Our Ground Water. U.S. Environmental Protection Agency, Office of Public Affairs, 401 M St. SW, Washington, District of Columbia 20460. (202) 260-2090. 1990.

Removal of Heavy Metals from Groundwaters. Robert W. Peters. Lewis Publishers, 2000 Corporate Blvd., N.W., Boca Raton, Florida 33431. (407) 994-0555 or (800) 272-7737. 1991. Describes the sources of heavy metal contamination, classification of metals by industry, extent of the contamination problem, toxicity associated with various heavy metals, effects of heavy metals in biological wastewater treatment operations, leaching of heavy metals from sludges, modeling of heavy metals in the saturated and unsaturated zones, and other related areas.

Summary of the U.S. Geological Survey and U.S. Bureau of Land Management National Coal-Hydrology Program. L.J. Britton. U.S. G.P.O., Washington, District of Columbia 20401. (202) 512-0000. 1990. Environmental aspects of coal and coal mining.

Understanding Ground-Water Contamination: An Orientation Manual. Paul E. Bailey and William D. Ward, eds. PennWell Books, PO Box 21288, Tulsa, Oklahoma 74121. (918) 831-9421; (800) 752-9764. 1990. Orientation manual for businesses, their counsel, local and regional officials, and government agencies, that must make decisions regarding groundwater.

Urban Stormwater Management and Technology. John A. Lager. U.S. G.P.O., Washington, District of Columbia 20401. (202) 512-0000. 1975. Technology relating to runoff and combined sewers.

Urban Stormwater Runoff. Gary T. Fisher. U.S. Geological Survey, 12201 Sunrise Valley Dr., Reston, Virginia 22092. (703) 648-4460. 1989. Selected background information and techniques for problem assessment.

The Washington Conference on Underground Storage, July 15-16, 1985, Stouffer Concourse. Center for Energy and Environmental Management, Washington, District of Columbia (202) 543-3939.

Water Quality Modeling. Brian Henderson-Sellere, et al. CRC Press, 2000 Corporate Blvd. N.W., Boca Raton, Florida 33431. (407) 994-0555; (800) 272-7737. 1990. Issues in four volumes. Discusses water supply and treatment and water resources engineering.

Wetlands: A Threatened Landscape. Michael Williams. B. Blackwell, 3 Cambridge Ctr., Suite 208, Cambridge, Massachusetts 02142. (617) 225-0401. 1990. Explores the evolution and composition of wetlands and their physical and biological dynamics, considers the impact of agriculture, industry, urbanization, and recreation upon them, and examines what steps we are taking and what steps should be considered to manage and preserve wetlands.

GOVERNMENTAL ORGANIZATIONS

U.S. Environmental Protection Agency: Office of Ground Water Protection. 401 M St., S.W., Washington, District of Columbia 20460. (202) 382-7077.

U.S. Environmental Protection Agency: Office of Underground Storage Tanks. 401 M St., S.W., Washington, District of Columbia 20460. (202) 382-4517.

HANDBOOKS AND MANUALS

The Global Ecology Handbook: What You Can Do about the Environmental Crisis. Walter H. Corson, ed. The Global Tomorrow Coalition, Beacon Pr., 25 Beacon St., Boston, Massachusetts 02108-2800. (617) 742-2110. 1990. Covers environment, energy policy, population growth and other issues. It includes chapters on tropical rain forests, garbage, oceans and coasts, global warming, population growth, agriculture, biological diversity, fresh water, hazardous wastes, and environment and development.

Ground Water Age–Handbook Issue. National Trade Publications, Inc., 13 Century Hill, Latham, New York 12110. (518) 783-1281.

Ground Water Handbook. Government Institutes, Inc., 4 Research Pl., Ste 200, Rockville, Maryland 20850. (301) 921-2300. 1989. Includes highlights of chapters on ground water contamination, use of models in managing ground water protection programs, ground water restoration, ground water quality investigations, basic hydrogeology, monitoring well design and construction, ground water sampling, ground water tracers and basic geology.

Ground Water Manual: A Guide for the Investigation, Development, and Management of Ground Water Resources. U.S. G.P.O., Washington, District of Columbia 20401. (202) 512-0000. 1981. Underground water resources in the water states.

Groundwater Chemicals Desk Reference. John H. Montgomery. Lewis Publishers, 2000 Corporate Blvd. NW, Boca Raton, Florida 33431. (407) 994-0555 or (800)272-7737. 1990. Protection and remediation of the groundwater environment. Includes profiles of chemical compounds promulgated by the EPA under the Clean Water Act of 1977.

Groundwater Chemicals Desk Reference, Volume II. John Montgomery. Lewis Publishers, 2000 Corporate Blvd., N.W., Boca Raton, Florida 33431. (407) 994-0555 or (800) 272-7737. 1991. Contains abbreviations, symbols, chemicals, conversion factors, CAS index, RTECS number index empirical formula, and synonym index.

Guide to the Management of Hazardous Waste: A Handbook for the Businessman and the Concerned Citizen. J. William Haun. Fulcrum Publishing, 350 Indiana St., Ste. 350, Golden, Colorado 80401. (303) 277-1623. 1991. Fact book on hazardous waste management, including factory and trade waste, and hazardous waste law and legislation in the United States.

Handbook of Drinking Water Quality: Standards and Controls. John De Zuane. Van Nostrand Reinhold, 115 5th Ave., New York, New York 10003. (212) 254-3232. 1990. Aids in evaluating water quality control at every stage of the water path, from source to treatment plant, from distribution system to consumer.

Handbook of Ground Water Development. The Roscoe Moss Company. John Wiley & Sons, Inc., 605 3rd Ave.,

New York, New York 10158-0012. (212) 850-6000. 1989. Guide to current theories and techniques for the exploration, extraction, use and management of ground water. Covers the physical geology and hydrodynamics of water in the ground, the exploitation of ground water and well design and construction, and the management of wells and well field operations.

How to Bottle Rainstorms. Bauer Engineering Inc. Metropolitan Water Reclamation District of Greater Chicago, 100 E. Erie, Chicago, Illinois 60611. (312) 751-5600. 1974. Urban runoff, sewage disposal and sanitation.

Is Your Water Safe to Drink?. Raymond Gabler. Consumer Union U.S., New York, New York 1988. Health, microbial, inorganic, and organic hazards in drinking water, chlorination, bottled water, and water shortages.

Modern Sewer Design. American Iron and Steel Institute, 1133 15th St., NW, Washington, District of Columbia 20005. 1980. Manual for sheet steel producers.

Our National Wetland Heritage. Jon A. Kusler. Environmental Law Institute, 1616 P St., NW, Suite 200, Washington, District of Columbia 20036. (202) 328-5150. 1983. Discusses practical ways to preserve and protect wetlands and their benefits, which include recreation, wildlife habitat, pollution and flood control, scientific research and groundwater recharge.

Practical Handbook of Ground Water Monitoring. David M. Nielsen. Lewis Publishers, 2000 Corporate Blvd., N.W., Boca Raton, Florida 33431. (407) 994-0555 or (800) 272-7737. 1991. Covers the complete spectrum of state-of-the-science technology applied to investigations of ground water quality. Emphasis is placed on the practical application of current technology, and minimum theory is discussed.

Storm Water: Guidance Manual for the Preparation of NPDES Permit Applications for Storm Water Discharges Associated with Industrial Activity. Government Institutes, Inc., 4 Research Pl., Ste. 200, Rockville, Maryland 20850. (301) 921-2300. 1991. Provides an overview of the new EPA regulations; contains an overview of the permitting process and information regarding the permit application requirements.

ONLINE DATA BASES

Enviro/Energyline Abstracts Plus. R. R. Bowker Co., 121 Chanlon Rd., New Providence, New Jersey 07974. (908) 464-6800.

Environmental Periodicals Bibliography. National Information Services Corp., Ste. 6, Wyman Towers, 3100 St. Paul St., Baltimore, Maryland 21218. (410)243-0797. Online version of abstract of same name.

Ground Water Federal Register Notices. National Ground Water Information Center, National Water Well Association, 6375 Riverside Dr., Dublin, Ohio 43017. (614) 761-1711.

Ground Water Industry Standards. National Ground Water Information Center, National Water Well Association, 6375 Riverside Dr., Dublin, Ohio 43017. (614) 761-1711.

Ground Water Job Mart. National Ground Water Information Center, National Water Well Association, 6375 Riverside Dr., Dublin, Ohio 43017. (614) 761-1711.

Ground Water Monitor. Business Publishers, Inc., 951 Pershing Dr., Silver Spring, Maryland 20910. (301) 587-6300. Online version of periodical of the same name.

Ground Water On-Line. National Water Well Association, National Ground Water Information Center, 6375 Riverside Dr., Dublin, Ohio 43017. (614) 761-1711. Technical literature covering all aspects of groundwater and well technology.

Ground Water Regulations. National Ground Water Information Center, National Water Well Association, 6375 Riverside Dr., Dublin, Ohio 43017. (614) 761-1711.

Monthly Catalog of United States Government Publications. U.S. G.P.O., Supt. of Docs., PO Box 371954, Pittsburgh, Pennsylvania 15250-7954. (202) 512-0000.

National Stream Quality Accounting Network. National Water Data Exchange, U.S. Geological Survey, 421 National Center, Reston, Virginia 22092. (703) 648-4000. 150 hydrologic measurements collected at daily, monthly and quarterly intervals from more than 500 monitoring stations in the U.S.

National Technical Information Service. U.S. Department of Commerce, National Technical Information Service, Office of Data Base Services, 5285 Port Royal Rd., Springfield, Virginia 22161. (703) 487-4807. Bibliographic database of government sponsored research and technical reports.

SCISEARCH. Institute for Scientific Information, University City Science Center, 3501 Market St., Philadelphia, Pennsylvania 19104. (215) 386-0100.

PERIODICALS AND NEWSLETTERS

Civil Engineering ASCE. American Society of Civil Engineers, 345 E 47th St., New York, New York 10017. (212) 705-7288; (800) 548-2723. Monthly. Professional journal that offers a forum for free exchange of ideas relevant to the profession of civil engineering. Covers in regular columns, engineering news, legal trends in engineering, calendar of events, membership news, publications and other items of interest to civil engineers. Formerly, Civil Engineering.

Earth Science. American Geological Institute, 4220 King Street, Alexandria, Virginia 22302. (703) 379-2480. Quarterly. Covers geological issues.

Ecological Applications. Ecological Society of America, Center for Environmental Studies, Arizona State University, Tempe, Arizona 85287. (602) 965-3000. 1991-. Quarterly. Emphasizes the application of basic ecological concepts to a wide range of problems.

Editorially Speaking about Ground Water: Its First Quarter Century. Jay H. Lehr and Anita B. Stanley. National Water Well Association, 6375 Riverside Dr., Dublin, Ohio 43017. (614) 761-1711. 1988. A collection of editorials from the Journal of Ground Water which traces the evolution of ground water science during the journal's first 25 years of publication.

GEM Notes: an Update of the Groundwater Education in Michigan Program. Groundwater Education in Michigan, Institute of Water Research, Michigan State University, 25 Manly Miles Bldg., 1405 S. Harrison Rd., East Lansing, Michigan 48824. (517) 355-9543. 1988-. Irregular.

Ground Water. Water Well Journal Publishing Co., 6375 Riverside Dr., Dublin, Ohio 43017. (614) 761-3222. Bimonthly. Contains technical papers for NWWA.

Ground Water Age. National Trade Publications, Inc., 13 Century Hill, Latham, New York 12110. (518) 783-1281. Monthly. Covers product and literature developments and industry news.

Ground Water Monitor. Business Publishers, Inc., 951 Pershing Dr., Silver Spring, Maryland 20910-4464. (301) 587-6300. Biweekly. Legislation, litigation, regulations and quality problems on ground water. Also available online.

Ground Water Monitoring Review. Water Well Journal Publishing Co. National Water Well Association, 6375 Riverside Drive, Dublin, Ohio 43017. (614) 761-3222. Quarterly. Covers protection and restoration of ground water.

Ground Water Newsletter. Water Information Center, Inc., 125 East Bethpage Road, Plainview, New York 11803. (516) 249-7634. Biweekly. Covers ground water exploration, development, and management.

Ground Water Pollution News. Buraff Publications, 1350 Connecticut Ave., NW, Washington, District of Columbia 20036. (202) 862-0990. Biweekly. Legislation, regulation and litigation concerning ground water pollution.

The Groundwater Newsletter. Water Information Center, Inc., 125 E. Bethpage Rd., Plainview, New York 11803. (516) 249-7634. Semimonthly.

Hydrosoft. Computational Mechanics Publications Inc., 400 W. Cummings Park, Suite 6200, Woburn, Massachusetts 01801. Quarterly. Covers software for hydraulics, hydrology and hydrodynamics.

Journal of Groundwater. Association of Ground Water Scientists and Engineers, Division of National Water Well Association, 6375 Riverside Dr., Dublin, Ohio 43017. (614) 761-1711. 1963-. Bimonthly. Serial dealing with all forms of ground water and its quality.

Journal of Hydraulic Engineering. American Society of Civil Engineers, 345 E. 47th St., New York, New York 10017. (212) 705-7288; (800) 548-2723. 1983-. Monthly. Papers describe the analysis and solutions of problems in hydraulic engineering, hydrology and water resources. Emphasizes concepts, methods, techniques and results that advance knowledge in the hydraulic engineering profession.

Michigan State University. Dept. of Resource Development. Water Bulletin. Dept. of Resource Development, Michigan State University, 302 Natural Resources Bldg., East Lansing, Michigan 48824-1222. (517) 355-0100. Monthly.

Newsletter of Association of Ground Water Scientists and Engineers. Association of Groundwater Scientists and Engineers, 6375 Riverside Drive, Dublin, Ohio 43017. (614) 761-1711. Bimonthly. Reports on events, activities, courses and conferences of AGSE.

Well Log. National Water Well Association, 500 W. Wilson Bridge Rd., Worthington, Ohio 43085. (614) 761-1711. Eight numbers a year. Newsletter of the National Water Well Association

RESEARCH CENTERS AND INSTITUTES

Antioch University, Environmental Studies Center. Yellow Springs, Ohio 45387. (513) 767-7331.

Aridland Watershed Management Research Unit. 2000 East Allen Road, Tucson, Arizona 85719. (602) 629-6381.

Edwards Aquifer Research and Data Center. 248 Freeman Building, Southwest Texas State University, San Marcos, Texas 78666-4616. (512) 245-2329.

Groundwater Research Center. University of Cincinnati, College of Engineering, Mail Location 18, Cincinnati, Ohio 45221-0018. (513) 475-2933.

Sanitary Engineering and Environmental Health Research Laboratory. University of California, Berkeley, 1301 South 46th, Building 112, Richmond, California 94804. (415) 231-9449.

Scripps Institution of Oceanography, Hydrolics Laboratory. University of California, San Diego, 9500 Gilman Dr., La Jolla, California 92093. (619) 534-0595.

State University of New York at Plattsburg, Center for Earth and Environmental Science. Plattsburg, New York 12901. (518) 564-2028.

Texas Tech University, Water Resources Center. Box 4630, Lubbock, Texas 79409. (806) 742-3597.

U.S. Forest Service, Forest Hydrology Laboratory. Southern Forest Experiment Station, P.O. Box 947, Oxford, Mississippi 38655. (601) 234-2744.

University of Georgia, Savanna River Ecology Laboratory. P.O. Box Drawer E, Aiken, South Carolina 29801. (803) 725-2472.

University of Kansas, Water Resources Institute. Lawrence, Kansas 66045. (913) 864-3807.

University of Michigan, Wetland Ecosystem Research Group. Department of Chemical Engineering, 3094 Dow Building, Ann Arbor, Michigan 48109. (313) 764-3362.

University of Minnesota, Water Resources Research Center. 1518 Cleveland Ave., Ste. 302, St. Paul, Minnesota 55108. (612) 624-9282.

University of Missouri-Rolla, Institute of River Studies. 111 Civil Engineering, Rolla, Missouri 65401. (314) 341-4476.

University of Montana, Montana Forest and Conservation Experiment Station. Missoula, Montana 59812. (406) 243-5521.

University of Nevada-Reno, Desert Research Institute, Water Resources Center. P.O. Box 60220, Reno, Nevada 89506-0220. (703) 673-7365.

University of North Dakota, Institute for Remote Sensing. Geography Department, Grand Folks, North Dakota 58202. (701) 777-4246.

University of Oklahoma, Environmental & Ground Water Institute. 200 Felgar Street, Room 127, Norman, Oklahoma 73019-0470. (405) 325-5202.

USDA Water Conservation Laboratory. 4331 East Broadway, Phoenix, Arizona 85040. (602) 379-4356.

Utah State University, Utah Water Research Laboratory. Logan, Utah 84322-8200. (801) 750-3200.

Vineyard Environmental Research Institute. RFD 862, Martha's Vineyard Airport, Tisbury, Massachusetts 02568. (508) 693-4632.

Virginia Water Resources Research Center. Virginia Polytech Institute and State University, 617 North Main Street, Blacksburg, Virginia 24060. (703) 231-5624.

Water and Energy Research Institute of the Western Pacific (*WERI*). University of Guam, UOG Station, Guam 96923. (617) 734-3132.

Water Resources Institute. Grand Valley State University, Allendale, Michigan 49401. (616) 895-3749.

STATISTICS SOURCES

Ecology: Community Profiles. U.S. Fish and Wildlife Service. National Technical Information Service, 5285 Port Royal Road, Springfield, Virginia 22161. (703) 487-4650. Irregular. Data on coastal and inland ecosystems, including wetlands, tidal-flats, near-shore seagrasses, sand dunes, drilling platforms, oyster reefs, estuaries, rivers and streams.

Economic and Technical Adjustments in Irrigation Due to Declining Ground Water. U.S. G.P.O, Washington, District of Columbia 20402-9325. (202) 512-0000. 1990. Impact of declining ground water levels on irrigation use and costs.

Environmental Data Compendium. OECD Publications and Information Center, 2001 L St., N.W., Suite 700, Washington, District of Columbia 20036. (202) 785-6323. 1989.

Environmental Indicators. OECD Publications and Information Center, 2001 L St., N.W., Suite 700, Washington, District of Columbia 20036. (202) 785-6323. 1991.

Environmental Quality. Council on Environmental Quality. U.S. G.P.O., Washington, District of Columbia 20401. (202) 512-0000. Annual.

National Water Summary. U.S. G.P.O, Washington, District of Columbia 20402-9325. (202) 512-0000. Annual. Hydrological events and issues, including floods, drought, inland oil spills, and water supply and use.

The State of the Environment. OECD Publications and Information Center, 2001 L St., N.W., Suite 700, Washington, District of Columbia 20036. (202) 785-6323. 1991.

Water Resources Data. U.S. Geological Survey. U.S. G.P.O., Washington, District of Columbia 20401. (202) 512-0000. Annual. Data on water supply and quality of streams, lakes and reservoirs for individual states by water year.

TRADE ASSOCIATIONS AND PROFESSIONAL SOCIETIES

American Cave Conservation Association. 131 Main and Cave Sts., P.O. Box 409, Horse Cave, Kentucky 42749. (502) 786-1466.

American Geophysical Union. 2000 Florida Ave., N.W., Washington, District of Columbia 20009. (202) 462-6900.

American Institute of Hydrology. 3416 University Ave., S.E., Suite 200, Minneapolis, Minnesota 55414. (612) 379-1030.

American Society of Agricultural Engineers. 2950 Niles Rd., St Joseph, Michigan 49085. (616) 429-0300.

American Water Resources Association. 5410 Grosvenor Lane, Suite 220, Bethesda, Maryland 20814. (301) 493-8600.

Association of Ground Water Scientists and Engineers. PO Box 1248, Hardwick, Vermont 05843. (803) 472-6956.

Association of State Drinking Water Administrators. 1911 N. Fort Myer Dr., Suite 400, Arlington, Virginia 22209. (703) 524-2428.

Ground Water Institute. P.O. Box 580981, Minneapolis, Minnesota 55458-0981. (612) 636-3204.

Groundwater Management Caucus. Box 637, White Deer, Texas 79097. (806) 883-2501.

Groundwater Management Districts Association. 1125 Maize Rd., Colby, Kansas 67701. (913) 462-3915.

National Hydropower Association. 555 13th St., N.W., Suite 900 E., Washington, District of Columbia 20004. (202) 637-8115.

National Water Well Association. 6375 Riverside Dr., Dublin, Ohio 43107. (614) 761-1711.

HYPOLIMNION

See: LAKES

I

ICEBERGS

ABSTRACTING AND INDEXING SERVICES

Geographical Abstracts. London School of Economics, Dept. of Geography, Regency House, 34 Duke St., London, England 1966-. Continued by Geo Abstracts issued in 6 parts: Pt. A. Landforms and the quaternary; Pt. B. Biogeography and Climatology; Pt. C. Economic geography; Pt. D. Social geography and cartography; Pt. E. Sedimentology; Pt. F. Regional and community planning.

Science Citation Index. Institute for Scientific Information, 3501 Market St., Philadelphia, Pennsylvania 19104. 1961-.

ENCYCLOPEDIAS AND DICTIONARIES

Van Nostrand's Scientific Encyclopedia. Glenn D. Considine, ed. Van Nostrand Reinhold, 115 5th Ave., New York, New York 10003. (212) 254-3232. 1983. Sixth edition. Includes all broad subject areas in science.

GENERAL WORKS

Antarctic Icebergs as a Global Fresh Water Resource. John Hult. RAND, 1700 Main St., Santa Monica, California 90401. (310) 393-0411. 1973. Water supply in Antarctic regions.

Conference on Use of Icebergs. International Glaciological Society, 700 Lensfield Rd., Cambridge, England CB2 1ER. 1980.

ICHTHYOLOGY

See: AQUACULTURE

IDAHO ENVIRONMENTAL AGENCIES

GOVERNMENTAL ORGANIZATIONS

Department of Agriculture: Pesticide Registration. Chief, Bureau of Pesticides, 2270 Old Penitentiary Rd., Boise, Idaho 83712. (208) 334-3243.

Department of Fish and Game: Fish and Wildlife. Director, 600 South Walnut St., PO Box 25, Boise, Idaho 83707. (203) 334-5159.

Department of Health and Welfare: Environmental Protection. Division Administrator, Division of the Envi-

ronment, 450 West State St., Boise, Idaho 83720. (208) 334-5840.

Department of Health and Welfare: Water Quality. Chief, Bureau of Water Quality, 450 West State St., Boise, Idaho 83720. (208) 334-4250.

Department of Lands: Underground Storage Tanks. Petroleum Engineer, Water Quality Bureau, Oil and Gas Commission, 701 River Ave., Coeur d'Alene, Idaho 83814. (208) 664-2171.

Department of Water Resources: Groundwater Management. Administrator, Water Management Division, 1301 N. Orchard St., Boise, Idaho 83720. (208) 327-7902.

Division of Environmental Quality: Air Quality. Administrator, 450 West State St., Boise, Idaho 83720. (208) 334-5840.

Division of the Environment: Hazardous Waste Management. Chief, Bureau of Hazardous Materials, 450 West State St., Boise, Idaho 83720. (208) 334-5879.

Emergency Response Commission: Emergency Preparedness and Community Right-to-Know. Chair, State House, Boise, Idaho 83720. (208) 334-5888.

Labor and Industrial Services Department: Occupational Safety. Director, 317 Main St., Boise, Idaho 83720. (208) 334-3950.

U.S. EPA Region 10: Pollution Prevention. Chief, Hazardous Waste Policy Office, 1200 Sixth Ave., Seattle, Washington 98101. (206) 442-5810.

ILLINOIS ENVIRONMENTAL AGENCIES

GOVERNMENTAL ORGANIZATIONS

Department of Agriculture: Pesticide Registration. Bureau Chief, Plant and Apiary Protection, PO Box 19281, Springfield, Illinois 62794-9281. (217) 785-2427.

Department of Conservation: Fish and Wildlife. Director, Lincoln Tower Plaza, 524 South 2nd St., Springfield, Illinois 62701. (217) 782-6302.

Department of Energy and Natural Resources: Natural Resources. Director, 325 West Adams St., Springfield, Illinois 62704. (217) 785-2002.

Department of Energy and Natural Resources: Solid Waste Management. Director, 325 West Adams St., Springfield, Illinois 62704. (217) 785-2800.

Department of Energy and Natural Resources: Waste Minimization and Pollution Prevention. Director, Hazardous Waste Research and Information Center, 1 East Hazlewood Dr., Champaign, Illinois 61820. (217) 333-8940.

Department of Labor: Occupational Safety. Manager, #1 W. Old State Capitol Plaza, Springfield, Illinois 62706. (217) 782-9386.

Division of Water Resources: Coastal Zone Management. Section Chief, Lake Michigan Management Section, Division of Water Resources, 310 South Michigan, Room 1606, Chicago, Illinois 60604. (312) 793-3123.

Environmental Protection Agency: Air Quality. Director, 2200 Churchill Rd., Springfield, Illinois 62708. (217) 782-3397.

Environmental Protection Agency: Environmental Protection. Director, 2200 Churchill Rd., Springfield, Illinois 62708. (217) 782-3397.

Environmental Protection Agency: Groundwater Management. Director, 2200 Churchill Rd., Springfield, Illinois 62708. (217) 782-3397.

Environmental Protection Agency: Water Quality. Director, 2200 Churchill Rd., Springfield, Illinois 62708. (217) 782-3397.

Hazardous Waste Center: Hazardous Waste Management. Director, 1808 Woodfield Dr., Savoy, Illinois 61874. (217) 333-8941.

Illinois EPA: Emergency Preparedness and Community Right-to-Know. Chair, Emergency Planning Unit, PO Box 19276, 2200 Churchill Rd., Springfield, Illinois 62794-9276. (217) 782-3637.

State Fire Marshal: Underground Storage Tanks. 3150 Executive Park Dr., Springfield, Illinois 62703. (217) 785-0969.

ILLINOIS ENVIRONMENTAL LEGISLATION

GENERAL WORKS

Illinois Environmental Law Handbook. Government Institutes, Inc., 4 Research Pl., Ste. 200, Rockville, Maryland 20850. (301) 921-2300. 1989.

IMMUNOTOXICITY

See: TOXICITY

IMPOUNDMENTS

See: DAMS

INCINERATION

See also: COMBUSTION

ABSTRACTING AND INDEXING SERVICES

Air Pollution Titles. Pennsylvania State University, Center for Air Environmental Studies, 226 Fenske Laboratory, University Park, Pennsylvania 16802. (814) 865-1415. 1965. Bibliographic guide to current research literature on air environment, including monitoring and control of air pollution, health effects, effects on agriculture, forests, toxic air contaminants, and global atmospheric pro cases.

Air Pollution Translations. A Bibliography With Abstracts. U.S. Environmental Protection Agency, MD 75, Research Triangle Park, North Carolina 27711. (919) 541-2184. 1969.

Applied Science and Technology Index. H.W. Wilson Co., 950 University Ave., Bronx, New York 10452. (800) 367-6770. Formerly Industrial Arts Index.

Bulletin Signaletique: Eau et Assainissement, Pollution Atmospherique, Droit des Pollutions. Centre de Documentation, Centre National de la Recherche Scientifique, 15, quai Anatole France, Paris, France 75700. (1) 45 55 92 25. 1983-. Monthly. Indexes pollution periodicals including water, atmospheric and related pollutions.

Engineering Index. The Engineering Index Inc., 345 E. 47th St., New York, New York 10017. 1962-.

General Science Index. H. W. Wilson Co., 950 University Ave., Bronx, New York 10452. 1978-. Monthly, also issued in annual cumulation. Cumulative subject index to English language periodicals in the subject fields of astronomy, botany, chemistry, earth science, environment and conservation, food and nutrition, genetics, mathematics, medicine and health, microbiology, oceanography, physics, physiology and zoology.

Geographical Abstracts. London School of Economics, Dept. of Geography, Regency House, 34 Duke St., London, England 1966-. Continued by Geo Abstracts issued in 6 parts: Pt. A. Landforms and the quaternary; Pt. B. Biogeography and Climatology; Pt. C. Economic geography; Pt. D. Social geography and cartography; Pt. E. Sedimentology; Pt. F. Regional and community planning.

Index to Scientific Book Contents. Institute for Scientific Information, 3501 Market St., Philadelphia, Pennsylvania 19104. (800) 523-1857. 1985-. Annual. Gives contents of science books published.

Pollution Abstracts. Cambridge Scientific Abstracts, 5161 River Rd., Bethesda, Maryland 20816. (301) 961-6750. Six/year. Indexes worldwide technical literature on environmental pollution. Covers air pollution, marine and freshwater pollution, sewage and wastewater treatment, waste management, toxicology and health, noise pollution, radiation, land pollution, and environmental policies, programs, legislation, and education. Also available online.

Science Citation Index. Institute for Scientific Information, 3501 Market St., Philadelphia, Pennsylvania 19104. 1961-.

ENCYCLOPEDIAS AND DICTIONARIES

Dictionary of Environmental Engineering and Related Sciences: English-Spanish, Spanish-English. Jose T. Villate. Ediciones Universal, 3090 SW 8th St., Miami, Florida 33135. (305) 642-3355. 1979.

Encyclopedia of Chemical Processing and Design. John J. Mcketta and W. A. Cunningham. Marcel Dekker, Inc., 270 Madison Ave., New York, New York 10016. (212) 696-9000; (800) 228-1160. 1992. Thirty-eight volumes.

Encyclopedia of Environmental Science and Engineering. J.R. Pfafflin. Gordon and Breach Science Publishers, Inc., 270 8th Ave., New York, New York 10011. (212) 206-8900. 1992.

Kirk-Othmer Encyclopedia of Chemical Technology. J. I. Kroschwitz, ed. John Wiley & Sons, Inc., 605 3rd Ave., New York, New York 10158-0012. (212) 850-6000. 1992-. All articles in the new edition have been rewritten and updated adding new subjects such as biotechnology, computer topics, analytical techniques and instrumentation, environmental concerns, fuels and energy, inorganic and solid state chemistry; composite materials and material science in general, and pharmaceuticals. Also available online.

McGraw-Hill Encyclopedia of Environmental Science. Sybil P. Parker. McGraw-Hill Science & Engineering Books, 11 W. 19th St., New York, New York 10011. (212) 337-6010. 1980. Covers ecology, man's influence on nature, and environmental protection.

McGraw-Hill Encyclopedia of Science and Technology. McGraw-Hill, 1221 Avenue of the Americas, New York, New York 10020. (212) 512-2000 or (800) 262-4729. 1992. Seventh edition. Issued in multiple volumes including index. Includes all science and technology broad subject areas.

The New York Times Encyclopedic Dictionary of the Environment. Paul Sarnoff. Quadrangle Books, New York, New York 1971. Focuses on state-of-the-art methods of pollution control, abatement, prevention and removal.

Van Nostrand's Scientific Encyclopedia. Glenn D. Considine, ed. Van Nostrand Reinhold, 115 5th Ave., New York, New York 10003. (212) 254-3232. 1983. Sixth edition. Includes all broad subject areas in science.

GENERAL WORKS

Air Pollution Control. Howard E. Hesketh. Technomic Publishing Co., 851 New Holland Ave., Box 3535, Lancaster, Pennsylvania 17604. (717) 291-5609. 1991. Presents both theory and application data. Provides a background relevant to behavior theories and control techniques for capturing gaseous and particulate air pollutants.

Controlled Air Incineration. Frank L. Cross, Jr. and Howard E. Hesketh. Technomic Publishing Co., 851 New Holland Ave., Box 3535, Lancaster, Pennsylvania 17604. (717) 291-5609. 1985.

Environmentally Acceptable Incineration of Chlorinated Chemical Waste. Martin A. de Zeeuw. Coronet Books, 311 Bainbridge St., Philadelphia, Pennsylvania 19147. (215) 925-2762. 1987.

Fate of Trace Metals in a Rotary Kiln Incinerator with a Single-Stage Ionizing Wet Scrubber. D. J. Fournier and L. R. Waterland. National Technical Information Service, 5285 Port Royal Rd., Springfield, Virginia 22161. (703) 487-4650. 1991. Two volumes. Vol. 1 Technical results. vol. 2. Appendices.

Health Effects of Municipal Waste Incineration. Holly A. Hattemer-Frey and C. C. Travis. CRC Press, 2000

Corporate Blvd. N.W., Boca Raton, Florida 33431. (800) 272-7737. 1991.

Incinerating Hazardous Wastes. Harry M. Freeman, ed. Technomic Publishing Co., 851 New Holland Ave., Box 3535, Lancaster, Pennsylvania 17604. (717) 291-5609. 1988. Book provides the essence of the thermal destruction research program at the EPA Lab in Cincinnati, Ohio. Highlights papers that have represented significant contributions to the field of incineration research. Provides a general overview of the role of incineration in the United States today.

Incinerating Municipal and Industrial Waste; Fireside Problems and Prospects for Improvement. Richard W. Bryers. Hemisphere, 79 Madison Ave., Suite 1110, New York, New York 10016. (212) 725-1999; (800) 821-8312. 1991. Addresses the causes and possible cures for corrosion and deposits due to impurities in the combustion of industrial and municipal refuse.

Incineration for Site Cleanup and Destruction of Hazardous Wastes. Howard E. Hesketh. Technomic Publishing Co., 851 New Holland Ave., Box 3535, Lancaster, Pennsylvania 17604. (717) 291-5609; (800) 233-9936. 1990.

Municipal Waste Combustion Study: Assessment of Health Risks Associated with Municipal Waste Combustion Emissions. U.S. Environmental Protection Agency, 401 M St., S.W., 20460. (202) 260-2090. 1987.

Recycling and Incineration: Evaluating Choices. Richard A. Denison and John Ruston. Island Press, 1718 Connecticut Ave. N.W., Suite 300, Washington, District of Columbia 20009. (202) 232-7933. 1990. Presents the technology, economics, environmental concerns, and legal intricacies behind these two approaches. Includes basics of waste reduction, recycling, and incineration; cost comparisons of the two approaches; an evaluation of the health and environmental impacts.

Rush to Burn: Solving America's Garbage Crisis?. Island Press, 1718 Connecticut Ave. N.W., Suite 300, Washington, District of Columbia 20009. (202) 232-7933. 1989. Describes incineration, refuse and refuse disposal.

Treatment and Conditioning of Radioactive Incinerator Ashes. L. Crecille, ed. Elsevier Science Publishing Co., 655 Avenue of the Americas, New York, New York 10010. (212) 989-5800. 1991. Incineration of radioactive wastes and purification of fly ash.

HANDBOOKS AND MANUALS

CRC Handbook of Incineration of Hazardous Wastes. William S. Rickman, ed. CRC Press, 2000 Corporate Blvd. N.W., Boca Raton, Florida 33431. (800) 272-7737. 1991.

Handbook of Incineration Systems. Calvin R. Brunner. McGraw-Hill Science & Engineering Books, 11 West 19th St., New York, New York 10011. (212) 337-6010. 1991. Examines every type of modern incinerator, describes the analytical techniques required to utilize the equipment, explains the basic scientific principles involved, and defines the regulations that apply to various incineration facilities and procedures for upgrading existing facilities to conform to new, stricter operating standards.

Hazardous Waste Incineration Calculations. Joseph P. Reynolds. John Wiley & Sons, Inc., 605 3rd Ave., New York, New York 10158-0012. (212) 850-6000. 1991.

Medical Waste Incineration Handbook. C. C. Lee. Government Institutes, Inc., 4 Research Pl., Suite 200, Rockville, Maryland 20850. (301) 921-2300. 1990. Covers incineration, equipment, measurement techniques, potential emissions, maintenance, safety guidance, operational problems and solutions, and the federal and state regulatory framework. Includes a list of addresses and phone numbers of manufacturers of medical waste incinerators and manufacturers of air pollution control equipment.

Quality Assurance/Quality Control Procedures for Hazardous Waste Incineration. Center for Environmental Research Information. U.S. Environmental Protection Agency, 26 W. Martin Luther King Dr., Cincinnati, Ohio 45628. (513) 569-7931. 1990.

ONLINE DATA BASES

Computerized Engineering Index–COMPENDEX. Engineering Information Inc., 345 E. 47th St., New York, New York 10017. (212) 705-7600.

Kirk-Othmer Encyclopedia of Chemical Technology. John Wiley & Sons, Inc., 605 3rd Ave., 5th Floor, New York, New York 10158. (212) 850-6000. Online version of the publication of the same name.

PressNet Environmental Reports. Chemical Information Systems, Inc., 7215 York Rd., Baltimore, Maryland 21212. (301) 321-8440.

PERIODICALS AND NEWSLETTERS

Infectious Wastes News. Richard H. Freeman, Washington Sq., PO Box 65686, Washington, District of Columbia 20035-5686. (202) 861-0708. Biweekly. Disposal of infectious wastes, new methods and technologies, sterilization and incineration of waste, and environmental standards.

Information Kit. Coalition for Responsible Waste Incineration, 1330 Connecticut Ave. NW, Suite 300, Washington, District of Columbia 20036. (202) 659-0060. Irregular.

Management of World Wastes. Communication Channels, 6255 Barfield Road, Atlanta, Georgia 30328. (404) 256-9800. Monthly. Covers public and private waste operations.

STATISTICS SOURCES

Incineration of Industrial Wastes. FIND/SVP, 625 Avenue of the Americas, New York, New York 10011. (212) 645-4500. 1990. Present state of incineration technology–liquid injection, fume, fixed hearth, multiple hearth, rotary kiln, fluidized bed, circulating bed, infrared, plasma-arc, mobile/transportable, oxygen-enhanced, auxiliary systems–as well as emerging technologies.

TRADE ASSOCIATIONS AND PROFESSIONAL SOCIETIES

Coalition for Responsible Waste Incineration. 1330 Connecticut Ave., NW, Suite 300, Washington, District of Columbia 20036. (202) 659-0060.

INDIANA ENVIRONMENTAL AGENCIES

GOVERNMENTAL ORGANIZATIONS

Department of Environmental Management: Environmental Protection. Commissioner, 105 South Meridan St., Indianapolis, Indiana 46206. (317) 232-8162.

Department of Environmental Management: Groundwater Management. Deputy Commissioner, 105 South Meridan St., Indianapolis, Indiana 46206. (317) 232-8595.

Department of Environmental Management: Hazardous Waste Management. Branch Chief, Hazardous Waste Management Branch, 105 South Meridan St., Indianapolis, Indiana 46206. (317) 232-4458.

Department of Environmental Management: Solid Waste Management. Chief, Solid Waste Management Branch, 105 South Meridan St., Indianapolis, Indiana 46206. (317) 232-4473.

Department of Natural Resources: Coastal Zone Management. Assistant Director, Division of Water, 2475 Director's Row, Indianapolis, Indiana 46241. (317) 232-4221.

Department of Natural Resources: Fish and Wildlife. Director, Fish and Wildlife Division, 607 State Office Building, Indianapolis, Indiana 46204. (317) 232-4091.

Department of Natural Resources: Natural Resources. Director, 608 State Office Building, Indianapolis, Indiana 46204. (317) 232-4020.

Division of Labor: Occupational Safety. Commissioner, 1013 State Office Building, Indianapolis, Indiana 46204. (317) 232-2663.

Emergency Response Commission: Emergency Preparedness and Community Right-to-Know. Director, 5500 West Bradbury Ave., Indianapolis, Indiana 46241. (317) 243-5176.

State Board of Health: Air Quality. Acting Assistant Commissioner, Air Pollution Control Division, 105 South Meridan St., Indianapolis, Indiana 46206. (317) 232-8217.

State Chemist Office: Pesticide Registration. State Chemist, Purdue University, Department of Biochemistry, West Lafayette, Indiana 47907. (317) 494-1585.

U.S. EPA Region 5: Emergency Preparedness and Community Right-to-Know. Pesticides and Toxic Substances Branch, 230 South Dearborn St., Chicago, Illinois 60604. (312) 353-2000.

Water Quality Branch: Water Quality. Chief, 105 South Meridian St., Box 6015, Indianapolis, Indiana 46206. (317) 245-5028.

RESEARCH CENTERS AND INSTITUTES

Environmental Management and Education Program: Waste Minimization and Pollution Prevention. Office Director, Civil Engineering Boulevard, Room 2129, Purdue University, West Lafayette, Indiana 47907. (317) 494-5036.

INDUSTRIAL CHEMICALS

ABSTRACTING AND INDEXING SERVICES

Biological and Agricultural Index. H.W. Wilson Co., 950 University Ave., Bronx, New York 10452. (800) 367-6770. 1916-. Monthly.

Chemical Abstracts. Chemical Abstracts Service, 2540 Olentangy River Rd., PO Box 3012, Columbus, Ohio 43210. (800) 848-6533. 1907-.

Engineering Index. The Engineering Index Inc., 345 E. 47th St., New York, New York 10017. 1962-.

Environment Abstracts. Bowker A & I Publishing, 121 Chanlon Rd., New Providence, New Jersey 07974. (908) 464-6800. 1974-.

Environment Index. Environment Information Center, Index Research Department, 124 E. 39th St., New York, New York 10016. 1971-. Annual.

Environmental Information Connection–EIC. Planning Information Program, Dept. of Urban and Regional Planning, University of Illinois, 1003 West Nevada, Urbana, Illinois 61801. (217) 333-1369. Also available online.

Environmental Periodicals Bibliography. Environmental Studies Institute, International Academy at Santa Barbara, 800 Garden St., Suite D, Santa Barbara, California 93101. (805) 965-5010. Also available online.

General Science Index. H. W. Wilson Co., 950 University Ave., Bronx, New York 10452. 1978-. Monthly, also issued in annual cumulation. Cumulative subject index to English language periodicals in the subject fields of astronomy, botany, chemistry, earth science, environment and conservation, food and nutrition, genetics, mathematics, medicine and health, microbiology, oceanography, physics, physiology and zoology.

Pollution Abstracts. Cambridge Scientific Abstracts, 5161 River Rd., Bethesda, Maryland 20816. (301) 961-6750. Six/year. Indexes worldwide technical literature on environmental pollution. Covers air pollution, marine and freshwater pollution, sewage and wastewater treatment, waste management, toxicology and health, noise pollution, radiation, land pollution, and environmental policies, programs, legislation, and education. Also available online.

Science Citation Index. Institute for Scientific Information, 3501 Market St., Philadelphia, Pennsylvania 19104. 1961-.

BIBLIOGRAPHIES

EPA Publications Bibliography. U.S. Environmental Protection Agency, Library Systems Branch, 401 M St., SW, Washington, District of Columbia 20460. (202) 260-2090. Quarterly.

DIRECTORIES

Directory of Chemical Producers. Chemical Information Services, Inc., Stanford Research Institute, Menlo Park, California 94305-2235. 1973-. Lists both plants and products for 1,300 companies and approximately 10,000 commercial chemicals. Some information on capacity, process, and raw materials is included for major chemicals.

Hazardous Materials Control Directory. Hazardous Materials Control Research Institute, 9300 Columbia Blvd., Silver Spring, Maryland 20910. (301) 587-9390.

OPD Chemical Buyer's Directory. Chemical Marketing Reporter, Schnell Pub. Co., 80 Broad St., New York, New York 10004-2203. (212) 248-4177. 1992. Seventy-ninth edition. Known as the "Green Book", this buyer's directory includes an index of chemical suppliers, branch offices, a glossary, an 800 phone directory for quick supplier reference. Also includes the chemfile folio of company catalogs, chemicals and related materials listings, and other related data.

ENCYCLOPEDIAS AND DICTIONARIES

Chem Sources–USA. Chemical Sources International Inc., PO Box 1884, Ormond Beach, Florida 32175-1884. Annual. Includes chemical nomenclature of some 130,000 chemicals of all classifications, trade name index, classified/trade name, company directory, and company index. Also includes paid advertising.

Concise Encyclopedia of Industrial Chemical Additives. Michael Ash. VCH Publishers, 303 NW 12th Ave., Deerfield Beach, Florida 33442-1788. (305) 428-5566.

Encyclopedia of Environmental Control Technology. Paul N. Cheremisinoff, ed. Gulf Publishing Co., Book Division, PO Box 2608, Houston, Texas 77252. (713) 529-4301 or (800) 231-6275. 1992. Volume 1: Thermal Treatment of Hazardous Wastes; volume 2: Air Pollution Control; volume 3: Wastewater Treatment Technology; volume 4: Hazardous Waste Containment and Treatment; volumes 5 through 8 in progress. Provides in-depth coverage of specialized topics related to environmental and industrial pollution control problems and state-of-the-art information on technology and research as well as projections of future trends in the field.

Encyclopedia of Trademarks and Synonyms. H. Bennett, ed. Chemical Publishing Co., 80 Eighth Ave., New York, New York 10011. (212) 255-1950. 1981. Three volumes. Includes chemical compounds, compositions consisting of one or more chemicals and other products. Also included are abbreviated names and WHO free names.

Hazardous and Toxic Effects of Industrial Chemicals. Marshall Sittig. Noyes Publications, 120 Mill Rd., Park Ridge, New Jersey 07656. (201) 391-8484. 1979. Dictionary of poisons and industrial toxicology.

Hazardous Chemicals Desk Reference. Richard J. Lewis. Van Nostrand Reinhold, 115 Fifth Ave., New York, New York 10003. (212) 254-3232. 1991. Information on the hazardous properties of some 5500 chemicals commonly encountered in industry, laboratories, environment, and the workplace.

McGraw-Hill Encyclopedia of Environmental Science. Sybil P. Parker. McGraw-Hill Science & Engineering Books, 11 W. 19th St., New York, New York 10011.

(212) 337-6010. 1980. Covers ecology, man's influence on nature, and environmental protection.

Ullmanns Encyclopedia of Industrial Chemistry. Hans Jurgen Arpe and Wolfgang Gerhartz, eds. VCH Publishers, 303 NW 12th Ave., Deerfield Beach, Florida 33442-1788. (305) 428-5566. 1990. Designed to keep up with the broad spectrum of chemical technology. Thirty-six volumes of the encyclopedia have been divided into two sets: the 28 A volumes contain alphabetically arranged articles on chemicals, product groups, processes and technological concepts; and the 8 B volumes are compendia of basic knowledge in industrial chemistry.

GENERAL WORKS

Biological Monitoring Techniques for Human Exposure to Industrial Chemicals. L. Sheldon. Noyes Publications, 120 Mill Rd., Park Ridge, New Jersey 07656. (201) 391-8484. 1986.

Cutting Chemical Wastes. David J. Sarokin, et al. INFORM, 381 Park Ave. S., New York, New York 10016. (212) 689-4040. 1985. Describes the activities of 29 organic chemical plants that are trying to reduce hazardous chemical wastes.

Industrial Organic Chemicals in Perspective. Harold A. Wittcoff. John Wiley & Sons, Inc., 605 3rd Ave., New York, New York 10158-0012. (212) 850-6000. 1980. Raw materials and manufacturing in the chemicals industry.

Metals and Their Compounds in the Environment. Ernest Merian, ed. VCH Publishers, 303 NW 12th Ave., Deerfield Beach, Florida 33442-1788. (305) 428-5566. 1990.

Prosperity without Pollution. Joel S. Hirschhorn and Kirsten U. Oldenburg. Van Nostrand Reinhold, 115 5th Ave., New York, New York 10003. (212) 254-3232. 1991. Explains how to decrease pollution without making a sacrifice in our standard of living.

The Top Fifty Industrial Chemicals. Raymond Chang. Random House, Inc., 201 E. 50th St., New York, New York 10022. (212) 751-2600. 1988. Technical chemistry and chemical engineering.

Toxicological Evaluations. Volume 1: Potential Health Hazards of Existing Chemicals. B. G. Chemie, ed. Springer-Verlag, 115 5th Ave., New York, New York 10010. (212) 460-1500; (800) 777-4643. 1990. Identifies thousands of compounds which might possibly be toxic and to date several hundreds that have been investigated. Contains results of the first 57 reviews of the literature.

HANDBOOKS AND MANUALS

Catalog Handbook of Fine Chemicals. Aldrich Chemical Co., 1001 W. St. Paul Ave., Milwaukee, Wisconsin 53233. (414) 273-3850 or (800) 558-9160. 1990/1991. Contains more than 27,000 products of which over 4,000 are new. Includes: chemicals, equipment, glassware, books, software, research products, bulk quantities, new products, custom synthesis and rare chemicals.

Chemical Economics Handbook. SRI International, 333 Rovenswood Ave., Menlo Park, California 14025-3493. (415) 859-4771. 1983-. 33 vols. Provides an in-depth evaluation of the present and future economic status of major chemical substances

Chemical Information Manual. Government Institutes, Inc., 4 Research Pl., Ste. 200, Rockville, Maryland

20850. (301) 921-2300. 1991. Handbook presenting a variety of useful data on each chemical substances, including proper identification, OSHA exposure limits, description and physical properties, carcinogenic status, health effects and toxicology, sampling and analysis.

Chemical Products Desk Reference. Michael and Irene Ash. Chemical Publishing Co., 80 Eighth Ave., New York, New York 10011. (212) 255-1950. Contains over 32,000 entries of currently marketed commercial chemical trademark products.

Chemical Waste: Handling and Treatment. Springer-Verlag, 175 5th Ave., New York, New York 10010. (212) 460-1500. 1986.

Compendium of Safety Data Sheets for Research and Industrial Chemicals. L. H. Keith and D. B. Walters, eds. VCH Publishers, 303 NW 12th Ave., Deerfield Beach, Florida 33442-1788. (305) 428-5566. 1985. Seven volumes. Provides information of safety-oriented needs involving chemicals.

Riegel's Handbook of Industrial Chemistry. James A. Kent, ed. Van Nostrand Reinhold, 115 5th Ave., New York, New York 10020. (212) 254-3232. 1983. Eighth edition. Includes industries such as: wastewater technology, coal technology, phosphate fertilizers, synthetic plastics, man-made textiles, detergents, sugar, animal and vegetable oils, chemical explosives, dyes, nuclear industry, and much more.

Suspect Chemicals Sourcebook. Roytech Publications, Inc., 7910 Woodmont Ave., Ste. 902, Bethesda, Maryland 20814. (301) 654-4281. 1985-. Includes: chemical name index, CAS registry numbers; OSHA Chemical Hazard chemical name; Summary and full text of OSHA Chemical Hazard Communication Standard and history and overview. Also available online.

Synthetic Organic Chemicals. U.S. G.P.O., Washington, District of Columbia 20401. (202) 512-0000. 1967. An annual publication on production and sales in the U.S. for all synthetic organic chemicals produced commercially. About 800 chemicals and 800 manufacturers are included in the USITC surveys, but because of confidentiality requirements only parts of the data are published. U.S. Tariff Commission acts under the provisions of Section 332 of the Tariff Act of 1930, as amended.

Tables of Physical and Chemical Constants and Some Mathematical Functions. G. W. C. Kaye, et al. Longman Group Ltd., Longman House, Burnt Mill, Harlow, England CM20 2J6. 0279 426721. 1988. Fifteenth edition. Includes tables on mechanical properties, density, elasticity, viscosity, surface tension, temperature and heat. Also covers radiation, optics, chemistry, electrochemistry, astrophysics, and chemical thermodynamics.

ONLINE DATA BASES

CERCLIS. Chemical Information Systems, Inc., 7215 York Rd., Baltimore, Maryland 21212. (301) 321-8440. Information on hazardous waste disposal sites that have either been listed by the EPA on the National Priority List (NPL) or nominated for consideration for the NPL.

Chemical Abstracts-CA. Chemical Abstracts Service, 2540 Olentangy River Rd., P.O. Box 3012, Columbus, Ohio 43210. (800) 848-6533 or (614) 421-3600. Information sources include 9000 journals, patents from 27 countries, two industrial property organizations, new

books, conference proceedings, and government research reports.

Chemical Engineering. McGraw-Hill Science & Engineering Books, 11 W. 19th St., New York, New York 10011. (212) 337-6010. Online version of periodical of the same name.

Chemical Engineering and Biotechnology Abstracts–CEBA. Orbit Search Service, Maxwell Online Inc., 8000 W. Park Dr., McLean, Virginia 22102. (703) 442-0900 or (800) 456-7248. Monthly. Covers theoretical, practical and commercial material on all aspects of processing safety, and the environment. Also covers process and reaction engineering, measurement and process control, environmental protection and safety, plant design and equipment used in chemical engineering and biotechnology. More than 400 of the world's major primary chemical and process engineering journals are scanned to compile the database. Available from ORBIT.

Chemical Industry Notes–CHEMSIS. Chemical Abstracts Service, PO Box 3012, 2540 Olentangy River, Columbus, Ohio 43210. (614) 421-3600 or (800) 848-6533. Contains citations to business-oriented literature relating to the chemical processing industries. Includes pricing, production, products and processes, corporate and government activities, facilities and people from more than 80 worldwide business periodicals published since 1974. Available on DIALOG and ORBIT.

Computerized Engineering Index–COMPENDEX. Engineering Information Inc., 345 E. 47th St., New York, New York 10017. (212) 705-7600.

Enviro/Energyline Abstracts Plus. R. R. Bowker Co., 121 Chanlon Rd., New Providence, New Jersey 07974. (908) 464-6800.

Environmental Periodicals Bibliography. National Information Services Corp., Ste. 6, Wyman Towers, 3100 St. Paul St., Baltimore, Maryland 21218. (410)243-0797. Online version of abstract of same name.

PERIODICALS AND NEWSLETTERS

Analytical Chemistry. American Chemical Society, 1155 16th St. N.W., Washington, District of Columbia 20036. (800) 227-5558. 1929-. Bimonthly. Articles for chemists, life scientists and engineers.

ChemEcology. Chemical Manufacturers Association, 2501 M St. NW, Washington, District of Columbia 20037. (202) 887-1100. Monthly. Articles on how the chemical industry deals with environmental issues.

Chemical & Engineering News. American Chemical Society, 1155 16th St. N.W., Washington, District of Columbia 20036. (800) 227-5558. Weekly. Cites technical and business developments in the chemical process industry.

Chemical Engineering. McGraw-Hill Science & Engineering Books, 11 W. 19th St., New York, New York 10011. (212) 337-6010. Monthly. Articles on new engineering techniques and equipment. Also available online.

Chemical Engineering Progress Magazine. American Institute of Chemical Engineers, 345 E. 47th St., New York, New York 10017. (212) 705-7338. Monthly. Articles covering environmental controls for chemical and petrochemical industrial plants.

Chemical Times & Trends. Chemical Specialties Manufacturers Association, 1913 Eye Street, NW, Washington, District of Columbia 20006. (202) 872-8110. Quarterly. Discusses trends in manufacturing/selling of industrial, household, and personal care products.

Chemist. American Institute of Chemists, 7315 Wisconsin Avenue, Bethesda, Maryland 20814. (301) 652-2447. Monthly. Covers topics of professional interest to chemists and chemical engineers.

Community and Worker Right-to-Know News. Thompson Publishing Group, 1725 K St. NW, Washington, District of Columbia 20006. (800) 424-2959. Bimonthly. Reports on chemical disclosure requirements and industrial liability.

Flashpoint. National Association of Solvent Recyclers, 1333 New Hampshire Ave., N.W., No. 1100, Washington, District of Columbia 20036. (202) 463-6956. Biweekly. Overview of recycling hazardous waste fuel blending & related industries.

Halogenated Solvent Industry Alliance Newsletter. Halogenated Solvent Industry Alliance, 1225 19th Street, NW, Suite 300, Washington, District of Columbia 20036. (202) 223-5890. Bimonthly. Covers legislative and regulatory problems involving halogenated solvents.

Harvard Environmental Law Review. Environmental Law Review, c/o Publication Center, Harvard Law School, 202 Austin Hall, Cambridge, Massachusetts 02138. (617) 495-3110. Semiannual. Law reviews of cases involving the environment.

Hazardous Materials Control. Hazardous Materials Control Research Institute, 9300 Columbia Blvd., Silver Spring, Maryland 20910-1702. (301) 587-9390. Bimonthly. Information, innovations and articles in the hazardous materials field.

Hazardous Waste News. Business Publishers, Inc., 951 Pershing Drive, Silver Spring, Maryland 20910-4464. (301) 587-6300. Weekly. Covers legislative, regulatory and judicial decisions on hazardous waste. Also available online.

HAZCHEM Alert. Van Nostrand Reinhold, 115 Fifth Ave., New York, New York 10003. (212) 254-3232. Biweekly. Covers hazardous chemical news and information.

Journal of Analytical Toxicology. Preston Publications, PO Box 48312, 7800 Merrimac, Niles, Illinois 60648. (708) 965-0566. Bimonthly. Articles on industrial toxicology, environmental pollution and pharmaceuticals.

Journal of Environmental Science and Health. Marcel Dekker, Inc., 270 Madison Ave., New York, New York 10016. (212) 696-9000. Bimonthly. Concerns pesticides, food contaminants, chemical carcinogens, and agricultural wastes.

Synthetic Organic Chemical Manufacturers Association Newsletter. Synthetic Organic Chemical Manufacturers Association, 1330 Connecticut Avenue, NW, Washington, District of Columbia 20036. (202) 659-0060. Biweekly. Covers trade, environmental and safety issues.

TRADE ASSOCIATIONS AND PROFESSIONAL SOCIETIES

American Institute of Chemical Engineers. 345 East 47th St., New York, New York 10017. (212) 705-7338.

American Institute of Chemists. 7315 Wisconsin Ave., Bethesda, Maryland 20814. (301) 652-2447.

Chemical Manufacturers Association. 2501 M St., N.W., Washington, District of Columbia 20037. (202) 887-1100.

Halogenated Solvents Industry Alliance. 1225 19th St., N.W., Suite 300, Washington, District of Columbia 20036. (202) 223-5890.

Industrial Chemical Research Association. 1811 Monroe St., Dearborn, Michigan 48124. (313) 563-0360.

Methyl Chloride Industry Alliance. c/o Latham and Watkins, 1001 Pennsylvania Ave., N.W., #130, Washington, District of Columbia 20004. (202) 637-2200.

Synthetic Organic Chemical Manufacturers Association. 1330 Connecticut Ave., N.W., Suite 300, Washington, District of Columbia 20036. (202) 659-0060.

INDUSTRIAL COOLING SYSTEMS

See: COOLING SYSTEMS

INDUSTRIAL DISCHARGE

See: WASTE DISPOSAL

INDUSTRIAL HEATING

See: HEATING SYSTEMS

INDUSTRIAL HYGIENE

See also: HEALTH, ENVIRONMENTAL

ABSTRACTING AND INDEXING SERVICES

Biological and Agricultural Index. H.W. Wilson Co., 950 University Ave., Bronx, New York 10452. (800) 367-6770. 1916-. Monthly.

Bulletin Signaletique: Eau et Assainissement, Pollution Atmospherique, Droit des Pollutions. Centre de Documentation, Centre National de la Recherche Scientifique, 15, quai Anatole France, Paris, France 75700. (1) 45 55 92 25. 1983-. Monthly. Indexes pollution periodicals including water, atmospheric and related pollutions.

Environment Abstracts. Bowker A & I Publishing, 121 Chanlon Rd., New Providence, New Jersey 07974. (908) 464-6800. 1974-.

Environment Index. Environment Information Center, Index Research Department, 124 E. 39th St., New York, New York 10016. 1971-. Annual.

Environmental Information Connection–EIC. Planning Information Program, Dept. of Urban and Regional Planning, University of Illinois, 1003 West Nevada, Urbana, Illinois 61801. (217) 333-1369. Also available online.

Environmental Periodicals Bibliography. Environmental Studies Institute, International Academy at Santa Barbara, 800 Garden St., Suite D, Santa Barbara, California 93101. (805) 965-5010. Also available online.

Ergonomics Abstracts. Taylor & Francis, 4 John St., London, England WC1N 2ET. 1990-. Bimonthly. Provides details on recent additions to the international literature on human factors in human-machine systems and physical environmental influences.

Geographical Abstracts. London School of Economics, Dept. of Geography, Regency House, 34 Duke St., London, England 1966-. Continued by Geo Abstracts issued in 6 parts: Pt. A. Landforms and the quaternary; Pt. B. Biogeography and Climatology; Pt. C. Economic geography; Pt. D. Social geography and cartography; Pt. E. Sedimentology; Pt. F. Regional and community planning.

Index to Scientific Book Contents. Institute for Scientific Information, 3501 Market St., Philadelphia, Pennsylvania 19104. (800) 523-1857. 1985-. Annual. Gives contents of science books published.

Pollution Abstracts. Cambridge Scientific Abstracts, 5161 River Rd., Bethesda, Maryland 20816. (301) 961-6750. Six/year. Indexes worldwide technical literature on environmental pollution. Covers air pollution, marine and freshwater pollution, sewage and wastewater treatment, waste management, toxicology and health, noise pollution, radiation, land pollution, and environmental policies, programs, legislation, and education. Also available online.

Science Citation Index. Institute for Scientific Information, 3501 Market St., Philadelphia, Pennsylvania 19104. 1961-.

Selected References on Environmental Quality as It Relates to Health. National Library of Medicine, 8600 Rockville Pike, Bethesda, Maryland 20894. (800) 638-8480. 1977.

BIBLIOGRAPHIES

EPA Publications Bibliography. U.S. Environmental Protection Agency, Library Systems Branch, 401 M St., SW, Washington, District of Columbia 20460. (202) 260-2090. Quarterly.

DIRECTORIES

Who's Who in Environmental Engineering. American Academy of Environmental Engineers, 132 Holiday Court, Suite 206, Annapolis, Maryland 21401. (301) 266-3311. 1980. Annual. Directory of environmental engineers who are certified by the academy.

ENCYCLOPEDIAS AND DICTIONARIES

Dictionary of Environmental Engineering and Related Sciences: English-Spanish, Spanish-English. Jose T. Villate. Ediciones Universal, 3090 SW 8th St., Miami, Florida 33135. (305) 642-3355. 1979.

Encyclopedia of Environmental Science and Engineering. J.R. Pfafflin. Gordon and Breach Science Publishers, Inc., 270 8th Ave., New York, New York 10011. (212) 206-8900. 1992.

Encyclopedia of Occupational Health and Safety. Luigi Parmeggiani. International Labour Office, 49 Sheridan Ave., Albany, New York 12210. (518) 436-9686. 1983. Reference work concerned with workers' safety and health, information for those with no specialized medical or with technical knowledge.

McGraw-Hill Encyclopedia of Environmental Science. Sybil P. Parker. McGraw-Hill Science & Engineering Books, 11 W. 19th St., New York, New York 10011. (212) 337-6010. 1980. Covers ecology, man's influence on nature, and environmental protection.

GENERAL WORKS

Analyses of Hazardous Substances in Biological Materials. J. Angere, ed. VCH Publishers, 303 NW 12th Ave., Deerfield Beach, Florida 33442-1788. (305) 428-5566. 1991. Discusses industrial hygiene and the various toxic substances involved.

Carcinogens in Industry and the Environment. James M. Sontag, ed. M. Dekker, 270 Madison Ave., New York, New York 10016. (212) 696-9000. 1981. Environmentally induced diseases and industrial hygiene.

Chemical Hazards of the Work Place. Nick H. Proctor and edited by Gloria J. Hathaway, et al. Van Nostrand Reinhold, 115 5th Ave., New York, New York 10003. (212) 254-3232. 1991. 3d ed.

Computers in Health and Safety. American Industrial Hygiene Association, 345 White Pond Dr., Akron, Ohio 44320. (216) 873-2442. 1990. Presents state-of-the-art computer applications specifically directed toward high-lighting better ways of maintaining, manipulating, and disseminating information in the field of industrial hygiene.

Dangerous Premises: An Insider's View of OSHA Enforcement. ILR Press, Cornell University, Ithaca, New York 14851. (607) 255-3061. Grouped by hazard: asbestos, solvents, lead, noise, carbon monoxide, and formaldehyde.

Ecology and Management of Food Industry Pests. J. Richard Gorham. AOAC International, 2200 Wilson Blvd., Suite 400, Arlington, Virginia 22201-3301. (703) 522-3032.

Fire Protection Management for Hazardous Materials. Byron L. Briese, ed. Government Institutes, Inc., 4 Research Pl., Suite 200, Rockville, Maryland 20850. (301) 921-2300. 1991. Designed as a guide to the industry, this manual gives standard fire and building codes and a framework needed to manage the federal, state and local requirements and the specific technical needs of the individual facility.

Safety in the Use of Asbestos. International Labour Office, 49 Sheridan Ave., Albany, New York 12210. (518) 436-9686. 1990. An ILO code of practice. The first part of the code includes monitoring in the work place, preventive measures, the protection and supervision of the workers' health, and the packaging, handling, transport and disposal of asbestos waste. More detailed guidance on the limitation of exposure to asbestos in specific activities is given in the second part of the code, which includes sections on mining and milling, asbestos cement, textiles, friction materials, and the removal of asbestos-containing materials.

Safety in the Use of Mineral and Synthetic Fibers. International Labour Office, 49 Sheridan Ave., Albany, New York 12210. (518) 436-9686. 1990. Working document for, and report of, a meeting of experts set up by the ILO to study the questions contained in this book, including discussions of man-made fibers, natural mineral fibers other than asbestos, and synthetic organic fibers. The meeting defined certain preventive measures based on adopting safe working methods, controlling the working environment and the exposure of workers to mineral and synthetic fibers, and monitoring the health of the workers.

The Solution to Pollution in the Workplace. Laurence Sombke, et al. MasterMedia, 17 E. 89th St., New York, New York 10028. (212) 348-2020. 1991. Non-technical guidebook for cost-effective, practical tips and actions to help businesses, big and small, take a proactive role in solving pollution problems.

GOVERNMENTAL ORGANIZATIONS

Centers for Disease Control: National Institute for Occupational Safety and Health. D-36, 1600 Clifton Rd. N.E., Atlanta, Georgia 30333. (404) 639-3771.

Occupational Safety and Health Administration: Assistant Secretary for Occupational Safety and Health. 200 Constitution Ave., N.W., Washington, District of Columbia 20210. (202) 523-7162.

Occupational Safety and Health Administration: Directorate of Administrative Programs. 200 Constitution Ave., N.W., Washington, District of Columbia 20210. (202) 523-8576.

Occupational Safety and Health Administration: Directorate of Federal- State Operations. 200 Constitution Ave., N.W., Washington, District of Columbia 20210. (202) 523-7251.

Occupational Safety and Health Administration: Directorate of Health Standards Programs. 200 Constitution Ave., N.W., Washington, District of Columbia 20210. (202) 523-7075.

Occupational Safety and Health Administration: Information, Consumer Affairs and Freedom of Information. 200 Constitution Ave., N.W., Washington, District of Columbia 20210. (202) 523-8148.

Occupational Safety and Health Administration: Publications Office. 200 Constitution Ave., N.W., Room N3101, Washington, District of Columbia 20210. (202) 523-9668.

HANDBOOKS AND MANUALS

Chemical Information Manual. Government Institutes, Inc., 4 Research Pl., Ste. 200, Rockville, Maryland 20850. (301) 921-2300. 1991. Handbook presenting a variety of useful data on each chemical substances, including proper identification, OSHA exposure limits, description and physical properties, carcinogenic status, health effects and toxicology, sampling and analysis.

CRC Handbook of Chemistry and Physics. CRC Press, 2000 Corporate Blvd. N.W., Boca Raton, Florida 33431. (407) 994-0555; (800) 272-7737. 1988. 67th ed.

Documentation of the Threshold Limit Values. American Conference of Governmental Industrial Hygienists, 6500 Glenway, Building D-5, Cincinnati, Ohio 45211. 1991. Provides threshold limit value documentation for any physical phenomenon in the environment, including chemical substances and physical agents.

Hazard Communication Guide: Federal & State Right-to-Know Standards. J. J. Keller & Associates, Inc., 3003 W. Breezewood, PO Box 368, Neenah, Wisconsin 54957-0368. (414) 722-2848. 1985. Deals with legal aspects of industrial hygiene, hazardous substances, and industrial safety.

Hygiene Guide Series. American Industrial Hygiene Association, 345 White Pond Dr., Akron, Ohio 44320. (216) 873-2442. 1955-. 1 v. (loose-leaf).

Laboratory Chemical Standards: The Complete OSHA Compliance Manual. Bureau of National Affairs, 1231 25th St. N.W., Washington, District of Columbia 20037. (800) 372-1033. 1990. OSHA's new lab standard applies to laboratories that use hazardous chemicals and requires a written plan that satisfies federal guidelines.

Synthetic Organic Chemicals. U.S. G.P.O., Washington, District of Columbia 20401. (202) 512-0000. 1967. An annual publication on production and sales in the U.S. for all synthetic organic chemicals produced commercially. About 800 chemicals and 800 manufacturers are included in the USITC surveys, but because of confidentiality requirements only parts of the data are published. U.S. Tariff Commission acts under the provisions of Section 332 of the Tariff Act of 1930, as amended.

ONLINE DATA BASES

CERCLIS. Chemical Information Systems, Inc., 7215 York Rd., Baltimore, Maryland 21212. (301) 321-8440. Information on hazardous waste disposal sites that have either been listed by the EPA on the National Priority List (NPL) or nominated for consideration for the NPL.

Chemical Engineering. McGraw-Hill Science & Engineering Books, 11 W. 19th St., New York, New York 10011. (212) 337-6010. Online version of periodical of the same name.

Chemical Engineering and Biotechnology Abstracts–CEBA. Orbit Search Service, Maxwell Online Inc., 8000 W. Park Dr., McLean, Virginia 22102. (703) 442-0900 or (800) 456-7248. Monthly. Covers theoretical, practical and commercial material on all aspects of processing safety, and the environment. Also covers process and reaction engineering, measurement and process control, environmental protection and safety, plant design and equipment used in chemical engineering and biotechnology. More than 400 of the world's major primary chemical and process engineering journals are scanned to compile the database. Available from ORBIT.

Enviro/Energyline Abstracts Plus. R. R. Bowker Co., 121 Chanlon Rd., New Providence, New Jersey 07974. (908) 464-6800.

Environment Reporter. Bureau of National Affairs, 1231 25th St., N.W., Rm. 215, Washington, District of Columbia 20037. (800) 372-1033. Online version of periodical of the same name.

Environmental Health News. Occupational Health Services, Inc., 450 7th Ave., New York, New York 10123. (212) 967-1100. Online access to court decisions, regulatory changes, and medical and scientific news related to hazardous substances.

Environmental Periodicals Bibliography. National Information Services Corp., Ste. 6, Wyman Towers, 3100 St. Paul St., Baltimore, Maryland 21218. (410)243-0797. Online version of abstract of same name.

Industrial Health & Hazards Update. Merton Allen Associates, P.O. Box 15640, Plantation, Florida 33318-5640. (305) 473-9560.

Monthly Catalog of United States Government Publications. U.S. G.P.O., Supt. of Docs., PO Box 371954, Pittsburgh, Pennsylvania 15250-7954. (202) 512-0000.

National Technical Information Service. U.S. Department of Commerce, National Technical Information Service, Office of Data Base Services, 5285 Port Royal Rd., Springfield, Virginia 22161. (703) 487-4807. Bibliographic database of government sponsored research and technical reports.

SCISEARCH. Institute for Scientific Information, University City Science Center, 3501 Market St., Philadelphia, Pennsylvania 19104. (215) 386-0100.

PERIODICALS AND NEWSLETTERS

AIPE Facilities: The Journal of Plant and Facilities Management & Engineering. American Institute of Plant Engineers, 3975 Erie Avenue, Cincinnati, Ohio 45208. (513) 561-6000. Bimonthly. Articles about the management of manufacturing facilities.

American Industrial Hygiene Association Journal. American Industrial Hygiene Association, 345 White Pond Drive, Akron, Ohio 44320. (216) 873-2442. Monthly. Reports relating to occupational and environmental health hazards.

American Industrial Hygiene Council Quarterly. American Industrial Health Council, 1330 Connecticut Avenue, NW, Suite 300, Washington, District of Columbia 20036. (202) 659-0060. Quarterly. Scientific issues related to proposed standards for regulating products.

Briefing. National Association of Manufacturers, 1331 Pennsylvania Avenue, NW, Suite 1500 North, Washington, District of Columbia 20004. (202) 637-3000. Weekly. Environmental issues as they relate to manufacturing.

Chemical & Engineering News. American Chemical Society, 1155 16th St. N.W., Washington, District of Columbia 20036. (800) 227-5558. Weekly. Cites technical and business developments in the chemical process industry.

Chemical Engineering. McGraw-Hill Science & Engineering Books, 11 W. 19th St., New York, New York 10011. (212) 337-6010. Monthly. Articles on new engineering techniques and equipment. Also available online.

Environment Reporter. Bureau of National Affairs, 1231 25th St. NW, Washington, District of Columbia 20037. (800) 372-1033. Weekly. Issues of pollution control and environmental activity. Also available online.

Environmental Health Letter. Business Publishers, Inc., 951 Pershing Dr., Silver Spring, Maryland 20910-4464. (301) 587-6300. 1961-. Biweekly. Covers areas such as: indoor air, asbestos health effects, toxic substances testing, health problems at wastewater plants, risk-based sludge rules, medical waste, developmental toxicity risk assessment, animal carcinogen tests, pesticide risk, air toxics, aerospace chemicals, lead, radionuclide emissions, state right-to-know statutes, and incinerator emissions.

Environmental Health News. University of Washington, School of Public Health, Dept. of Environmental Health, Seattle, Washington 98195. (206) 543-3222. Quarterly. Occupational health, air pollution and safety.

Environmental Science and Technology. American Chemical Society, 1155 16th St. N.W., Washington, District of Columbia 20036. (800) 227-5558. 1967-. Monthly. Contains research articles on various aspects of environmental chemistry, interpretative articles by invited experts and commentary on the scientific aspects of environmental management.

Industrial Hygiene News. Rimbach Publishing, Inc., 8650 Babcock Boulevard, Pittsburgh, Pennsylvania 15237. (412) 364-5366. Bimonthly. Covers new products, literature, and product briefs.

Industrial Safety and Hygiene News. Chilton Book Co., 201 King of Prussia Rd., Radnor, Pennsylvania 19089. (215) 964-4000. Monthly. Covers fire protection, security, and emergency first aid equipment.

Journal of Environmental Science and Health. Marcel Dekker, Inc., 270 Madison Ave., New York, New York 10016. (212) 696-9000. Bimonthly. Concerns pesticides, food contaminants, chemical carcinogens, and agricultural wastes.

Journal of Occupational Medicine. Williams & Wilkins, P.O. Box 64380, Baltimore, Maryland 21264. (301) 528-4105. Monthly. Issues on the maintenance and improvement of the health of workers.

Occupational Hazards. Penton Publishing Co., 1100 Superior Ave., Cleveland, Ohio 44114. (216) 696-7000. Monthly. Covers safety management and plant protection.

Occupational Health and Safety. Stevens Publishing Co., P.O. Box 2604, Waco, Texas 76714. (817) 776-9000. Monthly. Covers occupational health and safety.

Occupational Safety and Health Reporter. Bureau of National Affairs, 1231 25th St. NW, Washington, District of Columbia 20037. (202) 452-4200. Weekly. Covers federal safety and health standards, regulations, and policies. Also available online.

Synthetic Organic Chemical Manufacturers Association Newsletter. Synthetic Organic Chemical Manufacturers Association, 1330 Connecticut Avenue, NW, Washington, District of Columbia 20036. (202) 659-0060. Biweekly. Covers trade, environmental and safety issues.

STATISTICS SOURCES

OSHA Regulated Hazardous Substances: Health, Toxicity, Economic, and Technological Data. U.S. Occupational Safety and Health Administration. Noyes Publications, 120 Mill Rd., Park Ridge, New Jersey 07656. (201) 391-8484. 1990. Provides industrial exposure data and control technologies for more than 650 substances currently regulated, or candidates for regulation, by the Occupational Safety and Health Administration.

TRADE ASSOCIATIONS AND PROFESSIONAL SOCIETIES

American Industrial Health Council. 1330 Connecticut Ave., N.W., Suite 300, Washington, District of Columbia 20036. (202) 659-0060.

American Industrial Hygiene Association. 345 White Pond Dr., PO Box 8390, Akron, Ohio 44320. (216) 873-2442.

American Institute of Biological Sciences. 730 11th St., N.W., Washington, District of Columbia 20001-4521. (202) 628-1500.

Industrial Safety Equipment Association. 1901 N. Moore St., Arlington, Virginia 22209. (703) 525-1695.

National Association of Manufacturers. 1331 Pennsylvania Ave., N.W., Suite 1500 North, Washington, District of Columbia 20004. (202) 637-3000.

National Environmental Health Association. South Tower, 720 S. Colorado Blvd., #970, Denver, Colorado 80222. (303) 756-9090.

Synthetic Organic Chemical Manufacturers Association. 1330 Connecticut Ave., N.W., Suite 300, Washington, District of Columbia 20036. (202) 659-0060.

United States Operating Committee on ETAD. 1330 Connecticut Ave., N.W., Suite 300, Washington, District of Columbia 20036-1702. (202) 659-0060.

INDUSTRIAL NOISE
See: NOISE POLLUTION

INDUSTRIAL REFUSE
See also: FACTORY AND TRADEWASTE; WASTE DISPOSAL

ABSTRACTING AND INDEXING SERVICES

Applied Science and Technology Index. H.W. Wilson Co., 950 University Ave., Bronx, New York 10452. (800) 367-6770. Formerly Industrial Arts Index.

Aqualine Abstracts. Water Research Centre. c/o Pergamon Microforms International, Inc., Fairview Park, Elmsford, New York 10523. (914) 592-7720. 1927-. Contains some 8,000 records annually on water and wastewater technology. Covers all aspects of water, wastewater, associated engineering services and the aquatic environment. Over 600 periodicals, as well as books, reports and conference proceedings and other publications from water related institutions worldwide are scanned. Also available online.

Biological and Agricultural Index. H.W. Wilson Co., 950 University Ave., Bronx, New York 10452. (800) 367-6770. 1916-. Monthly.

Bulletin Signaletique: Eau et Assainissement, Pollution Atmospherique, Droit des Pollutions. Centre de Documentation, Centre National de la Recherche Scientifique, 15, quai Anatole France, Paris, France 75700. (1) 45 55 92 25. 1983-. Monthly. Indexes pollution periodicals including water, atmospheric and related pollutions.

Chemical Abstracts. Chemical Abstracts Service, 2540 Olentangy River Rd., PO Box 3012, Columbus, Ohio 43210. (800) 848-6533. 1907-.

Engineering Index. The Engineering Index Inc., 345 E. 47th St., New York, New York 10017. 1962-.

Environment Abstracts. Bowker A & I Publishing, 121 Chanlon Rd., New Providence, New Jersey 07974. (908) 464-6800. 1974-.

Environment Index. Environment Information Center, Index Research Department, 124 E. 39th St., New York, New York 10016. 1971-. Annual.

Environmental Information Connection-EIC. Planning Information Program, Dept. of Urban and Regional Planning, University of Illinois, 1003 West Nevada,

Urbana, Illinois 61801. (217) 333-1369. Also available online.

Environmental Periodicals Bibliography. Environmental Studies Institute, International Academy at Santa Barbara, 800 Garden St., Suite D, Santa Barbara, California 93101. (805) 965-5010. Also available online.

General Science Index. H. W. Wilson Co., 950 University Ave., Bronx, New York 10452. 1978-. Monthly, also issued in annual cumulation. Cumulative subject index to English language periodicals in the subject fields of astronomy, botany, chemistry, earth science, environment and conservation, food and nutrition, genetics, mathematics, medicine and health, microbiology, oceanography, physics, physiology and zoology.

Index to Scientific Book Contents. Institute for Scientific Information, 3501 Market St., Philadelphia, Pennsylvania 19104. (800) 523-1857. 1985-. Annual. Gives contents of science books published.

Metals Abstracts. ASM International, 9639 Kinsman, Materials Park, Ohio 44073. (216) 338-5151. 1968-. Published jointly by the Institute of Metals, London and the American Society for Metals. Formed by the Union of Metallurgical Abstracts and Review of Metal Literature.

Pollution Abstracts. Cambridge Scientific Abstracts, 5161 River Rd., Bethesda, Maryland 20816. (301) 961-6750. Six/year. Indexes worldwide technical literature on environmental pollution. Covers air pollution, marine and freshwater pollution, sewage and wastewater treatment, waste management, toxicology and health, noise pollution, radiation, land pollution, and environmental policies, programs, legislation, and education. Also available online.

Science Citation Index. Institute for Scientific Information, 3501 Market St., Philadelphia, Pennsylvania 19104. 1961-.

BIBLIOGRAPHIES

Chemical Plant Wastes: A Bibliography. Vance Bibliographies, PO Box 229, 112 N. Charter St., Monticello, Illinois 61856. (217) 762-3831.

EPA Publications Bibliography. U.S. Environmental Protection Agency, Library Systems Branch, 401 M St., SW, Washington, District of Columbia 20460. (202) 260-2090. Quarterly.

DIRECTORIES

Industrial and Hazardous Waste Management Firms. Environmental Information Ltd., 4801 W. 81st St., No. 119, Minneapolis, Minnesota 55437-1111. (612) 831-2473.

Northeast Industrial Waste Exchange Listings Catalog. 90 Presidential Plaza, Suite 122, Syracuse, New York 13202. (315) 422-6572. Quarterly.

ENCYCLOPEDIAS AND DICTIONARIES

Dictionary of Environmental Engineering and Related Sciences: English-Spanish, Spanish-English. Jose T. Villate. Ediciones Universal, 3090 SW 8th St., Miami, Florida 33135. (305) 642-3355. 1979.

Encyclopedia of Environmental Science and Engineering. J.R. Pfafflin. Gordon and Breach Science Publishers, Inc., 270 8th Ave., New York, New York 10011. (212) 206-8900. 1992.

McGraw-Hill Encyclopedia of Environmental Science. Sybil P. Parker. McGraw-Hill Science & Engineering Books, 11 W. 19th St., New York, New York 10011. (212) 337-6010. 1980. Covers ecology, man's influence on nature, and environmental protection.

The New York Times Encyclopedic Dictionary of the Environment. Paul Sarnoff. Quadrangle Books, New York, New York 1971. Focuses on state-of-the-art methods of pollution control, abatement, prevention and removal.

GENERAL WORKS

Borrowed Earth, Borrowed Time: Healing America's Chemical Wounds. Glenn E. Schweitzer. Plenum Press, 233 Spring St., New York, New York 10013-1578. (212) 620-8000; (800) 221-9369. 1991. Deals with chemical contamination and the problem of industrial dumping.

Fire Protection Management for Hazardous Materials. Byron L. Briese, ed. Government Institutes, Inc., 4 Research Pl., Suite 200, Rockville, Maryland 20850. (301) 921-2300. 1991. Designed as a guide to the industry, this manual gives standard fire and building codes and a framework needed to manage the federal, state and local requirements and the specific technical needs of the individual facility.

Hazardous and Industrial Wastes, 1990. Joseph P. Martin, et al., eds. Technomic Publishing Co., 851 Holland Ave., Box 3535, Lancaster, Pennsylvania 17604. (717) 291-5609. 1990. Proceedings of the 22nd Mid-Atlantic Industrial Waste Conference, June 24-27, 1990, Drexel University, Philadelphia, PA. Fifty-one new reports on developments in industrial and hazardouswaste management, technology and regulation were presented.

Hazardous and Industrial Wastes, 1991. Technomic Publishing Co., 851 New Holland Ave., Box 3535, Lancaster, Pennsylvania 17604. (717) 291-5609. 1991. Proceedings of the 23rd Mid-Atlantic Industrial Waste Conference held at Drexel University, 1991.

Incinerating Municipal and Industrial Waste; Fireside Problems and Prospects for Improvement. Richard W. Bryers. Hemisphere, 79 Madison Ave., Suite 1110, New York, New York 10016. (212) 725-1999; (800) 821-8312. 1991. Addresses the causes and possible cures for corrosion and deposits due to impurities in the combustion of industrial and municipal refuse.

Industrial Waste Gases: Utilization and Minimization. RCG/Hagler Bailly Inc. Technomic Publishing Co., 851 New Holland Ave., Box 3535, Lancaster, Pennsylvania 17604. (717) 291-5609. 1990. Also released under title Industrial Waste Gas Management. Deals with factory and trade waste and the effluents that are released into the atmosphere.

Metal-Bearing Waste Streams: Mining, Recycling, and Treatment. Michael Meltzer, et al. Noyes Publications, 120 Mill Rd., Park Ridge, New Jersey 07656. (201) 391-8484. 1990. Examines the management of metal-bearing wastes. Covers an in-depth industry study of the generation of metal-bearing waste streams. Summaries of waste management practices in various metal operations, including foundry activities, metal cleaning and stripping, surface treatment and plating, coating, and auxiliary operations, are provided.

Metal Recovery from Industrial Waste. Clyde S. Brooks. Lewis Publishers, 2000 Corporate Blvd., N.W., Boca Raton, Florida 33431. (407) 994-0555 or (800) 272-7737. 1991. Gives details of industrial waste recycling in particular nonferrous metals.

New Developments in Industrial Wastewater Treatment. Aysen Turkman, ed. Kluwer Academic Publishers, 101 Philip Dr., Assinippi Park, Norwell, Massachusetts 02061-0358. (617) 871-6600. 1991. NATO Advanced Research Workshop, Oct-Nov. 1989.

Packaging and the Environment: Alternatives, Trends, and Solutions. Susan E. M. Selke. Technomic Publishing Co., 851 New Holland Ave., Box 3535, Lancaster, Pennsylvania 17604. (717) 291-5609. 1990. Review of the contribution of packaging to various environmental problems.

Proceedings of the 45th Industrial Waste Conference, May 1990 at Purdue University. Ross A. Duckworth. Lewis Publishers, 2000 Corporate Blvd., N.W., Boca Raton, Florida 33431. (407) 994-0555 or (800) 272-7737. 1991. Subject areas included in the conference were: site remediation, hazardous waste minimization and treatment, biological systems, aerobic processes, anaerobic processes, sludge treatment, respirometry, new processes, equipment, and applications.

Serious Reduction of Hazardous Waste: Summary. Congress of the U.S., c/o U.S. Government Printing Office, Office of Technology Assessment, N. Capitol & H Sts. NW, Washington, District of Columbia 20401. (202) 512-0000. 1986. Deals with waste reduction from factories and air pollution control.

Toxicology of Inhaled Materials. I.Y.R. Adamson. Springer-Verlag, 175 5th Ave., New York, New York 10010. (212) 460-1500. 1985. General principles of inhalation toxicology.

HANDBOOKS AND MANUALS

Industrial and Hazardous Waste Treatment. Nelson Leonard Nemerow and Avijit Dasgupta. Van Nostrand Reinhold, 115 5th Ave., New York, New York 10003. (212) 254-3232. 1991. Factory and trade waste, and hazardous waste purification.

Managing Industrial Hazardous Waste–Practical Handbook. Gary F. Lindgren. Lewis Publishers, 2000 Corporate Blvd., N.W., Boca Raton, Florida 33431. (407) 994-0555 or (800) 272-7737. 1989. Explains the regulations regarding identification and listing of hazardous wastes.

Superfund Manual: Legal and Management Strategies. Crowell & Moring. Government Institutes, Inc., 4 Research Pl., Suite 200, Rockville, Maryland 20850. (301) 921-2300. 1990. 4th ed. Industrial liability for hazardous waste and pollution damage at hazardous waste sites are explained. Explains the latest developments in the Superfund program. Includes the interrelationships between Superfund and RCRA; new regulations to implement Emergency Planning and the Community Right-to-Know Act; revisions to the National Contingency Plan; new EPA guidance documents relating to cleanup standards, site studies, and settlement procedures; court decisions and the special problems.

ONLINE DATA BASES

CERCLIS. Chemical Information Systems, Inc., 7215 York Rd., Baltimore, Maryland 21212. (301) 321-8440. Information on hazardous waste disposal sites that have either been listed by the EPA on the National Priority List (NPL) or nominated for consideration for the NPL.

Chemical Abstracts-CA. Chemical Abstracts Service, 2540 Olentangy River Rd., P.O. Box 3012, Columbus, Ohio 43210. (800) 848-6533 or (614) 421-3600. Information sources include 9000 journals, patents from 27 countries, two industrial property organizations, new books, conference proceedings, and government research reports.

The Chemical Monitor. NewsNet, Inc., 945 Haverford Rd., Bryn Mawr, Pennsylvania 19010. (800) 345-1301.

Computerized Engineering Index–COMPENDEX. Engineering Information Inc., 345 E. 47th St., New York, New York 10017. (212) 705-7600.

Enviro/Energyline Abstracts Plus. R. R. Bowker Co., 121 Chanlon Rd., New Providence, New Jersey 07974. (908) 464-6800.

Environmental Periodicals Bibliography. National Information Services Corp., Ste. 6, Wyman Towers, 3100 St. Paul St., Baltimore, Maryland 21218. (410)243-0797. Online version of abstract of same name.

Monthly Catalog of United States Government Publications. U.S. G.P.O., Supt. of Docs., PO Box 371954, Pittsburgh, Pennsylvania 15250-7954. (202) 512-0000.

National Technical Information Service. U.S. Department of Commerce, National Technical Information Service, Office of Data Base Services, 5285 Port Royal Rd., Springfield, Virginia 22161. (703) 487-4807. Bibliographic database of government sponsored research and technical reports.

Report on Defense Plant Wastes. Business Publishers, Inc., 951 Pershing Dr., Silver Spring, Maryland 20910-4464. (301) 587-6300. Laws, regulations, cleanup actions, contracts, and court actions affecting U.S. defense, weapons production, government hospitals and laboratories, and other government institutions. Online version of periodical of the same name.

PERIODICALS AND NEWSLETTERS

AIPE Facilities: The Journal of Plant and Facilities Management & Engineering. American Institute of Plant Engineers, 3975 Erie Avenue, Cincinnati, Ohio 45208. (513) 561-6000. Bimonthly. Articles about the management of manufacturing facilities.

Federal Water Quality Association Newsletter. Federal Water Quality Association, P.O. Box 44163, Washington, District of Columbia 20026. (202) 447-4925. Seven times a year. Concerns sewage and industrial waste treatment and disposal.

Official Bulletin of the North Dakota Water and Pollution Control Conference. North Dakota State Health Dept., Bismarck, North Dakota 58501. (701) 224-2354. Quarterly. Municipal water and waste systems and industrial wastes.

Report on Defense Plant Wastes. Business Publishers, Inc., 951 Pershing Dr., Silver Spring, Maryland 20910-4464. (301) 587-6300. 1989-. Biweekly. Reports on environmental laws, regulations, cleanups, contracts and court actions affecting U.S. defense weapons production, government hospitals and other government institutions. Also available online.

Waste Treatment Technology News. Business Communications Company, Inc., 25 Van Zant Street, Norwalk, Connecticut 06855. (203) 853-4266. Monthly. Covers effective management and handling of hazardous wastes.

Water and Wastes Digest. Scranton Gillette Communications, Inc., 380 Northwest Highway, Des Plaines, Illinois 60016. (708) 298-6622. Bimonthly. Covers publicly and privately owned water and sewage systems.

RESEARCH CENTERS AND INSTITUTES

University of Alabama, Alabama Waste Exchange. P.O. Box 870203, Tuscaloosa, Alabama 35487. (205) 348-5889.

STATISTICS SOURCES

Incineration of Industrial Wastes. FIND/SVP, 625 Avenue of the Americas, New York, New York 10011. (212) 645-4500. 1990. Present state of incineration technology–liquid injection, fume, fixed hearth, multiple hearth, rotary kiln, fluidized bed, circulating bed, infrared, plasma-arc, mobile/transportable, oxygen-enhanced, auxiliary systems–as well as emerging technologies.

TRADE ASSOCIATIONS AND PROFESSIONAL SOCIETIES

American Industrial Health Council. 1330 Connecticut Ave., N.W., Suite 300, Washington, District of Columbia 20036. (202) 659-0060.

American Industrial Hygiene Association. 345 White Pond Dr., PO Box 8390, Akron, Ohio 44320. (216) 873-2442.

Federal Water Quality Association. PO Box 44163, Washington, District of Columbia 20026. (202) 447-4925.

Flexible Packaging Association. 1090 Vermont Ave., N.W., Suite 500, Washington, District of Columbia 20005. (202) 842-3880.

INDUSTRIAL SAFETY

ABSTRACTING AND INDEXING SERVICES

Biological and Agricultural Index. H.W. Wilson Co., 950 University Ave., Bronx, New York 10452. (800) 367-6770. 1916-. Monthly.

Chemical Abstracts. Chemical Abstracts Service, 2540 Olentangy River Rd., PO Box 3012, Columbus, Ohio 43210. (800) 848-6533. 1907-.

Environment Abstracts. Bowker A & I Publishing, 121 Chanlon Rd., New Providence, New Jersey 07974. (908) 464-6800. 1974-.

Environment Index. Environment Information Center, Index Research Department, 124 E. 39th St., New York, New York 10016. 1971-. Annual.

Environmental Information Connection–EIC. Planning Information Program, Dept. of Urban and Regional Planning, University of Illinois, 1003 West Nevada, Urbana, Illinois 61801. (217) 333-1369. Also available online.

Environmental Periodicals Bibliography. Environmental Studies Institute, International Academy at Santa Barbara, 800 Garden St., Suite D, Santa Barbara, California 93101. (805) 965-5010. Also available online.

General Science Index. H. W. Wilson Co., 950 University Ave., Bronx, New York 10452. 1978-. Monthly, also issued in annual cumulation. Cumulative subject index to English language periodicals in the subject fields of astronomy, botany, chemistry, earth science, environment and conservation, food and nutrition, genetics, mathematics, medicine and health, microbiology, oceanography, physics, physiology and zoology.

Index to Scientific Book Contents. Institute for Scientific Information, 3501 Market St., Philadelphia, Pennsylvania 19104. (800) 523-1857. 1985-. Annual. Gives contents of science books published.

BIBLIOGRAPHIES

EPA Publications Bibliography. U.S. Environmental Protection Agency, Library Systems Branch, 401 M St., SW, Washington, District of Columbia 20460. (202) 260-2090. Quarterly.

ENCYCLOPEDIAS AND DICTIONARIES

McGraw-Hill Encyclopedia of Environmental Science. Sybil P. Parker. McGraw-Hill Science & Engineering Books, 11 W. 19th St., New York, New York 10011. (212) 337-6010. 1980. Covers ecology, man's influence on nature, and environmental protection.

GENERAL WORKS

Employers and the Environmental Challenge. Harry Z. Evan. International Labour Organization, H, rue des Morillons, Geneva, Switzerland CH-1211. 1986. Industrial hygiene, industrial safety and environmental health.

NIOSH Certified Equipment List as of December 31, 1991. National Institute for Occupational Safety and Health, 1600 Clifton Rd. NE, Atlanta, Georgia 30333. (404) 639-3286. 1991. DHHS (NIOSH) Publication No. 91-105. This list of personal equipment that has been tested, approved and certified as safe by NIOSH is updated on an annual basis. Users should request the new list annually if they are not currently on the NIOSH publications mailing list.

ONLINE DATA BASES

Chemical Abstracts-CA. Chemical Abstracts Service, 2540 Olentangy River Rd., P.O. Box 3012, Columbus, Ohio 43210. (800) 848-6533 or (614) 421-3600. Information sources include 9000 journals, patents from 27 countries, two industrial property organizations, new books, conference proceedings, and government research reports.

Enviro/Energyline Abstracts Plus. R. R. Bowker Co., 121 Chanlon Rd., New Providence, New Jersey 07974. (908) 464-6800.

Environmental Periodicals Bibliography. National Information Services Corp., Ste. 6, Wyman Towers, 3100 St.

Paul St., Baltimore, Maryland 21218. (410)243-0797. Online version of abstract of same name.

Monthly Catalog of United States Government Publications. U.S. G.P.O., Supt. of Docs., PO Box 371954, Pittsburgh, Pennsylvania 15250-7954. (202) 512-0000.

National Technical Information Service. U.S. Department of Commerce, National Technical Information Service, Office of Data Base Services, 5285 Port Royal Rd., Springfield, Virginia 22161. (703) 487-4807. Bibliographic database of government sponsored research and technical reports.

INHALATION TOXICOLOGY

See also: TOXICOLOGY

ABSTRACTING AND INDEXING SERVICES

Biological and Agricultural Index. H.W. Wilson Co., 950 University Ave., Bronx, New York 10452. (800) 367-6770. 1916-. Monthly.

Environment Abstracts. Bowker A & I Publishing, 121 Chanlon Rd., New Providence, New Jersey 07974. (908) 464-6800. 1974-.

Environment Index. Environment Information Center, Index Research Department, 124 E. 39th St., New York, New York 10016. 1971-. Annual.

Environmental Information Connection–EIC. Planning Information Program, Dept. of Urban and Regional Planning, University of Illinois, 1003 West Nevada, Urbana, Illinois 61801. (217) 333-1369. Also available online.

Environmental Periodicals Bibliography. Environmental Studies Institute, International Academy at Santa Barbara, 800 Garden St., Suite D, Santa Barbara, California 93101. (805) 965-5010. Also available online.

BIBLIOGRAPHIES

EPA Publications Bibliography. U.S. Environmental Protection Agency, Library Systems Branch, 401 M St., SW, Washington, District of Columbia 20460. (202) 260-2090. Quarterly.

ENCYCLOPEDIAS AND DICTIONARIES

McGraw-Hill Encyclopedia of Environmental Science. Sybil P. Parker. McGraw-Hill Science & Engineering Books, 11 W. 19th St., New York, New York 10011. (212) 337-6010. 1980. Covers ecology, man's influence on nature, and environmental protection.

GENERAL WORKS

Annual Report–Inhalation Toxicology Research Institute. Lovelace Foundation for Medical Education and Research, 5400 Gibson S.E., Albuquerque, New Mexico 87108. (505) 262-7000. Annual.

Inhalation Toxicology. D. Dungworth. Springer-Verlag, 175 5th Ave., New York, New York 10010. (212) 460-1500. 1988.

Inhalation Toxicology of Air Pollution. Robert Frank. ASTM, 1916 Race St., Philadelphia, Pennsylvania 19103-1187. (215) 299-5400. 1985.

ONLINE DATA BASES

Enviro/Energyline Abstracts Plus. R. R. Bowker Co., 121 Chanlon Rd., New Providence, New Jersey 07974. (908) 464-6800.

Environmental Periodicals Bibliography. National Information Services Corp., Ste. 6, Wyman Towers, 3100 St. Paul St., Baltimore, Maryland 21218. (410)243-0797. Online version of abstract of same name.

Monthly Catalog of United States Government Publications. U.S. G.P.O., Supt. of Docs., PO Box 371954, Pittsburgh, Pennsylvania 15250-7954. (202) 512-0000.

National Technical Information Service. U.S. Department of Commerce, National Technical Information Service, Office of Data Base Services, 5285 Port Royal Rd., Springfield, Virginia 22161. (703) 487-4807. Bibliographic database of government sponsored research and technical reports.

INORGANIC COMPOUNDS

ABSTRACTING AND INDEXING SERVICES

Chemical Abstracts. Chemical Abstracts Service, 2540 Olentangy River Rd., PO Box 3012, Columbus, Ohio 43210. (800) 848-6533. 1907-.

Environment Abstracts. Bowker A & I Publishing, 121 Chanlon Rd., New Providence, New Jersey 07974. (908) 464-6800. 1974-.

Environment Index. Environment Information Center, Index Research Department, 124 E. 39th St., New York, New York 10016. 1971-. Annual.

Environmental Information Connection–EIC. Planning Information Program, Dept. of Urban and Regional Planning, University of Illinois, 1003 West Nevada, Urbana, Illinois 61801. (217) 333-1369. Also available online.

Environmental Periodicals Bibliography. Environmental Studies Institute, International Academy at Santa Barbara, 800 Garden St., Suite D, Santa Barbara, California 93101. (805) 965-5010. Also available online.

General Science Index. H. W. Wilson Co., 950 University Ave., Bronx, New York 10452. 1978-. Monthly, also issued in annual cumulation. Cumulative subject index to English language periodicals in the subject fields of astronomy, botany, chemistry, earth science, environment and conservation, food and nutrition, genetics, mathematics, medicine and health, microbiology, oceanography, physics, physiology and zoology.

Science Citation Index. Institute for Scientific Information, 3501 Market St., Philadelphia, Pennsylvania 19104. 1961-.

BIBLIOGRAPHIES

Electrochemical Synthesis of Inorganic Compounds: A Bibliography. Zoltan Nagy. Plenum Press, 233 Spring St.,

New York, New York 10013-1578. (212) 620-8000; (800) 221-9369. 1985.

EPA Publications Bibliography. U.S. Environmental Protection Agency, Library Systems Branch, 401 M St., SW, Washington, District of Columbia 20460. (202) 260-2090. Quarterly.

ENCYCLOPEDIAS AND DICTIONARIES

Dictionary of Inorganic Compounds. Chapman & Hall, 29 West 35th St., New York, New York 10001-2291. (212) 244-3336. 1991. Arranged by formula but not divided into element sections.

Ullmanns Encyclopedia of Industrial Chemistry. Hans Jurgen Arpe and Wolfgang Gerhartz, eds. VCH Publishers, 303 NW 12th Ave., Deerfield Beach, Florida 33442-1788. (305) 428-5566. 1990. Designed to keep up with the broad spectrum of chemical technology. Thirty-six volumes of the encyclopedia have been divided into two sets: the 28 A volumes contain alphabetically arranged articles on chemicals, product groups, processes and technological concepts; and the 8 B volumes are compendia of basic knowledge in industrial chemistry.

GENERAL WORKS

Handbook on Toxicity of Inorganic Compounds. Marcel Dekker Inc., 270 Madison Ave., New York, New York 10016. (212) 696-9000; (800) 228-1160. 1988. Environmental aspects of inorganic compounds.

Inorganic Contaminants in the Vadose Zone. Springer-Verlag, 175 5th Ave., New York, New York 10010. (212) 460-1500. 1989. Soil pollution and zone of aeration.

Inorganic Contaminants of Surface Water; Research and Monitoring Priorities. James W. Moore. Springer-Verlag, 175 Fifth Ave., New York, New York 10010. (212) 460-1500 or (800) 777-4643. 1991. Inorganic contaminants of surface water in terms of production, sources, and residues, chemistry, bioacculation, toxic effects to aquatic organisms, health effects and drinking water.

ONLINE DATA BASES

CAS Source Index–CASSI. Chemical Abstracts Service, 2540 Olentangy River Rd., P.O. Box 3012, Columbus, Ohio 43210. (800) 848-6533 or (614) 421-3600. A listing of bibliographic and library holdings information for scientific and technical primary literature relevant to the chemical sciences.

Chemical Abstracts–CA. Chemical Abstracts Service, 2540 Olentangy River Rd., P.O. Box 3012, Columbus, Ohio 43210. (800) 848-6533 or (614) 421-3600. Information sources include 9000 journals, patents from 27 countries, two industrial property organizations, new books, conference proceedings, and government research reports.

Chemical Collection System/Request Tracking–CCS/ RTS. U.S. Environmental Protection Agency, Office of Pesticides and Toxic Substances, 401 M St., SW, Washington, District of Columbia 20460. (202) 260-2090. Contains information on various properties of a number of chemicals including environmental effects, test and analysis methods, and health effects. Available from EPA.

Chemical Dictionary Online–CHEMLINE. Chemical Abstracts Service, 2540 Olentangy River Rd., Columbus, Ohio 43210. (614) 421-3600 or (800) 848-6533. Part of MEDLINE of the National Library of Medicine (NLM). File of 900,000 names for chemical substances, representing 450,000 unique compounds. It contains such information as Chemical Abstracts (CA) Service Registry Numbers, molecular formulas, preferred chemical nomenclature, and generic and ring structure information. Available on NLM's ELHILL system.

Chemical Engineering and Biotechnology Abstracts–CEBA. Orbit Search Service, Maxwell Online Inc., 8000 W. Park Dr., McLean, Virginia 22102. (703) 442-0900 or (800) 456-7248. Monthly. Covers theoretical, practical and commercial material on all aspects of processing safety, and the environment. Also covers process and reaction engineering, measurement and process control, environmental protection and safety, plant design and equipment used in chemical engineering and biotechnology. More than 400 of the world's major primary chemical and process engineering journals are scanned to compile the database. Available from ORBIT.

Chemical Exposure. Science Applications International Corp., Health & Environmental Information, P.O. Box 2501, Oak Ridge, Tennessee 37831. (615) 482-9031. Database of chemicals that have been identified in both human tissues and body fluids and in feral and food animals. Contains reference to journal articles, conferences, and reports. Covers the whole fields of information related to human and animal exposure to food, air, and water contaminants and pharmaceuticals. Its records include information on chemical properties, formulas, tissues measured, analytical method used, demographics and more. Available on DIALOG.

Enviro/Energyline Abstracts Plus. R. R. Bowker Co., 121 Chanlon Rd., New Providence, New Jersey 07974. (908) 464-6800.

Environmental Periodicals Bibliography. National Information Services Corp., Ste. 6, Wyman Towers, 3100 St. Paul St., Baltimore, Maryland 21218. (410)243-0797. Online version of abstract of same name.

TRADE ASSOCIATIONS AND PROFESSIONAL SOCIETIES

American Chemical Society. 1155 16th St., N.W., Washington, District of Columbia 20036. (202) 872-4600.

INORGANIC WASTES

See: WASTE DISPOSAL

INSECTICIDES

See also: PESTICIDES

ABSTRACTING AND INDEXING SERVICES

Biological Abstracts. BIOSIS, 2100 Arch St., Philadelphia, Pennsylvania 19103-1399. (215) 587-4800. 1927-.

Biological and Agricultural Index. H.W. Wilson Co., 950 University Ave., Bronx, New York 10452. (800) 367-6770. 1916-. Monthly.

Chemical Abstracts. Chemical Abstracts Service, 2540 Olentangy River Rd., PO Box 3012, Columbus, Ohio 43210. (800) 848-6533. 1907-.

Environment Abstracts. Bowker A & I Publishing, 121 Chanlon Rd., New Providence, New Jersey 07974. (908) 464-6800. 1974-.

Environment Index. Environment Information Center, Index Research Department, 124 E. 39th St., New York, New York 10016. 1971-. Annual.

Environmental Information Connection–EIC. Planning Information Program, Dept. of Urban and Regional Planning, University of Illinois, 1003 West Nevada, Urbana, Illinois 61801. (217) 333-1369. Also available online.

Environmental Periodicals Bibliography. Environmental Studies Institute, International Academy at Santa Barbara, 800 Garden St., Suite D, Santa Barbara, California 93101. (805) 965-5010. Also available online.

General Science Index. H. W. Wilson Co., 950 University Ave., Bronx, New York 10452. 1978-. Monthly, also issued in annual cumulation. Cumulative subject index to English language periodicals in the subject fields of astronomy, botany, chemistry, earth science, environment and conservation, food and nutrition, genetics, mathematics, medicine and health, microbiology, oceanography, physics, physiology and zoology.

Pollution Abstracts. Cambridge Scientific Abstracts, 5161 River Rd., Bethesda, Maryland 20816. (301) 961-6750. Six/year. Indexes worldwide technical literature on environmental pollution. Covers air pollution, marine and freshwater pollution, sewage and wastewater treatment, waste management, toxicology and health, noise pollution, radiation, land pollution, and environmental policies, programs, legislation, and education. Also available online.

Science Citation Index. Institute for Scientific Information, 3501 Market St., Philadelphia, Pennsylvania 19104. 1961-.

BIBLIOGRAPHIES

EPA Publications Bibliography. U.S. Environmental Protection Agency, Library Systems Branch, 401 M St., SW, Washington, District of Columbia 20460. (202) 260-2090. Quarterly.

Pesticide Applicator Training Materials: A Bibliography. Barbara O. Stommel. National Agricultural Library, 10301 Baltimore Blvd, Beltsville, Maryland 20705-2351. (301) 504-5755. 1991.

DIRECTORIES

European Directory of Agrochemical Products. H. Kidd and D. James, eds. Royal Society of Chemistry, c/o CRC Press, 2000 Corporate Blvd. N.W., Boca Raton, Florida 33431-9868. (800) 272-7737. 1990. Provides comprehensive information on over 26,000 agrochemical products currently manufactured, marketed or used in 25 European countries.

ENCYCLOPEDIAS AND DICTIONARIES

Encyclopedia of Human Biology. Renato Dulbecco, ed. Academic Press, c/o Harcourt Brace Jovanovich Inc.,

6277 Sea Harbor Dr., Orlando, Florida 32887. (800) 346-8648. 1991. Eight volumes.

Macmillan Dictionary of Toxicology. Ernest Hodgson, et al. Van Nostrand Reinhold, 115 5th Ave., New York, New York 10003. (212) 254-3232. 1988. Intended as a "starting point" to the literature of toxicology. American spelling is used with cross references to British version of words. Contains a list of references. Signed entries give explanatory definitions and cross references.

McGraw-Hill Encyclopedia of Environmental Science. Sybil P. Parker. McGraw-Hill Science & Engineering Books, 11 W. 19th St., New York, New York 10011. (212) 337-6010. 1980. Covers ecology, man's influence on nature, and environmental protection.

Van Nostrand's Scientific Encyclopedia. Glenn D. Considine, ed. Van Nostrand Reinhold, 115 5th Ave., New York, New York 10003. (212) 254-3232. 1983. Sixth edition. Includes all broad subject areas in science.

GENERAL WORKS

Bioassay of Malathion for Possible Carcinogenicity. National Cancer Institute, Division of Cancer Cause and Prevention, 9030 Old Georgetown Rd., Bethesda, Maryland 20892. (301) 496-7403. 1979. Adverse effects of malathion and carcinogens.

Chemistry of Pesticides. K. H. Buchel, ed. John Wiley & Sons, Inc., 605 3rd Ave., New York, New York 10158-0012. (212) 850-6000. 1983.

Environmental Fact Sheet: Risk/Benefit Balancing Under the Federal Insecticide, Fungicide, and Rodenticide Act. U.S. Environmental Protection Agency, Office of Pesticides and Toxic Substances, 401 M St. SW, Washington, District of Columbia 20460. (202) 260-2090. 1990.

Insecticides, Mechanisms of Action and Resistance. D. Otto and B. Weber, eds. VCH Publishers, 303 NW 12th Ave., Deerfield Beach, Florida 33442-1788. (305) 428-5566. 1991. Covers development of new concepts for ecologically-oriented plant protection. Latest applied research on commercial insecticides and pesticides. Reports on worldwide research.

Insecticides of Plant Origin. J. T. Armason, et al., eds. American Chemical Society, 1155 16th St. N.W., Washington, District of Columbia 20036. (202) 872-4600; (800) 227-5558. 1989. Describes all about biochemical pesticides past, present and future.

Materials Evaluated as Insecticides and Acaricides at Brownsville, TX, September, 1955 to June, 1961. B. A. Butt and J. C. Keller. Agricultural Research Service, U.S. Dept. of Agriculture, PO Box 96456, Washington, District of Columbia 20250. (202) 720-8999. 1964.

Microbial Toxins in Focus and Feeds. Albert E. Pohland, et al., eds. Plenum Press, 233 Spring St., New York, New York 10013. (212) 620-8000; (800) 221-9369. 1990. Proceedings of a Symposium on Cellular and Molecular Mode of Action of Selected Microbial Toxins in Foods and Feeds, Oct. 31- Nov. 2, 1988, Chevy Chase, MD.

Naturally Occurring Pest Bioregulators. Paul A. Hedin. American Chemical Society, 1155 16th St. NW, Washington, District of Columbia 20036. (202) 872-4600; (800) 227-5558. 1991. Symposium papers on naturally occurring biologically active chemicals grouped in five general sections: bioregulation of insect behavior and development; allelochemicals for control of insects and other animals; phytoalexins and phototoxins in plant pest control; mechanisms of plant resistance to insects; and allelochemicals as plant disease control agents.

Safer Insecticides: Development and Use. Marcel Dekker, Inc., 270 Madison Ave., New York, New York 10016. (212) 696-9000; (800) 228-1160. 1990. Communicates practical data for designing new insecticides, nontoxic to the environment and the public, and emphasizes optimal food production with safer insecticides.

HANDBOOKS AND MANUALS

Agricultural Chemicals. William Thomas Thomson. Thomson Publications, Box 9335, Fresno, California 93791. (209) 435-2163. 1991. Book 1: Insecticides and acaricides. Book 2: Herbicides. Book 3: Fumigants, growth regulators, repellents and rodenticides. Book 4: Fungicides.

The Agrochemicals Handbook. H. Kidd and D. Hartlet, eds. Royal Society of Chemistry, c/o CRC Press, 2000 Corporate Blvd., N.W., Boca Raton, Florida 33431-9868. (800) 272-7737. 1991. 3rd ed. Contains comprehensive worldwide information and data on substances which are active components of agriculture chemical products currently used in crop protection and pest control.

CRC Handbook of Chemistry and Physics. CRC Press, 2000 Corporate Blvd. N.W., Boca Raton, Florida 33431. (407) 994-0555; (800) 272-7737. 1988. 67th ed.

European Directory of Agrochemical Products. Royal Society of Chemistry, Thomas Graham House, Science Park, Milton Rd., Cambridge, England CB4 4WF. 1990. 4th ed. Volume 1: Fungicides. Volume 2: Herbicides. Volume 3: Insecticides. Volume 4: Growth regulators including rodenticides; molluscicides; nematicides; repellents and synerists.

Handbook of Environmental Data on Organic Chemicals. Karel Verschueren. Van Nostrand Reinhold, 115 5th Ave., New York, New York 10003. (212) 254-3232. 1983. Covers individual substances as well as mixtures and preparations. The profiles include: properties, air pollution factors, water pollution factors, and biological effects.

Hazardous Chemicals Data Book. G. Weiss, ed. Noyes Publications, 120 Mill Rd., Park Ridge, New Jersey 07656. (201) 391-8484. 1986. 2d ed. Supplies instant information on 1015 hazardous chemicals. The data will provide rapid assistance to personnel involved with handling of hazardous chemical materials and related accidents.

ONLINE DATA BASES

BIOSIS Previews. BIOSIS, 2100 Arch St., Philadelphia, Pennsylvania 19103-1399. (215) 587-4800. Largest and most comprehensive database of research in the life sciences. Contains citations for nearly 9000 primary research journals, monographs, reviews, symposia, preliminary reports, semi-popular journals, selected institutional reports, government reports and research communications.

Chemical Abstracts-CA. Chemical Abstracts Service, 2540 Olentangy River Rd., P.O. Box 3012, Columbus, Ohio 43210. (800) 848-6533 or (614) 421-3600. Information sources include 9000 journals, patents from 27 countries, two industrial property organizations, new

books, conference proceedings, and government research reports.

Enviro/Energyline Abstracts Plus. R. R. Bowker Co., 121 Chanlon Rd., New Providence, New Jersey 07974. (908) 464-6800.

Environmental Periodicals Bibliography. National Information Services Corp., Ste. 6, Wyman Towers, 3100 St. Paul St., Baltimore, Maryland 21218. (410)243-0797. Online version of abstract of same name.

Monthly Catalog of United States Government Publications. U.S. G.P.O., Supt. of Docs., PO Box 371954, Pittsburgh, Pennsylvania 15250-7954. (202) 512-0000.

National Technical Information Service. U.S. Department of Commerce, National Technical Information Service, Office of Data Base Services, 5285 Port Royal Rd., Springfield, Virginia 22161. (703) 487-4807. Bibliographic database of government sponsored research and technical reports.

SCISEARCH. Institute for Scientific Information, University City Science Center, 3501 Market St., Philadelphia, Pennsylvania 19104. (215) 386-0100.

PERIODICALS AND NEWSLETTERS

Aquatic Toxicology. Elsevier Science Publishing Co., 655 Avenue of the Americas, New York, New York 10010. (212) 989-5800. 1981-. 6/year.

Environmental Science and Technology. American Chemical Society, 1155 16th St. N.W., Washington, District of Columbia 20036. (800) 227-5558. 1967-. Monthly. Contains research articles on various aspects of environmental chemistry, interpretative articles by invited experts and commentary on the scientific aspects of environmental management.

Journal of Environmental Quality. American Society of Agronomy, 677 S. Segoe Rd., Madison, Wisconsin 53711-1086. (608) 273-8080. 1972-. Quarterly. Reports and brief reviews of agricultural ecology, environmental engineering and pollution.

STATISTICS SOURCES

World Resources. World Resources Institute. 1709 New York Ave., N.W., Washington, District of Columbia 20006. (202) 638-6300. Annual. Statistical and textual analysis of world's natural resources and the effects of growth-caused environmental pollution.

TRADE ASSOCIATIONS AND PROFESSIONAL SOCIETIES

American Chemical Society. 1155 16th St., N.W., Washington, District of Columbia 20036. (202) 872-4600.

INSECTS

ABSTRACTING AND INDEXING SERVICES

Biological Abstracts. BIOSIS, 2100 Arch St., Philadelphia, Pennsylvania 19103-1399. (215) 587-4800. 1927-.

Biological and Agricultural Index. H.W. Wilson Co., 950 University Ave., Bronx, New York 10452. (800) 367-6770. 1916-. Monthly.

Biology Digest. Data Courier, Plexus Pub Inc., 143 Old Marlton Pike, Medford, New Jersey 08055. 1974-. Monthly. Abstracts biology periodicals.

Ecological Abstracts. Geo Abstracts Ltd. Elsevier Applied Science, Crown House, Linton Rd., Barking, England IG 11 8JU. 1974-. Derived from over 600 leading ecological and environmental journals, plus books, conference proceedings, reports and theses.

Ecology Abstracts. Cambridge Scientific Abstracts, 5161 River Rd., Bethesda, Maryland 20816. (301) 961-6750. Monthly.

Environment Abstracts. Bowker A & I Publishing, 121 Chanlon Rd., New Providence, New Jersey 07974. (908) 464-6800. 1974-.

Environment Index. Environment Information Center, Index Research Department, 124 E. 39th St., New York, New York 10016. 1971-. Annual.

Environmental Information Connection–EIC. Planning Information Program, Dept. of Urban and Regional Planning, University of Illinois, 1003 West Nevada, Urbana, Illinois 61801. (217) 333-1369. Also available online.

Environmental Periodicals Bibliography. Environmental Studies Institute, International Academy at Santa Barbara, 800 Garden St., Suite D, Santa Barbara, California 93101. (805) 965-5010. Also available online.

General Science Index. H. W. Wilson Co., 950 University Ave., Bronx, New York 10452. 1978-. Monthly, also issued in annual cumulation. Cumulative subject index to English language periodicals in the subject fields of astronomy, botany, chemistry, earth science, environment and conservation, food and nutrition, genetics, mathematics, medicine and health, microbiology, oceanography, physics, physiology and zoology.

Genetics Abstracts. Cambridge Scientific Abstracts, 5161 River Rd., Bethesda, Maryland 20816. (301) 961-6750. 1968-. Monthly. Formerly published by Information Retrieval Ltd., London England. Published by Cambridge Scientific Abstracts since 1982.

Index to Scientific Book Contents. Institute for Scientific Information, 3501 Market St., Philadelphia, Pennsylvania 19104. (800) 523-1857. 1985-. Annual. Gives contents of science books published.

Review of Agricultural Entomology. C. A. B. International, 845 North Park Ave., Tucson, Arizona 85719. (602) 621-7897 or (800) 528-4841. 1990. Monthly. Abstracts of the world literature on: insects and other arthropods as pests of cultivated plants, forest trees and stored products, beneficial arthropods such as parasites and predators, slugs and snails as agricultural pests.

Science Citation Index. Institute for Scientific Information, 3501 Market St., Philadelphia, Pennsylvania 19104. 1961-.

BIBLIOGRAPHIES

EPA Publications Bibliography. U.S. Environmental Protection Agency, Library Systems Branch, 401 M St., SW, Washington, District of Columbia 20460. (202) 260-2090. Quarterly.

Pesticide Applicator Training Materials: A Bibliography. Barbara O. Stommel. National Agricultural Library,

10301 Baltimore Blvd, Beltsville, Maryland 20705-2351. (301) 504-5755. 1991.

ENCYCLOPEDIAS AND DICTIONARIES

Cambridge Dictionary of Biology. Peter M. B. Walker. Cambridge University Press, 40 W. 20th St., New York, New York 10011. (212) 924-3900 or (800) 227-0247. 1989. Includes 10,000 terms in zoology, botany, biochemistry, molecular biology and genetics. Previously published under the title Chambers Biology Dictionary.

Cambridge Encyclopedia of Life Sciences. A. E. Friday and David S. Ingram. Cambridge University Press, 40 W 20th St., New York, New York 10011. (212) 924-3900 or (800) 227-0247. 1985. Includes all topics under biology and ecology.

A Concise Dictionary of Biology. Elizabeth Martin, ed. Oxford University Press, 200 Madison Ave., New York, New York 10016. (212) 679-7300 or (800) 334-4249. 1990. New edition. Derived from the Concise Science Dictionary, published in 1984.

Encyclopedia of Human Biology. Renato Dulbecco, ed. Academic Press, c/o Harcourt Brace Jovanovich Inc., 6277 Sea Harbor Dr., Orlando, Florida 32887. (800) 346-8648. 1991. Eight volumes.

Grzimek's Animal Life Encyclopedia. Van Nostrand Reinhold, 115 5th Ave., New York, New York 10003. (212) 254-3232. 1975. Thirteen volumes. Includes lower animals, insects, mollusks, fishes, amphibians, reptiles, birds, and mammals.

McGraw-Hill Encyclopedia of Environmental Science. Sybil P. Parker. McGraw-Hill Science & Engineering Books, 11 W. 19th St., New York, New York 10011. (212) 337-6010. 1980. Covers ecology, man's influence on nature, and environmental protection.

McGraw-Hill Encyclopedia of Science and Technology. McGraw-Hill, 1221 Avenue of the Americas, New York, New York 10020. (212) 512-2000 or (800) 262-4729. 1992. Seventh edition. Issued in multiple volumes including index. Includes all science and technology broad subject areas.

Remarkable Animals: A Unique Encyclopedia of Wildlife Wonders. Guinness Books, 33 London Rd., Enfield, England EN2 6DJ. 1987. Includes mammals, birds, fishes, amphibians, reptiles, insects, and arachnids.

Van Nostrand's Scientific Encyclopedia. Glenn D. Considine, ed. Van Nostrand Reinhold, 115 5th Ave., New York, New York 10003. (212) 254-3232. 1983. Sixth edition. Includes all broad subject areas in science.

GENERAL WORKS

The Ants. Bert Holldobler and Edward O. Wilson. Harvard University Press, 79 Garden St., Cambridge, Massachusetts 02138. (617) 495-2600. 1990. Reviews the anatomy, physiology, social organization, ecology and natural history of ants. Illustrates each of 292 living genera of ants and provides taxonomic keys to them.

The Biogeography of Ground Beetles. G. R. Noonan, et al., eds. VCH Publishers, 303 NW 12th Ave., Deerfield Beach, Florida 33442-1788. (305) 428-5566. 1991. Book summarizes knowledge about the biogeography of ground beetles of mountains and islands. It describes a diverse group of ecologically divergent species from areas of special interest to biogeographers.

Chemical Ecology of Insects. William J. Bell. Chapman & Hall, 29 W. 35th St., New York, New York 10001-2291. (212) 244-3336. 1984.

Ecological Approach to Pest Management. David J. Horn. Guilford Press, 72 Spring St., New York, New York 10012. (212) 431-9800. 1987. Insect pests, food production and natural resources.

The Ecology of Aquatic Insects. Vincent H. Resh. Praeger Publishers, 1 Madison Ave., New York, New York 10010-3603. (212) 685-5300. 1984.

Environmental Physiology and Biochemistry of Insects. Klaus Hoffman. Springer-Verlag, 175 5th Ave., New York, New York 10010. (212) 460-1500. 1987. Physiology and ecology of insects.

Ground Beetles: Their Role in Ecological and Environmental Studies. Nigel E. Stork, ed. VCH Publishers, 303 NW 12th Ave., Deerfield Beach, Florida 33442-1788. (305) 428-5566. 1990. Summarizes the latest advances in the use of beetles in a range of ecological studies.

Insect Pest Management. David Dent. C. A. B. International, Oxon, Wallingford, England OX10 8DE. (44) 0491 3211. 1991.

Magill's Survey of Science. Life Science Series. Frank N. Magill, ed. Salem Press, PO Box 50062, Pasadena, California 91105. 1991. Six volumes. Contents: v.1. A-Central and peripheral nervous system functions; v.2. Central metabolism regulation - eukaryotic transcriptional control; v.3. Positive and negative eukaryotic transcriptional control - mammalian hormones; v.4. Hormones and behavior - muscular contraction; v.5. Muscular contraction and relaxation - sexual reproduction in plants; v.6. Reproductive behavior and mating - X inactivation and the Lyon hypothesis.

Naturally Occurring Pest Bioregulators. Paul A. Hedin. American Chemical Society, 1155 16th St. NW, Washington, District of Columbia 20036. (202) 872-4600; (800) 227-5558. 1991. Symposium papers on naturally occurring biologically active chemicals grouped in five general sections: bioregulation of insect behavior and development; allelochemicals for control of insects and other animals; phytoalexins and phototoxins in plant pest control; mechanisms of plant resistance to insects; and allelochemicals as plant disease control agents.

Population Dynamics of Forest Insects. VCH Publishers, 303 NW 12th Ave., Deerfield Beach, Florida 33442-1788. (305) 428-5566. 1990. Reviews the current research from an international Congress of delegates which covers population models, pest management and insect natural enemy interaction on forest insects. Topics include the effects of industrial air pollutants and acid rain as well as reviews of the biology and population dynamics of most major forest insects.

The Role of Ground Beetles in Ecological and Environmental Studies. Nigel E. Stork. Intercept, PO Box 716, Andover, England SP10 1YG. Ecology of carabidae and beetles.

Social Insects and the Environment. G. K. Veeresh, et al., eds. E. J. Brill, PO Box 9000, Leiden, Netherlands 2300 PA. 1990. Proceedings of the 11th International Congress of IUSSI, 1990. Includes 370 papers presented, and topics covered include: evolution of sociality, polygyny, social polymorphism, kin-recognition, foraging strategies, reproductive strategies, the biogeography and phycogenetics of bees and ants, pollination ecology and the management of pestiferous social insects.

Success and Dominance in Ecosystems. Edward O. Wilson. Ecology Institute, Nordbunte 23, Oldendorf/Luhe, Germany 1990. Proposes that the success of a species is measured by its evolutionary longevity and its dominance by its ability to dominate or control the appropriation of biomass and energy in ecosystems. Explores how and why social insects, representing only 2 percent of insect species but accounting for one-half of insect biomass, became the ecological center of terrestrial ecosystems. Much of the social insects success is attributed to their ability to function as highly structured superorganisms.

HANDBOOKS AND MANUALS

American Insects: A Handbook of the Insects of America North of Mexico. Ross H. Arnett. Van Nostrand Reinhold, 1115 5th Ave., New York, New York 10030. (212) 254-3232. 1985. General taxonomic introduction and includes classification of insects by common name, families, genus, generic name, distribution and pest species.

The Audubon Society Handbook for Butterfly Watchers. Robert Michael Pyle. Scribner Educational Publishers, 866 3d Ave., New York, New York 10022. (212) 702-2000 or (800) 257-5755. 1984. Generously illustrated includes line drawings as well as color photography. Includes information on: the size, species, life cycle, flight, habitat and range of existence of the butterflies.

Handbook of Insect Pheromones and Sex Attractants. Marion S. Meyer and John R. McLaughlin. CRC Press, 2000 Corporate Blvd., N.W., Boca Raton, Florida 33431. (800) 272-7737. 1991. Guide to the literature published before 1988 on chemicals that effect aggregation for mating and/or elicit sexual behavior in insects, mites and ticks.

ONLINE DATA BASES

BIOSIS Previews. BIOSIS, 2100 Arch St., Philadelphia, Pennsylvania 19103-1399. (215) 587-4800. Largest and most comprehensive database of research in the life sciences. Contains citations for nearly 9000 primary research journals, monographs, reviews, symposia, preliminary reports, semi-popular journals, selected institutional reports, government reports and research communications.

Cambridge Scientific Abstracts Life Science–CSAL. Cambridge Scientific Abstracts, 5161 River Rd., Bethesda, Maryland 20816. (301) 961-6750. Provides access to the following abstracting services: "Life Sciences Collection," "Aquatic Sciences and Fisheries Abstracts," "Oceanic Abstracts," and "Pollution Abstracts."

Enviro/Energyline Abstracts Plus. R. R. Bowker Co., 121 Chanlon Rd., New Providence, New Jersey 07974. (908) 464-6800.

Environmental Periodicals Bibliography. National Information Services Corp., Ste. 6, Wyman Towers, 3100 St. Paul St., Baltimore, Maryland 21218. (410)243-0797. Online version of abstract of same name.

SCISEARCH. Institute for Scientific Information, University City Science Center, 3501 Market St., Philadelphia, Pennsylvania 19104. (215) 386-0100.

PERIODICALS AND NEWSLETTERS

American Midland Naturalist. University of Notre Dame, Notre Dame, Indiana 46556. (219) 239-7481. Quarterly. Basic research in biology including animal and plant ecology, systematics and entomology, mammalogy, ichthyology, parasitology, invertebrate zoology, and limnology.

Environmental Entomology. Entomological Society of America, 9301 Annapolis Road, Lanham, Maryland 20706. (301) 731-4538. Bimonthly. Covers ecology and population dynamics.

Journal of Insect Behavior. Plenum Press, 233 Spring St., New York, New York 0013-1578. (212) 620-8000. Quarterly. Agricultural and biological aspects of insect behavior.

RESEARCH CENTERS AND INSTITUTES

Center for Advanced Invertebrate Molecular Sciences. Texas A & M University, College Station, Texas 77843-2475. (409) 845-9730.

Center for Molecular Biology. Wayne State University, 5047 Gullen Mall, Detroit, Michigan 48202. (313) 577-0616.

Florida Medical Entomology Laboratory. University of Florida, Institute of Food and Agricultural Sciences, 200 9th Street, S.E., Vero Beach, Florida 32962. (407) 778-7200.

Institute for Environmental Management. Western Illinois University, College of Arts and Sciences, Macomb, Illinois 61455. (309) 298-1266.

Institute of Arthropodology and Parasitology. Georgia Southern University, Biology Department, Landrum Box 8042, Statesboro, Georgia 30460-8042. (912) 681-5564.

Maurice T. James Entomological Collection. Washington State University, Department of Entomology, Pullman, Washington 99164-6432. (509) 335-5504.

Mosquito Control Research Laboratory. University of California, Berkeley, 9240 S. Riverbend Ave., Parlier, California 93648. (209) 891-2581.

Mosquito Research Program. University of California, Department of Entomology, Davis, California 95616. (916) 752-6983.

Pennsylvania State University, Frost Entomological Museum. Patterson Building, Department of Entomology, University Park, Pennsylvania 16802. (814) 863-2863.

R. M. Bohart Museum of Entomology. University of California, Davis, Department of Entomology, Davis, California 95616. (916) 752-0493.

Rockefeller University, Laboratory of Molecular Parasitology. 1230 York Ave., New York, New York 10021-6399. (212) 570-7571.

Southeastern Massachusetts University, Southeastern New England Clinical Microbiology Research Group. North Dartmouth, Massachusetts 02747. (508) 999-8320.

Temple University, Insect Biocontrol Center. Department of Biology, Philadelphia, Pennsylvania 19122. (215) 787-8843.

Texas A&M University, Pecan Insect Laboratory. Department of Entomology, College Station, Texas 77843. (409) 845-9757.

U.S. Forest Service, Forestry Sciences Laboratory. Carlton Street, Athens, Georgia 30602. (404) 546-2441.

U.S. Forest Service, Intermountain Research Station. 324 25th Street, Ogden, Utah 84401. (801) 625-5431.

U.S. Forest Service, North Central Forest Experiment Station. 1407 South Harrison Road, Suite 220, East Lansing, Michigan 48823. (517) 355-7740.

U.S. Forest Service, Rocky Mountain Forest and Range Experiment Station. 240 West Prospect Road, Fort Collins, Colorado 80526-2098. (303) 498-1126.

University of Arizona, Arizona Research Laboratories Division of Neurobiology. 611 Gould-Simpson Science Building, Tucson, Arizona 85721. (602) 621-6628.

University of Arizona, Center for Insect Science. Tucson, Arizona 85721. (602) 621-5769.

University of Georgia, Southeastern Cooperative Wildlife Disease. College of Veterinary Medicine, Athens, Georgia 30602. (404) 542-3000.

University of Kansas, Snow Entomological Museum. Snow Hall, Lawrence, Kansas 66045. (913) 864-3065.

University of Missouri-Columbia, Wilber R. Enns Entomology Museum. 1-87 Agriculture Building, Department of Entomology, Columbia, Missouri 65211. (314) 882-2410.

University of Nebraska-Lincoln, Harold W. Manter Laboratory of Parasitology. W529 Nebraska Hall West, Lincoln, Nebraska 68588-0514. (402) 472-3334.

University of Notre Dame, Vector Biology Laboratory. Notre Dame, Indiana 46556. (219) 239-7366.

University of South Carolina at Columbia, International Center for Public Health Research. Wedge Plantation, P.O. Box 699, McClellanville, South Carolina 29458. (803) 527-1371.

University of Texas at Arlington, Center for Parasitology. Box 19498, Arlington, Texas 76019. (817) 273-2423.

University of Texas at Austin, Brackenridge Field Laboratory. Lake Austin Boulevard, Austin, Texas 78712. (512) 471-7131.

University of Texas at Austin, Brues-Wheeler-Sellards Archives for Entomology and Paleoentomology. Texas Memorial Museum, 2400 Trinity Street, Austin, Texas 78705. (512) 471-4823.

University of Utah, Entomology Research Collections. Utah Museum of Natural History, President Circle, Salt Lake City, Utah 84112. (801) 581-6927.

USDA Biological Control of Insects Research Laboratory. P.O. Box 7629, Columbia, Missouri 65205. (314) 875-5361.

TRADE ASSOCIATIONS AND PROFESSIONAL SOCIETIES

American Entomological Society. 1900 Race St., Philadelphia, Pennsylvania 19103. (215) 561-3978.

American Institute of Biological Sciences. 730 11th St., N.W., Washington, District of Columbia 20001-4521. (202) 628-1500.

American Mosquito Control Association. Box 5416, Lake Charles, Louisiana 70606. (318) 474-2723.

American Registry of Professional Entomologists. 9301 Annapolis Rd., Lanham, Maryland 20706. (301) 731-4541.

American Society of Naturalists. Department of Ecology and Evolation, State University of New York, Stony Brook, New York 11794. (516) 632-8589.

American Society of Parasitologists. Department of Biological Sciences, 500 W. University Ave., University of Texas, El Paso, El Paso, Texas 79968. (915) 747-5844.

Association of Applied Insect Ecologists. 1008 10th St., Ste. 549, Sacramento, California 95814. (916) 392-5721.

Entomological Society of America. 9301 Annapolis Rd., Lanham, Maryland 20706-3115. (301) 731-4535.

INSULATION

ABSTRACTING AND INDEXING SERVICES

Applied Science and Technology Index. H.W. Wilson Co., 950 University Ave., Bronx, New York 10452. (800) 367-6770. Formerly Industrial Arts Index.

Engineering Index. The Engineering Index Inc., 345 E. 47th St., New York, New York 10017. 1962-.

Environment Abstracts. Bowker A & I Publishing, 121 Chanlon Rd., New Providence, New Jersey 07974. (908) 464-6800. 1974-.

Environment Index. Environment Information Center, Index Research Department, 124 E. 39th St., New York, New York 10016. 1971-. Annual.

Environmental Information Connection–EIC. Planning Information Program, Dept. of Urban and Regional Planning, University of Illinois, 1003 West Nevada, Urbana, Illinois 61801. (217) 333-1369. Also available online.

Environmental Periodicals Bibliography. Environmental Studies Institute, International Academy at Santa Barbara, 800 Garden St., Suite D, Santa Barbara, California 93101. (805) 965-5010. Also available online.

Pollution Abstracts. Cambridge Scientific Abstracts, 5161 River Rd., Bethesda, Maryland 20816. (301) 961-6750. Six/year. Indexes worldwide technical literature on environmental pollution. Covers air pollution, marine and freshwater pollution, sewage and wastewater treatment, waste management, toxicology and health, noise pollution, radiation, land pollution, and environmental policies, programs, legislation, and education. Also available online.

Science Citation Index. Institute for Scientific Information, 3501 Market St., Philadelphia, Pennsylvania 19104. 1961-.

ALMANACS AND YEARBOOKS

Annual Book of ASTM Standards. American Society for Testing and Materials, 1916 S. Race St., Philadelphia, Pennsylvania 19103. (215) 299-5585. 1991.

BIBLIOGRAPHIES

EPA Publications Bibliography. U.S. Environmental Protection Agency, Library Systems Branch, 401 M St., SW, Washington, District of Columbia 20460. (202) 260-2090. Quarterly.

Insulating Materials and Insulation. Mary Vance. Vance Bibliographies, PO Box 229, 112 N. Charter St., Monticello, Illinois 61856. (217) 762-3831. 1981.

DIRECTORIES

National Insulation and Abatement Contractors Association–Membership Directory and Buyer's Guide. 99 Canal Center Plaza, No. 222, Alexandria, Virginia 22314. (703) 683-6422. Annual.

ENCYCLOPEDIAS AND DICTIONARIES

Encyclopedia of Chemical Processing and Design. John J. Mcketta and W. A. Cunningham. Marcel Dekker, Inc., 270 Madison Ave., New York, New York 10016. (212) 696-9000; (800) 228-1160. 1992. Thirty-eight volumes.

Encyclopedia of Physical Science and Technology. Robert A. Meyers, ed. Academic Press, c/o Harcourt Brace Jovanovich Inc., 6277 Sea Harbor Dr., Orlando, Florida 32887. (800) 346-8648. Dictionary of engineering, technology and physical sciences.

Illustrated Encyclopedia of Science and the Future. Mike Biscare, et al., ed. Marshall Cavendish, 58 Old Compton St., London, England 0W1V5 PA. 01-734 6710. 1983. Twenty volumes. Each volume has 5 sections: Frontiers, Electronics in Action, Medical Science, Military Technology, and Resources.

Kirk-Othmer Encyclopedia of Chemical Technology. J. I. Kroschwitz, ed. John Wiley & Sons, Inc., 605 3rd Ave., New York, New York 10158-0012. (212) 850-6000. 1992-. All articles in the new edition have been rewritten and updated adding new subjects such as biotechnology, computer topics, analytical techniques and instrumentation, environmental concerns, fuels and energy, inorganic and solid state chemistry; composite materials and material science in general, and pharmaceuticals. Also available online.

Van Nostrand's Scientific Encyclopedia. Glenn D. Considine, ed. Van Nostrand Reinhold, 115 5th Ave., New York, New York 10003. (212) 254-3232. 1983. Sixth edition. Includes all broad subject areas in science.

HANDBOOKS AND MANUALS

Handbook of Thermal Insulation Design Economics for Pipes and Equipment. William Turner. Krieger Publishing Co., Inc., PO Box 9542, Melbourne, Florida 32902. (407) 724-9542. 1980. Topics in energy conservation.

Thermal Insulation Handbook. William Turner. McGraw-Hill Science & Engineering Books, 11 W. 19th St., New York, New York 10011. (212) 337-6010. 1981.

ONLINE DATA BASES

Computerized Engineering Index–COMPENDEX. Engineering Information Inc., 345 E. 47th St., New York, New York 10017. (212) 705-7600.

Enviro/Energyline Abstracts Plus. R. R. Bowker Co., 121 Chanlon Rd., New Providence, New Jersey 07974. (908) 464-6800.

Environmental Periodicals Bibliography. National Information Services Corp., Ste. 6, Wyman Towers, 3100 St. Paul St., Baltimore, Maryland 21218. (410)243-0797. Online version of abstract of same name.

Kirk-Othmer Encyclopedia of Chemical Technology. John Wiley & Sons, Inc., 605 3rd Ave., 5th Floor, New York, New York 10158. (212) 850-6000. Online version of the publication of the same name.

TRADE ASSOCIATIONS AND PROFESSIONAL SOCIETIES

International Association of Heat & Frost Insulators & Asbestos Workers. 1300 Connecticut Ave., N.W., Suite 505, Washington, District of Columbia 20036. (202) 785-2388.

INTEGRATED PEST MANAGEMENT (IPM)

See also: AGRICULTURE; BIOLOGICAL CONTROL; GENETIC RESISTANCE; ORGANIC GARDENING AND FARMING; PEST CONTROL

ABSTRACTING AND INDEXING SERVICES

Agrindex. AGRIS Coordinating Center, Via delle Terme di Caracalla, Rome, Italy I-00100. 61 0181-FA01. 1975-.

Applied Ecology Abstracts Studies in Renewable Natural Resources. Information Retrieval Ltd., 1911 Jefferson Davis Highway, Arlington, Virginia 22202. 1975-. Monthly.

Biological Abstracts. BIOSIS, 2100 Arch St., Philadelphia, Pennsylvania 19103-1399. (215) 587-4800. 1927-.

Biological and Agricultural Index. H.W. Wilson Co., 950 University Ave., Bronx, New York 10452. (800) 367-6770. 1916-. Monthly.

Biology Digest. Data Courier, Plexus Pub Inc., 143 Old Marlton Pike, Medford, New Jersey 08055. 1974-. Monthly. Abstracts biology periodicals.

Ecological Abstracts. Geo Abstracts Ltd. Elsevier Applied Science, Crown House, Linton Rd., Barking, England IG 11 8JU. 1974-. Derived from over 600 leading ecological and environmental journals, plus books, conference proceedings, reports and theses.

Environment Abstracts. Bowker A & I Publishing, 121 Chanlon Rd., New Providence, New Jersey 07974. (908) 464-6800. 1974-.

Environment Index. Environment Information Center, Index Research Department, 124 E. 39th St., New York, New York 10016. 1971-. Annual.

Environmental Information Connection–EIC. Planning Information Program, Dept. of Urban and Regional Planning, University of Illinois, 1003 West Nevada, Urbana, Illinois 61801. (217) 333-1369. Also available online.

Environmental Periodicals Bibliography. Environmental Studies Institute, International Academy at Santa Barbara, 800 Garden St., Suite D, Santa Barbara, California 93101. (805) 965-5010. Also available online.

General Science Index. H. W. Wilson Co., 950 University Ave., Bronx, New York 10452. 1978-. Monthly, also issued in annual cumulation. Cumulative subject index to English language periodicals in the subject fields of astronomy, botany, chemistry, earth science, environment and conservation, food and nutrition, genetics, mathematics, medicine and health, microbiology, oceanography, physics, physiology and zoology.

Index to Scientific Book Contents. Institute for Scientific Information, 3501 Market St., Philadelphia, Pennsylvania 19104. (800) 523-1857. 1985-. Annual. Gives contents of science books published.

Multimedia Index to Ecology. National Information Center for Educational Media, University of Southern California, Los Angeles, California 90007.

Pesticides Abstracts. U.S. Environmental Protection Agency, Office of Pesticides Programs, 345 Curtland, Atlanta, Georgia 30365. (404) 347-2864. 1981. Monthly. Formerly: Health Aspects of Pesticides Abstracts Bulletin.

Science Citation Index. Institute for Scientific Information, 3501 Market St., Philadelphia, Pennsylvania 19104. 1961-.

BIBLIOGRAPHIES

Current Contents. Agriculture, Biology and Environmental Sciences. Institute for Scientific Information, 3501 Market St., Philadelphia, Pennsylvania 19104. (800) 523-1857. 1973-. Previous title: Current Contents. Agricultural, Food & Veterinary Sciences. Gives the table of contents of periodicals in the fields of agriculture, biology, environmental and related areas.

EPA Publications Bibliography. U.S. Environmental Protection Agency, Library Systems Branch, 401 M St., SW, Washington, District of Columbia 20460. (202) 260-2090. Quarterly.

Integrated Pest Management. Jayne T. Maclean. National Agricultural Library, 10301 Baltimore Blvd., Beltsville, Maryland 20705-2351. (301) 504-5755. 1985.

A List of Publications Issued by the Consortium for Integrated Pest Management. Perry Adkisson. Consortium for Integrated Pest Management, New York, New York 1988.

ENCYCLOPEDIAS AND DICTIONARIES

Cambridge Encyclopedia of Life Sciences. A. E. Friday and David S. Ingram. Cambridge University Press, 40 W 20th St., New York, New York 10011. (212) 924-3900 or (800) 227-0247. 1985. Includes all topics under biology and ecology.

Grzimek's Encyclopedia of Ecology. Bernhard Grzimek. Van Nostrand Reinhold, 115 5th Ave., New York, New York 10003. (212) 254-3232. 1976.

McGraw-Hill Encyclopedia of Environmental Science. Sybil P. Parker. McGraw-Hill Science & Engineering

Books, 11 W. 19th St., New York, New York 10011. (212) 337-6010. 1980. Covers ecology, man's influence on nature, and environmental protection.

McGraw-Hill Encyclopedia of Science and Technology. McGraw-Hill, 1221 Avenue of the Americas, New York, New York 10020. (212) 512-2000 or (800) 262-4729. 1992. Seventh edition. Issued in multiple volumes including index. Includes all science and technology broad subject areas.

North American Reference Encyclopedia of Ecology and Pollution. William White. North American Pub. Co., 401 N. Broad St., Philadelphia, Pennsylvania 19108. (215) 238-5300. 1972.

Van Nostrand's Scientific Encyclopedia. Glenn D. Considine, ed. Van Nostrand Reinhold, 115 5th Ave., New York, New York 10003. (212) 254-3232. 1983. Sixth edition. Includes all broad subject areas in science.

GENERAL WORKS

Common Sense Pest Control. William Olkowski, et al. Tauton Pr., 63 South Main St., Box 5506, Newton, Connecticut 06740-5506. 1991. Discusses ways to manage other living organisms that are regarded as pests.

Ecological Theory and Integrated Pest Management Practice. Marcos Kogan. John Wiley & Sons, Inc., 605 3rd Ave., New York, New York 10158-0012. (212) 850-6000. 1986.

Insect Pest Management. David Dent. C. A. B. International, Oxon, Wallingford, England OX10 8DE. (44) 0491 3211. 1991.

Integrated Pest Management for the Home and Garden. Robert L. Metcalf. University of Illinois, Urbana, Illinois 61801. 1980.

Monitoring and Integrated Management of Arthropod Pests of Small Fruit Crops. N. J. Bostanian, et al., eds. VCH Publishers, 303 NW 12th Ave., Deerfield Beach, Florida 33442-1788. (305) 428-5566. 1990. Examines the population models, pest management and insect- natural enemy interactions of pests of small fruit crops. It covers topics of major importance to those who grow strawberries, cranberries and other fruit crops.

National Park Service Integrated Pest Management Information Packages. National Park Service, Biological Research Division, Washington, District of Columbia 20013. (202) 208-6843. 1984.

Tortricid Pests: Their Biology, Natural Enemies, and Control. L.P.S. van der Geest. Elsevier Science Publishing Co., 655 Avenue of the Americas, New York, New York 10010. (212) 989-5800. 1991.

HANDBOOKS AND MANUALS

Integrated Pest Management. ANR Publications, University of California, 6701 San Pablo Ave., Oakland, California 94608-1239. (510) 642-2431. 1990-. Irregular. Provides and orderly, scientifically based system for diagnosing, recording, evaluating, preventing, and treating pest problems in a variety of crops.

A Source Book on Integrated Pest Management. Mary Louise Flint. U.S. G.P.O., Washington, District of Columbia 20401. (202) 512-0000. 1977.

The Standard Pesticide User's Guide. Bert L. Bohmont. Prentice Hall, Rte. 9W, Englewood Cliffs, New Jersey 07632. (201) 592-2000. 1990. Includes material on laws and requirements, labeling, soil, groundwater, and endangered species. Covers new equipment, pumps, and techniques, as well as transportation, storage, decontamination, and disposal. Also covers integrated pest management.

UC IPM Pest Management Guidelines. ANR Publications, University of California, 6701 San Pablo Avenue, Oakland, California 94608-1239. (510) 642-2431. Official guidelines for monitoring techniques, pesticide use, and alternatives in agricultural crops.

ONLINE DATA BASES

BIOSIS Previews. BIOSIS, 2100 Arch St., Philadelphia, Pennsylvania 19103-1399. (215) 587-4800. Largest and most comprehensive database of research in the life sciences. Contains citations for nearly 9000 primary research journals, monographs, reviews, symposia, preliminary reports, semi-popular journals, selected institutional reports, government reports and research communications.

Cambridge Scientific Abstracts Life Science–CSAL. Cambridge Scientific Abstracts, 5161 River Rd., Bethesda, Maryland 20816. (301) 961-6750. Provides access to the following abstracting services: "Life Sciences Collection," "Aquatic Sciences and Fisheries Abstracts," "Oceanic Abstracts," and "Pollution Abstracts."

Enviro/Energyline Abstracts Plus. R. R. Bowker Co., 121 Chanlon Rd., New Providence, New Jersey 07974. (908) 464-6800.

Environmental Periodicals Bibliography. National Information Services Corp., Ste. 6, Wyman Towers, 3100 St. Paul St., Baltimore, Maryland 21218. (410)243-0797. Online version of abstract of same name.

Monthly Catalog of United States Government Publications. U.S. G.P.O., Supt. of Docs., PO Box 371954, Pittsburgh, Pennsylvania 15250-7954. (202) 512-0000.

National Technical Information Service. U.S. Department of Commerce, National Technical Information Service, Office of Data Base Services, 5285 Port Royal Rd., Springfield, Virginia 22161. (703) 487-4807. Bibliographic database of government sponsored research and technical reports.

PressNet Environmental Reports. Chemical Information Systems, Inc., 7215 York Rd., Baltimore, Maryland 21212. (301) 321-8440.

SCISEARCH. Institute for Scientific Information, University City Science Center, 3501 Market St., Philadelphia, Pennsylvania 19104. (215) 386-0100.

PERIODICALS AND NEWSLETTERS

Common Sense Pest Control Quarterly. Bio-Integral Resource Center, PO Box 7414, Berkeley, California 94707. (415) 524-2567. Four times a year. Least-toxic management of pests on indoor plants, pests that damage paper, controlling fleas and ticks on pets, and garden pests.

RESEARCH CENTERS AND INSTITUTES

Rutgers University, Mosquito Research and Control. P.O. Box 231, New Jersey Agricultural Experiment Station, New Brunswick, New Jersey 08903. (908) 932-9437.

Urban Pest Control Research Group. Virginia Polytech Institute and State University, Department of Entomology, Glade Road, Blacksburg, Virginia 24061. (703) 961-4045.

TRADE ASSOCIATIONS AND PROFESSIONAL SOCIETIES

American Institute of Biological Sciences. 730 11th St., N.W., Washington, District of Columbia 20001-4521. (202) 628-1500.

American Society of Naturalists. Department of Ecology and Evolation, State University of New York, Stony Brook, New York 11794. (516) 632-8589.

INTENSIVE AGRICULTURE (MONOCULTURE)

See also: AGRICULTURE

ABSTRACTING AND INDEXING SERVICES

Biological and Agricultural Index. H.W. Wilson Co., 950 University Ave., Bronx, New York 10452. (800) 367-6770. 1916-. Monthly.

Ecological Abstracts. Geo Abstracts Ltd. Elsevier Applied Science, Crown House, Linton Rd., Barking, England IG 11 8JU. 1974-. Derived from over 600 leading ecological and environmental journals, plus books, conference proceedings, reports and theses.

Environment Abstracts. Bowker A & I Publishing, 121 Chanlon Rd., New Providence, New Jersey 07974. (908) 464-6800. 1974-.

Environment Index. Environment Information Center, Index Research Department, 124 E. 39th St., New York, New York 10016. 1971-. Annual.

Environmental Information Connection–EIC. Planning Information Program, Dept. of Urban and Regional Planning, University of Illinois, 1003 West Nevada, Urbana, Illinois 61801. (217) 333-1369. Also available online.

Environmental Periodicals Bibliography. Environmental Studies Institute, International Academy at Santa Barbara, 800 Garden St., Suite D, Santa Barbara, California 93101. (805) 965-5010. Also available online.

Field Crop Abstracts. C. A. B. International, 845 North Park Ave., Tucson, Arizona 85719. (602) 621-7897 or (800) 528-4841. 1948-. Monthly. Covers literature on agronomy, field production, crop botany and physiology of all annual field crops, both temperate and tropical.

General Science Index. H. W. Wilson Co., 950 University Ave., Bronx, New York 10452. 1978-. Monthly, also issued in annual cumulation. Cumulative subject index to English language periodicals in the subject fields of astronomy, botany, chemistry, earth science, environment and conservation, food and nutrition, genetics,

mathematics, medicine and health, microbiology, oceanography, physics, physiology and zoology.

Geographical Abstracts. London School of Economics, Dept. of Geography, Regency House, 34 Duke St., London, England 1966-. Continued by Geo Abstracts issued in 6 parts: Pt. A. Landforms and the quaternary; Pt. B. Biogeography and Climatology; Pt. C. Economic geography; Pt. D. Social geography and cartography; Pt. E. Sedimentology; Pt. F. Regional and community planning.

Index to Scientific Book Contents. Institute for Scientific Information, 3501 Market St., Philadelphia, Pennsylvania 19104. (800) 523-1857. 1985-. Annual. Gives contents of science books published.

Science Citation Index. Institute for Scientific Information, 3501 Market St., Philadelphia, Pennsylvania 19104. 1961-.

BIBLIOGRAPHIES

Current Contents. Agriculture, Biology and Environmental Sciences. Institute for Scientific Information, 3501 Market St., Philadelphia, Pennsylvania 19104. (800) 523-1857. 1973-. Previous title: Current Contents. Agricultural, Food & Veterinary Sciences. Gives the table of contents of periodicals in the fields of agriculture, biology, environmental and related areas.

EPA Publications Bibliography. U.S. Environmental Protection Agency, Library Systems Branch, 401 M St., SW, Washington, District of Columbia 20460. (202) 260-2090. Quarterly.

ENCYCLOPEDIAS AND DICTIONARIES

McGraw-Hill Encyclopedia of Environmental Science. Sybil P. Parker. McGraw-Hill Science & Engineering Books, 11 W. 19th St., New York, New York 10011. (212) 337-6010. 1980. Covers ecology, man's influence on nature, and environmental protection.

McGraw-Hill Encyclopedia of Science and Technology. McGraw-Hill, 1221 Avenue of the Americas, New York, New York 10020. (212) 512-2000 or (800) 262-4729. 1992. Seventh edition. Issued in multiple volumes including index. Includes all science and technology broad subject areas.

Van Nostrand's Scientific Encyclopedia. Glenn D. Considine, ed. Van Nostrand Reinhold, 115 5th Ave., New York, New York 10003. (212) 254-3232. 1983. Sixth edition. Includes all broad subject areas in science.

GENERAL WORKS

Agricultural Ecology. Joy Tivy. John Wiley & Sons, Inc., 605 3rd Ave., New York, New York 10158-0012. (212) 850-6000. 1990. Analyzes the nature of relationships between crops, livestock, and the biophysical environment, and the extent to which man has modified the products and environment to suit his own needs.

Chemistry, Agriculture and the Environment. Mervyn L. Richardson. Royal Society of Chemistry, Thomas Graham House, Science Park, Milton Rd., Cambridge, England CB4 4WF. 44(0)223420066. 1991. Provides an overview of the chemical pollution of the environment caused by modern agricultural practices worldwide, and describes the effects of agrochemicals used in intensive animal and crop production on the air, water, soil, plants, and animals including humans. Also available through CRC Press.

Resource and Environmental Effects of U.S. Agriculture. Resources for the Future, 1616 P St., NW, Washington, District of Columbia 20036. (202) 328-5086. 1982. Soil conservation and agricultural ecology.

ONLINE DATA BASES

Cambridge Scientific Abstracts Life Science–CSAL. Cambridge Scientific Abstracts, 5161 River Rd., Bethesda, Maryland 20816. (301) 961-6750. Provides access to the following abstracting services: "Life Sciences Collection," "Aquatic Sciences and Fisheries Abstracts," "Oceanic Abstracts," and "Pollution Abstracts."

Enviro/Energyline Abstracts Plus. R. R. Bowker Co., 121 Chanlon Rd., New Providence, New Jersey 07974. (908) 464-6800.

Environmental Periodicals Bibliography. National Information Services Corp., Ste. 6, Wyman Towers, 3100 St. Paul St., Baltimore, Maryland 21218. (410)243-0797. Online version of abstract of same name.

Monthly Catalog of United States Government Publications. U.S. G.P.O., Supt. of Docs., PO Box 371954, Pittsburgh, Pennsylvania 15250-7954. (202) 512-0000.

National Technical Information Service. U.S. Department of Commerce, National Technical Information Service, Office of Data Base Services, 5285 Port Royal Rd., Springfield, Virginia 22161. (703) 487-4807. Bibliographic database of government sponsored research and technical reports.

SCISEARCH. Institute for Scientific Information, University City Science Center, 3501 Market St., Philadelphia, Pennsylvania 19104. (215) 386-0100.

PERIODICALS AND NEWSLETTERS

Agro-Ecosystems. Elsevier Science Publishing Co., 655 Avenue of the Americas, New York, New York 10010. (212) 989-5800. 1982-. Quarterly. Journal of International Association for Ecology featuring ecological interactions between agricultural and managed forest systems.

Protection Ecology. Elsevier Science Publishing Co., Journal Information Center, 655 Avenue of the Americas, New York, New York 10010. (212) 989-5800. Livestock and agricultural ecology and pest control.

TRADE ASSOCIATIONS AND PROFESSIONAL SOCIETIES

American Institute of Biological Sciences. 730 11th St., N.W., Washington, District of Columbia 20001-4521. (202) 628-1500.

INTENSIVE MONITORING SURVEY

See: WATER QUALITY

INTERCEPTOR SEWERS

See also: SEWERS

ABSTRACTING AND INDEXING SERVICES

Biological and Agricultural Index. H.W. Wilson Co., 950 University Ave., Bronx, New York 10452. (800) 367-6770. 1916-. Monthly.

Engineering Index. The Engineering Index Inc., 345 E. 47th St., New York, New York 10017. 1962-.

Environment Abstracts. Bowker A & I Publishing, 121 Chanlon Rd., New Providence, New Jersey 07974. (908) 464-6800. 1974-.

Environment Index. Environment Information Center, Index Research Department, 124 E. 39th St., New York, New York 10016. 1971-. Annual.

Environmental Information Connection–EIC. Planning Information Program, Dept. of Urban and Regional Planning, University of Illinois, 1003 West Nevada, Urbana, Illinois 61801. (217) 333-1369. Also available online.

Environmental Periodicals Bibliography. Environmental Studies Institute, International Academy at Santa Barbara, 800 Garden St., Suite D, Santa Barbara, California 93101. (805) 965-5010. Also available online.

General Science Index. H. W. Wilson Co., 950 University Ave., Bronx, New York 10452. 1978-. Monthly, also issued in annual cumulation. Cumulative subject index to English language periodicals in the subject fields of astronomy, botany, chemistry, earth science, environment and conservation, food and nutrition, genetics, mathematics, medicine and health, microbiology, oceanography, physics, physiology and zoology.

Index to Scientific Book Contents. Institute for Scientific Information, 3501 Market St., Philadelphia, Pennsylvania 19104. (800) 523-1857. 1985-. Annual. Gives contents of science books published.

BIBLIOGRAPHIES

EPA Publications Bibliography. U.S. Environmental Protection Agency, Library Systems Branch, 401 M St., SW, Washington, District of Columbia 20460. (202) 260-2090. Quarterly.

ENCYCLOPEDIAS AND DICTIONARIES

Van Nostrand's Scientific Encyclopedia. Glenn D. Considine, ed. Van Nostrand Reinhold, 115 5th Ave., New York, New York 10003. (212) 254-3232. 1983. Sixth edition. Includes all broad subject areas in science.

GENERAL WORKS

Evaluation of the Report on Interceptor Sewers and Suburban Sprawl. U.S. Environmental Protection Agency, Office of Planning and Evaluation, 401 M St. SW, Washington, District of Columbia 20460. (202) 260-2090. 1975.

Interceptor Sewers and Suburban Sprawl. National Technical Information Service, 5285 Port Royal Rd., Springfield, Virginia 22161. (703) 487-4650. 1974. The impact of construction grants on residential land use.

Interceptor Sewers and Urban Sprawl. Clark Binkley. Lexington Books, 866 3rd Ave., New York, New York 10022. (212) 702-2000. 1975.

ONLINE DATA BASES

Computerized Engineering Index–COMPENDEX. Engineering Information Inc., 345 E. 47th St., New York, New York 10017. (212) 705-7600.

Enviro/Energyline Abstracts Plus. R. R. Bowker Co., 121 Chanlon Rd., New Providence, New Jersey 07974. (908) 464-6800.

Environmental Periodicals Bibliography. National Information Services Corp., Ste. 6, Wyman Towers, 3100 St. Paul St., Baltimore, Maryland 21218. (410)243-0797. Online version of abstract of same name.

SCISEARCH. Institute for Scientific Information, University City Science Center, 3501 Market St., Philadelphia, Pennsylvania 19104. (215) 386-0100.

TRADE ASSOCIATIONS AND PROFESSIONAL SOCIETIES

American Institute of Biological Sciences. 730 11th St., N.W., Washington, District of Columbia 20001-4521. (202) 628-1500.

INTERNATIONAL TREATIES

See also: ANTARCTIC; FISH AND FISHING; MINERAL EXPLORATION; WHALING

ABSTRACTING AND INDEXING SERVICES

Ecological Abstracts. Geo Abstracts Ltd. Elsevier Applied Science, Crown House, Linton Rd., Barking, England IG 11 8JU. 1974-. Derived from over 600 leading ecological and environmental journals, plus books, conference proceedings, reports and theses.

Environment Abstracts. Bowker A & I Publishing, 121 Chanlon Rd., New Providence, New Jersey 07974. (908) 464-6800. 1974-.

Environment Index. Environment Information Center, Index Research Department, 124 E. 39th St., New York, New York 10016. 1971-. Annual.

Environmental Information Connection–EIC. Planning Information Program, Dept. of Urban and Regional Planning, University of Illinois, 1003 West Nevada, Urbana, Illinois 61801. (217) 333-1369. Also available online.

Environmental Periodicals Bibliography. Environmental Studies Institute, International Academy at Santa Barbara, 800 Garden St., Suite D, Santa Barbara, California 93101. (805) 965-5010. Also available online.

Index to Scientific Book Contents. Institute for Scientific Information, 3501 Market St., Philadelphia, Pennsylvania 19104. (800) 523-1857. 1985-. Annual. Gives contents of science books published.

BIBLIOGRAPHIES

EPA Publications Bibliography. U.S. Environmental Protection Agency, Library Systems Branch, 401 M St., SW, Washington, District of Columbia 20460. (202) 260-2090. Quarterly.

ENCYCLOPEDIAS AND DICTIONARIES

The Encyclopedia of Animal Ecology. Peter D. Moore. Facts on File, Inc., 460 Park Ave. S., New York, New York 10016. (212) 683-2244. 1987.

Grzimek's Encyclopedia of Ecology. Bernhard Grzimek. Van Nostrand Reinhold, 115 5th Ave., New York, New York 10003. (212) 254-3232. 1976.

McGraw-Hill Encyclopedia of Environmental Science. Sybil P. Parker. McGraw-Hill Science & Engineering Books, 11 W. 19th St., New York, New York 10011. (212) 337-6010. 1980. Covers ecology, man's influence on nature, and environmental protection.

North American Reference Encyclopedia of Ecology and Pollution. William White. North American Pub. Co., 401 N. Broad St., Philadelphia, Pennsylvania 19108. (215) 238-5300. 1972.

GENERAL WORKS

Integrated Pollution Control in Europe and North America. Nigel Haigh. World Wildlife Fund, The Conservation Foundation, Publications Dept., 1250 Twenty-Fourth St., NW, Washington, District of Columbia 20037. (202) 203-4800. 1990.

International Environmental Diplomacy. John E. Carroll. Cambridge University Press, 40 W. 20th St., New York, New York 10011. (212) 924-3900. 1988.

International Environmental Policy: Emergence and Dimensions. Lynton Keith Caldwell. Duke University Press, College Sta., Box 6697, Durham, North Carolina 27708. (919) 684-2173. 1990.

International Joint Commission Report. International Joint Commission, 2001 S St. NW, 2nd floor, Washington, District of Columbia 20440. (202) 673-6222. Information on water quality in the Great Lakes system.

International Wildlife Trade: Whose Business Is It?. Sarah Fitzgerald. World Wildlife Fund, The Conservation Foundation, Publications Dept., 1250 Twenty-Fourth St., NW, Washington, District of Columbia 20037. (202) 293-4800. 1989.

Saving the Mediterranean: The Politics of International Environmental Cooperation. Peter M. Haas. Columbia University Press, 562 W. 113th St., New York, New York 10025. (212) 316-7100. 1990. Focuses on the international pollution management of the Mediterranean. Ninety scientists and international officials were interviewed to ascertain how the international community responded to this particular threat.

Unfulfilled Promises: A Citizen Review of the International Water Quality Agreement. Great Lakes United, State University College at Buffalo, Cassety Hall, 1300 Elmwood Ave., Buffalo, New York 14222. (716) 886-0142. 1990.

ONLINE DATA BASES

Enviro/Energyline Abstracts Plus. R. R. Bowker Co., 121 Chanlon Rd., New Providence, New Jersey 07974. (908) 464-6800.

Environmental Periodicals Bibliography. National Information Services Corp., Ste. 6, Wyman Towers, 3100 St. Paul St., Baltimore, Maryland 21218. (410)243-0797. Online version of abstract of same name.

Monthly Catalog of United States Government Publications. U.S. G.P.O., Supt. of Docs., PO Box 371954, Pittsburgh, Pennsylvania 15250-7954. (202) 512-0000.

Multinational Environmental Outlook. Business Publishers, Inc., 951 Pershing Dr., Silver Spring, Maryland 20910-4464. (301) 587-6300. Environmental problems and solutions in countries outside the United States and their impact on the United States.

National Technical Information Service. U.S. Department of Commerce, National Technical Information Service, Office of Data Base Services, 5285 Port Royal Rd., Springfield, Virginia 22161. (703) 487-4807. Bibliographic database of government sponsored research and technical reports.

PressNet Environmental Reports. Chemical Information Systems, Inc., 7215 York Rd., Baltimore, Maryland 21212. (301) 321-8440.

SCISEARCH. Institute for Scientific Information, University City Science Center, 3501 Market St., Philadelphia, Pennsylvania 19104. (215) 386-0100.

PERIODICALS AND NEWSLETTERS

Consolidated List of Products Whose Consumption and/ or Sale Have Been Banned, Withdrawn, Severely Restricted or not Approved by Governments. United Nations, 2 United Nations Plaza, Salis Section Rm. DC 2-853, New York, New York 10017. (800) 553-3210. Biennial.

Multinational Environmental Outlook. Business Publishers, Inc., 951 Pershing Dr., Silver Spring, Maryland 20910-4464. (301) 587-6300. 1974-. Biweekly. Covers developments in world environmental problems such as acid rain, deforestation, soil erosion, overfishing, threats to health, animal extinction, population growth, diminishing water supply and other related matters. Also available online.

TRAFFIC. World Wildlife Fund, 1250 24th St., NW, Washington, District of Columbia 20037. (202) 293-4800. Quarterly. International trade in wild plants and animals, with emphasis on endangered and threatened species; information on Convention on International Trade in Endangered Species.

RESEARCH CENTERS AND INSTITUTES

Alaska Fisheries Science Center. 7600 Sand Point Way NE, BIN C15700, Seattle, Washington 98115. (206) 526-4000.

TRADE ASSOCIATIONS AND PROFESSIONAL SOCIETIES

TRAFFIC, USA. c/o World Wildlife Fund, 1250 24th St., N.W., Washington, District of Columbia 20037. (202) 293-4800.

INTRODUCED SPECIES

ABSTRACTING AND INDEXING SERVICES

ASFA Aquaculture Abstracts. Cambridge Scientific Abstracts, Inc., 5161 River Rd., Bethesda, Maryland 20816. (301) 961-6750. 1984.

Biological Abstracts. BIOSIS, 2100 Arch St., Philadelphia, Pennsylvania 19103-1399. (215) 587-4800. 1927-.

Biological and Agricultural Index. H.W. Wilson Co., 950 University Ave., Bronx, New York 10452. (800) 367-6770. 1916-. Monthly.

Ecology Abstracts. Cambridge Scientific Abstracts, 5161 River Rd., Bethesda, Maryland 20816. (301) 961-6750. Monthly.

Environment Abstracts. Bowker A & I Publishing, 121 Chanlon Rd., New Providence, New Jersey 07974. (908) 464-6800. 1974-.

Environment Index. Environment Information Center, Index Research Department, 124 E. 39th St., New York, New York 10016. 1971-. Annual.

Environmental Information Connection–EIC. Planning Information Program, Dept. of Urban and Regional Planning, University of Illinois, 1003 West Nevada, Urbana, Illinois 61801. (217) 333-1369. Also available online.

Environmental Periodicals Bibliography. Environmental Studies Institute, International Academy at Santa Barbara, 800 Garden St., Suite D, Santa Barbara, California 93101. (805) 965-5010. Also available online.

General Science Index. H. W. Wilson Co., 950 University Ave., Bronx, New York 10452. 1978-. Monthly, also issued in annual cumulation. Cumulative subject index to English language periodicals in the subject fields of astronomy, botany, chemistry, earth science, environment and conservation, food and nutrition, genetics, mathematics, medicine and health, microbiology, oceanography, physics, physiology and zoology.

Index to Scientific Book Contents. Institute for Scientific Information, 3501 Market St., Philadelphia, Pennsylvania 19104. (800) 523-1857. 1985-. Annual. Gives contents of science books published.

BIBLIOGRAPHIES

Current Contents. Agriculture, Biology and Environmental Sciences. Institute for Scientific Information, 3501 Market St., Philadelphia, Pennsylvania 19104. (800) 523-1857. 1973-. Previous title: Current Contents. Agricultural, Food & Veterinary Sciences. Gives the table of contents of periodicals in the fields of agriculture, biology, environmental and related areas.

EPA Publications Bibliography. U.S. Environmental Protection Agency, Library Systems Branch, 401 M St., SW, Washington, District of Columbia 20460. (202) 260-2090. Quarterly.

ENCYCLOPEDIAS AND DICTIONARIES

Cambridge Encyclopedia of Life Sciences. A. E. Friday and David S. Ingram. Cambridge University Press, 40 W 20th St., New York, New York 10011. (212) 924-3900 or (800) 227-0247. 1985. Includes all topics under biology and ecology.

The Encyclopedia of Animal Ecology. Peter D. Moore. Facts on File, Inc., 460 Park Ave. S., New York, New York 10016. (212) 683-2244. 1987.

McGraw-Hill Encyclopedia of Science and Technology. McGraw-Hill, 1221 Avenue of the Americas, New York, New York 10020. (212) 512-2000 or (800) 262-4729.

1992. Seventh edition. Issued in multiple volumes including index. Includes all science and technology broad subject areas.

Van Nostrand's Scientific Encyclopedia. Glenn D. Considine, ed. Van Nostrand Reinhold, 115 5th Ave., New York, New York 10003. (212) 254-3232. 1983. Sixth edition. Includes all broad subject areas in science.

HANDBOOKS AND MANUALS

Trees of North America. Christian Frank Brockman. Western Publishing Co., 1220 Mound Ave., Racine, Wisconsin 53404. (414) 633-2431. 1986. A field guide to the major native and introduced species of North America.

ONLINE DATA BASES

BIOSIS Previews. BIOSIS, 2100 Arch St., Philadelphia, Pennsylvania 19103-1399. (215) 587-4800. Largest and most comprehensive database of research in the life sciences. Contains citations for nearly 9000 primary research journals, monographs, reviews, symposia, preliminary reports, semi-popular journals, selected institutional reports, government reports and research communications.

Cambridge Scientific Abstracts Life Science–CSAL. Cambridge Scientific Abstracts, 5161 River Rd., Bethesda, Maryland 20816. (301) 961-6750. Provides access to the following abstracting services: "Life Sciences Collection," "Aquatic Sciences and Fisheries Abstracts," "Oceanic Abstracts," and "Pollution Abstracts."

Enviro/Energyline Abstracts Plus. R. R. Bowker Co., 121 Chanlon Rd., New Providence, New Jersey 07974. (908) 464-6800.

Environmental Periodicals Bibliography. National Information Services Corp., Ste. 6, Wyman Towers, 3100 St. Paul St., Baltimore, Maryland 21218. (410)243-0797. Online version of abstract of same name.

SCISEARCH. Institute for Scientific Information, University City Science Center, 3501 Market St., Philadelphia, Pennsylvania 19104. (215) 386-0100.

TRADE ASSOCIATIONS AND PROFESSIONAL SOCIETIES

American Institute of Biological Sciences. 730 11th St., N.W., Washington, District of Columbia 20001-4521. (202) 628-1500.

American Society of Naturalists. Department of Ecology and Evolation, State University of New York, Stony Brook, New York 11794. (516) 632-8589.

INVADER PLANT SPECIES
See: PLANTS

IODINE

ABSTRACTING AND INDEXING SERVICES

Biological Abstracts. BIOSIS, 2100 Arch St., Philadelphia, Pennsylvania 19103-1399. (215) 587-4800. 1927-.

Chemical Abstracts. Chemical Abstracts Service, 2540 Olentangy River Rd., PO Box 3012, Columbus, Ohio 43210. (800) 848-6533. 1907-.

Pollution Abstracts. Cambridge Scientific Abstracts, 5161 River Rd., Bethesda, Maryland 20816. (301) 961-6750. Six/year. Indexes worldwide technical literature on environmental pollution. Covers air pollution, marine and freshwater pollution, sewage and wastewater treatment, waste management, toxicology and health, noise pollution, radiation, land pollution, and environmental policies, programs, legislation, and education. Also available online.

Science Citation Index. Institute for Scientific Information, 3501 Market St., Philadelphia, Pennsylvania 19104. 1961-.

ENCYCLOPEDIAS AND DICTIONARIES

Encyclopedia of Electrochemistry of Elements. A. J. Bard. Marcel Dekker, Inc., 270 Madison Ave., New York, New York 10016. (212) 696-9000 or (800) 228-1160. Encyclopedic treatment of the subject area of electrochemistry and related subjects.

Van Nostrand's Scientific Encyclopedia. Glenn D. Considine, ed. Van Nostrand Reinhold, 115 5th Ave., New York, New York 10003. (212) 254-3232. 1983. Sixth edition. Includes all broad subject areas in science.

GENERAL WORKS

Iodine Species in Reactor Effluents and in the Environment. Paul Voillegue. Electric Power Research Institute, 3412 Hillview Ave., Palo Alto, California 94304. (415) 965-4081. 1979. Environmental aspects of radioactive waste disposal.

Sources of Radioiodine at Pressurized Water Reactors. Charles A. Pelletier. Electric Power Research Institute, 3412 Hillview Ave., Palo Alto, California 94304. (415) 965-4081. 1978.

HANDBOOKS AND MANUALS

Complete Guide to Vitamins, Minerals and Supplements. H. Winter Griffith. Fisher Books, 3499 N. Campbell Ave., Suite 909, Tucson, Arizona 85712. (602) 325-5263. 1988. Includes name, brand name, reasons to use, who should use, recommended daily allowance, and other related data in the form of a chart.

ONLINE DATA BASES

BIOSIS Previews. BIOSIS, 2100 Arch St., Philadelphia, Pennsylvania 19103-1399. (215) 587-4800. Largest and most comprehensive database of research in the life sciences. Contains citations for nearly 9000 primary research journals, monographs, reviews, symposia, preliminary reports, semi-popular journals, selected institutional reports, government reports and research communications.

CAS Source Index–CASSI. Chemical Abstracts Service, 2540 Olentangy River Rd., P.O. Box 3012, Columbus, Ohio 43210. (800) 848-6533 or (614) 421-3600. A listing of bibliographic and library holdings information for scientific and technical primary literature relevant to the chemical sciences.

Chemical Abstracts-CA. Chemical Abstracts Service, 2540 Olentangy River Rd., P.O. Box 3012, Columbus, Ohio 43210. (800) 848-6533 or (614) 421-3600. Information sources include 9000 journals, patents from 27 countries, two industrial property organizations, new books, conference proceedings, and government research reports.

TRADE ASSOCIATIONS AND PROFESSIONAL SOCIETIES

American Chemical Society. 1155 16th St., N.W., Washington, District of Columbia 20036. (202) 872-4600.

IOWA ENVIRONMENTAL AGENCIES

GOVERNMENTAL ORGANIZATIONS

Department of Agriculture: Pesticide Registration. Secretary of Agriculture, Wallace State Office Building, Des Moines, Iowa 50319. (515) 281-5321.

Department of Employment Services: Occupational Services. Administrator, Occupational Safety and Health Administration, 1000 East Grand, Des Moines, Iowa 50319. (515) 281-3606.

Department of Natural Resources: Air Quality. Director, Air Quality and Solid Waste Protection Bureau, Wallace State Office Building, Des Moines, Iowa 50319. (515) 281-8852.

Department of Natural Resources: Emergency Preparedness and Community Right-to-Know. Chair, Records Department, 900 East Grand Ave., Des Moines, Iowa 50319. (515) 281-8852.

Department of Natural Resources: Fish and Wildlife. Administrator, Fish and Wildlife Division, Wallace State Office Building, Des Moines, Iowa 50319. (515) 281-5918.

Department of Natural Resources: Groundwater Management. Chief, Division of Law Enforcement, Wallace State Office Building, Des Moines, Iowa 50319. (515) 281-5385.

Department of Natural Resources: Hazardous Waste Management. Bureau Chief, Solid Waste Protection Bureau, Wallace State Office Building, Des Moines, Iowa 50319. (515) 281-8693.

Department of Natural Resources: Natural Resources. Chief, Division of Law Enforcement, Wallace State Office Building, Des Moines, Iowa 50319. (515) 281-5385.

Department of Natural Resources: Solid Waste Department. Chief, Air Quality and Solid Waste Protection Bureau, Wallace State Office Building, Des Moines, Iowa 50319. (515) 281-8693.

Department of Natural Resources: Underground Storage Tanks. Director, Air Quality and Solid Waste Bureau, Wallace State Office Building, Des Moines, Iowa 50319. (515) 281-8852.

Department of Natural Resources: Waste Minimization and Pollution Prevention. Director, Air Quality and Solid Waste Protection Bureau, Wallace State Office Building, 900 East 9th and Grand Ave., Des Moines, Iowa 50319-0034. (515) 281-8690.

IOWA ENVIRONMENTAL LEGISLATION

GENERAL WORKS

Iowa 1990 Environmental Resource Handbook. Environmental Advocates, Iowa City, Iowa 1990.

What Farmers Need to Know About Environmental Law. Drake University Agricultural Law Center, Des Moines, Iowa 50311. (515) 271-2065. 1990.

IRON

See: METALS AND METALLURGY

IRON WASTES

ABSTRACTING AND INDEXING SERVICES

Applied Science and Technology Index. H.W. Wilson Co., 950 University Ave., Bronx, New York 10452. (800) 367-6770. Formerly Industrial Arts Index.

Chemical Abstracts. Chemical Abstracts Service, 2540 Olentangy River Rd., PO Box 3012, Columbus, Ohio 43210. (800) 848-6533. 1907-.

Pollution Abstracts. Cambridge Scientific Abstracts, 5161 River Rd., Bethesda, Maryland 20816. (301) 961-6750. Six/year. Indexes worldwide technical literature on environmental pollution. Covers air pollution, marine and freshwater pollution, sewage and wastewater treatment, waste management, toxicology and health, noise pollution, radiation, land pollution, and environmental policies, programs, legislation, and education. Also available online.

GENERAL WORKS

Development Document for Proposed Effluent Limitations Guidelines, New Source Performance Standards and Pretreatment Standards for the Iron and Steel Manufacturing Point Source Category. U.S. Environmental Protection Agency, Office of Water and Waste Management, Effluent Guidelines Division, 401 M St. SW, Washington, District of Columbia 20460. (202) 260-2090. 1981.

Environmental Aspects of Iron and Steel Production: A Technical Review. Industry & Environment Office, United Nations Environment Programme, Paris, France 1986. Waste disposal in the iron and steel industry.

Sampling and Analysis of Wastes Generated by Gray Iron Foundries. W.F. Beckert. Center for Environmental Research Information, U.S. Environmental Protection Agency, 26 W. Martin Luther King Dr., Cincinnati, Ohio 45268. (513) 569-7931. 1981.

ONLINE DATA BASES

Chemical Abstracts-CA. Chemical Abstracts Service, 2540 Olentangy River Rd., P.O. Box 3012, Columbus, Ohio 43210. (800) 848-6533 or (614) 421-3600. Information sources include 9000 journals, patents from 27 countries, two industrial property organizations, new books, conference proceedings, and government research reports.

TRADE ASSOCIATIONS AND PROFESSIONAL SOCIETIES

American Iron & Steel Institute. 1101 17th St., N.W., Washington, District of Columbia 20036-4700. (202) 463-6573.

IRRADIATION

ABSTRACTING AND INDEXING SERVICES

Applied Science and Technology Index. H.W. Wilson Co., 950 University Ave., Bronx, New York 10452. (800) 367-6770. Formerly Industrial Arts Index.

Biological Abstracts. BIOSIS, 2100 Arch St., Philadelphia, Pennsylvania 19103-1399. (215) 587-4800. 1927-.

Civil Engineering Hydraulic Abstracts. BHRA Fluid Engineering, Air Science Co., PO Box 143, Corning, New York 14830. (607) 962-5591. Monthly. Abstracts of periodicals that publish in the areas of hydraulic engineering and other related topics.

Environment Abstracts. Bowker A & I Publishing, 121 Chanlon Rd., New Providence, New Jersey 07974. (908) 464-6800. 1974-.

Environment Index. Environment Information Center, Index Research Department, 124 E. 39th St., New York, New York 10016. 1971-. Annual.

Environmental Information Connection–EIC. Planning Information Program, Dept. of Urban and Regional Planning, University of Illinois, 1003 West Nevada, Urbana, Illinois 61801. (217) 333-1369. Also available online.

Environmental Periodicals Bibliography. Environmental Studies Institute, International Academy at Santa Barbara, 800 Garden St., Suite D, Santa Barbara, California 93101. (805) 965-5010. Also available online.

General Science Index. H. W. Wilson Co., 950 University Ave., Bronx, New York 10452. 1978-. Monthly, also issued in annual cumulation. Cumulative subject index to English language periodicals in the subject fields of astronomy, botany, chemistry, earth science, environment and conservation, food and nutrition, genetics, mathematics, medicine and health, microbiology, oceanography, physics, physiology and zoology.

Physics Briefs. Physikalische Berichte. Physik Verlag, Pappapelallee 3, Postfach 101161, Weinheim, Germany D-6940. 1979-. Semimonthly. In English. Volumes for 1979- issued by the Deutsche Physikalische Gesellschaft and the Fachinformationszentrum Energie Physik, Mathematik in cooperation with the American Institute of Physics.

Pollution Abstracts. Cambridge Scientific Abstracts, 5161 River Rd., Bethesda, Maryland 20816. (301) 961-6750. Six/year. Indexes worldwide technical literature on environmental pollution. Covers air pollution, marine and freshwater pollution, sewage and wastewater treatment, waste management, toxicology and health, noise pollution, radiation, land pollution, and environmental policies, programs, legislation, and education. Also available online.

Science Citation Index. Institute for Scientific Information, 3501 Market St., Philadelphia, Pennsylvania 19104. 1961-.

ALMANACS AND YEARBOOKS

Research in Radiobiology. National Technical Information Service, 5285 Port Royal Rd., Springfield, Virginia 22161. (703) 487-4650. Annual. Annual report of work in progress in the Internal Irradiation Program.

BIBLIOGRAPHIES

Bibliography of the Beneficial Uses/Sewage Sludge Irradiation Project. P.S. Homann. National Technical Information Service, 5285 Port Royal Rd., Springfield, Virginia 22161. (703) 487-4650. 1982. Wastewater treatment by disinfection.

EPA Publications Bibliography. U.S. Environmental Protection Agency, Library Systems Branch, 401 M St., SW, Washington, District of Columbia 20460. (202) 260-2090. Quarterly.

ENCYCLOPEDIAS AND DICTIONARIES

Encyclopedia of Physics. Rita G. Lerner and George L. Trigg. VCH Publishers, 303 NW 12th Ave., Deerfield Beach, Florida 33442-1788. (305) 428-5566. 1991. Second edition.

Glossary of Terms in Nuclear Science and Technology. American Nuclear Society, 555 North Kensington Ave., La Grange Park, Illinois 60525. (708) 352-6611. 1986. Prepared by the American Nuclear Society Standards Committee. Subcommittee ANS-9.

McGraw-Hill Encyclopedia of Science and Technology. McGraw-Hill, 1221 Avenue of the Americas, New York, New York 10020. (212) 512-2000 or (800) 262-4729. 1992. Seventh edition. Issued in multiple volumes including index. Includes all science and technology broad subject areas.

Van Nostrand's Scientific Encyclopedia. Glenn D. Considine, ed. Van Nostrand Reinhold, 115 5th Ave., New York, New York 10003. (212) 254-3232. 1983. Sixth edition. Includes all broad subject areas in science.

GENERAL WORKS

Food Irradiation. Walter M. Urbain. Academic Press, c/o Harcourt Brace Jovanovich Inc., 6277 Sea Harbor Dr., Orlando, Florida 32887. (800) 346-8648. 1986. Food science and technology relating to food preservation.

Issues in Food Irradiation. Susan Mills. Science Council of Canada, Publications Office, Ottawa, Ontario, Canada 1987.

Preservation of Food by Ionizing Radiation. Edward S. Josephson. CRC Press, 2000 Corporate Blvd. N.W., Boca Raton, Florida 33431. (800) 272-7737.

Training Manual on Food Irradiation Technology and Techniques. UNIPUB, 1982. Technical reports on radiation preservation of foods.

ONLINE DATA BASES

BIOSIS Previews. BIOSIS, 2100 Arch St., Philadelphia, Pennsylvania 19103-1399. (215) 587-4800. Largest and most comprehensive database of research in the life sciences. Contains citations for nearly 9000 primary research journals, monographs, reviews, symposia, preliminary reports, semi-popular journals, selected institu-

tional reports, government reports and research communications.

Enviro/Energyline Abstracts Plus. R. R. Bowker Co., 121 Chanlon Rd., New Providence, New Jersey 07974. (908) 464-6800.

Environmental Periodicals Bibliography. National Information Services Corp., Ste. 6, Wyman Towers, 3100 St. Paul St., Baltimore, Maryland 21218. (410)243-0797. Online version of abstract of same name.

IRRIGATION

See also: ALKALINIZATION OF SOILS; EROSION; RESERVOIRS; WATER MANAGEMENT

ABSTRACTING AND INDEXING SERVICES

Agricultural Engineering Abstracts. C. A. B. International, 845 North Park Ave., Tucson, Arizona 85719. (602) 621-7897 or (800) 528-4841. 1976-. Monthly. Informs about significant research developments in agricultural engineering and instrumentation. Some of the topics scanned for the abstracts include mechanical power, crop production, crop harvesting and threshing, crop processing and storage, aquaculture, land improvement, protected cultivation, handling and transport, and farm buildings and equipment.

Agrindex. AGRIS Coordinating Center, Via delle Terme di Caracalla, Rome, Italy I-00100. 61 0181-FA01. 1975-.

Applied Science and Technology Index. H.W. Wilson Co., 950 University Ave., Bronx, New York 10452. (800) 367-6770. Formerly Industrial Arts Index.

Aqualine Abstracts. Water Research Centre. c/o Pergamon Microforms International, Inc., Fairview Park, Elmsford, New York 10523. (914) 592-7720. 1927-. Contains some 8,000 records annually on water and wastewater technology. Covers all aspects of water, wastewater, associated engineering services and the aquatic environment. Over 600 periodicals, as well as books, reports and conference proceedings and other publications from water related institutions worldwide are scanned. Also available online.

Biological Abstracts. BIOSIS, 2100 Arch St., Philadelphia, Pennsylvania 19103-1399. (215) 587-4800. 1927-.

Biological and Agricultural Index. H.W. Wilson Co., 950 University Ave., Bronx, New York 10452. (800) 367-6770. 1916-. Monthly.

Ecological Abstracts. Geo Abstracts Ltd. Elsevier Applied Science, Crown House, Linton Rd., Barking, England IG 11 8JU. 1974-. Derived from over 600 leading ecological and environmental journals, plus books, conference proceedings, reports and theses.

Energy Information Abstracts Annual 1987 in Retrospect. EIC/Intelligence Inc., 121 Chanlon Rd., New Providence, New Jersey 07974. (908) 464-6800. 1988. Annual. Cumulative edition of the monthly Energy Information Abstracts. Monitors sources in the field of energy including the scientific, technical and business journal literature, conference and symposia proceedings, corporate, government and academic reports.

Engineering Index. The Engineering Index Inc., 345 E. 47th St., New York, New York 10017. 1962-.

Environment Abstracts. Bowker A & I Publishing, 121 Chanlon Rd., New Providence, New Jersey 07974. (908) 464-6800. 1974-.

Environment Index. Environment Information Center, Index Research Department, 124 E. 39th St., New York, New York 10016. 1971-. Annual.

Environmental Information Connection–EIC. Planning Information Program, Dept. of Urban and Regional Planning, University of Illinois, 1003 West Nevada, Urbana, Illinois 61801. (217) 333-1369. Also available online.

Environmental Periodicals Bibliography. Environmental Studies Institute, International Academy at Santa Barbara, 800 Garden St., Suite D, Santa Barbara, California 93101. (805) 965-5010. Also available online.

General Science Index. H. W. Wilson Co., 950 University Ave., Bronx, New York 10452. 1978-. Monthly, also issued in annual cumulation. Cumulative subject index to English language periodicals in the subject fields of astronomy, botany, chemistry, earth science, environment and conservation, food and nutrition, genetics, mathematics, medicine and health, microbiology, oceanography, physics, physiology and zoology.

Pollution Abstracts. Cambridge Scientific Abstracts, 5161 River Rd., Bethesda, Maryland 20816. (301) 961-6750. Six/year. Indexes worldwide technical literature on environmental pollution. Covers air pollution, marine and freshwater pollution, sewage and wastewater treatment, waste management, toxicology and health, noise pollution, radiation, land pollution, and environmental policies, programs, legislation, and education. Also available online.

Science Citation Index. Institute for Scientific Information, 3501 Market St., Philadelphia, Pennsylvania 19104. 1961-.

Sea Grant Abstracts. National Sea Grant Depository, Pell Laboratory Bldg., Bay Campus, University of Rhode Island, Narragansett, Rhode Island 02882. (401) 792-6114. 1986-. Quarterly. Published by the National Sea Grant Programs, this collection includes annual reports, serials and newsletters, charts and maps.

Soils and Fertilizers. C. A. B. International, 845 North Park Ave., Tucson, Arizona 85719. (602) 621-7897 or (800) 528-4841. 1937-. Monthly. Focuses on soil chemistry, soil physics, soil biology, soil fertility, soil management, soil classification, soil formation, soil conservation, land reclamation, irrigation and damage, fertilizer technology, fertilizer use, plant nutrition, plant water relations, and environmental aspects.

BIBLIOGRAPHIES

EPA Publications Bibliography. U.S. Environmental Protection Agency, Library Systems Branch, 401 M St., SW, Washington, District of Columbia 20460. (202) 260-2090. Quarterly.

DIRECTORIES

Irrigation: International Guide to Organizations and Institutions. International Irrigation Information Center, Distr: Pergamon Press, Maxwell House, Fairview Park,

Elmsford, New York 10523. (914) 592-7720. 1980. Includes 864 organizations from 109 countries concerned with irrigation.

ENCYCLOPEDIAS AND DICTIONARIES

Dictionary of Civil Engineering. John S. Scott. Halsted Press, Division of J. Wiley, 605 3rd Ave., New York, New York 10158. (212) 850-6000. 1981. Third edition.

Dictionary of Environmental Engineering and Related Sciences: English-Spanish, Spanish-English. Jose T. Villate. Ediciones Universal, 3090 SW 8th St., Miami, Florida 33135. (305) 642-3355. 1979.

Encyclopedia of Environmental Science and Engineering. J.R. Pfafflin. Gordon and Breach Science Publishers, Inc., 270 8th Ave., New York, New York 10011. (212) 206-8900. 1992.

McGraw-Hill Encyclopedia of Environmental Science. Sybil P. Parker. McGraw-Hill Science & Engineering Books, 11 W. 19th St., New York, New York 10011. (212) 337-6010. 1980. Covers ecology, man's influence on nature, and environmental protection.

McGraw-Hill Encyclopedia of Science and Technology. McGraw-Hill, 1221 Avenue of the Americas, New York, New York 10020. (212) 512-2000 or (800) 262-4729. 1992. Seventh edition. Issued in multiple volumes including index. Includes all science and technology broad subject areas.

Van Nostrand's Scientific Encyclopedia. Glenn D. Considine, ed. Van Nostrand Reinhold, 115 5th Ave., New York, New York 10003. (212) 254-3232. 1983. Sixth edition. Includes all broad subject areas in science.

GENERAL WORKS

Agricultural Ecology. Joy Tivy. John Wiley & Sons, Inc., 605 3rd Ave., New York, New York 10158-0012. (212) 850-6000. 1990. Analyzes the nature of relationships between crops, livestock, and the biophysical environment, and the extent to which man has modified the products and environment to suit his own needs.

Arid Land Irrigation in Developing Countries. E. Barton Worthington. Pergamon Microforms International, Inc., Fairview Park, Elmsford, New York 10523. (914) 592-7720. 1977. Environmental problems and effects.

Environmental Aspects of Irrigation and Drainage. American Society of Civil Engineers, 345 E. 47th St., New York, New York 10017. (212) 705-7288. 1976.

Irrigation-Induced Water Quality Problems. National Academy Press, 2101 Constitution Ave. NW, PO Box 285, Washington, District of Columbia 20418. (202) 334-3313. 1989.

Sprinkle and Trickle Irrigation. Jack Keller and Ron D. Bliesner. Van Nostrand Reinhold, 115 5th Ave., New York, New York 10003. (212) 254-3232. 1990. Analyses environmental demands (evapotranspiration, leaching, and irrigation water requirements) with moisture and infiltration characteristics of the soil and the various hydraulic, economic, and physical constraints of pressurized systems.

Winning with Water: Soil Moisture Monitoring for Efficient Irrigation. Gail Richardson. INFORM, Publications Dept., 381 Park Ave. S., New York, New York 10016. (212) 689-4040. 1988.

ONLINE DATA BASES

BIOSIS Previews. BIOSIS, 2100 Arch St., Philadelphia, Pennsylvania 19103-1399. (215) 587-4800. Largest and most comprehensive database of research in the life sciences. Contains citations for nearly 9000 primary research journals, monographs, reviews, symposia, preliminary reports, semi-popular journals, selected institutional reports, government reports and research communications.

Computerized Engineering Index–COMPENDEX. Engineering Information Inc., 345 E. 47th St., New York, New York 10017. (212) 705-7600.

Enviro/Energyline Abstracts Plus. R. R. Bowker Co., 121 Chanlon Rd., New Providence, New Jersey 07974. (908) 464-6800.

Environmental Periodicals Bibliography. National Information Services Corp., Ste. 6, Wyman Towers, 3100 St. Paul St., Baltimore, Maryland 21218. (410)243-0797. Online version of abstract of same name.

SCISEARCH. Institute for Scientific Information, University City Science Center, 3501 Market St., Philadelphia, Pennsylvania 19104. (215) 386-0100.

PERIODICALS AND NEWSLETTERS

Irrigation Science. Springer International, 44 Hartz Way, Seacaucus, New Jersey 07094. (201) 348-4033.

Journal of Hydraulic Engineering. American Society of Civil Engineers, 345 E. 47th St., New York, New York 10017. (212) 705-7288; (800) 548-2723. 1983-. Monthly. Papers describe the analysis and solutions of problems in hydraulic engineering, hydrology and water resources. Emphasizes concepts, methods, techniques and results that advance knowledge in the hydraulic engineering profession.

RESEARCH CENTERS AND INSTITUTES

Arkansas Water Resources Research Center. University of Arkansas, 113 Ozark Hall, Fayetteville, Arkansas 72701. (501) 575-4403.

University of Idaho, Idaho Water Resources Research Institute. Morrill Hall 106, Moscow, Idaho 83843. (208) 885-6429.

USDA Water Conservation Laboratory. 4331 East Broadway, Phoenix, Arizona 85040. (602) 379-4356.

TRADE ASSOCIATIONS AND PROFESSIONAL SOCIETIES

American Society of Agricultural Engineers. 2950 Niles Rd., St Joseph, Michigan 49085. (616) 429-0300.

Irrigation Association. 1911 N. Fort Myer Dr., Suite 1009, Arlington, Virginia 22209. (703) 524-1200.

U.S. Committee on Irrigation and Drainage. P.O. Box 15326, Denver, Colorado 80215. (303) 236-6960.

ISOTOPES

See also: C14 DATING; RADIOCARBON DATING

ABSTRACTING AND INDEXING SERVICES

Biological Abstracts. BIOSIS, 2100 Arch St., Philadelphia, Pennsylvania 19103-1399. (215) 587-4800. 1927-.

Biological and Agricultural Index. H.W. Wilson Co., 950 University Ave., Bronx, New York 10452. (800) 367-6770. 1916-. Monthly.

Ecological Abstracts. Geo Abstracts Ltd. Elsevier Applied Science, Crown House, Linton Rd., Barking, England IG 11 8JU. 1974-. Derived from over 600 leading ecological and environmental journals, plus books, conference proceedings, reports and theses.

Environment Abstracts. Bowker A & I Publishing, 121 Chanlon Rd., New Providence, New Jersey 07974. (908) 464-6800. 1974-.

Environment Index. Environment Information Center, Index Research Department, 124 E. 39th St., New York, New York 10016. 1971-. Annual.

Environmental Information Connection–EIC. Planning Information Program, Dept. of Urban and Regional Planning, University of Illinois, 1003 West Nevada, Urbana, Illinois 61801. (217) 333-1369. Also available online.

Environmental Periodicals Bibliography. Environmental Studies Institute, International Academy at Santa Barbara, 800 Garden St., Suite D, Santa Barbara, California 93101. (805) 965-5010. Also available online.

General Science Index. H. W. Wilson Co., 950 University Ave., Bronx, New York 10452. 1978-. Monthly, also issued in annual cumulation. Cumulative subject index to English language periodicals in the subject fields of astronomy, botany, chemistry, earth science, environment and conservation, food and nutrition, genetics, mathematics, medicine and health, microbiology, oceanography, physics, physiology and zoology.

INIS Atomindex. International Atomic Energy Agency, Wagramerstrasse 5, Vienna, Austria A-1400. 222 23606198. 1988-. Semiannual. Abstracts nuclear energy and nuclear physics topics from journals, conferences, technical reports and other related publications. Issued in 6 parts: Personal Author, Corporate Entry, Subject, Report, Standard Patent, Conference (by place), Conference (by date).

Mineralogical Abstracts. Mineralogical Society, 41 Queen's Gate, London, England SW7 5HR. 71 5847916. Quarterly. Abstracts of journal articles, conferences, technical reports and specialized books in the areas of minerals, clay minerals, economic minerals, ore deposits, environmental studies, experimental mineralogy, gemstones, geochemistry, petrology, lunar and planetary studies and other related areas in mineralogy.

Pollution Abstracts. Cambridge Scientific Abstracts, 5161 River Rd., Bethesda, Maryland 20816. (301) 961-6750. Six/year. Indexes worldwide technical literature on environmental pollution. Covers air pollution, marine and freshwater pollution, sewage and wastewater treatment, waste management, toxicology and health, noise pollution, radiation, land pollution, and environmental policies, programs, legislation, and education. Also available online.

Science Citation Index. Institute for Scientific Information, 3501 Market St., Philadelphia, Pennsylvania 19104. 1961-.

BIBLIOGRAPHIES

Current Contents. Agriculture, Biology and Environmental Sciences. Institute for Scientific Information, 3501 Market St., Philadelphia, Pennsylvania 19104. (800) 523-1857. 1973-. Previous title: Current Contents. Agricultural, Food & Veterinary Sciences. Gives the table of contents of periodicals in the fields of agriculture, biology, environmental and related areas.

EPA Publications Bibliography. U.S. Environmental Protection Agency, Library Systems Branch, 401 M St., SW, Washington, District of Columbia 20460. (202) 260-2090. Quarterly.

New Publications of the Geological Survey. U.S. Department of the Interior, Geological Survey, 119 National Center, Reston, Virginia 22092. (703) 648-4460. 1984-. Monthly. Bibliography of geological publications and related government documents published by the Geological Survey.

DIRECTORIES

World Nuclear Directory. Longman, Burnt Mill, Harlow, England CM 20 2J6. (0279) 26721. 1988. Eighth edition. Includes organizations that are involved in nuclear physics research.

ENCYCLOPEDIAS AND DICTIONARIES

Chem Address Book. F. W. Derz, ed. Walter De Gruyter, New York, New York 1974. Includes over 180000 names (synonyms) in alphabetical order for chemical compounds and chemicals, radioactive labelled compounds, isotopes, dyes, polymers, etc. and their molecular formulas.

Encyclopedia of Physics. Rita G. Lerner and George L. Trigg. VCH Publishers, 303 NW 12th Ave., Deerfield Beach, Florida 33442-1788. (305) 428-5566. 1991. Second edition.

Glossary of Terms in Nuclear Science and Technology. American Nuclear Society, 555 North Kensington Ave., La Grange Park, Illinois 60525. (708) 352-6611. 1986. Prepared by the American Nuclear Society Standards Committee. Subcommittee ANS-9.

McGraw-Hill Encyclopedia of Environmental Science. Sybil P. Parker. McGraw-Hill Science & Engineering Books, 11 W. 19th St., New York, New York 10011. (212) 337-6010. 1980. Covers ecology, man's influence on nature, and environmental protection.

McGraw-Hill Encyclopedia of Science and Technology. McGraw-Hill, 1221 Avenue of the Americas, New York, New York 10020. (212) 512-2000 or (800) 262-4729. 1992. Seventh edition. Issued in multiple volumes including index. Includes all science and technology broad subject areas.

Van Nostrand's Scientific Encyclopedia. Glenn D. Considine, ed. Van Nostrand Reinhold, 115 5th Ave., New York, New York 10003. (212) 254-3232. 1983. Sixth edition. Includes all broad subject areas in science.

GENERAL WORKS

Applied Isotope Hydrogeology: A Case Study in Northern Switzerland. F. J. Pearson, Jr., et al. Elsevier Science Publishing Co., Inc, 655 Avenue of the Americas, New York, New York 10010. (212) 989-5800. 1991. This is a case study in northern Switzerland about radioactive waste disposal in the ground. Includes bibliographical references and an index.

Magill's Survey of Science. Life Science Series. Frank N. Magill, ed. Salem Press, PO Box 50062, Pasadena, California 91105. 1991. Six volumes. Contents: v.1. A-Central and peripheral nervous system functions; v.2. Central metabolism regulation - eukaryotic transcriptional control; v.3. Positive and negative eukaryotic transcriptional control - mammalian hormones; v.4. Hormones and behavior - muscular contraction; v.5. Muscular contraction and relaxation - sexual reproduction in plants; v.6. Reproductive behavior and mating - X inactivation and the Lyon hypothesis.

Radon and Its Decay in Indoor Air. William W. Nazaroff and Anthony V. Nero. John Wiley & Sons, Inc., 605 3rd Ave., New York, New York 10158-0012. (212) 850-6000. 1988. Radon isotopes toxicology and hygienic aspects of indoor air pollution.

Stable Isotopes: Natural and Anthropogenic Sulphur in the Environment. R. R. Krouse and V. H. Grinenko, eds. John Wiley & Sons, Inc., 605 3rd Ave., New York, New York 10158-0012. (212) 850-6000. 1991. Published on behalf of the Scientific Committee on Problems of the Environment (SCOPE) of the International Council of Scientific Unions (ICSU) in collaboration with the United Nations Environment Programme. Addresses the important question of differentiating natural and anthropogenic sulphur in the environment. International experts explain how stable isotopes of sulphur and oxygen have been used to study the origin and transformations of sulphur in ecosystems.

HANDBOOKS AND MANUALS

13C NMR Spectroscopy: A Working Manual with Exercises. E. Breitmaier. Harwood Academic Publishers, PO Box 786, Cooper Sta., New York, New York 10276. (212) 206-8900. 1984.

CRC Handbook of Phosphorus-31 Nuclear Magnetic Resonance Data. John C. Tebby. CRC Press, 2000 Corporate Blvd. N.W., Boca Raton, Florida 33431. (800) 272-7737. 1991.

ONLINE DATA BASES

BIOSIS Previews. BIOSIS, 2100 Arch St., Philadelphia, Pennsylvania 19103-1399. (215) 587-4800. Largest and most comprehensive database of research in the life sciences. Contains citations for nearly 9000 primary research journals, monographs, reviews, symposia, preliminary reports, semi-popular journals, selected institutional reports, government reports and research communications.

CAS Source Index–CASSI. Chemical Abstracts Service, 2540 Olentangy River Rd., P.O. Box 3012, Columbus, Ohio 43210. (800) 848-6533 or (614) 421-3600. A listing of bibliographic and library holdings information for scientific and technical primary literature relevant to the chemical sciences.

Enviro/Energyline Abstracts Plus. R. R. Bowker Co., 121 Chanlon Rd., New Providence, New Jersey 07974. (908) 464-6800.

Environmental Periodicals Bibliography. National Information Services Corp., Ste. 6, Wyman Towers, 3100 St. Paul St., Baltimore, Maryland 21218. (410)243-0797. Online version of abstract of same name.

PERIODICALS AND NEWSLETTERS

Topics in Carbon-13 NMR Spectroscopy. John Wiley & Sons Inc., 605 3rd Ave., New York, New York 10158-0012. (212) 850-6000. 1974-. Irregular.

STATISTICS SOURCES

World Survey of Isotope Concentration in Precipitation. International Atomic Energy Agency, Wagramerastrasse 5, Vienna, Austria A-1400. 222 23606198. 1986. Isotopes, precipitation meteorology, and rain and rainfall.

ITES

See: ENDANGERED SPECIES

J

JUNKYARDS

See also: WASTE MANAGEMENT

ABSTRACTING AND INDEXING SERVICES

Biological and Agricultural Index. H.W. Wilson Co., 950 University Ave., Bronx, New York 10452. (800) 367-6770. 1916-. Monthly.

GENERAL WORKS

Junkyards: The Highway and Visual Quality. Randolph F. Blum. U.S. G.P.O., Washington, District of Columbia 20401. (202) 512-0000. 1979. Abandonment of automobiles and the environmental impact.

K

KANSAS ENVIRONMENTAL AGENCIES

GOVERNMENTAL ORGANIZATIONS

Department of Agriculture: Pesticide Registration. Director, Plant Health Division, 109 S.W. 9th St., Topeka, Kansas 66612-1281. (913) 292-2263.

Department of Health and Environment: Air Quality. Director, Air and Waste Management, Forbes Field, Building 740, Topeka, Kansas 66620. (913) 926-1593.

Department of Health and Environment: Emergency Preparedness and Community Right-to-Know. Manager, Right-to-Know Program, Forbes Field, Building 740, Topeka, Kansas 66620. (913) 296-1690.

Department of Health And Environment: Environmental Protection. Director, Division of Environment, Forbes Field, Building 740, Topeka, Kansas 66620. (913) 296-1535.

Department of Health and Environment: Natural Resources. Director, Division of Environment, Forbes Field, Building 740, Topeka, Kansas 66620. (913) 296-1535.

Department of Health and Environment: Solid Waste Management. Director, Division of Environment, Forbes Field, Building 740, Topeka, Kansas 66620. (913) 296-1535.

Department of Health and Environment: Waste Minimization and Pollution Prevention. Chief, Bureau of Air and Waste Management, Forbes Field, Building 740, Topeka, Kansas 66620. (913) 296-1607.

Department of Health and Environment: Water Quality. Director, Division of Environment, Forbes Field, Building 740, Topeka, Kansas 66620. (913) 296-5500.

Department of Human Resources: Occupational Safety. Director, Employment Standards and Labor Relations, 430 S.W. Topeka, 3rd Floor, Topeka, Kansas 66603. (913) 296-7475.

Department of Wildlife and Parks: Fish and Wildlife. Secretary, Landon State Office Building, 900 S.W. Jackson St., Room 502, Topeka, Kansas 66612-1220. (913) 296-2281.

KANSAS ENVIRONMENTAL LEGISLATION

GENERAL WORKS

Kansas Environmental Law Handbook. Government Institutes, Inc., 4 Research Pl., Ste. 200, Rockville, Maryland 20850. (301) 921-2300. 1990.

KELP

ABSTRACTING AND INDEXING SERVICES

Applied Ecology Abstracts Studies in Renewable Natural Resources. Information Retrieval Ltd., 1911 Jefferson Davis Highway, Arlington, Virginia 22202. 1975-. Monthly.

ASFA Aquaculture Abstracts. Cambridge Scientific Abstracts, Inc., 5161 River Rd., Bethesda, Maryland 20816. (301) 961-6750. 1984.

Biological Abstracts. BIOSIS, 2100 Arch St., Philadelphia, Pennsylvania 19103-1399. (215) 587-4800. 1927-.

Biological and Agricultural Index. H.W. Wilson Co., 950 University Ave., Bronx, New York 10452. (800) 367-6770. 1916-. Monthly.

Ecological Abstracts. Geo Abstracts Ltd. Elsevier Applied Science, Crown House, Linton Rd., Barking, England IG 11 8JU. 1974-. Derived from over 600 leading ecological and environmental journals, plus books, conference proceedings, reports and theses.

Environment Abstracts. Bowker A & I Publishing, 121 Chanlon Rd., New Providence, New Jersey 07974. (908) 464-6800. 1974-.

Environment Index. Environment Information Center, Index Research Department, 124 E. 39th St., New York, New York 10016. 1971-. Annual.

Environmental Information Connection–EIC. Planning Information Program, Dept. of Urban and Regional Planning, University of Illinois, 1003 West Nevada, Urbana, Illinois 61801. (217) 333-1369. Also available online.

Environmental Periodicals Bibliography. Environmental Studies Institute, International Academy at Santa Barbara, 800 Garden St., Suite D, Santa Barbara, California 93101. (805) 965-5010. Also available online.

General Science Index. H. W. Wilson Co., 950 University Ave., Bronx, New York 10452. 1978-. Monthly, also issued in annual cumulation. Cumulative subject index

to English language periodicals in the subject fields of astronomy, botany, chemistry, earth science, environment and conservation, food and nutrition, genetics, mathematics, medicine and health, microbiology, oceanography, physics, physiology and zoology.

Multimedia Index to Ecology. National Information Center for Educational Media, University of Southern California, Los Angeles, California 90007.

Science Citation Index. Institute for Scientific Information, 3501 Market St., Philadelphia, Pennsylvania 19104. 1961-.

BIBLIOGRAPHIES

EPA Publications Bibliography. U.S. Environmental Protection Agency, Library Systems Branch, 401 M St., SW, Washington, District of Columbia 20460. (202) 260-2090. Quarterly.

ENCYCLOPEDIAS AND DICTIONARIES

Cambridge Encyclopedia of Life Sciences. A. E. Friday and David S. Ingram. Cambridge University Press, 40 W 20th St., New York, New York 10011. (212) 924-3900 or (800) 227-0247. 1985. Includes all topics under biology and ecology.

McGraw-Hill Encyclopedia of Science and Technology. McGraw-Hill, 1221 Avenue of the Americas, New York, New York 10020. (212) 512-2000 or (800) 262-4729. 1992. Seventh edition. Issued in multiple volumes including index. Includes all science and technology broad subject areas.

Van Nostrand's Scientific Encyclopedia. Glenn D. Considine, ed. Van Nostrand Reinhold, 115 5th Ave., New York, New York 10003. (212) 254-3232. 1983. Sixth edition. Includes all broad subject areas in science.

GENERAL WORKS

The Ecology of Giant Kelp Forests in California. Michael S. Foster. U.S. Department of the Interior, U.S. Fish and Wildlife Service, Washington, District of Columbia 20240. (202) 343-5634. 1985. Macrocystis pyrifera, marine ecology and kelp bed ecology.

Kelp Biomass Production. M. Neushul. Gas Research Institute, National Technical Information Service, 5285 Port Royal Rd., Springfield, Virginia 22161. (703) 487-4650. Annual.

Kelp Forests. Judith Connor. Monterey Bay Aquarium Foundation, Monterey, California (408) 648-4888. 1989.

ONLINE DATA BASES

BIOSIS Previews. BIOSIS, 2100 Arch St., Philadelphia, Pennsylvania 19103-1399. (215) 587-4800. Largest and most comprehensive database of research in the life sciences. Contains citations for nearly 9000 primary research journals, monographs, reviews, symposia, preliminary reports, semi-popular journals, selected institutional reports, government reports and research communications.

Cambridge Scientific Abstracts Life Science–CSAL. Cambridge Scientific Abstracts, 5161 River Rd., Bethesda, Maryland 20816. (301) 961-6750. Provides access to the following abstracting services: "Life Sciences Collec-

tion," "Aquatic Sciences and Fisheries Abstracts," "Oceanic Abstracts," and "Pollution Abstracts."

Enviro/Energyline Abstracts Plus. R. R. Bowker Co., 121 Chanlon Rd., New Providence, New Jersey 07974. (908) 464-6800.

Environmental Periodicals Bibliography. National Information Services Corp., Ste. 6, Wyman Towers, 3100 St. Paul St., Baltimore, Maryland 21218. (410)243-0797. Online version of abstract of same name.

SCISEARCH. Institute for Scientific Information, University City Science Center, 3501 Market St., Philadelphia, Pennsylvania 19104. (215) 386-0100.

KENTUCKY ENVIRONMENTAL AGENCIES

GOVERNMENTAL ORGANIZATIONS

Department of Agriculture: Pesticide Registration. Director, Division of Pesticides, 109 S.W. 9th St., Frankfurt, Kentucky 66612-1281. (502) 564-7274.

Department of Environmental Protection: Emergency Preparedness and Community Right-to-Know. Chair, 18 Reilly Rd., Frankfurt, Kentucky 40601. (502) 564-2150.

Department of Labor: Occupational Safety. Secretary, The 127 Building, U.S. 127 South, Frankfurt, Kentucky 40601. (502) 564-2300.

Fish and Wildlife Department: Fish and Wildlife. Commissioner, Tourism Cabinet, #1 Game Farm Rd., Frankfurt, Kentucky 40601. (502) 564-3400.

Natural Resources and Environmental Protection: Air Quality. Director, Air Pollution Control Division, 18 Reilly Rd., Frankfurt, Kentucky 40601. (502) 564-3382.

Natural Resources and Environmental Protection Cabinet: Solid Waste Management. Director, Division of Waste Management, 18 Reilly Rd., Frankfurt, Kentucky 40601. (502) 564-6716.

Natural Resources and Environmental Protection Cabinet: Waste Minimization and Pollution Prevention. Public Information Officer, Division of Waste Management, 18 Reilly Rd., Frankfurt, Kentucky 40601. (502) 564-6716.

Natural Resources and Environmental Protection: Environmental Protection. Secretary, Capital Plaza Tower, 5th Floor, Frankfurt, Kentucky 40601. (502) 564-3350.

Natural Resources and Environmental Protection: Groundwater Management. Secretary, Capital Plaza, 5th Floor, Frankfurt, Kentucky 40601. (502) 564-3350.

Natural Resources and Environmental Protection: Hazardous Waste Management. Secretary, Capital Plaza, 5th Floor, Frankfurt, Kentucky 40601. (502) 564-3350.

Natural Resources and Environmental Protection: Natural Resources. Secretary, 107 Mero St., Frankfurt, Kentucky 40601. (502) 564-2184.

Natural Resources and Environmental Protection: Underground Storage Tanks. Secretary, Capitol Plaza Tower, 5th Floor, Frankfurt, Kentucky 40601. (502) 564-3350.

Natural Resources and Environmental Protection: Water Quality. Director, Division of Water, 18 Reilly Rd., Frankfort, Kentucky 40601. (502) 564-3410.

KENTUCKY ENVIRONMENTAL LEGISLATION

GENERAL WORKS

Kentucky Environmental Law Handbook. Government Institutes, Inc., 4 Research Pl., Ste. 200, Rockville, Maryland 20850. (301) 921-2300. 1991.

KEPONE

See also: CARCINOGENS; MIREX; ORGANOCHLORINES

ABSTRACTING AND INDEXING SERVICES

Applied Ecology Abstracts Studies in Renewable Natural Resources. Information Retrieval Ltd., 1911 Jefferson Davis Highway, Arlington, Virginia 22202. 1975-. Monthly.

Biological and Agricultural Index. H.W. Wilson Co., 950 University Ave., Bronx, New York 10452. (800) 367-6770. 1916-. Monthly.

General Science Index. H. W. Wilson Co., 950 University Ave., Bronx, New York 10452. 1978-. Monthly, also issued in annual cumulation. Cumulative subject index to English language periodicals in the subject fields of astronomy, botany, chemistry, earth science, environment and conservation, food and nutrition, genetics, mathematics, medicine and health, microbiology, oceanography, physics, physiology and zoology.

Multimedia Index to Ecology. National Information Center for Educational Media, University of Southern California, Los Angeles, California 90007.

Pollution Abstracts. Cambridge Scientific Abstracts, 5161 River Rd., Bethesda, Maryland 20816. (301) 961-6750. Six/year. Indexes worldwide technical literature on environmental pollution. Covers air pollution, marine and freshwater pollution, sewage and wastewater treatment, waste management, toxicology and health, noise pollution, radiation, land pollution, and environmental policies, programs, legislation, and education. Also available online.

Science Citation Index. Institute for Scientific Information, 3501 Market St., Philadelphia, Pennsylvania 19104. 1961-.

BIBLIOGRAPHIES

Kepone: A Literature Summary. James Edward Huff. National Technical Information Service, 5285 Port Royal Rd., Springfield, Virginia 22161. (703) 487-4650. 1977.

Kepone Toxicology. Silas Jackson. U.S. Department of Health and Human Services, Public Health Services, National Institutes of Health, 9000 Rockville Pike, Bethesda, Maryland 20892. (301) 496-4000. 1983.

GENERAL WORKS

Kepone, Mirex, Hexachlorocyclopentadine: An Environmental Assessment. National Research Council, National Academy of Sciences, 2101 Constitution Ave., NW, Washington, District of Columbia 20418. (202) 334-2000. 1978. Toxicology and environmental aspects of pesticides.

ONLINE DATA BASES

Chemical Carcinogenesis Research Information System–CCRIS. National Library of Medicine, 8600 Rockville Pike, Bethesda, Maryland 20894. (800) 638-8480. Individual assay results and test conditions for 1,451 chemicals in the areas of carcinogenicity, mutagenicity, tumor promotion, and cocarcinogenicity.

KEROSENE

ABSTRACTING AND INDEXING SERVICES

Applied Science and Technology Index. H.W. Wilson Co., 950 University Ave., Bronx, New York 10452. (800) 367-6770. Formerly Industrial Arts Index.

Engineering Index. The Engineering Index Inc., 345 E. 47th St., New York, New York 10017. 1962-.

General Science Index. H. W. Wilson Co., 950 University Ave., Bronx, New York 10452. 1978-. Monthly, also issued in annual cumulation. Cumulative subject index to English language periodicals in the subject fields of astronomy, botany, chemistry, earth science, environment and conservation, food and nutrition, genetics, mathematics, medicine and health, microbiology, oceanography, physics, physiology and zoology.

Pollution Abstracts. Cambridge Scientific Abstracts, 5161 River Rd., Bethesda, Maryland 20816. (301) 961-6750. Six/year. Indexes worldwide technical literature on environmental pollution. Covers air pollution, marine and freshwater pollution, sewage and wastewater treatment, waste management, toxicology and health, noise pollution, radiation, land pollution, and environmental policies, programs, legislation, and education. Also available online.

Science Citation Index. Institute for Scientific Information, 3501 Market St., Philadelphia, Pennsylvania 19104. 1961-.

DIRECTORIES

Kerosine-Retail. American Business Directories, Inc., 5711 S. 86th Circle, Omaha, Nebraska 68127. (402) 593-4600.

ENCYCLOPEDIAS AND DICTIONARIES

Van Nostrand's Scientific Encyclopedia. Glenn D. Considine, ed. Van Nostrand Reinhold, 115 5th Ave., New York, New York 10003. (212) 254-3232. 1983. Sixth edition. Includes all broad subject areas in science.

GENERAL WORKS

A Consumer's Guide to Kerosene Heaters. Consumer Information Center, 18 F St. NW, Rm. G-142, Washington, District of Columbia 20405. (202) 501-1794. 1982.

Kerosene Heaters. U.S. Consumer Product Safety Commission, 5401 Westbord Ave., Bethesda, Maryland 20207. (301) 492-6580. 1984. Product safety fact sheet.

ONLINE DATA BASES

Computerized Engineering Index–COMPENDEX. Engineering Information Inc., 345 E. 47th St., New York, New York 10017. (212) 705-7600.

TRADE ASSOCIATIONS AND PROFESSIONAL SOCIETIES

National Kerosene Heater Association. First American Center, #15, Nashville, Tennessee 37238. (615) 254-1961.

L

LAGOONS

ABSTRACTING AND INDEXING SERVICES

Abstracts of Air and Water Conservation Literature. American Petroleum Institute. Central Abstracting and Indexing Service, 275 Madison Avenue, New York, New York 10016. 1972.

Applied Ecology Abstracts Studies in Renewable Natural Resources. Information Retrieval Ltd., 1911 Jefferson Davis Highway, Arlington, Virginia 22202. 1975-. Monthly.

Biological Abstracts. BIOSIS, 2100 Arch St., Philadelphia, Pennsylvania 19103-1399. (215) 587-4800. 1927-.

Biological and Agricultural Index. H.W. Wilson Co., 950 University Ave., Bronx, New York 10452. (800) 367-6770. 1916-. Monthly.

Engineering Index. The Engineering Index Inc., 345 E. 47th St., New York, New York 10017. 1962-.

Environment Abstracts. Bowker A & I Publishing, 121 Chanlon Rd., New Providence, New Jersey 07974. (908) 464-6800. 1974-.

Environment Index. Environment Information Center, Index Research Department, 124 E. 39th St., New York, New York 10016. 1971-. Annual.

Environmental Information Connection–EIC. Planning Information Program, Dept. of Urban and Regional Planning, University of Illinois, 1003 West Nevada, Urbana, Illinois 61801. (217) 333-1369. Also available online.

Environmental Periodicals Bibliography. Environmental Studies Institute, International Academy at Santa Barbara, 800 Garden St., Suite D, Santa Barbara, California 93101. (805) 965-5010. Also available online.

General Science Index. H. W. Wilson Co., 950 University Ave., Bronx, New York 10452. 1978-. Monthly, also issued in annual cumulation. Cumulative subject index to English language periodicals in the subject fields of astronomy, botany, chemistry, earth science, environment and conservation, food and nutrition, genetics, mathematics, medicine and health, microbiology, oceanography, physics, physiology and zoology.

Multimedia Index to Ecology. National Information Center for Educational Media, University of Southern California, Los Angeles, California 90007.

Pollution Abstracts. Cambridge Scientific Abstracts, 5161 River Rd., Bethesda, Maryland 20816. (301) 961-6750. Six/year. Indexes worldwide technical literature on environmental pollution. Covers air pollution, marine and freshwater pollution, sewage and wastewater treatment, waste management, toxicology and health, noise pollution, radiation, land pollution, and environmental policies, programs, legislation, and education. Also available online.

Science Citation Index. Institute for Scientific Information, 3501 Market St., Philadelphia, Pennsylvania 19104. 1961-.

BIBLIOGRAPHIES

Current Contents. Agriculture, Biology and Environmental Sciences. Institute for Scientific Information, 3501 Market St., Philadelphia, Pennsylvania 19104. (800) 523-1857. 1973-. Previous title: Current Contents. Agricultural, Food & Veterinary Sciences. Gives the table of contents of periodicals in the fields of agriculture, biology, environmental and related areas.

EPA Publications Bibliography. U.S. Environmental Protection Agency, Library Systems Branch, 401 M St., SW, Washington, District of Columbia 20460. (202) 260-2090. Quarterly.

ENCYCLOPEDIAS AND DICTIONARIES

Van Nostrand's Scientific Encyclopedia. Glenn D. Considine, ed. Van Nostrand Reinhold, 115 5th Ave., New York, New York 10003. (212) 254-3232. 1983. Sixth edition. Includes all broad subject areas in science.

GENERAL WORKS

Sewage Lagoons in Cold Climates. Environmental Protection Service, Technical Service Branch, 425 St. Joseph Blvd., 3rd Fl., Hull, Quebec, Canada K1A 0H3. (613) 953-5921. 1985. Cold weather conditions in sewage lagoons.

Upgrading Lagoons. U.S. Environmental Protection Agency, Technology Transfer, 401 M St. SW, Washington, District of Columbia 20460. (202) 382-5480. 1973.

ONLINE DATA BASES

BIOSIS Previews. BIOSIS, 2100 Arch St., Philadelphia, Pennsylvania 19103-1399. (215) 587-4800. Largest and most comprehensive database of research in the life sciences. Contains citations for nearly 9000 primary research journals, monographs, reviews, symposia, preliminary reports, semi-popular journals, selected institutional reports, government reports and research communications.

Computerized Engineering Index–COMPENDEX. Engineering Information Inc., 345 E. 47th St., New York, New York 10017. (212) 705-7600.

Enviro/Energyline Abstracts Plus. R. R. Bowker Co., 121 Chanlon Rd., New Providence, New Jersey 07974. (908) 464-6800.

Environmental Periodicals Bibliography. National Information Services Corp., Ste. 6, Wyman Towers, 3100 St. Paul St., Baltimore, Maryland 21218. (410)243-0797. Online version of abstract of same name.

SCISEARCH. Institute for Scientific Information, University City Science Center, 3501 Market St., Philadelphia, Pennsylvania 19104. (215) 386-0100.

TRADE ASSOCIATIONS AND PROFESSIONAL SOCIETIES

American Institute of Biological Sciences. 730 11th St., N.W., Washington, District of Columbia 20001-4521. (202) 628-1500.

American Society of Naturalists. Department of Ecology and Evolation, State University of New York, Stony Brook, New York 11794. (516) 632-8589.

LAKES

ABSTRACTING AND INDEXING SERVICES

Abstracts of Air and Water Conservation Literature. American Petroleum Institute. Central Abstracting and Indexing Service, 275 Madison Avenue, New York, New York 10016. 1972.

Applied Ecology Abstracts Studies in Renewable Natural Resources. Information Retrieval Ltd., 1911 Jefferson Davis Highway, Arlington, Virginia 22202. 1975-. Monthly.

Aqualine Abstracts. Water Research Centre. c/o Pergamon Microforms International, Inc., Fairview Park, Elmsford, New York 10523. (914) 592-7720. 1927-. Contains some 8,000 records annually on water and wastewater technology. Covers all aspects of water, wastewater, associated engineering services and the aquatic environment. Over 600 periodicals, as well as books, reports and conference proceedings and other publications from water related institutions worldwide are scanned. Also available online.

ASFA Aquaculture Abstracts. Cambridge Scientific Abstracts, Inc., 5161 River Rd., Bethesda, Maryland 20816. (301) 961-6750. 1984.

Biological Abstracts. BIOSIS, 2100 Arch St., Philadelphia, Pennsylvania 19103-1399. (215) 587-4800. 1927-.

Biological and Agricultural Index. H.W. Wilson Co., 950 University Ave., Bronx, New York 10452. (800) 367-6770. 1916-. Monthly.

Civil Engineering Hydraulic Abstracts. BHRA Fluid Engineering, Air Science Co., PO Box 143, Corning, New York 14830. (607) 962-5591. Monthly. Abstracts of periodicals that publish in the areas of hydraulic engineering and other related topics.

Ecological Abstracts. Geo Abstracts Ltd. Elsevier Applied Science, Crown House, Linton Rd., Barking, England IG 11 8JU. 1974-. Derived from over 600 leading ecological and environmental journals, plus books, conference proceedings, reports and theses.

Ecology Abstracts. Cambridge Scientific Abstracts, 5161 River Rd., Bethesda, Maryland 20816. (301) 961-6750. Monthly.

Environmental Research Laboratories Publication Abstracts. National Oceanic and Atmospheric Administration. Environmental Research Laboratories, 325 Broadway, Boulder, Colorado 80303. 1990. Annual. Sixth annual bibliography of NOAA Environmental Research Laboratories staff publications, FY 89. Covers journal articles, official ERL reports, conference papers, and publications released in cooperation with universities and by ERL funded contractors.

General Science Index. H. W. Wilson Co., 950 University Ave., Bronx, New York 10452. 1978-. Monthly, also issued in annual cumulation. Cumulative subject index to English language periodicals in the subject fields of astronomy, botany, chemistry, earth science, environment and conservation, food and nutrition, genetics, mathematics, medicine and health, microbiology, oceanography, physics, physiology and zoology.

Geographical Abstracts. London School of Economics, Dept. of Geography, Regency House, 34 Duke St., London, England 1966-. Continued by Geo Abstracts issued in 6 parts: Pt. A. Landforms and the quaternary; Pt. B. Biogeography and Climatology; Pt. C. Economic geography; Pt. D. Social geography and cartography; Pt. E. Sedimentology; Pt. F. Regional and community planning.

Multimedia Index to Ecology. National Information Center for Educational Media, University of Southern California, Los Angeles, California 90007.

Pollution Abstracts. Cambridge Scientific Abstracts, 5161 River Rd., Bethesda, Maryland 20816. (301) 961-6750. Six/year. Indexes worldwide technical literature on environmental pollution. Covers air pollution, marine and freshwater pollution, sewage and wastewater treatment, waste management, toxicology and health, noise pollution, radiation, land pollution, and environmental policies, programs, legislation, and education. Also available online.

BIBLIOGRAPHIES

Bibliography and Index of Geology. American Geological Institute, 4220 King St., Alexandria, Virginia 22302. Monthly. Includes environmental geology and hydrogeology.

Current Contents. Agriculture, Biology and Environmental Sciences. Institute for Scientific Information, 3501 Market St., Philadelphia, Pennsylvania 19104. (800) 523-1857. 1973-. Previous title: Current Contents. Agricultural, Food & Veterinary Sciences. Gives the table of contents of periodicals in the fields of agriculture, biology, environmental and related areas.

Lake Studies: An Annotated Bibliography of Social Science Research on Lakes. Vance Bibliographies, PO Box 229, 112 N. Charter St., Monticello, Illinois 61856. (217) 762-3831. 1986.

DIRECTORIES

Great Lakes Red Book. Fishwater Press, Inc., 1701 E. 12th St., Suite 3KW, Cleveland, Ohio 44114. (216) 241-0373.

Great Lakes Region Biomass Energy Facilities Directory. Council of Great Lakes Governors, 310 S. Michigan, 10th Fl., Chicago, Illinois 60604. (312) 427-0092.

ENCYCLOPEDIAS AND DICTIONARIES

The Encyclopedia of Climatology. John E. Oliver and Rhodes W. Fairbridge, eds. Van Nostrand Reinhold, 115 5th Ave., New York, New York 10003. (212) 254-3232. 1987. Belongs in the series Encyclopedia of Earth Sciences, v.11.

Van Nostrand's Scientific Encyclopedia. Glenn D. Considine, ed. Van Nostrand Reinhold, 115 5th Ave., New York, New York 10003. (212) 254-3232. 1983. Sixth edition. Includes all broad subject areas in science.

GENERAL WORKS

The Control of Eutrophication of Lakes and Reservoirs. S. O. Ryding and W. Rast, eds. Parthenon Pub., Casterton Hall, Carnforth, England LA6 2LA. 1990. Volume 1 of the Man and the Biosphere series published jointly with UNESCO.

Erie the Lake that Survived. Noel M. Burns. Rowman & Littlefield, Publishers, Inc., 8705 Bollman Pl., Savage, Maryland 20763. (301) 306-0400. 1985. Describes a model for anyone concerned with large lakes.

Handbook of Limnology. J. Schwoerbel. John Wiley & Sons, Inc., 605 3rd Ave., New York, New York 10158. (212) 850-6000. 1987. Gives an evaluation of response to environmental problems relating to surface water systems, water quality pollution control and environmental concern.

Human Health Risks from Chemical Exposure: The Great Lakes Ecosystem. R. Warren Flint. Lewis Publishers, 2000 Corporate Blvd., N.W., Boca Raton, Florida 33431. (407) 994-0555 or (800) 272-7737. 1991. Gives background on toxic chemicals in the Great Lakes. Also describes the toxicology and environmental chemistry of exposure to toxic chemicals, environmental and wildlife toxicology, epidemiology, public health and other related areas.

Magill's Survey of Science. Earth Science Series. Frank N. Magill. Salem Press, PO Box 50062, Pasadena, California 91105. 1990-. Five volumes. Includes information on earth's crust, hot spots and volcanic island chains, physical properties of minerals, rock magnetism, physical properties of rocks, and index.

Modeling of Total Acid Precipitation Impacts. Jerald L. Schnoor. Butterworth-Heinemann, 80 Montvale Ave., Stoneham, Massachusetts 02180. (617) 438-8464. 1984.

Physical Behavior of PCBs in the Great Lakes. Donald Mackay. Ann Arbor Science, 230 Collingwood, Ann Arbor, Michigan 48106. 1983.

Sediments: Chemistry and Toxicity of In-Place Pollutants. Renato Baudo, et al., eds. Lewis Publishers, 200 Corporate Blvd. NW, Boca Raton, Florida 33431. (407) 994-0555 or (800)272-7737. 1990.

Stream, Lake, Estuary, and Ocean Pollution. Nelson Leonard Nemerow. Van Nostrand Reinhold, 115 5th Ave., New York, New York 10003. (800) 926-2665. 1991.

The Uses of Ecology: Lake Washington and Beyond. W. T. Edmondson. University of Washington Press, PO Box 50096, Seattle, Washington 98145-5096. (206) 543-4050; (800) 441-4115. 1991. Author delivered most of the contents of this book as a Danz lecture at the University of Washington. Gives an account of the pollution and recovery of Lake Washington and describes how communities worked and applied lessons learned from Lake Washington cleanup. Includes extensive documentation and bibliographies.

Water Quality Modeling. Brian Henderson-Sellere, et al. CRC Press, 2000 Corporate Blvd. N.W., Boca Raton, Florida 33431. (407) 994-0555; (800) 272-7737. 1990. Issues in four volumes. Discusses water supply and treatment and water resources engineering.

GOVERNMENTAL ORGANIZATIONS

Great Lakes Commission. The Argus II Bldg., 400 4th St., Ann Arbor, Michigan 48103-4816. (313) 665-9135.

ONLINE DATA BASES

BIOSIS Previews. BIOSIS, 2100 Arch St., Philadelphia, Pennsylvania 19103-1399. (215) 587-4800. Largest and most comprehensive database of research in the life sciences. Contains citations for nearly 9000 primary research journals, monographs, reviews, symposia, preliminary reports, semi-popular journals, selected institutional reports, government reports and research communications.

Great Lakes Water Quality Data Base. U.S. Environmental Protection Agency, Office of Research and Development, Large Lakes Research Station, 401 M St. SW, Washington, District of Columbia 20460. (202) 260-2090. Water data related to the Great Lakes and related tributaries and watersheds.

SCISEARCH. Institute for Scientific Information, University City Science Center, 3501 Market St., Philadelphia, Pennsylvania 19104. (215) 386-0100.

PERIODICALS AND NEWSLETTERS

Advisor. Great Lakes Commission, 2200 North Bonisteel Blvd., Ann Arbor, Michigan 48109. (313) 665-9135. 1956-. Monthly. Concerns current developments relating to activities of the Great Lakes Commission and its eight member states. Includes environment, economy, and Great Lakes related issues.

American Midland Naturalist. University of Notre Dame, Notre Dame, Indiana 46556. (219) 239-7481. Quarterly. Basic research in biology including animal and plant ecology, systematics and entomology, mammalogy, ichthyology, parasitology, invertebrate zoology, and limnology.

Focus on International Joint Commission Activities. IJC Great Lakes Regional Office, PO Box 32869, Detroit, Michigan 48232. (313) 226-2170. 1986-. Three issues a year. Provides information on Great Lakes water quality and quantity issues.

Great Lakes Exchange. Waste Systems Institute of Michigan, Inc., 470 Market, SW, Suite 100-A, Grand Rapids, Michigan 49503. (616) 363-3262. Bimonthly. Information on waste management and pollution control .

Great Lakes News Letter. Great Lakes Commission, The Argus II Bldg., 400 S. Fourth St., Ann Arbor, Michigan 48109. (313) 665-9135. 1956-. Bimonthly.

Great Lakes Troller. District Extension Sea Grant Agent, 333 Clinton, Grand Haven, Michigan 49417. (616) 846-8250. Quarterly. Issues concerning Great Lakes fisheries.

Journal of Great Lakes Research. International Association for Great Lakes Research, University of Michigan, 2200 Bonisteel Blvd., Ann Arbor, Michigan 48109-2099. (313) 763-1520. Quarterly. Research on lakes of the world.

Lake Line. North American Lake Management Society, 1000 Connecticut Ave., NW, Suite 300, Washington, District of Columbia 20036. (202) 466-8550. Bimonthly. Articles on developments in limnology and lake management.

Limnology and Oceanography. American Society of Limnology and Oceanography, Inc., PO Box 1897, Lawrence, Kansas 66044-8897. (913) 843-1221. Topics in aquatic disciplines.

Littoral Drift. University of Wisconsin Sea Grant Institute, 1800 University Ave., Madison, Wisconsin 53705. (608) 263-3259. Ten times a year. National Sea Grant program and current Great Lakes issues.

Michigan Waste Report. Michigan Waste Report, Inc., 400 Ann, SW, Suite 204, Grand Rapids, Michigan 49504. (616) 363-3262. Biweekly. Covers information about waste management.

RESEARCH CENTERS AND INSTITUTES

Adirondack Lakes Survey Corporation. New York State Dept. of Environmental Conservation, Ray Brook, New York 12977. (518) 891-2758.

Center for Limnology. University of Colorado-Boulder, Department of EPO Biology, Boulder, Colorado 80309-0334. (303) 492-6379.

Eagle Lake Field Station. Department of Biological Sciences, California State University, Chico, Chico, California 95929-0515. (916) 898-4490.

Katherine Ordway Preserve and the Swisher Memorial Sanctuary. University of Florida, School of Forest Resources and Conservation, Gainesville, Florida 32611. (904) 392-1721.

Michigan State University, Inland Lakes Research and Study Center. 334 Natural Resources Building, East Lansing, Michigan 48824. (517) 353-3742.

Ohio State University, Ohio Sea Grant College Program. 1541 Research Center, 1314 Kinnear Road, Columbus, Ohio 43212. (614) 292-8949.

Purdue University, Great Lakes Coastal Research Laboratory. School of Civil Engineering, West Lafayette, Indiana 47907. (317) 494-3713.

State University of New York at Buffalo, Great Lakes Laboratory. 1300 Elmwood Avenue, Buffalo, New York 14222. (716) 878-5422.

University of Kansas, Water Resources Institute. Lawrence, Kansas 66045. (913) 864-3807.

University of Michigan, Center for Great Lakes and Aquatic Sciences. 2200 Bonisteel Boulevard, Ann Arbor, Michigan 48109-2099. (313) 763-3515.

University of Minnesota, Lake Itasca Forestry and Biological Station. Post Office, Lake Itasca, Minnesota 56460. (218) 266-3345.

University of Minnesota, Limnological Research Center. Pillsbury Hall 220, 310 Pillsbury Drive Southeast, Minneapolis, Minnesota 55455. (612) 624-7005.

University of Minnesota, Minnesota Sea Grant College Program. 1518 Cleveland Ave., Ste. 302, St. Paul, Minnesota 55108. (612) 625-9288.

University of Minnesota, Water Resources Research Center. 1518 Cleveland Ave., Ste. 302, St. Paul, Minnesota 55108. (612) 624-9282.

University of Montana, Flathead Lake Biological Station. 311 Bio Station Lane, Polson, Montana 59860. (406) 982-3301.

University of Nevada-Las Vegas, Lake Mead Limnological Research Center. 4505 Maryland Parkway, Las Vegas, Nevada 89154. (702) 798-0580.

University of North Dakota, Devil's Lake Biological Station. Grand Forks, North Dakota 58202-8238. (701) 777-2621.

University of Notre Dame, Environmental Research Center. Department of Biological Sciences, Notre Dame, Indiana 46556. (219) 239-7186.

University of Pittsburgh, Pymatuning Laboratory of Ecology. R.R. #1, Box 7, Linesville, Pennsylvania 16424. (814) 683-5813.

University of Virginia, Mountain Lake Biological Station. Room 251, Gilmer Hall, Charlottesville, Virginia 22901. (804) 982-5486.

University of Wisconsin-Madison, Center for Limnology. 680 North Park Street, Madison, Wisconsin 53706. (608) 262-3014.

University of Wisconsin-Madison, Marine Studies Center. 1269 Engineering Building, 1415 Johnson Drive, Madison, Wisconsin 53706. (608) 262-3883.

University of Wisconsin-Madison, Sea Grant Advisory Services. Walkway Mall, 522 Bayshore Drive, Sister Bay, Wisconsin 54234. (414) 854-5329.

University of Wisconsin-Madison, Water Chemistry Program. 660 North Park Street, Madison, Wisconsin 53706. (608) 262-2470.

University of Wisconsin-Milwaukee, Center for Great Lakes Studies. Milwaukee, Wisconsin 53201. (414) 649-3000.

University of Wisconsin-Milwaukee, Herbarium. Department of Biological Sciences, Box 413, Milwaukee, Wisconsin 53201. (414) 229-6728.

University of Wisconsin-Superior, Center for Lake Superior Environmental Studies. 1800 Grand Avenue, Superior, Wisconsin 54880. (715) 394-8315.

University of Wisconsin, University of Wisconsin Sea Grant Institute. 1800 University Avenue, Madison, Wisconsin 53705. (608) 262-0905.

Utah State University, Bear Lake Biological Laboratory. c/o Department of Fisheries and Wildlife, Logan, Utah 84322-5210. (801) 753-2459.

Wisconsin Cooperative Wildlife Research Unit. University of Wisconsin, 266 Russell Laboratories, Madison, Wisconsin 53706. (608) 263-6882.

STATISTICS SOURCES

Cleaning Up Great Lakes Areas of Concern: How Much Will it Cost?. Northeast-Midwest Institute, Publications Office, 218 D St., SE, Washington, District of Columbia 20003. 1989.

Water Resources Data. U.S. Geological Survey. U.S. G.P.O., Washington, District of Columbia 20401. (202) 512-0000. Annual. Data on water supply and quality of streams, lakes and reservoirs for individual states by water year.

World Resources. World Resources Institute. 1709 New York Ave., N.W., Washington, District of Columbia 20006. (202) 638-6300. Annual. Statistical and textual analysis of world's natural resources and the effects of growth-caused environmental pollution.

TRADE ASSOCIATIONS AND PROFESSIONAL SOCIETIES

American Littoral Society. Sandy Hook, Highlands, New Jersey 07732. (908) 291-0055.

American Society of Civil Engineers. 345 East 47th St., New York, New York 10017. (212) 705-7496.

American Society of Naturalists. Department of Ecology and Evolation, State University of New York, Stony Brook, New York 11794. (516) 632-8589.

Great Lakes Sport Fishing Council. c/o Dan Thomas, 293 Berteau, Elmhurst, Illinois 60126. (708) 941-1351.

Great Lakes United. Cassety Hall, 1300 Elmwood Ave., State University College at Buffalo, Buffalo, New York 14222. (716) 886-0142.

Great Lakes Unlimited. 24 Agassiz Circle, Buffalo, New York 14214. (716) 886-0142.

International Association for Great Lakes Research. 2200 Bonisteel Blvd., University of Michigan, Ann Arbor, Michigan 48109-2099. (313) 747-1673.

International Association of Theoretical and Applied Limnology. c/o Dr. Robert G. Wetzel, Dept. of Biology, University of Michigan, Ann Arbor, Michigan 48109. (313) 936-3193.

North American Lake Management Society. 1 Progress Blvd., Box 27, Alachua, Florida 32615-9536. (904) 462-2554.

LAMPRICIDES

ABSTRACTING AND INDEXING SERVICES

Biological and Agricultural Index. H.W. Wilson Co., 950 University Ave., Bronx, New York 10452. (800) 367-6770. 1916-. Monthly.

Ecological Abstracts. Geo Abstracts Ltd. Elsevier Applied Science, Crown House, Linton Rd., Barking, England IG 11 8JU. 1974-. Derived from over 600 leading ecological and environmental journals, plus books, conference proceedings, reports and theses.

Environment Abstracts. Bowker A & I Publishing, 121 Chanlon Rd., New Providence, New Jersey 07974. (908) 464-6800. 1974-.

Environment Index. Environment Information Center, Index Research Department, 124 E. 39th St., New York, New York 10016. 1971-. Annual.

Environmental Information Connection–EIC. Planning Information Program, Dept. of Urban and Regional Planning, University of Illinois, 1003 West Nevada, Urbana, Illinois 61801. (217) 333-1369. Also available online.

Environmental Periodicals Bibliography. Environmental Studies Institute, International Academy at Santa Barbara, 800 Garden St., Suite D, Santa Barbara, California 93101. (805) 965-5010. Also available online.

Science Citation Index. Institute for Scientific Information, 3501 Market St., Philadelphia, Pennsylvania 19104. 1961-.

BIBLIOGRAPHIES

EPA Publications Bibliography. U.S. Environmental Protection Agency, Library Systems Branch, 401 M St., SW, Washington, District of Columbia 20460. (202) 260-2090. Quarterly.

ENCYCLOPEDIAS AND DICTIONARIES

Van Nostrand's Scientific Encyclopedia. Glenn D. Considine, ed. Van Nostrand Reinhold, 115 5th Ave., New York, New York 10003. (212) 254-3232. 1983. Sixth edition. Includes all broad subject areas in science.

GENERAL WORKS

Investigations in Fish Control. Verdel K. Dawson. U.S. Department of the Interior, Fish and Wildlife Service, Washington, District of Columbia 20240. (202) 343-5634. 1982. Effect of lampricides and rotenone on fishes.

ONLINE DATA BASES

CERCLIS. Chemical Information Systems, Inc., 7215 York Rd., Baltimore, Maryland 21212. (301) 321-8440. Information on hazardous waste disposal sites that have either been listed by the EPA on the National Priority List (NPL) or nominated for consideration for the NPL.

Enviro/Energyline Abstracts Plus. R. R. Bowker Co., 121 Chanlon Rd., New Providence, New Jersey 07974. (908) 464-6800.

Environmental Periodicals Bibliography. National Information Services Corp., Ste. 6, Wyman Towers, 3100 St.

Paul St., Baltimore, Maryland 21218. (410)243-0797. Online version of abstract of same name.

SCISEARCH. Institute for Scientific Information, University City Science Center, 3501 Market St., Philadelphia, Pennsylvania 19104. (215) 386-0100.

LAND POLLUTION
See: POLLUTION CONTROL

LAND RECLAMATION

ABSTRACTING AND INDEXING SERVICES

Abstracts of Air and Water Conservation Literature. American Petroleum Institute. Central Abstracting and Indexing Service, 275 Madison Avenue, New York, New York 10016. 1972.

Agrindex. AGRIS Coordinating Center, Via delle Terme di Caracalla, Rome, Italy I-00100. 61 0181-FA01. 1975-.

Applied Ecology Abstracts Studies in Renewable Natural Resources. Information Retrieval Ltd., 1911 Jefferson Davis Highway, Arlington, Virginia 22202. 1975-. Monthly.

Biological and Agricultural Index. H.W. Wilson Co., 950 University Ave., Bronx, New York 10452. (800) 367-6770. 1916-. Monthly.

Civil Engineering Hydraulic Abstracts. BHRA Fluid Engineering, Air Science Co., PO Box 143, Corning, New York 14830. (607) 962-5591. Monthly. Abstracts of periodicals that publish in the areas of hydraulic engineering and other related topics.

Current Advances in Ecological and Environmental Science. Pergamon Microforms International, Inc., Fairview Park, Elmsford, New York 10523. (914) 592-7720. 1989-. Monthly. Current literature searching service includingjournals, reports, abstracts, etc. This service is available online as part of the CABS database on the hosts BRS and ORBIT search service.

Ecological Abstracts. Geo Abstracts Ltd. Elsevier Applied Science, Crown House, Linton Rd., Barking, England IG 11 8JU. 1974-. Derived from over 600 leading ecological and environmental journals, plus books, conference proceedings, reports and theses.

Environment Abstracts. Bowker A & I Publishing, 121 Chanlon Rd., New Providence, New Jersey 07974. (908) 464-6800. 1974-.

Environment Index. Environment Information Center, Index Research Department, 124 E. 39th St., New York, New York 10016. 1971-. Annual.

Environmental Information Connection–EIC. Planning Information Program, Dept. of Urban and Regional Planning, University of Illinois, 1003 West Nevada, Urbana, Illinois 61801. (217) 333-1369. Also available online.

Environmental Periodicals Bibliography. Environmental Studies Institute, International Academy at Santa Barbara, 800 Garden St., Suite D, Santa Barbara, California 93101. (805) 965-5010. Also available online.

Forestry Abstracts. C. A. B. International, Wallingford, England OX10 8DE. (0491) 3211. 1939/40-. Monthly. Journal of abstracts of journal articles, conferences, technical reports in the subject areas of: silviculture, forest mensuration and management, physical environment, fire, plant biology, genetics and breeding, mycology and pathology, game and wildlife, fish, protection of forests and other related matter.

General Science Index. H. W. Wilson Co., 950 University Ave., Bronx, New York 10452. 1978-. Monthly, also issued in annual cumulation. Cumulative subject index to English language periodicals in the subject fields of astronomy, botany, chemistry, earth science, environment and conservation, food and nutrition, genetics, mathematics, medicine and health, microbiology, oceanography, physics, physiology and zoology.

Index to Scientific Book Contents. Institute for Scientific Information, 3501 Market St., Philadelphia, Pennsylvania 19104. (800) 523-1857. 1985-. Annual. Gives contents of science books published.

Multimedia Index to Ecology. National Information Center for Educational Media, University of Southern California, Los Angeles, California 90007.

Pollution Abstracts. Cambridge Scientific Abstracts, 5161 River Rd., Bethesda, Maryland 20816. (301) 961-6750. Six/year. Indexes worldwide technical literature on environmental pollution. Covers air pollution, marine and freshwater pollution, sewage and wastewater treatment, waste management, toxicology and health, noise pollution, radiation, land pollution, and environmental policies, programs, legislation, and education. Also available online.

Science Citation Index. Institute for Scientific Information, 3501 Market St., Philadelphia, Pennsylvania 19104. 1961-.

Soils and Fertilizers. C. A. B. International, 845 North Park Ave., Tucson, Arizona 85719. (602) 621-7897 or (800) 528-4841. 1937-. Monthly. Focuses on soil chemistry, soil physics, soil biology, soil fertility, soil management, soil classification, soil formation, soil conservation, land reclamation, irrigation and damage, fertilizer technology, fertilizer use, plant nutrition, plant water relations, and environmental aspects.

BIBLIOGRAPHIES

Bibliography and Index of Geology. American Geological Institute, 4220 King St., Alexandria, Virginia 22302. Monthly. Includes environmental geology and hydrogeology.

Bibliography on the Economics and Technology of Mined Land Reclamation. Henry N. McCarl. Vance Bibliographies, PO Box 229, 112 N. Charter St., Monticello, Illinois 61856. (217) 762-3831. 1983.

Current Contents. Agriculture, Biology and Environmental Sciences. Institute for Scientific Information, 3501 Market St., Philadelphia, Pennsylvania 19104. (800) 523-1857. 1973-. Previous title: Current Contents. Agricultural, Food & Veterinary Sciences. Gives the table of contents of periodicals in the fields of agriculture, biology, environmental and related areas.

Ecological Aspects of the Reclamation of Derelict and Disturbed Land: An Annotated Bibliography. Gordon T. Goodman. Geo Abstracts Ltd., c/o Elsevier Science

Publishers, Crown House, Linton Rd., Barking, England IG11 8JU. 1975.

EPA Publications Bibliography. U.S. Environmental Protection Agency, Library Systems Branch, 401 M St., SW, Washington, District of Columbia 20460. (202) 260-2090. Quarterly.

DIRECTORIES

Land Clearing and Leveling. 5711 S. 86th Circle, Omaha, Nebraska 68127. (402) 248-9510. Irregular.

ENCYCLOPEDIAS AND DICTIONARIES

Dictionary of Environmental Engineering and Related Sciences: English-Spanish, Spanish-English. Jose T. Villate. Ediciones Universal, 3090 SW 8th St., Miami, Florida 33135. (305) 642-3355. 1979.

Encyclopedia of Community Planning and Environmental Management. Marilyn Spigel Schultz. Facts on File, Inc., 460 Park Ave. S., New York, New York 10016. (212) 683-2244. 1984.

Encyclopedia of Environmental Science and Engineering. J.R. Pfafflin. Gordon and Breach Science Publishers, Inc., 270 8th Ave., New York, New York 10011. (212) 206-8900. 1992.

Van Nostrand's Scientific Encyclopedia. Glenn D. Considine, ed. Van Nostrand Reinhold, 115 5th Ave., New York, New York 10003. (212) 254-3232. 1983. Sixth edition. Includes all broad subject areas in science.

GENERAL WORKS

Bioengineering for Land Reclamation and Conservation. University of Alberta Press, Edmonton, Alberta, Canada T6G 2G2. (403) 432-3254. 1980.

Environmental Change in Iceland: Past and Present. Judith K. Maizels and Chris Caseldine, eds. Kluwer Academic Publishers, 101 Philip Dr., Assinippi Park, Norwell, Massachusetts 02061. (617) 871-6600. 1991. Describes the glacial landforms and paleoclimatology in Iceland. Volume 7 of the Glaciology and Quaternary Geology Series.

Land Reclamation: An End to Dereliction?. M. C. R. Davies, ed. Elsevier Applied Science, Crown House, Linton Rd., Barking, England IG11. (081) 594-7272. 1991. Proceedings of the 3rd International Conference on Land Reclamation held at Cardiff, Wales.

Land Reclamation and Biomass Production with Municipal Wastewater and Sludge. Pennsylvania State University Press, Barbara Bldg., Ste. C, University Park, Pennsylvania 16802. (814) 865-1372. 1982. Sewage and sewage sludge as fertilizer.

The Role of Land/Inland Water Ecotones in Landscape Management and Restoration. Robert J. Naiman, et al, eds. UNESCO, 7, place de Fontenoy, Paris, France F-75700. (331) 45 68 40 67. 1989. MAB Digest 4. This is a proposal for collaborative research dealing with land management and restoration.

GOVERNMENTAL ORGANIZATIONS

Office of Public Affairs: Bureau of Land Management. 18th and C St., N.W., Washington, District of Columbia 20240. (202) 208-3435.

HANDBOOKS AND MANUALS

Land Reclamation in Cities: A Guide to Methods of Establishment of Vegetation on Urban Waste Land. R. A. Dutton. HMSO, PO Box 276, London, England SW8 5DT. 1982.

ONLINE DATA BASES

Enviro/Energyline Abstracts Plus. R. R. Bowker Co., 121 Chanlon Rd., New Providence, New Jersey 07974. (908) 464-6800.

Environmental Periodicals Bibliography. National Information Services Corp., Ste. 6, Wyman Towers, 3100 St. Paul St., Baltimore, Maryland 21218. (410)243-0797. Online version of abstract of same name.

Monthly Catalog of United States Government Publications. U.S. G.P.O., Supt. of Docs., PO Box 371954, Pittsburgh, Pennsylvania 15250-7954. (202) 512-0000.

National Technical Information Service. U.S. Department of Commerce, National Technical Information Service, Office of Data Base Services, 5285 Port Royal Rd., Springfield, Virginia 22161. (703) 487-4807. Bibliographic database of government sponsored research and technical reports.

PressNet Environmental Reports. Chemical Information Systems, Inc., 7215 York Rd., Baltimore, Maryland 21212. (301) 321-8440.

SCISEARCH. Institute for Scientific Information, University City Science Center, 3501 Market St., Philadelphia, Pennsylvania 19104. (215) 386-0100.

PERIODICALS AND NEWSLETTERS

Environmental Geology & Water Sciences. Springer-Verlag, 175 Fifth Avenue, New York, New York 10010. (212) 460-1500. Bimonthly. Covers interactions between humanity and Earth.

Land Letter. The Conservation Fund, 1800 N. Kent St., Suite 1120, Arlington, Virginia 22209. (703) 522-8008. Thirty four times a year. National land use and conservation policy; legislative, regulatory, and legal developments; use of private and public lands.

Land Use and Environmental Law Review. Clark Boardman Callaghan, 155 Pfingsten Rd., Deerfield, Illinois 60015. (800) 221-9428. Annual. Reprints of articles that appear in law reviews.

Land Use Digest. Urban Land Institute, 625 Indiana Avenue, NW, Suite 400, Washington, District of Columbia 20004. (202) 624-7000. Monthly. Information for planners and developers.

Washington Report. Interstate Conference on Water Policy, 955 L'Enfant Plaza, 6th Floor, Washington, District of Columbia 20024. (202) 466-7287. Every six weeks. Covers water conservation, development and administration.

RESEARCH CENTERS AND INSTITUTES

Montana State University, Reclamation Research Unit. Animal & Range Science Department, Bozeman, Montana 59717. (406) 994-4821.

TRADE ASSOCIATIONS AND PROFESSIONAL SOCIETIES

American Land Resource Association. 1516 P St., N.W., Washington, District of Columbia 20033. (202) 265-5000.

National Association of Conservation Districts. 509 Capitol Court, N.E., Washington, District of Columbia 20002. (202) 547-6223.

National Association of State Land Reclamationists. 459 B Carlisle Dr., Herndon, Virginia 22070. (703) 709-8654.

LAND USE

See also: AGRICULTURAL CONSERVATION; AGRICULTURE; RECLAMATION; TRANSPORTATION; URBAN DESIGN AND PLANNING

ABSTRACTING AND INDEXING SERVICES

Abstracts of Air and Water Conservation Literature. American Petroleum Institute. Central Abstracting and Indexing Service, 275 Madison Avenue, New York, New York 10016. 1972.

Applied Ecology Abstracts Studies in Renewable Natural Resources. Information Retrieval Ltd., 1911 Jefferson Davis Highway, Arlington, Virginia 22202. 1975-. Monthly.

Biological and Agricultural Index. H.W. Wilson Co., 950 University Ave., Bronx, New York 10452. (800) 367-6770. 1916-. Monthly.

Current Advances in Ecological and Environmental Science. Pergamon Microforms International, Inc., Fairview Park, Elmsford, New York 10523. (914) 592-7720. 1989-. Monthly. Current literature searching service includingjournals, reports, abstracts, etc. This service is available online as part of the CABS database on the hosts BRS and ORBIT search service.

EIS: Digests of Environmental Impact Statements. Cambridge Scientific Abstracts, 5161 River Rd., Bethesda, Maryland 20816. (301) 951-1400. 1970-. Bimonthly. Provides detailed abstracts of all the environmental impact statements issued by the federal government each year and indexes them. Also extracts the key issues from the complex government released environmental impact statements. Contents include areas such as: air transportation, defense programs, energy, hazardous substances, land use, manufacturing, parks, refuges, forests, research and development, roads and railroads, urban and social programs, wastes, and water.

Energy Information Abstracts Annual 1987 in Retrospect. EIC/Intelligence Inc., 121 Chanlon Rd., New Providence, New Jersey 07974. (908) 464-6800. 1988. Annual. Cumulative edition of the monthly Energy Information Abstracts. Monitors sources in the field of energy including the scientific, technical and business journal literature, conference and symposia proceedings, corporate, government and academic reports.

Environment Abstracts. Bowker A & I Publishing, 121 Chanlon Rd., New Providence, New Jersey 07974. (908) 464-6800. 1974-.

Environment Index. Environment Information Center, Index Research Department, 124 E. 39th St., New York, New York 10016. 1971-. Annual.

Environmental Information Connection-EIC. Planning Information Program, Dept. of Urban and Regional Planning, University of Illinois, 1003 West Nevada, Urbana, Illinois 61801. (217) 333-1369. Also available online.

Environmental Periodicals Bibliography. Environmental Studies Institute, International Academy at Santa Barbara, 800 Garden St., Suite D, Santa Barbara, California 93101. (805) 965-5010. Also available online.

Forestry Abstracts. C. A. B. International, Wallingford, England OX10 8DE. (0491) 3211. 1939/40-. Monthly. Journal of abstracts of journal articles, conferences, technical reports in the subject areas of: silviculture, forest mensuration and management, physical environment, fire, plant biology, genetics and breeding, mycology and pathology, game and wildlife, fish, protection of forests and other related matter.

General Science Index. H. W. Wilson Co., 950 University Ave., Bronx, New York 10452. 1978-. Monthly, also issued in annual cumulation. Cumulative subject index to English language periodicals in the subject fields of astronomy, botany, chemistry, earth science, environment and conservation, food and nutrition, genetics, mathematics, medicine and health, microbiology, oceanography, physics, physiology and zoology.

Geographical Abstracts. London School of Economics, Dept. of Geography, Regency House, 34 Duke St., London, England 1966-. Continued by Geo Abstracts issued in 6 parts: Pt. A. Landforms and the quaternary; Pt. B. Biogeography and Climatology; Pt. C. Economic geography; Pt. D. Social geography and cartography; Pt. E. Sedimentology; Pt. F. Regional and community planning.

Herbage Abstracts. C. A. B. International, 845 North Park Ave., Tucson, Arizona 85719. (602) 621-7897 or (800) 528-4841. 1931-. Monthly. Covers management, productivity and economics of grasslands, rangelands and fodder crops, grassland ecology, seed production, toxic plants, land use and farming systems, weed control, agricultural meteorology, and other related areas.

Index to Scientific Book Contents. Institute for Scientific Information, 3501 Market St., Philadelphia, Pennsylvania 19104. (800) 523-1857. 1985-. Annual. Gives contents of science books published.

Irrigation and Drainage Abstracts. C. A. B. International, 845 North Park Ave., Tucson, Arizona 85719. (602) 621-7897 or (800) 258-4841. 1975-. Quarterly. Subject areas scanned are: water management, irrigation of crop plants, drainage, soil water relations, plant water relations, salinity and toxicity problems, soil condition, evaporotranspiration, evaporation, land use, streams, water quality, and other related areas.

Land Use Planning Abstracts. Environmental Information Center, Land Use Reference Dept., 292 Madison Ave., New York, New York 10017.

Multimedia Index to Ecology. National Information Center for Educational Media, University of Southern California, Los Angeles, California 90007.

Pollution Abstracts. Cambridge Scientific Abstracts, 5161 River Rd., Bethesda, Maryland 20816. (301) 961-6750. Six/year. Indexes worldwide technical literature on environmental pollution. Covers air pollution, marine and freshwater pollution, sewage and wastewater treatment, waste management, toxicology and health, noise pollu-

tion, radiation, land pollution, and environmental policies, programs, legislation, and education. Also available online.

Science Citation Index. Institute for Scientific Information, 3501 Market St., Philadelphia, Pennsylvania 19104. 1961-.

BIBLIOGRAPHIES

Bibliography and Index of Geology. American Geological Institute, 4220 King St., Alexandria, Virginia 22302. Monthly. Includes environmental geology and hydrogeology.

EPA Publications Bibliography. U.S. Environmental Protection Agency, Library Systems Branch, 401 M St., SW, Washington, District of Columbia 20460. (202) 260-2090. Quarterly.

A Selected Annotated Bibliography on Ecological Planning Resources. Fredrick Steiner. Vance Bibliographies, PO Box 229, 112 N. Charter St., Monticello, Illinois 61856. (217) 762-3831. 1983.

DIRECTORIES

National Directory of Conservation Land Trusts. Land Trust Exchange, 1017 Duke St., Alexandria, Virginia 22314. (207) 288-9751.

ENCYCLOPEDIAS AND DICTIONARIES

Dictionary of Environmental Engineering and Related Sciences: English-Spanish, Spanish-English. Jose T. Villate. Ediciones Universal, 3090 SW 8th St., Miami, Florida 33135. (305) 642-3355. 1979.

Encyclopedia of Community Planning and Environmental Management. Marilyn Spigel Schultz. Facts on File, Inc., 460 Park Ave. S., New York, New York 10016. (212) 683-2244. 1984.

Encyclopedia of Environmental Science and Engineering. J.R. Pfafflin. Gordon and Breach Science Publishers, Inc., 270 8th Ave., New York, New York 10011. (212) 206-8900. 1992.

Encyclopedia of Physical Science and Technology. Robert A. Meyers, ed. Academic Press, c/o Harcourt Brace Jovanovich Inc., 6277 Sea Harbor Dr., Orlando, Florida 32887. (800) 346-8648. Dictionary of engineering, technology and physical sciences.

Illustrated Encyclopedia of Science and the Future. Mike Biscare, et al., ed. Marshall Cavendish, 58 Old Compton St., London, England 0W1V5 PA. 01-734 6710. 1983. Twenty volumes. Each volume has 5 sections: Frontiers, Electronics in Action, Medical Science, Military Technology, and Resources.

McGraw-Hill Encyclopedia of Science and Technology. McGraw-Hill, 1221 Avenue of the Americas, New York, New York 10020. (212) 512-2000 or (800) 262-4729. 1992. Seventh edition. Issued in multiple volumes including index. Includes all science and technology broad subject areas.

The New York Times Encyclopedic Dictionary of the Environment. Paul Sarnoff. Quadrangle Books, New York, New York 1971. Focuses on state-of-the-art methods of pollution control, abatement, prevention and removal.

Van Nostrand's Scientific Encyclopedia. Glenn D. Considine, ed. Van Nostrand Reinhold, 115 5th Ave., New York, New York 10003. (212) 254-3232. 1983. Sixth edition. Includes all broad subject areas in science.

GENERAL WORKS

The Conservation Easement in California. Thomas S. Barrett & Putnam Livermore for the Trust for Public Land. Island Press, 1718 Connecticut Ave. N.W., Suite 300, Washington, District of Columbia 20009. (202) 232-7933. 1983. Conservation lawyers discuss techniques, tax implications and solutions to potential problems.

Creating Successful Communities. Michael A. Mantelli, et al. Island Press, 1718 Connecticut Ave. N.W., Suite 300, Washington, District of Columbia 20009. (202) 232-7933. 1990. Compendium of techniques for effective land use and growth management to help communities retain their individuality in the face of rapid growth.

Ecology and Land Management in Amazonia. Michael J. Eden. Belhaven Press, 136 S. Broadway, Irvington, New York 10533. (914) 591-9111. 1990. Deals with three major areas: the rain forest as a global resource and its role in sustaining life on the planet as a whole; needs of the countries with large tracts of tropical rain forest (including the factors that relate to how one can utilize land, the climate, geomorphology, hydrology, soils and ecology); and how the Amazonia rain forest can be conserved, including the role of national parks and management at the regional level.

Environmental Analysis: For Land Use and Site Planning. McGraw-Hill Science & Engineering Books, 11 W. 19th St., New York, New York 10011. (212) 337-6010. 1978.

Farms of Tomorrow. Trauger Groh. Bio-Dynamic Farming and Gardening Association, PO Box 550, Kimberton, Pennsylvania 19442. (215) 935-7797. 1990. Describes a new approach to farming called community supported agriculture (CSA). It is built upon the solid foundation of organic and biodynamic cultivation, but it focuses on the social and economic conditions that make farming possible.

Federal Lands: A Guide to Planning, Management, and State Revenues. Sally K. Fairfax. Island Press, 1718 Connecticut Ave. N.W., Suite 300, Washington, District of Columbia 20009. (202) 232-7933. 1987. Comprehensive reference on the management and allocation of revenues from public lands.

Land Reclamation: An End to Dereliction?. M. C. R. Davies, ed. Elsevier Applied Science, Crown House, Linton Rd., Barking, England IG11. (081) 594-7272. 1991. Proceedings of the 3rd International Conference on Land Reclamation held at Cardiff, Wales.

Land-Saving Action. Russell L. Brenneman and Sarah M. Bates, eds. Island Press, 1718 Connecticut Ave. N.W., Suite 300, Washington, District of Columbia 20009. (202) 232-7933. 1984. Guide to saving land and an explanation of the conservation tools and techniques developed by individuals and organizations across the country.

Land Use Planning and Coal Refuse Disposal. Robert P. Larkin. Oxford University Press, Gipsy Ln., Headington, Oxford, England OX3 0BP. 1980. Covers land use, coal mines and mining, and waste disposal.

Landscape Planning: Environmental Applications. William M. Marsh. John Wiley & Sons, Inc., 605 3rd Ave., New York, New York 10158-0012. (212) 850-6000. 1991. Second edition. Discusses landscape protection and the effective use of land and its environmental aspects.

The Living Landscape: An Ecological Approach to Landscape Planning. Frederick R. Steiner. McGraw-Hill, 1221 Avenue of the Americas, New York, New York 10020. (212) 512-2000 or (800) 262-4729. 1991. An ecological approach to landscape planning and landscape protection. Discusses the ways in which land could be effectively used taking into consideration the fragility of the environment.

Magill's Survey of Science. Earth Science Series. Frank N. Magill. Salem Press, PO Box 50062, Pasadena, California 91105. 1990-. Five volumes. Includes information on earth's crust, hot spots and volcanic island chains, physical properties of minerals, rock magnetism, physical properties of rocks, and index.

Our Common Lands: Defending the National Parks. David J. Simon, ed. Island Press, 1718 Connecticut Ave. N.W., Suite 300, Washington, District of Columbia 20009. (202) 232-7933. 1988. Explains the complexities of key environmental laws and how they can be used to protect our national parks. Includes discussion of successful and unsuccessful attempts to use the laws and how the courts interpret them.

Plowman's Folly. Edward H. Faulkner. Island Press, 1718 Connecticut Ave. N.W., Suite 300, Washington, District of Columbia 20009. (202) 232-7933. 1987.

Private Options: Tools and Concepts for Land Conservation. Montana Land Reliance, Land Trust Exchange. Island Press, 1718 Connecticut Ave. N.W., Suite 300, Washington, District of Columbia 20009. (202) 232-7933. 1982. Private land conservation experts offer their expertise on how individuals can help contain urban sprawl, conserve wetlands, and protect wildlife. This book covers estate planning, tax incentives, purchase options, conservation easements and land management.

The Role of Land/Inland Water Ecotones in Landscape Management and Restoration. Robert J. Naiman, et al, eds. UNESCO, 7, place de Fontenoy, Paris, France F-75700. (331) 45 68 40 67. 1989. MAB Digest 4. This is a proposal for collaborative research dealing with land management and restoration.

Rural Environment Planning for Sustainable Communities. Frederic O. Sargent, et al. Island Press, 1718 Connecticut Ave. N.W., Ste. 300, Washington, District of Columbia 20009. (202) 232-7933. 1991.

Tropical Resources: Ecology and Development. Jose I. Furtado, et al., eds. Harwood Academic Publishers, PO Box 786, Cooper Sta., New York, New York 10276. (212) 206-8900. 1990. Overview of global tropical resources, both terrestrial and aquatic. Subjects discussed include forest resources, wildlife resources, general land use, pasture resources, economic development, fisheries, marine resources, and aquaculture.

Turning the Tide: Saving the Chesapeake Bay. Tom Horton. Island Press, 1718 Connecticut Ave. N.W., Suite 300, Washington, District of Columbia 20009. (202) 232-7933. 1991. Presents a comprehensive look at two decades of efforts to save the Chesapeake Bay. It outlines which methods have worked, and which have not. Sets a new strategy for the future, calling for greater political coverage, environmental leadership and vision.

Water Engineering and Landscape: Water Control and Landscape Transformation in the Modern Period. D. Cosgrove and G. Petts, eds. Belhaven Press, 136 S. Broadway, Irvington, New York 10533. (914) 591-9111. 1990. Examines the role played by water management in the environment.

GOVERNMENTAL ORGANIZATIONS

Assistant Attorney General: Environment and Resources Division, Department of Justice. Room 2143, 10th St. and Constitution Ave., N.W., Washington, District of Columbia 20530. (202) 514-2701.

Office of Public Affairs: Bureau of Land Management. 18th and C St., N.W., Washington, District of Columbia 20240. (202) 208-3435.

HANDBOOKS AND MANUALS

The Economics of Coastal Zone Management: A Manual of Assessment Techniques. Edmund Penning-Rowsell, ed. Belhaven Press, 136 S. Broadway, Irvington, New York 10533. (914) 591-9111. 1991. Manual for assessing and pricing the procedures that protect vulnerable coastlines against flood, storm, high tide and other environmental damage.

Land Reclamation in Cities: A Guide to Methods of Establishment of Vegetation on Urban Waste Land. R. A. Dutton. HMSO, PO Box 276, London, England SW8 5DT. 1982.

Planning for Change. Columbia University, Teachers College, 525 W. 120th St., New York, New York 10027. (212) 678-3000. 1982.

ONLINE DATA BASES

Enviro/Energyline Abstracts Plus. R. R. Bowker Co., 121 Chanlon Rd., New Providence, New Jersey 07974. (908) 464-6800.

Environmental Periodicals Bibliography. National Information Services Corp., Ste. 6, Wyman Towers, 3100 St. Paul St., Baltimore, Maryland 21218. (410)243-0797. Online version of abstract of same name.

Monthly Catalog of United States Government Publications. U.S. G.P.O., Supt. of Docs., PO Box 371954, Pittsburgh, Pennsylvania 15250-7954. (202) 512-0000.

Multinational Environmental Outlook. Business Publishers, Inc., 951 Pershing Dr., Silver Spring, Maryland 20910-4464. (301) 587-6300. Environmental problems and solutions in countries outside the United States and their impact on the United States.

National Technical Information Service. U.S. Department of Commerce, National Technical Information Service, Office of Data Base Services, 5285 Port Royal Rd., Springfield, Virginia 22161. (703) 487-4807. Bibliographic database of government sponsored research and technical reports.

Natural Resources Metabase. National Information Services Corporation, Ste. 6, Wyman Towers, 3100 St. Paul St., Baltimore, Maryland 21218. (301) 243-0797. Published and unpublished reports and other materials dealing with natural resources and environmental issues released by U.S. and Canadian government agencies and organizations.

PressNet Environmental Reports. Chemical Information Systems, Inc., 7215 York Rd., Baltimore, Maryland 21212. (301) 321-8440.

SCISEARCH. Institute for Scientific Information, University City Science Center, 3501 Market St., Philadelphia, Pennsylvania 19104. (215) 386-0100.

PERIODICALS AND NEWSLETTERS

Eco/Log Week. Southam Business Information, 1450 Don Mills Rd., Don Mills, Ontario, Canada M3D 2X7. (416) 445-6641. Weekly. Effluent treatment, emission controls, waste disposal, and land use and reclamation.

Environment. Heldref Publications, 4000 Albemarle Street, NW, Washington, District of Columbia 20016. (202) 362-6445. Ten a year. Covers science and science policy.

Environmental Defense Fund Letter. Environmental Defense Fund, 257 Park Avenue South, New York, New York 10010. (212) 505-2100. 1971-. Bimonthly. Environmental issues of concern.

Environmental Geology & Water Sciences. Springer-Verlag, 175 Fifth Avenue, New York, New York 10010. (212) 460-1500. Bimonthly. Covers interactions between humanity and Earth.

Environmental Resources Research Institute, Newsletter. Environmental Resources Research Institute, Pennsylvania State University, University Park, Pennsylvania 16802. (814) 863-0291. Quarterly. Land, water, air, and mining.

Forest Notes. Society for the Protection of New Hampshire Forests, 54 Portsmouth St., Concord, New Hampshire 03301. (603) 224-9945. 1937-. Quarterly. Devoted to forestry, land protection and other issues affecting New Hampshire natural resources.

Hickory Stump. Middle Tennessee Land Trust, 8070 Regency Dr., Nashville, Tennessee 37221. (615) 645-6245. Quarterly. Land trusts and ecologically oriented lifestyles.

Institute for Research on Land and Water Resources, Newsletter. Institute for Research on Land and Water Resources, Pennsylvania State University, University Park, Pennsylvania 16802. 1970-. Bimonthly.

Journal of Soil and Water Conservation. Soil and Water Conservation Society, 7515 Northeast Ankeny Road, Ankeny, Iowa 50021. (515) 289-2331. Bimonthly. Promotes better land and water use and management.

Land & Water. Land & Water, Route 3, P.O. Box 1197, Fort Dodge, Iowa 50501. (515) 576-3191. Eight times a year. Covers soil conservation, new machines and products.

Land and Water Contracting. A. B. Morse Co., 200 James St., Barrington, Illinois 60010. Monthly.

Land Improvement Contractors of America News. LICA Service Corp., LICA News, 1300 Maybrook Dr., Maybrook, Illinois 60153. Monthly. Deals with erosion control, land use and improvement.

Land/Leaf Newsletter. Land Educational Association, 3368 Oak Ave., Stevens Point, Wisconsin 54481. (715)

344-6158. Bimonthly. Nuclear weapons and the environment.

Land Letter. The Conservation Fund, 1800 N. Kent St., Suite 1120, Arlington, Virginia 22209. (703) 522-8008. Thirty four times a year. National land use and conservation policy; legislative, regulatory, and legal developments; use of private and public lands.

Land Use and Environmental Law Review. Clark Boardman Callaghan, 155 Pfingsten Rd., Deerfield, Illinois 60015. (800) 221-9428. Annual. Reprints of articles that appear in law reviews.

Land Use Digest. Urban Land Institute, 625 Indiana Avenue, NW, Suite 400, Washington, District of Columbia 20004. (202) 624-7000. Monthly. Information for planners and developers.

Land Use Planning Report. Business Publishers, Inc., 951 Pershing Dr., Silver Spring, Maryland 20910-4464. (301) 587-6300. Biweekly. Issues affecting urban, suburban, agricultural, and natural resource land jurisdictions .

Mountain Research and Development. University of California Press, 2120 Berkeley Way, Berkeley, California 94720. (415) 642-7485; (800) 822-6657. Quarterly. Environmental & land use problems.

Our Public Lands. Superintendent of Documents, U.S. Government Printing Office, Washington, District of Columbia 20402. 1951-. Quarterly.

Probe Post. Pollution Probe Foundation, 12 Madison Ave., Toronto, Ontario, Canada M5R 2S1. (416) 926-1647. Quarterly. Acid rain, toxic waste, renewable energy, deep ecology, land use, and greenhouse effect.

Public Land News. Resources Publishing Co., 1010 Vermont Avenue, NW, Suite 708, Washington, District of Columbia 20005. (202) 638-7529. Biweekly. Covers land use and land development.

Public Lands Council-Washington Highlight Report. Public Lands Council, 1301 Penn Ave., NW, #300, Washington, District of Columbia 20004. (202) 347-5355. Quarterly.

U. S. Bureau of Land Management. Information Bulletins. Superintendent of Documents, U.S. Government Printing Office, Washington, District of Columbia 20402. Irregular.

Urban Land: News and Trends in Land Development. Urban Land Institute, 1200 18th St. N.W., Washington, District of Columbia 20036. 1941-. Ten times a year.

RESEARCH CENTERS AND INSTITUTES

Arkansas Water Resources Research Center. University of Arkansas, 113 Ozark Hall, Fayetteville, Arkansas 72701. (501) 575-4403.

Center for Remote Sensing. University of Delaware, College of Marine Studies, Newark, Delaware 19711. (302) 451-2336.

The Nature Conservancy. 1815 N. Lynn St., Arlington, Virginia 22209. (703) 841-5300.

Remote Sensing Center. Rutgers University, Department of Environmental Resources, Cook College, PO Box 231, New Brunswick, New Jersey 08903. (908) 932-9631.

Sherbrooke University, Centre for Remote Sensing Research and Applications. 2500 Boulevard Universite, Sherbrooke, Quebec, Canada J1K 2R1. (819) 821-7180.

University of Arizona, Arizona Remote Sensing Center. Office of Arid Lands Studies, 845 North Park Avenue, Tucson, Arizona 85719. (602) 621-7896.

University of Idaho, Remote Sensing Center. College of Forestry, Wildlife and Range Sciences, Moscow, Idaho 83843. (208) 885-7209.

University of Michigan, Wildland Management Center. School of Natural Resources, 430 East University, Ann Arbor, Michigan 48109-1115. (313) 763-1312.

University of Minnesota, Remote Sensing Laboratory. 1530 North Cleveland Avenue, St. Paul, Minnesota 55108. (612) 624-3400.

University of North Dakota, Institute for Remote Sensing. Geography Department, Grand Folks, North Dakota 58202. (701) 777-4246.

University of Oklahoma, Oklahoma Biological Survey. Sutton Hall, Room 303, 625 Elm Avenue, Norman, Oklahoma 73019. (405) 325-4034.

University of Wisconsin-Madison, Environmental Remote Sensing Center. 1225 West Dayton Street, Madison, Wisconsin 53706. (608) 263-3251.

Water Resources Association of the Delaware River Basin. Box 867, Davis Road, Valley Forge, Pennsylvania 19481. (215) 783-0634.

STATISTICS SOURCES

OECD Environmental Data Compendium 1989. OECD Publications and Information Center, 2001 L St. N.W., Suite 700, Washington, District of Columbia 20036. (202) 785-OECD. 1989. Provides statistical data for OECD countries on air pollution, water pollution, the marine environment, land use, forests, wildlife, solid waste, noise and radioactivity. Also provides data on the underlying pressures on the environment such as energy use, transportation, industrial activity and agriculture.

The State of the Environment. OECD Publications and Information Center, 2001 L St., N.W., Suite 700, Washington, District of Columbia 20036. (202) 785-6323. 1991.

TRADE ASSOCIATIONS AND PROFESSIONAL SOCIETIES

American Land Resource Association. 1516 P St., N.W., Washington, District of Columbia 20033. (202) 265-5000.

American Society of Landscape Architects. 4401 Connecticut Ave., N.W., Washington, District of Columbia 20008. (202) 686-2752.

Association of Environmental Engineering Professors. Department of Civil Engineering, Virginia Polytechnic Institute and State University, Blacksburg, Virginia 24061. (703) 231-6021.

Environmental Defense Fund. 257 Park Ave., S., New York, New York 10010. (212) 505-2100. Non-profit organization that was established more than 20 years ago. Its goals are to protect the earth's environment by providing lasting solutions to global environmental problems.

The Institute of the North American West. 110 Cherry St., Suite 202, Seattle, Washington 98104. (206) 623-9597.

Interstate Conference on Water Policy. 955 L'Enfant Plaza, 6th Floor, Washington, District of Columbia 20024. (202) 466-7287.

Land Improvement Contractors of America. P.O. Box 9, 1300 Maybrook Dr., Maywood, Illinois 60153. (708) 344-0700.

Land Trust Alliance. 900 17th St., NW, Suite 410, Washington, District of Columbia 20006. (202) 785-1410.

Land Trust Exchange. 1017 Duke St., Alexandria, Virginia 22314. (703) 683-7778.

National Landscape Association. 1250 I St., N.W., Ste. 500, Washington, District of Columbia 20005. (202) 789-2900.

Northern Plains Resource Council. 419 Stapleton Bldg., Billings, Montana 59101. (406) 248-1154.

Open Space Institute. 145 Main St., Ossining, New York 10562. (914) 762-4630.

Professional Grounds Management Society. 120 Cockeysville Rd., Ste. 104, Hunt Valley, Maryland 21031. (410) 667-1833.

Rails-to-Trails Conservancy. 1400 16th St., NW, Washington, District of Columbia 20036. (202) 797-5400.

Trust for Public Land. 116 New Montgomery St., 4th Floor, San Francisco, California 94105. (415) 495-5660.

Urban Land Institute. 625 Indiana Ave., N.W., Washington, District of Columbia 20004. (202) 624-7000.

LANDFILLS

See also: HAZARDOUS WASTE SITES; SANITARY LANDFILLS; SOLID WASTE DISPOSAL

ABSTRACTING AND INDEXING SERVICES

Abstracts of Air and Water Conservation Literature. American Petroleum Institute. Central Abstracting and Indexing Service, 275 Madison Avenue, New York, New York 10016. 1972.

Applied Ecology Abstracts Studies in Renewable Natural Resources. Information Retrieval Ltd., 1911 Jefferson Davis Highway, Arlington, Virginia 22202. 1975-. Monthly.

Biological Abstracts. BIOSIS, 2100 Arch St., Philadelphia, Pennsylvania 19103-1399. (215) 587-4800. 1927-.

Biological and Agricultural Index. H.W. Wilson Co., 950 University Ave., Bronx, New York 10452. (800) 367-6770. 1916-. Monthly.

Civil Engineering Hydraulic Abstracts. BHRA Fluid Engineering, Air Science Co., PO Box 143, Corning, New York 14830. (607) 962-5591. Monthly. Abstracts of periodicals that publish in the areas of hydraulic engineering and other related topics.

Ecological Abstracts. Geo Abstracts Ltd. Elsevier Applied Science, Crown House, Linton Rd., Barking, England IG

11 8JU. 1974-. Derived from over 600 leading ecological and environmental journals, plus books, conference proceedings, reports and theses.

Environment Abstracts. Bowker A & I Publishing, 121 Chanlon Rd., New Providence, New Jersey 07974. (908) 464-6800. 1974-.

Environment Index. Environment Information Center, Index Research Department, 124 E. 39th St., New York, New York 10016. 1971-. Annual.

Environmental Information Connection–EIC. Planning Information Program, Dept. of Urban and Regional Planning, University of Illinois, 1003 West Nevada, Urbana, Illinois 61801. (217) 333-1369. Also available online.

Environmental Periodicals Bibliography. Environmental Studies Institute, International Academy at Santa Barbara, 800 Garden St., Suite D, Santa Barbara, California 93101. (805) 965-5010. Also available online.

General Science Index. H. W. Wilson Co., 950 University Ave., Bronx, New York 10452. 1978-. Monthly, also issued in annual cumulation. Cumulative subject index to English language periodicals in the subject fields of astronomy, botany, chemistry, earth science, environment and conservation, food and nutrition, genetics, mathematics, medicine and health, microbiology, oceanography, physics, physiology and zoology.

Geographical Abstracts. London School of Economics, Dept. of Geography, Regency House, 34 Duke St., London, England 1966-. Continued by Geo Abstracts issued in 6 parts: Pt. A. Landforms and the quaternary; Pt. B. Biogeography and Climatology; Pt. C. Economic geography; Pt. D. Social geography and cartography; Pt. E. Sedimentology; Pt. F. Regional and community planning.

Index to Scientific Book Contents. Institute for Scientific Information, 3501 Market St., Philadelphia, Pennsylvania 19104. (800) 523-1857. 1985-. Annual. Gives contents of science books published.

Multimedia Index to Ecology. National Information Center for Educational Media, University of Southern California, Los Angeles, California 90007.

Pollution Abstracts. Cambridge Scientific Abstracts, 5161 River Rd., Bethesda, Maryland 20816. (301) 961-6750. Six/year. Indexes worldwide technical literature on environmental pollution. Covers air pollution, marine and freshwater pollution, sewage and wastewater treatment, waste management, toxicology and health, noise pollution, radiation, land pollution, and environmental policies, programs, legislation, and education. Also available online.

Science Citation Index. Institute for Scientific Information, 3501 Market St., Philadelphia, Pennsylvania 19104. 1961-.

BIBLIOGRAPHIES

Bibliography and Index of Geology. American Geological Institute, 4220 King St., Alexandria, Virginia 22302. Monthly. Includes environmental geology and hydrogeology.

EPA Publications Bibliography. U.S. Environmental Protection Agency, Library Systems Branch, 401 M St., SW,

Washington, District of Columbia 20460. (202) 260-2090. Quarterly.

DIRECTORIES

Gale Environmental Sourcebook. Karen Hill. Gale Research Co., 835 Penobscot Bldg., Detroit, Michigan 48226-4094. (313) 961-2242. Contacts, information sources, or general information on environmental topics.

ENCYCLOPEDIAS AND DICTIONARIES

McGraw-Hill Encyclopedia of Science and Technology. McGraw-Hill, 1221 Avenue of the Americas, New York, New York 10020. (212) 512-2000 or (800) 262-4729. 1992. Seventh edition. Issued in multiple volumes including index. Includes all science and technology broad subject areas.

The New York Times Encyclopedic Dictionary of the Environment. Paul Sarnoff. Quadrangle Books, New York, New York 1971. Focuses on state-of-the-art methods of pollution control, abatement, prevention and removal.

Van Nostrand's Scientific Encyclopedia. Glenn D. Considine, ed. Van Nostrand Reinhold, 115 5th Ave., New York, New York 10003. (212) 254-3232. 1983. Sixth edition. Includes all broad subject areas in science.

GENERAL WORKS

Air Emissions from Municipal Solid Waste Landfills. Environmental Protection Agency. National Technical Information Service, 5285 Port Royal Rd., Springfield, Virginia 22161. (703) 487-4650. 1991. Background information for proposed standards and guidelines. Order number PB91-197061LDM.

Characterization of Municipal Waste Combustor Ashes and Leachates from Municipal Solid Waste Landfills, Monofills, and Codisposal Sites. U.S. Environmental Protection Agency, Office of Solid Waste, 401 M St., S.W., Washington, District of Columbia 20460. (202) 260-2090. 1987.

Chemical Concepts in Pollutant Behavior. Ian J. Tinsley. John Wiley & Sons, Inc., 605 3rd Ave., New York, New York 10158-0012. (212) 850-6000. 1979.

Closed Waste Site Evaluation: Emsdale Landfill: Report. Ontario Waste Management Branch. Waste Site Evaluation Unit, Toronto. National Technical Information Service, 5285 Port Royal Rd., Springfield, Virginia 22161. (703) 487-4650. 1989. Order number MIC-91-03061LDM.

Design, Construction, and Monitoring of Sanitary Landfill. Amalendu Bagchi. John Wiley & Sons, Inc., 605 3rd Ave., New York, New York 10158-0012. (212) 850-6000. 1990. Handbook of theory, practice, and mathematical models of sanitary landfill technology and how they apply to waste disposal.

Hazard Assessment of Chemicals. Academic Press, c/o Harcourt Brace Jovanovich Inc., 6277 Sea Harbor Dr., Orlando, Florida 32887. (800) 346-8648. 1981-. Annually. Presents comprehensive authoritative reviews of new and significant developments in the area of hazard assessment of chemicals or chemical classes.

Incineration for Site Cleanup and Destruction of Hazardous Wastes. Howard E. Hesketh. Technomic Publishing

Co., 851 New Holland Ave., Box 3535, Lancaster, Pennsylvania 17604. (717) 291-5609; (800) 233-9936. 1990.

Landfill Capacity in the Year 2000. National Solid Waste Management Association, 1730 Rhode Island Ave., NW, Ste. 1000, Washington, District of Columbia 20036. (202) 659-4613. 1989.

Landfill Management. Salvadore J. Lucido. Management Information Service, Suite 500, 777 N. Capitol St., N.E., Washington, District of Columbia 20002-420. (800) 745-8780. 1990.

Madison Conference of Applied Research & Practice on Municipal & Industrial Waste. Dept. of Engineering Professional Development, University of Wisconsin-Madison, Madison, Wisconsin 53706. 1990. Annual. Sewage disposal, factory and trade waste, soil liners, ground water clean up, landfill leachate treatment, groundwater monitary systems, evaluation of groundwater and soil gas remedial action; leachate generation estimates and landfills.

Magill's Survey of Science. Earth Science Series. Frank N. Magill. Salem Press, PO Box 50062, Pasadena, California 91105. 1990-. Five volumes. Includes information on earth's crust, hot spots and volcanic island chains, physical properties of minerals, rock magnetism, physical properties of rocks, and index.

TAPPI Environmental Conference Proceedings, Seattle, WA, April 9-11, 1990. TAPPI Press, Technology Park/ Atlanta, PO Box 105113, Atlanta, Georgia 30348. (404) 446-1400. 1990. Contains 11 papers presented at the conference covering industrial pollution and its remedies.

Treatability Studies for Hazardous Waste Sites. Hazardous Waste Action Coalition, 1015 15th St. N.W., Suite 802, Washington, District of Columbia 20005. (202) 347-7474. 1990. Assesses the use of treatability studies for evaluating the effectiveness and cost of treatment technologies performed at hazardous waste sites.

HANDBOOKS AND MANUALS

Guidance for the Reregistration of Pesticide Products Containing Lindane as the Active Ingredient. U.S. Environmental Protection Agency, Office of the Pesticides and Toxic Substances, 401 M St., SW, Washington, District of Columbia 20460. (202) 260-2090. 1985. The Federal Insecticide, Fungicide, Rodenticide Act directs EPA to reregister all pesticides as expeditiously as possible. The guide helps the user to carry out this task and to participate in the EPA's registration standard program. Includes extensive tabular data to the pesticides and an extensive bibliography.

Handbook of Analytical Toxicology. Irving Sunshine, ed. CRC Press, 2000 Corporate Blvd. N.W., Boca Raton, Florida 33431. (407) 994-0555; (800) 272-7737. 1969.

Handbook of Environmental Data on Organic Chemicals. Karel Verschueren. Van Nostrand Reinhold, 115 5th Ave., New York, New York 10003. (212) 254-3232. 1983. Covers individual substances as well as mixtures and preparations. The profiles include: properties, air pollution factors, water pollution factors, and biological effects.

Siting Hazardous Waste Treatment Facilities; the Nimby Syndrome. Kent E. Portney. Auburn House, 14 Dedham St., Dover, Massachusetts 02030-0658. (800) 223-2665. 1991. Advice to producers of hazardous waste on how to overcome people's reluctance to have it shipped into their neighborhood.

ONLINE DATA BASES

BIOSIS Previews. BIOSIS, 2100 Arch St., Philadelphia, Pennsylvania 19103-1399. (215) 587-4800. Largest and most comprehensive database of research in the life sciences. Contains citations for nearly 9000 primary research journals, monographs, reviews, symposia, preliminary reports, semi-popular journals, selected institutional reports, government reports and research communications.

Enviro/Energyline Abstracts Plus. R. R. Bowker Co., 121 Chanlon Rd., New Providence, New Jersey 07974. (908) 464-6800.

Environmental Periodicals Bibliography. National Information Services Corp., Ste. 6, Wyman Towers, 3100 St. Paul St., Baltimore, Maryland 21218. (410)243-0797. Online version of abstract of same name.

Monthly Catalog of United States Government Publications. U.S. G.P.O., Supt. of Docs., PO Box 371954, Pittsburgh, Pennsylvania 15250-7954. (202) 512-0000.

National Technical Information Service. U.S. Department of Commerce, National Technical Information Service, Office of Data Base Services, 5285 Port Royal Rd., Springfield, Virginia 22161. (703) 487-4807. Bibliographic database of government sponsored research and technical reports.

PressNet Environmental Reports. Chemical Information Systems, Inc., 7215 York Rd., Baltimore, Maryland 21212. (301) 321-8440.

PERIODICALS AND NEWSLETTERS

Bulletin of Environmental Contamination and Toxicology. Springer-Verlag, 175 5th Ave., New York, New York 10010. (212) 460-1500; (800) 777-4643. 1966-. Frequency varies. Disseminates advances and discoveries in the areas of soil, air and food contamination and pollution.

Environmental Science and Technology. American Chemical Society, 1155 16th St. N.W., Washington, District of Columbia 20036. (800) 227-5558. 1967-. Monthly. Contains research articles on various aspects of environmental chemistry, interpretative articles by invited experts and commentary on the scientific aspects of environmental management.

Journal of Environmental Quality. American Society of Agronomy, 677 S. Segoe Rd., Madison, Wisconsin 53711-1086. (608) 273-8080. 1972-. Quarterly. Reports and brief reviews of agricultural ecology, environmental engineering and pollution.

Rachel's Hazardous Waste News. Environmental Research Foundation, PO Box 3541, Princeton, New Jersey 08543-3541. (609) 683-0707. Weekly. Topics include landfills, toxins, incinerators, health and the environment, grassroots lobbying, and community energy conservation.

STATISTICS SOURCES

Environmental Data Compendium. OECD Publications and Information Center, 2001 L St., N.W., Suite 700,

Washington, District of Columbia 20036. (202) 785-6323. 1989.

Environmental Indicators. OECD Publications and Information Center, 2001 L St., N.W., Suite 700, Washington, District of Columbia 20036. (202) 785-6323. 1991.

Environmental Quality. Council on Environmental Quality. U.S. G.P.O., Washington, District of Columbia 20401. (202) 512-0000. Annual.

Landfill Capacity in the U.S.: How Much Do We Really Have?. National Solid Wastes Management Association, 1730 Rhode Island Ave., NW, Suite 1000, Washington, District of Columbia 20036. 1988. Future landfill capacity needs, household/neighborhood business solid waste recycled, recovered through waste-to-energy combustion, and requiring landfill disposal.

The State of the Environment. OECD Publications and Information Center, 2001 L St., N.W., Suite 700, Washington, District of Columbia 20036. (202) 785-6323. 1991.

TRADE ASSOCIATIONS AND PROFESSIONAL SOCIETIES

American Public Works Association. 106 W. 11th St., Ste. 1800, Kansas City, Missouri 64105-1806. (816) 472-6100.

LARVICIDE APPLICATION

ABSTRACTING AND INDEXING SERVICES

Biological Abstracts. BIOSIS, 2100 Arch St., Philadelphia, Pennsylvania 19103-1399. (215) 587-4800. 1927-.

Biological and Agricultural Index. H.W. Wilson Co., 950 University Ave., Bronx, New York 10452. (800) 367-6770. 1916-. Monthly.

Ecological Abstracts. Geo Abstracts Ltd. Elsevier Applied Science, Crown House, Linton Rd., Barking, England IG 11 8JU. 1974-. Derived from over 600 leading ecological and environmental journals, plus books, conference proceedings, reports and theses.

Environment Abstracts. Bowker A & I Publishing, 121 Chanlon Rd., New Providence, New Jersey 07974. (908) 464-6800. 1974-.

Environment Index. Environment Information Center, Index Research Department, 124 E. 39th St., New York, New York 10016. 1971-. Annual.

Environmental Information Connection–EIC. Planning Information Program, Dept. of Urban and Regional Planning, University of Illinois, 1003 West Nevada, Urbana, Illinois 61801. (217) 333-1369. Also available online.

Environmental Periodicals Bibliography. Environmental Studies Institute, International Academy at Santa Barbara, 800 Garden St., Suite D, Santa Barbara, California 93101. (805) 965-5010. Also available online.

Science Citation Index. Institute for Scientific Information, 3501 Market St., Philadelphia, Pennsylvania 19104. 1961-.

BIBLIOGRAPHIES

EPA Publications Bibliography. U.S. Environmental Protection Agency, Library Systems Branch, 401 M St., SW, Washington, District of Columbia 20460. (202) 260-2090. Quarterly.

GENERAL WORKS

Biocontrol of Medical and Veterinary Pests. Marshall Laird. Praeger Publishers, 1 Madison Ave., New York, New York 10010-3603. (212) 685-5300. 1981.

ONLINE DATA BASES

BIOSIS Previews. BIOSIS, 2100 Arch St., Philadelphia, Pennsylvania 19103-1399. (215) 587-4800. Largest and most comprehensive database of research in the life sciences. Contains citations for nearly 9000 primary research journals, monographs, reviews, symposia, preliminary reports, semi-popular journals, selected institutional reports, government reports and research communications.

Enviro/Energyline Abstracts Plus. R. R. Bowker Co., 121 Chanlon Rd., New Providence, New Jersey 07974. (908) 464-6800.

Environmental Periodicals Bibliography. National Information Services Corp., Ste. 6, Wyman Towers, 3100 St. Paul St., Baltimore, Maryland 21218. (410)243-0797. Online version of abstract of same name.

PERIODICALS AND NEWSLETTERS

Journal of the American Mosquito Control Association. American Mosquito Control Association, PO Box 5416, Lake Charles, Louisiana 70606. (318) 474-2723. Quarterly.

LASERS

ABSTRACTING AND INDEXING SERVICES

Applied Science and Technology Index. H.W. Wilson Co., 950 University Ave., Bronx, New York 10452. (800) 367-6770. Formerly Industrial Arts Index.

Environment Abstracts. Bowker A & I Publishing, 121 Chanlon Rd., New Providence, New Jersey 07974. (908) 464-6800. 1974-.

Environment Index. Environment Information Center, Index Research Department, 124 E. 39th St., New York, New York 10016. 1971-. Annual.

Environmental Information Connection–EIC. Planning Information Program, Dept. of Urban and Regional Planning, University of Illinois, 1003 West Nevada, Urbana, Illinois 61801. (217) 333-1369. Also available online.

Environmental Periodicals Bibliography. Environmental Studies Institute, International Academy at Santa Barbara, 800 Garden St., Suite D, Santa Barbara, California 93101. (805) 965-5010. Also available online.

General Science Index. H. W. Wilson Co., 950 University Ave., Bronx, New York 10452. 1978-. Monthly, also issued in annual cumulation. Cumulative subject index to English language periodicals in the subject fields of astronomy, botany, chemistry, earth science, environment and conservation, food and nutrition, genetics, mathematics, medicine and health, microbiology, oceanography, physics, physiology and zoology.

Index to Scientific Book Contents. Institute for Scientific Information, 3501 Market St., Philadelphia, Pennsylvania 19104. (800) 523-1857. 1985-. Annual. Gives contents of science books published.

Physics Briefs. Physikalische Berichte. Physik Verlag, Pappapelallee 3, Postfach 101161, Weinheim, Germany D-6940. 1979-. Semimonthly. In English. Volumes for 1979- issued by the Deutsche Physikalische Gesellschaft and the Fachinformationszentrum Energie Physik, Mathematik in cooperation with the American Institute of Physics.

Pollution Abstracts. Cambridge Scientific Abstracts, 5161 River Rd., Bethesda, Maryland 20816. (301) 961-6750. Six/year. Indexes worldwide technical literature on environmental pollution. Covers air pollution, marine and freshwater pollution, sewage and wastewater treatment, waste management, toxicology and health, noise pollution, radiation, land pollution, and environmental policies, programs, legislation, and education. Also available online.

Science Citation Index. Institute for Scientific Information, 3501 Market St., Philadelphia, Pennsylvania 19104. 1961-.

BIBLIOGRAPHIES

EPA Publications Bibliography. U.S. Environmental Protection Agency, Library Systems Branch, 401 M St., SW, Washington, District of Columbia 20460. (202) 260-2090. Quarterly.

DIRECTORIES

Laser Focus/World Buyers' Guide. Advanced Technology Group/Penwell Publishing Company, One Technology Park Dr., Westford, Massachusetts 01886. (508) 692-0700.

Lasers & Optronics Buying Guide. Elsevier Communications, 301 Gibraltar Dr., Morris Plains, New Jersey 07950. (201) 292-5100.

Lasers in Materials Processing–A Summary and Forecast. Tech Tran Consultants, Box 220, Lake Geneva, Wisconsin 53147. (414) 248-9510. Irregular.

ENCYCLOPEDIAS AND DICTIONARIES

Encyclopedia of Physical Science and Technology. Robert A. Meyers, ed. Academic Press, c/o Harcourt Brace Jovanovich Inc., 6277 Sea Harbor Dr., Orlando, Florida 32887. (800) 346-8648. Dictionary of engineering, technology and physical sciences.

Encyclopedia of Physics. Rita G. Lerner and George L. Trigg. VCH Publishers, 303 NW 12th Ave., Deerfield Beach, Florida 33442-1788. (305) 428-5566. 1991. Second edition.

Van Nostrand's Scientific Encyclopedia. Glenn D. Considine, ed. Van Nostrand Reinhold, 115 5th Ave., New York, New York 10003. (212) 254-3232. 1983. Sixth edition. Includes all broad subject areas in science.

HANDBOOKS AND MANUALS

CRC Handbook of Laser Science and Technology. Marvin Weber. CRC Press, 2000 Corporate Blvd. N.W., Boca Raton, Florida 33431. (800) 272-7737. 1982.

The Laser Guidebook. McGraw-Hill Science & Engineering Books, 11 W. 19th St., New York, New York 10011. (212) 337-6010. 1992. Topics in optical and electro-optical engineering.

The Laser Handbook. McGraw-Hill Science & Engineering Books, 11 W. 19th St., New York, New York 10011. (212) 337-6010. 1986.

ONLINE DATA BASES

Enviro/Energyline Abstracts Plus. R. R. Bowker Co., 121 Chanlon Rd., New Providence, New Jersey 07974. (908) 464-6800.

Environmental Periodicals Bibliography. National Information Services Corp., Ste. 6, Wyman Towers, 3100 St. Paul St., Baltimore, Maryland 21218. (410)243-0797. Online version of abstract of same name.

TRADE ASSOCIATIONS AND PROFESSIONAL SOCIETIES

Laser Association of America. 72 Mars St., San Francisco, California 94114. (415) 621-5776.

Laser Institute of America. 12424 Research Pkwy., Suite 130, Orlando, Florida 32826. (407) 380-1553.

LAW ENFORCEMENT, ENVIRONMENTAL
See: ENVIRONMENTAL LEGISLATION

LEACHATE
See: SOLID WASTE MANAGEMENT

LEAD

ABSTRACTING AND INDEXING SERVICES

Applied Science and Technology Index. H.W. Wilson Co., 950 University Ave., Bronx, New York 10452. (800) 367-6770. Formerly Industrial Arts Index.

ASFA Aquaculture Abstracts. Cambridge Scientific Abstracts, Inc., 5161 River Rd., Bethesda, Maryland 20816. (301) 961-6750. 1984.

Chemical Abstracts. Chemical Abstracts Service, 2540 Olentangy River Rd., PO Box 3012, Columbus, Ohio 43210. (800) 848-6533. 1907-.

Ecology Abstracts. Cambridge Scientific Abstracts, 5161 River Rd., Bethesda, Maryland 20816. (301) 961-6750. Monthly.

Environment Abstracts. Bowker A & I Publishing, 121 Chanlon Rd., New Providence, New Jersey 07974. (908) 464-6800. 1974-.

Environment Index. Environment Information Center, Index Research Department, 124 E. 39th St., New York, New York 10016. 1971-. Annual.

Environmental Information Connection–EIC. Planning Information Program, Dept. of Urban and Regional Planning, University of Illinois, 1003 West Nevada, Urbana, Illinois 61801. (217) 333-1369. Also available online.

Environmental Periodicals Bibliography. Environmental Studies Institute, International Academy at Santa Barbara, 800 Garden St., Suite D, Santa Barbara, California 93101. (805) 965-5010. Also available online.

General Science Index. H. W. Wilson Co., 950 University Ave., Bronx, New York 10452. 1978-. Monthly, also issued in annual cumulation. Cumulative subject index to English language periodicals in the subject fields of astronomy, botany, chemistry, earth science, environment and conservation, food and nutrition, genetics, mathematics, medicine and health, microbiology, oceanography, physics, physiology and zoology.

Metals Abstracts. ASM International, 9639 Kinsman, Materials Park, Ohio 44073. (216) 338-5151. 1968-. Published jointly by the Institute of Metals, London and the American Society for Metals. Formed by the Union of Metallurgical Abstracts and Review of Metal Literature.

Physics Briefs. Physikalische Berichte. Physik Verlag, Pappapelallee 3, Postfach 101161, Weinheim, Germany D-6940. 1979-. Semimonthly. In English. Volumes for 1979- issued by the Deutsche Physikalische Gesellschaft and the Fachinformationszentrum Energie Physik, Mathematik in cooperation with the American Institute of Physics.

Pollution Abstracts. Cambridge Scientific Abstracts, 5161 River Rd., Bethesda, Maryland 20816. (301) 961-6750. Six/year. Indexes worldwide technical literature on environmental pollution. Covers air pollution, marine and freshwater pollution, sewage and wastewater treatment, waste management, toxicology and health, noise pollution, radiation, land pollution, and environmental policies, programs, legislation, and education. Also available online.

Science Citation Index. Institute for Scientific Information, 3501 Market St., Philadelphia, Pennsylvania 19104. 1961-.

BIBLIOGRAPHIES

EPA Publications Bibliography. U.S. Environmental Protection Agency, Library Systems Branch, 401 M St., SW, Washington, District of Columbia 20460. (202) 260-2090. Quarterly.

Lead Exposure: Public and Occupational Health Hazards. National Technical Information Service, 5285 Port Royal Rd., Springfield, Virginia 22161. (703) 487-4650. 1990. Bibliography of lead toxicology and pollution.

Lead in Agricultural Ecosystems. Robert Lewis Jones. University of Illinois, Department of Agronomy, Urbana, Illinois 61801. 1973.

Lead Pollution from Motor Vehicles. Penny Farmer. Elsevier Science Publishing Co., 655 Avenue of the Americas, New York, New York 10010. (212) 984-5800. 1987.

DIRECTORIES

Lead Contractors and Materials Suppliers. 295 Madison Ave., New York, New York 10017. (212) 578-4750. Irregular.

ENCYCLOPEDIAS AND DICTIONARIES

Encyclopedia of Chemical Processing and Design. John J. Mcketta and W. A. Cunningham. Marcel Dekker, Inc., 270 Madison Ave., New York, New York 10016. (212) 696-9000; (800) 228-1160. 1992. Thirty-eight volumes.

Encyclopedia of Electrochemistry of Elements. A. J. Bard. Marcel Dekker, Inc., 270 Madison Ave., New York, New York 10016. (212) 696-9000 or (800) 228-1160. Encyclopedic treatment of the subject area of electrochemistry and related subjects.

Encyclopedia of Physical Science and Technology. Robert A. Meyers, ed. Academic Press, c/o Harcourt Brace Jovanovich Inc., 6277 Sea Harbor Dr., Orlando, Florida 32887. (800) 346-8648. Dictionary of engineering, technology and physical sciences.

Illustrated Encyclopedia of Science and the Future. Mike Biscare, et al., ed. Marshall Cavendish, 58 Old Compton St., London, England 0W1V5 PA. 01-734 6710. 1983. Twenty volumes. Each volume has 5 sections: Frontiers, Electronics in Action, Medical Science, Military Technology, and Resources.

Kirk-Othmer Encyclopedia of Chemical Technology. J. I. Kroschwitz, ed. John Wiley & Sons, Inc., 605 3rd Ave., New York, New York 10158-0012. (212) 850-6000. 1992-. All articles in the new edition have been rewritten and updated adding new subjects such as biotechnology, computer topics, analytical techniques and instrumentation, environmental concerns, fuels and energy, inorganic and solid state chemistry; composite materials and material science in general, and pharmaceuticals. Also available online.

The New York Times Encyclopedic Dictionary of the Environment. Paul Sarnoff. Quadrangle Books, New York, New York 1971. Focuses on state-of-the-art methods of pollution control, abatement, prevention and removal.

Van Nostrand's Scientific Encyclopedia. Glenn D. Considine, ed. Van Nostrand Reinhold, 115 5th Ave., New York, New York 10003. (212) 254-3232. 1983. Sixth edition. Includes all broad subject areas in science.

GENERAL WORKS

The Biogeochemistry of Lead in the Environment. J. O. Nriagu. North-Holland, 655 Avenue of the Americas, New York, New York 10010. (212) 989-5800. 1978. Topics in environmental health, ecological cycles and biological effects.

The Citizen's Guide to Lead: Uncovering a Hidden Health Hazard. Barbara Wallace. NC Press, 345 Adelaide St. W., Ste. 400, Toronto, Ontario, Canada M5V 1R5. (416) 593-6284. 1986. Guide to the serious problems of environmental lead contamination. Describes how we are all exposed to lead and what can be done to reduce personal health risks and further environmental contamination.

Environmental Combination by Lead and Other Heavy Metals. University of Illinois, Institute for Environmental Studies, Urbana, Illinois 61801. 1977.

Healthy Homes, Healthy Kids. Joyce M. Schoemaker and Charity Y. Vitale. Island Press, 1718 Connecticut Ave. N.W., Suite 300, Washington, District of Columbia 20009. (202) 232-7933. 1991. Identifies many hazards that parents tend to overlook. It translates technical, scientific information into an accessible how-to guide to help parents protect children from even the most toxic substances.

Lead and Its Alloys. D. R. Blaskett. E. Horwood, 200 Old Tappan Rd., Old Tappan, New Jersey 07675. (800) 223-2348. 1990. Presents a comprehensive account of the historical evolution of the extraction, smelting, and refining of lead. Also covers its working and shaping, and its corrion behavior.

Lead in the Marine Environment. M. Branica and Z. Konrad, eds. Pergamon Microforms International, Inc., Fairview Park, Elmsford, New York 10523. (914) 592-7720. 1980. Proceedings of the International Experts Discussion, Rovinj, Yugoslavia, October 1977.

Lead Pollution Prevention. U.S. G.P.O, Washington, District of Columbia 20401. (202) 512-0000. 1991. Toxicology of lead, hazardous substances, and chemicals. Also covers pediatric toxicology.

Lead Versus Health. Michael Rutter. John Wiley & Sons, Inc., 605 3rd Ave., New York, New York 10158-0012. (212) 850-6000. 1983.

HANDBOOKS AND MANUALS

Tables of Physical and Chemical Constants and Some Mathematical Functions. G. W. C. Kaye, et al. Longman Group Ltd., Longman House, Burnt Mill, Harlow, England CM20 2J6. 0279 426721. 1988. Fifteenth edition. Includes tables on mechanical properties, density, elasticity, viscosity, surface tension, temperature and heat. Also covers radiation, optics, chemistry, electrochemistry, astrophysics, and chemical thermodynamics.

ONLINE DATA BASES

Chemical Abstracts-CA. Chemical Abstracts Service, 2540 Olentangy River Rd., P.O. Box 3012, Columbus, Ohio 43210. (800) 848-6533 or (614) 421-3600. Information sources include 9000 journals, patents from 27 countries, two industrial property organizations, new books, conference proceedings, and government research reports.

Enviro/Energyline Abstracts Plus. R. R. Bowker Co., 121 Chanlon Rd., New Providence, New Jersey 07974. (908) 464-6800.

Environmental Periodicals Bibliography. National Information Services Corp., Ste. 6, Wyman Towers, 3100 St. Paul St., Baltimore, Maryland 21218. (410)243-0797. Online version of abstract of same name.

Kirk-Othmer Encyclopedia of Chemical Technology. John Wiley & Sons, Inc., 605 3rd Ave., 5th Floor, New York, New York 10158. (212) 850-6000. Online version of the publication of the same name.

PERIODICALS AND NEWSLETTERS

Environmental Health Letter. Business Publishers, Inc., 951 Pershing Dr., Silver Spring, Maryland 20910-4464. (301) 587-6300. 1961-. Biweekly. Covers areas such as: indoor air, asbestos health effects, toxic substances

testing, health problems at wastewater plants, risk-based sludge rules, medical waste, developmental toxicity risk assessment, animal carcinogen tests, pesticide risk, air toxics, aerospace chemicals, lead, radionuclide emissions, state right-to-know statutes, and incinerator emissions.

Indoor Pollution News. Buraff Publications, 1350 Connecticut Ave., NW, Suite 100, Washington, District of Columbia 20036. (202) 862-0990. Biweekly. Air quality in buildings (including radon, formaldehyde, solvents and asbestos) or other air pollutions, such as lead in pipes.

Lead Abatement News. FIND/SVP, 625 Avenue of the Americas, New York, New York 10011. (800) 346-3787. Monthly. Government and business news involving the nationwide effort to remove lead from homes, drinking water, the air and the workplace.

STATISTICS SOURCES

Lead Based Paint Abatement. FIND/SVP, 625 Avenue of the Americas, New York, New York 10011. (800) 346-3787. 1991. Analyzes and forecasts to 1995 the market for lead-based paint abatement, focusing on the market potential for both contractors and consultants.

TRADE ASSOCIATIONS AND PROFESSIONAL SOCIETIES

American Chemical Society. 1155 16th St., N.W., Washington, District of Columbia 20036. (202) 872-4600.

International Lead Zinc Research Organization. 2525 Meridian Pkwy., P.O. Box 12036, Research Triangle Park, North Carolina 27709. (919) 361-4647.

Lead Industries Association. 292 Madison Ave., New York, New York 10017. (212) 578-4750.

United Association of Journeymen & Apprentices of the Plumbing & Pipe Fitting Industry of the United States & Canada. P.O. Box 37800, Washington, District of Columbia 20013. (202) 628-5823.

LEAD POISONING

See: TOXIC POLLUTANTS

LEGISLATION, ENVIRONMENTAL

See: ENVIRONMENTAL LEGISLATION

LICHENS

ABSTRACTING AND INDEXING SERVICES

Biological Abstracts. BIOSIS, 2100 Arch St., Philadelphia, Pennsylvania 19103-1399. (215) 587-4800. 1927-.

Biological and Agricultural Index. H.W. Wilson Co., 950 University Ave., Bronx, New York 10452. (800) 367-6770. 1916-. Monthly.

Ecology Abstracts. Cambridge Scientific Abstracts, 5161 River Rd., Bethesda, Maryland 20816. (301) 961-6750. Monthly.

Environment Abstracts. Bowker A & I Publishing, 121 Chanlon Rd., New Providence, New Jersey 07974. (908) 464-6800. 1974-.

Environment Index. Environment Information Center, Index Research Department, 124 E. 39th St., New York, New York 10016. 1971-. Annual.

Environmental Information Connection–EIC. Planning Information Program, Dept. of Urban and Regional Planning, University of Illinois, 1003 West Nevada, Urbana, Illinois 61801. (217) 333-1369. Also available online.

Environmental Periodicals Bibliography. Environmental Studies Institute, International Academy at Santa Barbara, 800 Garden St., Suite D, Santa Barbara, California 93101. (805) 965-5010. Also available online.

General Science Index. H. W. Wilson Co., 950 University Ave., Bronx, New York 10452. 1978-. Monthly, also issued in annual cumulation. Cumulative subject index to English language periodicals in the subject fields of astronomy, botany, chemistry, earth science, environment and conservation, food and nutrition, genetics, mathematics, medicine and health, microbiology, oceanography, physics, physiology and zoology.

Pollution Abstracts. Cambridge Scientific Abstracts, 5161 River Rd., Bethesda, Maryland 20816. (301) 961-6750. Six/year. Indexes worldwide technical literature on environmental pollution. Covers air pollution, marine and freshwater pollution, sewage and wastewater treatment, waste management, toxicology and health, noise pollution, radiation, land pollution, and environmental policies, programs, legislation, and education. Also available online.

Science Citation Index. Institute for Scientific Information, 3501 Market St., Philadelphia, Pennsylvania 19104. 1961-.

BIBLIOGRAPHIES

Current Contents. Agriculture, Biology and Environmental Sciences. Institute for Scientific Information, 3501 Market St., Philadelphia, Pennsylvania 19104. (800) 523-1857. 1973-. Previous title: Current Contents. Agricultural, Food & Veterinary Sciences. Gives the table of contents of periodicals in the fields of agriculture, biology, environmental and related areas.

EPA Publications Bibliography. U.S. Environmental Protection Agency, Library Systems Branch, 401 M St., SW, Washington, District of Columbia 20460. (202) 260-2090. Quarterly.

ENCYCLOPEDIAS AND DICTIONARIES

Cambridge Dictionary of Biology. Peter M. B. Walker. Cambridge University Press, 40 W. 20th St., New York, New York 10011. (212) 924-3900 or (800) 227-0247. 1989. Includes 10,000 terms in zoology, botany, biochemistry, molecular biology and genetics. Previously published under the title Chambers Biology Dictionary.

Cambridge Encyclopedia of Life Sciences. A. E. Friday and David S. Ingram. Cambridge University Press, 40 W 20th St., New York, New York 10011. (212) 924-3900 or (800) 227-0247. 1985. Includes all topics under biology and ecology.

A Concise Dictionary of Biology. Elizabeth Martin, ed. Oxford University Press, 200 Madison Ave., New York, New York 10016. (212) 679-7300 or (800) 334-4249. 1990. New edition. Derived from the Concise Science Dictionary, published in 1984.

McGraw-Hill Encyclopedia of Environmental Science. Sybil P. Parker. McGraw-Hill Science & Engineering Books, 11 W. 19th St., New York, New York 10011. (212) 337-6010. 1980. Covers ecology, man's influence on nature, and environmental protection.

McGraw-Hill Encyclopedia of Science and Technology. McGraw-Hill, 1221 Avenue of the Americas, New York, New York 10020. (212) 512-2000 or (800) 262-4729. 1992. Seventh edition. Issued in multiple volumes including index. Includes all science and technology broad subject areas.

Van Nostrand's Scientific Encyclopedia. Glenn D. Considine, ed. Van Nostrand Reinhold, 115 5th Ave., New York, New York 10003. (212) 254-3232. 1983. Sixth edition. Includes all broad subject areas in science.

GENERAL WORKS

Lichen Ecology. Mark Seaward. Academic Press, c/o Harcourt Brace Jovanovich Inc., 6277 Sea Harbor Dr., Orlando, Florida 32887. (800) 346-8648. 1977. Topics in botanical ecology.

Lichens and Air Pollution. Kenneth Metzler. State Geological and Natural History Survey of Connecticut, Hartford, Connecticut 1980.

Lichens as Pollution Monitors. D.L. Hawksworth. E. Arnold, 41 Bedford Sq., London, England 1976.

The Vanishing Lichens. David Richardson. David & Charles, Brunel House, Newton Abbot, England TQ12 4PU. 1975.

ONLINE DATA BASES

BIOSIS Previews. BIOSIS, 2100 Arch St., Philadelphia, Pennsylvania 19103-1399. (215) 587-4800. Largest and most comprehensive database of research in the life sciences. Contains citations for nearly 9000 primary research journals, monographs, reviews, symposia, preliminary reports, semi-popular journals, selected institutional reports, government reports and research communications.

Cambridge Scientific Abstracts Life Science–CSAL. Cambridge Scientific Abstracts, 5161 River Rd., Bethesda, Maryland 20816. (301) 961-6750. Provides access to the following abstracting services: "Life Sciences Collec-

tion," "Aquatic Sciences and Fisheries Abstracts," "Oceanic Abstracts," and "Pollution Abstracts."

Enviro/Energyline Abstracts Plus. R. R. Bowker Co., 121 Chanlon Rd., New Providence, New Jersey 07974. (908) 464-6800.

Environmental Periodicals Bibliography. National Information Services Corp., Ste. 6, Wyman Towers, 3100 St. Paul St., Baltimore, Maryland 21218. (410)243-0797. Online version of abstract of same name.

SCISEARCH. Institute for Scientific Information, University City Science Center, 3501 Market St., Philadelphia, Pennsylvania 19104. (215) 386-0100.

LIDAR

ABSTRACTING AND INDEXING SERVICES

Biological and Agricultural Index. H.W. Wilson Co., 950 University Ave., Bronx, New York 10452. (800) 367-6770. 1916-. Monthly.

Environment Abstracts. Bowker A & I Publishing, 121 Chanlon Rd., New Providence, New Jersey 07974. (908) 464-6800. 1974-.

Environment Index. Environment Information Center, Index Research Department, 124 E. 39th St., New York, New York 10016. 1971-. Annual.

Environmental Information Connection–EIC. Planning Information Program, Dept. of Urban and Regional Planning, University of Illinois, 1003 West Nevada, Urbana, Illinois 61801. (217) 333-1369. Also available online.

Environmental Periodicals Bibliography. Environmental Studies Institute, International Academy at Santa Barbara, 800 Garden St., Suite D, Santa Barbara, California 93101. (805) 965-5010. Also available online.

General Science Index. H. W. Wilson Co., 950 University Ave., Bronx, New York 10452. 1978-. Monthly, also issued in annual cumulation. Cumulative subject index to English language periodicals in the subject fields of astronomy, botany, chemistry, earth science, environment and conservation, food and nutrition, genetics, mathematics, medicine and health, microbiology, oceanography, physics, physiology and zoology.

Pollution Abstracts. Cambridge Scientific Abstracts, 5161 River Rd., Bethesda, Maryland 20816. (301) 961-6750. Six/year. Indexes worldwide technical literature on environmental pollution. Covers air pollution, marine and freshwater pollution, sewage and wastewater treatment, waste management, toxicology and health, noise pollution, radiation, land pollution, and environmental policies, programs, legislation, and education. Also available online.

Science Citation Index. Institute for Scientific Information, 3501 Market St., Philadelphia, Pennsylvania 19104. 1961-.

BIBLIOGRAPHIES

EPA Publications Bibliography. U.S. Environmental Protection Agency, Library Systems Branch, 401 M St., SW, Washington, District of Columbia 20460. (202) 260-2090. Quarterly.

ENCYCLOPEDIAS AND DICTIONARIES

McGraw-Hill Encyclopedia of Environmental Science. Sybil P. Parker. McGraw-Hill Science & Engineering Books, 11 W. 19th St., New York, New York 10011. (212) 337-6010. 1980. Covers ecology, man's influence on nature, and environmental protection.

Van Nostrand's Scientific Encyclopedia. Glenn D. Considine, ed. Van Nostrand Reinhold, 115 5th Ave., New York, New York 10003. (212) 254-3232. 1983. Sixth edition. Includes all broad subject areas in science.

GENERAL WORKS

Application of Lidar Techniques to Estimating Atmospheric Dispersion. Edward T. Uthe. National Technical Information Service, 5285 Port Royal Rd., Springfield, Virginia 22161. (703) 487-4650. 1980.

A Basic Comparison of Lidar and Radar for Remote Sensing of Clouds. V.E. Derr. Environmental Research Laboratories, 325 Broadway, Boulder, Colorado 80303. 1978.

ONLINE DATA BASES

Enviro/Energyline Abstracts Plus. R. R. Bowker Co., 121 Chanlon Rd., New Providence, New Jersey 07974. (908) 464-6800.

Environmental Periodicals Bibliography. National Information Services Corp., Ste. 6, Wyman Towers, 3100 St. Paul St., Baltimore, Maryland 21218. (410)243-0797. Online version of abstract of same name.

SCISEARCH. Institute for Scientific Information, University City Science Center, 3501 Market St., Philadelphia, Pennsylvania 19104. (215) 386-0100.

LIFT
See: SOLID WASTE MANAGEMENT

LIGHT WATER REACTORS
See: REACTORS

LIGHTNING
See: WEATHER

LIGNITE
See: COAL

LIME

ABSTRACTING AND INDEXING SERVICES

Chemical Abstracts. Chemical Abstracts Service, 2540 Olentangy River Rd., PO Box 3012, Columbus, Ohio 43210. (800) 848-6533. 1907-.

Environment Abstracts. Bowker A & I Publishing, 121 Chanlon Rd., New Providence, New Jersey 07974. (908) 464-6800. 1974-.

Environment Index. Environment Information Center, Index Research Department, 124 E. 39th St., New York, New York 10016. 1971-. Annual.

Environmental Information Connection–EIC. Planning Information Program, Dept. of Urban and Regional Planning, University of Illinois, 1003 West Nevada, Urbana, Illinois 61801. (217) 333-1369. Also available online.

Environmental Periodicals Bibliography. Environmental Studies Institute, International Academy at Santa Barbara, 800 Garden St., Suite D, Santa Barbara, California 93101. (805) 965-5010. Also available online.

General Science Index. H. W. Wilson Co., 950 University Ave., Bronx, New York 10452. 1978-. Monthly, also issued in annual cumulation. Cumulative subject index to English language periodicals in the subject fields of astronomy, botany, chemistry, earth science, environment and conservation, food and nutrition, genetics, mathematics, medicine and health, microbiology, oceanography, physics, physiology and zoology.

Pollution Abstracts. Cambridge Scientific Abstracts, 5161 River Rd., Bethesda, Maryland 20816. (301) 961-6750. Six/year. Indexes worldwide technical literature on environmental pollution. Covers air pollution, marine and freshwater pollution, sewage and wastewater treatment, waste management, toxicology and health, noise pollution, radiation, land pollution, and environmental policies, programs, legislation, and education. Also available online.

Science Citation Index. Institute for Scientific Information, 3501 Market St., Philadelphia, Pennsylvania 19104. 1961-.

BIBLIOGRAPHIES

EPA Publications Bibliography. U.S. Environmental Protection Agency, Library Systems Branch, 401 M St., SW, Washington, District of Columbia 20460. (202) 260-2090. Quarterly.

ENCYCLOPEDIAS AND DICTIONARIES

Van Nostrand's Scientific Encyclopedia. Glenn D. Considine, ed. Van Nostrand Reinhold, 115 5th Ave., New York, New York 10003. (212) 254-3232. 1983. Sixth edition. Includes all broad subject areas in science.

GENERAL WORKS

Chemistry and Technology of Lime and Limestone. John Wiley & Sons, Inc., 605 3rd Ave., New York, New York 10158-0012. (212) 850-6000. 1980.

Lime Use in Wastewater Treatment. Denny Parker. National Technical Information Service, 5285 Port Royal Rd., Springfield, Virginia 22161. (703) 487-4650. 1975.

Physical-Chemical Treatment of Raw Municipal Wastewater. Dolloff Bishop. U.S. G.P.O., Washington, District of Columbia 20401. (202) 512-0000. 1974.

ONLINE DATA BASES

Chemical Abstracts-CA. Chemical Abstracts Service, 2540 Olentangy River Rd., P.O. Box 3012, Columbus, Ohio 43210. (800) 848-6533 or (614) 421-3600. Information sources include 9000 journals, patents from 27 countries, two industrial property organizations, new books, conference proceedings, and government research reports.

Enviro/Energyline Abstracts Plus. R. R. Bowker Co., 121 Chanlon Rd., New Providence, New Jersey 07974. (908) 464-6800.

Environmental Periodicals Bibliography. National Information Services Corp., Ste. 6, Wyman Towers, 3100 St. Paul St., Baltimore, Maryland 21218. (410)243-0797. Online version of abstract of same name.

TRADE ASSOCIATIONS AND PROFESSIONAL SOCIETIES

National Lime Association. 3601 N. Fairfax Dr., Arlington, Virginia 22201. (703) 243-5463.

LIMNETIC

See: LAKES

LIMNOLOGY

See also: EUTROPHICATION; LAKES

ABSTRACTING AND INDEXING SERVICES

Ecological Abstracts. Geo Abstracts Ltd. Elsevier Applied Science, Crown House, Linton Rd., Barking, England IG 11 8JU. 1974-. Derived from over 600 leading ecological and environmental journals, plus books, conference proceedings, reports and theses.

Ecology Abstracts. Cambridge Scientific Abstracts, 5161 River Rd., Bethesda, Maryland 20816. (301) 961-6750. Monthly.

Environment Abstracts. Bowker A & I Publishing, 121 Chanlon Rd., New Providence, New Jersey 07974. (908) 464-6800. 1974-.

Environment Index. Environment Information Center, Index Research Department, 124 E. 39th St., New York, New York 10016. 1971-. Annual.

Environmental Information Connection–EIC. Planning Information Program, Dept. of Urban and Regional Planning, University of Illinois, 1003 West Nevada, Urbana, Illinois 61801. (217) 333-1369. Also available online.

Environmental Periodicals Bibliography. Environmental Studies Institute, International Academy at Santa Barbara, 800 Garden St., Suite D, Santa Barbara, California 93101. (805) 965-5010. Also available online.

General Science Index. H. W. Wilson Co., 950 University Ave., Bronx, New York 10452. 1978-. Monthly, also issued in annual cumulation. Cumulative subject index to English language periodicals in the subject fields of astronomy, botany, chemistry, earth science, environment and conservation, food and nutrition, genetics,

mathematics, medicine and health, microbiology, ocean-ography, physics, physiology and zoology.

Index to Scientific Book Contents. Institute for Scientific Information, 3501 Market St., Philadelphia, Pennsylvania 19104. (800) 523-1857. 1985-. Annual. Gives contents of science books published.

BIBLIOGRAPHIES

Current Contents. Agriculture, Biology and Environmental Sciences. Institute for Scientific Information, 3501 Market St., Philadelphia, Pennsylvania 19104. (800) 523-1857. 1973-. Previous title: Current Contents. Agricultural, Food & Veterinary Sciences. Gives the table of contents of periodicals in the fields of agriculture, biology, environmental and related areas.

EPA Publications Bibliography. U.S. Environmental Protection Agency, Library Systems Branch, 401 M St., SW, Washington, District of Columbia 20460. (202) 260-2090. Quarterly.

New Publications of the Geological Survey. U.S. Department of the Interior, Geological Survey, 119 National Center, Reston, Virginia 22092. (703) 648-4460. 1984-. Monthly. Bibliography of geological publications and related government documents published by the Geological Survey.

ENCYCLOPEDIAS AND DICTIONARIES

Cambridge Encyclopedia of Life Sciences. A. E. Friday and David S. Ingram. Cambridge University Press, 40 W 20th St., New York, New York 10011. (212) 924-3900 or (800) 227-0247. 1985. Includes all topics under biology and ecology.

McGraw-Hill Encyclopedia of Environmental Science. Sybil P. Parker. McGraw-Hill Science & Engineering Books, 11 W. 19th St., New York, New York 10011. (212) 337-6010. 1980. Covers ecology, man's influence on nature, and environmental protection.

Van Nostrand's Scientific Encyclopedia. Glenn D. Considine, ed. Van Nostrand Reinhold, 115 5th Ave., New York, New York 10003. (212) 254-3232. 1983. Sixth edition. Includes all broad subject areas in science.

GENERAL WORKS

The Lake Michigan Pollution Case. Cliff Mortimer. University of Wisconsin, Center for Great Lake Studies, 3203 N. Downer Ave., Milwaukee, Wisconsin 53211. 1981.

ONLINE DATA BASES

Enviro/Energyline Abstracts Plus. R. R. Bowker Co., 121 Chanlon Rd., New Providence, New Jersey 07974. (908) 464-6800.

Environmental Periodicals Bibliography. National Information Services Corp., Ste. 6, Wyman Towers, 3100 St. Paul St., Baltimore, Maryland 21218. (410)243-0797. Online version of abstract of same name.

Monthly Catalog of United States Government Publications. U.S. G.P.O., Supt. of Docs., PO Box 371954, Pittsburgh, Pennsylvania 15250-7954. (202) 512-0000.

National Technical Information Service. U.S. Department of Commerce, National Technical Information

Service, Office of Data Base Services, 5285 Port Royal Rd., Springfield, Virginia 22161. (703) 487-4807. Bibliographic database of government sponsored research and technical reports.

PERIODICALS AND NEWSLETTERS

Freshwater Biology. Blackwell Scientific Publications, PO Box 87, Oxford, England OX2 0DT. 44 0865 791155. Quarterly.

Limnology and Oceanography. American Society of Limnology and Oceanography, Inc., PO Box 1897, Lawrence, Kansas 66044-8897. (913) 843-1221. Topics in aquatic disciplines.

RESEARCH CENTERS AND INSTITUTES

Advanced Sciences Research and Development Corporation. P.O. Box 127, Lakemont, Georgia 30552. (404) 782-2092.

Murray State University, Handcock Biological Station. Murray, Kentucky 42071. (502) 474-2272.

Ohio State University, Franz Theodore Stone Laboratory. 1541 Research Center, 1314 Kinnear Road, Columbus, Ohio 43212. (614) 292-8949.

Rensselaer Polytechnic Institute, Rensselaer Fresh Water Institute. MRC 203, Troy, New York 12181-3590. (518) 276-6757.

Stroud Water Research Center. 512 Spencer Road, Avondale, Pennsylvania 19311. (215) 268-2153.

LINDANE

ABSTRACTING AND INDEXING SERVICES

Biological Abstracts. BIOSIS, 2100 Arch St., Philadelphia, Pennsylvania 19103-1399. (215) 587-4800. 1927-.

Chemical Abstracts. Chemical Abstracts Service, 2540 Olentangy River Rd., PO Box 3012, Columbus, Ohio 43210. (800) 848-6533. 1907-.

Environment Abstracts. Bowker A & I Publishing, 121 Chanlon Rd., New Providence, New Jersey 07974. (908) 464-6800. 1974-.

Environment Index. Environment Information Center, Index Research Department, 124 E. 39th St., New York, New York 10016. 1971-. Annual.

Environmental Information Connection–EIC. Planning Information Program, Dept. of Urban and Regional Planning, University of Illinois, 1003 West Nevada, Urbana, Illinois 61801. (217) 333-1369. Also available online.

Environmental Periodicals Bibliography. Environmental Studies Institute, International Academy at Santa Barbara, 800 Garden St., Suite D, Santa Barbara, California 93101. (805) 965-5010. Also available online.

General Science Index. H. W. Wilson Co., 950 University Ave., Bronx, New York 10452. 1978-. Monthly, also issued in annual cumulation. Cumulative subject index to English language periodicals in the subject fields of astronomy, botany, chemistry, earth science, environment and conservation, food and nutrition, genetics,

mathematics, medicine and health, microbiology, oceanography, physics, physiology and zoology.

Pollution Abstracts. Cambridge Scientific Abstracts, 5161 River Rd., Bethesda, Maryland 20816. (301) 961-6750. Six/year. Indexes worldwide technical literature on environmental pollution. Covers air pollution, marine and freshwater pollution, sewage and wastewater treatment, waste management, toxicology and health, noise pollution, radiation, land pollution, and environmental policies, programs, legislation, and education. Also available online.

Science Citation Index. Institute for Scientific Information, 3501 Market St., Philadelphia, Pennsylvania 19104. 1961-.

BIBLIOGRAPHIES

EPA Publications Bibliography. U.S. Environmental Protection Agency, Library Systems Branch, 401 M St., SW, Washington, District of Columbia 20460. (202) 260-2090. Quarterly.

ENCYCLOPEDIAS AND DICTIONARIES

Encyclopedia of Trademarks and Synonyms. H. Bennett, ed. Chemical Publishing Co., 80 Eighth Ave., New York, New York 10011. (212) 255-1950. 1981. Three volumes. Includes chemical compounds, compositions consisting of one or more chemicals and other products. Also included are abbreviated names and WHO free names.

Van Nostrand's Scientific Encyclopedia. Glenn D. Considine, ed. Van Nostrand Reinhold, 115 5th Ave., New York, New York 10003. (212) 254-3232. 1983. Sixth edition. Includes all broad subject areas in science.

GENERAL WORKS

The Biologic and Economic Assessment of Lindane. U.S. Department of Agriculture, 14th St. & Independence Ave., SW, Washington, District of Columbia 20250. (202) 447-2791. 1980.

HANDBOOKS AND MANUALS

CRC Handbook of Chemistry and Physics. CRC Press, 2000 Corporate Blvd. N.W., Boca Raton, Florida 33431. (407) 994-0555; (800) 272-7737. 1988. 67th ed.

Documentation of the Threshold Limit Values. American Conference of Governmental Industrial Hygienists, 6500 Glenway, Building D-5, Cincinnati, Ohio 45211. 1991. Provides threshold limit value documentation for any physical phenomenon in the environment, including chemical substances and physical agents.

Lindane Health and Safety Guide. World Health Organization, Ave. Appia, Geneva, Switzerland CH-1211. 1991. Chemical safety and toxicology of hexachlorobenzene.

NIOSH Pocket Guide to Chemical Hazards. National Institute for Occupational Safety and Health, 1600 Clifton Rd. NE, Atlanta, Georgia 30333. (404) 639-3286. 1990. Presents sources of general industrial hygiene and medical surveillance information for workers, employees and others. Presents key information and data in an abbreviated format for 398 individual chemicals or chemical types.

ONLINE DATA BASES

BIOSIS Previews. BIOSIS, 2100 Arch St., Philadelphia, Pennsylvania 19103-1399. (215) 587-4800. Largest and most comprehensive database of research in the life sciences. Contains citations for nearly 9000 primary research journals, monographs, reviews, symposia, preliminary reports, semi-popular journals, selected institutional reports, government reports and research communications.

Chemical Abstracts-CA. Chemical Abstracts Service, 2540 Olentangy River Rd., P.O. Box 3012, Columbus, Ohio 43210. (800) 848-6533 or (614) 421-3600. Information sources include 9000 journals, patents from 27 countries, two industrial property organizations, new books, conference proceedings, and government research reports.

Chemical Abstracts Chemical Name Directory-CHEM-NAME. Chemical Abstracts Service, 2540 Olentangy River Rd., P.O. Box 3012, Columbus, Ohio 43210. (800) 848-6533 or (614) 421-3600. Listing of chemical substances in a dictionary type file. The Chemical Abstracts (CAS) Registry Number, molecular formula, Chemical Abstracts (CA) Substance Index Name, available synonyms, ring data and other chemical substance information is given for each entry.

Chemical Carcinogenesis Research Information System–CCRIS. National Library of Medicine, 8600 Rockville Pike, Bethesda, Maryland 20894. (800) 638-8480. Individual assay results and test conditions for 1,451 chemicals in the areas of carcinogenicity, mutagenicity, tumor promotion, and cocarcinogenicity.

Enviro/Energyline Abstracts Plus. R. R. Bowker Co., 121 Chanlon Rd., New Providence, New Jersey 07974. (908) 464-6800.

Environmental Periodicals Bibliography. National Information Services Corp., Ste. 6, Wyman Towers, 3100 St. Paul St., Baltimore, Maryland 21218. (410)243-0797. Online version of abstract of same name.

PERIODICALS AND NEWSLETTERS

Environmental Science and Technology. American Chemical Society, 1155 16th St. N.W., Washington, District of Columbia 20036. (800) 227-5558. 1967-. Monthly. Contains research articles on various aspects of environmental chemistry, interpretative articles by invited experts and commentary on the scientific aspects of environmental management.

LIPIDS

ABSTRACTING AND INDEXING SERVICES

ASFA Aquaculture Abstracts. Cambridge Scientific Abstracts, Inc., 5161 River Rd., Bethesda, Maryland 20816. (301) 961-6750. 1984.

Biological Abstracts. BIOSIS, 2100 Arch St., Philadelphia, Pennsylvania 19103-1399. (215) 587-4800. 1927-.

Biological and Agricultural Index. H.W. Wilson Co., 950 University Ave., Bronx, New York 10452. (800) 367-6770. 1916-. Monthly.

Biotechnology Research Abstracts. Cambridge Scientific Abstracts, 5161 River Rd., Bethesda, Maryland 20816. (301) 961-6750. Monthly. Includes such broad areas as genetic intervention, biochemical genetics, and microbiological techniques.

Chemical Abstracts. Chemical Abstracts Service, 2540 Olentangy River Rd., PO Box 3012, Columbus, Ohio 43210. (800) 848-6533. 1907-.

Current Advances in Plant Science. Pergamon Microforms International, Inc., Fairview Park, Elmsford, New York 10523. (914) 592-7720. 1984-. Monthly. Current literature searching service including journals, reports, abstracts, etc. This service is available online as part of the CABS database on the hosts BRS and ORBIT search service.

Ecology Abstracts. Cambridge Scientific Abstracts, 5161 River Rd., Bethesda, Maryland 20816. (301) 961-6750. Monthly.

Environment Abstracts. Bowker A & I Publishing, 121 Chanlon Rd., New Providence, New Jersey 07974. (908) 464-6800. 1974-.

Environment Index. Environment Information Center, Index Research Department, 124 E. 39th St., New York, New York 10016. 1971-. Annual.

Environmental Information Connection–EIC. Planning Information Program, Dept. of Urban and Regional Planning, University of Illinois, 1003 West Nevada, Urbana, Illinois 61801. (217) 333-1369. Also available online.

Environmental Periodicals Bibliography. Environmental Studies Institute, International Academy at Santa Barbara, 800 Garden St., Suite D, Santa Barbara, California 93101. (805) 965-5010. Also available online.

Food Science and Technology Abstracts. International Food Information Service, c/o National Food Laboratory, 6363 Clark Ave., Dublin, California 94568. (800) 336-3782. 1969-.

General Science Index. H. W. Wilson Co., 950 University Ave., Bronx, New York 10452. 1978-. Monthly, also issued in annual cumulation. Cumulative subject index to English language periodicals in the subject fields of astronomy, botany, chemistry, earth science, environment and conservation, food and nutrition, genetics, mathematics, medicine and health, microbiology, oceanography, physics, physiology and zoology.

Pollution Abstracts. Cambridge Scientific Abstracts, 5161 River Rd., Bethesda, Maryland 20816. (301) 961-6750. Six/year. Indexes worldwide technical literature on environmental pollution. Covers air pollution, marine and freshwater pollution, sewage and wastewater treatment, waste management, toxicology and health, noise pollution, radiation, land pollution, and environmental policies, programs, legislation, and education. Also available online.

Science Citation Index. Institute for Scientific Information, 3501 Market St., Philadelphia, Pennsylvania 19104. 1961-.

BIBLIOGRAPHIES

EPA Publications Bibliography. U.S. Environmental Protection Agency, Library Systems Branch, 401 M St., SW, Washington, District of Columbia 20460. (202) 260-2090. Quarterly.

ENCYCLOPEDIAS AND DICTIONARIES

Cambridge Dictionary of Biology. Peter M. B. Walker. Cambridge University Press, 40 W. 20th St., New York, New York 10011. (212) 924-3900 or (800) 227-0247. 1989. Includes 10,000 terms in zoology, botany, biochemistry, molecular biology and genetics. Previously published under the title Chambers Biology Dictionary.

Cambridge Encyclopedia of Life Sciences. A. E. Friday and David S. Ingram. Cambridge University Press, 40 W 20th St., New York, New York 10011. (212) 924-3900 or (800) 227-0247. 1985. Includes all topics under biology and ecology.

A Concise Dictionary of Biology. Elizabeth Martin, ed. Oxford University Press, 200 Madison Ave., New York, New York 10016. (212) 679-7300 or (800) 334-4249. 1990. New edition. Derived from the Concise Science Dictionary, published in 1984.

The Dictionary of Cell Biology. J. M. Lackie and J. A. T. Dow, eds. Academic Press, c/o Harcourt Brace Jovanovich Inc., 6277 Sea Harbor Dr., Orlando, Florida 32887. (800) 346-8648. 1989. Covers the broad subject area of cell biology including lipid, vitamins, amino acid, lectins, proteins, and other related topics.

Encyclopedia of Human Biology. Renato Dulbecco, ed. Academic Press, c/o Harcourt Brace Jovanovich Inc., 6277 Sea Harbor Dr., Orlando, Florida 32887. (800) 346-8648. 1991. Eight volumes.

The Nutrition and Health Encyclopedia. David F. Tver and Percy Russell. Van Nostrand Reinhold, 115 5th Ave., New York, New York 10003. (212) 254-3232. 1989.

Van Nostrand's Scientific Encyclopedia. Glenn D. Considine, ed. Van Nostrand Reinhold, 115 5th Ave., New York, New York 10003. (212) 254-3232. 1983. Sixth edition. Includes all broad subject areas in science.

GENERAL WORKS

Coagulation and Lipids. CRC Press, 2000 Corporate Blvd. N.W., Boca Raton, Florida 33431. (800) 272-7737. 1989. Physiological effect of phospholipids.

Lipid Analysis. William W. Christie. Pergamon Microforms International, Inc., Fairview Park, Elmsford, New York 10523. (914) 592-7720. 1982. Isolation, separation, identification, and structural analysis of lipids.

Lipid Manual: Methodology Appropriate for Fatty Acid-Cholesterol Analysis. Alan J. Sheppard. U.S. Food and Drug Administration, Division of Nutrition, 5600 Fishers Ln., Rockville, Maryland 20857. (301) 443-1544. 1989. Analysis of oils, fats, and cholesterol.

Lipids. Helmut K. Mangold. CRC Press, 2000 Corporate Blvd. N.W., Boca Raton, Florida 33431. (800) 272-7737. 1984. Chromatographic analysis of lipids.

Magill's Survey of Science. Life Science Series. Frank N. Magill, ed. Salem Press, PO Box 50062, Pasadena, California 91105. 1991. Six volumes. Contents: v.1. A-Central and peripheral nervous system functions; v.2. Central metabolism regulation - eukaryotic transcriptional control; v.3. Positive and negative eukaryotic transcriptional control - mammalian hormones; v.4. Hor-

mones and behavior - muscular contraction; v.5. Muscular contraction and relaxation - sexual reproduction in plants; v.6. Reproductive behavior and mating - X inactivation and the Lyon hypothesis.

HANDBOOKS AND MANUALS

Handbook of Lipid Research. Plenum Press, 233 Spring St., New York, New York 10013-1578. (212) 620-8000; (800) 221-9369. 1978.

ONLINE DATA BASES

BIOSIS Previews. BIOSIS, 2100 Arch St., Philadelphia, Pennsylvania 19103-1399. (215) 587-4800. Largest and most comprehensive database of research in the life sciences. Contains citations for nearly 9000 primary research journals, monographs, reviews, symposia, preliminary reports, semi-popular journals, selected institutional reports, government reports and research communications.

Cambridge Scientific Abstracts Life Science–CSAL. Cambridge Scientific Abstracts, 5161 River Rd., Bethesda, Maryland 20816. (301) 961-6750. Provides access to the following abstracting services: "Life Sciences Collection," "Aquatic Sciences and Fisheries Abstracts," "Oceanic Abstracts," and "Pollution Abstracts."

Chemical Abstracts-CA. Chemical Abstracts Service, 2540 Olentangy River Rd., P.O. Box 3012, Columbus, Ohio 43210. (800) 848-6533 or (614) 421-3600. Information sources include 9000 journals, patents from 27 countries, two industrial property organizations, new books, conference proceedings, and government research reports.

Chemical Engineering and Biotechnology Abstracts–CEBA. Orbit Search Service, Maxwell Online Inc., 8000 W. Park Dr., McLean, Virginia 22102. (703) 442-0900 or (800) 456-7248. Monthly. Covers theoretical, practical and commercial material on all aspects of processing safety, and the environment. Also covers process and reaction engineering, measurement and process control, environmental protection and safety, plant design and equipment used in chemical engineering and biotechnology. More than 400 of the world's major primary chemical and process engineering journals are scanned to compile the database. Available from ORBIT.

Enviro/Energyline Abstracts Plus. R. R. Bowker Co., 121 Chanlon Rd., New Providence, New Jersey 07974. (908) 464-6800.

Environmental Periodicals Bibliography. National Information Services Corp., Ste. 6, Wyman Towers, 3100 St. Paul St., Baltimore, Maryland 21218. (410)243-0797. Online version of abstract of same name.

PERIODICALS AND NEWSLETTERS

Journal of Lipid Research. Federation of American Societies for Experimental Biology, 9650 Rockville Pike, Bethesda, Maryland 20814-3998. (301) 530-7000. Monthly. Chemistry, biochemistry, and metabolism of lipids. Includes morphological and clinical studies.

Lipids. American Oil Chemists' Society, PO Box 3489, 1608 Broadmoor Dr., Champaign, Illinois 61826-3489. (217) 359-2344. 1966-. Monthly.

RESEARCH CENTERS AND INSTITUTES

Michigan State University, Center for Genetic and Biochemical Alteration of Plant Lipids and Starch. c/o Department of Botany and Plant Pathology, East Lansing, Michigan 48824. (517) 353-0611.

Syracuse University, Biological Research Laboratories. 130 College Place, Syracuse, New York 13210. (315) 423-3186.

Texas A&M University, Lipid Research Laboratory. Department of Biochemistry, College Station, Texas 77843. (409) 845-5616.

TRADE ASSOCIATIONS AND PROFESSIONAL SOCIETIES

American Chemical Society. 1155 16th St., N.W., Washington, District of Columbia 20036. (202) 872-4600.

LIQUEFIED NATURAL GAS

ABSTRACTING AND INDEXING SERVICES

Applied Science and Technology Index. H.W. Wilson Co., 950 University Ave., Bronx, New York 10452. (800) 367-6770. Formerly Industrial Arts Index.

Environment Abstracts. Bowker A & I Publishing, 121 Chanlon Rd., New Providence, New Jersey 07974. (908) 464-6800. 1974-.

Environment Index. Environment Information Center, Index Research Department, 124 E. 39th St., New York, New York 10016. 1971-. Annual.

Environmental Information Connection–EIC. Planning Information Program, Dept. of Urban and Regional Planning, University of Illinois, 1003 West Nevada, Urbana, Illinois 61801. (217) 333-1369. Also available online.

Environmental Periodicals Bibliography. Environmental Studies Institute, International Academy at Santa Barbara, 800 Garden St., Suite D, Santa Barbara, California 93101. (805) 965-5010. Also available online.

General Science Index. H. W. Wilson Co., 950 University Ave., Bronx, New York 10452. 1978-. Monthly, also issued in annual cumulation. Cumulative subject index to English language periodicals in the subject fields of astronomy, botany, chemistry, earth science, environment and conservation, food and nutrition, genetics, mathematics, medicine and health, microbiology, oceanography, physics, physiology and zoology.

Pollution Abstracts. Cambridge Scientific Abstracts, 5161 River Rd., Bethesda, Maryland 20816. (301) 961-6750. Six/year. Indexes worldwide technical literature on environmental pollution. Covers air pollution, marine and freshwater pollution, sewage and wastewater treatment, waste management, toxicology and health, noise pollution, radiation, land pollution, and environmental policies, programs, legislation, and education. Also available online.

Science Citation Index. Institute for Scientific Information, 3501 Market St., Philadelphia, Pennsylvania 19104. 1961-.

BIBLIOGRAPHIES

EPA Publications Bibliography. U.S. Environmental Protection Agency, Library Systems Branch, 401 M St., SW, Washington, District of Columbia 20460. (202) 260-2090. Quarterly.

ENCYCLOPEDIAS AND DICTIONARIES

Encyclopedia of Chemical Processing and Design. John J. Mcketta and W. A. Cunningham. Marcel Dekker, Inc., 270 Madison Ave., New York, New York 10016. (212) 696-9000; (800) 228-1160. 1992. Thirty-eight volumes.

Energy Terminology: A Multilingual Glossary. Pergamon Microforms International, Inc., Fairview Park, Elmsford, New York 10523. (914) 592-7720. 1986. Second edition. Contains 1500 defined terms and concepts related to the field of energy together with an index of several thousand undefined keywords used in the definitions of these terms and concepts. Contents appear in four languages: English, French, German and Spanish.

Kirk-Othmer Encyclopedia of Chemical Technology. J. I. Kroschwitz, ed. John Wiley & Sons, Inc., 605 3rd Ave., New York, New York 10158-0012. (212) 850-6000. 1992-. All articles in the new edition have been rewritten and updated adding new subjects such as biotechnology, computer topics, analytical techniques and instrumentation, environmental concerns, fuels and energy, inorganic and solid state chemistry; composite materials and material science in general, and pharmaceuticals. Also available online.

GENERAL WORKS

Biomass, Catalysts and Liquid Fuels. Technomic Publishing Co., 851 New Holland Ave., Box 3535, Lancaster, Pennsylvania 17604. (717) 291-5609.

The Feasibility of Methods and Systems for Reducing LNG Tanker Fire Hazards. Arthur D. Little, Inc. U.S. Department of Energy, Division of Environmental Safety and Engineering, Washington, District of Columbia 1980. Liquefied natural gas accidents.

Hazards to Nuclear Power Plants from Large Liquefied Natural Gas Spills on Water. C.A. Kot. U.S. G.P.O., Washington, District of Columbia 20401. (202)512-0000. 1981.

HANDBOOKS AND MANUALS

Recommended Research on LNG Safety. R & D Associates. National Technical Information Service, 5285 Port Royal Rd., Springfield, Virginia 22161. (703) 487-4650. 1981.

ONLINE DATA BASES

Enviro/Energyline Abstracts Plus. R. R. Bowker Co., 121 Chanlon Rd., New Providence, New Jersey 07974. (908) 464-6800.

Environmental Periodicals Bibliography. National Information Services Corp., Ste. 6, Wyman Towers, 3100 St. Paul St., Baltimore, Maryland 21218. (410)243-0797. Online version of abstract of same name.

Kirk-Othmer Encyclopedia of Chemical Technology. John Wiley & Sons, Inc., 605 3rd Ave., 5th Floor, New York,

New York 10158. (212) 850-6000. Online version of the publication of the same name.

Liquified Petroleum Gas. I.P. Sharp Associates, a Reuter Company, Suite 1900, Exchange Tower, 2 First Canadian Place, Toronto, Ontario, Canada M5X 1E3. (800) 387-1588.

TRADE ASSOCIATIONS AND PROFESSIONAL SOCIETIES

Compressed Gas Association. Crystal Gateway #1, Suite 501, 1235 Jefferson Davis Hwy., Arlington, Virginia 22202. (703) 979-0900.

LIQUEFIED PETROLEUM GAS

ABSTRACTING AND INDEXING SERVICES

Applied Science and Technology Index. H.W. Wilson Co., 950 University Ave., Bronx, New York 10452. (800) 367-6770. Formerly Industrial Arts Index.

Environment Abstracts. Bowker A & I Publishing, 121 Chanlon Rd., New Providence, New Jersey 07974. (908) 464-6800. 1974-.

Environment Index. Environment Information Center, Index Research Department, 124 E. 39th St., New York, New York 10016. 1971-. Annual.

Environmental Information Connection–EIC. Planning Information Program, Dept. of Urban and Regional Planning, University of Illinois, 1003 West Nevada, Urbana, Illinois 61801. (217) 333-1369. Also available online.

Environmental Periodicals Bibliography. Environmental Studies Institute, International Academy at Santa Barbara, 800 Garden St., Suite D, Santa Barbara, California 93101. (805) 965-5010. Also available online.

General Science Index. H. W. Wilson Co., 950 University Ave., Bronx, New York 10452. 1978-. Monthly, also issued in annual cumulation. Cumulative subject index to English language periodicals in the subject fields of astronomy, botany, chemistry, earth science, environment and conservation, food and nutrition, genetics, mathematics, medicine and health, microbiology, oceanography, physics, physiology and zoology.

Science Citation Index. Institute for Scientific Information, 3501 Market St., Philadelphia, Pennsylvania 19104. 1961-.

BIBLIOGRAPHIES

EPA Publications Bibliography. U.S. Environmental Protection Agency, Library Systems Branch, 401 M St., SW, Washington, District of Columbia 20460. (202) 260-2090. Quarterly.

DIRECTORIES

Gas Liquified Petroleum Directory. American Business Directories, Inc., 5711 S. 86th Circle, Omaha, Nebraska 68127. (402) 593-4600.

ENCYCLOPEDIAS AND DICTIONARIES

Energy Terminology: A Multilingual Glossary. Pergamon Microforms International, Inc., Fairview Park, Elmsford, New York 10523. (914) 592-7720. 1986. Second edition. Contains 1500 defined terms and concepts related to the field of energy together with an index of several thousand undefined keywords used in the definitions of these terms and concepts. Contents appear in four languages: English, French, German and Spanish.

GENERAL WORKS

Biomass, Catalysts and Liquid Fuels. Technomic Publishing Co., 851 New Holland Ave., Box 3535, Lancaster, Pennsylvania 17604. (717) 291-5609.

Fire Safety of LPG in Marine Transportation. Applied Technology Corp. National Technical Information Service, 5285 Port Royal Rd., Springfield, Virginia 22161. (703) 487-4650. 1980. Fire prevention in shipping LPG.

An Introduction to LP-Gases. W.W. Clark. Butane-Propane News, 338 W. Foothill Blvd., Arcadia, California 91006. (818) 357-2168. 1983.

LPG Land Transportation and Storage Safety. Applied Technology Corp. National Technical Information Service, 5285 Port Royal Rd., Springfield, Virginia 22161. (703) 487-4650. 1981. Storage and transportation of liquid petroleum gas.

HANDBOOKS AND MANUALS

LPG Tanks, Inspection and Safety. U.S. Customs Service, Office of Inspection and Control, 1301 Constitution Ave. NW, Washington, District of Columbia 20229. (202) 927-2095. 1986. A handbook for the safe, effective inspection of liquefied petroleum gas fuel tanks in cars and pick-up trucks.

Physical and Chemical Properties. W.W. Clark. Butane-Propane News, 338 W. Foothill Blvd., Arcadia, California 91006. (818) 357-2168. 1983. Covers LP-gas, propane and butane.

ONLINE DATA BASES

Enviro/Energyline Abstracts Plus. R. R. Bowker Co., 121 Chanlon Rd., New Providence, New Jersey 07974. (908) 464-6800.

Environmental Periodicals Bibliography. National Information Services Corp., Ste. 6, Wyman Towers, 3100 St. Paul St., Baltimore, Maryland 21218. (410)243-0797. Online version of abstract of same name.

Liquified Petroleum Gas. I.P. Sharp Associates, a Reuter Company, Suite 1900, Exchange Tower, 2 First Canadian Place, Toronto, Ontario, Canada M5X 1E3. (800) 387-1588.

TRADE ASSOCIATIONS AND PROFESSIONAL SOCIETIES

Compressed Gas Association. Crystal Gateway #1, Suite 501, 1235 Jefferson Davis Hwy., Arlington, Virginia 22202. (703) 979-0900.

LIQUID CHROMATOGRAPHY
See: CHROMATOGRAPHY

LITHOLOGY

ABSTRACTING AND INDEXING SERVICES

Biological Abstracts. BIOSIS, 2100 Arch St., Philadelphia, Pennsylvania 19103-1399. (215) 587-4800. 1927-.

Biological and Agricultural Index. H.W. Wilson Co., 950 University Ave., Bronx, New York 10452. (800) 367-6770. 1916-. Monthly.

Environment Abstracts. Bowker A & I Publishing, 121 Chanlon Rd., New Providence, New Jersey 07974. (908) 464-6800. 1974-.

Environment Index. Environment Information Center, Index Research Department, 124 E. 39th St., New York, New York 10016. 1971-. Annual.

Environmental Information Connection–EIC. Planning Information Program, Dept. of Urban and Regional Planning, University of Illinois, 1003 West Nevada, Urbana, Illinois 61801. (217) 333-1369. Also available online.

Environmental Periodicals Bibliography. Environmental Studies Institute, International Academy at Santa Barbara, 800 Garden St., Suite D, Santa Barbara, California 93101. (805) 965-5010. Also available online.

General Science Index. H. W. Wilson Co., 950 University Ave., Bronx, New York 10452. 1978-. Monthly, also issued in annual cumulation. Cumulative subject index to English language periodicals in the subject fields of astronomy, botany, chemistry, earth science, environment and conservation, food and nutrition, genetics, mathematics, medicine and health, microbiology, oceanography, physics, physiology and zoology.

Science Citation Index. Institute for Scientific Information, 3501 Market St., Philadelphia, Pennsylvania 19104. 1961-.

ALMANACS AND YEARBOOKS

Progress in Protein-Lipid Interactions. Elsevier Science Publishing Co., 655 Avenue of the Americas, New York, New York 10010. (212) 984-5800. Annual. Review designed to critically evaluate actively developing areas of research in protein-lipid interactions.

BIBLIOGRAPHIES

Bibliography and Index of Geology. American Geological Institute, 4220 King St., Alexandria, Virginia 22302. Monthly. Includes environmental geology and hydrogeology.

Current Contents. Agriculture, Biology and Environmental Sciences. Institute for Scientific Information, 3501 Market St., Philadelphia, Pennsylvania 19104. (800) 523-1857. 1973-. Previous title: Current Contents. Agricultural, Food & Veterinary Sciences. Gives the table of contents of periodicals in the fields of agriculture, biology, environmental and related areas.

EPA Publications Bibliography. U.S. Environmental Protection Agency, Library Systems Branch, 401 M St., SW, Washington, District of Columbia 20460. (202) 260-2090. Quarterly.

ENCYCLOPEDIAS AND DICTIONARIES

Van Nostrand's Scientific Encyclopedia. Glenn D. Considine, ed. Van Nostrand Reinhold, 115 5th Ave., New York, New York 10003. (212) 254-3232. 1983. Sixth edition. Includes all broad subject areas in science.

GENERAL WORKS

Magill's Survey of Science. Earth Science Series. Frank N. Magill. Salem Press, PO Box 50062, Pasadena, California 91105. 1990-. Five volumes. Includes information on earth's crust, hot spots and volcanic island chains, physical properties of minerals, rock magnetism, physical properties of rocks, and index.

ONLINE DATA BASES

BIOSIS Previews. BIOSIS, 2100 Arch St., Philadelphia, Pennsylvania 19103-1399. (215) 587-4800. Largest and most comprehensive database of research in the life sciences. Contains citations for nearly 9000 primary research journals, monographs, reviews, symposia, preliminary reports, semi-popular journals, selected institutional reports, government reports and research communications.

Enviro/Energyline Abstracts Plus. R. R. Bowker Co., 121 Chanlon Rd., New Providence, New Jersey 07974. (908) 464-6800.

Environmental Periodicals Bibliography. National Information Services Corp., Ste. 6, Wyman Towers, 3100 St. Paul St., Baltimore, Maryland 21218. (410)243-0797. Online version of abstract of same name.

SCISEARCH. Institute for Scientific Information, University City Science Center, 3501 Market St., Philadelphia, Pennsylvania 19104. (215) 386-0100.

PERIODICALS AND NEWSLETTERS

Chemistry and Physics of Lipids. North Holland Pub. Co., Amsterdam, Netherlands Bimonthly.

Progress in Lipid Research. Pergamon Microforms International, Inc., Fairview Park, Elmsford, New York 10523. (914) 592-7720. Quarterly. Covers topics in the chemistry of fats and other lipids.

LITIGATION
See: ENVIRONMENTAL LEGISLATION

LITTER (TRASH)
See: SOLID WASTE

LITTORAL
See: LAKES

LIVESTOCK
See also: AGRICULTURE

ABSTRACTING AND INDEXING SERVICES

Agricultural Engineering Abstracts. C. A. B. International, 845 North Park Ave., Tucson, Arizona 85719. (602) 621-7897 or (800) 528-4841. 1976-. Monthly. Informs about significant research developments in agricultural engineering and instrumentation. Some of the topics scanned for the abstracts include mechanical power, crop production, crop harvesting and threshing, crop processing and storage, aquaculture, land improvement, protected cultivation, handling and transport, and farm buildings and equipment.

Animal Breeding Abstracts. C. A. B. International, 845 North Park Ave., Tucson, Arizona 85719. (602) 621-7897 or (800) 528-4841. 1933-. Monthly. Abstracts covers the literature on animal breeding, genetics, reproduction and production. Includes areas of biological research such as immunogenetics, genetic engineering and fertility improvement.

Biological and Agricultural Index. H.W. Wilson Co., 950 University Ave., Bronx, New York 10452. (800) 367-6770. 1916-. Monthly.

Biology Digest. Data Courier, Plexus Pub Inc., 143 Old Marlton Pike, Medford, New Jersey 08055. 1974-. Monthly. Abstracts biology periodicals.

Ecology Abstracts. Cambridge Scientific Abstracts, 5161 River Rd., Bethesda, Maryland 20816. (301) 961-6750. Monthly.

General Science Index. H. W. Wilson Co., 950 University Ave., Bronx, New York 10452. 1978-. Monthly, also issued in annual cumulation. Cumulative subject index to English language periodicals in the subject fields of astronomy, botany, chemistry, earth science, environment and conservation, food and nutrition, genetics, mathematics, medicine and health, microbiology, oceanography, physics, physiology and zoology.

Index to Scientific Book Contents. Institute for Scientific Information, 3501 Market St., Philadelphia, Pennsylvania 19104. (800) 523-1857. 1985-. Annual. Gives contents of science books published.

Pollution Abstracts. Cambridge Scientific Abstracts, 5161 River Rd., Bethesda, Maryland 20816. (301) 961-6750. Six/year. Indexes worldwide technical literature on environmental pollution. Covers air pollution, marine and freshwater pollution, sewage and wastewater treatment, waste management, toxicology and health, noise pollution, radiation, land pollution, and environmental policies, programs, legislation, and education. Also available online.

Science Citation Index. Institute for Scientific Information, 3501 Market St., Philadelphia, Pennsylvania 19104. 1961-.

BIBLIOGRAPHIES

Agricultural and Animal Sciences Journals and Serials: An Analytical Guide. Richard D. Jensen. Greenwood Publishing Group, Inc., 88 Post Rd. W., PO Box 5007, Westport, Connecticut 06881. (212) 226-3571. 1986.

Current Contents. Agriculture, Biology and Environmental Sciences. Institute for Scientific Information, 3501 Market St., Philadelphia, Pennsylvania 19104. (800) 523-1857. 1973-. Previous title: Current Contents. Agricultural, Food & Veterinary Sciences. Gives the table of

contents of periodicals in the fields of agriculture, biology, environmental and related areas.

Livestock Grazing Strategies: Environmental Considerations, January 1980 - May 1991. Janet E. Dombrowski. National Agricultural Library, 10301 Baltimore Blvd., Beltsville, Maryland 20705-2351. (301) 504-5755. 1991.

ENCYCLOPEDIAS AND DICTIONARIES

Encyclopedia of Human Biology. Renato Dulbecco, ed. Academic Press, c/o Harcourt Brace Jovanovich Inc., 6277 Sea Harbor Dr., Orlando, Florida 32887. (800) 346-8648. 1991. Eight volumes.

GENERAL WORKS

Agricultural Ecology. Joy Tivy. John Wiley & Sons, Inc., 605 3rd Ave., New York, New York 10158-0012. (212) 850-6000. 1990. Analyzes the nature of relationships between crops, livestock, and the biophysical environment, and the extent to which man has modified the products and environment to suit his own needs.

Effluents from Livestock. J. K. R. Gasser, et al., eds. Applied Science Publications, PO Box 5399, New York, New York 10163. (718) 756-6440. 1980. Proceedings of a seminar to discuss work carried out within the EEC under the programme Effluents from Intensive Livestock, organized by Prof. H. Vetter and held at Bad Zwischenahn, 2-5 October, 1979.

GOVERNMENTAL ORGANIZATIONS

National Agricultural Library. Route 1, Beltsville, Maryland 20705. (301) 344-4348.

HANDBOOKS AND MANUALS

Handbook of Livestock Management Techniques. Richard Battaglia. Burgess Publishing Co., 7110 Ohms Ln., Minneapolis, Minnesota 55439-2143. (612) 831-1344. 1981.

Livestock Waste Facilities Handbook. Midwest Plan Service, Ames, Iowa 1985. Deals with agricultural waste management and manure handling in livestock waste facilities.

ONLINE DATA BASES

AGRIS. Food and Agriculture Organization of the United Nations, Via delle Terme di Caracalla, Rome, Italy 00100. 61 0181-FA01.

Animal Disease Occurrence. C. A. B. International, Wallingford, England OX110 8DE. 44 (491) 32111.

Cambridge Scientific Abstracts Life Science–CSAL. Cambridge Scientific Abstracts, 5161 River Rd., Bethesda, Maryland 20816. (301) 961-6750. Provides access to the following abstracting services: "Life Sciences Collection," "Aquatic Sciences and Fisheries Abstracts," "Oceanic Abstracts," and "Pollution Abstracts."

STATISTICS SOURCES

World Resources. World Resources Institute. 1709 New York Ave., N.W., Washington, District of Columbia 20006. (202) 638-6300. Annual. Statistical and textual

analysis of world's natural resources and the effects of growth-caused environmental pollution.

TRADE ASSOCIATIONS AND PROFESSIONAL SOCIETIES

American Society of Animal Science. c/o Carl D. Johnson, 309 W. Clark St., Champaign, Illinois 61820. (217) 356-3182.

Livestock Conservation Institute. 6414 Copps Ave. #116, Madison, Wisconsin 53716. (608) 221-4848.

National Feed Ingredients Association. One Corporate Pl., Suite 375, West Des Moines, Iowa 50265. (515) 225-9611.

National Food and Conservation Through Swine. c/o Ronie Polen, Fox Run Rd., R.R. 4, Box 397, Sewell, New Jersey 08080. (609) 468-5447.

LIVESTOCK FEEDLOT RUNOFF

ABSTRACTING AND INDEXING SERVICES

Biological and Agricultural Index. H.W. Wilson Co., 950 University Ave., Bronx, New York 10452. (800) 367-6770. 1916-. Monthly.

BIBLIOGRAPHIES

Current Contents. Agriculture, Biology and Environmental Sciences. Institute for Scientific Information, 3501 Market St., Philadelphia, Pennsylvania 19104. (800) 523-1857. 1973-. Previous title: Current Contents. Agricultural, Food & Veterinary Sciences. Gives the table of contents of periodicals in the fields of agriculture, biology, environmental and related areas.

GENERAL WORKS

Livestock Feedlot Runoff Control by Vegetative Filters. Robert S. Kerr. National Technical Information Service, 5285 Port Royal Rd., Springfield, Virginia 22161. (703) 487-4650. 1979. Environmental protection technology relating to filters and filtration.

ONLINE DATA BASES

Cambridge Scientific Abstracts Life Science–CSAL. Cambridge Scientific Abstracts, 5161 River Rd., Bethesda, Maryland 20816. (301) 961-6750. Provides access to the following abstracting services: "Life Sciences Collection," "Aquatic Sciences and Fisheries Abstracts," "Oceanic Abstracts," and "Pollution Abstracts."

TRADE ASSOCIATIONS AND PROFESSIONAL SOCIETIES

American Society of Agricultural Engineers. 2950 Niles Rd., St Joseph, Michigan 49085. (616) 429-0300.

LIVESTOCK HOUSING

BIBLIOGRAPHIES

Current Contents. Agriculture, Biology and Environmental Sciences. Institute for Scientific Information, 3501 Market St., Philadelphia, Pennsylvania 19104. (800) 523-

1857. 1973-. Previous title: Current Contents. Agricultural, Food & Veterinary Sciences. Gives the table of contents of periodicals in the fields of agriculture, biology, environmental and related areas.

GENERAL WORKS

Environment Control for Animals and Plants. Louis D. Albright. American Society of Agricultural Engineers, 2950 Niles Rd., St. Joseph, Michigan 49085-9659. (616) 429-0300. 1990. Deals with the physical aspects of environmental control with some attention to biological factors relevant to successful environment control. Includes 10 executable computer programs that allow the user to explore design options.

Environmental Control for Confinement Livestock Housing. Don D. Jones. Purdue University, Cooperative Extension Service, West Lafayette, Indiana 47907. (317) 494-8489. 1980. Heating and ventilation of livestock housing.

In One Barn: Efficient Livestock Housing and Management. Lee Pelley. Countryman Press, PO Box 175, Woodstock, Vermont 05091-0175. (802) 457-1049. 1984.

Insulating Livestock and Other Farm Buildings. Don D. Jones. Purdue University, Cooperative Extension Service, AGAD Bldg., West Lafayette, Indiana 47907. (317) 494-8489. 1979.

Livestock Health Housing. David Sainsbury. Bailliere Tindall, 24-28 Oval Rd., London, England NW1 7DX. 1988. Prevention and control of animal disease.

Stray Voltage. Robert J. Gustafson. Energy Research and Development Division, Energy and Environmental Policy Department, National Rural Electric Cooperative Association, 1800 Massachusetts Ave., NW, Washington, District of Columbia 20036. (202) 857-9500. 1988. Seasonal variations in grounding and primary neutral-to-earth voltages.

ONLINE DATA BASES

Cambridge Scientific Abstracts Life Science–CSAL. Cambridge Scientific Abstracts, 5161 River Rd., Bethesda, Maryland 20816. (301) 961-6750. Provides access to the following abstracting services: "Life Sciences Collection," "Aquatic Sciences and Fisheries Abstracts," "Oceanic Abstracts," and "Pollution Abstracts."

TRADE ASSOCIATIONS AND PROFESSIONAL SOCIETIES

American Society of Agricultural Engineers. 2950 Niles Rd., St Joseph, Michigan 49085. (616) 429-0300.

LOGGING

See: FOREST MANAGEMENT

LOSS OF COOLANT ACCIDENTS

See: DISASTERS

LOUISIANA ENVIRONMENTAL AGENCIES

GOVERNMENTAL ORGANIZATIONS

Department of Agriculture: Pesticide Registration. Director, Pesticide and Environmental Programs, PO Box 44153, Capitol Station, Baton Rouge, Louisiana 70804-4153. (504) 925-3763.

Department of Environmental Quality: Air Quality. Assistant Secretary, Office of Air Quality, PO Box 44096, Baton Rouge, Louisiana 70804-7096. (504) 342-9047.

Department of Environmental Quality: Emergency Preparedness and Community Right-to-Know. Emergency Response Coordinator, PO Box 44066, 333 Laurel St., Baton Rouge, Louisiana 70804-4066. (504) 342-8617.

Department of Environmental Quality: Environmental Protection. Secretary, PO Box 15570, Baton Rouge, Louisiana 70895. (504) 342-1266.

Department of Environmental Quality: Groundwater Management. Assistant Secretary, Office of Water Resources, PO Box 44091, Baton Rouge, Louisiana 70804-4066. (504) 342-6363.

Department of Environmental Quality: Hazardous Waste Management. Administrator, Hazardous Waste Division, 438 Main St., Baton Rouge, Louisiana 70804. (504) 342-1216.

Department of Environmental Quality: Solid Waste Management. Administrator of Solid Waste, Hazardous and Solid Waste Office, PO Box 44307, Baton Rouge, Louisiana 70804-4307. (504) 342-1216.

Department of Environmental Quality: Water Quality. Assistant Secretary, Office of Water Resources, PO Box 44091, Baton Rouge, Louisiana 70804-4066. (504) 342-6363.

Department of Labor: Occupational Safety. Assistant Secretary, Office of Labor, PO Box 94094, Baton Rouge, Louisiana 70804-9094. (504) 925-4221.

Department of Natural Resources: Coastal Zone Management. Director, Office of Coastal Management, PO Box 44124, Baton Rouge, Louisiana 70804-4487. (504) 342-7591.

Department of Natural Resources: Natural Resources. Secretary, PO Box 94396, Baton Rouge, Louisiana 70804-9396. (504) 342-4500.

Transportation and Development Department: Underground Storage Tanks. Materials Division, PO Box 9425, Baton Rouge, Louisiana 70804. (504) 929-9131.

U.S. EPA Region 6: Pollution Prevention. Coordinator, 1445 Ross Ave., Suite 1200, Dallas, Texas 75202-2733. (214) 655-6444.

Wildlife and Fisheries Department: Fish and Wildlife. Secretary, PO Box 98000, Baton Rouge, Louisiana 70898-2803. (504) 765-2803.

LOUISIANA ENVIRONMENTAL LEGISLATION

GENERAL WORKS

Environmental Law in Louisiana. The Cambridge Institute, 1964 Gallows Rd., Vienna, Virginia 22182. (703) 893-8500. 1989.

LOW SULFUR COAL

See: COAL

LUBRICATING OILS

ABSTRACTING AND INDEXING SERVICES

Engineering Index. The Engineering Index Inc., 345 E. 47th St., New York, New York 10017. 1962-.

Environment Abstracts. Bowker A & I Publishing, 121 Chanlon Rd., New Providence, New Jersey 07974. (908) 464-6800. 1974-.

Environment Index. Environment Information Center, Index Research Department, 124 E. 39th St., New York, New York 10016. 1971-. Annual.

Environmental Information Connection–EIC. Planning Information Program, Dept. of Urban and Regional Planning, University of Illinois, 1003 West Nevada, Urbana, Illinois 61801. (217) 333-1369. Also available online.

Environmental Periodicals Bibliography. Environmental Studies Institute, International Academy at Santa Barbara, 800 Garden St., Suite D, Santa Barbara, California 93101. (805) 965-5010. Also available online.

General Science Index. H. W. Wilson Co., 950 University Ave., Bronx, New York 10452. 1978-. Monthly, also issued in annual cumulation. Cumulative subject index to English language periodicals in the subject fields of astronomy, botany, chemistry, earth science, environment and conservation, food and nutrition, genetics, mathematics, medicine and health, microbiology, oceanography, physics, physiology and zoology.

Pollution Abstracts. Cambridge Scientific Abstracts, 5161 River Rd., Bethesda, Maryland 20816. (301) 961-6750. Six/year. Indexes worldwide technical literature on environmental pollution. Covers air pollution, marine and freshwater pollution, sewage and wastewater treatment, waste management, toxicology and health, noise pollution, radiation, land pollution, and environmental policies, programs, legislation, and education. Also available online.

Science Citation Index. Institute for Scientific Information, 3501 Market St., Philadelphia, Pennsylvania 19104. 1961-.

BIBLIOGRAPHIES

EPA Publications Bibliography. U.S. Environmental Protection Agency, Library Systems Branch, 401 M St., SW, Washington, District of Columbia 20460. (202) 260-2090. Quarterly.

DIRECTORIES

McCutcheon's Functional Materials. Manufacturing Confectioner Publishing Co., 175 Rock Rd., Glen Rock, New Jersey 07451. (201) 652-2655. 1985. Annual.

ENCYCLOPEDIAS AND DICTIONARIES

Encyclopedia of Industrial Chemical Additives. Michael and Irene Ash. Chemical Publishing Co., 80 Eighth Ave., New York, New York 10011. (212) 255-1950. 1984-87. Four volumes. Comprehensive compilation of tradename products that function as additives in enhancing the properties of various major industrial products.

GENERAL WORKS

Basic Lubrication Theory. Alastair Cameron. Halsted Press, 605 3rd Ave., New York, New York 10158. (212) 850-6000. 1981.

Lubrication in Practice. W. S. Robertson. Macmillan Publishers Ltd., 4 Little Essex St., London, England WC2R 3LF. 1983.

HANDBOOKS AND MANUALS

Industrial Lubrication. Michael Billett. Pergamon Microforms International, Inc., Fairview Park, Elmsford, New York 10523. (914) 592-7720. 1979. A practical handbook for lubrication and production engineers.

Wear Control Handbook. M. B. Peterson. American Society of Mechanical Engineers, 345 E. 47th St., New York, New York 10017. (212) 705-7722. 1980. Mechanical wear remediation through lubrication and lubricants.

ONLINE DATA BASES

Computerized Engineering Index–COMPENDEX. Engineering Information Inc., 345 E. 47th St., New York, New York 10017. (212) 705-7600.

Enviro/Energyline Abstracts Plus. R. R. Bowker Co., 121 Chanlon Rd., New Providence, New Jersey 07974. (908) 464-6800.

Environmental Periodicals Bibliography. National Information Services Corp., Ste. 6, Wyman Towers, 3100 St. Paul St., Baltimore, Maryland 21218. (410)243-0797. Online version of abstract of same name.

PERIODICALS AND NEWSLETTERS

Journal of Tribology. American Society of Mechanical Engineers, 345 E. 47th St., New York, New York 10017. (212) 705-7722. Quarterly. Topics in lubrication and lubricants.

STATISTICS SOURCES

Automotive & Industrial Lubricants. FIND/SVP, 625 Avenue of the Americas, New York, New York 10011. (212) 645-4500. 1990.

TRADE ASSOCIATIONS AND PROFESSIONAL SOCIETIES

National Lubricating Grease Institute. 4635 Wyandotte St., Kansas City, Missouri 64112. (816) 931-9480.

M

MAGNESIUM

ABSTRACTING AND INDEXING SERVICES

ASFA Aquaculture Abstracts. Cambridge Scientific Abstracts, Inc., 5161 River Rd., Bethesda, Maryland 20816. (301) 961-6750. 1984.

Environment Abstracts. Bowker A & I Publishing, 121 Chanlon Rd., New Providence, New Jersey 07974. (908) 464-6800. 1974-.

Environment Index. Environment Information Center, Index Research Department, 124 E. 39th St., New York, New York 10016. 1971-. Annual.

Environmental Information Connection–EIC. Planning Information Program, Dept. of Urban and Regional Planning, University of Illinois, 1003 West Nevada, Urbana, Illinois 61801. (217) 333-1369. Also available online.

Environmental Periodicals Bibliography. Environmental Studies Institute, International Academy at Santa Barbara, 800 Garden St., Suite D, Santa Barbara, California 93101. (805) 965-5010. Also available online.

General Science Index. H. W. Wilson Co., 950 University Ave., Bronx, New York 10452. 1978-. Monthly, also issued in annual cumulation. Cumulative subject index to English language periodicals in the subject fields of astronomy, botany, chemistry, earth science, environment and conservation, food and nutrition, genetics, mathematics, medicine and health, microbiology, oceanography, physics, physiology and zoology.

Physics Briefs. Physikalische Berichte. Physik Verlag, Pappapelallee 3, Postfach 101161, Weinheim, Germany D-6940. 1979-. Semimonthly. In English. Volumes for 1979- issued by the Deutsche Physikalische Gesellschaft and the Fachinformationszentrum Energie Physik, Mathematik in cooperation with the American Institute of Physics.

Pollution Abstracts. Cambridge Scientific Abstracts, 5161 River Rd., Bethesda, Maryland 20816. (301) 961-6750. Six/year. Indexes worldwide technical literature on environmental pollution. Covers air pollution, marine and freshwater pollution, sewage and wastewater treatment, waste management, toxicology and health, noise pollution, radiation, land pollution, and environmental policies, programs, legislation, and education. Also available online.

Science Citation Index. Institute for Scientific Information, 3501 Market St., Philadelphia, Pennsylvania 19104. 1961-.

BIBLIOGRAPHIES

Bibliography and Index of Geology. American Geological Institute, 4220 King St., Alexandria, Virginia 22302. Monthly. Includes environmental geology and hydrogeology.

EPA Publications Bibliography. U.S. Environmental Protection Agency, Library Systems Branch, 401 M St., SW, Washington, District of Columbia 20460. (202) 260-2090. Quarterly.

ENCYCLOPEDIAS AND DICTIONARIES

Encyclopedia of Chemical Processing and Design. John J. Mcketta and W. A. Cunningham. Marcel Dekker, Inc., 270 Madison Ave., New York, New York 10016. (212) 696-9000; (800) 228-1160. 1992. Thirty-eight volumes.

Encyclopedia of Human Biology. Renato Dulbecco, ed. Academic Press, c/o Harcourt Brace Jovanovich Inc., 6277 Sea Harbor Dr., Orlando, Florida 32887. (800) 346-8648. 1991. Eight volumes.

Encyclopedia of Physical Science and Technology. Robert A. Meyers, ed. Academic Press, c/o Harcourt Brace Jovanovich Inc., 6277 Sea Harbor Dr., Orlando, Florida 32887. (800) 346-8648. Dictionary of engineering, technology and physical sciences.

Encyclopedia of Physics. Rita G. Lerner and George L. Trigg. VCH Publishers, 303 NW 12th Ave., Deerfield Beach, Florida 33442-1788. (305) 428-5566. 1991. Second edition.

Kirk-Othmer Encyclopedia of Chemical Technology. J. I. Kroschwitz, ed. John Wiley & Sons, Inc., 605 3rd Ave., New York, New York 10158-0012. (212) 850-6000. 1992-. All articles in the new edition have been rewritten and updated adding new subjects such as biotechnology, computer topics, analytical techniques and instrumentation, environmental concerns, fuels and energy, inorganic and solid state chemistry; composite materials and material science in general, and pharmaceuticals. Also available online.

Ullmanns Encyclopedia of Industrial Chemistry. Hans Jurgen Arpe and Wolfgang Gerhartz, eds. VCH Publishers, 303 NW 12th Ave., Deerfield Beach, Florida 33442-1788. (305) 428-5566. 1990. Designed to keep up with the broad spectrum of chemical technology. Thirty-six volumes of the encyclopedia have been divided into two sets: the 28 A volumes contain alphabetically arranged articles on chemicals, product groups, processes and technological concepts; and the 8 B volumes are compendia of basic knowledge in industrial chemistry.

Van Nostrand's Scientific Encyclopedia. Glenn D. Considine, ed. Van Nostrand Reinhold, 115 5th Ave., New York, New York 10003. (212) 254-3232. 1983. Sixth edition. Includes all broad subject areas in science.

GENERAL WORKS

Calcium Magnesium Acetate: An Emerging Bulk Chemical for Environmental Applications. D.L. Wise. Elsevier Science Publishing Co., 655 Avenue of the Americas, New York, New York 10010. (212) 989-5800. 1991.

Effects of Environment on Microhardness of Magnesium Oxide. Hiroyuki Ishigaki. National Technical Information Service, 5285 Port Royal Rd., Springfield, Virginia 22161. (703) 487-4650. 1982. Testing of magnesia.

Environmental Monitoring and Evaluation of Calcium Magnesium Acetate. Richard Ray Horner. Transportation Research Board, National Research Council, 2101 Constitution Ave. NW, Washington, District of Columbia 20418. 1988. Deicing chemicals and snow and ice control of roads.

Magill's Survey of Science. Earth Science Series. Frank N. Magill. Salem Press, PO Box 50062, Pasadena, California 91105. 1990-. Five volumes. Includes information on earth's crust, hot spots and volcanic island chains, physical properties of minerals, rock magnetism, physical properties of rocks, and index.

HANDBOOKS AND MANUALS

Complete Guide to Vitamins, Minerals and Supplements. H. Winter Griffith. Fisher Books, 3499 N. Campbell Ave., Suite 909, Tucson, Arizona 85712. (602) 325-5263. 1988. Includes name, brand name, reasons to use, who should use, recommended daily allowance, and other related data in the form of a chart.

Tables of Physical and Chemical Constants and Some Mathematical Functions. G. W. C. Kaye, et al. Longman Group Ltd., Longman House, Burnt Mill, Harlow, England CM20 2J6. 0279 426721. 1988. Fifteenth edition. Includes tables on mechanical properties, density, elasticity, viscosity, surface tension, temperature and heat. Also covers radiation, optics, chemistry, electrochemistry, astrophysics, and chemical thermodynamics.

ONLINE DATA BASES

CAS Source Index–CASSI. Chemical Abstracts Service, 2540 Olentangy River Rd., P.O. Box 3012, Columbus, Ohio 43210. (800) 848-6533 or (614) 421-3600. A listing of bibliographic and library holdings information for scientific and technical primary literature relevant to the chemical sciences.

Enviro/Energyline Abstracts Plus. R. R. Bowker Co., 121 Chanlon Rd., New Providence, New Jersey 07974. (908) 464-6800.

Environmental Periodicals Bibliography. National Information Services Corp., Ste. 6, Wyman Towers, 3100 St. Paul St., Baltimore, Maryland 21218. (410)243-0797. Online version of abstract of same name.

Kirk-Othmer Encyclopedia of Chemical Technology. John Wiley & Sons, Inc., 605 3rd Ave., 5th Floor, New York, New York 10158. (212) 850-6000. Online version of the publication of the same name.

MAGNESIUM PEROXIDES
See: MAGNESIUM

MAGNETOHYDRODYNAMICS
See: ENERGY RESOURCES

MAINE ENVIRONMENTAL AGENCIES

GOVERNMENTAL ORGANIZATIONS

Department of Agriculture: Pesticide Registration. Director, Board of Pesticide Control, State House Station #28, Augusta, Maine 04333. (207) 289-2731.

Department of Environmental Protection: Environmental Protection. Commissioner, State House Station #17, Augusta, Maine 04333. (207) 289-2812.

Department of Environmental Protection: Groundwater Management. Commissioner, State House Station #17, Augusta, Maine 04333. (207) 289-2811.

Department of Environmental Protection: Natural Resources. Commissioner, State House Station #17, Augusta, Maine 04333. (207) 289-2811.

Department of Environmental Protection: Solid Waste Management. Commissioner, State House Station #17, Augusta, Maine 04333. (207) 289-2811.

Department of Environmental Protection: Underground Storage Tanks. Commissioner, State House Station #17, Augusta, Maine 04333. (207) 289-2811.

Department of Environmental Protection: Water Quality Control Bureau. Commissioner, State House Station #17, Augusta, Maine 04333. (207) 289-3901.

Department of Inland Fisheries and Wildlife: Fish and Wildlife. Commissioner, State House Station #41, Augusta, Maine 04333. (207) 289-4471.

Department of Labor: Occupational Safety. Director, Bureau of Labor Statistics, State House Station #45, Augusta, Maine 04333. (207) 289-2015.

Emergency Response Commission: Emergency Preparedness and Community Right-to-Know. Chairman, Statehouse Station #11, 157 Capitol Street, Augusta, Maine 04333. (207) 289-4080.

Environmental Protection Division: Air Quality. Bureau of Air Quality Control, State House Station #17, Augusta, Maine 04333. (207) 289-2437.

State Planning Office: Coastal Zone Management. Director, State House Station #38, Augusta, Maine 04333. (207) 289-3261.

U.S. EPA Region 1: Pollution Prevention. Program Manager, JFK Federal Building, Boston, Massachusetts 02203. (617) 565-3715.

MAINE ENVIRONMENTAL LEGISLATION

GENERAL WORKS

Maine Environmental Law Handbook. Government Institutes, Inc., 4 Research Pl., Ste. 200, Rockville, Maryland 20850. (301) 921-2300. 1990.

MALATHION

ABSTRACTING AND INDEXING SERVICES

Applied Ecology Abstracts Studies in Renewable Natural Resources. Information Retrieval Ltd., 1911 Jefferson Davis Highway, Arlington, Virginia 22202. 1975-. Monthly.

Biological Abstracts. BIOSIS, 2100 Arch St., Philadelphia, Pennsylvania 19103-1399. (215) 587-4800. 1927-.

Chemical Abstracts. Chemical Abstracts Service, 2540 Olentangy River Rd., PO Box 3012, Columbus, Ohio 43210. (800) 848-6533. 1907-.

Multimedia Index to Ecology. National Information Center for Educational Media, University of Southern California, Los Angeles, California 90007.

Pollution Abstracts. Cambridge Scientific Abstracts, 5161 River Rd., Bethesda, Maryland 20816. (301) 961-6750. Six/year. Indexes worldwide technical literature on environmental pollution. Covers air pollution, marine and freshwater pollution, sewage and wastewater treatment, waste management, toxicology and health, noise pollution, radiation, land pollution, and environmental policies, programs, legislation, and education. Also available online.

Science Citation Index. Institute for Scientific Information, 3501 Market St., Philadelphia, Pennsylvania 19104. 1961-.

ENCYCLOPEDIAS AND DICTIONARIES

Encyclopedia of Human Biology. Renato Dulbecco, ed. Academic Press, c/o Harcourt Brace Jovanovich Inc., 6277 Sea Harbor Dr., Orlando, Florida 32887. (800) 346-8648. 1991. Eight volumes.

Encyclopedia of Trademarks and Synonyms. H. Bennett, ed. Chemical Publishing Co., 80 Eighth Ave., New York, New York 10011. (212) 255-1950. 1981. Three volumes. Includes chemical compounds, compositions consisting of one or more chemicals and other products. Also included are abbreviated names and WHO free names.

Macmillan Dictionary of Toxicology. Ernest Hodgson, et al. Van Nostrand Reinhold, 115 5th Ave., New York, New York 10003. (212) 254-3232. 1988. Intended as a "starting point" to the literature of toxicology. American spelling is used with cross references to British version of words. Contains a list of references. Signed entries give explanatory definitions and cross references.

GENERAL WORKS

Bioassay of Malathion for Possible Carcinogenicity. National Cancer Institute, Division of Cancer Cause and Prevention, 9030 Old Georgetown Rd., Bethesda, Maryland 20892. (301) 496-7403. 1979. Adverse effects of malathion and carcinogens.

Criteria for a Recommended Standard, Occupational Exposure to Malathion. U.S. Department of Health and Human Services, Public Health Service, National Institute for Occupational Safety and Health, Robert A. Taft Lab, 4676 Columbia Pkwy., Cincinnati, Ohio 45226. (513) 684-8465. 1976.

Distribution, Transport, and Fate of the Insecticides Malathion and Parathion in the Environment. Mir S. Mulla. Springer-Verlag, 175 5th Ave., New York, New York 10010. (212) 460-1500. 1981. Environmental health problems caused by insecticides.

Occupational Exposure to Malathion. National Institute for Occupational Safety and Health, 1600 Clifton Rd. NE, Atlanta, Georgia 30333. (404) 639-3286. 1976. Occupational diseases and environmental exposure to malathion.

ONLINE DATA BASES

BIOSIS Previews. BIOSIS, 2100 Arch St., Philadelphia, Pennsylvania 19103-1399. (215) 587-4800. Largest and most comprehensive database of research in the life sciences. Contains citations for nearly 9000 primary research journals, monographs, reviews, symposia, preliminary reports, semi-popular journals, selected institutional reports, government reports and research communications.

CERCLIS. Chemical Information Systems, Inc., 7215 York Rd., Baltimore, Maryland 21212. (301) 321-8440. Information on hazardous waste disposal sites that have either been listed by the EPA on the National Priority List (NPL) or nominated for consideration for the NPL.

Chemical Abstracts-CA. Chemical Abstracts Service, 2540 Olentangy River Rd., P.O. Box 3012, Columbus, Ohio 43210. (800) 848-6533 or (614) 421-3600. Information sources include 9000 journals, patents from 27 countries, two industrial property organizations, new books, conference proceedings, and government research reports.

Chemical Abstracts Chemical Name Directory-CHEM-NAME. Chemical Abstracts Service, 2540 Olentangy River Rd., P.O. Box 3012, Columbus, Ohio 43210. (800) 848-6533 or (614) 421-3600. Listing of chemical substances in a dictionary type file. The Chemical Abstracts (CAS) Registry Number, molecular formula, Chemical Abstracts (CA) Substance Index Name, available synonyms, ring data and other chemical substance information is given for each entry.

Chemical Carcinogenesis Research Information System–CCRIS. National Library of Medicine, 8600 Rockville Pike, Bethesda, Maryland 20894. (800) 638-8480. Individual assay results and test conditions for 1,451 chemicals in the areas of carcinogenicity, mutagenicity, tumor promotion, and cocarcinogenicity.

Chemical Collection System/Request Tracking–CCS/RTS. U.S. Environmental Protection Agency, Office of Pesticides and Toxic Substances, 401 M St., SW, Washington, District of Columbia 20460. (202) 260-2090. Contains information on various properties of a number of chemicals including environmental effects, test and analysis methods, and health effects. Available from EPA.

Chemical Dictionary Online–CHEMLINE. Chemical Abstracts Service, 2540 Olentangy River Rd., Columbus, Ohio 43210. (614) 421-3600 or (800) 848-6533. Part of MEDLINE of the National Library of Medicine (NLM). File of 900,000 names for chemical substances, representing 450,000 unique compounds. It contains such information as Chemical Abstracts (CA) Service Registry Numbers, molecular formulas, preferred chemical nomenclature, and generic and ring structure information. Available on NLM's ELHILL system.

Chemical Exposure. Science Applications International Corp., Health & Environmental Information, P.O. Box 2501, Oak Ridge, Tennessee 37831. (615) 482-9031. Database of chemicals that have been identified in both human tissues and body fluids and in feral and food animals. Contains reference to journal articles, conferences, and reports. Covers the whole fields of information related to human and animal exposure to food, air, and water contaminants and pharmaceuticals. Its records include information on chemical properties, formulas, tissues measured, analytical method used, demographics and more. Available on DIALOG.

TRADE ASSOCIATIONS AND PROFESSIONAL SOCIETIES

American Chemical Society. 1155 16th St., N.W., Washington, District of Columbia 20036. (202) 872-4600.

MALNUTRITION

See: NUTRITION

MALTHUSIANISM

See: POPULATION

MANGANESE

ABSTRACTING AND INDEXING SERVICES

Applied Science and Technology Index. H.W. Wilson Co., 950 University Ave., Bronx, New York 10452. (800) 367-6770. Formerly Industrial Arts Index.

Chemical Abstracts. Chemical Abstracts Service, 2540 Olentangy River Rd., PO Box 3012, Columbus, Ohio 43210. (800) 848-6533. 1907-.

General Science Index. H. W. Wilson Co., 950 University Ave., Bronx, New York 10452. 1978-. Monthly, also issued in annual cumulation. Cumulative subject index to English language periodicals in the subject fields of astronomy, botany, chemistry, earth science, environment and conservation, food and nutrition, genetics, mathematics, medicine and health, microbiology, oceanography, physics, physiology and zoology.

Physics Briefs. Physikalische Berichte. Physik Verlag, Pappapelallee 3, Postfach 101161, Weinheim, Germany D-6940. 1979-. Semimonthly. In English. Volumes for 1979- issued by the Deutsche Physikalische Gesellschaft and the Fachinformationszentrum Energie Physik, Mathematik in cooperation with the American Institute of Physics.

Pollution Abstracts. Cambridge Scientific Abstracts, 5161 River Rd., Bethesda, Maryland 20816. (301) 961-6750. Six/year. Indexes worldwide technical literature on environmental pollution. Covers air pollution, marine and freshwater pollution, sewage and wastewater treatment, waste management, toxicology and health, noise pollution, radiation, land pollution, and environmental policies, programs, legislation, and education. Also available online.

Science Citation Index. Institute for Scientific Information, 3501 Market St., Philadelphia, Pennsylvania 19104. 1961-.

BIBLIOGRAPHIES

Bibliography and Index of Geology. American Geological Institute, 4220 King St., Alexandria, Virginia 22302. Monthly. Includes environmental geology and hydrogeology.

ENCYCLOPEDIAS AND DICTIONARIES

Encyclopedia of Chemical Processing and Design. John J. Mcketta and W. A. Cunningham. Marcel Dekker, Inc., 270 Madison Ave., New York, New York 10016. (212) 696-9000; (800) 228-1160. 1992. Thirty-eight volumes.

Encyclopedia of Electrochemistry of Elements. A. J. Bard. Marcel Dekker, Inc., 270 Madison Ave., New York, New York 10016. (212) 696-9000 or (800) 228-1160. Encyclopedic treatment of the subject area of electrochemistry and related subjects.

Encyclopedia of Human Biology. Renato Dulbecco, ed. Academic Press, c/o Harcourt Brace Jovanovich Inc., 6277 Sea Harbor Dr., Orlando, Florida 32887. (800) 346-8648. 1991. Eight volumes.

Encyclopedia of Physics. Rita G. Lerner and George L. Trigg. VCH Publishers, 303 NW 12th Ave., Deerfield Beach, Florida 33442-1788. (305) 428-5566. 1991. Second edition.

Kirk-Othmer Encyclopedia of Chemical Technology. J. I. Kroschwitz, ed. John Wiley & Sons, Inc., 605 3rd Ave., New York, New York 10158-0012. (212) 850-6000. 1992-. All articles in the new edition have been rewritten and updated adding new subjects such as biotechnology, computer topics, analytical techniques and instrumentation, environmental concerns, fuels and energy, inorganic and solid state chemistry; composite materials and material science in general, and pharmaceuticals. Also available online.

Macmillan Dictionary of Toxicology. Ernest Hodgson, et al. Van Nostrand Reinhold, 115 5th Ave., New York, New York 10003. (212) 254-3232. 1988. Intended as a "starting point" to the literature of toxicology. American spelling is used with cross references to British version of words. Contains a list of references. Signed entries give explanatory definitions and cross references.

Ullmanns Encyclopedia of Industrial Chemistry. Hans Jurgen Arpe and Wolfgang Gerhartz, eds. VCH Publishers, 303 NW 12th Ave., Deerfield Beach, Florida 33442-1788. (305) 428-5566. 1990. Designed to keep up with the broad spectrum of chemical technology. Thirty-six volumes of the encyclopedia have been divided into two sets: the 28 A volumes contain alphabetically arranged articles on chemicals, product groups, processes and technological concepts; and the 8 B volumes are compendia of basic knowledge in industrial chemistry.

Van Nostrand's Scientific Encyclopedia. Glenn D. Considine, ed. Van Nostrand Reinhold, 115 5th Ave., New York, New York 10003. (212) 254-3232. 1983. Sixth edition. Includes all broad subject areas in science.

GENERAL WORKS

Description of Manganese Nodule Processing Activities for Environmental Studies. Dames & Moore. National Technical Information Service, 5285 Port Royal Rd., Springfield, Virginia 22161. (703) 487-4650. 1977. Technical analysis of transportation and waste disposal.

Environmental Investigations During Manganese Nodule Mining Tests in the North Equatorial Pacific. E. Ozturgut. Environmental Research Laboratories, Marine Ecosystems Analysis Program, 325 Broadway, Boulder, Colorado 80303. 1980. Environmental aspects of submarine manganese mines and mining.

Magill's Survey of Science. Earth Science Series. Frank N. Magill. Salem Press, PO Box 50062, Pasadena, California 91105. 1990-. Five volumes. Includes information on earth's crust, hot spots and volcanic island chains, physical properties of minerals, rock magnetism, physical properties of rocks, and index.

HANDBOOKS AND MANUALS

Tables of Physical and Chemical Constants and Some Mathematical Functions. G. W. C. Kaye, et al. Longman Group Ltd., Longman House, Burnt Mill, Harlow, England CM20 2J6. 0279 426721. 1988. Fifteenth edition. Includes tables on mechanical properties, density, elasticity, viscosity, surface tension, temperature and heat. Also covers radiation, optics, chemistry, electrochemistry, astrophysics, and chemical thermodynamics.

ONLINE DATA BASES

CAS Source Index–CASSI. Chemical Abstracts Service, 2540 Olentangy River Rd., P.O. Box 3012, Columbus, Ohio 43210. (800) 848-6533 or (614) 421-3600. A listing of bibliographic and library holdings information for scientific and technical primary literature relevant to the chemical sciences.

Chemical Abstracts-CA. Chemical Abstracts Service, 2540 Olentangy River Rd., P.O. Box 3012, Columbus, Ohio 43210. (800) 848-6533 or (614) 421-3600. Information sources include 9000 journals, patents from 27 countries, two industrial property organizations, new books, conference proceedings, and government research reports.

Kirk-Othmer Encyclopedia of Chemical Technology. John Wiley & Sons, Inc., 605 3rd Ave., 5th Floor, New York, New York 10158. (212) 850-6000. Online version of the publication of the same name.

MANURE

See: FERTILIZERS

MARICULTURE

ABSTRACTING AND INDEXING SERVICES

Applied Ecology Abstracts Studies in Renewable Natural Resources. Information Retrieval Ltd., 1911 Jefferson Davis Highway, Arlington, Virginia 22202. 1975-. Monthly.

ASFA Aquaculture Abstracts. Cambridge Scientific Abstracts, Inc., 5161 River Rd., Bethesda, Maryland 20816. (301) 961-6750. 1984.

Biological Abstracts. BIOSIS, 2100 Arch St., Philadelphia, Pennsylvania 19103-1399. (215) 587-4800. 1927-.

Biological and Agricultural Index. H.W. Wilson Co., 950 University Ave., Bronx, New York 10452. (800) 367-6770. 1916-. Monthly.

Civil Engineering Hydraulic Abstracts. BHRA Fluid Engineering, Air Science Co., PO Box 143, Corning, New York 14830. (607) 962-5591. Monthly. Abstracts of periodicals that publish in the areas of hydraulic engineering and other related topics.

General Science Index. H. W. Wilson Co., 950 University Ave., Bronx, New York 10452. 1978-. Monthly, also issued in annual cumulation. Cumulative subject index to English language periodicals in the subject fields of astronomy, botany, chemistry, earth science, environment and conservation, food and nutrition, genetics, mathematics, medicine and health, microbiology, oceanography, physics, physiology and zoology.

Geographical Abstracts. London School of Economics, Dept. of Geography, Regency House, 34 Duke St., London, England 1966-. Continued by Geo Abstracts issued in 6 parts: Pt. A. Landforms and the quaternary; Pt. B. Biogeography and Climatology; Pt. C. Economic geography; Pt. D. Social geography and cartography; Pt. E. Sedimentology; Pt. F. Regional and community planning.

Index to Scientific Book Contents. Institute for Scientific Information, 3501 Market St., Philadelphia, Pennsylvania 19104. (800) 523-1857. 1985-. Annual. Gives contents of science books published.

Multimedia Index to Ecology. National Information Center for Educational Media, University of Southern California, Los Angeles, California 90007.

Science Citation Index. Institute for Scientific Information, 3501 Market St., Philadelphia, Pennsylvania 19104. 1961-.

BIBLIOGRAPHIES

Shrimp Mariculture: January 1979 - January 1990. Eileen McVey. National Agricultural Library, 10301 Baltimore Blvd., Beltsville, Maryland 20705-2351. (301) 504-5755. 1990.

ENCYCLOPEDIAS AND DICTIONARIES

McGraw-Hill Encyclopedia of Environmental Science. Sybil P. Parker. McGraw-Hill Science & Engineering Books, 11 W. 19th St., New York, New York 10011. (212) 337-6010. 1980. Covers ecology, man's influence on nature, and environmental protection.

Van Nostrand's Scientific Encyclopedia. Glenn D. Considine, ed. Van Nostrand Reinhold, 115 5th Ave., New York, New York 10003. (212) 254-3232. 1983. Sixth edition. Includes all broad subject areas in science.

GENERAL WORKS

Clam Mariculture in North America. J. J. Manzi. Elsevier Science Publishing Co., 655 Avenue of the Americas, New York, New York 10010. (212) 984-5800. 1989.

Optoelectronics for Environmental Science. S. Martellucci and A. N. Chester, eds. Plenum Press, 233 Spring St., New York, New York 10013-1578. (212) 620-8000; (800) 221-9369. 1991. Contribution of lasers and the optical sciences to specific problems, in situ measurements, atmospheric ozone, lidar detection, wind velocity, oceanographic measurements, heavy metal detection, toxic metals, and trace analysis. Proceedings of the 14th course of the International School of Quantum Electronics on Optoelectronics for Environmental Sciences, held September 3-12, 1989, in Erice, Italy.

HANDBOOKS AND MANUALS

CRC Handbook of Mariculture. CRC Press, 2000 Corporate Blvd. N.W., Boca Raton, Florida 33431. (800) 272-7737. 1993. Covers crustacean aquaculture.

ONLINE DATA BASES

BIOSIS Previews. BIOSIS, 2100 Arch St., Philadelphia, Pennsylvania 19103-1399. (215) 587-4800. Largest and most comprehensive database of research in the life sciences. Contains citations for nearly 9000 primary research journals, monographs, reviews, symposia, preliminary reports, semi-popular journals, selected institutional reports, government reports and research communications.

Cambridge Scientific Abstracts Life Science–CSAL. Cambridge Scientific Abstracts, 5161 River Rd., Bethesda, Maryland 20816. (301) 961-6750. Provides access to the following abstracting services: "Life Sciences Collection," "Aquatic Sciences and Fisheries Abstracts," "Oceanic Abstracts," and "Pollution Abstracts."

SCISEARCH. Institute for Scientific Information, University City Science Center, 3501 Market St., Philadelphia, Pennsylvania 19104. (215) 386-0100.

PERIODICALS AND NEWSLETTERS

Journal of the World Mariculture Society. Louisiana State University, Division of Continuing Education, Baton Rouge, Louisiana Quarterly.

RESEARCH CENTERS AND INSTITUTES

Lewes Marine Studies Complex. University of Delaware, Lewes, Delaware 19958. (302) 645-4212.

MARINAS

See also: BEACHES; COASTS

ABSTRACTING AND INDEXING SERVICES

Applied Ecology Abstracts Studies in Renewable Natural Resources. Information Retrieval Ltd., 1911 Jefferson Davis Highway, Arlington, Virginia 22202. 1975-. Monthly.

Biological and Agricultural Index. H.W. Wilson Co., 950 University Ave., Bronx, New York 10452. (800) 367-6770. 1916-. Monthly.

Civil Engineering Hydraulic Abstracts. BHRA Fluid Engineering, Air Science Co., PO Box 143, Corning, New York 14830. (607) 962-5591. Monthly. Abstracts of periodicals that publish in the areas of hydraulic engineering and other related topics.

Current Advances in Ecological and Environmental Science. Pergamon Microforms International, Inc., Fairview Park, Elmsford, New York 10523. (914) 592-7720. 1989-. Monthly. Current literature searching service includingjournals, reports, abstracts, etc. This service is available online as part of the CABS database on the hosts BRS and ORBIT search service.

Environment Abstracts. Bowker A & I Publishing, 121 Chanlon Rd., New Providence, New Jersey 07974. (908) 464-6800. 1974-.

Environment Index. Environment Information Center, Index Research Department, 124 E. 39th St., New York, New York 10016. 1971-. Annual.

Environmental Information Connection–EIC. Planning Information Program, Dept. of Urban and Regional Planning, University of Illinois, 1003 West Nevada, Urbana, Illinois 61801. (217) 333-1369. Also available online.

Environmental Periodicals Bibliography. Environmental Studies Institute, International Academy at Santa Barbara, 800 Garden St., Suite D, Santa Barbara, California 93101. (805) 965-5010. Also available online.

General Science Index. H. W. Wilson Co., 950 University Ave., Bronx, New York 10452. 1978-. Monthly, also issued in annual cumulation. Cumulative subject index to English language periodicals in the subject fields of astronomy, botany, chemistry, earth science, environment and conservation, food and nutrition, genetics, mathematics, medicine and health, microbiology, oceanography, physics, physiology and zoology.

Geographical Abstracts. London School of Economics, Dept. of Geography, Regency House, 34 Duke St., London, England 1966-. Continued by Geo Abstracts issued in 6 parts: Pt. A. Landforms and the quaternary; Pt. B. Biogeography and Climatology; Pt. C. Economic geography; Pt. D. Social geography and cartography; Pt. E. Sedimentology; Pt. F. Regional and community planning.

Index to Scientific Book Contents. Institute for Scientific Information, 3501 Market St., Philadelphia, Pennsylvania 19104. (800) 523-1857. 1985-. Annual. Gives contents of science books published.

Multimedia Index to Ecology. National Information Center for Educational Media, University of Southern California, Los Angeles, California 90007.

Oceanic Abstracts. UMI Data Courier, 620 S. 3rd St., Louisville, Kentucky 40202. (800) 626-2823. Formerly: Oceanic Index and Oceanic Citation Journal.

BIBLIOGRAPHIES

Architecture of Docks, Harbor Buildings, Harbors and Marinas: A Bibliography. Coppa & Avery Consultants. Vance Bibliographies, PO Box 229, 112 N. Charter St., Monticello, Illinois 61856. (217) 762-3831. 1984.

Bibliography and Index of Geology. American Geological Institute, 4220 King St., Alexandria, Virginia 22302. Monthly. Includes environmental geology and hydrogeology.

EPA Publications Bibliography. U.S. Environmental Protection Agency, Library Systems Branch, 401 M St., SW, Washington, District of Columbia 20460. (202) 260-2090. Quarterly.

New Publications of the Geological Survey. U.S. Department of the Interior, Geological Survey, 119 National Center, Reston, Virginia 22092. (703) 648-4460. 1984-. Monthly. Bibliography of geological publications and related government documents published by the Geological Survey.

ENCYCLOPEDIAS AND DICTIONARIES

Cambridge Encyclopedia of Life Sciences. A. E. Friday and David S. Ingram. Cambridge University Press, 40 W 20th St., New York, New York 10011. (212) 924-3900 or (800) 227-0247. 1985. Includes all topics under biology and ecology.

The Encyclopedia of Beaches and Coastal Environments. Maurice L. Schwartz. Hutchinson Ross Pub. Co., Stroudsburg, Pennsylvania 1982.

McGraw-Hill Encyclopedia of Environmental Science. Sybil P. Parker. McGraw-Hill Science & Engineering Books, 11 W. 19th St., New York, New York 10011. (212) 337-6010. 1980. Covers ecology, man's influence on nature, and environmental protection.

The Times Atlas and Encyclopedia of the Sea. A.D. Couper. Harper & Row, 10 E. 53rd St., New York, New York 10022. (212) 207-7000; (800) 242-7737. 1990.

Van Nostrand's Scientific Encyclopedia. Glenn D. Considine, ed. Van Nostrand Reinhold, 115 5th Ave., New York, New York 10003. (212) 254-3232. 1983. Sixth edition. Includes all broad subject areas in science.

GENERAL WORKS

Developing with Recreational Amenities: Golf, Tennis, Skiing, Marinas. Patrick L. Phillips. Urban Land Institute, 625 Indiana Ave., N.W., Washington, District of Columbia 20004. (202) 624-7000. 1986. Recreation areas, resorts, retirement communities, condominiums, and vacation homes.

The Environmental Impacts of Marinas and Their Boats. Gail L. Chmura. Marine Advisory Service, University of Rhode Island, Narragansett, Rhode Island 02882. 1978. Environmental aspects of marinas, boats, and boating.

Magill's Survey of Science. Earth Science Series. Frank N. Magill. Salem Press, PO Box 50062, Pasadena, California 91105. 1990-. Five volumes. Includes information on earth's crust, hot spots and volcanic island chains, physical properties of minerals, rock magnetism, physical properties of rocks, and index.

Marinas: A Working Guide to Their Development and Design. Donald W. Adie. Nichols Publishing Co., PO Box 96, New York, New York 10024. 1984.

Marine Biology. Matthew Lerman. Benjamin/Cummings Publishing Co., 390 Bridge Pkwy., Redwood City, California 94065. (415) 594-4400. 1986. Environment, diversity and ecology.

HANDBOOKS AND MANUALS

CRC Handbook of Marine Science. F. G. Walton Smith. CRC Press, 2000 Corporate Blvd. N.W., Boca Raton, Florida 33431. (800) 272-7737. 1976. Topics in oceanography and ocean engineering.

ONLINE DATA BASES

Enviro/Energyline Abstracts Plus. R. R. Bowker Co., 121 Chanlon Rd., New Providence, New Jersey 07974. (908) 464-6800.

Environmental Periodicals Bibliography. National Information Services Corp., Ste. 6, Wyman Towers, 3100 St. Paul St., Baltimore, Maryland 21218. (410)243-0797. Online version of abstract of same name.

Monthly Catalog of United States Government Publications. U.S. G.P.O., Supt. of Docs., PO Box 371954, Pittsburgh, Pennsylvania 15250-7954. (202) 512-0000.

National Technical Information Service. U.S. Department of Commerce, National Technical Information Service, Office of Data Base Services, 5285 Port Royal Rd., Springfield, Virginia 22161. (703) 487-4807. Bibliographic database of government sponsored research and technical reports.

Oceanic Abstracts. Cambridge Scientific Abstracts, 5161 River Rd., Bethesda, Maryland 20816. (301) 961-6750. Online access.

SCISEARCH. Institute for Scientific Information, University City Science Center, 3501 Market St., Philadelphia, Pennsylvania 19104. (215) 386-0100.

PERIODICALS AND NEWSLETTERS

Biological Oceanography. Crane, Russak & Co., 70 Madison Ave., Suite 101, New York, New York 10016. (212) 725-1999. Quarterly. Marine ecology, biology, natural products, and biochemistry.

Bulletin of Marine Science. Rosenstiel School of Marine and Atmospheric Science, 4600 Rickenbacker Causeway, Miami, Florida 33149-1098. (305) 361-4000. Bimonthly.

TRADE ASSOCIATIONS AND PROFESSIONAL SOCIETIES

American Institute of Biological Sciences. 730 11th St., N.W., Washington, District of Columbia 20001-4521. (202) 628-1500.

MARINE ALGAE AS FOOD

ABSTRACTING AND INDEXING SERVICES

Applied Ecology Abstracts Studies in Renewable Natural Resources. Information Retrieval Ltd., 1911 Jefferson

Davis Highway, Arlington, Virginia 22202. 1975-. Monthly.

Biological and Agricultural Index. H.W. Wilson Co., 950 University Ave., Bronx, New York 10452. (800) 367-6770. 1916-. Monthly.

Current Advances in Ecological and Environmental Science. Pergamon Microforms International, Inc., Fairview Park, Elmsford, New York 10523. (914) 592-7720. 1989-. Monthly. Current literature searching service including journals, reports, abstracts, etc. This service is available online as part of the CABS database on the hosts BRS and ORBIT search service.

Ecological Abstracts. Geo Abstracts Ltd. Elsevier Applied Science, Crown House, Linton Rd., Barking, England IG 11 8JU. 1974-. Derived from over 600 leading ecological and environmental journals, plus books, conference proceedings, reports and theses.

Ecology Abstracts. Cambridge Scientific Abstracts, 5161 River Rd., Bethesda, Maryland 20816. (301) 961-6750. Monthly.

Environment Abstracts. Bowker A & I Publishing, 121 Chanlon Rd., New Providence, New Jersey 07974. (908) 464-6800. 1974-.

Environment Index. Environment Information Center, Index Research Department, 124 E. 39th St., New York, New York 10016. 1971-. Annual.

Environmental Information Connection–EIC. Planning Information Program, Dept. of Urban and Regional Planning, University of Illinois, 1003 West Nevada, Urbana, Illinois 61801. (217) 333-1369. Also available online.

Environmental Periodicals Bibliography. Environmental Studies Institute, International Academy at Santa Barbara, 800 Garden St., Suite D, Santa Barbara, California 93101. (805) 965-5010. Also available online.

General Science Index. H. W. Wilson Co., 950 University Ave., Bronx, New York 10452. 1978-. Monthly, also issued in annual cumulation. Cumulative subject index to English language periodicals in the subject fields of astronomy, botany, chemistry, earth science, environment and conservation, food and nutrition, genetics, mathematics, medicine and health, microbiology, oceanography, physics, physiology and zoology.

Index to Scientific Book Contents. Institute for Scientific Information, 3501 Market St., Philadelphia, Pennsylvania 19104. (800) 523-1857. 1985-. Annual. Gives contents of science books published.

Multimedia Index to Ecology. National Information Center for Educational Media, University of Southern California, Los Angeles, California 90007.

Oceanic Abstracts. UMI Data Courier, 620 S. 3rd St., Louisville, Kentucky 40202. (800) 626-2823. Formerly: Oceanic Index and Oceanic Citation Journal.

BIBLIOGRAPHIES

EPA Publications Bibliography. U.S. Environmental Protection Agency, Library Systems Branch, 401 M St., SW, Washington, District of Columbia 20460. (202) 260-2090. Quarterly.

New Publications of the Geological Survey. U.S. Department of the Interior, Geological Survey, 119 National Center, Reston, Virginia 22092. (703) 648-4460. 1984-. Monthly. Bibliography of geological publications and related government documents published by the Geological Survey.

ENCYCLOPEDIAS AND DICTIONARIES

Cambridge Encyclopedia of Life Sciences. A. E. Friday and David S. Ingram. Cambridge University Press, 40 W 20th St., New York, New York 10011. (212) 924-3900 or (800) 227-0247. 1985. Includes all topics under biology and ecology.

The Encyclopedia of Oceanography. Rhodes Whitmore Fairbridge. Reinhold Pub. Co., 115 5th Ave., New York, New York 10003. (212) 254-3232. 1966.

McGraw-Hill Encyclopedia of Environmental Science. Sybil P. Parker. McGraw-Hill Science & Engineering Books, 11 W. 19th St., New York, New York 10011. (212) 337-6010. 1980. Covers ecology, man's influence on nature, and environmental protection.

GENERAL WORKS

Production and Utilization of Products from Commercial Seaweeds. Dennis J. McHugh. Food and Agriculture Organization of the United Nations, Via delle Terme di Caracalla, Rome, Italy 00100. 61 0181-FA01. 1987. Marine algae as feed and food.

The Seavegetable Book. Judith Cooper Madlener. Crown Publishing Group, 201 E. 50th St., New York, New York 10022. (212) 751-2600. 1977. Marine algae as food.

Vegetables from the Sea. Seibin Arasaki. Kodansha International/USA, 114 5th Ave., New York, New York 10011. (212) 727-6460. 1983.

ONLINE DATA BASES

Enviro/Energyline Abstracts Plus. R. R. Bowker Co., 121 Chanlon Rd., New Providence, New Jersey 07974. (908) 464-6800.

Environmental Periodicals Bibliography. National Information Services Corp., Ste. 6, Wyman Towers, 3100 St. Paul St., Baltimore, Maryland 21218. (410)243-0797. Online version of abstract of same name.

Oceanic Abstracts. Cambridge Scientific Abstracts, 5161 River Rd., Bethesda, Maryland 20816. (301) 961-6750. Online access.

SCISEARCH. Institute for Scientific Information, University City Science Center, 3501 Market St., Philadelphia, Pennsylvania 19104. (215) 386-0100.

MARINE BIOLOGY

See also: DREDGING; MARINE ECOLOGY; MARINE RESOURCES

ABSTRACTING AND INDEXING SERVICES

Biological and Agricultural Index. H.W. Wilson Co., 950 University Ave., Bronx, New York 10452. (800) 367-6770. 1916-. Monthly.

Current Advances in Ecological and Environmental Science. Pergamon Microforms International, Inc., Fairview Park, Elmsford, New York 10523. (914) 592-7720. 1989-. Monthly. Current literature searching service includingjournals, reports, abstracts, etc. This service is available online as part of the CABS database on the hosts BRS and ORBIT search service.

Ecology Abstracts. Cambridge Scientific Abstracts, 5161 River Rd., Bethesda, Maryland 20816. (301) 961-6750. Monthly.

General Science Index. H. W. Wilson Co., 950 University Ave., Bronx, New York 10452. 1978-. Monthly, also issued in annual cumulation. Cumulative subject index to English language periodicals in the subject fields of astronomy, botany, chemistry, earth science, environment and conservation, food and nutrition, genetics, mathematics, medicine and health, microbiology, oceanography, physics, physiology and zoology.

Index to Scientific Book Contents. Institute for Scientific Information, 3501 Market St., Philadelphia, Pennsylvania 19104. (800) 523-1857. 1985-. Annual. Gives contents of science books published.

Oceanic Abstracts. UMI Data Courier, 620 S. 3rd St., Louisville, Kentucky 40202. (800) 626-2823. Formerly: Oceanic Index and Oceanic Citation Journal.

ENCYCLOPEDIAS AND DICTIONARIES

The Encyclopedia of Oceanography. Rhodes Whitmore Fairbridge. Reinhold Pub. Co., 115 5th Ave., New York, New York 10003. (212) 254-3232. 1966.

McGraw-Hill Encyclopedia of Environmental Science. Sybil P. Parker. McGraw-Hill Science & Engineering Books, 11 W. 19th St., New York, New York 10011. (212) 337-6010. 1980. Covers ecology, man's influence on nature, and environmental protection.

ONLINE DATA BASES

Monthly Catalog of United States Government Publications. U.S. G.P.O., Supt. of Docs., PO Box 371954, Pittsburgh, Pennsylvania 15250-7954. (202) 512-0000.

National Technical Information Service. U.S. Department of Commerce, National Technical Information Service, Office of Data Base Services, 5285 Port Royal Rd., Springfield, Virginia 22161. (703) 487-4807. Bibliographic database of government sponsored research and technical reports.

Oceanic Abstracts. Cambridge Scientific Abstracts, 5161 River Rd., Bethesda, Maryland 20816. (301) 961-6750. Online access.

MARINE COMMUNITIES

See also: BENTHOS

ABSTRACTING AND INDEXING SERVICES

Abstracts of Air and Water Conservation Literature. American Petroleum Institute. Central Abstracting and Indexing Service, 275 Madison Avenue, New York, New York 10016. 1972.

Applied Ecology Abstracts Studies in Renewable Natural Resources. Information Retrieval Ltd., 1911 Jefferson Davis Highway, Arlington, Virginia 22202. 1975-. Monthly.

ASFA Aquaculture Abstracts. Cambridge Scientific Abstracts, Inc., 5161 River Rd., Bethesda, Maryland 20816. (301) 961-6750. 1984.

Biological Abstracts. BIOSIS, 2100 Arch St., Philadelphia, Pennsylvania 19103-1399. (215) 587-4800. 1927-.

Biological and Agricultural Index. H.W. Wilson Co., 950 University Ave., Bronx, New York 10452. (800) 367-6770. 1916-. Monthly.

Current Advances in Ecological and Environmental Science. Pergamon Microforms International, Inc., Fairview Park, Elmsford, New York 10523. (914) 592-7720. 1989-. Monthly. Current literature searching service includingjournals, reports, abstracts, etc. This service is available online as part of the CABS database on the hosts BRS and ORBIT search service.

Ecological Abstracts. Geo Abstracts Ltd. Elsevier Applied Science, Crown House, Linton Rd., Barking, England IG 11 8JU. 1974-. Derived from over 600 leading ecological and environmental journals, plus books, conference proceedings, reports and theses.

Ecology Abstracts. Cambridge Scientific Abstracts, 5161 River Rd., Bethesda, Maryland 20816. (301) 961-6750. Monthly.

Environment Abstracts. Bowker A & I Publishing, 121 Chanlon Rd., New Providence, New Jersey 07974. (908) 464-6800. 1974-.

Environment Index. Environment Information Center, Index Research Department, 124 E. 39th St., New York, New York 10016. 1971-. Annual.

Environmental Information Connection–EIC. Planning Information Program, Dept. of Urban and Regional Planning, University of Illinois, 1003 West Nevada, Urbana, Illinois 61801. (217) 333-1369. Also available online.

Environmental Periodicals Bibliography. Environmental Studies Institute, International Academy at Santa Barbara, 800 Garden St., Suite D, Santa Barbara, California 93101. (805) 965-5010. Also available online.

General Science Index. H. W. Wilson Co., 950 University Ave., Bronx, New York 10452. 1978-. Monthly, also issued in annual cumulation. Cumulative subject index to English language periodicals in the subject fields of astronomy, botany, chemistry, earth science, environment and conservation, food and nutrition, genetics, mathematics, medicine and health, microbiology, oceanography, physics, physiology and zoology.

Geographical Abstracts. London School of Economics, Dept. of Geography, Regency House, 34 Duke St., London, England 1966-. Continued by Geo Abstracts issued in 6 parts: Pt. A. Landforms and the quaternary; Pt. B. Biogeography and Climatology; Pt. C. Economic geography; Pt. D. Social geography and cartography; Pt. E. Sedimentology; Pt. F. Regional and community planning.

Index to Scientific Book Contents. Institute for Scientific Information, 3501 Market St., Philadelphia, Pennsylvania 19104. (800) 523-1857. 1985-. Annual. Gives contents of science books published.

Multimedia Index to Ecology. National Information Center for Educational Media, University of Southern California, Los Angeles, California 90007.

Oceanic Abstracts. UMI Data Courier, 620 S. 3rd St., Louisville, Kentucky 40202. (800) 626-2823. Formerly: Oceanic Index and Oceanic Citation Journal.

Pollution Abstracts. Cambridge Scientific Abstracts, 5161 River Rd., Bethesda, Maryland 20816. (301) 961-6750. Six/year. Indexes worldwide technical literature on environmental pollution. Covers air pollution, marine and freshwater pollution, sewage and wastewater treatment, waste management, toxicology and health, noise pollution, radiation, land pollution, and environmental policies, programs, legislation, and education. Also available online.

Science Citation Index. Institute for Scientific Information, 3501 Market St., Philadelphia, Pennsylvania 19104. 1961-.

ALMANACS AND YEARBOOKS

Ocean Yearbook. The University of Chicago Press, Journals Division, PO Box 37005, Chicago, Illinois 60637. 1978-. Annual. A comprehensive guide to current research and data on living and nonliving resources, marine science and technological environmental, and coastal management.

BIBLIOGRAPHIES

Annotated Bibliography on Hydrology and Sedimentation. Carroll E. Bradberry. U.S. G.P.O., Washington, District of Columbia 20401. (202) 512-0000. Annual.

Bibliography, Environmental Geomorphology. Susan Caris. Council of Planning Librarians, 1313 E. 60th St., Chicago, Illinois 60637-2897. (312) 942-2163. 1975.

Comprehensive Bibliography. Outer Continental Shelf Environmental Assessment Program. U.S. Department of the Interior, 1849 C St., NW, Washington, District of Columbia 20240. (202) 208-3171. 1986.

EPA Publications Bibliography. U.S. Environmental Protection Agency, Library Systems Branch, 401 M St., SW, Washington, District of Columbia 20460. (202) 260-2090. Quarterly.

New Publications of the Geological Survey. U.S. Department of the Interior, Geological Survey, 119 National Center, Reston, Virginia 22092. (703) 648-4460. 1984-. Monthly. Bibliography of geological publications and related government documents published by the Geological Survey.

ENCYCLOPEDIAS AND DICTIONARIES

Cambridge Encyclopedia of Life Sciences. A. E. Friday and David S. Ingram. Cambridge University Press, 40 W 20th St., New York, New York 10011. (212) 924-3900 or (800) 227-0247. 1985. Includes all topics under biology and ecology.

The Encyclopedia of Oceanography. Rhodes Whitmore Fairbridge. Reinhold Pub. Co., 115 5th Ave., New York, New York 10003. (212) 254-3232. 1966.

Grzimek's Encyclopedia of Ecology. Bernhard Grzimek. Van Nostrand Reinhold, 115 5th Ave., New York, New York 10003. (212) 254-3232. 1976.

McGraw-Hill Encyclopedia of Environmental Science. Sybil P. Parker. McGraw-Hill Science & Engineering Books, 11 W. 19th St., New York, New York 10011. (212) 337-6010. 1980. Covers ecology, man's influence on nature, and environmental protection.

North American Reference Encyclopedia of Ecology and Pollution. William White. North American Pub. Co., 401 N. Broad St., Philadelphia, Pennsylvania 19108. (215) 238-5300. 1972.

The Times Atlas and Encyclopedia of the Sea. A.D. Couper. Harper & Row, 10 E. 53rd St., New York, New York 10022. (212) 207-7000; (800) 242-7737. 1990.

GENERAL WORKS

The Atlantic Barrier Reef Ecosystem at Carrie Bow Cay, Belize, I: Structure and Communities. Klaus Rutzler and Ian G. MacIntyre. Smithsonian Institution Press, 470 L'Enfant Plaza, No. 7100, Washington, District of Columbia 20560. (800) 782-4612. 1982.

Food Chain Yields, Models, and Management of Large Marine Ecosystems. Kenneth Sherman, et al., eds. Westview Press, 5500 Central Ave., Boulder, Colorado 80301. (303) 444-3541. 1991. Describes marine ecology, its productive resources and its management.

Guide to Information on Research in the Marine Science and Engineering. U.S. Department of Commerce, National Oceanic and Atmospheric Administration, Office of Ocean Engineering, 6010 Executive Blvd., Rockville, Maryland 20852. (301) 443-8344. 1978.

The Living Ocean. Boyce Thorne-Miller. Island Press, 1718 Connecticut Ave. N.W., Suite 300, Washington, District of Columbia 20009. (202) 232-7933. 1991. Discusses all marine ecosystems, including coastal benthic, shore systems, estuaries, wetlands, and coral reefs, coastal pelagic, deep-sea benthic, hydrothermal vents and others.

Managing Marine Environments. Richard A. Kenchington. Taylor & Francis, 1900 Frost Rd., Ste. 101, Bristol, Pennsylvania 19007. (215) 785-5800. 1990. Contemporary issues of multiple-use planning and management of marine environments and natural resources.

GOVERNMENTAL ORGANIZATIONS

National Marine Fisheries Service. 1825 Connecticut Ave., N.W., Washington, District of Columbia 20235. (202) 673-5450.

Office of Public Affairs: National Oceanic and Atmospheric Administration. 14th and Constitution Avenues, N.W., Washington, District of Columbia 20230. (202) 377-2985.

HANDBOOKS AND MANUALS

Handbook of Coastal and Ocean Engineering. John B. Herbich. Gulf Publishing Co., Book Division, PO Box 2608, Houston, Texas 77252. (713) 529-4301. 1991. Wave phenomena in coastal structures.

Marine Environmental Engineering Handbook. Frank L. Cross. Technomic Publishing, Co., 265 Post Rd. W, PO Box 8, Saug Station, Westport, Connecticut 06880. 1974. Marine pollution abatement technology.

ONLINE DATA BASES

BIOSIS Previews. BIOSIS, 2100 Arch St., Philadelphia, Pennsylvania 19103-1399. (215) 587-4800. Largest and most comprehensive database of research in the life sciences. Contains citations for nearly 9000 primary research journals, monographs, reviews, symposia, preliminary reports, semi-popular journals, selected institutional reports, government reports and research communications.

Cambridge Scientific Abstracts Life Science–CSAL. Cambridge Scientific Abstracts, 5161 River Rd., Bethesda, Maryland 20816. (301) 961-6750. Provides access to the following abstracting services: "Life Sciences Collection," "Aquatic Sciences and Fisheries Abstracts," "Oceanic Abstracts," and "Pollution Abstracts."

Enviro/Energyline Abstracts Plus. R. R. Bowker Co., 121 Chanlon Rd., New Providence, New Jersey 07974. (908) 464-6800.

Environmental Periodicals Bibliography. National Information Services Corp., Ste. 6, Wyman Towers, 3100 St. Paul St., Baltimore, Maryland 21218. (410)243-0797. Online version of abstract of same name.

MARINELINE. Informationszentrum Rohstoffgewinnwig Geowissenschaften Wasserwirtschaft, Bundesanstalt fuer Geowissenschaften und Rohstoffe, Postfach 510153, Stilleweg 2, Hanover 51, Germany D-3000. 49 (511) 643-2819.

NODC Data Inventory Data Base. U.S. National Environmental Satellite, Data, and Information Service, National Oceanographic Data Center, 1825 Connecticut Ave., N.W., Suite 406, Washington, District of Columbia 20235. (202) 673-5594. Information on National Oceanographic Data Center holdings.

Oceanic Abstracts. Cambridge Scientific Abstracts, 5161 River Rd., Bethesda, Maryland 20816. (301) 961-6750. Online access.

SCISEARCH. Institute for Scientific Information, University City Science Center, 3501 Market St., Philadelphia, Pennsylvania 19104. (215) 386-0100.

PERIODICALS AND NEWSLETTERS

Marine Biology. Springer-Verlag, 175 5th Ave., New York, New York 10010. (212)'461-1500; (800) 777-4643. Sixteen/year. Life in oceans and coastal waters.

Ocean Physics and Engineering. Marcel Dekker, Inc., 270 Madison Ave., New York, New York 10016. (212) 696-9000; (800) 228-1160. Quarterly.

RESEARCH CENTERS AND INSTITUTES

Alaska Fisheries Science Center. 7600 Sand Point Way NE, BIN C15700, Seattle, Washington 98115. (206) 526-4000.

Bodega Marine Laboratory. University of California, PO Box 247, Bodega Bay, California 94923. (707) 875-2010.

Boston University, Marine Program. Marine Biology Laboratory, Woods Hole, Massachusetts 02543. (508) 548-3705.

Center for Marine Conservation. 1725 DeSales St., NW, Suite 500, Washington, District of Columbia 20036. (202) 429-5609.

Lewes Marine Studies Complex. University of Delaware, Lewes, Delaware 19958. (302) 645-4212.

Marine/Freshwater Biomedical Center. Oregon State University, Department of Food Science, Corvallis, Oregon 97331. (503) 737-4193.

Marine Station. Walla Walla College, 174 Rosario Beach, Anacortes, Washington 98221. (206) 293-2326.

Oregon State University, Oceanographic & Geophysics Research Program. College of Oceanography, Oceanography Administration Building 104, Corvallis, Oregon 97331-5503. (503) 737-3504.

Point Reyes Bird Observatory. 4990 Shoreline Highway, Stinson Beach, California 94970. (415) 868-1221.

Provasoli-Guillard Center for Culture of Marine Phytoplankton. Bigelow Laboratory for Ocean Sciences, McKown Point, West Boothbay Harbor, Maine 04575. (207) 633-2173.

Texas A&M University, Sea Grant College Program. 1716 Briarcrest Dr., Ste. 702, College Station, Texas 77802. (409) 845-3854.

University of Florida, Whitney Laboratory. 9505 Ocean Shore Boulevard, St. Augustine, Florida 32086-8623. (904) 461-4000.

University of Guam. Marine Laboratory, UOG Station, Guam 96923. (671) 734-2421.

University of Massachusetts, Cooperative Marine Research Program. The Environmental Institute, Blaisdell House, Amherst, Massachusetts 01003-0040. (413) 545-2842.

University of Massachusetts, Marine Station. P.O. Box 7125, Lanesville Station, 932 Washington Street, Gloucester, Massachusetts 01930. (508) 281-1930.

University of Miami, Rosenstiel School of Marine and Atmospheric Science. 4600 Rickenbacker Causeway, Miami, Florida 33149. (305) 361-4000.

University of Rhode Island, Marine Ecosystems Research Laboratory. Graduate School of Oceanography, Narragansett, Rhode Island 02882. (401) 792-6104.

University of South Carolina at Columbia, Belle W. Baruch Institute for Marine Biology and Coastal Research. Columbia, South Carolina 29208. (803) 777-5288.

University of Southern California, Catalina Marine Science Center. P.O. Box 398, Avalon, California 90704. (213) 743-6792.

University of Southern California, Hancock Institute for Marine Studies. University Park, Los Angeles, California 90089-0373. (213) 740-6276.

University of Washington, Institute for Marine Studies. College of Ocean and Fishery Science, 3707 Brooklyn Avenue, N.E., Seattle, Washington 98195. (206) 543-7004.

TRADE ASSOCIATIONS AND PROFESSIONAL SOCIETIES

American Institute of Biological Sciences. 730 11th St., N.W., Washington, District of Columbia 20001-4521. (202) 628-1500.

Cousteau Society. Cousteau Society Membership Center, 930 W 21st St., Norfolk, Virginia 23517. In addition to carrying on the many research projects and explorations made famous by Jacques-Yves Cousteau, the Society publishes educational materials and numerous Technical publications as well as Calypso Log (monthly) and Dolphin Log (bimonthly children's publication).

Marine Technology Society. 1825 K. St., N.W., Suite 218, Washington, District of Columbia 20006. (202) 775-5966.

National Coalition for Marine Conservation, Inc. P.O. Box 23298, Savannah, Georgia 31403. (912) 234-8062.

National Marine Educators Association. P.O. Box 51215, Pacific Beach, California 93950. (408) 648-4841.

National Marine Manufacturers Association. 401 N. Michigan Ave., Chicago, Illinois 60611. (312) 836-4747.

The Sounds Conservancy, Inc. c/o Marine Sciences Institute, University of Connecticut, Groton, Connecticut 06340. (203) 445-1868.

MARINE ECOLOGY

See also: CORAL REEF ECOLOGY

ABSTRACTING AND INDEXING SERVICES

Biological and Agricultural Index. H.W. Wilson Co., 950 University Ave., Bronx, New York 10452. (800) 367-6770. 1916-. Monthly.

Current Advances in Ecological and Environmental Science. Pergamon Microforms International, Inc., Fairview Park, Elmsford, New York 10523. (914) 592-7720. 1989-. Monthly. Current literature searching service includingjournals, reports, abstracts, etc. This service is available online as part of the CABS database on the hosts BRS and ORBIT search service.

Ecological Abstracts. Geo Abstracts Ltd. Elsevier Applied Science, Crown House, Linton Rd., Barking, England IG 11 8JU. 1974-. Derived from over 600 leading ecological and environmental journals, plus books, conference proceedings, reports and theses.

Environment Abstracts. Bowker A & I Publishing, 121 Chanlon Rd., New Providence, New Jersey 07974. (908) 464-6800. 1974-.

Environment Index. Environment Information Center, Index Research Department, 124 E. 39th St., New York, New York 10016. 1971-. Annual.

Environmental Information Connection–EIC. Planning Information Program, Dept. of Urban and Regional Planning, University of Illinois, 1003 West Nevada, Urbana, Illinois 61801. (217) 333-1369. Also available online.

Environmental Periodicals Bibliography. Environmental Studies Institute, International Academy at Santa Barbara, 800 Garden St., Suite D, Santa Barbara, California 93101. (805) 965-5010. Also available online.

General Science Index. H. W. Wilson Co., 950 University Ave., Bronx, New York 10452. 1978-. Monthly, also issued in annual cumulation. Cumulative subject index to English language periodicals in the subject fields of

astronomy, botany, chemistry, earth science, environment and conservation, food and nutrition, genetics, mathematics, medicine and health, microbiology, oceanography, physics, physiology and zoology.

Geographical Abstracts. London School of Economics, Dept. of Geography, Regency House, 34 Duke St., London, England 1966-. Continued by Geo Abstracts issued in 6 parts: Pt. A. Landforms and the quaternary; Pt. B. Biogeography and Climatology; Pt. C. Economic geography; Pt. D. Social geography and cartography; Pt. E. Sedimentology; Pt. F. Regional and community planning.

Index to Scientific Book Contents. Institute for Scientific Information, 3501 Market St., Philadelphia, Pennsylvania 19104. (800) 523-1857. 1985-. Annual. Gives contents of science books published.

Oceanic Abstracts. UMI Data Courier, 620 S. 3rd St., Louisville, Kentucky 40202. (800) 626-2823. Formerly: Oceanic Index and Oceanic Citation Journal.

BIBLIOGRAPHIES

EPA Publications Bibliography. U.S. Environmental Protection Agency, Library Systems Branch, 401 M St., SW, Washington, District of Columbia 20460. (202) 260-2090. Quarterly.

New Publications of the Geological Survey. U.S. Department of the Interior, Geological Survey, 119 National Center, Reston, Virginia 22092. (703) 648-4460. 1984-. Monthly. Bibliography of geological publications and related government documents published by the Geological Survey.

ENCYCLOPEDIAS AND DICTIONARIES

Cambridge Encyclopedia of Life Sciences. A. E. Friday and David S. Ingram. Cambridge University Press, 40 W 20th St., New York, New York 10011. (212) 924-3900 or (800) 227-0247. 1985. Includes all topics under biology and ecology.

The Encyclopedia of Oceanography. Rhodes Whitmore Fairbridge. Reinhold Pub. Co., 115 5th Ave., New York, New York 10003. (212) 254-3232. 1966.

McGraw-Hill Encyclopedia of Environmental Science. Sybil P. Parker. McGraw-Hill Science & Engineering Books, 11 W. 19th St., New York, New York 10011. (212) 337-6010. 1980. Covers ecology, man's influence on nature, and environmental protection.

The Times Atlas and Encyclopedia of the Sea. A.D. Couper. Harper & Row, 10 E. 53rd St., New York, New York 10022. (212) 207-7000; (800) 242-7737. 1990.

GENERAL WORKS

Elements of Marine Ecology. Ronald Victor Tait. Butterworth-Heinemann, 80 Montvale Ave., Stoneham, Massachusetts 02180. (617) 438-8464. 1981.

Food Chain Yields, Models, and Management of Large Marine Ecosystems. Kenneth Sherman, et al., eds. Westview Press, 5500 Central Ave., Boulder, Colorado 80301. (303) 444-3541. 1991. Describes marine ecology, its productive resources and its management.

Marine Ecology. Jeffery S. Levinton. Prentice-Hall, Rte. 9W, Englewood Cliffs, New Jersey 07632. (201) 592-2000. 1982.

Marine Ecology: Selected Readings. J. Stanley Cobb. University Park Press, Baltimore, Maryland 1976.

ONLINE DATA BASES

Enviro/Energyline Abstracts Plus. R. R. Bowker Co., 121 Chanlon Rd., New Providence, New Jersey 07974. (908) 464-6800.

Environmental Periodicals Bibliography. National Information Services Corp., Ste. 6, Wyman Towers, 3100 St. Paul St., Baltimore, Maryland 21218. (410)243-0797. Online version of abstract of same name.

Monthly Catalog of United States Government Publications. U.S. G.P.O., Supt. of Docs., PO Box 371954, Pittsburgh, Pennsylvania 15250-7954. (202) 512-0000.

National Technical Information Service. U.S. Department of Commerce, National Technical Information Service, Office of Data Base Services, 5285 Port Royal Rd., Springfield, Virginia 22161. (703) 487-4807. Bibliographic database of government sponsored research and technical reports.

Oceanic Abstracts. Cambridge Scientific Abstracts, 5161 River Rd., Bethesda, Maryland 20816. (301) 961-6750. Online access.

SCISEARCH. Institute for Scientific Information, University City Science Center, 3501 Market St., Philadelphia, Pennsylvania 19104. (215) 386-0100.

PERIODICALS AND NEWSLETTERS

Marine Ecology. Paul Parey Scientific Publishers, P.O. Box 236, 150 East 27th Street, Suite 1A, New York, New York 10016. (212) 730-0518. Quarterly. Information on specific organisms in the environment.

Marine Ecology Research Highlights. U.S. Environmental Protection Agency, South Ferry Rd., Narragansett, Rhode Island 02882. Semiannual. Ocean research news.

RESEARCH CENTERS AND INSTITUTES

Marine Ecological Institute. 1200 Chesapeake Drive, Redwood City, California 94063. (415) 364-2760.

MARINE ENGINEERING

ABSTRACTING AND INDEXING SERVICES

Biological and Agricultural Index. H.W. Wilson Co., 950 University Ave., Bronx, New York 10452. (800) 367-6770. 1916-. Monthly.

Environment Abstracts. Bowker A & I Publishing, 121 Chanlon Rd., New Providence, New Jersey 07974. (908) 464-6800. 1974-.

Environment Index. Environment Information Center, Index Research Department, 124 E. 39th St., New York, New York 10016. 1971-. Annual.

Environmental Information Connection–EIC. Planning Information Program, Dept. of Urban and Regional Planning, University of Illinois, 1003 West Nevada, Urbana, Illinois 61801. (217) 333-1369. Also available online.

Environmental Periodicals Bibliography. Environmental Studies Institute, International Academy at Santa Barbara, 800 Garden St., Suite D, Santa Barbara, California 93101. (805) 965-5010. Also available online.

Index to Scientific Book Contents. Institute for Scientific Information, 3501 Market St., Philadelphia, Pennsylvania 19104. (800) 523-1857. 1985-. Annual. Gives contents of science books published.

Oceanic Abstracts. UMI Data Courier, 620 S. 3rd St., Louisville, Kentucky 40202. (800) 626-2823. Formerly: Oceanic Index and Oceanic Citation Journal.

Sea Grant Abstracts. National Sea Grant Depository, Pell Laboratory Bldg., Bay Campus, University of Rhode Island, Narragansett, Rhode Island 02882. (401) 792-6114. 1986-. Quarterly. Published by the National Sea Grant Programs, this collection includes annual reports, serials and newsletters, charts and maps.

BIBLIOGRAPHIES

EPA Publications Bibliography. U.S. Environmental Protection Agency, Library Systems Branch, 401 M St., SW, Washington, District of Columbia 20460. (202) 260-2090. Quarterly.

New Publications of the Geological Survey. U.S. Department of the Interior, Geological Survey, 119 National Center, Reston, Virginia 22092. (703) 648-4460. 1984-. Monthly. Bibliography of geological publications and related government documents published by the Geological Survey.

ENCYCLOPEDIAS AND DICTIONARIES

Cambridge Encyclopedia of Life Sciences. A. E. Friday and David S. Ingram. Cambridge University Press, 40 W 20th St., New York, New York 10011. (212) 924-3900 or (800) 227-0247. 1985. Includes all topics under biology and ecology.

Dictionary of Environmental Engineering and Related Sciences: English-Spanish, Spanish-English. Jose T. Villate. Ediciones Universal, 3090 SW 8th St., Miami, Florida 33135. (305) 642-3355. 1979.

Encyclopedia of Environmental Science and Engineering. J.R. Pfafflin. Gordon and Breach Science Publishers, Inc., 270 8th Ave., New York, New York 10011. (212) 206-8900. 1992.

The Encyclopedia of Oceanography. Rhodes Whitmore Fairbridge. Reinhold Pub. Co., 115 5th Ave., New York, New York 10003. (212) 254-3232. 1966.

McGraw-Hill Encyclopedia of Environmental Science. Sybil P. Parker. McGraw-Hill Science & Engineering Books, 11 W. 19th St., New York, New York 10011. (212) 337-6010. 1980. Covers ecology, man's influence on nature, and environmental protection.

The Times Atlas and Encyclopedia of the Sea. A.D. Couper. Harper & Row, 10 E. 53rd St., New York, New York 10022. (212) 207-7000; (800) 242-7737. 1990.

ONLINE DATA BASES

Enviro/Energyline Abstracts Plus. R. R. Bowker Co., 121 Chanlon Rd., New Providence, New Jersey 07974. (908) 464-6800.

Environmental Periodicals Bibliography. National Information Services Corp., Ste. 6, Wyman Towers, 3100 St. Paul St., Baltimore, Maryland 21218. (410)243-0797. Online version of abstract of same name.

Monthly Catalog of United States Government Publications. U.S. G.P.O., Supt. of Docs., PO Box 371954, Pittsburgh, Pennsylvania 15250-7954. (202) 512-0000.

National Technical Information Service. U.S. Department of Commerce, National Technical Information Service, Office of Data Base Services, 5285 Port Royal Rd., Springfield, Virginia 22161. (703) 487-4807. Bibliographic database of government sponsored research and technical reports.

Oceanic Abstracts. Cambridge Scientific Abstracts, 5161 River Rd., Bethesda, Maryland 20816. (301) 961-6750. Online access.

MARINE ENVIRONMENT AND ECOSYSTEMS

See also: BIOMES; ECOSYSTEMS

ABSTRACTING AND INDEXING SERVICES

Abstracts of Air and Water Conservation Literature. American Petroleum Institute. Central Abstracting and Indexing Service, 275 Madison Avenue, New York, New York 10016. 1972.

Applied Ecology Abstracts Studies in Renewable Natural Resources. Information Retrieval Ltd., 1911 Jefferson Davis Highway, Arlington, Virginia 22202. 1975-. Monthly.

Aqualine Abstracts. Water Research Centre. c/o Pergamon Microforms International, Inc., Fairview Park, Elmsford, New York 10523. (914) 592-7720. 1927-. Contains some 8,000 records annually on water and wastewater technology. Covers all aspects of water, wastewater, associated engineering services and the aquatic environment. Over 600 periodicals, as well as books, reports and conference proceedings and other publications from water related institutions worldwide are scanned. Also available online.

ASFA Aquaculture Abstracts. Cambridge Scientific Abstracts, Inc., 5161 River Rd., Bethesda, Maryland 20816. (301) 961-6750. 1984.

Biological Abstracts. BIOSIS, 2100 Arch St., Philadelphia, Pennsylvania 19103-1399. (215) 587-4800. 1927-.

Biological and Agricultural Index. H.W. Wilson Co., 950 University Ave., Bronx, New York 10452. (800) 367-6770. 1916-. Monthly.

Biology Digest. Data Courier, Plexus Pub Inc., 143 Old Marlton Pike, Medford, New Jersey 08055. 1974-. Monthly. Abstracts biology periodicals.

Current Advances in Ecological and Environmental Science. Pergamon Microforms International, Inc., Fairview Park, Elmsford, New York 10523. (914) 592-7720. 1989-. Monthly. Current literature searching service including journals, reports, abstracts, etc. This service is available online as part of the CABS database on the hosts BRS and ORBIT search service.

Ecological Abstracts. Geo Abstracts Ltd. Elsevier Applied Science, Crown House, Linton Rd., Barking, England IG 11 8JU. 1974-. Derived from over 600 leading ecological and environmental journals, plus books, conference proceedings, reports and theses.

Ecology Abstracts. Cambridge Scientific Abstracts, 5161 River Rd., Bethesda, Maryland 20816. (301) 961-6750. Monthly.

Environment Abstracts. Bowker A & I Publishing, 121 Chanlon Rd., New Providence, New Jersey 07974. (908) 464-6800. 1974-.

Environment Index. Environment Information Center, Index Research Department, 124 E. 39th St., New York, New York 10016. 1971-. Annual.

Environmental Information Connection–EIC. Planning Information Program, Dept. of Urban and Regional Planning, University of Illinois, 1003 West Nevada, Urbana, Illinois 61801. (217) 333-1369. Also available online.

Environmental Periodicals Bibliography. Environmental Studies Institute, International Academy at Santa Barbara, 800 Garden St., Suite D, Santa Barbara, California 93101. (805) 965-5010. Also available online.

Environmental Research Laboratories Publication Abstracts. National Oceanic and Atmospheric Administration. Environmental Research Laboratories, 325 Broadway, Boulder, Colorado 80303. 1990. Annual. Sixth annual bibliography of NOAA Environmental Research Laboratories staff publications, FY 89. Covers journal articles, official ERL reports, conference papers, and publications released in cooperation with universities and by ERL funded contractors.

General Science Index. H. W. Wilson Co., 950 University Ave., Bronx, New York 10452. 1978-. Monthly, also issued in annual cumulation. Cumulative subject index to English language periodicals in the subject fields of astronomy, botany, chemistry, earth science, environment and conservation, food and nutrition, genetics, mathematics, medicine and health, microbiology, oceanography, physics, physiology and zoology.

Geographical Abstracts. London School of Economics, Dept. of Geography, Regency House, 34 Duke St., London, England 1966-. Continued by Geo Abstracts issued in 6 parts: Pt. A. Landforms and the quaternary; Pt. B. Biogeography and Climatology; Pt. C. Economic geography; Pt. D. Social geography and cartography; Pt. E. Sedimentology; Pt. F. Regional and community planning.

Index to Scientific Book Contents. Institute for Scientific Information, 3501 Market St., Philadelphia, Pennsylvania 19104. (800) 523-1857. 1985-. Annual. Gives contents of science books published.

Multimedia Index to Ecology. National Information Center for Educational Media, University of Southern California, Los Angeles, California 90007.

Oceanic Abstracts. UMI Data Courier, 620 S. 3rd St., Louisville, Kentucky 40202. (800) 626-2823. Formerly: Oceanic Index and Oceanic Citation Journal.

Science Citation Index. Institute for Scientific Information, 3501 Market St., Philadelphia, Pennsylvania 19104. 1961-.

Sea Grant Abstracts. National Sea Grant Depository, Pell Laboratory Bldg., Bay Campus, University of Rhode Island, Narragansett, Rhode Island 02882. (401) 792-6114. 1986-. Quarterly. Published by the National Sea Grant Programs, this collection includes annual reports, serials and newsletters, charts and maps.

BIBLIOGRAPHIES

Coastal Land Use. Council of Planning Librarians, 1313 E. 60th St., Chicago, Illinois 60637-2897. (312) 942-2163. Bibliography of shore protection.

Current Contents. Agriculture, Biology and Environmental Sciences. Institute for Scientific Information, 3501 Market St., Philadelphia, Pennsylvania 19104. (800) 523-1857. 1973-. Previous title: Current Contents. Agricultural, Food & Veterinary Sciences. Gives the table of contents of periodicals in the fields of agriculture, biology, environmental and related areas.

Directory of Published Proceedings. Interdok Corp., 173 Halstead Ave., Harrison, New York 10528. (914) 835-3506. 1990. Monthly. This is a listing of published proceedings including the series SEMTE (Science/Medicine/Engineering/Technology) and the series SSH (Social Science/Humanities).

EPA Publications Bibliography. U.S. Environmental Protection Agency, Library Systems Branch, 401 M St., SW, Washington, District of Columbia 20460. (202) 260-2090. Quarterly.

Interactions of Aquaculture, Marine Coastal Ecosystems, and Near-Shore Waters: A Bibliography. Deborah T. Hanfman. National Agricultural Library, 10301 Baltimore Blvd., Beltsville, Maryland 20705-2351. (301) 504-5755. Covers coastal ecology.

New Publications of the Geological Survey. U.S. Department of the Interior, Geological Survey, 119 National Center, Reston, Virginia 22092. (703) 648-4460. 1984-. Monthly. Bibliography of geological publications and related government documents published by the Geological Survey.

DIRECTORIES

Gale Environmental Sourcebook. Karen Hill. Gale Research Co., 835 Penobscot Bldg., Detroit, Michigan 48226-4094. (313) 961-2242. Contacts, information sources, or general information on environmental topics.

ENCYCLOPEDIAS AND DICTIONARIES

Cambridge Encyclopedia of Life Sciences. A. E. Friday and David S. Ingram. Cambridge University Press, 40 W 20th St., New York, New York 10011. (212) 924-3900 or (800) 227-0247. 1985. Includes all topics under biology and ecology.

Dictionary of Environmental Engineering and Related Sciences: English-Spanish, Spanish-English. Jose T. Villate. Ediciones Universal, 3090 SW 8th St., Miami, Florida 33135. (305) 642-3355. 1979.

A Dictionary of Genetics. Robert C. King and William A. Stansfield. Oxford University Press, 200 Madison Ave., New York, New York 10016. (212) 679-7300 or (800) 334-4249. 1991. Fourth edition. Includes 7,100 definitions with 250 illustrations. Also includes bibliography of major sources.

Dictionary of Genetics and Cell Biology. Norman Maclean. New York University Press, 70 Washington Sq. S., New York, New York 10012. (212) 998-2575. 1987. Includes the subject areas of cytology and genetics.

Dictionary of Microbiology and Molecular Biology. Paul Singleton and Diana Sainsbury. John Wiley & Sons, Inc., 605 3rd Ave., New York, New York 10158-0012. (212) 850-6000. 1987. Second edition. Comprehensive dictionary with "classical descriptive aspects of microbiology to current developments in related areas of bioenergetics, biochemistry and molecular biology." Entries give synonyms, cross references, and references to pertinent works. Miscellaneous appendixes. Bibliography.

The Encyclopedia of Animal Ecology. Peter D. Moore. Facts on File, Inc., 460 Park Ave. S., New York, New York 10016. (212) 683-2244. 1987.

The Encyclopedia of Beaches and Coastal Environments. Maurice L. Schwartz. Hutchinson Ross Pub. Co., Stroudsburg, Pennsylvania 1982.

Encyclopedia of Environmental Science and Engineering. J.R. Pfafflin. Gordon and Breach Science Publishers, Inc., 270 8th Ave., New York, New York 10011. (212) 206-8900. 1992.

Encyclopedia of Human Biology. Renato Dulbecco, ed. Academic Press, c/o Harcourt Brace Jovanovich Inc., 6277 Sea Harbor Dr., Orlando, Florida 32887. (800) 346-8648. 1991. Eight volumes.

The Encyclopedia of Oceanography. Rhodes Whitmore Fairbridge. Reinhold Pub. Co., 115 5th Ave., New York, New York 10003. (212) 254-3232. 1966.

Encyclopedic Dictionary of Genetics: With German Term Equivalents and Extensive German/English Index. R. C. King and W. D. Stansfield. VCH Publishers, 303 NW 12th Ave., Deerfield Beach, Florida 33442-1788. (305) 428-5566. 1990. 4th ed. Revised edition of: A Dictionary of Genetics, third edition.

Glossary of Geology. Robert Latimer Bates and Julia A. Jackson, eds. American Geological Institute, 4220 King St., Alexandria, Virginia 22302-1507. (703) 379-2480 or (800) 336-4764. 1987. Third edition.

Grzimek's Encyclopedia of Ecology. Bernhard Grzimek. Van Nostrand Reinhold, 115 5th Ave., New York, New York 10003. (212) 254-3232. 1976.

McGraw-Hill Encyclopedia of Environmental Science. Sybil P. Parker. McGraw-Hill Science & Engineering Books, 11 W. 19th St., New York, New York 10011. (212) 337-6010. 1980. Covers ecology, man's influence on nature, and environmental protection.

McGraw-Hill Encyclopedia of Science and Technology. McGraw-Hill, 1221 Avenue of the Americas, New York, New York 10020. (212) 512-2000 or (800) 262-4729. 1992. Seventh edition. Issued in multiple volumes including index. Includes all science and technology broad subject areas.

McGraw-Hill Encyclopedia of the Geological Sciences. Sybil P. Parker, ed. McGraw-Hill, 1221 Avenue of the

Americas, New York, New York 10020. (212) 512-2000 or (800) 262-4729. 1988. Second edition. Published previously in the McGraw-Hill Encyclopedia of Science and Technology.

North American Reference Encyclopedia of Ecology and Pollution. William White. North American Pub. Co., 401 N. Broad St., Philadelphia, Pennsylvania 19108. (215) 238-5300. 1972.

The Times Atlas and Encyclopedia of the Sea. A.D. Couper. Harper & Row, 10 E. 53rd St., New York, New York 10022. (212) 207-7000; (800) 242-7737. 1990.

Van Nostrand's Scientific Encyclopedia. Glenn D. Considine, ed. Van Nostrand Reinhold, 115 5th Ave., New York, New York 10003. (212) 254-3232. 1983. Sixth edition. Includes all broad subject areas in science.

GENERAL WORKS

Analysis of Marine Ecosystems. A. R. Longhurst. Academic Press, c/o Harcourt Brace Jovanovich Inc., 6277 Sea Harbor Dr., Orlando, Florida 32887. (800) 346-8648. 1981. Topics in marine ecology.

The Atlantic Barrier Reef Ecosystem at Carrie Bow Cay, Belize, I: Structure and Communities. Klaus Rutzler and Ian G. MacIntyre. Smithsonian Institution Press, 470 L'Enfant Plaza, No. 7100, Washington, District of Columbia 20560. (800) 782-4612. 1982.

Biomass Yields and Geography of Large Marine Ecosystems. Kenneth Sherman. Westview Press, 5500 Central AVe., Boulder, Colorado 80301. (303) 444-3541. 1989. Environmental aspects of marine pollution, marine productivity, and marine ecology.

Ecosystems of Florida. Ronald L. Myers and John J. Ewel, eds. Central Florida University, Dist. by Univ. Presses of Florida, 15 N.W. 15th St., Gainesville, Florida 32603. (904) 392-1351. 1990. Presents an ecosystem setting with geology, geography and soils, climate, and 13 ecosystems in a broad human context of historical biogeography and current human influences. Also presents community vulnerability and management techniques and issues in conservation.

Environmental Aspects of Coasts and Islands. BAR, Oxford, England 1981. Maritime anthropology, coastal ecology and environmental ecology.

Facets of Modern Biogeochemistry. V. Ittekkott, et al. Springer-Verlag, 175 5th Ave., New York, New York 10010. (212) 460-1500; (800) 777-4643. 1990. Deals with the geochemistry of marine sediments and related areas.

Food Chain Yields, Models, and Management of Large Marine Ecosystems. Kenneth Sherman, et al., eds. Westview Press, 5500 Central Ave., Boulder, Colorado 80301. (303) 444-3541. 1991. Describes marine ecology, its productive resources and its management.

Guide to Information on Research in the Marine Science and Engineering. U.S. Department of Commerce, National Oceanic and Atmospheric Administration, Office of Ocean Engineering, 6010 Executive Blvd., Rockville, Maryland 20852. (301) 443-8344. 1978.

Heavy Metals in the Marine Environment. Robert W. Furness and Philip S. Rainbow. CRC Press, 2000 Corporate Blvd. N.W., Boca Raton, Florida 33431. (800) 272-7737. 1990. Includes heavy metals in the marine environment, trace metals in sea water, metals in the marine

atmosphere, processes affecting metal concentration in estuarine and coastal marine sediments, heavy metal levels in marine invertebrates, use of microalgae and invertebrates to monitor metal levels in estuaries and coastal waters, toxic effects of metals, and the incidence of metal pollution in marine ecosystems.

Large Marine Ecosystems: Patterns, Processes, and Yields. Kenneth Sherman, et al., eds. American Association for the Advancement of Science, 1333 H St. N.W., 8th Flr., Washington, District of Columbia 20005. (202) 326-6400. 1990. Deals with the conservation and management of vitally important components of the ecosphere.

The Living Ocean. Boyce Thorne-Miller. Island Press, 1718 Connecticut Ave. N.W., Suite 300, Washington, District of Columbia 20009. (202) 232-7933. 1991. Discusses all marine ecosystems, including coastal benthic, shore systems, estuaries, wetlands, and coral reefs, coastal pelagic, deep-sea benthic, hydrothermal vents and others.

Managing Marine Environments. Richard A. Kenchington. Taylor & Francis, 1900 Frost Rd., Ste. 101, Bristol, Pennsylvania 19007. (215) 785-5800. 1990. Contemporary issues of multiple-use planning and management of marine environments and natural resources.

Marine and Estuarine Protection: Programs and Activities. U.S. Environmental Protection Agency, Office of Water, 401 M St. SW, Washington, District of Columbia 20460. (202) 260-2090. 1989.

Marine Environment Law in the United Nations Environment Programme: An Emergent Ecoregime. P. H. Sand, ed. Cassell PLC, Publishers Distribution Center, PO Box C831, Rutherford, New Jersey 07070. (201) 939-6064; (201) 939-6065. 1988.

Microbial Enzymes in Aquatic Environments. Ryszard J. Chrost. Springer-Varlag, 175 5th Ave., New York, New York 10010. (212) 460-1500. 1991. Brings together studies on enzymatic degradation processes from disciplines as diverse as water and sediment research, bacterial and algal aquatic ecophysiology, eutrophication, nutrient cycling, and biogeochemistry, in both freshwater and marine ecosystem.

Oceans under Threat. Phillip Neal. London Dryad Press, Essex, England 1990. Marine pollution and marine ecology.

Primary Productivity in the Sea. Paul G. Falkowski. Plenum Press, 233 Spring St., New York, New York 10013-1578. (212) 620-8000; (800) 221-9369. 1980.

Reviews of Environmental Contamination and Toxicology: v. 120. George W. Ware, ed. Springer-Verlag, 175 5th Ave., New York, New York 10010. (212) 460-1500; (800) 777-4643. 1991. Covers organochlorine pesticides and polychlorinated biphenyls in human adipose tissue, pesticide residues in foods imported into the U.S., and selected trace elements and the use of biomonitors in subtropical and tropical marine ecosystems.

Sharks in Question: The Smithsonian Answer Book. Victor G. Springer and Joy P. Gold. Smithsonian Institution Press, 470 L'Enfant Plaza #7100, Washington, District of Columbia 20560. (800) 782-4612. 1989.

Variability and Management of Large Marine Ecosystems. Kenneth Sherman. Westview Press, 5500 Central

Ave., Boulder, Colorado 80301. (303) 444-3541. 1986. Managing marine resources and marine ecology.

GOVERNMENTAL ORGANIZATIONS

Coast Guard. Information Office, 2100 Second St., S.W., Washington, District of Columbia 20593. (202) 267-2229.

National Marine Fisheries Service. 1825 Connecticut Ave., N.W., Washington, District of Columbia 20235. (202) 673-5450.

Office of Public Affairs: National Oceanic and Atmospheric Administration. 14th and Constitution Avenues, N.W., Washington, District of Columbia 20230. (202) 377-2985.

ONLINE DATA BASES

BIOSIS Previews. BIOSIS, 2100 Arch St., Philadelphia, Pennsylvania 19103-1399. (215) 587-4800. Largest and most comprehensive database of research in the life sciences. Contains citations for nearly 9000 primary research journals, monographs, reviews, symposia, preliminary reports, semi-popular journals, selected institutional reports, government reports and research communications. .

Enviro/Energyline Abstracts Plus. R. R. Bowker Co., 121 Chanlon Rd., New Providence, New Jersey 07974. (908) 464-6800.

Environmental Periodicals Bibliography. National Information Services Corp., Ste. 6, Wyman Towers, 3100 St. Paul St., Baltimore, Maryland 21218. (410)243-0797. Online version of abstract of same name.

LEXIS Admiralty and Maritime Library. Mead Data Central, Inc., P.O. Box 933, Dayton, Ohio 45401. (800) 227-4908.

MARINELINE. Informationszentrum Rohstoffgewinnwig Geowissenschaften Wasserwirtschaft, Bundesanstalt fuer Geowissenschaften und Rohstoffe, Postfach 510153, Stilleweg 2, Hanover 51, Germany D-3000. 49 (511) 643-2819.

Monthly Catalog of United States Government Publications. U.S. G.P.O., Supt. of Docs., PO Box 371954, Pittsburgh, Pennsylvania 15250-7954. (202) 512-0000.

National Technical Information Service. U.S. Department of Commerce, National Technical Information Service, Office of Data Base Services, 5285 Port Royal Rd., Springfield, Virginia 22161. (703) 487-4807. Bibliographic database of government sponsored research and technical reports.

Oceanic Abstracts. Cambridge Scientific Abstracts, 5161 River Rd., Bethesda, Maryland 20816. (301) 961-6750. Online access.

PressNet Environmental Reports. Chemical Information Systems, Inc., 7215 York Rd., Baltimore, Maryland 21212. (301) 321-8440.

SCISEARCH. Institute for Scientific Information, University City Science Center, 3501 Market St., Philadelphia, Pennsylvania 19104. (215) 386-0100.

PERIODICALS AND NEWSLETTERS

Calypso Log. Cousteau Society Membership Center, 930 W 21st St., Norfolk, Virginia 23517. 6 issues a year. Presents articles for members about Cousteau Society expeditions, ecology, conservation, oceans and marine mammals.

Environment. Heldref Publications, 4000 Albemarle Street, NW, Washington, District of Columbia 20016. (202) 362-6445. Ten a year. Covers science and science policy.

Estuaries. Chesapeake Biological Laboratory, 1 William St., Solomons, Maryland 20688-0038. (410) 326-4281. Quarterly. Journal of the Estuarine Research Federation dealing with estuaries and estuarine biology.

Journal of Shoreline Management. Elsevier Science Publishing Co., 655 Avenue of the Americas, New York, New York 10010. (212) 989-5800. Two issues a year. Deals with coastal ecology, coastal zone management, and ocean and shoreline management.

Marine Biology. Springer-Verlag, 175 5th Ave., New York, New York 10010. (212) 461-1500; (800) 777-4643. Sixteen/year. Life in oceans and coastal waters.

Marine Conservation News. Center for Marine Conservation, 1725 Desales St., N.W., Suite 500, Washington, District of Columbia 20036. (202) 429-5609. Quarterly. Marine conservation issues: whales, seals, sea turtles, and habitat.

Marine Ecology. Paul Parey Scientific Publishers, P.O. Box 236, 150 East 27th Street, Suite 1A, New York, New York 10016. (212) 730-0518. Quarterly. Information on specific organisms in the environment.

Marine Ecology Research Highlights. U.S. Environmental Protection Agency, South Ferry Rd., Narragansett, Rhode Island 02882. Semiannual. Ocean research news.

Marine Environmental Research. ASP Ltd., Ripple Road, Barking, Essex, England Monthly. Covers marine pollution and marine ecology.

Marine Policy Reports. Center for the Study of Marine Policy, College of Marine Studies, University of Delaware, Newark, Delaware 19716. (302) 451-8086. Bimonthly. Ocean research.

Marine Resource Economics. Taylor & Francis, 1900 Frost Road, Suite 101, Bristol, Pennsylvania 19007. (800) 821-8312. Quarterly. Issues related to the economics of marine resources.

RESEARCH CENTERS AND INSTITUTES

Academy of Natural Sciences of Philadelphia, Division of Environmental Research. 19th Street and the Parkway, Philadelphia, Pennsylvania 19103. (215) 299-1081.

Bowdoin College, Marine Station. Department of Chemistry, Brunswick, Maine 04011. (207) 725-3166.

Center for Marine Conservation. 1725 DeSales St., NW, Suite 500, Washington, District of Columbia 20036. (202) 429-5609.

Center for Study of Marine Policy. University of Delaware, Newark, Delaware 19711. (302) 831-8086.

College of Marine Studies. University of Delaware, Newark, Delaware 19716. (302) 451-2841.

Connecticut Sea Grant College Program. University of Connecticut at Avery Point, 1084 Schennecossett Rd., Groton, Connecticut 06340. (203) 445-5108.

Earth Sciences Centre. University of Toronto, 33 Willcocks St., Toronto, Ontario, Canada M5S 3B3. (416) 978-3248.

Lewes Marine Studies Complex. University of Delaware, Lewes, Delaware 19958. (302) 645-4212.

Louisiana State University, Office of Sea Grant Development. Center for Wetland Resources, Baton Rouge, Louisiana 70803. (504) 388-6710.

Louisiana Universities Marine Consortium. Chauvin, Louisiana 70344. (504) 851-2800.

Marine Biological Laboratory. Woods Hole, Massachusetts 02543. (508) 548-3705.

Marine Biotechnology Center. University of California, Santa Barbara, Marine Science Institute, Santa Barbara, California 93106. (805) 893-3765.

Marine Ecological Institute. 1200 Chesapeake Drive, Redwood City, California 94063. (415) 364-2760.

Marine Laboratory. University of Florida, 313 Carr, Gainesville, Florida 32611. (904) 392-1097.

Marine Policy Center. Crowell House, Woods Hole Oceanographic Institution, Woods Hole, Massachusetts 02543. (508) 548-1400.

Marine Science Center. Educational Service District 114, State Superintendent of Public Instruction, 18743 Front St., N.E., P.O. Box 2079, Poulsbo, Washington 98370. (206) 779-5549.

Marine Science Institute. University of California, Santa Barbara, Santa Barbara, California 93106. (805) 893-3764.

Marine Sciences Institute. University of Connecticut at Avery Point, Groton, Connecticut 06340. (203) 445-4714.

Marine World Africa USA. Marine World Foundation, Marine World Parkway, Vallejo, California 94589. (707) 644-4000.

Massachusetts Institute of Technology, MIT Sea Grant College Program. E38-300, 292 Main St., Cambridge, Massachusetts 02139. (617) 253-7041.

Mississippi-Alabama Sea Grant Consortium. Caylor Building, Gulf Coast Research Laboratory, P.O. Box 7000, Ocean Springs, Mississippi 39564-7000. (601) 875-9341.

Mystic Marinelife Aquarium. 55 Coogan Boulevard, Exit 90, I-95, Mystic, Connecticut 06355-1997. (203) 536-9631.

National Sea Grant Depository. Pell Library Building, University of Rhode Island, Narragansett, Rhode Island 02882. (401) 792-6114.

New England Aquarium, Harold E. Edgerton Research Laboratory. Central Wharf, Boston, Massachusetts 02110. (617) 973-5252.

New Jersey Marine Sciences Consortium. Building 22, Fort Hancock, New Jersey 07732. (201) 872-1300.

New York Sea Grant Institute. Duchess Hall, State University of New York, Stony Brook, New York 11794-5001. (516) 632-6905.

Newfound Harbor Marine Institute. Route 3, Box 170, Big Pine Key, Florida 33043. (305) 872-2331.

Northeastern Research Center for Wildlife Diseases. University of Connecticut, Box U-89, Connecticut 06268. (203) 486-3737.

Northeastern University, Marine Science Center. East Point, Nahant, Massachusetts 01908. (617) 581-7370.

Nova University, Institute of Marine and Coastal Studies. 8000 North Ocean Drive, Dania, Florida 33004. (305) 920-1909.

Old Dominion University, Applied Marine Research Laboratory. Norfolk, Virginia 23529-0456. (804) 683-4195.

Oregon State University, Hatfield Marine Science Center. Marine Science Drive, Newport, Oregon 97365. (503) 867-3011.

Osborn Laboratories of Marine Sciences. New York Aquarium, Boardwalk and West 8th, Brooklyn, New York 11224. (718) 265-3400.

Rutgers University, Center for Coastal and Environmental Studies. 104 Doolittle Building, Busch Campus, New Brunswick, New Jersey 08903. (201) 932-3738.

San Diego State University, Center for Marine Studies. San Diego, California 92182. (619) 594-6523.

Saskatchewan Fisheries Laboratory. Saskatchewan Parks and Renewable Resources, 112 Research Drive, Saskatoon, Saskatchewan, Canada S7K 2H6. (306) 933-5776.

School for Field Studies. 16 Broadway, Box S, Beverly, Massachusetts 01915. (508) 927-7777.

Scripps Institution of Oceanography, Marine Biology Research Division. University of California, San Diego, A-0202, San Diego, California 92093-0202. (619) 534-7378.

Scripps Institution of Oceanography, Marine Life Research Group. University of California, San Diego, A-027, La Jolla, California 92093-0227. (619) 534-3565.

Scripps Institution of Oceanography, Physiological Research Laboratory. University of California, San Diego, A-0204, La Jolla, California 92093. (714) 534-2934.

Stanford University, Hopkins Marine Station. Pacific Grove, California 93950. (408) 655-6200.

State University of New York at Stony Brook, Marine Sciences Research Center. Stony Brook, New York 11794. (516) 632-8700.

University of Alaska Fairbanks, Seward Marine Center. P.O. Box 730, Seward, Alaska 99664. (907) 224-5261.

University of Georgia, Marine Institute. Sapelo, Georgia (912) 485-2221.

University of Georgia, Marine Sciences Program. Athens, Georgia 30602 (404) 542-7671.

University of Hawaii at Manoa Hawaii Cooperative Fishery Research Unit. 2538 The Mall, Honolulu, Hawaii 96822. (808) 956-8350.

University of Hawaii at Manoa Hawaii Institute of Marine Biology. Coconut Island, P.O. Box 1346, Kaneohe, Hawaii 96744-1346. (808) 236-7401.

University of Hawaii at Manoa Sea Grant College Program. 1000 Pope Road, MSB 220, Honolulu, Hawaii 96822. (808) 948-7031.

University of Maine, Ira C. Darling Center for Research Teaching and Service. Walpole, Maine 04573. (207) 563-3146.

University of Maine, Maine Sea Grant College Program. 14 Coburn Hall, University of Maine, Orono, Maine 04469-0114. (207) 581-1435.

University of Maryland, Center of Marine Biotechnology. 600 East Lombard Street, Baltimore, Maryland 21202. (301) 783-4800.

University of Michigan, Marine Geochemistry Laboratory. Department of Geological Sciences, 1006 C.C. Little Building, Ann Arbor, Michigan 48109. (313) 763-4593.

University of Michigan, Marine Geology Laboratory. Department of Geological Sciences, Ann Arbor, Michigan 48109-1063. (313) 936-0521.

University of New Hampshire, Coastal Marine Laboratory. Department of Zoology, Durham, New Hampshire 03824. (603) 862-2100.

University of New Hampshire, Diamond Island Engineering Center. Marine Systems Engineering Lab, Science and Engineering Building, Durham, New Hampshire 03824. (603) 862-4600.

University of New Hampshire, Institute of Marine Science and Ocean Engineering. Marine Programs Building, Durham, New Hampshire 03824. (603) 862-2995.

University of New Hampshire, Jackson Estuarine Laboratory. 85 Adams Point Road, Durham, New Hampshire 03824-3406. (603) 862-2175.

University of North Carolina at Wilmington, Center for Marine Research. 601 South College Road, Wilmington, North Carolina 28406. (919) 256-3721.

University of North Carolina, Institute of Marine Sciences. 3407 Arendell Street, Morehead City, North Carolina 28577. (919) 726-6841.

University of Oregon, Oregon Institute of Marine Biology. Charleston, Oregon 97420. (503) 888-2581.

University of Puerto Rico, Sea Grant College Program. Department of Marine Sciences, P.O. Box 5000, Mayaguez, Puerto Rico 00681-5000. (809) 832-3585.

University of Rhode Island, Marine Ecosystems Research Laboratory. Graduate School of Oceanography, Narragansett, Rhode Island 02882. (401) 792-6104.

University of Rhode Island, Sea Grant College Program. Graduate School of Oceanography, Narragansett, Rhode Island 02882-1197. (401) 792-6800.

University of South Carolina at Columbia, Belle W. Baruch Institute for Marine Biology and Coastal Research. Columbia, South Carolina 29208. (803) 777-5288.

University of Southern California, Catalina Marine Science Center. P.O. Box 398, Avalon, California 90704. (213) 743-6792.

University of Southern California, Fish Harbor Marine Research Laboratory. 820 South Seaside Avenue, Terminal Island, California 90731. (310) 830-4570.

University of Southern California, Hancock Institute for Marine Studies. University Park, Los Angeles, California 90089-0373. (213) 740-6276.

University of Southern Mississippi, Center for Marine Science. John C. Stennis Space Center, Stennis Space Center, Mississippi 39529. (601) 688-3177.

University of Texas at Austin, Marine Science Institute. Port Aransas, Texas 78373. (512) 749-6711.

University of Texas-Pan American, Coastal Studies Laboratory. P.O. Box 2591, South Padre Island, Texas 78597. (512) 761-2644.

University of Washington, Friday Harbor Laboratories. 620 University Road, Friday Harbor, Washington 98250. (206) 378-2165.

STATISTICS SOURCES

Environmental Data Compendium. OECD Publications and Information Center, 2001 L St., N.W., Suite 700, Washington, District of Columbia 20036. (202) 785-6323. 1989.

Environmental Indicators. OECD Publications and Information Center, 2001 L St., N.W., Suite 700, Washington, District of Columbia 20036. (202) 785-6323. 1991.

Environmental Quality. Council on Environmental Quality. U.S. G.P.O., Washington, District of Columbia 20401. (202) 512-0000. Annual.

OECD Environmental Data Compendium 1989. OECD Publications and Information Center, 2001 L St. N.W., Suite 700, Washington, District of Columbia 20036. (202) 785-OECD. 1989. Provides statistical data for OECD countries on air pollution, water pollution, the marine environment, land use, forests, wildlife, solid waste, noise and radioactivity. Also provides data on the underlying pressures on the environment such as energy use, transportation, industrial activity and agriculture.

The State of the Environment. OECD Publications and Information Center, 2001 L St., N.W., Suite 700, Washington, District of Columbia 20036. (202) 785-6323. 1991.

TRADE ASSOCIATIONS AND PROFESSIONAL SOCIETIES

American Cetacean Society. P.O. Box 2639, San Pedro, California 90731. (213) 548-6279.

American Geophysical Union. 2000 Florida Ave., N.W., Washington, District of Columbia 20009. (202) 462-6900.

American Institute of Biological Sciences. 730 11th St., N.W., Washington, District of Columbia 20001-4521. (202) 628-1500.

American Littoral Society. Sandy Hook, Highlands, New Jersey 07732. (908) 291-0055.

American Shore and Beach Preservation Association. P.O. 279, Middletown, California 95461. (707) 987-2385.

American Society of Civil Engineers. 345 East 47th St., New York, New York 10017. (212) 705-7496.

American Society of Naturalists. Department of Ecology and Evolation, State University of New York, Stony Brook, New York 11794. (516) 632-8589.

Bigelow Laboratory for Ocean Sciences, Division of Northeast Research Foundation, Inc. Mckown Point, West Boothbay Harbor, Maine 04575. (207) 633-2173.

Center for Coastal Studies. 59 Commercial St., P.O. Box 1036, Provincetown, Massachusetts 02657. (508) 487-3622.

Cousteau Society. Cousteau Society Membership Center, 930 W 21st St., Norfolk, Virginia 23517. In addition to carrying on the many research projects and explorations made famous by Jacques-Yves Cousteau, the Society publishes educational materials and numerous Technical publications as well as Calypso Log (monthly) and Dolphin Log (bimonthly children's publication).

International Marinelife Alliance. 94 Station St., Suite 645, Hingham, Massachusetts 02043. (617) 383-1209.

National Coalition for Marine Conservation, Inc. P.O. Box 23298, Savannah, Georgia 31403. (912) 234-8062.

National Marine Educators Association. P.O. Box 51215, Pacific Beach, California 93950. (408) 648-4841.

National Marine Manufacturers Association. 401 N. Michigan Ave., Chicago, Illinois 60611. (312) 836-4747.

Save the Bay. 434 Smith St., Providence, Rhode Island 02908. (401) 272-3540.

Sea Grant Association. c/o Dr. Christopher F. D'Elia, Maryland Sea Grant College, 1123 Taliaferro Hall, UMCP, College Park, Maryland 20742. (301) 405-6371.

Sea Shepherd Conservation Society. 1314 2nd St., Santa Monica, California 90401. (213) 394-3198.

Seafloor Geosciences Division. John C. Stennis Space Center, Bay St. Louis, Mississippi 39529-5004. (601) 688-4657.

Society of Marine Port Engineers. P.O. Box 466, Avenel, New Jersey 07001. (908) 381-7673.

The Sounds Conservancy, Inc. c/o Marine Sciences Institute, University of Connecticut, Groton, Connecticut 06340. (203) 445-1868.

MARINE EXPLORATION

ABSTRACTING AND INDEXING SERVICES

Abstracts of Air and Water Conservation Literature. American Petroleum Institute. Central Abstracting and Indexing Service, 275 Madison Avenue, New York, New York 10016. 1972.

Aqualine Abstracts. Water Research Centre. c/o Pergamon Microforms International, Inc., Fairview Park, Elmsford, New York 10523. (914) 592-7720. 1927-. Contains some 8,000 records annually on water and wastewater technology. Covers all aspects of water, wastewater, associated engineering services and the aquatic environment. Over 600 periodicals, as well as books, reports and conference proceedings and other publications from water related institutions worldwide are scanned. Also available online.

ASFA Aquaculture Abstracts. Cambridge Scientific Abstracts, Inc., 5161 River Rd., Bethesda, Maryland 20816. (301) 961-6750. 1984.

Biological Abstracts. BIOSIS, 2100 Arch St., Philadelphia, Pennsylvania 19103-1399. (215) 587-4800. 1927-.

Biological and Agricultural Index. H.W. Wilson Co., 950 University Ave., Bronx, New York 10452. (800) 367-6770. 1916-. Monthly.

Ecology Abstracts. Cambridge Scientific Abstracts, 5161 River Rd., Bethesda, Maryland 20816. (301) 961-6750. Monthly.

Environment Abstracts. Bowker A & I Publishing, 121 Chanlon Rd., New Providence, New Jersey 07974. (908) 464-6800. 1974-.

Environment Index. Environment Information Center, Index Research Department, 124 E. 39th St., New York, New York 10016. 1971-. Annual.

Environmental Information Connection-EIC. Planning Information Program, Dept. of Urban and Regional Planning, University of Illinois, 1003 West Nevada, Urbana, Illinois 61801. (217) 333-1369. Also available online.

Environmental Periodicals Bibliography. Environmental Studies Institute, International Academy at Santa Barbara, 800 Garden St., Suite D, Santa Barbara, California 93101. (805) 965-5010. Also available online.

Geographical Abstracts. London School of Economics, Dept. of Geography, Regency House, 34 Duke St., London, England 1966-. Continued by Geo Abstracts issued in 6 parts: Pt. A. Landforms and the quaternary; Pt. B. Biogeography and Climatology; Pt. C. Economic geography; Pt. D. Social geography and cartography; Pt. E. Sedimentology; Pt. F. Regional and community planning.

Oceanic Abstracts. UMI Data Courier, 620 S. 3rd St., Louisville, Kentucky 40202. (800) 626-2823. Formerly: Oceanic Index and Oceanic Citation Journal.

Science Citation Index. Institute for Scientific Information, 3501 Market St., Philadelphia, Pennsylvania 19104. 1961-.

Sea Grant Abstracts. National Sea Grant Depository, Pell Laboratory Bldg., Bay Campus, University of Rhode Island, Narragansett, Rhode Island 02882. (401) 792-6114. 1986-. Quarterly. Published by the National Sea Grant Programs, this collection includes annual reports, serials and newsletters, charts and maps.

BIBLIOGRAPHIES

Current Contents. Agriculture, Biology and Environmental Sciences. Institute for Scientific Information, 3501 Market St., Philadelphia, Pennsylvania 19104. (800) 523-1857. 1973-. Previous title: Current Contents. Agricultural, Food & Veterinary Sciences. Gives the table of contents of periodicals in the fields of agriculture, biology, environmental and related areas.

EPA Publications Bibliography. U.S. Environmental Protection Agency, Library Systems Branch, 401 M St., SW, Washington, District of Columbia 20460. (202) 260-2090. Quarterly.

New Publications of the Geological Survey. U.S. Department of the Interior, Geological Survey, 119 National

Center, Reston, Virginia 22092. (703) 648-4460. 1984-. Monthly. Bibliography of geological publications and related government documents published by the Geological Survey.

DIRECTORIES

Marine Equipment and Supplies. 5711 S. 86th Circle, Omaha, Nebraska 68127. (402) 593-4600. Annual.

Marine Equipment Catalog. Maritime Activity Reports, Inc., 118 E. 25th St., New York, New York 10010. (212) 477-6700. 1984. Annual.

Marine Industry Fax Directory. National Marine Representatives' Association, Box 957075, Hoffman Estates, Illinois 60195. (708) 213-0606. 1988. Annual.

Marine Products Directory. Underwriters' Laboratory, 333 Pfingston Rd., Northbrook, Illinois 60062-2096. (708) 272-8800. Annual.

ENCYCLOPEDIAS AND DICTIONARIES

Cambridge Encyclopedia of Life Sciences. A. E. Friday and David S. Ingram. Cambridge University Press, 40 W 20th St., New York, New York 10011. (212) 924-3900 or (800) 227-0247. 1985. Includes all topics under biology and ecology.

Dictionary of Environmental Engineering and Related Sciences: English-Spanish, Spanish-English. Jose T. Villate. Ediciones Universal, 3090 SW 8th St., Miami, Florida 33135. (305) 642-3355. 1979.

Encyclopedia of Environmental Science and Engineering. J.R. Pfafflin. Gordon and Breach Science Publishers, Inc., 270 8th Ave., New York, New York 10011. (212) 206-8900. 1992.

The Encyclopedia of Oceanography. Rhodes Whitmore Fairbridge. Reinhold Pub. Co., 115 5th Ave., New York, New York 10003. (212) 254-3232. 1966.

McGraw-Hill Encyclopedia of Environmental Science. Sybil P. Parker. McGraw-Hill Science & Engineering Books, 11 W. 19th St., New York, New York 10011. (212) 337-6010. 1980. Covers ecology, man's influence on nature, and environmental protection.

GENERAL WORKS

Environmental Aspects of Potential Petroleum Exploration and Exploitation in Antarctica. Katherine A. Green Hammond. National Technical Information Service, 5285 Port Royal Rd., Springfield, Virginia 22161. (703) 487-4650. 1982. Forecasting and evaluating risks.

Guide to Information on Research in the Marine Science and Engineering. U.S. Department of Commerce, National Oceanic and Atmospheric Administration, Office of Ocean Engineering, 6010 Executive Blvd., Rockville, Maryland 20852. (301) 443-8344. 1978.

Marine Mineral Exploration. H. Kunzendorf. Elsevier Science Publishing Co., 655 Avenue of the Americas, New York, New York 10010. (212) 984-5800. 1986. Geochemical prospecting, marine mineral resources, ore-deposits, and geophysical methods prospecting.

ONLINE DATA BASES

BIOSIS Previews. BIOSIS, 2100 Arch St., Philadelphia, Pennsylvania 19103-1399. (215) 587-4800. Largest and most comprehensive database of research in the life sciences. Contains citations for nearly 9000 primary research journals, monographs, reviews, symposia, preliminary reports, semi-popular journals, selected institutional reports, government reports and research communications.

Cambridge Scientific Abstracts Life Science–CSAL. Cambridge Scientific Abstracts, 5161 River Rd., Bethesda, Maryland 20816. (301) 961-6750. Provides access to the following abstracting services: "Life Sciences Collection," "Aquatic Sciences and Fisheries Abstracts," "Oceanic Abstracts," and "Pollution Abstracts."

Enviro/Energyline Abstracts Plus. R. R. Bowker Co., 121 Chanlon Rd., New Providence, New Jersey 07974. (908) 464-6800.

Environmental Periodicals Bibliography. National Information Services Corp., Ste. 6, Wyman Towers, 3100 St. Paul St., Baltimore, Maryland 21218. (410)243-0797. Online version of abstract of same name.

MARINELINE. Informationszentrum Rohstoffgewinnwig Geowissenschaften Wasserwirtschaft, Bundesanstalt fuer Geowissenschaften und Rohstoffe, Postfach 510153, Stilleweg 2, Hanover 51, Germany D-3000. 49 (511) 643-2819.

Monthly Catalog of United States Government Publications. U.S. G.P.O., Supt. of Docs., PO Box 371954, Pittsburgh, Pennsylvania 15250-7954. (202) 512-0000.

National Technical Information Service. U.S. Department of Commerce, National Technical Information Service, Office of Data Base Services, 5285 Port Royal Rd., Springfield, Virginia 22161. (703) 487-4807. Bibliographic database of government sponsored research and technical reports.

NODC Data Inventory Data Base. U.S. National Environmental Satellite, Data, and Information Service, National Oceanographic Data Center, 1825 Connecticut Ave., N.W., Suite 406, Washington, District of Columbia 20235. (202) 673-5594. Information on National Oceanographic Data Center holdings.

Oceanic Abstracts. Cambridge Scientific Abstracts, 5161 River Rd., Bethesda, Maryland 20816. (301) 961-6750. Online access.

SCISEARCH. Institute for Scientific Information, University City Science Center, 3501 Market St., Philadelphia, Pennsylvania 19104. (215) 386-0100.

PERIODICALS AND NEWSLETTERS

Analytical Biochemistry. Academic Press, 111 Fifth Ave., New York, New York 10003. (800) 346-8648. Covers biological and chemical topics relating to the environment.

Calypso Log. Cousteau Society Membership Center, 930 W 21st St., Norfolk, Virginia 23517. 6 issues a year. Presents articles for members about Cousteau Society expeditions, ecology, conservation, oceans and marine mammals.

Marine Biology. Springer-Verlag, 175 5th Ave., New York, New York 10010. (212) 461-1500; (800) 777-4643. Sixteen/year. Life in oceans and coastal waters.

Marine Technology. Society of Naval Architects and Marine Engineers, 601 Pavonia Ave., Jersey City, New Jersey 07306. (201) 498-4800. 1964-1987.

RESEARCH CENTERS AND INSTITUTES

Marine Policy Center. Crowell House, Woods Hole Oceanographic Institution, Woods Hole, Massachusetts 02543. (508) 548-1400.

Marine Resources Development Foundation. Koblick Marine Center, 51 Shoreland Drive, P.O. Box 787, Key Largo, Florida 33037. (305) 451-1139.

Marine Resources Research Institute. South Carolina Wildlife and Marine Resources Dept., Charleston, South Carolina 29412. (803) 795-6350.

Marine Science Institute. University of California, Santa Barbara, Santa Barbara, California 93106. (805) 893-3764.

Marine World Africa USA. Marine World Foundation, Marine World Parkway, Vallejo, California 94589. (707) 644-4000.

Northeastern University, Marine Science Center. East Point, Nahant, Massachusetts 01908. (617) 581-7370.

Sea Grant College Program. University of Delaware, 196 South College Avenue, Newark, Delaware 19716. (302) 451-8182.

Sea World Research Institute. 1700 south Shores Road, San Diego, California 92109. (619) 226-3870.

University of Hawaii at Manoa Sea Grant College Program. 1000 Pope Road, MSB 220, Honolulu, Hawaii 96822. (808) 948-7031.

University of Miami, Rosenstiel School of Marine and Atmospheric Science. 4600 Rickenbacker Causeway, Miami, Florida 33149. (305) 361-4000.

University of Rhode Island, International Center for Marine Resource Development (*ICMRD*). 126 Woodward Hall, Kingston, Rhode Island 02881. (401) 792-2479.

University of Rhode Island, Marine Ecosystems Research Laboratory. Graduate School of Oceanography, Narragansett, Rhode Island 02882. (401) 792-6104.

University of Washington, Institute for Marine Studies. College of Ocean and Fishery Science, 3707 Brooklyn Avenue, N.E., Seattle, Washington 98195. (206) 543-7004.

TRADE ASSOCIATIONS AND PROFESSIONAL SOCIETIES

American Institute of Biological Sciences. 730 11th St., N.W., Washington, District of Columbia 20001-4521. (202) 628-1500.

American Society of Naturalists. Department of Ecology and Evolation, State University of New York, Stony Brook, New York 11794. (516) 632-8589.

Cousteau Society. Cousteau Society Membership Center, 930 W 21st St., Norfolk, Virginia 23517. In addition to carrying on the many research projects and explorations

made famous by Jacques-Yves Cousteau, the Society publishes educational materials and numerous Technical publications as well as Calypso Log (monthly) and Dolphin Log (bimonthly children's publication).

Oceanic Society Expeditions. Ft. Mason Center, Bldg. E, San Francisco, California 94123. (415) 441-1106.

Sea Grant Association. c/o Dr. Christopher F. D'Elia, Maryland Sea Grant College, 1123 Taliaferro Hall, UMCP, College Park, Maryland 20742. (301) 405-6371.

MARINE INDUSTRIES

See also: MARINE RESOURCES

ABSTRACTING AND INDEXING SERVICES

Biological and Agricultural Index. H.W. Wilson Co., 950 University Ave., Bronx, New York 10452. (800) 367-6770. 1916-. Monthly.

Environment Abstracts. Bowker A & I Publishing, 121 Chanlon Rd., New Providence, New Jersey 07974. (908) 464-6800. 1974-.

Environment Index. Environment Information Center, Index Research Department, 124 E. 39th St., New York, New York 10016. 1971-. Annual.

Environmental Information Connection–EIC. Planning Information Program, Dept. of Urban and Regional Planning, University of Illinois, 1003 West Nevada, Urbana, Illinois 61801. (217) 333-1369. Also available online.

Environmental Periodicals Bibliography. Environmental Studies Institute, International Academy at Santa Barbara, 800 Garden St., Suite D, Santa Barbara, California 93101. (805) 965-5010. Also available online.

General Science Index. H. W. Wilson Co., 950 University Ave., Bronx, New York 10452. 1978-. Monthly, also issued in annual cumulation. Cumulative subject index to English language periodicals in the subject fields of astronomy, botany, chemistry, earth science, environment and conservation, food and nutrition, genetics, mathematics, medicine and health, microbiology, oceanography, physics, physiology and zoology.

Oceanic Abstracts. UMI Data Courier, 620 S. 3rd St., Louisville, Kentucky 40202. (800) 626-2823. Formerly: Oceanic Index and Oceanic Citation Journal.

Sea Grant Abstracts. National Sea Grant Depository, Pell Laboratory Bldg., Bay Campus, University of Rhode Island, Narragansett, Rhode Island 02882. (401) 792-6114. 1986-. Quarterly. Published by the National Sea Grant Programs, this collection includes annual reports, serials and newsletters, charts and maps.

BIBLIOGRAPHIES

EPA Publications Bibliography. U.S. Environmental Protection Agency, Library Systems Branch, 401 M St., SW, Washington, District of Columbia 20460. (202) 260-2090. Quarterly.

ENCYCLOPEDIAS AND DICTIONARIES

The Encyclopedia of Oceanography. Rhodes Whitmore Fairbridge. Reinhold Pub. Co., 115 5th Ave., New York, New York 10003. (212) 254-3232. 1966.

McGraw-Hill Encyclopedia of Environmental Science. Sybil P. Parker. McGraw-Hill Science & Engineering Books, 11 W. 19th St., New York, New York 10011. (212) 337-6010. 1980. Covers ecology, man's influence on nature, and environmental protection.

ONLINE DATA BASES

Enviro/Energyline Abstracts Plus. R. R. Bowker Co., 121 Chanlon Rd., New Providence, New Jersey 07974. (908) 464-6800.

Environmental Periodicals Bibliography. National Information Services Corp., Ste. 6, Wyman Towers, 3100 St. Paul St., Baltimore, Maryland 21218. (410)243-0797. Online version of abstract of same name.

Monthly Catalog of United States Government Publications. U.S. G.P.O., Supt. of Docs., PO Box 371954, Pittsburgh, Pennsylvania 15250-7954. (202) 512-0000.

National Technical Information Service. U.S. Department of Commerce, National Technical Information Service, Office of Data Base Services, 5285 Port Royal Rd., Springfield, Virginia 22161. (703) 487-4807. Bibliographic database of government sponsored research and technical reports.

MARINE MAMMALS

See also: FISH AND FISHERIES; GREENPEACE; WHALING

ABSTRACTING AND INDEXING SERVICES

Applied Ecology Abstracts Studies in Renewable Natural Resources. Information Retrieval Ltd., 1911 Jefferson Davis Highway, Arlington, Virginia 22202. 1975-. Monthly.

Aqualine Abstracts. Water Research Centre. c/o Pergamon Microforms International, Inc., Fairview Park, Elmsford, New York 10523. (914) 592-7720. 1927-. Contains some 8,000 records annually on water and wastewater technology. Covers all aspects of water, wastewater, associated engineering services and the aquatic environment. Over 600 periodicals, as well as books, reports and conference proceedings and other publications from water related institutions worldwide are scanned. Also available online.

ASFA Aquaculture Abstracts. Cambridge Scientific Abstracts, Inc., 5161 River Rd., Bethesda, Maryland 20816. (301) 961-6750. 1984.

Biological Abstracts. BIOSIS, 2100 Arch St., Philadelphia, Pennsylvania 19103-1399. (215) 587-4800. 1927-.

Biological and Agricultural Index. H.W. Wilson Co., 950 University Ave., Bronx, New York 10452. (800) 367-6770. 1916-. Monthly.

Biology Digest. Data Courier, Plexus Pub Inc., 143 Old Marlton Pike, Medford, New Jersey 08055. 1974-. Monthly. Abstracts biology periodicals.

Current Advances in Ecological and Environmental Science. Pergamon Microforms International, Inc., Fairview Park, Elmsford, New York 10523. (914) 592-7720. 1989-. Monthly. Current literature searching service includingjournals, reports, abstracts, etc. This service is available online as part of the CABS database on the hosts BRS and ORBIT search service.

Ecological Abstracts. Geo Abstracts Ltd. Elsevier Applied Science, Crown House, Linton Rd., Barking, England IG 11 8JU. 1974-. Derived from over 600 leading ecological and environmental journals, plus books, conference proceedings, reports and theses.

Ecology Abstracts. Cambridge Scientific Abstracts, 5161 River Rd., Bethesda, Maryland 20816. (301) 961-6750. Monthly.

Environment Abstracts. Bowker A & I Publishing, 121 Chanlon Rd., New Providence, New Jersey 07974. (908) 464-6800. 1974-.

Environment Index. Environment Information Center, Index Research Department, 124 E. 39th St., New York, New York 10016. 1971-. Annual.

Environmental Information Connection–EIC. Planning Information Program, Dept. of Urban and Regional Planning, University of Illinois, 1003 West Nevada, Urbana, Illinois 61801. (217) 333-1369. Also available online.

Environmental Periodicals Bibliography. Environmental Studies Institute, International Academy at Santa Barbara, 800 Garden St., Suite D, Santa Barbara, California 93101. (805) 965-5010. Also available online.

General Science Index. H. W. Wilson Co., 950 University Ave., Bronx, New York 10452. 1978-. Monthly, also issued in annual cumulation. Cumulative subject index to English language periodicals in the subject fields of astronomy, botany, chemistry, earth science, environment and conservation, food and nutrition, genetics, mathematics, medicine and health, microbiology, oceanography, physics, physiology and zoology.

Geographical Abstracts. London School of Economics, Dept. of Geography, Regency House, 34 Duke St., London, England 1966-. Continued by Geo Abstracts issued in 6 parts: Pt. A. Landforms and the quaternary; Pt. B. Biogeography and Climatology; Pt. C. Economic geography; Pt. D. Social geography and cartography; Pt. E. Sedimentology; Pt. F. Regional and community planning.

Index to Scientific Book Contents. Institute for Scientific Information, 3501 Market St., Philadelphia, Pennsylvania 19104. (800) 523-1857. 1985-. Annual. Gives contents of science books published.

Multimedia Index to Ecology. National Information Center for Educational Media, University of Southern California, Los Angeles, California 90007.

Oceanic Abstracts. UMI Data Courier, 620 S. 3rd St., Louisville, Kentucky 40202. (800) 626-2823. Formerly: Oceanic Index and Oceanic Citation Journal.

Science Citation Index. Institute for Scientific Information, 3501 Market St., Philadelphia, Pennsylvania 19104. 1961-.

Sea Grant Abstracts. National Sea Grant Depository, Pell Laboratory Bldg., Bay Campus, University of Rhode Island, Narragansett, Rhode Island 02882. (401) 792-

6114. 1986-. Quarterly. Published by the National Sea Grant Programs, this collection includes annual reports, serials and newsletters, charts and maps.

ALMANACS AND YEARBOOKS

Dolphins, Porpoises and Whales of the World: The IUCN Red Data Book. M. Klinowska. The World Conservation Union, IUCN Publications Services Unit, 181a Huntingdon Road, Cambridge, England CB3 0DJ. (0223) 277894. 1991. Reviews the status of all cetacean species. Detailed accounts are provided for each species, describing their distribution, population, threats, and the conservation measures required to ensure their survival.

BIBLIOGRAPHIES

Current Contents. Agriculture, Biology and Environmental Sciences. Institute for Scientific Information, 3501 Market St., Philadelphia, Pennsylvania 19104. (800) 523-1857. 1973-. Previous title: Current Contents. Agricultural, Food & Veterinary Sciences. Gives the table of contents of periodicals in the fields of agriculture, biology, environmental and related areas.

EPA Publications Bibliography. U.S. Environmental Protection Agency, Library Systems Branch, 401 M St., SW, Washington, District of Columbia 20460. (202) 260-2090. Quarterly.

ENCYCLOPEDIAS AND DICTIONARIES

The Encyclopedia of Animal Ecology. Peter D. Moore. Facts on File, Inc., 460 Park Ave. S., New York, New York 10016. (212) 683-2244. 1987.

Encyclopedia of Human Biology. Renato Dulbecco, ed. Academic Press, c/o Harcourt Brace Jovanovich Inc., 6277 Sea Harbor Dr., Orlando, Florida 32887. (800) 346-8648. 1991. Eight volumes.

Encyclopedia of Marine Invertebrates. Jerry G. Walls, ed. TFH Publications, 1 TFH Plaza, Union and 3rd Plaza, Neptune, New Jersey 07753. (908) 998-8400. 1982.

The Encyclopedia of Oceanography. Rhodes Whitmore Fairbridge. Reinhold Pub. Co., 115 5th Ave., New York, New York 10003. (212) 254-3232. 1966.

McGraw-Hill Encyclopedia of Environmental Science. Sybil P. Parker. McGraw-Hill Science & Engineering Books, 11 W. 19th St., New York, New York 10011. (212) 337-6010. 1980. Covers ecology, man's influence on nature, and environmental protection.

McGraw-Hill Encyclopedia of Science and Technology. McGraw-Hill, 1221 Avenue of the Americas, New York, New York 10020. (212) 512-2000 or (800) 262-4729. 1992. Seventh edition. Issued in multiple volumes including index. Includes all science and technology broad subject areas.

The Times Atlas and Encyclopedia of the Sea. A.D. Couper. Harper & Row, 10 E. 53rd St., New York, New York 10022. (212) 207-7000; (800) 242-7737. 1990.

GENERAL WORKS

International Regulation of Whaling. Patricia Birnie. Oceana Publications Inc., 75 Main St., Dobbs Ferry, New York 10522. (914) 693-8100. 1985. A chronological account of the development of international law pertaining to the regulation of whaling. Traces the growing relationship of the regulation of whaling to the development of other relevant laws and institutions for the conservation of migratory species.

A Natural History of Marine Mammals. Victor B. Scheffer. Scribner Educational Publishers, 866 3rd Ave., New York, New York 10022. (212) 702-2000. 1976.

Sea Mammals and Oil: Confronting the Risks. Joseph R. Geraci and David J. St. Aubin, eds. Academic Press, c/o Harcourt Brace Jovanovich Inc., 6277 Sea Harbor Dr., Orlando, Florida 32887. (800) 346-8648. 1990. Explores the effects of spilled petroleum on seals, whales, dolphins, sea otters, polar bears, and manatees, which inhabit the coastal water of North America where spills occur. They consider the constant low-level leakage of urban and industrial oil, large spills, and long-term as well as immediate effects.

Sharks in Question: The Smithsonian Answer Book. Victor G. Springer and Joy P. Gold. Smithsonian Institution Press, 470 L'Enfant Plaza #7100, Washington, District of Columbia 20560. (800) 782-4612. 1989.

An Updated World Review of Interactions between Marine Mammals and Fisheries. Simon P. Northridge. Food and Agriculture Organization of the United Nations, Via delle Terme di Caracalla, Rome, Italy 00100. 61 0181-FA01. 1991.

GOVERNMENTAL ORGANIZATIONS

National Marine Fisheries Service. 1825 Connecticut Ave., N.W., Washington, District of Columbia 20235. (202) 673-5450.

HANDBOOKS AND MANUALS

Handbook of Marine Mammals. Sam H. Ridgway. Academic Press, c/o Harcourt Brace Jovanovich Inc., 6277 Sea Harbor Dr., Orlando, Florida 32887. (800) 346-8648. 1989. Covers walruses, sea lions, fur seals, sea otters, seals, and the sirenians and baleen whales.

ONLINE DATA BASES

BIOSIS Previews. BIOSIS, 2100 Arch St., Philadelphia, Pennsylvania 19103-1399. (215) 587-4800. Largest and most comprehensive database of research in the life sciences. Contains citations for nearly 9000 primary research journals, monographs, reviews, symposia, preliminary reports, semi-popular journals, selected institutional reports, government reports and research communications.

Enviro/Energyline Abstracts Plus. R. R. Bowker Co., 121 Chanlon Rd., New Providence, New Jersey 07974. (908) 464-6800.

Environmental Periodicals Bibliography. National Information Services Corp., Ste. 6, Wyman Towers, 3100 St. Paul St., Baltimore, Maryland 21218. (410)243-0797. Online version of abstract of same name.

Monthly Catalog of United States Government Publications. U.S. G.P.O., Supt. of Docs., PO Box 371954, Pittsburgh, Pennsylvania 15250-7954. (202) 512-0000.

National Technical Information Service. U.S. Department of Commerce, National Technical Information Service, Office of Data Base Services, 5285 Port Royal Rd., Springfield, Virginia 22161. (703) 487-4807. Biblio-

graphic database of government sponsored research and technical reports.

Oceanic Abstracts. Cambridge Scientific Abstracts, 5161 River Rd., Bethesda, Maryland 20816. (301) 961-6750. Online access.

SCISEARCH. Institute for Scientific Information, University City Science Center, 3501 Market St., Philadelphia, Pennsylvania 19104. (215) 386-0100.

PERIODICALS AND NEWSLETTERS

Calypso Log. Cousteau Society Membership Center, 930 W 21st St., Norfolk, Virginia 23517. 6 issues a year. Presents articles for members about Cousteau Society expeditions, ecology, conservation, oceans and marine mammals.

Dolphin Log. Cousteau Society Inc., 8440 Santa Monica Blvd., Los Angeles, California 90069. (804) 627-1144. Six issues a year. Covers marine animals, the oceans, science, natural history, and the arts as they relate to global water system. Magazine is for ages 7-15.

Marine Biology. Springer-Verlag, 175 5th Ave., New York, New York 10010. (212) 461-1500; (800) 777-4643. Sixteen/year. Life in oceans and coastal waters.

Marine Conservation News. Center for Marine Conservation, 1725 Desales St., N.W., Suite 500, Washington, District of Columbia 20036. (202) 429-5609. Quarterly. Marine conservation issues: whales, seals, sea turtles, and habitat.

Marine Mammal News. Nautilus Press Inc., National Press Bldg., 1056 National Press Bldg., Washington, District of Columbia 20045. 1971-. Monthly.

Marine Mammal Science. Society for Marine Mammology, Lawrence, Kansas Quarterly. Covers marine mammal fossil and marine mammals.

RESEARCH CENTERS AND INSTITUTES

Archie Carr Center for Sea Turtle Research. University of Florida, Department of Zoology, Gainesville, Florida 32611. (904) 392-5194.

Center for Marine Conservation. 1725 DeSales St., NW, Suite 500, Washington, District of Columbia 20036. (202) 429-5609.

Joseph M. Long Marine Laboratory. University of California, Santa Cruz, 100 Shaffer, Santa Cruz, California 95060. (408) 459-2464.

Laboratory for Marine Animal Husbandry. University of Connecticut, Noank, Connecticut 06340.

Marine Sciences Institute. University of Connecticut at Avery Point, Groton, Connecticut 06340. (203) 445-4714.

Massachusetts Institute of Technology, MIT Sea Grant College Program. E38-300, 292 Main St., Cambridge, Massachusetts 02139. (617) 253-7041.

Project Circle. Marine World Africa USA, Marine World Parkway, Vallejo, California 94589. (707) 644-4000.

University of Hawaii at Manoa Kewalo Basin Marine Mammal Laboratory. 1129 Ala Moana Boulevard, Honolulu, Hawaii 96814. (808) 538-0067.

University of Maine, Center for Marine Studies. 14 Coburn Hall, Orono, Maine 04469. (207) 581-1435.

STATISTICS SOURCES

Annual Report of the Marine Mammal Commission. U.S. G.P.O., Washington, District of Columbia 20401. (202) 512-0000. Annual. Research on marine mammals and actions for marine mammal conservation, including international agreements.

Marine Fisheries Review. U.S. G.P.O, Washington, District of Columbia 20402-9325. (202) 512-0000. Quarterly. Marine fishery resources, development, and management. Covers fish, shellfish, and marine mammal populations.

Mass Mortality of Bottlenose Dolphins. U.S. House. Committee on Merchant Marine and Fisheries. U.S. G.P.O., Washington, District of Columbia 20401. (202) 512-0000. 1989. Dolphin deaths caused by brevetoxin produced by red-tide algae.

Synthesis of Effects of Oil on Marine Mammals. U.S. Dept. of Interior. Mineral Management Service. National Technical Information Service, 5285 Port Royal Road, Springfield, Virginia 22161. (703) 487-4650. 1988. Impacts of spills and spill-treating agents on marine and arctic land mammals.

World Resources. World Resources Institute. 1709 New York Ave., N.W., Washington, District of Columbia 20006. (202) 638-6300. Annual. Statistical and textual analysis of world's natural resources and the effects of growth-caused environmental pollution.

TRADE ASSOCIATIONS AND PROFESSIONAL SOCIETIES

American Institute of Biological Sciences. 730 11th St., N.W., Washington, District of Columbia 20001-4521. (202) 628-1500.

American Society of Naturalists. Department of Ecology and Evolation, State University of New York, Stony Brook, New York 11794. (516) 632-8589.

Center for Whale Research. P.O. Box 1577, Friday Harbor, Washington 98250. (206) 378-5835.

Cousteau Society. Cousteau Society Membership Center, 930 W 21st St., Norfolk, Virginia 23517. In addition to carrying on the many research projects and explorations made famous by Jacques-Yves Cousteau, the Society publishes educational materials and numerous Technical publications as well as Calypso Log (monthly) and Dolphin Log (bimonthly children's publication).

Pacific Whale Foundation. Kealia Beach Plaza, Ste. 25, 101 N. Kihei Rd., Kihei, Hawaii 96753. (808) 879-8811.

The Society for Marine Mammology. National Marine Fisheries Service, SW Fisheries Center, PO Box 271, La Jolla, California 92038. (619) 546-7096.

MARINE ORGANISMS

ABSTRACTING AND INDEXING SERVICES

Applied Ecology Abstracts Studies in Renewable Natural Resources. Information Retrieval Ltd., 1911 Jefferson

Davis Highway, Arlington, Virginia 22202. 1975-. Monthly.

Aqualine Abstracts. Water Research Centre. c/o Pergamon Microforms International, Inc., Fairview Park, Elmsford, New York 10523. (914) 592-7720. 1927-. Contains some 8,000 records annually on water and wastewater technology. Covers all aspects of water, wastewater, associated engineering services and the aquatic environment. Over 600 periodicals, as well as books, reports and conference proceedings and other publications from water related institutions worldwide are scanned. Also available online.

ASFA Aquaculture Abstracts. Cambridge Scientific Abstracts, Inc., 5161 River Rd., Bethesda, Maryland 20816. (301) 961-6750. 1984.

Biological Abstracts. BIOSIS, 2100 Arch St., Philadelphia, Pennsylvania 19103-1399. (215) 587-4800. 1927-.

Biological and Agricultural Index. H.W. Wilson Co., 950 University Ave., Bronx, New York 10452. (800) 367-6770. 1916-. Monthly.

Current Advances in Ecological and Environmental Science. Pergamon Microforms International, Inc., Fairview Park, Elmsford, New York 10523. (914) 592-7720. 1989-. Monthly. Current literature searching service includingjournals, reports, abstracts, etc. This service is available online as part of the CABS database on the hosts BRS and ORBIT search service.

Ecological Abstracts. Geo Abstracts Ltd. Elsevier Applied Science, Crown House, Linton Rd., Barking, England IG 11 8JU. 1974-. Derived from over 600 leading ecological and environmental journals, plus books, conference proceedings, reports and theses.

Ecology Abstracts. Cambridge Scientific Abstracts, 5161 River Rd., Bethesda, Maryland 20816. (301) 961-6750. Monthly.

Environment Abstracts. Bowker A & I Publishing, 121 Chanlon Rd., New Providence, New Jersey 07974. (908) 464-6800. 1974-.

Environment Index. Environment Information Center, Index Research Department, 124 E. 39th St., New York, New York 10016. 1971-. Annual.

Environmental Information Connection–EIC. Planning Information Program, Dept. of Urban and Regional Planning, University of Illinois, 1003 West Nevada, Urbana, Illinois 61801. (217) 333-1369. Also available online.

Environmental Periodicals Bibliography. Environmental Studies Institute, International Academy at Santa Barbara, 800 Garden St., Suite D, Santa Barbara, California 93101. (805) 965-5010. Also available online.

General Science Index. H. W. Wilson Co., 950 University Ave., Bronx, New York 10452. 1978-. Monthly, also issued in annual cumulation. Cumulative subject index to English language periodicals in the subject fields of astronomy, botany, chemistry, earth science, environment and conservation, food and nutrition, genetics, mathematics, medicine and health, microbiology, oceanography, physics, physiology and zoology.

Geographical Abstracts. London School of Economics, Dept. of Geography, Regency House, 34 Duke St., London, England 1966-. Continued by Geo Abstracts issued in 6 parts: Pt. A. Landforms and the quaternary;

Pt. B. Biogeography and Climatology; Pt. C. Economic geography; Pt. D. Social geography and cartography; Pt. E. Sedimentology; Pt. F. Regional and community planning.

Index to Scientific Book Contents. Institute for Scientific Information, 3501 Market St., Philadelphia, Pennsylvania 19104. (800) 523-1857. 1985-. Annual. Gives contents of science books published.

Multimedia Index to Ecology. National Information Center for Educational Media, University of Southern California, Los Angeles, California 90007.

Oceanic Abstracts. UMI Data Courier, 620 S. 3rd St., Louisville, Kentucky 40202. (800) 626-2823. Formerly: Oceanic Index and Oceanic Citation Journal.

Pollution Abstracts. Cambridge Scientific Abstracts, 5161 River Rd., Bethesda, Maryland 20816. (301) 961-6750. Six/year. Indexes worldwide technical literature on environmental pollution. Covers air pollution, marine and freshwater pollution, sewage and wastewater treatment, waste management, toxicology and health, noise pollution, radiation, land pollution, and environmental policies, programs, legislation, and education. Also available online.

Science Citation Index. Institute for Scientific Information, 3501 Market St., Philadelphia, Pennsylvania 19104. 1961-.

BIBLIOGRAPHIES

Current Contents. Agriculture, Biology and Environmental Sciences. Institute for Scientific Information, 3501 Market St., Philadelphia, Pennsylvania 19104. (800) 523-1857. 1973-. Previous title: Current Contents. Agricultural, Food & Veterinary Sciences. Gives the table of contents of periodicals in the fields of agriculture, biology, environmental and related areas.

EPA Publications Bibliography. U.S. Environmental Protection Agency, Library Systems Branch, 401 M St., SW, Washington, District of Columbia 20460. (202) 260-2090. Quarterly.

ENCYCLOPEDIAS AND DICTIONARIES

Cambridge Encyclopedia of Life Sciences. A. E. Friday and David S. Ingram. Cambridge University Press, 40 W 20th St., New York, New York 10011. (212) 924-3900 or (800) 227-0247. 1985. Includes all topics under biology and ecology.

The Encyclopedia of Animal Ecology. Peter D. Moore. Facts on File, Inc., 460 Park Ave. S., New York, New York 10016. (212) 683-2244. 1987.

Encyclopedia of Marine Invertebrates. Jerry G. Walls, ed. TFH Publications, 1 TFH Plaza, Union and 3rd Plaza, Neptune, New Jersey 07753. (908) 998-8400. 1982.

The Encyclopedia of Oceanography. Rhodes Whitmore Fairbridge. Reinhold Pub. Co., 115 5th Ave., New York, New York 10003. (212) 254-3232. 1966.

McGraw-Hill Encyclopedia of Environmental Science. Sybil P. Parker. McGraw-Hill Science & Engineering Books, 11 W. 19th St., New York, New York 10011. (212) 337-6010. 1980. Covers ecology, man's influence on nature, and environmental protection.

The Times Atlas and Encyclopedia of the Sea. A.D. Couper. Harper & Row, 10 E. 53rd St., New York, New York 10022. (212) 207-7000; (800) 242-7737. 1990.

GENERAL WORKS

Marine Organisms as Indicators. Dorothy F. Soule. Springer-Verlag, 175 5th Ave., New York, New York 10010. (212) 460-1500. 1988. Environmental aspects of marine ecology and marine pollution.

Methods for Measuring the Acute Toxicity of Effluents to Freshwater and Marine Organisms. William H. Peltier. Environmental Monitoring and Support Laboratory, Office of Research and Development, U.S. Environmental Protection Agency, 401 M St. SW, Washington, District of Columbia 20024. (202) 260-2090. 1985. Measurement of water pollution in the United States.

Pollutant Effects on Marine Organisms. C. S. Giam. Lexington Books, 866 3rd Ave., New York, New York 10022. (212) 702-2000. 1977. Effect of water pollution on aquatic animals.

Trace Metal Concentrations in Marine Organisms. Ronald Eisler. Pergamon Microforms International, Inc., Fairview Park, Elmsford, New York 10523. (914) 592-7720. 1981. Physiology of marine flora and fauna as well as trace elements in the body.

GOVERNMENTAL ORGANIZATIONS

National Marine Fisheries Service. 1825 Connecticut Ave., N.W., Washington, District of Columbia 20235. (202) 673-5450.

ONLINE DATA BASES

Aquatic Information Retrieval. Chemical Information Systems, Inc., 7215 York Rd., Baltimore, Maryland 21212. (301) 321-8440. Toxic effects of more than 5000 chemicals on 2400 freshwater and saltwater organisms, with the exclusion of bacteria, birds, and aquatic mammals.

BIOSIS Previews. BIOSIS, 2100 Arch St., Philadelphia, Pennsylvania 19103-1399. (215) 587-4800. Largest and most comprehensive database of research in the life sciences. Contains citations for nearly 9000 primary research journals, monographs, reviews, symposia, preliminary reports, semi-popular journals, selected institutional reports, government reports and research communications.

Cambridge Scientific Abstracts Life Science–CSAL. Cambridge Scientific Abstracts, 5161 River Rd., Bethesda, Maryland 20816. (301) 961-6750. Provides access to the following abstracting services: "Life Sciences Collection," "Aquatic Sciences and Fisheries Abstracts," "Oceanic Abstracts," and "Pollution Abstracts."

Enviro/Energyline Abstracts Plus. R. R. Bowker Co., 121 Chanlon Rd., New Providence, New Jersey 07974. (908) 464-6800.

Environmental Periodicals Bibliography. National Information Services Corp., Ste. 6, Wyman Towers, 3100 St. Paul St., Baltimore, Maryland 21218. (410)243-0797. Online version of abstract of same name.

Oceanic Abstracts. Cambridge Scientific Abstracts, 5161 River Rd., Bethesda, Maryland 20816. (301) 961-6750. Online access.

SCISEARCH. Institute for Scientific Information, University City Science Center, 3501 Market St., Philadelphia, Pennsylvania 19104. (215) 386-0100.

PERIODICALS AND NEWSLETTERS

Calypso Log. Cousteau Society Membership Center, 930 W 21st St., Norfolk, Virginia 23517. 6 issues a year. Presents articles for members about Cousteau Society expeditions, ecology, conservation, oceans and marine mammals.

Marine Biology. Springer-Verlag, 175 5th Ave., New York, New York 10010. (212) 461-1500; (800) 777-4643. Sixteen/year. Life in oceans and coastal waters.

Marine Bulletin. National Coalition for Marine Conservation, Box 23298, Savannah, Georgia 31403. (912) 234-8062. Monthly. Marine fisheries, biological research, marine environmental pollution, and the prevention of the over-exploitation of ocean fish.

Marine Ecology. Paul Parey Scientific Publishers, P.O. Box 236, 150 East 27th Street, Suite 1A, New York, New York 10016. (212) 730-0518. Quarterly. Information on specific organisms in the environment.

Marine Resource Economics. Taylor & Francis, 1900 Frost Road, Suite 101, Bristol, Pennsylvania 19007. (800) 821-8312. Quarterly. Issues related to the economics of marine resources.

RESEARCH CENTERS AND INSTITUTES

Center for Marine Conservation. 1725 DeSales St., NW, Suite 500, Washington, District of Columbia 20036. (202) 429-5609.

Chelonia Institute. P.O. Box 9174, Arlington, Virginia 22209. (703) 524-4900.

Joseph M. Long Marine Laboratory. University of California, Santa Cruz, 100 Shaffer, Santa Cruz, California 95060. (408) 459-2464.

Marine World Africa USA. Marine World Foundation, Marine World Parkway, Vallejo, California 94589. (707) 644-4000.

University of Maryland, Center of Marine Biotechnology. 600 East Lombard Street, Baltimore, Maryland 21202. (301) 783-4800.

University of Maryland, Sea Grant College. 1123 Taliaferro Hall, College Park, Maryland 20742. (301) 405-6371.

University of Miami, Rosenstiel School of Marine and Atmospheric Science. 4600 Rickenbacker Causeway, Miami, Florida 33149. (305) 361-4000.

University of Texas at Austin, Marine Science Institute. Port Aransas, Texas 78373. (512) 749-6711.

STATISTICS SOURCES

Synthesis of Effects of Oil on Marine Mammals. U.S. Dept. of Interior. Mineral Management Service. National Technical Information Service, 5285 Port Royal Road, Springfield, Virginia 22161. (703) 487-4650. 1988. Impacts of spills and spill-treating agents on marine and arctic land mammals.

TRADE ASSOCIATIONS AND PROFESSIONAL SOCIETIES

American Institute of Biological Sciences. 730 11th St., N.W., Washington, District of Columbia 20001-4521. (202) 628-1500.

American Society of Naturalists. Department of Ecology and Evolation, State University of New York, Stony Brook, New York 11794. (516) 632-8589.

Cousteau Society. Cousteau Society Membership Center, 930 W 21st St., Norfolk, Virginia 23517. In addition to carrying on the many research projects and explorations made famous by Jacques-Yves Cousteau, the Society publishes educational materials and numerous Technical publications as well as Calypso Log (monthly) and Dolphin Log (bimonthly children's publication).

The Society for Marine Mammology. National Marine Fisheries Service, SW Fisheries Center, PO Box 271, La Jolla, California 92038. (619) 546-7096.

MARINE PLANTS

ABSTRACTING AND INDEXING SERVICES

Applied Ecology Abstracts Studies in Renewable Natural Resources. Information Retrieval Ltd., 1911 Jefferson Davis Highway, Arlington, Virginia 22202. 1975-. Monthly.

Aqualine Abstracts. Water Research Centre. c/o Pergamon Microforms International, Inc., Fairview Park, Elmsford, New York 10523. (914) 592-7720. 1927-. Contains some 8,000 records annually on water and wastewater technology. Covers all aspects of water, wastewater, associated engineering services and the aquatic environment. Over 600 periodicals, as well as books, reports and conference proceedings and other publications from water related institutions worldwide are scanned. Also available online.

Biological Abstracts. BIOSIS, 2100 Arch St., Philadelphia, Pennsylvania 19103-1399. (215) 587-4800. 1927-.

Biological and Agricultural Index. H.W. Wilson Co., 950 University Ave., Bronx, New York 10452. (800) 367-6770. 1916-. Monthly.

Current Advances in Ecological and Environmental Science. Pergamon Microforms International, Inc., Fairview Park, Elmsford, New York 10523. (914) 592-7720. 1989-. Monthly. Current literature searching service includingjournals, reports, abstracts, etc. This service is available online as part of the CABS database on the hosts BRS and ORBIT search service.

Ecological Abstracts. Geo Abstracts Ltd. Elsevier Applied Science, Crown House, Linton Rd., Barking, England IG 11 8JU. 1974-. Derived from over 600 leading ecological and environmental journals, plus books, conference proceedings, reports and theses.

Ecology Abstracts. Cambridge Scientific Abstracts, 5161 River Rd., Bethesda, Maryland 20816. (301) 961-6750. Monthly.

Environment Abstracts. Bowker A & I Publishing, 121 Chanlon Rd., New Providence, New Jersey 07974. (908) 464-6800. 1974-.

Environment Index. Environment Information Center, Index Research Department, 124 E. 39th St., New York, New York 10016. 1971-. Annual.

Environmental Information Connection–EIC. Planning Information Program, Dept. of Urban and Regional Planning, University of Illinois, 1003 West Nevada, Urbana, Illinois 61801. (217) 333-1369. Also available online.

Environmental Periodicals Bibliography. Environmental Studies Institute, International Academy at Santa Barbara, 800 Garden St., Suite D, Santa Barbara, California 93101. (805) 965-5010. Also available online.

General Science Index. H. W. Wilson Co., 950 University Ave., Bronx, New York 10452. 1978-. Monthly, also issued in annual cumulation. Cumulative subject index to English language periodicals in the subject fields of astronomy, botany, chemistry, earth science, environment and conservation, food and nutrition, genetics, mathematics, medicine and health, microbiology, oceanography, physics, physiology and zoology.

Geographical Abstracts. London School of Economics, Dept. of Geography, Regency House, 34 Duke St., London, England 1966-. Continued by Geo Abstracts issued in 6 parts: Pt. A. Landforms and the quaternary; Pt. B. Biogeography and Climatology; Pt. C. Economic geography; Pt. D. Social geography and cartography; Pt. E. Sedimentology; Pt. F. Regional and community planning.

Index to Scientific Book Contents. Institute for Scientific Information, 3501 Market St., Philadelphia, Pennsylvania 19104. (800) 523-1857. 1985-. Annual. Gives contents of science books published.

Multimedia Index to Ecology. National Information Center for Educational Media, University of Southern California, Los Angeles, California 90007.

Oceanic Abstracts. UMI Data Courier, 620 S. 3rd St., Louisville, Kentucky 40202. (800) 626-2823. Formerly: Oceanic Index and Oceanic Citation Journal.

Science Citation Index. Institute for Scientific Information, 3501 Market St., Philadelphia, Pennsylvania 19104. 1961-.

BIBLIOGRAPHIES

Current Contents. Agriculture, Biology and Environmental Sciences. Institute for Scientific Information, 3501 Market St., Philadelphia, Pennsylvania 19104. (800) 523-1857. 1973-. Previous title: Current Contents. Agricultural, Food & Veterinary Sciences. Gives the table of contents of periodicals in the fields of agriculture, biology, environmental and related areas.

EPA Publications Bibliography. U.S. Environmental Protection Agency, Library Systems Branch, 401 M St., SW, Washington, District of Columbia 20460. (202) 260-2090. Quarterly.

ENCYCLOPEDIAS AND DICTIONARIES

Cambridge Encyclopedia of Life Sciences. A. E. Friday and David S. Ingram. Cambridge University Press, 40 W 20th St., New York, New York 10011. (212) 924-3900 or (800) 227-0247. 1985. Includes all topics under biology and ecology.

The Encyclopedia of Oceanography. Rhodes Whitmore Fairbridge. Reinhold Pub. Co., 115 5th Ave., New York, New York 10003. (212) 254-3232. 1966.

McGraw-Hill Encyclopedia of Environmental Science. Sybil P. Parker. McGraw-Hill Science & Engineering Books, 11 W. 19th St., New York, New York 10011. (212) 337-6010. 1980. Covers ecology, man's influence on nature, and environmental protection.

The Times Atlas and Encyclopedia of the Sea. A.D. Couper. Harper & Row, 10 E. 53rd St., New York, New York 10022. (212) 207-7000; (800) 242-7737. 1990.

GENERAL WORKS

The Biology of Marine Plants. M. J. Dring. E. Arnold, 41 Bedford Sq., London, England 1982. Deals with marine flora.

Diversity of Marine Plants. Bobby N. Irby. University Press of Mississippi, 3825 Ridgewood Rd., Jackson, Mississippi 39211. (601) 982-6205. 1984. Various marine plants, their adaptive characteristics, and the interdependence of flora and fauna.

Marine Invertebrates and Plants of the Living Reef. Patrick Lynn Colin. TFH Publications, 1 TFH Plaza, Neptune City, New Jersey 07753. (908) 988-8400. 1988. Identification of coral reef flora and marine invertebrates.

The Physiological Ecology of Seaweeds. Christopher S. Lobban. Cambridge University Press, 40 W. 20th St., New York, New York 10011. (212) 924-3900. 1985.

HANDBOOKS AND MANUALS

Methods for Toxicity Tests of Single Substances and Liquid Complex Wastes With Marine Unicellular Algae. Gerald E. Walsh. Environmental Protection Agency, U.S. Environmental Research Laboratory, 401 M St. SW, Washington, District of Columbia 20460. (202) 260-2090. 1988. Deals with the impact of factory and trade waste on the marine environment, especially on algae and other biological forms.

ONLINE DATA BASES

BIOSIS Previews. BIOSIS, 2100 Arch St., Philadelphia, Pennsylvania 19103-1399. (215) 587-4800. Largest and most comprehensive database of research in the life sciences. Contains citations for nearly 9000 primary research journals, monographs, reviews, symposia, preliminary reports, semi-popular journals, selected institutional reports, government reports and research communications.

Cambridge Scientific Abstracts Life Science–CSAL. Cambridge Scientific Abstracts, 5161 River Rd., Bethesda, Maryland 20816. (301) 961-6750. Provides access to the following abstracting services: "Life Sciences Collection," "Aquatic Sciences and Fisheries Abstracts," "Oceanic Abstracts," and "Pollution Abstracts."

Enviro/Energyline Abstracts Plus. R. R. Bowker Co., 121 Chanlon Rd., New Providence, New Jersey 07974. (908) 464-6800.

Environmental Periodicals Bibliography. National Information Services Corp., Ste. 6, Wyman Towers, 3100 St. Paul St., Baltimore, Maryland 21218. (410)243-0797. Online version of abstract of same name.

Oceanic Abstracts. Cambridge Scientific Abstracts, 5161 River Rd., Bethesda, Maryland 20816. (301) 961-6750. Online access.

SCISEARCH. Institute for Scientific Information, University City Science Center, 3501 Market St., Philadelphia, Pennsylvania 19104. (215) 386-0100.

PERIODICALS AND NEWSLETTERS

Calypso Log. Cousteau Society Membership Center, 930 W 21st St., Norfolk, Virginia 23517. 6 issues a year. Presents articles for members about Cousteau Society expeditions, ecology, conservation, oceans and marine mammals.

Marine Biology. Springer-Verlag, 175 5th Ave., New York, New York 10010. (212) 461-1500; (800) 777-4643. Sixteen/year. Life in oceans and coastal waters.

TRADE ASSOCIATIONS AND PROFESSIONAL SOCIETIES

American Institute of Biological Sciences. 730 11th St., N.W., Washington, District of Columbia 20001-4521. (202) 628-1500.

American Society of Naturalists. Department of Ecology and Evolation, State University of New York, Stony Brook, New York 11794. (516) 632-8589.

Cousteau Society. Cousteau Society Membership Center, 930 W 21st St., Norfolk, Virginia 23517. In addition to carrying on the many research projects and explorations made famous by Jacques-Yves Cousteau, the Society publishes educational materials and numerous Technical publications as well as Calypso Log (monthly) and Dolphin Log (bimonthly children's publication).

The Society for Marine Mammology. National Marine Fisheries Service, SW Fisheries Center, PO Box 271, La Jolla, California 92038. (619) 546-7096.

MARINE POLLUTION

ABSTRACTING AND INDEXING SERVICES

Abstracts of Air and Water Conservation Literature. American Petroleum Institute. Central Abstracting and Indexing Service, 275 Madison Avenue, New York, New York 10016. 1972.

Applied Ecology Abstracts Studies in Renewable Natural Resources. Information Retrieval Ltd., 1911 Jefferson Davis Highway, Arlington, Virginia 22202. 1975-. Monthly.

Aqualine Abstracts. Water Research Centre. c/o Pergamon Microforms International, Inc., Fairview Park, Elmsford, New York 10523. (914) 592-7720. 1927-. Contains some 8,000 records annually on water and wastewater technology. Covers all aspects of water, wastewater, associated engineering services and the aquatic environment. Over 600 periodicals, as well as books, reports and conference proceedings and other publications from water related institutions worldwide are scanned. Also available online.

ASFA Aquaculture Abstracts. Cambridge Scientific Abstracts, Inc., 5161 River Rd., Bethesda, Maryland 20816. (301) 961-6750. 1984.

Biological Abstracts. BIOSIS, 2100 Arch St., Philadelphia, Pennsylvania 19103-1399. (215) 587-4800. 1927-.

Biological and Agricultural Index. H.W. Wilson Co., 950 University Ave., Bronx, New York 10452. (800) 367-6770. 1916-. Monthly.

Bulletin Signaletique: Eau et Assainissement, Pollution Atmospherique, Droit des Pollutions. Centre de Documentation, Centre National de la Recherche Scientifique, 15, quai Anatole France, Paris, France 75700. (1) 45 55 92 25. 1983-. Monthly. Indexes pollution periodicals including water, atmospheric and related pollutions.

Current Advances in Ecological and Environmental Science. Pergamon Microforms International, Inc., Fairview Park, Elmsford, New York 10523. (914) 592-7720. 1989-. Monthly. Current literature searching service includingjournals, reports, abstracts, etc. This service is available online as part of the CABS database on the hosts BRS and ORBIT search service.

Ecological Abstracts. Geo Abstracts Ltd. Elsevier Applied Science, Crown House, Linton Rd., Barking, England IG 11 8JU. 1974-. Derived from over 600 leading ecological and environmental journals, plus books, conference proceedings, reports and theses.

Ecology Abstracts. Cambridge Scientific Abstracts, 5161 River Rd., Bethesda, Maryland 20816. (301) 961-6750. Monthly.

Environment Abstracts. Bowker A & I Publishing, 121 Chanlon Rd., New Providence, New Jersey 07974. (908) 464-6800. 1974-.

Environment Index. Environment Information Center, Index Research Department, 124 E. 39th St., New York, New York 10016. 1971-. Annual.

Environmental Information Connection–EIC. Planning Information Program, Dept. of Urban and Regional Planning, University of Illinois, 1003 West Nevada, Urbana, Illinois 61801. (217) 333-1369. Also available online.

Environmental Periodicals Bibliography. Environmental Studies Institute, International Academy at Santa Barbara, 800 Garden St., Suite D, Santa Barbara, California 93101. (805) 965-5010. Also available online.

General Science Index. H. W. Wilson Co., 950 University Ave., Bronx, New York 10452. 1978-. Monthly, also issued in annual cumulation. Cumulative subject index to English language periodicals in the subject fields of astronomy, botany, chemistry, earth science, environment and conservation, food and nutrition, genetics, mathematics, medicine and health, microbiology, oceanography, physics, physiology and zoology.

Geographical Abstracts. London School of Economics, Dept. of Geography, Regency House, 34 Duke St., London, England 1966-. Continued by Geo Abstracts issued in 6 parts: Pt. A. Landforms and the quaternary; Pt. B. Biogeography and Climatology; Pt. C. Economic geography; Pt. D. Social geography and cartography; Pt. E. Sedimentology; Pt. F. Regional and community planning.

Index to Scientific Book Contents. Institute for Scientific Information, 3501 Market St., Philadelphia, Pennsylvania 19104. (800) 523-1857. 1985-. Annual. Gives contents of science books published.

Multimedia Index to Ecology. National Information Center for Educational Media, University of Southern California, Los Angeles, California 90007.

Oceanic Abstracts. UMI Data Courier, 620 S. 3rd St., Louisville, Kentucky 40202. (800) 626-2823. Formerly: Oceanic Index and Oceanic Citation Journal.

Pollution Abstracts. Cambridge Scientific Abstracts, 5161 River Rd., Bethesda, Maryland 20816. (301) 961-6750. Six/year. Indexes worldwide technical literature on environmental pollution. Covers air pollution, marine and freshwater pollution, sewage and wastewater treatment, waste management, toxicology and health, noise pollution, radiation, land pollution, and environmental policies, programs, legislation, and education. Also available online.

Science Citation Index. Institute for Scientific Information, 3501 Market St., Philadelphia, Pennsylvania 19104. 1961-.

Sea Grant Abstracts. National Sea Grant Depository, Pell Laboratory Bldg., Bay Campus, University of Rhode Island, Narragansett, Rhode Island 02882. (401) 792-6114. 1986-. Quarterly. Published by the National Sea Grant Programs, this collection includes annual reports, serials and newsletters, charts and maps.

ALMANACS AND YEARBOOKS

ACOPS Yearbook 1986-87. Advisory Committee on Pollution of the Sea, eds. Pergamon Microforms International, Inc., Fairview Park, Elmsford, New York 10523. (914) 592-7720. 1987. An annual review of activities by governmental and non-governmental organizations concerning remedies for global pollution, together with scientific and technical reports containing surveys of pollution in the marine environment.

BIBLIOGRAPHIES

Current Contents. Agriculture, Biology and Environmental Sciences. Institute for Scientific Information, 3501 Market St., Philadelphia, Pennsylvania 19104. (800) 523-1857. 1973-. Previous title: Current Contents. Agricultural, Food & Veterinary Sciences. Gives the table of contents of periodicals in the fields of agriculture, biology, environmental and related areas.

EPA Publications Bibliography. U.S. Environmental Protection Agency, Library Systems Branch, 401 M St., SW, Washington, District of Columbia 20460. (202) 260-2090. Quarterly.

Marine Pollution: Monographs. Mary A. Vance. Vance Bibliographies, PO Box 229, 112 N. Charter St., Monticello, Illinois 61856. (217) 762-3831. 1985.

New Publications of the Geological Survey. U.S. Department of the Interior, Geological Survey, 119 National Center, Reston, Virginia 22092. (703) 648-4460. 1984-. Monthly. Bibliography of geological publications and related government documents published by the Geological Survey.

DIRECTORIES

Directory of Environmental Information Sources. Thomas F. P. Sullivan, ed. Government Institutes, Inc., 4 Research Pl., Ste. 200, Rockville, Maryland 20850. (301) 921-2300. 1992. 3d ed.

Summary of Federal Programs and Projects. National Marine Pollution Program Office, National Oceanic and Atmospheric Administration, 11400 Rockville Pike, Rm. 610, Rockville, Maryland 20852. (301) 443-8823. 1969.

ENCYCLOPEDIAS AND DICTIONARIES

Cambridge Encyclopedia of Life Sciences. A. E. Friday and David S. Ingram. Cambridge University Press, 40 W 20th St., New York, New York 10011. (212) 924-3900 or (800) 227-0247. 1985. Includes all topics under biology and ecology.

Dictionary of Environmental Engineering and Related Sciences: English-Spanish, Spanish-English. Jose T. Villate. Ediciones Universal, 3090 SW 8th St., Miami, Florida 33135. (305) 642-3355. 1979.

The Encyclopedia of Beaches and Coastal Environments. Maurice L. Schwartz. Hutchinson Ross Pub. Co., Stroudsburg, Pennsylvania 1982.

Encyclopedia of Environmental Science and Engineering. J.R. Pfafflin. Gordon and Breach Science Publishers, Inc., 270 8th Ave., New York, New York 10011. (212) 206-8900. 1992.

The Encyclopedia of Oceanography. Rhodes Whitmore Fairbridge. Reinhold Pub. Co., 115 5th Ave., New York, New York 10003. (212) 254-3232. 1966.

Grzimek's Encyclopedia of Ecology. Bernhard Grzimek. Van Nostrand Reinhold, 115 5th Ave., New York, New York 10003. (212) 254-3232. 1976.

McGraw-Hill Encyclopedia of Environmental Science. Sybil P. Parker. McGraw-Hill Science & Engineering Books, 11 W. 19th St., New York, New York 10011. (212) 337-6010. 1980. Covers ecology, man's influence on nature, and environmental protection.

McGraw-Hill Encyclopedia of Science and Technology. McGraw-Hill, 1221 Avenue of the Americas, New York, New York 10020. (212) 512-2000 or (800) 262-4729. 1992. Seventh edition. Issued in multiple volumes including index. Includes all science and technology broad subject areas.

North American Reference Encyclopedia of Ecology and Pollution. William White. North American Pub. Co., 401 N. Broad St., Philadelphia, Pennsylvania 19108. (215) 238-5300. 1972.

The Times Atlas and Encyclopedia of the Sea. A.D. Couper. Harper & Row, 10 E. 53rd St., New York, New York 10022. (212) 207-7000; (800) 242-7737. 1990.

GENERAL WORKS

Carcinogenic, Mutagenic, and Teratogenic Marine Pollutants. Portfolio Publishing Co., P.O. Box 7802, The Woodlands, Texas 77381. (713) 363-3577. 1990. Effects of marine pollution on aquatic organisms as well as human beings.

Classification of Floating CHRIS Chemicals for the Development of a Spill Response Manual. A. T. Szhula. National Technical Information Service, 5285 Port Royal Rd, Springfield, Virginia 22161. (703) 487-4650. Covers classification of chemical spills.

The International Control of Marine Pollution. J. Tiamgenis. Oceana Publications Inc., 75 Main St., Dobbs Ferry, New York 10522. (914) 693-8100. 1990. 2 vols. Focuses

on conventional law on marine pollution, particularly from dumping and ships, within the context of a wider law-making process. The main body of the book is devoted to an analysis of international conventions, with reference to some 450 books and articles on the subject.

Lead in the Marine Environment. M. Branica and Z. Konrad, eds. Pergamon Microforms International, Inc., Fairview Park, Elmsford, New York 10523. (914) 592-7720. 1980. Proceedings of the International Experts Discussion, Rovinj, Yugoslavia, October 1977.

Managing Troubled Water. National Academy Press, 2101 Constitution Ave., NW, PO Box 285, Washington, District of Columbia 20418. (202) 334-3313. 1990.

Marine Toxins: Origin, Structure, and Molecular Pharmacology. Sherwood Hall and Gary Strichartz, eds. American Chemical Society, 1155 16th St. N.W., Washington, District of Columbia 20036. (202) 872-4600; (800) 227-5558. 1990. Describes the history of marine toxins and their various properties and effects on the environment.

Marine Treatment of Sewage Sludge. Telford House, 1 Heron Quay, London, England E14 9XF. 1988.

National Marine Pollution Program Plan, Federal Plan for Ocean Pollution Research, Development and Monitoring. Fiscal Years 1988-1992. National Oceanic and Atmospheric Administration, U.S. Dept. of Commerce, Washington, District of Columbia 20230. (202) 377-2985. 1988.

National Marine Pollution Program. Summary of Federal Programs and Projects, FY 1988 Update. National Marine Pollution Program Office, National Oceanic and Atmospheric Administration, 11400 Rockville Pike, Rockville, Maryland 20852. 1990.

Response Manual for Combatting Spills of Floating Hazardous CHRIS Chemicals. National Technical Information Service, 5285 Port Royal Rd., Springfield, Virginia 22161. (703) 487-4650. Covers chemical spills, hazardous substance accidents, and marine pollution.

GOVERNMENTAL ORGANIZATIONS

Coast Guard. Information Office, 2100 Second St., S.W., Washington, District of Columbia 20593. (202) 267-2229.

HANDBOOKS AND MANUALS

Handbook for Preparing Office of Marine Assessment Reports. Rosa Lee Echard. National Oceanic and Atmospheric Administration, U.S. Department of Commerce, Washington, District of Columbia 20230. (202) 377-2895. 1982.

Handbook on Marine Pollution. Edgar Gold. Assuranceforeningen Gard, Postboks 1563 Myrene, Arendal, Norway N-4801. 1985. Law and legislation relative to marine pollution.

ONLINE DATA BASES

Alaskan Marine Contaminants Database. National Oceanic and Atmospheric Administration, National Ocean Service, 222 W. 8th Ave., Box 56, Anchorage, Alaska 99513. (907) 271-3033. Contains data on the occurrence of contaminants in faunal tissue and sediments in Alaskan marine waters.

BIOSIS Previews. BIOSIS, 2100 Arch St., Philadelphia, Pennsylvania 19103-1399. (215) 587-4800. Largest and most comprehensive database of research in the life sciences. Contains citations for nearly 9000 primary research journals, monographs, reviews, symposia, preliminary reports, semi-popular journals, selected institutional reports, government reports and research communications.

Enviro/Energyline Abstracts Plus. R. R. Bowker Co., 121 Chanlon Rd., New Providence, New Jersey 07974. (908) 464-6800.

Environmental Periodicals Bibliography. National Information Services Corp., Ste. 6, Wyman Towers, 3100 St. Paul St., Baltimore, Maryland 21218. (410)243-0797. Online version of abstract of same name.

MARINELINE. Informationszentrum Rohstoffgewinnwig Geowissenschaften Wasserwirtschaft, Bundesanstalt fuer Geowissenschaften und Rohstoffe, Postfach 510153, Stilleweg 2, Hanover 51, Germany D-3000. 49 (511) 643-2819.

Monthly Catalog of United States Government Publications. U.S. G.P.O., Supt. of Docs., PO Box 371954, Pittsburgh, Pennsylvania 15250-7954. (202) 512-0000.

National Technical Information Service. U.S. Department of Commerce, National Technical Information Service, Office of Data Base Services, 5285 Port Royal Rd., Springfield, Virginia 22161. (703) 487-4807. Bibliographic database of government sponsored research and technical reports.

NMPIS Database. U.S. National Environmental Satellite, Data, and Information Service, National Oceanographic Data Center, 1825 Connecticut Ave., N.W., Suite 406, Washington, District of Columbia 20235. (202) 673-5594. Marine pollution research, development, or monitoring projects conducted or funded by federal agencies.

NODC Data Inventory Data Base. U.S. National Environmental Satellite, Data, and Information Service, National Oceanographic Data Center, 1825 Connecticut Ave., N.W., Suite 406, Washington, District of Columbia 20235. (202) 673-5594. Information on National Oceanographic Data Center holdings.

Oceanic Abstracts. Cambridge Scientific Abstracts, 5161 River Rd., Bethesda, Maryland 20816. (301) 961-6750. Online access.

Oceanographic Literature Review. Woods Hole Data Base, Inc., PO Box 712, Woods Hole, Massachusetts 02574. (508) 548-2743. International periodical literature dealing with oceanography, ocean waste disposal and pollution.

SCISEARCH. Institute for Scientific Information, University City Science Center, 3501 Market St., Philadelphia, Pennsylvania 19104. (215) 386-0100.

PERIODICALS AND NEWSLETTERS

Calypso Log. Cousteau Society Membership Center, 930 W 21st St., Norfolk, Virginia 23517. 6 issues a year. Presents articles for members about Cousteau Society expeditions, ecology, conservation, oceans and marine mammals.

Coastal Ocean Pollution Assessment News. Marine Sciences Research Center, State University of New York, Stony Brook, New York 11790. Frequency varies. Man and the marine environment.

Marine Biology. Springer-Verlag, 175 5th Ave., New York, New York 10010. (212) 461-1500; (800) 777-4643. Sixteen/year. Life in oceans and coastal waters.

Marine Debris Newsletter. Center for Marine Conservation, 1725 DeSales St, NW, Suite 500, Washington, District of Columbia 20036. (202) 429-5609. Quarterly. Plastic debris and other nondegradable trash in oceans and waterways.

Marine Ecology. Paul Parey Scientific Publishers, P.O. Box 236, 150 East 27th Street, Suite 1A, New York, New York 10016. (212) 730-0518. Quarterly. Information on specific organisms in the environment.

Marine Environmental Research. ASP Ltd., Ripple Road, Barking, Essex, England Monthly. Covers marine pollution and marine ecology.

Marine Pollution Bulletin: The International Journal for Marine Environmentalists, Scientists, Engineers, Administrators, Politicians and Lawyers. Pergamon Microforms International, Inc., Fairview Park, Elmsford, New York 10523. (914) 592-7720. 1969-. Monthly. Concerned with the rational use of maritime and marine resources in estuaries, the seas and oceans. Covers pollution control, management and productivity of the marine environment in general.

Marine Resource Economics. Taylor & Francis, 1900 Frost Road, Suite 101, Bristol, Pennsylvania 19007. (800) 821-8312. Quarterly. Issues related to the economics of marine resources.

The Siren: News from UNEP's Regional Seas Programme (English Ed.). United Nations Environment Programme, Regional Seas Programme Activity Centre, Geneva, Switzerland 1978-. Three issues yearly since 1983. Covers marine pollution, environmental policy, and coastal zone management.

RESEARCH CENTERS AND INSTITUTES

Marine Sciences Institute. University of Connecticut at Avery Point, Groton, Connecticut 06340. (203) 445-4714.

University of Hawaii at Manoa Hawaii Undersea Research Laboratory. 1000 Pope Road, MSB 303, Honolulu, Hawaii 96822. (808) 956-6335.

University of Maine, Ira C. Darling Center for Research Teaching and Service. Walpole, Maine 04573. (207) 563-3146.

University of Washington, Institute for Marine Studies. College of Ocean and Fishery Science, 3707 Brooklyn Avenue, N.E., Seattle, Washington 98195. (206) 543-7004.

University of Wisconsin-Madison, Marine Studies Center. 1269 Engineering Building, 1415 Johnson Drive, Madison, Wisconsin 53706. (608) 262-3883.

STATISTICS SOURCES

America in the 21st Century: The Demographic Dimension: Environmental Concerns. Population Reference Bureau, P.O. Box 96152, Washington, District of Columbia 20090-6152. Distribution of pollution by source.

TRADE ASSOCIATIONS AND PROFESSIONAL SOCIETIES

American Institute of Biological Sciences. 730 11th St., N.W., Washington, District of Columbia 20001-4521. (202) 628-1500.

American Society of Naturalists. Department of Ecology and Evolation, State University of New York, Stony Brook, New York 11794. (516) 632-8589.

Cousteau Society. Cousteau Society Membership Center, 930 W 21st St., Norfolk, Virginia 23517. In addition to carrying on the many research projects and explorations made famous by Jacques-Yves Cousteau, the Society publishes educational materials and numerous Technical publications as well as Calypso Log (monthly) and Dolphin Log (bimonthly children's publication).

International Ocean Pollution Symposium. Department of Chemical and Environmental Engineering, Florida Institute of Tech., Melbourne, Florida 32901. (407) 768-8000.

MARINE RESOURCES

ABSTRACTING AND INDEXING SERVICES

Aqualine Abstracts. Water Research Centre. c/o Pergamon Microforms International, Inc., Fairview Park, Elmsford, New York 10523. (914) 592-7720. 1927-. Contains some 8,000 records annually on water and wastewater technology. Covers all aspects of water, wastewater, associated engineering services and the aquatic environment. Over 600 periodicals, as well as books, reports and conference proceedings and other publications from water related institutions worldwide are scanned. Also available online.

Biological Abstracts. BIOSIS, 2100 Arch St., Philadelphia, Pennsylvania 19103-1399. (215) 587-4800. 1927-.

Biological and Agricultural Index. H.W. Wilson Co., 950 University Ave., Bronx, New York 10452. (800) 367-6770. 1916-. Monthly.

Current Advances in Ecological and Environmental Science. Pergamon Microforms International, Inc., Fairview Park, Elmsford, New York 10523. (914) 592-7720. 1989-. Monthly. Current literature searching service includingjournals, reports, abstracts, etc. This service is available online as part of the CABS database on the hosts BRS and ORBIT search service.

Ecological Abstracts. Geo Abstracts Ltd. Elsevier Applied Science, Crown House, Linton Rd., Barking, England IG 11 8JU. 1974-. Derived from over 600 leading ecological and environmental journals, plus books, conference proceedings, reports and theses.

Ecology Abstracts. Cambridge Scientific Abstracts, 5161 River Rd., Bethesda, Maryland 20816. (301) 961-6750. Monthly.

Environment Abstracts. Bowker A & I Publishing, 121 Chanlon Rd., New Providence, New Jersey 07974. (908) 464-6800. 1974-.

Environment Index. Environment Information Center, Index Research Department, 124 E. 39th St., New York, New York 10016. 1971-. Annual.

Environmental Information Connection–EIC. Planning Information Program, Dept. of Urban and Regional Planning, University of Illinois, 1003 West Nevada, Urbana, Illinois 61801. (217) 333-1369. Also available online.

Environmental Periodicals Bibliography. Environmental Studies Institute, International Academy at Santa Barbara, 800 Garden St., Suite D, Santa Barbara, California 93101. (805) 965-5010. Also available online.

General Science Index. H. W. Wilson Co., 950 University Ave., Bronx, New York 10452. 1978-. Monthly, also issued in annual cumulation. Cumulative subject index to English language periodicals in the subject fields of astronomy, botany, chemistry, earth science, environment and conservation, food and nutrition, genetics, mathematics, medicine and health, microbiology, oceanography, physics, physiology and zoology.

Geographical Abstracts. London School of Economics, Dept. of Geography, Regency House, 34 Duke St., London, England 1966-. Continued by Geo Abstracts issued in 6 parts: Pt. A. Landforms and the quaternary; Pt. B. Biogeography and Climatology; Pt. C. Economic geography; Pt. D. Social geography and cartography; Pt. E. Sedimentology; Pt. F. Regional and community planning.

Index to Scientific Book Contents. Institute for Scientific Information, 3501 Market St., Philadelphia, Pennsylvania 19104. (800) 523-1857. 1985-. Annual. Gives contents of science books published.

Oceanic Abstracts. UMI Data Courier, 620 S. 3rd St., Louisville, Kentucky 40202. (800) 626-2823. Formerly: Oceanic Index and Oceanic Citation Journal.

Science Citation Index. Institute for Scientific Information, 3501 Market St., Philadelphia, Pennsylvania 19104. 1961-.

Sea Grant Abstracts. National Sea Grant Depository, Pell Laboratory Bldg., Bay Campus, University of Rhode Island, Narragansett, Rhode Island 02882. (401) 792-6114. 1986-. Quarterly. Published by the National Sea Grant Programs, this collection includes annual reports, serials and newsletters, charts and maps.

BIBLIOGRAPHIES

Bibliography and Index of Geology. American Geological Institute, 4220 King St., Alexandria, Virginia 22302. Monthly. Includes environmental geology and hydrogeology.

Bibliography of Living Marine Resources. Food and Agriculture Organization of the United Nations, Fishery Resources and Environment Division. Research Information Unit, Fishery and Environment Division, Rome, Italy 1976.

Current Contents. Agriculture, Biology and Environmental Sciences. Institute for Scientific Information, 3501 Market St., Philadelphia, Pennsylvania 19104. (800) 523-1857. 1973-. Previous title: Current Contents. Agricultural, Food & Veterinary Sciences. Gives the table of contents of periodicals in the fields of agriculture, biology, environmental and related areas.

EPA Publications Bibliography. U.S. Environmental Protection Agency, Library Systems Branch, 401 M St., SW, Washington, District of Columbia 20460. (202) 260-2090. Quarterly.

DIRECTORIES

Connections: A Guide to Marine Resources, Living Systems, and Field Trips. Sea Grant College Program, Sea Grant College Program, North Carolina State University at Raleigh, Box 8605, Raleigh, North Carolina 27695. (919) 737-2454.

ENCYCLOPEDIAS AND DICTIONARIES

Cambridge Encyclopedia of Life Sciences. A. E. Friday and David S. Ingram. Cambridge University Press, 40 W 20th St., New York, New York 10011. (212) 924-3900 or (800) 227-0247. 1985. Includes all topics under biology and ecology.

The Encyclopedia of Beaches and Coastal Environments. Maurice L. Schwartz. Hutchinson Ross Pub. Co., Stroudsburg, Pennsylvania 1982.

The Encyclopedia of Oceanography. Rhodes Whitmore Fairbridge. Reinhold Pub. Co., 115 5th Ave., New York, New York 10003. (212) 254-3232. 1966.

Glossary of Geology. Robert Latimer Bates and Julia A. Jackson, eds. American Geological Institute, 4220 King St., Alexandria, Virginia 22302-1507. (703) 379-2480 or (800) 336-4764. 1987. Third edition.

Grzimek's Encyclopedia of Ecology. Bernhard Grzimek. Van Nostrand Reinhold, 115 5th Ave., New York, New York 10003. (212) 254-3232. 1976.

Illustrated Encyclopedia of Science and the Future. Mike Biscare, et al., ed. Marshall Cavendish, 58 Old Compton St., London, England 0W1V5 PA. 01-734 6710. 1983. Twenty volumes. Each volume has 5 sections: Frontiers, Electronics in Action, Medical Science, Military Technology, and Resources.

McGraw-Hill Encyclopedia of Environmental Science. Sybil P. Parker. McGraw-Hill Science & Engineering Books, 11 W. 19th St., New York, New York 10011. (212) 337-6010. 1980. Covers ecology, man's influence on nature, and environmental protection.

McGraw-Hill Encyclopedia of the Geological Sciences. Sybil P. Parker, ed. McGraw-Hill, 1221 Avenue of the Americas, New York, New York 10020. (212) 512-2000 or (800) 262-4729. 1988. Second edition. Published previously in the McGraw-Hill Encyclopedia of Science and Technology.

North American Reference Encyclopedia of Ecology and Pollution. William White. North American Pub. Co., 401 N. Broad St., Philadelphia, Pennsylvania 19108. (215) 238-5300. 1972.

GENERAL WORKS

Food Chain Yields, Models, and Management of Large Marine Ecosystems. Kenneth Sherman, et al., eds. Westview Press, 5500 Central Ave., Boulder, Colorado 80301. (303) 444-3541. 1991. Describes marine ecology, its productive resources and its management.

Guide to Information on Research in the Marine Science and Engineering. U.S. Department of Commerce, National Oceanic and Atmospheric Administration, Office of Ocean Engineering, 6010 Executive Blvd., Rockville, Maryland 20852. (301) 443-8344. 1978.

Magill's Survey of Science. Earth Science Series. Frank N. Magill. Salem Press, PO Box 50062, Pasadena, California

91105. 1990-. Five volumes. Includes information on earth's crust, hot spots and volcanic island chains, physical properties of minerals, rock magnetism, physical properties of rocks, and index.

Managing Marine Environments. Richard A. Kenchington. Taylor & Francis, 1900 Frost Rd., Ste. 101, Bristol, Pennsylvania 19007. (215) 785-5800. 1990. Contemporary issues of multiple-use planning and management of marine environments and natural resources.

Mangone's Concise Marine Almanac. Gerard J. Mangone. Taylor & Francis, 1900 Frost Rd., Ste. 101, Bristol, Pennsylvania 19007. (215) 785-5800. 1991. Covers oceanography, marine resources, merchant marine, and fisheries.

Tropical Resources: Ecology and Development. Jose I. Furtado, et al., eds. Harwood Academic Publishers, PO Box 786, Cooper Sta., New York, New York 10276. (212) 206-8900. 1990. Overview of global tropical resources, both terrestrial and aquatic. Subjects discussed include forest resources, wildlife resources, general land use, pasture resources, economic development, fisheries, marine resources, and aquaculture.

GOVERNMENTAL ORGANIZATIONS

National Marine Fisheries Service. 1825 Connecticut Ave., N.W., Washington, District of Columbia 20235. (202) 673-5450.

HANDBOOKS AND MANUALS

Marine Resource Mapping: An Introductory Manual. M. J. A. Butler. Food and Agriculture Organization of the United Nations, Via delle Terme di Caracalla, Rome, Italy 00100. 61 0181-FA01. 1987. Topics in cartography relative to marine resources.

ONLINE DATA BASES

BIOSIS Previews. BIOSIS, 2100 Arch St., Philadelphia, Pennsylvania 19103-1399. (215) 587-4800. Largest and most comprehensive database of research in the life sciences. Contains citations for nearly 9000 primary research journals, monographs, reviews, symposia, preliminary reports, semi-popular journals, selected institutional reports, government reports and research communications.

Cambridge Scientific Abstracts Life Science–CSAL. Cambridge Scientific Abstracts, 5161 River Rd., Bethesda, Maryland 20816. (301) 961-6750. Provides access to the following abstracting services: "Life Sciences Collection," "Aquatic Sciences and Fisheries Abstracts," "Oceanic Abstracts," and "Pollution Abstracts."

Enviro/Energyline Abstracts Plus. R. R. Bowker Co., 121 Chanlon Rd., New Providence, New Jersey 07974. (908) 464-6800.

Environmental Periodicals Bibliography. National Information Services Corp., Ste. 6, Wyman Towers, 3100 St. Paul St., Baltimore, Maryland 21218. (410)243-0797. Online version of abstract of same name.

MARINELINE. Informationszentrum Rohstoffgewinnwig Geowissenschaften Wasserwirtschaft, Bundesanstalt fuer Geowissenschaften und Rohstoffe, Postfach 510153, Stilleweg 2, Hanover 51, Germany D-3000. 49 (511) 643-2819.

Monthly Catalog of United States Government Publications. U.S. G.P.O., Supt. of Docs., PO Box 371954, Pittsburgh, Pennsylvania 15250-7954. (202) 512-0000.

National Technical Information Service. U.S. Department of Commerce, National Technical Information Service, Office of Data Base Services, 5285 Port Royal Rd., Springfield, Virginia 22161. (703) 487-4807. Bibliographic database of government sponsored research and technical reports.

NODC Data Inventory Data Base. U.S. National Environmental Satellite, Data, and Information Service, National Oceanographic Data Center, 1825 Connecticut Ave., N.W., Suite 406, Washington, District of Columbia 20235. (202) 673-5594. Information on National Oceanographic Data Center holdings.

Oceanic Abstracts. Cambridge Scientific Abstracts, 5161 River Rd., Bethesda, Maryland 20816. (301) 961-6750. Online access.

SCISEARCH. Institute for Scientific Information, University City Science Center, 3501 Market St., Philadelphia, Pennsylvania 19104. (215) 386-0100.

PERIODICALS AND NEWSLETTERS

Calypso Log. Cousteau Society Membership Center, 930 W 21st St., Norfolk, Virginia 23517. 6 issues a year. Presents articles for members about Cousteau Society expeditions, ecology, conservation, oceans and marine mammals.

Marine Ecology. Paul Parey Scientific Publishers, P.O. Box 236, 150 East 27th Street, Suite 1A, New York, New York 10016. (212) 730-0518. Quarterly. Information on specific organisms in the environment.

Marine Fish Management. Nautillus Press Inc., 1056 National Press Bldg., Washington, District of Columbia 20045. Monthly.

Marine Resource Economics. Taylor & Francis, 1900 Frost Road, Suite 101, Bristol, Pennsylvania 19007. (800) 821-8312. Quarterly. Issues related to the economics of marine resources.

Marine Technology. Society of Naval Architects and Marine Engineers, 601 Pavonia Ave., Jersey City, New Jersey 07306. (201) 498-4800. 1964-1987.

Ocean Development and International Law Journal. Crane, Russak & Co., 79 Madison Ave., New York, New York 10016. (212) 725-1999. Quarterly. International law of marine resources.

RESEARCH CENTERS AND INSTITUTES

Institute of Marine Resources. University of California, La Jolla, California 92093-0228. (619) 534-2868.

Institute of Marine Sciences. University of California, Santa Cruz, Applied Sciences, Room 272, Santa Cruz, California 95064. (408) 459-4730.

Marine Resources Development Foundation. Koblick Marine Center, 51 Shoreland Drive, P.O. Box 787, Key Largo, Florida 33037. (305) 451-1139.

Marine Sciences Institute. University of Connecticut at Avery Point, Groton, Connecticut 06340. (203) 445-4714.

North Carolina Aquarium at Pine Knoll Shores. Atlantic Beach, North Carolina 28512. (919) 247-4003.

North Carolina Aquarium/Roanoke Island. P.O. Box 967, Airport Road, Manteo, North Carolina 27954. (919) 473-3493.

Oregon State University, Seafoods Laboratory. 250 36th Street, Astoria, Oregon 97103. (503) 325-4531.

Scripps Institution of Oceanography, Marine Physical Laboratory. University of California, San Diego, San Diego, California 92152-6400. (619) 534-1789.

Sea Grant College Program. University of Delaware, 196 South College Avenue, Newark, Delaware 19716. (302) 451-8182.

University of Alaska Fairbanks, Alaska Sea Grant College Program. 138 Irving II, Fairbanks, Alaska 99775-5040. (907) 474-7086.

University of Georgia, Marine Extension Service. P.O. Box 13687, Savannah, Georgia 31416. (912) 356-2496.

University of Georgia, Marine Institute. Sapelo, Georgia (912) 485-2221.

University of Georgia, Marine Sciences Program. Athens, Georgia 30602 (404) 542-7671.

University of Hawaii at Manoa Sea Grant College Program. 1000 Pope Road, MSB 220, Honolulu, Hawaii 96822. (808) 948-7031.

University of Maryland, Sea Grant College. 1123 Taliaferro Hall, College Park, Maryland 20742. (301) 405-6371.

University of New Hampshire, Complex Systems Research Center. Science and Engineering Research Building, Durham, New Hampshire 03824. (603) 862-1792.

University of North Carolina at Wilmington, Center for Marine Research. 601 South College Road, Wilmington, North Carolina 28406. (919) 256-3721.

University of Washington, Institute for Marine Studies. College of Ocean and Fishery Science, 3707 Brooklyn Avenue, N.E., Seattle, Washington 98195. (206) 543-7004.

University of Wisconsin-Madison, Marine Studies Center. 1269 Engineering Building, 1415 Johnson Drive, Madison, Wisconsin 53706. (608) 262-3883.

TRADE ASSOCIATIONS AND PROFESSIONAL SOCIETIES

American Institute of Biological Sciences. 730 11th St., N.W., Washington, District of Columbia 20001-4521. (202) 628-1500.

American Society of Naturalists. Department of Ecology and Evolation, State University of New York, Stony Brook, New York 11794. (516) 632-8589.

Cousteau Society. Cousteau Society Membership Center, 930 W 21st St., Norfolk, Virginia 23517. In addition to carrying on the many research projects and explorations made famous by Jacques-Yves Cousteau, the Society publishes educational materials and numerous Technical publications as well as Calypso Log (monthly) and Dolphin Log (bimonthly children's publication).

Emergency Committee to Save America's Marine Resources. c/o Allan J. Ristori, 1552 Osprey Ct., Manasquan Park, New Jersey 08736. (201) 223-5729.

Marine Technology Society. 1825 K. St., N.W., Suite 218, Washington, District of Columbia 20006. (202) 775-5966.

National Coalition for Marine Conservation, Inc. P.O. Box 23298, Savannah, Georgia 31403. (912) 234-8062.

Offshore Marine Service Association. 1440 Canal St., Suite 1709, New Orleans, Louisiana 70112. (504) 566-4577.

Sea Grant Association. c/o Dr. Christopher F. D'Elia, Maryland Sea Grant College, 1123 Taliaferro Hall, UMCP, College Park, Maryland 20742. (301) 405-6371.

The Society for Marine Mammology. National Marine Fisheries Service, SW Fisheries Center, PO Box 271, La Jolla, California 92038. (619) 546-7096.

MARINE SANCTUARY PROGRAMS

ABSTRACTING AND INDEXING SERVICES

Ecological Abstracts. Geo Abstracts Ltd. Elsevier Applied Science, Crown House, Linton Rd., Barking, England IG 11 8JU. 1974-. Derived from over 600 leading ecological and environmental journals, plus books, conference proceedings, reports and theses.

Geographical Abstracts. London School of Economics, Dept. of Geography, Regency House, 34 Duke St., London, England 1966-. Continued by Geo Abstracts issued in 6 parts: Pt. A. Landforms and the quaternary; Pt. B. Biogeography and Climatology; Pt. C. Economic geography; Pt. D. Social geography and cartography; Pt. E. Sedimentology; Pt. F. Regional and community planning.

BIBLIOGRAPHIES

Underwater and Marine Parks: An Indexed Bibliography. Don Huff. Vance Bibliographies, PO Box 229, 112 N. Charter St., Monticello, Illinois 61856. (217) 762-3831. 1983.

ENCYCLOPEDIAS AND DICTIONARIES

The Encyclopedia of Oceanography. Rhodes Whitmore Fairbridge. Reinhold Pub. Co., 115 5th Ave., New York, New York 10003. (212) 254-3232. 1966.

GENERAL WORKS

Managing Marine Environments. Richard A. Kenchington. Taylor & Francis, 1900 Frost Rd., Ste. 101, Bristol, Pennsylvania 19007. (215) 785-5800. 1990. Contemporary issues of multiple-use planning and management of marine environments and natural resources.

Managing Marine Protected Areas: An Action Plan. Nancy Foster. U.S. Man and the Biosphere Program, Washington, District of Columbia 1988. Management of marine parks and reserves.

National Marine Sanctuary Program: Program Development Plan. Sanctuary Programs Office, Office of Coastal Zone Management, National Oceanic and Atmospheric Administration, Department of Commerce, Washington, District of Columbia 20230. 1982. Marine parks and reserves in the United States.

GOVERNMENTAL ORGANIZATIONS

U.S. Environmental Protection Agency: Office of Drinking Water. 401 M St., S.W., Washington, District of Columbia 20460. (202) 382-5543.

U.S. Environmental Protection Agency: Office of Marine and Estuarine Protection. 401 M St., S.W., Washington, District of Columbia 20460. (202) 382-8580.

PERIODICALS AND NEWSLETTERS

Calypso Log. Cousteau Society Membership Center, 930 W 21st St., Norfolk, Virginia 23517. 6 issues a year. Presents articles for members about Cousteau Society expeditions, ecology, conservation, oceans and marine mammals.

Marine Biology. Springer-Verlag, 175 5th Ave., New York, New York 10010. (212) 461-1500; (800) 777-4643. Sixteen/year. Life in oceans and coastal waters.

Marine Policy Reports. Center for the Study of Marine Policy, College of Marine Studies, University of Delaware, Newark, Delaware 19716. (302) 451-8086. Bimonthly. Ocean research.

Marine Sanctuaries News. Center for Marine Conservation, 1725 DeSales St., NW, Suite 500, Washington, District of Columbia 20036. (202) 429-5609. Quarterly. Current issues regarding marine sanctuaries.

TRADE ASSOCIATIONS AND PROFESSIONAL SOCIETIES

American Institute of Biological Sciences. 730 11th St., N.W., Washington, District of Columbia 20001-4521. (202) 628-1500.

American Society of Naturalists. Department of Ecology and Evolation, State University of New York, Stony Brook, New York 11794. (516) 632-8589.

Cousteau Society. Cousteau Society Membership Center, 930 W 21st St., Norfolk, Virginia 23517. In addition to carrying on the many research projects and explorations made famous by Jacques-Yves Cousteau, the Society publishes educational materials and numerous Technical publications as well as Calypso Log (monthly) and Dolphin Log (bimonthly children's publication).

National Coalition for Marine Conservation, Inc. P.O. Box 23298, Savannah, Georgia 31403. (912) 234-8062.

Offshore Marine Service Association. 1440 Canal St., Suite 1709, New Orleans, Louisiana 70112. (504) 566-4577.

MARINE WATER ANALYSIS

See: WATER ANALYSIS

MARINE WATER TEMPERATURE

See: WATER TEMPERATURE

MARSHES

See also: EVERGLADES

ABSTRACTING AND INDEXING SERVICES

Abstracts of Air and Water Conservation Literature. American Petroleum Institute. Central Abstracting and Indexing Service, 275 Madison Avenue, New York, New York 10016. 1972.

Applied Ecology Abstracts Studies in Renewable Natural Resources. Information Retrieval Ltd., 1911 Jefferson Davis Highway, Arlington, Virginia 22202. 1975-. Monthly.

Biological Abstracts. BIOSIS, 2100 Arch St., Philadelphia, Pennsylvania 19103-1399. (215) 587-4800. 1927-.

Biological and Agricultural Index. H.W. Wilson Co., 950 University Ave., Bronx, New York 10452. (800) 367-6770. 1916-. Monthly.

Environment Abstracts. Bowker A & I Publishing, 121 Chanlon Rd., New Providence, New Jersey 07974. (908) 464-6800. 1974-.

Environment Index. Environment Information Center, Index Research Department, 124 E. 39th St., New York, New York 10016. 1971-. Annual.

Environmental Information Connection–EIC. Planning Information Program, Dept. of Urban and Regional Planning, University of Illinois, 1003 West Nevada, Urbana, Illinois 61801. (217) 333-1369. Also available online.

Environmental Periodicals Bibliography. Environmental Studies Institute, International Academy at Santa Barbara, 800 Garden St., Suite D, Santa Barbara, California 93101. (805) 965-5010. Also available online.

Multimedia Index to Ecology. National Information Center for Educational Media, University of Southern California, Los Angeles, California 90007.

Science Citation Index. Institute for Scientific Information, 3501 Market St., Philadelphia, Pennsylvania 19104. 1961-.

BIBLIOGRAPHIES

Bibliography and Index of Geology. American Geological Institute, 4220 King St., Alexandria, Virginia 22302. Monthly. Includes environmental geology and hydrogeology.

EPA Publications Bibliography. U.S. Environmental Protection Agency, Library Systems Branch, 401 M St., SW, Washington, District of Columbia 20460. (202) 260-2090. Quarterly.

GENERAL WORKS

Coastal Marshes: Ecology and Wildlife Management. R. H. Charbreck. University of Minnesota Press, 2037 University Ave., SE, Minneapolis, Minnesota 55414. (612) 624-2516. 1988. Tidemarsh ecology and wildlife management.

Freshwater Marshes: Ecology and Wildlife Management. Milton Webster Weller. University of Minnesota Press, 2037 University Ave., SE, Minneapolis, Minnesota 55414. (612) 624-2516. 1987.

Magill's Survey of Science. Earth Science Series. Frank N. Magill. Salem Press, PO Box 50062, Pasadena, California 91105. 1990-. Five volumes. Includes information on earth's crust, hot spots and volcanic island chains, physical properties of minerals, rock magnetism, physical properties of rocks, and index.

Marshes of the Ocean Shore: Development of an Ecological Ethic. Joseph Vincent Siry. Texas A & M University Press, College Station, Texas 77843. 1984. Coastal zone management and tidemarsh ecology.

Saltmarsh Ecology. Paul Adam. Cambridge University Press, 40 W. 20th St., New York, New York 10011. (212) 924-3900. 1991. Flora, fauna, vegetation, how saltmarsh biota copes with this stressful environment, life history studies, marshes as ecosystems.

ONLINE DATA BASES

BIOSIS Previews. BIOSIS, 2100 Arch St., Philadelphia, Pennsylvania 19103-1399. (215) 587-4800. Largest and most comprehensive database of research in the life sciences. Contains citations for nearly 9000 primary research journals, monographs, reviews, symposia, preliminary reports, semi-popular journals, selected institutional reports, government reports and research communications.

Cambridge Scientific Abstracts Life Science–CSAL. Cambridge Scientific Abstracts, 5161 River Rd., Bethesda, Maryland 20816. (301) 961-6750. Provides access to the following abstracting services: "Life Sciences Collection," "Aquatic Sciences and Fisheries Abstracts," "Oceanic Abstracts," and "Pollution Abstracts."

Enviro/Energyline Abstracts Plus. R. R. Bowker Co., 121 Chanlon Rd., New Providence, New Jersey 07974. (908) 464-6800.

Environmental Periodicals Bibliography. National Information Services Corp., Ste. 6, Wyman Towers, 3100 St. Paul St., Baltimore, Maryland 21218. (410)243-0797. Online version of abstract of same name.

SCISEARCH. Institute for Scientific Information, University City Science Center, 3501 Market St., Philadelphia, Pennsylvania 19104. (215) 386-0100.

TRADE ASSOCIATIONS AND PROFESSIONAL SOCIETIES

American Institute of Biological Sciences. 730 11th St., N.W., Washington, District of Columbia 20001-4521. (202) 628-1500.

American Society of Naturalists. Department of Ecology and Evolation, State University of New York, Stony Brook, New York 11794. (516) 632-8589.

MARSHES, SALT

See also: SALT

ABSTRACTING AND INDEXING SERVICES

Abstracts of Air and Water Conservation Literature. American Petroleum Institute. Central Abstracting and

Indexing Service, 275 Madison Avenue, New York, New York 10016. 1972.

Biological and Agricultural Index. H.W. Wilson Co., 950 University Ave., Bronx, New York 10452. (800) 367-6770. 1916-. Monthly.

GENERAL WORKS

Ecology of Salt Marshes and Sand Dunes. D. S. Ranwell. Chapman & Hall, 2-6 Boundary Row, London, England SE1 8HN. 1975. Seashore ecology, sand dunes, and tidemarsh ecology.

Saltmarsh Ecology. Paul Adam. Cambridge University Press, 40 W. 20th St., New York, New York 10011. (212) 924-3900. 1991. Flora, fauna, vegetation, how saltmarsh biota copes with this stressful environment, life history studies, marshes as ecosystems.

HANDBOOKS AND MANUALS

Life In and Around the Salt Marshes. Michael Ursin. Crowell, New York, New York 1972. A handbook of plant and animal life in and around the temperate Atlantic coastal marshes.

TRADE ASSOCIATIONS AND PROFESSIONAL SOCIETIES

American Society of Naturalists. Department of Ecology and Evolation, State University of New York, Stony Brook, New York 11794. (516) 632-8589.

MARYLAND ENVIRONMENTAL AGENCIES

GOVERNMENTAL ORGANIZATIONS

Department of Agriculture: Pesticide Registration. Assistant Secretary, Office of Plant Industries and Pest Management, 50 Harry S. Truman Pkwy., Annapolis, Maryland 21401. (301) 841-5870.

Department of Environment: Air Quality. Director, Air Management Association, 2500 Broening Highway, Baltimore, Maryland 21224. (301) 631-3225.

Department of Environment: Environmental Protection. Secretary, 2500 Broening Highway, Annapolis, Maryland 21224. (301) 631-3084.

Department of Environment: Hazardous Waste Management. Director, Hazardous and Solid Waste Management, 2500 Broening Highway, Baltimore, Maryland 21224. (301) 631-3304.

Department of Environment: Solid Waste Management. Director, Hazardous and Solid Waste Management, 2500 Broening Highway, Baltimore, Maryland 21224. (301) 631-3304.

Department of Natural Resources: Coastal Zone Management. Administrator, Tidewater Administration, Tawes State Office Bldg., Annapolis, Maryland 21401. (301) 974-2926.

Department of Natural Resources: Fish and Wildlife. Director, Tidewater Administration, Tawes State Office Building, Annapolis, Maryland 21401. (301) 974-2926.

Department of Natural Resources: Groundwater Management. Division Director, Water Supply Division, 580

Taylor Ave., Annapolis, Maryland 21401. (301) 974-3675.

Department of Natural Resources: Natural Resources. Secretary, Tawes State Office Bldg., Annapolis, Maryland 21401. (301) 974-3041.

Department of Natural Resources: Underground Storage Tanks. Director, Oil Control Division, 580 Taylor Ave., Annapolis, Maryland 21401. (301) 974-3551.

Department of the Environment: Emergency Preparedness and Community Right-to-Know. State Emergency Response Commission, Department of the Environment, Toxics Information Center, 2500 Broening Highway, Baltimore, Maryland 21224. (301) 631-3800.

Hazardous Waste Facilities Siting Board: Waste Minimization and Pollution Prevention. Director, 60 West St., Suite 200 A, Annapolis, Maryland 21401. (301) 974-3432.

Licensing and Regulation Department: Occupational Safety. Assistant Commissioner, Occupational Safety and Health, 501 St. Paul Place, Baltimore, Maryland 21202-272. (301) 333-4195.

Water Management Association: Water Quality. Health and Mental Hygiene Department, 201 West Preston St., 5th Floor, Baltimore, Maryland 21201. (301) 225-6300.

MARYLAND ENVIRONMENTAL LEGISLATION

GENERAL WORKS

Maryland Guide to Environmental Law. Maryland Chamber of Commerce, Annapolis St., Annapolis, Maryland 21401. (410)268-7676. 1989.

MASS TRANSPORTATION

See: TRANSPORTATION

MASSACHUSETTS ENVIRONMENTAL AGENCIES

GOVERNMENTAL ORGANIZATIONS

Department of Environmental Management: Groundwater Management. Director, Water Resources, 100 Cambridge St., Boston, Massachusetts 02202. (617) 727-3267.

Department of Environmental Management: Solid Waste Management. Director, Division of Solid Waste Disposal, 100 Cambridge St., Boston, Massachusetts 02202. (617) 727-3260.

Department of Environmental Management: Waste Minimization and Pollution Prevention. Program Director, Office of Safe Waste Management, 100 Cambridge St., Room 1904, Boston, Massachusetts 02202. (617) 727-3260.

Department of Environmental Quality Engineering: Air Quality. Commissioner, One Winter St., Boston, Massachusetts 02108. (617) 292-5856.

Department of Environmental Quality Engineering: Emergency Preparedness and Community Right-to-Know. Title III Emergency Response Commission, One Winter St., 10th Floor, Boston, Massachusetts 02108. (617) 292-5993.

Department of Environmental Quality Engineering: Underground Storage Tanks. Program Director, Underground Storage Tank Program, 1 Winter St., Boston, Massachusetts 02108. (617) 292-5500.

Department of Fisheries, Wildlife and Environmental Law Enforcement. Director, 100 Cambridge St., Boston, Massachusetts 02202. (617) 727-1614.

Department of Food and Agriculture: Pesticide Registration. Chief, Pesticide Bureau, 100 Cambridge St., 21st Floor, Boston, Massachusetts 02202. (617) 727-7712.

Department of Labor and Industry: Occupational Safety. Director, Division of Industrial Safety, 100 Cambridge St., Boston, Massachusetts 02202. (617) 727-3567.

Division of Waste Disposal: Hazardous Waste Management. Director, 100 Cambridge St., Boston, Massachusetts 02202. (617) 727-3260.

Environmental Quality Engineering: Water Quality. Director, Water Pollution, 1 Winter St., Boston, Massachusetts 02108. (617) 292-5636.

Executive Office of Environmental Affairs: Coastal Zone Management. Director, Coastal Zone Management, 100 Cambridge St., Boston, Massachusetts 02202. (617) 727-9530.

Executive Office of Environmental Affairs: Environmental Protection. Secretary, 100 Cambridge St., 20th Floor, Boston, Massachusetts 02202. (617) 727-9800.

Executive Office of Environmental Affairs: Natural Resources. Commissioner, Department of Environmental Management, 100 Cambridge St., Boston, Massachusetts 02202. (617) 727-3163.

MAXIMUM PERMISSIBLE EXPOSURE

See: RADIATION EXPOSURE

MAXIMUM SUSTAINABLE YIELD

See: SUSTAINABLE YIELD

MEAT PROCESSING

See: FOOD PROCESSING AND TREATMENT

MECHANICAL TURBULENCE

See: NOISE

MEDICAL WASTES

See also: HAZARDOUS WASTES

ABSTRACTING AND INDEXING SERVICES

Applied Ecology Abstracts Studies in Renewable Natural Resources. Information Retrieval Ltd., 1911 Jefferson Davis Highway, Arlington, Virginia 22202. 1975-. Monthly.

Biological and Agricultural Index. H.W. Wilson Co., 950 University Ave., Bronx, New York 10452. (800) 367-6770. 1916-. Monthly.

Chemical Abstracts. Chemical Abstracts Service, 2540 Olentangy River Rd., PO Box 3012, Columbus, Ohio 43210. (800) 848-6533. 1907-.

General Science Index. H. W. Wilson Co., 950 University Ave., Bronx, New York 10452. 1978-. Monthly, also issued in annual cumulation. Cumulative subject index to English language periodicals in the subject fields of astronomy, botany, chemistry, earth science, environment and conservation, food and nutrition, genetics, mathematics, medicine and health, microbiology, oceanography, physics, physiology and zoology.

Multimedia Index to Ecology. National Information Center for Educational Media, University of Southern California, Los Angeles, California 90007.

Pollution Abstracts. Cambridge Scientific Abstracts, 5161 River Rd., Bethesda, Maryland 20816. (301) 961-6750. Six/year. Indexes worldwide technical literature on environmental pollution. Covers air pollution, marine and freshwater pollution, sewage and wastewater treatment, waste management, toxicology and health, noise pollution, radiation, land pollution, and environmental policies, programs, legislation, and education. Also available online.

ENCYCLOPEDIAS AND DICTIONARIES

McGraw-Hill Encyclopedia of Environmental Science. Sybil P. Parker. McGraw-Hill Science & Engineering Books, 11 W. 19th St., New York, New York 10011. (212) 337-6010. 1980. Covers ecology, man's influence on nature, and environmental protection.

GENERAL WORKS

Infectious and Medical Waste Management. Peter A. Rinehardt and Judith G. Gordon. Lewis Publishers, 2000 Corporate Blvd., N.W., Boca Raton, Florida 33431. (407) 994-0555 or (800) 272-7737. 1991. Explains in detail how to safely comply with the complex regulations and how to set up an effective infectious and medical waste program (including AIDS and Hepatitis B viruses) so the right decisions can be made.

Medical Waste Handling for Health Care Facilities. John H. Keene. American Society for Healthcare Environmental Services of the American Hospital Association., 840 N. Lake Shore Dr., Chicago, Illinois 60611. (312) 280-

6245. 1989. Covers medical waste, refuse disposal, environmental exposure, accident prevention, and health facilities.

The Public Health Implications of Medical Waste: A Report to Congress. U.S. Department of Health and Human Services, Public Health Service, 200 Independence Ave. SW, Washington, District of Columbia 20201. (202) 619-1296. 1990. Covers infectious wastes and medical wastes.

The Report in the Medical Waste Policy Committee. Nelson A. Rockefeller Institute of Government, State University of New York, 411 State St., Albany, New York 12203-1003. (518) 443-5258. 1989. Waste disposal for health facilities and infectious wastes.

HANDBOOKS AND MANUALS

Handbook: Operation and Maintenance of Hospital Medical Waste Incinerators. U.S. Environmental Protection Agency, MD 75, Research Triangle Park, North Carolina 27711. 1990.

Hazardous Waste Management Strategies for Health Care Facilities. Nelson S. Slavik. American Hospital Association, 840 North Lake Shore Dr., Chicago, Illinois 60611. 1987. Contains helpful information for health care facilities in the management of their chemical, cytotoxic, infectious, and radiological wastes.

Medical Waste Incineration Handbook. C. C. Lee. Government Institutes, Inc., 4 Research Pl., Suite 200, Rockville, Maryland 20850. (301) 921-2300. 1990. Covers incineration, equipment, measurement techniques, potential emissions, maintenance, safety guidance, operational problems and solutions, and the federal and state regulatory framework. Includes a list of addresses and phone numbers of manufacturers of medical waste incinerators and manufacturers of air pollution control equipment.

Operation and Maintenance of Hospital Medical Waste Incinerators. U.S. Environmental Protection Agency–Office of Air Quality Planning and Standards. U.S. G.P.O, Washington, District of Columbia 20401. (202) 512-0000. 1990. A manual covering incineration of hazardous and medical wastes.

ONLINE DATA BASES

Chemical Abstracts-CA. Chemical Abstracts Service, 2540 Olentangy River Rd., P.O. Box 3012, Columbus, Ohio 43210. (800) 848-6533 or (614) 421-3600. Information sources include 9000 journals, patents from 27 countries, two industrial property organizations, new books, conference proceedings, and government research reports.

Medical Waste News. Business Publishers, Inc., 951 Pershing Dr., Silver Spring, Maryland 20910-4464. (301) 587-6300. Online access to regulation, legislation, and technological news and developments related to medical waste management and disposal. Online version of the periodical of the same name.

Monthly Catalog of United States Government Publications. U.S. G.P.O., Supt. of Docs., PO Box 371954, Pittsburgh, Pennsylvania 15250-7954. (202) 512-0000.

National Technical Information Service. U.S. Department of Commerce, National Technical Information Service, Office of Data Base Services, 5285 Port Royal Rd., Springfield, Virginia 22161. (703) 487-4807. Bibliographic database of government sponsored research and technical reports.

PERIODICALS AND NEWSLETTERS

Medical Waste News. Business Publishers, Inc., 951 Pershing Dr., Silver Spring, Maryland 20910-4464. (301) 587-6300. 1989-. Biweekly. Covers EPA regulations and actions, state and nationwide changes in the laws, which management firms are landing big contracts, and also reports on technology such as: incineration, autoclaving, microwaves, etc. Also available online.

STATISTICS SOURCES

Finding the Rx for Managing Medical Wastes. U.S. G.P.O., Washington, District of Columbia 20401. (202) 512-0000. 1990. Medical waste composition and management technologies. Includes human and animal products, discarded medical equipment and parts, radioactive waste, and wastes from surgery and selected clinical and laboratory procedures, including chemotherapy and dialysis.

The Market for Disposable Hospital Products. FIND/SVP, 625 Avenue of the Americas, New York, New York 10011. (212) 645-4500. 1991. Covers the disposable products: prepackaged kits and trays; surgical and examination gloves; syringes; intravenous IV disposables; catheters; and nebulizers.

Medical and Biomedical Waste Management Markets. FIND/SVP, 625 Avenue of the Americas, New York, New York 10011. (212) 645-4500. 1990. Discusses the increasing amount of waste as a result of the trend toward disposable instruments and clothing, and the establishment of more small clinics and health facilities.

MERCURY

See also: ENZYMES; TOXICITY

ABSTRACTING AND INDEXING SERVICES

ASFA Aquaculture Abstracts. Cambridge Scientific Abstracts, Inc., 5161 River Rd., Bethesda, Maryland 20816. (301) 961-6750. 1984.

Biological and Agricultural Index. H.W. Wilson Co., 950 University Ave., Bronx, New York 10452. (800) 367-6770. 1916-. Monthly.

Chemical Abstracts. Chemical Abstracts Service, 2540 Olentangy River Rd., PO Box 3012, Columbus, Ohio 43210. (800) 848-6533. 1907-.

Environment Abstracts. Bowker A & I Publishing, 121 Chanlon Rd., New Providence, New Jersey 07974. (908) 464-6800. 1974-.

Environment Index. Environment Information Center, Index Research Department, 124 E. 39th St., New York, New York 10016. 1971-. Annual.

Environmental Information Connection–EIC. Planning Information Program, Dept. of Urban and Regional Planning, University of Illinois, 1003 West Nevada, Urbana, Illinois 61801. (217) 333-1369. Also available online.

Environmental Periodicals Bibliography. Environmental Studies Institute, International Academy at Santa Barbara, 800 Garden St., Suite D, Santa Barbara, California 93101. (805) 965-5010. Also available online.

General Science Index. H. W. Wilson Co., 950 University Ave., Bronx, New York 10452. 1978-. Monthly, also issued in annual cumulation. Cumulative subject index to English language periodicals in the subject fields of astronomy, botany, chemistry, earth science, environment and conservation, food and nutrition, genetics, mathematics, medicine and health, microbiology, oceanography, physics, physiology and zoology.

Science Citation Index. Institute for Scientific Information, 3501 Market St., Philadelphia, Pennsylvania 19104. 1961-.

BIBLIOGRAPHIES

EPA Publications Bibliography. U.S. Environmental Protection Agency, Library Systems Branch, 401 M St., SW, Washington, District of Columbia 20460. (202) 260-2090. Quarterly.

A Selected Bibliography on Mercury in the Environment, with Subject Listing. Susan Robinson. Royal Ontario Museum, 100 Queens Park, Toronto, Ontario, Canada M5S 2C6. (416) 586-5581. 1974.

ENCYCLOPEDIAS AND DICTIONARIES

Encyclopedia of Chemical Processing and Design. John J. Mcketta and W. A. Cunningham. Marcel Dekker, Inc., 270 Madison Ave., New York, New York 10016. (212) 696-9000; (800) 228-1160. 1992. Thirty-eight volumes.

Encyclopedia of Human Biology. Renato Dulbecco, ed. Academic Press, c/o Harcourt Brace Jovanovich Inc., 6277 Sea Harbor Dr., Orlando, Florida 32887. (800) 346-8648. 1991. Eight volumes.

Kirk-Othmer Encyclopedia of Chemical Technology. J. I. Kroschwitz, ed. John Wiley & Sons, Inc., 605 3rd Ave., New York, New York 10158-0012. (212) 850-6000. 1992-. All articles in the new edition have been rewritten and updated adding new subjects such as biotechnology, computer topics, analytical techniques and instrumentation, environmental concerns, fuels and energy, inorganic and solid state chemistry; composite materials and material science in general, and pharmaceuticals. Also available online.

Van Nostrand's Scientific Encyclopedia. Glenn D. Considine, ed. Van Nostrand Reinhold, 115 5th Ave., New York, New York 10003. (212) 254-3232. 1983. Sixth edition. Includes all broad subject areas in science.

GENERAL WORKS

The Biogeochemistry of Mercury in the Environment. J.O. Nriagu. Elsevier Science Publishing Co., 655 Avenue of the Americas, New York, New York 10010. (212) 984-5800. 1979. Environmental aspects and toxicology of mercury.

Ethylmercury: Formation in Plant Tissues and Relation to Methylmercury Formation. L. Fortmann. National Technical Information Service, 5285 Port Royal Rd., Springfield, Virginia 22161. (703) 487-4650. 1978. Environmental aspects of mercury and botanical chemistry.

Lead, Mercury, Cadmium, and Arsenic in the Environment. T.C. Hutchinson. John Wiley & Sons, Inc., 605 3rd Ave., New York, New York 10158-0012. (212) 850-6000. 1987. Environmental aspects of mercury, lead and arsenic.

Magill's Survey of Science. Earth Science Series. Frank N. Magill. Salem Press, PO Box 50062, Pasadena, California 91105. 1990-. Five volumes. Includes information on earth's crust, hot spots and volcanic island chains, physical properties of minerals, rock magnetism, physical properties of rocks, and index.

Mercury: Environmental Aspects. World Health Organization, Ave. Appia, Geneva, Switzerland CH-1211. Environmental health criteria relating to toxicology of mercury.

Review of National Emission Standards for Mercury. National Technical Information Service, 5285 Port Royal Rd., Springfield, Virginia 22161. (703) 487-4650. 1987.

HANDBOOKS AND MANUALS

Tables of Physical and Chemical Constants and Some Mathematical Functions. G. W. C. Kaye, et al. Longman Group Ltd., Longman House, Burnt Mill, Harlow, England CM20 2J6. 0279 426721. 1988. Fifteenth edition. Includes tables on mechanical properties, density, elasticity, viscosity, surface tension, temperature and heat. Also covers radiation, optics, chemistry, electrochemistry, astrophysics, and chemical thermodynamics.

ONLINE DATA BASES

CERCLIS. Chemical Information Systems, Inc., 7215 York Rd., Baltimore, Maryland 21212. (301) 321-8440. Information on hazardous waste disposal sites that have either been listed by the EPA on the National Priority List (NPL) or nominated for consideration for the NPL.

Chemical Abstracts-CA. Chemical Abstracts Service, 2540 Olentangy River Rd., P.O. Box 3012, Columbus, Ohio 43210. (800) 848-6533 or (614) 421-3600. Information sources include 9000 journals, patents from 27 countries, two industrial property organizations, new books, conference proceedings, and government research reports.

Enviro/Energyline Abstracts Plus. R. R. Bowker Co., 121 Chanlon Rd., New Providence, New Jersey 07974. (908) 464-6800.

Environmental Periodicals Bibliography. National Information Services Corp., Ste. 6, Wyman Towers, 3100 St. Paul St., Baltimore, Maryland 21218. (410)243-0797. Online version of abstract of same name.

Kirk-Othmer Encyclopedia of Chemical Technology. John Wiley & Sons, Inc., 605 3rd Ave., 5th Floor, New York, New York 10158. (212) 850-6000. Online version of the publication of the same name.

MERCURY WASTES

See: MERCURY

METABOLIC EFFECTS

ABSTRACTING AND INDEXING SERVICES

Biological and Agricultural Index. H.W. Wilson Co., 950 University Ave., Bronx, New York 10452. (800) 367-6770. 1916-. Monthly.

Crop Physiology Abstracts. C. A. B. International, 845 North Park Ave., Tucson, Arizona 85719. (602) 621-7897 or (800) 528-4841. 1975-. Monthly. Abstracts focus on the physiology of all higher plants of economic importance. Aspects include germination, reproductive development, nitrogen fixation, metabolic inhibitors, salinity, radiobiology, enzymes, membranes and other related areas.

Ecological Abstracts. Geo Abstracts Ltd. Elsevier Applied Science, Crown House, Linton Rd., Barking, England IG 11 8JU. 1974-. Derived from over 600 leading ecological and environmental journals, plus books, conference proceedings, reports and theses.

General Science Index. H. W. Wilson Co., 950 University Ave., Bronx, New York 10452. 1978-. Monthly, also issued in annual cumulation. Cumulative subject index to English language periodicals in the subject fields of astronomy, botany, chemistry, earth science, environment and conservation, food and nutrition, genetics, mathematics, medicine and health, microbiology, oceanography, physics, physiology and zoology.

Science Citation Index. Institute for Scientific Information, 3501 Market St., Philadelphia, Pennsylvania 19104. 1961-.

ENCYCLOPEDIAS AND DICTIONARIES

The Nutrition and Health Encyclopedia. David F. Tver and Percy Russell. Van Nostrand Reinhold, 115 5th Ave., New York, New York 10003. (212) 254-3232. 1989.

GENERAL WORKS

Environmental and Metabolic Animal Physiology. C. Ladd Prosser, ed. John Wiley & Sons, Inc., Wiley-Liss Division, 605 3rd Ave., New York, New York 10158-0012. (212) 850-6000. 1991. 4th ed. Focuses on the various aspects of adaptive physiology, including environmental, biochemical, and regulatory topics. Examines the theory of adaptation, water and ions, temperature and hydrostatic pressure, nutrition, digestion, nitrogen metabolism, and energy transfer, respiration, O2 and CO2 transport and circulation.

Microbial Toxins in Focus and Feeds. Albert E. Pohland, et al., eds. Plenum Press, 233 Spring St., New York, New York 10013. (212) 620-8000; (800) 221-9369. 1990. Proceedings of a Symposium on Cellular and Molecular Mode of Action of Selected Microbial Toxins in Foods and Feeds, Oct. 31- Nov. 2, 1988, Chevy Chase, MD.

TRADE ASSOCIATIONS AND PROFESSIONAL SOCIETIES

American Institute of Biological Sciences. 730 11th St., N.W., Washington, District of Columbia 20001-4521. (202) 628-1500.

METABOLISM

ABSTRACTING AND INDEXING SERVICES

ASFA Aquaculture Abstracts. Cambridge Scientific Abstracts, Inc., 5161 River Rd., Bethesda, Maryland 20816. (301) 961-6750. 1984.

Biological and Agricultural Index. H.W. Wilson Co., 950 University Ave., Bronx, New York 10452. (800) 367-6770. 1916-. Monthly.

Current Advances in Plant Science. Pergamon Microforms International, Inc., Fairview Park, Elmsford, New York 10523. (914) 592-7720. 1984-. Monthly. Current literature searching service including journals, reports, abstracts, etc. This service is available online as part of the CABS database on the hosts BRS and ORBIT search service.

Ecological Abstracts. Geo Abstracts Ltd. Elsevier Applied Science, Crown House, Linton Rd., Barking, England IG 11 8JU. 1974-. Derived from over 600 leading ecological and environmental journals, plus books, conference proceedings, reports and theses.

Food Science and Technology Abstracts. International Food Information Service, c/o National Food Laboratory, 6363 Clark Ave., Dublin, California 94568. (800) 336-3782. 1969-.

General Science Index. H. W. Wilson Co., 950 University Ave., Bronx, New York 10452. 1978-. Monthly, also issued in annual cumulation. Cumulative subject index to English language periodicals in the subject fields of astronomy, botany, chemistry, earth science, environment and conservation, food and nutrition, genetics, mathematics, medicine and health, microbiology, oceanography, physics, physiology and zoology.

Pollution Abstracts. Cambridge Scientific Abstracts, 5161 River Rd., Bethesda, Maryland 20816. (301) 961-6750. Six/year. Indexes worldwide technical literature on environmental pollution. Covers air pollution, marine and freshwater pollution, sewage and wastewater treatment, waste management, toxicology and health, noise pollution, radiation, land pollution, and environmental policies, programs, legislation, and education. Also available online.

Science Citation Index. Institute for Scientific Information, 3501 Market St., Philadelphia, Pennsylvania 19104. 1961-.

ENCYCLOPEDIAS AND DICTIONARIES

Encyclopedia of Human Biology. Renato Dulbecco, ed. Academic Press, c/o Harcourt Brace Jovanovich Inc., 6277 Sea Harbor Dr., Orlando, Florida 32887. (800) 346-8648. 1991. Eight volumes.

The Nutrition and Health Encyclopedia. David F. Tver and Percy Russell. Van Nostrand Reinhold, 115 5th Ave., New York, New York 10003. (212) 254-3232. 1989.

Van Nostrand's Scientific Encyclopedia. Glenn D. Considine, ed. Van Nostrand Reinhold, 115 5th Ave., New York, New York 10003. (212) 254-3232. 1983. Sixth edition. Includes all broad subject areas in science.

GENERAL WORKS

The Biochemistry and Uses of Pesticides: Structure, Metabolism, Mode of Action, and Uses in Crop Protection. Kenneth A. Hassall. VCH Publishers, 303 NW 12th Ave., Deerfield Beach, Florida 33442-1788. (305) 428-5566. 1990. Reports the progress that has been made in the last few years towards an understanding of how pesticides function, how metabolism contributes to selectivity and safety and how the development of resistance is linked to biochemistry and molecular biology.

Calcium in Biological Systems. Ronald P. Rubin. Plenum Press, 233 Spring St., New York, New York 10013-1578. (212) 620-8000. 1985. Covers calcification and calcium channel blockers.

Cell ATP. William A. Bridger. John Wiley & Sons, Inc., 605 3rd Ave., New York, New York 10158-0012. (212) 850-6000. 1983. Discusses the metabolism of adenosine triphosphate including cell metabolism.

Environmental and Metabolic Animal Physiology. C. Ladd Prosser, ed. John Wiley & Sons, Inc., Wiley-Liss Division, 605 3rd Ave., New York, New York 10158-0012. (212) 850-6000. 1991. 4th ed. Focuses on the various aspects of adaptive physiology, including environmental, biochemical, and regulatory topics. Examines the theory of adaptation, water and ions, temperature and hydrostatic pressure, nutrition, digestion, nitrogen metabolism, and energy transfer, respiration, O2 and CO2 transport and circulation.

Instrumental Methods for Quality Assurance in Foods. Daniel Y. C. Fung and Richard F. Matthews. Marcell Dekker Inc., 270 Madison Ave., New York, New York 10016. (212) 696-9000; (800) 228-1160. 1991.

Magill's Survey of Science. Life Science Series. Frank N. Magill, ed. Salem Press, PO Box 50062, Pasadena, California 91105. 1991. Six volumes. Contents: v.1. A-Central and peripheral nervous system functions; v.2. Central metabolism regulation - eukaryotic transcriptional control; v.3. Positive and negative eukaryotic transcriptional control - mammalian hormones; v.4. Hormones and behavior - muscular contraction; v.5. Muscular contraction and relaxation - sexual reproduction in plants; v.6. Reproductive behavior and mating - X inactivation and the Lyon hypothesis.

Microbial Toxins in Focus and Feeds. Albert E. Pohland, et al., eds. Plenum Press, 233 Spring St., New York, New York 10013. (212) 620-8000; (800) 221-9369. 1990. Proceedings of a Symposium on Cellular and Molecular Mode of Action of Selected Microbial Toxins in Foods and Feeds, Oct. 31- Nov. 2, 1988, Chevy Chase, MD.

The Role of Calcium in Biological Systems. CRC Press, 2000 Corporate Blvd. N.W., Boca Raton, Florida 33431. (800) 272-7737. 1982-.

The Role of Calcium in Drug Action. Pergamon Microforms International Inc., Fairview Park, Elmsford, New York 10523. (914) 592-7720. 1987. Calcium, agonists and their therapeutic use.

Secondary Metabolism in Microorganisms, Plants and Animals. Martin Luckner. Springer-Verlag, 175 5th Ave., New York, New York 10010. (212) 460-1500. 1990. Includes reviews of the latest results on the biosynthesis for age and degradation of secondary metabolites and characteristics of compounds of specialized cells from all groups of organisms. Has new chapters on: the transport of secondary compounds with the producer organism; the significance of colored and toxic secondary products; and on the improvement of secondary product biosynthesis by genetical means.

HANDBOOKS AND MANUALS

Handbook of Toxic Fungal Metabolites. Richard J. Cole and Richard H. Cox. Academic Press, c/o Harcourt Brace Jovanovich Inc., 6277 Sea Harbor Dr., Orlando, Florida 32887. (800) 346-8648. Oriented toward fungal metabolites that elicit a toxic response in vertebrate animals. Also includes metabolites that show little or no known acute toxicity.

Manual of Clinical Endocrinology & Metabolism. James E. Griffin. McGraw-Hill Science & Engineering Books, 11 W. 19th St., New York, New York 10011. (212) 337-6010. 1982. Metabolism disorders and diseases of endocrine glands.

Metabolic Maps of Pesticides. Hiroyasu Aizawa. Academic Press, c/o Harcourt Brace Jovanovich Inc., 6277 Sea Harbor Dr., Orlando, Florida 32887. (800) 346-8648. 1982. Ecotoxicology and environmental quality of pesticides metabolism.

Preclinical Drug Disposition: A Laboratory Handbook. Francis L.S. Tse. Marcel Dekker, Inc., 270 Madison Ave., New York, New York 10016. (212) 696-9000; (800) 228-1160. 1991. Covers drug metabolism and pharmacokinetics.

PERIODICALS AND NEWSLETTERS

Cell Calcium. Churchill Livingstone, Inc., 650 Avenue of the Americas, New York, New York 10011. (212) 206-5000. Bimonthly. The international interdisciplinary forum for research on calcium.

RESEARCH CENTERS AND INSTITUTES

University of Georgia, Complex Carbohydrate Research Center. 220 Riverbend Road, Athens, Georgia 30602. (404) 542-4401.

University of Wisconsin-Madison, Biotechnology Center. 1710 University Avenue, Madison, Wisconsin 53705. (608) 262-8606.

TRADE ASSOCIATIONS AND PROFESSIONAL SOCIETIES

American Institute of Biological Sciences. 730 11th St., N.W., Washington, District of Columbia 20001-4521. (202) 628-1500.

METAL CONTAMINATION

See also: CONTAMINATION

ABSTRACTING AND INDEXING SERVICES

Aqualine Abstracts. Water Research Centre. c/o Pergamon Microforms International, Inc., Fairview Park, Elmsford, New York 10523. (914) 592-7720. 1927-. Contains some 8,000 records annually on water and wastewater technology. Covers all aspects of water, wastewater, associated engineering services and the aquatic environment. Over 600 periodicals, as well as books, reports and conference proceedings and other

publications from water related institutions worldwide are scanned. Also available online.

Biological and Agricultural Index. H.W. Wilson Co., 950 University Ave., Bronx, New York 10452. (800) 367-6770. 1916-. Monthly.

Chemical Abstracts. Chemical Abstracts Service, 2540 Olentangy River Rd., PO Box 3012, Columbus, Ohio 43210. (800) 848-6533. 1907-.

Environment Abstracts. Bowker A & I Publishing, 121 Chanlon Rd., New Providence, New Jersey 07974. (908) 464-6800. 1974-.

Environment Index. Environment Information Center, Index Research Department, 124 E. 39th St., New York, New York 10016. 1971-. Annual.

Environmental Information Connection–EIC. Planning Information Program, Dept. of Urban and Regional Planning, University of Illinois, 1003 West Nevada, Urbana, Illinois 61801. (217) 333-1369. Also available online.

Environmental Periodicals Bibliography. Environmental Studies Institute, International Academy at Santa Barbara, 800 Garden St., Suite D, Santa Barbara, California 93101. (805) 965-5010. Also available online.

General Science Index. H. W. Wilson Co., 950 University Ave., Bronx, New York 10452. 1978-. Monthly, also issued in annual cumulation. Cumulative subject index to English language periodicals in the subject fields of astronomy, botany, chemistry, earth science, environment and conservation, food and nutrition, genetics, mathematics, medicine and health, microbiology, oceanography, physics, physiology and zoology.

Science Citation Index. Institute for Scientific Information, 3501 Market St., Philadelphia, Pennsylvania 19104. 1961-.

BIBLIOGRAPHIES

EPA Publications Bibliography. U.S. Environmental Protection Agency, Library Systems Branch, 401 M St., SW, Washington, District of Columbia 20460. (202) 260-2090. Quarterly.

ENCYCLOPEDIAS AND DICTIONARIES

Encyclopedia of Human Biology. Renato Dulbecco, ed. Academic Press, c/o Harcourt Brace Jovanovich Inc., 6277 Sea Harbor Dr., Orlando, Florida 32887. (800) 346-8648. 1991. Eight volumes.

GENERAL WORKS

Ecotoxicology of Metals: Current Concepts and Applications. Michael C. Newman and Alan W. McIntosh. Lewis Publishers, 2000 Corporate Blvd., N.W., Boca Raton, Florida 33431. (407) 994-0555 or (800) 272-7737. 1991. Examines the influence of water chemistry on metal toxicity. Also includes a review of toxic effects on fish and other biological forms that exist in the water. Analyzes and presents alternatives to standard techniques. Describes present and future needs in sediment toxicity and community level response of stream organisms to heavy metals.

Metal-Bearing Waste Streams: Mining, Recycling, and Treatment. Michael Meltzer, et al. Noyes Publications,

120 Mill Rd., Park Ridge, New Jersey 07656. (201) 391-8484. 1990. Examines the management of metal-bearing wastes. Covers an in-depth industry study of the generation of metal-bearing waste streams. Summaries of waste management practices in various metal operations, including foundry activities, metal cleaning and stripping, surface treatment and plating, coating, and auxiliary operations, are provided.

Metal Contamination of Food. Conor Reilly. Elsevier Science Publishing Co., 655 Avenue of the Americas, New York, New York 10010. (212) 984-5800. 1991. Analysis of testing of metals in food.

Metal Recovery from Industrial Waste. Clyde S. Brooks. Lewis Publishers, 2000 Corporate Blvd., N.W., Boca Raton, Florida 33431. (407) 994-0555 or (800) 272-7737. 1991. Gives details of industrial waste recycling in particular nonferrous metals.

Metals and Their Compounds in the Environment. Ernest Merian, ed. VCH Publishers, 303 NW 12th Ave., Deerfield Beach, Florida 33442-1788. (305) 428-5566. 1990.

HANDBOOKS AND MANUALS

Guidelines for Can Manufacturers and Food Canners: Prevention of Metal Contamination of Canned Foods. Food and Agricultural Organization of the United Nations, Via delle Terme di Caracalla, Rome, Italy 00100. 61 0181 FAO1. 1986. Canned foods industry and food contamination.

ONLINE DATA BASES

CERCLIS. Chemical Information Systems, Inc., 7215 York Rd., Baltimore, Maryland 21212. (301) 321-8440. Information on hazardous waste disposal sites that have either been listed by the EPA on the National Priority List (NPL) or nominated for consideration for the NPL.

Chemical Abstracts-CA. Chemical Abstracts Service, 2540 Olentangy River Rd., P.O. Box 3012, Columbus, Ohio 43210. (800) 848-6533 or (614) 421-3600. Information sources include 9000 journals, patents from 27 countries, two industrial property organizations, new books, conference proceedings, and government research reports.

Enviro/Energyline Abstracts Plus. R. R. Bowker Co., 121 Chanlon Rd., New Providence, New Jersey 07974. (908) 464-6800.

Environmental Periodicals Bibliography. National Information Services Corp., Ste. 6, Wyman Towers, 3100 St. Paul St., Baltimore, Maryland 21218. (410)243-0797. Online version of abstract of same name.

METAL POISONING

See also: CONTAMINATION; LEAD POISONING

ABSTRACTING AND INDEXING SERVICES

Biological and Agricultural Index. H.W. Wilson Co., 950 University Ave., Bronx, New York 10452. (800) 367-6770. 1916-. Monthly.

Chemical Abstracts. Chemical Abstracts Service, 2540 Olentangy River Rd., PO Box 3012, Columbus, Ohio 43210. (800) 848-6533. 1907-.

Environment Abstracts. Bowker A & I Publishing, 121 Chanlon Rd., New Providence, New Jersey 07974. (908) 464-6800. 1974-.

Environment Index. Environment Information Center, Index Research Department, 124 E. 39th St., New York, New York 10016. 1971-. Annual.

Environmental Information Connection–EIC. Planning Information Program, Dept. of Urban and Regional Planning, University of Illinois, 1003 West Nevada, Urbana, Illinois 61801. (217) 333-1369. Also available online.

Environmental Periodicals Bibliography. Environmental Studies Institute, International Academy at Santa Barbara, 800 Garden St., Suite D, Santa Barbara, California 93101. (805) 965-5010. Also available online.

General Science Index. H. W. Wilson Co., 950 University Ave., Bronx, New York 10452. 1978-. Monthly, also issued in annual cumulation. Cumulative subject index to English language periodicals in the subject fields of astronomy, botany, chemistry, earth science, environment and conservation, food and nutrition, genetics, mathematics, medicine and health, microbiology, oceanography, physics, physiology and zoology.

Index to Scientific Book Contents. Institute for Scientific Information, 3501 Market St., Philadelphia, Pennsylvania 19104. (800) 523-1857. 1985-. Annual. Gives contents of science books published.

Pollution Abstracts. Cambridge Scientific Abstracts, 5161 River Rd., Bethesda, Maryland 20816. (301) 961-6750. Six/year. Indexes worldwide technical literature on environmental pollution. Covers air pollution, marine and freshwater pollution, sewage and wastewater treatment, waste management, toxicology and health, noise pollution, radiation, land pollution, and environmental policies, programs, legislation, and education. Also available online.

BIBLIOGRAPHIES

EPA Publications Bibliography. U.S. Environmental Protection Agency, Library Systems Branch, 401 M St., SW, Washington, District of Columbia 20460. (202) 260-2090. Quarterly.

ENCYCLOPEDIAS AND DICTIONARIES

McGraw-Hill Encyclopedia of Environmental Science. Sybil P. Parker. McGraw-Hill Science & Engineering Books, 11 W. 19th St., New York, New York 10011. (212) 337-6010. 1980. Covers ecology, man's influence on nature, and environmental protection.

GENERAL WORKS

Aluminum in Food and the Environment. Robert C. Massey. Royal Society of Chemistry, c/o CRC Press, 2000 Corporate Blvd. N.W., Boca Raton, Florida 33431-9868. (800)272-7737. 1990. Looks at the adverse health effects associated with aluminum. The evidence of aluminum's involvement in both dialysis dementia and Alzheimer's disease is reviewed and biochemical mecha-

nisms by which aluminum may exert its detrimental effects on brain tissue are discussed.

ONLINE DATA BASES

CERCLIS. Chemical Information Systems, Inc., 7215 York Rd., Baltimore, Maryland 21212. (301) 321-8440. Information on hazardous waste disposal sites that have either been listed by the EPA on the National Priority List (NPL) or nominated for consideration for the NPL.

Chemical Abstracts-CA. Chemical Abstracts Service, 2540 Olentangy River Rd., P.O. Box 3012, Columbus, Ohio 43210. (800) 848-6533 or (614) 421-3600. Information sources include 9000 journals, patents from 27 countries, two industrial property organizations, new books, conference proceedings, and government research reports.

Enviro/Energyline Abstracts Plus. R. R. Bowker Co., 121 Chanlon Rd., New Providence, New Jersey 07974. (908) 464-6800.

Environmental Periodicals Bibliography. National Information Services Corp., Ste. 6, Wyman Towers, 3100 St. Paul St., Baltimore, Maryland 21218. (410)243-0797. Online version of abstract of same name.

RESEARCH CENTERS AND INSTITUTES

University of Wyoming, Red Buttes Environmental Biology Laboratory. Box 3166, University Station, Laramie, Wyoming 82071. (307) 745-8504.

METAL STRIPMINING

See: METALS AND METALLURGY

METALLOTHIONEIN

See: BIOMARKER

METALS AND METALLURGY

ABSTRACTING AND INDEXING SERVICES

Applied Science and Technology Index. H.W. Wilson Co., 950 University Ave., Bronx, New York 10452. (800) 367-6770. Formerly Industrial Arts Index.

Chemical Abstracts. Chemical Abstracts Service, 2540 Olentangy River Rd., PO Box 3012, Columbus, Ohio 43210. (800) 848-6533. 1907-.

Engineering Index. The Engineering Index Inc., 345 E. 47th St., New York, New York 10017. 1962-.

Metals Abstracts. ASM International, 9639 Kinsman, Materials Park, Ohio 44073. (216) 338-5151. 1968-. Published jointly by the Institute of Metals, London and the American Society for Metals. Formed by the Union of Metallurgical Abstracts and Review of Metal Literature.

Physics Briefs. Physikalische Berichte. Physik Verlag, Pappapelallee 3, Postfach 101161, Weinheim, Germany D-6940. 1979-. Semimonthly. In English. Volumes for 1979- issued by the Deutsche Physikalische Gesellschaft and the Fachinformationszentrum Energie Physik, Mathematik in cooperation with the American Institute of Physics.

BIBLIOGRAPHIES

Bibliography and Index of Geology. American Geological Institute, 4220 King St., Alexandria, Virginia 22302. Monthly. Includes environmental geology and hydrogeology.

DIRECTORIES

33 Metal Producing–Buyer's Guide Issue. Penton Publishing Co., 1100 Superior Ave., Cleveland, Ohio 44114. (216) 696-7000.

Directory of Plastics Recycling Companies. Resource Recycling, Box 10540, Portland, Oregon 97210. (503) 227-1319.

Engineering and Mining Journal–Buying Directory Issue. Maclean Hunter Publishing Company, 29 North Wacker Dr., Chicago, Illinois 60606. (312) 726-2802.

Ferro–Alloy Directory and Databook. 220 5th Ave., 10th Fl., New York, New York 10001. (212) 213-6202. Irregular.

Institute of Scrap Recycling Industries–Membership Directory. Institute of Scrap Recycling Industries, 1627 K St., N.W., Suite 700, Washington, District of Columbia 20006. (202) 466-4050.

Metal Bulletin Prices and Data. Metal Bulletin Books Ltd., 220 5th St, 10th Fl, New York, New York 10001. (212) 213-6202. 1987-. Annual.

Metal Casting Industry Directory. 1100 Superior Ave., Cleveland, Ohio 44114. (216) 696-7000. Annual.

North American Directory of Non-Ferrous Foundries. 455 State St., Suite 100, Des Plaines, Illinois 60061. (708) 299-0950. Biennial.

Powder Metallurgy Consultant's Directory. Metal Powder Industries Federation, 105 College Rd. East, Princeton, New Jersey 08540. (609) 452-7700.

Powder Metallurgy Equipment Directory. Powder Metallurgy Equipment Association, 105 College Rd. East, Princeton, New Jersey 08540. (609) 452-7700.

Precious Metal Databook. Metal Bulletin Inc., 220 5th Ave., 10th Floor, New York, New York 10001. (212) 213-6202.

Primary Aluminium Smelters and Producers of the World. Aluminium-Verlag GmbH, P.O. Box 1207, Dusseldorf 1, Germany D-4000. 211 320821.

Primary Aluminum Plants, Worldwide. Department of the Interior, 810 7th St. NW, Washington, District of Columbia 20241. (202) 501-9649.

Sources for Metal Castings: A Buyers Guide and Directory of Members. American Cast Metals Association, 455 State St., Des Plaines, Illinois 60016. (312) 299-9160.

Stainless Steel Databook. Metal Bulletin Inc., 220 5th St, 10th Fl., New York, New York 10001. (212) 213-6202. 1988.

ENCYCLOPEDIAS AND DICTIONARIES

Elsevier's Dictionary of Metallurgy and Metal Working in Six Languages. W. E. Clason. Elsevier Science Publishing Co., 655 Avenue of the Americas, New York, New York 10010. (212) 989-5800. 1978. Text in English/American, French, Spanish, Italian, Dutch, and German.

An Encyclopaedia of Metallurgy and Materials. C. R. Tottle. Institute of Metals, MacDonald and Evans, Estover, England PL6 7PZ. 1984. Deals with thermoelectric properties and other related data on metals.

Encyclopedia of Chemical Processing and Design. John J. Mcketta and W. A. Cunningham. Marcel Dekker, Inc., 270 Madison Ave., New York, New York 10016. (212) 696-9000; (800) 228-1160. 1992. Thirty-eight volumes.

Kirk-Othmer Encyclopedia of Chemical Technology. J. I. Kroschwitz, ed. John Wiley & Sons, Inc., 605 3rd Ave., New York, New York 10158-0012. (212) 850-6000. 1992-. All articles in the new edition have been rewritten and updated adding new subjects such as biotechnology, computer topics, analytical techniques and instrumentation, environmental concerns, fuels and energy, inorganic and solid state chemistry; composite materials and material science in general, and pharmaceuticals. Also available online.

McGraw-Hill Encyclopedia of Environmental Science. Sybil P. Parker. McGraw-Hill Science & Engineering Books, 11 W. 19th St., New York, New York 10011. (212) 337-6010. 1980. Covers ecology, man's influence on nature, and environmental protection.

The Nutrition and Health Encyclopedia. David F. Tver and Percy Russell. Van Nostrand Reinhold, 115 5th Ave., New York, New York 10003. (212) 254-3232. 1989.

GENERAL WORKS

Environmental Chemistry and Toxicology of Aluminum. Timothy E. Lewis. Lewis Publishers, 2000 Corporate Blvd., N.W., Boca Raton, Florida 33431. (407) 994-0555 or (800) 272-7737. 1989. Examines the sources, fate, transport, and health effects of aluminum in aquatic and terrestrial environments. Also includes the latest advances in the study of aluminum in the environment; toxicity research–aquatic and terrestrial biota; neurotoxicity and possible links to Alzheimer's disease; different forms of aluminum in soils and soil water; coordination chemistry; specification and analytical methods.

How on Earth Do We Recycle Metal?. Rudy Kouhoupt. Millbrook Press, 2 Old New Milford Rd., PO Box 335, New York, New York 06804-0335. (203) 740-2220. 1992. Disposal and recycling of metal waste by creating objects such as jewelry, weather vanes, and Christmas ornaments.

Metal-Bearing Waste Streams: Mining, Recycling, and Treatment. Michael Meltzer, et al. Noyes Publications, 120 Mill Rd., Park Ridge, New Jersey 07656. (201) 391-8484. 1990. Examines the management of metal-bearing wastes. Covers an in-depth industry study of the generation of metal-bearing waste streams. Summaries of waste management practices in various metal operations, including foundry activities, metal cleaning and stripping, surface treatment and plating, coating, and auxiliary operations, are provided.

Sensitive Biochemical and Behavioral Indicators of Trace Substance Exposure. Edward J. Massaro. Center for Environmental Research Information, U.S. Environmental Protection Agency, 26 W. Martin Luther King Dr., Cincinnati, Ohio 45268. (518) 569-7931. 1981.

Toxicity of Industrial Metals. Ethel Browning. Butterworth-Heinemann, 80 Montvale Ave., Stoneham, Massachusetts 02180. (617) 438-8464; (800) 366-2665. 1969. 2d ed.

HANDBOOKS AND MANUALS

The Environmental Chemistry of Aluminum. Garrison Sposito. CRC Press, 2000 Corporate Blvd. N.W., Boca Raton, Florida 33431. (800) 272-7737. 1989. Environmental aspects of aluminum content in water, soil and acid deposition.

Guidance Manual for Aluminum, Copper, and Nonferrous Metals Forming and Metal Powders Pretreatment Standards. U.S. Environmental Protection Agency, 401 M St. SW, Washington, District of Columbia 20460. (202) 260-2090. Environmental aspects of metallurgy and nonferrous metals.

Handbook on the Toxicology of Metals. Lars Friberg. Elsevier Science Publishing Co., 655 Avenue of the Americas, New York, New York 10010. (212) 984-5800. 1986. Pharmacodynamics and toxicity of metals.

Smithells Metals Reference Book. Eric A. Brandes, ed. Butterworth-Heinemann, 80 Montvale Ave., Stoneham, Massachusetts 02180. (617) 438-8464 or (800) 366-2665. 1983. Sixth edition. Contains data, pertaining to metals, such as: thermochemical data, physical properties of molten salts, metallography, equilibrium diagrams, gas-metal systems, diffusion in metals, general physical properties, elastic properties, temperature measurement and other related data.

Tables of Physical and Chemical Constants and Some Mathematical Functions. G. W. C. Kaye, et al. Longman Group Ltd., Longman House, Burnt Mill, Harlow, England CM20 2J6. 0279 426721. 1988. Fifteenth edition. Includes tables on mechanical properties, density, elasticity, viscosity, surface tension, temperature and heat. Also covers radiation, optics, chemistry, electrochemistry, astrophysics, and chemical thermodynamics.

ONLINE DATA BASES

Advanced Composites Bulletin. Elsevier Advanced Technology Publications, Mayfield House, 256 Banbury Rd., Oxford, England OX2 7DH. 44 (865) 512242.

CAS Source Index–CASSI. Chemical Abstracts Service, 2540 Olentangy River Rd., P.O. Box 3012, Columbus, Ohio 43210. (800) 848-6533 or (614) 421-3600. A listing of bibliographic and library holdings information for scientific and technical primary literature relevant to the chemical sciences.

Chemical Abstracts-CA. Chemical Abstracts Service, 2540 Olentangy River Rd., P.O. Box 3012, Columbus, Ohio 43210. (800) 848-6533 or (614) 421-3600. Information sources include 9000 journals, patents from 27 countries, two industrial property organizations, new books, conference proceedings, and government research reports.

Chemical Age Project File. MBC Information Services Ltd., Paulton House, 8 Shepherdess Walk, London, England N1 7LB. 44 (71) 490-0049.

Computerized Engineering Index–COMPENDEX. Engineering Information Inc., 345 E. 47th St., New York, New York 10017. (212) 705-7600.

DOMIS. ECHO Service, BP 2373, Luxembourg L-1023. (352) 488041.

Engineering and Mining Journal. Maclean Hunter Publishing Company, 29 N. Wacker Dr., Chicago, Illinois 60606. (312) 726-2802.

IMMAGE. Institution of Mining & Metallurgy Library and Information Services, 44 Portland Place, London, England W1N 4BR. 44 (71) 580-3802.

Kirk-Othmer Encyclopedia of Chemical Technology. John Wiley & Sons, Inc., 605 3rd Ave., 5th Floor, New York, New York 10158. (212) 850-6000. Online version of the publication of the same name.

Metals Week. McGraw-Hill Financial Services Company, 25 Broadway, New York, New York 10004. (212) 208-8880.

Minesearch. Metals Economics Group, Ltd., 1722 14th St., Boulder, Colorado 80302. (303) 442-7501.

Nonferrous Metals Abstracts. British Non-Ferrous Metals Technology Centre, Grove Laboratories, Denchworth Rd., Wantage, Oxfordshire, England OX12 9BJ. 44 (2357) 2992.

PERIODICALS AND NEWSLETTERS

Journal of American Mining Congress. American Mining Congress, 1920 N Street, NW, Suite 300, Washington, District of Columbia 20036. (202) 861-2800. Monthly. Contains information on the mining industry.

Scrap Age. Three Sons Pub. Co., 6311 Gross Point Rd., Niles, Illinois 60648. Monthly.

RESEARCH CENTERS AND INSTITUTES

Institute of Scrap Recycling Industries. 1627 K St., N.W., Suite 700, Washington, District of Columbia 20006. (202) 466-4050.

STATISTICS SOURCES

Aluminum Situation. Aluminum Association, Publications Department, 900 19th St., NW, Washington, District of Columbia 20006. Monthly. Estimated quarterly aluminum production, shipments, order, inventories, and foreign trade.

Aluminum Statistical Review. Aluminum Association, Publications Department, 900 19th St., NW, Washington, District of Columbia 20006. Annual. Ingot and mill product shipments, end-use markets, capacity, plants, scrap recovery, foreign trade, and supply and demand.

Annual Data: Copper, Brass, Bronze; Copper Supply and Consumption. Copper Development Association, Greenwich Office Park 2, Box 1840, Greenwich, Connecticut 06836-1840. Annual. Supply and consumption of copper and copper alloy.

Annual Statistical Report, American Iron and Steel Institute. American Iron and Steel Institute, 1133 15th St.,

NW, Washington, District of Columbia 20005. Annual. Industry production, finances, employment, shipments, and foreign trade.

Non-Ferrous Metal Data. American Bureau of Metal Statistics, 400 Plaza Dr. (Harmon Meadow), P.O. Box 1405, Secaucus, New Jersey 07094-0405. Annual. Production and consumption, imports and exports, and exchange prices.

Nonferrous Metals: Industry Structure. U.S. G.P.O., Washington, District of Columbia 20401. (202) 512-0000. 1990. Nonferrous metal production facilities and copper facility sales and aluminum production and sales.

TRADE ASSOCIATIONS AND PROFESSIONAL SOCIETIES

American Bureau of Metal Statistics. P.O. Box 1405, 400 Plaza Dr., Secaucus, New Jersey 07094. (201) 863-6900.

American Iron & Steel Institute. 1101 17th St., N.W., Washington, District of Columbia 20036-4700. (202) 463-6573.

American Iron Ore Association. 915 Rockefeller Bldg., 614 Superior Ave., N.W., Cleveland, Ohio 44113. (216) 241-8261.

American Mining Congress. 1920 N St., N.W., Suite 300, Washington, District of Columbia 20036. (202) 861-2800.

ASM International. 9639 Kinsman, Materials Park, Ohio 44073. (216) 338-5151.

Association of Iron and Steel Engineers. Three Gateway Center, Suite 2350, Pittsburgh, Pennsylvania 15222. (412) 281-6323.

Can Manufacturers Institute. 1625 Massachusetts Ave., N.W., Washington, District of Columbia 20036. (202) 232-4677.

Ferrous Scrap Consumers Coalition. c/o Collier, Shannon, Rill, & Scott, 1055 Thomas Jefferson St., N.W., Suite 308, Washington, District of Columbia 20007. (202) 342-8485.

Industrial Metal Containers Section of the Material Handling Institute. c/o Material Handling Inst., IMC, 8720 Red Oak Blvd., Suite 201, Charlotte, North Carolina 28217. (704) 522-8644.

The Institute of Metals. North American Publications Center, Old Post Rd., Brookfield, Vermont 05036. (802) 276-3162.

Iron and Steel Society. 410 Commonwealth Dr., Warrendale, Pennsylvania 15086. (412) 776-1535.

Materials Technology Institute of the Chemical Process Industries. 12747 Olive Blvd., Suite 203, St. Louis, Missouri 63141. (314) 576-7712.

Minerals, Metals, and Materials Society. 420 Commonwealth Dr., Warrendale, Pennsylvania 15086. (412) 776-9000.

Mining and Metallurgical Society of America. 9 Escalle Lane, Larkspur, California 94939. (415) 924-7441.

National Association of Metal Finishers. 401 N. Michigan Ave., Chicago, Illinois 60611-4267. (312) 644-6610.

Sheet Metal Workers' International Association. 1750 New York Ave., N.W., Washington, District of Columbia 20006. (202) 783-5880.

United Steelworkers of America. 5 Gateway Center, Pittsburgh, Pennsylvania 15222. (412) 562-2400.

METHANE

See also: COAL; FERTILIZERS; NATURAL GAS; OZONE

ABSTRACTING AND INDEXING SERVICES

Applied Science and Technology Index. H.W. Wilson Co., 950 University Ave., Bronx, New York 10452. (800) 367-6770. Formerly Industrial Arts Index.

Biological and Agricultural Index. H.W. Wilson Co., 950 University Ave., Bronx, New York 10452. (800) 367-6770. 1916-. Monthly.

Biotechnology Research Abstracts. Cambridge Scientific Abstracts, 5161 River Rd., Bethesda, Maryland 20816. (301) 961-6750. Monthly. Includes such broad areas as genetic intervention, biochemical genetics, and microbiological techniques.

Chemical Abstracts. Chemical Abstracts Service, 2540 Olentangy River Rd., PO Box 3012, Columbus, Ohio 43210. (800) 848-6533. 1907-.

General Science Index. H. W. Wilson Co., 950 University Ave., Bronx, New York 10452. 1978-. Monthly, also issued in annual cumulation. Cumulative subject index to English language periodicals in the subject fields of astronomy, botany, chemistry, earth science, environment and conservation, food and nutrition, genetics, mathematics, medicine and health, microbiology, oceanography, physics, physiology and zoology.

Physics Briefs. Physikalische Berichte. Physik Verlag, Pappapelallee 3, Postfach 101161, Weinheim, Germany D-6940. 1979-. Semimonthly. In English. Volumes for 1979- issued by the Deutsche Physikalische Gesellschaft and the Fachinformationszentrum Energie Physik, Mathematik in cooperation with the American Institute of Physics.

Pollution Abstracts. Cambridge Scientific Abstracts, 5161 River Rd., Bethesda, Maryland 20816. (301) 961-6750. Six/year. Indexes worldwide technical literature on environmental pollution. Covers air pollution, marine and freshwater pollution, sewage and wastewater treatment, waste management, toxicology and health, noise pollution, radiation, land pollution, and environmental policies, programs, legislation, and education. Also available online.

Science Citation Index. Institute for Scientific Information, 3501 Market St., Philadelphia, Pennsylvania 19104. 1961-.

DIRECTORIES

Gale Environmental Sourcebook. Karen Hill. Gale Research Co., 835 Penobscot Bldg., Detroit, Michigan 48226-4094. (313) 961-2242. Contacts, information sources, or general information on environmental topics.

Methane Recovery from Landfill Yearbook. Robert N. Gould. Government Advisory Associates, 177 E. 87th

St., Suite 404, New York, New York 10128. (212) 410-4165. Biennial.

ENCYCLOPEDIAS AND DICTIONARIES

Van Nostrand's Scientific Encyclopedia. Glenn D. Considine, ed. Van Nostrand Reinhold, 115 5th Ave., New York, New York 10003. (212) 254-3232. 1983. Sixth edition. Includes all broad subject areas in science.

GENERAL WORKS

Bioenvironmental Systems. Donald L. Wise, ed. CRC Press, 2000 Corporate Blvd. N.W., Boca Raton, Florida 33431. (407) 994-0555; (800) 272-7737. 1987. 4 vols.

Healing the Environment. R. Nicole Warner. Center for Clean Air Policy, 444 N. Capitol St., Ste. 526, Washington, District of Columbia 20001. (202) 624-7709. 1991. A look at coalbed methane as a cost-effective means of addressing global climate change.

Livestock Waste, a Renewable Resource. American Society of Agricultural Engineers, 2950 Niles Rd., St. Joseph, Michigan 49085-9659. (616) 429-0300. 1981. Papers presented at the 4th International Symposium on Livestock Wastes, Amarillo, TX, 1980. Topics covered include: processing manure for feed, methane production, land application, lagoons, runoff, odors, economics, stabilization, treatment, collection and transport, storage and solid-liquid separation.

The Relative Role of Methane and Carbon Dioxide in the Greenhouse Effect: Final Report. Robert R. Gamache. American Gas Association, 1515 Wilson Blvd., Arlington, Virginia 22209. 1990.

ONLINE DATA BASES

Chemical Abstracts-CA. Chemical Abstracts Service, 2540 Olentangy River Rd., P.O. Box 3012, Columbus, Ohio 43210. (800) 848-6533 or (614) 421-3600. Information sources include 9000 journals, patents from 27 countries, two industrial property organizations, new books, conference proceedings, and government research reports.

Monthly Catalog of United States Government Publications. U.S. G.P.O., Supt. of Docs., PO Box 371954, Pittsburgh, Pennsylvania 15250-7954. (202) 512-0000.

National Technical Information Service. U.S. Department of Commerce, National Technical Information Service, Office of Data Base Services, 5285 Port Royal Rd., Springfield, Virginia 22161. (703) 487-4807. Bibliographic database of government sponsored research and technical reports.

STATISTICS SOURCES

Environmental Data Compendium. OECD Publications and Information Center, 2001 L St., N.W., Suite 700, Washington, District of Columbia 20036. (202) 785-6323. 1989.

Environmental Indicators. OECD Publications and Information Center, 2001 L St., N.W., Suite 700, Washington, District of Columbia 20036. (202) 785-6323. 1991.

Environmental Quality. Council on Environmental Quality. U.S. G.P.O., Washington, District of Columbia 20401. (202) 512-0000. Annual.

Reducing Methane Emissions from Livestock. U.S. Environmental Protection Agency. U.S. G.P.O., Washington, District of Columbia 20401. (202) 512-0000. 1989.

The State of the Environment. OECD Publications and Information Center, 2001 L St., N.W., Suite 700, Washington, District of Columbia 20036. (202) 785-6323. 1991.

Trends '90: A Compendium of Data on Global Change. Thomas A. Boden, et al. Carbon Dioxide Information Analysis Center, Environmental Sciences Division, Oak Ridge National Laboratory, Oak Ridge, Tennessee 37831-6335. 1990. Source of frequently used global change data. Includes estimates of global and national CO_2 emissions from the burning of fossil fuels and from the production of cement and other pollutants.

World Resources. World Resources Institute. 1709 New York Ave., N.W., Washington, District of Columbia 20006. (202) 638-6300. Annual. Statistical and textual analysis of world's natural resources and the effects of growth-caused environmental pollution.

METHANOL

See also: ENERGY RESOURCES; GASOLINE; HYDROGEN AS FUEL; METHANE; PETROLEUM

ABSTRACTING AND INDEXING SERVICES

Biological Abstracts. BIOSIS, 2100 Arch St., Philadelphia, Pennsylvania 19103-1399. (215) 587-4800. 1927-.

Biological and Agricultural Index. H.W. Wilson Co., 950 University Ave., Bronx, New York 10452. (800) 367-6770. 1916-. Monthly.

Biotechnology Research Abstracts. Cambridge Scientific Abstracts, 5161 River Rd., Bethesda, Maryland 20816. (301) 961-6750. Monthly. Includes such broad areas as genetic intervention, biochemical genetics, and microbiological techniques.

Chemical Abstracts. Chemical Abstracts Service, 2540 Olentangy River Rd., PO Box 3012, Columbus, Ohio 43210. (800) 848-6533. 1907-.

General Science Index. H. W. Wilson Co., 950 University Ave., Bronx, New York 10452. 1978-. Monthly, also issued in annual cumulation. Cumulative subject index to English language periodicals in the subject fields of astronomy, botany, chemistry, earth science, environment and conservation, food and nutrition, genetics, mathematics, medicine and health, microbiology, oceanography, physics, physiology and zoology.

Pollution Abstracts. Cambridge Scientific Abstracts, 5161 River Rd., Bethesda, Maryland 20816. (301) 961-6750. Six/year. Indexes worldwide technical literature on environmental pollution. Covers air pollution, marine and freshwater pollution, sewage and wastewater treatment, waste management, toxicology and health, noise pollution, radiation, land pollution, and environmental policies, programs, legislation, and education. Also available online.

Science Citation Index. Institute for Scientific Information, 3501 Market St., Philadelphia, Pennsylvania 19104. 1961-.

BIBLIOGRAPHIES

Gasohol Sourcebook: Literature Survey and Abstracts. N. P. Cheremisinoff and P. N. Cheremisinoff. Ann Arbor Science, 230 Collingwood, PO Box 1425, Ann Arbor, Michigan 48106. 1981. Volume includes: biotechnology and bioconversion; ethanol and methanol production; automotive and other fuels; production of chemical feedstocks; and economics of alcohol production.

A Selected Bibliography on Alcohol Fuels. Solar Energy Research Institute, 1617 Cole Blvd., Golden, Colorado 80401. 1982. Covers literature written about biomass derived ethyl and methyl alcohols, including production processes, economics, use as fuel, engine conversion, feedstocks, financing, government regulations, coproducts, environmental effects and safety. The main focus is on alcohol fuels.

DIRECTORIES

Gale Environmental Sourcebook. Karen Hill. Gale Research Co., 835 Penobscot Bldg., Detroit, Michigan 48226-4094. (313) 961-2242. Contacts, information sources, or general information on environmental topics.

ENCYCLOPEDIAS AND DICTIONARIES

Encyclopedia of Chemical Processing and Design. John J. Mcketta and W. A. Cunningham. Marcel Dekker, Inc., 270 Madison Ave., New York, New York 10016. (212) 696-9000; (800) 228-1160. 1992. Thirty-eight volumes.

Encyclopedia of Human Biology. Renato Dulbecco, ed. Academic Press, c/o Harcourt Brace Jovanovich Inc., 6277 Sea Harbor Dr., Orlando, Florida 32887. (800) 346-8648. 1991. Eight volumes.

Kaiman's Encyclopedia of Energy Topics. Lee Kaiman and J. Masloff. Environmental Design and Research Center, 26799 Elena Rd., Los Altos Hills, California 94022. 1983. Two volumes. Coverage of topics range from natural energy sources that are renewable to nonrenewable, and the application of these energy sources.

Kirk-Othmer Encyclopedia of Chemical Technology. J. I. Kroschwitz, ed. John Wiley & Sons, Inc., 605 3rd Ave., New York, New York 10158-0012. (212) 850-6000. 1992-. All articles in the new edition have been rewritten and updated adding new subjects such as biotechnology, computer topics, analytical techniques and instrumentation, environmental concerns, fuels and energy, inorganic and solid state chemistry; composite materials and material science in general, and pharmaceuticals. Also available online.

Van Nostrand's Scientific Encyclopedia. Glenn D. Considine, ed. Van Nostrand Reinhold, 115 5th Ave., New York, New York 10003. (212) 254-3232. 1983. Sixth edition. Includes all broad subject areas in science.

GENERAL WORKS

Converting Transit to Methanol. Stephenie Frederick. Institute of Transportation Studies, University of California, Irvine, California 92717. (714) 833-5989. 1987. Costs and benefits for California's South Coast Air Basin.

Drive for Clean Air: Natural Gas and Methane Vehicles. James Spencer Cannon. INFORM, 381 Park Ave. S., New York, New York 10016. (212) 689-4040. 1989.

Methanol. Environmental Protection Services, Environment Canada, 425 St. Joseph Blvd., 3rd Fl., Hull, Quebec, Canada K1A 0H3. (613) 953-5921. 1985. Environmental and technical information for problem spills.

Replacing Gasoline: Alternative Fuels for Light-Duty Vehicles. Congress of the U.S., c/o U.S. Government Printing Office, Office of Technology Assesment, N. Capitol & H Sts. NW, Washington, District of Columbia 20401. (202) 512-0000. 1990. Gives information on alternatives to standard gasoline. Some of the alternatives are: electricity, hydrogen, compressed natural gas, liquified natural gas, liquid propane gas, methanol, ethanol, and reformulated gasoline.

ONLINE DATA BASES

BIOSIS Previews. BIOSIS, 2100 Arch St., Philadelphia, Pennsylvania 19103-1399. (215) 587-4800. Largest and most comprehensive database of research in the life sciences. Contains citations for nearly 9000 primary research journals, monographs, reviews, symposia, preliminary reports, semi-popular journals, selected institutional reports, government reports and research communications.

Chemical Abstracts-CA. Chemical Abstracts Service, 2540 Olentangy River Rd., P.O. Box 3012, Columbus, Ohio 43210. (800) 848-6533 or (614) 421-3600. Information sources include 9000 journals, patents from 27 countries, two industrial property organizations, new books, conference proceedings, and government research reports.

Dewitt Petrochemical Newsletter. DeWitt and Company, 16800 Greenspoint Park, North Atrium Suite 120, Houston, Texas 77060. (713) 875-5525.

Kirk-Othmer Encyclopedia of Chemical Technology. John Wiley & Sons, Inc., 605 3rd Ave., 5th Floor, New York, New York 10158. (212) 850-6000. Online version of the publication of the same name.

Monthly Catalog of United States Government Publications. U.S. G.P.O., Supt. of Docs., PO Box 371954, Pittsburgh, Pennsylvania 15250-7954. (202) 512-0000.

National Technical Information Service. U.S. Department of Commerce, National Technical Information Service, Office of Data Base Services, 5285 Port Royal Rd., Springfield, Virginia 22161. (703) 487-4807. Bibliographic database of government sponsored research and technical reports.

STATISTICS SOURCES

Environmental Data Compendium. OECD Publications and Information Center, 2001 L St., N.W., Suite 700, Washington, District of Columbia 20036. (202) 785-6323. 1989.

Environmental Indicators. OECD Publications and Information Center, 2001 L St., N.W., Suite 700, Washington, District of Columbia 20036. (202) 785-6323. 1991.

Environmental Quality. Council on Environmental Quality. U.S. G.P.O., Washington, District of Columbia 20401. (202) 512-0000. Annual.

The State of the Environment. OECD Publications and Information Center, 2001 L St., N.W., Suite 700, Washington, District of Columbia 20036. (202) 785-6323. 1991.

TRADE ASSOCIATIONS AND PROFESSIONAL SOCIETIES

Oxygenated Fuels Association. 1330 Connecticut Ave., N.W., #300, Washington, District of Columbia 20036. (202) 822-6750.

METHIOCARB

ABSTRACTING AND INDEXING SERVICES

Biological Abstracts. BIOSIS, 2100 Arch St., Philadelphia, Pennsylvania 19103-1399. (215) 587-4800. 1927-.

Chemical Abstracts. Chemical Abstracts Service, 2540 Olentangy River Rd., PO Box 3012, Columbus, Ohio 43210. (800) 848-6533. 1907-.

ENCYCLOPEDIAS AND DICTIONARIES

Ullmanns Encyclopedia of Industrial Chemistry. Hans Jurgen Arpe and Wolfgang Gerhartz, eds. VCH Publishers, 303 NW 12th Ave., Deerfield Beach, Florida 33442-1788. (305) 428-5566. 1990. Designed to keep up with the broad spectrum of chemical technology. Thirty-six volumes of the encyclopedia have been divided into two sets: the 28 A volumes contain alphabetically arranged articles on chemicals, product groups, processes and technological concepts; and the 8 B volumes are compendia of basic knowledge in industrial chemistry.

ONLINE DATA BASES

BIOSIS Previews. BIOSIS, 2100 Arch St., Philadelphia, Pennsylvania 19103-1399. (215) 587-4800. Largest and most comprehensive database of research in the life sciences. Contains citations for nearly 9000 primary research journals, monographs, reviews, symposia, preliminary reports, semi-popular journals, selected institutional reports, government reports and research communications.

Chemical Abstracts-CA. Chemical Abstracts Service, 2540 Olentangy River Rd., P.O. Box 3012, Columbus, Ohio 43210. (800) 848-6533 or (614) 421-3600. Information sources include 9000 journals, patents from 27 countries, two industrial property organizations, new books, conference proceedings, and government research reports.

Chemical Abstracts Chemical Name Directory-CHEM-NAME. Chemical Abstracts Service, 2540 Olentangy River Rd., P.O. Box 3012, Columbus, Ohio 43210. (800) 848-6533 or (614) 421-3600. Listing of chemical substances in a dictionary type file. The Chemical Abstracts (CAS) Registry Number, molecular formula, Chemical Abstracts (CA) Substance Index Name, available synonyms, ring data and other chemical substance information is given for each entry.

Chemical Carcinogenesis Research Information System-CCRIS. National Library of Medicine, 8600 Rockville Pike, Bethesda, Maryland 20894. (800) 638-8480. Individual assay results and test conditions for 1,451 chemicals in the areas of carcinogenicity, mutagenicity, tumor promotion, and cocarcinogenicity.

Chemical Collection System/Request Tracking-CCS/RTS. U.S. Environmental Protection Agency, Office of Pesticides and Toxic Substances, 401 M St., SW, Washington, District of Columbia 20460. (202) 260-2090.

Contains information on various properties of a number of chemicals including environmental effects, test and analysis methods, and health effects. Available from EPA.

Chemical Dictionary Online-CHEMLINE. Chemical Abstracts Service, 2540 Olentangy River Rd., Columbus, Ohio 43210. (614) 421-3600 or (800) 848-6533. Part of MEDLINE of the National Library of Medicine (NLM). File of 900,000 names for chemical substances, representing 450,000 unique compounds. It contains such information as Chemical Abstracts (CA) Service Registry Numbers, molecular formulas, preferred chemical nomenclature, and generic and ring structure information. Available on NLM's ELHILL system.

Chemical Exposure. Science Applications International Corp., Health & Environmental Information, P.O. Box 2501, Oak Ridge, Tennessee 37831. (615) 482-9031. Database of chemicals that have been identified in both human tissues and body fluids and in feral and food animals. Contains reference to journal articles, conferences, and reports. Covers the whole fields of information related to human and animal exposure to food, air, and water contaminants and pharmaceuticals. Its records include information on chemical properties, formulas, tissues measured, analytical method used, demographics and more. Available on DIALOG.

TRADE ASSOCIATIONS AND PROFESSIONAL SOCIETIES

American Chemical Society. 1155 16th St., N.W., Washington, District of Columbia 20036. (202) 872-4600.

METHOMYL

ABSTRACTING AND INDEXING SERVICES

Biological Abstracts. BIOSIS, 2100 Arch St., Philadelphia, Pennsylvania 19103-1399. (215) 587-4800. 1927-.

Biotechnology Research Abstracts. Cambridge Scientific Abstracts, 5161 River Rd., Bethesda, Maryland 20816. (301) 961-6750. Monthly. Includes such broad areas as genetic intervention, biochemical genetics, and microbiological techniques.

Chemical Abstracts. Chemical Abstracts Service, 2540 Olentangy River Rd., PO Box 3012, Columbus, Ohio 43210. (800) 848-6533. 1907-.

Science Citation Index. Institute for Scientific Information, 3501 Market St., Philadelphia, Pennsylvania 19104. 1961-.

ENCYCLOPEDIAS AND DICTIONARIES

Ullmanns Encyclopedia of Industrial Chemistry. Hans Jurgen Arpe and Wolfgang Gerhartz, eds. VCH Publishers, 303 NW 12th Ave., Deerfield Beach, Florida 33442-1788. (305) 428-5566. 1990. Designed to keep up with the broad spectrum of chemical technology. Thirty-six volumes of the encyclopedia have been divided into two sets: the 28 A volumes contain alphabetically arranged articles on chemicals, product groups, processes and technological concepts; and the 8 B volumes are compendia of basic knowledge in industrial chemistry.

ONLINE DATA BASES

BIOSIS Previews. BIOSIS, 2100 Arch St., Philadelphia, Pennsylvania 19103-1399. (215) 587-4800. Largest and most comprehensive database of research in the life sciences. Contains citations for nearly 9000 primary research journals, monographs, reviews, symposia, preliminary reports, semi-popular journals, selected institutional reports, government reports and research communications.

Chemical Abstracts-CA. Chemical Abstracts Service, 2540 Olentangy River Rd., P.O. Box 3012, Columbus, Ohio 43210. (800) 848-6533 or (614) 421-3600. Information sources include 9000 journals, patents from 27 countries, two industrial property organizations, new books, conference proceedings, and government research reports.

Chemical Abstracts Chemical Name Directory-CHEM-NAME. Chemical Abstracts Service, 2540 Olentangy River Rd., P.O. Box 3012, Columbus, Ohio 43210. (800) 848-6533 or (614) 421-3600. Listing of chemical substances in a dictionary type file. The Chemical Abstracts (CAS) Registry Number, molecular formula, Chemical Abstracts (CA) Substance Index Name, available synonyms, ring data and other chemical substance information is given for each entry.

Chemical Carcinogenesis Research Information System-CCRIS. National Library of Medicine, 8600 Rockville Pike, Bethesda, Maryland 20894. (800) 638-8480. Individual assay results and test conditions for 1,451 chemicals in the areas of carcinogenicity, mutagenicity, tumor promotion, and cocarcinogenicity.

Chemical Collection System/Request Tracking-CCS/RTS. U.S. Environmental Protection Agency, Office of Pesticides and Toxic Substances, 401 M St., SW, Washington, District of Columbia 20460. (202) 260-2090. Contains information on various properties of a number of chemicals including environmental effects, test and analysis methods, and health effects. Available from EPA.

Chemical Dictionary Online-CHEMLINE. Chemical Abstracts Service, 2540 Olentangy River Rd., Columbus, Ohio 43210. (614) 421-3600 or (800) 848-6533. Part of MEDLINE of the National Library of Medicine (NLM). File of 900,000 names for chemical substances, representing 450,000 unique compounds. It contains such information as Chemical Abstracts (CA) Service Registry Numbers, molecular formulas, preferred chemical nomenclature, and generic and ring structure information. Available on NLM's ELHILL system.

Chemical Exposure. Science Applications International Corp., Health & Environmental Information, P.O. Box 2501, Oak Ridge, Tennessee 37831. (615) 482-9031. Database of chemicals that have been identified in both human tissues and body fluids and in feral and food animals. Contains reference to journal articles, conferences, and reports. Covers the whole fields of information related to human and animal exposure to food, air, and water contaminants and pharmaceuticals. Its records include information on chemical properties, formulas, tissues measured, analytical method used, demographics and more. Available on DIALOG.

TRADE ASSOCIATIONS AND PROFESSIONAL SOCIETIES

American Chemical Society. 1155 16th St., N.W., Washington, District of Columbia 20036. (202) 872-4600.

METHOXYCHLOR

ABSTRACTING AND INDEXING SERVICES

Biological Abstracts. BIOSIS, 2100 Arch St., Philadelphia, Pennsylvania 19103-1399. (215) 587-4800. 1927-.

Chemical Abstracts. Chemical Abstracts Service, 2540 Olentangy River Rd., PO Box 3012, Columbus, Ohio 43210. (800) 848-6533. 1907-.

Science Citation Index. Institute for Scientific Information, 3501 Market St., Philadelphia, Pennsylvania 19104. 1961-.

ENCYCLOPEDIAS AND DICTIONARIES

Ullmanns Encyclopedia of Industrial Chemistry. Hans Jurgen Arpe and Wolfgang Gerhartz, eds. VCH Publishers, 303 NW 12th Ave., Deerfield Beach, Florida 33442-1788. (305) 428-5566. 1990. Designed to keep up with the broad spectrum of chemical technology. Thirty-six volumes of the encyclopedia have been divided into two sets: the 28 A volumes contain alphabetically arranged articles on chemicals, product groups, processes and technological concepts; and the 8 B volumes are compendia of basic knowledge in industrial chemistry.

GENERAL WORKS

Environment Impact of Nonpoint Source Pollution. Michael R. Overcash and James M. Davidson, eds. Ann Arbor Science, 230 Collingwood, Ann Arbor, Michigan 48106. 1980.

HANDBOOKS AND MANUALS

CRC Handbook of Chemistry and Physics. CRC Press, 2000 Corporate Blvd. N.W., Boca Raton, Florida 33431. (407) 994-0555; (800) 272-7737. 1988. 67th ed.

Documentation of the Threshold Limit Values. American Conference of Governmental Industrial Hygienists, 6500 Glenway, Building D-5, Cincinnati, Ohio 45211. 1991. Provides threshold limit value documentation for any physical phenomenon in the environment, including chemical substances and physical agents.

Handbook of Analytical Toxicology. Irving Sunshine, ed. CRC Press, 2000 Corporate Blvd. N.W., Boca Raton, Florida 33431. (407) 994-0555; (800) 272-7737. 1969.

Handbook of Environmental Data on Organic Chemicals. Karel Verschueren. Van Nostrand Reinhold, 115 5th Ave., New York, New York 10003. (212) 254-3232. 1983. Covers individual substances as well as mixtures and preparations. The profiles include: properties, air pollution factors, water pollution factors, and biological effects.

Hazardous Chemicals Data Book. G. Weiss, ed. Noyes Publications, 120 Mill Rd., Park Ridge, New Jersey 07656. (201) 391-8484. 1986. 2d ed. Supplies instant information on 1015 hazardous chemicals. The data will provide rapid assistance to personnel involved with handling of hazardous chemical materials and related accidents.

ONLINE DATA BASES

BIOSIS Previews. BIOSIS, 2100 Arch St., Philadelphia, Pennsylvania 19103-1399. (215) 587-4800. Largest and most comprehensive database of research in the life sciences. Contains citations for nearly 9000 primary research journals, monographs, reviews, symposia, preliminary reports, semi-popular journals, selected institutional reports, government reports and research communications.

Chemical Abstracts-CA. Chemical Abstracts Service, 2540 Olentangy River Rd., P.O. Box 3012, Columbus, Ohio 43210. (800) 848-6533 or (614) 421-3600. Information sources include 9000 journals, patents from 27 countries, two industrial property organizations, new books, conference proceedings, and government research reports.

Chemical Abstracts Chemical Name Directory-CHEM-NAME. Chemical Abstracts Service, 2540 Olentangy River Rd., P.O. Box 3012, Columbus, Ohio 43210. (800) 848-6533 or (614) 421-3600. Listing of chemical substances in a dictionary type file. The Chemical Abstracts (CAS) Registry Number, molecular formula, Chemical Abstracts (CA) Substance Index Name, available synonyms, ring data and other chemical substance information is given for each entry.

Chemical Carcinogenesis Research Information System–CCRIS. National Library of Medicine, 8600 Rockville Pike, Bethesda, Maryland 20894. (800) 638-8480. Individual assay results and test conditions for 1,451 chemicals in the areas of carcinogenicity, mutagenicity, tumor promotion, and cocarcinogenicity.

Chemical Collection System/Request Tracking–CCS/RTS. U.S. Environmental Protection Agency, Office of Pesticides and Toxic Substances, 401 M St., SW, Washington, District of Columbia 20460. (202) 260-2090. Contains information on various properties of a number of chemicals including environmental effects, test and analysis methods, and health effects. Available from EPA.

Chemical Dictionary Online–CHEMLINE. Chemical Abstracts Service, 2540 Olentangy River Rd., Columbus, Ohio 43210. (614) 421-3600 or (800) 848-6533. Part of MEDLINE of the National Library of Medicine (NLM). File of 900,000 names for chemical substances, representing 450,000 unique compounds. It contains such information as Chemical Abstracts (CA) Service Registry Numbers, molecular formulas, preferred chemical nomenclature, and generic and ring structure information. Available on NLM's ELHILL system.

Chemical Exposure. Science Applications International Corp., Health & Environmental Information, P.O. Box 2501, Oak Ridge, Tennessee 37831. (615) 482-9031. Database of chemicals that have been identified in both human tissues and body fluids and in feral and food animals. Contains reference to journal articles, conferences, and reports. Covers the whole fields of information related to human and animal exposure to food, air, and water contaminants and pharmaceuticals. Its records include information on chemical properties, formulas, tissues measured, analytical method used, demographics and more. Available on DIALOG.

PERIODICALS AND NEWSLETTERS

Aquatic Toxicology. Elsevier Science Publishing Co., 655 Avenue of the Americas, New York, New York 10010. (212) 989-5800. 1981-. 6/year.

IARC Monographs on the Evaluation of the Carcinogenic Risk of Chemicals to Man. International Agency for Research on Cancer, Q Corp., 49 Sheridan Ave., Albany, New York 12221. (518) 436-9686. 1972-. Irregular.

Journal of Agricultural and Food Chemistry. American Chemical Society, 1155 16th St. N.W., Washington, District of Columbia 20036. (202) 872-4600; (800) 227-5558. 1953-. Monthly. Contains documentation of significant advances in the science of agriculture and food chemistry.

Water Research. International Association on Water Pollution Research and Control. Pergamon Microforms International, Inc., Fairview Park, Elmsford, New York 10523. (914) 592-7720. 1966-. Monthly. Covers all aspects of the pollution of marine and fresh water and the management of water quality as well as water resources.

TRADE ASSOCIATIONS AND PROFESSIONAL SOCIETIES

American Chemical Society. 1155 16th St., N.W., Washington, District of Columbia 20036. (202) 872-4600.

METHYL ISOCYANATE

ABSTRACTING AND INDEXING SERVICES

Chemical Abstracts. Chemical Abstracts Service, 2540 Olentangy River Rd., PO Box 3012, Columbus, Ohio 43210. (800) 848-6533. 1907-.

Science Citation Index. Institute for Scientific Information, 3501 Market St., Philadelphia, Pennsylvania 19104. 1961-.

ENCYCLOPEDIAS AND DICTIONARIES

Ullmanns Encyclopedia of Industrial Chemistry. Hans Jurgen Arpe and Wolfgang Gerhartz, eds. VCH Publishers, 303 NW 12th Ave., Deerfield Beach, Florida 33442-1788. (305) 428-5566. 1990. Designed to keep up with the broad spectrum of chemical technology. Thirty-six volumes of the encyclopedia have been divided into two sets: the 28 A volumes contain alphabetically arranged articles on chemicals, product groups, processes and technological concepts; and the 8 B volumes are compendia of basic knowledge in industrial chemistry.

ONLINE DATA BASES

Chemical Abstracts-CA. Chemical Abstracts Service, 2540 Olentangy River Rd., P.O. Box 3012, Columbus, Ohio 43210. (800) 848-6533 or (614) 421-3600. Information sources include 9000 journals, patents from 27 countries, two industrial property organizations, new books, conference proceedings, and government research reports.

Chemical Abstracts Chemical Name Directory-CHEM-NAME. Chemical Abstracts Service, 2540 Olentangy River Rd., P.O. Box 3012, Columbus, Ohio 43210. (800) 848-6533 or (614) 421-3600. Listing of chemical substances in a dictionary type file. The Chemical Abstracts

(CAS) Registry Number, molecular formula, Chemical Abstracts (CA) Substance Index Name, available synonyms, ring data and other chemical substance information is given for each entry.

Chemical Carcinogenesis Research Information System–CCRIS. National Library of Medicine, 8600 Rockville Pike, Bethesda, Maryland 20894. (800) 638-8480. Individual assay results and test conditions for 1,451 chemicals in the areas of carcinogenicity, mutagenicity, tumor promotion, and cocarcinogenicity.

Chemical Collection System/Request Tracking–CCS/ RTS. U.S. Environmental Protection Agency, Office of Pesticides and Toxic Substances, 401 M St., SW, Washington, District of Columbia 20460. (202) 260-2090. Contains information on various properties of a number of chemicals including environmental effects, test and analysis methods, and health effects. Available from EPA.

Chemical Dictionary Online–CHEMLINE. Chemical Abstracts Service, 2540 Olentangy River Rd., Columbus, Ohio 43210. (614) 421-3600 or (800) 848-6533. Part of MEDLINE of the National Library of Medicine (NLM). File of 900,000 names for chemical substances, representing 450,000 unique compounds. It contains such information as Chemical Abstracts (CA) Service Registry Numbers, molecular formulas, preferred chemical nomenclature, and generic and ring structure information. Available on NLM's ELHILL system.

Chemical Exposure. Science Applications International Corp., Health & Environmental Information, P.O. Box 2501, Oak Ridge, Tennessee 37831. (615) 482-9031. Database of chemicals that have been identified in both human tissues and body fluids and in feral and food animals. Contains reference to journal articles, conferences, and reports. Covers the whole fields of information related to human and animal exposure to food, air, and water contaminants and pharmaceuticals. Its records include information on chemical properties, formulas, tissues measured, analytical method used, demographics and more. Available on DIALOG.

TRADE ASSOCIATIONS AND PROFESSIONAL SOCIETIES

American Chemical Society. 1155 16th St., N.W., Washington, District of Columbia 20036. (202) 872-4600.

METHYL PARTHION

See also: ORGANOCHLORINES; PARTHION

ABSTRACTING AND INDEXING SERVICES

Chemical Abstracts. Chemical Abstracts Service, 2540 Olentangy River Rd., PO Box 3012, Columbus, Ohio 43210. (800) 848-6533. 1907-.

Science Citation Index. Institute for Scientific Information, 3501 Market St., Philadelphia, Pennsylvania 19104. 1961-.

ENCYCLOPEDIAS AND DICTIONARIES

Ullmanns Encyclopedia of Industrial Chemistry. Hans Jurgen Arpe and Wolfgang Gerhartz, eds. VCH Publishers, 303 NW 12th Ave., Deerfield Beach, Florida 33442-

1788. (305) 428-5566. 1990. Designed to keep up with the broad spectrum of chemical technology. Thirty-six volumes of the encyclopedia have been divided into two sets: the 28 A volumes contain alphabetically arranged articles on chemicals, product groups, processes and technological concepts; and the 8 B volumes are compendia of basic knowledge in industrial chemistry.

ONLINE DATA BASES

Chemical Abstracts-CA. Chemical Abstracts Service, 2540 Olentangy River Rd., P.O. Box 3012, Columbus, Ohio 43210. (800) 848-6533 or (614) 421-3600. Information sources include 9000 journals, patents from 27 countries, two industrial property organizations, new books, conference proceedings, and government research reports.

Chemical Abstracts Chemical Name Directory-CHEM-NAME. Chemical Abstracts Service, 2540 Olentangy River Rd., P.O. Box 3012, Columbus, Ohio 43210. (800) 848-6533 or (614) 421-3600. Listing of chemical substances in a dictionary type file. The Chemical Abstracts (CAS) Registry Number, molecular formula, Chemical Abstracts (CA) Substance Index Name, available synonyms, ring data and other chemical substance information is given for each entry.

Chemical Carcinogenesis Research Information System–CCRIS. National Library of Medicine, 8600 Rockville Pike, Bethesda, Maryland 20894. (800) 638-8480. Individual assay results and test conditions for 1,451 chemicals in the areas of carcinogenicity, mutagenicity, tumor promotion, and cocarcinogenicity.

Chemical Collection System/Request Tracking–CCS/ RTS. U.S. Environmental Protection Agency, Office of Pesticides and Toxic Substances, 401 M St., SW, Washington, District of Columbia 20460. (202) 260-2090. Contains information on various properties of a number of chemicals including environmental effects, test and analysis methods, and health effects. Available from EPA.

Chemical Dictionary Online–CHEMLINE. Chemical Abstracts Service, 2540 Olentangy River Rd., Columbus, Ohio 43210. (614) 421-3600 or (800) 848-6533. Part of MEDLINE of the National Library of Medicine (NLM). File of 900,000 names for chemical substances, representing 450,000 unique compounds. It contains such information as Chemical Abstracts (CA) Service Registry Numbers, molecular formulas, preferred chemical nomenclature, and generic and ring structure information. Available on NLM's ELHILL system.

Chemical Exposure. Science Applications International Corp., Health & Environmental Information, P.O. Box 2501, Oak Ridge, Tennessee 37831. (615) 482-9031. Database of chemicals that have been identified in both human tissues and body fluids and in feral and food animals. Contains reference to journal articles, conferences, and reports. Covers the whole fields of information related to human and animal exposure to food, air, and water contaminants and pharmaceuticals. Its records include information on chemical properties, formulas, tissues measured, analytical method used, demographics and more. Available on DIALOG.

TRADE ASSOCIATIONS AND PROFESSIONAL SOCIETIES

American Chemical Society. 1155 16th St., N.W., Washington, District of Columbia 20036. (202) 872-4600.

METHYLMERCURY

See also: FUNGICIDES; MERCURY

ABSTRACTING AND INDEXING SERVICES

Science Citation Index. Institute for Scientific Information, 3501 Market St., Philadelphia, Pennsylvania 19104. 1961-.

GENERAL WORKS

Methylmercury. World Health Organization, Ave. Appia, Geneva, Switzerland CH-1211. 1990. Environmental health criteria relating to methylmercury.

The Toxicity of Methyl Mercury. Christine U. Eccles. Johns Hopkins University Press, 701 W. 40th St., Ste. 275, Baltimore, Maryland 21211. (410) 516-6900. 1987. Toxicology and physiological effects of methylmercury.

ONLINE DATA BASES

Chemical Collection System/Request Tracking–CCS/ RTS. U.S. Environmental Protection Agency, Office of Pesticides and Toxic Substances, 401 M St., SW, Washington, District of Columbia 20460. (202) 260-2090. Contains information on various properties of a number of chemicals including environmental effects, test and analysis methods, and health effects. Available from EPA.

Chemical Dictionary Online–CHEMLINE. Chemical Abstracts Service, 2540 Olentangy River Rd., Columbus, Ohio 43210. (614) 421-3600 or (800) 848-6533. Part of MEDLINE of the National Library of Medicine (NLM). File of 900,000 names for chemical substances, representing 450,000 unique compounds. It contains such information as Chemical Abstracts (CA) Service Registry Numbers, molecular formulas, preferred chemical nomenclature, and generic and ring structure information. Available on NLM's ELHILL system.

Chemical Exposure. Science Applications International Corp., Health & Environmental Information, P.O. Box 2501, Oak Ridge, Tennessee 37831. (615) 482-9031. Database of chemicals that have been identified in both human tissues and body fluids and in feral and food animals. Contains reference to journal articles, conferences, and reports. Covers the whole fields of information related to human and animal exposure to food, air, and water contaminants and pharmaceuticals. Its records include information on chemical properties, formulas, tissues measured, analytical method used, demographics and more. Available on DIALOG.

METOLACHLOR

ABSTRACTING AND INDEXING SERVICES

Biological Abstracts. BIOSIS, 2100 Arch St., Philadelphia, Pennsylvania 19103-1399. (215) 587-4800. 1927-.

Pollution Abstracts. Cambridge Scientific Abstracts, 5161 River Rd., Bethesda, Maryland 20816. (301) 961-6750. Six/year. Indexes worldwide technical literature on environmental pollution. Covers air pollution, marine and freshwater pollution, sewage and wastewater treatment, waste management, toxicology and health, noise pollution, radiation, land pollution, and environmental policies, programs, legislation, and education. Also available online.

Science Citation Index. Institute for Scientific Information, 3501 Market St., Philadelphia, Pennsylvania 19104. 1961-.

ENCYCLOPEDIAS AND DICTIONARIES

McGraw-Hill Encyclopedia of Science and Technology. McGraw-Hill, 1221 Avenue of the Americas, New York, New York 10020. (212) 512-2000 or (800) 262-4729. 1992. Seventh edition. Issued in multiple volumes including index. Includes all science and technology broad subject areas.

Ullmanns Encyclopedia of Industrial Chemistry. Hans Jurgen Arpe and Wolfgang Gerhartz, eds. VCH Publishers, 303 NW 12th Ave., Deerfield Beach, Florida 33442-1788. (305) 428-5566. 1990. Designed to keep up with the broad spectrum of chemical technology. Thirty-six volumes of the encyclopedia have been divided into two sets: the 28 A volumes contain alphabetically arranged articles on chemicals, product groups, processes and technological concepts; and the 8 B volumes are compendia of basic knowledge in industrial chemistry.

ONLINE DATA BASES

BIOSIS Previews. BIOSIS, 2100 Arch St., Philadelphia, Pennsylvania 19103-1399. (215) 587-4800. Largest and most comprehensive database of research in the life sciences. Contains citations for nearly 9000 primary research journals, monographs, reviews, symposia, preliminary reports, semi-popular journals, selected institutional reports, government reports and research communications.

Chemical Abstracts Chemical Name Directory-CHEMNAME. Chemical Abstracts Service, 2540 Olentangy River Rd., P.O. Box 3012, Columbus, Ohio 43210. (800) 848-6533 or (614) 421-3600. Listing of chemical substances in a dictionary type file. The Chemical Abstracts (CAS) Registry Number, molecular formula, Chemical Abstracts (CA) Substance Index Name, available synonyms, ring data and other chemical substance information is given for each entry.

Chemical Carcinogenesis Research Information System-CCRIS. National Library of Medicine, 8600 Rockville Pike, Bethesda, Maryland 20894. (800) 638-8480. Individual assay results and test conditions for 1,451 chemicals in the areas of carcinogenicity, mutagenicity, tumor promotion, and cocarcinogenicity.

Chemical Collection System/Request Tracking–CCS/ RTS. U.S. Environmental Protection Agency, Office of Pesticides and Toxic Substances, 401 M St., SW, Washington, District of Columbia 20460. (202) 260-2090. Contains information on various properties of a number of chemicals including environmental effects, test and analysis methods, and health effects. Available from EPA.

Chemical Dictionary Online–CHEMLINE. Chemical Abstracts Service, 2540 Olentangy River Rd., Columbus, Ohio 43210. (614) 421-3600 or (800) 848-6533. Part of MEDLINE of the National Library of Medicine (NLM). File of 900,000 names for chemical substances, representing 450,000 unique compounds. It contains such information as Chemical Abstracts (CA) Service Registry Numbers, molecular formulas, preferred chemical nomenclature, and generic and ring structure information. Available on NLM's ELHILL system.

Chemical Exposure. Science Applications International Corp., Health & Environmental Information, P.O. Box 2501, Oak Ridge, Tennessee 37831. (615) 482-9031. Database of chemicals that have been identified in both human tissues and body fluids and in feral and food animals. Contains reference to journal articles, conferences, and reports. Covers the whole fields of information related to human and animal exposure to food, air, and water contaminants and pharmaceuticals. Its records include information on chemical properties, formulas, tissues measured, analytical method used, demographics and more. Available on DIALOG.

PERIODICALS AND NEWSLETTERS

Biodegradation. Kluwer Academic Publishers, 101 Philip Dr., Assinippi Park, Norwell, Massachusetts 02061-0358. (617) 871-6600. 1990-. Quarterly. Covers all aspects of science pertaining to the detoxification, recycling, amelioration or treatment of waste materials and pollutants by naturally occurring microbial strains, associations, or recombinant microorganisms.

MHTGR

See: REACTORS

MICHIGAN ENVIRONMENTAL AGENCIES

GOVERNMENTAL ORGANIZATIONS

Department of Labor: Occupational Safety. Director, Bureau of Safety and Regulation, PO Box 30015, Lansing, Michigan 48909. (517) 322-1814.

Department of Natural Resources: Air Quality. Air Quality Division, 4th Floor Mason Bldg., PO Box 30028, Lansing, Michigan 48909. (517) 373-7023.

Department of Natural Resources: Coastal Zone Management. Chief, Great Lakes Shoreland Section, PO Box 30028, Lansing, Michigan 48909. (517) 373-1950.

Department of Natural Resources: Emergency Preparedness and Community Right-to-Know. Title III Coordinator, Environmental Response Division, Title III Notification, PO Box 30028, Lansing, Michigan 48909. (517) 373-8481.

Department of Natural Resources: Environmental Protection. Deputy Director, Environmental Protection Bureau, PO Box 30028, Lansing, Michigan 48909. (517) 373-7917.

Department of Natural Resources: Fish and Wildlife. Director, Mason Building, PO Box 30028, Lansing, Michigan 48909. (517) 373-1263.

Department of Natural Resources: Hazardous Waste Management. Chief, Waste Management Division, PO Box 30028, Lansing, Michigan 48909. (517) 373-2730.

Department of Natural Resources: Natural Resources. Director, Mason Building, PO Box 30028, Lansing, Michigan 48909. (517) 373-2329.

Department of Natural Resources: Solid Waste Management. Deputy Director, Environmental Protection Bureau, PO Box 30028, Lansing, Michigan 48909. (517) 373-7917.

Department of Natural Resources: Waste Minimization and Pollution Control. Division Chief, Waste Management Division, Resource Recovery Division, PO Box 30241, Lansing, Michigan 48909. (517) 373-0540.

Department of Natural Resources: Water Quality. Director, Mason Building, PO Box 30028, Lansing, Michigan 48909. (517) 373-2329.

Department of Regulation: Pesticide Registration. Director, Pesticide and Plant Management Division, PO Box 30017, Lansing, Michigan 48909. (517) 373-4540.

MICHIGAN ENVIRONMENTAL LEGISLATION

GENERAL WORKS

Environmental Quality and the Law. Michigan House of Representatives, Conservation, Recreation and Environment Committee, PO Box 30014, Lansing, Michigan 48909. (517)373-0135. 1990.

Michigan Environmental Law Letter. M. Lee Smith Publishers & Printers, 162 4th Ave., N., Box 2678, Arcade Sta., Nashville, Tennessee 37219. (615) 242-7395.

Michigan Environmental Management Directory. Michigan Waste Report, Inc., 400 Ann, SW, Ste. 204, Grand Rapids, Michigan 49504. (616) 363-3262. 1989.

Michigan Environmental Statutes and Regulations. State Bar of Michigan, 306 Townsend, Lansing, Michigan 48933. (517)372-9030. 1990.

MICROBES

See: SEWAGE ANALYSIS

MICROORGANISMS

ABSTRACTING AND INDEXING SERVICES

Applied Ecology Abstracts Studies in Renewable Natural Resources. Information Retrieval Ltd., 1911 Jefferson Davis Highway, Arlington, Virginia 22202. 1975-. Monthly.

Aqualine Abstracts. Water Research Centre. c/o Pergamon Microforms International, Inc., Fairview Park, Elmsford, New York 10523. (914) 592-7720. 1927-. Contains some 8,000 records annually on water and wastewater technology. Covers all aspects of water, wastewater, associated engineering services and the aquatic environment. Over 600 periodicals, as well as books, reports and conference proceedings and other publications from water related institutions worldwide are scanned. Also available online.

ASFA Aquaculture Abstracts. Cambridge Scientific Abstracts, Inc., 5161 River Rd., Bethesda, Maryland 20816. (301) 961-6750. 1984.

Biological Abstracts. BIOSIS, 2100 Arch St., Philadelphia, Pennsylvania 19103-1399. (215) 587-4800. 1927-.

Biological and Agricultural Index. H.W. Wilson Co., 950 University Ave., Bronx, New York 10452. (800) 367-6770. 1916-. Monthly.

Biology Digest. Data Courier, Plexus Pub Inc., 143 Old Marlton Pike, Medford, New Jersey 08055. 1974-. Monthly. Abstracts biology periodicals.

Biotechnology Research Abstracts. Cambridge Scientific Abstracts, 5161 River Rd., Bethesda, Maryland 20816. (301) 961-6750. Monthly. Includes such broad areas as genetic intervention, biochemical genetics, and microbiological techniques.

Ecological Abstracts. Geo Abstracts Ltd. Elsevier Applied Science, Crown House, Linton Rd., Barking, England IG 11 8JU. 1974-. Derived from over 600 leading ecological and environmental journals, plus books, conference proceedings, reports and theses.

Ecology Abstracts. Cambridge Scientific Abstracts, 5161 River Rd., Bethesda, Maryland 20816. (301) 961-6750. Monthly.

Environment Abstracts. Bowker A & I Publishing, 121 Chanlon Rd., New Providence, New Jersey 07974. (908) 464-6800. 1974-.

Environment Index. Environment Information Center, Index Research Department, 124 E. 39th St., New York, New York 10016. 1971-. Annual.

Environmental Information Connection–EIC. Planning Information Program, Dept. of Urban and Regional Planning, University of Illinois, 1003 West Nevada, Urbana, Illinois 61801. (217) 333-1369. Also available online.

Environmental Periodicals Bibliography. Environmental Studies Institute, International Academy at Santa Barbara, 800 Garden St., Suite D, Santa Barbara, California 93101. (805) 965-5010. Also available online.

Food Science and Technology Abstracts. International Food Information Service, c/o National Food Laboratory, 6363 Clark Ave., Dublin, California 94568. (800) 336-3782. 1969-.

General Science Index. H. W. Wilson Co., 950 University Ave., Bronx, New York 10452. 1978-. Monthly, also issued in annual cumulation. Cumulative subject index to English language periodicals in the subject fields of astronomy, botany, chemistry, earth science, environment and conservation, food and nutrition, genetics, mathematics, medicine and health, microbiology, oceanography, physics, physiology and zoology.

Microbiology Abstracts. Section A. Industrial and Applied Microbiology. Cambridge Scientific Abstracts, 5161 River Rd., Bethesda, Maryland 20816. (301) 961-6750. 1972-.

Multimedia Index to Ecology. National Information Center for Educational Media, University of Southern California, Los Angeles, California 90007.

Pollution Abstracts. Cambridge Scientific Abstracts, 5161 River Rd., Bethesda, Maryland 20816. (301) 961-6750. Six/year. Indexes worldwide technical literature on envi-

ronmental pollution. Covers air pollution, marine and freshwater pollution, sewage and wastewater treatment, waste management, toxicology and health, noise pollution, radiation, land pollution, and environmental policies, programs, legislation, and education. Also available online.

Science Citation Index. Institute for Scientific Information, 3501 Market St., Philadelphia, Pennsylvania 19104. 1961-.

ALMANACS AND YEARBOOKS

Advances in Microbial Ecology. Plenum Press, 233 Spring St., New York, New York 10013-1578. (212) 620-8000; (800) 221-9369. Annual.

BIBLIOGRAPHIES

Current Contents. Agriculture, Biology and Environmental Sciences. Institute for Scientific Information, 3501 Market St., Philadelphia, Pennsylvania 19104. (800) 523-1857. 1973-. Previous title: Current Contents. Agricultural, Food & Veterinary Sciences. Gives the table of contents of periodicals in the fields of agriculture, biology, environmental and related areas.

EPA Publications Bibliography. U.S. Environmental Protection Agency, Library Systems Branch, 401 M St., SW, Washington, District of Columbia 20460. (202) 260-2090. Quarterly.

ENCYCLOPEDIAS AND DICTIONARIES

The Agriculture Dictionary. Ray V. Herren and Roy L. Donahue. Delmar Publishers Inc., 2 Computer Dr. W., Albany, New York 12212. (518) 459-1150. 1991. Covers all the agricultural areas including acid rain, acid mine drainage, food additives, agricultural engineering, conservation of the natural resources, microorganisms, triticale and other related topics.

Cambridge Encyclopedia of Life Sciences. A. E. Friday and David S. Ingram. Cambridge University Press, 40 W 20th St., New York, New York 10011. (212) 924-3900 or (800) 227-0247. 1985. Includes all topics under biology and ecology.

Dictionary of Biotechnology. J. Coombs. Elsevier Science Publishing Co., 655 Avenue of the Americas, New York, New York 10010. (212) 984-5800. 1986. Areas covered in this dictionary include: fermentation; brewing; vaccines; plant tissue; culture; antibiotic production; production and use of enzymes; biomass; byproduct recovery and effluent treatment; equipment; processes; micro-organisms and biochemicals.

Dictionary of Microbiology and Molecular Biology. Paul Singleton and Diana Sainsbury. John Wiley & Sons, Inc., 605 3rd Ave., New York, New York 10158-0012. (212) 850-6000. 1987. Second edition. Comprehensive dictionary with "classical descriptive aspects of microbiology to current developments in related areas of bioenergetics, biochemistry and molecular biology." Entries give synonyms, cross references, and references to pertinent works. Miscellaneous appendixes. Bibliography.

McGraw-Hill Encyclopedia of Science and Technology. McGraw-Hill, 1221 Avenue of the Americas, New York, New York 10020. (212) 512-2000 or (800) 262-4729. 1992. Seventh edition. Issued in multiple volumes in-

cluding index. Includes all science and technology broad subject areas.

Van Nostrand's Scientific Encyclopedia. Glenn D. Considine, ed. Van Nostrand Reinhold, 115 5th Ave., New York, New York 10003. (212) 254-3232. 1983. Sixth edition. Includes all broad subject areas in science.

GENERAL WORKS

Assessing Ecological Risks of Biotechnology. Lev R. Ginzburg. Butterworth-Heinemann, 80 Montvale Ave., Stoneham, Massachusetts 02180. (617) 438-8464; (800) 366-2665. 1991. Presents an analysis of the ecological risk associated with genetically engineered microorganisms, organisms that, through gene splicing, have obtained additional genetic information.

Bacteria. L. R. Hill and B. E. Kirsop, eds. Cambridge University Press, 40 W. 20th St., New York, New York 10011. (212) 924-3900; (800) 227-0247. 1991. Directory and collection of bacteria type specimens.

Biodegradability of Organic Substances in the Aquatic Environment. Pavel Pitter, et al. CRC Press, 2000 Corporate Blvd. N.W., Boca Raton, Florida 33431. (800) 272-7737. 1990. Explains the principles and theories of biodegradation, primarily from an ecological standpoint. Current techniques used to evaluate the biodegradability of individual chemicals are reviewed.

Biological Wastewater Treatment Systems. N. J. Horan. John Wiley & Sons, Inc., 605 3rd Ave., New York, New York 10158-0012. (212) 850-6000. 1990. Introduces basic concepts of microbial growth and reactor engineering required to fully understand the design and operation of wastewater treatment systems. Topics include wastewater characteristics, microorganisms exploited in wastewater treatment, and microbial energy generation.

Biotechnology and Food Safety. Donald D. Bills. Butterworth-Heinemann, 80 Montvale Ave., Stoneham, Massachusetts 02180. (617) 438-8464. Natural control of microorganisms, detection of microorganisms, relation of the biological control of pests to food safety, and ingredients and food safety.

Comparative Ecology of Microorganisms and Macroorganisms. John H. Andrews. Springer-Verlag, 175 5th Ave., New York, New York 10010. (212) 460-1500. 1991. Constructs a format in which to compare the ecologies of large and small plant and animal organisms. Examines the differences between the sizes, and explores what similarities or parallels can be identified, and where they don't seem to exist. The ideas are illustrated by applying evolutionary principles to the individual organism.

Environmental Biotechnology. A. Balaozej and V. Prnivarovna, eds. Elsevier Science Publishing Co., 655 Avenue of the Americas, New York, New York 10010. (212) 989-5800. 1991. Proceedings of the International Symposium on Biotechnology, Bratislava, Czechoslovakia, June 27-29, 1990.

Environmental Biotechnology: Reducing Risks from Environmental Chemicals through Biotechnology. Gilbert S. Omenn. Plenum Press, 233 Spring St., New York, New York 10013-1578. (212) 620-8000. Covers environmental aspects of the chemical and biological treatment of sewage.

Micro-Organisms. Lilian E. Hawker. E. Arnold, 41 Bedford Sq., London, England 1979. Function, form, and environment of microbiology.

Microbial Control of Weeds. David O. TeBeest, ed. Chapman & Hall, 29 W. 35th St., New York, New York 10001-2291. (212) 244-3336. 1991. Summarizes the progress that has been made over the last 20 years in the biological control of weeds.

Microbial Ecology. Richard Campbell. Blackwell Scientific Publication, 3 Cambridge Ctr., Suite 208, Cambridge, Massachusetts 02142. (617) 225-0401. 1983.

Microbial Ecology. Morris A. Levin. McGraw-Hill Science & Engineering Books, 11 W. 19th St., New York, New York 10011. (212) 337-6010. 1992. Principles, methods, and applications.

Microbial Toxins in Focus and Feeds. Albert E. Pohland, et al., eds. Plenum Press, 233 Spring St., New York, New York 10013. (212) 620-8000; (800) 221-9369. 1990. Proceedings of a Symposium on Cellular and Molecular Mode of Action of Selected Microbial Toxins in Foods and Feeds, Oct. 31- Nov. 2, 1988, Chevy Chase, MD.

Modeling the Environmental Fate of Microorganisms. Criston J. Hurst. American Society for Microbiology, 1325 Massachusetts Ave. NW, Washington, District of Columbia 20005. (202) 737-3600. 1991. Mathematical models of microbial ecology.

Natural Microbial Communities: Ecological and Physiological Features. Tomomichi Yanagita. Springer-Verlag, 175 5th Ave., New York, New York 10010. (212) 460-1500; (800) 777-4643. 1990. Translation of a work which originally appeared in Japanese entitled Microbial Ecology.

Planetary Biology and Microbial Ecology. Lynn Margulis. National Aeronautics and Space Administration, Scientific and Technical Information Office, 5285 Port Royal Rd., Springfield, Virginia 22161. (703) 487-4650. 1983.

HANDBOOKS AND MANUALS

Practical Manual for Groundwater Microbiology. D. Roy Cullimore. Lewis Publishers, 2000 Corporate Blvd., N.W., Boca Raton, Florida 33431. (407) 994-0555 or (800) 272-7737. 1991. Describes the direct observation of microbial activities in groundwater, sampling procedures, indirect and direct microbiological examinations.

The Prokaryotes: A Handbook on Habitats, Isolation, and Identification of Bacteria. M. P. Starr. Springer-Verlag, 175 5th Ave., New York, New York 10010. (212) 460-1500. 1981. Identification of bacteria and cultures and culture media of bacteriology.

ONLINE DATA BASES

BIOSIS Previews. BIOSIS, 2100 Arch St., Philadelphia, Pennsylvania 19103-1399. (215) 587-4800. Largest and most comprehensive database of research in the life sciences. Contains citations for nearly 9000 primary research journals, monographs, reviews, symposia, preliminary reports, semi-popular journals, selected institutional reports, government reports and research communications.

Biotechnology Abstracts. Derwent Publications Ltd., 6845 Elm St., McLean, Virginia 22101. (703) 790-0400. Includes material on genetic manipulation, biochemical engineering, fermentation, biocatalysis, cell hybridization, in vitro plant propagation and industrial waste management.

Cambridge Scientific Abstracts Life Science–CSAL. Cambridge Scientific Abstracts, 5161 River Rd., Bethesda, Maryland 20816. (301) 961-6750. Provides access to the following abstracting services: "Life Sciences Collection," "Aquatic Sciences and Fisheries Abstracts," "Oceanic Abstracts," and "Pollution Abstracts."

Enviro/Energyline Abstracts Plus. R. R. Bowker Co., 121 Chanlon Rd., New Providence, New Jersey 07974. (908) 464-6800.

Environmental Periodicals Bibliography. National Information Services Corp., Ste. 6, Wyman Towers, 3100 St. Paul St., Baltimore, Maryland 21218. (410)243-0797. Online version of abstract of same name.

SCISEARCH. Institute for Scientific Information, University City Science Center, 3501 Market St., Philadelphia, Pennsylvania 19104. (215) 386-0100.

PERIODICALS AND NEWSLETTERS

Applied and Environmental Microbiology Journal. American Society for Microbiology, 1325 Massachusetts Avenue N.W., Washington, District of Columbia 20005. (202) 737-3600. Monthly. Articles on industrial and food microbiology and ecological studies.

Applied Microbiology and Biotechnology. Springer International, 44 Hartz Way, Seacaucus, New Jersey 07094. (201) 348-4033. Six times a year. Covers biotechnology, biochemical engineering, applied genetics and regulation, applied microbial and cell physiology, food biotechnology, and environmental biotechnology.

Biodegradation. Kluwer Academic Publishers, 101 Philip Dr., Assinippi Park, Norwell, Massachusetts 02061-0358. (617) 871-6600. 1990-. Quarterly. Covers all aspects of science pertaining to the detoxification, recycling, amelioration or treatment of waste materials and pollutants by naturally occurring microbial strains, associations, or recombinant microorganisms.

Biotechnology and Bioengineering. John Wiley & Sons, Inc., 605 3rd Ave., New York, New York 10158. (212) 850-6000. Monthly. Aerobic and anaerobic processes, systems involving biofilms, algal systems, detoxification and bioremediation and genetic aspects, biosensors, and cellular systems.

International Journal of Antimicrobial Agents. Elsevier Science Publishing Co., 655 Avenue of the Americas, New York, New York 10010. (212) 984-5800. Bimonthly. Physical, chemical, pharmacological, in vitro and clinical properties of individual antimicrobial agents, antiviral agents, antiparasitic agents, antibacterial agents, antifungal agents, and immunotherapy.

International Journal of Plant Nutrition, Plant Chemistry, Soil Microbiology and Soil-Bourne Plant Diseases. Kluwer Academic Publishers, 101 Philip Dr., Assinippi Park, Norwell, Massachusetts 02061. (617) 871-6600. 1948-.

Soil Biology and Biochemistry. Pergamon Microforms International, Inc., Fairview Park, Elmsford, New York 10523. (914) 592-7720. Eight times a year. Soil biology, soil biochemistry, nitrogen fixation, nitrogenase activity, sampling microorganisms in soil, soil compaction, and nutrient release in soils.

RESEARCH CENTERS AND INSTITUTES

Bioanalytical Center. Washington State University, Troy Hall, Pullman, Washington 99164. (509) 335-5126.

Lehigh University, Bioprocessing Institute. 111 Research Drive, Mountaintop Campus, Bethlehem, Pennsylvania 18015. (215) 758-4258.

Lehigh University, Center for Molecular Bioscience and Biotechnology. Mountaintop Campus, Building 111, Bethlehem, Pennsylvania 18015. (215) 758-5426.

University of Minnesota, Gray Freshwater Biological Institute. P.O. Box 100, Navarre, Minnesota 55392. (612) 471-8476.

University of Nebraska-Lincoln, Center for Microbial Ecology. Lincoln, Nebraska 68588-0343. (402) 472-2253.

TRADE ASSOCIATIONS AND PROFESSIONAL SOCIETIES

American Society for Microbiology. 1325 Massachusetts Ave., N.W., Washington, District of Columbia 20005. (202) 737-3600.

Society for Industrial Microbiology. Box 12534, Arlington, Virginia 22209. (703) 941-5373.

MICROWAVE ENERGY

ABSTRACTING AND INDEXING SERVICES

Applied Science and Technology Index. H.W. Wilson Co., 950 University Ave., Bronx, New York 10452. (800) 367-6770. Formerly Industrial Arts Index.

Energy Information Abstracts Annual 1987 in Retrospect. EIC/Intelligence Inc., 121 Chanlon Rd., New Providence, New Jersey 07974. (908) 464-6800. 1988. Annual. Cumulative edition of the monthly Energy Information Abstracts. Monitors sources in the field of energy including the scientific, technical and business journal literature, conference and symposia proceedings, corporate, government and academic reports.

Engineering Index. The Engineering Index Inc., 345 E. 47th St., New York, New York 10017. 1962-.

Environment Abstracts. Bowker A & I Publishing, 121 Chanlon Rd., New Providence, New Jersey 07974. (908) 464-6800. 1974-.

Environment Index. Environment Information Center, Index Research Department, 124 E. 39th St., New York, New York 10016. 1971-. Annual.

Environmental Information Connection–EIC. Planning Information Program, Dept. of Urban and Regional Planning, University of Illinois, 1003 West Nevada, Urbana, Illinois 61801. (217) 333-1369. Also available online.

Environmental Periodicals Bibliography. Environmental Studies Institute, International Academy at Santa Barbara, 800 Garden St., Suite D, Santa Barbara, California 93101. (805) 965-5010. Also available online.

General Science Index. H. W. Wilson Co., 950 University Ave., Bronx, New York 10452. 1978-. Monthly, also issued in annual cumulation. Cumulative subject index to English language periodicals in the subject fields of astronomy, botany, chemistry, earth science, environ-

ment and conservation, food and nutrition, genetics, mathematics, medicine and health, microbiology, oceanography, physics, physiology and zoology.

Physics Briefs. Physikalische Berichte. Physik Verlag, Pappapelallee 3, Postfach 101161, Weinheim, Germany D-6940. 1979-. Semimonthly. In English. Volumes for 1979- issued by the Deutsche Physikalische Gesellschaft and the Fachinformationszentrum Energie Physik, Mathematik in cooperation with the American Institute of Physics.

Science Citation Index. Institute for Scientific Information, 3501 Market St., Philadelphia, Pennsylvania 19104. 1961-.

BIBLIOGRAPHIES

EPA Publications Bibliography. U.S. Environmental Protection Agency, Library Systems Branch, 401 M St., SW, Washington, District of Columbia 20460. (202) 260-2090. Quarterly.

ENCYCLOPEDIAS AND DICTIONARIES

Encyclopedia of Physical Science and Technology. Robert A. Meyers, ed. Academic Press, c/o Harcourt Brace Jovanovich Inc., 6277 Sea Harbor Dr., Orlando, Florida 32887. (800) 346-8648. Dictionary of engineering, technology and physical sciences.

McGraw-Hill Encyclopedia of Science and Technology. McGraw-Hill, 1221 Avenue of the Americas, New York, New York 10020. (212) 512-2000 or (800) 262-4729. 1992. Seventh edition. Issued in multiple volumes including index. Includes all science and technology broad subject areas.

Van Nostrand's Scientific Encyclopedia. Glenn D. Considine, ed. Van Nostrand Reinhold, 115 5th Ave., New York, New York 10003. (212) 254-3232. 1983. Sixth edition. Includes all broad subject areas in science.

GENERAL WORKS

More Protection from Microwave Radiation Hazards Needed. U.S. General Accounting Office, 441 G St., NW, Washington, District of Columbia 1978. Health, environmental, and physiological effects of microwave devices.

The Zapping of America. Paul Brodeur. W. W. Norton & Co., Inc., 500 5th Ave., New York, New York 10110. (800) 223-4830. 1977.

ONLINE DATA BASES

Computerized Engineering Index–COMPENDEX. Engineering Information Inc., 345 E. 47th St., New York, New York 10017. (212) 705-7600.

Enviro/Energyline Abstracts Plus. R. R. Bowker Co., 121 Chanlon Rd., New Providence, New Jersey 07974. (908) 464-6800.

Environmental Periodicals Bibliography. National Information Services Corp., Ste. 6, Wyman Towers, 3100 St. Paul St., Baltimore, Maryland 21218. (410)243-0797. Online version of abstract of same name.

PERIODICALS AND NEWSLETTERS

Microwave Energy Applications Newsletter. International Microwave Power Institute. R. V. Decareau, PO Box 241, Amherst, New Hampshire 03031. (603) 673-2245. Irregular.

MIGRATION

ABSTRACTING AND INDEXING SERVICES

Applied Ecology Abstracts Studies in Renewable Natural Resources. Information Retrieval Ltd., 1911 Jefferson Davis Highway, Arlington, Virginia 22202. 1975-. Monthly.

ASFA Aquaculture Abstracts. Cambridge Scientific Abstracts, Inc., 5161 River Rd., Bethesda, Maryland 20816. (301) 961-6750. 1984.

Biological Abstracts. BIOSIS, 2100 Arch St., Philadelphia, Pennsylvania 19103-1399. (215) 587-4800. 1927-.

Biological and Agricultural Index. H.W. Wilson Co., 950 University Ave., Bronx, New York 10452. (800) 367-6770. 1916-. Monthly.

Current Advances in Ecological and Environmental Science. Pergamon Microforms International, Inc., Fairview Park, Elmsford, New York 10523. (914) 592-7720. 1989-. Monthly. Current literature searching service including journals, reports, abstracts, etc. This service is available online as part of the CABS database on the hosts BRS and ORBIT search service.

Ecological Abstracts. Geo Abstracts Ltd. Elsevier Applied Science, Crown House, Linton Rd., Barking, England IG 11 8JU. 1974-. Derived from over 600 leading ecological and environmental journals, plus books, conference proceedings, reports and theses.

Ecology Abstracts. Cambridge Scientific Abstracts, 5161 River Rd., Bethesda, Maryland 20816. (301) 961-6750. Monthly.

Environment Abstracts. Bowker A & I Publishing, 121 Chanlon Rd., New Providence, New Jersey 07974. (908) 464-6800. 1974-.

Environment Index. Environment Information Center, Index Research Department, 124 E. 39th St., New York, New York 10016. 1971-. Annual.

Environmental Information Connection–EIC. Planning Information Program, Dept. of Urban and Regional Planning, University of Illinois, 1003 West Nevada, Urbana, Illinois 61801. (217) 333-1369. Also available online.

Environmental Periodicals Bibliography. Environmental Studies Institute, International Academy at Santa Barbara, 800 Garden St., Suite D, Santa Barbara, California 93101. (805) 965-5010. Also available online.

General Science Index. H. W. Wilson Co., 950 University Ave., Bronx, New York 10452. 1978-. Monthly, also issued in annual cumulation. Cumulative subject index to English language periodicals in the subject fields of astronomy, botany, chemistry, earth science, environment and conservation, food and nutrition, genetics, mathematics, medicine and health, microbiology, oceanography, physics, physiology and zoology.

Geographical Abstracts. London School of Economics, Dept. of Geography, Regency House, 34 Duke St., London, England 1966-. Continued by Geo Abstracts issued in 6 parts: Pt. A. Landforms and the quaternary; Pt. B. Biogeography and Climatology; Pt. C. Economic geography; Pt. D. Social geography and cartography; Pt. E. Sedimentology; Pt. F. Regional and community planning.

Multimedia Index to Ecology. National Information Center for Educational Media, University of Southern California, Los Angeles, California 90007.

Science Citation Index. Institute for Scientific Information, 3501 Market St., Philadelphia, Pennsylvania 19104. 1961-.

BIBLIOGRAPHIES

Current Contents. Agriculture, Biology and Environmental Sciences. Institute for Scientific Information, 3501 Market St., Philadelphia, Pennsylvania 19104. (800) 523-1857. 1973-. Previous title: Current Contents. Agricultural, Food & Veterinary Sciences. Gives the table of contents of periodicals in the fields of agriculture, biology, environmental and related areas.

EPA Publications Bibliography. U.S. Environmental Protection Agency, Library Systems Branch, 401 M St., SW, Washington, District of Columbia 20460. (202) 260-2090. Quarterly.

ENCYCLOPEDIAS AND DICTIONARIES

Cambridge Encyclopedia of Life Sciences. A. E. Friday and David S. Ingram. Cambridge University Press, 40 W 20th St., New York, New York 10011. (212) 924-3900 or (800) 227-0247. 1985. Includes all topics under biology and ecology.

Encyclopedia of Human Biology. Renato Dulbecco, ed. Academic Press, c/o Harcourt Brace Jovanovich Inc., 6277 Sea Harbor Dr., Orlando, Florida 32887. (800) 346-8648. 1991. Eight volumes.

Van Nostrand's Scientific Encyclopedia. Glenn D. Considine, ed. Van Nostrand Reinhold, 115 5th Ave., New York, New York 10003. (212) 254-3232. 1983. Sixth edition. Includes all broad subject areas in science.

GENERAL WORKS

Migration Processes in the Soil and Groundwater Zone. Ludwig Luckner. Lewis Publishers, 2000 Corporate Blvd., N.W., Boca Raton, Florida 33431. (407) 994-0555 or (800) 272-7737. 1991. Discusses the significance of migration main objectives of migration simulation and some methods of mathematical modelling.

Where Have All the Birds Gone?. John Terborgh. Princeton University Press, 41 Williams St., Princeton, New Jersey 08540. (609) 258-4900. 1989. Includes topics such as: population monitoring, ecological consequences of fragmentation, evolution of migration, social and territorial behaviors of wintering songbirds.

ONLINE DATA BASES

BIOSIS Previews. BIOSIS, 2100 Arch St., Philadelphia, Pennsylvania 19103-1399. (215) 587-4800. Largest and most comprehensive database of research in the life sciences. Contains citations for nearly 9000 primary

research journals, monographs, reviews, symposia, preliminary reports, semi-popular journals, selected institutional reports, government reports and research communications.

Cambridge Scientific Abstracts Life Science–CSAL. Cambridge Scientific Abstracts, 5161 River Rd., Bethesda, Maryland 20816. (301) 961-6750. Provides access to the following abstracting services: "Life Sciences Collection," "Aquatic Sciences and Fisheries Abstracts," "Oceanic Abstracts," and "Pollution Abstracts."

Enviro/Energyline Abstracts Plus. R. R. Bowker Co., 121 Chanlon Rd., New Providence, New Jersey 07974. (908) 464-6800.

Environmental Periodicals Bibliography. National Information Services Corp., Ste. 6, Wyman Towers, 3100 St. Paul St., Baltimore, Maryland 21218. (410)243-0797. Online version of abstract of same name.

SCISEARCH. Institute for Scientific Information, University City Science Center, 3501 Market St., Philadelphia, Pennsylvania 19104. (215) 386-0100.

STATISTICS SOURCES

World Resources. World Resources Institute. 1709 New York Ave., N.W., Washington, District of Columbia 20006. (202) 638-6300. Annual. Statistical and textual analysis of world's natural resources and the effects of growth-caused environmental pollution.

TRADE ASSOCIATIONS AND PROFESSIONAL SOCIETIES

American Society of Naturalists. Department of Ecology and Evolation, State University of New York, Stony Brook, New York 11794. (516) 632-8589.

MINE DRAINAGE

ABSTRACTING AND INDEXING SERVICES

Chemical Abstracts. Chemical Abstracts Service, 2540 Olentangy River Rd., PO Box 3012, Columbus, Ohio 43210. (800) 848-6533. 1907-.

Environment Abstracts. Bowker A & I Publishing, 121 Chanlon Rd., New Providence, New Jersey 07974. (908) 464-6800. 1974-.

Environment Index. Environment Information Center, Index Research Department, 124 E. 39th St., New York, New York 10016. 1971-. Annual.

Environmental Information Connection–EIC. Planning Information Program, Dept. of Urban and Regional Planning, University of Illinois, 1003 West Nevada, Urbana, Illinois 61801. (217) 333-1369. Also available online.

Environmental Periodicals Bibliography. Environmental Studies Institute, International Academy at Santa Barbara, 800 Garden St., Suite D, Santa Barbara, California 93101. (805) 965-5010. Also available online.

Pollution Abstracts. Cambridge Scientific Abstracts, 5161 River Rd., Bethesda, Maryland 20816. (301) 961-6750. Six/year. Indexes worldwide technical literature on environmental pollution. Covers air pollution, marine and freshwater pollution, sewage and wastewater treatment,

waste management, toxicology and health, noise pollution, radiation, land pollution, and environmental policies, programs, legislation, and education. Also available online.

BIBLIOGRAPHIES

EPA Publications Bibliography. U.S. Environmental Protection Agency, Library Systems Branch, 401 M St., SW, Washington, District of Columbia 20460. (202) 260-2090. Quarterly.

Mine Drainage Bibliography. V.E. Gleason. National Technical Information Service, 5285 Port Royal Rd., Springfield, Virginia 22161. (703) 487-4650. Formation and effects of acid mine drainage; erosion and sedimentation; sediment control technology effects of coal mining on ground water quality and on hydrology; and drainage from coal storage piles.

ENCYCLOPEDIAS AND DICTIONARIES

Dictionary of Environmental Engineering and Related Sciences: English-Spanish, Spanish-English. Jose T. Villate. Ediciones Universal, 3090 SW 8th St., Miami, Florida 33135. (305) 642-3355. 1979.

Encyclopedia of Environmental Science and Engineering. J.R. Pfafflin. Gordon and Breach Science Publishers, Inc., 270 8th Ave., New York, New York 10011. (212) 206-8900. 1992.

HANDBOOKS AND MANUALS

Design Manual: Neutralization of Acid Mine Drainage. U.S. Environmental Protection Agency, Office of Research and Development, Industrial Environmental Research Laboratory, 26 W. Martin Luther King Dr., Cincinnati, Ohio 45268. (513) 569-7931. 1983. Acid mine drainage and the chemistry of neutralization.

Instructions, Drainway. U.S. Department of the Interior, Bureau of Mines, 810 7th St., NW, Washington, District of Columbia 20241. (202) 501-9649. 1988. Problems and exercises relating to mine drainage.

Surface Mining Water Diversion Manual. Li Simons & Associates, Inc. U.S. G.P.O., Washington, District of Columbia 20401. (202) 512-0000. 1982.

ONLINE DATA BASES

Chemical Abstracts-CA. Chemical Abstracts Service, 2540 Olentangy River Rd., P.O. Box 3012, Columbus, Ohio 43210. (800) 848-6533 or (614) 421-3600. Information sources include 9000 journals, patents from 27 countries, two industrial property organizations, new books, conference proceedings, and government research reports.

Enviro/Energyline Abstracts Plus. R. R. Bowker Co., 121 Chanlon Rd., New Providence, New Jersey 07974. (908) 464-6800.

Environmental Periodicals Bibliography. National Information Services Corp., Ste. 6, Wyman Towers, 3100 St. Paul St., Baltimore, Maryland 21218. (410)243-0797. Online version of abstract of same name.

PERIODICALS AND NEWSLETTERS

Journal of American Mining Congress. American Mining Congress, 1920 N Street, NW, Suite 300, Washington, District of Columbia 20036. (202) 861-2800. Monthly. Contains information on the mining industry.

TRADE ASSOCIATIONS AND PROFESSIONAL SOCIETIES

American Mining Congress. 1920 N St., N.W., Suite 300, Washington, District of Columbia 20036. (202) 861-2800.

MINERAL EXPLORATION AND EXTRACTION

ABSTRACTING AND INDEXING SERVICES

Applied Science and Technology Index. H.W. Wilson Co., 950 University Ave., Bronx, New York 10452. (800) 367-6770. Formerly Industrial Arts Index.

Engineering Index. The Engineering Index Inc., 345 E. 47th St., New York, New York 10017. 1962-.

Science Citation Index. Institute for Scientific Information, 3501 Market St., Philadelphia, Pennsylvania 19104. 1961-.

DIRECTORIES

Gale Environmental Sourcebook. Karen Hill. Gale Research Co., 835 Penobscot Bldg., Detroit, Michigan 48226-4094. (313) 961-2242. Contacts, information sources, or general information on environmental topics.

Mineral Industry Location System. Department of the Interior, 810 7th St. NW, Washington, District of Columbia 20241. (202) 501-9649.

Minerals Availability System. Bureau of Mines, Department of the Interior, Box 25086, Denver, Colorado 80225. (303) 236-5210.

Minerals Yearbook. Department of the Interior, 810 7th St. NW, Washington, District of Columbia 20241. (202) 501-9649.

ENCYCLOPEDIAS AND DICTIONARIES

Encyclopedia of Minerals. Willard Lincoln Roberts, et al. Van Nostrand Reinhold, 115 5th Ave., New York, New York 10003. (212) 254-3232 or (800) 926-2665. 1990. Second edition. Gives information on rare minerals, those minerals widely known and collected and those that are most attractive or visually diagnostic.

GOVERNMENTAL ORGANIZATIONS

Minerals Management Service. Room 1442, M5612, 18th and C St., N.W., Washington, District of Columbia 20240. (202) 208-3500.

Office of Public Information: Bureau of Mines. 2401 E St., N.W., Washington, District of Columbia 20241. (202) 501-9650.

Public Affairs Office: U.S. Geological Survey. 119 National Center, 12201 Sunrise Valley Dr., Reston, Virginia 22092. (703) 648-4460.

ONLINE DATA BASES

Computerized Engineering Index–COMPENDEX. Engineering Information Inc., 345 E. 47th St., New York, New York 10017. (212) 705-7600.

STATISTICS SOURCES

Environmental Data Compendium. OECD Publications and Information Center, 2001 L St., N.W., Suite 700, Washington, District of Columbia 20036. (202) 785-6323. 1989.

Environmental Indicators. OECD Publications and Information Center, 2001 L St., N.W., Suite 700, Washington, District of Columbia 20036. (202) 785-6323. 1991.

Environmental Quality. Council on Environmental Quality. U.S. G.P.O., Washington, District of Columbia 20401. (202) 512-0000. Annual.

Mineral Commodity Summaries. U.S. Bureau of Mines. U.S. G.P.O., Washington, District of Columbia 20401. (202) 512-0000. Annual. Market profiles of mineral commodities.

Mineral Industry Surveys. U.S. G.P.O, Washington, District of Columbia 20402-9325. (202) 512-0000. Annual. Mineral production, consumption, trade, and industry operations, by commodity.

Report on the Nation's Renewable Resources. U.S. Forest Service. U.S. G.P.O., Washington, District of Columbia 20401. (202) 512-0000. Quinquennial. Projections of resource use and supply from 1920 to 2040, covering wilderness, wildlife, fish, range, timber, water and minerals.

The State of the Environment. OECD Publications and Information Center, 2001 L St., N.W., Suite 700, Washington, District of Columbia 20036. (202) 785-6323. 1991.

TRADE ASSOCIATIONS AND PROFESSIONAL SOCIETIES

American Mining Congress. 1920 N St., N.W., Suite 300, Washington, District of Columbia 20036. (202) 861-2800.

Mineralogical Society of America. 1130 17th St., N.W., Suite 330, Washington, District of Columbia 20036. (202) 775-4344.

Society for Mining, Metallurgy, and Exploration, Inc. P.O. Box 625005, Littleton, Colorado 80162. (303) 973-9550.

Society of Mineral Analysts. P.O. Box 5416, Elko, Nevada 89802. (801) 569-7159.

MINERAL REFINING AND WASTES

ABSTRACTING AND INDEXING SERVICES

Applied Science and Technology Index. H.W. Wilson Co., 950 University Ave., Bronx, New York 10452. (800) 367-6770. Formerly Industrial Arts Index.

Engineering Index. The Engineering Index Inc., 345 E. 47th St., New York, New York 10017. 1962-.

General Science Index. H. W. Wilson Co., 950 University Ave., Bronx, New York 10452. 1978-. Monthly, also issued in annual cumulation. Cumulative subject index to English language periodicals in the subject fields of astronomy, botany, chemistry, earth science, environment and conservation, food and nutrition, genetics, mathematics, medicine and health, microbiology, oceanography, physics, physiology and zoology.

Mineralogical Abstracts. Mineralogical Society, 41 Queen's Gate, London, England SW7 5HR. 71 5847916. Quarterly. Abstracts of journal articles, conferences, technical reports and specialized books in the areas of minerals, clay minerals, economic minerals, ore deposits, environmental studies, experimental mineralogy, gemstones, geochemistry, petrology, lunar and planetary studies and other related areas in mineralogy.

Pollution Abstracts. Cambridge Scientific Abstracts, 5161 River Rd., Bethesda, Maryland 20816. (301) 961-6750. Six/year. Indexes worldwide technical literature on environmental pollution. Covers air pollution, marine and freshwater pollution, sewage and wastewater treatment, waste management, toxicology and health, noise pollution, radiation, land pollution, and environmental policies, programs, legislation, and education. Also available online.

Science Citation Index. Institute for Scientific Information, 3501 Market St., Philadelphia, Pennsylvania 19104. 1961-.

BIBLIOGRAPHIES

Bibliography and Index of Geology. American Geological Institute, 4220 King St., Alexandria, Virginia 22302. Monthly. Includes environmental geology and hydrogeology.

Bibliography on Disposal of Refuse from Coal Mines and Coal Cleaning Plants. Virginia E. Gleason. Industrial Environmental Research Laboratory, Office of Research and Development, U.S. Environmental Protection Agency, 242 Atlantic Ave., Raleigh, North Carolina 27604. (919) 834-4015. 1978.

New Publications: Bureau of Mines. U.S. Department of the Interior, 1849 C St. NW, Washington, District of Columbia 20240. (202) 208-3171. 1910-. Monthly. Subject areas included are mines and mineral resources, mining engineering and related areas.

New Publications of the Geological Survey. U.S. Department of the Interior, Geological Survey, 119 National Center, Reston, Virginia 22092. (703) 648-4460. 1984-. Monthly. Bibliography of geological publications and related government documents published by the Geological Survey.

DIRECTORIES

Industrial Minerals Directory: World Guide to Producers and Processors. Metal Bulletin, Inc., 220 5th Ave., 10th Fl., New York, New York 10001. (212) 213-6202. Includes mineral processing companies in addition to those which own and operate mines or quarries.

ENCYCLOPEDIAS AND DICTIONARIES

The Encyclopedia of Mineralogy. Hutchinson Ross Pub. Co., Stroudsburg, Pennsylvania 1981.

Encyclopedia of Minerals. Willard Lincoln Roberts, et al. Van Nostrand Reinhold, 115 5th Ave., New York, New York 10003. (212) 254-3232 or (800) 926-2665. 1990. Second edition. Gives information on rare minerals, those minerals widely known and collected and those that are most attractive or visually diagnostic.

Encyclopedia of Physical Science and Technology. Robert A. Meyers, ed. Academic Press, c/o Harcourt Brace Jovanovich Inc., 6277 Sea Harbor Dr., Orlando, Florida 32887. (800) 346-8648. Dictionary of engineering, technology and physical sciences.

Glossary of Geology. Robert Latimer Bates and Julia A. Jackson, eds. American Geological Institute, 4220 King St., Alexandria, Virginia 22302-1507. (703) 379-2480 or (800) 336-4764. 1987. Third edition.

McGraw-Hill Encyclopedia of the Geological Sciences. Sybil P. Parker, ed. McGraw-Hill, 1221 Avenue of the Americas, New York, New York 10020. (212) 512-2000 or (800) 262-4729. 1988. Second edition. Published previously in the McGraw-Hill Encyclopedia of Science and Technology.

GENERAL WORKS

Deep Coal Mining: Waste Disposal Technology. William S. Doyle. Noyes Publications, 120 Mill Rd., Park Ridge, New Jersey 07656. (201) 391-8484. 1976. Pollution technology review covering waste disposal in coal mining.

Evaluation of Treatment Technologies for Listed Petroleum Refinery Wastes. R. Rowe. American Petroleum Institute, 1220 L St. N.W., Washington, District of Columbia 20005. (202) 682-8000. 1987. Field studies conducted by the API Waste Technology Task Force on petroleum waste.

Land Use Planning and Coal Refuse Disposal. Robert P. Larkin. Oxford University Press, Gipsy Ln., Headington, Oxford, England OX3 0BP. 1980. Covers land use, coal mines and mining, and waste disposal.

Magill's Survey of Science. Earth Science Series. Frank N. Magill. Salem Press, PO Box 50062, Pasadena, California 91105. 1990-. Five volumes. Includes information on earth's crust, hot spots and volcanic island chains, physical properties of minerals, rock magnetism, physical properties of rocks, and index.

GOVERNMENTAL ORGANIZATIONS

Minerals Management Service. Room 1442, M5612, 18th and C St., N.W., Washington, District of Columbia 20240. (202) 208-3500.

Office of Public Information: Bureau of Mines. 2401 E St., N.W., Washington, District of Columbia 20241. (202) 501-9650.

Public Affairs Office: U.S. Geological Survey. 119 National Center, 12201 Sunrise Valley Dr., Reston, Virginia 22092. (703) 648-4460.

HANDBOOKS AND MANUALS

Coal Refuse Inspection Manual. U.S. Mining Enforcement and Safety Administration, Washington, District of Columbia 1976. Covers earthwork fills and coal mining waste.

Manual on Disposal of Refinery Wastes: Volume on Solid Wastes. American Petroleum Institute, 1220 L St. N.W., Washington, District of Columbia 20005. (202) 682-8000. 1980. Covers sewage disposal and petroleum waste.

ONLINE DATA BASES

Computerized Engineering Index–COMPENDEX. Engineering Information Inc., 345 E. 47th St., New York, New York 10017. (212) 705-7600.

PERIODICALS AND NEWSLETTERS

World Resource Review. SUPCON International, PO Box 5275, 1 Heritage Plaza, Woodridge, Illinois 60517. (708) 910-1551. 1981-. Quarterly. Covers all phases of policy discussions and their developments, including such topics as global change, energy production and use, ecosystem impacts of development activities, environmental law, solution of transnational environmental problems, global flow of strategic industrial materials, regional, national, and local resource management, natural resources, food, agriculture and forestry.

RESEARCH CENTERS AND INSTITUTES

University of Arizona, Arizona Cooperative Fish and Wildlife Research Unit. 210 Biological Sciences Building, Tucson, Arizona 85721. (602) 621-1959.

TRADE ASSOCIATIONS AND PROFESSIONAL SOCIETIES

American Mining Congress. 1920 N St., N.W., Suite 300, Washington, District of Columbia 20036. (202) 861-2800.

MINES AND MINERAL RESOURCES

ABSTRACTING AND INDEXING SERVICES

Applied Science and Technology Index. H.W. Wilson Co., 950 University Ave., Bronx, New York 10452. (800) 367-6770. Formerly Industrial Arts Index.

Chemical Abstracts. Chemical Abstracts Service, 2540 Olentangy River Rd., PO Box 3012, Columbus, Ohio 43210. (800) 848-6533. 1907-.

Ecology Abstracts. Cambridge Scientific Abstracts, 5161 River Rd., Bethesda, Maryland 20816. (301) 961-6750. Monthly.

Engineering Index. The Engineering Index Inc., 345 E. 47th St., New York, New York 10017. 1962-.

Food Science and Technology Abstracts. International Food Information Service, c/o National Food Laboratory, 6363 Clark Ave., Dublin, California 94568. (800) 336-3782. 1969-.

General Science Index. H. W. Wilson Co., 950 University Ave., Bronx, New York 10452. 1978-. Monthly, also issued in annual cumulation. Cumulative subject index to English language periodicals in the subject fields of astronomy, botany, chemistry, earth science, environment and conservation, food and nutrition, genetics, mathematics, medicine and health, microbiology, oceanography, physics, physiology and zoology.

Index to Scientific Book Contents. Institute for Scientific Information, 3501 Market St., Philadelphia, Pennsylvania 19104. (800) 523-1857. 1985-. Annual. Gives contents of science books published.

Mineralogical Abstracts. Mineralogical Society, 41 Queen's Gate, London, England SW7 5HR. 71 5847916. Quarterly. Abstracts of journal articles, conferences, technical reports and specialized books in the areas of minerals, clay minerals, economic minerals, ore deposits, environmental studies, experimental mineralogy, gemstones, geochemistry, petrology, lunar and planetary studies and other related areas in mineralogy.

Pollution Abstracts. Cambridge Scientific Abstracts, 5161 River Rd., Bethesda, Maryland 20816. (301) 961-6750. Six/year. Indexes worldwide technical literature on environmental pollution. Covers air pollution, marine and freshwater pollution, sewage and wastewater treatment, waste management, toxicology and health, noise pollution, radiation, land pollution, and environmental policies, programs, legislation, and education. Also available online.

Science Citation Index. Institute for Scientific Information, 3501 Market St., Philadelphia, Pennsylvania 19104. 1961-.

Sea Grant Abstracts. National Sea Grant Depository, Pell Laboratory Bldg., Bay Campus, University of Rhode Island, Narragansett, Rhode Island 02882. (401) 792-6114. 1986-. Quarterly. Published by the National Sea Grant Programs, this collection includes annual reports, serials and newsletters, charts and maps.

BIBLIOGRAPHIES

Bibliography and Index of Geology. American Geological Institute, 4220 King St., Alexandria, Virginia 22302. Monthly. Includes environmental geology and hydrogeology.

New Publications: Bureau of Mines. U.S. Department of the Interior, 1849 C St. NW, Washington, District of Columbia 20240. (202) 208-3171. 1910-. Monthly. Subject areas included are mines and mineral resources, mining engineering and related areas.

DIRECTORIES

Engineering and Mining Journal–Buying Directory Issue. Maclean Hunter Publishing Company, 29 North Wacker Dr., Chicago, Illinois 60606. (312) 726-2802.

Industrial Minerals Directory: World Guide to Producers and Processors. Metal Bulletin, Inc., 220 5th Ave., 10th Fl., New York, New York 10001. (212) 213-6202. Includes mineral processing companies in addition to those which own and operate mines or quarries.

Minerals Yearbook. Department of the Interior, 810 7th St. NW, Washington, District of Columbia 20241. (202) 501-9649.

Pit & Quarry–Buyers' Guide Issue. Edgell Communications, Inc., 7500 Old Oak Blvd., Cleveland, Ohio 44130. (216) 243-8100.

ENCYCLOPEDIAS AND DICTIONARIES

The Encyclopedia of Mineralogy. Hutchinson Ross Pub. Co., Stroudsburg, Pennsylvania 1981.

Encyclopedia of Physical Science and Technology. Robert A. Meyers, ed. Academic Press, c/o Harcourt Brace Jovanovich Inc., 6277 Sea Harbor Dr., Orlando, Florida 32887. (800) 346-8648. Dictionary of engineering, technology and physical sciences.

GENERAL WORKS

Comparative Dosimetry of Radon in Mines and Homes. Commission on Life Science, National Research Council. National Academy Press, 2101 Constitution Ave. N.W., PO Box 285, Washington, District of Columbia 20418. (202) 334-3313. 1991.

Magill's Survey of Science. Earth Science Series. Frank N. Magill. Salem Press, PO Box 50062, Pasadena, California 91105. 1990-. Five volumes. Includes information on earth's crust, hot spots and volcanic island chains, physical properties of minerals, rock magnetism, physical properties of rocks, and index.

GOVERNMENTAL ORGANIZATIONS

Minerals Management Service. Room 1442, M5612, 18th and C St., N.W., Washington, District of Columbia 20240. (202) 208-3500.

U.S. Department of Labor: Mine Safety and Health Administration. 4015 Wilson Blvd., Arlington, Virginia 22203. (703) 235-1452.

HANDBOOKS AND MANUALS

Complete Guide to Vitamins, Minerals and Supplements. H. Winter Griffith. Fisher Books, 3499 N. Campbell Ave., Suite 909, Tucson, Arizona 85712. (602) 325-5263. 1988. Includes name, brand name, reasons to use, who should use, recommended daily allowance, and other related data in the form of a chart.

ONLINE DATA BASES

Chemical Abstracts-CA. Chemical Abstracts Service, 2540 Olentangy River Rd., P.O. Box 3012, Columbus, Ohio 43210. (800) 848-6533 or (614) 421-3600. Information sources include 9000 journals, patents from 27 countries, two industrial property organizations, new books, conference proceedings, and government research reports.

Computerized Engineering Index–COMPENDEX. Engineering Information Inc., 345 E. 47th St., New York, New York 10017. (212) 705-7600.

Engineering and Mining Journal. Maclean Hunter Publishing Company, 29 N. Wacker Dr., Chicago, Illinois 60606. (312) 726-2802.

IMMAGE. Institution of Mining & Metallurgy Library and Information Services, 44 Portland Place, London, England W1N 4BR. 44 (71) 580-3802.

Minerals Data System & Rock Analysis Storage System. Geological Information Systems, c/o University of Oklahoma, 830 Van Fleet Oval, Norman, Oklahoma 73019. (405) 325-3031.

Minesearch. Metals Economics Group, Ltd., 1722 14th St., Boulder, Colorado 80302. (303) 442-7501.

PERIODICALS AND NEWSLETTERS

Journal of American Mining Congress. American Mining Congress, 1920 N Street, NW, Suite 300, Washington, District of Columbia 20036. (202) 861-2800. Monthly. Contains information on the mining industry.

STATISTICS SOURCES

Mineral Commodity Summaries. U.S. Bureau of Mines. U.S. G.P.O., Washington, District of Columbia 20401. (202) 512-0000. Annual. Market profiles of mineral commodities.

TRADE ASSOCIATIONS AND PROFESSIONAL SOCIETIES

American Institute of Mining, Metallurgical and Petroleum Engineers. 345 E. 47th St., 14th Fl., New York, New York 10017. (212) 705-7695.

American Mining Congress. 1920 N St., N.W., Suite 300, Washington, District of Columbia 20036. (202) 861-2800.

American Society for Surface Mining and Reclamation. 21 Grandview Dr., Princeton, New Jersey 24740. (304) 425-8332.

Center for Alternative Mining Development Policy. 210 Avon St., #9, La Crosse, Wisconsin 54603. (608) 784-4399.

Minerals, Metals, and Materials Society. 420 Commonwealth Dr., Warrendale, Pennsylvania 15086. (412) 776-9000.

Mining and Metallurgical Society of America. 9 Escalle Lane, Larkspur, California 94939. (415) 924-7441.

Society for Mining, Metallurgy, and Exploration, Inc. P.O. Box 625005, Littleton, Colorado 80162. (303) 973-9550.

Society of Mining Engineers. PO Box 625005, Littleton, Colorado 80162. (303) 973-9550.

United Mine Workers of America. 900 15th St., N.W., Washington, District of Columbia 20005. (202) 842-7200.

MINNESOTA ENVIRONMENTAL AGENCIES

GOVERNMENTAL ORGANIZATIONS

Department of Agriculture: Pesticide Registration. Director, Agronomy Services Division, 90 West Plato Blvd., St Paul, Minnesota 55107. (612) 297-2530.

Department of Labor and Industry: Occupational Safety. Director, Occupational Safety and Health Administration, 444 Lafayette Rd., St Paul, Minnesota 55101. (612) 296-2116.

Department of Natural Resources: Coastal Zone Management. Director, Water Division, 500 Lafayette Rd., St Paul, Minnesota 55155-4001. (612) 296-4810.

Department of Natural Resources: Fish and Wildlife. Director, Division of Fish and Wildlife, 500 Lafayette Rd., St Paul, Minnesota 55155-4001. (612) 296-1308.

Department of Natural Resources: Natural Resources. Commissioner, 500 Lafayette Rd., St Paul, Minnesota 55155-4001. (612) 296-2549.

Department of Natural Resources: Water Quality. Director, Waters Division, 500 Lafayette Rd., St. Paul, Minnesota 55155-4810. (612) 296-4800.

Division of Waters: Groundwater Management. Groundwater Division, 500 Lafayette Rd., St Paul, Minnesota 55155-4001. (612) 296-0436.

Emergency Preparedness and Community Right-to-Know. Director, 290 Bigelow Bldg., 450 North Syndicate, St Paul, Minnesota 55104. (612) 643-3000.

Office of Waste Management: Hazardous Waste Management. Director, 1350 Energy Lane, St Paul, Minnesota 55108. (612) 649-5741.

Pollution Control Agency: Air Quality. Director, Division of Air Quality, 520 Lafayette Rd., St Paul, Minnesota 55155. (612) 296-7731.

Pollution Control Agency: Environmental Protection. Commissioner, 520 Lafayette Rd., St Paul, Minnesota 55155. (612) 296-7301.

Pollution Control Agency: Solid Waste Management. Director, Solid and Hazardous Waste Division, 520 Lafayette Rd., St Paul, Minnesota 55155. (612) 643-3402.

Pollution Control Agency: Underground Storage Tanks. Director, Solid and Hazardous Waste Division, 520 Lafayette Rd., St Paul, Minnesota 55155. (612) 296-7282.

Pollution Control Agency: Waste Minimization and Pollution Prevention. Director, Solid and Hazardous Waste Minimization Division, 520 Lafayette Rd., St Paul, Minnesota 55155. (612) 296-6300.

MINNESOTA ENVIRONMENTAL LEGISLATION

GENERAL WORKS

Minnesota Environmental Law Handbook. Government Institutes, Inc., 4 Research Pl., Ste. 200, Rockville, Maryland 20850. (301) 921-2300. 1990.

MIREX

See also: KEPONE; ORGANOCHLORINE; PESTICIDES

ABSTRACTING AND INDEXING SERVICES

Applied Ecology Abstracts Studies in Renewable Natural Resources. Information Retrieval Ltd., 1911 Jefferson Davis Highway, Arlington, Virginia 22202. 1975-. Monthly.

Biological and Agricultural Index. H.W. Wilson Co., 950 University Ave., Bronx, New York 10452. (800) 367-6770. 1916-. Monthly.

Multimedia Index to Ecology. National Information Center for Educational Media, University of Southern California, Los Angeles, California 90007.

Pollution Abstracts. Cambridge Scientific Abstracts, 5161 River Rd., Bethesda, Maryland 20816. (301) 961-6750. Six/year. Indexes worldwide technical literature on environmental pollution. Covers air pollution, marine and freshwater pollution, sewage and wastewater treatment, waste management, toxicology and health, noise pollution, radiation, land pollution, and environmental policies, programs, legislation, and education. Also available online.

Science Citation Index. Institute for Scientific Information, 3501 Market St., Philadelphia, Pennsylvania 19104. 1961-.

ENCYCLOPEDIAS AND DICTIONARIES

McGraw-Hill Encyclopedia of Science and Technology. McGraw-Hill, 1221 Avenue of the Americas, New York, New York 10020. (212) 512-2000 or (800) 262-4729. 1992. Seventh edition. Issued in multiple volumes including index. Includes all science and technology broad subject areas.

Van Nostrand's Scientific Encyclopedia. Glenn D. Considine, ed. Van Nostrand Reinhold, 115 5th Ave., New York, New York 10003. (212) 254-3232. 1983. Sixth edition. Includes all broad subject areas in science.

GENERAL WORKS

Human Population Exposures to Mirex and Kepone. Benjamin E. Suta. National Technical Information Service, 5285 Port Royal Rd., Springfield, Virginia 22161. (703) 487-4650. 1978. Environmental aspects of pesticides, organochlorine, insecticides, and chlordecone.

Mirex. World Health Organization, Ave. Appia, Geneva, Switzerland CH-1211. 1984. Toxicology of mirex and insecticides.

Mirex Hazards to Fish, Wildlife, and Invertebrates: A Synoptic Review. Ronald Eisler. Fish and Wildlife Service, Department of the Interior, 18th and C Sts., NW, Washington, District of Columbia 20240. (202) 653-8750. 1985. Effect of water pollution on fish and wildlife and environmental aspects of mirex.

ONLINE DATA BASES

Chemical Carcinogenesis Research Information System–CCRIS. National Library of Medicine, 8600 Rockville Pike, Bethesda, Maryland 20894. (800) 638-8480. Individual assay results and test conditions for 1,451 chemicals in the areas of carcinogenicity, mutagenicity, tumor promotion, and cocarcinogenicity.

Chemical Collection System/Request Tracking–CCS/RTS. U.S. Environmental Protection Agency, Office of Pesticides and Toxic Substances, 401 M St., SW, Washington, District of Columbia 20460. (202) 260-2090. Contains information on various properties of a number of chemicals including environmental effects, test and analysis methods, and health effects. Available from EPA.

Chemical Dictionary Online–CHEMLINE. Chemical Abstracts Service, 2540 Olentangy River Rd., Columbus, Ohio 43210. (614) 421-3600 or (800) 848-6533. Part of

MEDLINE of the National Library of Medicine (NLM). File of 900,000 names for chemical substances, representing 450,000 unique compounds. It contains such information as Chemical Abstracts (CA) Service Registry Numbers, molecular formulas, preferred chemical nomenclature, and generic and ring structure information. Available on NLM's ELHILL system.

Chemical Exposure. Science Applications International Corp., Health & Environmental Information, P.O. Box 2501, Oak Ridge, Tennessee 37831. (615) 482-9031. Database of chemicals that have been identified in both human tissues and body fluids and in feral and food animals. Contains reference to journal articles, conferences, and reports. Covers the whole fields of information related to human and animal exposure to food, air, and water contaminants and pharmaceuticals. Its records include information on chemical properties, formulas, tissues measured, analytical method used, demographics and more. Available on DIALOG.

MISSISSIPPI ENVIRONMENTAL AGENCIES

GOVERNMENTAL ORGANIZATIONS

Bureau of Marine Resources: Coastal Zone Management. Director, 2620 W. Beach Blvd., Biloxi, Mississippi 39531. (601) 864-4602.

Commission of Environmental Quality: Air Quality. Director, Pollution Control Bureau, PO Box 10385, Jackson, Mississippi 39289-0385. (601) 961-5104.

Commission of Environmental Quality: Water Quality. Director, Pollution Control Bureau, PO Box 10385, Jackson, Mississippi 39289-0385. (601) 961-5100.

Department of Agriculture and Commerce: Pesticide Registration. State Entomologist/Director, Plant Industry Division, PO Box 5207, Mississippi State University, Mississippi 39762. (601) 325-3390.

Department of Environmental Quality: Hazardous Waste Management. Executive Director, Southport Mall, Jackson, Mississippi 39209. (601) 961-5000.

Department of Environmental Quality: Natural Resources. Executive Director, Southport Mall, Jackson, Mississippi 39209. (601) 961-5000.

Department of Health: Occupational Safety. Director, Occupational Safety and Health, 4443 I-55 North, Jackson, Mississippi 39211. (601) 982-6315.

Department of Natural Resources: Environmental Protection. Director, Pollution Control Bureau, Southport Mall, Jackson, Mississippi 39289-0385. (601) 961-5100.

Department of Natural Resources: Solid Waste Management. Chief, Division Director, Solid Waste Management Superfund, PO Box 40485, Jackson, Mississippi 39209. (601) 961-5062.

Department of Wildlife, Fisheries and Parks: Fish and Wildlife. Director, Division of Wildlife and Fisheries, PO Box 451, Jackson, Mississippi 39205. (601) 364-2015.

Emergency Management Agency: Emergency Preparedness and Community Right-to-Know. Emergency Response Commission, PO Box 4501, Fondren Station, Jackson, Mississippi 39296-4501. (601) 960-9973.

U.S. EPA Region 4: Pollution Prevention. Program Manager, 345 Courtland St., N.E., Atlanta, Georgia 30365. (404) 347-7109.

MISSISSIPPI ENVIRONMENTAL LEGISLATION

GENERAL WORKS

Natural Resources Law Update. University of Mississippi Law Center, Natural Resources Law Program, University, Mississippi 38677.

MISSOURI ENVIRONMENTAL AGENCIES

GOVERNMENTAL ORGANIZATIONS

Department of Agriculture: Pesticide Registration. Director, Plant Industries Division, PO Box 630, Jefferson City, Missouri 65102. (314) 751-2462.

Department of Conservation: Fish and Wildlife. Director, PO Box 180, Jefferson City, Missouri 65102-0180. (314) 751-4115.

Department of Natural Resources: Air Quality. Staff Director, Air Pollution Control Program, PO Box 176, Jefferson City, Missouri 65102. (314) 751-4817.

Department of Natural Resources: Emergency Preparedness and Community Right-to-Know. Emergency Response Commission, PO Box 3133, Jefferson City, MO, 65102. (314) 751-7929.

Department of Natural Resources: Environmental Protection. Director, Division of Environmental Quality, PO Box 176, Jefferson City, Missouri 65102. (314) 751-4810.

Department of Natural Resources: Groundwater Management. Director and State Geologist, Division of Geology and Land Survey, PO Box 250, Rolla, Missouri 65401. (314) 364-1752.

Department of Natural Resources: Natural Resources. Director, Jefferson State Office Building, 205 Jefferson St., Jefferson City, Missouri 65102. (314) 751-4422.

Department of Natural Resources: Waste Minimization and Pollution Prevention. Director, Environmental Quality Program, Waste Management Program, PO Box 176, Jefferson City, Missouri 65102. (314) 751-4919.

Division of Environmental Quality: Hazardous Waste Management. Director, Solid Waste Program, PO Box 176, Jefferson City, Missouri 65102. (314) 751-3176.

Division of Environmental Quality: Solid Waste Management. Director, Solid Waste Program, PO Box 176, Jefferson City, Missouri 65102. (314) 751-3176.

Division of Environmental Quality: Underground Storage Tanks. Director, Water Pollution Control Program, PO Box 176, Jefferson City, Missouri 65102. (314) 751-1300.

Division of Environmental Quality: Water Quality. Director, Water Pollution Control Program, PO Box 176, Jefferson City, Missouri 65102. (314) 751-1300.

Labor and Industrial Relations Department: Occupational Safety. Director, Division of Labor Standards, PO Box 449, Jefferson City, Missouri 65102. (314) 751-3403.

MISSOURI ENVIRONMENTAL LEGISLATION

GENERAL WORKS

Missouri Environmental Law Handbook. Government Institutes, Inc., 4 Research Pl., Ste. 200, Rockville, Maryland 20850. (301) 921-2300. 1990.

MOBILE SOURCE
See: AIR POLLUTION

MODULAR HIGH TEMPERATURE GAS COOLED REACTORS
See: REACTORS

MOLLUSCIDES
See: PESTICIDES

MOLYBDENUM

ABSTRACTING AND INDEXING SERVICES

Chemical Abstracts. Chemical Abstracts Service, 2540 Olentangy River Rd., PO Box 3012, Columbus, Ohio 43210. (800) 848-6533. 1907-.

Engineering Index. The Engineering Index Inc., 345 E. 47th St., New York, New York 10017. 1962-.

General Science Index. H. W. Wilson Co., 950 University Ave., Bronx, New York 10452. 1978-. Monthly, also issued in annual cumulation. Cumulative subject index to English language periodicals in the subject fields of astronomy, botany, chemistry, earth science, environment and conservation, food and nutrition, genetics, mathematics, medicine and health, microbiology, oceanography, physics, physiology and zoology.

Metals Abstracts. ASM International, 9639 Kinsman, Materials Park, Ohio 44073. (216) 338-5151. 1968-. Published jointly by the Institute of Metals, London and the American Society for Metals. Formed by the Union of Metallurgical Abstracts and Review of Metal Literature.

Physics Briefs. Physikalische Berichte. Physik Verlag, Pappapelallee 3, Postfach 101161, Weinheim, Germany D-6940. 1979-. Semimonthly. In English. Volumes for 1979- issued by the Deutsche Physikalische Gesellschaft and the Fachinformationszentrum Energie Physik, Mathematik in cooperation with the American Institute of Physics.

Pollution Abstracts. Cambridge Scientific Abstracts, 5161 River Rd., Bethesda, Maryland 20816. (301) 961-6750.

Six/year. Indexes worldwide technical literature on environmental pollution. Covers air pollution, marine and freshwater pollution, sewage and wastewater treatment, waste management, toxicology and health, noise pollution, radiation, land pollution, and environmental policies, programs, legislation, and education. Also available online.

Science Citation Index. Institute for Scientific Information, 3501 Market St., Philadelphia, Pennsylvania 19104. 1961-.

BIBLIOGRAPHIES

Molybdenum Catalyst Bibliography. Climax Molybdenum Co., 101 Merritt 7 Corporate Park, Norvalk, Connecticut 06851. (203) 845-3000. Irregular. Bibliography of catalysts.

Molybdenum in Agricultural Ecosystems: A Bibliography of the Literature 1950 through 1971. Robert L. Jones. Department of Agronomy, University of Illinois, Urbana, Illinois 61801. 1973. Environmental aspects of molybdenum and sewage sludge.

ENCYCLOPEDIAS AND DICTIONARIES

Encyclopedia of Human Biology. Renato Dulbecco, ed. Academic Press, c/o Harcourt Brace Jovanovich Inc., 6277 Sea Harbor Dr., Orlando, Florida 32887. (800) 346-8648. 1991. Eight volumes.

McGraw-Hill Encyclopedia of Science and Technology. McGraw-Hill, 1221 Avenue of the Americas, New York, New York 10020. (212) 512-2000 or (800) 262-4729. 1992. Seventh edition. Issued in multiple volumes including index. Includes all science and technology broad subject areas.

Van Nostrand's Scientific Encyclopedia. Glenn D. Considine, ed. Van Nostrand Reinhold, 115 5th Ave., New York, New York 10003. (212) 254-3232. 1983. Sixth edition. Includes all broad subject areas in science.

GENERAL WORKS

Molybdenum in the Environment. Willard R. Chappell. Marcel Dekker, Inc., 270 Madison Ave., New York, New York 10016. (212) 696-9000; (800) 228-1160. 1976. Physiological environmental and toxicological effects.

Molybdenum Removal from Concentration Waste Water. R. D. Dannenberg. U.S. Department of the Interior, Bureau of Mines, 810 7th St., NW, Washington, District of Columbia 20241. (202) 501-9649. 1982. Waste disposal and water purification relating to molybdenum.

ONLINE DATA BASES

CAS Source Index–CASSI. Chemical Abstracts Service, 2540 Olentangy River Rd., P.O. Box 3012, Columbus, Ohio 43210. (800) 848-6533 or (614) 421-3600. A listing of bibliographic and library holdings information for scientific and technical primary literature relevant to the chemical sciences.

Chemical Abstracts–CA. Chemical Abstracts Service, 2540 Olentangy River Rd., P.O. Box 3012, Columbus, Ohio 43210. (800) 848-6533 or (614) 421-3600. Information sources include 9000 journals, patents from 27 countries, two industrial property organizations, new

books, conference proceedings, and government research reports.

Computerized Engineering Index–COMPENDEX. Engineering Information Inc., 345 E. 47th St., New York, New York 10017. (212) 705-7600.

MONITORING, ENVIRONMENTAL

See also: POLLUTION CONTROL

ABSTRACTING AND INDEXING SERVICES

Ecological Abstracts. Geo Abstracts Ltd. Elsevier Applied Science, Crown House, Linton Rd., Barking, England IG 11 8JU. 1974-. Derived from over 600 leading ecological and environmental journals, plus books, conference proceedings, reports and theses.

Environment Abstracts. Bowker A & I Publishing, 121 Chanlon Rd., New Providence, New Jersey 07974. (908) 464-6800. 1974-.

Environment Index. Environment Information Center, Index Research Department, 124 E. 39th St., New York, New York 10016. 1971-. Annual.

Environmental Information Connection–EIC. Planning Information Program, Dept. of Urban and Regional Planning, University of Illinois, 1003 West Nevada, Urbana, Illinois 61801. (217) 333-1369. Also available online.

Environmental Periodicals Bibliography. Environmental Studies Institute, International Academy at Santa Barbara, 800 Garden St., Suite D, Santa Barbara, California 93101. (805) 965-5010. Also available online.

Index to Scientific Book Contents. Institute for Scientific Information, 3501 Market St., Philadelphia, Pennsylvania 19104. (800) 523-1857. 1985-. Annual. Gives contents of science books published.

BIBLIOGRAPHIES

EPA Publications Bibliography. U.S. Environmental Protection Agency, Library Systems Branch, 401 M St., SW, Washington, District of Columbia 20460. (202) 260-2090. Quarterly.

ENCYCLOPEDIAS AND DICTIONARIES

Dictionary of Environmental Protection. Otto E. Tutzauer. Fred B. Rothman, 10368 W. Centennial Rd., Littleton, California 80127. (303) 979-5657. 1979.

Dictionary of Environmental Protection Technology: In Four Languages, English, German, French, Russian. Egon Seidel. Elsevier Science Publishing Co., 655 Avenue of the Americas, New York, New York 10010. (212) 984-5800. 1988.

English-Russian Dictionary of Environmental Protection: About 14,000 Terms. E.L. Milovanov. Pergamon Microforms International, Inc., Fairview Park, Elmsford, New York 10523. (914) 592-7720. 1981.

Environmental Engineering Dictionary. C. C. Lee. Government Institutes, Inc., 4 Research Pl., Ste. 200, Rockville, Maryland 20850. (301) 921-2300. 1989. Defines over 6000 engineering terms relating to pollutioncontrol technologies, monitoring, risk assessment, sampling an-danalysis, quality control, permitting, and environmen-tally-regulated engineering and science. Includes biblio-graphical references (p. 612-627).

McGraw-Hill Encyclopedia of Environmental Science. Sybil P. Parker. McGraw-Hill Science & Engineering Books, 11 W. 19th St., New York, New York 10011. (212) 337-6010. 1980. Covers ecology, man's influence on nature, and environmental protection.

McGraw-Hill Encyclopedia of Science and Technology. McGraw-Hill, 1221 Avenue of the Americas, New York, New York 10020. (212) 512-2000 or (800) 262-4729. 1992. Seventh edition. Issued in multiple volumes in-cluding index. Includes all science and technology broad subject areas.

GENERAL WORKS

Environmental Monitoring: Meeting the Technical Chal-lenge. E. M. Cashell, ed. American Institute of Physics, 335 E 45th St., New York, New York 10017. (212) 661-9404. 1990. Proceedings of the International Conference organized by ISA International and held in Cork, Ireland, May 1990. Examines the current state of the technology and methodology employed by industry to fulfill its legal and public responsibilities, and looks at new innovative technologies which are likely to figure prominently in environmental monitoring in the future.

Principles of Sampling. B. G. Kratochvil and J. K. Taylor. Lewis Publishers, 2000 Corporate Blvd., N.W., Boca Raton, Florida 33431. (407) 994-0555 or (800) 272-7737. 1991. Contents include: sample modeling, sample plan-ning, calibration sampling, mechanism of sampling, sub-sampling, statistics of sampling, sample quality assur-ance, uncertainty of sampling, validation of samples, general sampling, acceptance sampling, and special sam-pling topics.

Quality Assurance of Environmental Measurements. H. G. Nowicki. Lewis Publishers, 2000 Corporate Blvd., N.W., Boca Raton, Florida 33431. (407) 994-0555 or (800) 272-7737. 1991. Includes an overview of costs/benefits of quality assurance, sample plans to match quality objectives, statistics for evaluating the numbers, agency required sample containers, program data for inorganic analysis, and designing and implementing and monitoring a quality assurance program.

ONLINE DATA BASES

Chemical Engineering and Biotechnology Ab-stracts–CEBA. Orbit Search Service, Maxwell Online Inc., 8000 W. Park Dr., McLean, Virginia 22102. (703) 442-0900 or (800) 456-7248. Monthly. Covers theoreti-cal, practical and commercial material on all aspects of processing safety, and the environment. Also covers process and reaction engineering, measurement and process control, environmental protection and safety, plant design and equipment used in chemical engineering and biotechnology. More than 400 of the world's major primary chemical and process engineering journals are scanned to compile the database. Available from ORBIT.

Enviro/Energyline Abstracts Plus. R. R. Bowker Co., 121 Chanlon Rd., New Providence, New Jersey 07974. (908) 464-6800.

Environmental Periodicals Bibliography. National Infor-mation Services Corp., Ste. 6, Wyman Towers, 3100 St.

Paul St., Baltimore, Maryland 21218. (410)243-0797. Online version of abstract of same name.

Monthly Catalog of United States Government Publica-tions. U.S. G.P.O., Supt. of Docs., PO Box 371954, Pittsburgh, Pennsylvania 15250-7954. (202) 512-0000.

National Technical Information Service. U.S. Depart-ment of Commerce, National Technical Information Service, Office of Data Base Services, 5285 Port Royal Rd., Springfield, Virginia 22161. (703) 487-4807. Biblio-graphic database of government sponsored research and technical reports.

PressNet Environmental Reports. Chemical Information Systems, Inc., 7215 York Rd., Baltimore, Maryland 21212. (301) 321-8440.

MONOCULTURE

See: INTENSIVE AGRICULTURE

MONOSODIUM GLUTAMATE

See: FOOD SCIENCE

MONTANA ENVIRONMENTAL AGENCIES

GOVERNMENTAL ORGANIZATIONS

Department of Agriculture: Pesticide Registration. Ad-ministrator, Environmental Management Division, Agri-culture/Livestock Building, Capitol Station, 6th and Roberts, Helena, Montana 59620-0201. (406) 444-2944.

Department of Health: Hazardous Waste Management. Chief, Solid and Hazardous Waste Bureau, State Capitol, Helena, Montana 59620. (406) 444-2821.

Department of Health: Solid Waste Management. Chief, Solid and Hazardous Waste Bureau, State Capitol, Hele-na, Montana 59620. (406) 444-2821.

Department of Health: Underground Storage Tanks. Chief, Solid and Hazardous Waste Bureau, State Capitol, Helena, Montana 59620. (406) 444-2821.

Department of Labor: Occupational Safety. Safety Bu-reau Chief, Worker's Compensation Division, 5 S. Last Chance Gulch, Helena, Montana 59601. (406) 444-6401.

Department of Natural Resources and Conservation: Natural Resources. Director, 1520 E. Sixth St., Helena, Montana 59620. (406) 444-6699.

Fish, Wildlife, and Parks Department: Fish and Wildlife. Director, 1420 E. Sixth Ave., Helena, Montana 59620. (406) 444-3186.

Fish, Wildlife, and Parks Department: Groundwater Management. Boating Law Administrator, 1420 E. Sixth Ave., Helena, Montana 59620. (406) 444-3186.

Health and Administrative Sciences Department: Emer-gency Preparedness And Community Right-to-Know. Co-Chair, Emergency Response Commission, Environ-mental Sciences Division, Cogswell Building, A-107, Helena, Montana 59620. (406) 444-6911.

Health and Environmental Sciences: Air Quality. Chief, Air Quality Bureau, Cogswell Building, Helena, Montana 59620. (406) 444-3454.

Health and Environmental Sciences: Environmental Protection. Administrator, Environmental Sciences Division, Cogswell Building, Helena, Montana 59620. (406) 444-3948.

Health and Environmental Sciences: Water Quality. Chief, Water Quality Bureau, Capitol Station, Helena, Montana 59620. (406) 444-2406.

U.S. EPA Region 8: Pollution Prevention. Senior Policy Advisor, 999 18th St., Suite 500, Denver, Colorado 80202-2405. (303) 293-1603.

MONTANA ENVIRONMENTAL LEGISLATION

GENERAL WORKS

River Protection in Montana: A Review of State Laws, Policies and Rules. Montana Department of Fish, Wildlife and Parks, 1420 E. 6th Ave., Helena, Montana 59620. (406)444-2535. 1990.

MOTOR VEHICLES

See: AUTOMOBILES

MOTORCYCLES

See: TRANSPORTATION

MUCK SOILS

See: FERTILIZERS

MULTIPLE-USE PHILOSOPHY/ PRINCIPLES

See also: FOREST MANAGEMENT; FORESTS; WILDERNESS

ABSTRACTING AND INDEXING SERVICES

Applied Ecology Abstracts Studies in Renewable Natural Resources. Information Retrieval Ltd., 1911 Jefferson Davis Highway, Arlington, Virginia 22202. 1975-. Monthly.

Environment Abstracts. Bowker A & I Publishing, 121 Chanlon Rd., New Providence, New Jersey 07974. (908) 464-6800. 1974-.

Environment Index. Environment Information Center, Index Research Department, 124 E. 39th St., New York, New York 10016. 1971-. Annual.

Environmental Information Connection–EIC. Planning Information Program, Dept. of Urban and Regional Planning, University of Illinois, 1003 West Nevada, Urbana, Illinois 61801. (217) 333-1369. Also available online.

Environmental Periodicals Bibliography. Environmental Studies Institute, International Academy at Santa Barbara, 800 Garden St., Suite D, Santa Barbara, California 93101. (805) 965-5010. Also available online.

Index to Scientific Book Contents. Institute for Scientific Information, 3501 Market St., Philadelphia, Pennsylvania 19104. (800) 523-1857. 1985-. Annual. Gives contents of science books published.

Multimedia Index to Ecology. National Information Center for Educational Media, University of Southern California, Los Angeles, California 90007.

BIBLIOGRAPHIES

EPA Publications Bibliography. U.S. Environmental Protection Agency, Library Systems Branch, 401 M St., SW, Washington, District of Columbia 20460. (202) 260-2090. Quarterly.

ENCYCLOPEDIAS AND DICTIONARIES

McGraw-Hill Encyclopedia of Environmental Science. Sybil P. Parker. McGraw-Hill Science & Engineering Books, 11 W. 19th St., New York, New York 10011. (212) 337-6010. 1980. Covers ecology, man's influence on nature, and environmental protection.

ONLINE DATA BASES

Enviro/Energyline Abstracts Plus. R. R. Bowker Co., 121 Chanlon Rd., New Providence, New Jersey 07974. (908) 464-6800.

Environmental Periodicals Bibliography. National Information Services Corp., Ste. 6, Wyman Towers, 3100 St. Paul St., Baltimore, Maryland 21218. (410)243-0797. Online version of abstract of same name.

Monthly Catalog of United States Government Publications. U.S. G.P.O., Supt. of Docs., PO Box 371954, Pittsburgh, Pennsylvania 15250-7954. (202) 512-0000.

National Technical Information Service. U.S. Department of Commerce, National Technical Information Service, Office of Data Base Services, 5285 Port Royal Rd., Springfield, Virginia 22161. (703) 487-4807. Bibliographic database of government sponsored research and technical reports.

MUNICIPAL RUNOFF

See also: RUNOFF; WATER POLLUTION

ABSTRACTING AND INDEXING SERVICES

Abstracts of Air and Water Conservation Literature. American Petroleum Institute. Central Abstracting and Indexing Service, 275 Madison Avenue, New York, New York 10016. 1972.

Environment Abstracts. Bowker A & I Publishing, 121 Chanlon Rd., New Providence, New Jersey 07974. (908) 464-6800. 1974-.

Environment Index. Environment Information Center, Index Research Department, 124 E. 39th St., New York, New York 10016. 1971-. Annual.

Environmental Information Connection–EIC. Planning Information Program, Dept. of Urban and Regional Planning, University of Illinois, 1003 West Nevada, Urbana, Illinois 61801. (217) 333-1369. Also available online.

Environmental Periodicals Bibliography. Environmental Studies Institute, International Academy at Santa Barbara, 800 Garden St., Suite D, Santa Barbara, California 93101. (805) 965-5010. Also available online.

Index to Scientific Book Contents. Institute for Scientific Information, 3501 Market St., Philadelphia, Pennsylvania 19104. (800) 523-1857. 1985-. Annual. Gives contents of science books published.

Science Citation Index. Institute for Scientific Information, 3501 Market St., Philadelphia, Pennsylvania 19104. 1961-.

BIBLIOGRAPHIES

Current Contents. Agriculture, Biology and Environmental Sciences. Institute for Scientific Information, 3501 Market St., Philadelphia, Pennsylvania 19104. (800) 523-1857. 1973-. Previous title: Current Contents. Agricultural, Food & Veterinary Sciences. Gives the table of contents of periodicals in the fields of agriculture, biology, environmental and related areas.

EPA Publications Bibliography. U.S. Environmental Protection Agency, Library Systems Branch, 401 M St., SW, Washington, District of Columbia 20460. (202) 260-2090. Quarterly.

ENCYCLOPEDIAS AND DICTIONARIES

Encyclopedia of Community Planning and Environmental Management. Marilyn Spigel Schultz. Facts on File, Inc., 460 Park Ave. S., New York, New York 10016. (212) 683-2244. 1984.

McGraw-Hill Encyclopedia of Environmental Science. Sybil P. Parker. McGraw-Hill Science & Engineering Books, 11 W. 19th St., New York, New York 10011. (212) 337-6010. 1980. Covers ecology, man's influence on nature, and environmental protection.

Van Nostrand's Scientific Encyclopedia. Glenn D. Considine, ed. Van Nostrand Reinhold, 115 5th Ave., New York, New York 10003. (212) 254-3232. 1983. Sixth edition. Includes all broad subject areas in science.

ONLINE DATA BASES

Enviro/Energyline Abstracts Plus. R. R. Bowker Co., 121 Chanlon Rd., New Providence, New Jersey 07974. (908) 464-6800.

Environmental Periodicals Bibliography. National Information Services Corp., Ste. 6, Wyman Towers, 3100 St. Paul St., Baltimore, Maryland 21218. (410)243-0797. Online version of abstract of same name.

Monthly Catalog of United States Government Publications. U.S. G.P.O., Supt. of Docs., PO Box 371954, Pittsburgh, Pennsylvania 15250-7954. (202) 512-0000.

National Technical Information Service. U.S. Department of Commerce, National Technical Information Service, Office of Data Base Services, 5285 Port Royal Rd., Springfield, Virginia 22161. (703) 487-4807. Bibliographic database of government sponsored research and technical reports.

SCISEARCH. Institute for Scientific Information, University City Science Center, 3501 Market St., Philadelphia, Pennsylvania 19104. (215) 386-0100.

TRADE ASSOCIATIONS AND PROFESSIONAL SOCIETIES

American Public Works Association. 106 W. 11th St., Ste. 1800, Kansas City, Missouri 64105-1806. (816) 472-6100.

MUNICIPAL SEWAGE

See: MUNICIPAL WASTES

MUNICIPAL WASTES

See also: LANDFILLS

ABSTRACTING AND INDEXING SERVICES

Biological and Agricultural Index. H.W. Wilson Co., 950 University Ave., Bronx, New York 10452. (800) 367-6770. 1916-. Monthly.

Energy from Biomass and Municipal Wastes. National Technical Information Service, 5285 Port Royal Rd., Springfield, Virginia 22161. (703) 487-4650. Monthly. Biomass production, conversion, and utilization for energy.

Engineering Index. The Engineering Index Inc., 345 E. 47th St., New York, New York 10017. 1962-.

Environment Abstracts. Bowker A & I Publishing, 121 Chanlon Rd., New Providence, New Jersey 07974. (908) 464-6800. 1974-.

Environment Index. Environment Information Center, Index Research Department, 124 E. 39th St., New York, New York 10016. 1971-. Annual.

Environmental Information Connection–EIC. Planning Information Program, Dept. of Urban and Regional Planning, University of Illinois, 1003 West Nevada, Urbana, Illinois 61801. (217) 333-1369. Also available online.

Environmental Periodicals Bibliography. Environmental Studies Institute, International Academy at Santa Barbara, 800 Garden St., Suite D, Santa Barbara, California 93101. (805) 965-5010. Also available online.

Geographical Abstracts. London School of Economics, Dept. of Geography, Regency House, 34 Duke St., London, England 1966-. Continued by Geo Abstracts issued in 6 parts: Pt. A. Landforms and the quaternary; Pt. B. Biogeography and Climatology; Pt. C. Economic geography; Pt. D. Social geography and cartography; Pt. E. Sedimentology; Pt. F. Regional and community planning.

Index to Scientific Book Contents. Institute for Scientific Information, 3501 Market St., Philadelphia, Pennsylvania 19104. (800) 523-1857. 1985-. Annual. Gives contents of science books published.

Pollution Abstracts. Cambridge Scientific Abstracts, 5161 River Rd., Bethesda, Maryland 20816. (301) 961-6750. Six/year. Indexes worldwide technical literature on environmental pollution. Covers air pollution, marine and freshwater pollution, sewage and wastewater treatment, waste management, toxicology and health, noise pollution, radiation, land pollution, and environmental policies, programs, legislation, and education. Also available online.

BIBLIOGRAPHIES

Current Contents. Agriculture, Biology and Environmental Sciences. Institute for Scientific Information, 3501 Market St., Philadelphia, Pennsylvania 19104. (800) 523-1857. 1973-. Previous title: Current Contents. Agricultural, Food & Veterinary Sciences. Gives the table of contents of periodicals in the fields of agriculture, biology, environmental and related areas.

EPA Publications Bibliography. U.S. Environmental Protection Agency, Library Systems Branch, 401 M St., SW, Washington, District of Columbia 20460. (202) 260-2090. Quarterly.

DIRECTORIES

Household Hazardous Waste: Solving the Disposal Dilemma. Golden Empire Health Planning Center, c/o Local Government Commission, 909 12th St., Suite 205, Sacramento, California 95814. (916) 448-1198.

Survey of Household Hazardous Wastes and Related Collection Programs. Waste Management Division/Office of Solid Waste, U.S. Environmental Protection Agency, 401 M St., S.W., Washington, District of Columbia 20460. (202) 382-2090.

ENCYCLOPEDIAS AND DICTIONARIES

Encyclopedia of Community Planning and Environmental Management. Marilyn Spigel Schultz. Facts on File, Inc., 460 Park Ave. S., New York, New York 10016. (212) 683-2244. 1984.

McGraw-Hill Encyclopedia of Environmental Science. Sybil P. Parker. McGraw-Hill Science & Engineering Books, 11 W. 19th St., New York, New York 10011. (212) 337-6010. 1980. Covers ecology, man's influence on nature, and environmental protection.

McGraw-Hill Encyclopedia of Science and Technology. McGraw-Hill, 1221 Avenue of the Americas, New York, New York 10020. (212) 512-2000 or (800) 262-4729. 1992. Seventh edition. Issued in multiple volumes including index. Includes all science and technology broad subject areas.

GENERAL WORKS

Discarding the Throwaway Society. John E. Young. Worldwatch Institute, 1776 Massachusetts Ave., N.W., Washington, District of Columbia 20036-1904. 1991.

Garbage in the Cities: Refuse, Reform, and the Environment, 1880-1980. Martin V. Melosi. Texas A & M University Press, College Station, Texas 77843. 1981.

Environmental history of refuse and refuse disposal in the United States.

Incinerating Municipal and Industrial Waste; Fireside Problems and Prospects for Improvement. Richard W. Bryers. Hemisphere, 79 Madison Ave., Suite 1110, New York, New York 10016. (212) 725-1999; (800) 821-8312. 1991. Addresses the causes and possible cures for corrosion and deposits due to impurities in the combustion of industrial and municipal refuse.

Mining Urban Wastes: The Potential for Recycling. Cynthia Pollock. Worldwatch Institute, 1776 Massachusetts Ave., N.W., Washington, District of Columbia 20036-1904. 1987.

Talking Trash: Municipal Solid Waste Mismanagement. Kenneth Chilton. Center for the Study of American Business, Washington University, Campus Box 1208, One Brookings Dr., St. Louis, Missouri 63130-4899. (314) 935-5630. 1990.

Who Should Take Out the Trash?. Kenneth Chilton. Center for the Study of American Business, Washington University, Campus Box 1208, One Brookings Dr., St. Louis, Missouri 63130-4899. (314) 935-5630. 1991.

HANDBOOKS AND MANUALS

Municipal Waste Disposal. Bela Liptak. Chilton Book Co., 201 King of Prussia Rd., Radnor, Pennsylvania 19089. (215) 964-4000. 1991.

ONLINE DATA BASES

Computerized Engineering Index–COMPENDEX. Engineering Information Inc., 345 E. 47th St., New York, New York 10017. (212) 705-7600.

Enviro/Energyline Abstracts Plus. R. R. Bowker Co., 121 Chanlon Rd., New Providence, New Jersey 07974. (908) 464-6800.

Environmental Periodicals Bibliography. National Information Services Corp., Ste. 6, Wyman Towers, 3100 St. Paul St., Baltimore, Maryland 21218. (410)243-0797. Online version of abstract of same name.

Monthly Catalog of United States Government Publications. U.S. G.P.O., Supt. of Docs., PO Box 371954, Pittsburgh, Pennsylvania 15250-7954. (202) 512-0000.

National Technical Information Service. U.S. Department of Commerce, National Technical Information Service, Office of Data Base Services, 5285 Port Royal Rd., Springfield, Virginia 22161. (703) 487-4807. Bibliographic database of government sponsored research and technical reports.

PressNet Environmental Reports. Chemical Information Systems, Inc., 7215 York Rd., Baltimore, Maryland 21212. (301) 321-8440.

SCISEARCH. Institute for Scientific Information, University City Science Center, 3501 Market St., Philadelphia, Pennsylvania 19104. (215) 386-0100.

STATISTICS SOURCES

Facing America's Trash: What Next for Municipal Solid Waste?. U.S. Office of Technology Assessment. Van Nostrand Reinhold, Washington, District of Columbia

20401. (202) 512-0000. 1991. Generation, composition and cost of recycling municipal solid waste.

The Feminine Hygiene Market. FIND/SVP, 625 Avenue of the Americas, New York, New York 10011. (212) 645-4500. 1990. Feminine hygiene market, including: tampons; napkins; douches, washes and wipes; and feminine deodorant sprays.

The Municipal Solid Waste Market. FIND/SVP, 625 Avenue of the Americas, New York, New York 10011. (212) 645-4500. 1991. Existing and emerging technologies (de-inking newsprint, recycling plastics, fluidized bed combustion, etc.) as well as applications and business opportunities in recycling and materials recovery, new waste-to-energy plant design, improved incineration technology, transportation of waste, compliance and landfill management.

Nonwoven Disposables in 1990s. FIND/SVP, 625 Avenue of the Americas, New York, New York 10011. (212) 645-4500. 1990. Analyzes to the years 1995 and 2000 for the market of nonwoven disposables.

The Overall Diaper Market. FIND/SVP, 625 Avenue of the Americas, New York, New York 10011. (212) 645-4500. 1990. Market for disposable and cloth diapers and diaper services.

TRADE ASSOCIATIONS AND PROFESSIONAL SOCIETIES

American Institute of Biological Sciences. 730 11th St., N.W., Washington, District of Columbia 20001-4521. (202) 628-1500.

American Public Works Association. 106 W. 11th St., Ste. 1800, Kansas City, Missouri 64105-1806. (816) 472-6100.

Foodservice and Packaging Institute. 1025 Connecticut Ave., N.W., Washington, District of Columbia 20036. (202) 822-6420.

Keep America Beautiful, Inc. 9 W. Broad St., Stamford, Connecticut 06902. (203) 323-8987.

MUTAGENIC AGENTS (MUTAGENS)

See also: CARCINOGENS; FOOD SCIENCE; INSECTICIDES; PESTICIDES

ABSTRACTING AND INDEXING SERVICES

Applied Ecology Abstracts Studies in Renewable Natural Resources. Information Retrieval Ltd., 1911 Jefferson Davis Highway, Arlington, Virginia 22202. 1975-. Monthly.

Biological Abstracts. BIOSIS, 2100 Arch St., Philadelphia, Pennsylvania 19103-1399. (215) 587-4800. 1927-.

Chemical Abstracts. Chemical Abstracts Service, 2540 Olentangy River Rd., PO Box 3012, Columbus, Ohio 43210. (800) 848-6533. 1907-.

Environment Abstracts. Bowker A & I Publishing, 121 Chanlon Rd., New Providence, New Jersey 07974. (908) 464-6800. 1974-.

Environment Index. Environment Information Center, Index Research Department, 124 E. 39th St., New York, New York 10016. 1971-. Annual.

Environmental Information Connection–EIC. Planning Information Program, Dept. of Urban and Regional Planning, University of Illinois, 1003 West Nevada, Urbana, Illinois 61801. (217) 333-1369. Also available online.

Environmental Periodicals Bibliography. Environmental Studies Institute, International Academy at Santa Barbara, 800 Garden St., Suite D, Santa Barbara, California 93101. (805) 965-5010. Also available online.

General Science Index. H. W. Wilson Co., 950 University Ave., Bronx, New York 10452. 1978-. Monthly, also issued in annual cumulation. Cumulative subject index to English language periodicals in the subject fields of astronomy, botany, chemistry, earth science, environment and conservation, food and nutrition, genetics, mathematics, medicine and health, microbiology, oceanography, physics, physiology and zoology.

Geographical Abstracts. London School of Economics, Dept. of Geography, Regency House, 34 Duke St., London, England 1966-. Continued by Geo Abstracts issued in 6 parts: Pt. A. Landforms and the quaternary; Pt. B. Biogeography and Climatology; Pt. C. Economic geography; Pt. D. Social geography and cartography; Pt. E. Sedimentology; Pt. F. Regional and community planning.

Multimedia Index to Ecology. National Information Center for Educational Media, University of Southern California, Los Angeles, California 90007.

Pesticides Abstracts. U.S. Environmental Protection Agency, Office of Pesticides Programs, 345 Curtland, Atlanta, Georgia 30365. (404) 347-2864. 1981. Monthly. Formerly: Health Aspects of Pesticides Abstracts Bulletin.

Pollution Abstracts. Cambridge Scientific Abstracts, 5161 River Rd., Bethesda, Maryland 20816. (301) 961-6750. Six/year. Indexes worldwide technical literature on environmental pollution. Covers air pollution, marine and freshwater pollution, sewage and wastewater treatment, waste management, toxicology and health, noise pollution, radiation, land pollution, and environmental policies, programs, legislation, and education. Also available online.

Science Citation Index. Institute for Scientific Information, 3501 Market St., Philadelphia, Pennsylvania 19104. 1961-.

BIBLIOGRAPHIES

Current Contents. Agriculture, Biology and Environmental Sciences. Institute for Scientific Information, 3501 Market St., Philadelphia, Pennsylvania 19104. (800) 523-1857. 1973-. Previous title: Current Contents. Agricultural, Food & Veterinary Sciences. Gives the table of contents of periodicals in the fields of agriculture, biology, environmental and related areas.

EPA Publications Bibliography. U.S. Environmental Protection Agency, Library Systems Branch, 401 M St., SW, Washington, District of Columbia 20460. (202) 260-2090. Quarterly.

ENCYCLOPEDIAS AND DICTIONARIES

Cambridge Dictionary of Biology. Peter M. B. Walker. Cambridge University Press, 40 W. 20th St., New York, New York 10011. (212) 924-3900 or (800) 227-0247.

1989. Includes 10,000 terms in zoology, botany, biochemistry, molecular biology and genetics. Previously published under the title Chambers Biology Dictionary.

A Concise Dictionary of Biology. Elizabeth Martin, ed. Oxford University Press, 200 Madison Ave., New York, New York 10016. (212) 679-7300 or (800) 334-4249. 1990. New edition. Derived from the Concise Science Dictionary, published in 1984.

Encyclopedia of Human Biology. Renato Dulbecco, ed. Academic Press, c/o Harcourt Brace Jovanovich Inc., 6277 Sea Harbor Dr., Orlando, Florida 32887. (800) 346-8648. 1991. Eight volumes.

Encyclopedic Dictionary of Genetics: With German Term Equivalents and Extensive German/English Index. R. C. King and W. D. Stansfield. VCH Publishers, 303 NW 12th Ave., Deerfield Beach, Florida 33442-1788. (305) 428-5566. 1990. 4th ed. Revised edition of: A Dictionary of Genetics, third edition.

McGraw-Hill Encyclopedia of Environmental Science. Sybil P. Parker. McGraw-Hill Science & Engineering Books, 11 W. 19th St., New York, New York 10011. (212) 337-6010. 1980. Covers ecology, man's influence on nature, and environmental protection.

Van Nostrand's Scientific Encyclopedia. Glenn D. Considine, ed. Van Nostrand Reinhold, 115 5th Ave., New York, New York 10003. (212) 254-3232. 1983. Sixth edition. Includes all broad subject areas in science.

GENERAL WORKS

CA Selects: Carcinogens, Mutagens & Teratogens. Chemical Abstracts Services, 2540 Olentangy River Rd., Columbus, Ohio 43210. (800) 848-6533. Irregular.

Carcinogenic, Mutagenic, and Teratogenic Marine Pollutants. Portfolio Publishing Co., P.O. Box 7802, The Woodlands, Texas 77381. (713) 363-3577. 1990. Effects of marine pollution on aquatic organisms as well as human beings.

Carcinogens and Mutagens in the Environment. Hans F. Stich, ed. CRC Press, 2000 Corporate Blvd. N.W., Boca Raton, Florida 33431. (800) 272-7737. 1982-. Naturally occurring compounds, endogenous modulation.

Comparative Chemical Mutagenesis. De Serres, Frederick J. Plenum Press, 233 Spring St., New York, New York 10013-1578. (212) 620-8000; (800) 221-9369. 1981. Mutagenicity tests and analysis of mutagens.

Environmental Mutagenesis, Carcinogenesis, and Plant Biology. Edward Klekowski. Praeger Publishers, 1 Madison Ave., New York, New York 10010-3603. (212) 685-5300. 1982. Plant metabolism and plant metabolites.

Mutagenicity, Carcinogenicity, and Teratogenicity of Industrial Pollutants. Micheline Krisch-Volders. Plenum Press, 233 Spring St., New York, New York 10013-1578. (212) 620-8000; (800) 221-9369. 1984. Industrial toxicology of teratogenic agents.

Potential Industrial Carcinogens and Mutagens. Lawrence Fishbein. Elsevier Science Publishing Co., 655 Avenue of the Americas, New York, New York 10010. (212) 984-5800. 1979.

Site-Directed Mutagenesis and Protein Engineering. M. Rafaat El-Gewely. Elsevier Science Publishing Co., 655

Avenue of the Americas, New York, New York 10010. (212) 989-5800. 1991.

HANDBOOKS AND MANUALS

Handbook of Environmental Genotoxicology. Eugene Sawicki. CRC Press, 2000 Corporate Blvd. N.W., Boca Raton, Florida 33431. (800) 272-7737. 1982. Human chromosome abnormalities, mutagenesis, carcinogenesis, and environmentally induced diseases.

ONLINE DATA BASES

BIOSIS Previews. BIOSIS, 2100 Arch St., Philadelphia, Pennsylvania 19103-1399. (215) 587-4800. Largest and most comprehensive database of research in the life sciences. Contains citations for nearly 9000 primary research journals, monographs, reviews, symposia, preliminary reports, semi-popular journals, selected institutional reports, government reports and research communications.

CESARS. State of Michigan, Department of Natural Resources, Great Lakes & Environmental Assessment Section, P.O. Box 30028, Lansing, Michigan 45909. (517) 373-2190.

Chemical Abstracts-CA. Chemical Abstracts Service, 2540 Olentangy River Rd., P.O. Box 3012, Columbus, Ohio 43210. (800) 848-6533 or (614) 421-3600. Information sources include 9000 journals, patents from 27 countries, two industrial property organizations, new books, conference proceedings, and government research reports.

Chemical Carcinogenesis Research Information System–CCRIS. National Library of Medicine, 8600 Rockville Pike, Bethesda, Maryland 20894. (800) 638-8480. Individual assay results and test conditions for 1,451 chemicals in the areas of carcinogenicity, mutagenicity, tumor promotion, and cocarcinogenicity.

Chemical Collection System/Request Tracking–CCS/RTS. U.S. Environmental Protection Agency, Office of Pesticides and Toxic Substances, 401 M St., SW, Washington, District of Columbia 20460. (202) 260-2090. Contains information on various properties of a number of chemicals including environmental effects, test and analysis methods, and health effects. Available from EPA.

Chemical Dictionary Online–CHEMLINE. Chemical Abstracts Service, 2540 Olentangy River Rd., Columbus, Ohio 43210. (614) 421-3600 or (800) 848-6533. Part of MEDLINE of the National Library of Medicine (NLM). File of 900,000 names for chemical substances, representing 450,000 unique compounds. It contains such information as Chemical Abstracts (CA) Service Registry Numbers, molecular formulas, preferred chemical nomenclature, and generic and ring structure information. Available on NLM's ELHILL system.

Chemical Engineering and Biotechnology Abstracts–CEBA. Orbit Search Service, Maxwell Online Inc., 8000 W. Park Dr., McLean, Virginia 22102. (703) 442-0900 or (800) 456-7248. Monthly. Covers theoretical, practical and commercial material on all aspects of processing safety, and the environment. Also covers process and reaction engineering, measurement and process control, environmental protection and safety, plant design and equipment used in chemical engineering and biotechnology. More than 400 of the world's major primary chemical and process engineering journals are scanned to compile the database. Available from ORBIT.

Chemical Evaluation Search and Retrieval System. Michigan State Department of Natural Resources, Surface Water Quality Division, Great Lakes and Environmental Assessment Section, Knapp's Office Center, PO Box 30028, Lansing, Michigan 48909. (517) 373-2190. Covers toxicology information on compounds of environmental concern, providing acute and chronic toxicity data for aquatic and terrestrial life as well as information on carcinogenicity, mutagenicity, and reproductive and developmental effects, bioconcentration, and environmental fate.

Chemical Exposure. Science Applications International Corp., Health & Environmental Information, P.O. Box 2501, Oak Ridge, Tennessee 37831. (615) 482-9031. Database of chemicals that have been identified in both human tissues and body fluids and in feral and food animals. Contains reference to journal articles, conferences, and reports. Covers the whole fields of information related to human and animal exposure to food, air, and water contaminants and pharmaceuticals. Its records include information on chemical properties, formulas, tissues measured, analytical method used, demographics and more. Available on DIALOG.

EMICBACK. Oak Ridge National Laboratory, Environmental Teratology Information Center, Building 2001, P.O. Box 2008, Oak Ridge, Tennessee 37831-6050. (615) 574-7871.

Enviro/Energyline Abstracts Plus. R. R. Bowker Co., 121 Chanlon Rd., New Providence, New Jersey 07974. (908) 464-6800.

Environmental Mutagen Information Center. U.S. Department of Energy, Oak Ridge National Laboratory, Environmental Mutagen Information Center, Bldg. 9224, PO Box Y, Oak Ridge, Tennessee 37830. (615) 574-7871. Chemical, biological and physical agents tested for mutagenicity.

Environmental Periodicals Bibliography. National Information Services Corp., Ste. 6, Wyman Towers, 3100 St. Paul St., Baltimore, Maryland 21218. (410)243-0797. Online version of abstract of same name.

Genetic Toxicity. U.S. Environmental Protection Agency, Office of Pesticides and Toxic Substances, 401 M St. SW, Washington, District of Columbia 20460. (202) 260-2090. Mutagenicity information on more than 2600 chemicals tested on 38 biological systems.

Medical Toxicology and Environmental Health. Department of Health and Social Security, Medical Toxiclology & Environmental Health Division, Hannibal House, Rm. 719, Elephant and Castle, London, England SE1 6TE. 44 (71) 972-2162.

Monthly Catalog of United States Government Publications. U.S. G.P.O., Supt. of Docs., PO Box 371954, Pittsburgh, Pennsylvania 15250-7954. (202) 512-0000.

National Technical Information Service. U.S. Department of Commerce, National Technical Information Service, Office of Data Base Services, 5285 Port Royal Rd., Springfield, Virginia 22161. (703) 487-4807. Bibliographic database of government sponsored research and technical reports.

SCISEARCH. Institute for Scientific Information, University City Science Center, 3501 Market St., Philadelphia, Pennsylvania 19104. (215) 386-0100.

PERIODICALS AND NEWSLETTERS

Environmental and Experimental Botany. Pergamon Microforms International, Inc., Fairview Park, Elmsford, New York 10523. (914) 592-7720. 1960-. An international journal covering radiation botany, photobotany, chemical mutagenesis, anatomy and morphology, cytogenetics and somatic cell genetics.

Environmental and Molecular Mutagenesis. Wiley-Liss, 605 3rd Ave., New York, New York 10158-0012. (212) 850-6000. 1974-. Eight issues per year. Provides an international forum for research on basic mechanisms of mutation, the detection of mutagens, and the implications of environmental mutagens for human health.

Environmental & Molecular Mutagenesis. Errol Zeiger. John Wiley & Sons, Inc., 605 3rd Ave., New York, New York 10158. Eight times a year. Covers environmentally induced diseases, carcinogenesis, mutagens and mutation.

Environmental Mutagen Society Newsletter. Dr. Virginia Houk. U.S. Environmental Protection Agency, M/D-68, Research Triangle Park, North Carolina 27711. (919) 541-2815. Twice a year. Studies of mutagens.

RESEARCH CENTERS AND INSTITUTES

University of Wisconsin-Madison, Drosophila Mutagenesis Laboratory. Zoology Department, Madison, Wisconsin 53706. (608) 263-7875.

TRADE ASSOCIATIONS AND PROFESSIONAL SOCIETIES

American Chemical Society. 1155 16th St., N.W., Washington, District of Columbia 20036. (202) 872-4600.

American Industrial Health Council. 1330 Connecticut Ave., N.W., Suite 300, Washington, District of Columbia 20036. (202) 659-0060.

American Industrial Hygiene Association. 345 White Pond Dr., PO Box 8390, Akron, Ohio 44320. (216) 873-2442.

American Institute of Biological Sciences. 730 11th St., N.W., Washington, District of Columbia 20001-4521. (202) 628-1500.

Environmental Mutagen Society. 1600 Wilson Blvd., Suite 905, Arlington, Virginia 22209. (703) 525-1191.

Genetic Toxicology Association. c/o Kerry Dearfield, USEPA, 401 M St., S.W., Washington, District of Columbia 20460. (703) 557-9780.

MYCOTOXINS

ABSTRACTING AND INDEXING SERVICES

Biological Abstracts. BIOSIS, 2100 Arch St., Philadelphia, Pennsylvania 19103-1399. (215) 587-4800. 1927-.

Biological and Agricultural Index. H.W. Wilson Co., 950 University Ave., Bronx, New York 10452. (800) 367-6770. 1916-. Monthly.

Chemical Abstracts. Chemical Abstracts Service, 2540 Olentangy River Rd., PO Box 3012, Columbus, Ohio 43210. (800) 848-6533. 1907-.

Current Advances in Ecological and Environmental Science. Pergamon Microforms International, Inc., Fairview Park, Elmsford, New York 10523. (914) 592-7720. 1989-. Monthly. Current literature searching service includingjournals, reports, abstracts, etc. This service is available online as part of the CABS database on the hosts BRS and ORBIT search service.

Ecological Abstracts. Geo Abstracts Ltd. Elsevier Applied Science, Crown House, Linton Rd., Barking, England IG 11 8JU. 1974-. Derived from over 600 leading ecological and environmental journals, plus books, conference proceedings, reports and theses.

Environment Abstracts. Bowker A & I Publishing, 121 Chanlon Rd., New Providence, New Jersey 07974. (908) 464-6800. 1974-.

Environment Index. Environment Information Center, Index Research Department, 124 E. 39th St., New York, New York 10016. 1971-. Annual.

Environmental Information Connection–EIC. Planning Information Program, Dept. of Urban and Regional Planning, University of Illinois, 1003 West Nevada, Urbana, Illinois 61801. (217) 333-1369. Also available online.

Environmental Periodicals Bibliography. Environmental Studies Institute, International Academy at Santa Barbara, 800 Garden St., Suite D, Santa Barbara, California 93101. (805) 965-5010. Also available online.

Food Science and Technology Abstracts. International Food Information Service, c/o National Food Laboratory, 6363 Clark Ave., Dublin, California 94568. (800) 336-3782. 1969-.

General Science Index. H. W. Wilson Co., 950 University Ave., Bronx, New York 10452. 1978-. Monthly, also issued in annual cumulation. Cumulative subject index to English language periodicals in the subject fields of astronomy, botany, chemistry, earth science, environment and conservation, food and nutrition, genetics, mathematics, medicine and health, microbiology, oceanography, physics, physiology and zoology.

Index to Scientific Book Contents. Institute for Scientific Information, 3501 Market St., Philadelphia, Pennsylvania 19104. (800) 523-1857. 1985-. Annual. Gives contents of science books published.

Science Citation Index. Institute for Scientific Information, 3501 Market St., Philadelphia, Pennsylvania 19104. 1961-.

Selected Abstracts on Aflatoxins and other Mycotoxins Carcinogenesis. U.S. Dept. of Health Education and Welfare. National Technical Information Service, 5285 Port Royal Rd., Springfield, Virginia 22161. (703) 487-4650. 1978. Prepared for the ICRDB Program by the Cancer Information Dissemination and Analysis Center for Carcinogenesis Information.

BIBLIOGRAPHIES

Current Contents. Agriculture, Biology and Environmental Sciences. Institute for Scientific Information, 3501 Market St., Philadelphia, Pennsylvania 19104. (800) 523-1857. 1973-. Previous title: Current Contents. Agricultur-al, Food & Veterinary Sciences. Gives the table of contents of periodicals in the fields of agriculture, biology, environmental and related areas.

EPA Publications Bibliography. U.S. Environmental Protection Agency, Library Systems Branch, 401 M St., SW, Washington, District of Columbia 20460. (202) 260-2090. Quarterly.

ENCYCLOPEDIAS AND DICTIONARIES

Dictionary of Microbiology and Molecular Biology. Paul Singleton and Diana Sainsbury. John Wiley & Sons, Inc., 605 3rd Ave., New York, New York 10158-0012. (212) 850-6000. 1987. Second edition. Comprehensive dictionary with "classical descriptive aspects of microbiology to current developments in related areas of bioenergetics, biochemistry and molecular biology." Entries give synonyms, cross references, and references to pertinent works. Miscellaneous appendixes. Bibliography.

Encyclopedia of Human Biology. Renato Dulbecco, ed. Academic Press, c/o Harcourt Brace Jovanovich Inc., 6277 Sea Harbor Dr., Orlando, Florida 32887. (800) 346-8648. 1991. Eight volumes.

McGraw-Hill Encyclopedia of Environmental Science. Sybil P. Parker. McGraw-Hill Science & Engineering Books, 11 W. 19th St., New York, New York 10011. (212) 337-6010. 1980. Covers ecology, man's influence on nature, and environmental protection.

McGraw-Hill Encyclopedia of Science and Technology. McGraw-Hill, 1221 Avenue of the Americas, New York, New York 10020. (212) 512-2000 or (800) 262-4729. 1992. Seventh edition. Issued in multiple volumes including index. Includes all science and technology broad subject areas.

Mycotoxic Fungi, Mycotoxins, Mycotoxicoses: An Encyclopedic Handbook. Thomas D. Wyllie and Lawrence G. Morehouse. Marcel Dekker, Inc., 270 Madison Ave., New York, New York 10016. (212) 696-9000; (800) 228-1160. 1977. Covers mycotoxic fungi and chemistry of mycotoxins, mycotoxicoses of domestic and laboratory animals, and mycotoxicoses of man and plants.

Van Nostrand's Scientific Encyclopedia. Glenn D. Considine, ed. Van Nostrand Reinhold, 115 5th Ave., New York, New York 10003. (212) 254-3232. 1983. Sixth edition. Includes all broad subject areas in science.

GENERAL WORKS

Mycotoxins. Vladimir Betina. Elsevier Science Publishing Co., 655 Avenue of the Americas, New York, New York 10010. (212) 984-5800. 1989. Chemical, biological, and environmental aspects of toxigenic fungi.

HANDBOOKS AND MANUALS

Handbook of Toxic Fungal Metabolites. Richard J. Cole and Richard H. Cox. Academic Press, c/o Harcourt Brace Jovanovich Inc., 6277 Sea Harbor Dr., Orlando, Florida 32887. (800) 346-8648. Oriented toward fungal metabolites that elicit a toxic response in vertebrate animals. Also includes metabolites that show little or no known acute toxicity.

ONLINE DATA BASES

BIOSIS Previews. BIOSIS, 2100 Arch St., Philadelphia, Pennsylvania 19103-1399. (215) 587-4800. Largest and most comprehensive database of research in the life sciences. Contains citations for nearly 9000 primary research journals, monographs, reviews, symposia, preliminary reports, semi-popular journals, selected institutional reports, government reports and research communications.

Cambridge Scientific Abstracts Life Science–CSAL. Cambridge Scientific Abstracts, 5161 River Rd., Bethesda, Maryland 20816. (301) 961-6750. Provides access to the following abstracting services: "Life Sciences Collection," "Aquatic Sciences and Fisheries Abstracts," "Oceanic Abstracts," and "Pollution Abstracts."

CERCLIS. Chemical Information Systems, Inc., 7215 York Rd., Baltimore, Maryland 21212. (301) 321-8440. Information on hazardous waste disposal sites that have either been listed by the EPA on the National Priority List (NPL) or nominated for consideration for the NPL.

Chemical Abstracts-CA. Chemical Abstracts Service, 2540 Olentangy River Rd., P.O. Box 3012, Columbus, Ohio 43210. (800) 848-6533 or (614) 421-3600. Information sources include 9000 journals, patents from 27 countries, two industrial property organizations, new books, conference proceedings, and government research reports.

Chemical Carcinogenesis Research Information System–CCRIS. National Library of Medicine, 8600 Rockville Pike, Bethesda, Maryland 20894. (800) 638-8480. Individual assay results and test conditions for 1,451 chemicals in the areas of carcinogenicity, mutagenicity, tumor promotion, and cocarcinogenicity.

Enviro/Energyline Abstracts Plus. R. R. Bowker Co., 121 Chanlon Rd., New Providence, New Jersey 07974. (908) 464-6800.

Environmental Periodicals Bibliography. National Information Services Corp., Ste. 6, Wyman Towers, 3100 St. Paul St., Baltimore, Maryland 21218. (410)243-0797. Online version of abstract of same name.

SCISEARCH. Institute for Scientific Information, University City Science Center, 3501 Market St., Philadelphia, Pennsylvania 19104. (215) 386-0100.

RESEARCH CENTERS AND INSTITUTES

Mycological Herbarium. Washington State University, 345 Johnson Hall, Pullman, Washington 99164-6430. (509) 335-9541.

TRADE ASSOCIATIONS AND PROFESSIONAL SOCIETIES

American Institute of Biological Sciences. 730 11th St., N.W., Washington, District of Columbia 20001-4521. (202) 628-1500.

N

NAPHTHALENE

ABSTRACTING AND INDEXING SERVICES

Biological Abstracts. BIOSIS, 2100 Arch St., Philadelphia, Pennsylvania 19103-1399. (215) 587-4800. 1927-.

Biotechnology Research Abstracts. Cambridge Scientific Abstracts, 5161 River Rd., Bethesda, Maryland 20816. (301) 961-6750. Monthly. Includes such broad areas as genetic intervention, biochemical genetics, and microbiological techniques.

Chemical Abstracts. Chemical Abstracts Service, 2540 Olentangy River Rd., PO Box 3012, Columbus, Ohio 43210. (800) 848-6533. 1907-.

Environment Abstracts. Bowker A & I Publishing, 121 Chanlon Rd., New Providence, New Jersey 07974. (908) 464-6800. 1974-.

Environment Index. Environment Information Center, Index Research Department, 124 E. 39th St., New York, New York 10016. 1971-. Annual.

Environmental Information Connection–EIC. Planning Information Program, Dept. of Urban and Regional Planning, University of Illinois, 1003 West Nevada, Urbana, Illinois 61801. (217) 333-1369. Also available online.

Environmental Periodicals Bibliography. Environmental Studies Institute, International Academy at Santa Barbara, 800 Garden St., Suite D, Santa Barbara, California 93101. (805) 965-5010. Also available online.

General Science Index. H. W. Wilson Co., 950 University Ave., Bronx, New York 10452. 1978-. Monthly, also issued in annual cumulation. Cumulative subject index to English language periodicals in the subject fields of astronomy, botany, chemistry, earth science, environment and conservation, food and nutrition, genetics, mathematics, medicine and health, microbiology, oceanography, physics, physiology and zoology.

Pollution Abstracts. Cambridge Scientific Abstracts, 5161 River Rd., Bethesda, Maryland 20816. (301) 961-6750. Six/year. Indexes worldwide technical literature on environmental pollution. Covers air pollution, marine and freshwater pollution, sewage and wastewater treatment, waste management, toxicology and health, noise pollution, radiation, land pollution, and environmental policies, programs, legislation, and education. Also available online.

Science Citation Index. Institute for Scientific Information, 3501 Market St., Philadelphia, Pennsylvania 19104. 1961-.

BIBLIOGRAPHIES

EPA Publications Bibliography. U.S. Environmental Protection Agency, Library Systems Branch, 401 M St., SW, Washington, District of Columbia 20460. (202) 260-2090. Quarterly.

ENCYCLOPEDIAS AND DICTIONARIES

Encyclopedia of Chemical Technology. Raymond E. Kirk. John Wiley & Sons, Inc., 605 3rd Ave., New York, New York 10158-0012. (212) 850-6000. 1991-. 4th ed. Also known as Kirk Othmer Encyclopedia of Chemical Technology; consists of 26 volumes.

Ullmanns Encyclopedia of Industrial Chemistry. Hans Jurgen Arpe and Wolfgang Gerhartz, eds. VCH Publishers, 303 NW 12th Ave., Deerfield Beach, Florida 33442-1788. (305) 428-5566. 1990. Designed to keep up with the broad spectrum of chemical technology. Thirty-six volumes of the encyclopedia have been divided into two sets: the 28 A volumes contain alphabetically arranged articles on chemicals, product groups, processes and technological concepts; and the 8 B volumes are compendia of basic knowledge in industrial chemistry.

Van Nostrand's Scientific Encyclopedia. Glenn D. Considine, ed. Van Nostrand Reinhold, 115 5th Ave., New York, New York 10003. (212) 254-3232. 1983. Sixth edition. Includes all broad subject areas in science.

GENERAL WORKS

Ambient Water Quality Criteria for Chlorinated Naphthalene. National Technical Information Service, 5285 Port Royal Rd., Springfield, Virginia 22161. (703) 487-4650. 1980. Covers toxicology of naphthalene and water quality standards.

Degradation of Synthetic Organic Molecules in the Biosphere. National Academy of Sciences, 2101 Constitution Ave. N.W., Washington, District of Columbia 20418. (202) 334-2000. 1972. Proceedings of conference, San Francisco, CA, June 12-13, 1971, under the aegis of the National Research Council.

Naphthalene: Registration Standard. U.S. Environmental Protection Agency, Office of Pesticides and Toxic Substances, 401 M St., SW, Washington, District of Columbia 20460. (202) 260-2090. 1981. Naphthalene and pesticides law and legislation in the United States.

Toxicological Profile for Naphthalene and 2-Methylnaphthalene. Life System, Inc. Agency for Toxic Substances and Disease Registry, U.S. Public Health Service, 1600 Clifton Rd. NE, Atlanta, Georgia 30333. (404) 452-4111.

1990. Toxicology and physiological effect of methylnaphthalenes.

HANDBOOKS AND MANUALS

Handbook of Analytical Chemistry. Louis Meites, ed. McGraw-Hill Science & Engineering Books, 11 W. 19th St., New York, New York 10011. (212) 337-6010. 1963.

Handbook of Environmental Data on Organic Chemicals. Karel Verschueren. Van Nostrand Reinhold, 115 5th Ave., New York, New York 10003. (212) 254-3232. 1983. Covers individual substances as well as mixtures and preparations. The profiles include: properties, air pollution factors, water pollution factors, and biological effects.

Handbook of Vapor Pressures and Heats of Vaporization of Hydrocarbons and Related Compounds. Randolph C. Wilhoit. Thermodynamics Research Center, Dept. of Chemistry, Texas A & M Univ., Drawer C, Lewis St., University Campus, College Station, Texas 77843. (409) 845-1436. 1971. Covers data on vapor liquid equilibrium tables and hydrocarbon tables.

Lange's Handbook of Chemistry. John A. Dean, ed. McGraw-Hill Science & Engineering Books, 11 W. 19th St., New York, New York 10011. (212) 337-6010. 1973-. 11th ed.

NIOSH Pocket Guide to Chemical Hazards. National Institute for Occupational Safety and Health, 1600 Clifton Rd. NE, Atlanta, Georgia 30333. (404) 639-3286. 1990. Presents sources of general industrial hygiene and medical surveillance information for workers, employees and others. Presents key information and data in an abbreviated format for 398 individual chemicals or chemical types.

Tables of Physical and Chemical Constants and Some Mathematical Functions. G. W. C. Kaye, et al. Longman Group Ltd., Longman House, Burnt Mill, Harlow, England CM20 2J6. 0279 426721. 1988. Fifteenth edition. Includes tables on mechanical properties, density, elasticity, viscosity, surface tension, temperature and heat. Also covers radiation, optics, chemistry, electrochemistry, astrophysics, and chemical thermodynamics.

ONLINE DATA BASES

BIOSIS Previews. BIOSIS, 2100 Arch St., Philadelphia, Pennsylvania 19103-1399. (215) 587-4800. Largest and most comprehensive database of research in the life sciences. Contains citations for nearly 9000 primary research journals, monographs, reviews, symposia, preliminary reports, semi-popular journals, selected institutional reports, government reports and research communications.

CAS Source Index–CASSI. Chemical Abstracts Service, 2540 Olentangy River Rd., P.O. Box 3012, Columbus, Ohio 43210. (800) 848-6533 or (614) 421-3600. A listing of bibliographic and library holdings information for scientific and technical primary literature relevant to the chemical sciences.

Chemical Abstracts-CA. Chemical Abstracts Service, 2540 Olentangy River Rd., P.O. Box 3012, Columbus, Ohio 43210. (800) 848-6533 or (614) 421-3600. Information sources include 9000 journals, patents from 27 countries, two industrial property organizations, new books, conference proceedings, and government research reports.

Chemical Abstracts Chemical Name Directory-CHEM-NAME. Chemical Abstracts Service, 2540 Olentangy River Rd., P.O. Box 3012, Columbus, Ohio 43210. (800) 848-6533 or (614) 421-3600. Listing of chemical substances in a dictionary type file. The Chemical Abstracts (CAS) Registry Number, molecular formula, Chemical Abstracts (CA) Substance Index Name, available synonyms, ring data and other chemical substance information is given for each entry.

Chemical Collection System/Request Tracking–CCS/RTS. U.S. Environmental Protection Agency, Office of Pesticides and Toxic Substances, 401 M St., SW, Washington, District of Columbia 20460. (202) 260-2090. Contains information on various properties of a number of chemicals including environmental effects, test and analysis methods, and health effects. Available from EPA.

Chemical Dictionary Online–CHEMLINE. Chemical Abstracts Service, 2540 Olentangy River Rd., Columbus, Ohio 43210. (614) 421-3600 or (800) 848-6533. Part of MEDLINE of the National Library of Medicine (NLM). File of 900,000 names for chemical substances, representing 450,000 unique compounds. It contains such information as Chemical Abstracts (CA) Service Registry Numbers, molecular formulas, preferred chemical nomenclature, and generic and ring structure information. Available on NLM's ELHILL system.

Chemical Exposure. Science Applications International Corp., Health & Environmental Information, P.O. Box 2501, Oak Ridge, Tennessee 37831. (615) 482-9031. Database of chemicals that have been identified in both human tissues and body fluids and in feral and food animals. Contains reference to journal articles, conferences, and reports. Covers the whole fields of information related to human and animal exposure to food, air, and water contaminants and pharmaceuticals. Its records include information on chemical properties, formulas, tissues measured, analytical method used, demographics and more. Available on DIALOG.

Enviro/Energyline Abstracts Plus. R. R. Bowker Co., 121 Chanlon Rd., New Providence, New Jersey 07974. (908) 464-6800.

Environmental Periodicals Bibliography. National Information Services Corp., Ste. 6, Wyman Towers, 3100 St. Paul St., Baltimore, Maryland 21218. (410)243-0797. Online version of abstract of same name.

PERIODICALS AND NEWSLETTERS

Aquatic Toxicology. Elsevier Science Publishing Co., 655 Avenue of the Americas, New York, New York 10010. (212) 989-5800. 1981-. 6/year.

Bulletin of Environmental Contamination and Toxicology. Springer-Verlag, 175 5th Ave., New York, New York 10010. (212) 460-1500; (800) 777-4643. 1966-. Frequency varies. Disseminates advances and discoveries in the areas of soil, air and food contamination and pollution.

Chemosphere: Chemistry, Biology and Toxicology as Related to Environmental Problems. Pergamon Microforms International, Inc., Fairview Park, Elmsford, New York 10523. (914) 592-7720. 1970-. Offers maximum dissemination of investigations related to the health and safety of every aspect of life. Environmental protection encompasses a very wide field and relies on scientific research in chemistry, biology, physics, toxicology and inter-related disciplines.

Environmental Science and Technology. American Chemical Society, 1155 16th St. N.W., Washington, District of Columbia 20036. (800) 227-5558. 1967-. Monthly. Contains research articles on various aspects of environmental chemistry, interpretative articles by invited experts and commentary on the scientific aspects of environmental management.

Journal of Environmental Quality. American Society of Agronomy, 677 S. Segoe Rd., Madison, Wisconsin 53711-1086. (608) 273-8080. 1972-. Quarterly. Reports and brief reviews of agricultural ecology, environmental engineering and pollution.

Journal of the American Chemical Society. American Chemical Society, 1155 16th St. N.W., Washington, District of Columbia 20036. (202) 872-4600; (800) 227-5558. 1879-. Biweekly.

TRADE ASSOCIATIONS AND PROFESSIONAL SOCIETIES

American Chemical Society. 1155 16th St., N.W., Washington, District of Columbia 20036. (202) 872-4600.

NATIONAL FORESTS

See: FORESTS

NATIONAL PARKS AND RESERVES

See also: CONSERVATION OF NATURAL RESOURCES; FORESTS; RECREATIONAL AREAS

ABSTRACTING AND INDEXING SERVICES

Applied Ecology Abstracts Studies in Renewable Natural Resources. Information Retrieval Ltd., 1911 Jefferson Davis Highway, Arlington, Virginia 22202. 1975-. Monthly.

Biological Abstracts. BIOSIS, 2100 Arch St., Philadelphia, Pennsylvania 19103-1399. (215) 587-4800. 1927-.

Biological and Agricultural Index. H.W. Wilson Co., 950 University Ave., Bronx, New York 10452. (800) 367-6770. 1916-. Monthly.

EIS: Digests of Environmental Impact Statements. Cambridge Scientific Abstracts, 5161 River Rd., Bethesda, Maryland 20816. (301) 951-1400. 1970-. Bimonthly. Provides detailed abstracts of all the environmental impact statements issued by the federal government each year and indexes them. Also extracts the key issues from the complex government released environmental impact statements. Contents include areas such as: air transportation, defense programs, energy, hazardous substances, land use, manufacturing, parks, refuges, forests, research and development, roads and railroads, urban and social programs, wastes, and water.

Environment Abstracts. Bowker A & I Publishing, 121 Chanlon Rd., New Providence, New Jersey 07974. (908) 464-6800. 1974-.

Environment Index. Environment Information Center, Index Research Department, 124 E. 39th St., New York, New York 10016. 1971-. Annual.

Environmental Information Connection–EIC. Planning Information Program, Dept. of Urban and Regional Planning, University of Illinois, 1003 West Nevada, Urbana, Illinois 61801. (217) 333-1369. Also available online.

Environmental Periodicals Bibliography. Environmental Studies Institute, International Academy at Santa Barbara, 800 Garden St., Suite D, Santa Barbara, California 93101. (805) 965-5010. Also available online.

General Science Index. H. W. Wilson Co., 950 University Ave., Bronx, New York 10452. 1978-. Monthly, also issued in annual cumulation. Cumulative subject index to English language periodicals in the subject fields of astronomy, botany, chemistry, earth science, environment and conservation, food and nutrition, genetics, mathematics, medicine and health, microbiology, oceanography, physics, physiology and zoology.

Multimedia Index to Ecology. National Information Center for Educational Media, University of Southern California, Los Angeles, California 90007.

Science Citation Index. Institute for Scientific Information, 3501 Market St., Philadelphia, Pennsylvania 19104. 1961-.

BIBLIOGRAPHIES

EPA Publications Bibliography. U.S. Environmental Protection Agency, Library Systems Branch, 401 M St., SW, Washington, District of Columbia 20460. (202) 260-2090. Quarterly.

DIRECTORIES

Access America: An Atlas and Guide to the National Parks for Visitors with Disabilities. Northern Cartographic, Box 133, Burlington, Vermont 05402. (802) 860-2886. 1992. Irregular. National parks with facilities for visitors with mobility impairments, and hearing, visual, or developmental disabilities.

Complete Guide to America's National Parks: The Official Visitor's Guide of the National Park Foundation. National Park Foundation, 1101 17th St. NW, Suite 1008, Washington, District of Columbia 20036. (202) 785-4500. Biennial.

United Nations List of National Parks and Protected Areas. World Conservation Monitoring Centre. World Conservation Union, IUCN Publications Services Unit, 181a Huntingdon Road, Cambridge, England CB3 0DJ. (0223) 277894. 1990. Standard list of national parks and other protected areas. Includes lists of world heritage sites, biosphere reserves and wetlands of international importance.

ENCYCLOPEDIAS AND DICTIONARIES

McGraw-Hill Encyclopedia of Environmental Science. Sybil P. Parker. McGraw-Hill Science & Engineering Books, 11 W. 19th St., New York, New York 10011. (212) 337-6010. 1980. Covers ecology, man's influence on nature, and environmental protection.

GENERAL WORKS

Construction of Dams and Aircraft Overflights in National Park Units. U.S. Congress. House Committee on Interior and Insular Affairs. U.S. G.P.O., Washington, District of Columbia 20401. Covers national parks and reserves, environmental aspects of dams, airplane noise and air traffic rules.

The Forest and the Trees: A Guide to Excellent Forestry. Gordon Robinson. Island Press, 1718 Connecticut Ave. N.W., Suite 300, Washington, District of Columbia 20009. (202) 232-7933. 1988. Gives concerned citizens who are not foresters the technical information they need to compete with the experts when commenting on how our national forests should be managed.

Islands under Siege: National Parks and the Politics of External Threats. John C. Freemuth. University Press of Kansas, 329 Carruth, Lawrence, Kansas 66045. (913) 864-4154. 1991. Outlines a diverse set of political strategies, evaluating each in terms of environmental effectiveness and political feasibility.

Our Common Lands: Defending the National Parks. David J. Simon, ed. Island Press, 1718 Connecticut Ave. N.W., Suite 300, Washington, District of Columbia 20009. (202) 232-7933. 1988. Explains the complexities of key environmental laws and how they can be used to protect our national parks. Includes discussion of successful and unsuccessful attempts to use the laws and how the courts interpret them.

Yellowstone Vegetation, Consequences of Environment and History in a Natural Setting. Don G. Despain. Roberts Rinhart Pub., PO Box 666, Niwot, Colorado 80544. (303) 652-2921. 1990. Explores Yellowstone's vegetation types in their habitats and communities, in their origins and distribution, and in their succession after devastation by fire, wind, and insects.

ONLINE DATA BASES

BIOSIS Previews. BIOSIS, 2100 Arch St., Philadelphia, Pennsylvania 19103-1399. (215) 587-4800. Largest and most comprehensive database of research in the life sciences. Contains citations for nearly 9000 primary research journals, monographs, reviews, symposia, preliminary reports, semi-popular journals, selected institutional reports, government reports and research communications.

Enviro/Energyline Abstracts Plus. R. R. Bowker Co., 121 Chanlon Rd., New Providence, New Jersey 07974. (908) 464-6800.

Environmental Periodicals Bibliography. National Information Services Corp., Ste. 6, Wyman Towers, 3100 St. Paul St., Baltimore, Maryland 21218. (410)243-0797. Online version of abstract of same name.

Monthly Catalog of United States Government Publications. U.S. G.P.O., Supt. of Docs., PO Box 371954, Pittsburgh, Pennsylvania 15250-7954. (202) 512-0000.

National Technical Information Service. U.S. Department of Commerce, National Technical Information Service, Office of Data Base Services, 5285 Port Royal Rd., Springfield, Virginia 22161. (703) 487-4807. Bibliographic database of government sponsored research and technical reports.

PERIODICALS AND NEWSLETTERS

Clearing House Newsletter. National Inst. on Park and Grounds Management, PO Box 1936, Appleton, Wisconsin 54913. (414) 733-2301. Bimonthly. Management of large outdoor areas such as parks, campuses, and industrial areas.

ENFO. 1251-B Miller Ave., Winter Park, Florida 32789-4827. (407) 644-5377. Bimonthly. Water resources, parks, wildlife air quality, growth management, government and private actions.

Federal Parks and Recreation. Resources Publishing Co., 1010 Vermont Ave., NW, Suite 708, Washington, District of Columbia 20005. (202) 638-7529. Biweekly. Policy changes affecting national parks and federal, state, and local park and recreation areas.

From the State Capitals: Parks and Recreation Trends. Wakeman/Walworth, PO Box 1939, New Haven, Connecticut 06509. (203) 562-8518. Monthly. What states and municipalities are doing in conservation, land management and development, parks and recreational programs, wildlife preserves, state fisheries, river management, poaching and game restrictions, and systems of licensing and fees.

Outdoors Unlimited. Outdoor Writers Association of America, 4141 West Bradley Rd., Milwaukee, Wisconsin 53209. 1940-. Monthly.

Parks. Science Reviews Inc., 707 Foulk Road, Suite 102, Wilmington, Delaware 19803. Three times a year. The international magazine dedicated to the protected areas of the world.

STATISTICS SOURCES

National Park Service Statistical Abstract. U.S. G.P.O., Washington, District of Columbia 20401. (202) 512-0000. Annual. Recreation visits, acreages, areas administered visits and visitor use and overnight stays.

World Resources. World Resources Institute. 1709 New York Ave., N.W., Washington, District of Columbia 20006. (202) 638-6300. Annual. Statistical and textual analysis of world's natural resources and the effects of growth-caused environmental pollution.

TRADE ASSOCIATIONS AND PROFESSIONAL SOCIETIES

African Wildlife Foundation. 1717 Massachusetts Avenue, NW, Washington, District of Columbia 20036. (202) 265-8393.

American Recreation Coalition. 1331 Pennsylvania Ave., N.W., Suite 726, Washington, District of Columbia 20004. (202) 662-7420.

Association for Conservation Information. PO Box 10678, Reno, Nevada 89520. (702) 688-1500.

Greater Yellowstone Coalition. 13 S. Wilson, Bozeman, Montana 59715. (406) 586-1593.

National Association of State Park Directors. 126 Mill Branch Rd., Tallahassee, Florida 32312. (904) 893-4959.

National Institute on Park & Grounds Management. Box 1936, Appleton, Wisconsin 54913. (414) 733-2301.

National Park Foundation. 1101 17th St. N.W., Ste. 1102, Washington, District of Columbia 20036. (202) 785-4500.

National Parks and Conservation Association. 1015 31st St., N.W., Washington, District of Columbia 20007. (202) 944-8530.

National Recreation & Park Association. 3101 Park Center Dr., Alexandria, Virginia 22302. (703) 820-4940.

National Trails Council. Box 493, Brookings, South Dakota 57006.

North American Family Campers Association. 16 Evergreen Terr., North Reading, Massachusetts 01864. (508) 664-4294.

Scenic America. 216 Seventh St., S.E., Washington, District of Columbia 20003. (202) 546-1100.

NATURAL DISASTERS

See: DISASTERS

NATURAL GAS

See also: COAL; METHANE; PETROLEUM

ABSTRACTING AND INDEXING SERVICES

Ecological Abstracts. Geo Abstracts Ltd. Elsevier Applied Science, Crown House, Linton Rd., Barking, England IG 11 8JU. 1974-. Derived from over 600 leading ecological and environmental journals, plus books, conference proceedings, reports and theses.

Environment Abstracts. Bowker A & I Publishing, 121 Chanlon Rd., New Providence, New Jersey 07974. (908) 464-6800. 1974-.

Environment Index. Environment Information Center, Index Research Department, 124 E. 39th St., New York, New York 10016. 1971-. Annual.

Environmental Information Connection–EIC. Planning Information Program, Dept. of Urban and Regional Planning, University of Illinois, 1003 West Nevada, Urbana, Illinois 61801. (217) 333-1369. Also available online.

Environmental Periodicals Bibliography. Environmental Studies Institute, International Academy at Santa Barbara, 800 Garden St., Suite D, Santa Barbara, California 93101. (805) 965-5010. Also available online.

General Science Index. H. W. Wilson Co., 950 University Ave., Bronx, New York 10452. 1978-. Monthly, also issued in annual cumulation. Cumulative subject index to English language periodicals in the subject fields of astronomy, botany, chemistry, earth science, environment and conservation, food and nutrition, genetics, mathematics, medicine and health, microbiology, oceanography, physics, physiology and zoology.

Science Citation Index. Institute for Scientific Information, 3501 Market St., Philadelphia, Pennsylvania 19104. 1961-.

BIBLIOGRAPHIES

EPA Publications Bibliography. U.S. Environmental Protection Agency, Library Systems Branch, 401 M St., SW, Washington, District of Columbia 20460. (202) 260-2090. Quarterly.

DIRECTORIES

Brown's Directory of North American & International Gas Companies. Energy Publications Division/Edgell Communications, Inc., 10300 N. Central Expressway, Building V-58, Dallas, Texas 75231. (214) 691-3911.

Refining, Construction, Petrochemical & Natural Gas Processing Plants of the World. Midwest Register, Inc., 15 W. 6th St., Suite 1308, Tulsa, Oklahoma 74119-1501. (918) 582-2000.

ENCYCLOPEDIAS AND DICTIONARIES

Encyclopedia of Chemical Processing and Design. John J. Mcketta and W. A. Cunningham. Marcel Dekker, Inc., 270 Madison Ave., New York, New York 10016. (212) 696-9000; (800) 228-1160. 1992. Thirty-eight volumes.

Glossary of Geology. Robert Latimer Bates and Julia A. Jackson, eds. American Geological Institute, 4220 King St., Alexandria, Virginia 22302-1507. (703) 379-2480 or (800) 336-4764. 1987. Third edition.

Kirk-Othmer Encyclopedia of Chemical Technology. J. I. Kroschwitz, ed. John Wiley & Sons, Inc., 605 3rd Ave., New York, New York 10158-0012. (212) 850-6000. 1992-. All articles in the new edition have been rewritten and updated adding new subjects such as biotechnology, computer topics, analytical techniques and instrumentation, environmental concerns, fuels and energy, inorganic and solid state chemistry; composite materials and material science in general, and pharmaceuticals. Also available online.

McGraw-Hill Encyclopedia of the Geological Sciences. Sybil P. Parker, ed. McGraw-Hill, 1221 Avenue of the Americas, New York, New York 10020. (212) 512-2000 or (800) 262-4729. 1988. Second edition. Published previously in the McGraw-Hill Encyclopedia of Science and Technology.

GENERAL WORKS

Environment, Resources, and Conservation. Susan Owens and Peter L. Owens. Cambridge University Press, 40 W 20th St., New York, New York 10011. (212) 924-3900 or (800) 227-0247. 1991. The book studies three cases illuminating problems and policy responses at three levels of geographic scale–international, national, and local. The case of acid rain is used to illustrate a pollution problem with international dimensions; the British coal industry is analyzed as an example of national nonrenewable resource depletion; and renewable wetland ecosystem management illustrates a local concern by analyzing conservation measures.

Environmental Conservation: The Oil and Gas Industries: An Overview. National Petroleum Council, 1625 K St., NW, Washington, District of Columbia 20006. (202) 393-6100. 1981.

Guide to Natural Gas Cogeneration. Nelson E. Hay. The Association of Energy Engineers, 4025 Pleasantdale Rd., Suite 420, Atlanta, Georgia 30340. (404) 925-9558. 1991. Second edition. Details the engineering and economic aspects of gas fired cogeneration systems. Includes examination of equipment considerations and applications strategies for gas engines, gas turbines, steam engines, and electrical switch gear. Guidelines show you how to select the prime mover which is best suited for a specific type of application.

Natural Gas and the Environment: New Issues, New Opportunities. Gas Research Institute, National Technical Information Service, 5285 Port Royal Rd., Springfield, Virginia 22161. (703) 487-4650. 1987.

Natural Gas Applications for Air Pollution Control. Nelson E. Hay. Fairmont Press, 700 Indian Trail, Lilburn, Georgia 30247. (404) 925-9388. 1987. Natural gas-induced air pollution.

Replacing Gasoline: Alternative Fuels for Light-Duty Vehicles. Congress of the U.S., c/o U.S. Government Printing Office, Office of Technology Assesment, N. Capitol & H Sts. NW, Washington, District of Columbia 20401. (202) 512-0000. 1990. Gives information on alternatives to standard gasoline. Some of the alternatives are: electricity, hydrogen, compressed natural gas, liquified natural gas, liquid propane gas, methanol, ethanol, and reformulated gasoline.

Select Use of Gas: Regulator's Perspective. Ruth K. Kretschmer. Illinois Commerce Commission, 527 E. Capitol Ave., PO Box 14280, Springfield, Illinois 62794-9280. (217) 782-7295. 1985. Economic and environmental aspects of the natural gas industry.

Studies in Surface Science and Catalysis. Elsevier Science Publishing Co., 655 Avenue of the Americas, New York, New York 10010. (212) 989-5800. 1991.

ONLINE DATA BASES

Enviro/Energyline Abstracts Plus. R. R. Bowker Co., 121 Chanlon Rd., New Providence, New Jersey 07974. (908) 464-6800.

Environmental Periodicals Bibliography. National Information Services Corp., Ste. 6, Wyman Towers, 3100 St. Paul St., Baltimore, Maryland 21218. (410)243-0797. Online version of abstract of same name.

Kirk-Othmer Encyclopedia of Chemical Technology. John Wiley & Sons, Inc., 605 3rd Ave., 5th Floor, New York, New York 10158. (212) 850-6000. Online version of the publication of the same name.

STATISTICS SOURCES

Gas Facts, 1988 Data: A Statistical Record of the Gas Utility Industry. American Gas Association, 1515 Wilson Blvd., Arlington, Virginia 22209. 1989. Annual. Transmission, distribution, consumption, finances, and prices.

TRADE ASSOCIATIONS AND PROFESSIONAL SOCIETIES

American Gas Association. 1515 Wilson Blvd., Arlington, Virginia 22209. (703) 841-8400.

Gas Research Institute. 8600 W. Bryn Mawr Ave., Chicago, Illinois 60631. (312) 399-8100.

Interstate Natural Gas Association of America. 555 13thSt., N.W., Ste. 300 W., Washington, District of Columbia 20004. (202) 626-3200.

Natural Gas Supply Association. 1129 20th St., N.W., Suite 300, Washington, District of Columbia 20036. (202) 331-8900.

NATURAL RESOURCES

See also: CONSERVATION OF NATURAL RESOURCES; ENERGY RESOURCES; FISH AND FISHERIES; FORESTS; LAND RECLAMATION; MARINE RESOURCES; MINES AND MINERAL RESOURCES; RENEWABLE ENERGY RESOURCES; WATER RESOURCES

ABSTRACTING AND INDEXING SERVICES

Applied Ecology Abstracts Studies in Renewable Natural Resources. Information Retrieval Ltd., 1911 Jefferson Davis Highway, Arlington, Virginia 22202. 1975-. Monthly.

Biological Abstracts. BIOSIS, 2100 Arch St., Philadelphia, Pennsylvania 19103-1399. (215) 587-4800. 1927-.

Biological and Agricultural Index. H.W. Wilson Co., 950 University Ave., Bronx, New York 10452. (800) 367-6770. 1916-. Monthly.

Current Advances in Ecological and Environmental Science. Pergamon Microforms International, Inc., Fairview Park, Elmsford, New York 10523. (914) 592-7720. 1989-. Monthly. Current literature searching service includingjournals, reports, abstracts, etc. This service is available online as part of the CABS database on the hosts BRS and ORBIT search service.

Environment Abstracts. Bowker A & I Publishing, 121 Chanlon Rd., New Providence, New Jersey 07974. (908) 464-6800. 1974-.

Environment Index. Environment Information Center, Index Research Department, 124 E. 39th St., New York, New York 10016. 1971-. Annual.

Environmental Information Connection–EIC. Planning Information Program, Dept. of Urban and Regional Planning, University of Illinois, 1003 West Nevada, Urbana, Illinois 61801. (217) 333-1369. Also available online.

Environmental Periodicals Bibliography. Environmental Studies Institute, International Academy at Santa Barbara, 800 Garden St., Suite D, Santa Barbara, California 93101. (805) 965-5010. Also available online.

General Science Index. H. W. Wilson Co., 950 University Ave., Bronx, New York 10452. 1978-. Monthly, also issued in annual cumulation. Cumulative subject index to English language periodicals in the subject fields of astronomy, botany, chemistry, earth science, environment and conservation, food and nutrition, genetics, mathematics, medicine and health, microbiology, oceanography, physics, physiology and zoology.

Index to Scientific Book Contents. Institute for Scientific Information, 3501 Market St., Philadelphia, Pennsylvania 19104. (800) 523-1857. 1985-. Annual. Gives contents of science books published.

Multimedia Index to Ecology. National Information Center for Educational Media, University of Southern California, Los Angeles, California 90007.

Science Citation Index. Institute for Scientific Information, 3501 Market St., Philadelphia, Pennsylvania 19104. 1961-.

World Agricultural Economics and Rural Sociology Abstracts. C. A. B. International, 845 North Park Ave., Tucson, Arizona 85719. (602) 621-7897 or (800) 528-

4841. 1959-. Monthly. Abstracts include areas such as: agricultural economics, agricultural policy and development, agrarian reform, employment policy, environmental and natural resources policy, income policy, input industries, supply and demand and prices, and other related areas.

ALMANACS AND YEARBOOKS

Gale Environmental Almanac. Russ Hoyle. Gale Research Inc., 835 Penobscot Bldg., Detroit, Michigan 48226-4094. (313) 961-2242. 1993. Focuses on the U.S. and Canada, although worldwide and transboundary issues are discussed.

North Country Almanac: Journal of the Adirondack Seasons. Robert F. Hall. Purple Mountain Press, PO Box E-3, Fleischmanns, New York 12430. (914)254-4062. 1990. Essays on the conservation of nature and its resources.

BIBLIOGRAPHIES

Current Contents. Agriculture, Biology and Environmental Sciences. Institute for Scientific Information, 3501 Market St., Philadelphia, Pennsylvania 19104. (800) 523-1857. 1973-. Previous title: Current Contents. Agricultural, Food & Veterinary Sciences. Gives the table of contents of periodicals in the fields of agriculture, biology, environmental and related areas.

Directory of Country Environmental Studies: An Annotated Bibliography of Environmental and Natural Resources Profiles and Assessments. World Resources Institute, 1709 New York Ave., NW, Washington, District of Columbia 20006. 1990. Concentrates on studies of developing countries. Reports on the condition and trends of the major natural resources of a country and their condition and relationship to economic development.

Environmental Issues in the Third World: A Bibliography. Joan Nordquist. Reference and Research Services, 511 Lincoln St., Santa Cruz, California 95060. (408) 426-4479. 1991.

EPA Publications Bibliography. U.S. Environmental Protection Agency, Library Systems Branch, 401 M St., SW, Washington, District of Columbia 20460. (202) 260-2090. Quarterly.

DIRECTORIES

Canadian Environmental Directory. Canadian Almanac & Directory Publishing Co. Ltd., 134 Adelaide St. E., Ste. 27, Toronto, Ontario, Canada M5C 1K9. (416) 362-4088. 1992. Includes individuals, agencies, firms, and associations.

Conservation Directory. National Wildlife Federation, 1400 16th St. N.W., Washington, District of Columbia 20036-2266. (202) 797-6800. 1956-. Annually. Contains information on organizations, agencies, officials, and education programs in the natural resources management field.

A Directory of Natural Resources Management Organizations in Latin America and the Caribbean. Julie Buckley-Ess, ed. Tinker Foundation, Inc., 55 East 59th St., New York, New York 10022. 1988. Lists the public and private organizations working in each country. Describes

their activities, whom they work with, their funding sources and contact people.

Environmental Studies to Natural Resources Management: An Annotated Guide to University and Government Training Programs in the United States. Sierra Club. International Earthcare Center, 802 2nd Ave., New York, New York 10017. 1980.

ERMD Directory. Special Libraries Association, Environmental Resources Management Division, Forest Resources Lib., AQ-15, Seattle, Washington 98195. Irregular. Listing of membership, services, contact persons, and consultants in environmental areas.

The Great Lakes Directory of the Natural Resources Agencies and Organizations. Fresh Water Society. Center for the Great Lakes, 435 N Michigan Ave., Suite 1408, Chicago, Illinois 60611. 1984-. Biennially. Profiles hundreds of organizations working on natural resource management around the Great Lakes.

Guide to Experts in Forestry and Natural Resources. Northeastern Forest Experimentation Service/Forest Service/U.S. Department of Agriculture, 5 Radnor Corporate Center, Suite 200, Radnor, Pennsylvania 19087. (215) 975-4229.

The United States and the Global Environment: A Guide to American Organizations Concerned with International Environmental Issues. Thaddeus C. Trzyna. California Institute of Public Affairs, PO Box 10, Claremont, California 91711. (714) 624-5212. 1983. A guide to American organizations concerned with international environmental issues.

The World Environment Handbook. Mark Baker. World Environment Center, 605 3rd Ave., Suite 1704, New York, New York 10158. 1985. Directory of natural resource management agencies and non-governmental environmental organizations in 145 countries.

ENCYCLOPEDIAS AND DICTIONARIES

Dictionary of the Environment. Michael Allaby. New York University Press, 70 Washington Sq. S., New York, New York 10012. (212) 998-2575. 1989.

Encyclopedia of Environmental Studies. William Ashworth. Facts on File, Inc., 460 Park Ave. S., New York, New York 10016. (212) 683-2244. 1991.

Encyclopedia of Human Biology. Renato Dulbecco, ed. Academic Press, c/o Harcourt Brace Jovanovich Inc., 6277 Sea Harbor Dr., Orlando, Florida 32887. (800) 346-8648. 1991. Eight volumes.

Environmental Encyclopedia. William P. Cunningham, Terence Ball, et. al. Gale Research Inc., 835 Penobscot Bldg., Detroit, Michigan 48226-4094. (313) 961-2242. 1993.

Grzimek's Encyclopedia of Ecology. Bernhard Grzimek. Van Nostrand Reinhold, 115 5th Ave., New York, New York 10003. (212) 254-3232. 1976.

Illustrated Encyclopedia of Science and the Future. Mike Biscare, et al., ed. Marshall Cavendish, 58 Old Compton St., London, England 0W1V5 PA. 01-734 6710. 1983. Twenty volumes. Each volume has 5 sections: Frontiers, Electronics in Action, Medical Science, Military Technology, and Resources.

The Life of Prairies and Plains. Durward Leon Allen. McGraw-Hill Science & Engineering Books, 11 W. 19th St., New York, New York 10011. (212) 337-6010. 1967.

McGraw-Hill Encyclopedia of Environmental Science. Sybil P. Parker. McGraw-Hill Science & Engineering Books, 11 W. 19th St., New York, New York 10011. (212) 337-6010. 1980. Covers ecology, man's influence on nature, and environmental protection.

McGraw-Hill Encyclopedia of Science and Technology. McGraw-Hill, 1221 Avenue of the Americas, New York, New York 10020. (212) 512-2000 or (800) 262-4729. 1992. Seventh edition. Issued in multiple volumes including index. Includes all science and technology broad subject areas.

Natural Resources Glossary. Government Institutes, Inc., 4 Research Pl., Ste. 200, Rockville, Maryland 20850. (301) 921-2300. Defines and standardizes over 2,500 terms, abbreviations, and acronyms, all compiled directly from the Natural Resources Statutes and the code of Federal Regulations.

North American Reference Encyclopedia of Ecology and Pollution. William White. North American Pub. Co., 401 N. Broad St., Philadelphia, Pennsylvania 19108. (215) 238-5300. 1972.

GENERAL WORKS

Agriculture and Natural Resources: Planning for Educational Priorities for the Twenty-First Century. Wava G. Haney, ed. Conservation of Natural Resources, 5500 Central Ave., Boulder, Colorado 80301. 1991. A volume in the Social Behavior and Natural Resources Series. Text details the priorities in planning for the 21st century while conserving natural resources and the environment.

Atlas of the United States Environmental Issues. Robert J. Mason. Maxwell Macmillan International, 866 3rd Ave., New York, New York 10022. (212) 702-2000. Describes the texture of our environmental health using maps, photographs, charts, graphs, and diagrams.

Blueprint for a Green Economy: A Report. David William Pearce. Earthscan, 3 Endsleigh St., London, England 071-388 2117. 1989. Covers environmental policy, natural resources, and economic policy.

Breaking New Ground. Gifford Pinchot. Island Press, 1718 Connecticut Ave. N.W., Suite 300, Washington, District of Columbia 20009. (202) 232-7933. 1987. Expounds the views that our precious forests should be managed for maximum yield with minimum long-term negative impact.

The Complete Guide to Environmental Careers. CEIP Fund. Island Press, 1718 Connecticut Ave. N.W., Suite 300, Washington, District of Columbia 20009. (202) 232-7933. 1989. Presents information needed to plan any career search. Case studies discuss how environmental organizations, government, and industry are working to manage and protect natural resources.

The Conservation Easement in California. Thomas S. Barrett & Putnam Livermore for the Trust for Public Land. Island Press, 1718 Connecticut Ave. N.W., Suite 300, Washington, District of Columbia 20009. (202) 232-7933. 1983. Conservation lawyers discuss techniques, tax implications and solutions to potential problems.

Conservation of Natural Resources. Gary A. Klee. Prentice-Hall, Rte. 9W, Englewood Cliffs, New Jersey 07632.

(201) 592-2000; (800) 634-2863. 1991. Draws together current and useful tools, techniques, and policy strategies for students training to be natural resource managers.

Economics of Natural Resources and the Environment. David W. Pearce. Johns Hopkins University Press, 701 W. 40th St., Suite 275, Baltimore, Maryland 21211. (410) 516-6900. 1990.

Economics of Protected Areas: A New Look at Benefits and Costs. John A. Dixon and Paul B. Sherman. Island Press, 1718 Connecticut Ave. N.W., Suite 300, Washington, District of Columbia 20009. (202) 232-7933. 1990. Represents a ground-breaking effort to help government examine the costs and benefits of maintaining protected areas. Provides a methodology for assigning monetary values to nature and explains the economic techniques involved.

Environmental Economics and Management: Pollution and Natural Resources. Finn R. Forsund. Croom Helm, 51 Washington St., Dover, New Hampshire 03820. (603) 749-5038. 1988. Covers environmental policy, pollution, human ecology, and natural resources.

The Environmental Sourcebook. Edith Carol Stein. Lyons & Burford, 31 W. 21st St., New York, New York 10010. (212) 620-9580. 1992. Provides information on 11 specific environmental issues, including population; agriculture; energy; climate and atmosphere; biodiversity; water; oceans; solid waste; hazardous substances and waste; endangered lands; and development.

Environmental Viewpoints. Marie Lazzari. Gale Research Inc., 835 Penobscot Bldg., Detroit, Michigan 48226-4094. (313) 961-2242. 1992.

Free Market Environmentalism. Terry L. Anderson and Donald R. Leal. Westview Press, 5500 Central Ave., Boulder, Colorado 80301. (303) 444-3541. 1991. Examines the prospects and pitfalls of improving natural resource allocation and environmental quality through market processes.

Great Basin Drama. Darwin Lambert. Roberts Rinehart Pub., PO Box 666, Niwot, Colorado 80544. (303) 652-2921. 1991. Deals with conservation of natural resources and parks.

Heaven is Under Our Feet. Don Henley, ed. Longmeadow Press, 201 High Ridge Rd, PO Box 10218, Stamford, Connecticut 06904. (203) 352-2110. 1991. Describes the conservation of natural resources.

Holistic Resource Management. Allan Savory. Island Press, 1718 Connecticut Ave. N.W., Suite 300, Washington, District of Columbia 20009. (202) 232-7933. 1988. Presents a comprehensive planning model that treats people and their environment as a whole. Discusses the scientific and management principles of the model, followed by detailed descriptions of each tool and guideline.

Holistic Resource Management Work Book. Sam Bingham and Allan Savory. Island Press, 1718 Connecticut Ave. N.W., Suite 300, Washington, District of Columbia 20009. (202) 232-7933. 1989. Provides practical instruction in financial, biological, and land planning segments necessary to apply the holistic management model.

In the U.S. Interest: Resources, Growth, and Security in the Developing World. Janet Welsh Brown, ed. World Resources Institute, 1709 New York Ave. N.W., Washington, District of Columbia 20006. (800) 822-0504. 1990.

International Resource Management. S. Anderssen and Willy Ostreng, eds. Belhaven Press, 136 S. Broadway, Irvington, New York 10533. (914) 591-9111. 1990. Analyzes the relationship between scientific knowledge and policy in the management of natural resources at the international level. Presents current practice and problems. Problems such as ozone layer protection, whaling, and air pollution.

Natural Resources for the 21st Century. R. Neil Sampson and Dwight Hair, eds. Island Press, 1718 Connecticut Ave. N.W., Suite 300, Washington, District of Columbia 20009. (202) 232-7933. 1990. Looks at lost or diminished resources, as well as those that appear to be rebounding. It offers a reliable status report on water, croplands, soil, forests, wetlands, rangelands, fisheries, wildlife, and wilderness.

Our Common Lands: Defending the National Parks. David J. Simon, ed. Island Press, 1718 Connecticut Ave. N.W., Suite 300, Washington, District of Columbia 20009. (202) 232-7933. 1988. Explains the complexities of key environmental laws and how they can be used to protect our national parks. Includes discussion of successful and unsuccessful attempts to use the laws and how the courts interpret them.

Policies For Maximizing Nature Tourism's Contribution to Sustainable Development. Kreg Lindberg. World Resources Institute, 1709 New York Ave. N.W., Washington, District of Columbia 20006. (800) 822-0504. 1991. Examines how better economic management of nature tourism can promote development and conservation without degrading the natural resources on which development depends.

Pollution Prevention Pays: An Overview by the 3M Company of Low- and Non-Pollution Technology. World Environment Center, 419 Park Ave. S, Suite 1404, New York, New York 10016. (212) 683-4700. Covers natural resources, pollution and control.

Private Options: Tools and Concepts for Land Conservation. Montana Land Reliance, Land Trust Exchange. Island Press, 1718 Connecticut Ave. N.W., Suite 300, Washington, District of Columbia 20009. (202) 232-7933. 1982. Private land conservation experts offer their expertise on how individuals can help contain urban sprawl, conserve wetlands, and protect wildlife. This book covers estate planning, tax incentives, purchase options, conservation easements and land management.

Resource Accounting in Costa Rica. Wilfrido Cruz and Robert Repetto. World Resources Institute, 1709 New York Ave. N.W., Washington, District of Columbia 20006. (800) 822-0504. 1991.

The State of the Earth Atlas. Joni Seger, ed. Touchstone/ Simon and Schuster, Rockefeller Center, 1230 Avenue of the Americas, New York, New York 10020. 1990. Deals with environmental issues such as air quality, urban sprawl, toxic waste, tropical forests and tourism from a socioeconomic perspective.

Tourism Planning: An Integrated and Sustainable Development Approach. Van Nostrand Reinhold, 115 5th Ave., New York, New York 10003. (212) 254-3232. 1991. Provides guidelines and approaches for developing tourism that take environmental, socioeconomic and institutional issues into account.

Wasting Assets: Natural Resources in the National Income Accounts. Robert Repetto and William B. Magrath. World Resources Institute, 1709 New York Ave. N.W., Washington, District of Columbia 20006. (800) 822-0504. 1989. Using Indonesia's timber, petroleum and soils as examples, this report tests and applies a new methodology for integrating natural resource depletion into a revised national accounting system that can more accurately reflect economic reality.

Wetlands Protection: The Role of Economics. Paul F. Scodari. Environmental Law Institute, 1616 P St. N.W., Suite 200, Washington, District of Columbia 20036. (202) 328-5150. 1990. Discussion of market economics as applied to wetland functions and values. Key features include the science of wetland valuation, principles and methods of wetland valuation, principles and methods for valuing wetland goods, the implementation of wetland valuation, and the natural resource damage assessment.

World Guide to Environmental Issues and Organizations. Peter Brackley. Longman Group Ltd., Longman House, Burnt Mill, Harlow, Essex, England CM20 2J6. (0279) 426721. 1991.

Yellowstone Vegetation, Consequences of Environment and History in a Natural Setting. Don G. Despain. Roberts Rinhart Pub., PO Box 666, Niwot, Colorado 80544. (303) 652-2921. 1990. Explores Yellowstone's vegetation types in their habitats and communities, in their origins and distribution, and in their succession after devastation by fire, wind, and insects.

GOVERNMENTAL ORGANIZATIONS

Agricultural Research Service. Washington, District of Columbia 20250.

Assistant Attorney General: Environment and Resources Division, Department of Justice. Room 2143, 10th St. and Constitution Ave., N.W., Washington, District of Columbia 20530. (202) 514-2701.

Assistant Secretary for Natural Resources and Environment. Administrative Building, 12th St. and Jefferson Dr., S.W., Washington, District of Columbia 20250. (202) 447-7173.

Information and Communications: Extension Service. 14th and Independence Ave., S.W., Washington, District of Columbia 20250. (202) 447-3029.

Office of Environmental Affairs: Bureau of Reclamation. 18th and C St., N.W., Washington, District of Columbia 20240. (202) 343-4662.

Office of Public Information: Bureau of Mines. 2401 E St., N.W., Washington, District of Columbia 20241. (202) 501-9650.

Office of the Governor: Natural Resources. Natural Resources Analyst, State Planning Coordinator's Office, Herschler Building, Cheyenne, Wyoming 82002. (307) 777-7574.

Public Affairs Office: U.S. Army Corps of Engineers. Room 8137, 20 Massachusetts Ave., N.W., Washington, District of Columbia 20314. (202) 272-0010.

Public Affairs Office: U.S. Geological Survey. 119 National Center, 12201 Sunrise Valley Dr., Reston, Virginia 22092. (703) 648-4460.

HANDBOOKS AND MANUALS

The Economics of Coastal Zone Management: A Manual of Assessment Techniques. Edmund Penning-Rowsell, ed. Belhaven Press, 136 S. Broadway, Irvington, New York 10533. (914) 591-9111. 1991. Manual for assessing and pricing the procedures that protect vulnerable coastlines against flood, storm, high tide and other environmental damage.

Environmental Statistics Handbook: Europe. Allan Foster, Oksana Newman. Gale Research Inc., 835 Penobscot Bldg., Detroit, Michigan 48226-4094. (313) 961-2242. 1993.

Natural Resources Law Handbook. Government Institutes, Inc., 4 Research Pl., Ste. 200, Rockville, Maryland 20850. (301) 921-2300. Laws governing public lands, wildlife, forests, mining, fisheries, oil, gas and coal resources, and water rights.

Natural Resources Statutes. Government Institutes, Inc., 4 Research Pl., Ste. 200, Rockville, Maryland 20850. (301) 921-2300. Includes the statutes covering coastal zones, federal islands, fish and wildlife, forestry, minerals, soil and water, and endangered species.

Participatory Rural Appraisal Handbook. World Resources Institute, 1709 New York Ave. N.W., Washington, District of Columbia 20006. (800) 822-0504. 1990. A practical guide to resource management in rural African communities, the handbook offers proven methodologies for defining problems, ranking priorities and implementing a village based plan to manage the local natural resource base.

ONLINE DATA BASES

AGRIS. Food and Agriculture Organization of the United Nations, Via delle Terme di Caracalla, Rome, Italy 00100. 61 0181-FA01.

BIOSIS Previews. BIOSIS, 2100 Arch St., Philadelphia, Pennsylvania 19103-1399. (215) 587-4800. Largest and most comprehensive database of research in the life sciences. Contains citations for nearly 9000 primary research journals, monographs, reviews, symposia, preliminary reports, semi-popular journals, selected institutional reports, government reports and research communications.

Enviro/Energyline Abstracts Plus. R. R. Bowker Co., 121 Chanlon Rd., New Providence, New Jersey 07974. (908) 464-6800.

Environmental Periodicals Bibliography. National Information Services Corp., Ste. 6, Wyman Towers, 3100 St. Paul St., Baltimore, Maryland 21218. (410)243-0797. Online version of abstract of same name.

Life Sciences from NTIS. National Technical Information Center for the Utilization of Federal Technology, 5285 Port Royal Rd., Springfield, Virginia 22161. (703) 487-4650.

Monthly Catalog of United States Government Publications. U.S. G.P.O., Supt. of Docs., PO Box 371954, Pittsburgh, Pennsylvania 15250-7954. (202) 512-0000.

Multinational Environmental Outlook. Business Publishers, Inc., 951 Pershing Dr., Silver Spring, Maryland 20910-4464. (301) 587-6300. Environmental problems and solutions in countries outside the United States and their impact on the United States.

National Technical Information Service. U.S. Department of Commerce, National Technical Information Service, Office of Data Base Services, 5285 Port Royal Rd., Springfield, Virginia 22161. (703) 487-4807. Bibliographic database of government sponsored research and technical reports.

Natural Resources Metabase. National Information Services Corporation, Ste. 6, Wyman Towers, 3100 St. Paul St., Baltimore, Maryland 21218. (301) 243-0797. Published and unpublished reports and other materials dealing with natural resources and environmental issues released by U.S. and Canadian government agencies and organizations.

PressNet Environmental Reports. Chemical Information Systems, Inc., 7215 York Rd., Baltimore, Maryland 21212. (301) 321-8440.

SCISEARCH. Institute for Scientific Information, University City Science Center, 3501 Market St., Philadelphia, Pennsylvania 19104. (215) 386-0100.

PERIODICALS AND NEWSLETTERS

The Amicus Journal. Natural Resources Defense Council, 40 West 20th Street, New York, New York 10011. (212) 727-2700. Quarterly. Articles on environmental affairs.

The Balance Wheel. Association for Conservation Information, c/o Roy Edwards, Virginia Game Department, 4010 W. Broad St., Richmond, Virginia 23230-3916. (804) 367-1000. Quarterly.

CAW Waste Watch. Californians Against Waste, Box 289, Sacramento, California 95802. (916) 443-5422. 1978-. Quarterly. Newsletter about natural resources conservation, recycling, anti-litter issues in California and other related topics.

Delaware Conservationist. Delaware Dept. of Natural Resources, 89 Kings Hwy., Box 1401, Dover, Delaware 19903. (302) 736-4506. Quarterly. Natural resources in the state.

EARR: Environment and Natural Resources. Academic Publishers, Box 786, Cooper Station, New York, New York 10276. (212) 206-8900. Monthly. All aspects of environmental and natural resources.

The Earth Care Annual. Russell Wild, ed. Rodale Press, 33 E. Minon St., Emmaus, Pennsylvania 18098. (215) 967-5171; (800) 322-6333. 1990-. Annually. Organized in alphabetical sections such as garbage, greenhouse effect, oceans, ozone, toxic waste, and wildlife, the annual presents environmental problems and offers innovative working solutions.

Earth Work. The Student Conservation Association Inc., PO Box 550, Charlestown, New Hampshire 03603-0550. (603) 826-4301. 1991-. Monthly. Articles focus on the people, agencies, and the nonprofit organizations that protect our parks, refuges, forests and other lands. Carries a special feature entitled JobScan which provides the most comprehensive listing of natural resource and environmental job opportunities anywhere.

Ecological Monographs. Business Office of the Ecological Society of America, Center of Environmental Studies, Arizona State University, Tempe, Arizona 85287-1201. (602) 965-3000. Quarterly. Scientific journal of ecological issues.

The Ecologist. Ecosystems Ltd., Wadebridge, England Covers human ecology, pollution, and natural resources.

Ecology. Ecological Society of America, Center of Environmental Studies, Arizona State University, Tempe, Arizona 85287-1201. (602) 965-3000. Bimonthly. Information on the study of living things.

Ecology USA. Business Publishers, Inc., 951 Pershing Dr., Silver Spring, Maryland 20910-4464. (301) 587-6300. 1972-. Biweekly. Contains all the legislation, regulation, and litigation affecting efforts to conserve and protect America's unique environmental and ecological heritage.

Environmental Geology & Water Sciences. Springer-Verlag, 175 Fifth Avenue, New York, New York 10010. (212) 460-1500. Bimonthly. Covers interactions between humanity and Earth.

Environs. King Hall School of Law, University of California, Environmental Law Society, King Hall, University of California, Davis, California 95616. (916) 752-6703. Environmental law and natural resource management in the western United States.

Franc Nord. Union Quebecoise pour la conservation de la nature, 160, 76 rue est, 2nd fl., Charlesbourg, Quebec, Canada H1K 7H6. (418) 628-9600. 1984-. Quarterly. Devoted to the conservation of natural resources, and the pollution free environment.

High Country News. High Country Foundation, 124 Grand Ave., Box 1090, Paonia, Colorado 81428-1090. (303) 527-4898. Biweekly. Environmental and public-lands issues in the Rocky Mountain region.

Journal of Energy, Natural Resources & Environmental Law. College of Law, University of Utah, Salt Lake City, Utah 84112. Semiannual. Legal aspects of energy development, natural resources, and environment.

Land & Water. Land & Water, Route 3, P.O. Box 1197, Fort Dodge, Iowa 50501. (515) 576-3191. Eight times a year. Covers soil conservation, new machines and products.

Land Letter. The Conservation Fund, 1800 N. Kent St., Suite 1120, Arlington, Virginia 22209. (703) 522-8008. Thirty four times a year. National land use and conservation policy; legislative, regulatory, and legal developments; use of private and public lands.

League Leader. Izaak Walton League of America, 1401 Wilson Blvd., Level B, Arlington, Virginia 22209. (703) 528-1818. Bimonthly. Soil, forest, water, & other natural resources.

Maine Environment. Natural Resource Council of Maine, 20 Willow St., Augusta, Maine 04330. 1974-. Monthly. Environmental activities and problems in Maine.

Minnesota Out-of-Doors. Minnesota Conservation Federation, 1036-B Cleveland Ave., S., St. Paul, Minnesota 55116. (612) 690-3077. Monthly. Conservation, natural resources, hunting & fishing.

Minnesota Volunteer. Minnesota Dept. of Natural Resources, 500 Lafayette Rd., St. Paul, Minnesota 55155-4046. (612) 296-3336. Bimonthly. Natural resources & conservation education.

Natural Resources & Earth Sciences. NTIS, 5285 Port Royal Rd., Springfield, Virginia 22161. (703) 487-4650. Weekly. Mineral industry, natural resources manage-

ment, hydrology, limnology, soil conservation, watershed management, forestry, soil sciences, & geology.

Natural Resources Journal. University of New Mexico School of Law, 1117 Stanford, NE, Albuquerque, New Mexico 87131. (505) 277-4820. Quarterly. Study of natural and environmental research.

Natural Resources Technical Bulletin. Earthcare Network, c/o Douglas Wheeler, 730 Polk St., San Francisco, California 94109. (415) 981-8634. Quarterly.

Nature and Resources. Elsevier Science Publishing Co., 655 Avenue of the Americas, New York, New York 10010. (212) 989-5800. 1965-. Quarterly. Provides in-depth reviews of contemporary environmental issues from an international perspective.

Nebraska Resources. Nebraska Natural Resources Commission, 301 Centennial Mall South, Lincoln, Nebraska 68508. 1970-. Quarterly.

North American Wildlife and Natural Resources Conference, Transactions. Wildlife Management Institute, 1101 14th St., N.W., Ste. 725, Washington, District of Columbia 20005. (202) 371-1808. Annual. Natural resource conservation.

North Woods Call-Charlevoix. North Woods Call, 00509 Turkey Run, Charlevoix, Michigan 49720. (616) 547-9797. Biweekly. Issues involving natural resources.

Outdoor America. Izaak Walton League of America, 1401 Wilson Blvd., Level B, Arlington, Virginia 22209. (703) 528-1818. Quarterly. Outdoor recreation and natural resource conservation.

Resource Recovery Report. Frank McManus, 5313 38th St. N.W., Washington, District of Columbia 20015. (202)362-3034. Monthly.

Society and Natural Resources: An International Journal. Taylor & Francis, 1900 Frost Rd., Suite 101, Bristol, Pennsylvania 19007. (215) 785-5800. Quarterly. Social science research and the environment.

The UNESCO Courier. UNESCO, 7 place de Fontenoy, Paris, France F-75700. 1948-. Monthly. Each issue deals with a theme of universal interest including regular features on the environment, world heritage and UNESCO activities.

Washington Report. Interstate Conference on Water Policy, 955 L'Enfant Plaza, 6th Floor, Washington, District of Columbia 20024. (202) 466-7287. Every six weeks. Covers water conservation, development and administration.

Wildlife Society Bulletin. The Wildlife Society, 5410 Grosvenor Lane, Bethesda, Maryland 20814. (301) 897-9770. Quarterly. Covers wildlife management and conservation education.

The Wildlifer. The Wildlife Society, 5410 Grosvenor Lane, Bethesda, Maryland 20814. (301) 897-9770. Bimonthly. Covers protection of wildlife resources.

Wisconsin Natural Resources. Wisconsin Department of Natural Resources, Box 450, Madison, Wisconsin 53701. 1936-. Bimonthly.

World Resource Review. SUPCON International, PO Box 5275, 1 Heritage Plaza, Woodridge, Illinois 60517. (708) 910-1551. 1981-. Quarterly. Covers all phases of policy discussions and their developments, including such topics as global change, energy production and use, ecosystem impacts of development activities, environmental law, solution of transnational environmental problems, global flow of strategic industrial materials, regional, national, and local resource management, natural resources, food, agriculture and forestry.

RESEARCH CENTERS AND INSTITUTES

Center for Field Research. P.O. Box 403, 608 Mt. Auburn St., Watertown, Massachusetts 02272. (617) 926-8200.

Center for Natural Resources. University of Florida, 1066 McCarty Hall, Gainesville, Florida 32611. (904) 392-7622.

Cooperative National Park Resources Studies Unit. University of California, Davis, Institute of Ecology, Davis, California 95616. (916) 752-7119.

Natural Resources Law Center. University of Colorado-Boulder, Campus Box 401, Boulder, Colorado 80309-0401. (303) 492-1288.

Resources for the Future, Inc. Energy and Natural Resources Division. 1616 P Street, N.W., Washington, District of Columbia 20036. (202) 328-5000.

Rocky Mountain Institute. 1739 Snowmass Creek Rd, Snowmass, Colorado 81654. (303) 927-3128.

School for Field Studies. 16 Broadway, Box S, Beverly, Massachusetts 01915. (508) 927-7777.

University of Georgia, Institute for Natural Products Research. Chemistry Building, Athens, Georgia 30602. (404) 542-5800.

University of Hawaii at Manoa, Environmental Center. 2550 Campus Road, Honolulu, Hawaii 96822. (808) 956-7361.

University of Michigan, School of Natural Resources, Research Service. 430 East University, Ann Arbor, Michigan 48109. (313) 764-6823.

University of Minnesota, Center for Natural Resource Policy and Management. 110 Green Hall, 1530 North Cleveland Avenue, St. Paul, Minnesota 55108. (612) 624-9796.

University of Minnesota, Duluth, Natural Resources Research Institute. 5013 Miller Trunk Highway, Duluth, Minnesota 55811. (218) 720-4294.

University of Montana, Wilderness Institute. Forestry Building, Room 207, Missoula, Montana 59812. (406) 243-5361.

University of Nevada-Reno, Knudtsen Renewable Resources Center. Department of Range, Wildlife and Forestry, 1000 Valley Road, Reno, Nevada 89512. (702) 784-4000.

University of North Texas, Institute of Applied Sciences. P.O. Box 13078, Denton, Texas 76203. (817) 565-2694.

University of Wisconsin-Madison, Kemp Natural Resources Station. Agricultural Research Station, 620 Babcock Drive, Madison, Wisconsin 53706. (608) 262-2969.

Wisconsin Department of Natural Resources, Bureau of Research. Box 7921, Madison, Wisconsin 53707. (608) 266-8170.

World Resources Institute. 1709 New York Ave., N.W., Washington, District of Columbia 20006. (202) 638-6300.

STATISTICS SOURCES

Statistical Record of the Environment. Arsen J. Darnay. Gale Research Inc., 835 Penobscot Bldg., Detroit, Michigan 48226-4094. (313) 961-2242. 1992.

World Resources. World Resources Institute. 1709 New York Ave., N.W., Washington, District of Columbia 20006. (202) 638-6300. Annual. Statistical and textual analysis of world's natural resources and the effects of growth-caused environmental pollution.

TRADE ASSOCIATIONS AND PROFESSIONAL SOCIETIES

African Wildlife Foundation. 1717 Massachusetts Avenue, NW, Washington, District of Columbia 20036. (202) 265-8393.

American Nature Study Society. 5881 Cold Brook Rd., Homer, New York 13077. (607) 749-3655.

American Resources Group. Signet Bank Bldg., Suite 210, 374 Maple Ave. E., Vienna, Virginia 22180. (703) 255-2700.

American Society of Naturalists. Department of Ecology and Evolation, State University of New York, Stony Brook, New York 11794. (516) 632-8589.

Association for Conservation Information. PO Box 10678, Reno, Nevada 89520. (702) 688-1500.

Basic Foundation. PO Box 47012, St. Petersburg, Florida 33743. (813) 526-9562. Non-profit corporation that was founded to augment efforts at balancing population growth with natural resources.

Better World Society. 1100 17th St., NW, Suite 502, Washington, District of Columbia 20036. (202) 331-3770. International non-profit membership organization that attempts to increase individual awareness of global issues related to the sustainability of life on earth.

Environmental and Energy Study Institute. 122 C St., N.W., Suite 700, Washington, District of Columbia 20001. (202) 628-1400.

Foundation for Field Research. PO Box 2010, Alpine, California 92001-0020. (619) 445-9264.

Friends of the Earth. 218 D St., SE, Washington, District of Columbia 20003. (202) 544-2600.

The Institute of the North American West. 110 Cherry St., Suite 202, Seattle, Washington 98104. (206) 623-9597.

International Research Expeditions. 140 University Dr., Menlo Park, California 94025. (415) 323-4228.

National League of Cities, Natural Resources Committee. 1301 Pennsylvania Ave., N.W., 6th Floor, Washington, District of Columbia 20004. (202) 626-3000.

National Wildlife Federation. 1400 16th St., N.W., Washington, District of Columbia 20036. (202) 797-6800.

Natural Areas Association. 320 S. Third St., Rockford, Illinois 61104. (815) 964-6666.

Natural Resources Council of America. 801 Pennsylvania Ave., SE, Suite 410, Washington, District of Columbia 20003. (202) 547-7553.

Natural Resources Defense Council. 40 W. 20th St., New York, New York 10011. (212) 727-2700.

New England Natural Resources Center. 200 Lincoln St., Boston, Massachusetts 02111. (617) 541-3670.

Oregon Natural Resources Council. Yeon Building, Suite 1050, 522 Southwest Fifth Ave., Portland, Oregon 97204. (503) 223-9001.

Partners of the Americas. 1424 K St., N.W., #700, Washington, District of Columbia 20005. (202) 628-3300.

The Rights Livelihood Awards Foundation. P.O. Box 15072, S-10465, Stockholm, Sweden (08) 702 03 04.

Scenic America. 216 Seventh St., S.E., Washington, District of Columbia 20003. (202) 546-1100.

Sierra Club. 100 Bush St., San Francisco, California 94104. (415) 291-1600.

Student Conservation Association. P.O. Box 550, Charlestown, New Hampshire 03603. (603) 826-4301.

United States Conference of Mayors National Resource Recovery Association. 1620 Eye St., N.W., 4th Fl., Washington, District of Columbia 20006. (202) 293-7330.

Wildlife Society. 5410 Grosvenor Lane, Bethesda, Maryland 20814. (301) 897-9770.

World Nature Association, Inc. PO Box 673, Silver Spring, Maryland 20901. (301) 593-2522.

NATURAL SELECTION

ABSTRACTING AND INDEXING SERVICES

Biological Abstracts. BIOSIS, 2100 Arch St., Philadelphia, Pennsylvania 19103-1399. (215) 587-4800. 1927-.

Biological and Agricultural Index. H.W. Wilson Co., 950 University Ave., Bronx, New York 10452. (800) 367-6770. 1916-. Monthly.

Current Advances in Ecological and Environmental Science. Pergamon Microforms International, Inc., Fairview Park, Elmsford, New York 10523. (914) 592-7720. 1989-. Monthly. Current literature searching service includingjournals, reports, abstracts, etc. This service is available online as part of the CABS database on the hosts BRS and ORBIT search service.

Ecological Abstracts. Geo Abstracts Ltd. Elsevier Applied Science, Crown House, Linton Rd., Barking, England IG 11 8JU. 1974-. Derived from over 600 leading ecological and environmental journals, plus books, conference proceedings, reports and theses.

Ecology Abstracts. Cambridge Scientific Abstracts, 5161 River Rd., Bethesda, Maryland 20816. (301) 961-6750. Monthly.

Environment Abstracts. Bowker A & I Publishing, 121 Chanlon Rd., New Providence, New Jersey 07974. (908) 464-6800. 1974-.

Environment Index. Environment Information Center, Index Research Department, 124 E. 39th St., New York, New York 10016. 1971-. Annual.

Environmental Information Connection–EIC. Planning Information Program, Dept. of Urban and Regional Planning, University of Illinois, 1003 West Nevada, Urbana, Illinois 61801. (217) 333-1369. Also available online.

Environmental Periodicals Bibliography. Environmental Studies Institute, International Academy at Santa Barbara, 800 Garden St., Suite D, Santa Barbara, California 93101. (805) 965-5010. Also available online.

General Science Index. H. W. Wilson Co., 950 University Ave., Bronx, New York 10452. 1978-. Monthly, also issued in annual cumulation. Cumulative subject index to English language periodicals in the subject fields of astronomy, botany, chemistry, earth science, environment and conservation, food and nutrition, genetics, mathematics, medicine and health, microbiology, oceanography, physics, physiology and zoology.

Index to Scientific Book Contents. Institute for Scientific Information, 3501 Market St., Philadelphia, Pennsylvania 19104. (800) 523-1857. 1985-. Annual. Gives contents of science books published.

Science Citation Index. Institute for Scientific Information, 3501 Market St., Philadelphia, Pennsylvania 19104. 1961-.

BIBLIOGRAPHIES

Current Contents. Agriculture, Biology and Environmental Sciences. Institute for Scientific Information, 3501 Market St., Philadelphia, Pennsylvania 19104. (800) 523-1857. 1973-. Previous title: Current Contents. Agricultural, Food & Veterinary Sciences. Gives the table of contents of periodicals in the fields of agriculture, biology, environmental and related areas.

EPA Publications Bibliography. U.S. Environmental Protection Agency, Library Systems Branch, 401 M St., SW, Washington, District of Columbia 20460. (202) 260-2090. Quarterly.

ENCYCLOPEDIAS AND DICTIONARIES

Cambridge Dictionary of Biology. Peter M. B. Walker. Cambridge University Press, 40 W. 20th St., New York, New York 10011. (212) 924-3900 or (800) 227-0247. 1989. Includes 10,000 terms in zoology, botany, biochemistry, molecular biology and genetics. Previously published under the title Chambers Biology Dictionary.

A Concise Dictionary of Biology. Elizabeth Martin, ed. Oxford University Press, 200 Madison Ave., New York, New York 10016. (212) 679-7300 or (800) 334-4249. 1990. New edition. Derived from the Concise Science Dictionary, published in 1984.

Encyclopedia of Human Biology. Renato Dulbecco, ed. Academic Press, c/o Harcourt Brace Jovanovich Inc., 6277 Sea Harbor Dr., Orlando, Florida 32887. (800) 346-8648. 1991. Eight volumes.

McGraw-Hill Encyclopedia of Science and Technology. McGraw-Hill, 1221 Avenue of the Americas, New York, New York 10020. (212) 512-2000 or (800) 262-4729. 1992. Seventh edition. Issued in multiple volumes in-

cluding index. Includes all science and technology broad subject areas.

Van Nostrand's Scientific Encyclopedia. Glenn D. Considine, ed. Van Nostrand Reinhold, 115 5th Ave., New York, New York 10003. (212) 254-3232. 1983. Sixth edition. Includes all broad subject areas in science.

GENERAL WORKS

Magill's Survey of Science. Life Science Series. Frank N. Magill, ed. Salem Press, PO Box 50062, Pasadena, California 91105. 1991. Six volumes. Contents: v.1. A-Central and peripheral nervous system functions; v.2. Central metabolism regulation - eukaryotic transcriptional control; v.3. Positive and negative eukaryotic transcriptional control - mammalian hormones; v.4. Hormones and behavior - muscular contraction; v.5. Muscular contraction and relaxation - sexual reproduction in plants; v.6. Reproductive behavior and mating - X inactivation and the Lyon hypothesis.

ONLINE DATA BASES

BIOSIS Previews. BIOSIS, 2100 Arch St., Philadelphia, Pennsylvania 19103-1399. (215) 587-4800. Largest and most comprehensive database of research in the life sciences. Contains citations for nearly 9000 primary research journals, monographs, reviews, symposia, preliminary reports, semi-popular journals, selected institutional reports, government reports and research communications.

Enviro/Energyline Abstracts Plus. R. R. Bowker Co., 121 Chanlon Rd., New Providence, New Jersey 07974. (908) 464-6800.

Environmental Periodicals Bibliography. National Information Services Corp., Ste. 6, Wyman Towers, 3100 St. Paul St., Baltimore, Maryland 21218. (410)243-0797. Online version of abstract of same name.

TRADE ASSOCIATIONS AND PROFESSIONAL SOCIETIES

American Institute of Biological Sciences. 730 11th St., N.W., Washington, District of Columbia 20001-4521. (202) 628-1500.

American Nature Study Society. 5881 Cold Brook Rd., Homer, New York 13077. (607) 749-3655.

American Society of Naturalists. Department of Ecology and Evolation, State University of New York, Stony Brook, New York 11794. (516) 632-8589.

NATURE CONSERVANCY

ABSTRACTING AND INDEXING SERVICES

Applied Ecology Abstracts Studies in Renewable Natural Resources. Information Retrieval Ltd., 1911 Jefferson Davis Highway, Arlington, Virginia 22202. 1975-. Monthly.

Biological Abstracts. BIOSIS, 2100 Arch St., Philadelphia, Pennsylvania 19103-1399. (215) 587-4800. 1927-.

Biological and Agricultural Index. H.W. Wilson Co., 950 University Ave., Bronx, New York 10452. (800) 367-6770. 1916-. Monthly.

Current Advances in Ecological and Environmental Science. Pergamon Microforms International, Inc., Fairview Park, Elmsford, New York 10523. (914) 592-7720. 1989-. Monthly. Current literature searching service includingjournals, reports, abstracts, etc. This service is available online as part of the CABS database on the hosts BRS and ORBIT search service.

Ecological Abstracts. Geo Abstracts Ltd. Elsevier Applied Science, Crown House, Linton Rd., Barking, England IG 11 8JU. 1974-. Derived from over 600 leading ecological and environmental journals, plus books, conference proceedings, reports and theses.

Ecology Abstracts. Cambridge Scientific Abstracts, 5161 River Rd., Bethesda, Maryland 20816. (301) 961-6750. Monthly.

Environment Abstracts. Bowker A & I Publishing, 121 Chanlon Rd., New Providence, New Jersey 07974. (908) 464-6800. 1974-.

Environment Index. Environment Information Center, Index Research Department, 124 E. 39th St., New York, New York 10016. 1971-. Annual.

Environmental Information Connection–EIC. Planning Information Program, Dept. of Urban and Regional Planning, University of Illinois, 1003 West Nevada, Urbana, Illinois 61801. (217) 333-1369. Also available online.

Environmental Periodicals Bibliography. Environmental Studies Institute, International Academy at Santa Barbara, 800 Garden St., Suite D, Santa Barbara, California 93101. (805) 965-5010. Also available online.

Forestry Abstracts. C. A. B. International, Wallingford, England OX10 8DE. (0491) 3211. 1939/40-. Monthly. Journal of abstracts of journal articles, conferences, technical reports in the subject areas of: silviculture, forest mensuration and management, physical environment, fire, plant biology, genetics and breeding, mycology and pathology, game and wildlife, fish, protection of forests and other related matter.

General Science Index. H. W. Wilson Co., 950 University Ave., Bronx, New York 10452. 1978-. Monthly, also issued in annual cumulation. Cumulative subject index to English language periodicals in the subject fields of astronomy, botany, chemistry, earth science, environment and conservation, food and nutrition, genetics, mathematics, medicine and health, microbiology, oceanography, physics, physiology and zoology.

Index to Scientific Book Contents. Institute for Scientific Information, 3501 Market St., Philadelphia, Pennsylvania 19104. (800) 523-1857. 1985-. Annual. Gives contents of science books published.

Multimedia Index to Ecology. National Information Center for Educational Media, University of Southern California, Los Angeles, California 90007.

Science Citation Index. Institute for Scientific Information, 3501 Market St., Philadelphia, Pennsylvania 19104. 1961-.

BIBLIOGRAPHIES

Current Contents. Agriculture, Biology and Environmental Sciences. Institute for Scientific Information, 3501 Market St., Philadelphia, Pennsylvania 19104. (800) 523-1857. 1973-. Previous title: Current Contents. Agricultural, Food & Veterinary Sciences. Gives the table of contents of periodicals in the fields of agriculture, biology, environmental and related areas.

Environmental Values, 1860-1972: A Guide to Information Sources. Loren C. Owings. Gale Research Co., 835 Penobscot Bldg., Detroit, Michigan 48226-4094. (313) 961-2242. 1976. This bibliography includes the broad areas of human ecology, nature and outdoor life. It belongs in the series entitled Man and the Environment Information Guide Series, v.4.

EPA Publications Bibliography. U.S. Environmental Protection Agency, Library Systems Branch, 401 M St., SW, Washington, District of Columbia 20460. (202) 260-2090. Quarterly.

DIRECTORIES

A Directory of Natural Resources Management Organizations in Latin America and the Caribbean. Julie Buckley-Ess, ed. Tinker Foundation, Inc., 55 East 59th St., New York, New York 10022. 1988. Lists the public and private organizations working in each country. Describes their activities, whom they work with, their funding sources and contact people.

Ecological Society of America Bulletin–Directory of Members Issue. Ecological Society of America, c/o Dr. Duncan Patten, Center for Environmental Studies, Arizona State University, Tempe, Arizona 85287. (602) 965-3000.

Gale Environmental Sourcebook. Karen Hill. Gale Research Co., 835 Penobscot Bldg., Detroit, Michigan 48226-4094. (313) 961-2242. Contacts, information sources, or general information on environmental topics.

The United States and the Global Environment: A Guide to American Organizations Concerned with International Environmental Issues. Thaddeus C. Trzyna. California Institute of Public Affairs, PO Box 10, Claremont, California 91711. (714) 624-5212. 1983. A guide to American organizations concerned with international environmental issues.

World Directory of Environmental Organizations. Thaddeus C. Trzyna, ed. California Institute of Public Affairs, PO Box 10, Claremont, California 91711. (714) 624-5212. 1989. 3rd ed. Handbook of organizations and programs concerned with protecting the environment and managing natural resources. It covers national and international organizations, both governmental and non-governmental, in all parts of the world.

ENCYCLOPEDIAS AND DICTIONARIES

A Dictionary of Environmental Quotations. Barbara K. Rodes and Rice Odell. Simon and Schuster, 15 Columbus Circle, New York, New York 10023. (212) 373-7342. 1992. Collection of nearly 3000 quotations arranged by topic, such as air, noise, energy, nature, pollution, forests, oceans, and other subjects on the environment.

Grzimek's Encyclopedia of Ecology. Bernhard Grzimek. Van Nostrand Reinhold, 115 5th Ave., New York, New York 10003. (212) 254-3232. 1976.

The Life of Prairies and Plains. Durward Leon Allen. McGraw-Hill Science & Engineering Books, 11 W. 19th St., New York, New York 10011. (212) 337-6010. 1967.

The Life of the African Plains. Leslie Brown. McGraw-Hill Science & Engineering Books, 11 W. 19th St., New York, New York 10011. (212) 337-6010. 1972.

McGraw-Hill Encyclopedia of Environmental Science. Sybil P. Parker. McGraw-Hill Science & Engineering Books, 11 W. 19th St., New York, New York 10011. (212) 337-6010. 1980. Covers ecology, man's influence on nature, and environmental protection.

McGraw-Hill Encyclopedia of Science and Technology. McGraw-Hill, 1221 Avenue of the Americas, New York, New York 10020. (212) 512-2000 or (800) 262-4729. 1992. Seventh edition. Issued in multiple volumes including index. Includes all science and technology broad subject areas.

North American Reference Encyclopedia of Ecology and Pollution. William White. North American Pub. Co., 401 N. Broad St., Philadelphia, Pennsylvania 19108. (215) 238-5300. 1972.

GENERAL WORKS

50 Simple Things You Can Do to Save the Earth. G.K. Hall & Co., 70 Lincoln St., Boston, Massachusetts 02111. (617) 423-3990. 1991. Citizen participation in environmental protection.

Ancient Forests of the Pacific Northwest. Elliot A. Norse. Island Press, 1718 Connecticut Ave. N.W., Suite 300, Washington, District of Columbia 20009. (202) 232-7933. 1990. Comprehensive assessment of the biological value of the ancient forests, information about how logging and atmospheric changes threaten the forests, and convincing arguments that replicated ecosystems are too weak to support biodiversity.

Atlas of the United States Environmental Issues. Robert J. Mason. Maxwell Macmillan International, 866 3rd Ave., New York, New York 10022. (212) 702-2000. Describes the texture of our environmental health using maps, photographs, charts, graphs, and diagrams.

Bacteria in Their Natural Environments. Madilyn Fletcher, ed. Academic Press Ltd., 24-28 Oval Rd., London, England NW1 7DX. (071) 2674466. 1985.

Biodiversity in Sub-Saharan Africa and Its Islands. Simon N. Stuart, et al. International Union for Conservation of Nature and Natural Resources, Avenue du Mont-Blanc, Gland, Switzerland CH-1196. 1990. Contains a broadly based environmental strategy and outlines actions that are necessary at political, economic, social, ecological, biological, and developmental levels. Focuses on the conservation of wild species and natural ecosystems.

Biological Conservation. David W. Ehrenfeld. Holt, Rinehart and Winston, 6277 Sea Harbor Dr., Orlando, Florida 32887. (407) 345-2500. 1970.

The Conservation Atlas of Tropical Forests: Asia and the Pacific. N. Mark Collins, Jeffery A. Sayer, and Timothy C. Whitmore. Simon & Schuster, 1230 Avenue of the Americas, New York, New York 10020. (212) 689-7000. 1991. Focuses on closed canopy, and true rain forests. This Asian volume is the first of a set of three–tropical America and Africa being the next. Address such regional subjects as forest wildlife, human impacts on forest lands, and the tropical timber trade; and includes a "Tropical Forestry Action Plan" to conserve and protect important remaining stands. The second part of the atlas gives a detailed survey of 17 countries plus the island groups of

Fiji and the Solomons, but not those of New Caledonia, New Hebrides, or Micronesia.

Conservation of Living Nature and Resources: Problems, Trends, and Prospects. A. V. Yablokov. Springer-Verlag, 175 5th Ave., New York, New York 10010. (212) 460-1500 or (800) 777-4643. 1991. Deals with wildlife conservation, the associated problems, solutions, and its future.

Conservation of Natural Resources. Gary A. Klee. Prentice-Hall, Rte. 9W, Englewood Cliffs, New Jersey 07632. (201) 592-2000; (800) 634-2863. 1991. Draws together current and useful tools, techniques, and policy strategies for students training to be natural resource managers.

Crossroads: Environmental Priorities for the Future. Peter Borrelli, ed. Island Press, 1718 Connecticut Ave. N.W., Suite 300, Washington, District of Columbia 20009. (202) 232-7933. 1988. An assessment of the environmental movement written by some of the country's top environmental leaders, activists and authors.

The Dream of the Earth. Thomas Berry. Sierra Club Books, 100 Bush St., San Francisco, California 94104. (415) 291-1600. 1988. Describes the ecological fate from a species perspective.

Eco-Warriors: Understanding the Radical Environmental Movement. Rik Scarce. Noble Pr., 111 E. Chestnut, Suite 48 A, Chicago, Illinois 60611. (312) 880-0439. 1990. Recounts escapades of pro-ecology sabotage by self styled eco- warriors. Episodes such as the sinking of two whaling ships in Iceland, the botched attempt to hang a banner on Mt. Rushmore, a national tree-sitting week, and raids on research facilities by animal liberation activists.

Economics of Protected Areas: A New Look at Benefits and Costs. John A. Dixon and Paul B. Sherman. Island Press, 1718 Connecticut Ave. N.W., Suite 300, Washington, District of Columbia 20009. (202) 232-7933. 1990. Represents a ground-breaking effort to help government examine the costs and benefits of maintaining protected areas. Provides a methodology for assigning monetary values to nature and explains the economic techniques involved.

An Environmental Agenda for the Future. John H. Adams, et al. Island Press, 1718 Connecticut Ave. N.W., Washington, District of Columbia 20009. (202) 232-7933. 1985. Contains articles by the CEOs of the 10 largest environmental organizations in the United States.

From the Land. Nancy P. Pittman, ed. Island Press, 1718 Connecticut Ave. N.W., Suite 300, Washington, District of Columbia 20009. (202) 232-7933. 1988. Anthology comes from 13 years of the Land–a journal of conservation writings from the '40s and '50s. Through fiction, essay, poetry, and philosophy we learn how our small farms have given way to today's agribusiness.

Inside the Environmental Movement: Meeting the Leadership Challenge. Donald Snow, ed. Island Press, 1718 Connecticut Ave. N.W., Suite 300, Washington, District of Columbia 20009. (202) 232-7933. 1992. Book offers recommendations and concrete solutions which will make it an invaluable resource as the conservation community prepares to meet the formidable challenges that lie ahead.

International Environmental Information Sources. Pira, Randalls Rd., Leatherhead, England KT22 7RU. 0372 376161. 1990. Contains valuable business and technical

contacts for environmental information sources worldwide. Information sources cover the following subjects: Air, noise, water and land pollution; waste control and disposal; recycling; energy recovery; nature conservation. Informational sources include associations, research organizations, legislative/regulatory agencies, directories, statistics, on-line databases, magazines and news letters in 24 countries.

Making Peace with the Planet. Barry Commoner. Pantheon Books, 201 E. 50th St., New York, New York 10220. (212) 751-2000. 1990. Reviews the vast efforts made in the public and private sphere to address and control damage to the environment.

Natural Resources for the 21st Century. R. Neil Sampson and Dwight Hair, eds. Island Press, 1718 Connecticut Ave. N.W., Suite 300, Washington, District of Columbia 20009. (202) 232-7933. 1990. Looks at lost or diminished resources, as well as those that appear to be rebounding. It offers a reliable status report on water, croplands, soil, forests, wetlands, rangelands, fisheries, wildlife, and wilderness.

Nature Reserves: Island Theory and Conservation Practice. Craig L. Shafer. Smithsonian Institution Press, 470 L'Enfant Plaza, No. 7100, Washington, District of Columbia 20560. (800) 782-4612. 1991. Encompasses ecology, biogeography, evolutionary biology, genetics, paleobiology, as well as legal, social, and economic issues.

Nature Tourism: Managing for the Environment. Tensie Whelan. Island Press, 1718 Connecticut Ave. N.W., Suite 300, Washington, District of Columbia 20009. (202) 232-7933. 1991. Provides practical advice and models for planning and developing a nature tourism industry, evaluating economic benefits and marketing nature tourism.

Policies For Maximizing Nature Tourism's Contribution to Sustainable Development. Kreg Lindberg. World Resources Institute, 1709 New York Ave. N.W., Washington, District of Columbia 20006. (800) 822-0504. 1991. Examines how better economic management of nature tourism can promote development and conservation without degrading the natural resources on which development depends.

Preserving Communities and Corridors. Gay Mackintosh, ed. Defenders of Wildlife, 1244 19th St. N.W., Washington, District of Columbia 20036. (202) 659-9510. 1989.

Private Options: Tools and Concepts for Land Conservation. Montana Land Reliance, Land Trust Exchange. Island Press, 1718 Connecticut Ave. N.W., Suite 300, Washington, District of Columbia 20009. (202) 232-7933. 1982. Private land conservation experts offer their expertise on how individuals can help contain urban sprawl, conserve wetlands, and protect wildlife. This book covers estate planning, tax incentives, purchase options, conservation easements and land management.

Protecting Nontidal Wetlands. David G. Burke, et al. American Planning Association, 1776 Massachusetts Ave. N.W., Washington, District of Columbia 20036. (202) 872-0611. 1988. Describes wetlands types and values, looks at the current status of U.S. wetlands, and reviews federal, state, and local regulations to protect nontidal wetlands.

The Protection and Management of Our Natural Resources, Wildlife and Habitat. W. Jack Grosse. Oceana Publications Inc., 75 Main St., Dobbs Ferry, New York

10522. (914) 693-8100. 1992. Covers question of overall management, control and protection of wildlife and habitat. Additionally, as the federal government has recently created numerous acts which serve to control wildlife and habitat, many questions have emerged over shared and conflicting power with the states.

The River of the Mother of God and Other Essays. Aldo Leopold. University of Wisconsin Press, 114 N. Murray St., Madison, Wisconsin 53715. (608) 262-8782. 1991. Brings together 60 of Leopold's previously unpublished or illusive essays.

Save Our Planet: 750 Everyday Ways You Can Help Clean Up the Earth. Diane MacEachern. Dell Pub., 666 5th Ave., New York, New York 10103. (212) 765-6500; (800) 255-4133. 1990. Practical guide to ways in which everyone can help clean up the earth.

The Sierra Nevada: A Mountain Journey. Tim Palmer. Island Press, 1718 Connecticut Ave. N.W., Suite 300, Washington, District of Columbia 20009. (202) 232-7933. 1988. This natural history of the Sierra Nevadas deals with the range, the people, and the surrounding communities to life. It describes development from the Gold Rush days to modern battles over preservation, water quality, wildlife protection and logging.

Wilderness Management. John C. Hendee, et al. North American Press, 350 Indiana St., Ste. 350, Golden, Colorado 80401. (303) 277-1623. 1990. 2d ed. rev. The expertise of the main authors has been combined with that of 10 other authorities in wilderness related fields, and nearly 100 wilderness managers, scientists, educators, and citizen conservationists, to make this book a valuable tool of practical information.

Wildlife of the Florida Keys: A Natural History. James D. Lazell, Jr. Island Press, 1718 Connecticut Ave. N.W., Suite 300, Washington, District of Columbia 20009. (202) 232-7933. 1989. Identifies habits, behaviors, and histories of most of the species indigenous to the Keys.

GOVERNMENTAL ORGANIZATIONS

Assistant Attorney General: Environment and Resources Division, Department of Justice. Room 2143, 10th St. and Constitution Ave., N.W., Washington, District of Columbia 20530. (202) 514-2701.

Office of Public Affairs: Bureau of Land Management. 18th and C St., N.W., Washington, District of Columbia 20240. (202) 208-3435.

HANDBOOKS AND MANUALS

The Official World Wildlife Fund Guide to Endangered Species of North America. David W. Lowe, ed. Beacham Publishing, Inc., 2100 S. St. NW, Washington, District of Columbia 20008. (202) 234-0877. 1990. Two volumes. Guide to endangered plants and animals. Describes 540 endangered or threatened species including their habitat, behavior and, recovery. Includes: directories of the Offices of the U.S. Fish and Wildlife Service, Offices of the National Marine Fisheries Service, State Heritage Programs, Bureau of Land Management Offices, National Forest Service Offices, National Wildlife Refuges, Canadian agencies, and state offices.

ONLINE DATA BASES

BIOSIS Previews. BIOSIS, 2100 Arch St., Philadelphia, Pennsylvania 19103-1399. (215) 587-4800. Largest and most comprehensive database of research in the life sciences. Contains citations for nearly 9000 primary research journals, monographs, reviews, symposia, preliminary reports, semi-popular journals, selected institutional reports, government reports and research communications.

Cambridge Scientific Abstracts Life Science–CSAL. Cambridge Scientific Abstracts, 5161 River Rd., Bethesda, Maryland 20816. (301) 961-6750. Provides access to the following abstracting services: "Life Sciences Collection," "Aquatic Sciences and Fisheries Abstracts," "Oceanic Abstracts," and "Pollution Abstracts."

Enviro/Energyline Abstracts Plus. R. R. Bowker Co., 121 Chanlon Rd., New Providence, New Jersey 07974. (908) 464-6800.

Environmental Periodicals Bibliography. National Information Services Corp., Ste. 6, Wyman Towers, 3100 St. Paul St., Baltimore, Maryland 21218. (410)243-0797. Online version of abstract of same name.

Managed Area Basic Record. The Nature Conservancy, 1815 N. Lynn St., Arlington, Virginia 22209. (703) 841-5300. Database of about 3,100 nature preserves.

Monthly Catalog of United States Government Publications. U.S. G.P.O., Supt. of Docs., PO Box 371954, Pittsburgh, Pennsylvania 15250-7954. (202) 512-0000.

National Technical Information Service. U.S. Department of Commerce, National Technical Information Service, Office of Data Base Services, 5285 Port Royal Rd., Springfield, Virginia 22161. (703) 487-4807. Bibliographic database of government sponsored research and technical reports.

PressNet Environmental Reports. Chemical Information Systems, Inc., 7215 York Rd., Baltimore, Maryland 21212. (301) 321-8440.

SCISEARCH. Institute for Scientific Information, University City Science Center, 3501 Market St., Philadelphia, Pennsylvania 19104. (215) 386-0100.

PERIODICALS AND NEWSLETTERS

Alabama Conservation. Alabama Department of Conservation, 64 N. Union St., Montgomery, Alabama 36130. (205) 242-3151. 1929-. Bimonthly. Promotes the wise use of natural resources.

Alabama Department of Conservation Report. Alabama Department of Conservation, 64 N. Union St., Montgomery, Alabama 36130. (205) 242-3151. Annually.

The American Naturalist. Americana Society of Naturalists, Business Sciences, University of Kansas, Lawrence, Kansas 66045. (913) 864-3763. Monthly. Contains information by professionals of the biological sciences.

The Amicus Journal. Natural Resources Defense Council, 40 West 20th Street, New York, New York 10011. (212) 727-2700. Quarterly. Articles on environmental affairs.

Biological Conservation. Applied Science Publishers, 655 Avenue of the Americas, PO Box 5399, New York, New York 10163. (718) 756-6440. Quarterly. Conservation of biological and allied natural resources, plants and animals and their habitats.

Business Associate. Western Pennsylvania Conservancy, 316 4th Ave., Pittsburgh, Pennsylvania 15222. (412) 288-2777. 1984-. Semiannually. Reports on land conservation projects of the Western Pennsylvania Conservancy.

California Tomorrow. California Tomorrow, Ft. Mason Ctr., Building B, #315, San Francisco, California 94123. (415) 441-7631. 1965-. Quarterly. Illustrates need for system of comprehensive state/regional planning to protect and improve the Californian environment.

CAW Waste Watch. Californians Against Waste, Box 289, Sacramento, California 95802. (916) 443-5422. 1978-. Quarterly. Newsletter about natural resources conservation, recycling, anti-litter issues in California and other related topics.

Conservation Commission News. New Hampshire Association of Conservation Commissions, 54 Portsmouth St., Concord, New Hampshire 03301. (603) 224-7867. 1968-. Quarterly. Concerns national, state, local information and issues dealing with natural resources and the environment.

Conservation Education Association Newsletter. Conservation Education Association, c/o Conservation Education Center, RR 1, Box 153, Guthrie Center, Iowa 50115. (515) 747-8383. Quarterly. Promotes environmental conservation education.

Conservationist. New York State Dept. of Environmental Conservation, 50 Wolf Rd., Albany, New York 12233. (518) 457-6668. 1946-. Bimonthly. Covers all aspects of conservation and outdoor recreation, scientific information, art and history of New York State.

Conservative Contractor. Conservative Contractor, 214 Suncrest Dr., PO Box 45, Port Lavaca, Texas 77979. 1962-. Bimonthly. Official publication of Conservation Contractors of Texas, Inc.

Conserve. Western Pennsylvania Conservancy, 316 4th Ave., Pittsburgh, Pennsylvania 15222. (412) 288-2777. 1971-. Semiannually. Reports on land conservation projects of the western Pennsylvania Conservancy.

Delaware Conservationist. Delaware Dept. of Natural Resources, 89 Kings Hwy., Box 1401, Dover, Delaware 19903. (302) 736-4506. Quarterly. Natural resources in the state.

Earth Science. American Geological Institute, 4220 King Street, Alexandria, Virginia 22302. (703) 379-2480. Quarterly. Covers geological issues.

Earth Work. The Student Conservation Association Inc., PO Box 550, Charlestown, New Hampshire 03603-0550. (603) 826-4301. 1991-. Monthly. Articles focus on the people, agencies, and the nonprofit organizations that protect our parks, refuges, forests and other lands. Carries a special feature entitled JobScan which provides the most comprehensive listing of natural resource and environmental job opportunities anywhere.

ECOL News. Environmental Conservation Library, 300 Nicollet Mall, Minneapolis, Minnesota 55401. (612) 372-6570. Semiannual. Environmental update on the library.

Ecological Monographs. Business Office of the Ecological Society of America, Center of Environmental Studies, Arizona State University, Tempe, Arizona 85287-1201. (602) 965-3000. Quarterly. Scientific journal of ecological issues.

Ecological Society of America Bulletin. Ecological Society of America, Center of Environmental Studies, Arizona State University, Tempe, Arizona 85287-1201. (602) 965-3000. Quarterly. Study of living things in relation to their environments.

Ecology. Ecological Society of America, Center of Environmental Studies, Arizona State University, Tempe, Arizona 85287-1201. (602) 965-3000. Bimonthly. Information on the study of living things.

Ecology USA. Business Publishers, Inc., 951 Pershing Dr., Silver Spring, Maryland 20910-4464. (301) 587-6300. 1972-. Biweekly. Contains all the legislation, regulation, and litigation affecting efforts to conserve and protect America's unique environmental and ecological heritage.

Environments. Faculty of Environmental Studies, University of Waterloo, Waterloo, Ontario, Canada N2L 3G1. (519) 885-1211. Three times a year. People in manmade and natural environments.

The Everglades Reporter. Friends of the Everglades, 202 Park St., #4, Miami, Florida 33166. (305) 888-1230. Five times a year. Ecology and nature conservation of the Florida Everglades.

Florida Naturalist. Florida Audubon Society, PO Drawer 7, Maitland, Florida 32751. 1917-. Bimonthly.

Forest Conservation. Forestry Range Club, Washington State University, Pullman, Washington 99164-3200. 1958-. Annually. None published in 1974. Deals with forest conservation and related topics.

Forest Notes. Society for the Protection of New Hampshire Forests, 54 Portsmouth St., Concord, New Hampshire 03301. (603) 224-9945. 1937-. Quarterly. Devoted to forestry, land protection and other issues affecting New Hampshire natural resources.

Friend O'Wildlife. North Carolina Wildlife Federation,Inc., Box 10626, Raleigh, North Carolina 27605. (919) 833-1923. 1959-. Bimonthly. Covers North Carolina wildlife conservation and related hunting, fishing and boating activities and other environmental issues.

Geojourney. Florida Department of Natural Resources, 3900 Commonwealth Blvd., Tallahassee, Florida 32303. (904) 488-1234. 1980-. Quarterly. Covers activities on resource management, marine resources, parks and recreation, and subjects related to fishing, boating and all uses of Florida's natural resources.

Georgia Conservancy Newsletter. Georgia Conservancy, 3376 Peachtree Rd., NE, Suite 44, Atlanta, Georgia 30326. 1967-. Monthly.

Greenpeace Magazine. Greenpeace, 1436 U St., NW, Washington, District of Columbia 20009. (202) 462-1177. Bimonthly. Deals with nature and wildlife conservation, and environmental protection.

High Country News. High Country Foundation, 124 Grand Ave., Box 1090, Paonia, Colorado 81428-1090. (303) 527-4898. Biweekly. Environmental and public-lands issues in the Rocky Mountain region.

INFORM Reports. INFORM Inc., 381 Park Ave., So., New York, New York 10016. (212) 689-4040. Quarterly. INFORM is a nonprofit environmental research & education organization for the preservation and conservation of natural resources and public health.

Journal of Wild Culture. Society for the Preservation of Wild Culture, 158 Crawford St., Toronto, Ontario, Canada M6J 2V4. (416) 588-8266. Quarterly. Deals with wildlife preservation.

Land & Water. Land & Water, Route 3, P.O. Box 1197, Fort Dodge, Iowa 50501. (515) 576-3191. Eight times a year. Covers soil conservation, new machines and products.

Maine Legacy. Nature Conservancy, 1815 N Lynn St., Arlington, Virginia 22209. (207) 729-5181. Bimonthly. Nature conservancy projects in Maine.

Maryland Conservationist. Department of Natural Resources, Tawes State Office Bldg., C-2, Annapolis, Maryland 21401. 1924-. Bimonthly.

Natural Areas Journal. Natural Areas Association, 320 S. Third St., Rockford, Illinois 61104. (815) 964-6666. Quarterly. Information of interest to natural areas professionals.

Natural Resources Journal. University of New Mexico School of Law, 1117 Stanford, NE, Albuquerque, New Mexico 87131. (505) 277-4820. Quarterly. Study of natural and environmental research.

Nature and Resources. Elsevier Science Publishing Co., 655 Avenue of the Americas, New York, New York 10010. (212) 989-5800. 1965-. Quarterly. Provides in-depth reviews of contemporary environmental issues from an international perspective.

Nature Center News. National Audubon Society, Nature Center Planning Division, 950, 3d Ave., New York, New York 10022. (212) 832-3200. 1971-. Monthly.

Nature Conservancy Magazine. The Nature Conservancy, 1815 North Lynn St., Arlington, Virginia 22209. (703) 841-5300. 1951-. Bimonthly. Membership magazine covering biotic diversity and related conservation issues.

Network News. World Environment Center, 419 Park Avenue South, Suite 1403, New York, New York 10016. (212) 683-4700. Quarterly. Covers international environmental issues.

Orion Nature Quarterly. Myrin Institute, Inc., 136 E. 64th St., New York, New York 10021. (212) 758-6475. Quarterly. Natural world and man's relation to it.

Outdoor Indiana. Indiana State Dept. of Natural Resources, Box 6113, Indianapolis, Indiana 46204. (317) 232-4004. Ten times a year. Facilities, services, and state programs.

Pack & Paddie. Ozark Society, Box 2914, Little Rock, Arkansas 72203. (501) 225-1795. Quarterly. Regional conservation.

Totem. Department of Natural Resources, Public Lands Bldg., Olympia, Washington 98504. Monthly.

The UNESCO Courier. UNESCO, 7 place de Fontenoy, Paris, France F-75700. 1948-. Monthly. Each issue deals with a theme of universal interest including regular features on the environment, world heritage and UNESCO activities.

Wildlife Society Bulletin. The Wildlife Society, 5410 Grosvenor Lane, Bethesda, Maryland 20814. (301) 897-9770. Quarterly. Covers wildlife management and conservation education.

The Wildlifer. The Wildlife Society, 5410 Grosvenor Lane, Bethesda, Maryland 20814. (301) 897-9770. Bimonthly. Covers protection of wildlife resources.

RESEARCH CENTERS AND INSTITUTES

The Nature Conservancy. 1815 N. Lynn St., Arlington, Virginia 22209. (703) 841-5300.

North Carolina State University, Natural Resources Research Center. Box 8210, Raleigh, North Carolina 27695. (919) 515-5100.

World Resources Institute. 1709 New York Ave., N.W., Washington, District of Columbia 20006. (202) 638-6300.

STATISTICS SOURCES

Environmental Data Compendium. OECD Publications and Information Center, 2001 L St., N.W., Suite 700, Washington, District of Columbia 20036. (202) 785-6323. 1989.

Environmental Indicators. OECD Publications and Information Center, 2001 L St., N.W., Suite 700, Washington, District of Columbia 20036. (202) 785-6323. 1991.

Environmental Quality. Council on Environmental Quality. U.S. G.P.O., Washington, District of Columbia 20401. (202) 512-0000. Annual.

The State of the Environment. OECD Publications and Information Center, 2001 L St., N.W., Suite 700, Washington, District of Columbia 20036. (202) 785-6323. 1991.

TRADE ASSOCIATIONS AND PROFESSIONAL SOCIETIES

American Institute of Biological Sciences. 730 11th St., N.W., Washington, District of Columbia 20001-4521. (202) 628-1500.

American Nature Study Society. 5881 Cold Brook Rd., Homer, New York 13077. (607) 749-3655.

American Society of Naturalists. Department of Ecology and Evolation, State University of New York, Stony Brook, New York 11794. (516) 632-8589.

Association for Conservation Information. PO Box 10678, Reno, Nevada 89520. (702) 688-1500.

Association of Interpretive Naturalists. P.O. Box 1892, Ft. Collins, Colorado 80522. (303) 491-6434.

Ecological Society of America. Arizona State University, Center for Environmental Studies, Tempe, Arizona 85287. (602) 965-3000.

INFORM. 381 Park Avenue S., New York, New York 10016. (212) 689-4040.

National Association of Conservation Districts. 509 Capitol Court, N.E., Washington, District of Columbia 20002. (202) 547-6223.

Natural Area Council. 219 Shoreham Bldg., N.W., Washington, District of Columbia 20005. (202) 638-1649.

Natural Areas Association. 320 S. Third St., Rockford, Illinois 61104. (815) 964-6666.

Wildlife Society. 5410 Grosvenor Lane, Bethesda, Maryland 20814. (301) 897-9770.

NEBRASKA ENVIRONMENTAL AGENCIES

GOVERNMENTAL ORGANIZATIONS

Department of Agriculture: Pesticide Registration. Director, Bureau of Plant Industry, 301 Centennial Mall S., Lincoln, Nebraska 68509. (402) 471-2394.

Department of Environmental Control: Air Quality. Chief, Air Pollution Control Division, PO Box 98922, Lincoln, Nebraska 68509-8922. (402) 471-2189.

Department of Environmental Control: Emergency Preparedness and Community Right-to-Know. Coordinator, Emergency Response Commission, PO Box 98922, State House Station, Lincoln, Nebraska 68509-8922. (402) 471-2186.

Department of Environmental Control: Environmental Protection. Director, 301 Centennial Mall S., Box 94877, Lincoln, Nebraska 68509-4877. (402) 471-2186.

Department of Environmental Control: Solid Waste Management. Director, 301 Centennial Mall S., Box 94877, Lincoln, Nebraska 68509-4877. (402) 471-2186.

Department of Environmental Control: Water Quality. Director, 301 Centennial Mall S., PO Box 98922, Lincoln, Nebraska 68509-8922. (402) 471-4220.

Department of Labor: Occupational Safety. Director, Division of Safety, PO Box 95024, Lincoln, Nebraska 68509-5024. (402) 471-2239.

Department of Water Resources: Groundwater Management. Director, 301 Centennial Mall S., PO Box 94676, Lincoln, Nebraska 68509-4676. (402) 471-2363.

Environmental Control Department: Underground Storage Tanks. Division Chief, Land Quality Division, 301 Centennial Mall S., PO Box 94877, Lincoln, Nebraska 68509. (402) 471-2186.

Game and Park Commission: Fish and Wildlife. Director, 2200 North 33rd St., PO Box 30370, Lincoln, Nebraska 68503-0370. (402) 464-0641.

Natural Resources Commission: Natural Resources. Director, 301 Centennial Mall S., Box 94876, Lincoln, Nebraska 68509-4876. (402) 471-2081.

U.S. EPA Region 7: Pollution Prevention. Section Chief, State Programs Section, 726 Minnesota Ave., Kansas City, Missouri 66101. (913) 551-7006.

NEBRASKA ENVIRONMENTAL LEGISLATION

GENERAL WORKS

Agricultural Energy Conservation Project: Final Report. University of Nebraska, Cooperative Extension, Institute of Agriculture and Natural Resources, 214 Agricultural Hall, Lincoln, Nebraska 68583-0703. (402) 472-7211. 1989.

NECROSIS

See: PLANTS

NEMATOCIDES

See: PESTICIDES

NEMATODE DAMAGE

ABSTRACTING AND INDEXING SERVICES

Biological Abstracts. BIOSIS, 2100 Arch St., Philadelphia, Pennsylvania 19103-1399. (215) 587-4800. 1927-.

Biological and Agricultural Index. H.W. Wilson Co., 950 University Ave., Bronx, New York 10452. (800) 367-6770. 1916-. Monthly.

Ecology Abstracts. Cambridge Scientific Abstracts, 5161 River Rd., Bethesda, Maryland 20816. (301) 961-6750. Monthly.

Nematological Abstracts. C. A. B. International, 845 North Park Ave., Tucson, Arizona 85719. (602) 621-7897 or (800) 528-4841. 1932-. Quarterly. Abstracts of the world literature on: nematode parasitic on plants; free-living and marine nematodes; nematodes parasitic on insects or other invertebrates.

Science Citation Index. Institute for Scientific Information, 3501 Market St., Philadelphia, Pennsylvania 19104. 1961-.

ENCYCLOPEDIAS AND DICTIONARIES

Cambridge Encyclopedia of Life Sciences. A. E. Friday and David S. Ingram. Cambridge University Press, 40 W 20th St., New York, New York 10011. (212) 924-3900 or (800) 227-0247. 1985. Includes all topics under biology and ecology.

ONLINE DATA BASES

BIOSIS Previews. BIOSIS, 2100 Arch St., Philadelphia, Pennsylvania 19103-1399. (215) 587-4800. Largest and most comprehensive database of research in the life sciences. Contains citations for nearly 9000 primary research journals, monographs, reviews, symposia, preliminary reports, semi-popular journals, selected institutional reports, government reports and research communications.

TRADE ASSOCIATIONS AND PROFESSIONAL SOCIETIES

Society of Nematologists. c/o R.N. Huehel, Ph.D., USDA, ARS, Nematology Laboratory, Bldg. 011A BARC-W, Beetsville, Maryland 20705. (301) 344-3081.

NEMATODES (ROUNDWORM)

ABSTRACTING AND INDEXING SERVICES

Biological Abstracts. BIOSIS, 2100 Arch St., Philadelphia, Pennsylvania 19103-1399. (215) 587-4800. 1927-.

Biological and Agricultural Index. H.W. Wilson Co., 950 University Ave., Bronx, New York 10452. (800) 367-6770. 1916-. Monthly.

Biology Digest. Data Courier, Plexus Pub Inc., 143 Old Marlton Pike, Medford, New Jersey 08055. 1974-. Monthly. Abstracts biology periodicals.

Ecological Abstracts. Geo Abstracts Ltd. Elsevier Applied Science, Crown House, Linton Rd., Barking, England IG 11 8JU. 1974-. Derived from over 600 leading ecological and environmental journals, plus books, conference proceedings, reports and theses.

Ecology Abstracts. Cambridge Scientific Abstracts, 5161 River Rd., Bethesda, Maryland 20816. (301) 961-6750. Monthly.

General Science Index. H. W. Wilson Co., 950 University Ave., Bronx, New York 10452. 1978-. Monthly, also issued in annual cumulation. Cumulative subject index to English language periodicals in the subject fields of astronomy, botany, chemistry, earth science, environment and conservation, food and nutrition, genetics, mathematics, medicine and health, microbiology, oceanography, physics, physiology and zoology.

Genetics Abstracts. Cambridge Scientific Abstracts, 5161 River Rd., Bethesda, Maryland 20816. (301) 961-6750. 1968-. Monthly. Formerly published by Information Retrieval Ltd., London England. Published by Cambridge Scientific Abstracts since 1982.

Science Citation Index. Institute for Scientific Information, 3501 Market St., Philadelphia, Pennsylvania 19104. 1961-.

ENCYCLOPEDIAS AND DICTIONARIES

Cambridge Dictionary of Biology. Peter M. B. Walker. Cambridge University Press, 40 W. 20th St., New York, New York 10011. (212) 924-3900 or (800) 227-0247. 1989. Includes 10,000 terms in zoology, botany, biochemistry, molecular biology and genetics. Previously published under the title Chambers Biology Dictionary.

Cambridge Encyclopedia of Life Sciences. A. E. Friday and David S. Ingram. Cambridge University Press, 40 W 20th St., New York, New York 10011. (212) 924-3900 or (800) 227-0247. 1985. Includes all topics under biology and ecology.

A Concise Dictionary of Biology. Elizabeth Martin, ed. Oxford University Press, 200 Madison Ave., New York, New York 10016. (212) 679-7300 or (800) 334-4249. 1990. New edition. Derived from the Concise Science Dictionary, published in 1984.

Encyclopedia of Human Biology. Renato Dulbecco, ed. Academic Press, c/o Harcourt Brace Jovanovich Inc., 6277 Sea Harbor Dr., Orlando, Florida 32887. (800) 346-8648. 1991. Eight volumes.

McGraw-Hill Encyclopedia of Science and Technology. McGraw-Hill, 1221 Avenue of the Americas, New York, New York 10020. (212) 512-2000 or (800) 262-4729. 1992. Seventh edition. Issued in multiple volumes including index. Includes all science and technology broad subject areas.

Van Nostrand's Scientific Encyclopedia. Glenn D. Considine, ed. Van Nostrand Reinhold, 115 5th Ave., New York, New York 10003. (212) 254-3232. 1983. Sixth edition. Includes all broad subject areas in science.

GENERAL WORKS

Magill's Survey of Science. Life Science Series. Frank N. Magill, ed. Salem Press, PO Box 50062, Pasadena, California 91105. 1991. Six volumes. Contents: v.1. A-Central and peripheral nervous system functions; v.2. Central metabolism regulation - eukaryotic transcriptional control; v.3. Positive and negative eukaryotic transcriptional control - mammalian hormones; v.4. Hormones and behavior - muscular contraction; v.5. Muscular contraction and relaxation - sexual reproduction in plants; v.6. Reproductive behavior and mating - X inactivation and the Lyon hypothesis.

ONLINE DATA BASES

BIOSIS Previews. BIOSIS, 2100 Arch St., Philadelphia, Pennsylvania 19103-1399. (215) 587-4800. Largest and most comprehensive database of research in the life sciences. Contains citations for nearly 9000 primary research journals, monographs, reviews, symposia, preliminary reports, semi-popular journals, selected institutional reports, government reports and research communications.

TRADE ASSOCIATIONS AND PROFESSIONAL SOCIETIES

American Institute of Biological Sciences. 730 11th St., N.W., Washington, District of Columbia 20001-4521. (202) 628-1500.

Society of Nematologists. c/o R.N. Huehel, Ph.D., USDA, ARS, Nematology Laboratory, Bldg. 011A BARC-W, Beetsville, Maryland 20705. (301) 344-3081.

NEUROTOXICITY

See also: TOXICITY

ABSTRACTING AND INDEXING SERVICES

Chemical Abstracts. Chemical Abstracts Service, 2540 Olentangy River Rd., PO Box 3012, Columbus, Ohio 43210. (800) 848-6533. 1907-.

Environment Abstracts. Bowker A & I Publishing, 121 Chanlon Rd., New Providence, New Jersey 07974. (908) 464-6800. 1974-.

Environment Index. Environment Information Center, Index Research Department, 124 E. 39th St., New York, New York 10016. 1971-. Annual.

Environmental Information Connection–EIC. Planning Information Program, Dept. of Urban and Regional Planning, University of Illinois, 1003 West Nevada, Urbana, Illinois 61801. (217) 333-1369. Also available online.

Environmental Periodicals Bibliography. Environmental Studies Institute, International Academy at Santa Barbara, 800 Garden St., Suite D, Santa Barbara, California 93101. (805) 965-5010. Also available online.

Pollution Abstracts. Cambridge Scientific Abstracts, 5161 River Rd., Bethesda, Maryland 20816. (301) 961-6750. Six/year. Indexes worldwide technical literature on environmental pollution. Covers air pollution, marine and freshwater pollution, sewage and wastewater treatment, waste management, toxicology and health, noise pollu-

tion, radiation, land pollution, and environmental policies, programs, legislation, and education. Also available online.

BIBLIOGRAPHIES

EPA Publications Bibliography. U.S. Environmental Protection Agency, Library Systems Branch, 401 M St., SW, Washington, District of Columbia 20460. (202) 260-2090. Quarterly.

ENCYCLOPEDIAS AND DICTIONARIES

Encyclopedia of Human Biology. Renato Dulbecco, ed. Academic Press, c/o Harcourt Brace Jovanovich Inc., 6277 Sea Harbor Dr., Orlando, Florida 32887. (800) 346-8648. 1991. Eight volumes.

Van Nostrand's Scientific Encyclopedia. Glenn D. Considine, ed. Van Nostrand Reinhold, 115 5th Ave., New York, New York 10003. (212) 254-3232. 1983. Sixth edition. Includes all broad subject areas in science.

GENERAL WORKS

Animals and Alternatives in Toxicology: Present Status and Future Prospects. Michael Balls. VCH Publishers, 303 NW 12th Ave., Deerfield Beach, Florida 33442-1788. (305) 428-5566. 1991. Animals and Alternatives in Toxicology conference where invited speakers gathered to recommend and discuss the alternatives.

ONLINE DATA BASES

Chemical Abstracts-CA. Chemical Abstracts Service, 2540 Olentangy River Rd., P.O. Box 3012, Columbus, Ohio 43210. (800) 848-6533 or (614) 421-3600. Information sources include 9000 journals, patents from 27 countries, two industrial property organizations, new books, conference proceedings, and government research reports.

Enviro/Energyline Abstracts Plus. R. R. Bowker Co., 121 Chanlon Rd., New Providence, New Jersey 07974. (908) 464-6800.

Environmental Periodicals Bibliography. National Information Services Corp., Ste. 6, Wyman Towers, 3100 St. Paul St., Baltimore, Maryland 21218. (410)243-0797. Online version of abstract of same name.

RESEARCH CENTERS AND INSTITUTES

Neuroscience Research Institute. University of California, Santa Barbara, Santa Barbara, California 93106. (805) 893-3637.

TRADE ASSOCIATIONS AND PROFESSIONAL SOCIETIES

American Institute of Biological Sciences. 730 11th St., N.W., Washington, District of Columbia 20001-4521. (202) 628-1500.

NEVADA ENVIRONMENTAL AGENCIES

GOVERNMENTAL ORGANIZATIONS

Conservation and Natural Resources Department: Air Quality. Administrator, Environmental Protection Division, 201 South Fall St., Carson City, Nevada 89710. (702) 885-4670.

Conservation and Natural Resources Department: Environmental Protection. Administrator, Environmental Protection Division, 201 South Fall St., Carson City, Nevada 89710. (702) 885-4670.

Conservation and Natural Resources Department: Groundwater Management. Chief, Groundwater Section, Division of Water Resources, 201 South Fall St., Carson City, Nevada 89710. (702) 885-4380.

Conservation and Natural Resources Department: Hazardous Waste Management. Administrator, Environmental Protection Division, 201 South Fall St., Carson City, Nevada 89710. (702) 885-4670.

Conservation and Natural Resources Department: Natural Resources. Director, 201 South Fall St., Carson City, Nevada 89710. (702) 885-4360.

Conservation and Natural Resources Department: Solid Waste Management. Administrator, Environmental Protection Division, 201 South Fall St., Carson City, Nevada 89710. (702) 885-4670.

Conservation and Natural Resources Department: Underground Storage Tanks. Administrator, Environmental Protection Division, 201 South Fall St., Carson City, Nevada 89710. (702) 885-4670.

Conservation and Natural Resources Department: Water Quality. Administrator, Environmental Protection Division, 201 South Fall St., Carson City, Nevada 89710. (702) 885-4670.

Department of Agriculture: Pesticide Registration. Director, Division of Plant Industry, 350 Capitol Hill Ave., PO Box 11100, Reno, Nevada 89510-1100. (702) 789-0180.

Department of Industrial Relations: Occupational Safety. Administrator, Occupational Safety and Health, 1370 South Curry St., Carson City, Nevada 89710. (702) 885-5270.

Department of Wildlife: Fish and Wildlife. Director, PO Box 10678, Reno, Nevada 89520. (702) 688-1500.

Division of Emergency Management: Emergency Preparedness and Community Right-to-Know. Chair, 2525 South Carson St., Carson City, Nevada 89710. (702) 885-4240.

U.S. EPA Region 9: Pollution Prevention. Deputy Director, Hazardous Waste, 215 Fremont St., San Francisco, California 94105. (415) 556-6322.

NEW HAMPSHIRE ENVIRONMENTAL AGENCIES

GOVERNMENTAL ORGANIZATIONS

Air Resources Agency: Air Quality. Director, Health and Welfare Building, 22 Hazen Dr., Concord, New Hampshire 03301. (603) 271-4582.

Bureau of Hazardous Waste: Hazardous Waste Management. Deputy Commissioner, Compliance and Enforcement, 6 Hazen Drive, Concord, New Hampshire 03301. (603) 271-4608.

Bureau of Solid Waste: Solid Waste Management. Director, Compliance and Enforcement, 6 Hazen Drive, Concord, New Hampshire 03301. (603) 271-4586.

Department of Agriculture: Pesticide Registration. Director, Division of Pesticide Control, Caller Box 2042, Concord, New Hampshire 03301. (603) 271-3550.

Department of Environmental Services: Environmental Protection. Commissioner, 6 Hazen Dr., Concord, New Hampshire 03301. (603) 271-3503.

Department of Environmental Services: Underground Storage Tanks. Commissioner, 6 Hazen Dr., Concord, New Hampshire 03301. (603) 271-3503.

Department of Environmental Services: Water Quality. Commissioner, 6 Hazen Dr., Concord, New Hampshire 03301. (603) 271-3503.

Department of Labor: Occupational Safety. Commissioner, 19 Pillsbury St., Concord, New Hampshire 03301. (603) 271-3171.

Department of Resources and Economic Development: Natural Resources. Commissioner, PO Box 856, Concord, New Hampshire 03301. (603) 271-2411.

Environmental Services Department: Groundwater Management. Administrator, Groundwater Protection Bureau, Box 95, 6 Hazen Drive, Concord, New Hampshire 03301. (603) 271-3503.

Fish and Game Department: Fish and Wildlife. Director, 34 Bridge St., Concord, New Hampshire 03301. (603) 271-3512.

Office of State Planning: Coastal Zone Management. Director, 2-1/2 Beacon St., Concord, New Hampshire 03301. (603) 271-2155.

State Emergency Management Agency: Emergency Preparedness and Community Right-to-Know. Director, Title III Program, State Office Park South, 107 Pleasant St., Concord, New Hampshire 03301. (603) 271-2231.

U.S. EPA Region 1: Pollution Prevention. Program Manager, JFK Federal Building, Boston, Massachusetts 02203. (617) 565-3715.

NEW HAMPSHIRE ENVIRONMENTAL LEGISLATION

GENERAL WORKS

An Introductory Guide to the New Hampshire Department of Environmental Services. New Hampshire Dept. of Environmental Services, PO Box 95, Concord, New Hampshire 03301. (603)271-3503. 1988.

Natural Resource Management and Protection: A New Hampshire State Development Plan. Office of State Planning, 2 1/2 Beacon St., Concord, Connecticut 03301. (603)271-2155. 1988.

Rivers and Lakes Protection Program. Office of State Planning, 2 1/2 Beacon St., Concord, Connecticut 03301. (603)271-2155. 1988.

NEW JERSEY ENVIRONMENTAL AGENCIES

GOVERNMENTAL ORGANIZATIONS

Bureau of Underground Storage Tanks: Underground Storage Tanks. Chief, Division of Water Resources, 401 East State St., CN029, Trenton, New Jersey 08625. (609) 984-3156.

Department of Environmental Protection: Air Quality. Director, Environmental Quality, 401 East State St., 2nd Floor, Trenton, New Jersey 08625. (609) 292-5383.

Department of Environmental Protection: Solid Waste Disposal. Director, Division of Solid Waste Management, 401 East State St., CN 402, Trenton, New Jersey 08625. (609) 530-8591.

Department of Environmental Protection: Water Quality. Director, Division of Water Resources, 401 East State St., CN402, Trenton, New Jersey 08625. (609) 292-1637.

Department of Environmental Quality: Pesticide Registration. Director, Division of Environmental Quality, 401 East State St., CN027, Trenton, New Jersey 08625. (609) 292-5383.

Department of Labor: Occupational Safety. Assistant Commissioner, Division of Workplace Standards, John Fitch Plaza, CN386, Trenton, New Jersey 08625. (609) 292-2313.

Division of Water Resources: Groundwater Management. Chief, Groundwater Quality Management, 401 East State St., Trenton, New Jersey 08625. (609) 292-0424.

Emergency Response Commission: Emergency Preparedness and Community Right-to-Know. Department of Environmental Protection, Division of Environmental Quality, Bureau of Hazardous Substances Information, Trenton, New Jersey 08625. (609) 292-6714.

Environmental Protection Department: Coastal Zone Management. Director, Division of Control Resources, 401 East State St., CN401, Trenton, New Jersey 08625. (609) 292-2795.

Environmental Protection Department: Environmental Protection. Commissioner, CN 402, 401 E. State St., Trenton, New Jersey 08625. (609) 292-2885.

Environmental Protection Department: Fish and Wildlife. Director, Fish, Game, and Wildlife Division, CN 400, Trenton, New Jersey 08625. (609) 292-9410.

Environmental Protection Department: Hazardous Waste Management. Director, Division of Hazardous Waste Management, 401 East State St., Trenton, New Jersey 08625. (609) 633-1408.

Environmental Protection Department: Natural Resources. Assistant Commissioner, Natural Resources, John Fitch Plaza, CN 402, Trenton, New Jersey 08625. (609) 292-3541.

Hazardous Waste Facilities Siting Commission: Waste Minimization and Pollution Prevention. Director, Room 514, 28 West State St., CN028, Trenton, New Jersey 08625-0406. (609) 292-1459.

NEW JERSEY ENVIRONMENTAL LEGISLATION

GENERAL WORKS

New Jersey Environmental Law Handbook. Government Institutes, Inc., 4 Research Pl., Ste. 200, Rockville, Maryland 20850. (301) 921-2300. 1990.

NEW MEXICO ENVIRONMENTAL AGENCIES

GOVERNMENTAL ORGANIZATIONS

Department of Agriculture: Pesticide Registration. Director, Division of Agricultural and Environmental Services, Department 3150, PO Box 30005, New Mexico State University, Las Cruces, New Mexico 88003-0005. (505) 646-2674.

Department of Energy, Minerals, and Natural Resources: Natural Resources. Director, 525 Camino de los Marcos, Santa Fe, New Mexico 87503. (505) 827-7835.

Department of Health and Environment: Air Quality. Bureau Chief, Air Quality Bureau, 725 St. Michael Dr., Santa Fe, New Mexico 87503. (505) 827-0070.

Department of Health and Environment: Environmental Protection. Director, Environmental Improvement Division, PO Box 968, Santa Fe, New Mexico 87504. (505) 827-0020.

Department of Health and Environment: Groundwater Management. Deputy Director, Environmental Protection Division, PO Box 968, Santa Fe, New Mexico 87504-0968. (505) 827-2850.

Department of Health and Environment: Hazardous Waste Management. Director, Environmental Improvement Division, PO Box 968, Santa Fe, New Mexico 87504-0968. (505) 827-2850.

Department of Health and Environment: Occupational Safety. Bureau Chief, Occupational Health and Safety Bureau, PO Box 968, Santa Fe, New Mexico 87504-0968. (505) 827-2877.

Department of Health and Environment: Solid Waste Management. Deputy Director, Environmental Improvement Division, PO Box 968, Santa Fe, New Mexico 87504-0968. (505) 827-2850.

Department of Health and Environment: Water Quality. Chief, Surface Water Quality Bureau, PO Box 968, Santa Fe, New Mexico 87504-0968. (505) 827-2793.

Department of Public Safety: Emergency Preparedness and Community Right-to- Know. Director, Emergency Response Commission, PO Box 1628, Santa Fe, New Mexico 87504-1628. (505) 827-9226.

Game and Fish Department: Fish and Wildlife. Director, Villagra Building, Santa Fe, New Mexico 87503. (505) 827-7899.

Health and Environment Department: Underground Storage Tanks. Bureau Chief, Underground Storage Tanks Bureau, PO Box 968, Runnels Building, Santa Fe, New Mexico 87503. (505) 827-2894.

U.S. EPA Region 6: Pollution Prevention. Coordinator, 1445 Ross Ave., Suite 1200, Dallas, Texas 75202-2733. (214) 655-6444.

NEW MEXICO ENVIRONMENTAL LEGISLATION

GENERAL WORKS

New Mexico Environmental Law Handbook. Government Institutes, Inc., 4 Research Pl., Ste. 200, Rockville, Maryland 20850. (301) 921-2300. 1990.

NEW YORK ENVIRONMENTAL AGENCIES

GOVERNMENTAL ORGANIZATIONS

Department of Environmental Conservation: Air Quality. Commissioner, 50 Wolf Rd., Albany, New York 12233. (518) 457-7230.

Department of Environmental Conservation: Emergency Preparedness and Community Right-to-Know. Deputy Director, Emergency Response Commission, Bureau of Spill Response, 50 Wolf Rd., Room 326, Albany, New York 12233-3510. (518) 457-4107.

Department of Environmental Conservation: Environmental Protection. Commissioner, 50 Wolf Rd., Albany, New York 12233. (518) 457-3446.

Department of Environmental Conservation: Fish and Wildlife. Commissioner, 50 Wolf Rd., Albany, New York 12233. (518) 457-5690.

Department of Environmental Conservation: Groundwater Management. Commissioner, 50 Wolf Rd., Albany, New York 12233. (518) 457-3446.

Department of Environmental Conservation: Hazardous Waste Management. Commissioner, 50 Wolf Rd., Albany, New York 12233. (518) 457-6943.

Department of Environmental Conservation: Natural Resources. Commissioner, 50 Wolf Rd., Albany, New York 12233. (518) 457-3446.

Department of Environmental Conservation: Pesticide Registration. Director, Bureau of Pesticides, Room 404, 50 Wolf Rd., Albany, New York 12233-0001. (518) 457-7842.

Department of Environmental Conservation: Solid Waste Management. Commissioner, 50 Wolf Rd., Albany, New York 12233. (518) 457-6603.

Department of Environmental Conservation: Underground Storage Tanks. Commissioner, 50 Wolf Rd., Albany, New York 12233. (518) 457-3446.

Department of Environmental Conservation: Water Quality. Commissioner, 50 Wolf Rd., Albany, New York 12233. (518) 457-6674.

Department of Labor: Occupational Safety. Commissioner, Campus, State Office Building, Albany, New York 12240. (518) 457-2741.

Department of State: Coastal Zone Management. Secretary of State, 162 Washington Ave., Albany, New York 12231. (518) 474-4750.

State Environmental Facilities Corporation: Waste Minimization and Pollution Prevention. President, 50 Wolf Rd., Albany, New York 12205. (518) 457-4222.

NEW YORK ENVIRONMENTAL LEGISLATION

GENERAL WORKS

New York Environmental Law Handbook. Government Institutes, Inc., 4 Research Pl., Ste. 200, Rockville, Maryland 20850. (301) 921-2300. 1990.

NICKEL CARBONYL

See: CARBON MONOXIDE

NICOTINE

ABSTRACTING AND INDEXING SERVICES

Biological Abstracts. BIOSIS, 2100 Arch St., Philadelphia, Pennsylvania 19103-1399. (215) 587-4800. 1927-.

Biological and Agricultural Index. H.W. Wilson Co., 950 University Ave., Bronx, New York 10452. (800) 367-6770. 1916-. Monthly.

Biotechnology Research Abstracts. Cambridge Scientific Abstracts, 5161 River Rd., Bethesda, Maryland 20816. (301) 961-6750. Monthly. Includes such broad areas as genetic intervention, biochemical genetics, and microbiological techniques.

Chemical Abstracts. Chemical Abstracts Service, 2540 Olentangy River Rd., PO Box 3012, Columbus, Ohio 43210. (800) 848-6533. 1907-.

Environment Abstracts. Bowker A & I Publishing, 121 Chanlon Rd., New Providence, New Jersey 07974. (908) 464-6800. 1974-.

Environment Index. Environment Information Center, Index Research Department, 124 E. 39th St., New York, New York 10016. 1971-. Annual.

Environmental Information Connection–EIC. Planning Information Program, Dept. of Urban and Regional Planning, University of Illinois, 1003 West Nevada, Urbana, Illinois 61801. (217) 333-1369. Also available online.

Environmental Periodicals Bibliography. Environmental Studies Institute, International Academy at Santa Barbara, 800 Garden St., Suite D, Santa Barbara, California 93101. (805) 965-5010. Also available online.

General Science Index. H. W. Wilson Co., 950 University Ave., Bronx, New York 10452. 1978-. Monthly, also issued in annual cumulation. Cumulative subject index to English language periodicals in the subject fields of astronomy, botany, chemistry, earth science, environment and conservation, food and nutrition, genetics, mathematics, medicine and health, microbiology, oceanography, physics, physiology and zoology.

Science Citation Index. Institute for Scientific Information, 3501 Market St., Philadelphia, Pennsylvania 19104. 1961-.

BIBLIOGRAPHIES

EPA Publications Bibliography. U.S. Environmental Protection Agency, Library Systems Branch, 401 M St., SW, Washington, District of Columbia 20460. (202) 260-2090. Quarterly.

ENCYCLOPEDIAS AND DICTIONARIES

Encyclopedia of Human Biology. Renato Dulbecco, ed. Academic Press, c/o Harcourt Brace Jovanovich Inc., 6277 Sea Harbor Dr., Orlando, Florida 32887. (800) 346-8648. 1991. Eight volumes.

Van Nostrand's Scientific Encyclopedia. Glenn D. Considine, ed. Van Nostrand Reinhold, 115 5th Ave., New York, New York 10003. (212) 254-3232. 1983. Sixth edition. Includes all broad subject areas in science.

ONLINE DATA BASES

BIOSIS Previews. BIOSIS, 2100 Arch St., Philadelphia, Pennsylvania 19103-1399. (215) 587-4800. Largest and most comprehensive database of research in the life sciences. Contains citations for nearly 9000 primary research journals, monographs, reviews, symposia, preliminary reports, semi-popular journals, selected institutional reports, government reports and research communications.

CERCLIS. Chemical Information Systems, Inc., 7215 York Rd., Baltimore, Maryland 21212. (301) 321-8440. Information on hazardous waste disposal sites that have either been listed by the EPA on the National Priority List (NPL) or nominated for consideration for the NPL.

Chemical Abstracts-CA. Chemical Abstracts Service, 2540 Olentangy River Rd., P.O. Box 3012, Columbus, Ohio 43210. (800) 848-6533 or (614) 421-3600. Information sources include 9000 journals, patents from 27 countries, two industrial property organizations, new books, conference proceedings, and government research reports.

Enviro/Energyline Abstracts Plus. R. R. Bowker Co., 121 Chanlon Rd., New Providence, New Jersey 07974. (908) 464-6800.

Environmental Periodicals Bibliography. National Information Services Corp., Ste. 6, Wyman Towers, 3100 St. Paul St., Baltimore, Maryland 21218. (410)243-0797. Online version of abstract of same name.

Smoking and Health. U.S. Department of Health & Human Services. Center for Disease Control, Center for Chronic Disease Prevention & Health Promotion, Office on Smoking and Health, Technical Information Center, Park Building, Rm. 1-16, 5600 Fishers Lane, Rockville, Maryland 20857. (301) 443-1690.

Smoking in the Workplace: 1987 Update. Society for Human Resource Management, 606 N. Washington St., Alexandria, Virginia 22314. (703) 548-3440.

NITRIC OXIDE

ABSTRACTING AND INDEXING SERVICES

Biological Abstracts. BIOSIS, 2100 Arch St., Philadelphia, Pennsylvania 19103-1399. (215) 587-4800. 1927-.

Chemical Abstracts. Chemical Abstracts Service, 2540 Olentangy River Rd., PO Box 3012, Columbus, Ohio 43210. (800) 848-6533. 1907-.

Environment Abstracts. Bowker A & I Publishing, 121 Chanlon Rd., New Providence, New Jersey 07974. (908) 464-6800. 1974-.

Environment Index. Environment Information Center, Index Research Department, 124 E. 39th St., New York, New York 10016. 1971-. Annual.

Environmental Information Connection–EIC. Planning Information Program, Dept. of Urban and Regional Planning, University of Illinois, 1003 West Nevada, Urbana, Illinois 61801. (217) 333-1369. Also available online.

Environmental Periodicals Bibliography. Environmental Studies Institute, International Academy at Santa Barbara, 800 Garden St., Suite D, Santa Barbara, California 93101. (805) 965-5010. Also available online.

General Science Index. H. W. Wilson Co., 950 University Ave., Bronx, New York 10452. 1978-. Monthly, also issued in annual cumulation. Cumulative subject index to English language periodicals in the subject fields of astronomy, botany, chemistry, earth science, environment and conservation, food and nutrition, genetics, mathematics, medicine and health, microbiology, oceanography, physics, physiology and zoology.

Science Citation Index. Institute for Scientific Information, 3501 Market St., Philadelphia, Pennsylvania 19104. 1961-.

BIBLIOGRAPHIES

EPA Publications Bibliography. U.S. Environmental Protection Agency, Library Systems Branch, 401 M St., SW, Washington, District of Columbia 20460. (202) 260-2090. Quarterly.

GENERAL WORKS

Support Senate NOx Ozone Non-Attainment Provision: White Paper. American Gas Association, 1515 Wilson Blvd., Arlington, Virginia 22209. 1990. Covers environmental aspects of the gas industry, nitric oxide, and ozone layer depletion-law and legislation.

ONLINE DATA BASES

BIOSIS Previews. BIOSIS, 2100 Arch St., Philadelphia, Pennsylvania 19103-1399. (215) 587-4800. Largest and most comprehensive database of research in the life sciences. Contains citations for nearly 9000 primary research journals, monographs, reviews, symposia, preliminary reports, semi-popular journals, selected institutional reports, government reports and research communications.

CERCLIS. Chemical Information Systems, Inc., 7215 York Rd., Baltimore, Maryland 21212. (301) 321-8440. Information on hazardous waste disposal sites that have

either been listed by the EPA on the National Priority List (NPL) or nominated for consideration for the NPL.

Chemical Abstracts-CA. Chemical Abstracts Service, 2540 Olentangy River Rd., P.O. Box 3012, Columbus, Ohio 43210. (800) 848-6533 or (614) 421-3600. Information sources include 9000 journals, patents from 27 countries, two industrial property organizations, new books, conference proceedings, and government research reports.

Enviro/Energyline Abstracts Plus. R. R. Bowker Co., 121 Chanlon Rd., New Providence, New Jersey 07974. (908) 464-6800.

Environmental Periodicals Bibliography. National Information Services Corp., Ste. 6, Wyman Towers, 3100 St. Paul St., Baltimore, Maryland 21218. (410)243-0797. Online version of abstract of same name.

TRADE ASSOCIATIONS AND PROFESSIONAL SOCIETIES

American Chemical Society. 1155 16th St., N.W., Washington, District of Columbia 20036. (202) 872-4600.

NITRIFICATION

ABSTRACTING AND INDEXING SERVICES

Biological Abstracts. BIOSIS, 2100 Arch St., Philadelphia, Pennsylvania 19103-1399. (215) 587-4800. 1927-.

Chemical Abstracts. Chemical Abstracts Service, 2540 Olentangy River Rd., PO Box 3012, Columbus, Ohio 43210. (800) 848-6533. 1907-.

Ecology Abstracts. Cambridge Scientific Abstracts, 5161 River Rd., Bethesda, Maryland 20816. (301) 961-6750. Monthly.

Environment Abstracts. Bowker A & I Publishing, 121 Chanlon Rd., New Providence, New Jersey 07974. (908) 464-6800. 1974-.

Environment Index. Environment Information Center, Index Research Department, 124 E. 39th St., New York, New York 10016. 1971-. Annual.

Environmental Information Connection–EIC. Planning Information Program, Dept. of Urban and Regional Planning, University of Illinois, 1003 West Nevada, Urbana, Illinois 61801. (217) 333-1369. Also available online.

Environmental Periodicals Bibliography. Environmental Studies Institute, International Academy at Santa Barbara, 800 Garden St., Suite D, Santa Barbara, California 93101. (805) 965-5010. Also available online.

General Science Index. H. W. Wilson Co., 950 University Ave., Bronx, New York 10452. 1978-. Monthly, also issued in annual cumulation. Cumulative subject index to English language periodicals in the subject fields of astronomy, botany, chemistry, earth science, environment and conservation, food and nutrition, genetics, mathematics, medicine and health, microbiology, oceanography, physics, physiology and zoology.

Pollution Abstracts. Cambridge Scientific Abstracts, 5161 River Rd., Bethesda, Maryland 20816. (301) 961-6750. Six/year. Indexes worldwide technical literature on environmental pollution. Covers air pollution, marine and

freshwater pollution, sewage and wastewater treatment, waste management, toxicology and health, noise pollution, radiation, land pollution, and environmental policies, programs, legislation, and education. Also available online.

Science Citation Index. Institute for Scientific Information, 3501 Market St., Philadelphia, Pennsylvania 19104. 1961-.

BIBLIOGRAPHIES

EPA Publications Bibliography. U.S. Environmental Protection Agency, Library Systems Branch, 401 M St., SW, Washington, District of Columbia 20460. (202) 260-2090. Quarterly.

ENCYCLOPEDIAS AND DICTIONARIES

Cambridge Dictionary of Biology. Peter M. B. Walker. Cambridge University Press, 40 W. 20th St., New York, New York 10011. (212) 924-3900 or (800) 227-0247. 1989. Includes 10,000 terms in zoology, botany, biochemistry, molecular biology and genetics. Previously published under the title Chambers Biology Dictionary.

A Concise Dictionary of Biology. Elizabeth Martin, ed. Oxford University Press, 200 Madison Ave., New York, New York 10016. (212) 679-7300 or (800) 334-4249. 1990. New edition. Derived from the Concise Science Dictionary, published in 1984.

Van Nostrand's Scientific Encyclopedia. Glenn D. Considine, ed. Van Nostrand Reinhold, 115 5th Ave., New York, New York 10003. (212) 254-3232. 1983. Sixth edition. Includes all broad subject areas in science.

GENERAL WORKS

Denitrification, Nitrification, and Atmospheric Nitrous Oxide. C.C. Delwiche. John Wiley & Sons, Inc., 605 3rd Ave., New York, New York 10158-0012. (212) 850-6000. 1981. Covers nitrification, nitrogen cycle, and nitrous oxide.

Nitrification Inhibition Biokinetics. R.D. Neufeld. U.S. Environmental Protection Agency, Industrial Environmental Research Laboratory, MD 75, Research Triangle Park, North Carolina 27711. 1984. Water purification by biological treatment.

ONLINE DATA BASES

BIOSIS Previews. BIOSIS, 2100 Arch St., Philadelphia, Pennsylvania 19103-1399. (215) 587-4800. Largest and most comprehensive database of research in the life sciences. Contains citations for nearly 9000 primary research journals, monographs, reviews, symposia, preliminary reports, semi-popular journals, selected institutional reports, government reports and research communications.

Chemical Abstracts-CA. Chemical Abstracts Service, 2540 Olentangy River Rd., P.O. Box 3012, Columbus, Ohio 43210. (800) 848-6533 or (614) 421-3600. Information sources include 9000 journals, patents from 27 countries, two industrial property organizations, new books, conference proceedings, and government research reports.

Enviro/Energyline Abstracts Plus. R. R. Bowker Co., 121 Chanlon Rd., New Providence, New Jersey 07974. (908) 464-6800.

Environmental Periodicals Bibliography. National Information Services Corp., Ste. 6, Wyman Towers, 3100 St. Paul St., Baltimore, Maryland 21218. (410)243-0797. Online version of abstract of same name.

NITRITES

See also: CARCINOGENS

ABSTRACTING AND INDEXING SERVICES

Biological and Agricultural Index. H.W. Wilson Co., 950 University Ave., Bronx, New York 10452. (800) 367-6770. 1916-. Monthly.

Environment Abstracts. Bowker A & I Publishing, 121 Chanlon Rd., New Providence, New Jersey 07974. (908) 464-6800. 1974-.

Environment Index. Environment Information Center, Index Research Department, 124 E. 39th St., New York, New York 10016. 1971-. Annual.

Environmental Information Connection–EIC. Planning Information Program, Dept. of Urban and Regional Planning, University of Illinois, 1003 West Nevada, Urbana, Illinois 61801. (217) 333-1369. Also available online.

Environmental Periodicals Bibliography. Environmental Studies Institute, International Academy at Santa Barbara, 800 Garden St., Suite D, Santa Barbara, California 93101. (805) 965-5010. Also available online.

Pollution Abstracts. Cambridge Scientific Abstracts, 5161 River Rd., Bethesda, Maryland 20816. (301) 961-6750. Six/year. Indexes worldwide technical literature on environmental pollution. Covers air pollution, marine and freshwater pollution, sewage and wastewater treatment, waste management, toxicology and health, noise pollution, radiation, land pollution, and environmental policies, programs, legislation, and education. Also available online.

Science Citation Index. Institute for Scientific Information, 3501 Market St., Philadelphia, Pennsylvania 19104. 1961-.

BIBLIOGRAPHIES

Death Rush: Poppers & AIDS: With Annotated Bibliography. John Lauritsen. Pagan Press, 26 St. Mark's Pl., New York, New York 10003. (212) 674-3321. 1986. Chemically induced substance abuse including nitrites.

EPA Publications Bibliography. U.S. Environmental Protection Agency, Library Systems Branch, 401 M St., SW, Washington, District of Columbia 20460. (202) 260-2090. Quarterly.

GENERAL WORKS

Health Hazards of Nitrite Inhalants. Harry W. Haverkos and John A. Dougherty. National Institute on Drug Abuse, 5600 Fishers Ln., Rm. 10-15, Rockville, Maryland 20857. (301) 443-6487. 1988. Toxicology of nitrites.

Nitrate and Drinking Water. European Chemical Industry Ecology & Toxicology Centre, Brussels, Belgium 1988. Physiological effect of nitrites and water nitrogen content.

Nitrate and Nitrite in Vegetables. W. J. Corre. Centre for Agricultural Publishing and Documentation, Wageningen, Netherlands 1979. Toxicology and physiological effect of nitrates, minerals in the body and minerals in animal nutrition.

Selected Abstracts on the Role of Dietary Nitrate and Nitrite in Human Carcinogenesis. Steven R. Tannenbaum. National Technical Information Service, 5285 Port Royal Rd., Springfield, Virginia 22161. (703) 487-4650. 1982.

ONLINE DATA BASES

Enviro/Energyline Abstracts Plus. R. R. Bowker Co., 121 Chanlon Rd., New Providence, New Jersey 07974. (908) 464-6800.

Environmental Periodicals Bibliography. National Information Services Corp., Ste. 6, Wyman Towers, 3100 St. Paul St., Baltimore, Maryland 21218. (410)243-0797. Online version of abstract of same name.

NITROGEN

ABSTRACTING AND INDEXING SERVICES

Applied Science and Technology Index. H.W. Wilson Co., 950 University Ave., Bronx, New York 10452. (800) 367-6770. Formerly Industrial Arts Index.

Biological and Agricultural Index. H.W. Wilson Co., 950 University Ave., Bronx, New York 10452. (800) 367-6770. 1916-. Monthly.

Biotechnology Research Abstracts. Cambridge Scientific Abstracts, 5161 River Rd., Bethesda, Maryland 20816. (301) 961-6750. Monthly. Includes such broad areas as genetic intervention, biochemical genetics, and microbiological techniques.

Chemical Abstracts. Chemical Abstracts Service, 2540 Olentangy River Rd., PO Box 3012, Columbus, Ohio 43210. (800) 848-6533. 1907-.

Environment Abstracts. Bowker A & I Publishing, 121 Chanlon Rd., New Providence, New Jersey 07974. (908) 464-6800. 1974-.

Environment Index. Environment Information Center, Index Research Department, 124 E. 39th St., New York, New York 10016. 1971-. Annual.

Environmental Information Connection–EIC. Planning Information Program, Dept. of Urban and Regional Planning, University of Illinois, 1003 West Nevada, Urbana, Illinois 61801. (217) 333-1369. Also available online.

Environmental Periodicals Bibliography. Environmental Studies Institute, International Academy at Santa Barbara, 800 Garden St., Suite D, Santa Barbara, California 93101. (805) 965-5010. Also available online.

Food Science and Technology Abstracts. International Food Information Service, c/o National Food Laborato-

ry, 6363 Clark Ave., Dublin, California 94568. (800) 336-3782. 1969-.

General Science Index. H. W. Wilson Co., 950 University Ave., Bronx, New York 10452. 1978-. Monthly, also issued in annual cumulation. Cumulative subject index to English language periodicals in the subject fields of astronomy, botany, chemistry, earth science, environment and conservation, food and nutrition, genetics, mathematics, medicine and health, microbiology, oceanography, physics, physiology and zoology.

Physics Briefs. Physikalische Berichte. Physik Verlag, Pappapelallee 3, Postfach 101161, Weinheim, Germany D-6940. 1979-. Semimonthly. In English. Volumes for 1979- issued by the Deutsche Physikalische Gesellschaft and the Fachinformationszentrum Energie Physik, Mathematik in cooperation with the American Institute of Physics.

Pollution Abstracts. Cambridge Scientific Abstracts, 5161 River Rd., Bethesda, Maryland 20816. (301) 961-6750. Six/year. Indexes worldwide technical literature on environmental pollution. Covers air pollution, marine and freshwater pollution, sewage and wastewater treatment, waste management, toxicology and health, noise pollution, radiation, land pollution, and environmental policies, programs, legislation, and education. Also available online.

Science Citation Index. Institute for Scientific Information, 3501 Market St., Philadelphia, Pennsylvania 19104. 1961-.

BIBLIOGRAPHIES

Current Contents. Agriculture, Biology and Environmental Sciences. Institute for Scientific Information, 3501 Market St., Philadelphia, Pennsylvania 19104. (800) 523-1857. 1973-. Previous title: Current Contents. Agricultural, Food & Veterinary Sciences. Gives the table of contents of periodicals in the fields of agriculture, biology, environmental and related areas.

EPA Publications Bibliography. U.S. Environmental Protection Agency, Library Systems Branch, 401 M St., SW, Washington, District of Columbia 20460. (202) 260-2090. Quarterly.

DIRECTORIES

Gale Environmental Sourcebook. Karen Hill. Gale Research Co., 835 Penobscot Bldg., Detroit, Michigan 48226-4094. (313) 961-2242. Contacts, information sources, or general information on environmental topics.

ENCYCLOPEDIAS AND DICTIONARIES

Encyclopedia of Physical Science and Technology. Robert A. Meyers, ed. Academic Press, c/o Harcourt Brace Jovanovich Inc., 6277 Sea Harbor Dr., Orlando, Florida 32887. (800) 346-8648. Dictionary of engineering, technology and physical sciences.

Encyclopedia of Physics. Rita G. Lerner and George L. Trigg. VCH Publishers, 303 NW 12th Ave., Deerfield Beach, Florida 33442-1788. (305) 428-5566. 1991. Second edition.

Life Sciences on File. Diagram Group. Facts on File, Inc., 460 Park Ave. S., New York, New York 10016. (212) 683-2244. 1986. Encyclopedia of pictorial collection in life sciences. Deals with all major topics in life sciences including ecology.

Van Nostrand's Scientific Encyclopedia. Glenn D. Considine, ed. Van Nostrand Reinhold, 115 5th Ave., New York, New York 10003. (212) 254-3232. 1983. Sixth edition. Includes all broad subject areas in science.

GENERAL WORKS

Carbon, Nitrogen, and Sulfur Pollutants and Their Determination in Air and Water. Jerome C. Greyson. Marcel Dekker, Inc., 270 Madison Ave., New York, New York 10016. (212) 696-9000; (800) 228-1160. 1990. Measurement of air and water pollution and environmental aspects of sulphur and nitrogens.

Carbon Nitrogen Sulfur: Human Interference in Grand Biospheric Cycles. Vaclay Smil. Plenum Press, 233 Spring St., New York, New York 10013-1578. (212) 620-8000. 1985.

Ecology of Arable Land. Olof Andersen, et al., eds. Munksgaard International, PO Box 2148, Copenhagen K, Denmark DK-1016. 1990. Investigates and synthesizes the contributions of the soil organisms and nitrogen and carbon circulation in four contrasting cropping systems. Also looks into future challenges of agroecosystem research.

Nitrogen in the Environment. Donald R. Nielsen. Academic Press, c/o Harcourt Brace Jovanovich Inc., 6277 Sea Harbor Dr., Orlando, Florida 32887. (800) 346-8648. 1978. Nitrogen behavior in field soil and soil plant nitrogen relationship.

Nitrogen, Public Health, and the Environment: Some Tools for Critical Thought. John H. Timothy Winneberger. Ann Arbor Science, 230 Collingwood, Ann Arbor, Michigan 48106. 1982. Environmental aspects of nitrogen removal in sewage.

ONLINE DATA BASES

CAS Source Index–CASSI. Chemical Abstracts Service, 2540 Olentangy River Rd., P.O. Box 3012, Columbus, Ohio 43210. (800) 848-6533 or (614) 421-3600. A listing of bibliographic and library holdings information for scientific and technical primary literature relevant to the chemical sciences.

Chemical Abstracts-CA. Chemical Abstracts Service, 2540 Olentangy River Rd., P.O. Box 3012, Columbus, Ohio 43210. (800) 848-6533 or (614) 421-3600. Information sources include 9000 journals, patents from 27 countries, two industrial property organizations, new books, conference proceedings, and government research reports.

Enviro/Energyline Abstracts Plus. R. R. Bowker Co., 121 Chanlon Rd., New Providence, New Jersey 07974. (908) 464-6800.

Environmental Periodicals Bibliography. National Information Services Corp., Ste. 6, Wyman Towers, 3100 St. Paul St., Baltimore, Maryland 21218. (410)243-0797. Online version of abstract of same name.

NBSFLUIDS. National Institute of Standards & Technology, Office of Standard Reference Data, A323 Physics Building, Gaithersburg, Maryland 20899. (301) 975-2208.

RESEARCH CENTERS AND INSTITUTES

University of New Hampshire, Complex Systems Research Center. Science and Engineering Research Building, Durham, New Hampshire 03824. (603) 862-1792.

STATISTICS SOURCES

Environmental Data Compendium. OECD Publications and Information Center, 2001 L St., N.W., Suite 700, Washington, District of Columbia 20036. (202) 785-6323. 1989.

Environmental Indicators. OECD Publications and Information Center, 2001 L St., N.W., Suite 700, Washington, District of Columbia 20036. (202) 785-6323. 1991.

Environmental Quality. Council on Environmental Quality. U.S. G.P.O., Washington, District of Columbia 20401. (202) 512-0000. Annual.

The State of the Environment. OECD Publications and Information Center, 2001 L St., N.W., Suite 700, Washington, District of Columbia 20036. (202) 785-6323. 1991.

TRADE ASSOCIATIONS AND PROFESSIONAL SOCIETIES

American Chemical Society. 1155 16th St., N.W., Washington, District of Columbia 20036. (202) 872-4600.

American Institute of Biological Sciences. 730 11th St., N.W., Washington, District of Columbia 20001-4521. (202) 628-1500.

NITROGEN FIXATION

ABSTRACTING AND INDEXING SERVICES

Biological Abstracts. BIOSIS, 2100 Arch St., Philadelphia, Pennsylvania 19103-1399. (215) 587-4800. 1927-.

Biological and Agricultural Index. H.W. Wilson Co., 950 University Ave., Bronx, New York 10452. (800) 367-6770. 1916-. Monthly.

Biotechnology Research Abstracts. Cambridge Scientific Abstracts, 5161 River Rd., Bethesda, Maryland 20816. (301) 961-6750. Monthly. Includes such broad areas as genetic intervention, biochemical genetics, and microbiological techniques.

Chemical Abstracts. Chemical Abstracts Service, 2540 Olentangy River Rd., PO Box 3012, Columbus, Ohio 43210. (800) 848-6533. 1907-.

Crop Physiology Abstracts. C. A. B. International, 845 North Park Ave., Tucson, Arizona 85719. (602) 621-7897 or (800) 528-4841. 1975-. Monthly. Abstracts focus on the physiology of all higher plants of economic importance. Aspects include germination, reproductive development, nitrogen fixation, metabolic inhibitors, salinity, radiobiology, enzymes, membranes and other related areas.

Ecological Abstracts. Geo Abstracts Ltd. Elsevier Applied Science, Crown House, Linton Rd., Barking, England IG 11 8JU. 1974-. Derived from over 600 leading ecological and environmental journals, plus books, conference proceedings, reports and theses.

Ecology Abstracts. Cambridge Scientific Abstracts, 5161 River Rd., Bethesda, Maryland 20816. (301) 961-6750. Monthly.

Environment Abstracts. Bowker A & I Publishing, 121 Chanlon Rd., New Providence, New Jersey 07974. (908) 464-6800. 1974-.

Environment Index. Environment Information Center, Index Research Department, 124 E. 39th St., New York, New York 10016. 1971-. Annual.

Environmental Information Connection–EIC. Planning Information Program, Dept. of Urban and Regional Planning, University of Illinois, 1003 West Nevada, Urbana, Illinois 61801. (217) 333-1369. Also available online.

Environmental Periodicals Bibliography. Environmental Studies Institute, International Academy at Santa Barbara, 800 Garden St., Suite D, Santa Barbara, California 93101. (805) 965-5010. Also available online.

Pollution Abstracts. Cambridge Scientific Abstracts, 5161 River Rd., Bethesda, Maryland 20816. (301) 961-6750. Six/year. Indexes worldwide technical literature on environmental pollution. Covers air pollution, marine and freshwater pollution, sewage and wastewater treatment, waste management, toxicology and health, noise pollution, radiation, land pollution, and environmental policies, programs, legislation, and education. Also available online.

Science Citation Index. Institute for Scientific Information, 3501 Market St., Philadelphia, Pennsylvania 19104. 1961-.

BIBLIOGRAPHIES

Current Contents. Agriculture, Biology and Environmental Sciences. Institute for Scientific Information, 3501 Market St., Philadelphia, Pennsylvania 19104. (800) 523-1857. 1973-. Previous title: Current Contents. Agricultural, Food & Veterinary Sciences. Gives the table of contents of periodicals in the fields of agriculture, biology, environmental and related areas.

EPA Publications Bibliography. U.S. Environmental Protection Agency, Library Systems Branch, 401 M St., SW, Washington, District of Columbia 20460. (202) 260-2090. Quarterly.

ENCYCLOPEDIAS AND DICTIONARIES

Cambridge Dictionary of Biology. Peter M. B. Walker. Cambridge University Press, 40 W. 20th St., New York, New York 10011. (212) 924-3900 or (800) 227-0247. 1989. Includes 10,000 terms in zoology, botany, biochemistry, molecular biology and genetics. Previously published under the title Chambers Biology Dictionary.

Cambridge Encyclopedia of Life Sciences. A. E. Friday and David S. Ingram. Cambridge University Press, 40 W 20th St., New York, New York 10011. (212) 924-3900 or (800) 227-0247. 1985. Includes all topics under biology and ecology.

A Concise Dictionary of Biology. Elizabeth Martin, ed. Oxford University Press, 200 Madison Ave., New York, New York 10016. (212) 679-7300 or (800) 334-4249. 1990. New edition. Derived from the Concise Science Dictionary, published in 1984.

The Encyclopedia of Soil Science. Rhodes W. Fairbridge. Academic Press, c/o Harcourt Brace Jovanovich Inc., 6277 Sea Harbor Dr., Orlando, Florida 32887. (800) 346-8648. 1979-. Includes soil physics, soil chemistry, soil biology, soil fertility and plant nutrition, soil genesis, classification and cartography.

McGraw-Hill Encyclopedia of Science and Technology. McGraw-Hill, 1221 Avenue of the Americas, New York, New York 10020. (212) 512-2000 or (800) 262-4729. 1992. Seventh edition. Issued in multiple volumes including index. Includes all science and technology broad subject areas.

Van Nostrand's Scientific Encyclopedia. Glenn D. Considine, ed. Van Nostrand Reinhold, 115 5th Ave., New York, New York 10003. (212) 254-3232. 1983. Sixth edition. Includes all broad subject areas in science.

GENERAL WORKS

Environmental Role of Nitrogen-Fixing Blue-Green Algae and Asymbiotic Bacteria. U. Granhall. Swedish Natural Science Research Council, P.O. Box 6711, Stockholm, Sweden S-113 85. 08-15-1580. 1978. Deals with nitrogen-fixing microorganisms, nitrogen-fixing algae and cyanobacteria.

Magill's Survey of Science. Life Science Series. Frank N. Magill, ed. Salem Press, PO Box 50062, Pasadena, California 91105. 1991. Six volumes. Contents: v.1. A-Central and peripheral nervous system functions; v.2. Central metabolism regulation - eukaryotic transcriptional control; v.3. Positive and negative eukaryotic transcriptional control - mammalian hormones; v.4. Hormones and behavior - muscular contraction; v.5. Muscular contraction and relaxation - sexual reproduction in plants; v.6. Reproductive behavior and mating - X inactivation and the Lyon hypothesis.

New Trends in the Chemistry of Nitrogen Fixation. J. Chatt. Academic Press, c/o Harcourt Brace Jovanovich Inc., 6277 Sea Harbor Dr., Orlando, Florida 32887. (800) 346-8648. 1980.

Nitrogen Fixation. W. J. Broughton. Oxford University Press, 200 Madison Ave., New York, New York 10016. (212) 679-7300. 1981. Covers ecology, rhizobium, legumes, and molecular biology.

Nutrient Cycling in Terrestrial Ecosystems Field Methods. A. F. Harrison, et al. Elsevier Science Publishing Co., 655 Avenue of the Americas, New York, New York 10010. (212) 984-5800. 1990. Describes a wide range of methods for the estimation of nutrient fluxes. The book is divided into sections dealing with inputs, turnover, losses and plant uptake processes.

ONLINE DATA BASES

BIOSIS Previews. BIOSIS, 2100 Arch St., Philadelphia, Pennsylvania 19103-1399. (215) 587-4800. Largest and most comprehensive database of research in the life sciences. Contains citations for nearly 9000 primary research journals, monographs, reviews, symposia, preliminary reports, semi-popular journals, selected institutional reports, government reports and research communications.

Chemical Abstracts-CA. Chemical Abstracts Service, 2540 Olentangy River Rd., P.O. Box 3012, Columbus, Ohio 43210. (800) 848-6533 or (614) 421-3600. Information sources include 9000 journals, patents from 27 countries, two industrial property organizations, new books, conference proceedings, and government research reports.

Enviro/Energyline Abstracts Plus. R. R. Bowker Co., 121 Chanlon Rd., New Providence, New Jersey 07974. (908) 464-6800.

Environmental Periodicals Bibliography. National Information Services Corp., Ste. 6, Wyman Towers, 3100 St. Paul St., Baltimore, Maryland 21218. (410)243-0797. Online version of abstract of same name.

PERIODICALS AND NEWSLETTERS

Soil Biology and Biochemistry. Pergamon Microforms International, Inc., Fairview Park, Elmsford, New York 10523. (914) 592-7720. Eight times a year. Soil biology, soil biochemistry, nitrogen fixation, nitrogenase activity, sampling microorganisms in soil, soil compaction, and nutrient release in soils.

RESEARCH CENTERS AND INSTITUTES

Oregon State University, Laboratory for Nitrogen Fixation Research. Corvallis, Oregon 97331. (503) 737-4214.

University of Wisconsin-Madison, Center for the Study of Nitrogen Fixation. 420 Henry Mall, Department of Biochemistry, Madison, Wisconsin 53706. (608) 262-6859.

Virginia Polytechnic Institute and State University, Anaerobe Laboratory. Department of Anaerobic Microbiology, Blacksburg, Virginia 24061-0305. (703) 231-6935.

TRADE ASSOCIATIONS AND PROFESSIONAL SOCIETIES

American Institute of Biological Sciences. 730 11th St., N.W., Washington, District of Columbia 20001-4521. (202) 628-1500.

Nitrogen Fixing Tree Association. P.O. Box 680, 41-698 Ahiki St., Waimanalo, Hawaii 96795. (808) 259-8555.

NITROGEN SUPERSATURATION

See also: TOXICITY

GENERAL WORKS

Keeping Options Alive: The Scientific Basis for Conserving Biodiversity. Walter V. C. Reid and Kenton R. Miller. World Resources Institute, 1709 New York Ave. N.W., Washington, District of Columbia 20006. (800) 822-0504. 1989. Examines the fundamental questions and recommends policies based on the best available scientific information for conserving biodiversity.

PERIODICALS AND NEWSLETTERS

Conservation Voter. California League of Conservation Voters, 965 Mission St. #705, San Francisco, California 94103-2928. (415) 896-5330. 1974-. Quarterly. Environmental political affairs analysis.

Environmental Defense Fund Letter. Environmental Defense Fund, 257 Park Avenue South, New York, New York 10010. (212) 505-2100. 1971-. Bimonthly. Environmental issues of concern.

TRADE ASSOCIATIONS AND PROFESSIONAL SOCIETIES

Basic Foundation. PO Box 47012, St. Petersburg, Florida 33743. (813) 526-9562. Non-profit corporation that was founded to augment efforts at balancing population growth with natural resources.

Environmental Defense Fund. 257 Park Ave., S., New York, New York 10010. (212) 505-2100. Non-profit organization that was established more than 20 years ago. Its goals are to protect the earth's environment by providing lasting solutions to global environmental problems.

NITROGENOUS WASTES

See: FACTORY AND TRADE WASTES

NITROSAMINES

ABSTRACTING AND INDEXING SERVICES

Chemical Abstracts. Chemical Abstracts Service, 2540 Olentangy River Rd., PO Box 3012, Columbus, Ohio 43210. (800) 848-6533. 1907-.

Environment Abstracts. Bowker A & I Publishing, 121 Chanlon Rd., New Providence, New Jersey 07974. (908) 464-6800. 1974-.

Environment Index. Environment Information Center, Index Research Department, 124 E. 39th St., New York, New York 10016. 1971-. Annual.

Environmental Information Connection–EIC. Planning Information Program, Dept. of Urban and Regional Planning, University of Illinois, 1003 West Nevada, Urbana, Illinois 61801. (217) 333-1369. Also available online.

Environmental Periodicals Bibliography. Environmental Studies Institute, International Academy at Santa Barbara, 800 Garden St., Suite D, Santa Barbara, California 93101. (805) 965-5010. Also available online.

Science Citation Index. Institute for Scientific Information, 3501 Market St., Philadelphia, Pennsylvania 19104. 1961-.

BIBLIOGRAPHIES

EPA Publications Bibliography. U.S. Environmental Protection Agency, Library Systems Branch, 401 M St., SW, Washington, District of Columbia 20460. (202) 260-2090. Quarterly.

ENCYCLOPEDIAS AND DICTIONARIES

Encyclopedia of Human Biology. Renato Dulbecco, ed. Academic Press, c/o Harcourt Brace Jovanovich Inc., 6277 Sea Harbor Dr., Orlando, Florida 32887. (800) 346-8648. 1991. Eight volumes.

GENERAL WORKS

Nitrosamines and Human Cancer. Peter N. Magee. Cold Spring Harbor Laboratory Press, PO Box 100, Cold Spring Harbor, New York 11724. (800) 843-4388. 1982. Cover carcinogenesis, nitrosamines, neoplasms, and drug dose response relationships.

HANDBOOKS AND MANUALS

FDA Food Additives Analytical Manual. C. Warner, et al., eds. Association of Official Analytical Chemists, 2200 Wilson Blvd., Suite 400-P, Arlington, Virginia 22201-3301. (703) 522-3032. 1983-1987. 2 vols. Provides methodology for determining compliance with food additive regulations. Contains analytical methods that have been evaluated by the FDA or found to operate satisfactorily in at least two laboratories.

ONLINE DATA BASES

CAS Source Index–CASSI. Chemical Abstracts Service, 2540 Olentangy River Rd., P.O. Box 3012, Columbus, Ohio 43210. (800) 848-6533 or (614) 421-3600. A listing of bibliographic and library holdings information for scientific and technical primary literature relevant to the chemical sciences.

Chemical Abstracts-CA. Chemical Abstracts Service, 2540 Olentangy River Rd., P.O. Box 3012, Columbus, Ohio 43210. (800) 848-6533 or (614) 421-3600. Information sources include 9000 journals, patents from 27 countries, two industrial property organizations, new books, conference proceedings, and government research reports.

Enviro/Energyline Abstracts Plus. R. R. Bowker Co., 121 Chanlon Rd., New Providence, New Jersey 07974. (908) 464-6800.

Environmental Periodicals Bibliography. National Information Services Corp., Ste. 6, Wyman Towers, 3100 St. Paul St., Baltimore, Maryland 21218. (410)243-0797. Online version of abstract of same name.

TRADE ASSOCIATIONS AND PROFESSIONAL SOCIETIES

American Chemical Society. 1155 16th St., N.W., Washington, District of Columbia 20036. (202) 872-4600.

NITROUS OXIDE

ABSTRACTING AND INDEXING SERVICES

Chemical Abstracts. Chemical Abstracts Service, 2540 Olentangy River Rd., PO Box 3012, Columbus, Ohio 43210. (800) 848-6533. 1907-.

Environment Abstracts. Bowker A & I Publishing, 121 Chanlon Rd., New Providence, New Jersey 07974. (908) 464-6800. 1974-.

Environment Index. Environment Information Center, Index Research Department, 124 E. 39th St., New York, New York 10016. 1971-. Annual.

Environmental Information Connection–EIC. Planning Information Program, Dept. of Urban and Regional Planning, University of Illinois, 1003 West Nevada,

Urbana, Illinois 61801. (217) 333-1369. Also available online.

Environmental Periodicals Bibliography. Environmental Studies Institute, International Academy at Santa Barbara, 800 Garden St., Suite D, Santa Barbara, California 93101. (805) 965-5010. Also available online.

General Science Index. H. W. Wilson Co., 950 University Ave., Bronx, New York 10452. 1978-. Monthly, also issued in annual cumulation. Cumulative subject index to English language periodicals in the subject fields of astronomy, botany, chemistry, earth science, environment and conservation, food and nutrition, genetics, mathematics, medicine and health, microbiology, oceanography, physics, physiology and zoology.

Pollution Abstracts. Cambridge Scientific Abstracts, 5161 River Rd., Bethesda, Maryland 20816. (301) 961-6750. Six/year. Indexes worldwide technical literature on environmental pollution. Covers air pollution, marine and freshwater pollution, sewage and wastewater treatment, waste management, toxicology and health, noise pollution, radiation, land pollution, and environmental policies, programs, legislation, and education. Also available online.

Science Citation Index. Institute for Scientific Information, 3501 Market St., Philadelphia, Pennsylvania 19104. 1961-.

BIBLIOGRAPHIES

EPA Publications Bibliography. U.S. Environmental Protection Agency, Library Systems Branch, 401 M St., SW, Washington, District of Columbia 20460. (202) 260-2090. Quarterly.

GENERAL WORKS

Nitrous Oxide/N20. Edmond I. Eger. Elsevier Science Publishing Co., 655 Avenue of the Americas, New York, New York 10010. (212) 984-5800. 1985.

Under the Influence: A History of Nitrous Oxide and Oxygen Anaesthesia. W.D.A. Smith. Wood Library-Museum of Anesthesiology, 515 Busse Hwy., Park Ridge, Illinois 60068. (708) 825-5586. 1982.

ONLINE DATA BASES

Chemical Abstracts-CA. Chemical Abstracts Service, 2540 Olentangy River Rd., P.O. Box 3012, Columbus, Ohio 43210. (800) 848-6533 or (614) 421-3600. Information sources include 9000 journals, patents from 27 countries, two industrial property organizations, new books, conference proceedings, and government research reports.

Enviro/Energyline Abstracts Plus. R. R. Bowker Co., 121 Chanlon Rd., New Providence, New Jersey 07974. (908) 464-6800.

Environmental Periodicals Bibliography. National Information Services Corp., Ste. 6, Wyman Towers, 3100 St. Paul St., Baltimore, Maryland 21218. (410)243-0797. Online version of abstract of same name.

TRADE ASSOCIATIONS AND PROFESSIONAL SOCIETIES

American Chemical Society. 1155 16th St., N.W., Washington, District of Columbia 20036. (202) 872-4600.

NMR

See: NUCLEAR MAGNETIC RESONANCE

NODULES

ABSTRACTING AND INDEXING SERVICES

Biological Abstracts. BIOSIS, 2100 Arch St., Philadelphia, Pennsylvania 19103-1399. (215) 587-4800. 1927-.

Biotechnology Research Abstracts. Cambridge Scientific Abstracts, 5161 River Rd., Bethesda, Maryland 20816. (301) 961-6750. Monthly. Includes such broad areas as genetic intervention, biochemical genetics, and microbiological techniques.

Ecology Abstracts. Cambridge Scientific Abstracts, 5161 River Rd., Bethesda, Maryland 20816. (301) 961-6750. Monthly.

Environment Abstracts. Bowker A & I Publishing, 121 Chanlon Rd., New Providence, New Jersey 07974. (908) 464-6800. 1974-.

Environment Index. Environment Information Center, Index Research Department, 124 E. 39th St., New York, New York 10016. 1971-. Annual.

Environmental Information Connection–EIC. Planning Information Program, Dept. of Urban and Regional Planning, University of Illinois, 1003 West Nevada, Urbana, Illinois 61801. (217) 333-1369. Also available online.

Environmental Periodicals Bibliography. Environmental Studies Institute, International Academy at Santa Barbara, 800 Garden St., Suite D, Santa Barbara, California 93101. (805) 965-5010. Also available online.

General Science Index. H. W. Wilson Co., 950 University Ave., Bronx, New York 10452. 1978-. Monthly, also issued in annual cumulation. Cumulative subject index to English language periodicals in the subject fields of astronomy, botany, chemistry, earth science, environment and conservation, food and nutrition, genetics, mathematics, medicine and health, microbiology, oceanography, physics, physiology and zoology.

Science Citation Index. Institute for Scientific Information, 3501 Market St., Philadelphia, Pennsylvania 19104. 1961-.

BIBLIOGRAPHIES

EPA Publications Bibliography. U.S. Environmental Protection Agency, Library Systems Branch, 401 M St., SW, Washington, District of Columbia 20460. (202) 260-2090. Quarterly.

ENCYCLOPEDIAS AND DICTIONARIES

Van Nostrand's Scientific Encyclopedia. Glenn D. Considine, ed. Van Nostrand Reinhold, 115 5th Ave., New York, New York 10003. (212) 254-3232. 1983. Sixth edition. Includes all broad subject areas in science.

ONLINE DATA BASES

BIOSIS Previews. BIOSIS, 2100 Arch St., Philadelphia, Pennsylvania 19103-1399. (215) 587-4800. Largest and most comprehensive database of research in the life sciences. Contains citations for nearly 9000 primary research journals, monographs, reviews, symposia, preliminary reports, semi-popular journals, selected institutional reports, government reports and research communications.

Enviro/Energyline Abstracts Plus. R. R. Bowker Co., 121 Chanlon Rd., New Providence, New Jersey 07974. (908) 464-6800.

Environmental Periodicals Bibliography. National Information Services Corp., Ste. 6, Wyman Towers, 3100 St. Paul St., Baltimore, Maryland 21218. (410)243-0797. Online version of abstract of same name.

NOISE

ABSTRACTING AND INDEXING SERVICES

Acoustics Abstracts. Multi-Science Publishing Co. Ltd., 107 High St., Brentwood, England CM14 4RX. (0277) 224632. Monthly. Covers the world's major periodical literature, conference proceedings, unpublished reports, and book notices on acoustics.

Applied Science and Technology Index. H.W. Wilson Co., 950 University Ave., Bronx, New York 10452. (800) 367-6770. Formerly Industrial Arts Index.

Biological Abstracts. BIOSIS, 2100 Arch St., Philadelphia, Pennsylvania 19103-1399. (215) 587-4800. 1927-.

Civil Engineering Hydraulic Abstracts. BHRA Fluid Engineering, Air Science Co., PO Box 143, Corning, New York 14830. (607) 962-5591. Monthly. Abstracts of periodicals that publish in the areas of hydraulic engineering and other related topics.

Engineering Index. The Engineering Index Inc., 345 E. 47th St., New York, New York 10017. 1962-.

Environment Abstracts. Bowker A & I Publishing, 121 Chanlon Rd., New Providence, New Jersey 07974. (908) 464-6800. 1974-.

Environment Index. Environment Information Center, Index Research Department, 124 E. 39th St., New York, New York 10016. 1971-. Annual.

Environmental Information Connection–EIC. Planning Information Program, Dept. of Urban and Regional Planning, University of Illinois, 1003 West Nevada, Urbana, Illinois 61801. (217) 333-1369. Also available online.

Environmental Periodicals Bibliography. Environmental Studies Institute, International Academy at Santa Barbara, 800 Garden St., Suite D, Santa Barbara, California 93101. (805) 965-5010. Also available online.

Ergonomics Abstracts. Taylor & Francis, 4 John St., London, England WC1N 2ET. 1990-. Bimonthly. Provides details on recent additions to the international literature on human factors in human-machine systems and physical environmental influences.

General Science Index. H. W. Wilson Co., 950 University Ave., Bronx, New York 10452. 1978-. Monthly, also issued in annual cumulation. Cumulative subject index to English language periodicals in the subject fields of astronomy, botany, chemistry, earth science, environment and conservation, food and nutrition, genetics,

mathematics, medicine and health, microbiology, oceanography, physics, physiology and zoology.

Physics Briefs. Physikalische Berichte. Physik Verlag, Pappapelallee 3, Postfach 101161, Weinheim, Germany D-6940. 1979-. Semimonthly. In English. Volumes for 1979- issued by the Deutsche Physikalische Gesellschaft and the Fachinformationszentrum Energie Physik, Mathematik in cooperation with the American Institute of Physics.

Science Citation Index. Institute for Scientific Information, 3501 Market St., Philadelphia, Pennsylvania 19104. 1961-.

BIBLIOGRAPHIES

EPA Publications Bibliography. U.S. Environmental Protection Agency, Library Systems Branch, 401 M St., SW, Washington, District of Columbia 20460. (202) 260-2090. Quarterly.

DIRECTORIES

Acoustical Society of America–Biennial Membership List. Acoustical Society of America, 500 Sunnyside Blvd., Woodbury, New York 11797. (516) 349-7800.

ENCYCLOPEDIAS AND DICTIONARIES

Encyclopedia of Physical Science and Technology. Robert A. Meyers, ed. Academic Press, c/o Harcourt Brace Jovanovich Inc., 6277 Sea Harbor Dr., Orlando, Florida 32887. (800) 346-8648. Dictionary of engineering, technology and physical sciences.

Encyclopedia of Physics. Rita G. Lerner and George L. Trigg. VCH Publishers, 303 NW 12th Ave., Deerfield Beach, Florida 33442-1788. (305) 428-5566. 1991. Second edition.

Van Nostrand's Scientific Encyclopedia. Glenn D. Considine, ed. Van Nostrand Reinhold, 115 5th Ave., New York, New York 10003. (212) 254-3232. 1983. Sixth edition. Includes all broad subject areas in science.

GENERAL WORKS

Fighting Noise in 1990s. Organisation for Economic Cooperation and Development. OECD Publication and Information Center, 2001 L. St. N.W., Suite 700, Washington, District of Columbia 20036. (202) 785-6323. 1991. Deals with transportation noise pollution. Includes the economic impacts and relevant legislation.

Hearing Conservation Programs: Practical Guidelines for Success. Julia D. Royster and Larry H. Royster. Lewis Publishers, 2000 Corporate Blvd., N.W., Boca Raton, Florida 33431. (407) 994-0555 or (800) 272-7737. 1990. Essentials for creating an effective hearing conservation program, details how to best organize to get the job done, and identifies the specific aspects within each phase of the program that spell the difference between success and failure.

Noise Control in Building Services. Pergamon Microforms International, Inc., Fairview Park, Elmsford, New York 10523. (914) 592-7720. 1988. Soundproofing techniques in buildings.

Sound Analysis and Noise Control. Van Nostrand Reinhold, 115 Fifth Ave., New York, New York 10003. (212)

254-3232. 1990. Discusses the physics of sound, the mechanism of hearing and the application of those principles to specific problems.

HANDBOOKS AND MANUALS

Noise, Buildings, and People. Derek J. Croome. Pergamon Microforms International, Inc., Fairview Park, Elmsford, New York 10523. (914) 592-7720. 1977. Soundproofing techniques in buildings.

Noise Control Manual. David A. Harris. Van Nostrand Reinhold, 115 5th Ave., New York, New York 10003. (212) 254-3232. 1991. Guidelines for problem-solving in the industrial/commercial acoustical environment.

ONLINE DATA BASES

BIOSIS Previews. BIOSIS, 2100 Arch St., Philadelphia, Pennsylvania 19103-1399. (215) 587-4800. Largest and most comprehensive database of research in the life sciences. Contains citations for nearly 9000 primary research journals, monographs, reviews, symposia, preliminary reports, semi-popular journals, selected institutional reports, government reports and research communications.

Computerized Engineering Index–COMPENDEX. Engineering Information Inc., 345 E. 47th St., New York, New York 10017. (212) 705-7600.

Enviro/Energyline Abstracts Plus. R. R. Bowker Co., 121 Chanlon Rd., New Providence, New Jersey 07974. (908) 464-6800.

Environmental Periodicals Bibliography. National Information Services Corp., Ste. 6, Wyman Towers, 3100 St. Paul St., Baltimore, Maryland 21218. (410)243-0797. Online version of abstract of same name.

Medical Toxicology and Environmental Health. Department of Health and Social Security, Medical Toxiclology & Environmental Health Division, Hannibal House, Rm. 719, Elephant and Castle, London, England SE1 6TE. 44 (71) 972-2162.

Noise Levels. Canadian Centre for Occupational Health & Safety, 250 Main St., East, Hamilton, Ontario, Canada L8N 1H6. (800) 263-8276.

PERIODICALS AND NEWSLETTERS

Applied Acoustics. Elsevier Science Publishing Co., 655 Avenue of the Americas, New York, New York 10010. (212) 989-5800. Quarterly. Acoustics of musical instruments and of sound propagation through the atmosphere and underwater.

Environment Midwest. U.S. Environmental Protection Agency, 230 S. Dearborn, Chicago, Illinois 60604. (312) 353-2072. Monthly. Programs for fighting air and water pollution, hazardous and solid wastes, toxicants, pesticides, noise, and radiation.

EPA Journal. U.S. Environmental Protection Agency, 401 M St., S.W., A-107, Washington, District of Columbia 20460. (202) 382-4393. Bimonthly. Air and water pollution, pesticides, noise, solid waste.

Journal of Low Frequency Noise & Vibration. Multi-Science Publishing Co. Ltd., 107 High St., Brentwood, Essex, England CM14 4RX. 0277-224632. Quarterly.

Noise and Vibration Bulletin. Multi-Science Publishing Co. Ltd., 1070 High St., Brentwood, Essex, England CM14 4RX. 0227-224632. Monthly. Effects of noise on the human and animal organism, instrumentation, standards and regulations; mechanisms involved in road and rail transport, aircraft, domestic and other sources, reduction and control.

Noise and Vibration in Industry. Multi-Science Publishing Co. Ltd., 107 High St., Brentwood, Essex, England CM14 4RX. 0227-224632. Quarterly. Effects of noise and vibration on individuals at work, the effects of vibration on machines and buildings, the impact of industrially-generated noise on the community, hearing protection, audiology and audiometry.

Noise Control Engineering Journal. Institute of Noise Control Engineering, Department of M.E., Auburn University, Auburn, Alabama 36849. (205) 826-4820. Bimonthly. Covers local, state and federal standards for noise control.

Noise/News. Institute of Noise Control Engineering, PO Box 1758, Poughkeepsie, New York 12601. 1972-. Bimonthly.

Noise Regulation Report. Business Publishers, Inc., 951 Pershing Dr., Silver Spring, Maryland 20910-4464. (301) 587-6300. 1974-. Biweekly. Focuses exclusively on noise abatement and control. Covers developments in this field, news from the federal government including regulatory activities at key federal agencies such as FAA and OSHA. Also covers hard to find information on which state and local governments are doing to enforce noise abatement laws.

Vibrations. National Association of Noise Control Officials, 53 Cubberly Rd., Trenton, New Jersey 08690. (609) 984-4161. Monthly. Covers technical advancements in the environmental noise control area.

STATISTICS SOURCES

OECD Environmental Data Compendium 1989. OECD Publications and Information Center, 2001 L St. N.W., Suite 700, Washington, District of Columbia 20036. (202) 785-OECD. 1989. Provides statistical data for OECD countries on air pollution, water pollution, the marine environment, land use, forests, wildlife, solid waste, noise and radioactivity. Also provides data on the underlying pressures on the environment such as energy use, transportation, industrial activity and agriculture.

TRADE ASSOCIATIONS AND PROFESSIONAL SOCIETIES

Acoustical Society of America. 500 Sunnyside Blvd., Woodbury, New York 11797. (516) 349-7800.

Institute of Noise Control Engineering. Box 3206, Arlington Branch, Poughkeepsie, New York 12603. (914) 462-4006.

National Association of Noise Control Officials. 53 Cubberly Rd., Trenton, New Jersey 08690. (609) 984-4161.

National Hearing Conservation Association. 900 Des Moines St., Suite 200, Des Moines, Iowa 50309. (515) 266-2189.

Noise Control Products and Materials Association. 104 Cresta Verde Dr., Rolling Hills, California 90274. (213) 377-9958.

NOISE POLLUTION

ABSTRACTING AND INDEXING SERVICES

Applied Science and Technology Index. H.W. Wilson Co., 950 University Ave., Bronx, New York 10452. (800) 367-6770. Formerly Industrial Arts Index.

Biological Abstracts. BIOSIS, 2100 Arch St., Philadelphia, Pennsylvania 19103-1399. (215) 587-4800. 1927-.

Engineering Index. The Engineering Index Inc., 345 E. 47th St., New York, New York 10017. 1962-.

Environment Abstracts. Bowker A & I Publishing, 121 Chanlon Rd., New Providence, New Jersey 07974. (908) 464-6800. 1974-.

Environment Index. Environment Information Center, Index Research Department, 124 E. 39th St., New York, New York 10016. 1971-. Annual.

Environmental Information Connection–EIC. Planning Information Program, Dept. of Urban and Regional Planning, University of Illinois, 1003 West Nevada, Urbana, Illinois 61801. (217) 333-1369. Also available online.

Environmental Periodicals Bibliography. Environmental Studies Institute, International Academy at Santa Barbara, 800 Garden St., Suite D, Santa Barbara, California 93101. (805) 965-5010. Also available online.

General Science Index. H. W. Wilson Co., 950 University Ave., Bronx, New York 10452. 1978-. Monthly, also issued in annual cumulation. Cumulative subject index to English language periodicals in the subject fields of astronomy, botany, chemistry, earth science, environment and conservation, food and nutrition, genetics, mathematics, medicine and health, microbiology, oceanography, physics, physiology and zoology.

Geographical Abstracts. London School of Economics, Dept. of Geography, Regency House, 34 Duke St., London, England 1966-. Continued by Geo Abstracts issued in 6 parts: Pt. A. Landforms and the quaternary; Pt. B. Biogeography and Climatology; Pt. C. Economic geography; Pt. D. Social geography and cartography; Pt. E. Sedimentology; Pt. F. Regional and community planning.

Index to Scientific Book Contents. Institute for Scientific Information, 3501 Market St., Philadelphia, Pennsylvania 19104. (800) 523-1857. 1985-. Annual. Gives contents of science books published.

Pollution Abstracts. Cambridge Scientific Abstracts, 5161 River Rd., Bethesda, Maryland 20816. (301) 961-6750. Six/year. Indexes worldwide technical literature on environmental pollution. Covers air pollution, marine and freshwater pollution, sewage and wastewater treatment, waste management, toxicology and health, noise pollution, radiation, land pollution, and environmental policies, programs, legislation, and education. Also available online.

Science Citation Index. Institute for Scientific Information, 3501 Market St., Philadelphia, Pennsylvania 19104. 1961-.

BIBLIOGRAPHIES

EPA Publications Bibliography. U.S. Environmental Protection Agency, Library Systems Branch, 401 M St., SW, Washington, District of Columbia 20460. (202) 260-2090. Quarterly.

Noise Pollution: A Guide to Information Sources. Clifford R. Bragdon. Gale Research Co., 835 Penobscot Bldg., Detroit, Michigan 48226-4094. (313) 961-2242. 1979. Part of the series entitled Man and the Environment Information Guides series, v.5.

ENCYCLOPEDIAS AND DICTIONARIES

Encyclopedia of Physical Science and Technology. Robert A. Meyers, ed. Academic Press, c/o Harcourt Brace Jovanovich Inc., 6277 Sea Harbor Dr., Orlando, Florida 32887. (800) 346-8648. Dictionary of engineering, technology and physical sciences.

McGraw-Hill Encyclopedia of Environmental Science. Sybil P. Parker. McGraw-Hill Science & Engineering Books, 11 W. 19th St., New York, New York 10011. (212) 337-6010. 1980. Covers ecology, man's influence on nature, and environmental protection.

McGraw-Hill Encyclopedia of Science and Technology. McGraw-Hill, 1221 Avenue of the Americas, New York, New York 10020. (212) 512-2000 or (800) 262-4729. 1992. Seventh edition. Issued in multiple volumes including index. Includes all science and technology broad subject areas.

The New York Times Encyclopedic Dictionary of the Environment. Paul Sarnoff. Quadrangle Books, New York, New York 1971. Focuses on state-of-the-art methods of pollution control, abatement, prevention and removal.

GENERAL WORKS

Construction of Dams and Aircraft Overflights in National Park Units. U.S. Congress. House Committee on Interior and Insular Affairs. U.S. G.P.O., Washington, District of Columbia 20401. Covers national parks and reserves, environmental aspects of dams, airplane noise and air traffic rules.

Environmental Engineering and Sanitation. Joseph A. Salvato. John Wiley & Sons, Inc., 605 3rd Ave., New York, New York 10158-0012. (212) 850-6000. 1992. 3d ed. Applies principles of sanitary science and engineering to sanitation and environmental health. It includes design, construction, maintenance, and operations of sanitation plants and structures. Provides state-of-the-art information on environmental factors associated with chronic and non-infectious diseases; environmental engineering planning and impact analysis; waste management and control; food sanitation; administration of health and sanitation programs; acid rain; noise control; campground sanitation, etc.

Fighting Noise in 1990s. Organisation for Economic Cooperation and Development. OECD Publication and Information Center, 2001 L. St. N.W., Suite 700, Washington, District of Columbia 20036. (202) 785-6323. 1991. Deals with transportation noise pollution. Includes the economic impacts and relevant legislation.

International Environmental Information Sources. Pira, Randalls Rd., Leatherhead, England KT22 7RU. 0372 376161. 1990. Contains valuable business and technical contacts for environmental information sources worldwide. Information sources cover the following subjects: Air, noise, water and land pollution; waste control and disposal; recycling; energy recovery; nature conservation. Informational sources include associations, research organizations, legislative/regulatory agencies, directories, statistics, on-line databases, magazines and news letters in 24 countries.

Sound Analysis and Noise Control. Van Nostrand Reinhold, 115 Fifth Ave., New York, New York 10003. (212) 254-3232. 1990. Discusses the physics of sound, the mechanism of hearing and the application of those principles to specific problems.

HANDBOOKS AND MANUALS

Handbook of Highway Engineering. Robert F. Baker, ed. R. E. Krieger Publishing Co., 115 5th Ave., New York, New York 10003. (212) 254-3232. 1982. Provides reference data on the application of technology to highway transportation.

ONLINE DATA BASES

BIOSIS Previews. BIOSIS, 2100 Arch St., Philadelphia, Pennsylvania 19103-1399. (215) 587-4800. Largest and most comprehensive database of research in the life sciences. Contains citations for nearly 9000 primary research journals, monographs, reviews, symposia, preliminary reports, semi-popular journals, selected institutional reports, government reports and research communications.

Computerized Engineering Index–COMPENDEX. Engineering Information Inc., 345 E. 47th St., New York, New York 10017. (212) 705-7600.

Enviro/Energyline Abstracts Plus. R. R. Bowker Co., 121 Chanlon Rd., New Providence, New Jersey 07974. (908) 464-6800.

Enviroline. R. R. Bowker Co., Bowker Electronic Publishing, 121 Chanlon Rd., New Providence, New Jersey 07974. (800) 521-8110.

Environmental Bibliography. Environmental Studies Institute, International Academy at Santa Barbara, 800 Garden St., Ste. D, Santa Barbara, California 93101. (805) 965-5010. International periodical literature dealing with environmental topics such as air pollution, water treatment, energy conservation, noise abatement, soil mechanics, wildlife preservation, and chemical wastes.

Environmental Periodicals Bibliography. National Information Services Corp., Ste. 6, Wyman Towers, 3100 St. Paul St., Baltimore, Maryland 21218. (410)243-0797. Online version of abstract of same name.

Medical Toxicology and Environmental Health. Department of Health and Social Security, Medical Toxiclology & Environmental Health Division, Hannibal House, Rm. 719, Elephant and Castle, London, England SE1 6TE. 44 (71) 972-2162.

Monthly Catalog of United States Government Publications. U.S. G.P.O., Supt. of Docs., PO Box 371954, Pittsburgh, Pennsylvania 15250-7954. (202) 512-0000.

National Technical Information Service. U.S. Department of Commerce, National Technical Information Service, Office of Data Base Services, 5285 Port Royal Rd., Springfield, Virginia 22161. (703) 487-4807. Biblio-

graphic database of government sponsored research and technical reports.

Noise Levels. Canadian Centre for Occupational Health & Safety, 250 Main St., East, Hamilton, Ontario, Canada L8N 1H6. (800) 263-8276.

PERIODICALS AND NEWSLETTERS

Environmental Pollution & Control. National Technical Information Service, 5285 Port Royal Rd., Springfield, Virginia 22161. (703) 487-4650. Weekly. Covers air, noise, solid waste, water pollution, radiation, environmental health and safety, pesticide pollution and control.

Multinational Environmental Outlook. Business Publishers, Inc., 951 Pershing Dr., Silver Spring, Maryland 20910-4464. (301) 587-6300. 1974-. Biweekly. Covers developments in world environmental problems such as acid rain, deforestation, soil erosion, overfishing, threats to health, animal extinction, population growth, diminishing water supply and other related matters. Also available online.

Noise Control Engineering Journal. Institute of Noise Control Engineering, Department of M.E., Auburn University, Auburn, Alabama 36849. (205) 826-4820. Bimonthly. Covers local, state and federal standards for noise control.

Noise Regulation Report. Business Publishers, Inc., 951 Pershing Dr., Silver Spring, Maryland 20910-4464. (301) 587-6300. 1974-. Biweekly. Focuses exclusively on noise abatement and control. Covers developments in this field, news from the federal government including regulatory activities at key federal agencies such as FAA and OSHA. Also covers hard to find information on which state and local governments are doing to enforce noise abatement laws.

Vibrations. National Association of Noise Control Officials, 53 Cubberly Rd., Trenton, New Jersey 08690. (609) 984-4161. Monthly. Covers technical advancements in the environmental noise control area.

TRADE ASSOCIATIONS AND PROFESSIONAL SOCIETIES

Automotive Exhaust Systems Manufacturers Council. 300 Sylvan Ave., Englewood Cliffs, New Jersey 07632. (201) 569-8500.

Citizens for a Quieter City. 300 E. 42nd St., New York, New York 10017. (212) 986-6590.

Institute of Noise Control Engineering. Box 3206, Arlington Branch, Poughkeepsie, New York 12603. (914) 462-4006.

National Association of Noise Control Officials. 53 Cubberly Rd., Trenton, New Jersey 08690. (609) 984-4161.

National Hearing Conservation Association. 900 Des Moines St., Suite 200, Des Moines, Iowa 50309. (515) 266-2189.

National Organization to Insure a Sound-Controlled Environment. 1620 I St., N.W., Suite 300, Washington, District of Columbia 20006. (202) 429-0166.

NONPOINT SOURCE POLLUTION

See also: RUNOFF

ABSTRACTING AND INDEXING SERVICES

Biological and Agricultural Index. H.W. Wilson Co., 950 University Ave., Bronx, New York 10452. (800) 367-6770. 1916-. Monthly.

Ecological Abstracts. Geo Abstracts Ltd. Elsevier Applied Science, Crown House, Linton Rd., Barking, England IG 11 8JU. 1974-. Derived from over 600 leading ecological and environmental journals, plus books, conference proceedings, reports and theses.

Environment Abstracts. Bowker A & I Publishing, 121 Chanlon Rd., New Providence, New Jersey 07974. (908) 464-6800. 1974-.

Environment Index. Environment Information Center, Index Research Department, 124 E. 39th St., New York, New York 10016. 1971-. Annual.

Environmental Information Connection–EIC. Planning Information Program, Dept. of Urban and Regional Planning, University of Illinois, 1003 West Nevada, Urbana, Illinois 61801. (217) 333-1369. Also available online.

Environmental Periodicals Bibliography. Environmental Studies Institute, International Academy at Santa Barbara, 800 Garden St., Suite D, Santa Barbara, California 93101. (805) 965-5010. Also available online.

Index to Scientific Book Contents. Institute for Scientific Information, 3501 Market St., Philadelphia, Pennsylvania 19104. (800) 523-1857. 1985-. Annual. Gives contents of science books published.

Pollution Abstracts. Cambridge Scientific Abstracts, 5161 River Rd., Bethesda, Maryland 20816. (301) 961-6750. Six/year. Indexes worldwide technical literature on environmental pollution. Covers air pollution, marine and freshwater pollution, sewage and wastewater treatment, waste management, toxicology and health, noise pollution, radiation, land pollution, and environmental policies, programs, legislation, and education. Also available online.

BIBLIOGRAPHIES

EPA Publications Bibliography. U.S. Environmental Protection Agency, Library Systems Branch, 401 M St., SW, Washington, District of Columbia 20460. (202) 260-2090. Quarterly.

Nonpoint Source Pollution, an Agricultural Concern, 1983-1987. National Agricultural Library, 10301 Baltimore Blvd., Beltsville, Maryland 20705-2351. (301) 504-5755. 1986.

GENERAL WORKS

Environmental Impact of Nonpoint Source Pollution. Ann Arbor Science, 230 Collingwood, Ann Arbor, Michigan 48106. 1980.

Nonpoint Source Pollution. Bruce W. Vigon. American Water Resources Association, 5410 Grosvenor Lane, Suite 220, Bethesda, Maryland 20814. (301) 493-8600.

1985. Water quality management and water pollution in the U.S.

Nonpoint Source Pollution: Land Use and Water Quality. Anne Weinberg. University of Wisconsin-Extension, 432 N. Lake St., Madison, Wisconsin 53706. 1979. Covers water pollution and water quality management.

Poison Runoff: A Guide to State and Local Control of Nonpoint Source Water Pollution. Paul Thompson. Natural Resources Defense Council, 40 W. 20th St., New York, New York 10011. (212) 727-2700. 1989. How-to-book addressing pollution in agricultural lands, urban development and construction, logging, mining and grazing.

ONLINE DATA BASES

Enviro/Energyline Abstracts Plus. R. R. Bowker Co., 121 Chanlon Rd., New Providence, New Jersey 07974. (908) 464-6800.

Environmental Periodicals Bibliography. National Information Services Corp., Ste. 6, Wyman Towers, 3100 St. Paul St., Baltimore, Maryland 21218. (410)243-0797. Online version of abstract of same name.

Monthly Catalog of United States Government Publications. U.S. G.P.O., Supt. of Docs., PO Box 371954, Pittsburgh, Pennsylvania 15250-7954. (202) 512-0000.

National Technical Information Service. U.S. Department of Commerce, National Technical Information Service, Office of Data Base Services, 5285 Port Royal Rd., Springfield, Virginia 22161. (703) 487-4807. Bibliographic database of government sponsored research and technical reports.

PERIODICALS AND NEWSLETTERS

Clean Water Report. Business Publishers, Inc., 951 Pershing Dr., Silver Spring, Maryland 20910-4464. (301) 587-6300. 1964-. Biweekly. Key information source for environmental professionals, covering the important issues: groundwater, drinking water, wastewater treatment, drought, wetlands, coastal protection, dioxin, non-point source pollution, agrichemical contamination, cleanup versus prevention issues, and related topics.

STATISTICS SOURCES

World Resources. World Resources Institute. 1709 New York Ave., N.W., Washington, District of Columbia 20006. (202) 638-6300. Annual. Statistical and textual analysis of world's natural resources and the effects of growth-caused environmental pollution.

NONRENEWABLE RESOURCES

ABSTRACTING AND INDEXING SERVICES

Biological and Agricultural Index. H.W. Wilson Co., 950 University Ave., Bronx, New York 10452. (800) 367-6770. 1916-. Monthly.

Engineering Index. The Engineering Index Inc., 345 E. 47th St., New York, New York 10017. 1962-.

Environment Abstracts. Bowker A & I Publishing, 121 Chanlon Rd., New Providence, New Jersey 07974. (908) 464-6800. 1974-.

Environment Index. Environment Information Center, Index Research Department, 124 E. 39th St., New York, New York 10016. 1971-. Annual.

Environmental Information Connection-EIC. Planning Information Program, Dept. of Urban and Regional Planning, University of Illinois, 1003 West Nevada, Urbana, Illinois 61801. (217) 333-1369. Also available online.

Environmental Periodicals Bibliography. Environmental Studies Institute, International Academy at Santa Barbara, 800 Garden St., Suite D, Santa Barbara, California 93101. (805) 965-5010. Also available online.

Index to Scientific Book Contents. Institute for Scientific Information, 3501 Market St., Philadelphia, Pennsylvania 19104. (800) 523-1857. 1985-. Annual. Gives contents of science books published.

BIBLIOGRAPHIES

EPA Publications Bibliography. U.S. Environmental Protection Agency, Library Systems Branch, 401 M St., SW, Washington, District of Columbia 20460. (202) 260-2090. Quarterly.

ENCYCLOPEDIAS AND DICTIONARIES

McGraw-Hill Encyclopedia of Environmental Science. Sybil P. Parker. McGraw-Hill Science & Engineering Books, 11 W. 19th St., New York, New York 10011. (212) 337-6010. 1980. Covers ecology, man's influence on nature, and environmental protection.

McGraw-Hill Encyclopedia of Science and Technology. McGraw-Hill, 1221 Avenue of the Americas, New York, New York 10020. (212) 512-2000 or (800) 262-4729. 1992. Seventh edition. Issued in multiple volumes including index. Includes all science and technology broad subject areas.

Van Nostrand's Scientific Encyclopedia. Glenn D. Considine, ed. Van Nostrand Reinhold, 115 5th Ave., New York, New York 10003. (212) 254-3232. 1983. Sixth edition. Includes all broad subject areas in science.

ONLINE DATA BASES

Computerized Engineering Index-COMPENDEX. Engineering Information Inc., 345 E. 47th St., New York, New York 10017. (212) 705-7600.

Enviro/Energyline Abstracts Plus. R. R. Bowker Co., 121 Chanlon Rd., New Providence, New Jersey 07974. (908) 464-6800.

Environmental Periodicals Bibliography. National Information Services Corp., Ste. 6, Wyman Towers, 3100 St. Paul St., Baltimore, Maryland 21218. (410)243-0797. Online version of abstract of same name.

Monthly Catalog of United States Government Publications. U.S. G.P.O., Supt. of Docs., PO Box 371954, Pittsburgh, Pennsylvania 15250-7954. (202) 512-0000.

National Technical Information Service. U.S. Department of Commerce, National Technical Information Service, Office of Data Base Services, 5285 Port Royal

Rd., Springfield, Virginia 22161. (703) 487-4807. Bibliographic database of government sponsored research and technical reports.

PressNet Environmental Reports. Chemical Information Systems, Inc., 7215 York Rd., Baltimore, Maryland 21212. (301) 321-8440.

SCISEARCH. Institute for Scientific Information, University City Science Center, 3501 Market St., Philadelphia, Pennsylvania 19104. (215) 386-0100.

NONTOXIC COMPOUNDS

ABSTRACTING AND INDEXING SERVICES

Biological and Agricultural Index. H.W. Wilson Co., 950 University Ave., Bronx, New York 10452. (800) 367-6770. 1916-. Monthly.

Environment Abstracts. Bowker A & I Publishing, 121 Chanlon Rd., New Providence, New Jersey 07974. (908) 464-6800. 1974-.

Environment Index. Environment Information Center, Index Research Department, 124 E. 39th St., New York, New York 10016. 1971-. Annual.

Environmental Information Connection–EIC. Planning Information Program, Dept. of Urban and Regional Planning, University of Illinois, 1003 West Nevada, Urbana, Illinois 61801. (217) 333-1369. Also available online.

Environmental Periodicals Bibliography. Environmental Studies Institute, International Academy at Santa Barbara, 800 Garden St., Suite D, Santa Barbara, California 93101. (805) 965-5010. Also available online.

BIBLIOGRAPHIES

EPA Publications Bibliography. U.S. Environmental Protection Agency, Library Systems Branch, 401 M St., SW, Washington, District of Columbia 20460. (202) 260-2090. Quarterly.

GENERAL WORKS

Making the Switch. Sacramento League of Women Voters. Golden Empire Health Planning Center, P.O. Box 649, Sacramento, California 98120. (916) 448-1198. 1988. Alternatives to using toxic chemicals in the home.

Nontoxic, Natural and Earthwise: How to Protect Yourself and Your Family from Harmful Products and Live in Harmony with the Earth. Debra Lynn Dadd. Jeremy P. Tarcher, 5858 Wilshire Blvd., Ste. 200, Los Angeles, California 90036. (213) 935-9980. 1990. Evaluation of household products and recommendations as to natural and homemade alternatives.

HANDBOOKS AND MANUALS

Tables of Physical and Chemical Constants and Some Mathematical Functions. G. W. C. Kaye, et al. Longman Group Ltd., Longman House, Burnt Mill, Harlow, England CM20 2J6. 0279 426721. 1988. Fifteenth edition. Includes tables on mechanical properties, density, elasticity, viscosity, surface tension, temperature and heat. Also

covers radiation, optics, chemistry, electrochemistry, astrophysics, and chemical thermodynamics.

ONLINE DATA BASES

Enviro/Energyline Abstracts Plus. R. R. Bowker Co., 121 Chanlon Rd., New Providence, New Jersey 07974. (908) 464-6800.

Environmental Periodicals Bibliography. National Information Services Corp., Ste. 6, Wyman Towers, 3100 St. Paul St., Baltimore, Maryland 21218. (410)243-0797. Online version of abstract of same name.

NORTH CAROLINA ENVIRONMENTAL AGENCIES

GENERAL WORKS

North Carolina Environmental and Natural Resources Law Directory. Radian Corp., PO Box 13000, Research Triangle Park, North Carolina 27709. (919) 481-0212. 1990.

NORTH CAROLINA ENVIRONMENTAL AGENCIES

GOVERNMENTAL ORGANIZATIONS

Department of Agriculture: Pesticide Registration. Pesticide Administrator, Food and Drug Protection Division, PO Box 27647, Raleigh, North Carolina 27611-0647. (919) 733-3556.

Department of Human Resources: Hazardous Waste Management. Chief, Solid Waste Management Section, 401 Oberlin Rd., Raleigh, North Carolina 27605. (919) 733-4996.

Department of Human Resources: Solid Waste Management. Chief, Solid Waste Management Section, 401 Oberlin Rd., Raleigh, North Carolina 27605. (919) 733-4966.

Department of Labor: Occupational Safety. Commissioner, 4 West Edenton St., Raleigh, North Carolina 27601-1092. (919) 733-7166.

Department of Natural Resources and Community Development: Underground Storage Tanks. Director, Environmental Management, 512 North Salisbury St., Raleigh, North Carolina 27604-1148. (919) 733-7015.

Division of Emergency Management: Emergency Preparedness and Community Right-to-Know. Chair, Emergency Response Commission, 116 West Jones St., Raleigh, North Carolina 27603-1335. (919) 733-3867.

Environment, Health and Natural Resources Department: Air Quality. Director, Environmental Management, PO Box 27687, Raleigh, North Carolina 27611. (919) 733-7015.

Environment, Health and Natural Resources Department: Coastal Zone Management. Director, Coastal Management Division, PO Box 27687, Raleigh, North Carolina 27611. (919) 733-2293.

Environment, Health and Natural Resources Department: Environmental Protection. Secretary, PO Box 27687, Raleigh, North Carolina 27611. (919) 733-4984.

Environment, Health and Natural Resources Department: Fish and Wildlife. Executive Director, Wildlife Resources Division, PO Box 27687, Raleigh, North Carolina 27611. (919) 733-3391.

Environment, Health and Natural Resources Department: Groundwater Management. Groundwater Chief, Division of Environment Management, PO Box 27687, Raleigh, North Carolina 27611. (919) 733-3221.

Environment, Health and Natural Resources Department: Natural Resources. Secretary, PO Box 27687, Raleigh, North Carolina 27611. (919) 733-4984.

Environment, Health and Natural Resources Department: Waste Minimization and Pollution Prevention. Information Officer, Pollution Prevention Pays Program, PO Box 27687, Raleigh, North Carolina 27611. (919) 733-7015.

Environment, Health and Natural Resources Department: Water Quality. Director, Environmental Management, 512 North Salisbury St., Raleigh, North Carolina 27604-1148. (919) 733-7015.

NORTH DAKOTA ENVIRONMENTAL AGENCIES

GOVERNMENTAL ORGANIZATIONS

Department of Health and Consolidated Laboratories: Air Quality. Director, Environmental Engineering Division, 1200 Missouri Ave., Bismarck, North Dakota 58501. (701) 224-2348.

Department of Health and Consolidated Laboratories: Emergency Preparedness and Community Right-to-Know. Coordinator, SARA Title III Coordinator, 1200 Missouri Ave., PO Box 5520, Bismark, North Dakota 58502-5520. (701) 224-2374.

Department of Health and Consolidated Laboratories: Pesticide Registration. Assistant Director, PO Box 937, Bismark, North Dakota 58505-0020. (701) 221-6146.

Department of Health: Environmental Protection. Director, Environmental Health Section, 1200 Missouri Ave., Bismark, North Dakota 58501. (701) 224-2374.

Division of Hazardous Waste Management and Special Studies: Hazardous Waste Management. Director, 1200 Missouri Ave., Bismark, North Dakota 58502-5520. (701) 224-2366.

Division of Hazardous Waste Management and Special Studies: Solid Waste Management. Director, 1200 Missouri Ave., Bismark, North Dakota 58502-5520. (701) 224-2366.

Division of Hazardous Waste Management and Special Studies: Underground Storage Tanks. Director, 1200 Missouri Ave., Bismark, North Dakota 58502-5502. (701) 224-2366.

Game and Fish Department: Fish and Wildlife. Commissioner, 100 North Bismark Expressway, Bismark, North Dakota 58501. (701) 221-6300.

State Water Commission: Groundwater Management. State Office Building, 900 East Blvd., Bismark, North Dakota 58505. (701) 224-2750.

U.S. EPA Region 8: Pollution Prevention. Senior Policy Advisor, 999 18th St., Suite 500, Denver, Colorado 80202-2405. (303) 293-1603.

Water Supply and Pollution Control Division: Water Quality. Director, 1200 Missouri Ave., Bismark, North Dakota 58501. (701) 224-2354.

Workmen's Compensation Bureau: Occupational Safety. Safety Director, 4007 North State St., Bismark, North Dakota 58501. (701) 224-2700.

NUCLEAR ACCIDENTS

ABSTRACTING AND INDEXING SERVICES

Applied Science and Technology Index. H.W. Wilson Co., 950 University Ave., Bronx, New York 10452. (800) 367-6770. Formerly Industrial Arts Index.

Energy Information Abstracts Annual 1987 in Retrospect. EIC/Intelligence Inc., 121 Chanlon Rd., New Providence, New Jersey 07974. (908) 464-6800. 1988. Annual. Cumulative edition of the monthly Energy Information Abstracts. Monitors sources in the field of energy including the scientific, technical and business journal literature, conference and symposia proceedings, corporate, government and academic reports.

Engineering Index. The Engineering Index Inc., 345 E. 47th St., New York, New York 10017. 1962-.

Environment Abstracts. Bowker A & I Publishing, 121 Chanlon Rd., New Providence, New Jersey 07974. (908) 464-6800. 1974-.

Environment Index. Environment Information Center, Index Research Department, 124 E. 39th St., New York, New York 10016. 1971-. Annual.

Environmental Information Connection–EIC. Planning Information Program, Dept. of Urban and Regional Planning, University of Illinois, 1003 West Nevada, Urbana, Illinois 61801. (217) 333-1369. Also available online.

Environmental Periodicals Bibliography. Environmental Studies Institute, International Academy at Santa Barbara, 800 Garden St., Suite D, Santa Barbara, California 93101. (805) 965-5010. Also available online.

General Science Index. H. W. Wilson Co., 950 University Ave., Bronx, New York 10452. 1978-. Monthly, also issued in annual cumulation. Cumulative subject index to English language periodicals in the subject fields of astronomy, botany, chemistry, earth science, environment and conservation, food and nutrition, genetics, mathematics, medicine and health, microbiology, oceanography, physics, physiology and zoology.

INIS Atomindex. International Atomic Energy Agency, Wagramerstrasse 5, Vienna, Austria A-1400. 222 23606198. 1988-. Semiannual. Abstracts nuclear energy and nuclear physics topics from journals, conferences, technical reports and other related publications. Issued in 6 parts: Personal Author, Corporate Entry, Subject, Report, Standard Patent, Conference (by place), Conference (by date).

Science Citation Index. Institute for Scientific Information, 3501 Market St., Philadelphia, Pennsylvania 19104. 1961-.

BIBLIOGRAPHIES

EPA Publications Bibliography. U.S. Environmental Protection Agency, Library Systems Branch, 401 M St., SW, Washington, District of Columbia 20460. (202) 260-2090. Quarterly.

ENCYCLOPEDIAS AND DICTIONARIES

Encyclopedia of Physical Science and Technology. Robert A. Meyers, ed. Academic Press, c/o Harcourt Brace Jovanovich Inc., 6277 Sea Harbor Dr., Orlando, Florida 32887. (800) 346-8648. Dictionary of engineering, technology and physical sciences.

Van Nostrand's Scientific Encyclopedia. Glenn D. Considine, ed. Van Nostrand Reinhold, 115 5th Ave., New York, New York 10003. (212) 254-3232. 1983. Sixth edition. Includes all broad subject areas in science.

GENERAL WORKS

Environmental Contamination Following a Major Nuclear Accident. STI/PUB, UNIPUB, 4611-F Assembly Dr., Lanham, Maryland 20706. (301) 459-7666 or (800) 274-4888. 1991. Two volumes. Reviews the extent and magnitude of environmental contamination occurring after a massive release of radioactive materials.

Fire in the Rain. Peter Gould. Carolina Biological Supply Company, 2700 York Rd., Burlington, North Carolina 27215. (919) 584-0381. 1990. Describes the Chernobyl accident.

Observed Behavior of Cesium, Iodine, and Tellurium in the ORNL Fission Product Release Program. J.L. Collins. U.S. Nuclear Regulatory Commission, Office of Nuclear Regulatory Research, Washington, District of Columbia 20555. (301) 492-7000. 1985.

Reactor Accidents: Nuclear Safety and the Role of Institutional Failure. David Mosey. Nuclear Engineering International Special Publications, c/o Butterworth-Heinemann, 80 Montvale Ave., Stoneham, Massachusetts 02180. (617) 438-8464; (800) 366-2665. 1990.

GOVERNMENTAL ORGANIZATIONS

Office of Public Affairs. 1717 H St., N.W., Washington, District of Columbia 20555. (301) 492-7715.

HANDBOOKS AND MANUALS

Aerosol Science. Pergamon Microforms International, Inc., Fairview Park, Elmsford, New York 10523. (914) 592-7720. 1991. Radioactive pollution of the atmosphere, nuclear reactor accidents and radioactive aerosols.

ONLINE DATA BASES

Computerized Engineering Index–COMPENDEX. Engineering Information Inc., 345 E. 47th St., New York, New York 10017. (212) 705-7600.

Enviro/Energyline Abstracts Plus. R. R. Bowker Co., 121 Chanlon Rd., New Providence, New Jersey 07974. (908) 464-6800.

Environment Week. NewsNet, Inc., 945 Haverford Rd., Bryn Mawr, Pennsylvania 19010. (800) 345-1301. Online version of periodical of same name.

Environmental Periodicals Bibliography. National Information Services Corp., Ste. 6, Wyman Towers, 3100 St. Paul St., Baltimore, Maryland 21218. (410)243-0797. Online version of abstract of same name.

International Nuclear Information System. International Atomic Energy Agency, INIS Section, Vienna International Centre, P.O. Box 100, Vienna, Austria A-1400. 43 (222) 23602882.

Monthly Catalog of United States Government Publications. U.S. G.P.O., Supt. of Docs., PO Box 371954, Pittsburgh, Pennsylvania 15250-7954. (202) 512-0000.

National Technical Information Service. U.S. Department of Commerce, National Technical Information Service, Office of Data Base Services, 5285 Port Royal Rd., Springfield, Virginia 22161. (703) 487-4807. Bibliographic database of government sponsored research and technical reports.

Nuclear Science Abstracts. U.S. Department of Energy, Office of Scientific & Technical Information, P.O. Box 62, Oak Ridge, Tennessee 37831. (615) 576-6299.

Nuclear Waste News–Online. Business Publishers, Inc., 951 Pershing Dr., Silver Spring, Maryland 20910-4464. (301) 587-6300. Federal and legislation regulation and research and development activities concerning the generation, packaging, transportation, processing, and disposal of nuclear wastes.

PressNet Environmental Reports. Chemical Information Systems, Inc., 7215 York Rd., Baltimore, Maryland 21212. (301) 321-8440.

TRADE ASSOCIATIONS AND PROFESSIONAL SOCIETIES

Friends of the Earth. 218 D St., SE, Washington, District of Columbia 20003. (202) 544-2600.

Task Force Against Nuclear Pollution. P.O. Box 1817, Washington, District of Columbia 20013. (301) 474-8311.

Three Mile Island Alert. 315 Peffer St., Harrisburg, Pennsylvania 17102. (717) 233-3072.

NUCLEAR ENERGY

See: NUCLEAR POWER

NUCLEAR EXPLOSIONS

See: NUCLEAR ACCIDENTS

NUCLEAR FUEL

ABSTRACTING AND INDEXING SERVICES

Applied Science and Technology Index. H.W. Wilson Co., 950 University Ave., Bronx, New York 10452. (800) 367-6770. Formerly Industrial Arts Index.

Energy Information Abstracts Annual 1987 in Retrospect. EIC/Intelligence Inc., 121 Chanlon Rd., New Providence, New Jersey 07974. (908) 464-6800. 1988. Annual. Cumulative edition of the monthly Energy Information Abstracts. Monitors sources in the field of energy including the scientific, technical and business journal literature, conference and symposia proceedings, corporate, government and academic reports.

Engineering Index. The Engineering Index Inc., 345 E. 47th St., New York, New York 10017. 1962-.

Environment Abstracts. Bowker A & I Publishing, 121 Chanlon Rd., New Providence, New Jersey 07974. (908) 464-6800. 1974-.

Environment Index. Environment Information Center, Index Research Department, 124 E. 39th St., New York, New York 10016. 1971-. Annual.

Environmental Information Connection–EIC. Planning Information Program, Dept. of Urban and Regional Planning, University of Illinois, 1003 West Nevada, Urbana, Illinois 61801. (217) 333-1369. Also available online.

Environmental Periodicals Bibliography. Environmental Studies Institute, International Academy at Santa Barbara, 800 Garden St., Suite D, Santa Barbara, California 93101. (805) 965-5010. Also available online.

General Science Index. H. W. Wilson Co., 950 University Ave., Bronx, New York 10452. 1978-. Monthly, also issued in annual cumulation. Cumulative subject index to English language periodicals in the subject fields of astronomy, botany, chemistry, earth science, environment and conservation, food and nutrition, genetics, mathematics, medicine and health, microbiology, oceanography, physics, physiology and zoology.

Index to Scientific Book Contents. Institute for Scientific Information, 3501 Market St., Philadelphia, Pennsylvania 19104. (800) 523-1857. 1985-. Annual. Gives contents of science books published.

INIS Atomindex. International Atomic Energy Agency, Wagramerstrasse 5, Vienna, Austria A-1400. 222 23606198. 1988-. Semiannual. Abstracts nuclear energy and nuclear physics topics from journals, conferences, technical reports and other related publications. Issued in 6 parts: Personal Author, Corporate Entry, Subject, Report, Standard Patent, Conference (by place), Conference (by date).

Physics Briefs. Physikalische Berichte. Physik Verlag, Pappapelallee 3, Postfach 101161, Weinheim, Germany D-6940. 1979-. Semimonthly. In English. Volumes for 1979- issued by the Deutsche Physikalische Gesellschaft and the Fachinformationszentrum Energie Physik, Mathematik in cooperation with the American Institute of Physics.

Pollution Abstracts. Cambridge Scientific Abstracts, 5161 River Rd., Bethesda, Maryland 20816. (301) 961-6750. Six/year. Indexes worldwide technical literature on environmental pollution. Covers air pollution, marine and freshwater pollution, sewage and wastewater treatment, waste management, toxicology and health, noise pollution, radiation, land pollution, and environmental policies, programs, legislation, and education. Also available online.

Science Citation Index. Institute for Scientific Information, 3501 Market St., Philadelphia, Pennsylvania 19104. 1961-.

BIBLIOGRAPHIES

EPA Publications Bibliography. U.S. Environmental Protection Agency, Library Systems Branch, 401 M St., SW, Washington, District of Columbia 20460. (202) 260-2090. Quarterly.

Nuclear Facility Decommissioning and Site Remedial Actions: A Selected Bibliography. National Technical Information Service, 5285 Port Royal Rd., Springfield, Virginia 22161. (703) 487-4650. Annual. Nuclear facility decommissioning, uranium mill tailings management, and radioactive waste site remedial actions.

DIRECTORIES

The Nuclear Fuel Cycle Information System. International Atomic Energy Agency, Wagramerstrasse 5, Vienna, Austria A-1400. 222 2360 6198.

Nuclear Fusion–World Survey of Activities in Controlled Fusion Research Special Supplement. International Atomic Energy Agency, Wagramerstrasse 5, Vienna, Austria A-1400. 222 23606198.

World Nuclear Directory. Longman, Burnt Mill, Harlow, England CM 20 2J6. (0279) 26721. 1988. Eighth edition. Includes organizations that are involved in nuclear physics research.

ENCYCLOPEDIAS AND DICTIONARIES

Encyclopedia of Physical Science and Technology. Robert A. Meyers, ed. Academic Press, c/o Harcourt Brace Jovanovich Inc., 6277 Sea Harbor Dr., Orlando, Florida 32887. (800) 346-8648. Dictionary of engineering, technology and physical sciences.

Encyclopedia of Physics. Rita G. Lerner and George L. Trigg. VCH Publishers, 303 NW 12th Ave., Deerfield Beach, Florida 33442-1788. (305) 428-5566. 1991. Second edition.

Glossary of Terms in Nuclear Science and Technology. American Nuclear Society, 555 North Kensington Ave., La Grange Park, Illinois 60525. (708) 352-6611. 1986. Prepared by the American Nuclear Society Standards Committee. Subcommittee ANS-9.

Van Nostrand's Scientific Encyclopedia. Glenn D. Considine, ed. Van Nostrand Reinhold, 115 5th Ave., New York, New York 10003. (212) 254-3232. 1983. Sixth edition. Includes all broad subject areas in science.

GENERAL WORKS

Power Generation and the Environment. P. S. Liss and P. A. H. Saunders. Oxford University Press, 200 Madison Ave., New York, New York 10016. (212) 679-7300; (800) 334-4249. 1990. Analyses the problems and possibilities inherent in producing electricity on a large scale.

ONLINE DATA BASES

Computerized Engineering Index–COMPENDEX. Engineering Information Inc., 345 E. 47th St., New York, New York 10017. (212) 705-7600.

EBIB. Texas A & M University, Sterling C. Evans Library, Reference Division, College Station, Texas 77843. (409) 845-5741.

Electric Power Industry Abstracts. Utility Data Institute, 1700 K St., N.W., Suite 400, Washington, District of Columbia 20006. (800) 466-3660.

Enviro/Energyline Abstracts Plus. R. R. Bowker Co., 121 Chanlon Rd., New Providence, New Jersey 07974. (908) 464-6800.

Environmental Periodicals Bibliography. National Information Services Corp., Ste. 6, Wyman Towers, 3100 St. Paul St., Baltimore, Maryland 21218. (410)243-0797. Online version of abstract of same name.

International Nuclear Information System. International Atomic Energy Agency, INIS Section, Vienna International Centre, P.O. Box 100, Vienna, Austria A-1400. 43 (222) 23602882.

Monthly Catalog of United States Government Publications. U.S. G.P.O., Supt. of Docs., PO Box 371954, Pittsburgh, Pennsylvania 15250-7954. (202) 512-0000.

National Technical Information Service. U.S. Department of Commerce, National Technical Information Service, Office of Data Base Services, 5285 Port Royal Rd., Springfield, Virginia 22161. (703) 487-4807. Bibliographic database of government sponsored research and technical reports.

Nuclear Fuel. McGraw-Hill Science & Engineering Books, 11 W. 19th St., New York, New York 10011. (212) 337-6010.

Nuclear News. American Nuclear Society, 555 N. Kensington Ave., LaGrange Park, Illinois 60525. (708) 352-6611.

Nuclear Science Abstracts. U.S. Department of Energy, Office of Scientific & Technical Information, P.O. Box 62, Oak Ridge, Tennessee 37831. (615) 576-6299.

STATISTICS SOURCES

Focus: Quarterly Report on the Nuclear Fuel Cycle. Nuclear Assurance Corp., 6251 Crooked Creek Road, Norcross, Georgia 30092. Quarterly. Data on nuclear reactor and fuel cycle operations; uranium project profile and Fuel-Trac summary.

Spent Fuel Storage Requirements. U.S. Dept. of Energy. Nuclear Energy Office. National Technical Information Service, 5285 Port Royal Road, Springfield, Virginia 22161. (703) 487-4650. 1980. Annual. Required storage capacity for spent fuel discharges to the year 2020.

Spent Nuclear Fuel Discharges from U.S. Reactors. U.S. G.P.O., Washington, District of Columbia 20402-9325. (202) 512-0000. 1991. Commercial nuclear power plant spent fuel discharges, shipments, storage capacity, and inventory.

TRADE ASSOCIATIONS AND PROFESSIONAL SOCIETIES

American Nuclear Energy Council. 410 First St., S.E., Washington, District of Columbia 20003. (202) 484-2670.

American Physical Society. 335 E. 45th St., New York, New York 10017. (212) 682-7341.

Nuclear Recycling Consultants. P.O. Box 819, Provincetown, Massachusetts 02657. (508) 487-1930.

NUCLEAR MAGNETIC RESONANCE

ABSTRACTING AND INDEXING SERVICES

Applied Science and Technology Index. H.W. Wilson Co., 950 University Ave., Bronx, New York 10452. (800) 367-6770. Formerly Industrial Arts Index.

Chemical Abstracts. Chemical Abstracts Service, 2540 Olentangy River Rd., PO Box 3012, Columbus, Ohio 43210. (800) 848-6533. 1907-.

Environment Abstracts. Bowker A & I Publishing, 121 Chanlon Rd., New Providence, New Jersey 07974. (908) 464-6800. 1974-.

Environment Index. Environment Information Center, Index Research Department, 124 E. 39th St., New York, New York 10016. 1971-. Annual.

Environmental Information Connection–EIC. Planning Information Program, Dept. of Urban and Regional Planning, University of Illinois, 1003 West Nevada, Urbana, Illinois 61801. (217) 333-1369. Also available online.

Environmental Periodicals Bibliography. Environmental Studies Institute, International Academy at Santa Barbara, 800 Garden St., Suite D, Santa Barbara, California 93101. (805) 965-5010. Also available online.

Food Science and Technology Abstracts. International Food Information Service, c/o National Food Laboratory, 6363 Clark Ave., Dublin, California 94568. (800) 336-3782. 1969-.

General Science Index. H. W. Wilson Co., 950 University Ave., Bronx, New York 10452. 1978-. Monthly, also issued in annual cumulation. Cumulative subject index to English language periodicals in the subject fields of astronomy, botany, chemistry, earth science, environment and conservation, food and nutrition, genetics, mathematics, medicine and health, microbiology, oceanography, physics, physiology and zoology.

Index to Scientific Book Contents. Institute for Scientific Information, 3501 Market St., Philadelphia, Pennsylvania 19104. (800) 523-1857. 1985-. Annual. Gives contents of science books published.

Physics Briefs. Physikalische Berichte. Physik Verlag, Pappapelallee 3, Postfach 101161, Weinheim, Germany D-6940. 1979-. Semimonthly. In English. Volumes for 1979- issued by the Deutsche Physikalische Gesellschaft and the Fachinformationszentrum Energie Physik, Mathematik in cooperation with the American Institute of Physics.

Science Citation Index. Institute for Scientific Information, 3501 Market St., Philadelphia, Pennsylvania 19104. 1961-.

BIBLIOGRAPHIES

EPA Publications Bibliography. U.S. Environmental Protection Agency, Library Systems Branch, 401 M St., SW, Washington, District of Columbia 20460. (202) 260-2090. Quarterly.

ENCYCLOPEDIAS AND DICTIONARIES

Cambridge Dictionary of Biology. Peter M. B. Walker. Cambridge University Press, 40 W. 20th St., New York, New York 10011. (212) 924-3900 or (800) 227-0247. 1989. Includes 10,000 terms in zoology, botany, biochemistry, molecular biology and genetics. Previously published under the title Chambers Biology Dictionary.

A Concise Dictionary of Biology. Elizabeth Martin, ed. Oxford University Press, 200 Madison Ave., New York, New York 10016. (212) 679-7300 or (800) 334-4249. 1990. New edition. Derived from the Concise Science Dictionary, published in 1984.

Encyclopedia of Physical Science and Technology. Robert A. Meyers, ed. Academic Press, c/o Harcourt Brace Jovanovich Inc., 6277 Sea Harbor Dr., Orlando, Florida 32887. (800) 346-8648. Dictionary of engineering, technology and physical sciences.

Encyclopedia of Physics. Rita G. Lerner and George L. Trigg. VCH Publishers, 303 NW 12th Ave., Deerfield Beach, Florida 33442-1788. (305) 428-5566. 1991. Second edition.

McGraw-Hill Encyclopedia of Science and Technology. McGraw-Hill, 1221 Avenue of the Americas, New York, New York 10020. (212) 512-2000 or (800) 262-4729. 1992. Seventh edition. Issued in multiple volumes including index. Includes all science and technology broad subject areas.

Van Nostrand's Scientific Encyclopedia. Glenn D. Considine, ed. Van Nostrand Reinhold, 115 5th Ave., New York, New York 10003. (212) 254-3232. 1983. Sixth edition. Includes all broad subject areas in science.

ONLINE DATA BASES

C13 Nuclear Magnetic Resonance/Infrared Data Base. BASF AG, D-ZHV-B9, Ludwigshafen, Germany D-6700. 49 (621) 6028401.

CAS Source Index–CASSI. Chemical Abstracts Service, 2540 Olentangy River Rd., P.O. Box 3012, Columbus, Ohio 43210. (800) 848-6533 or (614) 421-3600. A listing of bibliographic and library holdings information for scientific and technical primary literature relevant to the chemical sciences.

Chemical Abstracts-CA. Chemical Abstracts Service, 2540 Olentangy River Rd., P.O. Box 3012, Columbus, Ohio 43210. (800) 848-6533 or (614) 421-3600. Information sources include 9000 journals, patents from 27 countries, two industrial property organizations, new books, conference proceedings, and government research reports.

Enviro/Energyline Abstracts Plus. R. R. Bowker Co., 121 Chanlon Rd., New Providence, New Jersey 07974. (908) 464-6800.

Environmental Periodicals Bibliography. National Information Services Corp., Ste. 6, Wyman Towers, 3100 St.

Paul St., Baltimore, Maryland 21218. (410)243-0797. Online version of abstract of same name.

HODOC: Handbook of Data on Organic Compounds. CRC Press, 2000 Corporate Blvd. N.W., Boca Raton, Florida 33431. (800) 727-7737.

PERIODICALS AND NEWSLETTERS

Topics in Carbon-13 NMR Spectroscopy. John Wiley & Sons Inc., 605 3rd Ave., New York, New York 10158-0012. (212) 850-6000. 1974-. Irregular.

RESEARCH CENTERS AND INSTITUTES

Nuclear Magnetic Resonance Facility. University of California, Davis, Davis, California 95616. (916) 752-7677.

University of Georgia, Institute for Natural Products Research. Chemistry Building, Athens, Georgia 30602. (404) 542-5800.

University of Iowa, High Field Nuclear Magnetic Resonance Facility. Department of Chemistry, Room 77 Chemistry-Botany Building, Iowa City, Iowa 52242. (319) 335-3669.

TRADE ASSOCIATIONS AND PROFESSIONAL SOCIETIES

American Institute of Physics. 335 E. 45th St., New York, New York 10017. (212) 661-9404.

Union of Concerned Scientists. 26 Church St., Cambridge, Massachusetts 02238. (617) 547-5552.

NUCLEAR POWER

See also: ENERGY RESOURCES; POWER GENERATION; REACTORS

ABSTRACTING AND INDEXING SERVICES

Applied Science and Technology Index. H.W. Wilson Co., 950 University Ave., Bronx, New York 10452. (800) 367-6770. Formerly Industrial Arts Index.

Engineering Index. The Engineering Index Inc., 345 E. 47th St., New York, New York 10017. 1962-.

Environment Abstracts. Bowker A & I Publishing, 121 Chanlon Rd., New Providence, New Jersey 07974. (908) 464-6800. 1974-.

Environment Index. Environment Information Center, Index Research Department, 124 E. 39th St., New York, New York 10016. 1971-. Annual.

Environmental Information Connection–EIC. Planning Information Program, Dept. of Urban and Regional Planning, University of Illinois, 1003 West Nevada, Urbana, Illinois 61801. (217) 333-1369. Also available online.

Environmental Periodicals Bibliography. Environmental Studies Institute, International Academy at Santa Barbara, 800 Garden St., Suite D, Santa Barbara, California 93101. (805) 965-5010. Also available online.

ERDA Research Abstracts. U.S. ERDA Technical Information Center, Box 62, Oak Ridge, Tennessee 37830.

General Science Index. H. W. Wilson Co., 950 University Ave., Bronx, New York 10452. 1978-. Monthly, also issued in annual cumulation. Cumulative subject index to English language periodicals in the subject fields of astronomy, botany, chemistry, earth science, environment and conservation, food and nutrition, genetics, mathematics, medicine and health, microbiology, oceanography, physics, physiology and zoology.

Geographical Abstracts. London School of Economics, Dept. of Geography, Regency House, 34 Duke St., London, England 1966-. Continued by Geo Abstracts issued in 6 parts: Pt. A. Landforms and the quaternary; Pt. B. Biogeography and Climatology; Pt. C. Economic geography; Pt. D. Social geography and cartography; Pt. E. Sedimentology; Pt. F. Regional and community planning.

Index to Scientific Book Contents. Institute for Scientific Information, 3501 Market St., Philadelphia, Pennsylvania 19104. (800) 523-1857. 1985-. Annual. Gives contents of science books published.

INIS Atomindex. International Atomic Energy Agency, Wagramerstrasse 5, Vienna, Austria A-1400. 222 23606198. 1988-. Semiannual. Abstracts nuclear energy and nuclear physics topics from journals, conferences, technical reports and other related publications. Issued in 6 parts: Personal Author, Corporate Entry, Subject, Report, Standard Patent, Conference (by place), Conference (by date).

Physics Briefs. Physikalische Berichte. Physik Verlag, Pappapelallee 3, Postfach 101161, Weinheim, Germany D-6940. 1979-. Semimonthly. In English. Volumes for 1979- issued by the Deutsche Physikalische Gesellschaft and the Fachinformationszentrum Energie Physik, Mathematik in cooperation with the American Institute of Physics.

Science Citation Index. Institute for Scientific Information, 3501 Market St., Philadelphia, Pennsylvania 19104. 1961-.

ALMANACS AND YEARBOOKS

Gale Environmental Almanac. Russ Hoyle. Gale Research Inc., 835 Penobscot Bldg., Detroit, Michigan 48226-4094. (313) 961-2242. 1993. Focuses on the U.S. and Canada, although worldwide and transboundary issues are discussed.

BIBLIOGRAPHIES

EPA Publications Bibliography. U.S. Environmental Protection Agency, Library Systems Branch, 401 M St., SW, Washington, District of Columbia 20460. (202) 260-2090. Quarterly.

DIRECTORIES

Canadian Environmental Directory. Canadian Almanac & Directory Publishing Co. Ltd., 134 Adelaide St. E., Ste. 27, Toronto, Ontario, Canada M5C 1K9. (416) 362-4088. 1992. Includes individuals, agencies, firms, and associations.

Fusion Facilities Directory. Fusion Power Associates, 2 Professional Dr., Suite 248, Gaithersburg, Maryland 20879. (301) 258-0545. Biennial. Government and private institutions and laboratories involved in atomic fusion research.

The Green Encyclopedia. Irene Franck, David Brownstone. Prentice-Hall, Rte. 9W, Englewood Cliffs, New York 07632. (201) 592-2000. 1992. Covers environmental organizations.

International Who's Who in Energy and Nuclear Sciences. Longman Editorial Team. Longman, c/o Gale Research Inc., 835 Penobscot Bldg., Detroit, Michigan 48226-4094. (313) 961-2242. 1983. Deals with the subject areas of energy and nuclear science. Gives professional biographical profiles of over 3800 individuals arranged by surname from A to Z. Also includes a country and topic list of the same people.

World Nuclear Directory. Longman, Burnt Mill, Harlow, England CM 20 2J6. (0279) 26721. 1988. Eighth edition. Includes organizations that are involved in nuclear physics research.

ENCYCLOPEDIAS AND DICTIONARIES

Encyclopedia of Physical Science and Technology. Robert A. Meyers, ed. Academic Press, c/o Harcourt Brace Jovanovich Inc., 6277 Sea Harbor Dr., Orlando, Florida 32887. (800) 346-8648. Dictionary of engineering, technology and physical sciences.

Encyclopedia of Physics. Rita G. Lerner and George L. Trigg. VCH Publishers, 303 NW 12th Ave., Deerfield Beach, Florida 33442-1788. (305) 428-5566. 1991. Second edition.

Energy Terminology: A Multilingual Glossary. Pergamon Microforms International, Inc., Fairview Park, Elmsford, New York 10523. (914) 592-7720. 1986. Second edition. Contains 1500 defined terms and concepts related to the field of energy together with an index of several thousand undefined keywords used in the definitions of these terms and concepts. Contents appear in four languages: English, French, German and Spanish.

Environmental Encyclopedia. William P. Cunningham, Terence Ball, et. al. Gale Research Inc., 835 Penobscot Bldg., Detroit, Michigan 48226-4094. (313) 961-2242. 1993.

Glossary of Terms in Nuclear Science and Technology. American Nuclear Society, 555 North Kensington Ave., La Grange Park, Illinois 60525. (708) 352-6611. 1986. Prepared by the American Nuclear Society Standards Committee. Subcommittee ANS-9.

Kaiman's Encyclopedia of Energy Topics. Lee Kaiman and J. Masloff. Environmental Design and Research Center, 26799 Elena Rd., Los Altos Hills, California 94022. 1983. Two volumes. Coverage of topics range from natural energy sources that are renewable to nonrenewable, and the application of these energy sources.

McGraw-Hill Encyclopedia of Science and Technology. McGraw-Hill, 1221 Avenue of the Americas, New York, New York 10020. (212) 512-2000 or (800) 262-4729. 1992. Seventh edition. Issued in multiple volumes including index. Includes all science and technology broad subject areas.

Van Nostrand's Scientific Encyclopedia. Glenn D. Considine, ed. Van Nostrand Reinhold, 115 5th Ave., New York, New York 10003. (212) 254-3232. 1983. Sixth edition. Includes all broad subject areas in science.

GENERAL WORKS

BWR Cobalt Source Identification. C.F. Falk. General Electric Co., P.O. Box 861, Gainesville, Florida 32602-0861. (904) 462-3911. 1982. Safety measures in boiling water reactors.

Environmental Viewpoints. Marie Lazzari. Gale Research Inc., 835 Penobscot Bldg., Detroit, Michigan 48226-4094. (313) 961-2242. 1992.

Indirect Solar, Geothermal, and Nuclear Energy. T. Nejat Veziroglu, ed. Nova Science Publishers Inc., 283 Commack Rd., Suite 300, Commack, New York 11725-3401. (516) 499-3103; (516) 499-3106. 1991. Presents several focussed sectors of the energy spectrum: wind energy, ocean energy, gravitational energy, I.C. engines, and fluidized beds and looks at nuclear energy.

The Nuclear Energy Option: An Alternative for the 90s. Bernard L. Cohen. Plenum Press, 233 Spring St., New York, New York 10013-1578. (212) 620-8000; (800) 221-9369. 1990. Sets out to redress what is perceived as unbalanced negative media reporting on the risks of nuclear power.

Nuclear Power Plants Worldwide. Peter D. Dresser. Gale Research Inc., 835 Penobscot Bldg., Detroit, Michigan 48226-4094. (313) 961-2242. 1993.

Predicting Nuclear and Other Technological Disasters. Christopher Lampton. F. Watts, 387 Park Ave. S., New York, New York 10016. (800) 672-6672. 1989. Discusses risks involved in state-of-the-art technology.

Reassessing Nuclear Power: The Fallout from Chernobyl. Christopher Flavin. Worldwatch Institute, 1776 Massachusetts Ave., N.W., Washington, District of Columbia 20036-1904. 1987.

Safety in the Process Industries. Butterworth-Heinemann, 80 Montvale Ave., Stoneham, Massachusetts 02180. (617) 438-8464. 1990. Hazards of process plants, and causes of accidents and how they may be controlled.

World Guide to Environmental Issues and Organizations. Peter Brackley. Longman Group Ltd., Longman House, Burnt Mill, Harlow, Essex, England CM20 2J6. (0279) 426721. 1991.

World Nuclear Power. Peter R. Mounfield. Routledge, 29 W 35th St., New York, New York 10001-2291. (212) 244-3336. 1991. Gives an encyclopedic treatment of nuclear power–history of technology, nuclear physics, reactor engineering, safety considerations, energy economics and regional and international issues.

GOVERNMENTAL ORGANIZATIONS

Bureau of Oceans and International Environmental and Scientific Affairs. 2201 C St., N.W., Washington, District of Columbia 20520. (202) 647-1554.

Office of Public Affairs. 1717 H St., N.W., Washington, District of Columbia 20555. (301) 492-7715.

Office of Public Affairs: Fish and Wildlife Service. 18th and C St., N.W., Washington, District of Columbia 20240. (202) 343-5634.

HANDBOOKS AND MANUALS

Environmental Statistics Handbook: Europe. Allan Foster, Oksana Newman. Gale Research Inc., 835 Penobscot

Bldg., Detroit, Michigan 48226-4094. (313) 961-2242. 1993.

Riegel's Handbook of Industrial Chemistry. James A. Kent, ed. Van Nostrand Reinhold, 115 5th Ave., New York, New York 10020. (212) 254-3232. 1983. Eighth edition. Includes industries such as: wastewater technology, coal technology, phosphate fertilizers, synthetic plastics, man-made textiles, detergents, sugar, animal and vegetable oils, chemical explosives, dyes, nuclear industry, and much more.

ONLINE DATA BASES

Computerized Engineering Index–COMPENDEX. Engineering Information Inc., 345 E. 47th St., New York, New York 10017. (212) 705-7600.

EBIB. Texas A & M University, Sterling C. Evans Library, Reference Division, College Station, Texas 77843. (409) 845-5741.

ENSDF-NSR. Brookhaven National Laboratory, National Nuclear Data Center, Building 197D, Upton, New York 11973. (516) 282-2901.

Enviro/Energyline Abstracts Plus. R. R. Bowker Co., 121 Chanlon Rd., New Providence, New Jersey 07974. (908) 464-6800.

Environmental Periodicals Bibliography. National Information Services Corp., Ste. 6, Wyman Towers, 3100 St. Paul St., Baltimore, Maryland 21218. (410)243-0797. Online version of abstract of same name.

International Nuclear Information System. International Atomic Energy Agency, INIS Section, Vienna International Centre, P.O. Box 100, Vienna, Austria A-1400. 43 (222) 23602882.

Monthly Catalog of United States Government Publications. U.S. G.P.O., Supt. of Docs., PO Box 371954, Pittsburgh, Pennsylvania 15250-7954. (202) 512-0000.

National Technical Information Service. U.S. Department of Commerce, National Technical Information Service, Office of Data Base Services, 5285 Port Royal Rd., Springfield, Virginia 22161. (703) 487-4807. Bibliographic database of government sponsored research and technical reports.

Nuclear News. American Nuclear Society, 555 N. Kensington Ave., LaGrange Park, Illinois 60525. (708) 352-6611.

Nuclear Science Abstracts. U.S. Department of Energy, Office of Scientific & Technical Information, P.O. Box 62, Oak Ridge, Tennessee 37831. (615) 576-6299.

PERIODICALS AND NEWSLETTERS

Analytical Chemistry. American Chemical Society, 1155 16th St. N.W., Washington, District of Columbia 20036. (800) 227-5558. 1929-. Bimonthly. Articles for chemists, life scientists and engineers.

Atomic Energy Clearing House. Congressional Information Bureau, Inc., 1325 G St., NW, Suite 1005, Washington, District of Columbia 20005. (202) 347-2275. Weekly. Peaceful uses of nuclear energy, licensing, inspection, and legislation, waste legislation, medical uses of radioactive isotopes, and new plant construction.

Critical Mass Energy Bulletin. Public Citizen Critical Mass Energy Project, 215 Pennsylvania Ave, SE, Washington, District of Columbia 20003. (202) 546-4996. Bimonthly. Nuclear power, nuclear waste, nuclear weapons facilities, renewable energy, solar technologies, energy conservation and energy efficiency, and global warming.

Fusion Power Report. Business Publishers, Inc., 951 Pershing Dr., Silver Spring, Maryland 20910. (301) 587-6300. Monthly. Scientific, engineering, economic, and political developments in the field of fusion energy.

STATISTICS SOURCES

Statistical Record of the Environment. Arsen J. Darnay. Gale Research Inc., 835 Penobscot Bldg., Detroit, Michigan 48226-4094. (313) 961-2242. 1992.

World Resources. World Resources Institute. 1709 New York Ave., N.W., Washington, District of Columbia 20006. (202) 638-6300. Annual. Statistical and textual analysis of world's natural resources and the effects of growth-caused environmental pollution.

TRADE ASSOCIATIONS AND PROFESSIONAL SOCIETIES

Abalone Alliance. 2940 16th St., Suite 310, San Francisco, California 94103. (415) 861-0592.

American Institute of Physics. 335 E. 45th St., New York, New York 10017. (212) 661-9404.

American Nuclear Society. 555 N. Kensington Ave., La Grange Park, Illinois 60525. (708) 352-6611.

American Physical Society. 335 E. 45th St., New York, New York 10017. (212) 682-7341.

Americans for Nuclear Energy. 2525 Wilson Blvd., Arlington, Virginia 22201. (703) 528-4430.

Center for Religion, Ethics and Social Policy. Anabel Taylor Hall, Cornell University, Ithaca, New York 14853. (607) 255-6486.

Citizen's Call. P.O. Box 1722, Cedar City, Utah 84720. (801) 586-4808.

Citizen's Energy Council. 77 Homewood Ave., Allendale, New Jersey 07401. (201) 327-3914.

Committee of Atomic Bomb Survivors in the U.S. 1109 Shellgate Pl., Alameda, California 94501. (415) 523-5617.

Critical Mass Energy Project of Public Citizen. 215 Pennsylvania Ave., S.E., Washington, District of Columbia 20003. (202) 546-4996.

Environmental Coalition on Nuclear Power. 433 Orlando Ave., State College, Pennsylvania 16803. (814) 237-3900.

Fusion Power Associates. Two Professional Dr., Suite 248, Gaithersburg, Maryland 20879. (301) 258-0545.

Institute of Nuclear Materials Management. 60 Revere Dr., Suite 500, Northbrook, Illinois 60062. (708) 480-9080.

Institute of Nuclear Power Operations. 1100 Circle 75 Pkwy., Suite 1500, Atlanta, Georgia 30339. (040) 953-3600.

Nuclear Action Project. 2020 Pennsylvania Ave., Suite 103, Washington, District of Columbia 20006. (202) 331-9831.

Nuclear Free America. 325 E. 25th St., Baltimore, Maryland 21218. (301) 235-3575.

Nuclear Information and Records Management. 210 Fifth Ave., New York, New York 10010. (212) 683-9221.

Nuclear Information and Resource Service. 1424 16th St., N.W., #601, Washington, District of Columbia 20036. (202) 328-0002.

Safe Energy Communication Council. 1717 Massachusetts Ave., N.W., LL215, Washington, District of Columbia 20036. (202) 483-8491.

Seacoast Anti-Pollution League. Five Market St., Portsmouth, New Hampshire 03801. (603) 431-5089.

Union of Concerned Scientists. 26 Church St., Cambridge, Massachusetts 02238. (617) 547-5552.

NUCLEAR POWER PLANTS

See: REACTORS

NUCLEAR REACTORS

See: REACTORS

NUCLEAR SAFETY

ABSTRACTING AND INDEXING SERVICES

Applied Science and Technology Index. H.W. Wilson Co., 950 University Ave., Bronx, New York 10452. (800) 367-6770. Formerly Industrial Arts Index.

Engineering Index. The Engineering Index Inc., 345 E. 47th St., New York, New York 10017. 1962-.

Environment Abstracts. Bowker A & I Publishing, 121 Chanlon Rd., New Providence, New Jersey 07974. (908) 464-6800. 1974-.

Environment Index. Environment Information Center, Index Research Department, 124 E. 39th St., New York, New York 10016. 1971-. Annual.

Environmental Information Connection–EIC. Planning Information Program, Dept. of Urban and Regional Planning, University of Illinois, 1003 West Nevada, Urbana, Illinois 61801. (217) 333-1369. Also available online.

Environmental Periodicals Bibliography. Environmental Studies Institute, International Academy at Santa Barbara, 800 Garden St., Suite D, Santa Barbara, California 93101. (805) 965-5010. Also available online.

Geographical Abstracts. London School of Economics, Dept. of Geography, Regency House, 34 Duke St., London, England 1966-. Continued by Geo Abstracts issued in 6 parts: Pt. A. Landforms and the quaternary; Pt. B. Biogeography and Climatology; Pt. C. Economic geography; Pt. D. Social geography and cartography; Pt. E. Sedimentology; Pt. F. Regional and community planning.

Index to Scientific Book Contents. Institute for Scientific Information, 3501 Market St., Philadelphia, Pennsylvania 19104. (800) 523-1857. 1985-. Annual. Gives contents of science books published.

INIS Atomindex. International Atomic Energy Agency, Wagramerstrasse 5, Vienna, Austria A-1400. 222 23606198. 1988-. Semiannual. Abstracts nuclear energy and nuclear physics topics from journals, conferences, technical reports and other related publications. Issued in 6 parts: Personal Author, Corporate Entry, Subject, Report, Standard Patent, Conference (by place), Conference (by date).

BIBLIOGRAPHIES

EPA Publications Bibliography. U.S. Environmental Protection Agency, Library Systems Branch, 401 M St., SW, Washington, District of Columbia 20460. (202) 260-2090. Quarterly.

DIRECTORIES

World Nuclear Directory. Longman, Burnt Mill, Harlow, England CM 20 2J6. (0279) 26721. 1988. Eighth edition. Includes organizations that are involved in nuclear physics research.

ENCYCLOPEDIAS AND DICTIONARIES

Encyclopedia of Physical Science and Technology. Robert A. Meyers, ed. Academic Press, c/o Harcourt Brace Jovanovich Inc., 6277 Sea Harbor Dr., Orlando, Florida 32887. (800) 346-8648. Dictionary of engineering, technology and physical sciences.

Encyclopedia of Physics. Rita G. Lerner and George L. Trigg. VCH Publishers, 303 NW 12th Ave., Deerfield Beach, Florida 33442-1788. (305) 428-5566. 1991. Second edition.

Glossary of Terms in Nuclear Science and Technology. American Nuclear Society, 555 North Kensington Ave., La Grange Park, Illinois 60525. (708) 352-6611. 1986. Prepared by the American Nuclear Society Standards Committee. Subcommittee ANS-9.

GENERAL WORKS

Smoking Guns. Nuclear Regulatory Commission, Advisory Committee on Nuclear Facility Safety, 1717 H St., NW, Washington, District of Columbia 20555. (301) 492-7000. 1991. Deals with the Energy Department's campaign to improve safety and environmental compliance at its nuclear weapons plants.

ONLINE DATA BASES

Computerized Engineering Index–COMPENDEX. Engineering Information Inc., 345 E. 47th St., New York, New York 10017. (212) 705-7600.

Enviro/Energyline Abstracts Plus. R. R. Bowker Co., 121 Chanlon Rd., New Providence, New Jersey 07974. (908) 464-6800.

Environmental Periodicals Bibliography. National Information Services Corp., Ste. 6, Wyman Towers, 3100 St. Paul St., Baltimore, Maryland 21218. (410)243-0797. Online version of abstract of same name.

International Nuclear Information System. International Atomic Energy Agency, INIS Section, Vienna International Centre, P.O. Box 100, Vienna, Austria A-1400. 43 (222) 23602882.

Monthly Catalog of United States Government Publications. U.S. G.P.O., Supt. of Docs., PO Box 371954, Pittsburgh, Pennsylvania 15250-7954. (202) 512-0000.

National Technical Information Service. U.S. Department of Commerce, National Technical Information Service, Office of Data Base Services, 5285 Port Royal Rd., Springfield, Virginia 22161. (703) 487-4807. Bibliographic database of government sponsored research and technical reports.

Nuclear Science Abstracts. U.S. Department of Energy, Office of Scientific & Technical Information, P.O. Box 62, Oak Ridge, Tennessee 37831. (615) 576-6299.

PERIODICALS AND NEWSLETTERS

Groundswell. Nuclear Information and Resource Service, Inc., 1424 16th St., NW, No. 601, Washington, District of Columbia 20036. (202) 328-0002. Quarterly. Hazards of nuclear energy and safe alternative sources; legislative and regulatory trends, policies of utility corporations, and funding.

New Abolitionist. Nuclear Free America, 325 E. 25th St., Baltimore, Massachusetts 21218. (301) 235-3575. Quarterly. Nuclear free zone movement.

TRADE ASSOCIATIONS AND PROFESSIONAL SOCIETIES

Natural Resources Defense Council. 40 W. 20th St., New York, New York 10011. (212) 727-2700.

Union of Concerned Scientists. 26 Church St., Cambridge, Massachusetts 02238. (617) 547-5552.

NUCLEAR WEAPONS

ABSTRACTING AND INDEXING SERVICES

Applied Science and Technology Index. H.W. Wilson Co., 950 University Ave., Bronx, New York 10452. (800) 367-6770. Formerly Industrial Arts Index.

Engineering Index. The Engineering Index Inc., 345 E. 47th St., New York, New York 10017. 1962-.

ERDA Research Abstracts. U.S. ERDA Technical Information Center, Box 62, Oak Ridge, Tennessee 37830.

General Science Index. H. W. Wilson Co., 950 University Ave., Bronx, New York 10452. 1978-. Monthly, also issued in annual cumulation. Cumulative subject index to English language periodicals in the subject fields of astronomy, botany, chemistry, earth science, environment and conservation, food and nutrition, genetics, mathematics, medicine and health, microbiology, oceanography, physics, physiology and zoology.

Geographical Abstracts. London School of Economics, Dept. of Geography, Regency House, 34 Duke St., London, England 1966-. Continued by Geo Abstracts issued in 6 parts: Pt. A. Landforms and the quaternary; Pt. B. Biogeography and Climatology; Pt. C. Economic geography; Pt. D. Social geography and cartography; Pt.

E. Sedimentology; Pt. F. Regional and community planning.

Index to Scientific Book Contents. Institute for Scientific Information, 3501 Market St., Philadelphia, Pennsylvania 19104. (800) 523-1857. 1985-. Annual. Gives contents of science books published.

INIS Atomindex. International Atomic Energy Agency, Wagramerstrasse 5, Vienna, Austria A-1400. 222 23606198. 1988-. Semiannual. Abstracts nuclear energy and nuclear physics topics from journals, conferences, technical reports and other related publications. Issued in 6 parts: Personal Author, Corporate Entry, Subject, Report, Standard Patent, Conference (by place), Conference (by date).

Science Citation Index. Institute for Scientific Information, 3501 Market St., Philadelphia, Pennsylvania 19104. 1961-.

DIRECTORIES

World Nuclear Directory. Longman, Burnt Mill, Harlow, England CM 20 2J6. (0279) 26721. 1988. Eighth edition. Includes organizations that are involved in nuclear physics research.

ENCYCLOPEDIAS AND DICTIONARIES

Glossary of Terms in Nuclear Science and Technology. American Nuclear Society, 555 North Kensington Ave., La Grange Park, Illinois 60525. (708) 352-6611. 1986. Prepared by the American Nuclear Society Standards Committee. Subcommittee ANS-9.

GENERAL WORKS

Environmental Crimes at DOE's Nuclear Weapons Facilities. House Committee on Energy and Commerce. U.S. G.P.O., Washington, District of Columbia 20401. (202) 512-0000. 1990. Management of nuclear facilities, safety regulations, and environmental health.

Environmental Problems at the Department of Energy's Nuclear Weapons Complex. J. Dexter Peach. U.S. General Accounting Office, 441 G St., NW, Washington, District of Columbia 20548. (202) 275-5067. 1989. Environmental aspects of nuclear weapons industry and nuclear facilities.

Nuclear Free: The New Zealand Way. David Lange. Penguin Books, 375 Hudson St., New York, New York 10014. (212) 366-2000; (800) 253-2304. 1990. Provides a first-hand account of the behind-the-scenes story of how one small country in the South Pacific found the political will to say "no" to nuclear weapons.

The Nuclear Weapons Complex. National Research Council. National Academy Press, 2101 Constitution Ave., NW, PO Box 285, Washington, District of Columbia 20418. (202) 334-3313. 1989. Management for health, safety, and the environment.

Radioactive Heaven and Earth. The Apex Press, c/o Council on International and Public Affairs, 777 United Nations Plaza, Suite 3C, New York, New York 10017. (212) 953-6920. 1991. The health and environmental effects of nuclear weapons testing in, on, and above the Earth.

ONLINE DATA BASES

Computerized Engineering Index–COMPENDEX. Engineering Information Inc., 345 E. 47th St., New York, New York 10017. (212) 705-7600.

International Nuclear Information System. International Atomic Energy Agency, INIS Section, Vienna International Centre, P.O. Box 100, Vienna, Austria A-1400. 43 (222) 23602882.

Life Sciences from NTIS. National Technical Information Center for the Utilization of Federal Technology, 5285 Port Royal Rd., Springfield, Virginia 22161. (703) 487-4650.

Monthly Catalog of United States Government Publications. U.S. G.P.O., Supt. of Docs., PO Box 371954, Pittsburgh, Pennsylvania 15250-7954. (202) 512-0000.

National Technical Information Service. U.S. Department of Commerce, National Technical Information Service, Office of Data Base Services, 5285 Port Royal Rd., Springfield, Virginia 22161. (703) 487-4807. Bibliographic database of government sponsored research and technical reports.

Nuclear Science Abstracts. U.S. Department of Energy, Office of Scientific & Technical Information, P.O. Box 62, Oak Ridge, Tennessee 37831. (615) 576-6299.

PressNet Environmental Reports. Chemical Information Systems, Inc., 7215 York Rd., Baltimore, Maryland 21212. (301) 321-8440.

TRADE ASSOCIATIONS AND PROFESSIONAL SOCIETIES

Abalone Alliance. 2940 16th St., Suite 310, San Francisco, California 94103. (415) 861-0592.

Accidental Nuclear War Prevention Project. 1187 Coast Village Rd., Suite 123, Santa Barbara, California 93108. (805) 965-3443.

Friends of the Earth. 218 D St., SE, Washington, District of Columbia 20003. (202) 544-2600.

Greenpeace. 1436 U St., NW, Washington, District of Columbia 20009. (202) 462-1177.

Nukewatch. P.O. Box 2658, Madison, Wisconsin 53701-2658. (608) 256-4146.

Physicians for Social Responsibility. 1000 16th St., NW, Suite 810, Washington, District of Columbia 20036. (202) 785-3777.

Union of Concerned Scientists. 26 Church St., Cambridge, Massachusetts 02238. (617) 547-5552.

NUCLEAR WINTER

ABSTRACTING AND INDEXING SERVICES

Environment Abstracts. Bowker A & I Publishing, 121 Chanlon Rd., New Providence, New Jersey 07974. (908) 464-6800. 1974-.

Environment Index. Environment Information Center, Index Research Department, 124 E. 39th St., New York, New York 10016. 1971-. Annual.

Environmental Information Connection–EIC. Planning Information Program, Dept. of Urban and Regional Planning, University of Illinois, 1003 West Nevada, Urbana, Illinois 61801. (217) 333-1369. Also available online.

Environmental Periodicals Bibliography. Environmental Studies Institute, International Academy at Santa Barbara, 800 Garden St., Suite D, Santa Barbara, California 93101. (805) 965-5010. Also available online.

ERDA Research Abstracts. U.S. ERDA Technical Information Center, Box 62, Oak Ridge, Tennessee 37830.

Geographical Abstracts. London School of Economics, Dept. of Geography, Regency House, 34 Duke St., London, England 1966-. Continued by Geo Abstracts issued in 6 parts: Pt. A. Landforms and the quaternary; Pt. B. Biogeography and Climatology; Pt. C. Economic geography; Pt. D. Social geography and cartography; Pt. E. Sedimentology; Pt. F. Regional and community planning.

Index to Scientific Book Contents. Institute for Scientific Information, 3501 Market St., Philadelphia, Pennsylvania 19104. (800) 523-1857. 1985-. Annual. Gives contents of science books published.

BIBLIOGRAPHIES

EPA Publications Bibliography. U.S. Environmental Protection Agency, Library Systems Branch, 401 M St., SW, Washington, District of Columbia 20460. (202) 260-2090. Quarterly.

Nuclear Winter: A Bibliography. Robert W. Lockerby. Vance Bibliographies, PO Box 229, 112 N. Charter St., Monticello, Illinois 61856. (217) 762-3831. 1986.

DIRECTORIES

World Nuclear Directory. Longman, Burnt Mill, Harlow, England CM 20 2J6. (0279) 26721. 1988. Eighth edition. Includes organizations that are involved in nuclear physics research.

ENCYCLOPEDIAS AND DICTIONARIES

The Encyclopedia of Climatology. John E. Oliver and Rhodes W. Fairbridge, eds. Van Nostrand Reinhold, 115 5th Ave., New York, New York 10003. (212) 254-3232. 1987. Belongs in the series Encyclopedia of Earth Sciences, v.11.

GENERAL WORKS

Europhysics Study Conference on Induced Critical Conditions in the Atmosphere. A. Tartaglia. World Scientific, 687 Hartwell St., Teaneck, New Jersey 07666. (800) 227-7562. 1990. Deals with climatology, nuclear winter, ozone layer depletion, and the greenhouse effect.

Fire and Ice: The Nuclear Winter. Michael Rowan-Robinson. Longman Group Ltd., Longman House, Burnt Mill, Harlow, England CM20 2J6. (0279) 426721. 1985.

Global Air Pollution: Problems for the 1990s. Howard Bridgman. Belhaven Press, 136 S. Broadway, Irvington, New York 10533. (914) 591-9111. 1990. Addresses the environmental problems caused by human activities resulting in change and deterioration of the earth's atmosphere.

Nuclear Winter: The Evidence and the Risks. Owen Greene. B. Blackwell, 3 Cambridge Ctr., Suite 208, Cambridge, Massachusetts 02142. (617) 225-0401. 1985. Environmental aspects of nuclear warfare.

A Path Where No Man Thought. Carl Sagan. Random House Inc., 201 E. 50th St., New York, New York 10022. (212) 751-2600. 1990.

ONLINE DATA BASES

Enviro/Energyline Abstracts Plus. R. R. Bowker Co., 121 Chanlon Rd., New Providence, New Jersey 07974. (908) 464-6800.

Environmental Periodicals Bibliography. National Information Services Corp., Ste. 6, Wyman Towers, 3100 St. Paul St., Baltimore, Maryland 21218. (410)243-0797. Online version of abstract of same name.

Monthly Catalog of United States Government Publications. U.S. G.P.O., Supt. of Docs., PO Box 371954, Pittsburgh, Pennsylvania 15250-7954. (202) 512-0000.

National Technical Information Service. U.S. Department of Commerce, National Technical Information Service, Office of Data Base Services, 5285 Port Royal Rd., Springfield, Virginia 22161. (703) 487-4807. Bibliographic database of government sponsored research and technical reports.

Nuclear Science Abstracts. U.S. Department of Energy, Office of Scientific & Technical Information, P.O. Box 62, Oak Ridge, Tennessee 37831. (615) 576-6299.

PressNet Environmental Reports. Chemical Information Systems, Inc., 7215 York Rd., Baltimore, Maryland 21212. (301) 321-8440.

TRADE ASSOCIATIONS AND PROFESSIONAL SOCIETIES

Union of Concerned Scientists. 26 Church St., Cambridge, Massachusetts 02238. (617) 547-5552.

NUTRIENTS

ABSTRACTING AND INDEXING SERVICES

ASFA Aquaculture Abstracts. Cambridge Scientific Abstracts, Inc., 5161 River Rd., Bethesda, Maryland 20816. (301) 961-6750. 1984.

Biological Abstracts. BIOSIS, 2100 Arch St., Philadelphia, Pennsylvania 19103-1399. (215) 587-4800. 1927-.

Biological and Agricultural Index. H.W. Wilson Co., 950 University Ave., Bronx, New York 10452. (800) 367-6770. 1916-. Monthly.

Biotechnology Research Abstracts. Cambridge Scientific Abstracts, 5161 River Rd., Bethesda, Maryland 20816. (301) 961-6750. Monthly. Includes such broad areas as genetic intervention, biochemical genetics, and microbiological techniques.

Consumer Health and Nutrition Index. Oryx Press, 4041 N. Central at Indian School Rd., Ste. 700, Phoenix, Arizona 85012-3397. (602) 265-2651. Quarterly. Includes articles in 35 popular level health and nutrition magazines and newsletters. Many of these periodicals are not indexed elsewhere. Includes articles in nutrition, health and related areas.

Ecological Abstracts. Geo Abstracts Ltd. Elsevier Applied Science, Crown House, Linton Rd., Barking, England IG 11 8JU. 1974-. Derived from over 600 leading ecological and environmental journals, plus books, conference proceedings, reports and theses.

Ecology Abstracts. Cambridge Scientific Abstracts, 5161 River Rd., Bethesda, Maryland 20816. (301) 961-6750. Monthly.

Environment Abstracts. Bowker A & I Publishing, 121 Chanlon Rd., New Providence, New Jersey 07974. (908) 464-6800. 1974-.

Environment Index. Environment Information Center, Index Research Department, 124 E. 39th St., New York, New York 10016. 1971-. Annual.

Environmental Information Connection–EIC. Planning Information Program, Dept. of Urban and Regional Planning, University of Illinois, 1003 West Nevada, Urbana, Illinois 61801. (217) 333-1369. Also available online.

Environmental Periodicals Bibliography. Environmental Studies Institute, International Academy at Santa Barbara, 800 Garden St., Suite D, Santa Barbara, California 93101. (805) 965-5010. Also available online.

Food and Nutrition Quarterly Index. Oryx Press, 4041 N. Central at Indian School Rd., Ste. 700, Phoenix, Arizona 85012-3397. (602) 265-2651. 1985-. Quarterly. Abstracting service succeeds the Food and Nutrition Bibliography which was issued from 1980-1984 and covered the literature from 1978-1980, and was a continuation of the FNIC catalog and its supplements.

Food Science and Technology Abstracts. International Food Information Service, c/o National Food Laboratory, 6363 Clark Ave., Dublin, California 94568. (800) 336-3782. 1969-.

General Science Index. H. W. Wilson Co., 950 University Ave., Bronx, New York 10452. 1978-. Monthly, also issued in annual cumulation. Cumulative subject index to English language periodicals in the subject fields of astronomy, botany, chemistry, earth science, environment and conservation, food and nutrition, genetics, mathematics, medicine and health, microbiology, oceanography, physics, physiology and zoology.

Geographical Abstracts. London School of Economics, Dept. of Geography, Regency House, 34 Duke St., London, England 1966-. Continued by Geo Abstracts issued in 6 parts: Pt. A. Landforms and the quaternary; Pt. B. Biogeography and Climatology; Pt. C. Economic geography; Pt. D. Social geography and cartography; Pt. E. Sedimentology; Pt. F. Regional and community planning.

Pollution Abstracts. Cambridge Scientific Abstracts, 5161 River Rd., Bethesda, Maryland 20816. (301) 961-6750. Six/year. Indexes worldwide technical literature on environmental pollution. Covers air pollution, marine and freshwater pollution, sewage and wastewater treatment, waste management, toxicology and health, noise pollution, radiation, land pollution, and environmental policies, programs, legislation, and education. Also available online.

Science Citation Index. Institute for Scientific Information, 3501 Market St., Philadelphia, Pennsylvania 19104. 1961-.

BIBLIOGRAPHIES

EPA Publications Bibliography. U.S. Environmental Protection Agency, Library Systems Branch, 401 M St., SW, Washington, District of Columbia 20460. (202) 260-2090. Quarterly.

Food and Nutrition Information Guide. Paula Szilard. Libraries Unlimited, Inc., PO Box 6633, Englewood, Colorado 80155-6633. (303) 770-1220. 1987. Focuses on reference materials on human nutrition dietetics, food science and technology, and related subjects such as food service. It covers chiefly English-language materials published in the last ten years.

ENCYCLOPEDIAS AND DICTIONARIES

Dictionary of Nutrition. R. Ashley and H. Duggal. St. Martin's Press, 175 5th Ave., New York, New York 10010. (212) 674-5151. 1975.

Dictionary of Nutrition and Food Technology. Arnold E. Bender. Butterworth-Heinemann, 80 Montvale Ave., Stoneham, Massachusetts 02180. (617) 438-8464. Equipment and techniques, abbreviations, proper names, and the composition of common foods; covers agriculture, engineering, microbiology, biochemistry, and aspects of medicine.

Encyclopedia of Human Biology. Renato Dulbecco, ed. Academic Press, c/o Harcourt Brace Jovanovich Inc., 6277 Sea Harbor Dr., Orlando, Florida 32887. (800) 346-8648. 1991. Eight volumes.

Food and Nutrition Encyclopedia. A. H. Ensminger, et al. Pegus Press, 648 W. Sierra Ave, Clovis, California 93612. 1983. Two volumes. Covers commodities, nutrients, concepts, nutrition disorders and simple nutritional biochemistry with both brief and extensive entries.

McGraw-Hill Encyclopedia of Science and Technology. McGraw-Hill, 1221 Avenue of the Americas, New York, New York 10020. (212) 512-2000 or (800) 262-4729. 1992. Seventh edition. Issued in multiple volumes including index. Includes all science and technology broad subject areas.

The Nutrition and Health Encyclopedia. David F. Tver and Percy Russell. Van Nostrand Reinhold, 115 5th Ave., New York, New York 10003. (212) 254-3232. 1989.

Van Nostrand's Scientific Encyclopedia. Glenn D. Considine, ed. Van Nostrand Reinhold, 115 5th Ave., New York, New York 10003. (212) 254-3232. 1983. Sixth edition. Includes all broad subject areas in science.

GENERAL WORKS

Agricultural Ecology. Joy Tivy. John Wiley & Sons, Inc., 605 3rd Ave., New York, New York 10158-0012. (212) 850-6000. 1990. Analyzes the nature of relationships between crops, livestock, and the biophysical environment, and the extent to which man has modified the products and environment to suit his own needs.

Agriculture and Fertilizers. Oluf Chr. Bockman. Agricultural Group, Norsk Hydro, Oslo, Norway 1990. Fertilizers in perspective, their role in feeding the world, environmental challenges, and alternatives.

How to Protect Your Child Against Pesticides in Food. Anne Witte Garland. Natural Resources Defense Council, 40 W. 20th St., New York, New York 10011. (212) 727-2700. 1989. Food contamination, pesticide residues in food, and children's health and hygiene.

Microbial Enzymes in Aquatic Environments. Ryszard J. Chrost. Springer-Varlag, 175 5th Ave., New York, New York 10010. (212) 460-1500. 1991. Brings together studies on enzymatic degradation processes from disciplines as diverse as water and sediment research, bacterial and algal aquatic ecophysiology, eutrophication, nutrient cycling, and biogeochemistry, in both freshwater and marine ecosystem.

Nutrient Cycling in Terrestrial Ecosystems Field Methods. A. F. Harrison, et al. Elsevier Science Publishing Co., 655 Avenue of the Americas, New York, New York 10010. (212) 984-5800. 1990. Describes a wide range of methods for the estimation of nutrient fluxes. The book is divided into sections dealing with inputs, turnover, losses and plant uptake processes.

HANDBOOKS AND MANUALS

Fertile Soil: A Grower's Guide to Organic and Inorganic Fertilizers. Robert Parnes. AgAccess, PO Box 2008, Davis, California 95617. (916) 756-7177. 1990. Comprehensive technical resource on creating fertile soils using a balanced program that does not rely on chemical fertilizers.

Internal Nutrition. University of Iowa Hospitals and Clinics. Iowa State University Press, 2121 S. State Ave., Ames, Iowa 50010. (515) 292-0140. 1990. A handbook for dieticians and health professionals.

ONLINE DATA BASES

AGRICOLA. U.S. Department of Agriculture, Office of Public Affairs, 14 Independence Ave., S.W., Washington, District of Columbia 20250. (202) 447-7454.

BIOSIS Previews. BIOSIS, 2100 Arch St., Philadelphia, Pennsylvania 19103-1399. (215) 587-4800. Largest and most comprehensive database of research in the life sciences. Contains citations for nearly 9000 primary research journals, monographs, reviews, symposia, preliminary reports, semi-popular journals, selected institutional reports, government reports and research communications.

Enviro/Energyline Abstracts Plus. R. R. Bowker Co., 121 Chanlon Rd., New Providence, New Jersey 07974. (908) 464-6800.

Environmental Periodicals Bibliography. National Information Services Corp., Ste. 6, Wyman Towers, 3100 St. Paul St., Baltimore, Maryland 21218. (410)243-0797. Online version of abstract of same name.

Oil & Gas Journal Energy Database. PennWell Books, PO Box 1260, Tulsa, Oklahoma 74101. (918) 835-3161.

SCISEARCH. Institute for Scientific Information, University City Science Center, 3501 Market St., Philadelphia, Pennsylvania 19104. (215) 386-0100.

PERIODICALS AND NEWSLETTERS

Environmental Nutrition. Environmental Nutrition, Inc., 52 Riverside Dr., 15th Fl., New York, New York 10024. (212) 362-0424. Monthly.

The Journal of Biological Chemistry. American Society of Biological Chemists, 428 E. Preston St., Baltimore, Maryland 21202. Three times a month. Biological, agricultural, and energy aspects of the environment.

STATISTICS SOURCES

Quality Assurance Data for Routine Water Analysis. U.S. Geological Survey. U.S. G.P.O., Washington, District of Columbia 20401. (202) 512-0000. Annual. Test results determining alkalinity, inorganic ion, trace metal and organic nutrients.

TRADE ASSOCIATIONS AND PROFESSIONAL SOCIETIES

American Institute of Biological Sciences. 730 11th St., N.W., Washington, District of Columbia 20001-4521. (202) 628-1500.

NUTRITION

ABSTRACTING AND INDEXING SERVICES

ASFA Aquaculture Abstracts. Cambridge Scientific Abstracts, Inc., 5161 River Rd., Bethesda, Maryland 20816. (301) 961-6750. 1984.

Biological Abstracts. BIOSIS, 2100 Arch St., Philadelphia, Pennsylvania 19103-1399. (215) 587-4800. 1927-.

Biological and Agricultural Index. H.W. Wilson Co., 950 University Ave., Bronx, New York 10452. (800) 367-6770. 1916-. Monthly.

Biotechnology Research Abstracts. Cambridge Scientific Abstracts, 5161 River Rd., Bethesda, Maryland 20816. (301) 961-6750. Monthly. Includes such broad areas as genetic intervention, biochemical genetics, and microbiological techniques.

Consumer Health and Nutrition Index. Oryx Press, 4041 N. Central at Indian School Rd., Ste. 700, Phoenix, Arizona 85012-3397. (602) 265-2651. Quarterly. Includes articles in 35 popular level health and nutrition magazines and newsletters. Many of these periodicals are not indexed elsewhere. Includes articles in nutrition, health and related areas.

Crop Physiology Abstracts. C. A. B. International, 845 North Park Ave., Tucson, Arizona 85719. (602) 621-7897 or (800) 528-4841. 1975-. Monthly. Abstracts focus on the physiology of all higher plants of economic importance. Aspects include germination, reproductive development, nitrogen fixation, metabolic inhibitors, salinity, radiobiology, enzymes, membranes and other related areas.

Ecological Abstracts. Geo Abstracts Ltd. Elsevier Applied Science, Crown House, Linton Rd., Barking, England IG 11 8JU. 1974-. Derived from over 600 leading ecological and environmental journals, plus books, conference proceedings, reports and theses.

Ecology Abstracts. Cambridge Scientific Abstracts, 5161 River Rd., Bethesda, Maryland 20816. (301) 961-6750. Monthly.

Environment Abstracts. Bowker A & I Publishing, 121 Chanlon Rd., New Providence, New Jersey 07974. (908) 464-6800. 1974-.

Environment Index. Environment Information Center, Index Research Department, 124 E. 39th St., New York, New York 10016. 1971-. Annual.

Environmental Information Connection–EIC. Planning Information Program, Dept. of Urban and Regional Planning, University of Illinois, 1003 West Nevada, Urbana, Illinois 61801. (217) 333-1369. Also available online.

Environmental Periodicals Bibliography. Environmental Studies Institute, International Academy at Santa Barbara, 800 Garden St., Suite D, Santa Barbara, California 93101. (805) 965-5010. Also available online.

Food and Nutrition Quarterly Index. Oryx Press, 4041 N. Central at Indian School Rd., Ste. 700, Phoenix, Arizona 85012-3397. (602) 265-2651. 1985-. Quarterly. Abstracting service succeeds the Food and Nutrition Bibliography which was issued from 1980-1984 and covered the literature from 1978-1980, and was a continuation of the FNIC catalog and its supplements.

Food Science and Technology Abstracts. International Food Information Service, c/o National Food Laboratory, 6363 Clark Ave., Dublin, California 94568. (800) 336-3782. 1969-.

General Science Index. H. W. Wilson Co., 950 University Ave., Bronx, New York 10452. 1978-. Monthly, also issued in annual cumulation. Cumulative subject index to English language periodicals in the subject fields of astronomy, botany, chemistry, earth science, environment and conservation, food and nutrition, genetics, mathematics, medicine and health, microbiology, oceanography, physics, physiology and zoology.

Index to Scientific Book Contents. Institute for Scientific Information, 3501 Market St., Philadelphia, Pennsylvania 19104. (800) 523-1857. 1985-. Annual. Gives contents of science books published.

Pollution Abstracts. Cambridge Scientific Abstracts, 5161 River Rd., Bethesda, Maryland 20816. (301) 961-6750. Six/year. Indexes worldwide technical literature on environmental pollution. Covers air pollution, marine and freshwater pollution, sewage and wastewater treatment, waste management, toxicology and health, noise pollution, radiation, land pollution, and environmental policies, programs, legislation, and education. Also available online.

Science Citation Index. Institute for Scientific Information, 3501 Market St., Philadelphia, Pennsylvania 19104. 1961-.

ALMANACS AND YEARBOOKS

Environmental Almanac. World Resources Institute. Houghton Mifflin, 1 Beacon St., Boston, Massachusetts 02108. (617) 725-5000; (800) 225-3362. 1991. Covers consumer products, energy, endangered species, food safety, global warming, solid wastes, toxics, wetlands and other related areas. Also included are the names and addresses of the chief environmental executives for all 50 states.

BIBLIOGRAPHIES

Cholesterol in Foods and Its Effects on Animals and Humans. National Technical Information Service, 5285 Port Royal Rd., Springfield, Virginia 22161. (703) 487-4650.

Current Contents. Agriculture, Biology and Environmental Sciences. Institute for Scientific Information, 3501 Market St., Philadelphia, Pennsylvania 19104. (800) 523-1857. 1973-. Previous title: Current Contents. Agricultural, Food & Veterinary Sciences. Gives the table of contents of periodicals in the fields of agriculture, biology, environmental and related areas.

Dietary Cholesterol: Health Concerns and the Food Industry. National Technical Information Service, 5285 Port Royal Rd., Springfield, Virginia 22161. (703) 487-4650. 1989.

EPA Publications Bibliography. U.S. Environmental Protection Agency, Library Systems Branch, 401 M St., SW, Washington, District of Columbia 20460. (202) 260-2090. Quarterly.

Food and Nutrition Information Guide. Paula Szilard. Libraries Unlimited, Inc., PO Box 6633, Englewood, Colorado 80155-6633. (303) 770-1220. 1987. Focuses on reference materials on human nutrition dietetics, food science and technology, and related subjects such as food service. It covers chiefly English-language materials published in the last ten years.

Nutrition Education Resource Guide: An Annotated Bibliography of Education Materials. Food and Nutrition Information Center. National Agricultural Library, 10301 Baltimore Blvd., Beltsville, Maryland 20705-2351. (301) 504-5755. 1991.

DIRECTORIES

Community Guide to Cholesterol Resources. U.S. G.P.O., Washington, District of Columbia 20401. (202) 512-0000. 1988. Directory of low-cholesterol diet and community health services.

National Cholesterol Education Program Coordinating Committee Members Activities and Materials Directory. U.S. Department of Health and Human Services, 200 Independence Ave. SW, Washington, District of Columbia 20201. (202) 619-0257. 1991. Heart disease prevention and health promotion directories.

ENCYCLOPEDIAS AND DICTIONARIES

Cambridge Encyclopedia of Life Sciences. A. E. Friday and David S. Ingram. Cambridge University Press, 40 W 20th St., New York, New York 10011. (212) 924-3900 or (800) 227-0247. 1985. Includes all topics under biology and ecology.

Dictionary of Nutrition. R. Ashley and H. Duggal. St. Martin's Press, 175 5th Ave., New York, New York 10010. (212) 674-5151. 1975.

Dictionary of Nutrition and Food Technology. Arnold E. Bender. Butterworth-Heinemann, 80 Montvale Ave., Stoneham, Massachusetts 02180. (617) 438-8464. Equipment and techniques, abbreviations, proper names, and the composition of common foods; covers agriculture, engineering, microbiology, biochemistry, and aspects of medicine.

The Dictionary of Sodium, Fats, and Cholesterol. Barbara Kraus. Putnam Berkley Group, 200 Madison Ave., New York, New York 10016. (212) 951-8400. 1990. Food composition, fat, cholesterol, and sodium.

Encyclopedia of Human Biology. Renato Dulbecco, ed. Academic Press, c/o Harcourt Brace Jovanovich Inc.,

6277 Sea Harbor Dr., Orlando, Florida 32887. (800) 346-8648. 1991. Eight volumes.

Food and Nutrition Encyclopedia. A. H. Ensminger, et al. Pegus Press, 648 W. Sierra Ave, Clovis, California 93612. 1983. Two volumes. Covers commodities, nutrients, concepts, nutrition disorders and simple nutritional biochemistry with both brief and extensive entries.

Life Sciences on File. Diagram Group. Facts on File, Inc., 460 Park Ave. S., New York, New York 10016. (212) 683-2244. 1986. Encyclopedia of pictorial collection in life sciences. Deals with all major topics in life sciences including ecology.

The Nutrition and Health Encyclopedia. David F. Tver and Percy Russell. Van Nostrand Reinhold, 115 5th Ave., New York, New York 10003. (212) 254-3232. 1989.

The Prentice-Hall Dictionary of Nutrition and Health. K. Anderson and L. Harmon. Prentice Hall, Rte 9 W, Englewood Cliffs, New Jersey 07632. (201) 592-2000 or (800) 634-2863. 1985. Focuses on health rather than nutrition. Includes 900 to 1000 entries.

Van Nostrand's Scientific Encyclopedia. Glenn D. Considine, ed. Van Nostrand Reinhold, 115 5th Ave., New York, New York 10003. (212) 254-3232. 1983. Sixth edition. Includes all broad subject areas in science.

GENERAL WORKS

Beyond Cholesterol. Peter Kwiterovich. Knightsbridge Pub. Co., 701 W. 40th St., Suite 275, Baltimore, Maryland 21211. (410) 516-6900. 1991. Coronary heart disease prevention.

Chelated Mineral Nutrition in Plants, Animals, and Man. Charles C. Thomas Publishers, 2600 S. First, Springfield, Illinois 62794-9265. (217) 789-8980. 217-789-8980.

Chelates in Nutrition. F. Howard Kratzer. CRC Press, 2000 Corporate Blvd. N.W., Boca Raton, Florida 33431. (800) 272-7737. 1986. Mineral in human nutrition and chelation therapy.

Cholesterol Metabolism, LDL, and the LDL Receptor. N.B. Myant. Academic Press, c/o Harcourt Brace Jovanovich Inc., 6277 Sea Harbor Dr., Orlando, Florida 32887. (800) 346-8648. 1990.

Conversations on Chelation and Mineral Nutrition. H. DeWayne Ashmead. Keats Publishing Inc., P.O. Box 876, New Canaan, Connecticut 06840. (203) 966-8721. 1989. Physiological effect of malnutrition.

Environmental and Metabolic Animal Physiology. C. Ladd Prosser, ed. John Wiley & Sons, Inc., Wiley-Liss Division, 605 3rd Ave., New York, New York 10158-0012. (212) 850-6000. 1991. 4th ed. Focuses on the various aspects of adaptive physiology, including environmental, biochemical, and regulatory topics. Examines the theory of adaptation, water and ions, temperature and hydrostatic pressure, nutrition, digestion, nitrogen metabolism, and energy transfer, respiration, O2 and CO2 transport and circulation.

Feeding Tomorrow's World. Albert Sasson. Centre for Agriculture and Rural Cooperation and UNESCO, 7 Place de Fontenoy, Paris, France 1990. Analyzes Green Revolution and biotechnological revolution and tries to answer other pressing questions through a pluridisciplinary approach to human nutrition and food production.

Synthesizes the scientific, economic, socioeconomic and environmental aspects of nutrition throughout the world.

Grocery Shopping Guide: A Consumer's Manual for Selecting Foods Lower in Dietary Saturated Fat and Cholesterol. Nelda Mercer. University of Michigan Medical Center, 1500 E. Medical Center Dr., Ann Arbor, Michigan 48109. (313) 936-4000. 1989. Fat content, sodium content, and cholesterol content of food.

Lipid Manual: Methodology Appropriate for Fatty Acid-Cholesterol Analysis. Alan J. Sheppard. U.S. Food and Drug Administration, Division of Nutrition, 5600 Fishers Ln., Rockville, Maryland 20857. (301) 443-1544. 1989. Analysis of oils, fats, and cholesterol.

HANDBOOKS AND MANUALS

Cholesterol Handbook. Beekman Publishers Inc., P.O. Box 888, Woodstock, New York 12498. (914) 679-2300. 1989.

Complete Guide to Vitamins, Minerals and Supplements. H. Winter Griffith. Fisher Books, 3499 N. Campbell Ave., Suite 909, Tucson, Arizona 85712. (602) 325-5263. 1988. Includes name, brand name, reasons to use, who should use, recommended daily allowance, and other related data in the form of a chart.

ONLINE DATA BASES

AGRICOLA. U.S. Department of Agriculture, Office of Public Affairs, 14 Independence Ave., S.W., Washington, District of Columbia 20250. (202) 447-7454.

BIOSIS Previews. BIOSIS, 2100 Arch St., Philadelphia, Pennsylvania 19103-1399. (215) 587-4800. Largest and most comprehensive database of research in the life sciences. Contains citations for nearly 9000 primary research journals, monographs, reviews, symposia, preliminary reports, semi-popular journals, selected institutional reports, government reports and research communications.

CRIS/USDA. U.S. Department of Agriculture, Cooperative State Research Service, Current Research Information System, National Agricultural Library Building, 5th Fl., 10301 Baltimore Blvd., Beltsville, Maryland 20705. (301) 344-3850. Agricultural, food and nutrition, and forestry research projects.

Enviro/Energyline Abstracts Plus. R. R. Bowker Co., 121 Chanlon Rd., New Providence, New Jersey 07974. (908) 464-6800.

Environmental Periodicals Bibliography. National Information Services Corp., Ste. 6, Wyman Towers, 3100 St. Paul St., Baltimore, Maryland 21218. (410)243-0797. Online version of abstract of same name.

FROSTI: Food RA Online Scientific and Technical Information. Leatherhead Food Research Association, Randalls Rd., Leatherhead, Surrey, England KT22 7RY. 44 (372) 376761.

FSTA: Food Science and Technology Abstracts. International Food Information Service, Melibocusstrasse 52, 6000 Frankfurt, Germany 49 (69) 669007-8.

SCISEARCH. Institute for Scientific Information, University City Science Center, 3501 Market St., Philadelphia, Pennsylvania 19104. (215) 386-0100.

PERIODICALS AND NEWSLETTERS

Ecology of Food and Nutrition. Gordon & Breach Science Publishers, Inc., 270 8th Ave., New York, New York 10011. (212) 206-8900. Quarterly.

International Journal of Biosocial and Medical Research. Life Sciences Press, P.O. Box 1174, Takoma, Washington 98401-1174. (206) 922-0442. Semiannual. Deals with psychological and psychobiological aspects of environments.

The Journal of Biological Chemistry. American Society of Biological Chemists, 428 E. Preston St., Baltimore, Maryland 21202. Three times a month. Biological, agricultural, and energy aspects of the environment.

RESEARCH CENTERS AND INSTITUTES

Institute for Molecular Biology and Nutrition. Biology Department, MH 282, California State University, Fullerton, Fullerton, California 92634. (714) 773-3637.

Northern Illinois University, Center for Biochemical and Biophysical Studies. Faraday Hall, DeKalb, Illinois 60115. (815) 753-6866.

Shannon Point Marine Center. Western Washington University, 1900 Shannon Point Rd., Anacortes, Washington 98221. (206) 293-2188.

University of Georgia, Complex Carbohydrate Research Center. 220 Riverbend Road, Athens, Georgia 30602. (404) 542-4401.

TRADE ASSOCIATIONS AND PROFESSIONAL SOCIETIES

American Dietetic Association. 216 W. Jackson Blvd., Suite 800, Chicago, Illinois 60606. (312) 899-0040.

American Institute of Biological Sciences. 730 11th St., N.W., Washington, District of Columbia 20001-4521. (202) 628-1500.

American Institute of Nutrition. 9650 Rockville Pike, Bethesda, Maryland 20814. (301) 530-7050.

Center for Science in the Public Interest. 1875 Connecticut Ave., NW, Suite 300, Washington, District of Columbia 20009. (202) 332-9110.

EarthSave. 706 Frederick St., Santa Cruz, California 95062. (408) 423-4069.

O

OCCUPATIONAL HEALTH

See also: HEALTH, ENVIRONMENTAL

ABSTRACTING AND INDEXING SERVICES

Engineering Index. The Engineering Index Inc., 345 E. 47th St., New York, New York 10017. 1962-.

Environment Abstracts. Bowker A & I Publishing, 121 Chanlon Rd., New Providence, New Jersey 07974. (908) 464-6800. 1974-.

Environment Index. Environment Information Center, Index Research Department, 124 E. 39th St., New York, New York 10016. 1971-. Annual.

Environmental Information Connection–EIC. Planning Information Program, Dept. of Urban and Regional Planning, University of Illinois, 1003 West Nevada, Urbana, Illinois 61801. (217) 333-1369. Also available online.

Environmental Periodicals Bibliography. Environmental Studies Institute, International Academy at Santa Barbara, 800 Garden St., Suite D, Santa Barbara, California 93101. (805) 965-5010. Also available online.

General Science Index. H. W. Wilson Co., 950 University Ave., Bronx, New York 10452. 1978-. Monthly, also issued in annual cumulation. Cumulative subject index to English language periodicals in the subject fields of astronomy, botany, chemistry, earth science, environment and conservation, food and nutrition, genetics, mathematics, medicine and health, microbiology, oceanography, physics, physiology and zoology.

Geographical Abstracts. London School of Economics, Dept. of Geography, Regency House, 34 Duke St., London, England 1966-. Continued by Geo Abstracts issued in 6 parts: Pt. A. Landforms and the quaternary; Pt. B. Biogeography and Climatology; Pt. C. Economic geography; Pt. D. Social geography and cartography; Pt. E. Sedimentology; Pt. F. Regional and community planning.

Index to Scientific Book Contents. Institute for Scientific Information, 3501 Market St., Philadelphia, Pennsylvania 19104. (800) 523-1857. 1985-. Annual. Gives contents of science books published.

INIS Atomindex. International Atomic Energy Agency, Wagramerstrasse 5, Vienna, Austria A-1400. 222 23606198. 1988-. Semiannual. Abstracts nuclear energy and nuclear physics topics from journals, conferences, technical reports and other related publications. Issued in 6 parts: Personal Author, Corporate Entry, Subject, Report, Standard Patent, Conference (by place), Conference (by date).

Pollution Abstracts. Cambridge Scientific Abstracts, 5161 River Rd., Bethesda, Maryland 20816. (301) 961-6750. Six/year. Indexes worldwide technical literature on environmental pollution. Covers air pollution, marine and freshwater pollution, sewage and wastewater treatment, waste management, toxicology and health, noise pollution, radiation, land pollution, and environmental policies, programs, legislation, and education. Also available online.

Science Citation Index. Institute for Scientific Information, 3501 Market St., Philadelphia, Pennsylvania 19104. 1961-.

Selected References on Environmental Quality as It Relates to Health. National Library of Medicine, 8600 Rockville Pike, Bethesda, Maryland 20894. (800) 638-8480. 1977.

BIBLIOGRAPHIES

EPA Publications Bibliography. U.S. Environmental Protection Agency, Library Systems Branch, 401 M St., SW, Washington, District of Columbia 20460. (202) 260-2090. Quarterly.

DIRECTORIES

International Directory of Occupational Safety and Health Institutions. International Labour Office, 49 Sheridan Ave., Albany, New York 12210. (518) 436-9686. 1990.

ENCYCLOPEDIAS AND DICTIONARIES

Encyclopedia of Occupational Health and Safety. Luigi Parmeggiani. International Labour Office, 49 Sheridan Ave., Albany, New York 12210. (518) 436-9686. 1983. Reference work concerned with workers' safety and health, information for those with no specialized medical or with technical knowledge.

McGraw-Hill Encyclopedia of Environmental Science. Sybil P. Parker. McGraw-Hill Science & Engineering Books, 11 W. 19th St., New York, New York 10011. (212) 337-6010. 1980. Covers ecology, man's influence on nature, and environmental protection.

McGraw-Hill Encyclopedia of Science and Technology. McGraw-Hill, 1221 Avenue of the Americas, New York, New York 10020. (212) 512-2000 or (800) 262-4729. 1992. Seventh edition. Issued in multiple volumes including index. Includes all science and technology broad subject areas.

Van Nostrand's Scientific Encyclopedia. Glenn D. Considine, ed. Van Nostrand Reinhold, 115 5th Ave., New York, New York 10003. (212) 254-3232. 1983. Sixth edition. Includes all broad subject areas in science.

GENERAL WORKS

Advances in Neurobehavioral Toxicology: Applications in Environmental and Occupational Health. Barry L. Johnson, et al. Lewis Publishers, 2000 Corporate Blvd., N.W., Boca Raton, Florida 33431. (407) 994-0555 or (800) 272-7737. 1991. Focuses on neurobehavioral methods and their development and application in environmental and occupational health. Includes new methods to assess human neurotoxicity; human exposure to, and health effects of, neurotoxic substances; and animal methods that model human toxicity.

Chemical Protective Clothing. American Industrial Hygiene Association, 345 White Pond Dr., Akron, Ohio 44320. (216) 873-2442. 1990. 2 vols. Volume 1 reviews basic polymer chemistry and permeation theory and types, construction, and use of protective materials; specific test methods, selection guidelines and decontamination. Volume 2 contains product performance evaluation data and information on physical property test methods, permeation data, chemicals, products and vendors, and encapsulating suit ensembles.

Criteria for a Recommended Standard, Occupational Exposure to Malathion. U.S. Department of Health and Human Services, Public Health Service, National Institute for Occupational Safety and Health, Robert A. Taft Lab, 4676 Columbia Pkwy., Cincinnati, Ohio 45226. (513) 684-8465. 1976.

Criteria for Controlling Occupational Exposure to Cobalt. U.S. Department of Health and Human Services, 200 Independence Ave., SW, Room 34AF, Washington, District of Columbia 20201. (202) 472-5543. 1982.

Deadly Dust: Silicosis and the Politics of Occupational Disease in Twentieth-Century America. David Rosner and Gerald Markowitz. Princeton University Press, 41 Williams St., Princeton, New Jersey 08540. (609) 258-4900. 1991. Case study of how occupational diseases are defined and addressed.

Electrical Hazards and Accidents: Their Cause and Prevention. E. K. Greenwald, ed. Global Professional Publications, 2805 McGraw Ave., PO Box 19539, Irvine, California 92713-9539. (800) 854-7179. 1991. Workplace hazards associated with electricity and proven design, maintenance, and operating procedures for preventing them.

Environmental Issues: An Anthology of 1989. Thomas W. Joyce, ed. TAPPI Press, Technology Park/Atlanta, PO Box 105113, Atlanta, Georgia 30348. (404) 446-1400. 1990. Contains 39 papers on environmental, safety and occupational health concerns from 11 TAPPI, CPPA and AIChE meetings held during 1989. Also included is a literature review of over 200 papers published in 1989.

Environmental Tobacco Smoke in the Workplace: Lung Cancer and Other Health Effects. National Institute for Occupational Safety and Health, 1600 Clifton Rd. NE, Atlanta, Georgia 30333. (404) 639-3286. 1992. Current Intelligence Bulletin No. 54. DHHS (NIOSH) Publication No. 91-108.

LOGAN Workplace Exposure Evaluation System. American Industrial Hygiene Association, 345 White Pond Dr.,

Akron, Ohio 44320. (216) 873-2442. 1987. A computerized software package, presents statistical method for characterizing employee exposure to chemicals, noise, and other environmental hazards.

Measurement Techniques for Carcinogenic Agents in Workplace Air. Royal Society of Chemistry, c/o CRC Press, 2000 Corporate Blvd. N.W., Boca Raton, Florida 33431-9868. (800) 272-7737. 1989. Covers 31 substances with known or suspected carcinogenic properties and describes recommended analytical methods for each substance when present in workplace air. It provides information including CAS Registry number, synonyms, manufacture, uses and determination (with recommended sampling and measuring procedures, and performance characteristics), plus a review of other methods used.

Microcomputer Applications in Occupational Health and Safety. Lewis Publishers, 2000 Corporate Blvd., N.W., Boca Raton, Florida 33431. (407) 994-0555 or (800) 272-7737. 1987. Practical software use in the "real world" of occupational health and safety is the main theme of this book.

NEG (Nordic Expert Group for Documentation of Occupational Exposure Limits) and NIOSH Basis for an Occupational Safety and Health Standard: Propylene Glycol Ethers and Their Acetates. National Institute for Occupation Safety and Health, 4676 Columbia Parkway, Cincinnati, Ohio 45226-1998. (513) 533-8287. 1991. DHHS (NIOSH) Publication No. 91-103.

Occupational Epidemiology. Richard R. Monson. CRC Press, 2000 Corporate Blvd. N.W., Boca Raton, Florida 33431. (800) 272-7737. 1990. 2d ed. Updates and extends the first edition. Includes basic introduction to epidemiology in the occupational context and introduces new analytic methods.

Occupational Toxicants. VCH Publishers, 303 NW 12th Ave., Deerfield Beach, Florida 33442-1788. (305) 428-5566. 1991. Contains critical data evaluation for MAK values and classification of carcinogens. Also has standards for hazardous chemical compounds in the work area.

Proctor and Hughes' Chemical Hazards of the Workplace. G. J. Hathaway, et al. Global Professional Publications, 2805 McGraw Ave., PO Box 19539, Irvine, California 92713-9539. (800) 854-7179. 1991. Third edition. Includes 100 new chemicals and the new 1991 Threshold Limit Values. Gives a practical easy-to-use introduction to toxicology and hazards of over 600 chemicals most likely to be encountered in the workplace.

Radiation Exposure and Occupational Risks. G. Keller, et al. Springer-Verlag, 175 5th Ave., New York, New York 10010. (212) 460-1500; (800) 777-4643. 1990. Discusses radiation exposure injuries in the workplace and prevention.

Risk Factors for Cancer in the Workplace. Jack Siemia Tycki. CRC Press, 2000 Corporate Blvd., N.W., Boca Raton, Florida 33431. (407) 994-0555 or (800) 272-7737. 1991. Describes occupational risks from contamination and precautions.

Safety in the Use of Asbestos. International Labour Office, 49 Sheridan Ave., Albany, New York 12210. (518) 436-9686. 1990. An ILO code of practice. The first part of the code includes monitoring in the work place, preventive measures, the protection and supervision of the workers' health, and the packaging, handling, transport and disposal of asbestos waste. More detailed guidance on the limitation of exposure to asbestos in specific activities is given in the second part of the code, which includes sections on mining and milling, asbestos cement, textiles, friction materials, and the removal of asbestos-containing materials.

Safety in the Use of Mineral and Synthetic Fibers. International Labour Office, 49 Sheridan Ave., Albany, New York 12210. (518) 436-9686. 1990. Working document for, and report of, a meeting of experts set up by the ILO to study the questions contained in this book, including discussions of man-made fibers, natural mineral fibers other than asbestos, and synthetic organic fibers. The meeting defined certain preventive measures based on adopting safe working methods, controlling the working environment and the exposure of workers to mineral and synthetic fibers, and monitoring the health of the workers.

Silica, Silicosis, and Cancer: Controversy in Occupational Medicine. Praeger Publishers, 1 Madison Ave., New York, New York 10010-3603. (212) 685-5300. Covers lung cancer and the toxicology of silica.

Skin Penetration; Hazardous Chemicals at Work. Philippe Grandjean. Taylor & Francis, 79 Madison Ave., New York, New York 10016. (212) 725-1999 or (800) 821-8312. 1990. Mechanisms of percutaneous absorption and methods of evaluating its significance. Reviews different classes of chemicals, emphasizing those considered major skin hazards.

A Strategy for Occupational Exposure Assessment. American Industrial Hygiene Association, 345 White Pond Dr., Akron, Ohio 44320. (216) 873-2442. 1991. Highlights the considerations to be made in determining priorities for monitoring work exposures.

The Work Environment, V.1. Occupational Health Fundamentals. Doan J. Hansen. Lewis Publishers, 2000 Corporate Blvd., N.W., Boca Raton, Florida 33431. (407) 994-0555 or (800) 272-7737. 1991. Addresses topics in occupational safety and health and safety issues, including worker and community right-to-know issues, worker health and safety training, and other contemporary issues.

Workplace Environmental Exposure Level Guide. American Industrial Hygiene Association, 345 White Pond Dr., Akron, Ohio 44320. (216) 873-2442. 1991-. Includes guidelines for benzophenone, butyraldehyde, sodium hypochlorite, and vinylcyclohexene.

GOVERNMENTAL ORGANIZATIONS

Centers for Disease Control: National Institute for Occupational Safety and Health. D-36, 1600 Clifton Rd. N.E., Atlanta, Georgia 30333. (404) 639-3771.

Department of Labor and Statistics: Occupational Safety. Commissioner, Occupational Health and Safety, Herschler Building, Cheyenne, Wyoming 82002. (307) 777-7261.

Occupational Safety and Health Administration: Directorate for Policy. 200 Constitution Ave., N.W., Washington, District of Columbia 20210. (202) 523-8021.

Occupational Safety and Health Administration: Directorate of Safety Standards Programs. 200 Constitution Ave., N.W., Washington, District of Columbia 20210. (202) 523-8063.

Occupational Safety and Health Administration: Directorate of Technical Support. 200 Constitution Ave., N.W., Washington, District of Columbia 20210. (202) 523-7031.

Occupational Safety and Health Administration: Information, Consumer Affairs and Freedom of Information. 200 Constitution Ave., N.W., Washington, District of Columbia 20210. (202) 523-8148.

Occupational Safety and Health Administration: Office and Field Operations. 3rd St. and Constitution Ave., N.W., Washington, District of Columbia 20210. (202) 523-7725.

HANDBOOKS AND MANUALS

Dangerous Properties of Industrial Materials. Irving Newton Sax. Van Nostrand Reinhold, 115 5th Ave., New York, New York 10003. (212) 254-3232. 1989. 7th ed. Deals with hazardous substances and chemically induced occupational diseases.

Laboratory Chemical Standards: The Complete OSHA Compliance Manual. Bureau of National Affairs, 1231 25th St. N.W., Washington, District of Columbia 20037. (800) 372-1033. 1990. OSHA's new lab standard applies to laboratories that use hazardous chemicals and requires a written plan that satisfies federal guidelines.

OSHA Technical Manual. Government Institutes, Inc., 4 Research Pl., Ste. 200, Rockville, Maryland 20850. (301) 921-2300. 1991. Covers both health and safety inspections and procedures.

ONLINE DATA BASES

Chemical Information File. OSHA Salt Lake City Analytical Laboratory, 1781 S. 300 W., Salt Lake City, Utah 84165-0200. (801) 524-5287. Database is part of the OSHA Computerized Information System (OCIS) and contains chemical substances found in the workplace with current information on identification, exposure limits, compliance sampling methods, and analytical methods.

CHEMINFO. Canadian Centre for Occupational Health & Safety, 250 Main St., East, Hamilton, Ontario, Canada L8N 1H6. (800) 263-8276.

CISDOC. International Occupational Safety & Health Information Centre, International Labour Office, Geneva 22, Switzerland CH-1211. 41 (22) 996740.

Computerized Engineering Index–COMPENDEX. Engineering Information Inc., 345 E. 47th St., New York, New York 10017. (212) 705-7600.

Enviro/Energyline Abstracts Plus. R. R. Bowker Co., 121 Chanlon Rd., New Providence, New Jersey 07974. (908) 464-6800.

Environmental Fate Databases. Syracuse Research Cooperation, Merrill Lane, Syracuse, New York 13210. (312) 426-3200. Environmental fate of chemicals.

Environmental Health News. Occupational Health Services, Inc., 450 7th Ave., New York, New York 10123. (212) 967-1100. Online access to court decisions, regulatory changes, and medical and scientific news related to hazardous substances.

Environmental Periodicals Bibliography. National Information Services Corp., Ste. 6, Wyman Towers, 3100 St.

Paul St., Baltimore, Maryland 21218. (410)243-0797. Online version of abstract of same name.

Industrial Health & Hazards Update. Merton Allen Associates, P.O. Box 15640, Plantation, Florida 33318-5640. (305) 473-9560.

INFOTOX. Centre de Documentation, Commission de la Sante et de la Securite du Travail (CSST), 1199 rue de Bueury, 4th Floor, C.P. 6067 succ "A", Montreal, Quebec, Canada H3C 4E2. (514) 873-2297.

KEMI-INFO. Danish National Institute of Occupational Health, Produktregestret, Lerso Parkalle 105, Copenhagen 0, Denmark 45 (31) 299711.

Material Safety Data Sheets Reference Files–MSDS. NPIRS (National Pesticide Information Retrieval System) User Services Manager, Entomology Hall, Purdue University, West Lafayette, Indiana 47907. (317) 494-6614.

Monthly Catalog of United States Government Publications. U.S. G.P.O., Supt. of Docs., PO Box 371954, Pittsburgh, Pennsylvania 15250-7954. (202) 512-0000.

National Technical Information Service. U.S. Department of Commerce, National Technical Information Service, Office of Data Base Services, 5285 Port Royal Rd., Springfield, Virginia 22161. (703) 487-4807. Bibliographic database of government sponsored research and technical reports.

NIOSHTIC. U.S. Department of Health and Human Services, Centers for Disease Control, National Institute for Occupational Safety and Health, 4676 Columbia Parkway, Cincinnati, Ohio 45226. (513) 533-8317.

Occupational Health and Safety: Seven Critical Issues. Bureau of National Affairs, BNA PLUS, 1231 25th St., N.W., Rm. 215, Washington, District of Columbia 20037. (800) 452-7773.

Occupational Safety and Health. National Institute for Occupational Safety and Health, Standards Development and Technology Transfer Division, 4676 Columbia Pkwy., Cincinnati, Ohio 45226. (513) 684-8326. Hazardous agents and waste, unsafe workplace environment, toxicology, chemistry,and control technology.

Occupational Safety and Health Reporter. Bureau of National Affairs, BNA PLUS, 1231 25th St., N.W., Rm. 215, Washington, District of Columbia 20037. (800) 452-7773. Online version of the periodical of the same name.

PressNet Environmental Reports. Chemical Information Systems, Inc., 7215 York Rd., Baltimore, Maryland 21212. (301) 321-8440.

SCISEARCH. Institute for Scientific Information, University City Science Center, 3501 Market St., Philadelphia, Pennsylvania 19104. (215) 386-0100.

PERIODICALS AND NEWSLETTERS

American Industrial Hygiene Association Journal. American Industrial Hygiene Association, 345 White Pond Drive, Akron, Ohio 44320. (216) 873-2442. Monthly. Reports relating to occupational and environmental health hazards.

Analytical Chemistry. American Chemical Society, 1155 16th St. N.W., Washington, District of Columbia 20036. (800) 227-5558. 1929-. Bimonthly. Articles for chemists, life scientists and engineers.

Asbestos Control Report. Business Publishers, Inc., 951 Pershing Drive, Silver Spring, Maryland 20910-4464. (301) 587-6300. Biweekly. Information on asbestos control techniques, research, and regulations. Also available online.

Briefing. National Association of Manufacturers, 1331 Pennsylvania Avenue, NW, Suite 1500 North, Washington, District of Columbia 20004. (202) 637-3000. Weekly. Environmental issues as they relate to manufacturing.

Dangerous Properties of Industrial Materials Report. Van Nostrand Reinhold, 115 5th Avenue, New York, New York 10003. (212) 254-3232. Bimonthly. Chemical and environmental review of hazardous industrial materials.

Environmental Health News. University of Washington, School of Public Health, Dept. of Environmental Health, Seattle, Washington 98195. (206) 543-3222. Quarterly. Occupational health, air pollution and safety.

Journal of Occupational Medicine. Williams & Wilkins, P.O. Box 64380, Baltimore, Maryland 21264. (301) 528-4105. Monthly. Issues on the maintenance and improvement of the health of workers.

Occupational Hazards. Penton Publishing Co., 1100 Superior Ave., Cleveland, Ohio 44114. (216) 696-7000. Monthly. Covers safety management and plant protection.

Occupational Health and Safety. Stevens Publishing Co., P.O. Box 2604, Waco, Texas 76714. (817) 776-9000. Monthly. Covers occupational health and safety.

STATISTICS SOURCES

OSHA Regulated Hazardous Substances: Health, Toxicity, Economic, and Technological Data. U.S. Occupational Safety and Health Administration. Noyes Publications, 120 Mill Rd., Park Ridge, New Jersey 07656. (201) 391-8484. 1990. Provides industrial exposure data and control technologies for more than 650 substances currently regulated, or candidates for regulation, by the Occupational Safety and Health Administration.

OCCUPATIONAL SAFETY AND HEALTH GENERAL OFFICES

GENERAL WORKS

Safety in the Process Industries. Butterworth-Heinemann, 80 Montvale Ave., Stoneham, Massachusetts 02180. (617) 438-8464. 1990. Hazards of process plants, and causes of accidents and how they may be controlled.

GOVERNMENTAL ORGANIZATIONS

Department of Labor, Occupational Safety and Health Administration: Docket Room. 200 Constitution Ave., N.W., Room N3670, Washington, District of Columbia 20210. (202) 523-7894.

Department of Labor: Technical Data Center. 200 Constitution Ave., N.W., Washington, District of Columbia 20210. (202) 523-9700.

Occupational Safety and Health Administration: Information, Consumer Affairs and Freedom of Information.

200 Constitution Ave., N.W., Washington, District of Columbia 20210. (202) 523-8148.

Occupational Safety and Health Administration: Publications Office. 200 Constitution Ave., N.W., Room N3101, Washington, District of Columbia 20210. (202) 523-9668.

OCCUPATIONAL SAFETY AND HEALTH REGIONAL OFFICES

GOVERNMENTAL ORGANIZATIONS

Occupational Safety and Health Administration: Region 1 Office. 133 Portland St., Boston, Massachusetts 02114. (617) 565-7164.

Occupational Safety and Health Administration: Region 10 Office. 1111 Third Ave., Suite 715, Seattle, Washington 98101-3212. (206) 442-5930.

Occupational Safety and Health Administration: Region 2 Office. 201 Varick St., New York, New York 10014. (212) 337-2378.

Occupational Safety and Health Administration: Region 3 Office. 3535 Market St., Philadelphia, Pennsylvania 19104. (215) 596-1201.

Occupational Safety and Health Administration: Region 4 Office. 1375 Peachtree St., N.E., Suite 587, Atlanta, Georgia (404) 347-3573.

Occupational Safety and Health Administration: Region 5 Office. 230 S. Dearborn St., Room 3244, Chicago, Illinois 60604. (312) 353-2220.

Occupational Safety and Health Administration: Region 6 Office. Federal Building, 525 Griffen St., Dallas, Texas 75202. (214) 767-4764.

Occupational Safety and Health Administration: Region 7 Office. 911 Walnut St., Kansas City, Missouri 64106. (816) 426-5861.

Occupational Safety and Health Administration: Region 8 Office. Federal Building, 1961 Stout St., Room 1576, Denver, Colorado 80294. (303) 844-3061.

Occupational Safety and Health Administration: Region 9 Office. 71 Stevenson St., Suite 415, San Francisco, California 94105. (415) 744-7102.

OCEAN-ATMOSPHERE INTERACTION

ABSTRACTING AND INDEXING SERVICES

Environment Abstracts. Bowker A & I Publishing, 121 Chanlon Rd., New Providence, New Jersey 07974. (908) 464-6800. 1974-.

Environment Index. Environment Information Center, Index Research Department, 124 E. 39th St., New York, New York 10016. 1971-. Annual.

Environmental Information Connection–EIC. Planning Information Program, Dept. of Urban and Regional Planning, University of Illinois, 1003 West Nevada, Urbana, Illinois 61801. (217) 333-1369. Also available online.

Environmental Periodicals Bibliography. Environmental Studies Institute, International Academy at Santa Barbara, 800 Garden St., Suite D, Santa Barbara, California 93101. (805) 965-5010. Also available online.

General Science Index. H. W. Wilson Co., 950 University Ave., Bronx, New York 10452. 1978-. Monthly, also issued in annual cumulation. Cumulative subject index to English language periodicals in the subject fields of astronomy, botany, chemistry, earth science, environment and conservation, food and nutrition, genetics, mathematics, medicine and health, microbiology, oceanography, physics, physiology and zoology.

Geographical Abstracts. London School of Economics, Dept. of Geography, Regency House, 34 Duke St., London, England 1966-. Continued by Geo Abstracts issued in 6 parts: Pt. A. Landforms and the quaternary; Pt. B. Biogeography and Climatology; Pt. C. Economic geography; Pt. D. Social geography and cartography; Pt. E. Sedimentology; Pt. F. Regional and community planning.

Index to Scientific Book Contents. Institute for Scientific Information, 3501 Market St., Philadelphia, Pennsylvania 19104. (800) 523-1857. 1985-. Annual. Gives contents of science books published.

Oceanic Abstracts. UMI Data Courier, 620 S. 3rd St., Louisville, Kentucky 40202. (800) 626-2823. Formerly: Oceanic Index and Oceanic Citation Journal.

BIBLIOGRAPHIES

EPA Publications Bibliography. U.S. Environmental Protection Agency, Library Systems Branch, 401 M St., SW, Washington, District of Columbia 20460. (202) 260-2090. Quarterly.

ENCYCLOPEDIAS AND DICTIONARIES

The Encyclopedia of Climatology. John E. Oliver and Rhodes W. Fairbridge, eds. Van Nostrand Reinhold, 115 5th Ave., New York, New York 10003. (212) 254-3232. 1987. Belongs in the series Encyclopedia of Earth Sciences, v.11.

McGraw-Hill Encyclopedia of Environmental Science. Sybil P. Parker. McGraw-Hill Science & Engineering Books, 11 W. 19th St., New York, New York 10011. (212) 337-6010. 1980. Covers ecology, man's influence on nature, and environmental protection.

The Times Atlas and Encyclopedia of the Sea. A.D. Couper. Harper & Row, 10 E. 53rd St., New York, New York 10022. (212) 207-7000; (800) 242-7737. 1990.

GENERAL WORKS

Atmosphere and Ocean: Our Fluid Environments. John G. Harvey. Artemis Press, Sedgwick Park, Horsham, England RH13 6QH. 1976. Ocean-atmosphere interaction and oceanography.

Atmosphere-Ocean Dynamics. Adrian, E. Gill. Academic Press, c/o Harcourt Brace Jovanovich Inc., 6277 Sea Harbor Dr., Orlando, Florida 32887. (800) 346-8648. 1982. Geophysical topics covering ocean-atmosphere interaction.

Marine Interfaces Ecohydrodynamics. J.C.J. Nihoul. Elsevier Science Publishing Co., 655 Avenue of the Americas,

New York, New York 10010. (212) 984-5800. 1986. Ocean-atmosphere interaction and marine ecology.

ONLINE DATA BASES

Enviro/Energyline Abstracts Plus. R. R. Bowker Co., 121 Chanlon Rd., New Providence, New Jersey 07974. (908) 464-6800.

Environmental Periodicals Bibliography. National Information Services Corp., Ste. 6, Wyman Towers, 3100 St. Paul St., Baltimore, Maryland 21218. (410)243-0797. Online version of abstract of same name.

Oceanic Abstracts. Cambridge Scientific Abstracts, 5161 River Rd., Bethesda, Maryland 20816. (301) 961-6750. Online access.

OCEAN CURRENTS

See: OCEANS

OCEAN DUMPING

ABSTRACTING AND INDEXING SERVICES

Abstracts of Air and Water Conservation Literature. American Petroleum Institute. Central Abstracting and Indexing Service, 275 Madison Avenue, New York, New York 10016. 1972.

Applied Ecology Abstracts Studies in Renewable Natural Resources. Information Retrieval Ltd., 1911 Jefferson Davis Highway, Arlington, Virginia 22202. 1975-. Monthly.

Engineering Index. The Engineering Index Inc., 345 E. 47th St., New York, New York 10017. 1962-.

Environment Abstracts. Bowker A & I Publishing, 121 Chanlon Rd., New Providence, New Jersey 07974. (908) 464-6800. 1974-.

Environment Index. Environment Information Center, Index Research Department, 124 E. 39th St., New York, New York 10016. 1971-. Annual.

Environmental Information Connection–EIC. Planning Information Program, Dept. of Urban and Regional Planning, University of Illinois, 1003 West Nevada, Urbana, Illinois 61801. (217) 333-1369. Also available online.

Environmental Periodicals Bibliography. Environmental Studies Institute, International Academy at Santa Barbara, 800 Garden St., Suite D, Santa Barbara, California 93101. (805) 965-5010. Also available online.

Index to Scientific Book Contents. Institute for Scientific Information, 3501 Market St., Philadelphia, Pennsylvania 19104. (800) 523-1857. 1985-. Annual. Gives contents of science books published.

Multimedia Index to Ecology. National Information Center for Educational Media, University of Southern California, Los Angeles, California 90007.

Oceanic Abstracts. UMI Data Courier, 620 S. 3rd St., Louisville, Kentucky 40202. (800) 626-2823. Formerly: Oceanic Index and Oceanic Citation Journal.

Pollution Abstracts. Cambridge Scientific Abstracts, 5161 River Rd., Bethesda, Maryland 20816. (301) 961-6750. Six/year. Indexes worldwide technical literature on environmental pollution. Covers air pollution, marine and freshwater pollution, sewage and wastewater treatment, waste management, toxicology and health, noise pollution, radiation, land pollution, and environmental policies, programs, legislation, and education. Also available online.

Science Citation Index. Institute for Scientific Information, 3501 Market St., Philadelphia, Pennsylvania 19104. 1961-.

Sea Grant Abstracts. National Sea Grant Depository, Pell Laboratory Bldg., Bay Campus, University of Rhode Island, Narragansett, Rhode Island 02882. (401) 792-6114. 1986-. Quarterly. Published by the National Sea Grant Programs, this collection includes annual reports, serials and newsletters, charts and maps.

BIBLIOGRAPHIES

EPA Publications Bibliography. U.S. Environmental Protection Agency, Library Systems Branch, 401 M St., SW, Washington, District of Columbia 20460. (202) 260-2090. Quarterly.

Global Marine Pollution Bibliography: Ocean Dumping of Municipal and Industrial Wastes. Michael A. Champ. IFI/Plenum, 233 Spring St., New York, New York 10013. (800) 221-9369. 1982.

ENCYCLOPEDIAS AND DICTIONARIES

Dictionary of Environmental Protection Technology: In Four Languages, English, German, French, Russian. Egon Seidel. Elsevier Science Publishing Co., 655 Avenue of the Americas, New York, New York 10010. (212) 984-5800. 1988.

The Encyclopedia of Oceanography. Rhodes Whitmore Fairbridge. Reinhold Pub. Co., 115 5th Ave., New York, New York 10003. (212) 254-3232. 1966.

English-Russian Dictionary of Environmental Protection: About 14,000 Terms. E.L. Milovanov. Pergamon Microforms International, Inc., Fairview Park, Elmsford, New York 10523. (914) 592-7720. 1981.

Environmental Engineering Dictionary. C. C. Lee. Government Institutes, Inc., 4 Research Pl., Ste. 200, Rockville, Maryland 20850. (301) 921-2300. 1989. Defines over 6000 engineering terms relating to pollutioncontrol technologies, monitoring, risk assessment, sampling andanalysis, quality control, permitting, and environmentally-regulated engineering and science. Includes bibliographical references (p. 612-627).

McGraw-Hill Encyclopedia of Environmental Science. Sybil P. Parker. McGraw-Hill Science & Engineering Books, 11 W. 19th St., New York, New York 10011. (212) 337-6010. 1980. Covers ecology, man's influence on nature, and environmental protection.

GENERAL WORKS

Dying Oceans. Paula Hogan. Gareth Stevens, Inc., 7317 W. Green Tree Rd., Milwaukee, Wisconsin 53223. (414) 466-7550. 1991. Ecological balance of life in the oceans endangered by pollution.

Geotechnical Engineering of Ocean Waste Disposal. Kenneth R. Demars and Ronald C. Chaney. ASTM, 1916 Race St., Philadelphia, Pennsylvania 19103-1187. (215) 299-5400. 1990. Proceedings of the symposium held in Orlando, FL, Jan 1989. Reviews geotechnical test methods and procedures for site evaluation, design, construction, and monitoring of both contaminated areas and waste disposal facilities in the marine environment.

Long Range Transport of Pesticides. David A. Kurtz. Lewis Publishers, 2000 Corporate Blvd., N.W., Boca Raton, Florida 33431. (407) 994-0555 or (800) 272-7737. 1990. Presents the latest vital information on long range transport of pesticides. Includes sources of pesticides from lakes, oceans, and soil, circulation on global and regional basis, deposition, and fate of pesticides.

Marine Treatment of Sewage Sludge. Telford House, 1 Heron Quay, London, England E14 9XF. 1988.

Ocean Dumping and Marine Pollution. Van Nostrand Reinhold, Information Services, 115 5th Ave., New York, New York 10003. (212) 254-3232. 1979. Geological aspects of waste disposal in the ocean and marine pollution.

The Ocean Dumping Quandary. Donald Fleming Squires. State University of New York Press, State University Plaza, Albany, New York 12246. (518) 472-5000. 1983. Waste disposal in the New York Bight.

GOVERNMENTAL ORGANIZATIONS

Office of Public Affairs: National Ocean Service. 6013 Herbert C. Hoover Building, 14th and Constitution Avenues, N.W., Washington, District of Columbia 20230. (202) 673-5111.

ONLINE DATA BASES

Computerized Engineering Index–COMPENDEX. Engineering Information Inc., 345 E. 47th St., New York, New York 10017. (212) 705-7600.

Enviro/Energyline Abstracts Plus. R. R. Bowker Co., 121 Chanlon Rd., New Providence, New Jersey 07974. (908) 464-6800.

Environmental Periodicals Bibliography. National Information Services Corp., Ste. 6, Wyman Towers, 3100 St. Paul St., Baltimore, Maryland 21218. (410)243-0797. Online version of abstract of same name.

Oceanic Abstracts. Cambridge Scientific Abstracts, 5161 River Rd., Bethesda, Maryland 20816. (301) 961-6750. Online access.

SCISEARCH. Institute for Scientific Information, University City Science Center, 3501 Market St., Philadelphia, Pennsylvania 19104. (215) 386-0100.

RESEARCH CENTERS AND INSTITUTES

Institute of Marine Resources. University of California, La Jolla, California 92093-0228. (619) 534-2868.

OCEAN ENGINEERING
See: MARINE ENGINEERING

OCEAN MINING
See: OCEANS

OCEANS

ABSTRACTING AND INDEXING SERVICES

Abstracts of Air and Water Conservation Literature. American Petroleum Institute. Central Abstracting and Indexing Service, 275 Madison Avenue, New York, New York 10016. 1972.

Biological Abstracts. BIOSIS, 2100 Arch St., Philadelphia, Pennsylvania 19103-1399. (215) 587-4800. 1927-.

Civil Engineering Hydraulic Abstracts. BHRA Fluid Engineering, Air Science Co., PO Box 143, Corning, New York 14830. (607) 962-5591. Monthly. Abstracts of periodicals that publish in the areas of hydraulic engineering and other related topics.

Ecological Abstracts. Geo Abstracts Ltd. Elsevier Applied Science, Crown House, Linton Rd., Barking, England IG 11 8JU. 1974-. Derived from over 600 leading ecological and environmental journals, plus books, conference proceedings, reports and theses.

Engineering Index. The Engineering Index Inc., 345 E. 47th St., New York, New York 10017. 1962-.

Environment Abstracts. Bowker A & I Publishing, 121 Chanlon Rd., New Providence, New Jersey 07974. (908) 464-6800. 1974-.

Environment Index. Environment Information Center, Index Research Department, 124 E. 39th St., New York, New York 10016. 1971-. Annual.

Environmental Information Connection–EIC. Planning Information Program, Dept. of Urban and Regional Planning, University of Illinois, 1003 West Nevada, Urbana, Illinois 61801. (217) 333-1369. Also available online.

Environmental Periodicals Bibliography. Environmental Studies Institute, International Academy at Santa Barbara, 800 Garden St., Suite D, Santa Barbara, California 93101. (805) 965-5010. Also available online.

Environmental Research Laboratories Publication Abstracts. National Oceanic and Atmospheric Administration. Environmental Research Laboratories, 325 Broadway, Boulder, Colorado 80303. 1990. Annual. Sixth annual bibliography of NOAA Environmental Research Laboratories staff publications, FY 89. Covers journal articles, official ERL reports, conference papers, and publications released in cooperation with universities and by ERL funded contractors.

General Science Index. H. W. Wilson Co., 950 University Ave., Bronx, New York 10452. 1978-. Monthly, also issued in annual cumulation. Cumulative subject index to English language periodicals in the subject fields of astronomy, botany, chemistry, earth science, environment and conservation, food and nutrition, genetics, mathematics, medicine and health, microbiology, oceanography, physics, physiology and zoology.

Index to Scientific Book Contents. Institute for Scientific Information, 3501 Market St., Philadelphia, Pennsylva-

nia 19104. (800) 523-1857. 1985-. Annual. Gives contents of science books published.

Meteorological and Geoastrophysical Abstracts. American Meteorological Society, 45 Beacon St., Boston, Massachusetts 02108. (617) 227-2425.

Ocean Wave and Tidal Energy. National Technical Information Service, 5285 Port Royal Rd., Springfield, Virginia 22161. (703) 487-4650. 1988. Bimonthly. Ocean thermal energy conversion systems; salinity gradient power systems.

Oceanic Abstracts. UMI Data Courier, 620 S. 3rd St., Louisville, Kentucky 40202. (800) 626-2823. Formerly: Oceanic Index and Oceanic Citation Journal.

Pollution Abstracts. Cambridge Scientific Abstracts, 5161 River Rd., Bethesda, Maryland 20816. (301) 961-6750. Six/year. Indexes worldwide technical literature on environmental pollution. Covers air pollution, marine and freshwater pollution, sewage and wastewater treatment, waste management, toxicology and health, noise pollution, radiation, land pollution, and environmental policies, programs, legislation, and education. Also available online.

Sea Grant Abstracts. National Sea Grant Depository, Pell Laboratory Bldg., Bay Campus, University of Rhode Island, Narragansett, Rhode Island 02882. (401) 792-6114. 1986-. Quarterly. Published by the National Sea Grant Programs, this collection includes annual reports, serials and newsletters, charts and maps.

ALMANACS AND YEARBOOKS

Ocean Yearbook. The University of Chicago Press, Journals Division, PO Box 37005, Chicago, Illinois 60637. 1978-. Annual. A comprehensive guide to current research and data on living and nonliving resources, marine science and technological environmental, and coastal management.

BIBLIOGRAPHIES

Bibliography and Index of Geology. American Geological Institute, 4220 King St., Alexandria, Virginia 22302. Monthly. Includes environmental geology and hydrogeology.

EPA Publications Bibliography. U.S. Environmental Protection Agency, Library Systems Branch, 401 M St., SW, Washington, District of Columbia 20460. (202) 260-2090. Quarterly.

Marine Science Newsletters–1977: An Annotated Bibliography. Charlotte M. Ashby. National Oceanic and Atmospheric Administration, National Environmental Data Referral Service, Washington, District of Columbia 1977. NOAA Technical Memorandum EDS NODC; 5.

New Publications of the Geological Survey. U.S. Department of the Interior, Geological Survey, 119 National Center, Reston, Virginia 22092. (703) 648-4460. 1984-. Monthly. Bibliography of geological publications and related government documents published by the Geological Survey.

DIRECTORIES

Ocean Industry–Marine Drilling Rigs Directory Issue. Gulf Publishing Co., Book Division, PO Box 2608, Houston, Texas 77252. (713) 529-4301.

ENCYCLOPEDIAS AND DICTIONARIES

Cambridge Encyclopedia of Life Sciences. A. E. Friday and David S. Ingram. Cambridge University Press, 40 W 20th St., New York, New York 10011. (212) 924-3900 or (800) 227-0247. 1985. Includes all topics under biology and ecology.

A Dictionary of Environmental Quotations. Barbara K. Rodes and Rice Odell. Simon and Schuster, 15 Columbus Circle, New York, New York 10023. (212) 373-7342. 1992. Collection of nearly 3000 quotations arranged by topic, such as air, noise, energy, nature, pollution, forests, oceans, and other subjects on the environment.

The Encyclopedia of Oceanography. Rhodes Whitmore Fairbridge. Reinhold Pub. Co., 115 5th Ave., New York, New York 10003. (212) 254-3232. 1966.

McGraw-Hill Encyclopedia of Environmental Science. Sybil P. Parker. McGraw-Hill Science & Engineering Books, 11 W. 19th St., New York, New York 10011. (212) 337-6010. 1980. Covers ecology, man's influence on nature, and environmental protection.

McGraw-Hill Encyclopedia of Science and Technology. McGraw-Hill, 1221 Avenue of the Americas, New York, New York 10020. (212) 512-2000 or (800) 262-4729. 1992. Seventh edition. Issued in multiple volumes including index. Includes all science and technology broad subject areas.

The Times Atlas and Encyclopedia of the Sea. A.D. Couper. Harper & Row, 10 E. 53rd St., New York, New York 10022. (212) 207-7000; (800) 242-7737. 1990.

GENERAL WORKS

Guide to Information on Research in the Marine Science and Engineering. U.S. Department of Commerce, National Oceanic and Atmospheric Administration, Office of Ocean Engineering, 6010 Executive Blvd., Rockville, Maryland 20852. (301) 443-8344. 1978.

The Living Ocean. Boyce Thorne-Miller. Island Press, 1718 Connecticut Ave. N.W., Suite 300, Washington, District of Columbia 20009. (202) 232-7933. 1991. Discusses all marine ecosystems, including coastal benthic, shore systems, estuaries, wetlands, and coral reefs, coastal pelagic, deep-sea benthic, hydrothermal vents and others.

Magill's Survey of Science. Earth Science Series. Frank N. Magill. Salem Press, PO Box 50062, Pasadena, California 91105. 1990-. Five volumes. Includes information on earth's crust, hot spots and volcanic island chains, physical properties of minerals, rock magnetism, physical properties of rocks, and index.

The Ocean in Human Affairs. S. Fred Singer, ed. Paragon House Publishers, 90 5th Ave., New York, New York 10011. (212) 620-2820. 1990. Describes the role of the oceans on climate, its resources, energy and water projects in the eastern Mediterranean and other related essays on marine topics.

Optoelectronics for Environmental Science. S. Martellucci and A. N. Chester, eds. Plenum Press, 233 Spring St., New York, New York 10013-1578. (212) 620-8000; (800) 221-9369. 1991. Contribution of lasers and the optical sciences to specific problems, in situ measurements, atmospheric ozone, lidar detection, wind velocity, oceanographic measurements, heavy metal detection, toxic metals, and trace analysis. Proceedings of the 14th course of the International School of Quantum Electronics on Optoelectronics for Environmental Sciences, held September 3-12, 1989, in Erice, Italy.

Stream, Lake, Estuary, and Ocean Pollution. Nelson Leonard Nemerow. Van Nostrand Reinhold, 115 5th Ave., New York, New York 10003. (800) 926-2665. 1991.

GOVERNMENTAL ORGANIZATIONS

Bureau of Oceans and International Environmental and Scientific Affairs. 2201 C St., N.W., Washington, District of Columbia 20520. (202) 647-1554.

Coast Guard. Information Office, 2100 Second St., S.W., Washington, District of Columbia 20593. (202) 267-2229.

Office of Public Affairs: National Ocean Service. 6013 Herbert C. Hoover Building, 14th and Constitution Avenues, N.W., Washington, District of Columbia 20230. (202) 673-5111.

Office of Public Affairs: National Oceanic and Atmospheric Administration. 14th and Constitution Avenues, N.W., Washington, District of Columbia 20230. (202) 377-2985.

ONLINE DATA BASES

BIOSIS Previews. BIOSIS, 2100 Arch St., Philadelphia, Pennsylvania 19103-1399. (215) 587-4800. Largest and most comprehensive database of research in the life sciences. Contains citations for nearly 9000 primary research journals, monographs, reviews, symposia, preliminary reports, semi-popular journals, selected institutional reports, government reports and research communications.

Civil Engineering Database. American Society of Civil Engineers, 345 E. 47th St., New York, New York 10017. (800) 548-2723.

Computerized Engineering Index–COMPENDEX. Engineering Information Inc., 345 E. 47th St., New York, New York 10017. (212) 705-7600.

Enviro/Energyline Abstracts Plus. R. R. Bowker Co., 121 Chanlon Rd., New Providence, New Jersey 07974. (908) 464-6800.

Enviroline. R. R. Bowker Co., Bowker Electronic Publishing, 121 Chanlon Rd., New Providence, New Jersey 07974. (800) 521-8110.

Environmental Bibliography. Environmental Studies Institute, International Academy at Santa Barbara, 800 Garden St., Ste. D, Santa Barbara, California 93101. (805) 965-5010. International periodical literature dealing with environmental topics such as air pollution, water treatment, energy conservation, noise abatement, soil mechanics, wildlife preservation, and chemical wastes.

Environmental Periodicals Bibliography. National Information Services Corp., Ste. 6, Wyman Towers, 3100 St. Paul St., Baltimore, Maryland 21218. (410)243-0797. Online version of abstract of same name.

MARINELINE. Informationszentrum Rohstoffgewinnwig Geowissenschaften Wasserwirtschaft, Bundesanstalt fuer Geowissenschaften und Rohstoffe, Postfach 510153, Stilleweg 2, Hanover 51, Germany D-3000. 49 (511) 643-2819.

Monthly Catalog of United States Government Publications. U.S. G.P.O., Supt. of Docs., PO Box 371954, Pittsburgh, Pennsylvania 15250-7954. (202) 512-0000.

National Technical Information Service. U.S. Department of Commerce, National Technical Information Service, Office of Data Base Services, 5285 Port Royal Rd., Springfield, Virginia 22161. (703) 487-4807. Bibliographic database of government sponsored research and technical reports.

NODC Data Inventory Data Base. U.S. National Environmental Satellite, Data, and Information Service, National Oceanographic Data Center, 1825 Connecticut Ave., N.W., Suite 406, Washington, District of Columbia 20235. (202) 673-5594. Information on National Oceanographic Data Center holdings.

Oceanic Abstracts. Cambridge Scientific Abstracts, 5161 River Rd., Bethesda, Maryland 20816. (301) 961-6750. Online access.

Oceanographic Literature Review. Woods Hole Data Base, Inc., PO Box 712, Woods Hole, Massachusetts 02574. (508) 548-2743. International periodical literature dealing with oceanography, ocean waste disposal and pollution.

SCISEARCH. Institute for Scientific Information, University City Science Center, 3501 Market St., Philadelphia, Pennsylvania 19104. (215) 386-0100.

PERIODICALS AND NEWSLETTERS

Analytical Chemistry. American Chemical Society, 1155 16th St. N.W., Washington, District of Columbia 20036. (800) 227-5558. 1929-. Bimonthly. Articles for chemists, life scientists and engineers.

Earth Science. American Geological Institute, 4220 King Street, Alexandria, Virginia 22302. (703) 379-2480. Quarterly. Covers geological issues.

Limnology and Oceanography. American Society of Limnology and Oceanography, Inc., PO Box 1897, Lawrence, Kansas 66044-8897. (913) 843-1221. Topics in aquatic disciplines.

MIT Sea Grant Quarterly Report. Sea Grant College Program, Bldg. E38-320, Cambridge, Massachusetts 02139. (617) 235-3461. Quarterly. Ocean related research.

Ocean & Shoreline Management. Elsevier Science Publishing Co., 655 Avenue of the Americas, New York, New York 10010. (212) 989-5800. Bimonthly.

Ocean Science News. Nautilus Press Inc., 1056 National Press Bldg., Washington, District of Columbia 20045. 1970-. Weekly.

RESEARCH CENTERS AND INSTITUTES

California Sea Grant College Program. University of California, La Jolla, California 92093. (619) 534-4440.

Institute of Marine Resources. University of California, La Jolla, California 92093-0228. (619) 534-2868.

Institute of Marine Sciences. University of California, Santa Cruz, Applied Sciences, Room 272, Santa Cruz, California 95064. (408) 459-4730.

National Sea Grant Depository. Pell Library Building, University of Rhode Island, Narragansett, Rhode Island 02882. (401) 792-6114.

National Undersea Research Center. University of Connecticut at Avery Point, Groton, Connecticut 06340. (203) 445-4714.

Nova University, Oceanographic Center. 8000 North Ocean Drive, Dania, Florida 33004. (305) 920-1909.

Ocean Studies Institute. PH1-114, California State University, Long Beach, Long Beach, California 90840. (310) 985-5343.

Oceanic Society. 218 D St., S.E., Washington, District of Columbia 20003. (202) 544-2600.

Okeanos Ocean Research Foundation, Inc. P.O. Box 776, Hamptons Bays, New York 11946. (516) 728-4522.

Oregon State University, Oceanographic & Geophysics Research Program. College of Oceanography, Oceanography Administration Building 104, Corvallis, Oregon 97331-5503. (503) 737-3504.

Scripps Institution of Oceanography. University of California, San Diego, Mail Code 0210, La Jolla, California 92093. (619) 534-3624.

Scripps Institution of Oceanography, Division of Ship Operations and Marine Technical Support. University of California, San Diego, Mail Code A-010, La Jolla, California 92093. (619) 534-2853.

Scripps Institution of Oceanography, Hydrolics Laboratory. University of California, San Diego, 9500 Gilman Dr., La Jolla, California 92093. (619) 534-0595.

Scripps Institution of Oceanography, Marine Biology Research Division. University of California, San Diego, A-0202, San Diego, California 92093-0202. (619) 534-7378.

Scripps Institution of Oceanography, Marine Life Research Group. University of California, San Diego, A-027, La Jolla, California 92093-0227. (619) 534-3565.

Scripps Institution of Oceanography, Marine Physical Laboratory. University of California, San Diego, San Diego, California 92152-6400. (619) 534-1789.

Scripps Institution of Oceanography, Physical Oceanography Research Division. University of California, San Diego, La Jolla, California 92093. (619) 534-1876.

Sea Grant College Program. University of Delaware, 196 South College Avenue, Newark, Delaware 19716. (302) 451-8182.

Skidaway Institute of Oceanography. P.O. Box 13687, McWhorter Drive, Skidaway Island, Savannah, Georgia 31416. (912) 356-2453.

University of Alaska Fairbanks, Seward Marine Center. P.O.Box 730, Seward, Alaska 99664. (907) 224-5261.

University of Maine, Center for Marine Studies. 14 Coburn Hall, Orono, Maine 04469. (207) 581-1435.

University of Miami, Cooperative Institute for Marine and Atmospheric Studies. 4600 Rickenbacker Causeway, Miami, Florida 33149. (305) 361-4159.

University of New Hampshire, Diamond Island Engineering Center. Marine Systems Engineering Lab, Science and Engineering Building, Durham, New Hampshire 03824. (603) 862-4600.

University of New Hampshire, Ocean Process Analysis Laboratory. Science and Engineering Research Building, Durham, New Hampshire 03824. (603) 862-3505.

University of North Carolina at Wilmington, Center for Marine Research. 601 South College Road, Wilmington, North Carolina 28406. (919) 256-3721.

University of North Carolina at Wilmington, NOAA National Undersea Research Center. 7205 Wrightsville Avenue, Wilmington, North Carolina 28403. (919) 256-5133.

University of Puerto Rico, Sea Grant College Program. Department of Marine Sciences, P.O. Box 5000, Mayaguez, Puerto Rico 00681-5000. (809) 832-3585.

University of Rhode Island, Graduate School of Oceanography. Narragansett Bay Campus, Narragansett, Rhode Island 02882-1197. (401) 792-6222.

University of Southern California, Hancock Institute for Marine Studies. University Park, Los Angeles, California 90089-0373. (213) 740-6276.

University of Washington, Washington Sea Grant College Program. 3716 Brooklyn Avenue N.E., Seattle, Washington 98195. (206) 543-6600.

STATISTICS SOURCES

Regional Tide and Tidal Current Tables. U.S. G.P.O, Washington, District of Columbia 20402-9325. (202) 512-0000. Annual.

Tide Tables 1991, High and Low Water Predictions. U.S. G.P.O, Washington, District of Columbia 20402-9325. (202) 512-0000. Annual. Daily tide heights and times for 200 reference ports worldwide.

TRADE ASSOCIATIONS AND PROFESSIONAL SOCIETIES

American Geophysical Union. 2000 Florida Ave., N.W., Washington, District of Columbia 20009. (202) 462-6900.

American Institute of Biological Sciences. 730 11th St., N.W., Washington, District of Columbia 20001-4521. (202) 628-1500.

American Meteorological Society. 45 Beacon St., Boston, Massachusetts 02108. (617) 227-2425.

American Oceanic Organization. National Ocean Service, Herbert C. Hoover Bldg., Rm. 4021, 14th St. and Constitution Ave., Washington, District of Columbia 20230.

American Society of Limnology and Oceanography. Virginia Institute of Marine Science, College of William and Mary, Gloucester Point, Virginia 23062. (804) 642-7242.

American Society of Naval Engineers. 1452 Duke St., Alexandria, Virginia 22314. (703) 836-6727.

Bigelow Laboratory for Ocean Sciences, Division of Northeast Research Foundation, Inc. Mckown Point, West Boothbay Harbor, Maine 04575. (207) 633-2173.

Center for Oceans Law and Policy. School of Law, University of Virginia, Charlottesville, Virginia 22901. (804) 924-7441.

Coast Alliance. 235 Pennsylvania Ave., SE, Washington, District of Columbia 20003. (202) 546-9554.

Council on Ocean Law. 1709 New York Ave., NW, Suite 700, Washington, District of Columbia 20006. (202) 347-3766.

Friends of the Earth. 218 D St., SE, Washington, District of Columbia 20003. (202) 544-2600.

Greenpeace. 1436 U St., NW, Washington, District of Columbia 20009. (202) 462-1177.

International Ocean Pollution Symposium. Department of Chemical and Environmental Engineering, Florida Institute of Tech., Melbourne, Florida 32901. (407) 768-8000.

International Oceanographic Foundation. 4600 Rickenbacker Causeway, P.O. Box 499900, Miami, Florida 33149-9900. (305) 361-4888.

National Ocean Industries Association. 1120 G St., N.W., Suite 900, Washington, District of Columbia 20005. (202) 347-6900.

Ocean Outlook. 1230 31st St., N.W., #5, Washington, District of Columbia 20007. (202) 333-1188.

Sea Grant Association. c/o Dr. Christopher F. D'Elia, Maryland Sea Grant College, 1123 Taliaferro Hall, UMCP, College Park, Maryland 20742. (301) 405-6371.

U.S. National Committee for the Scientific Committee on Oceanic Research. Ocean Studies Blvd., 2001 Wisconsin Ave., N.W., Rm. MH550, Washington, District of Columbia 20007. (202) 334-2714.

OCTANE RATING

See also: CARBON MONOXIDE; GASOLINE

ABSTRACTING AND INDEXING SERVICES

Chemical Abstracts. Chemical Abstracts Service, 2540 Olentangy River Rd., PO Box 3012, Columbus, Ohio 43210. (800) 848-6533. 1907-.

Engineering Index. The Engineering Index Inc., 345 E. 47th St., New York, New York 10017. 1962-.

Environment Abstracts. Bowker A & I Publishing, 121 Chanlon Rd., New Providence, New Jersey 07974. (908) 464-6800. 1974-.

Environment Index. Environment Information Center, Index Research Department, 124 E. 39th St., New York, New York 10016. 1971-. Annual.

Environmental Information Connection–EIC. Planning Information Program, Dept. of Urban and Regional Planning, University of Illinois, 1003 West Nevada, Urbana, Illinois 61801. (217) 333-1369. Also available online.

Environmental Periodicals Bibliography. Environmental Studies Institute, International Academy at Santa Barbara, 800 Garden St., Suite D, Santa Barbara, California 93101. (805) 965-5010. Also available online.

Science Citation Index. Institute for Scientific Information, 3501 Market St., Philadelphia, Pennsylvania 19104. 1961-.

BIBLIOGRAPHIES

EPA Publications Bibliography. U.S. Environmental Protection Agency, Library Systems Branch, 401 M St., SW, Washington, District of Columbia 20460. (202) 260-2090. Quarterly.

ENCYCLOPEDIAS AND DICTIONARIES

McGraw-Hill Encyclopedia of Science and Technology. McGraw-Hill, 1221 Avenue of the Americas, New York, New York 10020. (212) 512-2000 or (800) 262-4729. 1992. Seventh edition. Issued in multiple volumes including index. Includes all science and technology broad subject areas.

ONLINE DATA BASES

Chemical Abstracts-CA. Chemical Abstracts Service, 2540 Olentangy River Rd., P.O. Box 3012, Columbus, Ohio 43210. (800) 848-6533 or (614) 421-3600. Information sources include 9000 journals, patents from 27 countries, two industrial property organizations, new books, conference proceedings, and government research reports.

Computerized Engineering Index–COMPENDEX. Engineering Information Inc., 345 E. 47th St., New York, New York 10017. (212) 705-7600.

Enviro/Energyline Abstracts Plus. R. R. Bowker Co., 121 Chanlon Rd., New Providence, New Jersey 07974. (908) 464-6800.

Environmental Periodicals Bibliography. National Information Services Corp., Ste. 6, Wyman Towers, 3100 St. Paul St., Baltimore, Maryland 21218. (410)243-0797. Online version of abstract of same name.

ODOR CONTROL

See: ODORS

ODORS

See also: FERTILIZERS; ORGANIC WASTE

ABSTRACTING AND INDEXING SERVICES

Applied Ecology Abstracts Studies in Renewable Natural Resources. Information Retrieval Ltd., 1911 Jefferson Davis Highway, Arlington, Virginia 22202. 1975-. Monthly.

Biological Abstracts. BIOSIS, 2100 Arch St., Philadelphia, Pennsylvania 19103-1399. (215) 587-4800. 1927-.

Biological and Agricultural Index. H.W. Wilson Co., 950 University Ave., Bronx, New York 10452. (800) 367-6770. 1916-. Monthly.

Biotechnology Research Abstracts. Cambridge Scientific Abstracts, 5161 River Rd., Bethesda, Maryland 20816. (301) 961-6750. Monthly. Includes such broad areas as genetic intervention, biochemical genetics, and microbiological techniques.

Environment Abstracts. Bowker A & I Publishing, 121 Chanlon Rd., New Providence, New Jersey 07974. (908) 464-6800. 1974-.

Environment Index. Environment Information Center, Index Research Department, 124 E. 39th St., New York, New York 10016. 1971-. Annual.

Environmental Information Connection–EIC. Planning Information Program, Dept. of Urban and Regional Planning, University of Illinois, 1003 West Nevada, Urbana, Illinois 61801. (217) 333-1369. Also available online.

Environmental Periodicals Bibliography. Environmental Studies Institute, International Academy at Santa Barbara, 800 Garden St., Suite D, Santa Barbara, California 93101. (805) 965-5010. Also available online.

General Science Index. H. W. Wilson Co., 950 University Ave., Bronx, New York 10452. 1978-. Monthly, also issued in annual cumulation. Cumulative subject index to English language periodicals in the subject fields of astronomy, botany, chemistry, earth science, environment and conservation, food and nutrition, genetics, mathematics, medicine and health, microbiology, oceanography, physics, physiology and zoology.

Multimedia Index to Ecology. National Information Center for Educational Media, University of Southern California, Los Angeles, California 90007.

Pollution Abstracts. Cambridge Scientific Abstracts, 5161 River Rd., Bethesda, Maryland 20816. (301) 961-6750. Six/year. Indexes worldwide technical literature on environmental pollution. Covers air pollution, marine and freshwater pollution, sewage and wastewater treatment, waste management, toxicology and health, noise pollution, radiation, land pollution, and environmental policies, programs, legislation, and education. Also available online.

BIBLIOGRAPHIES

EPA Publications Bibliography. U.S. Environmental Protection Agency, Library Systems Branch, 401 M St., SW, Washington, District of Columbia 20460. (202) 260-2090. Quarterly.

ENCYCLOPEDIAS AND DICTIONARIES

Encyclopedia of Chemical Processing and Design. John J. Mcketta and W. A. Cunningham. Marcel Dekker, Inc., 270 Madison Ave., New York, New York 10016. (212) 696-9000; (800) 228-1160. 1992. Thirty-eight volumes.

Kirk-Othmer Encyclopedia of Chemical Technology. J. I. Kroschwitz, ed. John Wiley & Sons, Inc., 605 3rd Ave., New York, New York 10158-0012. (212) 850-6000. 1992-. All articles in the new edition have been rewritten and updated adding new subjects such as biotechnology, computer topics, analytical techniques and instrumentation, environmental concerns, fuels and energy, inorganic and solid state chemistry; composite materials and material science in general, and pharmaceuticals. Also available online.

Van Nostrand's Scientific Encyclopedia. Glenn D. Considine, ed. Van Nostrand Reinhold, 115 5th Ave., New

York, New York 10003. (212) 254-3232. 1983. Sixth edition. Includes all broad subject areas in science.

GENERAL WORKS

Agricultural Waste Utilization and Management. American Society of Agricultural Engineers, 2950 Niles Rd., St. Joseph, Michigan 49085-9659. (616) 429-0300. 1985. Proceedings of the Fifth International Symposium on Agricultural Wastes, December 16-17, 1985, Chicago, IL. Covers topics such as liquid manure storage and transportation, energy recovery from wastes, digester types and design, recycling for feed, fuel and fertilizer, land applications and odor control.

The Fragrant Path. Louise Wilder. Collier Books, 866 3rd Ave., New York, New York 10022. (212) 702-2000. 1990. Aromatic plants and flower odor as well as fragrant gardens.

Livestock Waste, a Renewable Resource. American Society of Agricultural Engineers, 2950 Niles Rd., St. Joseph, Michigan 49085-9659. (616) 429-0300. 1981. Papers presented at the 4th International Symposium on Livestock Wastes, Amarillo, TX, 1980. Topics covered include: processing manure for feed, methane production, land application, lagoons, runoff, odors, economics, stabilization, treatment, collection and transport, storage and solid-liquid separation.

Odor and Corrosion Control in Sanitary Sewerage Systems and Treatment Plants: Design Manual. U.S. Environmental Protection Agency, 401 M St., S.W., Washington, District of Columbia 20460. (202) 260-2090. 1985. Sewage disposal plants and odor control.

Thermal Generation of Aromas. Thomas H. Parliment. American Chemical Society, 1155 16th St. N.W., Washington, District of Columbia 20036. (800) 227-5558. 1989. Food odor and effect of heat on food.

HANDBOOKS AND MANUALS

Atlas of Odor Character Profiles. Andrew Dravnieks. ASTM, 1916 Race St., Philadelphia, Pennsylvania 19103-1187. (215) 299-5400. Analytic chemistry and odor control.

Odor Control and Olfaction: A Handbook. James P. Cox. Pollution Sciences Publishing Company, Lynden, Washington 1975.

ONLINE DATA BASES

BIOSIS Previews. BIOSIS, 2100 Arch St., Philadelphia, Pennsylvania 19103-1399. (215) 587-4800. Largest and most comprehensive database of research in the life sciences. Contains citations for nearly 9000 primary research journals, monographs, reviews, symposia, preliminary reports, semi-popular journals, selected institutional reports, government reports and research communications.

Enviro/Energyline Abstracts Plus. R. R. Bowker Co., 121 Chanlon Rd., New Providence, New Jersey 07974. (908) 464-6800.

Environmental Periodicals Bibliography. National Information Services Corp., Ste. 6, Wyman Towers, 3100 St. Paul St., Baltimore, Maryland 21218. (410)243-0797. Online version of abstract of same name.

Kirk-Othmer Encyclopedia of Chemical Technology. John Wiley & Sons, Inc., 605 3rd Ave., 5th Floor, New York, New York 10158. (212) 850-6000. Online version of the publication of the same name.

TRADE ASSOCIATIONS AND PROFESSIONAL SOCIETIES

American Institute of Biological Sciences. 730 11th St., N.W., Washington, District of Columbia 20001-4521. (202) 628-1500.

OFF ROAD VEHICLES
See: TRANSPORTATION

OFFSHORE ACTIVITIES
See: DRILLING

OHIO ENVIRONMENTAL AGENCIES

GOVERNMENTAL ORGANIZATIONS

Department of Agriculture: Occupational Safety. Chief, Division of Plant Industry, 8995 East Main St., Reynoldsburg, Ohio 43068-3399. (614) 866-6361, Ext. 285.

Department of Agriculture: Pesticide Registration. Pesticide Regulation, 8995 East Main St., Reynoldsburg, Ohio 43068. (614) 866-6361.

Department of Commerce: Underground Storage Tanks. State Fire Marshal, Division of State Fire Marshal, 8895 East Main St., Reynoldsburg, Ohio 43068. (614) 466-2416.

Department of Natural Resources: Coastal Zone Management. Chief, Division of Water, Fountain Square, Building E, Columbus, Ohio 43224. (614) 265-6712.

Department of Natural Resources: Fish and Wildlife. Clayton Lakes, Chief, Division of Wildlife, Fountain Square, Building C-4, Columbus, Ohio 43224. (614) 265-6305.

Department of Natural Resources: Natural Resources. Director, Fountain Square, Building D-3, Columbus, Ohio 43224. (614) 265-6875.

Division of Air Pollution Control: Emergency Preparedness and Community Right-to-Know. Coordinator, 1800 Watermark Dr., Columbus, Ohio 43215. (614) 644-2266.

Environmental Protection Agency: Air Quality. Chief, Air Pollution Control Division, 1800 Watermark Dr., Columbus, Ohio 43266-0149. (614) 644-2270.

Environmental Protection Agency: Environmental Protection. Director, 1800 Watermark Dr., Columbus, Ohio 43266-0149. (614) 481-7050.

Environmental Protection Agency: Groundwater Management. Chief, Division of Groundwater, 1800 Watermark Dr., Columbus, Ohio 43266-0149. (614) 644-2905.

Environmental Protection Agency: Hazardous Waste Management. Chief, Division of Solid and Hazardous Waste Management, 1800 Watermark Dr., Columbus, Ohio 43266-0149. (614) 644-2917.

Environmental Protection Agency: Solid Waste Management. Chief, Division of Solid and Hazardous Waste, 1800 Watermark Dr., Columbus, Ohio 43266-0149. (614) 644-2917.

Environmental Protection Agency: Waste Minimization and Pollution Protection. Chief, Solid Waste Section, PO Box 1049, 1800 Watermark Dr., Columbus, Ohio 43266-0149. (614) 644-2917.

Environmental Protection Agency: Water Quality. Chief, 1800 Watermark Dr., Columbus, Ohio 43266-0149. (614) 644-2856.

OHIO ENVIRONMENTAL LEGISLATION

GENERAL WORKS

Ohio Environmental Law Handbook. Government Institutes, Inc., 4 Research Pl., Ste. 200, Rockville, Maryland 20850. (301) 921-2300. 1990.

OIL DISCHARGE

ABSTRACTING AND INDEXING SERVICES

ASFA Aquaculture Abstracts. Cambridge Scientific Abstracts, Inc., 5161 River Rd., Bethesda, Maryland 20816. (301) 961-6750. 1984.

Biological Abstracts. BIOSIS, 2100 Arch St., Philadelphia, Pennsylvania 19103-1399. (215) 587-4800. 1927-.

Engineering Index. The Engineering Index Inc., 345 E. 47th St., New York, New York 10017. 1962-.

General Science Index. H. W. Wilson Co., 950 University Ave., Bronx, New York 10452. 1978-. Monthly, also issued in annual cumulation. Cumulative subject index to English language periodicals in the subject fields of astronomy, botany, chemistry, earth science, environment and conservation, food and nutrition, genetics, mathematics, medicine and health, microbiology, oceanography, physics, physiology and zoology.

Pollution Abstracts. Cambridge Scientific Abstracts, 5161 River Rd., Bethesda, Maryland 20816. (301) 961-6750. Six/year. Indexes worldwide technical literature on environmental pollution. Covers air pollution, marine and freshwater pollution, sewage and wastewater treatment, waste management, toxicology and health, noise pollution, radiation, land pollution, and environmental policies, programs, legislation, and education. Also available online.

GENERAL WORKS

Assessment of Environmental Fate and Effects of Discharges from Offshore Oil and Gas Operations. U.S. Environmental Protection Agency, Office of Water Regulations and Standards, 401 M St., S.W., Washington, District of Columbia 20460. (202) 260-2090. 1985. Environmental aspects of offshore oil and gas industry.

Coast Guard Enforcement of Environmental Laws. House Committee on Merchant Marine and Fisheries. U.S.

G.P.O., Washington, District of Columbia 20401. (202) 512-0000. 1990.

ONLINE DATA BASES

BIOSIS Previews. BIOSIS, 2100 Arch St., Philadelphia, Pennsylvania 19103-1399. (215) 587-4800. Largest and most comprehensive database of research in the life sciences. Contains citations for nearly 9000 primary research journals, monographs, reviews, symposia, preliminary reports, semi-popular journals, selected institutional reports, government reports and research communications.

Computerized Engineering Index–COMPENDEX. Engineering Information Inc., 345 E. 47th St., New York, New York 10017. (212) 705-7600.

PERIODICALS AND NEWSLETTERS

Oil Spill Intelligence Report. Cahners Publishing Co., 249 W. 17th St., New York, New York 10011. (212) 645-0067. Irregular. Global information on oil spill cleanup, prevention control.

OIL DRILLING

See: OIL EXPLORATION

OIL EXPLORATION

ABSTRACTING AND INDEXING SERVICES

Energy Information Abstracts Annual 1987 in Retrospect. EIC/Intelligence Inc., 121 Chanlon Rd., New Providence, New Jersey 07974. (908) 464-6800. 1988. Annual. Cumulative edition of the monthly Energy Information Abstracts. Monitors sources in the field of energy including the scientific, technical and business journal literature, conference and symposia proceedings, corporate, government and academic reports.

Engineering Index. The Engineering Index Inc., 345 E. 47th St., New York, New York 10017. 1962-.

Environment Abstracts. Bowker A & I Publishing, 121 Chanlon Rd., New Providence, New Jersey 07974. (908) 464-6800. 1974-.

Environment Index. Environment Information Center, Index Research Department, 124 E. 39th St., New York, New York 10016. 1971-. Annual.

Environmental Information Connection–EIC. Planning Information Program, Dept. of Urban and Regional Planning, University of Illinois, 1003 West Nevada, Urbana, Illinois 61801. (217) 333-1369. Also available online.

Environmental Periodicals Bibliography. Environmental Studies Institute, International Academy at Santa Barbara, 800 Garden St., Suite D, Santa Barbara, California 93101. (805) 965-5010. Also available online.

General Science Index. H. W. Wilson Co., 950 University Ave., Bronx, New York 10452. 1978-. Monthly, also issued in annual cumulation. Cumulative subject index to English language periodicals in the subject fields of astronomy, botany, chemistry, earth science, environ-

ment and conservation, food and nutrition, genetics, mathematics, medicine and health, microbiology, oceanography, physics, physiology and zoology.

BIBLIOGRAPHIES

EPA Publications Bibliography. U.S. Environmental Protection Agency, Library Systems Branch, 401 M St., SW, Washington, District of Columbia 20460. (202) 260-2090. Quarterly.

DIRECTORIES

American Oil and Gas Reporter–American Drilling Rig Directory Issues. National Publishers Group, Inc., Box 343, Derby, Kansas 67037. (316) 681-3560.

American Oil and Gas Reporter–American Well Servicing Rig Directory Issues. National Publishers Group, Inc., Box 343, Derby, Kansas 63037. (316) 681-3560.

Armstrong Oil Directories. Armstrong Oil Directory, 1606 Jackson St., Amarillo, Texas 79102. (806) 374-1818.

Contracts for Field Projects and Supporting Research on Enhanced Oil Recovery and Improved Drilling Technology. Bartlesville Energy Technology Center, Box 1398, Bartlesville, Oklahoma 74005. (918) 336-2400.

Directory of Oil Well Drilling Contractors. Midwest Register, Inc., 15 W. 6th St., Suite 1308, Tulsa, Oklahoma 74119-1505. (918) 582-2000.

The Oil and Gas Directory; Regional and Worldwide. Oil and Gas Directory, 2200 Welch Ave., PO Box 13508, Houston, Texas 77219. (713) 529-8789. 1987-88. Eighteenth edition. Comprehensive listing of all companies and individuals directly connected with or engaged in petroleum exploration, drilling, and production.

ENCYCLOPEDIAS AND DICTIONARIES

Dictionary of Environmental Engineering and Related Sciences: English-Spanish, Spanish-English. Jose T. Villate. Ediciones Universal, 3090 SW 8th St., Miami, Florida 33135. (305) 642-3355. 1979.

Encyclopedia of Environmental Science and Engineering. J.R. Pfafflin. Gordon and Breach Science Publishers, Inc., 270 8th Ave., New York, New York 10011. (212) 206-8900. 1992.

Handbook of Oil Industry Terms and Phrases. R. D. Langenkamp. PennWell Books, PO Box 1260, Tulsa, Oklahoma 74101. (918) 835-3161. 1984. Fourth edition. Includes more than 700 new entries relating to geology, new equipment, advances in drilling technology and operating methods, investment funds, operating interests, royalty interests, nondrilling leases, top leases, joint leases, implied covenants and "escape clauses" and other related topics.

Oil Terms: A Dictionary of Terms Used in Oil Exploration and Development. Leo Crook. International Pub Service, 114 E 32d St., New York, New York 10016. 1975.

GENERAL WORKS

Coast Alert: Scientists Speak Out. Daniel W. Anderson. Coast Alliance by Friends of the Earth, San Francisco, California 1981. Coastal ecology and oil pollution of water.

Environmental Impacts from Offshore Exploration and Production of Oil and Gas. OECD Publications and Information Center, 2 rue Andre Pascal, Paris, France F-75775. 1977. Oil pollution of water and petroleum in submerged lands.

Oil and Gas Law: The North Sea Exploration. Kenneth R. Simmonds. Oceana Publications Inc., 75 Main St., Dobbs Ferry, New York 10522. (914) 693-8100. 1988. Surveys the legal framework within which operators have to carry out the exploration and exploitation of North Sea oil and gas resources.

Oil/Water Separation: State-of-the-Art. Fidelis A. Osamor. National Technical Information Service, 5285 Port Royal Rd., Springfield, Virginia 22161. (703) 487-4650. 1978. Oil pollution of water, rivers, and harbors and the technology of abatement.

HANDBOOKS AND MANUALS

Handbook for Oil Spill Protection and Cleanup Priorities. Municipal Environmental Research Laboratory, U.S. Environmental Protection Agency, 26 W Martin Luther King Dr., Cincinnati, Ohio 45268. (513) 569-7931. 1981. Environmental aspects of oil pollution of water and oil spills.

ONLINE DATA BASES

Computerized Engineering Index–COMPENDEX. Engineering Information Inc., 345 E. 47th St., New York, New York 10017. (212) 705-7600.

Enviro/Energyline Abstracts Plus. R. R. Bowker Co., 121 Chanlon Rd., New Providence, New Jersey 07974. (908) 464-6800.

Environmental Periodicals Bibliography. National Information Services Corp., Ste. 6, Wyman Towers, 3100 St. Paul St., Baltimore, Maryland 21218. (410)243-0797. Online version of abstract of same name.

International Petroleum Abstracts. John Wiley & Sons, Ltd., Baffers Lane, Chichester, Sussex, England PO1 91UD. 44 (243) 770215.

International Petroleum Annual. U.S. Department of Energy, Integrated Technical Information System, P.O. Box 62, Oak Ridge, Tennessee 37831. (615) 576-1222.

TRADE ASSOCIATIONS AND PROFESSIONAL SOCIETIES

American Petroleum Institute. 1220 L St., N.W., Washington, District of Columbia 20005. (202) 682-8000.

American Society of Petroleum Operations Engineers. PO Box 956, Richmond, Virginia 23207. (703) 768-4159.

Oil Field Haulers Association. 700 E. 11th St., Box 1669, Austin, Texas 78767. (512) 478-2541.

OIL FIELDS

DIRECTORIES

Interstate Oil Compact Commission 1990 Directory. Interstate Oil and Gas Compact Commission, 990 NE 23d St., PO Box 53127, Oklahoma City, Oklahoma 73152. (405) 525-3556 or (800) 822-4015. 1990. Includes addresses and telephone numbers of members.

ENCYCLOPEDIAS AND DICTIONARIES

Elsevier's Oil and Gas Field Dictionary. L. Y. Caballe, et al, eds. Elsevier Science Publishing Co., 655 Avenue of the Americas, New York, New York 10010. (212) 989-5800. 1980. The text is in English/American, French, Spanish, Italian, Dutch, German, Arabic supplement. Includes terms used in oil and gas field operations.

Handbook of Oil Industry Terms and Phrases. R. D. Langenkamp. PennWell Books, PO Box 1260, Tulsa, Oklahoma 74101. (918) 835-3161. 1984. Fourth edition. Includes more than 700 new entries relating to geology, new equipment, advances in drilling technology and operating methods, investment funds, operating interests, royalty interests, nondrilling leases, top leases, joint leases, implied covenants and "escape clauses" and other related topics.

ONLINE DATA BASES

International Petroleum Abstracts. John Wiley & Sons, Ltd., Baffers Lane, Chichester, Sussex, England PO1 91UD. 44 (243) 770215.

International Petroleum Annual. U.S. Department of Energy, Integrated Technical Information System, P.O. Box 62, Oak Ridge, Tennessee 37831. (615) 576-1222.

TRADE ASSOCIATIONS AND PROFESSIONAL SOCIETIES

American Petroleum Institute. 1220 L St., N.W., Washington, District of Columbia 20005. (202) 682-8000.

American Society of Petroleum Operations Engineers. PO Box 956, Richmond, Virginia 23207. (703) 768-4159.

Interstate Oil Compact Commission. Box 53127, Oklahoma City, Oklahoma 73152. (405) 525-3556 OR (800) 822-4015.

OIL IMPURITIES

See: OIL

OIL (PETROLEUM)

ABSTRACTING AND INDEXING SERVICES

ASFA Aquaculture Abstracts. Cambridge Scientific Abstracts, Inc., 5161 River Rd., Bethesda, Maryland 20816. (301) 961-6750. 1984.

Biological Abstracts. BIOSIS, 2100 Arch St., Philadelphia, Pennsylvania 19103-1399. (215) 587-4800. 1927-.

Biotechnology Research Abstracts. Cambridge Scientific Abstracts, 5161 River Rd., Bethesda, Maryland 20816. (301) 961-6750. Monthly. Includes such broad areas as genetic intervention, biochemical genetics, and microbiological techniques.

Engineering Index. The Engineering Index Inc., 345 E. 47th St., New York, New York 10017. 1962-.

Mineralogical Abstracts. Mineralogical Society, 41 Queen's Gate, London, England SW7 5HR. 71 5847916. Quarterly. Abstracts of journal articles, conferences, technical reports and specialized books in the areas of minerals, clay minerals, economic minerals, ore deposits, environmental studies, experimental mineralogy, gemstones, geochemistry, petrology, lunar and planetary studies and other related areas in mineralogy.

Pollution Abstracts. Cambridge Scientific Abstracts, 5161 River Rd., Bethesda, Maryland 20816. (301) 961-6750. Six/year. Indexes worldwide technical literature on environmental pollution. Covers air pollution, marine and freshwater pollution, sewage and wastewater treatment, waste management, toxicology and health, noise pollution, radiation, land pollution, and environmental policies, programs, legislation, and education. Also available online.

Science Citation Index. Institute for Scientific Information, 3501 Market St., Philadelphia, Pennsylvania 19104. 1961-.

BIBLIOGRAPHIES

Bibliography and Index of Geology. American Geological Institute, 4220 King St., Alexandria, Virginia 22302. Monthly. Includes environmental geology and hydrogeology.

Biological Effects of Oil Pollution: A Comprehensive Bibliography with Abstracts. Melvin Light. U.S. Coast Guard, Office of Research and Development, 2100 Second St., N.W., R,. 5410 C, Springfield, Virginia 20593. (202) 267-1042. 1978.

Oil Pollution Abstracts. Industrial Environmental Research Laboratory, Office of Research and Development, U.S. Environmental Protection Agency, 2412 Atlantic Ave., Raleigh, North Carolina 27604. (919) 834-4015. 1979.

DIRECTORIES

Financial Times Who's Who in World Oil and Gas. Longman Group UK Ltd., Westgate House, 6th Fl., The High, Harlow, England CM20 1NE. 279 442601.

Interstate Oil Compact Commission 1990 Directory. Interstate Oil and Gas Compact Commission, 990 NE 23d St., PO Box 53127, Oklahoma City, Oklahoma 73152. (405) 525-3556 or (800) 822-4015. 1990. Includes addresses and telephone numbers of members.

The Oil and Gas Directory; Regional and Worldwide. Oil and Gas Directory, 2200 Welch Ave., PO Box 13508, Houston, Texas 77219. (713) 529-8789. 1987-88. Eighteenth edition. Comprehensive listing of all companies and individuals directly connected with or engaged in petroleum exploration, drilling, and production.

ENCYCLOPEDIAS AND DICTIONARIES

Elsevier's Oil and Gas Field Dictionary. L. Y. Caballe, et al, eds. Elsevier Science Publishing Co., 655 Avenue of the Americas, New York, New York 10010. (212) 989-5800. 1980. The text is in English/American, French, Spanish, Italian, Dutch, German, Arabic supplement. Includes terms used in oil and gas field operations.

Encyclopedia of Chemical Processing and Design. John J. Mcketta and W. A. Cunningham. Marcel Dekker, Inc., 270 Madison Ave., New York, New York 10016. (212) 696-9000; (800) 228-1160. 1992. Thirty-eight volumes.

Glossary of Geology. Robert Latimer Bates and Julia A. Jackson, eds. American Geological Institute, 4220 King

St., Alexandria, Virginia 22302-1507. (703) 379-2480 or (800) 336-4764. 1987. Third edition.

Handbook of Oil Industry Terms and Phrases. R. D. Langenkamp. PennWell Books, PO Box 1260, Tulsa, Oklahoma 74101. (918) 835-3161. 1984. Fourth edition. Includes more than 700 new entries relating to geology, new equipment, advances in drilling technology and operating methods, investment funds, operating interests, royalty interests, nondrilling leases, top leases, joint leases, implied covenants and "escape clauses" and other related topics.

Illustrated Encyclopedia of Science and the Future. Mike Biscare, et al., ed. Marshall Cavendish, 58 Old Compton St., London, England 0W1V5 PA. 01-734 6710. 1983. Twenty volumes. Each volume has 5 sections: Frontiers, Electronics in Action, Medical Science, Military Technology, and Resources.

Kirk-Othmer Encyclopedia of Chemical Technology. J. I. Kroschwitz, ed. John Wiley & Sons, Inc., 605 3rd Ave., New York, New York 10158-0012. (212) 850-6000. 1992-. All articles in the new edition have been rewritten and updated adding new subjects such as biotechnology, computer topics, analytical techniques and instrumentation, environmental concerns, fuels and energy, inorganic and solid state chemistry; composite materials and material science in general, and pharmaceuticals. Also available online.

McGraw-Hill Encyclopedia of Science and Technology. McGraw-Hill, 1221 Avenue of the Americas, New York, New York 10020. (212) 512-2000 or (800) 262-4729. 1992. Seventh edition. Issued in multiple volumes including index. Includes all science and technology broad subject areas.

McGraw-Hill Encyclopedia of the Geological Sciences. Sybil P. Parker, ed. McGraw-Hill, 1221 Avenue of the Americas, New York, New York 10020. (212) 512-2000 or (800) 262-4729. 1988. Second edition. Published previously in the McGraw-Hill Encyclopedia of Science and Technology.

Van Nostrand's Scientific Encyclopedia. Glenn D. Considine, ed. Van Nostrand Reinhold, 115 5th Ave., New York, New York 10003. (212) 254-3232. 1983. Sixth edition. Includes all broad subject areas in science.

GENERAL WORKS

Law and Practice Relating to Oil Pollution from Ships. D.W. Abecassis. Stevens & Sons, South Quay Plaza, 183 Marsh Wall, London, England E14 9FT. 1985. International, United Kingdom, and United States law and practice.

Magill's Survey of Science. Earth Science Series. Frank N. Magill. Salem Press, PO Box 50062, Pasadena, California 91105. 1990-. Five volumes. Includes information on earth's crust, hot spots and volcanic island chains, physical properties of minerals, rock magnetism, physical properties of rocks, and index.

Oil Pollution Act of 1990: Special Report. Government Institutes, Inc., 4 Research Pl., Ste. 200, Rockville, Maryland 20850. (301) 921-2300. 1991. Gives complete coverage of the Oil Pollution Act for the Government Institutes' conference.

Oil Pollution from Tanker Operations; Causes, Costs, Controls. W.G. Waters. Centre for Transportation Studies, University of British Columbia, 1924 W. Mall, Rm. 100, Vancouver, British Columbia, Canada V6I 1Z2. (604) 822-4977. 1980. Tanker safety measures, costs, and oil pollution of the sea.

ONLINE DATA BASES

Active Well Data On-Line. Petroleum Information Cooperation, 4100 E. Dry Creek Road, Littleton, Colorado 80122. (800) 525-5569.

APILIT. American Petroleum Institute, 1220 L St. N.W., Washington, District of Columbia 20005. (202) 682-8000.

APIPAT. American Petroleum Institute, 1220 L St. N.W., Washington, District of Columbia 20005. (202) 682-8000.

BIOSIS Previews. BIOSIS, 2100 Arch St., Philadelphia, Pennsylvania 19103-1399. (215) 587-4800. Largest and most comprehensive database of research in the life sciences. Contains citations for nearly 9000 primary research journals, monographs, reviews, symposia, preliminary reports, semi-popular journals, selected institutional reports, government reports and research communications.

Computerized Engineering Index–COMPENDEX. Engineering Information Inc., 345 E. 47th St., New York, New York 10017. (212) 705-7600.

EMIS. TECNON (U.K.) Limited, 12 Calico House, Plantation Wharf, York Place, Battersea, London, England SW11 3TN. 44 (71) 924-3955.

International Petroleum Abstracts. John Wiley & Sons, Ltd., Baffers Lane, Chichester, Sussex, England PO1 91UD. 44 (243) 770215.

International Petroleum Annual. U.S. Department of Energy, Integrated Technical Information System, P.O. Box 62, Oak Ridge, Tennessee 37831. (615) 576-1222.

Kirk-Othmer Encyclopedia of Chemical Technology. John Wiley & Sons, Inc., 605 3rd Ave., 5th Floor, New York, New York 10158. (212) 850-6000. Online version of the publication of the same name.

Oil & Gas Journal Energy Database. PennWell Books, PO Box 1260, Tulsa, Oklahoma 74101. (918) 835-3161.

PERIODICALS AND NEWSLETTERS

American Oil Chemists Society Journal. The American Oil Chemists Society, P.O. Box 3489, Champaign, Illinois 61820. (217) 359-2344. 1917-. Monthly.

STATISTICS SOURCES

World Resources. World Resources Institute. 1709 New York Ave., N.W., Washington, District of Columbia 20006. (202) 638-6300. Annual. Statistical and textual analysis of world's natural resources and the effects of growth-caused environmental pollution.

TRADE ASSOCIATIONS AND PROFESSIONAL SOCIETIES

American Oil Chemists Society. P.O. Box 3489, Champaign, Illinois 61820. (217) 359-2344.

American Petroleum Institute. 1220 L St., N.W., Washington, District of Columbia 20005. (202) 682-8000.

Association of Diesel Specialists. 9140 Ward Pkwy., Kansas City, Missouri 64114. (816) 444-3500.

Interstate Oil Compact Commission. Box 53127, Oklahoma City, Oklahoma 73152. (405) 525-3556 OR (800) 822-4015.

Mid-Continent Oil & Gas Association. 801 Pennsylvania Ave. N.W., Ste. 840, Washington, District of Columbia 20004-2604. (202) 638-4400.

National Oil Recyclers Association. 805 15th St., N.W., Suite 900, Washington, District of Columbia 20005. (202) 962-3020.

National Stripper Well Association. 801 Petroleum Bldg., Wichita, Texas 76301. (817) 766-3870.

Oil, Chemical, & Atomic Workers International Union. Box 2812, Denver, Colorado 80201. (303) 987-2229.

Oil Field Haulers Association. 700 E. 11th St., Box 1669, Austin, Texas 78767. (512) 478-2541.

Western Oil & Gas Association. 505 N. Brand Ave., Suite 1400, Glendale, California 91203. (818) 545-4105.

OIL POLLUTION

See also: OIL SPILLS

ABSTRACTING AND INDEXING SERVICES

Environment Abstracts. Bowker A & I Publishing, 121 Chanlon Rd., New Providence, New Jersey 07974. (908) 464-6800. 1974-.

Environment Index. Environment Information Center, Index Research Department, 124 E. 39th St., New York, New York 10016. 1971-. Annual.

Environmental Information Connection–EIC. Planning Information Program, Dept. of Urban and Regional Planning, University of Illinois, 1003 West Nevada, Urbana, Illinois 61801. (217) 333-1369. Also available online.

Environmental Periodicals Bibliography. Environmental Studies Institute, International Academy at Santa Barbara, 800 Garden St., Suite D, Santa Barbara, California 93101. (805) 965-5010. Also available online.

General Science Index. H. W. Wilson Co., 950 University Ave., Bronx, New York 10452. 1978-. Monthly, also issued in annual cumulation. Cumulative subject index to English language periodicals in the subject fields of astronomy, botany, chemistry, earth science, environment and conservation, food and nutrition, genetics, mathematics, medicine and health, microbiology, oceanography, physics, physiology and zoology.

BIBLIOGRAPHIES

EPA Publications Bibliography. U.S. Environmental Protection Agency, Library Systems Branch, 401 M St., SW, Washington, District of Columbia 20460. (202) 260-2090. Quarterly.

GENERAL WORKS

Hydrocarbon Contaminated Soils and Groundwater: Analysis, Fate, Environmental and Public Health Effects, and Remediation. Paul T. Kostecki and Edward J. Calabrese. Lewis Publishers, 2000 Corporate Blvd.,N.W., Boca Raton, Florida 33431. (407) 994-0555 or (800) 272-7737. 1991. Describes perspectives and emerging issues, analytical techniques and site assessments, environmental fate and modeling.

Petroleum Contaminated Soils: Remediation Techniques, Environmental Fate and Risk Assessment. Paul T. Kostecki and Edward J. Calabrese. Lewis Publishers, 200 Corporate Blvd. NW, Boca Raton, Florida 33431. (407) 994-0555 or (800)272-7737. 1991. Three volumes. Provides valuable information to determine feasible solutions to petroleum contaminated soils.

ONLINE DATA BASES

Enviro/Energyline Abstracts Plus. R. R. Bowker Co., 121 Chanlon Rd., New Providence, New Jersey 07974. (908) 464-6800.

Environmental Periodicals Bibliography. National Information Services Corp., Ste. 6, Wyman Towers, 3100 St. Paul St., Baltimore, Maryland 21218. (410)243-0797. Online version of abstract of same name.

OIL REFINERIES

ABSTRACTING AND INDEXING SERVICES

Engineering Index. The Engineering Index Inc., 345 E. 47th St., New York, New York 10017. 1962-.

DIRECTORIES

Directory of Oil Refineries: Construction, Engineers, Petrochemical and Natural Gas Processing Plants. Midwest Oil Register, 15 W. 6th St., Ste. 1308, Tulsa, Oklahoma 74119-1505. (918) 582-2000. Annual.

ONLINE DATA BASES

APILIT. American Petroleum Institute, 1220 L St. N.W., Washington, District of Columbia 20005. (202) 682-8000.

APIPAT. American Petroleum Institute, 1220 L St. N.W., Washington, District of Columbia 20005. (202) 682-8000.

Chemical Age Project File. MBC Information Services Ltd., Paulton House, 8 Shepherdess Walk, London, England N1 7LB. 44 (71) 490-0049.

Computerized Engineering Index–COMPENDEX. Engineering Information Inc., 345 E. 47th St., New York, New York 10017. (212) 705-7600.

PERIODICALS AND NEWSLETTERS

American Oil Chemists Society Journal. The American Oil Chemists Society, P.O. Box 3489, Champaign, Illinois 61820. (217) 359-2344. 1917-. Monthly.

TRADE ASSOCIATIONS AND PROFESSIONAL SOCIETIES

American Oil Chemists Society. P.O. Box 3489, Champaign, Illinois 61820. (217) 359-2344.

American Petroleum Institute. 1220 L St., N.W., Washington, District of Columbia 20005. (202) 682-8000.

OIL RESOURCES
See: OIL

OIL SANDS
See also: PETROLEUM

ABSTRACTING AND INDEXING SERVICES

General Science Index. H. W. Wilson Co., 950 University Ave., Bronx, New York 10452. 1978-. Monthly, also issued in annual cumulation. Cumulative subject index to English language periodicals in the subject fields of astronomy, botany, chemistry, earth science, environment and conservation, food and nutrition, genetics, mathematics, medicine and health, microbiology, oceanography, physics, physiology and zoology.

BIBLIOGRAPHIES

Bibliography and Index of Geology. American Geological Institute, 4220 King St., Alexandria, Virginia 22302. Monthly. Includes environmental geology and hydrogeology.

ENCYCLOPEDIAS AND DICTIONARIES

Glossary of Geology. Robert Latimer Bates and Julia A. Jackson, eds. American Geological Institute, 4220 King St., Alexandria, Virginia 22302-1507. (703) 379-2480 or (800) 336-4764. 1987. Third edition.

McGraw-Hill Encyclopedia of the Geological Sciences. Sybil P. Parker, ed. McGraw-Hill, 1221 Avenue of the Americas, New York, New York 10020. (212) 512-2000 or (800) 262-4729. 1988. Second edition. Published previously in the McGraw-Hill Encyclopedia of Science and Technology.

GENERAL WORKS

Magill's Survey of Science. Earth Science Series. Frank N. Magill. Salem Press, PO Box 50062, Pasadena, California 91105. 1990-. Five volumes. Includes information on earth's crust, hot spots and volcanic island chains, physical properties of minerals, rock magnetism, physical properties of rocks, and index.

Production and Processing of U.S. Tar Sands, An Environmental Assessment. N.A. Frazier. National Technical Information Service, 5285 Port Royal Rd., Springfield, Virginia 22161. (703) 487-4650. 1980. Bitumen geology and environmental aspects of oil sands.

Surface Mining of Non-Coal Minerals: Appendix II, Mining and Processing of Oil Shale and Tar Sands. National Research Council. National Academy of Sciences, 2101 Constitution Ave., NW, Washington, District of Columbia 20418. (202) 334-2000. 1980. Environmental aspects of oil shale industry, strip mining, and mining law.

Tar Sands and Oil Shales. Walter Ruhl. Enke, Rudigerstr. 14, Stuttgart, Germany D-7000. 1982. Deals with the geology of petroleum.

TRADE ASSOCIATIONS AND PROFESSIONAL SOCIETIES

American Petroleum Institute. 1220 L St., N.W., Washington, District of Columbia 20005. (202) 682-8000.

OIL SKIMMERS

ABSTRACTING AND INDEXING SERVICES

Biological Abstracts. BIOSIS, 2100 Arch St., Philadelphia, Pennsylvania 19103-1399. (215) 587-4800. 1927-.

Engineering Index. The Engineering Index Inc., 345 E. 47th St., New York, New York 10017. 1962-.

Oceanic Abstracts. UMI Data Courier, 620 S. 3rd St., Louisville, Kentucky 40202. (800) 626-2823. Formerly: Oceanic Index and Oceanic Citation Journal.

ENCYCLOPEDIAS AND DICTIONARIES

Van Nostrand's Scientific Encyclopedia. Glenn D. Considine, ed. Van Nostrand Reinhold, 115 5th Ave., New York, New York 10003. (212) 254-3232. 1983. Sixth edition. Includes all broad subject areas in science.

GENERAL WORKS

Performance Tests of Four Selected Oil Spill Skimmers. Robert W. Urban. National Technical Information Service, 5285 Port Royal Rd., Springfield, Virginia 22161. (703) 487-4650. 1978.

ONLINE DATA BASES

BIOSIS Previews. BIOSIS, 2100 Arch St., Philadelphia, Pennsylvania 19103-1399. (215) 587-4800. Largest and most comprehensive database of research in the life sciences. Contains citations for nearly 9000 primary research journals, monographs, reviews, symposia, preliminary reports, semi-popular journals, selected institutional reports, government reports and research communications.

Computerized Engineering Index–COMPENDEX. Engineering Information Inc., 345 E. 47th St., New York, New York 10017. (212) 705-7600.

Oceanic Abstracts. Cambridge Scientific Abstracts, 5161 River Rd., Bethesda, Maryland 20816. (301) 961-6750. Online access.

PERIODICALS AND NEWSLETTERS

Oil Spill Intelligence Report. Cahners Publishing Co., 249 W. 17th St., New York, New York 10011. (212) 645-0067. Irregular. Global information on oil spill cleanup, prevention control.

TRADE ASSOCIATIONS AND PROFESSIONAL SOCIETIES

American Institute of Biological Sciences. 730 11th St., N.W., Washington, District of Columbia 20001-4521. (202) 628-1500.

American Petroleum Institute. 1220 L St., N.W., Washington, District of Columbia 20005. (202) 682-8000.

Spill Control Association of America. 400 Renaissance Center, Suite 1900, Detroit, Michigan 48243. (313) 567-0500.

OIL SPILL ANALYSIS
See: OIL SPILLS

OIL SPILL CLEANUP
See: OIL SPILLS

OIL SPILLS
See also: PETROLEUM; WATER POLLUTION

ABSTRACTING AND INDEXING SERVICES

Applied Ecology Abstracts Studies in Renewable Natural Resources. Information Retrieval Ltd., 1911 Jefferson Davis Highway, Arlington, Virginia 22202. 1975-. Monthly.

Bulletin Signaletique: Eau et Assainissement, Pollution Atmospherique, Droit des Pollutions. Centre de Documentation, Centre National de la Recherche Scientifique, 15, quai Anatole France, Paris, France 75700. (1) 45 55 92 25. 1983-. Monthly. Indexes pollution periodicals including water, atmospheric and related pollutions.

Ecological Abstracts. Geo Abstracts Ltd. Elsevier Applied Science, Crown House, Linton Rd., Barking, England IG 11 8JU. 1974-. Derived from over 600 leading ecological and environmental journals, plus books, conference proceedings, reports and theses.

Ecology Abstracts. Cambridge Scientific Abstracts, 5161 River Rd., Bethesda, Maryland 20816. (301) 961-6750. Monthly.

General Science Index. H. W. Wilson Co., 950 University Ave., Bronx, New York 10452. 1978-. Monthly, also issued in annual cumulation. Cumulative subject index to English language periodicals in the subject fields of astronomy, botany, chemistry, earth science, environment and conservation, food and nutrition, genetics, mathematics, medicine and health, microbiology, oceanography, physics, physiology and zoology.

Geographical Abstracts. London School of Economics, Dept. of Geography, Regency House, 34 Duke St., London, England 1966-. Continued by Geo Abstracts issued in 6 parts: Pt. A. Landforms and the quaternary; Pt. B. Biogeography and Climatology; Pt. C. Economic geography; Pt. D. Social geography and cartography; Pt. E. Sedimentology; Pt. F. Regional and community planning.

Index to Scientific Book Contents. Institute for Scientific Information, 3501 Market St., Philadelphia, Pennsylvania 19104. (800) 523-1857. 1985-. Annual. Gives contents of science books published.

Multimedia Index to Ecology. National Information Center for Educational Media, University of Southern California, Los Angeles, California 90007.

Oceanic Abstracts. UMI Data Courier, 620 S. 3rd St., Louisville, Kentucky 40202. (800) 626-2823. Formerly: Oceanic Index and Oceanic Citation Journal.

Pollution Abstracts. Cambridge Scientific Abstracts, 5161 River Rd., Bethesda, Maryland 20816. (301) 961-6750. Six/year. Indexes worldwide technical literature on environmental pollution. Covers air pollution, marine and freshwater pollution, sewage and wastewater treatment, waste management, toxicology and health, noise pollution, radiation, land pollution, and environmental policies, programs, legislation, and education. Also available online.

Science Citation Index. Institute for Scientific Information, 3501 Market St., Philadelphia, Pennsylvania 19104. 1961-.

BIBLIOGRAPHIES

Bibliography and Index of Geology. American Geological Institute, 4220 King St., Alexandria, Virginia 22302. Monthly. Includes environmental geology and hydrogeology.

Biodegradation of Oil Spills: Citations from the NTIS Bibliographic Database. National Technical Information Service, 5285 Port Royal Road, Springfield, Virginia 22161. (703) 487-4650. 1990.

Current Contents. Agriculture, Biology and Environmental Sciences. Institute for Scientific Information, 3501 Market St., Philadelphia, Pennsylvania 19104. (800) 523-1857. 1973-. Previous title: Current Contents. Agricultural, Food & Veterinary Sciences. Gives the table of contents of periodicals in the fields of agriculture, biology, environmental and related areas.

DIRECTORIES

Gale Environmental Sourcebook. Karen Hill. Gale Research Co., 835 Penobscot Bldg., Detroit, Michigan 48226-4094. (313) 961-2242. Contacts, information sources, or general information on environmental topics.

Oil Spill Data Base. Center for Short-Lived Phenomena, Box 199, Harvard Square Station, Cambridge, Massachusetts 02238. (617) 492-3310.

ENCYCLOPEDIAS AND DICTIONARIES

Hazardous Materials Dictionary. Ronny J. Coleman and Kara Hewson Williams. Technomic Publishing Co., 851 New Holland Ave., Box 3535, Lancaster, Pennsylvania 17604. (717) 291-5609. 1988. Defines more than 2600 specialized words which are critical for communication, especially under the stressful circumstances of an emer-

gency. Identifies many of the unique terms that apply to the handling of hazardous materials emergencies.

McGraw-Hill Encyclopedia of Science and Technology. McGraw-Hill, 1221 Avenue of the Americas, New York, New York 10020. (212) 512-2000 or (800) 262-4729. 1992. Seventh edition. Issued in multiple volumes including index. Includes all science and technology broad subject areas.

Van Nostrand's Scientific Encyclopedia. Glenn D. Considine, ed. Van Nostrand Reinhold, 115 5th Ave., New York, New York 10003. (212) 254-3232. 1983. Sixth edition. Includes all broad subject areas in science.

GENERAL WORKS

Energy, the Environment, and Public Policy: Issues for the 1990s. David L. McKee, ed. Praeger Publishers, 1 Madison Ave., New York, New York 10010-3603. (212) 685-5300. 1991. Addresses the extent and gravity of our environmental situation, from industrial waste to acid rain, from the Alaskan oil spill to the destruction of the rain forests.

Exxon Oil Spill: Hearing Before the Committee on Commerce, Science, Transportation, U. S. Senate, 101st Congress, First Session on Exxon Valdez Oil Spill and Its Environmental and Maritime Implications. U.S. G.P.O., Washington, District of Columbia 20401. (202) 512-0000. 1989.

Exxon Oil Spill: Hearing Before the National Ocean Policy Study and the Subcommittee on Merchant Marine of the Committee on Commerce, Science, and Transportation, U. S. Senate 101st Congress First Session on Cleanup,... U.S. G.P.O., Washington, District of Columbia 20401. (202) 512-0000. 1989.

In the Wake of the Exxon Valdez: Devastating Impact of Alaska's Oil Spill. Art Davidson. Sierra Club Books, 100 Bush St., San Francisco, California 94104. (415) 291-1600. 1990. Story of environmental risk and the consequences that arise.

Magill's Survey of Science. Earth Science Series. Frank N. Magill. Salem Press, PO Box 50062, Pasadena, California 91105. 1990-. Five volumes. Includes information on earth's crust, hot spots and volcanic island chains, physical properties of minerals, rock magnetism, physical properties of rocks, and index.

Microbial Hydrocarbon Degradation in Sediments Impacted by the Exxon Valdez Oil Spill; Final Report. Water Research Center, University of Alaska, Fairbanks, 460 Duckering Bldg., Fairbanks, Alaska 99775. (907) 474-7350. 1990.

Oil Spill Response Guide. Robert J. Meyers & Associates and Research Planning Institute, Inc. Noyes Publications, 120 Mill Rd., Park Ridge, New Jersey 07656. (201) 391-8484. 1989. Describes equipment, techniques and logistics for responding to oil spills. It is designed to serve as a planning guide which will help the on-scene coordinator (OSC) identify the steps and priorities for responding to major oil spill, or oil well blowouts associated with petroleum activity.

Out of the Channel: The Exxon Valdez Oil Spill in Prince William Sound. John Keeble. Harper & Row, 10 E. 53rd St., New York, New York 10022. (212) 207-7000. 1991. Presents a detailed account of the disaster, its implications and ramifications.

Response Manual for Combatting Spills of Floating Hazardous CHRIS Chemicals. National Technical Information Service, 5285 Port Royal Rd., Springfield, Virginia 22161. (703) 487-4650. Covers chemical spills, hazardous substance accidents, and marine pollution.

Sea Mammals and Oil: Confronting the Risks. Joseph R. Geraci and David J. St. Aubin, eds. Academic Press, c/o Harcourt Brace Jovanovich Inc., 6277 Sea Harbor Dr., Orlando, Florida 32887. (800) 346-8648. 1990. Explores the effects of spilled petroleum on seals, whales, dolphins, sea otters, polar bears, and manatees, which inhabit the coastal water of North America where spills occur. They consider the constant low-level leakage of urban and industrial oil, large spills, and long-term as well as immediate effects.

GOVERNMENTAL ORGANIZATIONS

Office of Pipeline Safety Regulation. 400 7th St., S.W., Washington, District of Columbia 20590. (202) 366-4595.

U.S. Environmental Protection Agency: Office of Emergency and Remedial Response. Emergency Response Division, 401 M St., S.W., Washington, District of Columbia 20460. (202) 382-2180.

U.S. Environmental Protection Agency, TS-799: Toxic Assistance Office. 401 M St., S.W., Washington, District of Columbia 20460. (202) 382-3790.

HANDBOOKS AND MANUALS

Bioremediation for Marine Oil Spills. U.S. Congress, Office of Technology Assessment, 600 Pennsylvania Ave. SE, Washington, District of Columbia 20003. (202) 224-8996. 1991.

Spill Reporting Procedures Guide. Robert E. Abbott. Bureau of National Affairs, 1231 25th St. N.W., Washington, District of Columbia 20037. (202) 452-4200. 1990. This aid to fulfilling the requisite federal, state, and local reporting requirements contains the verbal and written reporting requirements for oil, hazardous substances, hazardous wastes, hazardous materials, excess air emissions, wastewater excursions, underground tank leaks, and SARA Title III.

ONLINE DATA BASES

Monthly Catalog of United States Government Publications. U.S. G.P.O., Supt. of Docs., PO Box 371954, Pittsburgh, Pennsylvania 15250-7954. (202) 512-0000.

National Technical Information Service. U.S. Department of Commerce, National Technical Information Service, Office of Data Base Services, 5285 Port Royal Rd., Springfield, Virginia 22161. (703) 487-4807. Bibliographic database of government sponsored research and technical reports.

Oceanic Abstracts. Cambridge Scientific Abstracts, 5161 River Rd., Bethesda, Maryland 20816. (301) 961-6750. Online access.

Oil Spill Intelligence Report. Cutter Information Corp., 37 Broadway, Arlington, Massachusetts 02174-5539. (617) 648-8700. Oil spills and cleanup efforts, contingency planning and response, legislative and regulatory developments and technologies. Online version of periodical of same name.

PressNet Environmental Reports. Chemical Information Systems, Inc., 7215 York Rd., Baltimore, Maryland 21212. (301) 321-8440.

SCISEARCH. Institute for Scientific Information, University City Science Center, 3501 Market St., Philadelphia, Pennsylvania 19104. (215) 386-0100.

PERIODICALS AND NEWSLETTERS

Newsletter. Spill Control Association of America, 400 Renaissance Center, Suite 1900, Detroit, Michigan 48243-1509. (313) 567-0500. Biweekly. Oil and hazardous substance spill control technology.

Oil and Chemical Pollution. Elsevier Science Publishing Co., 655 Avenue of the Americas, New York, New York 10010. (212) 989-5800. Technology of spills and cleanups.

Oil Spill Intelligence Report. Cahners Publishing Co., 249 W. 17th St., New York, New York 10011. (212) 645-0067. Irregular. Global information on oil spill cleanup, prevention control.

Spill Control Association of America News Brief. Spill Control Association of America, 400 Renaissance Center, Suite 1900, Detroit, Michigan 48243. (313) 567-0500. Monthly. Covers spill control, clean-up, and protection.

RESEARCH CENTERS AND INSTITUTES

Bemidji State University, Center for Environmental Studies. Bemidji, Minnesota 56601. (218) 755-2910.

Large Experimental Aquifer Program. Oregon Graduate Institute of Science and Technology, 19600 N.W. Von Neumann Dr., Beaverton, Oregon 97006. (503) 690-1193.

Shannon Point Marine Center. Western Washington University, 1900 Shannon Point Rd., Anacortes, Washington 98221. (206) 293-2188.

STATISTICS SOURCES

Coping with an Oiled Sea: An Analysis of Oil Spill Response Technologies. U.S. Government Printing Office, Washington, District of Columbia 20402-9325. (202) 512-0000. 1990. Oil spill volume, date, location, cause, and vessel or other spill source, for individual major spills.

Ecology: Community Profiles. U.S. Fish and Wildlife Service. National Technical Information Service, 5285 Port Royal Road, Springfield, Virginia 22161. (703) 487-4650. Irregular. Data on coastal and inland ecosystems, including wetlands, tidal-flats, near-shore seagrasses, sand dunes, drilling platforms, oyster reefs, estuaries, rivers and streams.

Environmental Data Compendium. OECD Publications and Information Center, 2001 L St., N.W., Suite 700, Washington, District of Columbia 20036. (202) 785-6323. 1989.

Environmental Indicators. OECD Publications and Information Center, 2001 L St., N.W., Suite 700, Washington, District of Columbia 20036. (202) 785-6323. 1991.

Environmental Quality. Council on Environmental Quality. U.S. G.P.O., Washington, District of Columbia 20401. (202) 512-0000. Annual.

Federal Offshore Statistics. U.S. Dept. of Interior. Minerals Management Service. U.S. G.P.O., Washington, District of Columbia 20401. (202) 512-0000. Annual. Oil, gas and mineral exploration, production, well blowouts and spills.

Sorbent Material for Spills & Other Liquid Pickups. FIND/SVP, 625 Avenue of the Americas, New York, New York 10011. (800) 346-3787. 1991. Analysis of regulations, economic variables, players, technologies, manufacturing processes and market strategies.

The State of the Environment. OECD Publications and Information Center, 2001 L St., N.W., Suite 700, Washington, District of Columbia 20036. (202) 785-6323. 1991.

Synthesis of Effects of Oil on Marine Mammals. U.S. Dept. of Interior. Mineral Management Service. National Technical Information Service, 5285 Port Royal Road, Springfield, Virginia 22161. (703) 487-4650. 1988. Impacts of spills and spill-treating agents on marine and arctic land mammals.

TRADE ASSOCIATIONS AND PROFESSIONAL SOCIETIES

American Petroleum Institute. 1220 L St., N.W., Washington, District of Columbia 20005. (202) 682-8000.

Association of American Plant Food Control Officals. Division of Reg. Services, University of Kentucky, 103 Regional Services Bldg., Lexington, Kentucky 40546. (606) 257-2668.

Center for Short Lived Phenomena. P.O. Box 199, Harvard Sq. Station, Cambridge, Massachusetts 02238. (617) 492-3310.

Chemical Referral Center. c/o Chemical Manufacturers Association, 2501 M St., N.W., Washington, District of Columbia 20037. (202) 887-1100.

Clean Harbors Cooperative. P.O. Box 1375, 1200 State St., Perth Amboy, New Jersey 08862. (201) 738-2438.

OIL STORAGE

ABSTRACTING AND INDEXING SERVICES

Engineering Index. The Engineering Index Inc., 345 E. 47th St., New York, New York 10017. 1962-.

Geographical Abstracts. London School of Economics, Dept. of Geography, Regency House, 34 Duke St., London, England 1966-. Continued by Geo Abstracts issued in 6 parts: Pt. A. Landforms and the quaternary; Pt. B. Biogeography and Climatology; Pt. C. Economic geography; Pt. D. Social geography and cartography; Pt. E. Sedimentology; Pt. F. Regional and community planning.

DIRECTORIES

Bulk Liquid Terminals Directory. 1133 15th St., N.W., Washington, District of Columbia 20005. (202) 659-2301. Annual.

GENERAL WORKS

Standard for Flame Arrestors for Use on Vents of Storage Tanks for Petroleum Oil and Gasoline. American Nation-

al Standards Institute. Underwriters' Laboratories, 333 Pfingsten Rd., Northbrook, Illinois 60062. (708) 272-8800. 1984. Standards for fire prevention in oil and gasoline storage tanks.

Underground Storage of Oil and Gas in Salt Deposits and Other Non-Hard Rocks. Wolfgang Dreyer. Enke, Rudigerstr. 14, Stuttgart, Germany D-7000. 1982. Petroleum and natural gas underground storage and salt deposits.

Welded Steel Tanks for Oil Storage. American Petroleum Institute, 1220 L St. N.W., Washington, District of Columbia 20005. (202) 682-8000. 1980. Petroleum storage and standards for design and construction for oil storage tanks.

ONLINE DATA BASES

Computerized Engineering Index–COMPENDEX. Engineering Information Inc., 345 E. 47th St., New York, New York 10017. (212) 705-7600.

TRADE ASSOCIATIONS AND PROFESSIONAL SOCIETIES

American Petroleum Institute. 1220 L St., N.W., Washington, District of Columbia 20005. (202) 682-8000.

OIL TANKERS

ABSTRACTING AND INDEXING SERVICES

Engineering Index. The Engineering Index Inc., 345 E. 47th St., New York, New York 10017. 1962-.

ENCYCLOPEDIAS AND DICTIONARIES

Encyclopedia of Physical Science and Technology. Robert A. Meyers, ed. Academic Press, c/o Harcourt Brace Jovanovich Inc., 6277 Sea Harbor Dr., Orlando, Florida 32887. (800) 346-8648. Dictionary of engineering, technology and physical sciences.

GENERAL WORKS

Oil Transportation by Tankers. United States Congress Office of Technology Assessment. U.S. G.P.O., Washington, District of Columbia 20401. (202) 512-0000. 1975. An analysis of marine pollution and safety measures.

Product Tankers and Their Market Role. Michael Grey. Fairplay, London, England 1982. Economic aspects of petroleum transportation and tankers.

ONLINE DATA BASES

Computerized Engineering Index–COMPENDEX. Engineering Information Inc., 345 E. 47th St., New York, New York 10017. (212) 705-7600.

PressNet Environmental Reports. Chemical Information Systems, Inc., 7215 York Rd., Baltimore, Maryland 21212. (301) 321-8440.

TRADE ASSOCIATIONS AND PROFESSIONAL SOCIETIES

American Petroleum Institute. 1220 L St., N.W., Washington, District of Columbia 20005. (202) 682-8000.

National Tank Truck Carriers. 2200 Mill Rd., Alexandria, Virginia 22314. (703) 838-1960.

OIL USAGE

See: OIL

OIL WELL EQUIPMENT

See: OIL

OILY WASTES

GENERAL WORKS

Guidance and Procedures for Administering and Enforcing the Oily Waste Reception Facility Program. U.S. Coast Guard, 2100 Second St., N.W., Rm. 5410 C, Washington, District of Columbia 20593. (202) 267-1042. 1985. Oil pollution of the sea and law relating to ship waste disposal.

Guide to Oil Waste Management Alternatives for Used Oil, Oily Wastewater, Oily Sludge, and Other Wastes Resulting from the Use of Oil Products. Robert H. Salvesen Associates. Energy and Environmental Research Corporation, Irvine, California 1988. Recycling of hazardous and petroleum waste.

Land Treatment of an Oily Waste–Degradation, Immobilization, and Bioaccumulation. R.C. Loehr. U.S. Environmental Protection Agency, Robert S. Kerr Environmental Research Laboratory, Ada, Oklahoma 1985. Refuse and refuse disposal, factory and trade waste, and sewage irrigation.

Used Oil: Disposal Options, Management Practices and Potential Liability. John J. Nolan, et al. Government Institutes, Inc., 4 Research Pl., Suite 200, Rockville, Maryland 20850. (301) 921-2300. 1990. 3d ed. Helps with developing a plan to store and manage the handling of used oil that affects thousands of generators, collectors, processors, marketers and burners.

Waste Oil: Reclaiming Technology, Utilization and Disposal. Mueller Associates Inc. Noyes Publications, 120 Mill Rd., Park Ridge, New Jersey 07656. (201) 391-8484. 1989. Describes and assesses the current status of the technologies and environmental information associated with the waste oil industry.

TRADE ASSOCIATIONS AND PROFESSIONAL SOCIETIES

American Petroleum Institute. 1220 L St., N.W., Washington, District of Columbia 20005. (202) 682-8000.

OKLAHOMA ENVIRONMENTAL AGENCIES

GOVERNMENTAL ORGANIZATIONS

Corporation Commission: Underground Storage Tanks. Chairman, Jim Thorpe Building, Oklahoma City, Oklahoma 73105. (405) 521-2264.

Department of Agriculture: Pesticide Registration. Director, Plant Industry Division, 2800 North Lincoln Blvd., Oklahoma City, Oklahoma 73105. (405) 521-3864.

Department of Health: Air Quality. Chief, Air Quality Service, 1000 N.E. 10th St., PO Box 53551, Oklahoma City, Oklahoma 73152. (405) 271-4468.

Department of Health: Emergency Preparedness and Community Right-to-Know. Director, PO Box 53504, Oklahoma City, Oklahoma 73152. (405) 271-4468.

Department of Health: Hazardous Waste Management. Chief, Waste Management Service, 1000 N.E. 10th St., PO Box 53551, Oklahoma City, Oklahoma 73152. (405) 271-5338.

Department of Health: Solid Waste Management. Chief, Waste Management Service, 1000 N.E. 10th St., PO Box 53551, Oklahoma City, Oklahoma 73152. (405) 271-5338.

Department of Health: Waste Minimization and Pollution Prevention. Service Chief, Waste Minimization Service, PO Box 53551, Oklahoma City, Oklahoma 73152. (405) 271-7047.

Department of Labor: Occupational Safety. Supervisor, Safety Standards Division, 1315 Broadway Place, Oklahoma City, Oklahoma 73103. (405) 521-2461.

Department of Pollution Control: Environmental Protection. Director, 1000 N.E. 10th St., PO Box 53504, Oklahoma City, Oklahoma 73152. (405) 271-4677.

Department of Wildlife Conservation: Fish and Wildlife. Director, PO Box 53476, Oklahoma City, Oklahoma 73152. (405) 521-3851.

Water Resources Board: Water Quality. Chief, Water Quality Division, 1000 N.E. 10th St., PO Box 53585, Oklahoma City, Oklahoma 73152. (405) 271-2540.

OKLAHOMA ENVIRONMENTAL LEGISLATION

GENERAL WORKS

Environmental Law Update from Various Perspectives. Oklahoma Bar Association, Dept. of Continuing Education, PO Box 53036, Oklahoma City, Oklahoma 73152. 1990.

OLEFINS

ABSTRACTING AND INDEXING SERVICES

Biological Abstracts. BIOSIS, 2100 Arch St., Philadelphia, Pennsylvania 19103-1399. (215) 587-4800. 1927-.

Chemical Abstracts. Chemical Abstracts Service, 2540 Olentangy River Rd., PO Box 3012, Columbus, Ohio 43210. (800) 848-6533. 1907-.

Science Citation Index. Institute for Scientific Information, 3501 Market St., Philadelphia, Pennsylvania 19104. 1961-.

ENCYCLOPEDIAS AND DICTIONARIES

Van Nostrand's Scientific Encyclopedia. Glenn D. Considine, ed. Van Nostrand Reinhold, 115 5th Ave., New York, New York 10003. (212) 254-3232. 1983. Sixth edition. Includes all broad subject areas in science.

GENERAL WORKS

Olefins: Manufacture and Derivatives. Marshall Sittig. Noyes Publications, 120 Mill Rd., Park Ridge, New Jersey 07656. (201) 391-8484. 1968.

HANDBOOKS AND MANUALS

Alpha Olefins Applications Handbook. George R. Lappin. Marcel Dekker, Inc., 270 Madison Ave., New York, New York 10016. (212) 696-9000; (800) 228-1160. 1989.

ONLINE DATA BASES

BIOSIS Previews. BIOSIS, 2100 Arch St., Philadelphia, Pennsylvania 19103-1399. (215) 587-4800. Largest and most comprehensive database of research in the life sciences. Contains citations for nearly 9000 primary research journals, monographs, reviews, symposia, preliminary reports, semi-popular journals, selected institutional reports, government reports and research communications.

Chemical Abstracts-CA. Chemical Abstracts Service, 2540 Olentangy River Rd., P.O. Box 3012, Columbus, Ohio 43210. (800) 848-6533 or (614) 421-3600. Information sources include 9000 journals, patents from 27 countries, two industrial property organizations, new books, conference proceedings, and government research reports.

Chemical Collection System/Request Tracking–CCS/RTS. U.S. Environmental Protection Agency, Office of Pesticides and Toxic Substances, 401 M St., SW, Washington, District of Columbia 20460. (202) 260-2090. Contains information on various properties of a number of chemicals including environmental effects, test and analysis methods, and health effects. Available from EPA.

Chemical Dictionary Online–CHEMLINE. Chemical Abstracts Service, 2540 Olentangy River Rd., Columbus, Ohio 43210. (614) 421-3600 or (800) 848-6533. Part of MEDLINE of the National Library of Medicine (NLM). File of 900,000 names for chemical substances, representing 450,000 unique compounds. It contains such information as Chemical Abstracts (CA) Service Registry Numbers, molecular formulas, preferred chemical nomenclature, and generic and ring structure information. Available on NLM's ELHILL system.

Chemical Exposure. Science Applications International Corp., Health & Environmental Information, P.O. Box 2501, Oak Ridge, Tennessee 37831. (615) 482-9031. Database of chemicals that have been identified in both human tissues and body fluids and in feral and food animals. Contains reference to journal articles, conferences, and reports. Covers the whole fields of information related to human and animal exposure to food, air, and water contaminants and pharmaceuticals. Its records include information on chemical properties, formulas, tissues measured, analytical method used, demographics and more. Available on DIALOG.

OPEN BURNING

See: AIR POLLUTION

OPEN DUMPS

ABSTRACTING AND INDEXING SERVICES

Applied Ecology Abstracts Studies in Renewable Natural Resources. Information Retrieval Ltd., 1911 Jefferson Davis Highway, Arlington, Virginia 22202. 1975-. Monthly.

Index to Scientific Book Contents. Institute for Scientific Information, 3501 Market St., Philadelphia, Pennsylvania 19104. (800) 523-1857. 1985-. Annual. Gives contents of science books published.

Multimedia Index to Ecology. National Information Center for Educational Media, University of Southern California, Los Angeles, California 90007.

DIRECTORIES

Inventory of Open Dumps. Office of Solid Waste, Environmental Protection Agency, Washington, District of Columbia 20460. (202) 475-8710. 1984. Covers factory and trade waste and refuse and refuse disposal.

ENCYCLOPEDIAS AND DICTIONARIES

The New York Times Encyclopedic Dictionary of the Environment. Paul Sarnoff. Quadrangle Books, New York, New York 1971. Focuses on state-of-the-art methods of pollution control, abatement, prevention and removal.

ONLINE DATA BASES

PressNet Environmental Reports. Chemical Information Systems, Inc., 7215 York Rd., Baltimore, Maryland 21212. (301) 321-8440.

SCISEARCH. Institute for Scientific Information, University City Science Center, 3501 Market St., Philadelphia, Pennsylvania 19104. (215) 386-0100.

OPEN FIELD AGRICULTURE

See: AGRICULTURE

OREGON ENVIRONMENTAL AGENCIES

GOVERNMENTAL ORGANIZATIONS

Department of Agriculture: Pesticide Registration. Administrator, Plant Division, 635 Capitol St., N.E., Salem, Oregon 97310. (503) 378-3776.

Department of Environmental Quality: Air Quality. Director, 811 S.W. Sixth Ave., Portland, Oregon 97204. (503) 229-5397.

Department of Environmental Quality: Environmental Protection. Director, 811 S.W. Sixth Ave., Portland, Oregon 97204. (503) 229-5696.

Department of Environmental Quality: Hazardous Waste Management. Director, 811 S.W. Sixth Ave., Portland, Oregon 97204. (503) 229-5696.

Department of Environmental Quality: Solid Waste Management. Director, 811 S.W. Sixth Ave., Portland, Oregon 97204. (503) 229-5696.

Department of Environmental Quality: Underground Storage Tanks. Director, 811 S.W. Sixth Ave., Portland, Oregon 97204. (503) 229-5696.

Department of Environmental Quality: Waste Minimization and Pollution Prevention. Waste Reduction Manager, Hazardous Waste Reduction Program, 811 Southwest Sixth Ave., Portland, Oregon 97204. (503) 229-5913.

Department of Environmental Quality: Water Quality. Director, 811 S.W. Sixth Ave., Portland, Oregon 97204. (503) 229-5324.

Department of Fish and Game: Fish and Wildlife. Director, PO Box 59, Portland, Oregon 97207. (503) 229-6339.

Department of Insurance and Finance: Occupational Safety. Administrator, Accident Prevention Division, 21 Labor and Industries Bldg., Salem, Oregon 97310. (503) 378-3272.

Department of Land Conservation and Development: Coastal Zone Management. Director, 1175 Court St., N.E., Salem, Oregon 97310. (503) 378-4928.

Emergency Response Commission: Emergency Preparedness and Community Right-to-Know. Director, c/o State Fire Marshal, 3000 Market Street Plaza, Suite 534, Salem, Oregon 97310. (503) 378-2885.

Office of the Governor: Natural Resources. 160 State Capitol, Salem, Oregon 97310. (503) 378-3548.

Water Resources Department: Groundwater Management. Manager, Groundwater Division, 3850 Portland Rd., N.E., Salem, Oregon 97310. (503) 378-3671.

OREGON ENVIRONMENTAL LEGISLATION

GENERAL WORKS

Environmental Law for Oregon Practitioners. Oregon Law Institute, 921 SW Morrison St., Ste. 409, Portland, Oregon 97205. (503) 243-3326. 1991.

Save Oregon: An Environmental Resource Directory. Chronicle Books, 275 5th Ave., San Francisco, California 94103. (415) 777-7240. 1991.

ORGANIC AGRICULTURE

See: AGRICULTURE

ORGANIC COMPOUNDS

ABSTRACTING AND INDEXING SERVICES

Biological and Agricultural Index. H.W. Wilson Co., 950 University Ave., Bronx, New York 10452. (800) 367-6770. 1916-. Monthly.

Chemical Abstracts. Chemical Abstracts Service, 2540 Olentangy River Rd., PO Box 3012, Columbus, Ohio 43210. (800) 848-6533. 1907-.

ENCYCLOPEDIAS AND DICTIONARIES

Dictionary of Organic Compounds. Chapman & Hall, 29 West 35th St, New York, New York 10001-2291. (212) 244-3336. 1991. Continually updated system of information on most important inorganic chemical substances.

Dictionary of Organometallic Compounds. Chapman & Hall, 29 West 35th St., New York, New York 10001-2291. (212) 244-3336. 1989. Entries arranged by molecular formula within separate element section according to the Hill Convention.

Dictionary of Organophosphorus Compounds. Chapman & Hall, 29 West 35th St., New York, New York 10001-2291. (212) 244-3336. 1988.

Encyclopedia of Terpenoids. John S. Glasby. John Wiley & Sons, Inc., 605 3rd Ave., New York, New York 10158-0012. (212) 850-6000. 1982. Two volumes. Compendium of organic compounds found in nature, embracing a wide range of substances from the simple monoterpenoids to the highly complex triterpenoids and cartenoids, which are used in perfumes, antibiotics, cytotoxic agents and antifeedeants. Covers literature to the end of 1979.

Encyclopedia of the Alkaloids. Johns S. Glasby. Plenum Press, 233 Spring St., New York, New York 10013-1578. (212) 620-8000 or (800) 221-9369. 1975-. Compendium of plant alkaloids, with their origin and structure, molecular formula, and toxic properties. Also includes references to original papers. Covers the literature to the end of 1981.

GENERAL WORKS

Identification and Analysis of Organic Pollutants in Air. Lawrence Keith. Butterworth-Heinemann, 80 Montvale Ave., Stoneham, Massachusetts 02180. (617) 438-8464. 1984. Analysis of organic compounds and air pollution measurement.

Methods for Determination of Toxic Organic Compounds in Air; EPA Methods. William T. Winberry, et al. Noyes Publications, 120 Mill Rd., Park Ridge, New Jersey 07656. (201) 391-8484. 1990. Contains 14 procedures in a standardized format; five were selected to cover as many compounds as possible, and the others are targeted toward specific compounds.

Organic Chemistry of the Earth's Atmosphere. Valerii A. Isidorov. Springer-Verlag, 175 5th Ave., New York, New York 10010. (212) 460-1500; (800) 777-4643. 1990. Describes the composition of atmosphere; distribution of organic components in space and time; natural sources; human- created sources; atmosphere organic reactions methods of analysis.

HANDBOOKS AND MANUALS

Handbook of Environmental Data on Organic Chemicals. Karel Verschueren. Van Nostrand Reinhold, 115 5th Ave., New York, New York 10003. (212) 254-3232. 1983. Covers individual substances as well as mixtures and preparations. The profiles include: properties, air pollution factors, water pollution factors, and biological effects.

ONLINE DATA BASES

Chemical Abstracts-CA. Chemical Abstracts Service, 2540 Olentangy River Rd., P.O. Box 3012, Columbus, Ohio 43210. (800) 848-6533 or (614) 421-3600. Information sources include 9000 journals, patents from 27 countries, two industrial property organizations, new books, conference proceedings, and government research reports.

Information System for Hazardous Organics in Water. U.S. Environmental Protection Agency, Office of Pesticides & Toxic Substances, 401 M St., S.W., Washington, District of Columbia 20460. (202) 260-2090.

ORGANIC FERTILIZERS
See: FERTILIZERS

ORGANIC GARDENING AND FARMING
See also: AGRICULTURE; CROPS; PESTICIDES

ABSTRACTING AND INDEXING SERVICES

Applied Ecology Abstracts Studies in Renewable Natural Resources. Information Retrieval Ltd., 1911 Jefferson Davis Highway, Arlington, Virginia 22202. 1975-. Monthly.

Biological and Agricultural Index. H.W. Wilson Co., 950 University Ave., Bronx, New York 10452. (800) 367-6770. 1916-. Monthly.

Ecological Abstracts. Geo Abstracts Ltd. Elsevier Applied Science, Crown House, Linton Rd., Barking, England IG 11 8JU. 1974-. Derived from over 600 leading ecological and environmental journals, plus books, conference proceedings, reports and theses.

Ecology Abstracts. Cambridge Scientific Abstracts, 5161 River Rd., Bethesda, Maryland 20816. (301) 961-6750. Monthly.

Environment Abstracts. Bowker A & I Publishing, 121 Chanlon Rd., New Providence, New Jersey 07974. (908) 464-6800. 1974-.

Environment Index. Environment Information Center, Index Research Department, 124 E. 39th St., New York, New York 10016. 1971-. Annual.

Environmental Information Connection-EIC. Planning Information Program, Dept. of Urban and Regional Planning, University of Illinois, 1003 West Nevada, Urbana, Illinois 61801. (217) 333-1369. Also available online.

Environmental Periodicals Bibliography. Environmental Studies Institute, International Academy at Santa Barbara, 800 Garden St., Suite D, Santa Barbara, California 93101. (805) 965-5010. Also available online.

General Science Index. H. W. Wilson Co., 950 University Ave., Bronx, New York 10452. 1978-. Monthly, also issued in annual cumulation. Cumulative subject index to English language periodicals in the subject fields of astronomy, botany, chemistry, earth science, environment and conservation, food and nutrition, genetics, mathematics, medicine and health, microbiology, oceanography, physics, physiology and zoology.

Index to Scientific Book Contents. Institute for Scientific Information, 3501 Market St., Philadelphia, Pennsylvania 19104. (800) 523-1857. 1985-. Annual. Gives contents of science books published.

Multimedia Index to Ecology. National Information Center for Educational Media, University of Southern California, Los Angeles, California 90007.

BIBLIOGRAPHIES

Current Contents. Agriculture, Biology and Environmental Sciences. Institute for Scientific Information, 3501 Market St., Philadelphia, Pennsylvania 19104. (800) 523-1857. 1973-. Previous title: Current Contents. Agricultural, Food & Veterinary Sciences. Gives the table of contents of periodicals in the fields of agriculture, biology, environmental and related areas.

EPA Publications Bibliography. U.S. Environmental Protection Agency, Library Systems Branch, 401 M St., SW, Washington, District of Columbia 20460. (202) 260-2090. Quarterly.

Integrated Pest Management. Jayne T. Maclean. National Agricultural Library, 10301 Baltimore Blvd., Beltsville, Maryland 20705-2351. (301) 504-5755. 1985.

Organic Farming: A Bibliography. CPL Bibliographies, 1313 E. 60th St., Chicago, Illinois 60637-2897. (312) 942-2163. 1984.

Organic Farming and Gardening. Jayne T. MacLean. National Agricultural Library, 10301 Baltimore Blvd., Beltsville, Maryland 20705-2351. (301) 504-5755. 1987.

DIRECTORIES

Healthy Harvest II: A Directory of Sustainable Agriculture and Horticulture Organizations 1987-1988. Susan J. Sanzone, et al., eds. Potomac Valley Press, Suite 105, 1424 16th St. NW, Washington, District of Columbia 20036. 1987.

ENCYCLOPEDIAS AND DICTIONARIES

Cambridge Encyclopedia of Life Sciences. A. E. Friday and David S. Ingram. Cambridge University Press, 40 W 20th St., New York, New York 10011. (212) 924-3900 or (800) 227-0247. 1985. Includes all topics under biology and ecology.

Grzimek's Encyclopedia of Ecology. Bernhard Grzimek. Van Nostrand Reinhold, 115 5th Ave., New York, New York 10003. (212) 254-3232. 1976.

The Marshall Cavendish Encyclopedia of Gardening. Marshall Cavendish, 58 Old Compton St., London, England W1V 5PA. 01-734 6710. 1971. Seven volumes.

Encyclopedic treatment of garden plants and advise on how to grow them.

McGraw-Hill Encyclopedia of Environmental Science. Sybil P. Parker. McGraw-Hill Science & Engineering Books, 11 W. 19th St., New York, New York 10011. (212) 337-6010. 1980. Covers ecology, man's influence on nature, and environmental protection.

McGraw-Hill Encyclopedia of Science and Technology. McGraw-Hill, 1221 Avenue of the Americas, New York, New York 10020. (212) 512-2000 or (800) 262-4729. 1992. Seventh edition. Issued in multiple volumes including index. Includes all science and technology broad subject areas.

North American Reference Encyclopedia of Ecology and Pollution. William White. North American Pub. Co., 401 N. Broad St., Philadelphia, Pennsylvania 19108. (215) 238-5300. 1972.

GENERAL WORKS

The Biodynamic Farm. Herbert H. Koepf. Anthroposophic Press, RR 4 Box 94 A1, Hudson, New York 12534. (518) 851-2054. 1989. Deals with agricultural ecology and with the conservation of natural resources.

Biological Husbandry. Bernard Stonehouse. Butterworth-Heinemann, 80 Montvale Ave., Stoneham, Massachusetts 02180. (617) 438-8464. 1981. A scientific approach to organic farming.

Bugs, Slugs and Other Thugs: Controlling Garden Pests Organically. Rhonda Massingham Hart. Garden Way Pub., Schoolhouse Rd., Pownal, Vermont 05261. (802) 823-5811; (800) 441-5700. 1991.

Building a Healthy Lawn. Stuart Franklin. Garden Way Pub., Storey Communications Inc., Schoolhouse Rd., Pownal, Vermont 05261. (802) 823-5811; (800) 827-8673. 1988.

The Chemical Free Lawn. Warren Schultz. Rodale Press, 33 E. Minor St., Emmaus, Pennsylvania 18098. (215) 967-5171; (800) 322-6333. 1989. Describes how to grow lush hardy grass without pesticides, herbicides or chemical fertilizers.

Composting: the Organic Natural Way. Dick Kitto. Thornsons Publishing Ltd., Wellingborough, Northamptonshire, England NN82RQ. 1988. Covers principles of compost making and its uses.

Ecological Fruit Production in the North. Bart Hall-Beyer, and Jean Richard. B. Hall-Beyer, RR #3, Scotstown, Quebec, Canada J0B 3J0. 1983. Deals with the production of tree fruits and small fruits in North America. Discusses methods of ecological agriculture.

The Ecology of a Garden: The First Fifteen Years. Jennifer Owen. Cambridge University Press, 40 W. 20th St., New York, New York 10011. (212) 924-3900; (800) 227-0247. 1991.

The Environmental Gardener: The Solution to Pollution for Lawns and Gardens. Laurence Sombke. MasterMedia, 17 E. 89th St., New York, New York 10128. (212) 348-2020. 1991.

Farming in Nature's Image. Judith A. Soule. Island Press, 1718 Connecticut Ave. N.W., Suite 300, Washington, District of Columbia 20009. (202) 232-7933. 1992. Gives a detailed look into the pioneering work of the Land

Institute, the leading educational and research organization for sustainable agriculture.

The New Organic Grower. Eliot Coleman. Chelsea Green Publishing, PO Box 130, Post Mills, Vermont 05058-0130. (802) 333-9073. 1989. Covers crop rotation, green manures, tillage, seeding, transplanting, cultivation, and garden pests.

Organic Garden Vegetables. George F. Van Patten. Van Patten Pub., PO Box 82009, Portland, Oregon 97202. (503) 775-3815. 1991.

HANDBOOKS AND MANUALS

Integrated Pest Management. ANR Publications, University of California, 6701 San Pablo Ave., Oakland, California 94608-1239. (510) 642-2431. 1990-. Irregular. Provides and orderly, scientifically based system for diagnosing, recording, evaluating, preventing, and treating pest problems in a variety of crops.

ONLINE DATA BASES

Enviro/Energyline Abstracts Plus. R. R. Bowker Co., 121 Chanlon Rd., New Providence, New Jersey 07974. (908) 464-6800.

Environmental Periodicals Bibliography. National Information Services Corp., Ste. 6, Wyman Towers, 3100 St. Paul St., Baltimore, Maryland 21218. (410)243-0797. Online version of abstract of same name.

Monthly Catalog of United States Government Publications. U.S. G.P.O., Supt. of Docs., PO Box 371954, Pittsburgh, Pennsylvania 15250-7954. (202) 512-0000.

National Technical Information Service. U.S. Department of Commerce, National Technical Information Service, Office of Data Base Services, 5285 Port Royal Rd., Springfield, Virginia 22161. (703) 487-4807. Bibliographic database of government sponsored research and technical reports.

PressNet Environmental Reports. Chemical Information Systems, Inc., 7215 York Rd., Baltimore, Maryland 21212. (301) 321-8440.

SCISEARCH. Institute for Scientific Information, University City Science Center, 3501 Market St., Philadelphia, Pennsylvania 19104. (215) 386-0100.

PERIODICALS AND NEWSLETTERS

Biodynamics. Bio Dynamic Farming and Gardening Association, PO Box 550, Kimberton, Pennsylvania 19442-0550. (215) 935-7797. Quarterly. Soil conservation and organic agriculture.

Home, Yard and Garden Pest Newsletter. Agriculture Newsletter Service, University of Illinois, 116 Mumford Hall, 1301 W. Gregory Dr., Urbana, Illinois 61801. Twenty times a year. Pest controls, application equipment and methods, and storage and disposal of pesticides for the yard and garden.

Organic Gardening. Rodale Press, 33 E. Minor St., Emmaus, Pennsylvania 18098. (215) 967-5171.

TRADE ASSOCIATIONS AND PROFESSIONAL SOCIETIES

American Institute of Biological Sciences. 730 11th St., N.W., Washington, District of Columbia 20001-4521. (202) 628-1500.

New Alchemy Institute. 237 Hatchville Rd., East Falmouth, Massachusetts 02536. (508) 564-6301.

ORGANIC WASTE

See also: COMPOST

ABSTRACTING AND INDEXING SERVICES

Applied Ecology Abstracts Studies in Renewable Natural Resources. Information Retrieval Ltd., 1911 Jefferson Davis Highway, Arlington, Virginia 22202. 1975-. Monthly.

ASFA Aquaculture Abstracts. Cambridge Scientific Abstracts, Inc., 5161 River Rd., Bethesda, Maryland 20816. (301) 961-6750. 1984.

Biological and Agricultural Index. H.W. Wilson Co., 950 University Ave., Bronx, New York 10452. (800) 367-6770. 1916-. Monthly.

Ecological Abstracts. Geo Abstracts Ltd. Elsevier Applied Science, Crown House, Linton Rd., Barking, England IG 11 8JU. 1974-. Derived from over 600 leading ecological and environmental journals, plus books, conference proceedings, reports and theses.

Ecology Abstracts. Cambridge Scientific Abstracts, 5161 River Rd., Bethesda, Maryland 20816. (301) 961-6750. Monthly.

Environment Abstracts. Bowker A & I Publishing, 121 Chanlon Rd., New Providence, New Jersey 07974. (908) 464-6800. 1974-.

Environment Index. Environment Information Center, Index Research Department, 124 E. 39th St., New York, New York 10016. 1971-. Annual.

Environmental Information Connection–EIC. Planning Information Program, Dept. of Urban and Regional Planning, University of Illinois, 1003 West Nevada, Urbana, Illinois 61801. (217) 333-1369. Also available online.

Environmental Periodicals Bibliography. Environmental Studies Institute, International Academy at Santa Barbara, 800 Garden St., Suite D, Santa Barbara, California 93101. (805) 965-5010. Also available online.

Index to Scientific Book Contents. Institute for Scientific Information, 3501 Market St., Philadelphia, Pennsylvania 19104. (800) 523-1857. 1985-. Annual. Gives contents of science books published.

Multimedia Index to Ecology. National Information Center for Educational Media, University of Southern California, Los Angeles, California 90007.

Pollution Abstracts. Cambridge Scientific Abstracts, 5161 River Rd., Bethesda, Maryland 20816. (301) 961-6750. Six/year. Indexes worldwide technical literature on environmental pollution. Covers air pollution, marine and freshwater pollution, sewage and wastewater treatment, waste management, toxicology and health, noise pollu-

tion, radiation, land pollution, and environmental policies, programs, legislation, and education. Also available online.

BIBLIOGRAPHIES

Composts and Composting of Organic Wastes. Jayne T. Maclean. U.S. Department of Agriculture, National Agricultural Library, 10301 Baltimore Blvd., Beltsville, Maryland 20705-2351. (301) 504-5755. 1991.

Current Contents. Agriculture, Biology and Environmental Sciences. Institute for Scientific Information, 3501 Market St., Philadelphia, Pennsylvania 19104. (800) 523-1857. 1973-. Previous title: Current Contents. Agricultural, Food & Veterinary Sciences. Gives the table of contents of periodicals in the fields of agriculture, biology, environmental and related areas.

EPA Publications Bibliography. U.S. Environmental Protection Agency, Library Systems Branch, 401 M St., SW, Washington, District of Columbia 20460. (202) 260-2090. Quarterly.

Recycling Organic Wastes on the Land: A Bibliography. Diane E. Kirtz. Institute for Environmental Studies, University of Wisconsin, Madison, Wisconsin 53706. 1975.

ENCYCLOPEDIAS AND DICTIONARIES

Cambridge Encyclopedia of Life Sciences. A. E. Friday and David S. Ingram. Cambridge University Press, 40 W 20th St., New York, New York 10011. (212) 924-3900 or (800) 227-0247. 1985. Includes all topics under biology and ecology.

Grzimek's Encyclopedia of Ecology. Bernhard Grzimek. Van Nostrand Reinhold, 115 5th Ave., New York, New York 10003. (212) 254-3232. 1976.

McGraw-Hill Encyclopedia of Environmental Science. Sybil P. Parker. McGraw-Hill Science & Engineering Books, 11 W. 19th St., New York, New York 10011. (212) 337-6010. 1980. Covers ecology, man's influence on nature, and environmental protection.

North American Reference Encyclopedia of Ecology and Pollution. William White. North American Pub. Co., 401 N. Broad St., Philadelphia, Pennsylvania 19108. (215) 238-5300. 1972.

Van Nostrand's Scientific Encyclopedia. Glenn D. Considine, ed. Van Nostrand Reinhold, 115 5th Ave., New York, New York 10003. (212) 254-3232. 1983. Sixth edition. Includes all broad subject areas in science.

GENERAL WORKS

Environmental Toxicology. J. K. Fawell and S. Hunt. John Wiley & Sons, Inc., 605 3rd Ave., New York, New York 10158. (212) 850-6000. 1988. Information on the toxicology of contaminants in drinking water, upland surface water and ground water. Analysis is done using gas chromatography and mass spectrometry.

Food, Fuel, and Fertilizer from Organic Wastes. National Research Council. National Academy Press, 2101 Constitution Ave. NW, PO Box 285, Washington, District of Columbia 20418. (202) 334-3313. 1981. Recycling of organic wastes.

Livestock Waste, a Renewable Resource. American Society of Agricultural Engineers, 2950 Niles Rd., St. Joseph, Michigan 49085-9659. (616) 429-0300. 1981. Papers presented at the 4th International Symposium on Livestock Wastes, Amarillo, TX, 1980. Topics covered include: processing manure for feed, methane production, land application, lagoons, runoff, odors, economics, stabilization, treatment, collection and transport, storage and solid-liquid separation.

Nitrogen in Organic Wastes Applied to Soils. Academic Press, c/o Harcourt Brace Jovanovich Inc., 6277 Sea Harbor Dr., Orlando, Florida 32887. (800) 346-8648. 1989. Nitrogen fertilizers and organic wastes as fertilizer.

Organic Waste Recycling. Chongrak Polprasert. John Wiley & Sons, Inc., 605 Third Ave., New York, New York 10158. (212) 850-6000. 1989. Covers technologies for treating human waste, animal manure, agricultural residues and wastewater, sludge, algae, aquatic weeds and others.

HANDBOOKS AND MANUALS

Synthetic Organic Chemicals. U.S. G.P.O., Washington, District of Columbia 20401. (202) 512-0000. 1967. An annual publication on production and sales in the U.S. for all synthetic organic chemicals produced commercially. About 800 chemicals and 800 manufacturers are included in the USITC surveys, but because of confidentiality requirements only parts of the data are published. U.S. Tariff Commission acts under the provisions of Section 332 of the Tariff Act of 1930, as amended.

ONLINE DATA BASES

Enviro/Energyline Abstracts Plus. R. R. Bowker Co., 121 Chanlon Rd., New Providence, New Jersey 07974. (908) 464-6800.

Environmental Periodicals Bibliography. National Information Services Corp., Ste. 6, Wyman Towers, 3100 St. Paul St., Baltimore, Maryland 21218. (410)243-0797. Online version of abstract of same name.

Monthly Catalog of United States Government Publications. U.S. G.P.O., Supt. of Docs., PO Box 371954, Pittsburgh, Pennsylvania 15250-7954. (202) 512-0000.

National Technical Information Service. U.S. Department of Commerce, National Technical Information Service, Office of Data Base Services, 5285 Port Royal Rd., Springfield, Virginia 22161. (703) 487-4807. Bibliographic database of government sponsored research and technical reports.

PressNet Environmental Reports. Chemical Information Systems, Inc., 7215 York Rd., Baltimore, Maryland 21212. (301) 321-8440.

SCISEARCH. Institute for Scientific Information, University City Science Center, 3501 Market St., Philadelphia, Pennsylvania 19104. (215) 386-0100.

PERIODICALS AND NEWSLETTERS

Synthetic Organic Chemical Manufacturers Association Newsletter. Synthetic Organic Chemical Manufacturers Association, 1330 Connecticut Avenue, NW, Washington, District of Columbia 20036. (202) 659-0060. Biweekly. Covers trade, environmental and safety issues.

TRADE ASSOCIATIONS AND PROFESSIONAL SOCIETIES

American Institute of Biological Sciences. 730 11th St., N.W., Washington, District of Columbia 20001-4521. (202) 628-1500.

Synthetic Organic Chemical Manufacturers Association. 1330 Connecticut Ave., N.W., Suite 300, Washington, District of Columbia 20036. (202) 659-0060.

ORGANOCHLORINE PESTICIDES

See: PESTICIDES

ORGANOMERCURY COMPOUNDS

See: MERCURY

ORGANOPHOSPHATE PESTICIDES

See: PESTICIDES

ORNITHOLOGY

ABSTRACTING AND INDEXING SERVICES

Biological and Agricultural Index. H.W. Wilson Co., 950 University Ave., Bronx, New York 10452. (800) 367-6770. 1916-. Monthly.

General Science Index. H. W. Wilson Co., 950 University Ave., Bronx, New York 10452. 1978-. Monthly, also issued in annual cumulation. Cumulative subject index to English language periodicals in the subject fields of astronomy, botany, chemistry, earth science, environment and conservation, food and nutrition, genetics, mathematics, medicine and health, microbiology, oceanography, physics, physiology and zoology.

ENCYCLOPEDIAS AND DICTIONARIES

The Audubon Society Encyclopedia of North American Birds. Alfred A. Knopf, Inc., 201 E. 50th St., New York, New York 10022. (212) 726-0600. 1980.

The Cambridge Encyclopedia of Ornithology. Michael Brooke. Cambridge University Press, 40 W. 20th St., Cambridge, New York 10011. (212) 924-3900 or (800) 227-0247. 1991. Covers all aspects of avian biology with a text-like treatise. Includes bird anatomy, physiology, reproduction, evolution, behavior, migration, ecology, conservation, and more.

A Dictionary of Birds. Bruce Campbell. Buteo Books, PO Box 425, Friday Harbor, Washington 98250. (206) 378-6146. 1985.

The Encyclopedia of North American Wildlife. Stanley Klein. Facts on File, Inc., 460 Park Ave. S., New York, New York 10016. (212) 683-2244. 1983. Includes mammals, birds, reptiles, amphibians, and fish. Appendices include information on wildlife conservation organizations, a bibliographical list of endangered species and an index of Latin names.

Grzimek's Animal Life Encyclopedia. Van Nostrand Reinhold, 115 5th Ave., New York, New York 10003. (212) 254-3232. 1975. Thirteen volumes. Includes lower animals, insects, mollusks, fishes, amphibians, reptiles, birds, and mammals.

The Illustrated Encyclopedia of Birds: The Definitive Reference to Birds of the World. Prentice Hall, Rte. 9W, Englewood Cliffs, New York 07632. (201) 592-2000. 1991. Includes a short summary of basic bird biology, an illustrated catalog of about 1,200 species representing all living orders and families, and a checklist of all 9,300-plus currently recognized species.

Macmillan Illustrated Animal Encyclopedia. Philip Whitfield, ed. Macmillan Publishing Co., 866 3rd Ave., New York, New York 10022. (212) 702-2000. 1984. Provides a comprehensive catalog of the staggering range of animal types within the vertebrate group. Also the IUCN endangered species are noted and includes common names, range and habitat. Includes mammals, birds, reptiles, amphibians, and fish.

Remarkable Animals: A Unique Encyclopedia of Wildlife Wonders. Guinness Books, 33 London Rd., Enfield, England EN2 6DJ. 1987. Includes mammals, birds, fishes, amphibians, reptiles, insects, and arachnids.

GENERAL WORKS

Current Ornithology. Richard F. Johnston. Plenum Press, 233 Spring St., New York, New York 10013-1578. (212) 620-8000; (800) 221-9369. 1983.

HANDBOOKS AND MANUALS

Distribution and Taxonomy of Birds of the World. Charles G. Sibley and Burt L. Monroe. Yale University Press, 92 A Yale Station, 302 Temple St., New Haven, Connecticut 06520. (203) 432-0960. 1990. An up-to-date delineation of the present distribution of the species of birds arranged in a classification based primarily on evidence of phytogenetic relationships from comparison of the DNAs. Includes a list of scientific and English names of species.

RESEARCH CENTERS AND INSTITUTES

Manomet Bird Observatory. P.O. Box 1770, Manomet, Massachusetts 02345. (508) 224-6521.

Point Reyes Bird Observatory. 4990 Shoreline Highway, Stinson Beach, California 94970. (415) 868-1221.

University of Wisconsin-Milwaukee, Field Station. 3095 Blue Goose Road, Saukville, Wisconsin 53080. (414) 675-6844.

ORTHOPHOSPHATE

ABSTRACTING AND INDEXING SERVICES

Biological Abstracts. BIOSIS, 2100 Arch St., Philadelphia, Pennsylvania 19103-1399. (215) 587-4800. 1927-.

Biological and Agricultural Index. H.W. Wilson Co., 950 University Ave., Bronx, New York 10452. (800) 367-6770. 1916-. Monthly.

Chemical Abstracts. Chemical Abstracts Service, 2540 Olentangy River Rd., PO Box 3012, Columbus, Ohio 43210. (800) 848-6533. 1907-.

Pollution Abstracts. Cambridge Scientific Abstracts, 5161 River Rd., Bethesda, Maryland 20816. (301) 961-6750. Six/year. Indexes worldwide technical literature on environmental pollution. Covers air pollution, marine and freshwater pollution, sewage and wastewater treatment, waste management, toxicology and health, noise pollution, radiation, land pollution, and environmental policies, programs, legislation, and education. Also available online.

ENCYCLOPEDIAS AND DICTIONARIES

Ullmanns Encyclopedia of Industrial Chemistry. Hans Jurgen Arpe and Wolfgang Gerhartz, eds. VCH Publishers, 303 NW 12th Ave., Deerfield Beach, Florida 33442-1788. (305) 428-5566. 1990. Designed to keep up with the broad spectrum of chemical technology. Thirty-six volumes of the encyclopedia have been divided into two sets: the 28 A volumes contain alphabetically arranged articles on chemicals, product groups, processes and technological concepts; and the 8 B volumes are compendia of basic knowledge in industrial chemistry.

Van Nostrand's Scientific Encyclopedia. Glenn D. Considine, ed. Van Nostrand Reinhold, 115 5th Ave., New York, New York 10003. (212) 254-3232. 1983. Sixth edition. Includes all broad subject areas in science.

GENERAL WORKS

Kinetic Model for Orthophosphate Reactions in Mineral Soils. Carl George Enfield. U.S. G.P.O., Washington, District of Columbia 20401. (202) 512-0000.

ONLINE DATA BASES

BIOSIS Previews. BIOSIS, 2100 Arch St., Philadelphia, Pennsylvania 19103-1399. (215) 587-4800. Largest and most comprehensive database of research in the life sciences. Contains citations for nearly 9000 primary research journals, monographs, reviews, symposia, preliminary reports, semi-popular journals, selected institutional reports, government reports and research communications.

CAS Source Index–CASSI. Chemical Abstracts Service, 2540 Olentangy River Rd., P.O. Box 3012, Columbus, Ohio 43210. (800) 848-6533 or (614) 421-3600. A listing of bibliographic and library holdings information for scientific and technical primary literature relevant to the chemical sciences.

Chemical Abstracts-CA. Chemical Abstracts Service, 2540 Olentangy River Rd., P.O. Box 3012, Columbus, Ohio 43210. (800) 848-6533 or (614) 421-3600. Information sources include 9000 journals, patents from 27 countries, two industrial property organizations, new books, conference proceedings, and government research reports.

Chemical Collection System/Request Tracking–CCS/RTS. U.S. Environmental Protection Agency, Office of Pesticides and Toxic Substances, 401 M St., SW, Washington, District of Columbia 20460. (202) 260-2090. Contains information on various properties of a number of chemicals including environmental effects, test and analysis methods, and health effects. Available from EPA.

Chemical Dictionary Online–CHEMLINE. Chemical Abstracts Service, 2540 Olentangy River Rd., Columbus, Ohio 43210. (614) 421-3600 or (800) 848-6533. Part of MEDLINE of the National Library of Medicine (NLM). File of 900,000 names for chemical substances, representing 450,000 unique compounds. It contains such information as Chemical Abstracts (CA) Service Registry Numbers, molecular formulas, preferred chemical nomenclature, and generic and ring structure information. Available on NLM's ELHILL system.

Chemical Exposure. Science Applications International Corp., Health & Environmental Information, P.O. Box 2501, Oak Ridge, Tennessee 37831. (615) 482-9031. Database of chemicals that have been identified in both human tissues and body fluids and in feral and food animals. Contains reference to journal articles, conferences, and reports. Covers the whole fields of information related to human and animal exposure to food, air, and water contaminants and pharmaceuticals. Its records include information on chemical properties, formulas, tissues measured, analytical method used, demographics and more. Available on DIALOG.

PERIODICALS AND NEWSLETTERS

The Journal of Biological Chemistry. American Society of Biological Chemists, 428 E. Preston St., Baltimore, Maryland 21202. Three times a month. Biological, agricultural, and energy aspects of the environment.

TRADE ASSOCIATIONS AND PROFESSIONAL SOCIETIES

American Chemical Society. 1155 16th St., N.W., Washington, District of Columbia 20036. (202) 872-4600.

OSMOSIS

ABSTRACTING AND INDEXING SERVICES

Biological Abstracts. BIOSIS, 2100 Arch St., Philadelphia, Pennsylvania 19103-1399. (215) 587-4800. 1927-.

Biological and Agricultural Index. H.W. Wilson Co., 950 University Ave., Bronx, New York 10452. (800) 367-6770. 1916-. Monthly.

Biotechnology Research Abstracts. Cambridge Scientific Abstracts, 5161 River Rd., Bethesda, Maryland 20816. (301) 961-6750. Monthly. Includes such broad areas as genetic intervention, biochemical genetics, and microbiological techniques.

Chemical Abstracts. Chemical Abstracts Service, 2540 Olentangy River Rd., PO Box 3012, Columbus, Ohio 43210. (800) 848-6533. 1907-.

General Science Index. H. W. Wilson Co., 950 University Ave., Bronx, New York 10452. 1978-. Monthly, also issued in annual cumulation. Cumulative subject index to English language periodicals in the subject fields of astronomy, botany, chemistry, earth science, environment and conservation, food and nutrition, genetics, mathematics, medicine and health, microbiology, oceanography, physics, physiology and zoology.

Physics Briefs. Physikalische Berichte. Physik Verlag, Pappapelallee 3, Postfach 101161, Weinheim, Germany D-6940. 1979-. Semimonthly. In English. Volumes for 1979- issued by the Deutsche Physikalische Gesellschaft and the Fachinformationszentrum Energie Physik, Mathematik in cooperation with the American Institute of Physics.

Science Citation Index. Institute for Scientific Information, 3501 Market St., Philadelphia, Pennsylvania 19104. 1961-.

ENCYCLOPEDIAS AND DICTIONARIES

Cambridge Dictionary of Biology. Peter M. B. Walker. Cambridge University Press, 40 W. 20th St., New York, New York 10011. (212) 924-3900 or (800) 227-0247. 1989. Includes 10,000 terms in zoology, botany, biochemistry, molecular biology and genetics. Previously published under the title Chambers Biology Dictionary.

Cambridge Encyclopedia of Life Sciences. A. E. Friday and David S. Ingram. Cambridge University Press, 40 W 20th St., New York, New York 10011. (212) 924-3900 or (800) 227-0247. 1985. Includes all topics under biology and ecology.

A Concise Dictionary of Biology. Elizabeth Martin, ed. Oxford University Press, 200 Madison Ave., New York, New York 10016. (212) 679-7300 or (800) 334-4249. 1990. New edition. Derived from the Concise Science Dictionary, published in 1984.

Encyclopedia of Physics. Rita G. Lerner and George L. Trigg. VCH Publishers, 303 NW 12th Ave., Deerfield Beach, Florida 33442-1788. (305) 428-5566. 1991. Second edition.

McGraw-Hill Encyclopedia of Science and Technology. McGraw-Hill, 1221 Avenue of the Americas, New York, New York 10020. (212) 512-2000 or (800) 262-4729. 1992. Seventh edition. Issued in multiple volumes including index. Includes all science and technology broad subject areas.

GENERAL WORKS

Magill's Survey of Science. Life Science Series. Frank N. Magill, ed. Salem Press, PO Box 50062, Pasadena, California 91105. 1991. Six volumes. Contents: v.1. A-Central and peripheral nervous system functions; v.2. Central metabolism regulation - eukaryotic transcriptional control; v.3. Positive and negative eukaryotic transcriptional control - mammalian hormones; v.4. Hormones and behavior - muscular contraction; v.5. Muscular contraction and relaxation - sexual reproduction in plants; v.6. Reproductive behavior and mating - X inactivation and the Lyon hypothesis.

Removal of Heavy Metals from Wastewaters. Stephen Beszedits. B and L Information Services, PO Box 458, Station L, Toronto, Ontario, Canada M6E 2W4. (416) 657-1197. 1980. Covers wastewater treatment, electrodialysis, heavy metals, ultrafication, ozonization, foam separation, and ion exchange process.

Reverse Osmosis Technology. Bipin S. Parekh. Marcel Dekker, Inc., 270 Madison Ave., New York, New York 10016. (212) 696-9000; (800) 228-1160. 1988. Applications for high-purity-water production.

Reverse Osmosis Treatment of Drinking Water. Talbert N. Eisenberg. Butterworth-Heinemann, 80 Montvale Ave., Stoneham, Massachusetts 02180. (617) 438-8464. 1986.

HANDBOOKS AND MANUALS

Reverse Osmosis Technical Manual. U.S. Department of the Interior, Office of Water Research and Technology, 1849 C St. NW, Washington, District of Columbia 20240. (202) 208-3171. 1979.

ONLINE DATA BASES

BIOSIS Previews. BIOSIS, 2100 Arch St., Philadelphia, Pennsylvania 19103-1399. (215) 587-4800. Largest and most comprehensive database of research in the life sciences. Contains citations for nearly 9000 primary research journals, monographs, reviews, symposia, preliminary reports, semi-popular journals, selected institutional reports, government reports and research communications.

Chemical Abstracts-CA. Chemical Abstracts Service, 2540 Olentangy River Rd., P.O. Box 3012, Columbus, Ohio 43210. (800) 848-6533 or (614) 421-3600. Information sources include 9000 journals, patents from 27 countries, two industrial property organizations, new books, conference proceedings, and government research reports.

Chemical Engineering and Biotechnology Abstracts–CEBA. Orbit Search Service, Maxwell Online Inc., 8000 W. Park Dr., McLean, Virginia 22102. (703) 442-0900 or (800) 456-7248. Monthly. Covers theoretical, practical and commercial material on all aspects of processing safety, and the environment. Also covers process and reaction engineering, measurement and process control, environmental protection and safety, plant design and equipment used in chemical engineering and biotechnology. More than 400 of the world's major primary chemical and process engineering journals are scanned to compile the database. Available from ORBIT.

SCISEARCH. Institute for Scientific Information, University City Science Center, 3501 Market St., Philadelphia, Pennsylvania 19104. (215) 386-0100.

TRADE ASSOCIATIONS AND PROFESSIONAL SOCIETIES

American Institute of Chemical Engineers. 345 East 47th St., New York, New York 10017. (212) 705-7338.

American Institute of Chemists. 7315 Wisconsin Ave., Bethesda, Maryland 20814. (301) 652-2447.

OSMOTIC PUMPS

See: OSMOSIS

OUTER CONTINENTAL SHELF

DIRECTORIES

Gale Environmental Sourcebook. Karen Hill. Gale Research Co., 835 Penobscot Bldg., Detroit, Michigan 48226-4094. (313) 961-2242. Contacts, information sources, or general information on environmental topics.

OCS Directory: Federal and State Agencies Involved in the Outer Continental Shelf Oil and Gas Program. Minerals Management Science, Department of the Interior, 381 Elden St., Herndon, Virginia 22070. (703) 787-1028.

ENCYCLOPEDIAS AND DICTIONARIES

McGraw-Hill Encyclopedia of Science and Technology. McGraw-Hill, 1221 Avenue of the Americas, New York, New York 10020. (212) 512-2000 or (800) 262-4729. 1992. Seventh edition. Issued in multiple volumes including index. Includes all science and technology broad subject areas.

PERIODICALS AND NEWSLETTERS

Earth Science. American Geological Institute, 4220 King Street, Alexandria, Virginia 22302. (703) 379-2480. Quarterly. Covers geological issues.

STATISTICS SOURCES

Environmental Data Compendium. OECD Publications and Information Center, 2001 L St., N.W., Suite 700, Washington, District of Columbia 20036. (202) 785-6323. 1989.

Environmental Indicators. OECD Publications and Information Center, 2001 L St., N.W., Suite 700, Washington, District of Columbia 20036. (202) 785-6323. 1991.

Environmental Quality. Council on Environmental Quality. U.S. G.P.O., Washington, District of Columbia 20401. (202) 512-0000. Annual.

Outer Continental Shelf Environmental Assessment Program. U.S. NOAA. National Ocean Service. U.S. G.P.O., Washington, District of Columbia 20401. (202) 512-0000. 1991. Irregular. Environmental impacts of pollutants, including petroleum hydrocarbons and trace metals in marine biota, sediments and water.

Outer Continental Shelf Oil and Gas Activities. U.S. Dept. of Interior. Mineral Management Service. U.S. G.P.O., Washington, District of Columbia 20401. (202) 512-0000. 1980. Annual. Data on oil and gas drilling, production and reserves.

The State of the Environment. OECD Publications and Information Center, 2001 L St., N.W., Suite 700, Washington, District of Columbia 20036. (202) 785-6323. 1991.

OUTFALL

See: SEWERS

OVERFIRE AIR

See: INCINERATION

OVERHEAD TRANSMISSION LINES

See also: DISTRIBUTION LINES

ABSTRACTING AND INDEXING SERVICES

Engineering Index. The Engineering Index Inc., 345 E. 47th St., New York, New York 10017. 1962-.

BIBLIOGRAPHIES

Biological and Electrical Effects of Power Lines: A Worldwide Research Compilation. Interdisciplinary Environmental Associates, Minneapolis, Minnesota 1984.

Birds and Power Lines: A Bibliography. Charles A. Goulty. Council of Planning Librarians, 1313 E. 60th St., Chicago, Illinois 60637-2897. (312) 942-2163. 1988. Bird mortality due to electric lines.

ENCYCLOPEDIAS AND DICTIONARIES

Encyclopedia of Physical Science and Technology. Robert A. Meyers, ed. Academic Press, c/o Harcourt Brace Jovanovich Inc., 6277 Sea Harbor Dr., Orlando, Florida 32887. (800) 346-8648. Dictionary of engineering, technology and physical sciences.

McGraw-Hill Encyclopedia of Environmental Science. Sybil P. Parker. McGraw-Hill Science & Engineering Books, 11 W. 19th St., New York, New York 10011. (212) 337-6010. 1980. Covers ecology, man's influence on nature, and environmental protection.

ONLINE DATA BASES

Computerized Engineering Index–COMPENDEX. Engineering Information Inc., 345 E. 47th St., New York, New York 10017. (212) 705-7600.

OXIDANTS

See also: PHOTOCHEMICAL SMOG

ABSTRACTING AND INDEXING SERVICES

Applied Science and Technology Index. H.W. Wilson Co., 950 University Ave., Bronx, New York 10452. (800) 367-6770. Formerly Industrial Arts Index.

Biological and Agricultural Index. H.W. Wilson Co., 950 University Ave., Bronx, New York 10452. (800) 367-6770. 1916-. Monthly.

Chemical Abstracts. Chemical Abstracts Service, 2540 Olentangy River Rd., PO Box 3012, Columbus, Ohio 43210. (800) 848-6533. 1907-.

Environment Abstracts. Bowker A & I Publishing, 121 Chanlon Rd., New Providence, New Jersey 07974. (908) 464-6800. 1974-.

Environment Index. Environment Information Center, Index Research Department, 124 E. 39th St., New York, New York 10016. 1971-. Annual.

Environmental Information Connection–EIC. Planning Information Program, Dept. of Urban and Regional Planning, University of Illinois, 1003 West Nevada, Urbana, Illinois 61801. (217) 333-1369. Also available online.

Environmental Periodicals Bibliography. Environmental Studies Institute, International Academy at Santa Barbara, 800 Garden St., Suite D, Santa Barbara, California 93101. (805) 965-5010. Also available online.

Pollution Abstracts. Cambridge Scientific Abstracts, 5161 River Rd., Bethesda, Maryland 20816. (301) 961-6750. Six/year. Indexes worldwide technical literature on environmental pollution. Covers air pollution, marine and freshwater pollution, sewage and wastewater treatment, waste management, toxicology and health, noise pollution, radiation, land pollution, and environmental policies, programs, legislation, and education. Also available online.

Science Citation Index. Institute for Scientific Information, 3501 Market St., Philadelphia, Pennsylvania 19104. 1961-.

BIBLIOGRAPHIES

EPA Publications Bibliography. U.S. Environmental Protection Agency, Library Systems Branch, 401 M St., SW, Washington, District of Columbia 20460. (202) 260-2090. Quarterly.

ENCYCLOPEDIAS AND DICTIONARIES

Van Nostrand's Scientific Encyclopedia. Glenn D. Considine, ed. Van Nostrand Reinhold, 115 5th Ave., New York, New York 10003. (212) 254-3232. 1983. Sixth edition. Includes all broad subject areas in science.

GENERAL WORKS

Air Pollution by Photochemical Oxidants. Robert Guderian. Springer-Verlag, 175 5th Ave., New York, New York 10010. (212) 460-1500. 1985. Formation, transport, control, and effects on plants of photochemical oxidants.

Air Quality Criteria for Ozone and Other Photochemical Oxidants. U.S. Environmental Protection Agency, MD 75, Research Triangle Park, North Carolina 27711. 1986. Physiological effect of atmospheric ozone and effect of air pollution on plants.

Photochemical Oxidants. World Health Organization, Ave. Appia, Geneva, Switzerland CH-1211. 1979.

ONLINE DATA BASES

CAS Source Index–CASSI. Chemical Abstracts Service, 2540 Olentangy River Rd., P.O. Box 3012, Columbus, Ohio 43210. (800) 848-6533 or (614) 421-3600. A listing of bibliographic and library holdings information for scientific and technical primary literature relevant to the chemical sciences.

Chemical Abstracts-CA. Chemical Abstracts Service, 2540 Olentangy River Rd., P.O. Box 3012, Columbus, Ohio 43210. (800) 848-6533 or (614) 421-3600. Information sources include 9000 journals, patents from 27 countries, two industrial property organizations, new books, conference proceedings, and government research reports.

Enviro/Energyline Abstracts Plus. R. R. Bowker Co., 121 Chanlon Rd., New Providence, New Jersey 07974. (908) 464-6800.

Environmental Periodicals Bibliography. National Information Services Corp., Ste. 6, Wyman Towers, 3100 St. Paul St., Baltimore, Maryland 21218. (410)243-0797. Online version of abstract of same name.

OXIDATION

See also: WASTEWATER TREATMENT

ABSTRACTING AND INDEXING SERVICES

Biological and Agricultural Index. H.W. Wilson Co., 950 University Ave., Bronx, New York 10452. (800) 367-6770. 1916-. Monthly.

Chemical Abstracts. Chemical Abstracts Service, 2540 Olentangy River Rd., PO Box 3012, Columbus, Ohio 43210. (800) 848-6533. 1907-.

Environment Abstracts. Bowker A & I Publishing, 121 Chanlon Rd., New Providence, New Jersey 07974. (908) 464-6800. 1974-.

Environment Index. Environment Information Center, Index Research Department, 124 E. 39th St., New York, New York 10016. 1971-. Annual.

Environmental Information Connection–EIC. Planning Information Program, Dept. of Urban and Regional Planning, University of Illinois, 1003 West Nevada, Urbana, Illinois 61801. (217) 333-1369. Also available online.

Environmental Periodicals Bibliography. Environmental Studies Institute, International Academy at Santa Barbara, 800 Garden St., Suite D, Santa Barbara, California 93101. (805) 965-5010. Also available online.

General Science Index. H. W. Wilson Co., 950 University Ave., Bronx, New York 10452. 1978-. Monthly, also issued in annual cumulation. Cumulative subject index to English language periodicals in the subject fields of astronomy, botany, chemistry, earth science, environment and conservation, food and nutrition, genetics, mathematics, medicine and health, microbiology, oceanography, physics, physiology and zoology.

Pollution Abstracts. Cambridge Scientific Abstracts, 5161 River Rd., Bethesda, Maryland 20816. (301) 961-6750. Six/year. Indexes worldwide technical literature on environmental pollution. Covers air pollution, marine and freshwater pollution, sewage and wastewater treatment, waste management, toxicology and health, noise pollution, radiation, land pollution, and environmental policies, programs, legislation, and education. Also available online.

Science Citation Index. Institute for Scientific Information, 3501 Market St., Philadelphia, Pennsylvania 19104. 1961-.

BIBLIOGRAPHIES

EPA Publications Bibliography. U.S. Environmental Protection Agency, Library Systems Branch, 401 M St., SW, Washington, District of Columbia 20460. (202) 260-2090. Quarterly.

ENCYCLOPEDIAS AND DICTIONARIES

Cambridge Dictionary of Biology. Peter M. B. Walker. Cambridge University Press, 40 W. 20th St., New York, New York 10011. (212) 924-3900 or (800) 227-0247. 1989. Includes 10,000 terms in zoology, botany, biochemistry, molecular biology and genetics. Previously published under the title Chambers Biology Dictionary.

A Concise Dictionary of Biology. Elizabeth Martin, ed. Oxford University Press, 200 Madison Ave., New York, New York 10016. (212) 679-7300 or (800) 334-4249. 1990. New edition. Derived from the Concise Science Dictionary, published in 1984.

Van Nostrand's Scientific Encyclopedia. Glenn D. Considine, ed. Van Nostrand Reinhold, 115 5th Ave., New York, New York 10003. (212) 254-3232. 1983. Sixth edition. Includes all broad subject areas in science.

GENERAL WORKS

Ozone and Chlorine Dioxide Technology for Disinfection of Drinking Water. J. Katz. Noyes Publications, 120 Mill Rd., Park Ridge, New Jersey 07656. (201) 391-8484. 1980. Purification of drinking water through oxidation, chlorination, and ozonization.

Vapor-Phase Organic Pollutants: Volatile Hydrocarbons and Oxidation Products. National Research Council. National Academy of Sciences, 2101 Constitution Ave., NW, Washington, District of Columbia 20418. (202) 334-2000. 1976. Medical and biologic effects of environmental pollutants.

ONLINE DATA BASES

CERCLIS. Chemical Information Systems, Inc., 7215 York Rd., Baltimore, Maryland 21212. (301) 321-8440. Information on hazardous waste disposal sites that have either been listed by the EPA on the National Priority List (NPL) or nominated for consideration for the NPL.

Chemical Abstracts-CA. Chemical Abstracts Service, 2540 Olentangy River Rd., P.O. Box 3012, Columbus, Ohio 43210. (800) 848-6533 or (614) 421-3600. Information sources include 9000 journals, patents from 27 countries, two industrial property organizations, new books, conference proceedings, and government research reports.

Enviro/Energyline Abstracts Plus. R. R. Bowker Co., 121 Chanlon Rd., New Providence, New Jersey 07974. (908) 464-6800.

Environmental Periodicals Bibliography. National Information Services Corp., Ste. 6, Wyman Towers, 3100 St. Paul St., Baltimore, Maryland 21218. (410)243-0797. Online version of abstract of same name.

PERIODICALS AND NEWSLETTERS

Oxidation Communications. Elsevier, Box 211, Amsterdam, Netherlands 1000 AE. 020-5803-911. Quarterly.

TRADE ASSOCIATIONS AND PROFESSIONAL SOCIETIES

American Chemical Society. 1155 16th St., N.W., Washington, District of Columbia 20036. (202) 872-4600.

Natural Resources Defense Council. 40 W. 20th St., New York, New York 10011. (212) 727-2700.

Resource Policy Institute. c/o Dr. Arthur H. Purcell, 1745 Selby, Ste. 11, Los Angeles, California 90024. (213) 475-1684.

OXIDATION POND

See also: BACTERIA; LAKES

ABSTRACTING AND INDEXING SERVICES

Biological and Agricultural Index. H.W. Wilson Co., 950 University Ave., Bronx, New York 10452. (800) 367-6770. 1916-. Monthly.

Environment Abstracts. Bowker A & I Publishing, 121 Chanlon Rd., New Providence, New Jersey 07974. (908) 464-6800. 1974-.

Environment Index. Environment Information Center, Index Research Department, 124 E. 39th St., New York, New York 10016. 1971-. Annual.

Environmental Information Connection–EIC. Planning Information Program, Dept. of Urban and Regional Planning, University of Illinois, 1003 West Nevada, Urbana, Illinois 61801. (217) 333-1369. Also available online.

Environmental Periodicals Bibliography. Environmental Studies Institute, International Academy at Santa Barbara, 800 Garden St., Suite D, Santa Barbara, California 93101. (805) 965-5010. Also available online.

BIBLIOGRAPHIES

EPA Publications Bibliography. U.S. Environmental Protection Agency, Library Systems Branch, 401 M St., SW, Washington, District of Columbia 20460. (202) 260-2090. Quarterly.

ENCYCLOPEDIAS AND DICTIONARIES

Van Nostrand's Scientific Encyclopedia. Glenn D. Considine, ed. Van Nostrand Reinhold, 115 5th Ave., New York, New York 10003. (212) 254-3232. 1983. Sixth edition. Includes all broad subject areas in science.

GENERAL WORKS

Generic Facilities Plan for a Small Community: Stabilization Pond and Oxidation Ditch. Elaine Stanley. U.S. Environmental Protection Agency, 401 M St., S.W., Washington, District of Columbia 20460. (202) 260-2090. 1981. Design and construction of sewage disposal plants.

ONLINE DATA BASES

Enviro/Energyline Abstracts Plus. R. R. Bowker Co., 121 Chanlon Rd., New Providence, New Jersey 07974. (908) 464-6800.

Environmental Periodicals Bibliography. National Information Services Corp., Ste. 6, Wyman Towers, 3100 St. Paul St., Baltimore, Maryland 21218. (410)243-0797. Online version of abstract of same name.

TRADE ASSOCIATIONS AND PROFESSIONAL SOCIETIES

American Institute of Biological Sciences. 730 11th St., N.W., Washington, District of Columbia 20001-4521. (202) 628-1500.

OXIDES

ABSTRACTING AND INDEXING SERVICES

Chemical Abstracts. Chemical Abstracts Service, 2540 Olentangy River Rd., PO Box 3012, Columbus, Ohio 43210. (800) 848-6533. 1907-.

Environment Abstracts. Bowker A & I Publishing, 121 Chanlon Rd., New Providence, New Jersey 07974. (908) 464-6800. 1974-.

Environment Index. Environment Information Center, Index Research Department, 124 E. 39th St., New York, New York 10016. 1971-. Annual.

Environmental Information Connection–EIC. Planning Information Program, Dept. of Urban and Regional Planning, University of Illinois, 1003 West Nevada, Urbana, Illinois 61801. (217) 333-1369. Also available online.

Environmental Periodicals Bibliography. Environmental Studies Institute, International Academy at Santa Barbara, 800 Garden St., Suite D, Santa Barbara, California 93101. (805) 965-5010. Also available online.

General Science Index. H. W. Wilson Co., 950 University Ave., Bronx, New York 10452. 1978-. Monthly, also issued in annual cumulation. Cumulative subject index to English language periodicals in the subject fields of astronomy, botany, chemistry, earth science, environment and conservation, food and nutrition, genetics, mathematics, medicine and health, microbiology, oceanography, physics, physiology and zoology.

Science Citation Index. Institute for Scientific Information, 3501 Market St., Philadelphia, Pennsylvania 19104. 1961-.

BIBLIOGRAPHIES

EPA Publications Bibliography. U.S. Environmental Protection Agency, Library Systems Branch, 401 M St., SW, Washington, District of Columbia 20460. (202) 260-2090. Quarterly.

ENCYCLOPEDIAS AND DICTIONARIES

Van Nostrand's Scientific Encyclopedia. Glenn D. Considine, ed. Van Nostrand Reinhold, 115 5th Ave., New York, New York 10003. (212) 254-3232. 1983. Sixth edition. Includes all broad subject areas in science.

GENERAL WORKS

Calcium Oxide and Hydroxide. Environmental Protection Service, 425 St. Joseph Blvd., 3rd Fl., Hull, Quebec, Canada K1A 0H3. (613) 953-5921. 1984. Covers environmental and technical information for problem spills.

Propylene Oxide. Environmental Protection Service, 425 St. Joseph Blvd., 3rd Fl., Hull, Quebec, Canada K1A 0H3. (613) 953-5921. 1985. Environmental aspects of oxides.

ONLINE DATA BASES

CAS Source Index–CASSI. Chemical Abstracts Service, 2540 Olentangy River Rd., P.O. Box 3012, Columbus, Ohio 43210. (800) 848-6533 or (614) 421-3600. A listing of bibliographic and library holdings information for

scientific and technical primary literature relevant to the chemical sciences.

Chemical Abstracts-CA. Chemical Abstracts Service, 2540 Olentangy River Rd., P.O. Box 3012, Columbus, Ohio 43210. (800) 848-6533 or (614) 421-3600. Information sources include 9000 journals, patents from 27 countries, two industrial property organizations, new books, conference proceedings, and government research reports.

Enviro/Energyline Abstracts Plus. R. R. Bowker Co., 121 Chanlon Rd., New Providence, New Jersey 07974. (908) 464-6800.

Environmental Periodicals Bibliography. National Information Services Corp., Ste. 6, Wyman Towers, 3100 St. Paul St., Baltimore, Maryland 21218. (410)243-0797. Online version of abstract of same name.

STATISTICS SOURCES

Propylene Oxide & Derivatives. FIND/SVP, 625 Avenue of the Americas, New York, New York 10011. (212) 645-4500. 1991.

TRADE ASSOCIATIONS AND PROFESSIONAL SOCIETIES

American Chemical Society. 1155 16th St., N.W., Washington, District of Columbia 20036. (202) 872-4600.

OXIDIZABLE MATTER

See: BIOCHEMICAL OXYGEN DEMAND

OXYGEN DEBT

See also: OXYGEN DEPLETION

ONLINE DATA BASES

Solid Waste Report. NewsNet, Inc., 945 Haverford Rd., Bryn Mawr, Pennsylvania 19010. (800) 345-1301. Online version of the periodical of the same name.

OXYGEN DEPLETION

ABSTRACTING AND INDEXING SERVICES

Biotechnology Research Abstracts. Cambridge Scientific Abstracts, 5161 River Rd., Bethesda, Maryland 20816. (301) 961-6750. Monthly. Includes such broad areas as genetic intervention, biochemical genetics, and microbiological techniques.

Chemical Abstracts. Chemical Abstracts Service, 2540 Olentangy River Rd., PO Box 3012, Columbus, Ohio 43210. (800) 848-6533. 1907-.

Science Citation Index. Institute for Scientific Information, 3501 Market St., Philadelphia, Pennsylvania 19104. 1961-.

GENERAL WORKS

Living Without Oxygen: Closed and Open Systems in Hypoxia Tolerance. Peter W. Hochachka. Harvard University Press, 79 Garden St., Cambridge, Massachusetts 02138. (617) 495-2600. 1980. Covers anaerobiosis, anoxemia glycolysis, anoxia and glycolysis.

Oxygen Depletion and Associated Benthic Mortalities in New York Bight. R. Lawrence Swanson. National Oceanic and Atmospheric Administration, U.S. Department of Commerce, Washington, District of Columbia 20230. (202) 377-2985. 1980. Covers anoxemia, marine pollution, and dissolved oxygen in water.

ONLINE DATA BASES

Chemical Abstracts-CA. Chemical Abstracts Service, 2540 Olentangy River Rd., P.O. Box 3012, Columbus, Ohio 43210. (800) 848-6533 or (614) 421-3600. Information sources include 9000 journals, patents from 27 countries, two industrial property organizations, new books, conference proceedings, and government research reports.

Solid Waste Report. NewsNet, Inc., 945 Haverford Rd., Bryn Mawr, Pennsylvania 19010. (800) 345-1301. Online version of the periodical of the same name.

OXYGENATION

ABSTRACTING AND INDEXING SERVICES

Biological Abstracts. BIOSIS, 2100 Arch St., Philadelphia, Pennsylvania 19103-1399. (215) 587-4800. 1927-.

Biotechnology Research Abstracts. Cambridge Scientific Abstracts, 5161 River Rd., Bethesda, Maryland 20816. (301) 961-6750. Monthly. Includes such broad areas as genetic intervention, biochemical genetics, and microbiological techniques.

Chemical Abstracts. Chemical Abstracts Service, 2540 Olentangy River Rd., PO Box 3012, Columbus, Ohio 43210. (800) 848-6533. 1907-.

General Science Index. H. W. Wilson Co., 950 University Ave., Bronx, New York 10452. 1978-. Monthly, also issued in annual cumulation. Cumulative subject index to English language periodicals in the subject fields of astronomy, botany, chemistry, earth science, environment and conservation, food and nutrition, genetics, mathematics, medicine and health, microbiology, oceanography, physics, physiology and zoology.

Meteorological and Geoastrophysical Abstracts. American Meteorological Society, 45 Beacon St., Boston, Massachusetts 02108. (617) 227-2425.

Science Citation Index. Institute for Scientific Information, 3501 Market St., Philadelphia, Pennsylvania 19104. 1961-.

ENCYCLOPEDIAS AND DICTIONARIES

Van Nostrand's Scientific Encyclopedia. Glenn D. Considine, ed. Van Nostrand Reinhold, 115 5th Ave., New York, New York 10003. (212) 254-3232. 1983. Sixth edition. Includes all broad subject areas in science.

GENERAL WORKS

Environmental Aspects of Artificial Aeration and Oxygenation of Reservoirs: A Review of Theory, Techniques, and Experiences. Robert A. Pastorok. National Technical Information Service, 5285 Port Royal Rd., Springfield, Virginia 22161. (703) 487-4650. 1982. Environmental and water quality operation studies, and impact analysis relating to aeration treatment of wastewater.

ONLINE DATA BASES

BIOSIS Previews. BIOSIS, 2100 Arch St., Philadelphia, Pennsylvania 19103-1399. (215) 587-4800. Largest and most comprehensive database of research in the life sciences. Contains citations for nearly 9000 primary research journals, monographs, reviews, symposia, preliminary reports, semi-popular journals, selected institutional reports, government reports and research communications.

CAS Source Index–CASSI. Chemical Abstracts Service, 2540 Olentangy River Rd., P.O. Box 3012, Columbus, Ohio 43210. (800) 848-6533 or (614) 421-3600. A listing of bibliographic and library holdings information for scientific and technical primary literature relevant to the chemical sciences.

Chemical Abstracts-CA. Chemical Abstracts Service, 2540 Olentangy River Rd., P.O. Box 3012, Columbus, Ohio 43210. (800) 848-6533 or (614) 421-3600. Information sources include 9000 journals, patents from 27 countries, two industrial property organizations, new books, conference proceedings, and government research reports.

Dewitt Petrochemical Newsletter. DeWitt and Company, 16800 Greenspoint Park, North Atrium Suite 120, Houston, Texas 77060. (713) 875-5525.

Metracom Data. Metracom, Inc., P.O. Box 23498, Oklahoma City, Oklahoma 73132. (415) 721-0207.

NBSFLUIDS. National Institute of Standards & Technology, Office of Standard Reference Data, A323 Physics Building, Gaithersburg, Maryland 20899. (301) 975-2208.

Solid Waste Report. NewsNet, Inc., 945 Haverford Rd., Bryn Mawr, Pennsylvania 19010. (800) 345-1301. Online version of the periodical of the same name.

STATISTICS SOURCES

Forest Industries. Forest Industries, 500 Howard St., San Francisco, California 94105. Monthly. Concerned with logging, pulpwood and forest management, and the manufacture of lumber, plywood, board, and pulp.

Pulp and Paper. Forest Industries, 500 Howard St., San Francisco, California 94105. Monthly. Production, engineering/maintenance, management, and marketing.

TRADE ASSOCIATIONS AND PROFESSIONAL SOCIETIES

International Oxygen Manufacturers Association. P.O. Box 16248, Cleveland, Ohio 44116-0248. (216) 228-2166.

OZONE

See also: AEROSOLS; AIR POLLUTION; ATMOSPHERE; CHLOROFLUOROCARBONS (CFCS); COAL; FREON; GLOBAL WARMING; GREENHOUSE EFFECT; METHANE; OZONE LAYER; SMOG; STRATOSPHERE

ABSTRACTING AND INDEXING SERVICES

Air Pollution Titles. Pennsylvania State University, Center for Air Environmental Studies, 226 Fenske Laboratory, University Park, Pennsylvania 16802. (814) 865-1415. 1965. Bibliographic guide to current research literature on air environment, including monitoring and control of air pollution, health effects, effects on agriculture, forests, toxic air contaminants, and global atmospheric pro cases.

Air Pollution Translations. A Bibliography With Abstracts. U.S. Environmental Protection Agency, MD 75, Research Triangle Park, North Carolina 27711. (919) 541-2184. 1969.

Applied Ecology Abstracts Studies in Renewable Natural Resources. Information Retrieval Ltd., 1911 Jefferson Davis Highway, Arlington, Virginia 22202. 1975-. Monthly.

Applied Science and Technology Index. H.W. Wilson Co., 950 University Ave., Bronx, New York 10452. (800) 367-6770. Formerly Industrial Arts Index.

Biological and Agricultural Index. H.W. Wilson Co., 950 University Ave., Bronx, New York 10452. (800) 367-6770. 1916-. Monthly.

Biotechnology Research Abstracts. Cambridge Scientific Abstracts, 5161 River Rd., Bethesda, Maryland 20816. (301) 961-6750. Monthly. Includes such broad areas as genetic intervention, biochemical genetics, and microbiological techniques.

Bulletin Signaletique: Eau et Assainissement, Pollution Atmospherique, Droit des Pollutions. Centre de Documentation, Centre National de la Recherche Scientifique, 15, quai Anatole France, Paris, France 75700. (1) 45 55 92 25. 1983-. Monthly. Indexes pollution periodicals including water, atmospheric and related pollutions.

Chemical Abstracts. Chemical Abstracts Service, 2540 Olentangy River Rd., PO Box 3012, Columbus, Ohio 43210. (800) 848-6533. 1907-.

Current Advances in Ecological and Environmental Science. Pergamon Microforms International, Inc., Fairview Park, Elmsford, New York 10523. (914) 592-7720. 1989-. Monthly. Current literature searching service including journals, reports, abstracts, etc. This service is available online as part of the CABS database on the hosts BRS and ORBIT search service.

Ecological Abstracts. Geo Abstracts Ltd. Elsevier Applied Science, Crown House, Linton Rd., Barking, England IG 11 8JU. 1974-. Derived from over 600 leading ecological and environmental journals, plus books, conference proceedings, reports and theses.

Environment Abstracts. Bowker A & I Publishing, 121 Chanlon Rd., New Providence, New Jersey 07974. (908) 464-6800. 1974-.

Environment Index. Environment Information Center, Index Research Department, 124 E. 39th St., New York, New York 10016. 1971-. Annual.

Environmental Information Connection–EIC. Planning Information Program, Dept. of Urban and Regional Planning, University of Illinois, 1003 West Nevada, Urbana, Illinois 61801. (217) 333-1369. Also available online.

Environmental Periodicals Bibliography. Environmental Studies Institute, International Academy at Santa Barbara, 800 Garden St., Suite D, Santa Barbara, California 93101. (805) 965-5010. Also available online.

General Science Index. H. W. Wilson Co., 950 University Ave., Bronx, New York 10452. 1978-. Monthly, also issued in annual cumulation. Cumulative subject index to English language periodicals in the subject fields of astronomy, botany, chemistry, earth science, environment and conservation, food and nutrition, genetics, mathematics, medicine and health, microbiology, oceanography, physics, physiology and zoology.

Index to Scientific Book Contents. Institute for Scientific Information, 3501 Market St., Philadelphia, Pennsylvania 19104. (800) 523-1857. 1985-. Annual. Gives contents of science books published.

Mineralogical Abstracts. Mineralogical Society, 41 Queen's Gate, London, England SW7 5HR. 71 5847916. Quarterly. Abstracts of journal articles, conferences, technical reports and specialized books in the areas of minerals, clay minerals, economic minerals, ore deposits, environmental studies, experimental mineralogy, gemstones, geochemistry, petrology, lunar and planetary studies and other related areas in mineralogy.

Multimedia Index to Ecology. National Information Center for Educational Media, University of Southern California, Los Angeles, California 90007.

Physics Briefs. Physikalische Berichte. Physik Verlag, Pappapelallee 3, Postfach 101161, Weinheim, Germany D-6940. 1979-. Semimonthly. In English. Volumes for 1979- issued by the Deutsche Physikalische Gesellschaft and the Fachinformationszentrum Energie Physik, Mathematik in cooperation with the American Institute of Physics.

Pollution Abstracts. Cambridge Scientific Abstracts, 5161 River Rd., Bethesda, Maryland 20816. (301) 961-6750. Six/year. Indexes worldwide technical literature on environmental pollution. Covers air pollution, marine and freshwater pollution, sewage and wastewater treatment, waste management, toxicology and health, noise pollution, radiation, land pollution, and environmental policies, programs, legislation, and education. Also available online.

Science Citation Index. Institute for Scientific Information, 3501 Market St., Philadelphia, Pennsylvania 19104. 1961-.

BIBLIOGRAPHIES

Current Contents. Agriculture, Biology and Environmental Sciences. Institute for Scientific Information, 3501 Market St., Philadelphia, Pennsylvania 19104. (800) 523-1857. 1973-. Previous title: Current Contents. Agricultural, Food & Veterinary Sciences. Gives the table of contents of periodicals in the fields of agriculture, biology, environmental and related areas.

EPA Publications Bibliography. U.S. Environmental Protection Agency, Library Systems Branch, 401 M St., SW, Washington, District of Columbia 20460. (202) 260-2090. Quarterly.

Global Climate Change: Recent Publications. Library of the Department of State. The Library, 2201 C St. N.W., Washington, District of Columbia 20520. 1989.

DIRECTORIES

Gale Environmental Sourcebook. Karen Hill. Gale Research Co., 835 Penobscot Bldg., Detroit, Michigan 48226-4094. (313) 961-2242. Contacts, information sources, or general information on environmental topics.

ENCYCLOPEDIAS AND DICTIONARIES

Cambridge Dictionary of Biology. Peter M. B. Walker. Cambridge University Press, 40 W. 20th St., New York, New York 10011. (212) 924-3900 or (800) 227-0247. 1989. Includes 10,000 terms in zoology, botany, biochemistry, molecular biology and genetics. Previously published under the title Chambers Biology Dictionary.

Cambridge Encyclopedia of Life Sciences. A. E. Friday and David S. Ingram. Cambridge University Press, 40 W 20th St., New York, New York 10011. (212) 924-3900 or (800) 227-0247. 1985. Includes all topics under biology and ecology.

A Concise Dictionary of Biology. Elizabeth Martin, ed. Oxford University Press, 200 Madison Ave., New York, New York 10016. (212) 679-7300 or (800) 334-4249. 1990. New edition. Derived from the Concise Science Dictionary, published in 1984.

The Encyclopedia of Climatology. John E. Oliver and Rhodes W. Fairbridge, eds. Van Nostrand Reinhold, 115 5th Ave., New York, New York 10003. (212) 254-3232. 1987. Belongs in the series Encyclopedia of Earth Sciences, v.11.

The Encyclopedia of Geochemistry and Environmental Sciences. Rhodes Whitmore Fairbridge. Van Nostrand Reinhold Co., 115 5th Ave., New York, New York 10003. (212) 254-3232. 1972.

Encyclopedia of Physical Science and Technology. Robert A. Meyers, ed. Academic Press, c/o Harcourt Brace Jovanovich Inc., 6277 Sea Harbor Dr., Orlando, Florida 32887. (800) 346-8648. Dictionary of engineering, technology and physical sciences.

Encyclopedia of Physics. Rita G. Lerner and George L. Trigg. VCH Publishers, 303 NW 12th Ave., Deerfield Beach, Florida 33442-1788. (305) 428-5566. 1991. Second edition.

Grzimek's Encyclopedia of Ecology. Bernhard Grzimek. Van Nostrand Reinhold, 115 5th Ave., New York, New York 10003. (212) 254-3232. 1976.

McGraw-Hill Encyclopedia of Environmental Science. Sybil P. Parker. McGraw-Hill Science & Engineering Books, 11 W. 19th St., New York, New York 10011. (212) 337-6010. 1980. Covers ecology, man's influence on nature, and environmental protection.

McGraw-Hill Encyclopedia of Science and Technology. McGraw-Hill, 1221 Avenue of the Americas, New York, New York 10020. (212) 512-2000 or (800) 262-4729. 1992. Seventh edition. Issued in multiple volumes in-

cluding index. Includes all science and technology broad subject areas.

North American Reference Encyclopedia of Ecology and Pollution. William White. North American Pub. Co., 401 N. Broad St., Philadelphia, Pennsylvania 19108. (215) 238-5300. 1972.

Van Nostrand's Scientific Encyclopedia. Glenn D. Considine, ed. Van Nostrand Reinhold, 115 5th Ave., New York, New York 10003. (212) 254-3232. 1983. Sixth edition. Includes all broad subject areas in science.

GENERAL WORKS

The Challenge of Global Warming. Dean Edwin Abrahamson, ed. Island Press, 1718 Connecticut Ave. N.W., Suite 300, Washington, District of Columbia 20009. (202) 232-7933. 1989. Focuses on the causes, effects, policy implications, and possible solutions to global warming

The Changing Atmosphere: A Global Challenge. John Firor. Yale University Press, 302 Temple St., 92 A Yale Sta., New Haven, Connecticut 06520. (203) 432-0960. 1990. Examines three atmospheric problems: Acid rain, ozone depletion, and climate heating.

Environment in Peril. Anthony B. Wolbarst, ed. Smithsonian Institution Press, 470 L'Enfant Plaza, No. 7100, Washington, District of Columbia 20560. (800) 782-4612. 1991. Brings together in one volume the primary concerns of eleven of the world's leaders in conservation, ecology and public policy. Broad environmental issues covered are: ozone depletion, overpopulation, global warming, thinning forests, extinction of species, spreading deserts, toxic chemicals, and various pollutants.

The Environment: Problems and Solutions. Stuart Bruchey, ed. Garland Publishing, Inc., 1000A Sherman Ave., Hamden, Connecticut 06514. (203) 281-4487. 1991. Topics covered: forested wetlands and agriculture, the political economy of smog in southern California, environmental limits to growth in world agriculture, the tradeoff between cost and risk in hazardous waste management, and the protection of groundwater from agricultural pollution.

Global Air Pollution: Problems for the 1990s. Howard Bridgman. Belhaven Press, 136 S. Broadway, Irvington, New York 10533. (914) 591-9111. 1990. Addresses the environmental problems caused by human activities resulting in change and deterioration of the earth's atmosphere.

Greenhouse Warming: Negotiating a Global Regime. Jessica Tuchman Mathews, ed. World Resources Institute, 1709 New York Ave. N.W., Washington, District of Columbia 20006. (800) 822-0504. 1991. Offers specific suggestions for formulating, implementing, and enforcing a global regime to combat greenhouse warming.

Magill's Survey of Science. Life Science Series. Frank N. Magill, ed. Salem Press, PO Box 50062, Pasadena, California 91105. 1991. Six volumes. Contents: v.1. A-Central and peripheral nervous system functions; v.2. Central metabolism regulation - eukaryotic transcriptional control; v.3. Positive and negative eukaryotic transcriptional control - mammalian hormones; v.4. Hormones and behavior - muscular contraction; v.5. Muscular contraction and relaxation - sexual reproduction in plants; v.6. Reproductive behavior and mating - X inactivation and the Lyon hypothesis.

Optoelectronics for Environmental Science. S. Martellucci and A. N. Chester, eds. Plenum Press, 233 Spring St., New York, New York 10013-1578. (212) 620-8000; (800) 221-9369. 1991. Contribution of lasers and the optical sciences to specific problems, in situ measurements, atmospheric ozone, lidar detection, wind velocity, oceanographic measurements, heavy metal detection, toxic metals, and trace analysis. Proceedings of the 14th course of the International School of Quantum Electronics on Optoelectronics for Environmental Sciences, held September 3-12, 1989, in Erice, Italy.

Ozone Crisis: The 15-Year Evolution of a Sudden Global Emergency. Sharon L. Roan. John Wiley & Sons, Inc., 605 3rd Ave., New York, New York 10158-0012. (212) 850-6000. 1989. Chronicles the experiences of F. Sherwood Rowland and Mario Molina, the scientists who first made the ozone depletion discovery.

Ozone in the Atmosphere: Proceedings of the Quadrennial Ozone Symposium 1988 and Tropospheric Ozone Workshop, Gottingen, Germany, August 4-13, 1988. Rumen D. Bojkov and Peter Fabian, eds. A. Deepak, 101 Research Dr., Hampton, Virginia 23666-1340. 1989. Covers the topics: tropospheric ozone, polar ozone, ozone observations (from ground and space), observations of relevant trace constituents, reaction kinetics, mesospheric ozone, chemical- radiative-dynamic models, and new observational techniques.

Ozone in Water Treatment; Application and Engineering. Lewis Publishers, 200 Corporate Blvd. NW, Boca Raton, Florida 33431. (407) 994-0555 or (800)272-7737. 1991. Ozone technology as it is applied to drinking water production.

Ozone Risk Communication and Management. Edward J. Calabrese and Charles Gilbert. Lewis Publishers, 2000 Corporate Blvd., N.W., Boca Raton, Florida 33431. (407) 994-0555 or (800) 272-7737. 1990. Covers the non-attainment of EPS goals for ozone. Targets specific examples of environmental, agricultural, and public health implications of this non-compliance.

Panel Report on Ozone. United Nations Environment Program. United Nations Environment Programme, Box 30552, Nairobi, Kenya 1991.

Present State of Knowledge of the Upper Atmosphere. R.T. Watson. National Aeronautics and Space Administration, Scientific and Technical Information Office, 5285 Port Royal Rd., Springfield, Virginia 22161. (703) 487-4805. 1988. Atmospheric ozone and atmospheric chemistry.

Preserving the Global Environment: The Challenge of Shared Leadership. Jessica Tuchman Mathews, ed. World Resources Institute, 1709 New York Ave. N.W., Washington, District of Columbia 20006. (800) 822-0504. 1990. Includes findings on population growth, deforestation and the loss of biological diversity, the ozone layer, energy and climate change, economics, and other critical trends spell out new approaches to international cooperation and regulation in response to the shift from traditional security concerns to a focus on collective global security.

A Primer on Greenhouse Effect Gases. Donald J. Wuebbles and Jae Edmonds. Lewis Publishers, 200 Corporate Blvd. NW, Boca Raton, Florida 33431. (407) 994-0555 or (800)272-7737. 1991. Brings together the most current information available on greenhouse gases. Reveals information critical to developing an understanding of the role of energy and atmospheric chemical and radiative processes in determining atmospheric concentrations of greenhouse gases.

Protecting Life on Earth: Steps to Save the Ozone Layer. Cynthia Pollock Shea. Worldwatch Institute, 1776 Massachusetts Ave., N.W., Washington, District of Columbia 20036-1904. 1988. Reduction of air pollution and atmospheric ozone.

Stones in a Glass House: CFCs and Ozone Depletion. Douglas G. Cogan. Investor Responsibility Research Center, 1755 Massachusetts Ave., NW, Suite 600, Washington, District of Columbia 20036. (202) 234-7500. 1988. Environmental aspects of air pollution.

Surface-Level Ozone Exposures and Their Effects on Vegetation. A. S. Lefohn. Lewis Publishers, 2000 Corporate Blvd., N.W., Boca Raton, Florida 33431. (407) 994-0555 or (800) 272-7737. 1992. Discusses the tropospheric ozone, the characterization of ambient ozone exposures, experimental methodology, and effects on crops, trees and vegetation.

A Who's Who of American Ozone Depleters: A Guide to 3,014 Factories Emitting Three Ozone-Depleting Chemicals. Natural Resources Defense Council, 40 W. 20th St., New York, New York 10011. (212) 727-2700. 1990.

World on Fire: Saving the Endangered Earth. George J. Mitchell. Scribner Educational Publishers, 866 3d Ave., New York, New York 10022. (212) 702-2000; (800) 257-5755. 1991. Discusses the problems entailed with the issues of greenhouse effect, acid rain, the rift in the stratosphere ozone layer, and the destruction of tropical rain forests.

HANDBOOKS AND MANUALS

Handbook of Geophysics and the Space Environment. Adolph S. Jursa, ed. Air Force Geophysics Laboratory, Air Force Systems Command, United States Air Force, c/o National Technical Information Service, 5285 Port Royal Rd., Springfield, Virginia 22161. (703) 487-4650. 1985. Two volumes. Broad subject areas covered are space, atmosphere, and terrestrial environment. Includes topics such as solar radiation, sunspots, solar wind, geomagnetic fields, radiation belts, cosmic radiation, atmospheric gases, etc.

Ozone Drinking Water Treatment Handbook. Rip G. Rice. Lewis Publishers, 2000 Corporate Blvd., N.W., Boca Raton, Florida 33431. (407) 994-0555 or (800) 272-7737. 1991. Explains how ozone can be used to provide primary disinfection, while minimizing halogenated by-products.

ONLINE DATA BASES

CAS Source Index–CASSI. Chemical Abstracts Service, 2540 Olentangy River Rd., P.O. Box 3012, Columbus, Ohio 43210. (800) 848-6533 or (614) 421-3600. A listing of bibliographic and library holdings information for scientific and technical primary literature relevant to the chemical sciences.

Chemical Abstracts-CA. Chemical Abstracts Service, 2540 Olentangy River Rd., P.O. Box 3012, Columbus, Ohio 43210. (800) 848-6533 or (614) 421-3600. Information sources include 9000 journals, patents from 27 countries, two industrial property organizations, new

books, conference proceedings, and government research reports.

Enviro/Energyline Abstracts Plus. R. R. Bowker Co., 121 Chanlon Rd., New Providence, New Jersey 07974. (908) 464-6800.

Environmental Periodicals Bibliography. National Information Services Corp., Ste. 6, Wyman Towers, 3100 St. Paul St., Baltimore, Maryland 21218. (410)243-0797. Online version of abstract of same name.

Global Environmental Change Report. Cutter Information Corp., 37 Broadway, Arlington, Massachusetts 02174-5539. (617) 648-8700. Online access to environmental issues worldwide, including global warming, ozone depletion, deforestation, and acid rain. Online version of periodical of the same name.

PressNet Environmental Reports. Chemical Information Systems, Inc., 7215 York Rd., Baltimore, Maryland 21212. (301) 321-8440.

SCISEARCH. Institute for Scientific Information, University City Science Center, 3501 Market St., Philadelphia, Pennsylvania 19104. (215) 386-0100.

Solid Waste Report. NewsNet, Inc., 945 Haverford Rd., Bryn Mawr, Pennsylvania 19010. (800) 345-1301. Online version of the periodical of the same name.

PERIODICALS AND NEWSLETTERS

Atmospheres. Friends of the Earth, 218 D St. SE, Washington, District of Columbia 20003. (202) 544-2600. Quarterly. Reports on ozone depletion.

Atmospheric Environment. Pergamon Microforms International, Inc., Fairview Park, Elmsford, New York 10523. (914) 592-7720. 1966-. Publishes papers on all aspects of man's interactions with his atmospheric environment, including the administrative, economic and political aspects of these interactions. Air pollution research and its applications are covered, taking into account changes in the atmospheric flow patterns, temperature distributions and chemical constitution caused by natural and artificial variations in the earth's surface.

Global Climate Change Digest. Elsevier Science Publishing Co., 655 Avenue of the Americas, New York, New York 10010. (212) 984-5800. Monthly. Topics dealing with ozone depletion and the large-scale climatic changes linked to industrial activity, industrial by-products, and man-made substances.

Global Environmental Change Report. Cutter Information Corp., 37 Broadway, Arlington, Massachusetts 02174-5539. (617) 648-8700. Biweekly. Focus on global warming, ozone depletion, deforestation, and acid rain. Also available online.

International Environmental Affairs. University Press of New England, 17 1/2 Lebanon Street, Hanover, New Hampshire 03755. (603) 646-3340. Quarterly. Issues on management of natural resources.

Ozone: Science and Engineering. Rip G. Rice, ed. Lewis Publishers, 2000 Corporate Blvd., N.W., Boca Raton, Florida 33431. (407) 994-0555 or (800) 272-7737. 1979-. Six times a year. Exchanges information concerning ozone and other oxygen-related species between scientific disciplines.

STATISTICS SOURCES

Environmental Data Compendium. OECD Publications and Information Center, 2001 L St., N.W., Suite 700, Washington, District of Columbia 20036. (202) 785-6323. 1989.

Environmental Indicators. OECD Publications and Information Center, 2001 L St., N.W., Suite 700, Washington, District of Columbia 20036. (202) 785-6323. 1991.

Environmental Quality. Council on Environmental Quality. U.S. G.P.O., Washington, District of Columbia 20401. (202) 512-0000. Annual.

Ozone and Carbon Monoxide Air Quality Design Values. U.S. G.P.O., Washington, District of Columbia 20401. (202) 512-0000. Annual. National Ambient Air Quality Standards for Ozone and Carbon Monoxide Concentrations.

Progress in the Prevention and Control of Air Pollution. U.S. Environmental Protection Agency. National Technical Information Service, Springfield, Virginia 22161. (703) 487-4650. Annual. Covers air quality trends and control of radon, suspended particulates, sulfur and nitrogen oxides, carbon monoxide, ozone and lead.

The State of the Environment. OECD Publications and Information Center, 2001 L St., N.W., Suite 700, Washington, District of Columbia 20036. (202) 785-6323. 1991.

World Resources. World Resources Institute. 1709 New York Ave., N.W., Washington, District of Columbia 20006. (202) 638-6300. Annual. Statistical and textual analysis of world's natural resources and the effects of growth-caused environmental pollution.

TRADE ASSOCIATIONS AND PROFESSIONAL SOCIETIES

American Institute of Biological Sciences. 730 11th St., N.W., Washington, District of Columbia 20001-4521. (202) 628-1500.

International Ozone Association. Pan American Committee, 83 Oakwood Ave., Norwalk, Connecticut 06850. (203) 847-8169.

OZONE LAYER

ABSTRACTING AND INDEXING SERVICES

Air Pollution Titles. Pennsylvania State University, Center for Air Environmental Studies, 226 Fenske Laboratory, University Park, Pennsylvania 16802. (814) 865-1415. 1965. Bibliographic guide to current research literature on air environment, including monitoring and control of air pollution, health effects, effects on agriculture, forests, toxic air contaminants, and global atmospheric pro cases.

Air Pollution Translations. A Bibliography With Abstracts. U.S. Environmental Protection Agency, MD 75, Research Triangle Park, North Carolina 27711. (919) 541-2184. 1969.

Applied Ecology Abstracts Studies in Renewable Natural Resources. Information Retrieval Ltd., 1911 Jefferson Davis Highway, Arlington, Virginia 22202. 1975-. Monthly.

Biological and Agricultural Index. H.W. Wilson Co., 950 University Ave., Bronx, New York 10452. (800) 367-6770. 1916-. Monthly.

Bulletin Signaletique: Eau et Assainissement, Pollution Atmospherique, Droit des Pollutions. Centre de Documentation, Centre National de la Recherche Scientifique, 15, quai Anatole France, Paris, France 75700. (1) 45 55 92 25. 1983-. Monthly. Indexes pollution periodicals including water, atmospheric and related pollutions.

Chemical Abstracts. Chemical Abstracts Service, 2540 Olentangy River Rd., PO Box 3012, Columbus, Ohio 43210. (800) 848-6533. 1907-.

Current Advances in Ecological and Environmental Science. Pergamon Microforms International, Inc., Fairview Park, Elmsford, New York 10523. (914) 592-7720. 1989-. Monthly. Current literature searching service including journals, reports, abstracts, etc. This service is available online as part of the CABS database on the hosts BRS and ORBIT search service.

Environment Abstracts. Bowker A & I Publishing, 121 Chanlon Rd., New Providence, New Jersey 07974. (908) 464-6800. 1974-.

Environment Index. Environment Information Center, Index Research Department, 124 E. 39th St., New York, New York 10016. 1971-. Annual.

Environmental Information Connection–EIC. Planning Information Program, Dept. of Urban and Regional Planning, University of Illinois, 1003 West Nevada, Urbana, Illinois 61801. (217) 333-1369. Also available online.

Environmental Periodicals Bibliography. Environmental Studies Institute, International Academy at Santa Barbara, 800 Garden St., Suite D, Santa Barbara, California 93101. (805) 965-5010. Also available online.

Mineralogical Abstracts. Mineralogical Society, 41 Queen's Gate, London, England SW7 5HR. 71 5847916. Quarterly. Abstracts of journal articles, conferences, technical reports and specialized books in the areas of minerals, clay minerals, economic minerals, ore deposits, environmental studies, experimental mineralogy, gemstones, geochemistry, petrology, lunar and planetary studies and other related areas in mineralogy.

Multimedia Index to Ecology. National Information Center for Educational Media, University of Southern California, Los Angeles, California 90007.

Physics Briefs. Physikalische Berichte. Physik Verlag, Pappapelallee 3, Postfach 101161, Weinheim, Germany D-6940. 1979-. Semimonthly. In English. Volumes for 1979- issued by the Deutsche Physikalische Gesellschaft and the Fachinformationszentrum Energie Physik, Mathematik in cooperation with the American Institute of Physics.

Science Citation Index. Institute for Scientific Information, 3501 Market St., Philadelphia, Pennsylvania 19104. 1961-.

BIBLIOGRAPHIES

Current Contents. Agriculture, Biology and Environmental Sciences. Institute for Scientific Information, 3501 Market St., Philadelphia, Pennsylvania 19104. (800) 523-1857. 1973-. Previous title: Current Contents. Agricultural, Food & Veterinary Sciences. Gives the table of

contents of periodicals in the fields of agriculture, biology, environmental and related areas.

EPA Publications Bibliography. U.S. Environmental Protection Agency, Library Systems Branch, 401 M St., SW, Washington, District of Columbia 20460. (202) 260-2090. Quarterly.

ENCYCLOPEDIAS AND DICTIONARIES

Grzimek's Encyclopedia of Ecology. Bernhard Grzimek. Van Nostrand Reinhold, 115 5th Ave., New York, New York 10003. (212) 254-3232. 1976.

McGraw-Hill Encyclopedia of Environmental Science. Sybil P. Parker. McGraw-Hill Science & Engineering Books, 11 W. 19th St., New York, New York 10011. (212) 337-6010. 1980. Covers ecology, man's influence on nature, and environmental protection.

North American Reference Encyclopedia of Ecology and Pollution. William White. North American Pub. Co., 401 N. Broad St., Philadelphia, Pennsylvania 19108. (215) 238-5300. 1972.

GENERAL WORKS

Europhysics Study Conference on Induced Critical Conditions in the Atmosphere. A. Tartaglia. World Scientific, 687 Hartwell St., Teaneck, New Jersey 07666. (800) 227-7562. 1990. Deals with climatology, nuclear winter, ozone layer depletion, and the greenhouse effect.

The Greenhouse Effect and Ozone Layer. Philip Neal. Dryad, 15 Sherman Ave., Takoma Park, Maryland 20912. (301) 891-3729. 1989. Covers atmospheric carbon dioxide and effects of carbon dioxide on climate.

The Hole in the Sky: Man's Threat to the Ozone Layer. John R. Gribbin. Bantam Books, 666 5th Ave., New York, New York 10103. (212) 765-6500; (800) 223-6834. 1988. Scientific revelations about the ozone layer and global warming.

International Resource Management. S. Anderssen and Willy Ostreng, eds. Belhaven Press, 136 S. Broadway, Irvington, New York 10533. (914) 591-9111. 1990. Analyzes the relationship between scientific knowledge and policy in the management of natural resources at the international level. Presents current practice and problems. Problems such as ozone layer protection, whaling, and air pollution.

The Next One Hundred Years: Shaping the Fate of Our Living Earth. Jonathan Weiner. Bantam Books, 666 5th Ave., New York, New York 10103. (212) 765-6500; (800) 223-6834. 1991. Explores the following issues: the greenhouse effect, deforestation, the destruction of the ozone layer, the human population explosion and the onset of mass extinctions.

Ozone. Kathryn Gay. Franklin Watts, 387 Park Ave. S., New York, New York 10016. (212) 686-7070. 1989. Environmental aspects of chlorofluorocarbons.

Ozone Depletion: Health and Environmental Consequences. John Wiley & Sons, Inc., 605 3rd Ave., New York, New York 10158-0012. (212) 850-6000. 1989.

The Ozone Layer. Jane Duden. Crestwood House, Inc., c/o Macmillan Publishing Co., Front & Brown Streets, Riverside, New Jersey 08075. (609) 461-6500. 1990. Describes the ozone layer and its important function in protecting the earth from dangerous ultraviolet rays. Also

examines the threats posed to the ozone layer by chlorofluorocarbons and other pollutants.

Preserving the Global Environment: The Challenge of Shared Leadership. Jessica Tuchman Mathews, ed. World Resources Institute, 1709 New York Ave. N.W., Washington, District of Columbia 20006. (800) 822-0504. 1990. Includes findings on population growth, deforestation and the loss of biological diversity, the ozone layer, energy and climate change, economics, and other critical trends spell out new approaches to international cooperation and regulation in response to the shift from traditional security concerns to a focus on collective global security.

HANDBOOKS AND MANUALS

Handbook of Geophysics and the Space Environment. Adolph S. Jursa, ed. Air Force Geophysics Laboratory, Air Force Systems Command, United States Air Force, c/o National Technical Information Service, 5285 Port Royal Rd., Springfield, Virginia 22161. (703) 487-4650. 1985. Two volumes. Broad subject areas covered are space, atmosphere, and terrestrial environment. Includes topics such as solar radiation, sunspots, solar wind, geomagnetic fields, radiation belts, cosmic radiation, atmospheric gases, etc.

ONLINE DATA BASES

Chemical Abstracts-CA. Chemical Abstracts Service, 2540 Olentangy River Rd., P.O. Box 3012, Columbus, Ohio 43210. (800) 848-6533 or (614) 421-3600. Information sources include 9000 journals, patents from 27 countries, two industrial property organizations, new books, conference proceedings, and government research reports.

Enviro/Energyline Abstracts Plus. R. R. Bowker Co., 121 Chanlon Rd., New Providence, New Jersey 07974. (908) 464-6800.

Environmental Periodicals Bibliography. National Information Services Corp., Ste. 6, Wyman Towers, 3100 St. Paul St., Baltimore, Maryland 21218. (410)243-0797. Online version of abstract of same name.

Global Environmental Change Report. Cutter Information Corp., 37 Broadway, Arlington, Massachusetts 02174-5539. (617) 648-8700. Online access to environmental issues worldwide, including global warming, ozone depletion, deforestation, and acid rain. Online version of periodical of the same name.

PressNet Environmental Reports. Chemical Information Systems, Inc., 7215 York Rd., Baltimore, Maryland 21212. (301) 321-8440.

SCISEARCH. Institute for Scientific Information, University City Science Center, 3501 Market St., Philadelphia, Pennsylvania 19104. (215) 386-0100.

PERIODICALS AND NEWSLETTERS

Atmospheric Environment. Pergamon Microforms International, Inc., Fairview Park, Elmsford, New York 10523. (914) 592-7720. 1966-. Publishes papers on all aspects of man's interactions with his atmospheric environment, including the administrative, economic and political aspects of these interactions. Air pollution research and its applications are covered, taking into account changes in the atmospheric flow patterns, temperature distributions and chemical constitution caused by natural and artificial variations in the earth's surface.

Global Climate Change Digest. Elsevier Science Publishing Co., 655 Avenue of the Americas, New York, New York 10010. (212) 984-5800. Monthly. Topics dealing with ozone depletion and the large-scale climatic changes linked to industrial activity, industrial by-products, and man-made substances.

Global Environmental Change Report. Cutter Information Corp., 37 Broadway, Arlington, Massachusetts 02174-5539. (617) 648-8700. Biweekly. Focus on global warming, ozone depletion, deforestation, and acid rain. Also available online.

TRADE ASSOCIATIONS AND PROFESSIONAL SOCIETIES

American Institute of Biological Sciences. 730 11th St., N.W., Washington, District of Columbia 20001-4521. (202) 628-1500.

P

PACKAGE PLANT

See also: WASTEWATER TREATMENT

ABSTRACTING AND INDEXING SERVICES

Engineering Index. The Engineering Index Inc., 345 E. 47th St., New York, New York 10017. 1962-.

Science Citation Index. Institute for Scientific Information, 3501 Market St., Philadelphia, Pennsylvania 19104. 1961-.

GENERAL WORKS

Packaging and the Environment: Alternatives, Trends, and Solutions. Susan E. M. Selke. Technomic Publishing Co., 851 New Holland Ave., Box 3535, Lancaster, Pennsylvania 17604. (717) 291-5609. 1990. Review of the contribution of packaging to various environmental problems.

Plastics: America's Packaging Dilemma. Nancy A. Wolf and Ellen D. Feldman. Island Press, 1718 Connecticut Ave. N.W., Ste. 300, Washington, District of Columbia 20009. (202) 232-7933. 1991. Source books on plastics deal with packaging, building materials, consumer goods, electrical products, transportation, industrial machinery, adhesives, legislative and regulatory issues. Also covers the controversies over plastics incineration, degradability, and recyclability.

ONLINE DATA BASES

Computerized Engineering Index–COMPENDEX. Engineering Information Inc., 345 E. 47th St., New York, New York 10017. (212) 705-7600.

STATISTICS SOURCES

Packaging. Cahners Publishing Co., 249 W. 17th St., New York, New York 10011. (212) 645-0067. Monthly. Manufacturing, R&D, marketing, and consumption.

TRADE ASSOCIATIONS AND PROFESSIONAL SOCIETIES

Council on Plastics and Packaging in the Environment. 1001 Connecticut Ave., N.W., Suite 401, Washington, District of Columbia 20036. (202) 331-0099.

Packaging Institute International. Institute of Packaging Professionals, 481 Carlisle Dr., Herndon, Virginia 22070. (703) 318-8970.

Paperboard Packaging Council. 1101 Vermont Ave., N.W., Suite 411, Washington, District of Columbia 20005. (202) 289-4100.

Textile Bay & Packaging Association. 1024 W. Kinzie Ave., Chicago, Illinois 60622. (312) 733-3660.

PACKAGING

See: INDUSTRIAL REFUSE

PAINT

See also: LEAD

ABSTRACTING AND INDEXING SERVICES

Chemical Abstracts. Chemical Abstracts Service, 2540 Olentangy River Rd., PO Box 3012, Columbus, Ohio 43210. (800) 848-6533. 1907-.

General Science Index. H. W. Wilson Co., 950 University Ave., Bronx, New York 10452. 1978-. Monthly, also issued in annual cumulation. Cumulative subject index to English language periodicals in the subject fields of astronomy, botany, chemistry, earth science, environment and conservation, food and nutrition, genetics, mathematics, medicine and health, microbiology, oceanography, physics, physiology and zoology.

Pollution Abstracts. Cambridge Scientific Abstracts, 5161 River Rd., Bethesda, Maryland 20816. (301) 961-6750. Six/year. Indexes worldwide technical literature on environmental pollution. Covers air pollution, marine and freshwater pollution, sewage and wastewater treatment, waste management, toxicology and health, noise pollution, radiation, land pollution, and environmental policies, programs, legislation, and education. Also available online.

Science Citation Index. Institute for Scientific Information, 3501 Market St., Philadelphia, Pennsylvania 19104. 1961-.

BIBLIOGRAPHIES

Lead Paint Poisoning in Urban Children. Council of Planning Librarians, 1313 E. 60th St., Chicago, Illinois 60637-2897. (312) 942-2163. 1976.

DIRECTORIES

American Paint and Coatings Journal–Directory of Raw Material Distributors & Manufacturers' Agents Issue. 2911 Washington Ave., St. Louis, Missouri 63103. (314) 534-0301. Annual.

Coal Preparation Plant Association–Buyer's Guide. 5711 S. 86th Circle, Omaha, Nebraska 68127. (402) 593-4600. Annual.

Directory of the Paint and Coatings Industry. Communication Channels, 6255 Barfield Rd., Atlanta, Georgia 30328. (404) 256-9800. 1987. Annual.

Paint & Coatings Industry–Raw Materials & Equipment Source Directory & Buyers Guide Issue. Business News, 60 Industrial Way, Brisbane, California 94005. (415) 468-7786.

Paint, Body & Equipment Association–Membership Roster. Paint, Body & Equipment Association, 9140 Ward Parkway, Kansas City, Missouri 64114. (816) 444-3500.

Target Marketing Directory: U.S. Paint and Coating Manufacturers. Mannsville Chemical Products Corporation, Box 271, Asbury Park, New Jersey 07712. (908) 776-7888.

GENERAL WORKS

Acid Rain and Ozone Layer Depletion. Jutta Brunnee. Transnational Publishers, PO Box 7282, Ardsley-on-Hudson, New York 10503. (914) 693-0089. 1988. International law and regulation relating to air pollution.

Air Pollution Damage to Man-Made Materials: Physical and Economic Estimates. A.R. Stankunas. Electric Power Research Institute, 3412 Hillview Ave., Palo Alto, California 94304. (415) 965-4081. 1983. Environmental aspects of paint, galvanized steel and concrete.

Analysis of Pollution Controls for Bridge Painting Contracts. Lloyd Smith. National Technical Information Service, 5285 Port Royal Rd., Springfield, Virginia 22161. (703) 487-4650. 1991. Monitoring pollution caused by structural painting.

Destruction of VOCs by a Catalytic Paint Drying Device. C. David Cooper. U.S. Environmental Protection Agency, Air and Energy Engineering Research Laboratory, MD 75, Research Triangle Park, North Carolina 27711. 1985. Environmental aspects of drying paint and infrared drying equipment.

Environmental Fact Sheet: Mercury Biocides in Paint. U.S. Environmental Protection Agency, Office of Pesticides and Toxic Substances, 401 M St. SW, Washington, District of Columbia 20460. (202) 260-2090. 1990.

Hazardous Waste Minimization Audit Studies on the Paint Manufacturing Industry. Jacobs Engineering Group, Inc., S. Lake Ave., Pasadena, California 91171. (818)449-2171. 1987. Factory and trade wastes and disposal in the paint industry.

The Hole in the Sky: Man's Threat to the Ozone Layer. John R. Gribbin. Bantam Books, 666 5th Ave., New York, New York 10103. (212) 765-6500; (800) 223-6834. 1988. Scientific revelations about the ozone layer and global warming.

Lead Poisoning. National Park Service Housing, Washington, District of Columbia 20013. (202) 208-6843.

1991. Lead toxicology, health aspects of paints and children's health safety.

Long-Term Neurotoxic Effects of Paint Solvents. Royal Society of Chemistry, c/o CRC Press, 2000 Corporate Blvd. N.W., Boca Raton, Florida 33431-9868. (800) 272-7737. 1990. Various components of oil-based decorative paints are described, as are studies that have been made on the neurotoxicity of the individual solvents. The relative advantages and disadvantages of oil-based and water-based paints are described.

Paint Formulation: Principles and Practice. J. Boxall. Industrial Press, 200 Madison Ave., New York, New York 10016. (212) 889-6330. 1981.

Protecting Life on Earth: Steps to Save the Ozone Layer. Cynthia Pollock Shea. Worldwatch Institute, 1776 Massachusetts Ave., N.W., Washington, District of Columbia 20036-1904. 1988. Reduction of air pollution and atmospheric ozone.

The Sky is the Limit: Strategies for Protecting the Ozone Layer. Alan S. Miller. World Resources Institute, 1709 New York Ave., N.W., Washington, District of Columbia 20006. (800) 822-0504. 1986. Law and legislation relating to chlorofluorocarbons and atmospheric ozone reduction.

The Toxicities of Selected Bridge Painting Materials and Guidelines for Bridge Painting Projects. Harold G. Hunt. National Technical Information Service, 5285 Port Royal Rd., Springfield, Virginia 22161. (703) 487-4650. 1990. Environmental aspects of maintenance and repair of bridges.

HANDBOOKS AND MANUALS

Guidelines for Environmental Pollution Controls for Bridge Painting Contracts. Lloyd Smith. Department of Transportation, Office of Research & Special Studies, 400 7th St. SW, Washington, District of Columbia 20590. (202) 366-4433. 1991. Environmental aspects of protective coatings and structural painting.

Guides to Pollution Prevention. U.S. Environmental Protection Agency, 26 W. Martin Luther King Dr., Cincinnati, Ohio 45220. 1990. Waste disposal in the paint industry and trade and U.S. environmental aspects.

Paint Handbook. McGraw-Hill Science & Engineering Books, 11 W. 19th St., New York, New York 10011. (212) 337-6010. 1981. Covers industrial painting and paint.

Paint Manual. U.S. G.P.O., Washington, District of Columbia 20401. (202) 512-0000. 1976. Covers protective coatings and industrial painting.

ONLINE DATA BASES

Advanced Coatings & Surface Technology. NewsNet, Inc., 945 Haverford Rd., Bryn Mawr, Pennsylvania 19010. (800) 345-1301.

Chemical Abstracts-CA. Chemical Abstracts Service, 2540 Olentangy River Rd., P.O. Box 3012, Columbus, Ohio 43210. (800) 848-6533 or (614) 421-3600. Information sources include 9000 journals, patents from 27 countries, two industrial property organizations, new books, conference proceedings, and government research reports.

ChemQuest. Molecular Design Ltd., 2132 Farrallon Dr., San Leandro, California 94577. (415) 895-1313.

DOMIS. ECHO Service, BP 2373, Luxembourg L-1023. (352) 488041.

PERIODICALS AND NEWSLETTERS

Progress in Organic Coatings. Elsevier Sequoia, 50, ave. de la Gare, PO Box 564, Lausanne, Switzerland CH-1001. Covers protective coatings, polymers and polymerization.

STATISTICS SOURCES

Advances in Coating Materials, Techniques & Equipment. FIND/SVP, 625 Avenue of the Americas, New York, New York 10011. (212) 645-4500. 1991. Development of sophisticated materials, operating systems and surface modification techniques in areas as diverse as aerospace, lawn-mower components and microelectrics.

Guide to the U.S. Paint Industry. FIND/SVP, 625 Avenue of the Americas, New York, New York 10011. (212) 645-4500. 1991. Shipment trends/forecasts; company performances; profitability; prices; productivity; geographical patterns; transportation; distribution; foreign trade; and world production/trade.

Powder Coatings. FIND/SVP, 625 Avenue of the Americas, New York, New York 10011. (212) 645-4500. 1991. Comprehensive of the U.S. market for powder coatings by material type.

TRADE ASSOCIATIONS AND PROFESSIONAL SOCIETIES

Basic Acrylic Monomer Manufacturers Association. 1330 Connecticut Ave., N.W., Washington, District of Columbia 20036. (202) 659-0060.

Chemical Coaters Association. P.O. Box 44275, Cincinnati, Ohio 45244. (513) 232-5055.

Color Association of the United States. 343 Lexington Ave., New York, New York 10016. (212) 683-9531.

Dry Color Manufacturers Association. P.O. Box 20839, Alexandria, Virginia 22320. (703) 684-4044.

PALEOECOLOGY

See also: BIOGEOGRAPHY

ABSTRACTING AND INDEXING SERVICES

Biological Abstracts. BIOSIS, 2100 Arch St., Philadelphia, Pennsylvania 19103-1399. (215) 587-4800. 1927-.

Biological and Agricultural Index. H.W. Wilson Co., 950 University Ave., Bronx, New York 10452. (800) 367-6770. 1916-. Monthly.

Current Advances in Ecological and Environmental Science. Pergamon Microforms International, Inc., Fairview Park, Elmsford, New York 10523. (914) 592-7720. 1989-. Monthly. Current literature searching service includingjournals, reports, abstracts, etc. This service is available online as part of the CABS database on the hosts BRS and ORBIT search service.

Ecology Abstracts. Cambridge Scientific Abstracts, 5161 River Rd., Bethesda, Maryland 20816. (301) 961-6750. Monthly.

General Science Index. H. W. Wilson Co., 950 University Ave., Bronx, New York 10452. 1978-. Monthly, also issued in annual cumulation. Cumulative subject index to English language periodicals in the subject fields of astronomy, botany, chemistry, earth science, environment and conservation, food and nutrition, genetics, mathematics, medicine and health, microbiology, oceanography, physics, physiology and zoology.

Pollution Abstracts. Cambridge Scientific Abstracts, 5161 River Rd., Bethesda, Maryland 20816. (301) 961-6750. Six/year. Indexes worldwide technical literature on environmental pollution. Covers air pollution, marine and freshwater pollution, sewage and wastewater treatment, waste management, toxicology and health, noise pollution, radiation, land pollution, and environmental policies, programs, legislation, and education. Also available , online.

ALMANACS AND YEARBOOKS

Current Research in the Pleistocene. Center for the Study of Early Man, University of Maine at Orono, Orono, Maine 04473. 1985-.

ENCYCLOPEDIAS AND DICTIONARIES

Cambridge Dictionary of Biology. Peter M. B. Walker. Cambridge University Press, 40 W. 20th St., New York, New York 10011. (212) 924-3900 or (800) 227-0247. 1989. Includes 10,000 terms in zoology, botany, biochemistry, molecular biology and genetics. Previously published under the title Chambers Biology Dictionary.

A Concise Dictionary of Biology. Elizabeth Martin, ed. Oxford University Press, 200 Madison Ave., New York, New York 10016. (212) 679-7300 or (800) 334-4249. 1990. New edition. Derived from the Concise Science Dictionary, published in 1984.

Glossary of Geology. Robert Latimer Bates and Julia A. Jackson, eds. American Geological Institute, 4220 King St., Alexandria, Virginia 22302-1507. (703) 379-2480 or (800) 336-4764. 1987. Third edition.

McGraw-Hill Encyclopedia of Environmental Science. Sybil P. Parker. McGraw-Hill Science & Engineering Books, 11 W. 19th St., New York, New York 10011. (212) 337-6010. 1980. Covers ecology, man's influence on nature, and environmental protection.

McGraw-Hill Encyclopedia of the Geological Sciences. Sybil P. Parker, ed. McGraw-Hill, 1221 Avenue of the Americas, New York, New York 10020. (212) 512-2000 or (800) 262-4729. 1988. Second edition. Published previously in the McGraw-Hill Encyclopedia of Science and Technology.

Van Nostrand's Scientific Encyclopedia. Glenn D. Considine, ed. Van Nostrand Reinhold, 115 5th Ave., New York, New York 10003. (212) 254-3232. 1983. Sixth edition. Includes all broad subject areas in science.

GENERAL WORKS

Life History of a Fossil: An Introduction to Taphonomy and Paleoecology. Harvard University Press, 79 Garden

St., Cambridge, Massachusetts 02138. (617) 495-2600. 1981.

Paleobotany, Paleoecology, and Evolution. Praeger Publishers, 1 Madison Ave., New York, New York 10010-3603. (212) 685-5300. 1981.

Paleoecology, Concepts and Applications. John Wiley & Sons, Inc., 605 3rd Ave., New York, New York 10158-0012. (212) 850-6000. 1990.

HANDBOOKS AND MANUALS

Handbook of Holocene Palaeoecology and Palaeohydrology. B.E. Berglund. John Wiley & Sons, Inc., 605 3rd Ave., New York, New York 10158-0012. (212) 850-6000. 1986. Topics in straligraphic geology.

ONLINE DATA BASES

BIOSIS Previews. BIOSIS, 2100 Arch St., Philadelphia, Pennsylvania 19103-1399. (215) 587-4800. Largest and most comprehensive database of research in the life sciences. Contains citations for nearly 9000 primary research journals, monographs, reviews, symposia, preliminary reports, semi-popular journals, selected institutional reports, government reports and research communications.

GeoRef. American Geological Institute, 4220 King St., Alexandria, Virginia 22302. (703) 379-2480.

RESEARCH CENTERS AND INSTITUTES

University of Texas at El Paso, Laboratory for Environmental Biology. Department of Biology, EL Paso, Texas 79968. (915) 747-5164.

PALLADIUM

See: METALS AND METALLURGY

PALLUSTRINE

See: SWAMPS

PAN PEROXYACETYL NITRATE

See: PHOTOCHEMICAL SMOG

PAPER

See also: FORESTS; RECYCLING

ABSTRACTING AND INDEXING SERVICES

Applied Science and Technology Index. H.W. Wilson Co., 950 University Ave., Bronx, New York 10452. (800) 367-6770. Formerly Industrial Arts Index.

Biological Abstracts. BIOSIS, 2100 Arch St., Philadelphia, Pennsylvania 19103-1399. (215) 587-4800. 1927-.

General Science Index. H. W. Wilson Co., 950 University Ave., Bronx, New York 10452. 1978-. Monthly, also

issued in annual cumulation. Cumulative subject index to English language periodicals in the subject fields of astronomy, botany, chemistry, earth science, environment and conservation, food and nutrition, genetics, mathematics, medicine and health, microbiology, oceanography, physics, physiology and zoology.

Science Citation Index. Institute for Scientific Information, 3501 Market St., Philadelphia, Pennsylvania 19104. 1961-.

DIRECTORIES

American Papermaker–Mill and Personnel Directory Issue. 6 Piedmont Center, Suite 300, Atlanta, Georgia 30305. (404) 841-3333. Annual.

Lockwood-Post's Directory of the Pulp, Paper and Allied Trades. Miller Freeman Publications, 370 Lexington Ave., New York, New York 10017. (212) 683-9294. 1987. Annual.

Paper Products–Wholesale. American Business Directories, Inc., 5711 S. 86th Circle, Omaha, Nebraska 68127. (402) 593-4600.

Paper Year Book. Edgell Communications, Inc., 7500 Old Oak Blvd., Cleveland, Ohio 44130. (218) 243-8100.

PaperBase: Paper Industry Information Service. Communication & Information Services, 2399 Eugene Court, Concord, California 94518. (415) 687-4303.

Pulp and Paper–Buyer's Guide Issue. Miller Freeman Publications, Inc., 500 Howard Street, San Francisco, California 94105. (415) 397-1881.

Sources of Supply/Buyers Guide. Advertisers & Publishers Service, Inc., 300 N. Prospect Ave., Park Ridge, Illinois 60068. (708) 823-3145.

GENERAL WORKS

The Greenpeace Guide to Paper. Greenpeace, 1436 U St., NW, Washington, District of Columbia 20009. (202) 462-1177. 1990. Waste paper recycling and environmental aspects of paper industry.

How on Earth Do We Recycle Paper?. Helen Jill Fletcher. Millbrook Press, 2 Old New Milford Rd., PO Box 335, Brookfield, Connecticut 06804-0335. (203) 740-2220. 1992. How paper is produced and recycled. Presents crafts projects using paper discards.

The Mighty Rain Forest. John Nicol. Sterling Pub. Co. Inc., 387 Park Ave. S., New York, New York 10016. (212) 532-7160; (800) 367-9692. 1990. Focuses on the emotive debate on the environment regarding rainforests and the paper manufacturers. Includes a bibliography and a list of organizations working in rainforest conservation.

Paper Production and Processing. Robert Soklow. U.S. Environmental Protection Agency, Industrial Environmental Research Laboratory, 26 W. Martin Luther King Dr., Cincinnati, Ohio 45268. (513) 569-7931. 1984. Occupational exposure and environmental release study.

Pulp and Paper Industry Corrosion Problems. National Association of Corrosion Engineers, P.O. Box 218340, Houston, Texas 77218. (713) 492-0535. 1982.

Recycling Paper: From Fiber to Finished Product. Matthew J. Coleman. TAPPI Press, Technology Park/Atlanta, PO Box 105113, Atlanta, Georgia 30348. (404) 446-1400. 1991.

Your Office Paper Recycling Guide. San Francisco Recycling Program, Room 271 City Hall, San Francisco, California 94102. (415) 554-6193. 1990.

HANDBOOKS AND MANUALS

Recycler's Handbook: Everything You Need to Make Recycling a Part of Your Life. Earthworks Press, 1400 Shattuck Ave., No. 25, Berkeley, California 94709. (510) 652-8533. 1990.

ONLINE DATA BASES

BIOSIS Previews. BIOSIS, 2100 Arch St., Philadelphia, Pennsylvania 19103-1399. (215) 587-4800. Largest and most comprehensive database of research in the life sciences. Contains citations for nearly 9000 primary research journals, monographs, reviews, symposia, preliminary reports, semi-popular journals, selected institutional reports, government reports and research communications.

Chemical Industry Notes–CHEMSIS. Chemical Abstracts Service, PO Box 3012, 2540 Olentangy River, Columbus, Ohio 43210. (614) 421-3600 or (800) 848-6533. Contains citations to business-oriented literature relating to the chemical processing industries. Includes pricing, production, products and processes, corporate and government activities, facilities and people from more than 80 worldwide business periodicals published since 1974. Available on DIALOG and ORBIT.

FOREST. Forest Products Research Society, 2801 Marshall Court, Madison, Wisconsin 53705. (608) 231-1361.

PAPERCHEM. Institute of Paper Science & Technology, Inc., 575 14th St., N.W., Atlanta, Georgia 30318. (404) 853-9500.

Pulp and Paper Data Bank. Resource Information Systems, 110 Great Rd., Bedford, Massachusetts 01730. (617) 271-0030.

RISI Forest Products. Resource Information Systems, 110 Great Rd., Bedford, Massachusetts 01730. (617) 271-0030.

Solid Waste Report. NewsNet, Inc., 945 Haverford Rd., Bryn Mawr, Pennsylvania 19010. (800) 345-1301. Online version of the periodical of the same name.

PERIODICALS AND NEWSLETTERS

Environmental Conference. TAPPI Press, Technology Park/Atlanta, PO Box 105113, Atlanta, Georgia 30348. (404) 446-1400. 1980-. Annually. Conference papers include topics relating to the environment such as: landfill permitting; bleach plant emissions; environmental control; sludge dewatering; air toxics regulations and risk assessment as they relate to pulp and paper industry; water reuse and load control; water toxins; air modeling; and other pertinent environmental topics.

Paper Stock Report. McEntee Media Corp., 13727 Holland Rd., Cleveland, Ohio 44142-3920. (216) 362-7979. Weekly. Paper recycling markets and prices of various grades of waste paper.

TAPPI Journal. Technical Association of the Pulp and Paper Industry, Box 105113, Atlanta, Georgia 30348-

5113. (404) 446-1400. Monthly. Covers new technology and advancements in the pulp and paper industry.

STATISTICS SOURCES

Disposable Paper Products. FIND/SVP, 625 Avenue of the Americas, New York, New York 10011. (212) 645-4500. 1990. Addresses the problems and questions facing marketers of disposable paper products–facial tissue, paper towels, toilet paper and paper napkins.

Facing America's Trash: What Next for Municipal Solid Waste?. U.S. Office of Technology Assessment. Van Nostrand Reinhold, Washington, District of Columbia 20401. (202) 512-0000. 1991. Generation, composition and cost of recycling municipal solid waste.

Newsprint Division Monthly Statistical Report. American Paper Institute, 260 Madison Ave., New York, New York 10016. Monthly. Newsprint production, shipments, inventory, and plant capacity.

Paper, Paperboard, and Wood Pulp: Monthly Statistical Summary. American Paper Institute, 260 Madison Ave., New York, New York 10016. Monthly.

Pulp and Paper. Forest Industries, 500 Howard St., San Francisco, California 94105. Monthly. Production, engineering/maintenance, management, and marketing.

TRADE ASSOCIATIONS AND PROFESSIONAL SOCIETIES

American Paper Institute. 260 Madison Ave., New York, New York 10016. (212) 340-0600.

Institute of Paper Chemistry. 1043 E. South River St., Appleton, Wisconsin 54915. (414) 734-9251.

National Council of the Paper Industry for Air and Stream Improvements. 260 Madison Ave., New York, New York 10016. (212) 532-9000.

National Paperbox and Packaging Association. 1201 E. Abingdon Dr., Ste. 203, Alexandria, Virginia 22314. (703) 684-2212.

Paper Industry Management Association. 2400 E. Oakton St., Suite 100, Arlington Hts., Illinois 60005. (708) 956-0250.

Technical Association of the Pulp and Paper Industry. Box 105113, Atlanta, Georgia 30348-5113. (404) 446-1400.

United Paperworkers International Union. PO Box 1475, Nashville, Tennessee 37202. (615) 834-8590.

PAPER PULP MILLS

See also: WASTEWATER TREATMENT

ABSTRACTING AND INDEXING SERVICES

Engineering Index. The Engineering Index Inc., 345 E. 47th St., New York, New York 10017. 1962-.

Pollution Abstracts. Cambridge Scientific Abstracts, 5161 River Rd., Bethesda, Maryland 20816. (301) 961-6750. Six/year. Indexes worldwide technical literature on environmental pollution. Covers air pollution, marine and freshwater pollution, sewage and wastewater treatment,

waste management, toxicology and health, noise pollution, radiation, land pollution, and environmental policies, programs, legislation, and education. Also available online.

DIRECTORIES

Lockwood-Post's Directory of the Pulp, Paper and Allied Trades. Miller Freeman Publications, 370 Lexington Ave., New York, New York 10017. (212) 683-9294. 1987. Annual.

Powder/Bulk Solids Guide and Directory. Gordon Publications, 301 Gibraltar Dr., Morris Plains, New Jersey 07950. (201) 292-5100.

PPI International Pulp & Paper Directory. Miller Freeman Publications, Inc., 500 Howard St., San Francisco, California 94105. (415) 397-1881.

ENCYCLOPEDIAS AND DICTIONARIES

Encyclopedia of Chemical Processing and Design. John J. Mcketta and W. A. Cunningham. Marcel Dekker, Inc., 270 Madison Ave., New York, New York 10016. (212) 696-9000; (800) 228-1160. 1992. Thirty-eight volumes.

Kirk-Othmer Encyclopedia of Chemical Technology. J. I. Kroschwitz, ed. John Wiley & Sons, Inc., 605 3rd Ave., New York, New York 10158-0012. (212) 850-6000. 1992-. All articles in the new edition have been rewritten and updated adding new subjects such as biotechnology, computer topics, analytical techniques and instrumentation, environmental concerns, fuels and energy, inorganic and solid state chemistry; composite materials and material science in general, and pharmaceuticals. Also available online.

McGraw-Hill Encyclopedia of Environmental Science. Sybil P. Parker. McGraw-Hill Science & Engineering Books, 11 W. 19th St., New York, New York 10011. (212) 337-6010. 1980. Covers ecology, man's influence on nature, and environmental protection.

GENERAL WORKS

Efficiency in Environmental Regulation: A Benefit-Cost Analysis of Alternative Approaches. Kluwer Academic Publishers, 101 Philip Dr., Assinippi Park, Norwell, Massachusetts 02061-0358. (617) 871-6600. Quantitative assessment of the efficiency of the EPA's regulation of conventional air and water pollutants from the pulp and paper industry.

Environmental Issues: An Anthology of 1989. Thomas W. Joyce, ed. TAPPI Press, Technology Park/Atlanta, PO Box 105113, Atlanta, Georgia 30348. (404) 446-1400. 1990. Contains 39 papers on environmental, safety and occupational health concerns from 11 TAPPI, CPPA and AIChE meetings held during 1989. Also included is a literature review of over 200 papers published in 1989.

Industrial Environmental Control. A. M. Springer. John Wiley & Sons, Inc., 605 3rd Ave., New York, New York 10158-0012. (212) 850-6000. 1986. Covers in great detail all the basic information regarding industrial pollution and its treatment.

The Mighty Rain Forest. John Nicol. Sterling Pub. Co. Inc., 387 Park Ave. S., New York, New York 10016. (212) 532-7160; (800) 367-9692. 1990. Focuses on the emotive debate on the environment regarding rainforests

and the paper manufacturers. Includes a bibliography and a list of organizations working in rainforest conservation.

State-of-the-Art of the Pulp and Paper Industry. Neil McCubbin. Environmental Protection Service, 425 St. Joseph Blvd., 3rd Fl., Hull, Quebec, Canada K1A 0H3. (613) 953-5921. 1984. Control technology of the wood-pulp industry; paper making and trade.

HANDBOOKS AND MANUALS

Environmental Control for Pulp and Paper Mills. Howard Edde. Noyes Publications, 120 Mill Rd., Park Ridge, New Jersey 07656. (201) 391-8484. 1984. Pollution technology review of pulp and paper making and trade.

ONLINE DATA BASES

Computerized Engineering Index–COMPENDEX. Engineering Information Inc., 345 E. 47th St., New York, New York 10017. (212) 705-7600.

FOREST. Forest Products Research Society, 2801 Marshall Court, Madison, Wisconsin 53705. (608) 231-1361.

Kirk-Othmer Encyclopedia of Chemical Technology. John Wiley & Sons, Inc., 605 3rd Ave., 5th Floor, New York, New York 10158. (212) 850-6000. Online version of the publication of the same name.

PAPERCHEM. Institute of Paper Science & Technology, Inc., 575 14th St., N.W., Atlanta, Georgia 30318. (404) 853-9500.

Pulp and Paper Data Bank. Resource Information Systems, 110 Great Rd., Bedford, Massachusetts 01730. (617) 271-0030.

RISI Forest Products. Resource Information Systems, 110 Great Rd., Bedford, Massachusetts 01730. (617) 271-0030.

SCISEARCH. Institute for Scientific Information, University City Science Center, 3501 Market St., Philadelphia, Pennsylvania 19104. (215) 386-0100.

PERIODICALS AND NEWSLETTERS

Bulletin Board. National Council of the Paper Industry for Air and Stream Improvements, 260 Madison Avenue, New York, New York 10016. (212) 532-9000. Biweekly. Issues of interest to the paper industry.

Environmental Conference. TAPPI Press, Technology Park/Atlanta, PO Box 105113, Atlanta, Georgia 30348. (404) 446-1400. 1980-. Annually. Conference papers include topics relating to the environment such as: landfill permitting; bleach plant emissions; environmental control; sludge dewatering; air toxics regulations and risk assessment as they relate to pulp and paper industry; water reuse and load control; water toxins; air modeling; and other pertinent environmental topics.

TAPPI Journal. Technical Association of the Pulp and Paper Industry, Box 105113, Atlanta, Georgia 30348-5113. (404) 446-1400. Monthly. Covers new technology and advancements in the pulp and paper industry.

TRADE ASSOCIATIONS AND PROFESSIONAL SOCIETIES

Institute of Paper Chemistry. 1043 E. South River St., Appleton, Wisconsin 54915. (414) 734-9251.

National Council of the Paper Industry for Air and Stream Improvements. 260 Madison Ave., New York, New York 10016. (212) 532-9000.

National Paperbox and Packaging Association. 1201 E. Abingdon Dr., Ste. 203, Alexandria, Virginia 22314. (703) 684-2212.

Paper Industry Management Association. 2400 E. Oakton St., Suite 100, Arlington Hts., Illinois 60005. (708) 956-0250.

Technical Association of the Pulp and Paper Industry. Box 105113, Atlanta, Georgia 30348-5113. (404) 446-1400.

United Paperworkers International Union. PO Box 1475, Nashville, Tennessee 37202. (615) 834-8590.

PARAQUAT

ABSTRACTING AND INDEXING SERVICES

Biological Abstracts. BIOSIS, 2100 Arch St., Philadelphia, Pennsylvania 19103-1399. (215) 587-4800. 1927-.

Chemical Abstracts. Chemical Abstracts Service, 2540 Olentangy River Rd., PO Box 3012, Columbus, Ohio 43210. (800) 848-6533. 1907-.

Pollution Abstracts. Cambridge Scientific Abstracts, 5161 River Rd., Bethesda, Maryland 20816. (301) 961-6750. Six/year. Indexes worldwide technical literature on environmental pollution. Covers air pollution, marine and freshwater pollution, sewage and wastewater treatment, waste management, toxicology and health, noise pollution, radiation, land pollution, and environmental policies, programs, legislation, and education. Also available online.

Science Citation Index. Institute for Scientific Information, 3501 Market St., Philadelphia, Pennsylvania 19104. 1961-.

ENCYCLOPEDIAS AND DICTIONARIES

Encyclopedia of Trademarks and Synonyms. H. Bennett, ed. Chemical Publishing Co., 80 Eighth Ave., New York, New York 10011. (212) 255-1950. 1981. Three volumes. Includes chemical compounds, compositions consisting of one or more chemicals and other products. Also included are abbreviated names and WHO free names.

McGraw-Hill Encyclopedia of Science and Technology. McGraw-Hill, 1221 Avenue of the Americas, New York, New York 10020. (212) 512-2000 or (800) 262-4729. 1992. Seventh edition. Issued in multiple volumes including index. Includes all science and technology broad subject areas.

Van Nostrand's Scientific Encyclopedia. Glenn D. Considine, ed. Van Nostrand Reinhold, 115 5th Ave., New York, New York 10003. (212) 254-3232. 1983. Sixth edition. Includes all broad subject areas in science.

GENERAL WORKS

Biochemical Mechanisms of Paraquat Toxicity. Anne Pomeroy Autor, ed. Academic Press, c/o Harcourt Brace Jovanovich Inc., 6277 Sea Harbor Dr., Orlando, Florida 32887. (800) 346-8648. 1977. Proceedings of the Iowa Symposium on Toxic Mechanisms, 1st, 1976, Iowa City, IA.

Eradication of Marijuana with Paraquat. U.S. G.P.O., Washington, District of Columbia 20401. (202) 512-0000. 1985. Hearings before the Subcommittee on Crime of the Judiciary Committee, House of Representatives, 98th Congress, 1st session, October 5 and November 17, 1983.

Is Paraquat Sprayed Marihuana Harmful or Not?. U.S. G.P.O., Washington, District of Columbia 20401. (202) 512-0000. 1980. Hearing before the select committee on Narcotics and Abuse Control, House of Representatives, 96th Congress, first session, November 29, 1979. Discusses the effects of sprayed marihuana effects on humans.

Paraquat and Diquat. World Health Organization, Ave. Appia, Geneva, Switzerland CH-1211. 1984. Covers toxicology and environmental aspects of herbicides and heterocyclic compounds.

Paraquat Hazards to Fish, Wildlife, and Invertebrates. U.S. Department of the Interior, Fish and Wildlife Service, 1849 C St. NW, Washington, District of Columbia 20240. (202) 208-3171. 1990.

Toxicological and Teratogenic Studies with Paraquat. Northern Illinois University, Department of Biological Sciences, Dekalb, Illinois 60115. 1984.

The Toxicology of Paraquat, Diquat and Morfamquat. Aurelio Pasi. Hans Huber, Langgasstr. 76, Bern, Switzerland D-3000. 1978. The toxicology of paraquat and pyridinium compounds is described.

The Use of Paraquat to Eradicate Illicit Marihuana Crops and the Health Implications of Paraquat-Contaminated Marihuana on the U.S. Market. Select Committee on Narcotics and Abuse Control, U.S. Government Printing Office, Washington, District of Columbia 2042-9325. (202) 783-3238. 1980. A report of the Select Committee on Narcotics and Abuse Control, 96th Congress, 2nd session.

ONLINE DATA BASES

BIOSIS Previews. BIOSIS, 2100 Arch St., Philadelphia, Pennsylvania 19103-1399. (215) 587-4800. Largest and most comprehensive database of research in the life sciences. Contains citations for nearly 9000 primary research journals, monographs, reviews, symposia, preliminary reports, semi-popular journals, selected institutional reports, government reports and research communications.

CERCLIS. Chemical Information Systems, Inc., 7215 York Rd., Baltimore, Maryland 21212. (301) 321-8440. Information on hazardous waste disposal sites that have either been listed by the EPA on the National Priority List (NPL) or nominated for consideration for the NPL.

Chemical Abstracts-CA. Chemical Abstracts Service, 2540 Olentangy River Rd., P.O. Box 3012, Columbus, Ohio 43210. (800) 848-6533 or (614) 421-3600. Information sources include 9000 journals, patents from 27 countries, two industrial property organizations, new books, conference proceedings, and government research reports.

Chemical Abstracts Chemical Name Directory-CHEMNAME. Chemical Abstracts Service, 2540 Olentangy River Rd., P.O. Box 3012, Columbus, Ohio 43210. (800)

848-6533 or (614) 421-3600. Listing of chemical substances in a dictionary type file. The Chemical Abstracts (CAS) Registry Number, molecular formula, Chemical Abstracts (CA) Substance Index Name, available synonyms, ring data and other chemical substance information is given for each entry.

Chemical Carcinogenesis Research Information System–CCRIS. National Library of Medicine, 8600 Rockville Pike, Bethesda, Maryland 20894. (800) 638-8480. Individual assay results and test conditions for 1,451 chemicals in the areas of carcinogenicity, mutagenicity, tumor promotion, and cocarcinogenicity.

SCISEARCH. Institute for Scientific Information, University City Science Center, 3501 Market St., Philadelphia, Pennsylvania 19104. (215) 386-0100.

PARASITES

See: INSECTS

PARATHION

ABSTRACTING AND INDEXING SERVICES

Applied Ecology Abstracts Studies in Renewable Natural Resources. Information Retrieval Ltd., 1911 Jefferson Davis Highway, Arlington, Virginia 22202. 1975-. Monthly.

Biological Abstracts. BIOSIS, 2100 Arch St., Philadelphia, Pennsylvania 19103-1399. (215) 587-4800. 1927-.

Biotechnology Research Abstracts. Cambridge Scientific Abstracts, 5161 River Rd., Bethesda, Maryland 20816. (301) 961-6750. Monthly. Includes such broad areas as genetic intervention, biochemical genetics, and microbiological techniques.

Chemical Abstracts. Chemical Abstracts Service, 2540 Olentangy River Rd., PO Box 3012, Columbus, Ohio 43210. (800) 848-6533. 1907-.

Multimedia Index to Ecology. National Information Center for Educational Media, University of Southern California, Los Angeles, California 90007.

Pollution Abstracts. Cambridge Scientific Abstracts, 5161 River Rd., Bethesda, Maryland 20816. (301) 961-6750. Six/year. Indexes worldwide technical literature on environmental pollution. Covers air pollution, marine and freshwater pollution, sewage and wastewater treatment, waste management, toxicology and health, noise pollution, radiation, land pollution, and environmental policies, programs, legislation, and education. Also available online.

Science Citation Index. Institute for Scientific Information, 3501 Market St., Philadelphia, Pennsylvania 19104. 1961-.

ENCYCLOPEDIAS AND DICTIONARIES

Encyclopedia of Human Biology. Renato Dulbecco, ed. Academic Press, c/o Harcourt Brace Jovanovich Inc., 6277 Sea Harbor Dr., Orlando, Florida 32887. (800) 346-8648. 1991. Eight volumes.

Encyclopedia of Trademarks and Synonyms. H. Bennett, ed. Chemical Publishing Co., 80 Eighth Ave., New York, New York 10011. (212) 255-1950. 1981. Three volumes. Includes chemical compounds, compositions consisting of one or more chemicals and other products. Also included are abbreviated names and WHO free names.

McGraw-Hill Encyclopedia of Science and Technology. McGraw-Hill, 1221 Avenue of the Americas, New York, New York 10020. (212) 512-2000 or (800) 262-4729. 1992. Seventh edition. Issued in multiple volumes including index. Includes all science and technology broad subject areas.

Van Nostrand's Scientific Encyclopedia. Glenn D. Considine, ed. Van Nostrand Reinhold, 115 5th Ave., New York, New York 10003. (212) 254-3232. 1983. Sixth edition. Includes all broad subject areas in science.

GENERAL WORKS

Ecological Impact of Parathion in Soybeans. U.S. Department of Agriculture, Agricultural Research Service, 14 Independence Ave. SW, Washington, District of Columbia 20250. (202) 447-7454. 1982.

Toxicological Evaluation of Parathion and Azinphosmethyl in Freshwater Model Ecosystems. Centre for Agricultural Publishing and Documentation, Wageningen, Netherlands 1980. Covers water pollution and environmental aspects of pesticides.

ONLINE DATA BASES

BIOSIS Previews. BIOSIS, 2100 Arch St., Philadelphia, Pennsylvania 19103-1399. (215) 587-4800. Largest and most comprehensive database of research in the life sciences. Contains citations for nearly 9000 primary research journals, monographs, reviews, symposia, preliminary reports, semi-popular journals, selected institutional reports, government reports and research communications.

CERCLIS. Chemical Information Systems, Inc., 7215 York Rd., Baltimore, Maryland 21212. (301) 321-8440. Information on hazardous waste disposal sites that have either been listed by the EPA on the National Priority List (NPL) or nominated for consideration for the NPL.

Chemical Abstracts-CA. Chemical Abstracts Service, 2540 Olentangy River Rd., P.O. Box 3012, Columbus, Ohio 43210. (800) 848-6533 or (614) 421-3600. Information sources include 9000 journals, patents from 27 countries, two industrial property organizations, new books, conference proceedings, and government research reports.

Chemical Abstracts Chemical Name Directory-CHEMNAME. Chemical Abstracts Service, 2540 Olentangy River Rd., P.O. Box 3012, Columbus, Ohio 43210. (800) 848-6533 or (614) 421-3600. Listing of chemical substances in a dictionary type file. The Chemical Abstracts (CAS) Registry Number, molecular formula, Chemical Abstracts (CA) Substance Index Name, available synonyms, ring data and other chemical substance information is given for each entry.

Chemical Carcinogenesis Research Information System–CCRIS. National Library of Medicine, 8600 Rockville Pike, Bethesda, Maryland 20894. (800) 638-8480. Individual assay results and test conditions for 1,451 chemicals in the areas of carcinogenicity, mutagenicity, tumor promotion, and cocarcinogenicity.

Chemical Collection System/Request Tracking–CCS/RTS. U.S. Environmental Protection Agency, Office of Pesticides and Toxic Substances, 401 M St., SW, Washington, District of Columbia 20460. (202) 260-2090. Contains information on various properties of a number of chemicals including environmental effects, test and analysis methods, and health effects. Available from EPA.

Chemical Dictionary Online–CHEMLINE. Chemical Abstracts Service, 2540 Olentangy River Rd., Columbus, Ohio 43210. (614) 421-3600 or (800) 848-6533. Part of MEDLINE of the National Library of Medicine (NLM). File of 900,000 names for chemical substances, representing 450,000 unique compounds. It contains such information as Chemical Abstracts (CA) Service Registry Numbers, molecular formulas, preferred chemical nomenclature, and generic and ring structure information. Available on NLM's ELHILL system.

Chemical Exposure. Science Applications International Corp., Health & Environmental Information, P.O. Box 2501, Oak Ridge, Tennessee 37831. (615) 482-9031. Database of chemicals that have been identified in both human tissues and body fluids and in feral and food animals. Contains reference to journal articles, conferences, and reports. Covers the whole fields of information related to human and animal exposure to food, air, and water contaminants and pharmaceuticals. Its records include information on chemical properties, formulas, tissues measured, analytical method used, demographics and more. Available on DIALOG.

PARATRANSIT

See: TRANSPORTATION

PARTICULATES

See also: AIR POLLUTION

ABSTRACTING AND INDEXING SERVICES

Biological Abstracts. BIOSIS, 2100 Arch St., Philadelphia, Pennsylvania 19103-1399. (215) 587-4800. 1927-.

Chemical Abstracts. Chemical Abstracts Service, 2540 Olentangy River Rd., PO Box 3012, Columbus, Ohio 43210. (800) 848-6533. 1907-.

Current Awareness in Particle Technology. Particle Technology Information Service, University of Technology, Loughborough, England LE11 3TU. (0509) 222528. Monthly. Includes particles, sampling, instrumentation, occupational health, powder and compact properties, handling and mixing, sintering, porous media flow gas filtration,drying, colloids, and other related subjects. Scans over 292 journals on the subjects and retrieves relevant citations on the subject.

Environment Abstracts. Bowker A & I Publishing, 121 Chanlon Rd., New Providence, New Jersey 07974. (908) 464-6800. 1974-.

Environment Index. Environment Information Center, Index Research Department, 124 E. 39th St., New York, New York 10016. 1971-. Annual.

Environmental Information Connection–EIC. Planning Information Program, Dept. of Urban and Regional Planning, University of Illinois, 1003 West Nevada, Urbana, Illinois 61801. (217) 333-1369. Also available online.

Environmental Periodicals Bibliography. Environmental Studies Institute, International Academy at Santa Barbara, 800 Garden St., Suite D, Santa Barbara, California 93101. (805) 965-5010. Also available online.

Pollution Abstracts. Cambridge Scientific Abstracts, 5161 River Rd., Bethesda, Maryland 20816. (301) 961-6750. Six/year. Indexes worldwide technical literature on environmental pollution. Covers air pollution, marine and freshwater pollution, sewage and wastewater treatment, waste management, toxicology and health, noise pollution, radiation, land pollution, and environmental policies, programs, legislation, and education. Also available online.

Science Citation Index. Institute for Scientific Information, 3501 Market St., Philadelphia, Pennsylvania 19104. 1961-.

BIBLIOGRAPHIES

EPA Publications Bibliography. U.S. Environmental Protection Agency, Library Systems Branch, 401 M St., SW, Washington, District of Columbia 20460. (202) 260-2090. Quarterly.

Particulates and Air Pollution: An Annotated Bibliography. U.S. Environmental Protection Agency, Office of Air Quality Planning Standards, Research Triangle Park, North Carolina 27711. 1977.

ENCYCLOPEDIAS AND DICTIONARIES

Dictionary of Colloid and Surface Science. Paul Becher. Marcel Dekker, Inc., 270 Madison Ave., New York, New York 10016. (212) 696-9000; (800) 228-1160. 1990. Dictionary deals with the areas of colloids, surface chemistry, and the physics and technology involved with surfaces.

Encyclopedia of Chemical Processing and Design. John J. Mcketta and W. A. Cunningham. Marcel Dekker, Inc., 270 Madison Ave., New York, New York 10016. (212) 696-9000; (800) 228-1160. 1992. Thirty-eight volumes.

Kirk-Othmer Encyclopedia of Chemical Technology. J. I. Kroschwitz, ed. John Wiley & Sons, Inc., 605 3rd Ave., New York, New York 10158-0012. (212) 850-6000. 1992-. All articles in the new edition have been rewritten and updated adding new subjects such as biotechnology, computer topics, analytical techniques and instrumentation, environmental concerns, fuels and energy, inorganic and solid state chemistry; composite materials and material science in general, and pharmaceuticals. Also available online.

Van Nostrand's Scientific Encyclopedia. Glenn D. Considine, ed. Van Nostrand Reinhold, 115 5th Ave., New York, New York 10003. (212) 254-3232. 1983. Sixth edition. Includes all broad subject areas in science.

GENERAL WORKS

Aerosol Sampling: Science and Practice. J. H. Vincent. John Wiley & Sons, Inc., 605 3rd Ave., New York, New York 10158-0012. (212) 850-6000. 1989. Details the sampling of aerosols with a "real world" approach. Makes the connection between theory and practice.

Air Pollution Control. Howard E. Hesketh. Technomic Publishing Co., 851 New Holland Ave., Box 3535, Lancaster, Pennsylvania 17604. (717) 291-5609. 1991. Presents both theory and application data. Provides a background relevant to behavior theories and control techniques for capturing gaseous and particulate air pollutants.

Characterization of Urban and Rural Inhalable Particulates. Donald F. Gatz. Illinois Department of Energy and Natural Resources, 325 W. Adams St., Rm. 300, Springfield, Illinois 62706. (217) 785-2800. 1983. Covers the measurement of dust and environmental monitoring of air pollution.

Industrial Environmental Control. A. M. Springer. John Wiley & Sons, Inc., 605 3rd Ave., New York, New York 10158-0012. (212) 850-6000. 1986. Covers in great detail all the basic information regarding industrial pollution and its treatment.

Particulates and Fine Dust Removal: Processes and Equipment. Marshall Sittig. Noyes Publications, 120 Mill Rd., Park Ridge, New Jersey 07656. (201) 391-8484. 1977. Exhaust systems and dust removal.

Particulates in Water. Michael Kavanaugh. American Chemical Society, 1155 16th St. N.W., Washington, District of Columbia 20036. (800) 227-5558. 1980. Characterizations, fate, effects, and removal.

ONLINE DATA BASES

BIOSIS Previews. BIOSIS, 2100 Arch St., Philadelphia, Pennsylvania 19103-1399. (215) 587-4800. Largest and most comprehensive database of research in the life sciences. Contains citations for nearly 9000 primary research journals, monographs, reviews, symposia, preliminary reports, semi-popular journals, selected institutional reports, government reports and research communications.

Chemical Abstracts-CA. Chemical Abstracts Service, 2540 Olentangy River Rd., P.O. Box 3012, Columbus, Ohio 43210. (800) 848-6533 or (614) 421-3600. Information sources include 9000 journals, patents from 27 countries, two industrial property organizations, new books, conference proceedings, and government research reports.

Enviro/Energyline Abstracts Plus. R. R. Bowker Co., 121 Chanlon Rd., New Providence, New Jersey 07974. (908) 464-6800.

Environmental Periodicals Bibliography. National Information Services Corp., Ste. 6, Wyman Towers, 3100 St. Paul St., Baltimore, Maryland 21218. (410)243-0797. Online version of abstract of same name.

Kirk-Othmer Encyclopedia of Chemical Technology. John Wiley & Sons, Inc., 605 3rd Ave., 5th Floor, New York, New York 10158. (212) 850-6000. Online version of the publication of the same name.

Monthly Catalog of United States Government Publications. U.S. G.P.O., Supt. of Docs., PO Box 371954, Pittsburgh, Pennsylvania 15250-7954. (202) 512-0000.

National Technical Information Service. U.S. Department of Commerce, National Technical Information Service, Office of Data Base Services, 5285 Port Royal Rd., Springfield, Virginia 22161. (703) 487-4807. Bibliographic database of government sponsored research and technical reports.

STATISTICS SOURCES

Progress in the Prevention and Control of Air Pollution. U.S. Environmental Protection Agency. National Technical Information Service, Springfield, Virginia 22161. (703) 487-4650. Annual. Covers air quality trends and control of radon, suspended particulates, sulfur and nitrogen oxides, carbon monoxide, ozone and lead.

PASSENGER TRANSPORTATION

See: TRANSPORTATION

PCBS

ABSTRACTING AND INDEXING SERVICES

ASFA Aquaculture Abstracts. Cambridge Scientific Abstracts, Inc., 5161 River Rd., Bethesda, Maryland 20816. (301) 961-6750. 1984.

Chemical Abstracts. Chemical Abstracts Service, 2540 Olentangy River Rd., PO Box 3012, Columbus, Ohio 43210. (800) 848-6533. 1907-.

Ecology Abstracts. Cambridge Scientific Abstracts, 5161 River Rd., Bethesda, Maryland 20816. (301) 961-6750. Monthly.

Engineering Index. The Engineering Index Inc., 345 E. 47th St., New York, New York 10017. 1962-.

Environment Abstracts. Bowker A & I Publishing, 121 Chanlon Rd., New Providence, New Jersey 07974. (908) 464-6800. 1974-.

Environment Index. Environment Information Center, Index Research Department, 124 E. 39th St., New York, New York 10016. 1971-. Annual.

Environmental Information Connection-EIC. Planning Information Program, Dept. of Urban and Regional Planning, University of Illinois, 1003 West Nevada, Urbana, Illinois 61801. (217) 333-1369. Also available online.

Environmental Periodicals Bibliography. Environmental Studies Institute, International Academy at Santa Barbara, 800 Garden St., Suite D, Santa Barbara, California 93101. (805) 965-5010. Also available online.

General Science Index. H. W. Wilson Co., 950 University Ave., Bronx, New York 10452. 1978-. Monthly, also issued in annual cumulation. Cumulative subject index to English language periodicals in the subject fields of astronomy, botany, chemistry, earth science, environment and conservation, food and nutrition, genetics, mathematics, medicine and health, microbiology, oceanography, physics, physiology and zoology.

Pollution Abstracts. Cambridge Scientific Abstracts, 5161 River Rd., Bethesda, Maryland 20816. (301) 961-6750. Six/year. Indexes worldwide technical literature on environmental pollution. Covers air pollution, marine and freshwater pollution, sewage and wastewater treatment, waste management, toxicology and health, noise pollution, radiation, land pollution, and environmental policies, programs, legislation, and education. Also available online.

Science Citation Index. Institute for Scientific Information, 3501 Market St., Philadelphia, Pennsylvania 19104. 1961-.

BIBLIOGRAPHIES

EPA Publications Bibliography. U.S. Environmental Protection Agency, Library Systems Branch, 401 M St., SW, Washington, District of Columbia 20460. (202) 260-2090. Quarterly.

Toxicology of Polychlorinated Biphenyl Compounds. S. Jackson. U.S. Department of Health and Human Services, Public Health Services, National Institutes of Health, 9000 Rockville Pike, Bethesda, Maryland 20892. (301) 496-4000. 1981.

ENCYCLOPEDIAS AND DICTIONARIES

Encyclopedia of Chemical Technology. Raymond E. Kirk. John Wiley & Sons, Inc., 605 3rd Ave., New York, New York 10158-0012. (212) 850-6000. 1991-. 4th ed. Also known as Kirk Othmer Encyclopedia of Chemical Technology; consists of 26 volumes.

Handbook of Hazardous Chemicals and Carcinogens. Marshall Sittig. Noyes Publications, 120 Mill Rd., Park Ridge, New Jersey 07656. (201) 391-8484. 1985.

McGraw-Hill Encyclopedia of Science and Technology. McGraw-Hill, 1221 Avenue of the Americas, New York, New York 10020. (212) 512-2000 or (800) 262-4729. 1992. Seventh edition. Issued in multiple volumes including index. Includes all science and technology broad subject areas.

GENERAL WORKS

Applying for a Permit to Destroy PCB Waste Oil. S. G. Zelenski. Center for Environmental Research Information, U.S. Environmental Protection Agency, 26 W. Martin Luther King Dr., Cincinnati, Ohio 45268. (513) 569-7931. 1981. Covers hazardous wastes, incineration licenses, and polychlorinated biphenyls.

The Chemistry of PCBs. O. Hutzinger, et al. CRC Press, 2000 Corporate Blvd. N.W., Boca Raton, Florida 33431. (407) 994-0555; (800) 272-7737. 1983.

EPA's Final PCB Ban Rule. U.S. Environmental Protection Agency, Industrial Assistance Office and Chemical Control Division, Office of Toxic Substances, 401 M St., S.W., Washington, District of Columbia 20460. (202) 260-2090. 1980.

Locating and Estimating Air Emission from Sources of Polychlorinated Biphenyls. U.S. Environmental Protection Agency, MD 75, Research Triangle Park, North Carolina 27711. 1987. Environmental aspects of Polychlorinated Biphenyls.

Measurement of PCB Emissions from Combustion Sources. Philip L. Levins. National Technical Information Service, 5285 Port Royal Rd., Springfield, Virginia 22161. (703) 487-4650. 1979. Covers combustion measurement, polychlorinated biphenyls and emission spectroscopy.

PCB Compliance Guide for Electrical Equipment. John W. Coryell. Bureau of National Affairs, 1231 25th St. N.W., Washington, District of Columbia 20037. (202) 452-4200. 1991.

PCBs and the Environment. John S. Waid, ed. CRC Press, 2000 Corporate Blvd. N.W., Boca Raton, Florida 33431. (407) 994-0555; (800) 272-7737. 1987. 3 vols.

PCBs: Human and Environmental Hazards. Frank M. D'itri and Michael A. Kamrin, eds. Ann Arbor Science, 230 Collingwood, Ann Arbor, Michigan 48106. 1983.

Physical Behavior of PCBs in the Great Lakes. Donald Mackay. Ann Arbor Science, 230 Collingwood, Ann Arbor, Michigan 48106. 1983.

GOVERNMENTAL ORGANIZATIONS

U.S. Environmental Protection Agency, TS-799: Toxic Assistance Office. 401 M St., S.W., Washington, District of Columbia 20460. (202) 382-3790.

HANDBOOKS AND MANUALS

Handbook of Chemical Property Estimation Methods. Warren J. Lyman, et al. McGraw-Hill Science & Engineering Books, 11 W. 19th St., New York, New York 10011. (212) 337-6010. 1982.

Handbook of Environmental Data on Organic Chemicals. Karel Verschueren. Van Nostrand Reinhold, 115 5th Ave., New York, New York 10003. (212) 254-3232. 1983. Covers individual substances as well as mixtures and preparations. The profiles include: properties, air pollution factors, water pollution factors, and biological effects.

NIOSH Pocket Guide to Chemical Hazards. National Institute for Occupational Safety and Health, 1600 Clifton Rd. NE, Atlanta, Georgia 30333. (404) 639-3286. 1990. Presents sources of general industrial hygiene and medical surveillance information for workers, employees and others. Presents key information and data in an abbreviated format for 398 individual chemicals or chemical types.

PCB Regulation Manual. Glenn Kuntz. PennWell Books, PO Box 21288, Tulsa, Oklahoma 74121. (918) 831-9421; (800) 752-9764. 1990. 3rd ed. Provides the corporate environmental manager or plant engineer with a practical guide to compliance with PCB regulations.

Treatability Manual. U.S. Environmental Protection Agency, Office of Research and Development, 401 M St., SW, Washington, District of Columbia 20460. (202) 260-2090. 1983-. V.1 Treatability data. v.2 Change 2. Industrial Descriptions. v.3 Change 2. Technology for Control/removal of pollutants. v.4. Cost estimating. v.5. Change 2 summary.

User's Guide to the EPA PCB Spill Cleanup Policy. Glenn Kuntz. National Rural Electric Cooperative Assoc., 1800 Massachusetts Ave., NW, Washington, District of Columbia 20036. (202) 857-9598. 1988. Guide for PCB spill cleanup. Includes detailed review of published and unpublished information on the subject. This is NRECA research project 87-3.

ONLINE DATA BASES

CERCLIS. Chemical Information Systems, Inc., 7215 York Rd., Baltimore, Maryland 21212. (301) 321-8440. Information on hazardous waste disposal sites that have either been listed by the EPA on the National Priority List (NPL) or nominated for consideration for the NPL.

Chemical Abstracts-CA. Chemical Abstracts Service, 2540 Olentangy River Rd., P.O. Box 3012, Columbus, Ohio 43210. (800) 848-6533 or (614) 421-3600. Information sources include 9000 journals, patents from 27 countries, two industrial property organizations, new books, conference proceedings, and government research reports.

Chemical Carcinogenesis Research Information System–CCRIS. National Library of Medicine, 8600 Rockville Pike, Bethesda, Maryland 20894. (800) 638-8480. Individual assay results and test conditions for 1,451 chemicals in the areas of carcinogenicity, mutagenicity, tumor promotion, and cocarcinogenicity.

Computerized Engineering Index–COMPENDEX. Engineering Information Inc., 345 E. 47th St., New York, New York 10017. (212) 705-7600.

Enviro/Energyline Abstracts Plus. R. R. Bowker Co., 121 Chanlon Rd., New Providence, New Jersey 07974. (908) 464-6800.

Environmental Periodicals Bibliography. National Information Services Corp., Ste. 6, Wyman Towers, 3100 St. Paul St., Baltimore, Maryland 21218. (410)243-0797. Online version of abstract of same name.

Monthly Catalog of United States Government Publications. U.S. G.P.O., Supt. of Docs., PO Box 371954, Pittsburgh, Pennsylvania 15250-7954. (202) 512-0000.

National Technical Information Service. U.S. Department of Commerce, National Technical Information Service, Office of Data Base Services, 5285 Port Royal Rd., Springfield, Virginia 22161. (703) 487-4807. Bibliographic database of government sponsored research and technical reports.

PressNet Environmental Reports. Chemical Information Systems, Inc., 7215 York Rd., Baltimore, Maryland 21212. (301) 321-8440.

PERIODICALS AND NEWSLETTERS

Aquatic Toxicology. Elsevier Science Publishing Co., 655 Avenue of the Americas, New York, New York 10010. (212) 989-5800. 1981-. 6/year.

Bulletin of Environmental Contamination and Toxicology. Springer-Verlag, 175 5th Ave., New York, New York 10010. (212) 460-1500; (800) 777-4643. 1966-. Frequency varies. Disseminates advances and discoveries in the areas of soil, air and food contamination and pollution.

Chemosphere: Chemistry, Biology and Toxicology as Related to Environmental Problems. Pergamon Microforms International, Inc., Fairview Park, Elmsford, New York 10523. (914) 592-7720. 1970-. Offers maximum dissemination of investigations related to the health and safety of every aspect of life. Environmental protection encompasses a very wide field and relies on scientific research in chemistry, biology, physics, toxicology and inter-related disciplines.

Environmental Science and Technology. American Chemical Society, 1155 16th St. N.W., Washington, District of Columbia 20036. (800) 227-5558. 1967-. Monthly. Contains research articles on various aspects of environmental chemistry, interpretative articles by invited experts and commentary on the scientific aspects of environmental management.

TRADE ASSOCIATIONS AND PROFESSIONAL SOCIETIES

American Chemical Society. 1155 16th St., N.W., Washington, District of Columbia 20036. (202) 872-4600.

PEAK DEMAND

See: POWER PLANTS

PEAKING CAPACITY

See: POWER PLANTS

PEAKLOAD PLANT

See: POWER PLANTS

PEAT

See also: FUELS

ABSTRACTING AND INDEXING SERVICES

Biological and Agricultural Index. H.W. Wilson Co., 950 University Ave., Bronx, New York 10452. (800) 367-6770. 1916-. Monthly.

Engineering Index. The Engineering Index Inc., 345 E. 47th St., New York, New York 10017. 1962-.

General Science Index. H. W. Wilson Co., 950 University Ave., Bronx, New York 10452. 1978-. Monthly, also issued in annual cumulation. Cumulative subject index to English language periodicals in the subject fields of astronomy, botany, chemistry, earth science, environment and conservation, food and nutrition, genetics, mathematics, medicine and health, microbiology, oceanography, physics, physiology and zoology.

Science Citation Index. Institute for Scientific Information, 3501 Market St., Philadelphia, Pennsylvania 19104. 1961-.

BIBLIOGRAPHIES

Current Contents. Agriculture, Biology and Environmental Sciences. Institute for Scientific Information, 3501 Market St., Philadelphia, Pennsylvania 19104. (800) 523-1857. 1973-. Previous title: Current Contents. Agricultural, Food & Veterinary Sciences. Gives the table of contents of periodicals in the fields of agriculture, biology, environmental and related areas.

ENCYCLOPEDIAS AND DICTIONARIES

Cambridge Dictionary of Biology. Peter M. B. Walker. Cambridge University Press, 40 W. 20th St., New York, New York 10011. (212) 924-3900 or (800) 227-0247. 1989. Includes 10,000 terms in zoology, botany, biochemistry, molecular biology and genetics. Previously published under the title Chambers Biology Dictionary.

A Concise Dictionary of Biology. Elizabeth Martin, ed. Oxford University Press, 200 Madison Ave., New York, New York 10016. (212) 679-7300 or (800) 334-4249. 1990. New edition. Derived from the Concise Science Dictionary, published in 1984.

Van Nostrand's Scientific Encyclopedia. Glenn D. Considine, ed. Van Nostrand Reinhold, 115 5th Ave., New York, New York 10003. (212) 254-3232. 1983. Sixth edition. Includes all broad subject areas in science.

GENERAL WORKS

Peat and Water: Aspects of Water Retention and Dewatering in Peat. Elsevier Science Publishing Co., 655 Avenue of the Americas, New York, New York 10010. (212) 984-5800. 1986. Covers peat, peat bogs, and soil moisture.

HANDBOOKS AND MANUALS

Peat, Industrial Chemistry and Technology. Charles H. Fuchsman. Academic Press, c/o Harcourt Brace Jovanovich Inc., 6277 Sea Harbor Dr., Orlando, Florida 32887. (800) 346-8648. 1980.

ONLINE DATA BASES

Computerized Engineering Index–COMPENDEX. Engineering Information Inc., 345 E. 47th St., New York, New York 10017. (212) 705-7600.

Monthly Catalog of United States Government Publications. U.S. G.P.O., Supt. of Docs., PO Box 371954, Pittsburgh, Pennsylvania 15250-7954. (202) 512-0000.

National Technical Information Service. U.S. Department of Commerce, National Technical Information Service, Office of Data Base Services, 5285 Port Royal Rd., Springfield, Virginia 22161. (703) 487-4807. Bibliographic database of government sponsored research and technical reports.

RESEARCH CENTERS AND INSTITUTES

Bemidji State University, Center for Environmental Studies. Bemidji, Minnesota 56601. (218) 755-2910.

STATISTICS SOURCES

Peat Producers in the United States. U.S. Department of the Interior, Bureau of Mines, 810 7th St. NW, Washington, District of Columbia 20241. (202) 501-9649. Annual. Statistical data in the peat industry in the United States.

TRADE ASSOCIATIONS AND PROFESSIONAL SOCIETIES

United States National Committee of the International Peat Society. P.O. Box 441, Eveleth, Minnesota 55734. (218) 744-2993.

PEDIMENTS
See: EROSION

PELAGIC ZONES
See: OCEANS

PENNSYLVANIA ENVIRONMENTAL AGENCIES

GOVERNMENTAL ORGANIZATIONS

Department of Agriculture: Pesticide Bureau. Chief, Bureau of Plant Industry, Division of Agronomic Services, 2301 North Cameron St., Harrisburg, Pennsylvania 17110-9408. (717) 787-4843.

Department of Labor and Industry: Occupational Safety. Director, Occupational and Industry Safety, 1529 Labor and Industry Bldg., Harrisburg, Pennsylvania 17120. (717) 787-3323.

Environmental Resources Department: Air Quality. Director, Bureau of Air Quality Control, PO Box 2063, Harrisburg, Pennsylvania 17105. (717) 787-9702.

Environmental Resources Department: Coastal Zone Management. Director, Bureau of Water Resources Management, Room 208, Evangelical Press Building, Harrisburg, Pennsylvania 17120. (717) 787-6750.

Environmental Resources Department: Natural Resources. Secretary, PO Box 2063, Harrisburg, Pennsylvania 17105. (717) 787-2814.

Environmental Resources Department: Solid Waste Management. Director, Bureau of Solid Waste Management, PO Box 2063, Harrisburg, Pennsylvania 17105. (717) 787-9870.

Environmental Resources Department: Underground Storage Tanks. Director, Bureau of Water Quality Management, PO Box 2063, Harrisburg, Pennsylvania 17105. (717) 787-2666.

Environmental Resources Department: Water Quality. Director, Bureau of Water Quality Management, PO Box 2063, Harrisburg, Pennsylvania 17105. (717) 787-2666.

PENNSYLVANIA ENVIRONMENTAL LEGISLATION

GENERAL WORKS

Pennsylvania Environmental Law Handbook. Government Institutes, Inc., 4 Research Pl., Ste. 200, Rockville, Maryland 20850. (301) 921-2300. 1991.

PENTACHLOROPHENOL

ABSTRACTING AND INDEXING SERVICES

Biological Abstracts. BIOSIS, 2100 Arch St., Philadelphia, Pennsylvania 19103-1399. (215) 587-4800. 1927-.

Chemical Abstracts. Chemical Abstracts Service, 2540 Olentangy River Rd., PO Box 3012, Columbus, Ohio 43210. (800) 848-6533. 1907-.

General Science Index. H. W. Wilson Co., 950 University Ave., Bronx, New York 10452. 1978-. Monthly, also issued in annual cumulation. Cumulative subject index to English language periodicals in the subject fields of astronomy, botany, chemistry, earth science, environment and conservation, food and nutrition, genetics, mathematics, medicine and health, microbiology, oceanography, physics, physiology and zoology.

Science Citation Index. Institute for Scientific Information, 3501 Market St., Philadelphia, Pennsylvania 19104. 1961-.

BIBLIOGRAPHIES

Adsorption of Energy-Related Organic Pollutants. K. A. Reinbold, et al. National Technical Information Service, 5285 Port Royal Rd., Springfield, Virginia 22161. (703) 487-4650. 1979. Research reporting series #3, Ecological Research; EPA-600/3- 79-086.

ENCYCLOPEDIAS AND DICTIONARIES

Van Nostrand's Scientific Encyclopedia. Glenn D. Considine, ed. Van Nostrand Reinhold, 115 5th Ave., New York, New York 10003. (212) 254-3232. 1983. Sixth edition. Includes all broad subject areas in science.

GENERAL WORKS

Chemistry of Pesticides. K. H. Buchel, ed. John Wiley & Sons, Inc., 605 3rd Ave., New York, New York 10158-0012. (212) 850-6000. 1983.

Environment Impact of Nonpoint Source Pollution. Michael R. Overcash and James M. Davidson, eds. Ann Arbor Science, 230 Collingwood, Ann Arbor, Michigan 48106. 1980.

Herbicides: Chemistry, Degradation, and Mode of Action. P. C. Kearney and D. D. Kaufman, eds. Marcel Dekker, Inc., 270 Madison Ave., New York, New York 10016. (212) 696-9000; (800) 228-1160. 1988. 2d ed.

NTP Technical Report on the Toxicology and Carcinogenesis Studies of Two Pentachlorophenol Technical-Grade Mixtures. National Toxicology Program, U.S. Dept. of Health and Human Services, 9000 Rockville Pike, Research Triangle Park, North Carolina 20892. (301)496-4000. 1989.

Pentachlorophenol Hazards to Fish, Wildlife, and Invertebrates: A Synoptic Review. Ronald Eisler. U.S. Department of the Interior, Fish and Wildlife Service, 1849 C St. NW, 20240. (202)208-5634. 1989. Covers organochlorine compounds, herbicide toxicology, and pesticides and wildlife.

Pentachlorophenol Health and Safety Guide. World Health Organization, Ave. Appia, Geneva, Switzerland CH-1221. (518) 436-9686. 1989.

Water Quality Assessment. W. B. Mills, et al. U.S. Environmental Protection Agency, Office of Research and Development, Environmental Research Laboratory, 401 M St. SW, Washington, District of Columbia 20460. (202) 260-2090. 1985. 2 vols.

HANDBOOKS AND MANUALS

The Biologic and Economic Assessment of Pentachlorophenol, Inorganic Arsenicals, Creosote. U.S. Department of Agriculture, 14 Independence Ave. SW, Washington, District of Columbia 20250. (202) 447-7454. 1980. Covers wood preservative standards.

CRC Handbook of Chemistry and Physics. CRC Press, 2000 Corporate Blvd. N.W., Boca Raton, Florida 33431. (407) 994-0555; (800) 272-7737. 1988. 67th ed.

Handbook of Chemical Property Estimation Methods. Warren J. Lyman, et al. McGraw-Hill Science & Engineering Books, 11 W. 19th St., New York, New York 10011. (212) 337-6010. 1982.

Handbook of Environmental Data on Organic Chemicals. Karel Verschueren. Van Nostrand Reinhold, 115 5th Ave., New York, New York 10003. (212) 254-3232. 1983. Covers individual substances as well as mixtures and preparations. The profiles include: properties, air pollution factors, water pollution factors, and biological effects.

NIOSH Pocket Guide to Chemical Hazards. National Institute for Occupational Safety and Health, 1600 Clifton Rd. NE, Atlanta, Georgia 30333. (404) 639-3286. 1990. Presents sources of general industrial hygiene and medical surveillance information for workers, employees and others. Presents key information and data in an abbreviated format for 398 individual chemicals or chemical types.

Pentachlorophenol. World Health Organization, Ave. Appia, Geneva, Switzerland CH-1211. (518) 436-9686. 1987.

Pentachlorophenol: Chemistry, Pharmacology, and Environmental Toxicology. K. Ranga Rao. Plenum Press, 233 Spring St., New York, New York 10013-1578. (212) 620-8000; (800) 221-9369. 1978.

ONLINE DATA BASES

BIOSIS Previews. BIOSIS, 2100 Arch St., Philadelphia, Pennsylvania 19103-1399. (215) 587-4800. Largest and most comprehensive database of research in the life sciences. Contains citations for nearly 9000 primary research journals, monographs, reviews, symposia, preliminary reports, semi-popular journals, selected institutional reports, government reports and research communications.

Chemical Abstracts-CA. Chemical Abstracts Service, 2540 Olentangy River Rd., P.O. Box 3012, Columbus, Ohio 43210. (800) 848-6533 or (614) 421-3600. Information sources include 9000 journals, patents from 27 countries, two industrial property organizations, new books, conference proceedings, and government research reports.

Chemical Collection System/Request Tracking–CCS/RTS. U.S. Environmental Protection Agency, Office of Pesticides and Toxic Substances, 401 M St., SW, Washington, District of Columbia 20460. (202) 260-2090. Contains information on various properties of a number of chemicals including environmental effects, test and analysis methods, and health effects. Available from EPA.

Chemical Dictionary Online–CHEMLINE. Chemical Abstracts Service, 2540 Olentangy River Rd., Columbus, Ohio 43210. (614) 421-3600 or (800) 848-6533. Part of MEDLINE of the National Library of Medicine (NLM). File of 900,000 names for chemical substances, representing 450,000 unique compounds. It contains such information as Chemical Abstracts (CA) Service Registry Numbers, molecular formulas, preferred chemical nomenclature, and generic and ring structure information. Available on NLM's ELHILL system.

PERIODICALS AND NEWSLETTERS

Chemosphere: Chemistry, Biology and Toxicology as Related to Environmental Problems. Pergamon Microforms International, Inc., Fairview Park, Elmsford, New York 10523. (914) 592-7720. 1970-. Offers maximum dissemination of investigations related to the health and safety of every aspect of life. Environmental protection encompasses a very wide field and relies on scientific research in chemistry, biology, physics, toxicology and inter-related disciplines.

Ecotoxicology and Environmental Safety. Academic Press, c/o Harcourt Brace Jovanovich Inc., 6277 Sea Harbor Dr., Orlando, Florida 32887. (800) 346-8648. 1977-. Bimonthly.

EHP, Environmental Health Perspectives. National Institute of Environmental Health Sciences, National Institutes of Health, Dept. of Health Education and Welfare, Box 12233, Bldg. 101, Rm. A 259, Research Triangle Park, North Carolina 27709. (919) 541-3406. 1972-. Bimonthly.

Environmental Science and Technology. American Chemical Society, 1155 16th St. N.W., Washington, District of Columbia 20036. (800) 227-5558. 1967-. Monthly. Contains research articles on various aspects of environmental chemistry, interpretative articles by invited experts and commentary on the scientific aspects of environmental management.

IARC Monographs on the Evaluation of the Carcinogenic Risk of Chemicals to Man. International Agency for Research on Cancer, Q Corp., 49 Sheridan Ave., Albany, New York 12221. (518) 436-9686. 1972-. Irregular.

Journal of Agricultural and Food Chemistry. American Chemical Society, 1155 16th St. N.W., Washington, District of Columbia 20036. (202) 872-4600; (800) 227-5558. 1953-. Monthly. Contains documentation of significant advances in the science of agriculture and food chemistry.

TRADE ASSOCIATIONS AND PROFESSIONAL SOCIETIES

American Chemical Society. 1155 16th St., N.W., Washington, District of Columbia 20036. (202) 872-4600.

PERCOLATION

See: WATER TREATMENT

PERMAFROST

See: ARCTIC TUNDRAS

PERSISTENT INSECTICIDES

See: INSECTICIDES

PEST CONTROL

ABSTRACTING AND INDEXING SERVICES

Agrindex. AGRIS Coordinating Center, Via delle Terme di Caracalla, Rome, Italy I-00100. 61 0181-FA01. 1975-.

Biological Abstracts. BIOSIS, 2100 Arch St., Philadelphia, Pennsylvania 19103-1399. (215) 587-4800. 1927-.

Biological and Agricultural Index. H.W. Wilson Co., 950 University Ave., Bronx, New York 10452. (800) 367-6770. 1916-. Monthly.

Biology Digest. Data Courier, Plexus Pub Inc., 143 Old Marlton Pike, Medford, New Jersey 08055. 1974-. Monthly. Abstracts biology periodicals.

Biotechnology Research Abstracts. Cambridge Scientific Abstracts, 5161 River Rd., Bethesda, Maryland 20816. (301) 961-6750. Monthly. Includes such broad areas as genetic intervention, biochemical genetics, and microbiological techniques.

Chemical Abstracts. Chemical Abstracts Service, 2540 Olentangy River Rd., PO Box 3012, Columbus, Ohio 43210. (800) 848-6533. 1907-.

Current Advances in Ecological and Environmental Science. Pergamon Microforms International, Inc., Fairview Park, Elmsford, New York 10523. (914) 592-7720. 1989-. Monthly. Current literature searching service including journals, reports, abstracts, etc. This service is available online as part of the CABS database on the hosts BRS and ORBIT search service.

FDA Surveillance Index for Pesticides. National Technical Information Service, 5285 Port Royal Rd., Springfield, Virginia 22161. (703) 487-4650. Monthly. Health risks of individual pesticides from a dietary exposure standpoint; FDA monitoring; chemical, biological, and toxicological data.

General Science Index. H. W. Wilson Co., 950 University Ave., Bronx, New York 10452. 1978-. Monthly, also issued in annual cumulation. Cumulative subject index to English language periodicals in the subject fields of astronomy, botany, chemistry, earth science, environment and conservation, food and nutrition, genetics, mathematics, medicine and health, microbiology, oceanography, physics, physiology and zoology.

INIS Atomindex. International Atomic Energy Agency, Wagramerstrasse 5, Vienna, Austria A-1400. 222 23606198. 1988-. Semiannual. Abstracts nuclear energy and nuclear physics topics from journals, conferences, technical reports and other related publications. Issued in 6 parts: Personal Author, Corporate Entry, Subject, Report, Standard Patent, Conference (by place), Conference (by date).

Pollution Abstracts. Cambridge Scientific Abstracts, 5161 River Rd., Bethesda, Maryland 20816. (301) 961-6750. Six/year. Indexes worldwide technical literature on environmental pollution. Covers air pollution, marine and freshwater pollution, sewage and wastewater treatment, waste management, toxicology and health, noise pollution, radiation, land pollution, and environmental policies, programs, legislation, and education. Also available online.

Science Citation Index. Institute for Scientific Information, 3501 Market St., Philadelphia, Pennsylvania 19104. 1961-.

BIBLIOGRAPHIES

The Economics of Agricultural Pest Control. U.S. Department of Agriculture, Economics and Statistics Service, 14 Independence Ave. SW, Washington, District of Columbia 20250. (202) 447-7454. 1981.

Integrated Pest Management. Jayne T. Maclean. National Agricultural Library, 10301 Baltimore Blvd., Beltsville, Maryland 20705-2351. (301) 504-5755. 1985.

Pesticide Applicator Training Materials: A Bibliography. Barbara O. Stommel. National Agricultural Library, 10301 Baltimore Blvd, Beltsville, Maryland 20705-2351. (301) 504-5755. 1991.

DIRECTORIES

Resources for Organic Pest Control. Rodale Press, 33 E. Minor St., Emmaus, Pennsylvania 18098. (215) 967-5171. Biennial.

ENCYCLOPEDIAS AND DICTIONARIES

Cambridge Encyclopedia of Life Sciences. A. E. Friday and David S. Ingram. Cambridge University Press, 40 W 20th St., New York, New York 10011. (212) 924-3900 or (800) 227-0247. 1985. Includes all topics under biology and ecology.

The Dictionary of Pest Control. Sandra K. Kraft. Pinto, 914 Hillcrest Dr., Vienna, Virginia 22180. 1985. Deals with terms that relate to household, structural, industrial, commercial, and institutional pest control.

Grzimek's Encyclopedia of Ecology. Bernhard Grzimek. Van Nostrand Reinhold, 115 5th Ave., New York, New York 10003. (212) 254-3232. 1976.

North American Reference Encyclopedia of Ecology and Pollution. William White. North American Pub. Co., 401 N. Broad St., Philadelphia, Pennsylvania 19108. (215) 238-5300. 1972.

Van Nostrand's Scientific Encyclopedia. Glenn D. Considine, ed. Van Nostrand Reinhold, 115 5th Ave., New York, New York 10003. (212) 254-3232. 1983. Sixth edition. Includes all broad subject areas in science.

GENERAL WORKS

Biotechnology for Biological Control of Pests and Vectors. Karl Maramorosch. CRC Press, 2000 Corporate Blvd. N.W., Boca Raton, Florida 33431. (407) 994-0555; (800) 272-7737. 1991.

Common Sense Pest Control. William Olkowski, et al. Tauton Pr., 63 South Main St., Box 5506, Newton,

Connecticut 06740-5506. 1991. Discusses ways to manage other living organisms that are regarded as pests.

Controlling Vegetable Pests. Cynthia Putnam. Ortho Information Services, PO Box 5047, San Ramon, California 94583. (415) 842-5537. 1991. Describes pest control in horticultural crops.

Critical Issues in Biological Control. Simon Fraser, et al., eds. VCH Publishers, 303 NW 12th Ave., Deerfield Beach, Florida 33442-1788. (305) 428-5566. 1990. Analyzes the current concerns about the risks that synthetic pesticides pose to the environment and human health. As a potentially powerful forum of pest control that has few environmental disadvantages, biological control is an attractive alternative which has increased the urgency for more research into non-chemical methods of crop and food production.

Crop Protection Chemicals. B. G. Lever. E. Horwood, 1230 Avenue of the Americas, New York, New York 10020. (212) 698-7000; (800) 223-2348. 1990. Overview of crop protection technology. Traces the evolution of pest control as an integral part of crop production. Focuses on the requirements of governments and society regarding the safety of products to users, food consumers and the environment.

Ecology and Management of Food Industry Pests. J. Richard Gorham. AOAC International, 2200 Wilson Blvd., Suite 400, Arlington, Virginia 22201-3301. (703) 522-3032.

Insect Pest Management. David Dent. C. A. B. International, Oxon, Wallingford, England OX10 8DE. (44) 0491 3211. 1991.

Integrated Pest Management for the Home and Garden. Robert L. Metcalf. University of Illinois, Urbana, Illinois 61801. 1980.

Management and Control of Invertebrate Crop Pests. Gordon E. Russell, ed. VCH Publishers, 303 NW 12th Ave., Deerfield Beach, Florida 33442-1788. (305) 428-5566. 1989. Review articles covering important aspects of the management and control of several important insect and nematode pests of crop plants, selected from the multi-disciplinary series of annual review books Agricultural Zoology Reviews and Biotechnology & Genetic Engineering Reviews.

Managing Resistance to Agrochemicals: From Fundamental Research to Practical Strategies. Maurice B. Green, et al., eds. American Chemical Society, 1155 16th St. N.W., Washington, District of Columbia 20036. (800) 227-5558. 1990. A compilation of chapters written by some of the foremost scientists in pesticide and pest management research today.

Monitoring and Integrated Management of Arthropod Pests of Small Fruit Crops. N. J. Bostanian, et al., eds. VCH Publishers, 303 NW 12th Ave., Deerfield Beach, Florida 33442-1788. (305) 428-5566. 1990. Examines the population models, pest management and insect- natural enemy interactions of pests of small fruit crops. It covers topics of major importance to those who grow strawberries, cranberries and other fruit crops.

Naturally Occurring Pest Bioregulators. Paul A. Hedin. American Chemical Society, 1155 16th St. NW, Washington, District of Columbia 20036. (202) 872-4600; (800) 227-5558. 1991. Symposium papers on naturally occurring biologically active chemicals grouped in five general sections: bioregulation of insect behavior and development; allelochemicals for control of insects and other animals; phytoalexins and phototoxins in plant pest control; mechanisms of plant resistance to insects; and allelochemicals as plant disease control agents.

Pest Management in Rice. B. T. Grayson, et al., eds. Elsevier Science Publishing Co., 655 Avenue of the Americas, New York, New York 10010. (212) 989-5800. 1990.

Pesticides and Non-Target Invertebrates. Paul C. Jepson, ed. VCH Publishers, 303 NW 12th Ave., Deerfield Beach, Florida 33442-1788. (305) 428-5566. 1990. Current state of research into the side-effects of pesticides on non-target insects.

Population Dynamics of Forest Insects. VCH Publishers, 303 NW 12th Ave., Deerfield Beach, Florida 33442-1788. (305) 428-5566. 1990. Reviews the current research from an international Congress of delegates which covers population models, pest management and insect natural enemy interaction on forest insects. Topics include the effects of industrial air pollutants and acid rain as well as reviews of the biology and population dynamics of most major forest insects.

Tortricid Pests: Their Biology, Natural Enemies, and Control. L.P.S. van der Geest. Elsevier Science Publishing Co., 655 Avenue of the Americas, New York, New York 10010. (212) 989-5800. 1991.

Use of Pathogens in Scarab Pest Management. Trevor A. Jackson and Travis R. Glare, eds. VCH Publishers, 303 NW 12th Ave., Deerfield Beach, Florida 33442-1788. (305) 428-5566. 1991. Provides a concise up-to-date reference on alternate controls such as pathogens in pest management.

Whiteflies: Their Bionomics, Pest Status and Management. Dan Gerling, ed. VCH Publishers, 303 NW 12th Ave., Deerfield Beach, Florida 33442-1788. (305) 428-5566. 1990. Covers the many aspects of whitefly study from evolution and morphology, to biology, natural enemies, sampling, modeling and control.

HANDBOOKS AND MANUALS

Handbook of Pest Control: The Behavior, Life History, and Control of Household Pests. Arnold Mallis. Franzak & Foster, 4012 Bridge Ave., Cleveland, Ohio 44113. (216) 961-4134. 1982. Covers injurious and beneficial insects.

Integrated Pest Management. ANR Publications, University of California, 6701 San Pablo Ave., Oakland, California 94608-1239. (510) 642-2431. 1990-. Irregular. Provides and orderly, scientifically based system for diagnosing, recording, evaluating, preventing, and treating pest problems in a variety of crops.

Pest and Disease Control Handbook. Nigel Scopes. BCPC Publications, Bear Farm, Binfield, Brocknell, England RG12 5QE. 1983. Covers pest control and plant diseases.

The Standard Pesticide User's Guide. Bert L. Bohmont. Prentice Hall, Rte. 9W, Englewood Cliffs, New Jersey 07632. (201) 592-2000. 1990. Includes material on laws and requirements, labeling, soil, groundwater, and endangered species. Covers new equipment, pumps, and techniques, as well as transportation, storage, decontamination, and disposal. Also covers integrated pest management.

UC IPM Pest Management Guidelines. ANR Publications, University of California, 6701 San Pablo Avenue, Oakland, California 94608-1239. (510) 642-2431. Official guidelines for monitoring techniques, pesticide use, and alternatives in agricultural crops.

ONLINE DATA BASES

BIOSIS Previews. BIOSIS, 2100 Arch St., Philadelphia, Pennsylvania 19103-1399. (215) 587-4800. Largest and most comprehensive database of research in the life sciences. Contains citations for nearly 9000 primary research journals, monographs, reviews, symposia, preliminary reports, semi-popular journals, selected institutional reports, government reports and research communications.

Chemical Abstracts-CA. Chemical Abstracts Service, 2540 Olentangy River Rd., P.O. Box 3012, Columbus, Ohio 43210. (800) 848-6533 or (614) 421-3600. Information sources include 9000 journals, patents from 27 countries, two industrial property organizations, new books, conference proceedings, and government research reports.

Monthly Catalog of United States Government Publications. U.S. G.P.O., Supt. of Docs., PO Box 371954, Pittsburgh, Pennsylvania 15250-7954. (202) 512-0000.

National Pesticide Information Retrieval System. Entomology Hall, Purdue University, West Lafayette, Indiana 47907. (317) 494-6616. Pesticide products registered with the Environmental Protection Agency, as well as similar information from 36 states.

National Technical Information Service. U.S. Department of Commerce, National Technical Information Service, Office of Data Base Services, 5285 Port Royal Rd., Springfield, Virginia 22161. (703) 487-4807. Bibliographic database of government sponsored research and technical reports.

Pest Control Literature Documentation. Derwent Publications, Ltd., 6845 Elm St., McLean, Virginia 22101. (703) 790-0400.

Pest Management Research Information System. Agriculture Canada Research Branch, K.W. Neatby Building, Rm. 1135, Ottawa, Ontario, Canada K1A OC6. (613) 995-7084 x7254.

PESTDOC. Derwent Publications, Ltd., Rochdale House, 128 Theobalds Rd., London, England WC1X BRP. 44 (71) 242-5823.

PESTDOC II. Derwent Publications, Ltd., Rochdale House, 128 Theobalds Rd., London, England WC1X BRP. 44 (71) 242-5823.

Pesticide & Toxic Chemical News. Food Chemical News, Inc., 1101 Pennsylvania Ave., S.E., Washington, District of Columbia 20003. (202) 544-1980. Online version of the periodical of the same name.

SCISEARCH. Institute for Scientific Information, University City Science Center, 3501 Market St., Philadelphia, Pennsylvania 19104. (215) 386-0100.

PERIODICALS AND NEWSLETTERS

Common Sense Pest Control Quarterly. Bio-Integral Resource Center, PO Box 7414, Berkeley, California 94707. (415) 524-2567. Four times a year. Least-toxic management of pests on indoor plants, pests that damage paper, controlling fleas and ticks on pets, and garden pests.

Economic Poisons Report. New Mexico Dept. of Agriculture, Las Cruces, New Mexico 1979. Annual. Covers pesticides, pest control, and pesticides industry.

Pest Control Technology. Gei, Inc., 4012 Bridge Ave., Cleveland, Ohio 44113. (316) 961-4130. Monthly. Articles on pests and pesticides.

Pesticide Biochemistry and Physiology. Academic Press, c/o Harcourt Brace Jovanovich Inc., 6277 Sea Harbor Dr., Orlando, Florida 32887. (800) 346-8648. Nine times a year. Covers biochemistry and physiology of insecticides, herbicides and similar compounds.

Pesticide Science: An International Journal on Crop Protection and Pest Control. Elsevier Science Publishing Co., 655 Avenue of the Americas, New York, New York 10010. (212) 989-5800. 1970-. Monthly. Topics covered: Synthesis, screening, structure/activity and biochemical mode of action studies of compounds; physicochemical properties of new compounds; metabolism, degradation, field performance, environmental studies and safety in use of new and existing products; synthetic and naturally occurring insecticides; ecological implications of pesticide applications.

RESEARCH CENTERS AND INSTITUTES

Bio-Integral Resource Center. P.O. Box 7414, Berkeley, California 94707. (415) 524-2567.

Center for Urban Pest Management. Purdue University, Ag Research Building, West Lafayette, Indiana 47907. (317) 494-4554.

Simon Fraser University, Centre for Pest Management. Burnaby Mountain, Burnaby, British Columbia, Canada V5 A1S6. (607) 291-3705.

Urban Pest Control Research Group. Virginia Polytech Institute and State University, Department of Entomology, Glade Road, Blacksburg, Virginia 24061. (703) 961-4045.

TRADE ASSOCIATIONS AND PROFESSIONAL SOCIETIES

American Institute of Biological Sciences. 730 11th St., N.W., Washington, District of Columbia 20001-4521. (202) 628-1500.

Association of American Pesticide Control Officials. Office of the Secretary, P.O. Box 1249, Hardwick, Vermont 05843. (802) 472-6956.

Electronic Pest Control Association. 710 E. Ogden, Suite 113, Naperville, Illinois 60563. (708) 369-2406.

National Association of Insect Electrocutor Manufacturers. P.O. Box 439, Medina, New York 14103-0439.

National Pest Control Association. 8100 Oak St., Dunn Loring, Virginia 22027. (703) 573-8330.

PESTICIDE RUNOFF

See: WASTE DISPOSAL

PESTICIDE TOLERANCE

ABSTRACTING AND INDEXING SERVICES

Agrindex. AGRIS Coordinating Center, Via delle Terme di Caracalla, Rome, Italy I-00100. 61 0181-FA01. 1975-.

Biological and Agricultural Index. H.W. Wilson Co., 950 University Ave., Bronx, New York 10452. (800) 367-6770. 1916-. Monthly.

Chemical Abstracts. Chemical Abstracts Service, 2540 Olentangy River Rd., PO Box 3012, Columbus, Ohio 43210. (800) 848-6533. 1907-.

Environment Abstracts. Bowker A & I Publishing, 121 Chanlon Rd., New Providence, New Jersey 07974. (908) 464-6800. 1974-.

Environment Index. Environment Information Center, Index Research Department, 124 E. 39th St., New York, New York 10016. 1971-. Annual.

Environmental Information Connection–EIC. Planning Information Program, Dept. of Urban and Regional Planning, University of Illinois, 1003 West Nevada, Urbana, Illinois 61801. (217) 333-1369. Also available online.

Environmental Periodicals Bibliography. Environmental Studies Institute, International Academy at Santa Barbara, 800 Garden St., Suite D, Santa Barbara, California 93101. (805) 965-5010. Also available online.

Pesticides Abstracts. U.S. Environmental Protection Agency, Office of Pesticides Programs, 345 Curtland, Atlanta, Georgia 30365. (404) 347-2864. 1981. Monthly. Formerly: Health Aspects of Pesticides Abstracts Bulletin.

Science Citation Index. Institute for Scientific Information, 3501 Market St., Philadelphia, Pennsylvania 19104. 1961-.

BIBLIOGRAPHIES

EPA Publications Bibliography. U.S. Environmental Protection Agency, Library Systems Branch, 401 M St., SW, Washington, District of Columbia 20460. (202) 260-2090. Quarterly.

Pesticide Applicator Training Materials: A Bibliography. Barbara O. Stommel. National Agricultural Library, 10301 Baltimore Blvd, Beltsville, Maryland 20705-2351. (301) 504-5755. 1991.

ENCYCLOPEDIAS AND DICTIONARIES

McGraw-Hill Encyclopedia of Environmental Science. Sybil P. Parker. McGraw-Hill Science & Engineering Books, 11 W. 19th St., New York, New York 10011. (212) 337-6010. 1980. Covers ecology, man's influence on nature, and environmental protection.

Van Nostrand's Scientific Encyclopedia. Glenn D. Considine, ed. Van Nostrand Reinhold, 115 5th Ave., New York, New York 10003. (212) 254-3232. 1983. Sixth edition. Includes all broad subject areas in science.

GENERAL WORKS

Environmental Fact Sheet: Pesticide Tolerances. U.S. Environmental Protection Agency, Office of Pesticides and Toxic Substances, 401 M St. SW, Washington, District of Columbia 20460. (202) 260-2090. 1990.

Pesticide Tolerance Legislation. U.S. G.P.O., Washington, District of Columbia 20401. (202) 512-0000. 1984.

Pesticides and Non-Target Invertebrates. Paul C. Jepson, ed. VCH Publishers, 303 NW 12th Ave., Deerfield Beach, Florida 33442-1788. (305) 428-5566. 1990. Current state of research into the side-effects of pesticides on non-target insects.

HANDBOOKS AND MANUALS

Guidance for the Reregistration of Pesticide Products Containing Lindane as the Active Ingredient. U.S. Environmental Protection Agency, Office of the Pesticides and Toxic Substances, 401 M St., SW, Washington, District of Columbia 20460. (202) 260-2090. 1985. The Federal Insecticide, Fungicide, Rodenticide Act directs EPA to reregister all pesticides as expeditiously as possible. The guide helps the user to carry out this task and to participate in the EPA's registration standard program. Includes extensive tabular data to the pesticides and an extensive bibliography.

ONLINE DATA BASES

CERCLIS. Chemical Information Systems, Inc., 7215 York Rd., Baltimore, Maryland 21212. (301) 321-8440. Information on hazardous waste disposal sites that have either been listed by the EPA on the National Priority List (NPL) or nominated for consideration for the NPL.

Chemical Abstracts-CA. Chemical Abstracts Service, 2540 Olentangy River Rd., P.O. Box 3012, Columbus, Ohio 43210. (800) 848-6533 or (614) 421-3600. Information sources include 9000 journals, patents from 27 countries, two industrial property organizations, new books, conference proceedings, and government research reports.

Enviro/Energyline Abstracts Plus. R. R. Bowker Co., 121 Chanlon Rd., New Providence, New Jersey 07974. (908) 464-6800.

Environmental Periodicals Bibliography. National Information Services Corp., Ste. 6, Wyman Towers, 3100 St. Paul St., Baltimore, Maryland 21218. (410)243-0797. Online version of abstract of same name.

EPA Fact Sheet Program. National Pesticide Information Retrieval System (NPIRS) Services Manager, Purdue University, Entomology Hall, West Lafayette, Indiana 47907. (317) 494-6616.

National Pesticide Information Retrieval System. Entomology Hall, Purdue University, West Lafayette, Indiana 47907. (317) 494-6616. Pesticide products registered with the Environmental Protection Agency, as well as similar information from 36 states.

Pest Management Research Information System. Agriculture Canada Research Branch, K.W. Neatby Building,

Rm. 1135, Ottawa, Ontario, Canada K1A OC6. (613) 995-7084 x7254.

PESTDOC. Derwent Publications, Ltd., Rochdale House, 128 Theobalds Rd., London, England WC1X 8RP. 44 (71) 242-5823.

PESTDOC II. Derwent Publications, Ltd., Rochdale House, 128 Theobalds Rd., London, England WC1X 8RP. 44 (71) 242-5823.

Pesticide & Toxic Chemical News. Food Chemical News, Inc., 1101 Pennsylvania Ave., S.E., Washington, District of Columbia 20003. (202) 544-1980. Online version of the periodical of the same name.

SCISEARCH. Institute for Scientific Information, University City Science Center, 3501 Market St., Philadelphia, Pennsylvania 19104. (215) 386-0100.

Tolerance Database. NPIRS (National Pesticide Information Retrieval System) User Services Manager, Entomology Hall, Purdue University, West Lafayette, Indiana 47907. (317) 494-6614.

PERIODICALS AND NEWSLETTERS

Journal of Environmental Science and Health. Marcel Dekker, Inc., 270 Madison Ave., New York, New York 10016. (212) 696-9000. Bimonthly. Concerns pesticides, food contaminants, chemical carcinogens, and agricultural wastes.

Pesticide Science: An International Journal on Crop Protection and Pest Control. Elsevier Science Publishing Co., 655 Avenue of the Americas, New York, New York 10010. (212) 989-5800. 1970-. Monthly. Topics covered: Synthesis, screening, structure/activity and biochemical mode of action studies of compounds; physicochemical properties of new compounds; metabolism, degradation, field performance, environmental studies and safety in use of new and existing products; synthetic and naturally occurring insecticides; ecological implications of pesticide applications.

TRADE ASSOCIATIONS AND PROFESSIONAL SOCIETIES

American Institute of Biological Sciences. 730 11th St., N.W., Washington, District of Columbia 20001-4521. (202) 628-1500.

Association of American Pesticide Control Officials. Office of the Secretary, P.O. Box 1249, Hardwick, Vermont 05843. (802) 472-6956.

International Pesticide Applicators Association. Box 1377, Milton, Washington 98354. (206) 922-9437.

PESTICIDES

ABSTRACTING AND INDEXING SERVICES

Applied Ecology Abstracts Studies in Renewable Natural Resources. Information Retrieval Ltd., 1911 Jefferson Davis Highway, Arlington, Virginia 22202. 1975-. Monthly.

Applied Science and Technology Index. H.W. Wilson Co., 950 University Ave., Bronx, New York 10452. (800) 367-6770. Formerly Industrial Arts Index.

Aqualine Abstracts. Water Research Centre. c/o Pergamon Microforms International, Inc., Fairview Park, Elmsford, New York 10523. (914) 592-7720. 1927-. Contains some 8,000 records annually on water and wastewater technology. Covers all aspects of water, wastewater, associated engineering services and the aquatic environment. Over 600 periodicals, as well as books, reports and conference proceedings and other publications from water related institutions worldwide are scanned. Also available online.

ASFA Aquaculture Abstracts. Cambridge Scientific Abstracts, Inc., 5161 River Rd., Bethesda, Maryland 20816. (301) 961-6750. 1984.

Biological Abstracts. BIOSIS, 2100 Arch St., Philadelphia, Pennsylvania 19103-1399. (215) 587-4800. 1927-.

Biological and Agricultural Index. H.W. Wilson Co., 950 University Ave., Bronx, New York 10452. (800) 367-6770. 1916-. Monthly.

Biotechnology Research Abstracts. Cambridge Scientific Abstracts, 5161 River Rd., Bethesda, Maryland 20816. (301) 961-6750. Monthly. Includes such broad areas as genetic intervention, biochemical genetics, and microbiological techniques.

Chemical Abstracts. Chemical Abstracts Service, 2540 Olentangy River Rd., PO Box 3012, Columbus, Ohio 43210. (800) 848-6533. 1907-.

Ecological Abstracts. Geo Abstracts Ltd. Elsevier Applied Science, Crown House, Linton Rd., Barking, England IG 11 8JU. 1974-. Derived from over 600 leading ecological and environmental journals, plus books, conference proceedings, reports and theses.

Ecology Abstracts. Cambridge Scientific Abstracts, 5161 River Rd., Bethesda, Maryland 20816. (301) 961-6750. Monthly.

Environment Abstracts. Bowker A & I Publishing, 121 Chanlon Rd., New Providence, New Jersey 07974. (908) 464-6800. 1974-.

Environment Index. Environment Information Center, Index Research Department, 124 E. 39th St., New York, New York 10016. 1971-. Annual.

Environmental Information Connection–EIC. Planning Information Program, Dept. of Urban and Regional Planning, University of Illinois, 1003 West Nevada, Urbana, Illinois 61801. (217) 333-1369. Also available online.

Environmental Periodicals Bibliography. Environmental Studies Institute, International Academy at Santa Barbara, 800 Garden St., Suite D, Santa Barbara, California 93101. (805) 965-5010. Also available online.

FDA Surveillance Index for Pesticides. National Technical Information Service, 5285 Port Royal Rd., Springfield, Virginia 22161. (703) 487-4650. Monthly. Health risks of individual pesticides from a dietary exposure standpoint; FDA monitoring; chemical, biological, and toxicological data.

Food Science and Technology Abstracts. International Food Information Service, c/o National Food Laboratory, 6363 Clark Ave., Dublin, California 94568. (800) 336-3782. 1969-.

General Science Index. H. W. Wilson Co., 950 University Ave., Bronx, New York 10452. 1978-. Monthly, also

issued in annual cumulation. Cumulative subject index to English language periodicals in the subject fields of astronomy, botany, chemistry, earth science, environment and conservation, food and nutrition, genetics, mathematics, medicine and health, microbiology, oceanography, physics, physiology and zoology.

Index to Scientific Book Contents. Institute for Scientific Information, 3501 Market St., Philadelphia, Pennsylvania 19104. (800) 523-1857. 1985-. Annual. Gives contents of science books published.

Multimedia Index to Ecology. National Information Center for Educational Media, University of Southern California, Los Angeles, California 90007.

Pesticide Index. H. Kidd and D. Hartley, eds. Royal Society of Chemistry, c/o CRC Press, 2000 Corporate Blvd. N.W., Boca Raton, Florida 33431-9868. (800) 272-7737. 1988. A quick guide to chemical, common and trade names of pesticides and related crop-protection products world-wide. About 800 active-ingredients are included with about 25,000 trade names of pesticides containing these ingredients.

Pesticides Abstracts. U.S. Environmental Protection Agency, Office of Pesticides Programs, 345 Curtland, Atlanta, Georgia 30365. (404) 347-2864. 1981. Monthly. Formerly: Health Aspects of Pesticides Abstracts Bulletin.

Pollution Abstracts. Cambridge Scientific Abstracts, 5161 River Rd., Bethesda, Maryland 20816. (301) 961-6750. Six/year. Indexes worldwide technical literature on environmental pollution. Covers air pollution, marine and freshwater pollution, sewage and wastewater treatment, waste management, toxicology and health, noise pollution, radiation, land pollution, and environmental policies, programs, legislation, and education. Also available online.

Science Citation Index. Institute for Scientific Information, 3501 Market St., Philadelphia, Pennsylvania 19104. 1961-.

BIBLIOGRAPHIES

Arthropods as Final Hosts of Nematodes and Nematomorphs: An Annotated Bibliography. M.R.N. Shepard. Commonwealth Agricultural Bureaux, Wallingford, England OX10 8DE. 1974.

Current Contents. Agriculture, Biology and Environmental Sciences. Institute for Scientific Information, 3501 Market St., Philadelphia, Pennsylvania 19104. (800) 523-1857. 1973-. Previous title: Current Contents. Agricultural, Food & Veterinary Sciences. Gives the table of contents of periodicals in the fields of agriculture, biology, environmental and related areas.

Environmental Toxicology. Robert L. Rudd. Gale Research Co., 835 Penobscot Bldg., Detroit, Michigan 48226-4094. (313) 961-2242. 1977. Includes the broad areas of pollution, pesticides, and their effects. This bibliography is part of the series entitled Man and the Environment Information Guide Series, v.7.

EPA Publications Bibliography. U.S. Environmental Protection Agency, Library Systems Branch, 401 M St., SW, Washington, District of Columbia 20460. (202) 260-2090. Quarterly.

Pesticide Applicator Training Materials: A Bibliography. Barbara O. Stommel. National Agricultural Library,

10301 Baltimore Blvd, Beltsville, Maryland 20705-2351. (301) 504-5755. 1991.

Toxic Hazards of Certain Pesticides to Man, Together with a Select Bibliography on the Toxicology of Pesticides in Man and Mammals. World Health Organization, Ave. Appia, Geneva, Switzerland CH-1211. 1953. Toxicology and toxicity of pesticides and insecticides.

DIRECTORIES

The Pesticide Directory. Lori Thomson Harvey and W. T. Thomson. Thomson Publications, PO Box 9335, Fresno, California 93791. (209) 435-2163. 1990. A guide to producers and products, regulators, researchers, and associations in the U.S. Detailed listings (name, addresses, telephone numbers, key personnel, products or services) in four sections: chemicals, research, regulatory and miscellaneous.

Pesticides: A Community Action Guide. Concern, Inc., 1794 Columbia Rd., N.W., Washington, District of Columbia 20009. (202) 328-8160.

World Directory of Pesticide Control Organisations. H. Kidd and D. Hartley, eds. Royal Society of Chemistry, c/o CRC Press, 2000 Corporate Blvd. N.W., Boca Raton, Florida 33431-9868. (800) 272-7737. 1989. A directory of international organizations, associations and programmes in the field of pesticide control. It is arranged alphabetically for all the organizations listed including telephone numbers and telex numbers to encourage the easy establishment of contact.

ENCYCLOPEDIAS AND DICTIONARIES

Dictionary of Pesticides. Meister Publishing Co., 37733 Euclid Ave., Willoughby, Ohio 44094. (216) 942-2000. 1972.

Encyclopedia of Human Biology. Renato Dulbecco, ed. Academic Press, c/o Harcourt Brace Jovanovich Inc., 6277 Sea Harbor Dr., Orlando, Florida 32887. (800) 346-8648. 1991. Eight volumes.

Glossary of Pesticide Toxicology and Related Terms. Naeem Eesa. Thomson Publications, PO Box 9335, Fresno, California 93791. (209) 435-2163. 1984.

Grzimek's Encyclopedia of Ecology. Bernhard Grzimek. Van Nostrand Reinhold, 115 5th Ave., New York, New York 10003. (212) 254-3232. 1976.

McGraw-Hill Encyclopedia of Environmental Science. Sybil P. Parker. McGraw-Hill Science & Engineering Books, 11 W. 19th St., New York, New York 10011. (212) 337-6010. 1980. Covers ecology, man's influence on nature, and environmental protection.

McGraw-Hill Encyclopedia of Science and Technology. McGraw-Hill, 1221 Avenue of the Americas, New York, New York 10020. (212) 512-2000 or (800) 262-4729. 1992. Seventh edition. Issued in multiple volumes including index. Includes all science and technology broad subject areas.

North American Reference Encyclopedia of Ecology and Pollution. William White. North American Pub. Co., 401 N. Broad St., Philadelphia, Pennsylvania 19108. (215) 238-5300. 1972.

Ullmanns Encyclopedia of Industrial Chemistry. Hans Jurgen Arpe and Wolfgang Gerhartz, eds. VCH Publishers, 303 NW 12th Ave., Deerfield Beach, Florida 33442-

1788. (305) 428-5566. 1990. Designed to keep up with the broad spectrum of chemical technology. Thirty-six volumes of the encyclopedia have been divided into two sets: the 28 A volumes contain alphabetically arranged articles on chemicals, product groups, processes and technological concepts; and the 8 B volumes are compendia of basic knowledge in industrial chemistry.

GENERAL WORKS

Aquatic Toxicology. Jerome O. Nriagu. John Wiley & Sons, Inc., 605 3rd Ave., New York, New York 10158-0012. (212) 850-6000. 1989.

Basic Science Forcing Laws & Regulatory Case Studies. Devra Lee Lewis. Environmental Law Institute, 1616 P St., NW, Suite 200, Washington, District of Columbia 20036. (202) 328-5150. 1980. Environmental aspects and toxicology of pesticides.

Bioassay of Endrin for Possible Carcinogenicity. National Cancer Institute, Div. of Cancer Cause and Prevention, Carcinogenesis Testing Program, NIH Bldg. 31, Room 10A 24, 9030 Old Georgetown Rd., Bethesda, Maryland 20892. (301) 496-7403. 1978.

The Biochemistry and Uses of Pesticides: Structure, Metabolism, Mode of Action, and Uses in Crop Protection. Kenneth A. Hassall. VCH Publishers, 303 NW 12th Ave., Deerfield Beach, Florida 33442-1788. (305) 428-5566. 1990. Reports the progress that has been made in the last few years towards an understanding of how pesticides function, how metabolism contributes to selectivity and safety and how the development of resistance is linked to biochemistry and molecular biology.

Bound Pesticide Residues. Shahamat U. Khan. CRC Press, 2000 Corporate Blvd. N.W., Boca Raton, Florida 33431. (800) 272-7737. 1991. Overview of pesticide residues in soils and plants, its bioavailability, isolation and identification, toxicological significance and the regulatory aspects.

Carcinogenicity and Pesticides. Nancy N. Ragsdale and Robert E. Menzer, eds. American Chemical Society, 1155 16th St. N.W., Washington, District of Columbia 20036. (202) 872-4600; (800) 227-5558. 1989. Discusses the role of structure activity relationship analysis in evaluation of pesticides for potential carcinogenicity. Also traces the background, pesticide regulations, assessment of hazard and risk, and epidemiological studies of cancer and pesticide exposure.

Chemicals in the Human Food Chain. Carl K. Winter, et al. Van Nostrand Reinhold, 115 5th Ave., New York, New York 10003. (212) 254-3232. 1990. Deals with prevention of food contamination by pesticides and other toxic chemicals.

Chemicals Tested as Acaricides to Control One-Host Ticks, U.S. Livestock Insects Laboratory, 1962-77. R. O. Drummond. U.S. Livestock Insects Laboratory, PO Box 232, Kerrville, Texas 78029-0232. (512) 257-3566. 1979.

Chemistry, Agriculture and the Environment. Mervyn L. Richardson. Royal Society of Chemistry, Thomas Graham House, Science Park, Milton Rd., Cambridge, England CB4 4WF. 44(0)223420066. 1991. Provides an overview of the chemical pollution of the environment caused by modern agricultural practices worldwide, and describes the effects of agrochemicals used in intensive animal and crop production on the air, water, soil, plants, and animals including humans. Also available through CRC Press.

Chemistry of Pesticides. K. H. Buchel, ed. John Wiley & Sons, Inc., 605 3rd Ave., New York, New York 10158-0012. (212) 850-6000. 1983.

Common Sense Pest Control. William Olkowski, et al. Tauton Pr., 63 South Main St., Box 5506, Newton, Connecticut 06740-5506. 1991. Discusses ways to manage other living organisms that are regarded as pests.

CRC Handbook of Natural Pesticides. Volume V: Microbial Insecticides. Carlo M. Ignoffo. CRC Press, 2000 Corporate Blvd. N.W., Boca Raton, Florida 33431. (800) 272-7737. 1991. Review of the use of entomopathogenic microorganisms to control insects and other arthropod pests.

Degradation of Synthetic Organic Molecules in the Biosphere. National Academy of Sciences, 2101 Constitution Ave. N.W., Washington, District of Columbia 20418. (202) 334-2000. 1972. Proceedings of conference, San Francisco, CA, June 12-13, 1971, under the aegis of the National Research Council.

Enhanced Biodegradation of Pesticides in the Environment. Kenneth D. Racke and Joel R. Coats, eds. American Chemical Society, 1155 16th St. N.W., Washington, District of Columbia 20036. (202) 872-4600; (800) 227-5558. 1990. Discusses pesticides in the soil, microbial ecosystems, and the effects of long term application of herbicides on the soil.

Entomogenous Nematodes. George O. Polnar. Brill, Plantijnstraat 2, Postbus 9000, Leiden, Netherlands 2321 JC. 31 071 312 624. 1975. A manual and host list of insect-nematode associations.

Environmental Fact Sheet: Pesticide Reregistration. U.S. Environmental Protection Agency, Office of Pesticides and Toxic Substances, 401 M St. SW, Washington, District of Columbia 20460. (202) 260-2090. 1990.

Environmental Fact Sheet: Pesticide Tolerances. U.S. Environmental Protection Agency, Office of Pesticides and Toxic Substances, 401 M St. SW, Washington, District of Columbia 20460. (202) 260-2090. 1990.

Environmental Fact Sheet: Risk/Benefit Balancing Under the Federal Insecticide, Fungicide, and Rodenticide Act. U.S. Environmental Protection Agency, Office of Pesticides and Toxic Substances, 401 M St. SW, Washington, District of Columbia 20460. (202) 260-2090. 1990.

Environmental Fact Sheet: The Delaney Paradox and Negligible Risk. U.S. Environmental Protection Agency, Office of Pesticides and Toxic Substances, 401 M St. SW, Washington, District of Columbia 20460. (202) 260-2090. 1990.

Environmental Protection and Biological Forms of Control of Pest Organisms. B. Lundholm. Swedish National Science Research Council, Editorial Service, P.O. Box 6711, Stockholm, Sweden S-113 85. 08-15-1580. 1980. Environmental aspects of pests and natural pesticides.

Fate of Pesticides and Chemicals in the Environment. Jerald L. Schnoor, ed. John Wiley & Sons, Inc., 605 3rd Ave., New York, New York 10158-0012. (212) 850-6000. 1992. Focuses on the necessity to improve our deteriorating standards of public health, environmental science and technology with a total systems approach through the pooled talents of scientists and engineers.

Green Fields Forever. Charles E. Little. Island Press, 1718 Connecticut Ave. N.W., Suite 300, Washington, District of Columbia 20009. (202) 232-7933. 1987. An objective look at the costs and benefits of conservation tillage, a promising solution to agricultural problems such as decreased yields, soil erosion and reliance on pesticides and herbicides.

Harvest of Hope. Jennifer Curtis, et al. Natural Resources Defense Council, 40 W. 20th St., New York, New York 10011. (212) 727-2700. 1991. Details potential reductions in pesticide use and offers recommendations for reform in research, farm programs, marketing policy and water pricing.

Human Toxicology of Pesticides. Fina P. Kaloyanova and Mostafa A. El Batawi. CRC Press, 2000 Corporate Blvd. NW, Boca Raton, Florida 33431. (407) 994-0555; (800) 272-7737. 1991. Describes how pesticides affect humans.

Insecticides of Plant Origin. J. T. Armason, et al., eds. American Chemical Society, 1155 16th St. N.W., Washington, District of Columbia 20036. (202) 872-4600; (800) 227-5558. 1989. Describes all about biochemical pesticides past, present and future.

Long Range Transport of Pesticides. David A. Kurtz. Lewis Publishers, 2000 Corporate Blvd., N.W., Boca Raton, Florida 33431. (407) 994-0555 or (800) 272-7737. 1990. Presents the latest vital information on long range transport of pesticides. Includes sources of pesticides from lakes, oceans, and soil, circulation on global and regional basis, deposition, and fate of pesticides.

Managing Resistance to Agrochemicals: From Fundamental Research to Practical Strategies. Maurice B. Green, et al., eds. American Chemical Society, 1155 16th St. N.W., Washington, District of Columbia 20036. (800) 227-5558. 1990. A compilation of chapters written by some of the foremost scientists in pesticide and pest management research today.

Materials Evaluated as Insecticides and Acaricides at Brownsville, TX, September, 1955 to June, 1961. B. A. Butt and J. C. Keller. Agricultural Research Service, U.S. Dept. of Agriculture, PO Box 96456, Washington, District of Columbia 20250. (202) 720-8999. 1964.

Microbes and Microbial Products as Herbicides. Robert E. Hoagland, ed. American Chemical Society, 1155 16th St. N.W., Washington, District of Columbia 20036. (202) 872-4600; (800) 227-5558. 1990. Discusses the suitability of host specific phytotoxins, synthetic derivatives of abcisic acid, phytoalexins, pathogens, soilborne fungi, its biochemistry and other potential microbial product herbicides.

MSDS Reference for Crop Protection Chemicals. John Wiley & Sons, Inc., 605 3rd Ave., New York, New York 10158-0012. (212) 850-6000. 1990. 3d ed. Covering over 650 brand name pesticides and related products from 19 manufacturers, their reference reproduces the manufacturers' information exactly, in a standardized typeset format.

National Pesticide Survey: Fact Sheets. U.S. Environmental Protection Agency, Office of Pesticides and Toxic Substances, 401 M St. SW, Washington, District of Columbia 20460. (202) 260-2090. 1990.

National Pesticide Survey: Phase I Report. U.S. Environmental Protection Agency, Office of Pesticides and Toxic Substances, 401 M St. SW, Washington, District of Columbia 20460. (202) 260-2090. 1990.

National Pesticide Survey: Project Summary. U.S. Environmental Protection Agency, Office of Pesticides and Toxic Substances, 401 M St. SW, Washington, District of Columbia 20460. (202) 260-2090. 1990.

National Pesticide Survey: Summary Results of EPA's National Survey of Pesticides in Drinking Water Wells. U.S. Environmental Protection Agency, Office of Pesticides and Toxic Substances, 401 M St. SW, Washington, District of Columbia 20460. (202) 260-2090. 1990.

The Natural History of Nematodes. George O. Polanr. Prentice-Hall, Rte. 9W, Englewood Cliffs, New Jersey 07632. (201) 592-2000. 1983.

Naturally Occurring Pest Bioregulators. Paul A. Hedin. American Chemical Society, 1155 16th St. NW, Washington, District of Columbia 20036. (202) 872-4600; (800) 227-5558. 1991. Symposium papers on naturally occurring biologically active chemicals grouped in five general sections: bioregulation of insect behavior and development; allelochemicals for control of insects and other animals; phytoalexins and phototoxins in plant pest control; mechanisms of plant resistance to insects; and allelochemicals as plant disease control agents.

Nematodes in Soil Ecosystems. Diana W. Freckman. University of Texas Press, PO Box 7819, Austin, Texas 78713-7819. (512) 471-7233 or (800) 252-3206. 1982.

North Central Weed Science Society. Research Report. Michael Barrett, ed. North Central Weed Science Society, 309 W. Clark St., Champaign, Illinois 61820. (217) 356-3182. 1990.

Pest Management in Rice. B. T. Grayson, et al., eds. Elsevier Science Publishing Co., 655 Avenue of the Americas, New York, New York 10010. (212) 989-5800. 1990.

Pesticide Alert. Lawrie Mott, Karen Snyder. Sierra Club Books, 100 Bush St., San Francisco, California 94104. (415) 291-1600. 1987.

Pesticide Bioassays with Arthropods. Jacqueline Robertson. Lewis Publishers, 2000 Corporate Blvd., N.W., Boca Raton, Florida 33431. (407) 994-0555 or (800) 272-7737. 1992. Describes the experimental design of pesticide bioassays, tests with pesticides in an arthropod's natural environment, with unnatural environments, and international quarantine regulations.

Pesticide Chemistry: Advances in International Research, Development, and Legislation. Helmut Frehse. VCH Publishers, 303 NW 12th Ave., Deerfield Beach, Florida 33442-1788. (305) 428-5566.

Pesticide Development: Structure Activity Relationships. Wilfried Draber and Toshio Fujita. Lewis Publishers, 2000 Corporate Blvd., N.W., Boca Raton, Florida 33431. (407) 994-0555 or (800) 272-7737. 1991. Describes the physiochemical approach, biorational approach and the design of herbicides, fungicides, and insecticides.

Pesticide Formulations and Application Systems. ASTM, 1916 Race St., Philadelphia, Pennsylvania 19103-1187. (215) 299-5400. Perspectives on pesticide risks, formulation technology and characteristics of uptake, and application systems.

Pesticide Management for Local Governments. Anne R. Leslie. International City Management Association, 777 N. Capital St., NE, Suite 500, Washington, District of Columbia 20002-4201. (800) 745-8780. 1989. Case studies of integrated pest management and its application in local government operations. Includes turf grass management and mosquito control.

Pesticide Residues and Food Safety: A Harvest of Viewpoints. B. G. Tweedy, et al., eds. American Chemical Society, 1155 16th St. N.W., Washington, District of Columbia 20036. (202) 872-4600; (800) 227-5558. 1991. Discusses all the issues raised in connection with the use of pesticides in the United States. Some of the issues are the economic and social aspects, impact assessment programs, food safety, consumer attitude, pesticide free fruit crops, integrated pest management, EPA's program for validation of pesticides, and other related matters.

Pesticide Residues in Food. Food and Agriculture Organization of the United Nations, 4611-F Assembly Dr., Lanham, Maryland 20706-4391. (800) 274-4888. 1990.

Pesticide Transformation Products: Fate and Significance in the Environment: Papers. L. Somasundaram and Joel R. Coats, eds. American Chemical Society, 1155 16th St. N.W., Washington, District of Columbia 20036. (202) 872-4600; (800) 227-5558. 1991. The significance and impact of pesticide products on the environment is discussed.

Pesticide Waste Disposal Technology. James S. Bridges and Clyde R. Dempsey, eds. Noyes Publications, 120 Mill Rd., Park Ridge, New Jersey 07656. (201) 391-8484. 1988. Defines practical solutions to pesticide users' disposal problems.

Pesticides and Non-Target Invertebrates. Paul C. Jepson, ed. VCH Publishers, 303 NW 12th Ave., Deerfield Beach, Florida 33442-1788. (305) 428-5566. 1990. Current state of research into the side-effects of pesticides on non-target insects.

Phytotoxicity of Insecticides and Acaricides to Anthuriums. Trent Y. Hata. HITAHR, College of Tropical Agriculture and Human Resources, University of Hawaii, 2840 Kolowalu St., Honolulu, Hawaii 96822. (808) 948-8255. 1988.

Regulation of Agrochemicals: A Driving Force in Their Evolution. Gino J. Marco, et al., eds. American Chemical Society, 1155 16th St. N.W., Washington, District of Columbia 20036. (800) 227-5558. 1991. Agrochemicals and the regulatory process before 1970, subsequent regulations and their impact on pesticide chemistry.

Regulation of Pesticides: Science, Law and the Media. Government Institutes, Inc., 4 Research Pl., Ste. 200, Rockville, Maryland 20850. (301) 921-2300. Includes regulatory process, risk perception and risk communication, laboratory practices, and the weighing of risks and benefits.

Reviews of Environmental Contamination and Toxicology: v. 120. George W. Ware, ed. Springer-Verlag, 175 5th Ave., New York, New York 10010. (212) 460-1500; (800) 777-4643. 1991. Covers organochlorine pesticides and polychlorinated biphenyls in human adipose tissue, pesticide residues in foods imported into the U.S., and selected trace elements and the use of biomonitors in subtropical and tropical marine ecosystems.

Safer Insecticides: Development and Use. Marcel Dekker, Inc., 270 Madison Ave., New York, New York 10016. (212) 696-9000; (800) 228-1160. 1990. Communicates practical data for designing new insecticides, nontoxic to the environment and the public, and emphasizes optimal food production with safer insecticides.

Silent Spring Revisited. Gino J. Marco, et al., eds. American Chemical Society, 1155 16th St. N.W., Washington, District of Columbia 20036. (202) 872-4600; (800) 227-5558. 1987. Discusses Rachel Carson's vision and legacy. Traces the evolution of government regulations and the current pesticide registration criteria. Critically appraises the existing conditions and evaluates hazards.

Suspended, Cancelled, and Restricted Pesticides. U.S. Environmental Protection Agency, Office of Pesticides and Toxic Substances, 401 M St. SW, Washington, District of Columbia 20460. (202) 260-2090. 1990.

Synthesis and Chemistry of Agrochemicals II. Don R. Baker, et al., eds. American Chemical Society, 1155 16th St. N.W., Washington, District of Columbia 20036. (202) 872-4600; (800) 227-5558. 1991. Trends in synthesis and chemistry of agrochemicals.

Toxicological Profile for Carbon Tetrachloride. Agency for Toxic Substances and Disease Registry, U.S. Public Health Service, 1600 Clifton Rd. NE, Atlanta, Georgia 30333. (404) 452-4111. 1989.

UK Pesticides for Farmers and Growers. H. Kidd and D. Hartley, eds. Royal Society of Chemistry, c/o CRC Press, 2000 Corporate Blvd. N.W., Boca Raton, Florida 33431-9868. (800) 272-7737. 1987. Practical guide to pesticides designed specifically to meet the needs of farmers and growers.

Wildlife Toxicology. Tony J. Peterle. Van Nostrand Reinhold, 115 5th Ave., New York, New York 10003. (212) 354-3232. 1991. Presents an historical overview of the toxicology problem and summarizes the principal laws, testing protocols, and roles of leading U.S. federal agencies, especially EPA. Examines state and local issues, monitoring programs, and contains an unique section on the regulation of toxic substances overseas.

GOVERNMENTAL ORGANIZATIONS

Department of Agriculture: Pesticide Registration. Manager, Pesticide Control Division, 2219 Carey Ave., Cheyenne, Wyoming 82002-0100. (307) 777-6590.

Information and Communications: Extension Service. 14th and Independence Ave., S.W., Washington, District of Columbia 20250. (202) 447-3029.

Office of Public Affairs: Fish and Wildlife Service. 18th and C St., N.W., Washington, District of Columbia 20240. (202) 343-5634.

U.S. Environmental Protection Agency: Assistant Administrator for Enforcement. 401 M St., S.W., Washington, District of Columbia 20460. (202) 382-4134.

U.S. Environmental Protection Agency: Assistant Administrator for Pesticides and Toxic Substances. 401 M St., S.W., Washington, District of Columbia 20460. (202) 382-2902.

U.S. Environmental Protection Agency: Office of Civil Enforcement. 401 M St., S.W., Washington, District of Columbia 20460. (202) 382-4544.

U.S. Environmental Protection Agency: Office of Pesticide Programs. 401 M St., S.W., Washington, District of Columbia 20460. (202) 557-7090.

HANDBOOKS AND MANUALS

The Agrochemicals Handbook. H. Kidd and D. Hartlet, eds. Royal Society of Chemistry, c/o CRC Press, 2000 Corporate Blvd., N.W., Boca Raton, Florida 33431-9868. (800) 272-7737. 1991. 3rd ed. Contains comprehensive worldwide information and data on substances which are active components of agriculture chemical products currently used in crop protection and pest control.

CRC Handbook of Chemistry and Physics. CRC Press, 2000 Corporate Blvd. N.W., Boca Raton, Florida 33431. (407) 994-0555; (800) 272-7737. 1988. 67th ed.

CRC Handbook of Chromatography. CRC Press, 2000 Corporate Blvd. N.W., Boca Raton, Florida 33431. (800) 272-7737. Pesticides and related organic chemicals.

Crop Protection Chemical Reference. Chemical and Pharmaceutical Press/Wiley, 605 3rd Ave., New York, New York 10158-0012. (212) 850-6000. 1991. 7th ed. Updated annual edition of a standard reference on label information on crop protection chemicals contains the complete text of some 540 product labels, which provide detailed information concerning what products can be used to treat a certain crop for certain problems, using what quantities of the chemical and under what restrictions and precautions. Appendices provide useful information on such matters as coding required when transporting products, safety practices, calibrations, etc.

Farm Chemical Handbook. Meister Publishing Co., 37733 Euclid Ave., Willoughby, Ohio 44094. (216) 942-2000. Annual. Covers fertilizers and manures.

Guidance for the Reregistration of Pesticide Products Containing Lindane as the Active Ingredient. U.S. Environmental Protection Agency, Office of the Pesticides and Toxic Substances, 401 M St., SW, Washington, District of Columbia 20460. (202) 260-2090. 1985. The Federal Insecticide, Fungicide, Rodenticide Act directs EPA to reregister all pesticides as expeditiously as possible. The guide helps the user to carry out this task and to participate in the EPA's registration standard program. Includes extensive tabular data to the pesticides and an extensive bibliography.

Handbook of Environmental Data on Organic Chemicals. Karel Verschueren. Van Nostrand Reinhold, 115 5th Ave., New York, New York 10003. (212) 254-3232. 1983. Covers individual substances as well as mixtures and preparations. The profiles include: properties, air pollution factors, water pollution factors, and biological effects.

Handbook of Pesticide Toxicology. Wayland J. Hayes and Edward R. Laws, eds. Academic Press, c/o Harcourt Brace Jovanovich Inc., 6277 Sea Harbor Dr., Orlando, Florida 32887. (800) 346-8648. 1991. Three volumes. Covers various types of toxicity, nature of injury, reversibility, various methods of quantitating dose response, metabolism of toxins, factors affecting toxicity, absorption, and elimination.

Handbook of Toxicity of Pesticides to Wildlife. U.S. Department of the Interior, Fish and Wildlife Service, 1849 C St. NW, Washington, District of Columbia 20240. (202) 208-3171. 1984.

Hazardous Chemicals Data Book. G. Weiss, ed. Noyes Publications, 120 Mill Rd., Park Ridge, New Jersey 07656. (201) 391-8484. 1986. 2d ed. Supplies instant information on 1015 hazardous chemicals. The data will provide rapid assistance to personnel involved with handling of hazardous chemical materials and related accidents.

The Insecticide, Herbicide, Fungicide Quick Guide and Data Book. B. G. Page and N. T. Thomson. Thomson Publications, PO Box 9335, Fresno, California 93791. (209) 435-2163. 1984. Annually.

Manual of Acute Pesticide Toxicity. Guidotti. CRC Press, 2000 Corporate Blvd. N.W., Boca Raton, Florida 33431. (800) 272-7737. 1991.

Manual of Pesticide Residue Analysis. Hans-Peter Thier and Hans Zeumer, eds. VCH Publishers, 303 NW 12th Ave., Deerfield Beach, Florida 33442-1788. (305) 428-5566. 1989. Describes methods for analyzing pesticide residues representing those proven methods that are of the most value to the analyst. It presents 23 compound specific analytical methods.

Pesticide Fact Handbook. U. S. Environmental Protection Agency. Noyes Publications, 120 Mill Rd., Park Ridge, New Jersey 07656. (201) 391-8484. 1988-1990. Two volumes. Contains over 217 currently available pesticide fact sheets issued by the EPA. Each listing includes a description of the chemical use patterns and formulations, scientific findings, a summary of the Agency's regulatory position/rationale, toxicology, and a summary of major data gaps. Also covers trade name pesticides.

Pesticide Handbook. Peter Hurst. Journeyman Press, 955 Massachusetts Ave., Cambridge, Massachusetts 02139. (617) 868-3305. 1990.

Pesticide Handbook–Entoma. Entomological Society of America, 9301 Annapolis Rd., Lanham, Maryland 20706. (301) 731-4538. 1965-. Annual.

The Pesticide Handbook: Profiles for Action. International Organization of Consumers Unions, Emmastraat 9, The Hague, Netherlands 2595 EG. 1989.

Pesticide Poisonings Handbook: Recognition and Management of Pesticide Poisonings. Government Institutes, Inc., 4 Research Pl., Ste. 200, Rockville, Maryland 20850. (301) 921-2300. Provides current information on health hazards of pesticides and consensus recommendation for management of poisonings.

Pesticides Inspection Manual. Government Institutes, Inc., 4 Research Pl., Ste. 200, Rockville, Maryland 20850. (301) 921-2300. Provides all of the necessary guidance to carry out the standard field procedures including Pesticide law and definitions.

The Safe and Effective Use of Pesticides. Patrick J. Marer, et al. University of California Statewide Integrated Pest Management Project, Division of Agriculture and Natural Resources, Dist: Thomson Pub., PO Box 9335, Fresno, CA 93791, Oakland, California (209) 435-2163. 1988. Includes general information on pesticides, chemical pest control, and other pest management methods. Can be used as a study guide for the pest applicator test.

The Standard Pesticide User's Guide. Bert L. Bohmont. Prentice Hall, Rte. 9W, Englewood Cliffs, New Jersey 07632. (201) 592-2000. 1990. Includes material on laws and requirements, labeling, soil, groundwater, and endangered species. Covers new equipment, pumps, and techniques, as well as transportation, storage, decontamination, and disposal. Also covers integrated pest management.

Turf and Ornamental Chemicals Reference. John Wiley & Sons, Inc., 605 3rd Ave., New York, New York 10158-0012. (212) 850-6000. 1990. Provides with a consolidated and fully cross-indexed set of chemical product labels and material safety data sheets (MSDA's) in one easily accessible source. Products are indexed in 6 separate color coded indexes as follows: Brand name quick reference; manufacturer; product category; common and chemical name; and plant and site use and pet use.

UC IPM Pest Management Guidelines. ANR Publications, University of California, 6701 San Pablo Avenue, Oakland, California 94608-1239. (510) 642-2431. Official guidelines for monitoring techniques, pesticide use, and alternatives in agricultural crops.

ONLINE DATA BASES

AGRICOLA. U.S. Department of Agriculture, Office of Public Affairs, 14 Independence Ave., S.W., Washington, District of Columbia 20250. (202) 447-7454.

BioBusiness. Dialog Information Services, Inc., Marketing Dept., 3460 Hillview Avenue, Palo Alto, California 94304. (800) 334-2564 or (415) 858-3810. Provides information based on evaluations of the economic and business aspects of biological and biomedical research.

BIOSIS Previews. BIOSIS, 2100 Arch St., Philadelphia, Pennsylvania 19103-1399. (215) 587-4800. Largest and most comprehensive database of research in the life sciences. Contains citations for nearly 9000 primary research journals, monographs, reviews, symposia, preliminary reports, semi-popular journals, selected institutional reports, government reports and research communications.

Cambridge Scientific Abstracts Life Science–CSAL. Cambridge Scientific Abstracts, 5161 River Rd., Bethesda, Maryland 20816. (301) 961-6750. Provides access to the following abstracting services: "Life Sciences Collection," "Aquatic Sciences and Fisheries Abstracts," "Oceanic Abstracts," and "Pollution Abstracts."

CERCLIS. Chemical Information Systems, Inc., 7215 York Rd., Baltimore, Maryland 21212. (301) 321-8440. Information on hazardous waste disposal sites that have either been listed by the EPA on the National Priority List (NPL) or nominated for consideration for the NPL.

Chemical Abstracts-CA. Chemical Abstracts Service, 2540 Olentangy River Rd., P.O. Box 3012, Columbus, Ohio 43210. (800) 848-6533 or (614) 421-3600. Information sources include 9000 journals, patents from 27 countries, two industrial property organizations, new books, conference proceedings, and government research reports.

Chemical Carcinogenesis Research Information System–CCRIS. National Library of Medicine, 8600 Rockville Pike, Bethesda, Maryland 20894. (800) 638-8480. Individual assay results and test conditions for 1,451 chemicals in the areas of carcinogenicity, mutagenicity, tumor promotion, and cocarcinogenicity.

Chemical Collection System/Request Tracking–CCS/RTS. U.S. Environmental Protection Agency, Office of Pesticides and Toxic Substances, 401 M St., SW, Washington, District of Columbia 20460. (202) 260-2090. Contains information on various properties of a number of chemicals including environmental effects, test and analysis methods, and health effects. Available from EPA.

Chemical Dictionary Online–CHEMLINE. Chemical Abstracts Service, 2540 Olentangy River Rd., Columbus, Ohio 43210. (614) 421-3600 or (800) 848-6533. Part of MEDLINE of the National Library of Medicine (NLM). File of 900,000 names for chemical substances, representing 450,000 unique compounds. It contains such information as Chemical Abstracts (CA) Service Registry Numbers, molecular formulas, preferred chemical nomenclature, and generic and ring structure information. Available on NLM's ELHILL system.

Chemical Exposure. Science Applications International Corp., Health & Environmental Information, P.O. Box 2501, Oak Ridge, Tennessee 37831. (615) 482-9031. Database of chemicals that have been identified in both human tissues and body fluids and in feral and food animals. Contains reference to journal articles, conferences, and reports. Covers the whole fields of information related to human and animal exposure to food, air, and water contaminants and pharmaceuticals. Its records include information on chemical properties, formulas, tissues measured, analytical method used, demographics and more. Available on DIALOG.

Chemical Regulation Reporter. Bureau of National Affairs, BNA PLUS, 1231 25th St., N.W., Room 215, Washington, District of Columbia 20037. (800) 452-7773. Online version of periodicals of the same name.

Chemical Substance Control. Bureau of National Affairs, BNA PLUS, 1231 25th ST., N.W., Rm. 215, Washington, District of Columbia 20037. (800) 452-7773. Online version of periodical of the same name.

Enviro/Energyline Abstracts Plus. R. R. Bowker Co., 121 Chanlon Rd., New Providence, New Jersey 07974. (908) 464-6800.

Environmental Health News. Occupational Health Services, Inc., 450 7th Ave., New York, New York 10123. (212) 967-1100. Online access to court decisions, regulatory changes, and medical and scientific news related to hazardous substances.

Environmental Periodicals Bibliography. National Information Services Corp., Ste. 6, Wyman Towers, 3100 St. Paul St., Baltimore, Maryland 21218. (410)243-0797. Online version of abstract of same name.

EPA Fact Sheet Program. National Pesticide Information Retrieval System (NPIRS) Services Manager, Purdue University, Entomology Hall, West Lafayette, Indiana 47907. (317) 494-6616.

EPA Product Data Base. National Pesticide Information Retrieval System (NPIRS) Services Manager, Purdue University, Entomology Hall, West Lafayette, Indiana 47907. (317) 494-6616.

Farmer's Own Network for Education. Rodale Institute, 222 Main St., Emmaus, Pennsylvania 18098. (215) 967-5171. Efforts/results of farmers who have cut chemical use, diversified their farms, and adopted other regenerative agricultural techniques.

FIFRA and TSCA Enforcement System–FATES. U.S. Environmental Protection Agency, Office of Compliance and Monitoring, 401 M St., S.W., Washington, District of Columbia 20460. (202) 260-2090.

Industrial Studies Data Base–ISDB. U.S. Environmental Protection Agency, Office of Solid Waste, 401 M St., N.W., Washington, District of Columbia 20460. (202) 260-2090.

Medical Toxicology and Environmental Health. Department of Health and Social Security, Medical Toxiclology & Environmental Health Division, Hannibal House, Rm. 719, Elephant and Castle, London, England SE1 6TE. 44 (71) 972-2162.

The Merck Index Online. Merck & Company, Inc., Box 2000, Building 86-0900, Rahway, New Jersey 07065-0900. (201) 855-4558.

Monthly Catalog of United States Government Publications. U.S. G.P.O., Supt. of Docs., PO Box 371954, Pittsburgh, Pennsylvania 15250-7954. (202) 512-0000.

National Pesticide Information Retrieval System. Entomology Hall, Purdue University, West Lafayette, Indiana 47907. (317) 494-6616. Pesticide products registered with the Environmental Protection Agency, as well as similar information from 36 states.

National Stream Quality Accounting Network. National Water Data Exchange, U.S. Geological Survey, 421 National Center, Reston, Virginia 22092. (703) 648-4000. 150 hydrologic measurements collected at daily, monthly and quarterly intervals from more than 500 monitoring stations in the U.S.

National Technical Information Service. U.S. Department of Commerce, National Technical Information Service, Office of Data Base Services, 5285 Port Royal Rd., Springfield, Virginia 22161. (703) 487-4807. Bibliographic database of government sponsored research and technical reports.

NPIRS Pesticide and Hazardous Chemical Databases. National Pesticide Information Retrieval System, Purdue University, Entomology Hall, West Lafayette, Indiana 47907. (317) 494-6616. Covers more than 60,000 pesticides registered with the Environmental Protection Agency and with state government agencies.

Pest Management Research Information System. Agriculture Canada Research Branch, K.W. Neatby Building, Rm. 1135, Ottawa, Ontario, Canada K1A OC6. (613) 995-7084 x7254.

PESTDOC. Derwent Publications, Ltd., Rochdale House, 128 Theobalds Rd., London, England WC1X BRP. 44 (71) 242-5823.

PESTDOC II. Derwent Publications, Ltd., Rochdale House, 128 Theobalds Rd., London, England WC1X BRP. 44 (71) 242-5823.

Pesticide & Toxic Chemical News. Food Chemical News, Inc., 1101 Pennsylvania Ave., S.E., Washington, District of Columbia 20003. (202) 544-1980. Online version of the periodical of the same name.

PressNet Environmental Reports. Chemical Information Systems, Inc., 7215 York Rd., Baltimore, Maryland 21212. (301) 321-8440.

SCISEARCH. Institute for Scientific Information, University City Science Center, 3501 Market St., Philadelphia, Pennsylvania 19104. (215) 386-0100.

Standard Pesticide File. Derwent Publications, Ltd., 6845 Elm St., McLean, Virginia 22101. (703) 790-0400.

Tolerance Database. NPIRS (National Pesticide Information Retrieval System) User Services Manager, Entomology Hall, Purdue University, West Lafayette, Indiana 47907. (317) 494-6614.

PERIODICALS AND NEWSLETTERS

Agrarian Advocate. California Action Network, Box 464, Davis, California 95617. (916) 756-8518. 1978-. Quarterly. Includes issues of concern to rural California residents such as groundwater pollution, pesticides, and sustainable agriculture.

Agrichemical Age Magazine. HBJ Farm Publications, 731 Market Street, San Francisco, California 94103-2011. (415) 495-3340. Eleven times a year. Use and application of agricultural chemicals.

Alabama Pesticide News. Auburn University, Cooperative Extension Service, Extension Hall, Auburn, Alabama 36849. (205) 844-1592. Monthly.

Aquatic Toxicology. Elsevier Science Publishing Co., 655 Avenue of the Americas, New York, New York 10010. (212) 989-5800. 1981-. 6/year.

Between the Issues. Ecology Action Center, 1657 Barrington St., #520, Halifax, Nova Scotia, Canada B3J 2A1. (506) 422-4311. 1975-. Bimonthly. Newsletter that deals with environmental protection, uranium mining, waste, energy, agriculture, forestry, pesticides, and urban planning.

Chemical Regulation Reporter. Bureau of National Affairs, 1231 25th St. NW, Washington, District of Columbia 20037. (202) 452-4200. Weekly. Periodical covering legislative, regulatory, and industry action affecting controls on pesticides. Also available online.

Chemical Substances Control. Bureau of National Affairs, 1231 25th St. NW, Washington, District of Columbia 20037. (202) 452-4200. Biweekly. Periodical covering regulatory compliance and management of chemicals. Also available online.

Common Sense Pest Control Quarterly. Bio-Integral Resource Center, PO Box 7414, Berkeley, California 94707. (415) 524-2567. Four times a year. Least-toxic management of pests on indoor plants, pests that damage paper, controlling fleas and ticks on pets, and garden pests.

Drug and Chemical Toxicology. Marcel Dekker, Inc., 270 Madison Ave., New York, New York 10016. (212) 696-9000. Quarterly. Covers safety evaluations of drugs and chemicals.

Economic Poisons Report. New Mexico Dept. of Agriculture, Las Cruces, New Mexico 1979. Annual. Covers pesticides, pest control, and pesticides industry.

Environment Midwest. U.S. Environmental Protection Agency, 230 S. Dearborn, Chicago, Illinois 60604. (312) 353-2072. Monthly. Programs for fighting air and water pollution, hazardous and solid wastes, toxicants, pesticides, noise, and radiation.

Environmental Entomology. Entomological Society of America, 9301 Annapolis Road, Lanham, Maryland 20706. (301) 731-4538. Bimonthly. Covers ecology and population dynamics.

Environmental Health Letter. Business Publishers, Inc., 951 Pershing Dr., Silver Spring, Maryland 20910-4464.

(301) 587-6300. 1961-. Biweekly. Covers areas such as: indoor air, asbestos health effects, toxic substances testing, health problems at wastewater plants, risk-based sludge rules, medical waste, developmental toxicity risk assessment, animal carcinogen tests, pesticide risk, air toxics, aerospace chemicals, lead, radionuclide emissions, state right-to-know statutes, and incinerator emissions.

Environmental Health News. University of Washington, School of Public Health, Dept. of Environmental Health, Seattle, Washington 98195. (206) 543-3222. Quarterly. Occupational health, air pollution and safety.

Environmental Pollution & Control. National Technical Information Service, 5285 Port Royal Rd., Springfield, Virginia 22161. (703) 487-4650. Weekly. Covers air, noise, solid waste, water pollution, radiation, environmental health and safety, pesticide pollution and control.

Environmental Science and Technology. American Chemical Society, 1155 16th St. N.W., Washington, District of Columbia 20036. (800) 227-5558. 1967-. Monthly. Contains research articles on various aspects of environmental chemistry, interpretative articles by invited experts and commentary on the scientific aspects of environmental management.

EPA Journal. U.S. Environmental Protection Agency, 401 M St., S.W., A-107, Washington, District of Columbia 20460. (202) 382-4393. Bimonthly. Air and water pollution, pesticides, noise, solid waste.

Farm Chemicals Magazine. Meister Publishing Co., 37733 Euclid Avenue, Willoughby, Ohio 44094. (216) 942-2000. Monthly. Covers the production, marketing and application of fertilizers and crop protection chemicals.

Hilgardia: A Journal of Agricultural Science. California Agricultural Experiment Station, 2120 University Ave., Berkeley, California 94720. 1925-.

Insecticide and Acaricide Tests. Entomological Society of America, 9301 Annapolis Rd., Lanham, Maryland 20706-3115. (301) 731-4538. Irregular.

Journal of Environmental Quality. American Society of Agronomy, 677 S. Segoe Rd., Madison, Wisconsin 53711-1086. (608) 273-8080. 1972-. Quarterly. Reports and brief reviews of agricultural ecology, environmental engineering and pollution.

Journal of Environmental Science and Health. Marcel Dekker, Inc., 270 Madison Ave., New York, New York 10016. (212) 696-9000. Bimonthly. Concerns pesticides, food contaminants, chemical carcinogens, and agricultural wastes.

Journal of Pesticide Science. Elsevier Science Publishing Co., Journal Information Center, 655 Avenue of the Americas, New York, New York 10010. (212) 989-5800. Quarterly. Pesticide science in general, agrochemistry and chemistry of biologically active natural products.

The Merck Index. Merck Co., Inc., Box 2000, Rahway, New Jersey 07065. (201) 855-4558. Data on chemicals, drugs, and biological substances.

NCAMP's Technical Report. National Coalition Against the Misuse of Pesticides, 530 7th St., S.E., Washington, District of Columbia 20003. (202) 543-5450. Monthly. Actions on state & federal levels, legislation & litigation.

Pest Control Technology. Gei, Inc., 4012 Bridge Ave., Cleveland, Ohio 44113. (316) 961-4130. Monthly. Articles on pests and pesticides.

Pesticide. U.S. Department of the Interior, Natural Resource Library, 1849 C St. NW, Washington, District of Columbia 20240. (202) 208-3171. Annual.

Pesticide & Toxic Chemical News. Food Chemical News, Inc., 1101 Pennsylvania Avenue, SE, Washington, District of Columbia 20003. (202) 544-1980. Weekly. Covers government regulations of chemical pollution, transportation, disposal and occupational health. Also available online.

Pesticide Biochemistry and Physiology. Academic Press, c/o Harcourt Brace Jovanovich Inc., 6277 Sea Harbor Dr., Orlando, Florida 32887. (800) 346-8648. Nine times a year. Covers biochemistry and physiology of insecticides, herbicides and similar compounds.

Pesticide Science: An International Journal on Crop Protection and Pest Control. Elsevier Science Publishing Co., 655 Avenue of the Americas, New York, New York 10010. (212) 989-5800. 1970-. Monthly. Topics covered: Synthesis, screening, structure/activity and biochemical mode of action studies of compounds; physicochemical properties of new compounds; metabolism, degradation, field performance, environmental studies and safety in use of new and existing products; synthetic and naturally occurring insecticides; ecological implications of pesticide applications.

Pesticides and You. National Coalition Against the Misuse of Pesticides, 701 E St., S.E., Washington, District of Columbia 20003. (202) 543-5450. Five times a year. Analysis of pesticides and issues concerning urban and rural uses.

Technical Report. National Coalition Against the Misuse of Pesticides, 701 E St., SE, Washington, District of Columbia 20003. (202) 543-5450. Monthly. Congressional rulings and legislative action taken on pesticides.

RESEARCH CENTERS AND INSTITUTES

Benedict Estuarine Research Laboratory. Academy of Natural Sciences, Benedict Avenue, Benedict, Maryland 20612. (301) 274-3134.

Massachusetts Institute of Technology, Center for Fisheries Engineering Research. Sea Grant College Program, Building E38-376, 292 Main Street, Cambridge, Massachusetts 02139. (617) 253-7079.

Mississippi State Chemical Laboratory. Mississippi State University, P.O. Box CR, Mississippi State, Mississippi 39762. (601) 325-3324.

Pennsylvania State University, Pesticide Research Laboratory and Graduate Study Center. Department of Entomology, University Park, Pennsylvania 16802. (814) 863-7345.

Simon Fraser University, Centre for Pest Management. Burnaby Mountain, Burnaby, British Columbia, Canada V5 A1S6. (607) 291-3705.

Tri-State Bird Rescue and Research, Inc. 110 Possum Hollow Road, Wilmington, Delaware 19711. (302) 737-9543.

STATISTICS SOURCES

Agricultural Pesticide Use Trends and Policy Issues. U.S. G.P.O, Washington, District of Columbia 20402-9325. (202) 512-0000. Irregular. Farm use of pesticides and potential impact of alternative environmental protection.

The Insect Repellent Market. FIND/SVP, 625 Avenue of the Americas, New York, New York 10011. (212) 645-4500. 1991. Insect repellents marketed as aerosols, lotions and roll-on sticks.

The Market for Agricultural Chemicals. FIND/SVP, 625 Avenue of the Americas, New York, New York 10011. (212) 645-4500. 1990. Covers the markets for three types of agricultural chemicals: fertilizers, pesticide and natural and biotechnology products.

TRADE ASSOCIATIONS AND PROFESSIONAL SOCIETIES

American Chemical Society. 1155 16th St., N.W., Washington, District of Columbia 20036. (202) 872-4600.

American Institute of Biological Sciences. 730 11th St., N.W., Washington, District of Columbia 20001-4521. (202) 628-1500.

Association of American Pesticide Control Officials. Office of the Secretary, P.O. Box 1249, Hardwick, Vermont 05843. (802) 472-6956.

Chemical Producers and Distributors Association. 1220 19th St., N.W., Suite 202, Washington, District of Columbia 20036. (202) 785-2732.

Chemical Specialties Manufacturers Association. 1913 I St., N.W., Washington, District of Columbia 20006. (202) 872-8110.

Coalition to Keep Alaska Oil. 1667 K St., N.W., Suite 660, Washington, District of Columbia 20006. (202) 775-1796.

CONCERN, Inc. 1794 Columbia Rd, NW, Washington, District of Columbia 20009. (202) 328-8160.

Conservation and Research Foundation Inc. 240 Arapahal E., Lake Quivira, Kansas 66106. (913) 268-0076.

Conservation Districts Foundation, Inc. Conservation Film Service, Davis Conservation Library. 404 E. Main, P.O. Box 776, League City, Texas 77573. (713) 332-3404.

Industrial Chemical Research Association. 1811 Monroe St., Dearborn, Michigan 48124. (313) 563-0360.

International Pesticide Applicators Association. Box 1377, Milton, Washington 98354. (206) 922-9437.

National Agricultural Chemicals Association. 1155 15th St., N.W., Madison Building, Suite 900, Washington, District of Columbia 20005. (202) 296-1585.

National Coalition Against the Misuse of Pesticides. 701 E St., SE, Suite 200, Washington, District of Columbia 20003. (202) 543-5450.

National Council for Environmental Balance. 4169 Westport Rd., P.O. Box 7732, Louisville, Kentucky 40207. (502) 896-8731.

National Pest Control Association. 8100 Oak St., Dunn Loring, Virginia 22027. (703) 573-8330.

Natural Resources Defense Council. 40 W. 20th St., New York, New York 10011. (212) 727-2700.

Pesticide Producers Association. c/o Robert Bor, Bishop, Cook, Purcell, and Reynolds, 1400 L St., N.W., Suite 800, Washington, District of Columbia 20005. (202) 371-5700.

United Pesticide Formulators & Distributors Association. Prentiss Drug & Chemical, 3609 Shallowford Rd., Atlanta, Georgia 30340. (404) 458-1055.

PESTS

ABSTRACTING AND INDEXING SERVICES

Agrindex. AGRIS Coordinating Center, Via delle Terme di Caracalla, Rome, Italy I-00100. 61 0181-FA01. 1975-.

Biological Abstracts. BIOSIS, 2100 Arch St., Philadelphia, Pennsylvania 19103-1399. (215) 587-4800. 1927-.

Biological and Agricultural Index. H.W. Wilson Co., 950 University Ave., Bronx, New York 10452. (800) 367-6770. 1916-. Monthly.

Biology Digest. Data Courier, Plexus Pub Inc., 143 Old Marlton Pike, Medford, New Jersey 08055. 1974-. Monthly. Abstracts biology periodicals.

Biotechnology Research Abstracts. Cambridge Scientific Abstracts, 5161 River Rd., Bethesda, Maryland 20816. (301) 961-6750. Monthly. Includes such broad areas as genetic intervention, biochemical genetics, and microbiological techniques.

Ecology Abstracts. Cambridge Scientific Abstracts, 5161 River Rd., Bethesda, Maryland 20816. (301) 961-6750. Monthly.

Environment Abstracts. Bowker A & I Publishing, 121 Chanlon Rd., New Providence, New Jersey 07974. (908) 464-6800. 1974-.

Environment Index. Environment Information Center, Index Research Department, 124 E. 39th St., New York, New York 10016. 1971-. Annual.

Environmental Information Connection–EIC. Planning Information Program, Dept. of Urban and Regional Planning, University of Illinois, 1003 West Nevada, Urbana, Illinois 61801. (217) 333-1369. Also available online.

Environmental Periodicals Bibliography. Environmental Studies Institute, International Academy at Santa Barbara, 800 Garden St., Suite D, Santa Barbara, California 93101. (805) 965-5010. Also available online.

Field Crop Abstracts. C. A. B. International, 845 North Park Ave., Tucson, Arizona 85719. (602) 621-7897 or (800) 528-4841. 1948-. Monthly. Covers literature on agronomy, field production, crop botany and physiology of all annual field crops, both temperate and tropical.

Food Science and Technology Abstracts. International Food Information Service, c/o National Food Laboratory, 6363 Clark Ave., Dublin, California 94568. (800) 336-3782. 1969-.

Forestry Abstracts. C. A. B. International, Wallingford, England OX10 8DE. (0491) 3211. 1939/40-. Monthly. Journal of abstracts of journal articles, conferences, technical reports in the subject areas of: silviculture, forest mensuration and management, physical environment, fire, plant biology, genetics and breeding, mycolo-gy and pathology, game and wildlife, fish, protection of forests and other related matter.

Pesticides Abstracts. U.S. Environmental Protection Agency, Office of Pesticides Programs, 345 Curtland, Atlanta, Georgia 30365. (404) 347-2864. 1981. Monthly. Formerly: Health Aspects of Pesticides Abstracts Bulletin.

Science Citation Index. Institute for Scientific Information, 3501 Market St., Philadelphia, Pennsylvania 19104. 1961-.

BIBLIOGRAPHIES

Current Contents. Agriculture, Biology and Environmental Sciences. Institute for Scientific Information, 3501 Market St., Philadelphia, Pennsylvania 19104. (800) 523-1857. 1973-. Previous title: Current Contents. Agricultural, Food & Veterinary Sciences. Gives the table of contents of periodicals in the fields of agriculture, biology, environmental and related areas.

EPA Publications Bibliography. U.S. Environmental Protection Agency, Library Systems Branch, 401 M St., SW, Washington, District of Columbia 20460. (202) 260-2090. Quarterly.

Pesticide Applicator Training Materials: A Bibliography. Barbara O. Stommel. National Agricultural Library, 10301 Baltimore Blvd, Beltsville, Maryland 20705-2351. (301) 504-5755. 1991.

The Protection of Peanuts. Charles N. Bebee. National Agricultural Library, 10301 Baltimore Blvd., Beltsville, Maryland 20705-2351. (301) 504-5755. 1991. Citations from AGRICOLA concerning diseases and other environmental considerations.

The Protection of Tomatoes, Egg Plants and Peppers. Charles N. Bebee. National Agricultural Library, 10301 Baltimore Blvd., Beltsville, Maryland 20705-2351. (301) 504-5755. 1991. Citations from AGRICOLA concerning diseases and other environmental considerations.

DIRECTORIES

Gale Environmental Sourcebook. Karen Hill. Gale Research Co., 835 Penobscot Bldg., Detroit, Michigan 48226-4094. (313) 961-2242. Contacts, information sources, or general information on environmental topics.

ENCYCLOPEDIAS AND DICTIONARIES

Cambridge Encyclopedia of Life Sciences. A. E. Friday and David S. Ingram. Cambridge University Press, 40 W 20th St., New York, New York 10011. (212) 924-3900 or (800) 227-0247. 1985. Includes all topics under biology and ecology.

Dictionary of Forestry in Five Languages. Johannes Weck, et al. Elsevier Science Publishing Co., 655 Avenue of the Americas, New York, New York 10010. (212) 989-5800. 1966. Contains definitions in German, English, French, Spanish, and Russian.

The Dictionary of Pest Control. Sandra K. Kraft. Pinto, 914 Hillcrest Dr., Vienna, Virginia 22180. 1985. Deals with terms that relate to household, structural, industrial, commercial, and institutional pest control.

Grzimek's Encyclopedia of Ecology. Bernhard Grzimek. Van Nostrand Reinhold, 115 5th Ave., New York, New York 10003. (212) 254-3232. 1976.

McGraw-Hill Encyclopedia of Environmental Science. Sybil P. Parker. McGraw-Hill Science & Engineering Books, 11 W. 19th St., New York, New York 10011. (212) 337-6010. 1980. Covers ecology, man's influence on nature, and environmental protection.

North American Reference Encyclopedia of Ecology and Pollution. William White. North American Pub. Co., 401 N. Broad St., Philadelphia, Pennsylvania 19108. (215) 238-5300. 1972.

Van Nostrand's Scientific Encyclopedia. Glenn D. Considine, ed. Van Nostrand Reinhold, 115 5th Ave., New York, New York 10003. (212) 254-3232. 1983. Sixth edition. Includes all broad subject areas in science.

GENERAL WORKS

Biotechnology for Biological Control of Pests and Vectors. Karl Maramorosch. CRC Press, 2000 Corporate Blvd. N.W., Boca Raton, Florida 33431. (407) 994-0555; (800) 272-7737. 1991.

Bugs, Slugs and Other Thugs: Controlling Garden Pests Organically. Rhonda Massingham Hart. Garden Way Pub., Schoolhouse Rd., Pownal, Vermont 05261. (802) 823-5811; (800) 441-5700. 1991.

Common Sense Pest Control. William Olkowski, et al. Tauton Pr., 63 South Main St., Box 5506, Newton, Connecticut 06740-5506. 1991. Discusses ways to manage other living organisms that are regarded as pests.

Ecological Implications of Contemporary Agriculture. H. Eijsackers and A. Quispel, eds. Munksgaard International, PO Box 2148, Copenhagen K, Denmark DK-1016. 1988. Proceedings of the 4th European Symposium, September 7-12, 1986, Wageningen. Ecological bulletins are published in cooperation with ecological journals; holarctic ecology and Oikos. They consist of monographs, reports, and symposium proceedings on topics of international interest.

Environmental Protection and Biological Forms of Control of Pest Organisms. B. Lundholm. Swedish National Science Research Council, Editorial Service, P.O. Box 6711, Stockholm, Sweden S-113 85. 08-15-1580. 1980. Environmental aspects of pests and natural pesticides.

Influence of Environmental Factors on the Control of Grape, Pests, Diseases and Weeds. R. Cavalloro. A. A. Balkema, Old Post Rd., Brookfield, Vermont 05036. (802) 276-3162. 1989. Influence of environmental factors on cultivation of vines, and impact of insects, mites, diseases and weeds and pesticides.

Managing Resistance to Agrochemicals: From Fundamental Research to Practical Strategies. Maurice B. Green, et al., eds. American Chemical Society, 1155 16th St. N.W., Washington, District of Columbia 20036. (800) 227-5558. 1990. A compilation of chapters written by some of the foremost scientists in pesticide and pest management research today.

HANDBOOKS AND MANUALS

CRC Handbook of Pest Management in Agriculture. David Pimentel. CRC Press, 2000 Corporate Blvd. N.W., Boca Raton, Florida 33431. (800) 272-7737. 1991. 2d ed.

Examines the interdependency of agricultural pest management strategies.

ONLINE DATA BASES

BIOSIS Previews. BIOSIS, 2100 Arch St., Philadelphia, Pennsylvania 19103-1399. (215) 587-4800. Largest and most comprehensive database of research in the life sciences. Contains citations for nearly 9000 primary research journals, monographs, reviews, symposia, preliminary reports, semi-popular journals, selected institutional reports, government reports and research communications.

Enviro/Energyline Abstracts Plus. R. R. Bowker Co., 121 Chanlon Rd., New Providence, New Jersey 07974. (908) 464-6800.

Environmental Periodicals Bibliography. National Information Services Corp., Ste. 6, Wyman Towers, 3100 St. Paul St., Baltimore, Maryland 21218. (410)243-0797. Online version of abstract of same name.

Monthly Catalog of United States Government Publications. U.S. G.P.O., Supt. of Docs., PO Box 371954, Pittsburgh, Pennsylvania 15250-7954. (202) 512-0000.

National Technical Information Service. U.S. Department of Commerce, National Technical Information Service, Office of Data Base Services, 5285 Port Royal Rd., Springfield, Virginia 22161. (703) 487-4807. Bibliographic database of government sponsored research and technical reports.

Pest Management Research Information System. Agriculture Canada Research Branch, K.W. Neatby Building, Rm. 1135, Ottawa, Ontario, Canada K1A OC6. (613) 995-7084 x7254.

PESTDOC. Derwent Publications, Ltd., Rochdale House, 128 Theobalds Rd., London, England WC1X BRP. 44 (71) 242-5823.

PESTDOC II. Derwent Publications, Ltd., Rochdale House, 128 Theobalds Rd., London, England WC1X BRP. 44 (71) 242-5823.

Pesticide & Toxic Chemical News. Food Chemical News, Inc., 1101 Pennsylvania Ave., S.E., Washington, District of Columbia 20003. (202) 544-1980. Online version of the periodical of the same name.

SCISEARCH. Institute for Scientific Information, University City Science Center, 3501 Market St., Philadelphia, Pennsylvania 19104. (215) 386-0100.

Tolerance Database. NPIRS (National Pesticide Information Retrieval System) User Services Manager, Entomology Hall, Purdue University, West Lafayette, Indiana 47907. (317) 494-6614.

PERIODICALS AND NEWSLETTERS

Common Sense Pest Control Quarterly. Bio-Integral Resource Center, PO Box 7414, Berkeley, California 94707. (415) 524-2567. Four times a year. Least-toxic management of pests on indoor plants, pests that damage paper, controlling fleas and ticks on pets, and garden pests.

Home, Yard and Garden Pest Newsletter. Agriculture Newsletter Service, University of Illinois, 116 Mumford Hall, 1301 W. Gregory Dr., Urbana, Illinois 61801. Twenty times a year. Pest controls, application equipment and methods, and storage and disposal of pesticides for the yard and garden.

Journal of Environmental Science and Health. Marcel Dekker, Inc., 270 Madison Ave., New York, New York 10016. (212) 696-9000. Bimonthly. Concerns pesticides, food contaminants, chemical carcinogens, and agricultural wastes.

Pest Control Technology. Gei, Inc., 4012 Bridge Ave., Cleveland, Ohio 44113. (316) 961-4130. Monthly. Articles on pests and pesticides.

STATISTICS SOURCES

Environmental Data Compendium. OECD Publications and Information Center, 2001 L St., N.W., Suite 700, Washington, District of Columbia 20036. (202) 785-6323. 1989.

Environmental Indicators. OECD Publications and Information Center, 2001 L St., N.W., Suite 700, Washington, District of Columbia 20036. (202) 785-6323. 1991.

Environmental Quality. Council on Environmental Quality. U.S. G.P.O., Washington, District of Columbia 20401. (202) 512-0000. Annual.

The State of the Environment. OECD Publications and Information Center, 2001 L St., N.W., Suite 700, Washington, District of Columbia 20036. (202) 785-6323. 1991.

TRADE ASSOCIATIONS AND PROFESSIONAL SOCIETIES

American Entomological Society. 1900 Race St., Philadelphia, Pennsylvania 19103. (215) 561-3978.

American Institute of Biological Sciences. 730 11th St., N.W., Washington, District of Columbia 20001-4521. (202) 628-1500.

American Registry of Professional Entomologists. 9301 Annapolis Rd., Lanham, Maryland 20706. (301) 731-4541.

Association of American Pesticide Control Officials. Office of the Secretary, P.O. Box 1249, Hardwick, Vermont 05843. (802) 472-6956.

Entomological Society of America. 9301 Annapolis Rd., Lanham, Maryland 20706-3115. (301) 731-4535.

National Pest Control Association. 8100 Oak St., Dunn Loring, Virginia 22027. (703) 573-8330.

PETROLEUM

ABSTRACTING AND INDEXING SERVICES

Applied Science and Technology Index. H.W. Wilson Co., 950 University Ave., Bronx, New York 10452. (800) 367-6770. Formerly Industrial Arts Index.

Chemical Abstracts. Chemical Abstracts Service, 2540 Olentangy River Rd., PO Box 3012, Columbus, Ohio 43210. (800) 848-6533. 1907-.

Environment Abstracts. Bowker A & I Publishing, 121 Chanlon Rd., New Providence, New Jersey 07974. (908) 464-6800. 1974-.

Environment Index. Environment Information Center, Index Research Department, 124 E. 39th St., New York, New York 10016. 1971-. Annual.

Environmental Information Connection–EIC. Planning Information Program, Dept. of Urban and Regional Planning, University of Illinois, 1003 West Nevada, Urbana, Illinois 61801. (217) 333-1369. Also available online.

Environmental Periodicals Bibliography. Environmental Studies Institute, International Academy at Santa Barbara, 800 Garden St., Suite D, Santa Barbara, California 93101. (805) 965-5010. Also available online.

General Science Index. H. W. Wilson Co., 950 University Ave., Bronx, New York 10452. 1978-. Monthly, also issued in annual cumulation. Cumulative subject index to English language periodicals in the subject fields of astronomy, botany, chemistry, earth science, environment and conservation, food and nutrition, genetics, mathematics, medicine and health, microbiology, oceanography, physics, physiology and zoology.

BIBLIOGRAPHIES

Bibliography and Index of Geology. American Geological Institute, 4220 King St., Alexandria, Virginia 22302. Monthly. Includes environmental geology and hydrogeology.

EPA Publications Bibliography. U.S. Environmental Protection Agency, Library Systems Branch, 401 M St., SW, Washington, District of Columbia 20460. (202) 260-2090. Quarterly.

Guide to the Petroleum Reference Literature. Barbara C. Pearson and Katharine B. Ellwood. Libraries Unlimited, Inc., PO Box 6633, Englewood, Colorado 80155-6633. (303) 770-1220. 1987. Focuses on petroleum sources, also includes some major works in these related disciplines as they apply to the petroleum industry.

DIRECTORIES

Petroleum Engineering and Technology School. Society of Petroleum Engineers, PO Box 833836, Richardson, Texas 75083-3836. (214) 669-3377. 1987. Resource document for educational institutions and petroleum companies. Includes information about students, courses of study and institutional size and other related data.

Petroleum Marketer–Self-Service Equipment Directory. McKeand Publications, Inc., 636 First Ave., West Haven, Connecticut 06516. (203) 934-5288.

ENCYCLOPEDIAS AND DICTIONARIES

Dictionary of Petroleum Technology: English/French and French/English. M. Moureau and G. Brace. Editions Technip, 27 rue Giroux, Paris, France F-75737. Cedex 15 1979. Second edition. Includes approximately 50,000 terms and expressions. Multidisciplinary dictionary dealing with subject areas of: geology, geophysics, drilling, production, reservoir engineering, refining, petrochemicals, transportation, applications, engines, pollution economics, safety data processing and alternative energies.

A Dictionary of Petroleum Terms. Jodie Leecraft, ed. Petroleum Extension Service, Division of Continuing Education, The University of Texas at Austin, Austin, Texas 78712. 1983. Third edition.

The Encyclopedia of Geochemistry and Environmental Sciences. Rhodes Whitmore Fairbridge. Van Nostrand Reinhold Co., 115 5th Ave., New York, New York 10003. (212) 254-3232. 1972.

The Illustrated Petroleum Reference Dictionary. Robert D. Langenkamp. PennWell Books, PO Box 1260, Tulsa, Oklahoma 74101. (918) 835-3161. 1985. Third edition. Includes terms relating to petroleum. Special features of this dictionary include: D & D Standard Oil abbreviator and Universal Conversion Factor list.

McGraw-Hill Encyclopedia of Science and Technology. McGraw-Hill, 1221 Avenue of the Americas, New York, New York 10020. (212) 512-2000 or (800) 262-4729. 1992. Seventh edition. Issued in multiple volumes including index. Includes all science and technology broad subject areas.

Oil Terms: A Dictionary of Terms Used in Oil Exploration and Development. Leo Crook. International Pub Service, 114 E 32d St., New York, New York 10016. 1975.

Van Nostrand's Scientific Encyclopedia. Glenn D. Considine, ed. Van Nostrand Reinhold, 115 5th Ave., New York, New York 10003. (212) 254-3232. 1983. Sixth edition. Includes all broad subject areas in science.

GENERAL WORKS

Acute Lethality Data for Ontario's Petroleum Refinery Effluents Covering the Period from December 1988 to May 1989. Ontario Ministry of Environment, c/o National Technical Information Service, 5285 Port Royal Rd., Springfield, Virginia 22161. (703) 487-4650. 1990. Order number MIC-91-02537 LDM.

Acute Lethality Data for Ontario's Petroleum Refinery Effluents covering the Period June 1989 to November 1989. J. T. Lee. Ontario Ministry of the Environment, c/o National Technical Information Service, 5285 Port Royal Rd., Springfield, Virginia 22161. (703) 487-4650. 1989. Order number MIC-91-02523 LDM.

Leaking Underground Storage Tanks Containing Motor Fuels: A Chemical Advisory. U.S. Environmental Protection Agency, Office of Toxic Substances, 401 M St., S.W., Washington, District of Columbia 20460. (202) 260-2090. 1984. Underground storage of petroleum products.

Magill's Survey of Science. Earth Science Series. Frank N. Magill. Salem Press, PO Box 50062, Pasadena, California 91105. 1990-. Five volumes. Includes information on earth's crust, hot spots and volcanic island chains, physical properties of minerals, rock magnetism, physical properties of rocks, and index.

Petroleum Transportation and Production: Oil Spill and Pollution Control. Marshall Sittig. Noyes Publications, 120 Mill Rd., Park Ridge, New Jersey 07656. (201) 391-8484. 1978. Environmental aspects of petroleum industry and trade; oil spills and petroleum transportation.

Refinery System Safety for Contractors: A Six Volume Set. Fluke & Associates, Inc. PennWell Books, PO Box 21288, Tulsa, Oklahoma 74121. (918) 831-9421; (800) 752-9764. 1991. Employee-training and documentation manuals that comply with the safety regulations of OSHA and insurance carriers.

Restoration of Petroleum-Contaminated Aquifers. Stephen M. Testa and Duane L. Winegardner. Lewis Publishers, 200 Corporate Blvd. NW, Boca Raton, Florida 33431. (407) 994-0555 or (800)272-7737. 1991. Presents information on restoring aquifers contaminated by petroleum products and derivatives. Discusses the regulatory environment and framework within which environmental issues are addressed and explains the geochemistry of petroleum.

U.S. Petroleum Strategies in the Decade of the Environment. Bob Williams. PennWell Books, PO Box 21288, Tulsa, Oklahoma 74121. (918) 831-9421; (800) 752-9764. 1991.

Used Oil: Disposal Options, Management Practices and Potential Liability. John J. Nolan, et al. Government Institutes, Inc., 4 Research Pl., Suite 200, Rockville, Maryland 20850. (301) 921-2300. 1990. 3d ed. Helps with developing a plan to store and manage the handling of used oil that affects thousands of generators, collectors, processors, marketers and burners.

HANDBOOKS AND MANUALS

Petroleum Engineering Handbook. Howard B. Bradley, ed. Society of Petroleum Engineers, PO Box 833836, Richardson, Texas 75083-3836. (214) 669-3377. 1987. Revised edition. Compilation of practical information and data covering production equipment and reservoir engineering.

ONLINE DATA BASES

Active Well Data On-Line. Petroleum Information Cooperation, 4100 E. Dry Creek Road, Littleton, Colorado 80122. (800) 525-5569.

APILIT. American Petroleum Institute, 1220 L St. N.W., Washington, District of Columbia 20005. (202) 682-8000.

APIPAT. American Petroleum Institute, 1220 L St. N.W., Washington, District of Columbia 20005. (202) 682-8000.

Chemical Abstracts-CA. Chemical Abstracts Service, 2540 Olentangy River Rd., P.O. Box 3012, Columbus, Ohio 43210. (800) 848-6533 or (614) 421-3600. Information sources include 9000 journals, patents from 27 countries, two industrial property organizations, new books, conference proceedings, and government research reports.

Chemical Market Associates Petrochemical Market Reports. Chemical Market Associates, Inc., 11757 Daty Freeway, Suite 750, Houston, Texas 77079. (713) 531-4660.

Electric Power Industry Abstracts. Utility Data Institute, 1700 K St., N.W., Suite 400, Washington, District of Columbia 20006. (800) 466-3660.

EMIS. TECNON (U.K.) Limited, 12 Calico House, Plantation Wharf, York Place, Battersea, London, England SW11 3TN. 44 (71) 924-3955.

Enviro/Energyline Abstracts Plus. R. R. Bowker Co., 121 Chanlon Rd., New Providence, New Jersey 07974. (908) 464-6800.

Environmental Periodicals Bibliography. National Information Services Corp., Ste. 6, Wyman Towers, 3100 St. Paul St., Baltimore, Maryland 21218. (410)243-0797. Online version of abstract of same name.

Green Markets. McGraw-Hill Science & Engineering Books, 11 W. 19th St., New York, New York 10011. (212) 337-6010.

International Petroleum Abstracts. John Wiley & Sons, Ltd., Baffers Lane, Chichester, Sussex, England PO1 91UD. 44 (243) 770215.

International Petroleum Annual. U.S. Department of Energy, Integrated Technical Information System, P.O. Box 62, Oak Ridge, Tennessee 37831. (615) 576-1222.

Oil & Gas Journal Energy Database. PennWell Books, PO Box 1260, Tulsa, Oklahoma 74101. (918) 835-3161.

STATISTICS SOURCES

Basic Petroleum Data Book: Petroleum Industry Statistics. American Petroleum Institute, 1220 L St. N.W., Washington, District of Columbia 20005. (202) 682-8000. Three times a year. Oil and gas industry exploration, production, refining, demand, financial condition, prices, and reserves.

Monthly Completion Report: Report on Well Completions in the U.S. American Petroleum Institute, 1220 L St. N.W., Washington, District of Columbia 20005. (202) 682-8000. Monthly. Exploratory and development oil and gas well drilling.

Monthly Statistical Report, Estimated U.S. Petroleum Balance. American Petroleum Institute, 1220 L St. N.W., Washington, District of Columbia 20005. (202) 682-8000. Monthly. Petroleum supply and demand.

Oil and Gas Information. International Energy Agency. OECD Pub., Suite 700, 2001 L St. N.W., Washington, District of Columbia 20036-4905. (202) 785-6323. 1989-. Annually. IEA's annual statistical reference (in French and English) on oil and gas supply and demand. Contains statistics for OECD member countries on production, trade, demand, prices, refining capacity, and reserves. Data on world production, trade, and consumption of major oil products and natural gas are shown in summary tables.

Weekly Statistical Bulletin. American Petroleum Institute, 1220 L St. N.W., Washington, District of Columbia 20005. (202) 682-8000. 1962-. Weekly. Crude oil and refined product daily average production and imports, and end-of-week stocks.

TRADE ASSOCIATIONS AND PROFESSIONAL SOCIETIES

American Association of Petroleum Geologists. Box 979, Tulsa, Oklahoma 74101. (918) 584-2555.

American Association of Petroleum Landmen. 4100 Fossil Creek Blvd., Fort Worth, Texas 76137. (817) 847-7700.

American Independent Refiners Association. 649 S. Olive St., Suite 500, Los Angeles, California 20005. (202) 682-8000.

American Petroleum Institute. 1220 L St., N.W., Washington, District of Columbia 20005. (202) 682-8000.

International Union of Petroleum & Industrial Workers. 8131 E. Rosencrans Ave., Paramount, California 90723. (213) 630-6232.

National Petroleum Council. 1625 K St., N.W., Suite 601, Washington, District of Columbia 20006. (202) 393-6100.

National Petroleum Refiners Association. 1899 L St., N.W., Suite 1000, Washington, District of Columbia 20036. (202) 457-0480.

Society of Petroleum Engineers. P.O. Box 833836, Richardson, Texas 75083. (214) 669-3377.

pH (HYDROGEN ION CONCENTRATION)

ABSTRACTING AND INDEXING SERVICES

ASFA Aquaculture Abstracts. Cambridge Scientific Abstracts, Inc., 5161 River Rd., Bethesda, Maryland 20816. (301) 961-6750. 1984.

Biological and Agricultural Index. H.W. Wilson Co., 950 University Ave., Bronx, New York 10452. (800) 367-6770. 1916-. Monthly.

Biotechnology Research Abstracts. Cambridge Scientific Abstracts, 5161 River Rd., Bethesda, Maryland 20816. (301) 961-6750. Monthly. Includes such broad areas as genetic intervention, biochemical genetics, and microbiological techniques.

Chemical Abstracts. Chemical Abstracts Service, 2540 Olentangy River Rd., PO Box 3012, Columbus, Ohio 43210. (800) 848-6533. 1907-.

Environment Abstracts. Bowker A & I Publishing, 121 Chanlon Rd., New Providence, New Jersey 07974. (908) 464-6800. 1974-.

Environment Index. Environment Information Center, Index Research Department, 124 E. 39th St., New York, New York 10016. 1971-. Annual.

Environmental Information Connection–EIC. Planning Information Program, Dept. of Urban and Regional Planning, University of Illinois, 1003 West Nevada, Urbana, Illinois 61801. (217) 333-1369. Also available online.

Environmental Periodicals Bibliography. Environmental Studies Institute, International Academy at Santa Barbara, 800 Garden St., Suite D, Santa Barbara, California 93101. (805) 965-5010. Also available online.

General Science Index. H. W. Wilson Co., 950 University Ave., Bronx, New York 10452. 1978-. Monthly, also issued in annual cumulation. Cumulative subject index to English language periodicals in the subject fields of astronomy, botany, chemistry, earth science, environment and conservation, food and nutrition, genetics, mathematics, medicine and health, microbiology, oceanography, physics, physiology and zoology.

Physics Briefs. Physikalische Berichte. Physik Verlag, Pappapelallee 3, Postfach 101161, Weinheim, Germany D-6940. 1979-. Semimonthly. In English. Volumes for 1979- issued by the Deutsche Physikalische Gesellschaft and the Fachinformationszentrum Energie Physik, Mathematik in cooperation with the American Institute of Physics.

Science Citation Index. Institute for Scientific Information, 3501 Market St., Philadelphia, Pennsylvania 19104. 1961-.

BIBLIOGRAPHIES

Bibliography and Index of Geology. American Geological Institute, 4220 King St., Alexandria, Virginia 22302. Monthly. Includes environmental geology and hydrogeology.

EPA Publications Bibliography. U.S. Environmental Protection Agency, Library Systems Branch, 401 M St., SW, Washington, District of Columbia 20460. (202) 260-2090. Quarterly.

ENCYCLOPEDIAS AND DICTIONARIES

Dictionary of Alkaloids. J. Buckingham Southon. Chapman & Hall, 29 West 35th St., New York, New York 10001-2291. (212) 244-3336. 1989.

Encyclopedia of Human Biology. Renato Dulbecco, ed. Academic Press, c/o Harcourt Brace Jovanovich Inc., 6277 Sea Harbor Dr., Orlando, Florida 32887. (800) 346-8648. 1991. Eight volumes.

Encyclopedia of Physics. Rita G. Lerner and George L. Trigg. VCH Publishers, 303 NW 12th Ave., Deerfield Beach, Florida 33442-1788. (305) 428-5566. 1991. Second edition.

McGraw-Hill Encyclopedia of Science and Technology. McGraw-Hill, 1221 Avenue of the Americas, New York, New York 10020. (212) 512-2000 or (800) 262-4729. 1992. Seventh edition. Issued in multiple volumes including index. Includes all science and technology broad subject areas.

Van Nostrand's Scientific Encyclopedia. Glenn D. Considine, ed. Van Nostrand Reinhold, 115 5th Ave., New York, New York 10003. (212) 254-3232. 1983. Sixth edition. Includes all broad subject areas in science.

GENERAL WORKS

Acidic Deposition and Forest Soils. Dan Binkley. Springer-Verlag, 175 Fifth Ave., New York, New York 10010. (212) 460-1500 or (800) 777-4643. 1990. Environmental aspects of acid deposition, forest soils and soil acidity.

Alkalinity, pH Changes with Temperature for Waters in Industrial Systems. A.G.D. Emerson. Halsted Press, 605 3rd Ave., New York, New York 10158. (212) 850-6000. 1986. Water and wastewater technology topics.

Magill's Survey of Science. Earth Science Series. Frank N. Magill. Salem Press, PO Box 50062, Pasadena, California 91105. 1990-. Five volumes. Includes information on earth's crust, hot spots and volcanic island chains, physical properties of minerals, rock magnetism, physical properties of rocks, and index.

ONLINE DATA BASES

CAS Source Index–CASSI. Chemical Abstracts Service, 2540 Olentangy River Rd., P.O. Box 3012, Columbus, Ohio 43210. (800) 848-6533 or (614) 421-3600. A listing of bibliographic and library holdings information for scientific and technical primary literature relevant to the chemical sciences.

Chemical Abstracts-CA. Chemical Abstracts Service, 2540 Olentangy River Rd., P.O. Box 3012, Columbus, Ohio 43210. (800) 848-6533 or (614) 421-3600. Information sources include 9000 journals, patents from 27 countries, two industrial property organizations, new

books, conference proceedings, and government research reports.

Enviro/Energyline Abstracts Plus. R. R. Bowker Co., 121 Chanlon Rd., New Providence, New Jersey 07974. (908) 464-6800.

Environmental Periodicals Bibliography. National Information Services Corp., Ste. 6, Wyman Towers, 3100 St. Paul St., Baltimore, Maryland 21218. (410)243-0797. Online version of abstract of same name.

RESEARCH CENTERS AND INSTITUTES

Adirondack Lakes Survey Corporation. New York State Dept. of Environmental Conservation, Ray Brook, New York 12977. (518) 891-2758.

TRADE ASSOCIATIONS AND PROFESSIONAL SOCIETIES

American Chemical Society. 1155 16th St., N.W., Washington, District of Columbia 20036. (202) 872-4600.

PHARMACEUTICAL WASTES

See also: MEDICAL WASTES

ABSTRACTING AND INDEXING SERVICES

Chemical Abstracts. Chemical Abstracts Service, 2540 Olentangy River Rd., PO Box 3012, Columbus, Ohio 43210. (800) 848-6533. 1907-.

Environment Abstracts. Bowker A & I Publishing, 121 Chanlon Rd., New Providence, New Jersey 07974. (908) 464-6800. 1974-.

Environment Index. Environment Information Center, Index Research Department, 124 E. 39th St., New York, New York 10016. 1971-. Annual.

Environmental Information Connection–EIC. Planning Information Program, Dept. of Urban and Regional Planning, University of Illinois, 1003 West Nevada, Urbana, Illinois 61801. (217) 333-1369. Also available online.

Environmental Periodicals Bibliography. Environmental Studies Institute, International Academy at Santa Barbara, 800 Garden St., Suite D, Santa Barbara, California 93101. (805) 965-5010. Also available online.

Pollution Abstracts. Cambridge Scientific Abstracts, 5161 River Rd., Bethesda, Maryland 20816. (301) 961-6750. Six/year. Indexes worldwide technical literature on environmental pollution. Covers air pollution, marine and freshwater pollution, sewage and wastewater treatment, waste management, toxicology and health, noise pollution, radiation, land pollution, and environmental policies, programs, legislation, and education. Also available online.

BIBLIOGRAPHIES

EPA Publications Bibliography. U.S. Environmental Protection Agency, Library Systems Branch, 401 M St., SW, Washington, District of Columbia 20460. (202) 260-2090. Quarterly.

DIRECTORIES

Pharmaceutical Manufacturers of the U.S. Noyes Publications, 120 Mill Rd., Park Ridge, New Jersey 07656. (201) 391-8484. 1977.

Pharmaceutical Products–Wholesalers & Manufacturers. American Business Directories, Inc., 5711 S. 86th Circle, Omaha, Nebraska 68127. (402) 593-4600.

ENCYCLOPEDIAS AND DICTIONARIES

Van Nostrand's Scientific Encyclopedia. Glenn D. Considine, ed. Van Nostrand Reinhold, 115 5th Ave., New York, New York 10003. (212) 254-3232. 1983. Sixth edition. Includes all broad subject areas in science.

GENERAL WORKS

Pharmaceutical Industry: Hazardous Waste Generation, Treatment, and Disposal. U.S. Environmental Protection Agency, 401 M St., S.W., Washington, District of Columbia 20460. (202) 260-2090. 1976. Pollutants in the pharmaceutical industry.

ONLINE DATA BASES

Chemical Abstracts-CA. Chemical Abstracts Service, 2540 Olentangy River Rd., P.O. Box 3012, Columbus, Ohio 43210. (800) 848-6533 or (614) 421-3600. Information sources include 9000 journals, patents from 27 countries, two industrial property organizations, new books, conference proceedings, and government research reports.

Enviro/Energyline Abstracts Plus. R. R. Bowker Co., 121 Chanlon Rd., New Providence, New Jersey 07974. (908) 464-6800.

Environmental Periodicals Bibliography. National Information Services Corp., Ste. 6, Wyman Towers, 3100 St. Paul St., Baltimore, Maryland 21218. (410)243-0797. Online version of abstract of same name.

Medical Waste News. Business Publishers, Inc., 951 Pershing Dr., Silver Spring, Maryland 20910-4464. (301) 587-6300. Online access to regulation, legislation, and technological news and developments related to medical waste management and disposal. Online version of the periodical of the same name.

PressNet Environmental Reports. Chemical Information Systems, Inc., 7215 York Rd., Baltimore, Maryland 21212. (301) 321-8440.

PERIODICALS AND NEWSLETTERS

Medical Waste News. Business Publishers, Inc., 951 Pershing Dr., Silver Spring, Maryland 20910-4464. (301) 587-6300. 1989-. Biweekly. Covers EPA regulations and actions, state and nationwide changes in the laws, which management firms are landing big contracts, and also reports on technology such as: incineration, autoclaving, microwaves, etc. Also available online.

TRADE ASSOCIATIONS AND PROFESSIONAL SOCIETIES

American Pharmaceutical Association. 2215 Constitution Ave., N.W., Washington, District of Columbia 20037. (202) 628-4410.

National Association of Pharmaceutical Manufacturers. 747 Third Ave., New York, New York 10017. (212) 838-3720.

Pharmaceutical Manufacturers Association. 110 15th St., N.W., Washington, District of Columbia 20005. (202) 835-3400.

PHENOL

See also: PETROLEUM

ABSTRACTING AND INDEXING SERVICES

Chemical Abstracts. Chemical Abstracts Service, 2540 Olentangy River Rd., PO Box 3012, Columbus, Ohio 43210. (800) 848-6533. 1907-.

General Science Index. H. W. Wilson Co., 950 University Ave., Bronx, New York 10452. 1978-. Monthly, also issued in annual cumulation. Cumulative subject index to English language periodicals in the subject fields of astronomy, botany, chemistry, earth science, environment and conservation, food and nutrition, genetics, mathematics, medicine and health, microbiology, oceanography, physics, physiology and zoology.

BIBLIOGRAPHIES

Adsorption of Energy-Related Organic Pollutants. K. A. Reinbold, et al. National Technical Information Service, 5285 Port Royal Rd., Springfield, Virginia 22161. (703) 487-4650. 1979. Research reporting series #3, Ecological Research; EPA-600/3- 79-086.

ENCYCLOPEDIAS AND DICTIONARIES

Encyclopedia of Chemical Processing and Design. John J. Mcketta and W. A. Cunningham. Marcel Dekker, Inc., 270 Madison Ave., New York, New York 10016. (212) 696-9000; (800) 228-1160. 1992. Thirty-eight volumes.

Encyclopedia of Chemical Technology. Raymond E. Kirk. John Wiley & Sons, Inc., 605 3rd Ave., New York, New York 10158-0012. (212) 850-6000. 1991-. 4th ed. Also known as Kirk Othmer Encyclopedia of Chemical Technology; consists of 26 volumes.

Glossary of Geology. Robert Latimer Bates and Julia A. Jackson, eds. American Geological Institute, 4220 King St., Alexandria, Virginia 22302-1507. (703) 379-2480 or (800) 336-4764. 1987. Third edition.

Kirk-Othmer Encyclopedia of Chemical Technology. J. I. Kroschwitz, ed. John Wiley & Sons, Inc., 605 3rd Ave., New York, New York 10158-0012. (212) 850-6000. 1992-. All articles in the new edition have been rewritten and updated adding new subjects such as biotechnology, computer topics, analytical techniques and instrumentation, environmental concerns, fuels and energy, inorganic and solid state chemistry; composite materials and material science in general, and pharmaceuticals. Also available online.

McGraw-Hill Encyclopedia of the Geological Sciences. Sybil P. Parker, ed. McGraw-Hill, 1221 Avenue of the Americas, New York, New York 10020. (212) 512-2000 or (800) 262-4729. 1988. Second edition. Published previously in the McGraw-Hill Encyclopedia of Science and Technology.

Van Nostrand's Scientific Encyclopedia. Glenn D. Considine, ed. Van Nostrand Reinhold, 115 5th Ave., New York, New York 10003. (212) 254-3232. 1983. Sixth edition. Includes all broad subject areas in science.

GENERAL WORKS

Organic Solvents: Physical Properties and Methods of Solvents. John A. Riddick, et al. John Wiley & Sons, Inc., 605 3rd Ave., New York, New York 10158-0012. (212) 850-6000. 1986. 4th ed.

Solubilities of Inorganic and Organic Compounds. H. Stephen and T. Stephen, eds. Macmillan Publishing Co., 866 3rd Ave., New York, New York 10022. (212) 702-2000; (800) 257-5755. 1963-67.

HANDBOOKS AND MANUALS

Documentation of the Threshold Limit Values. American Conference of Governmental Industrial Hygienists, 6500 Glenway, Building D-5, Cincinnati, Ohio 45211. 1991. Provides threshold limit value documentation for any physical phenomenon in the environment, including chemical substances and physical agents.

Handbook of Chemistry and Physics. CRC Press, 2000 Corporate Blvd. N.W., Boca Raton, Florida 33431. (800) 272-7737. Annually.

Handbook of Environmental Data on Organic Chemicals. Karel Verschueren. Van Nostrand Reinhold, 115 5th Ave., New York, New York 10003. (212) 254-3232. 1983. Covers individual substances as well as mixtures and preparations. The profiles include: properties, air pollution factors, water pollution factors, and biological effects.

Hazardous Chemicals Data Book. G. Weiss, ed. Noyes Publications, 120 Mill Rd., Park Ridge, New Jersey 07656. (201) 391-8484. 1986. 2d ed. Supplies instant information on 1015 hazardous chemicals. The data will provide rapid assistance to personnel involved with handling of hazardous chemical materials and related accidents.

Lange's Handbook of Chemistry. John A. Dean, ed. McGraw-Hill Science & Engineering Books, 11 W. 19th St., New York, New York 10011. (212) 337-6010. 1973-. 11th ed.

NIOSH Pocket Guide to Chemical Hazards. National Institute for Occupational Safety and Health, 1600 Clifton Rd. NE, Atlanta, Georgia 30333. (404) 639-3286. 1990. Presents sources of general industrial hygiene and medical surveillance information for workers, employees and others. Presents key information and data in an abbreviated format for 398 individual chemicals or chemical types.

ONLINE DATA BASES

Chemical Abstracts-CA. Chemical Abstracts Service, 2540 Olentangy River Rd., P.O. Box 3012, Columbus, Ohio 43210. (800) 848-6533 or (614) 421-3600. Information sources include 9000 journals, patents from 27 countries, two industrial property organizations, new books, conference proceedings, and government research reports.

Kirk-Othmer Encyclopedia of Chemical Technology. John Wiley & Sons, Inc., 605 3rd Ave., 5th Floor, New York,

New York 10158. (212) 850-6000. Online version of the publication of the same name.

PERIODICALS AND NEWSLETTERS

Biogenic Amines. Pergamon Microforms International, Inc., Fairview Park, Elmsford, New York 10523. (914) 592-7720. 1984-. Bimonthly. Journal including of all aspects of research on biogenic amines and amino acid transmitters, their relating compounds and their interaction phenomena.

Environmental Science and Technology. American Chemical Society, 1155 16th St. N.W., Washington, District of Columbia 20036. (800) 227-5558. 1967-. Monthly. Contains research articles on various aspects of environmental chemistry, interpretative articles by invited experts and commentary on the scientific aspects of environmental management.

Journal of Agricultural and Food Chemistry. American Chemical Society, 1155 16th St. N.W., Washington, District of Columbia 20036. (202) 872-4600; (800) 227-5558. 1953-. Monthly. Contains documentation of significant advances in the science of agriculture and food chemistry.

Journal of Chemical and Engineering Data. American Chemical Society, 1155 16th St. N.W., Washington, District of Columbia 20036. (202) 872-4600; (800) 227-5558. 1959-. Quarterly.

Journal of Colloid and Interface Science. Academic Press, c/o Harcourt Brace Jovanovich Inc., 6277 Sea Harbor Dr., Orlando, Florida 32887. (800) 346-8648. 1946-. Fourteen times a year.

Journal of Environmental Quality. American Society of Agronomy, 677 S. Segoe Rd., Madison, Wisconsin 53711-1086. (608) 273-8080. 1972-. Quarterly. Reports and brief reviews of agricultural ecology, environmental engineering and pollution.

Journal of Organic Chemistry. American Chemical Society, 1155 16th St. N.W., Washington, District of Columbia 20036. (202) 872-4600; (800) 227-5558. 1936-.

TRADE ASSOCIATIONS AND PROFESSIONAL SOCIETIES

American Chemical Society. 1155 16th St., N.W., Washington, District of Columbia 20036. (202) 872-4600.

PHORATE

ABSTRACTING AND INDEXING SERVICES

Biological Abstracts. BIOSIS, 2100 Arch St., Philadelphia, Pennsylvania 19103-1399. (215) 587-4800. 1927-.

Chemical Abstracts. Chemical Abstracts Service, 2540 Olentangy River Rd., PO Box 3012, Columbus, Ohio 43210. (800) 848-6533. 1907-.

ENCYCLOPEDIAS AND DICTIONARIES

Van Nostrand's Scientific Encyclopedia. Glenn D. Considine, ed. Van Nostrand Reinhold, 115 5th Ave., New York, New York 10003. (212) 254-3232. 1983. Sixth edition. Includes all broad subject areas in science.

ONLINE DATA BASES

BIOSIS Previews. BIOSIS, 2100 Arch St., Philadelphia, Pennsylvania 19103-1399. (215) 587-4800. Largest and most comprehensive database of research in the life sciences. Contains citations for nearly 9000 primary research journals, monographs, reviews, symposia, preliminary reports, semi-popular journals, selected institutional reports, government reports and research communications.

CAS Source Index–CASSI. Chemical Abstracts Service, 2540 Olentangy River Rd., P.O. Box 3012, Columbus, Ohio 43210. (800) 848-6533 or (614) 421-3600. A listing of bibliographic and library holdings information for scientific and technical primary literature relevant to the chemical sciences.

Chemical Abstracts-CA. Chemical Abstracts Service, 2540 Olentangy River Rd., P.O. Box 3012, Columbus, Ohio 43210. (800) 848-6533 or (614) 421-3600. Information sources include 9000 journals, patents from 27 countries, two industrial property organizations, new books, conference proceedings, and government research reports.

Chemical Carcinogenesis Research Information System–CCRIS. National Library of Medicine, 8600 Rockville Pike, Bethesda, Maryland 20894. (800) 638-8480. Individual assay results and test conditions for 1,451 chemicals in the areas of carcinogenicity, mutagenicity, tumor promotion, and cocarcinogenicity.

Chemical Collection System/Request Tracking–CCS/RTS. U.S. Environmental Protection Agency, Office of Pesticides and Toxic Substances, 401 M St., SW, Washington, District of Columbia 20460. (202) 260-2090. Contains information on various properties of a number of chemicals including environmental effects, test and analysis methods, and health effects. Available from EPA.

Chemical Dictionary Online–CHEMLINE. Chemical Abstracts Service, 2540 Olentangy River Rd., Columbus, Ohio 43210. (614) 421-3600 or (800) 848-6533. Part of MEDLINE of the National Library of Medicine (NLM). File of 900,000 names for chemical substances, representing 450,000 unique compounds. It contains such information as Chemical Abstracts (CA) Service Registry Numbers, molecular formulas, preferred chemical nomenclature, and generic and ring structure information. Available on NLM's ELHILL system.

Chemical Exposure. Science Applications International Corp., Health & Environmental Information, P.O. Box 2501, Oak Ridge, Tennessee 37831. (615) 482-9031. Database of chemicals that have been identified in both human tissues and body fluids and in feral and food animals. Contains reference to journal articles, conferences, and reports. Covers the whole fields of information related to human and animal exposure to food, air, and water contaminants and pharmaceuticals. Its records include information on chemical properties, formulas, tissues measured, analytical method used, demographics and more. Available on DIALOG.

TRADE ASSOCIATIONS AND PROFESSIONAL SOCIETIES

American Chemical Society. 1155 16th St., N.W., Washington, District of Columbia 20036. (202) 872-4600.

PHOSALONE

ABSTRACTING AND INDEXING SERVICES

Chemical Abstracts. Chemical Abstracts Service, 2540 Olentangy River Rd., PO Box 3012, Columbus, Ohio 43210. (800) 848-6533. 1907-.

Science Citation Index. Institute for Scientific Information, 3501 Market St., Philadelphia, Pennsylvania 19104. 1961-.

ENCYCLOPEDIAS AND DICTIONARIES

Encyclopedia of Trademarks and Synonyms. H. Bennett, ed. Chemical Publishing Co., 80 Eighth Ave., New York, New York 10011. (212) 255-1950. 1981. Three volumes. Includes chemical compounds, compositions consisting of one or more chemicals and other products. Also included are abbreviated names and WHO free names.

Van Nostrand's Scientific Encyclopedia. Glenn D. Considine, ed. Van Nostrand Reinhold, 115 5th Ave., New York, New York 10003. (212) 254-3232. 1983. Sixth edition. Includes all broad subject areas in science.

ONLINE DATA BASES

Chemical Abstracts-CA. Chemical Abstracts Service, 2540 Olentangy River Rd., P.O. Box 3012, Columbus, Ohio 43210. (800) 848-6533 or (614) 421-3600. Information sources include 9000 journals, patents from 27 countries, two industrial property organizations, new books, conference proceedings, and government research reports.

Chemical Abstracts Chemical Name Directory-CHEMNAME. Chemical Abstracts Service, 2540 Olentangy River Rd., P.O. Box 3012, Columbus, Ohio 43210. (800) 848-6533 or (614) 421-3600. Listing of chemical substances in a dictionary type file. The Chemical Abstracts (CAS) Registry Number, molecular formula, Chemical Abstracts (CA) Substance Index Name, available synonyms, ring data and other chemical substance information is given for each entry.

Chemical Carcinogenesis Research Information System–CCRIS. National Library of Medicine, 8600 Rockville Pike, Bethesda, Maryland 20894. (800) 638-8480. Individual assay results and test conditions for 1,451 chemicals in the areas of carcinogenicity, mutagenicity, tumor promotion, and cocarcinogenicity.

Chemical Dictionary Online–CHEMLINE. Chemical Abstracts Service, 2540 Olentangy River Rd., Columbus, Ohio 43210. (614) 421-3600 or (800) 848-6533. Part of MEDLINE of the National Library of Medicine (NLM). File of 900,000 names for chemical substances, representing 450,000 unique compounds. It contains such information as Chemical Abstracts (CA) Service Registry Numbers, molecular formulas, preferred chemical nomenclature, and generic and ring structure information. Available on NLM's ELHILL system.

Chemical Exposure. Science Applications International Corp., Health & Environmental Information, P.O. Box 2501, Oak Ridge, Tennessee 37831. (615) 482-9031. Database of chemicals that have been identified in both human tissues and body fluids and in feral and food animals. Contains reference to journal articles, conferences, and reports. Covers the whole fields of informa-

tion related to human and animal exposure to food, air, and water contaminants and pharmaceuticals. Its records include information on chemical properties, formulas, tissues measured, analytical method used, demographics and more. Available on DIALOG.

TRADE ASSOCIATIONS AND PROFESSIONAL SOCIETIES

American Chemical Society. 1155 16th St., N.W., Washington, District of Columbia 20036. (202) 872-4600.

PHOSPHATES

ABSTRACTING AND INDEXING SERVICES

Biotechnology Research Abstracts. Cambridge Scientific Abstracts, 5161 River Rd., Bethesda, Maryland 20816. (301) 961-6750. Monthly. Includes such broad areas as genetic intervention, biochemical genetics, and microbiological techniques.

Chemical Abstracts. Chemical Abstracts Service, 2540 Olentangy River Rd., PO Box 3012, Columbus, Ohio 43210. (800) 848-6533. 1907-.

General Science Index. H. W. Wilson Co., 950 University Ave., Bronx, New York 10452. 1978-. Monthly, also issued in annual cumulation. Cumulative subject index to English language periodicals in the subject fields of astronomy, botany, chemistry, earth science, environment and conservation, food and nutrition, genetics, mathematics, medicine and health, microbiology, oceanography, physics, physiology and zoology.

Science Citation Index. Institute for Scientific Information, 3501 Market St., Philadelphia, Pennsylvania 19104. 1961-.

DIRECTORIES

Gale Environmental Sourcebook. Karen Hill. Gale Research Co., 835 Penobscot Bldg., Detroit, Michigan 48226-4094. (313) 961-2242. Contacts, information sources, or general information on environmental topics.

ENCYCLOPEDIAS AND DICTIONARIES

Ullmanns Encyclopedia of Industrial Chemistry. Hans Jurgen Arpe and Wolfgang Gerhartz, eds. VCH Publishers, 303 NW 12th Ave., Deerfield Beach, Florida 33442-1788. (305) 428-5566. 1990. Designed to keep up with the broad spectrum of chemical technology. Thirty-six volumes of the encyclopedia have been divided into two sets: the 28 A volumes contain alphabetically arranged articles on chemicals, product groups, processes and technological concepts; and the 8 B volumes are compendia of basic knowledge in industrial chemistry.

Van Nostrand's Scientific Encyclopedia. Glenn D. Considine, ed. Van Nostrand Reinhold, 115 5th Ave., New York, New York 10003. (212) 254-3232. 1983. Sixth edition. Includes all broad subject areas in science.

GENERAL WORKS

The Impact of Inorganic Phosphates in the Environment. Justine Welch. U.S. Environmental Protection Agency, Office of Pesticides and Toxic Substances, 401 M St., SW, Washington, District of Columbia 20460. (202) 260-

2090. 1978. Eutrophication of phosphorus in the environment.

Removal and Recovery of Metals and Phosphates from Municipal Sewage Sludge. Donald S. Scott. U.S. Environmental Protection Agency, Office of Research and Development, Municipal Environmental Research Laboratory, 26 W. Martin Luther King Dr., Cincinnati, Ohio 45268. (513) 569-7931. 1980.

Status Assessment of Toxic Chemicals: Phosphates. J. C. Ochsner. National Technical Information Service, 5285 Port Royal Rd., Springfield, Virginia 22161. (703) 487-4650. 1980.

HANDBOOKS AND MANUALS

Phosphates and Phosphoric Acid: Raw Materials, Technology, and Economics of the Wet Process. Pierre Becker. Marcel Dekker, Inc., 270 Madison Ave., New York, New York 10016. (212) 696-9000; (800) 228-1160. 1983.

Riegel's Handbook of Industrial Chemistry. James A. Kent, ed. Van Nostrand Reinhold, 115 5th Ave., New York, New York 10020. (212) 254-3232. 1983. Eighth edition. Includes industries such as: wastewater technology, coal technology, phosphate fertilizers, synthetic plastics, man-made textiles, detergents, sugar, animal and vegetable oils, chemical explosives, dyes, nuclear industry, and much more.

ONLINE DATA BASES

CAS Source Index–CASSI. Chemical Abstracts Service, 2540 Olentangy River Rd., P.O. Box 3012, Columbus, Ohio 43210. (800) 848-6533 or (614) 421-3600. A listing of bibliographic and library holdings information for scientific and technical primary literature relevant to the chemical sciences.

Chemical Abstracts–CA. Chemical Abstracts Service, 2540 Olentangy River Rd., P.O. Box 3012, Columbus, Ohio 43210. (800) 848-6533 or (614) 421-3600. Information sources include 9000 journals, patents from 27 countries, two industrial property organizations, new books, conference proceedings, and government research reports.

Chemical Collection System/Request Tracking–CCS/RTS. U.S. Environmental Protection Agency, Office of Pesticides and Toxic Substances, 401 M St., SW, Washington, District of Columbia 20460. (202) 260-2090. Contains information on various properties of a number of chemicals including environmental effects, test and analysis methods, and health effects. Available from EPA.

Chemical Dictionary Online–CHEMLINE. Chemical Abstracts Service, 2540 Olentangy River Rd., Columbus, Ohio 43210. (614) 421-3600 or (800) 848-6533. Part of MEDLINE of the National Library of Medicine (NLM). File of 900,000 names for chemical substances, representing 450,000 unique compounds. It contains such information as Chemical Abstracts (CA) Service Registry Numbers, molecular formulas, preferred chemical nomenclature, and generic and ring structure information. Available on NLM's ELHILL system.

Chemical Exposure. Science Applications International Corp., Health & Environmental Information, P.O. Box 2501, Oak Ridge, Tennessee 37831. (615) 482-9031. Database of chemicals that have been identified in both human tissues and body fluids and in feral and food animals. Contains reference to journal articles, conferences, and reports. Covers the whole fields of information related to human and animal exposure to food, air, and water contaminants and pharmaceuticals. Its records include information on chemical properties, formulas, tissues measured, analytical method used, demographics and more. Available on DIALOG.

STATISTICS SOURCES

Environmental Data Compendium. OECD Publications and Information Center, 2001 L St., N.W., Suite 700, Washington, District of Columbia 20036. (202) 785-6323. 1989.

Environmental Indicators. OECD Publications and Information Center, 2001 L St., N.W., Suite 700, Washington, District of Columbia 20036. (202) 785-6323. 1991.

Environmental Quality. Council on Environmental Quality. U.S. G.P.O., Washington, District of Columbia 20401. (202) 512-0000. Annual.

The State of the Environment. OECD Publications and Information Center, 2001 L St., N.W., Suite 700, Washington, District of Columbia 20036. (202) 785-6323. 1991.

TRADE ASSOCIATIONS AND PROFESSIONAL SOCIETIES

American Chemical Society. 1155 16th St., N.W., Washington, District of Columbia 20036. (202) 872-4600.

American Institute of Chemical Engineers. 345 East 47th St., New York, New York 10017. (212) 705-7338.

American Institute of Chemists. 7315 Wisconsin Ave., Bethesda, Maryland 20814. (301) 652-2447.

Phosphate Chemicals Export Association. 8750 W. Bryn Mawr Ave., Suite 1200, Chicago, Illinois 60631. (312) 399-1010.

Potash and Phosphate Institute. c/o R.T. Roberts, 2801 Buford Hwy., N.E., No. 401, Atlanta, Georgia 30329. (404) 634-4274.

PHOSPHOROUS

ABSTRACTING AND INDEXING SERVICES

Biological Abstracts. BIOSIS, 2100 Arch St., Philadelphia, Pennsylvania 19103-1399. (215) 587-4800. 1927-.

Chemical Abstracts. Chemical Abstracts Service, 2540 Olentangy River Rd., PO Box 3012, Columbus, Ohio 43210. (800) 848-6533. 1907-.

Environment Abstracts. Bowker A & I Publishing, 121 Chanlon Rd., New Providence, New Jersey 07974. (908) 464-6800. 1974-.

Environment Index. Environment Information Center, Index Research Department, 124 E. 39th St., New York, New York 10016. 1971-. Annual.

Environmental Information Connection–EIC. Planning Information Program, Dept. of Urban and Regional Planning, University of Illinois, 1003 West Nevada, Urbana, Illinois 61801. (217) 333-1369. Also available online.

Environmental Periodicals Bibliography. Environmental Studies Institute, International Academy at Santa Barbara, 800 Garden St., Suite D, Santa Barbara, California 93101. (805) 965-5010. Also available online.

Science Citation Index. Institute for Scientific Information, 3501 Market St., Philadelphia, Pennsylvania 19104. 1961-.

BIBLIOGRAPHIES

EPA Publications Bibliography. U.S. Environmental Protection Agency, Library Systems Branch, 401 M St., SW, Washington, District of Columbia 20460. (202) 260-2090. Quarterly.

Phosphorus in Agriculture. C. A. B. International, 845 North Park Ave., Tucson, Arizona 85719. (602) 621-7897 or (800) 528-4841. 1991. Two volumes. Contains 1,100 citations.

ENCYCLOPEDIAS AND DICTIONARIES

Van Nostrand's Scientific Encyclopedia. Glenn D. Considine, ed. Van Nostrand Reinhold, 115 5th Ave., New York, New York 10003. (212) 254-3232. 1983. Sixth edition. Includes all broad subject areas in science.

GENERAL WORKS

Phosphorus Chemistry in Everyday Living. Arthur Dock Fon Toy. American Chemical Society, 1155 16th St. N.W., Washington, District of Columbia 20036. (800) 227-5558. 1987.

HANDBOOKS AND MANUALS

Phosphorus: An Outline of Its Chemistry, Biochemistry, and Technology. Elsevier Science Publishing Co., 655 Avenue of the Americas, New York, New York 10010. (212) 984-5800. 1985. Covers organophosphorus and phosphorus compounds.

ONLINE DATA BASES

BIOSIS Previews. BIOSIS, 2100 Arch St., Philadelphia, Pennsylvania 19103-1399. (215) 587-4800. Largest and most comprehensive database of research in the life sciences. Contains citations for nearly 9000 primary research journals, monographs, reviews, symposia, preliminary reports, semi-popular journals, selected institutional reports, government reports and research communications.

CAS Source Index–CASSI. Chemical Abstracts Service, 2540 Olentangy River Rd., P.O. Box 3012, Columbus, Ohio 43210. (800) 848-6533 or (614) 421-3600. A listing of bibliographic and library holdings information for scientific and technical primary literature relevant to the chemical sciences.

Chemical Abstracts-CA. Chemical Abstracts Service, 2540 Olentangy River Rd., P.O. Box 3012, Columbus, Ohio 43210. (800) 848-6533 or (614) 421-3600. Information sources include 9000 journals, patents from 27 countries, two industrial property organizations, new books, conference proceedings, and government research reports.

Chemical Collection System/Request Tracking–CCS/RTS. U.S. Environmental Protection Agency, Office of

Pesticides and Toxic Substances, 401 M St., SW, Washington, District of Columbia 20460. (202) 260-2090. Contains information on various properties of a number of chemicals including environmental effects, test and analysis methods, and health effects. Available from EPA.

Chemical Dictionary Online–CHEMLINE. Chemical Abstracts Service, 2540 Olentangy River Rd., Columbus, Ohio 43210. (614) 421-3600 or (800) 848-6533. Part of MEDLINE of the National Library of Medicine (NLM). File of 900,000 names for chemical substances, representing 450,000 unique compounds. It contains such information as Chemical Abstracts (CA) Service Registry Numbers, molecular formulas, preferred chemical nomenclature, and generic and ring structure information. Available on NLM's ELHILL system.

Chemical Exposure. Science Applications International Corp., Health & Environmental Information, P.O. Box 2501, Oak Ridge, Tennessee 37831. (615) 482-9031. Database of chemicals that have been identified in both human tissues and body fluids and in feral and food animals. Contains reference to journal articles, conferences, and reports. Covers the whole fields of information related to human and animal exposure to food, air, and water contaminants and pharmaceuticals. Its records include information on chemical properties, formulas, tissues measured, analytical method used, demographics and more. Available on DIALOG.

Enviro/Energyline Abstracts Plus. R. R. Bowker Co., 121 Chanlon Rd., New Providence, New Jersey 07974. (908) 464-6800.

Environmental Periodicals Bibliography. National Information Services Corp., Ste. 6, Wyman Towers, 3100 St. Paul St., Baltimore, Maryland 21218. (410)243-0797. Online version of abstract of same name.

TRADE ASSOCIATIONS AND PROFESSIONAL SOCIETIES

American Chemical Society. 1155 16th St., N.W., Washington, District of Columbia 20036. (202) 872-4600.

American Institute of Chemical Engineers. 345 East 47th St., New York, New York 10017. (212) 705-7338.

American Institute of Chemists. 7315 Wisconsin Ave., Bethesda, Maryland 20814. (301) 652-2447.

Phosphate Chemicals Export Association. 8750 W. Bryn Mawr Ave., Suite 1200, Chicago, Illinois 60631. (312) 399-1010.

PHOTOCHEMICAL SMOG

See also: OXIDANTS

ABSTRACTING AND INDEXING SERVICES

Biological Abstracts. BIOSIS, 2100 Arch St., Philadelphia, Pennsylvania 19103-1399. (215) 587-4800. 1927-.

Biological and Agricultural Index. H.W. Wilson Co., 950 University Ave., Bronx, New York 10452. (800) 367-6770. 1916-. Monthly.

Chemical Abstracts. Chemical Abstracts Service, 2540 Olentangy River Rd., PO Box 3012, Columbus, Ohio 43210. (800) 848-6533. 1907-.

Environment Abstracts. Bowker A & I Publishing, 121 Chanlon Rd., New Providence, New Jersey 07974. (908) 464-6800. 1974-.

Environment Index. Environment Information Center, Index Research Department, 124 E. 39th St., New York, New York 10016. 1971-. Annual.

Environmental Information Connection–EIC. Planning Information Program, Dept. of Urban and Regional Planning, University of Illinois, 1003 West Nevada, Urbana, Illinois 61801. (217) 333-1369. Also available online.

Environmental Periodicals Bibliography. Environmental Studies Institute, International Academy at Santa Barbara, 800 Garden St., Suite D, Santa Barbara, California 93101. (805) 965-5010. Also available online.

Science Citation Index. Institute for Scientific Information, 3501 Market St., Philadelphia, Pennsylvania 19104. 1961-.

BIBLIOGRAPHIES

EPA Publications Bibliography. U.S. Environmental Protection Agency, Library Systems Branch, 401 M St., SW, Washington, District of Columbia 20460. (202) 260-2090. Quarterly.

ENCYCLOPEDIAS AND DICTIONARIES

Van Nostrand's Scientific Encyclopedia. Glenn D. Considine, ed. Van Nostrand Reinhold, 115 5th Ave., New York, New York 10003. (212) 254-3232. 1983. Sixth edition. Includes all broad subject areas in science.

GENERAL WORKS

Photochemical Oxidants. World Health Organization, Ave. Appia, Geneva, Switzerland CH-1211. 1979.

Photochemical Smog and Ozone Reaction. American Chemical Society, 1155 16th St. N.W., Washington, District of Columbia 20036. (800) 227-5558. 1972.

Photochemical Smog: Contribution of Volatile Organic Compounds. OECD Publications and Information Center, 2001 L St., NW, Washington, District of Columbia 20036. (202) 785-6323. 1982. Covers smog resulting from hydrocarbons and gasoline.

ONLINE DATA BASES

BIOSIS Previews. BIOSIS, 2100 Arch St., Philadelphia, Pennsylvania 19103-1399. (215) 587-4800. Largest and most comprehensive database of research in the life sciences. Contains citations for nearly 9000 primary research journals, monographs, reviews, symposia, preliminary reports, semi-popular journals, selected institutional reports, government reports and research communications.

Chemical Abstracts-CA. Chemical Abstracts Service, 2540 Olentangy River Rd., P.O. Box 3012, Columbus, Ohio 43210. (800) 848-6533 or (614) 421-3600. Information sources include 9000 journals, patents from 27 countries, two industrial property organizations, new books, conference proceedings, and government research reports.

Enviro/Energyline Abstracts Plus. R. R. Bowker Co., 121 Chanlon Rd., New Providence, New Jersey 07974. (908) 464-6800.

Environmental Periodicals Bibliography. National Information Services Corp., Ste. 6, Wyman Towers, 3100 St. Paul St., Baltimore, Maryland 21218. (410)243-0797. Online version of abstract of same name.

Monthly Catalog of United States Government Publications. U.S. G.P.O., Supt. of Docs., PO Box 371954, Pittsburgh, Pennsylvania 15250-7954. (202) 512-0000.

National Technical Information Service. U.S. Department of Commerce, National Technical Information Service, Office of Data Base Services, 5285 Port Royal Rd., Springfield, Virginia 22161. (703) 487-4807. Bibliographic database of government sponsored research and technical reports.

Solid Waste Report. NewsNet, Inc., 945 Haverford Rd., Bryn Mawr, Pennsylvania 19010. (800) 345-1301. Online version of the periodical of the same name.

PHOTOCHEMISTRY

ABSTRACTING AND INDEXING SERVICES

Applied Science and Technology Index. H.W. Wilson Co., 950 University Ave., Bronx, New York 10452. (800) 367-6770. Formerly Industrial Arts Index.

Biological Abstracts. BIOSIS, 2100 Arch St., Philadelphia, Pennsylvania 19103-1399. (215) 587-4800. 1927-.

Biological and Agricultural Index. H.W. Wilson Co., 950 University Ave., Bronx, New York 10452. (800) 367-6770. 1916-. Monthly.

Chemical Abstracts. Chemical Abstracts Service, 2540 Olentangy River Rd., PO Box 3012, Columbus, Ohio 43210. (800) 848-6533. 1907-.

Environment Abstracts. Bowker A & I Publishing, 121 Chanlon Rd., New Providence, New Jersey 07974. (908) 464-6800. 1974-.

Environment Index. Environment Information Center, Index Research Department, 124 E. 39th St., New York, New York 10016. 1971-. Annual.

Environmental Information Connection–EIC. Planning Information Program, Dept. of Urban and Regional Planning, University of Illinois, 1003 West Nevada, Urbana, Illinois 61801. (217) 333-1369. Also available online.

Environmental Periodicals Bibliography. Environmental Studies Institute, International Academy at Santa Barbara, 800 Garden St., Suite D, Santa Barbara, California 93101. (805) 965-5010. Also available online.

General Science Index. H. W. Wilson Co., 950 University Ave., Bronx, New York 10452. 1978-. Monthly, also issued in annual cumulation. Cumulative subject index to English language periodicals in the subject fields of astronomy, botany, chemistry, earth science, environment and conservation, food and nutrition, genetics, mathematics, medicine and health, microbiology, oceanography, physics, physiology and zoology.

Physics Briefs. Physikalische Berichte. Physik Verlag, Pappapelallee 3, Postfach 101161, Weinheim, Germany

D-6940. 1979-. Semimonthly. In English. Volumes for 1979- issued by the Deutsche Physikalische Gesellschaft and the Fachinformationszentrum Energie Physik, Mathematik in cooperation with the American Institute of Physics.

Science Citation Index. Institute for Scientific Information, 3501 Market St., Philadelphia, Pennsylvania 19104. 1961-.

BIBLIOGRAPHIES

Bibliography and Index of Geology. American Geological Institute, 4220 King St., Alexandria, Virginia 22302. Monthly. Includes environmental geology and hydrogeology.

EPA Publications Bibliography. U.S. Environmental Protection Agency, Library Systems Branch, 401 M St., SW, Washington, District of Columbia 20460. (202) 260-2090. Quarterly.

ENCYCLOPEDIAS AND DICTIONARIES

McGraw-Hill Encyclopedia of Science and Technology. McGraw-Hill, 1221 Avenue of the Americas, New York, New York 10020. (212) 512-2000 or (800) 262-4729. 1992. Seventh edition. Issued in multiple volumes including index. Includes all science and technology broad subject areas.

Van Nostrand's Scientific Encyclopedia. Glenn D. Considine, ed. Van Nostrand Reinhold, 115 5th Ave., New York, New York 10003. (212) 254-3232. 1983. Sixth edition. Includes all broad subject areas in science.

GENERAL WORKS

Control Strategies for Photochemical Oxidants Across Europe. OECD Publications and Information Center, 2001 L St. N.W., Suite 700, Washington, District of Columbia 20036. (202) 785-OECD. 1990. Describes the emissions causing high photochemical oxidant levels, analyzes possible emission control technologies and their costs, evaluates the impact of economically feasible control scenarios.

Environmental Pathways of Selected Chemicals in Freshwater Systems. J. H. Smit. U.S. Environmental Protection Agency, Office of Research and Development, 960 College Sation Rd., Athens, Georgia 30605. (706) 546-3154. 1978. Mathematical models of water pollution, fresh water analysis and photochemistry.

Magill's Survey of Science. Earth Science Series. Frank N. Magill. Salem Press, PO Box 50062, Pasadena, California 91105. 1990-. Five volumes. Includes information on earth's crust, hot spots and volcanic island chains, physical properties of minerals, rock magnetism, physical properties of rocks, and index.

Photochemistry of Environmental Aquatic Systems. Rod G. Zika. American Chemical Society, 1155 16th St. N.W., Washington, District of Columbia 20036. (800) 227-5558. 1987.

Sources and Applications of Ultraviolet Radiation. Academic Press, c/o Harcourt Brace Jovanovich Inc., 6277 Sea Harbor Dr., Orlando, Florida 32887. (800) 346-8648. 1983. Topics in photochemistry.

ONLINE DATA BASES

BIOSIS Previews. BIOSIS, 2100 Arch St., Philadelphia, Pennsylvania 19103-1399. (215) 587-4800. Largest and most comprehensive database of research in the life sciences. Contains citations for nearly 9000 primary research journals, monographs, reviews, symposia, preliminary reports, semi-popular journals, selected institutional reports, government reports and research communications.

CAS Source Index–CASSI. Chemical Abstracts Service, 2540 Olentangy River Rd., P.O. Box 3012, Columbus, Ohio 43210. (800) 848-6533 or (614) 421-3600. A listing of bibliographic and library holdings information for scientific and technical primary literature relevant to the chemical sciences.

Chemical Abstracts-CA. Chemical Abstracts Service, 2540 Olentangy River Rd., P.O. Box 3012, Columbus, Ohio 43210. (800) 848-6533 or (614) 421-3600. Information sources include 9000 journals, patents from 27 countries, two industrial property organizations, new books, conference proceedings, and government research reports.

Enviro/Energyline Abstracts Plus. R. R. Bowker Co., 121 Chanlon Rd., New Providence, New Jersey 07974. (908) 464-6800.

Environmental Periodicals Bibliography. National Information Services Corp., Ste. 6, Wyman Towers, 3100 St. Paul St., Baltimore, Maryland 21218. (410)243-0797. Online version of abstract of same name.

TRADE ASSOCIATIONS AND PROFESSIONAL SOCIETIES

American Chemical Society. 1155 16th St., N.W., Washington, District of Columbia 20036. (202) 872-4600.

American Institute of Chemical Engineers. 345 East 47th St., New York, New York 10017. (212) 705-7338.

American Institute of Chemists. 7315 Wisconsin Ave., Bethesda, Maryland 20814. (301) 652-2447.

Photo Chemical Machining Institute. 4113 Barberry Dr., Lafayette Hills, Pennsylvania 19444. (215) 825-2506.

PHOTODEGRADATION

ABSTRACTING AND INDEXING SERVICES

Biological Abstracts. BIOSIS, 2100 Arch St., Philadelphia, Pennsylvania 19103-1399. (215) 587-4800. 1927-.

Environment Abstracts. Bowker A & I Publishing, 121 Chanlon Rd., New Providence, New Jersey 07974. (908) 464-6800. 1974-.

Environment Index. Environment Information Center, Index Research Department, 124 E. 39th St., New York, New York 10016. 1971-. Annual.

Environmental Information Connection–EIC. Planning Information Program, Dept. of Urban and Regional Planning, University of Illinois, 1003 West Nevada, Urbana, Illinois 61801. (217) 333-1369. Also available online.

Environmental Periodicals Bibliography. Environmental Studies Institute, International Academy at Santa Barba-

ra, 800 Garden St., Suite D, Santa Barbara, California 93101. (805) 965-5010. Also available online.

Science Citation Index. Institute for Scientific Information, 3501 Market St., Philadelphia, Pennsylvania 19104. 1961-.

BIBLIOGRAPHIES

EPA Publications Bibliography. U.S. Environmental Protection Agency, Library Systems Branch, 401 M St., SW, Washington, District of Columbia 20460. (202) 260-2090. Quarterly.

ENCYCLOPEDIAS AND DICTIONARIES

Van Nostrand's Scientific Encyclopedia. Glenn D. Considine, ed. Van Nostrand Reinhold, 115 5th Ave., New York, New York 10003. (212) 254-3232. 1983. Sixth edition. Includes all broad subject areas in science.

GENERAL WORKS

Amine-Enhanced Photodegradation of Polychlorinated Biphenyls. J. M. Meuser. Electric Power Research Institute, 3412 Hillview Ave., Palo Alto, California 94304. (415) 965-4081. 1982. Capacitors, soil pollution testing and electric transformers.

A Study of the Photodegradation of Commercial Dyes. John J. Porter. U.S. G.P.O., Washington, District of Columbia 20401. (202) 512-0000. 1973. Textile waste, dyes and dyeing in terms of their chemistry and waste disposal.

ONLINE DATA BASES

BIOSIS Previews. BIOSIS, 2100 Arch St., Philadelphia, Pennsylvania 19103-1399. (215) 587-4800. Largest and most comprehensive database of research in the life sciences. Contains citations for nearly 9000 primary research journals, monographs, reviews, symposia, preliminary reports, semi-popular journals, selected institutional reports, government reports and research communications.

Enviro/Energyline Abstracts Plus. R. R. Bowker Co., 121 Chanlon Rd., New Providence, New Jersey 07974. (908) 464-6800.

Environmental Periodicals Bibliography. National Information Services Corp., Ste. 6, Wyman Towers, 3100 St. Paul St., Baltimore, Maryland 21218. (410)243-0797. Online version of abstract of same name.

SCISEARCH. Institute for Scientific Information, University City Science Center, 3501 Market St., Philadelphia, Pennsylvania 19104. (215) 386-0100.

TRADE ASSOCIATIONS AND PROFESSIONAL SOCIETIES

American Institute of Biological Sciences. 730 11th St., N.W., Washington, District of Columbia 20001-4521. (202) 628-1500.

PHOTOGRAPHY, AERIAL

BIBLIOGRAPHIES

Aerial Photography: Monographs. Mary A. Vance. Vance Bibliographies, PO Box 229, 112 N. Charter St., Monticello, Illinois 61856. (217) 762-3831. 1984.

GENERAL WORKS

Aerial Photography and Image Interpretation for Resource Management. David P. Paine. John Wiley & Sons, Inc., 605 3rd Ave., New York, New York 10158-0012. (212) 850-6000. 1981. Photographic interpretation and aerial photography in forestry.

Aerial Photography and Remote Sensing for Soil Survey. Leslie Paul White. Clarendon Press, Oxford, England 1977.

HANDBOOKS AND MANUALS

Index of Selected Aerial Photography of the United States. U.S. Fish and Wildlife Service, Office of Biological Services. U.S. Department of the Interior, Fish and Wildlife Service, 1849 C St. NW, Washington, District of Columbia 20240. (202) 208-5634. 1976.

Manual of Aerial Photography. Ron Graham. Focal Press, 80 Montvale Ave., Stoneham, Massachusetts 02180. (617) 438-8464. 1986.

PHOTOPERIODISM

ABSTRACTING AND INDEXING SERVICES

ASFA Aquaculture Abstracts. Cambridge Scientific Abstracts, Inc., 5161 River Rd., Bethesda, Maryland 20816. (301) 961-6750. 1984.

Biological Abstracts. BIOSIS, 2100 Arch St., Philadelphia, Pennsylvania 19103-1399. (215) 587-4800. 1927-.

Environment Abstracts. Bowker A & I Publishing, 121 Chanlon Rd., New Providence, New Jersey 07974. (908) 464-6800. 1974-.

Environment Index. Environment Information Center, Index Research Department, 124 E. 39th St., New York, New York 10016. 1971-. Annual.

Environmental Information Connection–EIC. Planning Information Program, Dept. of Urban and Regional Planning, University of Illinois, 1003 West Nevada, Urbana, Illinois 61801. (217) 333-1369. Also available online.

Environmental Periodicals Bibliography. Environmental Studies Institute, International Academy at Santa Barbara, 800 Garden St., Suite D, Santa Barbara, California 93101. (805) 965-5010. Also available online.

Science Citation Index. Institute for Scientific Information, 3501 Market St., Philadelphia, Pennsylvania 19104. 1961-.

BIBLIOGRAPHIES

EPA Publications Bibliography. U.S. Environmental Protection Agency, Library Systems Branch, 401 M St., SW,

Washington, District of Columbia 20460. (202) 260-2090. Quarterly.

ENCYCLOPEDIAS AND DICTIONARIES

Van Nostrand's Scientific Encyclopedia. Glenn D. Considine, ed. Van Nostrand Reinhold, 115 5th Ave., New York, New York 10003. (212) 254-3232. 1983. Sixth edition. Includes all broad subject areas in science.

GENERAL WORKS

Development of Circadian Rhythmicity and Photoperiodism in Mammals. Steven M. Reppert. Perinatology Press, 507 Cayuga Heights Rd., Ithaca, New York 14850. (607) 257-3278. 1989. Comparative physiology of mammals development.

Insect Photoperiodism. Stanley Beck. Academic Press, c/o Harcourt Brace Jovanovich Inc., 6277 Sea Harbor Dr., Orlando, Florida 32887. (800) 346-8648. 1980.

Photoperiodism in Plants and Animals. William S. Hillman. Scientific Publications Division, Carolina Biological Supply Co., 2700 York Rd., Burlington, North Carolina 27215. (919) 584-0381. 1979.

ONLINE DATA BASES

BIOSIS Previews. BIOSIS, 2100 Arch St., Philadelphia, Pennsylvania 19103-1399. (215) 587-4800. Largest and most comprehensive database of research in the life sciences. Contains citations for nearly 9000 primary research journals, monographs, reviews, symposia, preliminary reports, semi-popular journals, selected institutional reports, government reports and research communications.

Enviro/Energyline Abstracts Plus. R. R. Bowker Co., 121 Chanlon Rd., New Providence, New Jersey 07974. (908) 464-6800.

Environmental Periodicals Bibliography. National Information Services Corp., Ste. 6, Wyman Towers, 3100 St. Paul St., Baltimore, Maryland 21218. (410)243-0797. Online version of abstract of same name.

SCISEARCH. Institute for Scientific Information, University City Science Center, 3501 Market St., Philadelphia, Pennsylvania 19104. (215) 386-0100.

TRADE ASSOCIATIONS AND PROFESSIONAL SOCIETIES

American Institute of Biological Sciences. 730 11th St., N.W., Washington, District of Columbia 20001-4521. (202) 628-1500.

PHOTOSYNTHESIS

ABSTRACTING AND INDEXING SERVICES

Biological Abstracts. BIOSIS, 2100 Arch St., Philadelphia, Pennsylvania 19103-1399. (215) 587-4800. 1927-.

Biological and Agricultural Index. H.W. Wilson Co., 950 University Ave., Bronx, New York 10452. (800) 367-6770. 1916-. Monthly.

Biotechnology Research Abstracts. Cambridge Scientific Abstracts, 5161 River Rd., Bethesda, Maryland 20816.

(301) 961-6750. Monthly. Includes such broad areas as genetic intervention, biochemical genetics, and microbiological techniques.

Chemical Abstracts. Chemical Abstracts Service, 2540 Olentangy River Rd., PO Box 3012, Columbus, Ohio 43210. (800) 848-6533. 1907-.

Crop Physiology Abstracts. C. A. B. International, 845 North Park Ave., Tucson, Arizona 85719. (602) 621-7897 or (800) 528-4841. 1975-. Monthly. Abstracts focus on the physiology of all higher plants of economic importance. Aspects include germination, reproductive development, nitrogen fixation, metabolic inhibitors, salinity, radiobiology, enzymes, membranes and other related areas.

Current Advances in Plant Science. Pergamon Microforms International, Inc., Fairview Park, Elmsford, New York 10523. (914) 592-7720. 1984-. Monthly. Current literature searching service including journals, reports, abstracts, etc. This service is available online as part of the CABS database on the hosts BRS and ORBIT search service.

Ecology Abstracts. Cambridge Scientific Abstracts, 5161 River Rd., Bethesda, Maryland 20816. (301) 961-6750. Monthly.

Environment Abstracts. Bowker A & I Publishing, 121 Chanlon Rd., New Providence, New Jersey 07974. (908) 464-6800. 1974-.

Environment Index. Environment Information Center, Index Research Department, 124 E. 39th St., New York, New York 10016. 1971-. Annual.

Environmental Information Connection–EIC. Planning Information Program, Dept. of Urban and Regional Planning, University of Illinois, 1003 West Nevada, Urbana, Illinois 61801. (217) 333-1369. Also available online.

Environmental Periodicals Bibliography. Environmental Studies Institute, International Academy at Santa Barbara, 800 Garden St., Suite D, Santa Barbara, California 93101. (805) 965-5010. Also available online.

General Science Index. H. W. Wilson Co., 950 University Ave., Bronx, New York 10452. 1978-. Monthly, also issued in annual cumulation. Cumulative subject index to English language periodicals in the subject fields of astronomy, botany, chemistry, earth science, environment and conservation, food and nutrition, genetics, mathematics, medicine and health, microbiology, oceanography, physics, physiology and zoology.

Science Citation Index. Institute for Scientific Information, 3501 Market St., Philadelphia, Pennsylvania 19104. 1961-.

BIBLIOGRAPHIES

Bibliography and Index of Geology. American Geological Institute, 4220 King St., Alexandria, Virginia 22302. Monthly. Includes environmental geology and hydrogeology.

EPA Publications Bibliography. U.S. Environmental Protection Agency, Library Systems Branch, 401 M St., SW, Washington, District of Columbia 20460. (202) 260-2090. Quarterly.

ENCYCLOPEDIAS AND DICTIONARIES

Cambridge Dictionary of Biology. Peter M. B. Walker. Cambridge University Press, 40 W. 20th St., New York, New York 10011. (212) 924-3900 or (800) 227-0247. 1989. Includes 10,000 terms in zoology, botany, biochemistry, molecular biology and genetics. Previously published under the title Chambers Biology Dictionary.

Cambridge Encyclopedia of Life Sciences. A. E. Friday and David S. Ingram. Cambridge University Press, 40 W 20th St., New York, New York 10011. (212) 924-3900 or (800) 227-0247. 1985. Includes all topics under biology and ecology.

A Concise Dictionary of Biology. Elizabeth Martin, ed. Oxford University Press, 200 Madison Ave., New York, New York 10016. (212) 679-7300 or (800) 334-4249. 1990. New edition. Derived from the Concise Science Dictionary, published in 1984.

Encyclopedia of Human Biology. Renato Dulbecco, ed. Academic Press, c/o Harcourt Brace Jovanovich Inc., 6277 Sea Harbor Dr., Orlando, Florida 32887. (800) 346-8648. 1991. Eight volumes.

McGraw-Hill Encyclopedia of Science and Technology. McGraw-Hill, 1221 Avenue of the Americas, New York, New York 10020. (212) 512-2000 or (800) 262-4729. 1992. Seventh edition. Issued in multiple volumes including index. Includes all science and technology broad subject areas.

Van Nostrand's Scientific Encyclopedia. Glenn D. Considine, ed. Van Nostrand Reinhold, 115 5th Ave., New York, New York 10003. (212) 254-3232. 1983. Sixth edition. Includes all broad subject areas in science.

GENERAL WORKS

Ecology of Photosynthesis in Sun and Shade. J. R. Evans, et al. CSIRO, PO Box 89, East Melbourne, VIC, Australia 3002. 1988. The popular topic of function analysis of the photosynthetic apparatus in response to irradiance, and problems of acclimation and photoinhibition are also discussed.

Magill's Survey of Science. Earth Science Series. Frank N. Magill. Salem Press, PO Box 50062, Pasadena, California 91105. 1990-. Five volumes. Includes information on earth's crust, hot spots and volcanic island chains, physical properties of minerals, rock magnetism, physical properties of rocks, and index.

Magill's Survey of Science. Life Science Series. Frank N. Magill, ed. Salem Press, PO Box 50062, Pasadena, California 91105. 1991. Six volumes. Contents: v.1. A-Central and peripheral nervous system functions; v.2. Central metabolism regulation - eukaryotic transcriptional control; v.3. Positive and negative eukaryotic transcriptional control - mammalian hormones; v.4. Hormones and behavior - muscular contraction; v.5. Muscular contraction and relaxation - sexual reproduction in plants; v.6. Reproductive behavior and mating - X inactivation and the Lyon hypothesis.

Marine Photosynthesis: With Special Emphasis on the Ecological Aspects. E. Steema Nielsne. Elsevier Science Publishing Co., 655 Avenue of the Americas, New York, New York 10010. (212) 984-5800. 1975. Marine ecology and primary productivity.

Photosynthesis. Academic Press, c/o Harcourt Brace Jovanovich Inc., 6277 Sea Harbor Dr., Orlando, Florida 32887. (800) 346-8648. 1982.

Predicting Photosynthesis for Ecosystem Models. J. D. Hesketh. CRC Press, 2000 Corporate Blvd. N.W., Boca Raton, Florida 33431. (800) 272-7737. 1980. Simulation methods in photosynthesis.

ONLINE DATA BASES

BIOSIS Previews. BIOSIS, 2100 Arch St., Philadelphia, Pennsylvania 19103-1399. (215) 587-4800. Largest and most comprehensive database of research in the life sciences. Contains citations for nearly 9000 primary research journals, monographs, reviews, symposia, preliminary reports, semi-popular journals, selected institutional reports, government reports and research communications.

Chemical Abstracts-CA. Chemical Abstracts Service, 2540 Olentangy River Rd., P.O. Box 3012, Columbus, Ohio 43210. (800) 848-6533 or (614) 421-3600. Information sources include 9000 journals, patents from 27 countries, two industrial property organizations, new books, conference proceedings, and government research reports.

Enviro/Energyline Abstracts Plus. R. R. Bowker Co., 121 Chanlon Rd., New Providence, New Jersey 07974. (908) 464-6800.

Environmental Periodicals Bibliography. National Information Services Corp., Ste. 6, Wyman Towers, 3100 St. Paul St., Baltimore, Maryland 21218. (410)243-0797. Online version of abstract of same name.

SCISEARCH. Institute for Scientific Information, University City Science Center, 3501 Market St., Philadelphia, Pennsylvania 19104. (215) 386-0100.

RESEARCH CENTERS AND INSTITUTES

Arizona State University, Center for the Study of Early Events in Photosynthesis. Department of Chemistry, Tempe, Arizona 85278-1604. (602) 965-1963.

New Mexico State University, Center for Biochemical Engineering Research. Department of Chemical Engineering, Box 30001, Dept. 3805, Las Cruces, New Mexico 88003-0001. (505) 646-1214.

Rockefeller University, Laboratory of Biophysics. 1230 York Avenue, New York, New York 10021-6399. (212) 570-8000.

State University of New York at Plattsburg, Biochemistry/Biophysics Program. Plattsburg, New York 12901. (518) 564-3159.

University of Illinois, Laboratory of Plant Pigment Biochemistry and Photobiology. 1302 West Pennsylvania, Urbana, Illinois 61801. (217) 333-1968.

TRADE ASSOCIATIONS AND PROFESSIONAL SOCIETIES

American Institute of Biological Sciences. 730 11th St., N.W., Washington, District of Columbia 20001-4521. (202) 628-1500.

PHOTOTROPISM

ABSTRACTING AND INDEXING SERVICES

Biological Abstracts. BIOSIS, 2100 Arch St., Philadelphia, Pennsylvania 19103-1399. (215) 587-4800. 1927-.

Environment Abstracts. Bowker A & I Publishing, 121 Chanlon Rd., New Providence, New Jersey 07974. (908) 464-6800. 1974-.

Environment Index. Environment Information Center, Index Research Department, 124 E. 39th St., New York, New York 10016. 1971-. Annual.

Environmental Information Connection–EIC. Planning Information Program, Dept. of Urban and Regional Planning, University of Illinois, 1003 West Nevada, Urbana, Illinois 61801. (217) 333-1369. Also available online.

Environmental Periodicals Bibliography. Environmental Studies Institute, International Academy at Santa Barbara, 800 Garden St., Suite D, Santa Barbara, California 93101. (805) 965-5010. Also available online.

Science Citation Index. Institute for Scientific Information, 3501 Market St., Philadelphia, Pennsylvania 19104. 1961-.

BIBLIOGRAPHIES

EPA Publications Bibliography. U.S. Environmental Protection Agency, Library Systems Branch, 401 M St., SW, Washington, District of Columbia 20460. (202) 260-2090. Quarterly.

ENCYCLOPEDIAS AND DICTIONARIES

Van Nostrand's Scientific Encyclopedia. Glenn D. Considine, ed. Van Nostrand Reinhold, 115 5th Ave., New York, New York 10003. (212) 254-3232. 1983. Sixth edition. Includes all broad subject areas in science.

GENERAL WORKS

Planetary Biology and Microbial Ecology. Lynn Margulis. National Aeronautics and Space Administration, Scientific and Technical Information Office, 5285 Port Royal Rd., Springfield, Virginia 22161. (703) 487-4650. 1983.

ONLINE DATA BASES

BIOSIS Previews. BIOSIS, 2100 Arch St., Philadelphia, Pennsylvania 19103-1399. (215) 587-4800. Largest and most comprehensive database of research in the life sciences. Contains citations for nearly 9000 primary research journals, monographs, reviews, symposia, preliminary reports, semi-popular journals, selected institutional reports, government reports and research communications.

Enviro/Energyline Abstracts Plus. R. R. Bowker Co., 121 Chanlon Rd., New Providence, New Jersey 07974. (908) 464-6800.

Environmental Periodicals Bibliography. National Information Services Corp., Ste. 6, Wyman Towers, 3100 St. Paul St., Baltimore, Maryland 21218. (410)243-0797. Online version of abstract of same name.

SCISEARCH. Institute for Scientific Information, University City Science Center, 3501 Market St., Philadelphia, Pennsylvania 19104. (215) 386-0100.

PHYSICAL CONTROL

ABSTRACTING AND INDEXING SERVICES

Environment Abstracts. Bowker A & I Publishing, 121 Chanlon Rd., New Providence, New Jersey 07974. (908) 464-6800. 1974-.

Environment Index. Environment Information Center, Index Research Department, 124 E. 39th St., New York, New York 10016. 1971-. Annual.

Environmental Information Connection–EIC. Planning Information Program, Dept. of Urban and Regional Planning, University of Illinois, 1003 West Nevada, Urbana, Illinois 61801. (217) 333-1369. Also available online.

Environmental Periodicals Bibliography. Environmental Studies Institute, International Academy at Santa Barbara, 800 Garden St., Suite D, Santa Barbara, California 93101. (805) 965-5010. Also available online.

BIBLIOGRAPHIES

EPA Publications Bibliography. U.S. Environmental Protection Agency, Library Systems Branch, 401 M St., SW, Washington, District of Columbia 20460. (202) 260-2090. Quarterly.

ENCYCLOPEDIAS AND DICTIONARIES

Van Nostrand's Scientific Encyclopedia. Glenn D. Considine, ed. Van Nostrand Reinhold, 115 5th Ave., New York, New York 10003. (212) 254-3232. 1983. Sixth edition. Includes all broad subject areas in science.

ONLINE DATA BASES

Enviro/Energyline Abstracts Plus. R. R. Bowker Co., 121 Chanlon Rd., New Providence, New Jersey 07974. (908) 464-6800.

Environmental Periodicals Bibliography. National Information Services Corp., Ste. 6, Wyman Towers, 3100 St. Paul St., Baltimore, Maryland 21218. (410)243-0797. Online version of abstract of same name.

PHYTOPLANKTON

See: PLANKTON

PHYTOTOXICITY

See: TOXICITY

PIPELINE OIL SPILLS

See: OIL SPILLS

PIPELINES

ABSTRACTING AND INDEXING SERVICES

Engineering Index. The Engineering Index Inc., 345 E. 47th St., New York, New York 10017. 1962-.

Environment Abstracts. Bowker A & I Publishing, 121 Chanlon Rd., New Providence, New Jersey 07974. (908) 464-6800. 1974-.

Environment Index. Environment Information Center, Index Research Department, 124 E. 39th St., New York, New York 10016. 1971-. Annual.

Environmental Information Connection–EIC. Planning Information Program, Dept. of Urban and Regional Planning, University of Illinois, 1003 West Nevada, Urbana, Illinois 61801. (217) 333-1369. Also available online.

Environmental Periodicals Bibliography. Environmental Studies Institute, International Academy at Santa Barbara, 800 Garden St., Suite D, Santa Barbara, California 93101. (805) 965-5010. Also available online.

BIBLIOGRAPHIES

EPA Publications Bibliography. U.S. Environmental Protection Agency, Library Systems Branch, 401 M St., SW, Washington, District of Columbia 20460. (202) 260-2090. Quarterly.

DIRECTORIES

Pipe Line Industries. American Business Directories, Inc., 5711 S. 86th Circle, Omaha, Nebraska 68127. (402) 593-4600.

Pipeline & Gas Journal–Buyer's Guide Issue. Energy Publications Division/Edgell Communications, Inc., 10300 N. Central Expressway, Building V-580, Dallas, Texas 75231. (214) 691-3911.

Pipeline & Gas Journal–P&GJ 500 Issue. Energy Publications Division/Edgell Communications, Inc., 10300 N. Central Expressway, Building V-580, Dallas, Texas 75231. (214) 691-3911.

Pipeline–Directory of Pipelines and Equipment Issue. Oildom Publishing Company of Texas, Inc., 3314 Mercer, Houston, Texas 77027. (713) 622-0676.

ENCYCLOPEDIAS AND DICTIONARIES

Encyclopedia of Chemical Processing and Design. John J. Mcketta and W. A. Cunningham. Marcel Dekker, Inc., 270 Madison Ave., New York, New York 10016. (212) 696-9000; (800) 228-1160. 1992. Thirty-eight volumes.

Kirk-Othmer Encyclopedia of Chemical Technology. J. I. Kroschwitz, ed. John Wiley & Sons, Inc., 605 3rd Ave., New York, New York 10158-0012. (212) 850-6000. 1992-. All articles in the new edition have been rewritten and updated adding new subjects such as biotechnology, computer topics, analytical techniques and instrumentation, environmental concerns, fuels and energy, inorganic and solid state chemistry; composite materials and material science in general, and pharmaceuticals. Also available online.

Van Nostrand's Scientific Encyclopedia. Glenn D. Considine, ed. Van Nostrand Reinhold, 115 5th Ave., New York, New York 10003. (212) 254-3232. 1983. Sixth edition. Includes all broad subject areas in science.

GENERAL WORKS

Pipelines and the Environment. J. N. H. Tiratsoo. Pipeline Industries Guild, 17 Grosvenor Crescent, London, England SW1X 7ES. 1984.

Seminar on Emissions and Air Quality at Natural Gas Pipeline Installations. American Gas Association, 1515 Wilson Blvd., Arlington, Virginia 22209. 1981. Compressor emissions, nitrogen oxides, and natural gas pipelines.

The Trans-Alaska Pipeline Controversy: Technology, Conservation, and the Frontier. Peter A. Coates. Lehigh University Press, 302 Linderman Library 30, Bethlehem, Pennsylvania 18015-3067. (215) 758-3933. 1991. Question of oil extraction from the Arctic National Wildlife Refuge.

GOVERNMENTAL ORGANIZATIONS

Office of Pipeline Safety Regulation. 400 7th St., S.W., Washington, District of Columbia 20590. (202) 366-4595.

ONLINE DATA BASES

Computerized Engineering Index–COMPENDEX. Engineering Information Inc., 345 E. 47th St., New York, New York 10017. (212) 705-7600.

Enviro/Energyline Abstracts Plus. R. R. Bowker Co., 121 Chanlon Rd., New Providence, New Jersey 07974. (908) 464-6800.

Environmental Periodicals Bibliography. National Information Services Corp., Ste. 6, Wyman Towers, 3100 St. Paul St., Baltimore, Maryland 21218. (410)243-0797. Online version of abstract of same name.

Kirk-Othmer Encyclopedia of Chemical Technology. John Wiley & Sons, Inc., 605 3rd Ave., 5th Floor, New York, New York 10158. (212) 850-6000. Online version of the publication of the same name.

TRADE ASSOCIATIONS AND PROFESSIONAL SOCIETIES

United Association of Journeymen & Apprentices of the Plumbing & Pipe Fitting Industry of the United States & Canada. P.O. Box 37800, Washington, District of Columbia 20013. (202) 628-5823.

PLANKTON

ABSTRACTING AND INDEXING SERVICES

Applied Ecology Abstracts Studies in Renewable Natural Resources. Information Retrieval Ltd., 1911 Jefferson Davis Highway, Arlington, Virginia 22202. 1975-. Monthly.

ASFA Aquaculture Abstracts. Cambridge Scientific Abstracts, Inc., 5161 River Rd., Bethesda, Maryland 20816. (301) 961-6750. 1984.

Biological and Agricultural Index. H.W. Wilson Co., 950 University Ave., Bronx, New York 10452. (800) 367-6770. 1916-. Monthly.

Ecology Abstracts. Cambridge Scientific Abstracts, 5161 River Rd., Bethesda, Maryland 20816. (301) 961-6750. Monthly.

Environment Abstracts. Bowker A & I Publishing, 121 Chanlon Rd., New Providence, New Jersey 07974. (908) 464-6800. 1974-.

Environment Index. Environment Information Center, Index Research Department, 124 E. 39th St., New York, New York 10016. 1971-. Annual.

Environmental Information Connection–EIC. Planning Information Program, Dept. of Urban and Regional Planning, University of Illinois, 1003 West Nevada, Urbana, Illinois 61801. (217) 333-1369. Also available online.

Environmental Periodicals Bibliography. Environmental Studies Institute, International Academy at Santa Barbara, 800 Garden St., Suite D, Santa Barbara, California 93101. (805) 965-5010. Also available online.

General Science Index. H. W. Wilson Co., 950 University Ave., Bronx, New York 10452. 1978-. Monthly, also issued in annual cumulation. Cumulative subject index to English language periodicals in the subject fields of astronomy, botany, chemistry, earth science, environment and conservation, food and nutrition, genetics, mathematics, medicine and health, microbiology, oceanography, physics, physiology and zoology.

Multimedia Index to Ecology. National Information Center for Educational Media, University of Southern California, Los Angeles, California 90007.

Science Citation Index. Institute for Scientific Information, 3501 Market St., Philadelphia, Pennsylvania 19104. 1961-.

BIBLIOGRAPHIES

EPA Publications Bibliography. U.S. Environmental Protection Agency, Library Systems Branch, 401 M St., SW, Washington, District of Columbia 20460. (202) 260-2090. Quarterly.

ENCYCLOPEDIAS AND DICTIONARIES

Cambridge Dictionary of Biology. Peter M. B. Walker. Cambridge University Press, 40 W. 20th St., New York, New York 10011. (212) 924-3900 or (800) 227-0247. 1989. Includes 10,000 terms in zoology, botany, biochemistry, molecular biology and genetics. Previously published under the title Chambers Biology Dictionary.

Cambridge Encyclopedia of Life Sciences. A. E. Friday and David S. Ingram. Cambridge University Press, 40 W 20th St., New York, New York 10011. (212) 924-3900 or (800) 227-0247. 1985. Includes all topics under biology and ecology.

A Concise Dictionary of Biology. Elizabeth Martin, ed. Oxford University Press, 200 Madison Ave., New York, New York 10016. (212) 679-7300 or (800) 334-4249. 1990. New edition. Derived from the Concise Science Dictionary, published in 1984.

Encyclopedia of Human Biology. Renato Dulbecco, ed. Academic Press, c/o Harcourt Brace Jovanovich Inc.,

6277 Sea Harbor Dr., Orlando, Florida 32887. (800) 346-8648. 1991. Eight volumes.

McGraw-Hill Encyclopedia of Science and Technology. McGraw-Hill, 1221 Avenue of the Americas, New York, New York 10020. (212) 512-2000 or (800) 262-4729. 1992. Seventh edition. Issued in multiple volumes including index. Includes all science and technology broad subject areas.

Van Nostrand's Scientific Encyclopedia. Glenn D. Considine, ed. Van Nostrand Reinhold, 115 5th Ave., New York, New York 10003. (212) 254-3232. 1983. Sixth edition. Includes all broad subject areas in science.

GENERAL WORKS

Marine Plankton Ecology. Paul Bougis. Elsevier Science Publishing Co., 655 Ave. of the Americas, New York, New York 10010. (212) 989-5800. 1976.

Marine Toxins: Origin, Structure, and Molecular Pharmacology. Sherwood Hall and Gary Strichartz, eds. American Chemical Society, 1155 16th St. N.W., Washington, District of Columbia 20036. (202) 872-4600; (800) 227-5558. 1990. Describes the history of marine toxins and their various properties and effects on the environment.

Plankton and Productivity in the Oceans. John E. G. Raymont. Pergamon Microforms International, Inc., Fairview Park, Elmsford, New York 10523. (914) 592-7720. 1980. Covers phytoplankton and zooplankton.

Toxic Marine Phytoplankton. Edna Graneli. Elsevier Science Publishing Co., 655 Avenue of the Americas, New York, New York 10010. (212) 984-5800. 1990. Covers toxicology of marine phytoplankton.

Zoogeography and Diversity of Plankton. S. van der Spoel. Halsted Press, 605 3rd Ave., New York, New York 10158. (212) 850-6000. 1979. Ecology and variation in marine zooplankton and its geographical distribution.

HANDBOOKS AND MANUALS

User Manual for Two-Dimensional Multi-Class Phytoplankton Model with Internal Nutrient Pool Kinetics. U.S. Environmental Protection Agency, Office of Research and Development, Environmental Research Laboratory, 401 M St. SW, Washington, District of Columbia 20460. (202) 260-2090. 1986. Covers phytoplankton and eutrophication.

ONLINE DATA BASES

Enviro/Energyline Abstracts Plus. R. R. Bowker Co., 121 Chanlon Rd., New Providence, New Jersey 07974. (908) 464-6800.

Environmental Periodicals Bibliography. National Information Services Corp., Ste. 6, Wyman Towers, 3100 St. Paul St., Baltimore, Maryland 21218. (410)243-0797. Online version of abstract of same name.

SCISEARCH. Institute for Scientific Information, University City Science Center, 3501 Market St., Philadelphia, Pennsylvania 19104. (215) 386-0100.

RESEARCH CENTERS AND INSTITUTES

Alice L. Kibbe Life Science Station. Western Illinois University, Department of Biological Sciences, Macomb, Illinois 61455. (309) 298-1553.

Benedict Estuarine Research Laboratory. Academy of Natural Sciences, Benedict Avenue, Benedict, Maryland 20612. (301) 274-3134.

Boston University, Marine Program. Marine Biology Laboratory, Woods Hole, Massachusetts 02543. (508) 548-3705.

University of Maine, Ira C. Darling Center for Research Teaching and Service. Walpole, Maine 04573. (207) 563-3146.

University of Puerto Rico, Sea Grant College Program. Department of Marine Sciences, P.O. Box 5000, Mayaguez, Puerto Rico 00681-5000. (809) 832-3585.

University of Texas at Austin, Culture Collection of Algae. Department of Botany, Austin, Texas 78713. (512) 471-4019.

University of Wisconsin-Madison, Center for Biotic Systems. 1042 WARF Office Building, 610 Walnut Street, Madison, Wisconsin 53705. (608) 262-9937.

TRADE ASSOCIATIONS AND PROFESSIONAL SOCIETIES

American Institute of Biological Sciences. 730 11th St., N.W., Washington, District of Columbia 20001-4521. (202) 628-1500.

PLANNED URBAN DEVELOPMENT

See also: URBAN DESIGN AND PLANNING

ABSTRACTING AND INDEXING SERVICES

Environment Abstracts. Bowker A & I Publishing, 121 Chanlon Rd., New Providence, New Jersey 07974. (908) 464-6800. 1974-.

Environment Index. Environment Information Center, Index Research Department, 124 E. 39th St., New York, New York 10016. 1971-. Annual.

Environmental Information Connection–EIC. Planning Information Program, Dept. of Urban and Regional Planning, University of Illinois, 1003 West Nevada, Urbana, Illinois 61801. (217) 333-1369. Also available online.

Environmental Periodicals Bibliography. Environmental Studies Institute, International Academy at Santa Barbara, 800 Garden St., Suite D, Santa Barbara, California 93101. (805) 965-5010. Also available online.

BIBLIOGRAPHIES

EPA Publications Bibliography. U.S. Environmental Protection Agency, Library Systems Branch, 401 M St., SW, Washington, District of Columbia 20460. (202) 260-2090. Quarterly.

ENCYCLOPEDIAS AND DICTIONARIES

McGraw-Hill Encyclopedia of Environmental Science. Sybil P. Parker. McGraw-Hill Science & Engineering Books, 11 W. 19th St., New York, New York 10011. (212) 337-6010. 1980. Covers ecology, man's influence on nature, and environmental protection.

ONLINE DATA BASES

Enviro/Energyline Abstracts Plus. R. R. Bowker Co., 121 Chanlon Rd., New Providence, New Jersey 07974. (908) 464-6800.

Environmental Periodicals Bibliography. National Information Services Corp., Ste. 6, Wyman Towers, 3100 St. Paul St., Baltimore, Maryland 21218. (410)243-0797. Online version of abstract of same name.

Monthly Catalog of United States Government Publications. U.S. G.P.O., Supt. of Docs., PO Box 371954, Pittsburgh, Pennsylvania 15250-7954. (202) 512-0000.

National Technical Information Service. U.S. Department of Commerce, National Technical Information Service, Office of Data Base Services, 5285 Port Royal Rd., Springfield, Virginia 22161. (703) 487-4807. Bibliographic database of government sponsored research and technical reports.

PERIODICALS AND NEWSLETTERS

Journal of American Planning Association. American Planning Association, 1776 Massachusetts Avenue, NW, Suite 704, Washington, District of Columbia 20036. (202) 872-0611. Quarterly. Represents the interests of professional urban and regional planners.

PLANT COMMUNITIES

ENCYCLOPEDIAS AND DICTIONARIES

Cambridge Encyclopedia of Life Sciences. A. E. Friday and David S. Ingram. Cambridge University Press, 40 W 20th St., New York, New York 10011. (212) 924-3900 or (800) 227-0247. 1985. Includes all topics under biology and ecology.

Van Nostrand's Scientific Encyclopedia. Glenn D. Considine, ed. Van Nostrand Reinhold, 115 5th Ave., New York, New York 10003. (212) 254-3232. 1983. Sixth edition. Includes all broad subject areas in science.

GENERAL WORKS

Diversity and Pattern in Plant Communities. H. J. During. SPB Academic Publishing, Postbus 97747, The Hague, Netherlands 1988. Vegetation dynamics and plant communities.

Natural Landscaping: Designing with Native Plant Communities. John Diekelmann. McGraw-Hill Science & Engineering Books, 11 W. 19th St., New York, New York 10011. (212) 337-6010. 1982. Wild flower and landscape gardening.

HANDBOOKS AND MANUALS

Classification of Plant Communities. Robert H. Whittaker. W. Junk, 101 Phelps Dr., Norwell, Massachusetts 02061. (617) 871-6600. 1978. Handbook of vegetation science, with emphasis on vegetation classification.

PLANT CONSERVATION

See also: CONSERVATION OF NATURAL RESOURCES

ABSTRACTING AND INDEXING SERVICES

Current Advances in Ecological and Environmental Science. Pergamon Microforms International, Inc., Fairview Park, Elmsford, New York 10523. (914) 592-7720. 1989-. Monthly. Current literature searching service includingjournals, reports, abstracts, etc. This service is available online as part of the CABS database on the hosts BRS and ORBIT search service.

Index to Scientific Book Contents. Institute for Scientific Information, 3501 Market St., Philadelphia, Pennsylvania 19104. (800) 523-1857. 1985-. Annual. Gives contents of science books published.

ENCYCLOPEDIAS AND DICTIONARIES

McGraw-Hill Encyclopedia of Science and Technology. McGraw-Hill, 1221 Avenue of the Americas, New York, New York 10020. (212) 512-2000 or (800) 262-4729. 1992. Seventh edition. Issued in multiple volumes including index. Includes all science and technology broad subject areas.

Van Nostrand's Scientific Encyclopedia. Glenn D. Considine, ed. Van Nostrand Reinhold, 115 5th Ave., New York, New York 10003. (212) 254-3232. 1983. Sixth edition. Includes all broad subject areas in science.

GENERAL WORKS

The Biological Aspects of Rare Plant Conservation. Hugh Synge. John Wiley & Sons, Inc., 605 3rd Ave., New York, New York 10158-0012. (212) 850-6000. 1981.

Plant Genetic Resources: A Conservation Imperative. Christopher W. Yeatman. Westview Press, 5500 Central Ave., Boulder, Colorado 80301. (303) 444-3541. 1984.

Rare Plant Conservation: Geographical Data Organization. Larry E. Morse. New York Botanical Garden, Scientific Publications Dept., Bronx, New York 10458-5126. (212) 220-8721. 1981.

HANDBOOKS AND MANUALS

Genetics and Conservation: A Reference for Managing Wild Animal and Plant Populations. Christine M. Schonewald-Cox. Benjamin/Cummings Publishing Co., 390 Bridge Pkwy., Redwood City, California 94065. (415) 594-4400. 1983. Germplasm resources and population genetics.

STATISTICS SOURCES

World Resources. World Resources Institute. 1709 New York Ave., N.W., Washington, District of Columbia 20006. (202) 638-6300. Annual. Statistical and textual analysis of world's natural resources and the effects of growth-caused environmental pollution.

PLANT COVER

See: PLANTS

PLANT ECOLOGY

See also: BOTANICAL ECOLOGY

ABSTRACTING AND INDEXING SERVICES

Current Advances in Ecological and Environmental Science. Pergamon Microforms International, Inc., Fairview Park, Elmsford, New York 10523. (914) 592-7720. 1989-. Monthly. Current literature searching service includingjournals, reports, abstracts, etc. This service is available online as part of the CABS database on the hosts BRS and ORBIT search service.

Pollution Abstracts. Cambridge Scientific Abstracts, 5161 River Rd., Bethesda, Maryland 20816. (301) 961-6750. Six/year. Indexes worldwide technical literature on environmental pollution. Covers air pollution, marine and freshwater pollution, sewage and wastewater treatment, waste management, toxicology and health, noise pollution, radiation, land pollution, and environmental policies, programs, legislation, and education. Also available online.

ENCYCLOPEDIAS AND DICTIONARIES

McGraw-Hill Encyclopedia of Science and Technology. McGraw-Hill, 1221 Avenue of the Americas, New York, New York 10020. (212) 512-2000 or (800) 262-4729. 1992. Seventh edition. Issued in multiple volumes including index. Includes all science and technology broad subject areas.

PLANT GENETICS

See: GENETICS

PLANT NUTRITION

ABSTRACTING AND INDEXING SERVICES

Biological Abstracts. BIOSIS, 2100 Arch St., Philadelphia, Pennsylvania 19103-1399. (215) 587-4800. 1927-.

Biological and Agricultural Index. H.W. Wilson Co., 950 University Ave., Bronx, New York 10452. (800) 367-6770. 1916-. Monthly.

Current Advances in Ecological and Environmental Science. Pergamon Microforms International, Inc., Fairview Park, Elmsford, New York 10523. (914) 592-7720. 1989-. Monthly. Current literature searching service includingjournals, reports, abstracts, etc. This service is available online as part of the CABS database on the hosts BRS and ORBIT search service.

Environment Abstracts. Bowker A & I Publishing, 121 Chanlon Rd., New Providence, New Jersey 07974. (908) 464-6800. 1974-.

Environment Index. Environment Information Center, Index Research Department, 124 E. 39th St., New York, New York 10016. 1971-. Annual.

Environmental Information Connection–EIC. Planning Information Program, Dept. of Urban and Regional Planning, University of Illinois, 1003 West Nevada, Urbana, Illinois 61801. (217) 333-1369. Also available online.

Environmental Periodicals Bibliography. Environmental Studies Institute, International Academy at Santa Barbara, 800 Garden St., Suite D, Santa Barbara, California 93101. (805) 965-5010. Also available online.

Plant Growth Regulator Abstracts. Plant Growth Regulator Society of America, Boyce Thompson Institute, Tower Rd., Ithaca, New York 14850. Quarterly. Papers on applied and basic aspects of plant growth regulation by either natural or synthetic substances are accepted for publication.

Science Citation Index. Institute for Scientific Information, 3501 Market St., Philadelphia, Pennsylvania 19104. 1961-.

BIBLIOGRAPHIES

EPA Publications Bibliography. U.S. Environmental Protection Agency, Library Systems Branch, 401 M St., SW, Washington, District of Columbia 20460. (202) 260-2090. Quarterly.

ENCYCLOPEDIAS AND DICTIONARIES

Cambridge Encyclopedia of Life Sciences. A. E. Friday and David S. Ingram. Cambridge University Press, 40 W 20th St., New York, New York 10011. (212) 924-3900 or (800) 227-0247. 1985. Includes all topics under biology and ecology.

The Encyclopedia of Soil Science. Rhodes W. Fairbridge. Academic Press, c/o Harcourt Brace Jovanovich Inc., 6277 Sea Harbor Dr., Orlando, Florida 32887. (800) 346-8648. 1979-. Includes soil physics, soil chemistry, soil biology, soil fertility and plant nutrition, soil genesis, classification and cartography.

The Marshall Cavendish Illustrated Encyclopedia of Plants and Earth Sciences. Marshall Cavendish Corp., 2415 Jerusalem Ave., North Bellmore, New York 11710. (516) 826-4200. 1988.

McGraw-Hill Encyclopedia of Science and Technology. McGraw-Hill, 1221 Avenue of the Americas, New York, New York 10020. (212) 512-2000 or (800) 262-4729. 1992. Seventh edition. Issued in multiple volumes including index. Includes all science and technology broad subject areas.

Van Nostrand's Scientific Encyclopedia. Glenn D. Considine, ed. Van Nostrand Reinhold, 115 5th Ave., New York, New York 10003. (212) 254-3232. 1983. Sixth edition. Includes all broad subject areas in science.

GENERAL WORKS

Energy in Plant Nutrition and Pest Control. Zane R. Helsel. Elsevier Science Publishing Co., 655 Avenue of the Americas, New York, New York 10010. (212) 984-5800. 1987. Fertilizer and pesticides industry energy consumption.

Genetic Aspects of Plant Mineral Nutrition. N. El Bassam, et al., eds. Kluwer Academic Publishers, 101 Philip Dr., Assinippi Park, Norwell, Massachusetts 02061. (617) 871-6600. 1990. Proceedings of the 3rd International Symposium on Genetic Aspects of Plant Mineral Nutritions, Braunschweig, 1988. Papers discuss the fact that many nutritional characteristics are independently inherited and could be selected for a breeding program. Discusses development of plant breeding techniques. Special features include papers on genetic variation in symbiotic systems and a timely section on the creation of genotypes with increased efficiency of ion absorption under conditions of low input agriculture.

Principles of Plant Nutrition. Konrad Mengel. International Potash Institute, Postfach 121, Worblaufen, Bern, Switzerland CH-3048. 1978. Eight volumes.

ONLINE DATA BASES

BIOSIS Previews. BIOSIS, 2100 Arch St., Philadelphia, Pennsylvania 19103-1399. (215) 587-4800. Largest and most comprehensive database of research in the life sciences. Contains citations for nearly 9000 primary research journals, monographs, reviews, symposia, preliminary reports, semi-popular journals, selected institutional reports, government reports and research communications.

Cambridge Scientific Abstracts Life Science–CSAL. Cambridge Scientific Abstracts, 5161 River Rd., Bethesda, Maryland 20816. (301) 961-6750. Provides access to the following abstracting services: "Life Sciences Collection," "Aquatic Sciences and Fisheries Abstracts," "Oceanic Abstracts," and "Pollution Abstracts."

Enviro/Energyline Abstracts Plus. R. R. Bowker Co., 121 Chanlon Rd., New Providence, New Jersey 07974. (908) 464-6800.

Environmental Periodicals Bibliography. National Information Services Corp., Ste. 6, Wyman Towers, 3100 St. Paul St., Baltimore, Maryland 21218. (410)243-0797. Online version of abstract of same name.

PHYTOMED. Biologische Bundesanstalt fuer Land-und Forstwirtschaft, Dokumentationstelle fuer Phytomedizin, Koenign-Luise-Strasse 19, Berlin, Germany D-1000. 49 (30) 83041.

SCISEARCH. Institute for Scientific Information, University City Science Center, 3501 Market St., Philadelphia, Pennsylvania 19104. (215) 386-0100.

PERIODICALS AND NEWSLETTERS

American Midland Naturalist. University of Notre Dame, Notre Dame, Indiana 46556. (219) 239-7481. Quarterly. Basic research in biology including animal and plant ecology, systematics and entomology, mammalogy, ichthyology, parasitology, invertebrate zoology, and limnology.

FAO Fertilizer and Plant Nutrition Bulletin. Food and Agriculture Organization of the United Nations, Via delle Terme di Caracalla, Rome, Italy 00100. 61 0181-FA01. 1981-.

Journal of Plant Nutrition. Marcel Dekker, Inc., 270 Madison Ave., New York, New York 10016. (212) 696-9000; (800) 228-1160. Quarterly.

TRADE ASSOCIATIONS AND PROFESSIONAL SOCIETIES

American Institute of Biological Sciences. 730 11th St., N.W., Washington, District of Columbia 20001-4521. (202) 628-1500.

American Society of Agronomy. 677 South Segoe Rd., Madison, Wisconsin 53711. (608) 273-8080.

Association of American Plant Food Control Officals. Division of Reg. Services, University of Kentucky, 103 Regional Services Bldg., Lexington, Kentucky 40546. (606) 257-2668.

PLANT PATHOLOGY

See: PLANTS

PLANTS

ABSTRACTING AND INDEXING SERVICES

Biological Abstracts. BIOSIS, 2100 Arch St., Philadelphia, Pennsylvania 19103-1399. (215) 587-4800. 1927-.

Biological and Agricultural Index. H.W. Wilson Co., 950 University Ave., Bronx, New York 10452. (800) 367-6770. 1916-. Monthly.

Biotechnology Research Abstracts. Cambridge Scientific Abstracts, 5161 River Rd., Bethesda, Maryland 20816. (301) 961-6750. Monthly. Includes such broad areas as genetic intervention, biochemical genetics, and microbiological techniques.

Current Advances in Ecological and Environmental Science. Pergamon Microforms International, Inc., Fairview Park, Elmsford, New York 10523. (914) 592-7720. 1989-. Monthly. Current literature searching service includingjournals, reports, abstracts, etc. This service is available online as part of the CABS database on the hosts BRS and ORBIT search service.

Current Advances in Plant Science. Pergamon Microforms International, Inc., Fairview Park, Elmsford, New York 10523. (914) 592-7720. 1984-. Monthly. Current literature searching service including journals, reports, abstracts, etc. This service is available online as part of the CABS database on the hosts BRS and ORBIT search service.

Ecological Abstracts. Geo Abstracts Ltd. Elsevier Applied Science, Crown House, Linton Rd., Barking, England IG 11 8JU. 1974-. Derived from over 600 leading ecological and environmental journals, plus books, conference proceedings, reports and theses.

Ecology Abstracts. Cambridge Scientific Abstracts, 5161 River Rd., Bethesda, Maryland 20816. (301) 961-6750. Monthly.

Environment Abstracts. Bowker A & I Publishing, 121 Chanlon Rd., New Providence, New Jersey 07974. (908) 464-6800. 1974-.

Environment Index. Environment Information Center, Index Research Department, 124 E. 39th St., New York, New York 10016. 1971-. Annual.

Environmental Information Connection–EIC. Planning Information Program, Dept. of Urban and Regional

Planning, University of Illinois, 1003 West Nevada, Urbana, Illinois 61801. (217) 333-1369. Also available online.

Environmental Periodicals Bibliography. Environmental Studies Institute, International Academy at Santa Barbara, 800 Garden St., Suite D, Santa Barbara, California 93101. (805) 965-5010. Also available online.

Field Crop Abstracts. C. A. B. International, 845 North Park Ave., Tucson, Arizona 85719. (602) 621-7897 or (800) 528-4841. 1948-. Monthly. Covers literature on agronomy, field production, crop botany and physiology of all annual field crops, both temperate and tropical.

General Science Index. H. W. Wilson Co., 950 University Ave., Bronx, New York 10452. 1978-. Monthly, also issued in annual cumulation. Cumulative subject index to English language periodicals in the subject fields of astronomy, botany, chemistry, earth science, environment and conservation, food and nutrition, genetics, mathematics, medicine and health, microbiology, oceanography, physics, physiology and zoology.

Herbage Abstracts. C. A. B. International, 845 North Park Ave., Tucson, Arizona 85719. (602) 621-7897 or (800) 528-4841. 1931-. Monthly. Covers management, productivity and economics of grasslands, rangelands and fodder crops, grassland ecology, seed production, toxic plants, land use and farming systems, weed control, agricultural meteorology, and other related areas.

Nematological Abstracts. C. A. B. International, 845 North Park Ave., Tucson, Arizona 85719. (602) 621-7897 or (800) 528-4841. 1932-. Quarterly. Abstracts of the world literature on: nematode parasitic on plants; free-living and marine nematodes; nematodes parasitic on insects or other invertebrates.

Plant Growth Regulator Abstracts. Plant Growth Regulator Society of America, Boyce Thompson Institute, Tower Rd., Ithaca, New York 14850. Quarterly. Papers on applied and basic aspects of plant growth regulation by either natural or synthetic substances are accepted for publication.

Science Citation Index. Institute for Scientific Information, 3501 Market St., Philadelphia, Pennsylvania 19104. 1961-.

BIBLIOGRAPHIES

EPA Publications Bibliography. U.S. Environmental Protection Agency, Library Systems Branch, 401 M St., SW, Washington, District of Columbia 20460. (202) 260-2090. Quarterly.

Excerpta Botanica. Section A. Taxonomica et Chorologica. G. Fischer, 220E 23d St., Ste. 909, New York, New York 10010-4606. (212) 683-8333 or (800) 422-8824. 1959-.

The Protection of Peanuts. Charles N. Bebee. National Agricultural Library, 10301 Baltimore Blvd., Beltsville, Maryland 20705-2351. (301) 504-5755. 1991. Citations from AGRICOLA concerning diseases and other environmental considerations.

The Protection of Tomatoes, Egg Plants and Peppers. Charles N. Bebee. National Agricultural Library, 10301 Baltimore Blvd., Beltsville, Maryland 20705-2351. (301) 504-5755. 1991. Citations from AGRICOLA concerning diseases and other environmental considerations.

World Plant Conservation Bibliography. World Conservation Monitoring Centre. World Conservation Union, IUCN Publications Services Unit, 181a Huntingdon Road, Cambridge, England CB3 0DJ. (0223) 277894. 1990. Over 10,000 reference citations by country, author and plant name, and includes substantial geographical and plant family indexes for easy access.

DIRECTORIES

Agricultural Information Resource Centers, a World Directory 1990. Rita C. Fisher. IAALD World Directory Working Group, 716 W. Indiana Ave., Urbana, Illinois 61801-4836. (217) 333-7687. 1990. Includes 3,971 information resource centers that have agriculture related collection and/or information services.

ENCYCLOPEDIAS AND DICTIONARIES

Cambridge Encyclopedia of Life Sciences. A. E. Friday and David S. Ingram. Cambridge University Press, 40 W 20th St., New York, New York 10011. (212) 924-3900 or (800) 227-0247. 1985. Includes all topics under biology and ecology.

Elsevier's Dictionary of Horticultural and Agricultural Plant Production in Ten Languages. Elsevier Science Publishing Co., 655 Avenue of Americas, New York, New York 10010. (212) 989-5800. 1990. Language of the text: English, Dutch, French, German, Danish, Swedish, Italian, Spanish, Portuguese and Latin.

Elsevier's Dictionary of Wild and Cultivated Plants in Latin, English, French, Italian, Dutch, and German. W. E. Clason. Elsevier Science Publishing Co., 655 Avenue of the Americas, New York, New York 10010. (212) 989-5800. 1989. This dictionary consists of the scientific names of wild and cultivated plants found in Europe.

Life Sciences on File. Diagram Group. Facts on File, Inc., 460 Park Ave. S., New York, New York 10016. (212) 683-2244. 1986. Encyclopedia of pictorial collection in life sciences. Deals with all major topics in life sciences including ecology.

The Marshall Cavendish Illustrated Encyclopedia of Plants and Earth Sciences. Marshall Cavendish Corp., 2415 Jerusalem Ave., North Bellmore, New York 11710. (516) 826-4200. 1988.

McGraw-Hill Encyclopedia of Science and Technology. McGraw-Hill, 1221 Avenue of the Americas, New York, New York 10020. (212) 512-2000 or (800) 262-4729. 1992. Seventh edition. Issued in multiple volumes including index. Includes all science and technology broad subject areas.

Nature in America Your A-Z Guide to Our Country's Animals, Plants, Landforms and Other Natural Features. Readers Digest Association, 260 Madison Ave., New York, New York 10016. 1991. Reference guide of nature in North America. Explores plants, animals, weather, land forms, and wildlife habitats. Includes over 1000 photographs and illustrations for some 1200 entries.

Role of Environment Factors. R. P. Pharis, et al. Springer-Verlag, 175 5th Ave., New York, New York 10010. (212) 460-1500 or (800) 777-4643. 1985. Encyclopedia of plant physiology.

Van Nostrand's Scientific Encyclopedia. Glenn D. Considine, ed. Van Nostrand Reinhold, 115 5th Ave., New

York, New York 10003. (212) 254-3232. 1983. Sixth edition. Includes all broad subject areas in science.

GENERAL WORKS

The Biochemistry and Uses of Pesticides: Structure, Metabolism, Mode of Action, and Uses in Crop Protection. Kenneth A. Hassall. VCH Publishers, 303 NW 12th Ave., Deerfield Beach, Florida 33442-1788. (305) 428-5566. 1990. Reports the progress that has been made in the last few years towards an understanding of how pesticides function, how metabolism contributes to selectivity and safety and how the development of resistance is linked to biochemistry and molecular biology.

Bugs, Slugs and Other Thugs: Controlling Garden Pests Organically. Rhonda Massingham Hart. Garden Way Pub., Schoolhouse Rd., Pownal, Vermont 05261. (802) 823-5811; (800) 441-5700. 1991.

Climatic Change and Plant Genetic Resources. M. T. Jackson, et al., eds. Belhaven Press, 136 S. Broadway, Irvington, New York 10533. (914) 591-9111. 1990. Cities concerns about the effect of global warming on biological diversity of species is the main thrust of this text. Major portion of the book comes from the second international workshop on plant genetic resources held in 1989.

Conservation of Medicinal Plants. O. Akerele. World Conservation Union, IUCN Publications Services Unit, 181a Huntingdon Road, Cambridge, England CB3 0DJ. (0223) 277894. 1991. Plants identified as having medicinal properties.

Crop Protection Chemicals. B. G. Lever. E. Horwood, 1230 Avenue of the Americas, New York, New York 10020. (212) 698-7000; (800) 223-2348. 1990. Overview of crop protection technology. Traces the evolution of pest control as an integral part of crop production. Focuses on the requirements of governments and society regarding the safety of products to users, food consumers and the environment.

Ecology of Photosynthesis in Sun and Shade. J. R. Evans, et al. CSIRO, PO Box 89, East Melbourne, VIC, Australia 3002. 1988. The popular topic of function analysis of the photosynthetic apparatus in response to irradiance, and problems of acclimation and photoinhibition are also discussed.

Environmental Physiology of Plants. A. H. Fitter and R. K. M. Hay. Academic Press, c/o Harcourt Brace Jovanovich Inc., 6277 Sea Harbor Dr., Orlando, Florida 32887. (800) 346-8648. 1987. 2d ed. Discusses the interaction of plants with the environment. Also outlines the adaptation of plants to the environment and concepts such as optimization. Covers geographical areas of North America and Europe. Has an extensive reference section.

Genetic Aspects of Plant Mineral Nutrition. N. El Bassam, et al., eds. Kluwer Academic Publishers, 101 Philip Dr., Assinippi Park, Norwell, Massachusetts 02061. (617) 871-6600. 1990. Proceedings of the 3rd International Symposium on Genetic Aspects of Plant Mineral Nutritions, Braunschweig, 1988. Papers discuss the fact that many nutritional characteristics are independently inherited and could be selected for a breeding program. Discusses development of plant breeding techniques. Special features include papers on genetic variation in symbiotic systems and a timely section on the creation of genotypes with increased efficiency of ion absorption under conditions of low input agriculture.

Guidelines for the Control of Insect and Mite Pest of Foods, Fibers, Feeds, Ornamentals, Livestock, and Households. Agricultural Research Service. U.S. G.P.O., Washington, District of Columbia 20401. (202) 7512-0000. 1982. Plant diseases and pests, mites, and insect control.

Influence of Environmental Factors on the Control of Grape, Pests, Diseases and Weeds. R. Cavalloro. A. A. Balkema, Old Post Rd., Brookfield, Vermont 05036. (802) 276-3162. 1989. Influence of environmental factors on cultivation of vines, and impact of insects, mites, diseases and weeds and pesticides.

Magill's Survey of Science. Life Science Series. Frank N. Magill, ed. Salem Press, PO Box 50062, Pasadena, California 91105. 1991. Six volumes. Contents: v.1. A-Central and peripheral nervous system functions; v.2. Central metabolism regulation - eukaryotic transcriptional control; v.3. Positive and negative eukaryotic transcriptional control - mammalian hormones; v.4. Hormones and behavior - muscular contraction; v.5. Muscular contraction and relaxation - sexual reproduction in plants; v.6. Reproductive behavior and mating - X inactivation and the Lyon hypothesis.

Molecular Strategies of Pathogens and Host Plants. Suresh S. Patil, et al., eds. Springer-Verlag, 175 5th Ave, New York, New York 10010. (212) 460-1500. 1991. Papers from an April seminar in Honolulu discusses the molecular interactions between plant pathogens and their hosts, considering the strategies of various bacteria and fungi, the plant's response, and an approach to breeding disease-resistant plants.

Physiological Plant Ecology. O. L. Lange, et al., eds. Springer-Verlag, 175 5th Ave., New York, New York 10010. (212) 460-1500; (800) 777-4643. 1981-1983. Contents: Volume 1 - Responses to the physical environment; Volume 2 - Water relations and carbon assimilation; Volume 3 - Responses to the chemical and biological environment; Volume 4 - Ecosystem processes (mineral cycling, productivity, and man's influence).

Plant Demography in Vegetation Succession. Krystyna Falinska. Kluwer Academic Publishers, 101 Philip Dr., Assinippi Park, Norwell, Massachusetts 02061. (617) 871-6600. 1991.

Plant Growth: Interactions with Nutrition and Environment. J.R. Porter. Cambridge University Press, 40 W. 20th St., New York, New York 10011. (212) 924-3900. 1991. Plant growth, nutrition, and ecology.

Plants in Danger: What Do We Know?. Stephen Davis. World Conservation Union, IUCN Publications Services Unit, 181a Huntingdon Road, Cambridge, England CB3 0DJ. (0223) 277894. 1988. Indicates which plants are known to be threatened, where further information can be found, and which organizations can be contacted.

Pocket Flora of the Redwood Forest. Rudolf Willem Becking. Island Press, 1718 Connecticut Ave. N.W., Suite 300, Washington, District of Columbia 20009. (202) 232-7933. 1982. Guide to 212 of the most frequently seen plants in the Redwood Forest of the Pacific Coast. It is interspersed with accurate drawing color photographs and systematic keys to plant identification.

Responses of Plants to Environmental Stresses. J. Levitt. Academic Press, c/o Harcourt Brace Jovanovich Inc., 6277 Sea Harbor Dr., Orlando, Florida 32887. (800) 346-8648. 1980. 2nd ed. Volume 1 covers chilling, freezing and high temperature. Volume 2 contains water, radiation, salt, and other stresses.

Risk Assessment in Genetic Engineering; Environmental Release of Organisms. Morris A. Levin and Harlee Strauss. McGraw-Hill, 1221 Avenue of the Americas, New York, New York 10020. (212) 512-2000; (800) 262-4729. 1991. Investigates issues such as the transport of microorganisms via air, water, and soil; the persistence and establishment of viruses, bacteria, and plants; and the genetic transfer via viruses.

Yellowstone Vegetation, Consequences of Environment and History in a Natural Setting. Don G. Despain. Roberts Rinhart Pub., PO Box 666, Niwot, Colorado 80544. (303) 652-2921. 1990. Explores Yellowstone's vegetation types in their habitats and communities, in their origins and distribution, and in their succession after devastation by fire, wind, and insects.

GOVERNMENTAL ORGANIZATIONS

National Agricultural Library. Route 1, Beltsville, Maryland 20705. (301) 344-4348.

HANDBOOKS AND MANUALS

Crop Protection Chemical Reference. Chemical and Pharmaceutical Press/Wiley, 605 3rd Ave., New York, New York 10158-0012. (212) 850-6000. 1991. 7th ed. Updated annual edition of a standard reference on label information on crop protection chemicals contains the complete text of some 540 product labels, which provide detailed information concerning what products can be used to treat a certain crop for certain problems, using what quantities of the chemical and under what restrictions and precautions. Appendices provide useful information on such matters as coding required when transporting products, safety practices, calibrations, etc.

Index Hortensis: A Modern Nomenclator for Botanists, Horticulturalists, Plantsmen, and the Serious Gardener. Piers Trehane. Quarterjack Publishing, Hampreston Manor Farm, Wimborne, England BH21 7LX. 1989-. List of plants alphabetically arranged by genus indicating the correct name, hybrid species, botanical epithet and the family name and other related information. Volume 1 contains: perennials, including border plants, herbs, bulbous plants, non-woody alpines, aquatic plants, outdoor ferns and ornamental grasses.

The Official World Wildlife Fund Guide to Endangered Species of North America. David W. Lowe, ed. Beacham Publishing, Inc., 2100 S. St. NW, Washington, District of Columbia 20008. (202) 234-0877. 1990. Two volumes. Guide to endangered plants and animals. Describes 540 endangered or threatened species including their habitat, behavior and, recovery. Includes: directories of the Offices of the U.S. Fish and Wildlife Service, Offices of the National Marine Fisheries Service, State Heritage Programs, Bureau of Land Management Offices, National Forest Service Offices, National Wildlife Refuges, Canadian agencies, and state offices.

Plant Molecular Biology Manual. Stanton B. Gelvin. Kluwer Academic Publishers, 101 Philip Dr., Assinippi Park, Norwell, Massachusetts 02061. (617) 871-6600. 1988.

Poisonous Plants of Eastern North America. Randy G. Westbrooks and James W. Preacher. University of South Carolina Press, Columbia, South Carolina 29208. (803)

777-5243. 1986. List of poisonous plants which include species of plants, the plant part (leaf, root, fruit), the amount of plant material involved, the stage of development of the plant, and the soil type and growing conditions.

ONLINE DATA BASES

BIOSIS Previews. BIOSIS, 2100 Arch St., Philadelphia, Pennsylvania 19103-1399. (215) 587-4800. Largest and most comprehensive database of research in the life sciences. Contains citations for nearly 9000 primary research journals, monographs, reviews, symposia, preliminary reports, semi-popular journals, selected institutional reports, government reports and research communications.

Cambridge Scientific Abstracts Life Science–CSAL. Cambridge Scientific Abstracts, 5161 River Rd., Bethesda, Maryland 20816. (301) 961-6750. Provides access to the following abstracting services: "Life Sciences Collection," "Aquatic Sciences and Fisheries Abstracts," "Oceanic Abstracts," and "Pollution Abstracts."

Enviro/Energyline Abstracts Plus. R. R. Bowker Co., 121 Chanlon Rd., New Providence, New Jersey 07974. (908) 464-6800.

Environmental Periodicals Bibliography. National Information Services Corp., Ste. 6, Wyman Towers, 3100 St. Paul St., Baltimore, Maryland 21218. (410)243-0797. Online version of abstract of same name.

Life Sciences from NTIS. National Technical Information Center for the Utilization of Federal Technology, 5285 Port Royal Rd., Springfield, Virginia 22161. (703) 487-4650.

PHYTOMED. Biologische Bundesanstalt fuer Land-und Forstwirtschaft, Dokumentationstelle fuer Phytomedizin, Koenign-Luise-Strasse 19, Berlin, Germany D-1000. 49 (30) 83041.

Plant Toxicity Data. University of Oklahoma, Department of Botany & Microbiology, 770 Van Fleet Oval, Room 135, Norman, Oklahoma 73019. (405) 325-3174.

SCISEARCH. Institute for Scientific Information, University City Science Center, 3501 Market St., Philadelphia, Pennsylvania 19104. (215) 386-0100.

PERIODICALS AND NEWSLETTERS

American Midland Naturalist. University of Notre Dame, Notre Dame, Indiana 46556. (219) 239-7481. Quarterly. Basic research in biology including animal and plant ecology, systematics and entomology, mammalogy, ichthyology, parasitology, invertebrate zoology, and limnology.

Communications in Soil Science and Plant Analysis. M. Dekker, 270 Madison Ave., New York, New York 10016. (212) 696-9000; (800) 228-1160. 1970-.

Evolutionary Trends in Plants. Evolutionary Trends in Plants, Zurich, Switzerland Quarterly.

International Journal of Plant Nutrition, Plant Chemistry, Soil Microbiology and Soil-Bourne Plant Diseases. Kluwer Academic Publishers, 101 Philip Dr., Assinippi Park, Norwell, Massachusetts 02061. (617) 871-6600. 1948-.

Journal of Plant Growth Regulation. Springer-Verlag, 175 5th Ave., New York, New York 10010. (212) 460-1500. Quarterly. Growth and development of plants.

RESEARCH CENTERS AND INSTITUTES

Arboretum. University of California, Davis, Davis, California 95616. (916) 752-2498.

Blandy Experimental Farm and Orland E. White Arboretum. State Arboretum of Virginia, P.O. Box 175, Boyce, Virginia 22620. (703) 837-1758.

Boyce Thompson Institute for Plant Research. Cornell University, Tower Road, Ithaca, New York 14853. (607) 254-1234.

Center for Plant Conservation. 3115 S. Grand, P.O. Box 299, St. Louis, Missouri 63166. (314) 577-9450.

Committee on Evolutionary Biology. University of Chicago, 915 East 57th Street, Chicago, Illinois 60637. (312) 702-8940.

Hastings Natural History Reservation. University of California, Berkeley, 38601 E. Carmel Valley Rd., Carmel Valley, California 93924. (408) 659-2664.

Herbarium. University of California, Los Angeles, 405 Hilgard Avenue, Los Angeles, California 90024. (213) 825-3620.

Herbarium. University of Colorado, Campus Box 350, Boulder, Colorado 80309. (303) 492-5074.

Herbarium. University of Florida, 209 Rolfs Hall, Gainesville, Florida 32611. (904) 392-1767.

Herbarium. West Virginia University, Brooks Hall, Morgantown, West Virginia 26506. (304) 293-5201.

Herbarium. William Jewell College, Liberty, Missouri 64068. (816) 781-7700.

Herbarium. Yale University, 550 Osborn Memorial Laboratory, Biology Department, PO Box 6666, New Haven, Connecticut 06511. (203) 432-3904.

Institute of Biological Chemistry. Washington State University, Clark Hall, Pullman, Washington 99164. (509) 335-3412.

Joint Facility for Regional Ecosystem Analysis. University of Colorado-Boulder, Boulder, Colorado 80309. (303) 492-7303.

Louisiana State University, Mycological Herbarium. Department of Botany, Room 305, Life Sciences Building, Baton Rouge, Louisiana 70803. (504) 388-8487.

Marion Ownbey Herbarium. Washington State University, Pullman, Washington 99164-4309. (509) 335-3250.

Marsh Botanical Garden. Yale University, PO Box 6666, Biology Department, New Haven, Connecticut 06511-8112. (203) 432-3906.

Massachusetts College of Pharmacy and Allied Health Sciences, Herbarium. 179 Longwood Avenue, Boston, Massachusetts 02115. (617) 732-2960.

Michigan State University, Center for Environmental Toxicology. C 231 Holden Hall, East Lansing, Michigan 48824. (517) 353-6469.

Michigan State University, Center for Genetic and Biochemical Alteration of Plant Lipids and Starch. c/o

Department of Botany and Plant Pathology, East Lansing, Michigan 48824. (517) 353-0611.

Michigan State University, MSU-DOE Plant Research Laboratory. 106 Plant Biology Building, East Lansing, Michigan 48824-1312. (517) 353-2270.

Michigan State University, W.J. Beal Botanical Garden. 412 Olds Hall, East Lansing, Michigan 48824-1047. (517) 355-9582.

Missouri Botanical Garden. P.O. Box 299, St. Louis, Missouri 63166-0299. (314) 577-5100.

Montana State University, Herbarium. Bozeman, Montana 59717. (406) 994-4424.

Montana State University, Plant Growth Center. Bozeman, Montana 59717-0002. (406) 994-4821.

Morton Arboretum. Route 53, Lisle, Illinois 60532. (708) 968-0074.

Mycological Herbarium. Washington State University, 345 Johnson Hall, Pullman, Washington 99164-6430. (509) 335-9541.

New York Botanical Garden, Institute of Economic Botany. Bronx, New York 10458-5126. (212) 220-8763.

North Carolina State University, Southeastern Plant Environment Laboratory. Box 7618, Gardner, Raleigh, North Carolina 27695. (919) 737-2778.

North Dakota State University, Herbarium. State University Station, Fargo, North Dakota 58102. (701) 237-7222.

Northern Illinois University, Plant Molecular Biology Center. Department of Biological Sciences, Montgomery Hall, DeKalb, Illinois 60115-2861. (815) 753-7841.

Oberlin College, Herbarium. Kettering Hall, Oberlin, Ohio 44074. (216) 775-8315.

Ohio State University, Secrest Arboretum. 1680 Madison Avenue, Wooster, Ohio 44691. (216) 263-3761.

Oklahoma State University, Herbarium. Stillwater, Oklahoma 74078. (405) 744-9558.

Oklahoma State University, Plant Disease Diagnostic Laboratory. Department of Plant Pathology, 119 Noble Research Center, Stillwater, Oklahoma 74078. (405) 744-9961.

Oregon State University, Herbarium. Corvallis, Oregon 97331-2910. (503) 737-4106.

Purdue University, Arthur Herbarium. Department of Botany and Plant Pathology, 115 S. Lilly Hall, Rm. 1-423, West Lafayette, Indiana 47907. (317) 494-4623.

Rancho Santa Ana Botanic Garden. 1500 North College Avenue, Claremont, California 91711. (714) 626-3922.

Rockefeller University, Laboratory of Plant Biochemistry. 1230 York Ave, New York, New York 10021-6399. (212) 570-8000.

Rockefeller University, Laboratory of Plant Molecular Biology. 1230 York Ave, Box 301, New York, New York 10021-6399. (212) 570-8126.

Southern Methodist University, Herbarium. Science Information Center, Dallas, Texas (214) 692-2257.

Southwest Consortium on Plant Genetics and Water Resources. New Mexico State University, Box 3GL, Las Cruces, New Mexico 88003. (505) 646-5453.

State University of New York at Plattsburg, Biochemistry/Biophysics Program. Plattsburg, New York 12901. (518) 564-3159.

State University of New York College of Environmental Science and Forestry. Cellulose Research Institute, Baker Laboratory, Syracuse, New York 13210. (315) 470-6851.

Texas A&I University, Caesar Kleberg Wildlife Research Institute. College of Agriculture & Home Economics, Campus Box 218, Kingsville, Texas 78363. (512) 595-3922.

Texas A&I University, Herbarium. Kingsville, Texas 78363. (512) 595-3803.

Texas A&I University, South Texas Plant Materials Center. Caesar Kleberg Wildlife Research Institute, Campus Box 218, Kingsville, Texas 78363. (512) 595-3960.

Texas A&M University, Paleoethnobotanical Laboratory. Department of Anthropology, College Station, Texas 77843. (409) 845-9334.

Texas A&M University, S.M. Tracy Herbarium. College Station, Texas 77843. (409) 845-4328.

Texas Tech University, Brush Control Research Center. Goddard Range and Wildlife Building, Lubbock, Texas 79409. (806) 742-2841.

Texas Tech University, Herbarium. Texas Tech Museum, P.O. Box 4149, Lubbock, Texas 79409. (806) 742-3222.

Texas Woman's University, Biology Science Research Laboratory. Denton, Texas 76204. (817) 898-2351.

Triangle Universities Consortium for Research and Education in Plant Molecular Biology. North Carolina Biotechnology Center, P.O. Box 13547, Research Triangle Park, North Carolina 27709. (919) 541-9366.

U.S. Forest Service, Forestry Sciences Laboratory. 860 North 1200 East, Logan, Utah 84321. (801) 752-1311.

University and Jepson Herbaria. University of California, Berkeley, Berkeley, California 94720. (415) 642-2463.

University of Alabama, Arboretum. Box 870344, Tuscaloosa, Alabama 35487-0344. (205) 553-3278.

University of Arizona, Boyce Thompson Arboretum. P.O. Box AB, Superior, Arizona 85723. (602) 689-2811.

University of Arizona, Herbarium. 113 Shantz Building, Tucson, Arizona 85721. (602) 621-7243.

University of Georgia, Center for Advanced Ultrastructural Research. Barrow Hall, Athens, Georgia 30602. (404) 542-4080.

University of Georgia, Herbarium. Athens, Georgia 30602. (404) 542-1823.

University of Georgia, Julian H. Miller Mycological Herbarium. Department of Plant Pathology, Plant Sciences Building, Athens, Georgia 30602. (404) 542-1280.

University of Georgia, State Botanical Garden of Georgia. 2450 South Milledge Avenue, Athens, Georgia 30605. (404) 542-1244.

University of Hawaii at Manoa Harold L. Lyon Center. 3860 Manoa Road, Honolulu, Hawaii 96822. (808) 988-3177.

University of Idaho Herbarium. Department of Biological Sciences, Moscow, Idaho 83843. (208) 885-6798.

University of Illinois, Herbarium. Department of Plant Biology, 505 S. Goodwin Ave., Urbana, Illinois 61801. (217) 333-2522.

University of Illinois, Laboratory of Plant Pigment Biochemistry and Photobiology. 1302 West Pennsylvania, Urbana, Illinois 61801. (217) 333-1968.

University of Iowa, Herbarium. Department of Botany, Iowa City, Iowa 52242. (319) 335-1320.

University of Kansas, Kansas Biological Survey. 2041 Constant Avenue-Foley Hall, Lawrence, Kansas 66047-2906. (913) 864-7725.

University of Kansas, Kansas Ecological Reserves. Lawrence, Kansas 66045. (913) 864-3236.

University of Kansas, McGregor Herbarium. Joseph S. Bridwell Botanical Research Laboratory, 2045 Constant Ave., Campus West, Lawrence, Kansas 66047. (913) 864-4493.

University of Kentucky, Herbarium. School of Biological Science, Room 216 Funkhouser, Morgan 101, Lexington, Kentucky 40506. (606) 257-3240.

University of Maine, Herbarium. Department of Botany & Plant Pathology, Orono, Maine 04469. (207) 581-2976.

University of Massachusetts, Herbarium. Amherst, Massachusetts 01003. (413) 545-2775.

University of Miami, Morton Collectanea. Box 8204, Coral Gables, Florida 33124. (305) 284-3741.

University of Michigan, Herbarium. North University Building, Ann Arbor, Michigan 48109-1057. (313) 764-2407.

University of Michigan, Matthaei Botanical Gardens. 1800 North Dixboro Road, Ann Arbor, Michigan 48105. (313) 763-7060.

University of Michigan, Nichols Arboretum. Ann Arbor, Michigan 48109-1115. (313) 763-9315.

University of Minnesota, Cedar Creek Natural History Area. 2660 Fawn Lake Drive NE, Bethel, Minnesota 55005. (612) 434-5131.

University of Minnesota, Herbarium. St. Paul, Minnesota 55108. (612) 625-1234.

University of Mississippi, Biological Field Station. Department of Biology, University, Mississippi 38677. (601) 232-5479.

University of Mississippi, Herbarium. Department of Biology, University, Mississippi 38677. (601) 232-7215.

University of Missouri-Columbia, Herbarium. 226 Tucker Hall, Columbia, Missouri 65211. (314) 882-6519.

University of North Carolina at Chapel Hill, Herbarium. 401 Coker Hall 010A, CB 3280, Chapel Hill, North Carolina 27599-3280. (919) 962-6931.

University of North Carolina at Chapel Hill, North Carolina Botanical Garden. CB #3375 Totten Center, Chapel Hill, North Carolina 27599. (919) 962-0522.

University of Notre Dame, Greene-Nieuwland Herbarium. Department of Biological Sciences, Notre Dame, Indiana 46556. (219) 239-6684.

University of Oklahoma, Biological Station. Star Route B, Kingston, Oklahoma 73439. (405) 564-2463.

University of Oklahoma, Hebb Herbarium. Department of Botany and Microbiology, 770 Van Vleet Oval, Norman, Oklahoma 73019-0245. (405) 325-6443.

University of Oregon, Herbarium. Department of Biology, Eugene, Oregon 97403. (503) 346-3033.

University of Pennsylvania, Morris Arboretum. 9414 Meadowbrook Avenue, Philadelphia, Pennsylvania 19118. (215) 247-5777.

University of South Dakota, South Dakota Herbarium. Biology Department, Vermillion, South Dakota 57069. (605) 677-6176.

University of South Florida, Herbarium. Biology Department, Tampa, Florida 33620. (813) 974-2359.

University of Tennessee at Knoxville, Tennessee State Herbarium. Knoxville, Tennessee 37916. (615) 974-6212.

University of Texas at Austin, Brackenridge Field Laboratory. Lake Austin Boulevard, Austin, Texas 78712. (512) 471-7131.

University of Texas at Austin, Plant Resources Center. Department of Botany, Main Building 228, Austin, Texas 78712. (512) 471-5128.

University of Vermont, Pringle Herbarium. Burlington, Vermont 05405. (802) 656-3221.

University of Washington, Center for Urban Horticulture. Seattle, Washington 98195. (206) 543-8616.

University of Washington, Herbarium. Seattle, Washington 98195. (206) 543-8850.

University of Wisconsin-Madison, Center for the Study of Nitrogen Fixation. 420 Henry Mall, Department of Biochemistry, Madison, Wisconsin 53706. (608) 262-6859.

University of Wisconsin-Madison, Herbarium. Birge Hall, Madison, Wisconsin 53706. (608) 262-2792.

University of Wisconsin-Madison, Institute of Plant Development. B121 Birge Hall, Department of Botany, Madison, Wisconsin 53706. (608) 262-9997.

University of Wisconsin-Milwaukee, Herbarium. Department of Biological Sciences, Box 413, Milwaukee, Wisconsin 53201. (414) 229-6728.

University of Wyoming, Rocky Mountain Herbarium. Aven Nelson Building, 3165 University Station, Laramie, Wyoming 82071. (307) 766-2236.

University of Wyoming, Wilhelm G. Solheim Mycological Herbarium. 3165 University Station, Laramie, Wyoming 82071. (307) 766-2236.

USDA Plant Gene Expression Center. 800 Buchanan Street, Albany, California 94710. (510) 559-5900.

Utah State University, Intermountain Herbarium. UMC 55, Department of Biology, Logan, Utah 84322. (801) 750-1586.

Virus Laboratory. University of California, Berkeley, 229 Stanley Hall, Berkeley, California 94720. (510) 642-1722.

TRADE ASSOCIATIONS AND PROFESSIONAL SOCIETIES

American Association of Botanical Gardens and Arboreta. 786 Church Rd., Wayne, Pennsylvania 19087. (215) 688-1120.

American Institute of Biological Sciences. 730 11th St., N.W., Washington, District of Columbia 20001-4521. (202) 628-1500.

American Society of Agronomy. 677 South Segoe Rd., Madison, Wisconsin 53711. (608) 273-8080.

American Society of Plant Taxonomists. c/o Dr. Samuel Jones, Dept. of Botany, University of Georgia, Athens, Georgia 30602. (404) 542-1802.

Botanical Society of America. c/o Christopher Haufler, Department of Botany, University of Kansas, Lawrence, Kansas 66045-2106. (913) 864-4301.

Deciduous Tree Fruit Disease Workers. c/o David Sugar, Southern Oregon Expt. Sta., 569 Hanley Rd., Medford, Oregon 97502. (503) 772-5165.

International Plant Biotech Network. c/o TCCP, Dept. of Biology, Colorado State University, Fort Collins, Colorado 80523. (303) 491-6996.

International Society for Plant Molecular Biology. Biochemistry Dept., University of Georgia, Athens, Georgia 30602. (404) 542-3239.

National Council of Commercial Plant Breeders. 601 13th St., N.W., Suite 570, Washington, District of Columbia 20005. (202) 638-3128.

Society of Nematologists. c/o R.N. Huehel, Ph.D., USDA, ARS, Nematology Laboratory, Bldg. 011A BARC-W, Beetsville, Maryland 20705. (301) 344-3081.

PLASTICS

See also: PCBS; RECYCLING; WASTE MANAGEMENT

ABSTRACTING AND INDEXING SERVICES

Green Engineering: A Current Awareness Bulletin. Institution of Mechanical Engineers, 1 Birdcage Walk, Westminster, London, England SW1H 9JJ. 71973 1266/7. 1991. Monthly. Covers acid rain, aerosol technology, biotechnology chlorofluorocarbons, chemical and process engineering, environmental protection, energy conservation, energy generation, greenhouse effect, materials, pollution, recycling, waste disposal, and other environmental topics.

Science Citation Index. Institute for Scientific Information, 3501 Market St., Philadelphia, Pennsylvania 19104. 1961-.

BIBLIOGRAPHIES

CFCs & the Polyurethane Industry: A Compilation of Technical Publications. Society of the Plastics Industry, Polyurethane Division, 355 Lexington Ave., New York, New York 10017. (212)351-5425. 1992. Bibliography of plastic foams, chlorofluorocarbons and polyurethanes.

DIRECTORIES

American Society of Electroplated Plastics–Directory. 1101 14th St., N.W., Suite 1100, Washington, District of Columbia 20005. (202) 371-1323. Annual.

Directory of U.S. and Canadian Scrap Plastics Processors and Buyers. Jerry Powell. Resource Recycling, Box 10540, Portland, Oregon 97210. (503) 227-1319. Annual. Recycled plastics processors and end users.

List of PET Recyclers in the United States and Canada. National Assn. for Plastic Container Recovery, 4828 Pkwy. Plaza Blvd., Suite 260, Charlotte, North Carolina 28217. (704) 357-3250. Monthly.

Plastic Bottle Recycling Directory and Reference Guide. Plastic Bottle Information Bureau, 1275 K St. N.W., Suite 400, Washington, District of Columbia 20005. (202) 371-5200.

Plastics Compounding Redbook. Edgell Communications, Inc., 7500 Old Oak Blvd., Cleveland, Ohio 44130. (216) 243-8100.

Plastics–Fabricating, Finishing & Decor. American Business Directories, Inc., 5711 S. 86th Circle, Omaha, Nebraska 68127. (402) 593-4600.

Plastics Technology Manufacturing Handbook and Buyers' Guide. Bill Communications, Inc., 633 Third Ave., New York, New York 10017. (212) 986-4800.

Society of the Plastics Industry–Membership Directory and Buyers' Guide. Society of the Plastics Industry, Inc., 1275 K St.,N.W., Washington, District of Columbia 20005. (202) 371-5200.

ENCYCLOPEDIAS AND DICTIONARIES

Encyclopedia of Chemical Processing and Design. John J. Mcketta and W. A. Cunningham. Marcel Dekker, Inc., 270 Madison Ave., New York, New York 10016. (212) 696-9000; (800) 228-1160. 1992. Thirty-eight volumes.

Encyclopedia of Polymer Science and Engineering. Herman F. Mark, et al., eds. John Wiley & Sons, Inc., 605 3rd Ave., New York, New York 10158-0012. (212) 850-6000. 1985-. Seventeen volumes and two supplements.

Kirk-Othmer Encyclopedia of Chemical Technology. J. I. Kroschwitz, ed. John Wiley & Sons, Inc., 605 3rd Ave., New York, New York 10158-0012. (212) 850-6000. 1992-. All articles in the new edition have been rewritten and updated adding new subjects such as biotechnology, computer topics, analytical techniques and instrumentation, environmental concerns, fuels and energy, inorganic and solid state chemistry; composite materials and material science in general, and pharmaceuticals. Also available online.

McGraw-Hill Encyclopedia of Science and Technology. McGraw-Hill, 1221 Avenue of the Americas, New York, New York 10020. (212) 512-2000 or (800) 262-4729. 1992. Seventh edition. Issued in multiple volumes including index. Includes all science and technology broad subject areas.

Modern Plastics Encyclopedia. Modern Plastics Encyclopedia, PO Box 602, Highstown, New Jersey 08520-9955. 1992. Contains information on a broad range of topics from resin manufacture to semi finished materials. Includes environmental and safety regulations, on manufacture, use,and recycling and related matter.

Plastics Engineering Dictionary German/English. M. S. Welling. Hanser International, Scientific and Technical Books, Macmillan Pub. Co, 866 3d Ave., New York, New York 10022. 1982.

GENERAL WORKS

A Citizen's Guide to Plastics in the Ocean. Kathryn J. O'Hara and Suzanne Iudicello. Center for Marine Conservation, 1725 DeSales St, NW, Suite 500, Washington, District of Columbia 20036. (202) 429-5609. 1988.

How on Earth Do We Recycle Plastic?. Janet D'Amato. Millbrook Press, 2 Old New Milford Rd., PO Box 335, Brookfield, Connecticut 06804-0335. (203) 740-2220. 1992. Manufacture and disposal of plastic and how it can be recycled.

Plastics: America's Packaging Dilemma. Nancy A. Wolf and Ellen D. Feldman. Island Press, 1718 Connecticut Ave. N.W., Ste. 300, Washington, District of Columbia 20009. (202) 232-7933. 1991. Source books on plastics deal with packaging, building materials, consumer goods, electrical products, transportation, industrial machinery, adhesives, legislative and regulatory issues. Also covers the controversies over plastics incineration, degradability, and recyclability.

Popping the Plastics Question: Plastics Recycling and Bans on Plastics - Contacts, Resources and Legislation. Joan Mullany. National League of Cities, 1301 Pennsylvania Ave. N.W., Washington, District of Columbia 20004. (202) 626-3150. 1990.

Secondary Reclamation of Plastics Waste. Plastics Institute of America, Stevens Institute of Technology, Castle Point, Hoboken, New Jersey 07030. (201) 420-5553. 1987. Research report on Phase I development of techniques for preparation and formulation for recycling plastic scrap.

HANDBOOKS AND MANUALS

Riegel's Handbook of Industrial Chemistry. James A. Kent, ed. Van Nostrand Reinhold, 115 5th Ave., New York, New York 10020. (212) 254-3232. 1983. Eighth edition. Includes industries such as: wastewater technology, coal technology, phosphate fertilizers, synthetic plastics, man-made textiles, detergents, sugar, animal and vegetable oils, chemical explosives, dyes, nuclear industry, and much more.

ONLINE DATA BASES

DOMIS. ECHO Service, BP 2373, Luxembourg L-1023. (352) 488041.

Kirk-Othmer Encyclopedia of Chemical Technology. John Wiley & Sons, Inc., 605 3rd Ave., 5th Floor, New York, New York 10158. (212) 850-6000. Online version of the publication of the same name.

Monthly Catalog of United States Government Publications. U.S. G.P.O., Supt. of Docs., PO Box 371954, Pittsburgh, Pennsylvania 15250-7954. (202) 512-0000.

National Technical Information Service. U.S. Department of Commerce, National Technical Information Service, Office of Data Base Services, 5285 Port Royal Rd., Springfield, Virginia 22161. (703) 487-4807. Bibliographic database of government sponsored research and technical reports.

RAPRA Abstracts. RAPRA Technology Limited, Shawbury, Shrewsbury, England SY4 4NR. 44 (939) 250383.

SPI/ERS Plastics Data Base. Ernst & Young, 1225 Connecticut Ave., N.W., Washington, District of Columbia 20036. (202) 862-6042. Time series on the production and sales of plastic resins in the United States.

PERIODICALS AND NEWSLETTERS

The Plastic Bottle Reporter. Plastic Bottle Information Bureau, 1275 K St. NW, Suite 400, Washington, District of Columbia 20005. (202) 371-5200. Quarterly. Recycling technology and plastic bottle applications.

Plastic Waste Strategies. Washington Business Information, Inc., 1117 N. 19th St., Suite 200, Arlington, Virginia 22209-1798. (703) 247-3422. Monthly. Recycling, degradability, incineration, and alternative methods of handling solid and plastic waste.

Plastics Recycling Update. Resource Recycling, Box 10540, Portland, Oregon 97210. (503) 227-1319. Monthly.

Quarterly. Council on Plastics and Packaging in the Environment, 1275 K St. NW, Suite 900, Washington, District of Columbia 20005. (202) 789-1310. Quarterly.

Reuse/Recycle. Technomic Publishing Co., 851 New Holland Ave., Box 3535, Lancaster, Pennsylvania 17604. (717) 291-5609. 1970-. Monthly. Monthly newsletter of resource recycling reports on new technology, uses and markets for recycled materials, advances in recycling plants and equipment, and the changing infrastructure of the plastics recycling industry.

Update. Council on Plastics and Packaging in the Environment, 1275 K St. NW, Suite 900, Washington, District of Columbia 20005. (202) 789-1310. Recycling research and legislation.

RESEARCH CENTERS AND INSTITUTES

Plastics Recycling Institute. Rutgers Univ., PO Box 909, Piscataway, New Jersey 08854. (201) 932-4420.

STATISTICS SOURCES

Engineered Plastics to 1995. FIND/SVP, 625 Avenue of the Americas, New York, New York 10011. (212) 645-4500. 1991. Market for engineered plastics, historical data, and forecasts by type and market.

Facing America's Trash: What Next for Municipal Solid Waste?. U.S. Office of Technology Assessment. Van Nostrand Reinhold, Washington, District of Columbia 20401. (202) 512-0000. 1991. Generation, composition and cost of recycling municipal solid waste.

Facts and Figures of the U.S. Plastics Industry. Society of the Plastics Industry, Statistical Department, 1275 K St., NW, Suite 400, Washington, District of Columbia 20005. (202) 371-5200. Annual. Capacity, production, sales, markets, and foreign trade, by resin type.

Foamed Plastics Market. FIND/SVP, 625 Avenue of the Americas, New York, New York 10011. (212) 645-4500. 1991. Historical (1980, 1985, 1990) and forecast (1995 and 2000) data for foamed urethanes, foamed styrenes and other foamed types.

Modern Plastics. Modern Plastics, Circulation Department, 777 14th St., NW, Suite 8000, Washington, District of Columbia 20005. (202) 639-8040. Monthly. Plastics manufacturing, management, R&D, marketing, and consumption.

Plastics Recycling in the Industrial Sector. National Technical Information Service, 5285 Port Royal Rd., Springfield, Virginia 22161. (703) 487-4650. Potential for development of plastic waste recycling industry, with projections to 2000 and background data from 1973.

Polypropylene in North America. FIND/SVP, 625 Avenue of the Americas, New York, New York 10011. (212) 645-4500. 1991. Market for polypropylene to the years 1995 and 2000; analyzes pricing and capacity data, recent developments in manufacturing technology and production processes.

Rauch Guide to the U.S. Plastics Industry. Rauch Associates, P.O. Box 6802, Bridgewater, New Jersey 08807. Recurring. Economic structure, production of basic materials, processing, and end use markets.

The U.S. Plastics Industry. FIND/SVP, 625 Avenue of the Americas, New York, New York 10011. (212) 645-4500. 1990. Data on plastics additives production and use of major polymers, including engineering plastics, and processing equipment.

World Plastics to 1995. FIND/SVP, 625 Avenue of the Americas, New York, New York 10011. (212) 645-4500. 1991. Forecasts are given for plastics consumption, net exports and production of commodity thermoplastics and thermosets in over 30 countries and regions.

World Resources. World Resources Institute. 1709 New York Ave., N.W., Washington, District of Columbia 20006. (202) 638-6300. Annual. Statistical and textual analysis of world's natural resources and the effects of growth-caused environmental pollution.

TRADE ASSOCIATIONS AND PROFESSIONAL SOCIETIES

Chlorinated Paraffins Industry Association. 655 15th St., N.W., Suite 1200, Washington, District of Columbia 20005. (202) 879-5130.

Council on Plastics and Packaging in the Environment. 1001 Connecticut Ave., N.W., Suite 401, Washington, District of Columbia 20036. (202) 331-0099.

Glass, Pottery, Plastics, & Allied Workers International Union. 608 E. Baltimore Pike, Box 607, Media, Pennsylvania 19063. (215) 565-5051.

National Agricultural Plastics Association. P.O. Box 860238, St. Augustine, Florida 32086. (904) 829-1667.

National Association for Plastic Container Recovery. 4828 Parkway Plaza Blvd., Suite 260, Charlotte, North Carolina 28217. (704) 357-3250.

Plastic Bag Association. 505 White Plains Rd., #206, Tarrytown, New York 10591. (914) 631-0909.

Plastic Bottle Institute. 1275 K St., N.W., Suite 400, Washington, District of Columbia 20005. (202) 371-5244.

Plastics Education Foundation. 14 Fairfield Dr., Brookfield Center, Connecticut 06804. (203) 775-0471.

Plastics Recycling Foundation. 1275 K St., N.W., Suite 400, Washington, District of Columbia 20005. (202) 371-5200.

Society of Plastics Engineers. 14 Fairfield Dr., Brookfield Center, Connecticut 06805. (203) 775-0471.

Society of the Plastics Industry. 1275 K St., N.W., Suite 400, Washington, District of Columbia 20005. (202) 371-5200.

United Rubber, Cork, Linoleum, & Plastic Workers of America. 570 White Pond Dr., Akron, Ohio 44320. (216) 376-6181.

PLATINUM

See: METALS AND METALLURGY

PLUTONIUM

ABSTRACTING AND INDEXING SERVICES

Chemical Abstracts. Chemical Abstracts Service, 2540 Olentangy River Rd., PO Box 3012, Columbus, Ohio 43210. (800) 848-6533. 1907-.

Environment Abstracts. Bowker A & I Publishing, 121 Chanlon Rd., New Providence, New Jersey 07974. (908) 464-6800. 1974-.

Environment Index. Environment Information Center, Index Research Department, 124 E. 39th St., New York, New York 10016. 1971-. Annual.

Environmental Information Connection–EIC. Planning Information Program, Dept. of Urban and Regional Planning, University of Illinois, 1003 West Nevada, Urbana, Illinois 61801. (217) 333-1369. Also available online.

Environmental Periodicals Bibliography. Environmental Studies Institute, International Academy at Santa Barbara, 800 Garden St., Suite D, Santa Barbara, California 93101. (805) 965-5010. Also available online.

General Science Index. H. W. Wilson Co., 950 University Ave., Bronx, New York 10452. 1978-. Monthly, also issued in annual cumulation. Cumulative subject index to English language periodicals in the subject fields of astronomy, botany, chemistry, earth science, environment and conservation, food and nutrition, genetics, mathematics, medicine and health, microbiology, oceanography, physics, physiology and zoology.

Physics Briefs. Physikalische Berichte. Physik Verlag, Pappapelallee 3, Postfach 101161, Weinheim, Germany D-6940. 1979-. Semimonthly. In English. Volumes for 1979- issued by the Deutsche Physikalische Gesellschaft and the Fachinformationszentrum Energie Physik, Mathematik in cooperation with the American Institute of Physics.

Science Citation Index. Institute for Scientific Information, 3501 Market St., Philadelphia, Pennsylvania 19104. 1961-.

BIBLIOGRAPHIES

EPA Publications Bibliography. U.S. Environmental Protection Agency, Library Systems Branch, 401 M St., SW, Washington, District of Columbia 20460. (202) 260-2090. Quarterly.

ENCYCLOPEDIAS AND DICTIONARIES

Encyclopedia of Physics. Rita G. Lerner and George L. Trigg. VCH Publishers, 303 NW 12th Ave., Deerfield Beach, Florida 33442-1788. (305) 428-5566. 1991. Second edition.

McGraw-Hill Encyclopedia of Science and Technology. McGraw-Hill, 1221 Avenue of the Americas, New York, New York 10020. (212) 512-2000 or (800) 262-4729. 1992. Seventh edition. Issued in multiple volumes including index. Includes all science and technology broad subject areas.

Van Nostrand's Scientific Encyclopedia. Glenn D. Considine, ed. Van Nostrand Reinhold, 115 5th Ave., New York, New York 10003. (212) 254-3232. 1983. Sixth edition. Includes all broad subject areas in science.

GENERAL WORKS

The Environmental and Biological Behavior of Plutonium and Some Other Transuranium Elements. NEA Group of Experts. OECD Publications and Information Center, 2 rue Andre Pascal, Paris, France F-75775. 1981. Environmental aspects of transuranium elements and transuranium and plutonium elements in the body.

Plutonium in the Environment. U.S. Energy Research and Development Administration, Office of Public Affairs, 1000 Independence Ave. SW, Washington, District of Columbia 20585. (202) 586-4940. 1976. Safety and environmental aspects of plutonium.

ONLINE DATA BASES

CAS Source Index–CASSI. Chemical Abstracts Service, 2540 Olentangy River Rd., P.O. Box 3012, Columbus, Ohio 43210. (800) 848-6533 or (614) 421-3600. A listing of bibliographic and library holdings information for scientific and technical primary literature relevant to the chemical sciences.

Chemical Abstracts-CA. Chemical Abstracts Service, 2540 Olentangy River Rd., P.O. Box 3012, Columbus, Ohio 43210. (800) 848-6533 or (614) 421-3600. Information sources include 9000 journals, patents from 27 countries, two industrial property organizations, new books, conference proceedings, and government research reports.

Enviro/Energyline Abstracts Plus. R. R. Bowker Co., 121 Chanlon Rd., New Providence, New Jersey 07974. (908) 464-6800.

Environmental Periodicals Bibliography. National Information Services Corp., Ste. 6, Wyman Towers, 3100 St. Paul St., Baltimore, Maryland 21218. (410)243-0797. Online version of abstract of same name.

Monthly Catalog of United States Government Publications. U.S. G.P.O., Supt. of Docs., PO Box 371954, Pittsburgh, Pennsylvania 15250-7954. (202) 512-0000.

National Technical Information Service. U.S. Department of Commerce, National Technical Information Service, Office of Data Base Services, 5285 Port Royal Rd., Springfield, Virginia 22161. (703) 487-4807. Bibliographic database of government sponsored research and technical reports.

POISONS–ENVIRONMENTAL ASPECTS

See also: TOXICOLOGY

ABSTRACTING AND INDEXING SERVICES

Environment Abstracts. Bowker A & I Publishing, 121 Chanlon Rd., New Providence, New Jersey 07974. (908) 464-6800. 1974-.

Environment Index. Environment Information Center, Index Research Department, 124 E. 39th St., New York, New York 10016. 1971-. Annual.

Environmental Information Connection–EIC. Planning Information Program, Dept. of Urban and Regional Planning, University of Illinois, 1003 West Nevada, Urbana, Illinois 61801. (217) 333-1369. Also available online.

Environmental Periodicals Bibliography. Environmental Studies Institute, International Academy at Santa Barbara, 800 Garden St., Suite D, Santa Barbara, California 93101. (805) 965-5010. Also available online.

General Science Index. H. W. Wilson Co., 950 University Ave., Bronx, New York 10452. 1978-. Monthly, also issued in annual cumulation. Cumulative subject index to English language periodicals in the subject fields of astronomy, botany, chemistry, earth science, environment and conservation, food and nutrition, genetics, mathematics, medicine and health, microbiology, oceanography, physics, physiology and zoology.

Pollution Abstracts. Cambridge Scientific Abstracts, 5161 River Rd., Bethesda, Maryland 20816. (301) 961-6750. Six/year. Indexes worldwide technical literature on environmental pollution. Covers air pollution, marine and freshwater pollution, sewage and wastewater treatment, waste management, toxicology and health, noise pollution, radiation, land pollution, and environmental policies, programs, legislation, and education. Also available online.

Science Citation Index. Institute for Scientific Information, 3501 Market St., Philadelphia, Pennsylvania 19104. 1961-.

ALMANACS AND YEARBOOKS

Registry of Toxic Effects of Chemical Substances. Doris V. Sweet, ed. U.S. Department of Health and Human Services, National Institute for Occupational Safety and Health, Washington, District of Columbia 20402-9325. (202) 783-3238. 1988. Contains information on over 35,000 chemicals.

Toxic Substances Sourcebook. Environment Information Center, 124 E. 39th St., New York, New York 10016.

1980. Includes hazardous substances, poisons, and pollution.

BIBLIOGRAPHIES

EPA Publications Bibliography. U.S. Environmental Protection Agency, Library Systems Branch, 401 M St., SW, Washington, District of Columbia 20460. (202) 260-2090. Quarterly.

ENCYCLOPEDIAS AND DICTIONARIES

Handbook of Hazardous Chemicals and Carcinogens. Marshall Sittig. Noyes Publications, 120 Mill Rd., Park Ridge, New Jersey 07656. (201) 391-8484. 1985.

Handbook of Toxic and Hazardous Chemicals and Carcinogens. Marshall Sittig. Noyes Publications, 120 Mill Rd., Park Ridge, New Jersey 07656. (201) 391-8484. 1991.

McGraw-Hill Encyclopedia of Environmental Science. Sybil P. Parker. McGraw-Hill Science & Engineering Books, 11 W. 19th St., New York, New York 10011. (212) 337-6010. 1980. Covers ecology, man's influence on nature, and environmental protection.

Van Nostrand's Scientific Encyclopedia. Glenn D. Considine, ed. Van Nostrand Reinhold, 115 5th Ave., New York, New York 10003. (212) 254-3232. 1983. Sixth edition. Includes all broad subject areas in science.

GENERAL WORKS

AMA Handbook of Poisonous and Injurious Plants. American Medical Association, 515 N. State St., Chicago, Illinois 60610. (312) 464-4818. 1985. Toxicology of poisonous plants and skin inflammation.

Toxic Chemicals. Earon S. Davis. Farmworker Justice Fund, Inc., 2001 S St., NW, Ste. 210, Washington, District of Columbia 20009. (202) 462-8192. 1980. The interface between law and science: an introduction to scientific methods of demonstrating causation of diseases.

Toxic Chemicals and Public Protection. Toxic Substances Strategy Committee. U.S. G.P.O., Washington, District of Columbia 20201. (202) 512-0000. 1980.

The Toxic Substances Control Act. U.S. G.P.O., Washington, District of Columbia 20401. (202) 512-0000. 1981.

Toxicity of Industrial Metals. Ethel Browning. Butterworth-Heinemann, 80 Montvale Ave., Stoneham, Massachusetts 02180. (617) 438-8464; (800) 366-2665. 1969. 2d ed.

Toxics/Organics. Arthur D. Little, Inc. U.S. G.P.O., Washington, District of Columbia 204021. (202) 512-0000. 1979. Environmental considerations of selected energy conserving manufacturing process options.

HANDBOOKS AND MANUALS

Handbook of Analytical Toxicology. Irving Sunshine, ed. CRC Press, 2000 Corporate Blvd. N.W., Boca Raton, Florida 33431. (407) 994-0555; (800) 272-7737. 1969.

Handbook of Carcinogens and Hazardous Substances: Chemical and Trace Analysis. Malcolm C. Bowman, ed. M. Dekker, 270 Madison Ave., New York, New York 10016. (212) 696-9000. 1982. Alkylating agents, aromatic amines and azo compounds, estrogens, mycotoxins, N-nitrosamines and n-nitroso compounds, pesticides and related substances and hydrocarbons.

Handbook of Pesticide Toxicology. Wayland J. Hayes and Edward R. Laws, eds. Academic Press, c/o Harcourt Brace Jovanovich Inc., 6277 Sea Harbor Dr., Orlando, Florida 32887. (800) 346-8648. 1991. Three volumes. Covers various types of toxicity, nature of injury, reversibility, various methods of quantitating dose response, metabolism of toxins, factors affecting toxicity, absorption, and elimination.

Handbook of Toxicologic Pathology. Wanda M. Haschek and Colin G. Rosseaux, eds. Academic Press, c/o Harcourt Brace Jovanovich Inc., 6277 Sea Harbor Dr., Orlando, Florida 32887. (800) 346-8648. 1991. Handbook describing experimental methods and animal models for toxicological assessment.

Poisonous Plants of Eastern North America. Randy G. Westbrooks and James W. Preacher. University of South Carolina Press, Columbia, South Carolina 29208. (803) 777-5243. 1986. List of poisonous plants which include species of plants, the plant part (leaf, root, fruit), the amount of plant material involved, the stage of development of the plant, and the soil type and growing conditions.

ONLINE DATA BASES

Enviro/Energyline Abstracts Plus. R. R. Bowker Co., 121 Chanlon Rd., New Providence, New Jersey 07974. (908) 464-6800.

Environmental Periodicals Bibliography. National Information Services Corp., Ste. 6, Wyman Towers, 3100 St. Paul St., Baltimore, Maryland 21218. (410)243-0797. Online version of abstract of same name.

Monthly Catalog of United States Government Publications. U.S. G.P.O., Supt. of Docs., PO Box 371954, Pittsburgh, Pennsylvania 15250-7954. (202) 512-0000.

National Technical Information Service. U.S. Department of Commerce, National Technical Information Service, Office of Data Base Services, 5285 Port Royal Rd., Springfield, Virginia 22161. (703) 487-4807. Bibliographic database of government sponsored research and technical reports.

SCISEARCH. Institute for Scientific Information, University City Science Center, 3501 Market St., Philadelphia, Pennsylvania 19104. (215) 386-0100.

TRADE ASSOCIATIONS AND PROFESSIONAL SOCIETIES

American Association of Poison Control Centers. Arizona Poison and Drug Information Center, Health Sciences Center, Rm. 3204K, 1501 N. Campbell, Tucson, Arizona 85725. (602) 626-7899.

POLAR REGIONS

See also: ARCTIC ECOLOGY; COLD ENVIRONMENTS

ABSTRACTING AND INDEXING SERVICES

Polar and Glaciological Abstracts. Cambridge University Press, 40 W. 20th St., New York, New York 10011. (212)

924-3900. 1990. Quarterly. Contains abstracts selected from the SPRILIB bibliographic database maintained by the Library of the Scott Polar Research Institute.

GENERAL WORKS

Polar Oceanography. Walker O. Smith. Academic Press, c/o Harcourt Brace Jovanovich Inc., 6277 Sea Harbor Dr., Orlando, Florida 32887. (800) 346-8648. 1990.

Transport of Oil under Smooth Ice. M. S. Ozuner. Corvallis Environmental Research Laboratory, 200 S.W. 35th, Corvallis, Oregon 97333. (503) 754-4600. 1979. Environmental aspects of oil spills in polar regions.

PERIODICALS AND NEWSLETTERS

NOAA Environmental Digest. National Oceanic and Atmospheric Administration, U.S. Department of Commerce, Washington, District of Columbia 20230. (202) 377-2985. Irregular. Selected environmental indicators of the United States and the global environment.

Polar Geography and Geology. V. H. Winston, Washington, District of Columbia Quarterly.

POLLINATION

ABSTRACTING AND INDEXING SERVICES

Environment Abstracts. Bowker A & I Publishing, 121 Chanlon Rd., New Providence, New Jersey 07974. (908) 464-6800. 1974-.

Environment Index. Environment Information Center, Index Research Department, 124 E. 39th St., New York, New York 10016. 1971-. Annual.

Environmental Information Connection-EIC. Planning Information Program, Dept. of Urban and Regional Planning, University of Illinois, 1003 West Nevada, Urbana, Illinois 61801. (217) 333-1369. Also available online.

Environmental Periodicals Bibliography. Environmental Studies Institute, International Academy at Santa Barbara, 800 Garden St., Suite D, Santa Barbara, California 93101. (805) 965-5010. Also available online.

General Science Index. H. W. Wilson Co., 950 University Ave., Bronx, New York 10452. 1978-. Monthly, also issued in annual cumulation. Cumulative subject index to English language periodicals in the subject fields of astronomy, botany, chemistry, earth science, environment and conservation, food and nutrition, genetics, mathematics, medicine and health, microbiology, oceanography, physics, physiology and zoology.

Science Citation Index. Institute for Scientific Information, 3501 Market St., Philadelphia, Pennsylvania 19104. 1961-.

BIBLIOGRAPHIES

EPA Publications Bibliography. U.S. Environmental Protection Agency, Library Systems Branch, 401 M St., SW, Washington, District of Columbia 20460. (202) 260-2090. Quarterly.

ENCYCLOPEDIAS AND DICTIONARIES

Cambridge Dictionary of Biology. Peter M. B. Walker. Cambridge University Press, 40 W. 20th St., New York, New York 10011. (212) 924-3900 or (800) 227-0247. 1989. Includes 10,000 terms in zoology, botany, biochemistry, molecular biology and genetics. Previously published under the title Chambers Biology Dictionary.

A Concise Dictionary of Biology. Elizabeth Martin, ed. Oxford University Press, 200 Madison Ave., New York, New York 10016. (212) 679-7300 or (800) 334-4249. 1990. New edition. Derived from the Concise Science Dictionary, published in 1984.

Life Sciences on File. Diagram Group. Facts on File, Inc., 460 Park Ave. S., New York, New York 10016. (212) 683-2244. 1986. Encyclopedia of pictorial collection in life sciences. Deals with all major topics in life sciences including ecology.

Van Nostrand's Scientific Encyclopedia. Glenn D. Considine, ed. Van Nostrand Reinhold, 115 5th Ave., New York, New York 10003. (212) 254-3232. 1983. Sixth edition. Includes all broad subject areas in science.

ONLINE DATA BASES

Enviro/Energyline Abstracts Plus. R. R. Bowker Co., 121 Chanlon Rd., New Providence, New Jersey 07974. (908) 464-6800.

Environmental Periodicals Bibliography. National Information Services Corp., Ste. 6, Wyman Towers, 3100 St. Paul St., Baltimore, Maryland 21218. (410)243-0797. Online version of abstract of same name.

POLLONIUM

ABSTRACTING AND INDEXING SERVICES

Environment Abstracts. Bowker A & I Publishing, 121 Chanlon Rd., New Providence, New Jersey 07974. (908) 464-6800. 1974-.

Environment Index. Environment Information Center, Index Research Department, 124 E. 39th St., New York, New York 10016. 1971-. Annual.

Environmental Information Connection–EIC. Planning Information Program, Dept. of Urban and Regional Planning, University of Illinois, 1003 West Nevada, Urbana, Illinois 61801. (217) 333-1369. Also available online.

Environmental Periodicals Bibliography. Environmental Studies Institute, International Academy at Santa Barbara, 800 Garden St., Suite D, Santa Barbara, California 93101. (805) 965-5010. Also available online.

Physics Briefs. Physikalische Berichte. Physik Verlag, Pappapelallee 3, Postfach 101161, Weinheim, Germany D-6940. 1979-. Semimonthly. In English. Volumes for 1979- issued by the Deutsche Physikalische Gesellschaft and the Fachinformationszentrum Energie Physik, Mathematik in cooperation with the American Institute of Physics.

BIBLIOGRAPHIES

EPA Publications Bibliography. U.S. Environmental Protection Agency, Library Systems Branch, 401 M St., SW, Washington, District of Columbia 20460. (202) 260-2090. Quarterly.

ENCYCLOPEDIAS AND DICTIONARIES

Van Nostrand's Scientific Encyclopedia. Glenn D. Considine, ed. Van Nostrand Reinhold, 115 5th Ave., New York, New York 10003. (212) 254-3232. 1983. Sixth edition. Includes all broad subject areas in science.

GENERAL WORKS

The Chemistry of Sulphur, Selenium, Tellurium and Polonium. M. Schmidt. Pergamon Microforms International, Inc., Fairview Park, Elmsford, New York 10523. (914) 592-7720. 1975.

The Environmental Properties of Polonium-218. Scott D. Goldstein. University of Illinois at Urbana-Champaign, Urbana, Illinois 61801. 1984.

ONLINE DATA BASES

Enviro/Energyline Abstracts Plus. R. R. Bowker Co., 121 Chanlon Rd., New Providence, New Jersey 07974. (908) 464-6800.

Environmental Periodicals Bibliography. National Information Services Corp., Ste. 6, Wyman Towers, 3100 St. Paul St., Baltimore, Maryland 21218. (410)243-0797. Online version of abstract of same name.

POLLUTANTS

See also: AIR POLLUTION; ATMOSPHERE; ENVIRONMENTAL CONDITION

ABSTRACTING AND INDEXING SERVICES

Abstracts of Air and Water Conservation Literature. American Petroleum Institute. Central Abstracting and Indexing Service, 275 Madison Avenue, New York, New York 10016. 1972.

Abstracts on Health Effects of Environmental Pollutants. BIOSIS, 2100 Arch St., Philadelphia, Pennsylvania 19103. (215) 587-4800; (800) 523-4806.

Agrindex. AGRIS Coordinating Center, Via delle Terme di Caracalla, Rome, Italy I-00100. 61 0181-FA01. 1975-.

Air Pollution Technical Publications of the United States Environmental Protection Agency. U.S. Environmental Protection Agency, Mail Drop 75, Research Triangle Park, North Carolina 27711. (919) 541-2184. 1976. Quarterly.

Air Pollution Titles. Pennsylvania State University, Center for Air Environmental Studies, 226 Fenske Laboratory, University Park, Pennsylvania 16802. (814) 865-1415. 1965. Bibliographic guide to current research literature on air environment, including monitoring and control of air pollution, health effects, effects on agriculture, forests, toxic air contaminants, and global atmospheric pro cases.

Air Pollution Translations. A Bibliography With Abstracts. U.S. Environmental Protection Agency, MD 75, Research Triangle Park, North Carolina 27711. (919) 541-2184. 1969.

Applied Ecology Abstracts Studies in Renewable Natural Resources. Information Retrieval Ltd., 1911 Jefferson Davis Highway, Arlington, Virginia 22202. 1975-. Monthly.

Bulletin Signaletique: Eau et Assainissement, Pollution Atmospherique, Droit des Pollutions. Centre de Documentation, Centre National de la Recherche Scientifique, 15, quai Anatole France, Paris, France 75700. (1) 45 55 92 25. 1983-. Monthly. Indexes pollution periodicals including water, atmospheric and related pollutions.

Chemical Abstracts. Chemical Abstracts Service, 2540 Olentangy River Rd., PO Box 3012, Columbus, Ohio 43210. (800) 848-6533. 1907-.

Civil Engineering Hydraulic Abstracts. BHRA Fluid Engineering, Air Science Co., PO Box 143, Corning, New York 14830. (607) 962-5591. Monthly. Abstracts of periodicals that publish in the areas of hydraulic engineering and other related topics.

Ecological Abstracts. Geo Abstracts Ltd. Elsevier Applied Science, Crown House, Linton Rd., Barking, England IG 11 8JU. 1974-. Derived from over 600 leading ecological and environmental journals, plus books, conference proceedings, reports and theses.

Ecology Abstracts. Cambridge Scientific Abstracts, 5161 River Rd., Bethesda, Maryland 20816. (301) 961-6750. Monthly.

Engineering Index. The Engineering Index Inc., 345 E. 47th St., New York, New York 10017. 1962-.

Environment Abstracts. Bowker A & I Publishing, 121 Chanlon Rd., New Providence, New Jersey 07974. (908) 464-6800. 1974-.

Environment Index. Environment Information Center, Index Research Department, 124 E. 39th St., New York, New York 10016. 1971-. Annual.

Environmental Information Connection–EIC. Planning Information Program, Dept. of Urban and Regional Planning, University of Illinois, 1003 West Nevada, Urbana, Illinois 61801. (217) 333-1369. Also available online.

Environmental Periodicals Bibliography. Environmental Studies Institute, International Academy at Santa Barbara, 800 Garden St., Suite D, Santa Barbara, California 93101. (805) 965-5010. Also available online.

Index to Scientific Book Contents. Institute for Scientific Information, 3501 Market St., Philadelphia, Pennsylvania 19104. (800) 523-1857. 1985-. Annual. Gives contents of science books published.

Multimedia Index to Ecology. National Information Center for Educational Media, University of Southern California, Los Angeles, California 90007.

Pollution Abstracts. Cambridge Scientific Abstracts, 5161 River Rd., Bethesda, Maryland 20816. (301) 961-6750. Six/year. Indexes worldwide technical literature on environmental pollution. Covers air pollution, marine and freshwater pollution, sewage and wastewater treatment, waste management, toxicology and health, noise pollution, radiation, land pollution, and environmental poli-

cies, programs, legislation, and education. Also available online.

Science Citation Index. Institute for Scientific Information, 3501 Market St., Philadelphia, Pennsylvania 19104. 1961-.

BIBLIOGRAPHIES

EPA Publications Bibliography. U.S. Environmental Protection Agency, Library Systems Branch, 401 M St., SW, Washington, District of Columbia 20460. (202) 260-2090. Quarterly.

ENCYCLOPEDIAS AND DICTIONARIES

Encyclopedia of Physical Science and Technology. Robert A. Meyers, ed. Academic Press, c/o Harcourt Brace Jovanovich Inc., 6277 Sea Harbor Dr., Orlando, Florida 32887. (800) 346-8648. Dictionary of engineering, technology and physical sciences.

Grzimek's Encyclopedia of Ecology. Bernhard Grzimek. Van Nostrand Reinhold, 115 5th Ave., New York, New York 10003. (212) 254-3232. 1976.

McGraw-Hill Encyclopedia of Environmental Science. Sybil P. Parker. McGraw-Hill Science & Engineering Books, 11 W. 19th St., New York, New York 10011. (212) 337-6010. 1980. Covers ecology, man's influence on nature, and environmental protection.

McGraw-Hill Encyclopedia of Science and Technology. McGraw-Hill, 1221 Avenue of the Americas, New York, New York 10020. (212) 512-2000 or (800) 262-4729. 1992. Seventh edition. Issued in multiple volumes including index. Includes all science and technology broad subject areas.

North American Reference Encyclopedia of Ecology and Pollution. William White. North American Pub. Co., 401 N. Broad St., Philadelphia, Pennsylvania 19108. (215) 238-5300. 1972.

Van Nostrand's Scientific Encyclopedia. Glenn D. Considine, ed. Van Nostrand Reinhold, 115 5th Ave., New York, New York 10003. (212) 254-3232. 1983. Sixth edition. Includes all broad subject areas in science.

GENERAL WORKS

Carcinogens and Mutagens in the Environment. Hans F. Stich, ed. CRC Press, 2000 Corporate Blvd. N.W., Boca Raton, Florida 33431. (800) 272-7737. 1982-. Naturally occurring compounds, endogenous modulation.

Chemical Ecotoxicology. Jaakko Paasivirta. Lewis Publishers, 200 Corporate Blvd. NW, Boca Raton, Florida 33431. (407) 994-0555 or (800)272-7737. 1991. Presents an in-depth discussion of risk assessment, chemical cycles, structure-activity relationships, organohalogens, oil residues, mercury, sampling and analysis of trace chemicals, and emissions from the forest industry. Outlines the chemical basis for applied research in environmental protection and provides important data regarding the fate and effects of various chemicals on wildlife.

Ecotoxicology and Climate. Philippe Bordeaux, et al., eds. John Wiley & Sons, Inc., 605 3rd Ave., New York, New York 10158-0012. (212) 850-6000. 1989. Describes environmental chemistry of toxic pollutants in hot and cold climates. Includes bibliographical references and an index.

Food Contamination from Environmental Sources. J. O. Nriagu and M. S. Simmons, eds. John Wiley & Sons, Inc., 605 3rd Ave., New York, New York 10158-0012. (212) 850-6000. 1990. Discusses the accumulation and transfer of contaminants through the food chain to the consumer.

Global Air Pollution: Problems for the 1990s. Howard Bridgman. Belhaven Press, 136 S. Broadway, Irvington, New York 10533. (914) 591-9111. 1990. Addresses the environmental problems caused by human activities resulting in change and deterioration of the earth's atmosphere.

Hazardous and Industrial Wastes, 1991. Technomic Publishing Co., 851 New Holland Ave., Box 3535, Lancaster, Pennsylvania 17604. (717) 291-5609. 1991. Proceedings of the 23rd Mid-Atlantic Industrial Waste Conference held at Drexel University, 1991.

Heavy Metals in the Environment: International Conference. J. P. Vernet. CEP Consultants, 26 Albany St., Edinburgh, Scotland EH1 3QH. 1989.

Human Exposure Assessment for Airborne Pollutants: Advances and Opportunities. National Research Council (U.S.) Board of Environmental Studies and Toxicology. National Academy of Sciences, 2101 Constitution Ave. NW., Washington, District of Columbia 20418. (202) 334-2000 or (800) 624-6242. 1991. Provides a technical account of the principles and methodology of exposure assessment applied to air pollutants. Also provides valuable information for students on how to study air pollutant exposure and health effects through questionnaires, through air sampling, and through modeling.

Immunochemical Methods for Environmental Analysis. Jeanette M. Van Emon and Ralph O. Mumma, eds. American Chemical Society, 1155 16th St. N.W., Washington, District of Columbia 20036. (202) 872-4600; (800) 227-5558. 1990. Describes antibodies used as analytical tools to study environmentally important compounds. Discusses various applications in food industry, environmental analysis, and applications in agriculture.

Instrumental Analysis of Pollutants. C. N. Hewitt, ed. Elsevier Science Publishing Co., 655 Avenue of the Americas, New York, New York 10010. (212) 989-5800. 1991.

Metals and Their Compounds in the Environment. Ernest Merian, ed. VCH Publishers, 303 NW 12th Ave., Deerfield Beach, Florida 33442-1788. (305) 428-5566. 1990.

Persistent Pollutants: Economics and Policy. Hans Opschoor, ed. Kluwer Academic Publishers, 101 Philip Dr., Assinippi Park, Norwell, Massachusetts 02061. (617) 871-6600. 1991. Discusses environmental pollution and the studies conducted in that area.

Pollution: Causes, Effects and Control. Roy Michael Harrison. Royal Society of Chemistry, c/o CRC Press, 2000 Corporate Blvd. N.W., Boca Raton, Florida 33431. (800) 272-7737. 1990. 2nd ed. Deals with environmental pollution and its associated problems and legal ramifications.

Toxicological Profile for Carbon Tetrachloride. Agency for Toxic Substances and Disease Registry, U.S. Public Health Service, 1600 Clifton Rd. NE, Atlanta, Georgia 30333. (404) 452-4111. 1989.

HANDBOOKS AND MANUALS

Ambient Air Pollutants from Industrial Sources: A Reference Handbook. Michael J. Suess. Elsevier Science Publishing Co., 655 Avenue of the Americas, New York, New York 10010. (212) 984-5800. 1985. Adverse effects of occupational air pollutants.

Cross-Reference Index of Hazardous Chemicals, Synonyms, and CAS Registry Numbers. The Forum for Scientific Excellence. J. B. Lippincott, 227 E. Washington Sq., Philadelphia, Pennsylvania 19105. (215) 238-4200; (800) 982-4377. 1990. Contains more than 50,000 synonyms for the hazardous chemicals and environmental pollutants identified. Comprehensive resource title available for properly identifying common names, chemical names and product names associated with these chemicals.

ERT Handbook on Requirements for Industrial Facilities under the Clear Air Act: New–Information on Toxic Air Pollutants. Environmental Research & Technology, Concord, Massachusetts 1984. Air pollution law and legislation in the United States and environmental aspects of industry.

Handbook: Control Technologies for Hazardous Air Pollutants. Air and Energy Research Laboratory, U.S. Environmental Protection Agency, Research Triangle Park, North Carolina 27711. (919) 541-2350. 1986. Environmental research information relative to hazardous wastes.

Handbook of Control Technologies for Hazardous Air Pollutants. Robert Y. Purcell. Science Information Resource Center, Cambridge, Massachusetts 1988. Evaluation of control technologies for hazardous air pollutants.

Handbook of Environmental Degradation Rates. Philip H. Howard, et al. Lewis Publishers, 2000 Corporate Blvd., N.W., Boca Raton, Florida 33431. (407) 994-0555 or (800) 272-7737. 1991. Provides rate constant and half-life ranges for various processes and combines them into ranges for different media (air, groundwater, surface water, soils) which can be directly entered into various models.

The Infrared Spectra Handbook of Priority Pollutants and Toxic Chemicals. Sadtler Research Laboratories, 3316 Spring Garden St., Philadelphia, Pennsylvania 19104. (215) 382-7800. 1982. Chemicals spectra, hazardous substances spectra, gases spectra, and toxic chemicals.

ONLINE DATA BASES

CAS Source Index–CASSI. Chemical Abstracts Service, 2540 Olentangy River Rd., P.O. Box 3012, Columbus, Ohio 43210. (800) 848-6533 or (614) 421-3600. A listing of bibliographic and library holdings information for scientific and technical primary literature relevant to the chemical sciences.

Chemical Abstracts-CA. Chemical Abstracts Service, 2540 Olentangy River Rd., P.O. Box 3012, Columbus, Ohio 43210. (800) 848-6533 or (614) 421-3600. Information sources include 9000 journals, patents from 27 countries, two industrial property organizations, new books, conference proceedings, and government research reports.

Computerized Engineering Index–COMPENDEX. Engineering Information Inc., 345 E. 47th St., New York, New York 10017. (212) 705-7600.

Enviro/Energyline Abstracts Plus. R. R. Bowker Co., 121 Chanlon Rd., New Providence, New Jersey 07974. (908) 464-6800.

Environmental Periodicals Bibliography. National Information Services Corp., Ste. 6, Wyman Towers, 3100 St. Paul St., Baltimore, Maryland 21218. (410)243-0797. Online version of abstract of same name.

Los Angeles Catalytic Study–LACS. U.S. Environmental Protection Agency, Office of Monitoring Systems and Quality Assurance, 401 M St., S.W., Washington, District of Columbia 20460. (202) 260-2090.

Monthly Catalog of United States Government Publications. U.S. G.P.O., Supt. of Docs., PO Box 371954, Pittsburgh, Pennsylvania 15250-7954. (202) 512-0000.

National Technical Information Service. U.S. Department of Commerce, National Technical Information Service, Office of Data Base Services, 5285 Port Royal Rd., Springfield, Virginia 22161. (703) 487-4807. Bibliographic database of government sponsored research and technical reports.

SCISEARCH. Institute for Scientific Information, University City Science Center, 3501 Market St., Philadelphia, Pennsylvania 19104. (215) 386-0100.

PERIODICALS AND NEWSLETTERS

Archives of Environmental Contamination. Springer-Verlag, 175 5th Ave., New York, New York 10010. (212) 460-1500. 1972-. Bimonthly.

Bulletin of Environmental Contamination and Toxicology. Springer-Verlag, 175 5th Ave., New York, New York 10010. (212) 460-1500; (800) 777-4643. 1966-. Frequency varies. Disseminates advances and discoveries in the areas of soil, air and food contamination and pollution.

Environmental & Molecular Mutagenesis. Errol Zeiger. John Wiley & Sons, Inc., 605 3rd Ave., New York, New York 10158. Eight times a year. Covers environmentally induced diseases, carcinogenesis, mutagens and mutation.

Environmental Geology & Water Sciences. Springer-Verlag, 175 Fifth Avenue, New York, New York 10010. (212) 460-1500. Bimonthly. Covers interactions between humanity and Earth.

Environmental Professional. National Association of Environmental Professionals, P.O. Box 15210, Alexandria, Virginia 22309-0210. (703) 660-2364. Quarterly. Covers effective impact assessment, regulation, and environmental protection.

Environmental Research. Academic Press, 1250 6th Ave., San Diego, California 92101. (619) 231-0926. Bimonthly. Toxic effects of environmental agents in humans and animals.

International Journal of Energy, Environment, Economics. Nova Science Publishers, Inc., 283 Commack Rd., Ste. 300, Commack, New York 11725. (516) 499-3103. 1991-. Quarterly. Aims to provide a vehicle for the multidisciplinary field of energy-environment economics between research scientists, engineers and economists. The areas covered would be technological, environmental, economic and social feasibility.

Journal of Environmental Science and Health. Marcel Dekker, Inc., 270 Madison Ave., New York, New York

10016. (212) 696-9000. Bimonthly. Concerns pesticides, food contaminants, chemical carcinogens, and agricultural wastes.

National Air Toxics Information Clearinghouse Newsletter. National Air Toxic Information Clearinghouse, P.O. Box 13000, Research Triangle Park, North Carolina 27709. (919) 541-9100. Bimonthly. Covers noncriteria pollutant emissions.

TRADE ASSOCIATIONS AND PROFESSIONAL SOCIETIES

Association of Local Air Pollution Control Officials. 444 North Capitol St., N.W., Washington, District of Columbia 20001 (202) 624-7864.

POLLUTANTS, ATMOSPHERIC

See: ATMOSPHERE

POLLUTION

See also: AIR POLLUTION; ENVIRONMENTAL CONDITION; ENVIRONMENTAL ENGINEERING; MARINE POLLUTION; NOISE POLLUTION; RADIOACTIVE POLLUTION; WATER POLLUTION; WATER QUALITY

ABSTRACTING AND INDEXING SERVICES

Abstracts of Air and Water Conservation Literature. American Petroleum Institute. Central Abstracting and Indexing Service, 275 Madison Avenue, New York, New York 10016. 1972.

Abstracts on Health Effects of Environmental Pollutants. BIOSIS, 2100 Arch St., Philadelphia, Pennsylvania 19103. (215) 587-4800; (800) 523-4806.

Air Pollution Technical Publications of the United States Environmental Protection Agency. U.S. Environmental Protection Agency, Mail Drop 75, Research Triangle Park, North Carolina 27711. (919) 541-2184. 1976. Quarterly.

Air Pollution Titles. Pennsylvania State University, Center for Air Environmental Studies, 226 Fenske Laboratory, University Park, Pennsylvania 16802. (814) 865-1415. 1965. Bibliographic guide to current research literature on air environment, including monitoring and control of air pollution, health effects, effects on agriculture, forests, toxic air contaminants, and global atmospheric pro cases.

Air Pollution Translations. A Bibliography With Abstracts. U.S. Environmental Protection Agency, MD 75, Research Triangle Park, North Carolina 27711. (919) 541-2184. 1969.

Applied Ecology Abstracts Studies in Renewable Natural Resources. Information Retrieval Ltd., 1911 Jefferson Davis Highway, Arlington, Virginia 22202. 1975-. Monthly.

Aqualine Abstracts. Water Research Centre. c/o Pergamon Microforms International, Inc., Fairview Park, Elmsford, New York 10523. (914) 592-7720. 1927-. Contains some 8,000 records annually on water and wastewater technology. Covers all aspects of water, wastewater, associated engineering services and the aquatic environment. Over 600 periodicals, as well as books, reports and conference proceedings and other publications from water related institutions worldwide are scanned. Also available online.

ASFA Aquaculture Abstracts. Cambridge Scientific Abstracts, Inc., 5161 River Rd., Bethesda, Maryland 20816. (301) 961-6750. 1984.

Biological and Agricultural Index. H.W. Wilson Co., 950 University Ave., Bronx, New York 10452. (800) 367-6770. 1916-. Monthly.

Biotechnology Research Abstracts. Cambridge Scientific Abstracts, 5161 River Rd., Bethesda, Maryland 20816. (301) 961-6750. Monthly. Includes such broad areas as genetic intervention, biochemical genetics, and microbiological techniques.

Bulletin Signaletique: Eau et Assainissement, Pollution Atmospherique, Droit des Pollutions. Centre de Documentation, Centre National de la Recherche Scientifique, 15, quai Anatole France, Paris, France 75700. (1) 45 55 92 25. 1983-. Monthly. Indexes pollution periodicals including water, atmospheric and related pollutions.

Civil Engineering Hydraulic Abstracts. BHRA Fluid Engineering, Air Science Co., PO Box 143, Corning, New York 14830. (607) 962-5591. Monthly. Abstracts of periodicals that publish in the areas of hydraulic engineering and other related topics.

Current Advances in Ecological and Environmental Science. Pergamon Microforms International, Inc., Fairview Park, Elmsford, New York 10523. (914) 592-7720. 1989-. Monthly. Current literature searching service includingjournals, reports, abstracts, etc. This service is available online as part of the CABS database on the hosts BRS and ORBIT search service.

Ecological Abstracts. Geo Abstracts Ltd. Elsevier Applied Science, Crown House, Linton Rd., Barking, England IG 11 8JU. 1974-. Derived from over 600 leading ecological and environmental journals, plus books, conference proceedings, reports and theses.

Ecology Abstracts. Cambridge Scientific Abstracts, 5161 River Rd., Bethesda, Maryland 20816. (301) 961-6750. Monthly.

EIS: Digests of Environmental Impact Statements. Cambridge Scientific Abstracts, 5161 River Rd., Bethesda, Maryland 20816. (301) 951-1400. 1970-. Bimonthly. Provides detailed abstracts of all the environmental impact statements issued by the federal government each year and indexes them. Also extracts the key issues from the complex government released environmental impact statements. Contents include areas such as: air transportation, defense programs, energy, hazardous substances, land use, manufacturing, parks, refuges, forests, research and development, roads and railroads, urban and social programs, wastes, and water.

Engineering Index. The Engineering Index Inc., 345 E. 47th St., New York, New York 10017. 1962-.

Environment Abstracts. Bowker A & I Publishing, 121 Chanlon Rd., New Providence, New Jersey 07974. (908) 464-6800. 1974-.

Environment Index. Environment Information Center, Index Research Department, 124 E. 39th St., New York, New York 10016. 1971-. Annual.

Environmental Information Connection–EIC. Planning Information Program, Dept. of Urban and Regional Planning, University of Illinois, 1003 West Nevada, Urbana, Illinois 61801. (217) 333-1369. Also available online.

Environmental Periodicals Bibliography. Environmental Studies Institute, International Academy at Santa Barbara, 800 Garden St., Suite D, Santa Barbara, California 93101. (805) 965-5010. Also available online.

General Science Index. H. W. Wilson Co., 950 University Ave., Bronx, New York 10452. 1978-. Monthly, also issued in annual cumulation. Cumulative subject index to English language periodicals in the subject fields of astronomy, botany, chemistry, earth science, environment and conservation, food and nutrition, genetics, mathematics, medicine and health, microbiology, oceanography, physics, physiology and zoology.

Microbiology Abstracts. Section A. Industrial and Applied Microbiology. Cambridge Scientific Abstracts, 5161 River Rd., Bethesda, Maryland 20816. (301) 961-6750. 1972-.

Multimedia Index to Ecology. National Information Center for Educational Media, University of Southern California, Los Angeles, California 90007.

Pollution Abstracts. Cambridge Scientific Abstracts, 5161 River Rd., Bethesda, Maryland 20816. (301) 961-6750. Six/year. Indexes worldwide technical literature on environmental pollution. Covers air pollution, marine and freshwater pollution, sewage and wastewater treatment, waste management, toxicology and health, noise pollution, radiation, land pollution, and environmental policies, programs, legislation, and education. Also available online.

Pollution Research Index: A Guide to World Research in Environment Pollution. A. I. Sors and D. Coleman. Francis Hodgson, Longman House, Burnt Mill, Harlow, England CM20 2JE. 1979. Second edition. Provides a detailed insight of pollution research. Includes over 2000 entries related to government departments, universities, research institutions and manufacturing industry from over 100 countries throughout the world.

Science Citation Index. Institute for Scientific Information, 3501 Market St., Philadelphia, Pennsylvania 19104. 1961-.

Summaries of Foreign Government Environmental Reports. U.S. Environmental Protection Agency, 401 M St., S.W., Washington, District of Columbia 20460. (202) 260-2090.

ALMANACS AND YEARBOOKS

Gale Environmental Almanac. Russ Hoyle. Gale Research Inc., 835 Penobscot Bldg., Detroit, Michigan 48226-4094. (313) 961-2242. 1993. Focuses on the U.S. and Canada, although worldwide and transboundary issues are discussed.

BIBLIOGRAPHIES

Asbestos and Silicate Pollution: Citations from the Engineering Index Data Base. Diane M. Cavagnaro. National Technical Information Service, 5285 Port Royal Rd., Springfield, Virginia 22161. (703) 487-4650. 1980. Deals with asbestos pollution and silicate pollution and their effects on the environment.

Bibliography and Index of Geology. American Geological Institute, 4220 King St., Alexandria, Virginia 22302. Monthly. Includes environmental geology and hydrogeology.

Environmental Toxicology. Robert L. Rudd. Gale Research Co., 835 Penobscot Bldg., Detroit, Michigan 48226-4094. (313) 961-2242. 1977. Includes the broad areas of pollution, pesticides, and their effects. This bibliography is part of the series entitled Man and the Environment Information Guide Series, v.7.

EPA Publications Bibliography. U.S. Environmental Protection Agency, Library Systems Branch, 401 M St., SW, Washington, District of Columbia 20460. (202) 260-2090. Quarterly.

DIRECTORIES

Canadian Environmental Directory. Canadian Almanac & Directory Publishing Co. Ltd., 134 Adelaide St. E., Ste. 27, Toronto, Ontario, Canada M5C 1K9. (416) 362-4088. 1992. Includes individuals, agencies, firms, and associations.

Criteria Pollutant Point Source Directory. North American Water Office, Box 174, Lake Elmo, Minnesota 55042. (612) 770-3861. Biennial. Utilities, smelters, refineries, and other facilities that emit more than 1000 tons of particulates, sulfur oxides, nitrogen oxides, volatile organic compounds, or carbon monoxide.

Directory of Computer Software Applications. Environmental Pollution and Control. National Technical Information Service, 5285 Port Royal Rd., Springfield, Virginia 22161. (703) 487-4650. 1977-1980.

Directory of Environmental Information Sources. Thomas F. P. Sullivan, ed. Government Institutes, Inc., 4 Research Pl., Ste. 200, Rockville, Maryland 20850. (301) 921-2300. 1992. 3d ed.

Environmental Software Directory. Donley Technology, PO Box 335, Garrisonville, Virginia 22463. (703) 659-1954. 1989-. Annually. Provides descriptive access to commercial and government databases, software and online systems related to hazardous materials management, water and wastewater, groundwater, soils, mapping, air pollution and ecology.

The Green Encyclopedia. Irene Franck, David Brownstone. Prentice-Hall, Rte. 9W, Englewood Cliffs, New York 07632. (201) 592-2000. 1992. Covers environmental organizations.

ENCYCLOPEDIAS AND DICTIONARIES

Cambridge Dictionary of Biology. Peter M. B. Walker. Cambridge University Press, 40 W. 20th St., New York, New York 10011. (212) 924-3900 or (800) 227-0247. 1989. Includes 10,000 terms in zoology, botany, biochemistry, molecular biology and genetics. Previously published under the title Chambers Biology Dictionary.

A Concise Dictionary of Biology. Elizabeth Martin, ed. Oxford University Press, 200 Madison Ave., New York, New York 10016. (212) 679-7300 or (800) 334-4249. 1990. New edition. Derived from the Concise Science Dictionary, published in 1984.

Dictionary of Dangerous Pollutants, Ecology, and Environment. David F. Tver. Industrial Press, 200 Madison

Ave., New York, New York 10016. (212) 889-6330. 1981.

Dictionary of Environmental Science and Technology. Andrew Porteous. John Wiley & Sons, Inc., 605 3rd Ave., New York, New York 10158-0012. (212) 850-6000. 1992.

Dictionary of the Environment. Michael Allaby. New York University Press, 70 Washington Sq. S., New York, New York 10012. (212) 998-2575. 1989.

Encyclopedia of Environmental Studies. William Ashworth. Facts on File, Inc., 460 Park Ave. S., New York, New York 10016. (212) 683-2244. 1991.

Encyclopedia of Physical Science and Technology. Robert A. Meyers, ed. Academic Press, c/o Harcourt Brace Jovanovich Inc., 6277 Sea Harbor Dr., Orlando, Florida 32887. (800) 346-8648. Dictionary of engineering, technology and physical sciences.

Environmental Encyclopedia. William P. Cunningham, Terence Ball, et. al. Gale Research Inc., 835 Penobscot Bldg., Detroit, Michigan 48226-4094. (313) 961-2242. 1993.

McGraw-Hill Encyclopedia of Science and Technology. McGraw-Hill, 1221 Avenue of the Americas, New York, New York 10020. (212) 512-2000 or (800) 262-4729. 1992. Seventh edition. Issued in multiple volumes including index. Includes all science and technology broad subject areas.

NSCA Environmental Glossary. J. Dunmore. National Society for Clean Air, 136 North Street, Brighton, England BN1 1RG. 1905. Covers air pollution, noise, water pollution, wastes and radiation.

Van Nostrand's Scientific Encyclopedia. Glenn D. Considine, ed. Van Nostrand Reinhold, 115 5th Ave., New York, New York 10003. (212) 254-3232. 1983. Sixth edition. Includes all broad subject areas in science.

GENERAL WORKS

50 Simple Things You Can Do to Save the Earth. G.K. Hall & Co., 70 Lincoln St., Boston, Massachusetts 02111. (617) 423-3990. 1991. Citizen participation in environmental protection.

Atlas of the United States Environmental Issues. Robert J. Mason. Maxwell Macmillan International, 866 3rd Ave., New York, New York 10022. (212) 702-2000. Describes the texture of our environmental health using maps, photographs, charts, graphs, and diagrams.

Biomarkers of Environmental Contamination. John F. McCarthy and Lee R. Shugart. Lewis Publishers, 2000 Corporate Blvd., Boca Raton, Florida 33431. (800) 272-7737. 1990. Reviews the use of biological markers in animals and plants as an innovative approach to evaluating the ecological and physiological effects of environmental contamination.

Chemical Concepts in Pollutant Behavior. Ian J. Tinsley. John Wiley & Sons, Inc., 605 3rd Ave., New York, New York 10158-0012. (212) 850-6000. 1979.

Chemical Contamination in the Human Environment. Morton Lippmann. Oxford University Press, 200 Madison Ave., New York, New York 10016. (212) 679-7300. 1979. Deals with pollution and environmental health.

Chemical Waste Disposal: Chemicals Identified in Terrestrial and Aquatic Waste Disposal Processes; a Selected Bibliography with Abstracts, 1964-1979. J. G. Pruett. Federation of American Societies for Experimental Biology, 9650 Rockville Pike, Bethesda, Maryland 20814. (301) 530-7000. 1980.

Compilation of EPA's Sampling and Analysis Methods. William Mueller, et al. Lewis Publishers, 2000 Corporate Blvd., N.W., Boca Raton, Florida 33431. (407) 994-0555 or (800) 272-7737. 1991. Aids with rapid searching of sampling and analytical method summaries. More than 650 method/analytical summaries from the database are included in this volume.

Computer Graphics and Environmental Planning. Prentice-Hall, Rte. 9 W, Englewood Cliffs, New Jersey 07632. (201) 592-2000. 1983.

Design for a Livable Planet: How You Can Help Clean Up the Environment. Jon Naar. Perennial Library, 10 E. 53d St., New York, New York 10022. (212) 207-7000; (800) 242-7737. 1990. Explains the dangers we present to our environment and what we can do about it. Also available from Carolina Biological Supply Co., 2700 York Rd., Burlington, NC.

Ecotoxicology and Climate. Philippe Bordeaux, et al., eds. John Wiley & Sons, Inc., 605 3rd Ave., New York, New York 10158-0012. (212) 850-6000. 1989. Describes environmental chemistry of toxic pollutants in hot and cold climates. Includes bibliographical references and an index.

Environmental Biotechnology: Reducing Risks from Environmental Chemicals through Biotechnology. Gilbert S. Omenn. Plenum Press, 233 Spring St., New York, New York 10013-1578. (212) 620-8000. Covers environmental aspects of the chemical and biological treatment of sewage.

Environmental Pollution. Inderscience Enterprises Ltd., World Trade Center Bldg., 110 Avenue Louis Casai, Case Postale 306, Geneva-Airport, Switzerland CH-1215. (44) 908-314248. 1991. Special issue of the International Journal of Environment and Pollution. Proceedings of the 1st International Conference on Environmental Pollution held at the Congress Centre, Lisbon, April 15-19, 1991.

The Environmental Sourcebook. Edith Carol Stein. Lyons & Burford, 31 W. 21st St., New York, New York 10010. (212) 620-9580. 1992. Provides information on 11 specific environmental issues, including population; agriculture; energy; climate and atmosphere; biodiversity; water; oceans; solid waste; hazardous substances and waste; endangered lands; and development.

Environmental Viewpoints. Marie Lazzari. Gale Research Inc., 835 Penobscot Bldg., Detroit, Michigan 48226-4094. (313) 961-2242. 1992.

Envirosoft 86. P. Zanetti, ed. Computational Mechanics Inc., 25 Bridge St., Billerica, Massachusetts 01821. 1986. Environmental software part of the proceedings of the International Conference on Development and Applications of Computer Techniques to Environmental Studies, Los Angeles, 1986.

Evaluation of Environmental Data for Regulatory and Impact Assessment. S. Ramamoorthy and E. Baddaloo. Elsevier Science Publishing Co., 655 Avenue of the Americas, New York, New York 10010. (212) 984-5800. 1991.

Fighting Toxics. Gary Cohen and John O'Connor, eds. Island Press, 1718 Connecticut Ave. N.W., Suite 300, Washington, District of Columbia 20009. (202) 232-7933. 1990. Investigates the toxic hazards in the community, determining the health risks they pose, and launching an effective campaign to eliminate them.

Impact Models to Assess Regional Acidification. Juha Kamari. Kluwer Academic Publishers, 101 Philip Dr., Assinippi Park, Norwell, Massachusetts 02061. (617) 871-6600. 1990. Contains a description of the development and use of the Regional Acidification Information and Simulation (RAINS) model, an integrated assessment model of developing and determining control strategies to reduce regional acidification in Europe.

Imperiled Planet: Restoring Our Endangered Ecosystems. Edward Goldsmith, et al. MIT Press, 55 Hayward St., Cambridge, Massachusetts 02142. (617) 253-2884; (800) 356-0343. 1990. Presentation of a wide range of ecosystems, showing how they work, the traditional forms of human use, threats and losses, causes of destruction, and preservation attempts.

Integrated Approaches to Water Pollution. Joao Bau. Elsevier Science Publishing Co., 655 Avenue of the Americas, New York, New York 10010. (212) 984-5800. 1991. Integrated management strategies, policies for pollution control, groundwater pollution resulting from industrial, agricultural and urban sources, data and measurement.

An Introduction to Environmental Pattern Analysis. P. J. A. Howard. Parthenon Group Inc., 120 Mill Rd., Park Ridge, New Jersey 07656. (201) 391-6796. 1991. Explains the basic mathematics of the most widely used ordination and cluster analysis methods, types of data to which they are suited and their advantages and disadvantages.

Islands under Siege: National Parks and the Politics of External Threats. John C. Freemuth. University Press of Kansas, 329 Carruth, Lawrence, Kansas 66045. (913) 864-4154. 1991. Outlines a diverse set of political strategies, evaluating each in terms of environmental effectiveness and political feasibility.

Land Degradation: Development and Breakdown of Terrestrial Environments. C. J. Barrow. Cambridge University Press, 40 W. 20th St., New York, New York 10011. (212) 924-3900; (800) 227-0247. 1991.

Magill's Survey of Science. Earth Science Series. Frank N. Magill. Salem Press, PO Box 50062, Pasadena, California 91105. 1990-. Five volumes. Includes information on earth's crust, hot spots and volcanic island chains, physical properties of minerals, rock magnetism, physical properties of rocks, and index.

Making Peace with the Planet. Barry Commoner. Pantheon Books, 201 E. 50th St., New York, New York 10220. (212) 751-2000. 1990. Reviews the vast efforts made in the public and private sphere to address and control damage to the environment.

Multispecies Toxicity Testing. John Cairns, Jr. Pergamon Microforms International, Inc., Fairview Park, Clumsford, New York 10523. (914) 592-7720. Toxicity tests in the safety assessments of chemicals.

Optoelectronics for Environmental Science. S. Martellucci and A. N. Chester, eds. Plenum Press, 233 Spring St., New York, New York 10013-1578. (212) 620-8000; (800) 221-9369. 1991. Contribution of lasers and the optical sciences to specific problems, in situ measurements, atmospheric ozone, lidar detection, wind velocity, oceanographic measurements, heavy metal detection, toxic metals, and trace analysis. Proceedings of the 14th course of the International School of Quantum Electronics on Optoelectronics for Environmental Sciences, held September 3-12, 1989, in Erice, Italy.

PCBs: Human and Environmental Hazards. Frank M. D'itri and Michael A. Kamrin, eds. Ann Arbor Science, 230 Collingwood, Ann Arbor, Michigan 48106. 1983.

Pollution: Causes, Effects and Control. Roy Michael Harrison. Royal Society of Chemistry, c/o CRC Press, 2000 Corporate Blvd. N.W., Boca Raton, Florida 33431. (800) 272-7737. 1990. 2nd ed. Deals with environmental pollution and its associated problems and legal ramifications.

Pollution Prevention Pays: An Overview by the 3M Company of Low- and Non-Pollution Technology. World Environment Center, 419 Park Ave. S, Suite 1404, New York, New York 10016. (212) 683-4700. Covers natural resources, pollution and control.

Preventing Pollution Through Technical Assistance: One State's Experience. Mark H. Dorfman, et al. INFORM Inc., 381 Park Ave. S., New York, New York 10016. (212) 689-4040. 1990. Examines the state of North Carolina's voluntary program aimed at assisting the industry in pollution prevention. It also includes a glossary, a bibliography of information sources and helpful statistical tables of data collected.

Prosperity without Pollution. Joel S. Hirschhorn and Kirsten U. Oldenburg. Van Nostrand Reinhold, 115 5th Ave., New York, New York 10003. (212) 254-3232. 1991. Explains how to decrease pollution without making a sacrifice in our standard of living.

Saving the Mediterranean: The Politics of International Environmental Cooperation. Peter M. Haas. Columbia University Press, 562 W. 113th St., New York, New York 10025. (212) 316-7100. 1990. Focuses on the international pollution management of the Mediterranean. Ninety scientists and international officials were interviewed to ascertain how the international community responded to this particular threat.

The Solution to Pollution in the Workplace. Laurence Sombke, et al. MasterMedia, 17 E. 89th St., New York, New York 10028. (212) 348-2020. 1991. Non-technical guidebook for cost-effective, practical tips and actions to help businesses, big and small, take a proactive role in solving pollution problems.

Wildlife Toxicology. Tony J. Peterle. Van Nostrand Reinhold, 115 5th Ave., New York, New York 10003. (212) 354-3232. 1991. Presents an historical overview of the toxicology problem and summarizes the principal laws, testing protocols, and roles of leading U.S. federal agencies, especially EPA. Examines state and local issues, monitoring programs, and contains an unique section on the regulation of toxic substances overseas.

The World Bank and the Environment: A Progress Report, Fiscal 1991. World Bank, UNIPUB, 4611-F Assembly Dr., Lanham, Maryland 20706. (301) 459-7666 or (800) 274-4888. 1991. Describes specific environmental strategies and environmental lending in the Bank's four operational regions: Asia, Europe, the Middle East and North Africa, and Latin America and the Caribbean.

World Guide to Environmental Issues and Organizations. Peter Brackley. Longman Group Ltd., Longman House, Burnt Mill, Harlow, Essex, England CM20 2J6. (0279) 426721. 1991.

The World Watch Reader on Global Environmental Issues. W. W. Norton & Co., Inc., 500 5th Ave., New York, New York 10110. (800) 223-4830. 1991.

GOVERNMENTAL ORGANIZATIONS

Public Information Office: Soil Conservation Service. 12th and Independence Ave., S.W., PO Box 2890, Washington, District of Columbia 20013. (202) 447-4543.

U.S. Environmental Protection Agency: Office of Pollution Prevention. 401 M St., S.W., Washington, District of Columbia 20460.

HANDBOOKS AND MANUALS

Energy Technology Characterizations Handbook. National Technical Information Service, 5285 Port Royal Rd., Springfield, Virginia 22161. (703) 487-4650. 1983. Environmental pollution and control factors.

Environment in Key Words: A Multilingual Handbook of the Environment: English-French-German-Russian. Isaac Paenson. Pergamon Microforms International, Inc., Fairview Park, Elmsford, New York 10523. (914) 592-7720. 1990. Two volumes. Terminology in the areas of ecology, environmental protection, pollution, conservation of natural resources and related areas.

Environmental Statistics Handbook: Europe. Allan Foster, Oksana Newman. Gale Research Inc., 835 Penobscot Bldg., Detroit, Michigan 48226-4094. (313) 961-2242. 1993.

The Handbook of Environmental Chemistry. O. Hutzinger. Springer-Verlag, 175 5th Ave., New York, New York 10010. (212) 460-1500. Irregular. Distribution and equilibria between environmental compartments, pathways, thermodynamics and kinetics.

Our National Wetland Heritage. Jon A. Kusler. Environmental Law Institute, 1616 P St., NW, Suite 200, Washington, District of Columbia 20036. (202) 328-5150. 1983. Discusses practical ways to preserve and protect wetlands and their benefits, which include recreation, wildlife habitat, pollution and flood control, scientific research and groundwater recharge.

Plant Engineers' Pollution Control Handbook. Richard A. Young. American Institute of Plant Engineers, 3975 Erie Ave., Cincinnati, Ohio 45208. (513) 561-6000. 1973.

Pollution Law Handbook. Sidney M. Wolf. Quorum Books, Div. of Greenwood Press, Inc., 88 Post Rd. W., Box 5007, Westport, Connecticut 06881. (203) 226-3571. 1988. A guide to federal environmental laws.

ONLINE DATA BASES

Computerized Engineering Index–COMPENDEX. Engineering Information Inc., 345 E. 47th St., New York, New York 10017. (212) 705-7600.

Enviro/Energyline Abstracts Plus. R. R. Bowker Co., 121 Chanlon Rd., New Providence, New Jersey 07974. (908) 464-6800.

Environmental Periodicals Bibliography. National Information Services Corp., Ste. 6, Wyman Towers, 3100 St. Paul St., Baltimore, Maryland 21218. (410)243-0797. Online version of abstract of same name.

Los Angeles Catalytic Study–LACS. U.S. Environmental Protection Agency, Office of Monitoring Systems and Quality Assurance, 401 M St., S.W., Washington, District of Columbia 20460. (202) 260-2090.

Monthly Catalog of United States Government Publications. U.S. G.P.O., Supt. of Docs., PO Box 371954, Pittsburgh, Pennsylvania 15250-7954. (202) 512-0000.

Multispectral Scanner and Photographic Imagery. U.S. Environmental Protection Agency, Office of Modeling and Monitoring Systems and Quality Assurance, 401 M St., S.W., Washington, District of Columbia 20460. (202) 260-2090. An index for various data tapes containing multispectral imagery from aircraft and satellites relating to sources of pollution.

National Technical Information Service. U.S. Department of Commerce, National Technical Information Service, Office of Data Base Services, 5285 Port Royal Rd., Springfield, Virginia 22161. (703) 487-4807. Bibliographic database of government sponsored research and technical reports.

SCISEARCH. Institute for Scientific Information, University City Science Center, 3501 Market St., Philadelphia, Pennsylvania 19104. (215) 386-0100.

SIRS Social Issues and Critical Issues CD-ROM. Social Issues Resources Series, Inc., PO Box 2348, Boca Raton, Florida 33427-2348. (407) 994-0079. Pollution, population, and the atmosphere.

PERIODICALS AND NEWSLETTERS

Bulletin l'Environment. Societe pour Vaincre la Pollution, 445 rue St. Francois Xavier, Montreal, Quebec, Canada H3H 2T1. 1973-. Quarterly.

Bulletin of Environmental Contamination and Toxicology. Springer-Verlag, 175 5th Ave., New York, New York 10010. (212) 460-1500; (800) 777-4643. 1966-. Frequency varies. Disseminates advances and discoveries in the areas of soil, air and food contamination and pollution.

CA Selects: Environment Pollution. Chemical Abstracts Services, 2540 Olentangy River Rd., Box 3012, Columbus, Ohio 43210. (800) 848-6533. 1978-. Biweekly. Abstracts on pollution of the environment by gaseous, liquid, solid and radioactive wastes.

City Sierran. Sierra Club-NYC Group, 625 Broadway, 2nd Fl., New York, New York 10012. (212) 473-7841. 1984-. Quarterly. Reports environmental news to Sierra Club members in New York City. Writers are activists and experts on acid rain, pollution, toxic wastes, recycling, endangered species, etc.

The Earth Care Annual. Russell Wild, ed. Rodale Press, 33 E. Minon St., Emmaus, Pennsylvania 18098. (215) 967-5171; (800) 322-6333. 1990-. Annually. Organized in alphabetical sections such as garbage, greenhouse effect, oceans, ozone, toxic waste, and wildlife, the annual presents environmental problems and offers innovative working solutions.

Ecological Applications. Ecological Society of America, Center for Environmental Studies, Arizona State University, Tempe, Arizona 85287. (602) 965-3000. 1991-. Quarterly. Emphasizes the application of basic ecological concepts to a wide range of problems.

Environment International: A Journal of Science, Technology, Health, Monitoring and Policy. Pergamon Microforms International, Inc., Fairview Park, Elmsford, New York 10523. (914) 592-7720. 1974-. Bimonthly. Includes vital data, causes of pollution, and methods for protection, covering the entire field of environmental protection.

Environmental Action. Environmental Action Foundation, 6930 Carroll Ave., Ste. 600, Takoma Park, Maryland 20912. (301) 891-1100. Bimonthly. Impact of humans and industry on the environment.

Environmental Pollution. Applied Science Publications, PO Box 5399, New York, New York 10163. (718) 756-6440. 1987-.

Environmental Science and Technology. American Chemical Society, 1155 16th St. N.W., Washington, District of Columbia 20036. (800) 227-5558. 1967-. Monthly. Contains research articles on various aspects of environmental chemistry, interpretative articles by invited experts and commentary on the scientific aspects of environmental management.

Environmental Spectrum. New Jersey Cooperative Extension Service, Cook College, Rutgers University, P.O. Box 231, New Brunswick, New Jersey 08903. 1968-. Bimonthly. Emphasis on air/noise pollution, energy, water and other environmental topics.

The Highlands Voice. West Virginia Highlands, 1205 Quarrier St. Lower Level, Charleston, West Virginia 25301. Monthly. Covers environmental topics in the Appalachian area of West Virginia.

International Journal of Environment and Pollution. Inderscience Enterprises Ltd., World Trade Center Bldg., 110 Avenue Louis Casai, Case Postale 306, Geneva-Airport, Switzerland CH-1215. (44) 908-314248. 1991-. Publishes original state-of-the-art articles, book reviews, and technical papers in the areas of: Environmental policies, protection, institutional aspects of pollution, risk assessments of all forms of pollution, protection of soil and ground water, waste disposal strategies, ecological impact of pollutants and other related topics.

Journal of Environmental Biology. Academy of Environmental Biology, 657-5 Civil Lines (south), Muzaffarnagar, India 251001. 1980-. Quarterly. An international journal concerned with toxicology and the interrelations of organisms and their environment.

Journal of Environmental Quality. American Society of Agronomy, 677 S. Segoe Rd., Madison, Wisconsin 53711-1086. (608) 273-8080. 1972-. Quarterly. Reports and brief reviews of agricultural ecology, environmental engineering and pollution.

Multinational Environmental Outlook. Business Publishers, Inc., 951 Pershing Dr., Silver Spring, Maryland 20910-4464. (301) 587-6300. 1974-. Biweekly. Covers developments in world environmental problems such as acid rain, deforestation, soil erosion, overfishing, threats to health, animal extinction, population growth, diminishing water supply and other related matters. Also available online.

Pollution Equipment News. Rimbach Publishing, Inc., 8650 Babcock Boulevard, Pittsburgh, Pennsylvania

15237. (412) 364-5366. Bimonthly. Covers new products, techniques, and literature.

Pollution Prevention. Executive Enterprises Publications Co., Inc., 22 W. 21st St., New York, New York 10010-6990. (212) 645-7880 or (800) 332-8804. 1991. Quarterly. Includes practical approaches to reducing waste, case studies of successful waste reduction programs and the saving they provide, analyses of new technologies and their efficacy in reducing waste, and updates of federal and state legislative initiatives and their impacts on industries.

RESEARCH CENTERS AND INSTITUTES

U.S. EPA Test and Evaluation Facility. 26 W. Martin Luther King Dr., Cincinnati, Ohio 45268. (513) 684-2621.

World Resources Institute. 1709 New York Ave., N.W., Washington, District of Columbia 20006. (202) 638-6300.

STATISTICS SOURCES

Statistical Methods for the Environmental Sciences. A.H. El-Shaarwi, ed. Kluwer Academic Publishers, 101 Philip Dr., Assinippi Pk., Norwell, Massachusetts 02061. (617) 871-6600. 1991.

Statistical Record of the Environment. Arsen J. Darnay. Gale Research Inc., 835 Penobscot Bldg., Detroit, Michigan 48226-4094. (313) 961-2242. 1992.

World Resources. World Resources Institute. 1709 New York Ave., N.W., Washington, District of Columbia 20006. (202) 638-6300. Annual. Statistical and textual analysis of world's natural resources and the effects of growth-caused environmental pollution.

TRADE ASSOCIATIONS AND PROFESSIONAL SOCIETIES

Association of Local Air Pollution Control Officials. 444 North Capitol St., N.W., Washington, District of Columbia 20001 (202) 624-7864.

Citizen's Clearinghouse for Hazardous Wastes, Inc. P.O. Box 6806, Falls Church, Virginia 22040. (703) 237-2249.

Community Environmental Council. 930 Miramonte Drive, Santa Barbara, California 93109. (805) 963-0583.

Kids for a Clean Environment. P.O. Box 158254, Nashville, Tennessee 37215. (615) 331-0708.

National Audubon Society. 950 Third Ave., New York, New York 10022. (212) 832-3200.

National Coalition Against the Misuse of Pesticides. 701 E St., SE, Suite 200, Washington, District of Columbia 20003. (202) 543-5450.

National Toxics Campaign. 1168 Commonwealth Ave., Boston, Massachusetts 02134. (617) 232-0327.

Pesticide Action Network. North America Regional Center, 965 Mission St., Suite 514, San Francisco, California 94103. (415) 541-9140.

Pollution Liability Insurance Association. 1333 Butterfield Rd., Suite 100, Downers Grove, Illinois 60515. (312) 969-5300.

POLLUTION CONTROL

ABSTRACTING AND INDEXING SERVICES

Abstracts of Air and Water Conservation Literature. American Petroleum Institute. Central Abstracting and Indexing Service, 275 Madison Avenue, New York, New York 10016. 1972.

Agrindex. AGRIS Coordinating Center, Via delle Terme di Caracalla, Rome, Italy I-00100. 61 0181-FA01. 1975-.

Air Pollution Technical Publications of the United States Environmental Protection Agency. U.S. Environmental Protection Agency, Mail Drop 75, Research Triangle Park, North Carolina 27711. (919) 541-2184. 1976. Quarterly.

Air Pollution Titles. Pennsylvania State University, Center for Air Environmental Studies, 226 Fenske Laboratory, University Park, Pennsylvania 16802. (814) 865-1415. 1965. Bibliographic guide to current research literature on air environment, including monitoring and control of air pollution, health effects, effects on agriculture, forests, toxic air contaminants, and global atmospheric pro cases.

Air Pollution Translations. A Bibliography With Abstracts. U.S. Environmental Protection Agency, MD 75, Research Triangle Park, North Carolina 27711. (919) 541-2184. 1969.

Applied Ecology Abstracts Studies in Renewable Natural Resources. Information Retrieval Ltd., 1911 Jefferson Davis Highway, Arlington, Virginia 22202. 1975-. Monthly.

Applied Science and Technology Index. H.W. Wilson Co., 950 University Ave., Bronx, New York 10452. (800) 367-6770. Formerly Industrial Arts Index.

Aqualine Abstracts. Water Research Centre. c/o Pergamon Microforms International, Inc., Fairview Park, Elmsford, New York 10523. (914) 592-7720. 1927-. Contains some 8,000 records annually on water and wastewater technology. Covers all aspects of water, wastewater, associated engineering services and the aquatic environment. Over 600 periodicals, as well as books, reports and conference proceedings and other publications from water related institutions worldwide are scanned. Also available online.

ASFA Aquaculture Abstracts. Cambridge Scientific Abstracts, Inc., 5161 River Rd., Bethesda, Maryland 20816. (301) 961-6750. 1984.

Biological and Agricultural Index. H.W. Wilson Co., 950 University Ave., Bronx, New York 10452. (800) 367-6770. 1916-. Monthly.

Bulletin Signaletique: Eau et Assainissement, Pollution Atmospherique, Droit des Pollutions. Centre de Documentation, Centre National de la Recherche Scientifique, 15, quai Anatole France, Paris, France 75700. (1) 45 55 92 25. 1983-. Monthly. Indexes pollution periodicals including water, atmospheric and related pollutions.

Ecological Abstracts. Geo Abstracts Ltd. Elsevier Applied Science, Crown House, Linton Rd., Barking, England IG 11 8JU. 1974-. Derived from over 600 leading ecological and environmental journals, plus books, conference proceedings, reports and theses.

Ecology Abstracts. Cambridge Scientific Abstracts, 5161 River Rd., Bethesda, Maryland 20816. (301) 961-6750. Monthly.

Engineering Index. The Engineering Index Inc., 345 E. 47th St., New York, New York 10017. 1962-.

Environment Abstracts. Bowker A & I Publishing, 121 Chanlon Rd., New Providence, New Jersey 07974. (908) 464-6800. 1974-.

Environment Index. Environment Information Center, Index Research Department, 124 E. 39th St., New York, New York 10016. 1971-. Annual.

Environmental Information Connection-EIC. Planning Information Program, Dept. of Urban and Regional Planning, University of Illinois, 1003 West Nevada, Urbana, Illinois 61801. (217) 333-1369. Also available online.

Environmental Periodicals Bibliography. Environmental Studies Institute, International Academy at Santa Barbara, 800 Garden St., Suite D, Santa Barbara, California 93101. (805) 965-5010. Also available online.

Multimedia Index to Ecology. National Information Center for Educational Media, University of Southern California, Los Angeles, California 90007.

Pollution Abstracts. Cambridge Scientific Abstracts, 5161 River Rd., Bethesda, Maryland 20816. (301) 961-6750. Six/year. Indexes worldwide technical literature on environmental pollution. Covers air pollution, marine and freshwater pollution, sewage and wastewater treatment, waste management, toxicology and health, noise pollution, radiation, land pollution, and environmental policies, programs, legislation, and education. Also available online.

Science Citation Index. Institute for Scientific Information, 3501 Market St., Philadelphia, Pennsylvania 19104. 1961-.

BIBLIOGRAPHIES

Current Contents. Agriculture, Biology and Environmental Sciences. Institute for Scientific Information, 3501 Market St., Philadelphia, Pennsylvania 19104. (800) 523-1857. 1973-. Previous title: Current Contents. Agricultural, Food & Veterinary Sciences. Gives the table of contents of periodicals in the fields of agriculture, biology, environmental and related areas.

EPA Publications Bibliography. U.S. Environmental Protection Agency, Library Systems Branch, 401 M St., SW, Washington, District of Columbia 20460. (202) 260-2090. Quarterly.

DIRECTORIES

Best's Safety Directory. Ambest Rd., Oldwick, New Jersey 08858. (201) 439-2200. Annual.

ECO Technics: International Pollution Control Directory. ECO-Verlags A G, Josefstrasse 8, Zurich, Switzerland CH-8021.

Pollution Engineering Locator. Cahners Publishing Co., 249 W. 17th St., New York, New York 10011. (212) 645-0067.

Pollution Engineering-Yellow Pages Telephone Directory Issue. Pudvan Publishing Company, Inc., 1935 Shermer Rd., Northbrook, Illinois 60062. (708) 498-9840.

Pollution Equipment News-Buyer's Guide Issue. Rimbach Publishing, Inc., 8650 Babcock Blvd., Pittsburgh, Pennsylvania 15237. (412) 364-5366.

The World Environment Handbook. Mark Baker. World Environment Center, 605 3rd Ave., Suite 1704, New York, New York 10158. 1985. Directory of natural resource management agencies and non-governmental environmental organizations in 145 countries.

ENCYCLOPEDIAS AND DICTIONARIES

Cambridge Encyclopedia of Life Sciences. A. E. Friday and David S. Ingram. Cambridge University Press, 40 W 20th St., New York, New York 10011. (212) 924-3900 or (800) 227-0247. 1985. Includes all topics under biology and ecology.

Dictionary of Environmental Engineering and Related Sciences: English-Spanish, Spanish-English. Jose T. Villate. Ediciones Universal, 3090 SW 8th St., Miami, Florida 33135. (305) 642-3355. 1979.

Dictionary of Environmental Protection. Otto E. Tutzauer. Fred B. Rothman, 10368 W. Centennial Rd., Littleton, California 80127. (303) 979-5657. 1979.

Dictionary of Environmental Protection Technology: In Four Languages, English, German, French, Russian. Egon Seidel. Elsevier Science Publishing Co., 655 Avenue of the Americas, New York, New York 10010. (212) 984-5800. 1988.

Encyclopedia of Chemical Processing and Design. John J. Mcketta and W. A. Cunningham. Marcel Dekker, Inc., 270 Madison Ave., New York, New York 10016. (212) 696-9000; (800) 228-1160. 1992. Thirty-eight volumes.

Encyclopedia of Environmental Control Technology. Paul N. Cheremisinoff, ed. Gulf Publishing Co., Book Division, PO Box 2608, Houston, Texas 77252. (713) 529-4301 or (800) 231-6275. 1992. Volume 1: Thermal Treatment of Hazardous Wastes; volume 2: Air Pollution Control; volume 3: Wastewater Treatment Technology; volume 4: Hazardous Waste Containment and Treatment; volumes 5 through 8 in progress. Provides in-depth coverage of specialized topics related to environmental and industrial pollution control problems and state-of-the-art information on technology and research as well as projections of future trends in the field.

Encyclopedia of Environmental Science and Engineering. J.R. Pfafflin. Gordon and Breach Science Publishers, Inc., 270 8th Ave., New York, New York 10011. (212) 206-8900. 1992.

Encyclopedia of Physical Science and Technology. Robert A. Meyers, ed. Academic Press, c/o Harcourt Brace Jovanovich Inc., 6277 Sea Harbor Dr., Orlando, Florida 32887. (800) 346-8648. Dictionary of engineering, technology and physical sciences.

English-Russian Dictionary of Environmental Protection: About 14,000 Terms. E.L. Milovanov. Pergamon Microforms International, Inc., Fairview Park, Elmsford, New York 10523. (914) 592-7720. 1981.

Environmental Engineering Dictionary. C. C. Lee. Government Institutes, Inc., 4 Research Pl., Ste. 200, Rockville, Maryland 20850. (301) 921-2300. 1989. Defines over 6000 engineering terms relating to pollutioncontrol technologies, monitoring, risk assessment, sampling andanalysis, quality control, permitting, and environmentally-regulated engineering and science. Includes bibliographical references (p. 612-627).

Grzimek's Encyclopedia of Ecology. Bernhard Grzimek. Van Nostrand Reinhold, 115 5th Ave., New York, New York 10003. (212) 254-3232. 1976.

Kirk-Othmer Encyclopedia of Chemical Technology. J. I. Kroschwitz, ed. John Wiley & Sons, Inc., 605 3rd Ave., New York, New York 10158-0012. (212) 850-6000. 1992-. All articles in the new edition have been rewritten and updated adding new subjects such as biotechnology, computer topics, analytical techniques and instrumentation, environmental concerns, fuels and energy, inorganic and solid state chemistry; composite materials and material science in general, and pharmaceuticals. Also available online.

McGraw-Hill Encyclopedia of Environmental Science. Sybil P. Parker. McGraw-Hill Science & Engineering Books, 11 W. 19th St., New York, New York 10011. (212) 337-6010. 1980. Covers ecology, man's influence on nature, and environmental protection.

McGraw-Hill Encyclopedia of Science and Technology. McGraw-Hill, 1221 Avenue of the Americas, New York, New York 10020. (212) 512-2000 or (800) 262-4729. 1992. Seventh edition. Issued in multiple volumes including index. Includes all science and technology broad subject areas.

The New York Times Encyclopedic Dictionary of the Environment. Paul Sarnoff. Quadrangle Books, New York, New York 1971. Focuses on state-of-the-art methods of pollution control, abatement, prevention and removal.

North American Reference Encyclopedia of Ecology and Pollution. William White. North American Pub. Co., 401 N. Broad St., Philadelphia, Pennsylvania 19108. (215) 238-5300. 1972.

Van Nostrand's Scientific Encyclopedia. Glenn D. Considine, ed. Van Nostrand Reinhold, 115 5th Ave., New York, New York 10003. (212) 254-3232. 1983. Sixth edition. Includes all broad subject areas in science.

GENERAL WORKS

Acute Toxicology Testing: Perspectives and Horizons. Shayne C. Gad and Christopher P. Chengelis. Telford Press, PO Box 287, West Caldwell, New Jersey 07006. (201) 228-7744. 1989.

Air Monitoring for Toxic Exposure. Shirley A. Ness. Van Nostrand Reinhold, 115 5th Ave., New York, New York 10003. (212) 354-3232. 1991. Explains the procedures for evaluating potentially harmful exposure to people from hazardous materials including chemicals, radon and bioaerosols. Presents practical information on how to perform air sampling, collect biological and bulk samples, evaluate dermal exposures, and determine the advantages and limitations of a given method.

Air Pollution Control. Howard E. Hesketh. Technomic Publishing Co., 851 New Holland Ave., Box 3535, Lancaster, Pennsylvania 17604. (717) 291-5609. 1991. Presents both theory and application data. Provides a background relevant to behavior theories and control techniques for capturing gaseous and particulate air pollutants.

Air Toxics and Risk Assessment. Edward J. Calabrese and Elaina M. Kenyon. Lewis Publishers, 200 Corporate Blvd. NW, Boca Raton, Florida 33431. (407) 994-0555 or (800)272-7737. 1991. Does risk assessments for more than 110 chemicals that are confirmed or probable air toxics. All chemicals are analyzed with a scientifically sound methodology to assess public health risks.

Antarctica and Global Climatic Change. Colin M. Harris. Lewis Publishers, 2000 Corporate Blvd., NW, Boca Raton, Florida 33431. (800) 272-7737. 1991. A guide to recent literature on climatic changes and environmental monitoring.

Biomarkers of Environmental Contamination. John F. McCarthy and Lee R. Shugart. Lewis Publishers, 2000 Corporate Blvd., Boca Raton, Florida 33431. (800) 272-7737. 1990. Reviews the use of biological markers in animals and plants as an innovative approach to evaluating the ecological and physiological effects of environmental contamination.

Compilation of EPA's Sampling and Analysis Methods. William Mueller, et al. Lewis Publishers, 2000 Corporate Blvd., N.W., Boca Raton, Florida 33431. (407) 994-0555 or (800) 272-7737. 1991. Aids with rapid searching of sampling and analytical method summaries. More than 650 method/analytical summaries from the database are included in this volume.

Development Document for the Effluent Monitoring Regulation for the Metal Casting Sector. Ontario Ministry of the Environment, Toronto. National Technical Information Service, 5285 Port Royal Rd., Springfield, Virginia 22161. (703) 487-4650. 1990.

Environment and Energy. T. Nejat Veziroglu, ed. Nova Science Publishers, Inc., 283 Commack Rd., Ste. 300, Commack, New York 11725. (516) 499-3103. 1991. Based on a conference and a volume in the series Energy and Environmental Progress-I, Vol F. Deals mostly with environmental pollution engineering and the energy technology involved in the process.

Environmental Monitoring and Evaluation of Calcium Magnesium Acetate. Richard Ray Horner. Transportation Research Board, National Research Council, 2101 Constitution Ave. NW, Washington, District of Columbia 20418. 1988. Deicing chemicals and snow and ice control of roads.

Environmental Monitoring: Meeting the Technical Challenge. E. M. Cashell, ed. American Institute of Physics, 335 E 45th St., New York, New York 10017. (212) 661-9404. 1990. Proceedings of the International Conference organized by ISA International and held in Cork, Ireland, May 1990. Examines the current state of the technology and methodology employed by industry to fulfill its legal and public responsibilities, and looks at new innovative technologies which are likely to figure prominently in environmental monitoring in the future.

Environmental Monitoring, Restoration, and Assessment: What Have We Learned?. Handord Symposium on Health and Environment, 28th, 1989, Richmond, WA. Battelle Press, 505 King Ave., Columbus, Ohio 43201. (614) 424-6393. 1990. Evaluates some of the monitoring and assessment programs that have been conducted or are currently in place. Focuses on radiological monitoring and its expenditures.

Environmental Pollution and Control. P. Aarne Vesiling, et al. Butterworth-Heinemann, 80 Montvale Ave., Stoneham, Massachusetts 02180. (617) 438-8468; (800) 366-2665. 1990. Describes the more important aspects of environmental engineering science and technology.

Estimating Costs of Air Pollution Control. William M. Vatavuk. Lewis Publishers, 2000 Corporate Blvd., N.W., Boca Raton, Florida 33431. (407) 994-0555 or (800) 272-7737. 1990. Deals with information to select, size, and estimate budget/study level capital and annual costs for a variety of air pollution control equipment.

Feasibility of Environmental Monitoring and Exposure Assessment for a Municipal Waste Combustor. C. Sonich-Mullin. U.S. Environmental Protection Agency, 401 M St., SW, Washington, District of Columbia 20460. (202) 260-2090. 1991.

Hazardous Waste Measurements. Milagros S. Simmons, ed. Lewis Publishers, 200 Corporate Blvd. NW, Boca Raton, Florida 33431. (407) 994-0555 or (800)272-7737. 1991. Focuses on recent developments in field testing methods and quality assurance.

Industrial Environmental Control. A. M. Springer. John Wiley & Sons, Inc., 605 3rd Ave., New York, New York 10158-0012. (212) 850-6000. 1986. Covers in great detail all the basic information regarding industrial pollution and its treatment.

Industrial Ventilation Workbook; Indoor Air Quality Workbook; Laboratory Ventilation Workbook. American Industrial Hygiene Association, 345 White Pond Dr., Akron, Ohio 44320. (216) 873-2442. 1990-1991. Includes expanded coverage of introductory concepts through advanced materials and discussions of the state-of-the-art hood and duct design, loss factors, dilution ventilation, etc. Also describes HVAC in simple understandable terms. The Lab workbook describes lab hood exhaust systems and associated HVAC systems.

Instrumental Analysis of Pollutants. C. N. Hewitt, ed. Elsevier Science Publishing Co., 655 Avenue of the Americas, New York, New York 10010. (212) 989-5800. 1991.

International Environmental Information Sources. Pira, Randalls Rd., Leatherhead, England KT22 7RU. 0372 376161. 1990. Contains valuable business and technical contacts for environmental information sources worldwide. Information sources cover the following subjects: Air, noise, water and land pollution; waste control and disposal; recycling; energy recovery; nature conservation. Informational sources include associations, research organizations, legislative/regulatory agencies, directories, statistics, on-line databases, magazines and news letters in 24 countries.

Meeting Environmental Work Force Needs. Information Dynamics, 111 Claybrook Dr., Silver Spring, Maryland 20902. 1985. Proceedings of the Second National Conference on Meeting Environmental Workforce Needs, April 1-3, 1985: Education and Training to Assure a Qualified Work Force.

Meteorology of Air Pollution: Implications for the Environment and Its Future. R. S. Scorer. E. Horwood, 66 Wood Lane End, Hemel Hempstead, England HP2 4RG. 1990. Discusses methods of air pollution measurement and future expectations.

Methods for Assessing Exposure of Human and Non-Human Biota. R. G. Tardiff and B. D. Goldstein, eds.

John Wiley & Sons, Inc., 605 3rd Ave., New York, New York 10158-0012. (212) 850-6000. 1991. Provides a critical and collective evaluation of approaches to chemical exposure assessment.

Natural Gas Applications for Air Pollution Control. Nelson E. Hay. Fairmont Press, 700 Indian Trail, Lilburn, Georgia 30247. (404) 925-9388. 1987. Natural gas-induced air pollution.

Optoelectronics for Environmental Science. S. Martellucci and A. N. Chester, eds. Plenum Press, 233 Spring St., New York, New York 10013-1578. (212) 620-8000; (800) 221-9369. 1991. Contribution of lasers and the optical sciences to specific problems, in situ measurements, atmospheric ozone, lidar detection, wind velocity, oceanographic measurements, heavy metal detection, toxic metals, and trace analysis. Proceedings of the 14th course of the International School of Quantum Electronics on Optoelectronics for Environmental Sciences, held September 3-12, 1989, in Erice, Italy.

Particulate Carbon, Atmospheric Life Cycle. Plenum Press, 233 Spring St., New York, New York 10013-1578. (212) 620-8000. 1982.

Pollution and Its Containment. Institution of Civil Engineers Infrastructure Policy Group. Telford, 1 Heron Quay, London, England E14 9XF. (071) 987-6999. 1990.

Pollution: Causes, Effects and Control. Roy Michael Harrison. Royal Society of Chemistry, c/o CRC Press, 2000 Corporate Blvd. N.W., Boca Raton, Florida 33431. (800) 272-7737. 1990. 2nd ed. Deals with environmental pollution and its associated problems and legal ramifications.

Pollution Control and Conservation. M. Kovacs, ed. John Wiley & Sons, Inc., 605 3rd Ave., New York, New York 10158. (212) 850-6000. 1985. Comprehensive view on current knowledge and research in the area of effective protection of air, water, soil and living matter and pollution control.

Preventing Pollution Through Technical Assistance: One State's Experience. Mark H. Dorfman, et al. INFORM Inc., 381 Park Ave. S., New York, New York 10016. (212) 689-4040. 1990. Examines the state of North Carolina's voluntary program aimed at assisting the industry in pollution prevention. It also includes a glossary, a bibliography of information sources and helpful statistical tables of data collected.

TAPPI Environmental Conference Proceedings, Seattle, WA, April 9-11, 1990. TAPPI Press, Technology Park/Atlanta, PO Box 105113, Atlanta, Georgia 30348. (404) 446-1400. 1990. Contains 11 papers presented at the conference covering industrial pollution and its remedies.

Technology of Environmental Pollution Control. Esber I. Shaheen. PennWell Books, PO Box 21288, Tulsa, Oklahoma 74121. (918) 831-9421; (800) 752-9764. 1992. 2d ed. Covers the environmental spectrum in an attempt to update the reader on new technologies and topics regarding pollution control.

Treatability Studies for Hazardous Waste Sites. Hazardous Waste Action Coalition, 1015 15th St. N.W., Suite 802, Washington, District of Columbia 20005. (202) 347-7474. 1990. Assesses the use of treatability studies for evaluating the effectiveness and cost of treatment technologies performed at hazardous waste sites.

Water Pollution Biology. P. D. Abel. John Wiley & Sons, Inc., 605 3rd Ave., New York, New York 10158. (212) 850-6000. 1988. State-of-the-art information on methods of investigating water pollution problems and critically assesses the literature on water pollution. Also included is a discussion on the role of toxicological studies in the monitoring and control of water pollution.

GOVERNMENTAL ORGANIZATIONS

Technical Assistance Program: Waste Minimization and Pollution Prevention. Chief, Technical Assistance Program, 248 Calder Way, 307 University Park, Pennsylvania 16810. (814) 865-0427.

U.S. Environmental Protection Agency: Assistant Administrator for Policy, Planning and Evaluation. 401 M St., S.W., Washington, District of Columbia 20460. (202) 382-4332.

U.S. Environmental Protection Agency: Assistant Administrator for Research and Development. 401 M St., S.W., Washington, District of Columbia 20460. (202) 382-7676.

U.S. Environmental Protection Agency: Office of Modeling and Monitoring Systems and Quality Assurance. 401 M St., S.W., Washington, District of Columbia 20460. (202) 382-5767.

U.S. Environmental Protection Agency: Office of Municipal Pollution Control. 401 M St., S.W., Washington, District of Columbia 20460. (202) 382-5850.

U.S. Environmental Protection Agency: Office of Pollution Prevention. 401 M St., S.W., Washington, District of Columbia 20460.

U.S. Environmental Protection Agency: RCRA Enforcement Division. 401 M St., S.W., Washington, District of Columbia 20460. (202) 382-4808.

HANDBOOKS AND MANUALS

Environmental Sampling and Analysis: A Practical Guide. Lewis Publishers, 200 Corporate Blvd. NW, Boca Raton, Florida 33431. (407) 994-0555 or (800)272-7737. 1991. Topics in environmental monitoring and environmental chemistry.

Indoor Air Quality Design Guidebook. Milton Meckler. Fairmont Press, 700 Indian Trail, Lilburn, Georgia 30247. (404) 925-9388. 1991. Air cleaning systems, the carbon dioxide method, health lead/lag procedure, desiccants, contaminant absorption, effects of sick buildings, assessment of measurement techniques, indoor air quality simulation with computer models, and system design and maintenance techniques. Also available through the Association of Energy Engineers.

Practical Handbook of Ground Water Monitoring. David M. Nielsen. Lewis Publishers, 2000 Corporate Blvd., N.W., Boca Raton, Florida 33431. (407) 994-0555 or (800) 272-7737. 1991. Covers the complete spectrum of state-of-the-science technology applied to investigations of ground water quality. Emphasis is placed on the practical application of current technology, and minimum theory is discussed.

Treatability Manual. U.S. Environmental Protection Agency, Office of Research and Development, 401 M St., SW, Washington, District of Columbia 20460. (202) 260-2090. 1983-. V.1 Treatability data. v.2 Change 2. Indus-

trial Descriptions. v.3 Change 2. Technology for Control/removal of pollutants. v.4. Cost estimating. v.5. Change 2 summary.

ONLINE DATA BASES

Air Pollution Technical Information Center File. U.S. Environmental Protection Agency, Library Services Office, Air Information Center (MD-35), 401 M St. SW, Washington, District of Columbia 20460. (202) 260-2090. Citations and abstracts of the world's literature on air quality and air pollution prevention and control.

CERCLIS. Chemical Information Systems, Inc., 7215 York Rd., Baltimore, Maryland 21212. (301) 321-8440. Information on hazardous waste disposal sites that have either been listed by the EPA on the National Priority List (NPL) or nominated for consideration for the NPL.

Chemical Engineering. McGraw-Hill Science & Engineering Books, 11 W. 19th St., New York, New York 10011. (212) 337-6010. Online version of periodical of the same name.

Chemical Engineering and Biotechnology Abstracts–CEBA. Orbit Search Service, Maxwell Online Inc., 8000 W. Park Dr., McLean, Virginia 22102. (703) 442-0900 or (800) 456-7248. Monthly. Covers theoretical, practical and commercial material on all aspects of processing safety, and the environment. Also covers process and reaction engineering, measurement and process control, environmental protection and safety, plant design and equipment used in chemical engineering and biotechnology. More than 400 of the world's major primary chemical and process engineering journals are scanned to compile the database. Available from ORBIT.

The Chemical Monitor. NewsNet, Inc., 945 Haverford Rd., Bryn Mawr, Pennsylvania 19010. (800) 345-1301.

Computerized Engineering Index–COMPENDEX. Engineering Information Inc., 345 E. 47th St., New York, New York 10017. (212) 705-7600.

Enviro/Energyline Abstracts Plus. R. R. Bowker Co., 121 Chanlon Rd., New Providence, New Jersey 07974. (908) 464-6800.

Environment Reporter. Bureau of National Affairs, 1231 25th St., N.W., Rm. 215, Washington, District of Columbia 20037. (800) 372-1033. Online version of periodical of the same name.

Environmental Periodicals Bibliography. National Information Services Corp., Ste. 6, Wyman Towers, 3100 St. Paul St., Baltimore, Maryland 21218. (410)243-0797. Online version of abstract of same name.

Innovative/Alternative Pollution Control Technology Facility File–IADB. U.S. Environmental Protection Agency, Office of Water Program Operations, 401 M St., S.W., Washington, District of Columbia 20460. (202) 260-2090.

Kirk-Othmer Encyclopedia of Chemical Technology. John Wiley & Sons, Inc., 605 3rd Ave., 5th Floor, New York, New York 10158. (212) 850-6000. Online version of the publication of the same name.

Life Sciences from NTIS. National Technical Information Center for the Utilization of Federal Technology, 5285 Port Royal Rd., Springfield, Virginia 22161. (703) 487-4650.

Los Angeles Catalytic Study–LACS. U.S. Environmental Protection Agency, Office of Monitoring Systems and Quality Assurance, 401 M St., S.W., Washington, District of Columbia 20460. (202) 260-2090.

Membrane & Separation Technology News. NewsNet, Inc., 945 Haverford Rd., Bryn Mawr, Pennsylvania 19010. (800) 345-1301.

Monthly Catalog of United States Government Publications. U.S. G.P.O., Supt. of Docs., PO Box 371954, Pittsburgh, Pennsylvania 15250-7954. (202) 512-0000.

Multinational Environmental Outlook. Business Publishers, Inc., 951 Pershing Dr., Silver Spring, Maryland 20910-4464. (301) 587-6300. Environmental problems and solutions in countries outside the United States and their impact on the United States.

National Technical Information Service. U.S. Department of Commerce, National Technical Information Service, Office of Data Base Services, 5285 Port Royal Rd., Springfield, Virginia 22161. (703) 487-4807. Bibliographic database of government sponsored research and technical reports.

Nuclear Facility Decommissioning and Site Remedial Actions. Oak Ridge National Laboratory, Remedial Action Program Information Center, PO Box 2008, Bldg. 2001, Oak Ridge, Tennessee 37831-6050. (615) 576-0568. Radioactively contaminated facilities and site remedial actions.

PressNet Environmental Reports. Chemical Information Systems, Inc., 7215 York Rd., Baltimore, Maryland 21212. (301) 321-8440.

SCISEARCH. Institute for Scientific Information, University City Science Center, 3501 Market St., Philadelphia, Pennsylvania 19104. (215) 386-0100.

PERIODICALS AND NEWSLETTERS

Air and Water Pollution Control. Bureau of National Affairs, 1231 25th St. N.W., Washington, District of Columbia 20037. (202) 452-4200. 1986-. Biweekly. Review of developments in pollution laws, regulations and trends in government and industry.

Air Pollution Control. Bureau of National Affairs, 1231 25th St. NW, Washington, District of Columbia 20037. (202) 452-4200. Biweekly. A reference and advisory service on the control of air pollution, designed to meet the information needs of individuals responsible for complying with EPA and state air pollution control regulations.

Air Pollution Monitoring and Sampling Newsletter. McIlvaine Co., 2970 Maria Ave., Northbrook, Illinois 60062. (708) 272-0010. 1980-. Monthly. Information on air pollution monitoring and sampling equipment and service.

Air/Water Pollution Report. Business Publishers, Inc., 951 Pershing Dr., Silver Spring, Maryland 20910-4464. (301) 587-6300. 1963-. Weekly. Reports on the hard news and in-depth features for practical use by environmental managers. It keeps readers informed on the latest news from government and industry. Also available online.

Analytical Chemistry. American Chemical Society, 1155 16th St. N.W., Washington, District of Columbia 20036. (800) 227-5558. 1929-. Bimonthly. Articles for chemists, life scientists and engineers.

Atmospheric Environment. Pergamon Microforms International, Inc., Fairview Park, Elmsford, New York 10523. (914) 592-7720. 1966-. Publishes papers on all aspects of man's interactions with his atmospheric environment, including the administrative, economic and political aspects of these interactions. Air pollution research and its applications are covered, taking into account changes in the atmospheric flow patterns, temperature distributions and chemical constitution caused by natural and artificial variations in the earth's surface.

CA Selects: Air Pollution (Books and Reviews). Chemical Abstracts Services, 2540 Olentangy River Rd., Box 3012, Columbus, Ohio 43210. (800) 848-6533. Biweekly. Abstracts on pollution in the atmosphere by fixed and mobile sources; effects of air pollution on animals and vegetation.

CA Selects: Pollution Monitoring. Chemical Abstracts Services, 2540 Olentangy River Rd., Box 3012, Columbus, Ohio 43210. (800) 848-6533. 1978-. Biweekly. Abstracts on the analytical techniques and equipment relating to monitoring pollution.

Chemical & Engineering News. American Chemical Society, 1155 16th St. N.W., Washington, District of Columbia 20036. (800) 227-5558. Weekly. Cites technical and business developments in the chemical process industry.

Chemical Engineering. McGraw-Hill Science & Engineering Books, 11 W. 19th St., New York, New York 10011. (212) 337-6010. Monthly. Articles on new engineering techniques and equipment. Also available online.

Conservationist. New York State Dept. of Environmental Conservation, 50 Wolf Rd., Albany, New York 12233. (518) 457-6668. 1946-. Bimonthly. Covers all aspects of conservation and outdoor recreation, scientific information, art and history of New York State.

CRC Critical Reviews in Environmental Control. CRC Press, 2000 Corporate Blvd. N.W., Boca Raton, Florida 33431. (800) 272-7737. 1970-. Quarterly. Provides qualitative reviews of scientific literature published in the discipline.

Current Industrial Reports. U.S. G.P.O., Washington, District of Columbia 20401. (202) 512-0000. Annual. Statistical data on air pollution control industry.

Dickey Data. W.S. Dickey Clay Mfg. Co., Box 6, Pittsburgh, Kansas 66762. (316) 231-1400. Quarterly. Wastewater facilities, drainage, plumbing, pollution control and building materials industry.

The Earth Care Annual. Russell Wild, ed. Rodale Press, 33 E. Minon St., Emmaus, Pennsylvania 18098. (215) 967-5171; (800) 322-6333. 1990-. Annually. Organized in alphabetical sections such as garbage, greenhouse effect, oceans, ozone, toxic waste, and wildlife, the annual presents environmental problems and offers innovative working solutions.

Environment Report. Trends Publishing, Inc., 1079 National Press Bldg., Washington, District of Columbia 20045. (202) 393-0031. Semimonthly. Developments in environment, ecology and pollution abatement, with emphasis on policy, research, and development.

Environment Reporter. Bureau of National Affairs, 1231 25th St. NW, Washington, District of Columbia 20037. (800) 372-1033. Weekly. Issues of pollution control and environmental activity. Also available online.

Environmental and Experimental Botany. Pergamon Microforms International, Inc., Fairview Park, Elmsford, New York 10523. (914) 592-7720. 1960-. An international journal covering radiation botany, photobotany, chemical mutagenesis, anatomy and morphology, cytogenetics and somatic cell genetics.

Environmental Geology & Water Sciences. Springer-Verlag, 175 Fifth Avenue, New York, New York 10010. (212) 460-1500. Bimonthly. Covers interactions between humanity and Earth.

Environmental Health Letter. Business Publishers, Inc., 951 Pershing Dr., Silver Spring, Maryland 20910-4464. (301) 587-6300. 1961-. Biweekly. Covers areas such as: indoor air, asbestos health effects, toxic substances testing, health problems at wastewater plants, risk-based sludge rules, medical waste, developmental toxicity risk assessment, animal carcinogen tests, pesticide risk, air toxics, aerospace chemicals, lead, radionuclide emissions, state right-to-know statutes, and incinerator emissions.

Environmental Pollution & Control. National Technical Information Service, 5285 Port Royal Rd., Springfield, Virginia 22161. (703) 487-4650. Weekly. Covers air, noise, solid waste, water pollution, radiation, environmental health and safety, pesticide pollution and control.

Environmental Professional. National Association of Environmental Professionals, P.O. Box 15210, Alexandria, Virginia 22309-0210. (703) 660-2364. Quarterly. Covers effective impact assessment, regulation, and environmental protection.

Environmental Progress. American Institute of Chemical Engineers, 345 E. 47th St., New York, New York 10017. (212) 705-7338. Quarterly. Deals with environmental policies, protection and management-especially relating to chemicals.

Environmental Science & Technology. American Chemical Society, 1155 16th St. N.W., Washington, District of Columbia 20036. (800) 227-5558. Covers pollution, sanitary chemistry and environmental engineering.

Environmental Software. Computational Mechanics Publications Inc., Suite 6200, 400 W. Cummings Park, Woburn, Massachusetts 01801. Quarterly. Computer programs for environmental monitoring.

Environmental Toxicology and Chemistry. Society of Environmental Toxicology and Chemistry. Pergamon Microforms International, Inc., Fairview Park, Elmsford, New York 10523. (914) 592-7720. 1981-. Monthly. Contains information on environmental toxicology, and chemistry, including the application of science to hazard assessment.

Georgia Operator. Georgia Water and Pollution Control Association, 2532 Bolton Rd. N.W., Atlanta, Georgia 30318. 1963-. Quarterly.

International Pollution Control. Scranton Pub. Co., 434 S. Wabash Ave., Chicago, Illinois 60605. 1972-. Quarterly.

Journal of Analytical Toxicology. Preston Publications, PO Box 48312, 7800 Merrimac, Niles, Illinois 60648. (708) 965-0566. Bimonthly. Articles on industrial toxicology, environmental pollution and pharmaceuticals.

Journal of Atmospheric Sciences. American Meteorology Society, 45 Beacon Street, Boston, Massachusetts 02108.

(617) 227-2425. Biweekly. Articles on the atmosphere of the earth and other planets.

Journal of Environmental Science and Health. Marcel Dekker, Inc., 270 Madison Ave., New York, New York 10016. (212) 696-9000. Bimonthly. Concerns pesticides, food contaminants, chemical carcinogens, and agricultural wastes.

Michigan Waste Report. Michigan Waste Report, Inc., 400 Ann, SW, Suite 204, Grand Rapids, Michigan 49504. (616) 363-3262. Biweekly. Covers information about waste management.

National Environmental Enforcement Journal. National Association of Attorneys General, 444 N. Capitol, N.W., Suite 403, Washington, District of Columbia 20001. Monthly. Litigation and inventive settlements in cases of waste dumping and pollution.

Pollution Engineering. Cahners Publishing Co., 249 W. 17th St., New York, New York 10011. (212) 645-0067. 1969-. Monthly.

Pollution Equipment News Catalog and Buyers' Guide. Rimbach Publishing, Inc., 8650 Babcock Blvd., Pittsburgh, Pennsylvania 15237. (412) 364-5366. Annual. Product/service supplier information including specification, purchase, installation, and maintenance of pollution control equipment.

Texas Pollution Report. Report Publications, P.O. Box 12368, Austin, Texas 78711. (512) 478-5663. Weekly. Covers regulatory activity, court decisions and legislation.

Water and Pollution Control. Southam Business Pub. Inc., 1450 Don Mills Rd., Don Mills, Ontario, Canada M3B 2X7. 1893-. Monthly. Formerly Canada Municipal Utilities.

RESEARCH CENTERS AND INSTITUTES

Center for Air Pollution Impact and Trend Analysis. Washington University, Campus Box 1124, 319 Urbauer, St. Louis, Missouri 63130. (314) 889-6099.

Engineering Research Center for Hazardous Substances Control. University of California, Los Angeles, 6722 Boelter Hall, Los Angeles, California 90024. (213) 206-3071.

Environmental Engineering and Sciences Department. Virginia Polytech Institute and State University, 330 Norris Hall, Department of Civil Engineering, Blacksburg, Virginia 24061. (703) 961-6635.

Mississippi State University, Research Center. John C. Stennis Space Center, Stennis Space Center, Mississippi 39529-6000. (601) 688-3227.

National Center for Intermedia Transport Research. University of California, Los Angeles, 5531 Boelter, Department of Chemical Engineering, Los Angeles, California 90024-1592. (213) 825-9741.

Tufts University. Curtis Hall, 474 Boston Avenue, Medford, Massachusetts 02155. (617) 381-3486.

University of Wisconsin-Madison, Center for Human Systems. 1042 WARF Building, 610 North Walnut Street, Madison, Wisconsin 53705. (608) 262-9937.

STATISTICS SOURCES

Pollution Control. FIND/SVP, 625 Avenue of the Americas, New York, New York 10011. (212) 645-4500. 1991.

Tracking Toxic Substances at Industrial Facilities: Engineering Mass Balance Versus Materials Accounting. National Research Council–Committee to Evaluate Mass Balance Information for Facilities Handling Toxic Substances. National Academy Press, 2101 Constitution Ave., NW, Washington, District of Columbia 20418. (202) 334-3343. 1990. Covers measurement of factory and trade waste and hazardous substances.

TRADE ASSOCIATIONS AND PROFESSIONAL SOCIETIES

Air and Waste Management Association. Box 2861, Pittsburgh, Pennsylvania 15230. (412) 232-3444.

American Academy of Environmental Engineers. 130 Holiday Court, #100, Annapolis, Maryland 21404. (301) 266-3311.

American Institute of Chemical Engineers. 345 East 47th St., New York, New York 10017. (212) 705-7338.

American Institute of Chemists. 7315 Wisconsin Ave., Bethesda, Maryland 20814. (301) 652-2447.

American Land Resource Association. 1516 P St., N.W., Washington, District of Columbia 20033. (202) 265-5000.

Association of Environmental Engineering Professors. Department of Civil Engineering, Virginia Polytechnic Institute and State University, Blacksburg, Virginia 24061. (703) 231-6021.

Association of Local Air Pollution Control Officials. 444 North Capitol St., N.W., Washington, District of Columbia 20001 (202) 624-7864.

Association of State and Interstate Water Pollution Control Administrators. 444 N. Capitol St., N.W., Suite 330, Washington, District of Columbia 20001. (202) 624-7782.

CEIP Fund. 68 Harrison Ave., 5th Fl., Boston, Massachusetts 02111. (617) 426-4375.

Center for Environmental Management. Tufts University, Curtis Hall, 474 Boston Ave., Medford, Massachusetts 02155. (617) 381-3486.

Community Environmental Council. 930 Miramonte Drive, Santa Barbara, California 93109. (805) 963-0583.

Council of Pollution Control Financing Agencies. 1225 I. St., N.W., Suite 300, Washington, District of Columbia 20005. (202) 682-3996.

Environmental Industry Council. 1825 K St., N.W., Suite 210, Washington, District of Columbia 20006. (202) 331-7706.

Industrial Gas Clearing Institute. 1707 L St., N.W., Suite 570, Washington, District of Columbia 20036. (202) 457-0911.

International Society for Ecological Modeling/North American Chapter. Water Quality Division, South Florida Water Management District, PO Box 24680, West Palm Beach, Florida 33416. (407) 686-8800.

Intersociety Committee on Methods for Air Sampling and Analysis. 12113 Shropshire Blvd., Austin, Texas 78753. (512) 835-5118.

Manufacturers of Emission Controls Association. 1707 L St., N.W., Suite 570, Washington, District of Columbia 20036. (202) 296-4797.

National Air Toxics Information Clearinghouse. Research Triangle Park, North Carolina 27711. (919) 541-0850.

State and Territorial Air Pollution Program Administrators. 444 North Capitol St., Washington, District of Columbia 20001. (202) 624-7864.

Waste Systems Institute of Michigan, Inc. 400 Ann, N.W., Suite 204, Grand Rapids, Michigan 49504. (616) 363-3262.

POLLUTION, ENVIRONMENTAL EFFECTS OF
See: POLLUTION

POLLUTION, RADIATION
See: RADIATION POLLUTION

POLYCHLORINATED BIPHENYLS
See: PCBS

POLYCULTURE
See also: AGRICULTURE; INTENSIVE AGRICULTURE; ORGANIC GARDENING AND FARMING

ABSTRACTING AND INDEXING SERVICES

Agrindex. AGRIS Coordinating Center, Via delle Terme di Caracalla, Rome, Italy I-00100. 61 0181-FA01. 1975-.

ASFA Aquaculture Abstracts. Cambridge Scientific Abstracts, Inc., 5161 River Rd., Bethesda, Maryland 20816. (301) 961-6750. 1984.

Environment Abstracts. Bowker A & I Publishing, 121 Chanlon Rd., New Providence, New Jersey 07974. (908) 464-6800. 1974-.

Environment Index. Environment Information Center, Index Research Department, 124 E. 39th St., New York, New York 10016. 1971-. Annual.

Environmental Information Connection–EIC. Planning Information Program, Dept. of Urban and Regional Planning, University of Illinois, 1003 West Nevada, Urbana, Illinois 61801. (217) 333-1369. Also available online.

Environmental Periodicals Bibliography. Environmental Studies Institute, International Academy at Santa Barbara, 800 Garden St., Suite D, Santa Barbara, California 93101. (805) 965-5010. Also available online.

BIBLIOGRAPHIES

EPA Publications Bibliography. U.S. Environmental Protection Agency, Library Systems Branch, 401 M St., SW, Washington, District of Columbia 20460. (202) 260-2090. Quarterly.

ENCYCLOPEDIAS AND DICTIONARIES

Van Nostrand's Scientific Encyclopedia. Glenn D. Considine, ed. Van Nostrand Reinhold, 115 5th Ave., New York, New York 10003. (212) 254-3232. 1983. Sixth edition. Includes all broad subject areas in science.

ONLINE DATA BASES

Enviro/Energyline Abstracts Plus. R. R. Bowker Co., 121 Chanlon Rd., New Providence, New Jersey 07974. (908) 464-6800.

Environmental Periodicals Bibliography. National Information Services Corp., Ste. 6, Wyman Towers, 3100 St. Paul St., Baltimore, Maryland 21218. (410)243-0797. Online version of abstract of same name.

POLYOLEFINS

ABSTRACTING AND INDEXING SERVICES

Chemical Abstracts. Chemical Abstracts Service, 2540 Olentangy River Rd., PO Box 3012, Columbus, Ohio 43210. (800) 848-6533. 1907-.

Environment Abstracts. Bowker A & I Publishing, 121 Chanlon Rd., New Providence, New Jersey 07974. (908) 464-6800. 1974-.

Environment Index. Environment Information Center, Index Research Department, 124 E. 39th St., New York, New York 10016. 1971-. Annual.

Environmental Information Connection–EIC. Planning Information Program, Dept. of Urban and Regional Planning, University of Illinois, 1003 West Nevada, Urbana, Illinois 61801. (217) 333-1369. Also available online.

Environmental Periodicals Bibliography. Environmental Studies Institute, International Academy at Santa Barbara, 800 Garden St., Suite D, Santa Barbara, California 93101. (805) 965-5010. Also available online.

Science Citation Index. Institute for Scientific Information, 3501 Market St., Philadelphia, Pennsylvania 19104. 1961-.

BIBLIOGRAPHIES

EPA Publications Bibliography. U.S. Environmental Protection Agency, Library Systems Branch, 401 M St., SW, Washington, District of Columbia 20460. (202) 260-2090. Quarterly.

ENCYCLOPEDIAS AND DICTIONARIES

Van Nostrand's Scientific Encyclopedia. Glenn D. Considine, ed. Van Nostrand Reinhold, 115 5th Ave., New York, New York 10003. (212) 254-3232. 1983. Sixth edition. Includes all broad subject areas in science.

GENERAL WORKS

Degradation and Stabilization of Polyolefins. Norman S. Allen. Applied Science Publications, 655 Avenue of the Americas, New York, New York 10010. (212) 989-5800. 1983.

History of Polyolefins. Raymond B. Seymour. Kluwer Academic Publishers, 101 Philip Dr., Assinippi Park, Norwell, Massachusetts 02061. (617) 871-6600. 1987.

ONLINE DATA BASES

CAS Source Index–CASSI. Chemical Abstracts Service, 2540 Olentangy River Rd., P.O. Box 3012, Columbus, Ohio 43210. (800) 848-6533 or (614) 421-3600. A listing of bibliographic and library holdings information for scientific and technical primary literature relevant to the chemical sciences.

Chemical Abstracts-CA. Chemical Abstracts Service, 2540 Olentangy River Rd., P.O. Box 3012, Columbus, Ohio 43210. (800) 848-6533 or (614) 421-3600. Information sources include 9000 journals, patents from 27 countries, two industrial property organizations, new books, conference proceedings, and government research reports.

Enviro/Energyline Abstracts Plus. R. R. Bowker Co., 121 Chanlon Rd., New Providence, New Jersey 07974. (908) 464-6800.

Environmental Periodicals Bibliography. National Information Services Corp., Ste. 6, Wyman Towers, 3100 St. Paul St., Baltimore, Maryland 21218. (410)243-0797. Online version of abstract of same name.

TRADE ASSOCIATIONS AND PROFESSIONAL SOCIETIES

American Chemical Society. 1155 16th St., N.W., Washington, District of Columbia 20036. (202) 872-4600.

POLYURETHANE FOAM

ABSTRACTING AND INDEXING SERVICES

Biotechnology Research Abstracts. Cambridge Scientific Abstracts, 5161 River Rd., Bethesda, Maryland 20816. (301) 961-6750. Monthly. Includes such broad areas as genetic intervention, biochemical genetics, and microbiological techniques.

Chemical Abstracts. Chemical Abstracts Service, 2540 Olentangy River Rd., PO Box 3012, Columbus, Ohio 43210. (800) 848-6533. 1907-.

Environment Abstracts. Bowker A & I Publishing, 121 Chanlon Rd., New Providence, New Jersey 07974. (908) 464-6800. 1974-.

Environment Index. Environment Information Center, Index Research Department, 124 E. 39th St., New York, New York 10016. 1971-. Annual.

Environmental Information Connection–EIC. Planning Information Program, Dept. of Urban and Regional Planning, University of Illinois, 1003 West Nevada, Urbana, Illinois 61801. (217) 333-1369. Also available online.

Environmental Periodicals Bibliography. Environmental Studies Institute, International Academy at Santa Barba-

ra, 800 Garden St., Suite D, Santa Barbara, California 93101. (805) 965-5010. Also available online.

Science Citation Index. Institute for Scientific Information, 3501 Market St., Philadelphia, Pennsylvania 19104. 1961-.

BIBLIOGRAPHIES

CFCs & the Polyurethane Industry: A Compilation of Technical Publications. Society of the Plastics Industry, Polyurethane Division, 355 Lexington Ave., New York, New York 10017. (212)351-5425. 1992. Bibliography of plastic foams, chlorofluorocarbons and polyurethanes.

EPA Publications Bibliography. U.S. Environmental Protection Agency, Library Systems Branch, 401 M St., SW, Washington, District of Columbia 20460. (202) 260-2090. Quarterly.

A Summary of the NBS Literature Reviews on the Chemical Nature and Toxicity of the Pyrolysis and Combustion Products from Seven Plastics. Barbara C. Levin. National Technical Information Service, 5285 Port Royal Rd., Springfield, Virginia 22161. (703) 487-4650. 1986. Acrylonitrile-butadiene-styrenes (ABS), nylons, polyesters, polyethylenes, polystyrenes, poly(vinyl chlorides), and rigid polyurethane foams.

ENCYCLOPEDIAS AND DICTIONARIES

Van Nostrand's Scientific Encyclopedia. Glenn D. Considine, ed. Van Nostrand Reinhold, 115 5th Ave., New York, New York 10003. (212) 254-3232. 1983. Sixth edition. Includes all broad subject areas in science.

GENERAL WORKS

Advances in Food Emulsions and Foams. Elsevier Science Publishing Co., 655 Avenue of the Americas, New York, New York 10010. (212) 984-5800. 1989.

Foams: Physics, Chemistry, and Structure. A. J. Wilson. Springer-Verlag, 175 5th Ave., New York, New York 10010. (212) 460-1500. 1989.

Isolating Organic Water Pollutants: XAD Resins, Urethane Foams, Solvent Extraction. Ronald G. Webb. National Environmental Research Center, Corvallis, Oregon 1975. Isolation and purification of water pollutants.

ONLINE DATA BASES

Chemical Abstracts-CA. Chemical Abstracts Service, 2540 Olentangy River Rd., P.O. Box 3012, Columbus, Ohio 43210. (800) 848-6533 or (614) 421-3600. Information sources include 9000 journals, patents from 27 countries, two industrial property organizations, new books, conference proceedings, and government research reports.

Enviro/Energyline Abstracts Plus. R. R. Bowker Co., 121 Chanlon Rd., New Providence, New Jersey 07974. (908) 464-6800.

Environmental Periodicals Bibliography. National Information Services Corp., Ste. 6, Wyman Towers, 3100 St. Paul St., Baltimore, Maryland 21218. (410)243-0797. Online version of abstract of same name.

TRADE ASSOCIATIONS AND PROFESSIONAL SOCIETIES

Polyurethane Division, Society of the Plastics Industry. 355 Lexington Ave., New York, New York 10017. (212) 351-5425.

Polyurethane Foam Association. P.O. Box 1459, Wayne, New Jersey 07470. (201) 633-9044.

Polyurethane Manufacturers Association. 800 Roosevelt Rd., Bldg. C, Suite 20, Glen Ellyn, Illinois 61037. (708) 858-2670.

POLYVINYL ACETATE

ABSTRACTING AND INDEXING SERVICES

Biotechnology Research Abstracts. Cambridge Scientific Abstracts, 5161 River Rd., Bethesda, Maryland 20816. (301) 961-6750. Monthly. Includes such broad areas as genetic intervention, biochemical genetics, and microbiological techniques.

Chemical Abstracts. Chemical Abstracts Service, 2540 Olentangy River Rd., PO Box 3012, Columbus, Ohio 43210. (800) 848-6533. 1907-.

Environment Abstracts. Bowker A & I Publishing, 121 Chanlon Rd., New Providence, New Jersey 07974. (908) 464-6800. 1974-.

Environment Index. Environment Information Center, Index Research Department, 124 E. 39th St., New York, New York 10016. 1971-. Annual.

Environmental Information Connection–EIC. Planning Information Program, Dept. of Urban and Regional Planning, University of Illinois, 1003 West Nevada, Urbana, Illinois 61801. (217) 333-1369. Also available online.

Environmental Periodicals Bibliography. Environmental Studies Institute, International Academy at Santa Barbara, 800 Garden St., Suite D, Santa Barbara, California 93101. (805) 965-5010. Also available online.

Science Citation Index. Institute for Scientific Information, 3501 Market St., Philadelphia, Pennsylvania 19104. 1961-.

BIBLIOGRAPHIES

EPA Publications Bibliography. U.S. Environmental Protection Agency, Library Systems Branch, 401 M St., SW, Washington, District of Columbia 20460. (202) 260-2090. Quarterly.

ENCYCLOPEDIAS AND DICTIONARIES

Ullmanns Encyclopedia of Industrial Chemistry. Hans Jurgen Arpe and Wolfgang Gerhartz, eds. VCH Publishers, 303 NW 12th Ave., Deerfield Beach, Florida 33442-1788. (305) 428-5566. 1990. Designed to keep up with the broad spectrum of chemical technology. Thirty-six volumes of the encyclopedia have been divided into two sets: the 28 A volumes contain alphabetically arranged articles on chemicals, product groups, processes and technological concepts; and the 8 B volumes are compendia of basic knowledge in industrial chemistry.

Van Nostrand's Scientific Encyclopedia. Glenn D. Considine, ed. Van Nostrand Reinhold, 115 5th Ave., New

York, New York 10003. (212) 254-3232. 1983. Sixth edition. Includes all broad subject areas in science.

ONLINE DATA BASES

CAS Source Index–CASSI. Chemical Abstracts Service, 2540 Olentangy River Rd., P.O. Box 3012, Columbus, Ohio 43210. (800) 848-6533 or (614) 421-3600. A listing of bibliographic and library holdings information for scientific and technical primary literature relevant to the chemical sciences.

Chemical Abstracts-CA. Chemical Abstracts Service, 2540 Olentangy River Rd., P.O. Box 3012, Columbus, Ohio 43210. (800) 848-6533 or (614) 421-3600. Information sources include 9000 journals, patents from 27 countries, two industrial property organizations, new books, conference proceedings, and government research reports.

Enviro/Energyline Abstracts Plus. R. R. Bowker Co., 121 Chanlon Rd., New Providence, New Jersey 07974. (908) 464-6800.

Environmental Periodicals Bibliography. National Information Services Corp., Ste. 6, Wyman Towers, 3100 St. Paul St., Baltimore, Maryland 21218. (410)243-0797. Online version of abstract of same name.

TRADE ASSOCIATIONS AND PROFESSIONAL SOCIETIES

American Chemical Society. 1155 16th St., N.W., Washington, District of Columbia 20036. (202) 872-4600.

POLYVINYL CHLORINE

ABSTRACTING AND INDEXING SERVICES

Chemical Abstracts. Chemical Abstracts Service, 2540 Olentangy River Rd., PO Box 3012, Columbus, Ohio 43210. (800) 848-6533. 1907-.

Environment Abstracts. Bowker A & I Publishing, 121 Chanlon Rd., New Providence, New Jersey 07974. (908) 464-6800. 1974-.

Environment Index. Environment Information Center, Index Research Department, 124 E. 39th St., New York, New York 10016. 1971-. Annual.

Environmental Information Connection–EIC. Planning Information Program, Dept. of Urban and Regional Planning, University of Illinois, 1003 West Nevada, Urbana, Illinois 61801. (217) 333-1369. Also available online.

Environmental Periodicals Bibliography. Environmental Studies Institute, International Academy at Santa Barbara, 800 Garden St., Suite D, Santa Barbara, California 93101. (805) 965-5010. Also available online.

Science Citation Index. Institute for Scientific Information, 3501 Market St., Philadelphia, Pennsylvania 19104. 1961-.

BIBLIOGRAPHIES

EPA Publications Bibliography. U.S. Environmental Protection Agency, Library Systems Branch, 401 M St., SW, Washington, District of Columbia 20460. (202) 260-2090. Quarterly.

ENCYCLOPEDIAS AND DICTIONARIES

Ullmanns Encyclopedia of Industrial Chemistry. Hans Jurgen Arpe and Wolfgang Gerhartz, eds. VCH Publishers, 303 NW 12th Ave., Deerfield Beach, Florida 33442-1788. (305) 428-5566. 1990. Designed to keep up with the broad spectrum of chemical technology. Thirty-six volumes of the encyclopedia have been divided into two sets: the 28 A volumes contain alphabetically arranged articles on chemicals, product groups, processes and technological concepts; and the 8 B volumes are compendia of basic knowledge in industrial chemistry.

Van Nostrand's Scientific Encyclopedia. Glenn D. Considine, ed. Van Nostrand Reinhold, 115 5th Ave., New York, New York 10003. (212) 254-3232. 1983. Sixth edition. Includes all broad subject areas in science.

ONLINE DATA BASES

CAS Source Index–CASSI. Chemical Abstracts Service, 2540 Olentangy River Rd., P.O. Box 3012, Columbus, Ohio 43210. (800) 848-6533 or (614) 421-3600. A listing of bibliographic and library holdings information for scientific and technical primary literature relevant to the chemical sciences.

Chemical Abstracts-CA. Chemical Abstracts Service, 2540 Olentangy River Rd., P.O. Box 3012, Columbus, Ohio 43210. (800) 848-6533 or (614) 421-3600. Information sources include 9000 journals, patents from 27 countries, two industrial property organizations, new books, conference proceedings, and government research reports.

Enviro/Energyline Abstracts Plus. R. R. Bowker Co., 121 Chanlon Rd., New Providence, New Jersey 07974. (908) 464-6800.

Environmental Periodicals Bibliography. National Information Services Corp., Ste. 6, Wyman Towers, 3100 St. Paul St., Baltimore, Maryland 21218. (410)243-0797. Online version of abstract of same name.

TRADE ASSOCIATIONS AND PROFESSIONAL SOCIETIES

American Chemical Society. 1155 16th St., N.W., Washington, District of Columbia 20036. (202) 872-4600.

POPULATION

ABSTRACTING AND INDEXING SERVICES

Applied Ecology Abstracts Studies in Renewable Natural Resources. Information Retrieval Ltd., 1911 Jefferson Davis Highway, Arlington, Virginia 22202. 1975-. Monthly.

ASFA Aquaculture Abstracts. Cambridge Scientific Abstracts, Inc., 5161 River Rd., Bethesda, Maryland 20816. (301) 961-6750. 1984.

Biological Abstracts. BIOSIS, 2100 Arch St., Philadelphia, Pennsylvania 19103-1399. (215) 587-4800. 1927-.

Biological and Agricultural Index. H.W. Wilson Co., 950 University Ave., Bronx, New York 10452. (800) 367-6770. 1916-. Monthly.

Biology Digest. Data Courier, Plexus Pub Inc., 143 Old Marlton Pike, Medford, New Jersey 08055. 1974-. Monthly. Abstracts biology periodicals.

Biotechnology Research Abstracts. Cambridge Scientific Abstracts, 5161 River Rd., Bethesda, Maryland 20816. (301) 961-6750. Monthly. Includes such broad areas as genetic intervention, biochemical genetics, and microbiological techniques.

Current Advances in Ecological and Environmental Science. Pergamon Microforms International, Inc., Fairview Park, Elmsford, New York 10523. (914) 592-7720. 1989-. Monthly. Current literature searching service includingjournals, reports, abstracts, etc. This service is available online as part of the CABS database on the hosts BRS and ORBIT search service.

Ecological Abstracts. Geo Abstracts Ltd. Elsevier Applied Science, Crown House, Linton Rd., Barking, England IG 11 8JU. 1974-. Derived from over 600 leading ecological and environmental journals, plus books, conference proceedings, reports and theses.

Ecology Abstracts. Cambridge Scientific Abstracts, 5161 River Rd., Bethesda, Maryland 20816. (301) 961-6750. Monthly.

Environment Abstracts. Bowker A & I Publishing, 121 Chanlon Rd., New Providence, New Jersey 07974. (908) 464-6800. 1974-.

Environment Index. Environment Information Center, Index Research Department, 124 E. 39th St., New York, New York 10016. 1971-. Annual.

Environmental Information Connection-EIC. Planning Information Program, Dept. of Urban and Regional Planning, University of Illinois, 1003 West Nevada, Urbana, Illinois 61801. (217) 333-1369. Also available online.

Environmental Periodicals Bibliography. Environmental Studies Institute, International Academy at Santa Barbara, 800 Garden St., Suite D, Santa Barbara, California 93101. (805) 965-5010. Also available online.

General Science Index. H. W. Wilson Co., 950 University Ave., Bronx, New York 10452. 1978-. Monthly, also issued in annual cumulation. Cumulative subject index to English language periodicals in the subject fields of astronomy, botany, chemistry, earth science, environment and conservation, food and nutrition, genetics, mathematics, medicine and health, microbiology, oceanography, physics, physiology and zoology.

Genetics Abstracts. Cambridge Scientific Abstracts, 5161 River Rd., Bethesda, Maryland 20816. (301) 961-6750. 1968-. Monthly. Formerly published by Information Retrieval Ltd., London England. Published by Cambridge Scientific Abstracts since 1982.

Geographical Abstracts. London School of Economics, Dept. of Geography, Regency House, 34 Duke St., London, England 1966-. Continued by Geo Abstracts issued in 6 parts: Pt. A. Landforms and the quaternary; Pt. B. Biogeography and Climatology; Pt. C. Economic geography; Pt. D. Social geography and cartography; Pt. E. Sedimentology; Pt. F. Regional and community planning.

Multimedia Index to Ecology. National Information Center for Educational Media, University of Southern California, Los Angeles, California 90007.

Pollution Abstracts. Cambridge Scientific Abstracts, 5161 River Rd., Bethesda, Maryland 20816. (301) 961-6750. Six/year. Indexes worldwide technical literature on environmental pollution. Covers air pollution, marine and freshwater pollution, sewage and wastewater treatment, waste management, toxicology and health, noise pollution, radiation, land pollution, and environmental policies, programs, legislation, and education. Also available online.

BIBLIOGRAPHIES

A Bibliographic Guide to Population Geography. Wilbur Zelinsky. University of Chicago Press, 5801 Ellis Ave., 4th Fl., Chicago, Illinois 60637. (312) 702-7700; (800) 621-2736. 1976.

Current Contents. Agriculture, Biology and Environmental Sciences. Institute for Scientific Information, 3501 Market St., Philadelphia, Pennsylvania 19104. (800) 523-1857. 1973-. Previous title: Current Contents. Agricultural, Food & Veterinary Sciences. Gives the table of contents of periodicals in the fields of agriculture, biology, environmental and related areas.

EPA Publications Bibliography. U.S. Environmental Protection Agency, Library Systems Branch, 401 M St., SW, Washington, District of Columbia 20460. (202) 260-2090. Quarterly.

Population Education: Sources and Resources. Judith Seltzer and John Robinson. Population Reference Bureau, 777 14th St. N.W., Washington, District of Columbia 20005. (202) 639-8040. 1979.

A Retrospective Bibliography of American Demographic History from Colonial Times to 1983. David R. Gerhan and Robert V. Wells. Greenwood Publishing Group, Inc., 88 Post Rd. W., Box 5007, Westport, Connecticut 06881. (203) 226-3571. 1989.

DIRECTORIES

Ecological Society of America Bulletin–Directory of Members Issue. Ecological Society of America, c/o Dr. Duncan Patten, Center for Environmental Studies, Arizona State University, Tempe, Arizona 85287. (602) 965-3000.

ENCYCLOPEDIAS AND DICTIONARIES

Cambridge Dictionary of Biology. Peter M. B. Walker. Cambridge University Press, 40 W. 20th St., New York, New York 10011. (212) 924-3900 or (800) 227-0247. 1989. Includes 10,000 terms in zoology, botany, biochemistry, molecular biology and genetics. Previously published under the title Chambers Biology Dictionary.

Cambridge Encyclopedia of Life Sciences. A. E. Friday and David S. Ingram. Cambridge University Press, 40 W 20th St., New York, New York 10011. (212) 924-3900 or (800) 227-0247. 1985. Includes all topics under biology and ecology.

A Concise Dictionary of Biology. Elizabeth Martin, ed. Oxford University Press, 200 Madison Ave., New York, New York 10016. (212) 679-7300 or (800) 334-4249. 1990. New edition. Derived from the Concise Science Dictionary, published in 1984.

Encyclopedia of Bioethics. Warren T. Reich, ed. Free Press, 866 3rd Ave., New York, New York 10022. (212) 702-2004 or (800) 257-5755. 1978. Four volumes. Includes review articles in the field of bioethics by 330 reviewers representing fields such as: surgery, Islamic studies, pediatrics, philosophy, environmental sciences, theology, psychiatry, etc.

Grzimek's Encyclopedia of Ecology. Bernhard Grzimek. Van Nostrand Reinhold, 115 5th Ave., New York, New York 10003. (212) 254-3232. 1976.

McGraw-Hill Encyclopedia of Environmental Science. Sybil P. Parker. McGraw-Hill Science & Engineering Books, 11 W. 19th St., New York, New York 10011. (212) 337-6010. 1980. Covers ecology, man's influence on nature, and environmental protection.

McGraw-Hill Encyclopedia of Science and Technology. McGraw-Hill, 1221 Avenue of the Americas, New York, New York 10020. (212) 512-2000 or (800) 262-4729. 1992. Seventh edition. Issued in multiple volumes including index. Includes all science and technology broad subject areas.

North American Reference Encyclopedia of Ecology and Pollution. William White. North American Pub. Co., 401 N. Broad St., Philadelphia, Pennsylvania 19108. (215) 238-5300. 1972.

Van Nostrand's Scientific Encyclopedia. Glenn D. Considine, ed. Van Nostrand Reinhold, 115 5th Ave., New York, New York 10003. (212) 254-3232. 1983. Sixth edition. Includes all broad subject areas in science.

GENERAL WORKS

Distributional Aspects of Human Fertility: A Global Comparative Study. Wolfgang Lutz. Academic Press, c/o Harcourt Brace Jovanovich Inc., 6277 Sea Harbor Dr., Orlando, Florida 32887. (800) 346-8648. 1989. Studies in population dealing with family characteristics, population growth, birth intervals, fertility and maternal age.

Life History and Ecology of the Slider Turtle. J. Whitfield Gibbons. Smithsonian Institution Press, 470 L'Enfant Plaza #7100, Washington, District of Columbia 20560. (800) 782-4612. 1990. Deals with all that is known about a species, its taxonomic status and genetics, reproduction and growth, population structure and demography, population ecology, and bioenergetics.

Magill's Survey of Science. Life Science Series. Frank N. Magill, ed. Salem Press, PO Box 50062, Pasadena, California 91105. 1991. Six volumes. Contents: v.1. A-Central and peripheral nervous system functions; v.2. Central metabolism regulation - eukaryotic transcriptional control; v.3. Positive and negative eukaryotic transcriptional control - mammalian hormones; v.4. Hormones and behavior - muscular contraction; v.5. Muscular contraction and relaxation - sexual reproduction in plants; v.6. Reproductive behavior and mating - X inactivation and the Lyon hypothesis.

Research Priorities for Conservation Biology. Michael E. Soulfe and Kathryn A. Kohm, eds. Island Press, 1718 Connecticut Ave. N.W., Suite 300, Washington, District of Columbia 20009. (202) 232-7933. 1989. Proposes an urgent research agenda to improve our understanding and preservation of biological diversity.

Turtles of the World. Carl H. Ernst and Roger W. Barbour. Smithsonian Institution Press, 470 L'Enfant Plaza #7100, Washington, District of Columbia 20560. (800) 782-4612. 1989. Comprehensive coverage of the world's 257 turtle species.

Where Have All the Birds Gone?. John Terborgh. Princeton University Press, 41 Williams St., Princeton, New Jersey 08540. (609) 258-4900. 1989. Includes topics such as: population monitoring, ecological consequences of fragmentation, evolution of migration, social and territorial behaviors of wintering songbirds.

GOVERNMENTAL ORGANIZATIONS

Bureau of Oceans and International Environmental and Scientific Affairs. 2201 C St., N.W., Washington, District of Columbia 20520. (202) 647-1554.

National Center for Health Statistics: Public Health Service. 6525 Belcrest Rd., Hyattsville, Maryland 20782. (301) 436-7016.

HANDBOOKS AND MANUALS

Demography for Agricultural Planners. D. S. Baldwin. Food and Agriculture Organization of the United Nations, 4611-F, Assembly Dr., Lanham, Maryland 20706-4391. (301) 459-7666; (800) 274-4888. 1975. Deals with the rural population demography and agricultural economics.

Population Growth Estimation: A Handbook of Vital Statistics Measurement. Eli Samplin Marks. Population Council, 1 Dag Hammarskjold Plaza, New York, New York 10017. (212) 644-1300. 1974. Handbook covers population forecasting and other vital statistics.

ONLINE DATA BASES

BIOSIS Previews. BIOSIS, 2100 Arch St., Philadelphia, Pennsylvania 19103-1399. (215) 587-4800. Largest and most comprehensive database of research in the life sciences. Contains citations for nearly 9000 primary research journals, monographs, reviews, symposia, preliminary reports, semi-popular journals, selected institutional reports, government reports and research communications.

Biotechnology Abstracts. Derwent Publications Ltd., 6845 Elm St., McLean, Virginia 22101. (703) 790-0400. Includes material on genetic manipulation, biochemical engineering, fermentation, biocatalysis, cell hybridization, in vitro plant propagation and industrial waste management.

Cambridge Scientific Abstracts Life Science–CSAL. Cambridge Scientific Abstracts, 5161 River Rd., Bethesda, Maryland 20816. (301) 961-6750. Provides access to the following abstracting services: "Life Sciences Collection," "Aquatic Sciences and Fisheries Abstracts," "Oceanic Abstracts," and "Pollution Abstracts."

Enviro/Energyline Abstracts Plus. R. R. Bowker Co., 121 Chanlon Rd., New Providence, New Jersey 07974. (908) 464-6800.

Enviroline. R. R. Bowker Co., Bowker Electronic Publishing, 121 Chanlon Rd., New Providence, New Jersey 07974. (800) 521-8110.

Environmental Bibliography. Environmental Studies Institute, International Academy at Santa Barbara, 800 Garden St., Ste. D, Santa Barbara, California 93101. (805) 965-5010. International periodical literature dealing with environmental topics such as air pollution, water treatment, energy conservation, noise abatement, soil mechanics, wildlife preservation, and chemical wastes.

Environmental Periodicals Bibliography. National Information Services Corp., Ste. 6, Wyman Towers, 3100 St. Paul St., Baltimore, Maryland 21218. (410)243-0797. Online version of abstract of same name.

Monthly Catalog of United States Government Publications. U.S. G.P.O., Supt. of Docs., PO Box 371954, Pittsburgh, Pennsylvania 15250-7954. (202) 512-0000.

National Technical Information Service. U.S. Department of Commerce, National Technical Information Service, Office of Data Base Services, 5285 Port Royal Rd., Springfield, Virginia 22161. (703) 487-4807. Bibliographic database of government sponsored research and technical reports.

POPLINE. Johns Hopkins University, Population Information Program, 701 W. 40th St., Ste. 275, Baltimore, Maryland 21211. (410) 516-6900.

SCISEARCH. Institute for Scientific Information, University City Science Center, 3501 Market St., Philadelphia, Pennsylvania 19104. (215) 386-0100.

PERIODICALS AND NEWSLETTERS

Balance Report. Population Environment Balance, 1325 6th St. N.W., #1003, Washington, District of Columbia 20005. (202) 879-3000. Quarterly.

Ecological Society of America Bulletin. Ecological Society of America, Center of Environmental Studies, Arizona State University, Tempe, Arizona 85287-1201. (602) 965-3000. Quarterly. Study of living things in relation to their environments.

Ecology. Ecological Society of America, Center of Environmental Studies, Arizona State University, Tempe, Arizona 85287-1201. (602) 965-3000. Bimonthly. Information on the study of living things.

Ecology USA. Business Publishers, Inc., 951 Pershing Dr., Silver Spring, Maryland 20910-4464. (301) 587-6300. 1972-. Biweekly. Contains all the legislation, regulation, and litigation affecting efforts to conserve and protect America's unique environmental and ecological heritage.

Environmental Fund. Population-Environment Balance, 1325 6th St., N.W., #1003, Washington, District of Columbia 20005. Population-environment balance.

USSR Report. Human Resources. Foreign Broadcast Information Service. National Technical Information Service, 5285 Port Royal Rd., Springfield, Virginia 22161. (703) 487-4650. 1980-. Irregular.

RESEARCH CENTERS AND INSTITUTES

Committee on Evolutionary Biology. University of Chicago, 915 East 57th Street, Chicago, Illinois 60637. (312) 702-8940.

Earth Sciences Centre. University of Toronto, 33 Willcocks St., Toronto, Ontario, Canada M5S 3B3. (416) 978-3248.

Population Crisis Committee. 1120 19th St., N.W., Washington, District of Columbia 20036. (202) 659-1833.

Population Institute. 110 Maryland Ave., N.E., Washington, District of Columbia 20002. (202) 544-3300.

Stanford University, Jasper Ridge-Herrin Labs. Room 223, Stanford, California 94305. (415) 723-1589.

University of Houston Coastal Center. c/o Office of the Senior Vice President, Houston, Texas 77204-5502. (713) 749-2351.

University of Kansas, John H. Nelson Environmental Study Area. Division of Biological Sciences, Lawrence, Kansas 66045. (913) 864-3236.

University of Massachusetts, Cooperative Marine Research Program. The Environmental Institute, Blaisdell House, Amherst, Massachusetts 01003-0040. (413) 545-2842.

University of Missouri-Columbia, Gaylord Memorial Laboratory. Puxico, Missouri 63960. (314) 222-3531.

University of Montana, Montana Cooperative Wildlife Research Unit. Missoula, Montana 59812. (406) 243-5372.

Utah State University, Ecology Center. Logan, Utah 84322-5200. (801) 750-2555.

Wisconsin Cooperative Wildlife Research Unit. University of Wisconsin, 266 Russell Laboratories, Madison, Wisconsin 53706. (608) 263-6882.

STATISTICS SOURCES

A Community Researcher's Guide to Rural Data. Priscilla Salant. Island Press, 1718 Connecticut Ave. N.W., Suite 300, Washington, District of Columbia 20009. (202) 232-7933. 1990. Comprehensive manual intended for those less familiar with statistical data on rural America. Identifies a wealth of data sources such as the decennial census of population and housing, population reports and surveys, and labor market information.

Population Today. Population Reference Bureau, Circulation Department, 777 14th St., NW, Suite 800, Washington, District of Columbia 20005. (202) 639-8040. Monthly. Data on international population size and growth.

World Population Data Sheet. Population Reference Bureau, Circulation Department, 777 14th St., NW, Suite 800, Washington, District of Columbia 20005. (202) 639-8040. Annual. Population size and characteristics for countries, arranged by world region.

World Resources. World Resources Institute. 1709 New York Ave., N.W., Washington, District of Columbia 20006. (202) 638-6300. Annual. Statistical and textual analysis of world's natural resources and the effects of growth-caused environmental pollution.

TRADE ASSOCIATIONS AND PROFESSIONAL SOCIETIES

The Alan Guttmacher Institute. 111 5th Avenue, New York, New York 10003. (212) 254-5656.

American Institute of Biological Sciences. 730 11th St., N.W., Washington, District of Columbia 20001-4521. (202) 628-1500.

American Psychological Association. Division 34, Department of Psychology, University of Utah, Salt Lake City, Utah 84112.

Better World Society. 1100 17th St., NW, Suite 502, Washington, District of Columbia 20036. (202) 331-3770. International non-profit membership organization that attempts to increase individual awareness of global issues related to the sustainability of life on earth.

Center for Population Options. 1025 Vermont Ave., NW, Suite 210, Washington, District of Columbia 20005. (202) 347-5700.

Ecological Society of America. Arizona State University, Center for Environmental Studies, Tempe, Arizona 85287. (602) 965-3000.

Global Tomorrow Coalition. 1325 G St., N.W., Suite 915, Washington, District of Columbia 20005-3103. (202) 628-4016.

The Jessie Smith Noyes Foundation. 16 E. 34th St., New York, New York 10016. (212) 684-6577.

Negative Population Growth, Inc. 210 The Plaza, P.O. Box 1206, Teaneck, New Jersey 07666. (201) 837-3555.

The Pathfinder Fund. 9 Galen St., Suite 217, Watertown, Massachusetts 02172. (617) 924-7200.

Population Communication. 1489 E. Colorado Blvd., Suite 202, Pasadena, California 91106. (818) 793-4750.

The Population Council. 1 Dag Hammarskjold Plaza, New York, New York 10017. (212) 644-1300.

Population-Environment Balance. 1325 G St., N.W., Suite 1003, Washington, District of Columbia 20005. (202) 879-3000.

Windstar Foundation. 2317 Snowmass Creek Rd., Snowmass, Colorado 81654. (303) 927-4777. Foundation begun by John Denver offering information on a wide range of personal-action issues.

World Population Society. 1333 H St., Suite 760, Washington, District of Columbia 20005. (202) 898-1303.

Zero Population Growth. 1400 16th St., N.W., Ste. 320, Washington, District of Columbia 20036. (202) 332-2200.

POPULATION CONTROL

See also: DEMOGRAPHY

ABSTRACTING AND INDEXING SERVICES

Applied Ecology Abstracts Studies in Renewable Natural Resources. Information Retrieval Ltd., 1911 Jefferson Davis Highway, Arlington, Virginia 22202. 1975-. Monthly.

Biological and Agricultural Index. H.W. Wilson Co., 950 University Ave., Bronx, New York 10452. (800) 367-6770. 1916-. Monthly.

Biology Digest. Data Courier, Plexus Pub Inc., 143 Old Marlton Pike, Medford, New Jersey 08055. 1974-. Monthly. Abstracts biology periodicals.

Biotechnology Research Abstracts. Cambridge Scientific Abstracts, 5161 River Rd., Bethesda, Maryland 20816. (301) 961-6750. Monthly. Includes such broad areas as genetic intervention, biochemical genetics, and microbiological techniques.

Current Advances in Ecological and Environmental Science. Pergamon Microforms International, Inc., Fairview Park, Elmsford, New York 10523. (914) 592-7720. 1989-.

Monthly. Current literature searching service including journals, reports, abstracts, etc. This service is available online as part of the CABS database on the hosts BRS and ORBIT search service.

Ecological Abstracts. Geo Abstracts Ltd. Elsevier Applied Science, Crown House, Linton Rd., Barking, England IG 11 8JU. 1974-. Derived from over 600 leading ecological and environmental journals, plus books, conference proceedings, reports and theses.

Ecology Abstracts. Cambridge Scientific Abstracts, 5161 River Rd., Bethesda, Maryland 20816. (301) 961-6750. Monthly.

Environment Abstracts. Bowker A & I Publishing, 121 Chanlon Rd., New Providence, New Jersey 07974. (908) 464-6800. 1974-.

Environment Index. Environment Information Center, Index Research Department, 124 E. 39th St., New York, New York 10016. 1971-. Annual.

Environmental Information Connection–EIC. Planning Information Program, Dept. of Urban and Regional Planning, University of Illinois, 1003 West Nevada, Urbana, Illinois 61801. (217) 333-1369. Also available online.

Environmental Periodicals Bibliography. Environmental Studies Institute, International Academy at Santa Barbara, 800 Garden St., Suite D, Santa Barbara, California 93101. (805) 965-5010. Also available online.

Genetics Abstracts. Cambridge Scientific Abstracts, 5161 River Rd., Bethesda, Maryland 20816. (301) 961-6750. 1968-. Monthly. Formerly published by Information Retrieval Ltd., London England. Published by Cambridge Scientific Abstracts since 1982.

Geographical Abstracts. London School of Economics, Dept. of Geography, Regency House, 34 Duke St., London, England 1966-. Continued by Geo Abstracts issued in 6 parts: Pt. A. Landforms and the quaternary; Pt. B. Biogeography and Climatology; Pt. C. Economic geography; Pt. D. Social geography and cartography; Pt. E. Sedimentology; Pt. F. Regional and community planning.

Multimedia Index to Ecology. National Information Center for Educational Media, University of Southern California, Los Angeles, California 90007.

Science Citation Index. Institute for Scientific Information, 3501 Market St., Philadelphia, Pennsylvania 19104. 1961-.

BIBLIOGRAPHIES

Current Contents. Agriculture, Biology and Environmental Sciences. Institute for Scientific Information, 3501 Market St., Philadelphia, Pennsylvania 19104. (800) 523-1857. 1973-. Previous title: Current Contents. Agricultural, Food & Veterinary Sciences. Gives the table of contents of periodicals in the fields of agriculture, biology, environmental and related areas.

EPA Publications Bibliography. U.S. Environmental Protection Agency, Library Systems Branch, 401 M St., SW, Washington, District of Columbia 20460. (202) 260-2090. Quarterly.

ENCYCLOPEDIAS AND DICTIONARIES

Cambridge Encyclopedia of Life Sciences. A. E. Friday and David S. Ingram. Cambridge University Press, 40 W 20th St., New York, New York 10011. (212) 924-3900 or (800) 227-0247. 1985. Includes all topics under biology and ecology.

Encyclopedia of Bioethics. Warren T. Reich, ed. Free Press, 866 3rd Ave., New York, New York 10022. (212) 702-2004 or (800) 257-5755. 1978. Four volumes. Includes review articles in the field of bioethics by 330 reviewers representing fields such as: surgery, Islamic studies, pediatrics, philosophy, environmental sciences, theology, psychiatry, etc.

Grzimek's Encyclopedia of Ecology. Bernhard Grzimek. Van Nostrand Reinhold, 115 5th Ave., New York, New York 10003. (212) 254-3232. 1976.

McGraw-Hill Encyclopedia of Environmental Science. Sybil P. Parker. McGraw-Hill Science & Engineering Books, 11 W. 19th St., New York, New York 10011. (212) 337-6010. 1980. Covers ecology, man's influence on nature, and environmental protection.

North American Reference Encyclopedia of Ecology and Pollution. William White. North American Pub. Co., 401 N. Broad St., Philadelphia, Pennsylvania 19108. (215) 238-5300. 1972.

GENERAL WORKS

Magill's Survey of Science. Life Science Series. Frank N. Magill, ed. Salem Press, PO Box 50062, Pasadena, California 91105. 1991. Six volumes. Contents: v.1. A-Central and peripheral nervous system functions; v.2. Central metabolism regulation - eukaryotic transcriptional control; v.3. Positive and negative eukaryotic transcriptional control - mammalian hormones; v.4. Hormones and behavior - muscular contraction; v.5. Muscular contraction and relaxation - sexual reproduction in plants; v.6. Reproductive behavior and mating - X inactivation and the Lyon hypothesis.

GOVERNMENTAL ORGANIZATIONS

National Center for Health Statistics: Public Health Service. 6525 Belcrest Rd., Hyattsville, Maryland 20782. (301) 436-7016.

ONLINE DATA BASES

Biotechnology Abstracts. Derwent Publications Ltd., 6845 Elm St., McLean, Virginia 22101. (703) 790-0400. Includes material on genetic manipulation, biochemical engineering, fermentation, biocatalysis, cell hybridization, in vitro plant propagation and industrial waste management.

Cambridge Scientific Abstracts Life Science–CSAL. Cambridge Scientific Abstracts, 5161 River Rd., Bethesda, Maryland 20816. (301) 961-6750. Provides access to the following abstracting services: "Life Sciences Collection," "Aquatic Sciences and Fisheries Abstracts," "Oceanic Abstracts," and "Pollution Abstracts."

Enviro/Energyline Abstracts Plus. R. R. Bowker Co., 121 Chanlon Rd., New Providence, New Jersey 07974. (908) 464-6800.

Environmental Periodicals Bibliography. National Information Services Corp., Ste. 6, Wyman Towers, 3100 St.

Paul St., Baltimore, Maryland 21218. (410)243-0797. Online version of abstract of same name.

Monthly Catalog of United States Government Publications. U.S. G.P.O., Supt. of Docs., PO Box 371954, Pittsburgh, Pennsylvania 15250-7954. (202) 512-0000.

National Technical Information Service. U.S. Department of Commerce, National Technical Information Service, Office of Data Base Services, 5285 Port Royal Rd., Springfield, Virginia 22161. (703) 487-4807. Bibliographic database of government sponsored research and technical reports.

PressNet Environmental Reports. Chemical Information Systems, Inc., 7215 York Rd., Baltimore, Maryland 21212. (301) 321-8440.

SCISEARCH. Institute for Scientific Information, University City Science Center, 3501 Market St., Philadelphia, Pennsylvania 19104. (215) 386-0100.

RESEARCH CENTERS AND INSTITUTES

Population Institute. 110 Maryland Ave., N.E., Washington, District of Columbia 20002. (202) 544-3300.

TRADE ASSOCIATIONS AND PROFESSIONAL SOCIETIES

American Institute of Biological Sciences. 730 11th St., N.W., Washington, District of Columbia 20001-4521. (202) 628-1500.

Population-Environment Balance. 1325 G St., N.W., Suite 1003, Washington, District of Columbia 20005. (202) 879-3000.

World Population Society. 1333 H St., Suite 760, Washington, District of Columbia 20005. (202) 898-1303.

POPULATION DYNAMICS

ABSTRACTING AND INDEXING SERVICES

Applied Ecology Abstracts Studies in Renewable Natural Resources. Information Retrieval Ltd., 1911 Jefferson Davis Highway, Arlington, Virginia 22202. 1975-. Monthly.

ASFA Aquaculture Abstracts. Cambridge Scientific Abstracts, Inc., 5161 River Rd., Bethesda, Maryland 20816. (301) 961-6750. 1984.

Biological Abstracts. BIOSIS, 2100 Arch St., Philadelphia, Pennsylvania 19103-1399. (215) 587-4800. 1927-.

Biological and Agricultural Index. H.W. Wilson Co., 950 University Ave., Bronx, New York 10452. (800) 367-6770. 1916-. Monthly.

Biology Digest. Data Courier, Plexus Pub Inc., 143 Old Marlton Pike, Medford, New Jersey 08055. 1974-. Monthly. Abstracts biology periodicals.

Biotechnology Research Abstracts. Cambridge Scientific Abstracts, 5161 River Rd., Bethesda, Maryland 20816. (301) 961-6750. Monthly. Includes such broad areas as genetic intervention, biochemical genetics, and microbiological techniques.

Current Advances in Ecological and Environmental Science. Pergamon Microforms International, Inc., Fairview

Park, Elmsford, New York 10523. (914) 592-7720. 1989-. Monthly. Current literature searching service includingjournals, reports, abstracts, etc. This service is available online as part of the CABS database on the hosts BRS and ORBIT search service.

Ecological Abstracts. Geo Abstracts Ltd. Elsevier Applied Science, Crown House, Linton Rd., Barking, England IG 11 8JU. 1974-. Derived from over 600 leading ecological and environmental journals, plus books, conference proceedings, reports and theses.

Ecology Abstracts. Cambridge Scientific Abstracts, 5161 River Rd., Bethesda, Maryland 20816. (301) 961-6750. Monthly.

Environment Abstracts. Bowker A & I Publishing, 121 Chanlon Rd., New Providence, New Jersey 07974. (908) 464-6800. 1974-.

Environment Index. Environment Information Center, Index Research Department, 124 E. 39th St., New York, New York 10016. 1971-. Annual.

Environmental Information Connection–EIC. Planning Information Program, Dept. of Urban and Regional Planning, University of Illinois, 1003 West Nevada, Urbana, Illinois 61801. (217) 333-1369. Also available online.

Environmental Periodicals Bibliography. Environmental Studies Institute, International Academy at Santa Barbara, 800 Garden St., Suite D, Santa Barbara, California 93101. (805) 965-5010. Also available online.

Genetics Abstracts. Cambridge Scientific Abstracts, 5161 River Rd., Bethesda, Maryland 20816. (301) 961-6750. 1968-. Monthly. Formerly published by Information Retrieval Ltd., London England. Published by Cambridge Scientific Abstracts since 1982.

Geographical Abstracts. London School of Economics, Dept. of Geography, Regency House, 34 Duke St., London, England 1966-. Continued by Geo Abstracts issued in 6 parts: Pt. A. Landforms and the quaternary; Pt. B. Biogeography and Climatology; Pt. C. Economic geography; Pt. D. Social geography and cartography; Pt. E. Sedimentology; Pt. F. Regional and community planning.

Multimedia Index to Ecology. National Information Center for Educational Media, University of Southern California, Los Angeles, California 90007.

Science Citation Index. Institute for Scientific Information, 3501 Market St., Philadelphia, Pennsylvania 19104. 1961-.

BIBLIOGRAPHIES

Current Contents. Agriculture, Biology and Environmental Sciences. Institute for Scientific Information, 3501 Market St., Philadelphia, Pennsylvania 19104. (800) 523-1857. 1973-. Previous title: Current Contents. Agricultural, Food & Veterinary Sciences. Gives the table of contents of periodicals in the fields of agriculture, biology, environmental and related areas.

EPA Publications Bibliography. U.S. Environmental Protection Agency, Library Systems Branch, 401 M St., SW, Washington, District of Columbia 20460. (202) 260-2090. Quarterly.

ENCYCLOPEDIAS AND DICTIONARIES

Cambridge Dictionary of Biology. Peter M. B. Walker. Cambridge University Press, 40 W. 20th St., New York, New York 10011. (212) 924-3900 or (800) 227-0247. 1989. Includes 10,000 terms in zoology, botany, biochemistry, molecular biology and genetics. Previously published under the title Chambers Biology Dictionary.

Cambridge Encyclopedia of Life Sciences. A. E. Friday and David S. Ingram. Cambridge University Press, 40 W 20th St., New York, New York 10011. (212) 924-3900 or (800) 227-0247. 1985. Includes all topics under biology and ecology.

A Concise Dictionary of Biology. Elizabeth Martin, ed. Oxford University Press, 200 Madison Ave., New York, New York 10016. (212) 679-7300 or (800) 334-4249. 1990. New edition. Derived from the Concise Science Dictionary, published in 1984.

Encyclopedia of Bioethics. Warren T. Reich, ed. Free Press, 866 3rd Ave., New York, New York 10022. (212) 702-2004 or (800) 257-5755. 1978. Four volumes. Includes review articles in the field of bioethics by 330 reviewers representing fields such as: surgery, Islamic studies, pediatrics, philosophy, environmental sciences, theology, psychiatry, etc.

Grzimek's Encyclopedia of Ecology. Bernhard Grzimek. Van Nostrand Reinhold, 115 5th Ave., New York, New York 10003. (212) 254-3232. 1976.

McGraw-Hill Encyclopedia of Environmental Science. Sybil P. Parker. McGraw-Hill Science & Engineering Books, 11 W. 19th St., New York, New York 10011. (212) 337-6010. 1980. Covers ecology, man's influence on nature, and environmental protection.

North American Reference Encyclopedia of Ecology and Pollution. William White. North American Pub. Co., 401 N. Broad St., Philadelphia, Pennsylvania 19108. (215) 238-5300. 1972.

GENERAL WORKS

And the Poor Get Children: Radical Perspectives on Population Dynamics. Karen L. Michaelson. Monthly Review Press, 122 W. 27th St., New York, New York 10001. (212) 691-2555. 1981. Population, family size, and internal migration.

Ecological Heterogeneity. Jurek Kolasa, et al., eds. Springer-Verlag, 175 5th Ave., New York, New York 10010. (212) 460-1500. 1991. Examines the meaning of heterogeneity in a particular environment and its consequences for individuals, populations, and communities of plants and animals. Among the topics of the 14 papers are the causes of heterogeneity, system and observer dependence, dimension and scale, ecosystem organization, temporal and spatial changes, new models of competition and landscape patterns, and applications in desert, temperate, and marine areas.

The Next One Hundred Years: Shaping the Fate of Our Living Earth. Jonathan Weiner. Bantam Books, 666 5th Ave., New York, New York 10103. (212) 765-6500; (800) 223-6834. 1991. Explores the following issues: the greenhouse effect, deforestation, the destruction of the ozone layer, the human population explosion and the onset of mass extinctions.

Population Dynamics of Forest Insects. VCH Publishers, 303 NW 12th Ave., Deerfield Beach, Florida 33442-

1788. (305) 428-5566. 1990. Reviews the current research from an international Congress of delegates which covers population models, pest management and insect natural enemy interaction on forest insects. Topics include the effects of industrial air pollutants and acid rain as well as reviews of the biology and population dynamics of most major forest insects.

HANDBOOKS AND MANUALS

The Population Reference Bureau's Population Handbook. Arthur Haupt. Population Reference Bureau, 1875 Connecticut Ave., Ste. 520, Washington, District of Columbia 20009. (202) 483-1100. 1991. A quick guide to population dynamics for journalists, policymakers, teachers, students, and other people interested in population.

ONLINE DATA BASES

BIOSIS Previews. BIOSIS, 2100 Arch St., Philadelphia, Pennsylvania 19103-1399. (215) 587-4800. Largest and most comprehensive database of research in the life sciences. Contains citations for nearly 9000 primary research journals, monographs, reviews, symposia, preliminary reports, semi-popular journals, selected institutional reports, government reports and research communications.

Biotechnology Abstracts. Derwent Publications Ltd., 6845 Elm St., McLean, Virginia 22101. (703) 790-0400. Includes material on genetic manipulation, biochemical engineering, fermentation, biocatalysis, cell hybridization, in vitro plant propagation and industrial waste management.

Cambridge Scientific Abstracts Life Science–CSAL. Cambridge Scientific Abstracts, 5161 River Rd., Bethesda, Maryland 20816. (301) 961-6750. Provides access to the following abstracting services: "Life Sciences Collection," "Aquatic Sciences and Fisheries Abstracts," "Oceanic Abstracts," and "Pollution Abstracts."

Enviro/Energyline Abstracts Plus. R. R. Bowker Co., 121 Chanlon Rd., New Providence, New Jersey 07974. (908) 464-6800.

Environmental Periodicals Bibliography. National Information Services Corp., Ste. 6, Wyman Towers, 3100 St. Paul St., Baltimore, Maryland 21218. (410)243-0797. Online version of abstract of same name.

Monthly Catalog of United States Government Publications. U.S. G.P.O., Supt. of Docs., PO Box 371954, Pittsburgh, Pennsylvania 15250-7954. (202) 512-0000.

National Technical Information Service. U.S. Department of Commerce, National Technical Information Service, Office of Data Base Services, 5285 Port Royal Rd., Springfield, Virginia 22161. (703) 487-4807. Bibliographic database of government sponsored research and technical reports.

SCISEARCH. Institute for Scientific Information, University City Science Center, 3501 Market St., Philadelphia, Pennsylvania 19104. (215) 386-0100.

PERIODICALS AND NEWSLETTERS

Environmental Entomology. Entomological Society of America, 9301 Annapolis Road, Lanham, Maryland 20706. (301) 731-4538. Bimonthly. Covers ecology and population dynamics.

RESEARCH CENTERS AND INSTITUTES

Katherine Ordway Preserve and the Swisher Memorial Sanctuary. University of Florida, School of Forest Resources and Conservation, Gainesville, Florida 32611. (904) 392-1721.

Population Reference Bureau. 1875 Connecticut Ave., Suite 520, Washington, District of Columbia 20009. (202) 483-1100.

State University of New York at Stony Brook, Ecology Laboratory. Stony Brook, New York 11797-5245. (516) 623-8600.

University of Kansas, Kansas Ecological Reserves. Lawrence, Kansas 66045. (913) 864-3236.

University of Montana, Montana Cooperative Wildlife Research Unit. Missoula, Montana 59812. (406) 243-5372.

University of Washington, Fisheries Research Institute. School of Fisheries, WH-10, Seattle, Washington 98195. (206) 543-4650.

TRADE ASSOCIATIONS AND PROFESSIONAL SOCIETIES

American Institute of Biological Sciences. 730 11th St., N.W., Washington, District of Columbia 20001-4521. (202) 628-1500.

World Population Society. 1333 H St., Suite 760, Washington, District of Columbia 20005. (202) 898-1303.

POPULATION GROWTH

ABSTRACTING AND INDEXING SERVICES

Applied Ecology Abstracts Studies in Renewable Natural Resources. Information Retrieval Ltd., 1911 Jefferson Davis Highway, Arlington, Virginia 22202. 1975-. Monthly.

ASFA Aquaculture Abstracts. Cambridge Scientific Abstracts, Inc., 5161 River Rd., Bethesda, Maryland 20816. (301) 961-6750. 1984.

Biological Abstracts. BIOSIS, 2100 Arch St., Philadelphia, Pennsylvania 19103-1399. (215) 587-4800. 1927-.

Biological and Agricultural Index. H.W. Wilson Co., 950 University Ave., Bronx, New York 10452. (800) 367-6770. 1916-. Monthly.

Biology Digest. Data Courier, Plexus Pub Inc., 143 Old Marlton Pike, Medford, New Jersey 08055. 1974-. Monthly. Abstracts biology periodicals.

Biotechnology Research Abstracts. Cambridge Scientific Abstracts, 5161 River Rd., Bethesda, Maryland 20816. (301) 961-6750. Monthly. Includes such broad areas as genetic intervention, biochemical genetics, and microbiological techniques.

Current Advances in Ecological and Environmental Science. Pergamon Microforms International, Inc., Fairview Park, Elmsford, New York 10523. (914) 592-7720. 1989-. Monthly. Current literature searching service includingjournals, reports, abstracts, etc. This service is available online as part of the CABS database on the hosts BRS and ORBIT search service.

Ecological Abstracts. Geo Abstracts Ltd. Elsevier Applied Science, Crown House, Linton Rd., Barking, England IG 11 8JU. 1974-. Derived from over 600 leading ecological and environmental journals, plus books, conference proceedings, reports and theses.

Ecology Abstracts. Cambridge Scientific Abstracts, 5161 River Rd., Bethesda, Maryland 20816. (301) 961-6750. Monthly.

Environment Abstracts. Bowker A & I Publishing, 121 Chanlon Rd., New Providence, New Jersey 07974. (908) 464-6800. 1974-.

Environment Index. Environment Information Center, Index Research Department, 124 E. 39th St., New York, New York 10016. 1971-. Annual.

Environmental Information Connection–EIC. Planning Information Program, Dept. of Urban and Regional Planning, University of Illinois, 1003 West Nevada, Urbana, Illinois 61801. (217) 333-1369. Also available online.

Environmental Periodicals Bibliography. Environmental Studies Institute, International Academy at Santa Barbara, 800 Garden St., Suite D, Santa Barbara, California 93101. (805) 965-5010. Also available online.

Genetics Abstracts. Cambridge Scientific Abstracts, 5161 River Rd., Bethesda, Maryland 20816. (301) 961-6750. 1968-. Monthly. Formerly published by Information Retrieval Ltd., London England. Published by Cambridge Scientific Abstracts since 1982.

Geographical Abstracts. London School of Economics, Dept. of Geography, Regency House, 34 Duke St., London, England 1966-. Continued by Geo Abstracts issued in 6 parts: Pt. A. Landforms and the quaternary; Pt. B. Biogeography and Climatology; Pt. C. Economic geography; Pt. D. Social geography and cartography; Pt. E. Sedimentology; Pt. F. Regional and community planning.

Multimedia Index to Ecology. National Information Center for Educational Media, University of Southern California, Los Angeles, California 90007.

Science Citation Index. Institute for Scientific Information, 3501 Market St., Philadelphia, Pennsylvania 19104. 1961-.

ALMANACS AND YEARBOOKS

Environmental Almanac. World Resources Institute. Houghton Mifflin, 1 Beacon St., Boston, Massachusetts 02108. (617) 725-5000; (800) 225-3362. 1991. Covers consumer products, energy, endangered species, food safety, global warming, solid wastes, toxics, wetlands and other related areas. Also included are the names and addresses of the chief environmental executives for all 50 states.

BIBLIOGRAPHIES

Current Contents. Agriculture, Biology and Environmental Sciences. Institute for Scientific Information, 3501 Market St., Philadelphia, Pennsylvania 19104. (800) 523-1857. 1973-. Previous title: Current Contents. Agricultural, Food & Veterinary Sciences. Gives the table of contents of periodicals in the fields of agriculture, biology, environmental and related areas.

EPA Publications Bibliography. U.S. Environmental Protection Agency, Library Systems Branch, 401 M St., SW, Washington, District of Columbia 20460. (202) 260-2090. Quarterly.

ENCYCLOPEDIAS AND DICTIONARIES

Cambridge Encyclopedia of Life Sciences. A. E. Friday and David S. Ingram. Cambridge University Press, 40 W 20th St., New York, New York 10011. (212) 924-3900 or (800) 227-0247. 1985. Includes all topics under biology and ecology.

Encyclopedia of Bioethics. Warren T. Reich, ed. Free Press, 866 3rd Ave., New York, New York 10022. (212) 702-2004 or (800) 257-5755. 1978. Four volumes. Includes review articles in the field of bioethics by 330 reviewers representing fields such as: surgery, Islamic studies, pediatrics, philosophy, environmental sciences, theology, psychiatry, etc.

Grzimek's Encyclopedia of Ecology. Bernhard Grzimek. Van Nostrand Reinhold, 115 5th Ave., New York, New York 10003. (212) 254-3232. 1976.

McGraw-Hill Encyclopedia of Environmental Science. Sybil P. Parker. McGraw-Hill Science & Engineering Books, 11 W. 19th St., New York, New York 10011. (212) 337-6010. 1980. Covers ecology, man's influence on nature, and environmental protection.

North American Reference Encyclopedia of Ecology and Pollution. William White. North American Pub. Co., 401 N. Broad St., Philadelphia, Pennsylvania 19108. (215) 238-5300. 1972.

GENERAL WORKS

More?. League of Women Voters of the United States, 1730 M St., NW, Washington, District of Columbia 20036. (202) 429-1965. 1972. The interfaces between population, economic growth, and the environment.

Resource and Environmental Consequences of Population and Economic Growth. Ronald Gene Ridker. Resources for the Future, 1616 P St., NW, Washington, District of Columbia 20036. (202) 328-5086. 1979.

HANDBOOKS AND MANUALS

The Global Ecology Handbook: What You Can Do about the Environmental Crisis. Walter H. Corson, ed. The Global Tomorrow Coalition, Beacon Pr., 25 Beacon St., Boston, Massachusetts 02108-2800. (617) 742-2110. 1990. Covers environment, energy policy, population growth and other issues. It includes chapters on tropical rain forests, garbage, oceans and coasts, global warming, population growth, agriculture, biological diversity, fresh water, hazardous wastes, and environment and development.

ONLINE DATA BASES

BIOSIS Previews. BIOSIS, 2100 Arch St., Philadelphia, Pennsylvania 19103-1399. (215) 587-4800. Largest and most comprehensive database of research in the life sciences. Contains citations for nearly 9000 primary research journals, monographs, reviews, symposia, preliminary reports, semi-popular journals, selected institutional reports, government reports and research communications.

Biotechnology Abstracts. Derwent Publications Ltd., 6845 Elm St., McLean, Virginia 22101. (703) 790-0400. Includes material on genetic manipulation, biochemical engineering, fermentation, biocatalysis, cell hybridization, in vitro plant propagation and industrial waste management.

Cambridge Scientific Abstracts Life Science–CSAL. Cambridge Scientific Abstracts, 5161 River Rd., Bethesda, Maryland 20816. (301) 961-6750. Provides access to the following abstracting services: "Life Sciences Collection," "Aquatic Sciences and Fisheries Abstracts," "Oceanic Abstracts," and "Pollution Abstracts."

Enviro/Energyline Abstracts Plus. R. R. Bowker Co., 121 Chanlon Rd., New Providence, New Jersey 07974. (908) 464-6800.

Environmental Periodicals Bibliography. National Information Services Corp., Ste. 6, Wyman Towers, 3100 St. Paul St., Baltimore, Maryland 21218. (410)243-0797. Online version of abstract of same name.

Monthly Catalog of United States Government Publications. U.S. G.P.O., Supt. of Docs., PO Box 371954, Pittsburgh, Pennsylvania 15250-7954. (202) 512-0000.

National Technical Information Service. U.S. Department of Commerce, National Technical Information Service, Office of Data Base Services, 5285 Port Royal Rd., Springfield, Virginia 22161. (703) 487-4807. Bibliographic database of government sponsored research and technical reports.

SCISEARCH. Institute for Scientific Information, University City Science Center, 3501 Market St., Philadelphia, Pennsylvania 19104. (215) 386-0100.

PERIODICALS AND NEWSLETTERS

Ecology USA. Business Publishers, Inc., 951 Pershing Dr., Silver Spring, Maryland 20910-4464. (301) 587-6300. 1972-. Biweekly. Contains all the legislation, regulation, and litigation affecting efforts to conserve and protect America's unique environmental and ecological heritage.

RESEARCH CENTERS AND INSTITUTES

Population Resource Center. 500 E. 62nd St., New York, New York 10021. (212) 888-2820.

TRADE ASSOCIATIONS AND PROFESSIONAL SOCIETIES

American Institute of Biological Sciences. 730 11th St., N.W., Washington, District of Columbia 20001-4521. (202) 628-1500.

Institute for 21st Century Studies. 1611 N. Kent St., Suite 610, Arlington, Virginia 22209. (703) 841-0048.

World Population Society. 1333 H St., Suite 760, Washington, District of Columbia 20005. (202) 898-1303.

Zero Population Growth. 1400 16th St., N.W., Ste. 320, Washington, District of Columbia 20036. (202) 332-2200.

PORPOISES

See also: MARINE MAMMALS

ABSTRACTING AND INDEXING SERVICES

Applied Ecology Abstracts Studies in Renewable Natural Resources. Information Retrieval Ltd., 1911 Jefferson Davis Highway, Arlington, Virginia 22202. 1975-. Monthly.

Biological Abstracts. BIOSIS, 2100 Arch St., Philadelphia, Pennsylvania 19103-1399. (215) 587-4800. 1927-.

Biological and Agricultural Index. H.W. Wilson Co., 950 University Ave., Bronx, New York 10452. (800) 367-6770. 1916-. Monthly.

Biology Digest. Data Courier, Plexus Pub Inc., 143 Old Marlton Pike, Medford, New Jersey 08055. 1974-. Monthly. Abstracts biology periodicals.

Ecological Abstracts. Geo Abstracts Ltd. Elsevier Applied Science, Crown House, Linton Rd., Barking, England IG 11 8JU. 1974-. Derived from over 600 leading ecological and environmental journals, plus books, conference proceedings, reports and theses.

Environment Abstracts. Bowker A & I Publishing, 121 Chanlon Rd., New Providence, New Jersey 07974. (908) 464-6800. 1974-.

Environment Index. Environment Information Center, Index Research Department, 124 E. 39th St., New York, New York 10016. 1971-. Annual.

Environmental Information Connection–EIC. Planning Information Program, Dept. of Urban and Regional Planning, University of Illinois, 1003 West Nevada, Urbana, Illinois 61801. (217) 333-1369. Also available online.

Environmental Periodicals Bibliography. Environmental Studies Institute, International Academy at Santa Barbara, 800 Garden St., Suite D, Santa Barbara, California 93101. (805) 965-5010. Also available online.

Index to Scientific Book Contents. Institute for Scientific Information, 3501 Market St., Philadelphia, Pennsylvania 19104. (800) 523-1857. 1985-. Annual. Gives contents of science books published.

Multimedia Index to Ecology. National Information Center for Educational Media, University of Southern California, Los Angeles, California 90007.

Science Citation Index. Institute for Scientific Information, 3501 Market St., Philadelphia, Pennsylvania 19104. 1961-.

ALMANACS AND YEARBOOKS

Dolphins, Porpoises and Whales of the World: The IUCN Red Data Book. M. Klinowska. The World Conservation Union, IUCN Publications Services Unit, 181a Huntingdon Road, Cambridge, England CB3 0DJ. (0223) 277894. 1991. Reviews the status of all cetacean species. Detailed accounts are provided for each species, describing their distribution, population, threats, and the conservation measures required to ensure their survival.

BIBLIOGRAPHIES

Current Contents. Agriculture, Biology and Environmental Sciences. Institute for Scientific Information, 3501 Market St., Philadelphia, Pennsylvania 19104. (800) 523-1857. 1973-. Previous title: Current Contents. Agricultural, Food & Veterinary Sciences. Gives the table of

contents of periodicals in the fields of agriculture, biology, environmental and related areas.

EPA Publications Bibliography. U.S. Environmental Protection Agency, Library Systems Branch, 401 M St., SW, Washington, District of Columbia 20460. (202) 260-2090. Quarterly.

ENCYCLOPEDIAS AND DICTIONARIES

Cambridge Encyclopedia of Life Sciences. A. E. Friday and David S. Ingram. Cambridge University Press, 40 W 20th St., New York, New York 10011. (212) 924-3900 or (800) 227-0247. 1985. Includes all topics under biology and ecology.

Grzimek's Encyclopedia of Ecology. Bernhard Grzimek. Van Nostrand Reinhold, 115 5th Ave., New York, New York 10003. (212) 254-3232. 1976.

McGraw-Hill Encyclopedia of Environmental Science. Sybil P. Parker. McGraw-Hill Science & Engineering Books, 11 W. 19th St., New York, New York 10011. (212) 337-6010. 1980. Covers ecology, man's influence on nature, and environmental protection.

McGraw-Hill Encyclopedia of Science and Technology. McGraw-Hill, 1221 Avenue of the Americas, New York, New York 10020. (212) 512-2000 or (800) 262-4729. 1992. Seventh edition. Issued in multiple volumes including index. Includes all science and technology broad subject areas.

North American Reference Encyclopedia of Ecology and Pollution. William White. North American Pub. Co., 401 N. Broad St., Philadelphia, Pennsylvania 19108. (215) 238-5300. 1972.

Van Nostrand's Scientific Encyclopedia. Glenn D. Considine, ed. Van Nostrand Reinhold, 115 5th Ave., New York, New York 10003. (212) 254-3232. 1983. Sixth edition. Includes all broad subject areas in science.

GENERAL WORKS

The Mid-Net Zipper Ridge a Possible Cause of Unobserved Porpoise Mortality. David B. Holts. National Oceanic and Atmospheric Administration, U.S. Department of Commerce, Washington, District of Columbia 20230. (202) 377-2985. 1980. Effects of purse seining.

Porpoise, Dolphin and Small Whale Fisheries of the World: Status and Problems. Edward Mitchell. International Union for Conservation of Nature and Natural Resources, Avenue du Mont-Blanc, Gland, Switzerland CH-1196. 1975.

ONLINE DATA BASES

BIOSIS Previews. BIOSIS, 2100 Arch St., Philadelphia, Pennsylvania 19103-1399. (215) 587-4800. Largest and most comprehensive database of research in the life sciences. Contains citations for nearly 9000 primary research journals, monographs, reviews, symposia, preliminary reports, semi-popular journals, selected institutional reports, government reports and research communications.

Cambridge Scientific Abstracts Life Science–CSAL. Cambridge Scientific Abstracts, 5161 River Rd., Bethesda, Maryland 20816. (301) 961-6750. Provides access to the following abstracting services: "Life Sciences Collec-

tion," "Aquatic Sciences and Fisheries Abstracts," "Oceanic Abstracts," and "Pollution Abstracts."

Enviro/Energyline Abstracts Plus. R. R. Bowker Co., 121 Chanlon Rd., New Providence, New Jersey 07974. (908) 464-6800.

Environmental Periodicals Bibliography. National Information Services Corp., Ste. 6, Wyman Towers, 3100 St. Paul St., Baltimore, Maryland 21218. (410)243-0797. Online version of abstract of same name.

SCISEARCH. Institute for Scientific Information, University City Science Center, 3501 Market St., Philadelphia, Pennsylvania 19104. (215) 386-0100.

PERIODICALS AND NEWSLETTERS

Dolphin Log. Cousteau Society Inc., 8440 Santa Monica Blvd., Los Angeles, California 90069. (804) 627-1144. Six issues a year. Covers marine animals, the oceans, science, natural history, and the arts as they relate to global water system. Magazine is for ages 7-15.

TRADE ASSOCIATIONS AND PROFESSIONAL SOCIETIES

American Institute of Biological Sciences. 730 11th St., N.W., Washington, District of Columbia 20001-4521. (202) 628-1500.

Cousteau Society. Cousteau Society Membership Center, 930 W 21st St., Norfolk, Virginia 23517. In addition to carrying on the many research projects and explorations made famous by Jacques-Yves Cousteau, the Society publishes educational materials and numerous Technical publications as well as Calypso Log (monthly) and Dolphin Log (bimonthly children's publication).

PORTS
See: HARBORS

POSTEMERGENCE HERBICIDES
See: HERBICIDES

POTASSIUM

ABSTRACTING AND INDEXING SERVICES

ASFA Aquaculture Abstracts. Cambridge Scientific Abstracts, Inc., 5161 River Rd., Bethesda, Maryland 20816. (301) 961-6750. 1984.

Chemical Abstracts. Chemical Abstracts Service, 2540 Olentangy River Rd., PO Box 3012, Columbus, Ohio 43210. (800) 848-6533. 1907-.

Environment Abstracts. Bowker A & I Publishing, 121 Chanlon Rd., New Providence, New Jersey 07974. (908) 464-6800. 1974-.

Environment Index. Environment Information Center, Index Research Department, 124 E. 39th St., New York, New York 10016. 1971-. Annual.

Environmental Information Connection–EIC. Planning Information Program, Dept. of Urban and Regional

Planning, University of Illinois, 1003 West Nevada, Urbana, Illinois 61801. (217) 333-1369. Also available online.

Environmental Periodicals Bibliography. Environmental Studies Institute, International Academy at Santa Barbara, 800 Garden St., Suite D, Santa Barbara, California 93101. (805) 965-5010. Also available online.

Science Citation Index. Institute for Scientific Information, 3501 Market St., Philadelphia, Pennsylvania 19104. 1961-.

BIBLIOGRAPHIES

EPA Publications Bibliography. U.S. Environmental Protection Agency, Library Systems Branch, 401 M St., SW, Washington, District of Columbia 20460. (202) 260-2090. Quarterly.

ENCYCLOPEDIAS AND DICTIONARIES

Cambridge Dictionary of Biology. Peter M. B. Walker. Cambridge University Press, 40 W. 20th St., New York, New York 10011. (212) 924-3900 or (800) 227-0247. 1989. Includes 10,000 terms in zoology, botany, biochemistry, molecular biology and genetics. Previously published under the title Chambers Biology Dictionary.

A Concise Dictionary of Biology. Elizabeth Martin, ed. Oxford University Press, 200 Madison Ave., New York, New York 10016. (212) 679-7300 or (800) 334-4249. 1990. New edition. Derived from the Concise Science Dictionary, published in 1984.

McGraw-Hill Encyclopedia of Science and Technology. McGraw-Hill, 1221 Avenue of the Americas, New York, New York 10020. (212) 512-2000 or (800) 262-4729. 1992. Seventh edition. Issued in multiple volumes including index. Includes all science and technology broad subject areas.

Van Nostrand's Scientific Encyclopedia. Glenn D. Considine, ed. Van Nostrand Reinhold, 115 5th Ave., New York, New York 10003. (212) 254-3232. 1983. Sixth edition. Includes all broad subject areas in science.

GENERAL WORKS

Potassium, its Biologic Significance. Robert Whang. CRC Press, 2000 Corporate Blvd. N.W., Boca Raton, Florida 33431. (800) 272-7737. 1983.

Potassium: Keeping a Delicate Balance. U.S. Department of Health and Human Services, Public Health Service, Food and Drug Administration, 900 Rockville Pike, Rockville, Maryland 20892. (301) 406-4000. 1984.

Test and Evaluation of Potassium Sensors in Fresh and Saltwater. Gary K. Ward. National Ocean Survey, National Oceanic and Atmospheric Administration, 11400 Rockville Pike, Rockville, Maryland 20852. (301) 443-8823. 1979.

ONLINE DATA BASES

Chemical Abstracts-CA. Chemical Abstracts Service, 2540 Olentangy River Rd., P.O. Box 3012, Columbus, Ohio 43210. (800) 848-6533 or (614) 421-3600. Information sources include 9000 journals, patents from 27 countries, two industrial property organizations, new

books, conference proceedings, and government research reports.

Enviro/Energyline Abstracts Plus. R. R. Bowker Co., 121 Chanlon Rd., New Providence, New Jersey 07974. (908) 464-6800.

Environmental Periodicals Bibliography. National Information Services Corp., Ste. 6, Wyman Towers, 3100 St. Paul St., Baltimore, Maryland 21218. (410)243-0797. Online version of abstract of same name.

STATISTICS SOURCES

Statistical Report. Potash and Phosphate Institute, 2801 Buford Hwy., NE, Suite 401, Atlanta, Georgia 30329-2199. Monthly. Production, sales, imports, and exports.

TRADE ASSOCIATIONS AND PROFESSIONAL SOCIETIES

American Chemical Society. 1155 16th St., N.W., Washington, District of Columbia 20036. (202) 872-4600.

American Institute of Chemical Engineers. 345 East 47th St., New York, New York 10017. (212) 705-7338.

American Institute of Chemists. 7315 Wisconsin Ave., Bethesda, Maryland 20814. (301) 652-2447.

POWER GENERATION

See also: BIOMASS; DAMS; HYDROELECTRIC POWER; NUCLEAR POWER

ABSTRACTING AND INDEXING SERVICES

Applied Science and Technology Index. H.W. Wilson Co., 950 University Ave., Bronx, New York 10452. (800) 367-6770. Formerly Industrial Arts Index.

Biological and Agricultural Index. H.W. Wilson Co., 950 University Ave., Bronx, New York 10452. (800) 367-6770. 1916-. Monthly.

Civil Engineering Hydraulic Abstracts. BHRA Fluid Engineering, Air Science Co., PO Box 143, Corning, New York 14830. (607) 962-5591. Monthly. Abstracts of periodicals that publish in the areas of hydraulic engineering and other related topics.

Engineering Index. The Engineering Index Inc., 345 E. 47th St., New York, New York 10017. 1962-.

Environment Index. Environment Information Center, Index Research Department, 124 E. 39th St., New York, New York 10016. 1971-. Annual.

Environmental Information Connection–EIC. Planning Information Program, Dept. of Urban and Regional Planning, University of Illinois, 1003 West Nevada, Urbana, Illinois 61801. (217) 333-1369. Also available online.

Environmental Periodicals Bibliography. Environmental Studies Institute, International Academy at Santa Barbara, 800 Garden St., Suite D, Santa Barbara, California 93101. (805) 965-5010. Also available online.

ERDA Research Abstracts. U.S. ERDA Technical Information Center, Box 62, Oak Ridge, Tennessee 37830.

Index to Scientific Book Contents. Institute for Scientific Information, 3501 Market St., Philadelphia, Pennsylvania 19104. (800) 523-1857. 1985-. Annual. Gives contents of science books published.

BIBLIOGRAPHIES

EPA Publications Bibliography. U.S. Environmental Protection Agency, Library Systems Branch, 401 M St., SW, Washington, District of Columbia 20460. (202) 260-2090. Quarterly.

ENCYCLOPEDIAS AND DICTIONARIES

Dictionary of Environmental Engineering and Related Sciences: English-Spanish, Spanish-English. Jose T. Villate. Ediciones Universal, 3090 SW 8th St., Miami, Florida 33135. (305) 642-3355. 1979.

Encyclopedia of Environmental Science and Engineering. J.R. Pfafflin. Gordon and Breach Science Publishers, Inc., 270 8th Ave., New York, New York 10011. (212) 206-8900. 1992.

Encyclopedia of Physical Science and Technology. Robert A. Meyers, ed. Academic Press, c/o Harcourt Brace Jovanovich Inc., 6277 Sea Harbor Dr., Orlando, Florida 32887. (800) 346-8648. Dictionary of engineering, technology and physical sciences.

McGraw-Hill Encyclopedia of Environmental Science. Sybil P. Parker. McGraw-Hill Science & Engineering Books, 11 W. 19th St., New York, New York 10011. (212) 337-6010. 1980. Covers ecology, man's influence on nature, and environmental protection.

McGraw-Hill Encyclopedia of Science and Technology. McGraw-Hill, 1221 Avenue of the Americas, New York, New York 10020. (212) 512-2000 or (800) 262-4729. 1992. Seventh edition. Issued in multiple volumes including index. Includes all science and technology broad subject areas.

Van Nostrand's Scientific Encyclopedia. Glenn D. Considine, ed. Van Nostrand Reinhold, 115 5th Ave., New York, New York 10003. (212) 254-3232. 1983. Sixth edition. Includes all broad subject areas in science.

GENERAL WORKS

Conservation and Heat Transfer. Nejat T. Veziroglu, ed. Nova Science Publishers Inc., 283 Commack Rd., Suite 300, Commack, New York 11725-3104. (516) 499-3103; (516) 499-3106. 1991. Describes methods of conservation and heat transfer.

The Environmental Impact of Electrical Power Generation: Nuclear and Fossil. Pennsylvania Department of Education. U.S. G.P.O., Washington, District of Columbia 20401. (202) 512-0000. 1975. Environmental aspects of electric power production.

Hydrogen Energy and Power Generation. T. Nejat Veziroglu, ed. Nova Science Publishers Inc., 283 Commack Rd., Suite 300, Commack, New York 11725-3104. (516) 499-3103; (516) 499-3106. 1991. Deals with clean energy and with other new and increasingly significant forms of energy generation, i.e. cogeneration, waste energy. Defines the role of hydrogen energy in the upcoming decade.

Power Generation and the Environment. P. S. Liss and P. A. H. Saunders. Oxford University Press, 200 Madison Ave., New York, New York 10016. (212) 679-7300; (800)

334-4249. 1990. Analyses the problems and possibilities inherent in producing electricity on a large scale.

Some Aspects of the Environment and Electric Power Generation. Sylvain Denis. RAND, 1700 Main St., Santa Monica, California 90401. (310) 393-0411. 1972. Thermal pollution of rivers, lakes, and electric power-plants.

GOVERNMENTAL ORGANIZATIONS

TVA Public Information Office. 400 West Summit Hill Dr., Knoxville, Tennessee 37902. (615) 632-8000.

HANDBOOKS AND MANUALS

Power Generation, Energy Management and Environmental Sourcebook. Marilyn Jackson. The Association of Energy Engineers, 4025 Pleasantdale Rd., Suite 420, Atlanta, Georgia 30340. (404) 925-9558. 1992. Includes practical solutions to energy and environmental problems.

ONLINE DATA BASES

Computerized Engineering Index–COMPENDEX. Engineering Information Inc., 345 E. 47th St., New York, New York 10017. (212) 705-7600.

Enviro/Energyline Abstracts Plus. R. R. Bowker Co., 121 Chanlon Rd., New Providence, New Jersey 07974. (908) 464-6800.

Environmental Periodicals Bibliography. National Information Services Corp., Ste. 6, Wyman Towers, 3100 St. Paul St., Baltimore, Maryland 21218. (410)243-0797. Online version of abstract of same name.

Monthly Catalog of United States Government Publications. U.S. G.P.O., Supt. of Docs., PO Box 371954, Pittsburgh, Pennsylvania 15250-7954. (202) 512-0000.

National Technical Information Service. U.S. Department of Commerce, National Technical Information Service, Office of Data Base Services, 5285 Port Royal Rd., Springfield, Virginia 22161. (703) 487-4807. Bibliographic database of government sponsored research and technical reports.

PERIODICALS AND NEWSLETTERS

The Cogeneration Journal. Cogeneration Journal, PO Box 14227, Atlanta, Georgia 30324. 1985-. Quarterly. Provides facts and data needed to evaluate the market, assess technologies, develop new projects and make key decisions.

The Cogeneration Letter: The Monthly Newsletter on Cogeneration. Energy Engineering, 700 Indian Trail, Lilburn, Georgia 30247. 1985-. Monthly. Covers the information of importance to the power generation industry.

TRADE ASSOCIATIONS AND PROFESSIONAL SOCIETIES

Middle States Independent Power. 320 Walnut St., Suite 105, Philadelphia, Pennsylvania 19106. (215) 627-0307.

National Association of Power Engineers. 2350 E. Devon Ave., Suite 115, Des Plaines, Illinois 60018. (718) 298-0600.

National Hydropower Association. 555 13th St., N.W., Suite 900 E., Washington, District of Columbia 20004. (202) 637-8115.

POWER LINES
See: ELECTRIC POWER LINES–ENVIRONMENTAL ASPECTS

POWER OUTAGE

ABSTRACTING AND INDEXING SERVICES

Applied Science and Technology Index. H.W. Wilson Co., 950 University Ave., Bronx, New York 10452. (800) 367-6770. Formerly Industrial Arts Index.

Engineering Index. The Engineering Index Inc., 345 E. 47th St., New York, New York 10017. 1962-.

ENCYCLOPEDIAS AND DICTIONARIES

Dictionary of Environmental Engineering and Related Sciences: English-Spanish, Spanish-English. Jose T. Villate. Ediciones Universal, 3090 SW 8th St., Miami, Florida 33135. (305) 642-3355. 1979.

Encyclopedia of Environmental Science and Engineering. J.R. Pfafflin. Gordon and Breach Science Publishers, Inc., 270 8th Ave., New York, New York 10011. (212) 206-8900. 1992.

Encyclopedia of Physical Science and Technology. Robert A. Meyers, ed. Academic Press, c/o Harcourt Brace Jovanovich Inc., 6277 Sea Harbor Dr., Orlando, Florida 32887. (800) 346-8648. Dictionary of engineering, technology and physical sciences.

ONLINE DATA BASES

Computerized Engineering Index–COMPENDEX. Engineering Information Inc., 345 E. 47th St., New York, New York 10017. (212) 705-7600.

EBIB. Texas A & M University, Sterling C. Evans Library, Reference Division, College Station, Texas 77843. (409) 845-5741.

TRADE ASSOCIATIONS AND PROFESSIONAL SOCIETIES

American Water Resources Association. 5410 Grosvenor Lane, Suite 220, Bethesda, Maryland 20814. (301) 493-8600.

POWER PLANT EMISSIONS
See: EMISSIONS

POWER PLANTS

ABSTRACTING AND INDEXING SERVICES

Applied Science and Technology Index. H.W. Wilson Co., 950 University Ave., Bronx, New York 10452. (800) 367-6770. Formerly Industrial Arts Index.

Energy Information Abstracts Annual 1987 in Retrospect. EIC/Intelligence Inc., 121 Chanlon Rd., New Providence, New Jersey 07974. (908) 464-6800. 1988. Annual. Cumulative edition of the monthly Energy Information Abstracts. Monitors sources in the field of energy including the scientific, technical and business journal literature, conference and symposia proceedings, corporate, government and academic reports.

Engineering Index. The Engineering Index Inc., 345 E. 47th St., New York, New York 10017. 1962-.

Environment Abstracts. Bowker A & I Publishing, 121 Chanlon Rd., New Providence, New Jersey 07974. (908) 464-6800. 1974-.

Environment Index. Environment Information Center, Index Research Department, 124 E. 39th St., New York, New York 10016. 1971-. Annual.

Environmental Information Connection–EIC. Planning Information Program, Dept. of Urban and Regional Planning, University of Illinois, 1003 West Nevada, Urbana, Illinois 61801. (217) 333-1369. Also available online.

Environmental Periodicals Bibliography. Environmental Studies Institute, International Academy at Santa Barbara, 800 Garden St., Suite D, Santa Barbara, California 93101. (805) 965-5010. Also available online.

ERDA Research Abstracts. U.S. ERDA Technical Information Center, Box 62, Oak Ridge, Tennessee 37830.

Geographical Abstracts. London School of Economics, Dept. of Geography, Regency House, 34 Duke St., London, England 1966-. Continued by Geo Abstracts issued in 6 parts: Pt. A. Landforms and the quaternary; Pt. B. Biogeography and Climatology; Pt. C. Economic geography; Pt. D. Social geography and cartography; Pt. E. Sedimentology; Pt. F. Regional and community planning.

Index to Scientific Book Contents. Institute for Scientific Information, 3501 Market St., Philadelphia, Pennsylvania 19104. (800) 523-1857. 1985-. Annual. Gives contents of science books published.

BIBLIOGRAPHIES

EPA Publications Bibliography. U.S. Environmental Protection Agency, Library Systems Branch, 401 M St., SW, Washington, District of Columbia 20460. (202) 260-2090. Quarterly.

Siting of Power Lines and Communication Towers. Lynne De Merritt. Council of Planning Librarians, 1313 E. 60th St., Chicago, Illinois 60637-2897. (312) 942-2163. 1990. A bibliography on the potential health effects of electric and magnetic fields.

DIRECTORIES

Directory of Selected U.S. Cogeneration, Small Power, and Industrial Power Plants. Utility Data Institute, 1700 K St., N.W., Suite 400, Washington, District of Columbia 20006. (202) 466-3660.

Directory of U.S. Cogeneration, Small Power & Industrial Power Plants. FIND/SVP, 625 Avenue of the Americas, New York, New York 10011. (212) 645-4500. Semiannual. More than 4800 cogeneration, small power and industrial power projects, refuse-to-energy plants, gas turbine and combined-cycle facilities, geothermal units, coal and wood-fired plants, wind and solar installations and a variety of other plant types.

Inventory of Power Plants in the United States. Department of Energy, 1000 Independence Ave., N.W., Washington, District of Columbia 20585. (202) 586-8800. Annual. Inventory of individual electric power plants operating, added, and retired and planned for operation. Includes information on ownership, capacity, and energy source.

Public Power Directory of Local Publicly Owned Electric Utilities. American Public Power Association, 2301 M St., N.W., Washington, District of Columbia 20037. (202) 467-2900.

ENCYCLOPEDIAS AND DICTIONARIES

Dictionary of Environmental Engineering and Related Sciences: English-Spanish, Spanish-English. Jose T. Villate. Ediciones Universal, 3090 SW 8th St., Miami, Florida 33135. (305) 642-3355. 1979.

Encyclopedia of Environmental Science and Engineering. J.R. Pfafflin. Gordon and Breach Science Publishers, Inc., 270 8th Ave., New York, New York 10011. (212) 206-8900. 1992.

Encyclopedia of Physical Science and Technology. Robert A. Meyers, ed. Academic Press, c/o Harcourt Brace Jovanovich Inc., 6277 Sea Harbor Dr., Orlando, Florida 32887. (800) 346-8648. Dictionary of engineering, technology and physical sciences.

Encyclopedia of Physics. Rita G. Lerner and George L. Trigg. VCH Publishers, 303 NW 12th Ave., Deerfield Beach, Florida 33442-1788. (305) 428-5566. 1991. Second edition.

McGraw-Hill Encyclopedia of Environmental Science. Sybil P. Parker. McGraw-Hill Science & Engineering Books, 11 W. 19th St., New York, New York 10011. (212) 337-6010. 1980. Covers ecology, man's influence on nature, and environmental protection.

McGraw-Hill Encyclopedia of Science and Technology. McGraw-Hill, 1221 Avenue of the Americas, New York, New York 10020. (212) 512-2000 or (800) 262-4729. 1992. Seventh edition. Issued in multiple volumes including index. Includes all science and technology broad subject areas.

Van Nostrand's Scientific Encyclopedia. Glenn D. Considine, ed. Van Nostrand Reinhold, 115 5th Ave., New York, New York 10003. (212) 254-3232. 1983. Sixth edition. Includes all broad subject areas in science.

GENERAL WORKS

Be Your Own Power Company. David J. Morris. Rodale Press, 33 E. Minor St., Emmaus, Pennsylvania 18098. (215) 967-5171; (800) 322-6333. 1983. This book is a technical aid to those entering the power production business. Stresses that conservation is cheaper than production. Includes bibliography.

Coal Ash Disposal: Solid Waste Impacts. Raymond A. Tripodi and Paul N. Cheremisinoff. Technomic Publishing Co., 851 New Holland Ave., Box 3535, Lancaster, Pennsylvania 17604. (717) 291-5609. 1980.

Ecological Effects of Thermal Discharges. T.E. Langford. Elsevier Science Publishing Co., 655 Avenue of the Americas, New York, New York 10010. (212) 984-5800.

1990. Review of the biological studies which have been carried out in various habitats and in response to a variety of problems related to cooling water usage, particularly on the large scale such as in thermal power stations.

Extension of the Principles of Radiation Protection to ... International Atomic Energy Agency. UNIPUB, 4611-F Assembly Dr., Lanham, Maryland 20706-4391. (301) 459-7666; (800) 274-4888. 1990.

Large Power Plant Effluent Study. Francis A. Schiermeier. U.S. National Air Pollution Control Administration, Raleigh, North Carolina 1970. Electric power plants and air pollution in the United States.

Reactor Accidents: Nuclear Safety and the Role of Institutional Failure. David Mosey. Nuclear Engineering International Special Publications, c/o Butterworth-Heinemann, 80 Montvale Ave., Stoneham, Massachusetts 02180. (617) 438-8464; (800) 366-2665. 1990.

Surveillance of Items Important to Safety in Nuclear Power Plants. International Atomic Energy Agency. UNIPUB, 4611-F Assembly Dr., Lanham, Maryland 20706-4391. (301) 459-7666; (800) 270-4888. 1990. Discusses the safety measures observed at atomic power plants.

ONLINE DATA BASES

Computerized Engineering Index–COMPENDEX. Engineering Information Inc., 345 E. 47th St., New York, New York 10017. (212) 705-7600.

Enviro/Energyline Abstracts Plus. R. R. Bowker Co., 121 Chanlon Rd., New Providence, New Jersey 07974. (908) 464-6800.

Environmental Periodicals Bibliography. National Information Services Corp., Ste. 6, Wyman Towers, 3100 St. Paul St., Baltimore, Maryland 21218. (410)243-0797. Online version of abstract of same name.

Monthly Catalog of United States Government Publications. U.S. G.P.O., Supt. of Docs., PO Box 371954, Pittsburgh, Pennsylvania 15250-7954. (202) 512-0000.

National Technical Information Service. U.S. Department of Commerce, National Technical Information Service, Office of Data Base Services, 5285 Port Royal Rd., Springfield, Virginia 22161. (703) 487-4807. Bibliographic database of government sponsored research and technical reports.

Registry of Toxic Effects of Chemical Substances–Online1. US Department of Health and Human Services, National Institute for Occupational Safety and Health, Washington, District of Columbia 20402-9325. (202) 783-3238. Tests on chemical substances: Substance Identification, Toxicity/Biomedical Effects, Toxicology and Carcinogenicity Review, and Exposure Standards and Regulations.

TRADE ASSOCIATIONS AND PROFESSIONAL SOCIETIES

National Association of Power Engineers. 2350 E. Devon Ave., Suite 115, Des Plaines, Illinois 60018. (718) 298-0600.

POWER REACTOR INHERENTLY SAFE MODULES

See: REACTORS

POWER RESOURCES

ABSTRACTING AND INDEXING SERVICES

Applied Science and Technology Index. H.W. Wilson Co., 950 University Ave., Bronx, New York 10452. (800) 367-6770. Formerly Industrial Arts Index.

Engineering Index. The Engineering Index Inc., 345 E. 47th St., New York, New York 10017. 1962-.

Environment Abstracts. Bowker A & I Publishing, 121 Chanlon Rd., New Providence, New Jersey 07974. (908) 464-6800. 1974-.

Environment Index. Environment Information Center, Index Research Department, 124 E. 39th St., New York, New York 10016. 1971-. Annual.

Environmental Information Connection–EIC. Planning Information Program, Dept. of Urban and Regional Planning, University of Illinois, 1003 West Nevada, Urbana, Illinois 61801. (217) 333-1369. Also available online.

Environmental Periodicals Bibliography. Environmental Studies Institute, International Academy at Santa Barbara, 800 Garden St., Suite D, Santa Barbara, California 93101. (805) 965-5010. Also available online.

ERDA Research Abstracts. U.S. ERDA Technical Information Center, Box 62, Oak Ridge, Tennessee 37830.

General Science Index. H. W. Wilson Co., 950 University Ave., Bronx, New York 10452. 1978-. Monthly, also issued in annual cumulation. Cumulative subject index to English language periodicals in the subject fields of astronomy, botany, chemistry, earth science, environment and conservation, food and nutrition, genetics, mathematics, medicine and health, microbiology, oceanography, physics, physiology and zoology.

Geographical Abstracts. London School of Economics, Dept. of Geography, Regency House, 34 Duke St., London, England 1966-. Continued by Geo Abstracts issued in 6 parts: Pt. A. Landforms and the quaternary; Pt. B. Biogeography and Climatology; Pt. C. Economic geography; Pt. D. Social geography and cartography; Pt. E. Sedimentology; Pt. F. Regional and community planning.

Index to Scientific Book Contents. Institute for Scientific Information, 3501 Market St., Philadelphia, Pennsylvania 19104. (800) 523-1857. 1985-. Annual. Gives contents of science books published.

BIBLIOGRAPHIES

Energy Guide: A Directory of Information Resources. Virginia Bemis, et al. Garland Publishers, 136 Madison Ave., New York, New York 10016. (212) 686-7492 or (800) 627-6273. 1977.

Energy Information Guide. R. David Weber. ABC-CLIO, PO Box 1911, Santa Barbara, California 93116-1911. (805) 963-4221. 1982. Three volumes. Includes more than 2000 reference works on energy and energy related topics. Volume 1: General and Alternative Energy Sources; volume 2: Nuclear and Electric Power: volume 3: Fossil Fuels.

Energy Research Guide Journals, Indexes and Abstracts. John Viola, et al. Ballinger Publishing Co., 10 E. 53rd St., New York, New York 10022. (212) 207-7581. 1983. Covers over 500 periodicals, indexes and abstracts covering energy or related fields. Section one: an alphabetical master list of all titles; section 2: subject list; section 3: description of each publication.

Energy Update: A Guide to Current Literature. R. David Weber. Energy Information Press, 1100 Industrial Suite 9, San Carlos, California 94070. (415) 594-0743. 1991. Some 1000 reference works are fully identified as well as 75 databases available for purchase or use on an online system. All forms of conventional and alternate energy sources are covered with consideration given to conservation and environmental impact.

EPA Publications Bibliography. U.S. Environmental Protection Agency, Library Systems Branch, 401 M St., SW, Washington, District of Columbia 20460. (202) 260-2090. Quarterly.

DIRECTORIES

Guide to Energy Specialists. Porter B. Bennett, ed. Center for International Environment Information, 300 E 42d St., New York, New York 10017. (212) 697-3232. 1979. Lists energy specialists who are willing to answer questions in the area of their expertise.

ENCYCLOPEDIAS AND DICTIONARIES

Dictionary of Dangerous Pollutants, Ecology, and Environment. David F. Tver. Industrial Press, 200 Madison Ave., New York, New York 10016. (212) 889-6330. 1981.

Dictionary of Environmental Engineering and Related Sciences: English-Spanish, Spanish-English. Jose T. Villate. Ediciones Universal, 3090 SW 8th St., Miami, Florida 33135. (305) 642-3355. 1979.

Encyclopedia of Environmental Science and Engineering. J.R. Pfafflin. Gordon and Breach Science Publishers, Inc., 270 8th Ave., New York, New York 10011. (212) 206-8900. 1992.

Encyclopedia of Physical Science and Technology. Robert A. Meyers, ed. Academic Press, c/o Harcourt Brace Jovanovich Inc., 6277 Sea Harbor Dr., Orlando, Florida 32887. (800) 346-8648. Dictionary of engineering, technology and physical sciences.

Energy Dictionary. V. Daniel Hunt. Van Nostrand Reinhold, 115 5th Ave., New York, New York 10003. (212) 254-3232. 1979. Covers the broad field of energy including fossil, nuclear, solar, geothermal, ocean, and wind energy.

Energy Terminology: A Multilingual Glossary. Pergamon Microforms International, Inc., Fairview Park, Elmsford, New York 10523. (914) 592-7720. 1986. Second edition. Contains 1500 defined terms and concepts related to the field of energy together with an index of several thousand undefined keywords used in the definitions of these terms and concepts. Contents appear in four languages: English, French, German and Spanish.

Kaiman's Encyclopedia of Energy Topics. Lee Kaiman and J. Masloff. Environmental Design and Research Center, 26799 Elena Rd., Los Altos Hills, California 94022. 1983. Two volumes. Coverage of topics range from natural energy sources that are renewable to nonrenewable, and the application of these energy sources.

McGraw Hill Encyclopedia of Energy. Sybil P. Parker. McGraw-Hill Science & Engineering Books, 1221 Avenue of Americas, New York, New York 10020. (212) 512-2000 or (800) 262-4729. 1981. Second edition. Major issues in energy are discussed in six feature articles. The second section has 300 alphabetically arranged entries relating to energy.

McGraw-Hill Encyclopedia of Science and Technology. McGraw-Hill, 1221 Avenue of the Americas, New York, New York 10020. (212) 512-2000 or (800) 262-4729. 1992. Seventh edition. Issued in multiple volumes including index. Includes all science and technology broad subject areas.

Van Nostrand's Scientific Encyclopedia. Glenn D. Considine, ed. Van Nostrand Reinhold, 115 5th Ave., New York, New York 10003. (212) 254-3232. 1983. Sixth edition. Includes all broad subject areas in science.

GENERAL WORKS

Be Your Own Power Company. David J. Morris. Rodale Press, 33 E. Minor St., Emmaus, Pennsylvania 18098. (215) 967-5171; (800) 322-6333. 1983. This book is a technical aid to those entering the power production business. Stresses that conservation is cheaper than production. Includes bibliography.

Energy and Environmental Strategies for the 1990's. Mary Jo Winer and Marilyn Jackson, eds. Fairmont Pr., 700 Indian Trail, Lilburn, Georgia 30247. (404) 925-9388. 1991. Papers from the 13th World Energy Engineering Congress and the World Environmental Engineering Congress organized by the Association of Energy Engineers and sponsored by the U.S. Department of Energy, Office of Institutional Programs.

Environmental Effects of Energy Systems: The OECD COMPASS Project. OECD Publications and Information Center, 2 rue Andre Pascal, Paris, France F-75775. 1983. Environmental aspects of energy development.

The Environmental Impacts of Production and Use of Energy: An Assessment. Essam E. el-Hinnawi. Tycooly Press, Dublin, Ireland 1981. Environmental aspects of energy consumption.

Least-Cost Energy: Solving the CO2 Problem. Amory B. Levins. Brick House Publishing Co., Inc., Francestown Tpke., New Boston, New Hampshire 03070. (603) 487-3718. 1982. Energy conservation and environmental aspects of carbon dioxide.

Sources for the Future. Wallace Oates. Resources for the Future, 1616 P St., NW, Washington, District of Columbia 20036. (202) 328-5086. Examines emissions taxes, abatement subsides, and transferable emission permits in a national, regional, and global context.

HANDBOOKS AND MANUALS

Energy Deskbook. Samuel Glasstone. Van Nostrand Reinhold, 115 5th Ave., New York, New York 10020. (212) 254-3232. 1983. Single volume reference covering all energy resources.

Energy Handbook. Robert L. Loftness. Van Nostrand Reinhold, 115 5th Ave., New York, New York 10003. (212) 254-3232. 1984. Second edition. Resource book on energy with current data taking into consideration the environmental control technologies. Includes an appendix with an energy conversion factor, a glossary and a general index.

Handbook of Energy Technology Trends and Perspectives. V. Daniel Hunt. Van Nostrand Reinhold, 115 5th Ave., New York, New York 10003. (212) 254-3232. 1982.

ONLINE DATA BASES

Computerized Engineering Index–COMPENDEX. Engineering Information Inc., 345 E. 47th St., New York, New York 10017. (212) 705-7600.

Enviro/Energyline Abstracts Plus. R. R. Bowker Co., 121 Chanlon Rd., New Providence, New Jersey 07974. (908) 464-6800.

Environmental Periodicals Bibliography. National Information Services Corp., Ste. 6, Wyman Towers, 3100 St. Paul St., Baltimore, Maryland 21218. (410)243-0797. Online version of abstract of same name.

Monthly Catalog of United States Government Publications. U.S. G.P.O., Supt. of Docs., PO Box 371954, Pittsburgh, Pennsylvania 15250-7954. (202) 512-0000.

National Technical Information Service. U.S. Department of Commerce, National Technical Information Service, Office of Data Base Services, 5285 Port Royal Rd., Springfield, Virginia 22161. (703) 487-4807. Bibliographic database of government sponsored research and technical reports.

PERIODICALS AND NEWSLETTERS

The Cogeneration Letter: The Monthly Newsletter on Cogeneration. Energy Engineering, 700 Indian Trail, Lilburn, Georgia 30247. 1985-. Monthly. Covers the information of importance to the power generation industry.

Energy Research Reports. ER Publications Inc., PO Box 157, 17 Langdon Ave., Watertown, Massachusetts 02172. (508) 872-8200. Twenty-two issues a year.

High Country News. High Country Foundation, 124 Grand Ave., Box 1090, Paonia, Colorado 81428-1090. (303) 527-4898. Biweekly. Environmental and publiclands issues in the Rocky Mountain region.

STATISTICS SOURCES

Energy: Facts and Future. Herbert F. Matare. CRC Press, 2000 Corporate Blvd. N.W., Boca Raton, Florida 33431. (800) 272-7737. 1989. Data on power resources and power mechanics.

World Energy Statistics and Balances. International Energy Agency. OECD Publications and Information Center, Suite 700, 2001 L St. N.W., Ste. 700, Washington, District of Columbia 20036. (202) 785-6323. 1989-. A compilation of energy production and consumption statistics for 85 non-OECD countries and regions, including developing countries, Central and Eastern European countries, and the Soviet Union.

POWER STORAGE

See: BATTERIES

PRAIRIE ECOLOGY

See also: ECOLOGY

ABSTRACTING AND INDEXING SERVICES

Applied Ecology Abstracts Studies in Renewable Natural Resources. Information Retrieval Ltd., 1911 Jefferson Davis Highway, Arlington, Virginia 22202. 1975-. Monthly.

Biological and Agricultural Index. H.W. Wilson Co., 950 University Ave., Bronx, New York 10452. (800) 367-6770. 1916-. Monthly.

Ecological Abstracts. Geo Abstracts Ltd. Elsevier Applied Science, Crown House, Linton Rd., Barking, England IG 11 8JU. 1974-. Derived from over 600 leading ecological and environmental journals, plus books, conference proceedings, reports and theses.

Ecology Abstracts. Cambridge Scientific Abstracts, 5161 River Rd., Bethesda, Maryland 20816. (301) 961-6750. Monthly.

Environment Abstracts. Bowker A & I Publishing, 121 Chanlon Rd., New Providence, New Jersey 07974. (908) 464-6800. 1974-.

Environment Index. Environment Information Center, Index Research Department, 124 E. 39th St., New York, New York 10016. 1971-. Annual.

Environmental Information Connection–EIC. Planning Information Program, Dept. of Urban and Regional Planning, University of Illinois, 1003 West Nevada, Urbana, Illinois 61801. (217) 333-1369. Also available online.

Environmental Periodicals Bibliography. Environmental Studies Institute, International Academy at Santa Barbara, 800 Garden St., Suite D, Santa Barbara, California 93101. (805) 965-5010. Also available online.

Index to Scientific Book Contents. Institute for Scientific Information, 3501 Market St., Philadelphia, Pennsylvania 19104. (800) 523-1857. 1985-. Annual. Gives contents of science books published.

Multimedia Index to Ecology. National Information Center for Educational Media, University of Southern California, Los Angeles, California 90007.

BIBLIOGRAPHIES

Current Contents. Agriculture, Biology and Environmental Sciences. Institute for Scientific Information, 3501 Market St., Philadelphia, Pennsylvania 19104. (800) 523-1857. 1973-. Previous title: Current Contents. Agricultural, Food & Veterinary Sciences. Gives the table of contents of periodicals in the fields of agriculture, biology, environmental and related areas.

EPA Publications Bibliography. U.S. Environmental Protection Agency, Library Systems Branch, 401 M St., SW, Washington, District of Columbia 20460. (202) 260-2090. Quarterly.

ENCYCLOPEDIAS AND DICTIONARIES

McGraw-Hill Encyclopedia of Environmental Science. Sybil P. Parker. McGraw-Hill Science & Engineering Books, 11 W. 19th St., New York, New York 10011. (212) 337-6010. 1980. Covers ecology, man's influence on nature, and environmental protection.

McGraw-Hill Encyclopedia of Science and Technology. McGraw-Hill, 1221 Avenue of the Americas, New York, New York 10020. (212) 512-2000 or (800) 262-4729. 1992. Seventh edition. Issued in multiple volumes including index. Includes all science and technology broad subject areas.

Van Nostrand's Scientific Encyclopedia. Glenn D. Considine, ed. Van Nostrand Reinhold, 115 5th Ave., New York, New York 10003. (212) 254-3232. 1983. Sixth edition. Includes all broad subject areas in science.

ONLINE DATA BASES

Enviro/Energyline Abstracts Plus. R. R. Bowker Co., 121 Chanlon Rd., New Providence, New Jersey 07974. (908) 464-6800.

Environmental Periodicals Bibliography. National Information Services Corp., Ste. 6, Wyman Towers, 3100 St. Paul St., Baltimore, Maryland 21218. (410)243-0797. Online version of abstract of same name.

Monthly Catalog of United States Government Publications. U.S. G.P.O., Supt. of Docs., PO Box 371954, Pittsburgh, Pennsylvania 15250-7954. (202) 512-0000.

National Technical Information Service. U.S. Department of Commerce, National Technical Information Service, Office of Data Base Services, 5285 Port Royal Rd., Springfield, Virginia 22161. (703) 487-4807. Bibliographic database of government sponsored research and technical reports.

SCISEARCH. Institute for Scientific Information, University City Science Center, 3501 Market St., Philadelphia, Pennsylvania 19104. (215) 386-0100.

PRESCRIBED BURNING

See: AIR POLLUTION

PRESERVES, ECOLOGICAL

See also: ECOLOGICAL RESERVES

ABSTRACTING AND INDEXING SERVICES

Applied Ecology Abstracts Studies in Renewable Natural Resources. Information Retrieval Ltd., 1911 Jefferson Davis Highway, Arlington, Virginia 22202. 1975-. Monthly.

Biological and Agricultural Index. H.W. Wilson Co., 950 University Ave., Bronx, New York 10452. (800) 367-6770. 1916-. Monthly.

Current Advances in Ecological and Environmental Science. Pergamon Microforms International, Inc., Fairview Park, Elmsford, New York 10523. (914) 592-7720. 1989-. Monthly. Current literature searching service including journals, reports, abstracts, etc. This service is available online as part of the CABS database on the hosts BRS and ORBIT search service.

Environment Abstracts. Bowker A & I Publishing, 121 Chanlon Rd., New Providence, New Jersey 07974. (908) 464-6800. 1974-.

Environment Index. Environment Information Center, Index Research Department, 124 E. 39th St., New York, New York 10016. 1971-. Annual.

Environmental Information Connection–EIC. Planning Information Program, Dept. of Urban and Regional Planning, University of Illinois, 1003 West Nevada, Urbana, Illinois 61801. (217) 333-1369. Also available online.

Environmental Periodicals Bibliography. Environmental Studies Institute, International Academy at Santa Barbara, 800 Garden St., Suite D, Santa Barbara, California 93101. (805) 965-5010. Also available online.

Geographical Abstracts. London School of Economics, Dept. of Geography, Regency House, 34 Duke St., London, England 1966-. Continued by Geo Abstracts issued in 6 parts: Pt. A. Landforms and the quaternary; Pt. B. Biogeography and Climatology; Pt. C. Economic geography; Pt. D. Social geography and cartography; Pt. E. Sedimentology; Pt. F. Regional and community planning.

Multimedia Index to Ecology. National Information Center for Educational Media, University of Southern California, Los Angeles, California 90007.

Science Citation Index. Institute for Scientific Information, 3501 Market St., Philadelphia, Pennsylvania 19104. 1961-.

BIBLIOGRAPHIES

Current Contents. Agriculture, Biology and Environmental Sciences. Institute for Scientific Information, 3501 Market St., Philadelphia, Pennsylvania 19104. (800) 523-1857. 1973-. Previous title: Current Contents. Agricultural, Food & Veterinary Sciences. Gives the table of contents of periodicals in the fields of agriculture, biology, environmental and related areas.

EPA Publications Bibliography. U.S. Environmental Protection Agency, Library Systems Branch, 401 M St., SW, Washington, District of Columbia 20460. (202) 260-2090. Quarterly.

ENCYCLOPEDIAS AND DICTIONARIES

Cambridge Encyclopedia of Life Sciences. A. E. Friday and David S. Ingram. Cambridge University Press, 40 W 20th St., New York, New York 10011. (212) 924-3900 or (800) 227-0247. 1985. Includes all topics under biology and ecology.

Grzimek's Encyclopedia of Ecology. Bernhard Grzimek. Van Nostrand Reinhold, 115 5th Ave., New York, New York 10003. (212) 254-3232. 1976.

McGraw-Hill Encyclopedia of Environmental Science. Sybil P. Parker. McGraw-Hill Science & Engineering Books, 11 W. 19th St., New York, New York 10011. (212) 337-6010. 1980. Covers ecology, man's influence on nature, and environmental protection.

McGraw-Hill Encyclopedia of Science and Technology. McGraw-Hill, 1221 Avenue of the Americas, New York, New York 10020. (212) 512-2000 or (800) 262-4729. 1992. Seventh edition. Issued in multiple volumes including index. Includes all science and technology broad subject areas.

North American Reference Encyclopedia of Ecology and Pollution. William White. North American Pub. Co., 401 N. Broad St., Philadelphia, Pennsylvania 19108. (215) 238-5300. 1972.

GENERAL WORKS

Biodiversity. E. O. Wilson. National Academy Press, 2101 Constitution Ave. N.W., PO Box 285, Washington, District of Columbia 20418. (202) 334-3313. 1988.

Preserving Communities and Corridors. Gay Mackintosh, ed. Defenders of Wildlife, 1244 19th St. N.W., Washington, District of Columbia 20036. (202) 659-9510. 1989.

HANDBOOKS AND MANUALS

Ecological Studies of Six Endangered Butterflies (Lepidoptera, Lycaenidea). Richard Arthur Arnold. University of California Press, 2120 Berkeley Way, Berkeley, California 94720. (415) 642-4247 (800) 822-6657. 1983. Island biogeography, patch dynamics, and the design of habitat preserves.

ONLINE DATA BASES

Enviro/Energyline Abstracts Plus. R. R. Bowker Co., 121 Chanlon Rd., New Providence, New Jersey 07974. (908) 464-6800.

Environmental Periodicals Bibliography. National Information Services Corp., Ste. 6, Wyman Towers, 3100 St. Paul St., Baltimore, Maryland 21218. (410)243-0797. Online version of abstract of same name.

Managed Area Basic Record. The Nature Conservancy, 1815 N. Lynn St., Arlington, Virginia 22209. (703) 841-5300. Database of about 3,100 nature preserves.

Monthly Catalog of United States Government Publications. U.S. G.P.O., Supt. of Docs., PO Box 371954, Pittsburgh, Pennsylvania 15250-7954. (202) 512-0000.

National Technical Information Service. U.S. Department of Commerce, National Technical Information Service, Office of Data Base Services, 5285 Port Royal Rd., Springfield, Virginia 22161. (703) 487-4807. Bibliographic database of government sponsored research and technical reports.

PERIODICALS AND NEWSLETTERS

NCSHPO Newsletter. National Conference of State Historic Preservation Offices, 444 North Capitol Street, NW, Suite 332, Washington, District of Columbia 20001. (202) 624-5465. Monthly. Covers state and federal historic preservation programs.

TRADE ASSOCIATIONS AND PROFESSIONAL SOCIETIES

American Institute of Biological Sciences. 730 11th St., N.W., Washington, District of Columbia 20001-4521. (202) 628-1500.

PRESSURE, ATMOSPHERIC

See: ATMOSPHERE

PRESSURIZED WATER REACTORS

See: REACTORS

PRETREATMENT, INDUSTRIAL

See: SEWAGE DISPOSAL

PRIME MOVERS

ABSTRACTING AND INDEXING SERVICES

Applied Science and Technology Index. H.W. Wilson Co., 950 University Ave., Bronx, New York 10452. (800) 367-6770. Formerly Industrial Arts Index.

Engineering Index. The Engineering Index Inc., 345 E. 47th St., New York, New York 10017. 1962-.

Environment Abstracts. Bowker A & I Publishing, 121 Chanlon Rd., New Providence, New Jersey 07974. (908) 464-6800. 1974-.

Environment Index. Environment Information Center, Index Research Department, 124 E. 39th St., New York, New York 10016. 1971-. Annual.

Environmental Information Connection–EIC. Planning Information Program, Dept. of Urban and Regional Planning, University of Illinois, 1003 West Nevada, Urbana, Illinois 61801. (217) 333-1369. Also available online.

Environmental Periodicals Bibliography. Environmental Studies Institute, International Academy at Santa Barbara, 800 Garden St., Suite D, Santa Barbara, California 93101. (805) 965-5010. Also available online.

ERDA Research Abstracts. U.S. ERDA Technical Information Center, Box 62, Oak Ridge, Tennessee 37830.

Physics Briefs. Physikalische Berichte. Physik Verlag, Pappapelallee 3, Postfach 101161, Weinheim, Germany D-6940. 1979-. Semimonthly. In English. Volumes for 1979- issued by the Deutsche Physikalische Gesellschaft and the Fachinformationszentrum Energie Physik, Mathematik in cooperation with the American Institute of Physics.

BIBLIOGRAPHIES

EPA Publications Bibliography. U.S. Environmental Protection Agency, Library Systems Branch, 401 M St., SW, Washington, District of Columbia 20460. (202) 260-2090. Quarterly.

ENCYCLOPEDIAS AND DICTIONARIES

Dictionary of Environmental Engineering and Related Sciences: English-Spanish, Spanish-English. Jose T. Villate. Ediciones Universal, 3090 SW 8th St., Miami, Florida 33135. (305) 642-3355. 1979.

Encyclopedia of Environmental Science and Engineering. J.R. Pfafflin. Gordon and Breach Science Publishers, Inc., 270 8th Ave., New York, New York 10011. (212) 206-8900. 1992.

Encyclopedia of Physical Science and Technology. Robert A. Meyers, ed. Academic Press, c/o Harcourt Brace Jovanovich Inc., 6277 Sea Harbor Dr., Orlando, Florida 32887. (800) 346-8648. Dictionary of engineering, technology and physical sciences.

Encyclopedia of Physics. Rita G. Lerner and George L. Trigg. VCH Publishers, 303 NW 12th Ave., Deerfield Beach, Florida 33442-1788. (305) 428-5566. 1991. Second edition.

McGraw-Hill Encyclopedia of Science and Technology. McGraw-Hill, 1221 Avenue of the Americas, New York, New York 10020. (212) 512-2000 or (800) 262-4729. 1992. Seventh edition. Issued in multiple volumes including index. Includes all science and technology broad subject areas.

Van Nostrand's Scientific Encyclopedia. Glenn D. Considine, ed. Van Nostrand Reinhold, 115 5th Ave., New York, New York 10003. (212) 254-3232. 1983. Sixth edition. Includes all broad subject areas in science.

ONLINE DATA BASES

Computerized Engineering Index–COMPENDEX. Engineering Information Inc., 345 E. 47th St., New York, New York 10017. (212) 705-7600.

Enviro/Energyline Abstracts Plus. R. R. Bowker Co., 121 Chanlon Rd., New Providence, New Jersey 07974. (908) 464-6800.

Environmental Periodicals Bibliography. National Information Services Corp., Ste. 6, Wyman Towers, 3100 St. Paul St., Baltimore, Maryland 21218. (410)243-0797. Online version of abstract of same name.

PRIORITY POLLUTANTS

GENERAL WORKS

Analytical Procedures for Determining Organic Priority Pollutants in Municipal Sludges. J.S. Warner. National Technical Information Service, 5285 Port Royal Rd., Springfield, Virginia 22161. (703) 487-4650. Topics in water pollution abatement.

Mass Spectrometry of Priority Pollutants. Brian S. Middleditch. Plenum Press, 233 Spring St., New York, New York 10013-1578. (212) 620-8000 or (800) 221-9369. 1981. Spectra relating to organic water pollutants.

HANDBOOKS AND MANUALS

The Infrared Spectra Handbook of Priority Pollutants and Toxic Chemicals. Sadtler Research Laboratories, 3316 Spring Garden St., Philadelphia, Pennsylvania 19104. (215) 382-7800. 1982. Chemicals spectra, hazardous substances spectra, gases spectra, and toxic chemicals.

PRISM

See: REACTORS

PRIVATE ELECTRIC UTILITIES
See: ELECTRIC UTILITIES

PROPANE

ABSTRACTING AND INDEXING SERVICES

Chemical Abstracts. Chemical Abstracts Service, 2540 Olentangy River Rd., PO Box 3012, Columbus, Ohio 43210. (800) 848-6533. 1907-.

Environment Abstracts. Bowker A & I Publishing, 121 Chanlon Rd., New Providence, New Jersey 07974. (908) 464-6800. 1974-.

Environment Index. Environment Information Center, Index Research Department, 124 E. 39th St., New York, New York 10016. 1971-. Annual.

Environmental Information Connection–EIC. Planning Information Program, Dept. of Urban and Regional Planning, University of Illinois, 1003 West Nevada, Urbana, Illinois 61801. (217) 333-1369. Also available online.

Environmental Periodicals Bibliography. Environmental Studies Institute, International Academy at Santa Barbara, 800 Garden St., Suite D, Santa Barbara, California 93101. (805) 965-5010. Also available online.

General Science Index. H. W. Wilson Co., 950 University Ave., Bronx, New York 10452. 1978-. Monthly, also issued in annual cumulation. Cumulative subject index to English language periodicals in the subject fields of astronomy, botany, chemistry, earth science, environment and conservation, food and nutrition, genetics, mathematics, medicine and health, microbiology, oceanography, physics, physiology and zoology.

Science Citation Index. Institute for Scientific Information, 3501 Market St., Philadelphia, Pennsylvania 19104. 1961-.

BIBLIOGRAPHIES

EPA Publications Bibliography. U.S. Environmental Protection Agency, Library Systems Branch, 401 M St., SW, Washington, District of Columbia 20460. (202) 260-2090. Quarterly.

ENCYCLOPEDIAS AND DICTIONARIES

Van Nostrand's Scientific Encyclopedia. Glenn D. Considine, ed. Van Nostrand Reinhold, 115 5th Ave., New York, New York 10003. (212) 254-3232. 1983. Sixth edition. Includes all broad subject areas in science.

GENERAL WORKS

Replacing Gasoline: Alternative Fuels for Light-Duty Vehicles. Congress of the U.S., c/o U.S. Government Printing Office, Office of Technology Assesment, N. Capitol & H Sts. NW, Washington, District of Columbia 20401. (202) 512-0000. 1990. Gives information on alternatives to standard gasoline. Some of the alternatives are: electricity, hydrogen, compressed natural gas, liquified natural gas, liquid propane gas, methanol, ethanol, and reformulated gasoline.

ONLINE DATA BASES

Chemical Abstracts-CA. Chemical Abstracts Service, 2540 Olentangy River Rd., P.O. Box 3012, Columbus, Ohio 43210. (800) 848-6533 or (614) 421-3600. Information sources include 9000 journals, patents from 27 countries, two industrial property organizations, new books, conference proceedings, and government research reports.

Enviro/Energyline Abstracts Plus. R. R. Bowker Co., 121 Chanlon Rd., New Providence, New Jersey 07974. (908) 464-6800.

Environmental Periodicals Bibliography. National Information Services Corp., Ste. 6, Wyman Towers, 3100 St. Paul St., Baltimore, Maryland 21218. (410)243-0797. Online version of abstract of same name.

NBSFLUIDS. National Institute of Standards & Technology, Office of Standard Reference Data, A323 Physics Building, Gaithersburg, Maryland 20899. (301) 975-2208.

Plant Toxicity Data. University of Oklahoma, Department of Botany & Microbiology, 770 Van Fleet Oval, Room 135, Norman, Oklahoma 73019. (405) 325-3174.

TRADE ASSOCIATIONS AND PROFESSIONAL SOCIETIES

American Chemical Society. 1155 16th St., N.W., Washington, District of Columbia 20036. (202) 872-4600.

American Institute of Chemical Engineers. 345 East 47th St., New York, New York 10017. (212) 705-7338.

American Institute of Chemists. 7315 Wisconsin Ave., Bethesda, Maryland 20814. (301) 652-2447.

National Propane Gas Association. 1600 Eisenhower Ln., Lisle, Illinois 60532. (708) 515-0600.

PROPELLANTS
See also: AEROSOLS

ABSTRACTING AND INDEXING SERVICES

Air Pollution Titles. Pennsylvania State University, Center for Air Environmental Studies, 226 Fenske Laboratory, University Park, Pennsylvania 16802. (814) 865-1415. 1965. Bibliographic guide to current research literature on air environment, including monitoring and control of air pollution, health effects, effects on agriculture, forests, toxic air contaminants, and global atmospheric pro cases.

Air Pollution Translations. A Bibliography With Abstracts. U.S. Environmental Protection Agency, MD 75, Research Triangle Park, North Carolina 27711. (919) 541-2184. 1969.

Engineering Index. The Engineering Index Inc., 345 E. 47th St., New York, New York 10017. 1962-.

General Science Index. H. W. Wilson Co., 950 University Ave., Bronx, New York 10452. 1978-. Monthly, also issued in annual cumulation. Cumulative subject index to English language periodicals in the subject fields of astronomy, botany, chemistry, earth science, environment and conservation, food and nutrition, genetics,

mathematics, medicine and health, microbiology, oceanography, physics, physiology and zoology.

Physics Briefs. Physikalische Berichte. Physik Verlag, Pappapelallee 3, Postfach 101161, Weinheim, Germany D-6940. 1979-. Semimonthly. In English. Volumes for 1979- issued by the Deutsche Physikalische Gesellschaft and the Fachinformationszentrum Energie Physik, Mathematik in cooperation with the American Institute of Physics.

Science Citation Index. Institute for Scientific Information, 3501 Market St., Philadelphia, Pennsylvania 19104. 1961-.

BIBLIOGRAPHIES

Current Contents. Agriculture, Biology and Environmental Sciences. Institute for Scientific Information, 3501 Market St., Philadelphia, Pennsylvania 19104. (800) 523-1857. 1973-. Previous title: Current Contents. Agricultural, Food & Veterinary Sciences. Gives the table of contents of periodicals in the fields of agriculture, biology, environmental and related areas.

ENCYCLOPEDIAS AND DICTIONARIES

Encyclopedia of Physical Science and Technology. Robert A. Meyers, ed. Academic Press, c/o Harcourt Brace Jovanovich Inc., 6277 Sea Harbor Dr., Orlando, Florida 32887. (800) 346-8648. Dictionary of engineering, technology and physical sciences.

Encyclopedia of Physics. Rita G. Lerner and George L. Trigg. VCH Publishers, 303 NW 12th Ave., Deerfield Beach, Florida 33442-1788. (305) 428-5566. 1991. Second edition.

McGraw-Hill Encyclopedia of Environmental Science. Sybil P. Parker. McGraw-Hill Science & Engineering Books, 11 W. 19th St., New York, New York 10011. (212) 337-6010. 1980. Covers ecology, man's influence on nature, and environmental protection.

McGraw-Hill Encyclopedia of Science and Technology. McGraw-Hill, 1221 Avenue of the Americas, New York, New York 10020. (212) 512-2000 or (800) 262-4729. 1992. Seventh edition. Issued in multiple volumes including index. Includes all science and technology broad subject areas.

Van Nostrand's Scientific Encyclopedia. Glenn D. Considine, ed. Van Nostrand Reinhold, 115 5th Ave., New York, New York 10003. (212) 254-3232. 1983. Sixth edition. Includes all broad subject areas in science.

GENERAL WORKS

Explosives, Propellants and Pyrotechnics. A. Bailey. Brassey's Defense Publishers, 8000 Westpark Dr., 1st Fl., McLean, Virginia 22102. (703) 442-4535. 1989. Military fireworks and explosives.

High Explosives and Propellants. Stanley Fordham. Pergamon Microforms International, Inc., Fairview Park, New York, New York 10523. (914) 592-7720. 1980. Science and technology of explosives.

Post-Accident Procedures for Chemicals and Propellants. Deborah K. Shaver. Noyes Publications, 120 Mill Rd., Park Ridge, New Jersey 07656. (201) 391-8484. 1984. Covers accidents occurring during transportation of hazardous substances.

ONLINE DATA BASES

Computerized Engineering Index–COMPENDEX. Engineering Information Inc., 345 E. 47th St., New York, New York 10017. (212) 705-7600.

Monthly Catalog of United States Government Publications. U.S. G.P.O., Supt. of Docs., PO Box 371954, Pittsburgh, Pennsylvania 15250-7954. (202) 512-0000.

National Technical Information Service. U.S. Department of Commerce, National Technical Information Service, Office of Data Base Services, 5285 Port Royal Rd., Springfield, Virginia 22161. (703) 487-4807. Bibliographic database of government sponsored research and technical reports.

PERIODICALS AND NEWSLETTERS

Propellants, Explosives, Pyrotechnics. VCH Publishers, 303 NW 12th Ave., Deerfield Beach, Florida 33442-1788. (305) 428-5566. Quarterly.

PROTECTED AREAS

ABSTRACTING AND INDEXING SERVICES

Environment Abstracts. Bowker A & I Publishing, 121 Chanlon Rd., New Providence, New Jersey 07974. (908) 464-6800. 1974-.

Environment Index. Environment Information Center, Index Research Department, 124 E. 39th St., New York, New York 10016. 1971-. Annual.

Environmental Information Connection–EIC. Planning Information Program, Dept. of Urban and Regional Planning, University of Illinois, 1003 West Nevada, Urbana, Illinois 61801. (217) 333-1369. Also available online.

Environmental Periodicals Bibliography. Environmental Studies Institute, International Academy at Santa Barbara, 800 Garden St., Suite D, Santa Barbara, California 93101. (805) 965-5010. Also available online.

BIBLIOGRAPHIES

EPA Publications Bibliography. U.S. Environmental Protection Agency, Library Systems Branch, 401 M St., SW, Washington, District of Columbia 20460. (202) 260-2090. Quarterly.

DIRECTORIES

United Nations List of National Parks and Protected Areas. World Conservation Monitoring Centre. World Conservation Union, IUCN Publications Services Unit, 181a Huntingdon Road, Cambridge, England CB3 0DJ. (0223) 277894. 1990. Standard list of national parks and other protected areas. Includes lists of world heritage sites, biosphere reserves and wetlands of international importance.

GENERAL WORKS

Marine and Coastal Protected Areas: A Guide for Planners and Managers. Rodney V. Salm. International Union for Conservation of Nature and Natural Resources, Avenue du Mont-Blanc, Gland, Switzerland CH-1196. 1984.

Case studies in coastal zone management and marine resources conservation.

Wildlife and Protected Areas: An Overview. United Nations Environment Program. UNIPUB, 1980.

HANDBOOKS AND MANUALS

Guidelines for Protected Areas Legislation. Barbara J. Lausche. International Union for Conservation of Nature and Natural Resources, Avenue du Mont-Blanc, Gland, Switzerland CH-1196. 1985. Manual on environmental policy and law.

ONLINE DATA BASES

Enviro/Energyline Abstracts Plus. R. R. Bowker Co., 121 Chanlon Rd., New Providence, New Jersey 07974. (908) 464-6800.

Environmental Periodicals Bibliography. National Information Services Corp., Ste. 6, Wyman Towers, 3100 St. Paul St., Baltimore, Maryland 21218. (410)243-0797. Online version of abstract of same name.

STATISTICS SOURCES

World Resources. World Resources Institute. 1709 New York Ave., N.W., Washington, District of Columbia 20006. (202) 638-6300. Annual. Statistical and textual analysis of world's natural resources and the effects of growth-caused environmental pollution.

PROTECTIVE CLOTHING

ABSTRACTING AND INDEXING SERVICES

Environment Abstracts. Bowker A & I Publishing, 121 Chanlon Rd., New Providence, New Jersey 07974. (908) 464-6800. 1974-.

Environment Index. Environment Information Center, Index Research Department, 124 E. 39th St., New York, New York 10016. 1971-. Annual.

Environmental Information Connection–EIC. Planning Information Program, Dept. of Urban and Regional Planning, University of Illinois, 1003 West Nevada, Urbana, Illinois 61801. (217) 333-1369. Also available online.

Environmental Periodicals Bibliography. Environmental Studies Institute, International Academy at Santa Barbara, 800 Garden St., Suite D, Santa Barbara, California 93101. (805) 965-5010. Also available online.

BIBLIOGRAPHIES

EPA Publications Bibliography. U.S. Environmental Protection Agency, Library Systems Branch, 401 M St., SW, Washington, District of Columbia 20460. (202) 260-2090. Quarterly.

GENERAL WORKS

Chemical Protective Clothing. American Industrial Hygiene Association, 345 White Pond Dr., Akron, Ohio 44320. (216) 873-2442. 1990. 2 vols. Volume 1 reviews basic polymer chemistry and permeation theory and types, construction, and use of protective materials; specific test methods, selection guidelines and decontamination. Volume 2 contains product performance evaluation data and information on physical property test methods, permeation data, chemicals, products and vendors, and encapsulating suit ensembles.

Chemical Protective Clothing Performance in Chemical Emergency Response. J.L. Perkins. Association for Testing and Materials (ASTM), 1916 Race St., Philadelphia, Pennsylvania 19103-1187. (215) 299-5400. 1989. Chemical engineering safety measures relating to protective clothing.

Protective Clothing for Hazardous Materials Incidents. National Fire Protection Association. Burclan Productions, Batterymarch Park, PO Box 9101, Quincy, Massachusetts 02269. (617) 770-3000. 1984. A sound cassette, slide and technical manual relating to protective clothing.

HANDBOOKS AND MANUALS

Chemical Protective Clothing Performance Index Book. Krister Fosberg. John Wiley & Sons, Inc., 605 3rd Ave., New York, New York 10158-0012. (212) 850-6000. 1989.

Guidelines for the Selection of Chemical Protective Clothing. Arthur D. Little Inc. U.S. Coast Guard, 2100 Second St., N.W., Rm. 5410 C, Washington, District of Columbia 20593. (202) 267-1042. 1987. A field guide and a technical and reference manual.

ONLINE DATA BASES

Enviro/Energyline Abstracts Plus. R. R. Bowker Co., 121 Chanlon Rd., New Providence, New Jersey 07974. (908) 464-6800.

Environmental Periodicals Bibliography. National Information Services Corp., Ste. 6, Wyman Towers, 3100 St. Paul St., Baltimore, Maryland 21218. (410)243-0797. Online version of abstract of same name.

PROTEIN

ABSTRACTING AND INDEXING SERVICES

Agrindex. AGRIS Coordinating Center, Via delle Terme di Caracalla, Rome, Italy I-00100. 61 0181-FA01. 1975-.

ASFA Aquaculture Abstracts. Cambridge Scientific Abstracts, Inc., 5161 River Rd., Bethesda, Maryland 20816. (301) 961-6750. 1984.

Biological Abstracts. BIOSIS, 2100 Arch St., Philadelphia, Pennsylvania 19103-1399. (215) 587-4800. 1927-.

Biological and Agricultural Index. H.W. Wilson Co., 950 University Ave., Bronx, New York 10452. (800) 367-6770. 1916-. Monthly.

Biotechnology Research Abstracts. Cambridge Scientific Abstracts, 5161 River Rd., Bethesda, Maryland 20816. (301) 961-6750. Monthly. Includes such broad areas as genetic intervention, biochemical genetics, and microbiological techniques.

Current Advances in Plant Science. Pergamon Microforms International, Inc., Fairview Park, Elmsford, New York 10523. (914) 592-7720. 1984-. Monthly. Current literature searching service including journals, reports, abstracts, etc. This service is available online as part of the CABS database on the hosts BRS and ORBIT search service.

Environment Abstracts. Bowker A & I Publishing, 121 Chanlon Rd., New Providence, New Jersey 07974. (908) 464-6800. 1974-.

Environment Index. Environment Information Center, Index Research Department, 124 E. 39th St., New York, New York 10016. 1971-. Annual.

Environmental Information Connection–EIC. Planning Information Program, Dept. of Urban and Regional Planning, University of Illinois, 1003 West Nevada, Urbana, Illinois 61801. (217) 333-1369. Also available online.

Environmental Periodicals Bibliography. Environmental Studies Institute, International Academy at Santa Barbara, 800 Garden St., Suite D, Santa Barbara, California 93101. (805) 965-5010. Also available online.

Food Science and Technology Abstracts. International Food Information Service, c/o National Food Laboratory, 6363 Clark Ave., Dublin, California 94568. (800) 336-3782. 1969-.

General Science Index. H. W. Wilson Co., 950 University Ave., Bronx, New York 10452. 1978-. Monthly, also issued in annual cumulation. Cumulative subject index to English language periodicals in the subject fields of astronomy, botany, chemistry, earth science, environment and conservation, food and nutrition, genetics, mathematics, medicine and health, microbiology, oceanography, physics, physiology and zoology.

Genetics Abstracts. Cambridge Scientific Abstracts, 5161 River Rd., Bethesda, Maryland 20816. (301) 961-6750. 1968-. Monthly. Formerly published by Information Retrieval Ltd., London England. Published by Cambridge Scientific Abstracts since 1982.

Science Citation Index. Institute for Scientific Information, 3501 Market St., Philadelphia, Pennsylvania 19104. 1961-.

ALMANACS AND YEARBOOKS

Progress in Protein-Lipid Interactions. Elsevier Science Publishing Co., 655 Avenue of the Americas, New York, New York 10010. (212) 984-5800. Annual. Review designed to critically evaluate actively developing areas of research in protein-lipid interactions.

BIBLIOGRAPHIES

Current Contents. Agriculture, Biology and Environmental Sciences. Institute for Scientific Information, 3501 Market St., Philadelphia, Pennsylvania 19104. (800) 523-1857. 1973-. Previous title: Current Contents. Agricultural, Food & Veterinary Sciences. Gives the table of contents of periodicals in the fields of agriculture, biology, environmental and related areas.

EPA Publications Bibliography. U.S. Environmental Protection Agency, Library Systems Branch, 401 M St., SW, Washington, District of Columbia 20460. (202) 260-2090. Quarterly.

ENCYCLOPEDIAS AND DICTIONARIES

Cambridge Dictionary of Biology. Peter M. B. Walker. Cambridge University Press, 40 W. 20th St., New York, New York 10011. (212) 924-3900 or (800) 227-0247. 1989. Includes 10,000 terms in zoology, botany, biochemistry, molecular biology and genetics. Previously published under the title Chambers Biology Dictionary.

Cambridge Encyclopedia of Life Sciences. A. E. Friday and David S. Ingram. Cambridge University Press, 40 W 20th St., New York, New York 10011. (212) 924-3900 or (800) 227-0247. 1985. Includes all topics under biology and ecology.

A Concise Dictionary of Biology. Elizabeth Martin, ed. Oxford University Press, 200 Madison Ave., New York, New York 10016. (212) 679-7300 or (800) 334-4249. 1990. New edition. Derived from the Concise Science Dictionary, published in 1984.

The Dictionary of Cell Biology. J. M. Lackie and J. A. T. Dow, eds. Academic Press, c/o Harcourt Brace Jovanovich Inc., 6277 Sea Harbor Dr., Orlando, Florida 32887. (800) 346-8648. 1989. Covers the broad subject area of cell biology including lipid, vitamins, amino acid, lectins, proteins, and other related topics.

Dictionary of Microbiology and Molecular Biology. Paul Singleton and Diana Sainsbury. John Wiley & Sons, Inc., 605 3rd Ave., New York, New York 10158-0012. (212) 850-6000. 1987. Second edition. Comprehensive dictionary with "classical descriptive aspects of microbiology to current developments in related areas of bioenergetics, biochemistry and molecular biology." Entries give synonyms, cross references, and references to pertinent works. Miscellaneous appendixes. Bibliography.

Encyclopedia of Human Biology. Renato Dulbecco, ed. Academic Press, c/o Harcourt Brace Jovanovich Inc., 6277 Sea Harbor Dr., Orlando, Florida 32887. (800) 346-8648. 1991. Eight volumes.

Enzyme Nomenclature 1984. Edwin C. Webb. Academic Press, c/o Harcourt Brace Jovanovich Inc., 6277 Sea Harbor Dr., Orlando, Florida 32887. (800) 346-8648. 1992. Fifth edition. "This edition is a revision of the Recommendations (1978) of the Nomenclature Committee of IUB, and has been approved for publication by the Executive Committee of the International Union of Biochemistry." Includes 2728 enzymes. It considers classification and nomenclature, their units of activity and standard methods of assay, together with symbols used in the description of enzyme kinetics.

Life Sciences on File. Diagram Group. Facts on File, Inc., 460 Park Ave. S., New York, New York 10016. (212) 683-2244. 1986. Encyclopedia of pictorial collection in life sciences. Deals with all major topics in life sciences including ecology.

Macmillan Dictionary of Toxicology. Ernest Hodgson, et al. Van Nostrand Reinhold, 115 5th Ave., New York, New York 10003. (212) 254-3232. 1988. Intended as a "starting point" to the literature of toxicology. American spelling is used with cross references to British version of words. Contains a list of references. Signed entries give explanatory definitions and cross references.

McGraw-Hill Encyclopedia of Science and Technology. McGraw-Hill, 1221 Avenue of the Americas, New York, New York 10020. (212) 512-2000 or (800) 262-4729. 1992. Seventh edition. Issued in multiple volumes in-

cluding index. Includes all science and technology broad subject areas.

Van Nostrand's Scientific Encyclopedia. Glenn D. Considine, ed. Van Nostrand Reinhold, 115 5th Ave., New York, New York 10003. (212) 254-3232. 1983. Sixth edition. Includes all broad subject areas in science.

GENERAL WORKS

Bioluminescence and Chemiluminescence: Instruments and Applications. Academic Press, c/o Harcourt Brace Jovanovich Inc., 6277 Sea Harbor Dr., Orlando, Florida 32887. (800) 346-8648. 1986.

Calcium, Cell Cycles, and Cancer. James F. Whitfield. CRC Press, 2000 Corporate Blvd. N.W., Boca Raton, Florida 33431. (800) 272-7737. 1990.

Gel Electrophoresis of Proteins. M.J. Dunn. IOP Pub. Ltd., Techno House, Radcliffe Way, Bristol, England BS1 6NX. 1990. Techniques of analytical gel electrophoresis.

Interactions of Food Proteins. Nicholas Parris and Robert Bradford, eds. American Chemical Society, 1155 16th St. N.W., Washington, District of Columbia 20036. (202) 872-4600; (800) 227-5558. 1991. Discusses food proteins in great detail such as their composition, functionality, stability, properties, and other useful features.

Magill's Survey of Science. Life Science Series. Frank N. Magill, ed. Salem Press, PO Box 50062, Pasadena, California 91105. 1991. Six volumes. Contents: v.1. A-Central and peripheral nervous system functions; v.2. Central metabolism regulation - eukaryotic transcriptional control; v.3. Positive and negative eukaryotic transcriptional control - mammalian hormones; v.4. Hormones and behavior - muscular contraction; v.5. Muscular contraction and relaxation - sexual reproduction in plants; v.6. Reproductive behavior and mating - X inactivation and the Lyon hypothesis.

Methods of Protein Analysis. Istavan Kerese. Halsted Press, 605 Third Ave., New York, New York 10158. (212) 850-6000. 1984. Deals with electrophoresis, proteins and chromatography.

Protein Production by Biotechnology. T. J. R. Harris, ed. Elsevier Science Publishing Co., 655 Avenue of the Americas, New York, New York 10010. (212) 984-5800. 1990. Describes the use of recombinant DNA techniques to produce proteins of therapeutic or other importance.

Protein Purification: Design and Scale Up of Downstreams Processing. Scott M. Wheelwright. Oxford University Press, 200 Madison Ave., New York, New York 10016. (212) 679-7300; (800) 334-4249. 1991.

Protein Refolding. George Georgiou and Eliana De Barnardez-Clark, eds. American Chemical Society, 1155 16th St. N.W., Washington, District of Columbia 20036. (202) 872-4600; (800) 227-5558. 1991. Studies protein recovery, aggregation, formation, structure, and other features.

Site-Directed Mutagenesis and Protein Engineering. M. Rafaat El-Gewely. Elsevier Science Publishing Co., 655 Avenue of the Americas, New York, New York 10010. (212) 989-5800. 1991.

HANDBOOKS AND MANUALS

Handbook of Protein Sequence Analysis. L.R. Croft. John Wiley & Sons, Inc., 605 3rd Ave., New York, New York

10158-0012. (212) 850-6000. 1980. A compilation of amino acid sequences with an introduction to the methodology.

Methods of Protein Microcharacterization. John E. Shively. Humana Press, PO Box 2148, Clifton, New Jersey 07015. (201) 773-4389. 1986. Peptides analysis, trace analysis and amino acid sequences.

Practical Protein Chemistry. A. Darbre. John Wiley & Sons, Inc., 605 3rd Ave., New York, New York 10158-0012. (212) 850-6000. 1986. A handbook on proteins.

ONLINE DATA BASES

BIOSIS Previews. BIOSIS, 2100 Arch St., Philadelphia, Pennsylvania 19103-1399. (215) 587-4800. Largest and most comprehensive database of research in the life sciences. Contains citations for nearly 9000 primary research journals, monographs, reviews, symposia, preliminary reports, semi-popular journals, selected institutional reports, government reports and research communications.

Cambridge Scientific Abstracts Life Science–CSAL. Cambridge Scientific Abstracts, 5161 River Rd., Bethesda, Maryland 20816. (301) 961-6750. Provides access to the following abstracting services: "Life Sciences Collection," "Aquatic Sciences and Fisheries Abstracts," "Oceanic Abstracts," and "Pollution Abstracts."

Enviro/Energyline Abstracts Plus. R. R. Bowker Co., 121 Chanlon Rd., New Providence, New Jersey 07974. (908) 464-6800.

Environmental Periodicals Bibliography. National Information Services Corp., Ste. 6, Wyman Towers, 3100 St. Paul St., Baltimore, Maryland 21218. (410)243-0797. Online version of abstract of same name.

SCISEARCH. Institute for Scientific Information, University City Science Center, 3501 Market St., Philadelphia, Pennsylvania 19104. (215) 386-0100.

PERIODICALS AND NEWSLETTERS

The Journal of Biological Chemistry. American Society of Biological Chemists, 428 E. Preston St., Baltimore, Maryland 21202. Three times a month. Biological, agricultural, and energy aspects of the environment.

RESEARCH CENTERS AND INSTITUTES

Center for Molecular Biology. Wayne State University, 5047 Gullen Mall, Detroit, Michigan 48202. (313) 577-0616.

Mineralization Center. University of South Alabama, Department of Biological Sciences, LSB, Room 214, Mobile, Alabama 36688. (205) 460-6331.

Molecular Biology Institute. University of California, Los Angeles, 405 Hilgard Avenue, Los Angeles, California 90024. (213) 825-1018.

State University of New York at Albany, Institute of Hemoproteins. Chemistry 131 A, 1400 Washington Avenue, Albany, New York 12222. (518) 442-4420.

University of Miami, Institute for Molecular Cellular Evolution. 12500 SW 152 Street, Miami, Florida 33177. (305) 284-7366.

University of Michigan, Protein Sequencing Facility. Department of Biological Chemistry, 1301 Catherine Road, Ann Arbor, Michigan 48109-0606. (313) 763-0289.

University of Minnesota, Industry/University Cooperative Research Center for Biocatalytic Processing. 240 Gortner Laboratory, 1479 Gortner Avenue, St. Paul, Minnesota 55108. (612) 624-6774.

University of Wisconsin-Madison, Institute for Enzyme Research. 1710 University Avenue, Madison, Wisconsin 53705. (608) 262-2140.

TRADE ASSOCIATIONS AND PROFESSIONAL SOCIETIES

American Chemical Society. 1155 16th St., N.W., Washington, District of Columbia 20036. (202) 872-4600.

American Institute of Biological Sciences. 730 11th St., N.W., Washington, District of Columbia 20001-4521. (202) 628-1500.

American Institute of Chemical Engineers. 345 East 47th St., New York, New York 10017. (212) 705-7338.

American Institute of Chemists. 7315 Wisconsin Ave., Bethesda, Maryland 20814. (301) 652-2447.

PUBLIC ELECTRIC UTILITIES

See: ELECTRIC UTILITIES

PUERTO RICO ENVIRONMENTAL AGENCIES

GOVERNMENTAL ORGANIZATIONS

Coastal Zone Division: Coastal Zone Management. Sub-Secretary, Puerta de Tierra, PO Box 5887, San Juan, Puerto Rico 00904. (809) 725-2769.

Department of Agriculture: Pesticide Registration. Director, Analysis and Registration of Agricultural Materials, PO Box 10163, Santurce, Puerto Rico 00908. (809) 796-1710.

Department of Labor and Human Resources: Occupational Safety. Secretary, 505 Munoz Rivera Ave., Hato Rey, Puerto Rico 00918. (809) 754-5353.

Department of Natural Resources: Fish and Wildlife. Secretary, PO Box 5887, San Juan, Puerto Rico 00906. (809) 724-8774.

Department of Natural Resources: Natural Resources. Secretary, PO Box 5887, San Juan, Puerto Rico 00906. (809) 724-8774.

Environmental Quality Board: Air Quality. Chairman, PO Box 11488, Santurce, Puerto Rico 00910. (809) 767-8056.

Environmental Quality Board: Environmental Protection. Chairman, PO Box 11488, Santurce, Puerto Rico 00910. (809) 725-5140.

Environmental Quality Board: Hazardous Waste Management. Chairman, PO Box 11488, Santurce, Puerto Rico 00910. (809) 725-5140.

Environmental Quality Board: Water Quality. Chairman, PO Box 11488, Santurce, Puerto Rico 00910. (809) 725-5140.

Puerto Rico Environmental Quality Board: Emergency Preparedness and Community Right-to-Know. SERC Commissioner, Title III-SARA Section 313, PO Box 11488, Sernades Juncos Station, Santurce, Puerto Rico 00910. (809) 722-0077.

Solid Waste Authority: Solid Waste Management. Executive Director, PO Box 40285, Minallas Station, San Juan, Puerto Rico 00940. (809) 765-7584.

U.S. EPA Region 2: Pollution Prevention. Regional Contact, 26 Federal Plaza, New York, New York 10278. (212) 264-2525.

PUERTO RICO ENVIRONMENTAL LEGISLATION

GENERAL WORKS

Puerto Rico Environmental Law Handbook. Government Institutes, Inc., 4 Research Pl., Ste. 200, Rockville, Maryland 20850. (301) 921-2300. 1990.

PULP AND PAPER TECHNOLOGY

ABSTRACTING AND INDEXING SERVICES

Environment Abstracts. Bowker A & I Publishing, 121 Chanlon Rd., New Providence, New Jersey 07974. (908) 464-6800. 1974-.

Environment Index. Environment Information Center, Index Research Department, 124 E. 39th St., New York, New York 10016. 1971-. Annual.

Environmental Information Connection–EIC. Planning Information Program, Dept. of Urban and Regional Planning, University of Illinois, 1003 West Nevada, Urbana, Illinois 61801. (217) 333-1369. Also available online.

Environmental Periodicals Bibliography. Environmental Studies Institute, International Academy at Santa Barbara, 800 Garden St., Suite D, Santa Barbara, California 93101. (805) 965-5010. Also available online.

Forest Products Abstracts. C. A. B. International, 845 North Park Ave., Tucson, Arizona 85719. (602) 621-7897 or (800) 528-4841. Bimonthly. Contains abstracts in the area of forest product industry; wood properties; timber extraction; conversion and measurement; damage to timber and timber production; utilization of wood; pulp industries and the chemical utilization of wood and other related areas.

Pollution Abstracts. Cambridge Scientific Abstracts, 5161 River Rd., Bethesda, Maryland 20816. (301) 961-6750. Six/year. Indexes worldwide technical literature on environmental pollution. Covers air pollution, marine and freshwater pollution, sewage and wastewater treatment, waste management, toxicology and health, noise pollution, radiation, land pollution, and environmental policies, programs, legislation, and education. Also available online.

BIBLIOGRAPHIES

EPA Publications Bibliography. U.S. Environmental Protection Agency, Library Systems Branch, 401 M St., SW, Washington, District of Columbia 20460. (202) 260-2090. Quarterly.

ENCYCLOPEDIAS AND DICTIONARIES

Dictionary of Environmental Engineering and Related Sciences: English-Spanish, Spanish-English. Jose T. Villate. Ediciones Universal, 3090 SW 8th St., Miami, Florida 33135. (305) 642-3355. 1979.

Encyclopedia of Environmental Science and Engineering. J.R. Pfafflin. Gordon and Breach Science Publishers, Inc., 270 8th Ave., New York, New York 10011. (212) 206-8900. 1992.

McGraw-Hill Encyclopedia of Science and Technology. McGraw-Hill, 1221 Avenue of the Americas, New York, New York 10020. (212) 512-2000 or (800) 262-4729. 1992. Seventh edition. Issued in multiple volumes including index. Includes all science and technology broad subject areas.

GENERAL WORKS

Advanced Pollution Abatement Technology in the Pulp and Paper Industry. Environment Directorate. OECD Publication and Information Centre, 2 rue Andre Pascal, Paris, France F-75775. 1973. Waste disposal in the paper and wood-pulp industry.

Pulp and Paper. James P. Casey. John Wiley & Sons, Inc., 605 3rd Ave., New York, New York 10158-0012. (212) 850-6000. 1980. Chemistry and chemical technology relating to paper making and wood-pulp.

Pulp Technology and Treatment for Paper. James Clark. Freeman Publications, 600 Harrison St., San Francisco, California 94107. (415) 905-2200. 1985.

ONLINE DATA BASES

Enviro/Energyline Abstracts Plus. R. R. Bowker Co., 121 Chanlon Rd., New Providence, New Jersey 07974. (908) 464-6800.

Environmental Periodicals Bibliography. National Information Services Corp., Ste. 6, Wyman Towers, 3100 St. Paul St., Baltimore, Maryland 21218. (410)243-0797. Online version of abstract of same name.

Monthly Catalog of United States Government Publications. U.S. G.P.O., Supt. of Docs., PO Box 371954, Pittsburgh, Pennsylvania 15250-7954. (202) 512-0000.

National Technical Information Service. U.S. Department of Commerce, National Technical Information Service, Office of Data Base Services, 5285 Port Royal Rd., Springfield, Virginia 22161. (703) 487-4807. Bibliographic database of government sponsored research and technical reports.

PULP MILL EFFLUENTS

See also: EFFLUENTS (DISCHARGE); EMISSION; WASTEWATER TREATMENT

ABSTRACTING AND INDEXING SERVICES

Applied Science and Technology Index. H.W. Wilson Co., 950 University Ave., Bronx, New York 10452. (800) 367-6770. Formerly Industrial Arts Index.

Aqualine Abstracts. Water Research Centre. c/o Pergamon Microforms International, Inc., Fairview Park, Elmsford, New York 10523. (914) 592-7720. 1927-. Contains some 8,000 records annually on water and wastewater technology. Covers all aspects of water, wastewater, associated engineering services and the aquatic environment. Over 600 periodicals, as well as books, reports and conference proceedings and other publications from water related institutions worldwide are scanned. Also available online.

ASFA Aquaculture Abstracts. Cambridge Scientific Abstracts, Inc., 5161 River Rd., Bethesda, Maryland 20816. (301) 961-6750. 1984.

Chemical Abstracts. Chemical Abstracts Service, 2540 Olentangy River Rd., PO Box 3012, Columbus, Ohio 43210. (800) 848-6533. 1907-.

Engineering Index. The Engineering Index Inc., 345 E. 47th St., New York, New York 10017. 1962-.

Environment Abstracts. Bowker A & I Publishing, 121 Chanlon Rd., New Providence, New Jersey 07974. (908) 464-6800. 1974-.

Environment Index. Environment Information Center, Index Research Department, 124 E. 39th St., New York, New York 10016. 1971-. Annual.

Environmental Information Connection–EIC. Planning Information Program, Dept. of Urban and Regional Planning, University of Illinois, 1003 West Nevada, Urbana, Illinois 61801. (217) 333-1369. Also available online.

Environmental Periodicals Bibliography. Environmental Studies Institute, International Academy at Santa Barbara, 800 Garden St., Suite D, Santa Barbara, California 93101. (805) 965-5010. Also available online.

Pollution Abstracts. Cambridge Scientific Abstracts, 5161 River Rd., Bethesda, Maryland 20816. (301) 961-6750. Six/year. Indexes worldwide technical literature on environmental pollution. Covers air pollution, marine and freshwater pollution, sewage and wastewater treatment, waste management, toxicology and health, noise pollution, radiation, land pollution, and environmental policies, programs, legislation, and education. Also available online.

BIBLIOGRAPHIES

EPA Publications Bibliography. U.S. Environmental Protection Agency, Library Systems Branch, 401 M St., SW, Washington, District of Columbia 20460. (202) 260-2090. Quarterly.

GENERAL WORKS

Development of a Chemical Toxicity Assay for Pulp Mill Effluents. J.M. Leach. U.S. Environmental Protection Agency, 401 M St., S.W., Washington, District of Columbia 20460. (202) 260-2090. 1981. Sulphate pulping process and effect of water pollution on fishes.

Efficiency in Environmental Regulation: A Benefit-Cost Analysis of Alternative Approaches. Kluwer Academic

Publishers, 101 Philip Dr., Assinippi Park, Norwell, Massachusetts 02061-0358. (617) 871-6600. Quantitative assessment of the efficiency of the EPA's regulation of conventional air and water pollutants from the pulp and paper industry.

Proceedings of the 44th Industrial Waste Conference May 1989, Purdue University. John W. Bell, ed. Lewis Publishers, 2000 Corporate Blvd., N.W., Boca Raton, Florida 33431. (407) 994-0555 or (800) 272-7737. 1990. Includes new research, case histories and operating data, on every conceivable facet of today's big problem with unparalleled appropriate, usable information and data for current industrial waste problems.

Pulp and Paper Industry Corrosion Problems. National Association of Corrosion Engineers, P.O. Box 218340, Houston, Texas 77218. (713) 492-0535. 1982.

HANDBOOKS AND MANUALS

Environmental Control for Pulp and Paper Mills. Howard Edde. Noyes Publications, 120 Mill Rd., Park Ridge, New Jersey 07656. (201) 391-8484. 1984. Pollution technology review of pulp and paper making and trade.

ONLINE DATA BASES

Chemical Abstracts-CA. Chemical Abstracts Service, 2540 Olentangy River Rd., P.O. Box 3012, Columbus, Ohio 43210. (800) 848-6533 or (614) 421-3600. Information sources include 9000 journals, patents from 27 countries, two industrial property organizations, new books, conference proceedings, and government research reports.

Computerized Engineering Index–COMPENDEX. Engineering Information Inc., 345 E. 47th St., New York, New York 10017. (212) 705-7600.

EBIB. Texas A & M University, Sterling C. Evans Library, Reference Division, College Station, Texas 77843. (409) 845-5741.

Enviro/Energyline Abstracts Plus. R. R. Bowker Co., 121 Chanlon Rd., New Providence, New Jersey 07974. (908) 464-6800.

Environmental Periodicals Bibliography. National Information Services Corp., Ste. 6, Wyman Towers, 3100 St. Paul St., Baltimore, Maryland 21218. (410)243-0797. Online version of abstract of same name.

FOREST. Forest Products Research Society, 2801 Marshall Court, Madison, Wisconsin 53705. (608) 231-1361.

Monthly Catalog of United States Government Publications. U.S. G.P.O., Supt. of Docs., PO Box 371954, Pittsburgh, Pennsylvania 15250-7954. (202) 512-0000.

National Technical Information Service. U.S. Department of Commerce, National Technical Information Service, Office of Data Base Services, 5285 Port Royal Rd., Springfield, Virginia 22161. (703) 487-4807. Bibliographic database of government sponsored research and technical reports.

TRADE ASSOCIATIONS AND PROFESSIONAL SOCIETIES

National Council of the Paper Industry for Air and Stream Improvements. 260 Madison Ave., New York, New York 10016. (212) 532-9000.

Pulp Chemicals Association. P.O. Box 105113, Atlanta, Georgia 30348. (404) 446-1290.

Technical Association of the Pulp and Paper Industry. Box 105113, Atlanta, Georgia 30348-5113. (404) 446-1400.

PULVERIZATION

ABSTRACTING AND INDEXING SERVICES

Science Citation Index. Institute for Scientific Information, 3501 Market St., Philadelphia, Pennsylvania 19104. 1961-.

ENCYCLOPEDIAS AND DICTIONARIES

Van Nostrand's Scientific Encyclopedia. Glenn D. Considine, ed. Van Nostrand Reinhold, 115 5th Ave., New York, New York 10003. (212) 254-3232. 1983. Sixth edition. Includes all broad subject areas in science.

PUMPED STORAGE

ABSTRACTING AND INDEXING SERVICES

Engineering Index. The Engineering Index Inc., 345 E. 47th St., New York, New York 10017. 1962-.

ENCYCLOPEDIAS AND DICTIONARIES

Van Nostrand's Scientific Encyclopedia. Glenn D. Considine, ed. Van Nostrand Reinhold, 115 5th Ave., New York, New York 10003. (212) 254-3232. 1983. Sixth edition. Includes all broad subject areas in science.

GENERAL WORKS

An Assessment of Hydroelectric Pumped Storage. Dames and Moore Co. Institute for Water Resources, c/o American Public Works Association, 1313 E. 60th St., Chicago, Illinois 60637. (312) 667-2200. 1982. National hydroelectric power resources study.

Hydroelectric and Pumped Storage Plants. M.G. Jog. John Wiley & Sons, Inc., 605 3rd Ave., New York, New York 10158-0012. (212) 850-6000. 1989. Design and construction of hydroelectric plants.

Operation and Maintenance Experiences of Pumped-Storage Plants. A. Borenstadt. Electric Power Research Institute, 3412 Hillview Ave., Palo Alto, California 94304. (415) 965-4081. 1991. Repair and maintenance of hydroelectric power plants.

HANDBOOKS AND MANUALS

Pumped-Storage Planning and Evaluation Guide. H.H. Chen. Electric Power Research Institute, 3412 Hillview Ave., Palo Alto, California 94304. (415) 965-4081. 1990. Economic aspects of electric power production.

ONLINE DATA BASES

Computerized Engineering Index–COMPENDEX. Engineering Information Inc., 345 E. 47th St., New York, New York 10017. (212) 705-7600.

PUMPING STATION
See: SEWAGE TREATMENT

PYRETHROID PESTICIDES

ABSTRACTING AND INDEXING SERVICES

Biological Abstracts. BIOSIS, 2100 Arch St., Philadelphia, Pennsylvania 19103-1399. (215) 587-4800. 1927-.

Chemical Abstracts. Chemical Abstracts Service, 2540 Olentangy River Rd., PO Box 3012, Columbus, Ohio 43210. (800) 848-6533. 1907-.

Science Citation Index. Institute for Scientific Information, 3501 Market St., Philadelphia, Pennsylvania 19104. 1961-.

ENCYCLOPEDIAS AND DICTIONARIES

McGraw-Hill Encyclopedia of Environmental Science. Sybil P. Parker. McGraw-Hill Science & Engineering Books, 11 W. 19th St., New York, New York 10011. (212) 337-6010. 1980. Covers ecology, man's influence on nature, and environmental protection.

Van Nostrand's Scientific Encyclopedia. Glenn D. Considine, ed. Van Nostrand Reinhold, 115 5th Ave., New York, New York 10003. (212) 254-3232. 1983. Sixth edition. Includes all broad subject areas in science.

GENERAL WORKS

The Pyrethroid Insecticides. John P. Leahey. Taylor & Francis, 1900 Frost Rd., Ste. 101, Philadelphia, Pennsylvania 19007. (215) 785-5800. 1985. Toxicology and environmental aspects of pyrethroids.

Pyrethroids Residues, Immunoassays for Low Molecular Weight Compounds. Wolfgang Blass. Springer-Verlag, 175 5th Ave., New York, New York 10010. (212) 460-1500. 1990. Chemistry of plant protection, and pesticide residues in food.

Synthetic Pyrethroid Insecticides. Klaus Naumann. Springer-Verlag, 175 5th Ave., New York, New York 10010. (212) 460-1500. 1990. Structure and properties of pyrethroids and their synthesis.

ONLINE DATA BASES

BIOSIS Previews. BIOSIS, 2100 Arch St., Philadelphia, Pennsylvania 19103-1399. (215) 587-4800. Largest and most comprehensive database of research in the life sciences. Contains citations for nearly 9000 primary research journals, monographs, reviews, symposia, preliminary reports, semi-popular journals, selected institutional reports, government reports and research communications.

Chemical Abstracts-CA. Chemical Abstracts Service, 2540 Olentangy River Rd., P.O. Box 3012, Columbus, Ohio 43210. (800) 848-6533 or (614) 421-3600. Information sources include 9000 journals, patents from 27 countries, two industrial property organizations, new books, conference proceedings, and government research reports.

Chemical Collection System/Request Tracking–CCS/RTS. U.S. Environmental Protection Agency, Office of Pesticides and Toxic Substances, 401 M St., SW, Washington, District of Columbia 20460. (202) 260-2090. Contains information on various properties of a number of chemicals including environmental effects, test and analysis methods, and health effects. Available from EPA.

Chemical Dictionary Online–CHEMLINE. Chemical Abstracts Service, 2540 Olentangy River Rd., Columbus, Ohio 43210. (614) 421-3600 or (800) 848-6533. Part of MEDLINE of the National Library of Medicine (NLM). File of 900,000 names for chemical substances, representing 450,000 unique compounds. It contains such information as Chemical Abstracts (CA) Service Registry Numbers, molecular formulas, preferred chemical nomenclature, and generic and ring structure information. Available on NLM's ELHILL system.

Chemical Exposure. Science Applications International Corp., Health & Environmental Information, P.O. Box 2501, Oak Ridge, Tennessee 37831. (615) 482-9031. Database of chemicals that have been identified in both human tissues and body fluids and in feral and food animals. Contains reference to journal articles, conferences, and reports. Covers the whole fields of information related to human and animal exposure to food, air, and water contaminants and pharmaceuticals. Its records include information on chemical properties, formulas, tissues measured, analytical method used, demographics and more. Available on DIALOG.

TRADE ASSOCIATIONS AND PROFESSIONAL SOCIETIES

American Chemical Society. 1155 16th St., N.W., Washington, District of Columbia 20036. (202) 872-4600.

PYRITE

ABSTRACTING AND INDEXING SERVICES

Chemical Abstracts. Chemical Abstracts Service, 2540 Olentangy River Rd., PO Box 3012, Columbus, Ohio 43210. (800) 848-6533. 1907-.

General Science Index. H. W. Wilson Co., 950 University Ave., Bronx, New York 10452. 1978-. Monthly, also issued in annual cumulation. Cumulative subject index to English language periodicals in the subject fields of astronomy, botany, chemistry, earth science, environment and conservation, food and nutrition, genetics, mathematics, medicine and health, microbiology, oceanography, physics, physiology and zoology.

Science Citation Index. Institute for Scientific Information, 3501 Market St., Philadelphia, Pennsylvania 19104. 1961-.

ENCYCLOPEDIAS AND DICTIONARIES

Van Nostrand's Scientific Encyclopedia. Glenn D. Considine, ed. Van Nostrand Reinhold, 115 5th Ave., New York, New York 10003. (212) 254-3232. 1983. Sixth edition. Includes all broad subject areas in science.

HANDBOOKS AND MANUALS

Guidelines for Handling Excavated Acid-Producing Materials. Federal Lands Highway Programs. U.S. Federal Highway Administration, 400 7th St., S.W., Washington, District of Columbia 20590. (202) 366-0630. 1990. Soil acidification, leaching and environmental aspects of sulphide minerals.

ONLINE DATA BASES

Chemical Abstracts-CA. Chemical Abstracts Service, 2540 Olentangy River Rd., P.O. Box 3012, Columbus, Ohio 43210. (800) 848-6533 or (614) 421-3600. Information sources include 9000 journals, patents from 27 countries, two industrial property organizations, new books, conference proceedings, and government research reports.

Chemical Collection System/Request Tracking–CCS/RTS. U.S. Environmental Protection Agency, Office of Pesticides and Toxic Substances, 401 M St., SW, Washington, District of Columbia 20460. (202) 260-2090. Contains information on various properties of a number of chemicals including environmental effects, test and analysis methods, and health effects. Available from EPA.

Chemical Dictionary Online–CHEMLINE. Chemical Abstracts Service, 2540 Olentangy River Rd., Columbus, Ohio 43210. (614) 421-3600 or (800) 848-6533. Part of MEDLINE of the National Library of Medicine (NLM). File of 900,000 names for chemical substances, representing 450,000 unique compounds. It contains such information as Chemical Abstracts (CA) Service Registry Numbers, molecular formulas, preferred chemical nomenclature, and generic and ring structure information. Available on NLM's ELHILL system.

TRADE ASSOCIATIONS AND PROFESSIONAL SOCIETIES

American Chemical Society. 1155 16th St., N.W., Washington, District of Columbia 20036. (202) 872-4600.

American Institute of Chemical Engineers. 345 East 47th St., New York, New York 10017. (212) 705-7338.

American Institute of Chemists. 7315 Wisconsin Ave., Bethesda, Maryland 20814. (301) 652-2447.

PYROPHOSPHATE

ABSTRACTING AND INDEXING SERVICES

Chemical Abstracts. Chemical Abstracts Service, 2540 Olentangy River Rd., PO Box 3012, Columbus, Ohio 43210. (800) 848-6533. 1907-.

General Science Index. H. W. Wilson Co., 950 University Ave., Bronx, New York 10452. 1978-. Monthly, also issued in annual cumulation. Cumulative subject index to English language periodicals in the subject fields of astronomy, botany, chemistry, earth science, environment and conservation, food and nutrition, genetics, mathematics, medicine and health, microbiology, oceanography, physics, physiology and zoology.

Science Citation Index. Institute for Scientific Information, 3501 Market St., Philadelphia, Pennsylvania 19104. 1961-.

ENCYCLOPEDIAS AND DICTIONARIES

Van Nostrand's Scientific Encyclopedia. Glenn D. Considine, ed. Van Nostrand Reinhold, 115 5th Ave., New York, New York 10003. (212) 254-3232. 1983. Sixth edition. Includes all broad subject areas in science.

HANDBOOKS AND MANUALS

Thiamin Pyrophosphate Biochemistry. Alfred Schellenberger. CRC Press, 2000 Corporate Blvd. N.W., Boca Raton, Florida 33431. (800) 272-7737. 1988. Fundamentals of pyruvate decarboxylase and transketolase and pyruvate dehydrogenace complex.

ONLINE DATA BASES

Chemical Abstracts-CA. Chemical Abstracts Service, 2540 Olentangy River Rd., P.O. Box 3012, Columbus, Ohio 43210. (800) 848-6533 or (614) 421-3600. Information sources include 9000 journals, patents from 27 countries, two industrial property organizations, new books, conference proceedings, and government research reports.

Chemical Collection System/Request Tracking–CCS/RTS. U.S. Environmental Protection Agency, Office of Pesticides and Toxic Substances, 401 M St., SW, Washington, District of Columbia 20460. (202) 260-2090. Contains information on various properties of a number of chemicals including environmental effects, test and analysis methods, and health effects. Available from EPA.

Chemical Dictionary Online–CHEMLINE. Chemical Abstracts Service, 2540 Olentangy River Rd., Columbus, Ohio 43210. (614) 421-3600 or (800) 848-6533. Part of MEDLINE of the National Library of Medicine (NLM). File of 900,000 names for chemical substances, representing 450,000 unique compounds. It contains such information as Chemical Abstracts (CA) Service Registry Numbers, molecular formulas, preferred chemical nomenclature, and generic and ring structure information. Available on NLM's ELHILL system.

Chemical Exposure. Science Applications International Corp., Health & Environmental Information, P.O. Box 2501, Oak Ridge, Tennessee 37831. (615) 482-9031. Database of chemicals that have been identified in both human tissues and body fluids and in feral and food animals. Contains reference to journal articles, conferences, and reports. Covers the whole fields of information related to human and animal exposure to food, air, and water contaminants and pharmaceuticals. Its records include information on chemical properties, formulas, tissues measured, analytical method used, demographics and more. Available on DIALOG.

TRADE ASSOCIATIONS AND PROFESSIONAL SOCIETIES

American Chemical Society. 1155 16th St., N.W., Washington, District of Columbia 20036. (202) 872-4600.

Q

QUENCH TANK

See: INCINERATION

QUINONES

ABSTRACTING AND INDEXING SERVICES

Biological Abstracts. BIOSIS, 2100 Arch St., Philadelphia, Pennsylvania 19103-1399. (215) 587-4800. 1927-.

General Science Index. H. W. Wilson Co., 950 University Ave., Bronx, New York 10452. 1978-. Monthly, also issued in annual cumulation. Cumulative subject index to English language periodicals in the subject fields of astronomy, botany, chemistry, earth science, environment and conservation, food and nutrition, genetics, mathematics, medicine and health, microbiology, oceanography, physics, physiology and zoology.

Science Citation Index. Institute for Scientific Information, 3501 Market St., Philadelphia, Pennsylvania 19104. 1961-.

ENCYCLOPEDIAS AND DICTIONARIES

Encyclopedia of Trademarks and Synonyms. H. Bennett, ed. Chemical Publishing Co., 80 Eighth Ave., New York, New York 10011. (212) 255-1950. 1981. Three volumes. Includes chemical compounds, compositions consisting of one or more chemicals and other products. Also included are abbreviated names and WHO free names.

Van Nostrand's Scientific Encyclopedia. Glenn D. Considine, ed. Van Nostrand Reinhold, 115 5th Ave., New York, New York 10003. (212) 254-3232. 1983. Sixth edition. Includes all broad subject areas in science.

GENERAL WORKS

Naturally Occurring Quinones. Ronald Hunter Thomson. Chapman & Hall, 29 W. 35th St., New York, New York 10001-2291. (212) 244-3336. 1987. Recent advances in quinone derivatives and spectra.

HANDBOOKS AND MANUALS

CRC Handbook of EPR Spectra from Quinones and Quinols. J.A. Pedersen. CRC Press, 200 Corporate Blvd. N.W., Boca Raton, Florida 33431. (800) 272-7737. 1985. Topics in electron paramagnetic resonance spectroscopy.

ONLINE DATA BASES

BIOSIS Previews. BIOSIS, 2100 Arch St., Philadelphia, Pennsylvania 19103-1399. (215) 587-4800. Largest and most comprehensive database of research in the life sciences. Contains citations for nearly 9000 primary research journals, monographs, reviews, symposia, preliminary reports, semi-popular journals, selected institutional reports, government reports and research communications.

TRADE ASSOCIATIONS AND PROFESSIONAL SOCIETIES

American Chemical Society. 1155 16th St., N.W., Washington, District of Columbia 20036. (202) 872-4600.

R

RADIATION, ELECTROMAGNETIC

ABSTRACTING AND INDEXING SERVICES

Applied Science and Technology Index. H.W. Wilson Co., 950 University Ave., Bronx, New York 10452. (800) 367-6770. Formerly Industrial Arts Index.

Chemical Abstracts. Chemical Abstracts Service, 2540 Olentangy River Rd., PO Box 3012, Columbus, Ohio 43210. (800) 848-6533. 1907-.

Ecological Abstracts. Geo Abstracts Ltd. Elsevier Applied Science, Crown House, Linton Rd., Barking, England IG 11 8JU. 1974-. Derived from over 600 leading ecological and environmental journals, plus books, conference proceedings, reports and theses.

General Science Index. H. W. Wilson Co., 950 University Ave., Bronx, New York 10452. 1978-. Monthly, also issued in annual cumulation. Cumulative subject index to English language periodicals in the subject fields of astronomy, botany, chemistry, earth science, environment and conservation, food and nutrition, genetics, mathematics, medicine and health, microbiology, oceanography, physics, physiology and zoology.

Index of Publications on Biological Effects of Electromagnetic Radiation. James B. Kinn. U.S. Environmental Protection Agency, Health Effects Research Laboratory, 401 M St., SW, Washington, District of Columbia 20460. (202) 260-2090. 1981.

INIS Atomindex. International Atomic Energy Agency, Wagramerstrasse 5, Vienna, Austria A-1400. 222 23606198. 1988-. Semiannual. Abstracts nuclear energy and nuclear physics topics from journals, conferences, technical reports and other related publications. Issued in 6 parts: Personal Author, Corporate Entry, Subject, Report, Standard Patent, Conference (by place), Conference (by date).

Physics Briefs. Physikalische Berichte. Physik Verlag, Pappapelallee 3, Postfach 101161, Weinheim, Germany D-6940. 1979-. Semimonthly. In English. Volumes for 1979- issued by the Deutsche Physikalische Gesellschaft and the Fachinformationszentrum Energie Physik, Mathematik in cooperation with the American Institute of Physics.

Science Citation Index. Institute for Scientific Information, 3501 Market St., Philadelphia, Pennsylvania 19104. 1961-.

ENCYCLOPEDIAS AND DICTIONARIES

Encyclopedia of Physical Science and Technology. Robert A. Meyers, ed. Academic Press, c/o Harcourt Brace Jovanovich Inc., 6277 Sea Harbor Dr., Orlando, Florida 32887. (800) 346-8648. Dictionary of engineering, technology and physical sciences.

Van Nostrand's Scientific Encyclopedia. Glenn D. Considine, ed. Van Nostrand Reinhold, 115 5th Ave., New York, New York 10003. (212) 254-3232. 1983. Sixth edition. Includes all broad subject areas in science.

GENERAL WORKS

Biological Effects of Electromagnetic Radiation. James W. Frazer. John Wiley & Sons, Inc., 605 3rd Ave., New York, New York 10158-0012. (212) 850-6000. 1983.

How to Live with Low-Level Radiation: A Nutritional Protection Plan. Leon Chaitow. Healing Arts Pr., 1 Park St., Rochester, Vermont 05767. (802) 767-3174. 1988. Discusses the problem of low-level radiation in depth and offers safe, nutritional measures to counteract this invisible hazard.

ONLINE DATA BASES

Chemical Abstracts-CA. Chemical Abstracts Service, 2540 Olentangy River Rd., P.O. Box 3012, Columbus, Ohio 43210. (800) 848-6533 or (614) 421-3600. Information sources include 9000 journals, patents from 27 countries, two industrial property organizations, new books, conference proceedings, and government research reports.

RESEARCH CENTERS AND INSTITUTES

University of Michigan, Radiation Safety Service. North University Building, Room 1101, Ann Arbor, Michigan 48109-1057. (313) 764-4420.

University of Washington, Laboratory of Radiation Ecology. Fisheries Research Center, College of Fisheries, Seattle, Washington 98195. (206) 543-4259.

TRADE ASSOCIATIONS AND PROFESSIONAL SOCIETIES

Radiation Research Society. American College of Radiology, 1101 Market St., 14th Fl., Philadelphia, Pennsylvania 19107. (215) 574-3153.

RADIATION EXPOSURE

ABSTRACTING AND INDEXING SERVICES

Applied Science and Technology Index. H.W. Wilson Co., 950 University Ave., Bronx, New York 10452. (800) 367-6770. Formerly Industrial Arts Index.

Biological Abstracts. BIOSIS, 2100 Arch St., Philadelphia, Pennsylvania 19103-1399. (215) 587-4800. 1927-.

Chemical Abstracts. Chemical Abstracts Service, 2540 Olentangy River Rd., PO Box 3012, Columbus, Ohio 43210. (800) 848-6533. 1907-.

Ecological Abstracts. Geo Abstracts Ltd. Elsevier Applied Science, Crown House, Linton Rd., Barking, England IG 11 8JU. 1974-. Derived from over 600 leading ecological and environmental journals, plus books, conference proceedings, reports and theses.

Environment Abstracts. Bowker A & I Publishing, 121 Chanlon Rd., New Providence, New Jersey 07974. (908) 464-6800. 1974-.

Environment Index. Environment Information Center, Index Research Department, 124 E. 39th St., New York, New York 10016. 1971-. Annual.

Environmental Information Connection–EIC. Planning Information Program, Dept. of Urban and Regional Planning, University of Illinois, 1003 West Nevada, Urbana, Illinois 61801. (217) 333-1369. Also available online.

Environmental Periodicals Bibliography. Environmental Studies Institute, International Academy at Santa Barbara, 800 Garden St., Suite D, Santa Barbara, California 93101. (805) 965-5010. Also available online.

INIS Atomindex. International Atomic Energy Agency, Wagramerstrasse 5, Vienna, Austria A-1400. 222 23606198. 1988-. Semiannual. Abstracts nuclear energy and nuclear physics topics from journals, conferences, technical reports and other related publications. Issued in 6 parts: Personal Author, Corporate Entry, Subject, Report, Standard Patent, Conference (by place), Conference (by date).

Science Citation Index. Institute for Scientific Information, 3501 Market St., Philadelphia, Pennsylvania 19104. 1961-.

Selected References on Environmental Quality as It Relates to Health. National Library of Medicine, 8600 Rockville Pike, Bethesda, Maryland 20894. (800) 638-8480. 1977.

BIBLIOGRAPHIES

EPA Publications Bibliography. U.S. Environmental Protection Agency, Library Systems Branch, 401 M St., SW, Washington, District of Columbia 20460. (202) 260-2090. Quarterly.

DIRECTORIES

World Directory of Environmental Organizations. Thaddeus C. Trzyna, ed. California Institute of Public Affairs, PO Box 10, Claremont, California 91711. (714) 624-5212. 1989. 3rd ed. Handbook of organizations and programs concerned with protecting the environment and managing natural resources. It covers national and

international organizations, both governmental and non-governmental, in all parts of the world.

ENCYCLOPEDIAS AND DICTIONARIES

Encyclopedia of Human Biology. Renato Dulbecco, ed. Academic Press, c/o Harcourt Brace Jovanovich Inc., 6277 Sea Harbor Dr., Orlando, Florida 32887. (800) 346-8648. 1991. Eight volumes.

Encyclopedia of Physical Science and Technology. Robert A. Meyers, ed. Academic Press, c/o Harcourt Brace Jovanovich Inc., 6277 Sea Harbor Dr., Orlando, Florida 32887. (800) 346-8648. Dictionary of engineering, technology and physical sciences.

Glossary of Terms in Nuclear Science and Technology. American Nuclear Society, 555 North Kensington Ave., La Grange Park, Illinois 60525. (708) 352-6611. 1986. Prepared by the American Nuclear Society Standards Committee. Subcommittee ANS-9.

Van Nostrand's Scientific Encyclopedia. Glenn D. Considine, ed. Van Nostrand Reinhold, 115 5th Ave., New York, New York 10003. (212) 254-3232. 1983. Sixth edition. Includes all broad subject areas in science.

GENERAL WORKS

Extension of the Principles of Radiation Protection to ... International Atomic Energy Agency. UNIPUB, 4611-F Assembly Dr., Lanham, Maryland 20706-4391. (301) 459-7666; (800) 274-4888. 1990.

Guidelines for the Radiation Protection of Workers in Industry, Ionising Radiations. International Labour Office, 49 Sheridan Ave., Albany, New York 12210. (518) 436-9686. 1989. Provides technical information on protection against radiation in specific installations and for specific equipment. Designed to be used in conjunction with the ILO code of practice Radiation Protection of Workers (ionising rations), they describe the requirements of workers engaged in radiation work with external sources and unsealed sources.

How to Live with Low-Level Radiation: A Nutritional Protection Plan. Leon Chaitow. Healing Arts Pr., 1 Park St., Rochester, Vermont 05767. (802) 767-3174. 1988. Discusses the problem of low-level radiation in depth and offers safe, nutritional measures to counteract this invisible hazard.

Problems in Assessing the Cancer Risks of Low-Level Ionizing Radiation Exposure. U.S. General Accounting office, 441 G St., NW, Washington, District of Columbia 20548. (202) 275-5067. 1981. Toxicology of radiation and radiation-induced neoplasms.

Proposed Federal Radiation Protection Guidance for Occupational Exposure. Office of radiation Programs. USEPA, Washington, District of Columbia 1981. Safety measures in the nuclear industry.

Radiation Exposure and Occupational Risks. G. Keller, et al. Springer-Verlag, 175 5th Ave., New York, New York 10010. (212) 460-1500; (800) 777-4643. 1990. Discusses radiation exposure injuries in the workplace and prevention.

Radioactive Aerosols. A. C. Chamberlin. Cambridge University Press, 40 W 20th St., New York, New York 10011. (212) 924-3900; (800) 227-0247. 1991. Describes radioactive gases and particles which are dispersed in the environment, either from natural causes or following nuclear test and accidental emissions.

A Review of Radiation Exposure Estimates from Normal Operations in the Management and Disposal of High-Level Radioactive Waste and Spent Nuclear Fuel. William F. Holcomb. U.S. Environmental Protection Agency, 401 M St., S.W, Washington, District of Columbia 20460. (202) 260-2090. 1980.

GOVERNMENTAL ORGANIZATIONS

U.S. Environmental Protection Agency: Office of Radiation Programs. 401 M St., S.W., Washington, District of Columbia 20460. (202) 557-9710.

ONLINE DATA BASES

BIOSIS Previews. BIOSIS, 2100 Arch St., Philadelphia, Pennsylvania 19103-1399. (215) 587-4800. Largest and most comprehensive database of research in the life sciences. Contains citations for nearly 9000 primary research journals, monographs, reviews, symposia, preliminary reports, semi-popular journals, selected institutional reports, government reports and research communications.

Chemical Abstracts-CA. Chemical Abstracts Service, 2540 Olentangy River Rd., P.O. Box 3012, Columbus, Ohio 43210. (800) 848-6533 or (614) 421-3600. Information sources include 9000 journals, patents from 27 countries, two industrial property organizations, new books, conference proceedings, and government research reports.

Enviro/Energyline Abstracts Plus. R. R. Bowker Co., 121 Chanlon Rd., New Providence, New Jersey 07974. (908) 464-6800.

Environmental Periodicals Bibliography. National Information Services Corp., Ste. 6, Wyman Towers, 3100 St. Paul St., Baltimore, Maryland 21218. (410)243-0797. Online version of abstract of same name.

Global Environmental Change Report. Cutter Information Corp., 37 Broadway, Arlington, Massachusetts 02174-5539. (617) 648-8700. Online access to environmental issues worldwide, including global warming, ozone depletion, deforestation, and acid rain. Online version of periodical of the same name.

HADB. National Library of Medicine, Toxicology Information Program, 8600 Rockville Pike, Bethesda, Maryland 20894. (800) 638-8480.

Non-Ionizing Radiation Levels. Canadian Centre for Occupational Health & Safety, 250 Main St. E., Hamilton, Ontario, Canada L8N 1H6. (800) 263-8276.

RCDC Bibliographic Database. University of Notre Dame, Radiation Chemistry Data Center, Radiation Laboratory, Notre Dame, Indiana 46556. (219) 239-6527.

PERIODICALS AND NEWSLETTERS

Environmental Health Letter. Business Publishers, Inc., 951 Pershing Dr., Silver Spring, Maryland 20910-4464. (301) 587-6300. 1961-. Biweekly. Covers areas such as: indoor air, asbestos health effects, toxic substances testing, health problems at wastewater plants, risk-based sludge rules, medical waste, developmental toxicity risk assessment, animal carcinogen tests, pesticide risk, air

toxics, aerospace chemicals, lead, radionuclide emissions, state right-to-know statutes, and incinerator emissions.

Global Environmental Change Report. Cutter Information Corp., 37 Broadway, Arlington, Massachusetts 02174-5539. (617) 648-8700. Biweekly. Focus on global warming, ozone depletion, deforestation, and acid rain. Also available online.

Journal of Environmental Health. National Environmental Health Association, 720 South Colorado Boulevard, Suite 970, Denver, Colorado 80222. (303) 756-9090. Bimonthly. Covers phases in environmental health.

TRADE ASSOCIATIONS AND PROFESSIONAL SOCIETIES

Conference of Radiation Control Program Directors. 205 Capital Ave., Frankfort, Kentucky 40601. (502) 227-4543.

National Committee for Radiation Victims. 6935 Laurel Ave., Takoma Park, Maryland 20912. (301) 891-3990.

National Council on Radiation Protection and Measurements. 7910 Woodmont Ave., Suite 800, Bethesda, Maryland 20814. (301) 657-2652.

Radiation Research Society. American College of Radiology, 1101 Market St., 14th Fl., Philadelphia, Pennsylvania 19107. (215) 574-3153.

RADIATION INSTRUMENTS

ABSTRACTING AND INDEXING SERVICES

Applied Science and Technology Index. H.W. Wilson Co., 950 University Ave., Bronx, New York 10452. (800) 367-6770. Formerly Industrial Arts Index.

Chemical Abstracts. Chemical Abstracts Service, 2540 Olentangy River Rd., PO Box 3012, Columbus, Ohio 43210. (800) 848-6533. 1907-.

INIS Atomindex. International Atomic Energy Agency, Wagramerstrasse 5, Vienna, Austria A-1400. 222 23606198. 1988-. Semiannual. Abstracts nuclear energy and nuclear physics topics from journals, conferences, technical reports and other related publications. Issued in 6 parts: Personal Author, Corporate Entry, Subject, Report, Standard Patent, Conference (by place), Conference (by date).

DIRECTORIES

World Nuclear Directory. Longman, Burnt Mill, Harlow, England CM 20 2J6. (0279) 26721. 1988. Eighth edition. Includes organizations that are involved in nuclear physics research.

ENCYCLOPEDIAS AND DICTIONARIES

Encyclopedia of Physical Science and Technology. Robert A. Meyers, ed. Academic Press, c/o Harcourt Brace Jovanovich Inc., 6277 Sea Harbor Dr., Orlando, Florida 32887. (800) 346-8648. Dictionary of engineering, technology and physical sciences.

Glossary of Terms in Nuclear Science and Technology. American Nuclear Society, 555 North Kensington Ave., La Grange Park, Illinois 60525. (708) 352-6611. 1986.

Prepared by the American Nuclear Society Standards Committee. Subcommittee ANS-9.

Van Nostrand's Scientific Encyclopedia. Glenn D. Considine, ed. Van Nostrand Reinhold, 115 5th Ave., New York, New York 10003. (212) 254-3232. 1983. Sixth edition. Includes all broad subject areas in science.

GENERAL WORKS

Assessment of the Adequacy of the Calibrations Performed by Commercial Calibration Services for Ionizing Radiation Survey Instruments. R.H. Cooke. U.S. Nuclear Regulatory Commission, Washington, District of Columbia 20555. (301) 492-7000. 1986.

HANDBOOKS AND MANUALS

Calibration Handbook. G. Lalos. U.S. G.P.O, Washington, District of Columbia 20401. (202) 512-0000. 1983. Covers ionizing radiation measuring instruments.

Radiation Safety in Shelters. Federal Emergency Management Agency, 500 C St. SW, Washington, District of Columbia 20472. (202) 646-4600. 1983. A handbook for finding and providing the best protection in shelters with the use of nuclear radiation-detecting instruments.

ONLINE DATA BASES

Chemical Abstracts-CA. Chemical Abstracts Service, 2540 Olentangy River Rd., P.O. Box 3012, Columbus, Ohio 43210. (800) 848-6533 or (614) 421-3600. Information sources include 9000 journals, patents from 27 countries, two industrial property organizations, new books, conference proceedings, and government research reports.

TRADE ASSOCIATIONS AND PROFESSIONAL SOCIETIES

International Commission on Radiation Units and Measurements. 7910 Woodmont Ave., Suite 800, Bethesda, Maryland 20814. (301) 657-2652.

National Council on Radiation Protection and Measurements. 7910 Woodmont Ave., Suite 800, Bethesda, Maryland 20814. (301) 657-2652.

RADIATION, NATURAL

ABSTRACTING AND INDEXING SERVICES

Applied Science and Technology Index. H.W. Wilson Co., 950 University Ave., Bronx, New York 10452. (800) 367-6770. Formerly Industrial Arts Index.

Biological Abstracts. BIOSIS, 2100 Arch St., Philadelphia, Pennsylvania 19103-1399. (215) 587-4800. 1927-.

Chemical Abstracts. Chemical Abstracts Service, 2540 Olentangy River Rd., PO Box 3012, Columbus, Ohio 43210. (800) 848-6533. 1907-.

Current Advances in Ecological and Environmental Science. Pergamon Microforms International, Inc., Fairview Park, Elmsford, New York 10523. (914) 592-7720. 1989-. Monthly. Current literature searching service includingjournals, reports, abstracts, etc. This service is available online as part of the CABS database on the hosts BRS and ORBIT search service.

Ecological Abstracts. Geo Abstracts Ltd. Elsevier Applied Science, Crown House, Linton Rd., Barking, England IG 11 8JU. 1974-. Derived from over 600 leading ecological and environmental journals, plus books, conference proceedings, reports and theses.

General Science Index. H. W. Wilson Co., 950 University Ave., Bronx, New York 10452. 1978-. Monthly, also issued in annual cumulation. Cumulative subject index to English language periodicals in the subject fields of astronomy, botany, chemistry, earth science, environment and conservation, food and nutrition, genetics, mathematics, medicine and health, microbiology, oceanography, physics, physiology and zoology.

INIS Atomindex. International Atomic Energy Agency, Wagramerstrasse 5, Vienna, Austria A-1400. 222 23606198. 1988-. Semiannual. Abstracts nuclear energy and nuclear physics topics from journals, conferences, technical reports and other related publications. Issued in 6 parts: Personal Author, Corporate Entry, Subject, Report, Standard Patent, Conference (by place), Conference (by date).

Science Citation Index. Institute for Scientific Information, 3501 Market St., Philadelphia, Pennsylvania 19104. 1961-.

BIBLIOGRAPHIES

Bibliography and Index of Geology. American Geological Institute, 4220 King St., Alexandria, Virginia 22302. Monthly. Includes environmental geology and hydrogeology.

Current Contents. Agriculture, Biology and Environmental Sciences. Institute for Scientific Information, 3501 Market St., Philadelphia, Pennsylvania 19104. (800) 523-1857. 1973-. Previous title: Current Contents. Agricultural, Food & Veterinary Sciences. Gives the table of contents of periodicals in the fields of agriculture, biology, environmental and related areas.

DIRECTORIES

World Nuclear Directory. Longman, Burnt Mill, Harlow, England CM 20 2J6. (0279) 26721. 1988. Eighth edition. Includes organizations that are involved in nuclear physics research.

ENCYCLOPEDIAS AND DICTIONARIES

Encyclopedia of Physical Science and Technology. Robert A. Meyers, ed. Academic Press, c/o Harcourt Brace Jovanovich Inc., 6277 Sea Harbor Dr., Orlando, Florida 32887. (800) 346-8648. Dictionary of engineering, technology and physical sciences.

Glossary of Geology. Robert Latimer Bates and Julia A. Jackson, eds. American Geological Institute, 4220 King St., Alexandria, Virginia 22302-1507. (703) 379-2480 or (800) 336-4764. 1987. Third edition.

McGraw-Hill Encyclopedia of the Geological Sciences. Sybil P. Parker, ed. McGraw-Hill, 1221 Avenue of the Americas, New York, New York 10020. (212) 512-2000 or (800) 262-4729. 1988. Second edition. Published previously in the McGraw-Hill Encyclopedia of Science and Technology.

Van Nostrand's Scientific Encyclopedia. Glenn D. Considine, ed. Van Nostrand Reinhold, 115 5th Ave., New

York, New York 10003. (212) 254-3232. 1983. Sixth edition. Includes all broad subject areas in science.

GENERAL WORKS

Comparative Dosimetry of Radon in Mines and Homes. Commission on Life Science, National Research Council. National Academy Press, 2101 Constitution Ave. N.W., PO Box 285, Washington, District of Columbia 20418. (202) 334-3313. 1991.

How to Live with Low-Level Radiation: A Nutritional Protection Plan. Leon Chaitow. Healing Arts Pr., 1 Park St., Rochester, Vermont 05767. (802) 767-3174. 1988. Discusses the problem of low-level radiation in depth and offers safe, nutritional measures to counteract this invisible hazard.

Magill's Survey of Science. Earth Science Series. Frank N. Magill. Salem Press, PO Box 50062, Pasadena, California 91105. 1990-. Five volumes. Includes information on earth's crust, hot spots and volcanic island chains, physical properties of minerals, rock magnetism, physical properties of rocks, and index.

Magill's Survey of Science. Life Science Series. Frank N. Magill, ed. Salem Press, PO Box 50062, Pasadena, California 91105. 1991. Six volumes. Contents: v.1. A-Central and peripheral nervous system functions; v.2. Central metabolism regulation - eukaryotic transcriptional control; v.3. Positive and negative eukaryotic transcriptional control - mammalian hormones; v.4. Hormones and behavior - muscular contraction; v.5. Muscular contraction and relaxation - sexual reproduction in plants; v.6. Reproductive behavior and mating - X inactivation and the Lyon hypothesis.

GOVERNMENTAL ORGANIZATIONS

U.S. Environmental Protection Agcncy. 401 M St., S.W., Washington, District of Columbia 20460. (202) 382-7400.

U.S. Environmental Protection Agency: Assistant Administrator for Enforcement. 401 M St., S.W., Washington, District of Columbia 20460. (202) 382-4134.

U.S. Environmental Protection Agency: Office of Radiation Programs. 401 M St., S.W., Washington, District of Columbia 20460. (202) 557-9710.

ONLINE DATA BASES

BIOSIS Previews. BIOSIS, 2100 Arch St., Philadelphia, Pennsylvania 19103-1399. (215) 587-4800. Largest and most comprehensive database of research in the life sciences. Contains citations for nearly 9000 primary research journals, monographs, reviews, symposia, preliminary reports, semi-popular journals, selected institutional reports, government reports and research communications.

CERCLIS. Chemical Information Systems, Inc., 7215 York Rd., Baltimore, Maryland 21212. (301) 321-8440. Information on hazardous waste disposal sites that have either been listed by the EPA on the National Priority List (NPL) or nominated for consideration for the NPL.

Chemical Abstracts-CA. Chemical Abstracts Service, 2540 Olentangy River Rd., P.O. Box 3012, Columbus, Ohio 43210. (800) 848-6533 or (614) 421-3600. Information sources include 9000 journals, patents from 27

countries, two industrial property organizations, new books, conference proceedings, and government research reports.

Non-Ionizing Radiation Levels. Canadian Centre for Occupational Health & Safety, 250 Main St. E., Hamilton, Ontario, Canada L8N 1H6. (800) 263-8276.

TRADE ASSOCIATIONS AND PROFESSIONAL SOCIETIES

Radiation Research Society. American College of Radiology, 1101 Market St., 14th Fl., Philadelphia, Pennsylvania 19107. (215) 574-3153.

RADIATION POLLUTION

ABSTRACTING AND INDEXING SERVICES

Air Pollution Technical Publications of the United States Environmental Protection Agency. U.S. Environmental Protection Agency, Mail Drop 75, Research Triangle Park, North Carolina 27711. (919) 541-2184. 1976. Quarterly.

Applied Ecology Abstracts Studies in Renewable Natural Resources. Information Retrieval Ltd., 1911 Jefferson Davis Highway, Arlington, Virginia 22202. 1975-. Monthly.

Applied Science and Technology Index. H.W. Wilson Co., 950 University Ave., Bronx, New York 10452. (800) 367-6770. Formerly Industrial Arts Index.

Aqualine Abstracts. Water Research Centre. c/o Pergamon Microforms International, Inc., Fairview Park, Elmsford, New York 10523. (914) 592-7720. 1927-. Contains some 8,000 records annually on water and wastewater tcchnology. Covers all aspects of water, wastewater, associated engineering services and the aquatic environment. Over 600 periodicals, as well as books, reports and conference proceedings and other publications from water related institutions worldwide are scanned. Also available online.

Biological Abstracts. BIOSIS, 2100 Arch St., Philadelphia, Pennsylvania 19103-1399. (215) 587-4800. 1927-.

Biological and Agricultural Index. H.W. Wilson Co., 950 University Ave., Bronx, New York 10452. (800) 367-6770. 1916-. Monthly.

Chemical Abstracts. Chemical Abstracts Service, 2540 Olentangy River Rd., PO Box 3012, Columbus, Ohio 43210. (800) 848-6533. 1907-.

Current Advances in Ecological and Environmental Science. Pergamon Microforms International, Inc., Fairview Park, Elmsford, New York 10523. (914) 592-7720. 1989-. Monthly. Current literature searching service includingjournals, reports, abstracts, etc. This service is available online as part of the CABS database on the hosts BRS and ORBIT search service.

Ecological Abstracts. Geo Abstracts Ltd. Elsevier Applied Science, Crown House, Linton Rd., Barking, England IG 11 8JU. 1974-. Derived from over 600 leading ecological and environmental journals, plus books, conference proceedings, reports and theses.

Environment Abstracts. Bowker A & I Publishing, 121 Chanlon Rd., New Providence, New Jersey 07974. (908) 464-6800. 1974-.

Environment Index. Environment Information Center, Index Research Department, 124 E. 39th St., New York, New York 10016. 1971-. Annual.

Environmental Information Connection–EIC. Planning Information Program, Dept. of Urban and Regional Planning, University of Illinois, 1003 West Nevada, Urbana, Illinois 61801. (217) 333-1369. Also available online.

Environmental Periodicals Bibliography. Environmental Studies Institute, International Academy at Santa Barbara, 800 Garden St., Suite D, Santa Barbara, California 93101. (805) 965-5010. Also available online.

General Science Index. H. W. Wilson Co., 950 University Ave., Bronx, New York 10452. 1978-. Monthly, also issued in annual cumulation. Cumulative subject index to English language periodicals in the subject fields of astronomy, botany, chemistry, earth science, environment and conservation, food and nutrition, genetics, mathematics, medicine and health, microbiology, oceanography, physics, physiology and zoology.

Geographical Abstracts. London School of Economics, Dept. of Geography, Regency House, 34 Duke St., London, England 1966-. Continued by Geo Abstracts issued in 6 parts: Pt. A. Landforms and the quaternary; Pt. B. Biogeography and Climatology; Pt. C. Economic geography; Pt. D. Social geography and cartography; Pt. E. Sedimentology; Pt. F. Regional and community planning.

Index to Scientific Book Contents. Institute for Scientific Information, 3501 Market St., Philadelphia, Pennsylvania 19104. (800) 523-1857. 1985-. Annual. Gives contents of science books published.

INIS Atomindex. International Atomic Energy Agency, Wagramerstrasse 5, Vienna, Austria A-1400. 222 23606198. 1988-. Semiannual. Abstracts nuclear energy and nuclear physics topics from journals, conferences, technical reports and other related publications. Issued in 6 parts: Personal Author, Corporate Entry, Subject, Report, Standard Patent, Conference (by place), Conference (by date).

Mineralogical Abstracts. Mineralogical Society, 41 Queen's Gate, London, England SW7 5HR. 71 5847916. Quarterly. Abstracts of journal articles, conferences, technical reports and specialized books in the areas of minerals, clay minerals, economic minerals, ore deposits, environmental studies, experimental mineralogy, gemstones, geochemistry, petrology, lunar and planetary studies and other related areas in mineralogy.

Multimedia Index to Ecology. National Information Center for Educational Media, University of Southern California, Los Angeles, California 90007.

Physics Briefs. Physikalische Berichte. Physik Verlag, Pappapelallee 3, Postfach 101161, Weinheim, Germany D-6940. 1979-. Semimonthly. In English. Volumes for 1979- issued by the Deutsche Physikalische Gesellschaft and the Fachinformationszentrum Energie Physik, Mathematik in cooperation with the American Institute of Physics.

Pollution Abstracts. Cambridge Scientific Abstracts, 5161 River Rd., Bethesda, Maryland 20816. (301) 961-6750. Six/year. Indexes worldwide technical literature on environmental pollution. Covers air pollution, marine and freshwater pollution, sewage and wastewater treatment, waste management, toxicology and health, noise pollu-

tion, radiation, land pollution, and environmental policies, programs, legislation, and education. Also available online.

Science Citation Index. Institute for Scientific Information, 3501 Market St., Philadelphia, Pennsylvania 19104. 1961-.

Selected References on Environmental Quality as It Relates to Health. National Library of Medicine, 8600 Rockville Pike, Bethesda, Maryland 20894. (800) 638-8480. 1977.

BIBLIOGRAPHIES

Bibliography and Index of Geology. American Geological Institute, 4220 King St., Alexandria, Virginia 22302. Monthly. Includes environmental geology and hydrogeology.

EPA Publications Bibliography. U.S. Environmental Protection Agency, Library Systems Branch, 401 M St., SW, Washington, District of Columbia 20460. (202) 260-2090. Quarterly.

New Publications of the Geological Survey. U.S. Department of the Interior, Geological Survey, 119 National Center, Reston, Virginia 22092. (703) 648-4460. 1984-. Monthly. Bibliography of geological publications and related government documents published by the Geological Survey.

DIRECTORIES

Who's Who in Environmental Engineering. American Academy of Environmental Engineers, 132 Holiday Court, Suite 206, Annapolis, Maryland 21401. (301) 266-3311. 1980. Annual. Directory of environmental engineers who are certified by the academy.

World Nuclear Directory. Longman, Burnt Mill, Harlow, England CM 20 2J6. (0279) 26721. 1988. Eighth edition. Includes organizations that are involved in nuclear physics research.

ENCYCLOPEDIAS AND DICTIONARIES

Cambridge Dictionary of Biology. Peter M. B. Walker. Cambridge University Press, 40 W. 20th St., New York, New York 10011. (212) 924-3900 or (800) 227-0247. 1989. Includes 10,000 terms in zoology, botany, biochemistry, molecular biology and genetics. Previously published under the title Chambers Biology Dictionary.

A Concise Dictionary of Biology. Elizabeth Martin, ed. Oxford University Press, 200 Madison Ave., New York, New York 10016. (212) 679-7300 or (800) 334-4249. 1990. New edition. Derived from the Concise Science Dictionary, published in 1984.

Encyclopedia of Physical Science and Technology. Robert A. Meyers, ed. Academic Press, c/o Harcourt Brace Jovanovich Inc., 6277 Sea Harbor Dr., Orlando, Florida 32887. (800) 346-8648. Dictionary of engineering, technology and physical sciences.

Glossary of Terms in Nuclear Science and Technology. American Nuclear Society, 555 North Kensington Ave., La Grange Park, Illinois 60525. (708) 352-6611. 1986. Prepared by the American Nuclear Society Standards Committee. Subcommittee ANS-9.

McGraw-Hill Encyclopedia of Environmental Science. Sybil P. Parker. McGraw-Hill Science & Engineering Books, 11 W. 19th St., New York, New York 10011. (212) 337-6010. 1980. Covers ecology, man's influence on nature, and environmental protection.

McGraw-Hill Encyclopedia of Science and Technology. McGraw-Hill, 1221 Avenue of the Americas, New York, New York 10020. (212) 512-2000 or (800) 262-4729. 1992. Seventh edition. Issued in multiple volumes including index. Includes all science and technology broad subject areas.

Van Nostrand's Scientific Encyclopedia. Glenn D. Considine, ed. Van Nostrand Reinhold, 115 5th Ave., New York, New York 10003. (212) 254-3232. 1983. Sixth edition. Includes all broad subject areas in science.

GENERAL WORKS

Bioindications of Chemical Radioactive Pollution. D. A. Krivolutsky. Lewis Publishers, 2000 Corporate Blvd. N.W., Boca Raton, Florida 33431. (800) 272-7737. 1991. Part of the Advances in Science and Technology in the USSR series.

Heat and Water Transport Properties in Conifer Duff and Humus. Michael A. Fosberg. Department of Agriculture Forest Service, Rocky Mountain Forest Experiment Station, 240 W Prospect Rd., Fort Collins, Colorado 80526-2098. (303) 498-1100. 1977. Forest soils and soil permeability.

Humus Chemistry: Genesis, Composition, Reactions. F. J. Stevenson. John Wiley & Sons, Inc., 605 3rd Ave., New York, New York 10158-0012. (212) 850-6000. 1982. Covers soil biochemistry.

Magill's Survey of Science. Earth Science Series. Frank N. Magill. Salem Press, PO Box 50062, Pasadena, California 91105. 1990-. Five volumes. Includes information on earth's crust, hot spots and volcanic island chains, physical properties of minerals, rock magnetism, physical properties of rocks, and index.

MILDOS–a Computer Program for Calculating Environmental Radiation Doses from Uranium Recovery Operations. D. L. Strenge. National Technical Information Service, 5285 Port Royal Rd., Springfield, Virginia 22161. (703) 487-4650. 1981.

Physical and Chemical Characteristics of Aquatic Humus. Egil T. Gjessing. Ann Arbor Science, 230 Collingwood, Ann Arbor, Michigan 48106. 1976.

Radiation Protection Research Training Programme. European Community Information Service (UNIPUB), 4611-F Assembly Dr., Lanham, Maryland 20706-4391. (800) 274-4888. 1990. Review of the radiation protection programme, 1960-89. Gives a synopsis of results 1985-89. Includes radiation safety and decontamination procedures.

Radioactive Aerosols. A. C. Chamberlin. Cambridge University Press, 40 W 20th St., New York, New York 10011. (212) 924-3900; (800) 227-0247. 1991. Describes radioactive gases and particles which are dispersed in the environment, either from natural causes or following nuclear test and accidental emissions.

Soil, Humus and Health: An Organic Guide. Wilfred Edward Shewell-Cooper. David & Charles, Inc., PO Box 257, North Pomfret, Vermont 05053. (802) 457-1911. 1975.

GOVERNMENTAL ORGANIZATIONS

U.S. Environmental Protection Agency: Office of Radiation Programs. 401 M St., S.W., Washington, District of Columbia 20460. (202) 557-9710.

ONLINE DATA BASES

BIOSIS Previews. BIOSIS, 2100 Arch St., Philadelphia, Pennsylvania 19103-1399. (215) 587-4800. Largest and most comprehensive database of research in the life sciences. Contains citations for nearly 9000 primary research journals, monographs, reviews, symposia, preliminary reports, semi-popular journals, selected institutional reports, government reports and research communications.

CERCLIS. Chemical Information Systems, Inc., 7215 York Rd., Baltimore, Maryland 21212. (301) 321-8440. Information on hazardous waste disposal sites that have either been listed by the EPA on the National Priority List (NPL) or nominated for consideration for the NPL.

Chemical Abstracts-CA. Chemical Abstracts Service, 2540 Olentangy River Rd., P.O. Box 3012, Columbus, Ohio 43210. (800) 848-6533 or (614) 421-3600. Information sources include 9000 journals, patents from 27 countries, two industrial property organizations, new books, conference proceedings, and government research reports.

Enviro/Energyline Abstracts Plus. R. R. Bowker Co., 121 Chanlon Rd., New Providence, New Jersey 07974. (908) 464-6800.

Environmental Periodicals Bibliography. National Information Services Corp., Ste. 6, Wyman Towers, 3100 St. Paul St., Baltimore, Maryland 21218. (410)243-0797. Online version of abstract of same name.

Medical Toxicology and Environmental Health. Department of Health and Social Security, Medical Toxiclology & Environmental Health Division, Hannibal House, Rm. 719, Elephant and Castle, London, England SE1 6TE. 44 (71) 972-2162.

Monthly Catalog of United States Government Publications. U.S. G.P.O., Supt. of Docs., PO Box 371954, Pittsburgh, Pennsylvania 15250-7954. (202) 512-0000.

National Technical Information Service. U.S. Department of Commerce, National Technical Information Service, Office of Data Base Services, 5285 Port Royal Rd., Springfield, Virginia 22161. (703) 487-4807. Bibliographic database of government sponsored research and technical reports.

Non-Ionizing Radiation Levels. Canadian Centre for Occupational Health & Safety, 250 Main St. E., Hamilton, Ontario, Canada L8N 1H6. (800) 263-8276.

PERIODICALS AND NEWSLETTERS

Environmental Pollution & Control. National Technical Information Service, 5285 Port Royal Rd., Springfield, Virginia 22161. (703) 487-4650. Weekly. Covers air, noise, solid waste, water pollution, radiation, environmental health and safety, pesticide pollution and control.

STATISTICS SOURCES

Environmental Monitoring and Disposal of Radioactive Wastes from U.S. Naval Nuclear-Powered Ships and their

Support Facilities. U.S. G.P.O, Washington, District of Columbia 20402-9325. (202) 512-0000. Annual. Generation and disposal of radioactive waste from pressurized water reactors aboard nuclear-powered submarines and surface ships, and estimated public radiation exposure.

Occupational Radiation Exposure from U.S. Naval Nuclear Propulsion Plants and Their Support Facilities. U.S. G.P.O, Washington, District of Columbia 20401. (202) 512-0000. Annual. Radiation exposure for personnel engaged in operation and maintenance of pressurized water reactors aboard nuclear-powered submarines and surface ships, on duty aboard tenders, and at support facilities.

Population Dose Commitments Due to Radioactive Releases from Nuclear Power Plant Sites. U.S. G.P.O, Washington, District of Columbia 20402-9325. (202) 512-0000. Annual.

TRADE ASSOCIATIONS AND PROFESSIONAL SOCIETIES

Conference of Radiation Control Program Directors. 205 Capital Ave., Frankfort, Kentucky 40601. (502) 227-4543.

Institute of Environmental Sciences. 940 E. Northwest Hwy., Mount Prospect, Illinois 60056. (708) 255-1561.

National Council on Radiation Protection and Measurements. 7910 Woodmont Ave., Suite 800, Bethesda, Maryland 20814. (301) 657-2652.

RADIOACTIVE DECONTAMINATION

ABSTRACTING AND INDEXING SERVICES

Applied Science and Technology Index. H.W. Wilson Co., 950 University Ave., Bronx, New York 10452. (800) 367-6770. Formerly Industrial Arts Index.

Aqualine Abstracts. Water Research Centre. c/o Pergamon Microforms International, Inc., Fairview Park, Elmsford, New York 10523. (914) 592-7720. 1927-. Contains some 8,000 records annually on water and wastewater technology. Covers all aspects of water, wastewater, associated engineering services and the aquatic environment. Over 600 periodicals, as well as books, reports and conference proceedings and other publications from water related institutions worldwide are scanned. Also available online.

Chemical Abstracts. Chemical Abstracts Service, 2540 Olentangy River Rd., PO Box 3012, Columbus, Ohio 43210. (800) 848-6533. 1907-.

Environment Abstracts. Bowker A & I Publishing, 121 Chanlon Rd., New Providence, New Jersey 07974. (908) 464-6800. 1974-.

Environment Index. Environment Information Center, Index Research Department, 124 E. 39th St., New York, New York 10016. 1971-. Annual.

Environmental Information Connection–EIC. Planning Information Program, Dept. of Urban and Regional Planning, University of Illinois, 1003 West Nevada, Urbana, Illinois 61801. (217) 333-1369. Also available online.

Environmental Periodicals Bibliography. Environmental Studies Institute, International Academy at Santa Barba-

ra, 800 Garden St., Suite D, Santa Barbara, California 93101. (805) 965-5010. Also available online.

General Science Index. H. W. Wilson Co., 950 University Ave., Bronx, New York 10452. 1978-. Monthly, also issued in annual cumulation. Cumulative subject index to English language periodicals in the subject fields of astronomy, botany, chemistry, earth science, environment and conservation, food and nutrition, genetics, mathematics, medicine and health, microbiology, oceanography, physics, physiology and zoology.

Pollution Abstracts. Cambridge Scientific Abstracts, 5161 River Rd., Bethesda, Maryland 20816. (301) 961-6750. Six/year. Indexes worldwide technical literature on environmental pollution. Covers air pollution, marine and freshwater pollution, sewage and wastewater treatment, waste management, toxicology and health, noise pollution, radiation, land pollution, and environmental policies, programs, legislation, and education. Also available online.

Science Citation Index. Institute for Scientific Information, 3501 Market St., Philadelphia, Pennsylvania 19104. 1961-.

BIBLIOGRAPHIES

Current Contents. Agriculture, Biology and Environmental Sciences. Institute for Scientific Information, 3501 Market St., Philadelphia, Pennsylvania 19104. (800) 523-1857. 1973-. Previous title: Current Contents. Agricultural, Food & Veterinary Sciences. Gives the table of contents of periodicals in the fields of agriculture, biology, environmental and related areas.

EPA Publications Bibliography. U.S. Environmental Protection Agency, Library Systems Branch, 401 M St., SW, Washington, District of Columbia 20460. (202) 260-2090. Quarterly.

DIRECTORIES

World Nuclear Directory. Longman, Burnt Mill, Harlow, England CM 20 2J6. (0279) 26721. 1988. Eighth edition. Includes organizations that are involved in nuclear physics research.

ENCYCLOPEDIAS AND DICTIONARIES

Encyclopedia of Physical Science and Technology. Robert A. Meyers, ed. Academic Press, c/o Harcourt Brace Jovanovich Inc., 6277 Sea Harbor Dr., Orlando, Florida 32887. (800) 346-8648. Dictionary of engineering, technology and physical sciences.

Glossary of Terms in Nuclear Science and Technology. American Nuclear Society, 555 North Kensington Ave., La Grange Park, Illinois 60525. (708) 352-6611. 1986. Prepared by the American Nuclear Society Standards Committee. Subcommittee ANS-9.

Van Nostrand's Scientific Encyclopedia. Glenn D. Considine, ed. Van Nostrand Reinhold, 115 5th Ave., New York, New York 10003. (212) 254-3232. 1983. Sixth edition. Includes all broad subject areas in science.

GENERAL WORKS

BWR Cobalt Source Identification. C.F. Falk. General Electric Co., P.O. Box 861, Gainesville, Florida 32602-

0861. (904) 462-3911. 1982. Safety measures in boiling water reactors.

Extension of the Principles of Radiation Protection to ... International Atomic Energy Agency. UNIPUB, 4611-F Assembly Dr., Lanham, Maryland 20706-4391. (301) 459-7666; (800) 274-4888. 1990.

HANDBOOKS AND MANUALS

Handbook of Engineering Control Methods for Occupational Radiation Protection. Michael K. Orn. Prentice Hall, Rte 9W, Englewood Cliffs, New Jersey 07632. (201) 592-2000 or (800) 922-0579. 1992. Deals with radiological safety in the workplace.

ONLINE DATA BASES

CERCLIS. Chemical Information Systems, Inc., 7215 York Rd., Baltimore, Maryland 21212. (301) 321-8440. Information on hazardous waste disposal sites that have either been listed by the EPA on the National Priority List (NPL) or nominated for consideration for the NPL.

Chemical Abstracts-CA. Chemical Abstracts Service, 2540 Olentangy River Rd., P.O. Box 3012, Columbus, Ohio 43210. (800) 848-6533 or (614) 421-3600. Information sources include 9000 journals, patents from 27 countries, two industrial property organizations, new books, conference proceedings, and government research reports.

Enviro/Energyline Abstracts Plus. R. R. Bowker Co., 121 Chanlon Rd., New Providence, New Jersey 07974. (908) 464-6800.

Environmental Periodicals Bibliography. National Information Services Corp., Ste. 6, Wyman Towers, 3100 St. Paul St., Baltimore, Maryland 21218. (410)243-0797. Online version of abstract of same name.

Non-Ionizing Radiation Levels. Canadian Centre for Occupational Health & Safety, 250 Main St. E., Hamilton, Ontario, Canada L8N 1H6. (800) 263-8276.

STATISTICS SOURCES

OECD Environmental Data Compendium 1989. OECD Publications and Information Center, 2001 L St. N.W., Suite 700, Washington, District of Columbia 20036. (202) 785-OECD. 1989. Provides statistical data for OECD countries on air pollution, water pollution, the marine environment, land use, forests, wildlife, solid waste, noise and radioactivity. Also provides data on the underlying pressures on the environment such as energy use, transportation, industrial activity and agriculture.

RADIOACTIVE POLLUTION

See: RADIATION POLLUTION

RADIOACTIVE WASTE DISPOSAL

See: HAZARDOUS WASTE DISPOSAL

RADIOACTIVE WASTE MANAGEMENT

ABSTRACTING AND INDEXING SERVICES

Applied Science and Technology Index. H.W. Wilson Co., 950 University Ave., Bronx, New York 10452. (800) 367-6770. Formerly Industrial Arts Index.

Aqualine Abstracts. Water Research Centre. c/o Pergamon Microforms International, Inc., Fairview Park, Elmsford, New York 10523. (914) 592-7720. 1927-. Contains some 8,000 records annually on water and wastewater technology. Covers all aspects of water, wastewater, associated engineering services and the aquatic environment. Over 600 periodicals, as well as books, reports and conference proceedings and other publications from water related institutions worldwide are scanned. Also available online.

Biological Abstracts. BIOSIS, 2100 Arch St., Philadelphia, Pennsylvania 19103-1399. (215) 587-4800. 1927-.

Chemical Abstracts. Chemical Abstracts Service, 2540 Olentangy River Rd., PO Box 3012, Columbus, Ohio 43210. (800) 848-6533. 1907-.

Ecological Abstracts. Geo Abstracts Ltd. Elsevier Applied Science, Crown House, Linton Rd., Barking, England IG 11 8JU. 1974-. Derived from over 600 leading ecological and environmental journals, plus books, conference proceedings, reports and theses.

Environment Abstracts. Bowker A & I Publishing, 121 Chanlon Rd., New Providence, New Jersey 07974. (908) 464-6800. 1974-.

Environment Index. Environment Information Center, Index Research Department, 124 E. 39th St., New York, New York 10016. 1971-. Annual.

Environmental Information Connection–EIC. Planning Information Program, Dept. of Urban and Regional Planning, University of Illinois, 1003 West Nevada, Urbana, Illinois 61801. (217) 333-1369. Also available online.

Environmental Periodicals Bibliography. Environmental Studies Institute, International Academy at Santa Barbara, 800 Garden St., Suite D, Santa Barbara, California 93101. (805) 965-5010. Also available online.

General Science Index. H. W. Wilson Co., 950 University Ave., Bronx, New York 10452. 1978-. Monthly, also issued in annual cumulation. Cumulative subject index to English language periodicals in the subject fields of astronomy, botany, chemistry, earth science, environment and conservation, food and nutrition, genetics, mathematics, medicine and health, microbiology, oceanography, physics, physiology and zoology.

Geographical Abstracts. London School of Economics, Dept. of Geography, Regency House, 34 Duke St., London, England 1966-. Continued by Geo Abstracts issued in 6 parts: Pt. A. Landforms and the quaternary; Pt. B. Biogeography and Climatology; Pt. C. Economic geography; Pt. D. Social geography and cartography; Pt. E. Sedimentology; Pt. F. Regional and community planning.

INIS Atomindex. International Atomic Energy Agency, Wagramerstrasse 5, Vienna, Austria A-1400. 222 23606198. 1988-. Semiannual. Abstracts nuclear energy and nuclear physics topics from journals, conferences, technical reports and other related publications. Issued in 6 parts: Personal Author, Corporate Entry, Subject, Report, Standard Patent, Conference (by place), Conference (by date).

Physics Briefs. Physikalische Berichte. Physik Verlag, Pappapelallee 3, Postfach 101161, Weinheim, Germany D-6940. 1979-. Semimonthly. In English. Volumes for 1979- issued by the Deutsche Physikalische Gesellschaft and the Fachinformationszentrum Energie Physik, Mathematik in cooperation with the American Institute of Physics.

Pollution Abstracts. Cambridge Scientific Abstracts, 5161 River Rd., Bethesda, Maryland 20816. (301) 961-6750. Six/year. Indexes worldwide technical literature on environmental pollution. Covers air pollution, marine and freshwater pollution, sewage and wastewater treatment, waste management, toxicology and health, noise pollution, radiation, land pollution, and environmental policies, programs, legislation, and education. Also available online.

Radioactive Waste Management. National Technical Information Service, 5285 Port Royal Rd., Springfield, Virginia 22161. (703) 487-4650. Monthly. Topics include spent-fuel transport and storage; radioactive effluents from nuclear facilities; and techniques of processing wastes, their storage, and ultimate disposal.

BIBLIOGRAPHIES

Current Contents. Agriculture, Biology and Environmental Sciences. Institute for Scientific Information, 3501 Market St., Philadelphia, Pennsylvania 19104. (800) 523-1857. 1973-. Previous title: Current Contents. Agricultural, Food & Veterinary Sciences. Gives the table of contents of periodicals in the fields of agriculture, biology, environmental and related areas.

EPA Publications Bibliography. U.S. Environmental Protection Agency, Library Systems Branch, 401 M St., SW, Washington, District of Columbia 20460. (202) 260-2090. Quarterly.

New Publications of the Geological Survey. U.S. Department of the Interior, Geological Survey, 119 National Center, Reston, Virginia 22092. (703) 648-4460. 1984-. Monthly. Bibliography of geological publications and related government documents published by the Geological Survey.

DIRECTORIES

World Nuclear Directory. Longman, Burnt Mill, Harlow, England CM 20 2J6. (0279) 26721. 1988. Eighth edition. Includes organizations that are involved in nuclear physics research.

ENCYCLOPEDIAS AND DICTIONARIES

Cambridge Dictionary of Biology. Peter M. B. Walker. Cambridge University Press, 40 W. 20th St., New York, New York 10011. (212) 924-3900 or (800) 227-0247. 1989. Includes 10,000 terms in zoology, botany, biochemistry, molecular biology and genetics. Previously published under the title Chambers Biology Dictionary.

A Concise Dictionary of Biology. Elizabeth Martin, ed. Oxford University Press, 200 Madison Ave., New York, New York 10016. (212) 679-7300 or (800) 334-4249.

1990. New edition. Derived from the Concise Science Dictionary, published in 1984.

Dictionary of Environmental Engineering and Related Sciences: English-Spanish, Spanish-English. Jose T. Villate. Ediciones Universal, 3090 SW 8th St., Miami, Florida 33135. (305) 642-3355. 1979.

Encyclopedia of Environmental Science and Engineering. J.R. Pfafflin. Gordon and Breach Science Publishers, Inc., 270 8th Ave., New York, New York 10011. (212) 206-8900. 1992.

Glossary of Terms in Nuclear Science and Technology. American Nuclear Society, 555 North Kensington Ave., La Grange Park, Illinois 60525. (708) 352-6611. 1986. Prepared by the American Nuclear Society Standards Committee. Subcommittee ANS-9.

McGraw-Hill Encyclopedia of Environmental Science. Sybil P. Parker. McGraw-Hill Science & Engineering Books, 11 W. 19th St., New York, New York 10011. (212) 337-6010. 1980. Covers ecology, man's influence on nature, and environmental protection.

GENERAL WORKS

Applied Isotope Hydrogeology: A Case Study in Northern Switzerland. F. J. Pearson, Jr., et al. Elsevier Science Publishing Co., Inc, 655 Avenue of the Americas, New York, New York 10010. (212) 989-5800. 1991. This is a case study in northern Switzerland about radioactive waste disposal in the ground. Includes bibliographical references and an index.

High Level Radioactive Waste Management. American Society of Civil Engineers, 345 E. 47th St., New York, New York 10017. (212) 705-7288; (800) 548-2723. 1991. Proceedings of International Topical Meeting hosted by the University of Nevada Las Vegas, April 8-12, 1990.

High Level Radioactive Waste Management. American Society of Civil Engineers, 345 E. 47th St., New York, New York 10017. (212) 705-7288; (800) 548-2723. 1992. Proceedings of the 2nd Annual International Conference, Las Vegas, Nevada, April 28-May 3, 1991.

The Management of Radioactive Waste. Uranium Institute, 12th Floor, Bowater House, 68 Knightsbridge, London, England SW1X 7LT. 071-225 0303. 1991. Discusses methods of disposal of radioactive wastes and the hazards involved.

New Separation Chemistry Techniques for Radioactive Waste and Other Specific Applications. L. Cecille. Elsevier Science Publishing Co., 655 Avenue of the Americas, New York, New York 10010. (212) 989-5800. 1991. Purification technology relating to radioactive wastes and sewage. Proceedings of a technical seminar jointly organized by the Commission of the European Communities, Directorate General for Science, Research and Development and the Italian Commission.

HANDBOOKS AND MANUALS

Environmental Hazards: Radioactive Materials and Wastes: A Reference Handbook. E. Willard Miller and Ruby M. Miller. ABC-Clio, 130 Cremona Dr., PO Box 1911, Santa Barbara, California 93116-1911. (805) 968-1911; (800) 422-2546. 1990. Information source on radioactive materials and wastes. Introductory chapters describe the nature and characteristics of both natural and manufactured radioactive materials. Also provides information on laws, regulations, and treaties about waste materials. Including a directory of private, governmental, and international organizations that deal with radioactive wastes.

ONLINE DATA BASES

BIOSIS Previews. BIOSIS, 2100 Arch St., Philadelphia, Pennsylvania 19103-1399. (215) 587-4800. Largest and most comprehensive database of research in the life sciences. Contains citations for nearly 9000 primary research journals, monographs, reviews, symposia, preliminary reports, semi-popular journals, selected institutional reports, government reports and research communications.

CERCLIS. Chemical Information Systems, Inc., 7215 York Rd., Baltimore, Maryland 21212. (301) 321-8440. Information on hazardous waste disposal sites that have either been listed by the EPA on the National Priority List (NPL) or nominated for consideration for the NPL.

Chemical Abstracts-CA. Chemical Abstracts Service, 2540 Olentangy River Rd., P.O. Box 3012, Columbus, Ohio 43210. (800) 848-6533 or (614) 421-3600. Information sources include 9000 journals, patents from 27 countries, two industrial property organizations, new books, conference proceedings, and government research reports.

Enviro/Energyline Abstracts Plus. R. R. Bowker Co., 121 Chanlon Rd., New Providence, New Jersey 07974. (908) 464-6800.

Environmental Periodicals Bibliography. National Information Services Corp., Ste. 6, Wyman Towers, 3100 St. Paul St., Baltimore, Maryland 21218. (410)243-0797. Online version of abstract of same name.

Monthly Catalog of United States Government Publications. U.S. G.P.O., Supt. of Docs., PO Box 371954, Pittsburgh, Pennsylvania 15250-7954. (202) 512-0000.

National Technical Information Service. U.S. Department of Commerce, National Technical Information Service, Office of Data Base Services, 5285 Port Royal Rd., Springfield, Virginia 22161. (703) 487-4807. Bibliographic database of government sponsored research and technical reports.

PERIODICALS AND NEWSLETTERS

Defense Cleanup. Pasha Publications, 1401 Wilson Blvd., Suite 900, Arlington, Virginia 22209. (703) 528-1244. Weekly. Reports on projects to analyze, recycle, and dispose of defense weapons.

Nuclear Waste News. Business Publishers, Inc., 951 Pershing Dr., Silver Spring, Maryland 20910-4464. (301) 587-6300. 1981-. Weekly. Covers up-to-the-minute information on radioactive wastes management. Includes facts on all aspects of radioactive wastes such as generation, packaging, transportation, processing, storage and disposal.

Texas Pollution Report. Report Publications, P.O. Box 12368, Austin, Texas 78711. (512) 478-5663. Weekly. Covers regulatory activity, court decisions and legislation.

TRADE ASSOCIATIONS AND PROFESSIONAL SOCIETIES

Institute of Nuclear Materials Management. 60 Revere Dr., Suite 500, Northbrook, Illinois 60062. (708) 480-9080.

RADIOACTIVE WASTE STANDARDS

ABSTRACTING AND INDEXING SERVICES

Environment Abstracts. Bowker A & I Publishing, 121 Chanlon Rd., New Providence, New Jersey 07974. (908) 464-6800. 1974-.

Environment Index. Environment Information Center, Index Research Department, 124 E. 39th St., New York, New York 10016. 1971-. Annual.

Environmental Information Connection–EIC. Planning Information Program, Dept. of Urban and Regional Planning, University of Illinois, 1003 West Nevada, Urbana, Illinois 61801. (217) 333-1369. Also available online.

Environmental Periodicals Bibliography. Environmental Studies Institute, International Academy at Santa Barbara, 800 Garden St., Suite D, Santa Barbara, California 93101. (805) 965-5010. Also available online.

BIBLIOGRAPHIES

EPA Publications Bibliography. U.S. Environmental Protection Agency, Library Systems Branch, 401 M St., SW, Washington, District of Columbia 20460. (202) 260-2090. Quarterly.

DIRECTORIES

World Nuclear Directory. Longman, Burnt Mill, Harlow, England CM 20 2J6. (0279) 26721. 1988. Eighth edition. Includes organizations that are involved in nuclear physics research.

ENCYCLOPEDIAS AND DICTIONARIES

Glossary of Terms in Nuclear Science and Technology. American Nuclear Society, 555 North Kensington Ave., La Grange Park, Illinois 60525. (708) 352-6611. 1986. Prepared by the American Nuclear Society Standards Committee. Subcommittee ANS-9.

GENERAL WORKS

Analysis of Urban Solid Waste Services. Ann Arbor Science, 230 Collingwood, Ann Arbor, Michigan 48106. 1978. System analysis and mathematical models in refuse and refuse disposal.

The Toilet Papers: Designs to Recycle Human Waste and Water. Capra Press, PO Box 2068, Santa Barbara, California 93120. (805) 966-4590. 1980. Environmental aspects of toilets and sewage disposal, privies, and sewage irrigation.

Urban Wastes in Coastal Marine Environments. Krieger Publishing Co., Inc., PO Box 9542, Melbourne, Florida 32902. (407) 724-9542. 1988. Deals with marine pollution, refuse and refuse disposal, factory and trade waste and waste disposal in the ocean.

ONLINE DATA BASES

CERCLIS. Chemical Information Systems, Inc., 7215 York Rd., Baltimore, Maryland 21212. (301) 321-8440. Information on hazardous waste disposal sites that have either been listed by the EPA on the National Priority List (NPL) or nominated for consideration for the NPL.

Enviro/Energyline Abstracts Plus. R. R. Bowker Co., 121 Chanlon Rd., New Providence, New Jersey 07974. (908) 464-6800.

Environmental Periodicals Bibliography. National Information Services Corp., Ste. 6, Wyman Towers, 3100 St. Paul St., Baltimore, Maryland 21218. (410)243-0797. Online version of abstract of same name.

PERIODICALS AND NEWSLETTERS

Nuclear Waste News. Business Publishers, Inc., 951 Pershing Dr., Silver Spring, Maryland 20910-4464. (301) 587-6300. 1981-. Weekly. Covers up-to-the-minute information on radioactive wastes management. Includes facts on all aspects of radioactive wastes such as generation, packaging, transportation, processing, storage and disposal.

RADIOACTIVE WASTE STORAGE

See also: HAZARDOUS WASTE DISPOSAL

ABSTRACTING AND INDEXING SERVICES

Applied Science and Technology Index. H.W. Wilson Co., 950 University Ave., Bronx, New York 10452. (800) 367-6770. Formerly Industrial Arts Index.

Environment Abstracts. Bowker A & I Publishing, 121 Chanlon Rd., New Providence, New Jersey 07974. (908) 464-6800. 1974-.

Environment Index. Environment Information Center, Index Research Department, 124 E. 39th St., New York, New York 10016. 1971-. Annual.

Environmental Information Connection–EIC. Planning Information Program, Dept. of Urban and Regional Planning, University of Illinois, 1003 West Nevada, Urbana, Illinois 61801. (217) 333-1369. Also available online.

Environmental Periodicals Bibliography. Environmental Studies Institute, International Academy at Santa Barbara, 800 Garden St., Suite D, Santa Barbara, California 93101. (805) 965-5010. Also available online.

Pollution Abstracts. Cambridge Scientific Abstracts, 5161 River Rd., Bethesda, Maryland 20816. (301) 961-6750. Six/year. Indexes worldwide technical literature on environmental pollution. Covers air pollution, marine and freshwater pollution, sewage and wastewater treatment, waste management, toxicology and health, noise pollution, radiation, land pollution, and environmental policies, programs, legislation, and education. Also available online.

BIBLIOGRAPHIES

Current Contents. Agriculture, Biology and Environmental Sciences. Institute for Scientific Information, 3501 Market St., Philadelphia, Pennsylvania 19104. (800) 523-1857. 1973-. Previous title: Current Contents. Agricultural, Food & Veterinary Sciences. Gives the table of contents of periodicals in the fields of agriculture, biology, environmental and related areas.

EPA Publications Bibliography. U.S. Environmental Protection Agency, Library Systems Branch, 401 M St., SW, Washington, District of Columbia 20460. (202) 260-2090. Quarterly.

DIRECTORIES

World Nuclear Directory. Longman, Burnt Mill, Harlow, England CM 20 2J6. (0279) 26721. 1988. Eighth edition. Includes organizations that are involved in nuclear physics research.

ENCYCLOPEDIAS AND DICTIONARIES

Dictionary of Environmental Engineering and Related Sciences: English-Spanish, Spanish-English. Jose T. Villate. Ediciones Universal, 3090 SW 8th St., Miami, Florida 33135. (305) 642-3355. 1979.

Encyclopedia of Environmental Science and Engineering. J.R. Pfafflin. Gordon and Breach Science Publishers, Inc., 270 8th Ave., New York, New York 10011. (212) 206-8900. 1992.

Glossary of Terms in Nuclear Science and Technology. American Nuclear Society, 555 North Kensington Ave., La Grange Park, Illinois 60525. (708) 352-6611. 1986. Prepared by the American Nuclear Society Standards Committee. Subcommittee ANS-9.

Van Nostrand's Scientific Encyclopedia. Glenn D. Considine, ed. Van Nostrand Reinhold, 115 5th Ave., New York, New York 10003. (212) 254-3232. 1983. Sixth edition. Includes all broad subject areas in science.

GENERAL WORKS

High Level Radioactive Waste Management. American Society of Civil Engineers, 345 E. 47th St., New York, New York 10017. (212) 705-7288; (800) 548-2723. 1991. Proceedings of International Topical Meeting hosted by the University of Nevada Las Vegas, April 8-12, 1990.

High Level Radioactive Waste Management. American Society of Civil Engineers, 345 E. 47th St., New York, New York 10017. (212) 705-7288; (800) 548-2723. 1992. Proceedings of the 2nd Annual International Conference, Las Vegas, Nevada, April 28-May 3, 1991.

ONLINE DATA BASES

CERCLIS. Chemical Information Systems, Inc., 7215 York Rd., Baltimore, Maryland 21212. (301) 321-8440. Information on hazardous waste disposal sites that have either been listed by the EPA on the National Priority List (NPL) or nominated for consideration for the NPL.

Enviro/Energyline Abstracts Plus. R. R. Bowker Co., 121 Chanlon Rd., New Providence, New Jersey 07974. (908) 464-6800.

Environmental Periodicals Bibliography. National Information Services Corp., Ste. 6, Wyman Towers, 3100 St. Paul St., Baltimore, Maryland 21218. (410)243-0797. Online version of abstract of same name.

Monthly Catalog of United States Government Publications. U.S. G.P.O., Supt. of Docs., PO Box 371954, Pittsburgh, Pennsylvania 15250-7954. (202) 512-0000.

National Technical Information Service. U.S. Department of Commerce, National Technical Information Service, Office of Data Base Services, 5285 Port Royal Rd., Springfield, Virginia 22161. (703) 487-4807. Bibliographic database of government sponsored research and technical reports.

PERIODICALS AND NEWSLETTERS

Hazmat News: The Authoritative News Resource for Hazardous Control and Waste Management. Stevens Publishing Co., PO Box 2604, Waco, Texas 76702-2604. (817) 776-9000. Semimonthly. Hazardous materials transportation, storage, and disposal.

STATISTICS SOURCES

Report on Low-Level Radioactive Waste Management Progress. U.S. Dept. of Energy. Nuclear Energy Office. National Technical Information Service, 5285 Port Royal Road, Springfield, Virginia 22161. (703) 487-4650. Annual. Disposal of waste generated by nuclear power plants and non-utility sources by states.

RADIOACTIVE WASTE TRANSPORTATION

See also: TRANSPORTATION

ABSTRACTING AND INDEXING SERVICES

Environment Abstracts. Bowker A & I Publishing, 121 Chanlon Rd., New Providence, New Jersey 07974. (908) 464-6800. 1974-.

Environment Index. Environment Information Center, Index Research Department, 124 E. 39th St., New York, New York 10016. 1971-. Annual.

Environmental Information Connection–EIC. Planning Information Program, Dept. of Urban and Regional Planning, University of Illinois, 1003 West Nevada, Urbana, Illinois 61801. (217) 333-1369. Also available online.

Environmental Periodicals Bibliography. Environmental Studies Institute, International Academy at Santa Barbara, 800 Garden St., Suite D, Santa Barbara, California 93101. (805) 965-5010. Also available online.

Pollution Abstracts. Cambridge Scientific Abstracts, 5161 River Rd., Bethesda, Maryland 20816. (301) 961-6750. Six/year. Indexes worldwide technical literature on environmental pollution. Covers air pollution, marine and freshwater pollution, sewage and wastewater treatment, waste management, toxicology and health, noise pollution, radiation, land pollution, and environmental policies, programs, legislation, and education. Also available online.

Radioactive Waste Management. National Technical Information Service, 5285 Port Royal Rd., Springfield, Virginia 22161. (703) 487-4650. Monthly. Topics include spent-fuel transport and storage; radioactive effluents from nuclear facilities; and techniques of processing wastes, their storage, and ultimate disposal.

BIBLIOGRAPHIES

EPA Publications Bibliography. U.S. Environmental Protection Agency, Library Systems Branch, 401 M St., SW, Washington, District of Columbia 20460. (202) 260-2090. Quarterly.

DIRECTORIES

Directory of Certificates of Compliance for Radioactive Materials Packages. Office of Nuclear Material Safety and Safeguards, U.S. Nuclear Regulatory Commission, Washington, District of Columbia 20555. (301) 492-7000.

World Nuclear Directory. Longman, Burnt Mill, Harlow, England CM 20 2J6. (0279) 26721. 1988. Eighth edition. Includes organizations that are involved in nuclear physics research.

ENCYCLOPEDIAS AND DICTIONARIES

Dictionary of Environmental Engineering and Related Sciences: English-Spanish, Spanish-English. Jose T. Villate. Ediciones Universal, 3090 SW 8th St., Miami, Florida 33135. (305) 642-3355. 1979.

Encyclopedia of Environmental Science and Engineering. J.R. Pfafflin. Gordon and Breach Science Publishers, Inc., 270 8th Ave., New York, New York 10011. (212) 206-8900. 1992.

Glossary of Terms in Nuclear Science and Technology. American Nuclear Society, 555 North Kensington Ave., La Grange Park, Illinois 60525. (708) 352-6611. 1986. Prepared by the American Nuclear Society Standards Committee. Subcommittee ANS-9.

Van Nostrand's Scientific Encyclopedia. Glenn D. Considine, ed. Van Nostrand Reinhold, 115 5th Ave., New York, New York 10003. (212) 254-3232. 1983. Sixth edition. Includes all broad subject areas in science.

ONLINE DATA BASES

Enviro/Energyline Abstracts Plus. R. R. Bowker Co., 121 Chanlon Rd., New Providence, New Jersey 07974. (908) 464-6800.

Environmental Periodicals Bibliography. National Information Services Corp., Ste. 6, Wyman Towers, 3100 St. Paul St., Baltimore, Maryland 21218. (410)243-0797. Online version of abstract of same name.

Monthly Catalog of United States Government Publications. U.S. G.P.O., Supt. of Docs., PO Box 371954, Pittsburgh, Pennsylvania 15250-7954. (202) 512-0000.

National Technical Information Service. U.S. Department of Commerce, National Technical Information Service, Office of Data Base Services, 5285 Port Royal Rd., Springfield, Virginia 22161. (703) 487-4807. Bibliographic database of government sponsored research and technical reports.

PressNet Environmental Reports. Chemical Information Systems, Inc., 7215 York Rd., Baltimore, Maryland 21212. (301) 321-8440.

STATISTICS SOURCES

Radioactive Material Released from Nuclear Power Plants. U.S. Nuclear Regulatory Commission. U.S.

G.P.O., Washington, District of Columbia 20401. (202) 512-0000. Annual. Data on radioactive content of airborne and liquid effluents and solid wastes from nuclear power plants.

RADIOACTIVE WASTES

See also: HAZARDOUS WASTES

ABSTRACTING AND INDEXING SERVICES

Applied Science and Technology Index. H.W. Wilson Co., 950 University Ave., Bronx, New York 10452. (800) 367-6770. Formerly Industrial Arts Index.

Aqualine Abstracts. Water Research Centre. c/o Pergamon Microforms International, Inc., Fairview Park, Elmsford, New York 10523. (914) 592-7720. 1927-. Contains some 8,000 records annually on water and wastewater technology. Covers all aspects of water, wastewater, associated engineering services and the aquatic environment. Over 600 periodicals, as well as books, reports and conference proceedings and other publications from water related institutions worldwide are scanned. Also available online.

Environment Abstracts. Bowker A & I Publishing, 121 Chanlon Rd., New Providence, New Jersey 07974. (908) 464-6800. 1974-.

Environment Index. Environment Information Center, Index Research Department, 124 E. 39th St., New York, New York 10016. 1971-. Annual.

Environmental Information Connection–EIC. Planning Information Program, Dept. of Urban and Regional Planning, University of Illinois, 1003 West Nevada, Urbana, Illinois 61801. (217) 333-1369. Also available online.

Environmental Periodicals Bibliography. Environmental Studies Institute, International Academy at Santa Barbara, 800 Garden St., Suite D, Santa Barbara, California 93101. (805) 965-5010. Also available online.

General Science Index. H. W. Wilson Co., 950 University Ave., Bronx, New York 10452. 1978-. Monthly, also issued in annual cumulation. Cumulative subject index to English language periodicals in the subject fields of astronomy, botany, chemistry, earth science, environment and conservation, food and nutrition, genetics, mathematics, medicine and health, microbiology, oceanography, physics, physiology and zoology.

Pollution Abstracts. Cambridge Scientific Abstracts, 5161 River Rd., Bethesda, Maryland 20816. (301) 961-6750. Six/year. Indexes worldwide technical literature on environmental pollution. Covers air pollution, marine and freshwater pollution, sewage and wastewater treatment, waste management, toxicology and health, noise pollution, radiation, land pollution, and environmental policies, programs, legislation, and education. Also available online.

Radioactive Waste Management. National Technical Information Service, 5285 Port Royal Rd., Springfield, Virginia 22161. (703) 487-4650. Monthly. Topics include spent-fuel transport and storage; radioactive effluents from nuclear facilities; and techniques of processing wastes, their storage, and ultimate disposal.

BIBLIOGRAPHIES

Current Contents. Agriculture, Biology and Environmental Sciences. Institute for Scientific Information, 3501 Market St., Philadelphia, Pennsylvania 19104. (800) 523-1857. 1973-. Previous title: Current Contents. Agricultural, Food & Veterinary Sciences. Gives the table of contents of periodicals in the fields of agriculture, biology, environmental and related areas.

EPA Publications Bibliography. U.S. Environmental Protection Agency, Library Systems Branch, 401 M St., SW, Washington, District of Columbia 20460. (202) 260-2090. Quarterly.

Radioactive Waste as a Social and Political Issue: A Bibliography. Frederick Frankena. AMS Press, 56 E. 13th St., New York, New York 10003. (212) 777-4700. 1991.

DIRECTORIES

World Nuclear Directory. Longman, Burnt Mill, Harlow, England CM 20 2J6. (0279) 26721. 1988. Eighth edition. Includes organizations that are involved in nuclear physics research.

ENCYCLOPEDIAS AND DICTIONARIES

Encyclopedia of Physical Science and Technology. Robert A. Meyers, ed. Academic Press, c/o Harcourt Brace Jovanovich Inc., 6277 Sea Harbor Dr., Orlando, Florida 32887. (800) 346-8648. Dictionary of engineering, technology and physical sciences.

Glossary of Terms in Nuclear Science and Technology. American Nuclear Society, 555 North Kensington Ave., La Grange Park, Illinois 60525. (708) 352-6611. 1986. Prepared by the American Nuclear Society Standards Committee. Subcommittee ANS-9.

The New York Times Encyclopedic Dictionary of the Environment. Paul Sarnoff. Quadrangle Books, New York, New York 1971. Focuses on state-of-the-art methods of pollution control, abatement, prevention and removal.

Van Nostrand's Scientific Encyclopedia. Glenn D. Considine, ed. Van Nostrand Reinhold, 115 5th Ave., New York, New York 10003. (212) 254-3232. 1983. Sixth edition. Includes all broad subject areas in science.

GENERAL WORKS

Hazardous Waste Law and Practice. John-Mark Stensvaag. John Wiley & Sons, Inc., 605 3rd Ave., New York, New York 10158-0012. (212) 850-6000. 1986-1989. 2 vols. Discusses the intricacies of defining hazardous wastes and shows potentially regulated entities how to make that determination. Guides the user through the listed hazardous wastes under the EPA's Subtitle C, discussing commercial chemical products, specific and nonspecific source wastes, derivative wastes, delisted wastes, and exclusions.

High Level Radioactive Waste Management. American Society of Civil Engineers, 345 E. 47th St., New York, New York 10017. (212) 705-7288; (800) 548-2723. 1991. Proceedings of International Topical Meeting hosted by the University of Nevada Las Vegas, April 8-12, 1990.

High Level Radioactive Waste Management. American Society of Civil Engineers, 345 E. 47th St., New York, New York 10017. (212) 705-7288; (800) 548-2723. 1992.

Proceedings of the 2nd Annual International Conference, Las Vegas, Nevada, April 28-May 3, 1991.

Management of Radioactive Waste: The Issues for Local Authorities. Stuart Kemp, ed. Telford, Telford House, 1 Heron Quay, London, England E14 9XF. (071) 987-6999. 1991. Proceedings of the conference organized by the National Steering Committee, Nuclear Free Local Authorities, and held in Manchester on February 12, 1991.

Scientific Basis for Nuclear Waste Management XII. Werner Lutze, ed. Materials Research Society, 9800 McKnight Rd., Pittsburgh, Pennsylvania 15237. (412) 367-3003. 1989. Symposium held in Berlin Germany October 1988. Volume 127 of the Materials Research society Symposium Proceedings.

Treatment and Conditioning of Radioactive Incinerator Ashes. L. Crecille, ed. Elsevier Science Publishing Co., 655 Avenue of the Americas, New York, New York 10010. (212) 989-5800. 1991. Incineration of radioactive wastes and purification of fly ash.

Treatment Technologies. Environment Protection Agency. Government Institutes, Inc., 4 Research Pl., Ste. 200, Rockville, Maryland 20850. (301)921-2300. 1991. 2nd ed. Provides a clear explanation of 24 treatment technologies and evaluates the effectiveness of the design and operations of each type of treatment. This new edition has more supporting numerical data, examples for a better understanding of the technology and an updated reference for specific industrial wastes.

GOVERNMENTAL ORGANIZATIONS

U.S. Environmental Protection Agency: Office of Emergency and Remedial Response. Emergency Response Division, 401 M St., S.W., Washington, District of Columbia 20460. (202) 382-2180.

HANDBOOKS AND MANUALS

Environmental Hazards: Radioactive Materials and Wastes: A Reference Handbook. E. Willard Miller and Ruby M. Miller. ABC-Clio, 130 Cremona Dr., PO Box 1911, Santa Barbara, California 93116-1911. (805) 968-1911; (800) 422-2546. 1990. Information source on radioactive materials and wastes. Introductory chapters describe the nature and characteristics of both natural and manufactured radioactive materials. Also provides information on laws, regulations, and treaties about waste materials. Including a directory of private, governmental, and international organizations that deal with radioactive wastes.

Hazardous Waste Management Strategies for Health Care Facilities. Nelson S. Slavik. American Hospital Association, 840 North Lake Shore Dr., Chicago, Illinois 60611. 1987. Contains helpful information for health care facilities in the management of their chemical, cytotoxic, infectious, and radiological wastes.

Low-Level Radioactive Waste: From Cradle to Grave. E. L. Gershey. Global Professional Publications, 2805 McGraw Ave., PO Box 19539, Irvine, California 92713-9539. (800) 854-7179.

ONLINE DATA BASES

CERCLIS. Chemical Information Systems, Inc., 7215 York Rd., Baltimore, Maryland 21212. (301) 321-8440.

Information on hazardous waste disposal sites that have either been listed by the EPA on the National Priority List (NPL) or nominated for consideration for the NPL.

Enviro/Energyline Abstracts Plus. R. R. Bowker Co., 121 Chanlon Rd., New Providence, New Jersey 07974. (908) 464-6800.

Environment Week. NewsNet, Inc., 945 Haverford Rd., Bryn Mawr, Pennsylvania 19010. (800) 345-1301. Online version of periodical of same name.

Environmental Fate Databases. Syracuse Research Cooperation, Merrill Lane, Syracuse, New York 13210. (312) 426-3200. Environmental fate of chemicals.

Environmental Periodicals Bibliography. National Information Services Corp., Ste. 6, Wyman Towers, 3100 St. Paul St., Baltimore, Maryland 21218. (410)243-0797. Online version of abstract of same name.

Hazardous Waste News. Business Publishers, Inc., 951 Pershing Dr., Silver Spring, Maryland 20910-4464. (301) 587-6300. Online access to legislative, regulatory, and judicial decisions at the federal and state levels relating to the field of hazardous waste management. Online version of the periodical of the same name.

HAZINF. University of Alberta, Department of Chemistry, Edmonton, Alberta, Canada T6G 2G2. (403) 432-3254.

Monthly Catalog of United States Government Publications. U.S. G.P.O., Supt. of Docs., PO Box 371954, Pittsburgh, Pennsylvania 15250-7954. (202) 512-0000.

National Technical Information Service. U.S. Department of Commerce, National Technical Information Service, Office of Data Base Services, 5285 Port Royal Rd., Springfield, Virginia 22161. (703) 487-4807. Bibliographic database of government sponsored research and technical reports.

Nuclear Waste News–Online. Business Publishers, Inc., 951 Pershing Dr., Silver Spring, Maryland 20910-4464. (301) 587-6300. Federal and legislation regulation and research and development activities concerning the generation, packaging, transportation, processing, and disposal of nuclear wastes.

PressNet Environmental Reports. Chemical Information Systems, Inc., 7215 York Rd., Baltimore, Maryland 21212. (301) 321-8440.

PERIODICALS AND NEWSLETTERS

CA Selects: Environment Pollution. Chemical Abstracts Services, 2540 Olentangy River Rd., Box 3012, Columbus, Ohio 43210. (800) 848-6533. 1978-. Biweekly. Abstracts on pollution of the environment by gaseous, liquid, solid and radioactive wastes.

State Environment Report: Toxic Substances & Hazardous Wastes. Business Publishers, Inc., 951 Pershing Drive, Silver Spring, Maryland 20910. (301) 587-6300. Weekly. Covers state legislative and regulatory initiatives.

RESEARCH CENTERS AND INSTITUTES

Environmental Research Center. Washington State University, 305 Troy Hall, Pullman, Washington 99164-4430. (509) 335-8536.

STATISTICS SOURCES

Radioactive Material Released from Nuclear Power Plants. U.S. Nuclear Regulatory Commission. U.S. G.P.O., Washington, District of Columbia 20401. (202) 512-0000. Annual. Data on radioactive content of airborne and liquid effluents and solid wastes from nuclear power plants.

TRADE ASSOCIATIONS AND PROFESSIONAL SOCIETIES

Can Manufacturers Institute. 1625 Massachusetts Ave., N.W., Washington, District of Columbia 20036. (202) 232-4677.

National Campaign for Radioactive Waste Safety. 105 Stanford SE, PO Box 4524, Albuquerque, New Mexico 87106. (505) 262-1862.

Native Americans for a Clean Environment. P.O. Box 40, Marble City, Oklahoma 74945. (918) 458-4322.

Radioactive Waste Campaign. 625 Broadway, 2nd Fl., New York, New York 10012-2611. (212) 473-7390.

RADIOBIOLOGY

ABSTRACTING AND INDEXING SERVICES

Applied Ecology Abstracts Studies in Renewable Natural Resources. Information Retrieval Ltd., 1911 Jefferson Davis Highway, Arlington, Virginia 22202. 1975-. Monthly.

Biological Abstracts. BIOSIS, 2100 Arch St., Philadelphia, Pennsylvania 19103-1399. (215) 587-4800. 1927-.

Biological and Agricultural Index. H.W. Wilson Co., 950 University Ave., Bronx, New York 10452. (800) 367-6770. 1916-. Monthly.

Chemical Abstracts. Chemical Abstracts Service, 2540 Olentangy River Rd., PO Box 3012, Columbus, Ohio 43210. (800) 848-6533. 1907-.

Crop Physiology Abstracts. C. A. B. International, 845 North Park Ave., Tucson, Arizona 85719. (602) 621-7897 or (800) 528-4841. 1975-. Monthly. Abstracts focus on the physiology of all higher plants of economic importance. Aspects include germination, reproductive development, nitrogen fixation, metabolic inhibitors, salinity, radiobiology, enzymes, membranes and other related areas.

Ecological Abstracts. Geo Abstracts Ltd. Elsevier Applied Science, Crown House, Linton Rd., Barking, England IG 11 8JU. 1974-. Derived from over 600 leading ecological and environmental journals, plus books, conference proceedings, reports and theses.

Environment Abstracts. Bowker A & I Publishing, 121 Chanlon Rd., New Providence, New Jersey 07974. (908) 464-6800. 1974-.

Environment Index. Environment Information Center, Index Research Department, 124 E. 39th St., New York, New York 10016. 1971-. Annual.

Environmental Information Connection–EIC. Planning Information Program, Dept. of Urban and Regional Planning, University of Illinois, 1003 West Nevada, Urbana, Illinois 61801. (217) 333-1369. Also available online.

Environmental Periodicals Bibliography. Environmental Studies Institute, International Academy at Santa Barbara, 800 Garden St., Suite D, Santa Barbara, California 93101. (805) 965-5010. Also available online.

General Science Index. H. W. Wilson Co., 950 University Ave., Bronx, New York 10452. 1978-. Monthly, also issued in annual cumulation. Cumulative subject index to English language periodicals in the subject fields of astronomy, botany, chemistry, earth science, environment and conservation, food and nutrition, genetics, mathematics, medicine and health, microbiology, oceanography, physics, physiology and zoology.

INIS Atomindex. International Atomic Energy Agency, Wagramerstrasse 5, Vienna, Austria A-1400. 222 23606198. 1988-. Semiannual. Abstracts nuclear energy and nuclear physics topics from journals, conferences, technical reports and other related publications. Issued in 6 parts: Personal Author, Corporate Entry, Subject, Report, Standard Patent, Conference (by place), Conference (by date).

Multimedia Index to Ecology. National Information Center for Educational Media, University of Southern California, Los Angeles, California 90007.

Pollution Abstracts. Cambridge Scientific Abstracts, 5161 River Rd., Bethesda, Maryland 20816. (301) 961-6750. Six/year. Indexes worldwide technical literature on environmental pollution. Covers air pollution, marine and freshwater pollution, sewage and wastewater treatment, waste management, toxicology and health, noise pollution, radiation, land pollution, and environmental policies, programs, legislation, and education. Also available online.

Science Citation Index. Institute for Scientific Information, 3501 Market St., Philadelphia, Pennsylvania 19104. 1961-.

ALMANACS AND YEARBOOKS

Research in Radiobiology. National Technical Information Service, 5285 Port Royal Rd., Springfield, Virginia 22161. (703) 487-4650. Annual. Annual report of work in progress in the Internal Irradiation Program.

BIBLIOGRAPHIES

Current Contents. Agriculture, Biology and Environmental Sciences. Institute for Scientific Information, 3501 Market St., Philadelphia, Pennsylvania 19104. (800) 523-1857. 1973-. Previous title: Current Contents. Agricultural, Food & Veterinary Sciences. Gives the table of contents of periodicals in the fields of agriculture, biology, environmental and related areas.

EPA Publications Bibliography. U.S. Environmental Protection Agency, Library Systems Branch, 401 M St., SW, Washington, District of Columbia 20460. (202) 260-2090. Quarterly.

DIRECTORIES

World Nuclear Directory. Longman, Burnt Mill, Harlow, England CM 20 2J6. (0279) 26721. 1988. Eighth edition. Includes organizations that are involved in nuclear physics research.

ENCYCLOPEDIAS AND DICTIONARIES

Encyclopedia of Human Biology. Renato Dulbecco, ed. Academic Press, c/o Harcourt Brace Jovanovich Inc., 6277 Sea Harbor Dr., Orlando, Florida 32887. (800) 346-8648. 1991. Eight volumes.

Glossary of Terms in Nuclear Science and Technology. American Nuclear Society, 555 North Kensington Ave., La Grange Park, Illinois 60525. (708) 352-6611. 1986. Prepared by the American Nuclear Society Standards Committee. Subcommittee ANS-9.

McGraw-Hill Encyclopedia of Environmental Science. Sybil P. Parker. McGraw-Hill Science & Engineering Books, 11 W. 19th St., New York, New York 10011. (212) 337-6010. 1980. Covers ecology, man's influence on nature, and environmental protection.

Van Nostrand's Scientific Encyclopedia. Glenn D. Considine, ed. Van Nostrand Reinhold, 115 5th Ave., New York, New York 10003. (212) 254-3232. 1983. Sixth edition. Includes all broad subject areas in science.

HANDBOOKS AND MANUALS

CRC Handbook of Radiobiology. K. N. Prasad. CRC Press, 2000 Corporate Blvd. N.W., Boca Raton, Florida 33431. (800) 272-7737. 1984. Covers ionizing radiation, radiology and dose response relationship.

ONLINE DATA BASES

BIOSIS Previews. BIOSIS, 2100 Arch St., Philadelphia, Pennsylvania 19103-1399. (215) 587-4800. Largest and most comprehensive database of research in the life sciences. Contains citations for nearly 9000 primary research journals, monographs, reviews, symposia, preliminary reports, semi-popular journals, selected institutional reports, government reports and research communications.

CERCLIS. Chemical Information Systems, Inc., 7215 York Rd., Baltimore, Maryland 21212. (301) 321-8440. Information on hazardous waste disposal sites that have either been listed by the EPA on the National Priority List (NPL) or nominated for consideration for the NPL.

Chemical Abstracts-CA. Chemical Abstracts Service, 2540 Olentangy River Rd., P.O. Box 3012, Columbus, Ohio 43210. (800) 848-6533 or (614) 421-3600. Information sources include 9000 journals, patents from 27 countries, two industrial property organizations, new books, conference proceedings, and government research reports.

Enviro/Energyline Abstracts Plus. R. R. Bowker Co., 121 Chanlon Rd., New Providence, New Jersey 07974. (908) 464-6800.

Environmental Periodicals Bibliography. National Information Services Corp., Ste. 6, Wyman Towers, 3100 St. Paul St., Baltimore, Maryland 21218. (410)243-0797. Online version of abstract of same name.

RADIOCARBON DATING

See also: C14 DATING

ABSTRACTING AND INDEXING SERVICES

Applied Ecology Abstracts Studies in Renewable Natural Resources. Information Retrieval Ltd., 1911 Jefferson Davis Highway, Arlington, Virginia 22202. 1975-. Monthly.

Applied Science and Technology Index. H.W. Wilson Co., 950 University Ave., Bronx, New York 10452. (800) 367-6770. Formerly Industrial Arts Index.

Biological Abstracts. BIOSIS, 2100 Arch St., Philadelphia, Pennsylvania 19103-1399. (215) 587-4800. 1927-.

Chemical Abstracts. Chemical Abstracts Service, 2540 Olentangy River Rd., PO Box 3012, Columbus, Ohio 43210. (800) 848-6533. 1907-.

Ecological Abstracts. Geo Abstracts Ltd. Elsevier Applied Science, Crown House, Linton Rd., Barking, England IG 11 8JU. 1974-. Derived from over 600 leading ecological and environmental journals, plus books, conference proceedings, reports and theses.

Environment Abstracts. Bowker A & I Publishing, 121 Chanlon Rd., New Providence, New Jersey 07974. (908) 464-6800. 1974-.

Environment Index. Environment Information Center, Index Research Department, 124 E. 39th St., New York, New York 10016. 1971-. Annual.

Environmental Information Connection–EIC. Planning Information Program, Dept. of Urban and Regional Planning, University of Illinois, 1003 West Nevada, Urbana, Illinois 61801. (217) 333-1369. Also available online.

Environmental Periodicals Bibliography. Environmental Studies Institute, International Academy at Santa Barbara, 800 Garden St., Suite D, Santa Barbara, California 93101. (805) 965-5010. Also available online.

General Science Index. H. W. Wilson Co., 950 University Ave., Bronx, New York 10452. 1978-. Monthly, also issued in annual cumulation. Cumulative subject index to English language periodicals in the subject fields of astronomy, botany, chemistry, earth science, environment and conservation, food and nutrition, genetics, mathematics, medicine and health, microbiology, oceanography, physics, physiology and zoology.

Geographical Abstracts. London School of Economics, Dept. of Geography, Regency House, 34 Duke St., London, England 1966-. Continued by Geo Abstracts issued in 6 parts: Pt. A. Landforms and the quaternary; Pt. B. Biogeography and Climatology; Pt. C. Economic geography; Pt. D. Social geography and cartography; Pt. E. Sedimentology; Pt. F. Regional and community planning.

Index to Scientific Book Contents. Institute for Scientific Information, 3501 Market St., Philadelphia, Pennsylvania 19104. (800) 523-1857. 1985-. Annual. Gives contents of science books published.

INIS Atomindex. International Atomic Energy Agency, Wagramerstrasse 5, Vienna, Austria A-1400. 222 23606198. 1988-. Semiannual. Abstracts nuclear energy and nuclear physics topics from journals, conferences, technical reports and other related publications. Issued in 6 parts: Personal Author, Corporate Entry, Subject, Report, Standard Patent, Conference (by place), Conference (by date).

Multimedia Index to Ecology. National Information Center for Educational Media, University of Southern California, Los Angeles, California 90007.

Physics Briefs. Physikalische Berichte. Physik Verlag, Pappapelallee 3, Postfach 101161, Weinheim, Germany D-6940. 1979-. Semimonthly. In English. Volumes for 1979- issued by the Deutsche Physikalische Gesellschaft and the Fachinformationszentrum Energie Physik, Mathematik in cooperation with the American Institute of Physics.

Pollution Abstracts. Cambridge Scientific Abstracts, 5161 River Rd., Bethesda, Maryland 20816. (301) 961-6750. Six/year. Indexes worldwide technical literature on environmental pollution. Covers air pollution, marine and freshwater pollution, sewage and wastewater treatment, waste management, toxicology and health, noise pollution, radiation, land pollution, and environmental policies, programs, legislation, and education. Also available online.

Science Citation Index. Institute for Scientific Information, 3501 Market St., Philadelphia, Pennsylvania 19104. 1961-.

BIBLIOGRAPHIES

Bibliography and Index of Geology. American Geological Institute, 4220 King St., Alexandria, Virginia 22302. Monthly. Includes environmental geology and hydrogeology.

Current Contents. Agriculture, Biology and Environmental Sciences. Institute for Scientific Information, 3501 Market St., Philadelphia, Pennsylvania 19104. (800) 523-1857. 1973-. Previous title: Current Contents. Agricultural, Food & Veterinary Sciences. Gives the table of contents of periodicals in the fields of agriculture, biology, environmental and related areas.

EPA Publications Bibliography. U.S. Environmental Protection Agency, Library Systems Branch, 401 M St., SW, Washington, District of Columbia 20460. (202) 260-2090. Quarterly.

New Publications of the Geological Survey. U.S. Department of the Interior, Geological Survey, 119 National Center, Reston, Virginia 22092. (703) 648-4460. 1984-. Monthly. Bibliography of geological publications and related government documents published by the Geological Survey.

Radiocarbon Dating Literature: The First 21 Years. Dilette Polach. Academic Press Inc., 24-28 Oval Rd., London, England NW1 7DX. 071-267 4466. 1988.

DIRECTORIES

World Nuclear Directory. Longman, Burnt Mill, Harlow, England CM 20 2J6. (0279) 26721. 1988. Eighth edition. Includes organizations that are involved in nuclear physics research.

ENCYCLOPEDIAS AND DICTIONARIES

Glossary of Geology. Robert Latimer Bates and Julia A. Jackson, eds. American Geological Institute, 4220 King St., Alexandria, Virginia 22302-1507. (703) 379-2480 or (800) 336-4764. 1987. Third edition.

Glossary of Terms in Nuclear Science and Technology. American Nuclear Society, 555 North Kensington Ave.,

La Grange Park, Illinois 60525. (708) 352-6611. 1986. Prepared by the American Nuclear Society Standards Committee. Subcommittee ANS-9.

McGraw-Hill Encyclopedia of Science and Technology. McGraw-Hill, 1221 Avenue of the Americas, New York, New York 10020. (212) 512-2000 or (800) 262-4729. 1992. Seventh edition. Issued in multiple volumes including index. Includes all science and technology broad subject areas.

McGraw-Hill Encyclopedia of the Geological Sciences. Sybil P. Parker, ed. McGraw-Hill, 1221 Avenue of the Americas, New York, New York 10020. (212) 512-2000 or (800) 262-4729. 1988. Second edition. Published previously in the McGraw-Hill Encyclopedia of Science and Technology.

Van Nostrand's Scientific Encyclopedia. Glenn D. Considine, ed. Van Nostrand Reinhold, 115 5th Ave., New York, New York 10003. (212) 254-3232. 1983. Sixth edition. Includes all broad subject areas in science.

GENERAL WORKS

Magill's Survey of Science. Earth Science Series. Frank N. Magill. Salem Press, PO Box 50062, Pasadena, California 91105. 1990-. Five volumes. Includes information on earth's crust, hot spots and volcanic island chains, physical properties of minerals, rock magnetism, physical properties of rocks, and index.

Radiocarbon Dating. Sheridan Bowman. British Museum Publications, 46 Bloomsbury St., London, England WC1B 3QQ. 44 071 323 1234. 1990.

ONLINE DATA BASES

BIOSIS Previews. BIOSIS, 2100 Arch St., Philadelphia, Pennsylvania 19103-1399. (215) 587-4800. Largest and most comprehensive database of research in the life sciences. Contains citations for nearly 9000 primary research journals, monographs, reviews, symposia, preliminary reports, semi-popular journals, selected institutional reports, government reports and research communications.

CERCLIS. Chemical Information Systems, Inc., 7215 York Rd., Baltimore, Maryland 21212. (301) 321-8440. Information on hazardous waste disposal sites that have either been listed by the EPA on the National Priority List (NPL) or nominated for consideration for the NPL.

Chemical Abstracts-CA. Chemical Abstracts Service, 2540 Olentangy River Rd., P.O. Box 3012, Columbus, Ohio 43210. (800) 848-6533 or (614) 421-3600. Information sources include 9000 journals, patents from 27 countries, two industrial property organizations, new books, conference proceedings, and government research reports.

Enviro/Energyline Abstracts Plus. R. R. Bowker Co., 121 Chanlon Rd., New Providence, New Jersey 07974. (908) 464-6800.

Environmental Periodicals Bibliography. National Information Services Corp., Ste. 6, Wyman Towers, 3100 St. Paul St., Baltimore, Maryland 21218. (410)243-0797. Online version of abstract of same name.

Monthly Catalog of United States Government Publications. U.S. G.P.O., Supt. of Docs., PO Box 371954, Pittsburgh, Pennsylvania 15250-7954. (202) 512-0000.

National Technical Information Service. U.S. Department of Commerce, National Technical Information Service, Office of Data Base Services, 5285 Port Royal Rd., Springfield, Virginia 22161. (703) 487-4807. Bibliographic database of government sponsored research and technical reports.

TRADE ASSOCIATIONS AND PROFESSIONAL SOCIETIES

American Chemical Society. 1155 16th St., N.W., Washington, District of Columbia 20036. (202) 872-4600.

RADIOECOLOGY

ABSTRACTING AND INDEXING SERVICES

Applied Ecology Abstracts Studies in Renewable Natural Resources. Information Retrieval Ltd., 1911 Jefferson Davis Highway, Arlington, Virginia 22202. 1975-. Monthly.

Applied Science and Technology Index. H.W. Wilson Co., 950 University Ave., Bronx, New York 10452. (800) 367-6770. Formerly Industrial Arts Index.

ASFA Aquaculture Abstracts. Cambridge Scientific Abstracts, Inc., 5161 River Rd., Bethesda, Maryland 20816. (301) 961-6750. 1984.

Biological Abstracts. BIOSIS, 2100 Arch St., Philadelphia, Pennsylvania 19103-1399. (215) 587-4800. 1927-.

Biological and Agricultural Index. H.W. Wilson Co., 950 University Ave., Bronx, New York 10452. (800) 367-6770. 1916-. Monthly.

Chemical Abstracts. Chemical Abstracts Service, 2540 Olentangy River Rd., PO Box 3012, Columbus, Ohio 43210. (800) 848-6533. 1907-.

Current Advances in Ecological and Environmental Science. Pergamon Microforms International, Inc., Fairview Park, Elmsford, New York 10523. (914) 592-7720. 1989-. Monthly. Current literature searching service includingjournals, reports, abstracts, etc. This service is available online as part of the CABS database on the hosts BRS and ORBIT search service.

Ecological Abstracts. Geo Abstracts Ltd. Elsevier Applied Science, Crown House, Linton Rd., Barking, England IG 11 8JU. 1974-. Derived from over 600 leading ecological and environmental journals, plus books, conference proceedings, reports and theses.

Environment Abstracts. Bowker A & I Publishing, 121 Chanlon Rd., New Providence, New Jersey 07974. (908) 464-6800. 1974-.

Environment Index. Environment Information Center, Index Research Department, 124 E. 39th St., New York, New York 10016. 1971-. Annual.

Environmental Information Connection-EIC. Planning Information Program, Dept. of Urban and Regional Planning, University of Illinois, 1003 West Nevada, Urbana, Illinois 61801. (217) 333-1369. Also available online.

Environmental Periodicals Bibliography. Environmental Studies Institute, International Academy at Santa Barbara, 800 Garden St., Suite D, Santa Barbara, California 93101. (805) 965-5010. Also available online.

Geographical Abstracts. London School of Economics, Dept. of Geography, Regency House, 34 Duke St., London, England 1966-. Continued by Geo Abstracts issued in 6 parts: Pt. A. Landforms and the quaternary; Pt. B. Biogeography and Climatology; Pt. C. Economic geography; Pt. D. Social geography and cartography; Pt. E. Sedimentology; Pt. F. Regional and community planning.

INIS Atomindex. International Atomic Energy Agency, Wagramerstrasse 5, Vienna, Austria A-1400. 222 23606198. 1988-. Semiannual. Abstracts nuclear energy and nuclear physics topics from journals, conferences, technical reports and other related publications. Issued in 6 parts: Personal Author, Corporate Entry, Subject, Report, Standard Patent, Conference (by place), Conference (by date).

Multimedia Index to Ecology. National Information Center for Educational Media, University of Southern California, Los Angeles, California 90007.

Pollution Abstracts. Cambridge Scientific Abstracts, 5161 River Rd., Bethesda, Maryland 20816. (301) 961-6750. Six/year. Indexes worldwide technical literature on environmental pollution. Covers air pollution, marine and freshwater pollution, sewage and wastewater treatment, waste management, toxicology and health, noise pollution, radiation, land pollution, and environmental policies, programs, legislation, and education. Also available online.

BIBLIOGRAPHIES

Current Contents. Agriculture, Biology and Environmental Sciences. Institute for Scientific Information, 3501 Market St., Philadelphia, Pennsylvania 19104. (800) 523-1857. 1973-. Previous title: Current Contents. Agricultural, Food & Veterinary Sciences. Gives the table of contents of periodicals in the fields of agriculture, biology, environmental and related areas.

EPA Publications Bibliography. U.S. Environmental Protection Agency, Library Systems Branch, 401 M St., SW, Washington, District of Columbia 20460. (202) 260-2090. Quarterly.

Freshwater and Terrestrial Radioecology: A Selected Bibliography. Alfred W. Klement. Hutchinson & Ross, Stroudsburg, Pennsylvania 1980. Bibliography of ecology and environmental pollution.

DIRECTORIES

World Nuclear Directory. Longman, Burnt Mill, Harlow, England CM 20 2J6. (0279) 26721. 1988. Eighth edition. Includes organizations that are involved in nuclear physics research.

ENCYCLOPEDIAS AND DICTIONARIES

Encyclopedia of Physical Science and Technology. Robert A. Meyers, ed. Academic Press, c/o Harcourt Brace Jovanovich Inc., 6277 Sea Harbor Dr., Orlando, Florida 32887. (800) 346-8648. Dictionary of engineering, technology and physical sciences.

Encyclopedia of Physics. Rita G. Lerner and George L. Trigg. VCH Publishers, 303 NW 12th Ave., Deerfield Beach, Florida 33442-1788. (305) 428-5566. 1991. Second edition.

Grzimek's Encyclopedia of Ecology. Bernhard Grzimek. Van Nostrand Reinhold, 115 5th Ave., New York, New York 10003. (212) 254-3232. 1976.

McGraw-Hill Encyclopedia of Environmental Science. Sybil P. Parker. McGraw-Hill Science & Engineering Books, 11 W. 19th St., New York, New York 10011. (212) 337-6010. 1980. Covers ecology, man's influence on nature, and environmental protection.

McGraw-Hill Encyclopedia of Science and Technology. McGraw-Hill, 1221 Avenue of the Americas, New York, New York 10020. (212) 512-2000 or (800) 262-4729. 1992. Seventh edition. Issued in multiple volumes including index. Includes all science and technology broad subject areas.

North American Reference Encyclopedia of Ecology and Pollution. William White. North American Pub. Co., 401 N. Broad St., Philadelphia, Pennsylvania 19108. (215) 238-5300. 1972.

Van Nostrand's Scientific Encyclopedia. Glenn D. Considine, ed. Van Nostrand Reinhold, 115 5th Ave., New York, New York 10003. (212) 254-3232. 1983. Sixth edition. Includes all broad subject areas in science.

GENERAL WORKS

Radioecology. Whicker F.Ward. CRC Press, 2000 Corporate Blvd. N.W., Boca Raton, Florida 33431. (800) 272-7737. 1982. Topics in nuclear energy and its environmental impact.

ONLINE DATA BASES

BIOSIS Previews. BIOSIS, 2100 Arch St., Philadelphia, Pennsylvania 19103-1399. (215) 587-4800. Largest and most comprehensive database of research in the life sciences. Contains citations for nearly 9000 primary research journals, monographs, reviews, symposia, preliminary reports, semi-popular journals, selected institutional reports, government reports and research communications.

Chemical Abstracts-CA. Chemical Abstracts Service, 2540 Olentangy River Rd., P.O. Box 3012, Columbus, Ohio 43210. (800) 848-6533 or (614) 421-3600. Information sources include 9000 journals, patents from 27 countries, two industrial property organizations, new books, conference proceedings, and government research reports.

Enviro/Energyline Abstracts Plus. R. R. Bowker Co., 121 Chanlon Rd., New Providence, New Jersey 07974. (908) 464-6800.

Environmental Periodicals Bibliography. National Information Services Corp., Ste. 6, Wyman Towers, 3100 St. Paul St., Baltimore, Maryland 21218. (410)243-0797. Online version of abstract of same name.

Monthly Catalog of United States Government Publications. U.S. G.P.O., Supt. of Docs., PO Box 371954, Pittsburgh, Pennsylvania 15250-7954. (202) 512-0000.

National Technical Information Service. U.S. Department of Commerce, National Technical Information Service, Office of Data Base Services, 5285 Port Royal Rd., Springfield, Virginia 22161. (703) 487-4807. Bibliographic database of government sponsored research and technical reports.

SCISEARCH. Institute for Scientific Information, University City Science Center, 3501 Market St., Philadelphia, Pennsylvania 19104. (215) 386-0100.

TRADE ASSOCIATIONS AND PROFESSIONAL SOCIETIES

American Chemical Society. 1155 16th St., N.W., Washington, District of Columbia 20036. (202) 872-4600.

RADIOISOTOPES
See: ISOTOPES

RADIOISOTOPIC TRACERS
See: ISOTOPES

RADIOLOGICAL APPLICATIONS

ABSTRACTING AND INDEXING SERVICES

Biological Abstracts. BIOSIS, 2100 Arch St., Philadelphia, Pennsylvania 19103-1399. (215) 587-4800. 1927-.

Biological and Agricultural Index. H.W. Wilson Co., 950 University Ave., Bronx, New York 10452. (800) 367-6770. 1916-. Monthly.

Ecological Abstracts. Geo Abstracts Ltd. Elsevier Applied Science, Crown House, Linton Rd., Barking, England IG 11 8JU. 1974-. Derived from over 600 leading ecological and environmental journals, plus books, conference proceedings, reports and theses.

Environment Abstracts. Bowker A & I Publishing, 121 Chanlon Rd., New Providence, New Jersey 07974. (908) 464-6800. 1974-.

Environment Index. Environment Information Center, Index Research Department, 124 E. 39th St., New York, New York 10016. 1971-. Annual.

Environmental Information Connection–EIC. Planning Information Program, Dept. of Urban and Regional Planning, University of Illinois, 1003 West Nevada, Urbana, Illinois 61801. (217) 333-1369. Also available online.

Environmental Periodicals Bibliography. Environmental Studies Institute, International Academy at Santa Barbara, 800 Garden St., Suite D, Santa Barbara, California 93101. (805) 965-5010. Also available online.

Index to Scientific Book Contents. Institute for Scientific Information, 3501 Market St., Philadelphia, Pennsylvania 19104. (800) 523-1857. 1985-. Annual. Gives contents of science books published.

INIS Atomindex. International Atomic Energy Agency, Wagramerstrasse 5, Vienna, Austria A-1400. 222 23606198. 1988-. Semiannual. Abstracts nuclear energy and nuclear physics topics from journals, conferences, technical reports and other related publications. Issued in 6 parts: Personal Author, Corporate Entry, Subject, Report, Standard Patent, Conference (by place), Conference (by date).

Science Citation Index. Institute for Scientific Information, 3501 Market St., Philadelphia, Pennsylvania 19104. 1961-.

BIBLIOGRAPHIES

EPA Publications Bibliography. U.S. Environmental Protection Agency, Library Systems Branch, 401 M St., SW, Washington, District of Columbia 20460. (202) 260-2090. Quarterly.

DIRECTORIES

World Nuclear Directory. Longman, Burnt Mill, Harlow, England CM 20 2J6. (0279) 26721. 1988. Eighth edition. Includes organizations that are involved in nuclear physics research.

ENCYCLOPEDIAS AND DICTIONARIES

Glossary of Terms in Nuclear Science and Technology. American Nuclear Society, 555 North Kensington Ave., La Grange Park, Illinois 60525. (708) 352-6611. 1986. Prepared by the American Nuclear Society Standards Committee. Subcommittee ANS-9.

ONLINE DATA BASES

BIOSIS Previews. BIOSIS, 2100 Arch St., Philadelphia, Pennsylvania 19103-1399. (215) 587-4800. Largest and most comprehensive database of research in the life sciences. Contains citations for nearly 9000 primary research journals, monographs, reviews, symposia, preliminary reports, semi-popular journals, selected institutional reports, government reports and research communications.

Enviro/Energyline Abstracts Plus. R. R. Bowker Co., 121 Chanlon Rd., New Providence, New Jersey 07974. (908) 464-6800.

Environmental Periodicals Bibliography. National Information Services Corp., Ste. 6, Wyman Towers, 3100 St. Paul St., Baltimore, Maryland 21218. (410)243-0797. Online version of abstract of same name.

TRADE ASSOCIATIONS AND PROFESSIONAL SOCIETIES

American Society of Radiologic Technologists. 15000 Central Ave., S.E., Albuquerque, New Mexico 87123. (505) 298-4500.

RADIOLOGICAL CONTAMINATION

ABSTRACTING AND INDEXING SERVICES

Applied Ecology Abstracts Studies in Renewable Natural Resources. Information Retrieval Ltd., 1911 Jefferson Davis Highway, Arlington, Virginia 22202. 1975-. Monthly.

Biological Abstracts. BIOSIS, 2100 Arch St., Philadelphia, Pennsylvania 19103-1399. (215) 587-4800. 1927-.

Bulletin Signaletique: Eau et Assainissement, Pollution Atmospherique, Droit des Pollutions. Centre de Documentation, Centre National de la Recherche Scientifique, 15, quai Anatole France, Paris, France 75700. (1) 45 55

92 25. 1983-. Monthly. Indexes pollution periodicals including water, atmospheric and related pollutions.

Ecological Abstracts. Geo Abstracts Ltd. Elsevier Applied Science, Crown House, Linton Rd., Barking, England IG 11 8JU. 1974-. Derived from over 600 leading ecological and environmental journals, plus books, conference proceedings, reports and theses.

Environment Abstracts. Bowker A & I Publishing, 121 Chanlon Rd., New Providence, New Jersey 07974. (908) 464-6800. 1974-.

Environment Index. Environment Information Center, Index Research Department, 124 E. 39th St., New York, New York 10016. 1971-. Annual.

Environmental Information Connection–EIC. Planning Information Program, Dept. of Urban and Regional Planning, University of Illinois, 1003 West Nevada, Urbana, Illinois 61801. (217) 333-1369. Also available online.

Environmental Periodicals Bibliography. Environmental Studies Institute, International Academy at Santa Barbara, 800 Garden St., Suite D, Santa Barbara, California 93101. (805) 965-5010. Also available online.

General Science Index. H. W. Wilson Co., 950 University Ave., Bronx, New York 10452. 1978-. Monthly, also issued in annual cumulation. Cumulative subject index to English language periodicals in the subject fields of astronomy, botany, chemistry, earth science, environment and conservation, food and nutrition, genetics, mathematics, medicine and health, microbiology, oceanography, physics, physiology and zoology.

Index to Scientific Book Contents. Institute for Scientific Information, 3501 Market St., Philadelphia, Pennsylvania 19104. (800) 523-1857. 1985-. Annual. Gives contents of science books published.

INIS Atomindex. International Atomic Energy Agency, Wagramerstrasse 5, Vienna, Austria A-1400. 222 23606198. 1988-. Semiannual. Abstracts nuclear energy and nuclear physics topics from journals, conferences, technical reports and other related publications. Issued in 6 parts: Personal Author, Corporate Entry, Subject, Report, Standard Patent, Conference (by place), Conference (by date).

Multimedia Index to Ecology. National Information Center for Educational Media, University of Southern California, Los Angeles, California 90007.

Pollution Abstracts. Cambridge Scientific Abstracts, 5161 River Rd., Bethesda, Maryland 20816. (301) 961-6750. Six/year. Indexes worldwide technical literature on environmental pollution. Covers air pollution, marine and freshwater pollution, sewage and wastewater treatment, waste management, toxicology and health, noise pollution, radiation, land pollution, and environmental policies, programs, legislation, and education. Also available online.

BIBLIOGRAPHIES

EPA Publications Bibliography. U.S. Environmental Protection Agency, Library Systems Branch, 401 M St., SW, Washington, District of Columbia 20460. (202) 260-2090. Quarterly.

DIRECTORIES

World Nuclear Directory. Longman, Burnt Mill, Harlow, England CM 20 2J6. (0279) 26721. 1988. Eighth edition. Includes organizations that are involved in nuclear physics research.

ENCYCLOPEDIAS AND DICTIONARIES

Glossary of Terms in Nuclear Science and Technology. American Nuclear Society, 555 North Kensington Ave., La Grange Park, Illinois 60525. (708) 352-6611. 1986. Prepared by the American Nuclear Society Standards Committee. Subcommittee ANS-9.

GENERAL WORKS

Chemical & Radionuclide Food Contamination. MSS Information Corp., Edison, New Jersey 1973. Covers radioactive contamination of food.

Fire in the Rain. Peter Gould. Carolina Biological Supply Company, 2700 York Rd., Burlington, North Carolina 27215. (919) 584-0381. 1990. Describes the Chernobyl accident.

How to Live with Low-Level Radiation: A Nutritional Protection Plan. Leon Chaitow. Healing Arts Pr., 1 Park St., Rochester, Vermont 05767. (802) 767-3174. 1988. Discusses the problem of low-level radiation in depth and offers safe, nutritional measures to counteract this invisible hazard.

ONLINE DATA BASES

BIOSIS Previews. BIOSIS, 2100 Arch St., Philadelphia, Pennsylvania 19103-1399. (215) 587-4800. Largest and most comprehensive database of research in the life sciences. Contains citations for nearly 9000 primary research journals, monographs, reviews, symposia, preliminary reports, semi-popular journals, selected institutional reports, government reports and research communications.

CERCLIS. Chemical Information Systems, Inc., 7215 York Rd., Baltimore, Maryland 21212. (301) 321-8440. Information on hazardous waste disposal sites that have either been listed by the EPA on the National Priority List (NPL) or nominated for consideration for the NPL.

Enviro/Energyline Abstracts Plus. R. R. Bowker Co., 121 Chanlon Rd., New Providence, New Jersey 07974. (908) 464-6800.

Environmental Periodicals Bibliography. National Information Services Corp., Ste. 6, Wyman Towers, 3100 St. Paul St., Baltimore, Maryland 21218. (410)243-0797. Online version of abstract of same name.

Monthly Catalog of United States Government Publications. U.S. G.P.O., Supt. of Docs., PO Box 371954, Pittsburgh, Pennsylvania 15250-7954. (202) 512-0000.

National Technical Information Service. U.S. Department of Commerce, National Technical Information Service, Office of Data Base Services, 5285 Port Royal Rd., Springfield, Virginia 22161. (703) 487-4807. Bibliographic database of government sponsored research and technical reports.

TRADE ASSOCIATIONS AND PROFESSIONAL SOCIETIES

American Board of Radiology. 300 Park, Suite 440, Birmingham, Michigan 48009. (313) 645-0600.

American College of Radiology. 1891 Preston White Dr., Reston, Virginia 22091. (703) 648-8900.

American Society of Radiologic Technologists. 15000 Central Ave., S.E., Albuquerque, New Mexico 87123. (505) 298-4500.

National Association of Radiation Survivors. P.O. Box 20749, Oakland, California 94620. (415) 655-4886.

Radiological Society of North America. 1415 W. 22nd St., Tower B, Oak Brook, Illinois 60521. (312) 571-2670.

RADIOLOGICAL CONTAMINATION INCIDENT

ABSTRACTING AND INDEXING SERVICES

Environment Abstracts. Bowker A & I Publishing, 121 Chanlon Rd., New Providence, New Jersey 07974. (908) 464-6800. 1974-.

Environment Index. Environment Information Center, Index Research Department, 124 E. 39th St., New York, New York 10016. 1971-. Annual.

Environmental Information Connection–EIC. Planning Information Program, Dept. of Urban and Regional Planning, University of Illinois, 1003 West Nevada, Urbana, Illinois 61801. (217) 333-1369. Also available online.

Environmental Periodicals Bibliography. Environmental Studies Institute, International Academy at Santa Barbara, 800 Garden St., Suite D, Santa Barbara, California 93101. (805) 965-5010. Also available online.

INIS Atomindex. International Atomic Energy Agency, Wagramerstrasse 5, Vienna, Austria A-1400. 222 23606198. 1988-. Semiannual. Abstracts nuclear energy and nuclear physics topics from journals, conferences, technical reports and other related publications. Issued in 6 parts: Personal Author, Corporate Entry, Subject, Report, Standard Patent, Conference (by place), Conference (by date).

BIBLIOGRAPHIES

EPA Publications Bibliography. U.S. Environmental Protection Agency, Library Systems Branch, 401 M St., SW, Washington, District of Columbia 20460. (202) 260-2090. Quarterly.

DIRECTORIES

World Nuclear Directory. Longman, Burnt Mill, Harlow, England CM 20 2J6. (0279) 26721. 1988. Eighth edition. Includes organizations that are involved in nuclear physics research.

ENCYCLOPEDIAS AND DICTIONARIES

Glossary of Terms in Nuclear Science and Technology. American Nuclear Society, 555 North Kensington Ave., La Grange Park, Illinois 60525. (708) 352-6611. 1986.

Prepared by the American Nuclear Society Standards Committee. Subcommittee ANS-9.

ONLINE DATA BASES

CERCLIS. Chemical Information Systems, Inc., 7215 York Rd., Baltimore, Maryland 21212. (301) 321-8440. Information on hazardous waste disposal sites that have either been listed by the EPA on the National Priority List (NPL) or nominated for consideration for the NPL.

Enviro/Energyline Abstracts Plus. R. R. Bowker Co., 121 Chanlon Rd., New Providence, New Jersey 07974. (908) 464-6800.

Environmental Periodicals Bibliography. National Information Services Corp., Ste. 6, Wyman Towers, 3100 St. Paul St., Baltimore, Maryland 21218. (410)243-0797. Online version of abstract of same name.

RADIOLOGICAL CONTAMINATION TREATMENT

See: RADIOACTIVE DECONTAMINATION

RADIONUCLIDES

ABSTRACTING AND INDEXING SERVICES

Bulletin Signaletique: Eau et Assainissement, Pollution Atmospherique, Droit des Pollutions. Centre de Documentation, Centre National de la Recherche Scientifique, 15, quai Anatole France, Paris, France 75700. (1) 45 55 92 25. 1983-. Monthly. Indexes pollution periodicals including water, atmospheric and related pollutions.

Chemical Abstracts. Chemical Abstracts Service, 2540 Olentangy River Rd., PO Box 3012, Columbus, Ohio 43210. (800) 848-6533. 1907-.

Ecological Abstracts. Geo Abstracts Ltd. Elsevier Applied Science, Crown House, Linton Rd., Barking, England IG 11 8JU. 1974-. Derived from over 600 leading ecological and environmental journals, plus books, conference proceedings, reports and theses.

Environment Abstracts. Bowker A & I Publishing, 121 Chanlon Rd., New Providence, New Jersey 07974. (908) 464-6800. 1974-.

Environment Index. Environment Information Center, Index Research Department, 124 E. 39th St., New York, New York 10016. 1971-. Annual.

Environmental Information Connection–EIC. Planning Information Program, Dept. of Urban and Regional Planning, University of Illinois, 1003 West Nevada, Urbana, Illinois 61801. (217) 333-1369. Also available online.

Environmental Periodicals Bibliography. Environmental Studies Institute, International Academy at Santa Barbara, 800 Garden St., Suite D, Santa Barbara, California 93101. (805) 965-5010. Also available online.

Food Science and Technology Abstracts. International Food Information Service, c/o National Food Laboratory, 6363 Clark Ave., Dublin, California 94568. (800) 336-3782. 1969-.

General Science Index. H. W. Wilson Co., 950 University Ave., Bronx, New York 10452. 1978-. Monthly, also issued in annual cumulation. Cumulative subject index to English language periodicals in the subject fields of astronomy, botany, chemistry, earth science, environment and conservation, food and nutrition, genetics, mathematics, medicine and health, microbiology, oceanography, physics, physiology and zoology.

INIS Atomindex. International Atomic Energy Agency, Wagramerstrasse 5, Vienna, Austria A-1400. 222 23606198. 1988-. Semiannual. Abstracts nuclear energy and nuclear physics topics from journals, conferences, technical reports and other related publications. Issued in 6 parts: Personal Author, Corporate Entry, Subject, Report, Standard Patent, Conference (by place), Conference (by date).

Physics Briefs. Physikalische Berichte. Physik Verlag, Pappapelallee 3, Postfach 101161, Weinheim, Germany D-6940. 1979-. Semimonthly. In English. Volumes for 1979- issued by the Deutsche Physikalische Gesellschaft and the Fachinformationszentrum Energie Physik, Mathematik in cooperation with the American Institute of Physics.

Science Citation Index. Institute for Scientific Information, 3501 Market St., Philadelphia, Pennsylvania 19104. 1961-.

BIBLIOGRAPHIES

EPA Publications Bibliography. U.S. Environmental Protection Agency, Library Systems Branch, 401 M St., SW, Washington, District of Columbia 20460. (202) 260-2090. Quarterly.

DIRECTORIES

World Nuclear Directory. Longman, Burnt Mill, Harlow, England CM 20 2J6. (0279) 26721. 1988. Eighth edition. Includes organizations that are involved in nuclear physics research.

ENCYCLOPEDIAS AND DICTIONARIES

Encyclopedia of Human Biology. Renato Dulbecco, ed. Academic Press, c/o Harcourt Brace Jovanovich Inc., 6277 Sea Harbor Dr., Orlando, Florida 32887. (800) 346-8648. 1991. Eight volumes.

Encyclopedia of Physics. Rita G. Lerner and George L. Trigg. VCH Publishers, 303 NW 12th Ave., Deerfield Beach, Florida 33442-1788. (305) 428-5566. 1991. Second edition.

Van Nostrand's Scientific Encyclopedia. Glenn D. Considine, ed. Van Nostrand Reinhold, 115 5th Ave., New York, New York 10003. (212) 254-3232. 1983. Sixth edition. Includes all broad subject areas in science.

GENERAL WORKS

Screening Techniques for Determining Compliance with Environmental Standards. National Council on Radiation Protection and Measurements, 7910 Woodmont Ave., Ste. 800, Bethesda, Maryland 20814. (301) 657-2652. 1986. Commentary on the release of radionuclides in the atmosphere.

Transportation of Urban Radionuclides in Urban Environs. Nancy C. Finlay. Nuclear Regulatory Commission,

1717 H St. NW, Washington, District of Columbia 20555. (301) 492-7000. 1980. Environmental aspects of transportation of radioactive substances.

Transuranic Elements in the Environment. Wayne C. Hanson. National Technical Information Service, 5285 Port Royal Rd., Springfield, Virginia 22161. (703) 487-4650. A summary of environmental research on transuranium radionuclides funded by USDOE.

ONLINE DATA BASES

Chemical Abstracts-CA. Chemical Abstracts Service, 2540 Olentangy River Rd., P.O. Box 3012, Columbus, Ohio 43210. (800) 848-6533 or (614) 421-3600. Information sources include 9000 journals, patents from 27 countries, two industrial property organizations, new books, conference proceedings, and government research reports.

Enviro/Energyline Abstracts Plus. R. R. Bowker Co., 121 Chanlon Rd., New Providence, New Jersey 07974. (908) 464-6800.

Environmental Periodicals Bibliography. National Information Services Corp., Ste. 6, Wyman Towers, 3100 St. Paul St., Baltimore, Maryland 21218. (410)243-0797. Online version of abstract of same name.

TRADE ASSOCIATIONS AND PROFESSIONAL SOCIETIES

American Chemical Society. 1155 16th St., N.W., Washington, District of Columbia 20036. (202) 872-4600.

RADIUM

ABSTRACTING AND INDEXING SERVICES

Applied Science and Technology Index. H.W. Wilson Co., 950 University Ave., Bronx, New York 10452. (800) 367-6770. Formerly Industrial Arts Index.

Chemical Abstracts. Chemical Abstracts Service, 2540 Olentangy River Rd., PO Box 3012, Columbus, Ohio 43210. (800) 848-6533. 1907-.

Ecological Abstracts. Geo Abstracts Ltd. Elsevier Applied Science, Crown House, Linton Rd., Barking, England IG 11 8JU. 1974-. Derived from over 600 leading ecological and environmental journals, plus books, conference proceedings, reports and theses.

Environment Abstracts. Bowker A & I Publishing, 121 Chanlon Rd., New Providence, New Jersey 07974. (908) 464-6800. 1974-.

Environment Index. Environment Information Center, Index Research Department, 124 E. 39th St., New York, New York 10016. 1971-. Annual.

Environmental Information Connection–EIC. Planning Information Program, Dept. of Urban and Regional Planning, University of Illinois, 1003 West Nevada, Urbana, Illinois 61801. (217) 333-1369. Also available online.

Environmental Periodicals Bibliography. Environmental Studies Institute, International Academy at Santa Barbara, 800 Garden St., Suite D, Santa Barbara, California 93101. (805) 965-5010. Also available online.

General Science Index. H. W. Wilson Co., 950 University Ave., Bronx, New York 10452. 1978-. Monthly, also issued in annual cumulation. Cumulative subject index to English language periodicals in the subject fields of astronomy, botany, chemistry, earth science, environment and conservation, food and nutrition, genetics, mathematics, medicine and health, microbiology, oceanography, physics, physiology and zoology.

INIS Atomindex. International Atomic Energy Agency, Wagramerstrasse 5, Vienna, Austria A-1400. 222 23606198. 1988-. Semiannual. Abstracts nuclear energy and nuclear physics topics from journals, conferences, technical reports and other related publications. Issued in 6 parts: Personal Author, Corporate Entry, Subject, Report, Standard Patent, Conference (by place), Conference (by date).

Physics Briefs. Physikalische Berichte. Physik Verlag, Pappapelallee 3, Postfach 101161, Weinheim, Germany D-6940. 1979-. Semimonthly. In English. Volumes for 1979- issued by the Deutsche Physikalische Gesellschaft and the Fachinformationszentrum Energie Physik, Mathematik in cooperation with the American Institute of Physics.

Science Citation Index. Institute for Scientific Information, 3501 Market St., Philadelphia, Pennsylvania 19104. 1961-.

BIBLIOGRAPHIES

Bibliography and Index of Geology. American Geological Institute, 4220 King St., Alexandria, Virginia 22302. Monthly. Includes environmental geology and hydrogeology.

EPA Publications Bibliography. U.S. Environmental Protection Agency, Library Systems Branch, 401 M St., SW, Washington, District of Columbia 20460. (202) 260-2090. Quarterly.

DIRECTORIES

World Nuclear Directory. Longman, Burnt Mill, Harlow, England CM 20 2J6. (0279) 26721. 1988. Eighth edition. Includes organizations that are involved in nuclear physics research.

ENCYCLOPEDIAS AND DICTIONARIES

Encyclopedia of Electrochemistry of Elements. A. J. Bard. Marcel Dekker, Inc., 270 Madison Ave., New York, New York 10016. (212) 696-9000 or (800) 228-1160. Encyclopedic treatment of the subject area of electrochemistry and related subjects.

Encyclopedia of Physics. Rita G. Lerner and George L. Trigg. VCH Publishers, 303 NW 12th Ave., Deerfield Beach, Florida 33442-1788. (305) 428-5566. 1991. Second edition.

Glossary of Terms in Nuclear Science and Technology. American Nuclear Society, 555 North Kensington Ave., La Grange Park, Illinois 60525. (708) 352-6611. 1986. Prepared by the American Nuclear Society Standards Committee. Subcommittee ANS-9.

McGraw-Hill Encyclopedia of Science and Technology. McGraw-Hill, 1221 Avenue of the Americas, New York, New York 10020. (212) 512-2000 or (800) 262-4729. 1992. Seventh edition. Issued in multiple volumes in-

cluding index. Includes all science and technology broad subject areas.

Van Nostrand's Scientific Encyclopedia. Glenn D. Considine, ed. Van Nostrand Reinhold, 115 5th Ave., New York, New York 10003. (212) 254-3232. 1983. Sixth edition. Includes all broad subject areas in science.

GENERAL WORKS

The Environmental Behaviour of Radium. International Atomic Energy Agency, Vienna International Centre, Wagromerstrasse 5, Postfach 100, Vienna, Austria A-1400. 1990. Covers radium measurement, environmental monitoring and impact analysis.

Magill's Survey of Science. Earth Science Series. Frank N. Magill. Salem Press, PO Box 50062, Pasadena, California 91105. 1990-. Five volumes. Includes information on earth's crust, hot spots and volcanic island chains, physical properties of minerals, rock magnetism, physical properties of rocks, and index.

Radon, Radium, and Uranium in Drinking Water. C. Richard Cothern and Paul Rebers. Lewis Publishers, 2000 Corporate Blvd., N.W., Boca Raton, Florida 33431. (407) 994-0555 or (800) 272-7737. 1990. Covers most aspects of radionuclides in drinking water.

Toxicological Profile of Radium. Life Systems Inc. Agency for Toxic Substances and Disease Registry, U.S. Public Health Service, 1600 Clifton Rd. NE, Atlanta, Georgia 30333. (404) 452-4111. 1990. Toxicology, physiological and environmental aspects of radium.

ONLINE DATA BASES

CERCLIS. Chemical Information Systems, Inc., 7215 York Rd., Baltimore, Maryland 21212. (301) 321-8440. Information on hazardous waste disposal sites that have either been listed by the EPA on the National Priority List (NPL) or nominated for consideration for the NPL.

Chemical Abstracts-CA. Chemical Abstracts Service, 2540 Olentangy River Rd., P.O. Box 3012, Columbus, Ohio 43210. (800) 848-6533 or (614) 421-3600. Information sources include 9000 journals, patents from 27 countries, two industrial property organizations, new books, conference proceedings, and government research reports.

Enviro/Energyline Abstracts Plus. R. R. Bowker Co., 121 Chanlon Rd., New Providence, New Jersey 07974. (908) 464-6800.

Environmental Periodicals Bibliography. National Information Services Corp., Ste. 6, Wyman Towers, 3100 St. Paul St., Baltimore, Maryland 21218. (410)243-0797. Online version of abstract of same name.

Monthly Catalog of United States Government Publications. U.S. G.P.O., Supt. of Docs., PO Box 371954, Pittsburgh, Pennsylvania 15250-7954. (202) 512-0000.

National Technical Information Service. U.S. Department of Commerce, National Technical Information Service, Office of Data Base Services, 5285 Port Royal Rd., Springfield, Virginia 22161. (703) 487-4807. Bibliographic database of government sponsored research and technical reports.

TRADE ASSOCIATIONS AND PROFESSIONAL SOCIETIES

American Institute of Chemical Engineers. 345 East 47th St., New York, New York 10017. (212) 705-7338.

American Institute of Chemists. 7315 Wisconsin Ave., Bethesda, Maryland 20814. (301) 652-2447.

American Radium Society. 1101 Market St., Philadelphia, Pennsylvania 19107. (215) 574-3179.

RADON

ABSTRACTING AND INDEXING SERVICES

Air Pollution Technical Publications of the United States Environmental Protection Agency. U.S. Environmental Protection Agency, Mail Drop 75, Research Triangle Park, North Carolina 27711. (919) 541-2184. 1976. Quarterly.

Applied Science and Technology Index. H.W. Wilson Co., 950 University Ave., Bronx, New York 10452. (800) 367-6770. Formerly Industrial Arts Index.

Biological and Agricultural Index. H.W. Wilson Co., 950 University Ave., Bronx, New York 10452. (800) 367-6770. 1916-. Monthly.

Bulletin Signaletique: Eau et Assainissement, Pollution Atmospherique, Droit des Pollutions. Centre de Documentation, Centre National de la Recherche Scientifique, 15, quai Anatole France, Paris, France 75700. (1) 45 55 92 25. 1983-. Monthly. Indexes pollution periodicals including water, atmospheric and related pollutions.

Chemical Abstracts. Chemical Abstracts Service, 2540 Olentangy River Rd., PO Box 3012, Columbus, Ohio 43210. (800) 848-6533. 1907-.

Ecological Abstracts. Geo Abstracts Ltd. Elsevier Applied Science, Crown House, Linton Rd., Barking, England IG 11 8JU. 1974-. Derived from over 600 leading ecological and environmental journals, plus books, conference proceedings, reports and theses.

Environment Abstracts. Bowker A & I Publishing, 121 Chanlon Rd., New Providence, New Jersey 07974. (908) 464-6800. 1974-.

Environment Index. Environment Information Center, Index Research Department, 124 E. 39th St., New York, New York 10016. 1971-. Annual.

Environmental Information Connection–EIC. Planning Information Program, Dept. of Urban and Regional Planning, University of Illinois, 1003 West Nevada, Urbana, Illinois 61801. (217) 333-1369. Also available online.

Environmental Periodicals Bibliography. Environmental Studies Institute, International Academy at Santa Barbara, 800 Garden St., Suite D, Santa Barbara, California 93101. (805) 965-5010. Also available online.

General Science Index. H. W. Wilson Co., 950 University Ave., Bronx, New York 10452. 1978-. Monthly, also issued in annual cumulation. Cumulative subject index to English language periodicals in the subject fields of astronomy, botany, chemistry, earth science, environment and conservation, food and nutrition, genetics, mathematics, medicine and health, microbiology, oceanography, physics, physiology and zoology.

Index to Scientific Book Contents. Institute for Scientific Information, 3501 Market St., Philadelphia, Pennsylvania 19104. (800) 523-1857. 1985-. Annual. Gives contents of science books published.

INIS Atomindex. International Atomic Energy Agency, Wagramerstrasse 5, Vienna, Austria A-1400. 222 23606198. 1988-. Semiannual. Abstracts nuclear energy and nuclear physics topics from journals, conferences, technical reports and other related publications. Issued in 6 parts: Personal Author, Corporate Entry, Subject, Report, Standard Patent, Conference (by place), Conference (by date).

Physics Briefs. Physikalische Berichte. Physik Verlag, Pappapelallee 3, Postfach 101161, Weinheim, Germany D-6940. 1979-. Semimonthly. In English. Volumes for 1979- issued by the Deutsche Physikalische Gesellschaft and the Fachinformationszentrum Energie Physik, Mathematik in cooperation with the American Institute of Physics.

Science Citation Index. Institute for Scientific Information, 3501 Market St., Philadelphia, Pennsylvania 19104. 1961-.

BIBLIOGRAPHIES

Bibliography and Index of Geology. American Geological Institute, 4220 King St., Alexandria, Virginia 22302. Monthly. Includes environmental geology and hydrogeology.

Current Contents. Agriculture, Biology and Environmental Sciences. Institute for Scientific Information, 3501 Market St., Philadelphia, Pennsylvania 19104. (800) 523-1857. 1973-. Previous title: Current Contents. Agricultural, Food & Veterinary Sciences. Gives the table of contents of periodicals in the fields of agriculture, biology, environmental and related areas.

EPA Publications Bibliography. U.S. Environmental Protection Agency, Library Systems Branch, 401 M St., SW, Washington, District of Columbia 20460. (202) 260-2090. Quarterly.

DIRECTORIES

Radon Directory. Radon Press, Inc., 500 N. Washington St., Alexandria, Virginia 22314. (703) 548-2756.

World Nuclear Directory. Longman, Burnt Mill, Harlow, England CM 20 2J6. (0279) 26721. 1988. Eighth edition. Includes organizations that are involved in nuclear physics research.

ENCYCLOPEDIAS AND DICTIONARIES

Encyclopedia of Physical Science and Technology. Robert A. Meyers, ed. Academic Press, c/o Harcourt Brace Jovanovich Inc., 6277 Sea Harbor Dr., Orlando, Florida 32887. (800) 346-8648. Dictionary of engineering, technology and physical sciences.

Encyclopedia of Physics. Rita G. Lerner and George L. Trigg. VCH Publishers, 303 NW 12th Ave., Deerfield Beach, Florida 33442-1788. (305) 428-5566. 1991. Second edition.

McGraw-Hill Encyclopedia of Environmental Science. Sybil P. Parker. McGraw-Hill Science & Engineering Books, 11 W. 19th St., New York, New York 10011.

(212) 337-6010. 1980. Covers ecology, man's influence on nature, and environmental protection.

McGraw-Hill Encyclopedia of Science and Technology. McGraw-Hill, 1221 Avenue of the Americas, New York, New York 10020. (212) 512-2000 or (800) 262-4729. 1992. Seventh edition. Issued in multiple volumes including index. Includes all science and technology broad subject areas.

Van Nostrand's Scientific Encyclopedia. Glenn D. Considine, ed. Van Nostrand Reinhold, 115 5th Ave., New York, New York 10003. (212) 254-3232. 1983. Sixth edition. Includes all broad subject areas in science.

GENERAL WORKS

Comparative Dosimetry of Radon in Mines and Homes. Commission on Life Science, National Research Council. National Academy Press, 2101 Constitution Ave. N.W., PO Box 285, Washington, District of Columbia 20418. (202) 334-3313. 1991.

Indoor Air Pollution: Radon, Bioaerosols, and VOCs. Jack G. Kay, et al. Lewis Publishers, 2000 Corporate Blvd., N.W., Boca Raton, Florida 33431. (407) 994-0555 or (800) 272-7737. 1991. Consists of two parts: Overview of the ACS Symposium on Indoor Air Pollution, and Radon overview

Magill's Survey of Science. Earth Science Series. Frank N. Magill. Salem Press, PO Box 50062, Pasadena, California 91105. 1990-. Five volumes. Includes information on earth's crust, hot spots and volcanic island chains, physical properties of minerals, rock magnetism, physical properties of rocks, and index.

Radon and Its Decay in Indoor Air. William W. Nazaroff and Anthony V. Nero. John Wiley & Sons, Inc., 605 3rd Ave., New York, New York 10158-0012. (212) 850-6000. 1988. Radon isotopes toxicology and hygienic aspects of indoor air pollution.

Radon in the Environment. M. Wilkening. Elsevier Science Publishing Co., 655 Avenue of the Americas, New York, New York 10010. (212) 989-5800. 1990. Describes the discovery of radon, its characteristics, and sources in the environment methods of control, as well as possible health effects.

Radon, Radium, and Uranium in Drinking Water. C. Richard Cothern and Paul Rebers. Lewis Publishers, 2000 Corporate Blvd., N.W., Boca Raton, Florida 33431. (407) 994-0555 or (800) 272-7737. 1990. Covers most aspects of radionuclides in drinking water.

HANDBOOKS AND MANUALS

Controlling Indoor Radon. Kenneth Q. Lao. Global Professional Publications, 2805 McGraw Ave., PO Box 19539, Irvine, California 92713-9539. (800) 854-7179.

Illinois Homeowner's Guide to Reduction of Indoor Radon. Illinois Department of Energy and Natural Resources, Office of Research and Planning, 325 W. Adams St., Rm. 300, Springfield, Illinois 62706. (217) 785-2800. 1989. Environmental and health aspects of indoor air pollution.

Radon Attenuation Handbook for Uranium Mill Tailings Cover Design. U.S. Nuclear Regulatory Commission, Division of Health, Siting and Waste Management,

Office of Nuclear Regulatory Research, Washington, District of Columbia 20555. (301) 492-7000. 1984.

ONLINE DATA BASES

Chemical Abstracts-CA. Chemical Abstracts Service, 2540 Olentangy River Rd., P.O. Box 3012, Columbus, Ohio 43210. (800) 848-6533 or (614) 421-3600. Information sources include 9000 journals, patents from 27 countries, two industrial property organizations, new books, conference proceedings, and government research reports.

Concentrations of Indoor Pollutants–CIP. CIP Database Coordinator, Building 90, Rm 3058, Lawrence Berkeley Lab., 1 Cyclotron Rd., Berkeley, California 94720. (415) 486-6591. Contains field data from studies monitoring indoor air quality in occupied buildings in U.S. and Canada.

Enviro/Energyline Abstracts Plus. R. R. Bowker Co., 121 Chanlon Rd., New Providence, New Jersey 07974. (908) 464-6800.

Environmental Periodicals Bibliography. National Information Services Corp., Ste. 6, Wyman Towers, 3100 St. Paul St., Baltimore, Maryland 21218. (410)243-0797. Online version of abstract of same name.

Monthly Catalog of United States Government Publications. U.S. G.P.O., Supt. of Docs., PO Box 371954, Pittsburgh, Pennsylvania 15250-7954. (202) 512-0000.

National Technical Information Service. U.S. Department of Commerce, National Technical Information Service, Office of Data Base Services, 5285 Port Royal Rd., Springfield, Virginia 22161. (703) 487-4807. Bibliographic database of government sponsored research and technical reports.

PressNet Environmental Reports. Chemical Information Systems, Inc., 7215 York Rd., Baltimore, Maryland 21212. (301) 321-8440.

PERIODICALS AND NEWSLETTERS

Atmospheric Environment. Pergamon Microforms International, Inc., Fairview Park, Elmsford, New York 10523. (914) 592-7720. 1966-. Publishes papers on all aspects of man's interactions with his atmospheric environment, including the administrative, economic and political aspects of these interactions. Air pollution research and its applications are covered, taking into account changes in the atmospheric flow patterns, temperature distributions and chemical constitution caused by natural and artificial variations in the earth's surface.

Indoor Pollution Law Report. Leader Publications, New York Law Publishing Co., 111 Eighth Ave., New York, New York 10011. (212) 463-5709. Monthly.

Indoor Pollution News. Buraff Publications, 1350 Connecticut Ave., NW, Suite 100, Washington, District of Columbia 20036. (202) 862-0990. Biweekly. Air quality in buildings (including radon, formaldehyde, solvents and asbestos) or other air pollutions, such as lead in pipes.

Radon News Digest. Hoosier Environmental Pubs., Box 709, Carmel, Indiana 46032. (317) 843-0788. Monthly. Testing, mitigation, legislation and market trends.

TRADE ASSOCIATIONS AND PROFESSIONAL SOCIETIES

American Public Works Association. 106 W. 11th St., Ste. 1800, Kansas City, Missouri 64105-1806. (816) 472-6100.

North American Radon Association. 8441 River Birch, Roswell, Georgia 30075. (404) 993-5033.

RAIL TRANSPORTATION

See: TRANSPORTATION

RAILROAD NOISE

See: NOISE

RAIN FORESTS

See also: TROPICAL FORESTS

ABSTRACTING AND INDEXING SERVICES

Applied Ecology Abstracts Studies in Renewable Natural Resources. Information Retrieval Ltd., 1911 Jefferson Davis Highway, Arlington, Virginia 22202. 1975-. Monthly.

Biological Abstracts. BIOSIS, 2100 Arch St., Philadelphia, Pennsylvania 19103-1399. (215) 587-4800. 1927-.

Biological and Agricultural Index. H.W. Wilson Co., 950 University Ave., Bronx, New York 10452. (800) 367-6770. 1916-. Monthly.

Ecological Abstracts. Geo Abstracts Ltd. Elsevier Applied Science, Crown House, Linton Rd., Barking, England IG 11 8JU. 1974-. Derived from over 600 leading ecological and environmental journals, plus books, conference proceedings, reports and theses.

Ecology Abstracts. Cambridge Scientific Abstracts, 5161 River Rd., Bethesda, Maryland 20816. (301) 961-6750. Monthly.

Environment Abstracts. Bowker A & I Publishing, 121 Chanlon Rd., New Providence, New Jersey 07974. (908) 464-6800. 1974-.

Environment Index. Environment Information Center, Index Research Department, 124 E. 39th St., New York, New York 10016. 1971-. Annual.

Environmental Information Connection–EIC. Planning Information Program, Dept. of Urban and Regional Planning, University of Illinois, 1003 West Nevada, Urbana, Illinois 61801. (217) 333-1369. Also available online.

Environmental Periodicals Bibliography. Environmental Studies Institute, International Academy at Santa Barbara, 800 Garden St., Suite D, Santa Barbara, California 93101. (805) 965-5010. Also available online.

General Science Index. H. W. Wilson Co., 950 University Ave., Bronx, New York 10452. 1978-. Monthly, also issued in annual cumulation. Cumulative subject index to English language periodicals in the subject fields of astronomy, botany, chemistry, earth science, environ-

ment and conservation, food and nutrition, genetics, mathematics, medicine and health, microbiology, oceanography, physics, physiology and zoology.

Index to Scientific Book Contents. Institute for Scientific Information, 3501 Market St., Philadelphia, Pennsylvania 19104. (800) 523-1857. 1985-. Annual. Gives contents of science books published.

Multimedia Index to Ecology. National Information Center for Educational Media, University of Southern California, Los Angeles, California 90007.

Science Citation Index. Institute for Scientific Information, 3501 Market St., Philadelphia, Pennsylvania 19104. 1961-.

ALMANACS AND YEARBOOKS

Gale Environmental Almanac. Russ Hoyle. Gale Research Inc., 835 Penobscot Bldg., Detroit, Michigan 48226-4094. (313) 961-2242. 1993. Focuses on the U.S. and Canada, although worldwide and transboundary issues are discussed.

BIBLIOGRAPHIES

Current Contents. Agriculture, Biology and Environmental Sciences. Institute for Scientific Information, 3501 Market St., Philadelphia, Pennsylvania 19104. (800) 523-1857. 1973-. Previous title: Current Contents. Agricultural, Food & Veterinary Sciences. Gives the table of contents of periodicals in the fields of agriculture, biology, environmental and related areas.

EPA Publications Bibliography. U.S. Environmental Protection Agency, Library Systems Branch, 401 M St., SW, Washington, District of Columbia 20460. (202) 260-2090. Quarterly.

DIRECTORIES

Canadian Environmental Directory. Canadian Almanac & Directory Publishing Co. Ltd., 134 Adelaide St. E., Ste. 27, Toronto, Ontario, Canada M5C 1K9. (416) 362-4088. 1992. Includes individuals, agencies, firms, and associations.

Gale Environmental Sourcebook. Karen Hill. Gale Research Co., 835 Penobscot Bldg., Detroit, Michigan 48226-4094. (313) 961-2242. Contacts, information sources, or general information on environmental topics.

ENCYCLOPEDIAS AND DICTIONARIES

Cambridge Encyclopedia of Life Sciences. A. E. Friday and David S. Ingram. Cambridge University Press, 40 W 20th St., New York, New York 10011. (212) 924-3900 or (800) 227-0247. 1985. Includes all topics under biology and ecology.

Dictionary of the Environment. Michael Allaby. New York University Press, 70 Washington Sq. S., New York, New York 10012. (212) 998-2575. 1989.

Environmental Encyclopedia. William P. Cunningham, Terence Ball, et. al. Gale Research Inc., 835 Penobscot Bldg., Detroit, Michigan 48226-4094. (313) 961-2242. 1993.

GENERAL WORKS

Alternatives to Deforestation: Steps Toward Sustainable Use of the Amazon Rain Forest. Anthony B. Anderson, ed. Columbia University Press, 562 W. 113th St., New York, New York 10025. (212) 316-7100. 1992. Based on papers presented at an international conference in Belem, Brazil, for scientists in several fields, as well as government policy makers and representatives from foundations who are interested in exploring possible sustainable use of the world's largest rain forest, the Amazon, which is now being destroyed on an unprecedented scale.

An Amazonian Forest. C. F. Jordan. Parthenon Pub., Casterton Hall, Carnforth, England LA6 2LA. 1990. Volume 2 in the Man and the Biosphere series published jointly with UNESCO.

Carbon, Nutrient and Water Balances of Tropical Rain Forest Ecosystems Subject to Disturbance: Management Implications and Research Proposals. Jonathan M. Anderson and Thomas Spencer. UNESCO, 7, place de Fontenoy, Paris, France F-75700. (331) 45 68 40 67. 1991. MAB Digest 7.

Cattle in the Cold Desert. James A. Young. Utah State University Press, Logan, Utah 84322. (801)750-13620017064. 1985. Covers history of grazing, ranch life and beef cattle in the Great Basin.

Ecology and Land Management in Amazonia. Michael J. Eden. Belhaven Press, 136 S. Broadway, Irvington, New York 10533. (914) 591-9111. 1990. Deals with three major areas: the rain forest as a global resource and its role in sustaining life on the planet as a whole; needs of the countries with large tracts of tropical rain forest (including the factors that relate to how one can utilize land, the climate, geomorphology, hydrology, soils and ecology); and how the Amazonia rain forest can be conserved, including the role of national parks and management at the regional level.

The Ecology of a Tropical Forest. Egbert J. Leigh, Jr., et al., eds. Smithsonian Institution Press, 470 L'Enfant Plaza, No. 7100, Washington, District of Columbia 20560. (800) 782-4612. 1983. Describes the rhythm of plant reproduction through the seasons and how it affects animal population.

Economic and Ecological Sustainability of Tropical Rain Forest Management. Kathrin Schreckenberg and Malcolm Hadley, eds. UNESCO, 7, place de Fontenoy, Paris, France F-75700. (331) 45 68 40 67. 1991.

Energy, the Environment, and Public Policy: Issues for the 1990s. David L. McKee, ed. Praeger Publishers, 1 Madison Ave., New York, New York 10010-3603. (212) 685-5300. 1991. Addresses the extent and gravity of our environmental situation, from industrial waste to acid rain, from the Alaskan oil spill to the destruction of the rain forests.

The Environmental Sourcebook. Edith Carol Stein. Lyons & Burford, 31 W. 21st St., New York, New York 10010. (212) 620-9580. 1992. Provides information on 11 specific environmental issues, including population; agriculture; energy; climate and atmosphere; biodiversity; water; oceans; solid waste; hazardous substances and waste; endangered lands; and development.

Environmental Viewpoints. Marie Lazzari. Gale Research Inc., 835 Penobscot Bldg., Detroit, Michigan 48226-4094. (313) 961-2242. 1992.

Grazing Management: An Ecological Perspective. R.K. Heitschmidt. Timber Press, 9999 SW Wilshire, Portland, Oregon 97225. (800) 327-5680. 1991. Environmental aspects of grazing and range management.

Into the Amazon: The Struggle for the Rain Forest. Augusta Dwyer. Sierra Club Books, 100 Bush St., San Francisco, California 94104. (415) 291-1600. 1991. Summarizes the life-styles of the various socioeconomic classes of people who live in the Amazon Basin.

An Introduction to Tropical Rain Forests. T. C. Whitmore. Oxford University Press, 200 Madison Ave., New York, New York 10016. (212) 679-7300; (800) 334-4249. 1990. Describes the world's tropical rainforests, their structure and functioning, their value to humans, and what is being done to them.

The Last Rain Forests: A World Conservation Atlas. Mark Collins, ed. Oxford University Press, 200 Madison Ave., New York, New York 10016. (212) 679-7300; (800) 334-4249. 1990. Containing more than 200 full color photos and maps, this is a guide to the people, flora and fauna of the richest habitats on earth. Maps the world's rain forests, spells out the problems facing these regions, and proposes concrete, realistic strategies for ensuring their survival.

The Mighty Rain Forest. John Nicol. Sterling Pub. Co. Inc., 387 Park Ave. S., New York, New York 10016. (212) 532-7160; (800) 367-9692. 1990. Focuses on the emotive debate on the environment regarding rainforests and the paper manufacturers. Includes a bibliography and a list of organizations working in rainforest conservation.

Portraits of the Rainforest. Adrian Forsyth. Firefly Books, PO Box 1325, Ellicot Sta., Buffalo, New York 14205. 1990. Explores the precarious contingencies that determine the nature of tropical life.

Race to Save the Tropics. Robert Goodland, ed. Island Press, 1718 Connecticut Ave. N.W., Suite 300, Washington, District of Columbia 20009. (202) 232-7933. 1990. Documents the conflict between economic development and protection of biological diversity in tropical countries.

Rain Forest Regeneration and Management. G. Pompa, et al., eds. Parthenon Group Inc., 120 Mill Rd., Park Ridge, New Jersey 07656. (201) 391-6796. 1991. Explores the management implications of present scientific knowledge on rain forest generation. Providing case studies.

Range and Pasture Research. U.S. Agricultural Research Service, Washington, District of Columbia 1986.

Taking Stock: The Tropical Forestry Action Plan After Five Years. Robert Winterbottom. World Resources Institute, 1709 New York Ave. N.W., Washington, District of Columbia 20006. (800) 822-0504. 1990. Analyzes Tropical Forestry Action Plan's accomplishments and shortcomings, drawing on the biannual meetings of the TFAP Forestry Advisors' groups, assessments by FAO, various aid agencies, and by such organizations as the World Rainforest Movement, Friends of the Earth, and World Life Fund.

Trees of Life: Saving Tropical Forests and their Biological Wealth. Kenton Miller and Laura Tangley. World Resources Institute, 1709 New York Ave. N.W., Washington, District of Columbia 20006. (800) 822-0504. 1991. Explains what deforestation is doing to the global environment and why rainforest preservation is valid to human welfare around the world.

Tropical Forest and Its Environment. Kenneth Alan Longman. Longman Scientific & Technical, 1560 Broadway, New York, New York 10036. (212) 819-5400. 1990. Rain forest and tropical ecology, ecosystems, and cycles.

Tropical Rainforest: A World Survey of Our Most Valuable Endangered Habitat With a Blueprint for its Survival. Arnold Newman. Facts on File, Inc., 460 Park Ave. S., New York, New York 10016. (212) 683-2244; (800) 322-8755. 1990. Considers threats to rain forests, including logging and slash and burn agricultural practices. Presents a variety of measures to preserve our valuable rain forests.

Vegetation and Environmental Features of Forest and Range Ecosystems. Garrison, George A. U.S. Forest Service, Box 96090, Washington, District of Columbia 20090. (202) 720-3760. 1977. Range and forest ecology and classification of vegetation.

World Guide to Environmental Issues and Organizations. Peter Brackley. Longman Group Ltd., Longman House, Burnt Mill, Harlow, Essex, England CM20 2J6. (0279) 426721. 1991.

HANDBOOKS AND MANUALS

Environmental Statistics Handbook: Europe. Allan Foster, Oksana Newman. Gale Research Inc., 835 Penobscot Bldg., Detroit, Michigan 48226-4094. (313) 961-2242. 1993.

ONLINE DATA BASES

BIOSIS Previews. BIOSIS, 2100 Arch St., Philadelphia, Pennsylvania 19103-1399. (215) 587-4800. Largest and most comprehensive database of research in the life sciences. Contains citations for nearly 9000 primary research journals, monographs, reviews, symposia, preliminary reports, semi-popular journals, selected institutional reports, government reports and research communications.

Enviro/Energyline Abstracts Plus. R. R. Bowker Co., 121 Chanlon Rd., New Providence, New Jersey 07974. (908) 464-6800.

Environmental Periodicals Bibliography. National Information Services Corp., Ste. 6, Wyman Towers, 3100 St. Paul St., Baltimore, Maryland 21218. (410)243-0797. Online version of abstract of same name.

PressNet Environmental Reports. Chemical Information Systems, Inc., 7215 York Rd., Baltimore, Maryland 21212. (301) 321-8440.

PERIODICALS AND NEWSLETTERS

Action Alert. Rainforest Action Network, 301 Broadway, Suite A, San Francisco, California 94133. (415) 398-4404. Monthly. Bulletin on issues requiring immediate public attention.

The Canopy. Rainforest Alliance, 270 Lafayette St., Suite 512, New York, New York 10012. (212) 941-1900. Quarterly.

Earth Island Journal. Earth Island Institute, 300 Broadway, #28, San Francisco, California 94133-3312. (415)

788-3666. Quarterly. Local news from around the world on environmental issues.

World Rainforest Report. Rainforest Action Network, 301 Broadway, Suite A, San Francisco, California 94133. (415) 398-4404. Quarterly. Programs, list of educational materials, and calendar of events.

STATISTICS SOURCES

Environmental Data Compendium. OECD Publications and Information Center, 2001 L St., N.W., Suite 700, Washington, District of Columbia 20036. (202) 785-6323. 1989.

Environmental Indicators. OECD Publications and Information Center, 2001 L St., N.W., Suite 700, Washington, District of Columbia 20036. (202) 785-6323. 1991.

Environmental Quality. Council on Environmental Quality. U.S. G.P.O., Washington, District of Columbia 20401. (202) 512-0000. Annual.

The State of the Environment. OECD Publications and Information Center, 2001 L St., N.W., Suite 700, Washington, District of Columbia 20036. (202) 785-6323. 1991.

Statistical Record of the Environment. Arsen J. Darnay. Gale Research Inc., 835 Penobscot Bldg., Detroit, Michigan 48226-4094. (313) 961-2242. 1992.

TRADE ASSOCIATIONS AND PROFESSIONAL SOCIETIES

American Institute of Biological Sciences. 730 11th St., N.W., Washington, District of Columbia 20001-4521. (202) 628-1500.

Better World Society. 1100 17th St., NW, Suite 502, Washington, District of Columbia 20036. (202) 331-3770. International non-profit membership organization that attempts to increase individual awareness of global issues related to the sustainability of life on earth.

Conservation International. 1015 18th St. N.W., Suite 1002, Washington, District of Columbia 20036. (202) 429-5660. Non-profit organization established in 1987. Provides resources and expertise to private organizations, government agencies and universities of Latin America and Caribbean countries in an effort to develop the capacity and preserve critical habitats.

Earth Island Institute. 300 Broadway, Suite 28, San Francisco, California 94133. (415) 788-3666.

EarthSave. 706 Frederick St., Santa Cruz, California 95062. (408) 423-4069.

Ethnobotany Specialist Group. c/o Prof. Richard Evans Schultes, Botanical Museum, Oxford St., Harvard University, Cambridge, Massachusetts 02138. (617) 495-2326.

International Society for the Preservation of the Tropical Rainforest. 3931 Camino de la Cumbre, Sherman Oaks, California 91423. (818) 788-2002.

International Society of Tropical Foresters, Inc. 5400 Grosvenor Ln., Bethesda, Maryland 20814. (301) 897-8720.

Learning Alliance. 494 Broadway, New York, New York 10012. (212) 226-7171.

Natural Resources Defense Council. 40 W. 20th St., New York, New York 10011. (212) 727-2700.

Rainforest Action Network. 301 Broadway, Suite 28, San Francisco, California 94133. (415) 398-4404.

Rainforest Alliance. 270 Lafayette St., Suite 512, New York, New York 10012. (212) 941-1900.

Rainforest Health Alliance. Fort Mason, Building E, San Francisco, California 94123. (415) 921-1203.

RARE Center for Tropical Bird Conservation. 15290 Walnut St., Philadelphia, Pennsylvania 19102. (215) 568-0420.

Tropical Forests Forever. PO Box 69583, Portland, Oregon 97201. (503) 227-4127.

World Peace University. P.O. Box 10869, Eugene, Oregon 97440. (503) 741-1794.

World Wildlife Fund & the Conservation Foundation. 1250 24th St., N.W., Washington, District of Columbia 20037. (202) 293-4800.

RAIN SHADOW

See: WEATHER

RAINFALL

See: WEATHER

RANGELANDS

See also: AGRICULTURE; FORESTS

ABSTRACTING AND INDEXING SERVICES

Applied Ecology Abstracts Studies in Renewable Natural Resources. Information Retrieval Ltd., 1911 Jefferson Davis Highway, Arlington, Virginia 22202. 1975-. Monthly.

Biological and Agricultural Index. H.W. Wilson Co., 950 University Ave., Bronx, New York 10452. (800) 367-6770. 1916-. Monthly.

Environment Abstracts. Bowker A & I Publishing, 121 Chanlon Rd., New Providence, New Jersey 07974. (908) 464-6800. 1974-.

Environment Index. Environment Information Center, Index Research Department, 124 E. 39th St., New York, New York 10016. 1971-. Annual.

Environmental Information Connection–EIC. Planning Information Program, Dept. of Urban and Regional Planning, University of Illinois, 1003 West Nevada, Urbana, Illinois 61801. (217) 333-1369. Also available online.

Environmental Periodicals Bibliography. Environmental Studies Institute, International Academy at Santa Barbara, 800 Garden St., Suite D, Santa Barbara, California 93101. (805) 965-5010. Also available online.

Multimedia Index to Ecology. National Information Center for Educational Media, University of Southern California, Los Angeles, California 90007.

BIBLIOGRAPHIES

EPA Publications Bibliography. U.S. Environmental Protection Agency, Library Systems Branch, 401 M St., SW, Washington, District of Columbia 20460. (202) 260-2090. Quarterly.

The Sociology of Range Management: A Bibliography. Jere Lee Gilles. CPL Bibliographies, 1313 E. 60th St., Chicago, Illinois 60637-2897. (312) 942-2163. 1982.

ENCYCLOPEDIAS AND DICTIONARIES

A Glossary of Terms Used in Range Management. Peter W. Jacoby. Society for Range Management, 1839 York St., Denver, Colorado 80206. (303) 355-7070. 1989. A definition of terms commonly used in range management.

McGraw-Hill Encyclopedia of Environmental Science. Sybil P. Parker. McGraw-Hill Science & Engineering Books, 11 W. 19th St., New York, New York 10011. (212) 337-6010. 1980. Covers ecology, man's influence on nature, and environmental protection.

GENERAL WORKS

Rangelands. Bruce A. Buchanan. University of New Mexico Press, 1720 Lomas Blvd., NE, Albuquerque, New Mexico 87131. (505) 277-2346. 1988. Profiles range ecology and range management in the West.

Towards Wiser Use of Our Forests and Rangelands. U.S. Forest Service, PO Box 96090, Washington, District of Columbia 20090. (202) 720-3760. 1982. Forest management in the United States.

U.S. Forest Service Grazing and Rangelands: A History. William D. Rowley. Texas A & M University Press, College Station, Texas 1985. Forest and range policy, forest reserves and grazing history.

ONLINE DATA BASES

Enviro/Energyline Abstracts Plus. R. R. Bowker Co., 121 Chanlon Rd., New Providence, New Jersey 07974. (908) 464-6800.

Environmental Periodicals Bibliography. National Information Services Corp., Ste. 6, Wyman Towers, 3100 St. Paul St., Baltimore, Maryland 21218. (410)243-0797. Online version of abstract of same name.

STATISTICS SOURCES

Managing Interior Northwest Rangelands. U.S. G.P.O, Washington, District of Columbia 20402-9325. (202) 512-0000. Irregular. Grazing management practices and their effects on herbage production, water resources, and local economic conditions.

Report on the Nation's Renewable Resources. U.S. Forest Service. U.S. G.P.O., Washington, District of Columbia 20401. (202) 512-0000. Quinquennial. Projections of resource use and supply from 1920 to 2040, covering wilderness, wildlife, fish, range, timber, water and minerals.

U.S. Timber Production, Trade, Consumption and Price Statistics. U.S. Forest Service. U.S. G.P.O., Washington, District of Columbia 20402-9325. (202) 783-3238. 1987. Annual. Covers the period from 1950 to present. Includes measures of economic growth.

World Resources. World Resources Institute. 1709 New York Ave., N.W., Washington, District of Columbia 20006. (202) 638-6300. Annual. Statistical and textual analysis of world's natural resources and the effects of growth-caused environmental pollution.

TRADE ASSOCIATIONS AND PROFESSIONAL SOCIETIES

Society for Range Management. 1839 York St., Denver, Colorado 80206. (303) 355-7070.

RASP

See: SOLID WASTES

RAW SEWAGE

See: SEWAGE

REACTOR COOLANTS

See also: REACTORS

ABSTRACTING AND INDEXING SERVICES

Applied Science and Technology Index. H.W. Wilson Co., 950 University Ave., Bronx, New York 10452. (800) 367-6770. Formerly Industrial Arts Index.

ERDA Research Abstracts. U.S. ERDA Technical Information Center, Box 62, Oak Ridge, Tennessee 37830.

Physics Briefs. Physikalische Berichte. Physik Verlag, Pappapelallee 3, Postfach 101161, Weinheim, Germany D-6940. 1979-. Semimonthly. In English. Volumes for 1979- issued by the Deutsche Physikalische Gesellschaft and the Fachinformationszentrum Energie Physik, Mathematik in cooperation with the American Institute of Physics.

ENCYCLOPEDIAS AND DICTIONARIES

Glossary of Terms in Nuclear Science and Technology. American Nuclear Society, 555 North Kensington Ave., La Grange Park, Illinois 60525. (708) 352-6611. 1986. Prepared by the American Nuclear Society Standards Committee. Subcommittee ANS-9.

REACTOR SAFETY

See: REACTORS

REACTORS

ABSTRACTING AND INDEXING SERVICES

Applied Science and Technology Index. H.W. Wilson Co., 950 University Ave., Bronx, New York 10452. (800) 367-6770. Formerly Industrial Arts Index.

Chemical Abstracts. Chemical Abstracts Service, 2540 Olentangy River Rd., PO Box 3012, Columbus, Ohio 43210. (800) 848-6533. 1907-.

Energy Information Abstracts Annual 1987 in Retrospect. EIC/Intelligence Inc., 121 Chanlon Rd., New Providence, New Jersey 07974. (908) 464-6800. 1988. Annual. Cumulative edition of the monthly Energy Information Abstracts. Monitors sources in the field of energy including the scientific, technical and business journal literature, conference and symposia proceedings, corporate, government and academic reports.

Engineering Index. The Engineering Index Inc., 345 E. 47th St., New York, New York 10017. 1962-.

Environment Abstracts. Bowker A & I Publishing, 121 Chanlon Rd., New Providence, New Jersey 07974. (908) 464-6800. 1974-.

Environment Index. Environment Information Center, Index Research Department, 124 E. 39th St., New York, New York 10016. 1971-. Annual.

Environmental Information Connection–EIC. Planning Information Program, Dept. of Urban and Regional Planning, University of Illinois, 1003 West Nevada, Urbana, Illinois 61801. (217) 333-1369. Also available online.

Environmental Periodicals Bibliography. Environmental Studies Institute, International Academy at Santa Barbara, 800 Garden St., Suite D, Santa Barbara, California 93101. (805) 965-5010. Also available online.

ERDA Research Abstracts. U.S. ERDA Technical Information Center, Box 62, Oak Ridge, Tennessee 37830.

General Science Index. H. W. Wilson Co., 950 University Ave., Bronx, New York 10452. 1978-. Monthly, also issued in annual cumulation. Cumulative subject index to English language periodicals in the subject fields of astronomy, botany, chemistry, earth science, environment and conservation, food and nutrition, genetics, mathematics, medicine and health, microbiology, oceanography, physics, physiology and zoology.

Index to Scientific Book Contents. Institute for Scientific Information, 3501 Market St., Philadelphia, Pennsylvania 19104. (800) 523-1857. 1985-. Annual. Gives contents of science books published.

INIS Atomindex. International Atomic Energy Agency, Wagramerstrasse 5, Vienna, Austria A-1400. 222 23606198. 1988-. Semiannual. Abstracts nuclear energy and nuclear physics topics from journals, conferences, technical reports and other related publications. Issued in 6 parts: Personal Author, Corporate Entry, Subject, Report, Standard Patent, Conference (by place), Conference (by date).

Physics Briefs. Physikalische Berichte. Physik Verlag, Pappapelallee 3, Postfach 101161, Weinheim, Germany D-6940. 1979-. Semimonthly. In English. Volumes for 1979- issued by the Deutsche Physikalische Gesellschaft and the Fachinformationszentrum Energie Physik, Mathematik in cooperation with the American Institute of Physics.

Science Citation Index. Institute for Scientific Information, 3501 Market St., Philadelphia, Pennsylvania 19104. 1961-.

BIBLIOGRAPHIES

EPA Publications Bibliography. U.S. Environmental Protection Agency, Library Systems Branch, 401 M St., SW, Washington, District of Columbia 20460. (202) 260-2090. Quarterly.

Nuclear Facility Decommissioning and Site Remedial Actions: A Selected Bibliography. National Technical Information Service, 5285 Port Royal Rd., Springfield, Virginia 22161. (703) 487-4650. Annual. Nuclear facility decommissioning, uranium mill tailings management, and radioactive waste site remedial actions.

DIRECTORIES

Nuclear News–World List of Nuclear Power Plants Issues. American Nuclear Society, 555 N. Kensington Ave., La Grange Park, Illinois 60525. (708) 352-6611.

Nuclear Power Plant Construction Activity. Energy Information Administration, Department of Energy, El 231, 1000 Independence Ave., S.W., Washington, District of Columbia 20585. (202) 586-8800. 1985.

Nuclear Reactors Built, Being Built, or Planned in the United States. Office of Scientific and Technological Information, Department of Energy, Box 62, Oak Ridge, Tennessee 37831. (615) 576-5637.

Nuclear Regulatory Commission: General Information, Addresses, Phone Numbers, and Personnel Listing. Nuclear Regulatory Commission, 1717 H St., N.W., Washington, District of Columbia 20555. (301) 492-7000. 1980.

Research, Training, Test and Production Reactor Directory: United States of America. America Nuclear Society, 555 N. Kensington Ave., La Grange Park, Illinois 60525. (708) 352-6611.

ENCYCLOPEDIAS AND DICTIONARIES

Dictionary of Environmental Engineering and Related Sciences: English-Spanish, Spanish-English. Jose T. Villate. Ediciones Universal, 3090 SW 8th St., Miami, Florida 33135. (305) 642-3355. 1979.

Encyclopedia of Environmental Science and Engineering. J.R. Pfafflin. Gordon and Breach Science Publishers, Inc., 270 8th Ave., New York, New York 10011. (212) 206-8900. 1992.

Encyclopedia of Physical Science and Technology. Robert A. Meyers, ed. Academic Press, c/o Harcourt Brace Jovanovich Inc., 6277 Sea Harbor Dr., Orlando, Florida 32887. (800) 346-8648. Dictionary of engineering, technology and physical sciences.

Encyclopedia of Physics. Rita G. Lerner and George L. Trigg. VCH Publishers, 303 NW 12th Ave., Deerfield Beach, Florida 33442-1788. (305) 428-5566. 1991. Second edition.

Glossary of Terms in Nuclear Science and Technology. American Nuclear Society, 555 North Kensington Ave., La Grange Park, Illinois 60525. (708) 352-6611. 1986.

Prepared by the American Nuclear Society Standards Committee. Subcommittee ANS-9.

Illustrated Encyclopedia of Science and the Future. Mike Biscare, et al., ed. Marshall Cavendish, 58 Old Compton St., London, England 0W1V5 PA. 01-734 6710. 1983. Twenty volumes. Each volume has 5 sections: Frontiers, Electronics in Action, Medical Science, Military Technology, and Resources.

McGraw-Hill Encyclopedia of Science and Technology. McGraw-Hill, 1221 Avenue of the Americas, New York, New York 10020. (212) 512-2000 or (800) 262-4729. 1992. Seventh edition. Issued in multiple volumes including index. Includes all science and technology broad subject areas.

Van Nostrand's Scientific Encyclopedia. Glenn D. Considine, ed. Van Nostrand Reinhold, 115 5th Ave., New York, New York 10003. (212) 254-3232. 1983. Sixth edition. Includes all broad subject areas in science.

GENERAL WORKS

BWR Cobalt Source Identification. C.F. Falk. General Electric Co., P.O. Box 861, Gainesville, Florida 32602-0861. (904) 462-3911. 1982. Safety measures in boiling water reactors.

Cobalt Reduction Guidelines. Electric Power Research Institute, 3412 Hillview Ave., Palo Alto, California 94304. (415) 965-4081. 1990. Deals with nuclear power plants, hard-facing alloys, stress corrosion, and cobalt alloys.

Decommisioning: Nuclear Power's Missing Link. Cynthia Pollock. Worldwatch Institute, 1776 Massachusetts Ave., N.W., Washington, District of Columbia 20036-1904. 1986.

Extension of the Principles of Radiation Protection to ... International Atomic Energy Agency. UNIPUB, 4611-F Assembly Dr., Lanham, Maryland 20706-4391. (301) 459-7666; (800) 274-4888. 1990.

Nuclear Power Plants Worldwide. Peter D. Dresser. Gale Research Inc., 835 Penobscot Bldg., Detroit, Michigan 48226-4094. (313) 961-2242. 1993.

Predicting Nuclear and Other Technological Disasters. Christopher Lampton. F. Watts, 387 Park Ave. S., New York, New York 10016. (800) 672-6672. 1989. Discusses risks involved in state-of-the-art technology.

Reactor Accidents: Nuclear Safety and the Role of Institutional Failure. David Mosey. Nuclear Engineering International Special Publications, c/o Butterworth-Heinemann, 80 Montvale Ave., Stoneham, Massachusetts 02180. (617) 438-8464; (800) 366-2665. 1990.

Smoking Guns. Nuclear Regulatory Commission, Advisory Committee on Nuclear Facility Safety, 1717 H St., NW, Washington, District of Columbia 20555. (301) 492-7000. 1991. Deals with the Energy Department's campaign to improve safety and environmental compliance at its nuclear weapons plants.

Surveillance of Items Important to Safety in Nuclear Power Plants. International Atomic Energy Agency. UNIPUB, 4611-F Assembly Dr., Lanham, Maryland 20706-4391. (301) 459-7666; (800) 270-4888. 1990. Discusses the safety measures observed at atomic power plants.

GOVERNMENTAL ORGANIZATIONS

Office of Public Affairs. 1717 H St., N.W., Washington, District of Columbia 20555. (301) 492-7715.

HANDBOOKS AND MANUALS

Energy Deskbook. Samuel Glasstone. Van Nostrand Reinhold, 115 5th Ave., New York, New York 10020. (212) 254-3232. 1983. Single volume reference covering all energy resources.

ONLINE DATA BASES

Chemical Abstracts-CA. Chemical Abstracts Service, 2540 Olentangy River Rd., P.O. Box 3012, Columbus, Ohio 43210. (800) 848-6533 or (614) 421-3600. Information sources include 9000 journals, patents from 27 countries, two industrial property organizations, new books, conference proceedings, and government research reports.

Computerized Engineering Index–COMPENDEX. Engineering Information Inc., 345 E. 47th St., New York, New York 10017. (212) 705-7600.

EBIB. Texas A & M University, Sterling C. Evans Library, Reference Division, College Station, Texas 77843. (409) 845-5741.

Enviro/Energyline Abstracts Plus. R. R. Bowker Co., 121 Chanlon Rd., New Providence, New Jersey 07974. (908) 464-6800.

Environmental Periodicals Bibliography. National Information Services Corp., Ste. 6, Wyman Towers, 3100 St. Paul St., Baltimore, Maryland 21218. (410)243-0797. Online version of abstract of same name.

International Nuclear Information System. International Atomic Energy Agency, INIS Section, Vienna International Centre, P.O. Box 100, Vienna, Austria A-1400. 43 (222) 23602882.

Nuclear Criticality Information Systems. Lawrence Livermore National Laboratory, Criticality Safety Office, Box 808, Livermore, California 94550. (415) 422-9799.

Nuclear Science Abstracts. U.S. Department of Energy, Office of Scientific & Technical Information, P.O. Box 62, Oak Ridge, Tennessee 37831. (615) 576-6299.

PressNet Environmental Reports. Chemical Information Systems, Inc., 7215 York Rd., Baltimore, Maryland 21212. (301) 321-8440.

PERIODICALS AND NEWSLETTERS

The Nuclear Monitor. Nuclear Information and Resource Service, Inc., 1424 16th St., NW, No. 601, Washington, District of Columbia 20036. (202) 328-0002. Biweekly. Tracks the records of nuclear utilities in both operation and construction.

Nucleus. Union of Concerned Scientists, 26 Church St., Cambridge, Massachusetts 02238. (617) 547-5552. Quarterly. Global warming, renewable energy, energy efficiency, nuclear reactor safety, and radioactive waste disposal.

STATISTICS SOURCES

Annual Report to Congress on Federal Government Energy Management and Conservation Programs, FY89. U.S.

Dept. of Energy. National Technical Information Service, 5285 Port Royal Rd., Springfield, Virginia 22161. (703) 487-4650. Federal agency energy use and progress in meeting conservation goals.

Characteristics of Potential Repository Wastes. National Technical Information Service, 5285 Port Royal Rd., Springfield, Virginia 22161. (703) 487-4650. 1990. Inventories and selected characteristics of commercial light- water reactors (LWR) and non-LWR spent fuel, immobilized high-level radioactive waste (HLW), and other wastes likely to be placed in permanent geologic repositories.

Gas Mileage Guide. U.S. Dept. of Energy. U.S. G.P.O, Washington, District of Columbia 20402-9325. (202) 512-0000. Annual. Fuel economy results for cars and light-duty trucks tested by EPA and meeting EPA emissions standards.

Nuclear Waste Fund Fee Adequacy: An Assessment. National Technical Information Service, 5285 Port Royal Rd., Springfield, Virginia 22161. (703) 487-4650. 1990. User fees paid by nuclear-generated electric utilities into the Nuclear Waste Fund.

World Resources. World Resources Institute. 1709 New York Ave., N.W., Washington, District of Columbia 20006. (202) 638-6300. Annual. Statistical and textual analysis of world's natural resources and the effects of growth-caused environmental pollution.

TRADE ASSOCIATIONS AND PROFESSIONAL SOCIETIES

American Institute of Chemical Engineers. 345 East 47th St., New York, New York 10017. (212) 705-7338.

American Institute of Chemists. 7315 Wisconsin Ave., Bethesda, Maryland 20814. (301) 652-2447.

American Institute of Physics. 335 E. 45th St., New York, New York 10017. (212) 661-9404.

American Physical Society. 335 E. 45th St., New York, New York 10017. (212) 682-7341.

American Society of Civil Engineers. 345 East 47th St., New York, New York 10017. (212) 705-7496.

Concerned Citizens for the Nuclear Breeder. P.O. Box 3, Ross, Ohio 45061. (513) 738-6750.

National Organization of Test, Research, & Training Reactors. c/o Francis DiMeglio, Rhode Island Nuclear Science Center, S. Ferry Rd., Narragansett, Rhode Island 02882-1197. (401) 789-9391.

Nuclear Management and Resources Council. 1776 I St., N.W., Suite 300, Washington, District of Columbia 20006. (202) 872-1280.

Professional Reactor Operators Society. Box 181, Mishicot, Wisconsin 54288. (414) 755-2725.

Safe Energy Communication Council. 1717 Massachusetts Ave., N.W., LL215, Washington, District of Columbia 20036. (202) 483-8491.

RECLAMATION

See also: CONSERVATION OF NATURAL RESOURCES; EROSION; LAND RECLAMATION; SAND DUNE ECOLOGY; WETLANDS

ABSTRACTING AND INDEXING SERVICES

Applied Ecology Abstracts Studies in Renewable Natural Resources. Information Retrieval Ltd., 1911 Jefferson Davis Highway, Arlington, Virginia 22202. 1975-. Monthly.

Applied Science and Technology Index. H.W. Wilson Co., 950 University Ave., Bronx, New York 10452. (800) 367-6770. Formerly Industrial Arts Index.

Environment Abstracts. Bowker A & I Publishing, 121 Chanlon Rd., New Providence, New Jersey 07974. (908) 464-6800. 1974-.

Environment Index. Environment Information Center, Index Research Department, 124 E. 39th St., New York, New York 10016. 1971-. Annual.

Environmental Information Connection–EIC. Planning Information Program, Dept. of Urban and Regional Planning, University of Illinois, 1003 West Nevada, Urbana, Illinois 61801. (217) 333-1369. Also available online.

Environmental Periodicals Bibliography. Environmental Studies Institute, International Academy at Santa Barbara, 800 Garden St., Suite D, Santa Barbara, California 93101. (805) 965-5010. Also available online.

General Science Index. H. W. Wilson Co., 950 University Ave., Bronx, New York 10452. 1978-. Monthly, also issued in annual cumulation. Cumulative subject index to English language periodicals in the subject fields of astronomy, botany, chemistry, earth science, environment and conservation, food and nutrition, genetics, mathematics, medicine and health, microbiology, oceanography, physics, physiology and zoology.

Geographical Abstracts. London School of Economics, Dept. of Geography, Regency House, 34 Duke St., London, England 1966-. Continued by Geo Abstracts issued in 6 parts: Pt. A. Landforms and the quaternary; Pt. B. Biogeography and Climatology; Pt. C. Economic geography; Pt. D. Social geography and cartography; Pt. E. Sedimentology; Pt. F. Regional and community planning.

Index to Scientific Book Contents. Institute for Scientific Information, 3501 Market St., Philadelphia, Pennsylvania 19104. (800) 523-1857. 1985-. Annual. Gives contents of science books published.

Multimedia Index to Ecology. National Information Center for Educational Media, University of Southern California, Los Angeles, California 90007.

Science Citation Index. Institute for Scientific Information, 3501 Market St., Philadelphia, Pennsylvania 19104. 1961-.

BIBLIOGRAPHIES

Bibliography on the Economics and Technology of Mined Land Reclamation. Henry N. McCarl. Vance Bibliographies, PO Box 229, 112 N. Charter St., Monticello, Illinois 61856. (217) 762-3831. 1983.

Ecological Aspects of the Reclamation of Derelict and Disturbed Land: An Annotated Bibliography. Gordon T. Goodman. Geo Abstracts Ltd., c/o Elsevier Science Publishers, Crown House, Linton Rd., Barking, England 1G11 8JU. 1975.

EPA Publications Bibliography. U.S. Environmental Protection Agency, Library Systems Branch, 401 M St., SW, Washington, District of Columbia 20460. (202) 260-2090. Quarterly.

ENCYCLOPEDIAS AND DICTIONARIES

Dictionary of Environmental Engineering and Related Sciences: English-Spanish, Spanish-English. Jose T. Villate. Ediciones Universal, 3090 SW 8th St., Miami, Florida 33135. (305) 642-3355. 1979.

Encyclopedia of Environmental Science and Engineering. J.R. Pfafflin. Gordon and Breach Science Publishers, Inc., 270 8th Ave., New York, New York 10011. (212) 206-8900. 1992.

The Encyclopedia of Geochemistry and Environmental Sciences. Rhodes Whitmore Fairbridge. Van Nostrand Reinhold Co., 115 5th Ave., New York, New York 10003. (212) 254-3232. 1972.

Encyclopedia of Physical Science and Technology. Robert A. Meyers, ed. Academic Press, c/o Harcourt Brace Jovanovich Inc., 6277 Sea Harbor Dr., Orlando, Florida 32887. (800) 346-8648. Dictionary of engineering, technology and physical sciences.

Grzimek's Encyclopedia of Ecology. Bernhard Grzimek. Van Nostrand Reinhold, 115 5th Ave., New York, New York 10003. (212) 254-3232. 1976.

McGraw-Hill Encyclopedia of Environmental Science. Sybil P. Parker. McGraw-Hill Science & Engineering Books, 11 W. 19th St., New York, New York 10011. (212) 337-6010. 1980. Covers ecology, man's influence on nature, and environmental protection.

North American Reference Encyclopedia of Ecology and Pollution. William White. North American Pub. Co., 401 N. Broad St., Philadelphia, Pennsylvania 19108. (215) 238-5300. 1972.

Van Nostrand's Scientific Encyclopedia. Glenn D. Considine, ed. Van Nostrand Reinhold, 115 5th Ave., New York, New York 10003. (212) 254-3232. 1983. Sixth edition. Includes all broad subject areas in science.

GENERAL WORKS

Environmental Restoration: Science and Strategies for Restoring the Earth. John J. Berger. Island Press, 1718 Connecticut Ave. N.W., Suite 300, Washington, District of Columbia 20009. (202) 232-7933. 1990. Overview techniques of restoration.

Land Reclamation and Biomass Production with Municipal Wastewater and Sludge. Pennsylvania State University Press, Barbara Bldg., Ste. C, University Park, Pennsylvania 16802. (814) 865-1372. 1982. Sewage and sewage sludge as fertilizer.

Practices and Problems of Land Reclamation in Western North America. Mohan K. Wali. University of North Dakota, Grand Forks, North Dakota 1975. Environmental aspects of stripmining and coal mines and mining.

GOVERNMENTAL ORGANIZATIONS

Office of Environmental Affairs: Bureau of Reclamation. 18th and C St., N.W., Washington, District of Columbia 20240. (202) 343-4662.

ONLINE DATA BASES

Enviro/Energyline Abstracts Plus. R. R. Bowker Co., 121 Chanlon Rd., New Providence, New Jersey 07974. (908) 464-6800.

Environmental Periodicals Bibliography. National Information Services Corp., Ste. 6, Wyman Towers, 3100 St. Paul St., Baltimore, Maryland 21218. (410)243-0797. Online version of abstract of same name.

Monthly Catalog of United States Government Publications. U.S. G.P.O., Supt. of Docs., PO Box 371954, Pittsburgh, Pennsylvania 15250-7954. (202) 512-0000.

National Technical Information Service. U.S. Department of Commerce, National Technical Information Service, Office of Data Base Services, 5285 Port Royal Rd., Springfield, Virginia 22161. (703) 487-4807. Bibliographic database of government sponsored research and technical reports.

TRADE ASSOCIATIONS AND PROFESSIONAL SOCIETIES

American Society for Surface Mining and Reclamation. 21 Grandview Dr., Princeton, New Jersey 24740. (304) 425-8332.

National Association of State Land Reclamationists. 459 B Carlisle Dr., Herndon, Virginia 22070. (703) 709-8654.

RECOVERY OF WASTE

See: RECYCLING (WASTE, ETC.)

RECREATIONAL AREAS

See also: NATIONAL PARKS; URBAN DESIGN AND PLANNING

ABSTRACTING AND INDEXING SERVICES

Biological and Agricultural Index. H.W. Wilson Co., 950 University Ave., Bronx, New York 10452. (800) 367-6770. 1916-. Monthly.

Geographical Abstracts. London School of Economics, Dept. of Geography, Regency House, 34 Duke St., London, England 1966-. Continued by Geo Abstracts issued in 6 parts: Pt. A. Landforms and the quaternary; Pt. B. Biogeography and Climatology; Pt. C. Economic geography; Pt. D. Social geography and cartography; Pt. E. Sedimentology; Pt. F. Regional and community planning.

Index to Scientific Book Contents. Institute for Scientific Information, 3501 Market St., Philadelphia, Pennsylvania 19104. (800) 523-1857. 1985-. Annual. Gives contents of science books published.

ONLINE DATA BASES

Monthly Catalog of United States Government Publications. U.S. G.P.O., Supt. of Docs., PO Box 371954, Pittsburgh, Pennsylvania 15250-7954. (202) 512-0000.

National Technical Information Service. U.S. Department of Commerce, National Technical Information Service, Office of Data Base Services, 5285 Port Royal

Rd., Springfield, Virginia 22161. (703) 487-4807. Bibliographic database of government sponsored research and technical reports.

Outdoors Forum. CompuServe Information Service, 5000 Arlington Centre Blvd., PO Box 20212, Columbus, Ohio 43220. (614) 457-8600. Outdoor sports, hobbies, and entertainment. Includes search and rescue, nature, wildlife, equipment, and park and campground information.

STATISTICS SOURCES

Land Areas of the National Forest System. U.S. Forest Service. U.S. G.P.O., Washington, District of Columbia 20401. (202) 512-0000. Annual. Data on wilderness, scenic-research, monument and recreation areas, and game refuges.

National Park Service Statistical Abstract. U.S. G.P.O., Washington, District of Columbia 20401. (202) 512-0000. Annual. Recreation visits, acreages, areas administered visits and visitor use and overnight stays.

U.S. Timber Production, Trade, Consumption and Price Statistics. U.S. Forest Service. U.S. G.P.O., Washington, District of Columbia 20402-9325. (202) 783-3238. 1987. Annual. Covers the period from 1950 to present. Includes measures of economic growth.

TRADE ASSOCIATIONS AND PROFESSIONAL SOCIETIES

American Institute of Biological Sciences. 730 11th St., N.W., Washington, District of Columbia 20001-4521. (202) 628-1500.

American Recreation Coalition. 1331 Pennsylvania Ave., N.W., Suite 726, Washington, District of Columbia 20004. (202) 662-7420.

California State Parks Foundation. 800 College Ave., P.O. Box 548, Kentfield, California 94914. (415) 258-9975.

National Association of State Outdoor Recreation Liaison Officers. c/o Ney C. Landrum, 126 Mill Branch Rd., Tallahassee, Florida 32312. (904) 893-4959.

National Association of State Recreation Planners. c/o Dick Westfall, Illinois Dept. of Conversation, Division of Planning, 524 S. 2nd St., Room 310, Springfield, Illinois 62701-1787. (217) 782-3715.

National Institute on Park & Grounds Management. Box 1936, Appleton, Wisconsin 54913. (414) 733-2301.

North American Family Campers Association. 16 Evergreen Terr., North Reading, Massachusetts 01864. (508) 664-4294.

Trumpeter Swan Society. 3800 County Rd. 24, Maple Plain, Minnesota 55359. (612) 476-4663.

RECYCLING (WASTE, ETC.)

See also: CONSERVATION OF NATURAL RESOURCES; GLASS; PAPER; PLASTICS; RUBBER; WASTE MANAGEMENT

ABSTRACTING AND INDEXING SERVICES

Applied Ecology Abstracts Studies in Renewable Natural Resources. Information Retrieval Ltd., 1911 Jefferson Davis Highway, Arlington, Virginia 22202. 1975-. Monthly.

Applied Science and Technology Index. H.W. Wilson Co., 950 University Ave., Bronx, New York 10452. (800) 367-6770. Formerly Industrial Arts Index.

Ecological Abstracts. Geo Abstracts Ltd. Elsevier Applied Science, Crown House, Linton Rd., Barking, England IG 11 8JU. 1974-. Derived from over 600 leading ecological and environmental journals, plus books, conference proceedings, reports and theses.

Engineering Index. The Engineering Index Inc., 345 E. 47th St., New York, New York 10017. 1962-.

Environment Abstracts. Bowker A & I Publishing, 121 Chanlon Rd., New Providence, New Jersey 07974. (908) 464-6800. 1974-.

Environment Index. Environment Information Center, Index Research Department, 124 E. 39th St., New York, New York 10016. 1971-. Annual.

Environmental Information Connection–EIC. Planning Information Program, Dept. of Urban and Regional Planning, University of Illinois, 1003 West Nevada, Urbana, Illinois 61801. (217) 333-1369. Also available online.

Environmental Periodicals Bibliography. Environmental Studies Institute, International Academy at Santa Barbara, 800 Garden St., Suite D, Santa Barbara, California 93101. (805) 965-5010. Also available online.

General Science Index. H. W. Wilson Co., 950 University Ave., Bronx, New York 10452. 1978-. Monthly, also issued in annual cumulation. Cumulative subject index to English language periodicals in the subject fields of astronomy, botany, chemistry, earth science, environment and conservation, food and nutrition, genetics, mathematics, medicine and health, microbiology, oceanography, physics, physiology and zoology.

Geographical Abstracts. London School of Economics, Dept. of Geography, Regency House, 34 Duke St., London, England 1966-. Continued by Geo Abstracts issued in 6 parts: Pt. A. Landforms and the quaternary; Pt. B. Biogeography and Climatology; Pt. C. Economic geography; Pt. D. Social geography and cartography; Pt. E. Sedimentology; Pt. F. Regional and community planning.

Green Engineering: A Current Awareness Bulletin. Institution of Mechanical Engineers, 1 Birdcage Walk, Westminster, London, England SW1H 9JJ. 71973 1266/7. 1991. Monthly. Covers acid rain, aerosol technology, biotechnology chlorofluorocarbons, chemical and process engineering, environmental protection, energy conservation, energy generation, greenhouse effect, materials, pollution, recycling, waste disposal, and other environmental topics.

Index to Scientific Book Contents. Institute for Scientific Information, 3501 Market St., Philadelphia, Pennsylvania 19104. (800) 523-1857. 1985-. Annual. Gives contents of science books published.

Multimedia Index to Ecology. National Information Center for Educational Media, University of Southern California, Los Angeles, California 90007.

Pollution Abstracts. Cambridge Scientific Abstracts, 5161 River Rd., Bethesda, Maryland 20816. (301) 961-6750. Six/year. Indexes worldwide technical literature on environmental pollution. Covers air pollution, marine and freshwater pollution, sewage and wastewater treatment, waste management, toxicology and health, noise pollution, radiation, land pollution, and environmental policies, programs, legislation, and education. Also available online.

Science Citation Index. Institute for Scientific Information, 3501 Market St., Philadelphia, Pennsylvania 19104. 1961-.

ALMANACS AND YEARBOOKS

Gale Environmental Almanac. Russ Hoyle. Gale Research Inc., 835 Penobscot Bldg., Detroit, Michigan 48226-4094. (313) 961-2242. 1993. Focuses on the U.S. and Canada, although worldwide and transboundary issues are discussed.

BIBLIOGRAPHIES

EPA Publications Bibliography. U.S. Environmental Protection Agency, Library Systems Branch, 401 M St., SW, Washington, District of Columbia 20460. (202) 260-2090. Quarterly.

DIRECTORIES

American Recycling Market Directory/Reference Manual. Recoup Publishing Ltd., PO Box 577, Ogdensburg, New York 13669. (315) 471-0707. Companies, centers, state and federal government agencies responsible for recycling, and industry associations.

Bumper Recycling Association of North America–Membership Directory. Bumper Recycling Association of North America, 216 Country Club Rd., South Glastonbury, Connecticut 06073. (203) 659-1762.

Canadian Environmental Directory. Canadian Almanac & Directory Publishing Co. Ltd., 134 Adelaide St. E., Ste. 27, Toronto, Ontario, Canada M5C 1K9. (416) 362-4088. 1992. Includes individuals, agencies, firms, and associations.

Directory of Plastics Recycling Companies. Resource Recycling, Box 10540, Portland, Oregon 97210. (503) 227-1319.

Fibre Market News–Directory of Paper Stock Dealers Issue. 4012 Bridge Ave., Cleveland, Ohio 44113. (216) 961-4130. Annual.

Gale Environmental Sourcebook. Karen Hill. Gale Research Co., 835 Penobscot Bldg., Detroit, Michigan 48226-4094. (313) 961-2242. Contacts, information sources, or general information on environmental topics.

The Green Encyclopedia. Irene Franck, David Brownstone. Prentice-Hall, Rte. 9W, Englewood Cliffs, New York 07632. (201) 592-2000. 1992. Covers environmental organizations.

Institute of Scrap Recycling Industries–Membership Directory. Institute of Scrap Recycling Industries, 1627 K St., N.W., Suite 700, Washington, District of Columbia 20006. (202) 466-4050.

International Oil Spill Control Directory. Cutter Information Corp., 37 Broadway, Arlington, Massachusetts 02174-5537. (617) 648-8700.

National Association of Solvent Recyclers–Membership List. National Association of Solvent Recyclers, 1875 Connecticut Ave., NW, Suite 1200, Washington, District of Columbia 20009. (202) 986-8150.

Promoting Recycling to the Public. National Soft Drink Association, 1101 16th St., N.W., Washington, District of Columbia 20036. (202) 463-6770.

Recycling Centers Directory. American Business Directories, Inc., 5711 S. 86th Circle, Omaha, Nebraska 68127. (402) 593-4600.

Recycling Sourcebook. Thomas J. Cichonski, Karen Hill. Gale Research Inc., 835 Penobscot Bldg., Detroit, Michigan 48226-4094. (313) 961-2242. 1992. Covers 3,000 U.S. recycling organizations, agencies, publications, etc.

Recycling Today–Equipment and Services Directory Issue. GIE Incorporated Publisher, 4012 Bridge Ave., Cleveland, Ohio 44113. (216) 961-4130.

Resource Recycling–Equipment Guide Issue. Resource Recycling, Box 10540, Portland, Oregon 97210. (503) 227-1319.

Solid Waste Education Recycling Directory. Teresa Jones, et al. Lewis Publishers, 200 Corporate Blvd. NW, Boca Raton, Florida 33431. (407) 994-0555 or (800)272-7737. 1990. Summarizes recycling education curricula for each state covering all levels, K-12. Provides names, addresses, phone numbers, information about the availability of materials, how you collect them, and how much they cost.

ENCYCLOPEDIAS AND DICTIONARIES

Concise Encyclopedia of Polymer Processing & Applications. P. J. Corish. Pergamon Microforms International Inc., Fairview Park, Elmsford, New York 10523. (914) 592-7720.

Dictionary of Environmental Protection. Otto E. Tutzauer. Fred B. Rothman, 10368 W. Centennial Rd., Littleton, California 80127. (303) 979-5657. 1979.

Dictionary of Environmental Protection Technology: In Four Languages, English, German, French, Russian. Egon Seidel. Elsevier Science Publishing Co., 655 Avenue of the Americas, New York, New York 10010. (212) 984-5800. 1988.

Dictionary of Environmental Science and Technology. Andrew Porteous. John Wiley & Sons, Inc., 605 3rd Ave., New York, New York 10158-0012. (212) 850-6000. 1992.

Dictionary of the Environment. Michael Allaby. New York University Press, 70 Washington Sq. S., New York, New York 10012. (212) 998-2575. 1989.

Encyclopedia of Environmental Studies. William Ashworth. Facts on File, Inc., 460 Park Ave. S., New York, New York 10016. (212) 683-2244. 1991.

Encyclopedia of Physical Science and Technology. Robert A. Meyers, ed. Academic Press, c/o Harcourt Brace Jovanovich Inc., 6277 Sea Harbor Dr., Orlando, Florida 32887. (800) 346-8648. Dictionary of engineering, technology and physical sciences.

English-Russian Dictionary of Environmental Protection: About 14,000 Terms. E.L. Milovanov. Pergamon Microforms International, Inc., Fairview Park, Elmsford, New York 10523. (914) 592-7720. 1981.

Environmental Encyclopedia. William P. Cunningham, Terence Ball, et. al. Gale Research Inc., 835 Penobscot Bldg., Detroit, Michigan 48226-4094. (313) 961-2242. 1993.

Environmental Engineering Dictionary. C. C. Lee. Government Institutes, Inc., 4 Research Pl., Ste. 200, Rockville, Maryland 20850. (301) 921-2300. 1989. Defines over 6000 engineering terms relating to pollutioncontrol technologies, monitoring, risk assessment, sampling andanalysis, quality control, permitting, and environmentally-regulated engineering and science. Includes bibliographical references (p. 612-627).

Grzimek's Encyclopedia of Ecology. Bernhard Grzimek. Van Nostrand Reinhold, 115 5th Ave., New York, New York 10003. (212) 254-3232. 1976.

McGraw-Hill Encyclopedia of Environmental Science. Sybil P. Parker. McGraw-Hill Science & Engineering Books, 11 W. 19th St., New York, New York 10011. (212) 337-6010. 1980. Covers ecology, man's influence on nature, and environmental protection.

McGraw-Hill Encyclopedia of Science and Technology. McGraw-Hill, 1221 Avenue of the Americas, New York, New York 10020. (212) 512-2000 or (800) 262-4729. 1992. Seventh edition. Issued in multiple volumes including index. Includes all science and technology broad subject areas.

North American Reference Encyclopedia of Ecology and Pollution. William White. North American Pub. Co., 401 N. Broad St., Philadelphia, Pennsylvania 19108. (215) 238-5300. 1972.

Van Nostrand's Scientific Encyclopedia. Glenn D. Considine, ed. Van Nostrand Reinhold, 115 5th Ave., New York, New York 10003. (212) 254-3232. 1983. Sixth edition. Includes all broad subject areas in science.

GENERAL WORKS

50 Simple Things You Can Do to Save the Earth. G.K. Hall & Co., 70 Lincoln St., Boston, Massachusetts 02111. (617) 423-3990. 1991. Citizen participation in environmental protection.

Beyond 40 Percent: Record-Setting Recycling and Composting Programs. Brenda Platt, et al. Island Press, 1718 Connecticut Ave. N.W., Suite 300, Washington, District of Columbia 20009. (202) 232-7933. 1991. Produced by the Institute for Local Self-Reliance, this volume documents the operating experience of 17 U.S. communities, from small rural towns to large cities, that are recovering between 32 and 57 percent of their waste.

Complete Guide to Recycling at Home. Gary D. Branson. Betterway Publications, Inc., PO Box 219, Crozet, Virginia 22932. (804) 823-5661. 1991. Major areas covered include recycling, paper, lawn and garden, plastics, water conservation, alternative energy, etc.

Ecopreneuring: The Complete Guide to Small Business Opportunities from the Environmental Revolution. Steven J. Bennett. John Wiley & Sons, Inc., 605 3rd Ave., New York, New York 10158-0012. (212) 850-6000. 1991. Covers opportunities in recycling, energy conservation, personal care products, safe foods, and investment ser-

vices. Offers practical information, including market size, growth potential, and capital requirement. Provides a directory of resources.

Environmental Issues: An Anthology of 1989. Thomas W. Joyce, ed. TAPPI Press, Technology Park/Atlanta, PO Box 105113, Atlanta, Georgia 30348. (404) 446-1400. 1990. Contains 39 papers on environmental, safety and occupational health concerns from 11 TAPPI, CPPA and AIChE meetings held during 1989. Also included is a literature review of over 200 papers published in 1989.

The Environmental Sourcebook. Edith Carol Stein. Lyons & Burford, 31 W. 21st St., New York, New York 10010. (212) 620-9580. 1992. Provides information on 11 specific environmental issues, including population; agriculture; energy; climate and atmosphere; biodiversity; water; oceans; solid waste; hazardous substances and waste; endangered lands; and development.

Environmental Viewpoints. Marie Lazzari. Gale Research Inc., 835 Penobscot Bldg., Detroit, Michigan 48226-4094. (313) 961-2242. 1992.

The Greenpeace Guide to Paper. Greenpeace, 1436 U St., NW, Washington, District of Columbia 20009. (202) 462-1177. 1990. Waste paper recycling and environmental aspects of paper industry.

Hazardous and Industrial Wastes, 1990. Joseph P. Martin, et al., eds. Technomic Publishing Co., 851 Holland Ave., Box 3535, Lancaster, Pennsylvania 17604. (717) 291-5609. 1990. Proceedings of the 22nd Mid-Atlantic Industrial Waste Conference, June 24-27, 1990, Drexel University, Philadelphia, PA. Fifty-one new reports on developments in industrial and hazardouswaste management, technology and regulation were presented.

International Environmental Information Sources. Pira, Randalls Rd., Leatherhead, England KT22 7RU. 0372 376161. 1990. Contains valuable business and technical contacts for environmental information sources worldwide. Information sources cover the following subjects: Air, noise, water and land pollution; waste control and disposal; recycling; energy recovery; nature conservation. Informational sources include associations, research organizations, legislative/regulatory agencies, directories, statistics, on-line databases, magazines and news letters in 24 countries.

Investigation of Shredded Pesticide Containers for Recycling. Materials and Testing Department, Alberta Research Council for Alberta Environment, National Technical Information Service, 5285 Port Royal Rd., Springfield, Virginia 22161. (703) 487-4650. 1990.

Mandatory Deposit Legislation and Alternatives for Managing Solid Waste: A Review of the Evidence. Joan Rohlfs. University of Maryland, College Park, Institute for Governmental Service, College Park, Maryland 20742. 1988.

Organic Waste Recycling. Chongrak Polprasert. John Wiley & Sons, Inc., 605 Third Ave., New York, New York 10158. (212) 850-6000. 1989. Covers technologies for treating human waste, animal manure, agricultural residues and wastewater, sludge, algae, aquatic weeds and others.

Packaging and the Environment: Alternatives, Trends, and Solutions. Susan E. M. Selke. Technomic Publishing Co., 851 New Holland Ave., Box 3535, Lancaster, Pennsylvania 17604. (717) 291-5609. 1990. Review of the contribution of packaging to various environmental problems.

Plastics: America's Packaging Dilemma. Nancy A. Wolf and Ellen D. Feldman. Island Press, 1718 Connecticut Ave. N.W., Ste. 300, Washington, District of Columbia 20009. (202) 232-7933. 1991. Source books on plastics deal with packaging, building materials, consumer goods, electrical products, transportation, industrial machinery, adhesives, legislative and regulatory issues. Also covers the controversies over plastics incineration, degradability, and recyclability.

Popping the Plastics Question: Plastics Recycling and Bans on Plastics - Contacts, Resources and Legislation. Joan Mullany. National League of Cities, 1301 Pennsylvania Ave. N.W., Washington, District of Columbia 20004. (202) 626-3150. 1990.

Recycling. HMSO, UNIPUB, 4611-F Assembly Dr., Lanham, Maryland 20706. (301) 459-7666 or (800) 274-4888. 1991. Provides guidance for devising and implementing statutory recycling strategies in Great Britain. Gives advice to waste collection authorities on recycling plant design and current ideology.

Recycling and Incineration: Evaluating Choices. Richard A. Denison and John Ruston. Island Press, 1718 Connecticut Ave. N.W., Suite 300, Washington, District of Columbia 20009. (202) 232-7933. 1990. Presents the technology, economics, environmental concerns, and legal intricacies behind these two approaches. Includes basics of waste reduction, recycling, and incineration; cost comparisons of the two approaches; an evaluation of the health and environmental impacts.

Recycling in America. Debi Kimball. ABC-CLIO, PO Box 1911, 130 Cremona Dr., Santa Barbara, California 93116-1911. (805) 963-4221. 1992. Includes a history of the recycling movement, a chronology, and biographies of people in the field of recycling. Also contains descriptions of widely recycled materials.

Recycling Solid Waste. Milou Carolan. International City Management Association, 777 N. Capital St., NE, Suite 500, Washington, District of Columbia 20002-4201. (800) 745-8780. 1989. Integrated approach to waste management, focussing on the components of a successful recycling program.

Secondary Reclamation of Plastics Waste. Plastics Institute of America, Stevens Institute of Technology, Castle Point, Hoboken, New Jersey 07030. (201) 420-5553. 1987. Research report on Phase I development of techniques for preparation and formulation for recycling plastic scrap.

TAPPI Environmental Conference Proceedings, Seattle, WA, April 9-11, 1990. TAPPI Press, Technology Park/Atlanta, PO Box 105113, Atlanta, Georgia 30348. (404) 446-1400. 1990. Contains 11 papers presented at the conference covering industrial pollution and its remedies.

Treatment Technologies. Environment Protection Agency. Government Institutes, Inc., 4 Research Pl., Ste. 200, Rockville, Maryland 20850. (301)921-2300. 1991. 2nd ed. Provides a clear explanation of 24 treatment technologies and evaluates the effectiveness of the design and operations of each type of treatment. This new edition has more supporting numerical data, examples for a better understanding of the technology and an updated reference for specific industrial wastes.

War on Waste: Can America Win its Battle With Garbage?. Louis Blumberg and Robert Gottlieb. Island Press, 1718 Connecticut Ave. N.W., Suite 300, Washington, District of Columbia 20009. (202) 232-7933. 1989. In-depth analysis of the waste disposal crisis.

Waste Management: Towards A Sustainable Society. Om Prakash Kharbanda and E. A. Stallworthy. Auburn House, 14 Dedham St., Dover, Massachusetts 02030-0658. (505) 785-2220; (800) 223-2665. 1990. Describes the generation of various types of hazardous and nonhazardous wastes, with a whole chapter devoted to acid rain.

World Guide to Environmental Issues and Organizations. Peter Brackley. Longman Group Ltd., Longman House, Burnt Mill, Harlow, Essex, England CM20 2J6. (0279) 426721. 1991.

Your Office Paper Recycling Guide. San Francisco Recycling Program, Room 271 City Hall, San Francisco, California 94102. (415) 554-6193. 1990.

HANDBOOKS AND MANUALS

Environmental Statistics Handbook: Europe. Allan Foster, Oksana Newman. Gale Research Inc., 835 Penobscot Bldg., Detroit, Michigan 48226-4094. (313) 961-2242. 1993.

Recycler's Handbook: Everything You Need to Make Recycling a Part of Your Life. Earthworks Press, 1400 Shattuck Ave., No. 25, Berkeley, California 94709. (510) 652-8533. 1990.

Resource Conservation and Recovery Act Handbook. ERT, Marketing Dept., 696 Virginia Road, Concord, Massachusetts 01742. Law relating to hazardous wastes and waste sites.

Resource Conservation and Recovery Act Inspection Manual. U.S. Environmental Protection Agency. Government Institutes, Inc., 4 Research Pl., Ste. 200, Rockville, Maryland 20850. (301) 921-2300. 1989.

Solid Waste Recycling; The Complete Resource Guide. Bureau of National Affairs, 1231 25th St. N.W., Washington, District of Columbia 20037. (800) 372-1033. 1990. Details federal and state laws and regulations, legal issues and local initiatives relating to waste crisis. Includes case studies of programs, surveys, studies, reports guidelines, recommendations, resources and references.

ONLINE DATA BASES

Cambridge Scientific Abstracts Life Science–CSAL. Cambridge Scientific Abstracts, 5161 River Rd., Bethesda, Maryland 20816. (301) 961-6750. Provides access to the following abstracting services: "Life Sciences Collection," "Aquatic Sciences and Fisheries Abstracts," "Oceanic Abstracts," and "Pollution Abstracts."

Computerized Engineering Index–COMPENDEX. Engineering Information Inc., 345 E. 47th St., New York, New York 10017. (212) 705-7600.

Directory of Used Oil Collectors Handlers and Recyclers Serving the Southeast. Project ROSE, Box 870203, University of Alabama, Tuscaloosa, Alabama 35487-0203. (205) 348-4878. Covers the states of Alabama, Florida, Georgia, Kentucky, Mississippi, North Carolina, South Carolina, and Tennessee.

Electronic Information Exchange System. Office of Research and Development, U.S. Environmental Protection Agency, RD-618, 401 M St., Washington, District of Columbia 20460. Legislative Tracking System, which tracks the status of both state and federal legislation pertaining to source reduction and recycling; and National Waste Exchange.

Enhanced Recovery Week. Pasha Publications, Inc., 1401 Wilson Blvd., Suite 900, Arlington, Virginia 22209. (800) 424-2908.

Enviro/Energyline Abstracts Plus. R. R. Bowker Co., 121 Chanlon Rd., New Providence, New Jersey 07974. (908) 464-6800.

Environment Week. NewsNet, Inc., 945 Haverford Rd., Bryn Mawr, Pennsylvania 19010. (800) 345-1301. Online version of periodical of same name.

Environmental Periodicals Bibliography. National Information Services Corp., Ste. 6, Wyman Towers, 3100 St. Paul St., Baltimore, Maryland 21218. (410)243-0797. Online version of abstract of same name.

Monthly Catalog of United States Government Publications. U.S. G.P.O., Supt. of Docs., PO Box 371954, Pittsburgh, Pennsylvania 15250-7954. (202) 512-0000.

National Technical Information Service. U.S. Department of Commerce, National Technical Information Service, Office of Data Base Services, 5285 Port Royal Rd., Springfield, Virginia 22161. (703) 487-4807. Bibliographic database of government sponsored research and technical reports.

SCISEARCH. Institute for Scientific Information, University City Science Center, 3501 Market St., Philadelphia, Pennsylvania 19104. (215) 386-0100.

Waste Information Digest. Environmental Studies Institute, International Academy at Santa Barbara, 800 Garden St., Suite D, Santa Barbara, California 93101-1552. (805) 965-5010. Online version of the periodical of the same name.

PERIODICALS AND NEWSLETTERS

BioCycle-Journal of Waste Recycling. The J.G. Press, Inc., Box 351, Emmaus, Pennsylvania 18049. (215) 967-4135. Monthly. Articles on the reuse of sludge, waste water, and recycled products.

Biodegradation. Kluwer Academic Publishers, 101 Philip Dr., Assinippi Park, Norwell, Massachusetts 02061-0358. (617) 871-6600. 1990-. Quarterly. Covers all aspects of science pertaining to the detoxification, recycling, amelioration or treatment of waste materials and pollutants by naturally occurring microbial strains, associations, or recombinant microorganisms.

Bottle/Can Recycling Update. Resource Recycling, Box 10540, Portland, Oregon 97210. (503) 227-1319. 1990-. Monthly. Includes all recycling such as glass and plastic bottles, and steel and aluminum cans. Also covers market trends, economics collection processes, equipment news, and industry actions.

Canadian Association of Recycling Industries, Newsletter. Canadian Association of Recycling Industries, 415 Yonge St., #1620, Toronto, Ontario, Canada M5B 2E7. 1976-. Monthly.

CAW Waste Watch. Californians Against Waste, Box 289, Sacramento, California 95802. (916) 443-5422. 1978-. Quarterly. Newsletter about natural resources conservation, recycling, anti-litter issues in California and other related topics.

City Sierran. Sierra Club-NYC Group, 625 Broadway, 2nd Fl., New York, New York 10012. (212) 473-7841. 1984-. Quarterly. Reports environmental news to Sierra Club members in New York City. Writers are activists and experts on acid rain, pollution, toxic wastes, recycling, endangered species, etc.

Cycle/The Waste Paper. Environmental Action Coalition, 625 Broadway, New York, New York 10012. (212) 677-1601. Irregular. Disposal of solid waste materials, such as paper, used containers, metal and garbage.

Defense Cleanup. Pasha Publications, 1401 Wilson Blvd., Suite 900, Arlington, Virginia 22209. (703) 528-1244. Weekly. Reports on projects to analyze, recycle, and dispose of defense weapons.

Earth Science. American Geological Institute, 4220 King Street, Alexandria, Virginia 22302. (703) 379-2480. Quarterly. Covers geological issues.

Flashpoint. National Association of Solvent Recyclers, 1333 New Hampshire Ave., N.W., No. 1100, Washington, District of Columbia 20036. (202) 463-6956. Biweekly. Overview of recycling hazardous waste fuel blending & related industries.

Green Library Journal: Environmental Topics in the Information World. Maria A. Jankowska, ed. Green Library, University of Idaho Library, Moscow, Idaho 83843. (208) 885-6260. Jan 1992-. Scope of the journal would include information sources about: conservation, ecologically balanced regional development, environmental protection, natural resources management, environmental issues in libraries, publishing industries, and information science.

Journal of Waste Recycling. Chemical Abstracts Service, PO Box 3012, Columbus, Ohio 43210. (614) 421-3600. Bimonthly. Covers compost science, land utilization, waste disposal in the ground and recycling.

Management of World Wastes. Communication Channels, 6255 Barfield Road, Atlanta, Georgia 30328. (404) 256-9800. Monthly. Covers public and private waste operations.

Paper Stock Report. McEntee Media Corp., 13727 Holland Rd., Cleveland, Ohio 44142-3920. (216) 362-7979. Weekly. Paper recycling markets and prices of various grades of waste paper.

Plastics Recycling Update. Resource Recycling, Box 10540, Portland, Oregon 97210. (503) 227-1319. Monthly.

Record Retention Requirements in the CFRs. Superintendent of Documents, U.S. Government Printing Office, Washington, District of Columbia 20402. (202) 783-3238. Irregular. Covers federal regulations relating to public records.

Recycling Times. Recycling Times, 5616 W. Cermak Road, Cicero, Illinois 60650. (202) 861-0708. Biweekly. Covers major recycled commodities markets in the U.S.

Recycling Today. GIE Incorporated Publisher, 4012 Bridge Ave., Cleveland, Ohio 44113-3320. (216) 961-4130. Monthly. Covers recycling of secondary raw materials and solid waste management. Formerly, entitled Secondary Raw Materials.

Recycling Update. Illinois Department of Energy and Natural Resources, 325 W. Adams, Room 300, Springfield, Illinois 62704-9950. (217) 785-0310 or (800) 252-8955. Weekly. Features articles and announces the availability of publications, videos and fact sheets on recycling.

Resource Recovery Report. Frank McManus, 5313 38th St. N.W., Washington, District of Columbia 20015. (202)362-3034. Monthly.

Resource Recycling. Resource Recycling, PO Box 10540, Portland, Oregon 97210. (503) 227-1319. 1989-. Seven times a year.

Resources, Conservation and Recycling. Pergamon Microforms International, Inc., Fairview Park, Elmsford, New York 10523. (914) 592-7720. 1985-. Quarterly. Contains analyses and reviews of the interdisciplinary aspects of renewable and nonrenewable resource management, particularly their conservation.

Returnable Times. Environmental Action Foundation, 6930 Carroll Ave., Ste. 600, Takoma Park, Maryland 20912. (301) 891-1100. Quarterly.

Reuse/Recycle. Technomic Publishing Co., 851 New Holland Ave., Box 3535, Lancaster, Pennsylvania 17604. (717) 291-5609. 1970-. Monthly. Monthly newsletter of resource recycling reports on new technology, uses and markets for recycled materials, advances in recycling plants and equipment, and the changing infrastructure of the plastics recycling industry.

Scrap Processing and Recycling. Institute of Scrap Recycling Industries, 1627 K Street, NW, Washington, District of Columbia 20006. (202) 466-4050. Bimonthly. Issues in the field of scrap processing and recycling.

Solid Waste Report. Business Publishers, Inc., 951 Pershing Dr., Silver Spring, Maryland 20910-4464. (301) 587-6300. 1970-. Weekly. Covers the generation, collection, transportation, processing, resource recovery, recycling and ultimate disposal of municipal, commercial, agricultural and nonhazardous industrial refuse. Also available online.

Waste Age. National Solid Waste Management Association, 1730 Rhode Island Avenue, NW, Ste. 1000, Washington, District of Columbia 20036. (202) 659-4613. Monthly. Covers control and use of solid, hazardous and liquid wastes.

Waste Information Digests. Environmental Studies Institute, International Academy at Santa Barbara, 800 Garden St., Suite D, Santa Barbara, California 93101-1552. (805) 965-5010. Eight times a year. Covers waste collection, management and recycling.

Waste Minimization & Recycling Report. Government Institutes, Inc., 4 Research Pl., Ste. 200, Rockville, Maryland 20850. (301) 921-2300. Monthly. Covers waste minimization, reduction and recycling strategies.

Waste Treatment Technology News. Business Communications Company, Inc., 25 Van Zant Street, Norwalk, Connecticut 06855. (203) 853-4266. Monthly. Covers effective management and handling of hazardous wastes.

RESEARCH CENTERS AND INSTITUTES

Institute of Scrap Recycling Industries. 1627 K St., N.W., Suite 700, Washington, District of Columbia 20006. (202) 466-4050.

University of Alabama, Project Rose. P.O. Box 870203, Tuscaloosa, Alabama 35487-0203. (205) 348-4878.

University of North Carolina at Charlotte, Southeast Waste Exchange. Charlotte, North Carolina 28223. (704) 547-2307.

STATISTICS SOURCES

Environmental Data Compendium. OECD Publications and Information Center, 2001 L St., N.W., Suite 700, Washington, District of Columbia 20036. (202) 785-6323. 1989.

Environmental Indicators. OECD Publications and Information Center, 2001 L St., N.W., Suite 700, Washington, District of Columbia 20036. (202) 785-6323. 1991.

Environmental Quality. Council on Environmental Quality. U.S. G.P.O., Washington, District of Columbia 20401. (202) 512-0000. Annual.

Facing America's Trash: What Next for Municipal Solid Waste?. U.S. Office of Technology Assessment. Van Nostrand Reinhold, Washington, District of Columbia 20401. (202) 512-0000. 1991. Generation, composition and cost of recycling municipal solid waste.

FACTS. Institute of Scrap Recycling Industries, 1627 K St., NW, Suite 700, Washington, District of Columbia 20006. (202) 466-4050. Annual. Scrap production, consumption, prices, and foreign trade, for ferrous and nonferrous metals, paper, and textiles.

The Market for Plastics Recycling & Degradable Products. FIND/SVP, 625 Avenue of the Americas, New York, New York 10011. (212) 645-4500. 1990. The market for all types of degradable products, including bio-and photodegradable; and the complex distribution channel that includes collection, hailing, sorting, bailing and transporting by type of plastic.

Plastics Recycling in the Industrial Sector. National Technical Information Service, 5285 Port Royal Rd., Springfield, Virginia 22161. (703) 487-4650. Potential for development of plastic waste recycling industry, with projections to 2000 and background data from 1973.

The State of the Environment. OECD Publications and Information Center, 2001 L St., N.W., Suite 700, Washington, District of Columbia 20036. (202) 785-6323. 1991.

Statistical Record of the Environment. Arsen J. Darnay. Gale Research Inc., 835 Penobscot Bldg., Detroit, Michigan 48226-4094. (313) 961-2242. 1992.

Waste Not, Want Not. Northeast-Midwest Institute, Publications Office, 218 D St., SE, Washington, District of Columbia 20003. 1989. State and federal roles in source reduction and recycling of solid waste.

World Resources. World Resources Institute. 1709 New York Ave., N.W., Washington, District of Columbia 20006. (202) 638-6300. Annual. Statistical and textual analysis of world's natural resources and the effects of growth-caused environmental pollution.

TRADE ASSOCIATIONS AND PROFESSIONAL SOCIETIES

Aluminum Recycling Association. 1000 16th St., N.W., Washington, District of Columbia 20036. (202) 785-0951.

American Institute of Chemical Engineers. 345 East 47th St., New York, New York 10017. (212) 705-7338.

American Institute of Chemists. 7315 Wisconsin Ave., Bethesda, Maryland 20814. (301) 652-2447.

American Public Works Association. 106 W. 11th St., Ste. 1800, Kansas City, Missouri 64105-1806. (816) 472-6100.

Asphalt Recycling & Reclaiming Association. 3 Church Cir., Suite 250, Annapolis, Maryland 21401. (301) 267-0023.

Automotive Dismantlers and Recyclers Association. 10400 Eaton Pl., Suite 203, Fairfax, Virginia 22030-2208. (703) 385-1001.

Citizens Against Throwaways. Florida Conservation Foundation, Inc., 1251-B Miller Ave., Winter Park, Florida 32789. (305) 644-5377.

Community Environmental Council. 930 Miramonte Drive, Santa Barbara, California 93109. (805) 963-0583.

Council on Plastics and Packaging in the Environment. 1001 Connecticut Ave., N.W., Suite 401, Washington, District of Columbia 20036. (202) 331-0099.

Institute for Local Self-Reliance. 2425 18th St., N.W., Washington, District of Columbia 20009. (202) 232-4108.

National Association for Plastic Container Recovery. 4828 Parkway Plaza Blvd., Suite 260, Charlotte, North Carolina 28217. (704) 357-3250.

National Association of Solvent Recyclers. 1875 Connecticut Ave., N.W., Suite 1200, Washington, District of Columbia 20009. (202) 986-8150.

National Oil Recyclers Association. 805 15th St., N.W., Suite 900, Washington, District of Columbia 20005. (202) 962-3020.

National Recycling Coalition. 1101 30th St., N.W., Washington, District of Columbia 20007. (202) 625-6406.

National Resource Recovery Association. 1620 Eye St., N.W., Washington, District of Columbia 20006. (202) 293-7330.

Plastics Recycling Foundation. 1275 K St., N.W., Suite 400, Washington, District of Columbia 20005. (202) 371-5200.

Steel Can Recycling Institute. Foster Plaza X, 680 Anderson Dr., Pittsburgh, Pennsylvania 15220. (412) 922-2772.

United Rubber, Cork, Linoleum, & Plastic Workers of America. 570 White Pond Dr., Akron, Ohio 44320. (216) 376-6181.

United States Conference of Mayors National Resource Recovery Association. 1620 Eye St., N.W., 4th Fl., Washington, District of Columbia 20006. (202) 293-7330.

RED TIDE

See: PLANKTON

REDOX REACTIONS

See: OXIDATION

REDUCTION, CHEMICAL

ABSTRACTING AND INDEXING SERVICES

General Science Index. H. W. Wilson Co., 950 University Ave., Bronx, New York 10452. 1978-. Monthly, also issued in annual cumulation. Cumulative subject index to English language periodicals in the subject fields of astronomy, botany, chemistry, earth science, environment and conservation, food and nutrition, genetics, mathematics, medicine and health, microbiology, oceanography, physics, physiology and zoology.

GENERAL WORKS

Product Risk Reduction in the Chemical Industry. Leonard A. Miller. Executive Enterprises Publications Co., Inc., 22 W. 21st St., New York, New York 10010-6990. (212) 645-7880. 1985. A handbook for managing product and regulatory liability.

Toxicity Reduction through Chemical and Biological Modification of Spent Pulp Bleaching Liquors. Carlton W. Dence. National Technical Information Service, 5285 Port Royal Rd., Springfield, Virginia 22161. (703) 487-4650. 1980. Chlorophenol toxicology, chemical reactions and biological assay.

TRADE ASSOCIATIONS AND PROFESSIONAL SOCIETIES

American Chemical Society. 1155 16th St., N.W., Washington, District of Columbia 20036. (202) 872-4600.

Institute for Local Self-Reliance. 2425 18th St., N.W., Washington, District of Columbia 20009. (202) 232-4108.

REEFS

See: CORAL REEF ECOLOGY

REFORESTATION

See: FORESTS

REFRIGERATION

See also: COOLING SYSTEMS

ABSTRACTING AND INDEXING SERVICES

Applied Science and Technology Index. H.W. Wilson Co., 950 University Ave., Bronx, New York 10452. (800) 367-6770. Formerly Industrial Arts Index.

Engineering Index. The Engineering Index Inc., 345 E. 47th St., New York, New York 10017. 1962-.

General Science Index. H. W. Wilson Co., 950 University Ave., Bronx, New York 10452. 1978-. Monthly, also issued in annual cumulation. Cumulative subject index to English language periodicals in the subject fields of astronomy, botany, chemistry, earth science, environment and conservation, food and nutrition, genetics, mathematics, medicine and health, microbiology, oceanography, physics, physiology and zoology.

DIRECTORIES

Air Conditioning, Heating & Refrigeration News. Directory Issue. Business News Publishing Co., PO Box 2600, Troy, Michigan 48007. (313) 362-3700 or (800) 247-2160. Annual.

National Council on Refrigeration Sales Association–Membership Directory. c/o Fernley & Fernley, Inc., 1900 Arch St., Philadelphia, Pennsylvania 19103. (215) 564-3484. Annual.

ENCYCLOPEDIAS AND DICTIONARIES

Dictionary of Refrigeration and Air Conditioning. K. M. Booth. Elsevier Science Publishing Co., 655 Avenue of the Americas, New York, New York 10010. (212) 989-5800. 1970.

Van Nostrand's Scientific Encyclopedia. Glenn D. Considine, ed. Van Nostrand Reinhold, 115 5th Ave., New York, New York 10003. (212) 254-3232. 1983. Sixth edition. Includes all broad subject areas in science.

ONLINE DATA BASES

Computerized Engineering Index–COMPENDEX. Engineering Information Inc., 345 E. 47th St., New York, New York 10017. (212) 705-7600.

REFUSE

See: SOLID WASTES

REFUSE RECLAMATION

See: SOLID WASTES

REGOLITH

See: SOIL SCIENCE

REGULATION, ENVIRONMENTAL

See: ENVIRONMENTAL LEGISLATION

REMOTE SENSING, NATURAL RESOURCES

ABSTRACTING AND INDEXING SERVICES

Current Advances in Ecological and Environmental Science. Pergamon Microforms International, Inc., Fairview Park, Elmsford, New York 10523. (914) 592-7720. 1989-. Monthly. Current literature searching service including journals, reports, abstracts, etc. This service is available online as part of the CABS database on the hosts BRS and ORBIT search service.

General Science Index. H. W. Wilson Co., 950 University Ave., Bronx, New York 10452. 1978-. Monthly, also issued in annual cumulation. Cumulative subject index to English language periodicals in the subject fields of astronomy, botany, chemistry, earth science, environment and conservation, food and nutrition, genetics, mathematics, medicine and health, microbiology, oceanography, physics, physiology and zoology.

Quarterly Literature Review of the Remote Sensing of Natural Resources. Technology Application Center, University of New Mexico, Albuquerque, New Mexico 87131. Quarterly.

BIBLIOGRAPHIES

An Annotated Bibliography of Remote Sensing for Highway Planning and Natural Resources. Daniel L. Civco. Storrs Agricultural Experiment Station, University of Connecticut, Storrs, Connecticut 06268. 1980.

Bibliography and Index of Geology. American Geological Institute, 4220 King St., Alexandria, Virginia 22302. Monthly. Includes environmental geology and hydrogeology.

The World Remote Sensing Bibliographic Index. Tensor Industries, Falls Church, Virginia 1976. Comprehensive geographic index bibliography to remote sensing site investigations of natural and agricultural resources throughout the world.

ENCYCLOPEDIAS AND DICTIONARIES

Dictionary of Environmental Engineering and Related Sciences: English-Spanish, Spanish-English. Jose T. Villate. Ediciones Universal, 3090 SW 8th St., Miami, Florida 33135. (305) 642-3355. 1979.

Encyclopedia of Environmental Science and Engineering. J.R. Pfafflin. Gordon and Breach Science Publishers, Inc., 270 8th Ave., New York, New York 10011. (212) 206-8900. 1992.

The Encyclopedia of Geochemistry and Environmental Sciences. Rhodes Whitmore Fairbridge. Van Nostrand Reinhold Co., 115 5th Ave., New York, New York 10003. (212) 254-3232. 1972.

Van Nostrand's Scientific Encyclopedia. Glenn D. Considine, ed. Van Nostrand Reinhold, 115 5th Ave., New York, New York 10003. (212) 254-3232. 1983. Sixth edition. Includes all broad subject areas in science.

GENERAL WORKS

Magill's Survey of Science. Earth Science Series. Frank N. Magill. Salem Press, PO Box 50062, Pasadena, California

91105. 1990-. Five volumes. Includes information on earth's crust, hot spots and volcanic island chains, physical properties of minerals, rock magnetism, physical properties of rocks, and index.

Remote Sensing of Biosphere Functioning. Springer-Verlag, 175 5th Ave., New York, New York 10010. (212) 460-1500. 1990. Ecological studies relating to biosphere sensing and biological aspects of remote sensing.

Remote Sensing of Natural Resources. Technology Application Center, University of New Mexico, Albuquerque, New Mexico 87131.

RESEARCH CENTERS AND INSTITUTES

Remote Sensing Center. Rutgers University, Department of Environmental Resources, Cook College, PO Box 231, New Brunswick, New Jersey 08903. (908) 932-9631.

University of Minnesota, Remote Sensing Laboratory. 1530 North Cleveland Avenue, St. Paul, Minnesota 55108. (612) 624-3400.

STATISTICS SOURCES

World Resources. World Resources Institute. 1709 New York Ave., N.W., Washington, District of Columbia 20006. (202) 638-6300. Annual. Statistical and textual analysis of world's natural resources and the effects of growth-caused environmental pollution.

RENEWABLE ENERGY RESOURCES

ABSTRACTING AND INDEXING SERVICES

Chemical Abstracts. Chemical Abstracts Service, 2540 Olentangy River Rd., PO Box 3012, Columbus, Ohio 43210. (800) 848-6533. 1907-.

ERDA Research Abstracts. U.S. ERDA Technical Information Center, Box 62, Oak Ridge, Tennessee 37830.

BIBLIOGRAPHIES

Bibliography and Index of Geology. American Geological Institute, 4220 King St., Alexandria, Virginia 22302. Monthly. Includes environmental geology and hydrogeology.

Conservation and Renewable Energy: Guide to Sources of Information. Robert Argue. Energy Mines and Resources Canada, 580 Booth, Ottawa, Ontario, Canada KIA OE4. 1980.

Current Contents. Agriculture, Biology and Environmental Sciences. Institute for Scientific Information, 3501 Market St., Philadelphia, Pennsylvania 19104. (800) 523-1857. 1973-. Previous title: Current Contents. Agricultural, Food & Veterinary Sciences. Gives the table of contents of periodicals in the fields of agriculture, biology, environmental and related areas.

DIRECTORIES

International Directory of New and Renewable Energy: Information Sources and Research Centres. UNESCO, 7 place de Fontenoy, 75700 Paris, France F-75700. 1986. Second edition. Contains a total of 3,956 entries representing 156 countries. Profiles of the organizations

associated with new and renewable energy areas are included.

ENCYCLOPEDIAS AND DICTIONARIES

The Encyclopedia of Geochemistry and Environmental Sciences. Rhodes Whitmore Fairbridge. Van Nostrand Reinhold Co., 115 5th Ave., New York, New York 10003. (212) 254-3232. 1972.

Van Nostrand's Scientific Encyclopedia. Glenn D. Considine, ed. Van Nostrand Reinhold, 115 5th Ave., New York, New York 10003. (212) 254-3232. 1983. Sixth edition. Includes all broad subject areas in science.

GENERAL WORKS

Magill's Survey of Science. Earth Science Series. Frank N. Magill. Salem Press, PO Box 50062, Pasadena, California 91105. 1990-. Five volumes. Includes information on earth's crust, hot spots and volcanic island chains, physical properties of minerals, rock magnetism, physical properties of rocks, and index.

Renewable Energy Sources. M. A. Laughton. Elsevier Science Publishing Co., 655 Avenue of the Americas, New York, New York 10010. (212) 984-5800. 1990.

ONLINE DATA BASES

Chemical Abstracts-CA. Chemical Abstracts Service, 2540 Olentangy River Rd., P.O. Box 3012, Columbus, Ohio 43210. (800) 848-6533 or (614) 421-3600. Information sources include 9000 journals, patents from 27 countries, two industrial property organizations, new books, conference proceedings, and government research reports.

Monthly Catalog of United States Government Publications. U.S. G.P.O., Supt. of Docs., PO Box 371954, Pittsburgh, Pennsylvania 15250-7954. (202) 512-0000.

National Technical Information Service. U.S. Department of Commerce, National Technical Information Service, Office of Data Base Services, 5285 Port Royal Rd., Springfield, Virginia 22161. (703) 487-4807. Bibliographic database of government sponsored research and technical reports.

STATISTICS SOURCES

World Resources. World Resources Institute. 1709 New York Ave., N.W., Washington, District of Columbia 20006. (202) 638-6300. Annual. Statistical and textual analysis of world's natural resources and the effects of growth-caused environmental pollution.

RENEWABLE RESOURCES

ABSTRACTING AND INDEXING SERVICES

Applied Science and Technology Index. H.W. Wilson Co., 950 University Ave., Bronx, New York 10452. (800) 367-6770. Formerly Industrial Arts Index.

Chemical Abstracts. Chemical Abstracts Service, 2540 Olentangy River Rd., PO Box 3012, Columbus, Ohio 43210. (800) 848-6533. 1907-.

Pollution Abstracts. Cambridge Scientific Abstracts, 5161 River Rd., Bethesda, Maryland 20816. (301) 961-6750. Six/year. Indexes worldwide technical literature on environmental pollution. Covers air pollution, marine and freshwater pollution, sewage and wastewater treatment, waste management, toxicology and health, noise pollution, radiation, land pollution, and environmental policies, programs, legislation, and education. Also available online.

BIBLIOGRAPHIES

Current Contents. Agriculture, Biology and Environmental Sciences. Institute for Scientific Information, 3501 Market St., Philadelphia, Pennsylvania 19104. (800) 523-1857. 1973-. Previous title: Current Contents. Agricultural, Food & Veterinary Sciences. Gives the table of contents of periodicals in the fields of agriculture, biology, environmental and related areas.

DIRECTORIES

Gale Environmental Sourcebook. Karen Hill. Gale Research Co., 835 Penobscot Bldg., Detroit, Michigan 48226-4094. (313) 961-2242. Contacts, information sources, or general information on environmental topics.

Recycling Today–Equipment and Services Directory Issue. GIE Incorporated Publisher, 4012 Bridge Ave., Cleveland, Ohio 44113. (216) 961-4130.

SYNERJY: A Directory of Renewable Energy. SYNERJY, Box 1854, Cathedral Station, New York, New York 10025. (212) 865-9595.

ENCYCLOPEDIAS AND DICTIONARIES

Grzimek's Encyclopedia of Ecology. Bernhard Grzimek. Van Nostrand Reinhold, 115 5th Ave., New York, New York 10003. (212) 254-3232. 1976.

McGraw-Hill Encyclopedia of Environmental Science. Sybil P. Parker. McGraw-Hill Science & Engineering Books, 11 W. 19th St., New York, New York 10011. (212) 337-6010. 1980. Covers ecology, man's influence on nature, and environmental protection.

McGraw-Hill Encyclopedia of Science and Technology. McGraw-Hill, 1221 Avenue of the Americas, New York, New York 10020. (212) 512-2000 or (800) 262-4729. 1992. Seventh edition. Issued in multiple volumes including index. Includes all science and technology broad subject areas.

North American Reference Encyclopedia of Ecology and Pollution. William White. North American Pub. Co., 401 N. Broad St., Philadelphia, Pennsylvania 19108. (215) 238-5300. 1972.

Van Nostrand's Scientific Encyclopedia. Glenn D. Considine, ed. Van Nostrand Reinhold, 115 5th Ave., New York, New York 10003. (212) 254-3232. 1983. Sixth edition. Includes all broad subject areas in science.

GENERAL WORKS

Cool Energy: The Renewable Solution to Global Warming. Michael Brower. Union of Concerned Scientists, 26 Church St., Cambridge, Massachusetts 02238. (617) 547-5552. 1990. Describes how fossil fuel and renewable energy sources could be used to avoid global warming and air pollution.

Driving Forces: Motor Vehicle Trends and Their Implications for Global Warming, Energy Strategies, and Transportation. James J. MacKenzie and Michael P. Walsh. World Resources Institute, 1709 New York Ave., Washington, District of Columbia 20006. (800) 822-0504. 1990. Overview of new-vehicle fuel efficiency, reductions in air pollution emissions, and overall improvements in transportation and land-use as they relate to global warming planning. Also available through State University of New York Press.

Energy and the Environment. J. Dunderdale, ed. Royal Society of Chemistry, c/o CRC Press, 2000 Corporate Blvd. N.W., Boca Raton, Florida 33431-9868. (800) 272-7737. 1990. Compares the environmental impact of the various energy producing and using processes. The book covers the types and quantities of pollutants produced by these processes, looks at the interaction of these pollutants with the atmosphere, and reviews the use of renewable sources as possible alternatives.

Natural Resources for the 21st Century. R. Neil Sampson and Dwight Hair, eds. Island Press, 1718 Connecticut Ave. N.W., Suite 300, Washington, District of Columbia 20009. (202) 232-7933. 1990. Looks at lost or diminished resources, as well as those that appear to be rebounding. It offers a reliable status report on water, croplands, soil, forests, wetlands, rangelands, fisheries, wildlife, and wilderness.

Power Generation and the Environment. P. S. Liss and P. A. H. Saunders. Oxford University Press, 200 Madison Ave., New York, New York 10016. (212) 679-7300; (800) 334-4249. 1990. Analyses the problems and possibilities inherent in producing electricity on a large scale.

Renewable Energy: Today's Contribution, Tomorrow's Promise. Cynthia Pollock Shea. Worldwatch Institute, 1776 Massachusetts Ave., N.W., Washington, District of Columbia 20036-1904. 1988.

Replacing Gasoline: Alternative Fuels for Light-Duty Vehicles. Congress of the U.S., c/o U.S. Government Printing Office, Office of Technology Assesment, N. Capitol & H Sts. NW, Washington, District of Columbia 20401. (202) 512-0000. 1990. Gives information on alternatives to standard gasoline. Some of the alternatives are: electricity, hydrogen, compressed natural gas, liquified natural gas, liquid propane gas, methanol, ethanol, and reformulated gasoline.

Report on Renewable Energy and Utility Regulation. National Association of Regulatory Utility Commissioners, 1102 ICC Bldg., PO Box 684, Washington, District of Columbia 20044-0684. (202) 898-2200. 1990. Recently released NARUC report that addresses some key questions and makes some basic conclusions about potential of renewable energy resources.

ONLINE DATA BASES

Chemical Abstracts-CA. Chemical Abstracts Service, 2540 Olentangy River Rd., P.O. Box 3012, Columbus, Ohio 43210. (800) 848-6533 or (614) 421-3600. Information sources include 9000 journals, patents from 27 countries, two industrial property organizations, new books, conference proceedings, and government research reports.

Monthly Catalog of United States Government Publications. U.S. G.P.O., Supt. of Docs., PO Box 371954, Pittsburgh, Pennsylvania 15250-7954. (202) 512-0000.

National Technical Information Service. U.S. Department of Commerce, National Technical Information Service, Office of Data Base Services, 5285 Port Royal Rd., Springfield, Virginia 22161. (703) 487-4807. Bibliographic database of government sponsored research and technical reports.

PressNet Environmental Reports. Chemical Information Systems, Inc., 7215 York Rd., Baltimore, Maryland 21212. (301) 321-8440.

PERIODICALS AND NEWSLETTERS

International Journal of Energy, Environment, Economics. Nova Science Publishers, Inc., 283 Commack Rd., Ste. 300, Commack, New York 11725. (516) 499-3103. 1991-. Quarterly. Aims to provide a vehicle for the multidisciplinary field of energy-environment economics between research scientists, engineers and economists. The areas covered would be technological, environmental, economic and social feasibility.

People, Food. People Food, 35751 Oak Springs Dr., Tollhouse, California 93667. (209) 855-3710. Annual.

Probe Post. Pollution Probe Foundation, 12 Madison Ave., Toronto, Ontario, Canada M5R 2S1. (416) 926-1647. Quarterly. Acid rain, toxic waste, renewable energy, deep ecology, land use, and greenhouse effect.

Recycling Today. GIE Incorporated Publisher, 4012 Bridge Ave., Cleveland, Ohio 44113-3320. (216) 961-4130. Monthly. Covers recycling of secondary raw materials and solid waste management. Formerly, entitled Secondary Raw Materials.

Renewable Energy: An International Journal. Pergamon Microforms International, Inc., Fairview Park, Elmsford, New York 10523. (914) 592-7720. 1991-. Six issues a year. Topics include environmental protection and renewable sources of energy.

Renewable Energy Bulletin. Multi-Science Publishing Co. Ltd., 107 High St., Brentwood, Essex, England CM14 4RX. 0277-224632. Six times a year.

RESEARCH CENTERS AND INSTITUTES

Environmental Policy Institute. 218 D St., S.E., Washington, District of Columbia 20003. (202) 544-2600.

Renew America. 17 16th Street, N. W., Suite 710, Washington, District of Columbia 20036. (202) 232-2252.

University of Nevada-Reno, Knudtsen Renewable Resources Center. Department of Range, Wildlife and Forestry, 1000 Valley Road, Reno, Nevada 89512. (702) 784-4000.

STATISTICS SOURCES

Environmental Data Compendium. OECD Publications and Information Center, 2001 L St., N.W., Suite 700, Washington, District of Columbia 20036. (202) 785-6323. 1989.

Environmental Indicators. OECD Publications and Information Center, 2001 L St., N.W., Suite 700, Washington, District of Columbia 20036. (202) 785-6323. 1991.

Environmental Quality. Council on Environmental Quality. U.S. G.P.O., Washington, District of Columbia 20401. (202) 512-0000. Annual.

Report on the Nation's Renewable Resources. U.S. Forest Service. U.S. G.P.O., Washington, District of Columbia 20401. (202) 512-0000. Quinquennial. Projections of resource use and supply from 1920 to 2040, covering wilderness, wildlife, fish, range, timber, water and minerals.

The State of the Environment. OECD Publications and Information Center, 2001 L St., N.W., Suite 700, Washington, District of Columbia 20036. (202) 785-6323. 1991.

TRADE ASSOCIATIONS AND PROFESSIONAL SOCIETIES

Conservation and Renewable Energy Inquiry and Referral Service. P.O. Box 8900, Silver Spring, Maryland 20907. (800) 523-2929.

Fund for Renewable Energy & the Environment. 1400 16th St., N.W., Suite 710, Washington, District of Columbia 20036. (202) 232-2252.

Renewable Energy Info Center. c/o Mindsight Corp., Eight W. Janss Rd., Thousand Oaks, California 91360-3325. (805) 388-3097.

Renewable Fuels Association. 201 Massachusetts Ave., N.E., Suite C-4, Washington, District of Columbia 20002. (202) 543-3802.

Renewable Natural Resources Foundation. 5430 Grosvenor Ln., Bethesda, Maryland 20814. (301) 493-9101.

RESERVES

See: ECOLOGICAL RESERVES

RESERVOIRS

See also: DAMS; IRRIGATION; WATER MANAGEMENT; WATER RESOURCES

ABSTRACTING AND INDEXING SERVICES

ASFA Aquaculture Abstracts. Cambridge Scientific Abstracts, Inc., 5161 River Rd., Bethesda, Maryland 20816. (301) 961-6750. 1984.

Biological and Agricultural Index. H.W. Wilson Co., 950 University Ave., Bronx, New York 10452. (800) 367-6770. 1916-. Monthly.

Environment Abstracts. Bowker A & I Publishing, 121 Chanlon Rd., New Providence, New Jersey 07974. (908) 464-6800. 1974-.

Environment Index. Environment Information Center, Index Research Department, 124 E. 39th St., New York, New York 10016. 1971-. Annual.

Environmental Information Connection–EIC. Planning Information Program, Dept. of Urban and Regional Planning, University of Illinois, 1003 West Nevada, Urbana, Illinois 61801. (217) 333-1369. Also available online.

Environmental Periodicals Bibliography. Environmental Studies Institute, International Academy at Santa Barbara, 800 Garden St., Suite D, Santa Barbara, California 93101. (805) 965-5010. Also available online.

Geographical Abstracts. London School of Economics, Dept. of Geography, Regency House, 34 Duke St., London, England 1966-. Continued by Geo Abstracts issued in 6 parts: Pt. A. Landforms and the quaternary; Pt. B. Biogeography and Climatology; Pt. C. Economic geography; Pt. D. Social geography and cartography; Pt. E. Sedimentology; Pt. F. Regional and community planning.

BIBLIOGRAPHIES

Bibliography and Index of Geology. American Geological Institute, 4220 King St., Alexandria, Virginia 22302. Monthly. Includes environmental geology and hydrogeology.

EPA Publications Bibliography. U.S. Environmental Protection Agency, Library Systems Branch, 401 M St., SW, Washington, District of Columbia 20460. (202) 260-2090. Quarterly.

ENCYCLOPEDIAS AND DICTIONARIES

Van Nostrand's Scientific Encyclopedia. Glenn D. Considine, ed. Van Nostrand Reinhold, 115 5th Ave., New York, New York 10003. (212) 254-3232. 1983. Sixth edition. Includes all broad subject areas in science.

The Water Encyclopedia. Lewis Publishers, 2000 Corporate Blvd. N.W., Boca Raton, Florida 33431. (800) 272-7737. 1990. 2d ed. Includes groundwater contamination, drinking water, floods, waterborne diseases, global warming, climate change, irrigation, water agencies and organizations, precipitation, oceans and seas, and river, lakes and waterfalls.

GENERAL WORKS

The Control of Eutrophication of Lakes and Reservoirs. S. O. Ryding and W. Rast, eds. Parthenon Pub., Casterton Hall, Carnforth, England LA6 2LA. 1990. Volume 1 of the Man and the Biosphere series published jointly with UNESCO.

Magill's Survey of Science. Earth Science Series. Frank N. Magill. Salem Press, PO Box 50062, Pasadena, California 91105. 1990-. Five volumes. Includes information on earth's crust, hot spots and volcanic island chains, physical properties of minerals, rock magnetism, physical properties of rocks, and index.

Man-Made Lakes and Human Health. N. F. Stanley. Academic Press, c/o Harcourt Brace Jovanovich Inc., 6277 Sea Harbor Dr., Orlando, Florida 32887. (800) 346-8648. 1975. Environmental and hygienic aspects of reservoirs.

Reservoir Management for Water Quality and THM Precursor Control. George Dennis Cooke. American Water Works Association, 6666 W. Quincy Ave., Denver, Colorado 80235. (303) 794-7711. 1989. Water quality management and environmental effects of trihalomethanes.

Water Quality Modeling. Brian Henderson-Sellere, et al. CRC Press, 2000 Corporate Blvd. N.W., Boca Raton, Florida 33431. (407) 994-0555; (800) 272-7737. 1990.

Issues in four volumes. Discusses water supply and treatment and water resources engineering.

HANDBOOKS AND MANUALS

Archeological Inundation Studies: Manual for Reservoir Managers. John A. Ware. National Technical Information Service, 5285 Port Royal Rd., Springfield, Virginia 22161. (703) 487-4650. 1989. Excavation safety and protection measures.

ONLINE DATA BASES

Enviro/Energyline Abstracts Plus. R. R. Bowker Co., 121 Chanlon Rd., New Providence, New Jersey 07974. (908) 464-6800.

Environmental Periodicals Bibliography. National Information Services Corp., Ste. 6, Wyman Towers, 3100 St. Paul St., Baltimore, Maryland 21218. (410)243-0797. Online version of abstract of same name.

RESEARCH CENTERS AND INSTITUTES

Murray State University, Center of Excellence for Reservoir Research. College of Science, Murray, Kentucky 42071. (502) 762-2886.

Murray State University, Handcock Biological Station. Murray, Kentucky 42071. (502) 474-2272.

RESIDUAL WASTE
See: WASTE MANAGEMENT

RESIDUE ANALYSIS

GENERAL WORKS

Bound Pesticide Residues. Shahamat U. Khan. CRC Press, 2000 Corporate Blvd. N.W., Boca Raton, Florida 33431. (800) 272-7737. 1991. Overview of pesticide residues in soils and plants, its bioavailability, isolation and identification, toxicological significance and the regulatory aspects.

Pesticide Residue Analysis with Special Reference to Ion Pairing Techniques. Malin Akerblom. National Laboratory for Agricultural Chemistry, Uppsala, Sweden 1990. Analysis of pesticides and pesticide residues in food.

Pesticide Residues and Food Safety: A Harvest of Viewpoints. B. G. Tweedy, et al., eds. American Chemical Society, 1155 16th St. N.W., Washington, District of Columbia 20036. (202) 872-4600; (800) 227-5558. 1991. Discusses all the issues raised in connection with the use of pesticides in the United States. Some of the issues are the economic and social aspects, impact assessment programs, food safety, consumer attitude, pesticide free fruit crops, integrated pest management, EPA's program for validation of pesticides, and other related matters.

Trace Residue Analysis. David A. Kurtz. American Chemical Society, 1155 16th St. N.W., Washington, District of Columbia 20036. (800) 227-5558. 1985. Chemometric estimations of sampling, amount and error.

HANDBOOKS AND MANUALS

Analysis of Insecticides and Acaricides. Francis A. Gunther. Interscience Publishers, New York, New York 1955. A treatise on sampling isolation, and determination, including residue methods.

Manual of Pesticide Residue Analysis. Hans-Peter Thier and Hans Zeumer, eds. VCH Publishers, 303 NW 12th Ave., Deerfield Beach, Florida 33442-1788. (305) 428-5566. 1989. Describes methods for analyzing pesticide residues representing those proven methods that are of the most value to the analyst. It presents 23 compound specific analytical methods.

TRADE ASSOCIATIONS AND PROFESSIONAL SOCIETIES

American Institute of Chemical Engineers. 345 East 47th St., New York, New York 10017. (212) 705-7338.

American Institute of Chemists. 7315 Wisconsin Ave., Bethesda, Maryland 20814. (301) 652-2447.

RESIDUE BURNING

See: AIR POLLUTION

RESIN

ABSTRACTING AND INDEXING SERVICES

Biotechnology Research Abstracts. Cambridge Scientific Abstracts, 5161 River Rd., Bethesda, Maryland 20816. (301) 961-6750. Monthly. Includes such broad areas as genetic intervention, biochemical genetics, and microbiological techniques.

Environment Abstracts. Bowker A & I Publishing, 121 Chanlon Rd., New Providence, New Jersey 07974. (908) 464-6800. 1974-.

Environment Index. Environment Information Center, Index Research Department, 124 E. 39th St., New York, New York 10016. 1971-. Annual.

Environmental Information Connection–EIC. Planning Information Program, Dept. of Urban and Regional Planning, University of Illinois, 1003 West Nevada, Urbana, Illinois 61801. (217) 333-1369. Also available online.

Environmental Periodicals Bibliography. Environmental Studies Institute, International Academy at Santa Barbara, 800 Garden St., Suite D, Santa Barbara, California 93101. (805) 965-5010. Also available online.

BIBLIOGRAPHIES

EPA Publications Bibliography. U.S. Environmental Protection Agency, Library Systems Branch, 401 M St., SW, Washington, District of Columbia 20460. (202) 260-2090. Quarterly.

ENCYCLOPEDIAS AND DICTIONARIES

Van Nostrand's Scientific Encyclopedia. Glenn D. Considine, ed. Van Nostrand Reinhold, 115 5th Ave., New York, New York 10003. (212) 254-3232. 1983. Sixth edition. Includes all broad subject areas in science.

GENERAL WORKS

EPICOR-II Resin Waste Form Testing. R. M. Neilson. Division of Waste Management, U.S. Nuclear Regulatory Commission, Washington, District of Columbia 20555. (301) 492-7000. 1986. Leaching radioactive waste disposal, and ion exchange resins.

Standard Tests for Toughened Resin Composites. National Technical Information Service, 5285 Port Royal Rd., Springfield, Virginia 22161. (703) 487-4650. 1983. Composite materials testing.

ONLINE DATA BASES

Enviro/Energyline Abstracts Plus. R. R. Bowker Co., 121 Chanlon Rd., New Providence, New Jersey 07974. (908) 464-6800.

Environmental Periodicals Bibliography. National Information Services Corp., Ste. 6, Wyman Towers, 3100 St. Paul St., Baltimore, Maryland 21218. (410)243-0797. Online version of abstract of same name.

Industrial Studies Data Base–ISDB. U.S. Environmental Protection Agency, Office of Solid Waste, 401 M St., N.W., Washington, District of Columbia 20460. (202) 260-2090.

SPI/ERS Plastics Data Base. Ernst & Young, 1225 Connecticut Ave., N.W., Washington, District of Columbia 20036. (202) 862-6042. Time series on the production and sales of plastic resins in the United States.

PERIODICALS AND NEWSLETTERS

Paint & Resin. Wheatland Journals Ltd., Penn House, Penn Place, Rickmansworth, England WD3 1FN. 1981.

RESISTANCE

See also: ECOSYSTEMS; GENETIC RESISTANCE

ABSTRACTING AND INDEXING SERVICES

Biological and Agricultural Index. H.W. Wilson Co., 950 University Ave., Bronx, New York 10452. (800) 367-6770. 1916-. Monthly.

Current Advances in Ecological and Environmental Science. Pergamon Microforms International, Inc., Fairview Park, Elmsford, New York 10523. (914) 592-7720. 1989-. Monthly. Current literature searching service including journals, reports, abstracts, etc. This service is available online as part of the CABS database on the hosts BRS and ORBIT search service.

Ecological Abstracts. Geo Abstracts Ltd. Elsevier Applied Science, Crown House, Linton Rd., Barking, England IG 11 8JU. 1974-. Derived from over 600 leading ecological and environmental journals, plus books, conference proceedings, reports and theses.

Environment Abstracts. Bowker A & I Publishing, 121 Chanlon Rd., New Providence, New Jersey 07974. (908) 464-6800. 1974-.

Environment Index. Environment Information Center, Index Research Department, 124 E. 39th St., New York, New York 10016. 1971-. Annual.

Environmental Information Connection–EIC. Planning Information Program, Dept. of Urban and Regional Planning, University of Illinois, 1003 West Nevada, Urbana, Illinois 61801. (217) 333-1369. Also available online.

Environmental Periodicals Bibliography. Environmental Studies Institute, International Academy at Santa Barbara, 800 Garden St., Suite D, Santa Barbara, California 93101. (805) 965-5010. Also available online.

Science Citation Index. Institute for Scientific Information, 3501 Market St., Philadelphia, Pennsylvania 19104. 1961-.

BIBLIOGRAPHIES

Current Contents. Agriculture, Biology and Environmental Sciences. Institute for Scientific Information, 3501 Market St., Philadelphia, Pennsylvania 19104. (800) 523-1857. 1973-. Previous title: Current Contents. Agricultural, Food & Veterinary Sciences. Gives the table of contents of periodicals in the fields of agriculture, biology, environmental and related areas.

EPA Publications Bibliography. U.S. Environmental Protection Agency, Library Systems Branch, 401 M St., SW, Washington, District of Columbia 20460. (202) 260-2090. Quarterly.

ENCYCLOPEDIAS AND DICTIONARIES

Cambridge Encyclopedia of Life Sciences. A. E. Friday and David S. Ingram. Cambridge University Press, 40 W 20th St., New York, New York 10011. (212) 924-3900 or (800) 227-0247. 1985. Includes all topics under biology and ecology.

Van Nostrand's Scientific Encyclopedia. Glenn D. Considine, ed. Van Nostrand Reinhold, 115 5th Ave., New York, New York 10003. (212) 254-3232. 1983. Sixth edition. Includes all broad subject areas in science.

GENERAL WORKS

Managing Resistance to Agrochemicals: From Fundamental Research to Practical Strategies. Maurice B. Green, et al., eds. American Chemical Society, 1155 16th St. N.W., Washington, District of Columbia 20036. (800) 227-5558. 1990. A compilation of chapters written by some of the foremost scientists in pesticide and pest management research today.

Naturally Occurring Pest Bioregulators. Paul A. Hedin. American Chemical Society, 1155 16th St. NW, Washington, District of Columbia 20036. (202) 872-4600; (800) 227-5558. 1991. Symposium papers on naturally occurring biologically active chemicals grouped in five general sections: bioregulation of insect behavior and development; allelochemicals for control of insects and other animals; phytoalexins and phototoxins in plant pest control; mechanisms of plant resistance to insects; and allelochemicals as plant disease control agents.

HANDBOOKS AND MANUALS

Chemical Compatability & Environmental Stress Crack Resistance. Plastics Design Library, 345 E. 54th St., Ste. 5E, New York, New York 10022. (212) 838-2817. 1990. Plastics deterioration and biodegradation.

ONLINE DATA BASES

Enviro/Energyline Abstracts Plus. R. R. Bowker Co., 121 Chanlon Rd., New Providence, New Jersey 07974. (908) 464-6800.

Environmental Periodicals Bibliography. National Information Services Corp., Ste. 6, Wyman Towers, 3100 St. Paul St., Baltimore, Maryland 21218. (410)243-0797. Online version of abstract of same name.

SCISEARCH. Institute for Scientific Information, University City Science Center, 3501 Market St., Philadelphia, Pennsylvania 19104. (215) 386-0100.

RESEARCH CENTERS AND INSTITUTES

USDA Plant Gene Expression Center. 800 Buchanan Street, Albany, California 94710. (510) 559-5900.

TRADE ASSOCIATIONS AND PROFESSIONAL SOCIETIES

American Institute of Biological Sciences. 730 11th St., N.W., Washington, District of Columbia 20001-4521. (202) 628-1500.

RESOURCE CONSERVATION

ABSTRACTING AND INDEXING SERVICES

Agrindex. AGRIS Coordinating Center, Via delle Terme di Caracalla, Rome, Italy I-00100. 61 0181-FA01. 1975-.

Applied Ecology Abstracts Studies in Renewable Natural Resources. Information Retrieval Ltd., 1911 Jefferson Davis Highway, Arlington, Virginia 22202. 1975-. Monthly.

Applied Science and Technology Index. H.W. Wilson Co., 950 University Ave., Bronx, New York 10452. (800) 367-6770. Formerly Industrial Arts Index.

ASFA Aquaculture Abstracts. Cambridge Scientific Abstracts, Inc., 5161 River Rd., Bethesda, Maryland 20816. (301) 961-6750. 1984.

Biological and Agricultural Index. H.W. Wilson Co., 950 University Ave., Bronx, New York 10452. (800) 367-6770. 1916-. Monthly.

Current Advances in Ecological and Environmental Science. Pergamon Microforms International, Inc., Fairview Park, Elmsford, New York 10523. (914) 592-7720. 1989-. Monthly. Current literature searching service includingjournals, reports, abstracts, etc. This service is available online as part of the CABS database on the hosts BRS and ORBIT search service.

Ecological Abstracts. Geo Abstracts Ltd. Elsevier Applied Science, Crown House, Linton Rd., Barking, England IG 11 8JU. 1974-. Derived from over 600 leading ecological and environmental journals, plus books, conference proceedings, reports and theses.

Ecology Abstracts. Cambridge Scientific Abstracts, 5161 River Rd., Bethesda, Maryland 20816. (301) 961-6750. Monthly.

Environment Abstracts. Bowker A & I Publishing, 121 Chanlon Rd., New Providence, New Jersey 07974. (908) 464-6800. 1974-.

Environment Index. Environment Information Center, Index Research Department, 124 E. 39th St., New York, New York 10016. 1971-. Annual.

Environmental Information Connection–EIC. Planning Information Program, Dept. of Urban and Regional Planning, University of Illinois, 1003 West Nevada, Urbana, Illinois 61801. (217) 333-1369. Also available online.

Environmental Periodicals Bibliography. Environmental Studies Institute, International Academy at Santa Barbara, 800 Garden St., Suite D, Santa Barbara, California 93101. (805) 965-5010. Also available online.

General Science Index. H. W. Wilson Co., 950 University Ave., Bronx, New York 10452. 1978-. Monthly, also issued in annual cumulation. Cumulative subject index to English language periodicals in the subject fields of astronomy, botany, chemistry, earth science, environment and conservation, food and nutrition, genetics, mathematics, medicine and health, microbiology, oceanography, physics, physiology and zoology.

Geographical Abstracts. London School of Economics, Dept. of Geography, Regency House, 34 Duke St., London, England 1966-. Continued by Geo Abstracts issued in 6 parts: Pt. A. Landforms and the quaternary; Pt. B. Biogeography and Climatology; Pt. C. Economic geography; Pt. D. Social geography and cartography; Pt. E. Sedimentology; Pt. F. Regional and community planning.

Index to Scientific Book Contents. Institute for Scientific Information, 3501 Market St., Philadelphia, Pennsylvania 19104. (800) 523-1857. 1985-. Annual. Gives contents of science books published.

Multimedia Index to Ecology. National Information Center for Educational Media, University of Southern California, Los Angeles, California 90007.

Pollution Abstracts. Cambridge Scientific Abstracts, 5161 River Rd., Bethesda, Maryland 20816. (301) 961-6750. Six/year. Indexes worldwide technical literature on environmental pollution. Covers air pollution, marine and freshwater pollution, sewage and wastewater treatment, waste management, toxicology and health, noise pollution, radiation, land pollution, and environmental policies, programs, legislation, and education. Also available online.

BIBLIOGRAPHIES

Current Contents. Agriculture, Biology and Environmental Sciences. Institute for Scientific Information, 3501 Market St., Philadelphia, Pennsylvania 19104. (800) 523-1857. 1973-. Previous title: Current Contents. Agricultural, Food & Veterinary Sciences. Gives the table of contents of periodicals in the fields of agriculture, biology, environmental and related areas.

EPA Publications Bibliography. U.S. Environmental Protection Agency, Library Systems Branch, 401 M St., SW, Washington, District of Columbia 20460. (202) 260-2090. Quarterly.

ENCYCLOPEDIAS AND DICTIONARIES

Cambridge Encyclopedia of Life Sciences. A. E. Friday and David S. Ingram. Cambridge University Press, 40 W 20th St., New York, New York 10011. (212) 924-3900 or

(800) 227-0247. 1985. Includes all topics under biology and ecology.

Grzimek's Encyclopedia of Ecology. Bernhard Grzimek. Van Nostrand Reinhold, 115 5th Ave., New York, New York 10003. (212) 254-3232. 1976.

McGraw-Hill Encyclopedia of Environmental Science. Sybil P. Parker. McGraw-Hill Science & Engineering Books, 11 W. 19th St., New York, New York 10011. (212) 337-6010. 1980. Covers ecology, man's influence on nature, and environmental protection.

McGraw-Hill Encyclopedia of Science and Technology. McGraw-Hill, 1221 Avenue of the Americas, New York, New York 10020. (212) 512-2000 or (800) 262-4729. 1992. Seventh edition. Issued in multiple volumes including index. Includes all science and technology broad subject areas.

North American Reference Encyclopedia of Ecology and Pollution. William White. North American Pub. Co., 401 N. Broad St., Philadelphia, Pennsylvania 19108. (215) 238-5300. 1972.

Resource Conservation Glossary. Soil and Water Conservation Society, 7515 Northeast Ankeny Rd., Ankeny, Iowa 50021. (515) 289-2331. 1982. Third edition. Includes 4,000 terms commonly used in resource management. Terms from 34 technologies are represented.

Van Nostrand's Scientific Encyclopedia. Glenn D. Considine, ed. Van Nostrand Reinhold, 115 5th Ave., New York, New York 10003. (212) 254-3232. 1983. Sixth edition. Includes all broad subject areas in science.

GENERAL WORKS

Energy, Resources and Environment. John Blunden and Alan Reddish, eds. Hodder & Stoughton, PO Box 257, North Pomfret, Vermont 05053. (802) 457-1911. 1991.

Human Investment and Resource Use: A New Research Orientation at the Environment/Economics Interface. Michael Young and Natarajan Ishwaran, eds. UNESCO, 7, place de Fontenoy, Paris, France F-75700. (331) 45 68 40 67. 1989. Explores the issue of the environment/economics interface, parcularly the effect of the level and nature of human investments in determining the manner in which natural resources are utilized.

Paying the Farm Bill: U.S. Agricultural Policy and the Transition to Sustainable Agriculture. Paul Faeth, et al. World Resources Institute, 1709 New York Ave. N.W., Washington, District of Columbia 20006. (800) 822-0504. 1991. Demonstrates that resource conserving agricultural systems are environmentally and economically superior to conventional systems over the long term.

Wetland Creation and Restoration: The Status of the Science. Jon A. Kusler and Mary E. Kentula, eds. Island Press, 1718 Connecticut Ave. N.W., Suite 300, Washington, District of Columbia 20009. (202) 232-7933. 1990. Eighty papers from leading scientists and technicians draw upon important new information and provide assessment by region of the capacity to implement a goal of no-net-loss of wetlands.

GOVERNMENTAL ORGANIZATIONS

Information and Communications: Extension Service. 14th and Independence Ave., S.W., Washington, District of Columbia 20250. (202) 447-3029.

HANDBOOKS AND MANUALS

Resource Conservation and Recovery Act Handbook. ERT, Marketing Dept., 696 Virginia Road, Concord, Massachusetts 01742. Law relating to hazardous wastes and waste sites.

Resource Conservation and Recovery Act Inspection Manual. U.S. Environmental Protection Agency. Government Institutes, Inc., 4 Research Pl., Ste. 200, Rockville, Maryland 20850. (301) 921-2300. 1989.

ONLINE DATA BASES

Cambridge Scientific Abstracts Life Science–CSAL. Cambridge Scientific Abstracts, 5161 River Rd., Bethesda, Maryland 20816. (301) 961-6750. Provides access to the following abstracting services: "Life Sciences Collection," "Aquatic Sciences and Fisheries Abstracts," "Oceanic Abstracts," and "Pollution Abstracts."

Enviro/Energyline Abstracts Plus. R. R. Bowker Co., 121 Chanlon Rd., New Providence, New Jersey 07974. (908) 464-6800.

Environmental Periodicals Bibliography. National Information Services Corp., Ste. 6, Wyman Towers, 3100 St. Paul St., Baltimore, Maryland 21218. (410)243-0797. Online version of abstract of same name.

Monthly Catalog of United States Government Publications. U.S. G.P.O., Supt. of Docs., PO Box 371954, Pittsburgh, Pennsylvania 15250-7954. (202) 512-0000.

National Technical Information Service. U.S. Department of Commerce, National Technical Information Service, Office of Data Base Services, 5285 Port Royal Rd., Springfield, Virginia 22161. (703) 487-4807. Bibliographic database of government sponsored research and technical reports.

SCISEARCH. Institute for Scientific Information, University City Science Center, 3501 Market St., Philadelphia, Pennsylvania 19104. (215) 386-0100.

PERIODICALS AND NEWSLETTERS

Carrying Capacity News. Carrying Capacity Network, 1325 G St. NW, Suite 1003, Washington, District of Columbia 20005-3104. (202) 879-3044. Irregular. Discusses links between environmental, population, resources, and economic issues.

Environmental Defense Fund Letter. Environmental Defense Fund, 257 Park Avenue South, New York, New York 10010. (212) 505-2100. 1971-. Bimonthly. Environmental issues of concern.

Multinational Environmental Outlook. Business Publishers, Inc., 951 Pershing Dr., Silver Spring, Maryland 20910-4464. (301) 587-6300. 1974-. Biweekly. Covers developments in world environmental problems such as acid rain, deforestation, soil erosion, overfishing, threats to health, animal extinction, population growth, diminishing water supply and other related matters. Also available online.

Resources. Resources for the Future Inc., 1616 P St., NW, Washington, District of Columbia 20036. (202) 328-5000. 1959-. Three times a year.

Resources, Conservation and Recycling. Pergamon Microforms International, Inc., Fairview Park, Elmsford, New York 10523. (914) 592-7720. 1985-. Quarterly. Contains analyses and reviews of the interdisciplinary aspects of renewable and nonrenewable resource management, particularly their conservation.

Reuse/Recycle. Technomic Publishing Co., 851 New Holland Ave., Box 3535, Lancaster, Pennsylvania 17604. (717) 291-5609. 1970-. Monthly. Monthly newsletter of resource recycling reports on new technology, uses and markets for recycled materials, advances in recycling plants and equipment, and the changing infrastructure of the plastics recycling industry.

State of California Resources Agency News and Views. State of California Resources Agency, Department of Parks and Recreation, 1416 9th St., Sacramento, California 95814. 1943-. Monthly.

Waste Minimization & Recycling Report. Government Institutes, Inc., 4 Research Pl., Ste. 200, Rockville, Maryland 20850. (301) 921-2300. Monthly. Covers waste minimization, reduction and recycling strategies.

RESEARCH CENTERS AND INSTITUTES

Clark University, Program for International Development and Social Change. 950 Main St., Worcester, Massachusetts 01610.

Institute for Resource Management. 262 S. 200 W., Salt Lake City, Utah 84101. (801) 322-0530.

Resources for the Future, Inc. 1616 P St., N.W., Washington, District of Columbia 20036. (202) 328-5000.

Resources for the Future, Inc. Energy and Natural Resources Division. 1616 P Street, N.W., Washington, District of Columbia 20036. (202) 328-5000.

Resources for the Future, Inc., Quality of the Environment Division. 1616 P Street, N.W., Washington, District of Columbia 20036. (202) 328-5000.

University of Wisconsin-Milwaukee, Center for Great Lakes Studies. Milwaukee, Wisconsin 53201. (414) 649-3000.

World Resources Institute. 1709 New York Ave., N.W., Washington, District of Columbia 20006. (202) 638-6300.

Worldwatch Institute. 1776 Massachusetts Ave., N.W., Washington, District of Columbia 20036. (202) 452-1999.

STATISTICS SOURCES

World Resources. World Resources Institute. 1709 New York Ave., N.W., Washington, District of Columbia 20006. (202) 638-6300. Annual. Statistical and textual analysis of world's natural resources and the effects of growth-caused environmental pollution.

TRADE ASSOCIATIONS AND PROFESSIONAL SOCIETIES

American Institute of Biological Sciences. 730 11th St., N.W., Washington, District of Columbia 20001-4521. (202) 628-1500.

American Resources Group. Signet Bank Bldg., Suite 210, 374 Maple Ave. E., Vienna, Virginia 22180. (703) 255-2700.

Center for Holistic Resource Management. P.O. Box 7128, Albuquerque, New Mexico 87194. (505) 344-3445.

Conservation Foundation. 1250 24th St., N.W., Washington, District of Columbia 20037. (202) 293-4800. The World Wildlife Fund absorbed the Conservation Foundation in 1990.

Environmental Defense Fund. 257 Park Ave., S., New York, New York 10010. (212) 505-2100. Non-profit organization that was established more than 20 years ago. Its goals are to protect the earth's environment by providing lasting solutions to global environmental problems.

Environmental Resource Center. Crowder College, Neosho, Missouri 64850. (417) 451-3583.

Global Tomorrow Coalition. 1325 G St., N.W., Suite 915, Washington, District of Columbia 20005-3103. (202) 628-4016.

Institute for 21st Century Studies. 1611 N. Kent St., Suite 610, Arlington, Virginia 22209. (703) 841-0048.

J. N. "Ding" Darling Foundation. P.O. Box 703, Des Moines, Iowa 50303. (305) 361-9788.

John Muir Institute for Environmental Studies. 743 Wilson St., Napa, California 94559. (707) 252-8333.

National Audubon Society. 950 Third Ave., New York, New York 10022. (212) 832-3200.

Safari Club International. 4800 W. Gates Pass Rd., Tucson, Arizona 85745. (602) 620-1220.

Sierra Club. 100 Bush St., San Francisco, California 94104. (415) 291-1600.

RESOURCE RECOVERY

See also: RECYCLING (WASTE, ETC.)

ABSTRACTING AND INDEXING SERVICES

Advanced Oil and Gas Recovery Technologies. National Technical Information Service, 5285 Port Royal Road, Springfield, Virginia 22161. (703) 487-4650. Monthly. Enhanced and unconventional recovery of petroleum and natural gas, oil shales and tar sands, natural gas production from coal mines, gas hydrates, and geopressured systems.

Agrindex. AGRIS Coordinating Center, Via delle Terme di Caracalla, Rome, Italy I-00100. 61 0181-FA01. 1975-.

Applied Ecology Abstracts Studies in Renewable Natural Resources. Information Retrieval Ltd., 1911 Jefferson Davis Highway, Arlington, Virginia 22202. 1975-. Monthly.

Applied Science and Technology Index. H.W. Wilson Co., 950 University Ave., Bronx, New York 10452. (800) 367-6770. Formerly Industrial Arts Index.

Current Advances in Ecological and Environmental Science. Pergamon Microforms International, Inc., Fairview Park, Elmsford, New York 10523. (914) 592-7720. 1989-. Monthly. Current literature searching service including journals, reports, abstracts, etc. This service is available online as part of the CABS database on the hosts BRS and ORBIT search service.

Ecological Abstracts. Geo Abstracts Ltd. Elsevier Applied Science, Crown House, Linton Rd., Barking, England IG

11 8JU. 1974-. Derived from over 600 leading ecological and environmental journals, plus books, conference proceedings, reports and theses.

Environment Abstracts. Bowker A & I Publishing, 121 Chanlon Rd., New Providence, New Jersey 07974. (908) 464-6800. 1974-.

Environment Index. Environment Information Center, Index Research Department, 124 E. 39th St., New York, New York 10016. 1971-. Annual.

Environmental Information Connection–EIC. Planning Information Program, Dept. of Urban and Regional Planning, University of Illinois, 1003 West Nevada, Urbana, Illinois 61801. (217) 333-1369. Also available online.

Environmental Periodicals Bibliography. Environmental Studies Institute, International Academy at Santa Barbara, 800 Garden St., Suite D, Santa Barbara, California 93101. (805) 965-5010. Also available online.

General Science Index. H. W. Wilson Co., 950 University Ave., Bronx, New York 10452. 1978-. Monthly, also issued in annual cumulation. Cumulative subject index to English language periodicals in the subject fields of astronomy, botany, chemistry, earth science, environment and conservation, food and nutrition, genetics, mathematics, medicine and health, microbiology, oceanography, physics, physiology and zoology.

Geographical Abstracts. London School of Economics, Dept. of Geography, Regency House, 34 Duke St., London, England 1966-. Continued by Geo Abstracts issued in 6 parts: Pt. A. Landforms and the quaternary; Pt. B. Biogeography and Climatology; Pt. C. Economic geography; Pt. D. Social geography and cartography; Pt. E. Sedimentology; Pt. F. Regional and community planning.

Index to Scientific Book Contents. Institute for Scientific Information, 3501 Market St., Philadelphia, Pennsylvania 19104. (800) 523-1857. 1985-. Annual. Gives contents of science books published.

Multimedia Index to Ecology. National Information Center for Educational Media, University of Southern California, Los Angeles, California 90007.

Pollution Abstracts. Cambridge Scientific Abstracts, 5161 River Rd., Bethesda, Maryland 20816. (301) 961-6750. Six/year. Indexes worldwide technical literature on environmental pollution. Covers air pollution, marine and freshwater pollution, sewage and wastewater treatment, waste management, toxicology and health, noise pollution, radiation, land pollution, and environmental policies, programs, legislation, and education. Also available online.

BIBLIOGRAPHIES

EPA Publications Bibliography. U.S. Environmental Protection Agency, Library Systems Branch, 401 M St., SW, Washington, District of Columbia 20460. (202) 260-2090. Quarterly.

DIRECTORIES

City Currents-Resource Recovery Activities Issue. Ronald W. Musselwhite. HCI Publications, 410 Archibald St., Kansas City, Missouri 64111. (816) 931-1311. Annual. Operating or proposed resource recovery plants.

Directory of Resource Recovery Projects and Services. Julie C. Grady. Institute of Resource Recovery, National Solid Wastes Management Association, 1730 Rhode Island Ave., NW, Suite 1000, Washington, District of Columbia 20036. (202) 659-4613. Annual. Firms active in recovering energy from solid waste materials.

Recycling Today–Equipment and Services Directory Issue. GIE Incorporated Publisher, 4012 Bridge Ave., Cleveland, Ohio 44113. (216) 961-4130.

Resource Recycling–Equipment Guide Issue. Resource Recycling, Box 10540, Portland, Oregon 97210. (503) 227-1319.

Who's Who in Energy Recovery from Waste. Biofuels and Municipal Waste Technology Division/Office of Renewable Energy Technologies, Office of Conservation and Renewable Energy, Department of Energy, Washington, District of Columbia 20585. (202) 586-6750. 1982.

ENCYCLOPEDIAS AND DICTIONARIES

Grzimek's Encyclopedia of Ecology. Bernhard Grzimek. Van Nostrand Reinhold, 115 5th Ave., New York, New York 10003. (212) 254-3232. 1976.

McGraw-Hill Encyclopedia of Environmental Science. Sybil P. Parker. McGraw-Hill Science & Engineering Books, 11 W. 19th St., New York, New York 10011. (212) 337-6010. 1980. Covers ecology, man's influence on nature, and environmental protection.

North American Reference Encyclopedia of Ecology and Pollution. William White. North American Pub. Co., 401 N. Broad St., Philadelphia, Pennsylvania 19108. (215) 238-5300. 1972.

Van Nostrand's Scientific Encyclopedia. Glenn D. Considine, ed. Van Nostrand Reinhold, 115 5th Ave., New York, New York 10003. (212) 254-3232. 1983. Sixth edition. Includes all broad subject areas in science.

GENERAL WORKS

The Greater Yellowstone Ecosystem. Robert B. Keiter and Mark S. Boyce, eds. Yale University Press, 302 Temple St., New Haven, Connecticut 06520. (203) 432-0960. 1991. Discusses key resource management issues in the greater Yellowstone ecosystem, using them as starting points to debate the manner in which humans should interact with the environment of this area.

Hazardous and Industrial Wastes, 1990. Joseph P. Martin, et al., eds. Technomic Publishing Co., 851 Holland Ave., Box 3535, Lancaster, Pennsylvania 17604. (717) 291-5609. 1990. Proceedings of the 22nd Mid-Atlantic Industrial Waste Conference, June 24-27, 1990, Drexel University, Philadelphia, PA. Fifty-one new reports on developments in industrial and hazardous waste management, technology and regulation were presented.

Management and Restoration of Human-Impacted Resources: Approaches to Ecosystem Rehabilitation. Kathrin Schreckenberg, et al, eds. UNESCO, 7, place de Fontenoy, Paris, France F-75700. (331) 45 68 40 67. 1990. MAB Digest 5.

Recoverable Materials and Energy from Industrial Waste Streams. Fran V. Kremer. American Water Works Association, 6666 W. Quincy Ave., Denver, Colorado 80235. (303) 794-7711. 1987.

Wetland Creation and Restoration: The Status of the Science. Jon A. Kusler and Mary E. Kentula, eds. Island Press, 1718 Connecticut Ave. N.W., Suite 300, Washington, District of Columbia 20009. (202) 232-7933. 1990. Eighty papers from leading scientists and technicians draw upon important new information and provide assessment by region of the capacity to implement a goal of no-net-loss of wetlands.

HANDBOOKS AND MANUALS

RCRA Hazardous Wastes Handbook. Crowell & Moring. Government Institutes, Inc., 4 Research Place, Suite 200, Rockville, Maryland 20850. (301) 921-2300. 1989. 8th ed. Analyzes the impact of the Resource Conservation and Recovery Act on the business, while incorporating the most recent regulatory changes to the RCRA. These include the final 1988 underground storage tank rules, the medical waste regulations, permit modification regulations, amendments regarding corrective action and closures, the exemption for "treatability tests," waste export rules, etc. Includes the complete test of the RCRA statute as currently amended.

Resource Conservation and Recovery Act Handbook. ERT, Marketing Dept., 696 Virginia Road, Concord, Massachusetts 01742. Law relating to hazardous wastes and waste sites.

Resource Conservation and Recovery Act Inspection Manual. U.S. Environmental Protection Agency. Government Institutes, Inc., 4 Research Pl., Ste. 200, Rockville, Maryland 20850. (301) 921-2300. 1989.

ONLINE DATA BASES

Enviro/Energyline Abstracts Plus. R. R. Bowker Co., 121 Chanlon Rd., New Providence, New Jersey 07974. (908) 464-6800.

Environmental Periodicals Bibliography. National Information Services Corp., Ste. 6, Wyman Towers, 3100 St. Paul St., Baltimore, Maryland 21218. (410)243-0797. Online version of abstract of same name.

Monthly Catalog of United States Government Publications. U.S. G.P.O., Supt. of Docs., PO Box 371954, Pittsburgh, Pennsylvania 15250-7954. (202) 512-0000.

National Technical Information Service. U.S. Department of Commerce, National Technical Information Service, Office of Data Base Services, 5285 Port Royal Rd., Springfield, Virginia 22161. (703) 487-4807. Bibliographic database of government sponsored research and technical reports.

SCISEARCH. Institute for Scientific Information, University City Science Center, 3501 Market St., Philadelphia, Pennsylvania 19104. (215) 386-0100.

Waste Management and Resource Recovery. International Research & Evaluation, 21098 IRE Control Center, Eagan, Minnesota 55121. (612) 888-9635.

PERIODICALS AND NEWSLETTERS

Newsletter. Coalition on Resource Recovery and the Environment, c/o Dr. Walter M. Schaub, U.S. Conference of Mayors, 1620 I St. NW, Suite 600, Washington, District of Columbia 20006. (202) 293-7330. Monthly.

Recycling Today. GIE Incorporated Publisher, 4012 Bridge Ave., Cleveland, Ohio 44113-3320. (216) 961-

4130. Monthly. Covers recycling of secondary raw materials and solid waste management. Formerly, entitled Secondary Raw Materials.

Resource Recovery Briefs. National Center for Resource Recovery Inc., 1211 Connecticut Ave., N.W., Washington, District of Columbia 20036. Monthly.

Resource Recovery Report. Frank McManus, 5313 38th St. N.W., Washington, District of Columbia 20015. (202)362-3034. Monthly.

Resource Recycling. Resource Recycling, PO Box 10540, Portland, Oregon 97210. (503) 227-1319. 1989-. Seven times a year.

Resources. Resources for the Future Inc., 1616 P St., NW, Washington, District of Columbia 20036. (202) 328-5000. 1959-. Three times a year.

Reuse/Recycle. Technomic Publishing Co., 851 New Holland Ave., Box 3535, Lancaster, Pennsylvania 17604. (717) 291-5609. 1970-. Monthly. Monthly newsletter of resource recycling reports on new technology, uses and markets for recycled materials, advances in recycling plants and equipment, and the changing infrastructure of the plastics recycling industry.

Waste Minimization & Recycling Report. Government Institutes, Inc., 4 Research Pl., Ste. 200, Rockville, Maryland 20850. (301) 921-2300. Monthly. Covers waste minimization, reduction and recycling strategies.

RESEARCH CENTERS AND INSTITUTES

Institute of Resource Recovery. 1730 Rhode Island Ave., N.W., Suite 1000, Washington, District of Columbia 20036. (202) 659-4613.

Resources for the Future, Inc. 1616 P St., N.W., Washington, District of Columbia 20036. (202) 328-5000.

Resources for the Future, Inc. Energy and Natural Resources Division. 1616 P Street, N.W., Washington, District of Columbia 20036. (202) 328-5000.

Resources for the Future, Inc., Quality of the Environment Division. 1616 P Street, N.W., Washington, District of Columbia 20036. (202) 328-5000.

Texas A & M University, Separation and Ingredient Sciences Laboratory. Food Protein Research and Development Center, College Station, Texas 77843-2476. (409) 845-2741.

University of Alabama, Hazardous Materials Management Resource Recovery. Department of Chemical Engineering, P.O. Box 870203, Tuscaloosa, Alabama 35487-0203. (205) 348-8401.

University of Alabama, Project Rose. P.O. Box 870203, Tuscaloosa, Alabama 35487-0203. (205) 348-4878.

University of Alaska Fairbanks, Alaska Sea Grant College Program. 138 Irving II, Fairbanks, Alaska 99775-5040. (907) 474-7086.

University of Arizona, Environmental Engineering Laboratory. Civil Engineering Department, Room 206, Tucson, Arizona 85721. (602) 621-6586.

TRADE ASSOCIATIONS AND PROFESSIONAL SOCIETIES

American Resources Group. Signet Bank Bldg., Suite 210, 374 Maple Ave. E., Vienna, Virginia 22180. (703) 255-2700.

Caribbean Conservation Corporation. PO Box 2866, Gainsville, Florida 32602. (904) 373-6441.

Coalition on Resource Recovery and the Environment. c/o Dr. Walter M. Shaub, U.S. Conference of Mayors, 1620 I St. NW, Suite 600, Washington, District of Columbia 20006. (202) 293-7330.

National Resource Recovery Association. 1620 Eye St., N.W., Washington, District of Columbia 20006. (202) 293-7330.

United States Conference of Mayors National Resource Recovery Association. 1620 Eye St., N.W., 4th Fl., Washington, District of Columbia 20006. (202) 293-7330.

RESPIRABLE DUST

See: AIR POLLUTION

RESPIRATION

See also: AEROBIC RESPIRATION; FERMENTATION; METABOLISM

ABSTRACTING AND INDEXING SERVICES

Air Pollution Technical Publications of the United States Environmental Protection Agency. U.S. Environmental Protection Agency, Mail Drop 75, Research Triangle Park, North Carolina 27711. (919) 541-2184. 1976. Quarterly.

Applied Ecology Abstracts Studies in Renewable Natural Resources. Information Retrieval Ltd., 1911 Jefferson Davis Highway, Arlington, Virginia 22202. 1975-. Monthly.

Applied Science and Technology Index. H.W. Wilson Co., 950 University Ave., Bronx, New York 10452. (800) 367-6770. Formerly Industrial Arts Index.

ASFA Aquaculture Abstracts. Cambridge Scientific Abstracts, Inc., 5161 River Rd., Bethesda, Maryland 20816. (301) 961-6750. 1984.

Biological Abstracts. BIOSIS, 2100 Arch St., Philadelphia, Pennsylvania 19103-1399. (215) 587-4800. 1927-.

Biological and Agricultural Index. H.W. Wilson Co., 950 University Ave., Bronx, New York 10452. (800) 367-6770. 1916-. Monthly.

Biology Digest. Data Courier, Plexus Pub Inc., 143 Old Marlton Pike, Medford, New Jersey 08055. 1974-. Monthly. Abstracts biology periodicals.

Biotechnology Research Abstracts. Cambridge Scientific Abstracts, 5161 River Rd., Bethesda, Maryland 20816. (301) 961-6750. Monthly. Includes such broad areas as genetic intervention, biochemical genetics, and microbiological techniques.

Current Advances in Plant Science. Pergamon Microforms International, Inc., Fairview Park, Elmsford, New York 10523. (914) 592-7720. 1984-. Monthly. Current literature searching service including journals, reports, abstracts, etc. This service is available online as part of the CABS database on the hosts BRS and ORBIT search service.

Ecological Abstracts. Geo Abstracts Ltd. Elsevier Applied Science, Crown House, Linton Rd., Barking, England IG 11 8JU. 1974-. Derived from over 600 leading ecological and environmental journals, plus books, conference proceedings, reports and theses.

Ecology Abstracts. Cambridge Scientific Abstracts, 5161 River Rd., Bethesda, Maryland 20816. (301) 961-6750. Monthly.

Environment Abstracts. Bowker A & I Publishing, 121 Chanlon Rd., New Providence, New Jersey 07974. (908) 464-6800. 1974-.

Environment Index. Environment Information Center, Index Research Department, 124 E. 39th St., New York, New York 10016. 1971-. Annual.

Environmental Information Connection–EIC. Planning Information Program, Dept. of Urban and Regional Planning, University of Illinois, 1003 West Nevada, Urbana, Illinois 61801. (217) 333-1369. Also available online.

Environmental Periodicals Bibliography. Environmental Studies Institute, International Academy at Santa Barbara, 800 Garden St., Suite D, Santa Barbara, California 93101. (805) 965-5010. Also available online.

General Science Index. H. W. Wilson Co., 950 University Ave., Bronx, New York 10452. 1978-. Monthly, also issued in annual cumulation. Cumulative subject index to English language periodicals in the subject fields of astronomy, botany, chemistry, earth science, environment and conservation, food and nutrition, genetics, mathematics, medicine and health, microbiology, oceanography, physics, physiology and zoology.

Multimedia Index to Ecology. National Information Center for Educational Media, University of Southern California, Los Angeles, California 90007.

Pollution Abstracts. Cambridge Scientific Abstracts, 5161 River Rd., Bethesda, Maryland 20816. (301) 961-6750. Six/year. Indexes worldwide technical literature on environmental pollution. Covers air pollution, marine and freshwater pollution, sewage and wastewater treatment, waste management, toxicology and health, noise pollution, radiation, land pollution, and environmental policies, programs, legislation, and education. Also available online.

Science Citation Index. Institute for Scientific Information, 3501 Market St., Philadelphia, Pennsylvania 19104. 1961-.

BIBLIOGRAPHIES

Bibliography and Index of Geology. American Geological Institute, 4220 King St., Alexandria, Virginia 22302. Monthly. Includes environmental geology and hydrogeology.

Current Contents. Agriculture, Biology and Environmental Sciences. Institute for Scientific Information, 3501 Market St., Philadelphia, Pennsylvania 19104. (800) 523-

1857. 1973-. Previous title: Current Contents. Agricultural, Food & Veterinary Sciences. Gives the table of contents of periodicals in the fields of agriculture, biology, environmental and related areas.

EPA Publications Bibliography. U.S. Environmental Protection Agency, Library Systems Branch, 401 M St., SW, Washington, District of Columbia 20460. (202) 260-2090. Quarterly.

ENCYCLOPEDIAS AND DICTIONARIES

Cambridge Dictionary of Biology. Peter M. B. Walker. Cambridge University Press, 40 W. 20th St., New York, New York 10011. (212) 924-3900 or (800) 227-0247. 1989. Includes 10,000 terms in zoology, botany, biochemistry, molecular biology and genetics. Previously published under the title Chambers Biology Dictionary.

Cambridge Encyclopedia of Life Sciences. A. E. Friday and David S. Ingram. Cambridge University Press, 40 W 20th St., New York, New York 10011. (212) 924-3900 or (800) 227-0247. 1985. Includes all topics under biology and ecology.

A Concise Dictionary of Biology. Elizabeth Martin, ed. Oxford University Press, 200 Madison Ave., New York, New York 10016. (212) 679-7300 or (800) 334-4249. 1990. New edition. Derived from the Concise Science Dictionary, published in 1984.

Encyclopedia of Human Biology. Renato Dulbecco, ed. Academic Press, c/o Harcourt Brace Jovanovich Inc., 6277 Sea Harbor Dr., Orlando, Florida 32887. (800) 346-8648. 1991. Eight volumes.

The Encyclopedia of Soil Science. Rhodes W. Fairbridge. Academic Press, c/o Harcourt Brace Jovanovich Inc., 6277 Sea Harbor Dr., Orlando, Florida 32887. (800) 346-8648. 1979-. Includes soil physics, soil chemistry, soil biology, soil fertility and plant nutrition, soil genesis, classification and cartography.

Life Sciences on File. Diagram Group. Facts on File, Inc., 460 Park Ave. S., New York, New York 10016. (212) 683-2244. 1986. Encyclopedia of pictorial collection in life sciences. Deals with all major topics in life sciences including ecology.

McGraw-Hill Encyclopedia of Environmental Science. Sybil P. Parker. McGraw-Hill Science & Engineering Books, 11 W. 19th St., New York, New York 10011. (212) 337-6010. 1980. Covers ecology, man's influence on nature, and environmental protection.

Van Nostrand's Scientific Encyclopedia. Glenn D. Considine, ed. Van Nostrand Reinhold, 115 5th Ave., New York, New York 10003. (212) 254-3232. 1983. Sixth edition. Includes all broad subject areas in science.

GENERAL WORKS

The Biology of Respiration. Christopher Bryant. E. Arnold, 41 Bedford Sq., London, England 1980. Studies in biology relating to tissue respiration.

Control of Respiration. D. J. Pallot. Oxford University Press, 200 Madison Ave., New York, New York 10016. (212) 679-7300. 1983. Peripheral arterial and central chemoreceptors, lung and airway receptors and tissue oxygen transport in health and disease.

Environmental and Metabolic Animal Physiology. C. Ladd Prosser, ed. John Wiley & Sons, Inc., Wiley-Liss

Division, 605 3rd Ave., New York, New York 10158-0012. (212) 850-6000. 1991. 4th ed. Focuses on the various aspects of adaptive physiology, including environmental, biochemical, and regulatory topics. Examines the theory of adaptation, water and ions, temperature and hydrostatic pressure, nutrition, digestion, nitrogen metabolism, and energy transfer, respiration, O2 and CO2 transport and circulation.

Magill's Survey of Science. Earth Science Series. Frank N. Magill. Salem Press, PO Box 50062, Pasadena, California 91105. 1990-. Five volumes. Includes information on earth's crust, hot spots and volcanic island chains, physical properties of minerals, rock magnetism, physical properties of rocks, and index.

Magill's Survey of Science. Life Science Series. Frank N. Magill, ed. Salem Press, PO Box 50062, Pasadena, California 91105. 1991. Six volumes. Contents: v.1. A-Central and peripheral nervous system functions; v.2. Central metabolism regulation - eukaryotic transcriptional control; v.3. Positive and negative eukaryotic transcriptional control - mammalian hormones; v.4. Hormones and behavior - muscular contraction; v.5. Muscular contraction and relaxation - sexual reproduction in plants; v.6. Reproductive behavior and mating - X inactivation and the Lyon hypothesis.

HANDBOOKS AND MANUALS

Respiratory Protection: A Manual and Guideline. American Industrial Hygiene Association, 345 White Pond Dr., PO Box 8390, Akron, Ohio 44320. (216) 873-2442. 1991. 2d ed. Provides practical guidelines for establishing and managing respiratory protection programs. Presents guidelines for establishing chemical cartridge field service life policies and audit criteria for evaluating respiratory protection programs. Contains validated qualitative life-testing protocols, new equipment for quantitative respiratory protection, and information on use and testing of supplied-air suits.

ONLINE DATA BASES

BIOSIS Previews. BIOSIS, 2100 Arch St., Philadelphia, Pennsylvania 19103-1399. (215) 587-4800. Largest and most comprehensive database of research in the life sciences. Contains citations for nearly 9000 primary research journals, monographs, reviews, symposia, preliminary reports, semi-popular journals, selected institutional reports, government reports and research communications.

Chemical Engineering and Biotechnology Abstracts–CEBA. Orbit Search Service, Maxwell Online Inc., 8000 W. Park Dr., McLean, Virginia 22102. (703) 442-0900 or (800) 456-7248. Monthly. Covers theoretical, practical and commercial material on all aspects of processing safety, and the environment. Also covers process and reaction engineering, measurement and process control, environmental protection and safety, plant design and equipment used in chemical engineering and biotechnology. More than 400 of the world's major primary chemical and process engineering journals are scanned to compile the database. Available from ORBIT.

Enviro/Energyline Abstracts Plus. R. R. Bowker Co., 121 Chanlon Rd., New Providence, New Jersey 07974. (908) 464-6800.

Environmental Periodicals Bibliography. National Information Services Corp., Ste. 6, Wyman Towers, 3100 St.

Paul St., Baltimore, Maryland 21218. (410)243-0797. Online version of abstract of same name.

SCISEARCH. Institute for Scientific Information, University City Science Center, 3501 Market St., Philadelphia, Pennsylvania 19104. (215) 386-0100.

PERIODICALS AND NEWSLETTERS

Journal of Applied Physiology. American Physiology Society, 9650 Rockville Pike, Bethesda, Maryland 20814-3991. Monthly. Covers physiological aspects of exercise, adaption, respiration, and exertion.

TRADE ASSOCIATIONS AND PROFESSIONAL SOCIETIES

American Institute of Biological Sciences. 730 11th St., N.W., Washington, District of Columbia 20001-4521. (202) 628-1500.

RESPIRATORY DISORDERS
See: AIR POLLUTION

REUSE
See: RECYCLING

REUTILIZATION
See: RECYCLING

REVEGETATION

ABSTRACTING AND INDEXING SERVICES

Applied Ecology Abstracts Studies in Renewable Natural Resources. Information Retrieval Ltd., 1911 Jefferson Davis Highway, Arlington, Virginia 22202. 1975-. Monthly.

Biological and Agricultural Index. H.W. Wilson Co., 950 University Ave., Bronx, New York 10452. (800) 367-6770. 1916-. Monthly.

Environment Abstracts. Bowker A & I Publishing, 121 Chanlon Rd., New Providence, New Jersey 07974. (908) 464-6800. 1974-.

Environment Index. Environment Information Center, Index Research Department, 124 E. 39th St., New York, New York 10016. 1971-. Annual.

Environmental Information Connection–EIC. Planning Information Program, Dept. of Urban and Regional Planning, University of Illinois, 1003 West Nevada, Urbana, Illinois 61801. (217) 333-1369. Also available online.

Environmental Periodicals Bibliography. Environmental Studies Institute, International Academy at Santa Barbara, 800 Garden St., Suite D, Santa Barbara, California 93101. (805) 965-5010. Also available online.

Multimedia Index to Ecology. National Information Center for Educational Media, University of Southern California, Los Angeles, California 90007.

Science Citation Index. Institute for Scientific Information, 3501 Market St., Philadelphia, Pennsylvania 19104. 1961-.

BIBLIOGRAPHIES

EPA Publications Bibliography. U.S. Environmental Protection Agency, Library Systems Branch, 401 M St., SW, Washington, District of Columbia 20460. (202) 260-2090. Quarterly.

Literature on the Revegetation of Coal-Mined Lands. David L. Veith. U.S. Department of the Interior, Bureau of Mines, Cochrans Mill Rd., 15236. (412) 892-6400. 1985.

ENCYCLOPEDIAS AND DICTIONARIES

Van Nostrand's Scientific Encyclopedia. Glenn D. Considine, ed. Van Nostrand Reinhold, 115 5th Ave., New York, New York 10003. (212) 254-3232. 1983. Sixth edition. Includes all broad subject areas in science.

GENERAL WORKS

Biodegradable Containers for Use in Revegetation of Highway Right-of-Way. Russell N. Rosenthal. Washington State Department of Transportation, PO Box 47300, Olympia, Washington 98504-7300. (206) 705-7000. 1981. Roadside flora and roadside improvement.

ONLINE DATA BASES

Cambridge Scientific Abstracts Life Science–CSAL. Cambridge Scientific Abstracts, 5161 River Rd., Bethesda, Maryland 20816. (301) 961-6750. Provides access to the following abstracting services: "Life Sciences Collection," "Aquatic Sciences and Fisheries Abstracts," "Oceanic Abstracts," and "Pollution Abstracts."

Enviro/Energyline Abstracts Plus. R. R. Bowker Co., 121 Chanlon Rd., New Providence, New Jersey 07974. (908) 464-6800.

Environmental Periodicals Bibliography. National Information Services Corp., Ste. 6, Wyman Towers, 3100 St. Paul St., Baltimore, Maryland 21218. (410)243-0797. Online version of abstract of same name.

SCISEARCH. Institute for Scientific Information, University City Science Center, 3501 Market St., Philadelphia, Pennsylvania 19104. (215) 386-0100.

PERIODICALS AND NEWSLETTERS

Reclamation & Revegetation Research. Elsevier, Box 211, Amsterdam, Netherlands 1000 AE. 020-5803-911. Quarterly.

TRADE ASSOCIATIONS AND PROFESSIONAL SOCIETIES

American Institute of Biological Sciences. 730 11th St., N.W., Washington, District of Columbia 20001-4521. (202) 628-1500.

REVERSE CHROMATOGRAPHY
See: CHROMATOGRAPHY

REVERSE OSMOSIS
See: OSMOSIS

REVETMENTS
See: EROSION

RHODE ISLAND ENVIRONMENTAL AGENCIES

GOVERNMENTAL ORGANIZATIONS

Department of Environmental Management: Air Quality. Chief, Air and Hazardous Materials Division, 75 Davis St., Providence, Rhode Island 02908. (401) 277-2808.

Department of Environmental Management: Coastal Zone Management. Chairman, Coastal Resources Management Council, 9 Hayes St., Providence, Rhode Island 02903. (401) 277-2476.

Department of Environmental Management: Emergency Preparedness and Community Right-to-Know. 291 Promenade St., Providence, Rhode Island 02908. (401) 277-2808.

Department of Environmental Management: Environmental Protection. Director, 9 Hayes St., Providence, Rhode Island 02908-5003. (401) 277-2771.

Department of Environmental Management: Fish and Wildlife. Chief, Fish and Wildlife Division, Washington County Government Center, South Kingstown, Rhode Island 02903. (401) 789-3094.

Department of Environmental Management: Hazardous Waste Management. Chief, Air and Hazardous Materials Division, 75 Davis St., Providence, Rhode Island 02908. (401) 277-2808.

Department of Environmental Management: Natural Resources. Director, 9 Hayes St., Providence, Rhode Island 02908. (401) 277-2771.

Department of Environmental Management: Pesticide Registration. Chief, Division of Agriculture, 22 Hayes St., Providence, Rhode Island 02908. (401) 277-2782.

Department of Environmental Management: Solid Waste Management. Executive Director, Solid Waste Management Corporation, 75 Davis St., Providence, Rhode Island 02908. (401) 277-2808.

Department of Environmental Management: Waste Minimization and Pollution Prevention. Chief, Office of Environmental Coordination, Ocean State Cleanup and Recycling Program and Hazardous Waste Reduction Program, 9 Hayes St., Providence, Rhode Island 02908-5003. (401) 277-3434.

Department of Labor: Occupational Safety. Administrator, Occupational Safety and Health, 220 Elmwood Ave., Providence, Rhode Island 02907. (401) 457-1800.

RHODE ISLAND ENVIRONMENTAL LEGISLATION

GENERAL WORKS

Rhode Island Environmental Law Handbook. Government Institutes, Inc., 4 Research Pl., Ste. 200, Rockville, Maryland 20820. (301) 921-2300. 1991.

RINGLEMANN CHART

See: EMISSIONS

RIPARIAN ECOLOGY

ABSTRACTING AND INDEXING SERVICES

Applied Ecology Abstracts Studies in Renewable Natural Resources. Information Retrieval Ltd., 1911 Jefferson Davis Highway, Arlington, Virginia 22202. 1975-. Monthly.

Biological and Agricultural Index. H.W. Wilson Co., 950 University Ave., Bronx, New York 10452. (800) 367-6770. 1916-. Monthly.

Ecology Abstracts. Cambridge Scientific Abstracts, 5161 River Rd., Bethesda, Maryland 20816. (301) 961-6750. Monthly.

Environment Abstracts. Bowker A & I Publishing, 121 Chanlon Rd., New Providence, New Jersey 07974. (908) 464-6800. 1974-.

Environment Index. Environment Information Center, Index Research Department, 124 E. 39th St., New York, New York 10016. 1971-. Annual.

Environmental Information Connection–EIC. Planning Information Program, Dept. of Urban and Regional Planning, University of Illinois, 1003 West Nevada, Urbana, Illinois 61801. (217) 333-1369. Also available online.

Environmental Periodicals Bibliography. Environmental Studies Institute, International Academy at Santa Barbara, 800 Garden St., Suite D, Santa Barbara, California 93101. (805) 965-5010. Also available online.

General Science Index. H. W. Wilson Co., 950 University Ave., Bronx, New York 10452. 1978-. Monthly, also issued in annual cumulation. Cumulative subject index to English language periodicals in the subject fields of astronomy, botany, chemistry, earth science, environment and conservation, food and nutrition, genetics, mathematics, medicine and health, microbiology, oceanography, physics, physiology and zoology.

Multimedia Index to Ecology. National Information Center for Educational Media, University of Southern California, Los Angeles, California 90007.

BIBLIOGRAPHIES

EPA Publications Bibliography. U.S. Environmental Protection Agency, Library Systems Branch, 401 M St., SW, Washington, District of Columbia 20460. (202) 260-2090. Quarterly.

ENCYCLOPEDIAS AND DICTIONARIES

Cambridge Encyclopedia of Life Sciences. A. E. Friday and David S. Ingram. Cambridge University Press, 40 W 20th St., New York, New York 10011. (212) 924-3900 or (800) 227-0247. 1985. Includes all topics under biology and ecology.

The Encyclopedia of Animal Ecology. Peter D. Moore. Facts on File, Inc., 460 Park Ave. S., New York, New York 10016. (212) 683-2244. 1987.

Grzimek's Encyclopedia of Ecology. Bernhard Grzimek. Van Nostrand Reinhold, 115 5th Ave., New York, New York 10003. (212) 254-3232. 1976.

McGraw-Hill Encyclopedia of Environmental Science. Sybil P. Parker. McGraw-Hill Science & Engineering Books, 11 W. 19th St., New York, New York 10011. (212) 337-6010. 1980. Covers ecology, man's influence on nature, and environmental protection.

North American Reference Encyclopedia of Ecology and Pollution. William White. North American Pub. Co., 401 N. Broad St., Philadelphia, Pennsylvania 19108. (215) 238-5300. 1972.

Van Nostrand's Scientific Encyclopedia. Glenn D. Considine, ed. Van Nostrand Reinhold, 115 5th Ave., New York, New York 10003. (212) 254-3232. 1983. Sixth edition. Includes all broad subject areas in science.

ONLINE DATA BASES

Enviro/Energyline Abstracts Plus. R. R. Bowker Co., 121 Chanlon Rd., New Providence, New Jersey 07974. (908) 464-6800.

Environmental Periodicals Bibliography. National Information Services Corp., Ste. 6, Wyman Towers, 3100 St. Paul St., Baltimore, Maryland 21218. (410)243-0797. Online version of abstract of same name.

SCISEARCH. Institute for Scientific Information, University City Science Center, 3501 Market St., Philadelphia, Pennsylvania 19104. (215) 386-0100.

RIPRAP

See: EROSION

RISK ANALYSIS

ABSTRACTING AND INDEXING SERVICES

ASFA Aquaculture Abstracts. Cambridge Scientific Abstracts, Inc., 5161 River Rd., Bethesda, Maryland 20816. (301) 961-6750. 1984.

Ecology Abstracts. Cambridge Scientific Abstracts, 5161 River Rd., Bethesda, Maryland 20816. (301) 961-6750. Monthly.

Environment Abstracts. Bowker A & I Publishing, 121 Chanlon Rd., New Providence, New Jersey 07974. (908) 464-6800. 1974-.

Environment Index. Environment Information Center, Index Research Department, 124 E. 39th St., New York, New York 10016. 1971-. Annual.

Environmental Information Connection–EIC. Planning Information Program, Dept. of Urban and Regional Planning, University of Illinois, 1003 West Nevada, Urbana, Illinois 61801. (217) 333-1369. Also available online.

Environmental Periodicals Bibliography. Environmental Studies Institute, International Academy at Santa Barbara, 800 Garden St., Suite D, Santa Barbara, California 93101. (805) 965-5010. Also available online.

General Science Index. H. W. Wilson Co., 950 University Ave., Bronx, New York 10452. 1978-. Monthly, also issued in annual cumulation. Cumulative subject index to English language periodicals in the subject fields of astronomy, botany, chemistry, earth science, environment and conservation, food and nutrition, genetics, mathematics, medicine and health, microbiology, oceanography, physics, physiology and zoology.

Science Citation Index. Institute for Scientific Information, 3501 Market St., Philadelphia, Pennsylvania 19104. 1961-.

BIBLIOGRAPHIES

EPA Publications Bibliography. U.S. Environmental Protection Agency, Library Systems Branch, 401 M St., SW, Washington, District of Columbia 20460. (202) 260-2090. Quarterly.

DIRECTORIES

Best's Safety Directory. Ambest Rd., Oldwick, New Jersey 08858. (201) 439-2200. Annual.

CCPS/AIChE Directory of Chemical Process Safety Services. American Institute of Chemical Engineers, 345 E. 47th St., New York, New York 10017. (212) 705-7338. 1991. Lists providers of various chemical process safety services. It is compiled from questionnaires returned by the service providers. Company profiles are included.

Risk Assessment Guidelines and Information Directory. Government Institutes, Inc., 4 Research Pl., Ste. 200, Rockville, Maryland 20850. (301) 921-2300. Contains both EPA guidance on the conduct of EPA risk assessments, as well as information on EPA and non-EPA databases, environmental and dose response models, manuals, directories, and periodicals applicable to each element of risk assessment.

ENCYCLOPEDIAS AND DICTIONARIES

McGraw-Hill Encyclopedia of Environmental Science. Sybil P. Parker. McGraw-Hill Science & Engineering Books, 11 W. 19th St., New York, New York 10011. (212) 337-6010. 1980. Covers ecology, man's influence on nature, and environmental protection.

North American Reference Encyclopedia of Ecology and Pollution. William White. North American Pub. Co., 401 N. Broad St., Philadelphia, Pennsylvania 19108. (215) 238-5300. 1972.

Van Nostrand's Scientific Encyclopedia. Glenn D. Considine, ed. Van Nostrand Reinhold, 115 5th Ave., New York, New York 10003. (212) 254-3232. 1983. Sixth edition. Includes all broad subject areas in science.

GENERAL WORKS

Acceptable Risk?: Making Decisions in a Toxic Environment. Lee Clarke. University of California Press, 2120 Berkeley Way, Berkeley, California 94720. (415) 642-4247 (800) 822-6657. 1991. 1991

Air Toxics and Risk Assessment. Edward J. Calabrese and Elaina M. Kenyon. Lewis Publishers, 200 Corporate Blvd. NW, Boca Raton, Florida 33431. (407) 994-0555 or (800)272-7737. 1991. Does risk assessments for more than 110 chemicals that are confirmed or probable air toxics. All chemicals are analyzed with a scientifically sound methodology to assess public health risks.

Altering the Earth's Chemistry: Assessing the Risks. Sandra Postel. Worldwatch Institute, 1776 Massachusetts Avenue, N.W., Washington, District of Columbia 20036-1904. 1986.

Assessing Ecological Risks of Biotechnology. Lev R. Ginzburg. Butterworth-Heinemann, 80 Montvale Ave., Stoneham, Massachusetts 02180. (617) 438-8464; (800) 366-2665. 1991. Presents an analysis of the ecological risk associated with genetically engineered microorganisms, organisms that, through gene splicing, have obtained additional genetic information.

Contingency Planning for Industrial Emergencies. Piero Armenante. Global Professional Publications, 2805 McGraw Ave., PO Box 19539, Irvine, California 92713-9539. (800) 854-7179. 1991. Addresses the potential environmental and human risks from large chemical industrial accidents, as well as emergency medical planning and long-term environmental monitoring following such an occurrence.

Evaluation of Environmental Data for Regulatory and Impact Assessment. S. Ramamoorthy and E. Baddaloo. Elsevier Science Publishing Co., 655 Avenue of the Americas, New York, New York 10010. (212) 984-5800. 1991.

Hazard Assessment and Control Technology in Semiconductor Manufacturing. The American Conference of Governmental Industrial Hygienists. Lewis Publishers, 2000 Corporate Blvd., N.W., Boca Raton, Florida 33431. (407) 994-0555 or (800) 272-7737. 1989. Covers health studies, hazard control technology of manufacturing processes, catastrophic releases, and emerging technologies.

Hazard Assessment of Chemicals. Academic Press, c/o Harcourt Brace Jovanovich Inc., 6277 Sea Harbor Dr., Orlando, Florida 32887. (800) 346-8648. 1981-. Annually. Presents comprehensive authoritative reviews of new and significant developments in the area of hazard assessment of chemicals or chemical classes.

Hazardous and Industrial Wastes, 1990. Joseph P. Martin, et al., eds. Technomic Publishing Co., 851 Holland Ave., Box 3535, Lancaster, Pennsylvania 17604. (717) 291-5609. 1990. Proceedings of the 22nd Mid-Atlantic Industrial Waste Conference, June 24-27, 1990, Drexel University, Philadelphia, PA. Fifty-one new reports on developments in industrial and hazardouswaste management, technology and regulation were presented.

Innovation and Environmental Risk. Lewis Roberts and Albert Wheale. Belhaven Press, 136 S. Broadway, Irvington, New York 10533. (914) 591-9111. 1991. Debates public policies and scientific issues concerning environmental problems. Stresses energy, radiological protection, biotechnology and the role of the media.

Methods for Assessing Exposure of Human and Non-Human Biota. R. G. Tardiff and B. D. Goldstein, eds. John Wiley & Sons, Inc., 605 3rd Ave., New York, New York 10158-0012. (212) 850-6000. 1991. Provides a critical and collective evaluation of approaches to chemical exposure assessment.

Monitoring Human Tissues for Toxic Substances. National Academy Press, 2101 Constitution Ave. N.W., PO Box 285, Washington, District of Columbia 20418. (202) 334-3313. 1991. Evaluates the National Human Monitoring Program.

Pesticide Residues and Food Safety: A Harvest of Viewpoints. B. G. Tweedy, et al., eds. American Chemical Society, 1155 16th St. N.W., Washington, District of Columbia 20036. (202) 872-4600; (800) 227-5558. 1991. Discusses all the issues raised in connection with the use of pesticides in the United States. Some of the issues are the economic and social aspects, impact assessment programs, food safety, consumer attitude, pesticide free fruit crops, integrated pest management, EPA's program for validation of pesticides, and other related matters.

Petroleum Contaminated Soils: Remediation Techniques, Environmental Fate and Risk Assessment. Paul T. Kostecki and Edward J. Calabrese. Lewis Publishers, 200 Corporate Blvd. NW, Boca Raton, Florida 33431. (407) 994-0555 or (800)272-7737. 1991. Three volumes. Provides valuable information to determine feasible solutions to petroleum contaminated soils.

Predicting Nuclear and Other Technological Disasters. Christopher Lampton. F. Watts, 387 Park Ave. S., New York, New York 10016. (800) 672-6672. 1989. Discusses risks involved in state-of-the-art technology.

Radiation Exposure and Occupational Risks. G. Keller, et al. Springer-Verlag, 175 5th Ave., New York, New York 10010. (212) 460-1500; (800) 777-4643. 1990. Discusses radiation exposure injuries in the workplace and prevention.

Risk Assessment for Hazardous Installations. J. C. Chicken. Pergamon Microforms International, Inc., Fairview Park, Elmsford, New York 10523. (914) 592-7720. 1986.

Site-Specific Risk Assessments. Frank A. Jones. Lewis Publishers, 2000 Corporate Blvd., N.W., Boca Raton, Florida 33431. (407) 994-0555 or (800) 272-7737. 1991. Describes site characterization, hazard characterization, exposure characterization, risk characterization, uncertainties and case studies.

Society of Risk Analysis. Plenum Press, 233 Spring St., New York, New York 10013-1578. (212) 620-8000; (800) 221-9369. 1990. Proceedings of the Annual Meeting of the Society for Risk Analysis, held November 9-12, 1986, in Boston, MA.

GOVERNMENTAL ORGANIZATIONS

U.S. Environmental Protection Agency: Assistant Administrator for Research and Development. 401 M St., S.W., Washington, District of Columbia 20460. (202) 382-7676.

U.S. Environmental Protection Agency: National Enforcement Investigations Center. Building 53, Box 25227, Denver, Colorado 80225. (303) 236-5100.

HANDBOOKS AND MANUALS

NIOSH Pocket Guide to Chemical Hazards. National Institute for Occupational Safety and Health, 1600 Clifton Rd. NE, Atlanta, Georgia 30333. (404) 639-3286. 1990. Presents sources of general industrial hygiene and medical surveillance information for workers, employees and others. Presents key information and data in an abbreviated format for 398 individual chemicals or chemical types.

ONLINE DATA BASES

Enviro/Energyline Abstracts Plus. R. R. Bowker Co., 121 Chanlon Rd., New Providence, New Jersey 07974. (908) 464-6800.

Environmental Periodicals Bibliography. National Information Services Corp., Ste. 6, Wyman Towers, 3100 St. Paul St., Baltimore, Maryland 21218. (410)243-0797. Online version of abstract of same name.

Integrated Risk Information System - IRIS. US Environomental Protection Agency. Toxicology Data Network (TOXNET), 8600 Rockville Pike, Bethesda, Maryland 20894. (301) 496-1131. Quarterly. Effects of chemicals on human health and information on reference doses and carcinogen assessments.

RISKLINE. Swedish National Chemicals Inspectorate, P.O. Box 1384, Solna, Sweden 171 27. 46 (8) 7305700.

PERIODICALS AND NEWSLETTERS

Fundamentals & Applied Toxicology. Academic Press, c/o Marcourt Brace, PO Box 6250, 6277 Sea Harbor Dr., Orlando, Florida 32887. (218) 723-9828. 8/year. Covers risk assessment and safety studies of toxic agents.

International Journal of Environment and Pollution. Inderscience Enterprises Ltd., World Trade Center Bldg., 110 Avenue Louis Casai, Case Postale 306, Geneva-Airport, Switzerland CH-1215. (44) 908-314248. 1991-. Publishes original state-of-the-art articles, book reviews, and technical papers in the areas of: Environmental policies, protection, institutional aspects of pollution, risk assessments of all forms of pollution, protection of soil and ground water, waste disposal strategies, ecological impact of pollutants and other related topics.

RESEARCH CENTERS AND INSTITUTES

Center for Technology, Environment, and Development. Clark University, 16 Claremont St., Worcester, Massachusetts 01610. (508) 751-4606.

TRADE ASSOCIATIONS AND PROFESSIONAL SOCIETIES

Academy of Hazard Control Management. 5010A Nicholson Ln., Rockville, Maryland 20852. (301) 984-8969.

American Society for Healthcare Risk Management. American Hospital Association, 840 N. Lake Shore Dr., Chicago, Illinois 60611. (312) 280-6425.

Board of Certified Hazard Control Management. 8009 Carita Ct., Bethesda, Maryland 20817. (301) 984-8969.

Center for Environmental Management. Tufts University, Curtis Hall, 474 Boston Ave., Medford, Massachusetts 02155. (617) 381-3486.

National Association of Environmental Risk Auditors. 4211 East Third St., Bloomington, Indiana 47401. (812) 333-0077.

National Safety Council. 444 N. Michigan Ave., Chicago, Illinois 60611. (312) 527-4800.

Pollution Liability Insurance Association. 1333 Butterfield Rd., Suite 100, Downers Grove, Illinois 60515. (312) 969-5300.

RIVERS

See also: ESTUARIES; WATER POLLUTION

ABSTRACTING AND INDEXING SERVICES

Abstracts of Air and Water Conservation Literature. American Petroleum Institute. Central Abstracting and Indexing Service, 275 Madison Avenue, New York, New York 10016. 1972.

Aqualine Abstracts. Water Research Centre. c/o Pergamon Microforms International, Inc., Fairview Park, Elmsford, New York 10523. (914) 592-7720. 1927-. Contains some 8,000 records annually on water and wastewater technology. Covers all aspects of water, wastewater, associated engineering services and the aquatic environment. Over 600 periodicals, as well as books, reports and conference proceedings and other publications from water related institutions worldwide are scanned. Also available online.

Biological and Agricultural Index. H.W. Wilson Co., 950 University Ave., Bronx, New York 10452. (800) 367-6770. 1916-. Monthly.

Civil Engineering Hydraulic Abstracts. BHRA Fluid Engineering, Air Science Co., PO Box 143, Corning, New York 14830. (607) 962-5591. Monthly. Abstracts of periodicals that publish in the areas of hydraulic engineering and other related topics.

Ecological Abstracts. Geo Abstracts Ltd. Elsevier Applied Science, Crown House, Linton Rd., Barking, England IG 11 8JU. 1974-. Derived from over 600 leading ecological and environmental journals, plus books, conference proceedings, reports and theses.

Ecology Abstracts. Cambridge Scientific Abstracts, 5161 River Rd., Bethesda, Maryland 20816. (301) 961-6750. Monthly.

Environment Abstracts. Bowker A & I Publishing, 121 Chanlon Rd., New Providence, New Jersey 07974. (908) 464-6800. 1974-.

Environment Index. Environment Information Center, Index Research Department, 124 E. 39th St., New York, New York 10016. 1971-. Annual.

Environmental Information Connection–EIC. Planning Information Program, Dept. of Urban and Regional Planning, University of Illinois, 1003 West Nevada, Urbana, Illinois 61801. (217) 333-1369. Also available online.

Environmental Periodicals Bibliography. Environmental Studies Institute, International Academy at Santa Barbara, 800 Garden St., Suite D, Santa Barbara, California 93101. (805) 965-5010. Also available online.

General Science Index. H. W. Wilson Co., 950 University Ave., Bronx, New York 10452. 1978-. Monthly, also issued in annual cumulation. Cumulative subject index to English language periodicals in the subject fields of astronomy, botany, chemistry, earth science, environment and conservation, food and nutrition, genetics, mathematics, medicine and health, microbiology, oceanography, physics, physiology and zoology.

Science Citation Index. Institute for Scientific Information, 3501 Market St., Philadelphia, Pennsylvania 19104. 1961-.

BIBLIOGRAPHIES

Bibliography and Index of Geology. American Geological Institute, 4220 King St., Alexandria, Virginia 22302. Monthly. Includes environmental geology and hydrogeology.

Current Contents. Agriculture, Biology and Environmental Sciences. Institute for Scientific Information, 3501 Market St., Philadelphia, Pennsylvania 19104. (800) 523-1857. 1973-. Previous title: Current Contents. Agricultural, Food & Veterinary Sciences. Gives the table of contents of periodicals in the fields of agriculture, biology, environmental and related areas.

EPA Publications Bibliography. U.S. Environmental Protection Agency, Library Systems Branch, 401 M St., SW, Washington, District of Columbia 20460. (202) 260-2090. Quarterly.

DIRECTORIES

River Conservation Directory. National Association for State River Conservation Programs, 801 Pennsylvania Ave., SE, Suite 302, Washington, District of Columbia 20003. (202) 543-2862. Biennial.

ENCYCLOPEDIAS AND DICTIONARIES

Cambridge Encyclopedia of Life Sciences. A. E. Friday and David S. Ingram. Cambridge University Press, 40 W 20th St., New York, New York 10011. (212) 924-3900 or (800) 227-0247. 1985. Includes all topics under biology and ecology.

McGraw-Hill Encyclopedia of Environmental Science. Sybil P. Parker. McGraw-Hill Science & Engineering Books, 11 W. 19th St., New York, New York 10011. (212) 337-6010. 1980. Covers ecology, man's influence on nature, and environmental protection.

Van Nostrand's Scientific Encyclopedia. Glenn D. Considine, ed. Van Nostrand Reinhold, 115 5th Ave., New York, New York 10003. (212) 254-3232. 1983. Sixth edition. Includes all broad subject areas in science.

The Water Encyclopedia. Lewis Publishers, 2000 Corporate Blvd. N.W., Boca Raton, Florida 33431. (800) 272-7737. 1990. 2d ed. Includes groundwater contamination, drinking water, floods, waterborne diseases, global warming, climate change, irrigation, water agencies and organizations, precipitation, oceans and seas, and river, lakes and waterfalls.

GENERAL WORKS

Alternatives in Regulated River Management. J. A. Gore and G. E. Petts, eds. CRC Press, 2000 Corporate Blvd. N.W., Boca Raton, Florida 33431. (800) 272-7737. 1989.

Provides an alternative to the emphasis on ecological effects of river regulation and is a source of alternatives for managerial decision making.

The American Rivers Outstanding Rivers List. Matthew H. Huntington. American Rivers, Inc., 801 Pennsylvania Ave. S.E., Suite 303, Washington, District of Columbia 20003. (202) 547-6900. 1991. 2d ed. A compilation of rivers across the United States which possess outstanding ecological, recreational, natural, cultural or scientific value.

Magill's Survey of Science. Earth Science Series. Frank N. Magill. Salem Press, PO Box 50062, Pasadena, California 91105. 1990-. Five volumes. Includes information on earth's crust, hot spots and volcanic island chains, physical properties of minerals, rock magnetism, physical properties of rocks, and index.

Protection of River Basins, Lakes, and Estuaries. Robert C. Ryans. American Fisheries Society, 5410 Grosvenor Lane, Bethesda, Maryland 20814. (301) 897-8616. 1988. Fifteen years of cooperation toward solving environmental problems in the USSR and USA.

River Pollution: An Ecological Perspective. S. M. Haslam. Belhaven Press, 136 S. Broadway, Irvington, New York 10533. (914) 591-9111. 1990. Describes the impact of natural and man-made pollution in the ecosystem of freshwater streams, stressing understanding of processes and techniques of measurement.

Rivers at Risk: The Concerned Citizen's Guide to Hydropower. John D. Echeverria. Island Press, 1718 Connecticut Ave., NW, Suite 300, Washington, District of Columbia 20009. (202) 232-7933. 1989. Offers practical understanding of how to influence government decisions about hydropower development on the nation's rivers.

Rivers, Ponds, and Lakes. Anita Ganeri. Dillon Press, Inc., 242 Portland Ave., S., Minneapolis, Minnesota 55415. (612) 333-2691. 1992. A guide to pond, river, and lake pollution globally and conservation of indigenous endangered species.

The Surface Water Acidification Programme. B. J. Mason, ed. Cambridge University Press, 40 W. 20th St., New York, New York 10011. (212) 924-3900; (800) 227-0247. 1991. Proceedings of the final Conference of the Surface Water Acidification Programme, held at the Royal Society in March 1990. Deals with the acid pollution of rivers and lakes and presents research results on watersheds in Great Britain and Scandinavia.

Water. Hans Silvester. Thomasson-Grant, 1 Morton Dr., Suite 500, Charlottesville, Virginia 22901. (804) 977-1780. 1990. Details the dangers posed by the industrial society to the flow of clean water

GOVERNMENTAL ORGANIZATIONS

Delaware River Basin Commission. 1100 L St., N.W., Room 5113, Washington, District of Columbia 20240. (202) 343-5761.

Public Affairs Office: U.S. Army Corps of Engineers. Room 8137, 20 Massachusetts Ave., N.W., Washington, District of Columbia 20314. (202) 272-0010.

Susquehanna River Basin Commission. Department of Interior Building, 1100 L St., N.W., Room 5113, Washington, District of Columbia 20240. (202) 343-4091.

ONLINE DATA BASES

Cambridge Scientific Abstracts Life Science–CSAL. Cambridge Scientific Abstracts, 5161 River Rd., Bethesda, Maryland 20816. (301) 961-6750. Provides access to the following abstracting services: "Life Sciences Collection," "Aquatic Sciences and Fisheries Abstracts," "Oceanic Abstracts," and "Pollution Abstracts."

Enviro/Energyline Abstracts Plus. R. R. Bowker Co., 121 Chanlon Rd., New Providence, New Jersey 07974. (908) 464-6800.

Environmental Periodicals Bibliography. National Information Services Corp., Ste. 6, Wyman Towers, 3100 St. Paul St., Baltimore, Maryland 21218. (410)243-0797. Online version of abstract of same name.

FLUIDEX. STI, a subsidiary of BHR Group Limited, Cranfield, Bedfordshire, England MK43 OAJ. 44 (234) 750422.

Great Lakes Water Quality Data Base. U.S. Environmental Protection Agency, Office of Research and Development, Large Lakes Research Station, 401 M St. SW, Washington, District of Columbia 20460. (202) 260-2090. Water data related to the Great Lakes and related tributaries and watersheds.

SCISEARCH. Institute for Scientific Information, University City Science Center, 3501 Market St., Philadelphia, Pennsylvania 19104. (215) 386-0100.

PERIODICALS AND NEWSLETTERS

American Rivers. American Rivers, 801 Pennsylvania Ave. S.E., #303, Washington, District of Columbia 20003. (202) 547-6900. 1970-. Semiannually. Reports on the activities of American Rivers, the nation's principal river-saving organization.

Earth Science. American Geological Institute, 4220 King Street, Alexandria, Virginia 22302. (703) 379-2480. Quarterly. Covers geological issues.

Headwaters. Friends of the River, Bldg. C, Ft. Mason Center, San Francisco, California 94123. (415) 771-0400. Biweekly. River conservation, recreation, and water politics.

World Rivers Review. The Tides Foundation, 1847 Berkeley Way, Berkeley, California 94703. (510) 848-1155. Bimonthly. Topics related to pollution of world's rivers and shores and news and developments covering steps to mitigate the effects of such pollution.

RESEARCH CENTERS AND INSTITUTES

University of Georgia, Institute of Ecology. 103 Ecology Building, Athens, Georgia 30602. (404) 542-2968.

University of Georgia, Savanna River Ecology Laboratory. P.O. Box Drawer E, Aiken, South Carolina 29801. (803) 725-2472.

University of Missouri-Rolla, Institute of River Studies. 111 Civil Engineering, Rolla, Missouri 65401. (314) 341-4476.

University of Wisconsin, River Studies Center. 4032 Cowley Hall, La Crosse, Wisconsin 54601. (608) 785-8232.

STATISTICS SOURCES

Ecology: Community Profiles. U.S. Fish and Wildlife Service. National Technical Information Service, 5285 Port Royal Road, Springfield, Virginia 22161. (703) 487-4650. Irregular. Data on coastal and inland ecosystems, including wetlands, tidal-flats, near-shore seagrasses, sand dunes, drilling platforms, oyster reefs, estuaries, rivers and streams.

World Resources. World Resources Institute. 1709 New York Ave., N.W., Washington, District of Columbia 20006. (202) 638-6300. Annual. Statistical and textual analysis of world's natural resources and the effects of growth-caused environmental pollution.

TRADE ASSOCIATIONS AND PROFESSIONAL SOCIETIES

American Rivers, Inc. 801 Pennsylvania Ave., S.E., Suite 303, Washington, District of Columbia 20003. (202) 547-6900.

Connecticut River Watershed Council, Inc. 125 Combs Rd., Easthampton, Massachusetts 01027. (413) 584-0057.

Friends of the River Foundation. Fort Mason Center, Bldg. C, San Francisco, California 94123. (415) 771-0400.

Inland River Ports & Terminals. 204 E. High St., Jefferson City, Missouri 65101. (314) 634-2028.

International Rivers Network. 301 Broadway, Suite B, San Francisco, California 94133. (415) 986-4694.

National Organization for River Sports. 314 N. 20th St., P.O. Box 6847, Colorado Springs, Colorado 80934. (719) 473-2466.

National Watershed Congress. c/o National Assn. of Conservation Districts, 509 Capital Ct., Washington, District of Columbia 20002. (202) 547-6223.

Susquehanna River Tri-State Association. Stark Learning Center, Rm. 441, Wilkes College, Wilkes-Barre, Pennsylvania 18702. (717) 824-5193.

Upper Mississippi River Conservation Committee. 1830 Second Ave., Rock Island, Illinois 61201. (309) 793-5800.

RODENTICIDES

See: PESTICIDES

RODENTS

ABSTRACTING AND INDEXING SERVICES

Biological Abstracts. BIOSIS, 2100 Arch St., Philadelphia, Pennsylvania 19103-1399. (215) 587-4800. 1927-.

Environment Abstracts. Bowker A & I Publishing, 121 Chanlon Rd., New Providence, New Jersey 07974. (908) 464-6800. 1974-.

Environment Index. Environment Information Center, Index Research Department, 124 E. 39th St., New York, New York 10016. 1971-. Annual.

Environmental Information Connection–EIC. Planning Information Program, Dept. of Urban and Regional Planning, University of Illinois, 1003 West Nevada, Urbana, Illinois 61801. (217) 333-1369. Also available online.

Environmental Periodicals Bibliography. Environmental Studies Institute, International Academy at Santa Barbara, 800 Garden St., Suite D, Santa Barbara, California 93101. (805) 965-5010. Also available online.

General Science Index. H. W. Wilson Co., 950 University Ave., Bronx, New York 10452. 1978-. Monthly, also issued in annual cumulation. Cumulative subject index to English language periodicals in the subject fields of astronomy, botany, chemistry, earth science, environment and conservation, food and nutrition, genetics, mathematics, medicine and health, microbiology, oceanography, physics, physiology and zoology.

Science Citation Index. Institute for Scientific Information, 3501 Market St., Philadelphia, Pennsylvania 19104. 1961-.

BIBLIOGRAPHIES

EPA Publications Bibliography. U.S. Environmental Protection Agency, Library Systems Branch, 401 M St., SW, Washington, District of Columbia 20460. (202) 260-2090. Quarterly.

ENCYCLOPEDIAS AND DICTIONARIES

Van Nostrand's Scientific Encyclopedia. Glenn D. Considine, ed. Van Nostrand Reinhold, 115 5th Ave., New York, New York 10003. (212) 254-3232. 1983. Sixth edition. Includes all broad subject areas in science.

HANDBOOKS AND MANUALS

The Agrochemicals Handbook. H. Kidd and D. Hartlet, eds. Royal Society of Chemistry, c/o CRC Press, 2000 Corporate Blvd., N.W., Boca Raton, Florida 33431-9868. (800) 272-7737. 1991. 3rd ed. Contains comprehensive worldwide information and data on substances which are active components of agriculture chemical products currently used in crop protection and pest control.

Rodent Control in Agriculture. J. H. Greaves. Food and Agriculture Organization of the United Nations, Via delle Terme di Caracalla, Rome, Italy 00100. 61 0181-FA01. 1982. A handbook on the biology and control of commensal rodents as agricultural pests.

The Rodent Handbook. Austin M. Frishman. Frishman, Farmingdale, New York 1974. Questions and answers on rats, mice, and other pest vertebrae.

ONLINE DATA BASES

BIOSIS Previews. BIOSIS, 2100 Arch St., Philadelphia, Pennsylvania 19103-1399. (215) 587-4800. Largest and most comprehensive database of research in the life sciences. Contains citations for nearly 9000 primary research journals, monographs, reviews, symposia, preliminary reports, semi-popular journals, selected institutional reports, government reports and research communications.

Cambridge Scientific Abstracts Life Science–CSAL. Cambridge Scientific Abstracts, 5161 River Rd., Bethesda, Maryland 20816. (301) 961-6750. Provides access to the following abstracting services: "Life Sciences Collection," "Aquatic Sciences and Fisheries Abstracts," "Oceanic Abstracts," and "Pollution Abstracts."

Enviro/Energyline Abstracts Plus. R. R. Bowker Co., 121 Chanlon Rd., New Providence, New Jersey 07974. (908) 464-6800.

Environmental Periodicals Bibliography. National Information Services Corp., Ste. 6, Wyman Towers, 3100 St. Paul St., Baltimore, Maryland 21218. (410)243-0797. Online version of abstract of same name.

SCISEARCH. Institute for Scientific Information, University City Science Center, 3501 Market St., Philadelphia, Pennsylvania 19104. (215) 386-0100.

TRADE ASSOCIATIONS AND PROFESSIONAL SOCIETIES

American Institute of Biological Sciences. 730 11th St., N.W., Washington, District of Columbia 20001-4521. (202) 628-1500.

ROOTS

See also: ABSORPTION; PLANT NUTRITION

ABSTRACTING AND INDEXING SERVICES

Environment Abstracts. Bowker A & I Publishing, 121 Chanlon Rd., New Providence, New Jersey 07974. (908) 464-6800. 1974-.

Environment Index. Environment Information Center, Index Research Department, 124 E. 39th St., New York, New York 10016. 1971-. Annual.

Environmental Information Connection–EIC. Planning Information Program, Dept. of Urban and Regional Planning, University of Illinois, 1003 West Nevada, Urbana, Illinois 61801. (217) 333-1369. Also available online.

Environmental Periodicals Bibliography. Environmental Studies Institute, International Academy at Santa Barbara, 800 Garden St., Suite D, Santa Barbara, California 93101. (805) 965-5010. Also available online.

General Science Index. H. W. Wilson Co., 950 University Ave., Bronx, New York 10452. 1978-. Monthly, also issued in annual cumulation. Cumulative subject index to English language periodicals in the subject fields of astronomy, botany, chemistry, earth science, environment and conservation, food and nutrition, genetics, mathematics, medicine and health, microbiology, oceanography, physics, physiology and zoology.

Science Citation Index. Institute for Scientific Information, 3501 Market St., Philadelphia, Pennsylvania 19104. 1961-.

BIBLIOGRAPHIES

EPA Publications Bibliography. U.S. Environmental Protection Agency, Library Systems Branch, 401 M St., SW, Washington, District of Columbia 20460. (202) 260-2090. Quarterly.

GENERAL WORKS

Modifying the Root Environment to Reduce Crop Stress. G. F. Arkin and H. M. Taylor, eds. American Society of Agricultural Engineers, 2950 Niles Rd., St. Joseph, Michigan 49085-9659. (616) 429-0300. 1981. Emphasizes the development and understanding of relationship between the plant and its subterranean environment and effect of modification of that environment on plant response.

ONLINE DATA BASES

Enviro/Energyline Abstracts Plus. R. R. Bowker Co., 121 Chanlon Rd., New Providence, New Jersey 07974. (908) 464-6800.

Environmental Periodicals Bibliography. National Information Services Corp., Ste. 6, Wyman Towers, 3100 St. Paul St., Baltimore, Maryland 21218. (410)243-0797. Online version of abstract of same name.

TRADE ASSOCIATIONS AND PROFESSIONAL SOCIETIES

American Institute of Biological Sciences. 730 11th St., N.W., Washington, District of Columbia 20001-4521. (202) 628-1500.

ROTARY DRILLING

See: DRILLING

RUBBER

See also: RECYCLING

ABSTRACTING AND INDEXING SERVICES

Applied Science and Technology Index. H.W. Wilson Co., 950 University Ave., Bronx, New York 10452. (800) 367-6770. Formerly Industrial Arts Index.

Environment Abstracts. Bowker A & I Publishing, 121 Chanlon Rd., New Providence, New Jersey 07974. (908) 464-6800. 1974-.

Environment Index. Environment Information Center, Index Research Department, 124 E. 39th St., New York, New York 10016. 1971-. Annual.

Environmental Information Connection–EIC. Planning Information Program, Dept. of Urban and Regional Planning, University of Illinois, 1003 West Nevada, Urbana, Illinois 61801. (217) 333-1369. Also available online.

Environmental Periodicals Bibliography. Environmental Studies Institute, International Academy at Santa Barbara, 800 Garden St., Suite D, Santa Barbara, California 93101. (805) 965-5010. Also available online.

Science Citation Index. Institute for Scientific Information, 3501 Market St., Philadelphia, Pennsylvania 19104. 1961-.

BIBLIOGRAPHIES

EPA Publications Bibliography. U.S. Environmental Protection Agency, Library Systems Branch, 401 M St., SW, Washington, District of Columbia 20460. (202) 260-2090. Quarterly.

DIRECTORIES

Rubber Red Book. Communication Channels, 6255 Barfield Rd., Atlanta, Georgia 30328. (404) 256-9800.

Rubber World Blue Book: Materials, Compounding Ingredients and Machinery for Rubber. Lippincott & Peto, Inc., 1867 W. Market St., Akron, Ohio 44313. (216) 864-2122.

Rubber World–Custom Mixers Directory Issue. Lippencott and Peto, Inc., 1867 W. Market St., Akron, Ohio 44313. (216) 864-2122.

Rubber World–Machinery Suppliers Issue. Lippincott & Peto, Inc., 1867 W. Market St., Akron, Ohio 44313. (216) 864-2122.

ENCYCLOPEDIAS AND DICTIONARIES

Van Nostrand's Scientific Encyclopedia. Glenn D. Considine, ed. Van Nostrand Reinhold, 115 5th Ave., New York, New York 10003. (212) 254-3232. 1983. Sixth edition. Includes all broad subject areas in science.

ONLINE DATA BASES

Chemical Plant Database. Chemical Intelligence Services, 39A Bowling Green Lane, London, England EC 1R OBJ. 44 (71) 833-3812.

DOMIS. ECHO Service, BP 2373, Luxembourg L-1023. (352) 488041.

Enviro/Energyline Abstracts Plus. R. R. Bowker Co., 121 Chanlon Rd., New Providence, New Jersey 07974. (908) 464-6800.

Environmental Periodicals Bibliography. National Information Services Corp., Ste. 6, Wyman Towers, 3100 St. Paul St., Baltimore, Maryland 21218. (410)243-0797. Online version of abstract of same name.

RAPRA Abstracts. RAPRA Technology Limited, Shawbury, Shrewsbury, England SY4 4NR. 44 (939) 250383.

PERIODICALS AND NEWSLETTERS

Rubber World. Lippincott & Peto, Inc., 1867 W. Market St., Akron, Ohio 44313. (216) 864-2122. Monthly. Tire, hose, carbon black, and other major rubber and rubber chemical industry sectors.

RESEARCH CENTERS AND INSTITUTES

Texas A & M University, Separation and Ingredient Sciences Laboratory. Food Protein Research and Development Center, College Station, Texas 77843-2476. (409) 845-2741.

STATISTICS SOURCES

The Economics of Salt. FIND/SVP, 625 Avenue of the Americas, New York, New York 10011. (212) 645-4500. 1991. Salt markets, the main influences on salt prices, the impact of environmental pressure on chlorine manufacturing, consumption by end use, international trade, prices, costs and freights, methods of recovery, occurrence and reserves and world production.

Facing America's Trash: What Next for Municipal Solid Waste?. U.S. Office of Technology Assessment. Van Nostrand Reinhold, Washington, District of Columbia 20401. (202) 512-0000. 1991. Generation, composition and cost of recycling municipal solid waste.

Monthly Rubber Consumption Report. Rubber Manufacturers Association, 1400 K St., NW, Washington, District of Columbia 20005. Monthly. Production, trade, consumption and stock.

Monthly Tire Report. Rubber Manufacturers Association, 1400 K St., NW, Washington, District of Columbia 20005. Monthly. Tire and inner tube shipments, production, trade, and inventories.

The Tire & Rubber Industry. FIND/SVP, 625 Avenue of the Americas, New York, New York 10011. (212) 645-4500. Covers pricing, demand and market share, the replacement and retread markets, the supply side, distribution and foreign producers.

TRADE ASSOCIATIONS AND PROFESSIONAL SOCIETIES

United Rubber, Cork, Linoleum, & Plastic Workers of America. 570 White Pond Dr., Akron, Ohio 44320. (216) 376-6181.

RUBBISH

See: WASTE

RUNOFF

See also: AGRICULTURE; EROSION; MUNICIPAL RUNOFF; WATER POLLUTION; WATER RESOURCES

ABSTRACTING AND INDEXING SERVICES

Abstracts of Air and Water Conservation Literature. American Petroleum Institute. Central Abstracting and Indexing Service, 275 Madison Avenue, New York, New York 10016. 1972.

Applied Science and Technology Index. H.W. Wilson Co., 950 University Ave., Bronx, New York 10452. (800) 367-6770. Formerly Industrial Arts Index.

Aqualine Abstracts. Water Research Centre. c/o Pergamon Microforms International, Inc., Fairview Park, Elmsford, New York 10523. (914) 592-7720. 1927-. Contains some 8,000 records annually on water and wastewater technology. Covers all aspects of water, wastewater, associated engineering services and the aquatic environment. Over 600 periodicals, as well as books, reports and conference proceedings and other publications from water related institutions worldwide are scanned. Also available online.

ASFA Aquaculture Abstracts. Cambridge Scientific Abstracts, Inc., 5161 River Rd., Bethesda, Maryland 20816. (301) 961-6750. 1984.

Biological and Agricultural Index. H.W. Wilson Co., 950 University Ave., Bronx, New York 10452. (800) 367-6770. 1916-. Monthly.

Civil Engineering Hydraulic Abstracts. BHRA Fluid Engineering, Air Science Co., PO Box 143, Corning, New York 14830. (607) 962-5591. Monthly. Abstracts of periodicals that publish in the areas of hydraulic engineering and other related topics.

Environment Abstracts. Bowker A & I Publishing, 121 Chanlon Rd., New Providence, New Jersey 07974. (908) 464-6800. 1974-.

Environment Index. Environment Information Center, Index Research Department, 124 E. 39th St., New York, New York 10016. 1971-. Annual.

Environmental Information Connection–EIC. Planning Information Program, Dept. of Urban and Regional Planning, University of Illinois, 1003 West Nevada, Urbana, Illinois 61801. (217) 333-1369. Also available online.

Environmental Periodicals Bibliography. Environmental Studies Institute, International Academy at Santa Barbara, 800 Garden St., Suite D, Santa Barbara, California 93101. (805) 965-5010. Also available online.

Index to Scientific Book Contents. Institute for Scientific Information, 3501 Market St., Philadelphia, Pennsylvania 19104. (800) 523-1857. 1985-. Annual. Gives contents of science books published.

Science Citation Index. Institute for Scientific Information, 3501 Market St., Philadelphia, Pennsylvania 19104. 1961-.

BIBLIOGRAPHIES

Bibliography and Index of Geology. American Geological Institute, 4220 King St., Alexandria, Virginia 22302. Monthly. Includes environmental geology and hydrogeology.

EPA Publications Bibliography. U.S. Environmental Protection Agency, Library Systems Branch, 401 M St., SW, Washington, District of Columbia 20460. (202) 260-2090. Quarterly.

ENCYCLOPEDIAS AND DICTIONARIES

McGraw-Hill Encyclopedia of Environmental Science. Sybil P. Parker. McGraw-Hill Science & Engineering Books, 11 W. 19th St., New York, New York 10011. (212) 337-6010. 1980. Covers ecology, man's influence on nature, and environmental protection.

Van Nostrand's Scientific Encyclopedia. Glenn D. Considine, ed. Van Nostrand Reinhold, 115 5th Ave., New York, New York 10003. (212) 254-3232. 1983. Sixth edition. Includes all broad subject areas in science.

GENERAL WORKS

Cover Crops for Clean Water. W. L. Hargrove, ed. Soil and Water Conservation Society, 7515 Northeast Ankeny Rd., Ankeny, Iowa 50021-9764. (515) 289-2331; (800) THE-SOIL. 1991. Includes the latest information on the role of cover crops in water quality management, including means of reducing water runoff, soil erosion, agrichemical loss in runoff, and nitrate leaching to groundwater.

Groundwater Contamination: Sources, Control, and Preventive Measures. Chester D. Rail. Technomic Publishing Co., 851 New Holland Ave., Box 3535, Lancaster, Pennsylvania 17604. (717) 291-5609. 1989. Reviews the presently known sources of groundwater contamination and its many complex interactions, including managerial and political implications.

Magill's Survey of Science. Earth Science Series. Frank N. Magill. Salem Press, PO Box 50062, Pasadena, California 91105. 1990-. Five volumes. Includes information on earth's crust, hot spots and volcanic island chains, physical properties of minerals, rock magnetism, physical properties of rocks, and index.

New Technologies in Urban Drainage. C. Maksimovic. Elsevier Science Publishing Co., 655 Avenue of the Americas, New York, New York 10010. (212) 984-5800. 1991. Advances in rainfall-runoff modelling, hydrodynamics and quality modelling of receiving waters, and urban drainage in specific climates.

ONLINE DATA BASES

CRIS/USDA. U.S. Department of Agriculture, Cooperative State Research Service, Current Research Information System, National Agricultural Library Building, 5th Fl., 10301 Baltimore Blvd., Beltsville, Maryland 20705. (301) 344-3850. Agricultural, food and nutrition, and forestry research projects.

Enviro/Energyline Abstracts Plus. R. R. Bowker Co., 121 Chanlon Rd., New Providence, New Jersey 07974. (908) 464-6800.

Environmental Periodicals Bibliography. National Information Services Corp., Ste. 6, Wyman Towers, 3100 St. Paul St., Baltimore, Maryland 21218. (410)243-0797. Online version of abstract of same name.

RESEARCH CENTERS AND INSTITUTES

University of Tennessee at Knoxville, Water Resources Research Center. Knoxville, Tennessee 37996. (615) 974-2151.

STATISTICS SOURCES

World Resources. World Resources Institute. 1709 New York Ave., N.W., Washington, District of Columbia 20006. (202) 638-6300. Annual. Statistical and textual analysis of world's natural resources and the effects of growth-caused environmental pollution.

TRADE ASSOCIATIONS AND PROFESSIONAL SOCIETIES

American Society of Agricultural Engineers. 2950 Niles Rd., St Joseph, Michigan 49085. (616) 429-0300.

RURAL ATMOSPHERE

See: ATMOSPHERE

RURAL WATER SUPPLY

See also: HYDROLOGY; WATER RESOURCES; WETLANDS

ABSTRACTING AND INDEXING SERVICES

Abstracts of Air and Water Conservation Literature. American Petroleum Institute. Central Abstracting and Indexing Service, 275 Madison Avenue, New York, New York 10016. 1972.

Agrindex. AGRIS Coordinating Center, Via delle Terme di Caracalla, Rome, Italy I-00100. 61 0181-FA01. 1975-.

Applied Ecology Abstracts Studies in Renewable Natural Resources. Information Retrieval Ltd., 1911 Jefferson Davis Highway, Arlington, Virginia 22202. 1975-. Monthly.

Applied Science and Technology Index. H.W. Wilson Co., 950 University Ave., Bronx, New York 10452. (800) 367-6770. Formerly Industrial Arts Index.

Aqualine Abstracts. Water Research Centre. c/o Pergamon Microforms International, Inc., Fairview Park, Elmsford, New York 10523. (914) 592-7720. 1927-. Contains some 8,000 records annually on water and wastewater technology. Covers all aspects of water, wastewater, associated engineering services and the aquatic environment. Over 600 periodicals, as well as books, reports and conference proceedings and other publications from water related institutions worldwide are scanned. Also available online.

Biological and Agricultural Index. H.W. Wilson Co., 950 University Ave., Bronx, New York 10452. (800) 367-6770. 1916-. Monthly.

Ecological Abstracts. Geo Abstracts Ltd. Elsevier Applied Science, Crown House, Linton Rd., Barking, England IG 11 8JU. 1974-. Derived from over 600 leading ecological and environmental journals, plus books, conference proceedings, reports and theses.

Ecology Abstracts. Cambridge Scientific Abstracts, 5161 River Rd., Bethesda, Maryland 20816. (301) 961-6750. Monthly.

Engineering Index. The Engineering Index Inc., 345 E. 47th St., New York, New York 10017. 1962-.

Environment Abstracts. Bowker A & I Publishing, 121 Chanlon Rd., New Providence, New Jersey 07974. (908) 464-6800. 1974-.

Environment Index. Environment Information Center, Index Research Department, 124 E. 39th St., New York, New York 10016. 1971-. Annual.

Environmental Information Connection-EIC. Planning Information Program, Dept. of Urban and Regional Planning, University of Illinois, 1003 West Nevada, Urbana, Illinois 61801. (217) 333-1369. Also available online.

Environmental Periodicals Bibliography. Environmental Studies Institute, International Academy at Santa Barbara, 800 Garden St., Suite D, Santa Barbara, California 93101. (805) 965-5010. Also available online.

Geographical Abstracts. London School of Economics, Dept. of Geography, Regency House, 34 Duke St., London, England 1966-. Continued by Geo Abstracts issued in 6 parts: Pt. A. Landforms and the quaternary; Pt. B. Biogeography and Climatology; Pt. C. Economic geography; Pt. D. Social geography and cartography; Pt. E. Sedimentology; Pt. F. Regional and community planning.

Index to Scientific Book Contents. Institute for Scientific Information, 3501 Market St., Philadelphia, Pennsylvania 19104. (800) 523-1857. 1985-. Annual. Gives contents of science books published.

Multimedia Index to Ecology. National Information Center for Educational Media, University of Southern California, Los Angeles, California 90007.

Science Citation Index. Institute for Scientific Information, 3501 Market St., Philadelphia, Pennsylvania 19104. 1961-.

BIBLIOGRAPHIES

Current Contents. Agriculture, Biology and Environmental Sciences. Institute for Scientific Information, 3501 Market St., Philadelphia, Pennsylvania 19104. (800) 523-1857. 1973-. Previous title: Current Contents. Agricultural, Food & Veterinary Sciences. Gives the table of contents of periodicals in the fields of agriculture, biology, environmental and related areas.

EPA Publications Bibliography. U.S. Environmental Protection Agency, Library Systems Branch, 401 M St., SW, Washington, District of Columbia 20460. (202) 260-2090. Quarterly.

ENCYCLOPEDIAS AND DICTIONARIES

Dictionary of Environmental Engineering and Related Sciences: English-Spanish, Spanish-English. Jose T. Villate. Ediciones Universal, 3090 SW 8th St., Miami, Florida 33135. (305) 642-3355. 1979.

Encyclopedia of Environmental Science and Engineering. J.R. Pfafflin. Gordon and Breach Science Publishers, Inc., 270 8th Ave., New York, New York 10011. (212) 206-8900. 1992.

Grzimek's Encyclopedia of Ecology. Bernhard Grzimek. Van Nostrand Reinhold, 115 5th Ave., New York, New York 10003. (212) 254-3232. 1976.

McGraw-Hill Encyclopedia of Environmental Science. Sybil P. Parker. McGraw-Hill Science & Engineering Books, 11 W. 19th St., New York, New York 10011. (212) 337-6010. 1980. Covers ecology, man's influence on nature, and environmental protection.

GENERAL WORKS

Earth Ponds: The Country Pond Maker's Guide. Tim Matson. Countryman Press, PO Box 175, Woodstock, Vermont 05091-0175. (802) 457-1049. 1991. How-to manual regarding pond making.

Ground Water. H. M. Raghunath. John Wiley & Sons, Inc., 605 3rd Ave., New York, New York 10158-0012. (212) 850-6000. 1987. Hydrogeology, ground water survey and pumping tests, rural water supply and irrigation systems.

Rural Environment Planning for Sustainable Communities. Frederic O. Sargent, et al. Island Press, 1718 Connecticut Ave. N.W., Ste. 300, Washington, District of Columbia 20009. (202) 232-7933. 1991.

Rural Water Supply and Sanitation: Time for a Change. Anthony A. Churchill. World Bank, 1818 H. St., N.W., 20433. (202) 477-1234. 1987. Rural water supplies in developing countries.

Saving America's Countryside: A Guide to Rural Conservation. Samuel N. Stokes. Johns Hopkins University Press, 701 W. 40th St., Suite 275, Baltimore, Maryland 21211. (410) 516-6900. 1989.

Surveillance of Drinking Water Quality in Rural Areas. Barry Lloyd. John Wiley & Sons, Inc., 605 3rd Ave, New York, New York 10158-0012. (212) 850-6000. 1991. Examines the human and technical resources required for monitoring, maintaining and improving the safety of rural water supply services. A practical guide to improving the quality of service from small water supplies, it describes the essential minimum of reliable methods of monitoring water quality and discusses new cost effective approaches to sanitary inspection of community water supplies.

ONLINE DATA BASES

Computerized Engineering Index–COMPENDEX. Engineering Information Inc., 345 E. 47th St., New York, New York 10017. (212) 705-7600.

Enviro/Energyline Abstracts Plus. R. R. Bowker Co., 121 Chanlon Rd., New Providence, New Jersey 07974. (908) 464-6800.

Environmental Periodicals Bibliography. National Information Services Corp., Ste. 6, Wyman Towers, 3100 St. Paul St., Baltimore, Maryland 21218. (410)243-0797. Online version of abstract of same name.

Monthly Catalog of United States Government Publications. U.S. G.P.O., Supt. of Docs., PO Box 371954, Pittsburgh, Pennsylvania 15250-7954. (202) 512-0000.

National Technical Information Service. U.S. Department of Commerce, National Technical Information Service, Office of Data Base Services, 5285 Port Royal Rd., Springfield, Virginia 22161. (703) 487-4807. Bibliographic database of government sponsored research and technical reports.

SCISEARCH. Institute for Scientific Information, University City Science Center, 3501 Market St., Philadelphia, Pennsylvania 19104. (215) 386-0100.

TRADE ASSOCIATIONS AND PROFESSIONAL SOCIETIES

American Water Resources Association. 5410 Grosvenor Lane, Suite 220, Bethesda, Maryland 20814. (301) 493-8600.

RUTHENIUM

ABSTRACTING AND INDEXING SERVICES

Environment Abstracts. Bowker A & I Publishing, 121 Chanlon Rd., New Providence, New Jersey 07974. (908) 464-6800. 1974-.

Environment Index. Environment Information Center, Index Research Department, 124 E. 39th St., New York, New York 10016. 1971-. Annual.

Environmental Information Connection–EIC. Planning Information Program, Dept. of Urban and Regional Planning, University of Illinois, 1003 West Nevada, Urbana, Illinois 61801. (217) 333-1369. Also available online.

Environmental Periodicals Bibliography. Environmental Studies Institute, International Academy at Santa Barbara, 800 Garden St., Suite D, Santa Barbara, California 93101. (805) 965-5010. Also available online.

General Science Index. H. W. Wilson Co., 950 University Ave., Bronx, New York 10452. 1978-. Monthly, also issued in annual cumulation. Cumulative subject index to English language periodicals in the subject fields of astronomy, botany, chemistry, earth science, environment and conservation, food and nutrition, genetics, mathematics, medicine and health, microbiology, oceanography, physics, physiology and zoology.

Science Citation Index. Institute for Scientific Information, 3501 Market St., Philadelphia, Pennsylvania 19104. 1961-.

BIBLIOGRAPHIES

Bibliography and Index of Geology. American Geological Institute, 4220 King St., Alexandria, Virginia 22302. Monthly. Includes environmental geology and hydrogeology.

EPA Publications Bibliography. U.S. Environmental Protection Agency, Library Systems Branch, 401 M St., SW, Washington, District of Columbia 20460. (202) 260-2090. Quarterly.

ENCYCLOPEDIAS AND DICTIONARIES

McGraw-Hill Encyclopedia of Science and Technology. McGraw-Hill, 1221 Avenue of the Americas, New York, New York 10020. (212) 512-2000 or (800) 262-4729. 1992. Seventh edition. Issued in multiple volumes including index. Includes all science and technology broad subject areas.

Van Nostrand's Scientific Encyclopedia. Glenn D. Considine, ed. Van Nostrand Reinhold, 115 5th Ave., New York, New York 10003. (212) 254-3232. 1983. Sixth edition. Includes all broad subject areas in science.

GENERAL WORKS

The Chemistry of Ruthenium. Elaine A. Seddon. Elsevier Science Publishing Co., 655 Avenue of the Americas, New York, New York 10010. (212) 984-5800. 1984.

Magill's Survey of Science. Earth Science Series. Frank N. Magill. Salem Press, PO Box 50062, Pasadena, California 91105. 1990-. Five volumes. Includes information on earth's crust, hot spots and volcanic island chains, physical properties of minerals, rock magnetism, physical properties of rocks, and index.

Ruthenium: Its Behavior in Plant and Soil Systems. K. W. Brown. National Technical Information Service, 5285 Port Royal Rd., Springfield, Virginia 22161. (703) 487-4650. 1976. Effect of radioactive pollution on plants and radioactive substances in soils.

ONLINE DATA BASES

Enviro/Energyline Abstracts Plus. R. R. Bowker Co., 121 Chanlon Rd., New Providence, New Jersey 07974. (908) 464-6800.

Environmental Periodicals Bibliography. National Information Services Corp., Ste. 6, Wyman Towers, 3100 St.

Paul St., Baltimore, Maryland 21218. (410)243-0797. Online version of abstract of same name.

S

SAFETY GUIDELINES

See also: EMERGENCY RESPONSE PLANNING

ABSTRACTING AND INDEXING SERVICES

Environment Abstracts. Bowker A & I Publishing, 121 Chanlon Rd., New Providence, New Jersey 07974. (908) 464-6800. 1974-.

Environment Index. Environment Information Center, Index Research Department, 124 E. 39th St., New York, New York 10016. 1971-. Annual.

Environmental Information Connection–EIC. Planning Information Program, Dept. of Urban and Regional Planning, University of Illinois, 1003 West Nevada, Urbana, Illinois 61801. (217) 333-1369. Also available online.

Environmental Periodicals Bibliography. Environmental Studies Institute, International Academy at Santa Barbara, 800 Garden St., Suite D, Santa Barbara, California 93101. (805) 965-5010. Also available online.

BIBLIOGRAPHIES

EPA Publications Bibliography. U.S. Environmental Protection Agency, Library Systems Branch, 401 M St., SW, Washington, District of Columbia 20460. (202) 260-2090. Quarterly.

DIRECTORIES

CCPS/AIChE Directory of Chemical Process Safety Services. American Institute of Chemical Engineers, 345 E. 47th St., New York, New York 10017. (212) 705-7338. 1991. Lists providers of various chemical process safety services. It is compiled from questionnaires returned by the service providers. Company profiles are included.

Safety & Health–Safety Equipment Buyers' Guide Issue. National Safety Council, 444 N. Michigan Ave., Chicago, Illinois 60611. (312) 527-4800.

Safety Equipment Distributors Association–Membership Roster. Safety Equipment Distributors Association, c/o Smith, Bucklin & Associates, Inc., 111 E. Wacker Dr., Chicago, Illinois 60601. (312) 644-6610.

GENERAL WORKS

Emergency Response Planning Guidelines Set 5. American Industrial Hygiene Association, 345 White Pond Dr., Akron, Ohio 44320. (216) 873-2442. 1991. Includes guidelines for acrylic acid, 1,3-butadiene, epichlorohydrin, tetrafluoroethylene, and vinyl acetate.

OSHA Systems Safety Inspection Guide. Government Institutes, Inc., 4 Research Pl., Ste. 200, Rockville, Maryland 20850. (301) 921-2300. 1989. Focuses on overall management of any operation in which hazardous chemicals are handled.

Safety in the Process Industries. Butterworth-Heinemann, 80 Montvale Ave., Stoneham, Massachusetts 02180. (617) 438-8464. 1990. Hazards of process plants, and causes of accidents and how they may be controlled.

Smoking Guns. Nuclear Regulatory Commission, Advisory Committee on Nuclear Facility Safety, 1717 H St., NW, Washington, District of Columbia 20555. (301) 492-7000. 1991. Deals with the Energy Department's campaign to improve safety and environmental compliance at its nuclear weapons plants.

Workplace Environmental Exposure Level Guide. American Industrial Hygiene Association, 345 White Pond Dr., Akron, Ohio 44320. (216) 873-2442. 1991-. Includes guidelines for benzophenone, butyraldehyde, sodium hypochlorite, and vinylcyclohexene.

HANDBOOKS AND MANUALS

Compendium of Safety Data Sheets for Research and Industrial Chemicals. L. H. Keith and D. B. Walters, eds. VCH Publishers, 303 NW 12th Ave., Deerfield Beach, Florida 33442-1788. (305) 428-5566. 1985. Seven volumes. Provides information of safety-oriented needs involving chemicals.

Facilities Evaluation Manual: Safety Fire Protection and Environmental Compliance. K. L. Petrocelly. The Association of Energy Engineers, 4025 Pleasantdale Rd., Suite 420, Atlanta, Georgia 30340. (404) 925-9558. 1991. Guide to help plant and facility managers conduct thorough inspections and evaluations of their facilities in order to pinpoint and solve problems in the areas of maintenance, safety, energy efficiency and environmental compliance.

Good Laboratory Practice Compliance Inspection Manual. Government Institutes, Inc., 4 Research Pl., Ste. 200, Rockville, Maryland 20850. (301) 921-2300. Laboratory inspection procedures to comply with TSCA and FIFRA.

Guide to Hazardous Products Around the Home: A Personal Action Manual for Protecting Your Health and Environment. Household Hazardous Waste Project, 901 S. National Ave., Box 87, Springfield, Missouri 65804. 1989. Covers hazardous substances, safety measures, home accidents, and prevention.

Handbook of Environmental Health and Safety, Principles and Practices. Herman Koren. Lewis Publishers, 2000 Corporate Blvd., N.W., Boca Raton, Florida 33431. (800) 272-7737. 1991. Two volumes. Current issues and regulations are presented. The broad spectrum of topics is presented outlining the relationship of the environment to humans and also environmental health emergencies and how to deal with them.

Manual for Review and Update of Hospital Department Safety, Environmental and Infection Control Policies. Frank D. Murphy. G.K. Hall & Co., 70 Lincoln St., Boston, Massachusetts 02111. (617) 423-3990. 1980. Administrative manuals for health care institutions, hospital departments relating to accident prevention and cross infection.

OSHA Field Operations Manual. Government Institutes, Inc., 4 Research Pl., Ste. 200, Rockville, Maryland 20850. (301) 921-2300. 4th edition. Step-by-step manual, developed by OSHA for use by its own compliance safety and health officers in carrying out inspections.

Product Safety Evaluation Handbook. Shayne Cox Gad. Dekker, 270 Madison Ave., New York, New York 10016. (212) 696-9000 or (800) 228-1160. 1988. Discusses toxicity testing of products such as drugs, chemicals, etc. Gives an evaluation of their safety for the consumer.

Respiratory Protection: A Manual and Guideline. American Industrial Hygiene Association, 345 White Pond Dr., PO Box 8390, Akron, Ohio 44320. (216) 873-2442. 1991. 2d ed. Provides practical guidelines for establishing and managing respiratory protection programs. Presents guidelines for establishing chemical cartridge field service life policies and audit criteria for evaluating respiratory protection programs. Contains validated qualitative life-testing protocols, new equipment for quantitative respiratory protection, and information on use and testing of supplied-air suits.

Sanitation Safety & Environmental Standards. Lewis J. Minor. AVI Pub. Co., 250 Post Rd., PO Box 831, Westport, Connecticut 06881. 1983. Environmental aspects of food industry and trade.

Suspect Chemicals Sourcebook. Roytech Publications, Inc., 7910 Woodmont Ave., Ste. 902, Bethesda, Maryland 20814. (301) 654-4281. 1985-. Includes: chemical name index, CAS registry numbers; OSHA Chemical Hazard chemical name; Summary and full text of OSHA Chemical Hazard Communication Standard and history and overview. Also available online.

ONLINE DATA BASES

Chemical Safety Newsbase. Royal Society of Chemistry, Thomas Graham House, Science Park, Milton Rd., Cambridge, England CB4 4WF. 44 (223) 420066.

CHEMSAFE. DECHEMA, Chemische Technick und Biotechnologie e.V., I & D Information Systems and Data Banks, Theodor-Heuss-Alle 25, Postfach 97 01 46, Frankfurt, Germany D-6000. 49 (69) 7564-248.

Enviro/Energyline Abstracts Plus. R. R. Bowker Co., 121 Chanlon Rd., New Providence, New Jersey 07974. (908) 464-6800.

Environmental Periodicals Bibliography. National Information Services Corp., Ste. 6, Wyman Towers, 3100 St. Paul St., Baltimore, Maryland 21218. (410)243-0797. Online version of abstract of same name.

HADB. National Library of Medicine, Toxicology Information Program, 8600 Rockville Pike, Bethesda, Maryland 20894. (800) 638-8480.

Industrial Health & Hazards Update. Merton Allen Associates, P.O. Box 15640, Plantation, Florida 33318-5640. (305) 473-9560.

Monthly Catalog of United States Government Publications. U.S. G.P.O., Supt. of Docs., PO Box 371954, Pittsburgh, Pennsylvania 15250-7954. (202) 512-0000.

National Technical Information Service. U.S. Department of Commerce, National Technical Information Service, Office of Data Base Services, 5285 Port Royal Rd., Springfield, Virginia 22161. (703) 487-4807. Bibliographic database of government sponsored research and technical reports.

PERIODICALS AND NEWSLETTERS

Ecotoxicology and Environmental Safety. Academic Press, c/o Harcourt Brace Jovanovich Inc., 6277 Sea Harbor Dr., Orlando, Florida 32887. (800) 346-8648. 1977-. Bimonthly.

SALINITY

See: SALT

SALMONELLA

ABSTRACTING AND INDEXING SERVICES

Biological and Agricultural Index. H.W. Wilson Co., 950 University Ave., Bronx, New York 10452. (800) 367-6770. 1916-. Monthly.

Biotechnology Research Abstracts. Cambridge Scientific Abstracts, 5161 River Rd., Bethesda, Maryland 20816. (301) 961-6750. Monthly. Includes such broad areas as genetic intervention, biochemical genetics, and microbiological techniques.

General Science Index. H. W. Wilson Co., 950 University Ave., Bronx, New York 10452. 1978-. Monthly, also issued in annual cumulation. Cumulative subject index to English language periodicals in the subject fields of astronomy, botany, chemistry, earth science, environment and conservation, food and nutrition, genetics, mathematics, medicine and health, microbiology, oceanography, physics, physiology and zoology.

Genetics Abstracts. Cambridge Scientific Abstracts, 5161 River Rd., Bethesda, Maryland 20816. (301) 961-6750. 1968-. Monthly. Formerly published by Information Retrieval Ltd., London England. Published by Cambridge Scientific Abstracts since 1982.

Science Citation Index. Institute for Scientific Information, 3501 Market St., Philadelphia, Pennsylvania 19104. 1961-.

BIBLIOGRAPHIES

Salmonellas in Laboratory Animals. Kevin Engler. National Agricultural Library, 10301 Baltimore Blvd., Beltsville, Maryland 20705-2351. (301) 504-5755. 1988.

ENCYCLOPEDIAS AND DICTIONARIES

Cambridge Dictionary of Biology. Peter M. B. Walker. Cambridge University Press, 40 W. 20th St., New York, New York 10011. (212) 924-3900 or (800) 227-0247. 1989. Includes 10,000 terms in zoology, botany, biochemistry, molecular biology and genetics. Previously published under the title Chambers Biology Dictionary.

Cambridge Encyclopedia of Life Sciences. A. E. Friday and David S. Ingram. Cambridge University Press, 40 W 20th St., New York, New York 10011. (212) 924-3900 or (800) 227-0247. 1985. Includes all topics under biology and ecology.

A Concise Dictionary of Biology. Elizabeth Martin, ed. Oxford University Press, 200 Madison Ave., New York, New York 10016. (212) 679-7300 or (800) 334-4249. 1990. New edition. Derived from the Concise Science Dictionary, published in 1984.

Encyclopedia of Human Biology. Renato Dulbecco, ed. Academic Press, c/o Harcourt Brace Jovanovich Inc., 6277 Sea Harbor Dr., Orlando, Florida 32887. (800) 346-8648. 1991. Eight volumes.

McGraw-Hill Encyclopedia of Science and Technology. McGraw-Hill, 1221 Avenue of the Americas, New York, New York 10020. (212) 512-2000 or (800) 262-4729. 1992. Seventh edition. Issued in multiple volumes including index. Includes all science and technology broad subject areas.

The Nutrition and Health Encyclopedia. David F. Tver and Percy Russell. Van Nostrand Reinhold, 115 5th Ave., New York, New York 10003. (212) 254-3232. 1989.

Van Nostrand's Scientific Encyclopedia. Glenn D. Considine, ed. Van Nostrand Reinhold, 115 5th Ave., New York, New York 10003. (212) 254-3232. 1983. Sixth edition. Includes all broad subject areas in science.

GENERAL WORKS

Potential Salmonella Virulence Factors. Suraj B. Baloda. College of Veterinary Medicine, Swedish University of Agricultural Sciences, Uppasal, Sweden 1987. Studies on toxins, cell-surface adhesions, enterotoxins and cell membranes.

The Salmonella Investigation. Lee Daniels. Illinois. House Republican Committee, Illinois Secretary's State's Office, Springfield, Illinois 1985. An agenda for governmental action to combat salmonella incidents.

TRADE ASSOCIATIONS AND PROFESSIONAL SOCIETIES

American Institute of Biological Sciences. 730 11th St., N.W., Washington, District of Columbia 20001-4521. (202) 628-1500.

SALT

ABSTRACTING AND INDEXING SERVICES

Applied Science and Technology Index. H.W. Wilson Co., 950 University Ave., Bronx, New York 10452. (800) 367-6770. Formerly Industrial Arts Index.

ASFA Aquaculture Abstracts. Cambridge Scientific Abstracts, Inc., 5161 River Rd., Bethesda, Maryland 20816. (301) 961-6750. 1984.

Chemical Abstracts. Chemical Abstracts Service, 2540 Olentangy River Rd., PO Box 3012, Columbus, Ohio 43210. (800) 848-6533. 1907-.

Food Science and Technology Abstracts. International Food Information Service, c/o National Food Laboratory, 6363 Clark Ave., Dublin, California 94568. (800) 336-3782. 1969-.

General Science Index. H. W. Wilson Co., 950 University Ave., Bronx, New York 10452. 1978-. Monthly, also issued in annual cumulation. Cumulative subject index to English language periodicals in the subject fields of astronomy, botany, chemistry, earth science, environment and conservation, food and nutrition, genetics, mathematics, medicine and health, microbiology, oceanography, physics, physiology and zoology.

Science Citation Index. Institute for Scientific Information, 3501 Market St., Philadelphia, Pennsylvania 19104. 1961-.

BIBLIOGRAPHIES

Bibliography and Index of Geology. American Geological Institute, 4220 King St., Alexandria, Virginia 22302. Monthly. Includes environmental geology and hydrogeology.

Salt, Evaporites, and Brines: An Annotated Bibliography. Vivian S. Hall and Mary R. Spencer. Oryx Press, 4041 N. Central Ave., #700, Phoenix, Arizona 85012. (602) 265-2651; (800) 279-6799. 1984.

DIRECTORIES

Directory of Companies Producing Salt in the United States. Department of the Interior, 810 7th St. NW, Washington, District of Columbia 20241. (202) 501-9649.

ENCYCLOPEDIAS AND DICTIONARIES

The Concise Russian-English Chemical Glossary: Acids, Esters, Ethers, and Salts. James F. Shipp. Wychwood Press, PO Box 10, College Park, Maryland 20740. 1983. Lists four of the basic substances commonly occurring in chemical and environmental literature: acids, esters, ethers and salts.

The Dictionary of Sodium, Fats, and Cholesterol. Barbara Kraus. Putnam Berkley Group, 200 Madison Ave., New York, New York 10016. (212) 951-8400. 1990. Food composition, fat, cholesterol, and sodium.

The Nutrition and Health Encyclopedia. David F. Tver and Percy Russell. Van Nostrand Reinhold, 115 5th Ave., New York, New York 10003. (212) 254-3232. 1989.

Van Nostrand's Scientific Encyclopedia. Glenn D. Considine, ed. Van Nostrand Reinhold, 115 5th Ave., New York, New York 10003. (212) 254-3232. 1983. Sixth edition. Includes all broad subject areas in science.

GENERAL WORKS

Cholesterol Metabolism, LDL, and the LDL Receptor. N.B. Myant. Academic Press, c/o Harcourt Brace Jovanovich Inc., 6277 Sea Harbor Dr., Orlando, Florida 32887. (800) 346-8648. 1990.

Magill's Survey of Science. Earth Science Series. Frank N. Magill. Salem Press, PO Box 50062, Pasadena, California 91105. 1990-. Five volumes. Includes information on earth's crust, hot spots and volcanic island chains, physical properties of minerals, rock magnetism, physical properties of rocks, and index.

Sodium Chloride. Environmental Protection Programs Directorate. Environmental Protection Service, 425 St. Joseph Blvd., 3rd Fl., Hull, Quebec, Canada K1A 0H3. (613) 953-5921. 1984. Environmental and technical information for problem spills.

HANDBOOKS AND MANUALS

The Salt Storage Handbook. The Salt Institute, Fairfax Plaza, Ste. 600, 700 N. Fairfax, Alexandria, Virginia 22314. (703) 549-4648. 1987. A practical guide for storing and handling de-icing salt.

ONLINE DATA BASES

Chemical Abstracts-CA. Chemical Abstracts Service, 2540 Olentangy River Rd., P.O. Box 3012, Columbus, Ohio 43210. (800) 848-6533 or (614) 421-3600. Information sources include 9000 journals, patents from 27 countries, two industrial property organizations, new books, conference proceedings, and government research reports.

PERIODICALS AND NEWSLETTERS

Salt and the Environment. Salt Institute, 206 North Washington St., Alexandria, Virginia 23314.

RESEARCH CENTERS AND INSTITUTES

University of Georgia, Marine Institute. Sapelo, Georgia (912) 485-2221.

TRADE ASSOCIATIONS AND PROFESSIONAL SOCIETIES

American Chemical Society. 1155 16th St., N.W., Washington, District of Columbia 20036. (202) 872-4600.

SALVAGE

See: WASTE MANAGEMENT

SAND DUNE ECOLOGY

ABSTRACTING AND INDEXING SERVICES

Applied Ecology Abstracts Studies in Renewable Natural Resources. Information Retrieval Ltd., 1911 Jefferson Davis Highway, Arlington, Virginia 22202. 1975-. Monthly.

Biological and Agricultural Index. H.W. Wilson Co., 950 University Ave., Bronx, New York 10452. (800) 367-6770. 1916-. Monthly.

Environment Abstracts. Bowker A & I Publishing, 121 Chanlon Rd., New Providence, New Jersey 07974. (908) 464-6800. 1974-.

Environment Index. Environment Information Center, Index Research Department, 124 E. 39th St., New York, New York 10016. 1971-. Annual.

Environmental Information Connection-EIC. Planning Information Program, Dept. of Urban and Regional Planning, University of Illinois, 1003 West Nevada, Urbana, Illinois 61801. (217) 333-1369. Also available online.

Environmental Periodicals Bibliography. Environmental Studies Institute, International Academy at Santa Barbara, 800 Garden St., Suite D, Santa Barbara, California 93101. (805) 965-5010. Also available online.

General Science Index. H. W. Wilson Co., 950 University Ave., Bronx, New York 10452. 1978-. Monthly, also issued in annual cumulation. Cumulative subject index to English language periodicals in the subject fields of astronomy, botany, chemistry, earth science, environment and conservation, food and nutrition, genetics, mathematics, medicine and health, microbiology, oceanography, physics, physiology and zoology.

Multimedia Index to Ecology. National Information Center for Educational Media, University of Southern California, Los Angeles, California 90007.

Science Citation Index. Institute for Scientific Information, 3501 Market St., Philadelphia, Pennsylvania 19104. 1961-.

BIBLIOGRAPHIES

EPA Publications Bibliography. U.S. Environmental Protection Agency, Library Systems Branch, 401 M St., SW, Washington, District of Columbia 20460. (202) 260-2090. Quarterly.

ENCYCLOPEDIAS AND DICTIONARIES

Van Nostrand's Scientific Encyclopedia. Glenn D. Considine, ed. Van Nostrand Reinhold, 115 5th Ave., New York, New York 10003. (212) 254-3232. 1983. Sixth edition. Includes all broad subject areas in science.

GENERAL WORKS

Ecology of Sandy Shores. A. C. Brown and A. Mclachlan. Elsevier Science Publishing Co., 655 Avenue of the Americas, New York, New York 10010. (212) 989-5800. 1990. Deals with the biological study of sandy beaches.

Sand Dune Ecology and Formation. Jan Gumprecht. Educational Images Ltd., PO Box 3456, Elmira, New York 14905. (607) 732-1090. 1986. Filmstrip describing the animate and inanimate composition of sand dunes.

ONLINE DATA BASES

Enviro/Energyline Abstracts Plus. R. R. Bowker Co., 121 Chanlon Rd., New Providence, New Jersey 07974. (908) 464-6800.

Environmental Periodicals Bibliography. National Information Services Corp., Ste. 6, Wyman Towers, 3100 St. Paul St., Baltimore, Maryland 21218. (410)243-0797. Online version of abstract of same name.

SANITARY ENGINEERING

See also: BUILDINGS, ENVIRONMENTAL ENGINEERING
OF; POLLUTION; WATER RESOURCES

ABSTRACTING AND INDEXING SERVICES

Biological and Agricultural Index. H.W. Wilson Co., 950
University Ave., Bronx, New York 10452. (800) 367-
6770. 1916-. Monthly.

Environment Abstracts. Bowker A & I Publishing, 121
Chanlon Rd., New Providence, New Jersey 07974. (908)
464-6800. 1974-.

Environment Index. Environment Information Center,
Index Research Department, 124 E. 39th St., New York,
New York 10016. 1971-. Annual.

Environmental Information Connection–EIC. Planning
Information Program, Dept. of Urban and Regional
Planning, University of Illinois, 1003 West Nevada,
Urbana, Illinois 61801. (217) 333-1369. Also available
online.

Environmental Periodicals Bibliography. Environmental
Studies Institute, International Academy at Santa Barbara, 800 Garden St., Suite D, Santa Barbara, California
93101. (805) 965-5010. Also available online.

General Science Index. H. W. Wilson Co., 950 University
Ave., Bronx, New York 10452. 1978-. Monthly, also
issued in annual cumulation. Cumulative subject index
to English language periodicals in the subject fields of
astronomy, botany, chemistry, earth science, environment and conservation, food and nutrition, genetics,
mathematics, medicine and health, microbiology, oceanography, physics, physiology and zoology.

Public Health Engineering Abstracts. U.S. G.P.O., Washington, District of Columbia 20401. (202) 512-0000.
Monthly.

BIBLIOGRAPHIES

EPA Publications Bibliography. U.S. Environmental Protection Agency, Library Systems Branch, 401 M St., SW,
Washington, District of Columbia 20460. (202) 260-
2090. Quarterly.

ONLINE DATA BASES

Enviro/Energyline Abstracts Plus. R. R. Bowker Co., 121
Chanlon Rd., New Providence, New Jersey 07974. (908)
464-6800.

Environmental Periodicals Bibliography. National Infor-
mation Services Corp., Ste. 6, Wyman Towers, 3100 St.
Paul St., Baltimore, Maryland 21218. (410)243-0797.
Online version of abstract of same name.

*Monthly Catalog of United States Government Publica-
tions.* U.S. G.P.O., Supt. of Docs., PO Box 371954,
Pittsburgh, Pennsylvania 15250-7954. (202) 512-0000.

National Technical Information Service. U.S. Department of Commerce, National Technical Information
Service, Office of Data Base Services, 5285 Port Royal
Rd., Springfield, Virginia 22161. (703) 487-4807. Bibliographic database of government sponsored research and
technical reports.

SANITARY LANDFILLS

See also: SOLID WASTE DISPOSAL

GENERAL WORKS

Air Emissions from Municipal Solid Waste Landfills.
Environmental Protection Agency. National Technical
Information Service, 5285 Port Royal Rd., Springfield,
Virginia 22161. (703) 487-4650. 1991. Background infor-
mation for proposed standards and guidelines. Order
number PB91-197061LDM.

*Characterization of Municipal Waste Combustor Ashes
and Leachates from Municipal Solid Waste Landfills,
Monofills, and Codisposal Sites.* U.S. Environmental
Protection Agency, Office of Solid Waste, 401 M St.,
S.W., Washington, District of Columbia 20460. (202)
260-2090. 1987.

*Chemical, Physical, and Biological Properties of Com-
pounds Present at Hazardous Waste Sites: Final Report.*
U.S. Environmental Protection Agency. Clement Associates Inc., Arlington, Virginia 1985.

Closed Waste Site Evaluation: Emsdale Landfill: Report.
Ontario Waste Management Branch. Waste Site Evaluation Unit, Toronto. National Technical Information
Service, 5285 Port Royal Rd., Springfield, Virginia
22161. (703) 487-4650. 1989. Order number MIC-91-
03061LDM.

*Design, Construction, and Monitoring of Sanitary Land-
fill.* Amalendu Bagchi. John Wiley & Sons, Inc., 605 3rd
Ave., New York, New York 10158-0012. (212) 850-6000.
1990. Handbook of theory, practice, and mathematical
models of sanitary landfill technology and how they
apply to waste disposal.

*How to Meet Requirements for Hazardous Waste Landfill
Design, Construction and Closure.* U. S. Environmental
Protection Agency. Noyes Publications, 120 Mill Rd.,
Park Ridge, New Jersey 07656. (201) 391-8484. 1990.
Outlines in detail the provisions of the minimum technology guidance regulations, and offers practical and
detailed technology transfer information on the construction of hazardous waste facilities that comply with these
requirements.

*Incineration for Site Cleanup and Destruction of Hazard-
ous Wastes.* Howard E. Hesketh. Technomic Publishing
Co., 851 New Holland Ave., Box 3535, Lancaster,
Pennsylvania 17604. (717) 291-5609; (800) 233-9936.
1990.

*International Technologies for Hazardous Waste Site
Cleanup.* Thomas Nunno, et al. Noyes Publications, 120
Mill Rd., Park Ridge, New Jersey 07656. (201) 391-8484.
1990. Identifies 95 international technologies that could
be utilized for hazardous waste site remediation within
the United States.

*Waste Containment Systems: Construction, Regulation
and Performance.* Rudolph Bonaparte, ed. American
Society of Civil Engineers, 345 E. 47th St., New York,
New York 10017. (212) 705-7288; (800) 548-2723. 1990.
Proceedings of a symposium sponsored by the Commit-
tee on Soil Improvement and Geosynthetics and the
Committee on Soil properties of the Geotechnical Engi-
neering Division, American Society of Civil Engineers in
conjunction with the ASCE National Convention, San
Francisco, CA, November 6-7, 1990.

HANDBOOKS AND MANUALS

Siting Hazardous Waste Treatment Facilities; the Nimby Syndrome. Kent E. Portney. Auburn House, 14 Dedham St., Dover, Massachusetts 02030-0658. (800) 223-2665. 1991. Advice to producers of hazardous waste on how to overcome people's reluctance to have it shipped into their neighborhood.

PERIODICALS AND NEWSLETTERS

Inside the EPA'S Superfund Report. Inside Washington Publishers, PO Box 7167, Ben Franklin Station, Washington, District of Columbia 20044. Biweekly. Liability for hazardous substances pollution and damages.

SANITARY SEWERS

See: SEWERS

SANITATION

ABSTRACTING AND INDEXING SERVICES

General Science Index. H. W. Wilson Co., 950 University Ave., Bronx, New York 10452. 1978-. Monthly, also issued in annual cumulation. Cumulative subject index to English language periodicals in the subject fields of astronomy, botany, chemistry, earth science, environment and conservation, food and nutrition, genetics, mathematics, medicine and health, microbiology, oceanography, physics, physiology and zoology.

Public Health Engineering Abstracts. U.S. G.P.O., Washington, District of Columbia 20401. (202) 512-0000. Monthly.

Science Citation Index. Institute for Scientific Information, 3501 Market St., Philadelphia, Pennsylvania 19104. 1961-.

BIBLIOGRAPHIES

Low-Cost Technology Options for Sanitation. W. Rybczynski. The World Bank, 1818 H. St., N.W., Washington, District of Columbia 20433. 1982. A state of the art review of toilets and sanitary engineering in underdeveloped countries.

DIRECTORIES

International Sanitary Supply Association–Membership Directory. 7373 N. Lincoln Ave., Lincolnwood, Illinois 60646. (708) 982-0800. Annual.

Sanitation Compliance and Enforcement Ratings of Interstate Milk Shippers. Milk Safety Branch/Food and Drug Administration, Department of Health and Human Services, Washington, District of Columbia 20204. (208) 485-0175. 1974.

Who's Who in Environmental Engineering. American Academy of Environmental Engineers, 132 Holiday Court, Suite 206, Annapolis, Maryland 21401. (301) 266-3311. 1980. Annual. Directory of environmental engineers who are certified by the academy.

ENCYCLOPEDIAS AND DICTIONARIES

Nomenclature Pertaining to Environmental Sanitation. Wilhelmena C. Carey. National Institute of Mental Health, 5600 Fishers Ln., Rm. 15CO5, Rockville, Maryland 20857. (301) 493-3877. 1980. Institutional housekeeping manual.

Van Nostrand's Scientific Encyclopedia. Glenn D. Considine, ed. Van Nostrand Reinhold, 115 5th Ave., New York, New York 10003. (212) 254-3232. 1983. Sixth edition. Includes all broad subject areas in science.

GENERAL WORKS

Appropriate Sanitation Alternatives. John M. Kalbermatten. Johns Hopkins University Press, 701 W. 40th St., Ste. 275, Baltimore, Maryland 21211. (410) 516-6900. 1983. Sanitary engineering in developing countries.

Environmental Engineering and Sanitation. Joseph A. Salvato. John Wiley & Sons, Inc., 605 3rd Ave., New York, New York 10158-0012. (212) 850-6000. 1992. 3d ed. Applies principles of sanitary science and engineering to sanitation and environmental health. It includes design, construction, maintenance, and operations of sanitation plants and structures. Provides state-of-the-art information on environmental factors associated with chronic and non-infectious diseases; environmental engineering planning and impact analysis; waste management and control; food sanitation; administration of health and sanitation programs; acid rain; noise control; campground sanitation, etc.

Environmental Health Components for Water Supply, Sanitation and Urban Projects. James A. Listorti. World Bank, 1818 H. St., N.W., Washington, District of Columbia 20433. (202) 477-1234. 1990. Sanitary engineering, with special reference to health related aspects of the water supply.

HANDBOOKS AND MANUALS

Guidance Manual for Sewerless Sanitary Devices and Recycling Methods. U.S. Department of Housing and Urban Development, 451 7th St. SW, Washington, District of Columbia 20410. (202) 708-1422. 1983. Sanitary engineering relating to rural sewage disposal.

Hazardous Waste Management Strategies for Health Care Facilities. Nelson S. Slavik. American Hospital Association, 840 North Lake Shore Dr., Chicago, Illinois 60611. 1987. Contains helpful information for health care facilities in the management of their chemical, cytotoxic, infectious, and radiological wastes.

Procedures Pertaining to Environmental Sanitation. Wilhelmina C. Carey. U.S. G.P.O., Washington, District of Columbia 20401. (202) 512-0000. 1976. A manual on hospital housekeeping procedures.

Sanitation Safety & Environmental Standards. Lewis J. Minor. AVI Pub. Co., 250 Post Rd., PO Box 831, Westport, Connecticut 06881. 1983. Environmental aspects of food industry and trade.

PERIODICALS AND NEWSLETTERS

Environmental Science and Technology. American Chemical Society, 1155 16th St. N.W., Washington, District of Columbia 20036. (800) 227-5558. 1967-. Monthly. Contains research articles on various aspects of environmental chemistry, interpretative articles by invited experts and commentary on the scientific aspects of environmental management.

Pollution Engineering. Cahners Publishing Co., 249 W. 17th St., New York, New York 10011. (212) 645-0067. 1969-. Monthly.

Water and Waste Treatment Journal. D.R. Publications, Faversham House, 111 St. James's Rd., Croydon, England CR9 2TH. Monthly. Sewage and water supply engineering topics.

STATISTICS SOURCES

World Resources. World Resources Institute. 1709 New York Ave., N.W., Washington, District of Columbia 20006. (202) 638-6300. Annual. Statistical and textual analysis of world's natural resources and the effects of growth-caused environmental pollution.

TRADE ASSOCIATIONS AND PROFESSIONAL SOCIETIES

American Academy of Environmental Engineers. 130 Holiday Court, #100, Annapolis, Maryland 21404. (301) 266-3311.

American Academy of Sanitarians. 14151 91st Ct., N.E., Bothell, Washington 98011. (206) 823-5810.

American Society of Plumbing Engineers. 3617 Thousand Oaks Blvd., #210, Westlake, California 91362. (805) 495-7120.

American Society of Sanitary Engineering. Box 40362, Bay Village, Ohio 44140. (216) 835-3040.

Chemical Specialties Manufacturers Association. 1913 I St., N.W., Washington, District of Columbia 20006. (202) 872-8110.

Environmental Management Association. 255 Detroit St., Suite 200, Denver, Colorado 80206. (303) 320-7855.

Industrial Chemical Research Association. 1811 Monroe St., Dearborn, Michigan 48124. (313) 563-0360.

Inter-American Association of Sanitary Engineering and Environmental Sciences. 18729 Considine Dr., Brookeville, Maryland 20833. (301) 492-7686.

International Association of Milk, Food, & Environmental Sanitarians. 502 E. Lincoln Way, Ames, Iowa 50010. (515) 232-6699.

National Sanitation Foundation. 3475 Plymouth Rd., P.O. Box 130140, Ann Arbor, Michigan 48105. (313) 769-8010.

National Society of Professional Sanitarians. 1224 Hoffman Dr., Jefferson City, Missouri 65101. (314) 751-6095.

Portable Sanitation Association International. 7800 Metro Pkwy., Suite 104, Bloomington, Minnesota 55420. (612) 854-8300.

SAPROPHYTE

See: WATER RESOURCES

SATELLITE APPLICATIONS

ABSTRACTING AND INDEXING SERVICES

General Science Index. H. W. Wilson Co., 950 University Ave., Bronx, New York 10452. 1978-. Monthly, also issued in annual cumulation. Cumulative subject index to English language periodicals in the subject fields of astronomy, botany, chemistry, earth science, environment and conservation, food and nutrition, genetics, mathematics, medicine and health, microbiology, oceanography, physics, physiology and zoology.

Science Citation Index. Institute for Scientific Information, 3501 Market St., Philadelphia, Pennsylvania 19104. 1961-.

ENCYCLOPEDIAS AND DICTIONARIES

Dictionary of Environmental Engineering and Related Sciences: English-Spanish, Spanish-English. Jose T. Villate. Ediciones Universal, 3090 SW 8th St., Miami, Florida 33135. (305) 642-3355. 1979.

Encyclopedia of Environmental Science and Engineering. J.R. Pfafflin. Gordon and Breach Science Publishers, Inc., 270 8th Ave., New York, New York 10011. (212) 206-8900. 1992.

GENERAL WORKS

The Geostationary Applications Satellite. Peter Berlin. Cambridge University Press, 40 W. 20th St., New York, New York 10011. (212) 924-3900. 1988. Environmental applications of satellite technology.

The Satellite as Microscope. R. S. Scorer. E. Horwood, 66 Wood Lane End, Hemel Hempstead, England HP2 4RG. 1990. Describes the use of artificial satellites in air pollution control.

Satellite Surveying. Gregory J. Hoar. Magnavox Advanced Products & Systems Co., 2529 Maricopa St., Torrance, California 90503. (310) 618-1200. 1982. Theory, geodesy, map projections, applications, equipment and operations.

Some Applications of Satellite Radiation Observations to Climate Studies. T.S. Chen. National Technical Information Service, 5285 Port Royal Rd., Springfield, Virginia 22161. (703) 487-4650. Detection of atmospheric radiation by meteorological satellites.

Weather from Above: America's Meteorological Satellites. Janice Hill. Smithsonian Institution Press, 470 L'Enfant Plaza, #7100, Washington, District of Columbia 20560. (800) 782-4612. 1991. Covers global weather systems. Describes instruments the satellites carried as well as images they returned to earth analyses how meteorological data are used to predict weather.

GOVERNMENTAL ORGANIZATIONS

National Environmental Satellite, Data, and Information Service. 1825 Connecticut Ave., N.W., Washington, District of Columbia 20235. (301) 763-7190.

ONLINE DATA BASES

Multispectral Scanner and Photographic Imagery. U.S. Environmental Protection Agency, Office of Modeling and Monitoring Systems and Quality Assurance, 401 M St., S.W., Washington, District of Columbia 20460. (202) 260-2090. An index for various data tapes containing multispectral imagery from aircraft and satellites relating to sources of pollution.

SCENIC PRESERVATION

ABSTRACTING AND INDEXING SERVICES

Applied Ecology Abstracts Studies in Renewable Natural Resources. Information Retrieval Ltd., 1911 Jefferson Davis Highway, Arlington, Virginia 22202. 1975-. Monthly.

Index to Scientific Book Contents. Institute for Scientific Information, 3501 Market St., Philadelphia, Pennsylvania 19104. (800) 523-1857. 1985-. Annual. Gives contents of science books published.

Multimedia Index to Ecology. National Information Center for Educational Media, University of Southern California, Los Angeles, California 90007.

Science Citation Index. Institute for Scientific Information, 3501 Market St., Philadelphia, Pennsylvania 19104. 1961-.

ENCYCLOPEDIAS AND DICTIONARIES

Van Nostrand's Scientific Encyclopedia. Glenn D. Considine, ed. Van Nostrand Reinhold, 115 5th Ave., New York, New York 10003. (212) 254-3232. 1983. Sixth edition. Includes all broad subject areas in science.

GENERAL WORKS

Evaluating the Benefits of Environmental Resources with Special Reference to Scenic Resources. John V. Krutilla. Centre for Resource Development, University of Guelph, Guelph, Ontario, Canada 1971. Economic measurement of natural resources.

Green-Line Parks. Library of Congress-Environmental Policy Division. U.S. G.P.O., Washington, District of Columbia 20401. (202) 512-0000. 1975. An approach to preserving recreational landscapes in urban areas.

Roads and Trails Study and Environmental Assessment. National Park Service. U.S. Department of the Interior, 1849 C St., NW, Washington, District of Columbia 20240. (202) 208-3171. 1991. Wild and scenic rivers and outdoor recreation.

Wild and Scenic River Economics. Richard D. Walsh. American Wildlands, 7600 E. Arapahoe Rd., Ste. 114, Englewood, Colorado 80112. (303) 771-0380. 1985. Economic aspects, recreation use and preservation values relating to reserves.

SCR

See: SELECTIVE CATALYTIC REDUCTION

SCRAP METAL

See: METALS AND METALLURGY

SCREENING

See: WASTE TREATMENT

SCRUBBERS, LIME

See: EROSION

SCRUBBERS, SPRAY SYSTEM

See: EMISSIONS

SCRUBLAND

See: DESERTS

SEA LEVEL

ABSTRACTING AND INDEXING SERVICES

General Science Index. H. W. Wilson Co., 950 University Ave., Bronx, New York 10452. 1978-. Monthly, also issued in annual cumulation. Cumulative subject index to English language periodicals in the subject fields of astronomy, botany, chemistry, earth science, environment and conservation, food and nutrition, genetics, mathematics, medicine and health, microbiology, oceanography, physics, physiology and zoology.

GENERAL WORKS

Greenhouse Effect, Sea Level Rise, and Coastal Wetlands. U.S. Environmental Protection Agency, 401 M St., S.W., Washington, District of Columbia 20460. (202) 260-2090. 1988. Deals with wetland conservation and atmospheric greenhouse effect.

On Possible Changes in Global Sealevel and Their Potential Causes. T.P. Barnett. National Technical Information Service, 5285 Port Royal Rd., Springfield, Virginia 22161. (703) 487-4650. A Scripps Institute of Oceanography study on climatic changes, global warming, etc.

Projecting Future Sealevel Rise. John S. Hoffman. Office of Policy and Resource Management, U.S. Environmental Protection Agency, 401 M St. SW, Washington, District of Columbia 20460. (202) 260-2090. 1983. Methodology, estimates of sealevel rise to the year 2100 and research needs on solar radiation and climatic change.

HANDBOOKS AND MANUALS

Sea Level Variation for the United States, 1855-1980. Steacy D. Hicks. National Oceanic and Atmospheric Administration, Department of Commerce, 20230. (202) 377-2985. 1983. Changes in tides and water levels over the years.

SEABED DISPOSAL

ABSTRACTING AND INDEXING SERVICES

Science Citation Index. Institute for Scientific Information, 3501 Market St., Philadelphia, Pennsylvania 19104. 1961-.

ENCYCLOPEDIAS AND DICTIONARIES

Van Nostrand's Scientific Encyclopedia. Glenn D. Considine, ed. Van Nostrand Reinhold, 115 5th Ave., New York, New York 10003. (212) 254-3232. 1983. Sixth edition. Includes all broad subject areas in science.

GENERAL WORKS

Feasibility of Disposal of High-Level Radioactive Waste into the Seabed. Nuclear Energy Agency. OECD Publication and Information Centre, 2 rue Andre Pascal, Paris, France F-75775. 1988. Radiological assessment, geoscience characterization, deep-sea biology, radiological processes and radiobiology, migration through deep-sea sediments and the review of the processes near a buried waste canister.

Nuclear Waste Disposal Under the Seabed. Edward L. Miles. Institute of International Studies, University of California, 215 Moses Hall, Berkeley, California 94720. (510) 642-2472. 1985. Assessment of government policy regarding the disposal in the ocean of radioactive waste.

Seabed Disposal of High-Level Radioactive Waste. Nuclear Energy Agency. OECD Publication and Information Centre, 2 rue Andre Pascal, Paris, France F-75775. 1984. A status report on the NEA-coordinated research program on the radioactive pollution of the ocean.

STATISTICS SOURCES

Ecology: Community Profiles. U.S. Fish and Wildlife Service. National Technical Information Service, 5285 Port Royal Road, Springfield, Virginia 22161. (703) 487-4650. Irregular. Data on coastal and inland ecosystems, including wetlands, tidal-flats, near-shore seagrasses, sand dunes, drilling platforms, oyster reefs, estuaries, rivers and streams.

SEASHORES

See also: BEACHES; COASTS

ABSTRACTING AND INDEXING SERVICES

Applied Science and Technology Index. H.W. Wilson Co., 950 University Ave., Bronx, New York 10452. (800) 367-6770. Formerly Industrial Arts Index.

Ecological Abstracts. Geo Abstracts Ltd. Elsevier Applied Science, Crown House, Linton Rd., Barking, England IG 11 8JU. 1974-. Derived from over 600 leading ecological and environmental journals, plus books, conference proceedings, reports and theses.

Ecology Abstracts. Cambridge Scientific Abstracts, 5161 River Rd., Bethesda, Maryland 20816. (301) 961-6750. Monthly.

Index to Scientific Book Contents. Institute for Scientific Information, 3501 Market St., Philadelphia, Pennsylvania 19104. (800) 523-1857. 1985-. Annual. Gives contents of science books published.

Science Citation Index. Institute for Scientific Information, 3501 Market St., Philadelphia, Pennsylvania 19104. 1961-.

ENCYCLOPEDIAS AND DICTIONARIES

McGraw-Hill Encyclopedia of Science and Technology. McGraw-Hill, 1221 Avenue of the Americas, New York, New York 10020. (212) 512-2000 or (800) 262-4729. 1992. Seventh edition. Issued in multiple volumes including index. Includes all science and technology broad subject areas.

GENERAL WORKS

Biogeochemical Processes at the Land-Sea Boundary. Pierre Lasserre. Elsevier Science Publishing Co., 655 Avenue of the Americas, New York, New York 10010. (212) 989-5800. 1988. Covers biogeochemical cycles, and seashore and coastal ecology.

Ecology of Sandy Shores. A. C. Brown and A. Mclachlan. Elsevier Science Publishing Co., 655 Avenue of the Americas, New York, New York 10010. (212) 989-5800. 1990. Deals with the biological study of sandy beaches.

The Shore Environment. J.H. Price. Academic Press, c/o Harcourt Brace Jovanovich Inc., 6277 Sea Harbor Dr., Orlando, Florida 32887. (800) 346-8648. 1980. Seashore ecology management methods.

HANDBOOKS AND MANUALS

America's Seashore Wonderlands. National Geographic Society, 17th & M Sts. NW, Washington, District of Columbia 20036. (202) 857-7000. 1985. A guide to North American coasts and seashore ecology.

Coastal Ecosystem Management. John Ray Clark. John Wiley & Sons, Inc., 605 3rd Ave., New York, New York 10158-0012. (212) 850-6000. 1983. A technical manual for the conservation of coastal resources.

SEAWATER

ABSTRACTING AND INDEXING SERVICES

Chemical Abstracts. Chemical Abstracts Service, 2540 Olentangy River Rd., PO Box 3012, Columbus, Ohio 43210. (800) 848-6533. 1907-.

Desalination Abstracts. National Center for Scientific and Technological Information, PO Box 20125, Tel-Aviv, Israel 1966-. Quarterly.

Ecology Abstracts. Cambridge Scientific Abstracts, 5161 River Rd., Bethesda, Maryland 20816. (301) 961-6750. Monthly.

General Science Index. H. W. Wilson Co., 950 University Ave., Bronx, New York 10452. 1978-. Monthly, also issued in annual cumulation. Cumulative subject index to English language periodicals in the subject fields of astronomy, botany, chemistry, earth science, environment and conservation, food and nutrition, genetics,

mathematics, medicine and health, microbiology, oceanography, physics, physiology and zoology.

Science Citation Index. Institute for Scientific Information, 3501 Market St., Philadelphia, Pennsylvania 19104. 1961-.

BIBLIOGRAPHIES

Bibliography and Index of Geology. American Geological Institute, 4220 King St., Alexandria, Virginia 22302. Monthly. Includes environmental geology and hydrogeology.

Desalination Technology. Vance Bibliographies, PO Box 229, 112 N. Charter St., Monticello, Illinois 61856. (217) 762-3831. 1981.

DIRECTORIES

Desalination Directory: Desalination and Water Purification. Elsevier Science Publishing Co., 655 Avenue of the Americas, New York, New York 10010. (212) 989-5800. 1981-.

ENCYCLOPEDIAS AND DICTIONARIES

McGraw-Hill Encyclopedia of Science and Technology. McGraw-Hill, 1221 Avenue of the Americas, New York, New York 10020. (212) 512-2000 or (800) 262-4729. 1992. Seventh edition. Issued in multiple volumes including index. Includes all science and technology broad subject areas.

Van Nostrand's Scientific Encyclopedia. Glenn D. Considine, ed. Van Nostrand Reinhold, 115 5th Ave., New York, New York 10003. (212) 254-3232. 1983. Sixth edition. Includes all broad subject areas in science.

GENERAL WORKS

Adsorption of Trace Metals by Hydrous Ferric Oxide in Seawater. K.C. Swallow. National Technical Information Service, 5285 Port Royal Rd., Springfield, Virginia 22161. (703) 487-4650. Water purification and trace elements in water.

Analysis of Seawater. Thomas Roy Crompton. Butterworth-Heinemann, 80 Montvale Ave., Stoneham, Massachusetts 02180. (617) 438-8464. 1989.

Assessment of the Effects of Chlorinated Seawater from Power Plants on Aquatic Organisms. R. Sung. National Technical Information Service, 5285 Port Royal Rd., Springfield, Virginia 22161. (703) 487-4650. Physiological effects of marine pollution and chlorine on aquatic animals.

Desalination Materials Manual. Dow Chemical Company. Office of Water Research and Technology, U.S. Dept. of the Interior, Washington, District of Columbia 20240. 1975.

Heavy Metals in the Marine Environment. Robert W. Furness and Philip S. Rainbow. CRC Press, 2000 Corporate Blvd. N.W., Boca Raton, Florida 33431. (800) 272-7737. 1990. Includes heavy metals in the marine environment, trace metals in sea water, metals in the marine atmosphere, processes affecting metal concentration in estuarine and coastal marine sediments, heavy metal levels in marine invertebrates, use of microalgae and invertebrates to monitor metal levels in estuaries and

coastal waters, toxic effects of metals, and the incidence of metal pollution in marine ecosystems.

Magill's Survey of Science. Earth Science Series. Frank N. Magill. Salem Press, PO Box 50062, Pasadena, California 91105. 1990-. Five volumes. Includes information on earth's crust, hot spots and volcanic island chains, physical properties of minerals, rock magnetism, physical properties of rocks, and index.

Saline Water Processing: Desalination and Treatment of Seawater, Brackish Water, and Industrial Waste Water. Hans-Gunter Heitmann, ed. VCH Publishers, 303 NW 12th Ave., Deerfield Beach, Florida 33442-1788. (305) 428-5566. 1990. Desalination and treatment of seawater, brackish water, and industrial waste water.

Seawater and Desalting. A. Delyannis. Springer-Verlag, 175 5th Ave., New York, New York 10010. (212) 460-1500. 1980. Topics in saline water conversion.

HANDBOOKS AND MANUALS

Desalination Processes and Multistage Flash Distillation Practice. Arshad Hassan Khan. Elsevier Science Publishing Co., 655 Avenue of the Americas, New York, New York 10010. (212) 984-5800. 1986. Saline water conservation through flash distillation process.

Desalting Handbook for Planners. Catalytic Inc. U.S. Department of the Interior, Office of Water Research and Technology, Washington, District of Columbia 20240. 1979. 2d ed.

ONLINE DATA BASES

Chemical Abstracts-CA. Chemical Abstracts Service, 2540 Olentangy River Rd., P.O. Box 3012, Columbus, Ohio 43210. (800) 848-6533 or (614) 421-3600. Information sources include 9000 journals, patents from 27 countries, two industrial property organizations, new books, conference proceedings, and government research reports.

SCISEARCH. Institute for Scientific Information, University City Science Center, 3501 Market St., Philadelphia, Pennsylvania 19104. (215) 386-0100.

PERIODICALS AND NEWSLETTERS

Desalination. Elsevier, Box 211, Amsterdam, Netherlands 1000 AE. 020-5803-911. 1966-. Forty-two times a year. The international journal on the science and technology of desalting and water purification. Formed by the merger of the Journal of Membrane Science and Desalination.

SECONDARY TREATMENT
See: WASTEWATER TREATMENT

SEDIMENT TRANSPORT
See also: RIVERS

ABSTRACTING AND INDEXING SERVICES

Biological and Agricultural Index. H.W. Wilson Co., 950 University Ave., Bronx, New York 10452. (800) 367-6770. 1916-. Monthly.

Civil Engineering Hydraulic Abstracts. BHRA Fluid Engineering, Air Science Co., PO Box 143, Corning, New York 14830. (607) 962-5591. Monthly. Abstracts of periodicals that publish in the areas of hydraulic engineering and other related topics.

Ecological Abstracts. Geo Abstracts Ltd. Elsevier Applied Science, Crown House, Linton Rd., Barking, England IG 11 8JU. 1974-. Derived from over 600 leading ecological and environmental journals, plus books, conference proceedings, reports and theses.

Ecology Abstracts. Cambridge Scientific Abstracts, 5161 River Rd., Bethesda, Maryland 20816. (301) 961-6750. Monthly.

BIBLIOGRAPHIES

Bibliography and Index of Geology. American Geological Institute, 4220 King St., Alexandria, Virginia 22302. Monthly. Includes environmental geology and hydrogeology.

New Publications of the Geological Survey. U.S. Department of the Interior, Geological Survey, 119 National Center, Reston, Virginia 22092. (703) 648-4460. 1984-. Monthly. Bibliography of geological publications and related government documents published by the Geological Survey.

ENCYCLOPEDIAS AND DICTIONARIES

Glossary of Geology. Robert Latimer Bates and Julia A. Jackson, eds. American Geological Institute, 4220 King St., Alexandria, Virginia 22302-1507. (703) 379-2480 or (800) 336-4764. 1987. Third edition.

McGraw-Hill Encyclopedia of the Geological Sciences. Sybil P. Parker, ed. McGraw-Hill, 1221 Avenue of the Americas, New York, New York 10020. (212) 512-2000 or (800) 262-4729. 1988. Second edition. Published previously in the McGraw-Hill Encyclopedia of Science and Technology.

Van Nostrand's Scientific Encyclopedia. Glenn D. Considine, ed. Van Nostrand Reinhold, 115 5th Ave., New York, New York 10003. (212) 254-3232. 1983. Sixth edition. Includes all broad subject areas in science.

GENERAL WORKS

Magill's Survey of Science. Earth Science Series. Frank N. Magill. Salem Press, PO Box 50062, Pasadena, California 91105. 1990-. Five volumes. Includes information on earth's crust, hot spots and volcanic island chains, physical properties of minerals, rock magnetism, physical properties of rocks, and index.

Mechanics of Sediment Transportation and Alluvial Stream Problems. R.J. Garde. John Wiley & Sons, Inc., 605 3rd Ave., New York, New York 10158-0012. (212) 850-6000. 1985.

Modern and Ancient Fluvial Systems. J.D. Collinson. Blackwell Scientific Publications, 3 Cambridge Ctr., Ste. 208, Boston, Massachusetts 02142. (617) 225-0401. 1983. Topics in sediment transport in rivers.

Sedimentary Dynamics of Continental Shelves. C.A. Nittrouer. Elsevier, Amsterdam, 1000 AE. 020-5803-911. 1981. Developments in sedimentology and marine sediments.

ONLINE DATA BASES

National Stream Quality Accounting Network. National Water Data Exchange, U.S. Geological Survey, 421 National Center, Reston, Virginia 22092. (703) 648-4000. 150 hydrologic measurements collected at daily, monthly and quarterly intervals from more than 500 monitoring stations in the U.S.

SEDIMENTATION AND DEPOSITION

See also: ACID PRECIPITATION; SEDIMENT TRANSPORT

ABSTRACTING AND INDEXING SERVICES

Agrindex. AGRIS Coordinating Center, Via delle Terme di Caracalla, Rome, Italy I-00100. 61 0181-FA01. 1975-.

Biological and Agricultural Index. H.W. Wilson Co., 950 University Ave., Bronx, New York 10452. (800) 367-6770. 1916-. Monthly.

Civil Engineering Hydraulic Abstracts. BHRA Fluid Engineering, Air Science Co., PO Box 143, Corning, New York 14830. (607) 962-5591. Monthly. Abstracts of periodicals that publish in the areas of hydraulic engineering and other related topics.

General Science Index. H. W. Wilson Co., 950 University Ave., Bronx, New York 10452. 1978-. Monthly, also issued in annual cumulation. Cumulative subject index to English language periodicals in the subject fields of astronomy, botany, chemistry, earth science, environment and conservation, food and nutrition, genetics, mathematics, medicine and health, microbiology, oceanography, physics, physiology and zoology.

DIRECTORIES

Certified Professional Erosion and Sediment Control Specialists– Directory. Office of the Registry/Certified Professional Erosion and Sediment Control Specialists, 677 S. Segoe Rd., Madison, Wisconsin 53711. (503) 326-2826.

GENERAL WORKS

Sedimentation Engineering. Vito A. Vanoni. American Society of Civil Engineers, 345 E. 47th St., New York, New York 10017. (212) 705-7288; (800) 548-2723. 1975. Hydraulic engineering aspects of sedimentation and deposition.

HANDBOOKS AND MANUALS

Coastal Sedimentation and Dredging. Naval Facilities Engineering Command. U.S. Department of the Navy, The Pentagon, Washington, District of Columbia 20350. (703) 545-6700. 1981. Design manual for dredging, sedimentation and deposition.

Handbook of Deltaic Facies. Donald C. Swanson. Swanson Petroleum Enterprises, Lafayette, Indiana 1980. A collection of practical and useful information and exercises for the subsurface geologist.

National Engineering Handbook. Section 3, Sedimentation. U.S. Department of Agriculture, Soil Conservation Service, 14 Independence Ave., SW, Washington, District of Columbia 20250. (202) 447-7454. 1983. Deals with sedimentation, deposition, and erosion in the United States.

ONLINE DATA BASES

National Stream Quality Accounting Network. National Water Data Exchange, U.S. Geological Survey, 421 National Center, Reston, Virginia 22092. (703) 648-4000. 150 hydrologic measurements collected at daily, monthly and quarterly intervals from more than 500 monitoring stations in the U.S.

SEEPAGE

See: SOIL SCIENCE

SELECTIVE CATALYTIC REDUCTION

ENCYCLOPEDIAS AND DICTIONARIES

Dictionary of Environmental Engineering and Related Sciences: English-Spanish, Spanish-English. Jose T. Villate. Ediciones Universal, 3090 SW 8th St., Miami, Florida 33135. (305) 642-3355. 1979.

Encyclopedia of Environmental Science and Engineering. J.R. Pfafflin. Gordon and Breach Science Publishers, Inc., 270 8th Ave., New York, New York 10011. (212) 206-8900. 1992.

SELECTIVE HERBICIDES

See: HERBICIDES

SELENIUM

ABSTRACTING AND INDEXING SERVICES

ASFA Aquaculture Abstracts. Cambridge Scientific Abstracts, Inc., 5161 River Rd., Bethesda, Maryland 20816. (301) 961-6750. 1984.

Chemical Abstracts. Chemical Abstracts Service, 2540 Olentangy River Rd., PO Box 3012, Columbus, Ohio 43210. (800) 848-6533. 1907-.

General Science Index. H. W. Wilson Co., 950 University Ave., Bronx, New York 10452. 1978-. Monthly, also issued in annual cumulation. Cumulative subject index to English language periodicals in the subject fields of astronomy, botany, chemistry, earth science, environment and conservation, food and nutrition, genetics, mathematics, medicine and health, microbiology, oceanography, physics, physiology and zoology.

Physics Briefs. Physikalische Berichte. Physik Verlag, Pappapelallee 3, Postfach 101161, Weinheim, Germany D-6940. 1979-. Semimonthly. In English. Volumes for

1979- issued by the Deutsche Physikalische Gesellschaft and the Fachinformationszentrum Energie Physik, Mathematik in cooperation with the American Institute of Physics.

Science Citation Index. Institute for Scientific Information, 3501 Market St., Philadelphia, Pennsylvania 19104. 1961-.

BIBLIOGRAPHIES

Selenium in Agricultural Ecosystems. Robert Lewis Jones. Department of Agronomy, University of Illinois, Urbana, Illinois 61801. 1971. A bibliography of literature, 1950 through 1971, covering environmental aspects of sewage sludge.

ENCYCLOPEDIAS AND DICTIONARIES

Encyclopedia of Human Biology. Renato Dulbecco, ed. Academic Press, c/o Harcourt Brace Jovanovich Inc., 6277 Sea Harbor Dr., Orlando, Florida 32887. (800) 346-8648. 1991. Eight volumes.

McGraw-Hill Encyclopedia of Science and Technology. McGraw-Hill, 1221 Avenue of the Americas, New York, New York 10020. (212) 512-2000 or (800) 262-4729. 1992. Seventh edition. Issued in multiple volumes including index. Includes all science and technology broad subject areas.

Van Nostrand's Scientific Encyclopedia. Glenn D. Considine, ed. Van Nostrand Reinhold, 115 5th Ave., New York, New York 10003. (212) 254-3232. 1983. Sixth edition. Includes all broad subject areas in science.

GENERAL WORKS

Aquatic Cycling of Selenium. Fish and Wildlife Service. U.S. Department of the Interior, 1849 C St., NW, Washington, District of Columbia 20240. (202) 208-3171. 1988. Implications for fish and wildlife from selenium in the environment.

Death in the Marsh. Tom Harris. Island Press, 1718 Connecticut Ave. N.W., Suite 300, Washington, District of Columbia 20009. (202) 232-7933. 1991. Explains how federal irrigation projects have altered the selenium's circulation in the environment, allowing it to accumulate in marshes, killing ecosystems and wildlife, and causing deformities in some animals.

Health Risks of Toxic Emissions from a Coal-Fired Power Plant. J.G. Bolten. RAND, 1700 Main St., Santa Monica, California 90401. (310) 393-0411. 1987. Toxicology of selenium and beryllium used in coal-fired power plants.

Selenium. Charles Grady Wilber. Charles C. Thomas Publishing Co., 2600 S. First St., Springfield, Illinois 62794-9265. (217) 789-8980. 1983. A potential environmental poison and a necessary food constituent.

Selenium Pretreatment Study. Lisa H. Rowley. Bureau of Reclamation, U.S. Department of the Interior, Washington, District of Columbia 202400. (202) 208-4662. 1991. Water purification using agricultural chemicals, especially selenium.

HANDBOOKS AND MANUALS

Complete Guide to Vitamins, Minerals and Supplements. H. Winter Griffith. Fisher Books, 3499 N. Campbell

Ave., Suite 909, Tucson, Arizona 85712. (602) 325-5263. 1988. Includes name, brand name, reasons to use, who should use, recommended daily allowance, and other related data in the form of a chart.

ONLINE DATA BASES

Chemical Abstracts-CA. Chemical Abstracts Service, 2540 Olentangy River Rd., P.O. Box 3012, Columbus, Ohio 43210. (800) 848-6533 or (614) 421-3600. Information sources include 9000 journals, patents from 27 countries, two industrial property organizations, new books, conference proceedings, and government research reports.

TRADE ASSOCIATIONS AND PROFESSIONAL SOCIETIES

Selenium-Tellurium Development Association. 301 Borgtstraat, B1850 Brimbergen, Belgium

SENESCENCE

See: LAKES

SEPTIC TANKS

ENCYCLOPEDIAS AND DICTIONARIES

Dictionary of Environmental Engineering and Related Sciences: English-Spanish, Spanish-English. Jose T. Villate. Ediciones Universal, 3090 SW 8th St., Miami, Florida 33135. (305) 642-3355. 1979.

Encyclopedia of Environmental Science and Engineering. J.R. Pfafflin. Gordon and Breach Science Publishers, Inc., 270 8th Ave., New York, New York 10011. (212) 206-8900. 1992.

Van Nostrand's Scientific Encyclopedia. Glenn D. Considine, ed. Van Nostrand Reinhold, 115 5th Ave., New York, New York 10003. (212) 254-3232. 1983. Sixth edition. Includes all broad subject areas in science.

HANDBOOKS AND MANUALS

Septic Systems Handbook. O. Benjamin Kaplan. Lewis Publishers, 2000 Corporate Blvd., N.W., Boca Raton, Florida 33431. (407) 994-0555 or (800) 272-7737. 1991. Discusses why public health agencies control the disposal of domestic sewage. The septic system, economics of leachfield size, soils at a glance, soil water movement, the percolation test, size of leachline, factors affecting failure of leachlines, size of seepage pits, various onsite sewage disposal technologies, degradation of groundwater by septic systems and related matters.

SETTLED SOLIDS

See: WASTEWATER TREATMENT

SETTLING TANK

See: WASTEWATER TREATMENT

SEWAGE

ABSTRACTING AND INDEXING SERVICES

Aqualine Abstracts. Water Research Centre. c/o Pergamon Microforms International, Inc., Fairview Park, Elmsford, New York 10523. (914) 592-7720. 1927-. Contains some 8,000 records annually on water and wastewater technology. Covers all aspects of water, wastewater, associated engineering services and the aquatic environment. Over 600 periodicals, as well as books, reports and conference proceedings and other publications from water related institutions worldwide are scanned. Also available online.

ASFA Aquaculture Abstracts. Cambridge Scientific Abstracts, Inc., 5161 River Rd., Bethesda, Maryland 20816. (301) 961-6750. 1984.

Biotechnology Research Abstracts. Cambridge Scientific Abstracts, 5161 River Rd., Bethesda, Maryland 20816. (301) 961-6750. Monthly. Includes such broad areas as genetic intervention, biochemical genetics, and microbiological techniques.

Chemical Abstracts. Chemical Abstracts Service, 2540 Olentangy River Rd., PO Box 3012, Columbus, Ohio 43210. (800) 848-6533. 1907-.

Civil Engineering Hydraulic Abstracts. BHRA Fluid Engineering, Air Science Co., PO Box 143, Corning, New York 14830. (607) 962-5591. Monthly. Abstracts of periodicals that publish in the areas of hydraulic engineering and other related topics.

General Science Index. H. W. Wilson Co., 950 University Ave., Bronx, New York 10452. 1978-. Monthly, also issued in annual cumulation. Cumulative subject index to English language periodicals in the subject fields of astronomy, botany, chemistry, earth science, environment and conservation, food and nutrition, genetics, mathematics, medicine and health, microbiology, oceanography, physics, physiology and zoology.

Science Citation Index. Institute for Scientific Information, 3501 Market St., Philadelphia, Pennsylvania 19104. 1961-.

BIBLIOGRAPHIES

Cobalt in Agricultural Ecosystems: A Bibliography of the Literature 1950 Through 1971. Robert Lewis Jones. Department of Agronomy, University of Illinois, Urbana, Illinois 61801. 1973.

Current Contents. Agriculture, Biology and Environmental Sciences. Institute for Scientific Information, 3501 Market St., Philadelphia, Pennsylvania 19104. (800) 523-1857. 1973-. Previous title: Current Contents. Agricultural, Food & Veterinary Sciences. Gives the table of contents of periodicals in the fields of agriculture, biology, environmental and related areas.

ENCYCLOPEDIAS AND DICTIONARIES

Dictionary of Environmental Engineering and Related Sciences: English-Spanish, Spanish-English. Jose T. Villate. Ediciones Universal, 3090 SW 8th St., Miami, Florida 33135. (305) 642-3355. 1979.

Dictionary of Waste and Water Treatment. Butterworth-Heinemann, 80 Montvale Ave., Stoneham, Massachusetts 02180. (617) 438-8464. 1981. Dictionary of sanitary engineering.

Dictionary of Water and Sewage Engineering. Fritz Meinck and Helmut Mohle. Elsevier Science Publishing Co., 655 Avenue of the Americas, New York, New York 10010. (212) 984-5800. 1977. Text is in German, English, French and Italian. Deals with water management engineering and sewage.

Encyclopedia of Environmental Science and Engineering. J.R. Pfafflin. Gordon and Breach Science Publishers, Inc., 270 8th Ave., New York, New York 10011. (212) 206-8900. 1992.

McGraw-Hill Encyclopedia of Environmental Science. Sybil P. Parker. McGraw-Hill Science & Engineering Books, 11 W. 19th St., New York, New York 10011. (212) 337-6010. 1980. Covers ecology, man's influence on nature, and environmental protection.

McGraw-Hill Encyclopedia of Science and Technology. McGraw-Hill, 1221 Avenue of the Americas, New York, New York 10020. (212) 512-2000 or (800) 262-4729. 1992. Seventh edition. Issued in multiple volumes including index. Includes all science and technology broad subject areas.

Van Nostrand's Scientific Encyclopedia. Glenn D. Considine, ed. Van Nostrand Reinhold, 115 5th Ave., New York, New York 10003. (212) 254-3232. 1983. Sixth edition. Includes all broad subject areas in science.

GENERAL WORKS

Bioenvironmental Systems. Donald L. Wise, ed. CRC Press, 2000 Corporate Blvd. N.W., Boca Raton, Florida 33431. (407) 994-0555; (800) 272-7737. 1987. 4 vols.

Biological Wastewater Treatment Systems. N. J. Horan. John Wiley & Sons, Inc., 605 3rd Ave., New York, New York 10158-0012. (212) 850-6000. 1990. Introduces basic concepts of microbial growth and reactor engineering required to fully understand the design and operation of wastewater treatment systems. Topics include wastewater characteristics, microorganisms exploited in wastewater treatment, and microbial energy generation.

Biomass Determination–a New Technique for Activated Sludge Control. U.S. Environmental Protection Agency, 401 M St. SW, Washington, District of Columbia 20460. (202) 260-2090. 1972. Includes an analysis of sewage sludge analysis by biomass determination. Also describes sewage disposal.

The Codisposal of Sewage Sludge and Refuse in the Purox System. Union Carbide Corporation. Municipal Environmental Research Laboratory, Office of Research and Development, U.S. Environmental Protection Agency, Cincinnati, Ohio 1978.

Constructed Wetlands for Wastewater Treatment. Donald A. Hammer. Lewis Publishers, 200 Corporate Blvd. NW, Boca Raton, Florida 33431. (407) 994-0555 or (800)272-7737. 1989. Presents general principles of wetland ecology, hydrology, soil chemistry, vegetation, microbiology, and wildlife dependence on wetlands. It provides management guidelines, beginning with policies and regulations, and including siting and construction and operations and monitoring of constructed wetland systems.

Emerging Technologies in Hazardous Waste Management. D. William Tedder and Frederick G. Pohland, eds. American Chemical Society, 1155 16th St. N.W., Wash-

ington, District of Columbia 20036. (202) 872-4600; (800) 227-5558. 1990. Hazardous waste management technology.

Emerging Technologies in Hazardous Waste Management II. D. William Tedder and Frederick G. Pohland, eds. American Chemical Society, 1155 16th St. N.W., Washington, District of Columbia 20036. (202) 872-4600; (800) 227-5558. 1991. Developed from a symposium sponsored by the Division of Industrial and Engineering Chemistry, Inc. of the American Chemical Society at the Industrial and Engineering Chemistry Special Symposium, Atlantic City, NJ, June 4-7, 1990.

Hazardous and Industrial Wastes, 1991. Technomic Publishing Co., 851 New Holland Ave., Box 3535, Lancaster, Pennsylvania 17604. (717) 291-5609. 1991. Proceedings of the 23rd Mid-Atlantic Industrial Waste Conference held at Drexel University, 1991.

Leaching and Hydraulic Properties of Retorted Oil Shale Including Effects from Codisposal of Wastewater. David B. McWhorter. U.S. Environmental Protection Agency, Air and Energy Engineering Research Laboratory, MD 75, Research Triangle Park, North Carolina 27711. (919) 541-2184. 1987.

River Pollution: An Ecological Perspective. S. M. Haslam. Belhaven Press, 136 S. Broadway, Irvington, New York 10533. (914) 591-9111. 1990. Describes the impact of natural and man-made pollution in the ecosystem of freshwater streams, stressing understanding of processes and techniques of measurement.

Sewage and the Bacterial Purification of Sewage. Samuel Rideal. John Wiley & Sons, Inc., 605 3rd Ave., New York, New York 10158-0012. (212) 850-6000. 1906. Publication on sewage purification with illustrations and colored plates.

Sewage Lagoons in Cold Climates. Environmental Protection Service, Technical Service Branch, 425 St. Joseph Blvd., 3rd Fl., Hull, Quebec, Canada K1A 0H3. (613) 953-5921. 1985. Cold weather conditions in sewage lagoons.

Wastewater Engineering: Treatment, Disposal, and Reuse. Metcalf & Eddy, Inc. McGraw-Hill Science & Engineering Books, 11 West 19th St., New York, New York 10011. (212) 337-6010. 1991. Reflects the impact of changing federal legislation on environmental quality control and sludge management. Gives a solid overall perspective on wastewater engineering.

HANDBOOKS AND MANUALS

Economic Analysis of Proposed Revised Effluent Guidelines and Standards for the Inorganic Chemicals Industry. National Technical Information Service, 5285 Port Royal Rd., Springfield, Virginia 22161. (703) 487-4650. 1980. Covers effluent quality and sewage purification technology.

Water and Wastewater Examination Manual. V. Dean Adams. Lewis Publishers, 2000 Corporate Blvd., N.W., Boca Raton, Florida 33431. (407) 994-0555 or (800) 272-7737. 1990. Guide and reference for water/wastewater quality analysis. Includes procedures for parameters frequently used in water quality analysis.

ONLINE DATA BASES

CERCLIS. Chemical Information Systems, Inc., 7215 York Rd., Baltimore, Maryland 21212. (301) 321-8440. Information on hazardous waste disposal sites that have either been listed by the EPA on the National Priority List (NPL) or nominated for consideration for the NPL.

Chemical Abstracts-CA. Chemical Abstracts Service, 2540 Olentangy River Rd., P.O. Box 3012, Columbus, Ohio 43210. (800) 848-6533 or (614) 421-3600. Information sources include 9000 journals, patents from 27 countries, two industrial property organizations, new books, conference proceedings, and government research reports.

Monthly Catalog of United States Government Publications. U.S. G.P.O., Supt. of Docs., PO Box 371954, Pittsburgh, Pennsylvania 15250-7954. (202) 512-0000.

National Technical Information Service. U.S. Department of Commerce, National Technical Information Service, Office of Data Base Services, 5285 Port Royal Rd., Springfield, Virginia 22161. (703) 487-4807. Bibliographic database of government sponsored research and technical reports.

PERIODICALS AND NEWSLETTERS

Association of Metropolitan Sewerage Agencies Monthly Report. Association of Metropolitan Sewerage Agencies, 1000 Connecticut Avenue, NW, Suite 1006, Washington, District of Columbia 20005. (202) 833-4653. Monthly. Data on environmental and regulatory matters.

Journal of the Water Pollution Control Federation. Water Pollution Control Federation, 801 Wythe St., Alexandria, Virginia 22314-1994. (703) 684-2400. Monthly. Deals with sewage and pollution.

Sewage and Waste Disposal. Sewage and Waste Disposal, 321 Sunset Ave., Asbury Park, New Jersey 07712. 1946-. Fourteen times a year.

STATISTICS SOURCES

World Resources. World Resources Institute. 1709 New York Ave., N.W., Washington, District of Columbia 20006. (202) 638-6300. Annual. Statistical and textual analysis of world's natural resources and the effects of growth-caused environmental pollution.

TRADE ASSOCIATIONS AND PROFESSIONAL SOCIETIES

American Public Works Association. 106 W. 11th St., Ste. 1800, Kansas City, Missouri 64105-1806. (816) 472-6100.

American Society of Sanitary Engineering. Box 40362, Bay Village, Ohio 44140. (216) 835-3040.

Association of Metropolitan Sewerage Agencies. 1000 Connecticut Ave., N.W., Suite 1006, Washington, District of Columbia 20036. (202) 833-4653.

SEWAGE ANALYSIS

ABSTRACTING AND INDEXING SERVICES

Aqualine Abstracts. Water Research Centre. c/o Pergamon Microforms International, Inc., Fairview Park,

Elmsford, New York 10523. (914) 592-7720. 1927-. Contains some 8,000 records annually on water and wastewater technology. Covers all aspects of water, wastewater, associated engineering services and the aquatic environment. Over 600 periodicals, as well as books, reports and conference proceedings and other publications from water related institutions worldwide are scanned. Also available online.

ASFA Aquaculture Abstracts. Cambridge Scientific Abstracts, Inc., 5161 River Rd., Bethesda, Maryland 20816. (301) 961-6750. 1984.

Biological and Agricultural Index. H.W. Wilson Co., 950 University Ave., Bronx, New York 10452. (800) 367-6770. 1916-. Monthly.

Biotechnology Research Abstracts. Cambridge Scientific Abstracts, 5161 River Rd., Bethesda, Maryland 20816. (301) 961-6750. Monthly. Includes such broad areas as genetic intervention, biochemical genetics, and microbiological techniques.

Chemical Abstracts. Chemical Abstracts Service, 2540 Olentangy River Rd., PO Box 3012, Columbus, Ohio 43210. (800) 848-6533. 1907-.

Engineering Index. The Engineering Index Inc., 345 E. 47th St., New York, New York 10017. 1962-.

General Science Index. H. W. Wilson Co., 950 University Ave., Bronx, New York 10452. 1978-. Monthly, also issued in annual cumulation. Cumulative subject index to English language periodicals in the subject fields of astronomy, botany, chemistry, earth science, environment and conservation, food and nutrition, genetics, mathematics, medicine and health, microbiology, oceanography, physics, physiology and zoology.

Pollution Abstracts. Cambridge Scientific Abstracts, 5161 River Rd., Bethesda, Maryland 20816. (301) 961-6750. Six/year. Indexes worldwide technical literature on environmental pollution. Covers air pollution, marine and freshwater pollution, sewage and wastewater treatment, waste management, toxicology and health, noise pollution, radiation, land pollution, and environmental policies, programs, legislation, and education. Also available online.

BIBLIOGRAPHIES

Current Contents. Agriculture, Biology and Environmental Sciences. Institute for Scientific Information, 3501 Market St., Philadelphia, Pennsylvania 19104. (800) 523-1857. 1973-. Previous title: Current Contents. Agricultural, Food & Veterinary Sciences. Gives the table of contents of periodicals in the fields of agriculture, biology, environmental and related areas.

ENCYCLOPEDIAS AND DICTIONARIES

Dictionary of Environmental Engineering and Related Sciences: English-Spanish, Spanish-English. Jose T. Villate. Ediciones Universal, 3090 SW 8th St., Miami, Florida 33135. (305) 642-3355. 1979.

Encyclopedia of Environmental Science and Engineering. J.R. Pfafflin. Gordon and Breach Science Publishers, Inc., 270 8th Ave., New York, New York 10011. (212) 206-8900. 1992.

Van Nostrand's Scientific Encyclopedia. Glenn D. Considine, ed. Van Nostrand Reinhold, 115 5th Ave., New

York, New York 10003. (212) 254-3232. 1983. Sixth edition. Includes all broad subject areas in science.

GENERAL WORKS

Applied Math for Wastewater Plant Operators. Joanne Kilpatrick Price. Technomic Publishing Co., 851 New Holland Ave., Box 3535, Lancaster, Pennsylvania 17604. (717) 291-5609. 1991.

Biological Wastewater Treatment Systems. N. J. Horan. John Wiley & Sons, Inc., 605 3rd Ave., New York, New York 10158-0012. (212) 850-6000. 1990. Introduces basic concepts of microbial growth and reactor engineering required to fully understand the design and operation of wastewater treatment systems. Topics include wastewater characteristics, microorganisms exploited in wastewater treatment, and microbial energy generation.

Chemical and Biological Characterization of Municipal Sludges, Sediments, Dredge Spoils, and Drilling Muds. James L. Lichtenberg, et al. American Society for Testing and Materials, 1916 S. Race St., Philadelphia, Pennsylvania 19103. (215) 299-5585. 1988. Deals with the environmental aspects of sewage disposal, analysis, health risk assessment, biological purification of sludge, and water quality management.

The Codisposal of Sewage Sludge and Refuse in the Purox System. Union Carbide Corporation. Municipal Environmental Research Laboratory, Office of Research and Development, U.S. Environmental Protection Agency, Cincinnati, Ohio 1978.

ONLINE DATA BASES

Chemical Abstracts-CA. Chemical Abstracts Service, 2540 Olentangy River Rd., P.O. Box 3012, Columbus, Ohio 43210. (800) 848-6533 or (614) 421-3600. Information sources include 9000 journals, patents from 27 countries, two industrial property organizations, new books, conference proceedings, and government research reports.

Computerized Engineering Index–COMPENDEX. Engineering Information Inc., 345 E. 47th St., New York, New York 10017. (212) 705-7600.

SCISEARCH. Institute for Scientific Information, University City Science Center, 3501 Market St., Philadelphia, Pennsylvania 19104. (215) 386-0100.

PERIODICALS AND NEWSLETTERS

Association of Metropolitan Sewerage Agencies Monthly Report. Association of Metropolitan Sewerage Agencies, 1000 Connecticut Avenue, NW, Suite 1006, Washington, District of Columbia 20005. (202) 833-4653. Monthly. Data on environmental and regulatory matters.

Law Digest. Association of Metropolitan Sewerage Agencies, 1000 Connecticut Avenue, NW, Suite 1006, Washington, District of Columbia 20036. (202) 833-2672. Monthly. Legal issues on environmental and regulatory matters.

RESEARCH CENTERS AND INSTITUTES

Center for Interfacial Microbial Process Engineering. Montana State University, College of Engineering, 409 Cobleigh Hall, Bozeman, Montana 59717-0007. (406) 994-4770.

Michigan State University, Microbial Ecology Center. 540 Plant and Soil Sciences Building, East Lansing, Michigan 48824-1325. (517) 353-9021.

New York University, Laboratory of Microbial Ecology. 735 Brown Building, New York, New York 10003. (212) 998-8268.

TRADE ASSOCIATIONS AND PROFESSIONAL SOCIETIES

American Public Works Association. 106 W. 11th St., Ste. 1800, Kansas City, Missouri 64105-1806. (816) 472-6100.

American Society of Sanitary Engineering. Box 40362, Bay Village, Ohio 44140. (216) 835-3040.

Association of Metropolitan Sewerage Agencies. 1000 Connecticut Ave., N.W., Suite 1006, Washington, District of Columbia 20036. (202) 833-4653.

SEWAGE DISPOSAL

See also: BIOFILTRATION; WASTEWATER TREATMENT

ABSTRACTING AND INDEXING SERVICES

Applied Science and Technology Index. H.W. Wilson Co., 950 University Ave., Bronx, New York 10452. (800) 367-6770. Formerly Industrial Arts Index.

Aqualine Abstracts. Water Research Centre. c/o Pergamon Microforms International, Inc., Fairview Park, Elmsford, New York 10523. (914) 592-7720. 1927-. Contains some 8,000 records annually on water and wastewater technology. Covers all aspects of water, wastewater, associated engineering services and the aquatic environment. Over 600 periodicals, as well as books, reports and conference proceedings and other publications from water related institutions worldwide are scanned. Also available online.

Biological Abstracts. BIOSIS, 2100 Arch St., Philadelphia, Pennsylvania 19103-1399. (215) 587-4800. 1927-.

Biological and Agricultural Index. H.W. Wilson Co., 950 University Ave., Bronx, New York 10452. (800) 367-6770. 1916-. Monthly.

Chemical Abstracts. Chemical Abstracts Service, 2540 Olentangy River Rd., PO Box 3012, Columbus, Ohio 43210. (800) 848-6533. 1907-.

Engineering Index. The Engineering Index Inc., 345 E. 47th St., New York, New York 10017. 1962-.

General Science Index. H. W. Wilson Co., 950 University Ave., Bronx, New York 10452. 1978-. Monthly, also issued in annual cumulation. Cumulative subject index to English language periodicals in the subject fields of astronomy, botany, chemistry, earth science, environment and conservation, food and nutrition, genetics, mathematics, medicine and health, microbiology, oceanography, physics, physiology and zoology.

Pollution Abstracts. Cambridge Scientific Abstracts, 5161 River Rd., Bethesda, Maryland 20816. (301) 961-6750. Six/year. Indexes worldwide technical literature on environmental pollution. Covers air pollution, marine and freshwater pollution, sewage and wastewater treatment, waste management, toxicology and health, noise pollu-

tion, radiation, land pollution, and environmental policies, programs, legislation, and education. Also available online.

Science Citation Index. Institute for Scientific Information, 3501 Market St., Philadelphia, Pennsylvania 19104. 1961-.

BIBLIOGRAPHIES

Current Contents. Agriculture, Biology and Environmental Sciences. Institute for Scientific Information, 3501 Market St., Philadelphia, Pennsylvania 19104. (800) 523-1857. 1973-. Previous title: Current Contents. Agricultural, Food & Veterinary Sciences. Gives the table of contents of periodicals in the fields of agriculture, biology, environmental and related areas.

Wastewater Management: A Guide to Information Sources. George Tchobanoglous, et al. Gale Research Co., 835 Penobscot Bldg., Detroit, Michigan 48226-4094. (313) 961-2242. 1976.

DIRECTORIES

Water Engineering & Management–Reference Handbook/Buyer's Guide Issue. Scranton Gillette Communications, Inc., 380 E. Northwest Hwy., Des Plaines, Illinois 60016. (708) 298-6622.

ENCYCLOPEDIAS AND DICTIONARIES

Dictionary of Civil Engineering. John S. Scott. Halsted Press, Division of J. Wiley, 605 3rd Ave., New York, New York 10158. (212) 850-6000. 1981. Third edition.

McGraw-Hill Encyclopedia of Science and Technology. McGraw-Hill, 1221 Avenue of the Americas, New York, New York 10020. (212) 512-2000 or (800) 262-4729. 1992. Seventh edition. Issued in multiple volumes including index. Includes all science and technology broad subject areas.

Van Nostrand's Scientific Encyclopedia. Glenn D. Considine, ed. Van Nostrand Reinhold, 115 5th Ave., New York, New York 10003. (212) 254-3232. 1983. Sixth edition. Includes all broad subject areas in science.

GENERAL WORKS

Applied Math for Wastewater Plant Operators. Joanne Kilpatrick Price. Technomic Publishing Co., 851 New Holland Ave., Box 3535, Lancaster, Pennsylvania 17604. (717) 291-5609. 1991.

Biological Wastewater Treatment Systems. N. J. Horan. John Wiley & Sons, Inc., 605 3rd Ave., New York, New York 10158-0012. (212) 850-6000. 1990. Introduces basic concepts of microbial growth and reactor engineering required to fully understand the design and operation of wastewater treatment systems. Topics include wastewater characteristics, microorganisms exploited in wastewater treatment, and microbial energy generation.

Biomass Determination–a New Technique for Activated Sludge Control. U.S. Environmental Protection Agency, 401 M St. SW, Washington, District of Columbia 20460. (202) 260-2090. 1972. Includes an analysis of sewage sludge analysis by biomass determination. Also describes sewage disposal.

Chemical and Biological Characterization of Municipal Sludges, Sediments, Dredge Spoils, and Drilling Muds. James L. Lichtenberg, et al. American Society for Testing and Materials, 1916 S. Race St., Philadelphia, Pennsylvania 19103. (215) 299-5585. 1988. Deals with the environmental aspects of sewage disposal, analysis, health risk assessment, biological purification of sludge, and water quality management.

Emerging Technologies in Hazardous Waste Management. D. William Tedder and Frederick G. Pohland, eds. American Chemical Society, 1155 16th St. N.W., Washington, District of Columbia 20036. (202) 872-4600; (800) 227-5558. 1990. Hazardous waste management technology.

Emerging Technologies in Hazardous Waste Management II. D. William Tedder and Frederick G. Pohland, eds. American Chemical Society, 1155 16th St. N.W., Washington, District of Columbia 20036. (202) 872-4600; (800) 227-5558. 1991. Developed from a symposium sponsored by the Division of Industrial and Engineering Chemistry, Inc. of the American Chemical Society at the Industrial and Engineering Chemistry Special Symposium, Atlantic City, NJ, June 4-7, 1990.

Madison Conference of Applied Research & Practice on Municipal & Industrial Waste. Dept. of Engineering Professional Development, University of Wisconsin-Madison, Madison, Wisconsin 53706. 1990. Annual. Sewage disposal, factory and trade waste, soil liners, ground water clean up, landfill leachate treatment, groundwater monitary systems, evaluation of groundwater and soil gas remedial action; leachate generation estimates and landfills.

Marine Treatment of Sewage Sludge. Telford House, 1 Heron Quay, London, England E14 9XF. 1988.

New Developments in Industrial Wastewater Treatment. Aysen Turkman, ed. Kluwer Academic Publishers, 101 Philip Dr., Assinippi Park, Norwell, Massachusetts 02061-0358. (617) 871-6600. 1991. NATO Advanced Research Workshop, Oct-Nov. 1989.

Proceedings of the 4th National Symposium on Individual and Small Community Sewage Systems. American Society of Agricultural Engineers, 2950 Niles Rd., St. Joseph, Michigan 49085-9659. (616) 429-0300. 1985. Includes current trends such as design, planning, management, and performance of large systems, the use of computers for on-site technology, site evaluation, etc. The 5th National Symposium held in 1987 further includes environmental effects of on-site disposal soil absorption/ system siting requirement and groundwater impact.

Sludge Management. W. F. Garber and D. R. Anderson, eds. Pergamon Microforms International, Inc., Fairview Park, Elmsford, New York 10523. (914) 592-7720. 1990. Proceedings of the IAWPRC Conference on Sludge Management, held at Loyola Marymount University, Los Angeles, California, 8-12 January 1990. Offers an insight into sludge management. Topics include: treatment plant planning and management, sludge melting, incineration, drying and dewatering, aerobic and anaerobic digestion, heavy metal contaminants, and the use of sludge products as construction materials.

Trihalomethane Removal by Coagulation Techniques in a Softening Process. U.S. Environmental Protection Agency, Municipal Environmental Research Laboratory, 26 W. Martin Luther King Dr., Cincinnati, Ohio 45268.

(513) 569-7931. 1983. Sewage purification through chlorination.

Wastewater Engineering: Treatment, Disposal, and Reuse. Metcalf & Eddy, Inc. McGraw-Hill Science & Engineering Books, 11 West 19th St., New York, New York 10011. (212) 337-6010. 1991. Reflects the impact of changing federal legislation on environmental quality control and sludge management. Gives a solid overall perspective on wastewater engineering.

HANDBOOKS AND MANUALS

Basic Mechanical Maintenance Procedures at Water and Wastewater Plants. Glenn M. Tillman. Lewis Publishers, 2000 Corporate Blvd., Boca Raton, Florida 33431. (407) 994-0555 or (800) 272-7737. 1991. Part Operator's Guide series. Includes standard mechanical drawing symbols for valves, gates, gate equipment, equipment lockout procedures, centrifugal pumps, positive displacement pumps, rotary pumps, coupling alignment, pumping systems, macerator blades, shear pins, lubrication, and appendices.

Operation of Municipal Wastewater Treatment Plants. Water Pollution Control Federation, 601 Wythe St., Alexandria, Virginia 22314. (800) 556-8700. 2nd ed.

ONLINE DATA BASES

BIOSIS Previews. BIOSIS, 2100 Arch St., Philadelphia, Pennsylvania 19103-1399. (215) 587-4800. Largest and most comprehensive database of research in the life sciences. Contains citations for nearly 9000 primary research journals, monographs, reviews, symposia, preliminary reports, semi-popular journals, selected institutional reports, government reports and research communications.

CERCLIS. Chemical Information Systems, Inc., 7215 York Rd., Baltimore, Maryland 21212. (301) 321-8440. Information on hazardous waste disposal sites that have either been listed by the EPA on the National Priority List (NPL) or nominated for consideration for the NPL.

Chemical Abstracts-CA. Chemical Abstracts Service, 2540 Olentangy River Rd., P.O. Box 3012, Columbus, Ohio 43210. (800) 848-6533 or (614) 421-3600. Information sources include 9000 journals, patents from 27 countries, two industrial property organizations, new books, conference proceedings, and government research reports.

Computerized Engineering Index–COMPENDEX. Engineering Information Inc., 345 E. 47th St., New York, New York 10017. (212) 705-7600.

Monthly Catalog of United States Government Publications. U.S. G.P.O., Supt. of Docs., PO Box 371954, Pittsburgh, Pennsylvania 15250-7954. (202) 512-0000.

National Technical Information Service. U.S. Department of Commerce, National Technical Information Service, Office of Data Base Services, 5285 Port Royal Rd., Springfield, Virginia 22161. (703) 487-4807. Bibliographic database of government sponsored research and technical reports.

PressNet Environmental Reports. Chemical Information Systems, Inc., 7215 York Rd., Baltimore, Maryland 21212. (301) 321-8440.

SCISEARCH. Institute for Scientific Information, University City Science Center, 3501 Market St., Philadelphia, Pennsylvania 19104. (215) 386-0100.

PERIODICALS AND NEWSLETTERS

Law Digest. Association of Metropolitan Sewerage Agencies, 1000 Connecticut Avenue, NW, Suite 1006, Washington, District of Columbia 20036. (202) 833-2672. Monthly. Legal issues on environmental and regulatory matters.

Pollution Engineering. Cahners Publishing Co., 249 W. 17th St., New York, New York 10011. (212) 645-0067. 1969-. Monthly.

Sewage and Waste Disposal. Sewage and Waste Disposal, 321 Sunset Ave., Asbury Park, New Jersey 07712. 1946-. Fourteen times a year.

Water Engineering & Management. Scranton Gillette Communications, Inc., 380 E. Northwest Hwy., Des Plaines, Illinois 60016-2282. (708) 298-6622. 1986-. Monthly. A professional trade publication which includes latest legislative news in the area of water quality, EPA criteria for drinking water, pesticides, and related standards. Includes articles of interest by water professionals and has regular news features such as forthcoming conferences, products at work, surveys, company profiles, etc.

TRADE ASSOCIATIONS AND PROFESSIONAL SOCIETIES

American Public Works Association. 106 W. 11th St., Ste. 1800, Kansas City, Missouri 64105-1806. (816) 472-6100.

American Society of Sanitary Engineering. Box 40362, Bay Village, Ohio 44140. (216) 835-3040.

Association of Metropolitan Sewerage Agencies. 1000 Connecticut Ave., N.W., Suite 1006, Washington, District of Columbia 20036. (202) 833-4653.

Sump and Sewage Pump Association. P.O. Box 298, Winnetka, Illinois 60093. (312) 835-8911.

SEWAGE LAGOONS

See: LAGOONS

SEWAGE SLUDGE

See: SLUDGE

SEWAGE TRANSPORT

See: TRANSPORTATION

SEWAGE TREATMENT

ABSTRACTING AND INDEXING SERVICES

Applied Science and Technology Index. H.W. Wilson Co., 950 University Ave., Bronx, New York 10452. (800) 367-6770. Formerly Industrial Arts Index.

Aqualine Abstracts. Water Research Centre. c/o Pergamon Microforms International, Inc., Fairview Park, Elmsford, New York 10523. (914) 592-7720. 1927-. Contains some 8,000 records annually on water and wastewater technology. Covers all aspects of water, wastewater, associated engineering services and the aquatic environment. Over 600 periodicals, as well as books, reports and conference proceedings and other publications from water related institutions worldwide are scanned. Also available online.

ASFA Aquaculture Abstracts. Cambridge Scientific Abstracts, Inc., 5161 River Rd., Bethesda, Maryland 20816. (301) 961-6750. 1984.

Biological Abstracts. BIOSIS, 2100 Arch St., Philadelphia, Pennsylvania 19103-1399. (215) 587-4800. 1927-.

Biological and Agricultural Index. H.W. Wilson Co., 950 University Ave., Bronx, New York 10452. (800) 367-6770. 1916-. Monthly.

Biotechnology Research Abstracts. Cambridge Scientific Abstracts, 5161 River Rd., Bethesda, Maryland 20816. (301) 961-6750. Monthly. Includes such broad areas as genetic intervention, biochemical genetics, and microbiological techniques.

Bulletin Signaletique: Eau et Assainissement, Pollution Atmospherique, Droit des Pollutions. Centre de Documentation, Centre National de la Recherche Scientifique, 15, quai Anatole France, Paris, France 75700. (1) 45 55 92 25. 1983-. Monthly. Indexes pollution periodicals including water, atmospheric and related pollutions.

Chemical Abstracts. Chemical Abstracts Service, 2540 Olentangy River Rd., PO Box 3012, Columbus, Ohio 43210. (800) 848-6533. 1907-.

Civil Engineering Hydraulic Abstracts. BHRA Fluid Engineering, Air Science Co., PO Box 143, Corning, New York 14830. (607) 962-5591. Monthly. Abstracts of periodicals that publish in the areas of hydraulic engineering and other related topics.

Engineering Index. The Engineering Index Inc., 345 E. 47th St., New York, New York 10017. 1962-.

Index to Scientific Book Contents. Institute for Scientific Information, 3501 Market St., Philadelphia, Pennsylvania 19104. (800) 523-1857. 1985-. Annual. Gives contents of science books published.

Pollution Abstracts. Cambridge Scientific Abstracts, 5161 River Rd., Bethesda, Maryland 20816. (301) 961-6750. Six/year. Indexes worldwide technical literature on environmental pollution. Covers air pollution, marine and freshwater pollution, sewage and wastewater treatment, waste management, toxicology and health, noise pollution, radiation, land pollution, and environmental policies, programs, legislation, and education. Also available online.

BIBLIOGRAPHIES

Current Contents. Agriculture, Biology and Environmental Sciences. Institute for Scientific Information, 3501 Market St., Philadelphia, Pennsylvania 19104. (800) 523-1857. 1973-. Previous title: Current Contents. Agricultural, Food & Veterinary Sciences. Gives the table of contents of periodicals in the fields of agriculture, biology, environmental and related areas.

Ozone in the Troposphere and the Stratosphere. Council of Planning Librarians, 1313 E. 60th St., Chicago, Illinois 60637-2897. (312) 942-2163. 1988. Atmospheric ozone bibliography.

Stabilization, Disinfection, and Odor Control in Sewage Sludge Treatment: An Annotated Bibliography Covering the Period 1950-1983. E. S. Connor. E. Horwood, 1230 Avenue of the Americas, New York, New York 10020. (212) 698-7000. 1984.

ENCYCLOPEDIAS AND DICTIONARIES

Dictionary of Civil Engineering. John S. Scott. Halsted Press, Division of J. Wiley, 605 3rd Ave., New York, New York 10158. (212) 850-6000. 1981. Third edition.

Dictionary of Environmental Engineering and Related Sciences: English-Spanish, Spanish-English. Jose T. Villate. Ediciones Universal, 3090 SW 8th St., Miami, Florida 33135. (305) 642-3355. 1979.

Dictionary of Environmental Protection Technology: In Four Languages, English, German, French, Russian. Egon Seidel. Elsevier Science Publishing Co., 655 Avenue of the Americas, New York, New York 10010. (212) 984-5800. 1988.

Dictionary of Waste and Water Treatment. Butterworth-Heinemann, 80 Montvale Ave., Stoneham, Massachusetts 02180. (617) 438-8464. 1981. Dictionary of sanitary engineering.

Dictionary of Water and Sewage Engineering. Fritz Meinck and Helmut Mohle. Elsevier Science Publishing Co., 655 Avenue of the Americas, New York, New York 10010. (212) 984-5800. 1977. Text is in German, English, French and Italian. Deals with water management engineering and sewage.

Encyclopedia of Environmental Science and Engineering. J.R. Pfafflin. Gordon and Breach Science Publishers, Inc., 270 8th Ave., New York, New York 10011. (212) 206-8900. 1992.

English-Russian Dictionary of Environmental Protection: About 14,000 Terms. E.L. Milovanov. Pergamon Microforms International, Inc., Fairview Park, Elmsford, New York 10523. (914) 592-7720. 1981.

Environmental Engineering Dictionary. C. C. Lee. Government Institutes, Inc., 4 Research Pl., Ste. 200, Rockville, Maryland 20850. (301) 921-2300. 1989. Defines over 6000 engineering terms relating to pollutioncontrol technologies, monitoring, risk assessment, sampling andanalysis, quality control, permitting, and environmentally-regulated engineering and science. Includes bibliographical references (p. 612-627).

McGraw-Hill Encyclopedia of Environmental Science. Sybil P. Parker. McGraw-Hill Science & Engineering Books, 11 W. 19th St., New York, New York 10011. (212) 337-6010. 1980. Covers ecology, man's influence on nature, and environmental protection.

McGraw-Hill Encyclopedia of Science and Technology. McGraw-Hill, 1221 Avenue of the Americas, New York, New York 10020. (212) 512-2000 or (800) 262-4729. 1992. Seventh edition. Issued in multiple volumes including index. Includes all science and technology broad subject areas.

Van Nostrand's Scientific Encyclopedia. Glenn D. Considine, ed. Van Nostrand Reinhold, 115 5th Ave., New

York, New York 10003. (212) 254-3232. 1983. Sixth edition. Includes all broad subject areas in science.

GENERAL WORKS

Applied Math for Wastewater Plant Operators. Joanne Kilpatrick Price. Technomic Publishing Co., 851 New Holland Ave., Box 3535, Lancaster, Pennsylvania 17604. (717) 291-5609. 1991.

Biodegradation of PCBs Sorbed to Sewage Sludge Lagoon Sediments in an Aerobic Digester. William Amdor Chantry. University of Wisconsin Press, 114 N. Murray St., Madison, Wisconsin 53715. (608) 262-8782. 1989.

Bioenvironmental Systems. Donald L. Wise, ed. CRC Press, 2000 Corporate Blvd. N.W., Boca Raton, Florida 33431. (407) 994-0555; (800) 272-7737. 1987. 4 vols.

Biological Wastewater Treatment Systems. N. J. Horan. John Wiley & Sons, Inc., 605 3rd Ave., New York, New York 10158-0012. (212) 850-6000. 1990. Introduces basic concepts of microbial growth and reactor engineering required to fully understand the design and operation of wastewater treatment systems. Topics include wastewater characteristics, microorganisms exploited in wastewater treatment, and microbial energy generation.

Chemical Primary Sludge Thickening and Dewatering. Di Gregorio, David. National Technical Information Service, 5285 Port Royal Rd., Springfield, Virginia 22161. (703) 487-4650. 1979.

Codisposal of Garbage and Sewage Sludge–a Promising Solution to Two Problems. U.S. General Accounting Office. U.S. G.P.O., Washington, District of Columbia 20401. (202) 512-0000. 1979.

Concentrated Mine Drainage Disposal into Sewage Treatment Systems. Environmental Protection Agency, 401 M St. SW, Washington, District of Columbia 20460. (202) 382-5480. 1971. Covers acid mine drainage and sewage purification.

Constructed Wetlands for Wastewater Treatment. Donald A. Hammer. Lewis Publishers, 200 Corporate Blvd. NW, Boca Raton, Florida 33431. (407) 994-0555 or (800)272-7737. 1989. Presents general principles of wetland ecology, hydrology, soil chemistry, vegetation, microbiology, and wildlife dependence on wetlands. It provides management guidelines, beginning with policies and regulations, and including siting and construction and operations and monitoring of constructed wetland systems.

Design and Operation of Sewage Treatment Plants in Coastal Tourist Areas. M. Nicolaou and I. Hadjivassilis, eds. Pergamon Microforms International, Inc., Fairview Park, Elmsford, New York 10523. (914) 592-7720. 1989. Proceedings of the IAWPRC Conference held in Limassol, Cyprus, November 3-4, 1987. Discusses problems associated with all aspects of water pollution prevention and control in coastal tourist areas. Also covers the reuse of treated wastewater, as shortage of freshwater is a problem in some countries which have a large seasonal demand for water through tourism.

Environmental Biotechnology: Reducing Risks from Environmental Chemicals through Biotechnology. Gilbert S. Omenn. Plenum Press, 233 Spring St., New York, New York 10013-1578. (212) 620-8000. Covers environmental aspects of the chemical and biological treatment of sewage.

Evaluation of a Pulsed Bed Filter for Filtration of Municipal Primary Effluent. Donald S. Brown. U.S. Environmental Protection Agency, 401 M St. SW, Washington, District of Columbia 20460. (202) 260-2090. Water treatment and purification plants.

Hazardous and Industrial Wastes, 1991. Technomic Publishing Co., 851 New Holland Ave., Box 3535, Lancaster, Pennsylvania 17604. (717) 291-5609. 1991. Proceedings of the 23rd Mid-Atlantic Industrial Waste Conference held at Drexel University, 1991.

Irrigation with Treated Sewage Effluent: Management for Environmental Protection. A. Feigin. Springer-Verlag, 175 5th Ave., New York, New York 10010. (212) 460-1500 or (800) 777-4643. 1991. Use of treated sewage effluent as an irrigation source for agriculture.

Marine Treatment of Sewage Sludge. Telford House, 1 Heron Quay, London, England E14 9XF. 1988.

Sewage and the Bacterial Purification of Sewage. Samuel Rideal. John Wiley & Sons, Inc., 605 3rd Ave., New York, New York 10158-0012. (212) 850-6000. 1906. Publication on sewage purification with illustrations and colored plates.

Sludge Management. W. F. Garber and D. R. Anderson, eds. Pergamon Microforms International, Inc., Fairview Park, Elmsford, New York 10523. (914) 592-7720. 1990. Proceedings of the IAWPRC Conference on Sludge Management, held at Loyola Marymount University, Los Angeles, California, 8-12 January 1990. Offers an insight into sludge management. Topics include: treatment plant planning and management, sludge melting, incineration, drying and dewatering, aerobic and anaerobic digestion, heavy metal contaminants, and the use of sludge products as construction materials.

Sources and Distribution of Nitrate in Ground Water at a Farmed Field Irrigated With Sewage Treatment Plant Effluent. Marian P. Berndt. Department of the Interior, U.S. Geological Survey, 119 National Center, Reston, Virginia 22092. (703) 648-4460. 1990. Covers underground water, sewage sludge as fertilizer, and nitrates.

Trihalomethane Removal by Coagulation Techniques in a Softening Process. U.S. Environmental Protection Agency, Municipal Environmental Research Laboratory, 26 W. Martin Luther King Dr., Cincinnati, Ohio 45268. (513) 569-7931. 1983. Sewage purification through chlorination.

HANDBOOKS AND MANUALS

Chemical Waste: Handling and Treatment. Springer-Verlag, 175 5th Ave., New York, New York 10010. (212) 460-1500. 1986.

Economic Analysis of Proposed Revised Effluent Guidelines and Standards for the Inorganic Chemicals Industry. National Technical Information Service, 5285 Port Royal Rd., Springfield, Virginia 22161. (703) 487-4650. 1980. Covers effluent quality and sewage purification technology.

Sewer and Water–Main Design Tables. L. B. Escrit. Maclaren and Sons Ltd., 7 Grape St., London, England WC2. 1969. Includes tables of flow in sewers, drains and water-mains in British and Metric units. Also includes tables of rainfall, run-off, repayment of loans, etc.

Water Treatment Handbook. Degremont s.a., 184, ave. du 18-Juin-1940, Rueil-Malmaison, France F-92500.

1991. Sixth edition. Part 1 is a general survey of water and its action on the materials with which it comes into contact, and theoretical principles of separation and correction processes used in water treatment. Part 2 describes the process and the treatment plant beginning with the separation process.

ONLINE DATA BASES

BIOSIS Previews. BIOSIS, 2100 Arch St., Philadelphia, Pennsylvania 19103-1399. (215) 587-4800. Largest and most comprehensive database of research in the life sciences. Contains citations for nearly 9000 primary research journals, monographs, reviews, symposia, preliminary reports, semi-popular journals, selected institutional reports, government reports and research communications.

CERCLIS. Chemical Information Systems, Inc., 7215 York Rd., Baltimore, Maryland 21212. (301) 321-8440. Information on hazardous waste disposal sites that have either been listed by the EPA on the National Priority List (NPL) or nominated for consideration for the NPL.

Chemical Abstracts-CA. Chemical Abstracts Service, 2540 Olentangy River Rd., P.O. Box 3012, Columbus, Ohio 43210. (800) 848-6533 or (614) 421-3600. Information sources include 9000 journals, patents from 27 countries, two industrial property organizations, new books, conference proceedings, and government research reports.

Computerized Engineering Index–COMPENDEX. Engineering Information Inc., 345 E. 47th St., New York, New York 10017. (212) 705-7600.

Environment Reporter. Bureau of National Affairs, 1231 25th St., N.W., Rm. 215, Washington, District of Columbia 20037. (800) 372-1033. Online version of periodical of the same name.

Monthly Catalog of United States Government Publications. U.S. G.P.O., Supt. of Docs., PO Box 371954, Pittsburgh, Pennsylvania 15250-7954. (202) 512-0000.

National Technical Information Service. U.S. Department of Commerce, National Technical Information Service, Office of Data Base Services, 5285 Port Royal Rd., Springfield, Virginia 22161. (703) 487-4807. Bibliographic database of government sponsored research and technical reports.

SCISEARCH. Institute for Scientific Information, University City Science Center, 3501 Market St., Philadelphia, Pennsylvania 19104. (215) 386-0100.

PERIODICALS AND NEWSLETTERS

Association of Metropolitan Sewerage Agencies Monthly Report. Association of Metropolitan Sewerage Agencies, 1000 Connecticut Avenue, NW, Suite 1006, Washington, District of Columbia 20005. (202) 833-4653. Monthly. Data on environmental and regulatory matters.

Biodegradation. Kluwer Academic Publishers, 101 Philip Dr., Assinippi Park, Norwell, Massachusetts 02061-0358. (617) 871-6600. 1990-. Quarterly. Covers all aspects of science pertaining to the detoxification, recycling, amelioration or treatment of waste materials and pollutants by naturally occurring microbial strains, associations, or recombinant microorganisms.

Environment Reporter. Bureau of National Affairs, 1231 25th St. NW, Washington, District of Columbia 20037. (800) 372-1033. Weekly. Issues of pollution control and environmental activity. Also available online.

Law Digest. Association of Metropolitan Sewerage Agencies, 1000 Connecticut Avenue, NW, Suite 1006, Washington, District of Columbia 20036. (202) 833-2672. Monthly. Legal issues on environmental and regulatory matters.

TRADE ASSOCIATIONS AND PROFESSIONAL SOCIETIES

American Public Works Association. 106 W. 11th St., Ste. 1800, Kansas City, Missouri 64105-1806. (816) 472-6100.

American Society of Sanitary Engineering. Box 40362, Bay Village, Ohio 44140. (216) 835-3040.

Association of Metropolitan Sewerage Agencies. 1000 Connecticut Ave., N.W., Suite 1006, Washington, District of Columbia 20036. (202) 833-4653.

SEWERS

ABSTRACTING AND INDEXING SERVICES

Applied Science and Technology Index. H.W. Wilson Co., 950 University Ave., Bronx, New York 10452. (800) 367-6770. Formerly Industrial Arts Index.

Aqualine Abstracts. Water Research Centre. c/o Pergamon Microforms International, Inc., Fairview Park, Elmsford, New York 10523. (914) 592-7720. 1927-. Contains some 8,000 records annually on water and wastewater technology. Covers all aspects of water, wastewater, associated engineering services and the aquatic environment. Over 600 periodicals, as well as books, reports and conference proceedings and other publications from water related institutions worldwide are scanned. Also available online.

ASFA Aquaculture Abstracts. Cambridge Scientific Abstracts, Inc., 5161 River Rd., Bethesda, Maryland 20816. (301) 961-6750. 1984.

Biological and Agricultural Index. H.W. Wilson Co., 950 University Ave., Bronx, New York 10452. (800) 367-6770. 1916-. Monthly.

Bulletin Signaletique: Eau et Assainissement, Pollution Atmospherique, Droit des Pollutions. Centre de Documentation, Centre National de la Recherche Scientifique, 15, quai Anatole France, Paris, France 75700. (1) 45 55 92 25. 1983-. Monthly. Indexes pollution periodicals including water, atmospheric and related pollutions.

Chemical Abstracts. Chemical Abstracts Service, 2540 Olentangy River Rd., PO Box 3012, Columbus, Ohio 43210. (800) 848-6533. 1907-.

Civil Engineering Hydraulic Abstracts. BHRA Fluid Engineering, Air Science Co., PO Box 143, Corning, New York 14830. (607) 962-5591. Monthly. Abstracts of periodicals that publish in the areas of hydraulic engineering and other related topics.

Pollution Abstracts. Cambridge Scientific Abstracts, 5161 River Rd., Bethesda, Maryland 20816. (301) 961-6750. Six/year. Indexes worldwide technical literature on environmental pollution. Covers air pollution, marine and

freshwater pollution, sewage and wastewater treatment, waste management, toxicology and health, noise pollution, radiation, land pollution, and environmental policies, programs, legislation, and education. Also available online.

Science Citation Index. Institute for Scientific Information, 3501 Market St., Philadelphia, Pennsylvania 19104. 1961-.

BIBLIOGRAPHIES

Current Contents. Agriculture, Biology and Environmental Sciences. Institute for Scientific Information, 3501 Market St., Philadelphia, Pennsylvania 19104. (800) 523-1857. 1973-. Previous title: Current Contents. Agricultural, Food & Veterinary Sciences. Gives the table of contents of periodicals in the fields of agriculture, biology, environmental and related areas.

ENCYCLOPEDIAS AND DICTIONARIES

Dictionary of Environmental Engineering and Related Sciences: English-Spanish, Spanish-English. Jose T. Villate. Ediciones Universal, 3090 SW 8th St., Miami, Florida 33135. (305) 642-3355. 1979.

Dictionary of Water and Sewage Engineering. Fritz Meinck and Helmut Mohle. Elsevier Science Publishing Co., 655 Avenue of the Americas, New York, New York 10010. (212) 984-5800. 1977. Text is in German, English, French and Italian. Deals with water management engineering and sewage.

Encyclopedia of Environmental Science and Engineering. J.R. Pfafflin. Gordon and Breach Science Publishers, Inc., 270 8th Ave., New York, New York 10011. (212) 206-8900. 1992.

McGraw-Hill Encyclopedia of Science and Technology. McGraw-Hill, 1221 Avenue of the Americas, New York, New York 10020. (212) 512-2000 or (800) 262-4729. 1992. Seventh edition. Issued in multiple volumes including index. Includes all science and technology broad subject areas.

Van Nostrand's Scientific Encyclopedia. Glenn D. Considine, ed. Van Nostrand Reinhold, 115 5th Ave., New York, New York 10003. (212) 254-3232. 1983. Sixth edition. Includes all broad subject areas in science.

HANDBOOKS AND MANUALS

New Generation Guide to the Birds of Britain and Europe. Christopher Perrins, ed. University of Texas Press, PO Box 7819, Austin, Texas 78713-7819. (512) 471-7233 or (800) 252-3206. 1987.

Sewer and Water–Main Design Tables. L. B. Escrit. Maclaren and Sons Ltd., 7 Grape St., London, England WC2. 1969. Includes tables of flow in sewers, drains and water-mains in British and Metric units. Also includes tables of rainfall, run-off, repayment of loans, etc.

ONLINE DATA BASES

CERCLIS. Chemical Information Systems, Inc., 7215 York Rd., Baltimore, Maryland 21212. (301) 321-8440. Information on hazardous waste disposal sites that have either been listed by the EPA on the National Priority List (NPL) or nominated for consideration for the NPL.

Chemical Abstracts-CA. Chemical Abstracts Service, 2540 Olentangy River Rd., P.O. Box 3012, Columbus, Ohio 43210. (800) 848-6533 or (614) 421-3600. Information sources include 9000 journals, patents from 27 countries, two industrial property organizations, new books, conference proceedings, and government research reports.

SCISEARCH. Institute for Scientific Information, University City Science Center, 3501 Market St., Philadelphia, Pennsylvania 19104. (215) 386-0100.

PERIODICALS AND NEWSLETTERS

Association of Metropolitan Sewerage Agencies Monthly Report. Association of Metropolitan Sewerage Agencies, 1000 Connecticut Avenue, NW, Suite 1006, Washington, District of Columbia 20005. (202) 833-4653. Monthly. Data on environmental and regulatory matters.

Pollution Engineering. Cahners Publishing Co., 249 W. 17th St., New York, New York 10011. (212) 645-0067. 1969-. Monthly.

TRADE ASSOCIATIONS AND PROFESSIONAL SOCIETIES

American Public Works Association. 106 W. 11th St., Ste. 1800, Kansas City, Missouri 64105-1806. (816) 472-6100.

American Society of Sanitary Engineering. Box 40362, Bay Village, Ohio 44140. (216) 835-3040.

Association of Metropolitan Sewerage Agencies. 1000 Connecticut Ave., N.W., Suite 1006, Washington, District of Columbia 20036. (202) 833-4653.

National Association of Sewer Service Companies. 101 Wymore Rd., Suite 521, Altamonte, Florida 32714. (407) 774-0304.

SHALE OIL

See: OIL

SHIELD

See: RADIATION POLLUTION

SHIP NOISE

See: NOISE

SHIPBOARD WASTES

See: WASTE TREATMENT

SHIPS

ABSTRACTING AND INDEXING SERVICES

General Science Index. H. W. Wilson Co., 950 University Ave., Bronx, New York 10452. 1978-. Monthly, also issued in annual cumulation. Cumulative subject index

to English language periodicals in the subject fields of astronomy, botany, chemistry, earth science, environment and conservation, food and nutrition, genetics, mathematics, medicine and health, microbiology, oceanography, physics, physiology and zoology.

GENERAL WORKS

The Challenge of Arctic Shipping. David L. VanderZwaag. McGill-Queen's University Press, 3430 McTavish St., Montreal, Quebec, Canada H3A 1X9. (514) 398-3750. 1990. Science, environmental assessment, and human values.

Exotic Species and the Shipping Industry. Great Lakes Fishery Commission, 2200 North Bonisteel Blvd., Ann Arbor, Michigan 481009. (313) 665-9135. 1990. The Great Lakes-St. Lawrence ecosystem at risk: a special report to the governments of the United States and Canada.

Longevity, Senescence, and the Genome. Caleb Ellicott Finch. University of Chicago Press, 5801 Ellis Ave., 4th Floor, Chicago, Illinois 60637. (800) 621-2736. 1990. Genetic aspects of aging and longevity.

A Medical Monitoring Program for the Marine Hazardous Chemical Worker. R.J. Prevost. U.S. Coast Guard, Office of Research and Development, 2100 Second St., N.W., Rm. 5410 C, Washington, District of Columbia 20593. (202) 267-1042. 1985. Safety measures and environmental effects of hazardous substances transportation.

Senescence and Aging in Plants. L.C. Nooden. Academic Press, c/o Harcourt Brace Jovanovich Inc., 6277 Sea Harbor Dr., Orlando, Florida 32887. (800) 346-8648. 1988.

SHREDDING

See also: RECYCLING

ABSTRACTING AND INDEXING SERVICES

Applied Science and Technology Index. H.W. Wilson Co., 950 University Ave., Bronx, New York 10452. (800) 367-6770. Formerly Industrial Arts Index.

Engineering Index. The Engineering Index Inc., 345 E. 47th St., New York, New York 10017. 1962-.

Pollution Abstracts. Cambridge Scientific Abstracts, 5161 River Rd., Bethesda, Maryland 20816. (301) 961-6750. Six/year. Indexes worldwide technical literature on environmental pollution. Covers air pollution, marine and freshwater pollution, sewage and wastewater treatment, waste management, toxicology and health, noise pollution, radiation, land pollution, and environmental policies, programs, legislation, and education. Also available online.

GENERAL WORKS

Resource Recovery Plant Cost Estimates: A Comparative Evaluation of Four Recent Dry-Shredding Designs. U.S. Environmental Protection Agency, 401 M St., S.W., Washington, District of Columbia 20460. (202) 260-2090. 1975.

Solid Waste Shredding and Shredder Selection. Harvey W. Rogers. U.S. Environmental Protection Agency, 401 M St., S.W., Washington, District of Columbia 20460. (202) 260-2090. 1974. Refuse and refuse disposal in the United States.

ONLINE DATA BASES

Computerized Engineering Index–COMPENDEX. Engineering Information Inc., 345 E. 47th St., New York, New York 10017. (212) 705-7600.

SHRIMP AND SHRIMP FISHERIES

See also: AQUACULTURE

ABSTRACTING AND INDEXING SERVICES

ASFA Aquaculture Abstracts. Cambridge Scientific Abstracts, Inc., 5161 River Rd., Bethesda, Maryland 20816. (301) 961-6750. 1984.

Biology Digest. Data Courier, Plexus Pub Inc., 143 Old Marlton Pike, Medford, New Jersey 08055. 1974-. Monthly. Abstracts biology periodicals.

General Science Index. H. W. Wilson Co., 950 University Ave., Bronx, New York 10452. 1978-. Monthly, also issued in annual cumulation. Cumulative subject index to English language periodicals in the subject fields of astronomy, botany, chemistry, earth science, environment and conservation, food and nutrition, genetics, mathematics, medicine and health, microbiology, oceanography, physics, physiology and zoology.

Science Citation Index. Institute for Scientific Information, 3501 Market St., Philadelphia, Pennsylvania 19104. 1961-.

BIBLIOGRAPHIES

Shrimp Mariculture: January 1979 - January 1990. Eileen McVey. National Agricultural Library, 10301 Baltimore Blvd., Beltsville, Maryland 20705-2351. (301) 504-5755. 1990.

GENERAL WORKS

Brine Shrimp and Their Habitat: An Environmental Investigation. National Wildlife Federation, 1400 16th St. NW, Washington, District of Columbia 20036-2266. (202) 797-6800. 1972.

Sea Turtle Conservation and the Shrimp Industry. Congress Committee on Merchant Marine and Fisheries. U.S. G.P.O., Washington, District of Columbia 20401. (202) 512-0000. 1990. Equipment and supplies used in the shrimp industry.

Species Profiles: Life Histories and Environmental Requirements of Coastal Fishes and Invertebrates, Pink Shrimp. Lourdes M. Bielsa. U.S. Department of the Interior, Fish and Wildlife Service, Washington, District of Columbia 20240. (202) 343-5634. 1983. Anatomy of invertebrates, fish, and shrimps.

ONLINE DATA BASES

FISHNET. Aquatic Data Center, 1100 Gentry St., North Kansas City, Missouri 64116. (816) 842-5936.

RESEARCH CENTERS AND INSTITUTES

Robert J. Bernard Biological Field Station. Claremont McKenna College, Claremont, California 91711. (714) 621-5425.

University of Miami, Cooperative Institute for Marine and Atmospheric Studies. 4600 Rickenbacker Causeway, Miami, Florida 33149. (305) 361-4159.

SIGNS AND BILLBOARDS

GENERAL WORKS

Billboards, Glass Houses, and the Law, and Other Land Use Fables: Zoning and Land Use Reflections. Richard F. Babcock. Shepard's Citations, 555 Middlecreek Pkwy., Colorado Springs, Colorado 80901. 1977. Citizen participation in preventing visual pollution.

God's Own Junkyard; The Planned Deterioration of America's Landscape. Peter Blake. Holt, Rinehart and Winston, 6277 Sea Harbor Dr., Orlando, Florida 32887. (407) 345-2500. 1964. Billboards and national monuments in the United States.

Highway Beautification: The Environmental Movement's Greatest Failure. Charles F. Floyd. Westview Press, 5500 Central AVe., Boulder, Colorado 80301. (303) 444-3541. 1979. Roadside improvement and law and legislation relating to signs and billboards.

HANDBOOKS AND MANUALS

Legal Handbook on Sign Control. Scenic America, 216 7th St. SE, Washington, District of Columbia 20003. (202) 546-1100. 1990.

Visual Pollution and Sign Control: A Legal Handbook on Billboard Reform. Southern Environmental Law Center, 201 W. Main St., Ste. 14, Charlottesville, Virginia 22901. (804) 977-4090. 1988.

SILICATES

ABSTRACTING AND INDEXING SERVICES

Chemical Abstracts. Chemical Abstracts Service, 2540 Olentangy River Rd., PO Box 3012, Columbus, Ohio 43210. (800) 848-6533. 1907-.

General Science Index. H. W. Wilson Co., 950 University Ave., Bronx, New York 10452. 1978-. Monthly, also issued in annual cumulation. Cumulative subject index to English language periodicals in the subject fields of astronomy, botany, chemistry, earth science, environment and conservation, food and nutrition, genetics, mathematics, medicine and health, microbiology, oceanography, physics, physiology and zoology.

Physics Briefs. Physikalische Berichte. Physik Verlag, Pappapelallee 3, Postfach 101161, Weinheim, Germany D-6940. 1979-. Semimonthly. In English. Volumes for 1979- issued by the Deutsche Physikalische Gesellschaft and the Fachinformationszentrum Energie Physik, Mathematik in cooperation with the American Institute of Physics.

Science Citation Index. Institute for Scientific Information, 3501 Market St., Philadelphia, Pennsylvania 19104. 1961-.

BIBLIOGRAPHIES

Asbestos and Silicate Pollution: Citations from the Engineering Index Data Base. Diane M. Cavagnaro. National Technical Information Service, 5285 Port Royal Rd., Springfield, Virginia 22161. (703) 487-4650. 1980. Deals with asbestos pollution and silicate pollution and their effects on the environment.

Bibliography and Index of Geology. American Geological Institute, 4220 King St., Alexandria, Virginia 22302. Monthly. Includes environmental geology and hydrogeology.

ENCYCLOPEDIAS AND DICTIONARIES

Encyclopedia of Physics. Rita G. Lerner and George L. Trigg. VCH Publishers, 303 NW 12th Ave., Deerfield Beach, Florida 33442-1788. (305) 428-5566. 1991. Second edition.

Glossary of Geology. Robert Latimer Bates and Julia A. Jackson, eds. American Geological Institute, 4220 King St., Alexandria, Virginia 22302-1507. (703) 379-2480 or (800) 336-4764. 1987. Third edition.

McGraw-Hill Encyclopedia of Science and Technology. McGraw-Hill, 1221 Avenue of the Americas, New York, New York 10020. (212) 512-2000 or (800) 262-4729. 1992. Seventh edition. Issued in multiple volumes including index. Includes all science and technology broad subject areas.

McGraw-Hill Encyclopedia of the Geological Sciences. Sybil P. Parker, ed. McGraw-Hill, 1221 Avenue of the Americas, New York, New York 10020. (212) 512-2000 or (800) 262-4729. 1988. Second edition. Published previously in the McGraw-Hill Encyclopedia of Science and Technology.

Van Nostrand's Scientific Encyclopedia. Glenn D. Considine, ed. Van Nostrand Reinhold, 115 5th Ave., New York, New York 10003. (212) 254-3232. 1983. Sixth edition. Includes all broad subject areas in science.

GENERAL WORKS

The Chemistry of Silica. Ralph K. Iler. John Wiley & Sons, Inc., 605 3rd Ave., New York, New York 10158-0012. (212) 850-6000. 1979. Solubility, polymerization, colloid and surface properties, and biochemistry.

Deadly Dust: Silicosis and the Politics of Occupational Disease in Twentieth-Century America. David Rosner and Gerald Markowitz. Princeton University Press, 41 Williams St., Princeton, New Jersey 08540. (609) 258-4900. 1991. Case study of how occupational diseases are defined and addressed.

Definition for Asbestos and Other Health-Related Silicates. American Society for Testing and Materials, 1916 S. Race St., Philadelphia, Pennsylvania 19103. (215) 299-5585. 1984. Toxicology of asbestos and silicates.

Magill's Survey of Science. Earth Science Series. Frank N. Magill. Salem Press, PO Box 50062, Pasadena, California 91105. 1990-. Five volumes. Includes information on earth's crust, hot spots and volcanic island chains, physical properties of minerals, rock magnetism, physical properties of rocks, and index.

Physical Chemistry of Magmas. Leonid L. Perchuk. Springer-Verlag, 175 5th Ave., New York, New York 10010. (212) 460-1500. 1991.

Silica, Silicosis, and Cancer: Controversy in Occupational Medicine. Praeger Publishers, 1 Madison Ave., New York, New York 10010-3603. (212) 685-5300. Covers lung cancer and the toxicology of silica.

ONLINE DATA BASES

Chemical Abstracts-CA. Chemical Abstracts Service, 2540 Olentangy River Rd., P.O. Box 3012, Columbus, Ohio 43210. (800) 848-6533 or (614) 421-3600. Information sources include 9000 journals, patents from 27 countries, two industrial property organizations, new books, conference proceedings, and government research reports.

TRADE ASSOCIATIONS AND PROFESSIONAL SOCIETIES

American Chemical Society. 1155 16th St., N.W., Washington, District of Columbia 20036. (202) 872-4600.

Silicones Health Council. 1330 Connecticut Ave., N.W., Suite 300, Washington, District of Columbia 20036. (202) 659-0060.

Synthetic Amorphous Silica an Silicates Industry Association. 1226 Cardinal Ave., Pittsburgh, Pennsylvania 15243. (201) 807-3173.

SILTATION

See: EROSION

SILVER RESOURCES

BIBLIOGRAPHIES

Silver in Agricultural Ecosystems: A Bibliography of the Literature 1950 through 1971. Robert L. Jones. Department of Agronomy, University of Illinois, Urbana, Illinois 61801. 1973.

GENERAL WORKS

Environmental Impacts of Artificial Ice Nucleating Agents. Donald A. Klein. Van Nostrand Reinhold, Information Services, 115 5th Ave., New York, New York 10003. (212) 254-3232. 1978. Environmental aspects of silver and silver compounds.

Toxicological Profile for Silver. Clement International Corporation. Agency for Toxic Substances and Disease Registry, U.S. Public Health Service, 1600 Clifton Rd. NE, Atlanta, Georgia 30333. (404) 452-4111. 1990. Toxicology and physiological effects and environmental aspects of silver.

SILVICULTURE

ABSTRACTING AND INDEXING SERVICES

Applied Ecology Abstracts Studies in Renewable Natural Resources. Information Retrieval Ltd., 1911 Jefferson Davis Highway, Arlington, Virginia 22202. 1975-. Monthly.

Biological and Agricultural Index. H.W. Wilson Co., 950 University Ave., Bronx, New York 10452. (800) 367-6770. 1916-. Monthly.

Forestry Abstracts. C. A. B. International, Wallingford, England OX10 8DE. (0491) 3211. 1939/40-. Monthly. Journal of abstracts of journal articles, conferences, technical reports in the subject areas of: silviculture, forest mensuration and management, physical environment, fire, plant biology, genetics and breeding, mycology and pathology, game and wildlife, fish, protection of forests and other related matter.

Multimedia Index to Ecology. National Information Center for Educational Media, University of Southern California, Los Angeles, California 90007.

Science Citation Index. Institute for Scientific Information, 3501 Market St., Philadelphia, Pennsylvania 19104. 1961-.

BIBLIOGRAPHIES

Current Contents. Agriculture, Biology and Environmental Sciences. Institute for Scientific Information, 3501 Market St., Philadelphia, Pennsylvania 19104. (800) 523-1857. 1973-. Previous title: Current Contents. Agricultural, Food & Veterinary Sciences. Gives the table of contents of periodicals in the fields of agriculture, biology, environmental and related areas.

ENCYCLOPEDIAS AND DICTIONARIES

McGraw-Hill Encyclopedia of Science and Technology. McGraw-Hill, 1221 Avenue of the Americas, New York, New York 10020. (212) 512-2000 or (800) 262-4729. 1992. Seventh edition. Issued in multiple volumes including index. Includes all science and technology broad subject areas.

Van Nostrand's Scientific Encyclopedia. Glenn D. Considine, ed. Van Nostrand Reinhold, 115 5th Ave., New York, New York 10003. (212) 254-3232. 1983. Sixth edition. Includes all broad subject areas in science.

ONLINE DATA BASES

SCISEARCH. Institute for Scientific Information, University City Science Center, 3501 Market St., Philadelphia, Pennsylvania 19104. (215) 386-0100.

RESEARCH CENTERS AND INSTITUTES

Department of Forest Resources. University of Arkansas at Monticello, Monticello, Arkansas 71655. (501) 460-1052.

State University of New York College of Environmental Science and Forestry. Syracuse Forest Experiment Station, 452 Lafayette Rd., Syracuse, New York 13205. (315) 469-3053.

University of Alabama, Arboretum. Box 870344, Tuscaloosa, Alabama 35487-0344. (205) 553-3278.

University of Maine, Cooperative Forestry Research Unit. College of Forest Resources, Orono, Maine 04469. (207) 581-2893.

SINK HOLES

ABSTRACTING AND INDEXING SERVICES

Applied Ecology Abstracts Studies in Renewable Natural Resources. Information Retrieval Ltd., 1911 Jefferson Davis Highway, Arlington, Virginia 22202. 1975-. Monthly.

Multimedia Index to Ecology. National Information Center for Educational Media, University of Southern California, Los Angeles, California 90007.

BIBLIOGRAPHIES

Bibliography and Index of Geology. American Geological Institute, 4220 King St., Alexandria, Virginia 22302. Monthly. Includes environmental geology and hydrogeology.

GENERAL WORKS

Caves and Other Groundwater Features. JLM Visuals, 1208 Bridge St., Grafton, Wisconsin 53024. (414) 377-7775. 1979. Slides of sinkholes, stalactites, stalagmites and caves.

Development of Sinkholes Resulting from Man's Activities in the Eastern United States. John G. Newton. U.S. Geological Survey, 12201 Sunrise Valley Dr., Reston, Virginia 22092. (703) 648-4460. 1987. Causes and environmental aspects of sinkholes.

Magill's Survey of Science. Earth Science Series. Frank N. Magill. Salem Press, PO Box 50062, Pasadena, California 91105. 1990-. Five volumes. Includes information on earth's crust, hot spots and volcanic island chains, physical properties of minerals, rock magnetism, physical properties of rocks, and index.

Sinkhole Type, Development and Distribution in Florida. William C. Sinclair. Department of Natural Resources, Bureau of Geology, 3900 Commonwealth Blvd., Tallahassee, Florida 32399. (904) 488-7131. 1985. Maps giving locations and descriptions of Florida sinkholes.

Sinkholes. Barry F. Beck. A. A. Balkema, Boston, Massachusetts 1984. Sinkhole geology, engineering and environmental impact.

SLAG

ABSTRACTING AND INDEXING SERVICES

Science Citation Index. Institute for Scientific Information, 3501 Market St., Philadelphia, Pennsylvania 19104. 1961-.

ENCYCLOPEDIAS AND DICTIONARIES

Van Nostrand's Scientific Encyclopedia. Glenn D. Considine, ed. Van Nostrand Reinhold, 115 5th Ave., New York, New York 10003. (212) 254-3232. 1983. Sixth edition. Includes all broad subject areas in science.

GENERAL WORKS

Blastfurnace and Steel Slag. A.R. Lee. John Wiley & Sons, Inc., 605 3rd Ave., New York, New York 10158-0012. (212) 850-6000. 1974. Covers production, properties and uses of slag.

Methods for the Analysis of Mineral Chromites and Ferrochrome Slag. Delbert A. Baker. U.S. Department of the Interior, 1849 C St., NW, Washington, District of Columbia 20240. (202) 208-3171. 1989. Analysis of chromium ores.

Phosphate Slag Risk. U.S. Congress, Senate Committee on Environment and Public Works, Subcommittee on Nuclear Regulation. U.S. G.P.O., Washington, District of Columbia 20401. (202) 512-0000. 1990.

ONLINE DATA BASES

Monthly Catalog of United States Government Publications. U.S. G.P.O., Supt. of Docs., PO Box 371954, Pittsburgh, Pennsylvania 15250-7954. (202) 512-0000.

National Technical Information Service. U.S. Department of Commerce, National Technical Information Service, Office of Data Base Services, 5285 Port Royal Rd., Springfield, Virginia 22161. (703) 487-4807. Bibliographic database of government sponsored research and technical reports.

TRADE ASSOCIATIONS AND PROFESSIONAL SOCIETIES

National Slag Association. 300 S. Washington St., Alexandria, Virginia 22314. (703) 549-3111.

SLUDGE

See also: WASTEWATER TREATMENT

ABSTRACTING AND INDEXING SERVICES

ASFA Aquaculture Abstracts. Cambridge Scientific Abstracts, Inc., 5161 River Rd., Bethesda, Maryland 20816. (301) 961-6750. 1984.

Biological and Agricultural Index. H.W. Wilson Co., 950 University Ave., Bronx, New York 10452. (800) 367-6770. 1916-. Monthly.

Biotechnology Research Abstracts. Cambridge Scientific Abstracts, 5161 River Rd., Bethesda, Maryland 20816. (301) 961-6750. Monthly. Includes such broad areas as genetic intervention, biochemical genetics, and microbiological techniques.

Bulletin Signaletique: Eau et Assainissement, Pollution Atmospherique, Droit des Pollutions. Centre de Documentation, Centre National de la Recherche Scientifique, 15, quai Anatole France, Paris, France 75700. (1) 45 55 92 25. 1983-. Monthly. Indexes pollution periodicals including water, atmospheric and related pollutions.

General Science Index. H. W. Wilson Co., 950 University Ave., Bronx, New York 10452. 1978-. Monthly, also issued in annual cumulation. Cumulative subject index to English language periodicals in the subject fields of astronomy, botany, chemistry, earth science, environment and conservation, food and nutrition, genetics, mathematics, medicine and health, microbiology, oceanography, physics, physiology and zoology.

Pollution Abstracts. Cambridge Scientific Abstracts, 5161 River Rd., Bethesda, Maryland 20816. (301) 961-6750. Six/year. Indexes worldwide technical literature on environmental pollution. Covers air pollution, marine and freshwater pollution, sewage and wastewater treatment, waste management, toxicology and health, noise pollution, radiation, land pollution, and environmental policies, programs, legislation, and education. Also available online.

Science Citation Index. Institute for Scientific Information, 3501 Market St., Philadelphia, Pennsylvania 19104. 1961-.

BIBLIOGRAPHIES

Bibliography of the Beneficial Uses/Sewage Sludge Irradiation Project. P.S. Homann. National Technical Information Service, 5285 Port Royal Rd., Springfield, Virginia 22161. (703) 487-4650. 1982. Wastewater treatment by disinfection.

Cobalt in Agricultural Ecosystems: A Bibliography of the Literature 1950 Through 1971. Robert Lewis Jones. Department of Agronomy, University of Illinois, Urbana, Illinois 61801. 1973.

Stabilization, Disinfection, and Odor Control in Sewage Sludge Treatment: An Annotated Bibliography Covering the Period 1950-1983. E. S. Connor. E. Horwood, 1230 Avenue of the Americas, New York, New York 10020. (212) 698-7000. 1984.

ENCYCLOPEDIAS AND DICTIONARIES

The Encyclopedia of Soil Science. Rhodes W. Fairbridge. Academic Press, c/o Harcourt Brace Jovanovich Inc., 6277 Sea Harbor Dr., Orlando, Florida 32887. (800) 346-8648. 1979-. Includes soil physics, soil chemistry, soil biology, soil fertility and plant nutrition, soil genesis, classification and cartography.

The New York Times Encyclopedic Dictionary of the Environment. Paul Sarnoff. Quadrangle Books, New York, New York 1971. Focuses on state-of-the-art methods of pollution control, abatement, prevention and removal.

Van Nostrand's Scientific Encyclopedia. Glenn D. Considine, ed. Van Nostrand Reinhold, 115 5th Ave., New York, New York 10003. (212) 254-3232. 1983. Sixth edition. Includes all broad subject areas in science.

GENERAL WORKS

Activated Sludge; Theory and Practice. N.F. Gray. Oxford University Press, 200 Madison Ave., New York, New York 10016. (212) 679-7300 or (800) 334-4249. 1990. Microbial theory and kinetics, process control, modes of operation and aeration methods, trouble shooting, bulking problems, and nutrient removal.

Adsorption Studies Evaluating Codisposal of Coal Gasification Ash with PAH-Containing Wastewater Sludges. John William Kilmer. University of Illinois at Urbana-Champaign, Urbana, Illinois 61801. 1986.

Chemical and Biological Characterization of Municipal Sludges, Sediments, Dredge Spoils, and Drilling Muds. James L. Lichtenberg, et al. American Society for Testing and Materials, 1916 S. Race St., Philadelphia, Pennsylvania 19103. (215) 299-5585. 1988. Deals with the environmental aspects of sewage disposal, analysis, health risk assessment, biological purification of sludge, and water quality management.

Codisposal of Municipal Solid Waste and Sewage Sludge: An Analysis of Constraints. Dick Baldwin. National Technical Information Service, 5285 Port Royal Rd., Springfield, Virginia 22161. (703) 487-4650. 1980.

The Codisposal of Sewage Sludge and Refuse in the Purox System. Union Carbide Corporation. Municipal Environmental Research Laboratory, Office of Research and Development, U.S. Environmental Protection Agency, Cincinnati, Ohio 1978.

Marine Treatment of Sewage Sludge. Telford House, 1 Heron Quay, London, England E14 9XF. 1988.

Sludge Treatment. W.W. Eckenfelder. Marcel Dekker Inc., 270 Madison Ave., New York, New York 10016. (212) 696-9000; (800) 228-1160. 1981. Design and construction of sewage disposal plants and sewage purification.

Sources and Distribution of Nitrate in Ground Water at a Farmed Field Irrigated With Sewage Treatment Plant Effluent. Marian P. Berndt. Department of the Interior, U.S. Geological Survey, 119 National Center, Reston, Virginia 22092. (703) 648-4460. 1990. Covers underground water, sewage sludge as fertilizer, and nitrates.

TAPPI Environmental Conference Proceedings, Seattle, WA, April 9-11, 1990. TAPPI Press, Technology Park/Atlanta, PO Box 105113, Atlanta, Georgia 30348. (404) 446-1400. 1990. Contains 11 papers presented at the conference covering industrial pollution and its remedies.

HANDBOOKS AND MANUALS

Manual on the Causes and Control of Activated Sludge Bulking and Foaming. David Jenkins. Water Research Commission, PO Box 824, Pretoria, Republic of #South Africa 0001. 1992. Handbook on sludge characterization.

ONLINE DATA BASES

Monthly Catalog of United States Government Publications. U.S. G.P.O., Supt. of Docs., PO Box 371954, Pittsburgh, Pennsylvania 15250-7954. (202) 512-0000.

National Technical Information Service. U.S. Department of Commerce, National Technical Information Service, Office of Data Base Services, 5285 Port Royal Rd., Springfield, Virginia 22161. (703) 487-4807. Bibliographic database of government sponsored research and technical reports.

SCISEARCH. Institute for Scientific Information, University City Science Center, 3501 Market St., Philadelphia, Pennsylvania 19104. (215) 386-0100.

Sludge. Business Publishers, Inc., 951 Pershing Dr., Silver Spring, Maryland 20910-4464. (301) 587-6300.

Management of sludge residuals and byproducts generated by industrial and municipal air and water pollution control measures.

PERIODICALS AND NEWSLETTERS

BioCycle-Journal of Waste Recycling. The J.G. Press, Inc., Box 351, Emmaus, Pennsylvania 18049. (215) 967-4135. Monthly. Articles on the reuse of sludge, waste water, and recycled products.

Environmental Health Letter. Business Publishers, Inc., 951 Pershing Dr., Silver Spring, Maryland 20910-4464. (301) 587-6300. 1961-. Biweekly. Covers areas such as: indoor air, asbestos health effects, toxic substances testing, health problems at wastewater plants, risk-based sludge rules, medical waste, developmental toxicity risk assessment, animal carcinogen tests, pesticide risk, air toxics, aerospace chemicals, lead, radionuclide emissions, state right-to-know statutes, and incinerator emissions.

Research Journal of the Water Pollution Control Federation. Water Pollution Control Federation, 601 Wythe St., Alexandria, Virginia 22314-1994. (800) 556-8700. Bimonthly. Covers area water pollution, sewage and sewage treatment.

Sludge Newsletter. Business Publishers, Inc., 951 Pershing Dr., Silver Spring, Maryland 20910-4464. (301) 587-6300. 1976-. Biweekly. Reports on continuing changes at EPA, plus an array of new hazardous waste management and industrial pretreatment requirements that will affect municipal sludge.

TRADE ASSOCIATIONS AND PROFESSIONAL SOCIETIES

American Society of Sanitary Engineering. Box 40362, Bay Village, Ohio 44140. (216) 835-3040.

SLUDGE TREATMENT

See also: WASTEWATER TREATMENT

ABSTRACTING AND INDEXING SERVICES

Abstracts of Air and Water Conservation Literature. American Petroleum Institute. Central Abstracting and Indexing Service, 275 Madison Avenue, New York, New York 10016. 1972.

ASFA Aquaculture Abstracts. Cambridge Scientific Abstracts, Inc., 5161 River Rd., Bethesda, Maryland 20816. (301) 961-6750. 1984.

Biological and Agricultural Index. H.W. Wilson Co., 950 University Ave., Bronx, New York 10452. (800) 367-6770. 1916-. Monthly.

Biotechnology Research Abstracts. Cambridge Scientific Abstracts, 5161 River Rd., Bethesda, Maryland 20816. (301) 961-6750. Monthly. Includes such broad areas as genetic intervention, biochemical genetics, and microbiological techniques.

Bulletin Signaletique: Eau et Assainissement, Pollution Atmospherique, Droit des Pollutions. Centre de Documentation, Centre National de la Recherche Scientifique, 15, quai Anatole France, Paris, France 75700. (1) 45 55

92 25. 1983-. Monthly. Indexes pollution periodicals including water, atmospheric and related pollutions.

Engineering Index. The Engineering Index Inc., 345 E. 47th St., New York, New York 10017. 1962-.

General Science Index. H. W. Wilson Co., 950 University Ave., Bronx, New York 10452. 1978-. Monthly, also issued in annual cumulation. Cumulative subject index to English language periodicals in the subject fields of astronomy, botany, chemistry, earth science, environment and conservation, food and nutrition, genetics, mathematics, medicine and health, microbiology, oceanography, physics, physiology and zoology.

Index to Scientific Book Contents. Institute for Scientific Information, 3501 Market St., Philadelphia, Pennsylvania 19104. (800) 523-1857. 1985-. Annual. Gives contents of science books published.

Science Citation Index. Institute for Scientific Information, 3501 Market St., Philadelphia, Pennsylvania 19104. 1961-.

ENCYCLOPEDIAS AND DICTIONARIES

Dictionary of Environmental Engineering and Related Sciences: English-Spanish, Spanish-English. Jose T. Villate. Ediciones Universal, 3090 SW 8th St., Miami, Florida 33135. (305) 642-3355. 1979.

Encyclopedia of Environmental Science and Engineering. J.R. Pfafflin. Gordon and Breach Science Publishers, Inc., 270 8th Ave., New York, New York 10011. (212) 206-8900. 1992.

The Encyclopedia of Soil Science. Rhodes W. Fairbridge. Academic Press, c/o Harcourt Brace Jovanovich Inc., 6277 Sea Harbor Dr., Orlando, Florida 32887. (800) 346-8648. 1979-. Includes soil physics, soil chemistry, soil biology, soil fertility and plant nutrition, soil genesis, classification and cartography.

McGraw-Hill Encyclopedia of Environmental Science. Sybil P. Parker. McGraw-Hill Science & Engineering Books, 11 W. 19th St., New York, New York 10011. (212) 337-6010. 1980. Covers ecology, man's influence on nature, and environmental protection.

McGraw-Hill Encyclopedia of Science and Technology. McGraw-Hill, 1221 Avenue of the Americas, New York, New York 10020. (212) 512-2000 or (800) 262-4729. 1992. Seventh edition. Issued in multiple volumes including index. Includes all science and technology broad subject areas.

GENERAL WORKS

Activated Sludge; Theory and Practice. N.F. Gray. Oxford University Press, 200 Madison Ave., New York, New York 10016. (212) 679-7300 or (800) 334-4249. 1990. Microbial theory and kinetics, process control, modes of operation and aeration methods, trouble shooting, bulking problems, and nutrient removal.

Alternatives for Solid Waste and Sewage Sludge Disposal. Carel C. DeWinkel. Institute for Environmental Studies, University of Wisconsin, Madison, Wisconsin 53706. 1973. Environmental specifications of refuse and refuse disposal.

Biodegradation of PCBs Sorbed to Sewage Sludge Lagoon Sediments in an Aerobic Digester. William Amdor Chantry. University of Wisconsin Press, 114 N. Murray St., Madison, Wisconsin 53715. (608) 262-8782. 1989.

Chemical and Biological Characterization of Municipal Sludges, Sediments, Dredge Spoils, and Drilling Muds. James L. Lichtenberg, et al. American Society for Testing and Materials, 1916 S. Race St., Philadelphia, Pennsylvania 19103. (215) 299-5585. 1988. Deals with the environmental aspects of sewage disposal, analysis, health risk assessment, biological purification of sludge, and water quality management.

Marine Treatment of Sewage Sludge. Telford House, 1 Heron Quay, London, England E14 9XF. 1988.

Principles of Water Quality Management. William Wesley Eckenfelder. CBI, Boston, Massachusetts 1980.

Sludge Management. W. F. Garber and D. R. Anderson, eds. Pergamon Microforms International, Inc., Fairview Park, Elmsford, New York 10523. (914) 592-7720. 1990. Proceedings of the IAWPRC Conference on Sludge Management, held at Loyola Marymount University, Los Angeles, California, 8-12 January 1990. Offers an insight into sludge management. Topics include: treatment plant planning and management, sludge melting, incineration, drying and dewatering, aerobic and anaerobic digestion, heavy metal contaminants, and the use of sludge products as construction materials.

Sludge Treatment. W.W. Eckenfelder. Marcel Dekker Inc., 270 Madison Ave., New York, New York 10016. (212) 696-9000; (800) 228-1160. 1981. Design and construction of sewage disposal plants and sewage purification.

Use of Soil for Treatment and Final Disposal of Effluents and Sludge. P. R. C. Oliveira and S. A. S. Almeida, eds. Pergamon Microforms International, Inc., Fairview Park, Elmsford, New York 10523. (914) 592-7720. 1988. Proceedings of an IAWPRC Seminar held in Salvador, Bahia, Brazil, August 13-15, 1986. Contains a broad scope of topics regarding the treatment and final disposal of effluents and sludge on land.

Wastewater Engineering: Treatment, Disposal, and Reuse. Metcalf & Eddy, Inc. McGraw-Hill Science & Engineering Books, 11 West 19th St., New York, New York 10011. (212) 337-6010. 1991. Reflects the impact of changing federal legislation on environmental quality control and sludge management. Gives a solid overall perspective on wastewater engineering.

HANDBOOKS AND MANUALS

Design Handbook for Automation of Activated Sludge Wastewater Treatment Plants. Alan W. Manning. National Technical Information Service, 5285 Port Royal Rd., Springfield, Virginia 22161. (703) 487-4650. 1980. Sewage purification and activated sludge process.

User's Guide for the Handling, Treatment, and Disposal of Oily Sludge. U.S. Naval Facilities Engineering Command, 200 Stovel St., Alexandria, Virginia 22332-2300. (703) 325-0589. 1986. Manual for waste disposal in the ocean.

Water Treatment Handbook. Degremont s.a., 184, ave. du 18-Juin-1940, Rueil-Malmaison, France F-92500. 1991. Sixth edition. Part 1 is a general survey of water and its action on the materials with which it comes into contact, and theoretical principles of separation and correction processes used in water treatment. Part 2

describes the process and the treatment plant beginning with the separation process.

ONLINE DATA BASES

CERCLIS. Chemical Information Systems, Inc., 7215 York Rd., Baltimore, Maryland 21212. (301) 321-8440. Information on hazardous waste disposal sites that have either been listed by the EPA on the National Priority List (NPL) or nominated for consideration for the NPL.

Computerized Engineering Index–COMPENDEX. Engineering Information Inc., 345 E. 47th St., New York, New York 10017. (212) 705-7600.

Monthly Catalog of United States Government Publications. U.S. G.P.O., Supt. of Docs., PO Box 371954, Pittsburgh, Pennsylvania 15250-7954. (202) 512-0000.

National Technical Information Service. U.S. Department of Commerce, National Technical Information Service, Office of Data Base Services, 5285 Port Royal Rd., Springfield, Virginia 22161. (703) 487-4807. Bibliographic database of government sponsored research and technical reports.

SCISEARCH. Institute for Scientific Information, University City Science Center, 3501 Market St., Philadelphia, Pennsylvania 19104. (215) 386-0100.

Sludge. Business Publishers, Inc., 951 Pershing Dr., Silver Spring, Maryland 20910-4464. (301) 587-6300. Management of sludge residuals and byproducts generated by industrial and municipal air and water pollution control measures.

PERIODICALS AND NEWSLETTERS

Sludge Newsletter. Business Publishers, Inc., 951 Pershing Dr., Silver Spring, Maryland 20910-4464. (301) 587-6300. 1976-. Biweekly. Reports on continuing changes at EPA, plus an array of new hazardous waste management and industrial pretreatment requirements that will affect municipal sludge.

TRADE ASSOCIATIONS AND PROFESSIONAL SOCIETIES

Acrylamide Producers Association. 1330 Connecticut Ave., N.W., Washington, District of Columbia 20036. (202) 659-0060.

American Chemical Society. 1155 16th St., N.W., Washington, District of Columbia 20036. (202) 872-4600.

American Public Works Association. 106 W. 11th St., Ste. 1800, Kansas City, Missouri 64105-1806. (816) 472-6100.

SLURRY

See: DAMS

SMALL FARMERS

See: AGRICULTURE

SMELTERS

ABSTRACTING AND INDEXING SERVICES

Engineering Index. The Engineering Index Inc., 345 E. 47th St., New York, New York 10017. 1962-.

General Science Index. H. W. Wilson Co., 950 University Ave., Bronx, New York 10452. 1978-. Monthly, also issued in annual cumulation. Cumulative subject index to English language periodicals in the subject fields of astronomy, botany, chemistry, earth science, environment and conservation, food and nutrition, genetics, mathematics, medicine and health, microbiology, oceanography, physics, physiology and zoology.

ENCYCLOPEDIAS AND DICTIONARIES

Van Nostrand's Scientific Encyclopedia. Glenn D. Considine, ed. Van Nostrand Reinhold, 115 5th Ave., New York, New York 10003. (212) 254-3232. 1983. Sixth edition. Includes all broad subject areas in science.

GENERAL WORKS

Environmental Impacts of Smelters. Jerome O. Nriagu. John Wiley & Sons, Inc., 605 3rd Ave., New York, New York 10158-0012. (212) 850-6000. 1984. Toxicity of water pollutants and environmental aspects of smelting furnaces.

Inorganic Arsenic Emissions from Primary Copper Smelters and Arsenic Plants. Office of Air Quality Planning and Standards. U.S. Environmental Protection Agency, 401 M St., S.W., Washington, District of Columbia 20460. (202) 260-2090. 1986. Background information for promulgated standards.

ONLINE DATA BASES

Computerized Engineering Index–COMPENDEX. Engineering Information Inc., 345 E. 47th St., New York, New York 10017. (212) 705-7600.

TRADE ASSOCIATIONS AND PROFESSIONAL SOCIETIES

Secondary Lead Smelters Association. 6000 Lake Forest Dr., Suite 350, Atlanta, Georgia 30328. (404) 257-9634.

SMOG

See also: AIR POLLUTION; AIR QUALITY

ABSTRACTING AND INDEXING SERVICES

Air Pollution Titles. Pennsylvania State University, Center for Air Environmental Studies, 226 Fenske Laboratory, University Park, Pennsylvania 16802. (814) 865-1415. 1965. Bibliographic guide to current research literature on air environment, including monitoring and control of air pollution, health effects, effects on agriculture, forests, toxic air contaminants, and global atmospheric pro cases.

Air Pollution Translations. A Bibliography With Abstracts. U.S. Environmental Protection Agency, MD 75, Research Triangle Park, North Carolina 27711. (919) 541-2184. 1969.

Pollution Abstracts. Cambridge Scientific Abstracts, 5161 River Rd., Bethesda, Maryland 20816. (301) 961-6750. Six/year. Indexes worldwide technical literature on environmental pollution. Covers air pollution, marine and freshwater pollution, sewage and wastewater treatment, waste management, toxicology and health, noise pollution, radiation, land pollution, and environmental policies, programs, legislation, and education. Also available online.

BIBLIOGRAPHIES

Bibliography and Index of Geology. American Geological Institute, 4220 King St., Alexandria, Virginia 22302. Monthly. Includes environmental geology and hydrogeology.

ENCYCLOPEDIAS AND DICTIONARIES

McGraw-Hill Encyclopedia of Environmental Science. Sybil P. Parker. McGraw-Hill Science & Engineering Books, 11 W. 19th St., New York, New York 10011. (212) 337-6010. 1980. Covers ecology, man's influence on nature, and environmental protection.

Van Nostrand's Scientific Encyclopedia. Glenn D. Considine, ed. Van Nostrand Reinhold, 115 5th Ave., New York, New York 10003. (212) 254-3232. 1983. Sixth edition. Includes all broad subject areas in science.

GENERAL WORKS

Battling Smog: A Plan for Action. Kenneth Chilton. Center for the Study of American Business, Washington University, Campus Box 1208, One Brookings Dr., St. Louis, Missouri 63130-4899. (314) 935-5630. 1989.

Human Health Damages from Mobile Source Air Pollution. Steve Leung. National Technical Information Service, 5285 Port Royal Rd., Springfield, Virginia 22161. (703) 487-4650. A delphi analysis of smog, air pollution, carbon monoxide and nitrogen dioxide poisoning.

Magill's Survey of Science. Earth Science Series. Frank N. Magill. Salem Press, PO Box 50062, Pasadena, California 91105. 1990-. Five volumes. Includes information on earth's crust, hot spots and volcanic island chains, physical properties of minerals, rock magnetism, physical properties of rocks, and index.

Ozone, Smog and You. Office of Public Information. Illinois Environmental Protection Agency, 2200 Churchill Rd., PO Box 19276, Springfield, Illinois 62794-9276. (217) 782-2829. 1987. Physiological effects of air pollution.

Political Economy of Smog in Southern California. Jeffry Fawcett. Garland Publishers, 136 Madison Ave., New York, New York 10016. (212) 686-7492; (800) 627-6273. 1990.

ONLINE DATA BASES

PressNet Environmental Reports. Chemical Information Systems, Inc., 7215 York Rd., Baltimore, Maryland 21212. (301) 321-8440.

SMOG CHAMBERS

See: AIR POLLUTION

SMOG, PHOTOCHEMICAL

ABSTRACTING AND INDEXING SERVICES

Air Pollution Titles. Pennsylvania State University, Center for Air Environmental Studies, 226 Fenske Laboratory, University Park, Pennsylvania 16802. (814) 865-1415. 1965. Bibliographic guide to current research literature on air environment, including monitoring and control of air pollution, health effects, effects on agriculture, forests, toxic air contaminants, and global atmospheric pro cases.

Air Pollution Translations. A Bibliography With Abstracts. U.S. Environmental Protection Agency, MD 75, Research Triangle Park, North Carolina 27711. (919) 541-2184. 1969.

Pollution Abstracts. Cambridge Scientific Abstracts, 5161 River Rd., Bethesda, Maryland 20816. (301) 961-6750. Six/year. Indexes worldwide technical literature on environmental pollution. Covers air pollution, marine and freshwater pollution, sewage and wastewater treatment, waste management, toxicology and health, noise pollution, radiation, land pollution, and environmental policies, programs, legislation, and education. Also available online.

ONLINE DATA BASES

SCISEARCH. Institute for Scientific Information, University City Science Center, 3501 Market St., Philadelphia, Pennsylvania 19104. (215) 386-0100.

SMOKE

ABSTRACTING AND INDEXING SERVICES

Air Pollution Technical Publications of the United States Environmental Protection Agency. U.S. Environmental Protection Agency, Mail Drop 75, Research Triangle Park, North Carolina 27711. (919) 541-2184. 1976. Quarterly.

Air Pollution Titles. Pennsylvania State University, Center for Air Environmental Studies, 226 Fenske Laboratory, University Park, Pennsylvania 16802. (814) 865-1415. 1965. Bibliographic guide to current research literature on air environment, including monitoring and control of air pollution, health effects, effects on agriculture, forests, toxic air contaminants, and global atmospheric pro cases.

Air Pollution Translations. A Bibliography With Abstracts. U.S. Environmental Protection Agency, MD 75, Research Triangle Park, North Carolina 27711. (919) 541-2184. 1969.

Bulletin Signaletique: Eau et Assainissement, Pollution Atmospherique, Droit des Pollutions. Centre de Documentation, Centre National de la Recherche Scientifique, 15, quai Anatole France, Paris, France 75700. (1) 45 55 92 25. 1983-. Monthly. Indexes pollution periodicals including water, atmospheric and related pollutions.

Science Citation Index. Institute for Scientific Information, 3501 Market St., Philadelphia, Pennsylvania 19104. 1961-.

ENCYCLOPEDIAS AND DICTIONARIES

Van Nostrand's Scientific Encyclopedia. Glenn D. Considine, ed. Van Nostrand Reinhold, 115 5th Ave., New York, New York 10003. (212) 254-3232. 1983. Sixth edition. Includes all broad subject areas in science.

GENERAL WORKS

Clearing the Air: Perspectives on Environmental Tobacco Smoke. Robert D. Tollison. Lexington Books, 866 3rd Ave., New York, New York 10022. (212) 702-2000. 1988. Smoking and air pollution, environmental air pollutants resulting from tobacco smoke.

Environmental Tobacco Smoke: A Guide to Workplace Smoking Policies. U.S. Environmental Protection Agency, 401 M St. SW, Washington, District of Columbia 20460. (202) 260-2090. 1990. Tobacco smoke pollution effects on atmospheric air, and indoor air and air radiation.

Environmental Tobacco Smoke and Cancer. William Weiss. U.S. G.P.O., Washington, District of Columbia 20401. (202) 512-0000. 1989. Passive smoking and lungs–cancer.

SMOKING

ABSTRACTING AND INDEXING SERVICES

Air Pollution Technical Publications of the United States Environmental Protection Agency. U.S. Environmental Protection Agency, Mail Drop 75, Research Triangle Park, North Carolina 27711. (919) 541-2184. 1976. Quarterly.

Air Pollution Titles. Pennsylvania State University, Center for Air Environmental Studies, 226 Fenske Laboratory, University Park, Pennsylvania 16802. (814) 865-1415. 1965. Bibliographic guide to current research literature on air environment, including monitoring and control of air pollution, health effects, effects on agriculture, forests, toxic air contaminants, and global atmospheric pro cases.

Air Pollution Translations. A Bibliography With Abstracts. U.S. Environmental Protection Agency, MD 75, Research Triangle Park, North Carolina 27711. (919) 541-2184. 1969.

Food Science and Technology Abstracts. International Food Information Service, c/o National Food Laboratory, 6363 Clark Ave., Dublin, California 94568. (800) 336-3782. 1969-.

General Science Index. H. W. Wilson Co., 950 University Ave., Bronx, New York 10452. 1978-. Monthly, also issued in annual cumulation. Cumulative subject index to English language periodicals in the subject fields of astronomy, botany, chemistry, earth science, environment and conservation, food and nutrition, genetics, mathematics, medicine and health, microbiology, oceanography, physics, physiology and zoology.

ENCYCLOPEDIAS AND DICTIONARIES

Encyclopedia of Human Biology. Renato Dulbecco, ed. Academic Press, c/o Harcourt Brace Jovanovich Inc.,

6277 Sea Harbor Dr., Orlando, Florida 32887. (800) 346-8648. 1991. Eight volumes.

GENERAL WORKS

Active and Passive Smoking Hazards in the Workplace. Judith A. Douville. Van Nostrand Reinhold, 115 5th Ave., 10003. (212) 254-3232. 1990.

Banishing Tobacco. William U. Chandler. Worldwatch Institute, 1776 Massachusetts Ave., N.W., Washington, District of Columbia 20036-1904. 1986.

ONLINE DATA BASES

Medical Toxicology and Environmental Health. Department of Health and Social Security, Medical Toxiclology & Environmental Health Division, Hannibal House, Rm. 719, Elephant and Castle, London, England SE1 6TE. 44 (71) 972-2162.

Smoking and Health. U.S. Department of Health & Human Services. Center for Disease Control, Center for Chronic Disease Prevention & Health Promotion, Office on Smoking and Health, Technical Information Center, Park Building, Rm. 1-16, 5600 Fishers Lane, Rockville, Maryland 20857. (301) 443-1690.

Smoking in the Workplace: 1987 Update. Society for Human Resource Management, 606 N. Washington St., Alexandria, Virginia 22314. (703) 548-3440.

Where There's Smoke: Problems and Policies Concerning Smoking in the Workplace. Bureau of National Affairs, 1231 25th St., N.W., Rm. 215, Washington, District of Columbia 20037. (800) 452-7773.

PERIODICALS AND NEWSLETTERS

Journal of the National Cancer Institute. National Institute of Health. U.S. G.P.O., Washington, District of Columbia 20401. (202) 512-0000. Semi-monthly. Covers epidemiology and biochemistry of cancer.

STATISTICS SOURCES

Smoking and Health, A National Status Report. U.S. Centers for Disease Control, c/o U.S. Government Printing Office, Washington, District of Columbia 20401. (202) 512-0000. 1986. Biennial. Smoking and health research, education, legislative and other intervention efforts, program outcomes, and smoking prevalence.

Smoking, Tobacco, and Health: A Fact Book. U.S. Centers for Disease Control. U.S. G.P.O., Washington, District of Columbia 20401. (202) 512-0000. 1987. Irregular. Smoking related death and illness rates, nicotine absorption and exposure levels.

TRADE ASSOCIATIONS AND PROFESSIONAL SOCIETIES

American Association for Cancer Education. Box 700, UAB Station, Birmingham, Alabama 35294. (205) 934-3054.

American Cancer Society. 1599 Clifton Rd., N.E., Atlanta, Georgia 30329. (404) 320-3333.

American Heart Association. 7320 Greenville Ave., Dallas, Texas 75231. (214) 373-6300.

American Lung Association. 1740 Broadway, New York, New York 10019. (212) 315-8700.

Americans United for a Smoke Free Society. 8701 Georgia Ave., Silver Spring, Maryland 20910. (202) 667-6653.

Association for the Care of Asthma. Jefferson Medical College, 1025 Walnut St., Rm. 727, Philadelphia, Pennsylvania 19107. (215) 955-8912.

Breathe-Free Plan to Stop Smoking. 12501 Old Columbia Pike, Silver Spring, Maryland 20904-6600.

Citizens Against Tobacco Smoke. P.O. Box 36236, Cincinnati, Ohio 45236. (513) 984-8833.

Coalition on Smoking or Health. 1607 New Hampshire Ave., N.W., Washington, District of Columbia 20009. (202) 234-9375.

Council for Tobacco Research–U.S.A. 900 Third Ave., New York, New York 10022. (212) 421-8885.

Cystic Fibrosis Foundation. 6931 Arlington Rd., #200, Bethesda, Maryland 20814. (301) 951-4422.

Emphysema Anonymous. P.O. Box 3224, Seminole, Florida 34642. (813) 391-9977.

Group Against Smokers' Pollution. P.O. Box 632, College Park, Maryland 20740. (301) 459-4791.

National Foundation for Asthma. P.O. Box 30069, Tucson, Arizona 85751. (602) 323-6046.

Respiratory Health Association. 55 Paramus Rd., Paramus, New Jersey 07652. (201) 843-4111.

Smoking Policy Institute. 218 Broadway E., Seattle, Washington 98102. (206) 324-4444.

Tobacco Institute. 1875 I St., N.W., Suite 800, Washington, District of Columbia 20006. (202) 457-4800.

United Cancer Council. 4010 W. 86th St., Suite H, Indianapolis, Indiana 46268. (317) 879-9900.

SOAPS

See: DETERGENTS AND SOAPS

SODIUM

ABSTRACTING AND INDEXING SERVICES

ASFA Aquaculture Abstracts. Cambridge Scientific Abstracts, Inc., 5161 River Rd., Bethesda, Maryland 20816. (301) 961-6750. 1984.

Physics Briefs. Physikalische Berichte. Physik Verlag, Pappapelallee 3, Postfach 101161, Weinheim, Germany D-6940. 1979-. Semimonthly. In English. Volumes for 1979- issued by the Deutsche Physikalische Gesellschaft and the Fachinformationszentrum Energie Physik, Mathematik in cooperation with the American Institute of Physics.

Science Citation Index. Institute for Scientific Information, 3501 Market St., Philadelphia, Pennsylvania 19104. 1961-.

ENCYCLOPEDIAS AND DICTIONARIES

The Dictionary of Sodium, Fats, and Cholesterol. Barbara Kraus. Putnam Berkley Group, 200 Madison Ave., New York, New York 10016. (212) 951-8400. 1990. Food composition, fat, cholesterol, and sodium.

GENERAL WORKS

Sodium, Its Biologic Significance. Solomon Papper. CRC Press, 2000 Corporate Blvd. N.W., Boca Raton, Florida 33431. (800) 272-7737. 1982. Sodium in the body, sodium metabolism disorders, complications and sequelae.

Sodium: Think About It. U.S. Department of Agriculture, Washington, District of Columbia 1982. Deals with sodium in the body.

STATISTICS SOURCES

Sodium Chemicals. FIND/SVP, 625 Avenue of the Americas, New York, New York 10011. (212) 645-4500. 1991. Historical production and demand data with forecasts to 1995 and 2000 for caustic soda; sodium chlorate; sodium bichromate; soda ash; sodium bicarbonate; STPP; silicates; and other chemicals.

TRADE ASSOCIATIONS AND PROFESSIONAL SOCIETIES

Association of American Cancer Institutes. 666 Elm St., Buffalo, New York 14263. (716) 845-3028.

SODIUM CHLORIDE

See: SALT

SODIUM COMPOUNDS

ABSTRACTING AND INDEXING SERVICES

ASFA Aquaculture Abstracts. Cambridge Scientific Abstracts, Inc., 5161 River Rd., Bethesda, Maryland 20816. (301) 961-6750. 1984.

General Science Index. H. W. Wilson Co., 950 University Ave., Bronx, New York 10452. 1978-. Monthly, also issued in annual cumulation. Cumulative subject index to English language periodicals in the subject fields of astronomy, botany, chemistry, earth science, environment and conservation, food and nutrition, genetics, mathematics, medicine and health, microbiology, oceanography, physics, physiology and zoology.

ENCYCLOPEDIAS AND DICTIONARIES

Van Nostrand's Scientific Encyclopedia. Glenn D. Considine, ed. Van Nostrand Reinhold, 115 5th Ave., New York, New York 10003. (212) 254-3232. 1983. Sixth edition. Includes all broad subject areas in science.

TRADE ASSOCIATIONS AND PROFESSIONAL SOCIETIES

American Chemical Society. 1155 16th St., N.W., Washington, District of Columbia 20036. (202) 872-4600.

American Institute of Chemical Engineers. 345 East 47th St., New York, New York 10017. (212) 705-7338.

American Institute of Chemists. 7315 Wisconsin Ave., Bethesda, Maryland 20814. (301) 652-2447.

SODIUM FLUOROCETATES

ONLINE DATA BASES

Chemical Carcinogenesis Research Information System–CCRIS. National Library of Medicine, 8600 Rockville Pike, Bethesda, Maryland 20894. (800) 638-8480. Individual assay results and test conditions for 1,451 chemicals in the areas of carcinogenicity, mutagenicity, tumor promotion, and cocarcinogenicity.

Chemical Collection System/Request Tracking–CCS/RTS. U.S. Environmental Protection Agency, Office of Pesticides and Toxic Substances, 401 M St., SW, Washington, District of Columbia 20460. (202) 260-2090. Contains information on various properties of a number of chemicals including environmental effects, test and analysis methods, and health effects. Available from EPA.

Chemical Dictionary Online–CHEMLINE. Chemical Abstracts Service, 2540 Olentangy River Rd., Columbus, Ohio 43210. (614) 421-3600 or (800) 848-6533. Part of MEDLINE of the National Library of Medicine (NLM). File of 900,000 names for chemical substances, representing 450,000 unique compounds. It contains such information as Chemical Abstracts (CA) Service Registry Numbers, molecular formulas, preferred chemical nomenclature, and generic and ring structure information. Available on NLM's ELHILL system.

Chemical Exposure. Science Applications International Corp., Health & Environmental Information, P.O. Box 2501, Oak Ridge, Tennessee 37831. (615) 482-9031. Database of chemicals that have been identified in both human tissues and body fluids and in feral and food animals. Contains reference to journal articles, conferences, and reports. Covers the whole fields of information related to human and animal exposure to food, air, and water contaminants and pharmaceuticals. Its records include information on chemical properties, formulas, tissues measured, analytical method used, demographics and more. Available on DIALOG.

TRADE ASSOCIATIONS AND PROFESSIONAL SOCIETIES

American Chemical Society. 1155 16th St., N.W., Washington, District of Columbia 20036. (202) 872-4600.

American Institute of Chemical Engineers. 345 East 47th St., New York, New York 10017. (212) 705-7338.

American Institute of Chemists. 7315 Wisconsin Ave., Bethesda, Maryland 20814. (301) 652-2447.

SODIUM HYDROXIDE

GENERAL WORKS

American Water Works Association Standard for Caustic Soda. American Water Works Association, 6666 W. Quincy Ave., Denver, Colorado 80235. (303) 794-7711. 1988. Standards for water purification using caustic soda.

Sodium Hydroxide. Environmental Protection Service, 425 St. Joseph Blvd., 3rd Fl., Hull, Quebec, Canada K1A 0H3. (613) 953-5921. 1984. Environmental and technical information for problem spills manuals.

ONLINE DATA BASES

Chemical Collection System/Request Tracking–CCS/ RTS. U.S. Environmental Protection Agency, Office of Pesticides and Toxic Substances, 401 M St., SW, Washington, District of Columbia 20460. (202) 260-2090. Contains information on various properties of a number of chemicals including environmental effects, test and analysis methods, and health effects. Available from EPA.

Chemical Dictionary Online–CHEMLINE. Chemical Abstracts Service, 2540 Olentangy River Rd., Columbus, Ohio 43210. (614) 421-3600 or (800) 848-6533. Part of MEDLINE of the National Library of Medicine (NLM). File of 900,000 names for chemical substances, representing 450,000 unique compounds. It contains such information as Chemical Abstracts (CA) Service Registry Numbers, molecular formulas, preferred chemical nomenclature, and generic and ring structure information. Available on NLM's ELHILL system.

Chemical Exposure. Science Applications International Corp., Health & Environmental Information, P.O. Box 2501, Oak Ridge, Tennessee 37831. (615) 482-9031. Database of chemicals that have been identified in both human tissues and body fluids and in feral and food animals. Contains reference to journal articles, conferences, and reports. Covers the whole fields of information related to human and animal exposure to food, air, and water contaminants and pharmaceuticals. Its records include information on chemical properties, formulas, tissues measured, analytical method used, demographics and more. Available on DIALOG.

TRADE ASSOCIATIONS AND PROFESSIONAL SOCIETIES

American Chemical Society. 1155 16th St., N.W., Washington, District of Columbia 20036. (202) 872-4600.

American Institute of Chemical Engineers. 345 East 47th St., New York, New York 10017. (212) 705-7338.

American Institute of Chemists. 7315 Wisconsin Ave., Bethesda, Maryland 20814. (301) 652-2447.

SOFT DETERGENTS

See: BIODEGRADABLE

SOIL ANALYSIS

ABSTRACTING AND INDEXING SERVICES

Abstracts of Air and Water Conservation Literature. American Petroleum Institute. Central Abstracting and Indexing Service, 275 Madison Avenue, New York, New York 10016. 1972.

ASFA Aquaculture Abstracts. Cambridge Scientific Abstracts, Inc., 5161 River Rd., Bethesda, Maryland 20816. (301) 961-6750. 1984.

Biological and Agricultural Index. H.W. Wilson Co., 950 University Ave., Bronx, New York 10452. (800) 367-6770. 1916-. Monthly.

Biotechnology Research Abstracts. Cambridge Scientific Abstracts, 5161 River Rd., Bethesda, Maryland 20816. (301) 961-6750. Monthly. Includes such broad areas as genetic intervention, biochemical genetics, and microbiological techniques.

Civil Engineering Hydraulic Abstracts. BHRA Fluid Engineering, Air Science Co., PO Box 143, Corning, New York 14830. (607) 962-5591. Monthly. Abstracts of periodicals that publish in the areas of hydraulic engineering and other related topics.

Environment Abstracts. Bowker A & I Publishing, 121 Chanlon Rd., New Providence, New Jersey 07974. (908) 464-6800. 1974-.

Environment Index. Environment Information Center, Index Research Department, 124 E. 39th St., New York, New York 10016. 1971-. Annual.

Environmental Information Connection–EIC. Planning Information Program, Dept. of Urban and Regional Planning, University of Illinois, 1003 West Nevada, Urbana, Illinois 61801. (217) 333-1369. Also available online.

Environmental Periodicals Bibliography. Environmental Studies Institute, International Academy at Santa Barbara, 800 Garden St., Suite D, Santa Barbara, California 93101. (805) 965-5010. Also available online.

General Science Index. H. W. Wilson Co., 950 University Ave., Bronx, New York 10452. 1978-. Monthly, also issued in annual cumulation. Cumulative subject index to English language periodicals in the subject fields of astronomy, botany, chemistry, earth science, environment and conservation, food and nutrition, genetics, mathematics, medicine and health, microbiology, oceanography, physics, physiology and zoology.

Physics Briefs. Physikalische Berichte. Physik Verlag, Pappapelallee 3, Postfach 101161, Weinheim, Germany D-6940. 1979-. Semimonthly. In English. Volumes for 1979- issued by the Deutsche Physikalische Gesellschaft and the Fachinformationszentrum Energie Physik, Mathematik in cooperation with the American Institute of Physics.

Science Citation Index. Institute for Scientific Information, 3501 Market St., Philadelphia, Pennsylvania 19104. 1961-.

Soils and Fertilizers. C. A. B. International, 845 North Park Ave., Tucson, Arizona 85719. (602) 621-7897 or (800) 528-4841. 1937-. Monthly. Focuses on soil chemistry, soil physics, soil biology, soil fertility, soil management, soil classification, soil formation, soil conservation, land reclamation, irrigation and damage, fertilizer technology, fertilizer use, plant nutrition, plant water relations, and environmental aspects.

BIBLIOGRAPHIES

Bibliography and Index of Geology. American Geological Institute, 4220 King St., Alexandria, Virginia 22302. Monthly. Includes environmental geology and hydrogeology.

EPA Publications Bibliography. U.S. Environmental Protection Agency, Library Systems Branch, 401 M St., SW,

Washington, District of Columbia 20460. (202) 260-2090. Quarterly.

New Publications of the Geological Survey. U.S. Department of the Interior, Geological Survey, 119 National Center, Reston, Virginia 22092. (703) 648-4460. 1984-. Monthly. Bibliography of geological publications and related government documents published by the Geological Survey.

ENCYCLOPEDIAS AND DICTIONARIES

Dictionary of Civil Engineering. John S. Scott. Halsted Press, Division of J. Wiley, 605 3rd Ave., New York, New York 10158. (212) 850-6000. 1981. Third edition.

Elsevier's Dictionary of Soil Mechanics and Geotechnical Engineering. J. D. Van Der Tuin. Elsevier Science Publishing Co., 655 Avenue of the Americas, New York, New York 10010. (212) 989-5800. 1989. The text is in English, French, Spanish, Dutch, and German.

The Encyclopedia of Geochemistry and Environmental Sciences. Rhodes Whitmore Fairbridge. Van Nostrand Reinhold Co., 115 5th Ave., New York, New York 10003. (212) 254-3232. 1972.

Encyclopedia of Physics. Rita G. Lerner and George L. Trigg. VCH Publishers, 303 NW 12th Ave., Deerfield Beach, Florida 33442-1788. (305) 428-5566. 1991. Second edition.

The Encyclopedia of Soil Science. Rhodes W. Fairbridge. Academic Press, c/o Harcourt Brace Jovanovich Inc., 6277 Sea Harbor Dr., Orlando, Florida 32887. (800) 346-8648. 1979-. Includes soil physics, soil chemistry, soil biology, soil fertility and plant nutrition, soil genesis, classification and cartography.

Glossary of Geology. Robert Latimer Bates and Julia A. Jackson, eds. American Geological Institute, 4220 King St., Alexandria, Virginia 22302-1507. (703) 379-2480 or (800) 336-4764. 1987. Third edition.

McGraw-Hill Encyclopedia of the Geological Sciences. Sybil P. Parker, ed. McGraw-Hill, 1221 Avenue of the Americas, New York, New York 10020. (212) 512-2000 or (800) 262-4729. 1988. Second edition. Published previously in the McGraw-Hill Encyclopedia of Science and Technology.

Van Nostrand's Scientific Encyclopedia. Glenn D. Considine, ed. Van Nostrand Reinhold, 115 5th Ave., New York, New York 10003. (212) 254-3232. 1983. Sixth edition. Includes all broad subject areas in science.

GENERAL WORKS

Acidic Deposition and Forest Soils. Dan Binkley. Springer-Verlag, 175 Fifth Ave., New York, New York 10010. (212) 460-1500 or (800) 777-4643. 1990. Environmental aspects of acid deposition, forest soils and soil acidity.

Chemical Analysis of Ecological Materials. Stewart E. Allen. John Wiley & Sons, Inc., 605 3rd Ave., New York, New York 10158-0012. (212) 850-6000. 1974.

Cycles of Soil: Carbon, Nitrogen, Phosphorus, Sulfur, Micronutrients. F.J. Stevenson. John Wiley & Sons Inc., 605 3rd Ave., New York, New York 10158-0012. (212) 850-6000. 1986.

Death in the Marsh. Tom Harris. Island Press, 1718 Connecticut Ave. N.W., Suite 300, Washington, District

of Columbia 20009. (202) 232-7933. 1991. Explains how federal irrigation projects have altered the selenium's circulation in the environment, allowing it to accumulate in marshes, killing ecosystems and wildlife, and causing deformities in some animals.

Ecological Implications of Contemporary Agriculture. H. Eijsackers and A. Quispel, eds. Munksgaard International, PO Box 2148, Copenhagen K, Denmark DK-1016. 1988. Proceedings of the 4th European Symposium, September 7-12, 1986, Wageningen. Ecological bulletins are published in cooperation with ecological journals; holarctic ecology and Oikos. They consist of monographs, reports, and symposium proceedings on topics of international interest.

Enhanced Biodegradation of Pesticides in the Environment. Kenneth D. Racke and Joel R. Coats, eds. American Chemical Society, 1155 16th St. N.W., Washington, District of Columbia 20036. (202) 872-4600; (800) 227-5558. 1990. Discusses pesticides in the soil, microbial ecosystems, and the effects of long term application of herbicides on the soil.

Magill's Survey of Science. Earth Science Series. Frank N. Magill. Salem Press, PO Box 50062, Pasadena, California 91105. 1990-. Five volumes. Includes information on earth's crust, hot spots and volcanic island chains, physical properties of minerals, rock magnetism, physical properties of rocks, and index.

Soil Analysis: Modern Instrumental Techniques. Keith A. Smith, ed. Marcel Dekker, Inc., 270 Madison Ave., New York, New York 10016. (212) 696-9000; (800) 228-1160. 1991. Covers instrumental analysis for soil chemists. The second edition combines the underlying principles of current techniques with discussions of sample preparation and matrix problems which critically reviewing applications in modern soil science and related disciplines.

Soil Testing and Plant Analysis. R. L. Westerman, et al., eds. Crop Science Society of America, 677 South Segoe Rd., Madison, Wisconsin 53711. (608) 273-8080. 1990. 3d ed. Standard source on the subject of soil testing. Summarizes current knowledge and experience as diagnostic tool for assessing nutritional requirements of crops, efficient fertilizer use, saline-sodic conditions, and toxicity of metals.

HANDBOOKS AND MANUALS

The Agricultural Notebook. Primrose McConnell; R. J. Halley, ed. Butterworth-Heinemann, 80 Montvale Ave., Stoneham, Massachusetts 02180. (617) 438-8464 or (800) 366-2665. 1982. Seventeenth edition. Includes data on the business of farming. Topics discussed include soils, drainage, crop physiology, crop nutrition, arable crops, grassland, trees on the farm, weed control, diseases of crops, pests of crops, grain preservation and storage, animal production, farm equipment, farm management, agricultural law, health and safety, and agricultural computers.

Handbook of Methods for Acid Deposition Studies: Laboratory Analyses for Soil Chemistry. L.J. Blume. Environmental Monitoring Systems Laboratory, PO Box 15027, Las Vegas, Nevada 89104. (702) 798-2000. 1990.

Methods of Soil Analysis. Arnold Klute. Soil Science Society of America, 677 S. Segoe Rd., Madison, Wisconsin 53611. (608) 273-8080. 1986. Physical and mineralogical methods and chemical and microbiological properties of soil.

ONLINE DATA BASES

Chemest. Technical Database Services, Inc., 10 Columbus Circle, New York, New York 10019. (212) 245-0044. Covers methods of estimating 11 important properties: water solubility, soil adsorption coefficient, bioconcentration factor, acid dissociation constant, activity coefficient, boiling point, vapor pressure, water volatilization rate, Henry's Law Constant, melting point, and liquid viscosity.

Enviro/Energyline Abstracts Plus. R. R. Bowker Co., 121 Chanlon Rd., New Providence, New Jersey 07974. (908) 464-6800.

Environmental Periodicals Bibliography. National Information Services Corp., Ste. 6, Wyman Towers, 3100 St. Paul St., Baltimore, Maryland 21218. (410)243-0797. Online version of abstract of same name.

Monthly Catalog of United States Government Publications. U.S. G.P.O., Supt. of Docs., PO Box 371954, Pittsburgh, Pennsylvania 15250-7954. (202) 512-0000.

National Technical Information Service. U.S. Department of Commerce, National Technical Information Service, Office of Data Base Services, 5285 Port Royal Rd., Springfield, Virginia 22161. (703) 487-4807. Bibliographic database of government sponsored research and technical reports.

SCISEARCH. Institute for Scientific Information, University City Science Center, 3501 Market St., Philadelphia, Pennsylvania 19104. (215) 386-0100.

PERIODICALS AND NEWSLETTERS

Fertilizer Research: An International Journal on Fertilizer Use and Technology. Kluwer Academic Publishers, 101 Philip Dr., Assinippi Park, Norwell, Massachusetts 02061. (617) 871-6600. Monthly. Soils, soil fertility, soil chemistry, crop and animal production and husbandry, crop quality and environment.

International Journal of Plant Nutrition, Plant Chemistry, Soil Microbiology and Soil-Bourne Plant Diseases. Kluwer Academic Publishers, 101 Philip Dr., Assinippi Park, Norwell, Massachusetts 02061. (617) 871-6600. 1948-.

Soil Biology and Biochemistry. Pergamon Microforms International, Inc., Fairview Park, Elmsford, New York 10523. (914) 592-7720. Eight times a year. Soil biology, soil biochemistry, nitrogen fixation, nitrogenase activity, sampling microorganisms in soil, soil compaction, and nutrient release in soils.

Water Research. International Association on Water Pollution Research and Control. Pergamon Microforms International, Inc., Fairview Park, Elmsford, New York 10523. (914) 592-7720. 1966-. Monthly. Covers all aspects of the pollution of marine and fresh water and the management of water quality as well as water resources.

RESEARCH CENTERS AND INSTITUTES

Northeast Louisiana University, Soil-Plant Analysis Laboratory. Room 117, Chemistry and Natural Sciences Building, Monroe, Louisiana 71209-0505. (318) 342-1948.

Northeast Watershed Research Center. 111 Research Building A, Pennsylvania State University, University Park, Pennsylvania 16802. (814) 865-2048.

Soil and Environmental Chemistry Lab. Pennsylvania State University, 104 Research Unit A, University Park, Pennsylvania 16802. (814) 865-1221.

University of Alaska Fairbanks, Forestry Soils Laboratory. Fairbanks, Alaska 99775. (907) 474-7114.

University of Puerto Rico, Central Analytical Laboratory. P.O. Box 21360, Rio Piedras, Puerto Rico 00928. (809) 767-9705.

TRADE ASSOCIATIONS AND PROFESSIONAL SOCIETIES

American Institute of Biological Sciences. 730 11th St., N.W., Washington, District of Columbia 20001-4521. (202) 628-1500.

American Institute of Chemical Engineers. 345 East 47th St., New York, New York 10017. (212) 705-7338.

American Institute of Chemists. 7315 Wisconsin Ave., Bethesda, Maryland 20814. (301) 652-2447.

American Society of Agronomy. 677 South Segoe Rd., Madison, Wisconsin 53711. (608) 273-8080.

Association of Soil & Foundation Engineers. 8811 Colesville Rd., Suite G106, Silver Spring, Maryland 20910. (301) 563-2733.

SOIL CEMENT

See: DAMS

SOIL CONDITIONER

See also: COMPOST; HUMUS

ABSTRACTING AND INDEXING SERVICES

Biological and Agricultural Index. H.W. Wilson Co., 950 University Ave., Bronx, New York 10452. (800) 367-6770. 1916-. Monthly.

Environment Abstracts. Bowker A & I Publishing, 121 Chanlon Rd., New Providence, New Jersey 07974. (908) 464-6800. 1974-.

Environment Index. Environment Information Center, Index Research Department, 124 E. 39th St., New York, New York 10016. 1971-. Annual.

Environmental Information Connection–EIC. Planning Information Program, Dept. of Urban and Regional Planning, University of Illinois, 1003 West Nevada, Urbana, Illinois 61801. (217) 333-1369. Also available online.

Environmental Periodicals Bibliography. Environmental Studies Institute, International Academy at Santa Barbara, 800 Garden St., Suite D, Santa Barbara, California 93101. (805) 965-5010. Also available online.

General Science Index. H. W. Wilson Co., 950 University Ave., Bronx, New York 10452. 1978-. Monthly, also issued in annual cumulation. Cumulative subject index

to English language periodicals in the subject fields of astronomy, botany, chemistry, earth science, environment and conservation, food and nutrition, genetics, mathematics, medicine and health, microbiology, oceanography, physics, physiology and zoology.

Science Citation Index. Institute for Scientific Information, 3501 Market St., Philadelphia, Pennsylvania 19104. 1961-.

BIBLIOGRAPHIES

Bibliography and Index of Geology. American Geological Institute, 4220 King St., Alexandria, Virginia 22302. Monthly. Includes environmental geology and hydrogeology.

EPA Publications Bibliography. U.S. Environmental Protection Agency, Library Systems Branch, 401 M St., SW, Washington, District of Columbia 20460. (202) 260-2090. Quarterly.

ENCYCLOPEDIAS AND DICTIONARIES

The Encyclopedia of Geochemistry and Environmental Sciences. Rhodes Whitmore Fairbridge. Van Nostrand Reinhold Co., 115 5th Ave., New York, New York 10003. (212) 254-3232. 1972.

Glossary of Geology. Robert Latimer Bates and Julia A. Jackson, eds. American Geological Institute, 4220 King St., Alexandria, Virginia 22302-1507. (703) 379-2480 or (800) 336-4764. 1987. Third edition.

McGraw-Hill Encyclopedia of the Geological Sciences. Sybil P. Parker, ed. McGraw-Hill, 1221 Avenue of the Americas, New York, New York 10020. (212) 512-2000 or (800) 262-4729. 1988. Second edition. Published previously in the McGraw-Hill Encyclopedia of Science and Technology.

GENERAL WORKS

The Effects of Agri-SC Soil Conditioner on Soil Physical Properties. Bryan C. Fitch. Southern Illinois University, Carbondale, Illinois 62901. 1988.

Magill's Survey of Science. Earth Science Series. Frank N. Magill. Salem Press, PO Box 50062, Pasadena, California 91105. 1990-. Five volumes. Includes information on earth's crust, hot spots and volcanic island chains, physical properties of minerals, rock magnetism, physical properties of rocks, and index.

Utilization of Sewage Sludge Compost as a Soil Conditioner and Fertilizer for Plant Growth. Agricultural Research service. U.S. G.P.O., Washington, District of Columbia 1984.

ONLINE DATA BASES

Cambridge Scientific Abstracts Life Science–CSAL. Cambridge Scientific Abstracts, 5161 River Rd., Bethesda, Maryland 20816. (301) 961-6750. Provides access to the following abstracting services: "Life Sciences Collection," "Aquatic Sciences and Fisheries Abstracts," "Oceanic Abstracts," and "Pollution Abstracts."

Enviro/Energyline Abstracts Plus. R. R. Bowker Co., 121 Chanlon Rd., New Providence, New Jersey 07974. (908) 464-6800.

Environmental Periodicals Bibliography. National Information Services Corp., Ste. 6, Wyman Towers, 3100 St. Paul St., Baltimore, Maryland 21218. (410)243-0797. Online version of abstract of same name.

SCISEARCH. Institute for Scientific Information, University City Science Center, 3501 Market St., Philadelphia, Pennsylvania 19104. (215) 386-0100.

TRADE ASSOCIATIONS AND PROFESSIONAL SOCIETIES

American Institute of Biological Sciences. 730 11th St., N.W., Washington, District of Columbia 20001-4521. (202) 628-1500.

American Institute of Chemical Engineers. 345 East 47th St., New York, New York 10017. (212) 705-7338.

American Institute of Chemists. 7315 Wisconsin Ave., Bethesda, Maryland 20814. (301) 652-2447.

American Society of Agronomy. 677 South Segoe Rd., Madison, Wisconsin 53711. (608) 273-8080.

Association of Soil & Foundation Engineers. 8811 Colesville Rd., Suite G106, Silver Spring, Maryland 20910. (301) 563-2733.

Soil Science Society of America. 677 S. Segoe Rd., Madison, Wisconsin 53711. (608) 273-8080.

SOIL CONSERVATION

See also: CONSERVATION OF NATURAL RESOURCES

ABSTRACTING AND INDEXING SERVICES

Abstracts of Air and Water Conservation Literature. American Petroleum Institute. Central Abstracting and Indexing Service, 275 Madison Avenue, New York, New York 10016. 1972.

Agricultural Engineering Abstracts. C. A. B. International, 845 North Park Ave., Tucson, Arizona 85719. (602) 621-7897 or (800) 528-4841. 1976-. Monthly. Informs about significant research developments in agricultural engineering and instrumentation. Some of the topics scanned for the abstracts include mechanical power, crop production, crop harvesting and threshing, crop processing and storage, aquaculture, land improvement, protected cultivation, handling and transport, and farm buildings and equipment.

Agrindex. AGRIS Coordinating Center, Via delle Terme di Caracalla, Rome, Italy I-00100. 61 0181-FA01. 1975-.

Applied Ecology Abstracts Studies in Renewable Natural Resources. Information Retrieval Ltd., 1911 Jefferson Davis Highway, Arlington, Virginia 22202. 1975-. Monthly.

Applied Science and Technology Index. H.W. Wilson Co., 950 University Ave., Bronx, New York 10452. (800) 367-6770. Formerly Industrial Arts Index.

Biological and Agricultural Index. H.W. Wilson Co., 950 University Ave., Bronx, New York 10452. (800) 367-6770. 1916-. Monthly.

Current Advances in Ecological and Environmental Science. Pergamon Microforms International, Inc., Fairview Park, Elmsford, New York 10523. (914) 592-7720. 1989-.

Monthly. Current literature searching service includingjournals, reports, abstracts, etc. This service is available online as part of the CABS database on the hosts BRS and ORBIT search service.

Ecology Abstracts. Cambridge Scientific Abstracts, 5161 River Rd., Bethesda, Maryland 20816. (301) 961-6750. Monthly.

Environment Abstracts. Bowker A & I Publishing, 121 Chanlon Rd., New Providence, New Jersey 07974. (908) 464-6800. 1974-.

Environment Index. Environment Information Center, Index Research Department, 124 E. 39th St., New York, New York 10016. 1971-. Annual.

Environmental Information Connection–EIC. Planning Information Program, Dept. of Urban and Regional Planning, University of Illinois, 1003 West Nevada, Urbana, Illinois 61801. (217) 333-1369. Also available online.

Environmental Periodicals Bibliography. Environmental Studies Institute, International Academy at Santa Barbara, 800 Garden St., Suite D, Santa Barbara, California 93101. (805) 965-5010. Also available online.

Field Crop Abstracts. C. A. B. International, 845 North Park Ave., Tucson, Arizona 85719. (602) 621-7897 or (800) 528-4841. 1948-. Monthly. Covers literature on agronomy, field production, crop botany and physiology of all annual field crops, both temperate and tropical.

Forestry Abstracts. C. A. B. International, Wallingford, England OX10 8DE. (0491) 3211. 1939/40-. Monthly. Journal of abstracts of journal articles, conferences, technical reports in the subject areas of: silviculture, forest mensuration and management, physical environment, fire, plant biology, genetics and breeding, mycology and pathology, game and wildlife, fish, protection of forests and other related matter.

General Science Index. H. W. Wilson Co., 950 University Ave., Bronx, New York 10452. 1978-. Monthly, also issued in annual cumulation. Cumulative subject index to English language periodicals in the subject fields of astronomy, botany, chemistry, earth science, environment and conservation, food and nutrition, genetics, mathematics, medicine and health, microbiology, oceanography, physics, physiology and zoology.

Geographical Abstracts. London School of Economics, Dept. of Geography, Regency House, 34 Duke St., London, England 1966-. Continued by Geo Abstracts issued in 6 parts: Pt. A. Landforms and the quaternary; Pt. B. Biogeography and Climatology; Pt. C. Economic geography; Pt. D. Social geography and cartography; Pt. E. Sedimentology; Pt. F. Regional and community planning.

Mineralogical Abstracts. Mineralogical Society, 41 Queen's Gate, London, England SW7 5HR. 71 5847916. Quarterly. Abstracts of journal articles, conferences, technical reports and specialized books in the areas of minerals, clay minerals, economic minerals, ore deposits, environmental studies, experimental mineralogy, gemstones, geochemistry, petrology, lunar and planetary studies and other related areas in mineralogy.

Multimedia Index to Ecology. National Information Center for Educational Media, University of Southern California, Los Angeles, California 90007.

Pollution Abstracts. Cambridge Scientific Abstracts, 5161 River Rd., Bethesda, Maryland 20816. (301) 961-6750. Six/year. Indexes worldwide technical literature on environmental pollution. Covers air pollution, marine and freshwater pollution, sewage and wastewater treatment, waste management, toxicology and health, noise pollution, radiation, land pollution, and environmental policies, programs, legislation, and education. Also available online.

Science Citation Index. Institute for Scientific Information, 3501 Market St., Philadelphia, Pennsylvania 19104. 1961-.

Soils and Fertilizers. C. A. B. International, 845 North Park Ave., Tucson, Arizona 85719. (602) 621-7897 or (800) 528-4841. 1937-. Monthly. Focuses on soil chemistry, soil physics, soil biology, soil fertility, soil management, soil classification, soil formation, soil conservation, land reclamation, irrigation and damage, fertilizer technology, fertilizer use, plant nutrition, plant water relations, and environmental aspects.

BIBLIOGRAPHIES

EPA Publications Bibliography. U.S. Environmental Protection Agency, Library Systems Branch, 401 M St., SW, Washington, District of Columbia 20460. (202) 260-2090. Quarterly.

New Publications of the Geological Survey. U.S. Department of the Interior, Geological Survey, 119 National Center, Reston, Virginia 22092. (703) 648-4460. 1984-. Monthly. Bibliography of geological publications and related government documents published by the Geological Survey.

ENCYCLOPEDIAS AND DICTIONARIES

Cambridge Encyclopedia of Life Sciences. A. E. Friday and David S. Ingram. Cambridge University Press, 40 W 20th St., New York, New York 10011. (212) 924-3900 or (800) 227-0247. 1985. Includes all topics under biology and ecology.

The Encyclopedia of Geochemistry and Environmental Sciences. Rhodes Whitmore Fairbridge. Van Nostrand Reinhold Co., 115 5th Ave., New York, New York 10003. (212) 254-3232. 1972.

Encyclopedia of Physical Science and Technology. Robert A. Meyers, ed. Academic Press, c/o Harcourt Brace Jovanovich Inc., 6277 Sea Harbor Dr., Orlando, Florida 32887. (800) 346-8648. Dictionary of engineering, technology and physical sciences.

The Encyclopedia of Soil Science. Rhodes W. Fairbridge. Academic Press, c/o Harcourt Brace Jovanovich Inc., 6277 Sea Harbor Dr., Orlando, Florida 32887. (800) 346-8648. 1979-. Includes soil physics, soil chemistry, soil biology, soil fertility and plant nutrition, soil genesis, classification and cartography.

Glossary of Geology. Robert Latimer Bates and Julia A. Jackson, eds. American Geological Institute, 4220 King St., Alexandria, Virginia 22302-1507. (703) 379-2480 or (800) 336-4764. 1987. Third edition.

Grzimek's Encyclopedia of Ecology. Bernhard Grzimek. Van Nostrand Reinhold, 115 5th Ave., New York, New York 10003. (212) 254-3232. 1976.

McGraw-Hill Encyclopedia of Science and Technology. McGraw-Hill, 1221 Avenue of the Americas, New York, New York 10020. (212) 512-2000 or (800) 262-4729. 1992. Seventh edition. Issued in multiple volumes including index. Includes all science and technology broad subject areas.

McGraw-Hill Encyclopedia of the Geological Sciences. Sybil P. Parker, ed. McGraw-Hill, 1221 Avenue of the Americas, New York, New York 10020. (212) 512-2000 or (800) 262-4729. 1988. Second edition. Published previously in the McGraw-Hill Encyclopedia of Science and Technology.

North American Reference Encyclopedia of Ecology and Pollution. William White. North American Pub. Co., 401 N. Broad St., Philadelphia, Pennsylvania 19108. (215) 238-5300. 1972.

Van Nostrand's Scientific Encyclopedia. Glenn D. Considine, ed. Van Nostrand Reinhold, 115 5th Ave., New York, New York 10003. (212) 254-3232. 1983. Sixth edition. Includes all broad subject areas in science.

GENERAL WORKS

Cycles of Soil: Carbon, Nitrogen, Phosphorus, Sulfur, Micronutrients. F.J. Stevenson. John Wiley & Sons Inc., 605 3rd Ave., New York, New York 10158-0012. (212) 850-6000. 1986.

From the Land. Nancy P. Pittman, ed. Island Press, 1718 Connecticut Ave. N.W., Suite 300, Washington, District of Columbia 20009. (202) 232-7933. 1988. Anthology comes from 13 years of the Land–a journal of conservation writings from the '40s and '50s. Through fiction, essay, poetry, and philosophy we learn how our small farms have given way to today's agribusiness.

Land Degradation: Development and Breakdown of Terrestrial Environments. C. J. Barrow. Cambridge University Press, 40 W. 20th St., New York, New York 10011. (212) 924-3900; (800) 227-0247. 1991.

Land-Saving Action. Russell L. Brenneman and Sarah M. Bates, eds. Island Press, 1718 Connecticut Ave. N.W., Suite 300, Washington, District of Columbia 20009. (202) 232-7933. 1984. Guide to saving land and an explanation of the conservation tools and techniques developed by individuals and organizations across the country.

Modifying the Root Environment to Reduce Crop Stress. G. F. Arkin and H. M. Taylor, eds. American Society of Agricultural Engineers, 2950 Niles Rd., St. Joseph, Michigan 49085-9659. (616) 429-0300. 1981. Emphasizes the development and understanding of relationship between the plant and its subterranean environment and effect of modification of that environment on plant response.

Plowman's Folly. Edward H. Faulkner. Island Press, 1718 Connecticut Ave. N.W., Suite 300, Washington, District of Columbia 20009. (202) 232-7933. 1987.

Private Options: Tools and Concepts for Land Conservation. Montana Land Reliance, Land Trust Exchange. Island Press, 1718 Connecticut Ave. N.W., Suite 300, Washington, District of Columbia 20009. (202) 232-7933. 1982. Private land conservation experts offer their expertise on how individuals can help contain urban sprawl, conserve wetlands, and protect wildlife. This book covers estate planning, tax incentives, purchase options, conservation easements and land management.

Soil and Water Conservation. Frederick R. Troeh, et al. Prentice-Hall, Rte. 9W, Englewood Cliffs, New Jersey 07632. (201) 592-2000; (800) 634-2863. 1991. 2d ed. Describes the hazards of erosion, sedimentation, and pollution, and the techniques needed to conserve soil and maintain environmental quality.

Soil Management for Sustainability. R. Lal and F. J. Pierce, eds. Soil and Water Conservation Society, 7515 NE Ankeny Rd., Ankeny, Iowa 50021-9764. (515) 289-2331. 1991. Topics discussed in the book include: soil structure, soil compaction, and predicting soil erosion and its effects on crop productivity. Also covered are the basic processes, management options, and policy issues and priorities. Published in cooperation with the World Association of Soil and Water Conservation and the Soil Science Society of America

Soil Organisms as Components of Ecosystems. U. Lohm. Swedish Natural Science Research Council, P.O. Box 6711, Stockholm, Sweden S-113 85. 08-15-1580. 1977. Covers soil ecology and soil fauna.

Soils and the Greenhouse Effect. A. F. Bouwman, ed. John Wiley & Sons, Inc., 605 3rd Ave., New York, New York 10158-0012. (212) 850-6000. 1990. Proceedings of the International Conference on Soils and the Greenhouse Effect, Wageningen, Netherlands, 1989. Covers the present status and future trends concerning the effect of soils and vegetation on the fluxes of greenhouse gases, the surface energy balance, and the water balance. Discusses the role of deforestation and management practices such as mulching, wetlands, agriculture and livestock.

Watershed Management Field Manual. Food and Agriculture Organization of the United Nations, 46110F Assembly Dr., Lanham, Maryland 20706-4391. (800) 274-4888. 1986.

GOVERNMENTAL ORGANIZATIONS

Agricultural Research Service. Washington, District of Columbia 20250.

Assistant Secretary for Natural Resources and Environment. Administrative Building, 12th St. and Jefferson Dr., S.W., Washington, District of Columbia 20250. (202) 447-7173.

Public Information Office: Soil Conservation Service. 12th and Independence Ave., S.W., PO Box 2890, Washington, District of Columbia 20013. (202) 447-4543.

HANDBOOKS AND MANUALS

The Agricultural Notebook. Primrose McConnell; R. J. Halley, ed. Butterworth-Heinemann, 80 Montvale Ave., Stoneham, Massachusetts 02180. (617) 438-8464 or (800) 366-2665. 1982. Seventeenth edition. Includes data on the business of farming. Topics discussed include soils, drainage, crop physiology, crop nutrition, arable crops, grassland, trees on the farm, weed control, diseases of crops, pests of crops, grain preservation and storage, animal production, farm equipment, farm management, agricultural law, health and safety, and agricultural computers.

The Earth Manual. Malcolm Margolin. Heyday Books, PO Box 9145, Berkeley, California 94709. (510) 549-3564. 1985. How to work on wild land without taming it.

Engineering Field Manual. U.S. Soil Conservation Service, PO Box 2890, Washington, District of Columbia 20013. (202) 205-0027. 1984. Procedures recommended for water and soil conservation.

Land Husbandry. T.F. Shaxson. Soil and Water Conservation Society, 7515 NE Ankeny Rd., Ankeney, Iowa (515) 289-2331. 1989. A framework for hill farming, soil and water conservation.

National Plant Material Manual. U.S. Soil Conservation Service, PO Box 2890, Washington, District of Columbia 20013. (202) 205-0027. 1984. Looseleaf.

Soil and Water Conservation Engineering. John Wiley & Sons, Inc., 605 3rd Ave., New York, New York 10158-0012. (212) 850-6000. 1981. Agricultural engineering and soil and water conservation.

ONLINE DATA BASES

Cambridge Scientific Abstracts Life Science–CSAL. Cambridge Scientific Abstracts, 5161 River Rd., Bethesda, Maryland 20816. (301) 961-6750. Provides access to the following abstracting services: "Life Sciences Collection," "Aquatic Sciences and Fisheries Abstracts," "Oceanic Abstracts," and "Pollution Abstracts."

Enviro/Energyline Abstracts Plus. R. R. Bowker Co., 121 Chanlon Rd., New Providence, New Jersey 07974. (908) 464-6800.

Environmental Periodicals Bibliography. National Information Services Corp., Ste. 6, Wyman Towers, 3100 St. Paul St., Baltimore, Maryland 21218. (410)243-0797. Online version of abstract of same name.

GeoRef. American Geological Institute, 4220 King St., Alexandria, Virginia 22302. (703) 379-2480.

Monthly Catalog of United States Government Publications. U.S. G.P.O., Supt. of Docs., PO Box 371954, Pittsburgh, Pennsylvania 15250-7954. (202) 512-0000.

National Technical Information Service. U.S. Department of Commerce, National Technical Information Service, Office of Data Base Services, 5285 Port Royal Rd., Springfield, Virginia 22161. (703) 487-4807. Bibliographic database of government sponsored research and technical reports.

SCISEARCH. Institute for Scientific Information, University City Science Center, 3501 Market St., Philadelphia, Pennsylvania 19104. (215) 386-0100.

PERIODICALS AND NEWSLETTERS

The American Land. American Land Resource Association, Washington, District of Columbia Five times a year. Covers topics in land use and conservation.

American Land Forum. American Land Forum, Bethesda, Maryland Quarterly. Research and opinion on land use and conservation of natural resources.

Biodynamics. Bio Dynamic Farming and Gardening Association, PO Box 550, Kimberton, Pennsylvania 19442-0550. (215) 935-7797. Quarterly. Soil conservation and organic agriculture.

Biology and Fertility of Soils. Springer International, 44 Hartz Way, Seacaucus, New Jersey 07094. (201) 348-4033. Quarterly. Biological functions, processes and interactions in soils, agriculture, deforestation and industrialization.

Earth Science. American Geological Institute, 4220 King Street, Alexandria, Virginia 22302. (703) 379-2480. Quarterly. Covers geological issues.

Ecological Applications. Ecological Society of America, Center for Environmental Studies, Arizona State University, Tempe, Arizona 85287. (602) 965-3000. 1991-. Quarterly. Emphasizes the application of basic ecological concepts to a wide range of problems.

Journal of Soil and Water Conservation. Soil and Water Conservation Society, 7515 Northeast Ankeny Road, Ankeny, Iowa 50021. (515) 289-2331. Bimonthly. Promotes better land and water use and management.

Kentucky Soil and Water News. Kentucky Division of Soil, 628 Teton Trail, Frankfort, Kentucky 40601. (502) 564-3080. Monthly. Water management issues and erosion in the state.

Nebraska Resources. Nebraska Natural Resources Commission, 301 Centennial Mall South, Lincoln, Nebraska 68508. 1970-. Quarterly.

Soil and Water Conservation News. U.S. Soil Conservation Service, PO Box 2890, Washington, District of Columbia 20013. (202) 205-0027. Monthly.

RESEARCH CENTERS AND INSTITUTES

North Central Soil Conservation Research Laboratory. North Iowa Avenue, Morris, Minnesota 56267. (612) 589-3411.

TRADE ASSOCIATIONS AND PROFESSIONAL SOCIETIES

American Institute of Chemical Engineers. 345 East 47th St., New York, New York 10017. (212) 705-7338.

American Institute of Chemists. 7315 Wisconsin Ave., Bethesda, Maryland 20814. (301) 652-2447.

American Registry of Certified Professionals in Agronomy, Crops and Soils. c/o American Society of Agronomy, 677 S. Segoe Rd., Madison, Wisconsin 53711. (608) 273-8080.

American Society of Agronomy. 677 South Segoe Rd., Madison, Wisconsin 53711. (608) 273-8080.

American Society of Civil Engineers. 345 East 47th St., New York, New York 10017. (212) 705-7496.

Association for Conservation Information. PO Box 10678, Reno, Nevada 89520. (702) 688-1500.

Association of Soil & Foundation Engineers. 8811 Colesville Rd., Suite G106, Silver Spring, Maryland 20910. (301) 563-2733.

Soil & Water Conservation Society. 7515 Northeast Ankeny Rd., Ankeny, Iowa 50021. (515) 289-2331.

Soil and Water Conservation Society of America. 7515 N.E. Ankeny Rd., Ankeny, Iowa 50021. (515) 289-2331.

Soil Science Society of America. 677 S. Segoe Rd., Madison, Wisconsin 53711. (608) 273-8080.

World Association of Soil and Water Conservation. 7515 N.E. Ankeny Rd., Ankeny, Iowa 50021. (515) 289-2331.

SOIL CONTAMINATION

ABSTRACTING AND INDEXING SERVICES

Abstracts of Air and Water Conservation Literature. American Petroleum Institute. Central Abstracting and Indexing Service, 275 Madison Avenue, New York, New York 10016. 1972.

Agrindex. AGRIS Coordinating Center, Via delle Terme di Caracalla, Rome, Italy I-00100. 61 0181-FA01. 1975-.

Applied Science and Technology Index. H.W. Wilson Co., 950 University Ave., Bronx, New York 10452. (800) 367-6770. Formerly Industrial Arts Index.

Biological and Agricultural Index. H.W. Wilson Co., 950 University Ave., Bronx, New York 10452. (800) 367-6770. 1916-. Monthly.

Biotechnology Research Abstracts. Cambridge Scientific Abstracts, 5161 River Rd., Bethesda, Maryland 20816. (301) 961-6750. Monthly. Includes such broad areas as genetic intervention, biochemical genetics, and microbiological techniques.

Environment Abstracts. Bowker A & I Publishing, 121 Chanlon Rd., New Providence, New Jersey 07974. (908) 464-6800. 1974-.

Environment Index. Environment Information Center, Index Research Department, 124 E. 39th St., New York, New York 10016. 1971-. Annual.

Environmental Information Connection–EIC. Planning Information Program, Dept. of Urban and Regional Planning, University of Illinois, 1003 West Nevada, Urbana, Illinois 61801. (217) 333-1369. Also available online.

Environmental Periodicals Bibliography. Environmental Studies Institute, International Academy at Santa Barbara, 800 Garden St., Suite D, Santa Barbara, California 93101. (805) 965-5010. Also available online.

Index to Scientific Book Contents. Institute for Scientific Information, 3501 Market St., Philadelphia, Pennsylvania 19104. (800) 523-1857. 1985-. Annual. Gives contents of science books published.

Mineralogical Abstracts. Mineralogical Society, 41 Queen's Gate, London, England SW7 5HR. 71 5847916. Quarterly. Abstracts of journal articles, conferences, technical reports and specialized books in the areas of minerals, clay minerals, economic minerals, ore deposits, environmental studies, experimental mineralogy, gemstones, geochemistry, petrology, lunar and planetary studies and other related areas in mineralogy.

Pollution Abstracts. Cambridge Scientific Abstracts, 5161 River Rd., Bethesda, Maryland 20816. (301) 961-6750. Six/year. Indexes worldwide technical literature on environmental pollution. Covers air pollution, marine and freshwater pollution, sewage and wastewater treatment, waste management, toxicology and health, noise pollution, radiation, land pollution, and environmental policies, programs, legislation, and education. Also available online.

Science Citation Index. Institute for Scientific Information, 3501 Market St., Philadelphia, Pennsylvania 19104. 1961-.

BIBLIOGRAPHIES

Bibliography and Index of Geology. American Geological Institute, 4220 King St., Alexandria, Virginia 22302. Monthly. Includes environmental geology and hydrogeology.

EPA Publications Bibliography. U.S. Environmental Protection Agency, Library Systems Branch, 401 M St., SW, Washington, District of Columbia 20460. (202) 260-2090. Quarterly.

New Publications of the Geological Survey. U.S. Department of the Interior, Geological Survey, 119 National Center, Reston, Virginia 22092. (703) 648-4460. 1984-. Monthly. Bibliography of geological publications and related government documents published by the Geological Survey.

ENCYCLOPEDIAS AND DICTIONARIES

Cambridge Encyclopedia of Life Sciences. A. E. Friday and David S. Ingram. Cambridge University Press, 40 W 20th St., New York, New York 10011. (212) 924-3900 or (800) 227-0247. 1985. Includes all topics under biology and ecology.

The Encyclopedia of Geochemistry and Environmental Sciences. Rhodes Whitmore Fairbridge. Van Nostrand Reinhold Co., 115 5th Ave., New York, New York 10003. (212) 254-3232. 1972.

Encyclopedia of Physical Science and Technology. Robert A. Meyers, ed. Academic Press, c/o Harcourt Brace Jovanovich Inc., 6277 Sea Harbor Dr., Orlando, Florida 32887. (800) 346-8648. Dictionary of engineering, technology and physical sciences.

The Encyclopedia of Soil Science. Rhodes W. Fairbridge. Academic Press, c/o Harcourt Brace Jovanovich Inc., 6277 Sea Harbor Dr., Orlando, Florida 32887. (800) 346-8648. 1979-. Includes soil physics, soil chemistry, soil biology, soil fertility and plant nutrition, soil genesis, classification and cartography.

Glossary of Geology. Robert Latimer Bates and Julia A. Jackson, eds. American Geological Institute, 4220 King St., Alexandria, Virginia 22302-1507. (703) 379-2480 or (800) 336-4764. 1987. Third edition.

McGraw-Hill Encyclopedia of Science and Technology. McGraw-Hill, 1221 Avenue of the Americas, New York, New York 10020. (212) 512-2000 or (800) 262-4729. 1992. Seventh edition. Issued in multiple volumes including index. Includes all science and technology broad subject areas.

McGraw-Hill Encyclopedia of the Geological Sciences. Sybil P. Parker, ed. McGraw-Hill, 1221 Avenue of the Americas, New York, New York 10020. (212) 512-2000 or (800) 262-4729. 1988. Second edition. Published previously in the McGraw-Hill Encyclopedia of Science and Technology.

Van Nostrand's Scientific Encyclopedia. Glenn D. Considine, ed. Van Nostrand Reinhold, 115 5th Ave., New York, New York 10003. (212) 254-3232. 1983. Sixth edition. Includes all broad subject areas in science.

GENERAL WORKS

Biotechnological Slurry Process for the Decontamination of Excavated Polluted Soils. R. Kleijintjens. National Technical Information Service, 5285 Port Royal Rd., Springfield, Virginia 22161. (703) 487-4650. 1991.

Cleanup of Petroleum Contaminated Soils at Underground Storage Tanks. Warren J. Lyman, et al. Noyes Publications, 120 Mill Rd., Park Ridge, New Jersey 07656. (201) 391-8484. Describes soil venting, biorestoration, soil flushing, hydraulic barriers, and vacuum extraction of non-aqueous phase liquids, and biorestoration for saturated zones.

Effects of Acid Rain on Soil and Water. E.C. Krug. Connecticut Agricultural Extension Station, PO Box 1106, New Haven, Connecticut 06504. (203) 789-7272. 1983. Topics in soil and water pollution.

Environmental Pollution. Inderscience Enterprises Ltd., World Trade Center Bldg., 110 Avenue Louis Casai, Case Postale 306, Geneva-Airport, Switzerland CH-1215. (44) 908-314248. 1991. Special issue of the International Journal of Environment and Pollution. Proceedings of the 1st International Conference on Environmental Pollution held at the Congress Centre, Lisbon, April 15-19, 1991.

Evaluating Soil Contamination. W. Nelson Beyer. U.S. Department of the Interior, Fish and Wildlife Service, Washington, District of Columbia 20240. (202) 343-5634. 1990. Biological analysis of soil pollution.

Groundwater and Soil Contamination Remediation. Water Science and Technology Board. National Academy Press, Washington, District of Columbia (202) 334-3343. 1990. Science, policy and public perception.

Hydrocarbon Contaminated Soils and Groundwater: Analysis, Fate, Environmental and Public Health Effects, and Remediation. Paul T. Kostecki and Edward J. Calabrese. Lewis Publishers, 2000 Corporate Blvd.,N.W., Boca Raton, Florida 33431. (407) 994-0555 or (800) 272-7737. 1991. Describes perspectives and emerging issues, analytical techniques and site assessments, environmental fate and modeling.

In Situ Immobilization of Heavy-Metal-Contaminated Soils. G. Czupyrna, et al. Noyes Publications, 120 Mill Rd., Park Ridge, New Jersey 07656. (201) 391-8484. 1989. Reports on an evaluation of various treatment chemicals for the in situ immobilization of heavy-metal-contaminated soils.

Magill's Survey of Science. Earth Science Series. Frank N. Magill. Salem Press, PO Box 50062, Pasadena, California 91105. 1990-. Five volumes. Includes information on earth's crust, hot spots and volcanic island chains, physical properties of minerals, rock magnetism, physical properties of rocks, and index.

Petroleum Contaminated Soils: Remediation Techniques, Environmental Fate and Risk Assessment. Paul T. Kostecki and Edward J. Calabrese. Lewis Publishers, 200 Corporate Blvd. NW, Boca Raton, Florida 33431. (407) 994-0555 or (800)272-7737. 1991. Three volumes. Provides valuable information to determine feasible solutions to petroleum contaminated soils.

Petroleum Contaminated Soils, Volume 2. Edward J. Calabrese and Paul T. Kostecki. Lewis Publishers, 200 Corporate Blvd. NW, Boca Raton, Florida 33431. (407) 994-0555 or (800)272-7737. 1989. Proceedings of the

Third National Conference on Petroleum Contaminated Soils held at the University of Massachusetts-Amherst, September 19-21, 1988.

Sediments: Chemistry and Toxicity of In-Place Pollutants. Renato Baudo, et al., eds. Lewis Publishers, 200 Corporate Blvd. NW, Boca Raton, Florida 33431. (407) 994-0555 or (800)272-7737. 1990.

The Soil Chemistry of Hazardous Materials. James Dragun. Hazardous Material Control Research Institute, 7737 Hanover Pkwy., Greenbelt, Maryland 20770. (301) 982-9500. 1988. Hazardous substances, soil absorption and adsorption.

Soil Management for Sustainability. R. Lal and F. J. Pierce, eds. Soil and Water Conservation Society, 7515 NE Ankeny Rd., Ankeny, Iowa 50021-9764. (515) 289-2331. 1991. Topics discussed in the book include: soil structure, soil compaction, and predicting soil erosion and its effects on crop productivity. Also covered are the basic processes, management options, and policy issues and priorities. Published in cooperation with the World Association of Soil and Water Conservation and the Soil Science Society of America

Trace Elements in Soils and Plants. Alina Kabata-Pendias and Henryk Pendias. CRC Press, 2000 Corporate Blvd. N.W., Boca Raton, Florida 33431. (800) 272-7737. 1991. 2d ed. Discusses the pollution of air, water, soil and plants, all about soil processes, and the involvement of trace elements in the soil and plants.

Treatment Potential for 56 EPA Listed Hazardous Chemicals in Soil. Ronald C. Sims, et al. Robert S. Kerr Environmental Research Laboratory, U.S. Environmental Protection Agency, PO Box 1198, Ada, Oklahoma 74820. (405) 332-8800. 1988.

The Use of Paraquat to Eradicate Illicit Marihuana Crops and the Health Implications of Paraquat-Contaminated Marihuana on the U.S. Market. Select Committee on Narcotics and Abuse Control, U.S. Government Printing Office, Washington, District of Columbia 2042-9325. (202) 783-3238. 1980. A report of the Select Committee on Narcotics and Abuse Control, 96th Congress, 2nd session.

Waste Containment Systems: Construction, Regulation and Performance. Rudolph Bonaparte, ed. American Society of Civil Engineers, 345 E. 47th St., New York, New York 10017. (212) 705-7288; (800) 548-2723. 1990. Proceedings of a symposium sponsored by the Committee on Soil Improvement and Geosynthetics and the Committee on Soil properties of the Geotechnical Engineering Division, American Society of Civil Engineers in conjunction with the ASCE National Convention, San Francisco, CA, November 6-7, 1990.

GOVERNMENTAL ORGANIZATIONS

Public Information Office: Soil Conservation Service. 12th and Independence Ave., S.W., PO Box 2890, Washington, District of Columbia 20013. (202) 447-4543.

ONLINE DATA BASES

Cambridge Scientific Abstracts Life Science–CSAL. Cambridge Scientific Abstracts, 5161 River Rd., Bethesda, Maryland 20816. (301) 961-6750. Provides access to the following abstracting services: "Life Sciences Collec-

tion," "Aquatic Sciences and Fisheries Abstracts," "Oceanic Abstracts," and "Pollution Abstracts."

Enviro/Energyline Abstracts Plus. R. R. Bowker Co., 121 Chanlon Rd., New Providence, New Jersey 07974. (908) 464-6800.

Environmental Periodicals Bibliography. National Information Services Corp., Ste. 6, Wyman Towers, 3100 St. Paul St., Baltimore, Maryland 21218. (410)243-0797. Online version of abstract of same name.

Monthly Catalog of United States Government Publications. U.S. G.P.O., Supt. of Docs., PO Box 371954, Pittsburgh, Pennsylvania 15250-7954. (202) 512-0000.

National Technical Information Service. U.S. Department of Commerce, National Technical Information Service, Office of Data Base Services, 5285 Port Royal Rd., Springfield, Virginia 22161. (703) 487-4807. Bibliographic database of government sponsored research and technical reports.

SCISEARCH. Institute for Scientific Information, University City Science Center, 3501 Market St., Philadelphia, Pennsylvania 19104. (215) 386-0100.

PERIODICALS AND NEWSLETTERS

Earth Science. American Geological Institute, 4220 King Street, Alexandria, Virginia 22302. (703) 379-2480. Quarterly. Covers geological issues.

International Journal of Environment and Pollution. Inderscience Enterprises Ltd., World Trade Center Bldg., 110 Avenue Louis Casai, Case Postale 306, Geneva-Airport, Switzerland CH-1215. (44) 908-314248. 1991-. Publishes original state-of-the-art articles, book reviews, and technical papers in the areas of: Environmental policies, protection, institutional aspects of pollution, risk assessments of all forms of pollution, protection of soil and ground water, waste disposal strategies, ecological impact of pollutants and other related topics.

Water, Air, and Soil Pollution. Kluwer Academic Publishers, 101 Philip Dr., Assinippi Park, Norwell, Massachusetts 02061. (617) 871-6600. Bimonthly. Covers water, soil, and air pollution. This is an international journal on environmental pollution dealing with all types of pollution including acid rain.

TRADE ASSOCIATIONS AND PROFESSIONAL SOCIETIES

American Institute of Biological Sciences. 730 11th St., N.W., Washington, District of Columbia 20001-4521. (202) 628-1500.

American Institute of Chemical Engineers. 345 East 47th St., New York, New York 10017. (212) 705-7338.

American Institute of Chemists. 7315 Wisconsin Ave., Bethesda, Maryland 20814. (301) 652-2447.

American Society of Agronomy. 677 South Segoe Rd., Madison, Wisconsin 53711. (608) 273-8080.

Association of Soil & Foundation Engineers. 8811 Colesville Rd., Suite G106, Silver Spring, Maryland 20910. (301) 563-2733.

Soil Science Society of America. 677 S. Segoe Rd., Madison, Wisconsin 53711. (608) 273-8080.

SOIL EROSION

See: EROSION

SOIL ORGANISMS

ABSTRACTING AND INDEXING SERVICES

Abstracts of Air and Water Conservation Literature. American Petroleum Institute. Central Abstracting and Indexing Service, 275 Madison Avenue, New York, New York 10016. 1972.

Biological and Agricultural Index. H.W. Wilson Co., 950 University Ave., Bronx, New York 10452. (800) 367-6770. 1916-. Monthly.

Biotechnology Research Abstracts. Cambridge Scientific Abstracts, 5161 River Rd., Bethesda, Maryland 20816. (301) 961-6750. Monthly. Includes such broad areas as genetic intervention, biochemical genetics, and microbiological techniques.

Ecology Abstracts. Cambridge Scientific Abstracts, 5161 River Rd., Bethesda, Maryland 20816. (301) 961-6750. Monthly.

Environment Abstracts. Bowker A & I Publishing, 121 Chanlon Rd., New Providence, New Jersey 07974. (908) 464-6800. 1974-.

Environment Index. Environment Information Center, Index Research Department, 124 E. 39th St., New York, New York 10016. 1971-. Annual.

Environmental Information Connection–EIC. Planning Information Program, Dept. of Urban and Regional Planning, University of Illinois, 1003 West Nevada, Urbana, Illinois 61801. (217) 333-1369. Also available online.

Environmental Periodicals Bibliography. Environmental Studies Institute, International Academy at Santa Barbara, 800 Garden St., Suite D, Santa Barbara, California 93101. (805) 965-5010. Also available online.

Forestry Abstracts. C. A. B. International, Wallingford, England OX10 8DE. (0491) 3211. 1939/40-. Monthly. Journal of abstracts of journal articles, conferences, technical reports in the subject areas of: silviculture, forest mensuration and management, physical environment, fire, plant biology, genetics and breeding, mycology and pathology, game and wildlife, fish, protection of forests and other related matter.

General Science Index. H. W. Wilson Co., 950 University Ave., Bronx, New York 10452. 1978-. Monthly, also issued in annual cumulation. Cumulative subject index to English language periodicals in the subject fields of astronomy, botany, chemistry, earth science, environment and conservation, food and nutrition, genetics, mathematics, medicine and health, microbiology, oceanography, physics, physiology and zoology.

Science Citation Index. Institute for Scientific Information, 3501 Market St., Philadelphia, Pennsylvania 19104. 1961-.

BIBLIOGRAPHIES

Bibliography and Index of Geology. American Geological Institute, 4220 King St., Alexandria, Virginia 22302. Monthly. Includes environmental geology and hydrogeology.

EPA Publications Bibliography. U.S. Environmental Protection Agency, Library Systems Branch, 401 M St., SW, Washington, District of Columbia 20460. (202) 260-2090. Quarterly.

ENCYCLOPEDIAS AND DICTIONARIES

Cambridge Encyclopedia of Life Sciences. A. E. Friday and David S. Ingram. Cambridge University Press, 40 W 20th St., New York, New York 10011. (212) 924-3900 or (800) 227-0247. 1985. Includes all topics under biology and ecology.

The Encyclopedia of Geochemistry and Environmental Sciences. Rhodes Whitmore Fairbridge. Van Nostrand Reinhold Co., 115 5th Ave., New York, New York 10003. (212) 254-3232. 1972.

The Encyclopedia of Soil Science. Rhodes W. Fairbridge. Academic Press, c/o Harcourt Brace Jovanovich Inc., 6277 Sea Harbor Dr., Orlando, Florida 32887. (800) 346-8648. 1979-. Includes soil physics, soil chemistry, soil biology, soil fertility and plant nutrition, soil genesis, classification and cartography.

Glossary of Geology. Robert Latimer Bates and Julia A. Jackson, eds. American Geological Institute, 4220 King St., Alexandria, Virginia 22302-1507. (703) 379-2480 or (800) 336-4764. 1987. Third edition.

McGraw-Hill Encyclopedia of the Geological Sciences. Sybil P. Parker, ed. McGraw-Hill, 1221 Avenue of the Americas, New York, New York 10020. (212) 512-2000 or (800) 262-4729. 1988. Second edition. Published previously in the McGraw-Hill Encyclopedia of Science and Technology.

GENERAL WORKS

Ecology of Soil Organisms. Brown Alison Leadley. Heinemann Educational, Holley Court, Jordan Hill, Oxford, England OX2 8EJ. 1978.

Enhanced Biodegradation of Pesticides in the Environment. Kenneth D. Racke and Joel R. Coats, eds. American Chemical Society, 1155 16th St. N.W., Washington, District of Columbia 20036. (202) 872-4600; (800) 227-5558. 1990. Discusses pesticides in the soil, microbial ecosystems, and the effects of long term application of herbicides on the soil.

Magill's Survey of Science. Earth Science Series. Frank N. Magill. Salem Press, PO Box 50062, Pasadena, California 91105. 1990-. Five volumes. Includes information on earth's crust, hot spots and volcanic island chains, physical properties of minerals, rock magnetism, physical properties of rocks, and index.

Soil Organisms as Components of Ecosystems. U. Lohm. Swedish Natural Science Research Council, P.O. Box 6711, Stockholm, Sweden S-113 85. 08-15-1580. 1977. Covers soil ecology and soil fauna.

ONLINE DATA BASES

Cambridge Scientific Abstracts Life Science–CSAL. Cambridge Scientific Abstracts, 5161 River Rd., Bethesda, Maryland 20816. (301) 961-6750. Provides access to the following abstracting services: "Life Sciences Collection," "Aquatic Sciences and Fisheries Abstracts," "Oceanic Abstracts," and "Pollution Abstracts."

Enviro/Energyline Abstracts Plus. R. R. Bowker Co., 121 Chanlon Rd., New Providence, New Jersey 07974. (908) 464-6800.

Environmental Periodicals Bibliography. National Information Services Corp., Ste. 6, Wyman Towers, 3100 St. Paul St., Baltimore, Maryland 21218. (410)243-0797. Online version of abstract of same name.

SCISEARCH. Institute for Scientific Information, University City Science Center, 3501 Market St., Philadelphia, Pennsylvania 19104. (215) 386-0100.

PERIODICALS AND NEWSLETTERS

International Journal of Plant Nutrition, Plant Chemistry, Soil Microbiology and Soil-Bourne Plant Diseases. Kluwer Academic Publishers, 101 Philip Dr., Assinippi Park, Norwell, Massachusetts 02061. (617) 871-6600. 1948-.

Soil Biology and Biochemistry. Pergamon Microforms International, Inc., Fairview Park, Elmsford, New York 10523. (914) 592-7720. Eight times a year. Soil biology, soil biochemistry, nitrogen fixation, nitrogenase activity, sampling microorganisms in soil, soil compaction, and nutrient release in soils.

TRADE ASSOCIATIONS AND PROFESSIONAL SOCIETIES

American Institute of Biological Sciences. 730 11th St., N.W., Washington, District of Columbia 20001-4521. (202) 628-1500.

Association of Soil & Foundation Engineers. 8811 Colesville Rd., Suite G106, Silver Spring, Maryland 20910. (301) 563-2733.

Soil Science Society of America. 677 S. Segoe Rd., Madison, Wisconsin 53711. (608) 273-8080.

SOIL POLLUTION

See: SOIL CONTAMINATION

SOIL SAMPLING

ABSTRACTING AND INDEXING SERVICES

Abstracts of Air and Water Conservation Literature. American Petroleum Institute. Central Abstracting and Indexing Service, 275 Madison Avenue, New York, New York 10016. 1972.

Biological and Agricultural Index. H.W. Wilson Co., 950 University Ave., Bronx, New York 10452. (800) 367-6770. 1916-. Monthly.

Biotechnology Research Abstracts. Cambridge Scientific Abstracts, 5161 River Rd., Bethesda, Maryland 20816. (301) 961-6750. Monthly. Includes such broad areas as genetic intervention, biochemical genetics, and microbiological techniques.

Environment Abstracts. Bowker A & I Publishing, 121 Chanlon Rd., New Providence, New Jersey 07974. (908) 464-6800. 1974-.

Environment Index. Environment Information Center, Index Research Department, 124 E. 39th St., New York, New York 10016. 1971-. Annual.

Environmental Information Connection–EIC. Planning Information Program, Dept. of Urban and Regional Planning, University of Illinois, 1003 West Nevada, Urbana, Illinois 61801. (217) 333-1369. Also available online.

Environmental Periodicals Bibliography. Environmental Studies Institute, International Academy at Santa Barbara, 800 Garden St., Suite D, Santa Barbara, California 93101. (805) 965-5010. Also available online.

Pollution Abstracts. Cambridge Scientific Abstracts, 5161 River Rd., Bethesda, Maryland 20816. (301) 961-6750. Six/year. Indexes worldwide technical literature on environmental pollution. Covers air pollution, marine and freshwater pollution, sewage and wastewater treatment, waste management, toxicology and health, noise pollution, radiation, land pollution, and environmental policies, programs, legislation, and education. Also available online.

Science Citation Index. Institute for Scientific Information, 3501 Market St., Philadelphia, Pennsylvania 19104. 1961-.

BIBLIOGRAPHIES

Bibliography and Index of Geology. American Geological Institute, 4220 King St., Alexandria, Virginia 22302. Monthly. Includes environmental geology and hydrogeology.

EPA Publications Bibliography. U.S. Environmental Protection Agency, Library Systems Branch, 401 M St., SW, Washington, District of Columbia 20460. (202) 260-2090. Quarterly.

New Publications of the Geological Survey. U.S. Department of the Interior, Geological Survey, 119 National Center, Reston, Virginia 22092. (703) 648-4460. 1984-. Monthly. Bibliography of geological publications and related government documents published by the Geological Survey.

ENCYCLOPEDIAS AND DICTIONARIES

The Encyclopedia of Geochemistry and Environmental Sciences. Rhodes Whitmore Fairbridge. Van Nostrand Reinhold Co., 115 5th Ave., New York, New York 10003. (212) 254-3232. 1972.

The Encyclopedia of Soil Science. Rhodes W. Fairbridge. Academic Press, c/o Harcourt Brace Jovanovich Inc., 6277 Sea Harbor Dr., Orlando, Florida 32887. (800) 346-8648. 1979-. Includes soil physics, soil chemistry, soil biology, soil fertility and plant nutrition, soil genesis, classification and cartography.

Glossary of Geology. Robert Latimer Bates and Julia A. Jackson, eds. American Geological Institute, 4220 King St., Alexandria, Virginia 22302-1507. (703) 379-2480 or (800) 336-4764. 1987. Third edition.

McGraw-Hill Encyclopedia of the Geological Sciences. Sybil P. Parker, ed. McGraw-Hill, 1221 Avenue of the Americas, New York, New York 10020. (212) 512-2000 or (800) 262-4729. 1988. Second edition. Published previously in the McGraw-Hill Encyclopedia of Science and Technology.

GENERAL WORKS

Basic Procedures for Soil Sampling and Core Drilling. W.L. Acker. Acker Drill Co., PO Box 830, Scranton, Pennsylvania 18501. (717) 586-2061. 1974. Covers soil testing procedures.

Constructed Wetlands for Wastewater Treatment. Donald A. Hammer. Lewis Publishers, 200 Corporate Blvd. NW, Boca Raton, Florida 33431. (407) 994-0555 or (800)272-7737. 1989. Presents general principles of wetland ecology, hydrology, soil chemistry, vegetation, microbiology, and wildlife dependence on wetlands. It provides management guidelines, beginning with policies and regulations, and including siting and construction and operations and monitoring of constructed wetland systems.

Death in the Marsh. Tom Harris. Island Press, 1718 Connecticut Ave. N.W., Suite 300, Washington, District of Columbia 20009. (202) 232-7933. 1991. Explains how federal irrigation projects have altered the selenium's circulation in the environment, allowing it to accumulate in marshes, killing ecosystems and wildlife, and causing deformities in some animals.

Magill's Survey of Science. Earth Science Series. Frank N. Magill. Salem Press, PO Box 50062, Pasadena, California 91105. 1990-. Five volumes. Includes information on earth's crust, hot spots and volcanic island chains, physical properties of minerals, rock magnetism, physical properties of rocks, and index.

Soil Sampling and Analysis for Volatile Organic Compounds. U.S. Environmental Protection Agency Center for Environmental Research Information, 26 W. Martin Luther King Dr., Cincinnati, Ohio 45268. (513) 569-7931. 1991. Organic compounds in the underground water and their testing.

Soil Sampling and Soil Description. J.M. Hodgson. Clarendon Press, Walton St., Oxford, England OX2 6DP. 1978. Topics in conducting soil surveys.

Statistical Methods in Soil and Land Resource Survey. R. Webster and M. A. Oliver. Oxford University Press, 200 Madison Ave., New York, New York 10016. (212) 679-7300; (800) 334-4249. 1990. Describes methods for making quantitative surveys, stressing the need for sound sampling, sensible and efficient estimation and proper planning.

GOVERNMENTAL ORGANIZATIONS

Public Information Office: Soil Conservation Service. 12th and Independence Ave., S.W., PO Box 2890, Washington, District of Columbia 20013. (202) 447-4543.

HANDBOOKS AND MANUALS

Compendium of ERT Soil Sampling and Surface Geophysics Procedures. National Technical Information Service, 5285 Port Royal Rd., Springfield, Virginia 22161. (703) 487-4650. Sampling of soil air and hazardous waste sites.

ONLINE DATA BASES

Cambridge Scientific Abstracts Life Science–CSAL. Cambridge Scientific Abstracts, 5161 River Rd., Bethesda, Maryland 20816. (301) 961-6750. Provides access to the following abstracting services: "Life Sciences Collection," "Aquatic Sciences and Fisheries Abstracts," "Oceanic Abstracts," and "Pollution Abstracts."

Enviro/Energyline Abstracts Plus. R. R. Bowker Co., 121 Chanlon Rd., New Providence, New Jersey 07974. (908) 464-6800.

Environmental Periodicals Bibliography. National Information Services Corp., Ste. 6, Wyman Towers, 3100 St. Paul St., Baltimore, Maryland 21218. (410)243-0797. Online version of abstract of same name.

SCISEARCH. Institute for Scientific Information, University City Science Center, 3501 Market St., Philadelphia, Pennsylvania 19104. (215) 386-0100.

TRADE ASSOCIATIONS AND PROFESSIONAL SOCIETIES

American Institute of Biological Sciences. 730 11th St., N.W., Washington, District of Columbia 20001-4521. (202) 628-1500.

American Institute of Chemical Engineers. 345 East 47th St., New York, New York 10017. (212) 705-7338.

American Institute of Chemists. 7315 Wisconsin Ave., Bethesda, Maryland 20814. (301) 652-2447.

American Society of Agronomy. 677 South Segoe Rd., Madison, Wisconsin 53711. (608) 273-8080.

American Society of Civil Engineers. 345 East 47th St., New York, New York 10017. (212) 705-7496.

Association of Soil & Foundation Engineers. 8811 Colesville Rd., Suite G106, Silver Spring, Maryland 20910. (301) 563-2733.

Soil Science Society of America. 677 S. Segoe Rd., Madison, Wisconsin 53711. (608) 273-8080.

SOIL SCIENCE

ABSTRACTING AND INDEXING SERVICES

Abstracts of Air and Water Conservation Literature. American Petroleum Institute. Central Abstracting and Indexing Service, 275 Madison Avenue, New York, New York 10016. 1972.

Agricultural Engineering Abstracts. C. A. B. International, 845 North Park Ave., Tucson, Arizona 85719. (602) 621-7897 or (800) 528-4841. 1976-. Monthly. Informs about significant research developments in agricultural engineering and instrumentation. Some of the topics scanned for the abstracts include mechanical power, crop production, crop harvesting and threshing, crop processing and storage, aquaculture, land improvement, protected cultivation, handling and transport, and farm buildings and equipment.

Agrindex. AGRIS Coordinating Center, Via delle Terme di Caracalla, Rome, Italy I-00100. 61 0181-FA01. 1975-.

Applied Science and Technology Index. H.W. Wilson Co., 950 University Ave., Bronx, New York 10452. (800) 367-6770. Formerly Industrial Arts Index.

Biological and Agricultural Index. H.W. Wilson Co., 950 University Ave., Bronx, New York 10452. (800) 367-6770. 1916-. Monthly.

Biotechnology Research Abstracts. Cambridge Scientific Abstracts, 5161 River Rd., Bethesda, Maryland 20816. (301) 961-6750. Monthly. Includes such broad areas as genetic intervention, biochemical genetics, and microbiological techniques.

Civil Engineering Hydraulic Abstracts. BHRA Fluid Engineering, Air Science Co., PO Box 143, Corning, New York 14830. (607) 962-5591. Monthly. Abstracts of periodicals that publish in the areas of hydraulic engineering and other related topics.

Ecology Abstracts. Cambridge Scientific Abstracts, 5161 River Rd., Bethesda, Maryland 20816. (301) 961-6750. Monthly.

Engineering Index. The Engineering Index Inc., 345 E. 47th St., New York, New York 10017. 1962-.

Environment Abstracts. Bowker A & I Publishing, 121 Chanlon Rd., New Providence, New Jersey 07974. (908) 464-6800. 1974-.

Environment Index. Environment Information Center, Index Research Department, 124 E. 39th St., New York, New York 10016. 1971-. Annual.

Environmental Information Connection–EIC. Planning Information Program, Dept. of Urban and Regional Planning, University of Illinois, 1003 West Nevada, Urbana, Illinois 61801. (217) 333-1369. Also available online.

Environmental Periodicals Bibliography. Environmental Studies Institute, International Academy at Santa Barbara, 800 Garden St., Suite D, Santa Barbara, California 93101. (805) 965-5010. Also available online.

General Science Index. H. W. Wilson Co., 950 University Ave., Bronx, New York 10452. 1978-. Monthly, also issued in annual cumulation. Cumulative subject index to English language periodicals in the subject fields of astronomy, botany, chemistry, earth science, environment and conservation, food and nutrition, genetics, mathematics, medicine and health, microbiology, oceanography, physics, physiology and zoology.

Geographical Abstracts. London School of Economics, Dept. of Geography, Regency House, 34 Duke St., London, England 1966-. Continued by Geo Abstracts issued in 6 parts: Pt. A. Landforms and the quaternary; Pt. B. Biogeography and Climatology; Pt. C. Economic geography; Pt. D. Social geography and cartography; Pt. E. Sedimentology; Pt. F. Regional and community planning.

Index to Scientific Book Contents. Institute for Scientific Information, 3501 Market St., Philadelphia, Pennsylvania 19104. (800) 523-1857. 1985-. Annual. Gives contents of science books published.

Irrigation and Drainage Abstracts. C. A. B. International, 845 North Park Ave., Tucson, Arizona 85719. (602) 621-7897 or (800) 258-4841. 1975-. Quarterly. Subject areas scanned are: water management, irrigation of crop plants, drainage, soil water relations, plant water relations, salinity and toxicity problems, soil condition, evaporotranspiration, evaporation, land use, streams, water quality, and other related areas.

Physics Briefs. Physikalische Berichte. Physik Verlag, Pappapelallee 3, Postfach 101161, Weinheim, Germany D-6940. 1979-. Semimonthly. In English. Volumes for 1979- issued by the Deutsche Physikalische Gesellschaft and the Fachinformationszentrum Energie Physik, Mathematik in cooperation with the American Institute of Physics.

Pollution Abstracts. Cambridge Scientific Abstracts, 5161 River Rd., Bethesda, Maryland 20816. (301) 961-6750. Six/year. Indexes worldwide technical literature on environmental pollution. Covers air pollution, marine and freshwater pollution, sewage and wastewater treatment, waste management, toxicology and health, noise pollution, radiation, land pollution, and environmental policies, programs, legislation, and education. Also available online.

Science Citation Index. Institute for Scientific Information, 3501 Market St., Philadelphia, Pennsylvania 19104. 1961-.

Soils and Fertilizers. C. A. B. International, 845 North Park Ave., Tucson, Arizona 85719. (602) 621-7897 or (800) 528-4841. 1937-. Monthly. Focuses on soil chemistry, soil physics, soil biology, soil fertility, soil management, soil classification, soil formation, soil conservation, land reclamation, irrigation and damage, fertilizer technology, fertilizer use, plant nutrition, plant water relations, and environmental aspects.

BIBLIOGRAPHIES

Bibliography and Index of Geology. American Geological Institute, 4220 King St., Alexandria, Virginia 22302. Monthly. Includes environmental geology and hydrogeology.

EPA Publications Bibliography. U.S. Environmental Protection Agency, Library Systems Branch, 401 M St., SW, Washington, District of Columbia 20460. (202) 260-2090. Quarterly.

New Publications of the Geological Survey. U.S. Department of the Interior, Geological Survey, 119 National Center, Reston, Virginia 22092. (703) 648-4460. 1984-. Monthly. Bibliography of geological publications and related government documents published by the Geological Survey.

DIRECTORIES

Agricultural Information Resource Centers, a World Directory 1990. Rita C. Fisher. IAALD World Directory Working Group, 716 W. Indiana Ave., Urbana, Illinois 61801-4836. (217) 333-7687. 1990. Includes 3,971 information resource centers that have agriculture related collection and/or information services.

Expanded Shale, Clay & Slate Institute–Roster of Members. 2225 E. Murray Holladay Rd., Suite 102, Salt Lake City, Utah 84117. (801) 272-7070. Annual.

ENCYCLOPEDIAS AND DICTIONARIES

Cambridge Encyclopedia of Life Sciences. A. E. Friday and David S. Ingram. Cambridge University Press, 40 W 20th St., New York, New York 10011. (212) 924-3900 or (800) 227-0247. 1985. Includes all topics under biology and ecology.

Dictionary of Civil Engineering. John S. Scott. Halsted Press, Division of J. Wiley, 605 3rd Ave., New York, New York 10158. (212) 850-6000. 1981. Third edition.

Elsevier's Dictionary of Soil Mechanics and Geotechnical Engineering. J. D. Van Der Tuin. Elsevier Science Publishing Co., 655 Avenue of the Americas, New York, New York 10010. (212) 989-5800. 1989. The text is in English, French, Spanish, Dutch, and German.

The Encyclopedia of Climatology. John E. Oliver and Rhodes W. Fairbridge, eds. Van Nostrand Reinhold, 115 5th Ave., New York, New York 10003. (212) 254-3232. 1987. Belongs in the series Encyclopedia of Earth Sciences, v.11.

The Encyclopedia of Geochemistry and Environmental Sciences. Rhodes Whitmore Fairbridge. Van Nostrand Reinhold Co., 115 5th Ave., New York, New York 10003. (212) 254-3232. 1972.

Encyclopedia of Human Biology. Renato Dulbecco, ed. Academic Press, c/o Harcourt Brace Jovanovich Inc., 6277 Sea Harbor Dr., Orlando, Florida 32887. (800) 346-8648. 1991. Eight volumes.

Encyclopedia of Physical Science and Technology. Robert A. Meyers, ed. Academic Press, c/o Harcourt Brace Jovanovich Inc., 6277 Sea Harbor Dr., Orlando, Florida 32887. (800) 346-8648. Dictionary of engineering, technology and physical sciences.

Encyclopedia of Physics. Rita G. Lerner and George L. Trigg. VCH Publishers, 303 NW 12th Ave., Deerfield Beach, Florida 33442-1788. (305) 428-5566. 1991. Second edition.

The Encyclopedia of Soil Science. Rhodes W. Fairbridge. Academic Press, c/o Harcourt Brace Jovanovich Inc., 6277 Sea Harbor Dr., Orlando, Florida 32887. (800) 346-8648. 1979-. Includes soil physics, soil chemistry, soil biology, soil fertility and plant nutrition, soil genesis, classification and cartography.

Glossary of Geology. Robert Latimer Bates and Julia A. Jackson, eds. American Geological Institute, 4220 King St., Alexandria, Virginia 22302-1507. (703) 379-2480 or (800) 336-4764. 1987. Third edition.

Illustrated Encyclopedia of Science and the Future. Mike Biscare, et al., ed. Marshall Cavendish, 58 Old Compton St., London, England 0W1V5 PA. 01-734 6710. 1983. Twenty volumes. Each volume has 5 sections: Frontiers, Electronics in Action, Medical Science, Military Technology, and Resources.

McGraw-Hill Encyclopedia of Science and Technology. McGraw-Hill, 1221 Avenue of the Americas, New York, New York 10020. (212) 512-2000 or (800) 262-4729. 1992. Seventh edition. Issued in multiple volumes including index. Includes all science and technology broad subject areas.

Van Nostrand's Scientific Encyclopedia. Glenn D. Considine, ed. Van Nostrand Reinhold, 115 5th Ave., New York, New York 10003. (212) 254-3232. 1983. Sixth edition. Includes all broad subject areas in science.

GENERAL WORKS

Agricultural Ecology. Joy Tivy. John Wiley & Sons, Inc., 605 3rd Ave., New York, New York 10158-0012. (212) 850-6000. 1990. Analyzes the nature of relationships between crops, livestock, and the biophysical environment, and the extent to which man has modified the products and environment to suit his own needs.

Alluvial Fans, Mudflows, and Mud Floods. Association of State Floodplain Managers, PO Box 2051, Madison, Wisconsin 53701-2051. (608) 266-1926. 1988.

Controlling Toxic Substances in Agricultural Drainage. U.S. Committee on Irrigation and Drainage, PO Box 15326, Denver, Colorado 80215. 1990. Looks at current technology on toxic substances and water treatment processes and techniques.

Dentrification in Soil and Sediment. Niels Peter Revsbech and Jan Sorensen, eds. Plenum Press, 233 Spring St., New York, New York 10013-1578. (212) 620-8000; (800) 221-9369. 1991. The process, its measurement, and its significance are analyzed in 20 papers from a June 1989 symposium in Ahrus, Denmark. Topics included are: biochemistry, genetics, ecophysiology, and the emission of nitrogen-oxygen compounds.

Ecology of Arable Land. Olof Andersen, et al., eds. Munksgaard International, PO Box 2148, Copenhagen K, Denmark DK-1016. 1990. Investigates and synthesizes the contributions of the soil organisms and nitrogen and carbon circulation in four contrasting cropping systems. Also looks into future challenges of agroecosystem research.

Fundamentals of Soil Science. Henry D. Foth. John Wiley & Sons, Inc., 605 3rd Ave., New York, New York 10158-0012. (212) 850-6000. 1992.

Global Patterns; Climate, Vegetation, and Soils. Wallace E. Akin. University of Oklahoma Press, 1005 Asp Ave., Norman, Oklahoma 73019. (405) 325-5111. 1991. Maps the three systems that dominate and shape life on earth in such a way as to clarify their interaction and combined effect.

Magill's Survey of Science. Earth Science Series. Frank N. Magill. Salem Press, PO Box 50062, Pasadena, California 91105. 1990-. Five volumes. Includes information on earth's crust, hot spots and volcanic island chains, physical properties of minerals, rock magnetism, physical properties of rocks, and index.

Poison Runoff: A Guide to State and Local Control of Nonpoint Source Water Pollution. Paul Thompson. Natural Resources Defense Council, 40 W. 20th St., New York, New York 10011. (212) 727-2700. 1989. How-to-book addressing pollution in agricultural lands, urban development and construction, logging, mining and grazing.

Soils and the Greenhouse Effect. A. F. Bouwman, ed. John Wiley & Sons, Inc., 605 3rd Ave., New York, New York 10158-0012. (212) 850-6000. 1990. Proceedings of the International Conference on Soils and the Greenhouse Effect, Wageningen, Netherlands, 1989. Covers the present status and future trends concerning the effect of soils and vegetation on the fluxes of greenhouse gases, the surface energy balance, and the water balance. Discusses the role of deforestation and management practices such as mulching, wetlands, agriculture and livestock.

Statistical Methods in Soil and Land Resource Survey. R. Webster and M. A. Oliver. Oxford University Press, 200 Madison Ave., New York, New York 10016. (212) 679-7300; (800) 334-4249. 1990. Describes methods for making quantitative surveys, stressing the need for sound sampling, sensible and efficient estimation and proper planning.

HANDBOOKS AND MANUALS

The Agricultural Notebook. Primrose McConnell; R. J. Halley, ed. Butterworth-Heinemann, 80 Montvale Ave., Stoneham, Massachusetts 02180. (617) 438-8464 or (800) 366-2665. 1982. Seventeenth edition. Includes data on the business of farming. Topics discussed include soils, drainage, crop physiology, crop nutrition, arable crops, grassland, trees on the farm, weed control, diseases of crops, pests of crops, grain preservation and storage, animal production, farm equipment, farm management, agricultural law, health and safety, and agricultural computers.

Fertile Soil: A Grower's Guide to Organic and Inorganic Fertilizers. Robert Parnes. AgAccess, PO Box 2008, Davis, California 95617. (916) 756-7177. 1990. Comprehensive technical resource on creating fertile soils using a balanced program that does not rely on chemical fertilizers.

Handbook of Highway Engineering. Robert F. Baker, ed. R. E. Krieger Publishing Co., 115 5th Ave., New York, New York 10003. (212) 254-3232. 1982. Provides reference data on the application of technology to highway transportation.

ONLINE DATA BASES

Computerized Engineering Index–COMPENDEX. Engineering Information Inc., 345 E. 47th St., New York, New York 10017. (212) 705-7600.

Enviro/Energyline Abstracts Plus. R. R. Bowker Co., 121 Chanlon Rd., New Providence, New Jersey 07974. (908) 464-6800.

Environmental Fate Databases. Syracuse Research Cooperation, Merrill Lane, Syracuse, New York 13210. (312) 426-3200. Environmental fate of chemicals.

Environmental Periodicals Bibliography. National Information Services Corp., Ste. 6, Wyman Towers, 3100 St. Paul St., Baltimore, Maryland 21218. (410)243-0797. Online version of abstract of same name.

GeoRef. American Geological Institute, 4220 King St., Alexandria, Virginia 22302. (703) 379-2480.

Monthly Catalog of United States Government Publications. U.S. G.P.O., Supt. of Docs., PO Box 371954, Pittsburgh, Pennsylvania 15250-7954. (202) 512-0000.

National Technical Information Service. U.S. Department of Commerce, National Technical Information Service, Office of Data Base Services, 5285 Port Royal Rd., Springfield, Virginia 22161. (703) 487-4807. Bibliographic database of government sponsored research and technical reports.

SCISEARCH. Institute for Scientific Information, University City Science Center, 3501 Market St., Philadelphia, Pennsylvania 19104. (215) 386-0100.

PERIODICALS AND NEWSLETTERS

Biodynamics. Bio Dynamic Farming and Gardening Association, PO Box 550, Kimberton, Pennsylvania 19442-0550. (215) 935-7797. Quarterly. Soil conservation and organic agriculture.

Biology and Fertility of Soils. Springer International, 44 Hartz Way, Seacaucus, New Jersey 07094. (201) 348-4033. Quarterly. Biological functions, processes and interactions in soils, agriculture, deforestation and industrialization.

Communications in Soil Science and Plant Analysis. M. Dekker, 270 Madison Ave., New York, New York 10016. (212) 696-9000; (800) 228-1160. 1970-.

Earth Science. American Geological Institute, 4220 King Street, Alexandria, Virginia 22302. (703) 379-2480. Quarterly. Covers geological issues.

The Journal of Soil Science. Clarendon Press, Walton St., Oxford, England OX2 6DP. Quarterly.

Natural Resources & Earth Sciences. NTIS, 5285 Port Royal Rd., Springfield, Virginia 22161. (703) 487-4650. Weekly. Mineral industry, natural resources management, hydrology, limnology, soil conservation, watershed management, forestry, soil sciences, & geology.

Soil Biology and Biochemistry. Pergamon Microforms International, Inc., Fairview Park, Elmsford, New York 10523. (914) 592-7720. Eight times a year. Soil biology, soil biochemistry, nitrogen fixation, nitrogenase activity, sampling microorganisms in soil, soil compaction, and nutrient release in soils.

Water Research. International Association on Water Pollution Research and Control. Pergamon Microforms International, Inc., Fairview Park, Elmsford, New York 10523. (914) 592-7720. 1966-. Monthly. Covers all aspects of the pollution of marine and fresh water and the management of water quality as well as water resources.

RESEARCH CENTERS AND INSTITUTES

State University of New York at Plattsburg, Center for Earth and Environmental Science. Plattsburg, New York 12901. (518) 564-2028.

U.S. Forest Service, Shrub Sciences Laboratory. 735 N. 500 E., Provo, Utah 84606. (801) 377-5717.

University of Idaho, Idaho Water Resources Research Institute. Morrill Hall 106, Moscow, Idaho 83843. (208) 885-6429.

University of Missouri-Columbia, Clair L. Kucera Research Station At Tucker Prairie. Columbia, Missouri 65211. (314) 882-7541.

STATISTICS SOURCES

Water Resources Data. U.S. Geological Survey. U.S. G.P.O., Washington, District of Columbia 20401. (202) 512-0000. Annual. Data on water supply and quality of streams, lakes and reservoirs for individual states by water year.

TRADE ASSOCIATIONS AND PROFESSIONAL SOCIETIES

American Institute of Chemical Engineers. 345 East 47th St., New York, New York 10017. (212) 705-7338.

American Institute of Chemists. 7315 Wisconsin Ave., Bethesda, Maryland 20814. (301) 652-2447.

American Registry of Certified Professionals in Agronomy, Crops and Soils. c/o American Society of Agronomy, 677 S. Segoe Rd., Madison, Wisconsin 53711. (608) 273-8080.

American Society of Agronomy. 677 South Segoe Rd., Madison, Wisconsin 53711. (608) 273-8080.

Association of Soil & Foundation Engineers. 8811 Colesville Rd., Suite G106, Silver Spring, Maryland 20910. (301) 563-2733.

Clay Minerals Society. P.O. Box 12210, Boulder, Colorado 80303. (303) 444-6405.

Council of Soil Testing and Plant Analysis. P.O. Box 2007, Georgia University Station, Athens, Georgia 30612. (404) 542-0782.

Crop Science Society of America. 677 S. Segoe Rd., Madison, Wisconsin 53711. (608) 273-8080.

Plumbing and Drainage Institute. c/o Sol Baker, 1106 W. 77th St., South Dr., Indianapolis, Indiana 46260. (317) 251-6970.

Plumbing Manufacturers Institute. Bldg. C, Suite 20, 800 Roosevelt Rd., Glen Ellyn, Illinois 60137. (312) 858-9172.

Soil Science Society of America. 677 S. Segoe Rd., Madison, Wisconsin 53711. (608) 273-8080.

SOIL WASTE

See: WASTE

SOLAR CELLS

See also: BATTERIES

ABSTRACTING AND INDEXING SERVICES

Applied Science and Technology Index. H.W. Wilson Co., 950 University Ave., Bronx, New York 10452. (800) 367-6770. Formerly Industrial Arts Index.

Biological and Agricultural Index. H.W. Wilson Co., 950 University Ave., Bronx, New York 10452. (800) 367-6770. 1916-. Monthly.

Energy Information Abstracts Annual 1987 in Retrospect. EIC/Intelligence Inc., 121 Chanlon Rd., New Providence, New Jersey 07974. (908) 464-6800. 1988. Annual. Cumulative edition of the monthly Energy Information Abstracts. Monitors sources in the field of energy including the scientific, technical and business journal literature, conference and symposia proceedings, corporate, government and academic reports.

Engineering Index. The Engineering Index Inc., 345 E. 47th St., New York, New York 10017. 1962-.

Physics Briefs. Physikalische Berichte. Physik Verlag, Pappapelallee 3, Postfach 101161, Weinheim, Germany D-6940. 1979-. Semimonthly. In English. Volumes for 1979- issued by the Deutsche Physikalische Gesellschaft and the Fachinformationszentrum Energie Physik, Mathematik in cooperation with the American Institute of Physics.

Science Citation Index. Institute for Scientific Information, 3501 Market St., Philadelphia, Pennsylvania 19104. 1961-.

Solar Energy Index: The Arizona State University Solar Energy Collection. George Machovic. Pergamon Microforms International, Inc., Fairview Park, Elmsford, New York 10523. (914) 592-7720. 1980. Includes over 10,500 citations covering from the late 1800's to 1979. Aimed primarily at researchers, graduate students and advanced undergraduates.

Solar Thermal Energy Technology. National Technical Information Service, 5285 Port Royal Road, Springfield, Virginia 22161. (703) 487-4650. 1983-. Bimonthly. Advanced concepts in materials research, concentrator and receiver technology, and salinity-gradient solar pond technology.

ALMANACS AND YEARBOOKS

The Solar Energy Almanac. Facts on File, Inc., 460 Park Ave. S., New York, New York 10016. (212) 683-2244. 1983. " Basic book about the use of solar energy by individuals, communities, and nations."

ENCYCLOPEDIAS AND DICTIONARIES

Elsevier's Dictionary of Solar Technology. K. Neutwig. Elsevier Science Publishing Co., 655 Avenue of the Americas, New York, New York 10010. (212) 989-5800. 1985. Text in English, German, French, Spanish and Italian. Specialized terms from the field of solar technology.

Solar Dictionary. C. Breuning and F. F. Evangel. Energy Store, PO Box 1120, San Juan Pueblo, New Mexico 87566. 1983. "Terms defined in the dictionary relate to solar energy and associated fields."

Van Nostrand's Scientific Encyclopedia. Glenn D. Considine, ed. Van Nostrand Reinhold, 115 5th Ave., New York, New York 10003. (212) 254-3232. 1983. Sixth edition. Includes all broad subject areas in science.

HANDBOOKS AND MANUALS

Solar Energy Sourcebook for the Home Owner, Commercial Builder and Manufacturer. Christopher Wells Martz. Solar Energy Institute of America, 1110 6th St. NW, Washington, District of Columbia 20001. (202) 667-6611. 1978. Second edition. Gives profiles of companies and their services in connection with the application of solar energy in everyday life.

ONLINE DATA BASES

Computerized Engineering Index–COMPENDEX. Engineering Information Inc., 345 E. 47th St., New York, New York 10017. (212) 705-7600.

Monthly Catalog of United States Government Publications. U.S. G.P.O., Supt. of Docs., PO Box 371954, Pittsburgh, Pennsylvania 15250-7954. (202) 512-0000.

National Technical Information Service. U.S. Department of Commerce, National Technical Information Service, Office of Data Base Services, 5285 Port Royal Rd., Springfield, Virginia 22161. (703) 487-4807. Bibliographic database of government sponsored research and technical reports.

PERIODICALS AND NEWSLETTERS

Applied Solar Energy. Allerton Press Inc., 150 5th Ave., New York, New York 10011. (212) 924-3950. 1965-. Six times a year.

TRADE ASSOCIATIONS AND PROFESSIONAL SOCIETIES

American Solar Energy Association. 1667 K St., N.W., Suite 395, Washington, District of Columbia 20006. (202) 347-2000.

American Solar Energy Society. 2400 Central Ave. B-1, Boulder, Colorado 80301. (303) 443-3130.

SOLAR ENERGY

ABSTRACTING AND INDEXING SERVICES

Agrindex. AGRIS Coordinating Center, Via delle Terme di Caracalla, Rome, Italy I-00100. 61 0181-FA01. 1975-.

Applied Science and Technology Index. H.W. Wilson Co., 950 University Ave., Bronx, New York 10452. (800) 367-6770. Formerly Industrial Arts Index.

Biological and Agricultural Index. H.W. Wilson Co., 950 University Ave., Bronx, New York 10452. (800) 367-6770. 1916-. Monthly.

Engineering Index. The Engineering Index Inc., 345 E. 47th St., New York, New York 10017. 1962-.

General Science Index. H. W. Wilson Co., 950 University Ave., Bronx, New York 10452. 1978-. Monthly, also issued in annual cumulation. Cumulative subject index to English language periodicals in the subject fields of astronomy, botany, chemistry, earth science, environment and conservation, food and nutrition, genetics, mathematics, medicine and health, microbiology, oceanography, physics, physiology and zoology.

Geographical Abstracts. London School of Economics, Dept. of Geography, Regency House, 34 Duke St., London, England 1966-. Continued by Geo Abstracts issued in 6 parts: Pt. A. Landforms and the quaternary; Pt. B. Biogeography and Climatology; Pt. C. Economic geography; Pt. D. Social geography and cartography; Pt. E. Sedimentology; Pt. F. Regional and community planning.

Physics Briefs. Physikalische Berichte. Physik Verlag, Pappapelallee 3, Postfach 101161, Weinheim, Germany D-6940. 1979-. Semimonthly. In English. Volumes for 1979- issued by the Deutsche Physikalische Gesellschaft and the Fachinformationszentrum Energie Physik, Mathematik in cooperation with the American Institute of Physics.

Science Citation Index. Institute for Scientific Information, 3501 Market St., Philadelphia, Pennsylvania 19104. 1961-.

Solar Energy Index: The Arizona State University Solar Energy Collection. George Machovic. Pergamon Microforms International, Inc., Fairview Park, Elmsford, New York 10523. (914) 592-7720. 1980. Includes over 10,500 citations covering from the late 1800's to 1979. Aimed primarily at researchers, graduate students and advanced undergraduates.

Solar Thermal Energy Technology. National Technical Information Service, 5285 Port Royal Road, Springfield, Virginia 22161. (703) 487-4650. 1983-. Bimonthly. Advanced concepts in materials research, concentrator and receiver technology, and salinity-gradient solar pond technology.

ALMANACS AND YEARBOOKS

The Solar Energy Almanac. Facts on File, Inc., 460 Park Ave. S., New York, New York 10016. (212) 683-2244. 1983. " Basic book about the use of solar energy by individuals, communities, and nations."

DIRECTORIES

Directory of Solar Rating and Certificating Corporation Certified Collectors and Solar Water Heating Systems Ratings. Solar Rating & Certification Corp., 777 N. Capital St., NE, Suite 805, Washington, District of Columbia 20002. (202) 408-0306. 1991. Manufacturers of solar collectors and water heaters certified by the organization.

Solar Energy Directory. Sandra Oddo, ed. Grey House Pub., 229 E. 79th St., Suite 3E, New York, New York 10010. 1983. Lists those U.S. organizations, institutions, agencies and industries working with the direct use of solar energy.

Solar Thermal Directory. Solar Energy Industries Association, 1730 N. Lynn St., Suite 610, Arlington, Virginia 22209. (703) 524-6100.

ENCYCLOPEDIAS AND DICTIONARIES

Encyclopedia of Physics. Rita G. Lerner and George L. Trigg. VCH Publishers, 303 NW 12th Ave., Deerfield Beach, Florida 33442-1788. (305) 428-5566. 1991. Second edition.

Energy Dictionary. V. Daniel Hunt. Van Nostrand Reinhold, 115 5th Ave., New York, New York 10003. (212) 254-3232. 1979. Covers the broad field of energy including fossil, nuclear, solar, geothermal, ocean, and wind energy.

Energy Terminology: A Multilingual Glossary. Pergamon Microforms International, Inc., Fairview Park, Elmsford, New York 10523. (914) 592-7720. 1986. Second edition. Contains 1500 defined terms and concepts related to the field of energy together with an index of several thousand undefined keywords used in the definitions of these terms and concepts. Contents appear in four languages: English, French, German and Spanish.

McGraw-Hill Encyclopedia of Science and Technology. McGraw-Hill, 1221 Avenue of the Americas, New York, New York 10020. (212) 512-2000 or (800) 262-4729. 1992. Seventh edition. Issued in multiple volumes including index. Includes all science and technology broad subject areas.

Solar Dictionary. C. Breuning and F. F. Evangel. Energy Store, PO Box 1120, San Juan Pueblo, New Mexico 87566. 1983. "Terms defined in the dictionary relate to solar energy and associated fields."

GENERAL WORKS

Direct Solar Energy. T. Nejat Veziroglu, ed. Nova Science Publishers. Inc, 283 Commack Rd., Suite 300, Commack, New York 11725-3104. (516) 499-3103; (516) 499-3106. 1991. Examines direct solar energy aspects such as solar radiation, greenhouses, water heaters, heat pumps, distillation/potable water and energy storage.

Indirect Solar, Geothermal, and Nuclear Energy. T. Nejat Veziroglu, ed. Nova Science Publishers Inc., 283 Commack Rd., Suite 300, Commack, New York 11725-3401.

(516) 499-3103; (516) 499-3106. 1991. Presents several focussed sectors of the energy spectrum: wind energy, ocean energy, gravitational energy, I.C. engines, and fluidized beds and looks at nuclear energy.

Solar Energy Application, Bioconversion and Synfuels. T. Nejat Veziroglu, ed. Nova Science Publishers Inc., 283 Commack Rd., Suite 300, Commack, New York 11725-3401. (516) 499-3103; (516) 499-3106. 1990. Deals with solar energy applications such as heating and cooking, energy transmission, photovoltaics and industrial applications. Also includes chapters on bioconversion and synfuels.

Solar Energy in Agriculture. Blaine F. Parker, ed. Elsevier Science Publishing Co., 655 Avenue of the Americas, New York, New York 10010. (212) 989-5800. 1991.

Solar-Hydrogen Energy Systems. Tokio Ohta. Pergamon Microforms International, Inc., Fairview Park, Elmsford, New York 10523. (914) 592-7720. 1979.

Solar Hydrogen: Moving Beyond Fossil Fuels. Joan M. Ogden and Robert H. Williams. World Resources Institute, 1709 New York Ave. N.W., Washington, District of Columbia 20006. (800) 822-0504. 1989. Traces the technical breakthroughs associated with solar hydrogen. Assesses the new fuel's potential as a replacement for oil, compares its costs and uses with those of both traditional and synthetic fuels, and charts a path for developing solar hydrogen markets.

The Solar Jobs Book. Katharine Ericson. Brick House Publishing Co., Inc., Francestown Tpke., New Boston, New Hampshire 03070. (603) 487-3718. 1980. How-to book that covers educational programs that teach how to participate in the new movement towards energy self-sufficiency.

HANDBOOKS AND MANUALS

Energy Deskbook. Samuel Glasstone. Van Nostrand Reinhold, 115 5th Ave., New York, New York 10020. (212) 254-3232. 1983. Single volume reference covering all energy resources.

Handbook of Geophysics and the Space Environment. Adolph S. Jursa, ed. Air Force Geophysics Laboratory, Air Force Systems Command, United States Air Force, c/o National Technical Information Service, 5285 Port Royal Rd., Springfield, Virginia 22161. (703) 487-4650. 1985. Two volumes. Broad subject areas covered are space, atmosphere, and terrestrial environment. Includes topics such as solar radiation, sunspots, solar wind, geomagnetic fields, radiation belts, cosmic radiation, atmospheric gases, etc.

Solar Energy Sourcebook for the Home Owner, Commercial Builder and Manufacturer. Christopher Wells Martz. Solar Energy Institute of America, 1110 6th St. NW, Washington, District of Columbia 20001. (202) 667-6611. 1978. Second edition. Gives profiles of companies and their services in connection with the application of solar energy in everyday life.

ONLINE DATA BASES

Computerized Engineering Index–COMPENDEX. Engineering Information Inc., 345 E. 47th St., New York, New York 10017. (212) 705-7600.

International Solar Energy Intelligence Report. Business Publishers, Inc., 951 Pershing Dr., Silver Spring, Maryland 20910. (301) 587-6300.

Monthly Catalog of United States Government Publications. U.S. G.P.O., Supt. of Docs., PO Box 371954, Pittsburgh, Pennsylvania 15250-7954. (202) 512-0000.

National Technical Information Service. U.S. Department of Commerce, National Technical Information Service, Office of Data Base Services, 5285 Port Royal Rd., Springfield, Virginia 22161. (703) 487-4807. Bibliographic database of government sponsored research and technical reports.

SCISEARCH. Institute for Scientific Information, University City Science Center, 3501 Market St., Philadelphia, Pennsylvania 19104. (215) 386-0100.

PERIODICALS AND NEWSLETTERS

Applied Solar Energy. Allerton Press Inc., 150 5th Ave., New York, New York 10011. (212) 924-3950. 1965-. Six times a year.

CA Selects: Solar Energy. Chemical Abstracts Services, 2540 Olentangy River Rd., Box 3012, Columbus, Ohio 43210. (800) 848-6533. 1978-. Biweekly. Abstracts on solar energy conversion devices, materials and processes.

Earth Science. American Geological Institute, 4220 King Street, Alexandria, Virginia 22302. (703) 379-2480. Quarterly. Covers geological issues.

Renewable Energy: An International Journal. Pergamon Microforms International, Inc., Fairview Park, Elmsford, New York 10523. (914) 592-7720. 1991-. Six issues a year. Topics include environmental protection and renewable sources of energy.

The Solar Collector. Florida Solar Energy Center, 300 State Rd., 401, Cape Canaveral, Florida 32920-4099. (407) 783-0300. Quarterly. Renewable energy research and technology.

Solar Energy: Official Journal of the International Solar Energy Society. Pergamon Microforms International Inc., Fairview Park, Elmsford, New York 10523. (914) 592-7720. Monthly. Science and technology of solar energy applications.

The Solar Thermal Report. Solar Liaison, Chicago, Illinois Quarterly. Covers solar energy and geothermal resources.

RESEARCH CENTERS AND INSTITUTES

Renew America. 17 16th Street, N. W., Suite 710, Washington, District of Columbia 20036. (202) 232-2252.

University of Arizona, Herbarium. 113 Shantz Building, Tucson, Arizona 85721. (602) 621-7243.

TRADE ASSOCIATIONS AND PROFESSIONAL SOCIETIES

American Solar Energy Association. 1667 K St., N.W., Suite 395, Washington, District of Columbia 20006. (202) 347-2000.

American Solar Energy Society. 2400 Central Ave. B-1, Boulder, Colorado 80301. (303) 443-3130.

Interstate Solar Coordination Council. 900 American Center Bldg., ST. Paul, Minnesota 55101. (612) 296-4737.

Passive Solar Industries Council. 1090 Vermont Ave., N.W., Suite 1200, Washington, District of Columbia 20005. (202) 371-0357.

Passive Solar Institute. P.O. Box 722, Bascom, Ohio 44809. (419) 937-2225.

Solar Energy Industries Association. 1730 N. Lynn St., Suite 610, Arlington, Virginia 22209. (703) 524-6100.

Solartherm. 1315 Apple Ave., Silver Spring, Maryland 20910. (301) 587-8686.

SOLAR HEATING

ABSTRACTING AND INDEXING SERVICES

Agrindex. AGRIS Coordinating Center, Via delle Terme di Caracalla, Rome, Italy I-00100. 61 0181-FA01. 1975-.

Applied Science and Technology Index. H.W. Wilson Co., 950 University Ave., Bronx, New York 10452. (800) 367-6770. Formerly Industrial Arts Index.

Biological and Agricultural Index. H.W. Wilson Co., 950 University Ave., Bronx, New York 10452. (800) 367-6770. 1916-. Monthly.

Engineering Index. The Engineering Index Inc., 345 E. 47th St., New York, New York 10017. 1962-.

Geographical Abstracts. London School of Economics, Dept. of Geography, Regency House, 34 Duke St., London, England 1966-. Continued by Geo Abstracts issued in 6 parts: Pt. A. Landforms and the quaternary; Pt. B. Biogeography and Climatology; Pt. C. Economic geography; Pt. D. Social geography and cartography; Pt. E. Sedimentology; Pt. F. Regional and community planning.

Physics Briefs. Physikalische Berichte. Physik Verlag, Pappapelallee 3, Postfach 101161, Weinheim, Germany D-6940. 1979-. Semimonthly. In English. Volumes for 1979- issued by the Deutsche Physikalische Gesellschaft and the Fachinformationszentrum Energie Physik, Mathematik in cooperation with the American Institute of Physics.

Science Citation Index. Institute for Scientific Information, 3501 Market St., Philadelphia, Pennsylvania 19104. 1961-.

Solar Buildings Technology. National Technical Information Service, 5285 Port Royal Road, Springfield, Virginia 22161. (703) 487-4650. 1988-. Bimonthly. Solar energy use in buildings, including desulfurization, photovoltaic systems, solar thermal, solar collectors, and heat storage.

Solar Energy Index: The Arizona State University Solar Energy Collection. George Machovic. Pergamon Microforms International, Inc., Fairview Park, Elmsford, New York 10523. (914) 592-7720. 1980. Includes over 10,500 citations covering from the late 1800's to 1979. Aimed primarily at researchers, graduate students and advanced undergraduates.

Solar Thermal Energy Technology. National Technical Information Service, 5285 Port Royal Road, Springfield, Virginia 22161. (703) 487-4650. 1983-. Bimonthly. Advanced concepts in materials research, concentrator and receiver technology, and salinity-gradient solar pond technology.

ALMANACS AND YEARBOOKS

The Solar Energy Almanac. Facts on File, Inc., 460 Park Ave. S., New York, New York 10016. (212) 683-2244. 1983. " Basic book about the use of solar energy by individuals, communities, and nations."

DIRECTORIES

Solar Thermal Directory. Solar Energy Industries Association, 1730 N. Lynn St., Suite 610, Arlington, Virginia 22209. (703) 524-6100.

ENCYCLOPEDIAS AND DICTIONARIES

Dictionary of Environmental Engineering and Related Sciences: English-Spanish, Spanish-English. Jose T. Villate. Ediciones Universal, 3090 SW 8th St., Miami, Florida 33135. (305) 642-3355. 1979.

Dictionary of Environmental Protection Technology: In Four Languages, English, German, French, Russian. Egon Seidel. Elsevier Science Publishing Co., 655 Avenue of the Americas, New York, New York 10010. (212) 984-5800. 1988.

Elsevier's Dictionary of Solar Technology. K. Neutwig. Elsevier Science Publishing Co., 655 Avenue of the Americas, New York, New York 10010. (212) 989-5800. 1985. Text in English, German, French, Spanish and Italian. Specialized terms from the field of solar technology.

Encyclopedia of Environmental Science and Engineering. J.R. Pfafflin. Gordon and Breach Science Publishers, Inc., 270 8th Ave., New York, New York 10011. (212) 206-8900. 1992.

Encyclopedia of Physical Science and Technology. Robert A. Meyers, ed. Academic Press, c/o Harcourt Brace Jovanovich Inc., 6277 Sea Harbor Dr., Orlando, Florida 32887. (800) 346-8648. Dictionary of engineering, technology and physical sciences.

English-Russian Dictionary of Environmental Protection: About 14,000 Terms. E.L. Milovanov. Pergamon Microforms International, Inc., Fairview Park, Elmsford, New York 10523. (914) 592-7720. 1981.

Environmental Engineering Dictionary. C. C. Lee. Government Institutes, Inc., 4 Research Pl., Ste. 200, Rockville, Maryland 20850. (301) 921-2300. 1989. Defines over 6000 engineering terms relating to pollutioncontrol technologies, monitoring, risk assessment, sampling andanalysis, quality control, permitting, and environmentally-regulated engineering and science. Includes bibliographical references (p. 612-627).

Solar Dictionary. C. Breuning and F. F. Evangel. Energy Store, PO Box 1120, San Juan Pueblo, New Mexico 87566. 1983. "Terms defined in the dictionary relate to solar energy and associated fields."

GENERAL WORKS

Affordable Passive Solar Homes. Richard Crowther. American Solar Energy Society, 2400 Central Ave., No.

B-1, Boulder, Colorado 80301. (303) 443-3130. 1983. Passive systems in solar energy.

HANDBOOKS AND MANUALS

Handbook of Geophysics and the Space Environment. Adolph S. Jursa, ed. Air Force Geophysics Laboratory, Air Force Systems Command, United States Air Force, c/o National Technical Information Service, 5285 Port Royal Rd., Springfield, Virginia 22161. (703) 487-4650. 1985. Two volumes. Broad subject areas covered are space, atmosphere, and terrestrial environment. Includes topics such as solar radiation, sunspots, solar wind, geomagnetic fields, radiation belts, cosmic radiation, atmospheric gases, etc.

Solar Energy Sourcebook for the Home Owner, Commercial Builder and Manufacturer. Christopher Wells Martz. Solar Energy Institute of America, 1110 6th St. NW, Washington, District of Columbia 20001. (202) 667-6611. 1978. Second edition. Gives profiles of companies and their services in connection with the application of solar energy in everyday life.

ONLINE DATA BASES

Computerized Engineering Index–COMPENDEX. Engineering Information Inc., 345 E. 47th St., New York, New York 10017. (212) 705-7600.

International Solar Energy Intelligence Report. Business Publishers, Inc., 951 Pershing Dr., Silver Spring, Maryland 20910. (301) 587-6300.

Monthly Catalog of United States Government Publications. U.S. G.P.O., Supt. of Docs., PO Box 371954, Pittsburgh, Pennsylvania 15250-7954. (202) 512-0000.

National Technical Information Service. U.S. Department of Commerce, National Technical Information Service, Office of Data Base Services, 5285 Port Royal Rd., Springfield, Virginia 22161. (703) 487-4807. Bibliographic database of government sponsored research and technical reports.

SCISEARCH. Institute for Scientific Information, University City Science Center, 3501 Market St., Philadelphia, Pennsylvania 19104. (215) 386-0100.

PERIODICALS AND NEWSLETTERS

Applied Solar Energy. Allerton Press Inc., 150 5th Ave., New York, New York 10011. (212) 924-3950. 1965-. Six times a year.

Earth Science. American Geological Institute, 4220 King Street, Alexandria, Virginia 22302. (703) 379-2480. Quarterly. Covers geological issues.

TRADE ASSOCIATIONS AND PROFESSIONAL SOCIETIES

American Solar Energy Association. 1667 K St., N.W., Suite 395, Washington, District of Columbia 20006. (202) 347-2000.

American Solar Energy Society. 2400 Central Ave. B-1, Boulder, Colorado 80301. (303) 443-3130.

SOLAR POWER

See also: POWER GENERATION; SOLAR ENERGY

ABSTRACTING AND INDEXING SERVICES

Agrindex. AGRIS Coordinating Center, Via delle Terme di Caracalla, Rome, Italy I-00100. 61 0181-FA01. 1975-.

Applied Ecology Abstracts Studies in Renewable Natural Resources. Information Retrieval Ltd., 1911 Jefferson Davis Highway, Arlington, Virginia 22202. 1975-. Monthly.

Applied Science and Technology Index. H.W. Wilson Co., 950 University Ave., Bronx, New York 10452. (800) 367-6770. Formerly Industrial Arts Index.

ASFA Aquaculture Abstracts. Cambridge Scientific Abstracts, Inc., 5161 River Rd., Bethesda, Maryland 20816. (301) 961-6750. 1984.

Biological and Agricultural Index. H.W. Wilson Co., 950 University Ave., Bronx, New York 10452. (800) 367-6770. 1916-. Monthly.

Engineering Index. The Engineering Index Inc., 345 E. 47th St., New York, New York 10017. 1962-.

General Science Index. H. W. Wilson Co., 950 University Ave., Bronx, New York 10452. 1978-. Monthly, also issued in annual cumulation. Cumulative subject index to English language periodicals in the subject fields of astronomy, botany, chemistry, earth science, environment and conservation, food and nutrition, genetics, mathematics, medicine and health, microbiology, oceanography, physics, physiology and zoology.

Geographical Abstracts. London School of Economics, Dept. of Geography, Regency House, 34 Duke St., London, England 1966-. Continued by Geo Abstracts issued in 6 parts: Pt. A. Landforms and the quaternary; Pt. B. Biogeography and Climatology; Pt. C. Economic geography; Pt. D. Social geography and cartography; Pt. E. Sedimentology; Pt. F. Regional and community planning.

Multimedia Index to Ecology. National Information Center for Educational Media, University of Southern California, Los Angeles, California 90007.

Physics Briefs. Physikalische Berichte. Physik Verlag, Pappapelallee 3, Postfach 101161, Weinheim, Germany D-6940. 1979-. Semimonthly. In English. Volumes for 1979- issued by the Deutsche Physikalische Gesellschaft and the Fachinformationszentrum Energie Physik, Mathematik in cooperation with the American Institute of Physics.

Science Citation Index. Institute for Scientific Information, 3501 Market St., Philadelphia, Pennsylvania 19104. 1961-.

Solar Energy Index: The Arizona State University Solar Energy Collection. George Machovic. Pergamon Microforms International, Inc., Fairview Park, Elmsford, New York 10523. (914) 592-7720. 1980. Includes over 10,500 citations covering from the late 1800's to 1979. Aimed primarily at researchers, graduate students and advanced undergraduates.

Solar Thermal Energy Technology. National Technical Information Service, 5285 Port Royal Road, Springfield, Virginia 22161. (703) 487-4650. 1983-. Bimonthly. Advanced concepts in materials research, concentrator and receiver technology, and salinity-gradient solar pond technology.

ALMANACS AND YEARBOOKS

The Solar Energy Almanac. Facts on File, Inc., 460 Park Ave. S., New York, New York 10016. (212) 683-2244. 1983. " Basic book about the use of solar energy by individuals, communities, and nations."

BIBLIOGRAPHIES

Bibliography and Index of Geology. American Geological Institute, 4220 King St., Alexandria, Virginia 22302. Monthly. Includes environmental geology and hydrogeology.

Sun Power: A Bibliography of United States Government Documents on Solar Energy. Sandra McAninch. Greenwood Publishing Group, Inc., 88 Post Rd. W., PO Box 5007, Westport, Connecticut 06881. (212) 226-3571. 1981. Has over 3600 citations.

DIRECTORIES

Directory of Solar Rating and Certificating Corporation Certified Collectors and Solar Water Heating Systems Ratings. Solar Rating & Certification Corp., 777 N. Capital St., NE, Suite 805, Washington, District of Columbia 20002. (202) 408-0306. 1991. Manufacturers of solar collectors and water heaters certified by the organization.

ENCYCLOPEDIAS AND DICTIONARIES

Dictionary of Environmental Engineering and Related Sciences: English-Spanish, Spanish-English. Jose T. Villate. Ediciones Universal, 3090 SW 8th St., Miami, Florida 33135. (305) 642-3355. 1979.

Dictionary of Environmental Protection Technology: In Four Languages, English, German, French, Russian. Egon Seidel. Elsevier Science Publishing Co., 655 Avenue of the Americas, New York, New York 10010. (212) 984-5800. 1988.

Elsevier's Dictionary of Solar Technology. K. Neutwig. Elsevier Science Publishing Co., 655 Avenue of the Americas, New York, New York 10010. (212) 989-5800. 1985. Text in English, German, French, Spanish and Italian. Specialized terms from the field of solar technology.

Encyclopedia of Environmental Science and Engineering. J.R. Pfafflin. Gordon and Breach Science Publishers, Inc., 270 8th Ave., New York, New York 10011. (212) 206-8900. 1992.

Encyclopedia of Physical Science and Technology. Robert A. Meyers, ed. Academic Press, c/o Harcourt Brace Jovanovich Inc., 6277 Sea Harbor Dr., Orlando, Florida 32887. (800) 346-8648. Dictionary of engineering, technology and physical sciences.

English-Russian Dictionary of Environmental Protection: About 14,000 Terms. E.L. Milovanov. Pergamon Microforms International, Inc., Fairview Park, Elmsford, New York 10523. (914) 592-7720. 1981.

Environmental Engineering Dictionary. C. C. Lee. Government Institutes, Inc., 4 Research Pl., Ste. 200, Rockville, Maryland 20850. (301) 921-2300. 1989. Defines over 6000 engineering terms relating to pollutioncontrol technologies, monitoring, risk assessment, sampling andanalysis, quality control, permitting, and environmentally-regulated engineering and science. Includes bibliographical references (p. 612-627).

McGraw-Hill Encyclopedia of Science and Technology. McGraw-Hill, 1221 Avenue of the Americas, New York, New York 10020. (212) 512-2000 or (800) 262-4729. 1992. Seventh edition. Issued in multiple volumes including index. Includes all science and technology broad subject areas.

Solar Dictionary. C. Breuning and F. F. Evangel. Energy Store, PO Box 1120, San Juan Pueblo, New Mexico 87566. 1983. "Terms defined in the dictionary relate to solar energy and associated fields."

Van Nostrand's Scientific Encyclopedia. Glenn D. Considine, ed. Van Nostrand Reinhold, 115 5th Ave., New York, New York 10003. (212) 254-3232. 1983. Sixth edition. Includes all broad subject areas in science.

GENERAL WORKS

Magill's Survey of Science. Earth Science Series. Frank N. Magill. Salem Press, PO Box 50062, Pasadena, California 91105. 1990-. Five volumes. Includes information on earth's crust, hot spots and volcanic island chains, physical properties of minerals, rock magnetism, physical properties of rocks, and index.

HANDBOOKS AND MANUALS

Handbook of Geophysics and the Space Environment. Adolph S. Jursa, ed. Air Force Geophysics Laboratory, Air Force Systems Command, United States Air Force, c/o National Technical Information Service, 5285 Port Royal Rd., Springfield, Virginia 22161. (703) 487-4650. 1985. Two volumes. Broad subject areas covered are space, atmosphere, and terrestrial environment. Includes topics such as solar radiation, sunspots, solar wind, geomagnetic fields, radiation belts, cosmic radiation, atmospheric gases, etc.

Solar Energy Sourcebook for the Home Owner, Commercial Builder and Manufacturer. Christopher Wells Martz. Solar Energy Institute of America, 1110 6th St. NW, Washington, District of Columbia 20001. (202) 667-6611. 1978. Second edition. Gives profiles of companies and their services in connection with the application of solar energy in everyday life.

ONLINE DATA BASES

Computerized Engineering Index–COMPENDEX. Engineering Information Inc., 345 E. 47th St., New York, New York 10017. (212) 705-7600.

International Solar Energy Intelligence Report. Business Publishers, Inc., 951 Pershing Dr., Silver Spring, Maryland 20910. (301) 587-6300.

Monthly Catalog of United States Government Publications. U.S. G.P.O., Supt. of Docs., PO Box 371954, Pittsburgh, Pennsylvania 15250-7954. (202) 512-0000.

National Technical Information Service. U.S. Department of Commerce, National Technical Information Service, Office of Data Base Services, 5285 Port Royal Rd., Springfield, Virginia 22161. (703) 487-4807. Bibliographic database of government sponsored research and technical reports.

PressNet Environmental Reports. Chemical Information Systems, Inc., 7215 York Rd., Baltimore, Maryland 21212. (301) 321-8440.

PERIODICALS AND NEWSLETTERS

Applied Solar Energy. Allerton Press Inc., 150 5th Ave., New York, New York 10011. (212) 924-3950. 1965-. Six times a year.

Earth Science. American Geological Institute, 4220 King Street, Alexandria, Virginia 22302. (703) 379-2480. Quarterly. Covers geological issues.

RESEARCH CENTERS AND INSTITUTES

University of Arizona, Herbarium. 113 Shantz Building, Tucson, Arizona 85721. (602) 621-7243.

TRADE ASSOCIATIONS AND PROFESSIONAL SOCIETIES

American Solar Energy Association. 1667 K St., N.W., Suite 395, Washington, District of Columbia 20006. (202) 347-2000.

American Solar Energy Society. 2400 Central Ave. B-1, Boulder, Colorado 80301. (303) 443-3130.

National Solid Wastes Management Association. 1730 Rhode Island Ave., N.W., Suite 1000, Washington, District of Columbia 20036. (202) 659-4613.

SOLAR RADIATION

ABSTRACTING AND INDEXING SERVICES

Agrindex. AGRIS Coordinating Center, Via delle Terme di Caracalla, Rome, Italy I-00100. 61 0181-FA01. 1975-.

Applied Science and Technology Index. H.W. Wilson Co., 950 University Ave., Bronx, New York 10452. (800) 367-6770. Formerly Industrial Arts Index.

Biological and Agricultural Index. H.W. Wilson Co., 950 University Ave., Bronx, New York 10452. (800) 367-6770. 1916-. Monthly.

Engineering Index. The Engineering Index Inc., 345 E. 47th St., New York, New York 10017. 1962-.

Geographical Abstracts. London School of Economics, Dept. of Geography, Regency House, 34 Duke St., London, England 1966-. Continued by Geo Abstracts issued in 6 parts: Pt. A. Landforms and the quaternary; Pt. B. Biogeography and Climatology; Pt. C. Economic geography; Pt. D. Social geography and cartography; Pt. E. Sedimentology; Pt. F. Regional and community planning.

Index to Scientific Book Contents. Institute for Scientific Information, 3501 Market St., Philadelphia, Pennsylvania 19104. (800) 523-1857. 1985-. Annual. Gives contents of science books published.

Physics Briefs. Physikalische Berichte. Physik Verlag, Pappapelallee 3, Postfach 101161, Weinheim, Germany D-6940. 1979-. Semimonthly. In English. Volumes for 1979- issued by the Deutsche Physikalische Gesellschaft and the Fachinformationszentrum Energie Physik, Mathematik in cooperation with the American Institute of Physics.

Science Citation Index. Institute for Scientific Information, 3501 Market St., Philadelphia, Pennsylvania 19104. 1961-.

Solar Energy Index: The Arizona State University Solar Energy Collection. George Machovic. Pergamon Microforms International, Inc., Fairview Park, Elmsford, New York 10523. (914) 592-7720. 1980. Includes over 10,500 citations covering from the late 1800's to 1979. Aimed primarily at researchers, graduate students and advanced undergraduates.

ALMANACS AND YEARBOOKS

The Solar Energy Almanac. Facts on File, Inc., 460 Park Ave. S., New York, New York 10016. (212) 683-2244. 1983. " Basic book about the use of solar energy by individuals, communities, and nations."

BIBLIOGRAPHIES

Bibliography and Index of Geology. American Geological Institute, 4220 King St., Alexandria, Virginia 22302. Monthly. Includes environmental geology and hydrogeology.

ENCYCLOPEDIAS AND DICTIONARIES

The Encyclopedia of Climatology. John E. Oliver and Rhodes W. Fairbridge, eds. Van Nostrand Reinhold, 115 5th Ave., New York, New York 10003. (212) 254-3232. 1987. Belongs in the series Encyclopedia of Earth Sciences, v.11.

McGraw-Hill Encyclopedia of Environmental Science. Sybil P. Parker. McGraw-Hill Science & Engineering Books, 11 W. 19th St., New York, New York 10011. (212) 337-6010. 1980. Covers ecology, man's influence on nature, and environmental protection.

Solar Dictionary. C. Breuning and F. F. Evangel. Energy Store, PO Box 1120, San Juan Pueblo, New Mexico 87566. 1983. "Terms defined in the dictionary relate to solar energy and associated fields."

Van Nostrand's Scientific Encyclopedia. Glenn D. Considine, ed. Van Nostrand Reinhold, 115 5th Ave., New York, New York 10003. (212) 254-3232. 1983. Sixth edition. Includes all broad subject areas in science.

GENERAL WORKS

Magill's Survey of Science. Earth Science Series. Frank N. Magill. Salem Press, PO Box 50062, Pasadena, California 91105. 1990-. Five volumes. Includes information on earth's crust, hot spots and volcanic island chains, physical properties of minerals, rock magnetism, physical properties of rocks, and index.

HANDBOOKS AND MANUALS

Handbook of Geophysics and the Space Environment. Adolph S. Jursa, ed. Air Force Geophysics Laboratory, Air Force Systems Command, United States Air Force, c/o National Technical Information Service, 5285 Port Royal Rd., Springfield, Virginia 22161. (703) 487-4650. 1985. Two volumes. Broad subject areas covered are space, atmosphere, and terrestrial environment. Includes topics such as solar radiation, sunspots, solar wind, geomagnetic fields, radiation belts, cosmic radiation, atmospheric gases, etc.

ONLINE DATA BASES

Computerized Engineering Index–COMPENDEX. Engineering Information Inc., 345 E. 47th St., New York, New York 10017. (212) 705-7600.

Monthly Catalog of United States Government Publications. U.S. G.P.O., Supt. of Docs., PO Box 371954, Pittsburgh, Pennsylvania 15250-7954. (202) 512-0000.

National Technical Information Service. U.S. Department of Commerce, National Technical Information Service, Office of Data Base Services, 5285 Port Royal Rd., Springfield, Virginia 22161. (703) 487-4807. Bibliographic database of government sponsored research and technical reports.

PERIODICALS AND NEWSLETTERS

Applied Solar Energy. Allerton Press Inc., 150 5th Ave., New York, New York 10011. (212) 924-3950. 1965-. Six times a year.

Earth Science. American Geological Institute, 4220 King Street, Alexandria, Virginia 22302. (703) 379-2480. Quarterly. Covers geological issues.

TRADE ASSOCIATIONS AND PROFESSIONAL SOCIETIES

American Solar Energy Association. 1667 K St., N.W., Suite 395, Washington, District of Columbia 20006. (202) 347-2000.

American Solar Energy Society. 2400 Central Ave. B-1, Boulder, Colorado 80301. (303) 443-3130.

SOLID WASTE DISPOSAL

See also: SOLID WASTES; WASTE DISPOSAL

ABSTRACTING AND INDEXING SERVICES

Applied Science and Technology Index. H.W. Wilson Co., 950 University Ave., Bronx, New York 10452. (800) 367-6770. Formerly Industrial Arts Index.

Biological and Agricultural Index. H.W. Wilson Co., 950 University Ave., Bronx, New York 10452. (800) 367-6770. 1916-. Monthly.

Chemical Abstracts. Chemical Abstracts Service, 2540 Olentangy River Rd., PO Box 3012, Columbus, Ohio 43210. (800) 848-6533. 1907-.

Engineering Index. The Engineering Index Inc., 345 E. 47th St., New York, New York 10017. 1962-.

Environment Abstracts. Bowker A & I Publishing, 121 Chanlon Rd., New Providence, New Jersey 07974. (908) 464-6800. 1974-.

Environment Index. Environment Information Center, Index Research Department, 124 E. 39th St., New York, New York 10016. 1971-. Annual.

Environmental Information Connection–EIC. Planning Information Program, Dept. of Urban and Regional Planning, University of Illinois, 1003 West Nevada, Urbana, Illinois 61801. (217) 333-1369. Also available online.

Environmental Periodicals Bibliography. Environmental Studies Institute, International Academy at Santa Barbara, 800 Garden St., Suite D, Santa Barbara, California 93101. (805) 965-5010. Also available online.

General Science Index. H. W. Wilson Co., 950 University Ave., Bronx, New York 10452. 1978-. Monthly, also issued in annual cumulation. Cumulative subject index to English language periodicals in the subject fields of astronomy, botany, chemistry, earth science, environment and conservation, food and nutrition, genetics, mathematics, medicine and health, microbiology, oceanography, physics, physiology and zoology.

Geographical Abstracts. London School of Economics, Dept. of Geography, Regency House, 34 Duke St., London, England 1966-. Continued by Geo Abstracts issued in 6 parts: Pt. A. Landforms and the quaternary; Pt. B. Biogeography and Climatology; Pt. C. Economic geography; Pt. D. Social geography and cartography; Pt. E. Sedimentology; Pt. F. Regional and community planning.

Index to Scientific Book Contents. Institute for Scientific Information, 3501 Market St., Philadelphia, Pennsylvania 19104. (800) 523-1857. 1985-. Annual. Gives contents of science books published.

Pollution Abstracts. Cambridge Scientific Abstracts, 5161 River Rd., Bethesda, Maryland 20816. (301) 961-6750. Six/year. Indexes worldwide technical literature on environmental pollution. Covers air pollution, marine and freshwater pollution, sewage and wastewater treatment, waste management, toxicology and health, noise pollution, radiation, land pollution, and environmental policies, programs, legislation, and education. Also available online.

Science Citation Index. Institute for Scientific Information, 3501 Market St., Philadelphia, Pennsylvania 19104. 1961-.

BIBLIOGRAPHIES

EPA Publications Bibliography. U.S. Environmental Protection Agency, Library Systems Branch, 401 M St., SW, Washington, District of Columbia 20460. (202) 260-2090. Quarterly.

DIRECTORIES

Environmental Software Directory. Donley Technology, PO Box 335, Garrisonville, Virginia 22463. (703) 659-1954. 1989-. Annually. Provides descriptive access to commercial and government databases, software and online systems related to hazardous materials management, water and wastewater, groundwater, soils, mapping, air pollution and ecology.

ENCYCLOPEDIAS AND DICTIONARIES

Dictionary of Environmental Engineering and Related Sciences: English-Spanish, Spanish-English. Jose T. Villate. Ediciones Universal, 3090 SW 8th St., Miami, Florida 33135. (305) 642-3355. 1979.

Encyclopedia of Environmental Science and Engineering. J.R. Pfafflin. Gordon and Breach Science Publishers, Inc., 270 8th Ave., New York, New York 10011. (212) 206-8900. 1992.

McGraw-Hill Encyclopedia of Environmental Science. Sybil P. Parker. McGraw-Hill Science & Engineering Books, 11 W. 19th St., New York, New York 10011. (212) 337-6010. 1980. Covers ecology, man's influence on nature, and environmental protection.

Van Nostrand's Scientific Encyclopedia. Glenn D. Considine, ed. Van Nostrand Reinhold, 115 5th Ave., New York, New York 10003. (212) 254-3232. 1983. Sixth edition. Includes all broad subject areas in science.

GENERAL WORKS

Air Emissions from Municipal Solid Waste Landfills. Environmental Protection Agency. National Technical Information Service, 5285 Port Royal Rd., Springfield, Virginia 22161. (703) 487-4650. 1991. Background information for proposed standards and guidelines. Order number PB91-197061LDM.

Beyond 40 Percent: Record-Setting Recycling and Composting Programs. Brenda Platt, et al. Island Press, 1718 Connecticut Ave. N.W., Suite 300, Washington, District of Columbia 20009. (202) 232-7933. 1991. Produced by the Institute for Local Self-Reliance, this volume documents the operating experience of 17 U.S. communities, from small rural towns to large cities, that are recovering between 32 and 57 percent of their waste.

Characterization of Municipal Waste Combustor Ashes and Leachates from Municipal Solid Waste Landfills, Monofills, and Codisposal Sites. U.S. Environmental Protection Agency, Office of Solid Waste, 401 M St., S.W., Washington, District of Columbia 20460. (202) 260-2090. 1987.

Chemical Waste Disposal: Chemicals Identified in Terrestrial and Aquatic Waste Disposal Processes; a Selected Bibliography with Abstracts, 1964-1979. J. G. Pruett. Federation of American Societies for Experimental Biology, 9650 Rockville Pike, Bethesda, Maryland 20814. (301) 530-7000. 1980.

Coal Ash Disposal: Solid Waste Impacts. Raymond A. Tripodi and Paul N. Cheremisinoff. Technomic Publishing Co., 851 New Holland Ave., Box 3535, Lancaster, Pennsylvania 17604. (717) 291-5609. 1980.

Codisposal of Garbage and Sewage Sludge–a Promising Solution to Two Problems. U.S. General Accounting Office. U.S. G.P.O., Washington, District of Columbia 20401. (202) 512-0000. 1979.

Codisposal of Municipal Solid Waste and Sewage Sludge: An Analysis of Constraints. Dick Baldwin. National Technical Information Service, 5285 Port Royal Rd., Springfield, Virginia 22161. (703) 487-4650. 1980.

Design, Construction, and Monitoring of Sanitary Landfill. Amalendu Bagchi. John Wiley & Sons, Inc., 605 3rd Ave., New York, New York 10158-0012. (212) 850-6000. 1990. Handbook of theory, practice, and mathematical models of sanitary landfill technology and how they apply to waste disposal.

Drinking Water and Groundwater Remediation Cost Evaluation: Air Stripping. Robert M. Clark and Jeffrey Q. Adams. Lewis Publishers, 2000 Corporate Blvd. N.W., Boca Raton, Florida 33431. (800) 272-7737. 1991. The new software program shows air stripping costs and performance of the remediation of hazardous waste sites or drinking water treatment. The program helps do cost comparisons of the technology against other available technologies.

Drinking Water and Groundwater Remediation Cost Evaluation: Granular Activated Carbon. Robert M. Clark and Jeffrey Q. Adams. Lewis Publishers, 2000 Corporate Blvd. N.W., Boca Raton, Florida 33431. (800) 272-7737. 1991. Shows GAC costs and performance forthe remediation of hazardous waste sites or drinking watertreatment. Compares the cost of the technology against other available technologies.

Environmental Issues: An Anthology of 1989. Thomas W. Joyce, ed. TAPPI Press, Technology Park/Atlanta, PO Box 105113, Atlanta, Georgia 30348. (404) 446-1400. 1990. Contains 39 papers on environmental, safety and occupational health concerns from 11 TAPPI, CPPA and AIChE meetings held during 1989. Also included is a literature review of over 200 papers published in 1989.

How to Meet Requirements for Hazardous Waste Landfill Design, Construction and Closure. U. S. Environmental Protection Agency. Noyes Publications, 120 Mill Rd., Park Ridge, New Jersey 07656. (201) 391-8484. 1990. Outlines in detail the provisions of the minimum technology guidance regulations, and offers practical and detailed technology transfer information on the construction of hazardous waste facilities that comply with these requirements.

Incineration for Site Cleanup and Destruction of Hazardous Wastes. Howard E. Hesketh. Technomic Publishing Co., 851 New Holland Ave., Box 3535, Lancaster, Pennsylvania 17604. (717) 291-5609; (800) 233-9936. 1990.

Municipal Solid Waste Incinerator Ash Management and Disposal Data Entries. The Institute, 2425 18th St., N.W., Washington, District of Columbia 20009. (202) 232-4108. Database on solid waste resources recovery and economic development, including municipal solid waste ash.

The New York Environment Book. Eric A. Goldstein. Island Press, 1718 Connecticut Ave. N.W., Suite 300, Washington, District of Columbia 20009. (202) 232-7933. 1990. Provides an in-depth analysis of New York City's environment. The five areas surveyed are: solid waste disposal, hazardous substances, water pollution, air quality, and drinking water quality. Discusses past cleanup efforts, and offers an agenda for the future. Describes and analyzes the general environment of urban areas, and offers solutions for their special environmental problems.

Recycling Solid Waste. Milou Carolan. International City Management Association, 777 N. Capital St., NE, Suite 500, Washington, District of Columbia 20002-4201. (800) 745-8780. 1989. Integrated approach to waste management, focussing on the components of a successful recycling program.

The Revised Hazard Ranking System: Os and As. U.S. Environmental Protection Agency, Office of Solid Waste and Emergency Response, 401 M St. SW, Washington, District of Columbia 20460. (202) 260-2090. 1990.

Rush to Burn: Solving America's Garbage Crisis?. Island Press, 1718 Connecticut Ave. N.W., Suite 300, Washington, District of Columbia 20009. (202) 232-7933. 1989. Describes incineration, refuse and refuse disposal.

Solid Waste Shredding and Shredder Selection. Harvey W. Rogers. U.S. Environmental Protection Agency, 401 M St., S.W., Washington, District of Columbia 20460.

(202) 260-2090. 1974. Refuse and refuse disposal in the United States.

State and Local Government Solid Waste Management. James T. O'Reilly. Clark Boardman Callaghan, 155 Pfingsten Rd., Deerfield, Illinois 60015. (800) 221-9428. 1991. To be revised annually. Focuses on municipal solid waste issues.

Staying Out of Trouble: What You Should Know about the New Hazardous Waste Law. National Association of Manufacturers, 1331 Pennsylvania Ave., NW, Suite 1500 N., Washington, District of Columbia 20004. (202) 637-3000. 1985. Hazardous waste laws and legislation in the United States. Also covers refuse and disposal.

TAPPI Environmental Conference Proceedings, Seattle, WA, April 9-11, 1990. TAPPI Press, Technology Park/ Atlanta, PO Box 105113, Atlanta, Georgia 30348. (404) 446-1400. 1990. Contains 11 papers presented at the conference covering industrial pollution and its remedies.

Treatability Studies for Hazardous Waste Sites. Hazardous Waste Action Coalition, 1015 15th St. N.W., Suite 802, Washington, District of Columbia 20005. (202) 347-7474. 1990. Assesses the use of treatability studies for evaluating the effectiveness and cost of treatment technologies performed at hazardous waste sites.

HANDBOOKS AND MANUALS

Final Covers on Hazardous Waste Landfills and Surface Impoundments. Office of Solid Waste and Emergency Response, U.S. Environment Protection Agency, U.S. G.P.O., Washington, District of Columbia 20402-9325. (202) 783-3238. 1989. Technical Guidance Document series EPA/530-SW-89-047. Shipping list no. 89-483-P.

Handbook of Incineration Systems. Calvin R. Brunner. McGraw-Hill Science & Engineering Books, 11 West 19th St., New York, New York 10011. (212) 337-6010. 1991. Examines every type of modern incinerator, describes the analytical techniques required to utilize the equipment, explains the basic scientific principles involved, and defines the regulations that apply to various incineration facilities and procedures for upgrading existing facilities to conform to new, stricter operating standards.

The Solid Waste Handbook: A Practical Guide. William D. Robinson, ed. John Wiley & Sons, Inc., 605 3rd Ave., New York, New York 10158-0012. (212) 850-6000. 1986. Covers the field of solid waste management, including legislation, regulation, planning, finance, technologies, operations, economics administration, and future trends.

Superfund Handbook. Sidley & Austin, 696 Virginia Road, Concord, Massachusetts 01742. 1987. Law and legislation relating to refuse, refuse disposal, and its environmental aspects.

ONLINE DATA BASES

CERCLIS. Chemical Information Systems, Inc., 7215 York Rd., Baltimore, Maryland 21212. (301) 321-8440. Information on hazardous waste disposal sites that have either been listed by the EPA on the National Priority List (NPL) or nominated for consideration for the NPL.

Chemical Abstracts-CA. Chemical Abstracts Service, 2540 Olentangy River Rd., P.O. Box 3012, Columbus,

Ohio 43210. (800) 848-6533 or (614) 421-3600. Information sources include 9000 journals, patents from 27 countries, two industrial property organizations, new books, conference proceedings, and government research reports.

Computerized Engineering Index–COMPENDEX. Engineering Information Inc., 345 E. 47th St., New York, New York 10017. (212) 705-7600.

Enviro/Energyline Abstracts Plus. R. R. Bowker Co., 121 Chanlon Rd., New Providence, New Jersey 07974. (908) 464-6800.

Environmental Periodicals Bibliography. National Information Services Corp., Ste. 6, Wyman Towers, 3100 St. Paul St., Baltimore, Maryland 21218. (410)243-0797. Online version of abstract of same name.

Monthly Catalog of United States Government Publications. U.S. G.P.O., Supt. of Docs., PO Box 371954, Pittsburgh, Pennsylvania 15250-7954. (202) 512-0000.

National Technical Information Service. U.S. Department of Commerce, National Technical Information Service, Office of Data Base Services, 5285 Port Royal Rd., Springfield, Virginia 22161. (703) 487-4807. Bibliographic database of government sponsored research and technical reports.

PressNet Environmental Reports. Chemical Information Systems, Inc., 7215 York Rd., Baltimore, Maryland 21212. (301) 321-8440.

SCISEARCH. Institute for Scientific Information, University City Science Center, 3501 Market St., Philadelphia, Pennsylvania 19104. (215) 386-0100.

PERIODICALS AND NEWSLETTERS

Biodegradation. Kluwer Academic Publishers, 101 Philip Dr., Assinippi Park, Norwell, Massachusetts 02061-0358. (617) 871-6600. 1990-. Quarterly. Covers all aspects of science pertaining to the detoxification, recycling, amelioration or treatment of waste materials and pollutants by naturally occurring microbial strains, associations, or recombinant microorganisms.

Environment Week. King Communications Group, Inc., 627 National Press Bldg., Washington, District of Columbia 20045. (202) 638-4260. Weekly. Covers acid rain, solid waste and disposal, clean coal, nuclear and hazardous waste. Also available online.

Garbage: The Practical Journal for the Environment. Old House Journal Corp., 2 Main St., Gloucester, Massachusetts 01930. (508) 283-4629. Bimonthly. Issues in municipal wastes.

Inside the EPA'S Superfund Report. Inside Washington Publishers, PO Box 7167, Ben Franklin Station, Washington, District of Columbia 20044. Biweekly. Liability for hazardous substances pollution and damages.

Pollution Engineering. Cahners Publishing Co., 249 W. 17th St., New York, New York 10011. (212) 645-0067. 1969-. Monthly.

Solid Waste Report. Business Publishers, Inc., 951 Pershing Dr., Silver Spring, Maryland 20910-4464. (301) 587-6300. 1970-. Weekly. Covers the generation, collection, transportation, processing, resource recovery, recycling and ultimate disposal of municipal, commercial,

agricultural and nonhazardous industrial refuse. Also available online.

Solid Waste Systems. Government Refuse Collection and Disposal Association, 444 North LaBrea Ave., Los Angeles, California 90036. Bimonthly.

RESEARCH CENTERS AND INSTITUTES

Sanitary Engineering and Environmental Health Research Laboratory. University of California, Berkeley, 1301 South 46th, Building 112, Richmond, California 94804. (415) 231-9449.

TRADE ASSOCIATIONS AND PROFESSIONAL SOCIETIES

American Public Works Association. 106 W. 11th St., Ste. 1800, Kansas City, Missouri 64105-1806. (816) 472-6100.

American Society of Sanitary Engineering. Box 40362, Bay Village, Ohio 44140. (216) 835-3040.

Association of State and Territorial Solid Waste Management Officials. 444 North Capitol St., N.W., Suite 388, Washington, District of Columbia 20001. (202) 624-5828.

Center for Environmental Management. Tufts University, Curtis Hall, 474 Boston Ave., Medford, Massachusetts 02155. (617) 381-3486.

Hazardous Waste Treatment Council. 1440 New York Ave., Suite 310, Washington, District of Columbia 20005. (202) 783-0870.

SOLID WASTE ENERGY

See also: ANIMAL WASTES; METHANE; WASTE-TO-ENERGY SYSTEMS

ABSTRACTING AND INDEXING SERVICES

Applied Science and Technology Index. H.W. Wilson Co., 950 University Ave., Bronx, New York 10452. (800) 367-6770. Formerly Industrial Arts Index.

Biological and Agricultural Index. H.W. Wilson Co., 950 University Ave., Bronx, New York 10452. (800) 367-6770. 1916-. Monthly.

Chemical Abstracts. Chemical Abstracts Service, 2540 Olentangy River Rd., PO Box 3012, Columbus, Ohio 43210. (800) 848-6533. 1907-.

Engineering Index. The Engineering Index Inc., 345 E. 47th St., New York, New York 10017. 1962-.

Environment Abstracts. Bowker A & I Publishing, 121 Chanlon Rd., New Providence, New Jersey 07974. (908) 464-6800. 1974-.

Environment Index. Environment Information Center, Index Research Department, 124 E. 39th St., New York, New York 10016. 1971-. Annual.

Environmental Information Connection–EIC. Planning Information Program, Dept. of Urban and Regional Planning, University of Illinois, 1003 West Nevada, Urbana, Illinois 61801. (217) 333-1369. Also available online.

Environmental Periodicals Bibliography. Environmental Studies Institute, International Academy at Santa Barbara, 800 Garden St., Suite D, Santa Barbara, California 93101. (805) 965-5010. Also available online.

Pollution Abstracts. Cambridge Scientific Abstracts, 5161 River Rd., Bethesda, Maryland 20816. (301) 961-6750. Six/year. Indexes worldwide technical literature on environmental pollution. Covers air pollution, marine and freshwater pollution, sewage and wastewater treatment, waste management, toxicology and health, noise pollution, radiation, land pollution, and environmental policies, programs, legislation, and education. Also available online.

Science Citation Index. Institute for Scientific Information, 3501 Market St., Philadelphia, Pennsylvania 19104. 1961-.

BIBLIOGRAPHIES

EPA Publications Bibliography. U.S. Environmental Protection Agency, Library Systems Branch, 401 M St., SW, Washington, District of Columbia 20460. (202) 260-2090. Quarterly.

DIRECTORIES

Solid Waste & Power–Waste-to-Energy Industry Directory Issue. HCI Publications, 410 Archibald St., Kansas City, Missouri 64111. (816) 931-1311.

ENCYCLOPEDIAS AND DICTIONARIES

Dictionary of Environmental Engineering and Related Sciences: English-Spanish, Spanish-English. Jose T. Villate. Ediciones Universal, 3090 SW 8th St., Miami, Florida 33135. (305) 642-3355. 1979.

Encyclopedia of Environmental Science and Engineering. J.R. Pfafflin. Gordon and Breach Science Publishers, Inc., 270 8th Ave., New York, New York 10011. (212) 206-8900. 1992.

McGraw-Hill Encyclopedia of Environmental Science. Sybil P. Parker. McGraw-Hill Science & Engineering Books, 11 W. 19th St., New York, New York 10011. (212) 337-6010. 1980. Covers ecology, man's influence on nature, and environmental protection.

ONLINE DATA BASES

CERCLIS. Chemical Information Systems, Inc., 7215 York Rd., Baltimore, Maryland 21212. (301) 321-8440. Information on hazardous waste disposal sites that have either been listed by the EPA on the National Priority List (NPL) or nominated for consideration for the NPL.

Chemical Abstracts-CA. Chemical Abstracts Service, 2540 Olentangy River Rd., P.O. Box 3012, Columbus, Ohio 43210. (800) 848-6533 or (614) 421-3600. Information sources include 9000 journals, patents from 27 countries, two industrial property organizations, new books, conference proceedings, and government research reports.

Computerized Engineering Index–COMPENDEX. Engineering Information Inc., 345 E. 47th St., New York, New York 10017. (212) 705-7600.

Enviro/Energyline Abstracts Plus. R. R. Bowker Co., 121 Chanlon Rd., New Providence, New Jersey 07974. (908) 464-6800.

Environmental Periodicals Bibliography. National Information Services Corp., Ste. 6, Wyman Towers, 3100 St. Paul St., Baltimore, Maryland 21218. (410)243-0797. Online version of abstract of same name.

Monthly Catalog of United States Government Publications. U.S. G.P.O., Supt. of Docs., PO Box 371954, Pittsburgh, Pennsylvania 15250-7954. (202) 512-0000.

National Technical Information Service. U.S. Department of Commerce, National Technical Information Service, Office of Data Base Services, 5285 Port Royal Rd., Springfield, Virginia 22161. (703) 487-4807. Bibliographic database of government sponsored research and technical reports.

SCISEARCH. Institute for Scientific Information, University City Science Center, 3501 Market St., Philadelphia, Pennsylvania 19104. (215) 386-0100.

PERIODICALS AND NEWSLETTERS

Solid Waste and Power: The Waste-To-Energy Magazine. HCI Publications, 410 Archibald St., Suite 100, Kansas City, Missouri 64111. (816) 931-1311. Six times a year. Environmental considerations and proven approaches for dealing with concerns and requirements.

TRADE ASSOCIATIONS AND PROFESSIONAL SOCIETIES

American Society of Civil Engineers. 345 East 47th St., New York, New York 10017. (212) 705-7496.

Institute for Local Self-Reliance. 2425 18th St., N.W., Washington, District of Columbia 20009. (202) 232-4108.

SOLID WASTE EQUIPMENT

ABSTRACTING AND INDEXING SERVICES

Applied Science and Technology Index. H.W. Wilson Co., 950 University Ave., Bronx, New York 10452. (800) 367-6770. Formerly Industrial Arts Index.

Biological and Agricultural Index. H.W. Wilson Co., 950 University Ave., Bronx, New York 10452. (800) 367-6770. 1916-. Monthly.

Chemical Abstracts. Chemical Abstracts Service, 2540 Olentangy River Rd., PO Box 3012, Columbus, Ohio 43210. (800) 848-6533. 1907-.

Engineering Index. The Engineering Index Inc., 345 E. 47th St., New York, New York 10017. 1962-.

Environment Abstracts. Bowker A & I Publishing, 121 Chanlon Rd., New Providence, New Jersey 07974. (908) 464-6800. 1974-.

Environment Index. Environment Information Center, Index Research Department, 124 E. 39th St., New York, New York 10016. 1971-. Annual.

Environmental Information Connection–EIC. Planning Information Program, Dept. of Urban and Regional Planning, University of Illinois, 1003 West Nevada,

Urbana, Illinois 61801. (217) 333-1369. Also available online.

Environmental Periodicals Bibliography. Environmental Studies Institute, International Academy at Santa Barbara, 800 Garden St., Suite D, Santa Barbara, California 93101. (805) 965-5010. Also available online.

Pollution Abstracts. Cambridge Scientific Abstracts, 5161 River Rd., Bethesda, Maryland 20816. (301) 961-6750. Six/year. Indexes worldwide technical literature on environmental pollution. Covers air pollution, marine and freshwater pollution, sewage and wastewater treatment, waste management, toxicology and health, noise pollution, radiation, land pollution, and environmental policies, programs, legislation, and education. Also available online.

BIBLIOGRAPHIES

EPA Publications Bibliography. U.S. Environmental Protection Agency, Library Systems Branch, 401 M St., SW, Washington, District of Columbia 20460. (202) 260-2090. Quarterly.

ENCYCLOPEDIAS AND DICTIONARIES

Dictionary of Environmental Engineering and Related Sciences: English-Spanish, Spanish-English. Jose T. Villate. Ediciones Universal, 3090 SW 8th St., Miami, Florida 33135. (305) 642-3355. 1979.

Encyclopedia of Environmental Science and Engineering. J.R. Pfafflin. Gordon and Breach Science Publishers, Inc., 270 8th Ave., New York, New York 10011. (212) 206-8900. 1992.

Encyclopedia of Physical Science and Technology. Robert A. Meyers, ed. Academic Press, c/o Harcourt Brace Jovanovich Inc., 6277 Sea Harbor Dr., Orlando, Florida 32887. (800) 346-8648. Dictionary of engineering, technology and physical sciences.

McGraw-Hill Encyclopedia of Environmental Science. Sybil P. Parker. McGraw-Hill Science & Engineering Books, 11 W. 19th St., New York, New York 10011. (212) 337-6010. 1980. Covers ecology, man's influence on nature, and environmental protection.

HANDBOOKS AND MANUALS

The Solid Waste Handbook: A Practical Guide. William D. Robinson, ed. John Wiley & Sons, Inc., 605 3rd Ave., New York, New York 10158-0012. (212) 850-6000. 1986. Covers the field of solid waste management, including legislation, regulation, planning, finance, technologies, operations, economics administration, and future trends.

ONLINE DATA BASES

Chemical Abstracts-CA. Chemical Abstracts Service, 2540 Olentangy River Rd., P.O. Box 3012, Columbus, Ohio 43210. (800) 848-6533 or (614) 421-3600. Information sources include 9000 journals, patents from 27 countries, two industrial property organizations, new books, conference proceedings, and government research reports.

Computerized Engineering Index–COMPENDEX. Engineering Information Inc., 345 E. 47th St., New York, New York 10017. (212) 705-7600.

Enviro/Energyline Abstracts Plus. R. R. Bowker Co., 121 Chanlon Rd., New Providence, New Jersey 07974. (908) 464-6800.

Environmental Periodicals Bibliography. National Information Services Corp., Ste. 6, Wyman Towers, 3100 St. Paul St., Baltimore, Maryland 21218. (410)243-0797. Online version of abstract of same name.

Monthly Catalog of United States Government Publications. U.S. G.P.O., Supt. of Docs., PO Box 371954, Pittsburgh, Pennsylvania 15250-7954. (202) 512-0000.

National Technical Information Service. U.S. Department of Commerce, National Technical Information Service, Office of Data Base Services, 5285 Port Royal Rd., Springfield, Virginia 22161. (703) 487-4807. Bibliographic database of government sponsored research and technical reports.

TRADE ASSOCIATIONS AND PROFESSIONAL SOCIETIES

American Institute of Chemical Engineers. 345 East 47th St., New York, New York 10017. (212) 705-7338.

American Institute of Chemists. 7315 Wisconsin Ave., Bethesda, Maryland 20814. (301) 652-2447.

SOLID WASTE FUEL

ABSTRACTING AND INDEXING SERVICES

Applied Science and Technology Index. H.W. Wilson Co., 950 University Ave., Bronx, New York 10452. (800) 367-6770. Formerly Industrial Arts Index.

Biological and Agricultural Index. H.W. Wilson Co., 950 University Ave., Bronx, New York 10452. (800) 367-6770. 1916-. Monthly.

Chemical Abstracts. Chemical Abstracts Service, 2540 Olentangy River Rd., PO Box 3012, Columbus, Ohio 43210. (800) 848-6533. 1907-.

Engineering Index. The Engineering Index Inc., 345 E. 47th St., New York, New York 10017. 1962-.

Environment Abstracts. Bowker A & I Publishing, 121 Chanlon Rd., New Providence, New Jersey 07974. (908) 464-6800. 1974-.

Environment Index. Environment Information Center, Index Research Department, 124 E. 39th St., New York, New York 10016. 1971-. Annual.

Environmental Information Connection–EIC. Planning Information Program, Dept. of Urban and Regional Planning, University of Illinois, 1003 West Nevada, Urbana, Illinois 61801. (217) 333-1369. Also available online.

Environmental Periodicals Bibliography. Environmental Studies Institute, International Academy at Santa Barbara, 800 Garden St., Suite D, Santa Barbara, California 93101. (805) 965-5010. Also available online.

Pollution Abstracts. Cambridge Scientific Abstracts, 5161 River Rd., Bethesda, Maryland 20816. (301) 961-6750. Six/year. Indexes worldwide technical literature on environmental pollution. Covers air pollution, marine and freshwater pollution, sewage and wastewater treatment, waste management, toxicology and health, noise pollu-

tion, radiation, land pollution, and environmental policies, programs, legislation, and education. Also available online.

Science Citation Index. Institute for Scientific Information, 3501 Market St., Philadelphia, Pennsylvania 19104. 1961-.

BIBLIOGRAPHIES

EPA Publications Bibliography. U.S. Environmental Protection Agency, Library Systems Branch, 401 M St., SW, Washington, District of Columbia 20460. (202) 260-2090. Quarterly.

ENCYCLOPEDIAS AND DICTIONARIES

Encyclopedia of Physical Science and Technology. Robert A. Meyers, ed. Academic Press, c/o Harcourt Brace Jovanovich Inc., 6277 Sea Harbor Dr., Orlando, Florida 32887. (800) 346-8648. Dictionary of engineering, technology and physical sciences.

McGraw-Hill Encyclopedia of Environmental Science. Sybil P. Parker. McGraw-Hill Science & Engineering Books, 11 W. 19th St., New York, New York 10011. (212) 337-6010. 1980. Covers ecology, man's influence on nature, and environmental protection.

ONLINE DATA BASES

Chemical Abstracts-CA. Chemical Abstracts Service, 2540 Olentangy River Rd., P.O. Box 3012, Columbus, Ohio 43210. (800) 848-6533 or (614) 421-3600. Information sources include 9000 journals, patents from 27 countries, two industrial property organizations, new books, conference proceedings, and government research reports.

Computerized Engineering Index–COMPENDEX. Engineering Information Inc., 345 E. 47th St., New York, New York 10017. (212) 705-7600.

Enviro/Energyline Abstracts Plus. R. R. Bowker Co., 121 Chanlon Rd., New Providence, New Jersey 07974. (908) 464-6800.

Environmental Periodicals Bibliography. National Information Services Corp., Ste. 6, Wyman Towers, 3100 St. Paul St., Baltimore, Maryland 21218. (410)243-0797. Online version of abstract of same name.

Monthly Catalog of United States Government Publications. U.S. G.P.O., Supt. of Docs., PO Box 371954, Pittsburgh, Pennsylvania 15250-7954. (202) 512-0000.

National Technical Information Service. U.S. Department of Commerce, National Technical Information Service, Office of Data Base Services, 5285 Port Royal Rd., Springfield, Virginia 22161. (703) 487-4807. Bibliographic database of government sponsored research and technical reports.

SCISEARCH. Institute for Scientific Information, University City Science Center, 3501 Market St., Philadelphia, Pennsylvania 19104. (215) 386-0100.

TRADE ASSOCIATIONS AND PROFESSIONAL SOCIETIES

American Institute of Chemical Engineers. 345 East 47th St., New York, New York 10017. (212) 705-7338.

American Institute of Chemists. 7315 Wisconsin Ave., Bethesda, Maryland 20814. (301) 652-2447.

SOLID WASTE MANAGEMENT

See also: HAZARDOUS WASTES; POLLUTION; RADIOACTIVE WASTES; RECYCLING (WASTES, ETC.)

ABSTRACTING AND INDEXING SERVICES

Applied Science and Technology Index. H.W. Wilson Co., 950 University Ave., Bronx, New York 10452. (800) 367-6770. Formerly Industrial Arts Index.

Biological and Agricultural Index. H.W. Wilson Co., 950 University Ave., Bronx, New York 10452. (800) 367-6770. 1916-. Monthly.

Chemical Abstracts. Chemical Abstracts Service, 2540 Olentangy River Rd., PO Box 3012, Columbus, Ohio 43210. (800) 848-6533. 1907-.

Engineering Index. The Engineering Index Inc., 345 E. 47th St., New York, New York 10017. 1962-.

Environment Abstracts. Bowker A & I Publishing, 121 Chanlon Rd., New Providence, New Jersey 07974. (908) 464-6800. 1974-.

Environment Index. Environment Information Center, Index Research Department, 124 E. 39th St., New York, New York 10016. 1971-. Annual.

Environmental Information Connection–EIC. Planning Information Program, Dept. of Urban and Regional Planning, University of Illinois, 1003 West Nevada, Urbana, Illinois 61801. (217) 333-1369. Also available online.

Environmental Periodicals Bibliography. Environmental Studies Institute, International Academy at Santa Barbara, 800 Garden St., Suite D, Santa Barbara, California 93101. (805) 965-5010. Also available online.

Geographical Abstracts. London School of Economics, Dept. of Geography, Regency House, 34 Duke St., London, England 1966-. Continued by Geo Abstracts issued in 6 parts: Pt. A. Landforms and the quaternary; Pt. B. Biogeography and Climatology; Pt. C. Economic geography; Pt. D. Social geography and cartography; Pt. E. Sedimentology; Pt. F. Regional and community planning.

INIS Atomindex. International Atomic Energy Agency, Wagramerstrasse 5, Vienna, Austria A-1400. 222 23606198. 1988-. Semiannual. Abstracts nuclear energy and nuclear physics topics from journals, conferences, technical reports and other related publications. Issued in 6 parts: Personal Author, Corporate Entry, Subject, Report, Standard Patent, Conference (by place), Conference (by date).

Pollution Abstracts. Cambridge Scientific Abstracts, 5161 River Rd., Bethesda, Maryland 20816. (301) 961-6750. Six/year. Indexes worldwide technical literature on environmental pollution. Covers air pollution, marine and freshwater pollution, sewage and wastewater treatment, waste management, toxicology and health, noise pollution, radiation, land pollution, and environmental policies, programs, legislation, and education. Also available online.

Science Citation Index. Institute for Scientific Information, 3501 Market St., Philadelphia, Pennsylvania 19104. 1961-.

BIBLIOGRAPHIES

EPA Publications Bibliography. U.S. Environmental Protection Agency, Library Systems Branch, 401 M St., SW, Washington, District of Columbia 20460. (202) 260-2090. Quarterly.

DIRECTORIES

Hazardous Waste Management Facilities Directory: Treatment, Storage, Disposal and Recycling. U. S. Environmental Protection Agency. Noyes Publications, 120 Mill Rd., Park Ridge, New Jersey 07656. (201) 391-8484. 1990. Provides geographical listings of 1045 commercial hazardous waste management facilities, along with information on the types of commercial services offered and types of wastes managed. It is a compilation of recent data from EPA data bases and includes the facility name, address, contact person, and phone number.

Solid Waste Education Recycling Directory. Teresa Jones, et al. Lewis Publishers, 200 Corporate Blvd. NW, Boca Raton, Florida 33431. (407) 994-0555 or (800)272-7737. 1990. Summarizes recycling education curricula for each state covering all levels, K-12. Provides names, addresses, phone numbers, information about the availability of materials, how you collect them, and how much they cost.

Waste Age–Directory to Waste Systems and Services Supplement. National Solid Waste Management Association, 1730 Rhode Island Ave., NW, Suite 1000, Washington, District of Columbia 20036. (202) 659-4613.

ENCYCLOPEDIAS AND DICTIONARIES

Dictionary of Environmental Engineering and Related Sciences: English-Spanish, Spanish-English. Jose T. Villate. Ediciones Universal, 3090 SW 8th St., Miami, Florida 33135. (305) 642-3355. 1979.

Encyclopedia of Environmental Science and Engineering. J.R. Pfafflin. Gordon and Breach Science Publishers, Inc., 270 8th Ave., New York, New York 10011. (212) 206-8900. 1992.

The Encyclopedia of Soil Science. Rhodes W. Fairbridge. Academic Press, c/o Harcourt Brace Jovanovich Inc., 6277 Sea Harbor Dr., Orlando, Florida 32887. (800) 346-8648. 1979-. Includes soil physics, soil chemistry, soil biology, soil fertility and plant nutrition, soil genesis, classification and cartography.

Grzimek's Encyclopedia of Ecology. Bernhard Grzimek. Van Nostrand Reinhold, 115 5th Ave., New York, New York 10003. (212) 254-3232. 1976.

McGraw-Hill Encyclopedia of Environmental Science. Sybil P. Parker. McGraw-Hill Science & Engineering Books, 11 W. 19th St., New York, New York 10011. (212) 337-6010. 1980. Covers ecology, man's influence on nature, and environmental protection.

McGraw-Hill Encyclopedia of Science and Technology. McGraw-Hill, 1221 Avenue of the Americas, New York, New York 10020. (212) 512-2000 or (800) 262-4729. 1992. Seventh edition. Issued in multiple volumes including index. Includes all science and technology broad subject areas.

North American Reference Encyclopedia of Ecology and Pollution. William White. North American Pub. Co., 401 N. Broad St., Philadelphia, Pennsylvania 19108. (215) 238-5300. 1972.

Van Nostrand's Scientific Encyclopedia. Glenn D. Considine, ed. Van Nostrand Reinhold, 115 5th Ave., New York, New York 10003. (212) 254-3232. 1983. Sixth edition. Includes all broad subject areas in science.

GENERAL WORKS

Characterization of Municipal Waste Combustor Ashes and Leachates from Municipal Solid Waste Landfills, Monofills, and Codisposal Sites. U.S. Environmental Protection Agency, Office of Solid Waste, 401 M St., S.W., Washington, District of Columbia 20460. (202) 260-2090. 1987.

The Environmental Challenge of the 1990's. U.S. Environmental Protection Agency, 401 M St. SW, Washington, District of Columbia 20009. (202) 260-2090. 1991. Provides an overview of past and present projects for pollution prevention, focusing on the promotion of clean technologies and clean products in both the public and private sectors. Covers new prevention ideas relating to solid and hazardous wastes, pesticides, drinking water, wastewater and toxic substances.

Hazardous Waste from Small Quantity Generators. Seymour I. Schwartz, et al. Island Press, 1718 Connecticut Ave. N.W., Suite 300, Washington, District of Columbia 20009. (202) 232-7933. 1990. Examines the role small businesses play in degrading the environment. Includes information on the extent and seriousness of the problem, regulations; and liability issues; national, state, and local programs for SQ Gas in California, analysis of methods for managing SQG waste; policy options for promoting legal methods; and discouraging illegal methods.

The Hazardous Waste System. U.S. Environmental Protection Agency, Office of Solid Waste and Emergency Response, 401 M St., SW April 9, 1992, Washington, District of Columbia 20460. (202) 382-4610. 1987. Hazardous wastes law and legislation in the United States.

Incineration for Site Cleanup and Destruction of Hazardous Wastes. Howard E. Hesketh. Technomic Publishing Co., 851 New Holland Ave., Box 3535, Lancaster, Pennsylvania 17604. (717) 291-5609; (800) 233-9936. 1990.

Industrial Environmental Control. A. M. Springer. John Wiley & Sons, Inc., 605 3rd Ave., New York, New York 10158-0012. (212) 850-6000. 1986. Covers in great detail all the basic information regarding industrial pollution and its treatment.

Leaching and Hydraulic Properties of Retorted Oil Shale Including Effects from Codisposal of Wastewater. David B. McWhorter. U.S. Environmental Protection Agency, Air and Energy Engineering Research Laboratory, MD 75, Research Triangle Park, North Carolina 27711. (919) 541-2184. 1987.

Madison Conference of Applied Research & Practice on Municipal & Industrial Waste. Dept. of Engineering Professional Development, University of Wisconsin-

Madison, Madison, Wisconsin 53706. 1990. Annual. Sewage disposal, factory and trade waste, soil liners, ground water clean up, landfill leachate treatment, groundwater monitary systems, evaluation of groundwater and soil gas remedial action; leachate generation estimates and landfills.

Packaging and the Environment: Alternatives, Trends, and Solutions. Susan E. M. Selke. Technomic Publishing Co., 851 New Holland Ave., Box 3535, Lancaster, Pennsylvania 17604. (717) 291-5609. 1990. Review of the contribution of packaging to various environmental problems.

Principles of Hazardous Materials Management. Roger D. Griffin. Lewis Publishers, 2000 Corporate Blvd., N.W., Boca Raton, Florida 33431. (407) 994-0555 or (800) 272-7737. 1988. Gives basic understanding of the principles involved in each major topic represented: risk assessment, air toxics, groundwater, management methods, federal laws, transportation, waste minimization, treatment and disposal, toxicology, and analytical methods.

The Revised Hazard Ranking System: Os and As. U.S. Environmental Protection Agency, Office of Solid Waste and Emergency Response, 401 M St. SW, Washington, District of Columbia 20460. (202) 260-2090. 1990.

The Solid Waste Dilemma: An Agenda for Action. U.S. Environmental Protection Agency, Office of Solid Waste and Emergency Response, 401 M St. SW, Washington, District of Columbia 20460. (202) 260-2090. 1989.

Solid Waste Management and the Environment: The Mounting Garbage and Trash Crisis. Homer A. Neal. Prentice-Hall, Rte. 9W, Englewood Cliffs, New Jersey 07632. (201) 592-2000. 1987. Environmental aspects of refuse and refuse disposal.

State and Local Government Solid Waste Management. James T. O'Reilly. Clark Boardman Callaghan, 155 Pfingsten Rd., Deerfield, Illinois 60015. (800) 221-9428. 1991. To be revised annually. Focuses on municipal solid waste issues.

Treatment Technologies. Environment Protection Agency. Government Institutes, Inc., 4 Research Pl., Ste. 200, Rockville, Maryland 20850. (301)921-2300. 1991. 2nd ed. Provides a clear explanation of 24 treatment technologies and evaluates the effectiveness of the design and operations of each type of treatment. This new edition has more supporting numerical data, examples for a better understanding of the technology and an updated reference for specific industrial wastes.

Waste Reduction: Policy and Practice. Waste Management Inc. and Piper & Marbury. Executive Enterprises Publications Co., Inc., 22 W. 21st St., New York, New York 10010-6990. (212) 645-7880. 1990. Examines waste reduction on a national level. Gives an overview of the makeup of hazardous waste and municipal solid waste streams and different means of reducing the generation of those streams. Case studies of waste reduction in industry are described.

GOVERNMENTAL ORGANIZATIONS

Solid Waste Authority: Solid Waste Management. Executive Director, PO Box 40285, Minallas Station, San Juan, Puerto Rico 00940. (809) 765-7584.

U.S. Environmental Protection Agency: National Enforcement Investigations Center. Building 53, Box 25227, Denver, Colorado 80225. (303) 236-5100.

U.S. Environmental Protection Agency: Office of Solid Waste. 401 M St., S.W., Washington, District of Columbia 20460. (202) 382-4627.

HANDBOOKS AND MANUALS

Guide to the Management of Hazardous Waste: A Handbook for the Businessman and the Concerned Citizen. J. William Haun. Fulcrum Publishing, 350 Indiana St., Ste. 350, Golden, Colorado 80401. (303) 277-1623. 1991. Fact book on hazardous waste management, including factory and trade waste, and hazardous waste law and legislation in the United States.

Handbook of Incineration Systems. Calvin R. Brunner. McGraw-Hill Science & Engineering Books, 11 West 19th St., New York, New York 10011. (212) 337-6010. 1991. Examines every type of modern incinerator, describes the analytical techniques required to utilize the equipment, explains the basic scientific principles involved, and defines the regulations that apply to various incineration facilities and procedures for upgrading existing facilities to conform to new, stricter operating standards.

The Solid Waste Handbook: A Practical Guide. William D. Robinson, ed. John Wiley & Sons, Inc., 605 3rd Ave., New York, New York 10158-0012. (212) 850-6000. 1986. Covers the field of solid waste management, including legislation, regulation, planning, finance, technologies, operations, economics administration, and future trends.

Solid Waste Recycling; The Complete Resource Guide. Bureau of National Affairs, 1231 25th St. N.W., Washington, District of Columbia 20037. (800) 372-1033. 1990. Details federal and state laws and regulations, legal issues and local initiatives relating to waste crisis. Includes case studies of programs, surveys, studies, reports guidelines, recommendations, resources and references.

Standard Handbook of Hazardous Waste Treatment and Disposal. Harry M. Freeman, ed. McGraw-Hill Science & Engineering Books, 11 West 19th St., New York, New York 10011. (212) 337-6010. 1989. A reference of alternatives and innovative technologies for managing hazardous waste and cleaning up abandoned disposal sites.

ONLINE DATA BASES

Chemical Abstracts-CA. Chemical Abstracts Service, 2540 Olentangy River Rd., P.O. Box 3012, Columbus, Ohio 43210. (800) 848-6533 or (614) 421-3600. Information sources include 9000 journals, patents from 27 countries, two industrial property organizations, new books, conference proceedings, and government research reports.

Computerized Engineering Index–COMPENDEX. Engineering Information Inc., 345 E. 47th St., New York, New York 10017. (212) 705-7600.

Enviro/Energyline Abstracts Plus. R. R. Bowker Co., 121 Chanlon Rd., New Providence, New Jersey 07974. (908) 464-6800.

Environmental Periodicals Bibliography. National Information Services Corp., Ste. 6, Wyman Towers, 3100 St.

Paul St., Baltimore, Maryland 21218. (410)243-0797. Online version of abstract of same name.

Monthly Catalog of United States Government Publications. U.S. G.P.O., Supt. of Docs., PO Box 371954, Pittsburgh, Pennsylvania 15250-7954. (202) 512-0000.

National Technical Information Service. U.S. Department of Commerce, National Technical Information Service, Office of Data Base Services, 5285 Port Royal Rd., Springfield, Virginia 22161. (703) 487-4807. Bibliographic database of government sponsored research and technical reports.

SCISEARCH. Institute for Scientific Information, University City Science Center, 3501 Market St., Philadelphia, Pennsylvania 19104. (215) 386-0100.

PERIODICALS AND NEWSLETTERS

Civil Engineering ASCE. American Society of Civil Engineers, 345 E 47th St., New York, New York 10017. (212) 705-7288; (800) 548-2723. Monthly. Professional journal that offers a forum for free exchange of ideas relevant to the profession of civil engineering. Covers in regular columns, engineering news, legal trends in engineering, calendar of events, membership news, publications and other items of interest to civil engineers. Formerly, Civil Engineering.

Hazardous Materials World. HazMat World, Circulation Dept., P.O. Box 3021, Wheaton, Illinois 60137. (708) 858-1888. Monthly. Covers biobusiness, hazardous wastes management, and hazardous substance safety measures.

INFORM Reports. INFORM Inc., 381 Park Ave., So., New York, New York 10016. (212) 689-4040. Quarterly. INFORM is a nonprofit environmental research & education organization for the preservation and conservation of natural resources and public health.

Management of World Wastes. Communication Channels, 6255 Barfield Road, Atlanta, Georgia 30328. (404) 256-9800. Monthly. Covers public and private waste operations.

Solid Waste Management Newsletter. Cook College, Rutgers University, New Brunswick, New Jersey 08903. Bimonthly.

The Solid Waste Management Newsletter. Office of Technology Transfer (M/C 922), School of Public Health, University of Illinois at Chicago, Box 6998, Chicago, Illinois 60680. (312) 996-6927. Monthly. Provides a summary of important aspects in solid waste management. Subject matter for the newsletter reflects the hierarchy of methods for waste management specified in the Illinois Solid Waste Management Act of 1986.

Solid Waste Report. Business Publishers, Inc., 951 Pershing Dr., Silver Spring, Maryland 20910-4464. (301) 587-6300. 1970-. Weekly. Covers the generation, collection, transportation, processing, resource recovery, recycling and ultimate disposal of municipal, commercial, agricultural and nonhazardous industrial refuse. Also available online.

Washington Update. Association of Local Air Pollution Control Officials, 444 N. Capitol St, NW, Suite 306, Washington, District of Columbia 20001. (202) 624-7864. Monthly. Congressional and Environmental Protection Agency activities, and current issues related to air pollution.

Waste Age. National Solid Waste Management Association, 1730 Rhode Island Avenue, NW, Ste. 1000, Washington, District of Columbia 20036. (202) 659-4613. Monthly. Covers control and use of solid, hazardous and liquid wastes.

RESEARCH CENTERS AND INSTITUTES

Renew America. 17 16th Street, N. W., Suite 710, Washington, District of Columbia 20036. (202) 232-2252.

STATISTICS SOURCES

Solid Waste Management in the Food Distribution Industry. Food Marketing Institute, Research Department, 1750 K St., NW, Washington, District of Columbia 20006. 1990.

TRADE ASSOCIATIONS AND PROFESSIONAL SOCIETIES

American Public Works Association. 106 W. 11th St., Ste. 1800, Kansas City, Missouri 64105-1806. (816) 472-6100.

American Society of Sanitary Engineering. Box 40362, Bay Village, Ohio 44140. (216) 835-3040.

Association of State and Territorial Solid Waste Management Officials. 444 North Capitol St., N.W., Suite 388, Washington, District of Columbia 20001. (202) 624-5828.

Chemical Waste Transportation Council. 1730 Rhode Island Ave., N.W., Suite 1000, Washington, District of Columbia 20036. (202) 659-4613.

INFORM. 381 Park Avenue S., New York, New York 10016. (212) 689-4040.

National Solid Wastes Management Association. 1730 Rhode Island Ave., N.W., Suite 1000, Washington, District of Columbia 20036. (202) 659-4613.

SOLID WASTE MILLING

See: SOLID WASTES

GENERAL WORKS

Rush to Burn: Solving America's Garbage Crisis?. Island Press, 1718 Connecticut Ave. N.W., Suite 300, Washington, District of Columbia 20009. (202) 232-7933. 1989. Describes incineration, refuse and refuse disposal.

SOLID WASTE REDUCTION

See: WASTE REDUCTION

SOLID WASTE REPROCESSING

See: WASTE REPROCESSING

SOLID WASTE STORAGE
See: WASTE STORAGE

SOLID WASTE TREATMENT

ABSTRACTING AND INDEXING SERVICES

Applied Science and Technology Index. H.W. Wilson Co., 950 University Ave., Bronx, New York 10452. (800) 367-6770. Formerly Industrial Arts Index.

Biological and Agricultural Index. H.W. Wilson Co., 950 University Ave., Bronx, New York 10452. (800) 367-6770. 1916-. Monthly.

Chemical Abstracts. Chemical Abstracts Service, 2540 Olentangy River Rd., PO Box 3012, Columbus, Ohio 43210. (800) 848-6533. 1907-.

Engineering Index. The Engineering Index Inc., 345 E. 47th St., New York, New York 10017. 1962-.

Environment Abstracts. Bowker A & I Publishing, 121 Chanlon Rd., New Providence, New Jersey 07974. (908) 464-6800. 1974-.

Environment Index. Environment Information Center, Index Research Department, 124 E. 39th St., New York, New York 10016. 1971-. Annual.

Environmental Information Connection–EIC. Planning Information Program, Dept. of Urban and Regional Planning, University of Illinois, 1003 West Nevada, Urbana, Illinois 61801. (217) 333-1369. Also available online.

Environmental Periodicals Bibliography. Environmental Studies Institute, International Academy at Santa Barbara, 800 Garden St., Suite D, Santa Barbara, California 93101. (805) 965-5010. Also available online.

General Science Index. H. W. Wilson Co., 950 University Ave., Bronx, New York 10452. 1978-. Monthly, also issued in annual cumulation. Cumulative subject index to English language periodicals in the subject fields of astronomy, botany, chemistry, earth science, environment and conservation, food and nutrition, genetics, mathematics, medicine and health, microbiology, oceanography, physics, physiology and zoology.

Index to Scientific Book Contents. Institute for Scientific Information, 3501 Market St., Philadelphia, Pennsylvania 19104. (800) 523-1857. 1985-. Annual. Gives contents of science books published.

Pollution Abstracts. Cambridge Scientific Abstracts, 5161 River Rd., Bethesda, Maryland 20816. (301) 961-6750. Six/year. Indexes worldwide technical literature on environmental pollution. Covers air pollution, marine and freshwater pollution, sewage and wastewater treatment, waste management, toxicology and health, noise pollution, radiation, land pollution, and environmental policies, programs, legislation, and education. Also available online.

Science Citation Index. Institute for Scientific Information, 3501 Market St., Philadelphia, Pennsylvania 19104. 1961-.

BIBLIOGRAPHIES

EPA Publications Bibliography. U.S. Environmental Protection Agency, Library Systems Branch, 401 M St., SW, Washington, District of Columbia 20460. (202) 260-2090. Quarterly.

DIRECTORIES

Waste Age–Directory to Waste Systems and Services Supplement. National Solid Waste Management Association, 1730 Rhode Island Ave., NW, Suite 1000, Washington, District of Columbia 20036. (202) 659-4613.

ENCYCLOPEDIAS AND DICTIONARIES

Dictionary of Environmental Engineering and Related Sciences: English-Spanish, Spanish-English. Jose T. Villate. Ediciones Universal, 3090 SW 8th St., Miami, Florida 33135. (305) 642-3355. 1979.

Dictionary of Environmental Protection Technology: In Four Languages, English, German, French, Russian. Egon Seidel. Elsevier Science Publishing Co., 655 Avenue of the Americas, New York, New York 10010. (212) 984-5800. 1988.

Encyclopedia of Environmental Science and Engineering. J.R. Pfafflin. Gordon and Breach Science Publishers, Inc., 270 8th Ave., New York, New York 10011. (212) 206-8900. 1992.

Encyclopedia of Physical Science and Technology. Robert A. Meyers, ed. Academic Press, c/o Harcourt Brace Jovanovich Inc., 6277 Sea Harbor Dr., Orlando, Florida 32887. (800) 346-8648. Dictionary of engineering, technology and physical sciences.

English-Russian Dictionary of Environmental Protection: About 14,000 Terms. E.L. Milovanov. Pergamon Microforms International, Inc., Fairview Park, Elmsford, New York 10523. (914) 592-7720. 1981.

Environmental Engineering Dictionary. C. C. Lee. Government Institutes, Inc., 4 Research Pl., Ste. 200, Rockville, Maryland 20850. (301) 921-2300. 1989. Defines over 6000 engineering terms relating to pollutioncontrol technologies, monitoring, risk assessment, sampling andanalysis, quality control, permitting, and environmentally-regulated engineering and science. Includes bibliographical references (p. 612-627).

McGraw-Hill Encyclopedia of Environmental Science. Sybil P. Parker. McGraw-Hill Science & Engineering Books, 11 W. 19th St., New York, New York 10011. (212) 337-6010. 1980. Covers ecology, man's influence on nature, and environmental protection.

McGraw-Hill Encyclopedia of Science and Technology. McGraw-Hill, 1221 Avenue of the Americas, New York, New York 10020. (212) 512-2000 or (800) 262-4729. 1992. Seventh edition. Issued in multiple volumes including index. Includes all science and technology broad subject areas.

Van Nostrand's Scientific Encyclopedia. Glenn D. Considine, ed. Van Nostrand Reinhold, 115 5th Ave., New York, New York 10003. (212) 254-3232. 1983. Sixth edition. Includes all broad subject areas in science.

GENERAL WORKS

Hazardous Waste from Small Quantity Generators. Seymour I. Schwartz, et al. Island Press, 1718 Connecticut Ave. N.W., Suite 300, Washington, District of Columbia 20009. (202) 232-7933. 1990. Examines the role small businesses play in degrading the environment. Includes information on the extent and seriousness of the problem, regulations; and liability issues; national, state, and local programs for SQ Gas in California, analysis of methods for managing SQG waste; policy options for promoting legal methods; and discouraging illegal methods.

How to Select Hazardous Waste Treatment Technologies for Soil and Sludges: Alternative, Innovative and Emerging Technologies. Tim Holden, et al. Noyes Publications, 120 Mill Rd., Park Ridge, New Jersey 07656. (201) 391-8484. 1989. Guide for screening feasible alternative, innovative and emerging treatment technologies for contaminated soils and sludges at CERCLA (Superfund) sites. The technology data were selected from individual treatment technology vendors.

Proceedings of the 44th Industrial Waste Conference May 1989, Purdue University. John W. Bell, ed. Lewis Publishers, 2000 Corporate Blvd., N.W., Boca Raton, Florida 33431. (407) 994-0555 or (800) 272-7737. 1990. Includes new research, case histories and operating data, on every conceivable facet of today's big problem with unparalleled appropriate, usable information and data for current industrial waste problems.

State and Local Government Solid Waste Management. James T. O'Reilly. Clark Boardman Callaghan, 155 Pfingsten Rd., Deerfield, Illinois 60015. (800) 221-9428. 1991. To be revised annually. Focuses on municipal solid waste issues.

Waste Reduction: Policy and Practice. Waste Management Inc. and Piper & Marbury. Executive Enterprises Publications Co., Inc., 22 W. 21st St., New York, New York 10010-6990. (212) 645-7880. 1990. Examines waste reduction on a national level. Gives an overview of the makeup of hazardous waste and municipal solid waste streams and different means of reducing the generation of those streams. Case studies of waste reduction in industry are described.

HANDBOOKS AND MANUALS

Industrial and Hazardous Waste Treatment. Nelson Leonard Nemerow and Avijit Dasgupta. Van Nostrand Reinhold, 115 5th Ave., New York, New York 10003. (212) 254-3232. 1991. Factory and trade waste, and hazardous waste purification.

Standard Handbook of Hazardous Waste Treatment and Disposal. Harry M. Freeman, ed. McGraw-Hill Science & Engineering Books, 11 West 19th St., New York, New York 10011. (212) 337-6010. 1989. A reference of alternatives and innovative technologies for managing hazardous waste and cleaning up abandoned disposal sites.

ONLINE DATA BASES

CERCLIS. Chemical Information Systems, Inc., 7215 York Rd., Baltimore, Maryland 21212. (301) 321-8440. Information on hazardous waste disposal sites that have either been listed by the EPA on the National Priority List (NPL) or nominated for consideration for the NPL.

Chemical Abstracts-CA. Chemical Abstracts Service, 2540 Olentangy River Rd., P.O. Box 3012, Columbus, Ohio 43210. (800) 848-6533 or (614) 421-3600. Information sources include 9000 journals, patents from 27 countries, two industrial property organizations, new books, conference proceedings, and government research reports.

Computerized Engineering Index–COMPENDEX. Engineering Information Inc., 345 E. 47th St., New York, New York 10017. (212) 705-7600.

Enviro/Energyline Abstracts Plus. R. R. Bowker Co., 121 Chanlon Rd., New Providence, New Jersey 07974. (908) 464-6800.

Environment Reporter. Bureau of National Affairs, 1231 25th St., N.W., Rm. 215, Washington, District of Columbia 20037. (800) 372-1033. Online version of periodical of the same name.

Environmental Periodicals Bibliography. National Information Services Corp., Ste. 6, Wyman Towers, 3100 St. Paul St., Baltimore, Maryland 21218. (410)243-0797. Online version of abstract of same name.

Monthly Catalog of United States Government Publications. U.S. G.P.O., Supt. of Docs., PO Box 371954, Pittsburgh, Pennsylvania 15250-7954. (202) 512-0000.

National Technical Information Service. U.S. Department of Commerce, National Technical Information Service, Office of Data Base Services, 5285 Port Royal Rd., Springfield, Virginia 22161. (703) 487-4807. Bibliographic database of government sponsored research and technical reports.

SCISEARCH. Institute for Scientific Information, University City Science Center, 3501 Market St., Philadelphia, Pennsylvania 19104. (215) 386-0100.

PERIODICALS AND NEWSLETTERS

Civil Engineering ASCE. American Society of Civil Engineers, 345 E 47th St., New York, New York 10017. (212) 705-7288; (800) 548-2723. Monthly. Professional journal that offers a forum for free exchange of ideas relevant to the profession of civil engineering. Covers in regular columns, engineering news, legal trends in engineering, calendar of events, membership news, publications and other items of interest to civil engineers. Formerly, Civil Engineering.

Defense Cleanup. Pasha Publications, 1401 Wilson Blvd., Suite 900, Arlington, Virginia 22209. (703) 528-1244. Weekly. Reports on projects to analyze, recycle, and dispose of defense weapons.

Environment Reporter. Bureau of National Affairs, 1231 25th St. NW, Washington, District of Columbia 20037. (800) 372-1033. Weekly. Issues of pollution control and environmental activity. Also available online.

Management of World Wastes. Communication Channels, 6255 Barfield Road, Atlanta, Georgia 30328. (404) 256-9800. Monthly. Covers public and private waste operations.

Solid Waste Report. Business Publishers, Inc., 951 Pershing Dr., Silver Spring, Maryland 20910-4464. (301) 587-6300. 1970-. Weekly. Covers the generation, collection, transportation, processing, resource recovery, recycling and ultimate disposal of municipal, commercial, agricultural and nonhazardous industrial refuse. Also available online.

Waste Age. National Solid Waste Management Association, 1730 Rhode Island Avenue, NW, Ste. 1000, Washington, District of Columbia 20036. (202) 659-4613. Monthly. Covers control and use of solid, hazardous and liquid wastes.

TRADE ASSOCIATIONS AND PROFESSIONAL SOCIETIES

American Public Works Association. 106 W. 11th St., Ste. 1800, Kansas City, Missouri 64105-1806. (816) 472-6100.

American Society of Sanitary Engineering. Box 40362, Bay Village, Ohio 44140. (216) 835-3040.

Association of State and Territorial Solid Waste Management Officials. 444 North Capitol St., N.W., Suite 388, Washington, District of Columbia 20001. (202) 624-5828.

Center for Environmental Management. Tufts University, Curtis Hall, 474 Boston Ave., Medford, Massachusetts 02155. (617) 381-3486.

Hazardous Waste Treatment Council. 1440 New York Ave., Suite 310, Washington, District of Columbia 20005. (202) 783-0870.

International Clearinghouse for Environmental Technologies. 12600 West Colfax Ave., Suite C-310, Lakewood, Colorado 80215. (303) 233-1248.

National Solid Wastes Management Association. 1730 Rhode Island Ave., N.W., Suite 1000, Washington, District of Columbia 20036. (202) 659-4613.

SOLID WASTES

See also: WASTE DISPOSAL

ABSTRACTING AND INDEXING SERVICES

Environment Abstracts. Bowker A & I Publishing, 121 Chanlon Rd., New Providence, New Jersey 07974. (908) 464-6800. 1974-.

Environmental Information Connection–EIC. Planning Information Program, Dept. of Urban and Regional Planning, University of Illinois, 1003 West Nevada, Urbana, Illinois 61801. (217) 333-1369. Also available online.

Environmental Periodicals Bibliography. Environmental Studies Institute, International Academy at Santa Barbara, 800 Garden St., Suite D, Santa Barbara, California 93101. (805) 965-5010. Also available online.

General Science Index. H. W. Wilson Co., 950 University Ave., Bronx, New York 10452. 1978-. Monthly, also issued in annual cumulation. Cumulative subject index to English language periodicals in the subject fields of astronomy, botany, chemistry, earth science, environment and conservation, food and nutrition, genetics, mathematics, medicine and health, microbiology, oceanography, physics, physiology and zoology.

ALMANACS AND YEARBOOKS

Environmental Almanac. World Resources Institute. Houghton Mifflin, 1 Beacon St., Boston, Massachusetts 02108. (617) 725-5000; (800) 225-3362. 1991. Covers consumer products, energy, endangered species, food safety, global warming, solid wastes, toxics, wetlands and other related areas. Also included are the names and addresses of the chief environmental executives for all 50 states.

BIBLIOGRAPHIES

EPA Publications Bibliography. U.S. Environmental Protection Agency, Library Systems Branch, 401 M St., SW, Washington, District of Columbia 20460. (202) 260-2090. Quarterly.

DIRECTORIES

Solid Waste Education Recycling Directory. Teresa Jones, et al. Lewis Publishers, 200 Corporate Blvd. NW, Boca Raton, Florida 33431. (407) 994-0555 or (800)272-7737. 1990. Summarizes recycling education curricula for each state covering all levels, K-12. Provides names, addresses, phone numbers, information about the availability of materials, how you collect them, and how much they cost.

ENCYCLOPEDIAS AND DICTIONARIES

Dictionary of Environmental Engineering and Related Sciences: English-Spanish, Spanish-English. Jose T. Villate. Ediciones Universal, 3090 SW 8th St., Miami, Florida 33135. (305) 642-3355. 1979.

Encyclopedia of Environmental Science and Engineering. J.R. Pfafflin. Gordon and Breach Science Publishers, Inc., 270 8th Ave., New York, New York 10011. (212) 206-8900. 1992.

McGraw-Hill Encyclopedia of Environmental Science. Sybil P. Parker. McGraw-Hill Science & Engineering Books, 11 W. 19th St., New York, New York 10011. (212) 337-6010. 1980. Covers ecology, man's influence on nature, and environmental protection.

Van Nostrand's Scientific Encyclopedia. Glenn D. Considine, ed. Van Nostrand Reinhold, 115 5th Ave., New York, New York 10003. (212) 254-3232. 1983. Sixth edition. Includes all broad subject areas in science.

GENERAL WORKS

Beyond 40 Percent: Record-Setting Recycling and Composting Programs. Brenda Platt, et al. Island Press, 1718 Connecticut Ave. N.W., Suite 300, Washington, District of Columbia 20009. (202) 232-7933. 1991. Produced by the Institute for Local Self-Reliance, this volume documents the operating experience of 17 U.S. communities, from small rural towns to large cities, that are recovering between 32 and 57 percent of their waste.

Design, Construction, and Monitoring of Sanitary Landfill. Amalendu Bagchi. John Wiley & Sons, Inc., 605 3rd Ave., New York, New York 10158-0012. (212) 850-6000. 1990. Handbook of theory, practice, and mathematical models of sanitary landfill technology and how they apply to waste disposal.

Emerging Technologies in Hazardous Waste Management. D. William Tedder and Frederick G. Pohland, eds.

American Chemical Society, 1155 16th St. N.W., Washington, District of Columbia 20036. (202) 872-4600; (800) 227-5558. 1990. Hazardous waste management technology.

Emerging Technologies in Hazardous Waste Management II. D. William Tedder and Frederick G. Pohland, eds. American Chemical Society, 1155 16th St. N.W., Washington, District of Columbia 20036. (202) 872-4600; (800) 227-5558. 1991. Developed from a symposium sponsored by the Division of Industrial and Engineering Chemistry, Inc. of the American Chemical Society at the Industrial and Engineering Chemistry Special Symposium, Atlantic City, NJ, June 4-7, 1990.

Environmental Issues: An Anthology of 1989. Thomas W. Joyce, ed. TAPPI Press, Technology Park/Atlanta, PO Box 105113, Atlanta, Georgia 30348. (404) 446-1400. 1990. Contains 39 papers on environmental, safety and occupational health concerns from 11 TAPPI, CPPA and AIChE meetings held during 1989. Also included is a literature review of over 200 papers published in 1989.

Rush to Burn: Solving America's Garbage Crisis?. Island Press, 1718 Connecticut Ave. N.W., Suite 300, Washington, District of Columbia 20009. (202) 232-7933. 1989. Describes incineration, refuse and refuse disposal.

War on Waste: Can America Win its Battle With Garbage?. Louis Blumberg and Robert Gottlieb. Island Press, 1718 Connecticut Ave. N.W., Suite 300, Washington, District of Columbia 20009. (202) 232-7933. 1989. In-depth analysis of the waste disposal crisis.

GOVERNMENTAL ORGANIZATIONS

U.S. Environmental Protection Agency: National Enforcement Investigations Center. Building 53, Box 25227, Denver, Colorado 80225. (303) 236-5100.

U.S. Environmental Protection Agency: Office of Environmental Engineering and Technology. 401 M St., S.W., Washington, District of Columbia 20460. (202) 382-2600.

U.S. Environmental Protection Agency: Office of Underground Storage Tanks. 401 M St., S.W., Washington, District of Columbia 20460. (202) 382-4517.

HANDBOOKS AND MANUALS

Final Covers on Hazardous Waste Landfills and Surface Impoundments. Office of Solid Waste and Emergency Response, U.S. Environment Protection Agency, U.S. G.P.O., Washington, District of Columbia 20402-9325. (202) 783-3238. 1989. Technical Guidance Document series EPA/530-SW-89-047. Shipping list no. 89-483-P.

The Solid Waste Handbook: A Practical Guide. William D. Robinson, ed. John Wiley & Sons, Inc., 605 3rd Ave., New York, New York 10158-0012. (212) 850-6000. 1986. Covers the field of solid waste management, including legislation, regulation, planning, finance, technologies, operations, economics administration, and future trends.

Solid Waste Recycling; The Complete Resource Guide. Bureau of National Affairs, 1231 25th St. N.W., Washington, District of Columbia 20037. (800) 372-1033. 1990. Details federal and state laws and regulations, legal issues and local initiatives relating to waste crisis. Includes case studies of programs, surveys, studies, reports guidelines, recommendations, resources and references.

Standard Handbook of Environmental Engineering. Robert A. Corbitt. McGraw-Hill, 1221 Ave. of the Americas, New York, New York 10020. (212) 512-2000 or (800) 262-4729. 1990. Hands-on reference to understand environmental engineering technology. Covers air quality control, water supply, wastewater disposal, waste management, stormwater and hazardous wastes.

ONLINE DATA BASES

Enviro/Energyline Abstracts Plus. R. R. Bowker Co., 121 Chanlon Rd., New Providence, New Jersey 07974. (908) 464-6800.

Environmental Periodicals Bibliography. National Information Services Corp., Ste. 6, Wyman Towers, 3100 St. Paul St., Baltimore, Maryland 21218. (410)243-0797. Online version of abstract of same name.

Greenwire. American Political Network, 282 North Washington St., Falls Church, Virginia 22046. (703) 237-5130. 1991. Daily. Daily electronic 12-page summary of the last 24 hours of news coverage of environmental issues worldwide. Monday through Friday at 10 am EST, it can be accessed by a PC, modem and an 800 number contains issues on environmental protection, energy/natural resources, business science, 50-state news, worldwide headlines, TV monitor, daily calendar, marketplace battles, Capitol Hill, spotlight story, global issues, environment and the law, solid waste and focus interviews.

PERIODICALS AND NEWSLETTERS

American Public Works Association Reporter. American Public Works Association, 106 W. 11th St., Ste. 1800, Kansas City, Missouri 64105-1806. (816 472-6100. Monthly. Articles for public works officials.

CA Selects: Environment Pollution. Chemical Abstracts Services, 2540 Olentangy River Rd., Box 3012, Columbus, Ohio 43210. (800) 848-6533. 1978-. Biweekly. Abstracts on pollution of the environment by gaseous, liquid, solid and radioactive wastes.

Civil Engineering ASCE. American Society of Civil Engineers, 345 E 47th St., New York, New York 10017. (212) 705-7288; (800) 548-2723. Monthly. Professional journal that offers a forum for free exchange of ideas relevant to the profession of civil engineering. Covers in regular columns, engineering news, legal trends in engineering, calendar of events, membership news, publications and other items of interest to civil engineers. Formerly, Civil Engineering.

Environment Midwest. U.S. Environmental Protection Agency, 230 S. Dearborn, Chicago, Illinois 60604. (312) 353-2072. Monthly. Programs for fighting air and water pollution, hazardous and solid wastes, toxicants, pesticides, noise, and radiation.

Environmental Pollution & Control. National Technical Information Service, 5285 Port Royal Rd., Springfield, Virginia 22161. (703) 487-4650. Weekly. Covers air, noise, solid waste, water pollution, radiation, environmental health and safety, pesticide pollution and control.

Environmental Progress. American Institute of Chemical Engineers, 345 E. 47th St., New York, New York 10017. (212) 705-7338. Quarterly. Deals with environmental policies, protection and management-especially relating to chemicals.

EPA Journal. U.S. Environmental Protection Agency, 401 M St., S.W., A-107, Washington, District of Columbia 20460. (202) 382-4393. Bimonthly. Air and water pollution, pesticides, noise, solid waste.

Florida Environments. Florida Environments Pub., 215 N. Main St., PO Box 1617, High Springs, Florida 32643. (904) 454-2007. Monthly. Florida's hazardous materials/wastes, wildlife, regulation, drinking/ground/surface waters, air, and solid waste.

Garbage: The Practical Journal for the Environment. Old House Journal Corp., 2 Main St., Gloucester, Massachusetts 01930. (508) 283-4629. Bimonthly. Issues in municipal wastes.

Management of World Wastes. Communication Channels, 6255 Barfield Road, Atlanta, Georgia 30328. (404) 256-9800. Monthly. Covers public and private waste operations.

Outdoors Unlittered Pitch-In News. Outdoors Unlittered, 200-1676 Martin Dr., White Rock, British Columbia, Canada V4A 6E7. (403) 429-0517. Semiannually. Solid waste and litter problems

Solid Waste Report. Business Publishers, Inc., 951 Pershing Dr., Silver Spring, Maryland 20910-4464. (301) 587-6300. 1970-. Weekly. Covers the generation, collection, transportation, processing, resource recovery, recycling and ultimate disposal of municipal, commercial, agricultural and nonhazardous industrial refuse. Also available online.

Waste Age. National Solid Waste Management Association, 1730 Rhode Island Avenue, NW, Ste. 1000, Washington, District of Columbia 20036. (202) 659-4613. Monthly. Covers control and use of solid, hazardous and liquid wastes.

RESEARCH CENTERS AND INSTITUTES

Center for Environmental Sciences. University of Colorado-Denver, P.O. Box 173364, Denver, Colorado 80217-3364. (303) 5556-4277.

State University of New York at Oswego, Research Center. King Hall, Oswego, New York 13126. (315) 341-3639.

STATISTICS SOURCES

OECD Environmental Data Compendium 1989. OECD Publications and Information Center, 2001 L St. N.W., Suite 700, Washington, District of Columbia 20036. (202) 785-OECD. 1989. Provides statistical data for OECD countries on air pollution, water pollution, the marine environment, land use, forests, wildlife, solid waste, noise and radioactivity. Also provides data on the underlying pressures on the environment such as energy use, transportation, industrial activity and agriculture.

TRADE ASSOCIATIONS AND PROFESSIONAL SOCIETIES

American Institute of Chemical Engineers. 345 East 47th St., New York, New York 10017. (212) 705-7338.

American Institute of Chemists. 7315 Wisconsin Ave., Bethesda, Maryland 20814. (301) 652-2447.

American Public Works Association. 106 W. 11th St., Ste. 1800, Kansas City, Missouri 64105-1806. (816) 472-6100.

American Society of Mechanical Engineers, Solid Waste Processing Division. 345 E. 47th St., New York, New York 10017. (212) 705-7722.

American Society of Sanitary Engineering. Box 40362, Bay Village, Ohio 44140. (216) 835-3040.

Center for Environmental Management. Tufts University, Curtis Hall, 474 Boston Ave., Medford, Massachusetts 02155. (617) 381-3486.

Government Refuse Collection & Disposal Association. 8750 Georgia Ave., Ste. 140, PO Box 7219, Silver Spring, Maryland 20910. (301) 585-2898.

INFORM. 381 Park Avenue S., New York, New York 10016. (212) 689-4040.

Keep America Beautiful, Inc. 9 W. Broad St., Stamford, Connecticut 06902. (203) 323-8987.

National Solid Wastes Management Association. 1730 Rhode Island Ave., N.W., Suite 1000, Washington, District of Columbia 20036. (202) 659-4613.

SONIC BOOM

ABSTRACTING AND INDEXING SERVICES

Applied Science and Technology Index. H.W. Wilson Co., 950 University Ave., Bronx, New York 10452. (800) 367-6770. Formerly Industrial Arts Index.

Environment Abstracts. Bowker A & I Publishing, 121 Chanlon Rd., New Providence, New Jersey 07974. (908) 464-6800. 1974-.

Environment Index. Environment Information Center, Index Research Department, 124 E. 39th St., New York, New York 10016. 1971-. Annual.

Environmental Information Connection–EIC. Planning Information Program, Dept. of Urban and Regional Planning, University of Illinois, 1003 West Nevada, Urbana, Illinois 61801. (217) 333-1369. Also available online.

Environmental Periodicals Bibliography. Environmental Studies Institute, International Academy at Santa Barbara, 800 Garden St., Suite D, Santa Barbara, California 93101. (805) 965-5010. Also available online.

Science Citation Index. Institute for Scientific Information, 3501 Market St., Philadelphia, Pennsylvania 19104. 1961-.

BIBLIOGRAPHIES

EPA Publications Bibliography. U.S. Environmental Protection Agency, Library Systems Branch, 401 M St., SW, Washington, District of Columbia 20460. (202) 260-2090. Quarterly.

ENCYCLOPEDIAS AND DICTIONARIES

Van Nostrand's Scientific Encyclopedia. Glenn D. Considine, ed. Van Nostrand Reinhold, 115 5th Ave., New York, New York 10003. (212) 254-3232. 1983. Sixth edition. Includes all broad subject areas in science.

ONLINE DATA BASES

Enviro/Energyline Abstracts Plus. R. R. Bowker Co., 121 Chanlon Rd., New Providence, New Jersey 07974. (908) 464-6800.

Environmental Periodicals Bibliography. National Information Services Corp., Ste. 6, Wyman Towers, 3100 St. Paul St., Baltimore, Maryland 21218. (410)243-0797. Online version of abstract of same name.

SOOT

ABSTRACTING AND INDEXING SERVICES

Air Pollution Titles. Pennsylvania State University, Center for Air Environmental Studies, 226 Fenske Laboratory, University Park, Pennsylvania 16802. (814) 865-1415. 1965. Bibliographic guide to current research literature on air environment, including monitoring and control of air pollution, health effects, effects on agriculture, forests, toxic air contaminants, and global atmospheric pro cases.

Air Pollution Translations. A Bibliography With Abstracts. U.S. Environmental Protection Agency, MD 75, Research Triangle Park, North Carolina 27711. (919) 541-2184. 1969.

Pollution Abstracts. Cambridge Scientific Abstracts, 5161 River Rd., Bethesda, Maryland 20816. (301) 961-6750. Six/year. Indexes worldwide technical literature on environmental pollution. Covers air pollution, marine and freshwater pollution, sewage and wastewater treatment, waste management, toxicology and health, noise pollution, radiation, land pollution, and environmental policies, programs, legislation, and education. Also available online.

Science Citation Index. Institute for Scientific Information, 3501 Market St., Philadelphia, Pennsylvania 19104. 1961-.

ENCYCLOPEDIAS AND DICTIONARIES

Van Nostrand's Scientific Encyclopedia. Glenn D. Considine, ed. Van Nostrand Reinhold, 115 5th Ave., New York, New York 10003. (212) 254-3232. 1983. Sixth edition. Includes all broad subject areas in science.

GENERAL WORKS

Black Carbon in the Environment. John Wiley and Sons, 605 Third Ave., New York, New York 10158-0012. (212) 850-6000. Environmental chemistry and environmental aspects of soot.

Particulate Carbon, Atmospheric Life Cycle. Plenum Press, 233 Spring St., New York, New York 10013-1578. (212) 620-8000. 1982.

SORGHUM

ABSTRACTING AND INDEXING SERVICES

Agrindex. AGRIS Coordinating Center, Via delle Terme di Caracalla, Rome, Italy I-00100. 61 0181-FA01. 1975-.

Biological and Agricultural Index. H.W. Wilson Co., 950 University Ave., Bronx, New York 10452. (800) 367-6770. 1916-. Monthly.

Field Crop Abstracts. C. A. B. International, 845 North Park Ave., Tucson, Arizona 85719. (602) 621-7897 or (800) 528-4841. 1948-. Monthly. Covers literature on agronomy, field production, crop botany and physiology of all annual field crops, both temperate and tropical.

Food Science and Technology Abstracts. International Food Information Service, c/o National Food Laboratory, 6363 Clark Ave., Dublin, California 94568. (800) 336-3782. 1969-.

Sorghum and Millets Abstracts. C. A. B. International, 845 North Park Ave., Tucson, Arizona 85719. (602) 621-7897 or (800) 528-4841. 1976-. Bimonthly. Covers studies from throughout the world in areas such as sorghum bicolor, eleusine coracana, panicum miliaceum, pennisetum americanum, and minor millets and related crops.

ENCYCLOPEDIAS AND DICTIONARIES

Van Nostrand's Scientific Encyclopedia. Glenn D. Considine, ed. Van Nostrand Reinhold, 115 5th Ave., New York, New York 10003. (212) 254-3232. 1983. Sixth edition. Includes all broad subject areas in science.

ONLINE DATA BASES

Cambridge Scientific Abstracts Life Science–CSAL. Cambridge Scientific Abstracts, 5161 River Rd., Bethesda, Maryland 20816. (301) 961-6750. Provides access to the following abstracting services: "Life Sciences Collection," "Aquatic Sciences and Fisheries Abstracts," "Oceanic Abstracts," and "Pollution Abstracts."

TRADE ASSOCIATIONS AND PROFESSIONAL SOCIETIES

American Institute of Biological Sciences. 730 11th St., N.W., Washington, District of Columbia 20001-4521. (202) 628-1500.

SORPTION

ABSTRACTING AND INDEXING SERVICES

ASFA Aquaculture Abstracts. Cambridge Scientific Abstracts, Inc., 5161 River Rd., Bethesda, Maryland 20816. (301) 961-6750. 1984.

Food Science and Technology Abstracts. International Food Information Service, c/o National Food Laboratory, 6363 Clark Ave., Dublin, California 94568. (800) 336-3782. 1969-.

General Science Index. H. W. Wilson Co., 950 University Ave., Bronx, New York 10452. 1978-. Monthly, also issued in annual cumulation. Cumulative subject index to English language periodicals in the subject fields of astronomy, botany, chemistry, earth science, environment and conservation, food and nutrition, genetics, mathematics, medicine and health, microbiology, oceanography, physics, physiology and zoology.

Science Citation Index. Institute for Scientific Information, 3501 Market St., Philadelphia, Pennsylvania 19104. 1961-.

ENCYCLOPEDIAS AND DICTIONARIES

Van Nostrand's Scientific Encyclopedia. Glenn D. Considine, ed. Van Nostrand Reinhold, 115 5th Ave., New York, New York 10003. (212) 254-3232. 1983. Sixth edition. Includes all broad subject areas in science.

SOUND INSULATION
See: INSULATION

SOUTH CAROLINA ENVIRONMENTAL AGENCIES

GOVERNMENTAL ORGANIZATIONS

Department of Labor: Occupational Safety. Director, Occupational Safety and Health, PO Box 11329, Columbia, South Carolina 29211. (803) 734-9644.

Energy, Agriculture, and Natural Resources: Natural Resources. Director, Governor's Office, 1205 Pendleton St., Columbia, South Carolina 29201. (803) 734-0445.

Health and Environmental Control Department: Underground Storage Tanks. Director, Groundwater Protection, 2600 Bull St., Columbia, South Carolina 29201. (803) 734-5331.

Health and Environmental Control: Groundwater Management. Director, Groundwater Protection, 2600 Bull St., Columbia, South Carolina 29201. (803) 734-5331.

Health and Environmental Control: Hazardous Waste Management. Chief, Solid and Hazardous Waste Management, 2600 Bull St., Columbia, South Carolina 29201. (803) 734-5213.

Health and Environmental Control: Solid Waste Management. Chief, Solid and Hazardous Waste Management, 2600 Bull St., Columbia, South Carolina 29201. (803) 734-5200.

Health and Environmental Control: Water Quality. Deputy Commissioner, Division of Environmental Quality Control, 2600 Bull St., Columbia, South Carolina 29201. (803) 734-5360.

Regulatory and Public Service Programs: Pesticide Registration. Director, 212 Barre Hall, Clemson University, Clemson, South Carolina 29634-2775. (803) 656-3005.

U.S. EPA Region 4: Pollution Prevention. Program Manager, 345 Courtland St., N.E., Atlanta, Georgia 30365. (404) 347-7109.

Wildlife and Marine Resources Department: Fish and Wildlife. Executive Director, PO Box 167, Columbia, South Carolina 29202. (803) 734-4007.

RESEARCH CENTERS AND INSTITUTES

South Carolina Sea Grant Consortium. 287 Meeting Street, Charleston, South Carolina 29401. (803) 727-2078.

SOUTH CAROLINA ENVIRONMENTAL LEGISLATION

GENERAL WORKS

South Carolina Environmental & Social Action Directory. Carolina Peace Resource Center, Columbia, South Carolina (803) 799-3640.

South Carolina Environmental Law Reporter. Environmental Law Society, University of South Carolina Law Center, 1244 Blossom St., Columbia, South Carolina 29208.

SOUTH DAKOTA ENVIRONMENTAL AGENCIES

GOVERNMENTAL ORGANIZATIONS

Department of Agriculture: Pesticide Registration. Administrator, Feed, Fertilizer and Pesticide Program, Division of Regulatory Services, Joe Foss Building, 523 E. Capital, Pierre, South Dakota 57501. (605) 773-3724.

Department of Fish, Game and Parks: Fish and Wildlife. Secretary, Joe Foss Building, 523 E. Capital, Pierre, South Dakota 57501. (605) 773-3387.

Department of Water and Natural Resources: Emergency Preparedness and Community Right-to-Know. Emergency Response Commission, Joe Foss Building, 523 East Capitol, Pierre, South Dakota 57501-3181. (605) 773-3153.

U.S. EPA Region 8: Pollution Prevention. Senior Policy Advisor, 999 18th St., Suite 500, Denver, Colorado 80202-2405. (303) 293-1603.

Water and Natural Resources Building: Natural Resources. Secretary, 2nd Floor, Joe Foss Building, 523 E. Capital, Pierre, South Dakota 57501. (605) 773-3151.

Water and Natural Resources Department: Air Quality. Administrator, Air Quality and Solid Waste, Joe Foss Building, 523 E. Capital, Pierre, South Dakota 57501. (605) 773-3329.

Water and Natural Resources Department: Environmental Protection. Director, Division of Environmental Health, Joe Foss Building, 523 E. Capital, Pierre, South Dakota 57501. (605) 773-3151.

Water and Natural Resources Department: Groundwater Management. Director, Division of Environmental Health, Joe Foss Building, 523 E. Capital, Pierre, South Dakota 57501. (605) 773-3151.

Water and Natural Resources Department: Hazardous Waste Management. Administrator, Air Quality and Solid Waste, Joe Foss Building, 523 E. Capital, Pierre, South Dakota 57501. (605) 773-3329.

Water and Natural Resources Department: Solid Waste Management. Director, Division of Environmental Health, Joe Foss Building, 523 E. Capital, Pierre, South Dakota 57501. (605) 773-3151.

Water and Natural Resources Department: Underground Storage Tanks. Director, Division of Environmental

Health, Joe Foss Building, 523 E. Capital, Pierre, South Dakota 57501. (605) 773-3151.

Water and Natural Resources Department: Water Quality. Director, Division of Environmental Health, Joe Foss Building, 523 E. Capital, Pierre, South Dakota 57501. (605) 773-3751.

RESEARCH CENTERS AND INSTITUTES

South Dakota State University, South Dakota Cooperative Fish and Wildlife Research Unit. P.O. Box 2206, Brookings, South Dakota 57007. (605) 688-6121.

South Dakota State University, Water Resources Institute. Brookings, South Dakota 57007. (605) 688-4910.

SPILL DETECTION
See: OIL SPILLS

SPRAY IRRIGATION
See: IRRIGATION

STABILIZATION PONDS

ABSTRACTING AND INDEXING SERVICES

Biological and Agricultural Index. H.W. Wilson Co., 950 University Ave., Bronx, New York 10452. (800) 367-6770. 1916-. Monthly.

Science Citation Index. Institute for Scientific Information, 3501 Market St., Philadelphia, Pennsylvania 19104. 1961-.

ENCYCLOPEDIAS AND DICTIONARIES

Van Nostrand's Scientific Encyclopedia. Glenn D. Considine, ed. Van Nostrand Reinhold, 115 5th Ave., New York, New York 10003. (212) 254-3232. 1983. Sixth edition. Includes all broad subject areas in science.

GENERAL WORKS

A Dynamic Nutrient Cycle Model for Waste Stabilization Ponds. R.A. Ferrara. MIT Department of Civil Engineering, 77 Massachusetts Ave., Cambridge, Massachusetts 02137. 1978. Hydraulic models pf sewage lagoons.

HANDBOOKS AND MANUALS

Municipal Wastewater Stabilization Ponds. Office of Water Program Operations. U.S. Environmental Protection Agency, 401 M St., S.W., Washington, District of Columbia 20460. (202) 260-2090. 1983. Design manual for sewage lagoons and aeration purification of sewage.

Practical Pedology. Stuart Gordon McRae. Halsted Press, 605 3rd Ave., New York, New York 10158. (212) 850-6000. 1988. Handbook for studying soils in the field.

STACK EMISSIONS
See: EMISSIONS

STATIONARY SOURCE
See: AIR POLLUTION

STEAM-ELECTRIC POWER PLANTS
See: POWER PLANTS

STEAM TURBINES
See: POWER PLANTS

STERILIZATION, ANIMAL

ABSTRACTING AND INDEXING SERVICES

Biological and Agricultural Index. H.W. Wilson Co., 950 University Ave., Bronx, New York 10452. (800) 367-6770. 1916-. Monthly.

Science Citation Index. Institute for Scientific Information, 3501 Market St., Philadelphia, Pennsylvania 19104. 1961-.

ENCYCLOPEDIAS AND DICTIONARIES

Encyclopedia of Bioethics. Warren T. Reich, ed. Free Press, 866 3rd Ave., New York, New York 10022. (212) 702-2004 or (800) 257-5755. 1978. Four volumes. Includes review articles in the field of bioethics by 330 reviewers representing fields such as: surgery, Islamic studies, pediatrics, philosophy, environmental sciences, theology, psychiatry, etc.

ONLINE DATA BASES

Monthly Catalog of United States Government Publications. U.S. G.P.O., Supt. of Docs., PO Box 371954, Pittsburgh, Pennsylvania 15250-7954. (202) 512-0000.

National Technical Information Service. U.S. Department of Commerce, National Technical Information Service, Office of Data Base Services, 5285 Port Royal Rd., Springfield, Virginia 22161. (703) 487-4807. Bibliographic database of government sponsored research and technical reports.

PERIODICALS AND NEWSLETTERS

Infectious Wastes News. Richard H. Freeman, Washington Sq., PO Box 65686, Washington, District of Columbia 20035-5686. (202) 861-0708. Biweekly. Disposal of infectious wastes, new methods and technologies, sterilization and incineration of waste, and environmental standards.

STERILIZATION, HUMAN

ABSTRACTING AND INDEXING SERVICES

Science Citation Index. Institute for Scientific Information, 3501 Market St., Philadelphia, Pennsylvania 19104. 1961-.

ENCYCLOPEDIAS AND DICTIONARIES

Encyclopedia of Bioethics. Warren T. Reich, ed. Free Press, 866 3rd Ave., New York, New York 10022. (212) 702-2004 or (800) 257-5755. 1978. Four volumes. Includes review articles in the field of bioethics by 330 reviewers representing fields such as: surgery, Islamic studies, pediatrics, philosophy, environmental sciences, theology, psychiatry, etc.

ONLINE DATA BASES

Monthly Catalog of United States Government Publications. U.S. G.P.O., Supt. of Docs., PO Box 371954, Pittsburgh, Pennsylvania 15250-7954. (202) 512-0000.

National Technical Information Service. U.S. Department of Commerce, National Technical Information Service, Office of Data Base Services, 5285 Port Royal Rd., Springfield, Virginia 22161. (703) 487-4807. Bibliographic database of government sponsored research and technical reports.

PERIODICALS AND NEWSLETTERS

Infectious Wastes News. Richard H. Freeman, Washington Sq., PO Box 65686, Washington, District of Columbia 20035-5686. (202) 861-0708. Biweekly. Disposal of infectious wastes, new methods and technologies, sterilization and incineration of waste, and environmental standards.

STERILIZATION, INSECT

ABSTRACTING AND INDEXING SERVICES

Agrindex. AGRIS Coordinating Center, Via delle Terme di Caracalla, Rome, Italy I-00100. 61 0181-FA01. 1975-.

Biological and Agricultural Index. H.W. Wilson Co., 950 University Ave., Bronx, New York 10452. (800) 367-6770. 1916-. Monthly.

Science Citation Index. Institute for Scientific Information, 3501 Market St., Philadelphia, Pennsylvania 19104. 1961-.

ENCYCLOPEDIAS AND DICTIONARIES

Encyclopedia of Bioethics. Warren T. Reich, ed. Free Press, 866 3rd Ave., New York, New York 10022. (212) 702-2004 or (800) 257-5755. 1978. Four volumes. Includes review articles in the field of bioethics by 330 reviewers representing fields such as: surgery, Islamic studies, pediatrics, philosophy, environmental sciences, theology, psychiatry, etc.

PERIODICALS AND NEWSLETTERS

Infectious Wastes News. Richard H. Freeman, Washington Sq., PO Box 65686, Washington, District of Columbia 20035-5686. (202) 861-0708. Biweekly. Disposal of infectious wastes, new methods and technologies, sterilization and incineration of waste, and environmental standards.

STORM RUNOFF
See: HYDROLOGY

STORM SEWERS
See: HYDROLOGY

STRATIFICATION
See: LAKES

STRATOSPHERE

ABSTRACTING AND INDEXING SERVICES

Index to Scientific Book Contents. Institute for Scientific Information, 3501 Market St., Philadelphia, Pennsylvania 19104. (800) 523-1857. 1985-. Annual. Gives contents of science books published.

Mineralogical Abstracts. Mineralogical Society, 41 Queen's Gate, London, England SW7 5HR. 71 5847916. Quarterly. Abstracts of journal articles, conferences, technical reports and specialized books in the areas of minerals, clay minerals, economic minerals, ore deposits, environmental studies, experimental mineralogy, gemstones, geochemistry, petrology, lunar and planetary studies and other related areas in mineralogy.

Science Citation Index. Institute for Scientific Information, 3501 Market St., Philadelphia, Pennsylvania 19104. 1961-.

ENCYCLOPEDIAS AND DICTIONARIES

The Encyclopedia of Atmospheric Sciences and Astrogeology. Rhodes Whitmore Fairbridge. Reinhold Pub. Co., 115 5th Ave., New York, New York 10003. (212) 254-3232. 1967.

The Encyclopedia of Climatology. John E. Oliver and Rhodes W. Fairbridge, eds. Van Nostrand Reinhold, 115 5th Ave., New York, New York 10003. (212) 254-3232. 1987. Belongs in the series Encyclopedia of Earth Sciences, v.11.

GENERAL WORKS

Air Quality. Lewis Publishers, 200 Corporate Blvd. NW, Boca Raton, Florida 33431. (407) 994-0555 or (800)272-7737. 2nd edition. Air pollution and control, stratosphere O3 depletion, global warming, and indoor air pollution.

Chlorofluoromethanes and the Stratosphere. Robert D. Hudson, ed. National Technical Information Service,

5285 Port Royal Rd., Springfield, Virginia 22161. (703) 487-4650. 1977.

Global Air Pollution: Problems for the 1990s. Howard Bridgman. Belhaven Press, 136 S. Broadway, Irvington, New York 10533. (914) 591-9111. 1990. Addresses the environmental problems caused by human activities resulting in change and deterioration of the earth's atmosphere.

Halocarbons: Environmental Effects of Chlorofluoromethane Release. National Research Council. Committee on Impacts of Stratospheric Change. National Academy of Sciences, 2101 Constitution Ave., NW, Washington, District of Columbia 20418. (202) 334-2000. 1976.

HANDBOOKS AND MANUALS

Handbook of Geophysics and the Space Environment. Adolph S. Jursa, ed. Air Force Geophysics Laboratory, Air Force Systems Command, United States Air Force, c/o National Technical Information Service, 5285 Port Royal Rd., Springfield, Virginia 22161. (703) 487-4650. 1985. Two volumes. Broad subject areas covered are space, atmosphere, and terrestrial environment. Includes topics such as solar radiation, sunspots, solar wind, geomagnetic fields, radiation belts, cosmic radiation, atmospheric gases, etc.

ONLINE DATA BASES

SCISEARCH. Institute for Scientific Information, University City Science Center, 3501 Market St., Philadelphia, Pennsylvania 19104. (215) 386-0100.

STATISTICS SOURCES

The State of the Environment. OECD Publications and Information Center, 2001 L St., N.W., Suite 700, Washington, District of Columbia 20036. (202) 785-6323. 1991.

STRAY VOLTAGE

See: ELECTRIC POWER LINES–ENVIRONMENTAL ASPECTS

STREAMS

See also: FRESHWATER ECOSYSTEMS

ABSTRACTING AND INDEXING SERVICES

Applied Ecology Abstracts Studies in Renewable Natural Resources. Information Retrieval Ltd., 1911 Jefferson Davis Highway, Arlington, Virginia 22202. 1975-. Monthly.

Applied Science and Technology Index. H.W. Wilson Co., 950 University Ave., Bronx, New York 10452. (800) 367-6770. Formerly Industrial Arts Index.

ASFA Aquaculture Abstracts. Cambridge Scientific Abstracts, Inc., 5161 River Rd., Bethesda, Maryland 20816. (301) 961-6750. 1984.

Civil Engineering Hydraulic Abstracts. BHRA Fluid Engineering, Air Science Co., PO Box 143, Corning, New York 14830. (607) 962-5591. Monthly. Abstracts of

periodicals that publish in the areas of hydraulic engineering and other related topics.

Ecology Abstracts. Cambridge Scientific Abstracts, 5161 River Rd., Bethesda, Maryland 20816. (301) 961-6750. Monthly.

Environment Abstracts. Bowker A & I Publishing, 121 Chanlon Rd., New Providence, New Jersey 07974. (908) 464-6800. 1974-.

Environment Index. Environment Information Center, Index Research Department, 124 E. 39th St., New York, New York 10016. 1971-. Annual.

Environmental Information Connection–EIC. Planning Information Program, Dept. of Urban and Regional Planning, University of Illinois, 1003 West Nevada, Urbana, Illinois 61801. (217) 333-1369. Also available online.

Environmental Periodicals Bibliography. Environmental Studies Institute, International Academy at Santa Barbara, 800 Garden St., Suite D, Santa Barbara, California 93101. (805) 965-5010. Also available online.

General Science Index. H. W. Wilson Co., 950 University Ave., Bronx, New York 10452. 1978-. Monthly, also issued in annual cumulation. Cumulative subject index to English language periodicals in the subject fields of astronomy, botany, chemistry, earth science, environment and conservation, food and nutrition, genetics, mathematics, medicine and health, microbiology, oceanography, physics, physiology and zoology.

Irrigation and Drainage Abstracts. C. A. B. International, 845 North Park Ave., Tucson, Arizona 85719. (602) 621-7897 or (800) 258-4841. 1975-. Quarterly. Subject areas scanned are: water management, irrigation of crop plants, drainage, soil water relations, plant water relations, salinity and toxicity problems, soil condition, evaporotranspiration, evaporation, land use, streams, water quality, and other related areas.

Multimedia Index to Ecology. National Information Center for Educational Media, University of Southern California, Los Angeles, California 90007.

Science Citation Index. Institute for Scientific Information, 3501 Market St., Philadelphia, Pennsylvania 19104. 1961-.

BIBLIOGRAPHIES

EPA Publications Bibliography. U.S. Environmental Protection Agency, Library Systems Branch, 401 M St., SW, Washington, District of Columbia 20460. (202) 260-2090. Quarterly.

New Publications of the Geological Survey. U.S. Department of the Interior, Geological Survey, 119 National Center, Reston, Virginia 22092. (703) 648-4460. 1984-. Monthly. Bibliography of geological publications and related government documents published by the Geological Survey.

ENCYCLOPEDIAS AND DICTIONARIES

Glossary of Geology. Robert Latimer Bates and Julia A. Jackson, eds. American Geological Institute, 4220 King St., Alexandria, Virginia 22302-1507. (703) 379-2480 or (800) 336-4764. 1987. Third edition.

McGraw-Hill Encyclopedia of Environmental Science. Sybil P. Parker. McGraw-Hill Science & Engineering Books, 11 W. 19th St., New York, New York 10011. (212) 337-6010. 1980. Covers ecology, man's influence on nature, and environmental protection.

McGraw-Hill Encyclopedia of the Geological Sciences. Sybil P. Parker, ed. McGraw-Hill, 1221 Avenue of the Americas, New York, New York 10020. (212) 512-2000 or (800) 262-4729. 1988. Second edition. Published previously in the McGraw-Hill Encyclopedia of Science and Technology.

Van Nostrand's Scientific Encyclopedia. Glenn D. Considine, ed. Van Nostrand Reinhold, 115 5th Ave., New York, New York 10003. (212) 254-3232. 1983. Sixth edition. Includes all broad subject areas in science.

GENERAL WORKS

Better Trout Habitat. Christopher J. Hunter. Island Press, 1718 Connecticut Ave. N.W., Suite 300, Washington, District of Columbia 20009. (202) 232-7933. 1991. Explains the physical, chemical and biological needs of trout, and shows how climate, geology, vegetation, and flowing water all help to create trout habitats. Book includes 14 detailed case studies of successful trout stream restoration projects.

Biogeochemistry of Major World Rivers. Egon T. Degens, et al. John Wiley & Sons, Inc., 605 3rd Ave., New York, New York 10158-0012. (212) 850-6000. 1991.

Cache la Poudre: The Natural History of Rocky Mountain River. Howard Ensign Evans and Mary Alice Evans. University Press of Colorado, PO Box 849, Niwot, Colorado 80544. (303) 530-5337. 1991. Includes a summary of the ecological and cultural values of the river corridor. Describes the corridor's flora, fauna, geology, insects, people and history.

Environmental Change in Iceland: Past and Present. Judith K. Maizels and Chris Caseldine, eds. Kluwer Academic Publishers, 101 Philip Dr., Assinippi Park, Norwell, Massachusetts 02061. (617) 871-6600. 1991. Describes the glacial landforms and paleoclimatology in Iceland. Volume 7 of the Glaciology and Quaternary Geology Series.

Impounded Rivers: Perspectives for Ecological Management. Geoffrey E. Petts. John Wiley & Sons, Inc., 605 3rd Ave., New York, New York 10158. (212) 850-6000. 1984. Environmental aspects of dams, stream ecology and stream conservation.

River Pollution: An Ecological Perspective. S. M. Haslam. Belhaven Press, 136 S. Broadway, Irvington, New York 10533. (914) 591-9111. 1990. Describes the impact of natural and man-made pollution in the ecosystem of freshwater streams, stressing understanding of processes and techniques of measurement.

Rivers at Risk: The Concerned Citizen's Guide to Hydropower. John D. Echeverria. Island Press, 1718 Connecticut Ave., NW, Suite 300, Washington, District of Columbia 20009. (202) 232-7933. 1989. Offers practical understanding of how to influence government decisions about hydropower development on the nation's rivers.

The Snake River: Window to the West. Tim Palmer. Island Press, 1718 Connecticut Ave. N.W., Suite 300, Washington, District of Columbia 20009. (202) 232-7933. 1991. Offers information about instream flows for fish and wildlife; groundwater management and quality; water conservation and efficiency; pollution of streams from agriculture and logging; small hydroelectric development; and reclamation of riparian habitat.

Stream, Lake, Estuary, and Ocean Pollution. Nelson Leonard Nemerow. Van Nostrand Reinhold, 115 5th Ave., New York, New York 10003. (800) 926-2665. 1991.

Water. Hans Silvester. Thomasson-Grant, 1 Morton Dr., Suite 500, Charlottesville, Virginia 22901. (804) 977-1780. 1990. Details the dangers posed by the industrial society to the flow of clean water

GOVERNMENTAL ORGANIZATIONS

Office of Public Affairs: Fish and Wildlife Service. 18th and C St., N.W., Washington, District of Columbia 20240. (202) 343-5634.

Public Affairs Office: U.S. Army Corps of Engineers. Room 8137, 20 Massachusetts Ave., N.W., Washington, District of Columbia 20314. (202) 272-0010.

ONLINE DATA BASES

Enviro/Energyline Abstracts Plus. R. R. Bowker Co., 121 Chanlon Rd., New Providence, New Jersey 07974. (908) 464-6800.

Environmental Periodicals Bibliography. National Information Services Corp., Ste. 6, Wyman Towers, 3100 St. Paul St., Baltimore, Maryland 21218. (410)243-0797. Online version of abstract of same name.

National Stream Quality Accounting Network. National Water Data Exchange, U.S. Geological Survey, 421 National Center, Reston, Virginia 22092. (703) 648-4000. 150 hydrologic measurements collected at daily, monthly and quarterly intervals from more than 500 monitoring stations in the U.S.

PERIODICALS AND NEWSLETTERS

Earth Science. American Geological Institute, 4220 King Street, Alexandria, Virginia 22302. (703) 379-2480. Quarterly. Covers geological issues.

RESEARCH CENTERS AND INSTITUTES

Massachusetts Institute of Technology Biotechnology Process Engineering Center. Room 20A-207, Cambridge, Massachusetts 02139. (617) 253-0805.

University of Pittsburgh, Pymatuning Laboratory of Ecology. R.R. #1, Box 7, Linesville, Pennsylvania 16424. (814) 683-5813.

Utah State University, Utah Cooperative Fish and Wildlife Research Unit. Logan, Utah 84322. (801) 750-2509.

STATISTICS SOURCES

Ecology: Community Profiles. U.S. Fish and Wildlife Service. National Technical Information Service, 5285 Port Royal Road, Springfield, Virginia 22161. (703) 487-4650. Irregular. Data on coastal and inland ecosystems, including wetlands, tidal-flats, near-shore seagrasses, sand dunes, drilling platforms, oyster reefs, estuaries, rivers and streams.

Water Resources Data. U.S. Geological Survey. U.S. G.P.O., Washington, District of Columbia 20401. (202) 512-0000. Annual. Data on water supply and quality of streams, lakes and reservoirs for individual states by water year.

STREET CLEANING

ABSTRACTING AND INDEXING SERVICES

Environment Abstracts. Bowker A & I Publishing, 121 Chanlon Rd., New Providence, New Jersey 07974. (908) 464-6800. 1974-.

Environment Index. Environment Information Center, Index Research Department, 124 E. 39th St., New York, New York 10016. 1971-. Annual.

Environmental Information Connection–EIC. Planning Information Program, Dept. of Urban and Regional Planning, University of Illinois, 1003 West Nevada, Urbana, Illinois 61801. (217) 333-1369. Also available online.

Environmental Periodicals Bibliography. Environmental Studies Institute, International Academy at Santa Barbara, 800 Garden St., Suite D, Santa Barbara, California 93101. (805) 965-5010. Also available online.

Science Citation Index. Institute for Scientific Information, 3501 Market St., Philadelphia, Pennsylvania 19104. 1961-.

BIBLIOGRAPHIES

EPA Publications Bibliography. U.S. Environmental Protection Agency, Library Systems Branch, 401 M St., SW, Washington, District of Columbia 20460. (202) 260-2090. Quarterly.

ENCYCLOPEDIAS AND DICTIONARIES

Van Nostrand's Scientific Encyclopedia. Glenn D. Considine, ed. Van Nostrand Reinhold, 115 5th Ave., New York, New York 10003. (212) 254-3232. 1983. Sixth edition. Includes all broad subject areas in science.

ONLINE DATA BASES

Enviro/Energyline Abstracts Plus. R. R. Bowker Co., 121 Chanlon Rd., New Providence, New Jersey 07974. (908) 464-6800.

Environmental Periodicals Bibliography. National Information Services Corp., Ste. 6, Wyman Towers, 3100 St. Paul St., Baltimore, Maryland 21218. (410)243-0797. Online version of abstract of same name.

STRIP CUTTING

ABSTRACTING AND INDEXING SERVICES

Science Citation Index. Institute for Scientific Information, 3501 Market St., Philadelphia, Pennsylvania 19104. 1961-.

ENCYCLOPEDIAS AND DICTIONARIES

Van Nostrand's Scientific Encyclopedia. Glenn D. Considine, ed. Van Nostrand Reinhold, 115 5th Ave., New York, New York 10003. (212) 254-3232. 1983. Sixth edition. Includes all broad subject areas in science.

STRONTIUM

ABSTRACTING AND INDEXING SERVICES

ASFA Aquaculture Abstracts. Cambridge Scientific Abstracts, Inc., 5161 River Rd., Bethesda, Maryland 20816. (301) 961-6750. 1984.

Chemical Abstracts. Chemical Abstracts Service, 2540 Olentangy River Rd., PO Box 3012, Columbus, Ohio 43210. (800) 848-6533. 1907-.

General Science Index. H. W. Wilson Co., 950 University Ave., Bronx, New York 10452. 1978-. Monthly, also issued in annual cumulation. Cumulative subject index to English language periodicals in the subject fields of astronomy, botany, chemistry, earth science, environment and conservation, food and nutrition, genetics, mathematics, medicine and health, microbiology, oceanography, physics, physiology and zoology.

Mineralogical Abstracts. Mineralogical Society, 41 Queen's Gate, London, England SW7 5HR. 71 5847916. Quarterly. Abstracts of journal articles, conferences, technical reports and specialized books in the areas of minerals, clay minerals, economic minerals, ore deposits, environmental mineralogy, experimental mineralogy, gemstones, geochemistry, petrology, lunar and planetary studies and other related areas in mineralogy.

Science Citation Index. Institute for Scientific Information, 3501 Market St., Philadelphia, Pennsylvania 19104. 1961-.

BIBLIOGRAPHIES

Bibliography and Index of Geology. American Geological Institute, 4220 King St., Alexandria, Virginia 22302. Monthly. Includes environmental geology and hydrogeology.

ENCYCLOPEDIAS AND DICTIONARIES

Encyclopedia of Electrochemistry of Elements. A. J. Bard. Marcel Dekker, Inc., 270 Madison Ave., New York, New York 10016. (212) 696-9000 or (800) 228-1160. Encyclopedic treatment of the subject area of electrochemistry and related subjects.

Encyclopedia of Minerals. Willard Lincoln Roberts, et al. Van Nostrand Reinhold, 115 5th Ave., New York, New York 10003. (212) 254-3232 or (800) 926-2665. 1990. Second edition. Gives information on rare minerals, those minerals widely known and collected and those that are most attractive or visually diagnostic.

McGraw-Hill Encyclopedia of Science and Technology. McGraw-Hill, 1221 Avenue of the Americas, New York, New York 10020. (212) 512-2000 or (800) 262-4729. 1992. Seventh edition. Issued in multiple volumes including index. Includes all science and technology broad subject areas.

Van Nostrand's Scientific Encyclopedia. Glenn D. Considine, ed. Van Nostrand Reinhold, 115 5th Ave., New York, New York 10003. (212) 254-3232. 1983. Sixth edition. Includes all broad subject areas in science.

GENERAL WORKS

Magill's Survey of Science. Earth Science Series. Frank N. Magill. Salem Press, PO Box 50062, Pasadena, California 91105. 1990-. Five volumes. Includes information on earth's crust, hot spots and volcanic island chains, physical properties of minerals, rock magnetism, physical properties of rocks, and index.

ONLINE DATA BASES

Chemical Abstracts-CA. Chemical Abstracts Service, 2540 Olentangy River Rd., P.O. Box 3012, Columbus, Ohio 43210. (800) 848-6533 or (614) 421-3600. Information sources include 9000 journals, patents from 27 countries, two industrial property organizations, new books, conference proceedings, and government research reports.

TRADE ASSOCIATIONS AND PROFESSIONAL SOCIETIES

American Chemical Society. 1155 16th St., N.W., Washington, District of Columbia 20036. (202) 872-4600.

STYRENE

ABSTRACTING AND INDEXING SERVICES

Chemical Abstracts. Chemical Abstracts Service, 2540 Olentangy River Rd., PO Box 3012, Columbus, Ohio 43210. (800) 848-6533. 1907-.

General Science Index. H. W. Wilson Co., 950 University Ave., Bronx, New York 10452. 1978-. Monthly, also issued in annual cumulation. Cumulative subject index to English language periodicals in the subject fields of astronomy, botany, chemistry, earth science, environment and conservation, food and nutrition, genetics, mathematics, medicine and health, microbiology, oceanography, physics, physiology and zoology.

Science Citation Index. Institute for Scientific Information, 3501 Market St., Philadelphia, Pennsylvania 19104. 1961-.

ENCYCLOPEDIAS AND DICTIONARIES

Encyclopedia of Chemical Technology. Raymond E. Kirk. John Wiley & Sons, Inc., 605 3rd Ave., New York, New York 10158-0012. (212) 850-6000. 1991-. 4th ed. Also known as Kirk Othmer Encyclopedia of Chemical Technology; consists of 26 volumes.

McGraw-Hill Encyclopedia of Science and Technology. McGraw-Hill, 1221 Avenue of the Americas, New York, New York 10020. (212) 512-2000 or (800) 262-4729. 1992. Seventh edition. Issued in multiple volumes including index. Includes all science and technology broad subject areas.

Ullmanns Encyclopedia of Industrial Chemistry. Hans Jurgen Arpe and Wolfgang Gerhartz, eds. VCH Publishers, 303 NW 12th Ave., Deerfield Beach, Florida 33442-1788. (305) 428-5566. 1990. Designed to keep up with

the broad spectrum of chemical technology. Thirty-six volumes of the encyclopedia have been divided into two sets: the 28 A volumes contain alphabetically arranged articles on chemicals, product groups, processes and technological concepts; and the 8 B volumes are compendia of basic knowledge in industrial chemistry.

Van Nostrand's Scientific Encyclopedia. Glenn D. Considine, ed. Van Nostrand Reinhold, 115 5th Ave., New York, New York 10003. (212) 254-3232. 1983. Sixth edition. Includes all broad subject areas in science.

GENERAL WORKS

Organic Solvents: Physical Properties and Methods of Solvents. John A. Riddick, et al. John Wiley & Sons, Inc., 605 3rd Ave., New York, New York 10158-0012. (212) 850-6000. 1986. 4th ed.

Teratologic Assessment of Butylene Oxide, Styrene Oxide and Methyl Bromide. Melvin R. Sikov. U.S. G.P.O., Washington, District of Columbia 20401. (202) 512-0000. 1981. Toxicology aspects of the following: butene, styrene, bromomethane, teratogenic agents, hydrocarbons, and ethers.

HANDBOOKS AND MANUALS

Documentation of the Threshold Limit Values. American Conference of Governmental Industrial Hygienists, 6500 Glenway, Building D-5, Cincinnati, Ohio 45211. 1991. Provides threshold limit value documentation for any physical phenomenon in the environment, including chemical substances and physical agents.

FDA Food Additives Analytical Manual. C. Warner, et al., eds. Association of Official Analytical Chemists, 2200 Wilson Blvd., Suite 400-P, Arlington, Virginia 22201-3301. (703) 522-3032. 1983-1987. 2 vols. Provides methodology for determining compliance with food additive regulations. Contains analytical methods that have been evaluated by the FDA or found to operate satisfactorily in at least two laboratories.

Handbook of Chemistry and Physics. CRC Press, 2000 Corporate Blvd. N.W., Boca Raton, Florida 33431. (800) 272-7737. Annually.

Handbook of Environmental Data on Organic Chemicals. Karel Verschueren. Van Nostrand Reinhold, 115 5th Ave., New York, New York 10003. (212) 254-3232. 1983. Covers individual substances as well as mixtures and preparations. The profiles include: properties, air pollution factors, water pollution factors, and biological effects.

NIOSH Pocket Guide to Chemical Hazards. National Institute for Occupational Safety and Health, 1600 Clifton Rd. NE, Atlanta, Georgia 30333. (404) 639-3286. 1990. Presents sources of general industrial hygiene and medical surveillance information for workers, employees and others. Presents key information and data in an abbreviated format for 398 individual chemicals or chemical types.

ONLINE DATA BASES

CAS Source Index–CASSI. Chemical Abstracts Service, 2540 Olentangy River Rd., P.O. Box 3012, Columbus, Ohio 43210. (800) 848-6533 or (614) 421-3600. A listing of bibliographic and library holdings information for

scientific and technical primary literature relevant to the chemical sciences.

Chemical Abstracts-CA. Chemical Abstracts Service, 2540 Olentangy River Rd., P.O. Box 3012, Columbus, Ohio 43210. (800) 848-6533 or (614) 421-3600. Information sources include 9000 journals, patents from 27 countries, two industrial property organizations, new books, conference proceedings, and government research reports.

Chemical Collection System/Request Tracking–CCS/ RTS. U.S. Environmental Protection Agency, Office of Pesticides and Toxic Substances, 401 M St., SW, Washington, District of Columbia 20460. (202) 260-2090. Contains information on various properties of a number of chemicals including environmental effects, test and analysis methods, and health effects. Available from EPA.

Chemical Dictionary Online–CHEMLINE. Chemical Abstracts Service, 2540 Olentangy River Rd., Columbus, Ohio 43210. (614) 421-3600 or (800) 848-6533. Part of MEDLINE of the National Library of Medicine (NLM). File of 900,000 names for chemical substances, representing 450,000 unique compounds. It contains such information as Chemical Abstracts (CA) Service Registry Numbers, molecular formulas, preferred chemical nomenclature, and generic and ring structure information. Available on NLM's ELHILL system.

Chemical Exposure. Science Applications International Corp., Health & Environmental Information, P.O. Box 2501, Oak Ridge, Tennessee 37831. (615) 482-9031. Database of chemicals that have been identified in both human tissues and body fluids and in feral and food animals. Contains reference to journal articles, conferences, and reports. Covers the whole fields of information related to human and animal exposure to food, air, and water contaminants and pharmaceuticals. Its records include information on chemical properties, formulas, tissues measured, analytical method used, demographics and more. Available on DIALOG.

PERIODICALS AND NEWSLETTERS

Environmental Science and Technology. American Chemical Society, 1155 16th St. N.W., Washington, District of Columbia 20036. (800) 227-5558. 1967-. Monthly. Contains research articles on various aspects of environmental chemistry, interpretative articles by invited experts and commentary on the scientific aspects of environmental management.

TRADE ASSOCIATIONS AND PROFESSIONAL SOCIETIES

American Chemical Society. 1155 16th St., N.W., Washington, District of Columbia 20036. (202) 872-4600.

Styrene and Ethylbenzene Association. c/o SOCMA, 1330 Connecticut Ave., N.W., Suite 300, Washington, District of Columbia 20036. (202) 659-0060.

Styrene Information and Research Center. 1275 K St., N.W., Suite 400, Washington, District of Columbia 20036. (202) 371-5314.

STYROFOAM

See also: CHLOROFLUOROCARBONS (CFCS); OZONE
LAYER

ABSTRACTING AND INDEXING SERVICES

Applied Science and Technology Index. H.W. Wilson Co., 950 University Ave., Bronx, New York 10452. (800) 367-6770. Formerly Industrial Arts Index.

Science Citation Index. Institute for Scientific Information, 3501 Market St., Philadelphia, Pennsylvania 19104. 1961-.

ENCYCLOPEDIAS AND DICTIONARIES

Van Nostrand's Scientific Encyclopedia. Glenn D. Considine, ed. Van Nostrand Reinhold, 115 5th Ave., New York, New York 10003. (212) 254-3232. 1983. Sixth edition. Includes all broad subject areas in science.

SUBITUMINOUS COAL

See: COAL

SULFANIMIDE FUNGICIDES

ABSTRACTING AND INDEXING SERVICES

Chemical Abstracts. Chemical Abstracts Service, 2540 Olentangy River Rd., PO Box 3012, Columbus, Ohio 43210. (800) 848-6533. 1907-.

Science Citation Index. Institute for Scientific Information, 3501 Market St., Philadelphia, Pennsylvania 19104. 1961-.

ENCYCLOPEDIAS AND DICTIONARIES

Van Nostrand's Scientific Encyclopedia. Glenn D. Considine, ed. Van Nostrand Reinhold, 115 5th Ave., New York, New York 10003. (212) 254-3232. 1983. Sixth edition. Includes all broad subject areas in science.

GENERAL WORKS

Synthesis and Chemistry of Agrochemicals II. Don R. Baker, et al., eds. American Chemical Society, 1155 16th St. N.W., Washington, District of Columbia 20036. (202) 872-4600; (800) 227-5558. 1991. Trends in synthesis and chemistry of agrochemicals.

ONLINE DATA BASES

Chemical Abstracts-CA. Chemical Abstracts Service, 2540 Olentangy River Rd., P.O. Box 3012, Columbus, Ohio 43210. (800) 848-6533 or (614) 421-3600. Information sources include 9000 journals, patents from 27 countries, two industrial property organizations, new books, conference proceedings, and government research reports.

Chemical Carcinogenesis Research Information System–CCRIS. National Library of Medicine, 8600 Rockville Pike, Bethesda, Maryland 20894. (800) 638-8480. Individual assay results and test conditions for 1,451 chemicals in the areas of carcinogenicity, mutagenicity, tumor promotion, and cocarcinogenicity.

Chemical Collection System/Request Tracking–CCS/ RTS. U.S. Environmental Protection Agency, Office of Pesticides and Toxic Substances, 401 M St., SW, Washington, District of Columbia 20460. (202) 260-2090. Contains information on various properties of a number of chemicals including environmental effects, test and analysis methods, and health effects. Available from EPA.

Chemical Dictionary Online–CHEMLINE. Chemical Abstracts Service, 2540 Olentangy River Rd., Columbus, Ohio 43210. (614) 421-3600 or (800) 848-6533. Part of MEDLINE of the National Library of Medicine (NLM). File of 900,000 names for chemical substances, representing 450,000 unique compounds. It contains such information as Chemical Abstracts (CA) Service Registry Numbers, molecular formulas, preferred chemical nomenclature, and generic and ring structure information. Available on NLM's ELHILL system.

Chemical Exposure. Science Applications International Corp., Health & Environmental Information, P.O. Box 2501, Oak Ridge, Tennessee 37831. (615) 482-9031. Database of chemicals that have been identified in both human tissues and body fluids and in feral and food animals. Contains reference to journal articles, conferences, and reports. Covers the whole fields of information related to human and animal exposure to food, air, and water contaminants and pharmaceuticals. Its records include information on chemical properties, formulas, tissues measured, analytical method used, demographics and more. Available on DIALOG.

PressNet Environmental Reports. Chemical Information Systems, Inc., 7215 York Rd., Baltimore, Maryland 21212. (301) 321-8440.

TRADE ASSOCIATIONS AND PROFESSIONAL SOCIETIES

American Chemical Society. 1155 16th St., N.W., Washington, District of Columbia 20036. (202) 872-4600.

SULFIDES

ABSTRACTING AND INDEXING SERVICES

Chemical Abstracts. Chemical Abstracts Service, 2540 Olentangy River Rd., PO Box 3012, Columbus, Ohio 43210. (800) 848-6533. 1907-.

Science Citation Index. Institute for Scientific Information, 3501 Market St., Philadelphia, Pennsylvania 19104. 1961-.

ENCYCLOPEDIAS AND DICTIONARIES

Ullmanns Encyclopedia of Industrial Chemistry. Hans Jurgen Arpe and Wolfgang Gerhartz, eds. VCH Publishers, 303 NW 12th Ave., Deerfield Beach, Florida 33442-1788. (305) 428-5566. 1990. Designed to keep up with the broad spectrum of chemical technology. Thirty-six volumes of the encyclopedia have been divided into two sets: the 28 A volumes contain alphabetically arranged articles on chemicals, product groups, processes and technological concepts; and the 8 B volumes are compendia of basic knowledge in industrial chemistry.

Van Nostrand's Scientific Encyclopedia. Glenn D. Considine, ed. Van Nostrand Reinhold, 115 5th Ave., New York, New York 10003. (212) 254-3232. 1983. Sixth edition. Includes all broad subject areas in science.

ONLINE DATA BASES

CAS Source Index–CASSI. Chemical Abstracts Service, 2540 Olentangy River Rd., P.O. Box 3012, Columbus, Ohio 43210. (800) 848-6533 or (614) 421-3600. A listing of bibliographic and library holdings information for scientific and technical primary literature relevant to the chemical sciences.

Chemical Abstracts-CA. Chemical Abstracts Service, 2540 Olentangy River Rd., P.O. Box 3012, Columbus, Ohio 43210. (800) 848-6533 or (614) 421-3600. Information sources include 9000 journals, patents from 27 countries, two industrial property organizations, new books, conference proceedings, and government research reports.

Chemical Collection System/Request Tracking–CCS/RTS. U.S. Environmental Protection Agency, Office of Pesticides and Toxic Substances, 401 M St., SW, Washington, District of Columbia 20460. (202) 260-2090. Contains information on various properties of a number of chemicals including environmental effects, test and analysis methods, and health effects. Available from EPA.

Chemical Dictionary Online–CHEMLINE. Chemical Abstracts Service, 2540 Olentangy River Rd., Columbus, Ohio 43210. (614) 421-3600 or (800) 848-6533. Part of MEDLINE of the National Library of Medicine (NLM). File of 900,000 names for chemical substances, representing 450,000 unique compounds. It contains such information as Chemical Abstracts (CA) Service Registry Numbers, molecular formulas, preferred chemical nomenclature, and generic and ring structure information. Available on NLM's ELHILL system.

Chemical Exposure. Science Applications International Corp., Health & Environmental Information, P.O. Box 2501, Oak Ridge, Tennessee 37831. (615) 482-9031. Database of chemicals that have been identified in both human tissues and body fluids and in feral and food animals. Contains reference to journal articles, conferences, and reports. Covers the whole fields of information related to human and animal exposure to food, air, and water contaminants and pharmaceuticals. Its records include information on chemical properties, formulas, tissues measured, analytical method used, demographics and more. Available on DIALOG.

TRADE ASSOCIATIONS AND PROFESSIONAL SOCIETIES

American Chemical Society. 1155 16th St., N.W., Washington, District of Columbia 20036. (202) 872-4600.

SULFITES

ABSTRACTING AND INDEXING SERVICES

Chemical Abstracts. Chemical Abstracts Service, 2540 Olentangy River Rd., PO Box 3012, Columbus, Ohio 43210. (800) 848-6533. 1907-.

Science Citation Index. Institute for Scientific Information, 3501 Market St., Philadelphia, Pennsylvania 19104. 1961-.

ENCYCLOPEDIAS AND DICTIONARIES

Ullmanns Encyclopedia of Industrial Chemistry. Hans Jurgen Arpe and Wolfgang Gerhartz, eds. VCH Publishers, 303 NW 12th Ave., Deerfield Beach, Florida 33442-1788. (305) 428-5566. 1990. Designed to keep up with the broad spectrum of chemical technology. Thirty-six volumes of the encyclopedia have been divided into two sets: the 28 A volumes contain alphabetically arranged articles on chemicals, product groups, processes and technological concepts; and the 8 B volumes are compendia of basic knowledge in industrial chemistry.

Van Nostrand's Scientific Encyclopedia. Glenn D. Considine, ed. Van Nostrand Reinhold, 115 5th Ave., New York, New York 10003. (212) 254-3232. 1983. Sixth edition. Includes all broad subject areas in science.

ONLINE DATA BASES

CAS Source Index–CASSI. Chemical Abstracts Service, 2540 Olentangy River Rd., P.O. Box 3012, Columbus, Ohio 43210. (800) 848-6533 or (614) 421-3600. A listing of bibliographic and library holdings information for scientific and technical primary literature relevant to the chemical sciences.

Chemical Abstracts–CA. Chemical Abstracts Service, 2540 Olentangy River Rd., P.O. Box 3012, Columbus, Ohio 43210. (800) 848-6533 or (614) 421-3600. Information sources include 9000 journals, patents from 27 countries, two industrial property organizations, new books, conference proceedings, and government research reports.

Chemical Collection System/Request Tracking–CCS/ RTS. U.S. Environmental Protection Agency, Office of Pesticides and Toxic Substances, 401 M St., SW, Washington, District of Columbia 20460. (202) 260-2090. Contains information on various properties of a number of chemicals including environmental effects, test and analysis methods, and health effects. Available from EPA.

Chemical Dictionary Online–CHEMLINE. Chemical Abstracts Service, 2540 Olentangy River Rd., Columbus, Ohio 43210. (614) 421-3600 or (800) 848-6533. Part of MEDLINE of the National Library of Medicine (NLM). File of 900,000 names for chemical substances, representing 450,000 unique compounds. It contains such information as Chemical Abstracts (CA) Service Registry Numbers, molecular formulas, preferred chemical nomenclature, and generic and ring structure information. Available on NLM's ELHILL system.

Chemical Exposure. Science Applications International Corp., Health & Environmental Information, P.O. Box 2501, Oak Ridge, Tennessee 37831. (615) 482-9031. Database of chemicals that have been identified in both human tissues and body fluids and in feral and food animals. Contains reference to journal articles, conferences, and reports. Covers the whole fields of information related to human and animal exposure to food, air, and water contaminants and pharmaceuticals. Its records include information on chemical properties, formulas, tissues measured, analytical method used, demographics and more. Available on DIALOG.

TRADE ASSOCIATIONS AND PROFESSIONAL SOCIETIES

American Chemical Society. 1155 16th St., N.W., Washington, District of Columbia 20036. (202) 872-4600.

SULFUR

ABSTRACTING AND INDEXING SERVICES

Biotechnology Research Abstracts. Cambridge Scientific Abstracts, 5161 River Rd., Bethesda, Maryland 20816. (301) 961-6750. Monthly. Includes such broad areas as genetic intervention, biochemical genetics, and microbiological techniques.

Chemical Abstracts. Chemical Abstracts Service, 2540 Olentangy River Rd., PO Box 3012, Columbus, Ohio 43210. (800) 848-6533. 1907-.

General Science Index. H. W. Wilson Co., 950 University Ave., Bronx, New York 10452. 1978-. Monthly, also issued in annual cumulation. Cumulative subject index to English language periodicals in the subject fields of astronomy, botany, chemistry, earth science, environment and conservation, food and nutrition, genetics, mathematics, medicine and health, microbiology, oceanography, physics, physiology and zoology.

INIS Atomindex. International Atomic Energy Agency, Wagramerstrasse 5, Vienna, Austria A-1400. 222 23606198. 1988-. Semiannual. Abstracts nuclear energy and nuclear physics topics from journals, conferences, technical reports and other related publications. Issued in 6 parts: Personal Author, Corporate Entry, Subject, Report, Standard Patent, Conference (by place), Conference (by date).

Science Citation Index. Institute for Scientific Information, 3501 Market St., Philadelphia, Pennsylvania 19104. 1961-.

DIRECTORIES

Gale Environmental Sourcebook. Karen Hill. Gale Research Co., 835 Penobscot Bldg., Detroit, Michigan 48226-4094. (313) 961-2242. Contacts, information sources, or general information on environmental topics.

ENCYCLOPEDIAS AND DICTIONARIES

McGraw-Hill Encyclopedia of Science and Technology. McGraw-Hill, 1221 Avenue of the Americas, New York, New York 10020. (212) 512-2000 or (800) 262-4729. 1992. Seventh edition. Issued in multiple volumes including index. Includes all science and technology broad subject areas.

Ullmanns Encyclopedia of Industrial Chemistry. Hans Jurgen Arpe and Wolfgang Gerhartz, eds. VCH Publishers, 303 NW 12th Ave., Deerfield Beach, Florida 33442-1788. (305) 428-5566. 1990. Designed to keep up with the broad spectrum of chemical technology. Thirty-six volumes of the encyclopedia have been divided into two sets: the 28 A volumes contain alphabetically arranged articles on chemicals, product groups, processes and technological concepts; and the 8 B volumes are compendia of basic knowledge in industrial chemistry.

Van Nostrand's Scientific Encyclopedia. Glenn D. Considine, ed. Van Nostrand Reinhold, 115 5th Ave., New York, New York 10003. (212) 254-3232. 1983. Sixth edition. Includes all broad subject areas in science.

GENERAL WORKS

Stable Isotopes: Natural and Anthropogenic Sulphur in the Environment. R. R. Krouse and V. H. Grinenko, eds. John Wiley & Sons, Inc., 605 3rd Ave., New York, New York 10158-0012. (212) 850-6000. 1991. Published on behalf of the Scientific Committee on Problems of the Environment (SCOPE) of the International Council of Scientific Unions (ICSU) in collaboration with the United Nations Environment Programme. Addresses the important question of differentiating natural and anthropogenic sulphur in the environment. International experts explain how stable isotopes of sulphur and oxygen have been used to study the origin and transformations of sulphur in ecosystems.

ONLINE DATA BASES

CAS Source Index–CASSI. Chemical Abstracts Service, 2540 Olentangy River Rd., P.O. Box 3012, Columbus, Ohio 43210. (800) 848-6533 or (614) 421-3600. A listing of bibliographic and library holdings information for scientific and technical primary literature relevant to the chemical sciences.

Chemical Abstracts–CA. Chemical Abstracts Service, 2540 Olentangy River Rd., P.O. Box 3012, Columbus, Ohio 43210. (800) 848-6533 or (614) 421-3600. Information sources include 9000 journals, patents from 27 countries, two industrial property organizations, new books, conference proceedings, and government research reports.

Chemical Collection System/Request Tracking–CCS/ RTS. U.S. Environmental Protection Agency, Office of Pesticides and Toxic Substances, 401 M St., SW, Washington, District of Columbia 20460. (202) 260-2090. Contains information on various properties of a number of chemicals including environmental effects, test and analysis methods, and health effects. Available from EPA.

Chemical Dictionary Online–CHEMLINE. Chemical Abstracts Service, 2540 Olentangy River Rd., Columbus, Ohio 43210. (614) 421-3600 or (800) 848-6533. Part of MEDLINE of the National Library of Medicine (NLM). File of 900,000 names for chemical substances, representing 450,000 unique compounds. It contains such information as Chemical Abstracts (CA) Service Registry Numbers, molecular formulas, preferred chemical nomenclature, and generic and ring structure information. Available on NLM's ELHILL system.

Chemical Exposure. Science Applications International Corp., Health & Environmental Information, P.O. Box 2501, Oak Ridge, Tennessee 37831. (615) 482-9031. Database of chemicals that have been identified in both human tissues and body fluids and in feral and food animals. Contains reference to journal articles, conferences, and reports. Covers the whole fields of information related to human and animal exposure to food, air, and water contaminants and pharmaceuticals. Its records include information on chemical properties, formulas, tissues measured, analytical method used, demographics and more. Available on DIALOG.

STATISTICS SOURCES

Environmental Data Compendium. OECD Publications and Information Center, 2001 L St., N.W., Suite 700, Washington, District of Columbia 20036. (202) 785-6323. 1989.

Environmental Indicators. OECD Publications and Information Center, 2001 L St., N.W., Suite 700, Washington, District of Columbia 20036. (202) 785-6323. 1991.

Environmental Quality. Council on Environmental Quality. U.S. G.P.O., Washington, District of Columbia 20401. (202) 512-0000. Annual.

The State of the Environment. OECD Publications and Information Center, 2001 L St., N.W., Suite 700, Washington, District of Columbia 20036. (202) 785-6323. 1991.

World Resources. World Resources Institute. 1709 New York Ave., N.W., Washington, District of Columbia 20006. (202) 638-6300. Annual. Statistical and textual analysis of world's natural resources and the effects of growth-caused environmental pollution.

TRADE ASSOCIATIONS AND PROFESSIONAL SOCIETIES

American Chemical Society. 1155 16th St., N.W., Washington, District of Columbia 20036. (202) 872-4600.

Sulphur Institute. 1725 K St., N.W., Suite 508, Washington, District of Columbia 20006. (202) 331-9660.

SULFUR COMPOUNDS
See: SULFUR

SULFUR DIOXIDE
See also: SULFUR

ABSTRACTING AND INDEXING SERVICES

Air Pollution Technical Publications of the United States Environmental Protection Agency. U.S. Environmental Protection Agency, Mail Drop 75, Research Triangle Park, North Carolina 27711. (919) 541-2184. 1976. Quarterly.

Air Pollution Titles. Pennsylvania State University, Center for Air Environmental Studies, 226 Fenske Laboratory, University Park, Pennsylvania 16802. (814) 865-1415. 1965. Bibliographic guide to current research literature on air environment, including monitoring and control of air pollution, health effects, effects on agriculture, forests, toxic air contaminants, and global atmospheric pro cases.

Air Pollution Translations. A Bibliography With Abstracts. U.S. Environmental Protection Agency, MD 75, Research Triangle Park, North Carolina 27711. (919) 541-2184. 1969.

Applied Science and Technology Index. H.W. Wilson Co., 950 University Ave., Bronx, New York 10452. (800) 367-6770. Formerly Industrial Arts Index.

Bulletin Signaletique: Eau et Assainissement, Pollution Atmospherique, Droit des Pollutions. Centre de Documentation, Centre National de la Recherche Scientifique, 15, quai Anatole France, Paris, France 75700. (1) 45 55 92 25. 1983-. Monthly. Indexes pollution periodicals including water, atmospheric and related pollutions.

Chemical Abstracts. Chemical Abstracts Service, 2540 Olentangy River Rd., PO Box 3012, Columbus, Ohio 43210. (800) 848-6533. 1907-.

Environment Abstracts. Bowker A & I Publishing, 121 Chanlon Rd., New Providence, New Jersey 07974. (908) 464-6800. 1974-.

Environment Index. Environment Information Center, Index Research Department, 124 E. 39th St., New York, New York 10016. 1971-. Annual.

Environmental Information Connection–EIC. Planning Information Program, Dept. of Urban and Regional Planning, University of Illinois, 1003 West Nevada, Urbana, Illinois 61801. (217) 333-1369. Also available online.

Environmental Periodicals Bibliography. Environmental Studies Institute, International Academy at Santa Barbara, 800 Garden St., Suite D, Santa Barbara, California 93101. (805) 965-5010. Also available online.

Science Citation Index. Institute for Scientific Information, 3501 Market St., Philadelphia, Pennsylvania 19104. 1961-.

BIBLIOGRAPHIES

Bibliography and Index of Geology. American Geological Institute, 4220 King St., Alexandria, Virginia 22302. Monthly. Includes environmental geology and hydrogeology.

EPA Publications Bibliography. U.S. Environmental Protection Agency, Library Systems Branch, 401 M St., SW, Washington, District of Columbia 20460. (202) 260-2090. Quarterly.

ENCYCLOPEDIAS AND DICTIONARIES

Van Nostrand's Scientific Encyclopedia. Glenn D. Considine, ed. Van Nostrand Reinhold, 115 5th Ave., New York, New York 10003. (212) 254-3232. 1983. Sixth edition. Includes all broad subject areas in science.

GENERAL WORKS

Magill's Survey of Science. Earth Science Series. Frank N. Magill. Salem Press, PO Box 50062, Pasadena, California 91105. 1990-. Five volumes. Includes information on earth's crust, hot spots and volcanic island chains, physical properties of minerals, rock magnetism, physical properties of rocks, and index.

ONLINE DATA BASES

Chemical Abstracts-CA. Chemical Abstracts Service, 2540 Olentangy River Rd., P.O. Box 3012, Columbus, Ohio 43210. (800) 848-6533 or (614) 421-3600. Information sources include 9000 journals, patents from 27 countries, two industrial property organizations, new books, conference proceedings, and government research reports.

Enviro/Energyline Abstracts Plus. R. R. Bowker Co., 121 Chanlon Rd., New Providence, New Jersey 07974. (908) 464-6800.

Environmental Periodicals Bibliography. National Information Services Corp., Ste. 6, Wyman Towers, 3100 St. Paul St., Baltimore, Maryland 21218. (410)243-0797. Online version of abstract of same name.

PERIODICALS AND NEWSLETTERS

Atmospheric Environment. Pergamon Microforms International, Inc., Fairview Park, Elmsford, New York 10523. (914) 592-7720. 1966-. Publishes papers on all aspects of man's interactions with his atmospheric environment, including the administrative, economic and political aspects of these interactions. Air pollution research and its applications are covered, taking into account changes in the atmospheric flow patterns, temperature distributions and chemical constitution caused by natural and artificial variations in the earth's surface.

TRADE ASSOCIATIONS AND PROFESSIONAL SOCIETIES

American Chemical Society. 1155 16th St., N.W., Washington, District of Columbia 20036. (202) 872-4600.

American Institute of Chemical Engineers. 345 East 47th St., New York, New York 10017. (212) 705-7338.

American Institute of Chemists. 7315 Wisconsin Ave., Bethesda, Maryland 20814. (301) 652-2447.

SULFUR RECOVERY

See: SULFUR

SULFUR RESOURCES

See: SULFUR

SULFUR TRIOXIDE

See: SULFUR

SULFURIC ACID

ABSTRACTING AND INDEXING SERVICES

Chemical Abstracts. Chemical Abstracts Service, 2540 Olentangy River Rd., PO Box 3012, Columbus, Ohio 43210. (800) 848-6533. 1907-.

Science Citation Index. Institute for Scientific Information, 3501 Market St., Philadelphia, Pennsylvania 19104. 1961-.

ENCYCLOPEDIAS AND DICTIONARIES

Van Nostrand's Scientific Encyclopedia. Glenn D. Considine, ed. Van Nostrand Reinhold, 115 5th Ave., New York, New York 10003. (212) 254-3232. 1983. Sixth edition. Includes all broad subject areas in science.

ONLINE DATA BASES

CAS Source Index–CASSI. Chemical Abstracts Service, 2540 Olentangy River Rd., P.O. Box 3012, Columbus, Ohio 43210. (800) 848-6533 or (614) 421-3600. A listing of bibliographic and library holdings information for scientific and technical primary literature relevant to the chemical sciences.

Chemical Abstracts-CA. Chemical Abstracts Service, 2540 Olentangy River Rd., P.O. Box 3012, Columbus, Ohio 43210. (800) 848-6533 or (614) 421-3600. Information sources include 9000 journals, patents from 27 countries, two industrial property organizations, new books, conference proceedings, and government research reports.

TRADE ASSOCIATIONS AND PROFESSIONAL SOCIETIES

American Chemical Society. 1155 16th St., N.W., Washington, District of Columbia 20036. (202) 872-4600.

American Institute of Chemical Engineers. 345 East 47th St., New York, New York 10017. (212) 705-7338.

American Institute of Chemists. 7315 Wisconsin Ave., Bethesda, Maryland 20814. (301) 652-2447.

SUPERCONDUCTORS

ABSTRACTING AND INDEXING SERVICES

Chemical Abstracts. Chemical Abstracts Service, 2540 Olentangy River Rd., PO Box 3012, Columbus, Ohio 43210. (800) 848-6533. 1907-.

Science Citation Index. Institute for Scientific Information, 3501 Market St., Philadelphia, Pennsylvania 19104. 1961-.

ENCYCLOPEDIAS AND DICTIONARIES

McGraw-Hill Encyclopedia of Science and Technology. McGraw-Hill, 1221 Avenue of the Americas, New York, New York 10020. (212) 512-2000 or (800) 262-4729. 1992. Seventh edition. Issued in multiple volumes including index. Includes all science and technology broad subject areas.

Van Nostrand's Scientific Encyclopedia. Glenn D. Considine, ed. Van Nostrand Reinhold, 115 5th Ave., New York, New York 10003. (212) 254-3232. 1983. Sixth edition. Includes all broad subject areas in science.

ONLINE DATA BASES

Chemical Abstracts-CA. Chemical Abstracts Service, 2540 Olentangy River Rd., P.O. Box 3012, Columbus, Ohio 43210. (800) 848-6533 or (614) 421-3600. Information sources include 9000 journals, patents from 27 countries, two industrial property organizations, new books, conference proceedings, and government research reports.

Solid State and Superconductivity Abstracts. Cambridge Scientific Abstracts, 5161 River Rd., Bethesda, Maryland 20816. (301) 961-6750.

Superconductor Week. NewsNet, Inc., 945 Haverford Rd., Bryn Mawr, Pennsylvania 19010. (800) 345-1301.

SUPERFUND

ABSTRACTING AND INDEXING SERVICES

Chemical Abstracts. Chemical Abstracts Service, 2540 Olentangy River Rd., PO Box 3012, Columbus, Ohio 43210. (800) 848-6533. 1907-.

General Science Index. H. W. Wilson Co., 950 University Ave., Bronx, New York 10452. 1978-. Monthly, also issued in annual cumulation. Cumulative subject index to English language periodicals in the subject fields of astronomy, botany, chemistry, earth science, environment and conservation, food and nutrition, genetics, mathematics, medicine and health, microbiology, oceanography, physics, physiology and zoology.

DIRECTORIES

Gale Environmental Sourcebook. Karen Hill. Gale Research Co., 835 Penobscot Bldg., Detroit, Michigan 48226-4094. (313) 961-2242. Contacts, information sources, or general information on environmental topics.

Reference Directory to Hazardous, Toxic, and Superfund Services. Rimbach Publishing, Inc., 8650 Babcock Blvd., Pittsburgh, Pennsylvania 15237. (412) 364-5366.

ENCYCLOPEDIAS AND DICTIONARIES

McGraw-Hill Encyclopedia of Environmental Science. Sybil P. Parker. McGraw-Hill Science & Engineering Books, 11 W. 19th St., New York, New York 10011. (212) 337-6010. 1980. Covers ecology, man's influence on nature, and environmental protection.

McGraw-Hill Encyclopedia of Science and Technology. McGraw-Hill, 1221 Avenue of the Americas, New York, New York 10020. (212) 512-2000 or (800) 262-4729. 1992. Seventh edition. Issued in multiple volumes including index. Includes all science and technology broad subject areas.

Van Nostrand's Scientific Encyclopedia. Glenn D. Considine, ed. Van Nostrand Reinhold, 115 5th Ave., New York, New York 10003. (212) 254-3232. 1983. Sixth edition. Includes all broad subject areas in science.

GENERAL WORKS

Air/Superfund National Technical Guidance Study Series. Database of Emission Rate Measurement Projects. B. Eklund, et al. U.S. Environmental Protection Agency, 401 M St. SW, Washington, District of Columbia 20460. (202) 260-2090. 1991. Emission rate measurements of polluted air conducted at different projects and compiled into a database.

Air/Superfund National Technical Guidance Study Series. Emission Factors for Superfund Remediation Technologies. P. Thompson, et al. Radian Corporation, Austin, TX., National Technical Information Service, 5285 Port Royal Rd., Springfield, Virginia 22161. (703) 487-4650. Order number PB 91-190975 LDM.

EPA's RCRA/Superfund & EPCRA Hotlines: Questions and Answers. Government Institutes, Inc., 4 Research Pl., Suite 200, Rockville, Maryland 20850. (301) 921-2300. 1991. Actual test of the Significant Questions and Resolved Issues internal EPA reports released each month by the RCRA/Superfund Industrial assistance

Hotline, and the Emergency Planning and Community Right-to-Know Industrial Hotline covering 1989 and 1990.

Extremely Hazardous Substances: Superfund Chemical Profiles. U. S. Environment Protection Agency. Noyes Publications, 120 Mill Rd., Park Ridge, New Jersey 07656. (201) 391-8484. 1988. Contains chemical profiles for each of the 366 chemicals listed as extremely hazardous substances by the USEPA in 1988. The EPA developed this set of documents for use in dealing with Section 302 of Title III of the Superfund Amendments and Reauthorization Act (SARA). Each profile contains a summary of documented information which has been reviewed for accuracy and completeness.

Financing the Cleanup of Hazardous Wastes: The National Environmental Trust Fund. American International Group, New York, New York 1989.

The New Superfund: What It Is, How It Works. U.S. Environmental Protection Agency, 401 M St. SW, Washington, District of Columbia 20460. (202) 260-2090. 1987.

GOVERNMENTAL ORGANIZATIONS

U.S. Environmental Protection Agency: Office of Environmental Engineering and Technology. 401 M St., S.W., Washington, District of Columbia 20460. (202) 382-2600.

U.S. Environmental Protection Agency: RCRA/Superfund Hotline. 401 M St., S.W., Washington, District of Columbia 20460. (202) 382-9346.

HANDBOOKS AND MANUALS

Superfund Handbook. Sidley & Austin, 696 Virginia Road, Concord, Massachusetts 01742. 1987. Law and legislation relating to refuse, refuse disposal, and its environmental aspects.

Superfund Manual: Legal and Management Strategies. Crowell & Moring. Government Institutes, Inc., 4 Research Pl., Suite 200, Rockville, Maryland 20850. (301) 921-2300. 1990. 4th ed. Industrial liability for hazardous waste and pollution damage at hazardous waste sites are explained. Explains the latest developments in the Superfund program. Includes the interrelationships between Superfund and RCRA; new regulations to implement Emergency Planning and the Community Right-to-Know Act; revisions to the National Contingency Plan; new EPA guidance documents relating to cleanup standards, site studies, and settlement procedures; court decisions and the special problems.

ONLINE DATA BASES

CERCLIS. Chemical Information Systems, Inc., 7215 York Rd., Baltimore, Maryland 21212. (301) 321-8440. Information on hazardous waste disposal sites that have either been listed by the EPA on the National Priority List (NPL) or nominated for consideration for the NPL.

Chemical Abstracts-CA. Chemical Abstracts Service, 2540 Olentangy River Rd., P.O. Box 3012, Columbus, Ohio 43210. (800) 848-6533 or (614) 421-3600. Information sources include 9000 journals, patents from 27 countries, two industrial property organizations, new books, conference proceedings, and government research reports.

Superfund. NewsNet, Inc., 945 Haverford Rd., Bryn Mawr, Pennsylvania 19010. (800) 345-1301.

PERIODICALS AND NEWSLETTERS

Inside the EPA'S Superfund Report. Inside Washington Publishers, PO Box 7167, Ben Franklin Station, Washington, District of Columbia 20044. Biweekly. Liability for hazardous substances pollution and damages.

Washington Bulletin. Water Pollution Control Federation, 601 Wythe Street, Alexandria, Virginia 22314-1994. (703) 684-2400. Monthly. Covers legislative issues in the water control industry.

RESEARCH CENTERS AND INSTITUTES

Montana State University, Reclamation Research Unit. Animal & Range Science Department, Bozeman, Montana 59717. (406) 994-4821.

STATISTICS SOURCES

Analysis of State Superfund Programs: 50 State Study. U.S. G.P.O., Washington, District of Columbia 20401. (202) 512-0000. 1989. Report on state Superfund hazardous waste cleanup programs.

Annual Report. U.S. Environmental Protection Agency. U.S. G.P.O., Washington, District of Columbia 20401. (202) 512-0000. Annual. Data on the activities under the Superfund legislation.

Environmental Data Compendium. OECD Publications and Information Center, 2001 L St., N.W., Suite 700, Washington, District of Columbia 20036. (202) 785-6323. 1989.

Environmental Indicators. OECD Publications and Information Center, 2001 L St., N.W., Suite 700, Washington, District of Columbia 20036. (202) 785-6323. 1991.

Environmental Quality. Council on Environmental Quality. U.S. G.P.O., Washington, District of Columbia 20401. (202) 512-0000. Annual.

The State of the Environment. OECD Publications and Information Center, 2001 L St., N.W., Suite 700, Washington, District of Columbia 20036. (202) 785-6323. 1991.

SUPERFUND: A More Vigorous and Better Managed Enforcement Program Is Needed. U.S. G.P.O., Washington, District of Columbia 20401. (202) 512-0000. 1989. Irregular. Superfund hazardous waste site cleanup enforcement and cost recovery activities.

SURFACTANTS

ABSTRACTING AND INDEXING SERVICES

Chemical Abstracts. Chemical Abstracts Service, 2540 Olentangy River Rd., PO Box 3012, Columbus, Ohio 43210. (800) 848-6533. 1907-.

General Science Index. H. W. Wilson Co., 950 University Ave., Bronx, New York 10452. 1978-. Monthly, also issued in annual cumulation. Cumulative subject index to English language periodicals in the subject fields of astronomy, botany, chemistry, earth science, environment and conservation, food and nutrition, genetics,

mathematics, medicine and health, microbiology, oceanography, physics, physiology and zoology.

Metals Abstracts. ASM International, 9639 Kinsman, Materials Park, Ohio 44073. (216) 338-5151. 1968-. Published jointly by the Institute of Metals, London and the American Society for Metals. Formed by the Union of Metallurgical Abstracts and Review of Metal Literature.

Science Citation Index. Institute for Scientific Information, 3501 Market St., Philadelphia, Pennsylvania 19104. 1961-.

ENCYCLOPEDIAS AND DICTIONARIES

Cambridge Encyclopedia of Life Sciences. A. E. Friday and David S. Ingram. Cambridge University Press, 40 W 20th St., New York, New York 10011. (212) 924-3900 or (800) 227-0247. 1985. Includes all topics under biology and ecology.

The Condensed Encyclopedia of Surfactants. Michael and Irene Ash. Chemical Publishing Co., 80 Eighth Ave., New York, New York 10011. (212) 255-1950. Contains over 12,000 entries with the first section devoted to trademarks containing short entries that appear in volumes 1-4. Also includes chemical component and manufacturer cross reference.

Dictionary of Colloid and Surface Science. Paul Becher. Marcel Dekker, Inc., 270 Madison Ave., New York, New York 10016. (212) 696-9000; (800) 228-1160. 1990. Dictionary deals with the areas of colloids, surface chemistry, and the physics and technology involved with surfaces.

Dictionary of Surfactants. Kurt Siekmann, J. Falbe, ed. Springer Verlag, 175 5th Ave., New York, New York 10010. (212) 460-1500 or (800) 777-4643. 1986. Supplement to Surfactants in Consumer Products.

Encyclopedia of Surfactants. Michael Ash and Irene Ash. Chemical Pub. Co., 80 8th Ave., New York, New York 10011. (212) 255-1950. 1980-1985. Four volumes. Provides information on each trade name product including chemical ingredients, properties, form and applications.

McGraw-Hill Encyclopedia of Science and Technology. McGraw-Hill, 1221 Avenue of the Americas, New York, New York 10020. (212) 512-2000 or (800) 262-4729. 1992. Seventh edition. Issued in multiple volumes including index. Includes all science and technology broad subject areas.

Van Nostrand's Scientific Encyclopedia. Glenn D. Considine, ed. Van Nostrand Reinhold, 115 5th Ave., New York, New York 10003. (212) 254-3232. 1983. Sixth edition. Includes all broad subject areas in science.

GENERAL WORKS

River Pollution: An Ecological Perspective. S. M. Haslam. Belhaven Press, 136 S. Broadway, Irvington, New York 10533. (914) 591-9111. 1990. Describes the impact of natural and man-made pollution in the ecosystem of freshwater streams, stressing understanding of processes and techniques of measurement.

ONLINE DATA BASES

Chemical Abstracts-CA. Chemical Abstracts Service, 2540 Olentangy River Rd., P.O. Box 3012, Columbus,

Ohio 43210. (800) 848-6533 or (614) 421-3600. Information sources include 9000 journals, patents from 27 countries, two industrial property organizations, new books, conference proceedings, and government research reports.

STATISTICS SOURCES

Advances in Surface Enhancement Technology. FIND/SVP, 625 Avenue of the Americas, New York, New York 10011. (212) 645-4500. 1991.

The Role of Surfactants in U.S., W. European & Japanese Household/Personal Care Market. FIND/SVP, 625 Avenue of the Americas, New York, New York 10011. (212) 645-4500. 1991.

Surfactants to 1995. FIND/SVP, 625 Avenue of the Americas, New York, New York 10011. (212) 645-4500. 1991. Analyzes four major types of surfactants used in over a dozen markets.

SUSCEPTIBILITY

ABSTRACTING AND INDEXING SERVICES

Physics Briefs. Physikalische Berichte. Physik Verlag, Pappapelallee 3, Postfach 101161, Weinheim, Germany D-6940. 1979-. Semimonthly. In English. Volumes for 1979- issued by the Deutsche Physikalische Gesellschaft and the Fachinformationszentrum Energie Physik, Mathematik in cooperation with the American Institute of Physics.

Science Citation Index. Institute for Scientific Information, 3501 Market St., Philadelphia, Pennsylvania 19104. 1961-.

ENCYCLOPEDIAS AND DICTIONARIES

Encyclopedia of Physics. Rita G. Lerner and George L. Trigg. VCH Publishers, 303 NW 12th Ave., Deerfield Beach, Florida 33442-1788. (305) 428-5566. 1991. Second edition.

Van Nostrand's Scientific Encyclopedia. Glenn D. Considine, ed. Van Nostrand Reinhold, 115 5th Ave., New York, New York 10003. (212) 254-3232. 1983. Sixth edition. Includes all broad subject areas in science.

SUSPENDED SOLIDS

See: PARTICULATES

SUSTAINABLE AGRICULTURE

See also: AGRICULTURE

ABSTRACTING AND INDEXING SERVICES

Biological and Agricultural Index. H.W. Wilson Co., 950 University Ave., Bronx, New York 10452. (800) 367-6770. 1916-. Monthly.

SUSTAINABLE RESOURCES

ABSTRACTING AND INDEXING SERVICES

Biological and Agricultural Index. H.W. Wilson Co., 950 University Ave., Bronx, New York 10452. (800) 367-6770. 1916-. Monthly.

Science Citation Index. Institute for Scientific Information, 3501 Market St., Philadelphia, Pennsylvania 19104. 1961-.

DIRECTORIES

Committee for Sustainable Agriculture-Ecological Farming Directory. Otis Wollan. Committee for Sustainable Agriculture, Box 1300, Colfax, California 95713. (916) 346-2777. Annual. Organic farmers, farm suppliers and consultants, produce handlers, researchers, extension agents, students, organization representatives.

International Green Front Report. Michael Pilarski. Friends of the Trees, PO Box 1064, Tonasket, Washington 98855. (509) 486-4726. 1988. Irregular. Organizations and periodicals dealing with sustainable forestry and agriculture.

ENCYCLOPEDIAS AND DICTIONARIES

Grzimek's Encyclopedia of Ecology. Bernhard Grzimek. Van Nostrand Reinhold, 115 5th Ave., New York, New York 10003. (212) 254-3232. 1976.

North American Reference Encyclopedia of Ecology and Pollution. William White. North American Pub. Co., 401 N. Broad St., Philadelphia, Pennsylvania 19108. (215) 238-5300. 1972.

GENERAL WORKS

Alternatives to Deforestation: Steps Toward Sustainable Use of the Amazon Rain Forest. Anthony B. Anderson, ed. Columbia University Press, 562 W. 113th St., New York, New York 10025. (212) 316-7100. 1992. Based on papers presented at an international conference in Belem, Brazil, for scientists in several fields, as well as government policy makers and representatives from foundations who are interested in exploring possible sustainable use of the world's largest rain forest, the Amazon, which is now being destroyed on an unprecedented scale.

Rural Environment Planning for Sustainable Communities. Frederic O. Sargent, et al. Island Press, 1718 Connecticut Ave. N.W., Ste. 300, Washington, District of Columbia 20009. (202) 232-7933. 1991.

Saving the Tropical Forests. Judith Gradwohl and Russell Greenberg. Island Press, 1718 Connecticut Ave. N.W., Suite 300, Washington, District of Columbia 20009. (202) 232-7933. 1988. Sourcebook about the causes and effects of tropical deforestation, with case studies, examples of sustainable agriculture and forestry, and a section on the restoration of tropical rain forests.

Sustainable Development and Environmental Management of Small Islands. W. Beller, et al., eds. Parthenon Pub., Casterton Hall, Carnforth, England LA6 2LA. 1990. Volume 5 in the Man and the Biosphere series published jointly with UNESCO.

PERIODICALS AND NEWSLETTERS

International Journal of Sustainable Development. Inderscience Enterprises Ltd., World Trade Center Building, 110 Avenue Louis Casai, Case Postale 306, Geneva-Aeroport, Switzerland CH 1215. (44) 908-314248. Quarterly. Forum to provide and authoritative source of information in the field of sustainable development and related fields.

The New Alchemy Quarterly. New Alchemy Inst., Inc., 237 Hatchville Rd., East Falmouth, Massachusetts 02536. (508) 564-6301. Quarterly. Sustainable technologies for providing food, energy, shelter, landscape design, and bioshelters.

RESEARCH CENTERS AND INSTITUTES

Coolidge Center for Environmental Leadership. 1675 Massachusetts Ave., Suite 4, Cambridge, Massachusetts 02138. (617) 864-5085.

STATISTICS SOURCES

World Resources. World Resources Institute. 1709 New York Ave., N.W., Washington, District of Columbia 20006. (202) 638-6300. Annual. Statistical and textual analysis of world's natural resources and the effects of growth-caused environmental pollution.

TRADE ASSOCIATIONS AND PROFESSIONAL SOCIETIES

Bolton Institute for a Sustainable Future, Inc. 4 Linden Square, Wellesley, Massachusetts 02181. (617) 235-5320.

The Centre for Our Common Future. Palais Wilson, 52, rue des Paquis, 1201, Geneva, Switzerland (41) 2-732-7117.

Steering Committee for Sustainable Agriculture. P.O. Box 1300, Colfax, California 95713. (916) 346-2777.

SUSTAINED YIELD

ABSTRACTING AND INDEXING SERVICES

Biological and Agricultural Index. H.W. Wilson Co., 950 University Ave., Bronx, New York 10452. (800) 367-6770. 1916-. Monthly.

Science Citation Index. Institute for Scientific Information, 3501 Market St., Philadelphia, Pennsylvania 19104. 1961-.

TRADE ASSOCIATIONS AND PROFESSIONAL SOCIETIES

Bolton Institute for a Sustainable Future, Inc. 4 Linden Square, Wellesley, Massachusetts 02181. (617) 235-5320.

SWAMPS

See: WETLANDS

SYNECOLOGY

See: ECOSYSTEMS

SYNERGISTIC EFFECTS

ABSTRACTING AND INDEXING SERVICES

Science Citation Index. Institute for Scientific Information, 3501 Market St., Philadelphia, Pennsylvania 19104. 1961-.

HANDBOOKS AND MANUALS

The Agrochemicals Handbook. H. Kidd and D. Hartlet, eds. Royal Society of Chemistry, c/o CRC Press, 2000 Corporate Blvd., N.W., Boca Raton, Florida 33431-9868. (800) 272-7737. 1991. 3rd ed. Contains comprehensive worldwide information and data on substances which are active components of agriculture chemical products currently used in crop protection and pest control.

SYNERGY

ABSTRACTING AND INDEXING SERVICES

General Science Index. H. W. Wilson Co., 950 University Ave., Bronx, New York 10452. 1978-. Monthly, also issued in annual cumulation. Cumulative subject index to English language periodicals in the subject fields of astronomy, botany, chemistry, earth science, environment and conservation, food and nutrition, genetics, mathematics, medicine and health, microbiology, oceanography, physics, physiology and zoology.

Mineralogical Abstracts. Mineralogical Society, 41 Queen's Gate, London, England SW7 5HR. 71 5847916. Quarterly. Abstracts of journal articles, conferences, technical reports and specialized books in the areas of minerals, clay minerals, economic minerals, ore deposits, environmental studies, experimental mineralogy, gemstones, geochemistry, petrology, lunar and planetary studies and other related areas in mineralogy.

Science Citation Index. Institute for Scientific Information, 3501 Market St., Philadelphia, Pennsylvania 19104. 1961-.

DIRECTORIES

SYNERJY: A Directory of Renewable Energy. SYNERJY, Box 1854, Cathedral Station, New York, New York 10025. (212) 865-9595.

ENCYCLOPEDIAS AND DICTIONARIES

McGraw-Hill Encyclopedia of Science and Technology. McGraw-Hill, 1221 Avenue of the Americas, New York, New York 10020. (212) 512-2000 or (800) 262-4729. 1992. Seventh edition. Issued in multiple volumes including index. Includes all science and technology broad subject areas.

Van Nostrand's Scientific Encyclopedia. Glenn D. Considine, ed. Van Nostrand Reinhold, 115 5th Ave., New York, New York 10003. (212) 254-3232. 1983. Sixth edition. Includes all broad subject areas in science.

GENERAL WORKS

Magill's Survey of Science. Life Science Series. Frank N. Magill, ed. Salem Press, PO Box 50062, Pasadena,

California 91105. 1991. Six volumes. Contents: v.1. A-Central and peripheral nervous system functions; v.2. Central metabolism regulation - eukaryotic transcriptional control; v.3. Positive and negative eukaryotic transcriptional control - mammalian hormones; v.4. Hormones and behavior - muscular contraction; v.5. Muscular contraction and relaxation - sexual reproduction in plants; v.6. Reproductive behavior and mating - X inactivation and the Lyon hypothesis.

HANDBOOKS AND MANUALS

The Agrochemicals Handbook. H. Kidd and D. Hartlet, eds. Royal Society of Chemistry, c/o CRC Press, 2000 Corporate Blvd., N.W., Boca Raton, Florida 33431-9868. (800) 272-7737. 1991. 3rd ed. Contains comprehensive worldwide information and data on substances which are active components of agriculture chemical products currently used in crop protection and pest control.

SYNTHETIC ECOLOGY
See: ECOSYSTEMS

SYNTHETIC FIBERS

ABSTRACTING AND INDEXING SERVICES

Science Citation Index. Institute for Scientific Information, 3501 Market St., Philadelphia, Pennsylvania 19104. 1961-.

DIRECTORIES

Fiber Organon–Directory of U.S. Manufactured Fiber Products Issue. 101 Eisenhower Parkway, Roseland, New Jersey 07068. (201) 228-1107. Annual.

GENERAL WORKS

Safety in the Use of Mineral and Synthetic Fibers. International Labour Office, 49 Sheridan Ave., Albany, New York 12210. (518) 436-9686. 1990. Working document for, and report of, a meeting of experts set up by the ILO to study the questions contained in this book, including discussions of man-made fibers, natural mineral fibers other than asbestos, and synthetic organic fibers. The meeting defined certain preventive measures based on adopting safe working methods, controlling the working environment and the exposure of workers to mineral and synthetic fibers, and monitoring the health of the workers.

ONLINE DATA BASES

Chemical Plant Database. Chemical Intelligence Services, 39A Bowling Green Lane, London, England EC 1R OBJ. 44 (71) 833-3812.

SYNTHETIC FUEL

ABSTRACTING AND INDEXING SERVICES

Engineering Index. The Engineering Index Inc., 345 E. 47th St., New York, New York 10017. 1962-.

Science Citation Index. Institute for Scientific Information, 3501 Market St., Philadelphia, Pennsylvania 19104. 1961-.

DIRECTORIES

Synthetic Fuels and Alternate Energy Worldwide Directory. PennWell Books, PO Box 1260, Tulsa, Oklahoma 74101. (918) 663-4225. 1984. Third edition. Provides a complete list of companies, organizations, individuals, government agencies and educational institutions involved in the development of and the application of synthetic fuels and alternate energy sources.

GENERAL WORKS

A Matrix Approach to Biological Investigation of Synthetic Fuels. U.S. Environmental Protection Agency, Health Effects Research Laboratory, Office of Research and Development, MD 75, Research Triangle Park, North Carolina (919) 541-2184. Covers toxicology of shale oils, diesel fuels, jet planes, and synthetic fuels.

Solar Energy Application, Bioconversion and Synfuels. T. Nejat Veziroglu, ed. Nova Science Publishers Inc., 283 Commack Rd., Suite 300, Commack, New York 11725-3401. (516) 499-3103; (516) 499-3106. 1990. Deals with solar energy applications such as heating and cooking, energy transmission, photovoltaics and industrial applications. Also includes chapters on bioconversion and synfuels.

Studies in Surface Science and Catalysis. Elsevier Science Publishing Co., 655 Avenue of the Americas, New York, New York 10010. (212) 989-5800. 1991.

HANDBOOKS AND MANUALS

Synfuels Handbook. Including the Yellow Pages of Synfuels. McGraw-Hill Science & Engineering Books, 1221 Avenue of the Americas, New York, New York 10020. (212) 512-2000 or (800) 262-4729. 1980. Specific aspects included in this handbook are: coal gasification and liquefaction, oil shale, overview, process development, materials, synfuels, and other products, mining and environmental aspects.

ONLINE DATA BASES

Clean-Coal/Synfuels Letter. McGraw-Hill Science & Engineering Books, 11 W. 19th St., New York, New York 10011. (212) 337-6010.

Computerized Engineering Index–COMPENDEX. Engineering Information Inc., 345 E. 47th St., New York, New York 10017. (212) 705-7600.

Monthly Catalog of United States Government Publications. U.S. G.P.O., Supt. of Docs., PO Box 371954, Pittsburgh, Pennsylvania 15250-7954. (202) 512-0000.

National Technical Information Service. U.S. Department of Commerce, National Technical Information Service, Office of Data Base Services, 5285 Port Royal Rd., Springfield, Virginia 22161. (703) 487-4807. Bibliographic database of government sponsored research and technical reports.

SYSTEMIC PESTICIDES

See: PESTICIDES

T

TAIGA

See: FORESTS

TAILINGS

See: WASTE TREATMENT

TANKER ACCIDENTS

See: OIL SPILLS

TANKER OIL SPILLS

See: OIL SPILLS

TAR

See: PETROLEUM

TDS

See: TOTAL DISSOLVED SOLIDS

TECHNETIUM

ABSTRACTING AND INDEXING SERVICES

General Science Index. H. W. Wilson Co., 950 University Ave., Bronx, New York 10452. 1978-. Monthly, also issued in annual cumulation. Cumulative subject index to English language periodicals in the subject fields of astronomy, botany, chemistry, earth science, environment and conservation, food and nutrition, genetics, mathematics, medicine and health, microbiology, oceanography, physics, physiology and zoology.

Science Citation Index. Institute for Scientific Information, 3501 Market St., Philadelphia, Pennsylvania 19104. 1961-.

ENCYCLOPEDIAS AND DICTIONARIES

McGraw-Hill Encyclopedia of Science and Technology. McGraw-Hill, 1221 Avenue of the Americas, New York, New York 10020. (212) 512-2000 or (800) 262-4729. 1992. Seventh edition. Issued in multiple volumes including index. Includes all science and technology broad subject areas.

Van Nostrand's Scientific Encyclopedia. Glenn D. Considine, ed. Van Nostrand Reinhold, 115 5th Ave., New York, New York 10003. (212) 254-3232. 1983. Sixth edition. Includes all broad subject areas in science.

HANDBOOKS AND MANUALS

The Chemistry of Manganese, Technetium and Rhenium. R. D. W. Kemmitt. Pergamon Microforms International, Inc., Fairview Park, Elmsford, New York 10523. (914) 592-7720. 1975.

Environmental Effects of the Uranium Fuel Cycle; A Review of Data for Technetium. J. E. Till. U.S. Nuclear Regulatory Commission, Office for Nuclear Reactor Regulation, Division of Systems Integration, Washington, District of Columbia 20555. (301) 492-7000. 1985. Environmental aspects of the uranium industry, particularly technetium.

TECHNOLOGY AND THE ENVIRONMENT

ABSTRACTING AND INDEXING SERVICES

Applied Ecology Abstracts Studies in Renewable Natural Resources. Information Retrieval Ltd., 1911 Jefferson Davis Highway, Arlington, Virginia 22202. 1975-. Monthly.

Applied Science and Technology Index. H.W. Wilson Co., 950 University Ave., Bronx, New York 10452. (800) 367-6770. Formerly Industrial Arts Index.

Engineering Index. The Engineering Index Inc., 345 E. 47th St., New York, New York 10017. 1962-.

Index to Scientific Book Contents. Institute for Scientific Information, 3501 Market St., Philadelphia, Pennsylvania 19104. (800) 523-1857. 1985-. Annual. Gives contents of science books published.

Multimedia Index to Ecology. National Information Center for Educational Media, University of Southern California, Los Angeles, California 90007.

Science Citation Index. Institute for Scientific Information, 3501 Market St., Philadelphia, Pennsylvania 19104. 1961-.

DIRECTORIES

Directory of Institutions and Individuals Active in Environmentally-Sound and Appropriate Technologies. Pergamon Press, Headington Hill Hall, Headington, Oxford, England OX3 0BW. 1979.

ENCYCLOPEDIAS AND DICTIONARIES

Concise Encyclopedia of Biological & Biomedical Measurement Systems. Peter A. Payne. Pergamon Microforms International Inc., Fairview Park, Elmsford, New York 10523. (914) 592-7720. Comprehensive survey of the measurement systems and descriptions of the biological systems and subsystems.

Dictionary of Environmental Engineering and Related Sciences: English-Spanish, Spanish-English. Jose T. Villate. Ediciones Universal, 3090 SW 8th St., Miami, Florida 33135. (305) 642-3355. 1979.

Dictionary of Environmental Protection. Otto E. Tutzauer. Fred B. Rothman, 10368 W. Centennial Rd., Littleton, California 80127. (303) 979-5657. 1979.

Dictionary of Environmental Protection Technology: In Four Languages, English, German, French, Russian. Egon Seidel. Elsevier Science Publishing Co., 655 Avenue of the Americas, New York, New York 10010. (212) 984-5800. 1988.

Dictionary of Environmental Science and Technology. Andrew Porteous. John Wiley & Sons, Inc., 605 3rd Ave., New York, New York 10158-0012. (212) 850-6000. 1992.

Encyclopedia of Environmental Control Technology. Paul N. Cheremisinoff, ed. Gulf Publishing Co., Book Division, PO Box 2608, Houston, Texas 77252. (713) 529-4301 or (800) 231-6275. 1992. Volume 1: Thermal Treatment of Hazardous Wastes; volume 2: Air Pollution Control; volume 3: Wastewater Treatment Technology; volume 4: Hazardous Waste Containment and Treatment; volumes 5 through 8 in progress. Provides in-depth coverage of specialized topics related to environmental and industrial pollution control problems and state-of-the-art information on technology and research as well as projections of future trends in the field.

Encyclopedia of Environmental Science and Engineering. J.R. Pfafflin. Gordon and Breach Science Publishers, Inc., 270 8th Ave., New York, New York 10011. (212) 206-8900. 1992.

Encyclopedia of Physical Science and Technology. Robert A. Meyers, ed. Academic Press, c/o Harcourt Brace Jovanovich Inc., 6277 Sea Harbor Dr., Orlando, Florida 32887. (800) 346-8648. Dictionary of engineering, technology and physical sciences.

Illustrated Encyclopedia of Science and the Future. Mike Biscare, et al., ed. Marshall Cavendish, 58 Old Compton St., London, England 0W1V5 PA. 01-734 6710. 1983. Twenty volumes. Each volume has 5 sections: Frontiers,

Electronics in Action, Medical Science, Military Technology, and Resources.

McGraw-Hill Encyclopedia of Environmental Science. Sybil P. Parker. McGraw-Hill Science & Engineering Books, 11 W. 19th St., New York, New York 10011. (212) 337-6010. 1980. Covers ecology, man's influence on nature, and environmental protection.

McGraw-Hill Encyclopedia of Science and Technology. McGraw-Hill, 1221 Avenue of the Americas, New York, New York 10020. (212) 512-2000 or (800) 262-4729. 1992. Seventh edition. Issued in multiple volumes including index. Includes all science and technology broad subject areas.

GENERAL WORKS

Analytical Instrumentation for the Water Industry. T. R. Crompton. Butterworth-Heinemann, Linacre House, Jordan Hill, Oxford, England OX2 8DP. (0865) 310366. 1990.

Emerging Technologies in Hazardous Waste Management. D. William Tedder and Frederick G. Pohland, eds. American Chemical Society, 1155 16th St. N.W., Washington, District of Columbia 20036. (202) 872-4600; (800) 227-5558. 1990. Hazardous waste management technology.

Emerging Technologies in Hazardous Waste Management II. D. William Tedder and Frederick G. Pohland, eds. American Chemical Society, 1155 16th St. N.W., Washington, District of Columbia 20036. (202) 872-4600; (800) 227-5558. 1991. Developed from a symposium sponsored by the Division of Industrial and Engineering Chemistry, Inc. of the American Chemical Society at the Industrial and Engineering Chemistry Special Symposium, Atlantic City, NJ, June 4-7, 1990.

Environmental Pollution and Control. P. Aarne Vesiling, et al. Butterworth-Heinemann, 80 Montvale Ave., Stoneham, Massachusetts 02180. (617) 438-8468; (800) 366-2665. 1990. Describes the more important aspects of environmental engineering science and technology.

Health Effects of Drinking Water Treatment Technologies. Lewis Publishers, 200 Corporate Blvd. NW, Boca Raton, Florida 33431. (407) 994-0555 or (800)272-7737. 1989. Evaluates the public health impact from the most widespread drinking water treatment technologies, with particular emphasis on disinfection. Focuses solely on the most common treatment technologies and practices used today.

New Separation Chemistry Techniques for Radioactive Waste and Other Specific Applications. L. Cecille. Elsevier Science Publishing Co., 655 Avenue of the Americas, New York, New York 10010. (212) 989-5800. 1991. Purification technology relating to radioactive wastes and sewage. Proceedings of a technical seminar jointly organized by the Commission of the European Communities, Directorate General for Science, Research and Development and the Italian Commission.

Pollution Prevention Pays: An Overview by the 3M Company of Low- and Non-Pollution Technology. World Environment Center, 419 Park Ave. S, Suite 1404, New York, New York 10016. (212) 683-4700. Covers natural resources, pollution and control.

Society of Risk Analysis. Plenum Press, 233 Spring St., New York, New York 10013-1578. (212) 620-8000; (800)

221-9369. 1990. Proceedings of the Annual Meeting of the Society for Risk Analysis, held November 9-12, 1986, in Boston, MA.

Substitute Fuels for Road Transport: A Technology Assessment. OECD Publications and Information Center, 2001 L. St., N.W., Suite 700, Washington, District of Columbia 20036. (202) 785-OECD. 1990. Report analyzes the availability, economics, technical problems and effects on the environment from the use of substitute fuels.

Transforming Technology: An Agenda for Environmentally Sustainable Growth in the Twenty-First Century. George Heaton, et al. World Resources Institute, 1709 New York Ave. N.W., Washington, District of Columbia 20006. (800) 822-0504. 1991. Explores the extraordinarily rich potential of new technologies to resolve environmental and economic problems.

GOVERNMENTAL ORGANIZATIONS

Bureau of Oceans and International Environmental and Scientific Affairs. 2201 C St., N.W., Washington, District of Columbia 20520. (202) 647-1554.

U.S. Environmental Protection Agency: Office of Technology Transfer and Regulatory Support. 401 M St., S.W., Washington, District of Columbia 20460.

HANDBOOKS AND MANUALS

Prevention Reference Manual: Control Technologies. Daniel S. Davis. Air and Energy Research Laboratory, U.S. Environmental Protection Agency, Research Triangle Park, North Carolina 27711. (919) 541-2350. 1987-. Accidents caused by hazardous substances and chemicals.

ONLINE DATA BASES

Computerized Engineering Index–COMPENDEX. Engineering Information Inc., 345 E. 47th St., New York, New York 10017. (212) 705-7600.

DECHEMA Environmental Technology Equipment Data–DETEQ. STN International, c/o Chemical Abstracts Service, 2540 Olentangy River Road, P.O. Box 3012, Columbus, Ohio 43210. Information on the manufacturers of apparatus and technical equipment in the field of environmental engineering. Corresponds to the "ACHEMA Handbook Pollution Control."

Innovative/Alternative Pollution Control Technology Facility File–IADB. U.S. Environmental Protection Agency, Office of Water Program Operations, 401 M St., S.W., Washington, District of Columbia 20460. (202) 260-2090.

Monthly Catalog of United States Government Publications. U.S. G.P.O., Supt. of Docs., PO Box 371954, Pittsburgh, Pennsylvania 15250-7954. (202) 512-0000.

National Technical Information Service. U.S. Department of Commerce, National Technical Information Service, Office of Data Base Services, 5285 Port Royal Rd., Springfield, Virginia 22161. (703) 487-4807. Bibliographic database of government sponsored research and technical reports.

PERIODICALS AND NEWSLETTERS

Applied Microbiology and Biotechnology. Springer International, 44 Hartz Way, Seacacus, New Jersey 07094. (201) 348-4033. Six times a year. Covers biotechnology, biochemical engineering, applied genetics and regulation, applied microbial and cell physiology, food biotechnology, and environmental biotechnology.

Pollution Equipment News. Rimbach Publishing, Inc., 8650 Babcock Boulevard, Pittsburgh, Pennsylvania 15237. (412) 364-5366. Bimonthly. Covers new products, techniques, and literature.

Pollution Equipment News Catalog and Buyers' Guide. Rimbach Publishing, Inc., 8650 Babcock Blvd., Pittsburgh, Pennsylvania 15237. (412) 364-5366. Annual. Product/service supplier information including specification, purchase, installation, and maintenance of pollution control equipment.

RESEARCH CENTERS AND INSTITUTES

Advanced Environmental Technology Research Center. University of Illinois at Urbana-Champaign, Urbana, Illinois 61801. (217) 333-3822.

Facility for Advanced Instrumentation. University of California Davis, Davis, California 95616. (916) 752-0284.

Utah State University, Center for Bio-Catalysis Science and Technology. Logan, Utah 84322-4630. (801) 750-2033.

Wisconsin Applied Water Pollution Research Consortium. University of Wisconsin-Madison, 3204 Engineering Building, 1415 Johnson Dr., Madison, Wisconsin 53706. (608) 262-7248.

STATISTICS SOURCES

Air Pollution Control Equipment & Services Market. FIND/SVP, 625 Avenue of the Americas, New York, New York 10011. (212) 645-4500. 1991. Technologies currently used to combat particulate and gaseous pollutants–gravity settlers, centrifugal separators, electrostatic precipitators, fabric filters, wet scrubbers, adsorption and absorption devices, and incinerators.

Environmental Sensors & Monitoring. FIND/SVP, 625 Avenue of the Americas, New York, New York 10011. (212) 645-4500. Step-by-step guide to a group of biosensor, optic sensor and mass sensor technologies, patents and regulations.

Industrial Air Pollution Control Equipment. FIND/SVP, 625 Avenue of the Americas, New York, New York 10011. (212) 645-4500. 1991.

TRADE ASSOCIATIONS AND PROFESSIONAL SOCIETIES

Environmental Technology Seminar. P.O. Box 391, Bethpage, New York 11714. (516) 931-3200.

Federation of Environmental Technologists. P.O. Box 185, Milwaukee, Wisconsin 53201. (414) 251-8163.

Manufacturers of Emission Controls Association. 1707 L St., N.W., Suite 570, Washington, District of Columbia 20036. (202) 296-4797.

TED (TURTLE EXCLUDER DEVICES)

See also: ENDANGERED SPECIES; FISH AND FISHING

ABSTRACTING AND INDEXING SERVICES

Applied Ecology Abstracts Studies in Renewable Natural Resources. Information Retrieval Ltd., 1911 Jefferson Davis Highway, Arlington, Virginia 22202. 1975-. Monthly.

Multimedia Index to Ecology. National Information Center for Educational Media, University of Southern California, Los Angeles, California 90007.

Science Citation Index. Institute for Scientific Information, 3501 Market St., Philadelphia, Pennsylvania 19104. 1961-.

ENCYCLOPEDIAS AND DICTIONARIES

McGraw-Hill Encyclopedia of Environmental Science. Sybil P. Parker. McGraw-Hill Science & Engineering Books, 11 W. 19th St., New York, New York 10011. (212) 337-6010. 1980. Covers ecology, man's influence on nature, and environmental protection.

GENERAL WORKS

Construction, Installation, and Handling Procedure for National Marine Fisheries Service's Sea Turtle Excluder Device. U.S. Department of Commerce, National Oceanic and Atmospheric Administration, National Marine Service, Southeast Fisheries Center, 3209 Frederick St., Pascagoula, Mississippi 39568. (601) 762-4591. 1981. Covers equipment and supplies of trawls and trawling.

ONLINE DATA BASES

Monthly Catalog of United States Government Publications. U.S. G.P.O., Supt. of Docs., PO Box 371954, Pittsburgh, Pennsylvania 15250-7954. (202) 512-0000.

National Technical Information Service. U.S. Department of Commerce, National Technical Information Service, Office of Data Base Services, 5285 Port Royal Rd., Springfield, Virginia 22161. (703) 487-4807. Bibliographic database of government sponsored research and technical reports.

TEFLON

ABSTRACTING AND INDEXING SERVICES

Applied Science and Technology Index. H.W. Wilson Co., 950 University Ave., Bronx, New York 10452. (800) 367-6770. Formerly Industrial Arts Index.

General Science Index. H. W. Wilson Co., 950 University Ave., Bronx, New York 10452. 1978-. Monthly, also issued in annual cumulation. Cumulative subject index to English language periodicals in the subject fields of astronomy, botany, chemistry, earth science, environment and conservation, food and nutrition, genetics, mathematics, medicine and health, microbiology, oceanography, physics, physiology and zoology.

Science Citation Index. Institute for Scientific Information, 3501 Market St., Philadelphia, Pennsylvania 19104. 1961-.

ENCYCLOPEDIAS AND DICTIONARIES

Van Nostrand's Scientific Encyclopedia. Glenn D. Considine, ed. Van Nostrand Reinhold, 115 5th Ave., New York, New York 10003. (212) 254-3232. 1983. Sixth edition. Includes all broad subject areas in science.

ONLINE DATA BASES

CAS Source Index–CASSI. Chemical Abstracts Service, 2540 Olentangy River Rd., P.O. Box 3012, Columbus, Ohio 43210. (800) 848-6533 or (614) 421-3600. A listing of bibliographic and library holdings information for scientific and technical primary literature relevant to the chemical sciences.

TELLURIUM

ABSTRACTING AND INDEXING SERVICES

Applied Science and Technology Index. H.W. Wilson Co., 950 University Ave., Bronx, New York 10452. (800) 367-6770. Formerly Industrial Arts Index.

General Science Index. H. W. Wilson Co., 950 University Ave., Bronx, New York 10452. 1978-. Monthly, also issued in annual cumulation. Cumulative subject index to English language periodicals in the subject fields of astronomy, botany, chemistry, earth science, environment and conservation, food and nutrition, genetics, mathematics, medicine and health, microbiology, oceanography, physics, physiology and zoology.

Mineralogical Abstracts. Mineralogical Society, 41 Queen's Gate, London, England SW7 5HR. 71 5847916. Quarterly. Abstracts of journal articles, conferences, technical reports and specialized books in the areas of minerals, clay minerals, economic minerals, ore deposits, environmental studies, experimental mineralogy, gemstones, geochemistry, petrology, lunar and planetary studies and other related areas in mineralogy.

Science Citation Index. Institute for Scientific Information, 3501 Market St., Philadelphia, Pennsylvania 19104. 1961-.

ENCYCLOPEDIAS AND DICTIONARIES

Encyclopedia of Minerals. Willard Lincoln Roberts, et al. Van Nostrand Reinhold, 115 5th Ave., New York, New York 10003. (212) 254-3232 or (800) 926-2665. 1990. Second edition. Gives information on rare minerals, those minerals widely known and collected and those that are most attractive or visually diagnostic.

McGraw-Hill Encyclopedia of Science and Technology. McGraw-Hill, 1221 Avenue of the Americas, New York, New York 10020. (212) 512-2000 or (800) 262-4729. 1992. Seventh edition. Issued in multiple volumes including index. Includes all science and technology broad subject areas.

Van Nostrand's Scientific Encyclopedia. Glenn D. Considine, ed. Van Nostrand Reinhold, 115 5th Ave., New York, New York 10003. (212) 254-3232. 1983. Sixth edition. Includes all broad subject areas in science.

TRADE ASSOCIATIONS AND PROFESSIONAL SOCIETIES

Selenium-Tellurium Development Association. 301 Borgtstraat, B1850 Brimbergen, Belgium

TEMEPHOS

ABSTRACTING AND INDEXING SERVICES

Science Citation Index. Institute for Scientific Information, 3501 Market St., Philadelphia, Pennsylvania 19104. 1961-.

ENCYCLOPEDIAS AND DICTIONARIES

Van Nostrand's Scientific Encyclopedia. Glenn D. Considine, ed. Van Nostrand Reinhold, 115 5th Ave., New York, New York 10003. (212) 254-3232. 1983. Sixth edition. Includes all broad subject areas in science.

GENERAL WORKS

Temephos. U.S. Environmental Protection Agency, Office of Pesticides and Toxic Substances, 401 M St., S.W., Washington, District of Columbia 20460. (202) 260-2090. 1981. Covers mosquito control and pesticide law and legislation.

TENNESSEE ENVIRONMENTAL AGENCIES

GOVERNMENTAL ORGANIZATIONS

Department of Agriculture: Pesticide Registration. Director, Division of Plant Industries, PO Box 40627, Melrose Station, Nashville, Tennessee 37204. (615) 360-0130.

Department of Conservation: Natural Resources. Commissioner, 701 Broadway, Nashville, Tennessee 37243-0345. (615) 742-6747.

Department of Health and Environment: Air Quality. Director, Air Pollution Control Board, TERRA Building, 150 Ninth Ave., N., Nashville, Tennessee 37247-3001. (615) 741-3931.

Department of Health and Environment: Environmental Protection. Assistant Commissioner, Bureau of Environment, 4th Floor, Customs House, Nashville, Tennessee 37203. (615) 741-3424.

Department of Health and Environment: Hazardous Waste Management. Director, Solid Waste Management Division, 4th Floor, Customs House, Nashville, Tennessee 37203. (615) 741-3424.

Department of Health and Environment: Solid Waste Management. Director, Solid Waste Management Division, 4th Floor, Customs House, Nashville, Tennessee 37203. (615) 741-3424.

Department of Health and Environment: Underground Storage Electronics. Director, Underground Storage Tank Program, 150 Ninth Ave., N., Nashville, Tennessee 37219. (615) 741-0690.

Department of Health and Environment: Water Quality. Administrator, Water Quality Control Bureau, TERRA

Building, 150 Ninth St., N., Nashville, Tennessee 37204. (615) 741-4608.

Department of Labor: Occupational Safety. Occupational Safety Division, 501 Union Bldg., Nashville, Tennessee 37219. (615) 741-2793.

Emergency Response Commission: Emergency Preparedness and Community Right-to-Know. Chair, 3041 Sidco, Nashville, Tennessee 37204. (615) 252-3300.

Hazardous Waste Extension Program: Waste Minimization and Pollution Prevention. Program Director, Center for Industrial Services, 226 Capitol Boulevard Bldg., Suite 401, University of Tennessee, Nashville, Tennessee 37219-1804. (615) 242-2456.

Wildlife Resources Agency: Fish and Wildlife. Executive Director, PO Box 40747, Nashville, Tennessee 37204. (615) 781-6552.

TENNESSEE ENVIRONMENTAL LEGISLATION

GENERAL WORKS

Tennessee Environmental Law Letter. Lee Smith Publishers & Printers, Nashville, Tennessee 1989.

TERATOGENIC AGENTS

ABSTRACTING AND INDEXING SERVICES

Science Citation Index. Institute for Scientific Information, 3501 Market St., Philadelphia, Pennsylvania 19104. 1961-.

GENERAL WORKS

CA Selects: Carcinogens, Mutagens & Teratogens. Chemical Abstracts Services, 2540 Olentangy River Rd., Columbus, Ohio 43210. (800) 848-6533. Irregular.

Carcinogenic, Mutagenic, and Teratogenic Marine Pollutants. Portfolio Publishing Co., P.O. Box 7802, The Woodlands, Texas 77381. (713) 363-3577. 1990. Effects of marine pollution on aquatic organisms as well as human beings.

Teratologic Assessment of Butylene Oxide, Styrene Oxide and Methyl Bromide. Melvin R. Sikov. U.S. G.P.O., Washington, District of Columbia 20401. (202) 512-0000. 1981. Toxicology aspects of the following: butene, styrene, bromomethane, teratogenic agents, hydrocarbons, and ethers.

HANDBOOKS AND MANUALS

Catalog of Teratogenic Agents. Thomas H. Shephard. Johns Hopkins University Press, 701 W. 40th St., Ste. 275, Baltimore, Maryland 21211. (410) 516-6900. 1992. Drug-induced abnormalities and teratogens.

Reproductively Active Chemicals: A Reference Guide. Richard J. Lewis, Sr. Van Nostrand Reinhold, 115 5th Ave., New York, New York 10003. (212) 254-3232. 1991. Provides the dose, species exposed, a brief characterization of the exposure conditions, and a reference to the source of the data.

ONLINE DATA BASES

CAS Source Index–CASSI. Chemical Abstracts Service, 2540 Olentangy River Rd., P.O. Box 3012, Columbus, Ohio 43210. (800) 848-6533 or (614) 421-3600. A listing of bibliographic and library holdings information for scientific and technical primary literature relevant to the chemical sciences.

Chemical Carcinogenesis Research Information System–CCRIS. National Library of Medicine, 8600 Rockville Pike, Bethesda, Maryland 20894. (800) 638-8480. Individual assay results and test conditions for 1,451 chemicals in the areas of carcinogenicity, mutagenicity, tumor promotion, and cocarcinogenicity.

REPRORISK System. Micromedex, Inc., 600 Grant St., Denver, Colorado 80203. (800) 525-9083 or (303) 831-1400. Reproductive risks to females and males caused by drugs, chemicals, and physical and environmental agents. Includes the Teratogen Information System (TERIS), which deals with the teratogenicity of over 700 drugs and environmental agents that affect a fetus. One of the additional modules under development is the REPRO-TEXT database, containing a ranking system for reproductive hazards and the general toxicity of over 600 chemicals, emphasizing chronic occupational exposures.

TERMITES

ABSTRACTING AND INDEXING SERVICES

Biological Abstracts. BIOSIS, 2100 Arch St., Philadelphia, Pennsylvania 19103-1399. (215) 587-4800. 1927-.

Science Citation Index. Institute for Scientific Information, 3501 Market St., Philadelphia, Pennsylvania 19104. 1961-.

ENCYCLOPEDIAS AND DICTIONARIES

Van Nostrand's Scientific Encyclopedia. Glenn D. Considine, ed. Van Nostrand Reinhold, 115 5th Ave., New York, New York 10003. (212) 254-3232. 1983. Sixth edition. Includes all broad subject areas in science.

GENERAL WORKS

Subterranean Termites. Raymond H. Beal. U.S. Department of Agriculture, c/o U.S. Government Printing Office, Washington, District of Columbia 20401. (202) 512-0000. 1989.

ONLINE DATA BASES

BIOSIS Previews. BIOSIS, 2100 Arch St., Philadelphia, Pennsylvania 19103-1399. (215) 587-4800. Largest and most comprehensive database of research in the life sciences. Contains citations for nearly 9000 primary research journals, monographs, reviews, symposia, preliminary reports, semi-popular journals, selected institutional reports, government reports and research communications.

RESEARCH CENTERS AND INSTITUTES

Center for Urban Pest Management. Purdue University, Ag Research Building, West Lafayette, Indiana 47907. (317) 494-4554.

TRADE ASSOCIATIONS AND PROFESSIONAL SOCIETIES

American Institute of Biological Sciences. 730 11th St., N.W., Washington, District of Columbia 20001-4521. (202) 628-1500.

TERRACING

ABSTRACTING AND INDEXING SERVICES

Science Citation Index. Institute for Scientific Information, 3501 Market St., Philadelphia, Pennsylvania 19104. 1961-.

ENCYCLOPEDIAS AND DICTIONARIES

Van Nostrand's Scientific Encyclopedia. Glenn D. Considine, ed. Van Nostrand Reinhold, 115 5th Ave., New York, New York 10003. (212) 254-3232. 1983. Sixth edition. Includes all broad subject areas in science.

GENERAL WORKS

Soil Erosion by Water as Related to Management of Tillage and Surface Residues, Terracing, and Contouring in Eastern Oregon. R. R. Allmaras. U.S. Department of Agriculture, Science and Education Administration, Agricultural Research, 800 Buchanan St., Albany, California 94710. (510) 559-6082. 1980. Covers soil erosion and soil management and tillage.

TERRESTRIAL ECOSYSTEMS
See: ECOSYSTEMS

TERTIARY TREATMENT
See: SEWAGE TREATMENT

TETRAALKYL LEAD
See: LEAD

TETRACHLORODIARYLMETHANES

ABSTRACTING AND INDEXING SERVICES

Science Citation Index. Institute for Scientific Information, 3501 Market St., Philadelphia, Pennsylvania 19104. 1961-.

BIBLIOGRAPHIES

Agent Orange Dioxin, TCDD. Trellis C. Wright. Library of Congress, Science and Technology Division, Reference Section, Washington, District of Columbia 20540. (202) 738-3238. 1979.

Dioxin Bibliography. Kay Flowers. TCT Engineers, 1908 Inner Belt Business Center Dr., St. Louis, Missouri 63114-5700. (314) 426-0880. 1984.

GENERAL WORKS

Determination of TCDD in Industrial and Municipal Wastewaters. U.S. Environmental Protection Agency, Environmental Monitoring and Support Laboratory, Center for Environmental Research Information, 26 W. Martin Luther King Dr., Cincinnati, Ohio 45268. (513) 569-7931. 1982. Covers sewage purification through chlorination, particularly tetrachlorodibenzodioxin.

Hot Flue Gas Spiking and Recovery Study for Tetrachlorodibenzodioxins Using Modified Method 5 and SASS Sampling with a Simulated Incinerator. Marcus Cooke. U.S. Environmental Protection Agency, Industrial Environmental Research Laboratory, MD 75, Research Triangle Park, North Carolina 27711. 1984. Covers environmental aspects of flue gases, steamboilers, and tetrachlorodibenzodioxin.

ONLINE DATA BASES

CAS Source Index–CASSI. Chemical Abstracts Service, 2540 Olentangy River Rd., P.O. Box 3012, Columbus, Ohio 43210. (800) 848-6533 or (614) 421-3600. A listing of bibliographic and library holdings information for scientific and technical primary literature relevant to the chemical sciences.

Chemical Abstracts Chemical Name Directory–CHEMNAME. Chemical Abstracts Service, 2540 Olentangy River Rd., P.O. Box 3012, Columbus, Ohio 43210. (800) 848-6533 or (614) 421-3600. Listing of chemical substances in a dictionary type file. The Chemical Abstracts (CAS) Registry Number, molecular formula, Chemical Abstracts (CA) Substance Index Name, available synonyms, ring data and other chemical substance information is given for each entry.

Chemical Collection System/Request Tracking–CCS/RTS. U.S. Environmental Protection Agency, Office of Pesticides and Toxic Substances, 401 M St., SW, Washington, District of Columbia 20460. (202) 260-2090. Contains information on various properties of a number of chemicals including environmental effects, test and analysis methods, and health effects. Available from EPA.

Chemical Dictionary Online–CHEMLINE. Chemical Abstracts Service, 2540 Olentangy River Rd., Columbus, Ohio 43210. (614) 421-3600 or (800) 848-6533. Part of MEDLINE of the National Library of Medicine (NLM). File of 900,000 names for chemical substances, representing 450,000 unique compounds. It contains such information as Chemical Abstracts (CA) Service Registry Numbers, molecular formulas, preferred chemical nomenclature, and generic and ring structure information. Available on NLM's ELHILL system.

Chemical Exposure. Science Applications International Corp., Health & Environmental Information, P.O. Box 2501, Oak Ridge, Tennessee 37831. (615) 482-9031.

Database of chemicals that have been identified in both human tissues and body fluids and in feral and food animals. Contains reference to journal articles, conferences, and reports. Covers the whole fields of information related to human and animal exposure to food, air, and water contaminants and pharmaceuticals. Its records include information on chemical properties, formulas, tissues measured, analytical method used, demographics and more. Available on DIALOG.

TRADE ASSOCIATIONS AND PROFESSIONAL SOCIETIES

American Chemical Society. 1155 16th St., N.W., Washington, District of Columbia 20036. (202) 872-4600.

TETRACHLORODIBENZODIOXINS

ABSTRACTING AND INDEXING SERVICES

Science Citation Index. Institute for Scientific Information, 3501 Market St., Philadelphia, Pennsylvania 19104. 1961-.

ONLINE DATA BASES

Chemical Collection System/Request Tracking–CCS/RTS. U.S. Environmental Protection Agency, Office of Pesticides and Toxic Substances, 401 M St., SW, Washington, District of Columbia 20460. (202) 260-2090. Contains information on various properties of a number of chemicals including environmental effects, test and analysis methods, and health effects. Available from EPA.

Chemical Dictionary Online–CHEMLINE. Chemical Abstracts Service, 2540 Olentangy River Rd., Columbus, Ohio 43210. (614) 421-3600 or (800) 848-6533. Part of MEDLINE of the National Library of Medicine (NLM). File of 900,000 names for chemical substances, representing 450,000 unique compounds. It contains such information as Chemical Abstracts (CA) Service Registry Numbers, molecular formulas, preferred chemical nomenclature, and generic and ring structure information. Available on NLM's ELHILL system.

Chemical Exposure. Science Applications International Corp., Health & Environmental Information, P.O. Box 2501, Oak Ridge, Tennessee 37831. (615) 482-9031. Database of chemicals that have been identified in both human tissues and body fluids and in feral and food animals. Contains reference to journal articles, conferences, and reports. Covers the whole fields of information related to human and animal exposure to food, air, and water contaminants and pharmaceuticals. Its records include information on chemical properties, formulas, tissues measured, analytical method used, demographics and more. Available on DIALOG.

STATISTICS SOURCES

Comparison of Serum Levels of 2,3,7,8- Tetrachlorodibenzo-p-Dioxin with Indirect Estimates of Agent Orange Exposure Among Vietnam Veterans. U.S. Center for Disease Control, c/o U.S. Government Printing Office, Washington, District of Columbia 20401. (202) 512-0000. 1989. Results of a study on blood serum dioxin concentration of army combat veterans exposed to Agent Orange while serving in Vietnam.

TRADE ASSOCIATIONS AND PROFESSIONAL SOCIETIES

American Chemical Society. 1155 16th St., N.W., Washington, District of Columbia 20036. (202) 872-4600.

TEXAS ENVIRONMENTAL AGENCIES

GOVERNMENTAL ORGANIZATIONS

Air Control Board: Air Quality. Executive Director, 6330 Highway 290 E., Austin, Texas 78723. (512) 451-5711.

Department of Agriculture: Pesticide Registration. Director, Agriculture and Environmental Sciences Division, PO Box 12847, Austin, Texas 78711. (512) 463-7534.

Department of Health: Environmental Protection. Associate Commissioner, Environment and Consumer Health Protection, 100 West 49th St., Austin, Texas 78756. (512) 458-7541.

Department of Health: Occupational Safety. Commissioner, 1100 West 49th St., Austin, Texas 78756. (512) 458-7375.

Department of Health: Solid Waste Management. Director, Division of Solid Waste Management, 1100 West 49th St., Austin, Texas 78756. (512) 458-7271.

Governor's Office of Budget and Planning: Coastal Zone Management. Director, Box 12428, Capitol Station, Austin, Texas 78711. (512) 463-1778.

Parks and Wildlife Department: Fish and Wildlife. Executive Director, 4200 Smith School Rd., Austin, Texas 78744. (512) 389-4800.

Railroad Commission: Underground Storage Tanks. Assistant Director, Oil and Gas Division, PO Box 12967, Capitol Station, Austin, Texas 78711. (512) 463-6922.

Texas Water Commission: Emergency Preparedness and Community Right-to-Know. Supervisor, Emergency Response Unit, PO Box 13087 Capitol Station, 1100 West 49th St., Austin, Texas 78756. (512) 458-7410.

Texas Water Development Board: Water Quality. Executive Director, Box 13231, Austin, Texas 78711. (512) 463-7847.

U.S. EPA Region 6: Pollution Prevention. Coordinator, 1445 Ross Ave., Suite 1200, Dallas, Texas 75202-2733. (214) 655-6444.

Water Commission: Groundwater Management. Chief, Groundwater Management, Box 13087, Capitol Station, Austin, Texas 78711. (512) 463-4969.

Water Commission: Hazardous Waste Management. Director, Hazardous and Solid Waste Management, PO Box 13087, Capitol Station, Austin, Texas 78711. (512) 463-7760.

Water Commission: Natural Resources. Executive Director, Box 13087, Capitol Station, Austin, Texas 78711. (512) 463-7898.

TEXAS ENVIRONMENTAL LEGISLATION

GENERAL WORKS

Texas Environmental Law Handbook. Government Institutes, Inc., 4 Research Pl., Ste. 200, Rockville, Maryland 20850. (301) 921-2300. 1990.

THALLIUM

ABSTRACTING AND INDEXING SERVICES

Chemical Abstracts. Chemical Abstracts Service, 2540 Olentangy River Rd., PO Box 3012, Columbus, Ohio 43210. (800) 848-6533. 1907-.

General Science Index. H. W. Wilson Co., 950 University Ave., Bronx, New York 10452. 1978-. Monthly, also issued in annual cumulation. Cumulative subject index to English language periodicals in the subject fields of astronomy, botany, chemistry, earth science, environment and conservation, food and nutrition, genetics, mathematics, medicine and health, microbiology, oceanography, physics, physiology and zoology.

Science Citation Index. Institute for Scientific Information, 3501 Market St., Philadelphia, Pennsylvania 19104. 1961-.

BIBLIOGRAPHIES

Thallium Toxicology. S. Jackson. Department of Health and Human Services, Public Health Service, National Institutes of Health, National Library of Medicine, 9000 Rockville Pike, Bethesda, Maryland 20892. (301) 496-4000. 1977.

ENCYCLOPEDIAS AND DICTIONARIES

McGraw-Hill Encyclopedia of Science and Technology. McGraw-Hill, 1221 Avenue of the Americas, New York, New York 10020. (212) 512-2000 or (800) 262-4729. 1992. Seventh edition. Issued in multiple volumes including index. Includes all science and technology broad subject areas.

Van Nostrand's Scientific Encyclopedia. Glenn D. Considine, ed. Van Nostrand Reinhold, 115 5th Ave., New York, New York 10003. (212) 254-3232. 1983. Sixth edition. Includes all broad subject areas in science.

GENERAL WORKS

Ambient Water Quality Criteria for Thallium. National Technical Information Service, 5285 Port Royal Rd., Springfield, Virginia 22161. (703) 487-4650. 1980. Covers thallium and water quality standards.

Organometallic Compounds of Aluminum, Gallium, Indium, and Thallium. A. McKillog. Chapman & Hall, 29 W. 35th St., New York, New York 10001-2291. (212) 244-3336. 1985. Covers organoaluminum, organogallium and organothallium compounds.

ONLINE DATA BASES

Chemical Abstracts-CA. Chemical Abstracts Service, 2540 Olentangy River Rd., P.O. Box 3012, Columbus, Ohio 43210. (800) 848-6533 or (614) 421-3600. Information sources include 9000 journals, patents from 27 countries, two industrial property organizations, new books, conference proceedings, and government research reports.

THALWEG

See: RIVERS

THERMAL ANALYSIS

ABSTRACTING AND INDEXING SERVICES

Biological and Agricultural Index. H.W. Wilson Co., 950 University Ave., Bronx, New York 10452. (800) 367-6770. 1916-. Monthly.

Ecological Abstracts. Geo Abstracts Ltd. Elsevier Applied Science, Crown House, Linton Rd., Barking, England IG 11 8JU. 1974-. Derived from over 600 leading ecological and environmental journals, plus books, conference proceedings, reports and theses.

Energy Information Abstracts Annual 1987 in Retrospect. EIC/Intelligence Inc., 121 Chanlon Rd., New Providence, New Jersey 07974. (908) 464-6800. 1988. Annual. Cumulative edition of the monthly Energy Information Abstracts. Monitors sources in the field of energy including the scientific, technical and business journal literature, conference and symposia proceedings, corporate, government and academic reports.

Engineering Index. The Engineering Index Inc., 345 E. 47th St., New York, New York 10017. 1962-.

Physics Briefs. Physikalische Berichte. Physik Verlag, Pappapelallee 3, Postfach 101161, Weinheim, Germany D-6940. 1979-. Semimonthly. In English. Volumes for 1979- issued by the Deutsche Physikalische Gesellschaft and the Fachinformationszentrum Energie Physik, Mathematik in cooperation with the American Institute of Physics.

Science Citation Index. Institute for Scientific Information, 3501 Market St., Philadelphia, Pennsylvania 19104. 1961-.

ENCYCLOPEDIAS AND DICTIONARIES

Dictionary of Environmental Engineering and Related Sciences: English-Spanish, Spanish-English. Jose T. Villate. Ediciones Universal, 3090 SW 8th St., Miami, Florida 33135. (305) 642-3355. 1979.

Encyclopedia of Environmental Science and Engineering. J.R. Pfafflin. Gordon and Breach Science Publishers, Inc., 270 8th Ave., New York, New York 10011. (212) 206-8900. 1992.

Encyclopedia of Physical Science and Technology. Robert A. Meyers, ed. Academic Press, c/o Harcourt Brace Jovanovich Inc., 6277 Sea Harbor Dr., Orlando, Florida 32887. (800) 346-8648. Dictionary of engineering, technology and physical sciences.

Encyclopedia of Physics. Rita G. Lerner and George L. Trigg. VCH Publishers, 303 NW 12th Ave., Deerfield Beach, Florida 33442-1788. (305) 428-5566. 1991. Second edition.

GENERAL WORKS

Ecological Effects of Thermal Discharges. T.E. Langford. Elsevier Science Publishing Co., 655 Avenue of the Americas, New York, New York 10010. (212) 984-5800. 1990. Review of the biological studies which have been carried out in various habitats and in response to a variety of problems related to cooling water usage, particularly on the large scale such as in thermal power stations.

Thermal Analysis. W. W. Wendlandt. Halsted Press, 605 3rd Ave., New York, New York 10158. (212) 850-6000. 1976. Topics in analytical chemistry.

HANDBOOKS AND MANUALS

Introduction to Thermal Analysis: Techniques and Applications. Michael E. Brown. Chapman & Hall, 29 W. 35th St., New York, New York 10001-2291. (212) 244-3336. 1988.

Tables of Physical and Chemical Constants and Some Mathematical Functions. G. W. C. Kaye, et al. Longman Group Ltd., Longman House, Burnt Mill, Harlow, England CM20 2J6. 0279 426721. 1988. Fifteenth edition. Includes tables on mechanical properties, density, elasticity, viscosity, surface tension, temperature and heat. Also covers radiation, optics, chemistry, electrochemistry, astrophysics, and chemical thermodynamics.

Thermal Analysis Research Program Reference Manual. George N. Walton. National Technical Information Service, 5285 Port Royal Rd., Springfield, Virginia 22161. (703) 487-4650. 1983. Mathematical models in heat transmission.

ONLINE DATA BASES

Computerized Engineering Index–COMPENDEX. Engineering Information Inc., 345 E. 47th St., New York, New York 10017. (212) 705-7600.

Multispectral Scanner and Photographic Imagery. U.S. Environmental Protection Agency, Office of Modeling and Monitoring Systems and Quality Assurance, 401 M St., S.W., Washington, District of Columbia 20460. (202) 260-2090. An index for various data tapes containing multispectral imagery from aircraft and satellites relating to sources of pollution.

PERIODICALS AND NEWSLETTERS

Journal of Thermal Analysis. Akademiai Kiado, Prielle Kornelia ut 19-35, Budapest, Hungary H-1117. 36 01 181 21 31. An international forum for communications on thermal investigations.

THERMAL PLUMES

ABSTRACTING AND INDEXING SERVICES

Science Citation Index. Institute for Scientific Information, 3501 Market St., Philadelphia, Pennsylvania 19104. 1961-.

ENCYCLOPEDIAS AND DICTIONARIES

Dictionary of Environmental Engineering and Related Sciences: English-Spanish, Spanish-English. Jose T. Villate. Ediciones Universal, 3090 SW 8th St., Miami, Florida 33135. (305) 642-3355. 1979.

Encyclopedia of Environmental Science and Engineering. J.R. Pfafflin. Gordon and Breach Science Publishers, Inc., 270 8th Ave., New York, New York 10011. (212) 206-8900. 1992.

Encyclopedia of Physical Science and Technology. Robert A. Meyers, ed. Academic Press, c/o Harcourt Brace Jovanovich Inc., 6277 Sea Harbor Dr., Orlando, Florida 32887. (800) 346-8648. Dictionary of engineering, technology and physical sciences.

GENERAL WORKS

A Review of Thermal Plume Modeling. Lorin R. Davis. U.S. Environmental Protection Agency, Corvallis Environmental Research Laboratory, Office of Research and Development, 200 SW 35th St., Corvallis, Oregon 97333. (503) 754-4600. 1978. Environmental implications of electric power plants and thermal pollution of rivers and lakes.

River Pollution: An Ecological Perspective. S. M. Haslam. Belhaven Press, 136 S. Broadway, Irvington, New York 10533. (914) 591-9111. 1990. Describes the impact of natural and man-made pollution in the ecosystem of freshwater streams, stressing understanding of processes and techniques of measurement.

HANDBOOKS AND MANUALS

Workbook of Thermal Plume Prediction. Mostafa A. Shirazi. U.S. Environmental Protection Agency, National Environmental Research Center, Office of Research and Monitoring, 401 M St., S.W., Washington, District of Columbia 20460. (202) 260-2090. 1972. Water-jets, waste heat and thermal pollution of rivers and lakes.

THERMAL RADIATION

ABSTRACTING AND INDEXING SERVICES

Applied Science and Technology Index. H.W. Wilson Co., 950 University Ave., Bronx, New York 10452. (800) 367-6770. Formerly Industrial Arts Index.

Physics Briefs. Physikalische Berichte. Physik Verlag, Pappapelallee 3, Postfach 101161, Weinheim, Germany D-6940. 1979-. Semimonthly. In English. Volumes for 1979- issued by the Deutsche Physikalische Gesellschaft and the Fachinformationszentrum Energie Physik, Mathematik in cooperation with the American Institute of Physics.

Science Citation Index. Institute for Scientific Information, 3501 Market St., Philadelphia, Pennsylvania 19104. 1961-.

ENCYCLOPEDIAS AND DICTIONARIES

Dictionary of Environmental Engineering and Related Sciences: English-Spanish, Spanish-English. Jose T. Villate. Ediciones Universal, 3090 SW 8th St., Miami, Florida 33135. (305) 642-3355. 1979.

Encyclopedia of Environmental Science and Engineering. J.R. Pfafflin. Gordon and Breach Science Publishers, Inc., 270 8th Ave., New York, New York 10011. (212) 206-8900. 1992.

Encyclopedia of Physical Science and Technology. Robert A. Meyers, ed. Academic Press, c/o Harcourt Brace Jovanovich Inc., 6277 Sea Harbor Dr., Orlando, Florida 32887. (800) 346-8648. Dictionary of engineering, technology and physical sciences.

Encyclopedia of Physics. Rita G. Lerner and George L. Trigg. VCH Publishers, 303 NW 12th Ave., Deerfield Beach, Florida 33442-1788. (305) 428-5566. 1991. Second edition.

Van Nostrand's Scientific Encyclopedia. Glenn D. Considine, ed. Van Nostrand Reinhold, 115 5th Ave., New York, New York 10003. (212) 254-3232. 1983. Sixth edition. Includes all broad subject areas in science.

HANDBOOKS AND MANUALS

Tables of Physical and Chemical Constants and Some Mathematical Functions. G. W. C. Kaye, et al. Longman Group Ltd., Longman House, Burnt Mill, Harlow, England CM20 2J6. 0279 426721. 1988. Fifteenth edition. Includes tables on mechanical properties, density, elasticity, viscosity, surface tension, temperature and heat. Also covers radiation, optics, chemistry, electrochemistry, astrophysics, and chemical thermodynamics.

THERMOCLINE

See: LAKES

THIN LAYER CHROMATOGRAPHY

See: CHROMATOGRAPHY

THIOCARBAMATES

ABSTRACTING AND INDEXING SERVICES

Chemical Abstracts. Chemical Abstracts Service, 2540 Olentangy River Rd., PO Box 3012, Columbus, Ohio 43210. (800) 848-6533. 1907-.

Science Citation Index. Institute for Scientific Information, 3501 Market St., Philadelphia, Pennsylvania 19104. 1961-.

ENCYCLOPEDIAS AND DICTIONARIES

Van Nostrand's Scientific Encyclopedia. Glenn D. Considine, ed. Van Nostrand Reinhold, 115 5th Ave., New York, New York 10003. (212) 254-3232. 1983. Sixth edition. Includes all broad subject areas in science.

GENERAL WORKS

Synthetically Useful Dipole-Stabilized Carbonions from Thioesters and Thiocarbamates. Peter Donald Becker. University of Illinois, Urbana, Illinois 61801. 1982.

ONLINE DATA BASES

CAS Source Index–CASSI. Chemical Abstracts Service, 2540 Olentangy River Rd., P.O. Box 3012, Columbus, Ohio 43210. (800) 848-6533 or (614) 421-3600. A listing of bibliographic and library holdings information for scientific and technical primary literature relevant to the chemical sciences.

Chemical Abstracts-CA. Chemical Abstracts Service, 2540 Olentangy River Rd., P.O. Box 3012, Columbus, Ohio 43210. (800) 848-6533 or (614) 421-3600. Information sources include 9000 journals, patents from 27 countries, two industrial property organizations, new books, conference proceedings, and government research reports.

Chemical Abstracts Chemical Name Directory-CHEM-NAME. Chemical Abstracts Service, 2540 Olentangy River Rd., P.O. Box 3012, Columbus, Ohio 43210. (800) 848-6533 or (614) 421-3600. Listing of chemical substances in a dictionary type file. The Chemical Abstracts (CAS) Registry Number, molecular formula, Chemical Abstracts (CA) Substance Index Name, available synonyms, ring data and other chemical substance information is given for each entry.

Chemical Collection System/Request Tracking–CCS/RTS. U.S. Environmental Protection Agency, Office of Pesticides and Toxic Substances, 401 M St., SW, Washington, District of Columbia 20460. (202) 260-2090. Contains information on various properties of a number of chemicals including environmental effects, test and analysis methods, and health effects. Available from EPA.

Chemical Dictionary Online–CHEMLINE. Chemical Abstracts Service, 2540 Olentangy River Rd., Columbus, Ohio 43210. (614) 421-3600 or (800) 848-6533. Part of MEDLINE of the National Library of Medicine (NLM). File of 900,000 names for chemical substances, representing 450,000 unique compounds. It contains such information as Chemical Abstracts (CA) Service Registry Numbers, molecular formulas, preferred chemical nomenclature, and generic and ring structure information. Available on NLM's ELHILL system.

Chemical Exposure. Science Applications International Corp., Health & Environmental Information, P.O. Box 2501, Oak Ridge, Tennessee 37831. (615) 482-9031. Database of chemicals that have been identified in both human tissues and body fluids and in feral and food animals. Contains reference to journal articles, conferences, and reports. Covers the whole fields of information related to human and animal exposure to food, air, and water contaminants and pharmaceuticals. Its records include information on chemical properties, formulas, tissues measured, analytical method used, demographics and more. Available on DIALOG.

TRADE ASSOCIATIONS AND PROFESSIONAL SOCIETIES

American Chemical Society. 1155 16th St., N.W., Washington, District of Columbia 20036. (202) 872-4600.

THORIUM

ABSTRACTING AND INDEXING SERVICES

Chemical Abstracts. Chemical Abstracts Service, 2540 Olentangy River Rd., PO Box 3012, Columbus, Ohio 43210. (800) 848-6533. 1907-.

General Science Index. H. W. Wilson Co., 950 University Ave., Bronx, New York 10452. 1978-. Monthly, also issued in annual cumulation. Cumulative subject index to English language periodicals in the subject fields of astronomy, botany, chemistry, earth science, environment and conservation, food and nutrition, genetics, mathematics, medicine and health, microbiology, oceanography, physics, physiology and zoology.

ENCYCLOPEDIAS AND DICTIONARIES

Encyclopedia of Physics. Rita G. Lerner and George L. Trigg. VCH Publishers, 303 NW 12th Ave., Deerfield Beach, Florida 33442-1788. (305) 428-5566. 1991. Second edition.

McGraw-Hill Encyclopedia of Science and Technology. McGraw-Hill, 1221 Avenue of the Americas, New York, New York 10020. (212) 512-2000 or (800) 262-4729. 1992. Seventh edition. Issued in multiple volumes including index. Includes all science and technology broad subject areas.

Van Nostrand's Scientific Encyclopedia. Glenn D. Considine, ed. Van Nostrand Reinhold, 115 5th Ave., New York, New York 10003. (212) 254-3232. 1983. Sixth edition. Includes all broad subject areas in science.

ONLINE DATA BASES

CAS Source Index–CASSI. Chemical Abstracts Service, 2540 Olentangy River Rd., P.O. Box 3012, Columbus, Ohio 43210. (800) 848-6533 or (614) 421-3600. A listing of bibliographic and library holdings information for scientific and technical primary literature relevant to the chemical sciences.

Chemical Abstracts-CA. Chemical Abstracts Service, 2540 Olentangy River Rd., P.O. Box 3012, Columbus, Ohio 43210. (800) 848-6533 or (614) 421-3600. Information sources include 9000 journals, patents from 27 countries, two industrial property organizations, new books, conference proceedings, and government research reports.

TRADE ASSOCIATIONS AND PROFESSIONAL SOCIETIES

American Chemical Society. 1155 16th St., N.W., Washington, District of Columbia 20036. (202) 872-4600.

American Institute of Chemical Engineers. 345 East 47th St., New York, New York 10017. (212) 705-7338.

American Institute of Chemists. 7315 Wisconsin Ave., Bethesda, Maryland 20814. (301) 652-2447.

THREATENED SPECIES
See: ENDANGERED SPECIES

THROWAWAY CONTAINERS

See also: RECYCLING

ABSTRACTING AND INDEXING SERVICES

Applied Ecology Abstracts Studies in Renewable Natural Resources. Information Retrieval Ltd., 1911 Jefferson Davis Highway, Arlington, Virginia 22202. 1975-. Monthly.

Index to Scientific Book Contents. Institute for Scientific Information, 3501 Market St., Philadelphia, Pennsylvania 19104. (800) 523-1857. 1985-. Annual. Gives contents of science books published.

Multimedia Index to Ecology. National Information Center for Educational Media, University of Southern California, Los Angeles, California 90007.

ONLINE DATA BASES

Monthly Catalog of United States Government Publications. U.S. G.P.O., Supt. of Docs., PO Box 371954, Pittsburgh, Pennsylvania 15250-7954. (202) 512-0000.

National Technical Information Service. U.S. Department of Commerce, National Technical Information Service, Office of Data Base Services, 5285 Port Royal Rd., Springfield, Virginia 22161. (703) 487-4807. Bibliographic database of government sponsored research and technical reports.

PressNet Environmental Reports. Chemical Information Systems, Inc., 7215 York Rd., Baltimore, Maryland 21212. (301) 321-8440.

SCISEARCH. Institute for Scientific Information, University City Science Center, 3501 Market St., Philadelphia, Pennsylvania 19104. (215) 386-0100.

THYROID FUNCTION

ABSTRACTING AND INDEXING SERVICES

Science Citation Index. Institute for Scientific Information, 3501 Market St., Philadelphia, Pennsylvania 19104. 1961-.

ENCYCLOPEDIAS AND DICTIONARIES

Encyclopedia of Human Biology. Renato Dulbecco, ed. Academic Press, c/o Harcourt Brace Jovanovich Inc., 6277 Sea Harbor Dr., Orlando, Florida 32887. (800) 346-8648. 1991. Eight volumes.

McGraw-Hill Encyclopedia of Science and Technology. McGraw-Hill, 1221 Avenue of the Americas, New York, New York 10020. (212) 512-2000 or (800) 262-4729. 1992. Seventh edition. Issued in multiple volumes including index. Includes all science and technology broad subject areas.

Van Nostrand's Scientific Encyclopedia. Glenn D. Considine, ed. Van Nostrand Reinhold, 115 5th Ave., New York, New York 10003. (212) 254-3232. 1983. Sixth edition. Includes all broad subject areas in science.

GENERAL WORKS

Thyroid Function and Disease. W. B. Saunders, Curtis Center, Independence Sq. W., Philadelphia, Pennsylvania 19106. (215) 238-7800. 1989. Physiology of thyroid gland.

HANDBOOKS AND MANUALS

Control of the Thyroid Gland: Regulation of its Normal Function and Growth. Plenum Press, 233 Spring St., New York, New York 10013-1578. (212) 620-8000; (800) 221-9369. 1989. Physiology of thyroid hormones and receptors.

TIDAL MARSHES

ABSTRACTING AND INDEXING SERVICES

Science Citation Index. Institute for Scientific Information, 3501 Market St., Philadelphia, Pennsylvania 19104. 1961-.

BIBLIOGRAPHIES

Bibliography and Index of Geology. American Geological Institute, 4220 King St., Alexandria, Virginia 22302. Monthly. Includes environmental geology and hydrogeology.

ENCYCLOPEDIAS AND DICTIONARIES

McGraw-Hill Encyclopedia of Science and Technology. McGraw-Hill, 1221 Avenue of the Americas, New York, New York 10020. (212) 512-2000 or (800) 262-4729. 1992. Seventh edition. Issued in multiple volumes including index. Includes all science and technology broad subject areas.

Van Nostrand's Scientific Encyclopedia. Glenn D. Considine, ed. Van Nostrand Reinhold, 115 5th Ave., New York, New York 10003. (212) 254-3232. 1983. Sixth edition. Includes all broad subject areas in science.

GENERAL WORKS

Conservation of Tidal Marshes. Franklin C. Daiber. Van Nostrand Reinhold, 115 Fifth Ave., New York, New York 10003. (212) 254-3232. 1986. Topics in wetland conservation.

Estuaries and Tidal Marshes. National Institute for Urban Wildlife, 10921 Trotting Ridge Way, Columbia, Maryland 21044. (301) 596-3311. 1986. Topics in estuarine and tidemarsh ecology.

Magill's Survey of Science. Earth Science Series. Frank N. Magill. Salem Press, PO Box 50062, Pasadena, California 91105. 1990-. Five volumes. Includes information on earth's crust, hot spots and volcanic island chains, physical properties of minerals, rock magnetism, physical properties of rocks, and index.

STATISTICS SOURCES

Ecology: Community Profiles. U.S. Fish and Wildlife Service. National Technical Information Service, 5285 Port Royal Road, Springfield, Virginia 22161. (703) 487-4650. Irregular. Data on coastal and inland ecosystems, including wetlands, tidal-flats, near-shore seagrasses, sand dunes, drilling platforms, oyster reefs, estuaries, rivers and streams.

TIMBER

See also: WOOD

ABSTRACTING AND INDEXING SERVICES

Forest Products Abstracts. C. A. B. International, 845 North Park Ave., Tucson, Arizona 85719. (602) 621-7897 or (800) 528-4841. Bimonthly. Contains abstracts in the area of forest product industry; wood properties; timber extraction; conversion and measurement; damage to timber and timber production; utilization of wood; pulp industries and the chemical utilization of wood and other related areas.

General Science Index. H. W. Wilson Co., 950 University Ave., Bronx, New York 10452. 1978-. Monthly, also issued in annual cumulation. Cumulative subject index to English language periodicals in the subject fields of astronomy, botany, chemistry, earth science, environment and conservation, food and nutrition, genetics, mathematics, medicine and health, microbiology, oceanography, physics, physiology and zoology.

ENCYCLOPEDIAS AND DICTIONARIES

Van Nostrand's Scientific Encyclopedia. Glenn D. Considine, ed. Van Nostrand Reinhold, 115 5th Ave., New York, New York 10003. (212) 254-3232. 1983. Sixth edition. Includes all broad subject areas in science.

TIRES

ABSTRACTING AND INDEXING SERVICES

Science Citation Index. Institute for Scientific Information, 3501 Market St., Philadelphia, Pennsylvania 19104. 1961-.

ENCYCLOPEDIAS AND DICTIONARIES

Van Nostrand's Scientific Encyclopedia. Glenn D. Considine, ed. Van Nostrand Reinhold, 115 5th Ave., New York, New York 10003. (212) 254-3232. 1983. Sixth edition. Includes all broad subject areas in science.

STATISTICS SOURCES

The Tire & Rubber Industry. FIND/SVP, 625 Avenue of the Americas, New York, New York 10011. (212) 645-4500. Covers pricing, demand and market share, the replacement and retread markets, the supply side, distribution and foreign producers.

TRADE ASSOCIATIONS AND PROFESSIONAL SOCIETIES

Tire and Rim Association. 175 Montrose Ave., W., Copely, Ohio 44321. (216) 666-8121.

Tire Industry Safety Council. National Press Bldg., Suite 844, Washington, District of Columbia 20045. (202) 783-1022.

TITANIUM

ABSTRACTING AND INDEXING SERVICES

Chemical Abstracts. Chemical Abstracts Service, 2540 Olentangy River Rd., PO Box 3012, Columbus, Ohio 43210. (800) 848-6533. 1907-.

General Science Index. H. W. Wilson Co., 950 University Ave., Bronx, New York 10452. 1978-. Monthly, also issued in annual cumulation. Cumulative subject index to English language periodicals in the subject fields of astronomy, botany, chemistry, earth science, environment and conservation, food and nutrition, genetics, mathematics, medicine and health, microbiology, oceanography, physics, physiology and zoology.

Metals Abstracts. ASM International, 9639 Kinsman, Materials Park, Ohio 44073. (216) 338-5151. 1968-. Published jointly by the Institute of Metals, London and the American Society for Metals. Formed by the Union of Metallurgical Abstracts and Review of Metal Literature.

Physics Briefs. Physikalische Berichte. Physik Verlag, Pappapelallee 3, Postfach 101161, Weinheim, Germany D-6940. 1979-. Semimonthly. In English. Volumes for 1979- issued by the Deutsche Physikalische Gesellschaft and the Fachinformationszentrum Energie Physik, Mathematik in cooperation with the American Institute of Physics.

Science Citation Index. Institute for Scientific Information, 3501 Market St., Philadelphia, Pennsylvania 19104. 1961-.

BIBLIOGRAPHIES

Bibliography and Index of Geology. American Geological Institute, 4220 King St., Alexandria, Virginia 22302. Monthly. Includes environmental geology and hydrogeology.

DIRECTORIES

Titanium Development Association–Buyers Guide. Titanium Development Association, 4141 Arapahoe Ave., Ste. 100, Boulder, Colorado 80303. (303) 443-7515. 1984-.

ENCYCLOPEDIAS AND DICTIONARIES

Van Nostrand's Scientific Encyclopedia. Glenn D. Considine, ed. Van Nostrand Reinhold, 115 5th Ave., New York, New York 10003. (212) 254-3232. 1983. Sixth edition. Includes all broad subject areas in science.

GENERAL WORKS

Magill's Survey of Science. Earth Science Series. Frank N. Magill. Salem Press, PO Box 50062, Pasadena, California 91105. 1990-. Five volumes. Includes information on earth's crust, hot spots and volcanic island chains, physical properties of minerals, rock magnetism, physical properties of rocks, and index.

HANDBOOKS AND MANUALS

Tables of Physical and Chemical Constants and Some Mathematical Functions. G. W. C. Kaye, et al. Longman

Group Ltd., Longman House, Burnt Mill, Harlow, England CM20 2J6. 0279 426721. 1988. Fifteenth edition. Includes tables on mechanical properties, density, elasticity, viscosity, surface tension, temperature and heat. Also covers radiation, optics, chemistry, electrochemistry, astrophysics, and chemical thermodynamics.

ONLINE DATA BASES

CAS Source Index–CASSI. Chemical Abstracts Service, 2540 Olentangy River Rd., P.O. Box 3012, Columbus, Ohio 43210. (800) 848-6533 or (614) 421-3600. A listing of bibliographic and library holdings information for scientific and technical primary literature relevant to the chemical sciences.

Chemical Abstracts-CA. Chemical Abstracts Service, 2540 Olentangy River Rd., P.O. Box 3012, Columbus, Ohio 43210. (800) 848-6533 or (614) 421-3600. Information sources include 9000 journals, patents from 27 countries, two industrial property organizations, new books, conference proceedings, and government research reports.

STATISTICS SOURCES

Tritium Deposition in the Continental U.S. U.S. G.P.O, Washington, District of Columbia 20402-9325. (202) 512-0000. Irregular. Showing precipitation and tritium deposition, by location.

World Titanium Dioxide Market. FIND/SVP, 625 Avenue of the Americas, New York, New York 10011. (212) 645-4500. 1991.

TRADE ASSOCIATIONS AND PROFESSIONAL SOCIETIES

American Institute of Chemical Engineers. 345 East 47th St., New York, New York 10017. (212) 705-7338.

American Institute of Chemists. 7315 Wisconsin Ave., Bethesda, Maryland 20814. (301) 652-2447.

Titanium Development Association. 4141 Arapahoe Ave., Ste. 100, Boulder, Colorado 80303. (303) 443-7515.

TITANIUM DIOXIDE

ABSTRACTING AND INDEXING SERVICES

Chemical Abstracts. Chemical Abstracts Service, 2540 Olentangy River Rd., PO Box 3012, Columbus, Ohio 43210. (800) 848-6533. 1907-.

Science Citation Index. Institute for Scientific Information, 3501 Market St., Philadelphia, Pennsylvania 19104. 1961-.

ENCYCLOPEDIAS AND DICTIONARIES

McGraw-Hill Encyclopedia of Science and Technology. McGraw-Hill, 1221 Avenue of the Americas, New York, New York 10020. (212) 512-2000 or (800) 262-4729. 1992. Seventh edition. Issued in multiple volumes including index. Includes all science and technology broad subject areas.

Van Nostrand's Scientific Encyclopedia. Glenn D. Considine, ed. Van Nostrand Reinhold, 115 5th Ave., New

York, New York 10003. (212) 254-3232. 1983. Sixth edition. Includes all broad subject areas in science.

ONLINE DATA BASES

CAS Source Index–CASSI. Chemical Abstracts Service, 2540 Olentangy River Rd., P.O. Box 3012, Columbus, Ohio 43210. (800) 848-6533 or (614) 421-3600. A listing of bibliographic and library holdings information for scientific and technical primary literature relevant to the chemical sciences.

Chemical Abstracts-CA. Chemical Abstracts Service, 2540 Olentangy River Rd., P.O. Box 3012, Columbus, Ohio 43210. (800) 848-6533 or (614) 421-3600. Information sources include 9000 journals, patents from 27 countries, two industrial property organizations, new books, conference proceedings, and government research reports.

Chemical Abstracts Chemical Name Directory-CHEM-NAME. Chemical Abstracts Service, 2540 Olentangy River Rd., P.O. Box 3012, Columbus, Ohio 43210. (800) 848-6533 or (614) 421-3600. Listing of chemical substances in a dictionary type file. The Chemical Abstracts (CAS) Registry Number, molecular formula, Chemical Abstracts (CA) Substance Index Name, available synonyms, ring data and other chemical substance information is given for each entry.

Chemical Collection System/Request Tracking–CCS/RTS. U.S. Environmental Protection Agency, Office of Pesticides and Toxic Substances, 401 M St., SW, Washington, District of Columbia 20460. (202) 260-2090. Contains information on various properties of a number of chemicals including environmental effects, test and analysis methods, and health effects. Available from EPA.

Chemical Dictionary Online–CHEMLINE. Chemical Abstracts Service, 2540 Olentangy River Rd., Columbus, Ohio 43210. (614) 421-3600 or (800) 848-6533. Part of MEDLINE of the National Library of Medicine (NLM). File of 900,000 names for chemical substances, representing 450,000 unique compounds. It contains such information as Chemical Abstracts (CA) Service Registry Numbers, molecular formulas, preferred chemical nomenclature, and generic and ring structure information. Available on NLM's ELHILL system.

Chemical Exposure. Science Applications International Corp., Health & Environmental Information, P.O. Box 2501, Oak Ridge, Tennessee 37831. (615) 482-9031. Database of chemicals that have been identified in both human tissues and body fluids and in feral and food animals. Contains reference to journal articles, conferences, and reports. Covers the whole fields of information related to human and animal exposure to food, air, and water contaminants and pharmaceuticals. Its records include information on chemical properties, formulas, tissues measured, analytical method used, demographics and more. Available on DIALOG.

TRADE ASSOCIATIONS AND PROFESSIONAL SOCIETIES

American Chemical Society. 1155 16th St., N.W., Washington, District of Columbia 20036. (202) 872-4600.

TITANIUM RESOURCES

ABSTRACTING AND INDEXING SERVICES

Chemical Abstracts. Chemical Abstracts Service, 2540 Olentangy River Rd., PO Box 3012, Columbus, Ohio 43210. (800) 848-6533. 1907-.

Science Citation Index. Institute for Scientific Information, 3501 Market St., Philadelphia, Pennsylvania 19104. 1961-.

ONLINE DATA BASES

CAS Source Index–CASSI. Chemical Abstracts Service, 2540 Olentangy River Rd., P.O. Box 3012, Columbus, Ohio 43210. (800) 848-6533 or (614) 421-3600. A listing of bibliographic and library holdings information for scientific and technical primary literature relevant to the chemical sciences.

Chemical Abstracts-CA. Chemical Abstracts Service, 2540 Olentangy River Rd., P.O. Box 3012, Columbus, Ohio 43210. (800) 848-6533 or (614) 421-3600. Information sources include 9000 journals, patents from 27 countries, two industrial property organizations, new books, conference proceedings, and government research reports.

TRADE ASSOCIATIONS AND PROFESSIONAL SOCIETIES

American Chemical Society. 1155 16th St., N.W., Washington, District of Columbia 20036. (202) 872-4600.

TOBACCO SMOKE

ABSTRACTING AND INDEXING SERVICES

General Science Index. H. W. Wilson Co., 950 University Ave., Bronx, New York 10452. 1978-. Monthly, also issued in annual cumulation. Cumulative subject index to English language periodicals in the subject fields of astronomy, botany, chemistry, earth science, environment and conservation, food and nutrition, genetics, mathematics, medicine and health, microbiology, oceanography, physics, physiology and zoology.

Science Citation Index. Institute for Scientific Information, 3501 Market St., Philadelphia, Pennsylvania 19104. 1961-.

ENCYCLOPEDIAS AND DICTIONARIES

McGraw-Hill Encyclopedia of Science and Technology. McGraw-Hill, 1221 Avenue of the Americas, New York, New York 10020. (212) 512-2000 or (800) 262-4729. 1992. Seventh edition. Issued in multiple volumes including index. Includes all science and technology broad subject areas.

ONLINE DATA BASES

PressNet Environmental Reports. Chemical Information Systems, Inc., 7215 York Rd., Baltimore, Maryland 21212. (301) 321-8440.

TOLERANCE LEVELS

See also: PESTICIDE TOLERANCE

ABSTRACTING AND INDEXING SERVICES

Chemical Abstracts. Chemical Abstracts Service, 2540 Olentangy River Rd., PO Box 3012, Columbus, Ohio 43210. (800) 848-6533. 1907-.

Science Citation Index. Institute for Scientific Information, 3501 Market St., Philadelphia, Pennsylvania 19104. 1961-.

ONLINE DATA BASES

Chemical Abstracts-CA. Chemical Abstracts Service, 2540 Olentangy River Rd., P.O. Box 3012, Columbus, Ohio 43210. (800) 848-6533 or (614) 421-3600. Information sources include 9000 journals, patents from 27 countries, two industrial property organizations, new books, conference proceedings, and government research reports.

TOLUENE

ABSTRACTING AND INDEXING SERVICES

Chemical Abstracts. Chemical Abstracts Service, 2540 Olentangy River Rd., PO Box 3012, Columbus, Ohio 43210. (800) 848-6533. 1907-.

General Science Index. H. W. Wilson Co., 950 University Ave., Bronx, New York 10452. 1978-. Monthly, also issued in annual cumulation. Cumulative subject index to English language periodicals in the subject fields of astronomy, botany, chemistry, earth science, environment and conservation, food and nutrition, genetics, mathematics, medicine and health, microbiology, oceanography, physics, physiology and zoology.

ENCYCLOPEDIAS AND DICTIONARIES

Ullmanns Encyclopedia of Industrial Chemistry. Hans Jurgen Arpe and Wolfgang Gerhartz, eds. VCH Publishers, 303 NW 12th Ave., Deerfield Beach, Florida 33442-1788. (305) 428-5566. 1990. Designed to keep up with the broad spectrum of chemical technology. Thirty-six volumes of the encyclopedia have been divided into two sets: the 28 A volumes contain alphabetically arranged articles on chemicals, product groups, processes and technological concepts; and the 8 B volumes are compendia of basic knowledge in industrial chemistry.

Van Nostrand's Scientific Encyclopedia. Glenn D. Considine, ed. Van Nostrand Reinhold, 115 5th Ave., New York, New York 10003. (212) 254-3232. 1983. Sixth edition. Includes all broad subject areas in science.

GENERAL WORKS

Hazardous Wastes and Hazardous Materials. Hazardous Materials Control Research Institute, 9300 Columbia Blvd., Silver Spring, Maryland 20910. (301) 587-9390. 1987.

Practical Aspects of Groundwater Modeling. William Clarence Walton. National Water Well Association, 6375

Riverside Dr., Dublin, Ohio 43017. (614) 761-1711. 1985. Practical aspects of groundwater computer models. Deals with flow, mass and heat transport and subsidence.

Solubilities of Inorganic and Organic Compounds. H. Stephen and T. Stephen, eds. Macmillan Publishing Co., 866 3rd Ave., New York, New York 10022. (212) 702-2000; (800) 257-5755. 1963-67.

HANDBOOKS AND MANUALS

Documentation of the Threshold Limit Values. American Conference of Governmental Industrial Hygienists, 6500 Glenway, Building D-5, Cincinnati, Ohio 45211. 1991. Provides threshold limit value documentation for any physical phenomenon in the environment, including chemical substances and physical agents.

FDA Food Additives Analytical Manual. C. Warner, et al., eds. Association of Official Analytical Chemists, 2200 Wilson Blvd., Suite 400-P, Arlington, Virginia 22201-3301. (703) 522-3032. 1983-1987. 2 vols. Provides methodology for determining compliance with food additive regulations. Contains analytical methods that have been evaluated by the FDA or found to operate satisfactorily in at least two laboratories.

Handbook of Analytical Chemistry. Louis Meites, ed. McGraw-Hill Science & Engineering Books, 11 W. 19th St., New York, New York 10011. (212) 337-6010. 1963.

Handbook of Chemistry and Physics. CRC Press, 2000 Corporate Blvd. N.W., Boca Raton, Florida 33431. (800) 272-7737. Annually.

Handbook of Environmental Data on Organic Chemicals. Karel Verschueren. Van Nostrand Reinhold, 115 5th Ave., New York, New York 10003. (212) 254-3232. 1983. Covers individual substances as well as mixtures and preparations. The profiles include: properties, air pollution factors, water pollution factors, and biological effects.

NIOSH Pocket Guide to Chemical Hazards. National Institute for Occupational Safety and Health, 1600 Clifton Rd. NE, Atlanta, Georgia 30333. (404) 639-3286. 1990. Presents sources of general industrial hygiene and medical surveillance information for workers, employees and others. Presents key information and data in an abbreviated format for 398 individual chemicals or chemical types.

ONLINE DATA BASES

CAS Source Index–CASSI. Chemical Abstracts Service, 2540 Olentangy River Rd., P.O. Box 3012, Columbus, Ohio 43210. (800) 848-6533 or (614) 421-3600. A listing of bibliographic and library holdings information for scientific and technical primary literature relevant to the chemical sciences.

Chemical Abstracts-CA. Chemical Abstracts Service, 2540 Olentangy River Rd., P.O. Box 3012, Columbus, Ohio 43210. (800) 848-6533 or (614) 421-3600. Information sources include 9000 journals, patents from 27 countries, two industrial property organizations, new books, conference proceedings, and government research reports.

Chemical Abstracts Chemical Name Directory-CHEM-NAME. Chemical Abstracts Service, 2540 Olentangy River Rd., P.O. Box 3012, Columbus, Ohio 43210. (800) 848-6533 or (614) 421-3600. Listing of chemical sub-

stances in a dictionary type file. The Chemical Abstracts (CAS) Registry Number, molecular formula, Chemical Abstracts (CA) Substance Index Name, available synonyms, ring data and other chemical substance information is given for each entry.

Chemical Collection System/Request Tracking–CCS/RTS. U.S. Environmental Protection Agency, Office of Pesticides and Toxic Substances, 401 M St., SW, Washington, District of Columbia 20460. (202) 260-2090. Contains information on various properties of a number of chemicals including environmental effects, test and analysis methods, and health effects. Available from EPA.

Chemical Exposure. Science Applications International Corp., Health & Environmental Information, P.O. Box 2501, Oak Ridge, Tennessee 37831. (615) 482-9031. Database of chemicals that have been identified in both human tissues and body fluids and in feral and food animals. Contains reference to journal articles, conferences, and reports. Covers the whole fields of information related to human and animal exposure to food, air, and water contaminants and pharmaceuticals. Its records include information on chemical properties, formulas, tissues measured, analytical method used, demographics and more. Available on DIALOG.

Dewitt Petrochemical Newsletter. DeWitt and Company, 16800 Greenspoint Park, North Atrium Suite 120, Houston, Texas 77060. (713) 875-5525.

PERIODICALS AND NEWSLETTERS

Aquatic Toxicology. Elsevier Science Publishing Co., 655 Avenue of the Americas, New York, New York 10010. (212) 989-5800. 1981-. 6/year.

Environmental Science and Technology. American Chemical Society, 1155 16th St. N.W., Washington, District of Columbia 20036. (800) 227-5558. 1967-. Monthly. Contains research articles on various aspects of environmental chemistry, interpretative articles by invited experts and commentary on the scientific aspects of environmental management.

Journal of Chemical and Engineering Data. American Chemical Society, 1155 16th St. N.W., Washington, District of Columbia 20036. (202) 872-4600; (800) 227-5558. 1959-. Quarterly.

Journal of Organic Chemistry. American Chemical Society, 1155 16th St. N.W., Washington, District of Columbia 20036. (202) 872-4600; (800) 227-5558. 1936-.

Journal of the American Chemical Society. American Chemical Society, 1155 16th St. N.W., Washington, District of Columbia 20036. (202) 872-4600; (800) 227-5558. 1879-. Biweekly.

TRADE ASSOCIATIONS AND PROFESSIONAL SOCIETIES

American Chemical Society. 1155 16th St., N.W., Washington, District of Columbia 20036. (202) 872-4600.

TOP SOIL

ABSTRACTING AND INDEXING SERVICES

Abstracts of Air and Water Conservation Literature. American Petroleum Institute. Central Abstracting and

Indexing Service, 275 Madison Avenue, New York, New York 10016. 1972.

Biological and Agricultural Index. H.W. Wilson Co., 950 University Ave., Bronx, New York 10452. (800) 367-6770. 1916-. Monthly.

Ecological Abstracts. Geo Abstracts Ltd. Elsevier Applied Science, Crown House, Linton Rd., Barking, England IG 11 8JU. 1974-. Derived from over 600 leading ecological and environmental journals, plus books, conference proceedings, reports and theses.

Engineering Index. The Engineering Index Inc., 345 E. 47th St., New York, New York 10017. 1962-.

Science Citation Index. Institute for Scientific Information, 3501 Market St., Philadelphia, Pennsylvania 19104. 1961-.

BIBLIOGRAPHIES

Bibliography and Index of Geology. American Geological Institute, 4220 King St., Alexandria, Virginia 22302. Monthly. Includes environmental geology and hydrogeology.

DIRECTORIES

Gale Environmental Sourcebook. Karen Hill. Gale Research Co., 835 Penobscot Bldg., Detroit, Michigan 48226-4094. (313) 961-2242. Contacts, information sources, or general information on environmental topics.

ENCYCLOPEDIAS AND DICTIONARIES

The Encyclopedia of Geochemistry and Environmental Sciences. Rhodes Whitmore Fairbridge. Van Nostrand Reinhold Co., 115 5th Ave., New York, New York 10003. (212) 254-3232. 1972.

Van Nostrand's Scientific Encyclopedia. Glenn D. Considine, ed. Van Nostrand Reinhold, 115 5th Ave., New York, New York 10003. (212) 254-3232. 1983. Sixth edition. Includes all broad subject areas in science.

GENERAL WORKS

Magill's Survey of Science. Earth Science Series. Frank N. Magill. Salem Press, PO Box 50062, Pasadena, California 91105. 1990-. Five volumes. Includes information on earth's crust, hot spots and volcanic island chains, physical properties of minerals, rock magnetism, physical properties of rocks, and index.

ONLINE DATA BASES

Computerized Engineering Index–COMPENDEX. Engineering Information Inc., 345 E. 47th St., New York, New York 10017. (212) 705-7600.

STATISTICS SOURCES

Environmental Data Compendium. OECD Publications and Information Center, 2001 L St., N.W., Suite 700, Washington, District of Columbia 20036. (202) 785-6323. 1989.

Environmental Indicators. OECD Publications and Information Center, 2001 L St., N.W., Suite 700, Washington, District of Columbia 20036. (202) 785-6323. 1991.

Environmental Quality. Council on Environmental Quality. U.S. G.P.O., Washington, District of Columbia 20401. (202) 512-0000. Annual.

The State of the Environment. OECD Publications and Information Center, 2001 L St., N.W., Suite 700, Washington, District of Columbia 20036. (202) 785-6323. 1991.

TRADE ASSOCIATIONS AND PROFESSIONAL SOCIETIES

American Society of Agronomy. 677 South Segoe Rd., Madison, Wisconsin 53711. (608) 273-8080.

TOTAL DISSOLVED SOLIDS

ABSTRACTING AND INDEXING SERVICES

Abstracts of Air and Water Conservation Literature. American Petroleum Institute. Central Abstracting and Indexing Service, 275 Madison Avenue, New York, New York 10016. 1972.

Chemical Abstracts. Chemical Abstracts Service, 2540 Olentangy River Rd., PO Box 3012, Columbus, Ohio 43210. (800) 848-6533. 1907-.

BIBLIOGRAPHIES

Bibliography and Index of Geology. American Geological Institute, 4220 King St., Alexandria, Virginia 22302. Monthly. Includes environmental geology and hydrogeology.

ENCYCLOPEDIAS AND DICTIONARIES

Van Nostrand's Scientific Encyclopedia. Glenn D. Considine, ed. Van Nostrand Reinhold, 115 5th Ave., New York, New York 10003. (212) 254-3232. 1983. Sixth edition. Includes all broad subject areas in science.

GENERAL WORKS

Magill's Survey of Science. Earth Science Series. Frank N. Magill. Salem Press, PO Box 50062, Pasadena, California 91105. 1990-. Five volumes. Includes information on earth's crust, hot spots and volcanic island chains, physical properties of minerals, rock magnetism, physical properties of rocks, and index.

ONLINE DATA BASES

CAS Source Index–CASSI. Chemical Abstracts Service, 2540 Olentangy River Rd., P.O. Box 3012, Columbus, Ohio 43210. (800) 848-6533 or (614) 421-3600. A listing of bibliographic and library holdings information for scientific and technical primary literature relevant to the chemical sciences.

Chemical Abstracts-CA. Chemical Abstracts Service, 2540 Olentangy River Rd., P.O. Box 3012, Columbus, Ohio 43210. (800) 848-6533 or (614) 421-3600. Information sources include 9000 journals, patents from 27 countries, two industrial property organizations, new books, conference proceedings, and government research reports.

TOTAL ORGANIC CARBON

ABSTRACTING AND INDEXING SERVICES

Chemical Abstracts. Chemical Abstracts Service, 2540 Olentangy River Rd., PO Box 3012, Columbus, Ohio 43210. (800) 848-6533. 1907-.

ONLINE DATA BASES

Chemical Abstracts-CA. Chemical Abstracts Service, 2540 Olentangy River Rd., P.O. Box 3012, Columbus, Ohio 43210. (800) 848-6533 or (614) 421-3600. Information sources include 9000 journals, patents from 27 countries, two industrial property organizations, new books, conference proceedings, and government research reports.

TRADE ASSOCIATIONS AND PROFESSIONAL SOCIETIES

American Chemical Society. 1155 16th St., N.W., Washington, District of Columbia 20036. (202) 872-4600.

TOTAL OXYGEN DEMAND

ABSTRACTING AND INDEXING SERVICES

Chemical Abstracts. Chemical Abstracts Service, 2540 Olentangy River Rd., PO Box 3012, Columbus, Ohio 43210. (800) 848-6533. 1907-.

ENCYCLOPEDIAS AND DICTIONARIES

Van Nostrand's Scientific Encyclopedia. Glenn D. Considine, ed. Van Nostrand Reinhold, 115 5th Ave., New York, New York 10003. (212) 254-3232. 1983. Sixth edition. Includes all broad subject areas in science.

ONLINE DATA BASES

Chemical Abstracts-CA. Chemical Abstracts Service, 2540 Olentangy River Rd., P.O. Box 3012, Columbus, Ohio 43210. (800) 848-6533 or (614) 421-3600. Information sources include 9000 journals, patents from 27 countries, two industrial property organizations, new books, conference proceedings, and government research reports.

TRADE ASSOCIATIONS AND PROFESSIONAL SOCIETIES

American Chemical Society. 1155 16th St., N.W., Washington, District of Columbia 20036. (202) 872-4600.

TOXAPHENE

ABSTRACTING AND INDEXING SERVICES

Chemical Abstracts. Chemical Abstracts Service, 2540 Olentangy River Rd., PO Box 3012, Columbus, Ohio 43210. (800) 848-6533. 1907-.

Science Citation Index. Institute for Scientific Information, 3501 Market St., Philadelphia, Pennsylvania 19104. 1961-.

BIBLIOGRAPHIES

Biochemical Oxygen Demand. National Technical Information Service, 5285 Port Royal Rd., Springfield, Virginia 22161. (703) 487-4650. 1973.

ENCYCLOPEDIAS AND DICTIONARIES

Van Nostrand's Scientific Encyclopedia. Glenn D. Considine, ed. Van Nostrand Reinhold, 115 5th Ave., New York, New York 10003. (212) 254-3232. 1983. Sixth edition. Includes all broad subject areas in science.

GENERAL WORKS

Sediment Oxygen Demand in Streams Receiving Sewage Effluent. Eastern Illinois University, Department of Botany, Charleston, Illinois 61920. 1984. Covers sewage irrigation and sediment control.

HANDBOOKS AND MANUALS

Documentation of the Threshold Limit Values. American Conference of Governmental Industrial Hygienists, 6500 Glenway, Building D-5, Cincinnati, Ohio 45211. 1991. Provides threshold limit value documentation for any physical phenomenon in the environment, including chemical substances and physical agents.

NIOSH Pocket Guide to Chemical Hazards. National Institute for Occupational Safety and Health, 1600 Clifton Rd. NE, Atlanta, Georgia 30333. (404) 639-3286. 1990. Presents sources of general industrial hygiene and medical surveillance information for workers, employees and others. Presents key information and data in an abbreviated format for 398 individual chemicals or chemical types.

Treatability Manual. U.S. Environmental Protection Agency, Office of Research and Development, 401 M St., SW, Washington, District of Columbia 20460. (202) 260-2090. 1983-. V.1 Treatability data. v.2 Change 2. Industrial Descriptions. v.3 Change 2. Technology for Control/removal of pollutants. v.4. Cost estimating. v.5. Change 2 summary.

ONLINE DATA BASES

CAS Source Index–CASSI. Chemical Abstracts Service, 2540 Olentangy River Rd., P.O. Box 3012, Columbus, Ohio 43210. (800) 848-6533 or (614) 421-3600. A listing of bibliographic and library holdings information for scientific and technical primary literature relevant to the chemical sciences.

CERCLIS. Chemical Information Systems, Inc., 7215 York Rd., Baltimore, Maryland 21212. (301) 321-8440. Information on hazardous waste disposal sites that have either been listed by the EPA on the National Priority List (NPL) or nominated for consideration for the NPL.

Chemical Abstracts-CA. Chemical Abstracts Service, 2540 Olentangy River Rd., P.O. Box 3012, Columbus, Ohio 43210. (800) 848-6533 or (614) 421-3600. Information sources include 9000 journals, patents from 27 countries, two industrial property organizations, new books, conference proceedings, and government research reports.

Chemical Abstracts Chemical Name Directory-CHEMNAME. Chemical Abstracts Service, 2540 Olentangy River Rd., P.O. Box 3012, Columbus, Ohio 43210. (800)

848-6533 or (614) 421-3600. Listing of chemical substances in a dictionary type file. The Chemical Abstracts (CAS) Registry Number, molecular formula, Chemical Abstracts (CA) Substance Index Name, available synonyms, ring data and other chemical substance information is given for each entry.

Chemical Carcinogenesis Research Information System–CCRIS. National Library of Medicine, 8600 Rockville Pike, Bethesda, Maryland 20894. (800) 638-8480. Individual assay results and test conditions for 1,451 chemicals in the areas of carcinogenicity, mutagenicity, tumor promotion, and cocarcinogenicity.

Chemical Collection System/Request Tracking–CCS/RTS. U.S. Environmental Protection Agency, Office of Pesticides and Toxic Substances, 401 M St., SW, Washington, District of Columbia 20460. (202) 260-2090. Contains information on various properties of a number of chemicals including environmental effects, test and analysis methods, and health effects. Available from EPA.

Chemical Dictionary Online–CHEMLINE. Chemical Abstracts Service, 2540 Olentangy River Rd., Columbus, Ohio 43210. (614) 421-3600 or (800) 848-6533. Part of MEDLINE of the National Library of Medicine (NLM). File of 900,000 names for chemical substances, representing 450,000 unique compounds. It contains such information as Chemical Abstracts (CA) Service Registry Numbers, molecular formulas, preferred chemical nomenclature, and generic and ring structure information. Available on NLM's ELHILL system.

Chemical Exposure. Science Applications International Corp., Health & Environmental Information, P.O. Box 2501, Oak Ridge, Tennessee 37831. (615) 482-9031. Database of chemicals that have been identified in both human tissues and body fluids and in feral and food animals. Contains reference to journal articles, conferences, and reports. Covers the whole fields of information related to human and animal exposure to food, air, and water contaminants and pharmaceuticals. Its records include information on chemical properties, formulas, tissues measured, analytical method used, demographics and more. Available on DIALOG.

PERIODICALS AND NEWSLETTERS

Aquatic Toxicology. Elsevier Science Publishing Co., 655 Avenue of the Americas, New York, New York 10010. (212) 989-5800. 1981-. 6/year.

Bulletin of Environmental Contamination and Toxicology. Springer-Verlag, 175 5th Ave., New York, New York 10010. (212) 460-1500; (800) 777-4643. 1966-. Frequency varies. Disseminates advances and discoveries in the areas of soil, air and food contamination and pollution.

Environmental Science and Technology. American Chemical Society, 1155 16th St. N.W., Washington, District of Columbia 20036. (800) 227-5558. 1967-. Monthly. Contains research articles on various aspects of environmental chemistry, interpretative articles by invited experts and commentary on the scientific aspects of environmental management.

TRADE ASSOCIATIONS AND PROFESSIONAL SOCIETIES

American Chemical Society. 1155 16th St., N.W., Washington, District of Columbia 20036. (202) 872-4600.

TOXIC POLLUTANTS

See also: HAZARDOUS WASTES

ABSTRACTING AND INDEXING SERVICES

Applied Science and Technology Index. H.W. Wilson Co., 950 University Ave., Bronx, New York 10452. (800) 367-6770. Formerly Industrial Arts Index.

Chemical Abstracts. Chemical Abstracts Service, 2540 Olentangy River Rd., PO Box 3012, Columbus, Ohio 43210. (800) 848-6533. 1907-.

Ecological Abstracts. Geo Abstracts Ltd. Elsevier Applied Science, Crown House, Linton Rd., Barking, England IG 11 8JU. 1974-. Derived from over 600 leading ecological and environmental journals, plus books, conference proceedings, reports and theses.

Engineering Index. The Engineering Index Inc., 345 E. 47th St., New York, New York 10017. 1962-.

Index to Scientific Book Contents. Institute for Scientific Information, 3501 Market St., Philadelphia, Pennsylvania 19104. (800) 523-1857. 1985-. Annual. Gives contents of science books published.

Pollution Abstracts. Cambridge Scientific Abstracts, 5161 River Rd., Bethesda, Maryland 20816. (301) 961-6750. Six/year. Indexes worldwide technical literature on environmental pollution. Covers air pollution, marine and freshwater pollution, sewage and wastewater treatment, waste management, toxicology and health, noise pollution, radiation, land pollution, and environmental policies, programs, legislation, and education. Also available online.

Science Citation Index. Institute for Scientific Information, 3501 Market St., Philadelphia, Pennsylvania 19104. 1961-.

Selected References on Environmental Quality as It Relates to Health. National Library of Medicine, 8600 Rockville Pike, Bethesda, Maryland 20894. (800) 638-8480. 1977.

ALMANACS AND YEARBOOKS

Administration of the Toxic Substances Control Act. U.S. Environmental Protection Agency. Washington, District of Columbia Annual. Law and legislation regarding hazardous substances, chemicals, and poisons.

BIBLIOGRAPHIES

Current Contents. Agriculture, Biology and Environmental Sciences. Institute for Scientific Information, 3501 Market St., Philadelphia, Pennsylvania 19104. (800) 523-1857. 1973-. Previous title: Current Contents. Agricultural, Food & Veterinary Sciences. Gives the table of contents of periodicals in the fields of agriculture, biology, environmental and related areas.

Lead Paint Poisoning in Urban Children. Council of Planning Librarians, 1313 E. 60th St., Chicago, Illinois 60637-2897. (312) 942-2163. 1976.

Lead Poisoning: A Selected Bibliography. Vance Bibliographies, PO Box 229, 112 N. Charter St., Monticello, Illinois 61856. (217) 762-3831. 1988. Bibliography of lead toxicology.

DIRECTORIES

Toxic Chemical Release Inventory. U.S. National Library of Medicine/Toxicology Information Program, 8600 Rockville Pike, Bethesda, Maryland 20894. (301) 496-1131.

ENCYCLOPEDIAS AND DICTIONARIES

McGraw-Hill Encyclopedia of Environmental Science. Sybil P. Parker. McGraw-Hill Science & Engineering Books, 11 W. 19th St., New York, New York 10011. (212) 337-6010. 1980. Covers ecology, man's influence on nature, and environmental protection.

Van Nostrand's Scientific Encyclopedia. Glenn D. Considine, ed. Van Nostrand Reinhold, 115 5th Ave., New York, New York 10003. (212) 254-3232. 1983. Sixth edition. Includes all broad subject areas in science.

GENERAL WORKS

Acute Toxicology Testing: Perspectives and Horizons. Shayne C. Gad and Christopher P. Chengelis. Telford Press, PO Box 287, West Caldwell, New Jersey 07006. (201) 228-7744. 1989.

Chemical Ecotoxicology. Jaakko Paasivirta. Lewis Publishers, 200 Corporate Blvd. NW, Boca Raton, Florida 33431. (407) 994-0555 or (800)272-7737. 1991. Presents an in-depth discussion of risk assessment, chemical cycles, structure-activity relationships, organohalogens, oil residues, mercury, sampling and analysis of trace chemicals, and emissions from the forest industry. Outlines the chemical basis for applied research in environmental protection and provides important data regarding the fate and effects of various chemicals on wildlife.

Chemical, Physical, and Biological Properties of Compounds Present at Hazardous Waste Sites: Final Report. U.S. Environmental Protection Agency. Clement Associates Inc., Arlington, Virginia 1985.

Criteria for a Recommended Standard: Occupational Exposure to Carbon Tetrachloride. National Institute for Occupational Safety and Health, 1600 Clifton Rd. NE, Atlanta, Georgia 30333. (404) 639-3286. 1976.

Defusing the Toxics Threat: Controlling Pesticides and Industrial Waste. Sandra Postel. Worldwatch Institute, 1776 Massachusetts Ave., N.W., Washington, District of Columbia 20036-1904. 1987.

Ecotoxicology and Climate. Philippe Bordeaux, et al., eds. John Wiley & Sons, Inc., 605 3rd Ave., New York, New York 10158-0012. (212) 850-6000. 1989. Describes environmental chemistry of toxic pollutants in hot and cold climates. Includes bibliographical references and an index.

The Environmental Challenge of the 1990's. U.S. Environmental Protection Agency, 401 M St. SW, Washington, District of Columbia 20460. (202) 260-2090. 1991. Provides an overview of past and present projects for pollution prevention, focusing on the promotion of clean technologies and clean products in both the public and private sectors. Covers new prevention ideas relating to solid and hazardous wastes, pesticides, drinking water, wastewater and toxic substances.

Hazardous and Industrial Wastes, 1990. Joseph P. Martin, et al., eds. Technomic Publishing Co., 851 Holland Ave., Box 3535, Lancaster, Pennsylvania 17604. (717)

291-5609. 1990. Proceedings of the 22nd Mid-Atlantic Industrial Waste Conference, June 24-27, 1990, Drexel University, Philadelphia, PA. Fifty-one new reports on developments in industrial and hazardouswaste management, technology and regulation were presented.

Hazardous Substances Resource Guide. Richard Pohanish, Stanley Greene. Gale Research Inc., 835 Penobscot Bldg., Detroit, Michigan 48226-4094. (313) 961-2242. 1993.

Hazardous Waste Measurements. Milagros S. Simmons, ed. Lewis Publishers, 200 Corporate Blvd. NW, Boca Raton, Florida 33431. (407) 994-0555 or (800)272-7737. 1991. Focuses on recent developments in field testing methods and quality assurance.

Health Assessment Document for Carbon Tetrachloride. U.S. Environmental Protection Agency, 401 M St., SW, Washington, District of Columbia 20460. (202) 260-2090. 1984.

Healthy Homes, Healthy Kids. Joyce M. Schoemaker and Charity Y. Vitale. Island Press, 1718 Connecticut Ave. N.W., Suite 300, Washington, District of Columbia 20009. (202) 232-7933. 1991. Identifies many hazards that parents tend to overlook. It translates technical, scientific information into an accessible how-to guide to help parents protect children from even the most toxic substances.

Inorganic Contaminants of Surface Water; Research and Monitoring Priorities. James W. Moore. Springer-Verlag, 175 Fifth Ave., New York, New York 10010. (212) 460-1500 or (800) 777-4643. 1991. Inorganic contaminants of surface water in terms of production, sources, and residues, chemistry, bioacculation, toxic effects to aquatic organisms, health effects and drinking water.

Lead Poisoning. National Park Service Housing, Washington, District of Columbia 20013. (202) 208-6843. 1991. Lead toxicology, health aspects of paints and children's health safety.

Long-Term Neurotoxic Effects of Paint Solvents. Royal Society of Chemistry, c/o CRC Press, 2000 Corporate Blvd. N.W., Boca Raton, Florida 33431-9868. (800) 272-7737. 1990. Various components of oil-based decorative paints are described, as are studies that have been made on the neurotoxicity of the individual solvents. The relative advantages and disadvantages of oil-based and water-based paints are described.

Measurement Techniques for Carcinogenic Agents in Workplace Air. Royal Society of Chemistry, c/o CRC Press, 2000 Corporate Blvd. N.W., Boca Raton, Florida 33431-9868. (800) 272-7737. 1989. Covers 31 substances with known or suspended carcinogenic properties and describes recommended analytical methods for each substance when present in workplace air. It provides information including CAS Registry number, synonyms, manufacture, uses and determination (with recommended sampling and measuring procedures, and performance characteristics), plus a review of other methods used.

Physicochemical and Biological Detoxification of Hazardous Wastes. Yeun C. Wu, ed. Technomic Publishing Co., 851 New Holland Ave., Box 3535, Lancaster, Pennsylvania 17604. (717) 291-5609. 1989. 2 volume set. Proceedings of the International Conference of Physicochemical and Biological Detoxification of Hazardous Wastes, May 3-5, 1988, Atlantic City, NJ. Provides new information on a variety of established, new and in-development methods for treating a wide range of industrial and municipal hazardous wastes.

Toxic Air Pollution–A Comprehensive Study of Non-Criteria Air Pollutants. Paul J. Lioy and Joan M. Daisey. Lewis Publishers, 2000 Corporate Blvd., N.W., Boca Raton, Florida 33431. (407) 994-0555 or (800) 272-7737. 1987. Provides historical data base of ambient toxic air pollution measurements for future trend analysis, assessment of total exposure and indoor air pollution relationships.

The Toxic Substances Control Act. U.S. G.P.O., Washington, District of Columbia 20401. (202) 512-0000. 1981.

GOVERNMENTAL ORGANIZATIONS

Office of Hazardous Materials Transportation. 400 7th St., S.W., Washington, District of Columbia 20590. (202) 366-0656.

U.S. Environmental Protection Agency: Assistant Administrator for Enforcement. 401 M St., S.W., Washington, District of Columbia 20460. (202) 382-4134.

HANDBOOKS AND MANUALS

Handbook of Analytical Toxicology. Irving Sunshine, ed. CRC Press, 2000 Corporate Blvd. N.W., Boca Raton, Florida 33431. (407) 994-0555; (800) 272-7737. 1969.

Toxic Release Inventory CD-ROM Retrieval User Guide. Environmental Protection Agency. U.S. G.P.O, Washington, District of Columbia 20402-9325. (202) 512-0000. 1990. Data on industrial facilities that intentionally or accidently release toxic chemicals into the environment.

TSCA Handbook. Government Institutes, Inc., 4 Research Pl., Ste. 200, Rockville, Maryland 20850. (301) 921-2300. 1989. 2nd edition. Details existing chemical regulation under TSCA; EPA's program for evaluating and regulating new chemical substances; PMN preparations and follow through; civil and criminal liability; inspections and audits; required testing of chemical substances and mixtures and exemptions from PMN requirements.

ONLINE DATA BASES

BNA Toxics Law Daily. Bureau of National Affairs, BNA PLUS, 1231 25th St., N.W., Rm. 215, Washington, District of Columbia 20037. (800) 454-7773.

CERCLIS. Chemical Information Systems, Inc., 7215 York Rd., Baltimore, Maryland 21212. (301) 321-8440. Information on hazardous waste disposal sites that have either been listed by the EPA on the National Priority List (NPL) or nominated for consideration for the NPL.

Chemical Abstracts-CA. Chemical Abstracts Service, 2540 Olentangy River Rd., P.O. Box 3012, Columbus, Ohio 43210. (800) 848-6533 or (614) 421-3600. Information sources include 9000 journals, patents from 27 countries, two industrial property organizations, new books, conference proceedings, and government research reports.

Chemical Carcinogenesis Research Information System–CCRIS. National Library of Medicine, 8600 Rockville Pike, Bethesda, Maryland 20894. (800) 638-8480. Individual assay results and test conditions for 1,451 chemicals in the areas of carcinogenicity, mutagenicity, tumor promotion, and cocarcinogenicity.

Chemical Collection System/Request Tracking–CCS/RTS. U.S. Environmental Protection Agency, Office of Pesticides and Toxic Substances, 401 M St., SW, Washington, District of Columbia 20460. (202) 260-2090. Contains information on various properties of a number of chemicals including environmental effects, test and analysis methods, and health effects. Available from EPA.

Chemical Dictionary Online–CHEMLINE. Chemical Abstracts Service, 2540 Olentangy River Rd., Columbus, Ohio 43210. (614) 421-3600 or (800) 848-6533. Part of MEDLINE of the National Library of Medicine (NLM). File of 900,000 names for chemical substances, representing 450,000 unique compounds. It contains such information as Chemical Abstracts (CA) Service Registry Numbers, molecular formulas, preferred chemical nomenclature, and generic and ring structure information. Available on NLM's ELHILL system.

Chemical Evaluation Search and Retrieval System. Michigan State Department of Natural Resources, Surface Water Quality Division, Great Lakes and Environmental Assessment Section, Knapp's Office Center, PO Box 30028, Lansing, Michigan 48909. (517) 373-2190. Covers toxicology information on compounds of environmental concern, providing acute and chronic toxicity data for aquatic and terrestrial life as well as information on carcinogenicity, mutagenicity, and reproductive and developmental effects, bioconcentration, and environmental fate.

Chemical Exposure. Science Applications International Corp., Health & Environmental Information, P.O. Box 2501, Oak Ridge, Tennessee 37831. (615) 482-9031. Database of chemicals that have been identified in both human tissues and body fluids and in feral and food animals. Contains reference to journal articles, conferences, and reports. Covers the whole fields of information related to human and animal exposure to food, air, and water contaminants and pharmaceuticals. Its records include information on chemical properties, formulas, tissues measured, analytical method used, demographics and more. Available on DIALOG.

CHEMLINE. National Library of Medicine, Toxicology Information Program, 8600 Rockville Pike, Bethesda, Maryland 20894. (800) 638-8480.

Computerized Engineering Index–COMPENDEX. Engineering Information Inc., 345 E. 47th St., New York, New York 10017. (212) 705-7600.

CTCP. Dartmouth Medical School, Department of Pharmacology and Toxicology, Hanover, New Hampshire 03755.

Epidemiology Information System. Oak Ridge National Laboratory, Toxicology Information Response Center, Building 2001, P.O. Box 2008, Oak Ridge, Tennessee 37831-6050. (615) 576-1746.

ETICBACK: Environmental Teratology Information Center Backfile. Oak Ridge National Laboratory, Environmental Teratology Information Center, Building 2001, P.O. Box 2008, Oak Ridge, Tennessee 37831-6050. (615) 574-7871.

HADB. National Library of Medicine, Toxicology Information Program, 8600 Rockville Pike, Bethesda, Maryland 20894. (800) 638-8480.

Information System for Hazardous Organics in Water. U.S. Environmental Protection Agency, Office of Pesticides & Toxic Substances, 401 M St., S.W., Washington, District of Columbia 20460. (202) 260-2090.

Medical Toxicology and Environmental Health. Department of Health and Social Security, Medical Toxiclology & Environmental Health Division, Hannibal House, Rm. 719, Elephant and Castle, London, England SE1 6TE. 44 (71) 972-2162.

MSDS Solution/Suspect Chemicals Sourcebook Database. Logical Technology, Inc., PO Box 3655, 1422 W. Main, Peoria, Illinois 61614. (309) 655-0223.

Registry of Toxic Effects of Chemical Substances–Online1. US Department of Health and Human Services, National Institute for Occupational Safety and Health, Washington, District of Columbia 20402-9325. (202) 783-3238. Tests on chemical substances: Substance Identification, Toxicity/Biomedical Effects, Toxicology and Carcinogenicity Review, and Exposure Standards and Regulations.

SCISEARCH. Institute for Scientific Information, University City Science Center, 3501 Market St., Philadelphia, Pennsylvania 19104. (215) 386-0100.

TOXALL. National Library of Medicine, Specialized Information Services Division, 8600 Rockville Pike, Bethesda, Maryland 20894. (301) 496-6531.

Toxic Chemical Release Inventory. Office of Research and Development, U.S. Environmental Protection Agency, RD-689, 401 M St., S.W., Washington, District of Columbia 20460. Releases of toxic chemicals to the environment. Includes names and addresses of the facilities and the amount of certain toxic chemicals they release to the air, water, or land.

Toxic Materials News. Business Publishers, Inc., 951 Pershing Dr., Silver Spring, Maryland 20910-4464. (301) 587-6300. Legislation, regulations, and litigation concerning toxic substances. Online version of periodical of the same name.

Toxic Substances Control Act Chemical Substances Inventory. U.S. Environmental Protection Agency, Office of Pesticides and Toxic Substances, 401 M St., S.W., Washington, District of Columbia 20460. (202) 260-2090. Lists chemical substances manufactured, imported, or processed in the United States for commercial purposes.

Toxic Substances Control Act Test Submissions. Chemical Information Systems, Inc., 7215 York Rd., Baltimore, Maryland 21212. (301) 321-8440. An index of unpublished health and safety studies submitted to the U.S. Environmental Protection Agency under the Toxic Substances Control Act.

TOXLIT. National Library of Medicine, Toxicology Information Program, 8600 Rockville Pike, Bethesda, Maryland 20894. (800) 638-8480.

TSCA Chemical Substances Inventory. U.S. Environmental Protection Agency, Office of Pesticides and Toxic Substances, 401 M St., S.W., Washington, District of Columbia 20460. (202) 260-2090.

TSCATS. U.S. Environmental Protection Agency, Office of Pesticides and Toxic Substances, 401 M St., S.W., Washington, District of Columbia 20460. (202) 382-3524.

Vapor Pressure Database. Texas A & M University, Thermodynamics Research Center, College Station, Texas 77843-3111. (409) 845-4940.

PERIODICALS AND NEWSLETTERS

City Sierran. Sierra Club-NYC Group, 625 Broadway, 2nd Fl., New York, New York 10012. (212) 473-7841. 1984-. Quarterly. Reports environmental news to Sierra Club members in New York City. Writers are activists and experts on acid rain, pollution, toxic wastes, recycling, endangered species, etc.

Environmental Action. Environmental Action Foundation, 6930 Carroll Ave., Ste. 600, Takoma Park, Maryland 20912. (301) 891-1100. Bimonthly. Impact of humans and industry on the environment.

Environmental Defense Fund Letter. Environmental Defense Fund, 257 Park Avenue South, New York, New York 10010. (212) 505-2100. 1971-. Bimonthly. Environmental issues of concern.

Fundamentals & Applied Toxicology. Academic Press, c/o Marcourt Brace, PO Box 6250, 6277 Sea Harbor Dr., Orlando, Florida 32887. (218) 723-9828. 8/year. Covers risk assessment and safety studies of toxic agents.

Indoor Pollution News. Buraff Publications, 1350 Connecticut Ave., NW, Suite 100, Washington, District of Columbia 20036. (202) 862-0990. Biweekly. Air quality in buildings (including radon, formaldehyde, solvents and asbestos) or other air pollutions, such as lead in pipes.

Toxic Materials News. Business Publishers, Inc., 951 Pershing Dr., Silver Spring, Maryland 20910-4464. (301) 587-6300. 1974-. Weekly. Informs on regulations governing the manufacture, handling, transport, distribution and disposal of toxic chemicals and pesticides. Also available online.

TSCA Chemicals on Progress Bulletin. TSCA Assistance Office, Office of Pesticide & Toxic Substances, U.S. EPA, Washington, District of Columbia 20460. (202) 554-1404. Quarterly. Covers happenings in the EPA.

RESEARCH CENTERS AND INSTITUTES

University Center for Environmental and Hazardous Materials Studies. Virginia Polytech Institute and State University, 1020 Derring Hall, Blacksburg, Virginia 24061. (703) 951-5538.

University of Missouri-Rolla, Environmental Research Center. Rolla, Missouri 65401. (314) 341-4485.

Water Pollution Control Federation Research Foundation. 601 Wythe St., Alexandria, Virginia 22314-1994. (703) 684-2400.

STATISTICS SOURCES

National Water Quality Inventory. U.S. G.P.O., Washington, District of Columbia 20401. (202) 512-0000. Biennial. Water pollution problems and control activities by states.

Toxic Air Pollutant Emission Factors. U.S. Environmental Protection Agency. National Technical Information Service, Springfield, Virginia 22161. (703) 487-4650. 1990. Irregular. Data on emissions by source, SIC code, combustion material and pollutant process.

Tracking Toxic Substances at Industrial Facilities: Engineering Mass Balance Versus Materials Accounting. National Research Council–Committee to Evaluate Mass Balance Information for Facilities Handling Toxic Substances. National Academy Press, 2101 Constitution Ave., NW, Washington, District of Columbia 20418. (202) 334-3343. 1990. Covers measurement of factory and trade waste and hazardous substances.

TRADE ASSOCIATIONS AND PROFESSIONAL SOCIETIES

American Chemical Society. 1155 16th St., N.W., Washington, District of Columbia 20036. (202) 872-4600.

American College of Toxicology. 9650 Rockville Pike, Bethesda, Maryland 20814. (301) 571-1840.

Chlorobenzene Producers Association. 1330 Connecticut Ave., N.W., Washington, District of Columbia 20036. (202) 659-0060.

Conservation Foundation. 1250 24th St., N.W., Washington, District of Columbia 20037. (202) 293-4800. The World Wildlife Fund absorbed the Conservation Foundation in 1990.

Environmental Defense Fund. 257 Park Ave., S., New York, New York 10010. (212) 505-2100. Non-profit organization that was established more than 20 years ago. Its goals are to protect the earth's environment by providing lasting solutions to global environmental problems.

Environmental Quality Industrial Resources Center. The Ohio State University, 1200 Chambers Rd., Room 310, Columbus, Ohio 43212. (614) 292-6717.

National Toxics Campaign. 1168 Commonwealth Ave., Boston, Massachusetts 02134. (617) 232-0327.

Pesticide Action Network. North America Regional Center, 965 Mission St., Suite 514, San Francisco, California 94103. (415) 541-9140.

United States Public Interest Research Group. 215 Pennsylvania Ave., SE, Washington, District of Columbia 20003. (202) 546-9707.

Waste Systems Institute of Michigan, Inc. 400 Ann, N.W., Suite 204, Grand Rapids, Michigan 49504. (616) 363-3262.

TOXIC WASTES
See: HAZARDOUS WASTES

ONLINE DATA BASES

Toxic Chemical Release Inventory. Office of Research and Development, U.S. Environmental Protection Agency, RD-689, 401 M St., S.W., Washington, District of Columbia 20460. Releases of toxic chemicals to the environment. Includes names and addresses of the facilities and the amount of certain toxic chemicals they release to the air, water, or land.

PERIODICALS AND NEWSLETTERS

Toxic Substances Journal. Hemisphere Publishing Co., 79 Madison Ave., Suite 1110, New York, New York

10016. (212) 725-1999. Quarterly. Legislation, testing, and guidelines relating to toxic substances.

RESEARCH CENTERS AND INSTITUTES

Pennsylvania State University, Environmental Resources Research Institute. 100 Land and Water Resource Building, University Park, Pennsylvania 16802. (814) 863-0291.

TOXICITY

ABSTRACTING AND INDEXING SERVICES

Applied Science and Technology Index. H.W. Wilson Co., 950 University Ave., Bronx, New York 10452. (800) 367-6770. Formerly Industrial Arts Index.

ASFA Aquaculture Abstracts. Cambridge Scientific Abstracts, Inc., 5161 River Rd., Bethesda, Maryland 20816. (301) 961-6750. 1984.

Biological and Agricultural Index. H.W. Wilson Co., 950 University Ave., Bronx, New York 10452. (800) 367-6770. 1916-. Monthly.

Chemical Abstracts. Chemical Abstracts Service, 2540 Olentangy River Rd., PO Box 3012, Columbus, Ohio 43210. (800) 848-6533. 1907-.

Ecological Abstracts. Geo Abstracts Ltd. Elsevier Applied Science, Crown House, Linton Rd., Barking, England IG 11 8JU. 1974-. Derived from over 600 leading ecological and environmental journals, plus books, conference proceedings, reports and theses.

Engineering Index. The Engineering Index Inc., 345 E. 47th St., New York, New York 10017. 1962-.

Index to Scientific Book Contents. Institute for Scientific Information, 3501 Market St., Philadelphia, Pennsylvania 19104. (800) 523-1857. 1985-. Annual. Gives contents of science books published.

Science Citation Index. Institute for Scientific Information, 3501 Market St., Philadelphia, Pennsylvania 19104. 1961-.

Selected Abstracts on Aflatoxins and other Mycotoxins Carcinogenesis. U.S. Dept. of Health Education and Welfare. National Technical Information Service, 5285 Port Royal Rd., Springfield, Virginia 22161. (703) 487-4650. 1978. Prepared for the ICRDB Program by the Cancer Information Dissemination and Analysis Center for Carcinogenesis Information.

BIBLIOGRAPHIES

The Draize Eye-Irritancy Test. Janice C. Swanson. National Agricultural Library, 10301 Baltimore Blvd., Beltsville, Maryland 20705-2351. (301) 504-5755. 1990. Citations in the area of toxicity testing using rabbits as laboratory animals and the resulting eye diseases due to toxicity. This bibliography updates an earlier publications numbered SRB 89- 02.

Information Resources in Toxicology. Elsevier Science Publishing Co., 655 Avenue of the Americas, New York, New York 10010. (212) 984-5800. 1988. Toxicology directory, bibliography and societies.

The LD50 and LC50 Toxicity Tests, January 1980-August 1990. Karen J. Clingerman. National Agricultural Library, 10301 Baltimore Blvd., Beltsville, Maryland 20705-2351. (301) 504-5755. 1990.

DIRECTORIES

CCPS/AIChE Directory of Chemical Process Safety Services. American Institute of Chemical Engineers, 345 E. 47th St., New York, New York 10017. (212) 705-7338. 1991. Lists providers of various chemical process safety services. It is compiled from questionnaires returned by the service providers. Company profiles are included.

Gale Environmental Sourcebook. Karen Hill. Gale Research Co., 835 Penobscot Bldg., Detroit, Michigan 48226-4094. (313) 961-2242. Contacts, information sources, or general information on environmental topics.

International Directory of Contract Laboratories. Edward M. Jackson. Marcel Dekker, Inc., 270 Madison Ave., New York, New York 10016. (212) 696-9000; (800) 228-1160. 1989. List of toxicology laboratories that list specific tests conducted on chemicals, foods, prescription drugs, over-the-counter drugs, cosmetics, and household products. Alphabetical arrangement by names of laboratories. Each entry gives address, year founded, and tests. Contains geographical listing. Miscellaneous indexes.

ENCYCLOPEDIAS AND DICTIONARIES

Compendium of Hazardous Chemicals in Schools and Colleges. Forum for Scientific Excellence. J. B. Lippincott, 227 E. Washington Sq., Philadelphia, Pennsylvania 19105. (215) 238-4200; (800) 982-4377. 1990. Encyclopedia of more than 950 hazardous chemicals found in academic institutions. Contains all the data necessary for identifying these chemicals and their hazardous effects.

Encyclopedia of Terpenoids. John S. Glasby. John Wiley & Sons, Inc., 605 3rd Ave., New York, New York 10158-0012. (212) 850-6000. 1982. Two volumes. Compendium of organic compounds found in nature, embracing a wide range of substances from the simple monoterpenoids to the highly complex triterpenoids and cartenoids, which are used in perfumes, antibiotics, cytotoxic agents and antifeedants. Covers literature to the end of 1979.

Encyclopedia of the Alkaloids. Johns S. Glasby. Plenum Press, 233 Spring St., New York, New York 10013-1578. (212) 620-8000 or (800) 221-9369. 1975-. Compendium of plant alkaloids, with their origin and structure, molecular formula, and toxic properties. Also includes references to original papers. Covers the literature to the end of 1981.

Handbook of Hazardous Chemicals and Carcinogens. Marshall Sittig. Noyes Publications, 120 Mill Rd., Park Ridge, New Jersey 07656. (201) 391-8484. 1985.

McGraw-Hill Encyclopedia of Environmental Science. Sybil P. Parker. McGraw-Hill Science & Engineering Books, 11 W. 19th St., New York, New York 10011. (212) 337-6010. 1980. Covers ecology, man's influence on nature, and environmental protection.

McGraw-Hill Encyclopedia of Science and Technology. McGraw-Hill, 1221 Avenue of the Americas, New York, New York 10020. (212) 512-2000 or (800) 262-4729. 1992. Seventh edition. Issued in multiple volumes including index. Includes all science and technology broad subject areas.

Ullmanns Encyclopedia of Industrial Chemistry. Hans Jurgen Arpe and Wolfgang Gerhartz, eds. VCH Publishers, 303 NW 12th Ave., Deerfield Beach, Florida 33442-1788. (305) 428-5566. 1990. Designed to keep up with the broad spectrum of chemical technology. Thirty-six volumes of the encyclopedia have been divided into two sets: the 28 A volumes contain alphabetically arranged articles on chemicals, product groups, processes and technological concepts; and the 8 B volumes are compendia of basic knowledge in industrial chemistry.

Van Nostrand's Scientific Encyclopedia. Glenn D. Considine, ed. Van Nostrand Reinhold, 115 5th Ave., New York, New York 10003. (212) 254-3232. 1983. Sixth edition. Includes all broad subject areas in science.

GENERAL WORKS

Acute and Sub-Acute Toxicology. Vernon K. Brown. E. Arnold, 41 Bedford Square, London, England WC1B 3DQ. 1988. Explains the effect of toxicants on vertebrate species, including man.

Acute Toxicology Testing: Perspectives and Horizons. Shayne C. Gad and Christopher P. Chengelis. Telford Press, PO Box 287, West Caldwell, New Jersey 07006. (201) 228-7744. 1989.

Bacterial Toxins. W. E. Van Heyningen. Charles C. Thomas Publisher, 2600 S. First St., Springfield, Illinois 62794-9265. (217) 789-8980. Covers bacterial toxins and antitoxins.

The Biochemistry and Uses of Pesticides: Structure, Metabolism, Mode of Action, and Uses in Crop Protection. Kenneth A. Hassall. VCH Publishers, 303 NW 12th Ave., Deerfield Beach, Florida 33442-1788. (305) 428-5566. 1990. Reports the progress that has been made in the last few years towards an understanding of how pesticides function, how metabolism contributes to selectivity and safety and how the development of resistance is linked to biochemistry and molecular biology.

Biological Assessment of Toxicity Caused by Chemical Constituents Eluted from Site Soils Collected at the Drake Chemical Superfund Site, Lock Haven, Clinton Co., Pennsylvania. J. Greene. National Technical Information Service, 5285 Port Royal Rd., Springfield, Virginia 22161. (703) 487-4650. 1991. Order number PB91-186965 LDM

Chemical Ecotoxicology. Jaakko Paasivirta. Lewis Publishers, 200 Corporate Blvd. NW, Boca Raton, Florida 33431. (407) 994-0555 or (800)272-7737. 1991. Presents an in-depth discussion of risk assessment, chemical cycles, structure-activity relationships, organohalogens, oil residues, mercury, sampling and analysis of trace chemicals, and emissions from the forest industry. Outlines the chemical basis for applied research in environmental protection and provides important data regarding the fate and effects of various chemicals on wildlife.

Chemical Hazards of the Work Place. Nick H. Proctor and edited by Gloria J. Hathaway, et al. Van Nostrand Reinhold, 115 5th Ave., New York, New York 10003. (212) 254-3232. 1991. 3d ed.

Chemicals in the Human Food Chain. Carl K. Winter, et al. Van Nostrand Reinhold, 115 5th Ave., New York, New York 10003. (212) 254-3232. 1990. Deals with prevention of food contamination by pesticides and other toxic chemicals.

A Citizen's Guide to Promoting Toxic Waste Reduction. Lauren Kenworthy and Eric Schaeffer. INFORM, 381 Park Ave. S., New York, New York 10016. (212) 689-4040. 1990. The how-to manual describes source reduction and its benefits, five strategies plants can use to reduce their hazardous wastes at the source, a step-by-step process for gathering background facts, and interviewing company representatives and analyzing data.

Controlling Toxic Substances in Agricultural Drainage. U.S. Committee on Irrigation and Drainage, PO Box 15326, Denver, Colorado 80215. 1990. Looks at current technology on toxic substances and water treatment processes and techniques.

Criteria for a Recommended Standard: Occupational Exposure to Carbon Tetrachloride. National Institute for Occupational Safety and Health, 1600 Clifton Rd. NE, Atlanta, Georgia 30333. (404) 639-3286. 1976.

Dermatotoxicology. Francis N. Marzulli and Howard I. Maibach, eds. Hemisphere Publishing Co., 79 Madison Ave., Suite 1110, New York, New York 10016. (212) 725-1999; (800) 821-8312. 1991. 4th ed. Provides information on theoretical aspects and practical test methods, including both in vitro and in vivo approaches. Pays attention to the worldwide movement for the development of suitable alternatives to animals when feasible.

Ecotoxicology and Climate. Philippe Bordeaux, et al., eds. John Wiley & Sons, Inc., 605 3rd Ave., New York, New York 10158-0012. (212) 850-6000. 1989. Describes environmental chemistry of toxic pollutants in hot and cold climates. Includes bibliographical references and an index.

The Environmental Challenge of the 1990's. U.S. Environmental Protection Agency, 401 M St. SW, Washington, District of Columbia 20460. (202) 260-2090. 1991. Provides an overview of past and present projects for pollution prevention, focusing on the promotion of clean technologies and clean products in both the public and private sectors. Covers new prevention ideas relating to solid and hazardous wastes, pesticides, drinking water, wastewater and toxic substances.

Environmental Fact Sheet: The Delaney Paradox and Negligible Risk. U.S. Environmental Protection Agency, Office of Pesticides and Toxic Substances, 401 M St. SW, Washington, District of Columbia 20460. (202) 260-2090. 1990.

Healthy Homes, Healthy Kids. Joyce M. Schoemaker and Charity Y. Vitale. Island Press, 1718 Connecticut Ave. N.W., Suite 300, Washington, District of Columbia 20009. (202) 232-7933. 1991. Identifies many hazards that parents tend to overlook. It translates technical, scientific information into an accessible how-to guide to help parents protect children from even the most toxic substances.

Heavy Metals in the Marine Environment. Robert W. Furness and Philip S. Rainbow. CRC Press, 2000 Corporate Blvd. N.W., Boca Raton, Florida 33431. (800) 272-7737. 1990. Includes heavy metals in the marine environment, trace metals in sea water, metals in the marine atmosphere, processes affecting metal concentration in estuarine and coastal marine sediments, heavy metal levels in marine invertebrates, use of microalgae and invertebrates to monitor metal levels in estuaries and coastal waters, toxic effects of metals, and the incidence of metal pollution in marine ecosystems.

Heptachlor. World Health Organization, Q Corp., 49 Sheridan Ave., Albany, New York 12221. (518) 436-9686. 1984. Toxicity and environmental physiological effects.

Immunoassays for Trace Chemical Analysis; Monitoring Toxic Chemicals in Humans, Food, and the Environment. Martin Vandelaan, et al. American Chemical Society, 1155 16th St., N.W., Washington, District of Columbia 20036. (202) 872-4600; (800) 227-5558. Deals with the use of immunoassays as alternative methods for conducting sampling for chemical residues in food and the environment, for natural toxins, and for monitoring human exposure to toxic chemicals.

Industrial Environmental Control. A. M. Springer. John Wiley & Sons, Inc., 605 3rd Ave., New York, New York 10158-0012. (212) 850-6000. 1986. Covers in great detail all the basic information regarding industrial pollution and its treatment.

Long-Term Neurotoxic Effects of Paint Solvents. Royal Society of Chemistry, c/o CRC Press, 2000 Corporate Blvd. N.W., Boca Raton, Florida 33431-9868. (800) 272-7737. 1990. Various components of oil-based decorative paints are described, as are studies that have been made on the neurotoxicity of the individual solvents. The relative advantages and disadvantages of oil-based and water-based paints are described.

Methods for Determination of Toxic Organic Compounds in Air; EPA Methods. William T. Winberry, et al. Noyes Publications, 120 Mill Rd., Park Ridge, New Jersey 07656. (201) 391-8484. 1990. Contains 14 procedures in a standardized format; five were selected to cover as many compounds as possible, and the others are targeted toward specific compounds.

Microbial Toxins in Focus and Feeds. Albert E. Pohland, et al., eds. Plenum Press, 233 Spring St., New York, New York 10013. (212) 620-8000; (800) 221-9369. 1990. Proceedings of a Symposium on Cellular and Molecular Mode of Action of Selected Microbial Toxins in Foods and Feeds, Oct. 31- Nov. 2, 1988, Chevy Chase, MD.

Multispecies Toxicity Testing. John Cairns, Jr. Pergamon Microforms International, Inc., Fairview Park, Clumsford, New York 10523. (914) 592-7720. Toxicity tests in the safety assessments of chemicals.

NTP Technical Report on the Toxicology and Carcinogenesis Studies of Two Pentachlorophenol Technical-Grade Mixtures. National Toxicology Program, U.S. Dept. of Health and Human Services, 9000 Rockville Pike, Research Triangle Park, North Carolina 20892. (301)496-4000. 1989.

Pesticide Transformation Products: Fate and Significance in the Environment: Papers. L. Somasundaram and Joel R. Coats, eds. American Chemical Society, 1155 16th St. N.W., Washington, District of Columbia 20036. (202) 872-4600; (800) 227-5558. 1991. The significance and impact of pesticide products on the environment is discussed.

Physicochemical and Biological Detoxification of Hazardous Wastes. Yeun C. Wu, ed. Technomic Publishing Co., 851 New Holland Ave., Box 3535, Lancaster, Pennsylvania 17604. (717) 291-5609. 1989. 2 volume set. Proceedings of the International Conference of Physicochemical and Biological Detoxification of Hazardous Wastes, May 3-5, 1988, Atlantic City, NJ. Provides new information on a variety of established, new and in-development methods for treating a wide range of industrial and municipal hazardous wastes.

Principles of Animal Extrapolation. Edward J. Calabrese. Lewis Publishers, 2000 Corporate Blvd., Boca Raton, Florida 33431. (800) 272-7737. 1991. Animal models for toxicity testing are described. Also includes statistical methods in experimental toxicology.

Proof of Causation and Damages in Toxic Chemical, Hazardous Waste, and Drug Cases. Sheila L. Birnbaum. Practicing Law Institute, 810 7th Ave., New York, New York 10019. (212) 765-5700. 1987.

Silent Spring. Rachel Carson. Carolina Biological Supply Company, 2700 York Rd., Burlington, North Carolina 27215. (919) 584-0381. 1987.

Silent Spring Revisited. Gino J. Marco, et al., eds. American Chemical Society, 1155 16th St. N.W., Washington, District of Columbia 20036. (202) 872-4600; (800) 227-5558. 1987. Discusses Rachel Carson's vision and legacy. Traces the evolution of government regulations and the current pesticide registration criteria. Critically appraises the existing conditions and evaluates hazards.

The State of the Earth Atlas. Joni Seger, ed. Touchstone/ Simon and Schuster, Rockefeller Center, 1230 Avenue of the Americas, New York, New York 10020. 1990. Deals with environmental issues such as air quality, urban sprawl, toxic waste, tropical forests and tourism from a socioeconomic perspective.

Toxic Chemical Releases and Your "Right-To-Know". U.S. Environmental Protection Agency, 401 M St. SW, Washington, District of Columbia 20460. (202) 260-2090. 1988.

Toxic Hazard Assessment of Chemicals. M. L. Richardson. Royal Society of Chemistry, c/o CRC Press, 2000 Corporate Blvd. N.W., Boca Raton, Florida 33431-9868. (800) 272-7737. 1989. Provides basic guidance on means of retrieving, validating, and interpreting data in order to make a toxicological hazard assessment upon a chemical.

Toxicity and Metabolism of Industrial Solvents. Ethel Browning. Elsevier Science Publishing Co., 655 Avenue of the Americas, New York, New York 10010. (212) 984-5800. 1965.

Toxicity of Industrial Metals. Ethel Browning. Butterworth-Heinemann, 80 Montvale Ave., Stoneham, Massachusetts 02180. (617) 438-8464; (800) 366-2665. 1969. 2d ed.

Toxicity Reduction in Industrial Effluents. Perry W. Lanford, et al. Van Nostrand Reinhold, 115 5th Ave., New York, New York 10003. (212) 254-3232. 1990. Overview of aquatic toxicology and toxicity reduction. Specific treatment technologies that can be used to reduce toxicity, such as aerobic and anaerobic biological treatment, air and steam stripping of volatile organics, granulated carbon absorption, powdered activated carbon treatment and chemical oxidation, are discussed in detail.

Toxicological Chemistry: A Guide to Toxic Substances in Chemistry. Stanley E. Manahan. Lewis Publishers, 200 Corporate Blvd. NW, Boca Raton, Florida 33431. (407) 994-0555 or (800)272-7737. 1989. Defines toxicological chemistry and gives information on its origin and use. Emphasizes the chemical formulas, structures, and reactions of toxic substances.

Toxicological Profile for Chloroform. National Technical Information Service, 5285 Port Royal Rd., Springfield, Virginia 22161. (703) 487-4650. 1989.

Toxics in the Community: National and Local Perspectives. U.S. Environmental Protection Agency, Offices of Pesticides and Toxic Substances, 401 M St. SW, Washington, District of Columbia 20460. (202) 260-2090. 1990.

The Toxics Release Inventory: Executive Summary. U.S. Environmental Protection Agency, Office of Pesticides and Toxic Substances, 401 M St. SW, Washington, District of Columbia 20460. (202) 260-2090. 1989.

TSCA Policy Compendium. Government Institutes, Inc., 4 Research Pl., Ste. 200, Rockville, Maryland 20850. (301) 921-2300. 1985. Clarifies inspection and enforcement requirements with the official EPA supporting documents.

Waste Management: Towards A Sustainable Society. Om Prakash Kharbanda and E. A. Stallworthy. Auburn House, 14 Dedham St., Dover, Massachusetts 02030-0658. (505) 785-2220; (800) 223-2665. 1990. Describes the generation of various types of hazardous and nonhazardous wastes, with a whole chapter devoted to acid rain.

GOVERNMENTAL ORGANIZATIONS

U.S. Environmental Protection Agency: Assistant Administrator for Pesticides and Toxic Substances. 401 M St., S.W., Washington, District of Columbia 20460. (202) 382-2902.

U.S. Environmental Protection Agency: Office of Civil Enforcement. 401 M St., S.W., Washington, District of Columbia 20460. (202) 382-4544.

U.S. Environmental Protection Agency: Office of Pesticide Programs. 401 M St., S.W., Washington, District of Columbia 20460. (202) 557-7090.

U.S. Environmental Protection Agency: Office of Toxic Substances. 401 M St., S.W., Washington, District of Columbia 20460. (202) 382-3813.

U.S. Environmental Protection Agency, TS-799: Toxic Assistance Office. 401 M St., S.W., Washington, District of Columbia 20460. (202) 382-3790.

HANDBOOKS AND MANUALS

Concise Manual of Chemical and Environmental Safety in Schools and Colleges. Forum for Scientific Excellence. J. B. Lippincott, 227 E. Washington Sq., Philadelphia, Pennsylvania 19105. (215) 238-4200; (800) 982-4377. 1991.

Handbook of Acute Toxicity of Chemicals to Fish and Aquatic Invertebrates. Waynon W. Johnson and Mack T. Finley. U.S. Department of the Interior, Fish and Wildlife Service, Washington, District of Columbia 20240. (202) 208-5634. 1980. Fisheries Research Laboratory, 1965-78; Resource publication/U.S. Fish and Wildlife Service, no. 137.

Handbook of In Vivo Toxicity Testing. Academic Press, c/o Harcourt Brace Jovanovich Inc., 6277 Sea Harbor Dr., Orlando, Florida 32887. (800) 346-8648. 1990.

Handbook of Poisoning: Prevention, Diagnosis, and Treatment. Lange Medical Publications, Los Altos, California 1983.

Handbook of Toxicity of Pesticides to Wildlife. U.S. Department of the Interior, Fish and Wildlife Service, 1849 C St. NW, Washington, District of Columbia 20240. (202) 208-3171. 1984.

Handbook on Toxicity of Organic Compounds. Marcel Dekker, Inc., 270 Madison Ave., New York, New York 10016. (212) 696-9000; (800) 228-1160. 1988.

Immunotoxicology of Drugs and Chemicals. Elsevier Science Publishing Co., 655 Avenue of the Americas, New York, New York 10010. (212) 984-5800. 1988.

Methods for Toxicity Tests of Single Substances and Liquid Complex Wastes With Marine Unicellular Algae. Gerald E. Walsh. Environmental Protection Agency, U.S. Environmental Research Laboratory, 401 M St. SW, Washington, District of Columbia 20460. (202) 260-2090. 1988. Deals with the impact of factory and trade waste on the marine environment, especially on algae and other biological forms.

Pentachlorophenol. World Health Organization, Ave. Appia, Geneva, Switzerland CH-1211. (518) 436-9686. 1987.

Product Safety Evaluation Handbook. Shayne Cox Gad. Dekker, 270 Madison Ave., New York, New York 10016. (212) 696-9000 or (800) 228-1160. 1988. Discusses toxicity testing of products such as drugs, chemicals, etc. Gives an evaluation of their safety for the consumer.

TSCA Compliance/Enforcement Guidance Manual. Government Institutes, Inc., 4 Research Pl., Ste. 200, Rockville, Maryland 20850. (301) 921-2300. 1984. Includes analyzing evidence collected during a compliance inspection.

TSCA Inspection Manual. Government Institutes, Inc., 4 Research Pl., Ste. 200, Rockville, Maryland 20850. (301) 921-2300. Forms and procedures to ensure your compliance with the Toxic Substances Control Act.

ONLINE DATA BASES

Air Toxics Report. Business Publishers, Inc., 951 Pershing Dr., Silver Spring, Maryland 20910. (301) 587-6300. Online version of periodical of the same name.

ANEUPLOIDY. Oak Ridge National Laboratory, Environmental Mutagen Information Center, Building 2001, P.O. Box 2008, Oak Ridge, Tennessee 37831-6050. (615) 574-7871.

BNA Toxics Law Daily. Bureau of National Affairs, BNA PLUS, 1231 25th St., N.W., Rm. 215, Washington, District of Columbia 20037. (800) 454-7773.

CERCLIS. Chemical Information Systems, Inc., 7215 York Rd., Baltimore, Maryland 21212. (301) 321-8440. Information on hazardous waste disposal sites that have either been listed by the EPA on the National Priority List (NPL) or nominated for consideration for the NPL.

CESARS. State of Michigan, Department of Natural Resources, Great Lakes & Environmental Assessment Section, P.O. Box 30028, Lansing, Michigan 45909. (517) 373-2190.

Chemical Abstracts-CA. Chemical Abstracts Service, 2540 Olentangy River Rd., P.O. Box 3012, Columbus, Ohio 43210. (800) 848-6533 or (614) 421-3600. Information sources include 9000 journals, patents from 27 countries, two industrial property organizations, new books, conference proceedings, and government research reports.

Chemical Carcinogenesis Research Information System–CCRIS. National Library of Medicine, 8600 Rockville Pike, Bethesda, Maryland 20894. (800) 638-8480. Individual assay results and test conditions for 1,451 chemicals in the areas of carcinogenicity, mutagenicity, tumor promotion, and cocarcinogenicity.

Chemical Collection System/Request Tracking–CCS/RTS. U.S. Environmental Protection Agency, Office of Pesticides and Toxic Substances, 401 M St., SW, Washington, District of Columbia 20460. (202) 260-2090. Contains information on various properties of a number of chemicals including environmental effects, test and analysis methods, and health effects. Available from EPA.

Chemical Dictionary Online–CHEMLINE. Chemical Abstracts Service, 2540 Olentangy River Rd., Columbus, Ohio 43210. (614) 421-3600 or (800) 848-6533. Part of MEDLINE of the National Library of Medicine (NLM). File of 900,000 names for chemical substances, representing 450,000 unique compounds. It contains such information as Chemical Abstracts (CA) Service Registry Numbers, molecular formulas, preferred chemical nomenclature, and generic and ring structure information. Available on NLM's ELHILL system.

Chemical Evaluation Search and Retrieval System. Michigan State Department of Natural Resources, Surface Water Quality Division, Great Lakes and Environmental Assessment Section, Knapp's Office Center, PO Box 30028, Lansing, Michigan 48909. (517) 373-2190. Covers toxicology information on compounds of environmental concern, providing acute and chronic toxicity data for aquatic and terrestrial life as well as information on carcinogenicity, mutagenicity, and reproductive and developmental effects, bioconcentration, and environmental fate.

Chemical Exposure. Science Applications International Corp., Health & Environmental Information, P.O. Box 2501, Oak Ridge, Tennessee 37831. (615) 482-9031. Database of chemicals that have been identified in both human tissues and body fluids and in feral and food animals. Contains reference to journal articles, conferences, and reports. Covers the whole fields of information related to human and animal exposure to food, air, and water contaminants and pharmaceuticals. Its records include information on chemical properties, formulas, tissues measured, analytical method used, demographics and more. Available on DIALOG.

Chemical Substance Control. Bureau of National Affairs, BNA PLUS, 1231 25th ST., N.W., Rm. 215, Washington, District of Columbia 20037. (800) 452-7773. Online version of periodical of the same name.

CHEMLINE. National Library of Medicine, Toxicology Information Program, 8600 Rockville Pike, Bethesda, Maryland 20894. (800) 638-8480.

CHEMLIST. American Petroleum Institute, Central Abstracting & Indexing Service, 275 7th Ave., New York, New York 10001. (212) 366-4040.

Computerized Engineering Index–COMPENDEX. Engineering Information Inc., 345 E. 47th St., New York, New York 10017. (212) 705-7600.

CTCP. Dartmouth Medical School, Department of Pharmacology and Toxicology, Hanover, New Hampshire 03755.

Dermal Absorption. U.S. Environmental Protection Agency, Office of Pesticides and Toxic Substances, 401 M St., SW, Washington, District of Columbia 20460. (202) 260-2090. Toxic effects, absorption, distribution, metabolism, and excretion relation to the dermal absorption of 655 chemicals.

Epidemiology Information System. Oak Ridge National Laboratory, Toxicology Information Response Center, Building 2001, P.O. Box 2008, Oak Ridge, Tennessee 37831-6050. (615) 576-1746.

ETICBACK: Environmental Teratology Information Center Backfile. Oak Ridge National Laboratory, Environmental Teratology Information Center, Building 2001, P.O. Box 2008, Oak Ridge, Tennessee 37831-6050. (615) 574-7871.

Forensic Science Database. Home Office Forensic Science Service, Central Research and Support Establishment, Aldermaston, Reading, Berkshire, England RG7 4PN. 44 (734) 814100.

Global Indexing System. U.S. Environmental Protection Agency, 401 M St., S.W., Washington, District of Columbia 20460. (202) 260-2090. International information on various qualities of chemicals.

HADB. National Library of Medicine, Toxicology Information Program, 8600 Rockville Pike, Bethesda, Maryland 20894. (800) 638-8480.

Industrial Health & Hazards Update. Merton Allen Associates, P.O. Box 15640, Plantation, Florida 33318-5640. (305) 473-9560.

Medical Toxicology and Environmental Health. Department of Health and Social Security, Medical Toxiclology & Environmental Health Division, Hannibal House, Rm. 719, Elephant and Castle, London, England SE1 6TE. 44 (71) 972-2162.

The Merck Index Online. Merck & Company, Inc., Box 2000, Building 86-0900, Rahway, New Jersey 07065-0900. (201) 855-4558.

NIOSHTIC. U.S. Department of Health and Human Services, Centers for Disease Control, National Institute for Occupational Safety and Health, 4676 Columbia Parkway, Cincinnati, Ohio 45226. (513) 533-8317.

Registry of Toxic Effects of Chemical Substances–Online1. US Department of Health and Human Services, National Institute for Occupational Safety and Health, Washington, District of Columbia 20402-9325. (202) 783-3238. Tests on chemical substances: Substance Identification, Toxicity/Biomedical Effects, Toxicology and Carcinogenicity Review, and Exposure Standards and Regulations.

REPRORISK System. Micromedex, Inc., 600 Grant St., Denver, Colorado 80203. (800) 525-9083 or (303) 831-1400. Reproductive risks to females and males caused by drugs, chemicals, and physical and environmental agents. Includes the Teratogen Information System (TERIS), which deals with the teratogenicity of over 700 drugs and environmental agents that affect a fetus. One of the

additional modules under development is the REPRO-TEXT database, containing a ranking system for reproductive hazards and the general toxicity of over 600 chemicals, emphasizing chronic occupational exposures.

SCISEARCH. Institute for Scientific Information, University City Science Center, 3501 Market St., Philadelphia, Pennsylvania 19104. (215) 386-0100.

TOXALL. National Library of Medicine, Specialized Information Services Division, 8600 Rockville Pike, Bethesda, Maryland 20894. (301) 496-6531.

Toxic Chemical Release Inventory. Office of Research and Development, U.S. Environmental Protection Agency, RD-689, 401 M St., S.W., Washington, District of Columbia 20460. Releases of toxic chemicals to the environment. Includes names and addresses of the facilities and the amount of certain toxic chemicals they release to the air, water, or land.

Toxic Materials News. Business Publishers, Inc., 951 Pershing Dr., Silver Spring, Maryland 20910-4464. (301) 587-6300. Legislation, regulations, and litigation concerning toxic substances. Online version of periodical of the same name.

TOXLIT. National Library of Medicine, Toxicology Information Program, 8600 Rockville Pike, Bethesda, Maryland 20894. (800) 638-8480.

TSCA Chemical Substances Inventory. U.S. Environmental Protection Agency, Office of Pesticides and Toxic Substances, 401 M St., S.W., Washington, District of Columbia 20460. (202) 260-2090.

TSCATS. U.S. Environmental Protection Agency, Office of Pesticides and Toxic Substances, 401 M St., S.W., Washington, District of Columbia 20460. (202) 382-3524.

PERIODICALS AND NEWSLETTERS

Air Toxics Report. Business Publishers, Inc., 951 Pershing Dr., Silver Spring, Maryland 20910-4464. (301) 587-6300. 1988-. Monthly. Directed towards organizations and facilities that are or may be affected by regulations under the Clean Air Act and National Emission Standards for Hazardous Air Pollutants, with articles on government regulation, studies, compliance, violations and legal actions. Also available online.

Archives of Environmental Health: An International Journal. Heldref Publications, Helen Dwight Reid Educational Foundation, 4000 Albemarle St., NW, Washington, District of Columbia 20016-1851. Bimonthly. Documentation on the effects of environmental agents on human health.

Bulletin of Environmental Contamination and Toxicology. Springer-Verlag, 175 5th Ave., New York, New York 10010. (212) 460-1500; (800) 777-4643. 1966-. Frequency varies. Disseminates advances and discoveries in the areas of soil, air and food contamination and pollution.

Chemical Substances Control. Bureau of National Affairs, 1231 25th St. NW, Washington, District of Columbia 20037. (202) 452-4200. Biweekly. Periodical covering regulatory compliance and management of chemicals. Also available online.

Ecological Monographs. Business Office of the Ecological Society of America, Center of Environmental Studies, Arizona State University, Tempe, Arizona 85287-1201.

(602) 965-3000. Quarterly. Scientific journal of ecological issues.

Environment Midwest. U.S. Environmental Protection Agency, 230 S. Dearborn, Chicago, Illinois 60604. (312) 353-2072. Monthly. Programs for fighting air and water pollution, hazardous and solid wastes, toxicants, pesticides, noise, and radiation.

Environment Week. King Communications Group, Inc., 627 National Press Bldg., Washington, District of Columbia 20045. (202) 638-4260. Weekly. Covers acid rain, solid waste and disposal, clean coal, nuclear and hazardous waste. Also available online.

Environmental Action. Environmental Action Foundation, 6930 Carroll Ave., Ste. 600, Takoma Park, Maryland 20912. (301) 891-1100. Bimonthly. Impact of humans and industry on the environment.

Environmental Health Letter. Business Publishers, Inc., 951 Pershing Dr., Silver Spring, Maryland 20910-4464. (301) 587-6300. 1961-. Biweekly. Covers areas such as: indoor air, asbestos health effects, toxic substances testing, health problems at wastewater plants, risk-based sludge rules, medical waste, developmental toxicity risk assessment, animal carcinogen tests, pesticide risk, air toxics, aerospace chemicals, lead, radionuclide emissions, state right-to-know statutes, and incinerator emissions.

Environmental Research. Academic Press, 1250 6th Ave., San Diego, California 92101. (619) 231-0926. Bimonthly. Toxic effects of environmental agents in humans and animals.

Environmental Toxicology and Chemistry. Society of Environmental Toxicology and Chemistry. Pergamon Microforms International, Inc., Fairview Park, Elmsford, New York 10523. (914) 592-7720. 1981-. Monthly. Contains information on environmental toxicology, and chemistry, including the application of science to hazard assessment.

Environmental Toxicology and Water Quality. John Wiley & Sons, Inc., 605 3rd Ave., New York, New York 10158-0012. (212) 850-6000. Quarterly. Covers water pollution toxicology, microbiological assay, water quality bioassay and toxicity testing.

Food and Chemical Toxicology. Pergamon Microforms International Inc., Fairview Park, Elmsford, New York 10523. (914) 592-7720. Monthly. Information and risks of food and chemicals.

Fundamentals & Applied Toxicology. Academic Press, c/o Marcourt Brace, PO Box 6250, 6277 Sea Harbor Dr., Orlando, Florida 32887. (218) 723-9828. 8/year. Covers risk assessment and safety studies of toxic agents.

Hazardous Waste Consultant. McCoy & Associates, 13701 West Jewell Avenue, Suite 202, Lakewood, Colorado 80228. (303) 987-0333. Bimonthly. Information on hazardous and toxic waste issues.

Journal of Analytical Toxicology. Preston Publications, PO Box 48312, 7800 Merrimac, Niles, Illinois 60648. (708) 965-0566. Bimonthly. Articles on industrial toxicology, environmental pollution and pharmaceuticals.

Journal of Environmental Health. National Environmental Health Association, 720 South Colorado Boulevard, Suite 970, Denver, Colorado 80222. (303) 756-9090. Bimonthly. Covers phases in environmental health.

The Merck Index. Merck Co., Inc., Box 2000, Rahway, New Jersey 07065. (201) 855-4558. Data on chemicals, drugs, and biological substances.

Michigan Waste Report. Michigan Waste Report, Inc., 400 Ann, SW, Suite 204, Grand Rapids, Michigan 49504. (616) 363-3262. Biweekly. Covers information about waste management.

Pesticide & Toxic Chemical News. Food Chemical News, Inc., 1101 Pennsylvania Avenue, SE, Washington, District of Columbia 20003. (202) 544-1980. Weekly. Covers government regulations of chemical pollution, transportation, disposal and occupational health. Also available online.

Toxic Materials News. Business Publishers, Inc., 951 Pershing Dr., Silver Spring, Maryland 20910-4464. (301) 587-6300. 1974-. Weekly. Informs on regulations governing the manufacture, handling, transport, distribution and disposal of toxic chemicals and pesticides. Also available online.

Toxics Law Reporter. Bureau of National Affairs, 1231 25th St. NW, Washington, District of Columbia 20037. (202) 452-4200. Weekly. Covers legal developments of toxic tort.

TSCA Chemicals on Progress Bulletin. TSCA Assistance Office, Office of Pesticide & Toxic Substances, U.S. EPA, Washington, District of Columbia 20460. (202) 554-1404. Quarterly. Covers happenings in the EPA.

Waste Disposal and Pollution Control. Wakeman/Walworth, P.O. Box 1939, New Haven, Connecticut 06509. (203) 562-8518. Monthly. Covers air and water pollution, toxic waste, and acid rain.

RESEARCH CENTERS AND INSTITUTES

Mississippi State Chemical Laboratory. Mississippi State University, P.O. Box CR, Mississippi State, Mississippi 39762. (601) 325-3324.

University of Nevada-Las Vegas, Environmental Research Center. 4505 S. Maryland Parkway, Las Vegas, Nevada 89154-4009. (702) 739-3382.

STATISTICS SOURCES

Environmental Data Compendium. OECD Publications and Information Center, 2001 L St., N.W., Suite 700, Washington, District of Columbia 20036. (202) 785-6323. 1989.

Environmental Indicators. OECD Publications and Information Center, 2001 L St., N.W., Suite 700, Washington, District of Columbia 20036. (202) 785-6323. 1991.

Environmental Quality. Council on Environmental Quality. U.S. G.P.O., Washington, District of Columbia 20401. (202) 512-0000. Annual.

The State of the Environment. OECD Publications and Information Center, 2001 L St., N.W., Suite 700, Washington, District of Columbia 20036. (202) 785-6323. 1991.

TRADE ASSOCIATIONS AND PROFESSIONAL SOCIETIES

American Chemical Society. 1155 16th St., N.W., Washington, District of Columbia 20036. (202) 872-4600.

American College of Toxicology. 9650 Rockville Pike, Bethesda, Maryland 20814. (301) 571-1840.

American Institute of Chemical Engineers. 345 East 47th St., New York, New York 10017. (212) 705-7338.

American Institute of Chemists. 7315 Wisconsin Ave., Bethesda, Maryland 20814. (301) 652-2447.

Better World Society. 1100 17th St., NW, Suite 502, Washington, District of Columbia 20036. (202) 331-3770. International non-profit membership organization that attempts to increase individual awareness of global issues related to the sustainability of life on earth.

Chemical Industry Institute of Toxicology. P.O. Box 12137, Research Triangle Park, North Carolina 27709. (919) 541-2070.

Citizen's Clearinghouse for Hazardous Wastes, Inc. P.O. Box 6806, Falls Church, Virginia 22040. (703) 237-2249.

Clean Water Action Project. c/o David Zwick, 1320 18th St. N.W., Washington, District of Columbia 20003. (202) 457-1286.

Friends of the Earth. 218 D St., SE, Washington, District of Columbia 20003. (202) 544-2600.

Genetic Toxicology Association. c/o Kerry Dearfield, USEPA, 401 M St., S.W., Washington, District of Columbia 20460. (703) 557-9780.

National Air Toxics Information Clearinghouse. Research Triangle Park, North Carolina 27711. (919) 541-0850.

National Coalition Against the Misuse of Pesticides. 701 E St., SE, Suite 200, Washington, District of Columbia 20003. (202) 543-5450.

National Toxics Campaign. 1168 Commonwealth Ave., Boston, Massachusetts 02134. (617) 232-0327.

Natural Resources Defense Council. 40 W. 20th St., New York, New York 10011. (212) 727-2700.

Pesticide Action Network. North America Regional Center, 965 Mission St., Suite 514, San Francisco, California 94103. (415) 541-9140.

Waste Systems Institute of Michigan, Inc. 400 Ann, N.W., Suite 204, Grand Rapids, Michigan 49504. (616) 363-3262.

TOXICOLOGY

See also: POISONS–ENVIRONMENTAL ASPECTS

ABSTRACTING AND INDEXING SERVICES

Abstracts on Health Effects of Environmental Pollutants. BIOSIS, 2100 Arch St., Philadelphia, Pennsylvania 19103. (215) 587-4800; (800) 523-4806.

Applied Science and Technology Index. H.W. Wilson Co., 950 University Ave., Bronx, New York 10452. (800) 367-6770. Formerly Industrial Arts Index.

ASFA Aquaculture Abstracts. Cambridge Scientific Abstracts, Inc., 5161 River Rd., Bethesda, Maryland 20816. (301) 961-6750. 1984.

Biological and Agricultural Index. H.W. Wilson Co., 950 University Ave., Bronx, New York 10452. (800) 367-6770. 1916-. Monthly.

Chemical Abstracts. Chemical Abstracts Service, 2540 Olentangy River Rd., PO Box 3012, Columbus, Ohio 43210. (800) 848-6533. 1907-.

Ecological Abstracts. Geo Abstracts Ltd. Elsevier Applied Science, Crown House, Linton Rd., Barking, England IG 11 8JU. 1974-. Derived from over 600 leading ecological and environmental journals, plus books, conference proceedings, reports and theses.

General Science Index. H. W. Wilson Co., 950 University Ave., Bronx, New York 10452. 1978-. Monthly, also issued in annual cumulation. Cumulative subject index to English language periodicals in the subject fields of astronomy, botany, chemistry, earth science, environment and conservation, food and nutrition, genetics, mathematics, medicine and health, microbiology, oceanography, physics, physiology and zoology.

Index to Scientific Book Contents. Institute for Scientific Information, 3501 Market St., Philadelphia, Pennsylvania 19104. (800) 523-1857. 1985-. Annual. Gives contents of science books published.

Science Citation Index. Institute for Scientific Information, 3501 Market St., Philadelphia, Pennsylvania 19104. 1961-.

ALMANACS AND YEARBOOKS

Registry of Toxic Effects of Chemical Substances. Doris V. Sweet, ed. U.S. Department of Health and Human Services, National Institute for Occupational Safety and Health, Washington, District of Columbia 20402-9325. (202) 783-3238. 1988. Contains information on over 35,000 chemicals.

Toxic Substances Sourcebook. Environment Information Center, 124 E. 39th St., New York, New York 10016. 1980. Includes hazardous substances, poisons, and pollution.

BIBLIOGRAPHIES

Adverse Effects of Aluminum. U.S. Department of Health and Human Services, Public Health Services, National Institutes of Health, 9000 Rockville Pike, Bethesda, Maryland 20892. (301) 496-4000. 1984. Covers toxicology of aluminum and occupational diseases.

Bismuth Toxicology. National Institutes of Health, National Library of Medicine, Department of Health and Human Services, 8600 Rockville Pike, Bethesda, Maryland 20894. (301) 496-6308. 1977.

The Effects of Environmental Chemicals on the Immune System: A Selected Bibliography with Abstracts. Federation of American Societies for Experimental Biology, 9650 Rockville Pike, Bethesda, Maryland 20814. (301) 530-7000. 1981. Chemically induced immunologic diseases and environmental carcinogens.

Environmental Health and Toxicology. Centers for Disease Control, Center for Environmental Health and Injury Control, Chamblee 27 F-29, Atlanta, Georgia 30333. (404) 488-4588. 1991. A selected bibliography of printed information sources.

Environmental Toxicology. Robert L. Rudd. Gale Research Co., 835 Penobscot Bldg., Detroit, Michigan

48226-4094. (313) 961-2242. 1977. Includes the broad areas of pollution, pesticides, and their effects. This bibliography is part of the series entitled Man and the Environment Information Guide Series, v.7.

Environmental Toxins. Cheryl Brown Travis. American Physiological Society, 9650 Rockville Pike, Bethesda, Maryland 20814. (301) 530-7164. 1989. Bibliography of toxicity in environmental pollutants.

Food Safety, 1990: An Annotated Bibliography of the Literature. Dorothy C. Gosting, et al. Butterworth-Heinemann, 80 Montvale Ave., Stoneham, Massachusetts 02180. (617) 438-8464 or (800) 366-2665. 1991. Deals with the areas of environmental health and toxicology in relation to food safety and preservation. The bibliography is divided into three major parts headed "Diet and Health," "Safety of Food Components," and "Foodborne Microbial Illness." The appendix is titled "Food-and-Water-Associated Viruses."

Health Aspects of Chloroform. National Technical Information Center, 5285 Port Royal Rd., Springfield, Virginia 22161. (703) 487-4650. 1977.

Information Resources in Toxicology. Elsevier Science Publishing Co., 655 Avenue of the Americas, New York, New York 10010. (212) 984-5800. 1988. Toxicology directory, bibliography and societies.

National Toxicology Program. U.S. G.P.O., Washington, District of Columbia 20401. (202) 512-0000. Annual. Effort to strengthen and coordinate research and testing of toxic chemicals.

Steel Shot and Lead Poisoning in Waterfowl. National Wildlife Federation, Resources Conservation Department, 1400 16th St. NW, Washington, District of Columbia 20036-2266. (202) 797-6800. 1983. Covers waterfowl shooting, veterinary toxicology and lead poisoning.

Toxic Hazards of Certain Pesticides to Man, Together with a Select Bibliography on the Toxicology of Pesticides in Man and Mammals. World Health Organization, Ave. Appia, Geneva, Switzerland CH-1211. 1953. Toxicology and toxicity of pesticides and insecticides.

Toxicological / Environmental Health Information Source Update. Centers for Disease Control, 1600 Clifton Rd. NE, Atlanta, Georgia 30333. (404) 488-4588. Lists recent online bibliographic databases relating to environmental health and toxicology.

DIRECTORIES

Chemical Times & Trends–Directory of Toxicology Testing Laboratories Issue. Chemical Specialties Manufacturers Association, 1913 Eye St. N.W., Washington, District of Columbia 20006. (202) 872-8110.

Directory of Toxicological and Related Testing Laboratories. Regulatory Assistance Corporation. Taylor & Francis, 1900 Frost Road, Suite 101, Bristol, Pennsylvania 19007-1598. (800) 821-8312. 1991. Lists toxicology, ecotoxicology, environmental, analytical, and support service laboratories in the United States.

International Directory of Contract Laboratories. Edward M. Jackson. Marcel Dekker, Inc., 270 Madison Ave., New York, New York 10016. (212) 696-9000; (800) 228-1160. 1989. List of toxicology laboratories that list specific tests conducted on chemicals, foods, prescription drugs, over-the-counter drugs, cosmetics, and household products. Alphabetical arrangement by names of labora-

tories. Each entry gives address, year founded, and tests. Contains geographical listing. Miscellaneous indexes.

Toxic Chemical Release Inventory. U.S. National Library of Medicine/Toxicology Information Program, 8600 Rockville Pike, Bethesda, Maryland 20894. (301) 496-1131.

Toxicology Research Projects Directory. Toxicology Information Subcommittee of the DHEW. National Technical Information Service, 5285 Port Royal Rd., Springfield, Virginia 22161. (703) 487-4650. 1976-. Monthly, with annual cumulation. Monthly publication containing selections from the Smithsonian Science Information Exchange data base. Provides on going project summaries related to toxicology manuals.

ENCYCLOPEDIAS AND DICTIONARIES

Macmillan Dictionary of Toxicology. Ernest Hodgson, et al. Van Nostrand Reinhold, 115 5th Ave., New York, New York 10003. (212) 254-3232. 1988. Intended as a "starting point" to the literature of toxicology. American spelling is used with cross references to British version of words. Contains a list of references. Signed entries give explanatory definitions and cross references.

McGraw-Hill Encyclopedia of Environmental Science. Sybil P. Parker. McGraw-Hill Science & Engineering Books, 11 W. 19th St., New York, New York 10011. (212) 337-6010. 1980. Covers ecology, man's influence on nature, and environmental protection.

McGraw-Hill Encyclopedia of Science and Technology. McGraw-Hill, 1221 Avenue of the Americas, New York, New York 10020. (212) 512-2000 or (800) 262-4729. 1992. Seventh edition. Issued in multiple volumes including index. Includes all science and technology broad subject areas.

Toxics A to Z: A Guide to Everyday Pollution Hazards. University of California Press, 2120 Berkeley Way, Berkeley, California 94720. (510) 642-4247 (900) 822-6657. 1991. A consumer guide to toxicology and poisons.

Van Nostrand's Scientific Encyclopedia. Glenn D. Considine, ed. Van Nostrand Reinhold, 115 5th Ave., New York, New York 10003. (212) 254-3232. 1983. Sixth edition. Includes all broad subject areas in science.

GENERAL WORKS

Acesulfame-K. D. G. Mayer, ed. Marcel Dekker, Inc., 270 Madison Ave., New York, New York 10016. (212) 696-9000; (800) 228-1160. 1991. Food and Science Technology series, vol. 47

Acute and Sub-Acute Toxicology. Vernon K. Brown. E. Arnold, 41 Bedford Square, London, England WC1B 3DQ. 1988. Explains the effect of toxicants on vertebrate species, including man.

Aflatoxins: Chemical and Biological Aspects. John Godfrey Heathcote and J. R. Hibbert. Elsevier Science Publishing Co., 655 Avenue of the Americas, New York, New York 10010. (212) 989-5800. 1978. Discusses the properties of aflatoxins, their toxicology and physiological effects.

Air Toxics and Risk Assessment. Edward J. Calabrese and Elaina M. Kenyon. Lewis Publishers, 200 Corporate Blvd. NW, Boca Raton, Florida 33431. (407) 994-0555 or (800)272-7737. 1991. Does risk assessments for more than 110 chemicals that are confirmed or probable air toxics. All chemicals are analyzed with a scientifically sound methodology to assess public health risks.

Animals and Alternatives in Toxicology: Present Status and Future Prospects. Michael Balls. VCH Publishers, 303 NW 12th Ave., Deerfield Beach, Florida 33442-1788. (305) 428-5566. 1991. Animals and Alternatives in Toxicology conference where invited speakers gathered to recommend and discuss the alternatives.

Annual Report on Carcinogens. Summary. U.S. Department of Health and Human Services, Public Health Service, 9000 Rockville Pike, Bethesda, Maryland 20892. (301) 496-4000. Annual.

Aquatic Toxicology. Jerome O. Nriagu. John Wiley & Sons, Inc., 605 3rd Ave., New York, New York 10158-0012. (212) 850-6000. 1989.

Bioassay of Endrin for Possible Carcinogenicity. National Cancer Institute, Div. of Cancer Cause and Prevention, Carcinogenesis Testing Program, NIH Bldg. 31, Room 10A 24, 9030 Old Georgetown Rd., Bethesda, Maryland 20892. (301) 496-7403. 1978.

Bioassay of Fenthion for Possible Carcinogenicity. Department of Health and Human Services, 200 Independence Ave. SW, Washington, District of Columbia 20201. (202) 619-0257. 1979. Covers carcinogens and organophosphorus compounds and toxicology of insecticides.

Bioassay of Hexachlorophene for Possible Carcinogenicity. National Cancer Institute, Cancer Cause and Prevention Division, 9030 Old Georgetown Rd., Bethesda, Maryland 20892. (301) 496-7403. 1978.

Bioassay of Malathion for Possible Carcinogenicity. National Cancer Institute, Division of Cancer Cause and Prevention, 9030 Old Georgetown Rd., Bethesda, Maryland 20892. (301) 496-7403. 1979. Adverse effects of malathion and carcinogens.

Biochemical Mechanisms of Paraquat Toxicity. Anne Pomeroy Autor, ed. Academic Press, c/o Harcourt Brace Jovanovich Inc., 6277 Sea Harbor Dr., Orlando, Florida 32887. (800) 346-8648. 1977. Proceedings of the Iowa Symposium on Toxic Mechanisms, 1st, 1976, Iowa City, IA.

The Caffeine Book. Frances Sheridan Goulart. Mead Publishing Corp., 1515 S. Commerce St., Las Vegas, Nevada 81902-2703. (702) 387-8750. 1984.

Caffeine: Perspectives from Recent Research. P.B. Dews, ed. Springer-Verlag, 175 5th Ave., New York, New York 10010. (212) 460-1500. 1984.

Chemical Contamination and Its Victims: Medical Remedies, Legal Redress, and Public Policy. David W. Schnare, ed. Greenwood Publishing Group, Inc., 88 Post Rd., W., Box 5007, Westport, Connecticut 06881. (203) 226-3571. 1989. Covers toxicology, hazardous waste, and liability for hazardous substances pollution damages.

Chemical Ecotoxicology. Jaakko Paasivirta. Lewis Publishers, 200 Corporate Blvd. NW, Boca Raton, Florida 33431. (407) 994-0555 or (800)272-7737. 1991. Presents an in-depth discussion of risk assessment, chemical cycles, structure-activity relationships, organohalogens, oil residues, mercury, sampling and analysis of trace chemicals, and emissions from the forest industry. Outlines the chemical basis for applied research in environ-

mental protection and provides important data regarding the fate and effects of various chemicals on wildlife.

Chemical Hazards in the Workplace. Ronald M. Scott. Lewis Publishers, 200 Corporate Blvd. NW, Boca Raton, Florida 33431. (407) 994-0555 or (800)272-7737. 1989. Presents basics of toxicology. Reports a sampling of the accumulated knowledge of the hazards of specific compounds in the workplace. Also discusses the federal regulatory agencies charged with worker protection and the specific practices involved in maintaining safety and regulatory compliance.

Chemical, Physical, and Biological Properties of Compounds Present at Hazardous Waste Sites: Final Report. U.S. Environmental Protection Agency. Clement Associates Inc., Arlington, Virginia 1985.

Chlorinated Dioxins and Dibenzofurans in the Total Environment. Gangadhar Chordhary, Lawrence H. Keith, and Christoffer Rappe. Butterworth-Heinemann, 80 Montvale Ave., Stoneham, Massachusetts 02180. (617) 438-8464. 1985. Environmental aspects and toxicology of tetrachlorodibenzodioxin and dibenzofurans.

Chlorophenols Other than Pentachlorophenol. World Health Organization, Ave. Appia, Geneva, Switzerland CH-1211. (518) 436-9686. 1989.

Combustion Toxicology. Shane C. Gad and Rosalind C. Anderson. CRC Press, 2000 Corporate Blvd., N.W., Boca Raton, Florida 33431. (407) 994-0555; (800) 272-7737. 1990. Evaluates the health hazards of the decomposition products formed when plastics are heated. Coverage includes the basics of inhalation toxicology and heat stress physiology, toxicity of smoke and combustion gases, combustion toxicity testing, regulations, toxicity of polymers by class, flame retardants and other additives, current issues and directions.

Controlling Chemical Hazards: Fundamentals of the Management of Toxic Chemicals. Raymond P. Cote and Peter G. Wells, eds. Unwin Hyman, 77/85 Fulham Palace Rd., London, England W6 8JB. 081 741 7070. 1991. Gives an overview of the properties, fate of, and dilemmas involving hazardous chemicals.

Criteria for a Recommended Standard, Occupational Exposure to Malathion. U.S. Department of Health and Human Services, Public Health Service, National Institute for Occupational Safety and Health, Robert A. Taft Lab, 4676 Columbia Pkwy., Cincinnati, Ohio 45226. (513) 684-8465. 1976.

Criteria for Controlling Occupational Exposure to Cobalt. U.S. Department of Health and Human Services, 200 Independence Ave., SW, Room 34AF, Washington, District of Columbia 20201. (202) 472-5543. 1982.

Death in the Marsh. Tom Harris. Island Press, 1718 Connecticut Ave. N.W., Suite 300, Washington, District of Columbia 20009. (202) 232-7933. 1991. Explains how federal irrigation projects have altered the selenium's circulation in the environment, allowing it to accumulate in marshes, killing ecosystems and wildlife, and causing deformities in some animals.

Dermatotoxicology. Francis N. Marzulli and Howard I. Maibach, eds. Hemisphere Publishing Co., 79 Madison Ave., Suite 1110, New York, New York 10016. (212) 725-1999; (800) 821-8312. 1991. 4th ed. Provides information on theoretical aspects and practical test methods, including both in vitro and in vivo approaches. Pays attention to the worldwide movement for the development of suitable alternatives to animals when feasible.

Econometric and Dynamic Modelling–Exemplified by Caesium in Lakes after Chernobyl. Lars Hakanson. Springer-Verlag, 175 5th Ave., New York, New York 10010. (212) 460-1500 or (800) 777-4643. 1991. Details methods to establish representative and compatible lake data models and load after the Chernobyl accident. Deals with ecotoxicology and hydrogeology.

Ecotoxicology and Climate. Philippe Bordeaux, et al., eds. John Wiley & Sons, Inc., 605 3rd Ave., New York, New York 10158-0012. (212) 850-6000. 1989. Describes environmental chemistry of toxic pollutants in hot and cold climates. Includes bibliographical references and an index.

Ecotoxicology of Metals: Current Concepts and Applications. Michael C. Newman and Alan W. McIntosh. Lewis Publishers, 2000 Corporate Blvd., N.W., Boca Raton, Florida 33431. (407) 994-0555 or (800) 272-7737. 1991. Examines the influence of water chemistry on metal toxicity. Also includes a review of toxic effects on fish and other biological forms that exist in the water. Analyzes and presents alternatives to standard techniques. Describes present and future needs in sediment toxicity and community level response of stream organisms to heavy metals.

Environment in Peril. Anthony B. Wolbarst, ed. Smithsonian Institution Press, 470 L'Enfant Plaza, No. 7100, Washington, District of Columbia 20560. (800) 782-4612. 1991. Brings together in one volume the primary concerns of eleven of the world's leaders in conservation, ecology and public policy. Broad environmental issues covered are: ozone depletion, overpopulation, global warming, thinning forests, extinction of species, spreading deserts, toxic chemicals, and various pollutants.

Environmental Chemistry and Toxicology of Aluminum. Timothy E. Lewis. Lewis Publishers, 2000 Corporate Blvd., N.W., Boca Raton, Florida 33431. (407) 994-0555 or (800) 272-7737. 1989. Examines the sources, fate, transport, and health effects of aluminum in aquatic and terrestrial environments. Also includes the latest advances in the study of aluminum in the environment; toxicity research–aquatic and terrestrial biota; neurotoxicity and possible links to Alzheimer's disease; different forms of aluminum in soils and soil water; coordination chemistry; specification and analytical methods.

Environmental Health-Related Information: A Bibliographic Guide to Federal Sources for the Health Professional. Interagency Education Program Liaison Group, Task Force on Environmental Cancer and Heart and Lung Disease, Maryland 1984.

Experimental Toxicology: The Basic Issues. Diana Anderson and D. M. Conning, eds. Royal Society of Chemistry, c/o CRC Press, 2000 Corporate Blvd. N.W., Boca Raton, Florida 33431-9868. (800) 272-7737. 1988. Addresses the basic issues concerned with the practice of experimental toxicology.

Fighting Toxics. Gary Cohen and John O'Connor, eds. Island Press, 1718 Connecticut Ave. N.W., Suite 300, Washington, District of Columbia 20009. (202) 232-7933. 1990. Investigates the toxic hazards in the community, determining the health risks they pose, and launching an effective campaign to eliminate them.

Ground Water and Toxicological Risk. Jenifer S. Heath. Lewis Publishers, 2000 Corporate Blvd., N.W., Boca Raton, Florida 33431. (407) 994-0555 or (800) 272-7737. 1991. Discusses the nature of ground water, the nature of toxicology, risk assessment, basics of risk perception and two case studies of reaction.

Groundwater Contamination: Sources, Control, and Preventive Measures. Chester D. Rail. Technomic Publishing Co., 851 New Holland Ave., Box 3535, Lancaster, Pennsylvania 17604. (717) 291-5609. 1989. Reviews the presently known sources of groundwater contamination and its many complex interactions, including managerial and political implications.

Hazardous Waste Chemistry, Toxicology and Treatment. Stanley E. Manahan. Lewis Publishers, 2000 Corporate Blvd., N.W., Boca Raton, Florida 33431. (407) 994-0555 or (800) 272-7737. 1990. Reviews hazardous wastes, their chemistry and toxicology. Gives a basic coverage of chemistry and biochemistry, environmental chemical processes, and toxicology.

Hazardous Waste Measurements. Milagros S. Simmons, ed. Lewis Publishers, 200 Corporate Blvd. NW, Boca Raton, Florida 33431. (407) 994-0555 or (800)272-7737. 1991. Focuses on recent developments in field testing methods and quality assurance.

Human Toxicology of Pesticides. Fina P. Kaloyanova and Mostafa A. El Batawi. CRC Press, 2000 Corporate Blvd. NW, Boca Raton, Florida 33431. (407) 994-0555; (800) 272-7737. 1991. Describes how pesticides affect humans.

Interim Procedures for Estimating Risks Associated with Exposures to Mixtures of Chlorinated Dibenzo-RHO-Dioxins-and- Dibenzofurans. Judith S. Bellin. U.S. Environmental Protection Agency, 401 M St., SW, Washington, District of Columbia 20460. (202) 260-2090.

Marine Toxins: Origin, Structure, and Molecular Pharmacology. Sherwood Hall and Gary Strichartz, eds. American Chemical Society, 1155 16th St. N.W., Washington, District of Columbia 20036. (202) 872-4600; (800) 227-5558. 1990. Describes the history of marine toxins and their various properties and effects on the environment.

A Matrix Approach to Biological Investigation of Synthetic Fuels. U.S. Environmental Protection Agency, Health Effects Research Laboratory, Office of Research and Development, MD 75, Research Triangle Park, North Carolina (919) 541-2184. Covers toxicology of shale oils, diesel fuels, jet planes, and synthetic fuels.

Molecular Aspects of Monooxygenases and Bioactivation of Toxic Compounds. Emel Arinc, ed. Plenum Press, 233 Spring St., New York, New York 10013-1578. (212) 620-8000 or (800) 221-9369. 1991. Proceedings of the NATO Advanced Study Institute on Molecular Aspects of Monooxgenases and Bioactivation held in August-September, 1989.

Occupational Exposure Limits for Airborne Toxic Substances. International Labour Office, 49 Sheridan Ave., Albany, New York 12210. (518) 436-9686. 1991.

Occupational Exposures to Diisocyanates. National Institute for Occupational Safety and Health. Department of Health and Human Services, Public Health Service, Center for Disease Control, National Institute for Occupational Safety and Health, 200 Independence Ave. SW, Cincinnati, Ohio 20201. (202) 619-1296. 1978. Discusses toxicology of isocyanates and safety measures that are in practice.

Occupational Toxicants. VCH Publishers, 303 NW 12th Ave., Deerfield Beach, Florida 33442-1788. (305) 428-5566. 1991. Contains critical data evaluation for MAK values and classification of carcinogens. Also has standards for hazardous chemical compounds in the work area.

Poison Runoff: A Guide to State and Local Control of Nonpoint Source Water Pollution. Paul Thompson. Natural Resources Defense Council, 40 W. 20th St., New York, New York 10011. (212) 727-2700. 1989. How-to-book addressing pollution in agricultural lands, urban development and construction, logging, mining and grazing.

Principles of Air Toxics. Roger D. Griffin. Lewis Publishers, 2000 Corporate Blvd., N.W., Boca Raton, Florida 33431. (407) 994-0555 or (800) 272-7737. 1991. Includes health effects of air pollutants, meteorology, pollutant transport and dispersion, types and definitions, sources and emissions, air emission characteristics, control and mitigation approaches, stationary source control technology, mobile source control, ambient air quality, and regulatory approaches.

Principles of Animal Extrapolation. Edward J. Calabrese. Lewis Publishers, 2000 Corporate Blvd., Boca Raton, Florida 33431. (800) 272-7737. 1991. Animal models for toxicity testing are described. Also includes statistical methods in experimental toxicology.

Proctor and Hughes' Chemical Hazards of the Workplace. G. J. Hathaway, et al. Global Professional Publications, 2805 McGraw Ave., PO Box 19539, Irvine, California 92713-9539. (800) 854-7179. 1991. Third edition. Includes 100 new chemicals and the new 1991 Threshold Limit Values. Gives a practical easy-to-use introduction to toxicology and hazards of over 600 chemicals most likely to be encountered in the workplace.

Reviews of Environmental Contamination and Toxicology: v. 120. George W. Ware, ed. Springer-Verlag, 175 5th Ave., New York, New York 10010. (212) 460-1500; (800) 777-4643. 1991. Covers organochlorine pesticides and polychlorinated biphenyls in human adipose tissue, pesticide residues in foods imported into the U.S., and selected trace elements and the use of biomonitors in subtropical and tropical marine ecosystems.

Risk Assessment in Genetic Engineering; Environmental Release of Organisms. Morris A. Levin and Harlee Strauss. McGraw-Hill, 1221 Avenue of the Americas, New York, New York 10020. (212) 512-2000; (800) 262-4729. 1991. Investigates issues such as the transport of microorganisms via air, water, and soil; the persistence and establishment of viruses, bacteria, and plants; and the genetic transfer via viruses.

Sensitive Biochemical and Behavioral Indicators of Trace Substance Exposure. Edward J. Massaro. Center for Environmental Research Information, U.S. Environmental Protection Agency, 26 W. Martin Luther King Dr., Cincinnati, Ohio 45268. (518) 569-7931. 1981.

Silica, Silicosis, and Cancer: Controversy in Occupational Medicine. Praeger Publishers, 1 Madison Ave., New York, New York 10010-3603. (212) 685-5300. Covers lung cancer and the toxicology of silica.

Toxic Marine Phytoplankton. Edna Graneli. Elsevier Science Publishing Co., 655 Avenue of the Americas, New York, New York 10010. (212) 984-5800. 1990. Covers toxicology of marine phytoplankton.

Toxicity and Metabolism of Industrial Solvents. Ethel Browning. Elsevier Science Publishing Co., 655 Avenue of the Americas, New York, New York 10010. (212) 984-5800. 1965.

Toxicity of Industrial Metals. Ethel Browning. Butterworth-Heinemann, 80 Montvale Ave., Stoneham, Massachusetts 02180. (617) 438-8464; (800) 366-2665. 1969. 2d ed.

Toxicity Reduction in Industrial Effluents. Perry W. Lanford, et al. Van Nostrand Reinhold, 115 5th Ave., New York, New York 10003. (212) 254-3232. 1990. Overview of aquatic toxicology and toxicity reduction. Specific treatment technologies that can be used to reduce toxicity, such as aerobic and anaerobic biological treatment, air and steam stripping of volatile organics, granulated carbon absorption, powdered activated carbon treatment and chemical oxidation, are discussed in detail.

Toxicological Chemistry: A Guide to Toxic Substances in Chemistry. Stanley E. Manahan. Lewis Publishers, 200 Corporate Blvd. NW, Boca Raton, Florida 33431. (407) 994-0555 or (800)272-7737. 1989. Defines toxicological chemistry and gives information on its origin and use. Emphasizes the chemical formulas, structures, and reactions of toxic substances.

Toxicological Evaluations. Volume 1: Potential Health Hazards of Existing Chemicals. B. G. Chemie, ed. Springer-Verlag, 115 5th Ave., New York, New York 10010. (212) 460-1500; (800) 777-4643. 1990. Identifies thousands of compounds which might possibly be toxic and to date several hundreds that have been investigated. Contains results of the first 57 reviews of the literature.

Toxicology of Inhaled Materials. I.Y.R. Adamson. Springer-Verlag, 175 5th Ave., New York, New York 10010. (212) 460-1500. 1985. General principles of inhalation toxicology.

The Toxicology of Paraquat, Diquat and Morfamquat. Aurelio Pasi. Hans Huber, Langgasstr. 76, Bern, Switzerland D-3000. 1978. The toxicology of paraquat and pyridinium compounds is described.

Trace Elements in Soils and Plants. Alina Kabata-Pendias and Henryk Pendias. CRC Press, 2000 Corporate Blvd. N.W., Boca Raton, Florida 33431. (800) 272-7737. 1991. 2d ed. Discusses the pollution of air, water, soil and plants, all about soil processes, and the involvement of trace elements in the soil and plants.

Understanding Cell Toxicology: Principles and Practice. Erik Walum, Kjell Stenberg and Dag Jenssen. E. Horwood, 200 Old Tappan Rd., Old Tappan, New Jersey 07675. (800) 223-2348. 1990. Surveys the uses of mammalian cell assays to evaluate the toxic actions of chemical and physical agents.

Wildlife Toxicology. Tony J. Peterle. Van Nostrand Reinhold, 115 5th Ave., New York, New York 10003. (212) 354-3232. 1991. Presents an historical overview of the toxicology problem and summarizes the principal laws, testing protocols, and roles of leading U.S. federal agencies, especially EPA. Examines state and local issues, monitoring programs, and contains an unique section on the regulation of toxic substances overseas.

GOVERNMENTAL ORGANIZATIONS

U.S. Environmental Protection Agency: Assistant Administrator for Pesticides and Toxic Substances. 401 M St., S.W., Washington, District of Columbia 20460. (202) 382-2902.

U.S. Environmental Protection Agency: National Enforcement Investigations Center. Building 53, Box 25227, Denver, Colorado 80225. (303) 236-5100.

U.S. Environmental Protection Agency: Office of Toxic Substances. 401 M St., S.W., Washington, District of Columbia 20460. (202) 382-3813.

HANDBOOKS AND MANUALS

Casarett and Doull's Toxicology. Pergamon Microforms International, Inc., Fairview Park, Elmsford, New York 10523. (914) 592-7720. 1991. Covers toxicology, poisoning and poisons.

CRC Handbook of Chemistry and Physics. CRC Press, 2000 Corporate Blvd. N.W., Boca Raton, Florida 33431. (407) 994-0555; (800) 272-7737. 1988. 67th ed.

Documentation of the Threshold Limit Values. American Conference of Governmental Industrial Hygienists, 6500 Glenway, Building D-5, Cincinnati, Ohio 45211. 1991. Provides threshold limit value documentation for any physical phenomenon in the environment, including chemical substances and physical agents.

Guidance for the Reregistration of Pesticide Products Containing Lindane as the Active Ingredient. U.S. Environmental Protection Agency, Office of the Pesticides and Toxic Substances, 401 M St., SW, Washington, District of Columbia 20460. (202) 260-2090. 1985. The Federal Insecticide, Fungicide, Rodenticide Act directs EPA to reregister all pesticides as expeditiously as possible. The guide helps the user to carry out this task and to participate in the EPA's registration standard program. Includes extensive tabular data to the pesticides and an extensive bibliography.

Handbook of Analytical Toxicology. Irving Sunshine, ed. CRC Press, 2000 Corporate Blvd. N.W., Boca Raton, Florida 33431. (407) 994-0555; (800) 272-7737. 1969.

Handbook of Pesticide Toxicology. Wayland J. Hayes and Edward R. Laws, eds. Academic Press, c/o Harcourt Brace Jovanovich Inc., 6277 Sea Harbor Dr., Orlando, Florida 32887. (800) 346-8648. 1991. Three volumes. Covers various types of toxicity, nature of injury, reversibility, various methods of quantitating dose response, metabolism of toxins, factors affecting toxicity, absorption, and elimination.

Handbook of Toxicologic Pathology. Wanda M. Haschek and Colin G. Rosseaux, eds. Academic Press, c/o Harcourt Brace Jovanovich Inc., 6277 Sea Harbor Dr., Orlando, Florida 32887. (800) 346-8648. 1991. Handbook describing experimental methods and animal models for toxicological assessment.

Handbook of Toxicology. W. Thomas Shier and Dietrich Mebs. Marcel Dekker, Inc., 270 Madison Ave., New York, New York 10016. (212) 696-9000; (800) 228-1160. 1990. Covers most toxins for which sufficient research has been done to clearly establish the identity and characteristics of the toxin.

Pesticide Handbook. Peter Hurst. Journeyman Press, 955 Massachusetts Ave., Cambridge, Massachusetts 02139. (617) 868-3305. 1990.

Poisonous Plants of Eastern North America. Randy G. Westbrooks and James W. Preacher. University of South Carolina Press, Columbia, South Carolina 29208. (803) 777-5243. 1986. List of poisonous plants which include species of plants, the plant part (leaf, root, fruit), the amount of plant material involved, the stage of development of the plant, and the soil type and growing conditions.

Toxicology Handbook. Government Institutes, Inc., 4 Research Pl., Ste. 200, Rockville, Maryland 20850. (301) 921-2300. 1986. Contains a list of key acronyms, glossary of terms, and chapters on Fundamental Concepts; Toxicity Assessments; Protocols in Toxicology Studies; Exposure Assessment; Risk Assessment and dioxing.

ONLINE DATA BASES

ANEUPLOIDY. Oak Ridge National Laboratory, Environmental Mutagen Information Center, Building 2001, P.O. Box 2008, Oak Ridge, Tennessee 37831-6050. (615) 574-7871.

BioBusiness. Dialog Information Services, Inc., Marketing Dept., 3460 Hillview Avenue, Palo Alto, California 94304. (800) 334-2564 or (415) 858-3810. Provides information based on evaluations of the economic and business aspects of biological and biomedical research.

BNA Toxics Law Daily. Bureau of National Affairs, BNA PLUS, 1231 25th St., N.W., Rm. 215, Washington, District of Columbia 20037. (800) 454-7773.

CERCLIS. Chemical Information Systems, Inc., 7215 York Rd., Baltimore, Maryland 21212. (301) 321-8440. Information on hazardous waste disposal sites that have either been listed by the EPA on the National Priority List (NPL) or nominated for consideration for the NPL.

Chemical Abstracts-CA. Chemical Abstracts Service, 2540 Olentangy River Rd., P.O. Box 3012, Columbus, Ohio 43210. (800) 848-6533 or (614) 421-3600. Information sources include 9000 journals, patents from 27 countries, two industrial property organizations, new books, conference proceedings, and government research reports.

Chemical Carcinogenesis Research Information System–CCRIS. National Library of Medicine, 8600 Rockville Pike, Bethesda, Maryland 20894. (800) 638-8480. Individual assay results and test conditions for 1,451 chemicals in the areas of carcinogenicity, mutagenicity, tumor promotion, and cocarcinogenicity.

Chemical Engineering and Biotechnology Abstracts–CEBA. Orbit Search Service, Maxwell Online Inc., 8000 W. Park Dr., McLean, Virginia 22102. (703) 442-0900 or (800) 456-7248. Monthly. Covers theoretical, practical and commercial material on all aspects of processing safety, and the environment. Also covers process and reaction engineering, measurement and process control, environmental protection and safety, plant design and equipment used in chemical engineering and biotechnology. More than 400 of the world's major primary chemical and process engineering journals are scanned to compile the database. Available from ORBIT.

Chemical Evaluation Search and Retrieval System. Michigan State Department of Natural Resources, Surface

Water Quality Division, Great Lakes and Environmental Assessment Section, Knapp's Office Center, PO Box 30028, Lansing, Michigan 48909. (517) 373-2190. Covers toxicology information on compounds of environmental concern, providing acute and chronic toxicity data for aquatic and terrestrial life as well as information on carcinogenicity, mutagenicity, and reproductive and developmental effects, bioconcentration, and environmental fate.

ChemID. National Library of Medicine, Toxicology Information Program, 8600 Rockville Pike, Bethesda, Maryland 20894. (800) 638-8480.

CHEMLINE. National Library of Medicine, Toxicology Information Program, 8600 Rockville Pike, Bethesda, Maryland 20894. (800) 638-8480.

CHEMLIST. American Petroleum Institute, Central Abstracting & Indexing Service, 275 7th Ave., New York, New York 10001. (212) 366-4040.

CTCP. Dartmouth Medical School, Department of Pharmacology and Toxicology, Hanover, New Hampshire 03755.

Dermal Absorption. U.S. Environmental Protection Agency, Office of Pesticides and Toxic Substances, 401 M St., SW, Washington, District of Columbia 20460. (202) 260-2090. Toxic effects, absorption, distribution, metabolism, and excretion relation to the dermal absorption of 655 chemicals.

EMICBACK. Oak Ridge National Laboratory, Environmental Teratology Information Center, Building 2001, P.O. Box 2008, Oak Ridge, Tennessee 37831-6050. (615) 574-7871.

Epidemiology Information System. Oak Ridge National Laboratory, Toxicology Information Response Center, Building 2001, P.O. Box 2008, Oak Ridge, Tennessee 37831-6050. (615) 576-1746.

ETICBACK: Environmental Teratology Information Center Backfile. Oak Ridge National Laboratory, Environmental Teratology Information Center, Building 2001, P.O. Box 2008, Oak Ridge, Tennessee 37831-6050. (615) 574-7871.

Forensic Science Database. Home Office Forensic Science Service, Central Research and Support Establishment, Aldermaston, Reading, Berkshire, England RG7 4PN. 44 (734) 814100.

Global Indexing System. U.S. Environmental Protection Agency, 401 M St., S.W., Washington, District of Columbia 20460. (202) 260-2090. International information on various qualities of chemicals.

HADB. National Library of Medicine, Toxicology Information Program, 8600 Rockville Pike, Bethesda, Maryland 20894. (800) 638-8480.

INFOTOX. Centre de Documentation, Commission de la Sante et de la Securite du Travail (CSST), 1199 rue de Bueury, 4th Floor, C.P. 6067 succ "A", Montreal, Quebec, Canada H3C 4E2. (514) 873-2297.

Medical Toxicology and Environmental Health. Department of Health and Social Security, Medical Toxiclology & Environmental Health Division, Hannibal House, Rm. 719, Elephant and Castle, London, England SE1 6TE. 44 (71) 972-2162.

The Merck Index Online. Merck & Company, Inc., Box 2000, Building 86-0900, Rahway, New Jersey 07065-0900. (201) 855-4558.

Monthly Catalog of United States Government Publications. U.S. G.P.O., Supt. of Docs., PO Box 371954, Pittsburgh, Pennsylvania 15250-7954. (202) 512-0000.

National Technical Information Service. U.S. Department of Commerce, National Technical Information Service, Office of Data Base Services, 5285 Port Royal Rd., Springfield, Virginia 22161. (703) 487-4807. Bibliographic database of government sponsored research and technical reports.

NIOSHTIC. U.S. Department of Health and Human Services, Centers for Disease Control, National Institute for Occupational Safety and Health, 4676 Columbia Parkway, Cincinnati, Ohio 45226. (513) 533-8317.

Registry of Toxic Effects of Chemical Substances–Online1. US Department of Health and Human Services, National Institute for Occupational Safety and Health, Washington, District of Columbia 20402-9325. (202) 783-3238. Tests on chemical substances: Substance Identification, Toxicity/Biomedical Effects, Toxicology and Carcinogenicity Review, and Exposure Standards and Regulations.

REPRORISK System. Micromedex, Inc., 600 Grant St., Denver, Colorado 80203. (800) 525-9083 or (303) 831-1400. Reproductive risks to females and males caused by drugs, chemicals, and physical and environmental agents. Includes the Teratogen Information System (TERIS), which deals with the teratogenicity of over 700 drugs and environmental agents that affect a fetus. One of the additional modules under development is the REPROTEXT database, containing a ranking system for reproductive hazards and the general toxicity of over 600 chemicals, emphasizing chronic occupational exposures.

SCISEARCH. Institute for Scientific Information, University City Science Center, 3501 Market St., Philadelphia, Pennsylvania 19104. (215) 386-0100.

TOXALL. National Library of Medicine, Specialized Information Services Division, 8600 Rockville Pike, Bethesda, Maryland 20894. (301) 496-6531.

Toxic Chemical Release Inventory. Office of Research and Development, U.S. Environmental Protection Agency, RD-689, 401 M St., S.W., Washington, District of Columbia 20460. Releases of toxic chemicals to the environment. Includes names and addresses of the facilities and the amount of certain toxic chemicals they release to the air, water, or land.

Toxic Materials News. Business Publishers, Inc., 951 Pershing Dr., Silver Spring, Maryland 20910-4464. (301) 587-6300. Legislation, regulations, and litigation concerning toxic substances. Online version of periodical of the same name.

TOXLIT. National Library of Medicine, Toxicology Information Program, 8600 Rockville Pike, Bethesda, Maryland 20894. (800) 638-8480.

TSCA Chemical Substances Inventory. U.S. Environmental Protection Agency, Office of Pesticides and Toxic Substances, 401 M St., S.W., Washington, District of Columbia 20460. (202) 260-2090.

TSCATS. U.S. Environmental Protection Agency, Office of Pesticides and Toxic Substances, 401 M St., S.W.,

Washington, District of Columbia 20460. (202) 382-3524.

PERIODICALS AND NEWSLETTERS

Advances in Analytical Toxicology. Biomedical Publications, PO Box 8209, Foster City, California 94404. (415) 573-6224. Annual. Analysis of toxins and poisons.

American College of Toxicology Newsletter. American College of Toxicology, 9650 Rockville Pike, Rockville, Maryland 20814. (301) 571-1840. Quarterly. Information on toxicology.

Annual Report of the Inhalation Toxicology Research Institute. Inhalation Toxicology Research Institute. Lovelace Biomedical and Environmental Research Institute, 5285 Port Royal Rd., Springfield, Virginia 22161. (703) 487-4650. 1972/73-. Annual. Deals with aerosols, poisonous gases and radioactive substances. Describes the impact on inhalation of these hazardous substances.

Annual Review of Pharmacology and Toxicology. Annual Reviews Inc., 4139 El Camino Way, Palo Alto, California 94303-0897. (800) 523-8635. Annual.

Aquatic Toxicology. Elsevier Science Publishing Co., 655 Avenue of the Americas, New York, New York 10010. (212) 989-5800. 1981-. 6/year.

Aquatic Toxicology and Risk Assessment. ASTM, 1916 Race St., Philadelphia, Pennsylvania 19103. (215) 299-5400. Annual. Covers aquatic animals, aquatic plants, water pollution, and water quality bioassay.

Archives of Environmental Health: An International Journal. Heldref Publications, Helen Dwight Reid Educational Foundation, 4000 Albemarle St., NW, Washington, District of Columbia 20016-1851. Bimonthly. Documentation on the effects of environmental agents on human health.

Archives of Toxicology. Springer-Verlag, 175 5th Ave., New York, New York 10010. (212) 460-1500.

Bulletin. U.S. Department of Health and Human Services, Public Health Service, Food and Drug Administration, 9000 Rockville Pike, Bethesda, Maryland 20892. (301) 496-4000. Safety measures and physiological effects of poisons.

Bulletin of Environmental Contamination and Toxicology. Springer-Verlag, 175 5th Ave., New York, New York 10010. (212) 460-1500; (800) 777-4643. 1966-. Frequency varies. Disseminates advances and discoveries in the areas of soil, air and food contamination and pollution.

Chemical Research in Toxicology. American Chemical Society, 1155 16th St. N.W., Washington, District of Columbia 20036. (800) 227-5558. Bimonthly. Deals with chemical analysis and reactive intermediates.

Chemosphere: Chemistry, Biology and Toxicology as Related to Environmental Problems. Pergamon Microforms International, Inc., Fairview Park, Elmsford, New York 10523. (914) 592-7720. 1970-. Offers maximum dissemination of investigations related to the health and safety of every aspect of life. Environmental protection encompasses a very wide field and relies on scientific research in chemistry, biology, physics, toxicology and inter-related disciplines.

Clinical Toxicology. Marcel Dekker, Inc., 270 Madison Ave., New York, New York 10016. (212) 696-9000; (800)

228-1160. Quarterly. Toxicology and poison related topics.

Current Advances in Pharmacology & Toxicology. Pergamon Microforms International, Inc., Fairview Park, Elmsford, New York 10523. (914) 592-7720. 1984. Current awareness in biological sciences including toxicology and pharmacology.

Drug and Chemical Toxicology. Marcel Dekker, Inc., 270 Madison Ave., New York, New York 10016. (212) 696-9000. Quarterly. Covers safety evaluations of drugs and chemicals.

Ecotoxicology and Environmental Safety. Academic Press, c/o Harcourt Brace Jovanovich Inc., 6277 Sea Harbor Dr., Orlando, Florida 32887. (800) 346-8648. 1977-. Bimonthly.

Environmental Action. Environmental Action Foundation, 6930 Carroll Ave., Ste. 600, Takoma Park, Maryland 20912. (301) 891-1100. Bimonthly. Impact of humans and industry on the environment.

Environmental Health Letter. Business Publishers, Inc., 951 Pershing Dr., Silver Spring, Maryland 20910-4464. (301) 587-6300. 1961-. Biweekly. Covers areas such as: indoor air, asbestos health effects, toxic substances testing, health problems at wastewater plants, risk-based sludge rules, medical waste, developmental toxicity risk assessment, animal carcinogen tests, pesticide risk, air toxics, aerospace chemicals, lead, radionuclide emissions, state right-to-know statutes, and incinerator emissions.

Environmental Research. Academic Press, 1250 6th Ave., San Diego, California 92101. (619) 231-0926. Bimonthly. Toxic effects of environmental agents in humans and animals.

Environmental Toxicology and Chemistry. Society of Environmental Toxicology and Chemistry. Pergamon Microforms International, Inc., Fairview Park, Elmsford, New York 10523. (914) 592-7720. 1981-. Monthly. Contains information on environmental toxicology, and chemistry, including the application of science to hazard assessment.

Food and Chemical Toxicology. Pergamon Microforms International Inc., Fairview Park, Elmsford, New York 10523. (914) 592-7720. Monthly. Information and risks of food and chemicals.

Fundamentals & Applied Toxicology. Academic Press, c/o Marcourt Brace, PO Box 6250, 6277 Sea Harbor Dr., Orlando, Florida 32887. (218) 723-9828. 8/year. Covers risk assessment and safety studies of toxic agents.

Hazardous Waste Consultant. McCoy & Associates, 13701 West Jewell Avenue, Suite 202, Lakewood, Colorado 80228. (303) 987-0333. Bimonthly. Information on hazardous and toxic waste issues.

Industrial Hygiene News. Rimbach Publishing, Inc., 8650 Babcock Boulevard, Pittsburgh, Pennsylvania 15237. (412) 364-5366. Bimonthly. Covers new products, literature, and product briefs.

Journal of Analytical Toxicology. Preston Publications, PO Box 48312, 7800 Merrimac, Niles, Illinois 60648. (708) 965-0566. Bimonthly. Articles on industrial toxicology, environmental pollution and pharmaceuticals.

Journal of Biochemical Toxicology. VCH Publishers, 303 NW 12th Ave., Deerfield Beach, Florida 33442-1788.

(305) 428-5566. 1986. Topics in biochemistry and biochemical toxicology.

Journal of Environmental Biology. Academy of Environmental Biology, 657-5 Civil Lines (south), Muzaffarnagar, India 251001. 1980-. Quarterly. An international journal concerned with toxicology and the interrelations of organisms and their environment.

Journal of Environmental Health. National Environmental Health Association, 720 South Colorado Boulevard, Suite 970, Denver, Colorado 80222. (303) 756-9090. Bimonthly. Covers phases in environmental health.

Journal of Environmental Pathology, Toxicology, and Oncology. Chem-Orbital, PO Box 134, Park Forest, Illinois 60466. (708) 748-0440. Six times a year. Official organ of the International Society for Environmental Toxicology and Cancer, covering environmentally induced diseases and carcinogens.

Journal of the American College of Toxicology. Mary Ann Liebert, Inc. Publishers, 1651 Third Avenue, New York, New York 10128. (202) 289-2300. Bimonthly. Issues and events that influence the field of toxicology.

Journal of Toxicology. Marcel Dekker, Inc., 270 Madison Ave., New York, New York 10016. (212) 696-9000; (800) 228-1160. Ten times a year.

Journal of Toxicology and Environmental Health. Taylor & Francis, 1900 Frost Road, Suite 101, Bristol, Pennsylvania 19007. (800) 821-8312. Monthly. Covers toxilogical effects of environmental pollution.

Journal of Toxicology: Clinical Toxicology. Marcel Dekker, Inc., 270 Madison Ave., New York, New York 10016. (212) 696-9000. Bimonthly. Covers all facets of medical toxicology.

Journal of Toxicology: Cutaneous and Ocular Toxicology. Marcel Dekker, Inc., 270 Madison Ave., New York, New York 10016. (212) 696-9000. Quarterly. Covers dermatological, toxicological, and ophthalmological studies.

Journal of Toxicology: Toxin Reviews. Marcel Dekker, Inc., 270 Madison Ave., New York, New York 10016. (212) 696-9000. Three times a year. Covers new underutilized substances.

Lithium and Animal Behavior. Eden Press, Montreal, Quebec, Canada Annual. Toxicology and therapeutic use of lithium.

The Merck Index. Merck Co., Inc., Box 2000, Rahway, New Jersey 07065. (201) 855-4558. Data on chemicals, drugs, and biological substances.

Multinational Environmental Outlook. Business Publishers, Inc., 951 Pershing Dr., Silver Spring, Maryland 20910-4464. (301) 587-6300. 1974-. Biweekly. Covers developments in world environmental problems such as acid rain, deforestation, soil erosion, overfishing, threats to health, animal extinction, population growth, diminishing water supply and other related matters. Also available online.

Pesticide & Toxic Chemical News. Food Chemical News, Inc., 1101 Pennsylvania Avenue, SE, Washington, District of Columbia 20003. (202) 544-1980. Weekly. Covers government regulations of chemical pollution, transportation, disposal and occupational health. Also available online.

Publications Index. U.S. G.P.O., Washington, District of Columbia 20401. (202) 512-0000. Annual. Covers radiation toxicology and radiation management.

State Environment Report: Toxic Substances & Hazardous Wastes. Business Publishers, Inc., 951 Pershing Drive, Silver Spring, Maryland 20910. (301) 587-6300. Weekly. Covers state legislative and regulatory initiatives.

Toxic Materials News. Business Publishers, Inc., 951 Pershing Dr., Silver Spring, Maryland 20910-4464. (301) 587-6300. 1974-. Weekly. Informs on regulations governing the manufacture, handling, transport, distribution and disposal of toxic chemicals and pesticides. Also available online.

Toxicology & Applied Pharmacology. Academic Press, P.O. Box 6250, c/o Harcourt Brace, 6277 Sea Harbor Dr., Orlando, Florida 32887. (218) 723-9828. Fifteen times a year. Covers the effects of chemicals on living organisms.

Toxicology and Environmental Chemistry. Gordon and Breach Science Publishers, Inc., 270 8th Ave., New York, New York 10011. (212) 206-8900. 1984.

Toxicology Letters. Elsevier, PO Box 211, Amsterdam, Netherlands 1000 AE. 020-5803-911. 1977.

Toxicology Methods. Raven Press, 1185 Avenue of the Americas, New York, New York 10036. (212) 930-9500. Quarterly.

Toxics Law Reporter. Bureau of National Affairs, 1231 25th St. NW, Washington, District of Columbia 20037. (202) 452-4200. Weekly. Covers legal developments of toxic tort.

TSCA Chemicals on Progress Bulletin. TSCA Assistance Office, Office of Pesticide & Toxic Substances, U.S. EPA, Washington, District of Columbia 20460. (202) 554-1404. Quarterly. Covers happenings in the EPA.

Veterinary and Human Toxicology. College of Veterinary Medicine, Drawer V, Mississippi State, Mississippi 39762. (601) 325-1106.

Waste Disposal and Pollution Control. Wakeman/Walworth, P.O. Box 1939, New Haven, Connecticut 06509. (203) 562-8518. Monthly. Covers air and water pollution, toxic waste, and acid rain.

RESEARCH CENTERS AND INSTITUTES

Bemidji State University, Center for Environmental Studies. Bemidji, Minnesota 56601. (218) 755-2910.

Michigan State University, Center for Environmental Toxicology. C 231 Holden Hall, East Lansing, Michigan 48824. (517) 353-6469.

Mississippi State Chemical Laboratory. Mississippi State University, P.O. Box CR, Mississippi State, Mississippi 39762. (601) 325-3324.

National Center for Toxicological Research Associated Universities, Inc. 4301 W. Markham, UAMS 522, Little Rock, Arkansas 72205. (501) 686-6501.

State University of New York at Buffalo, Toxicology Research Center. 102 Faber Hall, Buffalo, New York 14214. (716) 831-2125.

Texas Woman's University, Biology Science Research Laboratory. Denton, Texas 76204. (817) 898-2351.

University of San Francisco, Institute of Chemical Biology. Ignarian Heights, Room H342, San Francisco, California 94117-1080. (415) 666-6415.

University of Tennessee at Knoxville, Biology Consortium. M303 Walters Life Sciences Building, Knoxville, Tennessee 37996. (615) 974-6841.

TRADE ASSOCIATIONS AND PROFESSIONAL SOCIETIES

American Academy of Clinical Toxicology. Comparative Toxicology Laboratories, Kansas State University, Manhattan, Kansas 66506. (913) 532-5679.

American Board of Medical Toxicology. Primary Children Center, 320 12th Ave., Salt Lake City, Utah 84103. (801) 521-1536.

American Chemical Society. 1155 16th St., N.W., Washington, District of Columbia 20036. (202) 872-4600.

American College of Toxicology. 9650 Rockville Pike, Bethesda, Maryland 20814. (301) 571-1840.

Chemical Industry Institute of Toxicology. P.O. Box 12137, Research Triangle Park, North Carolina 27709. (919) 541-2070.

Clean Water Action Project. c/o David Zwick, 1320 18th St. N.W., Washington, District of Columbia 20003. (202) 457-1286.

Genetic Toxicology Association. c/o Kerry Dearfield, USEPA, 401 M St., S.W., Washington, District of Columbia 20460. (703) 557-9780.

Greenpeace. 1436 U St., NW, Washington, District of Columbia 20009. (202) 462-1177.

International Society for Environmental Toxicology and Cancer. P.O. Box 134, Park Forest, Illinois 60466. (312) 755-2080.

International Society of Toxinology. Dept. of Pharmacology and Toxicology, School of Pharmacy, University of Connecticut, Storrs, Connecticut 06269. (203) 486-2213.

National Air Toxics Information Clearinghouse. Research Triangle Park, North Carolina 27711. (919) 541-0850.

Society of Forensic Toxicologists. 1013 Three Mile Dr., Grosse Pointe Park, Michigan 48230. (313) 884-4718.

Society of Toxicology. 1101 14th St., N.W., Suite 1100, Washington, District of Columbia 20005. (202) 371-1393.

Toxicology Forum. 1575 I St., N.W., 5th Fl., Washington, District of Columbia 20005. (202) 659-0030.

United States Operating Committee on ETAD. 1330 Connecticut Ave., N.W., Suite 300, Washington, District of Columbia 20036-1702. (202) 659-0060.

TRACE METALS

ABSTRACTING AND INDEXING SERVICES

Applied Ecology Abstracts Studies in Renewable Natural Resources. Information Retrieval Ltd., 1911 Jefferson Davis Highway, Arlington, Virginia 22202. 1975-. Monthly.

Applied Science and Technology Index. H.W. Wilson Co., 950 University Ave., Bronx, New York 10452. (800) 367-6770. Formerly Industrial Arts Index.

Biological and Agricultural Index. H.W. Wilson Co., 950 University Ave., Bronx, New York 10452. (800) 367-6770. 1916-. Monthly.

Chemical Abstracts. Chemical Abstracts Service, 2540 Olentangy River Rd., PO Box 3012, Columbus, Ohio 43210. (800) 848-6533. 1907-.

Ecological Abstracts. Geo Abstracts Ltd. Elsevier Applied Science, Crown House, Linton Rd., Barking, England IG 11 8JU. 1974-. Derived from over 600 leading ecological and environmental journals, plus books, conference proceedings, reports and theses.

Engineering Index. The Engineering Index Inc., 345 E. 47th St., New York, New York 10017. 1962-.

General Science Index. H. W. Wilson Co., 950 University Ave., Bronx, New York 10452. 1978-. Monthly, also issued in annual cumulation. Cumulative subject index to English language periodicals in the subject fields of astronomy, botany, chemistry, earth science, environment and conservation, food and nutrition, genetics, mathematics, medicine and health, microbiology, oceanography, physics, physiology and zoology.

Index to Scientific Book Contents. Institute for Scientific Information, 3501 Market St., Philadelphia, Pennsylvania 19104. (800) 523-1857. 1985-. Annual. Gives contents of science books published.

Multimedia Index to Ecology. National Information Center for Educational Media, University of Southern California, Los Angeles, California 90007.

Physics Briefs. Physikalische Berichte. Physik Verlag, Pappapelallee 3, Postfach 101161, Weinheim, Germany D-6940. 1979-. Semimonthly. In English. Volumes for 1979- issued by the Deutsche Physikalische Gesellschaft and the Fachinformationszentrum Energie Physik, Mathematik in cooperation with the American Institute of Physics.

Pollution Abstracts. Cambridge Scientific Abstracts, 5161 River Rd., Bethesda, Maryland 20816. (301) 961-6750. Six/year. Indexes worldwide technical literature on environmental pollution. Covers air pollution, marine and freshwater pollution, sewage and wastewater treatment, waste management, toxicology and health, noise pollution, radiation, land pollution, and environmental policies, programs, legislation, and education. Also available online.

Science Citation Index. Institute for Scientific Information, 3501 Market St., Philadelphia, Pennsylvania 19104. 1961-.

BIBLIOGRAPHIES

New Publications of the Geological Survey. U.S. Department of the Interior, Geological Survey, 119 National Center, Reston, Virginia 22092. (703) 648-4460. 1984-. Monthly. Bibliography of geological publications and related government documents published by the Geological Survey.

ENCYCLOPEDIAS AND DICTIONARIES

Dictionary of Environmental Engineering and Related Sciences: English-Spanish, Spanish-English. Jose T. Villate. Ediciones Universal, 3090 SW 8th St., Miami, Florida 33135. (305) 642-3355. 1979.

Encyclopedia of Environmental Science and Engineering. J.R. Pfafflin. Gordon and Breach Science Publishers, Inc., 270 8th Ave., New York, New York 10011. (212) 206-8900. 1992.

Encyclopedia of Physical Science and Technology. Robert A. Meyers, ed. Academic Press, c/o Harcourt Brace Jovanovich Inc., 6277 Sea Harbor Dr., Orlando, Florida 32887. (800) 346-8648. Dictionary of engineering, technology and physical sciences.

The Encyclopedia of Soil Science. Rhodes W. Fairbridge. Academic Press, c/o Harcourt Brace Jovanovich Inc., 6277 Sea Harbor Dr., Orlando, Florida 32887. (800) 346-8648. 1979-. Includes soil physics, soil chemistry, soil biology, soil fertility and plant nutrition, soil genesis, classification and cartography.

Grzimek's Encyclopedia of Ecology. Bernhard Grzimek. Van Nostrand Reinhold, 115 5th Ave., New York, New York 10003. (212) 254-3232. 1976.

McGraw-Hill Encyclopedia of Environmental Science. Sybil P. Parker. McGraw-Hill Science & Engineering Books, 11 W. 19th St., New York, New York 10011. (212) 337-6010. 1980. Covers ecology, man's influence on nature, and environmental protection.

North American Reference Encyclopedia of Ecology and Pollution. William White. North American Pub. Co., 401 N. Broad St., Philadelphia, Pennsylvania 19108. (215) 238-5300. 1972.

Van Nostrand's Scientific Encyclopedia. Glenn D. Considine, ed. Van Nostrand Reinhold, 115 5th Ave., New York, New York 10003. (212) 254-3232. 1983. Sixth edition. Includes all broad subject areas in science.

GENERAL WORKS

Fate of Trace Metals in a Rotary Kiln Incinerator with a Single-Stage Ionizing Wet Scrubber. D. J. Fournier and L. R. Waterland. National Technical Information Service, 5285 Port Royal Rd., Springfield, Virginia 22161. (703) 487-4650. 1991. Two volumes. Vol. 1 Technical results. vol. 2. Appendices.

Heavy Metals in the Marine Environment. Robert W. Furness and Philip S. Rainbow. CRC Press, 2000 Corporate Blvd. N.W., Boca Raton, Florida 33431. (800) 272-7737. 1990. Includes heavy metals in the marine environment, trace metals in sea water, metals in the marine atmosphere, processes affecting metal concentration in estuarine and coastal marine sediments, heavy metal levels in marine invertebrates, use of microalgae and invertebrates to monitor metal levels in estuaries and coastal waters, toxic effects of metals, and the incidence of metal pollution in marine ecosystems.

Metals in Groundwater. Herbert E. Allen. Lewis Publishers, 2000 Corporate Blvd., N.W., Boca Raton, Florida 33431. (407) 994-0555 or (800) 272-7737. 1991. Discusses in depth the state of the knowledge of metal sorption by aquifer materials. The status of chemical partitioning, hydrologic transport models is also considered. Includes agricultural, wastewater, and mining field-site examples.

Optoelectronics for Environmental Science. S. Martellucci and A. N. Chester, eds. Plenum Press, 233 Spring St., New York, New York 10013-1578. (212) 620-8000; (800)

221-9369. 1991. Contribution of lasers and the optical sciences to specific problems, in situ measurements, atmospheric ozone, lidar detection, wind velocity, oceanographic measurements, heavy metal detection, toxic metals, and trace analysis. Proceedings of the 14th course of the International School of Quantum Electronics on Optoelectronics for Environmental Sciences, held September 3-12, 1989, in Erice, Italy.

Trace Elements in Health and Disease. A. Aitio, et al., eds. Royal Society of Chemistry, c/o CRC Press, 2000 Corporate Blvd. N.W., Boca Raton, Florida 33431-9868. (800) 272-7737. 1991. Reviews the newest data available on both nutritional and toxicological aspects of trace elements. Assesses the current state of knowledge on the relationship between trace elements and human health and disease.

Trace Elements in Soils and Plants. Alina Kabata-Pendias and Henryk Pendias. CRC Press, 2000 Corporate Blvd. N.W., Boca Raton, Florida 33431. (800) 272-7737. 1991. 2d ed. Discusses the pollution of air, water, soil and plants, all about soil processes, and the involvement of trace elements in the soil and plants.

HANDBOOKS AND MANUALS

Tables of Physical and Chemical Constants and Some Mathematical Functions. G. W. C. Kaye, et al. Longman Group Ltd., Longman House, Burnt Mill, Harlow, England CM20 2J6. 0279 426721. 1988. Fifteenth edition. Includes tables on mechanical properties, density, elasticity, viscosity, surface tension, temperature and heat. Also covers radiation, optics, chemistry, electrochemistry, astrophysics, and chemical thermodynamics.

ONLINE DATA BASES

CERCLIS. Chemical Information Systems, Inc., 7215 York Rd., Baltimore, Maryland 21212. (301) 321-8440. Information on hazardous waste disposal sites that have either been listed by the EPA on the National Priority List (NPL) or nominated for consideration for the NPL.

Chemical Abstracts-CA. Chemical Abstracts Service, 2540 Olentangy River Rd., P.O. Box 3012, Columbus, Ohio 43210. (800) 848-6533 or (614) 421-3600. Information sources include 9000 journals, patents from 27 countries, two industrial property organizations, new books, conference proceedings, and government research reports.

Chemical Collection System/Request Tracking–CCS/ RTS. U.S. Environmental Protection Agency, Office of Pesticides and Toxic Substances, 401 M St., SW, Washington, District of Columbia 20460. (202) 260-2090. Contains information on various properties of a number of chemicals including environmental effects, test and analysis methods, and health effects. Available from EPA.

Chemical Dictionary Online–CHEMLINE. Chemical Abstracts Service, 2540 Olentangy River Rd., Columbus, Ohio 43210. (614) 421-3600 or (800) 848-6533. Part of MEDLINE of the National Library of Medicine (NLM). File of 900,000 names for chemical substances, representing 450,000 unique compounds. It contains such information as Chemical Abstracts (CA) Service Registry Numbers, molecular formulas, preferred chemical nomenclature, and generic and ring structure information. Available on NLM's ELHILL system.

Chemical Exposure. Science Applications International Corp., Health & Environmental Information, P.O. Box 2501, Oak Ridge, Tennessee 37831. (615) 482-9031. Database of chemicals that have been identified in both human tissues and body fluids and in feral and food animals. Contains reference to journal articles, conferences, and reports. Covers the whole fields of information related to human and animal exposure to food, air, and water contaminants and pharmaceuticals. Its records include information on chemical properties, formulas, tissues measured, analytical method used, demographics and more. Available on DIALOG.

Computerized Engineering Index–COMPENDEX. Engineering Information Inc., 345 E. 47th St., New York, New York 10017. (212) 705-7600.

Monthly Catalog of United States Government Publications. U.S. G.P.O., Supt. of Docs., PO Box 371954, Pittsburgh, Pennsylvania 15250-7954. (202) 512-0000.

National Technical Information Service. U.S. Department of Commerce, National Technical Information Service, Office of Data Base Services, 5285 Port Royal Rd., Springfield, Virginia 22161. (703) 487-4807. Bibliographic database of government sponsored research and technical reports.

RESEARCH CENTERS AND INSTITUTES

Soil and Environmental Chemistry Lab. Pennsylvania State University, 104 Research Unit A, University Park, Pennsylvania 16802. (814) 865-1221.

University of Michigan, Wetland Ecosystem Research Group. Department of Chemical Engineering, 3094 Dow Building, Ann Arbor, Michigan 48109. (313) 764-3362.

University of Missouri, Environmental Trace Substances Research Center. 5450 South Sinclair Road, Columbia, Missouri 65203. (314) 882-2151.

University of Southern Mississippi, Center for Marine Science. John C. Stennis Space Center, Stennis Space Center, Mississippi 39529. (601) 688-3177.

Water Quality Laboratory. Western Illinois University, Department of Chemistry, Macomb, Illinois 61455. (309) 298-1356.

STATISTICS SOURCES

Quality Assurance Data for Routine Water Analysis. U.S. Geological Survey. U.S. G.P.O., Washington, District of Columbia 20401. (202) 512-0000. Annual. Test results determining alkalinity, inorganic ion, trace metal and organic nutrients.

TRADE ASSOCIATIONS AND PROFESSIONAL SOCIETIES

American Chemical Society. 1155 16th St., N.W., Washington, District of Columbia 20036. (202) 872-4600.

TRANSFORMERS

ABSTRACTING AND INDEXING SERVICES

Applied Science and Technology Index. H.W. Wilson Co., 950 University Ave., Bronx, New York 10452. (800) 367-6770. Formerly Industrial Arts Index.

Engineering Index. The Engineering Index Inc., 345 E. 47th St., New York, New York 10017. 1962-.

Science Citation Index. Institute for Scientific Information, 3501 Market St., Philadelphia, Pennsylvania 19104. 1961-.

ENCYCLOPEDIAS AND DICTIONARIES

Encyclopedia of Physical Science and Technology. Robert A. Meyers, ed. Academic Press, c/o Harcourt Brace Jovanovich Inc., 6277 Sea Harbor Dr., Orlando, Florida 32887. (800) 346-8648. Dictionary of engineering, technology and physical sciences.

McGraw-Hill Encyclopedia of Science and Technology. McGraw-Hill, 1221 Avenue of the Americas, New York, New York 10020. (212) 512-2000 or (800) 262-4729. 1992. Seventh edition. Issued in multiple volumes including index. Includes all science and technology broad subject areas.

Van Nostrand's Scientific Encyclopedia. Glenn D. Considine, ed. Van Nostrand Reinhold, 115 5th Ave., New York, New York 10003. (212) 254-3232. 1983. Sixth edition. Includes all broad subject areas in science.

ONLINE DATA BASES

Computerized Engineering Index–COMPENDEX. Engineering Information Inc., 345 E. 47th St., New York, New York 10017. (212) 705-7600.

TRANSMISSION LINES

See: ELECTRIC POWER LINES–ENVIRONMENTAL ASPECTS

TRANSPIRATION

See also: CLIMATE; HYDROLOGY; PLANTS

ABSTRACTING AND INDEXING SERVICES

Engineering Index. The Engineering Index Inc., 345 E. 47th St., New York, New York 10017. 1962-.

Science Citation Index. Institute for Scientific Information, 3501 Market St., Philadelphia, Pennsylvania 19104. 1961-.

ENCYCLOPEDIAS AND DICTIONARIES

Van Nostrand's Scientific Encyclopedia. Glenn D. Considine, ed. Van Nostrand Reinhold, 115 5th Ave., New York, New York 10003. (212) 254-3232. 1983. Sixth edition. Includes all broad subject areas in science.

ONLINE DATA BASES

Computerized Engineering Index–COMPENDEX. Engineering Information Inc., 345 E. 47th St., New York, New York 10017. (212) 705-7600.

RESEARCH CENTERS AND INSTITUTES

University of Wisconsin-Superior, Center for Lake Superior Environmental Studies. 1800 Grand Avenue, Superior, Wisconsin 54880. (715) 394-8315.

TRANSPORTATION

ABSTRACTING AND INDEXING SERVICES

Applied Science and Technology Index. H.W. Wilson Co., 950 University Ave., Bronx, New York 10452. (800) 367-6770. Formerly Industrial Arts Index.

Engineering Index. The Engineering Index Inc., 345 E. 47th St., New York, New York 10017. 1962-.

Green Engineering: A Current Awareness Bulletin. Institution of Mechanical Engineers, 1 Birdcage Walk, Westminster, London, England SW1H 9JJ. 71973 1266/7. 1991. Monthly. Covers acid rain, aerosol technology, biotechnology chlorofluorocarbons, chemical and process engineering, environmental protection, energy conservation, energy generation, greenhouse effect, materials, pollution, recycling, waste disposal, and other environmental topics.

Science Citation Index. Institute for Scientific Information, 3501 Market St., Philadelphia, Pennsylvania 19104. 1961-.

Transportation Energy Research. National Technical Information Service, 5285 Port Royal Rd., Springfield, Virginia 22161. (703) 487-4650. 1986-. Monthly. Engineering and design of energy-efficient advanced automotive propulsion systems and other aspects of energy conservation measures involving transportation .

Transportation Research News. National Academy of Science, Transportation Research Board, Box 289, Washington, District of Columbia 20055. (202) 334-3213. 1982. Monthly.

DIRECTORIES

Directory of the Transportation Research Board. Jewelene Gaskins, ed. Transportation Research Board, National Research Council, 2101 Constitution Ave. NW, Washington, District of Columbia 20418. (202) 334-2934. 1991. Gives information on committees and membership. Includes alphabetical listing of (U.S. and foreign) committee members and associates, and a list of TRB awards and recipients.

ENCYCLOPEDIAS AND DICTIONARIES

Dictionary of Environmental Engineering and Related Sciences: English-Spanish, Spanish-English. Jose T. Villate. Ediciones Universal, 3090 SW 8th St., Miami, Florida 33135. (305) 642-3355. 1979.

Encyclopedia of Environmental Science and Engineering. J.R. Pfafflin. Gordon and Breach Science Publishers, Inc., 270 8th Ave., New York, New York 10011. (212) 206-8900. 1992.

Encyclopedia of Physical Science and Technology. Robert A. Meyers, ed. Academic Press, c/o Harcourt Brace Jovanovich Inc., 6277 Sea Harbor Dr., Orlando, Florida 32887. (800) 346-8648. Dictionary of engineering, technology and physical sciences.

McGraw-Hill Encyclopedia of Science and Technology. McGraw-Hill, 1221 Avenue of the Americas, New York, New York 10020. (212) 512-2000 or (800) 262-4729. 1992. Seventh edition. Issued in multiple volumes including index. Includes all science and technology broad subject areas.

Van Nostrand's Scientific Encyclopedia. Glenn D. Considine, ed. Van Nostrand Reinhold, 115 5th Ave., New York, New York 10003. (212) 254-3232. 1983. Sixth edition. Includes all broad subject areas in science.

GENERAL WORKS

Alternatives to the Automobile: Transport for Livable Cities. Marcia D. Lowe. Worldwatch Institute, 1776 Massachusetts Ave., N.W., Washington, District of Columbia 20036-1904. 1990.

The Bicycle: Vehicle for a Small Planet. Marcia D. Lowe. Worldwatch Institute, 1776 Massachusetts Ave., N.W., Washington, District of Columbia 20036-1904. 1989.

Car Trouble. James J. MacKenzie, et al. World Resources Institute, 1709 New York Ave., N.W., Washington, District of Columbia 20006. 1992. Reviews the technical options for air purification, cleaner fuels, more flexible transportation systems, and more intelligent city planning, among others.

Drive for Clean Air: Natural Gas and Methane Vehicles. James Spencer Cannon. INFORM, 381 Park Ave. S., New York, New York 10016. (212) 689-4040. 1989.

Driving Forces: Motor Vehicle Trends and Their Implications for Global Warming, Energy Strategies, and Transportation. James J. MacKenzie and Michael P. Walsh. World Resources Institute, 1709 New York Ave., Washington, District of Columbia 20006. (800) 822-0504. 1990. Overview of new-vehicle fuel efficiency, reductions in air pollution emissions, and overall improvements in transportation and land-use as they relate to global warming planning. Also available through State University of New York Press.

Fighting Noise in 1990s. Organisation for Economic Cooperation and Development. OECD Publication and Information Center, 2001 L. St. N.W., Suite 700, Washington, District of Columbia 20036. (202) 785-6323. 1991. Deals with transportation noise pollution. Includes the economic impacts and relevant legislation.

Hazardous Materials Transportation Accidents. National Fire Protection Association, 1 Battery Park, Quincy, Massachusetts 02269. (617) 770-3000; (800) 344-3555. 1978. Compilation of articles from Fire Journal and Fire Command. Deals with transportation of hazardous substances, their combustibility during accidents and preventive measures.

Steering a New Course: Transportation, Energy and the Environment. Deborah Gordon. Island Press, 1718 Connecticut Ave. N.W., Suite 300, Washington, District of Columbia 20009. (202) 232-7933. 1991. Includes a history of modern American transportation, an overview of the U.S. transportation sector, and an in-depth discussion of the strategies that hold the most promise for the future. Also has information on alternative fuels, advances in mass transit, ultra fuel efficient vehicles, high-occupancy vehicle facilities and telecommuting and alternative work schedules.

Transport and the Environment. OECD Publications and Information Center, 2001 L St., N.W., Suite 700, Washington, District of Columbia 20036. (202) 785-OECD. 1988. Comprehensive overview of the impact on the environment of road transport. Assesses the efficacy of technical changes to motor vehicles to reduce air pollution and noise and evaluates innovations in the management of the transport systems of ten large cities in OECD countries.

Transport Policy and the Environment. OECD Publications and Information Center, 2001 L St., N.W., Suite 700, Washington, District of Columbia 20036. (202) 785-OECD. 1990. Describes how the government is addressing the adverse environmental effects of transport and the challenges that lie ahead.

HANDBOOKS AND MANUALS

A National Compendium of Freshwater Fish and Water Temperature Data. Kenneth E. Biesinger. U.S. Environmental Protection Agency, Environmental Research Laboratory, Office of Research and Development, 6201 Congdon Blvd., Duluth, Minnesota 55804. (218) 720-5500. 1979. River temperature, thermal pollution of rivers and lakes, and freshwater fishes.

ONLINE DATA BASES

Computerized Engineering Index–COMPENDEX. Engineering Information Inc., 345 E. 47th St., New York, New York 10017. (212) 705-7600.

Enviroline. R. R. Bowker Co., Bowker Electronic Publishing, 121 Chanlon Rd., New Providence, New Jersey 07974. (800) 521-8110.

Environmental Bibliography. Environmental Studies Institute, International Academy at Santa Barbara, 800 Garden St., Ste. D, Santa Barbara, California 93101. (805) 965-5010. International periodical literature dealing with environmental topics such as air pollution, water treatment, energy conservation, noise abatement, soil mechanics, wildlife preservation, and chemical wastes.

Monthly Catalog of United States Government Publications. U.S. G.P.O., Supt. of Docs., PO Box 371954, Pittsburgh, Pennsylvania 15250-7954. (202) 512-0000.

National Technical Information Service. U.S. Department of Commerce, National Technical Information Service, Office of Data Base Services, 5285 Port Royal Rd., Springfield, Virginia 22161. (703) 487-4807. Bibliographic database of government sponsored research and technical reports.

Transportation Research Information Service–TRIS. Transportation Research Board, Box 289, Washington, District of Columbia 20055. (202) 334-3213.

PERIODICALS AND NEWSLETTERS

Highways and Transportation: Journal of the Institution of Highways and Transportation & HTTA. The Institution of Highways and Transportation, 3 Lygon Place, Elbury St., London, England SW1 0JS. (01) 730-5245. 1983-. Monthly. Information on roads and traffic for highway and transportation engineers.

Journal of Environmental Science and Health. Marcel Dekker, Inc., 270 Madison Ave., New York, New York 10016. (212) 696-9000. Bimonthly. Concerns pesticides, food contaminants, chemical carcinogens, and agricultural wastes.

Journal of the Transportation Research Forum. Transportation Research Forum, 103 S. Howard St., Box 405, Oxford, Indiana 47971. 1962-. Annual. Continues Transportation Research Forum Proceedings.

Pedestrian Research. American Pedestrian Assn., PO Box 624, Forest Hills, New York 11375. Quarterly. Pedestrian environment and protection against vehicular encroachments.

Transportation Science. Operations Research Society of America, Mount Royal and Guilford Ave., Baltimore, Maryland 21202. (301) 528-4146. 1967-. Quarterly.

RESEARCH CENTERS AND INSTITUTES

Institute of Transportation Engineers. 525 School St., S.W., Suite 410, Washington, District of Columbia 20024. (202) 554-8050.

STATISTICS SOURCES

Air Transport, 1990. Air Transport Association of America, 1709 New York Ave., NW, Washington, District of Columbia 20006-5206. Annual. Statistics on finances and operations of scheduled air carriers.

FAA Aviation Forecasts. U.S. Federal Aviation Administration. U.S. G.P.O., Washington, District of Columbia 20401. (202) 512-0000. Annual. Data on air traffic activity at major hubs projected to 2005.

FAA Statistical Handbook of Aviation. U.S. G.P.O., Washington, District of Columbia 20401. (202) 512-0000. Annual. Detailed and comprehensive data on all phases of aviation- related regulated by the FAA.

National Urban Mass Transportation Statistics. U.S. Urban Mass Transportation Administration. U.S. G.P.O., Washington, District of Columbia 20401. (202) 512-0000. Annual. Data on public transit use by type, including car and van pools.

OECD Environmental Data Compendium 1989. OECD Publications and Information Center, 2001 L St. N.W., Suite 700, Washington, District of Columbia 20036. (202) 785-OECD. 1989. Provides statistical data for OECD countries on air pollution, water pollution, the marine environment, land use, forests, wildlife, solid waste, noise and radioactivity. Also provides data on the underlying pressures on the environment such as energy use, transportation, industrial activity and agriculture.

Selected Highway Statistics and Charts. U.S. Federal Highway Administration. U.S. G.P.O., Washington, District of Columbia 20401. (202) 512-0000. Annual. Travel mileage on public roads and motor fuel use.

Transit Fact Book. American Public Transit Association, 1201 New York Ave., NW, Suite 400, Washington, District of Columbia 20005. 1975-. Annual. Mass transportation systems finances, operations, equipment, employment, energy use, and governmental assistance.

Transport Statistics in the United States. U.S. Interstate Commerce Commission. U.S. GPO, Washington, District of Columbia 20401. (202) 512-0000. Annual. Data on intercity motor carriers and railroads and water services.

Transportation Energy Data Book. Stacy C. Davis and Patricia S. Hu. Oak Ridge National Laboratory, Transportation Energy Group, PO Box 2008, Oak Ridge, Tennessee 37831-6050. (615) 576-1746. 1991. Eleventh edition. Data book represents an assembly and display of statistics that characterize transportation activity and presents data on other factors that influence transportation energy use.

Urban Rail Transit Projects. U.S. Urban Mass Transportation Administration. U.S. G.P.O., Washington, District of Columbia 20401. (202) 512-0000. 1989. Data on actual ridership, costs, mileage, areas served and impacts.

TRADE ASSOCIATIONS AND PROFESSIONAL SOCIETIES

Advanced Transit Association. 1200 18th St., N.W., Suite 610, Washington, District of Columbia 20036. (703) 591-8328.

American Railway Engineering Association. 50 F St., N.W., Suite 7702, Washington, District of Columbia 20001. (202) 639-2190.

American Society of Civil Engineers. 345 East 47th St., New York, New York 10017. (212) 705-7496.

Association of American Railroads. 50 F St., N.W., Washington, District of Columbia 20001. (202) 639-2333.

Chemical Waste Transportation Council. 1730 Rhode Island Ave., N.W., Suite 1000, Washington, District of Columbia 20036. (202) 659-4613.

Committee for Better Transit. P.O. Box 3106, Long Island, New York 11103. (718) 278-0650.

National Defense Transportation Association. 50 S. Pickett St., Suite 220, Alexandria, Virginia 22304-3008. (703) 571-5011.

National Industrial Transportation League. 1700 N. Moore St., Suite 1900, Arlington, Virginia 22209-1904. (703) 524-5011.

National Utility Contractors Association. 1235 Jefferson Davis Hwy., Suite 606, Arlington, Virginia 22202. (703) 486-2100.

Project Lighthawk. P.O. Box 8163, Santa Fe, New Mexico 87504. (505) 982-9656.

Railway Fuel & Operating Officers Association. Box 8496, Springfield, Illinois 62791. (217) 544-7834.

Recreation Vehicle Industry Association. 1896 Preston White Dr., Reston, Virginia 22090. (703) 620-6003.

Specialty Vehicle Institute of America. 2 Jenner St., Ste. 150, Irvine, California 92718. (714) 727-3727.

Transportation Alternatives. 494 Broadway, New York, New York 10012. (212) 941-4600.

Transportation Institute. 5201 Auth Way, Camp Springs, Maryland 20746. (301) 423-3335.

Transportation Research Board. Box 289, Washington, District of Columbia 20055. (202) 334-3213.

Transportation Research Forum. 1600 Wilson Blvd., #905, Arlington, Virginia 22209. (703) 525-1191.

TRANSPORTATION EMISSIONS
See: EMISSIONS

TRANSPORTATION NOISE
See: NOISE

TRANSPORTATION OF HAZARDOUS MATERIALS
See also: HAZARDOUS MATERIALS; HAZARDOUS WASTES

ABSTRACTING AND INDEXING SERVICES

Applied Science and Technology Index. H.W. Wilson Co., 950 University Ave., Bronx, New York 10452. (800) 367-6770. Formerly Industrial Arts Index.

Biological and Agricultural Index. H.W. Wilson Co., 950 University Ave., Bronx, New York 10452. (800) 367-6770. 1916-. Monthly.

Engineering Index. The Engineering Index Inc., 345 E. 47th St., New York, New York 10017. 1962-.

Index to Scientific Book Contents. Institute for Scientific Information, 3501 Market St., Philadelphia, Pennsylvania 19104. (800) 523-1857. 1985-. Annual. Gives contents of science books published.

INIS Atomindex. International Atomic Energy Agency, Wagramerstrasse 5, Vienna, Austria A-1400. 222 23606198. 1988-. Semiannual. Abstracts nuclear energy and nuclear physics topics from journals, conferences, technical reports and other related publications. Issued in 6 parts: Personal Author, Corporate Entry, Subject, Report, Standard Patent, Conference (by place), Conference (by date).

Pollution Abstracts. Cambridge Scientific Abstracts, 5161 River Rd., Bethesda, Maryland 20816. (301) 961-6750. Six/year. Indexes worldwide technical literature on environmental pollution. Covers air pollution, marine and freshwater pollution, sewage and wastewater treatment, waste management, toxicology and health, noise pollution, radiation, land pollution, and environmental policies, programs, legislation, and education. Also available online.

Radioactive Waste Management. National Technical Information Service, 5285 Port Royal Rd., Springfield, Virginia 22161. (703) 487-4650. Monthly. Topics include spent-fuel transport and storage; radioactive effluents from nuclear facilities; and techniques of processing wastes, their storage, and ultimate disposal.

Science Citation Index. Institute for Scientific Information, 3501 Market St., Philadelphia, Pennsylvania 19104. 1961-.

Transportation Research News. National Academy of Science, Transportation Research Board, Box 289, Washington, District of Columbia 20055. (202) 334-3213. 1982. Monthly.

BIBLIOGRAPHIES

Hazardous Materials: Sources of Information on Their Transportation. Nigel Lees. British Library Science Reference and Information Service, London, England 1990.

The Transportation of Hazardous Materials. Joseph Lee Cook. Vance Bibliographies, PO Box 229, 112 N. Charter St., Monticello, Illinois 61856. (217) 762-3831. 1986.

DIRECTORIES

Directory of Chemical Waste Transporters. Chemical Waste Transport Institute. National Solid Waste Management Association, 1730 Rhode Island Ave. N.W., Suite 1000, Washington, District of Columbia 20036. (202) 659-4613. 1989.

Hazardous Materials Advisory Council–Directory. Hazardous Materials Advisory Council, 1110 Vermont Ave., N.W., Suite 250, Washington, District of Columbia 20005. (202) 728-1460.

Official Guide for the Transportation of Hazardous Materials. K III Press, 424 W. 33rd St., 11th Fl., New York, New York 10001. (212) 714-3100. Directory of services available to transport hazardous material.

ENCYCLOPEDIAS AND DICTIONARIES

Dictionary of Environmental Engineering and Related Sciences: English-Spanish, Spanish-English. Jose T. Villate. Ediciones Universal, 3090 SW 8th St., Miami, Florida 33135. (305) 642-3355. 1979.

Encyclopedia of Environmental Science and Engineering. J.R. Pfafflin. Gordon and Breach Science Publishers, Inc., 270 8th Ave., New York, New York 10011. (212) 206-8900. 1992.

Grzimek's Encyclopedia of Ecology. Bernhard Grzimek. Van Nostrand Reinhold, 115 5th Ave., New York, New York 10003. (212) 254-3232. 1976.

McGraw-Hill Encyclopedia of Environmental Science. Sybil P. Parker. McGraw-Hill Science & Engineering Books, 11 W. 19th St., New York, New York 10011. (212) 337-6010. 1980. Covers ecology, man's influence on nature, and environmental protection.

North American Reference Encyclopedia of Ecology and Pollution. William White. North American Pub. Co., 401 N. Broad St., Philadelphia, Pennsylvania 19108. (215) 238-5300. 1972.

Van Nostrand's Scientific Encyclopedia. Glenn D. Considine, ed. Van Nostrand Reinhold, 115 5th Ave., New York, New York 10003. (212) 254-3232. 1983. Sixth edition. Includes all broad subject areas in science.

GENERAL WORKS

Hazardous Materials Transportation. Department of California Highway Patrol, PO Box 94298, Sacramento, California 94298-0001. (916) 445-1865. 1985. Hazardous substances transportation law and legislation in California.

Hazardous Waste Management. S. Maltezou, et al., eds. Cassell PLC, Publishers Distribution Center, PO Box C831, Rutherford, New Jersey 07070. (201) 939-6064; (201) 939-6065. 1989.

Mailing of Biological Toxins and Etiologic Agents. Washington, District of Columbia 1990. Hazardous substances transportation through the postal service.

Safety in the Use of Asbestos. International Labour Office, 49 Sheridan Ave., Albany, New York 12210. (518) 436-9686. 1990. An ILO code of practice. The first part of the code includes monitoring in the work place, preventive measures, the protection and supervision of the workers' health, and the packaging, handling, transport and disposal of asbestos waste. More detailed guidance on the limitation of exposure to asbestos in specific activities is given in the second part of the code, which includes sections on mining and milling, asbestos cement, textiles, friction materials, and the removal of asbestos-containing materials.

Transportation of Hazardous Materials: A Management Guide for Generators and Manufactuerers. William E. Kenworthy. Government Institutes, Inc., 4 Research Pl., Suite 200, Rockville, Maryland 20850. (301) 921-2300. 1989. A management guide for generators of hazardous waste. Covers of hazardous materials regulation, alternative shipping methods for generators, and useful approaches for achieving compliance.

Transportation of Urban Radionuclides in Urban Environs. Nancy C. Finlay. Nuclear Regulatory Commission, 1717 H St. NW, Washington, District of Columbia 20555. (301) 492-7000. 1980. Environmental aspects of transportation of radioactive substances.

GOVERNMENTAL ORGANIZATIONS

Office of Hazardous Materials Transportation. 400 7th St., S.W., Washington, District of Columbia 20590. (202) 366-0656.

HANDBOOKS AND MANUALS

Hazardous Materials Guide: Shipping, Materials Handling, and Transportation. J. J. Keller & Associates, Inc., 3003 W. Breezewood, PO Box 368, Neenah, Wisconsin 54957-0368. (414) 722-2848. Laws and procedures relating to the packing and transportation of hazardous substances.

Recommendations of the Transport of Dangerous Goods: Test and Criteria. United Nations Publications, Sales Section, Room DC2-0853, Department 733, New York, New York 10017. (800) 253-9646. Companion to the ORANGE BOOK which provides technical guidelines on the transport of dangerous explosive substances and organic peroxides.

Storage, Shipment, Handling, and Disposal of Chemical Agents and Hazardous Chemicals. Department of the Army, The Pentagon, Washington, District of Columbia 20310. (202) 545-6700. 1989. Safety measures and transportation of chemicals.

ONLINE DATA BASES

Chemical Hazard Response Information System–CHRIS. U.S. Coast Guard. Office of Research and Development, 2100 2d St., NW., Rm. 5410 C, Washington, District of Columbia 20593. (202) 783-3238. Contains information needed to respond to emergencies that occur during the transport of hazardous chemicals, as well as information that can help prevent emergency situations. Each of the approximately 1,300 records include information on physical and chemical properties, health and fire hazards, labeling, chemical reactivity, hazard classification and water pollution. Available on CIS and on Microdex's TOMES Plus series.

Computerized Engineering Index–COMPENDEX. Engineering Information Inc., 345 E. 47th St., New York, New York 10017. (212) 705-7600.

Monthly Catalog of United States Government Publications. U.S. G.P.O., Supt. of Docs., PO Box 371954, Pittsburgh, Pennsylvania 15250-7954. (202) 512-0000.

National Technical Information Service. U.S. Department of Commerce, National Technical Information Service, Office of Data Base Services, 5285 Port Royal Rd., Springfield, Virginia 22161. (703) 487-4807. Bibliographic database of government sponsored research and technical reports.

PressNet Environmental Reports. Chemical Information Systems, Inc., 7215 York Rd., Baltimore, Maryland 21212. (301) 321-8440.

SCISEARCH. Institute for Scientific Information, University City Science Center, 3501 Market St., Philadelphia, Pennsylvania 19104. (215) 386-0100.

Transportation Legislative Data Base. Battelle Memorial Institute, Office of Transportation Systems and Planning, 505 King Ave., Columbus, Ohio 43201-2693. (614) 424-5606. Shipment of radioactive materials which have been introduced, enacted, or denied at U.S. federal, state, or local levels of government.

Transportation Research Information Service–TRIS. Transportation Research Board, Box 289, Washington, District of Columbia 20055. (202) 334-3213.

TSCA Plant and Production Data. Chemical Information Systems, Inc., 7215 York Rd., Baltimore, Maryland 21212. (301) 321-8440. Unique substances data, which represents the non-confidential portion of reports received by the Environmental Protection Agency as a result of the U.S. Toxic Substances Control Act.

PERIODICALS AND NEWSLETTERS

Hazardous Materials Transportation. Bureau of National Affairs, 1231 25th St. NW, Washington, District of Columbia 20037. (202) 452-4200. Monthly. Covers rules and regulations governing the shipment of hazardous materials in the U.S.

Hazmat News: The Authoritative News Resource for Hazardous Control and Waste Management. Stevens Publishing Co., PO Box 2604, Waco, Texas 76702-2604. (817) 776-9000. Semimonthly. Hazardous materials transportation, storage, and disposal.

Toxic Materials Transport. Business Publishers, Inc., 951 Pershing Dr., Silver Spring, Maryland 20910. (301) 587-6300. Biweekly. Covers new laws and regulations at federal, state and local levels.

STATISTICS SOURCES

Annual Report on Hazardous Materials Transportation. U.S. Department of Transportation, Research and Transportation Bureau. U.S. G.P.O., Washington, District of Columbia Annual.

TRADE ASSOCIATIONS AND PROFESSIONAL SOCIETIES

Chemical Waste Transportation Council. 1730 Rhode Island Ave., N.W., Suite 1000, Washington, District of Columbia 20036. (202) 659-4613.

Chemical Waste Transportation Institute. c/o National Solid Wastes Management Association, 1730 Rhode Island Ave., N.W., 10th Floor, Washington, District of Columbia 20036. (202) 659-4613.

Conference on Safe Transportation of Hazardous Articles. c/o Lawrence W. Bierlein, 2300 N. St., N.W., Washington, District of Columbia 20037. (202) 663-9245.

Hazardous Materials Advisory Council. 1110 Vermont Ave. N.W., Ste. 250, Washington, District of Columbia 20005. (202) 728-1460.

Transportation Research Board. Box 289, Washington, District of Columbia 20055. (202) 334-3213.

TRASH

See: MUNICIPAL WASTES

TREATIES

See: INTERNATIONAL TREATIES

TREATMENT

See: WASTEWATER TREATMENT

TREE RINGS

See also: WOOD

ABSTRACTING AND INDEXING SERVICES

Applied Ecology Abstracts Studies in Renewable Natural Resources. Information Retrieval Ltd., 1911 Jefferson Davis Highway, Arlington, Virginia 22202. 1975-. Monthly.

Biological and Agricultural Index. H.W. Wilson Co., 950 University Ave., Bronx, New York 10452. (800) 367-6770. 1916-. Monthly.

Ecological Abstracts. Geo Abstracts Ltd. Elsevier Applied Science, Crown House, Linton Rd., Barking, England IG 11 8JU. 1974-. Derived from over 600 leading ecological and environmental journals, plus books, conference proceedings, reports and theses.

Multimedia Index to Ecology. National Information Center for Educational Media, University of Southern California, Los Angeles, California 90007.

Science Citation Index. Institute for Scientific Information, 3501 Market St., Philadelphia, Pennsylvania 19104. 1961-.

ENCYCLOPEDIAS AND DICTIONARIES

The Encyclopedia of Climatology. John E. Oliver and Rhodes W. Fairbridge, eds. Van Nostrand Reinhold, 115 5th Ave., New York, New York 10003. (212) 254-3232. 1987. Belongs in the series Encyclopedia of Earth Sciences, v.11.

McGraw-Hill Encyclopedia of Science and Technology. McGraw-Hill, 1221 Avenue of the Americas, New York, New York 10020. (212) 512-2000 or (800) 262-4729. 1992. Seventh edition. Issued in multiple volumes including index. Includes all science and technology broad subject areas.

Van Nostrand's Scientific Encyclopedia. Glenn D. Considine, ed. Van Nostrand Reinhold, 115 5th Ave., New York, New York 10003. (212) 254-3232. 1983. Sixth edition. Includes all broad subject areas in science.

RESEARCH CENTERS AND INSTITUTES

University of Arizona, Laboratory of Tree-Ring Research. Tucson, Arizona 85721. (602) 621-2191.

TRADE ASSOCIATIONS AND PROFESSIONAL SOCIETIES

American Institute of Biological Sciences. 730 11th St., N.W., Washington, District of Columbia 20001-4521. (202) 628-1500.

Tree-Ring Society. Tree-Ring Research Laboratory, University of Arizona, Tucson, Arizona 85721. (602) 621-2191.

TRICHLOROETHYLENE

ABSTRACTING AND INDEXING SERVICES

General Science Index. H. W. Wilson Co., 950 University Ave., Bronx, New York 10452. 1978-. Monthly, also issued in annual cumulation. Cumulative subject index to English language periodicals in the subject fields of astronomy, botany, chemistry, earth science, environment and conservation, food and nutrition, genetics, mathematics, medicine and health, microbiology, oceanography, physics, physiology and zoology.

Science Citation Index. Institute for Scientific Information, 3501 Market St., Philadelphia, Pennsylvania 19104. 1961-.

ENCYCLOPEDIAS AND DICTIONARIES

Encyclopedia of Chemical Technology. Raymond E. Kirk. John Wiley & Sons, Inc., 605 3rd Ave., New York, New York 10158-0012. (212) 850-6000. 1991-. 4th ed. Also known as Kirk Othmer Encyclopedia of Chemical Technology; consists of 26 volumes.

Ullmanns Encyclopedia of Industrial Chemistry. Hans Jurgen Arpe and Wolfgang Gerhartz, eds. VCH Publishers, 303 NW 12th Ave., Deerfield Beach, Florida 33442-1788. (305) 428-5566. 1990. Designed to keep up with the broad spectrum of chemical technology. Thirty-six volumes of the encyclopedia have been divided into two sets: the 28 A volumes contain alphabetically arranged articles on chemicals, product groups, processes and technological concepts; and the 8 B volumes are compendia of basic knowledge in industrial chemistry.

Van Nostrand's Scientific Encyclopedia. Glenn D. Considine, ed. Van Nostrand Reinhold, 115 5th Ave., New York, New York 10003. (212) 254-3232. 1983. Sixth edition. Includes all broad subject areas in science.

GENERAL WORKS

NTP Technical Report on the Toxicology and Carcinogenesis Studies of Trichloroethylene. National Technical Information Service, 5285 Port Royal Rd., Springfield, Virginia 22161. (703)487-4650. 1988. Deals with toxicology of trichloroethylene and ethylene.

Organic Solvents: Physical Properties and Methods of Solvents. John A. Riddick, et al. John Wiley & Sons, Inc., 605 3rd Ave., New York, New York 10158-0012. (212) 850-6000. 1986. 4th ed.

HANDBOOKS AND MANUALS

Catalog Handbook of Fine Chemicals. Aldrich Chemical Co., 1001 W. St. Paul Ave., Milwaukee, Wisconsin 53233. (414) 273-3850 or (800) 558-9160. 1990/1991. Contains more than 27,000 products of which over 4,000 are new. Includes: chemicals, equipment, glassware, books, software, research products, bulk quantities, new products, custom synthesis and rare chemicals.

Documentation of the Threshold Limit Values. American Conference of Governmental Industrial Hygienists, 6500 Glenway, Building D-5, Cincinnati, Ohio 45211. 1991. Provides threshold limit value documentation for any physical phenomenon in the environment, including chemical substances and physical agents.

FDA Food Additives Analytical Manual. C. Warner, et al., eds. Association of Official Analytical Chemists, 2200 Wilson Blvd., Suite 400-P, Arlington, Virginia 22201-3301. (703) 522-3032. 1983-1987. 2 vols. Provides methodology for determining compliance with food additive regulations. Contains analytical methods that have been evaluated by the FDA or found to operate satisfactorily in at least two laboratories.

Handbook of Analytical Chemistry. Louis Meites, ed. McGraw-Hill Science & Engineering Books, 11 W. 19th St., New York, New York 10011. (212) 337-6010. 1963.

Handbook of Environmental Data on Organic Chemicals. Karel Verschueren. Van Nostrand Reinhold, 115 5th Ave., New York, New York 10003. (212) 254-3232. 1983. Covers individual substances as well as mixtures and preparations. The profiles include: properties, air pollution factors, water pollution factors, and biological effects.

Hazardous Chemicals Data Book. G. Weiss, ed. Noyes Publications, 120 Mill Rd., Park Ridge, New Jersey 07656. (201) 391-8484. 1986. 2d ed. Supplies instant information on 1015 hazardous chemicals. The data will provide rapid assistance to personnel involved with handling of hazardous chemical materials and related accidents.

Lange's Handbook of Chemistry. John A. Dean, ed. McGraw-Hill Science & Engineering Books, 11 W. 19th St., New York, New York 10011. (212) 337-6010. 1973-. 11th ed.

NIOSH Pocket Guide to Chemical Hazards. National Institute for Occupational Safety and Health, 1600 Clifton Rd. NE, Atlanta, Georgia 30333. (404) 639-3286. 1990. Presents sources of general industrial hygiene and medical surveillance information for workers, employees and others. Presents key information and data in an abbreviated format for 398 individual chemicals or chemical types.

Treatability Manual. U.S. Environmental Protection Agency, Office of Research and Development, 401 M St., SW, Washington, District of Columbia 20460. (202) 260-2090. 1983-. V.1 Treatability data. v.2 Change 2. Industrial Descriptions. v.3 Change 2. Technology for Control/removal of pollutants. v.4. Cost estimating. v.5. Change 2 summary.

ONLINE DATA BASES

CERCLIS. Chemical Information Systems, Inc., 7215 York Rd., Baltimore, Maryland 21212. (301) 321-8440. Information on hazardous waste disposal sites that have either been listed by the EPA on the National Priority List (NPL) or nominated for consideration for the NPL.

Chemical Abstracts Chemical Name Directory-CHEM-NAME. Chemical Abstracts Service, 2540 Olentangy River Rd., P.O. Box 3012, Columbus, Ohio 43210. (800) 848-6533 or (614) 421-3600. Listing of chemical substances in a dictionary type file. The Chemical Abstracts (CAS) Registry Number, molecular formula, Chemical Abstracts (CA) Substance Index Name, available synonyms, ring data and other chemical substance information is given for each entry.

Chemical Collection System/Request Tracking–CCS/RTS. U.S. Environmental Protection Agency, Office of Pesticides and Toxic Substances, 401 M St., SW, Washington, District of Columbia 20460. (202) 260-2090. Contains information on various properties of a number of chemicals including environmental effects, test and analysis methods, and health effects. Available from EPA.

Chemical Dictionary Online–CHEMLINE. Chemical Abstracts Service, 2540 Olentangy River Rd., Columbus, Ohio 43210. (614) 421-3600 or (800) 848-6533. Part of MEDLINE of the National Library of Medicine (NLM). File of 900,000 names for chemical substances, representing 450,000 unique compounds. It contains such information as Chemical Abstracts (CA) Service Registry Numbers, molecular formulas, preferred chemical nomenclature, and generic and ring structure information. Available on NLM's ELHILL system.

Chemical Exposure. Science Applications International Corp., Health & Environmental Information, P.O. Box 2501, Oak Ridge, Tennessee 37831. (615) 482-9031. Database of chemicals that have been identified in both human tissues and body fluids and in feral and food animals. Contains reference to journal articles, conferences, and reports. Covers the whole fields of information related to human and animal exposure to food, air, and water contaminants and pharmaceuticals. Its records include information on chemical properties, formulas, tissues measured, analytical method used, demographics and more. Available on DIALOG.

PERIODICALS AND NEWSLETTERS

Chemosphere: Chemistry, Biology and Toxicology as Related to Environmental Problems. Pergamon Microforms International, Inc., Fairview Park, Elmsford, New York 10523. (914) 592-7720. 1970-. Offers maximum dissemination of investigations related to the health and safety of every aspect of life. Environmental protection

encompasses a very wide field and relies on scientific research in chemistry, biology, physics, toxicology and inter-related disciplines.

Ecotoxicology and Environmental Safety. Academic Press, c/o Harcourt Brace Jovanovich Inc., 6277 Sea Harbor Dr., Orlando, Florida 32887. (800) 346-8648. 1977-. Bimonthly.

Environmental Science and Technology. American Chemical Society, 1155 16th St. N.W., Washington, District of Columbia 20036. (800) 227-5558. 1967-. Monthly. Contains research articles on various aspects of environmental chemistry, interpretative articles by invited experts and commentary on the scientific aspects of environmental management.

TRADE ASSOCIATIONS AND PROFESSIONAL SOCIETIES

American Chemical Society. 1155 16th St., N.W., Washington, District of Columbia 20036. (202) 872-4600.

American Institute of Chemical Engineers. 345 East 47th St., New York, New York 10017. (212) 705-7338.

American Institute of Chemists. 7315 Wisconsin Ave., Bethesda, Maryland 20814. (301) 652-2447.

TRICKLING FILTERS

See: WASTEWATER TREATMENT

TRIHALOMETHANE

ABSTRACTING AND INDEXING SERVICES

Chemical Abstracts. Chemical Abstracts Service, 2540 Olentangy River Rd., PO Box 3012, Columbus, Ohio 43210. (800) 848-6533. 1907-.

Science Citation Index. Institute for Scientific Information, 3501 Market St., Philadelphia, Pennsylvania 19104. 1961-.

ENCYCLOPEDIAS AND DICTIONARIES

Ullmanns Encyclopedia of Industrial Chemistry. Hans Jurgen Arpe and Wolfgang Gerhartz, eds. VCH Publishers, 303 NW 12th Ave., Deerfield Beach, Florida 33442-1788. (305) 428-5566. 1990. Designed to keep up with the broad spectrum of chemical technology. Thirty-six volumes of the encyclopedia have been divided into two sets: the 28 A volumes contain alphabetically arranged articles on chemicals, product groups, processes and technological concepts; and the 8 B volumes are compendia of basic knowledge in industrial chemistry.

Van Nostrand's Scientific Encyclopedia. Glenn D. Considine, ed. Van Nostrand Reinhold, 115 5th Ave., New York, New York 10003. (212) 254-3232. 1983. Sixth edition. Includes all broad subject areas in science.

ONLINE DATA BASES

CAS Source Index–CASSI. Chemical Abstracts Service, 2540 Olentangy River Rd., P.O. Box 3012, Columbus, Ohio 43210. (800) 848-6533 or (614) 421-3600. A listing of bibliographic and library holdings information for

scientific and technical primary literature relevant to the chemical sciences.

Chemical Abstracts-CA. Chemical Abstracts Service, 2540 Olentangy River Rd., P.O. Box 3012, Columbus, Ohio 43210. (800) 848-6533 or (614) 421-3600. Information sources include 9000 journals, patents from 27 countries, two industrial property organizations, new books, conference proceedings, and government research reports.

Chemical Abstracts Chemical Name Directory-CHEM-NAME. Chemical Abstracts Service, 2540 Olentangy River Rd., P.O. Box 3012, Columbus, Ohio 43210. (800) 848-6533 or (614) 421-3600. Listing of chemical substances in a dictionary type file. The Chemical Abstracts (CAS) Registry Number, molecular formula, Chemical Abstracts (CA) Substance Index Name, available synonyms, ring data and other chemical substance information is given for each entry.

Chemical Carcinogenesis Research Information System-CCRIS. National Library of Medicine, 8600 Rockville Pike, Bethesda, Maryland 20894. (800) 638-8480. Individual assay results and test conditions for 1,451 chemicals in the areas of carcinogenicity, mutagenicity, tumor promotion, and cocarcinogenicity.

Chemical Dictionary Online-CHEMLINE. Chemical Abstracts Service, 2540 Olentangy River Rd., Columbus, Ohio 43210. (614) 421-3600 or (800) 848-6533. Part of MEDLINE of the National Library of Medicine (NLM). File of 900,000 names for chemical substances, representing 450,000 unique compounds. It contains such information as Chemical Abstracts (CA) Service Registry Numbers, molecular formulas, preferred chemical nomenclature, and generic and ring structure information. Available on NLM's ELHILL system.

Chemical Exposure. Science Applications International Corp., Health & Environmental Information, P.O. Box 2501, Oak Ridge, Tennessee 37831. (615) 482-9031. Database of chemicals that have been identified in both human tissues and body fluids and in feral and food animals. Contains reference to journal articles, conferences, and reports. Covers the whole fields of information related to human and animal exposure to food, air, and water contaminants and pharmaceuticals. Its records include information on chemical properties, formulas, tissues measured, analytical method used, demographics and more. Available on DIALOG.

TRADE ASSOCIATIONS AND PROFESSIONAL SOCIETIES

American Chemical Society. 1155 16th St., N.W., Washington, District of Columbia 20036. (202) 872-4600.

American Institute of Chemical Engineers. 345 East 47th St., New York, New York 10017. (212) 705-7338.

American Institute of Chemists. 7315 Wisconsin Ave., Bethesda, Maryland 20814. (301) 652-2447.

TRITICALE

ABSTRACTING AND INDEXING SERVICES

Chemical Abstracts. Chemical Abstracts Service, 2540 Olentangy River Rd., PO Box 3012, Columbus, Ohio 43210. (800) 848-6533. 1907-.

Field Crop Abstracts. C. A. B. International, 845 North Park Ave., Tucson, Arizona 85719. (602) 621-7897 or (800) 528-4841. 1948-. Monthly. Covers literature on agronomy, field production, crop botany and physiology of all annual field crops, both temperate and tropical.

Science Citation Index. Institute for Scientific Information, 3501 Market St., Philadelphia, Pennsylvania 19104. 1961-.

Wheat, Barley, and Triticale. C. A. B. International, 845 North Park Ave., Tucson, Arizona 85719. (602) 621-7897 or (800) 528-4841. 1984-. Bimonthly. Abstracts the world literature in the areas of: Plant breeding and genetics; plant physiology; soil science; pests and diseases; agriculture engineering and other related areas focusing on wheat barley and triticale.

ENCYCLOPEDIAS AND DICTIONARIES

The Agriculture Dictionary. Ray V. Herren and Roy L. Donahue. Delmar Publishers Inc., 2 Computer Dr. W., Albany, New York 12212. (518) 459-1150. 1991. Covers all the agricultural areas including acid rain, acid mine drainage, food additives, agricultural engineering, conservation of the natural resources, microorganisms, triticale and other related topics.

Encyclopedia of Trademarks and Synonyms. H. Bennett, ed. Chemical Publishing Co., 80 Eighth Ave., New York, New York 10011. (212) 255-1950. 1981. Three volumes. Includes chemical compounds, compositions consisting of one or more chemicals and other products. Also included are abbreviated names and WHO free names.

Ullmanns Encyclopedia of Industrial Chemistry. Hans Jurgen Arpe and Wolfgang Gerhartz, eds. VCH Publishers, 303 NW 12th Ave., Deerfield Beach, Florida 33442-1788. (305) 428-5566. 1990. Designed to keep up with the broad spectrum of chemical technology. Thirty-six volumes of the encyclopedia have been divided into two sets: the 28 A volumes contain alphabetically arranged articles on chemicals, product groups, processes and technological concepts; and the 8 B volumes are compendia of basic knowledge in industrial chemistry.

Van Nostrand's Scientific Encyclopedia. Glenn D. Considine, ed. Van Nostrand Reinhold, 115 5th Ave., New York, New York 10003. (212) 254-3232. 1983. Sixth edition. Includes all broad subject areas in science.

ONLINE DATA BASES

Chemical Abstracts-CA. Chemical Abstracts Service, 2540 Olentangy River Rd., P.O. Box 3012, Columbus, Ohio 43210. (800) 848-6533 or (614) 421-3600. Information sources include 9000 journals, patents from 27 countries, two industrial property organizations, new books, conference proceedings, and government research reports.

Chemical Abstracts Chemical Name Directory-CHEM-NAME. Chemical Abstracts Service, 2540 Olentangy River Rd., P.O. Box 3012, Columbus, Ohio 43210. (800) 848-6533 or (614) 421-3600. Listing of chemical substances in a dictionary type file. The Chemical Abstracts (CAS) Registry Number, molecular formula, Chemical Abstracts (CA) Substance Index Name, available synonyms, ring data and other chemical substance information is given for each entry.

Chemical Carcinogenesis Research Information System–CCRIS. National Library of Medicine, 8600 Rockville Pike, Bethesda, Maryland 20894. (800) 638-8480. Individual assay results and test conditions for 1,451 chemicals in the areas of carcinogenicity, mutagenicity, tumor promotion, and cocarcinogenicity.

Chemical Collection System/Request Tracking–CCS/RTS. U.S. Environmental Protection Agency, Office of Pesticides and Toxic Substances, 401 M St., SW, Washington, District of Columbia 20460. (202) 260-2090. Contains information on various properties of a number of chemicals including environmental effects, test and analysis methods, and health effects. Available from EPA.

Chemical Dictionary Online–CHEMLINE. Chemical Abstracts Service, 2540 Olentangy River Rd., Columbus, Ohio 43210. (614) 421-3600 or (800) 848-6533. Part of MEDLINE of the National Library of Medicine (NLM). File of 900,000 names for chemical substances, representing 450,000 unique compounds. It contains such information as Chemical Abstracts (CA) Service Registry Numbers, molecular formulas, preferred chemical nomenclature, and generic and ring structure information. Available on NLM's ELHILL system.

Chemical Exposure. Science Applications International Corp., Health & Environmental Information, P.O. Box 2501, Oak Ridge, Tennessee 37831. (615) 482-9031. Database of chemicals that have been identified in both human tissues and body fluids and in feral and food animals. Contains reference to journal articles, conferences, and reports. Covers the whole fields of information related to human and animal exposure to food, air, and water contaminants and pharmaceuticals. Its records include information on chemical properties, formulas, tissues measured, analytical method used, demographics and more. Available on DIALOG.

TRADE ASSOCIATIONS AND PROFESSIONAL SOCIETIES

American Chemical Society. 1155 16th St., N.W., Washington, District of Columbia 20036. (202) 872-4600.

American Institute of Chemical Engineers. 345 East 47th St., New York, New York 10017. (212) 705-7338.

American Institute of Chemists. 7315 Wisconsin Ave., Bethesda, Maryland 20814. (301) 652-2447.

TRITIUM

ABSTRACTING AND INDEXING SERVICES

Chemical Abstracts. Chemical Abstracts Service, 2540 Olentangy River Rd., PO Box 3012, Columbus, Ohio 43210. (800) 848-6533. 1907-.

Science Citation Index. Institute for Scientific Information, 3501 Market St., Philadelphia, Pennsylvania 19104. 1961-.

ENCYCLOPEDIAS AND DICTIONARIES

McGraw-Hill Encyclopedia of Science and Technology. McGraw-Hill, 1221 Avenue of the Americas, New York, New York 10020. (212) 512-2000 or (800) 262-4729. 1992. Seventh edition. Issued in multiple volumes in-

cluding index. Includes all science and technology broad subject areas.

Ullmanns Encyclopedia of Industrial Chemistry. Hans Jurgen Arpe and Wolfgang Gerhartz, eds. VCH Publishers, 303 NW 12th Ave., Deerfield Beach, Florida 33442-1788. (305) 428-5566. 1990. Designed to keep up with the broad spectrum of chemical technology. Thirty-six volumes of the encyclopedia have been divided into two sets: the 28 A volumes contain alphabetically arranged articles on chemicals, product groups, processes and technological concepts; and the 8 B volumes are compendia of basic knowledge in industrial chemistry.

Van Nostrand's Scientific Encyclopedia. Glenn D. Considine, ed. Van Nostrand Reinhold, 115 5th Ave., New York, New York 10003. (212) 254-3232. 1983. Sixth edition. Includes all broad subject areas in science.

GENERAL WORKS

Magill's Survey of Science. Life Science Series. Frank N. Magill, ed. Salem Press, PO Box 50062, Pasadena, California 91105. 1991. Six volumes. Contents: v.1. A-Central and peripheral nervous system functions; v.2. Central metabolism regulation - eukaryotic transcriptional control; v.3. Positive and negative eukaryotic transcriptional control - mammalian hormones; v.4. Hormones and behavior - muscular contraction; v.5. Muscular contraction and relaxation - sexual reproduction in plants; v.6. Reproductive behavior and mating - X inactivation and the Lyon hypothesis.

ONLINE DATA BASES

Chemical Abstracts-CA. Chemical Abstracts Service, 2540 Olentangy River Rd., P.O. Box 3012, Columbus, Ohio 43210. (800) 848-6533 or (614) 421-3600. Information sources include 9000 journals, patents from 27 countries, two industrial property organizations, new books, conference proceedings, and government research reports.

Chemical Abstracts Chemical Name Directory-CHEMNAME. Chemical Abstracts Service, 2540 Olentangy River Rd., P.O. Box 3012, Columbus, Ohio 43210. (800) 848-6533 or (614) 421-3600. Listing of chemical substances in a dictionary type file. The Chemical Abstracts (CAS) Registry Number, molecular formula, Chemical Abstracts (CA) Substance Index Name, available synonyms, ring data and other chemical substance information is given for each entry.

TRADE ASSOCIATIONS AND PROFESSIONAL SOCIETIES

American Institute of Chemical Engineers. 345 East 47th St., New York, New York 10017. (212) 705-7338.

American Institute of Chemists. 7315 Wisconsin Ave., Bethesda, Maryland 20814. (301) 652-2447.

TROPICAL ECOLOGY

ABSTRACTING AND INDEXING SERVICES

ASFA Aquaculture Abstracts. Cambridge Scientific Abstracts, Inc., 5161 River Rd., Bethesda, Maryland 20816. (301) 961-6750. 1984.

Biological and Agricultural Index. H.W. Wilson Co., 950 University Ave., Bronx, New York 10452. (800) 367-6770. 1916-. Monthly.

Ecological Abstracts. Geo Abstracts Ltd. Elsevier Applied Science, Crown House, Linton Rd., Barking, England IG 11 8JU. 1974-. Derived from over 600 leading ecological and environmental journals, plus books, conference proceedings, reports and theses.

Index to Scientific Book Contents. Institute for Scientific Information, 3501 Market St., Philadelphia, Pennsylvania 19104. (800) 523-1857. 1985-. Annual. Gives contents of science books published.

Science Citation Index. Institute for Scientific Information, 3501 Market St., Philadelphia, Pennsylvania 19104. 1961-.

ENCYCLOPEDIAS AND DICTIONARIES

Cambridge Encyclopedia of Life Sciences. A. E. Friday and David S. Ingram. Cambridge University Press, 40 W 20th St., New York, New York 10011. (212) 924-3900 or (800) 227-0247. 1985. Includes all topics under biology and ecology.

Grzimek's Encyclopedia of Ecology. Bernhard Grzimek. Van Nostrand Reinhold, 115 5th Ave., New York, New York 10003. (212) 254-3232. 1976.

McGraw-Hill Encyclopedia of Environmental Science. Sybil P. Parker. McGraw-Hill Science & Engineering Books, 11 W. 19th St., New York, New York 10011. (212) 337-6010. 1980. Covers ecology, man's influence on nature, and environmental protection.

North American Reference Encyclopedia of Ecology and Pollution. William White. North American Pub. Co., 401 N. Broad St., Philadelphia, Pennsylvania 19108. (215) 238-5300. 1972.

Van Nostrand's Scientific Encyclopedia. Glenn D. Considine, ed. Van Nostrand Reinhold, 115 5th Ave., New York, New York 10003. (212) 254-3232. 1983. Sixth edition. Includes all broad subject areas in science.

GENERAL WORKS

Alternatives to Deforestation: Steps Toward Sustainable Use of the Amazon Rain Forest. Anthony B. Anderson, ed. Columbia University Press, 562 W. 113th St., New York, New York 10025. (212) 316-7100. 1992. Based on papers presented at an international conference in Belem, Brazil, for scientists in several fields, as well as government policy makers and representatives from foundations who are interested in exploring possible sustainable use of the world's largest rain forest, the Amazon, which is now being destroyed on an unprecedented scale.

An Amazonian Forest. C. F. Jordan. Parthenon Pub., Casterton Hall, Carnforth, England LA6 2LA. 1990. Volume 2 in the Man and the Biosphere series published jointly with UNESCO.

Carbon, Nutrient and Water Balances of Tropical Rain Forest Ecosystems Subject to Disturbance: Management Implications and Research Proposals. Jonathan M. Anderson and Thomas Spencer. UNESCO, 7, place de Fontenoy, Paris, France F-75700. (331) 45 68 40 67. 1991. MAB Digest 7.

Contributing to Sustained Resource Use in the Humid and Sub- Humid Tropics: Some Research Approaches and

Insights. Malcolm Hadley and Kathrin Schreckenberg. UNESCO, 7, place de Fontenoy, Paris, France F-75700. (331)45 68 40 67. 1989. Overview of recent, ongoing and planned activities with in the framework of MAB relating to the ecology of humid and sub-humid tropical ecosystems, principally forests and savannas.

Cutting Our Losses: Policy Reform to Sustain Tropical Forest Resources. Charles V. Barber. World Resources Institute, 1709 New York Ave. N.W., Washington, District of Columbia 20006. (800) 822-0504. 1991. Focuses on the underlying economic social and political forces that drive forest conversation and exploitation.

Ecology and Land Management in Amazonia. Michael J. Eden. Belhaven Press, 136 S. Broadway, Irvington, New York 10533. (914) 591-9111. 1990. Deals with three major areas: the rain forest as a global resource and its role in sustaining life on the planet as a whole; needs of the countries with large tracts of tropical rain forest (including the factors that relate to how one can utilize land, the climate, geomorphology, hydrology, soils and ecology); and how the Amazonia rain forest can be conserved, including the role of national parks and management at the regional level.

The Ecology of a Tropical Forest. Egbert J. Leigh, Jr., et al., eds. Smithsonian Institution Press, 470 L'Enfant Plaza, No. 7100, Washington, District of Columbia 20560. (800) 782-4612. 1983. Describes the rhythm of plant reproduction through the seasons and how it affects animal population.

Exploring the Tropical Rain Forest. D. Lamb. Parthenon Pub., Casterton Hall, Carnforth, England LA6 2LA. 1990. Volume 3 of the Man and the Biosphere series published jointly with UNESCO.

Keeping It Green: Tropical Forestry and the Mitigation of Global Warming. Mark C. Trexler. World Resources Institute, 1709 New York Ave. N.W., Washington, District of Columbia 20006. (800) 822-0504. 1991. Report links knowledge gained from past tropical forestry initiatives with expectations for their future effectiveness in the mitigation of global warming.

The Last Rain Forests: A World Conservation Atlas. Mark Collins, ed. Oxford University Press, 200 Madison Ave., New York, New York 10016. (212) 679-7300; (800) 334-4249. 1990. Containing more than 200 full color photos and maps, this is a guide to the people, flora and fauna of the richest habitats on earth. Maps the world's rain forests, spells out the problems facing these regions, and proposes concrete, realistic strategies for ensuring their survival.

The Last Tree: Reclaiming the Environment in Tropical Asia. James Rush. Asia Society, Distr: Westview, 5500 Central Ave., Boulder, Colorado 80301. (303) 444-3541. 1991. Traces the history of tropical Asia to make the point that "without an alternative, people will cut the last tree." Also describes the many nongovernmental agencies and grass-roots organizations that are working to conserve tropical forests.

Plant-Animal Interactions; Evolutionary Ecology in Tropical and Temperate Regions. Peter W. Price, et al. John Wiley & Sons, Inc., 605 3rd Ave., New York, New York 10158-0012. (212) 850-6000. 1991. Comprises a comparative analysis of the existing ecological systems of temperate and tropical regions.

Race to Save the Tropics. Robert Goodland, ed. Island Press, 1718 Connecticut Ave. N.W., Suite 300, Washington, District of Columbia 20009. (202) 232-7933. 1990. Documents the conflict between economic development and protection of biological diversity in tropical countries.

Rain Forest Regeneration and Management. G. Pompa, et al., eds. Parthenon Group Inc., 120 Mill Rd., Park Ridge, New Jersey 07656. (201) 391-6796. 1991. Explores the management implications of present scientific knowledge on rain forest generation. Providing case studies.

Reproductive Ecology of Tropical Forest Plants. K. Bawa and M. Hadley, eds. Parthenon Pub., Casterton Hall, Carnforth, England LA6 2LA. 1990. Volume 7 in the "Man and the Biosphere" series jointly published with UNESCO.

Taking Stock: The Tropical Forestry Action Plan After Five Years. Robert Winterbottom. World Resources Institute, 1709 New York Ave. N.W., Washington, District of Columbia 20006. (800) 822-0504. 1990. Analyzes Tropical Forestry Action Plan's accomplishments and shortcomings, drawing on the biannual meetings of the TFAP Forestry Advisors' groups, assessments by FAO, various aid agencies, and by such organizations as the World Rainforest Movement, Friends of the Earth, and World Life Fund.

Trees of Life: Saving Tropical Forests and their Biological Wealth. Kenton Miller and Laura Tangley. World Resources Institute, 1709 New York Ave. N.W., Washington, District of Columbia 20006. (800) 822-0504. 1991. Explains what deforestation is doing to the global environment and why rainforest preservation is valid to human welfare around the world.

Tropical Resources: Ecology and Development. Jose I. Furtado, et al., eds. Harwood Academic Publishers, PO Box 786, Cooper Sta., New York, New York 10276. (212) 206-8900. 1990. Overview of global tropical resources, both terrestrial and aquatic. Subjects discussed include forest resources, wildlife resources, general land use, pasture resources, economic development, fisheries, marine resources, and aquaculture.

Vertebrate Ecology in Northern Neotropics. John F. Esenberg, ed. Smithsonian Institution Press, 470 L'Enfant Plaza, No. 7100, Washington, District of Columbia 20560. (800) 782-4612. 1979. Comparison of faunas found in tropical forests covering several mammalian species, including the red howler monkey, crab-eating fox, cebus monkey, and the didelphid marsupials.

ONLINE DATA BASES

Monthly Catalog of United States Government Publications. U.S. G.P.O., Supt. of Docs., PO Box 371954, Pittsburgh, Pennsylvania 15250-7954. (202) 512-0000.

National Technical Information Service. U.S. Department of Commerce, National Technical Information Service, Office of Data Base Services, 5285 Port Royal Rd., Springfield, Virginia 22161. (703) 487-4807. Bibliographic database of government sponsored research and technical reports.

SCISEARCH. Institute for Scientific Information, University City Science Center, 3501 Market St., Philadelphia, Pennsylvania 19104. (215) 386-0100.

PERIODICALS AND NEWSLETTERS

Hot Topics from the Tropics. Rainforest Alliance, 270 Lafayette St., Suite 512, New York, New York 10012. (212) 941-1900. Bimonthly.

RESEARCH CENTERS AND INSTITUTES

Organization for Tropical Studies, Inc. P.O. Box DM, Duke Station, Durham, North Carolina 27706. (919) 684-5774.

Tropical Resources Institute. Yale University, School of Forestry and Environmental Studies, 205 Prospect St., New Haven, Connecticut 06511. (203) 432-5109.

University of the Virgin Islands, Environmental Research Center. St. Thomas, Virgin Islands 00802. (809) 776-9200.

TRADE ASSOCIATIONS AND PROFESSIONAL SOCIETIES

American Institute of Biological Sciences. 730 11th St., N.W., Washington, District of Columbia 20001-4521. (202) 628-1500.

Biological Institute of Tropical America. P.O. Box 2585, Menlo Park, California 94026. (415) 593-9024.

The Jessie Smith Noyes Foundation. 16 E. 34th St., New York, New York 10016. (212) 684-6577.

Rainforest Action Network. 301 Broadway, Suite 28, San Francisco, California 94133. (415) 398-4404.

Tropical Forests Working Group. 1350 New York Ave., N.W., Washington, District of Columbia 20005.

TROPICAL FORESTS

See also: BIOMES; DEFORESTATION; LAND USE; RAIN FORESTS

ABSTRACTING AND INDEXING SERVICES

Science Citation Index. Institute for Scientific Information, 3501 Market St., Philadelphia, Pennsylvania 19104. 1961-.

ALMANACS AND YEARBOOKS

Environmental Almanac. World Resources Institute. Houghton Mifflin, 1 Beacon St., Boston, Massachusetts 02108. (617) 725-5000; (800) 225-3362. 1991. Covers consumer products, energy, endangered species, food safety, global warming, solid wastes, toxics, wetlands and other related areas. Also included are the names and addresses of the chief environmental executives for all 50 states.

GENERAL WORKS

Alternatives to Deforestation: Steps Toward Sustainable Use of the Amazon Rain Forest. Anthony B. Anderson, ed. Columbia University Press, 562 W. 113th St., New York, New York 10025. (212) 316-7100. 1992. Based on papers presented at an international conference in Belem, Brazil, for scientists in several fields, as well as government policy makers and representatives from foundations who are interested in exploring possible sustainable use of the world's largest rain forest, the Amazon, which is now being destroyed on an unprecedented scale.

An Amazonian Forest. C. F. Jordan. Parthenon Pub., Casterton Hall, Carnforth, England LA6 2LA. 1990. Volume 2 in the Man and the Biosphere series published jointly with UNESCO.

Carbon, Nutrient and Water Balances of Tropical Rain Forest Ecosystems Subject to Disturbance: Management Implications and Research Proposals. Jonathan M. Anderson and Thomas Spencer. UNESCO, 7, place de Fontenoy, Paris, France F-75700. (331) 45 68 40 67. 1991. MAB Digest 7.

The Conservation Atlas of Tropical Forests: Asia and the Pacific. N. Mark Collins, Jeffery A. Sayer, and Timothy C. Whitmore. Simon & Schuster, 1230 Avenue of the Americas, New York, New York 10020. (212) 689-7000. 1991. Focuses on closed canopy, and true rain forests. This Asian volume is the first of a set of three–tropical America and Africa being the next. Address such regional subjects as forest wildlife, human impacts on forest lands, and the tropical timber trade; and includes a "Tropical Forestry Action Plan" to conserve and protect important remaining stands. The second part of the atlas gives a detailed survey of 17 countries plus the island groups of Fiji and the Solomons, but not those of New Caledonia, New Hebrides, or Micronesia.

Cutting Our Losses: Policy Reform to Sustain Tropical Forest Resources. Charles V. Barber. World Resources Institute, 1709 New York Ave. N.W., Washington, District of Columbia 20006. (800) 822-0504. 1991. Focuses on the underlying economic social and political forces that drive forest conversation and exploitation.

Ecology and Land Management in Amazonia. Michael J. Eden. Belhaven Press, 136 S. Broadway, Irvington, New York 10533. (914) 591-9111. 1990. Deals with three major areas: the rain forest as a global resource and its role in sustaining life on the planet as a whole; needs of the countries with large tracts of tropical rain forest (including the factors that relate to how one can utilize land, the climate, geomorphology, hydrology, soils and ecology); and how the Amazonia rain forest can be conserved, including the role of national parks and management at the regional level.

The Ecology of a Tropical Forest. Egbert J. Leigh, Jr., et al., eds. Smithsonian Institution Press, 470 L'Enfant Plaza, No. 7100, Washington, District of Columbia 20560. (800) 782-4612. 1983. Describes the rhythm of plant reproduction through the seasons and how it affects animal population.

Exploring the Tropical Rain Forest. D. Lamb. Parthenon Pub., Casterton Hall, Carnforth, England LA6 2LA. 1990. Volume 3 of the Man and the Biosphere series published jointly with UNESCO.

An Introduction to Tropical Rain Forests. T. C. Whitmore. Oxford University Press, 200 Madison Ave., New York, New York 10016. (212) 679-7300; (800) 334-4249. 1990. Describes the world's tropical rainforests, their structure and functioning, their value to humans, and what is being done to them.

Keeping It Green: Tropical Forestry and the Mitigation of Global Warming. Mark C. Trexler. World Resources Institute, 1709 New York Ave. N.W., Washington, District of Columbia 20006. (800) 822-0504. 1991. Report links knowledge gained from past tropical forestry

initiatives with expectations for their future effectiveness in the mitigation of global warming.

The Last Rain Forests: A World Conservation Atlas. Mark Collins, ed. Oxford University Press, 200 Madison Ave., New York, New York 10016. (212) 679-7300; (800) 334-4249. 1990. Containing more than 200 full color photos and maps, this is a guide to the people, flora and fauna of the richest habitats on earth. Maps the world's rain forests, spells out the problems facing these regions, and proposes concrete, realistic strategies for ensuring their survival.

Magill's Survey of Science. Life Science Series. Frank N. Magill, ed. Salem Press, PO Box 50062, Pasadena, California 91105. 1991. Six volumes. Contents: v.1. A-Central and peripheral nervous system functions; v.2. Central metabolism regulation - eukaryotic transcriptional control; v.3. Positive and negative eukaryotic transcriptional control - mammalian hormones; v.4. Hormones and behavior - muscular contraction; v.5. Muscular contraction and relaxation - sexual reproduction in plants; v.6. Reproductive behavior and mating - X inactivation and the Lyon hypothesis.

Portraits of the Rainforest. Adrian Forsyth. Firefly Books, PO Box 1325, Ellicot Sta., Buffalo, New York 14205. 1990. Explores the precarious contingencies that determine the nature of tropical life.

Public Policies and the Misuse of Forest Resources. Robert Repetto and Malcolm Gillis, eds. Cambridge University Press, 40 W. 20th St., New York, New York 10011. (212) 924-3900; (800) 227-0247. 1988. Case studies of forest policies in developing countries. Also deals with deforestation problems from the environmental point of view.

Race to Save the Tropics. Robert Goodland, cd. Island Press, 1718 Connecticut Ave. N.W., Suite 300, Washington, District of Columbia 20009. (202) 232-7933. 1990. Documents the conflict between economic development and protection of biological diversity in tropical countries.

Rain Forest Regeneration and Management. G. Pompa, et al., eds. Parthenon Group Inc., 120 Mill Rd., Park Ridge, New Jersey 07656. (201) 391-6796. 1991. Explores the management implications of present scientific knowledge on rain forest generation. Providing case studies.

Reproductive Ecology of Tropical Forest Plants. K. Bawa and M. Hadley, eds. Parthenon Pub., Casterton Hall, Carnforth, England LA6 2LA. 1990. Volume 7 in the "Man and the Biosphere" series jointly published with UNESCO.

The State of the Earth Atlas. Joni Seger, ed. Touchstone/ Simon and Schuster, Rockefeller Center, 1230 Avenue of the Americas, New York, New York 10020. 1990. Deals with environmental issues such as air quality, urban sprawl, toxic waste, tropical forests and tourism from a socioeconomic perspective.

Taking Stock: The Tropical Forestry Action Plan After Five Years. Robert Winterbottom. World Resources Institute, 1709 New York Ave. N.W., Washington, District of Columbia 20006. (800) 822-0504. 1990. Analyzes Tropical Forestry Action Plan's accomplishments and shortcomings, drawing on the biannual meetings of the TFAP Forestry Advisors' groups, assessments by FAO, various aid agencies, and by such organizations as the World Rainforest Movement, Friends of the Earth, and World Life Fund.

Trees of Life: Saving Tropical Forests and their Biological Wealth. Kenton Miller and Laura Tangley. World Resources Institute, 1709 New York Ave. N.W., Washington, District of Columbia 20006. (800) 822-0504. 1991. Explains what deforestation is doing to the global environment and why rainforest preservation is valid to human welfare around the world.

Tropical Forest and Its Environment. Kenneth Alan Longman. Longman Scientific & Technical, 1560 Broadway, New York, New York 10036. (212) 819 5400. 1990. Rain forest and tropical ecology, ecosystems, and cycles.

Tropical Rain Forests and the World Atmosphere. T. Ghillean. Westview Press, 5500 Central Ave., Boulder, Colorado 80301. (303) 444-3541. 1986. Deals with vegetation and climate in the tropics. Also describes the weather patterns in that part of the world.

Tropical Rainforest: A World Survey of Our Most Valuable Endangered Habitat With a Blueprint for its Survival. Arnold Newman. Facts on File, Inc., 460 Park Ave. S., New York, New York 10016. (212) 683-2244; (800) 322-8755. 1990. Considers threats to rain forests, including logging and slash and burn agricultural practices. Presents a variety of measures to preserve our valuable rain forests.

Tropical Resources: Ecology and Development. Jose I. Furtado, et al., eds. Harwood Academic Publishers, PO Box 786, Cooper Sta., New York, New York 10276. (212) 206-8900. 1990. Overview of global tropical resources, both terrestrial and aquatic. Subjects discussed include forest resources, wildlife resources, general land use, pasture resources, economic development, fisheries, marine resources, and aquaculture.

Vertebrate Ecology in Northern Neotropics. John F. Esenberg, ed. Smithsonian Institution Press, 470 L'Enfant Plaza, No. 7100, Washington, District of Columbia 20560. (800) 782-4612. 1979. Comparison of faunas found in tropical forests covering several mammalian species, including the red howler monkey, crab-eating fox, cebus monkey, and the didelphid marsupials.

World on Fire: Saving the Endangered Earth. George J. Mitchell. Scribner Educational Publishers, 866 3d Ave., New York, New York 10022. (212) 702-2000; (800) 257-5755. 1991. Discusses the problems entailed with the issues of greenhouse effect, acid rain, the rift in the stratosphere ozone layer, and the destruction of tropical rain forests.

HANDBOOKS AND MANUALS

The Conservation Atlas of Tropical Forests. N. Mark Collins. Simon & Schuster, 1230 Avenue of the Americas, New York, New York 10020. (212) 689-7000. 1991. Detailed and authoritative study of the issues surrounding deforestation-and the first complete visual analysis in country-by- country maps.

The Global Ecology Handbook: What You Can Do about the Environmental Crisis. Walter H. Corson, ed. The Global Tomorrow Coalition, Beacon Pr., 25 Beacon St., Boston, Massachusetts 02108-2800. (617) 742-2110. 1990. Covers environment, energy policy, population growth and other issues. It includes chapters on tropical rain forests, garbage, oceans and coasts, global warming, population growth, agriculture, biological diversity, fresh water, hazardous wastes, and environment and development.

ONLINE DATA BASES

SCISEARCH. Institute for Scientific Information, University City Science Center, 3501 Market St., Philadelphia, Pennsylvania 19104. (215) 386-0100.

TRADE ASSOCIATIONS AND PROFESSIONAL SOCIETIES

Greenpeace. 1436 U St., NW, Washington, District of Columbia 20009. (202) 462-1177.

International Society for the Preservation of the Tropical Rainforest. 3931 Camino de la Cumbre, Sherman Oaks, California 91423. (818) 788-2002.

International Society of Tropical Foresters, Inc. 5400 Grosvenor Ln., Bethesda, Maryland 20814. (301) 897-8720.

Rainforest Action Network. 301 Broadway, Suite 28, San Francisco, California 94133. (415) 398-4404.

Threshold, International Center for Environmental Renewal. Drawer CU, Bisbee, Arizona 85603. (602) 432-7353.

Tropical Forests Working Group. 1350 New York Ave., N.W., Washington, District of Columbia 20005.

TROPICAL LAKES

See: LAKES

TROPOSPHERE

ABSTRACTING AND INDEXING SERVICES

Science Citation Index. Institute for Scientific Information, 3501 Market St., Philadelphia, Pennsylvania 19104. 1961-.

BIBLIOGRAPHIES

Bibliography and Index of Geology. American Geological Institute, 4220 King St., Alexandria, Virginia 22302. Monthly. Includes environmental geology and hydrogeology.

ENCYCLOPEDIAS AND DICTIONARIES

The Encyclopedia of Climatology. John E. Oliver and Rhodes W. Fairbridge, eds. Van Nostrand Reinhold, 115 5th Ave., New York, New York 10003. (212) 254-3232. 1987. Belongs in the series Encyclopedia of Earth Sciences, v.11.

Van Nostrand's Scientific Encyclopedia. Glenn D. Considine, ed. Van Nostrand Reinhold, 115 5th Ave., New York, New York 10003. (212) 254-3232. 1983. Sixth edition. Includes all broad subject areas in science.

GENERAL WORKS

Fields, Currents, and Aerosols in the Lower Troposphere. A. A. Balkema, Rotterdam, Netherlands 1986.

Magill's Survey of Science. Earth Science Series. Frank N. Magill. Salem Press, PO Box 50062, Pasadena, California 91105. 1990-. Five volumes. Includes information on earth's crust, hot spots and volcanic island chains, physical properties of minerals, rock magnetism, physical properties of rocks, and index.

Man's Impact of the Troposphere: Lectures in Tropospheric Chemistry. National Technical Information Service, 5285 Port Royal Rd., Springfield, Virginia 22161. (703) 487-4650. 1978. Man's influence on nature and air pollution and atmospheric chemistry.

Natural and Anthropogenic Sources of Oxides of Nitrogen for the Troposphere. National Technical Information Service, 5285 Port Royal Rd., Springfield, Virginia 22161. (703) 487-4650. 1982. Covers nitrogen oxides, troposphere, and aircraft exhaust emissions.

ONLINE DATA BASES

SCISEARCH. Institute for Scientific Information, University City Science Center, 3501 Market St., Philadelphia, Pennsylvania 19104. (215) 386-0100.

TRADE ASSOCIATIONS AND PROFESSIONAL SOCIETIES

American Institute of Biological Sciences. 730 11th St., N.W., Washington, District of Columbia 20001-4521. (202) 628-1500.

TRUCKS AND TRANSPORTATION

ABSTRACTING AND INDEXING SERVICES

Engineering Index. The Engineering Index Inc., 345 E. 47th St., New York, New York 10017. 1962-.

ENCYCLOPEDIAS AND DICTIONARIES

Dictionary of Environmental Engineering and Related Sciences: English-Spanish, Spanish-English. Jose T. Villate. Ediciones Universal, 3090 SW 8th St., Miami, Florida 33135. (305) 642-3355. 1979.

Encyclopedia of Environmental Science and Engineering. J.R. Pfafflin. Gordon and Breach Science Publishers, Inc., 270 8th Ave., New York, New York 10011. (212) 206-8900. 1992.

ONLINE DATA BASES

Computerized Engineering Index–COMPENDEX. Engineering Information Inc., 345 E. 47th St., New York, New York 10017. (212) 705-7600.

TRADE ASSOCIATIONS AND PROFESSIONAL SOCIETIES

American Trucking Associations. 2200 Mill Rd., Alexandria, Virginia 22314. (703) 838-1700.

TUNDRA BIOMES

See also: ALPINE TUNDRAS; ARCTIC TUNDRAS

ABSTRACTING AND INDEXING SERVICES

Biological Abstracts. BIOSIS, 2100 Arch St., Philadelphia, Pennsylvania 19103-1399. (215) 587-4800. 1927-.

Biological and Agricultural Index. H.W. Wilson Co., 950 University Ave., Bronx, New York 10452. (800) 367-6770. 1916-. Monthly.

Ecological Abstracts. Geo Abstracts Ltd. Elsevier Applied Science, Crown House, Linton Rd., Barking, England IG 11 8JU. 1974-. Derived from over 600 leading ecological and environmental journals, plus books, conference proceedings, reports and theses.

Geographical Abstracts. London School of Economics, Dept. of Geography, Regency House, 34 Duke St., London, England 1966-. Continued by Geo Abstracts issued in 6 parts: Pt. A. Landforms and the quaternary; Pt. B. Biogeography and Climatology; Pt. C. Economic geography; Pt. D. Social geography and cartography; Pt. E. Sedimentology; Pt. F. Regional and community planning.

Science Citation Index. Institute for Scientific Information, 3501 Market St., Philadelphia, Pennsylvania 19104. 1961-.

BIBLIOGRAPHIES

U.S. Tundra Biome Publication List. U.S. Army Corps of Engineers, Cold Regions Research and Engineering Laboratory, 22 Lyme Rd., Hanover, New Hampshire 03755-1290. (603) 646-4221. 1983. Bibliography of the U.S. Tundra Biome International Biological Program

ENCYCLOPEDIAS AND DICTIONARIES

The Encyclopedia of Climatology. John E. Oliver and Rhodes W. Fairbridge, eds. Van Nostrand Reinhold, 115 5th Ave., New York, New York 10003. (212) 254-3232. 1987. Belongs in the series Encyclopedia of Earth Sciences, v.11.

McGraw-Hill Encyclopedia of Environmental Science. Sybil P. Parker. McGraw-Hill Science & Engineering Books, 11 W. 19th St., New York, New York 10011. (212) 337-6010. 1980. Covers ecology, man's influence on nature, and environmental protection.

Van Nostrand's Scientific Encyclopedia. Glenn D. Considine, ed. Van Nostrand Reinhold, 115 5th Ave., New York, New York 10003. (212) 254-3232. 1983. Sixth edition. Includes all broad subject areas in science.

GENERAL WORKS

Ecology of a Subarctic Mire. Swedish Natural Science Research Council, PO Box 6711, Stockholm, Sweden S-113 85. 08-15-1580. 1980. Topics in tundra ecology.

Tundra Ecosystems: A Comparative Analysis. Cambridge University Press, 40 W. 20th St., New York, New York 10011. (212) 924-3900. 1981. Report of the International Biological Programme on tundra ecology.

ONLINE DATA BASES

BIOSIS Previews. BIOSIS, 2100 Arch St., Philadelphia, Pennsylvania 19103-1399. (215) 587-4800. Largest and most comprehensive database of research in the life sciences. Contains citations for nearly 9000 primary research journals, monographs, reviews, symposia, preliminary reports, semi-popular journals, selected institutional reports, government reports and research communications.

Monthly Catalog of United States Government Publications. U.S. G.P.O., Supt. of Docs., PO Box 371954, Pittsburgh, Pennsylvania 15250-7954. (202) 512-0000.

National Technical Information Service. U.S. Department of Commerce, National Technical Information Service, Office of Data Base Services, 5285 Port Royal Rd., Springfield, Virginia 22161. (703) 487-4807. Bibliographic database of government sponsored research and technical reports.

SCISEARCH. Institute for Scientific Information, University City Science Center, 3501 Market St., Philadelphia, Pennsylvania 19104. (215) 386-0100.

RESEARCH CENTERS AND INSTITUTES

University of Alaska Anchorage, Arctic Environmental Information and Data Center. 707 A Street, Anchorage, Alaska 99501. (907) 257-2733.

TUNGSTEN
See: METALS AND METALLURGY

TURBIDITY
See: AIR POLLUTION

TURBINE ENGINES
See: POWER PLANTS

U

ULTRAFILTRATION

See: WASTEWATER TREATMENT

ULTRASONIC APPLICATIONS

ABSTRACTING AND INDEXING SERVICES

Acoustics Abstracts. Multi-Science Publishing Co. Ltd., 107 High St., Brentwood, England CM14 4RX. (0277) 224632. Monthly. Covers the world's major periodical literature, conference proceedings, unpublished reports, and book notices on acoustics.

Engineering Index. The Engineering Index Inc., 345 E. 47th St., New York, New York 10017. 1962-.

General Science Index. H. W. Wilson Co., 950 University Ave., Bronx, New York 10452. 1978-. Monthly, also issued in annual cumulation. Cumulative subject index to English language periodicals in the subject fields of astronomy, botany, chemistry, earth science, environment and conservation, food and nutrition, genetics, mathematics, medicine and health, microbiology, oceanography, physics, physiology and zoology.

Index to Scientific Book Contents. Institute for Scientific Information, 3501 Market St., Philadelphia, Pennsylvania 19104. (800) 523-1857. 1985-. Annual. Gives contents of science books published.

Science Citation Index. Institute for Scientific Information, 3501 Market St., Philadelphia, Pennsylvania 19104. 1961-.

ENCYCLOPEDIAS AND DICTIONARIES

Dictionary of Environmental Engineering and Related Sciences: English-Spanish, Spanish-English. Jose T. Villate. Ediciones Universal, 3090 SW 8th St., Miami, Florida 33135. (305) 642-3355. 1979.

Encyclopedia of Environmental Science and Engineering. J.R. Pfafflin. Gordon and Breach Science Publishers, Inc., 270 8th Ave., New York, New York 10011. (212) 206-8900. 1992.

Van Nostrand's Scientific Encyclopedia. Glenn D. Considine, ed. Van Nostrand Reinhold, 115 5th Ave., New York, New York 10003. (212) 254-3232. 1983. Sixth edition. Includes all broad subject areas in science.

ONLINE DATA BASES

Computerized Engineering Index–COMPENDEX. Engineering Information Inc., 345 E. 47th St., New York, New York 10017. (212) 705-7600.

ULTRAVIOLET RADIATION

ABSTRACTING AND INDEXING SERVICES

ASFA Aquaculture Abstracts. Cambridge Scientific Abstracts, Inc., 5161 River Rd., Bethesda, Maryland 20816. (301) 961-6750. 1984.

Engineering Index. The Engineering Index Inc., 345 E. 47th St., New York, New York 10017. 1962-.

General Science Index. H. W. Wilson Co., 950 University Ave., Bronx, New York 10452. 1978-. Monthly, also issued in annual cumulation. Cumulative subject index to English language periodicals in the subject fields of astronomy, botany, chemistry, earth science, environment and conservation, food and nutrition, genetics, mathematics, medicine and health, microbiology, oceanography, physics, physiology and zoology.

Science Citation Index. Institute for Scientific Information, 3501 Market St., Philadelphia, Pennsylvania 19104. 1961-.

BIBLIOGRAPHIES

Sunlight, Ultraviolet Radiation, and the Skin. U.S. Department of Health and Human Services, Public Health Services, National Institutes of Health, 9000 Rockville Pike, Bethesda, Maryland 20892. (301) 496-4000. 1989. Bibliography of the physiological effects of solar and ultraviolet radiation.

Ultra-violet Rays: Factors & Adverse Effects. ABBE Publishers Association of Washington DC, 4111 Gallows Rd., Annandale, Virginia 22003-1862. 1987. Bibliography of the physiological effects of ultraviolet radiation.

ENCYCLOPEDIAS AND DICTIONARIES

The Encyclopedia of Climatology. John E. Oliver and Rhodes W. Fairbridge, eds. Van Nostrand Reinhold, 115 5th Ave., New York, New York 10003. (212) 254-3232. 1987. Belongs in the series Encyclopedia of Earth Sciences, v.11.

Encyclopedia of Physical Science and Technology. Robert A. Meyers, ed. Academic Press, c/o Harcourt Brace Jovanovich Inc., 6277 Sea Harbor Dr., Orlando, Florida

32887. (800) 346-8648. Dictionary of engineering, technology and physical sciences.

GENERAL WORKS

Biological Effects of Ultraviolet Radiation. Cambridge University Press, 40 W. 20th St., New York, New York 10011. (212) 924-3900. 1980. Physiological effect of ultraviolet radiation and radiogenetics.

On the Linkage of Solar Ultraviolet Radiation to Skin Cancer. Department of Transportation, Federal Aviation Administration, Office of Environmental Quality, 800 Independence Ave. SW, Washington, District of Columbia 20591. (202) 267-3484. 1978. Effect of radiation on the skin.

Ozone and Ultraviolet Radiation Disinfection for Small Community Water Systems. Municipal Environmental Research Laboratory, Office of Research and Development, U.S. Environmental Protection Agency, 26 W. Martin Luther King Dr., Cincinnati, Ohio 45268. 1979. Water purification through ultraviolet treatment, water quality management and water purification ozonization.

Panel Report on Ozone. United Nations Environment Program. United Nations Environment Programme, Box 30552, Nairobi, Kenya 1991.

Sources and Applications of Ultraviolet Radiation. Academic Press, c/o Harcourt Brace Jovanovich Inc., 6277 Sea Harbor Dr., Orlando, Florida 32887. (800) 346-8648. 1983. Topics in photochemistry.

Ultraviolet Radiation. American Industrial Hygiene Association, 345 White Pond Dr., Akron, Ohio 44320. (216) 873-2442. 1991. Offers updated and expanded information on ultraviolet radiations' physical characteristics; generation, uses, and sources; interaction with matter; biological effects; exposure criteria; instrumentation; evaluation and measurement; and controls and their practical applications.

ONLINE DATA BASES

Computerized Engineering Index–COMPENDEX. Engineering Information Inc., 345 E. 47th St., New York, New York 10017. (212) 705-7600.

UNDERGROUND MINING

ABSTRACTING AND INDEXING SERVICES

Engineering Index. The Engineering Index Inc., 345 E. 47th St., New York, New York 10017. 1962-.

ENCYCLOPEDIAS AND DICTIONARIES

Dictionary of Environmental Engineering and Related Sciences: English-Spanish, Spanish-English. Jose T. Villate. Ediciones Universal, 3090 SW 8th St., Miami, Florida 33135. (305) 642-3355. 1979.

Encyclopedia of Environmental Science and Engineering. J.R. Pfafflin. Gordon and Breach Science Publishers, Inc., 270 8th Ave., New York, New York 10011. (212) 206-8900. 1992.

Encyclopedia of Physical Science and Technology. Robert A. Meyers, ed. Academic Press, c/o Harcourt Brace

Jovanovich Inc., 6277 Sea Harbor Dr., Orlando, Florida 32887. (800) 346-8648. Dictionary of engineering, technology and physical sciences.

GENERAL WORKS

Diesels in Underground Mining. U.S. Department of the Interior, Bureau of Mines, Avondale, Maryland 1984. Investigation of diesel motor safety measures, diesel motor exhaust gas, mine ventilation, air quality measurement, coal mines and mining, equipment and supplies.

Safety and Health Standards Applicable to Underground Metal and Nonmetal Mining and Milling Operations. U.S. G.P.O., Washington, District of Columbia 20401. (202) 512-0000. 1985. Mine safety law and legislation in the United States.

Subsidence from Underground Mining. U.S. Geological Survey, 12201 Sunrise Valley Dr., Reston, Virginia 22092. (703) 648-4460. 1983. Environmental aspects of mine subsidence.

HANDBOOKS AND MANUALS

Coal Age Operating Handbook of Underground Mining. Coal Age Mining Informational Services, New York, New York 1978. Coal mines and mining method manual.

E/MJ Operating Handbook of Mineral Underground Mining. E/MJ Mining Informational Services, New York, New York 1978.

Underground Mining Methods Handbook. Society for Mining, Metallurgy and Exploration Inc., PO Box 625005, Littleton, Colorado 80162. (303) 973-9550. 1982. A manual of mining engineering.

ONLINE DATA BASES

Computerized Engineering Index–COMPENDEX. Engineering Information Inc., 345 E. 47th St., New York, New York 10017. (212) 705-7600.

TRADE ASSOCIATIONS AND PROFESSIONAL SOCIETIES

Underground Injection Practices Council. 525 Central Park Dr., Suite 304, Oklahoma City, Oklahoma 73105. (405) 525-6146.

UNDERGROUND STORAGE

ABSTRACTING AND INDEXING SERVICES

Engineering Index. The Engineering Index Inc., 345 E. 47th St., New York, New York 10017. 1962-.

BIBLIOGRAPHIES

Underground Storage of Gaseous Fuels. American Gas Association, 1515 Wilson Blvd., Arlington, Virginia 22209. 1981. Underground storage of natural gas and petroleum products.

DIRECTORIES

Gale Environmental Sourcebook. Karen Hill. Gale Research Co., 835 Penobscot Bldg., Detroit, Michigan

48226-4094. (313) 961-2242. Contacts, information sources, or general information on environmental topics.

ENCYCLOPEDIAS AND DICTIONARIES

Dictionary of Environmental Engineering and Related Sciences: English-Spanish, Spanish-English. Jose T. Villate. Ediciones Universal, 3090 SW 8th St., Miami, Florida 33135. (305) 642-3355. 1979.

Encyclopedia of Environmental Science and Engineering. J.R. Pfafflin. Gordon and Breach Science Publishers, Inc., 270 8th Ave., New York, New York 10011. (212) 206-8900. 1992.

Encyclopedia of Physical Science and Technology. Robert A. Meyers, ed. Academic Press, c/o Harcourt Brace Jovanovich Inc., 6277 Sea Harbor Dr., Orlando, Florida 32887. (800) 346-8648. Dictionary of engineering, technology and physical sciences.

GENERAL WORKS

Cleanup of Petroleum Contaminated Soils at Underground Storage Tanks. Warren J. Lyman, et al. Noyes Publications, 120 Mill Rd., Park Ridge, New Jersey 07656. (201) 391-8484. Describes soil venting, biorestoration, soil flushing, hydraulic barriers, and vacuum extraction of non-aqueous phase liquids, and biorestoration for saturated zones.

Corrective Action Response Guide for Leaking Underground Storage Tanks. Albert D. Young, Jr. Government Institutes, Inc., 4 Research Pl., Suite 200, Rockville, Maryland 20850. (301) 921-2300. 1990. Comprehensive resource for preparing for or preventing an uncontrolled release in underground storage tanks.

Groundwater Remediation and Petroleum: A Guide for Underground Storage Tanks. David C. Noonan and James T. Curtis. PennWell Books, PO Box 21288, Tulsa, Oklahoma 74121. (918) 831-9421; (800) 752-9764. 1990. Guide for personnel charged with the responsibility of addressing contamination caused by leaking underground storage tanks.

Leak Prevention and Corrective Action Technology for Underground Storage Tanks. Noyes Publications, 120 Mill Rd., Park Ridge, New Jersey 07656. (201) 391-8484. 1988. Oil storage tanks safety measures and technology.

Leaking Underground Storage Tanks Containing Motor Fuels: A Chemical Advisory. U.S. Environmental Protection Agency, Office of Toxic Substances, 401 M St., S.W., Washington, District of Columbia 20460. (202) 260-2090. 1984. Underground storage of petroleum products.

More About Leaking Underground Storage Tanks: A Background Booklet for the Chemical Advisory. U.S. Environmental Protection Agency, 401 M St., S.W., Washington, District of Columbia 20460. (202) 260-2090. 1984. Covers underground storage and drinking water contamination.

Release Detection for Underground Storage Tank Piping System. Roy F. Weston Inc. Electric Power Research Institute, 3412 Hillview Ave., Palo Alto, California 94304. (415) 965-4081. 1990. Discusses leak detection systems for suction and pressurized piping.

TAPPI Environmental Conference Proceedings, Seattle, WA, April 9-11, 1990. TAPPI Press, Technology Park/Atlanta, PO Box 105113, Atlanta, Georgia 30348. (404)

446-1400. 1990. Contains 11 papers presented at the conference covering industrial pollution and its remedies.

Underground Storage of Natural Gas: Theory and Practice. Kluwer Academic Publishers, 101 Philip Dr., Assinippi Park, Norwell, Massachusetts 02061. (617) 871-6600. 1989.

Underground Storage of Oil and Gas in Salt Deposits and Other Non-Hard Rocks. Wolfgang Dreyer. Enke, Rudigerstr. 14, Stuttgart, Germany D-7000. 1982. Petroleum and natural gas underground storage and salt deposits.

Underground Storage Tank Guide. Jeffrey L. Leiter, ed. PennWell Books, PO Box 21288, Tulsa, Oklahoma 74121. (918) 831-9421; (800) 752-9764. Monthly. Describes exactly what EPA's underground storage tank regulations require. Lists contacts and requirements for each state's underground storage tank program.

Underground Storage Tank Management: A Practical Guide. Hart Environmental Management Corp. Government Institutes Inc., 4 Research Place, Suite 200, Rockville, Maryland 20850. (301) 921-2300. 1991. 3rd ed. Presents the latest in the state-of-the-art tank design, how to predict tank leaks, test tank integrity, avoid costly tank replacement through low-cost retrofit and maintenance techniques, and how to respond to leaks.

Underground Storage Tanks: A Primer on the New Federal Regulatory Program. American Bar Association, 750 N. Lake Shore Dr., Chicago, Illinois 60611. (312) 988-5000. 1989. Environmental law relative to hazardous waste sites, waste disposal sites and underground storage.

Volumetric Leak Detection Methods for Underground Fuel Storage Tanks. Joseph E. Maresca, et al. Noyes Publications, 120 Mill Rd., Park Ridge, New Jersey 07656. (201) 391-8484. 1990. Summarizes the results of the USEPA's research program to evaluate the current performance of commercially available volumetric test methods for the detection of small leaks in underground fuel storage tanks.

The Washington Conference on Underground Storage, July 15-16, 1985, Stouffer Concourse. Center for Energy and Environmental Management, Washington, District of Columbia (202) 543-3939.

GOVERNMENTAL ORGANIZATIONS

U.S. Environmental Protection Agency: Office of Underground Storage Tanks. 401 M St., S.W., Washington, District of Columbia 20460. (202) 382-4517.

HANDBOOKS AND MANUALS

Handbook of Underground Storage Tank Safety and Correction Technology. Hemisphere Publishing Co., Science Information Resource Center, 79 Madison Ave., Ste. 1110, New York, New York 10016. (212) 725-1999. 1988.

Underground Storage Tank Compliance Manual. IMA and Rooks, Pitts and Poust, Chicago, Illinois 1988. Underground storage, maintenance and repair, and waste disposal.

ONLINE DATA BASES

Computerized Engineering Index–COMPENDEX. Engineering Information Inc., 345 E. 47th St., New York, New York 10017. (212) 705-7600.

STATISTICS SOURCES

Environmental Data Compendium. OECD Publications and Information Center, 2001 L St., N.W., Suite 700, Washington, District of Columbia 20036. (202) 785-6323. 1989.

Environmental Indicators. OECD Publications and Information Center, 2001 L St., N.W., Suite 700, Washington, District of Columbia 20036. (202) 785-6323. 1991.

Environmental Quality. Council on Environmental Quality. U.S. G.P.O., Washington, District of Columbia 20401. (202) 512-0000. Annual.

The State of the Environment. OECD Publications and Information Center, 2001 L St., N.W., Suite 700, Washington, District of Columbia 20036. (202) 785-6323. 1991.

TRADE ASSOCIATIONS AND PROFESSIONAL SOCIETIES

American Society of Agricultural Engineers. 2950 Niles Rd., St Joseph, Michigan 49085. (616) 429-0300.

Association for Composite Tanks. 3000 Chestnut St., Suite 331, Baltimore, Maryland 21211. (301) 235-6000.

Leak Detection Technology Association. 1801 K St., N.W., Suite 800, Washington, District of Columbia 20006. (202) 835-2355.

Underground Injection Practices Council. 525 Central Park Dr., Suite 304, Oklahoma City, Oklahoma 73105. (405) 525-6146.

UPPER ATMOSPHERE

See: ATMOSPHERE

URANIUM

ABSTRACTING AND INDEXING SERVICES

Chemical Abstracts. Chemical Abstracts Service, 2540 Olentangy River Rd., PO Box 3012, Columbus, Ohio 43210. (800) 848-6533. 1907-.

Energy Information Abstracts Annual 1987 in Retrospect. EIC/Intelligence Inc., 121 Chanlon Rd., New Providence, New Jersey 07974. (908) 464-6800. 1988. Annual. Cumulative edition of the monthly Energy Information Abstracts. Monitors sources in the field of energy including the scientific, technical and business journal literature, conference and symposia proceedings, corporate, government and academic reports.

Engineering Index. The Engineering Index Inc., 345 E. 47th St., New York, New York 10017. 1962-.

General Science Index. H. W. Wilson Co., 950 University Ave., Bronx, New York 10452. 1978-. Monthly, also issued in annual cumulation. Cumulative subject index to English language periodicals in the subject fields of

astronomy, botany, chemistry, earth science, environment and conservation, food and nutrition, genetics, mathematics, medicine and health, microbiology, oceanography, physics, physiology and zoology.

INIS Atomindex. International Atomic Energy Agency, Wagramerstrasse 5, Vienna, Austria A-1400. 222 23606198. 1988-. Semiannual. Abstracts nuclear energy and nuclear physics topics from journals, conferences, technical reports and other related publications. Issued in 6 parts: Personal Author, Corporate Entry, Subject, Report, Standard Patent, Conference (by place), Conference (by date).

Physics Briefs. Physikalische Berichte. Physik Verlag, Pappapelallee 3, Postfach 101161, Weinheim, Germany D-6940. 1979-. Semimonthly. In English. Volumes for 1979- issued by the Deutsche Physikalische Gesellschaft and the Fachinformationszentrum Energie Physik, Mathematik in cooperation with the American Institute of Physics.

Science Citation Index. Institute for Scientific Information, 3501 Market St., Philadelphia, Pennsylvania 19104. 1961-.

BIBLIOGRAPHIES

Bibliography and Index of Geology. American Geological Institute, 4220 King St., Alexandria, Virginia 22302. Monthly. Includes environmental geology and hydrogeology.

New Publications of the Geological Survey. U.S. Department of the Interior, Geological Survey, 119 National Center, Reston, Virginia 22092. (703) 648-4460. 1984-. Monthly. Bibliography of geological publications and related government documents published by the Geological Survey.

ENCYCLOPEDIAS AND DICTIONARIES

Encyclopedia of Physical Science and Technology. Robert A. Meyers, ed. Academic Press, c/o Harcourt Brace Jovanovich Inc., 6277 Sea Harbor Dr., Orlando, Florida 32887. (800) 346-8648. Dictionary of engineering, technology and physical sciences.

Encyclopedia of Physics. Rita G. Lerner and George L. Trigg. VCH Publishers, 303 NW 12th Ave., Deerfield Beach, Florida 33442-1788. (305) 428-5566. 1991. Second edition.

Glossary of Terms in Nuclear Science and Technology. American Nuclear Society, 555 North Kensington Ave., La Grange Park, Illinois 60525. (708) 352-6611. 1986. Prepared by the American Nuclear Society Standards Committee. Subcommittee ANS-9.

Van Nostrand's Scientific Encyclopedia. Glenn D. Considine, ed. Van Nostrand Reinhold, 115 5th Ave., New York, New York 10003. (212) 254-3232. 1983. Sixth edition. Includes all broad subject areas in science.

GENERAL WORKS

Magill's Survey of Science. Earth Science Series. Frank N. Magill. Salem Press, PO Box 50062, Pasadena, California 91105. 1990-. Five volumes. Includes information on earth's crust, hot spots and volcanic island chains, physical properties of minerals, rock magnetism, physical properties of rocks, and index.

Population Risks from Uranium Ore Bodies. U.S. Environmental Protection Agency, Office of Radiation Programs, 401 M St., S.W., Washington, District of Columbia 20460. (202) 260-2090. 1980.

Radon, Radium, and Uranium in Drinking Water. C. Richard Cothern and Paul Rebers. Lewis Publishers, 2000 Corporate Blvd., N.W., Boca Raton, Florida 33431. (407) 994-0555 or (800) 272-7737. 1990. Covers most aspects of radionuclides in drinking water.

Toxicological Profile for Uranium. Agency for Toxic Substances and Disease Registry, U.S. Public Health Service, 1600 Clifton Rd. NE, Atlanta, Georgia 30333. (404) 452-4111. 1990. Physiological effects, environmental aspects and toxicology of uranium compounds.

Uranium Series Disequilibrium. Clarendon Press, Walton St., Oxford, England OX2 6DP. 1982. Environmental aspects of uranium isotopes decay.

HANDBOOKS AND MANUALS

Environmental Effects of the Uranium Fuel Cycle; A Review of Data for Technetium. J. E. Till. U.S. Nuclear Regulatory Commission, Office for Nuclear Reactor Regulation, Division of Systems Integration, Washington, District of Columbia 20555. (301) 492-7000. 1985. Environmental aspects of the uranium industry, particularly technetium.

Radon Attenuation Handbook for Uranium Mill Tailings Cover Design. U.S. Nuclear Regulatory Commission, Division of Health, Siting and Waste Management, Office of Nuclear Regulatory Research, Washington, District of Columbia 20555. (301) 492-7000. 1984.

Tables of Physical and Chemical Constants and Some Mathematical Functions. G. W. C. Kaye, et al. Longman Group Ltd., Longman House, Burnt Mill, Harlow, England CM20 2J6. 0279 426721. 1988. Fifteenth edition. Includes tables on mechanical properties, density, elasticity, viscosity, surface tension, temperature and heat. Also covers radiation, optics, chemistry, electrochemistry, astrophysics, and chemical thermodynamics.

ONLINE DATA BASES

CAS Source Index–CASSI. Chemical Abstracts Service, 2540 Olentangy River Rd., P.O. Box 3012, Columbus, Ohio 43210. (800) 848-6533 or (614) 421-3600. A listing of bibliographic and library holdings information for scientific and technical primary literature relevant to the chemical sciences.

CERCLIS. Chemical Information Systems, Inc., 7215 York Rd., Baltimore, Maryland 21212. (301) 321-8440. Information on hazardous waste disposal sites that have either been listed by the EPA on the National Priority List (NPL) or nominated for consideration for the NPL.

Chemical Abstracts-CA. Chemical Abstracts Service, 2540 Olentangy River Rd., P.O. Box 3012, Columbus, Ohio 43210. (800) 848-6533 or (614) 421-3600. Information sources include 9000 journals, patents from 27 countries, two industrial property organizations, new books, conference proceedings, and government research reports.

Computerized Engineering Index–COMPENDEX. Engineering Information Inc., 345 E. 47th St., New York, New York 10017. (212) 705-7600.

STATISTICS SOURCES

The Economics of Uranium 1991. FIND/SVP, 625 Avenue of the Americas, New York, New York 10011. (212) 645-4500. 1991. Analyzes uranium and nuclear activities within 39 countries with subsections on the roles played by 28 leading companies.

Focus: Quarterly Report on the Nuclear Fuel Cycle. Nuclear Assurance Corp., 6251 Crooked Creek Road, Norcross, Georgia 30092. Quarterly. Data on nuclear reactor and fuel cycle operations; uranium project profile and Fuel-Trac summary.

Uranium Industry Annual. U.S. G.P.O, Washington, District of Columbia 20402-9325. (202) 512-0000. 1984. Annual. Reserves, exploration, mining and milling operations, prices, and marketing.

URANIUM WASTES

See: RADIOACTIVE WASTES

URBAN DESIGN AND PLANNING

ABSTRACTING AND INDEXING SERVICES

Applied Science and Technology Index. H.W. Wilson Co., 950 University Ave., Bronx, New York 10452. (800) 367-6770. Formerly Industrial Arts Index.

Chicorel Index to Urban Planning and Environmental Design. Marietta Chicorel. Chicorel Library Pub. Corp., New York, New York Irregular. Covers cities and towns planning.

Engineering Index. The Engineering Index Inc., 345 E. 47th St., New York, New York 10017. 1962-.

Index to Scientific Book Contents. Institute for Scientific Information, 3501 Market St., Philadelphia, Pennsylvania 19104. (800) 523-1857. 1985-. Annual. Gives contents of science books published.

Transportation Research News. National Academy of Science, Transportation Research Board, Box 289, Washington, District of Columbia 20055. (202) 334-3213. 1982. Monthly.

Urban Affairs Abstracts. National League of Cities, 1301 Pennsylvania Ave., NW, Washington, District of Columbia 20004. (202) 626-3150. 1977-. Weekly.

ALMANACS AND YEARBOOKS

Livable Cities Almanac. J.T. Marlin. Harper Perennial, New York, New York 1992. How over 100 metropolitan areas compare in economic health, air quality, water quality, life expectancy and health services.

BIBLIOGRAPHIES

Social Network Analysis: A Man/Environment Approach to Urban Design and Planning. Council of Planning Librarians, 1313 E. 60th St., Chicago, Illinois 60637-2897. (312) 942-2163. 1978. Bibliography of city planning and social structure.

Urban Design. Vance Bibliographies, PO Box 229, 112 N. Charter St., Monticello, Illinois 61856. (217) 762-3831. 1983.

Urbanization and Changing Land Uses: A Bibliography of Selected References, 1950-58. Elizabeth Gould Davis. U.S. Department of Agriculture, 14 Independence Ave. SW, Washington, District of Columbia 20250. (202) 447-7454. 1960. Bibliography of land utilization and urban growth.

DIRECTORIES

American Society of Consulting Planners–Membership Directory. 1015 15th St., N.W., Suite 600, Washington, District of Columbia 20005. (202) 789-2200.

Society of Environmental Graphic Designers–Corporate Directory. Society of Environmental Graphic Designers, 47 Third St., Cambridge, Massachusetts 02141. (617) 577-8225.

Society of Environmental Graphic Designers–Professional Firm Directory. Society of Environmental Graphic Designers, 47 Third St., Cambridge, Massachusetts 02141. (617) 577-8225.

ENCYCLOPEDIAS AND DICTIONARIES

Dictionary of Environmental Engineering and Related Sciences: English-Spanish, Spanish-English. Jose T. Villate. Ediciones Universal, 3090 SW 8th St., Miami, Florida 33135. (305) 642-3355. 1979.

Encyclopedia of Community Planning and Environmental Management. Marilyn Spigel Schultz. Facts on File, Inc., 460 Park Ave. S., New York, New York 10016. (212) 683-2244. 1984.

Encyclopedia of Environmental Science and Engineering. J.R. Pfafflin. Gordon and Breach Science Publishers, Inc., 270 8th Ave., New York, New York 10011. (212) 206-8900. 1992.

Encyclopedia of Physical Science and Technology. Robert A. Meyers, ed. Academic Press, c/o Harcourt Brace Jovanovich Inc., 6277 Sea Harbor Dr., Orlando, Florida 32887. (800) 346-8648. Dictionary of engineering, technology and physical sciences.

McGraw-Hill Encyclopedia of Environmental Science. Sybil P. Parker. McGraw-Hill Science & Engineering Books, 11 W. 19th St., New York, New York 10011. (212) 337-6010. 1980. Covers ecology, man's influence on nature, and environmental protection.

Van Nostrand's Scientific Encyclopedia. Glenn D. Considine, ed. Van Nostrand Reinhold, 115 5th Ave., New York, New York 10003. (212) 254-3232. 1983. Sixth edition. Includes all broad subject areas in science.

GENERAL WORKS

America's Downtowns: Growth, Politics, and Preservation. Richard C. Collins. Preservation Press, National Trust for Historic Preservation, 1785 Massachusetts Ave. NW, Washington, District of Columbia 20036. (202) 673-4058. 1991. Examines the efforts of 10 major American cities to integrate preservation values into the local policies that shape downtown growth and development.

Comparative Urbanization: Divergent Paths in the Twentieth Century. Brian J. L. Berry. St. Martin's Press, 175 5th Ave., New York, New York 10010. (212) 674-5151. 1981.

Creating Successful Communities. Michael A. Mantelli, et al. Island Press, 1718 Connecticut Ave. N.W., Suite 300, Washington, District of Columbia 20009. (202) 232-7933. 1990. Compendium of techniques for effective land use and growth management to help communities retain their individuality in the face of rapid growth.

The Future of Urbanization: Facing the Ecological and Economic Constraints. Lester R. Brown, Jodi L. Jacobson. Worldwatch Institute, 1776 Massachusetts Ave., N.W., Washington, District of Columbia 20036-1904. 1987.

Human Aspects of Urban Form: Towards a Man-Environment Approach to Urban Form and Design. Pergamon Microforms International, Inc., Fairview Park, Elmsford, New York 10523. (914) 592-7720. 1977. Human factors in city planning, geographical perception and environmental aspects of architecture.

Livable Cities. Marcia D. Lowe. Worldwatch Institute, 1776 Massachusetts Ave., N.W., Washington, District of Columbia 20036-1904.

Nature in Cities: The Natural Environment in the Design and Development of Urban Green Space. John Wiley & Sons, Inc., 605 3rd Ave., New York, New York 10158-0012. (212) 850-6000. 1979. Urban ecology, city planning, and urban beautification.

Planning for an Urban World. MIT Press, 55 Hayward St., Cambridge, Massachusetts 02142. (617) 253-2884. 1974.

The Politics of Park Design. MIT Press, 55 Hayward St., Cambridge, Massachusetts 02142. (617) 253-2884. 1982. Lists history, design and construction of parks in the United States.

Trees in Urban Design. Van Nostrand Reinhold, 115 Fifth Ave., New York, New York 10003. (212) 254-3232. 1993. Trees in cities and urban beautification.

Urbanization and Cities: Historical and Comparative Perspectives in Our Urbanizing World. Hilda H. Golden. D. C. Heath, 125 Spring St., Lexington, Massachusetts 02173. (617) 862-6650. 1991. Urban sociology and urbanization.

Urbanization and Environmental Quality. Isao Orishimo. Kluwer Academic Publishers, 101 Philip Dr., Assinippi Park, Norwell, Massachusetts 02061. (617) 871-6600. 1982. Covers central places, pollution, quality of life, residential mobility, and urbanization.

The World Bank and the Environment: A Progress Report, Fiscal 1991. World Bank, UNIPUB, 4611-F Assembly Dr., Lanham, Maryland 20706. (301) 459-7666 or (800) 274-4888. 1991. Describes specific environmental strategies and environmental lending in the Bank's four operational regions: Asia, Europe, the Middle East and North Africa, and Latin America and the Caribbean.

ONLINE DATA BASES

Civil Engineering Database. American Society of Civil Engineers, 345 E. 47th St., New York, New York 10017. (800) 548-2723.

Computerized Engineering Index–COMPENDEX. Engineering Information Inc., 345 E. 47th St., New York, New York 10017. (212) 705-7600.

Enviroline. R. R. Bowker Co., Bowker Electronic Publishing, 121 Chanlon Rd., New Providence, New Jersey 07974. (800) 521-8110.

Environmental Bibliography. Environmental Studies Institute, International Academy at Santa Barbara, 800 Garden St., Ste. D, Santa Barbara, California 93101. (805) 965-5010. International periodical literature dealing with environmental topics such as air pollution, water treatment, energy conservation, noise abatement, soil mechanics, wildlife preservation, and chemical wastes.

Monthly Catalog of United States Government Publications. U.S. G.P.O., Supt. of Docs., PO Box 371954, Pittsburgh, Pennsylvania 15250-7954. (202) 512-0000.

National Technical Information Service. U.S. Department of Commerce, National Technical Information Service, Office of Data Base Services, 5285 Port Royal Rd., Springfield, Virginia 22161. (703) 487-4807. Bibliographic database of government sponsored research and technical reports.

SCISEARCH. Institute for Scientific Information, University City Science Center, 3501 Market St., Philadelphia, Pennsylvania 19104. (215) 386-0100.

Transportation Research Information Service–TRIS. Transportation Research Board, Box 289, Washington, District of Columbia 20055. (202) 334-3213.

PERIODICALS AND NEWSLETTERS

Between the Issues. Ecology Action Center, 1657 Barrington St., #520, Halifax, Nova Scotia, Canada B3J 2A1. (506) 422-4311. 1975-. Bimonthly. Newsletter that deals with environmental protection, uranium mining, waste, energy, agriculture, forestry, pesticides, and urban planning.

CERP. Dana Silk, ed. UNESCO, 7, place de Fontenoy, Paris, France F-75700. (331) 45 68 40 67. Discusses forest and agroforestry ecosystems, urban development and planning.

Design Research News. Environmental Design Research Assn., PO Box 24083, Oklahoma City, Oklahoma 73124. (405) 232-2655. Quarterly. Environmental policy, planning, design, and education; human behavior and implications for environmental designing.

Journal of American Planning Association. American Planning Association, 1776 Massachusetts Avenue, NW, Suite 704, Washington, District of Columbia 20036. (202) 872-0611. Quarterly. Represents the interests of professional urban and regional planners.

TRADE ASSOCIATIONS AND PROFESSIONAL SOCIETIES

American Institute of Certified Planners. 1776 Massachusetts Ave., N.W., Washington, District of Columbia 20036. (202) 872-0611.

American Planning Association. 1776 Massachusetts Ave., N.W., Suite 704, Washington, District of Columbia 20036. (202) 872-0611.

Association for Rational Environmental Alternatives. 256 Alpine Rd., West Palm Beach, Florida 33405. (407) 585-7841.

Environic Foundation International. 916 St. Vincent St., South Bend, Indiana 46617. (219) 259-9976.

Greensward Foundation. 104 Prospect Park, W., Brooklyn, New York 11215.

Institute for Community Design Analysis. 66 Clover Dr., Great Neck, New York 11021. (516) 773-4727.

International Center for the Solution of Environmental Problems. 535 Lovett Blvd., Houston, Texas 77006. (713) 527-8711.

Interprofessional Council on Environmental Design. c/o Israel Stallman, American Institute of Certified Planners, 1776 Massachusetts Ave., N.W., Washington, District of Columbia 20036. (202) 872-0611.

Metropolitan Tree Improvement Alliance. c/o Andrew Todd, Division of Forestry, Ohio Dept. of Natural Resources, Fountain Square Bldg. B-3, Columbus, Ohio 43224. (614) 265-6707.

National Arborist Association. The Meeting Place Mall, Rt. 101, P.O. Box 1094, Amherst, New Hampshire 03031. (603) 673-3311.

National Center for Urban Environmental Studies. 516 N. Charles St., Suite 501, Baltimore, Maryland 21201. (301) 727-6212.

National Institute for Urban Wildlife. 10921 Trotting Ridge Way, Columbia, Maryland 21044. (301) 596-3311.

National Landscape Association. 1250 I St., N.W., Ste. 500, Washington, District of Columbia 20005. (202) 789-2900.

National Planning Association. 1424 16th St., N.W., Suite 700, Washington, District of Columbia 20036. (202) 265-7685.

Partners for Liveable Places. 1429 21st St., N.W., Washington, District of Columbia 20036. (202) 887-5990.

Professional Grounds Management Society. 120 Cockeysville Rd., Ste. 104, Hunt Valley, Maryland 21031. (410) 667-1833.

Scenic America. 216 Seventh St., S.E., Washington, District of Columbia 20003. (202) 546-1100.

Transportation Research Board. Box 289, Washington, District of Columbia 20055. (202) 334-3213.

ULI–The Urban Land Institute. 625 Indiana Ave., N.W., Washington, District of Columbia 20004. (202) 624-7000.

United New Conservationists. P.O. Box 362, Campbell, California 95009. (408) 241-5769.

Urban Environment Conference. 7620 Morningside Dr., N.W., Washington, District of Columbia 20012. (202) 726-8111.

Urban Initiatives. 530 W. 25th St., New York, New York 10001. (212) 620-9773.

Urban Land Institute. 625 Indiana Ave., N.W., Washington, District of Columbia 20004. (202) 624-7000.

World Future Society. 4916 St. Elmo Ave., Bethesda, Maryland 20814. (301) 656-8274.

URBAN ECOSYSTEMS

See: ECOSYSTEMS

URBAN RUNOFF

ABSTRACTING AND INDEXING SERVICES

Abstracts of Air and Water Conservation Literature. American Petroleum Institute. Central Abstracting and Indexing Service, 275 Madison Avenue, New York, New York 10016. 1972.

Applied Science and Technology Index. H.W. Wilson Co., 950 University Ave., Bronx, New York 10452. (800) 367-6770. Formerly Industrial Arts Index.

Biological and Agricultural Index. H.W. Wilson Co., 950 University Ave., Bronx, New York 10452. (800) 367-6770. 1916-. Monthly.

Engineering Index. The Engineering Index Inc., 345 E. 47th St., New York, New York 10017. 1962-.

Geographical Abstracts. London School of Economics, Dept. of Geography, Regency House, 34 Duke St., London, England 1966-. Continued by Geo Abstracts issued in 6 parts: Pt. A. Landforms and the quaternary; Pt. B. Biogeography and Climatology; Pt. C. Economic geography; Pt. D. Social geography and cartography; Pt. E. Sedimentology; Pt. F. Regional and community planning.

Urban Affairs Abstracts. National League of Cities, 1301 Pennsylvania Ave., NW, Washington, District of Columbia 20004. (202) 626-3150. 1977-. Weekly.

ENCYCLOPEDIAS AND DICTIONARIES

Encyclopedia of Community Planning and Environmental Management. Marilyn Spigel Schultz. Facts on File, Inc., 460 Park Ave. S., New York, New York 10016. (212) 683-2244. 1984.

McGraw-Hill Encyclopedia of Environmental Science. Sybil P. Parker. McGraw-Hill Science & Engineering Books, 11 W. 19th St., New York, New York 10011. (212) 337-6010. 1980. Covers ecology, man's influence on nature, and environmental protection.

Van Nostrand's Scientific Encyclopedia. Glenn D. Considine, ed. Van Nostrand Reinhold, 115 5th Ave., New York, New York 10003. (212) 254-3232. 1983. Sixth edition. Includes all broad subject areas in science.

GENERAL WORKS

New Technologies in Urban Drainage. C. Maksimovic. Elsevier Science Publishing Co., 655 Avenue of the Americas, New York, New York 10010. (212) 984-5800. 1991. Advances in rainfall-runoff modelling, hydrodynamics and quality modelling of receiving waters, and urban drainage in specific climates.

Real Time Control of Urban Drainage Systems, the State-of-the-Art. Wolfgang Schilling, ed. Pergamon Microforms International, Inc., Fairview Park, Elmsford, New York 10523. (914) 592-7720. 1989. Report by the IAWPRC Task Group on real-time control of drainage systems.

Urban Discharges and Receiving Water Quality Impacts. J. B. Ellis, ed. Pergamon Microforms International, Inc., Fairview Park, Elmsford, New York 10523. (914) 592-7720. 1989. Proceedings of a seminar organized by the IAWPRC/IAHR Sub Committee for Urban Runoff Quality Data, as part of the IAWPRC 14th biennial conference, Brighton, UK, July 18-21, 1988.

ONLINE DATA BASES

Computerized Engineering Index–COMPENDEX. Engineering Information Inc., 345 E. 47th St., New York, New York 10017. (212) 705-7600.

Monthly Catalog of United States Government Publications. U.S. G.P.O., Supt. of Docs., PO Box 371954, Pittsburgh, Pennsylvania 15250-7954. (202) 512-0000.

National Technical Information Service. U.S. Department of Commerce, National Technical Information Service, Office of Data Base Services, 5285 Port Royal Rd., Springfield, Virginia 22161. (703) 487-4807. Bibliographic database of government sponsored research and technical reports.

SCISEARCH. Institute for Scientific Information, University City Science Center, 3501 Market St., Philadelphia, Pennsylvania 19104. (215) 386-0100.

PERIODICALS AND NEWSLETTERS

Association of Metropolitan Sewerage Agencies Monthly Report. Association of Metropolitan Sewerage Agencies, 1000 Connecticut Avenue, NW, Suite 1006, Washington, District of Columbia 20005. (202) 833-4653. Monthly. Data on environmental and regulatory matters.

TRADE ASSOCIATIONS AND PROFESSIONAL SOCIETIES

American Public Works Association. 106 W. 11th St., Ste. 1800, Kansas City, Missouri 64105-1806. (816) 472-6100.

American Society of Agricultural Engineers. 2950 Niles Rd., St Joseph, Michigan 49085. (616) 429-0300.

URBAN WATER RESOURCES

ABSTRACTING AND INDEXING SERVICES

Abstracts of Air and Water Conservation Literature. American Petroleum Institute. Central Abstracting and Indexing Service, 275 Madison Avenue, New York, New York 10016. 1972.

Applied Science and Technology Index. H.W. Wilson Co., 950 University Ave., Bronx, New York 10452. (800) 367-6770. Formerly Industrial Arts Index.

Aqualine Abstracts. Water Research Centre. c/o Pergamon Microforms International, Inc., Fairview Park, Elmsford, New York 10523. (914) 592-7720. 1927-. Contains some 8,000 records annually on water and wastewater technology. Covers all aspects of water, wastewater, associated engineering services and the aquatic environment. Over 600 periodicals, as well as books, reports and conference proceedings and other publications from water related institutions worldwide are scanned. Also available online.

Biological and Agricultural Index. H.W. Wilson Co., 950 University Ave., Bronx, New York 10452. (800) 367-6770. 1916-. Monthly.

Ecological Abstracts. Geo Abstracts Ltd. Elsevier Applied Science, Crown House, Linton Rd., Barking, England IG 11 8JU. 1974-. Derived from over 600 leading ecological and environmental journals, plus books, conference proceedings, reports and theses.

Engineering Index. The Engineering Index Inc., 345 E. 47th St., New York, New York 10017. 1962-.

Geographical Abstracts. London School of Economics, Dept. of Geography, Regency House, 34 Duke St., London, England 1966-. Continued by Geo Abstracts issued in 6 parts: Pt. A. Landforms and the quaternary; Pt. B. Biogeography and Climatology; Pt. C. Economic geography; Pt. D. Social geography and cartography; Pt. E. Sedimentology; Pt. F. Regional and community planning.

Index to Scientific Book Contents. Institute for Scientific Information, 3501 Market St., Philadelphia, Pennsylvania 19104. (800) 523-1857. 1985-. Annual. Gives contents of science books published.

Urban Affairs Abstracts. National League of Cities, 1301 Pennsylvania Ave., NW, Washington, District of Columbia 20004. (202) 626-3150. 1977-. Weekly.

ENCYCLOPEDIAS AND DICTIONARIES

Encyclopedia of Community Planning and Environmental Management. Marilyn Spigel Schultz. Facts on File, Inc., 460 Park Ave. S., New York, New York 10016. (212) 683-2244. 1984.

McGraw-Hill Encyclopedia of Environmental Science. Sybil P. Parker. McGraw-Hill Science & Engineering Books, 11 W. 19th St., New York, New York 10011. (212) 337-6010. 1980. Covers ecology, man's influence on nature, and environmental protection.

GENERAL WORKS

New Technologies in Urban Drainage. C. Maksimovic. Elsevier Science Publishing Co., 655 Avenue of the Americas, New York, New York 10010. (212) 984-5800. 1991. Advances in rainfall-runoff modelling, hydrodynamics and quality modelling of receiving waters, and urban drainage in specific climates.

ONLINE DATA BASES

Computerized Engineering Index–COMPENDEX. Engineering Information Inc., 345 E. 47th St., New York, New York 10017. (212) 705-7600.

Monthly Catalog of United States Government Publications. U.S. G.P.O., Supt. of Docs., PO Box 371954, Pittsburgh, Pennsylvania 15250-7954. (202) 512-0000.

National Technical Information Service. U.S. Department of Commerce, National Technical Information Service, Office of Data Base Services, 5285 Port Royal Rd., Springfield, Virginia 22161. (703) 487-4807. Bibliographic database of government sponsored research and technical reports.

SCISEARCH. Institute for Scientific Information, University City Science Center, 3501 Market St., Philadelphia, Pennsylvania 19104. (215) 386-0100.

TRADE ASSOCIATIONS AND PROFESSIONAL SOCIETIES

American Public Works Association. 106 W. 11th St., Ste. 1800, Kansas City, Missouri 64105-1806. (816) 472-6100.

American Society of Agricultural Engineers. 2950 Niles Rd., St Joseph, Michigan 49085. (616) 429-0300.

American Society of Civil Engineers. 345 East 47th St., New York, New York 10017. (212) 705-7496.

American Water Resources Association. 5410 Grosvenor Lane, Suite 220, Bethesda, Maryland 20814. (301) 493-8600.

URBANIZATION

ABSTRACTING AND INDEXING SERVICES

Applied Science and Technology Index. H.W. Wilson Co., 950 University Ave., Bronx, New York 10452. (800) 367-6770. Formerly Industrial Arts Index.

Engineering Index. The Engineering Index Inc., 345 E. 47th St., New York, New York 10017. 1962-.

Urban Affairs Abstracts. National League of Cities, 1301 Pennsylvania Ave., NW, Washington, District of Columbia 20004. (202) 626-3150. 1977-. Weekly.

ENCYCLOPEDIAS AND DICTIONARIES

Encyclopedia of Community Planning and Environmental Management. Marilyn Spigel Schultz. Facts on File, Inc., 460 Park Ave. S., New York, New York 10016. (212) 683-2244. 1984.

McGraw-Hill Encyclopedia of Environmental Science. Sybil P. Parker. McGraw-Hill Science & Engineering Books, 11 W. 19th St., New York, New York 10011. (212) 337-6010. 1980. Covers ecology, man's influence on nature, and environmental protection.

Van Nostrand's Scientific Encyclopedia. Glenn D. Considine, ed. Van Nostrand Reinhold, 115 5th Ave., New York, New York 10003. (212) 254-3232. 1983. Sixth edition. Includes all broad subject areas in science.

ONLINE DATA BASES

Computerized Engineering Index–COMPENDEX. Engineering Information Inc., 345 E. 47th St., New York, New York 10017. (212) 705-7600.

Monthly Catalog of United States Government Publications. U.S. G.P.O., Supt. of Docs., PO Box 371954, Pittsburgh, Pennsylvania 15250-7954. (202) 512-0000.

National Technical Information Service. U.S. Department of Commerce, National Technical Information Service, Office of Data Base Services, 5285 Port Royal Rd., Springfield, Virginia 22161. (703) 487-4807. Bibliographic database of government sponsored research and technical reports.

PERIODICALS AND NEWSLETTERS

Journal of American Planning Association. American Planning Association, 1776 Massachusetts Avenue, NW, Suite 704, Washington, District of Columbia 20036.

(202) 872-0611. Quarterly. Represents the interests of professional urban and regional planners.

STATISTICS SOURCES

World Resources. World Resources Institute. 1709 New York Ave., N.W., Washington, District of Columbia 20006. (202) 638-6300. Annual. Statistical and textual analysis of world's natural resources and the effects of growth-caused environmental pollution.

TRADE ASSOCIATIONS AND PROFESSIONAL SOCIETIES

American Public Works Association. 106 W. 11th St., Ste. 1800, Kansas City, Missouri 64105-1806. (816) 472-6100.

URIC ACID

ABSTRACTING AND INDEXING SERVICES

Chemical Abstracts. Chemical Abstracts Service, 2540 Olentangy River Rd., PO Box 3012, Columbus, Ohio 43210. (800) 848-6533. 1907-.

General Science Index. H. W. Wilson Co., 950 University Ave., Bronx, New York 10452. 1978-. Monthly, also issued in annual cumulation. Cumulative subject index to English language periodicals in the subject fields of astronomy, botany, chemistry, earth science, environment and conservation, food and nutrition, genetics, mathematics, medicine and health, microbiology, oceanography, physics, physiology and zoology.

Science Citation Index. Institute for Scientific Information, 3501 Market St., Philadelphia, Pennsylvania 19104. 1961-.

ENCYCLOPEDIAS AND DICTIONARIES

A Dictionary of Genetics. Robert C. King and William A. Stansfield. Oxford University Press, 200 Madison Ave., New York, New York 10016. (212) 679-7300 or (800) 334-4249. 1991. Fourth edition. Includes 7,100 definitions with 250 illustrations. Also includes bibliography of major sources.

Dictionary of Genetics and Cell Biology. Norman Maclean. New York University Press, 70 Washington Sq. S., New York, New York 10012. (212) 998-2575. 1987. Includes the subject areas of cytology and genetics.

Encyclopedia of Human Biology. Renato Dulbecco, ed. Academic Press, c/o Harcourt Brace Jovanovich Inc., 6277 Sea Harbor Dr., Orlando, Florida 32887. (800) 346-8648. 1991. Eight volumes.

Encyclopedic Dictionary of Genetics: With German Term Equivalents and Extensive German/English Index. R. C. King and W. D. Stansfield. VCH Publishers, 303 NW 12th Ave., Deerfield Beach, Florida 33442-1788. (305) 428-5566. 1990. 4th ed. Revised edition of: A Dictionary of Genetics, third edition.

Van Nostrand's Scientific Encyclopedia. Glenn D. Considine, ed. Van Nostrand Reinhold, 115 5th Ave., New York, New York 10003. (212) 254-3232. 1983. Sixth edition. Includes all broad subject areas in science.

ONLINE DATA BASES

CAS Source Index–CASSI. Chemical Abstracts Service, 2540 Olentangy River Rd., P.O. Box 3012, Columbus, Ohio 43210. (800) 848-6533 or (614) 421-3600. A listing of bibliographic and library holdings information for scientific and technical primary literature relevant to the chemical sciences.

Chemical Abstracts-CA. Chemical Abstracts Service, 2540 Olentangy River Rd., P.O. Box 3012, Columbus, Ohio 43210. (800) 848-6533 or (614) 421-3600. Information sources include 9000 journals, patents from 27 countries, two industrial property organizations, new books, conference proceedings, and government research reports.

TRADE ASSOCIATIONS AND PROFESSIONAL SOCIETIES

American Chemical Society. 1155 16th St., N.W., Washington, District of Columbia 20036. (202) 872-4600.

UTAH ENVIRONMENTAL AGENCIES

GOVERNMENTAL ORGANIZATIONS

Department of Agriculture: Pesticide Registration. Director, Division of Plant Industry, 350 North Redwood Rd., Salt Lake City, Utah 84116. (801) 538-7128.

Department of Health: Air Quality. Director, Bureau of Air Quality, 288 North 1460 West, Salt Lake City, Utah 84116. (801) 538-6108.

Department of Health: Environmental Protection. Director, Division of Environmental Health, 288 North 1460 W., PO Box 16690, Salt Lake City, Utah 84116-1690. (801) 538-0700.

Department of Health: Water Quality. Director, Drinking Water/Sanitation Bureau, 288 North 1460 W., PO Box 16690, Salt Lake City, Utah 84116-0700. (801) 538-6159.

Department of Natural Resources and Energy: Fish and Wildlife. Director, Division of Wildlife Resources, 1596 N.W. Temple, Salt Lake City, Utah 84116. (801) 530-4700.

Department of Natural Resources and Energy: Natural Resources. Executive Director, 1636 N.W. Temple, Room 316, Salt Lake City, Utah 84116. (801) 538-7200.

Department of Natural Resources: Groundwater Management. State Engineer, Division of Water Rights, 1636 N.W. Temple, Salt Lake City, Utah 84116. (801) 538-7240.

Division of Environmental Health: Emergency Preparedness and Community Right-to-Know. Director, Division of Wildlife Resources, 1596 N.W. Temple, Salt Lake City, Utah 84116. (801) 530-1245.

Division of Environmental Health: Hazardous Waste Management. Director, Bureau of Hazardous Waste Management, 288 North 1460 W., PO Box 16690, Salt Lake City, Utah 84116-0700. (801) 538-6170.

Division of Environmental Health: Solid Waste Management. Director, Bureau of Hazardous Waste Management, 288 North 1460 W., Box 16690, Salt Lake City, Utah 84116-0700. (801) 538-6170.

Division of Environmental Health: Underground Storage Tanks. Director, Bureau of Hazardous Waste Management, 288 North 1460 W., PO Box 16690, Salt Lake City, Utah 84116-0700. (801) 538-6170.

Industrial Commission: Occupational Safety. Administrator, Occupational Safety and Health Division, 160 East 300 S., Salt Lake City, Utah 84110-5800. (801) 530-6901.

U.S. EPA Region 8: Pollution Prevention. Senior Policy Advisor, 999 18th St., Suite 500, Denver, Colorado 80202-2405. (303) 293-1603.

V

VACCINES

ABSTRACTING AND INDEXING SERVICES

ASFA Aquaculture Abstracts. Cambridge Scientific Abstracts, Inc., 5161 River Rd., Bethesda, Maryland 20816. (301) 961-6750. 1984.

General Science Index. H. W. Wilson Co., 950 University Ave., Bronx, New York 10452. 1978-. Monthly, also issued in annual cumulation. Cumulative subject index to English language periodicals in the subject fields of astronomy, botany, chemistry, earth science, environment and conservation, food and nutrition, genetics, mathematics, medicine and health, microbiology, oceanography, physics, physiology and zoology.

Science Citation Index. Institute for Scientific Information, 3501 Market St., Philadelphia, Pennsylvania 19104. 1961-.

ENCYCLOPEDIAS AND DICTIONARIES

Encyclopedia of Human Biology. Renato Dulbecco, ed. Academic Press, c/o Harcourt Brace Jovanovich Inc., 6277 Sea Harbor Dr., Orlando, Florida 32887. (800) 346-8648. 1991. Eight volumes.

Van Nostrand's Scientific Encyclopedia. Glenn D. Considine, ed. Van Nostrand Reinhold, 115 5th Ave., New York, New York 10003. (212) 254-3232. 1983. Sixth edition. Includes all broad subject areas in science.

HANDBOOKS AND MANUALS

Handbook of Toxicology. W. Thomas Shier and Dietrich Mebs. Marcel Dekker, Inc., 270 Madison Ave., New York, New York 10016. (212) 696-9000; (800) 228-1160. 1990. Covers most toxins for which sufficient research has been done to clearly establish the identity and characteristics of the toxin.

VANADIUM

See: METALS AND METALLURGY

VAPORIZATION

See: AIR POLLUTION

VAPORS, TOXIC

See: TOXIC POLLUTANTS

VEGETATION MAPPING

GENERAL WORKS

Yellowstone Vegetation, Consequences of Environment and History in a Natural Setting. Don G. Despain. Roberts Rinhart Pub., PO Box 666, Niwot, Colorado 80544. (303) 652-2921. 1990. Explores Yellowstone's vegetation types in their habitats and communities, in their origins and distribution, and in their succession after devastation by fire, wind, and insects.

VEHICLE INSPECTION

See: TRANSPORTATION

VENTURI SCRUBBERS

See: EMISSIONS

VERMONT ENVIRONMENTAL AGENCIES

GOVERNMENTAL ORGANIZATIONS

Agency of Natural Resources: Air Quality. Director, Air Pollution Control Division, 103 South Wissell, Waterbury, Vermont 05676. (802) 244-8731.

Agency of Natural Resources: Environmental Protection. Secretary, 103 South Wissell, Waterbury, Vermont 05676. (802) 244-7347.

Agency of Natural Resources: Fish and Wildlife. Commissioner, Department of Fish and Wildlife, 103 South Wissell, Waterbury, Vermont 05676. (802) 224-7331.

Agency of Natural Resources: Natural Resources. Secretary, 103 South Wissell, Waterbury, Vermont 05676. (802) 244-7347.

Agency of Natural Resources: Solid Waste Management. Director, Solid Waste Programs, 103 South Wissell, Waterbury, Vermont 05676. (802) 244-7831.

Department of Agriculture: Pesticide Registration. Director, Plant Industry, Laboratory and Standards Division,

116 State St., Montpelier, Vermont 05602. (802) 828-2431.

Department of Environmental Conservation: Groundwater Management. Commissioner, Agency of Natural Resources, 103 South Wissell, Waterbury, Vermont 05676. (802) 244-8755.

Department of Environmental Conservation: Hazardous Waste Management. Commissioner, 103 South Wissell, Waterbury, Vermont 05676. (802) 244-5141.

Department of Environmental Conservation: Underground Storage Tanks. Commissioner, Agency of Natural Resources, 103 South Wissell, Waterbury, Vermont 05676. (802) 244-8755.

Department of Environmental Conservation: Water Quality. Director, Water Quality Division, 103 South Wissell, Waterbury, Vermont 05676. (802) 244-6951.

Department of Health: Emergency Preparedness and Community Right-to-Know. Commissioner, 60 Main St., PO Box 70, Montpelier, Vermont 05402. (802) 863-7281.

Department of Labor and Industry: Occupational Safety. Manager, VOSHA Division, 5 Court St., Montpelier, Vermont 05602. (802) 828-2765.

Office of Water Resources Management: Groundwater Management. Groundwater Management Program, State Water Control Board, PO Box 11143, Richmond, Virginia 23230. (804) 367-6387.

VERMONT ENVIRONMENTAL LEGISLATION

GENERAL WORKS

Vermont Environmental Law Handbook. Vermont Bar Association, PO Box 100, Montpelier, Vermont 05601. (802) 223-2020. 1990.

Vermont Environmental Services Directory. Putney Press, PO Box 935, Brattleboro, Vermont 05302. (802)257-7305. 1991.

VNRC Legislative Bulletin. Vermont Natural Resources Council, 9 Bailey Ave., Montpelier, Vermont 05602. (802) 223-2328.

VINYL CHLORIDES

ABSTRACTING AND INDEXING SERVICES

General Science Index. H. W. Wilson Co., 950 University Ave., Bronx, New York 10452. 1978-. Monthly, also issued in annual cumulation. Cumulative subject index to English language periodicals in the subject fields of astronomy, botany, chemistry, earth science, environment and conservation, food and nutrition, genetics, mathematics, medicine and health, microbiology, oceanography, physics, physiology and zoology.

Science Citation Index. Institute for Scientific Information, 3501 Market St., Philadelphia, Pennsylvania 19104. 1961-.

BIBLIOGRAPHIES

A Summary of the NBS Literature Reviews on the Chemical Nature and Toxicity of the Pyrolysis and Combustion Products from Seven Plastics. Barbara C. Levin. National Technical Information Service, 5285 Port Royal Rd., Springfield, Virginia 22161. (703) 487-4650. 1986. Acrylonitrile-butadiene-styrenes (ABS), nylons, polyesters, polyethylenes, polystyrenes, poly(vinyl chlorides), and rigid polyurethane foams.

Vinyl Chloride Toxicology. U.S. Department of Health and Human Services, Public Health Services, National Institutes of Health, 9000 Rockville Pike, Bethesda, Maryland 20892. (301) 496-4000. 1980.

ENCYCLOPEDIAS AND DICTIONARIES

Encyclopedia of Chemical Technology. Raymond E. Kirk. John Wiley & Sons, Inc., 605 3rd Ave., New York, New York 10158-0012. (212) 850-6000. 1991-. 4th ed. Also known as Kirk Othmer Encyclopedia of Chemical Technology; consists of 26 volumes.

Encyclopedia of Polymer Science and Engineering. Herman F. Mark, et al., eds. John Wiley & Sons, Inc., 605 3rd Ave., New York, New York 10158-0012. (212) 850-6000. 1985-. Seventeen volumes and two supplements.

GENERAL WORKS

Biochemical and Physiological Aspects of Ethylene Production in Lower and Higher Plants. H. Clijsters. Kluwer Academic Publishers, 101 Philip Dr., Assinippi Park, Norwell, Massachusetts 02061. (617) 871-6600. 1989. Covers ethylene synthesis and metabolism.

Research and Development. National Technical Information Service, 5285 Port Royal Rd., Springfield, Virginia 22161. (703) 487-4650. 1980. Environmental effects of dichlorethylene.

HANDBOOKS AND MANUALS

Documentation of the Threshold Limit Values. American Conference of Governmental Industrial Hygienists, 6500 Glenway, Building D-5, Cincinnati, Ohio 45211. 1991. Provides threshold limit value documentation for any physical phenomenon in the environment, including chemical substances and physical agents.

FDA Food Additives Analytical Manual. C. Warner, et al., eds. Association of Official Analytical Chemists, 2200 Wilson Blvd., Suite 400-P, Arlington, Virginia 22201-3301. (703) 522-3032. 1983-1987. 2 vols. Provides methodology for determining compliance with food additive regulations. Contains analytical methods that have been evaluated by the FDA or found to operate satisfactorily in at least two laboratories.

Handbook of Chemistry and Physics. CRC Press, 2000 Corporate Blvd. N.W., Boca Raton, Florida 33431. (800) 272-7737. Annually.

Handbook of Environmental Data on Organic Chemicals. Karel Verschueren. Van Nostrand Reinhold, 115 5th Ave., New York, New York 10003. (212) 254-3232. 1983. Covers individual substances as well as mixtures and preparations. The profiles include: properties, air pollution factors, water pollution factors, and biological effects.

Hazardous Chemicals Data Book. G. Weiss, ed. Noyes Publications, 120 Mill Rd., Park Ridge, New Jersey 07656. (201) 391-8484. 1986. 2d ed. Supplies instant information on 1015 hazardous chemicals. The data will provide rapid assistance to personnel involved with handling of hazardous chemical materials and related accidents.

NIOSH Pocket Guide to Chemical Hazards. National Institute for Occupational Safety and Health, 1600 Clifton Rd. NE, Atlanta, Georgia 30333. (404) 639-3286. 1990. Presents sources of general industrial hygiene and medical surveillance information for workers, employees and others. Presents key information and data in an abbreviated format for 398 individual chemicals or chemical types.

ONLINE DATA BASES

CERCLIS. Chemical Information Systems, Inc., 7215 York Rd., Baltimore, Maryland 21212. (301) 321-8440. Information on hazardous waste disposal sites that have either been listed by the EPA on the National Priority List (NPL) or nominated for consideration for the NPL.

Chemical Collection System/Request Tracking–CCS/RTS. U.S. Environmental Protection Agency, Office of Pesticides and Toxic Substances, 401 M St., SW, Washington, District of Columbia 20460. (202) 260-2090. Contains information on various properties of a number of chemicals including environmental effects, test and analysis methods, and health effects. Available from EPA.

Chemical Dictionary Online–CHEMLINE. Chemical Abstracts Service, 2540 Olentangy River Rd., Columbus, Ohio 43210. (614) 421-3600 or (800) 848-6533. Part of MEDLINE of the National Library of Medicine (NLM). File of 900,000 names for chemical substances, representing 450,000 unique compounds. It contains such information as Chemical Abstracts (CA) Service Registry Numbers, molecular formulas, preferred chemical nomenclature, and generic and ring structure information. Available on NLM's ELHILL system.

Chemical Exposure. Science Applications International Corp., Health & Environmental Information, P.O. Box 2501, Oak Ridge, Tennessee 37831. (615) 482-9031. Database of chemicals that have been identified in both human tissues and body fluids and in feral and food animals. Contains reference to journal articles, conferences, and reports. Covers the whole fields of information related to human and animal exposure to food, air, and water contaminants and pharmaceuticals. Its records include information on chemical properties, formulas, tissues measured, analytical method used, demographics and more. Available on DIALOG.

PERIODICALS AND NEWSLETTERS

Environmental Science and Technology. American Chemical Society, 1155 16th St. N.W., Washington, District of Columbia 20036. (800) 227-5558. 1967-. Monthly. Contains research articles on various aspects of environmental chemistry, interpretative articles by invited experts and commentary on the scientific aspects of environmental management.

Journal of Environmental Quality. American Society of Agronomy, 677 S. Segoe Rd., Madison, Wisconsin 53711-1086. (608) 273-8080. 1972-. Quarterly. Reports and brief reviews of agricultural ecology, environmental engineering and pollution.

TRADE ASSOCIATIONS AND PROFESSIONAL SOCIETIES

American Chemical Society. 1155 16th St., N.W., Washington, District of Columbia 20036. (202) 872-4600.

American Institute of Chemical Engineers. 345 East 47th St., New York, New York 10017. (212) 705-7338.

American Institute of Chemists. 7315 Wisconsin Ave., Bethesda, Maryland 20814. (301) 652-2447.

VIRGINIA ENVIRONMENTAL AGENCIES

GOVERNMENTAL ORGANIZATIONS

Council on the Environment: Coastal Zone Management. Administrator, Ninth Street Office Bldg., Room 903, Richmond, Virginia 23219. (804) 786-4500.

Council on the Environment: Environmental Protection. Administrator, Ninth Street Office Bldg., Room 903, Richmond, Virginia 23219. (804) 786-4500.

Department of Agriculture and Consumer Services: Pesticide Registration. Supervisor, Office of Pesticide Registration, PO Box 1163, Richmond, Virginia 23209. (804) 786-3162.

Department of Community Development: Emergency Preparedness and Community Right-to-Know. Emergency Response Commission, 9th and Columbia Bldg., Olympia, Washington 98504. (206) 459-9191.

Department of Labor and Industry: Occupational Safety. Commissioner, PO Box 12064, Richmond, Virginia 23219. (804) 786-2377.

Department of Waste Management: Air Quality. Director, Emergency Response Council, James Monroe Building, 14th Floor, 101 North 14th St., Richmond, Virginia 23219. (804) 225-2997.

Department of Waste Management: Emergency Preparedness and Community Right-to-Know. State Emergency Response Council, James Monroe Bldg., 11th Floor, 101 North 14th St., Richmond, Virginia 23219. (804) 225-2667.

Department of Waste Management: Hazardous Waste Management. Executive Director, 101 North 14th St., 11th Floor, Richmond, Virginia 23219. (804) 225-2667.

Department of Waste Management: Solid Waste Management. Executive Director, 101 North 14th St., 11th Floor, Richmond, Virginia 23219. (804) 225-2667.

Department of Waste Management: Waste Minimization and Pollution Prevention. Director, Office of Policy and Planning, 11th Floor, Monroe Bldg., 101 North 14th St., Richmond, Virginia 23219. (804) 225-2667.

Game and Inland Fisheries Department: Fish and Wildlife. Executive Director, Fresh Water, 4010 W. Broad St., Richmond, Virginia 23230. (804) 367-9231.

Office of the Secretary of Natural Resources: Natural Resources. Secretary, 733 Ninth St., Richmond, Virginia 23212. (804) 786-0044.

State Water Control Board: Underground Storage Tanks. Director, Office of Water Resources Management, PO Box 11143, Richmond, Virginia 23230. (804) 367-6383.

State Water Control Board: Water Quality. Executive Director, PO Box 11143, Richmond, Virginia 23230. (804) 257-6384.

VIRGINIA ENVIRONMENTAL LEGISLATION

GENERAL WORKS

Virginia Environmental Law Handbook. Government Institutes, Inc., 4 Research Pl., Ste. 200, Rockville, Maryland 20850. (301) 921-2300. 1990.

VISIBILITY

ABSTRACTING AND INDEXING SERVICES

Physics Briefs. Physikalische Berichte. Physik Verlag, Pappapelallee 3, Postfach 101161, Weinheim, Germany D-6940. 1979-. Semimonthly. In English. Volumes for 1979- issued by the Deutsche Physikalische Gesellschaft and the Fachinformationszentrum Energie Physik, Mathematik in cooperation with the American Institute of Physics.

Science Citation Index. Institute for Scientific Information, 3501 Market St., Philadelphia, Pennsylvania 19104. 1961-.

ENCYCLOPEDIAS AND DICTIONARIES

The Encyclopedia of Climatology. John E. Oliver and Rhodes W. Fairbridge, eds. Van Nostrand Reinhold, 115 5th Ave., New York, New York 10003. (212) 254-3232. 1987. Belongs in the series Encyclopedia of Earth Sciences, v.11.

VISUAL POLLUTION

See: AIR POLLUTION

VITAMINS

See also: FOOD SCIENCE; NUTRITION

ABSTRACTING AND INDEXING SERVICES

Food Science and Technology Abstracts. International Food Information Service, c/o National Food Laboratory, 6363 Clark Ave., Dublin, California 94568. (800) 336-3782. 1969-.

General Science Index. H. W. Wilson Co., 950 University Ave., Bronx, New York 10452. 1978-. Monthly, also issued in annual cumulation. Cumulative subject index to English language periodicals in the subject fields of astronomy, botany, chemistry, earth science, environment and conservation, food and nutrition, genetics,

mathematics, medicine and health, microbiology, oceanography, physics, physiology and zoology.

Science Citation Index. Institute for Scientific Information, 3501 Market St., Philadelphia, Pennsylvania 19104. 1961-.

Vitamin E Abstracts. Max K. Horwitt. VERIS–Vitamin E Research & Information Service, 5325 S. 9th Ave., La Grange, Illinois 60525. (800) 328-6199. 1980-. Annual. Gives information of current interest on Vitamin E. Answers to questions about Vitamin E; Vitamin E related research findings; Annual comprehensive Vitamin E research Abstracts; and Vitamin E for university research.

ENCYCLOPEDIAS AND DICTIONARIES

Cambridge Dictionary of Biology. Peter M. B. Walker. Cambridge University Press, 40 W. 20th St., New York, New York 10011. (212) 924-3900 or (800) 227-0247. 1989. Includes 10,000 terms in zoology, botany, biochemistry, molecular biology and genetics. Previously published under the title Chambers Biology Dictionary.

A Concise Dictionary of Biology. Elizabeth Martin, ed. Oxford University Press, 200 Madison Ave., New York, New York 10016. (212) 679-7300 or (800) 334-4249. 1990. New edition. Derived from the Concise Science Dictionary, published in 1984.

The Dictionary of Cell Biology. J. M. Lackie and J. A. T. Dow, eds. Academic Press, c/o Harcourt Brace Jovanovich Inc., 6277 Sea Harbor Dr., Orlando, Florida 32887. (800) 346-8648. 1989. Covers the broad subject area of cell biology including lipid, vitamins, amino acid, lectins, proteins, and other related topics.

The Nutrition and Health Encyclopedia. David F. Tver and Percy Russell. Van Nostrand Reinhold, 115 5th Ave., New York, New York 10003. (212) 254-3232. 1989.

Van Nostrand's Scientific Encyclopedia. Glenn D. Considine, ed. Van Nostrand Reinhold, 115 5th Ave., New York, New York 10003. (212) 254-3232. 1983. Sixth edition. Includes all broad subject areas in science.

GENERAL WORKS

The Complete Book of Vitamins. Rodale Press, 33 E. Minor St., Emmaus, Pennsylvania 18098. (215) 967-5171. 1984.

Magill's Survey of Science. Life Science Series. Frank N. Magill, ed. Salem Press, PO Box 50062, Pasadena, California 91105. 1991. Six volumes. Contents: v.1. A-Central and peripheral nervous system functions; v.2. Central metabolism regulation - eukaryotic transcriptional control; v.3. Positive and negative eukaryotic transcriptional control - mammalian hormones; v.4. Hormones and behavior - muscular contraction; v.5. Muscular contraction and relaxation - sexual reproduction in plants; v.6. Reproductive behavior and mating - X inactivation and the Lyon hypothesis.

Vitamins and "Health" Foods. Victor Herbert. George F. Stickley Co., Philadelphia, Pennsylvania 1981. Vitamins, dietary supplements and nutrition as well as inherent dangers of quackery.

Vitamins and Minerals: Help or Harm?. Charles W. Marshall. George F. Stickley Co., Philadelphia, Pennsylvania 1983.

Vitamins in Human Biology and Medicine. Michael H. Briggs. CRC Press, 2000 Corporate Blvd. N.W., Boca Raton, Florida 33431. (800) 272-7737. 1981. Deals with physiological effects of vitamins and vitamins in human nutrition.

HANDBOOKS AND MANUALS

Complete Guide to Vitamins, Minerals and Supplements. H. Winter Griffith. Fisher Books, 3499 N. Campbell Ave., Suite 909, Tucson, Arizona 85712. (602) 325-5263. 1988. Includes name, brand name, reasons to use, who should use, recommended daily allowance, and other related data in the form of a chart.

CRC Handbook of Hormones, Vitamins, and Radiopaques. Matthew Verderame. CRC Press, 2000 Corporate Blvd. N.W., Boca Raton, Florida 33431. (800) 272-7737. 1986. Covers contrast media, hormones, and vitamins.

Handbook of Toxicology. W. Thomas Shier and Dietrich Mebs. Marcel Dekker, Inc., 270 Madison Ave., New York, New York 10016. (212) 696-9000; (800) 228-1160. 1990. Covers most toxins for which sufficient research has been done to clearly establish the identity and characteristics of the toxin.

Handbook of Vitamins. Lawrence J. Machlin. Marcel Dekker, Inc., 270 Madison Ave., New York, New York 10016. (212) 696-9000; (800) 228-1160. 1991. Food science and technology of vitamins in human nutrition.

Handbook of Vitamins, Minerals, and Hormones. Roman J. Kutsky. Van Nostrand Reinhold, 115 5th Ave., New York, New York 10003. (212) 254-3232. 1981. Covers vitamins, hormones and minerals in the body.

TRADE ASSOCIATIONS AND PROFESSIONAL SOCIETIES

American Chemical Society. 1155 16th St., N.W., Washington, District of Columbia 20036. (202) 872-4600.

North American Benthological Society. c/o Cheryl R. Black, Savannah River Ecology Laboratory, Drawer E, Aiken, South Carolina 29802. (803) 925-7425.

VITRIFICATION

ABSTRACTING AND INDEXING SERVICES

General Science Index. H. W. Wilson Co., 950 University Ave., Bronx, New York 10452. 1978-. Monthly, also issued in annual cumulation. Cumulative subject index to English language periodicals in the subject fields of astronomy, botany, chemistry, earth science, environment and conservation, food and nutrition, genetics, mathematics, medicine and health, microbiology, oceanography, physics, physiology and zoology.

Science Citation Index. Institute for Scientific Information, 3501 Market St., Philadelphia, Pennsylvania 19104. 1961-.

GENERAL WORKS

In Situ Vitrification of PCB-Contaminated Soils. Battelle, Pacific Northwest Laboratories. Electric Power Research Institute, 3412 Hillview Ave., Palo Alto, California 94304. (415) 965-4081. 1986. Covers polychlorinated biphenyls and soil contamination.

VOLATILE ORGANIC COMPOUNDS

ABSTRACTING AND INDEXING SERVICES

General Science Index. H. W. Wilson Co., 950 University Ave., Bronx, New York 10452. 1978-. Monthly, also issued in annual cumulation. Cumulative subject index to English language periodicals in the subject fields of astronomy, botany, chemistry, earth science, environment and conservation, food and nutrition, genetics, mathematics, medicine and health, microbiology, oceanography, physics, physiology and zoology.

Science Citation Index. Institute for Scientific Information, 3501 Market St., Philadelphia, Pennsylvania 19104. 1961-.

GENERAL WORKS

Emissions of Reactive Volatile Organic Compounds from Utility Broilers. National Technical Information Service, 5285 Port Royal Rd., Springfield, Virginia 22161. (703) 487-4650. 1980. Air pollution management, electrical power plants, and flue gases.

Guidance to State and Local Agencies in Preparing Regulations to Control Volatile Organic Compounds from Ten Stationary Source Categories. National Technical Information Service, 5285 Port Royal Rd., Springfield, Virginia 22161. (703) 487-4650. 1979. Environmental aspects of organic compounds and air pollution standards.

Procedures for the Preparation of Emission Inventories for Volatile Organic Compounds. National Technical Information Service, 5285 Port Royal Rd., Springfield, Virginia 22161. (703) 487-4650. 1980. Air pollution measurement and air quality management.

Significance and Treatment of Volatile Organic Compounds in Water Supplies. Neil M. Ram, et al. Lewis Publishers, 2000 Corporate Blvd., N.W., Boca Raton, Florida 33431. (407) 994-0555 or (800) 272-7737. 1990. Includes EPA approved analytical methods for VOC analysis, QA/QC, data quality objectives and limits of detection. Covers current methods for the assessment of health effects, including toxicity and carcinogenicity.

Treatment of Volatile Organic Compounds in Drinking Water. U.S. Environmental Protection Agency, Municipal Environmental Research Laboratory, Office of Research and Development, 26 W. Martin Luther King Dr., Cincinnati, Ohio 45268. (513) 569-7931. 1983. Drinking water purification methods.

Volatile Organic Compounds. Lewis Publishers, 200 Corporate Blvd. NW, Boca Raton, Florida 33431. (407) 994-0555 or (800)272-7737. 1991. Covers health aspects of drinking water, organic water pollutants, water purification and organic compounds removal.

HANDBOOKS AND MANUALS

Manual of Determination of Volatile Organic Compounds in Paints, Inks, and Related Coating Products. J. John Brezinski. ASTM, 1916 Race St., Philadelphia, Pennsylvania 19103-1187. (215) 299-5400. 1989. Analysis of solvents.

National Ambient Volatile Organic Compounds. U.S. Environmental Protection Agency, Atmospheric Sciences Research Laboratory, MD 75, Research Triangle Park, North Carolina 27711. 1988.

Volatile Organic Compound Species Data Manual. National Technical Information Service, 5285 Port Royal Rd., Springfield, Virginia 22161. (703) 487-4650. 1980. Covers air pollution standards in the United States.

ONLINE DATA BASES

CAS Source Index–CASSI. Chemical Abstracts Service, 2540 Olentangy River Rd., P.O. Box 3012, Columbus, Ohio 43210. (800) 848-6533 or (614) 421-3600. A listing of bibliographic and library holdings information for scientific and technical primary literature relevant to the chemical sciences.

TRADE ASSOCIATIONS AND PROFESSIONAL SOCIETIES

American Chemical Society. 1155 16th St., N.W., Washington, District of Columbia 20036. (202) 872-4600.

VOLCANOES

ABSTRACTING AND INDEXING SERVICES

General Science Index. H. W. Wilson Co., 950 University Ave., Bronx, New York 10452. 1978-. Monthly, also issued in annual cumulation. Cumulative subject index to English language periodicals in the subject fields of astronomy, botany, chemistry, earth science, environment and conservation, food and nutrition, genetics, mathematics, medicine and health, microbiology, oceanography, physics, physiology and zoology.

Science Citation Index. Institute for Scientific Information, 3501 Market St., Philadelphia, Pennsylvania 19104. 1961-.

BIBLIOGRAPHIES

Bibliography and Index of Geology. American Geological Institute, 4220 King St., Alexandria, Virginia 22302. Monthly. Includes environmental geology and hydrogeology.

ENCYCLOPEDIAS AND DICTIONARIES

The Encyclopedia of Climatology. John E. Oliver and Rhodes W. Fairbridge, eds. Van Nostrand Reinhold, 115 5th Ave., New York, New York 10003. (212) 254-3232. 1987. Belongs in the series Encyclopedia of Earth Sciences, v.11.

The Encyclopedia of Geochemistry and Environmental Sciences. Rhodes Whitmore Fairbridge. Van Nostrand Reinhold Co., 115 5th Ave., New York, New York 10003. (212) 254-3232. 1972.

Glossary of Geology. Robert Latimer Bates and Julia A. Jackson, eds. American Geological Institute, 4220 King St., Alexandria, Virginia 22302-1507. (703) 379-2480 or (800) 336-4764. 1987. Third edition.

McGraw-Hill Encyclopedia of the Geological Sciences. Sybil P. Parker, ed. McGraw-Hill, 1221 Avenue of the Americas, New York, New York 10020. (212) 512-2000 or (800) 262-4729. 1988. Second edition. Published previously in the McGraw-Hill Encyclopedia of Science and Technology.

Van Nostrand's Scientific Encyclopedia. Glenn D. Considine, ed. Van Nostrand Reinhold, 115 5th Ave., New York, New York 10003. (212) 254-3232. 1983. Sixth edition. Includes all broad subject areas in science.

GENERAL WORKS

Magill's Survey of Science. Earth Science Series. Frank N. Magill. Salem Press, PO Box 50062, Pasadena, California 91105. 1990-. Five volumes. Includes information on earth's crust, hot spots and volcanic island chains, physical properties of minerals, rock magnetism, physical properties of rocks, and index.

Volcanoes. Susanna Van Rose and Ian Mercer. Harvard University Press, 79 Garden St., Cambridge, Massachusetts 02138. (617) 495-2600. 1991. Second edition.

PERIODICALS AND NEWSLETTERS

Earthquakes & Volcanos. Geological Survey. U.S. Geological Survey, 12201 Sunrise Valley Dr., Reston, Virginia 22092. (703) 648-4460. Bimonthly. Earthquake information bulletin.

W

WAR–ENVIRONMENTAL EFFECTS

See: DISASTERS

WARMING

See: GLOBAL WARMING

WASHINGTON ENVIRONMENTAL AGENCIES

GOVERNMENTAL ORGANIZATIONS

Department of Agriculture: Pesticide Registration. Director, Chemical and Plant Division, 406 General Administration Bldg., GT-12, Olympia, Washington 98504. (206) 753-5062.

Department of Ecology: Air Quality. Air Program Manager, Air Program Division, Mail Stop PV-11, Olympia, Washington 98504. (206) 459-6255.

Department of Ecology: Environmental Protection. Director, Mail Stop PV-11, Olympia, Washington 98504. (206) 459-6168.

Department of Ecology: Hazardous Waste Management. Program Manager, Solid and Hazardous Waste, Mail Stop PV-11, Olympia, Washington 98504. (206) 459-6316.

Department of Ecology: Solid Waste Management. Section Head, Solid Waste Support, 4224 Sixth Ave., S.E., Row 6, Building 4, Mail Stop PV-11, Lacey, Washington 98503. (206) 459-6259.

Department of Ecology: Underground Storage Tanks. Unit Supervisor, Underground Storage Tank Program, 4224 Sixth Ave., S.E., Mail Stop PV-11, Lacey, Washington 98504. (206) 459-6272.

Department of Ecology: Waste Minimization and Pollution Prevention. Program Manager, Hazardous Waste Section, 4424 6th Ave., S.E., Olympia, Washington 98504-8711. (206) 459-6322.

Department of Ecology: Water Quality. Assistant Director, Water and Shorelands, Mail Stop PV-11, Olympia, Washington 98504-8711. (206) 438-7090.

Department of Labor and Industry: Occupational Safety. Assistant Director, Industrial Safety and Health, 805 Plum St., S.E., Mail Stop HC-402, Olympia, Washington 98504

Department of Natural Resources: Natural Resources. Commissioner of Public Lands, 201 John A. Cherburg Bldg., Mail Stop QW-21, Olympia, Washington 98504. (206) 753-5317.

Department of Wildlife: Fish and Wildlife. Director, 600 North Capitol Way, Olympia, Washington 98501-1091. (206) 753-5710.

WASHINGTON ENVIRONMENTAL LEGISLATION

GENERAL WORKS

Washington Environmental Law Handbook. Government Institutes, Inc., 4 Research Pl., Ste. 200, Rockville, Maryland 20850. (301) 921-2300. 1990.

WASTE

See also: GARBAGE; SOLID WASTES

ABSTRACTING AND INDEXING SERVICES

Applied Ecology Abstracts Studies in Renewable Natural Resources. Information Retrieval Ltd., 1911 Jefferson Davis Highway, Arlington, Virginia 22202. 1975-. Monthly.

Applied Science and Technology Index. H.W. Wilson Co., 950 University Ave., Bronx, New York 10452. (800) 367-6770. Formerly Industrial Arts Index.

EIS: Digests of Environmental Impact Statements. Cambridge Scientific Abstracts, 5161 River Rd., Bethesda, Maryland 20816. (301) 951-1400. 1970-. Bimonthly. Provides detailed abstracts of all the environmental impact statements issued by the federal government each year and indexes them. Also extracts the key issues from the complex government released environmental impact statements. Contents include areas such as: air transportation, defense programs, energy, hazardous substances, land use, manufacturing, parks, refuges, forests, research and development, roads and railroads, urban and social programs, wastes, and water.

Multimedia Index to Ecology. National Information Center for Educational Media, University of Southern California, Los Angeles, California 90007.

Public Health Engineering Abstracts. U.S. G.P.O., Washington, District of Columbia 20401. (202) 512-0000. Monthly.

Science Citation Index. Institute for Scientific Information, 3501 Market St., Philadelphia, Pennsylvania 19104. 1961-.

DIRECTORIES

Gale Environmental Sourcebook. Karen Hill. Gale Research Co., 835 Penobscot Bldg., Detroit, Michigan 48226-4094. (313) 961-2242. Contacts, information sources, or general information on environmental topics.

ENCYCLOPEDIAS AND DICTIONARIES

Dictionary of Environmental Protection Technology: In Four Languages, English, German, French, Russian. Egon Seidel. Elsevier Science Publishing Co., 655 Avenue of the Americas, New York, New York 10010. (212) 984-5800. 1988.

English-Russian Dictionary of Environmental Protection: About 14,000 Terms. E.L. Milovanov. Pergamon Microforms International, Inc., Fairview Park, Elmsford, New York 10523. (914) 592-7720. 1981.

Environmental Engineering Dictionary. C. C. Lee. Government Institutes, Inc., 4 Research Pl., Ste. 200, Rockville, Maryland 20850. (301) 921-2300. 1989. Defines over 6000 engineering terms relating to pollutioncontrol technologies, monitoring, risk assessment, sampling andanalysis, quality control, permitting, and environmentally-regulated engineering and science. Includes bibliographical references (p. 612-627).

GENERAL WORKS

Managing Health Care Hazards. Linda F. Chaff. Labelmaster, 574 N. Pulaski Rd., Chicago, Illinois 60646. (312) 478-0900. 1988.

ONLINE DATA BASES

Monthly Catalog of United States Government Publications. U.S. G.P.O., Supt. of Docs., PO Box 371954, Pittsburgh, Pennsylvania 15250-7954. (202) 512-0000.

National Technical Information Service. U.S. Department of Commerce, National Technical Information Service, Office of Data Base Services, 5285 Port Royal Rd., Springfield, Virginia 22161. (703) 487-4807. Bibliographic database of government sponsored research and technical reports.

National Waste Exchange Data Base. Northeast Industrial Waste Exchange, 90 Presidential Plaza, Ste. 122, Syracuse, New York 13202. (315) 422-6572. Computerized catalog of waste materials listed with the Northeast Industrial Exchange.

Report on Defense Plant Wastes. Business Publishers, Inc., 951 Pershing Dr., Silver Spring, Maryland 20910-4464. (301) 587-6300. Laws, regulations, cleanup actions, contracts, and court actions affecting U.S. defense, weapons production, government hospitals and laboratories, and other government institutions. Online version of periodical of the same name.

Waste Information Digest. Environmental Studies Institute, International Academy at Santa Barbara, 800 Gar-

den St., Suite D, Santa Barbara, California 93101-1552. (805) 965-5010. Online version of the periodical of the same name.

Waste Management and Resource Recovery. International Research & Evaluation, 21098 IRE Control Center, Eagan, Minnesota 55121. (612) 888-9635.

WasteInfo. Waste Management Information Bureau, United Kingdom Atomic Energy Authority, Building 46J, Harwell Laboratory, Harwell, Oxfordshire, England OX11 ORB. 44 (235) 24141.

PERIODICALS AND NEWSLETTERS

Official Bulletin of the North Dakota Water and Pollution Control Conference. North Dakota State Health Dept., Bismarck, North Dakota 58501. (701) 224-2354. Quarterly. Municipal water and waste systems and industrial wastes.

Report on Defense Plant Wastes. Business Publishers, Inc., 951 Pershing Dr., Silver Spring, Maryland 20910-4464. (301) 587-6300. 1989-. Biweekly. Reports on environmental laws, regulations, cleanups, contracts and court actions affecting U.S. defense weapons production, government hospitals and other government institutions. Also available online.

Waste Information Digests. Environmental Studies Institute, International Academy at Santa Barbara, 800 Garden St., Suite D, Santa Barbara, California 93101-1552. (805) 965-5010. Eight times a year. Covers waste collection, management and recycling.

Waste Watch Magazine. Massachusetts Department of Environmental Quality Control, Division of Solid Waste Management, 1 Winter Street, 4th Floor, Boston, Massachusetts 02108. (617) 292-5989. Quarterly. Covers issues and events in solid waste disposal.

STATISTICS SOURCES

Environmental Data Compendium. OECD Publications and Information Center, 2001 L St., N.W., Suite 700, Washington, District of Columbia 20036. (202) 785-6323. 1989.

Environmental Indicators. OECD Publications and Information Center, 2001 L St., N.W., Suite 700, Washington, District of Columbia 20036. (202) 785-6323. 1991.

Environmental Quality. Council on Environmental Quality. U.S. G.P.O., Washington, District of Columbia 20401. (202) 512-0000. Annual.

The State of the Environment. OECD Publications and Information Center, 2001 L St., N.W., Suite 700, Washington, District of Columbia 20036. (202) 785-6323. 1991.

TRADE ASSOCIATIONS AND PROFESSIONAL SOCIETIES

Association of Soil & Foundation Engineers. 8811 Colesville Rd., Suite G106, Silver Spring, Maryland 20910. (301) 563-2733.

CONCERN, Inc. 1794 Columbia Rd, NW, Washington, District of Columbia 20009. (202) 328-8160.

Waste Systems Institute of Michigan, Inc. 400 Ann, N.W., Suite 204, Grand Rapids, Michigan 49504. (616) 363-3262.

Waste Watch. P.O. Box 298, Livingston, Kentucky 40445.

WASTE DISPOSAL

ABSTRACTING AND INDEXING SERVICES

Applied Ecology Abstracts Studies in Renewable Natural Resources. Information Retrieval Ltd., 1911 Jefferson Davis Highway, Arlington, Virginia 22202. 1975-. Monthly.

Applied Science and Technology Index. H.W. Wilson Co., 950 University Ave., Bronx, New York 10452. (800) 367-6770. Formerly Industrial Arts Index.

ASFA Aquaculture Abstracts. Cambridge Scientific Abstracts, Inc., 5161 River Rd., Bethesda, Maryland 20816. (301) 961-6750. 1984.

Biological and Agricultural Index. H.W. Wilson Co., 950 University Ave., Bronx, New York 10452. (800) 367-6770. 1916-. Monthly.

Civil Engineering Hydraulic Abstracts. BHRA Fluid Engineering, Air Science Co., PO Box 143, Corning, New York 14830. (607) 962-5591. Monthly. Abstracts of periodicals that publish in the areas of hydraulic engineering and other related topics.

Current Advances in Ecological and Environmental Science. Pergamon Microforms International, Inc., Fairview Park, Elmsford, New York 10523. (914) 592-7720. 1989-. Monthly. Current literature searching service includingjournals, reports, abstracts, etc. This service is available online as part of the CABS database on the hosts BRS and ORBIT search service.

Energy Information Abstracts Annual 1987 in Retrospect. EIC/Intelligence Inc., 121 Chanlon Rd., New Providence, New Jersey 07974. (908) 464-6800. 1988. Annual. Cumulative edition of the monthly Energy Information Abstracts. Monitors sources in the field of energy including the scientific, technical and business journal literature, conference and symposia proceedings, corporate, government and academic reports.

Engineering Index. The Engineering Index Inc., 345 E. 47th St., New York, New York 10017. 1962-.

General Science Index. H. W. Wilson Co., 950 University Ave., Bronx, New York 10452. 1978-. Monthly, also issued in annual cumulation. Cumulative subject index to English language periodicals in the subject fields of astronomy, botany, chemistry, earth science, environment and conservation, food and nutrition, genetics, mathematics, medicine and health, microbiology, oceanography, physics, physiology and zoology.

Geographical Abstracts. London School of Economics, Dept. of Geography, Regency House, 34 Duke St., London, England 1966-. Continued by Geo Abstracts issued in 6 parts: Pt. A. Landforms and the quaternary; Pt. B. Biogeography and Climatology; Pt. C. Economic geography; Pt. D. Social geography and cartography; Pt. E. Sedimentology; Pt. F. Regional and community planning.

Multimedia Index to Ecology. National Information Center for Educational Media, University of Southern California, Los Angeles, California 90007.

Pollution Abstracts. Cambridge Scientific Abstracts, 5161 River Rd., Bethesda, Maryland 20816. (301) 961-6750. Six/year. Indexes worldwide technical literature on environmental pollution. Covers air pollution, marine and freshwater pollution, sewage and wastewater treatment, waste management, toxicology and health, noise pollution, radiation, land pollution, and environmental policies, programs, legislation, and education. Also available online.

Public Health Engineering Abstracts. U.S. G.P.O., Washington, District of Columbia 20401. (202) 512-0000. Monthly.

Radioactive Waste Management. National Technical Information Service, 5285 Port Royal Rd., Springfield, Virginia 22161. (703) 487-4650. Monthly. Topics include spent-fuel transport and storage; radioactive effluents from nuclear facilities; and techniques of processing wastes, their storage, and ultimate disposal.

Science Citation Index. Institute for Scientific Information, 3501 Market St., Philadelphia, Pennsylvania 19104. 1961-.

Urban Affairs Abstracts. National League of Cities, 1301 Pennsylvania Ave., NW, Washington, District of Columbia 20004. (202) 626-3150. 1977-. Weekly.

BIBLIOGRAPHIES

Bibliography of Livestock Waste Management. U.S. Government Printing Office, Washington, District of Columbia 20402-9325. (202) 783-3238. 1972. Covers agricultural and animal waste, manure handling, and feedlots.

New Publications of the Geological Survey. U.S. Department of the Interior, Geological Survey, 119 National Center, Reston, Virginia 22092. (703) 648-4460. 1984-. Monthly. Bibliography of geological publications and related government documents published by the Geological Survey.

DIRECTORIES

Directory of Waste Equipment Manufacturers. Waste Equipment Manufacturers Institute/National Solid Wastes Management Association, 1730 Rhode Island Ave., N.W., Suite 1000, Washington, District of Columbia 20036. (202) 659-4613.

Directory of Waste Utilization Technologies in Europe and the United States. Institute for Local Self-Reliance, 2425 18th St., N.W., Washington, District of Columbia 20009. (202) 232-4108.

Waste Age–Directory to Waste Systems and Services Supplement. National Solid Waste Management Association, 1730 Rhode Island Ave., NW, Suite 1000, Washington, District of Columbia 20036. (202) 659-4613.

Waste Industry Buyer Guide. National Solid Wastes Management Association, 1730 Rhode Island Ave., N.W., Suite 1000, Washington, District of Columbia 20036. (202) 659-4613.

ENCYCLOPEDIAS AND DICTIONARIES

Dictionary of Ecology and Environment. P. H. Collin. Collin Pub., 8 The Causeway, Teddington, England TW11 0HE. 1988. Vocabulary of 5,000 words and expressions covering a range of topics relating to ecology, including: climate, vegetation, pollution, waste disposal, and energy conservation.

Dictionary of Environmental Engineering and Related Sciences: English-Spanish, Spanish-English. Jose T. Villate. Ediciones Universal, 3090 SW 8th St., Miami, Florida 33135. (305) 642-3355. 1979.

Dictionary of Environmental Protection. Otto E. Tutzauer. Fred B. Rothman, 10368 W. Centennial Rd., Littleton, California 80127. (303) 979-5657. 1979.

Dictionary of Environmental Protection Technology: In Four Languages, English, German, French, Russian. Egon Seidel. Elsevier Science Publishing Co., 655 Avenue of the Americas, New York, New York 10010. (212) 984-5800. 1988.

Encyclopedia of Environmental Control Technology. Paul N. Cheremisinoff, ed. Gulf Publishing Co., Book Division, PO Box 2608, Houston, Texas 77252. (713) 529-4301 or (800) 231-6275. 1992. Volume 1: Thermal Treatment of Hazardous Wastes; volume 2: Air Pollution Control; volume 3: Wastewater Treatment Technology; volume 4: Hazardous Waste Containment and Treatment; volumes 5 through 8 in progress. Provides in-depth coverage of specialized topics related to environmental and industrial pollution control problems and state-of-the-art information on technology and research as well as projections of future trends in the field.

Encyclopedia of Environmental Science and Engineering. J.R. Pfafflin. Gordon and Breach Science Publishers, Inc., 270 8th Ave., New York, New York 10011. (212) 206-8900. 1992.

English-Russian Dictionary of Environmental Protection: About 14,000 Terms. E.L. Milovanov. Pergamon Microforms International, Inc., Fairview Park, Elmsford, New York 10523. (914) 592-7720. 1981.

Environmental Engineering Dictionary. C. C. Lee. Government Institutes, Inc., 4 Research Pl., Ste. 200, Rockville, Maryland 20850. (301) 921-2300. 1989. Defines over 6000 engineering terms relating to pollutioncontrol technologies, monitoring, risk assessment, sampling andanalysis, quality control, permitting, and environmentally-regulated engineering and science. Includes bibliographical references (p. 612-627).

McGraw-Hill Encyclopedia of Environmental Science. Sybil P. Parker. McGraw-Hill Science & Engineering Books, 11 W. 19th St., New York, New York 10011. (212) 337-6010. 1980. Covers ecology, man's influence on nature, and environmental protection.

McGraw-Hill Encyclopedia of Science and Technology. McGraw-Hill, 1221 Avenue of the Americas, New York, New York 10020. (212) 512-2000 or (800) 262-4729. 1992. Seventh edition. Issued in multiple volumes including index. Includes all science and technology broad subject areas.

The New York Times Encyclopedic Dictionary of the Environment. Paul Sarnoff. Quadrangle Books, New York, New York 1971. Focuses on state-of-the-art methods of pollution control, abatement, prevention and removal.

Van Nostrand's Scientific Encyclopedia. Glenn D. Considine, ed. Van Nostrand Reinhold, 115 5th Ave., New York, New York 10003. (212) 254-3232. 1983. Sixth edition. Includes all broad subject areas in science.

GENERAL WORKS

Beyond 40 Percent: Record-Setting Recycling and Composting Programs. Brenda Platt, et al. Island Press, 1718 Connecticut Ave. N.W., Suite 300, Washington, District of Columbia 20009. (202) 232-7933. 1991. Produced by the Institute for Local Self-Reliance, this volume documents the operating experience of 17 U.S. communities, from small rural towns to large cities, that are recovering between 32 and 57 percent of their waste.

Burning Garbage in the U.S.: Practice vs. State of the Art. Marjorie J. Clarke. INFORM, 381 Park Ave. S, New York, New York 10016. (212) 689-4040. 1991. Deals with the state of the art in waste disposal methods.

Coal Ash Disposal: Solid Waste Impacts. Raymond A. Tripodi and Paul N. Cheremisinoff. Technomic Publishing Co., 851 New Holland Ave., Box 3535, Lancaster, Pennsylvania 17604. (717) 291-5609. 1980.

Design, Construction, and Monitoring of Sanitary Landfill. Amalendu Bagchi. John Wiley & Sons, Inc., 605 3rd Ave., New York, New York 10158-0012. (212) 850-6000. 1990. Handbook of theory, practice, and mathematical models of sanitary landfill technology and how they apply to waste disposal.

Disposal of Flue Gas Desulfurization Wastes. P.R. Hurt. U.S. Environmental Protection Agency, 401 M St. SW, Washington, District of Columbia 20460. (202) 260-2090. 1981.

Environmental Impacts of Hazardous Waste Treatment, Storage and Disposal Facilities. Rodolfo N. Salcedo, et al. Technomic Publishing Co., 851 New Holland Ave., Box 3535, Lancaster, Pennsylvania 17604. (717) 291-5609. 1989. Provides guidance in dealing with the many obstacles and preliminary requirements in siting TSD facilities.

Environmental Issues: An Anthology of 1989. Thomas W. Joyce, ed. TAPPI Press, Technology Park/Atlanta, PO Box 105113, Atlanta, Georgia 30348. (404) 446-1400. 1990. Contains 39 papers on environmental, safety and occupational health concerns from 11 TAPPI, CPPA and AIChE meetings held during 1989. Also included is a literature review of over 200 papers published in 1989.

Geotechnical Engineering of Ocean Waste Disposal. Kenneth R. Demars and Ronald C. Chaney. ASTM, 1916 Race St., Philadelphia, Pennsylvania 19103-1187. (215) 299-5400. 1990. Proceedings of the symposium held in Orlando, FL, Jan 1989. Reviews geotechnical test methods and procedures for site evaluation, design, construction, and monitoring of both contaminated areas and waste disposal facilities in the marine environment.

Groundwater Contamination: Sources, Control, and Preventive Measures. Chester D. Rail. Technomic Publishing Co., 851 New Holland Ave., Box 3535, Lancaster, Pennsylvania 17604. (717) 291-5609. 1989. Reviews the presently known sources of groundwater contamination and its many complex interactions, including managerial and political implications.

Hazardous and Industrial Wastes, 1990. Joseph P. Martin, et al., eds. Technomic Publishing Co., 851 Holland Ave., Box 3535, Lancaster, Pennsylvania 17604. (717) 291-5609. 1990. Proceedings of the 22nd Mid-Atlantic Industrial Waste Conference, June 24-27, 1990, Drexel University, Philadelphia, PA. Fifty-one new reports on developments in industrial and hazardouswaste management, technology and regulation were presented.

High Level Radioactive Waste Management. American Society of Civil Engineers, 345 E. 47th St., New York, New York 10017. (212) 705-7288; (800) 548-2723. 1991. Proceedings of International Topical Meeting hosted by the University of Nevada Las Vegas, April 8-12, 1990.

High Level Radioactive Waste Management. American Society of Civil Engineers, 345 E. 47th St., New York, New York 10017. (212) 705-7288; (800) 548-2723. 1992. Proceedings of the 2nd Annual International Conference, Las Vegas, Nevada, April 28-May 3, 1991.

Industrial Environmental Control. A. M. Springer. John Wiley & Sons, Inc., 605 3rd Ave., New York, New York 10158-0012. (212) 850-6000. 1986. Covers in great detail all the basic information regarding industrial pollution and its treatment.

Infectious Waste Management. Frank L. Cross. Technomic Publishing Co., 851 New Holland Ave., Box 3535, Lancaster, Pennsylvania 17604. (717) 291-5609; (800) 233-9936. 1990.

Rush to Burn: Solving America's Garbage Crisis?. Island Press, 1718 Connecticut Ave. N.W., Suite 300, Washington, District of Columbia 20009. (202) 232-7933. 1989. Describes incineration, refuse and refuse disposal.

Techniques for Hazardous Chemical and Waste Spill Control. L. Albert Weaver. L.A. Weaver, 308 E. Jones St., Raleigh, North Carolina 27601. 1983.

War on Waste: Can America Win its Battle With Garbage?. Louis Blumberg and Robert Gottlieb. Island Press, 1718 Connecticut Ave. N.W., Suite 300, Washington, District of Columbia 20009. (202) 232-7933. 1989. In-depth analysis of the waste disposal crisis.

Waste Disposal in Academic Institutions. James A. Kaufman. Lewis Publishers, 2000 Corporate Blvd., N.W., Boca Raton, Florida 33431. (407) 994-0555 or (800) 272-7737. 1990. Discusses academic waste disposal programs, identifies unknown chemicals, discusses methods for handling and treating wastes, and waste disposal practices.

Waste Management: Towards A Sustainable Society. Om Prakash Kharbanda and E. A. Stallworthy. Auburn House, 14 Dedham St., Dover, Massachusetts 02030-0658. (505) 785-2220; (800) 223-2665. 1990. Describes the generation of various types of hazardous and nonhazardous wastes, with a whole chapter devoted to acid rain.

Waste Reduction: Policy and Practice. Waste Management Inc. and Piper & Marbury. Executive Enterprises Publications Co., Inc., 22 W. 21st St., New York, New York 10010-6990. (212) 645-7880. 1990. Examines waste reduction on a national level. Gives an overview of the makeup of hazardous waste and municipal solid waste streams and different means of reducing the generation of those streams. Case studies of waste reduction in industry are described.

HANDBOOKS AND MANUALS

Final Covers on Hazardous Waste Landfills and Surface Impoundments. Office of Solid Waste and Emergency Response, U.S. Environment Protection Agency, U.S. G.P.O., Washington, District of Columbia 20402-9325. (202) 783-3238. 1989. Technical Guidance Document series EPA/530-SW-89-047. Shipping list no. 89-483-P.

The Global Ecology Handbook: What You Can Do about the Environmental Crisis. Walter H. Corson, ed. The Global Tomorrow Coalition, Beacon Pr., 25 Beacon St., Boston, Massachusetts 02108-2800. (617) 742-2110. 1990. Covers environment, energy policy, population growth and other issues. It includes chapters on tropical rain forests, garbage, oceans and coasts, global warming, population growth, agriculture, biological diversity, fresh water, hazardous wastes, and environment and development.

Handbook of Incineration Systems. Calvin R. Brunner. McGraw-Hill Science & Engineering Books, 11 West 19th St., New York, New York 10011. (212) 337-6010. 1991. Examines every type of modern incinerator, describes the analytical techniques required to utilize the equipment, explains the basic scientific principles involved, and defines the regulations that apply to various incineration facilities and procedures for upgrading existing facilities to conform to new, stricter operating standards.

Livestock Waste Facilities Handbook. Midwest Plan Service, Ames, Iowa 1985. Deals with agricultural waste management and manure handling in livestock waste facilities.

Resource Conservation and Recovery Act Handbook. ERT, Marketing Dept., 696 Virginia Road, Concord, Massachusetts 01742. Law relating to hazardous wastes and waste sites.

Resource Conservation and Recovery Act Inspection Manual. U.S. Environmental Protection Agency. Government Institutes, Inc., 4 Research Pl., Ste. 200, Rockville, Maryland 20850. (301) 921-2300. 1989.

ONLINE DATA BASES

Biotechnology Abstracts. Derwent Publications Ltd., 6845 Elm St., McLean, Virginia 22101. (703) 790-0400. Includes material on genetic manipulation, biochemical engineering, fermentation, biocatalysis, cell hybridization, in vitro plant propagation and industrial waste management.

The Chemical Monitor. NewsNet, Inc., 945 Haverford Rd., Bryn Mawr, Pennsylvania 19010. (800) 345-1301.

Computerized Engineering Index–COMPENDEX. Engineering Information Inc., 345 E. 47th St., New York, New York 10017. (212) 705-7600.

Environment Week. NewsNet, Inc., 945 Haverford Rd., Bryn Mawr, Pennsylvania 19010. (800) 345-1301. Online version of periodical of same name.

Monthly Catalog of United States Government Publications. U.S. G.P.O., Supt. of Docs., PO Box 371954, Pittsburgh, Pennsylvania 15250-7954. (202) 512-0000.

National Technical Information Service. U.S. Department of Commerce, National Technical Information Service, Office of Data Base Services, 5285 Port Royal Rd., Springfield, Virginia 22161. (703) 487-4807. Bibliographic database of government sponsored research and technical reports.

Report on Defense Plant Wastes. Business Publishers, Inc., 951 Pershing Dr., Silver Spring, Maryland 20910-4464. (301) 587-6300. Laws, regulations, cleanup actions, contracts, and court actions affecting U.S. defense, weapons production, government hospitals and laboratories, and other government institutions. Online version of periodical of the same name.

SCISEARCH. Institute for Scientific Information, University City Science Center, 3501 Market St., Philadelphia, Pennsylvania 19104. (215) 386-0100.

Waste Information Digest. Environmental Studies Institute, International Academy at Santa Barbara, 800 Garden St., Suite D, Santa Barbara, California 93101-1552. (805) 965-5010. Online version of the periodical of the same name.

Waste Management and Resource Recovery. International Research & Evaluation, 21098 IRE Control Center, Eagan, Minnesota 55121. (612) 888-9635.

WasteInfo. Waste Management Information Bureau, United Kingdom Atomic Energy Authority, Building 46J, Harwell Laboratory, Harwell, Oxfordshire, England OX11 ORB. 44 (235) 24141.

PERIODICALS AND NEWSLETTERS

Cycle/The Waste Paper. Environmental Action Coalition, 625 Broadway, New York, New York 10012. (212) 677-1601. Irregular. Disposal of solid waste materials, such as paper, used containers, metal and garbage.

Defense Cleanup. Pasha Publications, 1401 Wilson Blvd., Suite 900, Arlington, Virginia 22209. (703) 528-1244. Weekly. Reports on projects to analyze, recycle, and dispose of defense weapons.

Eco/Log Week. Southam Business Information, 1450 Don Mills Rd., Don Mills, Ontario, Canada M3D 2X7. (416) 445-6641. Weekly. Effluent treatment, emission controls, waste disposal, and land use and reclamation.

EI Digest. Environmental Information Ltd., 7400 Metro Blvd., Ste. 400, Minneapolis, Minnesota 55435. (612) 831-2473. Monthly. Industrial and hazardous waste management regulations & technologies.

Environmental Liability Monitor. Business Publishers, Inc., 951 Pershing Dr., Silver Spring, Maryland 20910-4464. (301) 587-6300. 1990-. Monthly. Reports about environmental liability in all areas.

Environmental Regulation From the State Capital: Waste Disposal and Pollution Control. Wakeman/Walworth, 300 N. Washington St., Alexandria, Virginia 22314. (703) 549-8606. Legislative action concerning pollution control.

International Journal of Environment and Pollution. Inderscience Enterprises Ltd., World Trade Center Bldg., 110 Avenue Louis Casai, Case Postale 306, Geneva-Airport, Switzerland CH-1215. (44) 908-314248. 1991-. Publishes original state-of-the-art articles, book reviews, and technical papers in the areas of: Environmental policies, protection, institutional aspects of pollution, risk assessments of all forms of pollution, protection of soil and ground water, waste disposal strategies, ecological impact of pollutants and other related topics.

Journal of Environmental Science and Health. Marcel Dekker, Inc., 270 Madison Ave., New York, New York 10016. (212) 696-9000. Bimonthly. Concerns pesticides, food contaminants, chemical carcinogens, and agricultural wastes.

Management of World Wastes. Communication Channels, 6255 Barfield Road, Atlanta, Georgia 30328. (404)

256-9800. Monthly. Covers public and private waste operations.

Multinational Environmental Outlook. Business Publishers, Inc., 951 Pershing Dr., Silver Spring, Maryland 20910-4464. (301) 587-6300. 1974-. Biweekly. Covers developments in world environmental problems such as acid rain, deforestation, soil erosion, overfishing, threats to health, animal extinction, population growth, diminishing water supply and other related matters. Also available online.

National Environmental Enforcement Journal. National Association of Attorneys General, 444 N. Capitol, N.W., Suite 403, Washington, District of Columbia 20001. Monthly. Litigation and inventive settlements in cases of waste dumping and pollution.

Report on Defense Plant Wastes. Business Publishers, Inc., 951 Pershing Dr., Silver Spring, Maryland 20910-4464. (301) 587-6300. 1989-. Biweekly. Reports on environmental laws, regulations, cleanups, contracts and court actions affecting U.S. defense weapons production, government hospitals and other government institutions. Also available online.

Sewage and Waste Disposal. Sewage and Waste Disposal, 321 Sunset Ave., Asbury Park, New Jersey 07712. 1946-. Fourteen times a year.

Solid Waste Report. Business Publishers, Inc., 951 Pershing Dr., Silver Spring, Maryland 20910-4464. (301) 587-6300. 1970-. Weekly. Covers the generation, collection, transportation, processing, resource recovery, recycling and ultimate disposal of municipal, commercial, agricultural and nonhazardous industrial refuse. Also available online.

Texas Water Report. Report Publications, P.O. Box 12368, Austin, Texas 78711. (512) 478-5663. Weekly. Covers water pollution, waste, and conservation.

Waste Age. National Solid Waste Management Association, 1730 Rhode Island Avenue, NW, Ste. 1000, Washington, District of Columbia 20036. (202) 659-4613. Monthly. Covers control and use of solid, hazardous and liquid wastes.

Waste Disposal and Pollution Control. Wakeman/Walworth, P.O. Box 1939, New Haven, Connecticut 06509. (203) 562-8518. Monthly. Covers air and water pollution, toxic waste, and acid rain.

Waste Information Digests. Environmental Studies Institute, International Academy at Santa Barbara, 800 Garden St., Suite D, Santa Barbara, California 93101-1552. (805) 965-5010. Eight times a year. Covers waste collection, management and recycling.

Waste Treatment Technology News. Business Communications Company, Inc., 25 Van Zant Street, Norwalk, Connecticut 06855. (203) 853-4266. Monthly. Covers effective management and handling of hazardous wastes.

Waste Watch Magazine. Massachusetts Department of Environmental Quality Control, Division of Solid Waste Management, 1 Winter Street, 4th Floor, Boston, Massachusetts 02108. (617) 292-5989. Quarterly. Covers issues and events in solid waste disposal.

RESEARCH CENTERS AND INSTITUTES

U.S. EPA Test and Evaluation Facility. 26 W. Martin Luther King Dr., Cincinnati, Ohio 45268. (513) 684-2621.

STATISTICS SOURCES

National Priorities List. U.S. G.P.O., Washington, District of Columbia 20401. (202) 512-0000. Annual. Inventories of hazardous waste sites included in the EPA National Priorities List (NPL) and proposed for addition to and removal from the list.

Radioactive Material Released from Nuclear Power Plants. U.S. Nuclear Regulatory Commission. U.S. G.P.O., Washington, District of Columbia 20401. (202) 512-0000. Annual. Data on radioactive content of airborne and liquid effluents and solid wastes from nuclear power plants.

The State of the Environment. OECD Publications and Information Center, 2001 L St., N.W., Suite 700, Washington, District of Columbia 20036. (202) 785-6323. 1991.

World Resources. World Resources Institute. 1709 New York Ave., N.W., Washington, District of Columbia 20006. (202) 638-6300. Annual. Statistical and textual analysis of world's natural resources and the effects of growth-caused environmental pollution.

TRADE ASSOCIATIONS AND PROFESSIONAL SOCIETIES

American Industrial Health Council. 1330 Connecticut Ave., N.W., Suite 300, Washington, District of Columbia 20036. (202) 659-0060.

American Industrial Hygiene Association. 345 White Pond Dr., PO Box 8390, Akron, Ohio 44320. (216) 873-2442.

American Society of Sanitary Engineering. Box 40362, Bay Village, Ohio 44140. (216) 835-3040.

Fertilizer Institute. 501 2nd Ave., N.E., Washington, District of Columbia 20002. (202) 675-8250.

Society for Industrial Microbiology. Box 12534, Arlington, Virginia 22209. (703) 941-5373.

United States Operating Committee on ETAD. 1330 Connecticut Ave., N.W., Suite 300, Washington, District of Columbia 20036-1702. (202) 659-0060.

Waste Systems Institute of Michigan, Inc. 400 Ann, N.W., Suite 204, Grand Rapids, Michigan 49504. (616) 363-3262.

WASTE MANAGEMENT

ABSTRACTING AND INDEXING SERVICES

AgBiotech News and Information. C. A. B. International, 845 North Park Ave., Tucson, Arizona 85719. (602) 621-7897 or (800) 528-4841. 1989-. Bimonthly. Includes news items on topics such as research, companies, products, patents, books, education, diary, people, equipment, and legal issues. Also reviews articles and conference reports. Abstracts journal articles, reports, conferences, and books. Also includes biological control, bioenvironmental interactions and stress resistance and genetics.

Applied Ecology Abstracts Studies in Renewable Natural Resources. Information Retrieval Ltd., 1911 Jefferson Davis Highway, Arlington, Virginia 22202. 1975-. Monthly.

Applied Science and Technology Index. H.W. Wilson Co., 950 University Ave., Bronx, New York 10452. (800) 367-6770. Formerly Industrial Arts Index.

Biological and Agricultural Index. H.W. Wilson Co., 950 University Ave., Bronx, New York 10452. (800) 367-6770. 1916-. Monthly.

Current Advances in Ecological and Environmental Science. Pergamon Microforms International, Inc., Fairview Park, Elmsford, New York 10523. (914) 592-7720. 1989-. Monthly. Current literature searching service including journals, reports, abstracts, etc. This service is available online as part of the CABS database on the hosts BRS and ORBIT search service.

Engineering Index. The Engineering Index Inc., 345 E. 47th St., New York, New York 10017. 1962-.

General Science Index. H. W. Wilson Co., 950 University Ave., Bronx, New York 10452. 1978-. Monthly, also issued in annual cumulation. Cumulative subject index to English language periodicals in the subject fields of astronomy, botany, chemistry, earth science, environment and conservation, food and nutrition, genetics, mathematics, medicine and health, microbiology, oceanography, physics, physiology and zoology.

Geographical Abstracts. London School of Economics, Dept. of Geography, Regency House, 34 Duke St., London, England 1966-. Continued by Geo Abstracts issued in 6 parts: Pt. A. Landforms and the quaternary; Pt. B. Biogeography and Climatology; Pt. C. Economic geography; Pt. D. Social geography and cartography; Pt. E. Sedimentology; Pt. F. Regional and community planning.

Index to Scientific Book Contents. Institute for Scientific Information, 3501 Market St., Philadelphia, Pennsylvania 19104. (800) 523-1857. 1985-. Annual. Gives contents of science books published.

INIS Atomindex. International Atomic Energy Agency, Wagramerstrasse 5, Vienna, Austria A-1400. 222 23606198. 1988-. Semiannual. Abstracts nuclear energy and nuclear physics topics from journals, conferences, technical reports and other related publications. Issued in 6 parts: Personal Author, Corporate Entry, Subject, Report, Standard Patent, Conference (by place), Conference (by date).

Multimedia Index to Ecology. National Information Center for Educational Media, University of Southern California, Los Angeles, California 90007.

Pollution Abstracts. Cambridge Scientific Abstracts, 5161 River Rd., Bethesda, Maryland 20816. (301) 961-6750. Six/year. Indexes worldwide technical literature on environmental pollution. Covers air pollution, marine and freshwater pollution, sewage and wastewater treatment, waste management, toxicology and health, noise pollution, radiation, land pollution, and environmental policies, programs, legislation, and education. Also available online.

Proceedings Digests. Air and Waste Management Association, PO Box 2861, Pittsburgh, Pennsylvania 15230. (412) 232-3444. Annual.

Science Citation Index. Institute for Scientific Information, 3501 Market St., Philadelphia, Pennsylvania 19104. 1961-.

Urban Affairs Abstracts. National League of Cities, 1301 Pennsylvania Ave., NW, Washington, District of Columbia 20004. (202) 626-3150. 1977-. Weekly.

BIBLIOGRAPHIES

Bibliography and Index of Geology. American Geological Institute, 4220 King St., Alexandria, Virginia 22302. Monthly. Includes environmental geology and hydrogeology.

Hazardous and Toxic Waste Management January 1979-May 1989. Louise Reynnells. U.S. Department of Agriculture Library, Beltsville, Maryland 1989.

Hazardous Waste Minimization Bibliography. Waste Programs Planning Section, Office of Waste Programs, Arizona Dept. of Environmental Quality, 3033 N. Central, Phoenix, Arizona 85012. (602) 207-2381. 1990.

DIRECTORIES

ACEC Engineering Services Directory for Waste Management. American Consulting Engineering Council Research & Management Foundation, 1015 15th St., N.W., Washington, District of Columbia 20005. (202) 347-7575.

Air and Waste Management Association Directory and Resource Book. Air and Waste Management Association, PO Box 2861, Pittsburgh, Pennsylvania 15230. (412) 232-3444. Annual.

Civic Public Works–Waste Management Reference Manual and Buyers Guide Issue. Maclean-Hunter Ltd., 777 Bay St., Toronto, Ontario, Canada M5W 1A7. (416) 596-5953.

Directory of Professional Services. Professional Services Institute/National Solid Wastes Management Association, 1730 Rhode Island Ave, N.W., Suite 1000, Washington, District of Columbia 20036. (202) 659-4613.

Directory of State Waste Management Program Officials. Association of State Territorial Solid Waste Management Officials, 444 N. Capitol St., Suite 388, Washington, District of Columbia 20001. (202) 624-5828.

Industrial and Hazardous Waste Management Firms. Environmental Information Ltd., 4801 W. 81st St., No. 119, Minneapolis, Minnesota 55437-1111. (612) 831-2473.

Management of World Wastes–Buyers' Guide Issue. Communication Channels, 6255 Barfield Rd., Atlanta, Georgia 30328. (404) 256-9800.

Recycling Sourcebook. Thomas J. Cichonski, Karen Hill. Gale Research Inc., 835 Penobscot Bldg., Detroit, Michigan 48226-4094. (313) 961-2242. 1992. Covers 3,000 U.S. recycling organizations, agencies, publications, etc.

ENCYCLOPEDIAS AND DICTIONARIES

Dictionary of Environmental Engineering and Related Sciences: English-Spanish, Spanish-English. Jose T. Villate. Ediciones Universal, 3090 SW 8th St., Miami, Florida 33135. (305) 642-3355. 1979.

Dictionary of Environmental Protection. Otto E. Tutzauer. Fred B. Rothman, 10368 W. Centennial Rd., Littleton, California 80127. (303) 979-5657. 1979.

Dictionary of Environmental Protection Technology: In Four Languages, English, German, French, Russian. Egon Seidel. Elsevier Science Publishing Co., 655 Avenue of the Americas, New York, New York 10010. (212) 984-5800. 1988.

Encyclopedia of Environmental Science and Engineering. J.R. Pfafflin. Gordon and Breach Science Publishers, Inc., 270 8th Ave., New York, New York 10011. (212) 206-8900. 1992.

English-Russian Dictionary of Environmental Protection: About 14,000 Terms. E.L. Milovanov. Pergamon Microforms International, Inc., Fairview Park, Elmsford, New York 10523. (914) 592-7720. 1981.

Environmental Engineering Dictionary. C. C. Lee. Government Institutes, Inc., 4 Research Pl., Ste. 200, Rockville, Maryland 20850. (301) 921-2300. 1989. Defines over 6000 engineering terms relating to pollutioncontrol technologies, monitoring, risk assessment, sampling andanalysis, quality control, permitting, and environmentally-regulated engineering and science. Includes bibliographical references (p. 612-627).

McGraw-Hill Encyclopedia of Environmental Science. Sybil P. Parker. McGraw-Hill Science & Engineering Books, 11 W. 19th St., New York, New York 10011. (212) 337-6010. 1980. Covers ecology, man's influence on nature, and environmental protection.

The New York Times Encyclopedic Dictionary of the Environment. Paul Sarnoff. Quadrangle Books, New York, New York 1971. Focuses on state-of-the-art methods of pollution control, abatement, prevention and removal.

Van Nostrand's Scientific Encyclopedia. Glenn D. Considine, ed. Van Nostrand Reinhold, 115 5th Ave., New York, New York 10003. (212) 254-3232. 1983. Sixth edition. Includes all broad subject areas in science.

GENERAL WORKS

Beyond 40 Percent: Record-Setting Recycling and Composting Programs. Brenda Platt, et al. Island Press, 1718 Connecticut Ave. N.W., Suite 300, Washington, District of Columbia 20009. (202) 232-7933. 1991. Produced by the Institute for Local Self-Reliance, this volume documents the operating experience of 17 U.S. communities, from small rural towns to large cities, that are recovering between 32 and 57 percent of their waste.

The Biocycle Guide to Yard Waste Composting. The Staff of Biocycle, Journal of Waste Recycling. JG Press, Box 351, Emmaus, Pennsylvania 18049. (215)967-4010. 1989. Contains chapters on: planning yard waste utilization programs; collection-evaluation options and methods; cost and economics; composting yard waste with other materials; waste reduction implemented backyard composting; and collection and composting equipment.

A Citizen's Guide to Promoting Toxic Waste Reduction. Lauren Kenworthy and Eric Schaeffer. INFORM, 381 Park Ave. S., New York, New York 10016. (212) 689-4040. 1990. The how-to manual describes source reduction and its benefits, five strategies plants can use to reduce their hazardous wastes at the source, a step-by-step process for gathering background facts, and interviewing company representatives and analyzing data.

Clay Liners for Waste Management Facilities; Design, Construction, and Evaluation. L. J. Goldman, et al. Noyes Publications, 120 Mill Rd., Park Ridge, New Jersey 07656. (201) 391-8484. 1990. Compilation of all of the available information on the design, construction, and evaluation of clay liners for waste landfills, surface impoundments, and wastepiles.

Complete Guide to Recycling at Home. Gary D. Branson. Betterway Publications, Inc., PO Box 219, Crozet, Virginia 22932. (804) 823-5661. 1991. Major areas covered include recycling, paper, lawn and garden, plastics, water conservation, alternative energy, etc.

Design, Construction, and Monitoring of Sanitary Landfill. Amalendu Bagchi. John Wiley & Sons, Inc., 605 3rd Ave., New York, New York 10158-0012. (212) 850-6000. 1990. Handbook of theory, practice, and mathematical models of sanitary landfill technology and how they apply to waste disposal.

Design, Construction, and Operation of Hazardous and Non-Hazardous Waste Surface Impoundments. R. P. Hartley. National Technical Information Service, 5285 Port Royal Rd., Springfield, Virginia 22161. (703) 487-4650. 1991.

DOE Model Conference on Waste Management and Environmental Restoration: Proceedings. National Technical Information Service, 5285 Port Royal Rd., Springfield, Virginia 22161. (703) 487-4650. 1990.

Emerging Technologies in Hazardous Waste Management. D. William Tedder and Frederick G. Pohland, eds. American Chemical Society, 1155 16th St. N.W., Washington, District of Columbia 20036. (202) 872-4600; (800) 227-5558. 1990. Hazardous waste management technology.

Emerging Technologies in Hazardous Waste Management II. D. William Tedder and Frederick G. Pohland, eds. American Chemical Society, 1155 16th St. N.W., Washington, District of Columbia 20036. (202) 872-4600; (800) 227-5558. 1991. Developed from a symposium sponsored by the Division of Industrial and Engineering Chemistry, Inc. of the American Chemical Society at the Industrial and Engineering Chemistry Special Symposium, Atlantic City, NJ, June 4-7, 1990.

Environmental Engineering and Sanitation. Joseph A. Salvato. John Wiley & Sons, Inc., 605 3rd Ave., New York, New York 10158-0012. (212) 850-6000. 1992. 3d ed. Applies principles of sanitary science and engineering to sanitation and environmental health. It includes design, construction, maintenance, and operations of sanitation plants and structures. Provides state-of-the-art information on environmental factors associated with chronic and non-infectious diseases; environmental engineering planning and impact analysis; waste management and control; food sanitation; administration of health and sanitation programs; acid rain; noise control; campground sanitation, etc.

Environmentally Acceptable Incineration of Chlorinated Chemical Waste. Martin A. de Zeeuw. Coronet Books, 311 Bainbridge St., Philadelphia, Pennsylvania 19147. (215) 925-2762. 1987.

Geosynthetic Testing for Waste Containment Applications. Robert M. Koerner, ed. ASTM, 1916 Race St., Philadelphia, Pennsylvania 19103-1187. (215) 299-5400.

1990. Contains papers presented at the symposium held in Las Vegas, January 1990. Examines the selection, testing design, and use of geosynthetics.

Hazardous and Industrial Wastes, 1990. Joseph P. Martin, et al., eds. Technomic Publishing Co., 851 Holland Ave., Box 3535, Lancaster, Pennsylvania 17604. (717) 291-5609. 1990. Proceedings of the 22nd Mid-Atlantic Industrial Waste Conference, June 24-27, 1990, Drexel University, Philadelphia, PA. Fifty-one new reports on developments in industrial and hazardouswaste management, technology and regulation were presented.

Hazardous Waste Management. S. Maltezou, et al., eds. Cassell PLC, Publishers Distribution Center, PO Box C831, Rutherford, New Jersey 07070. (201) 939-6064; (201) 939-6065. 1989.

Hazardous Waste Management: New Regulation and New Technology. Brian Price. Financial Times Bus. Info. Ltd., 50-64 Broadway, 7th Fl., London, England 071-799 2002. 1990.

Hazardous Waste Management: Reducing the Risk. Council on Economic Priorities. Island Press, 1718 Connecticut Ave. N.W., Suite 300, Washington, District of Columbia 20009. (202) 232-7933. 1986. Includes information for regulatory agencies, waste generators, host communities, and public officials. Topics include compliance, liabilities, technologies, corporate and public relations, groundwater monitoring, key laws and recommendations.

Hazardous Waste Minimization Assessment, Fort Carson, CO. Seshasayi Dharmavaram, et al. National Technical Information Service, 5285 Port Royal Rd., Springfield, Virginia 22161. (703) 487-4650. 1991.

Hazardous Waste Minimization Assessment, Fort Meade, MD. Seshasayi Dharmavaram and Bernard A. Donahue. National Technical Information Service, 5285 Port Royal Rd., Springfield, Virginia 22161. (703) 487-4650. 1991.

High Level Radioactive Waste Management. American Society of Civil Engineers, 345 E. 47th St., New York, New York 10017. (212) 705-7288; (800) 548-2723. 1991. Proceedings of International Topical Meeting hosted by the University of Nevada Las Vegas, April 8-12, 1990.

High Level Radioactive Waste Management. American Society of Civil Engineers, 345 E. 47th St., New York, New York 10017. (212) 705-7288; (800) 548-2723. 1992. Proceedings of the 2nd Annual International Conference, Las Vegas, Nevada, April 28-May 3, 1991.

Industrial Waste Gases: Utilization and Minimization. RCG/Hagler Bailly Inc. Technomic Publishing Co., 851 New Holland Ave., Box 3535, Lancaster, Pennsylvania 17604. (717) 291-5609. 1990. Also released under title Industrial Waste Gas Management. Deals with factory and trade waste and the effluents that are released into the atmosphere.

Infectious Waste Management. Frank L. Cross. Technomic Publishing Co., 851 New Holland Ave., Box 3535, Lancaster, Pennsylvania 17604. (717) 291-5609; (800) 233-9936. 1990.

Investigation of Shredded Pesticide Containers for Recycling. Materials and Testing Department, Alberta Research Council for Alberta Environment, National Technical Information Service, 5285 Port Royal Rd., Springfield, Virginia 22161. (703) 487-4650. 1990.

An Investigation of the International Toxic Waste Trade. Christoph Hilz. Van Nostrand Reinhold, 115 Fifth Ave., New York, New York 10003. (212) 254-3232. 1992. Hazardous waste management industry, environmental aspects, and law and legislation.

Magill's Survey of Science. Earth Science Series. Frank N. Magill. Salem Press, PO Box 50062, Pasadena, California 91105. 1990-. Five volumes. Includes information on earth's crust, hot spots and volcanic island chains, physical properties of minerals, rock magnetism, physical properties of rocks, and index.

Metal-Bearing Waste Streams: Mining, Recycling, and Treatment. Michael Meltzer, et al. Noyes Publications, 120 Mill Rd., Park Ridge, New Jersey 07656. (201) 391-8484. 1990. Examines the management of metal-bearing wastes. Covers an in-depth industry study of the generation of metal-bearing waste streams. Summaries of waste management practices in various metal operations, including foundry activities, metal cleaning and stripping, surface treatment and plating, coating, and auxiliary operations, are provided.

Popping the Plastics Question: Plastics Recycling and Bans on Plastics - Contacts, Resources and Legislation. Joan Mullany. National League of Cities, 1301 Pennsylvania Ave. N.W., Washington, District of Columbia 20004. (202) 626-3150. 1990.

Preventing Pollution Through Technical Assistance: One State's Experience. Mark H. Dorfman, et al. INFORM Inc., 381 Park Ave. S., New York, New York 10016. (212) 689-4040. 1990. Examines the state of North Carolina's voluntary program aimed at assisting the industry in pollution prevention. It also includes a glossary, a bibliography of information sources and helpful statistical tables of data collected.

Recycling and Incineration: Evaluating Choices. Richard A. Denison and John Ruston. Island Press, 1718 Connecticut Ave. N.W., Suite 300, Washington, District of Columbia 20009. (202) 232-7933. 1990. Presents the technology, economics, environmental concerns, and legal intricacies behind these two approaches. Includes basics of waste reduction, recycling, and incineration; cost comparisons of the two approaches; an evaluation of the health and environmental impacts.

Recycling in America. Debi Kimball. ABC-CLIO, PO Box 1911, 130 Cremona Dr., Santa Barbara, California 93116-1911. (805) 963-4221. 1992. Includes a history of the recycling movement, a chronology, and biographies of people in the field of recycling. Also contains descriptions of widely recycled materials.

Safe Disposal of Hazardous Wastes. Roger Batstone, ed. The World Bank, 1818 H. St. N.W., Washington, District of Columbia 20433. 1990. Describes the special needs and problem of the management of hazardous wastes in developing countries.

Scientific Basis for Nuclear Waste Management XII. Werner Lutze, ed. Materials Research Society, 9800 McKnight Rd., Pittsburgh, Pennsylvania 15237. (412) 367-3003. 1989. Symposium held in Berlin Germany October 1988. Volume 127 of the Materials Research society Symposium Proceedings.

Waste Containment Systems: Construction, Regulation and Performance. Rudolph Bonaparte, ed. American Society of Civil Engineers, 345 E. 47th St., New York, New York 10017. (212) 705-7288; (800) 548-2723. 1990.

Proceedings of a symposium sponsored by the Committee on Soil Improvement and Geosynthetics and the Committee on Soil properties of the Geotechnical Engineering Division, American Society of Civil Engineers in conjunction with the ASCE National Convention, San Francisco, CA, November 6-7, 1990.

Waste Management: Towards A Sustainable Society. Om Prakash Kharbanda and E. A. Stallworthy. Auburn House, 14 Dedham St., Dover, Massachusetts 02030-0658. (505) 785-2220; (800) 223-2665. 1990. Describes the generation of various types of hazardous and nonhazardous wastes, with a whole chapter devoted to acid rain.

Waste Minimization: Manufacturer's Strategies for Success. National Association of Manufacturers, 1331 Pennsylvania Ave., NW, Suite 1500 N., Washington, District of Columbia 20004. (202) 637-3000. 1989.

Waste Reduction: Policy and Practice. Waste Management Inc. and Piper & Marbury. Executive Enterprises Publications Co., Inc., 22 W. 21st St., New York, New York 10010-6990. (212) 645-7880. 1990. Examines waste reduction on a national level. Gives an overview of the makeup of hazardous waste and municipal solid waste streams and different means of reducing the generation of those streams. Case studies of waste reduction in industry are described.

GOVERNMENTAL ORGANIZATIONS

U.S. Environmental Protection Agency: Assistant Administrator for Research and Development. 401 M St., S.W., Washington, District of Columbia 20460. (202) 382-7676.

U.S. Environmental Protection Agency: Office of Solid Waste. 401 M St., S.W., Washington, District of Columbia 20460. (202) 382-4627.

HANDBOOKS AND MANUALS

The Generator's Guide to Hazardous Materials/Waste Management. Leo H. Traverse. Van Nostrand Reinhold, 115 5th Ave., New York, New York 10003. (212) 254-3232. 1991. Comprehensive information source for hazardous waste and hazardous materials management.

Guide to the Management of Hazardous Waste: A Handbook for the Businessman and the Concerned Citizen. J. William Haun. Fulcrum Publishing, 350 Indiana St., Ste. 350, Golden, Colorado 80401. (303) 277-1623. 1991. Fact book on hazardous waste management, including factory and trade waste, and hazardous waste law and legislation in the United States.

Handbook of Hazardous Waste Management for Small Quantity Generators. Russell W. Phifer and William R. McTigue, Jr. Lewis Publishers, 2000 Corporate Blvd., N.W., Boca Raton, Florida 33431. (407) 994-0555 or (800) 272-7737. 1988. Includes practical "how to" instructions, state/federal regulations, overview, lab waste management, interpretations of regulation, enforcement, generator checklist, etc.

Hazardous Waste Management Strategies for Health Care Facilities. Nelson S. Slavik. American Hospital Association, 840 North Lake Shore Dr., Chicago, Illinois 60611. 1987. Contains helpful information for health care facilities in the management of their chemical, cytotoxic, infectious, and radiological wastes.

Hazardous Waste Minimization Handbook. Thomas E. Higgins, et al. Lewis Publishers, 2000 Corporate Blvd., Boca Raton, Florida 33431. (407) 994-0555 or (800) 272-7737. 1989. Describes how to make changes in waste handling, manufacturing, and purchasing to reduce costs and liabilities of waste disposal.

Resource Conservation and Recovery Act Handbook. ERT, Marketing Dept., 696 Virginia Road, Concord, Massachusetts 01742. Law relating to hazardous wastes and waste sites.

Resource Conservation and Recovery Act Inspection Manual. U.S. Environmental Protection Agency. Government Institutes, Inc., 4 Research Pl., Ste. 200, Rockville, Maryland 20850. (301) 921-2300. 1989.

The Solid Waste Handbook: A Practical Guide. William D. Robinson, ed. John Wiley & Sons, Inc., 605 3rd Ave., New York, New York 10158-0012. (212) 850-6000. 1986. Covers the field of solid waste management, including legislation, regulation, planning, finance, technologies, operations, economics administration, and future trends.

Standard Handbook of Environmental Engineering. Robert A. Corbitt. McGraw-Hill, 1221 Ave. of the Americas, New York, New York 10020. (212) 512-2000 or (800) 262-4729. 1990. Hands-on reference to understand environmental engineering technology. Covers air quality control, water supply, wastewater disposal, waste management, stormwater and hazardous wastes.

ONLINE DATA BASES

Biotechnology Abstracts. Derwent Publications Ltd., 6845 Elm St., McLean, Virginia 22101. (703) 790-0400. Includes material on genetic manipulation, biochemical engineering, fermentation, biocatalysis, cell hybridization, in vitro plant propagation and industrial waste management.

Computerized Engineering Index–COMPENDEX. Engineering Information Inc., 345 E. 47th St., New York, New York 10017. (212) 705-7600.

ENSI. Asian Institute of Technology, Environmental Sanitation Information Center, P.O. Box 2754, Bangkok, Thailand 10501. 66 (2) 5290100-13-X2870.

Hazardous Waste News. Business Publishers, Inc., 951 Pershing Dr., Silver Spring, Maryland 20910-4464. (301) 587-6300. Online access to legislative, regulatory, and judicial decisions at the federal and state levels relating to the field of hazardous waste management. Online version of the periodical of the same name.

Industrial Studies Data Base–ISDB. U.S. Environmental Protection Agency, Office of Solid Waste, 401 M St., N.W., Washington, District of Columbia 20460. (202) 260-2090.

Monthly Catalog of United States Government Publications. U.S. G.P.O., Supt. of Docs., PO Box 371954, Pittsburgh, Pennsylvania 15250-7954. (202) 512-0000.

National Technical Information Service. U.S. Department of Commerce, National Technical Information Service, Office of Data Base Services, 5285 Port Royal Rd., Springfield, Virginia 22161. (703) 487-4807. Bibliographic database of government sponsored research and technical reports.

PressNet Environmental Reports. Chemical Information Systems, Inc., 7215 York Rd., Baltimore, Maryland 21212. (301) 321-8440.

SCISEARCH. Institute for Scientific Information, University City Science Center, 3501 Market St., Philadelphia, Pennsylvania 19104. (215) 386-0100.

Waste Information Digest. Environmental Studies Institute, International Academy at Santa Barbara, 800 Garden St., Suite D, Santa Barbara, California 93101-1552. (805) 965-5010. Online version of the periodical of the same name.

Waste Management and Resource Recovery. International Research & Evaluation, 21098 IRE Control Center, Eagan, Minnesota 55121. (612) 888-9635.

WasteInfo. Waste Management Information Bureau, United Kingdom Atomic Energy Authority, Building 46J, Harwell Laboratory, Harwell, Oxfordshire, England OX11 ORB. 44 (235) 24141.

PERIODICALS AND NEWSLETTERS

APCA Messenger. Mid Atlantic States Section, Air and Waste Management Assn., Box 2861, Pittsburgh, Pennsylvania 15230. (412) 621-1090. 1970-. Three times a year.

Beaver Defenders. Unexpected Wildlife Refuge, Box 765, Newfield, New Jersey 08344. (609) 697-3541. 1971-. Quarterly. Newsletter about the unexpected wildlife refuge and about issues regarding beavers everywhere.

EI Digest. Environmental Information Ltd., 7400 Metro Blvd., Ste. 400, Minneapolis, Minnesota 55435. (612) 831-2473. Monthly. Industrial and hazardous waste management regulations & technologies.

Hazardous Materials World. HazMat World, Circulation Dept., P.O. Box 3021, Wheaton, Illinois 60137. (708) 858-1888. Monthly. Covers biobusiness, hazardous wastes management, and hazardous substance safety measures.

Journal of Air and Waste Management Association. Air and Waste Management Association, P.O. Box 2861, Pittsburgh, Pennsylvania 15230. (412) 232-3444. Monthly. Current events in air pollution control and hazardous wastes.

Management of World Wastes. Communication Channels, 6255 Barfield Road, Atlanta, Georgia 30328. (404) 256-9800. Monthly. Covers public and private waste operations.

Michigan Waste Report. Michigan Waste Report, Inc., 400 Ann, SW, Suite 204, Grand Rapids, Michigan 49504. (616) 363-3262. Biweekly. Covers information about waste management.

Multinational Environmental Outlook. Business Publishers, Inc., 951 Pershing Dr., Silver Spring, Maryland 20910-4464. (301) 587-6300. 1974-. Biweekly. Covers developments in world environmental problems such as acid rain, deforestation, soil erosion, overfishing, threats to health, animal extinction, population growth, diminishing water supply and other related matters. Also available online.

New Jersey Air, Water, & Waste Management Times. New Jersey State Department of Health, Division of

Clean Air & Water, John Fitch Plaza, Trenton, New Jersey 08625. Bimonthly.

Pollution Equipment News. Rimbach Publishing, Inc., 8650 Babcock Boulevard, Pittsburgh, Pennsylvania 15237. (412) 364-5366. Bimonthly. Covers new products, techniques, and literature.

Solid Waste Report. Business Publishers, Inc., 951 Pershing Dr., Silver Spring, Maryland 20910-4464. (301) 587-6300. 1970-. Weekly. Covers the generation, collection, transportation, processing, resource recovery, recycling and ultimate disposal of municipal, commercial, agricultural and nonhazardous industrial refuse. Also available online.

Waste Information Digests. Environmental Studies Institute, International Academy at Santa Barbara, 800 Garden St., Suite D, Santa Barbara, California 93101-1552. (805) 965-5010. Eight times a year. Covers waste collection, management and recycling.

Waste Management: Nuclear, Chemical, Biological, Municipal. Pergamon Microforms International, Inc., Fairview Park, Elmsford, New York 10523. (914) 592-7720. 1980-. Quarterly. Formerly Nuclear and Chemical Waste Management. Presents information encompassing the entire field of waste disposal, including radioactive and transuranic waste.

Waste Minimization & Recycling Report. Government Institutes, Inc., 4 Research Pl., Ste. 200, Rockville, Maryland 20850. (301) 921-2300. Monthly. Covers waste minimization, reduction and recycling strategies.

Waste Watch Magazine. Massachusetts Department of Environmental Quality Control, Division of Solid Waste Management, 1 Winter Street, 4th Floor, Boston, Massachusetts 02108. (617) 292-5989. Quarterly. Covers issues and events in solid waste disposal.

RESEARCH CENTERS AND INSTITUTES

Center for Environmental Research. Cornell University, 470 Hollister Hall, Ithaca, New York 14853-3501. (607) 255-7535.

Center for Waste Minimization and Management. Department of Chemical Engineering, North Carolina State University, PO Box 7905, Raleigh, North Carolina 27695-7905. (919) 737-2325.

Institute of Waste Equipment Distributors. 1730 Rhode Island Ave., N.W., Suite 1000, Washington, District of Columbia 20036. (202) 659-4613.

Pennsylvania State University, Office of Hazardous and Toxic Waste Management. Environmental Resources Research Institute, University Park, Pennsylvania 16802. (814) 863-0291.

University of Alabama, Alabama Waste Exchange. P.O. Box 870203, Tuscaloosa, Alabama 35487. (205) 348-5889.

University of Alabama, Environmental Institute for Waste Management Studies. P.O. Box 870203, Tuscaloosa, Alabama 35487-0203. (205) 348-8401.

University of North Carolina at Charlotte, Southeast Waste Exchange. Charlotte, North Carolina 28223. (704) 547-2307.

University of Tennessee at Knoxville, Waste Management Research and Education Institute. 327 South Stadium Hall, Knoxville, Tennessee 37996-0710. (615) 974-4251.

STATISTICS SOURCES

California Solid Waste Market. FIND/SVP, 625 Avenue of the Americas, New York, New York 10011. (800) 346-3787. 1991. Cites market structure, landfill capacity, primary market participants and other primary assets.

Hazardous Waste Management. FIND/SVP, 625 Avenue of the Americas, New York, New York 10011. (212) 645-4500. 1990. Hazardous materials handling costs and the potential threat of increased state and federal regulation.

Massachusetts Solid Waste Market. FIND/SVP, 625 Avenue of the Americas, New York, New York 10011. (800) 346-3787. 1991. Market structure, landfill capacity, primary market participants and other primary assets.

Ohio Solid Waste Market. FIND/SVP, 625 Avenue of the Americas, New York, New York 10011. (800) 346-3787. 1991. Market structure, landfill capacity, primary market participants and other primary assets.

Texas Solid Waste Market. FIND/SVP, 625 Avenue of the Americas, New York, New York 10011. (800) 346-3787. 1991. Market structure, landfill capacity, primary market participants and other primary assets.

Waste Service Industry Review. FIND/SVP, 625 Avenue of the Americas, New York, New York 10011. (800) 346-3787. 1991. Major components and current and future industry fundamentals and opportunities within each sector of the waste services industry.

TRADE ASSOCIATIONS AND PROFESSIONAL SOCIETIES

Air and Waste Management Association. Box 2861, Pittsburgh, Pennsylvania 15230. (412) 232-3444.

American Society of Civil Engineers. 345 East 47th St., New York, New York 10017. (212) 705-7496.

Association of State and Territorial Solid Waste Management Officials. 444 North Capitol St., N.W., Suite 388, Washington, District of Columbia 20001. (202) 624-5828.

Community Environmental Council. 930 Miramonte Drive, Santa Barbara, California 93109. (805) 963-0583.

Fertilizer Institute. 501 2nd Ave., N.E., Washington, District of Columbia 20002. (202) 675-8250.

Institute for Local Self-Reliance. 2425 18th St., N.W., Washington, District of Columbia 20009. (202) 232-4108.

Waste Systems Institute of Michigan, Inc. 400 Ann, N.W., Suite 204, Grand Rapids, Michigan 49504. (616) 363-3262.

WASTE OIL

ABSTRACTING AND INDEXING SERVICES

Engineering Index. The Engineering Index Inc., 345 E. 47th St., New York, New York 10017. 1962-.

Science Citation Index. Institute for Scientific Information, 3501 Market St., Philadelphia, Pennsylvania 19104. 1961-.

ENCYCLOPEDIAS AND DICTIONARIES

Van Nostrand's Scientific Encyclopedia. Glenn D. Considine, ed. Van Nostrand Reinhold, 115 5th Ave., New York, New York 10003. (212) 254-3232. 1983. Sixth edition. Includes all broad subject areas in science.

GENERAL WORKS

Environmental Resources Conservation, and Economic Aspects of Used Oil Recycling. D. W. Brinkman. Bartlesville Energy Technology Center, Box 1398, Bartlesville, Oklahoma 74005. (918) 336-2400. 1981. Recycling of petroleum waste and lubricating oils.

Industrial Energy Conservation. Federal Energy Administration, Conservation and Environment, Office of Industrial Programs, 1000 Independence Ave. SW, Washington, District of Columbia 20585. (202) 586-5000. 1975. Petroleum waste and petroleum recycling in the U.S.

Waste Oil: Reclaiming Technology, Utilization and Disposal. Mueller Associates Inc. Noyes Publications, 120 Mill Rd., Park Ridge, New Jersey 07656. (201) 391-8484. 1989. Describes and assesses the current status of the technologies and environmental information associated with the waste oil industry.

Waste Oil Recovery and Disposal. Noyes Publications, 120 Mill Rd., Park Ridge, New Jersey 07656. (201) 391-8484. 1975.

HANDBOOKS AND MANUALS

Program Guide to Used Oil Recycling. National Technical Information Service, 5285 Port Royal Rd., Springfield, Virginia 22161. (703) 487-4650. 1982.

ONLINE DATA BASES

Computerized Engineering Index–COMPENDEX. Engineering Information Inc., 345 E. 47th St., New York, New York 10017. (212) 705-7600.

SCISEARCH. Institute for Scientific Information, University City Science Center, 3501 Market St., Philadelphia, Pennsylvania 19104. (215) 386-0100.

Waste Information Digest. Environmental Studies Institute, International Academy at Santa Barbara, 800 Garden St., Suite D, Santa Barbara, California 93101-1552. (805) 965-5010. Online version of the periodical of the same name.

Waste Management and Resource Recovery. International Research & Evaluation, 21098 IRE Control Center, Eagan, Minnesota 55121. (612) 888-9635.

WasteInfo. Waste Management Information Bureau, United Kingdom Atomic Energy Authority, Building 46J, Harwell Laboratory, Harwell, Oxfordshire, England OX11 ORB. 44 (235) 24141.

WASTE PAPER

See: RECYCLING (WASTE, ETC.)

WASTE PRODUCTS

See also: RECYCLING (WASTE, ETC.)

ABSTRACTING AND INDEXING SERVICES

Applied Ecology Abstracts Studies in Renewable Natural Resources. Information Retrieval Ltd., 1911 Jefferson Davis Highway, Arlington, Virginia 22202. 1975-. Monthly.

Geographical Abstracts. London School of Economics, Dept. of Geography, Regency House, 34 Duke St., London, England 1966-. Continued by Geo Abstracts issued in 6 parts: Pt. A. Landforms and the quaternary; Pt. B. Biogeography and Climatology; Pt. C. Economic geography; Pt. D. Social geography and cartography; Pt. E. Sedimentology; Pt. F. Regional and community planning.

Multimedia Index to Ecology. National Information Center for Educational Media, University of Southern California, Los Angeles, California 90007.

Pollution Abstracts. Cambridge Scientific Abstracts, 5161 River Rd., Bethesda, Maryland 20816. (301) 961-6750. Six/year. Indexes worldwide technical literature on environmental pollution. Covers air pollution, marine and freshwater pollution, sewage and wastewater treatment, waste management, toxicology and health, noise pollution, radiation, land pollution, and environmental policies, programs, legislation, and education. Also available online.

Public Health Engineering Abstracts. U.S. G.P.O., Washington, District of Columbia 20401. (202) 512-0000. Monthly.

BIBLIOGRAPHIES

Current Contents. Agriculture, Biology and Environmental Sciences. Institute for Scientific Information, 3501 Market St., Philadelphia, Pennsylvania 19104. (800) 523-1857. 1973-. Previous title: Current Contents. Agricultural, Food & Veterinary Sciences. Gives the table of contents of periodicals in the fields of agriculture, biology, environmental and related areas.

ENCYCLOPEDIAS AND DICTIONARIES

McGraw-Hill Encyclopedia of Environmental Science. Sybil P. Parker. McGraw-Hill Science & Engineering Books, 11 W. 19th St., New York, New York 10011. (212) 337-6010. 1980. Covers ecology, man's influence on nature, and environmental protection.

Van Nostrand's Scientific Encyclopedia. Glenn D. Considine, ed. Van Nostrand Reinhold, 115 5th Ave., New York, New York 10003. (212) 254-3232. 1983. Sixth edition. Includes all broad subject areas in science.

ONLINE DATA BASES

Monthly Catalog of United States Government Publications. U.S. G.P.O., Supt. of Docs., PO Box 371954, Pittsburgh, Pennsylvania 15250-7954. (202) 512-0000.

National Technical Information Service. U.S. Department of Commerce, National Technical Information Service, Office of Data Base Services, 5285 Port Royal Rd., Springfield, Virginia 22161. (703) 487-4807. Biblio-

graphic database of government sponsored research and technical reports.

SCISEARCH. Institute for Scientific Information, University City Science Center, 3501 Market St., Philadelphia, Pennsylvania 19104. (215) 386-0100.

WASTE REDUCTION

See also: BIODEGRADABLE

ABSTRACTING AND INDEXING SERVICES

Applied Science and Technology Index. H.W. Wilson Co., 950 University Ave., Bronx, New York 10452. (800) 367-6770. Formerly Industrial Arts Index.

Biological and Agricultural Index. H.W. Wilson Co., 950 University Ave., Bronx, New York 10452. (800) 367-6770. 1916-. Monthly.

Current Advances in Ecological and Environmental Science. Pergamon Microforms International, Inc., Fairview Park, Elmsford, New York 10523. (914) 592-7720. 1989-. Monthly. Current literature searching service includingjournals, reports, abstracts, etc. This service is available online as part of the CABS database on the hosts BRS and ORBIT search service.

Engineering Index. The Engineering Index Inc., 345 E. 47th St., New York, New York 10017. 1962-.

Public Health Engineering Abstracts. U.S. G.P.O., Washington, District of Columbia 20401. (202) 512-0000. Monthly.

Science Citation Index. Institute for Scientific Information, 3501 Market St., Philadelphia, Pennsylvania 19104. 1961-.

BIBLIOGRAPHIES

Current Contents. Agriculture, Biology and Environmental Sciences. Institute for Scientific Information, 3501 Market St., Philadelphia, Pennsylvania 19104. (800) 523-1857. 1973-. Previous title: Current Contents. Agricultural, Food & Veterinary Sciences. Gives the table of contents of periodicals in the fields of agriculture, biology, environmental and related areas.

DIRECTORIES

Recycling Today–Equipment and Services Directory Issue. GIE Incorporated Publisher, 4012 Bridge Ave., Cleveland, Ohio 44113. (216) 961-4130.

ENCYCLOPEDIAS AND DICTIONARIES

Dictionary of Environmental Engineering and Related Sciences: English-Spanish, Spanish-English. Jose T. Villate. Ediciones Universal, 3090 SW 8th St., Miami, Florida 33135. (305) 642-3355. 1979.

Dictionary of Environmental Protection. Otto E. Tutzauer. Fred B. Rothman, 10368 W. Centennial Rd., Littleton, California 80127. (303) 979-5657. 1979.

Dictionary of Environmental Protection Technology: In Four Languages, English, German, French, Russian. Egon Seidel. Elsevier Science Publishing Co., 655 Avenue of the Americas, New York, New York 10010. (212) 984-5800. 1988.

Encyclopedia of Environmental Science and Engineering. J.R. Pfafflin. Gordon and Breach Science Publishers, Inc., 270 8th Ave., New York, New York 10011. (212) 206-8900. 1992.

English-Russian Dictionary of Environmental Protection: About 14,000 Terms. E.L. Milovanov. Pergamon Microforms International, Inc., Fairview Park, Elmsford, New York 10523. (914) 592-7720. 1981.

Environmental Engineering Dictionary. C. C. Lee. Government Institutes, Inc., 4 Research Pl., Ste. 200, Rockville, Maryland 20850. (301) 921-2300. 1989. Defines over 6000 engineering terms relating to pollutioncontrol technologies, monitoring, risk assessment, sampling andanalysis, quality control, permitting, and environmentally-regulated engineering and science. Includes bibliographical references (p. 612-627).

Grzimek's Encyclopedia of Ecology. Bernhard Grzimek. Van Nostrand Reinhold, 115 5th Ave., New York, New York 10003. (212) 254-3232. 1976.

McGraw-Hill Encyclopedia of Environmental Science. Sybil P. Parker. McGraw-Hill Science & Engineering Books, 11 W. 19th St., New York, New York 10011. (212) 337-6010. 1980. Covers ecology, man's influence on nature, and environmental protection.

The New York Times Encyclopedic Dictionary of the Environment. Paul Sarnoff. Quadrangle Books, New York, New York 1971. Focuses on state-of-the-art methods of pollution control, abatement, prevention and removal.

North American Reference Encyclopedia of Ecology and Pollution. William White. North American Pub. Co., 401 N. Broad St., Philadelphia, Pennsylvania 19108. (215) 238-5300. 1972.

Van Nostrand's Scientific Encyclopedia. Glenn D. Considine, ed. Van Nostrand Reinhold, 115 5th Ave., New York, New York 10003. (212) 254-3232. 1983. Sixth edition. Includes all broad subject areas in science.

GENERAL WORKS

A Citizen's Guide to Promoting Toxic Waste Reduction. Lauren Kenworthy and Eric Schaeffer. INFORM, 381 Park Ave. S., New York, New York 10016. (212) 689-4040. 1990. The how-to manual describes source reduction and its benefits, five strategies plants can use to reduce their hazardous wastes at the source, a step-by-step process for gathering background facts, and interviewing company representatives and analyzing data.

Cutting Chemical Wastes. David J. Sarokin, et al. INFORM, 381 Park Ave. S., New York, New York 10016. (212) 689-4040. 1985. Describes the activities of 29 organic chemical plants that are trying to reduce hazardous chemical wastes.

Hazardous and Industrial Wastes, 1990. Joseph P. Martin, et al., eds. Technomic Publishing Co., 851 Holland Ave., Box 3535, Lancaster, Pennsylvania 17604. (717) 291-5609. 1990. Proceedings of the 22nd Mid-Atlantic Industrial Waste Conference, June 24-27, 1990, Drexel University, Philadelphia, PA. Fifty-one new reports on developments in industrial and hazardouswaste management, technology and regulation were presented.

Metal-Bearing Waste Streams: Mining, Recycling, and Treatment. Michael Meltzer, et al. Noyes Publications, 120 Mill Rd., Park Ridge, New Jersey 07656. (201) 391-8484. 1990. Examines the management of metal-bearing wastes. Covers an in-depth industry study of the generation of metal-bearing waste streams. Summaries of waste management practices in various metal operations, including foundry activities, metal cleaning and stripping, surface treatment and plating, coating, and auxiliary operations, are provided.

Preventing Pollution Through Technical Assistance: One State's Experience. Mark H. Dorfman, et al. INFORM Inc., 381 Park Ave. S., New York, New York 10016. (212) 689-4040. 1990. Examines the state of North Carolina's voluntary program aimed at assisting the industry in pollution prevention. It also includes a glossary, a bibliography of information sources and helpful statistical tables of data collected.

Recycling and Incineration: Evaluating Choices. Richard A. Denison and John Ruston. Island Press, 1718 Connecticut Ave. N.W., Suite 300, Washington, District of Columbia 20009. (202) 232-7933. 1990. Presents the technology, economics, environmental concerns, and legal intricacies behind these two approaches. Includes basics of waste reduction, recycling, and incineration; cost comparisons of the two approaches; an evaluation of the health and environmental impacts.

Serious Reduction of Hazardous Waste: Summary. Congress of the U.S., c/o U.S. Government Printing Office, Office of Technology Assessment, N. Capitol & H Sts. NW, Washington, District of Columbia 20401. (202) 512-0000. 1986. Deals with waste reduction from factories and air pollution control.

Solvent Waste Reduction. Noyes Publications, 120 Mill Rd., Park Ridge, New Jersey 07656. (201) 391-8484. 1990. Alternatives for reducing or eliminating environmental risk from waste solvents, either by internal practices or processes, or by the treatment, reuse, or recycling of the material before its final disposition.

TAPPI Environmental Conference Proceedings, Seattle, WA, April 9-11, 1990. TAPPI Press, Technology Park/Atlanta, PO Box 105113, Atlanta, Georgia 30348. (404) 446-1400. 1990. Contains 11 papers presented at the conference covering industrial pollution and its remedies.

Waste Management: Towards A Sustainable Society. Om Prakash Kharbanda and E. A. Stallworthy. Auburn House, 14 Dedham St., Dover, Massachusetts 02030-0658. (505) 785-2220; (800) 223-2665. 1990. Describes the generation of various types of hazardous and nonhazardous wastes, with a whole chapter devoted to acid rain.

Waste Minimization: Manufacturer's Strategies for Success. National Association of Manufacturers, 1331 Pennsylvania Ave., NW, Suite 1500 N., Washington, District of Columbia 20004. (202) 637-3000. 1989.

Waste Reduction: Policy and Practice. Waste Management Inc. and Piper & Marbury. Executive Enterprises Publications Co., Inc., 22 W. 21st St., New York, New York 10010-6990. (212) 645-7880. 1990. Examines waste reduction on a national level. Gives an overview of the makeup of hazardous waste and municipal solid waste streams and different means of reducing the generation of those streams. Case studies of waste reduction in industry are described.

GOVERNMENTAL ORGANIZATIONS

Technical Assistance Program: Waste Minimization and Pollution Prevention. Chief, Technical Assistance Program, 248 Calder Way, 307 University Park, Pennsylvania 16810. (814) 865-0427.

Waste Minimization and Pollution Prevention. Director, Hazardous Material Management and Resource Recovery Program, PO Box 872203, Tuscaloosa, Alabama 35487-0203. (205) 348-8401.

HANDBOOKS AND MANUALS

The Generator's Guide to Hazardous Materials/Waste Management. Leo H. Traverse. Van Nostrand Reinhold, 115 5th Ave., New York, New York 10003. (212) 254-3232. 1991. Comprehensive information source for hazardous waste and hazardous materials management.

Hazardous Waste Minimization Handbook. Thomas E. Higgins, et al. Lewis Publishers, 2000 Corporate Blvd., Boca Raton, Florida 33431. (407) 994-0555 or (800) 272-7737. 1989. Describes how to make changes in waste handling, manufacturing, and purchasing to reduce costs and liabilities of waste disposal.

Waste Minimization Manual. Government Institutes, Inc., 4 Research Pl., Ste. 200, Rockville, Maryland 20850. (301) 921-2300.

Waste Minimization Opportunity Assessment Manual. Government Institutes, Inc., 4 Research Pl., Ste. 200, Rockville, Maryland 20850. (301) 921-2300. 1988. Deals with managing hazardous waste and its minimization.

ONLINE DATA BASES

Computerized Engineering Index–COMPENDEX. Engineering Information Inc., 345 E. 47th St., New York, New York 10017. (212) 705-7600.

SCISEARCH. Institute for Scientific Information, University City Science Center, 3501 Market St., Philadelphia, Pennsylvania 19104. (215) 386-0100.

Waste Information Digest. Environmental Studies Institute, International Academy at Santa Barbara, 800 Garden St., Suite D, Santa Barbara, California 93101-1552. (805) 965-5010. Online version of the periodical of the same name.

Waste Management and Resource Recovery. International Research & Evaluation, 21098 IRE Control Center, Eagan, Minnesota 55121. (612) 888-9635.

WasteInfo. Waste Management Information Bureau, United Kingdom Atomic Energy Authority, Building 46J, Harwell Laboratory, Harwell, Oxfordshire, England OX11 ORB. 44 (235) 24141.

PERIODICALS AND NEWSLETTERS

BioCycle-Journal of Waste Recycling. The J.G. Press, Inc., Box 351, Emmaus, Pennsylvania 18049. (215) 967-4135. Monthly. Articles on the reuse of sludge, waste water, and recycled products.

Biodegradation. Kluwer Academic Publishers, 101 Philip Dr., Assinippi Park, Norwell, Massachusetts 02061-0358. (617) 871-6600. 1990-. Quarterly. Covers all aspects of science pertaining to the detoxification, recycling, amelioration or treatment of waste materials and pollutants by naturally occurring microbial strains, associations, or recombinant microorganisms.

CAW Waste Watch. Californians Against Waste, Box 289, Sacramento, California 95802. (916) 443-5422. 1978-. Quarterly. Newsletter about natural resources conservation, recycling, anti-litter issues in California and other related topics.

Journal of Environmental Engineering. American Society for Civil Engineers, 345 East 47th Street, New York, New York 10017. (212) 705-7496. Bimonthly. Covers problems in the environment and sanitation.

Recycling Today. GIE Incorporated Publisher, 4012 Bridge Ave., Cleveland, Ohio 44113-3320. (216) 961-4130. Monthly. Covers recycling of secondary raw materials and solid waste management. Formerly, entitled Secondary Raw Materials.

Texas Water Report. Report Publications, P.O. Box 12368, Austin, Texas 78711. (512) 478-5663. Weekly. Covers water pollution, waste, and conservation.

Waste Minimization & Recycling Report. Government Institutes, Inc., 4 Research Pl., Ste. 200, Rockville, Maryland 20850. (301) 921-2300. Monthly. Covers waste minimization, reduction and recycling strategies.

RESEARCH CENTERS AND INSTITUTES

Center for Waste Reduction Technologies. American Institute of Chemical Engineers, 345 East 47th St., New York, New York 10017. (212) 705-7407.

University of Tennessee at Knoxville, Energy Environment and Resource Center. 327 South Stadium Hall, Knoxville, Tennessee 37996. (615) 974-4251.

TRADE ASSOCIATIONS AND PROFESSIONAL SOCIETIES

American Society of Civil Engineers. 345 East 47th St., New York, New York 10017. (212) 705-7496.

American Society of Sanitary Engineering. Box 40362, Bay Village, Ohio 44140. (216) 835-3040.

Institute for Local Self-Reliance. 2425 18th St., N.W., Washington, District of Columbia 20009. (202) 232-4108.

WASTE REPROCESSING

See also: RECYCLING

ABSTRACTING AND INDEXING SERVICES

Applied Ecology Abstracts Studies in Renewable Natural Resources. Information Retrieval Ltd., 1911 Jefferson Davis Highway, Arlington, Virginia 22202. 1975-. Monthly.

Biological and Agricultural Index. H.W. Wilson Co., 950 University Ave., Bronx, New York 10452. (800) 367-6770. 1916-. Monthly.

Engineering Index. The Engineering Index Inc., 345 E. 47th St., New York, New York 10017. 1962-.

Metals Abstracts. ASM International, 9639 Kinsman, Materials Park, Ohio 44073. (216) 338-5151. 1968-.

Published jointly by the Institute of Metals, London and the American Society for Metals. Formed by the Union of Metallurgical Abstracts and Review of Metal Literature.

Multimedia Index to Ecology. National Information Center for Educational Media, University of Southern California, Los Angeles, California 90007.

Pollution Abstracts. Cambridge Scientific Abstracts, 5161 River Rd., Bethesda, Maryland 20816. (301) 961-6750. Six/year. Indexes worldwide technical literature on environmental pollution. Covers air pollution, marine and freshwater pollution, sewage and wastewater treatment, waste management, toxicology and health, noise pollution, radiation, land pollution, and environmental policies, programs, legislation, and education. Also available online.

Public Health Engineering Abstracts. U.S. G.P.O., Washington, District of Columbia 20401. (202) 512-0000. Monthly.

Science Citation Index. Institute for Scientific Information, 3501 Market St., Philadelphia, Pennsylvania 19104. 1961-.

BIBLIOGRAPHIES

Current Contents. Agriculture, Biology and Environmental Sciences. Institute for Scientific Information, 3501 Market St., Philadelphia, Pennsylvania 19104. (800) 523-1857. 1973-. Previous title: Current Contents. Agricultural, Food & Veterinary Sciences. Gives the table of contents of periodicals in the fields of agriculture, biology, environmental and related areas.

DIRECTORIES

Beyond 25 Percent: Materials Recovery Comes of Age. Theresa Allan, Brenda Platt, and David Morris. Institute for Local Self-Reliance, 2425 18th St, NW, Washington, District of Columbia 20009. (202) 232-4108. 1989.

Recycling Today–Equipment and Services Directory Issue. GIE Incorporated Publisher, 4012 Bridge Ave., Cleveland, Ohio 44113. (216) 961-4130.

ENCYCLOPEDIAS AND DICTIONARIES

Dictionary of Environmental Engineering and Related Sciences: English-Spanish, Spanish-English. Jose T. Villate. Ediciones Universal, 3090 SW 8th St., Miami, Florida 33135. (305) 642-3355. 1979.

Dictionary of Environmental Protection. Otto E. Tutzauer. Fred B. Rothman, 10368 W. Centennial Rd., Littleton, California 80127. (303) 979-5657. 1979.

Dictionary of Environmental Protection Technology: In Four Languages, English, German, French, Russian. Egon Seidel. Elsevier Science Publishing Co., 655 Avenue of the Americas, New York, New York 10010. (212) 984-5800. 1988.

Encyclopedia of Environmental Science and Engineering. J.R. Pfafflin. Gordon and Breach Science Publishers, Inc., 270 8th Ave., New York, New York 10011. (212) 206-8900. 1992.

English-Russian Dictionary of Environmental Protection: About 14,000 Terms. E.L. Milovanov. Pergamon Microforms International, Inc., Fairview Park, Elmsford, New York 10523. (914) 592-7720. 1981.

Environmental Engineering Dictionary. C. C. Lee. Government Institutes, Inc., 4 Research Pl., Ste. 200, Rockville, Maryland 20850. (301) 921-2300. 1989. Defines over 6000 engineering terms relating to pollutioncontrol technologies, monitoring, risk assessment, sampling andanalysis, quality control, permitting, and environmentally-regulated engineering and science. Includes bibliographical references (p. 612-627).

McGraw-Hill Encyclopedia of Environmental Science. Sybil P. Parker. McGraw-Hill Science & Engineering Books, 11 W. 19th St., New York, New York 10011. (212) 337-6010. 1980. Covers ecology, man's influence on nature, and environmental protection.

GENERAL WORKS

Beyond 40 Percent: Record-Setting Recycling and Composting Programs. Brenda Platt, et al. Island Press, 1718 Connecticut Ave. N.W., Suite 300, Washington, District of Columbia 20009. (202) 232-7933. 1991. Produced by the Institute for Local Self-Reliance, this volume documents the operating experience of 17 U.S. communities, from small rural towns to large cities, that are recovering between 32 and 57 percent of their waste.

Metal-Bearing Waste Streams: Mining, Recycling, and Treatment. Michael Meltzer, et al. Noyes Publications, 120 Mill Rd., Park Ridge, New Jersey 07656. (201) 391-8484. 1990. Examines the management of metal-bearing wastes. Covers an in-depth industry study of the generation of metal-bearing waste streams. Summaries of waste management practices in various metal operations, including foundry activities, metal cleaning and stripping, surface treatment and plating, coating, and auxiliary operations, are provided.

Recycling and Incineration: Evaluating Choices. Richard A. Denison and John Ruston. Island Press, 1718 Connecticut Ave. N.W., Suite 300, Washington, District of Columbia 20009. (202) 232-7933. 1990. Presents the technology, economics, environmental concerns, and legal intricacies behind these two approaches. Includes basics of waste reduction, recycling, and incineration; cost comparisons of the two approaches; an evaluation of the health and environmental impacts.

War on Waste: Can America Win its Battle With Garbage?. Louis Blumberg and Robert Gottlieb. Island Press, 1718 Connecticut Ave. N.W., Suite 300, Washington, District of Columbia 20009. (202) 232-7933. 1989. In-depth analysis of the waste disposal crisis.

ONLINE DATA BASES

Computerized Engineering Index–COMPENDEX. Engineering Information Inc., 345 E. 47th St., New York, New York 10017. (212) 705-7600.

Monthly Catalog of United States Government Publications. U.S. G.P.O., Supt. of Docs., PO Box 371954, Pittsburgh, Pennsylvania 15250-7954. (202) 512-0000.

National Technical Information Service. U.S. Department of Commerce, National Technical Information Service, Office of Data Base Services, 5285 Port Royal Rd., Springfield, Virginia 22161. (703) 487-4807. Bibliographic database of government sponsored research and technical reports.

SCISEARCH. Institute for Scientific Information, University City Science Center, 3501 Market St., Philadelphia, Pennsylvania 19104. (215) 386-0100.

Waste Information Digest. Environmental Studies Institute, International Academy at Santa Barbara, 800 Garden St., Suite D, Santa Barbara, California 93101-1552. (805) 965-5010. Online version of the periodical of the same name.

Waste Management and Resource Recovery. International Research & Evaluation, 21098 IRE Control Center, Eagan, Minnesota 55121. (612) 888-9635.

WasteInfo. Waste Management Information Bureau, United Kingdom Atomic Energy Authority, Building 46J, Harwell Laboratory, Harwell, Oxfordshire, England OX11 ORB. 44 (235) 24141.

PERIODICALS AND NEWSLETTERS

BioCycle-Journal of Waste Recycling. The J.G. Press, Inc., Box 351, Emmaus, Pennsylvania 18049. (215) 967-4135. Monthly. Articles on the reuse of sludge, waste water, and recycled products.

Recycling Today. GIE Incorporated Publisher, 4012 Bridge Ave., Cleveland, Ohio 44113-3320. (216) 961-4130. Monthly. Covers recycling of secondary raw materials and solid waste management. Formerly, entitled Secondary Raw Materials.

TRADE ASSOCIATIONS AND PROFESSIONAL SOCIETIES

American Society of Mechanical Engineers, Solid Waste Processing Division. 345 E. 47th St., New York, New York 10017. (212) 705-7722.

American Society of Sanitary Engineering. Box 40362, Bay Village, Ohio 44140. (216) 835-3040.

Waste Equipment Manufacturers Institute. National Solid Waste, Mgmt. Association, 1730 Rhode Island Ave., N.W., Washington, District of Columbia 20036. (202) 659-4613.

Waste Systems Institute of Michigan, Inc. 400 Ann, N.W., Suite 204, Grand Rapids, Michigan 49504. (616) 363-3262.

WASTE STORAGE

ABSTRACTING AND INDEXING SERVICES

Applied Science and Technology Index. H.W. Wilson Co., 950 University Ave., Bronx, New York 10452. (800) 367-6770. Formerly Industrial Arts Index.

Biological and Agricultural Index. H.W. Wilson Co., 950 University Ave., Bronx, New York 10452. (800) 367-6770. 1916-. Monthly.

Engineering Index. The Engineering Index Inc., 345 E. 47th St., New York, New York 10017. 1962-.

Pollution Abstracts. Cambridge Scientific Abstracts, 5161 River Rd., Bethesda, Maryland 20816. (301) 961-6750. Six/year. Indexes worldwide technical literature on environmental pollution. Covers air pollution, marine and freshwater pollution, sewage and wastewater treatment, waste management, toxicology and health, noise pollution, radiation, land pollution, and environmental poli-

cies, programs, legislation, and education. Also available online.

Public Health Engineering Abstracts. U.S. G.P.O., Washington, District of Columbia 20401. (202) 512-0000. Monthly.

Radioactive Waste Management. National Technical Information Service, 5285 Port Royal Rd., Springfield, Virginia 22161. (703) 487-4650. Monthly. Topics include spent-fuel transport and storage; radioactive effluents from nuclear facilities; and techniques of processing wastes, their storage, and ultimate disposal.

Science Citation Index. Institute for Scientific Information, 3501 Market St., Philadelphia, Pennsylvania 19104. 1961-.

BIBLIOGRAPHIES

Current Contents. Agriculture, Biology and Environmental Sciences. Institute for Scientific Information, 3501 Market St., Philadelphia, Pennsylvania 19104. (800) 523-1857. 1973-. Previous title: Current Contents. Agricultural, Food & Veterinary Sciences. Gives the table of contents of periodicals in the fields of agriculture, biology, environmental and related areas.

DIRECTORIES

Hazardous Waste Management Facilities Directory: Treatment, Storage, Disposal and Recycling. U. S. Environmental Protection Agency. Noyes Publications, 120 Mill Rd., Park Ridge, New Jersey 07656. (201) 391-8484. 1990. Provides geographical listings of 1045 commercial hazardous waste management facilities, along with information on the types of commercial services offered and types of wastes managed. It is a compilation of recent data from EPA data bases and includes the facility name, address, contact person, and phone number.

ENCYCLOPEDIAS AND DICTIONARIES

Dictionary of Environmental Engineering and Related Sciences: English-Spanish, Spanish-English. Jose T. Villate. Ediciones Universal, 3090 SW 8th St., Miami, Florida 33135. (305) 642-3355. 1979.

Dictionary of Environmental Protection Technology: In Four Languages, English, German, French, Russian. Egon Seidel. Elsevier Science Publishing Co., 655 Avenue of the Americas, New York, New York 10010. (212) 984-5800. 1988.

Encyclopedia of Environmental Science and Engineering. J.R. Pfafflin. Gordon and Breach Science Publishers, Inc., 270 8th Ave., New York, New York 10011. (212) 206-8900. 1992.

English-Russian Dictionary of Environmental Protection: About 14,000 Terms. E.L. Milovanov. Pergamon Microforms International, Inc., Fairview Park, Elmsford, New York 10523. (914) 592-7720. 1981.

Environmental Engineering Dictionary. C. C. Lee. Government Institutes, Inc., 4 Research Pl., Ste. 200, Rockville, Maryland 20850. (301) 921-2300. 1989. Defines over 6000 engineering terms relating to pollutioncontrol technologies, monitoring, risk assessment, sampling andanalysis, quality control, permitting, and environmentally-regulated engineering and science. Includes bibliographical references (p. 612-627).

McGraw-Hill Encyclopedia of Environmental Science. Sybil P. Parker. McGraw-Hill Science & Engineering Books, 11 W. 19th St., New York, New York 10011. (212) 337-6010. 1980. Covers ecology, man's influence on nature, and environmental protection.

GENERAL WORKS

Characterization of Municipal Waste Combustor Ashes and Leachates from Municipal Solid Waste Landfills, Monofills, and Codisposal Sites. U.S. Environmental Protection Agency, Office of Solid Waste, 401 M St., S.W., Washington, District of Columbia 20460. (202) 260-2090. 1987.

Environmental Impacts of Hazardous Waste Treatment, Storage and Disposal Facilities. Rodolfo N. Salcedo, et al. Technomic Publishing Co., 851 New Holland Ave., Box 3535, Lancaster, Pennsylvania 17604. (717) 291-5609. 1989. Provides guidance in dealing with the many obstacles and preliminary requirements in siting TSD facilities.

War on Waste: Can America Win its Battle With Garbage?. Louis Blumberg and Robert Gottlieb. Island Press, 1718 Connecticut Ave. N.W., Suite 300, Washington, District of Columbia 20009. (202) 232-7933. 1989. In-depth analysis of the waste disposal crisis.

ONLINE DATA BASES

Computerized Engineering Index–COMPENDEX. Engineering Information Inc., 345 E. 47th St., New York, New York 10017. (212) 705-7600.

Monthly Catalog of United States Government Publications. U.S. G.P.O., Supt. of Docs., PO Box 371954, Pittsburgh, Pennsylvania 15250-7954. (202) 512-0000.

National Technical Information Service. U.S. Department of Commerce, National Technical Information Service, Office of Data Base Services, 5285 Port Royal Rd., Springfield, Virginia 22161. (703) 487-4807. Bibliographic database of government sponsored research and technical reports.

SCISEARCH. Institute for Scientific Information, University City Science Center, 3501 Market St., Philadelphia, Pennsylvania 19104. (215) 386-0100.

Waste Information Digest. Environmental Studies Institute, International Academy at Santa Barbara, 800 Garden St., Suite D, Santa Barbara, California 93101-1552. (805) 965-5010. Online version of the periodical of the same name.

Waste Management and Resource Recovery. International Research & Evaluation, 21098 IRE Control Center, Eagan, Minnesota 55121. (612) 888-9635.

WasteInfo. Waste Management Information Bureau, United Kingdom Atomic Energy Authority, Building 46J, Harwell Laboratory, Harwell, Oxfordshire, England OX11 ORB. 44 (235) 24141.

TRADE ASSOCIATIONS AND PROFESSIONAL SOCIETIES

American Society of Sanitary Engineering. Box 40362, Bay Village, Ohio 44140. (216) 835-3040.

WASTE-TO-ENERGY SYSTEMS

See also: ANIMAL WASTES; METHANE

ABSTRACTING AND INDEXING SERVICES

Applied Ecology Abstracts Studies in Renewable Natural Resources. Information Retrieval Ltd., 1911 Jefferson Davis Highway, Arlington, Virginia 22202. 1975-. Monthly.

Biological and Agricultural Index. H.W. Wilson Co., 950 University Ave., Bronx, New York 10452. (800) 367-6770. 1916-. Monthly.

Current Advances in Ecological and Environmental Science. Pergamon Microforms International, Inc., Fairview Park, Elmsford, New York 10523. (914) 592-7720. 1989-. Monthly. Current literature searching service includingjournals, reports, abstracts, etc. This service is available online as part of the CABS database on the hosts BRS and ORBIT search service.

Ecological Abstracts. Geo Abstracts Ltd. Elsevier Applied Science, Crown House, Linton Rd., Barking, England IG 11 8JU. 1974-. Derived from over 600 leading ecological and environmental journals, plus books, conference proceedings, reports and theses.

Engineering Index. The Engineering Index Inc., 345 E. 47th St., New York, New York 10017. 1962-.

ERDA Research Abstracts. U.S. ERDA Technical Information Center, Box 62, Oak Ridge, Tennessee 37830.

Geographical Abstracts. London School of Economics, Dept. of Geography, Regency House, 34 Duke St., London, England 1966-. Continued by Geo Abstracts issued in 6 parts: Pt. A. Landforms and the quaternary; Pt. B. Biogeography and Climatology; Pt. C. Economic geography; Pt. D. Social geography and cartography; Pt. E. Sedimentology; Pt. F. Regional and community planning.

Index to Scientific Book Contents. Institute for Scientific Information, 3501 Market St., Philadelphia, Pennsylvania 19104. (800) 523-1857. 1985-. Annual. Gives contents of science books published.

Multimedia Index to Ecology. National Information Center for Educational Media, University of Southern California, Los Angeles, California 90007.

Pollution Abstracts. Cambridge Scientific Abstracts, 5161 River Rd., Bethesda, Maryland 20816. (301) 961-6750. Six/year. Indexes worldwide technical literature on environmental pollution. Covers air pollution, marine and freshwater pollution, sewage and wastewater treatment, waste management, toxicology and health, noise pollution, radiation, land pollution, and environmental policies, programs, legislation, and education. Also available online.

Public Health Engineering Abstracts. U.S. G.P.O., Washington, District of Columbia 20401. (202) 512-0000. Monthly.

Science Citation Index. Institute for Scientific Information, 3501 Market St., Philadelphia, Pennsylvania 19104. 1961-.

Urban Affairs Abstracts. National League of Cities, 1301 Pennsylvania Ave., NW, Washington, District of Columbia 20004. (202) 626-3150. 1977-. Weekly.

BIBLIOGRAPHIES

Current Contents. Agriculture, Biology and Environmental Sciences. Institute for Scientific Information, 3501 Market St., Philadelphia, Pennsylvania 19104. (800) 523-1857. 1973-. Previous title: Current Contents. Agricultural, Food & Veterinary Sciences. Gives the table of contents of periodicals in the fields of agriculture, biology, environmental and related areas.

DIRECTORIES

Waste-to-Energy Facilities. National Publishing, Alexandria, Virginia 1986. Covers refuse as fuel and refuse disposal facilities in the United States.

ENCYCLOPEDIAS AND DICTIONARIES

Dictionary of Environmental Engineering and Related Sciences: English-Spanish, Spanish-English. Jose T. Villate. Ediciones Universal, 3090 SW 8th St., Miami, Florida 33135. (305) 642-3355. 1979.

Dictionary of Environmental Protection Technology: In Four Languages, English, German, French, Russian. Egon Seidel. Elsevier Science Publishing Co., 655 Avenue of the Americas, New York, New York 10010. (212) 984-5800. 1988.

Encyclopedia of Environmental Science and Engineering. J.R. Pfafflin. Gordon and Breach Science Publishers, Inc., 270 8th Ave., New York, New York 10011. (212) 206-8900. 1992.

Encyclopedia of Physical Science and Technology. Robert A. Meyers, ed. Academic Press, c/o Harcourt Brace Jovanovich Inc., 6277 Sea Harbor Dr., Orlando, Florida 32887. (800) 346-8648. Dictionary of engineering, technology and physical sciences.

English-Russian Dictionary of Environmental Protection: About 14,000 Terms. E.L. Milovanov. Pergamon Microforms International, Inc., Fairview Park, Elmsford, New York 10523. (914) 592-7720. 1981.

Environmental Engineering Dictionary. C. C. Lee. Government Institutes, Inc., 4 Research Pl., Ste. 200, Rockville, Maryland 20850. (301) 921-2300. 1989. Defines over 6000 engineering terms relating to pollutioncontrol technologies, monitoring, risk assessment, sampling andanalysis, quality control, permitting, and environmentally-regulated engineering and science. Includes bibliographical references (p. 612-627).

Grzimek's Encyclopedia of Ecology. Bernhard Grzimek. Van Nostrand Reinhold, 115 5th Ave., New York, New York 10003. (212) 254-3232. 1976.

McGraw-Hill Encyclopedia of Environmental Science. Sybil P. Parker. McGraw-Hill Science & Engineering Books, 11 W. 19th St., New York, New York 10011. (212) 337-6010. 1980. Covers ecology, man's influence on nature, and environmental protection.

North American Reference Encyclopedia of Ecology and Pollution. William White. North American Pub. Co., 401 N. Broad St., Philadelphia, Pennsylvania 19108. (215) 238-5300. 1972.

GENERAL WORKS

Agricultural Waste Utilization and Management. American Society of Agricultural Engineers, 2950 Niles Rd., St. Joseph, Michigan 49085-9659. (616) 429-0300. 1985. Proceedings of the Fifth International Symposium on Agricultural Wastes, December 16-17, 1985, Chicago, IL. Covers topics such as liquid manure storage and transportation, energy recovery from wastes, digester types and design, recycling for feed, fuel and fertilizer, land applications and odor control.

Case Studies of Waste-to-Energy Facilities. Illinois Department of Energy and Natural Resources, Office of Research and Planning, 325 W. Adams St., Rm. 300, Springfield, Illinois 62706. (217) 785-2800. 1989. Covers incinerators, resource recovery facilities, waste products as fuel and salvage of wastes.

Environmental Assessment of Waste-to-Energy Processes. National Technical Information Service, 5285 Port Royal Rd., Springfield, Virginia 22161. (703) 487-4650. 1977. Environmental aspects of refuse as fuel.

How to Implement Waste-to-Energy Projects. Noyes Publications, 120 Mill Rd., Park Ridge, New Jersey 07656. (201) 391-8484. 1987. Refuse and waste products as fuel.

Waste-to-Energy. The American Public Power Association, 2301 M St., NW, Washington, District of Columbia 20037. (202) 467-2900. 1986. Waste products as fuel and electric power production.

Waste-to-Energy Commercial Facilities Profiles; Technical, Operational, and Economic Perspectives. Dick Richards, et al. Noyes Publications, 120 Mill Rd., Park Ridge, New Jersey 07656. (201) 391-8484. 1990. Presents profiles of all commercial-scale facilities in the U.S. that are processing municipal solid waste to recover energy, as well as case studies for three of the facilities. Information comes from Waste-to-Energy revised edition 1988 prepared for the U.S. Dept. of Energy Dec 1988 and Case Studies of Waste-to-Energy Facilities prepared by the Illinois Dept. of Energy and Natural Resources, May 1989.

HANDBOOKS AND MANUALS

Waste-to-Energy Compendium. National Technical Information Service, 5285 Port Royal Rd., Springfield, Virginia 22161. (703) 487-4650. 1988. Deals with refuse and refuse disposal, waste product as fuel and factory and trade waste.

ONLINE DATA BASES

Computerized Engineering Index–COMPENDEX. Engineering Information Inc., 345 E. 47th St., New York, New York 10017. (212) 705-7600.

Monthly Catalog of United States Government Publications. U.S. G.P.O., Supt. of Docs., PO Box 371954, Pittsburgh, Pennsylvania 15250-7954. (202) 512-0000.

National Technical Information Service. U.S. Department of Commerce, National Technical Information Service, Office of Data Base Services, 5285 Port Royal Rd., Springfield, Virginia 22161. (703) 487-4807. Bibliographic database of government sponsored research and technical reports.

SCISEARCH. Institute for Scientific Information, University City Science Center, 3501 Market St., Philadelphia, Pennsylvania 19104. (215) 386-0100.

PERIODICALS AND NEWSLETTERS

Biomass and Bioenergy. Pergamon Microforms International, Inc., Fairview Park, Elmsford, New York 10523. (914) 592-7720. 1991-. Monthly. Key areas covered by this journal are: Biomass-sources, energy, crop production processes, genetic improvements, composition; biological residues: wastes from agricultural production and forestry, processing industries, and municipal sources; bioenergy processes: fermentations, thermochemical conversions, liquid and gaseous fuels, and petrochemical substitutes; bioenergy utilization: direct combustion gasification, electricity production, chemical processes, and by-product remediation. Also includes environmental management and economic aspects of biomass and bioenergy.

Solid Waste and Power: The Waste-To-Energy Magazine. HCI Publications, 410 Archibald St., Suite 100, Kansas City, Missouri 64111. (816) 931-1311. Six times a year. Environmental considerations and proven approaches for dealing with concerns and requirements.

STATISTICS SOURCES

Waste-to-Energy Industry. FIND/SVP, 625 Avenue of the Americas, New York, New York 10011. (212) 645-4500. Environment regulation of waste-to-energy; and competing means of solid waste disposal.

TRADE ASSOCIATIONS AND PROFESSIONAL SOCIETIES

American Institute of Biological Sciences. 730 11th St., N.W., Washington, District of Columbia 20001-4521. (202) 628-1500.

WASTE TREATMENT

ABSTRACTING AND INDEXING SERVICES

Applied Ecology Abstracts Studies in Renewable Natural Resources. Information Retrieval Ltd., 1911 Jefferson Davis Highway, Arlington, Virginia 22202. 1975-. Monthly.

Applied Science and Technology Index. H.W. Wilson Co., 950 University Ave., Bronx, New York 10452. (800) 367-6770. Formerly Industrial Arts Index.

Biological and Agricultural Index. H.W. Wilson Co., 950 University Ave., Bronx, New York 10452. (800) 367-6770. 1916-. Monthly.

Chemical Abstracts. Chemical Abstracts Service, 2540 Olentangy River Rd., PO Box 3012, Columbus, Ohio 43210. (800) 848-6533. 1907-.

Current Advances in Ecological and Environmental Science. Pergamon Microforms International, Inc., Fairview Park, Elmsford, New York 10523. (914) 592-7720. 1989-. Monthly. Current literature searching service including journals, reports, abstracts, etc. This service is available online as part of the CABS database on the hosts BRS and ORBIT search service.

Ecological Abstracts. Geo Abstracts Ltd. Elsevier Applied Science, Crown House, Linton Rd., Barking, England IG 11 8JU. 1974-. Derived from over 600 leading ecological and environmental journals, plus books, conference proceedings, reports and theses.

Engineering Index. The Engineering Index Inc., 345 E. 47th St., New York, New York 10017. 1962-.

General Science Index. H. W. Wilson Co., 950 University Ave., Bronx, New York 10452. 1978-. Monthly, also issued in annual cumulation. Cumulative subject index to English language periodicals in the subject fields of astronomy, botany, chemistry, earth science, environment and conservation, food and nutrition, genetics, mathematics, medicine and health, microbiology, oceanography, physics, physiology and zoology.

Green Engineering: A Current Awareness Bulletin. Institution of Mechanical Engineers, 1 Birdcage Walk, Westminster, London, England SW1H 9JJ. 71973 1266/7. 1991. Monthly. Covers acid rain, aerosol ·technology, biotechnology chlorofluorocarbons, chemical and process engineering, environmental protection, energy conservation, energy generation, greenhouse effect, materials, pollution, recycling, waste disposal, and other environmental topics.

Multimedia Index to Ecology. National Information Center for Educational Media, University of Southern California, Los Angeles, California 90007.

Pollution Abstracts. Cambridge Scientific Abstracts, 5161 River Rd., Bethesda, Maryland 20816. (301) 961-6750. Six/year. Indexes worldwide technical literature on environmental pollution. Covers air pollution, marine and freshwater pollution, sewage and wastewater treatment, waste management, toxicology and health, noise pollution, radiation, land pollution, and environmental policies, programs, legislation, and education. Also available online.

Public Health Engineering Abstracts. U.S. G.P.O., Washington, District of Columbia 20401. (202) 512-0000. Monthly.

Science Citation Index. Institute for Scientific Information, 3501 Market St., Philadelphia, Pennsylvania 19104. 1961-.

BIBLIOGRAPHIES

Bibliography and Index of Geology. American Geological Institute, 4220 King St., Alexandria, Virginia 22302. Monthly. Includes environmental geology and hydrogeology.

Current Contents. Agriculture, Biology and Environmental Sciences. Institute for Scientific Information, 3501 Market St., Philadelphia, Pennsylvania 19104. (800) 523-1857. 1973-. Previous title: Current Contents. Agricultural, Food & Veterinary Sciences. Gives the table of contents of periodicals in the fields of agriculture, biology, environmental and related areas.

DIRECTORIES

ICWM Directory of Hazardous Waste Treatment and Disposal Facilities. Institute of Chemical Waste Management/National Solid Wastes Management Association, 1730 Rhode Island Ave., N.W., Suite 1000, Washington, District of Columbia 20036. (202) 659-4613.

ENCYCLOPEDIAS AND DICTIONARIES

Dictionary of Environmental Engineering and Related Sciences: English-Spanish, Spanish-English. Jose T. Villate. Ediciones Universal, 3090 SW 8th St., Miami, Florida 33135. (305) 642-3355. 1979.

Dictionary of Environmental Protection. Otto E. Tutzauer. Fred B. Rothman, 10368 W. Centennial Rd., Littleton, California 80127. (303) 979-5657. 1979.

Dictionary of Environmental Protection Technology: In Four Languages, English, German, French, Russian. Egon Seidel. Elsevier Science Publishing Co., 655 Avenue of the Americas, New York, New York 10010. (212) 984-5800. 1988.

Dictionary of Waste and Water Treatment. Butterworth-Heinemann, 80 Montvale Ave., Stoneham, Massachusetts 02180. (617) 438-8464. 1981. Dictionary of sanitary engineering.

Dictionary of Water and Sewage Engineering. Fritz Meinck and Helmut Mohle. Elsevier Science Publishing Co., 655 Avenue of the Americas, New York, New York 10010. (212) 984-5800. 1977. Text is in German, English, French and Italian. Deals with water management engineering and sewage.

Encyclopedia of Environmental Control Technology. Paul N. Cheremisinoff, ed. Gulf Publishing Co., Book Division, PO Box 2608, Houston, Texas 77252. (713) 529-4301 or (800) 231-6275. 1992. Volume 1: Thermal Treatment of Hazardous Wastes; volume 2: Air Pollution Control; volume 3: Wastewater Treatment Technology; volume 4: Hazardous Waste Containment and Treatment; volumes 5 through 8 in progress. Provides in-depth coverage of specialized topics related to environmental and industrial pollution control problems and state-of-the-art information on technology and research as well as projections of future trends in the field.

Encyclopedia of Environmental Science and Engineering. J.R. Pfafflin. Gordon and Breach Science Publishers, Inc., 270 8th Ave., New York, New York 10011. (212) 206-8900. 1992.

English-Russian Dictionary of Environmental Protection: About 14,000 Terms. E.L. Milovanov. Pergamon Microforms International, Inc., Fairview Park, Elmsford, New York 10523. (914) 592-7720. 1981.

Environmental Engineering Dictionary. C. C. Lee. Government Institutes, Inc., 4 Research Pl., Ste. 200, Rockville, Maryland 20850. (301) 921-2300. 1989. Defines over 6000 engineering terms relating to pollutioncontrol technologies, monitoring, risk assessment, sampling andanalysis, quality control, permitting, and environmentally-regulated engineering and science. Includes bibliographical references (p. 612-627).

Grzimek's Encyclopedia of Ecology. Bernhard Grzimek. Van Nostrand Reinhold, 115 5th Ave., New York, New York 10003. (212) 254-3232. 1976.

McGraw-Hill Encyclopedia of Environmental Science. Sybil P. Parker. McGraw-Hill Science & Engineering Books, 11 W. 19th St., New York, New York 10011. (212) 337-6010. 1980. Covers ecology, man's influence on nature, and environmental protection.

North American Reference Encyclopedia of Ecology and Pollution. William White. North American Pub. Co., 401

N. Broad St., Philadelphia, Pennsylvania 19108. (215) 238-5300. 1972.

Van Nostrand's Scientific Encyclopedia. Glenn D. Considine, ed. Van Nostrand Reinhold, 115 5th Ave., New York, New York 10003. (212) 254-3232. 1983. Sixth edition. Includes all broad subject areas in science.

GENERAL WORKS

Anaerobic Digestion: A Waste Treatment Technology. Elsevier Science Publishing Co., 655 Avenue of the Americas, New York, New York 10010. (212) 984-5800. 1991. Refuse and refuse disposal, biodegradation, anaerobic bacteria and sewage sludges digestion.

Biotechnology Application in Hazardous Waste Treatment. Gordon Lewandowski. Engineering Foundation, 345 E. 47th St., New York, New York 10017. (212) 705-7835. 1989. Trends in hazardous waste treatment using biotechnological methods.

Burning Garbage in the U.S.: Practice vs. State of the Art. Marjorie J. Clarke. INFORM, 381 Park Ave. S, New York, New York 10016. (212) 689-4040. 1991. Deals with the state of the art in waste disposal methods.

Closed Waste Site Evaluation: Emsdale Landfill: Report. Ontario Waste Management Branch. Waste Site Evaluation Unit, Toronto. National Technical Information Service, 5285 Port Royal Rd., Springfield, Virginia 22161. (703) 487-4650. 1989. Order number MIC-91-03061LDM.

Desulphurisation 2: Technologies and Strategies for Reducing Sulphur Emissions. Hemisphere Publishing Co., 79 Madison Ave., Suite 1110, New York, New York 10016. (212) 725-1999. 1991. Proceedings of a Symposium held in Sheffield, March 1991.

Environmental Biotechnology for Waste Treatment. Gary S. Sayler, et al., eds. Plenum Press, 233 Spring St., New York, New York 10013-1578. (212) 620-8000. 1991. Symposium on Environmental Biotechnology: Moving from the Flask to the Field. Knoxville, TN, 1990.

The Environmental Challenge of the 1990's. U.S. Environmental Protection Agency, 401 M St. SW, Washington, District of Columbia 20460. (202) 260-2090. 1991. Provides an overview of past and present projects for pollution prevention, focusing on the promotion of clean technologies and clean products in both the public and private sectors. Covers new prevention ideas relating to solid and hazardous wastes, pesticides, drinking water, wastewater and toxic substances.

Environmental Impacts of Hazardous Waste Treatment, Storage and Disposal Facilities. Rodolfo N. Salcedo, et al. Technomic Publishing Co., 851 New Holland Ave., Box 3535, Lancaster, Pennsylvania 17604. (717) 291-5609. 1989. Provides guidance in dealing with the many obstacles and preliminary requirements in siting TSD facilities.

Hazardous Waste Chemistry, Toxicology and Treatment. Stanley E. Manahan. Lewis Publishers, 2000 Corporate Blvd., N.W., Boca Raton, Florida 33431. (407) 994-0555 or (800) 272-7737. 1990. Reviews hazardous wastes, their chemistry and toxicology. Gives a basic coverage of chemistry and biochemistry, environmental chemical processes, and toxicology.

Hazardous Waste Land Treatment. Municipal Environmental Research Laboratory, Office of Research and Development, U.S. Environmental Protection Agency, 26 W. Martin Luther King Dr., Cincinnati, Ohio 45268. (513) 569-7931. 1983. Covers hazardous wastes, sanitary landfills and waste disposal in the ground.

Hazardous Waste Treatment Technologies: Biological Treatment, Wet Air Oxidation, Chemical Fixation, Chemical Oxidation. Alan P. Jackman. Noyes Publications, 120 Mill Rd., Park Ridge, New Jersey 07656. (201) 391-8484. 1991. Purification of hazardous wastes.

Innovative Thermal Hazardous Organic Waste Treatment Processes. Noyes Publications, 120 Mill Rd., Park Ridge, New Jersey 07656. (201) 391-8484. 1985. Technological innovations in hazardous waste treatment.

Magill's Survey of Science. Earth Science Series. Frank N. Magill. Salem Press, PO Box 50062, Pasadena, California 91105. 1990-. Five volumes. Includes information on earth's crust, hot spots and volcanic island chains, physical properties of minerals, rock magnetism, physical properties of rocks, and index.

National Survey of Hazardous Waste Generators and Treatment, Storage, and Disposal Facilities Regulated Under RCRA in 1981. U.S. Environmental Protection Agency, Office of Solid Waste and Emergency Response, 401 M St., S.W., Washington, District of Columbia 20460. (202) 260-2090. 1984. Environmental aspects of hazardous substances and waste disposal in the ground.

Physicochemical and Biological Detoxification of Hazardous Wastes. Yeun C. Wu, ed. Technomic Publishing Co., 851 New Holland Ave., Box 3535, Lancaster, Pennsylvania 17604. (717) 291-5609. 1989. 2 volume set. Proceedings of the International Conference of Physicochemical and Biological Detoxification of Hazardous Wastes, May 3-5, 1988, Atlantic City, NJ. Provides new information on a variety of established, new and in-development methods for treating a wide range of industrial and municipal hazardous wastes.

Pollution: Causes, Effects and Control. Roy Michael Harrison. Royal Society of Chemistry, c/o CRC Press, 2000 Corporate Blvd. N.W., Boca Raton, Florida 33431. (800) 272-7737. 1990. 2nd ed. Deals with environmental pollution and its associated problems and legal ramifications.

Recycling and Incineration: Evaluating Choices. Richard A. Denison and John Ruston. Island Press, 1718 Connecticut Ave. N.W., Suite 300, Washington, District of Columbia 20009. (202) 232-7933. 1990. Presents the technology, economics, environmental concerns, and legal intricacies behind these two approaches. Includes basics of waste reduction, recycling, and incineration; cost comparisons of the two approaches; an evaluation of the health and environmental impacts.

Treatment Technologies. Environment Protection Agency. Government Institutes, Inc., 4 Research Pl., Ste. 200, Rockville, Maryland 20850. (301)921-2300. 1991. 2nd ed. Provides a clear explanation of 24 treatment technologies and evaluates the effectiveness of the design and operations of each type of treatment. This new edition has more supporting numerical data, examples for a better understanding of the technology and an updated reference for specific industrial wastes.

Water Pollution: Modelling, Measuring and Prediction. L.C. Wrobel. Elsevier Science Publishing Co., 655 Avenue of the Americas, New York, New York 10010. (212) 984-5800. 1991. Mathematical modelling data acquisition waste disposal and wastewater treatment chemical and biological problems.

GOVERNMENTAL ORGANIZATIONS

New England Interstate Water Pollution Control Commission. 85 Merrimac St., Boston, Massachusetts 02114. (617) 367-8522.

HANDBOOKS AND MANUALS

The Generator's Guide to Hazardous Materials/Waste Management. Leo H. Traverse. Van Nostrand Reinhold, 115 5th Ave., New York, New York 10003. (212) 254-3232. 1991. Comprehensive information source for hazardous waste and hazardous materials management.

Industrial and Hazardous Waste Treatment. Nelson Leonard Nemerow and Avijit Dasgupta. Van Nostrand Reinhold, 115 5th Ave., New York, New York 10003. (212) 254-3232. 1991. Factory and trade waste, and hazardous waste purification.

Standard Handbook of Hazardous Waste Treatment and Disposal. Harry M. Freeman, ed. McGraw-Hill Science & Engineering Books, 11 West 19th St., New York, New York 10011. (212) 337-6010. 1989. A reference of alternatives and innovative technologies for managing hazardous waste and cleaning up abandoned disposal sites.

ONLINE DATA BASES

Aqualine. Water Research Center, Medmenham Laboratory, Marlow, Buckinghamshire, England SL7 2HD. Literature on water and wastewater technology.

BioBusiness. Dialog Information Services, Inc., Marketing Dept., 3460 Hillview Avenue, Palo Alto, California 94304. (800) 334-2564 or (415) 858-3810. Provides information based on evaluations of the economic and business aspects of biological and biomedical research.

CERCLIS. Chemical Information Systems, Inc., 7215 York Rd., Baltimore, Maryland 21212. (301) 321-8440. Information on hazardous waste disposal sites that have either been listed by the EPA on the National Priority List (NPL) or nominated for consideration for the NPL.

Chemical Abstracts-CA. Chemical Abstracts Service, 2540 Olentangy River Rd., P.O. Box 3012, Columbus, Ohio 43210. (800) 848-6533 or (614) 421-3600. Information sources include 9000 journals, patents from 27 countries, two industrial property organizations, new books, conference proceedings, and government research reports.

Computerized Engineering Index–COMPENDEX. Engineering Information Inc., 345 E. 47th St., New York, New York 10017. (212) 705-7600.

Medical Waste News. Business Publishers, Inc., 951 Pershing Dr., Silver Spring, Maryland 20910-4464. (301) 587-6300. Online access to regulation, legislation, and technological news and developments related to medical waste management and disposal. Online version of the periodical of the same name.

Monthly Catalog of United States Government Publications. U.S. G.P.O., Supt. of Docs., PO Box 371954, Pittsburgh, Pennsylvania 15250-7954. (202) 512-0000.

National Technical Information Service. U.S. Department of Commerce, National Technical Information Service, Office of Data Base Services, 5285 Port Royal Rd., Springfield, Virginia 22161. (703) 487-4807. Bibliographic database of government sponsored research and technical reports.

SCISEARCH. Institute for Scientific Information, University City Science Center, 3501 Market St., Philadelphia, Pennsylvania 19104. (215) 386-0100.

Toxic Materials News. Business Publishers, Inc., 951 Pershing Dr., Silver Spring, Maryland 20910-4464. (301) 587-6300. Legislation, regulations, and litigation concerning toxic substances. Online version of periodical of the same name.

Waste Information Digest. Environmental Studies Institute, International Academy at Santa Barbara, 800 Garden St., Suite D, Santa Barbara, California 93101-1552. (805) 965-5010. Online version of the periodical of the same name.

Waste Management and Resource Recovery. International Research & Evaluation, 21098 IRE Control Center, Eagan, Minnesota 55121. (612) 888-9635.

WasteInfo. Waste Management Information Bureau, United Kingdom Atomic Energy Authority, Building 46J, Harwell Laboratory, Harwell, Oxfordshire, England OX11 0RB. 44 (235) 24141.

PERIODICALS AND NEWSLETTERS

BioCycle-Journal of Waste Recycling. The J.G. Press, Inc., Box 351, Emmaus, Pennsylvania 18049. (215) 967-4135. Monthly. Articles on the reuse of sludge, waste water, and recycled products.

Bioresource Technology. Elsevier Science Publishing Co., 655 Avenue of the Americas, New York, New York 10010. (212) 989-5800. Monthly. Disseminates knowledge in the related areas of biomass, biological waste treatment, bioscience systems analysis and in the technologies associated with production or conversion.

Defense Cleanup. Pasha Publications, 1401 Wilson Blvd., Suite 900, Arlington, Virginia 22209. (703) 528-1244. Weekly. Reports on projects to analyze, recycle, and dispose of defense weapons.

Digester/Over the Spillway. Illinois Environmental Protection Agency, 2200 Churchill Rd., Box 19276, Springfield, Illinois 62794-9276. (217) 782-5562. Bimonthly. Water & wastewater operators.

Ecological Monographs. Business Office of the Ecological Society of America, Center of Environmental Studies, Arizona State University, Tempe, Arizona 85287-1201. (602) 965-3000. Quarterly. Scientific journal of ecological issues.

Federal Water Quality Association Newsletter. Federal Water Quality Association, P.O. Box 44163, Washington, District of Columbia 20026. (202) 447-4925. Seven times a year. Concerns sewage and industrial waste treatment and disposal.

Management of World Wastes. Communication Channels, 6255 Barfield Road, Atlanta, Georgia 30328. (404) 256-9800. Monthly. Covers public and private waste operations.

Medical Waste News. Business Publishers, Inc., 951 Pershing Dr., Silver Spring, Maryland 20910-4464. (301) 587-6300. 1989-. Biweekly. Covers EPA regulations and actions, state and nationwide changes in the laws, which management firms are landing big contracts, and also reports on technology such as: incineration, autoclaving, microwaves, etc. Also available online.

Michigan Waste Report. Michigan Waste Report, Inc., 400 Ann, SW, Suite 204, Grand Rapids, Michigan 49504. (616) 363-3262. Biweekly. Covers information about waste management.

Multinational Environmental Outlook. Business Publishers, Inc., 951 Pershing Dr., Silver Spring, Maryland 20910-4464. (301) 587-6300. 1974-. Biweekly. Covers developments in world environmental problems such as acid rain, deforestation, soil erosion, overfishing, threats to health, animal extinction, population growth, diminishing water supply and other related matters. Also available online.

Resource Exchange and News. Waste Systems Institute of Michigan, 400 Ann, NW, Suite 204, Grand Rapids, Michigan 49503. (616) 363-3262. Bimonthly.

Toxic Materials News. Business Publishers, Inc., 951 Pershing Dr., Silver Spring, Maryland 20910-4464. (301) 587-6300. 1974-. Weekly. Informs on regulations governing the manufacture, handling, transport, distribution and disposal of toxic chemicals and pesticides. Also available online.

Waste Disposal and Pollution Control. Wakeman/Walworth, P.O. Box 1939, New Haven, Connecticut 06509. (203) 562-8518. Monthly. Covers air and water pollution, toxic waste, and acid rain.

Waste Minimization & Recycling Report. Government Institutes, Inc., 4 Research Pl., Ste. 200, Rockville, Maryland 20850. (301) 921-2300. Monthly. Covers waste minimization, reduction and recycling strategies.

Waste Treatment Technology News. Business Communications Company, Inc., 25 Van Zant Street, Norwalk, Connecticut 06855. (203) 853-4266. Monthly. Covers effective management and handling of hazardous wastes.

Water & Waste Treatment. D.R. Publications, Faversham House, 111 St. James's Rd., Croydon, England CR9 2TH. Monthly. Covers water-supply engineering, sewage and sanitary engineering.

RESEARCH CENTERS AND INSTITUTES

University of Missouri-Rolla, Environmental Research Center. Rolla, Missouri 65401. (314) 341-4485.

Wisconsin Applied Water Pollution Research Consortium. University of Wisconsin-Madison, 3204 Engineering Building, 1415 Johnson Dr., Madison, Wisconsin 53706. (608) 262-7248.

TRADE ASSOCIATIONS AND PROFESSIONAL SOCIETIES

American Public Works Association. 106 W. 11th St., Ste. 1800, Kansas City, Missouri 64105-1806. (816) 472-6100.

American Society of Civil Engineers. 345 East 47th St., New York, New York 10017. (212) 705-7496.

American Society of Sanitary Engineering. Box 40362, Bay Village, Ohio 44140. (216) 835-3040.

American Water Resources Association. 5410 Grosvenor Lane, Suite 220, Bethesda, Maryland 20814. (301) 493-8600.

Federal Water Quality Association. PO Box 44163, Washington, District of Columbia 20026. (202) 447-4925.

WASTEWATER TREATMENT

See also: BIOFILTRATION; SEWAGE DISPOSAL

ABSTRACTING AND INDEXING SERVICES

Applied Science and Technology Index. H.W. Wilson Co., 950 University Ave., Bronx, New York 10452. (800) 367-6770. Formerly Industrial Arts Index.

Aqualine Abstracts. Water Research Centre. c/o Pergamon Microforms International, Inc., Fairview Park, Elmsford, New York 10523. (914) 592-7720. 1927-. Contains some 8,000 records annually on water and wastewater technology. Covers all aspects of water, wastewater, associated engineering services and the aquatic environment. Over 600 periodicals, as well as books, reports and conference proceedings and other publications from water related institutions worldwide are scanned. Also available online.

ASFA Aquaculture Abstracts. Cambridge Scientific Abstracts, Inc., 5161 River Rd., Bethesda, Maryland 20816. (301) 961-6750. 1984.

Biological and Agricultural Index. H.W. Wilson Co., 950 University Ave., Bronx, New York 10452. (800) 367-6770. 1916-. Monthly.

Chemical Abstracts. Chemical Abstracts Service, 2540 Olentangy River Rd., PO Box 3012, Columbus, Ohio 43210. (800) 848-6533. 1907-.

Civil Engineering Hydraulic Abstracts. BHRA Fluid Engineering, Air Science Co., PO Box 143, Corning, New York 14830. (607) 962-5591. Monthly. Abstracts of periodicals that publish in the areas of hydraulic engineering and other related topics.

Current Advances in Ecological and Environmental Science. Pergamon Microforms International, Inc., Fairview Park, Elmsford, New York 10523. (914) 592-7720. 1989-. Monthly. Current literature searching service includingjournals, reports, abstracts, etc. This service is available online as part of the CABS database on the hosts BRS and ORBIT search service.

Ecological Abstracts. Geo Abstracts Ltd. Elsevier Applied Science, Crown House, Linton Rd., Barking, England IG 11 8JU. 1974-. Derived from over 600 leading ecological and environmental journals, plus books, conference proceedings, reports and theses.

Ecology Abstracts. Cambridge Scientific Abstracts, 5161 River Rd., Bethesda, Maryland 20816. (301) 961-6750. Monthly.

Engineering Index. The Engineering Index Inc., 345 E. 47th St., New York, New York 10017. 1962-.

Food Science and Technology Abstracts. International Food Information Service, c/o National Food Laboratory, 6363 Clark Ave., Dublin, California 94568. (800) 336-3782. 1969-.

Lagoon Information Source Book. E. J. Middlebrooks, et al. Ann Arbor Science, 230 Collingwood, Ann Arbor, Michigan 48106. 1978. Presents information on all aspects of lagoon performance, operation, maintenance, upgrading, construction, construction techniques and problems associated with this method of wastewater treatment. Includes abstracts of the articles reviewed.

Microbiology Abstracts. Section A. Industrial and Applied Microbiology. Cambridge Scientific Abstracts, 5161 River Rd., Bethesda, Maryland 20816. (301) 961-6750. 1972-.

Pollution Abstracts. Cambridge Scientific Abstracts, 5161 River Rd., Bethesda, Maryland 20816. (301) 961-6750. Six/year. Indexes worldwide technical literature on environmental pollution. Covers air pollution, marine and freshwater pollution, sewage and wastewater treatment, waste management, toxicology and health, noise pollution, radiation, land pollution, and environmental policies, programs, legislation, and education. Also available online.

Public Health Engineering Abstracts. U.S. G.P.O., Washington, District of Columbia 20401. (202) 512-0000. Monthly.

Science Citation Index. Institute for Scientific Information, 3501 Market St., Philadelphia, Pennsylvania 19104. 1961-.

ALMANACS AND YEARBOOKS

Water Supply and Wastewater Disposal International Almanac. A. Kepinske and W. A. S. Kepinski. Vulkan-Verlag, Dr. W. Classen Nacht, Gooiland 11, Netherlands 1976-1985. Seven volumes. Deals with all problems and aspects in the domain of water supply and wastewater disposal.

BIBLIOGRAPHIES

Bibliography on Coagulation and Sedimentation in Water and Sewage Treatment. U.S. Works Project Administration for the City of New York, New York, New York 1939. Selected problems in sewage treatment.

Cobalt in Agricultural Ecosystems: A Bibliography of the Literature 1950 Through 1971. Robert Lewis Jones. Department of Agronomy, University of Illinois, Urbana, Illinois 61801. 1973.

Current Contents. Agriculture, Biology and Environmental Sciences. Institute for Scientific Information, 3501 Market St., Philadelphia, Pennsylvania 19104. (800) 523-1857. 1973-. Previous title: Current Contents. Agricultural, Food & Veterinary Sciences. Gives the table of contents of periodicals in the fields of agriculture, biology, environmental and related areas.

Operation, Maintenance and Management of Wastewater Treatment Facilities. Municipal Operations Branch, Office of Water Program Operations, U.S. Environmental Protection Agency, 401 M St. SW, Washington, District of Columbia 20460. (202) 260-5856. 1978. Bibliography of operations and maintenance of wastewater treatment plants.

DIRECTORIES

Who's Who in Environmental Engineering. American Academy of Environmental Engineers, 132 Holiday Court, Suite 206, Annapolis, Maryland 21401. (301) 266-3311. 1980. Annual. Directory of environmental engineers who are certified by the academy.

ENCYCLOPEDIAS AND DICTIONARIES

Dictionary of Environmental Engineering and Related Sciences: English-Spanish, Spanish-English. Jose T. Villate. Ediciones Universal, 3090 SW 8th St., Miami, Florida 33135. (305) 642-3355. 1979.

Dictionary of Environmental Protection Technology: In Four Languages, English, German, French, Russian. Egon Seidel. Elsevier Science Publishing Co., 655 Avenue of the Americas, New York, New York 10010. (212) 984-5800. 1988.

Dictionary of Waste and Water Treatment. Butterworth-Heinemann, 80 Montvale Ave., Stoneham, Massachusetts 02180. (617) 438-8464. 1981. Dictionary of sanitary engineering.

Dictionary of Water and Sewage Engineering. Fritz Meinck and Helmut Mohle. Elsevier Science Publishing Co., 655 Avenue of the Americas, New York, New York 10010. (212) 984-5800. 1977. Text is in German, English, French and Italian. Deals with water management engineering and sewage.

Encyclopedia of Chemical Processing and Design. John J. Mcketta and W. A. Cunningham. Marcel Dekker, Inc., 270 Madison Ave., New York, New York 10016. (212) 696-9000; (800) 228-1160. 1992. Thirty-eight volumes.

Encyclopedia of Environmental Control Technology. Paul N. Cheremisinoff, ed. Gulf Publishing Co., Book Division, PO Box 2608, Houston, Texas 77252. (713) 529-4301 or (800) 231-6275. 1992. Volume 1: Thermal Treatment of Hazardous Wastes; volume 2: Air Pollution Control; volume 3: Wastewater Treatment Technology; volume 4: Hazardous Waste Containment and Treatment; volumes 5 through 8 in progress. Provides in-depth coverage of specialized topics related to environmental and industrial pollution control problems and state-of-the-art information on technology and research as well as projections of future trends in the field.

Encyclopedia of Environmental Science and Engineering. J.R. Pfafflin. Gordon and Breach Science Publishers, Inc., 270 8th Ave., New York, New York 10011. (212) 206-8900. 1992.

The Encyclopedia of Sedimentology. Rhodes W. Fairbridge. Van Nostrand Reinhold, Information Services, 115 5th Ave., New York, New York 10003. (212) 254-3232. 1978.

English-Russian Dictionary of Environmental Protection: About 14,000 Terms. E.L. Milovanov. Pergamon Microforms International, Inc., Fairview Park, Elmsford, New York 10523. (914) 592-7720. 1981.

Environmental Engineering Dictionary. C. C. Lee. Government Institutes, Inc., 4 Research Pl., Ste. 200, Rockville, Maryland 20850. (301) 921-2300. 1989. Defines over 6000 engineering terms relating to pollutioncontrol technologies, monitoring, risk assessment, sampling andanalysis, quality control, permitting, and environmentally-regulated engineering and science. Includes bibliographical references (p. 612-627).

Grzimek's Encyclopedia of Ecology. Bernhard Grzimek. Van Nostrand Reinhold, 115 5th Ave., New York, New York 10003. (212) 254-3232. 1976.

Kirk-Othmer Encyclopedia of Chemical Technology. J. I. Kroschwitz, ed. John Wiley & Sons, Inc., 605 3rd Ave., New York, New York 10158-0012. (212) 850-6000. 1992-. All articles in the new edition have been rewritten and updated adding new subjects such as biotechnology, computer topics, analytical techniques and instrumentation, environmental concerns, fuels and energy, inorganic and solid state chemistry; composite materials and material science in general, and pharmaceuticals. Also available online.

McGraw-Hill Encyclopedia of Environmental Science. Sybil P. Parker. McGraw-Hill Science & Engineering Books, 11 W. 19th St., New York, New York 10011. (212) 337-6010. 1980. Covers ecology, man's influence on nature, and environmental protection.

North American Reference Encyclopedia of Ecology and Pollution. William White. North American Pub. Co., 401 N. Broad St., Philadelphia, Pennsylvania 19108. (215) 238-5300. 1972.

Van Nostrand's Scientific Encyclopedia. Glenn D. Considine, ed. Van Nostrand Reinhold, 115 5th Ave., New York, New York 10003. (212) 254-3232. 1983. Sixth edition. Includes all broad subject areas in science.

GENERAL WORKS

Activated Sludge; Theory and Practice. N.F. Gray. Oxford University Press, 200 Madison Ave., New York, New York 10016. (212) 679-7300 or (800) 334-4249. 1990. Microbial theory and kinetics, process control, modes of operation and aeration methods, trouble shooting, bulking problems, and nutrient removal.

Adsorption Studies Evaluating Codisposal of Coal Gasification Ash with PAH-Containing Wastewater Sludges. John William Kilmer. University of Illinois at Urbana-Champaign, Urbana, Illinois 61801. 1986.

Applied Math for Wastewater Plant Operators. Joanne Kilpatrick Price. Technomic Publishing Co., 851 New Holland Ave., Box 3535, Lancaster, Pennsylvania 17604. (717) 291-5609. 1991.

The Arthur Young Guide to Water and Wastewater Finance and Pricing. George A. Raftelis. Lewis Publishers, 121 S. Main St., Chelsea, Michigan 48118. (313) 475-8619; (800) 525-7894. 1989. Covers virtually all aspects of establishing a financial planning and management program for a water or wastewater utility. Examines the development of capital plans, alternatives for securing capital funding and the options for a user charge system.

Basic Math Concepts for Water and Wastewater Plant Operators. Joanne Kirkpatrick Price. Technomic Publishing Co., 851 New Holland Ave., Box 3535, Lancaster, Pennsylvania 17604. (717) 291-5609. 1991.

Biodegradability of Organic Substances in the Aquatic Environment. Pavel Pitter, et al. CRC Press, 2000 Corporate Blvd. N.W., Boca Raton, Florida 33431. (800) 272-7737. 1990. Explains the principles and theories of biodegradation, primarily from an ecological standpoint. Current techniques used to evaluate the biodegradability of individual chemicals are reviewed.

Biological Wastewater Treatment Systems. N. J. Horan. John Wiley & Sons, Inc., 605 3rd Ave., New York, New York 10158-0012. (212) 850-6000. 1990. Introduces basic concepts of microbial growth and reactor engineering required to fully understand the design and operation

of wastewater treatment systems. Topics include wastewater characteristics, microorganisms exploited in wastewater treatment, and microbial energy generation.

Chemical Primary Sludge Thickening and Dewatering. Di Gregorio, David. National Technical Information Service, 5285 Port Royal Rd., Springfield, Virginia 22161. (703) 487-4650. 1979.

Codisposal of Garbage and Sewage Sludge–a Promising Solution to Two Problems. U.S. General Accounting Office. U.S. G.P.O., Washington, District of Columbia 20401. (202) 512-0000. 1979.

Constructed Wetlands for Wastewater Treatment. Donald A. Hammer. Lewis Publishers, 200 Corporate Blvd. NW, Boca Raton, Florida 33431. (407) 994-0555 or (800)272-7737. 1989. Presents general principles of wetland ecology, hydrology, soil chemistry, vegetation, microbiology, and wildlife dependence on wetlands. It provides management guidelines, beginning with policies and regulations, and including siting and construction and operations and monitoring of constructed wetland systems.

Controlling Volatile Organic Compound Emissions From Industrial Wastewater. Jeffrey Elliott and Sheryl Watkins. Noyes Publications, 120 Mill Rd., Park Ridge, New Jersey 07656. (201) 391-8484. 1990. Describes sources of organic containing wastewater, volatile organic compound emission estimation procedures for treatment and collection system units, and available volatile organic compound emission control strategies. Secondary impacts and the control costs associated with steam stripping are also presented.

Desalination and Water Re-Use. Miriam Balaban, ed. Institution of Chemical Engineers, c/o Hemisphere Pub., 1900 Frost Rd., Suite 101, Bristol, Pennsylvania 19007-1598. (215) 785-5800. 1991. Four volumes. Includes the papers presented at a four-day symposium organized by the Institution of Chemical Engineers (UK) on behalf of the European Federation of Chemical Engineers Working Parties on Desalination and Water Technology and the Membrane Society.

Determination of TCDD in Industrial and Municipal Wastewaters. U.S. Environmental Protection Agency, Environmental Monitoring and Support Laboratory, Center for Environmental Research Information, 26 W. Martin Luther King Dr., Cincinnati, Ohio 45268. (513) 569-7931. 1982. Covers sewage purification through chlorination, particularly tetrachlorodibenzodioxin.

Determining Wastewater Treatment Costs for Your Community. U.S. Environmental Protection Agency, Office of Water Program Operations, 401 M St., S.W., Washington, District of Columbia 20460. (202) 260-2090. 1979. Economic aspects of sewage disposal plants.

Developments in Design and Operation of Large Wastewater Treatment Plants. P. Benedek, et al., eds. Pergamon Microforms International, Inc., Fairview Park, Elmsford, New York 10523. (914) 592-7720. 1988. Proceedings of an IAWPRC Workshop held in Budapest, Hungary, September 14-18, 1987. Covers a wide range of topics of interest to designers, operators and researchers in the field of wastewater treatment plants. Includes practical applications of research work.

Dynamic Modeling and Expert Systems in Wastewater Engineering. Giles G. Patry and David Chapman. Lewis Publishers, 200 Corporate Blvd. NW, Boca Raton, Florida 33431. (407) 994-0555 or (800)272-7737. 1988. Result of a workshop held at McMaster University (May 19-20, 1988). Brings together current work on dynamic modelling and expert systems as applied to the design, operation and control of waste- water treatment systems.

Effluent Treatment and Waste Disposal. Institution of Chemical Engineers. Hemisphere Publishing Corp., 79 Madison Ave., Suite 1110, New York, New York 10016. (212) 725-1999. 1990. Provides a detailed analysis of the strides which industry has taken to address the pollution of waterways.

The Environmental Challenge of the 1990's. U.S. Environmental Protection Agency, 401 M St. SW, Washington, District of Columbia 20460. (202) 260-2090. 1991. Provides an overview of past and present projects for pollution prevention, focusing on the promotion of clean technologies and clean products in both the public and private sectors. Covers new prevention ideas relating to solid and hazardous wastes, pesticides, drinking water, wastewater and toxic substances.

Environmental Issues: An Anthology of 1989. Thomas W. Joyce, ed. TAPPI Press, Technology Park/Atlanta, PO Box 105113, Atlanta, Georgia 30348. (404) 446-1400. 1990. Contains 39 papers on environmental, safety and occupational health concerns from 11 TAPPI, CPPA and AIChE meetings held during 1989. Also included is a literature review of over 200 papers published in 1989.

Fine Pore Aeration for Wastewater Treatment. W. C. Boyle, et al. Noyes Publications, 120 Mill Rd., Park Ridge, New Jersey 07656. (201) 391-8484. 1990. Presents information from Design Manual prepared for the U.S. Environmental Protection Agency, Sept. 1989. Includes the following devices: porous ceramic plates, discs, domes, tubes, perforated membrane tubes and discs.

Handbook for Identification and Correction of Typical Design Deficiencies at Municipal Wastewater Treatment Facilities. U.S. Environmental Protection Agency, Office of Research and Development, Municipal Environmental Research Laboratory, 26 W. Martin Luther King Dr., Cincinnati, Ohio 45268. (513) 569-7931. 1982. Sewage purification and sewage disposal plants.

Health Effects Due to the Cessation of Chlorination of Wastewater Treatment Plant Effluent. Janet A. Holden. Institute of Natural Resources, Chicago, Illinois 1981.

Industrial Wastewater Heavy Metal Removal. Robert W. Peters. CRC Press, 2000 Corporate Blvd. N.W., Boca Raton, Florida 33431. (800) 272-7737. 1991. Includes heavy metal contamination episodes, metal speciation complexation, brief review of various unit operation processes used for removal of heavy metals from solution with approximate percentage of installations employing each technology. Also discusses the various technologies used and the new emerging techniques.

Inspector's Guide: To Be Used in the Evaluation of Municipal Wastewater Treatment Plants. U.S. G.P.O., Washington, District of Columbia 20401. (202) 512-0000. 1979. Sewage disposal plant evaluation and sewage purification.

Integrated Design of Water Treatment Facilities. Susumu Kawamura. John Wiley & Sons, Inc., 605 3rd Ave., New York, New York 10158-0012. (212) 850-6000. 1991. Covers research pilot studies and preliminary design studies, as well as the actual design, construction and plant management. Covers the entire project sequence, describing not only very basic and essential design

criteria, but also how to design each phase to maximize overall efficiency while minimizing operation and maintenance costs.

It's Your Choice: Small-Community Wastewater Options. U.S. Environmental Protection Agency, Office of Water, 401 M St. SW, Washington, District of Columbia 20460. (202) 260-2090. 1989.

New Developments in Industrial Wastewater Treatment. Aysen Turkman, ed. Kluwer Academic Publishers, 101 Philip Dr., Assinippi Park, Norwell, Massachusetts 02061-0358. (617) 871-6600. 1991. NATO Advanced Research Workshop, Oct.-Nov. 1989.

Organic Substances and Sediment in Water. Robert A. Baker. Lewis Publishers, 2000 Corporate Blvd., Boca Raton, Florida 33431. (407) 994-0555 or (800) 272-7737. 1991. vol. 1-3.

Phosphorous Removal From Wastewater. Robert P. G. Bowker and H. David Stensel. Noyes Publications, 120 Mill Rd., Park Ridge, New Jersey 07656. (201) 391-8484. 1990. Oriented toward design methods and operating procedures. Cost information from actual phosphorous removing installations is presented when available. Planning level cost estimates are also included.

Principles of Water Quality Management. William Wesley Eckenfelder. CBI, Boston, Massachusetts 1980.

Proceedings of the 4th National Symposium on Individual and Small Community Sewage Systems. American Society of Agricultural Engineers, 2950 Niles Rd., St. Joseph, Michigan 49085-9659. (616) 429-0300. 1985. Includes current trends such as design, planning, management, and performance of large systems, the use of computers for on-site technology, site evaluation, etc. The 5th National Symposium held in 1987 further includes environmental effects of on-site disposal soil absorption/ system siting requirement and groundwater impact.

Removal of Heavy Metals from Groundwaters. Robert W. Peters. Lewis Publishers, 2000 Corporate Blvd., N.W., Boca Raton, Florida 33431. (407) 994-0555 or (800) 272-7737. 1991. Describes the sources of heavy metal contamination, classification of metals by industry, extent of the contamination problem, toxicity associated with various heavy metals, effects of heavy metals in biological wastewater treatment operations, leaching of heavy metals from sludges, modeling of heavy metals in the saturated and unsaturated zones, and other related areas.

Removal of Heavy Metals from Wastewaters. Stephen Beszedits. B and L Information Services, PO Box 458, Station L, Toronto, Ontario, Canada M6E 2W4. (416) 657-1197. 1980. Covers wastewater treatment, electro-dialysis, heavy metals, ultrafication, ozonization, foam separation, and ion exchange process.

Sludge Management. W. F. Garber and D. R. Anderson, eds. Pergamon Microforms International, Inc., Fairview Park, Elmsford, New York 10523. (914) 592-7720. 1990. Proceedings of the IAWPRC Conference on Sludge Management, held at Loyola Marymount University, Los Angeles, California, 8-12 January 1990. Offers an insight into sludge management. Topics include: treatment plant planning and management, sludge melting, incineration, drying and dewatering, aerobic and anaerobic digestion, heavy metal contaminants, and the use of sludge products as construction materials.

Technologies for Small Water and Wastewater Systems. Edward J. Martin and Edward T. Martin. Van Nostrand

Reinhold, 115 5th Ave., New York, New York 10003. (212) 254-3232. 1991. Addresses how to exploit different water treatment technologies according to available resources. Includes extensive sections on costs and design of both established and new technologies with vital data on limitations, operations and maintenance, control and special factors.

Toxicity Reduction in Industrial Effluents. Perry W. Lanford, et al. Van Nostrand Reinhold, 115 5th Ave., New York, New York 10003. (212) 254-3232. 1990. Overview of aquatic toxicology and toxicity reduction. Specific treatment technologies that can be used to reduce toxicity, such as aerobic and anaerobic biological treatment, air and steam stripping of volatile organics, granulated carbon absorption, powdered activated carbon treatment and chemical oxidation, are discussed in detail.

The Use of Macrophytes in Water Pollution Control. D. Athie and C. C. Cerri, eds. Pergamon Microforms International, Inc., Fairview Park, Elmsford, New York 10523. (914) 592-7720. 1988. Proceedings of an IAWPRC specialized seminar held in Piracicaba, Brazil, August 24-28,1986. Describes the problem of river pollution, caused mainly by sewage and industrial effluents.

Wastewater Engineering: Treatment, Disposal, and Reuse. Metcalf & Eddy, Inc. McGraw-Hill Science & Engineering Books, 11 West 19th St., New York, New York 10011. (212) 337-6010. 1991. Reflects the impact of changing federal legislation on environmental quality control and sludge management. Gives a solid overall perspective on wastewater engineering.

Wastewater Treatment Using Flocculation, Coagulation, and Flotation; Citations from the American Petroleum Institute Data Base. National Technical Information Service, 5285 Port Royal Rd., Springfield, Virginia 22161. (703) 487-4650.

Water Pollution: Modelling, Measuring and Prediction. L.C. Wrobel. Elsevier Science Publishing Co., 655 Avenue of the Americas, New York, New York 10010. (212) 984-5800. 1991. Mathematical modelling data acquisition waste disposal and wastewater treatment chemical and biological problems.

GOVERNMENTAL ORGANIZATIONS

U.S. Environmental Protection Agency: Office of Wetlands Protection. 401 M St., S.W., Washington, District of Columbia 20460. (202) 382-7946.

HANDBOOKS AND MANUALS

Basic Mechanical Maintenance Procedures at Water and Wastewater Plants. Glenn M. Tillman. Lewis Publishers, 2000 Corporate Blvd., Boca Raton, Florida 33431. (407) 994-0555 or (800) 272-7737. 1991. Part Operator's Guide series. Includes standard mechanical drawing symbols for valves, gates, gate equipment, equipment lockout procedures, centrifugal pumps, positive displacement pumps, rotary pumps, coupling alignment, pumping systems, macerator blades, shear pins, lubrication, and appendices.

CRC Handbook of Techniques for Aquatic Sediments Sampling. Alena Murdoch and Scott D. MacKnight. CRC Press, 2000 Corporate Blvd., N.W., Boca Raton, Florida 33431. (407) 994-0555 or (800) 272-7737. 1991.

Contents includes: selection of bottom sediment sampling stations, bottom sediment sampling, sampling the settling and suspended particulate matter, sediment sample handling process, and sampling sediment pore water.

Design Handbook for Automation of Activated Sludge Wastewater Treatment Plants. Alan W. Manning. National Technical Information Service, 5285 Port Royal Rd., Springfield, Virginia 22161. (703) 487-4650. 1980. Sewage purification and activated sludge process.

The EPA Manual for Waste Minimization Opportunity Assessments. U.S. Environmental Protection Agency. Technomic Publishing Co., 851 New Holland Ave., Box 3535, Lancaster, Pennsylvania 17604. (717) 291-5609. 1990.

Handbook of Biological Wastewater Treatment. Garland Publishing, Inc., 1000A Sherman Ave., Hamden, Connecticut 06514. (203) 281-4487. 1980.

Handbook of Wastewater Collection and Treatment: Principles and Practice. Garland Publishing, Inc., 1000A Sherman Ave., Hamden, Connecticut 06514. (203) 281-4487. 1980. Sewage disposal and sewage purification.

Industrial Wastewater Source Control: An Inspection Guide. Nancy Rukonen. Technomic Pub. Co., 851 New Holland Ave., Box 3535, Lancaster, Pennsylvania 17604. (800) 233-9936. 1992. Comprehensive guide for industrial waste inspectors.

Instrumentation Handbook for Water & Wastewater Treatment Plants. Lewis Publishers, 121 S. Main St., Chelsea, Michigan 48118. (313) 475-8619. 1988. Water and sewage purification equipment and supplies.

Operation of Municipal Wastewater Treatment Plants. Water Pollution Control Federation, 601 Wythe St., Alexandria, Virginia 22314. (800) 556-8700. 2nd ed.

Riegel's Handbook of Industrial Chemistry. James A. Kent, ed. Van Nostrand Reinhold, 115 5th Ave., New York, New York 10020. (212) 254-3232. 1983. Eighth edition. Includes industries such as: wastewater technology, coal technology, phosphate fertilizers, synthetic plastics, man-made textiles, detergents, sugar, animal and vegetable oils, chemical explosives, dyes, nuclear industry, and much more.

Screening Equipment Handbook: For Industrial and Municipal Water and Wastewater Treatment. Tom M. Pankratz. Technomic Publishing Co., Lancaster, Pennsylvania 1988. Covers the water purification equipment industry, fish screens, and filters and filtration.

Standard Handbook of Environmental Engineering. Robert A. Corbitt. McGraw-Hill, 1221 Ave. of the Americas, New York, New York 10020. (212) 512-2000 or (800) 262-4729. 1990. Hands-on reference to understand environmental engineering technology. Covers air quality control, water supply, wastewater disposal, waste management, stormwater and hazardous wastes.

Wastewater Treatment Plant Instrumentation Handbook. National Technical Information Service, 5285 Port Royal Rd., Springfield, Virginia 22161. (703) 487-4650. 1985.

Wastewater Treatment: Pocket Handbook. Pudvan Publishing Co., Inc., 1935 Shermer Rd., Northbrook, Illinois 60062. (312) 498-9840. 1987. Covers sewage purification methods.

Water and Wastewater Examination Manual. V. Dean Adams. Lewis Publishers, 2000 Corporate Blvd., N.W., Boca Raton, Florida 33431. (407) 994-0555 or (800) 272-7737. 1990. Guide and reference for water/wastewater quality analysis. Includes procedures for parameters frequently used in water quality analysis.

Water Treatment Handbook. Degremont s.a., 184, ave. du 18-Juin-1940, Rueil-Malmaison, France F-92500. 1991. Sixth edition. Part 1 is a general survey of water and its action on the materials with which it comes into contact, and theoretical principles of separation and correction processes used in water treatment. Part 2 describes the process and the treatment plant beginning with the separation process.

ONLINE DATA BASES

Air/Water Pollution Report. NewsNet, Inc., 945 Haverford Rd., Bryn Mawr, Pennsylvania 19010. (800) 345-1301. Online version of periodical of same name.

CERCLIS. Chemical Information Systems, Inc., 7215 York Rd., Baltimore, Maryland 21212. (301) 321-8440. Information on hazardous waste disposal sites that have either been listed by the EPA on the National Priority List (NPL) or nominated for consideration for the NPL.

Chemical Abstracts-CA. Chemical Abstracts Service, 2540 Olentangy River Rd., P.O. Box 3012, Columbus, Ohio 43210. (800) 848-6533 or (614) 421-3600. Information sources include 9000 journals, patents from 27 countries, two industrial property organizations, new books, conference proceedings, and government research reports.

Computerized Engineering Index–COMPENDEX. Engineering Information Inc., 345 E. 47th St., New York, New York 10017. (212) 705-7600.

Great Lakes Water Quality Data Base. U.S. Environmental Protection Agency, Office of Research and Development, Large Lakes Research Station, 401 M St. SW, Washington, District of Columbia 20460. (202) 260-2090. Water data related to the Great Lakes and related tributaries and watersheds.

Innovative/Alternative Pollution Control Technology Facility File–IADB. U.S. Environmental Protection Agency, Office of Water Program Operations, 401 M St., S.W., Washington, District of Columbia 20460. (202) 260-2090.

Kirk-Othmer Encyclopedia of Chemical Technology. John Wiley & Sons, Inc., 605 3rd Ave., 5th Floor, New York, New York 10158. (212) 850-6000. Online version of the publication of the same name.

Monthly Catalog of United States Government Publications. U.S. G.P.O., Supt. of Docs., PO Box 371954, Pittsburgh, Pennsylvania 15250-7954. (202) 512-0000.

National Technical Information Service. U.S. Department of Commerce, National Technical Information Service, Office of Data Base Services, 5285 Port Royal Rd., Springfield, Virginia 22161. (703) 487-4807. Bibliographic database of government sponsored research and technical reports.

PressNet Environmental Reports. Chemical Information Systems, Inc., 7215 York Rd., Baltimore, Maryland 21212. (301) 321-8440.

SCISEARCH. Institute for Scientific Information, University City Science Center, 3501 Market St., Philadelphia, Pennsylvania 19104. (215) 386-0100.

Waste Information Digest. Environmental Studies Institute, International Academy at Santa Barbara, 800 Garden St., Suite D, Santa Barbara, California 93101-1552. (805) 965-5010. Online version of the periodical of the same name.

Waste Management and Resource Recovery. International Research & Evaluation, 21098 IRE Control Center, Eagan, Minnesota 55121. (612) 888-9635.

WasteInfo. Waste Management Information Bureau, United Kingdom Atomic Energy Authority, Building 46J, Harwell Laboratory, Harwell, Oxfordshire, England OX11 ORB. 44 (235) 24141.

PERIODICALS AND NEWSLETTERS

Analytical Biochemistry. Academic Press, 111 Fifth Ave., New York, New York 10003. (800) 346-8648. Covers biological and chemical topics relating to the environment.

Biodegradation. Kluwer Academic Publishers, 101 Philip Dr., Assinippi Park, Norwell, Massachusetts 02061-0358. (617) 871-6600. 1990-. Quarterly. Covers all aspects of science pertaining to the detoxification, recycling, amelioration or treatment of waste materials and pollutants by naturally occurring microbial strains, associations, or recombinant microorganisms.

Clean Water Report. Business Publishers, Inc., 951 Pershing Dr., Silver Spring, Maryland 20910-4464. (301) 587-6300. 1964-. Biweekly. Key information source for environmental professionals, covering the important issues: groundwater, drinking water, wastewater treatment, drought, wetlands, coastal protection, dioxin, non-point source pollution, agrichemical contamination, cleanup versus prevention issues, and related topics.

Clearwaters. New York Water Pollution Control Association, 90 Presidential Plaza, Suite 122, Syracuse, New York 13202. (315) 422-7811. 1971-. Quarterly. Articles on design methods, legislation, and innovations on wastewater treatment plants.

Desalination and Water Re-Use Technologies in Japan. Annual Report. Water Re-Use Promotion Center, Landix Akasaka Bldg, 2-3-4, Akasaka, Minato-ku, Tokyo, Japan 1981-. Annual.

Dickey Data. W.S. Dickey Clay Mfg. Co., Box 6, Pittsburgh, Kansas 66762. (316) 231-1400. Quarterly. Wastewater facilities, drainage, plumbing, pollution control and building materials industry.

Environmental Protection Magazine. Stevens Publishing Co., 225 New Road, PO Box 2604, Waco, Texas 76702-2573. (817) 776-9000. Air and water pollution, wastewater and hazardous materials.

Operations Forum. Water Pollution Control Federation, 601 Wythe Street, Alexandria, Virginia 22314-1994. (703) 684-2400. Monthly. Covers the advancement of practical knowledge in water quality control systems.

Pollution Equipment News. Rimbach Publishing, Inc., 8650 Babcock Boulevard, Pittsburgh, Pennsylvania 15237. (412) 364-5366. Bimonthly. Covers new products, techniques, and literature.

Sludge Newsletter. Business Publishers, Inc., 951 Pershing Dr., Silver Spring, Maryland 20910-4464. (301) 587-6300. 1976-. Biweekly. Reports on continuing changes at EPA, plus an array of new hazardous waste management and industrial pretreatment requirements that will affect municipal sludge.

Wastewater Works News. Michigan Department of Health, Wastewater Section, Division of Engineering, Lansing, Michigan 48914. Bimonthly.

Water and Wastes Digest. Scranton Gillette Communications, Inc., 380 Northwest Highway, Des Plaines, Illinois 60016. (708) 298-6622. Bimonthly. Covers publicly and privately owned water and sewage systems.

RESEARCH CENTERS AND INSTITUTES

Engineering Research Center for Hazardous Substances Control. University of California, Los Angeles, 6722 Boelter Hall, Los Angeles, California 90024. (213) 206-3071.

Environmental Engineering and Sciences Department. Virginia Polytech Institute and State University, 330 Norris Hall, Department of Civil Engineering, Blacksburg, Virginia 24061. (703) 961-6635.

Mississippi State University, Water Resources Research Institute. P.O. Drawer AD, Mississippi State, Mississippi 39762. (601) 325-3620.

Sanitary Engineering and Environmental Health Research Laboratory. University of California, Berkeley, 1301 South 46th, Building 112, Richmond, California 94804. (415) 231-9449.

University of Oklahoma, Bureau of Water and Environmental Resources Research. P.O. Box 2850, Norman, Oklahoma 73070. (405) 325-2960.

STATISTICS SOURCES

Ecology: Community Profiles. U.S. Fish and Wildlife Service. National Technical Information Service, 5285 Port Royal Road, Springfield, Virginia 22161. (703) 487-4650. Irregular. Data on coastal and inland ecosystems, including wetlands, tidal-flats, near-shore seagrasses, sand dunes, drilling platforms, oyster reefs, estuaries, rivers and streams.

Electron Beam Wastewater Treatment Removes Organics. FIND/SVP, 625 Avenue of the Americas, New York, New York 10011. (212) 645-4500. New low-cost, high-capacity method of effectively treating low-level contamination; the uses of electron-beam radiation (EBR); EBR potential in effluent lines of waste-producing factories; EBR treatment of low-level concentration and disinfection of sewage.

Notes on Sedimentation Activities. U.S. Geological Survey, 12201 Sunrise Valley Dr., Reston, Virginia 22092. (703) 648-4460. 1967-. Annual. Monitoring of suspended sediments, measurement of sediment loads and deposition, studies of erosion and sedimentation damage, and sediment removal projects.

TRADE ASSOCIATIONS AND PROFESSIONAL SOCIETIES

American Institute of Chemical Engineers. 345 East 47th St., New York, New York 10017. (212) 705-7338.

American Institute of Chemists. 7315 Wisconsin Ave., Bethesda, Maryland 20814. (301) 652-2447.

American Society of Sanitary Engineering. Box 40362, Bay Village, Ohio 44140. (216) 835-3040.

Association of Metropolitan Water Agencies. 1717 K St., N.W., Suite 1102, Washington, District of Columbia 20036. (202) 331-2820.

Environmental Quality Industrial Resources Center. The Ohio State University, 1200 Chambers Rd., Room 310, Columbus, Ohio 43212. (614) 292-6717.

National Council of the Paper Industry for Air and Stream Improvements. 260 Madison Ave., New York, New York 10016. (212) 532-9000.

Society for Industrial Microbiology. Box 12534, Arlington, Virginia 22209. (703) 941-5373.

Submersible Wastewater Pump Association. 600 Federal St., Suite 400, Chicago, Illinois 60605. (312) 922-6222.

Water Environment Federation. 601 Wythe St., Alexandria, Virginia 22314-1994. (703) 684-2400. Formerly, Water Pollution Control Federation.

WATER ANALYSIS

ABSTRACTING AND INDEXING SERVICES

Abstracts of Air and Water Conservation Literature. American Petroleum Institute. Central Abstracting and Indexing Service, 275 Madison Avenue, New York, New York 10016. 1972.

Applied Science and Technology Index. H.W. Wilson Co., 950 University Ave., Bronx, New York 10452. (800) 367-6770. Formerly Industrial Arts Index.

Aqualine Abstracts. Water Research Centre. c/o Pergamon Microforms International, Inc., Fairview Park, Elmsford, New York 10523. (914) 592-7720. 1927-. Contains some 8,000 records annually on water and wastewater technology. Covers all aspects of water, wastewater, associated engineering services and the aquatic environment. Over 600 periodicals, as well as books, reports and conference proceedings and other publications from water related institutions worldwide are scanned. Also available online.

ASFA Aquaculture Abstracts. Cambridge Scientific Abstracts, Inc., 5161 River Rd., Bethesda, Maryland 20816. (301) 961-6750. 1984.

Bulletin Signaletique: Eau et Assainissement, Pollution Atmospherique, Droit des Pollutions. Centre de Documentation, Centre National de la Recherche Scientifique, 15, quai Anatole France, Paris, France 75700. (1) 45 55 92 25. 1983-. Monthly. Indexes pollution periodicals including water, atmospheric and related pollutions.

Chemical Abstracts. Chemical Abstracts Service, 2540 Olentangy River Rd., PO Box 3012, Columbus, Ohio 43210. (800) 848-6533. 1907-.

EIS: Digests of Environmental Impact Statements. Cambridge Scientific Abstracts, 5161 River Rd., Bethesda, Maryland 20816. (301) 951-1400. 1970-. Bimonthly. Provides detailed abstracts of all the environmental impact statements issued by the federal government each year and indexes them. Also extracts the key issues from the complex government released environmental impact statements. Contents include areas such as: air transportation, defense programs, energy, hazardous substances, land use, manufacturing, parks, refuges, forests, research and development, roads and railroads, urban and social programs, wastes, and water.

Engineering Index. The Engineering Index Inc., 345 E. 47th St., New York, New York 10017. 1962-.

General Science Index. H. W. Wilson Co., 950 University Ave., Bronx, New York 10452. 1978-. Monthly, also issued in annual cumulation. Cumulative subject index to English language periodicals in the subject fields of astronomy, botany, chemistry, earth science, environment and conservation, food and nutrition, genetics, mathematics, medicine and health, microbiology, oceanography, physics, physiology and zoology.

Pollution Abstracts. Cambridge Scientific Abstracts, 5161 River Rd., Bethesda, Maryland 20816. (301) 961-6750. Six/year. Indexes worldwide technical literature on environmental pollution. Covers air pollution, marine and freshwater pollution, sewage and wastewater treatment, waste management, toxicology and health, noise pollution, radiation, land pollution, and environmental policies, programs, legislation, and education. Also available online.

Science Citation Index. Institute for Scientific Information, 3501 Market St., Philadelphia, Pennsylvania 19104. 1961-.

BIBLIOGRAPHIES

Chemical Analysis of Inorganic Constituents of Water. CRC Press, 2000 Corporate Blvd. N.W., Boca Raton, Florida 33431. (800) 272-7737. 1982.

Current Contents. Agriculture, Biology and Environmental Sciences. Institute for Scientific Information, 3501 Market St., Philadelphia, Pennsylvania 19104. (800) 523-1857. 1973-. Previous title: Current Contents. Agricultural, Food & Veterinary Sciences. Gives the table of contents of periodicals in the fields of agriculture, biology, environmental and related areas.

Public and Private Water Utility Treatment: Metals and Organics in Raw and Finished Waters. Vance Bibliographies, PO Box 229, 112 N. Charter St., Monticello, Illinois 61856. (217) 762-3831. 1980. Bibliography of water analysis, environmental aspects of metals and organic compounds.

DIRECTORIES

Hydro Review–Industry Directory Issue. HCI Publications, 410 Archibald St., Kansas City, Missouri 64111. (816) 931-1311.

ENCYCLOPEDIAS AND DICTIONARIES

Dictionary of Environmental Engineering and Related Sciences: English-Spanish, Spanish-English. Jose T. Villate. Ediciones Universal, 3090 SW 8th St., Miami, Florida 33135. (305) 642-3355. 1979.

Encyclopedia of Environmental Science and Engineering. J.R. Pfafflin. Gordon and Breach Science Publishers, Inc., 270 8th Ave., New York, New York 10011. (212) 206-8900. 1992.

GENERAL WORKS

Advances in Water Treatment and Environmental Management. George Thomas. Elsevier Science Publishing Co., 655 Avenue of the Americas, New York, New York 10010. (212) 984-5800. 1991. Measurement and control of groundwater quality, rivers, river management, estuaries, and beaches.

Biogeochemistry of Major World Rivers. Egon T. Degens, et al. John Wiley & Sons, Inc., 605 3rd Ave., New York, New York 10158-0012. (212) 850-6000. 1991.

The Chemical Analysis of Water: General Principles and Techniques. D. T. E. Hunt and A. L . Wilson. Royal Society of Chemistry, c/o CRC Press, 2000 Corporate Blvd. N.W., Boca Raton, Florida 33431-9868. (800) 272-7737. 1986. 2d ed. 2d reprint. Covers the measurement of water quality with particular reference to methods for estimating and controlling possible errors in analytical results.

Design of Water Quality Monitoring Systems. Robert C. Ward. Van Nostrand Reinhold, 115 5th Ave., New York, New York 10003. (212) 254-3232. 1990. Describes the essential tools to design a system that gets consistently valid results. Features the latest methods of sampling and lab analysis, data handling and analysis, reporting, and information utilization, and includes case studies of system design projects.

Ground Water and Toxicological Risk. Jenifer S. Heath. Lewis Publishers, 2000 Corporate Blvd., N.W., Boca Raton, Florida 33431. (407) 994-0555 or (800) 272-7737. 1991. Discusses the nature of ground water, the nature of toxicology, risk assessment, basics of risk perception and two case studies of reaction.

Groundwater Residue Sampling Design. Ralph G. Nash and Anne R. Leslie, eds. American Chemical Society, 1155 16th St. N.W., Washington, District of Columbia 20036. (202) 872-4600; (800) 227-5558. 1991. Gives an overview of the approach taken by government agencies and discusses in great detail the various techniques in sampling and analysis of groundwater.

Practical Aspects of Groundwater Modeling. William Clarence Walton. National Water Well Association, 6375 Riverside Dr., Dublin, Ohio 43017. (614) 761-1711. 1985. Practical aspects of groundwater computer models. Deals with flow, mass and heat transport and subsidence.

Stream, Lake, Estuary, and Ocean Pollution. Nelson Leonard Nemerow. Van Nostrand Reinhold, 115 5th Ave., New York, New York 10003. (800) 926-2665. 1991.

The Surface Water Acidification Programme. B. J. Mason, ed. Cambridge University Press, 40 W. 20th St., New York, New York 10011. (212) 924-3900; (800) 227-0247. 1991. Proceedings of the final Conference of the Surface Water Acidification Programme, held at the Royal Society in March 1990. Deals with the acid pollution of rivers and lakes and presents research results on watersheds in Great Britain and Scandinavia.

Technical Additions to Methods for Chemical Analysis of Water and Wastes. U.S. Environmental Protection Agency, Environmental Monitoring and Support Laboratory, 26 W. Martin Luther King Dr., Cincinnati, Ohio 45268. (513) 569-7931. 1983. Analysis of sewage and water.

Water Analysis. Academic Press, c/o Harcourt Brace Jovanovich Inc., 6277 Sea Harbor Dr., Orlando, Florida

32887. (800) 346-8648. 1982. Analysis of inorganic species in water.

HANDBOOKS AND MANUALS

Groundwater Chemicals Desk Reference, Volume II. John Montgomery. Lewis Publishers, 2000 Corporate Blvd., N.W., Boca Raton, Florida 33431. (407) 994-0555 or (800) 272-7737. 1991. Contains abbreviations, symbols, chemicals, conversion factors, CAS index, RTECS number index empirical formula, and synonym index.

Hach Water Analysis Handbook. Hach Chemical Co., P.O. Box 907, Ames, Iowa 50010. (515) 232-2533. 1973.

Handbook for Water Analysis for the Food Industry: Industrial, Potable, and Wastewater Systems for the Use of Food Processors and Packers. Avery Publishing Corp., 120 Old Broadway, Garden City Park, New York 11040. (201) 696-3359. 1982. A manual for water analysis for use in the food industry and trade.

Handbook of Drinking Water Quality: Standards and Controls. John De Zuane. Van Nostrand Reinhold, 115 5th Ave., New York, New York 10003. (212) 254-3232. 1990. Aids in evaluating water quality control at every stage of the water path, from source to treatment plant, from distribution system to consumer.

Industrial Wastewater Source Control: An Inspection Guide. Nancy Rukonen. Technomic Pub. Co., 851 New Holland Ave., Box 3535, Lancaster, Pennsylvania 17604. (800) 233-9936. 1992. Comprehensive guide for industrial waste inspectors.

Water and Wastewater Examination Manual. V. Dean Adams. Lewis Publishers, 2000 Corporate Blvd., N.W., Boca Raton, Florida 33431. (407) 994-0555 or (800) 272-7737. 1990. Guide and reference for water/wastewater quality analysis. Includes procedures for parameters frequently used in water quality analysis.

ONLINE DATA BASES

Chemest. Technical Database Services, Inc., 10 Columbus Circle, New York, New York 10019. (212) 245-0044. Covers methods of estimating 11 important properties: water solubility, soil adsorption coefficient, bioconcentration factor, acid dissociation constant, activity coefficient, boiling point, vapor pressure, water volatilization rate, Henry's Law Constant, melting point, and liquid viscosity.

Chemical Abstracts-CA. Chemical Abstracts Service, 2540 Olentangy River Rd., P.O. Box 3012, Columbus, Ohio 43210. (800) 848-6533 or (614) 421-3600. Information sources include 9000 journals, patents from 27 countries, two industrial property organizations, new books, conference proceedings, and government research reports.

Computerized Engineering Index–COMPENDEX. Engineering Information Inc., 345 E. 47th St., New York, New York 10017. (212) 705-7600.

Monthly Catalog of United States Government Publications. U.S. G.P.O., Supt. of Docs., PO Box 371954, Pittsburgh, Pennsylvania 15250-7954. (202) 512-0000.

National Technical Information Service. U.S. Department of Commerce, National Technical Information Service, Office of Data Base Services, 5285 Port Royal Rd., Springfield, Virginia 22161. (703) 487-4807. Biblio-

graphic database of government sponsored research and technical reports.

NOAA Weather Service. National Oceanic and Atmospheric Administration, National Environmental Data Referral Service, 1825 Connecticut Ave., N.W., Washington, District of Columbia 20235. (202) 673-5548.

SCISEARCH. Institute for Scientific Information, University City Science Center, 3501 Market St., Philadelphia, Pennsylvania 19104. (215) 386-0100.

PERIODICALS AND NEWSLETTERS

Analytical Biochemistry. Academic Press, 111 Fifth Ave., New York, New York 10003. (800) 346-8648. Covers biological and chemical topics relating to the environment.

Ground Water Monitoring Review. Water Well Journal Publishing Co. National Water Well Association, 6375 Riverside Drive, Dublin, Ohio 43017. (614) 761-3222. Quarterly. Covers protection and restoration of ground water.

Ground Water Newsletter. Water Information Center, Inc., 125 East Bethpage Road, Plainview, New York 11803. (516) 249-7634. Biweekly. Covers ground water exploration, development, and management.

Hydata News and Views. American Water Resources Association, 5410 Grosvenor Lane, Suite 220, Bethesda, Maryland 20814. (301) 493-8600. Six times a year. Research, planning and management in water resources.

Journal - American Water Works Association. American Water Works Association, 6666 W. Quincy Ave., Denver, Colorado 80235. (303) 794-7711. Monthly. Includes regulatory summaries, conference information and job listings. Has state chapters, annual meetings, and special publications.

Journal of Hydraulic Engineering. American Society of Civil Engineers, 345 E. 47th St., New York, New York 10017. (212) 705-7288; (800) 548-2723. 1983-. Monthly. Papers describe the analysis and solutions of problems in hydraulic engineering, hydrology and water resources. Emphasizes concepts, methods, techniques and results that advance knowledge in the hydraulic engineering profession.

Multinational Environmental Outlook. Business Publishers, Inc., 951 Pershing Dr., Silver Spring, Maryland 20910-4464. (301) 587-6300. 1974-. Biweekly. Covers developments in world environmental problems such as acid rain, deforestation, soil erosion, overfishing, threats to health, animal extinction, population growth, diminishing water supply and other related matters. Also available online.

Operations Forum. Water Pollution Control Federation, 601 Wythe Street, Alexandria, Virginia 22314-1994. (703) 684-2400. Monthly. Covers the advancement of practical knowledge in water quality control systems.

Washington Bulletin. Water Pollution Control Federation, 601 Wythe Street, Alexandria, Virginia 22314-1994. (703) 684-2400. Monthly. Covers legislative issues in the water control industry.

Water in the News. Soap and Detergent Association, 457 Park Ave. S., New York, New York 10016. (212) 725-1262. 1965-. Bimonthly.

RESEARCH CENTERS AND INSTITUTES

Adirondack Lakes Survey Corporation. New York State Dept. of Environmental Conservation, Ray Brook, New York 12977. (518) 891-2758.

Michigan State University, Institute of Water Research. 334 Natural Resources Building, East Lansing, Michigan 48824. (517) 353-3742.

Michigan Technological University, Environmental Engineering Center for Water and Waste Management. 1400 Townsend Rd., Houghton, Michigan 49931. (906) 487-2194.

National Center for Ground Water Research. University of Oklahoma, 200 Telgar St., Rm. 127, Norman, Oklahoma 73019-0470. (405) 325-5202.

Northeast Watershed Research Center. 111 Research Building A, Pennsylvania State University, University Park, Pennsylvania 16802. (814) 865-2048.

Oklahoma State University, University Center for Water Research. 003 Life Sciences East, Stillwater, Oklahoma 74078. (405) 744-9995.

Scripps Institution of Oceanography, Marine Physical Laboratory. University of California, San Diego, San Diego, California 92152-6400. (619) 534-1789.

Skidaway Institute of Oceanography. P.O. Box 13687, McWhorter Drive, Skidaway Island, Savannah, Georgia 31416. (912) 356-2453.

University of Alaska Fairbanks, Water Research Center. Fairbanks, Alaska 99775. (907) 474-7350.

University of Wisconsin-Madison, Water Chemistry Program. 660 North Park Street, Madison, Wisconsin 53706. (608) 262-2470.

University of Wyoming, Wyoming Water Research Center. Box 3067, University Station, Laramie, Wyoming 82071. (307) 766-2143.

Water Quality Laboratory. Western Illinois University, Department of Chemistry, Macomb, Illinois 61455. (309) 298-1356.

Water Research Institute. West Virginia University, Morgantown, West Virginia 26506. (304) 293-2757.

TRADE ASSOCIATIONS AND PROFESSIONAL SOCIETIES

American Chemical Society. 1155 16th St., N.W., Washington, District of Columbia 20036. (202) 872-4600.

American Institute of Biological Sciences. 730 11th St., N.W., Washington, District of Columbia 20001-4521. (202) 628-1500.

American Institute of Chemical Engineers. 345 East 47th St., New York, New York 10017. (212) 705-7338.

American Institute of Chemists. 7315 Wisconsin Ave., Bethesda, Maryland 20814. (301) 652-2447.

American Society of Civil Engineers. 345 East 47th St., New York, New York 10017. (212) 705-7496.

Industrial Water Conditioning Institute. c/o J.J. Jewett, III, One James Center, 6th Fl., Richmond, Virginia 23219. (804) 775-1005.

WATER CHEMISTRY
See: WATER ANALYSIS

WATER COLOR
See: WATER QUALITY

WATER CONSERVATION
See also: CONSERVATION OF NATURAL RESOURCES; WATER QUALITY; WATER RECLAMATION; WATER RESOURCES

ABSTRACTING AND INDEXING SERVICES

Abstracts of Air and Water Conservation Literature. American Petroleum Institute. Central Abstracting and Indexing Service, 275 Madison Avenue, New York, New York 10016. 1972.

Agricultural Engineering Abstracts. C. A. B. International, 845 North Park Ave., Tucson, Arizona 85719. (602) 621-7897 or (800) 528-4841. 1976-. Monthly. Informs about significant research developments in agricultural engineering and instrumentation. Some of the topics scanned for the abstracts include mechanical power, crop production, crop harvesting and threshing, crop processing and storage, aquaculture, land improvement, protected cultivation, handling and transport, and farm buildings and equipment.

Applied Science and Technology Index. H.W. Wilson Co., 950 University Ave., Bronx, New York 10452. (800) 367-6770. Formerly Industrial Arts Index.

Aqualine Abstracts. Water Research Centre. c/o Pergamon Microforms International, Inc., Fairview Park, Elmsford, New York 10523. (914) 592-7720. 1927-. Contains some 8,000 records annually on water and wastewater technology. Covers all aspects of water, wastewater, associated engineering services and the aquatic environment. Over 600 periodicals, as well as books, reports and conference proceedings and other publications from water related institutions worldwide are scanned. Also available online.

ASFA Aquaculture Abstracts. Cambridge Scientific Abstracts, Inc., 5161 River Rd., Bethesda, Maryland 20816. (301) 961-6750. 1984.

Chemical Abstracts. Chemical Abstracts Service, 2540 Olentangy River Rd., PO Box 3012, Columbus, Ohio 43210. (800) 848-6533. 1907-.

Ecology Abstracts. Cambridge Scientific Abstracts, 5161 River Rd., Bethesda, Maryland 20816. (301) 961-6750. Monthly.

Engineering Index. The Engineering Index Inc., 345 E. 47th St., New York, New York 10017. 1962-.

Field Crop Abstracts. C. A. B. International, 845 North Park Ave., Tucson, Arizona 85719. (602) 621-7897 or (800) 528-4841. 1948-. Monthly. Covers literature on agronomy, field production, crop botany and physiology of all annual field crops, both temperate and tropical.

General Science Index. H. W. Wilson Co., 950 University Ave., Bronx, New York 10452. 1978-. Monthly, also

issued in annual cumulation. Cumulative subject index to English language periodicals in the subject fields of astronomy, botany, chemistry, earth science, environment and conservation, food and nutrition, genetics, mathematics, medicine and health, microbiology, oceanography, physics, physiology and zoology.

Index to Scientific Book Contents. Institute for Scientific Information, 3501 Market St., Philadelphia, Pennsylvania 19104. (800) 523-1857. 1985-. Annual. Gives contents of science books published.

Pollution Abstracts. Cambridge Scientific Abstracts, 5161 River Rd., Bethesda, Maryland 20816. (301) 961-6750. Six/year. Indexes worldwide technical literature on environmental pollution. Covers air pollution, marine and freshwater pollution, sewage and wastewater treatment, waste management, toxicology and health, noise pollution, radiation, land pollution, and environmental policies, programs, legislation, and education. Also available online.

Science Citation Index. Institute for Scientific Information, 3501 Market St., Philadelphia, Pennsylvania 19104. 1961-.

BIBLIOGRAPHIES

Analytical Bibliography for Water Supply and Conservation Techniques. John Boland. U.S. Army Corps of Engineers, Institute for Water Resources, Fort Belvoir, Virginia 22060. (703) 780-2155. 1982.

An Annotated Bibliography on Water Conservation. National Technical Information Service, 5285 Port Royal Rd., Springfield, Virginia 22161. (703) 487-4650. 1979.

Municipal Water Conservation. Vance Bibliographies, PO Box 229, 112 N. Charter St., Monticello, Illinois 61856. (217) 762-3831. 1982.

Residential Water Conservation. U.S. Environmental Protection Agency, 401 M St., S.W., Washington, District of Columbia 20460. (202) 260-2090. 1980. Bibliography of water supply and water consumption

Residential Water Conservation: A Selected Research Bibliography. Marc J. Rogoff. Vance Bibliographies, PO Box 229, 112 N. Charter St., Monticello, Illinois 61856. (217) 762-3831. 1982.

DIRECTORIES

Water Engineering & Management–Reference Handbook/Buyer's Guide Issue. Scranton Gillette Communications, Inc., 380 E. Northwest Hwy., Des Plaines, Illinois 60016. (708) 298-6622.

ENCYCLOPEDIAS AND DICTIONARIES

Dictionary of Environmental Engineering and Related Sciences: English-Spanish, Spanish-English. Jose T. Villate. Ediciones Universal, 3090 SW 8th St., Miami, Florida 33135. (305) 642-3355. 1979.

Encyclopedia of Environmental Science and Engineering. J.R. Pfafflin. Gordon and Breach Science Publishers, Inc., 270 8th Ave., New York, New York 10011. (212) 206-8900. 1992.

McGraw-Hill Encyclopedia of Environmental Science. Sybil P. Parker. McGraw-Hill Science & Engineering Books, 11 W. 19th St., New York, New York 10011.

(212) 337-6010. 1980. Covers ecology, man's influence on nature, and environmental protection.

The Water Encyclopedia. Lewis Publishers, 2000 Corporate Blvd. N.W., Boca Raton, Florida 33431. (800) 272-7737. 1990. 2d ed. Includes groundwater contamination, drinking water, floods, waterborne diseases, global warming, climate change, irrigation, water agencies and organizations, precipitation, oceans and seas, and river, lakes and waterfalls.

GENERAL WORKS

Advances in Water Treatment and Environmental Management. George Thomas. Elsevier Science Publishing Co., 655 Avenue of the Americas, New York, New York 10010. (212) 984-5800. 1991. Measurement and control of groundwater quality, rivers, river management, estuaries, and beaches.

America's Soil and Water. U.S. Department of Agriculture, Soil Conservation Service, 14 Independence Ave. SW, Washington, District of Columbia 20250. (202) 447-7454. 1981. Covers water supply, land use, soil ecology, soil management, and water resources development.

Conserving Water: The Untapped Alternative. Postel, Sandra. Worldwatch Institute, 1776 Massachusetts Ave., N.W., Washington, District of Columbia 20036-1904. 1985.

Cover Crops for Clean Water. W. L. Hargrove, ed. Soil and Water Conservation Society, 7515 Northeast Ankeny Rd., Ankeny, Iowa 50021-9764. (515) 289-2331; (800) THE-SOIL. 1991. Includes the latest information on the role of cover crops in water quality management, including means of reducing water runoff, soil erosion, agrichemical loss in runoff, and nitrate leaching to groundwater.

Farmland of Wasteland. Rodale Press, 33 E. Minor St., Emmaus, Pennsylvania 18098. (215) 967-5171. 1981. Deals with soil conservation, agricultural water supply and land use.

Overtapped Oasis: Reform or Revolution for Western Water. Marc Reisner and Sarah Bates. Island Press, 1718 Connecticut Ave. N.W., Suite 300, Washington, District of Columbia 20009. (202) 232-7933. 1990. Comprehensive critique of the cardinal dogma of the American West: that the region is always running out of water and therefore must build more and more dams.

Soil and Water Conservation. Frederick R. Troeh, et al. Prentice-Hall, Rte. 9W, Englewood Cliffs, New Jersey 07632. (201) 592-2000; (800) 634-2863. 1991. 2d ed. Describes the hazards of erosion, sedimentation, and pollution, and the techniques needed to conserve soil and maintain environmental quality.

Wetlands: A Threatened Landscape. Michael Williams. B. Blackwell, 3 Cambridge Ctr., Suite 208, Cambridge, Massachusetts 02142. (617) 225-0401. 1990. Explores the evolution and composition of wetlands and their physical and biological dynamics, considers the impact of agriculture, industry, urbanization, and recreation upon them, and examines what steps we are taking and what steps should be considered to manage and preserve wetlands.

HANDBOOKS AND MANUALS

Before the Well Runs Dry. U.S. Geological Survey, 12201 Sunrise Valley Dr., Reston, Virginia 22092. (703) 648-

4460. 1981. A handbook for designing a local water conservation plan.

Goodbye to the Flush Toilet. Rodale Press, 33 E. Minor St., Emmaus, Pennsylvania 18098. (215) 967-5171. 1977.

Handbook of Methods for the Evaluation of Water Conservation for Municipal and Industrial Water Supply. Institute for Water Resources, c/o American Public Works Association, 1313 E. 60th St., Chicago, Illinois 60637. (312) 667-2200. 1985.

Soil and Water Conservation Engineering. John Wiley & Sons, Inc., 605 3rd Ave., New York, New York 10158-0012. (212) 850-6000. 1981. Agricultural engineering and soil and water conservation.

ONLINE DATA BASES

Chemical Abstracts-CA. Chemical Abstracts Service, 2540 Olentangy River Rd., P.O. Box 3012, Columbus, Ohio 43210. (800) 848-6533 or (614) 421-3600. Information sources include 9000 journals, patents from 27 countries, two industrial property organizations, new books, conference proceedings, and government research reports.

Computerized Engineering Index–COMPENDEX. Engineering Information Inc., 345 E. 47th St., New York, New York 10017. (212) 705-7600.

Monthly Catalog of United States Government Publications. U.S. G.P.O., Supt. of Docs., PO Box 371954, Pittsburgh, Pennsylvania 15250-7954. (202) 512-0000.

National Technical Information Service. U.S. Department of Commerce, National Technical Information Service, Office of Data Base Services, 5285 Port Royal Rd., Springfield, Virginia 22161. (703) 487-4807. Bibliographic database of government sponsored research and technical reports.

SCISEARCH. Institute for Scientific Information, University City Science Center, 3501 Market St., Philadelphia, Pennsylvania 19104. (215) 386-0100.

PERIODICALS AND NEWSLETTERS

Ecology USA. Business Publishers, Inc., 951 Pershing Dr., Silver Spring, Maryland 20910-4464. (301) 587-6300. 1972-. Biweekly. Contains all the legislation, regulation, and litigation affecting efforts to conserve and protect America's unique environmental and ecological heritage.

Editorially Speaking about Ground Water: Its First Quarter Century. Jay H. Lehr and Anita B. Stanley. National Water Well Association, 6375 Riverside Dr., Dublin, Ohio 43017. (614) 761-1711. 1988. A collection of editorials from the Journal of Ground Water which traces the evolution of ground water science during the journal's first 25 years of publication.

FAO Conservation Guide. Food and Agriculture Organization of the United Nations, Via delle Terme di Caracalla, Rome, Italy 00100. 61 0181-FA01. Annual. Covers soil and water conservation.

Ground Water Newsletter. Water Information Center, Inc., 125 East Bethpage Road, Plainview, New York 11803. (516) 249-7634. Biweekly. Covers ground water exploration, development, and management.

ICWP Policy Statement & Bylaws. Interstate Conference on Water Problems, 5300 M Street, NW, Suite 800, Washington, District of Columbia 20037. (202) 466-7287. Annual. Covers conservation and administration of water.

INFORM Reports. INFORM Inc., 381 Park Ave., So., New York, New York 10016. (212) 689-4040. Quarterly. INFORM is a nonprofit environmental research & education organization for the preservation and conservation of natural resources and public health.

Journal - American Water Works Association. American Water Works Association, 6666 W. Quincy Ave., Denver, Colorado 80235. (303) 794-7711. Monthly. Includes regulatory summaries, conference information and job listings. Has state chapters, annual meetings, and special publications.

Journal of Soil and Water Conservation. Soil and Water Conservation Society, 7515 Northeast Ankeny Road, Ankeny, Iowa 50021. (515) 289-2331. Bimonthly. Promotes better land and water use and management.

Kentucky Soil and Water News. Kentucky Division of Soil, 628 Teton Trail, Frankfort, Kentucky 40601. (502) 564-3080. Monthly. Water management issues and erosion in the state.

Land and Water Contracting. A. B. Morse Co., 200 James St., Barrington, Illinois 60010. Monthly.

Nebraska Resources. Nebraska Natural Resources Commission, 301 Centennial Mall South, Lincoln, Nebraska 68508. 1970-. Quarterly.

New York's Waters. New York State Department of Health, 84 Holland Ave., Albany, New York 12208. Quarterly.

Operations Forum. Water Pollution Control Federation, 601 Wythe Street, Alexandria, Virginia 22314-1994. (703) 684-2400. Monthly. Covers the advancement of practical knowledge in water quality control systems.

Soil and Water Conservation News. U.S. Soil Conservation Service, PO Box 2890, Washington, District of Columbia 20013. (202) 205-0027. Monthly.

U. S. Geological Survey. Water Supply Papers. Superintendent of Documents, U.S. Government Printing Office, Washington, District of Columbia 20402. 1896-. Irregular.

Washington Report. Interstate Conference on Water Policy, 955 L'Enfant Plaza, 6th Floor, Washington, District of Columbia 20024. (202) 466-7287. Every six weeks. Covers water conservation, development and administration.

Washington Waterline. Environmental Communication Corp., Box 1824, Washington, District of Columbia 20013. 1967-. Weekly.

Water Engineering & Management. Scranton Gillette Communications, Inc., 380 E. Northwest Hwy., Des Plaines, Illinois 60016-2282. (708) 298-6622. 1986-. Monthly. A professional trade publication which includes latest legislative news in the area of water quality, EPA criteria for drinking water, pesticides, and related standards. Includes articles of interest by water professionals and has regular news features such as forthcoming conferences, products at work, surveys, company profiles, etc.

Water Newsletter. Water Information Center Inc., 7 High St., Huntington, New York 11743. 1958-. Semimonthly. Includes news about water supply, waste, disposal, conservation and pollution.

Western Water. Western Water Education Foundation, 717 K St., Ste. 517, Sacramento, California 95814. (916) 444-6240. Bimonthly.

RESEARCH CENTERS AND INSTITUTES

Cooling Tower Institute. 530 Wells Fargo Dr., Suite 113, Houston, Texas 77273. (713) 583-4087.

Desert Turfgrass Research Facility. University of Arizona, Forbes Building, Tucson, Arizona 85721. (602) 621-1851.

North Central Soil Conservation Research Laboratory. North Iowa Avenue, Morris, Minnesota 56267. (612) 589-3411.

University of Minnesota, Duluth, Center for Water and The Environment. Natural Resources Research Institute, 5103 Miller Trunk Highway, Duluth, Minnesota 55811. (218) 720-4270.

University of Texas at Austin, Center for Research in Water Resources. Balcones Research Center, Building 119, Austin, Texas 78712. (512) 471-3131.

University of Wyoming, Wyoming Water Research Center. Box 3067, University Station, Laramie, Wyoming 82071. (307) 766-2143.

USDA National Sedimentation Laboratory. P.O.Box 1157, Oxford, Missouri 38655. (601) 232-2900.

USDA Water Conservation Laboratory. 4331 East Broadway, Phoenix, Arizona 85040. (602) 379-4356.

Water Resources Research Center. University of Arizona, Geology Building, Room 314, Tucson, Arizona 85721. (602) 621-7607.

STATISTICS SOURCES

Agricultural Conservation Program Statistical Summary. U.S. Agricultural Stabilization and Conservation Service, Dept. of Agriculture, Washington, District of Columbia 20013. (202) 512-0000. Annual. Deals with soil erosion control, water conservation, water quality and costs by state and county.

TRADE ASSOCIATIONS AND PROFESSIONAL SOCIETIES

American Institute of Biological Sciences. 730 11th St., N.W., Washington, District of Columbia 20001-4521. (202) 628-1500.

American Society of Civil Engineers. 345 East 47th St., New York, New York 10017. (212) 705-7496.

American Water Resources Association. 5410 Grosvenor Lane, Suite 220, Bethesda, Maryland 20814. (301) 493-8600.

CONCERN, Inc. 1794 Columbia Rd, NW, Washington, District of Columbia 20009. (202) 328-8160.

Food & Water, Inc. 225 Lafayette St., Suite 612, New York, New York 10012. (212) 941-9340.

INFORM. 381 Park Avenue S., New York, New York 10016. (212) 689-4040.

Interstate Conference on Water Policy. 955 L'Enfant Plaza, 6th Floor, Washington, District of Columbia 20024. (202) 466-7287.

The Izaak Walton League of America. 1401 Wilson Boulevard, Level B, Arlington, Virginia 22209. (703) 528-1818.

The Jessie Smith Noyes Foundation. 16 E. 34th St., New York, New York 10016. (212) 684-6577.

Kids for a Clean Environment. P.O. Box 158254, Nashville, Tennessee 37215. (615) 331-0708.

National Association of Conservation Districts. 509 Capitol Court, N.E., Washington, District of Columbia 20002. (202) 547-6223.

National Demonstration Water Project. Rural Community Assistance Program, 602 King St., Suite 402, Leesburg, Virginia 22075. (703) 771-8636.

Soil and Water Conservation Society of America. 7515 N.E. Ankeny Rd., Ankeny, Iowa 50021. (515) 289-2331.

Water Resources Congress. Courthouse Plaza II, 2300 Clarendon Blvd., Suite 404, Arlington, Virginia 22201. (703) 525-4881.

Western Water Education Foundation. 717 K St., Ste. 517, Sacramento, California 95814-3406. (916) 444-6240.

World Association of Soil and Water Conservation. 7515 N.E. Ankeny Rd., Ankeny, Iowa 50021. (515) 289-2331.

WATER CYCLE

See: HYDROLOGY

WATER EROSION

See: EROSION

WATER HARDNESS

See: WATER QUALITY

WATER MANAGEMENT

See also: HYDROELECTRIC POWER; IRRIGATION; RESERVOIRS

ABSTRACTING AND INDEXING SERVICES

Abstracts of Air and Water Conservation Literature. American Petroleum Institute. Central Abstracting and Indexing Service, 275 Madison Avenue, New York, New York 10016. 1972.

Agrindex. AGRIS Coordinating Center, Via delle Terme di Caracalla, Rome, Italy I-00100. 61 0181-FA01. 1975-.

Applied Ecology Abstracts Studies in Renewable Natural Resources. Information Retrieval Ltd., 1911 Jefferson

Davis Highway, Arlington, Virginia 22202. 1975-. Monthly.

Applied Science and Technology Index. H.W. Wilson Co., 950 University Ave., Bronx, New York 10452. (800) 367-6770. Formerly Industrial Arts Index.

Aqualine Abstracts. Water Research Centre. c/o Pergamon Microforms International, Inc., Fairview Park, Elmsford, New York 10523. (914) 592-7720. 1927-. Contains some 8,000 records annually on water and wastewater technology. Covers all aspects of water, wastewater, associated engineering services and the aquatic environment. Over 600 periodicals, as well as books, reports and conference proceedings and other publications from water related institutions worldwide are scanned. Also available online.

Biological and Agricultural Index. H.W. Wilson Co., 950 University Ave., Bronx, New York 10452. (800) 367-6770. 1916-. Monthly.

Chemical Abstracts. Chemical Abstracts Service, 2540 Olentangy River Rd., PO Box 3012, Columbus, Ohio 43210. (800) 848-6533. 1907-.

Civil Engineering Hydraulic Abstracts. BHRA Fluid Engineering, Air Science Co., PO Box 143, Corning, New York 14830. (607) 962-5591. Monthly. Abstracts of periodicals that publish in the areas of hydraulic engineering and other related topics.

Current Advances in Ecological and Environmental Science. Pergamon Microforms International, Inc., Fairview Park, Elmsford, New York 10523. (914) 592-7720. 1989-. Monthly. Current literature searching service includingjournals, reports, abstracts, etc. This service is available online as part of the CABS database on the hosts BRS and ORBIT search service.

Ecological Abstracts. Geo Abstracts Ltd. Elsevier Applied Science, Crown House, Linton Rd., Barking, England IG 11 8JU. 1974-. Derived from over 600 leading ecological and environmental journals, plus books, conference proceedings, reports and theses.

Ecology Abstracts. Cambridge Scientific Abstracts, 5161 River Rd., Bethesda, Maryland 20816. (301) 961-6750. Monthly.

Engineering Index. The Engineering Index Inc., 345 E. 47th St., New York, New York 10017. 1962-.

General Science Index. H. W. Wilson Co., 950 University Ave., Bronx, New York 10452. 1978-. Monthly, also issued in annual cumulation. Cumulative subject index to English language periodicals in the subject fields of astronomy, botany, chemistry, earth science, environment and conservation, food and nutrition, genetics, mathematics, medicine and health, microbiology, oceanography, physics, physiology and zoology.

Geographical Abstracts. London School of Economics, Dept. of Geography, Regency House, 34 Duke St., London, England 1966-. Continued by Geo Abstracts issued in 6 parts: Pt. A. Landforms and the quaternary; Pt. B. Biogeography and Climatology; Pt. C. Economic geography; Pt. D. Social geography and cartography; Pt. E. Sedimentology; Pt. F. Regional and community planning.

Index to Scientific Book Contents. Institute for Scientific Information, 3501 Market St., Philadelphia, Pennsylva-

nia 19104. (800) 523-1857. 1985-. Annual. Gives contents of science books published.

Irrigation and Drainage Abstracts. C. A. B. International, 845 North Park Ave., Tucson, Arizona 85719. (602) 621-7897 or (800) 258-4841. 1975-. Quarterly. Subject areas scanned are: water management, irrigation of crop plants, drainage, soil water relations, plant water relations, salinity and toxicity problems, soil condition, evaporotranspiration, evaporation, land use, streams, water quality, and other related areas.

Multimedia Index to Ecology. National Information Center for Educational Media, University of Southern California, Los Angeles, California 90007.

Pollution Abstracts. Cambridge Scientific Abstracts, 5161 River Rd., Bethesda, Maryland 20816. (301) 961-6750. Six/year. Indexes worldwide technical literature on environmental pollution. Covers air pollution, marine and freshwater pollution, sewage and wastewater treatment, waste management, toxicology and health, noise pollution, radiation, land pollution, and environmental policies, programs, legislation, and education. Also available online.

Science Citation Index. Institute for Scientific Information, 3501 Market St., Philadelphia, Pennsylvania 19104. 1961-.

BIBLIOGRAPHIES

Current Contents. Agriculture, Biology and Environmental Sciences. Institute for Scientific Information, 3501 Market St., Philadelphia, Pennsylvania 19104. (800) 523-1857. 1973-. Previous title: Current Contents. Agricultural, Food & Veterinary Sciences. Gives the table of contents of periodicals in the fields of agriculture, biology, environmental and related areas.

DIRECTORIES

American Water Works Association–Buyers' Guide Issue. American Water Works Association, 6666 W. Quincy Ave., Denver, Colorado 80235. (303) 794-7711.

Buyer Guide and Publications Catalog of American Water Works Association. American Water Works Association, 6666 W. Quincy Ave., Denver, Colorado 80235. (303) 794-7711. 1991. Includes directories of AWWA agent, representative and distributor members; AWWA manufacturers agents and distributor members; AWWA contract members; consultant members; and the supplier catalog.

EI Environmental Services Directory. Environmental Information Ltd., 4801 W. 81st St., No. 119, Minneapolis, Minnesota 55437-1111. (612) 831-2473.

IWED Guide to Waste Management Distributors. Institute of Waste Equipment Distributors, National Solid Wastes Management Association, 1730 Rhode Island Ave., N.W., Suite 1000, Washington, District of Columbia 20036. (202) 659-4613.

Water Engineering & Management–Reference Handbook/Buyer's Guide Issue. Scranton Gillette Communications, Inc., 380 E. Northwest Hwy., Des Plaines, Illinois 60016. (708) 298-6622.

Water Purification and Filteration Equipment. American Business Directories, Inc., 5711 S. 86th Circle, Omaha, Nebraska 68127. (402) 593-4600.

Water Technology–Directory of Manufacturers and Suppliers Issue. National Trade Publications, Inc., 13 Century Hill Dr., Latham, New York 12110. (518) 783-1281.

Water Technology–Planning & Purchasing Handbook Issue. National Trade Publications, Inc., 13 Century Hill Dr., Latham, New York 12110. (518) 783-1281.

Water Treatment Equipment Service/Supplies. American Business Directories, Inc., 5711 S. 86th Circle, Omaha, Nebraska 68127. (402) 593-4600.

ENCYCLOPEDIAS AND DICTIONARIES

Dictionary of Environmental Engineering and Related Sciences: English-Spanish, Spanish-English. Jose T. Villate. Ediciones Universal, 3090 SW 8th St., Miami, Florida 33135. (305) 642-3355. 1979.

Elsevier's Dictionary of Hydrology and Water Quality Management. J. D. Van der Tuin. Elsevier Science Publishing Co., 655 Avenue of the Americas, New York, New York 10010. (212) 989-5800. 1991. The languages are English, French, Spanish, Dutch, and German. Freshwater environment constitutes the main subject of this dictionary. Defines more than 37,000 terms.

Elsevier's Dictionary of Water and Hydraulic Engineering. J. D. Van Der Tuin. Elsevier Science Publishing Co., 655 Avenue of the Americas, New York, New York 10010. (212) 989-5800. 1987. The text is in English, Spanish, French, Dutch and German.

Encyclopedia of Environmental Science and Engineering. J.R. Pfafflin. Gordon and Breach Science Publishers, Inc., 270 8th Ave., New York, New York 10011. (212) 206-8900. 1992.

Encyclopedia of Physical Science and Technology. Robert A. Meyers, ed. Academic Press, c/o Harcourt Brace Jovanovich Inc., 6277 Sea Harbor Dr., Orlando, Florida 32887. (800) 346-8648. Dictionary of engineering, technology and physical sciences.

McGraw-Hill Encyclopedia of Environmental Science. Sybil P. Parker. McGraw-Hill Science & Engineering Books, 11 W. 19th St., New York, New York 10011. (212) 337-6010. 1980. Covers ecology, man's influence on nature, and environmental protection.

The Water Encyclopedia. Lewis Publishers, 2000 Corporate Blvd. N.W., Boca Raton, Florida 33431. (800) 272-7737. 1990. 2d ed. Includes groundwater contamination, drinking water, floods, waterborne diseases, global warming, climate change, irrigation, water agencies and organizations, precipitation, oceans and seas, and river, lakes and waterfalls.

GENERAL WORKS

Advances in Water Treatment and Environmental Management. George Thomas. Elsevier Science Publishing Co., 655 Avenue of the Americas, New York, New York 10010. (212) 984-5800. 1991. Measurement and control of groundwater quality, rivers, river management, estuaries, and beaches.

Alternatives in Regulated River Management. J. A. Gore and G. E. Petts, eds. CRC Press, 2000 Corporate Blvd. N.W., Boca Raton, Florida 33431. (800) 272-7737. 1989. Provides an alternative to the emphasis on ecological effects of river regulation and is a source of alternatives for managerial decision making.

The Arthur Young Guide to Water and Wastewater Finance and Pricing. George A. Raftelis. Lewis Publishers, 121 S. Main St., Chelsea, Michigan 48118. (313) 475-8619; (800) 525-7894. 1989. Covers virtually all aspects of establishing a financial planning and management program for a water or wastewater utility. Examines the development of capital plans, alternatives for securing capital funding and the options for a user charge system.

Chemical and Biological Characterization of Municipal Sludges, Sediments, Dredge Spoils, and Drilling Muds. James L. Lichtenberg, et al. American Society for Testing and Materials, 1916 S. Race St., Philadelphia, Pennsylvania 19103. (215) 299-5585. 1988. Deals with the environmental aspects of sewage disposal, analysis, health risk assessment, biological purification of sludge, and water quality management.

Climate Change and U.S. Water Resources. P. E. Waggoner, ed. John Wiley & Sons, Inc., 605 3rd Ave., New York, New York 10158-0012. (212) 850-6000. 1990. Covers latest research in climate changes and subsequent effects on water supply. Topics include future water use, statistics in forecasting, vulnerability of water systems, irrigation, urban water systems, and reallocation by markets and prices.

Design of Water Quality Monitoring Systems. Robert C. Ward. Van Nostrand Reinhold, 115 5th Ave., New York, New York 10003. (212) 254-3232. 1990. Describes the essential tools to design a system that gets consistently valid results. Features the latest methods of sampling and lab analysis, data handling and analysis, reporting, and information utilization, and includes case studies of system design projects.

Envirosoft 86. P. Zanetti, ed. Computational Mechanics Inc., 25 Bridge St., Billerica, Massachusetts 01821. 1986. Environmental software part of the proceedings of the International Conference on Development and Applications of Computer Techniques to Environmental Studies, Los Angeles, 1986.

Envirosoft 88: Computer Techniques in Environmental Studies. P. Zannetti, ed. Computational Mechanics Inc., 25 Bridge St., Billerica, Massachusetts 01821. (508) 667-5841. 1988. Proceedings of the 2nd International Conference, Envirosoft 88, covering the development and application of computer techniques to environmental problems.

Groundwater Contamination: Sources, Control, and Preventive Measures. Chester D. Rail. Technomic Publishing Co., 851 New Holland Ave., Box 3535, Lancaster, Pennsylvania 17604. (717) 291-5609. 1989. Reviews the presently known sources of groundwater contamination and its many complex interactions, including managerial and political implications.

Groundwater Protection: Local Success Stories. Milou Carolan. Internal City Management Association, 777 N. Capital St., NE, Suite 500, Washington, District of Columbia 20002-4201. (800) 745-8780. 1990. Case studies from local governments that have created effective programs for protecting the local water supply by evaluating contamination sources and developing community support.

Integrated Approaches to Water Pollution. Joao Bau. Elsevier Science Publishing Co., 655 Avenue of the Americas, New York, New York 10010. (212) 984-5800. 1991. Integrated management strategies, policies for pollution control, groundwater pollution resulting from industrial, agricultural and urban sources, data and measurement.

Integrated Water Management. Bruce Mitchell, ed. Belhaven Press, 136 S. Broadway, Irvington, New York 10533. (914) 591-9111. 1990. Using case studies from the United States, New Zealand, Canada, Japan, England, Poland and Nigeria, this book surveys the principles and the practice of water management.

Large-Scale Water Transfers: Emerging Environmental and Social Experiences. G. Golubev and A. Biswas, eds. Cassell PLC, Publishers Distribution Center, PO Box C831, Rutherford, New Jersey 07070. (201) 939-6064; (201) 939-6065. 1986.

Poison Runoff: A Guide to State and Local Control of Nonpoint Source Water Pollution. Paul Thompson. Natural Resources Defense Council, 40 W. 20th St., New York, New York 10011. (212) 727-2700. 1989. How-to-book addressing pollution in agricultural lands, urban development and construction, logging, mining and grazing.

Pricing of Water Services. OECD Publications and Information Center, 2001 L St., N.W., Suite 700, Washington, District of Columbia 20036. (202) 785-OECD. 1987. Reviews existing practices in various OECD countries and presents options for economically rational pricing practices which would also lead to environmentally acceptable results.

Promotion of Women's Participation in Water Resources Development. UNIPUB, 4611-F Assembly Dr., Lanham, Maryland 20706-4391. (301) 459-7666; (800) 274-4888. 1990.

Saving the Mediterranean: The Politics of International Environmental Cooperation. Peter M. Haas. Columbia University Press, 562 W. 113th St., New York, New York 10025. (212) 316-7100. 1990. Focuses on the international pollution management of the Mediterranean. Ninety scientists and international officials were interviewed to ascertain how the international community responded to this particular threat.

The Snake River: Window to the West. Tim Palmer. Island Press, 1718 Connecticut Ave. N.W., Suite 300, Washington, District of Columbia 20009. (202) 232-7933. 1991. Offers information about instream flows for fish and wildlife; groundwater management and quality; water conservation and efficiency; pollution of streams from agriculture and logging; small hydroelectric development; and reclamation of riparian habitat.

Surveillance of Drinking Water Quality in Rural Areas. Barry Lloyd. John Wiley & Sons, Inc., 605 3rd Ave, New York, New York 10158-0012. (212) 850-6000. 1991. Examines the human and technical resources required for monitoring, maintaining and improving the safety of rural water supply services. A practical guide to improving the quality of service from small water supplies, it describes the essential minimum of reliable methods of monitoring water quality and discusses new cost effective approaches to sanitary inspection of community water supplies.

System Analysis Applied to Management of Water Resource. M. Jellali, ed. Pergamon Microforms International, Inc., Fairview Park, Elmsford, New York 10523. (914) 592-7720. 1989. Proceedings of the Fourth IFAC Symposium, Rabat, Morocco, 11- 13 October 1988. Illustrates aspects of the application of systems analysis to water

resource management. Also included are theoretical discussions on mathematical modelling and the potential role of expert systems.

Technologies for Small Water and Wastewater Systems. Edward J. Martin and Edward T. Martin. Van Nostrand Reinhold, 115 5th Ave., New York, New York 10003. (212) 254-3232. 1991. Addresses how to exploit different water treatment technologies according to available resources. Includes extensive sections on costs and design of both established and new technologies with vital data on limitations, operations and maintenance, control and special factors.

Water Resource Management: Integrated Policies. OECD Publications and Information Center, 2001 L St., N.W., Suite 700, Washington, District of Columbia 20036. (202) 785-OECD. 1989. Report underlines the need for more effective policy integration within the water sector itself (in order to improve water quality and quantity, demand management, surface and groundwater supply).

Water Resources Planning. Andrew A. Dzurik. Rowman & Littlefield, Publishers, Inc., 8705 Bollman Pl., Savage, Maryland 20763. (301) 306-0400. 1990. Offers a comprehensive survey of all aspects of water resources planning and management.

Water: Rethinking Management in an Age of Scarcity. Sandra Postel. Worldwatch Institute, 1776 Massachusetts Ave., N.W., Washington, District of Columbia 20036-1904. 1984.

Watershed Management Field Manual. Food and Agriculture Organization of the United Nations, 46110F Assembly Dr., Lanham, Maryland 20706-4391. (800) 274-4888. 1986.

The World Bank and the Environment: A Progress Report, Fiscal 1991. World Bank, UNIPUB, 4611-F Assembly Dr., Lanham, Maryland 20706. (301) 459-7666 or (800) 274-4888. 1991. Describes specific environmental strategies and environmental lending in the Bank's four operational regions: Asia, Europe, the Middle East and North Africa, and Latin America and the Caribbean.

HANDBOOKS AND MANUALS

Handbook of Drinking Water Quality: Standards and Controls. John De Zuane. Van Nostrand Reinhold, 115 5th Ave., New York, New York 10003. (212) 254-3232. 1990. Aids in evaluating water quality control at every stage of the water path, from source to treatment plant, from distribution system to consumer.

High-Quality Industrial Water Management Manual. Paul N. Garay and Franklin M. Chn. The Association of Energy Engineers, 4025 Pleasantdale Rd., Suite 420, Atlanta, Georgia 30340. (404) 925-9558. 1992. Guide to managing water resources.

Standard Handbook of Environmental Engineering. Robert A. Corbitt. McGraw-Hill, 1221 Ave. of the Americas, New York, New York 10020. (212) 512-2000 or (800) 262-4729. 1990. Hands-on reference to understand environmental engineering technology. Covers air quality control, water supply, wastewater disposal, waste management, stormwater and hazardous wastes.

ONLINE DATA BASES

Chemical Abstracts-CA. Chemical Abstracts Service, 2540 Olentangy River Rd., P.O. Box 3012, Columbus,

Ohio 43210. (800) 848-6533 or (614) 421-3600. Information sources include 9000 journals, patents from 27 countries, two industrial property organizations, new books, conference proceedings, and government research reports.

Computerized Engineering Index–COMPENDEX. Engineering Information Inc., 345 E. 47th St., New York, New York 10017. (212) 705-7600.

Monthly Catalog of United States Government Publications. U.S. G.P.O., Supt. of Docs., PO Box 371954, Pittsburgh, Pennsylvania 15250-7954. (202) 512-0000.

National Technical Information Service. U.S. Department of Commerce, National Technical Information Service, Office of Data Base Services, 5285 Port Royal Rd., Springfield, Virginia 22161. (703) 487-4807. Bibliographic database of government sponsored research and technical reports.

SCISEARCH. Institute for Scientific Information, University City Science Center, 3501 Market St., Philadelphia, Pennsylvania 19104. (215) 386-0100.

PERIODICALS AND NEWSLETTERS

British Columbia Ministry of Environment, Annual Report. British Columbia, Ministry of Environment, 810 Blanchard, 1st Fl., Victoria, British Columbia, Canada (604) 387-9418. 1976-. Annually. Review of work carried out during the year by the Ministry of the Environment, including fish, wildlife, water management, and parks.

Focus on International Joint Commission Activities. IJC Great Lakes Regional Office, PO Box 32869, Detroit, Michigan 48232. (313) 226-2170. 1986-. Three issues a year. Provides information on Great Lakes water quality and quantity issues.

GEM Notes: an Update of the Groundwater Education in Michigan Program. Groundwater Education in Michigan, Institute of Water Research, Michigan State University, 25 Manly Miles Bldg., 1405 S. Harrison Rd., East Lansing, Michigan 48824. (517) 355-9543. 1988-. Irregular.

Ground Water Newsletter. Water Information Center, Inc., 125 East Bethpage Road, Plainview, New York 11803. (516) 249-7634. Biweekly. Covers ground water exploration, development, and management.

Headwaters. Friends of the River, Bldg. C, Ft. Mason Center, San Francisco, California 94123. (415) 771-0400. Biweekly. River conservation, recreation, and water politics.

Hydata News and Views. American Water Resources Association, 5410 Grosvenor Lane, Suite 220, Bethesda, Maryland 20814. (301) 493-8600. Six times a year. Research, planning and management in water resources.

Journal - American Water Works Association. American Water Works Association, 6666 W. Quincy Ave., Denver, Colorado 80235. (303) 794-7711. Monthly. Includes regulatory summaries, conference information and job listings. Has state chapters, annual meetings, and special publications.

Journal of Hydraulic Engineering. American Society of Civil Engineers, 345 E. 47th St., New York, New York 10017. (212) 705-7288; (800) 548-2723. 1983-. Monthly. Papers describe the analysis and solutions of problems in hydraulic engineering, hydrology and water resources.

Emphasizes concepts, methods, techniques and results that advance knowledge in the hydraulic engineering profession.

Journal of Soil and Water Conservation. Soil and Water Conservation Society, 7515 Northeast Ankeny Road, Ankeny, Iowa 50021. (515) 289-2331. Bimonthly. Promotes better land and water use and management.

Journal of Water Resources Planning and Management. American Society of Civil Engineers, Resource Planning and Management Division, 345 E. 47th St., New York, New York 10017. (212) 705-7288; (800) 548-2723. 1983-. Quarterly. Reports on all phases of planning and management of water resources. Examines social, economic, environmental, and administrative concerns relating to the use and conservation of water.

New Jersey Air, Water, & Waste Management Times. New Jersey State Department of Health, Division of Clean Air & Water, John Fitch Plaza, Trenton, New Jersey 08625. Bimonthly.

Washington Report. Interstate Conference on Water Policy, 955 L'Enfant Plaza, 6th Floor, Washington, District of Columbia 20024. (202) 466-7287. Every six weeks. Covers water conservation, development and administration.

Water Engineering & Management. Scranton Gillette Communications, Inc., 380 E. Northwest Hwy., Des Plaines, Illinois 60016-2282. (708) 298-6622. 1986-. Monthly. A professional trade publication which includes latest legislative news in the area of water quality, EPA criteria for drinking water, pesticides, and related standards. Includes articles of interest by water professionals and has regular news features such as forthcoming conferences, products at work, surveys, company profiles, etc.

Water Technology. National Trade Publications, Inc., 13 Century Hill Dr., Latham, New York 12110. (518) 783-1281. Monthly.

RESEARCH CENTERS AND INSTITUTES

Auburn University, Water Resources Research Institute. 202 Hargis Hall, Auburn University, Alabama 36849-5124. (205) 844-5080.

Michigan State University, Institute of Water Research. 334 Natural Resources Building, East Lansing, Michigan 48824. (517) 353-3742.

Michigan Technological University, Environmental Engineering Center for Water and Waste Management. 1400 Townsend Rd., Houghton, Michigan 49931. (906) 487-2194.

Utah State University, Watershed Science Unit. Range Science Department, Logan, Utah 84322-5250. (801) 750-2759.

STATISTICS SOURCES

Water Management Chemicals. FIND/SVP, 625 Avenue of the Americas, New York, New York 10011. (212) 645-4500. 1991. Analyzes U.S. consumption of water management chemicals.

TRADE ASSOCIATIONS AND PROFESSIONAL SOCIETIES

American Society of Civil Engineers. 345 East 47th St., New York, New York 10017. (212) 705-7496.

American Water Resources Association. 5410 Grosvenor Lane, Suite 220, Bethesda, Maryland 20814. (301) 493-8600.

Interstate Conference on Water Policy. 955 L'Enfant Plaza, 6th Floor, Washington, District of Columbia 20024. (202) 466-7287.

National Association of Water Companies. 1725 K St., N.W., Suite 1212, Washington, District of Columbia 20006. (202) 833-8383.

National Hydropower Association. 555 13th St., N.W., Suite 900 E., Washington, District of Columbia 20004. (202) 637-8115.

National Water Resources Association. 3800 N. Fairfax Dr., Suite 4, Arlington, Virginia 22203. (703) 524-1544.

Water & Wastewater Equipment Manufacturers Association. Box 17402, Dulles International Airport, Washington, District of Columbia 20041. (703) 444-1777.

WATER ODORS

See: WATER QUALITY

WATER POLLUTION

See also: ACID PRECIPITATION; AQUATIC ECOSYSTEMS; EUTROPHICATION; FISH AND WILDLIFE MANAGEMENT; MARINE POLLUTION; TOXIC POLLUTANTS; WASTEWATER TREATMENT; WATER QUALITY; WATER RESOURCES

ABSTRACTING AND INDEXING SERVICES

Abstracts of Air and Water Conservation Literature. American Petroleum Institute. Central Abstracting and Indexing Service, 275 Madison Avenue, New York, New York 10016. 1972.

Agrindex. AGRIS Coordinating Center, Via delle Terme di Caracalla, Rome, Italy I-00100. 61 0181-FA01. 1975-.

Applied Science and Technology Index. H.W. Wilson Co., 950 University Ave., Bronx, New York 10452. (800) 367-6770. Formerly Industrial Arts Index.

Aqualine Abstracts. Water Research Centre. c/o Pergamon Microforms International, Inc., Fairview Park, Elmsford, New York 10523. (914) 592-7720. 1927-. Contains some 8,000 records annually on water and wastewater technology. Covers all aspects of water, wastewater, associated engineering services and the aquatic environment. Over 600 periodicals, as well as books, reports and conference proceedings and other publications from water related institutions worldwide are scanned. Also available online.

ASFA Aquaculture Abstracts. Cambridge Scientific Abstracts, Inc., 5161 River Rd., Bethesda, Maryland 20816. (301) 961-6750. 1984.

Biological and Agricultural Index. H.W. Wilson Co., 950 University Ave., Bronx, New York 10452. (800) 367-6770. 1916-. Monthly.

Chemical Abstracts. Chemical Abstracts Service, 2540 Olentangy River Rd., PO Box 3012, Columbus, Ohio 43210. (800) 848-6533. 1907-.

Current Advances in Ecological and Environmental Science. Pergamon Microforms International, Inc., Fairview Park, Elmsford, New York 10523. (914) 592-7720. 1989-. Monthly. Current literature searching service including journals, reports, abstracts, etc. This service is available online as part of the CABS database on the hosts BRS and ORBIT search service.

Ecological Abstracts. Geo Abstracts Ltd. Elsevier Applied Science, Crown House, Linton Rd., Barking, England IG 11 8JU. 1974-. Derived from over 600 leading ecological and environmental journals, plus books, conference proceedings, reports and theses.

Engineering Index. The Engineering Index Inc., 345 E. 47th St., New York, New York 10017. 1962-.

Food Science and Technology Abstracts. International Food Information Service, c/o National Food Laboratory, 6363 Clark Ave., Dublin, California 94568. (800) 336-3782. 1969-.

General Science Index. H. W. Wilson Co., 950 University Ave., Bronx, New York 10452. 1978-. Monthly, also issued in annual cumulation. Cumulative subject index to English language periodicals in the subject fields of astronomy, botany, chemistry, earth science, environment and conservation, food and nutrition, genetics, mathematics, medicine and health, microbiology, oceanography, physics, physiology and zoology.

Geographical Abstracts. London School of Economics, Dept. of Geography, Regency House, 34 Duke St., London, England 1966-. Continued by Geo Abstracts issued in 6 parts: Pt. A. Landforms and the quaternary; Pt. B. Biogeography and Climatology; Pt. C. Economic geography; Pt. D. Social geography and cartography; Pt. E. Sedimentology; Pt. F. Regional and community planning.

Index to Scientific Book Contents. Institute for Scientific Information, 3501 Market St., Philadelphia, Pennsylvania 19104. (800) 523-1857. 1985-. Annual. Gives contents of science books published.

Irrigation and Drainage Abstracts. C. A. B. International, 845 North Park Ave., Tucson, Arizona 85719. (602) 621-7897 or (800) 258-4841. 1975-. Quarterly. Subject areas scanned are: water management, irrigation of crop plants, drainage, soil water relations, plant water relations, salinity and toxicity problems, soil condition, evaporotranspiration, evaporation, land use, streams, water quality, and other related areas.

Pollution Abstracts. Cambridge Scientific Abstracts, 5161 River Rd., Bethesda, Maryland 20816. (301) 961-6750. Six/year. Indexes worldwide technical literature on environmental pollution. Covers air pollution, marine and freshwater pollution, sewage and wastewater treatment, waste management, toxicology and health, noise pollution, radiation, land pollution, and environmental policies, programs, legislation, and education. Also available online.

Public Health Engineering Abstracts. U.S. G.P.O., Washington, District of Columbia 20401. (202) 512-0000. Monthly.

Science Citation Index. Institute for Scientific Information, 3501 Market St., Philadelphia, Pennsylvania 19104. 1961-.

BIBLIOGRAPHIES

Current Contents. Agriculture, Biology and Environmental Sciences. Institute for Scientific Information, 3501 Market St., Philadelphia, Pennsylvania 19104. (800) 523-1857. 1973-. Previous title: Current Contents. Agricultural, Food & Veterinary Sciences. Gives the table of contents of periodicals in the fields of agriculture, biology, environmental and related areas.

Geraghty & Miller's Groundwater Bibliography. Frits Van Der Leeden. Lewis Publishers, 200 Corporate Blvd. NW, Boca Raton, Florida 33431. (407) 994-0555 or (800)272-7737. 1991. 5th ed. Since the last edition, this essential research aid reflects increased interest in areas such as ground water contamination, modeling, and legal issues. Contains a listing of general bibliographies, periodicals, and books, followed by a subject section covering 3 specific aspects of hydrogeology.

Literature Review. Water Pollution Control Federation, 601 Wythe St., Alexandria, Virginia 22314-1994. (703) 684-2400.

New Publications of the Geological Survey. U.S. Department of the Interior, Geological Survey, 119 National Center, Reston, Virginia 22092. (703) 648-4460. 1984-. Monthly. Bibliography of geological publications and related government documents published by the Geological Survey.

Water Pollution: A Guide to Information Sources. Allen W. Knight and Mary Ann Simmons. Gale Research Co., 835 Penobscot Bldg., Detroit, Michigan 48226-4094. (313) 961-2242. 1980. Brings together a diverse set of information sources in the subject area of water pollution from the physical, social and natural sciences in the economic context of the environment planning and management process.

DIRECTORIES

American Water Works Association–Buyers' Guide Issue. American Water Works Association, 6666 W. Quincy Ave., Denver, Colorado 80235. (303) 794-7711.

American Water Works Association Directory. The Association, 6666 W. Quincy Ave., Denver, Colorado 80235. (303) 794-7711. Annual.

Directory of Environmental Information Sources. Thomas F. P. Sullivan, ed. Government Institutes, Inc., 4 Research Pl., Ste. 200, Rockville, Maryland 20850. (301) 921-2300. 1992. 3d ed.

List of Water Pollution Control Administrators. Association of State and Interstate Water Pollution Control Administrators, 444 N. Capitol St., N.W., Suite 330N, Washington, District of Columbia 20001. (202) 624-7782.

National Water Well Association–Membership Directory. National Water Well Association, 6375 Riverside Dr., Dublin, Ohio 43017. (614) 761-1711.

ENCYCLOPEDIAS AND DICTIONARIES

American Water Works Association Encyclopedia. American Water Works Association, 6666 W. Quincy Ave., Denver, Colorado 80235. (303) 794-7711. 1985. Subject headings used in water resources research and literature.

Cambridge Encyclopedia of Life Sciences. A. E. Friday and David S. Ingram. Cambridge University Press, 40 W 20th St., New York, New York 10011. (212) 924-3900 or (800) 227-0247. 1985. Includes all topics under biology and ecology.

Dictionary of Environmental Engineering and Related Sciences: English-Spanish, Spanish-English. Jose T. Villate. Ediciones Universal, 3090 SW 8th St., Miami, Florida 33135. (305) 642-3355. 1979.

Dictionary of Environmental Protection. Otto E. Tutzauer. Fred B. Rothman, 10368 W. Centennial Rd., Littleton, California 80127. (303) 979-5657. 1979.

Dictionary of Environmental Protection Technology: In Four Languages, English, German, French, Russian. Egon Seidel. Elsevier Science Publishing Co., 655 Avenue of the Americas, New York, New York 10010. (212) 984-5800. 1988.

Encyclopedia of Environmental Science and Engineering. J.R. Pfafflin. Gordon and Breach Science Publishers, Inc., 270 8th Ave., New York, New York 10011. (212) 206-8900. 1992.

The Encyclopedia of Geochemistry and Environmental Sciences. Rhodes Whitmore Fairbridge. Van Nostrand Reinhold Co., 115 5th Ave., New York, New York 10003. (212) 254-3232. 1972.

English-Russian Dictionary of Environmental Protection: About 14,000 Terms. E.L. Milovanov. Pergamon Microforms International, Inc., Fairview Park, Elmsford, New York 10523. (914) 592-7720. 1981.

Environmental Engineering Dictionary. C. C. Lee. Government Institutes, Inc., 4 Research Pl., Ste. 200, Rockville, Maryland 20850. (301) 921-2300. 1989. Defines over 6000 engineering terms relating to pollutioncontrol technologies, monitoring, risk assessment, sampling andanalysis, quality control, permitting, and environmentally-regulated engineering and science. Includes bibliographical references (p. 612-627).

McGraw-Hill Encyclopedia of Environmental Science. Sybil P. Parker. McGraw-Hill Science & Engineering Books, 11 W. 19th St., New York, New York 10011. (212) 337-6010. 1980. Covers ecology, man's influence on nature, and environmental protection.

Van Nostrand's Scientific Encyclopedia. Glenn D. Considine, ed. Van Nostrand Reinhold, 115 5th Ave., New York, New York 10003. (212) 254-3232. 1983. Sixth edition. Includes all broad subject areas in science.

GENERAL WORKS

Advances in Water Treatment and Environmental Management. George Thomas. Elsevier Science Publishing Co., 655 Avenue of the Americas, New York, New York 10010. (212) 984-5800. 1991. Measurement and control of groundwater quality, rivers, river management, estuaries, and beaches.

Aquatic Toxicology. Jerome O. Nriagu. John Wiley & Sons, Inc., 605 3rd Ave., New York, New York 10158-0012. (212) 850-6000. 1989.

Beneath the Bottom Line: Agricultural Approaches to Reduce Agrichemical Contamination of Groundwater. Office of Technology Assessment, U.S. Congress, Washington, District of Columbia 20510-8025. (202) 224-8996. 1991. Identifies ways to minimize contamination of ground water by agricultural chemicals.

Biology of Freshwater Pollution. C. F. Mason. Longman, Burnt Mill, Harlow, England CM20 2J6. (0279) 26721. 1991. Second edition. Deals with biological effects of pollution in water and the environment.

CDC Interference in Dioxin Water Standards. Committee on Government Operations. U.S. G.P.O., Washington, District of Columbia 20401. (202) 512-0000. 1991. Hearing before the Human Resources and Intergovernmental Relations Subcommittee of the Committee on Government Operations, House of Representatives, 101st Congress, 2d session, July 26, 1991. Provides the basic standards for dioxin content in water.

Contaminant Transport in Groundwater. H.E. Kobus and W. Kinzelbach. A. A. Balkema, Old Post Rd., Brookfield, Vermont 05036. (802) 276-3162. 1989. Describes physical and chemical processes, model building and application as well as remedial action.

Contamination of Ground Water Prevention, Assessment, Restoration. Michael Barcelona, et al. Noyes Publications, 120 Mill Rd., Park Ridge, New Jersey 07656. (201) 391-8484. 1990. Provides regulatory agencies and industry a convenient source of technical information on the management of contaminated ground water.

Controlling Toxic Substances in Agricultural Drainage. U.S. Committee on Irrigation and Drainage, PO Box 15326, Denver, Colorado 80215. 1990. Looks at current technology on toxic substances and water treatment processes and techniques.

Degradation, Retention and Dispersion of Pollutants in Groundwater. E. Arvin, ed. Pergamon Microforms International, Inc., Fairview Park, Elmsford, New York 10523. (914) 592-7720. 1985. Proceedings of the IAWPRC Seminar held in Copenhagen, Denmark, September 12-14, 1984.

Demanding Clean Food and Water. Plenum Press, 233 Spring St., New York, New York 10013. (212) 620-8000. Details specific chemicals to avoid in foods and discusses approaches for eradicating pests without polluting the environment.

Drinking Water Hazards: How to Know If There Are Toxic Chemicals in Your Water and What to Do If There Are. John Cary Stewart. Envirographics, PO Box 334, Hiram, Ohio 44234. (216) 527-5207. 1990. Documents the increase of cancer and other diseases that may be environmentally induced. Discusses the increases in the use of synthetic organic chemicals, and covers each group of drinking water contaminants in some detail: inorganic chemicals, heavy metals, bacteria and viruses, radionuclides, nitrates, and organic chemicals, including pesticides.

Efficiency in Environmental Regulation: A Benefit-Cost Analysis of Alternative Approaches. Kluwer Academic Publishers, 101 Philip Dr., Assinippi Park, Norwell, Massachusetts 02061-0358. (617) 871-6600. Quantitative assessment of the efficiency of the EPA's regulation of conventional air and water pollutants from the pulp and paper industry.

Environmental Hazard Assessment of Effluents. Pergamon Microforms International, Inc., Fairview Park, Elmsford, New York 10523. (914) 592-7720. Concepts of effluent testing, biomonitoring, hazard assessment, and disposal.

Fate of Pesticides and Chemicals in the Environment. Jerald L. Schnoor, ed. John Wiley & Sons, Inc., 605 3rd Ave., New York, New York 10158-0012. (212) 850-6000. 1992. Focuses on the necessity to improve our deteriorating standards of public health, environmental science and technology with a total systems approach through the pooled talents of scientists and engineers.

Ground Water and Vadose Zone Monitoring. David M. Nielsen and A. Ivan Johnson, eds. PennWell Books, PO Box 21288, Tulsa, Oklahoma 74121. (918) 831-9421; (800) 752-9764. 1988. Contains 22 papers presented at the symposium on standards and development for ground water and Vadose Zone monitoring investigations.

Groundwater Contamination: Sources, Control, and Preventive Measures. Chester D. Rail. Technomic Publishing Co., 851 New Holland Ave., Box 3535, Lancaster, Pennsylvania 17604. (717) 291-5609. 1989. Reviews the presently known sources of groundwater contamination and its many complex interactions, including managerial and political implications.

Groundwater Protection: Local Success Stories. Milou Carolan. Internal City Management Association, 777 N. Capital St., NE, Suite 500, Washington, District of Columbia 20002-4201. (800) 745-8780. 1990. Case studies from local governments that have created effective programs for protecting the local water supply by evaluating contamination sources and developing community support.

Groundwater Remediation and Petroleum: A Guide for Underground Storage Tanks. David C. Noonan and James T. Curtis. PennWell Books, PO Box 21288, Tulsa, Oklahoma 74121. (918) 831-9421; (800) 752-9764. 1990. Guide for personnel charged with the responsibility of addressing contamination caused by leaking underground storage tanks.

Hydrocarbon Contaminated Soils and Groundwater: Analysis, Fate, Environmental and Public Health Effects, and Remediation. Paul T. Kostecki and Edward J. Calabrese. Lewis Publishers, 2000 Corporate Blvd.,N.W., Boca Raton, Florida 33431. (407) 994-0555 or (800) 272-7737. 1991. Describes perspectives and emerging issues, analytical techniques and site assessments, environmental fate and modeling.

Industrial Environmental Control. A. M. Springer. John Wiley & Sons, Inc., 605 3rd Ave., New York, New York 10158-0012. (212) 850-6000. 1986. Covers in great detail all the basic information regarding industrial pollution and its treatment.

Integrated Approaches to Water Pollution. Joao Bau. Elsevier Science Publishing Co., 655 Avenue of the Americas, New York, New York 10010. (212) 984-5800. 1991. Integrated management strategies, policies for pollution control, groundwater pollution resulting from industrial, agricultural and urban sources, data and measurement.

International Environmental Information Sources. Pira, Randalls Rd., Leatherhead, England KT22 7RU. 0372 376161. 1990. Contains valuable business and technical contacts for environmental information sources worldwide. Information sources cover the following subjects: Air, noise, water and land pollution; waste control and disposal; recycling; energy recovery; nature conservation. Informational sources include associations, research organizations, legislative/regulatory agencies, directories, statistics, on-line databases, magazines and news letters in 24 countries.

Introduction to Water Quality Standards. U.S. Environmental Protection Agency, Office of Water, 401 M St. SW, Washington, District of Columbia 20460. (202) 260-2090. 1988.

Meeting Environmental Work Force Needs. Information Dynamics, 111 Claybrook Dr., Silver Spring, Maryland 20902. 1985. Proceedings of the Second National Conference on Meeting Environmental Workforce Needs, April 1-3, 1985: Education and Training to Assure a Qualified Work Force.

Methods for Assessing Exposure of Human and Non-Human Biota. R. G. Tardiff and B. D. Goldstein, eds. John Wiley & Sons, Inc., 605 3rd Ave., New York, New York 10158-0012. (212) 850-6000. 1991. Provides a critical and collective evaluation of approaches to chemical exposure assessment.

The New York Environment Book. Eric A. Goldstein. Island Press, 1718 Connecticut Ave. N.W., Suite 300, Washington, District of Columbia 20009. (202) 232-7933. 1990. Provides an in-depth analysis of New York City's environment. The five areas surveyed are: solid waste disposal, hazardous substances, water pollution, air quality, and drinking water quality. Discusses past cleanup efforts, and offers an agenda for the future. Describes and analyzes the general environment of urban areas, and offers solutions for their special environmental problems.

Organic Substances and Sediment in Water. Robert A. Baker. Lewis Publishers, 2000 Corporate Blvd., Boca Raton, Florida 33431. (407) 994-0555 or (800) 272-7737. 1991. vol. 1-3.

Poison Runoff: A Guide to State and Local Control of Nonpoint Source Water Pollution. Paul Thompson. Natural Resources Defense Council, 40 W. 20th St., New York, New York 10011. (212) 727-2700. 1989. How-to-book addressing pollution in agricultural lands, urban development and construction, logging, mining and grazing.

Pollution: Causes, Effects and Control. Roy Michael Harrison. Royal Society of Chemistry, c/o CRC Press, 2000 Corporate Blvd. N.W., Boca Raton, Florida 33431. (800) 272-7737. 1990. 2nd ed. Deals with environmental pollution and its associated problems and legal ramifications.

Pollution Control and Conservation. M. Kovacs, ed. John Wiley & Sons, Inc., 605 3rd Ave., New York, New York 10158. (212) 850-6000. 1985. Comprehensive view on current knowledge and research in the area of effective protection of air, water, soil and living matter and pollution control.

Position Statements. Association of State and Interstate Water Pollution Control Administrators, 444 N. Capitol St., NW, Suite 330, Washington, District of Columbia 20001. (202) 624-7782.

Power Generation and the Environment. P. S. Liss and P. A. H. Saunders. Oxford University Press, 200 Madison Ave., New York, New York 10016. (212) 679-7300; (800) 334-4249. 1990. Analyses the problems and possibilities inherent in producing electricity on a large scale.

Protecting the Nation's Groundwater from Contamination. U.S. G.P.O., Washington, District of Columbia 20401. 1984-. Covers underground water quality and pollution.

Removal of Heavy Metals from Groundwaters. Robert W. Peters. Lewis Publishers, 2000 Corporate Blvd., N.W., Boca Raton, Florida 33431. (407) 994-0555 or (800) 272-7737. 1991. Describes the sources of heavy metal contamination, classification of metals by industry, extent of the contamination problem, toxicity associated with various heavy metals, effects of heavy metals in biological wastewater treatment operations, leaching of heavy metals from sludges, modeling of heavy metals in the saturated and unsaturated zones, and other related areas.

Risk Assessment of Groundwater Pollution Control. William F. McTernan and Edward Kaplan, eds. American Society of Civil Engineers, 345 E. 47th St., New York, New York 10017. (212) 705-7288; (800) 548-2723. 1990.

River Pollution: An Ecological Perspective. S. M. Haslam. Belhaven Press, 136 S. Broadway, Irvington, New York 10533. (914) 591-9111. 1990. Describes the impact of natural and man-made pollution in the ecosystem of freshwater streams, stressing understanding of processes and techniques of measurement.

Sediments: Chemistry and Toxicity of In-Place Pollutants. Renato Baudo, et al., eds. Lewis Publishers, 200 Corporate Blvd. NW, Boca Raton, Florida 33431. (407) 994-0555 or (800)272-7737. 1990.

Some Economic Impacts of Freshwater Stream Effluent Discharge Limits on Selected Small Communities in Mississippi. Leo R. Cheatham. Water Resources Research Institute, Mississippi State University, Mississippi State, Mississippi 39762. Water supply, water pollution and drinking water contamination.

Stream, Lake, Estuary, and Ocean Pollution. Nelson Leonard Nemerow. Van Nostrand Reinhold, 115 5th Ave., New York, New York 10003. (800) 926-2665. 1991.

Subsurface Migration of Hazardous Wastes. Joseph S. Devinny. Van Nostrand Reinhold, 115 5th Ave., New York, New York 10003. (212) 254-3232. 1990. Environmental aspects of underground water pollution.

The Surface Water Acidification Programme. B. J. Mason, ed. Cambridge University Press, 40 W. 20th St., New York, New York 10011. (212) 924-3900; (800) 227-0247. 1991. Proceedings of the final Conference of the Surface Water Acidification Programme, held at the Royal Society in March 1990. Deals with the acid pollution of rivers and lakes and presents research results on watersheds in Great Britain and Scandinavia.

Understanding Ground-Water Contamination: An Orientation Manual. Paul E. Bailey and William D. Ward, eds. PennWell Books, PO Box 21288, Tulsa, Oklahoma 74121. (918) 831-9421; (800) 752-9764. 1990. Orientation manual for businesses, their counsel, local and regional officials, and government agencies, that must make decisions regarding groundwater.

The Use of Macrophytes in Water Pollution Control. D. Athie and C. C. Cerri, eds. Pergamon Microforms International, Inc., Fairview Park, Elmsford, New York 10523. (914) 592-7720. 1988. Proceedings of an IAWPRC specialized seminar held in Piracicaba, Brazil, August 24-28,1986. Describes the problem of river pollution, caused mainly by sewage and industrial effluents.

The Uses of Ecology: Lake Washington and Beyond. W. T. Edmondson. University of Washington Press, PO Box 50096, Seattle, Washington 98145-5096. (206) 543-4050; (800) 441-4115. 1991. Author delivered most of the contents of this book as a Danz lecture at the University of Washington. Gives an account of the pollution and recovery of Lake Washington and describes how communities worked and applied lessons learned from Lake Washington cleanup. Includes extensive documentation and bibliographies.

Waste Management in Petrochemical Complexes. S. A. S. Almeida, et al., eds. Pergamon Microforms International, Inc., Fairview Park, Elmsford, New York 10523. (914) 592-7720. 1989. Proceedings of an IAWPRC Seminar held in Porto Alegre, Rio Grande do Sul, Brazil, October 26-28, 1987. Covers a wide range of topics related to the processing and final disposal of effluents derived from the chemical and petrochemical industries.

Water Contamination by Viruses: Occurrence, Detection, Treatment. Charles P. Gerba, et al. Lewis Publishers, 2000 Corporate Blvd., N.W., Boca Raton, Florida 33431. (407) 994-0555 or (800) 272-7737. 1991. Describes the occurrence of viruses in the environment such as soil, sludge, drinking water, and rivers. Also gives details on how these viruses are detected, and their elimination by adsorption, irradiation, and other related methods.

Water Pollution Biology. P. D. Abel. John Wiley & Sons, Inc., 605 3rd Ave., New York, New York 10158. (212) 850-6000. 1988. State-of-the-art information on methods of investigating water pollution problems and critically assesses the literature on water pollution. Also included is a discussion on the role of toxicological studies in the monitoring and control of water pollution.

Water Pollution: Modelling, Measuring and Prediction. L.C. Wrobel. Elsevier Science Publishing Co., 655 Avenue of the Americas, New York, New York 10010. (212) 984-5800. 1991. Mathematical modelling data acquisition waste disposal and wastewater treatment chemical and biological problems.

Water Pollution Research and Control. L. Lijklema, ed. Pergamon Microforms International, Inc., Fairview Park, Elmsford, New York 10523. (914) 592-7720. 1989. Proceedings of the 14th biennial conference of the International Association on Water Pollution Research and Control held in Brighton, UK, July 18-21, 1988. Incorporates aspects of both research and practice in water pollution control, and contains valuable information for the abatement of water pollution and the enhancement of the quality of the water environment worldwide.

GOVERNMENTAL ORGANIZATIONS

Assistant Attorney General: Environment and Resources Division, Department of Justice. Room 2143, 10th St. and Constitution Ave., N.W., Washington, District of Columbia 20530. (202) 514-2701.

New England Interstate Water Pollution Control Commission. 85 Merrimac St., Boston, Massachusetts 02114. (617) 367-8522.

U.S. Environmental Protection Agency: Office of Drinking Water. 401 M St., S.W., Washington, District of Columbia 20460. (202) 382-5543.

U.S. Environmental Protection Agency: Office of Underground Storage Tanks. 401 M St., S.W., Washington, District of Columbia 20460. (202) 382-4517.

HANDBOOKS AND MANUALS

Clean Water Handbook. Government Institutes, Inc., 4 Research Pl., Ste. 200, Rockville, Maryland 20850. (301) 921-2300. 1990. Offers straightforward explanation on enforcement, toxics, water quality standards, efficient limitations, NPDES, stormwater and nonpoint discharge control.

Controlling Nonprofit-Source Water Pollution. National Audubon Society, 950 3rd Ave., New York, New York 10022. (212) 832-3200. 1988. Guide to citizen participation in water quality management.

Ground Water Handbook. Government Institutes, Inc., 4 Research Pl., Ste 200, Rockville, Maryland 20850. (301) 921-2300. 1989. Includes highlights of chapters on ground water contamination, use of models in managing ground water protection programs, ground water restoration, ground water quality investigations, basic hydrogeology, monitoring well design and construction, ground water sampling, ground water tracers and basic geology.

Handbook for the Identification, Location and Investigation of Pollution Sources Affecting Ground Water. National Water Well Association, 6375 Riverside Dr., Dublin, Ohio 43017. (614) 761-1711. 1989.

Handbook of Acute Toxicity of Chemicals to Fish and Aquatic Invertebrates. Waynon W. Johnson and Mack T. Finley. U.S. Department of the Interior, Fish and Wildlife Service, Washington, District of Columbia 20240. (202) 208-5634. 1980. Fisheries Research Laboratory, 1965-78; Resource publication/U.S. Fish and Wildlife Service, no. 137.

Hazardous Materials Spills Emergency Handbook. American Water Works Association, 6666 W. Quincy Ave., Denver, Colorado 80235. (303) 794-7711. Covers chemical safety measures, water pollution, and water purification.

Operation of Municipal Wastewater Treatment Plants. Water Pollution Control Federation, 601 Wythe St., Alexandria, Virginia 22314. (800) 556-8700. 2nd ed.

The Poisoned Well: New Strategies for Groundwater Protection. Eric P. Jorgensen, ed. Island Press, 1718 Connecticut Ave. N.W., Suite 300, Washington, District of Columbia 20009. (202) 232-7933. 1989. Explains how individuals can work with agencies and the courts to enforce water laws, how the major federal water laws, work what remedies exist for each type of groundwater contamination, and what state and local programs may be helpful.

Subsurface Contamination Reference Guide. Office of Emergency and Remedial Response, U.S. Environmental Protection Agency, 401 M St.,S.W., Washington, District of Columbia 1991. Underground water pollution and hazardous substances.

Water Pollution Biology: A Laboratory/Field Handbook. Robert A. Coler, John P. Rockwood. Technomic Publishing Co., 851 New Holland Ave., PO Box 3535, Lancaster, Pennsylvania 17604. (717) 291-5609. 1989. Overview of the types of surface water quality problems and the types of field and laboratory methodologies used to assess the impacts of those problems on aquatic biota.

ONLINE DATA BASES

Air/Water Pollution Report. NewsNet, Inc., 945 Haverford Rd., Bryn Mawr, Pennsylvania 19010. (800) 345-1301. Online version of periodical of same name.

Chemical Abstracts-CA. Chemical Abstracts Service, 2540 Olentangy River Rd., P.O. Box 3012, Columbus, Ohio 43210. (800) 848-6533 or (614) 421-3600. Information sources include 9000 journals, patents from 27 countries, two industrial property organizations, new books, conference proceedings, and government research reports.

Chemical Hazard Response Information System–CHRIS. U.S. Coast Guard. Office of Research and Development, 2100 2d St., NW., Rm. 5410 C, Washington, District of Columbia 20593. (202) 783-3238. Contains information needed to respond to emergencies that occur during the transport of hazardous chemicals, as well as information that can help prevent emergency situations. Each of the approximately 1,300 records include information on physical and chemical properties, health and fire hazards, labeling, chemical reactivity, hazard classification and water pollution. Available on CIS and on Microdex's TOMES Plus series.

Computerized Engineering Index–COMPENDEX. Engineering Information Inc., 345 E. 47th St., New York, New York 10017. (212) 705-7600.

Enviroline. R. R. Bowker Co., Bowker Electronic Publishing, 121 Chanlon Rd., New Providence, New Jersey 07974. (800) 521-8110.

Environment Reporter. Bureau of National Affairs, 1231 25th St., N.W., Rm. 215, Washington, District of Columbia 20037. (800) 372-1033. Online version of periodical of the same name.

Environmental Bibliography. Environmental Studies Institute, International Academy at Santa Barbara, 800 Garden St., Ste. D, Santa Barbara, California 93101. (805) 965-5010. International periodical literature dealing with environmental topics such as air pollution, water treatment, energy conservation, noise abatement, soil mechanics, wildlife preservation, and chemical wastes.

Information System for Hazardous Organics in Water. U.S. Environmental Protection Agency, Office of Pesticides & Toxic Substances, 401 M St., S.W., Washington, District of Columbia 20460. (202) 260-2090.

Monthly Catalog of United States Government Publications. U.S. G.P.O., Supt. of Docs., PO Box 371954, Pittsburgh, Pennsylvania 15250-7954. (202) 512-0000.

National Technical Information Service. U.S. Department of Commerce, National Technical Information Service, Office of Data Base Services, 5285 Port Royal Rd., Springfield, Virginia 22161. (703) 487-4807. Bibliographic database of government sponsored research and technical reports.

SCISEARCH. Institute for Scientific Information, University City Science Center, 3501 Market St., Philadelphia, Pennsylvania 19104. (215) 386-0100.

STORET. U.S. Environmental Protection Agency, Office of Information Resources Management, 401 M St., S.W., Washington, District of Columbia 20460. (202) 260-2090. Water pollution measurement data collected from more than 700,000 observation stations across the United States.

PERIODICALS AND NEWSLETTERS

Agrarian Advocate. California Action Network, Box 464, Davis, California 95617. (916) 756-8518. 1978-. Quarterly. Includes issues of concern to rural California residents such as groundwater pollution, pesticides, and sustainable agriculture.

Air and Water Pollution Control. Bureau of National Affairs, 1231 25th St. N.W., Washington, District of Columbia 20037. (202) 452-4200. 1986-. Biweekly. Review of developments in pollution laws, regulations and trends in government and industry.

Air/Water Pollution Report. Business Publishers, Inc., 951 Pershing Dr., Silver Spring, Maryland 20910-4464. (301) 587-6300. 1963-. Weekly. Reports on the hard news and in-depth features for practical use by environmental managers. It keeps readers informed on the latest news from government and industry. Also available online.

American Water Works Association Journal. American Water Works Association, 6666 W. Quincy Avenue, Denver, Colorado 80235. (303) 794-7711. Monthly. Articles on public water supply systems.

Aquatic Toxicology. Elsevier Science Publishing Co., 655 Avenue of the Americas, New York, New York 10010. (212) 989-5800. 1981-. 6/year.

The Bench Sheet. Water Pollution Control Federation, 601 Wythe Street, Alexandria, Virginia 22314-1994. (703) 684-2400. Bimonthly. Articles on water and wastewater laboratory analysis.

Bulletin of the California Water Pollution Control Association. California Water Pollution Control Association, Box 575, Lafayette, California 94549. (415) 284-1778. 1954-. Quarterly. Membership activity reports, environmental concerns and papers.

Buzzworm: The Environmental Journal. Buzzworm Inc., 2305 Canyon Blvd., No. 206, Boulder, Colorado 80302-5655. (303) 442-1969. 1988-. Quarterly. An independent environmental journal for the reader interested in nature, adventure, travel, the natural environment and the issues of conservation.

Clean Water. The Water Quality Bureau of the Division of Environment, Idaho Dept. of Health and Welfare, 450 W. State St., Boise, Idaho 83720. (208) 334-5855. Quarterly. Water quality and water pollution control in Idaho.

Clearwaters. New York Water Pollution Control Association, 90 Presidential Plaza, Suite 122, Syracuse, New York 13202. (315) 422-7811. 1971-. Quarterly. Articles on design methods, legislation, and innovations on wastewater treatment plants.

Environment Midwest. U.S. Environmental Protection Agency, 230 S. Dearborn, Chicago, Illinois 60604. (312) 353-2072. Monthly. Programs for fighting air and water pollution, hazardous and solid wastes, toxicants, pesticides, noise, and radiation.

Environment Ohio. Ohio Environmental Protection Agency, PO Box 1049, Columbus, Ohio 43216. (614) 644-2160. Bimonthly. Air, water, land pollution, and public water supply.

Environment Reporter. Bureau of National Affairs, 1231 25th St. NW, Washington, District of Columbia 20037. (800) 372-1033. Weekly. Issues of pollution control and environmental activity. Also available online.

Environmental Geology & Water Sciences. Springer-Verlag, 175 Fifth Avenue, New York, New York 10010. (212) 460-1500. Bimonthly. Covers interactions between humanity and Earth.

Environmental Health Letter. Business Publishers, Inc., 951 Pershing Dr., Silver Spring, Maryland 20910-4464. (301) 587-6300. 1961-. Biweekly. Covers areas such as: indoor air, asbestos health effects, toxic substances testing, health problems at wastewater plants, risk-based sludge rules, medical waste, developmental toxicity risk assessment, animal carcinogen tests, pesticide risk, air toxics, aerospace chemicals, lead, radionuclide emissions, state right-to-know statutes, and incinerator emissions.

Environmental Pollution & Control. National Technical Information Service, 5285 Port Royal Rd., Springfield, Virginia 22161. (703) 487-4650. Weekly. Covers air, noise, solid waste, water pollution, radiation, environmental health and safety, pesticide pollution and control.

Environmental Progress. American Institute of Chemical Engineers, 345 E. 47th St., New York, New York 10017. (212) 705-7338. Quarterly. Deals with environmental policies, protection and management-especially relating to chemicals.

Environmental Protection Magazine. Stevens Publishing Co., 225 New Road, PO Box 2604, Waco, Texas 76702-2573. (817) 776-9000. Air and water pollution, wastewater and hazardous materials.

Environmental Regulation From the State Capital: Waste Disposal and Pollution Control. Wakeman/Walworth, 300 N. Washington St., Alexandria, Virginia 22314. (703) 549-8606. Legislative action concerning pollution control.

Environmental Resources Research Institute, Newsletter. Environmental Resources Research Institute, Pennsylvania State University, University Park, Pennsylvania 16802. (814) 863-0291. Quarterly. Land, water, air, and mining.

Environmental Technology and Economics. Technomic Publishing Co., 750 Summer St., Stamford, Connecticut 06902. (717) 291-5609. 1966-. Semimonthly.

EPA Journal. U.S. Environmental Protection Agency, 401 M St., S.W., A-107, Washington, District of Columbia 20460. (202) 382-4393. Bimonthly. Air and water pollution, pesticides, noise, solid waste.

European Water Pollution Control. European Water Pollution Control Association, Elsevier Science Pub., PO Box 211, 1000 AE, Amsterdam, Netherlands 1991-. Bimonthly. Discussion of views, policies, strategies, directives and guidelines, design procedures, technical ideas and solutions, performance and experience in

construction, maintenance and operation of water pollution control.

Federal Water Quality Association Newsletter. Federal Water Quality Association, P.O. Box 44163, Washington, District of Columbia 20026. (202) 447-4925. Seven times a year. Concerns sewage and industrial waste treatment and disposal.

Federation Highlights. Water Pollution Control Federation, 601 Wythe St., Alexandria, Virginia 22314-1994. (703) 684-2400. Monthly. News and trends in water pollution control.

Georgia Operator. Georgia Water and Pollution Control Association, 2532 Bolton Rd. N.W., Atlanta, Georgia 30318. 1963-. Quarterly.

Ground Water Monitor. Business Publishers, Inc., 951 Pershing Dr., Silver Spring, Maryland 20910-4464. (301) 587-6300. Biweekly. Legislation, litigation, regulations and quality problems on ground water. Also available online.

Ground Water Monitoring Review. Water Well Journal Publishing Co. National Water Well Association, 6375 Riverside Drive, Dublin, Ohio 43017. (614) 761-3222. Quarterly. Covers protection and restoration of ground water.

Ground Water Newsletter. Water Information Center, Inc., 125 East Bethpage Road, Plainview, New York 11803. (516) 249-7634. Biweekly. Covers ground water exploration, development, and management.

Ground Water Pollution News. Buraff Publications, 1350 Connecticut Ave., NW, Washington, District of Columbia 20036. (202) 862-0990. Biweekly. Legislation, regulation and litigation concerning ground water pollution.

Journal of Environmental Engineering. American Society for Civil Engineers, 345 East 47th Street, New York, New York 10017. (212) 705-7496. Bimonthly. Covers problems in the environment and sanitation.

Journal of Environmental Health. National Environmental Health Association, 720 South Colorado Boulevard, Suite 970, Denver, Colorado 80222. (303) 756-9090. Bimonthly. Covers phases in environmental health.

Journal of the Water Pollution Control Federation. Water Pollution Control Federation, 801 Wythe St., Alexandria, Virginia 22314-1994. (703) 684-2400. Monthly. Deals with sewage and pollution.

Journal of Water Resources Planning and Management. American Society of Civil Engineers, Resource Planning and Management Division, 345 E. 47th St., New York, New York 10017. (212) 705-7288; (800) 548-2723. 1983-. Quarterly. Reports on all phases of planning and management of water resources. Examines social, economic, environmental, and administrative concerns relating to the use and conservation of water.

Multinational Environmental Outlook. Business Publishers, Inc., 951 Pershing Dr., Silver Spring, Maryland 20910-4464. (301) 587-6300. 1974-. Biweekly. Covers developments in world environmental problems such as acid rain, deforestation, soil erosion, overfishing, threats to health, animal extinction, population growth, diminishing water supply and other related matters. Also available online.

NEIWPCC Aqua News. New England Interstate Water Pollution Control Commission, 607 Boylston St., Boston, Massachusetts 02116. 1970-. Quarterly.

Official Bulletin of the North Dakota Water and Pollution Control Conference. North Dakota State Health Dept., Bismarck, North Dakota 58501. (701) 224-2354. Quarterly. Municipal water and waste systems and industrial wastes.

Pollution Engineering. Cahners Publishing Co., 249 W. 17th St., New York, New York 10011. (212) 645-0067. 1969-. Monthly.

Pollution Equipment News. Rimbach Publishing, Inc., 8650 Babcock Boulevard, Pittsburgh, Pennsylvania 15237. (412) 364-5366. Bimonthly. Covers new products, techniques, and literature.

Research Journal of the Water Pollution Control Federation. Water Pollution Control Federation, 601 Wythe St., Alexandria, Virginia 22314-1994. (800) 556-8700. Bimonthly. Covers area water pollution, sewage and sewage treatment.

Texas Water Report. Report Publications, P.O. Box 12368, Austin, Texas 78711. (512) 478-5663. Weekly. Covers water pollution, waste, and conservation.

Waste Disposal and Pollution Control. Wakeman/Walworth, P.O. Box 1939, New Haven, Connecticut 06509. (203) 562-8518. Monthly. Covers air and water pollution, toxic waste, and acid rain.

Water, Air, and Soil Pollution. Kluwer Academic Publishers, 101 Philip Dr., Assinippi Park, Norwell, Massachusetts 02061. (617) 871-6600. Bimonthly. Covers water, soil, and air pollution. This is an international journal on environmental pollution dealing with all types of pollution including acid rain.

Water and Pollution Control. Southam Business Pub. Inc., 1450 Don Mills Rd., Don Mills, Ontario, Canada M3B 2X7. 1893-. Monthly. Formerly Canada Municipal Utilities.

Water and Wastes Digest. Scranton Gillette Communications, Inc., 380 Northwest Highway, Des Plaines, Illinois 60016. (708) 298-6622. Bimonthly. Covers publicly and privately owned water and sewage systems.

Water Pollution Newsletter. Water Information Center Inc., 7 High St., Huntington, New York 11743.

Water Research. International Association on Water Pollution Research and Control. Pergamon Microforms International, Inc., Fairview Park, New York 10523. (914) 592-7720. 1966-. Monthly. Covers all aspects of the pollution of marine and fresh water and the management of water quality as well as water resources.

Water Science and Technology. Pergamon Microforms International Inc., Fairview Park, Elmsford, New York 10523. (914) 592-7720. Monthly. Covers water, pollution, sewage, purification, and water quality management.

RESEARCH CENTERS AND INSTITUTES

Auburn University, Water Resources Research Institute. 202 Hargis Hall, Auburn University, Alabama 36849-5124. (205) 844-5080.

Michigan State University, Institute of Water Research. 334 Natural Resources Building, East Lansing, Michigan 48824. (517) 353-3742.

Stella Duncan Memorial Research Institute. University of Montana, Missoula, Montana 59812. (406) 243-6676.

University of Nebraska-Lincoln, Water Center. 103 Natural Resources Hall, Lincoln, Nebraska 68503-0844. (402) 472-3305.

University of Southern California, Sea Grant Program. University Park, Los Angeles, California 90089-1231. (213) 740-1961.

University of Wyoming, Wyoming Water Research Center. Box 3067, University Station, Laramie, Wyoming 82071. (307) 766-2143.

Water Pollution Control Federation Research Foundation. 601 Wythe St., Alexandria, Virginia 22314-1994. (703) 684-2400.

Wisconsin Applied Water Pollution Research Consortium. University of Wisconsin-Madison, 3204 Engineering Building, 1415 Johnson Dr., Madison, Wisconsin 53706. (608) 262-7248.

STATISTICS SOURCES

America in the 21st Century: The Demographic Dimension: Environmental Concerns. Population Reference Bureau, P.O. Box 96152, Washington, District of Columbia 20090-6152. Distribution of pollution by source.

The Market for Water Pollution Control Equipment & Services. FIND/SVP, 625 Avenue of the Americas, New York, New York 10011. (212) 645-4500. Chemicals and supplies; equipment and instruments; engineering and analytical services.

OECD Environmental Data Compendium 1989. OECD Publications and Information Center, 2001 L St. N.W., Suite 700, Washington, District of Columbia 20036. (202) 785-OECD. 1989. Provides statistical data for OECD countries on air pollution, water pollution, the marine environment, land use, forests, wildlife, solid waste, noise and radioactivity. Also provides data on the underlying pressures on the environment such as energy use, transportation, industrial activity and agriculture.

The State of the Environment. OECD Publications and Information Center, 2001 L St., N.W., Suite 700, Washington, District of Columbia 20036. (202) 785-6323. 1991.

TRADE ASSOCIATIONS AND PROFESSIONAL SOCIETIES

American Society of Civil Engineers. 345 East 47th St., New York, New York 10017. (212) 705-7496.

American Society of Sanitary Engineering. Box 40362, Bay Village, Ohio 44140. (216) 835-3040.

American Water Resources Association. 5410 Grosvenor Lane, Suite 220, Bethesda, Maryland 20814. (301) 493-8600.

American Water Works Association. 6666 W. Quincy Ave., Denver, Colorado 80235. (303) 794-7711.

Association of Metropolitan Water Agencies. 1717 K St., N.W., Suite 1102, Washington, District of Columbia 20036. (202) 331-2820.

Association of the State and Interstate Water Pollution Control Administrators. 444 North Capitol St., N.W., Suite 330, Washington, District of Columbia 20001. (202) 624-7782.

Clean Water Action Project. c/o David Zwick, 1320 18th St. N.W., Washington, District of Columbia 20003. (202) 457-1286.

Federal Water Quality Association. PO Box 44163, Washington, District of Columbia 20026. (202) 447-4925.

Friends of the Earth. 218 D St., SE, Washington, District of Columbia 20003. (202) 544-2600.

Interstate Conference on Water Policy. 955 L'Enfant Plaza, 6th Floor, Washington, District of Columbia 20024. (202) 466-7287.

Natural Resources Defense Council. 40 W. 20th St., New York, New York 10011. (212) 727-2700.

Water Environment Federation. 601 Wythe St., Alexandria, Virginia 22314-1994. (703) 684-2400. Formerly, Water Pollution Control Federation.

WATER PURIFICATION

See also: BIOLOGICAL TREATMENT; WASTEWATER TREATMENT; WATER QUALITY; WETLANDS

ABSTRACTING AND INDEXING SERVICES

Abstracts of Air and Water Conservation Literature. American Petroleum Institute. Central Abstracting and Indexing Service, 275 Madison Avenue, New York, New York 10016. 1972.

Aqualine Abstracts. Water Research Centre. c/o Pergamon Microforms International, Inc., Fairview Park, Elmsford, New York 10523. (914) 592-7720. 1927-. Contains some 8,000 records annually on water and wastewater technology. Covers all aspects of water, wastewater, associated engineering services and the aquatic environment. Over 600 periodicals, as well as books, reports and conference proceedings and other publications from water related institutions worldwide are scanned. Also available online.

ASFA Aquaculture Abstracts. Cambridge Scientific Abstracts, Inc., 5161 River Rd., Bethesda, Maryland 20816. (301) 961-6750. 1984.

Bulletin Signaletique: Eau et Assainissement, Pollution Atmospherique, Droit des Pollutions. Centre de Documentation, Centre National de la Recherche Scientifique, 15, quai Anatole France, Paris, France 75700. (1) 45 55 92 25. 1983-. Monthly. Indexes pollution periodicals including water, atmospheric and related pollutions.

Chemical Abstracts. Chemical Abstracts Service, 2540 Olentangy River Rd., PO Box 3012, Columbus, Ohio 43210. (800) 848-6533. 1907-.

Current Advances in Ecological and Environmental Science. Pergamon Microforms International, Inc., Fairview Park, Elmsford, New York 10523. (914) 592-7720. 1989-. Monthly. Current literature searching service includingjournals, reports, abstracts, etc. This service is available online as part of the CABS database on the hosts BRS and ORBIT search service.

Desalination Abstracts. National Center for Scientific and Technological Information, PO Box 20125, Tel-Aviv, Israel 1966-. Quarterly.

Ecological Abstracts. Geo Abstracts Ltd. Elsevier Applied Science, Crown House, Linton Rd., Barking, England IG 11 8JU. 1974-. Derived from over 600 leading ecological and environmental journals, plus books, conference proceedings, reports and theses.

Engineering Index. The Engineering Index Inc., 345 E. 47th St., New York, New York 10017. 1962-.

General Science Index. H. W. Wilson Co., 950 University Ave., Bronx, New York 10452. 1978-. Monthly, also issued in annual cumulation. Cumulative subject index to English language periodicals in the subject fields of astronomy, botany, chemistry, earth science, environment and conservation, food and nutrition, genetics, mathematics, medicine and health, microbiology, oceanography, physics, physiology and zoology.

Index to Scientific Book Contents. Institute for Scientific Information, 3501 Market St., Philadelphia, Pennsylvania 19104. (800) 523-1857. 1985-. Annual. Gives contents of science books published.

Pollution Abstracts. Cambridge Scientific Abstracts, 5161 River Rd., Bethesda, Maryland 20816. (301) 961-6750. Six/year. Indexes worldwide technical literature on environmental pollution. Covers air pollution, marine and freshwater pollution, sewage and wastewater treatment, waste management, toxicology and health, noise pollution, radiation, land pollution, and environmental policies, programs, legislation, and education. Also available online.

Science Citation Index. Institute for Scientific Information, 3501 Market St., Philadelphia, Pennsylvania 19104. 1961-.

Urban Affairs Abstracts. National League of Cities, 1301 Pennsylvania Ave., NW, Washington, District of Columbia 20004. (202) 626-3150. 1977-. Weekly.

BIBLIOGRAPHIES

Current Contents. Agriculture, Biology and Environmental Sciences. Institute for Scientific Information, 3501 Market St., Philadelphia, Pennsylvania 19104. (800) 523-1857. 1973-. Previous title: Current Contents. Agricultural, Food & Veterinary Sciences. Gives the table of contents of periodicals in the fields of agriculture, biology, environmental and related areas.

Desalination Technology. Vance Bibliographies, PO Box 229, 112 N. Charter St., Monticello, Illinois 61856. (217) 762-3831. 1981.

DIRECTORIES

American Water Works Association–Buyers' Guide Issue. American Water Works Association, 6666 W. Quincy Ave., Denver, Colorado 80235. (303) 794-7711.

Desalination Directory: Desalination and Water Purification. Elsevier Science Publishing Co., 655 Avenue of the Americas, New York, New York 10010. (212) 989-5800. 1981-.

Water Conditioning & Purification–Buyers Guide Issue. Publicom, Inc., 4651 N. First Ave., Suite 101, Tucson, Arizona 85718. (602) 293-5446.

Water Environment & Technology–Buyer's Guide and Yearbook. Water Pollution Control Federation, 601 Wythe St., Alexandria, Virginia 22314-1994. (703) 684-2400.

Water Softening Equipment Service Directory. American Business Directories, Inc., 5711 S. 86th Circle, Omaha, Nebraska 68127. (402) 593-4600.

Water Systems Council and Pitless Adapter Division–Membership Directory. Pitless Adapter Division/ Water Systems Council, 600 S. Federal St., Suite 400, Chicago, Illinois 60605. (312) 922-6222.

Water Technology–Directory of Manufacturers and Suppliers Issue. National Trade Publications, Inc., 13 Century Hill Dr., Latham, New York 12110. (518) 783-1281.

Water Technology–Planning & Purchasing Handbook Issue. National Trade Publications, Inc., 13 Century Hill Dr., Latham, New York 12110. (518) 783-1281.

ENCYCLOPEDIAS AND DICTIONARIES

Dictionary of Environmental Engineering and Related Sciences: English-Spanish, Spanish-English. Jose T. Villate. Ediciones Universal, 3090 SW 8th St., Miami, Florida 33135. (305) 642-3355. 1979.

Dictionary of Environmental Protection Technology: In Four Languages, English, German, French, Russian. Egon Seidel. Elsevier Science Publishing Co., 655 Avenue of the Americas, New York, New York 10010. (212) 984-5800. 1988.

Encyclopedia of Environmental Science and Engineering. J.R. Pfafflin. Gordon and Breach Science Publishers, Inc., 270 8th Ave., New York, New York 10011. (212) 206-8900. 1992.

The Encyclopedia of Geochemistry and Environmental Sciences. Rhodes Whitmore Fairbridge. Van Nostrand Reinhold Co., 115 5th Ave., New York, New York 10003. (212) 254-3232. 1972.

Environmental Engineering Dictionary. C. C. Lee. Government Institutes, Inc., 4 Research Pl., Ste. 200, Rockville, Maryland 20850. (301) 921-2300. 1989. Defines over 6000 engineering terms relating to pollutioncontrol technologies, monitoring, risk assessment, sampling andanalysis, quality control, permitting, and environmentally-regulated engineering and science. Includes bibliographical references (p. 612-627).

Grzimek's Encyclopedia of Ecology. Bernhard Grzimek. Van Nostrand Reinhold, 115 5th Ave., New York, New York 10003. (212) 254-3232. 1976.

McGraw-Hill Encyclopedia of Environmental Science. Sybil P. Parker. McGraw-Hill Science & Engineering Books, 11 W. 19th St., New York, New York 10011. (212) 337-6010. 1980. Covers ecology, man's influence on nature, and environmental protection.

North American Reference Encyclopedia of Ecology and Pollution. William White. North American Pub. Co., 401 N. Broad St., Philadelphia, Pennsylvania 19108. (215) 238-5300. 1972.

Van Nostrand's Scientific Encyclopedia. Glenn D. Considine, ed. Van Nostrand Reinhold, 115 5th Ave., New York, New York 10003. (212) 254-3232. 1983. Sixth edition. Includes all broad subject areas in science.

GENERAL WORKS

Adsorption Technology for Air and Water Pollution Control. Kenneth E. Noll. Lewis Publishers, 200 Corporate Blvd. NW, Boca Raton, Florida 33431. (407) 994-0555 or (800)272-7737. 1991. Contains useful information on adsorption technology which can be applied in both air and water pollution.

AWWA Standard for Liquid Chlorine: American National Standard. American National Standards Institute. American Water Works Association, 6666 W. Quincy Ave., Denver, Colorado 80235. (303) 794-7711. 1987.

Basic Math Concepts for Water and Wastewater Plant Operators. Joanne Kirkpatrick Price. Technomic Publishing Co., 851 New Holland Ave., Box 3535, Lancaster, Pennsylvania 17604. (717) 291-5609. 1991.

Biofouling and Biocorrosion in Industrial Water Systems. Hans C. Flemming, ed. Springer-Verlag, 175 5th Ave., New York, New York 10010. (212) 460-1500. 1991.

The Chemistry of Chlorine and Chlorination. Frank Nickols. State of Illinois Environmental Protection Agency, 2200 Churchill Rd., Springfield, Illinois 62706. (217) 782-2829. 1990.

Contamination of Ground Water Prevention, Assessment, Restoration. Michael Barcelona, et al. Noyes Publications, 120 Mill Rd., Park Ridge, New Jersey 07656. (201) 391-8484. 1990. Provides regulatory agencies and industry a convenient source of technical information on the management of contaminated ground water.

Cover Crops for Clean Water. W. L. Hargrove, ed. Soil and Water Conservation Society, 7515 Northeast Ankeny Rd., Ankeny, Iowa 50021-9764. (515) 289-2331; (800) THE-SOIL. 1991. Includes the latest information on the role of cover crops in water quality management, including means of reducing water runoff, soil erosion, agrichemical loss in runoff, and nitrate leaching to groundwater.

Desalination and Water Re-Use. Miriam Balaban, ed. Institution of Chemical Engineers, c/o Hemisphere Pub., 1900 Frost Rd., Suite 101, Bristol, Pennsylvania 19007-1598. (215) 785-5800. 1991. Four volumes. Includes the papers presented at a four-day symposium organized by the Institution of Chemical Engineers (UK) on behalf of the European Federation of Chemical Engineers Working Parties on Desalination and Water Technology and the Membrane Society.

Desalination Materials Manual. Dow Chemical Company. Office of Water Research and Technology, U.S. Dept. of the Interior, Washington, District of Columbia 20240. 1975.

Design of Water Quality Monitoring Systems. Robert C. Ward. Van Nostrand Reinhold, 115 5th Ave., New York, New York 10003. (212) 254-3232. 1990. Describes the essential tools to design a system that gets consistently valid results. Features the latest methods of sampling and lab analysis, data handling and analysis, reporting, and information utilization, and includes case studies of system design projects.

Drinking Water and Groundwater Remediation Cost Evaluation: Air Stripping. Robert M. Clark and Jeffrey Q. Adams. Lewis Publishers, 2000 Corporate Blvd. N.W., Boca Raton, Florida 33431. (800) 272-7737. 1991. The new software program shows air stripping costs and performance of the remediation of hazardous waste sites or drinking water treatment. The program helps do cost comparisons of the technology against other available technologies.

Drinking Water and Groundwater Remediation Cost Evaluation: Granular Activated Carbon. Robert M. Clark and Jeffrey Q. Adams. Lewis Publishers, 2000 Corporate Blvd. N.W., Boca Raton, Florida 33431. (800) 272-7737. 1991. Shows GAC costs and performance forthe remediation of hazardous waste sites or drinking watertreatment. Compares the cost of the technology against other available technologies.

Drinking Water Treatment. P. Toft, et al., eds. Pergamon Microforms International, Inc., Fairview Park, Elmsford, New York 10523. (914) 592-7720. 1989. Proceedings of the 3d National Conference on Drinking Water, St. John's Newfoundland, Canada, June 12-14, 1988. Discussions concerned all aspects of design, construction and operation of small systems for the provision and treatment of drinking water.

Dynamic Modeling and Expert Systems in Wastewater Engineering. Giles G. Patry and David Chapman. Lewis Publishers, 200 Corporate Blvd. NW, Boca Raton, Florida 33431. (407) 994-0555 or (800)272-7737. 1988. Result of a workshop held at McMaster University (May 19-20, 1988). Brings together current work on dynamic modelling and expert systems as applied to the design, operation and control of waste- water treatment systems.

Environmental Impact and Health Effects of Wastewater Chlorination. Gary R. Brenniman. Institute of Natural Resources, Chicago, Illinois 1981. Physiological and environmental aspects of chlorination.

An Evaluation of Streaming Current Detectors. Steven Keith Dentel. AWWA Research Foundation, 6666 W. Quincy Ave., Denver, Colorado 80235. (303) 794-7711. 1988. Evaluation of water current meters.

Guidance Manual for Compliance with the Filtration and Disinfection Requirements for Public Water Systems Using Surface Water Sources. American Water Works Association, 6666 W. Quincy Ave., Denver, Colorado 80235. (303) 794-7711. 1991.

Health Effects of Drinking Water Treatment Technologies. Lewis Publishers, 200 Corporate Blvd. NW, Boca Raton, Florida 33431. (407) 994-0555 or (800)272-7737. 1989. Evaluates the public health impact from the most widespread drinking water treatment technologies, with particular emphasis on disinfection. Focuses solely on the most common treatment technologies and practices used today.

Integrated Design of Water Treatment Facilities. Susumu Kawamura. John Wiley & Sons, Inc., 605 3rd Ave, New York, New York 10158-0012. (212) 850-6000. 1991. Covers research pilot studies and preliminary design studies, as well as the actual design, construction and plant management. Covers the entire project sequence, describing not only very basic and essential design criteria, but also how to design each phase to maximize overall efficiency while minimizing operation and maintenance costs.

New Health Considerations in Water Treatment. Roger Holdsworth, ed. Avebury Technical, Gower House, Croft Rd., Aldershot, England GU11 3HR. (0252) 331551. 1991.

Point-of-Use/Entry Treatment of Drinking Water. Noyes Publications, 120 Mill Rd., Park Ridge, New Jersey 07656. (201) 391-8484. 1990. Covers the administrative and technical aspects of utilizing POU/POE systems to solve individual and small community drinking water problems.

Small Water Purification Systems. Richard B. Case. U.S. Department of the Interior, Bureau of Land Management, 2850 Youngfield St., Denver, Colorado 80215. (303) 239-3700. 1981. Covers water, purification, equipment, supplies, and drinking water standards.

Surveillance of Drinking Water Quality in Rural Areas. Barry Lloyd. John Wiley & Sons, Inc., 605 3rd Ave, New York, New York 10158-0012. (212) 850-6000. 1991. Examines the human and technical resources required for monitoring, maintaining and improving the safety of rural water supply services. A practical guide to improving the quality of service from small water supplies, it describes the essential minimum of reliable methods of monitoring water quality and discusses new cost effective approaches to sanitary inspection of community water supplies.

Technologies for Small Water and Wastewater Systems. Edward J. Martin and Edward T. Martin. Van Nostrand Reinhold, 115 5th Ave., New York, New York 10003. (212) 254-3232. 1991. Addresses how to exploit different water treatment technologies according to available resources. Includes extensive sections on costs and design of both established and new technologies with vital data on limitations, operations and maintenance, control and special factors.

Technologies for Upgrading Existing or Designing New Drinking Water Treatment Facilities. Office of Drinking Water, Center for Environmental Research Information, U.S. Environmental Protection Agency. Technomic Publishing Co., 851 New Holland Ave., Box 3535, Lancaster, Pennsylvania 17604. (717) 291-5609. 1991. Discusses drinking water treatment technologies that address contamination and contaminant categories regulated under the Safe Drinking Water Act and its 1986 amendments.

The Washington Conference on Underground Storage, July 15-16, 1985, Stouffer Concourse. Center for Energy and Environmental Management, Washington, District of Columbia (202) 543-3939.

Water Chlorination: Chemistry, Environmental Impact and Health Effects. Robert L. Jolley, et al., eds. Lewis Publishers, 2000 Corporate Blvd., N.W., Boca Raton, Florida 33431. (407) 994-0555 or (800) 272-7737. 1990. Proceedings of the 6th conference on Water Contamination held in Oak Ridge, Tennessee, May 3-8, 1987. Includes all the ramifications of water chlorination practice and presents the most significant original research and developments of recent occurrence.

Water Supply and Treatment. Jack G. Walters, ed. TAPPI Press, Technology Park/Atlanta, PO Box 105113, Atlanta, Georgia 30348. (404) 446-1400. 1989. In-depth study of water use in the pulp and paper industry. Covers selection of equipment for a water treatment system, raw water treatment, clarification, lime soda softening, filtration, demineralizers, cooling systems and cooling water treatment and pumping systems.

Water Treatment: Principles and Design. James M. Montgomery. John Wiley & Sons, Inc., 605 3rd Ave., New York, New York 10158-0012. (212) 850-6000. 1985. Offers a comprehensive coverage of the principles and design of water quality and treatment programs, plus plant operations.

GOVERNMENTAL ORGANIZATIONS

U.S. Environmental Protection Agency: Office of Wetlands Protection. 401 M St., S.W., Washington, District of Columbia 20460. (202) 382-7946.

HANDBOOKS AND MANUALS

Desalination Processes and Multistage Flash Distillation Practice. Arshad Hassan Khan. Elsevier Science Publishing Co., 655 Avenue of the Americas, New York, New York 10010. (212) 984-5800. 1986. Saline water conservation through flash distillation process.

Desalting Handbook for Planners. Catalytic Inc. U.S. Department of the Interior, Office of Water Research and Technology, Washington, District of Columbia 20240. 1979. 2d ed.

The Drinking Water Book: A Complete Guide to Safe Drinking Water. Colin Ingram. Ten Speed Press, P.O. Box 7123, Berkeley, California 94707. (800) 841-2665. 1991. Discusses potential pollutants and their sources in drinking water. Includes water testing and methods for reducing pollutants in the home water supply.

The EPA Manual for Waste Minimization Opportunity Assessments. U.S. Environmental Protection Agency. Technomic Publishing Co., 851 New Holland Ave., Box 3535, Lancaster, Pennsylvania 17604. (717) 291-5609. 1990.

Groundwater Chemicals Desk Reference. John H. Montgomery. Lewis Publishers, 2000 Corporate Blvd. NW, Boca Raton, Florida 33431. (407) 994-0555 or (800)272-7737. 1990. Protection and remediation of the groundwater environment. Includes profiles of chemical compounds promulgated by the EPA under the Clean Water Act of 1977.

The Handbook of Chlorination. George Clifford White. Van Nostrand Reinhold Co., 115 Fifth Ave., New York, New York 10003. (212) 254-3232. 1986. Water purification through chlorination.

Handbook of Methods for Acid Deposition Studies: Field Methods for Surface Water Chemistry. D. J. Chaloud, et al. U.S. Environmental Protection Agency, Office of Modeling, Monitoring Systems, and Quality Assurance, 401 M St., SW, Washington, District of Columbia 20460. (202) 260-2090. 1990-.

Handbook of Water Purification. Walter Lorch. Halsted Press, 605 3rd Ave., New York, New York 10158. (212) 850-6000.

Hazardous Materials Spills Emergency Handbook. American Water Works Association, 6666 W. Quincy Ave., Denver, Colorado 80235. (303) 794-7711. Covers chemical safety measures, water pollution, and water purification.

Is Your Water Safe to Drink?. Raymond Gabler. Consumer Union U.S., New York, New York 1988. Health, microbial, inorganic, and organic hazards in drinking water, chlorination, bottled water, and water shortages.

Practical Handbook of Ground Water Monitoring. David M. Nielsen. Lewis Publishers, 2000 Corporate Blvd., N.W., Boca Raton, Florida 33431. (407) 994-0555 or (800) 272-7737. 1991. Covers the complete spectrum of state-of-the-science technology applied to investigations of ground water quality. Emphasis is placed on the practical application of current technology, and minimum theory is discussed.

Water Treatment Handbook. Degremont s.a., 184, ave. du 18-Juin-1940, Rueil-Malmaison, France F-92500. 1991. Sixth edition. Part 1 is a general survey of water and its action on the materials with which it comes into contact, and theoretical principles of separation and correction processes used in water treatment. Part 2 describes the process and the treatment plant beginning with the separation process.

ONLINE DATA BASES

Chemical Abstracts-CA. Chemical Abstracts Service, 2540 Olentangy River Rd., P.O. Box 3012, Columbus, Ohio 43210. (800) 848-6533 or (614) 421-3600. Information sources include 9000 journals, patents from 27 countries, two industrial property organizations, new books, conference proceedings, and government research reports.

Computerized Engineering Index–COMPENDEX. Engineering Information Inc., 345 E. 47th St., New York, New York 10017. (212) 705-7600.

Environmental Fate Databases. Syracuse Research Cooperation, Merrill Lane, Syracuse, New York 13210. (312) 426-3200. Environmental fate of chemicals.

Monthly Catalog of United States Government Publications. U.S. G.P.O., Supt. of Docs., PO Box 371954, Pittsburgh, Pennsylvania 15250-7954. (202) 512-0000.

National Technical Information Service. U.S. Department of Commerce, National Technical Information Service, Office of Data Base Services, 5285 Port Royal Rd., Springfield, Virginia 22161. (703) 487-4807. Bibliographic database of government sponsored research and technical reports.

PressNet Environmental Reports. Chemical Information Systems, Inc., 7215 York Rd., Baltimore, Maryland 21212. (301) 321-8440.

SCISEARCH. Institute for Scientific Information, University City Science Center, 3501 Market St., Philadelphia, Pennsylvania 19104. (215) 386-0100.

PERIODICALS AND NEWSLETTERS

The Bench Sheet. Water Pollution Control Federation, 601 Wythe Street, Alexandria, Virginia 22314-1994. (703) 684-2400. Bimonthly. Articles on water and wastewater laboratory analysis.

Clean Water Action News. Clean Water Action Project, 317 Pennsylvania Ave. S.E., Washington, District of Columbia 20003. (202) 547-1196. 1976-. Quarterly. Features news and articles on environmental political issues.

Clean Water Report. Business Publishers, Inc., 951 Pershing Dr., Silver Spring, Maryland 20910-4464. (301) 587-6300. 1964-. Biweekly. Key information source for environmental professionals, covering the important issues: groundwater, drinking water, wastewater treatment, drought, wetlands, coastal protection, dioxin, non-point source pollution, agrichemical contamination, cleanup versus prevention issues, and related topics.

Clearwaters. New York Water Pollution Control Association, 90 Presidential Plaza, Suite 122, Syracuse, New York 13202. (315) 422-7811. 1971-. Quarterly. Articles on design methods, legislation, and innovations on wastewater treatment plants.

Desalination. Elsevier, Box 211, Amsterdam, Netherlands 1000 AE. 020-5803-911. 1966-. Forty-two times a year. The international journal on the science and technology of desalting and water purification. Formed by the merger of the Journal of Membrane Science and Desalination.

Desalination and Water Re-Use Technologies in Japan. Annual Report. Water Re-Use Promotion Center, Landix Akasaka Bldg, 2-3-4, Akasaka, Minato-ku, Tokyo, Japan 1981-. Annual.

Drinking Water & Backflow Prevention. Elizabeth Gold, PO Box 33209, Northglenn, Colorado 80233. (303) 451-0980. Monthly. Safety standards, water system protection, training programs, cross-connection control, and issues related to preventing the contamination of potable drinking water supplies with backflow prevention devices.

Environmental Progress. American Institute of Chemical Engineers, 345 E. 47th St., New York, New York 10017. (212) 705-7338. Quarterly. Deals with environmental policies, protection and management-especially relating to chemicals.

Federal Water Quality Association Newsletter. Federal Water Quality Association, P.O. Box 44163, Washington, District of Columbia 20026. (202) 447-4925. Seven times a year. Concerns sewage and industrial waste treatment and disposal.

International Water Report. Water Information Center, Inc., 125 East Bethpage Road, Plainview, New York 11803. (516) 249-7634. Quarterly. Covers water works and topics done in Europe, Asia, South America.

Pollution Engineering. Cahners Publishing Co., 249 W. 17th St., New York, New York 10011. (212) 645-0067. 1969-. Monthly.

Pure Water from the Sea. International Desalination Association, Box 328, Englewood, New Jersey 07631. (201) 567-0188. Bimonthly.

Water Conditioning and Purification. Publicom Inc., 4651 N. 1st Ave., Suite 101, Tucson, Arizona 85718. (602) 293-5446. Monthly.

Water, Environment, and Technology. Water Pollution Control Federation, 601 Wythe St., Alexandria, Virginia 22314-1994. (703) 684-2400. Monthly.

Water Technology. National Trade Publications, Inc., 13 Century Hill Dr., Latham, New York 12110. (518) 783-1281. Monthly.

STATISTICS SOURCES

Public Water Supply. FIND/SVP, 625 Avenue of the Americas, New York, New York 10011. (212) 645-4500. 1991. Market for equipment, supplies and services sold to public water utilities.

Residential Water Purification. FIND/SVP, 625 Avenue of the Americas, New York, New York 10011. (212) 645-4500. Examines equipment sales, services and supplies, as well as renting and leasing.

The Water Purification Market. FIND/SVP, 625 Avenue of the Americas, New York, New York 10011. (212) 645-4500. 1991. State-of-the-art technologies and equipment

sold into each market sector, and the cost effectiveness of various treatment methods.

TRADE ASSOCIATIONS AND PROFESSIONAL SOCIETIES

American Society of Sanitary Engineering. Box 40362, Bay Village, Ohio 44140. (216) 835-3040.

American Water Resources Association. 5410 Grosvenor Lane, Suite 220, Bethesda, Maryland 20814. (301) 493-8600.

Association of State Drinking Water Administrators. 1911 N. Fort Myer Dr., Suite 400, Arlington, Virginia 22209. (703) 524-2428.

Association of the State and Interstate Water Pollution Control Administrators. 444 North Capitol St., N.W., Suite 330, Washington, District of Columbia 20001. (202) 624-7782.

Federal Water Quality Association. PO Box 44163, Washington, District of Columbia 20026. (202) 447-4925.

Legal Environmental Assistance Foundation. 1115 N. Gadsden St., Tallahassee, Florida 32303. (904) 681-2591.

National Wetlands Technical Council. 1616 P St., N.W., 2nd floor, Washington, District of Columbia 20036. (202) 328-5150.

Water Environment Federation. 601 Wythe St., Alexandria, Virginia 22314-1994. (703) 684-2400. Formerly, Water Pollution Control Federation.

Water Systems Council. 600 S. Federal St., Suite 400, Chicago, Illinois 60605. (312) 922-6222.

WATER QUALITY

ABSTRACTING AND INDEXING SERVICES

Abstracts of Air and Water Conservation Literature. American Petroleum Institute. Central Abstracting and Indexing Service, 275 Madison Avenue, New York, New York 10016. 1972.

Agrindex. AGRIS Coordinating Center, Via delle Terme di Caracalla, Rome, Italy I-00100. 61 0181-FA01. 1975-.

Applied Ecology Abstracts Studies in Renewable Natural Resources. Information Retrieval Ltd., 1911 Jefferson Davis Highway, Arlington, Virginia 22202. 1975-. Monthly.

Applied Science and Technology Index. H.W. Wilson Co., 950 University Ave., Bronx, New York 10452. (800) 367-6770. Formerly Industrial Arts Index.

Aqualine Abstracts. Water Research Centre. c/o Pergamon Microforms International, Inc., Fairview Park, Elmsford, New York 10523. (914) 592-7720. 1927-. Contains some 8,000 records annually on water and wastewater technology. Covers all aspects of water, wastewater, associated engineering services and the aquatic environment. Over 600 periodicals, as well as books, reports and conference proceedings and other publications from water related institutions worldwide are scanned. Also available online.

ASFA Aquaculture Abstracts. Cambridge Scientific Abstracts, Inc., 5161 River Rd., Bethesda, Maryland 20816. (301) 961-6750. 1984.

Biological and Agricultural Index. H.W. Wilson Co., 950 University Ave., Bronx, New York 10452. (800) 367-6770. 1916-. Monthly.

Bulletin Signaletique: Eau et Assainissement, Pollution Atmospherique, Droit des Pollutions. Centre de Documentation, Centre National de la Recherche Scientifique, 15, quai Anatole France, Paris, France 75700. (1) 45 55 92 25. 1983-. Monthly. Indexes pollution periodicals including water, atmospheric and related pollutions.

Chemical Abstracts. Chemical Abstracts Service, 2540 Olentangy River Rd., PO Box 3012, Columbus, Ohio 43210. (800) 848-6533. 1907-.

Civil Engineering Hydraulic Abstracts. BHRA Fluid Engineering, Air Science Co., PO Box 143, Corning, New York 14830. (607) 962-5591. Monthly. Abstracts of periodicals that publish in the areas of hydraulic engineering and other related topics.

Current Advances in Ecological and Environmental Science. Pergamon Microforms International, Inc., Fairview Park, Elmsford, New York 10523. (914) 592-7720. 1989-. Monthly. Current literature searching service includingjournals, reports, abstracts, etc. This service is available online as part of the CABS database on the hosts BRS and ORBIT search service.

Ecological Abstracts. Geo Abstracts Ltd. Elsevier Applied Science, Crown House, Linton Rd., Barking, England IG 11 8JU. 1974-. Derived from over 600 leading ecological and environmental journals, plus books, conference proceedings, reports and theses.

Ecology Abstracts. Cambridge Scientific Abstracts, 5161 River Rd., Bethesda, Maryland 20816. (301) 961-6750. Monthly.

Engineering Index. The Engineering Index Inc., 345 E. 47th St., New York, New York 10017. 1962-.

Food Science and Technology Abstracts. International Food Information Service, c/o National Food Laboratory, 6363 Clark Ave., Dublin, California 94568. (800) 336-3782. 1969-.

General Science Index. H. W. Wilson Co., 950 University Ave., Bronx, New York 10452. 1978-. Monthly, also issued in annual cumulation. Cumulative subject index to English language periodicals in the subject fields of astronomy, botany, chemistry, earth science, environment and conservation, food and nutrition, genetics, mathematics, medicine and health, microbiology, oceanography, physics, physiology and zoology.

Geographical Abstracts. London School of Economics, Dept. of Geography, Regency House, 34 Duke St., London, England 1966-. Continued by Geo Abstracts issued in 6 parts: Pt. A. Landforms and the quaternary; Pt. B. Biogeography and Climatology; Pt. C. Economic geography; Pt. D. Social geography and cartography; Pt. E. Sedimentology; Pt. F. Regional and community planning.

Index to Scientific Book Contents. Institute for Scientific Information, 3501 Market St., Philadelphia, Pennsylvania 19104. (800) 523-1857. 1985-. Annual. Gives contents of science books published.

Irrigation and Drainage Abstracts. C. A. B. International, 845 North Park Ave., Tucson, Arizona 85719. (602) 621-7897 or (800) 258-4841. 1975-. Quarterly. Subject areas scanned are: water management, irrigation of crop plants, drainage, soil water relations, plant water relations, salinity and toxicity problems, soil condition, evaporotranspiration, evaporation, land use, streams, water quality, and other related areas.

Microbiology Abstracts. Section A. Industrial and Applied Microbiology. Cambridge Scientific Abstracts, 5161 River Rd., Bethesda, Maryland 20816. (301) 961-6750. 1972-.

Mineralogical Abstracts. Mineralogical Society, 41 Queen's Gate, London, England SW7 5HR. 71 5847916. Quarterly. Abstracts of journal articles, conferences, technical reports and specialized books in the areas of minerals, clay minerals, economic minerals, ore deposits, environmental studies, experimental mineralogy, gemstones, geochemistry, petrology, lunar and planetary studies and other related areas in mineralogy.

Multimedia Index to Ecology. National Information Center for Educational Media, University of Southern California, Los Angeles, California 90007.

Pollution Abstracts. Cambridge Scientific Abstracts, 5161 River Rd., Bethesda, Maryland 20816. (301) 961-6750. Six/year. Indexes worldwide technical literature on environmental pollution. Covers air pollution, marine and freshwater pollution, sewage and wastewater treatment, waste management, toxicology and health, noise pollution, radiation, land pollution, and environmental policies, programs, legislation, and education. Also available online.

Science Citation Index. Institute for Scientific Information, 3501 Market St., Philadelphia, Pennsylvania 19104. 1961-.

ALMANACS AND YEARBOOKS

Steam-Electric Plant Air and Water Quality Control Data for the Year Ended...Summary Report. Federal Energy Regulatory Commission, Office of Electrical Power Regulation, 825 N. Capitol St. NE, Washington, District of Columbia 20426. (202) 208-0200. 1969-1973. Covers electric power-plants, air quality, and water quality.

BIBLIOGRAPHIES

1986 Water Quality Implications of Conservation Tillage: A Reference Guide. The Center, West Lafayette, Indiana 1986.

Current Contents. Agriculture, Biology and Environmental Sciences. Institute for Scientific Information, 3501 Market St., Philadelphia, Pennsylvania 19104. (800) 523-1857. 1973-. Previous title: Current Contents. Agricultural, Food & Veterinary Sciences. Gives the table of contents of periodicals in the fields of agriculture, biology, environmental and related areas.

New Publications of the Geological Survey. U.S. Department of the Interior, Geological Survey, 119 National Center, Reston, Virginia 22092. (703) 648-4460. 1984-. Monthly. Bibliography of geological publications and related government documents published by the Geological Survey.

Water Quality and Forestry. Jodee Kuske. National Agricultural Library, 10301 Baltimore Blvd., Beltsville, Maryland 20705-2351. (301) 504-5755. 1991.

Water Quality in Agriculture. National Agricultural Library, 10301 Baltimore Blvd., Beltsville, Maryland 20705-2351. (301) 504-5755. 1990.

DIRECTORIES

American Water Works Association–Buyers' Guide Issue. American Water Works Association, 6666 W. Quincy Ave., Denver, Colorado 80235. (303) 794-7711.

Citizen's Directory for Water Quality Abuses. Karen Firehock. Izaak Walton League of America, 1401 Wilson Dr., Level B, Arlington, Virginia 22209. (703) 528-1818. Annual. Environmental agencies, including state and regional offices interested in providing quality control by eliminating pollution and dumping of wastes into water resources.

Directory of State Certification Officers for Drinking Water Laboratories. Association of State Drinking Water Administrators, 1911 N. Fort Myer Dr., Arlington, Virginia 22209. (703) 524-2428.

National Registry of Laboratories Certified to Test for Drinking Water Parameters. Association of State Drinking Water Administrators, 1911 N. Fort Myer Dr., Arlington, Virginia 22209. (703) 524-2428. 1990. Annual.

Water Quality Association Directory. Water Quality Association, 4151 Naperville Rd., Lisle, Illinois 60532. (708) 505-0160. Annual.

ENCYCLOPEDIAS AND DICTIONARIES

Cambridge Encyclopedia of Life Sciences. A. E. Friday and David S. Ingram. Cambridge University Press, 40 W 20th St., New York, New York 10011. (212) 924-3900 or (800) 227-0247. 1985. Includes all topics under biology and ecology.

Dictionary of Environmental Engineering and Related Sciences: English-Spanish, Spanish-English. Jose T. Villate. Ediciones Universal, 3090 SW 8th St., Miami, Florida 33135. (305) 642-3355. 1979.

Elsevier's Dictionary of Hydrology and Water Quality Management. J. D. Van der Tuin. Elsevier Science Publishing Co., 655 Avenue of the Americas, New York, New York 10010. (212) 989-5800. 1991. The languages are English, French, Spanish, Dutch, and German. Freshwater environment constitutes the main subject of this dictionary. Defines more than 37,000 terms.

Encyclopedia of Environmental Science and Engineering. J.R. Pfafflin. Gordon and Breach Science Publishers, Inc., 270 8th Ave., New York, New York 10011. (212) 206-8900. 1992.

The Encyclopedia of Geochemistry and Environmental Sciences. Rhodes Whitmore Fairbridge. Van Nostrand Reinhold Co., 115 5th Ave., New York, New York 10003. (212) 254-3232. 1972.

Encyclopedia of Physical Science and Technology. Robert A. Meyers, ed. Academic Press, c/o Harcourt Brace Jovanovich Inc., 6277 Sea Harbor Dr., Orlando, Florida 32887. (800) 346-8648. Dictionary of engineering, technology and physical sciences.

Grzimek's Encyclopedia of Ecology. Bernhard Grzimek. Van Nostrand Reinhold, 115 5th Ave., New York, New York 10003. (212) 254-3232. 1976.

McGraw-Hill Encyclopedia of Environmental Science. Sybil P. Parker. McGraw-Hill Science & Engineering Books, 11 W. 19th St., New York, New York 10011. (212) 337-6010. 1980. Covers ecology, man's influence on nature, and environmental protection.

North American Reference Encyclopedia of Ecology and Pollution. William White. North American Pub. Co., 401 N. Broad St., Philadelphia, Pennsylvania 19108. (215) 238-5300. 1972.

Van Nostrand's Scientific Encyclopedia. Glenn D. Considine, ed. Van Nostrand Reinhold, 115 5th Ave., New York, New York 10003. (212) 254-3232. 1983. Sixth edition. Includes all broad subject areas in science.

The Water Encyclopedia. Lewis Publishers, 2000 Corporate Blvd. N.W., Boca Raton, Florida 33431. (800) 272-7737. 1990. 2d ed. Includes groundwater contamination, drinking water, floods, waterborne diseases, global warming, climate change, irrigation, water agencies and organizations, precipitation, oceans and seas, and river, lakes and waterfalls.

GENERAL WORKS

Acidic Deposition and Aquatic Ecosystems. D. F. Charles and S. Christie, eds. Springer-Verlag, 175 5th Ave., New York, New York 10010. (212) 460-1500. 1991. Comprehensive integrated synthesis of available information on current and potential effects of acidic precipitation on lakes and streams in different geographic regions of the U.S. Examines the current status of water chemistry.

Advances in Water Treatment and Environmental Management. George Thomas. Elsevier Science Publishing Co., 655 Avenue of the Americas, New York, New York 10010. (212) 984-5800. 1991. Measurement and control of groundwater quality, rivers, river management, estuaries, and beaches.

Ambient Water Quality Criteria for 2, 4-Dichlorophenol. U. S. Environmental Protection Agency. National Technical Information Service, 5285 Port Royal Rd., Springfield, Virginia 22161. (703) 487-4650. 1980. Describes the regulations and standards criteria set by the EPA.

Ambient Water Quality Criteria for Carbon Tetrachloride. Office of Water Regulations and Standards. U.S. Environmental Protection Agency, 401 M St., SW, Washington, District of Columbia 20460. (202) 260-2090. 1980.

Automated Biomonitoring: Living Sensors as Environmental Monitors. D. Gruber. John Wiley & Sons, Inc., 605 3rd Ave., New York, New York 10158. (212) 850-6000. 1988. Papers presented deal with conceptual and historical issues of biological early warning systems. Studies using fish as sensors are presented as well as studies using other biological sensors. Not limited to water quality monitoring alone.

Biofouling and Biocorrosion in Industrial Water Systems. Hans C. Flemming, ed. Springer-Verlag, 175 5th Ave., New York, New York 10010. (212) 460-1500. 1991.

Chemical and Biological Characterization of Municipal Sludges, Sediments, Dredge Spoils, and Drilling Muds. James L. Lichtenberg, et al. American Society for Testing and Materials, 1916 S. Race St., Philadelphia, Pennsylvania 19103. (215) 299-5585. 1988. Deals with the environmental aspects of sewage disposal, analysis, health risk assessment, biological purification of sludge, and water quality management.

Chemical Quality of Water and the Hydrologic Cycle. Robert C. Averett and Diane M. McKnight. Lewis Publishers, 2000 Corporate Blvd. N.W., Boca Raton, Florida 33431. (407) 994-0555 or (800) 272-7737. 1987. Organized collection of papers dealing with changes in the quality of water as it moves through the world's hydrologic cycle.

Contaminant Transport in Groundwater. H.E. Kobus and W. Kinzelbach. A. A. Balkema, Old Post Rd., Brookfield, Vermont 05036. (802) 276-3162. 1989. Describes physical and chemical processes, model building and application as well as remedial action.

Contamination of Ground Water Prevention, Assessment, Restoration. Michael Barcelona, et al. Noyes Publications, 120 Mill Rd., Park Ridge, New Jersey 07656. (201) 391-8484. 1990. Provides regulatory agencies and industry a convenient source of technical information on the management of contaminated ground water.

Cover Crops for Clean Water. W. L. Hargrove, ed. Soil and Water Conservation Society, 7515 Northeast Ankeny Rd., Ankeny, Iowa 50021-9764. (515) 289-2331; (800) THE-SOIL. 1991. Includes the latest information on the role of cover crops in water quality management, including means of reducing water runoff, soil erosion, agrichemical loss in runoff, and nitrate leaching to groundwater.

Desalination and Water Re-Use. Miriam Balaban, ed. Institution of Chemical Engineers, c/o Hemisphere Pub., 1900 Frost Rd., Suite 101, Bristol, Pennsylvania 19007-1598. (215) 785-5800. 1991. Four volumes. Includes the papers presented at a four-day symposium organized by the Institution of Chemical Engineers (UK) on behalf of the European Federation of Chemical Engineers Working Parties on Desalination and Water Technology and the Membrane Society.

Design of Water Quality Monitoring Systems. Robert C. Ward. Van Nostrand Reinhold, 115 5th Ave., New York, New York 10003. (212) 254-3232. 1990. Describes the essential tools to design a system that gets consistently valid results. Features the latest methods of sampling and lab analysis, data handling and analysis, reporting, and information utilization, and includes case studies of system design projects.

Drinking Water and Groundwater Remediation Cost Evaluation: Air Stripping. Robert M. Clark and Jeffrey Q. Adams. Lewis Publishers, 2000 Corporate Blvd. N.W., Boca Raton, Florida 33431. (800) 272-7737. 1991. The new software program shows air stripping costs and performance of the remediation of hazardous waste sites or drinking water treatment. The program helps do cost comparisons of the technology against other available technologies.

Drinking Water and Groundwater Remediation Cost Evaluation: Granular Activated Carbon. Robert M. Clark and Jeffrey Q. Adams. Lewis Publishers, 2000 Corporate Blvd. N.W., Boca Raton, Florida 33431. (800) 272-7737. 1991. Shows GAC costs and performance forthe remediation of hazardous waste sites or drinking watertreatment. Compares the cost of the technology against other available technologies.

Drinking Water Hazards: How to Know If There Are Toxic Chemicals in Your Water and What to Do If There Are. John Cary Stewart. Envirographics, PO Box 334, Hiram, Ohio 44234. (216) 527-5207. 1990. Documents the increase of cancer and other diseases that may be environmentally induced. Discusses the increases in the use of synthetic organic chemicals, and covers each group of drinking water contaminants in some detail: inorganic chemicals, heavy metals, bacteria and viruses, radionuclides, nitrates, and organic chemicals, including pesticides.

Drinking Water Health Advisory: Volatile Organic Compounds. United States Environmental Protection Agency Office of Drinking Water. Lewis Publishers, 2000 Corporate Blvd., N.W., Boca Raton, Florida 33431. (407) 994-0555 or (800) 272-7737. 1991. Provides technical guidance to public health officials on health effects, analytical methodologies, and treatment technologies associated with drinking water contamination.

Drinking Water Treatment. P. Toft, et al., eds. Pergamon Microforms International, Inc., Fairview Park, Elmsford, New York 10523. (914) 592-7720. 1989. Proceedings of the 3d National Conference on Drinking Water, St. John's Newfoundland, Canada, June 12-14, 1988. Discussions concerned all aspects of design, construction and operation of small systems for the provision and treatment of drinking water.

Drinking Water Treatment Technologies: Comparative Health Effects Assessments. Government Institutes, Inc., 4 Research Pl., Ste. 200, Rockville, Maryland 20850. (301) 921-2300. 1990. Evaluates the relative benefits and risks of each of the common types of drinking water treatment technologies.

The Environmental Challenge of the 1990's. U.S. Environmental Protection Agency, 401 M St. SW, Washington, District of Columbia 20460. (202) 260-2090. 1991. Provides an overview of past and present projects for pollution prevention, focusing on the promotion of clean technologies and clean products in both the public and private sectors. Covers new prevention ideas relating to solid and hazardous wastes, pesticides, drinking water, wastewater and toxic substances.

Environmental Toxicology. J. K. Fawell and S. Hunt. John Wiley & Sons, Inc., 605 3rd Ave., New York, New York 10158. (212) 850-6000. 1988. Information on the toxicology of contaminants in drinking water, upland surface water and ground water. Analysis is done using gas chromatography and mass spectrometry.

Free Market Environmentalism. Terry L. Anderson and Donald R. Leal. Westview Press, 5500 Central Ave., Boulder, Colorado 80301. (303) 444-3541. 1991. Examines the prospects and pitfalls of improving natural resource allocation and environmental quality through market processes.

Groundwater Contamination: Sources, Control, and Preventive Measures. Chester D. Rail. Technomic Publishing Co., 851 New Holland Ave., Box 3535, Lancaster, Pennsylvania 17604. (717) 291-5609. 1989. Reviews the presently known sources of groundwater contamination and its many complex interactions, including managerial and political implications.

Groundwater Protection: Local Success Stories. Milou Carolan. Internal City Management Association, 777 N. Capital St., NE, Suite 500, Washington, District of Columbia 20002-4201. (800) 745-8780. 1990. Case studies from local governments that have created effective programs for protecting the local water supply by evaluating contamination sources and developing community support.

Groundwater Remediation and Petroleum: A Guide for Underground Storage Tanks. David C. Noonan and James T. Curtis. PennWell Books, PO Box 21288, Tulsa, Oklahoma 74121. (918) 831-9421; (800) 752-9764. 1990. Guide for personnel charged with the responsibility of addressing contamination caused by leaking underground storage tanks.

Groundwater Residue Sampling Design. Ralph G. Nash and Anne R. Leslie, eds. American Chemical Society, 1155 16th St. N.W., Washington, District of Columbia 20036. (202) 872-4600; (800) 227-5558. 1991. Gives an overview of the approach taken by government agencies and discusses in great detail the various techniques in sampling and analysis of groundwater.

Guidance Manual for Compliance with the Filtration and Disinfection Requirements for Public Water Systems Using Surface Water Sources. American Water Works Association, 6666 W. Quincy Ave., Denver, Colorado 80235. (303) 794-7711. 1991.

Health Assessment Document for Chloroform. U.S. Environmental Protection Agency, Office of Research and Development, MD 75, Research Triangle Park, North Carolina 27711. (919) 541-2184. 1985.

Inorganic Contaminants of Surface Water; Research and Monitoring Priorities. James W. Moore. Springer-Verlag, 175 Fifth Ave., New York, New York 10010. (212) 460-1500 or (800) 777-4643. 1991. Inorganic contaminants of surface water in terms of production, sources, and residues, chemistry, bioacculation, toxic effects to aquatic organisms, health effects and drinking water.

Integrated Approaches to Water Pollution. Joao Bau. Elsevier Science Publishing Co., 655 Avenue of the Americas, New York, New York 10010. (212) 984-5800. 1991. Integrated management strategies, policies for pollution control, groundwater pollution resulting from industrial, agricultural and urban sources, data and measurement.

Integrated Design of Water Treatment Facilities. Susumu Kawamura. John Wiley & Sons, Inc., 605 3rd Ave., New York, New York 10158-0012. (212) 850-6000. 1991. Covers research pilot studies and preliminary design studies, as well as the actual design, construction and plant management. Covers the entire project sequence, describing not only very basic and essential design criteria, but also how to design each phase to maximize overall efficiency while minimizing operation and maintenance costs.

Introduction to Water Quality Standards. U.S. Environmental Protection Agency, Office of Water, 401 M St. SW, Washington, District of Columbia 20460. (202) 260-2090. 1988.

Madison Conference of Applied Research & Practice on Municipal & Industrial Waste. Dept. of Engineering Professional Development, University of Wisconsin-Madison, Madison, Wisconsin 53706. 1990. Annual. Sewage disposal, factory and trade waste, soil liners, ground water clean up, landfill leachate treatment, groundwater monitary systems, evaluation of groundwater and soil gas remedial action; leachate generation estimates and landfills.

More About Leaking Underground Storage Tanks: A Background Booklet for the Chemical Advisory. U.S. Environmental Protection Agency, 401 M St., S.W., Washington, District of Columbia 20460. (202) 260-2090. 1984. Covers underground storage and drinking water contamination.

The New York Environment Book. Eric A. Goldstein. Island Press, 1718 Connecticut Ave. N.W., Suite 300, Washington, District of Columbia 20009. (202) 232-7933. 1990. Provides an in-depth analysis of New York City's environment. The five areas surveyed are: solid waste disposal, hazardous substances, water pollution, air quality, and drinking water quality. Discusses past clean-up efforts, and offers an agenda for the future. Describes and analyzes the general environment of urban areas, and offers solutions for their special environmental problems.

Point-of-Use/Entry Treatment of Drinking Water. Noyes Publications, 120 Mill Rd., Park Ridge, New Jersey 07656. (201) 391-8484. 1990. Covers the administrative and technical aspects of utilizing POU/POE systems to solve individual and small community drinking water problems.

Poison Runoff: A Guide to State and Local Control of Nonpoint Source Water Pollution. Paul Thompson. Natural Resources Defense Council, 40 W. 20th St., New York, New York 10011. (212) 727-2700. 1989. How-to-book addressing pollution in agricultural lands, urban development and construction, logging, mining and grazing.

Protecting the Nation's Groundwater from Contamination. U.S. G.P.O., Washington, District of Columbia 20401. 1984-. Covers underground water quality and pollution.

Radon, Radium, and Uranium in Drinking Water. C. Richard Cothern and Paul Rebers. Lewis Publishers, 2000 Corporate Blvd., N.W., Boca Raton, Florida 33431. (407) 994-0555 or (800) 272-7737. 1990. Covers most aspects of radionuclides in drinking water.

Saving the Mediterranean: The Politics of International Environmental Cooperation. Peter M. Haas. Columbia University Press, 562 W. 113th St., New York, New York 10025. (212) 316-7100. 1990. Focuses on the international pollution management of the Mediterranean. Ninety scientists and international officials were interviewed to ascertain how the international community responded to this particular threat.

A Science of Impurity: Water Analysis in Nineteenth Century Britain. Christopher Hamlin. University of California Press, Berkeley, California 94720. (510) 642-4247. 1990. Presents a series of biographies of scientists and government officials responsible for London's water quality during a period of pressing need and sparse scientific knowledge. Also presents some chemical information, placing chemical and epidemiological concepts in perspective, which is needed to grasp the inconsistencies of water analysis in 19th-century Britain.

Some Economic Impacts of Freshwater Stream Effluent Discharge Limits on Selected Small Communities in Mississippi. Leo R. Cheatham. Water Resources Research Institute, Mississippi State University, Mississippi State, Mississippi 39762. Water supply, water pollution and drinking water contamination.

Supplying Water and Saving the Environment for Six Billion People. Udai P. Singh and Otto J. Helweg, eds.

American Society of Civil Engineers, 345 E. 47th St., New York, New York 10017. (212) 705-7288; (800) 548-2723. 1990. Proceedings of selected sessions from the 1990 ASCE Convention, San Francisco, CA, Nov. 5-8, 1990. Sponsored by the Environmental Engineering Division, Irrigation and Drainage Division, Water Resources Planning and Management Division of the American Society of Civil Engineers.

The Surface Water Acidification Programme. B. J. Mason, ed. Cambridge University Press, 40 W. 20th St., New York, New York 10011. (212) 924-3900; (800) 227-0247. 1991. Proceedings of the final Conference of the Surface Water Acidification Programme, held at the Royal Society in March 1990. Deals with the acid pollution of rivers and lakes and presents research results on watersheds in Great Britain and Scandinavia.

Surveillance of Drinking Water Quality in Rural Areas. Barry Lloyd. John Wiley & Sons, Inc., 605 3rd Ave, New York, New York 10158-0012. (212) 850-6000. 1991. Examines the human and technical resources required for monitoring, maintaining and improving the safety of rural water supply services. A practical guide to improving the quality of service from small water supplies, it describes the essential minimum of reliable methods of monitoring water quality and discusses new cost effective approaches to sanitary inspection of community water supplies.

Symposium on Regeneration Research (1975: Gatlinburg, Tenn.) Proceedings. American Society of Civil Engineers, 345 E. 47th St., New York, New York 10017. (212) 705-7288. 1979. Papers presented dealt with water quality and dissolved oxygen in water and the water aeration process.

TAPPI Environmental Conference Proceedings, Seattle, WA, April 9-11, 1990. TAPPI Press, Technology Park/ Atlanta, PO Box 105113, Atlanta, Georgia 30348. (404) 446-1400. 1990. Contains 11 papers presented at the conference covering industrial pollution and its remedies.

Technologies for Upgrading Existing or Designing New Drinking Water Treatment Facilities. Office of Drinking Water, Center for Environmental Research Information, U.S. Environmental Protection Agency. Technomic Publishing Co., 851 New Holland Ave., Box 3535, Lancaster, Pennsylvania 17604. (717) 291-5609. 1991. Discusses drinking water treatment technologies that address contamination and contaminant categories regulated under the Safe Drinking Water Act and its 1986 amendments.

Turning the Tide: Saving the Chesapeake Bay. Tom Horton. Island Press, 1718 Connecticut Ave. N.W., Suite 300, Washington, District of Columbia 20009. (202) 232-7933. 1991. Presents a comprehensive look at two decades of efforts to save the Chesapeake Bay. It outlines which methods have worked, and which have not. Sets a new strategy for the future, calling for greater political coverage, environmental leadership and vision.

Urban Discharges and Receiving Water Quality Impacts. J. B. Ellis, ed. Pergamon Microforms International, Inc., Fairview Park, Elmsford, New York 10523. (914) 592-7720. 1989. Proceedings of a seminar organized by the IAWPRC/IAHR Sub Committee for Urban Runoff Quality Data, as part of the IAWPRC 14th biennial conference, Brighton, UK, July 18-21, 1988.

The Washington Conference on Underground Storage, July 15-16, 1985, Stouffer Concourse. Center for Energy

and Environmental Management, Washington, District of Columbia (202) 543-3939.

Water. Hans Silvester. Thomasson-Grant, 1 Morton Dr., Suite 500, Charlottesville, Virginia 22901. (804) 977-1780. 1990. Details the dangers posed by the industrial society to the flow of clean water

Water Chlorination: Chemistry, Environmental Impact and Health Effects. Robert L. Jolley, et al., eds. Lewis Publishers, 2000 Corporate Blvd., N.W., Boca Raton, Florida 33431. (407) 994-0555 or (800) 272-7737. 1990. Proceedings of the 6th conference on Water Contamination held in Oak Ridge, Tennessee, May 3-8, 1987. Includes all the ramifications of water chlorination practice and presents the most significant original research and developments of recent occurrence.

Water Pollution Biology. P. D. Abel. John Wiley & Sons, Inc., 605 3rd Ave., New York, New York 10158. (212) 850-6000. 1988. State-of-the-art information on methods of investigating water pollution problems and critically assesses the literature on water pollution. Also included is a discussion on the role of toxicological studies in the monitoring and control of water pollution.

Water Quality and Management for Recreation and Tourism. B. Rigden and L. Henry, eds. Pergamon Microforms International, Inc., Fairview Park, Elmsford, New York 10523. (914) 592-7720. 1989. Proceedings of the IAWPRC Conference held in Brisbane, Australia, July 10-15, 1988. Describes the problems associated with water quality and management for recreation tourism.

Water Quality and Treatment; A Handbook of Public Water Supplies. American Water Works Association. McGraw-Hill, 1221 Avenue of the Americas, New York, New York 10020. (212) 512-2000; (800) 262-4729. 1990. 4th ed. Revised and updated to reflect recent developments in the field. Addresses water quality issues for both municipal and industrial water supply, reports on the source of contaminants and other problems, and describes the treatment methods of choice.

Water Quality Modeling. Brian Henderson-Sellere, et al. CRC Press, 2000 Corporate Blvd. N.W., Boca Raton, Florida 33431. (407) 994-0555; (800) 272-7737. 1990. Issues in four volumes. Discusses water supply and treatment and water resources engineering.

GOVERNMENTAL ORGANIZATIONS

New England Interstate Water Pollution Control Commission. 85 Merrimac St., Boston, Massachusetts 02114. (617) 367-8522.

U.S. Environmental Protection Agency: Assistant Administrator for Water. 401 M St., S.W., Washington, District of Columbia 20460. (202) 382-5700.

U.S. Environmental Protection Agency: Office of Drinking Water. 401 M St., S.W., Washington, District of Columbia 20460. (202) 382-5543.

U.S. Environmental Protection Agency: Office of Water Enforcement and Permits. 401 M St., S.W., Washington, District of Columbia 20460. (202) 475-8488.

U.S. Environmental Protection Agency: Office of Water Regulations and Standards. 401 M St., S.W., Washington, District of Columbia 20460. (202) 382-5400.

Water Quality Branch: Water Quality. Chief, 105 South Meridian St., Box 6015, Indianapolis, Indiana 46206. (317) 245-5028.

Water Resources Board: Water Quality. Chief, Water Quality Division, 1000 N.E. 10th St., PO Box 53585, Oklahoma City, Oklahoma 73152. (405) 271-2540.

HANDBOOKS AND MANUALS

Basic Mechanical Maintenance Procedures at Water and Wastewater Plants. Glenn M. Tillman. Lewis Publishers, 2000 Corporate Blvd., Boca Raton, Florida 33431. (407) 994-0555 or (800) 272-7737. 1991. Part Operator's Guide series. Includes standard mechanical drawing symbols for valves, gates, gate equipment, equipment lockout procedures, centrifugal pumps, positive displacement pumps, rotary pumps, coupling alignment, pumping systems, macerator blades, shear pins, lubrication, and appendices.

Clean Water Handbook. Government Institutes, Inc., 4 Research Pl., Ste. 200, Rockville, Maryland 20850. (301) 921-2300. 1990. Offers straightforward explanation on enforcement, toxics, water quality standards, efficient limitations, NPDES, stormwater and nonpoint discharge control.

Drinking Water: A Community Action Guide. Concern, Inc., 1794 Columbia Rd., NW, Washington, District of Columbia 20009. (202) 328-8160. 1990.

The Drinking Water Book: A Complete Guide to Safe Drinking Water. Colin Ingram. Ten Speed Press, P.O. Box 7123, Berkeley, California 94707. (800) 841-2665. 1991. Discusses potential pollutants and their sources in drinking water. Includes water testing and methods for reducing pollutants in the home water supply.

The Economics of Improved Estuarine Water Quality: An NEP Manual for Measuring Benefits. U.S. Environmental Protection Agency, Office of Marine and Estuarine Protection, 401 M St., S.W., Washington, District of Columbia 20460. (202) 260-2090. 1990. Covers wetland conservation and estuarine ecology.

The EPA Manual for Waste Minimization Opportunity Assessments. U.S. Environmental Protection Agency. Technomic Publishing Co., 851 New Holland Ave., Box 3535, Lancaster, Pennsylvania 17604. (717) 291-5609. 1990.

Ground Water Handbook. Government Institutes, Inc., 4 Research Pl., Ste 200, Rockville, Maryland 20850. (301) 921-2300. 1989. Includes highlights of chapters on ground water contamination, use of models in managing ground water protection programs, ground water restoration, ground water quality investigations, basic hydrogeology, monitoring well design and construction, ground water sampling, ground water tracers and basic geology.

Groundwater Chemicals Desk Reference. John H. Montgomery. Lewis Publishers, 2000 Corporate Blvd. NW, Boca Raton, Florida 33431. (407) 994-0555 or (800)272-7737. 1990. Protection and remediation of the groundwater environment. Includes profiles of chemical compounds promulgated by the EPA under the Clean Water Act of 1977.

Handbook of Drinking Water Quality: Standards and Controls. John De Zuane. Van Nostrand Reinhold, 115 5th Ave., New York, New York 10003. (212) 254-3232. 1990. Aids in evaluating water quality control at every stage of the water path, from source to treatment plant, from distribution system to consumer.

High-Quality Industrial Water Management Manual. Paul N. Garay and Franklin M. Chn. The Association of Energy Engineers, 4025 Pleasantdale Rd., Suite 420, Atlanta, Georgia 30340. (404) 925-9558. 1992. Guide to managing water resources.

The Poisoned Well: New Strategies for Groundwater Protection. Eric P. Jorgensen, ed. Island Press, 1718 Connecticut Ave. N.W., Suite 300, Washington, District of Columbia 20009. (202) 232-7933. 1989. Explains how individuals can work with agencies and the courts to enforce water laws, how the major federal water laws, work what remedies exist for each type of groundwater contamination, and what state and local programs may be helpful.

Practical Handbook of Ground Water Monitoring. David M. Nielsen. Lewis Publishers, 2000 Corporate Blvd., N.W., Boca Raton, Florida 33431. (407) 994-0555 or (800) 272-7737. 1991. Covers the complete spectrum of state-of-the-science technology applied to investigations of ground water quality. Emphasis is placed on the practical application of current technology, and minimum theory is discussed.

Practical Manual for Groundwater Microbiology. D. Roy Cullimore. Lewis Publishers, 2000 Corporate Blvd., N.W., Boca Raton, Florida 33431. (407) 994-0555 or (800) 272-7737. 1991. Describes the direct observation of microbial activities in groundwater, sampling procedures, indirect and direct microbiological examinations.

Standard Handbook of Environmental Engineering. Robert A. Corbitt. McGraw-Hill, 1221 Ave. of the Americas, New York, New York 10020. (212) 512-2000 or (800) 262-4729. 1990. Hands-on reference to understand environmental engineering technology. Covers air quality control, water supply, wastewater disposal, waste management, stormwater and hazardous wastes.

Tables of Physical and Chemical Constants and Some Mathematical Functions. G. W. C. Kaye, et al. Longman Group Ltd., Longman House, Burnt Mill, Harlow, England CM20 2J6. 0279 426721. 1988. Fifteenth edition. Includes tables on mechanical properties, density, elasticity, viscosity, surface tension, temperature and heat. Also covers radiation, optics, chemistry, electrochemistry, astrophysics, and chemical thermodynamics.

Technical Guidance Manual for Performing Waste Load Allocations. U.S. Environmental Protection Agency, 401 M St., S.W., Washington, District of Columbia 20460. (202) 260-2090. 1984-.

Water Quality and Treatment: A Handbook of Community Water Supplies. McGraw-Hill Science & Engineering Books, 11 W. 19th St., New York, New York 10011. (212) 337-6010. 1990. Covers water purification and water supply in the United States.

Water Quality Standards Handbook. U.S. Environmental Protection Agency, Office of Water Regulations and Standards, 401 M St., S.W., Washington, District of Columbia 20460. (202) 260-2090. 1982. Covers water quality management in the United States.

ONLINE DATA BASES

Aqualine. Water Research Center, Medmenham Laboratory, Marlow, Buckinghamshire, England SL7 2HD. Literature on water and wastewater technology.

Chemical Abstracts-CA. Chemical Abstracts Service, 2540 Olentangy River Rd., P.O. Box 3012, Columbus, Ohio 43210. (800) 848-6533 or (614) 421-3600. Information sources include 9000 journals, patents from 27 countries, two industrial property organizations, new books, conference proceedings, and government research reports.

Computerized Engineering Index–COMPENDEX. Engineering Information Inc., 345 E. 47th St., New York, New York 10017. (212) 705-7600.

Great Lakes Water Quality Data Base. U.S. Environmental Protection Agency, Office of Research and Development, Large Lakes Research Station, 401 M St. SW, Washington, District of Columbia 20460. (202) 260-2090. Water data related to the Great Lakes and related tributaries and watersheds.

Ground Water Sampling Devices. National Ground Water Information Center, National Well Water Association, 6375 Riverside Dr., Dublin, Ohio 43017. (614) 761-1711.

Information System for Hazardous Organics in Water. U.S. Environmental Protection Agency, Office of Pesticides & Toxic Substances, 401 M St., S.W., Washington, District of Columbia 20460. (202) 260-2090.

Monthly Catalog of United States Government Publications. U.S. G.P.O., Supt. of Docs., PO Box 371954, Pittsburgh, Pennsylvania 15250-7954. (202) 512-0000.

National Technical Information Service. U.S. Department of Commerce, National Technical Information Service, Office of Data Base Services, 5285 Port Royal Rd., Springfield, Virginia 22161. (703) 487-4807. Bibliographic database of government sponsored research and technical reports.

Oil and Hazardous Materials Technical Assistance Data System. U.S. Environmental Protection Agency, Office of Solid Waste and Emergency Response, 401 M St., S.W., Washington, District of Columbia 20460. (202) 260-2090. Hazardous substances and their deleterious effects on water quality and other environmental media.

PressNet Environmental Reports. Chemical Information Systems, Inc., 7215 York Rd., Baltimore, Maryland 21212. (301) 321-8440.

SCISEARCH. Institute for Scientific Information, University City Science Center, 3501 Market St., Philadelphia, Pennsylvania 19104. (215) 386-0100.

PERIODICALS AND NEWSLETTERS

The Bench Sheet. Water Pollution Control Federation, 601 Wythe Street, Alexandria, Virginia 22314-1994. (703) 684-2400. Bimonthly. Articles on water and wastewater laboratory analysis.

Clean Water. The Water Quality Bureau of the Division of Environment, Idaho Dept. of Health and Welfare, 450 W. State St., Boise, Idaho 83720. (208) 334-5855. Quarterly. Water quality and water pollution control in Idaho.

Clean Water Action News. Clean Water Action Project, 317 Pennsylvania Ave. S.E., Washington, District of Columbia 20003. (202) 547-1196. 1976-. Quarterly. Features news and articles on environmental political issues.

Clean Water Report. Business Publishers, Inc., 951 Pershing Dr., Silver Spring, Maryland 20910-4464. (301) 587-6300. 1964-. Biweekly. Key information source for environmental professionals, covering the important issues: groundwater, drinking water, wastewater treatment, drought, wetlands, coastal protection, dioxin, non-point source pollution, agrichemical contamination, cleanup versus prevention issues, and related topics.

Clearwaters. New York Water Pollution Control Association, 90 Presidential Plaza, Suite 122, Syracuse, New York 13202. (315) 422-7811. 1971-. Quarterly. Articles on design methods, legislation, and innovations on wastewater treatment plants.

Desalination and Water Re-Use Technologies in Japan. Annual Report. Water Re-Use Promotion Center, Landix Akasaka Bldg, 2-3-4, Akasaka, Minato-ku, Tokyo, Japan 1981-. Annual.

Drinking Water News. Business Publishers, Inc., PO Box 1067, Blair Station, Silver Spring, Maryland 20910. (301) 587-6300. 1977-.

Ecological Monographs. Business Office of the Ecological Society of America, Center of Environmental Studies, Arizona State University, Tempe, Arizona 85287-1201. (602) 965-3000. Quarterly. Scientific journal of ecological issues.

European Water Pollution Control. European Water Pollution Control Association, Elsevier Science Pub., PO Box 211, 1000 AE, Amsterdam, Netherlands 1991-. Bimonthly. Discussion of views, policies, strategies, directives and guidelines, design procedures, technical ideas and solutions, performance and experience in construction, maintenance and operation of water pollution control.

Facets of Freshwater. Freshwater Biological Research Foundation, 2500 Shadywood Rd., Box 90, Navarre, Minnesota 55392. (612) 471-8407. 1970-. Quarterly. Topics in freshwater biological research.

Federal Water Quality Association Newsletter. Federal Water Quality Association, P.O. Box 44163, Washington, District of Columbia 20026. (202) 447-4925. Seven times a year. Concerns sewage and industrial waste treatment and disposal.

Focus on International Joint Commission Activities. IJC Great Lakes Regional Office, PO Box 32869, Detroit, Michigan 48232. (313) 226-2170. 1986-. Three issues a year. Provides information on Great Lakes water quality and quantity issues.

GEM Notes: an Update of the Groundwater Education in Michigan Program. Groundwater Education in Michigan, Institute of Water Research, Michigan State University, 25 Manly Miles Bldg., 1405 S. Harrison Rd., East Lansing, Michigan 48824. (517) 355-9543. 1988-. Irregular.

Georgia Operator. Georgia Water and Pollution Control Association, 2532 Bolton Rd. N.W., Atlanta, Georgia 30318. 1963-. Quarterly.

Ground Water Monitor. Business Publishers, Inc., 951 Pershing Dr., Silver Spring, Maryland 20910-4464. (301) 587-6300. Biweekly. Legislation, litigation, regulations and quality problems on ground water. Also available online.

Ground Water Monitoring Review. Water Well Journal Publishing Co. National Water Well Association, 6375 Riverside Drive, Dublin, Ohio 43017. (614) 761-3222. Quarterly. Covers protection and restoration of ground water.

Ground Water Newsletter. Water Information Center, Inc., 125 East Bethpage Road, Plainview, New York 11803. (516) 249-7634. Biweekly. Covers ground water exploration, development, and management.

ICWP Policy Statement & Bylaws. Interstate Conference on Water Problems, 5300 M Street, NW, Suite 800, Washington, District of Columbia 20037. (202) 466-7287. Annual. Covers conservation and administration of water.

International Water Report. Water Information Center, Inc., 125 East Bethpage Road, Plainview, New York 11803. (516) 249-7634. Quarterly. Covers water works and topics done in Europe, Asia, South America.

Journal - American Water Works Association. American Water Works Association, 6666 W. Quincy Ave., Denver, Colorado 80235. (303) 794-7711. Monthly. Includes regulatory summaries, conference information and job listings. Has state chapters, annual meetings, and special publications.

The Journal of Freshwater. Freshwater Biological Research Foundation, 2500 Shadywood Rd., Box 90, Navarre, Minnesota 55392. (612) 471-8407. 1977-. Quarterly.

Journal of Groundwater. Association of Ground Water Scientists and Engineers, Division of National Water Well Association, 6375 Riverside Dr., Dublin, Ohio 43017. (614) 761-1711. 1963-. Bimonthly. Serial dealing with all forms of ground water and its quality.

Journal of Hydraulic Engineering. American Society of Civil Engineers, 345 E. 47th St., New York, New York 10017. (212) 705-7288; (800) 548-2723. 1983-. Monthly. Papers describe the analysis and solutions of problems in hydraulic engineering, hydrology and water resources. Emphasizes concepts, methods, techniques and results that advance knowledge in the hydraulic engineering profession.

Monthly Report. Association of Metropolitan Water Agencies, 1717 K St. NW, Suite 1006, Washington, District of Columbia 20036. (202) 331-2820.

New Jersey Air, Water, & Waste Management Times. New Jersey State Department of Health, Division of Clean Air & Water, John Fitch Plaza, Trenton, New Jersey 08625. Bimonthly.

New York's Waters. New York State Department of Health, 84 Holland Ave., Albany, New York 12208. Quarterly.

Newsletter of Association of Ground Water Scientists and Engineers. Association of Groundwater Scientists and Engineers, 6375 Riverside Drive, Dublin, Ohio 43017. (614) 761-1711. Bimonthly. Reports on events, activities, courses and conferences of AGSE.

Operations Forum. Water Pollution Control Federation, 601 Wythe Street, Alexandria, Virginia 22314-1994. (703) 684-2400. Monthly. Covers the advancement of practical knowledge in water quality control systems.

Pure Water from the Sea. International Desalination Association, Box 328, Englewood, New Jersey 07631. (201) 567-0188. Bimonthly.

Texas Pollution Report. Report Publications, P.O. Box 12368, Austin, Texas 78711. (512) 478-5663. Weekly. Covers regulatory activity, court decisions and legislation.

Washington Bulletin. Water Pollution Control Federation, 601 Wythe Street, Alexandria, Virginia 22314-1994. (703) 684-2400. Monthly. Covers legislative issues in the water control industry.

Water Quality International. Pergamon Microforms International, Inc., Fairview Park, Elmsford, New York 10523. (914) 592-7720. 1990-. Quarterly. Contains news and information from IAWPRC conferences and Specialist and Task Groups, and other news.

RESEARCH CENTERS AND INSTITUTES

Academy of Natural Sciences of Philadelphia, Division of Environmental Research. 19th Street and the Parkway, Philadelphia, Pennsylvania 19103. (215) 299-1081.

Center for Environmental Sciences. University of Colorado-Denver, P.O. Box 173364, Denver, Colorado 80217-3364. (303) 5556-4277.

Edwards Aquifer Research and Data Center. 248 Freeman Building, Southwest Texas State University, San Marcos, Texas 78666-4616. (512) 245-2329.

Environmental Research Foundation. PO Box 3541, Princeton, New Jersey 08543-3541. (609) 683-0707.

Mississippi State University, Water Resources Research Institute. P.O. Drawer AD, Mississippi State, Mississippi 39762. (601) 325-3620.

North Dakota Water Resources Research Institute. North Dakota State University, Box 5626, Fargo, North Dakota 58105. (701) 237-7193.

Oklahoma State University, Water Quality Research Laboratory. Stillwater, Oklahoma 74078-0459. (405) 744-5551.

Resources for the Future, Inc., Quality of the Environment Division. 1616 P Street, N.W., Washington, District of Columbia 20036. (202) 328-5000.

Texas Tech University, Water Resources Center. Box 4630, Lubbock, Texas 79409. (806) 742-3597.

U.S. Forest Service, Aquatic Ecosystem Analysis Laboratory. 105 Page, Brigham Young University, Provo, Utah 84602. (801) 378-4928.

U.S. Forest Service, Redwood Science Laboratory. 1700 Bayview Dr., Arcata, California 95521. (707) 822-3691.

University of Arizona, Environmental Engineering Laboratory. Civil Engineering Department, Room 206, Tucson, Arizona 85721. (602) 621-6586.

University of Kansas, Water Resources Institute. Lawrence, Kansas 66045. (913) 864-3807.

University of Kentucky, Kentucky Water Resources Research Institute. 219 Anderson Hall, Lexington, Kentucky 40506-0046. (606) 257-1832.

University of Maryland, Sea Grant College. 1123 Taliaferro Hall, College Park, Maryland 20742. (301) 405-6371.

University of Minnesota, Center for Natural Resource Policy and Management. 110 Green Hall, 1530 North Cleveland Avenue, St. Paul, Minnesota 55108. (612) 624-9796.

University of Minnesota, Duluth, Center for Water and The Environment. Natural Resources Research Institute, 5103 Miller Trunk Highway, Duluth, Minnesota 55811. (218) 720-4270.

University of Missouri-Columbia, Missouri Water Resources Research Center. 0056 Engineering Complex, Columbia, Missouri 65211. (314) 882-3132.

University of Nebraska-Lincoln, Water Center. 103 Natural Resources Hall, Lincoln, Nebraska 68503-0844. (402) 472-3305.

University of Nevada-Reno, Desert Research Institute, Water Resources Center. P.O. Box 60220, Reno, Nevada 89506-0220. (703) 673-7365.

University of North Carolina, North Carolina Water Resources Research Institute. North Carolina State University, Box 7912, Raleigh, North Carolina 27695-7912. (919) 737-2815.

University of Rhode Island, Water Resources Center. 202 Bliss Hall, Kingston, Rhode Island 02881. (401) 792-2297.

University of Southern California, Sea Grant Program. University Park, Los Angeles, California 90089-1231. (213) 740-1961.

University of Texas at Austin, Center for Research in Water Resources. Balcones Research Center, Building 119, Austin, Texas 78712. (512) 471-3131.

University of Wisconsin-Madison, Sea Grant Advisory Services. Walkway Mall, 522 Bayshore Drive, Sister Bay, Wisconsin 54234. (414) 854-5329.

University of Wisconsin-Madison, Water Resources Center. 1975 Willow Drive, Madison, Wisconsin 53706. (608) 262-3577.

Utah State University, Institute for Land Rehabilitation. College of Natural Resources, Logan, Utah 84322-5230. (801) 750-2547.

Utah State University, Watershed Science Unit. Range Science Department, Logan, Utah 84322-5250. (801) 750-2759.

Water Quality Laboratory. Western Illinois University, Department of Chemistry, Macomb, Illinois 61455. (309) 298-1356.

STATISTICS SOURCES

Ecology: Community Profiles. U.S. Fish and Wildlife Service. National Technical Information Service, 5285 Port Royal Road, Springfield, Virginia 22161. (703) 487-4650. Irregular. Data on coastal and inland ecosystems, including wetlands, tidal-flats, near-shore seagrasses, sand dunes, drilling platforms, oyster reefs, estuaries, rivers and streams.

National Water Quality Inventory. U.S. G.P.O., Washington, District of Columbia 20401. (202) 512-0000. Bienni-al. Water pollution problems and control activities by states.

Quality Assurance Data for Routine Water Analysis. U.S. Geological Survey. U.S. G.P.O., Washington, District of Columbia 20401. (202) 512-0000. Annual. Test results determining alkalinity, inorganic ion, trace metal and organic nutrients.

Water Quality Standards Criteria Summaries. National Technical Information Service, 5285 Port Royal Rd., Springfield, Virginia 22161. (703) 487-4650. Maximum allowable pollutant concentrations, and limits for other properties. Includes agricultural chemicals, trace metals, and bacteria; or physical or chemical properties including acidity, temperature, and turbidity.

World Resources. World Resources Institute. 1709 New York Ave., N.W., Washington, District of Columbia 20006. (202) 638-6300. Annual. Statistical and textual analysis of world's natural resources and the effects of growth-caused environmental pollution.

TRADE ASSOCIATIONS AND PROFESSIONAL SOCIETIES

American Clean Water Association. 7308 Birch Ave., Tacoma Park, Maryland 20912. (301) 495-0746.

American Society of Civil Engineers. 345 East 47th St., New York, New York 10017. (212) 705-7496.

American Society of Sanitary Engineering. Box 40362, Bay Village, Ohio 44140. (216) 835-3040.

American Water Resources Association. 5410 Grosvenor Lane, Suite 220, Bethesda, Maryland 20814. (301) 493-8600.

Association of State Drinking Water Administrators. 1911 N. Fort Myer Dr., Suite 400, Arlington, Virginia 22209. (703) 524-2428.

Association of the State and Interstate Water Pollution Control Administrators. 444 North Capitol St., N.W., Suite 330, Washington, District of Columbia 20001. (202) 624-7782.

Clean Water Action Project. c/o David Zwick, 1320 18th St. N.W., Washington, District of Columbia 20003. (202) 457-1286.

Environmental Quality Industrial Resources Center. The Ohio State University, 1200 Chambers Rd., Room 310, Columbus, Ohio 43212. (614) 292-6717.

Federal Water Quality Association. PO Box 44163, Washington, District of Columbia 20026. (202) 447-4925.

Freshwater Foundation. spring Hill Center, 728 County Rd. 6, Wayzata, New Mexico 55391. (612) 449-0092.

International Bottled Water Association. 113 N. Henry St., Alexandria, Virginia 22314. (703) 683-5213.

National Environmental Training Association. 2930 E. Camelback Rd., Phoenix, Arizona 85016. (602) 956-6099.

Safe Water Coalition. 150 Woodland Ave., San Anselmo, California 94960. (415) 453-0158.

Water Environment Federation. 601 Wythe St., Alexandria, Virginia 22314-1994. (703) 684-2400. Formerly, Water Pollution Control Federation.

Water Quality Association. 4151 Naperville Rd., Lisle, Illinois 60532. (708) 505-0160.

Water Quality Research Council. 4151 Naperville Rd., Lisle, Illinois 60532. (708) 505-0160.

WATER RECLAMATION

See also: WATER USES

ABSTRACTING AND INDEXING SERVICES

Geographical Abstracts. London School of Economics, Dept. of Geography, Regency House, 34 Duke St., London, England 1966-. Continued by Geo Abstracts issued in 6 parts: Pt. A. Landforms and the quaternary; Pt. B. Biogeography and Climatology; Pt. C. Economic geography; Pt. D. Social geography and cartography; Pt. E. Sedimentology; Pt. F. Regional and community planning.

Pollution Abstracts. Cambridge Scientific Abstracts, 5161 River Rd., Bethesda, Maryland 20816. (301) 961-6750. Six/year. Indexes worldwide technical literature on environmental pollution. Covers air pollution, marine and freshwater pollution, sewage and wastewater treatment, waste management, toxicology and health, noise pollution, radiation, land pollution, and environmental policies, programs, legislation, and education. Also available online.

BIBLIOGRAPHIES

Current Contents. Agriculture, Biology and Environmental Sciences. Institute for Scientific Information, 3501 Market St., Philadelphia, Pennsylvania 19104. (800) 523-1857. 1973-. Previous title: Current Contents. Agricultural, Food & Veterinary Sciences. Gives the table of contents of periodicals in the fields of agriculture, biology, environmental and related areas.

ENCYCLOPEDIAS AND DICTIONARIES

McGraw-Hill Encyclopedia of Environmental Science. Sybil P. Parker. McGraw-Hill Science & Engineering Books, 11 W. 19th St., New York, New York 10011. (212) 337-6010. 1980. Covers ecology, man's influence on nature, and environmental protection.

ONLINE DATA BASES

Monthly Catalog of United States Government Publications. U.S. G.P.O., Supt. of Docs., PO Box 371954, Pittsburgh, Pennsylvania 15250-7954. (202) 512-0000.

National Technical Information Service. U.S. Department of Commerce, National Technical Information Service, Office of Data Base Services, 5285 Port Royal Rd., Springfield, Virginia 22161. (703) 487-4807. Bibliographic database of government sponsored research and technical reports.

SCISEARCH. Institute for Scientific Information, University City Science Center, 3501 Market St., Philadelphia, Pennsylvania 19104. (215) 386-0100.

WATER RESOURCES

See also: GROUNDWATER; RESERVOIRS; WATER CONSERVATION; WATER POLLUTION; WATER QUALITY; WATER RECLAMATION; WATER TREATMENT; WATER USES; WATER WELLS; WETLANDS

ABSTRACTING AND INDEXING SERVICES

Abstracts of Air and Water Conservation Literature. American Petroleum Institute. Central Abstracting and Indexing Service, 275 Madison Avenue, New York, New York 10016. 1972.

Applied Science and Technology Index. H.W. Wilson Co., 950 University Ave., Bronx, New York 10452. (800) 367-6770. Formerly Industrial Arts Index.

Aqualine Abstracts. Water Research Centre. c/o Pergamon Microforms International, Inc., Fairview Park, Elmsford, New York 10523. (914) 592-7720. 1927-. Contains some 8,000 records annually on water and wastewater technology. Covers all aspects of water, wastewater, associated engineering services and the aquatic environment. Over 600 periodicals, as well as books, reports and conference proceedings and other publications from water related institutions worldwide are scanned. Also available online.

ASFA Aquaculture Abstracts. Cambridge Scientific Abstracts, Inc., 5161 River Rd., Bethesda, Maryland 20816. (301) 961-6750. 1984.

Chemical Abstracts. Chemical Abstracts Service, 2540 Olentangy River Rd., PO Box 3012, Columbus, Ohio 43210. (800) 848-6533. 1907-.

Civil Engineering Hydraulic Abstracts. BHRA Fluid Engineering, Air Science Co., PO Box 143, Corning, New York 14830. (607) 962-5591. Monthly. Abstracts of periodicals that publish in the areas of hydraulic engineering and other related topics.

Engineering Index. The Engineering Index Inc., 345 E. 47th St., New York, New York 10017. 1962-.

General Science Index. H. W. Wilson Co., 950 University Ave., Bronx, New York 10452. 1978-. Monthly, also issued in annual cumulation. Cumulative subject index to English language periodicals in the subject fields of astronomy, botany, chemistry, earth science, environment and conservation, food and nutrition, genetics, mathematics, medicine and health, microbiology, oceanography, physics, physiology and zoology.

Geographical Abstracts. London School of Economics, Dept. of Geography, Regency House, 34 Duke St., London, England 1966-. Continued by Geo Abstracts issued in 6 parts: Pt. A. Landforms and the quaternary; Pt. B. Biogeography and Climatology; Pt. C. Economic geography; Pt. D. Social geography and cartography; Pt. E. Sedimentology; Pt. F. Regional and community planning.

Pollution Abstracts. Cambridge Scientific Abstracts, 5161 River Rd., Bethesda, Maryland 20816. (301) 961-6750. Six/year. Indexes worldwide technical literature on environmental pollution. Covers air pollution, marine and freshwater pollution, sewage and wastewater treatment, waste management, toxicology and health, noise pollution, radiation, land pollution, and environmental policies, programs, legislation, and education. Also available online.

Science Citation Index. Institute for Scientific Information, 3501 Market St., Philadelphia, Pennsylvania 19104. 1961-.

ALMANACS AND YEARBOOKS

Water Supply and Wastewater Disposal International Almanac. A. Kepinske and W. A. S. Kepinski. Vulkan-Verlag, Dr. W. Classen Nacht, Gooiland 11, Netherlands 1976-1985. Seven volumes. Deals with all problems and aspects in the domain of water supply and wastewater disposal.

BIBLIOGRAPHIES

Analytical Bibliography for Water Supply and Conservation Techniques. John Boland. U.S. Army Corps of Engineers, Institute for Water Resources, Fort Belvoir, Virginia 22060. (703) 780-2155. 1982.

Current Contents. Agriculture, Biology and Environmental Sciences. Institute for Scientific Information, 3501 Market St., Philadelphia, Pennsylvania 19104. (800) 523-1857. 1973-. Previous title: Current Contents. Agricultural, Food & Veterinary Sciences. Gives the table of contents of periodicals in the fields of agriculture, biology, environmental and related areas.

Geraghty & Miller's Groundwater Bibliography. Frits Van Der Leeden. Lewis Publishers, 200 Corporate Blvd. NW, Boca Raton, Florida 33431. (407) 994-0555 or (800)272-7737. 1991. 5th ed. Since the last edition, this essential research aid reflects increased interest in areas such as ground water contamination, modeling, and legal issues. Contains a listing of general bibliographies, periodicals, and books, followed by a subject section covering 3 specific aspects of hydrogeology.

New Publications of the Geological Survey. U.S. Department of the Interior, Geological Survey, 119 National Center, Reston, Virginia 22092. (703) 648-4460. 1984-. Monthly. Bibliography of geological publications and related government documents published by the Geological Survey.

DIRECTORIES

Agricultural Information Resource Centers, a World Directory 1990. Rita C. Fisher. IAALD World Directory Working Group, 716 W. Indiana Ave., Urbana, Illinois 61801-4836. (217) 333-7687. 1990. Includes 3,971 information resource centers that have agriculture related collection and/or information services.

American Water Works Association-Buyers' Guide Issue. American Water Works Association, 6666 W. Quincy Ave., Denver, Colorado 80235. (303) 794-7711.

American Water Works Association Directory. The Association, 6666 W. Quincy Ave., Denver, Colorado 80235. (303) 794-7711. Annual.

Buyer Guide and Publications Catalog of American Water Works Association. American Water Works Association, 6666 W. Quincy Ave., Denver, Colorado 80235. (303) 794-7711. 1991. Includes directories of AWWA agent, representative and distributor members; AWWA manufacturers agents and distributor members; AWWA contract members; consultant members; and the supplier catalog.

California Water Resources Directory: A Guide to Organizations and Information Sources. Roberta Childers, ed. California Institute of Public Affairs, PO Box 189040, Sacramento, California 95818. (916) 442-2472. 1991. Second edition. Describes water-related activities of national executive and independent government agencies in the state. Also includes details on the California state government.

Directory of Water Resources Expertise. California Water Resources Center, Rubidoux Hall, University of California, Riverside, California 92521. (714) 787-4327.

Water Systems Council and Pitless Adapter Division–Membership Directory. Pitless Adapter Division/ Water Systems Council, 600 S. Federal St., Suite 400, Chicago, Illinois 60605. (312) 922-6222.

ENCYCLOPEDIAS AND DICTIONARIES

American Water Works Association Encyclopedia. American Water Works Association, 6666 W. Quincy Ave., Denver, Colorado 80235. (303) 794-7711. 1985. Subject headings used in water resources research and literature.

Aqualine Thesaurus 2. Joyce G. Smith and Peter G. Jennings. Water Research Centre, Ellis Horwood, Market Cross House, Cooper St., Chichester, England PO19 1EB. 1987.

The Encyclopedia of Geochemistry and Environmental Sciences. Rhodes Whitmore Fairbridge. Van Nostrand Reinhold Co., 115 5th Ave., New York, New York 10003. (212) 254-3232. 1972.

Grzimek's Encyclopedia of Ecology. Bernhard Grzimek. Van Nostrand Reinhold, 115 5th Ave., New York, New York 10003. (212) 254-3232. 1976.

Illustrated Encyclopedia of Science and the Future. Mike Biscare, et al., ed. Marshall Cavendish, 58 Old Compton St., London, England 0W1V5 PA. 01-734 6710. 1983. Twenty volumes. Each volume has 5 sections: Frontiers, Electronics in Action, Medical Science, Military Technology, and Resources.

Life Sciences on File. Diagram Group. Facts on File, Inc., 460 Park Ave. S., New York, New York 10016. (212) 683-2244. 1986. Encyclopedia of pictorial collection in life sciences. Deals with all major topics in life sciences including ecology.

McGraw-Hill Encyclopedia of Environmental Science. Sybil P. Parker. McGraw-Hill Science & Engineering Books, 11 W. 19th St., New York, New York 10011. (212) 337-6010. 1980. Covers ecology, man's influence on nature, and environmental protection.

North American Reference Encyclopedia of Ecology and Pollution. William White. North American Pub. Co., 401 N. Broad St., Philadelphia, Pennsylvania 19108. (215) 238-5300. 1972.

Van Nostrand's Scientific Encyclopedia. Glenn D. Considine, ed. Van Nostrand Reinhold, 115 5th Ave., New York, New York 10003. (212) 254-3232. 1983. Sixth edition. Includes all broad subject areas in science.

The Water Encyclopedia. Lewis Publishers, 2000 Corporate Blvd. N.W., Boca Raton, Florida 33431. (800) 272-7737. 1990. 2d ed. Includes groundwater contamination, drinking water, floods, waterborne diseases, global warming, climate change, irrigation, water agencies and organizations, precipitation, oceans and seas, and river, lakes and waterfalls.

GENERAL WORKS

Advances in Water Treatment and Environmental Management. George Thomas. Elsevier Science Publishing Co., 655 Avenue of the Americas, New York, New York 10010. (212) 984-5800. 1991. Measurement and control of groundwater quality, rivers, river management, estuaries, and beaches.

Climate Change and U.S. Water Resources. P. E. Waggoner, ed. John Wiley & Sons, Inc., 605 3rd Ave., New York, New York 10158-0012. (212) 850-6000. 1990. Covers latest research in climate changes and subsequent effects on water supply. Topics include future water use, statistics in forecasting, vulnerability of water systems, irrigation, urban water systems, and reallocation by markets and prices.

Conservation of Water and Related Land Resources. Peter E. Black. Rowman & Littlefield, Publishers, Inc., 8705 Bollman Pl., Savage, Maryland 20763. (301) 306-0400. 1988. 2d ed. Analysis of the current status of water and land-water resources policy and programming in the United States.

Down by the River: The Impact of Federal Water Projects and Policies on Biological Diversity. Constance Elizabeth Hunt with Verne Huser. Island Press, 1718 Connecticut Ave. N.W., Suite 300, Washington, District of Columbia 20009. (202) 232-7933. 1988. Presents case studies of development projects on seven river systems, including the Columbia, the Delaware, the Missouri, and the rivers of Maine ,to illustrate their effect on biological diversity.

Earth Ponds: The Country Pond Maker's Guide. Tim Matson. Countryman Press, PO Box 175, Woodstock, Vermont 05091-0175. (802) 457-1049. 1991. How-to manual regarding pond making.

Geotechnical and Environmental Geophysics. Stanley H. Ward. Society of Exploration Geophysicists, PO Box 702740, Tulsa, Oklahoma 74170-2740. (918) 493-3516. 1990.

Integrated Water Management. Bruce Mitchell, ed. Belhaven Press, 136 S. Broadway, Irvington, New York 10533. (914) 591-9111. 1990. Using case studies from the United States, New Zealand, Canada, Japan, England, Poland and Nigeria, this book surveys the principles and the practice of water management.

Magill's Survey of Science. Life Science Series. Frank N. Magill, ed. Salem Press, PO Box 50062, Pasadena, California 91105. 1991. Six volumes. Contents: v.1. A-Central and peripheral nervous system functions; v.2. Central metabolism regulation - eukaryotic transcriptional control; v.3. Positive and negative eukaryotic transcriptional control - mammalian hormones; v.4. Hormones and behavior - muscular contraction; v.5. Muscular contraction and relaxation - sexual reproduction in plants; v.6. Reproductive behavior and mating - X inactivation and the Lyon hypothesis.

Microcomputer Applications in Water Resources. Otto J. Helweg. Prentice Hall, Rte. 9W, Englewood Cliffs, New Jersey 07632. (201) 592-2000; (800) 634-2863. 1991. Presents 14 programs for solving a range of water resource engineering problems on microcomputers. Includes a 5 1/4 inch disk containing the problems described in the text. Also includes a basic introduction to computers and to BASIC, in which the programs are written.

Overtapped Oasis: Reform or Revolution for Western Water. Marc Reisner and Sarah Bates. Island Press, 1718 Connecticut Ave. N.W., Suite 300, Washington, District of Columbia 20009. (202) 232-7933. 1990. Comprehensive critique of the cardinal dogma of the American West: that the region is always running out of water and therefore must build more and more dams.

Promotion of Women's Participation in Water Resources Development. UNIPUB, 4611-F Assembly Dr., Lanham, Maryland 20706-4391. (301) 459-7666; (800) 274-4888. 1990.

Reserved Water Rights Settlement Manual. Peter W. Sly. Island Press, 1718 Connecticut Ave. N.W., Suite 300, Washington, District of Columbia 20009. (202) 232-7933. 1988. Manual provides a negotiating process for settling water disputes between states and/or reservations.

Supplying Water and Saving the Environment for Six Billion People. Udai P. Singh and Otto J. Helweg, eds. American Society of Civil Engineers, 345 E. 47th St., New York, New York 10017. (212) 705-7288; (800) 548-2723. 1990. Proceedings of selected sessions from the 1990 ASCE Convention, San Francisco, CA, Nov. 5-8, 1990. Sponsored by the Environmental Engineering Division, Irrigation and Drainage Division, Water Resources Planning and Management Division of the American Society of Civil Engineers.

System Analysis Applied to Management of Water Resource. M. Jellali, ed. Pergamon Microforms International, Inc., Fairview Park, Elmsford, New York 10523. (914) 592-7720. 1989. Proceedings of the Fourth IFAC Symposium, Rabat, Morocco, 11- 13 October 1988. Illustrates aspects of the application of systems analysis to water resource management. Also included are theoretical discussions on mathematical modelling and the potential role of expert systems.

Water Law. William Goldfarb. Lewis Publishers, 200 Corporate Blvd. NW, Boca Raton, Florida 33431. (407) 994-0555 or (800)272-7737. 1988. Explains all legal terms and covers all aspects of water laws, including water pollution law.

Water Quality Modeling. Brian Henderson-Sellere, et al. CRC Press, 2000 Corporate Blvd. N.W., Boca Raton, Florida 33431. (407) 994-0555; (800) 272-7737. 1990. Issues in four volumes. Discusses water supply and treatment and water resources engineering.

Water Resource Management: Integrated Policies. OECD Publications and Information Center, 2001 L St., N.W., Suite 700, Washington, District of Columbia 20036. (202) 785-OECD. 1989. Report underlines the need for more effective policy integration within the water sector itself (in order to improve water quality and quantity, demand management, surface and groundwater supply).

Water Resources Planning. Andrew A. Dzurik. Rowman & Littlefield, Publishers, Inc., 8705 Bollman Pl., Savage, Maryland 20763. (301) 306-0400. 1990. Offers a comprehensive survey of all aspects of water resources planning and management.

Western Water Made Simple. Ed Marston, ed. Island Press, 1718 Connecticut Ave. N.W., Suite 300, Washington, District of Columbia 20009. (202) 232-7933. 1987.

Wetlands: Mitigating and Regulating Development Impacts. David Salvesen. The Urban Land Institute, 1090 Vermont Ave. N.W., Washington, District of Columbia 20005. (202) 289-8500; (800) 237-9196. 1990. Presents the latest examination of the conflicts surrounding development of wetlands. Explains both federal and state wetland regulations. Included is an up-to-date review of important wetlands case law and a detailed look at six of the toughest state programs.

GOVERNMENTAL ORGANIZATIONS

Assistant Attorney General: Environment and Resources Division, Department of Justice. Room 2143, 10th St. and Constitution Ave., N.W., Washington, District of Columbia 20530. (202) 514-2701.

Great Lakes Commission. The Argus II Bldg., 400 4th St., Ann Arbor, Michigan 48103-4816. (313) 665-9135.

Office of Environmental Affairs: Bureau of Reclamation. 18th and C St., N.W., Washington, District of Columbia 20240. (202) 343-4662.

HANDBOOKS AND MANUALS

Ground Water Age–Handbook Issue. National Trade Publications, Inc., 13 Century Hill, Latham, New York 12110. (518) 783-1281.

Ground Water Manual: A Guide for the Investigation, Development, and Management of Ground Water Resources. U.S. G.P.O., Washington, District of Columbia 20401. (202) 512-0000. 1981. Underground water resources in the water states.

Handbook of Water Resources and Pollution Control. Harry W. Gehm. Van Nostrand Reinhold, 115 Fifth Ave., New York, New York 10003. (212) 254-3232. 1976. Covers sewage disposal, water pollution, and water supply engineering.

The Poisoned Well: New Strategies for Groundwater Protection. Eric P. Jorgensen, ed. Island Press, 1718 Connecticut Ave. N.W., Suite 300, Washington, District of Columbia 20009. (202) 232-7933. 1989. Explains how individuals can work with agencies and the courts to enforce water laws, how the major federal water laws, work what remedies exist for each type of groundwater contamination, and what state and local programs may be helpful.

Practical Handbook of Ground Water Monitoring. David M. Nielsen. Lewis Publishers, 2000 Corporate Blvd., N.W., Boca Raton, Florida 33431. (407) 994-0555 or (800) 272-7737. 1991. Covers the complete spectrum of state-of-the-science technology applied to investigations of ground water quality. Emphasis is placed on the practical application of current technology, and minimum theory is discussed.

Public Involvement Manual: Involving the Public in Water and Power Resources Decisions. James L. Creighton. U.S. G.P.O., Washington, District of Columbia 20401. (202) 512-0000. Citizen participation in power development.

Standard Handbook of Environmental Engineering. Robert A. Corbitt. McGraw-Hill, 1221 Ave. of the Americas, New York, New York 10020. (212) 512-2000 or (800) 262-4729. 1990. Hands-on reference to understand environmental engineering technology. Covers air quality control, water supply, wastewater disposal, waste management, stormwater and hazardous wastes.

Water Resources Protection Technology. J. Toby Tourbier. Urban Land Institute, 625 Indiana Ave., NW, Ste. 400, Washington, District of Columbia 20004. (202) 624-7000. 1981. Covers urbanization and water resources development.

ONLINE DATA BASES

Chemical Abstracts-CA. Chemical Abstracts Service, 2540 Olentangy River Rd., P.O. Box 3012, Columbus, Ohio 43210. (800) 848-6533 or (614) 421-3600. Information sources include 9000 journals, patents from 27 countries, two industrial property organizations, new books, conference proceedings, and government research reports.

Computerized Engineering Index–COMPENDEX. Engineering Information Inc., 345 E. 47th St., New York, New York 10017. (212) 705-7600.

ENSI. Asian Institute of Technology, Environmental Sanitation Information Center, P.O. Box 2754, Bangkok, Thailand 10501. 66 (2) 5290100-13-X2870.

Master Water Data Index. U.S. Geological Survey, Water Resources Division, National Water Data Exchange, 12201 Sunrise Valley Dr., Reston, Virginia 22092. (703) 648-4460. Information on more than 450,000 water data collection sites.

National Stream Quality Accounting Network. National Water Data Exchange, U.S. Geological Survey, 421 National Center, Reston, Virginia 22092. (703) 648-4000. 150 hydrologic measurements collected at daily, monthly and quarterly intervals from more than 500 monitoring stations in the U.S.

National Water Data Exchange. National Water Data Exchange, U.S. Geological Survey, 421 National Center, Reston, Virginia 22092. (703) 648-4000. Identification, location, and acquisition of water data.

National Water Data Storage and Retrieval System. U.S. Geological Survey, Water Resources Division, 12201 Sunrise Valley Dr., Reston, Virginia 22092. (703) 648-4460. Surface and underground water resources of the United States.

SCISEARCH. Institute for Scientific Information, University City Science Center, 3501 Market St., Philadelphia, Pennsylvania 19104. (215) 386-0100.

Source of Water Supply. National Ground Water Information Center, National Water Well Association, 6375 Riverside Dr., Dublin, Ohio 43017. (614) 761-1711.

Water Resources Abstracts. U.S. Department of the Interior, Geological Survey, Water Resources Scientific Information Center, 119 National Center, Reston, Virginia 22092. (703) 648-4460.

PERIODICALS AND NEWSLETTERS

American Public Works Association Reporter. American Public Works Association, 106 W. 11th St., Ste. 1800, Kansas City, Missouri 64105-1806. (816 472-6100. Monthly. Articles for public works officials.

American Water Works Association Journal. American Water Works Association, 6666 W. Quincy Avenue, Denver, Colorado 80235. (303) 794-7711. Monthly. Articles on public water supply systems.

American Water Works Association Washington Report. American Water Works Association, 6666 W. Quincy Ave., Denver, Colorado 80235. (303) 794-7711. Monthly. News and developments affecting the water supply industry.

Divining Rod. New Mexico Water Resources Research Institute, Box 30001, Dept. 3167, Las Cruces, New Mexico 88003-0001. (505) 646-1813. Quarterly. Water issues & water research in New Mexico.

Ecological Monographs. Business Office of the Ecological Society of America, Center of Environmental Studies, Arizona State University, Tempe, Arizona 85287-1201. (602) 965-3000. Quarterly. Scientific journal of ecological issues.

Editorially Speaking about Ground Water: Its First Quarter Century. Jay H. Lehr and Anita B. Stanley. National Water Well Association, 6375 Riverside Dr., Dublin, Ohio 43017. (614) 761-1711. 1988. A collection of editorials from the Journal of Ground Water which traces the evolution of ground water science during the journal's first 25 years of publication.

ENFO. 1251-B Miller Ave., Winter Park, Florida 32789-4827. (407) 644-5377. Bimonthly. Water resources, parks, wildlife air quality, growth management, government and private actions.

Environment Ohio. Ohio Environmental Protection Agency, PO Box 1049, Columbus, Ohio 43216. (614) 644-2160. Bimonthly. Air, water, land pollution, and public water supply.

Environmental Defense Fund Letter. Environmental Defense Fund, 257 Park Avenue South, New York, New York 10010. (212) 505-2100. 1971-. Bimonthly. Environmental issues of concern.

Ground Water Monitoring Review. Water Well Journal Publishing Co. National Water Well Association, 6375 Riverside Drive, Dublin, Ohio 43017. (614) 761-3222. Quarterly. Covers protection and restoration of ground water.

Ground Water Newsletter. Water Information Center, Inc., 125 East Bethpage Road, Plainview, New York 11803. (516) 249-7634. Biweekly. Covers ground water exploration, development, and management.

Hydata News and Views. American Water Resources Association, 5410 Grosvenor Lane, Suite 220, Bethesda, Maryland 20814. (301) 493-8600. Six times a year. Research, planning and management in water resources.

ICWP Policy Statement & Bylaws. Interstate Conference on Water Problems, 5300 M Street, NW, Suite 800, Washington, District of Columbia 20037. (202) 466-7287. Annual. Covers conservation and administration of water.

Institute for Research on Land and Water Resources. Newsletter. Institute for Research on Land and Water Resources, Pennsylvania State University, University Park, Pennsylvania 16802. 1970-. Bimonthly.

International Water Report. Water Information Center, Inc., 125 East Bethpage Road, Plainview, New York 11803. (516) 249-7634. Quarterly. Covers water works and topics done in Europe, Asia, South America.

Journal of Water Resources Planning and Management. American Society of Civil Engineers, Resource Planning and Management Division, 345 E. 47th St., New York,

New York 10017. (212) 705-7288; (800) 548-2723. 1983-Quarterly. Reports on all phases of planning and management of water resources. Examines social, economic, environmental, and administrative concerns relating to the use and conservation of water.

Kansas Water News. Kansas Water Resources Board, Mills Bldg., 4th Floor, 109 West 9th, Topeka, Kansas 66612.

National Water Line. National Water Resources Association, 3800 North Fairfax Drive, #4, Arlington, Virginia 22203. (703) 524-1544. Monthly. Covers water resource development projects.

Notes on Water Research. Water Research Centre, Stevenage Laboratory, Elder Way, Stevenage, England SG1 1TH. 1975-. Bimonthly. Notes on water pollution.

Underwater Naturalist. American Littoral Society, Sandy Hook, Highlands, New Jersey 07732. (201) 291-0055. Monthly. Covers issues relating to coastal areas.

Universities Council on Water Resources Update. Universities Council on Water Resources, 4543 Faner Hall, Dept. of Geography, Southern Illinois University, Carbondale, Illinois 62901-4526. (618) 536-7571. Three times a year. Covers education, research, and legislation on water resources.

Washington Report. Interstate Conference on Water Policy, 955 L'Enfant Plaza, 6th Floor, Washington, District of Columbia 20024. (202) 466-7287. Every six weeks. Covers water conservation, development and administration.

Water and Air Resources in North Carolina. Department of Natural and Economic Resources, PO Box 27687, Raleigh, North Carolina 27611.

Water and Wastes Digest. Scranton Gillette Communications, Inc., 380 Northwest Highway, Des Plaines, Illinois 60016. (708) 298-6622. Bimonthly. Covers publicly and privately owned water and sewage systems.

Water Supply (from the State Capitals). Bethune Jones, 321 Sunset Ave., Asbury Park, New Jersey 07712. 1946-. Fourteen times a year. Provides water resource information from state capitals.

Water Supply Management. A. B. Morse Co., 200 James St., Barrington, Illinois 60010. 1927-. Monthly.

Waterworld News. American Water Works Association, 6666 West Quincy Ave., Denver, Colorado 80235. (303) 794-7711. Bimonthly. Articles on technological developments in the water industry.

Western Lands and Waters Series. Arthur H. Clark Co., 1264 S. Central Ave., Glendale, California 91204. 1959-. Irregular.

Western Water. Western Water Education Foundation, 717 K St., Ste. 517, Sacramento, California 95814. (916) 444-6240. Bimonthly.

RESEARCH CENTERS AND INSTITUTES

Arkansas Water Resources Research Center. University of Arkansas, 113 Ozark Hall, Fayetteville, Arkansas 72701. (501) 575-4403.

Auburn University, Water Resources Research Institute. 202 Hargis Hall, Auburn University, Alabama 36849-5124. (205) 844-5080.

California Water Resources Center. University of California, Riverside, California 92521. (714) 787-4327.

Environmental Systems Engineering Institute. University of Central Florida, Department of Civil Engineering and Environmental Science, PO Box 25000, Orlando, Florida 32816. (305) 275-2785.

Institute of Water Resources. University of Connecticut, U-18, Storrs, Connecticut 06269-4018. (203) 486-0335.

Mississippi State University, Water Resources Research Institute. P.O. Drawer AD, Mississippi State, Mississippi 39762. (601) 325-3620.

Montana University System Water Resources Center. 412 Cobleigh Hall, Bozeman, Montana 59715. (406) 994-6690.

New Mexico State University, Water Resources Research Institute. P.O. Box 30001 Dept. 3167, Las Cruces, New Mexico 88003. (505) 646-4337.

North Dakota Water Resources Research Institute. North Dakota State University, Box 5626, Fargo, North Dakota 58105. (701) 237-7193.

Ohio State University, Water Resources Center. 262 Agriculture Building, 590 Woody Hayes Drive, Columbus, Ohio 43210. (614) 292-2334.

Oklahoma State University, Oklahoma Water Resources Research Institute. University Center for Water Research, 003 Life Science East, Stillwater, Oklahoma 74078. (405) 744-9994.

Oklahoma State University, University Center for Water Research. 003 Life Sciences East, Stillwater, Oklahoma 74078. (405) 744-9995.

Oregon State University, Water Resources Research Institute. 210 Strand Agriculture Hall, Corvallis, Oregon 97331-2208. (503) 737-4022.

Pennsylvania State University, Environmental Resources Research Institute. 100 Land and Water Resource Building, University Park, Pennsylvania 16802. (814) 863-0291.

Puerto Rico Water Resources Research Institute. College of Engineering, University of Puerto Rico, P.O. Box 5000, Mayaguez, Puerto Rico 00709-5000. (809) 834-4040.

South Dakota State University, Water Resources Institute. Brookings, South Dakota 57007. (605) 688-4910.

Southwest Consortium on Plant Genetics and Water Resources. New Mexico State University, Box 3GL, Las Cruces, New Mexico 88003. (505) 646-5453.

State of Washington Water Research Center. Washington State University, Pullman, Washington 99164-3002. (509) 335-5531.

Texas A&M University Texas Water Resources Institute. College Station, Texas 77843-2118. (409) 845-1851.

Texas Tech University, Water Resources Center. Box 4630, Lubbock, Texas 79409. (806) 742-3597.

University of Florida, Water Resources Research Center. 424 Black Hall, Gainesville, Florida 32611. (904) 471-0684.

University of Hawaii at Manoa, Water Resources Research Center. 2540 Dole Street, Honolulu, Hawaii 96822. (808) 956-7847.

University of Idaho, Idaho Water Resources Research Institute. Morrill Hall 106, Moscow, Idaho 83843. (208) 885-6429.

University of Illinois, Water Resources Center. 2535 Hydrosystems Laboratory, 205 North Matthews Avenue, Urbana, Illinois 61801. (217) 333-0536.

University of Kansas, Water Resources Institute. Lawrence, Kansas 66045. (913) 864-3807.

University of Kentucky, Kentucky Water Resources Research Institute. 219 Anderson Hall, Lexington, Kentucky 40506-0046. (606) 257-1832.

University of Louisville, Water Resource Laboratory. Louisville, Kentucky 40292. (502) 588-6731.

University of Maine, Environmental Studies Center. Coburn Hall #11, Orono, Maine 04469. (207) 581-1490.

University of Maryland, Water Resources Research Center. 3101 Chemistry Bldg., College Park, Maryland 20742. (301) 405-6829.

University of Massachusetts, Massachusetts Water Resources Research Center. Blaisdell House, Amherst, Massachusetts 01003. (413) 545-2842.

University of Minnesota, Center for Natural Resource Policy and Management. 110 Green Hall, 1530 North Cleveland Avenue, St. Paul, Minnesota 55108. (612) 624-9796.

University of Minnesota, Water Resources Research Center. 1518 Cleveland Ave., Ste. 302, St. Paul, Minnesota 55108. (612) 624-9282.

University of Missouri-Columbia, Missouri Water Resources Research Center. 0056 Engineering Complex, Columbia, Missouri 65211. (314) 882-3132.

University of Nevada-Reno, Desert Research Institute, Water Resources Center. P.O. Box 60220, Reno, Nevada 89506-0220. (703) 673-7365.

University of New Hampshire, Water Resources Research Center. 218 Science & Engineering Research Building, Durham, New Hampshire 08324. (603) 862-2144.

University of North Carolina, North Carolina Water Resources Research Institute. North Carolina State University, Box 7912, Raleigh, North Carolina 27695-7912. (919) 737-2815.

University of North Texas, Institute of Applied Sciences. P.O. Box 13078, Denton, Texas 76203. (817) 565-2694.

University of Oklahoma, Bureau of Water and Environmental Resources Research. P.O. Box 2850, Norman, Oklahoma 73070. (405) 325-2960.

University of Rhode Island, Water Resources Center. 202 Bliss Hall, Kingston, Rhode Island 02881. (401) 792-2297.

University of Tennessee at Knoxville, Water Resources Research Center. Knoxville, Tennessee 37996. (615) 974-2151.

University of Texas at Austin, Center for Research in Water Resources. Balcones Research Center, Building 119, Austin, Texas 78712. (512) 471-3131.

University of Vermont, Vermont Water Resources Research Center. Aiken Center for Natural Resources, Burlington, Vermont 05405. (802) 656-4057.

University of Wisconsin-Madison, Center for Biotic Systems. 1042 WARF Office Building, 610 Walnut Street, Madison, Wisconsin 53705. (608) 262-9937.

University of Wisconsin-Madison, Water Resources Center. 1975 Willow Drive, Madison, Wisconsin 53706. (608) 262-3577.

Utah State University, Utah Water Research Laboratory. Logan, Utah 84322-8200. (801) 750-3200.

Virginia Water Resources Research Center. Virginia Polytech Institute and State University, 617 North Main Street, Blacksburg, Virginia 24060. (703) 231-5624.

Water Resources Association of the Delaware River Basin. Box 867, Davis Road, Valley Forge, Pennsylvania 19481. (215) 783-0634.

Water Resources Center. University of Delaware, 210 Hullihen Hall, Newark, Delaware 19716. (302) 451-2191.

Water Resources Institute. Grand Valley State University, Allendale, Michigan 49401. (616) 895-3749.

Water Resources Research Center. University of Arizona, Geology Building, Room 314, Tucson, Arizona 85721. (602) 621-7607.

STATISTICS SOURCES

Compendium on Water Supply, Drought, and Conservation. National Regulatory Research Institute. U.S. G.P.O, Washington, District of Columbia 20402-9325. (202) 512-0000. 1989. Water supply and demand, drought, conservation, utility ratemaking and regulatory issues.

National Water Summary. U.S. G.P.O, Washington, District of Columbia 20402-9325. (202) 512-0000. Annual. Hydrological events and issues, including floods, drought, inland oil spills, and water supply and use.

Report on the Nation's Renewable Resources. U.S. Forest Service. U.S. G.P.O., Washington, District of Columbia 20401. (202) 512-0000. Quinquennial. Projections of resource use and supply from 1920 to 2040, covering wilderness, wildlife, fish, range, timber, water and minerals.

Water Resources Data. U.S. Geological Survey. U.S. G.P.O., Washington, District of Columbia 20401. (202) 512-0000. Annual. Data on water supply and quality of streams, lakes and reservoirs for individual states by water year.

Water Resources Development. U.S. Army Core of Engineers. U.S. G.P.O., Washington, District of Columbia 20401. (202) 512-0000. Biennial. Data on the corporation's activities relating to flood control, erosion, shore protection and disaster relief.

TRADE ASSOCIATIONS AND PROFESSIONAL SOCIETIES

American Society of Irrigation Consultants. Four Union Sq., Suite C, Union City, California 94587. (415) 471-9244.

American Society of Sanitary Engineering. Box 40362, Bay Village, Ohio 44140. (216) 835-3040.

American Water Resources Association. 5410 Grosvenor Lane, Suite 220, Bethesda, Maryland 20814. (301) 493-8600.

American Water Works Association. 6666 W. Quincy Ave., Denver, Colorado 80235. (303) 794-7711.

Association of Environmental Engineering Professors. Department of Civil Engineering, Virginia Polytechnic Institute and State University, Blacksburg, Virginia 24061. (703) 231-6021.

Clean Water Action Project. c/o David Zwick, 1320 18th St. N.W., Washington, District of Columbia 20003. (202) 457-1286.

Conservation Foundation. 1250 24th St., N.W., Washington, District of Columbia 20037. (202) 293-4800. The World Wildlife Fund absorbed the Conservation Foundation in 1990.

Environmental Defense Fund. 257 Park Ave., S., New York, New York 10010. (212) 505-2100. Non-profit organization that was established more than 20 years ago. Its goals are to protect the earth's environment by providing lasting solutions to global environmental problems.

International Water Resources Association. 205 N. Mathews Ave., University of Illinois, Urbana, Illinois 61801. (217) 333-0536.

Interstate Conference on Water Policy. 955 L'Enfant Plaza, 6th Floor, Washington, District of Columbia 20024. (202) 466-7287.

National Association of Water Companies. 1725 K St., N.W., Suite 1212, Washington, District of Columbia 20006. (202) 833-8383.

National Association of Water Institute Directors. Water Resources Research Center, Blaisdell House, University of Massachusetts, Amherst, Massachusetts 01003. (413) 545-2842.

National Water Alliance. 1225 I St., N.W., Suite 300, Washington, District of Columbia 20005. (202) 646-0917.

National Water Center. P.O. Box 264, Eureka Springs, Arkansas 72632. (510) 253-9755.

National Water Resources Association. 3800 N. Fairfax Dr., Suite 4, Arlington, Virginia 22203. (703) 524-1544.

National Water Supply Improvement Association. P.O. Box 102, St. Leonard, Maryland 20865. (301) 855-1173.

Soil & Water Conservation Society. 7515 Northeast Ankeny Rd., Ankeny, Iowa 50021. (515) 289-2331.

Universities Council on Water Resources. 4543 Faner Hall, Dept. of Geography, Southern Illinois University, Carbondale, Illinois 62901. (618) 536-7571.

Water Resources Congress. Courthouse Plaza II, 2300 Clarendon Blvd., Suite 404, Arlington, Virginia 22201. (703) 525-4881.

Water Systems Council. 600 S. Federal St., Suite 400, Chicago, Illinois 60605. (312) 922-6222.

Western Snow Conference. P.O. Box 2646, Portland, Oregon 97208. (503) 326-2843.

Western Water Education Foundation. 717 K St., Ste. 517, Sacramento, California 95814-3406. (916) 444-6240.

WATER TABLE

See: HYDROLOGY

WATER TASTE

See: WATER QUALITY

WATER TEMPERATURE

See also: LAKES

ABSTRACTING AND INDEXING SERVICES

Abstracts of Air and Water Conservation Literature. American Petroleum Institute. Central Abstracting and Indexing Service, 275 Madison Avenue, New York, New York 10016. 1972.

Applied Science and Technology Index. H.W. Wilson Co., 950 University Ave., Bronx, New York 10452. (800) 367-6770. Formerly Industrial Arts Index.

Aqualine Abstracts. Water Research Centre. c/o Pergamon Microforms International, Inc., Fairview Park, Elmsford, New York 10523. (914) 592-7720. 1927-. Contains some 8,000 records annually on water and wastewater technology. Covers all aspects of water, wastewater, associated engineering services and the aquatic environment. Over 600 periodicals, as well as books, reports and conference proceedings and other publications from water related institutions worldwide are scanned. Also available online.

ASFA Aquaculture Abstracts. Cambridge Scientific Abstracts, Inc., 5161 River Rd., Bethesda, Maryland 20816. (301) 961-6750. 1984.

General Science Index. H. W. Wilson Co., 950 University Ave., Bronx, New York 10452. 1978-. Monthly, also issued in annual cumulation. Cumulative subject index to English language periodicals in the subject fields of astronomy, botany, chemistry, earth science, environment and conservation, food and nutrition, genetics, mathematics, medicine and health, microbiology, oceanography, physics, physiology and zoology.

Science Citation Index. Institute for Scientific Information, 3501 Market St., Philadelphia, Pennsylvania 19104. 1961-.

ONLINE DATA BASES

SCISEARCH. Institute for Scientific Information, University City Science Center, 3501 Market St., Philadelphia, Pennsylvania 19104. (215) 386-0100.

WATER TRANSPORT

See: TRANSPORTATION

WATER TREATMENT

See also: WATER PURIFICATION

ABSTRACTING AND INDEXING SERVICES

Abstracts of Air and Water Conservation Literature. American Petroleum Institute. Central Abstracting and Indexing Service, 275 Madison Avenue, New York, New York 10016. 1972.

Agrindex. AGRIS Coordinating Center, Via delle Terme di Caracalla, Rome, Italy I-00100. 61 0181-FA01. 1975-.

Applied Ecology Abstracts Studies in Renewable Natural Resources. Information Retrieval Ltd., 1911 Jefferson Davis Highway, Arlington, Virginia 22202. 1975-. Monthly.

Applied Science and Technology Index. H.W. Wilson Co., 950 University Ave., Bronx, New York 10452. (800) 367-6770. Formerly Industrial Arts Index.

Aqualine Abstracts. Water Research Centre. c/o Pergamon Microforms International, Inc., Fairview Park, Elmsford, New York 10523. (914) 592-7720. 1927-. Contains some 8,000 records annually on water and wastewater technology. Covers all aspects of water, wastewater, associated engineering services and the aquatic environment. Over 600 periodicals, as well as books, reports and conference proceedings and other publications from water related institutions worldwide are scanned. Also available online.

ASFA Aquaculture Abstracts. Cambridge Scientific Abstracts, Inc., 5161 River Rd., Bethesda, Maryland 20816. (301) 961-6750. 1984.

Biological and Agricultural Index. H.W. Wilson Co., 950 University Ave., Bronx, New York 10452. (800) 367-6770. 1916-. Monthly.

Bulletin Signaletique: Eau et Assainissement, Pollution Atmospherique, Droit des Pollutions. Centre de Documentation, Centre National de la Recherche Scientifique, 15, quai Anatole France, Paris, France 75700. (1) 45 55 92 25. 1983-. Monthly. Indexes pollution periodicals including water, atmospheric and related pollutions.

Chemical Abstracts. Chemical Abstracts Service, 2540 Olentangy River Rd., PO Box 3012, Columbus, Ohio 43210. (800) 848-6533. 1907-.

Engineering Index. The Engineering Index Inc., 345 E. 47th St., New York, New York 10017. 1962-.

General Science Index. H. W. Wilson Co., 950 University Ave., Bronx, New York 10452. 1978-. Monthly, also issued in annual cumulation. Cumulative subject index to English language periodicals in the subject fields of astronomy, botany, chemistry, earth science, environment and conservation, food and nutrition, genetics, mathematics, medicine and health, microbiology, oceanography, physics, physiology and zoology.

Geographical Abstracts. London School of Economics, Dept. of Geography, Regency House, 34 Duke St., London, England 1966-. Continued by Geo Abstracts issued in 6 parts: Pt. A. Landforms and the quaternary; Pt. B. Biogeography and Climatology; Pt. C. Economic geography; Pt. D. Social geography and cartography; Pt. E. Sedimentology; Pt. F. Regional and community planning.

Multimedia Index to Ecology. National Information Center for Educational Media, University of Southern California, Los Angeles, California 90007.

Pollution Abstracts. Cambridge Scientific Abstracts, 5161 River Rd., Bethesda, Maryland 20816. (301) 961-6750. Six/year. Indexes worldwide technical literature on environmental pollution. Covers air pollution, marine and freshwater pollution, sewage and wastewater treatment, waste management, toxicology and health, noise pollution, radiation, land pollution, and environmental policies, programs, legislation, and education. Also available online.

Public Health Engineering Abstracts. U.S. G.P.O., Washington, District of Columbia 20401. (202) 512-0000. Monthly.

Science Citation Index. Institute for Scientific Information, 3501 Market St., Philadelphia, Pennsylvania 19104. 1961-.

Urban Affairs Abstracts. National League of Cities, 1301 Pennsylvania Ave., NW, Washington, District of Columbia 20004. (202) 626-3150. 1977-. Weekly.

BIBLIOGRAPHIES

Current Contents. Agriculture, Biology and Environmental Sciences. Institute for Scientific Information, 3501 Market St., Philadelphia, Pennsylvania 19104. (800) 523-1857. 1973-. Previous title: Current Contents. Agricultural, Food & Veterinary Sciences. Gives the table of contents of periodicals in the fields of agriculture, biology, environmental and related areas.

DIRECTORIES

American Water Works Association–Buyers' Guide Issue. American Water Works Association, 6666 W. Quincy Ave., Denver, Colorado 80235. (303) 794-7711.

American Water Works Association Directory. The Association, 6666 W. Quincy Ave., Denver, Colorado 80235. (303) 794-7711. Annual.

Directory of Commercial Hazardous Waste Treatment and Recycling Facilities. Office of Solid Waste, Environmental Protection Agency, Washington, District of Columbia 20460. (202) 475-8710.

ENCYCLOPEDIAS AND DICTIONARIES

American Water Works Association Encyclopedia. American Water Works Association, 6666 W. Quincy Ave., Denver, Colorado 80235. (303) 794-7711. 1985. Subject headings used in water resources research and literature.

Dictionary of Civil Engineering. John S. Scott. Halsted Press, Division of J. Wiley, 605 3rd Ave., New York, New York 10158. (212) 850-6000. 1981. Third edition.

Dictionary of Environmental Engineering and Related Sciences: English-Spanish, Spanish-English. Jose T. Villate. Ediciones Universal, 3090 SW 8th St., Miami, Florida 33135. (305) 642-3355. 1979.

Dictionary of Environmental Protection Technology: In Four Languages, English, German, French, Russian. Egon Seidel. Elsevier Science Publishing Co., 655 Avenue of the Americas, New York, New York 10010. (212) 984-5800. 1988.

Encyclopedia of Environmental Science and Engineering. J.R. Pfafflin. Gordon and Breach Science Publishers, Inc., 270 8th Ave., New York, New York 10011. (212) 206-8900. 1992.

English-Russian Dictionary of Environmental Protection: About 14,000 Terms. E.L. Milovanov. Pergamon Microforms International, Inc., Fairview Park, Elmsford, New York 10523. (914) 592-7720. 1981.

Environmental Engineering Dictionary. C. C. Lee. Government Institutes, Inc., 4 Research Pl., Ste. 200, Rockville, Maryland 20850. (301) 921-2300. 1989. Defines over 6000 engineering terms relating to pollutioncontrol technologies, monitoring, risk assessment, sampling andanalysis, quality control, permitting, and environmentally-regulated engineering and science. Includes bibliographical references (p. 612-627).

Grzimek's Encyclopedia of Ecology. Bernhard Grzimek. Van Nostrand Reinhold, 115 5th Ave., New York, New York 10003. (212) 254-3232. 1976.

North American Reference Encyclopedia of Ecology and Pollution. William White. North American Pub. Co., 401 N. Broad St., Philadelphia, Pennsylvania 19108. (215) 238-5300. 1972.

Van Nostrand's Scientific Encyclopedia. Glenn D. Considine, ed. Van Nostrand Reinhold, 115 5th Ave., New York, New York 10003. (212) 254-3232. 1983. Sixth edition. Includes all broad subject areas in science.

The Water Encyclopedia. Lewis Publishers, 2000 Corporate Blvd. N.W., Boca Raton, Florida 33431. (800) 272-7737. 1990. 2d ed. Includes groundwater contamination, drinking water, floods, waterborne diseases, global warming, climate change, irrigation, water agencies and organizations, precipitation, oceans and seas, and river, lakes and waterfalls.

GENERAL WORKS

Advances in Water Treatment and Environmental Management. George Thomas. Elsevier Science Publishing Co., 655 Avenue of the Americas, New York, New York 10010. (212) 984-5800. 1991. Measurement and control of groundwater quality, rivers, river management, estuaries, and beaches.

Analytical Instrumentation for the Water Industry. T. R. Crompton. Butterworth-Heinemann, Linacre House, Jordan Hill, Oxford, England OX2 8DP. (0865) 310366. 1990.

Basic Math Concepts for Water and Wastewater Plant Operators. Joanne Kirkpatrick Price. Technomic Publishing Co., 851 New Holland Ave., Box 3535, Lancaster, Pennsylvania 17604. (717) 291-5609. 1991.

Contamination of Ground Water Prevention, Assessment, Restoration. Michael Barcelona, et al. Noyes Publications, 120 Mill Rd., Park Ridge, New Jersey 07656. (201) 391-8484. 1990. Provides regulatory agencies and industry a convenient source of technical information on the management of contaminated ground water.

Drinking Water and Groundwater Remediation Cost Evaluation: Air Stripping. Robert M. Clark and Jeffrey Q. Adams. Lewis Publishers, 2000 Corporate Blvd. N.W., Boca Raton, Florida 33431. (800) 272-7737. 1991. The new software program shows air stripping costs and performance of the remediation of hazardous waste sites or drinking water treatment. The program helps do cost comparisons of the technology against other available technologies.

Drinking Water and Groundwater Remediation Cost Evaluation: Granular Activated Carbon. Robert M. Clark and Jeffrey Q. Adams. Lewis Publishers, 2000 Corporate Blvd. N.W., Boca Raton, Florida 33431. (800) 272-7737. 1991. Shows GAC costs and performance for the remediation of hazardous waste sites or drinking water treatment. Compares the cost of the technology against other available technologies.

Drinking Water Hazards: How to Know If There Are Toxic Chemicals in Your Water and What to Do If There Are. John Cary Stewart. Envirographics, PO Box 334, Hiram, Ohio 44234. (216) 527-5207. 1990. Documents the increase of cancer and other diseases that may be environmentally induced. Discusses the increases in the use of synthetic organic chemicals, and covers each group of drinking water contaminants in some detail: inorganic chemicals, heavy metals, bacteria and viruses, radionuclides, nitrates, and organic chemicals, including pesticides.

Drinking Water Treatment Technologies: Comparative Health Effects Assessments. Government Institutes, Inc., 4 Research Pl., Ste. 200, Rockville, Maryland 20850. (301) 921-2300. 1990. Evaluates the relative benefits and risks of each of the common types of drinking water treatment technologies.

Dynamic Modeling and Expert Systems in Wastewater Engineering. Giles G. Patry and David Chapman. Lewis Publishers, 200 Corporate Blvd. NW, Boca Raton, Florida 33431. (407) 994-0555 or (800)272-7737. 1988. Result of a workshop held at McMaster University (May 19-20, 1988). Brings together current work on dynamic modelling and expert systems as applied to the design, operation and control of waste- water treatment systems.

Evaluation of a Pulsed Bed Filter for Filtration of Municipal Primary Effluent. Donald S. Brown. U.S. Environmental Protection Agency, 401 M St. SW, Washington, District of Columbia 20460. (202) 260-2090. Water treatment and purification plants.

An Evaluation of Streaming Current Detectors. Steven Keith Dentel. AWWA Research Foundation, 6666 W. Quincy Ave., Denver, Colorado 80235. (303) 794-7711. 1988. Evaluation of water current meters.

Groundwater Contamination: Sources, Control, and Preventive Measures. Chester D. Rail. Technomic Publishing Co., 851 New Holland Ave., Box 3535, Lancaster, Pennsylvania 17604. (717) 291-5609. 1989. Reviews the presently known sources of groundwater contamination and its many complex interactions, including managerial and political implications.

Health Effects of Drinking Water Treatment Technologies. Lewis Publishers, 200 Corporate Blvd. NW, Boca Raton, Florida 33431. (407) 994-0555 or (800)272-7737. 1989. Evaluates the public health impact from the most widespread drinking water treatment technologies, with particular emphasis on disinfection. Focuses solely on the most common treatment technologies and practices used today.

Industrial Wastewater Heavy Metal Removal. Robert W. Peters. CRC Press, 2000 Corporate Blvd. N.W., Boca Raton, Florida 33431. (800) 272-7737. 1991. Includes heavy metal contamination episodes, metal speciation complexation, brief review of various unit operation

processes used for removal of heavy metals from solution with approximate percentage of installations employing each technology. Also discusses the various technologies used and the new emerging techniques.

Integrated Design of Water Treatment Facilities. Susumu Kawamura. John Wiley & Sons, Inc., 605 3rd Ave., New York, New York 10158-0012. (212) 850-6000. 1991. Covers research pilot studies and preliminary design studies, as well as the actual design, construction and plant management. Covers the entire project sequence, describing not only very basic and essential design criteria, but also how to design each phase to maximize overall efficiency while minimizing operation and maintenance costs.

New Health Considerations in Water Treatment. Roger Holdsworth, ed. Avebury Technical, Gower House, Croft Rd., Aldershot, England GU11 3HR. (0252) 331551. 1991.

Ozone in Water Treatment; Application and Engineering. Lewis Publishers, 200 Corporate Blvd. NW, Boca Raton, Florida 33431. (407) 994-0555 or (800)272-7737. 1991. Ozone technology as it is applied to drinking water production.

Proceedings of the 4th National Symposium on Individual and Small Community Sewage Systems. American Society of Agricultural Engineers, 2950 Niles Rd., St. Joseph, Michigan 49085-9659. (616) 429-0300. 1985. Includes current trends such as design, planning, management, and performance of large systems, the use of computers for on-site technology, site evaluation, etc. The 5th National Symposium held in 1987 further includes environmental effects of on-site disposal soil absorption/ system siting requirement and groundwater impact.

Significance and Treatment of Volatile Organic Compounds in Water Supplies. Neil M. Ram, et al. Lewis Publishers, 2000 Corporate Blvd., N.W., Boca Raton, Florida 33431. (407) 994-0555 or (800) 272-7737. 1990. Includes EPA approved analytical methods for VOC analysis, QA/QC, data quality objectives and limits of detection. Covers current methods for the assessment of health effects, including toxicity and carcinogenicity.

Surveillance of Drinking Water Quality in Rural Areas. Barry Lloyd. John Wiley & Sons, Inc., 605 3rd Ave, New York, New York 10158-0012. (212) 850-6000. 1991. Examines the human and technical resources required for monitoring, maintaining and improving the safety of rural water supply services. A practical guide to improving the quality of service from small water supplies, it describes the essential minimum of reliable methods of monitoring water quality and discusses new cost effective approaches to sanitary inspection of community water supplies.

Technologies for Small Water and Wastewater Systems. Edward J. Martin and Edward T. Martin. Van Nostrand Reinhold, 115 5th Ave., New York, New York 10003. (212) 254-3232. 1991. Addresses how to exploit different water treatment technologies according to available resources. Includes extensive sections on costs and design of both established and new technologies with vital data on limitations, operations and maintenance, control and special factors.

Technologies for Upgrading Existing or Designing New Drinking Water Treatment Facilities. Office of Drinking Water, Center for Environmental Research Information, U.S. Environmental Protection Agency. Technomic Publishing Co., 851 New Holland Ave., Box 3535, Lancaster, Pennsylvania 17604. (717) 291-5609. 1991. Discusses drinking water treatment technologies that address contamination and contaminant categories regulated under the Safe Drinking Water Act and its 1986 amendments.

The Washington Conference on Underground Storage, July 15-16, 1985, Stouffer Concourse. Center for Energy and Environmental Management, Washington, District of Columbia (202) 543-3939.

Wastewater Engineering: Treatment, Disposal, and Reuse. Metcalf & Eddy, Inc. McGraw-Hill Science & Engineering Books, 11 West 19th St., New York, New York 10011. (212) 337-6010. 1991. Reflects the impact of changing federal legislation on environmental quality control and sludge management. Gives a solid overall perspective on wastewater engineering.

Water Supply and Treatment. Jack G. Walters, ed. TAPPI Press, Technology Park/Atlanta, PO Box 105113, Atlanta, Georgia 30348. (404) 446-1400. 1989. In-depth study of water use in the pulp and paper industry. Covers selection of equipment for a water treatment system, raw water treatment, clarification, lime soda softening, filtration, demineralizers, cooling systems and cooling water treatment and pumping systems.

Water Treatment: Principles and Design. James M. Montgomery. John Wiley & Sons, Inc., 605 3rd Ave., New York, New York 10158-0012. (212) 850-6000. 1985. Offers a comprehensive coverage of the principles and design of water quality and treatment programs, plus plant operations.

HANDBOOKS AND MANUALS

The EPA Manual for Waste Minimization Opportunity Assessments. U.S. Environmental Protection Agency. Technomic Publishing Co., 851 New Holland Ave., Box 3535, Lancaster, Pennsylvania 17604. (717) 291-5609. 1990.

Handbook of Drinking Water Quality: Standards and Controls. John De Zuane. Van Nostrand Reinhold, 115 5th Ave., New York, New York 10003. (212) 254-3232. 1990. Aids in evaluating water quality control at every stage of the water path, from source to treatment plant, from distribution system to consumer.

High-Quality Industrial Water Management Manual. Paul N. Garay and Franklin M. Chn. The Association of Energy Engineers, 4025 Pleasantdale Rd., Suite 420, Atlanta, Georgia 30340. (404) 925-9558. 1992. Guide to managing water resources.

Ozone Drinking Water Treatment Handbook. Rip G. Rice. Lewis Publishers, 2000 Corporate Blvd., N.W., Boca Raton, Florida 33431. (407) 994-0555 or (800) 272-7737. 1991. Explains how ozone can be used to provide primary disinfection, while minimizing halogenated by-products.

Water Treatment Handbook. Degremont s.a., 184, ave. du 18-Juin-1940, Rueil-Malmaison, France F-92500. 1991. Sixth edition. Part 1 is a general survey of water and its action on the materials with which it comes into contact, and theoretical principles of separation and correction processes used in water treatment. Part 2 describes the process and the treatment plant beginning with the separation process.

ONLINE DATA BASES

Chemical Abstracts-CA. Chemical Abstracts Service, 2540 Olentangy River Rd., P.O. Box 3012, Columbus, Ohio 43210. (800) 848-6533 or (614) 421-3600. Information sources include 9000 journals, patents from 27 countries, two industrial property organizations, new books, conference proceedings, and government research reports.

Computerized Engineering Index–COMPENDEX. Engineering Information Inc., 345 E. 47th St., New York, New York 10017. (212) 705-7600.

Ground Water Sampling Devices. National Ground Water Information Center, National Well Water Association, 6375 Riverside Dr., Dublin, Ohio 43017. (614) 761-1711.

Monthly Catalog of United States Government Publications. U.S. G.P.O., Supt. of Docs., PO Box 371954, Pittsburgh, Pennsylvania 15250-7954. (202) 512-0000.

National Technical Information Service. U.S. Department of Commerce, National Technical Information Service, Office of Data Base Services, 5285 Port Royal Rd., Springfield, Virginia 22161. (703) 487-4807. Bibliographic database of government sponsored research and technical reports.

SCISEARCH. Institute for Scientific Information, University City Science Center, 3501 Market St., Philadelphia, Pennsylvania 19104. (215) 386-0100.

Water Treatability. National Ground Water Information Center, National Well Water Association, 6375 Riverside Dr., Dublin, Ohio 43017. (614) 761-1711.

Waternet. American Water Works Association, Technical Library, 6666 W. Quincy Ave., Denver, Colorado 80235. (303) 794-7711.

PERIODICALS AND NEWSLETTERS

American Water Works Association Journal. American Water Works Association, 6666 W. Quincy Avenue, Denver, Colorado 80235. (303) 794-7711. Monthly. Articles on public water supply systems.

The Bench Sheet. Water Pollution Control Federation, 601 Wythe Street, Alexandria, Virginia 22314-1994. (703) 684-2400. Bimonthly. Articles on water and wastewater laboratory analysis.

Digester/Over the Spillway. Illinois Environmental Protection Agency, 2200 Churchill Rd., Box 19276, Springfield, Illinois 62794-9276. (217) 782-5562. Bimonthly. Water & wastewater operators.

European Water Pollution Control. European Water Pollution Control Association, Elsevier Science Pub., PO Box 211, 1000 AE, Amsterdam, Netherlands 1991-. Bimonthly. Discussion of views, policies, strategies, directives and guidelines, design procedures, technical ideas and solutions, performance and experience in construction, maintenance and operation of water pollution control.

Federal Water Quality Association Newsletter. Federal Water Quality Association, P.O. Box 44163, Washington, District of Columbia 20026. (202) 447-4925. Seven times a year. Concerns sewage and industrial waste treatment and disposal.

Ground Water Newsletter. Water Information Center, Inc., 125 East Bethpage Road, Plainview, New York 11803. (516) 249-7634. Biweekly. Covers ground water exploration, development, and management.

Journal of Hydraulic Engineering. American Society of Civil Engineers, 345 E. 47th St., New York, New York 10017. (212) 705-7288; (800) 548-2723. 1983-. Monthly. Papers describe the analysis and solutions of problems in hydraulic engineering, hydrology and water resources. Emphasizes concepts, methods, techniques and results that advance knowledge in the hydraulic engineering profession.

Pollution Engineering. Cahners Publishing Co., 249 W. 17th St., New York, New York 10011. (212) 645-0067. 1969-. Monthly.

Pollution Equipment News. Rimbach Publishing, Inc., 8650 Babcock Boulevard, Pittsburgh, Pennsylvania 15237. (412) 364-5366. Bimonthly. Covers new products, techniques, and literature.

Water and Wastes Digest. Scranton Gillette Communications, Inc., 380 Northwest Highway, Des Plaines, Illinois 60016. (708) 298-6622. Bimonthly. Covers publicly and privately owned water and sewage systems.

TRADE ASSOCIATIONS AND PROFESSIONAL SOCIETIES

American Institute of Chemical Engineers. 345 East 47th St., New York, New York 10017. (212) 705-7338.

American Institute of Chemists. 7315 Wisconsin Ave., Bethesda, Maryland 20814. (301) 652-2447.

American Society of Civil Engineers. 345 East 47th St., New York, New York 10017. (212) 705-7496.

American Water Resources Association. 5410 Grosvenor Lane, Suite 220, Bethesda, Maryland 20814. (301) 493-8600.

American Water Works Association. 6666 W. Quincy Ave., Denver, Colorado 80235. (303) 794-7711.

Associated Laboratories. 500 S. Vermont St., Palatine, Illinois 60067. (708) 358-7400.

Association of the State and Interstate Water Pollution Control Administrators. 444 North Capitol St., N.W., Suite 330, Washington, District of Columbia 20001. (202) 624-7782.

Federal Water Quality Association. PO Box 44163, Washington, District of Columbia 20026. (202) 447-4925.

WATER USES (AGRICULTURAL, DOMESTIC, INDUSTRIAL)

See also: AGRICULTURE; IRRIGATION

ABSTRACTING AND INDEXING SERVICES

Abstracts of Air and Water Conservation Literature. American Petroleum Institute. Central Abstracting and Indexing Service, 275 Madison Avenue, New York, New York 10016. 1972.

Agrindex. AGRIS Coordinating Center, Via delle Terme di Caracalla, Rome, Italy I-00100. 61 0181-FA01. 1975-.

Applied Ecology Abstracts Studies in Renewable Natural Resources. Information Retrieval Ltd., 1911 Jefferson Davis Highway, Arlington, Virginia 22202. 1975-. Monthly.

Applied Science and Technology Index. H.W. Wilson Co., 950 University Ave., Bronx, New York 10452. (800) 367-6770. Formerly Industrial Arts Index.

Aqualine Abstracts. Water Research Centre. c/o Pergamon Microforms International, Inc., Fairview Park, Elmsford, New York 10523. (914) 592-7720. 1927-. Contains some 8,000 records annually on water and wastewater technology. Covers all aspects of water, wastewater, associated engineering services and the aquatic environment. Over 600 periodicals, as well as books, reports and conference proceedings and other publications from water related institutions worldwide are scanned. Also available online.

Biological and Agricultural Index. H.W. Wilson Co., 950 University Ave., Bronx, New York 10452. (800) 367-6770. 1916-. Monthly.

Bulletin Signaletique: Eau et Assainissement, Pollution Atmospherique, Droit des Pollutions. Centre de Documentation, Centre National de la Recherche Scientifique, 15, quai Anatole France, Paris, France 75700. (1) 45 55 92 25. 1983-. Monthly. Indexes pollution periodicals including water, atmospheric and related pollutions.

Current Advances in Ecological and Environmental Science. Pergamon Microforms International, Inc., Fairview Park, Elmsford, New York 10523. (914) 592-7720. 1989-. Monthly. Current literature searching service includingjournals, reports, abstracts, etc. This service is available online as part of the CABS database on the hosts BRS and ORBIT search service.

Ecological Abstracts. Geo Abstracts Ltd. Elsevier Applied Science, Crown House, Linton Rd., Barking, England IG 11 8JU. 1974-. Derived from over 600 leading ecological and environmental journals, plus books, conference proceedings, reports and theses.

Engineering Index. The Engineering Index Inc., 345 E. 47th St., New York, New York 10017. 1962-.

General Science Index. H. W. Wilson Co., 950 University Ave., Bronx, New York 10452. 1978-. Monthly, also issued in annual cumulation. Cumulative subject index to English language periodicals in the subject fields of astronomy, botany, chemistry, earth science, environment and conservation, food and nutrition, genetics, mathematics, medicine and health, microbiology, oceanography, physics, physiology and zoology.

Geographical Abstracts. London School of Economics, Dept. of Geography, Regency House, 34 Duke St., London, England 1966-. Continued by Geo Abstracts issued in 6 parts: Pt. A. Landforms and the quaternary; Pt. B. Biogeography and Climatology; Pt. C. Economic geography; Pt. D. Social geography and cartography; Pt. E. Sedimentology; Pt. F. Regional and community planning.

Index to Scientific Book Contents. Institute for Scientific Information, 3501 Market St., Philadelphia, Pennsylvania 19104. (800) 523-1857. 1985-. Annual. Gives contents of science books published.

Multimedia Index to Ecology. National Information Center for Educational Media, University of Southern California, Los Angeles, California 90007.

Pollution Abstracts. Cambridge Scientific Abstracts, 5161 River Rd., Bethesda, Maryland 20816. (301) 961-6750. Six/year. Indexes worldwide technical literature on environmental pollution. Covers air pollution, marine and freshwater pollution, sewage and wastewater treatment, waste management, toxicology and health, noise pollution, radiation, land pollution, and environmental policies, programs, legislation, and education. Also available online.

Public Health Engineering Abstracts. U.S. G.P.O., Washington, District of Columbia 20401. (202) 512-0000. Monthly.

Science Citation Index. Institute for Scientific Information, 3501 Market St., Philadelphia, Pennsylvania 19104. 1961-.

Urban Affairs Abstracts. National League of Cities, 1301 Pennsylvania Ave., NW, Washington, District of Columbia 20004. (202) 626-3150. 1977-. Weekly.

BIBLIOGRAPHIES

Current Contents. Agriculture, Biology and Environmental Sciences. Institute for Scientific Information, 3501 Market St., Philadelphia, Pennsylvania 19104. (800) 523-1857. 1973-. Previous title: Current Contents. Agricultural, Food & Veterinary Sciences. Gives the table of contents of periodicals in the fields of agriculture, biology, environmental and related areas.

ENCYCLOPEDIAS AND DICTIONARIES

Dictionary of Environmental Engineering and Related Sciences: English-Spanish, Spanish-English. Jose T. Villate. Ediciones Universal, 3090 SW 8th St., Miami, Florida 33135. (305) 642-3355. 1979.

Dictionary of Environmental Protection Technology: In Four Languages, English, German, French, Russian. Egon Seidel. Elsevier Science Publishing Co., 655 Avenue of the Americas, New York, New York 10010. (212) 984-5800. 1988.

Encyclopedia of Environmental Science and Engineering. J.R. Pfafflin. Gordon and Breach Science Publishers, Inc., 270 8th Ave., New York, New York 10011. (212) 206-8900. 1992.

The Encyclopedia of Geochemistry and Environmental Sciences. Rhodes Whitmore Fairbridge. Van Nostrand Reinhold Co., 115 5th Ave., New York, New York 10003. (212) 254-3232. 1972.

Encyclopedia of Physical Science and Technology. Robert A. Meyers, ed. Academic Press, c/o Harcourt Brace Jovanovich Inc., 6277 Sea Harbor Dr., Orlando, Florida 32887. (800) 346-8648. Dictionary of engineering, technology and physical sciences.

English-Russian Dictionary of Environmental Protection: About 14,000 Terms. E.L. Milovanov. Pergamon Microforms International, Inc., Fairview Park, Elmsford, New York 10523. (914) 592-7720. 1981.

Environmental Engineering Dictionary. C. C. Lee. Government Institutes, Inc., 4 Research Pl., Ste. 200, Rockville, Maryland 20850. (301) 921-2300. 1989. Defines over 6000 engineering terms relating to pollutioncontrol

technologies, monitoring, risk assessment, sampling andanalysis, quality control, permitting, and environmentally-regulated engineering and science. Includes bibliographical references (p. 612-627).

Grzimek's Encyclopedia of Ecology. Bernhard Grzimek. Van Nostrand Reinhold, 115 5th Ave., New York, New York 10003. (212) 254-3232. 1976.

McGraw-Hill Encyclopedia of Environmental Science. Sybil P. Parker. McGraw-Hill Science & Engineering Books, 11 W. 19th St., New York, New York 10011. (212) 337-6010. 1980. Covers ecology, man's influence on nature, and environmental protection.

North American Reference Encyclopedia of Ecology and Pollution. William White. North American Pub. Co., 401 N. Broad St., Philadelphia, Pennsylvania 19108. (215) 238-5300. 1972.

Van Nostrand's Scientific Encyclopedia. Glenn D. Considine, ed. Van Nostrand Reinhold, 115 5th Ave., New York, New York 10003. (212) 254-3232. 1983. Sixth edition. Includes all broad subject areas in science.

The Water Encyclopedia. Lewis Publishers, 2000 Corporate Blvd. N.W., Boca Raton, Florida 33431. (800) 272-7737. 1990. 2d ed. Includes groundwater contamination, drinking water, floods, waterborne diseases, global warming, climate change, irrigation, water agencies and organizations, precipitation, oceans and seas, and river, lakes and waterfalls.

GENERAL WORKS

Advances in Water Treatment and Environmental Management. George Thomas. Elsevier Science Publishing Co., 655 Avenue of the Americas, New York, New York 10010. (212) 984-5800. 1991. Measurement and control of groundwater quality, rivers, river management, estuaries, and beaches.

Harvest of Hope. Jennifer Curtis, et al. Natural Resources Defense Council, 40 W. 20th St., New York, New York 10011. (212) 727-2700. 1991. Details potential reductions in pesticide use and offers recommendations for reform in research, farm programs, marketing policy and water pricing.

Wastewater Engineering: Treatment, Disposal, and Reuse. Metcalf & Eddy, Inc. McGraw-Hill Science & Engineering Books, 11 West 19th St., New York, New York 10011. (212) 337-6010. 1991. Reflects the impact of changing federal legislation on environmental quality control and sludge management. Gives a solid overall perspective on wastewater engineering.

ONLINE DATA BASES

Computerized Engineering Index–COMPENDEX. Engineering Information Inc., 345 E. 47th St., New York, New York 10017. (212) 705-7600.

Monthly Catalog of United States Government Publications. U.S. G.P.O., Supt. of Docs., PO Box 371954, Pittsburgh, Pennsylvania 15250-7954. (202) 512-0000.

National Technical Information Service. U.S. Department of Commerce, National Technical Information Service, Office of Data Base Services, 5285 Port Royal Rd., Springfield, Virginia 22161. (703) 487-4807. Bibliographic database of government sponsored research and technical reports.

PressNet Environmental Reports. Chemical Information Systems, Inc., 7215 York Rd., Baltimore, Maryland 21212. (301) 321-8440.

SCISEARCH. Institute for Scientific Information, University City Science Center, 3501 Market St., Philadelphia, Pennsylvania 19104. (215) 386-0100.

PERIODICALS AND NEWSLETTERS

Journal of Soil and Water Conservation. Soil and Water Conservation Society, 7515 Northeast Ankeny Road, Ankeny, Iowa 50021. (515) 289-2331. Bimonthly. Promotes better land and water use and management.

RESEARCH CENTERS AND INSTITUTES

University of Nebraska-Lincoln, Water Center. 103 Natural Resources Hall, Lincoln, Nebraska 68503-0844. (402) 472-3305.

TRADE ASSOCIATIONS AND PROFESSIONAL SOCIETIES

American Institute of Chemical Engineers. 345 East 47th St., New York, New York 10017. (212) 705-7338.

American Institute of Chemists. 7315 Wisconsin Ave., Bethesda, Maryland 20814. (301) 652-2447.

American Society of Agricultural Engineers. 2950 Niles Rd., St Joseph, Michigan 49085. (616) 429-0300.

American Society of Civil Engineers. 345 East 47th St., New York, New York 10017. (212) 705-7496.

American Society of Sanitary Engineering. Box 40362, Bay Village, Ohio 44140. (216) 835-3040.

American Water Resources Association. 5410 Grosvenor Lane, Suite 220, Bethesda, Maryland 20814. (301) 493-8600.

Association of the State and Interstate Water Pollution Control Administrators. 444 North Capitol St., N.W., Suite 330, Washington, District of Columbia 20001. (202) 624-7782.

Water Resources Congress. Courthouse Plaza II, 2300 Clarendon Blvd., Suite 404, Arlington, Virginia 22201. (703) 525-4881.

WATER WELLS

See also: HYDROLOGY

ABSTRACTING AND INDEXING SERVICES

Abstracts of Air and Water Conservation Literature. American Petroleum Institute. Central Abstracting and Indexing Service, 275 Madison Avenue, New York, New York 10016. 1972.

Agrindex. AGRIS Coordinating Center, Via delle Terme di Caracalla, Rome, Italy I-00100. 61 0181-FA01. 1975-.

Applied Ecology Abstracts Studies in Renewable Natural Resources. Information Retrieval Ltd., 1911 Jefferson Davis Highway, Arlington, Virginia 22202. 1975-. Monthly.

Applied Science and Technology Index. H.W. Wilson Co., 950 University Ave., Bronx, New York 10452. (800) 367-6770. Formerly Industrial Arts Index.

Aqualine Abstracts. Water Research Centre. c/o Pergamon Microforms International, Inc., Fairview Park, Elmsford, New York 10523. (914) 592-7720. 1927-. Contains some 8,000 records annually on water and wastewater technology. Covers all aspects of water, wastewater, associated engineering services and the aquatic environment. Over 600 periodicals, as well as books, reports and conference proceedings and other publications from water related institutions worldwide are scanned. Also available online.

Biological and Agricultural Index. H.W. Wilson Co., 950 University Ave., Bronx, New York 10452. (800) 367-6770. 1916-. Monthly.

Engineering Index. The Engineering Index Inc., 345 E. 47th St., New York, New York 10017. 1962-.

Geographical Abstracts. London School of Economics, Dept. of Geography, Regency House, 34 Duke St., London, England 1966-. Continued by Geo Abstracts issued in 6 parts: Pt. A. Landforms and the quaternary; Pt. B. Biogeography and Climatology; Pt. C. Economic geography; Pt. D. Social geography and cartography; Pt. E. Sedimentology; Pt. F. Regional and community planning.

Multimedia Index to Ecology. National Information Center for Educational Media, University of Southern California, Los Angeles, California 90007.

Pollution Abstracts. Cambridge Scientific Abstracts, 5161 River Rd., Bethesda, Maryland 20816. (301) 961-6750. Six/year. Indexes worldwide technical literature on environmental pollution. Covers air pollution, marine and freshwater pollution, sewage and wastewater treatment, waste management, toxicology and health, noise pollution, radiation, land pollution, and environmental policies, programs, legislation, and education. Also available online.

Science Citation Index. Institute for Scientific Information, 3501 Market St., Philadelphia, Pennsylvania 19104. 1961-.

Urban Affairs Abstracts. National League of Cities, 1301 Pennsylvania Ave., NW, Washington, District of Columbia 20004. (202) 626-3150. 1977-. Weekly.

BIBLIOGRAPHIES

Bibliography and Index of Geology. American Geological Institute, 4220 King St., Alexandria, Virginia 22302. Monthly. Includes environmental geology and hydrogeology.

Geraghty & Miller's Groundwater Bibliography. Frits Van Der Leeden. Lewis Publishers, 200 Corporate Blvd. NW, Boca Raton, Florida 33431. (407) 994-0555 or (800)272-7737. 1991. 5th ed. Since the last edition, this essential research aid reflects increased interest in areas such as ground water contamination, modeling, and legal issues. Contains a listing of general bibliographies, periodicals, and books, followed by a subject section covering 3 specific aspects of hydrogeology.

DIRECTORIES

Guide to U.S. Produced Water Well Drilling Rigs and Support Vehicles. National Water Well Association, 6375 Riverside Dr., Dublin, Ohio 43017. (614) 761-1711.

Nonprofit Sample and Core Repositories Open to the Public in the United States. Branch of Sedimentary Processes/U.S. Geological Survey, Department of the Interior, Box 25046, Denver Federal Center, MS975, Denver, Colorado 80225-0046. (303) 236-1930. 1984.

Water Well Drilling Directory. American Business Directories, Inc., 5711 S. 86th Circle, Omaha, Nebraska 68127. (402) 593-4600.

Water Well Regulations Data Base. National Water Well Association, 6375 Riverside Dr., Dublin, Ohio 43017. (614) 761-1711.

Well Drilling. American Business Directories, Inc., 5711 S. 86th Circle, Omaha, Nebraska 68127. (402) 593-4600.

ENCYCLOPEDIAS AND DICTIONARIES

Dictionary of Environmental Engineering and Related Sciences: English-Spanish, Spanish-English. Jose T. Villate. Ediciones Universal, 3090 SW 8th St., Miami, Florida 33135. (305) 642-3355. 1979.

Encyclopedia of Environmental Science and Engineering. J.R. Pfafflin. Gordon and Breach Science Publishers, Inc., 270 8th Ave., New York, New York 10011. (212) 206-8900. 1992.

The Encyclopedia of Geochemistry and Environmental Sciences. Rhodes Whitmore Fairbridge. Van Nostrand Reinhold Co., 115 5th Ave., New York, New York 10003. (212) 254-3232. 1972.

McGraw-Hill Encyclopedia of Environmental Science. Sybil P. Parker. McGraw-Hill Science & Engineering Books, 11 W. 19th St., New York, New York 10011. (212) 337-6010. 1980. Covers ecology, man's influence on nature, and environmental protection.

Van Nostrand's Scientific Encyclopedia. Glenn D. Considine, ed. Van Nostrand Reinhold, 115 5th Ave., New York, New York 10003. (212) 254-3232. 1983. Sixth edition. Includes all broad subject areas in science.

The Water Encyclopedia. Lewis Publishers, 2000 Corporate Blvd. N.W., Boca Raton, Florida 33431. (800) 272-7737. 1990. 2d ed. Includes groundwater contamination, drinking water, floods, waterborne diseases, global warming, climate change, irrigation, water agencies and organizations, precipitation, oceans and seas, and river, lakes and waterfalls.

GENERAL WORKS

Contamination of Ground Water Prevention, Assessment, Restoration. Michael Barcelona, et al. Noyes Publications, 120 Mill Rd., Park Ridge, New Jersey 07656. (201) 391-8484. 1990. Provides regulatory agencies and industry a convenient source of technical information on the management of contaminated ground water.

Evaluation of Longitudinal Dispersivity from Tracer Test Data. Claire Welty and Lynn W. Gelhar. Ralph M. Parsons Laboratory for Water Resources and Hydrodynamics, Massachusetts Institute of Technology, Cambridge, Massachusetts 02139. 1989. Groundwater flow, tracers, and diffusion in hydrology.

Field Comparison of Ground-Water Sampling Methods. Ronald Paul Blegen. National Technical Information Service, 5285 Port Royal, Springfield, Virginia 22161. (703) 487-4650. 1988. Thesis (M.S.)–Geoscience, University of Nevada, Las Vegas, 1988.

Ground Water and Vadose Zone Monitoring. David M. Nielsen and A. Ivan Johnson, eds. PennWell Books, PO Box 21288, Tulsa, Oklahoma 74121. (918) 831-9421; (800) 752-9764. 1988. Contains 22 papers presented at the symposium on standards and development for ground water and Vadose Zone monitoring investigations.

Magill's Survey of Science. Earth Science Series. Frank N. Magill. Salem Press, PO Box 50062, Pasadena, California 91105. 1990-. Five volumes. Includes information on earth's crust, hot spots and volcanic island chains, physical properties of minerals, rock magnetism, physical properties of rocks, and index.

National Pesticide Survey: Summary Results of EPA's National Survey of Pesticides in Drinking Water Wells. U.S. Environmental Protection Agency, Office of Pesticides and Toxic Substances, 401 M St. SW, Washington, District of Columbia 20460. (202) 260-2090. 1990.

Protecting the Nation's Groundwater from Contamination. U.S. G.P.O., Washington, District of Columbia 20401. 1984-. Covers underground water quality and pollution.

Technologies for Upgrading Existing or Designing New Drinking Water Treatment Facilities. Office of Drinking Water, Center for Environmental Research Information, U.S. Environmental Protection Agency. Technomic Publishing Co., 851 New Holland Ave., Box 3535, Lancaster, Pennsylvania 17604. (717) 291-5609. 1991. Discusses drinking water treatment technologies that address contamination and contaminant categories regulated under the Safe Drinking Water Act and its 1986 amendments.

HANDBOOKS AND MANUALS

Ground Water Handbook. Government Institutes, Inc., 4 Research Pl., Ste 200, Rockville, Maryland 20850. (301) 921-2300. 1989. Includes highlights of chapters on ground water contamination, use of models in managing ground water protection programs, ground water restoration, ground water quality investigations, basic hydrogeology, monitoring well design and construction, ground water sampling, ground water tracers and basic geology.

Handbook of Drinking Water Quality: Standards and Controls. John De Zuane. Van Nostrand Reinhold, 115 5th Ave., New York, New York 10003. (212) 254-3232. 1990. Aids in evaluating water quality control at every stage of the water path, from source to treatment plant, from distribution system to consumer.

Handbook of Ground Water Development. The Roscoe Moss Company. John Wiley & Sons, Inc., 605 3rd Ave., New York, New York 10158-0012. (212) 850-6000. 1989. Guide to current theories and techniques for the exploration, extraction, use and management of ground water. Covers the physical geology and hydrodynamics of water in the ground, the exploitation of ground water and well design and construction, and the management of wells and well field operations.

Our National Wetland Heritage. Jon A. Kusler. Environmental Law Institute, 1616 P St., NW, Suite 200, Washington, District of Columbia 20036. (202) 328-

5150. 1983. Discusses practical ways to preserve and protect wetlands and their benefits, which include recreation, wildlife habitat, pollution and flood control, scientific research and groundwater recharge.

The Poisoned Well: New Strategies for Groundwater Protection. Eric P. Jorgensen, ed. Island Press, 1718 Connecticut Ave. N.W., Suite 300, Washington, District of Columbia 20009. (202) 232-7933. 1989. Explains how individuals can work with agencies and the courts to enforce water laws, how the major federal water laws, work what remedies exist for each type of groundwater contamination, and what state and local programs may be helpful.

ONLINE DATA BASES

Computerized Engineering Index–COMPENDEX. Engineering Information Inc., 345 E. 47th St., New York, New York 10017. (212) 705-7600.

Ground Water Industry Standards. National Ground Water Information Center, National Water Well Association, 6375 Riverside Dr., Dublin, Ohio 43017. (614) 761-1711.

Ground Water Job Mart. National Ground Water Information Center, National Water Well Association, 6375 Riverside Dr., Dublin, Ohio 43017. (614) 761-1711.

Ground Water On-Line. National Water Well Association, National Ground Water Information Center, 6375 Riverside Dr., Dublin, Ohio 43017. (614) 761-1711. Technical literature covering all aspects of groundwater and well technology.

Ground Water Sampling Devices. National Ground Water Information Center, National Well Water Association, 6375 Riverside Dr., Dublin, Ohio 43017. (614) 761-1711.

Monthly Catalog of United States Government Publications. U.S. G.P.O., Supt. of Docs., PO Box 371954, Pittsburgh, Pennsylvania 15250-7954. (202) 512-0000.

National Technical Information Service. U.S. Department of Commerce, National Technical Information Service, Office of Data Base Services, 5285 Port Royal Rd., Springfield, Virginia 22161. (703) 487-4807. Bibliographic database of government sponsored research and technical reports.

SCISEARCH. Institute for Scientific Information, University City Science Center, 3501 Market St., Philadelphia, Pennsylvania 19104. (215) 386-0100.

PERIODICALS AND NEWSLETTERS

Editorially Speaking about Ground Water: Its First Quarter Century. Jay H. Lehr and Anita B. Stanley. National Water Well Association, 6375 Riverside Dr., Dublin, Ohio 43017. (614) 761-1711. 1988. A collection of editorials from the Journal of Ground Water which traces the evolution of ground water science during the journal's first 25 years of publication.

Ground Water. Water Well Journal Publishing Co., 6375 Riverside Dr., Dublin, Ohio 43017. (614) 761-3222. Bimonthly. Contains technical papers for NWWA.

Ground Water Age. National Trade Publications, Inc., 13 Century Hill, Latham, New York 12110. (518) 783-1281. Monthly. Covers product and literature developments and industry news.

Ground Water Monitoring Review. Water Well Journal Publishing Co. National Water Well Association, 6375 Riverside Drive, Dublin, Ohio 43017. (614) 761-3222. Quarterly. Covers protection and restoration of ground water.

Journal of Groundwater. Association of Ground Water Scientists and Engineers, Division of National Water Well Association, 6375 Riverside Dr., Dublin, Ohio 43017. (614) 761-1711. 1963-. Bimonthly. Serial dealing with all forms of ground water and its quality.

Newsletter of Association of Ground Water Scientists and Engineers. Association of Groundwater Scientists and Engineers, 6375 Riverside Drive, Dublin, Ohio 43017. (614) 761-1711. Bimonthly. Reports on events, activities, courses and conferences of AGSE.

Well Log. National Water Well Association, 500 W. Wilson Bridge Rd., Worthington, Ohio 43085. (614) 761-1711. Eight numbers a year. Newsletter of the National Water Well Association

TRADE ASSOCIATIONS AND PROFESSIONAL SOCIETIES

American Society of Civil Engineers. 345 East 47th St., New York, New York 10017. (212) 705-7496.

American Water Resources Association. 5410 Grosvenor Lane, Suite 220, Bethesda, Maryland 20814. (301) 493-8600.

Association of Ground Water Scientists and Engineers. PO Box 1248, Hardwick, Vermont 05843. (803) 472-6956.

Association of State Drinking Water Administrators. 1911 N. Fort Myer Dr., Suite 400, Arlington, Virginia 22209. (703) 524-2428.

National Water Resources Association. 3800 N. Fairfax Dr., Suite 4, Arlington, Virginia 22203. (703) 524-1544.

National Water Well Association. 6375 Riverside Dr., Dublin, Ohio 43107. (614) 761-1711.

Pitless Adapter Division of Water Council. 600 S. Federal St., Suite 400, Chicago, Illinois 60605. (312) 922-6222.

WATERWAYS

ABSTRACTING AND INDEXING SERVICES

Abstracts of Air and Water Conservation Literature. American Petroleum Institute. Central Abstracting and Indexing Service, 275 Madison Avenue, New York, New York 10016. 1972.

Applied Science and Technology Index. H.W. Wilson Co., 950 University Ave., Bronx, New York 10452. (800) 367-6770. Formerly Industrial Arts Index.

Aqualine Abstracts. Water Research Centre. c/o Pergamon Microforms International, Inc., Fairview Park, Elmsford, New York 10523. (914) 592-7720. 1927-. Contains some 8,000 records annually on water and wastewater technology. Covers all aspects of water, wastewater, associated engineering services and the aquatic environment. Over 600 periodicals, as well as books, reports and conference proceedings and other

publications from water related institutions worldwide are scanned. Also available online.

Biological and Agricultural Index. H.W. Wilson Co., 950 University Ave., Bronx, New York 10452. (800) 367-6770. 1916-. Monthly.

Engineering Index. The Engineering Index Inc., 345 E. 47th St., New York, New York 10017. 1962-.

Science Citation Index. Institute for Scientific Information, 3501 Market St., Philadelphia, Pennsylvania 19104. 1961-.

Urban Affairs Abstracts. National League of Cities, 1301 Pennsylvania Ave., NW, Washington, District of Columbia 20004. (202) 626-3150. 1977-. Weekly.

BIBLIOGRAPHIES

Current Contents. Agriculture, Biology and Environmental Sciences. Institute for Scientific Information, 3501 Market St., Philadelphia, Pennsylvania 19104. (800) 523-1857. 1973-. Previous title: Current Contents. Agricultural, Food & Veterinary Sciences. Gives the table of contents of periodicals in the fields of agriculture, biology, environmental and related areas.

ENCYCLOPEDIAS AND DICTIONARIES

Dictionary of Environmental Engineering and Related Sciences: English-Spanish, Spanish-English. Jose T. Villate. Ediciones Universal, 3090 SW 8th St., Miami, Florida 33135. (305) 642-3355. 1979.

Encyclopedia of Environmental Science and Engineering. J.R. Pfafflin. Gordon and Breach Science Publishers, Inc., 270 8th Ave., New York, New York 10011. (212) 206-8900. 1992.

GOVERNMENTAL ORGANIZATIONS

TVA Public Information Office. 400 West Summit Hill Dr., Knoxville, Tennessee 37902. (615) 632-8000.

ONLINE DATA BASES

Civil Engineering Database. American Society of Civil Engineers, 345 E. 47th St., New York, New York 10017. (800) 548-2723.

Computerized Engineering Index–COMPENDEX. Engineering Information Inc., 345 E. 47th St., New York, New York 10017. (212) 705-7600.

Monthly Catalog of United States Government Publications. U.S. G.P.O., Supt. of Docs., PO Box 371954, Pittsburgh, Pennsylvania 15250-7954. (202) 512-0000.

National Technical Information Service. U.S. Department of Commerce, National Technical Information Service, Office of Data Base Services, 5285 Port Royal Rd., Springfield, Virginia 22161. (703) 487-4807. Bibliographic database of government sponsored research and technical reports.

SCISEARCH. Institute for Scientific Information, University City Science Center, 3501 Market St., Philadelphia, Pennsylvania 19104. (215) 386-0100.

RESEARCH CENTERS AND INSTITUTES

University of Missouri-Columbia, University Forest. 1-30 Agriculture Building, Columbia, Missouri 65211. (314) 222-8373.

STATISTICS SOURCES

Waterborne Commerce of the U.S.: Waterways and Harbors. U.S. G.P.O, Washington, District of Columbia 20402-9325. (202) 512-0000. 1959. Annual. Freight, passengers, and vessels within or between coastal and noncontiguous U.S. ports, on inland waterways, and on the Great Lakes.

TRADE ASSOCIATIONS AND PROFESSIONAL SOCIETIES

American Society of Civil Engineers. 345 East 47th St., New York, New York 10017. (212) 705-7496.

American Society of Sanitary Engineering. Box 40362, Bay Village, Ohio 44140. (216) 835-3040.

American Water Resources Association. 5410 Grosvenor Lane, Suite 220, Bethesda, Maryland 20814. (301) 493-8600.

National Waterways Conference. 1130 17th St. N.W., Washington, District of Columbia 20036. (202) 296-4415.

WEATHER

ABSTRACTING AND INDEXING SERVICES

Applied Science and Technology Index. H.W. Wilson Co., 950 University Ave., Bronx, New York 10452. (800) 367-6770. Formerly Industrial Arts Index.

Biological and Agricultural Index. H.W. Wilson Co., 950 University Ave., Bronx, New York 10452. (800) 367-6770. 1916-. Monthly.

Environmental Research Laboratories Publication Abstracts. National Oceanic and Atmospheric Administration. Environmental Research Laboratories, 325 Broadway, Boulder, Colorado 80303. 1990. Annual. Sixth annual bibliography of NOAA Environmental Research Laboratories staff publications, FY 89. Covers journal articles, official ERL reports, conference papers, and publications released in cooperation with universities and by ERL funded contractors.

General Science Index. H. W. Wilson Co., 950 University Ave., Bronx, New York 10452. 1978-. Monthly, also issued in annual cumulation. Cumulative subject index to English language periodicals in the subject fields of astronomy, botany, chemistry, earth science, environment and conservation, food and nutrition, genetics, mathematics, medicine and health, microbiology, oceanography, physics, physiology and zoology.

Meteorological and Geoastrophysical Abstracts. American Meteorological Society, 45 Beacon St., Boston, Massachusetts 02108. (617) 227-2425.

Science Citation Index. Institute for Scientific Information, 3501 Market St., Philadelphia, Pennsylvania 19104. 1961-.

ALMANACS AND YEARBOOKS

The Weather Almanac. Frank E. Bair, ed. Gale Research Co., 835 Penobscot Bldg., Detroit, Michigan 48226-4094. (313) 961-2242. 1992. Sixth edition. A reference guide to weather, climate, and air quality in the United States and its key cities, compromising statistics, principles, and terminology.

BIBLIOGRAPHIES

Bibliography and Index of Geology. American Geological Institute, 4220 King St., Alexandria, Virginia 22302. Monthly. Includes environmental geology and hydrogeology.

New Publications of the Geological Survey. U.S. Department of the Interior, Geological Survey, 119 National Center, Reston, Virginia 22092. (703) 648-4460. 1984-. Monthly. Bibliography of geological publications and related government documents published by the Geological Survey.

DIRECTORIES

National Environmental Data Referral Service. National Oceanic and Atmospheric Administration, Department of Commerce, 1825 Connecticut Ave., N.W., Washington, District of Columbia 20235. (202) 673-5548. Also available online.

Who's Who in Ozone. International Ozone Association, c/o Wasserversorgung Zurich, Hardhaf 9, Postfach, Zurich, Switzerland CH-8023. 1 4352112.

ENCYCLOPEDIAS AND DICTIONARIES

The Encyclopedia of Atmospheric Sciences and Astrogeology. Rhodes Whitmore Fairbridge. Reinhold Pub. Co., 115 5th Ave., New York, New York 10003. (212) 254-3232. 1967.

The Encyclopedia of Climatology. John E. Oliver and Rhodes W. Fairbridge, eds. Van Nostrand Reinhold, 115 5th Ave., New York, New York 10003. (212) 254-3232. 1987. Belongs in the series Encyclopedia of Earth Sciences, v.11.

Encyclopedia of Physical Science and Technology. Robert A. Meyers, ed. Academic Press, c/o Harcourt Brace Jovanovich Inc., 6277 Sea Harbor Dr., Orlando, Florida 32887. (800) 346-8648. Dictionary of engineering, technology and physical sciences.

Nature in America Your A-Z Guide to Our Country's Animals, Plants, Landforms and Other Natural Features. Readers Digest Association, 260 Madison Ave., New York, New York 10016. 1991. Reference guide of nature in North America. Explores plants, animals, weather, land forms, and wildlife habitats. Includes over 1000 photographs and illustrations for some 1200 entries.

Van Nostrand's Scientific Encyclopedia. Glenn D. Considine, ed. Van Nostrand Reinhold, 115 5th Ave., New York, New York 10003. (212) 254-3232. 1983. Sixth edition. Includes all broad subject areas in science.

GENERAL WORKS

Be Your Own Power Company. David J. Morris. Rodale Press, 33 E. Minor St., Emmaus, Pennsylvania 18098. (215) 967-5171; (800) 322-6333. 1983. This book is a technical aid to those entering the power production business. Stresses that conservation is cheaper than production. Includes bibliography.

Climates of the States. Gale Research Inc., 835 Penobscot Bldg., Detroit, Michigan 48226-4094. (313) 961-2242. 1986. State-by-state summaries of climate based on first order weather reporting stations for the period 1951-1980.

Hydrological Application of Weather Radar. I. D. Cluckie and C. G. Collier, eds. E. Horwood, 66 Wood Lane End, Hemel Hempstead, England HP2 4RG. 1991.

Magill's Survey of Science. Earth Science Series. Frank N. Magill. Salem Press, PO Box 50062, Pasadena, California 91105. 1990-. Five volumes. Includes information on earth's crust, hot spots and volcanic island chains, physical properties of minerals, rock magnetism, physical properties of rocks, and index.

The Satellite as Microscope. R. S. Scorer. E. Horwood, 66 Wood Lane End, Hemel Hempstead, England HP2 4RG. 1990. Describes the use of artificial satellites in air pollution control.

Weather from Above: America's Meteorological Satellites. Janice Hill. Smithsonian Institution Press, 470 L'Enfant Plaza, #7100, Washington, District of Columbia 20560. (800) 782-4612. 1991. Covers global weather systems. Describes instruments the satellites carried as well as images they returned to earth analyses how meteorological data are used to predict weather.

Weather of U.S. Cities. Frank E. Bair. Gale Research Inc., 835 Penobscot Bldg., Detroit, Michigan 48226-4094. (313) 961-2242. 1992. Compilation of U.S. government weather data on 281 cities and weather observation stations.

GOVERNMENTAL ORGANIZATIONS

National Environmental Satellite, Data, and Information Service. 1825 Connecticut Ave., N.W., Washington, District of Columbia 20235. (301) 763-7190.

National Weather Service. 8060 13th St., Silver Spring, Maryland 20910. (301) 443-8910.

ONLINE DATA BASES

Enviroline. R. R. Bowker Co., Bowker Electronic Publishing, 121 Chanlon Rd., New Providence, New Jersey 07974. (800) 521-8110.

Environmental Bibliography. Environmental Studies Institute, International Academy at Santa Barbara, 800 Garden St., Ste. D, Santa Barbara, California 93101. (805) 965-5010. International periodical literature dealing with environmental topics such as air pollution, water treatment, energy conservation, noise abatement, soil mechanics, wildlife preservation, and chemical wastes.

National Environmental Data Referral Service Database. National Oceanic & Atmospheric Administration, Department of Commerce, 1825 Connecticut Ave., N.W., Washington, District of Columbia 20235. (202) 673-5548. Data files, published data sources, documentation references, and organizations that make environmental data available.

PERIODICALS AND NEWSLETTERS

Bulletin of American Meteorological Society. American Meteorological Society, 45 Beacon Street, Boston, Massachusetts 02108. (617) 227-2425. Monthly. Bulletin which certifies consulting meteorologists.

Journal of Applied Meteorology. American Meteorological Society, 45 Beacon Street, Boston, Massachusetts 02108. (617) 227-2425. Monthly. Articles on the relationship between weather and environment.

RESEARCH CENTERS AND INSTITUTES

State University of New York College of Environmental Science and Forestry. Syracuse Forest Experiment Station, 452 Lafayette Rd., Syracuse, New York 13205. (315) 469-3053.

STATISTICS SOURCES

Annual Tropical Cyclone Report. U.S. G.P.O, Washington, District of Columbia 20402-9325. (202) 512-0000. Annual. Tropical storm activity in the western Pacific and the Indian Ocean.

Comparative Climatic Data for the U.S. U.S. G.P.O, Washington, District of Columbia 20402-9325. (202) 512-0000. Annual. Monthly averages of surface weather data for U.S. and outlying areas.

Marine Fisheries Review. U.S. G.P.O, Washington, District of Columbia 20402-9325. (202) 512-0000. Quarterly. Marine fishery resources, development, and management. Covers fish, shellfish, and marine mammal populations.

National Marine Pollution Program. U.S. G.P.O, Washington, District of Columbia 20402-9325. (202) 512-0000. Annual. Federally funded programs for development, or monitoring activities related to marine pollution.

TRADE ASSOCIATIONS AND PROFESSIONAL SOCIETIES

American Institute of Biomedical Climatology. 1023 Welsh Rd., Philadelphia, Pennsylvania 19115. (215) 673-8368.

American Meteorological Society. 45 Beacon St., Boston, Massachusetts 02108. (617) 227-2425.

WEATHER FORECASTING

See: WEATHER

WEATHER MANAGEMENT

See: WEATHER

WEATHER MODIFICATION RESEARCH

See: WEATHER

WEATHERING

ABSTRACTING AND INDEXING SERVICES

Applied Science and Technology Index. H.W. Wilson Co., 950 University Ave., Bronx, New York 10452. (800) 367-6770. Formerly Industrial Arts Index.

General Science Index. H. W. Wilson Co., 950 University Ave., Bronx, New York 10452. 1978-. Monthly, also issued in annual cumulation. Cumulative subject index to English language periodicals in the subject fields of astronomy, botany, chemistry, earth science, environment and conservation, food and nutrition, genetics, mathematics, medicine and health, microbiology, oceanography, physics, physiology and zoology.

Science Citation Index. Institute for Scientific Information, 3501 Market St., Philadelphia, Pennsylvania 19104. 1961-.

BIBLIOGRAPHIES

Bibliography and Index of Geology. American Geological Institute, 4220 King St., Alexandria, Virginia 22302. Monthly. Includes environmental geology and hydrogeology.

New Publications of the Geological Survey. U.S. Department of the Interior, Geological Survey, 119 National Center, Reston, Virginia 22092. (703) 648-4460. 1984-. Monthly. Bibliography of geological publications and related government documents published by the Geological Survey.

ENCYCLOPEDIAS AND DICTIONARIES

Glossary of Geology. Robert Latimer Bates and Julia A. Jackson, eds. American Geological Institute, 4220 King St., Alexandria, Virginia 22302-1507. (703) 379-2480 or (800) 336-4764. 1987. Third edition.

McGraw-Hill Encyclopedia of the Geological Sciences. Sybil P. Parker, ed. McGraw-Hill, 1221 Avenue of the Americas, New York, New York 10020. (212) 512-2000 or (800) 262-4729. 1988. Second edition. Published previously in the McGraw-Hill Encyclopedia of Science and Technology.

Van Nostrand's Scientific Encyclopedia. Glenn D. Considine, ed. Van Nostrand Reinhold, 115 5th Ave., New York, New York 10003. (212) 254-3232. 1983. Sixth edition. Includes all broad subject areas in science.

GENERAL WORKS

Chemistry of Coal Weathering. Elsevier Science Publishing Co., 655 Avenue of the Americas, New York, New York 10010. (212) 984-5800. 1989. Discusses topics in coal science and technology.

Magill's Survey of Science. Earth Science Series. Frank N. Magill. Salem Press, PO Box 50062, Pasadena, California 91105. 1990-. Five volumes. Includes information on earth's crust, hot spots and volcanic island chains, physical properties of minerals, rock magnetism, physical properties of rocks, and index.

Residual Deposits. Blackwell Scientific Publications, 3 Cambridge Ctr., Suite 208, Cambridge, Massachusetts 02142. (617) 225-0401. 1983. Surface related weathering processes.

Soil Mineral Weathering. Van Nostrand Reinhold, 115 Fifth Ave., New York, New York 10003. (212) 254-3232. 1986. Topics in soil science and soil mineralogy.

Weathering. Longman Scientific & Technical, 1560 Broadway, New York, New York 10036. (212) 819-5400. 1984. Topics in geomorphology.

Weathering and Erosion. Butterworth-Heinemann, 80 Montvale Ave., Stoneham, Massachusetts 02180. (617) 438-8464. 1983. Techniques and methods used in weathering and the prevention of erosion.

WEATHERSTRIPPING

ABSTRACTING AND INDEXING SERVICES

Science Citation Index. Institute for Scientific Information, 3501 Market St., Philadelphia, Pennsylvania 19104. 1961-.

ONLINE DATA BASES

SCISEARCH. Institute for Scientific Information, University City Science Center, 3501 Market St., Philadelphia, Pennsylvania 19104. (215) 386-0100.

WEED CONTROL

See: HERBICIDES

WELDING FUMES

See: AIR POLLUTION

WEST VIRGINIA ENVIRONMENTAL AGENCIES

GOVERNMENTAL ORGANIZATIONS

Air Pollution Control Commission: Air Quality. Director, 1558 Washington St., E., Charleston, West Virginia 25311. (304) 348-4022.

Department of Agriculture: Pesticide Registration. Administrator, Regulatory and Inspection Division, Capitol Building, Charleston, West Virginia 25305. (304) 348-2208.

Department of Natural Resources: Fish and Wildlife. Chief, Division of Wildlife Resources, State Capitol Complex, Building 3, Room 669, Charleston, West Virginia 25305. (304) 348-2771.

Division of Health: Water Quality. Chief, Environmental Engineering Division, State Capital Complex, Building 3, Charleston, West Virginia 25305. (304) 348-2981.

Division of Labor: Occupational Safety. Commissioner, State Capitol Complex, Building 3, Charleston, West Virginia 25305. (304) 348-7890.

Division of Natural Resources: Environmental Protection. Director, State Capital Complex, Building 3, Room 669, Charleston, West Virginia 25305. (304) 348-2754.

Division of Natural Resources: Groundwater Management. Chairman, Groundwater Policy and Technical Advisory Commission, State Capital Complex, Charleston, West Virginia 25305. (304) 348-2754.

Division of Natural Resources: Natural Resources. Director, State Capital Complex, Building 3, Room 669, Charleston, West Virginia 25305. (304) 348-2754.

Division of Waste Management: Hazardous Waste Management. Division Chief, Solid Waste Management Section, 1201 Greenbrier St., Charleston, West Virginia 25311. (304) 348-5929.

Division of Waste Management: Solid Waste Management. Division Chief, Solid Waste Management Section, 1201 Greenbrier St., Charleston, West Virginia 25311. (304) 348-5929.

Division of Waste Management: Underground Storage Tanks. Division Chief, Solid Waste Management Section, 1201 Greenbrier St., Charleston, West Virginia 25311. (304) 348-5929.

Emergency Response Commission: Emergency Preparedness and Community Right-to-Know. Director, Office of Emergency Services, State Capitol Bldg. 1, Room EB-80, Charlestown, West Virginia 25305. (304) 348-5380.

U.S. EPA Region 3: Pollution Prevention. Program Manager, 841 Chestnut St., Philadelphia, Pennsylvania 19107. (215) 597-9800.

WEST VIRGINIA ENVIRONMENTAL LEGISLATION

GENERAL WORKS

West Virginia Environmental Law Handbook. Government Institutes, Inc., 4 Research Pl., Ste. 200, Rockville, Maryland 20850. (301) 921-2300. 1990.

WET SCRUBBERS

See also: EMISSIONS

DIRECTORIES

Directory of Astacologists. International Association of Astacology, c/o Jay V. Huner, Secretary-Treasurer, University of Southwestern Louisiana, Box 44650, Lafayette, Louisiana 70504. (318) 231-5239.

Gale Environmental Sourcebook. Karen Hill. Gale Research Co., 835 Penobscot Bldg., Detroit, Michigan 48226-4094. (313) 961-2242. Contacts, information sources, or general informational on environmental topics.

HANDBOOKS AND MANUALS

Handbook of Water Quality Management Planning. Van Nostrand Reinhold, 115 Fifth Ave., New York, New York 10003. (212) 254-3232. 1977. Topics in environmental engineering including water purification and water supply.

STATISTICS SOURCES

Environmental Data Compendium. OECD Publications and Information Center, 2001 L St., N.W., Suite 700, Washington, District of Columbia 20036. (202) 785-6323. 1989.

Environmental Indicators. OECD Publications and Information Center, 2001 L St., N.W., Suite 700, Washington, District of Columbia 20036. (202) 785-6323. 1991.

Environmental Quality. Council on Environmental Quality. U.S. G.P.O., Washington, District of Columbia 20401. (202) 512-0000. Annual.

The State of the Environment. OECD Publications and Information Center, 2001 L St., N.W., Suite 700, Washington, District of Columbia 20036. (202) 785-6323. 1991.

WETLANDS

See also: AQUATIC BIOMES; FISH AND WILDLIFE MANAGEMENT; WATER PURIFICATION; WATER RESOURCES

ABSTRACTING AND INDEXING SERVICES

Abstracts of Air and Water Conservation Literature. American Petroleum Institute. Central Abstracting and Indexing Service, 275 Madison Avenue, New York, New York 10016. 1972.

Agrindex. AGRIS Coordinating Center, Via delle Terme di Caracalla, Rome, Italy I-00100. 61 0181-FA01. 1975-.

Applied Ecology Abstracts Studies in Renewable Natural Resources. Information Retrieval Ltd., 1911 Jefferson Davis Highway, Arlington, Virginia 22202. 1975-. Monthly.

Applied Science and Technology Index. H.W. Wilson Co., 950 University Ave., Bronx, New York 10452. (800) 367-6770. Formerly Industrial Arts Index.

Aqualine Abstracts. Water Research Centre. c/o Pergamon Microforms International, Inc., Fairview Park, Elmsford, New York 10523. (914) 592-7720. 1927-. Contains some 8,000 records annually on water and wastewater technology. Covers all aspects of water, wastewater, associated engineering services and the aquatic environment. Over 600 periodicals, as well as books, reports and conference proceedings and other publications from water related institutions worldwide are scanned. Also available online.

Biological and Agricultural Index. H.W. Wilson Co., 950 University Ave., Bronx, New York 10452. (800) 367-6770. 1916-. Monthly.

Civil Engineering Hydraulic Abstracts. BHRA Fluid Engineering, Air Science Co., PO Box 143, Corning, New York 14830. (607) 962-5591. Monthly. Abstracts of periodicals that publish in the areas of hydraulic engineering and other related topics.

Current Advances in Ecological and Environmental Science. Pergamon Microforms International, Inc., Fairview Park, Elmsford, New York 10523. (914) 592-7720. 1989-. Monthly. Current literature searching service includingjournals, reports, abstracts, etc. This service is available online as part of the CABS database on the hosts BRS and ORBIT search service.

Ecological Abstracts. Geo Abstracts Ltd. Elsevier Applied Science, Crown House, Linton Rd., Barking, England IG 11 8JU. 1974-. Derived from over 600 leading ecological and environmental journals, plus books, conference proceedings, reports and theses.

Engineering Index. The Engineering Index Inc., 345 E. 47th St., New York, New York 10017. 1962-.

General Science Index. H. W. Wilson Co., 950 University Ave., Bronx, New York 10452. 1978-. Monthly, also issued in annual cumulation. Cumulative subject index to English language periodicals in the subject fields of astronomy, botany, chemistry, earth science, environment and conservation, food and nutrition, genetics, mathematics, medicine and health, microbiology, oceanography, physics, physiology and zoology.

Geographical Abstracts. London School of Economics, Dept. of Geography, Regency House, 34 Duke St., London, England 1966-. Continued by Geo Abstracts issued in 6 parts: Pt. A. Landforms and the quaternary; Pt. B. Biogeography and Climatology; Pt. C. Economic geography; Pt. D. Social geography and cartography; Pt. E. Sedimentology; Pt. F. Regional and community planning.

Index to Scientific Book Contents. Institute for Scientific Information, 3501 Market St., Philadelphia, Pennsylvania 19104. (800) 523-1857. 1985-. Annual. Gives contents of science books published.

Multimedia Index to Ecology. National Information Center for Educational Media, University of Southern California, Los Angeles, California 90007.

Science Citation Index. Institute for Scientific Information, 3501 Market St., Philadelphia, Pennsylvania 19104. 1961-.

ALMANACS AND YEARBOOKS

Environmental Almanac. World Resources Institute. Houghton Mifflin, 1 Beacon St., Boston, Massachusetts 02108. (617) 725-5000; (800) 225-3362. 1991. Covers consumer products, energy, endangered species, food safety, global warming, solid wastes, toxics, wetlands and other related areas. Also included are the names and addresses of the chief environmental executives for all 50 states.

BIBLIOGRAPHIES

An Annotated Wetland Bibliography. Wetlands Project, Massachusetts Audubon Society, South Great Rd., Lincoln, Massachusetts 01773. (617) 259-9500. 1976.

Current Contents. Agriculture, Biology and Environmental Sciences. Institute for Scientific Information, 3501 Market St., Philadelphia, Pennsylvania 19104. (800) 523-1857. 1973-. Previous title: Current Contents. Agricultural, Food & Veterinary Sciences. Gives the table of

contents of periodicals in the fields of agriculture, biology, environmental and related areas.

Geraghty & Miller's Groundwater Bibliography. Frits Van Der Leeden. Lewis Publishers, 200 Corporate Blvd. NW, Boca Raton, Florida 33431. (407) 994-0555 or (800)272-7737. 1991. 5th ed. Since the last edition, this essential research aid reflects increased interest in areas such as ground water contamination, modeling, and legal issues. Contains a listing of general bibliographies, periodicals, and books, followed by a subject section covering 3 specific aspects of hydrogeology.

Literature Review of Wetland Evaluation Methodologies. U.S. Environmental Protection Agency, 401 M St., S.W., Washington, District of Columbia 20460. (202) 260-2090. 1984.

New Publications of the Geological Survey. U.S. Department of the Interior, Geological Survey, 119 National Center, Reston, Virginia 22092. (703) 648-4460. 1984-. Monthly. Bibliography of geological publications and related government documents published by the Geological Survey.

Prairie Wetland Drainage Regulations. North Dakota State University, Agricultural Experiment Station, Fargo, North Dakota 58105. 1981.

Socioeconomic Values of Wetlands: Concepts, Research Methods, and Annotated Bibliography. North Dakota State University, Agricultural Experiment Station, Fargo, North Dakota 58105. 1981. Bibliography of wetland ecology; its economic aspects and recreational uses.

Soils, Microbiology and Chemistry of Prairie Wetlands. North Dakota State University, Agricultural Experiment Station, Fargo, North Dakota 58105. 1981. Annotated bibliography of soil science and wetlands.

Wetland Economics and Assessment. Garland Publishing Inc., 1000A Sherman Ave., Hamden, Connecticut 06514. (203) 281-4487. 1989. Bibliography of the social and economic aspects of wetland conservation.

Wetland Hydrology. North Dakota State University, Agricultural Experiment Station, Fargo, North Dakota 58105. 1981. Bibliography of hydrology of wetlands.

Wetlands. Council of Planning Librarians, 1313 E. 60th St., Chicago, Illinois 60637-2897. (312) 942-2163. 1991. Bibliography of wetland conservation.

DIRECTORIES

A Directory of Wetlands of International Importance. World Conservation Monitoring Centre. World Conservation Union, IUCN Publications Services Unit, 181a Huntingdon Road, Cambridge, England CB3 0DJ. (0223) 277894. 1990. Sites designated for the list of Wetlands of International Importance.

United Nations List of National Parks and Protected Areas. World Conservation Monitoring Centre. World Conservation Union, IUCN Publications Services Unit, 181a Huntingdon Road, Cambridge, England CB3 0DJ. (0223) 277894. 1990. Standard list of national parks and other protected areas. Includes lists of world heritage sites, biosphere reserves and wetlands of international importance.

ENCYCLOPEDIAS AND DICTIONARIES

Grzimek's Encyclopedia of Ecology. Bernhard Grzimek. Van Nostrand Reinhold, 115 5th Ave., New York, New York 10003. (212) 254-3232. 1976.

McGraw-Hill Encyclopedia of Environmental Science. Sybil P. Parker. McGraw-Hill Science & Engineering Books, 11 W. 19th St., New York, New York 10011. (212) 337-6010. 1980. Covers ecology, man's influence on nature, and environmental protection.

North American Reference Encyclopedia of Ecology and Pollution. William White. North American Pub. Co., 401 N. Broad St., Philadelphia, Pennsylvania 19108. (215) 238-5300. 1972.

Van Nostrand's Scientific Encyclopedia. Glenn D. Considine, ed. Van Nostrand Reinhold, 115 5th Ave., New York, New York 10003. (212) 254-3232. 1983. Sixth edition. Includes all broad subject areas in science.

GENERAL WORKS

Climate Change and U.S. Water Resources. P. E. Waggoner, ed. John Wiley & Sons, Inc., 605 3rd Ave., New York, New York 10158-0012. (212) 850-6000. 1990. Covers latest research in climate changes and subsequent effects on water supply. Topics include future water use, statistics in forecasting, vulnerability of water systems, irrigation, urban water systems, and reallocation by markets and prices.

Coastal Wetlands of the United States. Donald W. Field. U.S. Department of Commerce, National Oceanic and Atmospheric Administration, Washington, District of Columbia 20230. (202) 377-2985. 1991. A special NOAA 20th anniversary report published in cooperation with the National Wetlands Inventory.

Constructed Wetlands for Wastewater Treatment. Donald A. Hammer. Lewis Publishers, 200 Corporate Blvd. NW, Boca Raton, Florida 33431. (407) 994-0555 or (800)272-7737. 1989. Presents general principles of wetland ecology, hydrology, soil chemistry, vegetation, microbiology, and wildlife dependence on wetlands. It provides management guidelines, beginning with policies and regulations, and including siting and construction and operations and monitoring of constructed wetland systems.

Constructed Wetlands in Water Pollution Control. Pergamon Microforms International, Inc., Fairview Park, Elmsford, New York 10523. (914) 592-7720. 1990.

Creating Freshwater Wetlands. Donald A. Hammer. Lewis Publishers, 2000 Corporate Blvd., N.W., Boca Raton, Florida 33431. (407) 994-0555 or (800) 272-7737. 1992. Includes marshes, bogs, swamps, sloughs, fens, tules, bayous. Also describes methods for creating wetlands and a history of creation and restoration.

Earth Ponds: The Country Pond Maker's Guide. Tim Matson. Countryman Press, PO Box 175, Woodstock, Vermont 05091-0175. (802) 457-1049. 1991. How-to manual regarding pond making.

Ecological Processes and Cumulative Impacts Illustrated by Bottomland Harwood Wetland Ecosystems. James G. Gosselink, et al. Lewis Publishers, 2000 Corporate Blvd., N.W., Boca Raton, Florida 33431. (407) 994-0555 or (800) 272-7737. 1990. Covers the ecological processes in bottomland hardwood forests and relates these processes to human activities.

Ecosystems Experiments. H. A. Mooney, et al., eds. John Wiley & Sons, Inc., 605 3rd Ave., New York, New York 10158-0012. (212) 850-6000. 1991. Explores the potential ecosystem experimentation as a tool for understanding and predicting changes in the biosphere. Areas investigated include deforestation, desertification, El Nino phenomenon, acid rain, watersheds, wetlands, and aquatic and climatic changes.

The Environment: Problems and Solutions. Stuart Bruchey, ed. Garland Publishing, Inc., 1000A Sherman Ave., Hamden, Connecticut 06514. (203) 281-4487. 1991. Topics covered: forested wetlands and agriculture, the political economy of smog in southern California, environmental limits to growth in world agriculture, the tradeoff between cost and risk in hazardous waste management, and the protection of groundwater from agricultural pollution.

Environment, Resources, and Conservation. Susan Owens and Peter L. Owens. Cambridge University Press, 40 W 20th St., New York, New York 10011. (212) 924-3900 or (800) 227-0247. 1991. The book studies three cases illuminating problems and policy responses at three levels of geographic scale–international, national, and local. The case of acid rain is used to illustrate a pollution problem with international dimensions; the British coal industry is analyzed as an example of national nonrenewable resource depletion; and renewable wetland ecosystem management illustrates a local concern by analyzing conservation measures.

The Future of Wetlands: Assessing Visual-Cultural Values. Richard C. Smardon, ed. Rowman & Littlefield, Publishers, Inc., 8705 Bollman Pl., Savage, Maryland 20763. (301) 306-0400. 1983. Attempts to provide a systematic basis for incorporating migrational, aesthetic, social, and educational values into the decision-making processes involved in land-use allocation.

Geotechnical and Environmental Geophysics. Stanley H. Ward. Society of Exploration Geophysicists, PO Box 702740, Tulsa, Oklahoma 74170-2740. (918) 493-3516. 1990.

Greenhouse Effect, Sea Level Rise, and Coastal Wetlands. U.S. Environmental Protection Agency, 401 M St., S.W., Washington, District of Columbia 20460. (202) 260-2090. 1988. Deals with wetland conservation and atmospheric greenhouse effect.

Law of Wetlands Regulation. Clark Boardman Callaghan, 155 Pfingsten Rd., Deerfield, Illinois 60015. (800) 221-9428. 1990. Law and legislation in United States relating to wetlands.

The Living Ocean. Boyce Thorne-Miller. Island Press, 1718 Connecticut Ave. N.W., Suite 300, Washington, District of Columbia 20009. (202) 232-7933. 1991. Discusses all marine ecosystems, including coastal benthic, shore systems, estuaries, wetlands, and coral reefs, coastal pelagic, deep-sea benthic, hydrothermal vents and others.

Protecting America's Wetlands. Conservation Foundation, 1250 24th St. NW, Washington, District of Columbia 20037. (202) 293-4800. 1988. Final report of the National Wetlands Policy Forum.

Protecting Nontidal Wetlands. David G. Burke, et al. American Planning Association, 1776 Massachusetts Ave. N.W., Washington, District of Columbia 20036. (202) 872-0611. 1988. Describes wetlands types and

values, looks at the current status of U.S. wetlands, and reviews federal, state, and local regulations to protect nontidal wetlands.

Riparian and Wetland Classification Review. Karl Gebhardt. U.S. Department of the Interior, Bureau of Land Management, 2850 Youngfield St., Lakewood, Colorado 80215. (303) 239-3700. 1990.

Urban Runoff Treatment Methods. National Technical Information Service, 5285 Port Royal Rd., Springfield, Virginia 22161. (703) 487-4650. 1977. Environmental protection technology related to non-structural wetland treatment.

Wetland Creation and Restoration: The Status of the Science. Jon A. Kusler and Mary E. Kentula, eds. Island Press, 1718 Connecticut Ave. N.W., Suite 300, Washington, District of Columbia 20009. (202) 232-7933. 1990. Eighty papers from leading scientists and technicians draw upon important new information and provide assessment by region of the capacity to implement a goal of no-net-loss of wetlands.

Wetland Losses in the United States. U.S. Department of the Interior, Fish and Wildlife Service, 1849 C St. NW, Washington, District of Columbia 20240. (202) 208-5634. 1990. A National Wetlands Inventory Group report on wetland conservation.

Wetland Modelling. Elsevier Science Publishing Co., 655 Avenue of the Americas, New York, New York 10010. (212) 984-5800. 1988. Simulation methods in wetland ecology and wetlands.

Wetlands: A Threatened Landscape. Michael Williams. B. Blackwell, 3 Cambridge Ctr., Suite 208, Cambridge, Massachusetts 02142. (617) 225-0401. 1990. Explores the evolution and composition of wetlands and their physical and biological dynamics, considers the impact of agriculture, industry, urbanization, and recreation upon them, and examines what steps we are taking and what steps should be considered to manage and preserve wetlands.

Wetlands: Mitigating and Regulating Development Impacts. David Salvesen. The Urban Land Institute, 1090 Vermont Ave. N.W., Washington, District of Columbia 20005. (202) 289-8500; (800) 237-9196. 1990. Presents the latest examination of the conflicts surrounding development of wetlands. Explains both federal and state wetland regulations. Included is an up-to-date review of important wetlands case law and a detailed look at six of the toughest state programs.

Wetlands of North America. William A. Niering. Thomasson-Grant, 1 Morton Dr., Suite 500, Charlottesville, Virginia 22901. (804) 977-1780 or (800) 999-1780. 1991. Deals with wetlands ecology and the methods of its preservation.

Wetlands of the United States. National Wetlands Inventory, U.S. Department of the Interior, Fish and Wildlife Service, 1849 C St. NW, Washington, District of Columbia 20240. (202) 208-3171.

Wetlands Protection: The Role of Economics. Paul F. Scodari. Environmental Law Institute, 1616 P St. N.W., Suite 200, Washington, District of Columbia 20036. (202) 328-5150. 1990. Discussion of market economics as applied to wetland functions and values. Key features include the science of wetland valuation, principles and methods of wetland valuation, principles and methods for valuing wetland goods, the implementation of wetland valuation, and the natural resource damage assessment.

Wetlands, Their Use and Regulation. Congress of the U.S., Office of Technology Assessment, c/o U.S. Government Printing Office, N. Capitol & H Sts. NW, Washington, District of Columbia 20401. (202) 512-0000. 1984. Legal aspects of wetland conservation.

GOVERNMENTAL ORGANIZATIONS

Assistant Attorney General: Environment and Resources Division, Department of Justice. Room 2143, 10th St. and Constitution Ave., N.W., Washington, District of Columbia 20530. (202) 514-2701.

Public Affairs Office: U.S. Army Corps of Engineers. Room 8137, 20 Massachusetts Ave., N.W., Washington, District of Columbia 20314. (202) 272-0010.

U.S. Environmental Protection Agency: Office of Wetlands Protection. 401 M St., S.W., Washington, District of Columbia 20460. (202) 382-7946.

HANDBOOKS AND MANUALS

Our National Wetland Heritage. Jon A. Kusler. Environmental Law Institute, 1616 P St., NW, Suite 200, Washington, District of Columbia 20036. (202) 328-5150. 1983. Discusses practical ways to preserve and protect wetlands and their benefits, which include recreation, wildlife habitat, pollution and flood control, scientific research and groundwater recharge.

The Poisoned Well: New Strategies for Groundwater Protection. Eric P. Jorgensen, ed. Island Press, 1718 Connecticut Ave. N.W., Suite 300, Washington, District of Columbia 20009. (202) 232-7933. 1989. Explains how individuals can work with agencies and the courts to enforce water laws, how the major federal water laws, work what remedies exist for each type of groundwater contamination, and what state and local programs may be helpful.

Waterways and Wetlands. British Trust for Conservation Volunteers, Berkshire, Reading, England 1976. Covers conservation of natural resources, with special reference to wetlands.

ONLINE DATA BASES

Computerized Engineering Index–COMPENDEX. Engineering Information Inc., 345 E. 47th St., New York, New York 10017. (212) 705-7600.

Monthly Catalog of United States Government Publications. U.S. G.P.O., Supt. of Docs., PO Box 371954, Pittsburgh, Pennsylvania 15250-7954. (202) 512-0000.

National Technical Information Service. U.S. Department of Commerce, National Technical Information Service, Office of Data Base Services, 5285 Port Royal Rd., Springfield, Virginia 22161. (703) 487-4807. Bibliographic database of government sponsored research and technical reports.

PressNet Environmental Reports. Chemical Information Systems, Inc., 7215 York Rd., Baltimore, Maryland 21212. (301) 321-8440.

SCISEARCH. Institute for Scientific Information, University City Science Center, 3501 Market St., Philadelphia, Pennsylvania 19104. (215) 386-0100.

Wetland Values Bibliographic Database. U.S. Army Corps of Engineers, Waterways Experiment Station, Environmental Lab, P.O. Box 631, Vicksburg, Mississippi 39180. (601) 634-3774.

PERIODICALS AND NEWSLETTERS

Aquanotes. Louisiana State University, Office of Sea Grant Development Center for Wetland Resources, Baton Rouge, Louisiana 70803. (504) 385-6449. 1972-. Quarterly. Wetlands related topics covering Louisiana Sea Grant College Program research.

Clean Water Report. Business Publishers, Inc., 951 Pershing Dr., Silver Spring, Maryland 20910-4464. (301) 587-6300. 1964-. Biweekly. Key information source for environmental professionals, covering the important issues: groundwater, drinking water, wastewater treatment, drought, wetlands, coastal protection, dioxin, non-point source pollution, agrichemical contamination, cleanup versus prevention issues, and related topics.

Ground Water. Water Well Journal Publishing Co., 6375 Riverside Dr., Dublin, Ohio 43017. (614) 761-3222. Bimonthly. Contains technical papers for NWWA.

Ground Water Age. National Trade Publications, Inc., 13 Century Hill, Latham, New York 12110. (518) 783-1281. Monthly. Covers product and literature developments and industry news.

Ground Water Monitor. Business Publishers, Inc., 951 Pershing Dr., Silver Spring, Maryland 20910-4464. (301) 587-6300. Biweekly. Legislation, litigation, regulations and quality problems on ground water. Also available online.

Ground Water Monitoring Review. Water Well Journal Publishing Co. National Water Well Association, 6375 Riverside Drive, Dublin, Ohio 43017. (614) 761-3222. Quarterly. Covers protection and restoration of ground water.

National Water Line. National Water Resources Association, 3800 North Fairfax Drive, #4, Arlington, Virginia 22203. (703) 524-1544. Monthly. Covers water resource development projects.

National Wetlands Newsletter. Environmental Law Institute, 1616 P St., NW, Suite 200, Washington, District of Columbia 20036. (202) 328-5150. Bimonthly. Federal, state, and local laws, policies, and programs concerning wetlands, floodplains, and coastal water resources.

Wetland News. Association of State Wetland Managers, PO Box 2463, Berne, New York 12023. (518) 872-1804. Quarterly.

Wetlands. Society of the Wetlands Scientists, Wilmington, North Carolina Annual.

RESEARCH CENTERS AND INSTITUTES

Center for Environmental Research. Cornell University, 470 Hollister Hall, Ithaca, New York 14853-3501. (607) 255-7535.

Center for Remote Sensing. University of Delaware, College of Marine Studies, Newark, Delaware 19711. (302) 451-2336.

Center for Wetlands. University of Florida, Phelps Laboratory, Gainesville, Florida 32611. (904) 392-2424.

Mote Marine Laboratory. 1600 Thompson Park, Sarasota, Florida 34236. (813) 388-4441.

University of Michigan, Wetland Ecosystem Research Group. Department of Chemical Engineering, 3094 Dow Building, Ann Arbor, Michigan 48109. (313) 764-3362.

Urban Vegetation Laboratory. Morton Arboretum, Route 53, Lisle, Illinois 60532. (708) 968-0074.

Vineyard Environmental Research Institute. RFD 862, Martha's Vineyard Airport, Tisbury, Massachusetts 02568. (508) 693-4632.

Wetland Center. Duke University, School of Forestry and Environmental Studies, Durham, North Carolina 27706. (919) 684-8741.

Wetlands Institute. Stone Harbor Boulevard, Stone Harbor, New Jersey 08247. (609) 368-1211.

Wetlands Research Area. Unity College, Unity, Maine 04988. (207) 948-3131.

STATISTICS SOURCES

Ecology: Community Profiles. U.S. Fish and Wildlife Service. National Technical Information Service, 5285 Port Royal Road, Springfield, Virginia 22161. (703) 487-4650. Irregular. Data on coastal and inland ecosystems, including wetlands, tidal-flats, near-shore seagrasses, sand dunes, drilling platforms, oyster reefs, estuaries, rivers and streams.

National Water Quality Inventory. U.S. G.P.O., Washington, District of Columbia 20401. (202) 512-0000. Biennial. Water pollution problems and control activities by states.

Wetlands of the California Central Valley: Status and Trends 1939 to Mid-1980's. U.S. G.P.O., Washington, District of Columbia 20401. (202) 512-0000. 1989. Report on area of current wetlands, and former wetlands converted to other uses, in the California Central Valley.

World Resources. World Resources Institute. 1709 New York Ave., N.W., Washington, District of Columbia 20006. (202) 638-6300. Annual. Statistical and textual analysis of world's natural resources and the effects of growth-caused environmental pollution.

TRADE ASSOCIATIONS AND PROFESSIONAL SOCIETIES

American Institute of Biological Sciences. 730 11th St., N.W., Washington, District of Columbia 20001-4521. (202) 628-1500.

Association of State Wetland Managers. P.O. Box 2463, Berne, New York 12023. (518) 872-1804.

Great Swamp Research Institute. Lycoming College, Dean of the College, Washington Blvd., Williamsport, Pennsylvania 17701-5192. (717) 321-4102.

The Izaak Walton League of America. 1401 Wilson Boulevard, Level B, Arlington, Virginia 22209. (703) 528-1818.

National Water Resources Association. 3800 N. Fairfax Dr., Suite 4, Arlington, Virginia 22203. (703) 524-1544.

National Wetlands Technical Council. 1616 P St., N.W., 2nd floor, Washington, District of Columbia 20036. (202) 328-5150.

Wetlands for Wildlife, Inc. PO Box 344, West Bend, Wisconsin 53095. (414) 334-0327.

Whooping Crane Conservation Association, Inc. 1007 Carmel Ave., Lafayette, Louisiana 70501. (318) 234-6339.

WHALING

See also: MARINE MAMMALS

ABSTRACTING AND INDEXING SERVICES

Applied Science and Technology Index. H.W. Wilson Co., 950 University Ave., Bronx, New York 10452. (800) 367-6770. Formerly Industrial Arts Index.

Biological Abstracts. BIOSIS, 2100 Arch St., Philadelphia, Pennsylvania 19103-1399. (215) 587-4800. 1927-.

Biological and Agricultural Index. H.W. Wilson Co., 950 University Ave., Bronx, New York 10452. (800) 367-6770. 1916-. Monthly.

Ecological Abstracts. Geo Abstracts Ltd. Elsevier Applied Science, Crown House, Linton Rd., Barking, England IG 11 8JU. 1974-. Derived from over 600 leading ecological and environmental journals, plus books, conference proceedings, reports and theses.

General Science Index. H. W. Wilson Co., 950 University Ave., Bronx, New York 10452. 1978-. Monthly, also issued in annual cumulation. Cumulative subject index to English language periodicals in the subject fields of astronomy, botany, chemistry, earth science, environment and conservation, food and nutrition, genetics, mathcmatics, medicine and health, microbiology, oceanography, physics, physiology and zoology.

Science Citation Index. Institute for Scientific Information, 3501 Market St., Philadelphia, Pennsylvania 19104. 1961-.

ALMANACS AND YEARBOOKS

Dolphins, Porpoises and Whales of the World: The IUCN Red Data Book. M. Klinowska. The World Conservation Union, IUCN Publications Services Unit, 181a Huntingdon Road, Cambridge, England CB3 0DJ. (0223) 277894. 1991. Reviews the status of all cetacean species. Detailed accounts are provided for each species, describing their distribution, population, threats, and the conservation measures required to ensure their survival.

ENCYCLOPEDIAS AND DICTIONARIES

Grzimek's Encyclopedia of Ecology. Bernhard Grzimek. Van Nostrand Reinhold, 115 5th Ave., New York, New York 10003. (212) 254-3232. 1976.

North American Reference Encyclopedia of Ecology and Pollution. William White. North American Pub. Co., 401 N. Broad St., Philadelphia, Pennsylvania 19108. (215) 238-5300. 1972.

Van Nostrand's Scientific Encyclopedia. Glenn D. Considine, ed. Van Nostrand Reinhold, 115 5th Ave., New York, New York 10003. (212) 254-3232. 1983. Sixth edition. Includes all broad subject areas in science.

GENERAL WORKS

Can the Whales Be Saved?. Philip Whitfield. Viking Kestrel, 40 W 23rd St., New York, New York 10010. (212) 337-5200. 1989.

International Regulation of Whaling. Patricia Birnie. Oceana Publications Inc., 75 Main St., Dobbs Ferry, New York 10522. (914) 693-8100. 1985. A chronological account of the development of international law pertaining to the regulation of whaling. Traces the growing relationship of the regulation of whaling to the development of other relevant laws and institutions for the conservation of migratory species.

The Whale War. David Day. Sierra Club Books, 100 Bush St., San Francisco, California 94104. (415) 291-1600. 1987.

ONLINE DATA BASES

BIOSIS Previews. BIOSIS, 2100 Arch St., Philadelphia, Pennsylvania 19103-1399. (215) 587-4800. Largest and most comprehensive database of research in the life sciences. Contains citations for nearly 9000 primary research journals, monographs, reviews, symposia, preliminary reports, semi-popular journals, selected institutional reports, government reports and research communications.

PressNet Environmental Reports. Chemical Information Systems, Inc., 7215 York Rd., Baltimore, Maryland 21212. (301) 321-8440.

PERIODICALS AND NEWSLETTERS

Coastwatch. Center for Coastal Studies, 59 Commercial St., PO Box 1036, Provincetown, Massachusetts 02657. (508) 487-3622. Bimonthly. Coastal ecology and biology, whale research, and conservation issues.

STATISTICS SOURCES

World Resources. World Resources Institute. 1709 New York Ave., N.W., Washington, District of Columbia 20006. (202) 638-6300. Annual. Statistical and textual analysis of world's natural resources and the effects of growth-caused environmental pollution.

TRADE ASSOCIATIONS AND PROFESSIONAL SOCIETIES

American Institute of Biological Sciences. 730 11th St., N.W., Washington, District of Columbia 20001-4521. (202) 628-1500.

Center for Whale Research. P.O. Box 1577, Friday Harbor, Washington 98250. (206) 378-5835.

Pacific Whale Foundation. Kealia Beach Plaza, Ste. 25, 101 N. Kihei Rd., Kihei, Hawaii 96753. (808) 879-8811.

Whale Center. 3929 Piedmont Ave., Oakland, California 94611. (415) 654-6692.

WILDERNESS

ABSTRACTING AND INDEXING SERVICES

Applied Ecology Abstracts Studies in Renewable Natural Resources. Information Retrieval Ltd., 1911 Jefferson Davis Highway, Arlington, Virginia 22202. 1975-. Monthly.

Applied Science and Technology Index. H.W. Wilson Co., 950 University Ave., Bronx, New York 10452. (800) 367-6770. Formerly Industrial Arts Index.

Biological and Agricultural Index. H.W. Wilson Co., 950 University Ave., Bronx, New York 10452. (800) 367-6770. 1916-. Monthly.

Current Advances in Ecological and Environmental Science. Pergamon Microforms International, Inc., Fairview Park, Elmsford, New York 10523. (914) 592-7720. 1989-. Monthly. Current literature searching service including journals, reports, abstracts, etc. This service is available online as part of the CABS database on the hosts BRS and ORBIT search service.

Ecological Abstracts. Geo Abstracts Ltd. Elsevier Applied Science, Crown House, Linton Rd., Barking, England IG 11 8JU. 1974-. Derived from over 600 leading ecological and environmental journals, plus books, conference proceedings, reports and theses.

Multimedia Index to Ecology. National Information Center for Educational Media, University of Southern California, Los Angeles, California 90007.

Science Citation Index. Institute for Scientific Information, 3501 Market St., Philadelphia, Pennsylvania 19104. 1961-.

BIBLIOGRAPHIES

Changing Wilderness Values, 1930-1990: An Annotated Bibliography. Joan S. Elbers. Greenwood Publishing Group, Inc., 88 Post Rd. W., Box 5007, Westport, Connecticut 06881. (203) 226-3571. 1991. "Encompasses the different values Americans have sought in or attributed to the wilderness." Most of the entries fall into the areas of "wilderness experience."

DIRECTORIES

Gale Environmental Sourcebook. Karen Hill. Gale Research Co., 835 Penobscot Bldg., Detroit, Michigan 48226-4094. (313) 961-2242. Contacts, information sources, or general information on environmental topics.

ENCYCLOPEDIAS AND DICTIONARIES

Grzimek's Encyclopedia of Ecology. Bernhard Grzimek. Van Nostrand Reinhold, 115 5th Ave., New York, New York 10003. (212) 254-3232. 1976.

North American Reference Encyclopedia of Ecology and Pollution. William White. North American Pub. Co., 401 N. Broad St., Philadelphia, Pennsylvania 19108. (215) 238-5300. 1972.

Van Nostrand's Scientific Encyclopedia. Glenn D. Considine, ed. Van Nostrand Reinhold, 115 5th Ave., New York, New York 10003. (212) 254-3232. 1983. Sixth edition. Includes all broad subject areas in science.

GENERAL WORKS

Wilderness Management. John C. Hendee, et al. North American Press, 350 Indiana St., Ste. 350, Golden, Colorado 80401. (303) 277-1623. 1990. 2d ed. rev. The expertise of the main authors has been combined with that of 10 other authorities in wilderness related fields, and nearly 100 wilderness managers, scientists, educators, and citizen conservationists, to make this book a valuable tool of practical information.

Wilderness Preservation and the Sagebrush Rebellions. William L. Graf. Rowman & Littlefield, Publishers, Inc., 8705 Bollman Pl., Savage, Maryland 20763. (301) 306-0400. 1990. Narrates the emergence of wilderness preservation as part of American public land policy from the 1880s to the 1980s.

ONLINE DATA BASES

Cambridge Scientific Abstracts Life Science–CSAL. Cambridge Scientific Abstracts, 5161 River Rd., Bethesda, Maryland 20816. (301) 961-6750. Provides access to the following abstracting services: "Life Sciences Collection," "Aquatic Sciences and Fisheries Abstracts," "Oceanic Abstracts," and "Pollution Abstracts."

PERIODICALS AND NEWSLETTERS

It's Time to Go Wild. American Wildlands, 7600 E. Arapahoe Rd., Suite 114, Englewood, Colorado 80112. (303) 771-0380. Quarterly. Protection and proper use of wilderness lands and rivers.

Public Land News. Resources Publishing Co., 1010 Vermont Avenue, NW, Suite 708, Washington, District of Columbia 20005. (202) 638-7529. Biweekly. Covers land use and land development.

Wild America Magazine. American Wildlands, 7500 E. Arapahoe Rd., Suite 355, Englewood, Colorado 80112. (303) 771-0380. Annual.

Wilderness. The Wilderness Society, 900 17th St. NW, Washington, District of Columbia 20006. (202) 833-2300. Quarterly. Preserving wilderness and wildlife, protecting America's prime forests, parks, rivers, shorelands, and fostering an American land ethic.

RESEARCH CENTERS AND INSTITUTES

DC Water Resources Research Center. University of District of Columbia, 4200 Connecticut Avenue, NW, MB5004, Washington, District of Columbia 20008. (202) 673-3442.

Quetico-Superior Wilderness Research Center. Box 479, Minnesota

University of Idaho, Wilderness Research Center. Moscow, Idaho 83843. (208) 885-7911.

STATISTICS SOURCES

Environmental Data Compendium. OECD Publications and Information Center, 2001 L St., N.W., Suite 700, Washington, District of Columbia 20036. (202) 785-6323. 1989.

Environmental Indicators. OECD Publications and Information Center, 2001 L St., N.W., Suite 700, Washington, District of Columbia 20036. (202) 785-6323. 1991.

Environmental Quality. Council on Environmental Quality. U.S. G.P.O., Washington, District of Columbia 20401. (202) 512-0000. Annual.

Land Areas of the National Forest System. U.S. Forest Service. U.S. G.P.O., Washington, District of Columbia 20401. (202) 512-0000. Annual. Data on wilderness,

scenic-research, monument and recreation areas, and game refuges.

Managing the Nation's Public Lands. U.S. Bureau of Land Management. U.S. G.P.O., Washington, District of Columbia 20401. (202) 512-0000. Annual. Data on wilderness, wildlife, recreational resources, rangeland and forests.

The State of the Environment. OECD Publications and Information Center, 2001 L St., N.W., Suite 700, Washington, District of Columbia 20036. (202) 785-6323. 1991.

TRADE ASSOCIATIONS AND PROFESSIONAL SOCIETIES

American Institute of Biological Sciences. 730 11th St., N.W., Washington, District of Columbia 20001-4521. (202) 628-1500.

American Wilderness Alliance. 7500 E. Arapahoe Rd., Suite 355, Englewood, Colorado 80112. (303) 694-9047.

American Wilderness Leadership School. c/o 4800 Gates Pass Rd., Tucson, Arizona 85745. (606) 620-1220.

The Izaak Walton League of America. 1401 Wilson Boulevard, Level B, Arlington, Virginia 22209. (703) 528-1818.

Sierra Club. 100 Bush St., San Francisco, California 94104. (415) 291-1600.

Wilderness Flyers. c/o Seaplane Pilots Association, 421 Aviation Way, Frederick, Maryland 21701. (301) 695-2082.

Wilderness Society. 900 17th St., NW, Washington, District of Columbia 20006. (202) 833-2300.

Wilderness Watch. P.O. Box 782, Sturgeon Bay, Wisconsin 54235. (414) 743-1238.

WILDFIRES

See: FORESTS

WILDLIFE

ABSTRACTING AND INDEXING SERVICES

Applied Ecology Abstracts Studies in Renewable Natural Resources. Information Retrieval Ltd., 1911 Jefferson Davis Highway, Arlington, Virginia 22202. 1975-. Monthly.

Biological Abstracts. BIOSIS, 2100 Arch St., Philadelphia, Pennsylvania 19103-1399. (215) 587-4800. 1927-.

Biological and Agricultural Index. H.W. Wilson Co., 950 University Ave., Bronx, New York 10452. (800) 367-6770. 1916-. Monthly.

Biology Digest. Data Courier, Plexus Pub Inc., 143 Old Marlton Pike, Medford, New Jersey 08055. 1974-. Monthly. Abstracts biology periodicals.

Civil Engineering Hydraulic Abstracts. BHRA Fluid Engineering, Air Science Co., PO Box 143, Corning, New York 14830. (607) 962-5591. Monthly. Abstracts of periodicals that publish in the areas of hydraulic engineering and other related topics.

Current Advances in Ecological and Environmental Science. Pergamon Microforms International, Inc., Fairview Park, Elmsford, New York 10523. (914) 592-7720. 1989-. Monthly. Current literature searching service includingjournals, reports, abstracts, etc. This service is available online as part of the CABS database on the hosts BRS and ORBIT search service.

Ecological Abstracts. Geo Abstracts Ltd. Elsevier Applied Science, Crown House, Linton Rd., Barking, England IG 11 8JU. 1974-. Derived from over 600 leading ecological and environmental journals, plus books, conference proceedings, reports and theses.

General Science Index. H. W. Wilson Co., 950 University Ave., Bronx, New York 10452. 1978-. Monthly, also issued in annual cumulation. Cumulative subject index to English language periodicals in the subject fields of astronomy, botany, chemistry, earth science, environment and conservation, food and nutrition, genetics, mathematics, medicine and health, microbiology, oceanography, physics, physiology and zoology.

Index to Scientific Book Contents. Institute for Scientific Information, 3501 Market St., Philadelphia, Pennsylvania 19104. (800) 523-1857. 1985-. Annual. Gives contents of science books published.

Index Veterinarius. C. A. B. International, 845 North Park Ave., Tucson, Arizona 85719. (602) 621-7897 or (800) 528-4841. 1933-. Monthly. A monthly subject and author index to the world's veterinary literature. References are given to abstracts published in Veterinary Bulletin. Animals included in the index are: cattle, horses, sheep, goats, pigs, poultry, cats, dogs, rabbits, cagebirds, laboratory animals, wildlife, zoo animals, fish and other domestic animals.

Multimedia Index to Ecology. National Information Center for Educational Media, University of Southern California, Los Angeles, California 90007.

Science Citation Index. Institute for Scientific Information, 3501 Market St., Philadelphia, Pennsylvania 19104. 1961-.

BIBLIOGRAPHIES

Current Contents. Agriculture, Biology and Environmental Sciences. Institute for Scientific Information, 3501 Market St., Philadelphia, Pennsylvania 19104. (800) 523-1857. 1973-. Previous title: Current Contents. Agricultural, Food & Veterinary Sciences. Gives the table of contents of periodicals in the fields of agriculture, biology, environmental and related areas.

DIRECTORIES

Animal Organizations and Services Directory. Kathleen A. Reece. Animal Stories Pub., 16787 Beach Blvd., Huntington Beach, California 92647. 1990-91. Fourth edition. Devoted to animals, pets and wildlife.

Current Federal Aid Research Report: Wildlife. Claude Stephens. Department of the Interior, Fish & Wildlife Service, 1849 C St. NW, Washington, District of Columbia 20240. (202) 208-5634. Annual. Wildlife research projects funded by the Pittman-Robertson grant program.

List of National Wildlife Refuges. U.S. Dept. of Interior, Fish, Interior Dept., Washington, District of Columbia 20240. (202) 343-5634.

National Wildlife Refuges: A Visitor's Guide. Fish and Wildlife Service, Department of the Interior, 18th and C Sts., N.W., Washington, District of Columbia 20240. (202) 653-8750.

ENCYCLOPEDIAS AND DICTIONARIES

Cambridge Encyclopedia of Life Sciences. A. E. Friday and David S. Ingram. Cambridge University Press, 40 W 20th St., New York, New York 10011. (212) 924-3900 or (800) 227-0247. 1985. Includes all topics under biology and ecology.

Elsevier's Dictionary of the World's Game and Wildlife. G. Ferlin. Elsevier Science Publishing Co., 655 Avenue of the Americas, New York, New York 10010. (212) 989-5800. 1989. The languages included are English, Latin, French, German, Dutch, Spanish.

The Encyclopedia of North American Wildlife. Stanley Klein. Facts on File, Inc., 460 Park Ave. S., New York, New York 10016. (212) 683-2244. 1983. Includes mammals, birds, reptiles, amphibians, and fish. Appendices include information on wildlife conservation organizations, a bibliographical list of endangered species and an index of Latin names.

Grzimek's Encyclopedia of Ecology. Bernhard Grzimek. Van Nostrand Reinhold, 115 5th Ave., New York, New York 10003. (212) 254-3232. 1976.

Nature in America Your A-Z Guide to Our Country's Animals, Plants, Landforms and Other Natural Features. Readers Digest Association, 260 Madison Ave., New York, New York 10016. 1991. Reference guide of nature in North America. Explores plants, animals, weather, land forms, and wildlife habitats. Includes over 1000 photographs and illustrations for some 1200 entries.

The New International Wildlife Encyclopedia. Maurice Burton and Robert Burton, eds. N. C. L. S. Ltd., 150 Southampton Row, London, England WC1. 1980. Two volumes.

North American Reference Encyclopedia of Ecology and Pollution. William White. North American Pub. Co., 401 N. Broad St., Philadelphia, Pennsylvania 19108. (215) 238-5300. 1972.

Remarkable Animals: A Unique Encyclopedia of Wildlife Wonders. Guinness Books, 33 London Rd., Enfield, England EN2 6DJ. 1987. Includes mammals, birds, fishes, amphibians, reptiles, insects, and arachnids.

Van Nostrand's Scientific Encyclopedia. Glenn D. Considine, ed. Van Nostrand Reinhold, 115 5th Ave., New York, New York 10003. (212) 254-3232. 1983. Sixth edition. Includes all broad subject areas in science.

GENERAL WORKS

Atlas of the Environment. Geoffrey Lean, et al. Prentice Hall, Rte. 9W, Englewood Cliffs, New York 07632. (201) 592-2000. 1990. Guide to the major environmental issues around the world that makes good use of numerous maps and diagrams to present the increasing amount of information available in this field. Covers related subjects such as indigenous people and refugees, the education gap, natural and human induced disasters, wildlife trade, and migration routes.

Backyard Wildlife Habitat. National Wildlife Federation, 1400 16th St. N.W., Washington, District of Columbia 20036-2266. (202) 797-6800. 1989. Backyard Wildlife Habitat program run by the National Wildlife Federation. Participants in the program create backyard havens for native fauna.

Biological Conservation. David W. Ehrenfeld. Holt, Rinehart and Winston, 6277 Sea Harbor Dr., Orlando, Florida 32887. (407) 345-2500. 1970.

Common Sense Pest Control. William Olkowski, et al. Tauton Pr., 63 South Main St., Box 5506, Newton, Connecticut 06740-5506. 1991. Discusses ways to manage other living organisms that are regarded as pests.

Conservation of Living Nature and Resources: Problems, Trends, and Prospects. A. V. Yablokov. Springer-Verlag, 175 5th Ave., New York, New York 10010. (212) 460-1500 or (800) 777-4643. 1991. Deals with wildlife conservation, the associated problems, solutions, and its future.

The Endangered Kingdom: The Struggle to Save America's Wildlife. Roger L. DiSilvestro. John Wiley & Sons, Inc., 605 3rd Ave., New York, New York 10158-0012. (212) 850-6000. 1989. Describes the historical perspective and overview of present- day wildlife conservation. Included are game animals, endangered species, and nongame species.

Game Wars: The Undercover Pursuit of Wildlife Poachers. Marc Reisner. Academic Marketing, Penguin USA, 375 Hudson St., New York, New York 10014. (212) 366-2000; (800) 253-2304. 1991. Provides a first hand account of the life and dangers encountered by federal wildlife agents working for U.S. Fish and Wildlife Service: the elaborate covers they devise; the meticulous preparation necessary to pull off a successful sting; the weeks, months, even years they spend putting together their traps and cases; and the dangers they face as they impersonate big game hunters, ivory trades; and professional smugglers.

The Greater Yellowstone Ecosystem. Robert B. Keiter and Mark S. Boyce, eds. Yale University Press, 302 Temple St., New Haven, Connecticut 06520. (203) 432-0960. 1991. Discusses key resource management issues in the greater Yellowstone ecosystem, using them as starting points to debate the manner in which humans should interact with the environment of this area.

In the Wake of the Exxon Valdez: Devastating Impact of Alaska's Oil Spill. Art Davidson. Sierra Club Books, 100 Bush St., San Francisco, California 94104. (415) 291-1600. 1990. Story of environmental risk and the consequences that arise.

Magill's Survey of Science. Life Science Series. Frank N. Magill, ed. Salem Press, PO Box 50062, Pasadena, California 91105. 1991. Six volumes. Contents: v.1. A-Central and peripheral nervous system functions; v.2. Central metabolism regulation - eukaryotic transcriptional control; v.3. Positive and negative eukaryotic transcriptional control - mammalian hormones; v.4. Hormones and behavior - muscular contraction; v.5. Muscular contraction and relaxation - sexual reproduction in plants; v.6. Reproductive behavior and mating - X inactivation and the Lyon hypothesis.

Managing our Wildlife Resources. Stanley H. Anderson. Prentice-Hall, Rte. 9W, Englewood Cliffs, New Jersey 07632. (201) 592-2000; (800) 634-2863. 1991. Reviews wildlife management, history, population characteristic, and habitat intervention; emphasizes planning, developing programs, and the impact of pollutants.

Neotropical Wildlife Use and Conservation. John R. Robinson, ed. University of Chicago Press, 5801 Ellis Ave., 4th Fl., Chicago, Illinois 60637. (800) 621-2736. 1991. The importance of wildlife to people, impact of the use of wildlife on population or biological communities.

Oregon Wildlife. Oregon State Dept. of Fish, Box 59, Portland, Oregon 97207. (503) 229-5403. Bimonthly.

The Philosophy and Practice of Wildlife Management. Frederick F. Gilbert and Donald G. Dodds. Krieger Publishing Co., Inc., PO Box 9542, Melbourne, Florida 32902-9542. (407) 724-9542. 1992. Shows the mechanisms and historical foundations of wildlife management and traces the evolution of increasingly sophisticated approaches to the management of our natural fauna.

Preserving Communities and Corridors. Gay Mackintosh, ed. Defenders of Wildlife, 1244 19th St. N.W., Washington, District of Columbia 20036. (202) 659-9510. 1989.

The Protection and Management of Our Natural Resources, Wildlife and Habitat. W. Jack Grosse. Oceana Publications Inc., 75 Main St., Dobbs Ferry, New York 10522. (914) 693-8100. 1992. Covers question of overall management, control and protection of wildlife and habitat. Additionally, as the federal government has recently created numerous acts which serve to control wildlife and habitat, many questions have emerged over shared and conflicting power with the states.

Saving America's Wildlife. Thomas R. Dunlap. Princeton University Press, 41 Williams St., Princeton, New Jersey 08540. (609) 258-4900. 1988. Explores how we have deepened our commitment to and broadened the scope of animal conservation through the 1980s.

Taking Stock: The Tropical Forestry Action Plan After Five Years. Robert Winterbottom. World Resources Institute, 1709 New York Ave. N.W., Washington, District of Columbia 20006. (800) 822-0504. 1990. Analyzes Tropical Forestry Action Plan's accomplishments and shortcomings, drawing on the biannual meetings of the TFAP Forestry Advisors' groups, assessments by FAO, various aid agencies, and by such organizations as the World Rainforest Movement, Friends of the Earth, and World Life Fund.

Tropical Resources: Ecology and Development. Jose I. Furtado, et al., eds. Harwood Academic Publishers, PO Box 786, Cooper Sta., New York, New York 10276. (212) 206-8900. 1990. Overview of global tropical resources, both terrestrial and aquatic. Subjects discussed include forest resources, wildlife resources, general land use, pasture resources, economic development, fisheries, marine resources, and aquaculture.

Valuing Wildlife: Economic and Social Perspectives. Daniel J. Decker and Gary R. Goff, eds. Westview Press, 5500 Central Ave., Boulder, Colorado 80301. (303) 444-3541. 1987. State of the art guide to determining the value of wildlife, the application for environmental impact assessment, and strategies in wildlife planning and policy.

Wildlife and Habitat Law. Jack W. Grosse. Oceana Publications Inc., 75 Main St., Dobbs Ferry, New York

10522. (914) 693-8100. 1991. Covers questions of overall management, control and protection of wildlife and habitat. Issues of shared and conflicting power with the states are covered.

Wildlife and Protected Areas: An Overview. United Nations Environment Program. UNIPUB, 1980.

Wildlife Extinction. Charles L. Cadieux. Stone Wall Pr., 1241 30th St. N.W., Washington, District of Columbia 20007. (202) 333-1860. 1991. Presents a worldwide picture of animals in danger of extinction and addresses controversial issues such as exploding human population, the role of zoos and wildlife parks, hunting and poaching.

Wildlife, Forests, and Forestry. Malcolm L. Hunter, Jr. Prentice Hall, Rte 9W, Englewood Cliffs, New Jersey 07632. (201) 592-2000. 1990. Presents new ideas that will form the basis of forest wildlife management in years to come. It looks at the costs of managing wildlife, as well as national policies on forest wildlife management and quantitative techniques for measuring diversity.

Wildlife of the Florida Keys: A Natural History. James D. Lazell, Jr. Island Press, 1718 Connecticut Ave. N.W., Suite 300, Washington, District of Columbia 20009. (202) 232-7933. 1989. Identifies habits, behaviors, and histories of most of the species indigenous to the Keys.

Wildlife Reserves and Corridors in the Urban Environment. Lowell W. Adams. National Institute for Urban Wildlife, 10921 Trotting Ridge Way, Columbia, Maryland 21044. (301) 596-3311. 1989. Reviews the knowledge base on wildlife habitat reserves and corridors in urban and urbanizing areas. Provides guidelines and approaches to ecological landscape planning and wildlife conservation in these regions.

Wildlife Toxicology. Tony J. Peterle. Van Nostrand Reinhold, 115 5th Ave., New York, New York 10003. (212) 354-3232. 1991. Presents an historical overview of the toxicology problem and summarizes the principal laws, testing protocols, and roles of leading U.S. federal agencies, especially EPA. Examines state and local issues, monitoring programs, and contains an unique section on the regulation of toxic substances overseas.

GOVERNMENTAL ORGANIZATIONS

Assistant Attorney General: Environment and Resources Division, Department of Justice. Room 2143, 10th St. and Constitution Ave., N.W., Washington, District of Columbia 20530. (202) 514-2701.

Office of Public Affairs: Fish and Wildlife Service. 18th and C St., N.W., Washington, District of Columbia 20240. (202) 343-5634.

TVA Public Information Office. 400 West Summit Hill Dr., Knoxville, Tennessee 37902. (615) 632-8000.

Wildlife and Fisheries Department: Fish and Wildlife. Secretary, PO Box 98000, Baton Rouge, Louisiana 70898-2803. (504) 765-2803.

Wildlife and Marine Resources Department: Fish and Wildlife. Executive Director, PO Box 167, Columbia, South Carolina 29202. (803) 734-4007.

Wildlife Resources Agency: Fish and Wildlife. Executive Director, PO Box 40747, Nashville, Tennessee 37204. (615) 781-6552.

HANDBOOKS AND MANUALS

Collins Guide to the Rare Mammals of the World. John A. Burton and Vivian G. Burton. Collins, 77/85 Fulham Palace Rd., London, England W6 8JB. 071-493 7070. 1988. Includes all the mammal species which might be considered threatened.

The Official World Wildlife Fund Guide to Endangered Species of North America. David W. Lowe, ed. Beacham Publishing, Inc., 2100 S. St. NW, Washington, District of Columbia 20008. (202) 234-0877. 1990. Two volumes. Guide to endangered plants and animals. Describes 540 endangered or threatened species including their habitat, behavior and, recovery. Includes: directories of the Offices of the U.S. Fish and Wildlife Service, Offices ofthe National Marine Fisheries Service, State Heritage Programs, Bureau of Land Management Offices, National Forest Service Offices, National Wildlife Refuges, Canadian agencies, and state offices.

Prevention and Control of Wildlife Damage. Nebraska Cooperative Extension Service, Institute of Agricultural and Natural Resources, University of Nebraska, 211 Agricultural Hall, Lincoln, Nebraska 68583-0703. (402) 472-7211. 1983. Published in cooperation with Great Plains Agricultural Council Wildlife Resources Committee.

Wildlife and Fisheries Habitat Improvement Handbook. Neil F. Payne. Wildlife and Fisheries, Department of the Interior, 18th and C Sts. NW, Washington, District of Columbia 20240. (202) 653-8750. 1990.

ONLINE DATA BASES

BIOSIS Previews. BIOSIS, 2100 Arch St., Philadelphia, Pennsylvania 19103-1399. (215) 587-4800. Largest and most comprehensive database of research in the life sciences. Contains citations for nearly 9000 primary research journals, monographs, reviews, symposia, preliminary reports, semi-popular journals, selected institutional reports, government reports and research communications.

Cambridge Scientific Abstracts Life Science–CSAL. Cambridge Scientific Abstracts, 5161 River Rd., Bethesda, Maryland 20816. (301) 961-6750. Provides access to the following abstracting services: "Life Sciences Collection," "Aquatic Sciences and Fisheries Abstracts," "Oceanic Abstracts," and "Pollution Abstracts."

Enviroline. R. R. Bowker Co., Bowker Electronic Publishing, 121 Chanlon Rd., New Providence, New Jersey 07974. (800) 521-8110.

Environmental Bibliography. Environmental Studies Institute, International Academy at Santa Barbara, 800 Garden St., Ste. D, Santa Barbara, California 93101. (805) 965-5010. International periodical literature dealing with environmental topics such as air pollution, water treatment, energy conservation, noise abatement, soil mechanics, wildlife preservation, and chemical wastes.

Herman Wildlife Database. Julie Moore & Assoc., Box 5156, Riverside, California 92517. (714) 943-3863.

Natural Resources Metabase. National Information Services Corporation, Ste. 6, Wyman Towers, 3100 St. Paul St., Baltimore, Maryland 21218. (301) 243-0797. Published and unpublished reports and other materials dealing with natural resources and environmental issues released by U.S. and Canadian government agencies and organizations.

PressNet Environmental Reports. Chemical Information Systems, Inc., 7215 York Rd., Baltimore, Maryland 21212. (301) 321-8440.

SCISEARCH. Institute for Scientific Information, University City Science Center, 3501 Market St., Philadelphia, Pennsylvania 19104. (215) 386-0100.

Wildlife Data Base. Julie Moore & Associates, 9956 N. Highway 85, Los Cruces, New Mexico 88005. Scientific literature on wildlife, including North American waterfowl, shore and marsh birds, upland game birds, birds of prey, rodents and lagomorphs, carnivores and ungulates; international oceanic birds, marine mammals including whales, and bats.

PERIODICALS AND NEWSLETTERS

Activist Newsletter. Defenders of Wildlife, 1244 19th St. NW, Washington, District of Columbia 20036. (202) 659-9510. Quarterly.

Arizona Wildlife News. Arizona Wildlife Federation, 4330 N. 62nd St., #102, Scottsdale, Arizona 85251. (602) 946-6160. 1965-. Monthly.

The Balance Wheel. Association for Conservation Information, c/o Roy Edwards, Virginia Game Department, 4010 W. Broad St., Richmond, Virginia 23230-3916. (804) 367-1000. Quarterly.

Bear News. Great Bear Foundation, Box 2699, Missoula, Montana 59806. (406) 721-3009. Quarterly. Covers all topics about the world's wild bears and the lands necessary for their survival. Topics include climate change, pandas, mothers and cubs, forests, and economic conflict in bear habitats.

Beaver Defenders. Unexpected Wildlife Refuge, Box 765, Newfield, New Jersey 08344. (609) 697-3541. 1971-. Quarterly. Newsletter about the unexpected wildlife refuge and about issues regarding beavers everywhere.

Biological Conservation. Applied Science Publishers, 655 Avenue of the Americas, PO Box 5399, New York, New York 10163. (718) 756-6440. Quarterly. Conservation of biological and allied natural resources, plants and animals and their habitats.

Born Free News. Elsa Wild Animal Appeal, U.S.A., Box 4572, North Hollywood, California 91617-0572. (818) 761-8387. 1969-. News about wildlife.

Bounty News. Bounty Information Service, Stephens College Post Office, Columbia, Missouri 65215. (314) 876-7186. Biannual. Wildlife bounties in North America and methods for removing bounties.

Coalition to Protect Animals in Parks and Refuges. Coalition to Protect Animals in Parks and Refuges, Box 26, Swain, New York 14884. (607) 545-6213. 1983-. Quarterly. Primary concern is to eliminate the killing of wild animals for fun and profit in parks and National Wildlife refuges. Also covers more general wildlife and ecological issues.

Colorado Wildlife. Colorado Wildlife Federation, 1560 Broadway, Denver, Colorado 80202. (303) 830-2557. 1973-. Monthly.

Common Sense Pest Control Quarterly. Bio-Integral Resource Center, PO Box 7414, Berkeley, California

94707. (415) 524-2567. Four times a year. Least-toxic management of pests on indoor plants, pests that damage paper, controlling fleas and ticks on pets, and garden pests.

Defenders. Defenders of Wildlife, 1244 19th St. NW, Washington, District of Columbia 20036. (202) 659-9510. Bimonthly. Wildlife and conservation.

Divining Rod. New Mexico Water Resources Research Institute, Box 30001, Dept. 3167, Las Cruces, New Mexico 88003-0001. (505) 646-1813. Quarterly. Water issues & water research in New Mexico.

Duckological. Ducks Unlimited, 1 Waterfowl Way, Long Grove, Illinois 60047. (708) 438-4300. Bimonthly. Protection of ducks.

Eco-Humane Letter. International Ecology Society, 1471 Barcly St., St. Paul, Minnesota 55106-1405. (612) 774-4971. Irregular. Issues concerning animals, wildlife, and the environment.

Ecology USA. Business Publishers, Inc., 951 Pershing Dr., Silver Spring, Maryland 20910-4464. (301) 587-6300. 1972-. Biweekly. Contains all the legislation, regulation, and litigation affecting efforts to conserve and protect America's unique environmental and ecological heritage.

ENFO. 1251-B Miller Ave., Winter Park, Florida 32789-4827. (407) 644-5377. Bimonthly. Water resources, parks, wildlife air quality, growth management, government and private actions.

Environmental Defense Fund Letter. Environmental Defense Fund, 257 Park Avenue South, New York, New York 10010. (212) 505-2100. 1971-. Bimonthly. Environmental issues of concern.

The Eyas. Institute for Wildlife Research, National Wildlife Federation, 1412 16th St., NW, Washington, District of Columbia 20036-2266. (202) 797-6800. Semiannual. Research, education, and management programs about birds of prey in the United states, Canada, and Latin America.

Florida Environments. Florida Environments Pub., 215 N. Main St., PO Box 1617, High Springs, Florida 32643. (904) 454-2007. Monthly. Florida's hazardous materials/wastes, wildlife, regulation, drinking/ground/surface waters, air, and solid waste.

Florida Wildlife. Florida Game and Fresh Water Fish Commission, Florida State Game, 620 S. Meridian St., Tallahassee, Florida 32399-1600. (904) 488-5563. 1976-. Bimonthly. State wildlife conservation magazine.

Friend O'Wildlife. North Carolina Wildlife Federation,Inc., Box 10626, Raleigh, North Carolina 27605. (919) 833-1923. 1959-. Bimonthly. Covers North Carolina wildlife conservation and related hunting, fishing and boating activities and other environmental issues.

Greenpeace Magazine. Greenpeace, 1436 U St., NW, Washington, District of Columbia 20009. (202) 462-1177. Bimonthly. Deals with nature and wildlife conservation, and environmental protection.

Idaho Wildlife. Idaho Dept. of Fish and Game, P.O. Box 25, 600 S. Walnut, Boise, Idaho 83712. (208) 334-3746. Bimonthly. Covers conservation, wildlife management, fish and game operations and policies.

Illinois Wildlife. Illinois Wildlife Federation, 123 S. Chicago St., Rossville, Illinois 60963. (217) 748-6365. Bimonthly. Deals with outdoor recreational trends.

International Wildlife. National Wildlife Federation, 1400 16th Street, NW, Washington, District of Columbia 20036. (202) 797-6800. Bimonthly. Covers international conservation activities.

The Journal of Wildlife Management. The Wildlife Society, 5410 Grosvenor Ln., Bethesda, Maryland 20814. (301) 897-9770. Quarterly. Covers wildlife management and research.

Maine Audubon News. Maine Audubon Society, Old Route 1, Falmouth, Maine 04105. (207) 781-2330. Monthly. Wild life conservation, energy conservation, and alternative sources of energy.

Maryland Conservationist. Department of Natural Resources, Tawes State Office Bldg., C-2, Annapolis, Maryland 21401. 1924-. Bimonthly.

Massachusetts Audubon Newsletter. Massachusetts Audubon Society, S. Great Rd., Lincoln, Massachusetts 01773. (617) 259-9500. 1962-. Ten times a year.

Minnesota Wildlife Reports. Minnesota Dept. of Natural Resources, 500 Lafayette Rd., St. Paul, Minnesota 55155-4046. (612) 296-3344. Irregular. Wildlife research & surveys.

Missouri Conservationist. Missouri Deptartment of Conservation, Box 180, Jefferson City, Missouri 65102. (314) 751-4115. Monthly. Game, fish, and forestry management and hunting and fishing techniques.

Missouri Wildlife. Conservation Federation of Missouri, 728 W. Main St., Jefferson City, Missouri 65101. (314) 634-2322. Bimonthly. Conservation & environmental news and features.

Montana Outdoors. Montana Dept. of Fish, Wildlife, and Parks, 930 Custer Ave., W., Helena, Montana 59620. (406) 444-2474. Bimonthly. Wildlife and fisheries management.

National Wildlife. National Wildlife Federation, 1400 16th Street, NW, Washington, District of Columbia 20036. (202) 797-6800. Bimonthly. Covers all forms of conservation activities.

National Wildlife Newsletter. Sierra Club Books, 100 Bush St., San Francisco, California 94104. (415) 291-1600. 1976-. Monthly.

New Mexico Wildlife Magazine. N.M. Dept. of Game & Fish, Villagra Bldg., 408 Galisteo, Santa Fe, New Mexico 87503. (505) 827-7911. Irregular. Hunting, fishing, and wildlife management.

North American Wildlife and Natural Resources Conference, Transactions. Wildlife Management Institute, 1101 14th St., N.W., Ste. 725, Washington, District of Columbia 20005. (202) 371-1808. Annual. Natural resource conservation.

On the Edge. Wildlife Preservation Trust International, 34th St. & Girard Ave., Philadelphia, Pennsylvania 19104. (215) 222-2191. Semiannual. Animal conservation, endangered species and captive breeding.

Outdoor California. California State Dept. of Fish & Game, 1416 9th St., Sacramento, California 95814. (916) 445-3531. Bimonthly. Wildlife conservation.

Outdoor News Bulletin. Wildlife Management Institute, 1101 14th St., N.W., Suite 725, Washington, District of Columbia 20005. (202) 371-1808. Biweekly. Conservation and wildlife.

Outdoor Oklahoma. Oklahoma Dept. Wildlife Conservation, Box 53465, 1801 N. Lincoln, Oklahoma City, Oklahoma 73152. Bimonthly. Hunting, fishing, and outdoor activities.

Public Use of National Wildlife Refugees. U.S. Department of the Interior, Fish and Wildlife Service, 1849 C St. NW, Washington, District of Columbia 20240. (202) 208-5634. Annual.

TRAFFIC. World Wildlife Fund, 1250 24th St., NW, Washington, District of Columbia 20037. (202) 293-4800. Quarterly. International trade in wild plants and animals, with emphasis on endangered and threatened species; information on Convention on International Trade in Endangered Species.

Wilderness. The Wilderness Society, 900 17th St. NW, Washington, District of Columbia 20006. (202) 833-2300. Quarterly. Preserving wilderness and wildlife, protecting America's prime forests, parks, rivers, shorelands, and fostering an American land ethic.

Wildlife Conservation. Wildlife Conservation International, c/o New York Zoological Society, Bronx, New York 10460. (212) 220-5155. Bimonthly.

Wildlife Disease Association Journal. Wildlife Disease Assn., PO Box 886, Ames, Iowa 50010. (515) 233-1931. Quarterly.

Wildlife Society Bulletin. The Wildlife Society, 5410 Grosvenor Lane, Bethesda, Maryland 20814. (301) 897-9770. Quarterly. Covers wildlife management and conservation education.

The Wildlifer. The Wildlife Society, 5410 Grosvenor Lane, Bethesda, Maryland 20814. (301) 897-9770. Bimonthly. Covers protection of wildlife resources.

RESEARCH CENTERS AND INSTITUTES

Alaska Cooperative Fishery and Wildlife Research Unit. 138 Arctic Health Research Unit, University of Alaska-Fairbanks, Fairbanks, Alaska 99775-0110. (907) 474-7661.

Auburn University, Alabama Cooperative Fish and Wildlife Research Unit. 331 Funchess Hall, Auburn, Alabama 36849. (205) 844-4796.

Last Chance Forever. 506 Avenue A, San Antonio, Texas 78215. (512) 224-7228.

Max McGraw Wildlife Foundation. P.O. Box 9, Dundee, Illinois 60118. (708) 741-8000.

National Wild Turkey Federation. P.O. Box 530, Edgefield, South Carolina 29824. (803) 637-3106.

The Nature Conservancy. 1815 N. Lynn St., Arlington, Virginia 22209. (703) 841-5300.

North Carolina State University, Hope Valley Forest. Department of Forestry, Box 8002, Raleigh, North Carolina 27695. (919) 737-2891.

Northeastern Research Center for Wildlife Diseases. University of Connecticut, Box U-89, Connecticut 06268. (203) 486-3737.

Pennsylvania State University, Deer Research Center. Department of Dairy & Animal Science, 324 Henning Building, University Park, Pennsylvania 16802. (814) 865-1362.

Project in Conservation Science. University of California, San Diego, Department of Biology C-016, La Jolla, California 92093. (619) 534-2375.

Reynolds Homestead Agricultural Experiment Station. Virginia Polytech Institute and State University, PO Box 70, Critz, Virginia 24082. (703) 694-4135.

Rose Lake Wildlife Research Center. Michigan Department of Natural Resources, Wildlife Division, 8562 East Stoll Road, East Lansing, Michigan 48823. (517) 373-9358.

Southern Illinois University at Carbondale, Cooperative Wildlife Research Laboratory. Carbondale, Illinois 62901-6504. (618) 536-7766.

State University of New York College of Environmental Science and Forestry. Roosevelt Wildlife Institute, Syracuse, New York 13210. (315) 470-6741.

Tall Timbers Research Station. R.R. 1, Box 678, Tallahassee, Florida 32312. (904) 893-4153.

Texas A&I University, Caesar Kleberg Wildlife Research Institute. College of Agriculture & Home Economics, Campus Box 218, Kingsville, Texas 78363. (512) 595-3922.

Texas A&M University, Texas Cooperative Wildlife Collection. Maple Hall, Rm. 210, Mail Stop 2258, College Station, Texas 77843. (409) 845-5777.

Tucker Wildlife Sanctuary. Star Route, Box 858, Orange, California 92667. (714) 649-2760.

U.S. Forest Service, Forestry Sciences Laboratory. I-26 Agricultural Building, University of Missouri- Columbia, Columbia, Missouri 65211. (314) 875-5341.

U.S. Forest Service, Forestry Sciences Laboratory. South Dakota School of Mines and Technology, Rapid City, South Dakota 57701. (605) 394-1960.

U.S. Forest Service, San Joaquin Experimental Range. 24075 Highway 41, Coarsegold, California 93614. (209) 868-3349.

U.S. Forest Service, Wildlife Habitat and Silviculture Laboratory. Box 7600, SFA Sta., Nacogdoches, Texas 75962. (409) 569-7981.

University of Georgia, Southeastern Cooperative Wildlife Disease. College of Veterinary Medicine, Athens, Georgia 30602. (404) 542-3000.

University of Idaho Forest, Wildlife and Range Experiment Station. Moscow, Idaho 83843. (208) 885-6441.

University of Idaho, Remote Sensing Center. College of Forestry, Wildlife and Range Sciences, Moscow, Idaho 83843. (208) 885-7209.

University of Idaho, Wilderness Research Center. Moscow, Idaho 83843. (208) 885-7911.

University of Michigan, School of Natural Resources, Research Service. 430 East University, Ann Arbor, Michigan 48109. (313) 764-6823.

University of Michigan, Wildland Management Center. School of Natural Resources, 430 East University, Ann Arbor, Michigan 48109-1115. (313) 763-1312.

University of Missouri-Columbia, Gaylord Memorial Laboratory. Puxico, Missouri 63960. (314) 222-3531.

University of Missouri-Columbia, Thomas S. Baskett Wildlife Research and Education Center. 112 Stephens Hall, Columbia, Missouri 65201. (314) 882-3436.

University of Montana, Montana Cooperative Wildlife Research Unit. Missoula, Montana 59812. (406) 243-5372.

University of Montana, Wilderness Institute. Forestry Building, Room 207, Missoula, Montana 59812. (406) 243-5361.

University of Nevada-Reno, Knudtsen Renewable Resources Center. Department of Range, Wildlife and Forestry, 1000 Valley Road, Reno, Nevada 89512. (702) 784-4000.

University of Nevada-Reno, S-S Field Laboratory. Box 10, Wadsworth, Nevada 89442. (702) 575-1057.

University of North Dakota, Institute for Remote Sensing. Geography Department, Grand Folks, North Dakota 58202. (701) 777-4246.

Utah State University, Institute for Land Rehabilitation. College of Natural Resources, Logan, Utah 84322-5230. (801) 750-2547.

Washington Cooperative Fishery and Wildlife Research Unit. University of Washington, School of Fisheries, WH-10, Seattle, Washington 98195. (206) 543-6475.

Washington Department of Wildlife, Fisheries Management Division. 600 Capitol Way North, Olympia, Washington 98504-1091. (206) 753-5713.

Wildland Resources Center. University of California, 145 Walter Mulford Hall, Berkeley, California 94720. (415) 642-0263.

Wildlife Management Institute. 1101 14th Street, N.W., Suite 725, Washington, District of Columbia 20005. (202) 371-1808.

Wisconsin Cooperative Wildlife Research Unit. University of Wisconsin, 266 Russell Laboratories, Madison, Wisconsin 53706. (608) 263-6882.

Wyoming Cooperative Fishery and Wildlife Research Unit. University of Wyoming, Box 3166, University Station, Laramie, Wyoming 82071. (307) 766-5415.

STATISTICS SOURCES

Ecology: Community Profiles. U.S. Fish and Wildlife Service. National Technical Information Service, 5285 Port Royal Road, Springfield, Virginia 22161. (703) 487-4650. Irregular. Data on coastal and inland ecosystems, including wetlands, tidal-flats, near-shore seagrasses, sand dunes, drilling platforms, oyster reefs, estuaries, rivers and streams.

Managing the Nation's Public Lands. U.S. Bureau of Land Management. U.S. G.P.O., Washington, District of Columbia 20401. (202) 512-0000. Annual. Data on wilderness, wildlife, recreational resources, rangeland and forests.

OECD Environmental Data Compendium 1989. OECD Publications and Information Center, 2001 L St. N.W., Suite 700, Washington, District of Columbia 20036. (202) 785-OECD. 1989. Provides statistical data for OECD countries on air pollution, water pollution, the marine environment, land use, forests, wildlife, solid waste, noise and radioactivity. Also provides data on the underlying pressures on the environment such as energy use, transportation, industrial activity and agriculture.

Report on the Nation's Renewable Resources. U.S. Forest Service. U.S. G.P.O., Washington, District of Columbia 20401. (202) 512-0000. Quinquennial. Projections of resource use and supply from 1920 to 2040, covering wilderness, wildlife, fish, range, timber, water and minerals.

Statistical Summary of Fish and Wildlife Restoration. U.S. Fish and Wildlife Service. U.S. G.P.O., Washington, District of Columbia 20401. (202) 512-0000. Annual. Data on hunting, fishing activities, and restoration.

World Resources. World Resources Institute. 1709 New York Ave., N.W., Washington, District of Columbia 20006. (202) 638-6300. Annual. Statistical and textual analysis of world's natural resources and the effects of growth-caused environmental pollution.

TRADE ASSOCIATIONS AND PROFESSIONAL SOCIETIES

African Wildlife Foundation. 1717 Massachusetts Avenue, NW, Washington, District of Columbia 20036. (202) 265-8393.

Alaska Conservation Foundation. 430 West 7th St., Suite 215, Anchorage, Alaska 99501. (907) 276-1917.

American Association of Zoological Parks and Aquariums. Rt. 88, Oglebay Park, Wheeling, West Virginia 26003. (304) 242-2160.

American Committee for International Conservation. c/o Roger McManus, Secretary, Center for Marine Conservation, 1725 DeSales St., N.W., Washington, District of Columbia 20036. (202) 429-5609.

American Institute of Biological Sciences. 730 11th St., N.W., Washington, District of Columbia 20001-4521. (202) 628-1500.

American Ornithologists' Union. Smithsonian Institution, National Museum of Natural History, Washington, District of Columbia 20560. (202) 357-1970.

American Pheasant and Waterfowl Society. c/o Lloyd Ure, R.R. 1, Box 164-A, Granton, Wisconsin 54436. (715) 238-7291.

The American Society for the Prevention of Cruelty to Animals. 441 East 92nd St., New York, New York 10128. (212) 876-7700.

American Wilderness Leadership School. c/o 4800 Gates Pass Rd., Tucson, Arizona 85745. (606) 620-1220.

Atlantic Waterfowl Council. Division of Fish and Wildlife, P.O. Box 1401, Dover, Delaware 19903. (302) 739-5295.

Bat Conservation International. PO Box 162603, Austin, Texas 78716. (512) 327-9721. Bat Conservation International was established to educate people about the important role that bats play in the environment.

Boone and Crockett Club. 241 S. Farley Blvd., Dumfries, Virginia 22026. (703) 221-1888.

Brooks Bird Club. 707 Warwood Ave., Wheeling, West Virginia 26003. (304) 547-5253.

Canvasback Society. P.O. Box 101, Gates Mills, Ohio 44040. (216) 443-2340.

CEIP Fund. 68 Harrison Ave., 5th Fl., Boston, Massachusetts 02111. (617) 426-4375.

Colorado River Wildlife Council. 1596 W. North Temple, Salt Lake City, Utah 84116. (801) 533-9333.

Columbia Basin Fish & Wildlife Authority. 2000 SW First Ave., Suite 170, Portland, Oregon 97201. (503) 294-7031.

Committee for the Preservation of the Tule Elk. P.O. Box 3696, San Diego, California 92103. (619) 485-0626.

Conservation Foundation. 1250 24th St., N.W., Washington, District of Columbia 20037. (202) 293-4800. The World Wildlife Fund absorbed the Conservation Foundation in 1990.

Deer Unlimited of America. P.O. Box 1129, Abbeville, South Carolina 29620. (803) 391-2300.

Defenders of Wildlife. 1244 19th St., NW, Washington, District of Columbia 20036. (202) 659-9510.

Desert Bighorn Council. P.O. Box 5430, Riverside, California 92517. (714) 683-7523.

Desert Tortoise Council. P.O. Box 1738, Palm Desert, California 92261-1738. (619) 341-8449.

Ducks Unlimited. 1 Waterfowl Way, Long Grove, Illinois 60047. (708) 438-4300.

Elephant Interest Group. 106 E. Hickory Grove, Bloomfield Hills, Michigan 48013. (313) 540-3947.

Elsa Clubs of America. PO Box 4572, North Hollywood, California 91617-0572. (818) 761-8387.

Elsa Wild Animal Appeal-USA. P.O. Box 675, Elmhurst, Illinois 60126. (708) 833-8896.

Entanglement Network Coalition. c/o Dr. Albert Manville II, Defenders of Wildlife, 1244 19th St. NW, Washington, District of Columbia 20036. (202) 659-9510.

Environmental Defense Fund. 257 Park Ave., S., New York, New York 10010. (212) 505-2100. Non-profit organization that was established more than 20 years ago. Its goals are to protect the earth's environment by providing lasting solutions to global environmental problems.

Felicidades Wildlife Foundation. P.O. Box 490, Waynesville, North Carolina 28786. (704) 926-0192.

Foundation for North American Wild Sheep. 720 Allen Ave., Cody, Wyoming 82414-3402. (307) 527-6261.

The Friends of the Everglades. 101 Westward Dr., No. 2, Miami Springs, Florida 33166. (305) 888-1230.

Friends of the National Zoo. National Zoological Park, Washington, District of Columbia 20008. (202) 673-4950.

Game Conservation International. P.O. Box 17444, San Antonio, Texas 78217. (512) 824-7509.

Institute for Wildlife Research. c/o National Wildlife Fed., 1400 16th St., N.W., Washington, District of Columbia 20036. (703) 790-4483.

International Association for Bear Research and Management. ADF&G, 333 Raspberry Rd., Anchorage, Alaska 99518-1599. (907) 344-0541.

International Council for Bird Preservation, U.S. Section. c/o World Wildlife Fund, 1250 24th St. N.W., Washington, District of Columbia 20037. (202) 778-9563.

International Crane Foundation. E-11376 Shady Lane Rd., Baraboo, Wisconsin 53913-9778. (608) 356-9462.

The International Osprey Foundation. P.O. Box 250, Sanibel, Florida 33957. (813) 472-5218.

International Society for the Protection of Mustangs and Burros. c/o Helen A. Reilly, 11790 Deodar Way, Reno, Nevada 89506. (702) 972-1989.

International Wild Waterfowl Association. c/o Nancy Collins, Hidden Lake Waterfowl, 5614 River Styx Rd., Medina, Ohio 44256. (216) 725-8782.

International Wildlife Coalition. 634 N. Falmouth Hwy., P.O. Box 388, Falmouth, Massachusetts 02556. (508) 564-9980.

International Wildlife Rehabilitation Council. 1171 Kellog St., Suisun, California 94585. (707) 428-IWRC.

The Jane Goodall Institute for Wildlife Research, Education and Conservation. P.O. Box 41720, Tucson, Arizona 85717. (602) 325-1211.

National Association of Conservation Districts. 509 Capitol Court, N.E., Washington, District of Columbia 20002. (202) 547-6223.

National Audubon Society. 950 Third Ave., New York, New York 10022. (212) 832-3200.

National Institute for Urban Wildlife. 10921 Trotting Ridge Way, Columbia, Maryland 21044. (301) 596-3311.

National Waterfowl Alliance. Box 50, Waterfowl Bldg., Edgefield, South Carolina 29824. (803) 637-5767.

National Waterfowl Council. c/o Roger Holmes, Minnestoa Dept. of Natural Resources, 500 Lafayette Rd., St. Paul, Minnesota 55155. (612) 297-1308.

National Wildlife Federation. 1400 16th St., N.W., Washington, District of Columbia 20036. (202) 797-6800.

National Wildlife Federation Corporate Conservation Council. 1400 16th St., N.W., Washington, District of Columbia 20036. (202) 797-6800.

National Wildlife Health Foundation. c/o James L. Naviaux, 606 El Pintado Rd., Danville, California 94526. (415) 939-3456.

National Wildlife Refuge Association. 10824 Fox Hunt Ln., Potomac, Maryland 20854. (301) 983-1238.

National Wildlife Rehabilitators Association. c/o Carpenter Nature Center, 12805 St. Croix Trail, Hastings, Minnesota 55033. (612) 437-9194.

National Wildlife Rescue Team. 160 N.E. 165th St., North Miami Beach, Florida 33162.

Natural Resources Defense Council. 40 W. 20th St., New York, New York 10011. (212) 727-2700.

New York Zoological Society. The Zoological Park, Bronx, New York 10460. (212) 220-5100.

North American Wildlife Foundation. 102 Wilmot Rd., Suite 410, Deerfield, Illinois 60015. (708) 940-7776.

North American Wildlife Park Foundation. Wolf Park, Battle Ground, Indiana 47920. (317) 567-2265.

North American Wolf Society. P.O. Box 82950, Fairbanks, Alaska 99708. (907) 474-6117.

Organization of Wildlife Planners. 1420 E. 6th Ave., Helena, Montana 59620. (406) 444-4758.

Pacific Wildlife Project. P.O. Box 7673, Laguna Niguel, California 92607. (714) 831-1178.

RARE Center for Tropical Bird Conservation. 15290 Walnut St., Philadelphia, Pennsylvania 19102. (215) 568-0420.

Safari Club International. 4800 W. Gates Pass Rd., Tucson, Arizona 85745. (602) 620-1220.

Sea Shepherd Conservation Society. 1314 2nd St., Santa Monica, California 90401. (213) 394-3198.

Southeastern Cooperative Wildlife Disease Study. College of Veterinary Medicine, University of Georgia, Athens, Georgia 30602. (404) 548-1032.

TRAFFIC, USA. c/o World Wildlife Fund, 1250 24th St., N.W., Washington, District of Columbia 20037. (202) 293-4800.

Urban Wildlife Research Center. 10921 Trotting Ridge Way, Columbia, Maryland 21044. (301) 596-3311.

Wetlands for Wildlife, Inc. PO Box 344, West Bend, Wisconsin 53095. (414) 334-0327.

Wilderness Society. 900 17th St., NW, Washington, District of Columbia 20006. (202) 833-2300.

Wildlife Conservation Fund of America. 801 Kingsmill Pkwy., Columbus, Ohio 43229-1137. (614) 888-4868.

Wildlife Conservation International. c/o New York Zoological Society, Bronx, New York 10460. (212) 220-5155.

Wildlife Disease Association. Box 886, Ames, Iowa 50010. (515) 233-1931.

Wildlife Habitat Enhancement Council. 1010 Wayne Ave., Suite 1240, Silver Spring, Maryland 20910. (301) 588-8994.

Wildlife Information Center, Inc. 629 Green St., Allentown, Pennsylvania 18102. (215) 434-1637.

Wildlife Legislative Fund of America & The Wildlife Conservation. 50 W. Broad St., Columbus, Ohio 43215. (614) 221-2684.

Wildlife Preservation Trust International. 34th St. and Girard Ave., Philadelphia, Pennsylvania 19104. (215) 222-3636.

Wildlife Research Institute, Inc. Box 4446, Arcata, California 95521. (208) 456-2246.

Wildlife Society. 5410 Grosvenor Lane, Bethesda, Maryland 20814. (301) 897-9770.

World Center for Birds of Prey. 5666 W. Flying Hawk Ln., Boise, Idaho 83709. (208) 362-3716.

World Wildlife Fund & the Conservation Foundation. 1250 24th St., N.W., Washington, District of Columbia 20037. (202) 293-4800.

WILDLIFE REFUGES
See: WILDLIFE

WIND EROSION
See: EROSION

WISCONSIN ENVIRONMENTAL AGENCIES

GOVERNMENTAL ORGANIZATIONS

Bureau of Solid and Hazardous Waste Management: Waste Minimization and Pollution Prevention. Director, PO Box 7921, Madison, Wisconsin 53707. (608) 266-2111.

Department of Administration: Coastal Zone Management. Director, Coastal Management Section, PO Box 7864, Madison, Wisconsin 53707. (608) 266-3687.

Department of Agriculture, Trade and Consumer Protection: Pesticide Registration. Assistant Administrator, Agricultural Resources Management Division, Bureau of Plant Division, 801 West Badger Rd., Madison, Wisconsin 53708. (608) 266-7131.

Department of Natural Resources: Air Quality. Director, Bureau of Natural Resources, PO Box 7921, Madison, Wisconsin 53707. (608) 266-0603.

Department of Natural Resources: Emergency Preparedness and Community Right-to-Know. Director, PO Box 7921, Madison, Wisconsin 53707. (608) 266-9255.

Department of Natural Resources: Environmental Quality. Administrator, Division of Environmental Quality, PO Box 7921, Madison, Wisconsin 53707. (608) 266-1099.

Department of Natural Resources: Fish and Wildlife. Director, Bureau of Wildlife Management, PO Box 7921, Madison, Wisconsin 53707. (608) 266-2193.

Department of Natural Resources: Groundwater Management. Director, Bureau of Water Resources Management, PO Box 7921, Madison, Wisconsin 53707. (608) 266-8631.

Department of Natural Resources: Hazardous Waste Management. Director, Bureau of Solid Waste Management, PO Box 7921, Madison, Wisconsin 53707. (608) 266-1327.

Department of Natural Resources: Natural Resources. Secretary, PO Box 7921, Madison, Wisconsin 53707. (608) 266-2121.

Department of Natural Resources: Solid Waste Management. Director, Bureau of Solid Waste Management, PO Box 7921, Madison, Wisconsin 53707. (608) 266-1327.

Department of Natural Resources: Water Quality. Director, Bureau of Water Resources Management, PO Box 7921, Madison, Wisconsin 53707. (608) 266-8631.

Division of Safety and Buildings: Occupational Safety. Administrator, Industry, Labor, and Human Relations, PO Box 7969, Madison, Wisconsin 53707. (608) 266-1816.

Emergency Management Agency: Emergency Preparedness and Community Right-to-Know. Emergency Response Commission, Comprehensive Emergency Management, 5500 Bishop Blvd., Cheyenne, Wyoming 82009. (307) 777-7566.

Industrial Labor and Human Relations: Underground Storage Tanks. Director, Bureau of Petroleum Inspection, PO Box 7969, Madison, Wisconsin 53707. (608) 266-7605.

WISCONSIN ENVIRONMENTAL LEGISLATION

GENERAL WORKS

Wisconsin Environmental Law Handbook. Government Institutes, Inc., 4 Research Pl., Ste. 200, Rockville, Maryland 20850. (301) 921-2300. 1990.

WOMEN IN ENVIRONMENT

ABSTRACTING AND INDEXING SERVICES

Engineering Index. The Engineering Index Inc., 345 E. 47th St., New York, New York 10017. 1962-.

Index to Scientific Book Contents. Institute for Scientific Information, 3501 Market St., Philadelphia, Pennsylvania 19104. (800) 523-1857. 1985-. Annual. Gives contents of science books published.

Science Citation Index. Institute for Scientific Information, 3501 Market St., Philadelphia, Pennsylvania 19104. 1961-.

DIRECTORIES

Worldwide Directory of Women in Environment. World-WIDE, 1250 24th St., NW, 4th Fl., Washington, District of Columbia 20037. (202) 331-9863. 1988.

GENERAL WORKS

Promotion of Women's Participation in Water Resources Development. UNIPUB, 4611-F Assembly Dr., Lanham, Maryland 20706-4391. (301) 459-7666; (800) 274-4888. 1990.

Safeguarding the Land: Women at Work in Parks, Forests, and Rangelands. Harcourt Brace Jovanovich, Inc., 1250 6th Ave., San Diego, California 92101. (800) 346-8648. 1981.

ONLINE DATA BASES

Computerized Engineering Index–COMPENDEX. Engineering Information Inc., 345 E. 47th St., New York, New York 10017. (212) 705-7600.

TRADE ASSOCIATIONS AND PROFESSIONAL SOCIETIES

WorldWIDE. 1250 24th St., N.W., 4th Fl., Washington, District of Columbia 20037. (202) 331-9863.

WOOD

ABSTRACTING AND INDEXING SERVICES

Applied Science and Technology Index. H.W. Wilson Co., 950 University Ave., Bronx, New York 10452. (800) 367-6770. Formerly Industrial Arts Index.

Biological and Agricultural Index. H.W. Wilson Co., 950 University Ave., Bronx, New York 10452. (800) 367-6770. 1916-. Monthly.

Energy Information Abstracts Annual 1987 in Retrospect. EIC/Intelligence Inc., 121 Chanlon Rd., New Providence, New Jersey 07974. (908) 464-6800. 1988. Annual. Cumulative edition of the monthly Energy Information Abstracts. Monitors sources in the field of energy including the scientific, technical and business journal literature, conference and symposia proceedings, corporate, government and academic reports.

Engineering Index. The Engineering Index Inc., 345 E. 47th St., New York, New York 10017. 1962-.

Forest Products Abstracts. C. A. B. International, 845 North Park Ave., Tucson, Arizona 85719. (602) 621-7897 or (800) 528-4841. Bimonthly. Contains abstracts in the area of forest product industry; wood properties; timber extraction; conversion and measurement; damage to timber and timber production; utilization of wood; pulp industries and the chemical utilization of wood and other related areas.

General Science Index. H. W. Wilson Co., 950 University Ave., Bronx, New York 10452. 1978-. Monthly, also issued in annual cumulation. Cumulative subject index to English language periodicals in the subject fields of astronomy, botany, chemistry, earth science, environment and conservation, food and nutrition, genetics, mathematics, medicine and health, microbiology, oceanography, physics, physiology and zoology.

Microbiology Abstracts. Section A. Industrial and Applied Microbiology. Cambridge Scientific Abstracts, 5161 River Rd., Bethesda, Maryland 20816. (301) 961-6750. 1972-.

Science Citation Index. Institute for Scientific Information, 3501 Market St., Philadelphia, Pennsylvania 19104. 1961-.

DIRECTORIES

Alternative Energy Retailer–Solid Fuel Industry Buyer's Guide Issue. Zackin Publications, Inc., 70 Edwin Ave., Waterbury, Connecticut 06722. (203) 755-0158.

American Plywood Association–Member and Product Directory. American Plywood Association, PO Box 11700, Tacoma, Washington 98411. (206) 565-6600.

Dimension Buyer's Guide to Forest Products Industry. 1000 Johnson Ferry Rd., Suite A-130, Marietta, Georgia 30068. (404) 565-6660. Annual.

Directory of Hardwood Plywood Manufacturers in the United States and Canada. 1825 Michail Faraday Dr., Reston, Virginia 22090. (703) 435-2900. Irregular.

Firewood-Retail. American Business Directories, Inc., 5711 S. 86th Circle, Omaha, Nebraska 68127. (402) 593-4600.

Hardwood Plywood Manufacturers Association–Face Veneer Manufacturers List. Hardwood Plywood Manufacturers Association, 1825 Michael Faraday Dr., P.O. Box 2789, Reston, Virginia 22090. (703) 435-2900.

Hardwood Plywood Manufacturers Association–Lists of Manufacturers. Hardwood Plywood Manufacturers Association, 1825 Michael Faraday Dr., P.O. Box 2789, Reston, Virginia 22090. (703) 435-2900.

Lumber Retailers Directory. 5711 S. 86th Circle, Omaha, Nebraska 68127. (402) 593-4600. Annual.

National Hardwood Lumber Association–Members. Box 34518, Memphis, Tennessee 38184. (901) 377-1818. Annual.

North American Wholesale Lumber Association–Distribution Directory. 2340 S. Arlington Heights Rd., Suite 680, Arlington Heights, Illinois 60005. (708) 981-8630. Annual.

Plywood & Panel World–Directory and Buyers' Guide Issue. Hatten-Brown Publishers, Inc., P.O. Box 2268, Montgomery, Alabama 36102-2268. (205) 834-1170.

Timber & Timberland Companies. American Business Directories, Inc., 5711 S. 86th Circle, Omaha, Nebraska 68127. (402) 593-4600.

Who's Who in Industrial Woodworking Machinery Distribution. Woodworking Machinery Distributors' Association, 251 W. DeKalb Pike, King of Prussia, Pennsylvania 19406. (215) 265-6658.

Wood & Wood Products–Red Book Issue. Vance Publishing Corporation, Box 1400, Lincolnshire, Illinois 60069. (708) 634-2600. 1980-.

Wood Machinery Manufacturers of America–Buyer's Guide and Directory. Wood Machinery Manufacturers of America, 1900 Arch St., Philadelphia, Pennsylvania 19103. (215) 564-3484.

ENCYCLOPEDIAS AND DICTIONARIES

Kaiman's Encyclopedia of Energy Topics. Lee Kaiman and J. Masloff. Environmental Design and Research Center, 26799 Elena Rd., Los Altos Hills, California 94022. 1983. Two volumes. Coverage of topics range from natural energy sources that are renewable to nonrenewable, and the application of these energy sources.

GENERAL WORKS

The CSIRO Family Key to Hardwood Identification. C. J. Ilic. Commonwealth Scientific and Industrial Research Organisation, Private Bag 10, Clayton, Australia 3168. 1987. Describes the anatomical data of 152 families of Angiosperms for the identification of hardwoods using the microscope and the computer.

The Forest and the Trees: A Guide to Excellent Forestry. Gordon Robinson. Island Press, 1718 Connecticut Ave. N.W., Suite 300, Washington, District of Columbia 20009. (202) 232-7933. 1988. Gives concerned citizens who are not foresters the technical information they need to compete with the experts when commenting on how our national forests should be managed.

Pocket Flora of the Redwood Forest. Rudolf Willem Becking. Island Press, 1718 Connecticut Ave. N.W., Suite 300, Washington, District of Columbia 20009. (202) 232-7933. 1982. Guide to 212 of the most frequently seen plants in the Redwood Forest of the Pacific Coast. It is interspersed with accurate drawing color photographs and systematic keys to plant identification.

Wood Structure and Composition. Marcel Dekker, Inc., 270 Madison Ave., New York, New York 10016. (212) 696-9000; (800) 228-1160. 1991. Chemistry and anatomy of wood.

ONLINE DATA BASES

Computerized Engineering Index–COMPENDEX. Engineering Information Inc., 345 E. 47th St., New York, New York 10017. (212) 705-7600.

DOMIS. ECHO Service, BP 2373, Luxembourg L-1023. (352) 488041.

FOREST. Forest Products Research Society, 2801 Marshall Court, Madison, Wisconsin 53705. (608) 231-1361.

PERIODICALS AND NEWSLETTERS

Environmental Conference. TAPPI Press, Technology Park/Atlanta, PO Box 105113, Atlanta, Georgia 30348. (404) 446-1400. 1980-. Annually. Conference papers include topics relating to the environment such as: landfill permitting; bleach plant emissions; environmental control; sludge dewatering; air toxics regulations and risk assessment as they relate to pulp and paper industry; water reuse and load control; water toxins; air modeling; and other pertinent environmental topics.

RESEARCH CENTERS AND INSTITUTES

North Carolina State University, Wood Products Laboratory. Box 8005, Raleigh, North Carolina 27695. (919) 737-2881.

State University of New York College of Environmental Science and Forestry. Tropical Timber Information Center, 1 Forestry Dr., Syracuse, New York 13210-2786. (315) 470-6879.

U.S. Forest Service, Forestry Sciences Laboratory. Southern Illinois University at Carbondale, Carbondale, Illinois 62901-4630. (618) 453-2318.

U.S. Forest Service, Forestry Sciences Laboratory. Forest Hill Road, Houghton, Michigan 49931. (906) 482-6303.

University of Arizona, Laboratory of Tree-Ring Research. Tucson, Arizona 85721. (602) 621-2191.

University of Montana, Wood Chemistry Laboratory. Missoula, Montana 59812. (406) 243-6212.

Urban Pest Control Research Group. Virginia Polytech Institute and State University, Department of Entomology, Glade Road, Blacksburg, Virginia 24061. (703) 961-4045.

Winrock International Institute for Agricultural Development. Petit Jean Mountain, Morrillton, Arkansas 72110. (501) 727-5435.

Woods Hole Oceanographic Institution. Woods Hole, Massachusetts 02543. (617) 548-1400.

STATISTICS SOURCES

Estimates of Biofuels Consumption in the U.S. U.S. G.P.O, Washington, District of Columbia 20402-9325. (202) 512-0000. 1990. Consumption of energy from biofuels, including wood, solid waste, and ethanol. Waste energy types include mass burning, manufacturing wastes, refuse derived fuel and methane gas form landfills.

Forest Industries. Forest Industries, 500 Howard St., San Francisco, California 94105. Monthly. Concerned with logging, pulpwood and forest management, and the manufacture oflumber, plywood, board, and pulp.

New Perspectives on Silvicultural Management of Northern Hardwoods. U.S. G.P.O, Washington, District of Columbia 20402-9325. (202) 512-0000. 1989. Timber stand condition and other factors involved in selecting management strategies for northern U.S. and Canada hardwood forests.

Newsprint Division Monthly Statistical Report. American Paper Institute, 260 Madison Ave., New York, New York 10016. Monthly. Newsprint production, shipments, inventory, and plant capacity.

Paper, Paperboard, and Wood Pulp: Monthly Statistical Summary. American Paper Institute, 260 Madison Ave., New York, New York 10016. Monthly.

Pulp and Paper. Forest Industries, 500 Howard St., San Francisco, California 94105. Monthly. Production, engineering/maintenance, management, and marketing.

U.S. Timber Production, Trade, Consumption and Price Statistics. U.S. Forest Service. U.S. G.P.O., Washington, District of Columbia 20402-9325. (202) 783-3238. 1987. Annual. Covers the period from 1950 to present. Includes measures of economic growth.

TRADE ASSOCIATIONS AND PROFESSIONAL SOCIETIES

American Institute of Biological Sciences. 730 11th St., N.W., Washington, District of Columbia 20001-4521. (202) 628-1500.

American Plywood Association. P.O. Box 11700, Tacoma, Washington 98411. (206) 565-6600.

American Wood Council. 1250 Connecticut Ave., N.W., Suite 230, Washington, District of Columbia 20036. (202) 833-1595.

Appalachian Hardwood Manufacturers. Box 427, High Point, North Carolina 27261. (919) 885-8315.

Fine Hardwoods-American Walnut Association. 5603 W. Raymond St., Suite O, Indianapolis, Indiana 46241. (317) 244-3311.

Hardwood Manufacturers Association. 400 Penn Center Bldv., Pittsburgh, Pennsylvania 15235. (901) 346-2222.

Hardwood Plywood Manufacturers Association. 1825 Michael Faraday Dr., P.O. Box 2789, Reston, Virginia 22090. (703) 435-2900.

Hardwood Research Council. Box 34518, Memphis, Tennessee 38184. (901) 377-1824.

National Bark and Soil Producers Association. 13542 Union Village Circle, Clifton, Virginia 22024. (703) 830-5367.

National Hardwood Lumber Association. Box 34518, Memphis, Tennessee 38184. (901) 377-1818.

National Lumber Exporters Association. 1250 Connecticut Ave., N.W., Suite 200, Washington, District of Columbia 20036. (202) 463-2723.

National Wood Energy Association. 777 N. Capitol St. N.W., Suite 805, Washington, District of Columbia 20002. (202) 408-0664.

Save the Redwoods League. 114 Sansome St., Rm. 605, San Francisco, California 94104. (415) 362-2352.

Society of American Wood Preservers. 7297 Lee Hwy., Unit P, Falls Church, Virginia 22042. (703) 237-0900.

Society of Wood Science and Technology. One Gifford Pinchot Dr., Madison, Wisconsin 53705. (608) 231-9347.

Timber Operators Council. 6825 S.W. Sandburg St., Tigard, Oregon 97223. (503) 620-1710.

Timber Products Manufacturers. 951 E. Third Ave., Spokane, Washington 99202. (509) 535-4646.

Western Timber Association. California Forestry Association, 1311 I St., Ste. 1000, Sacramento, California 95814. (916) 444-6592.

X

X RAYS

ABSTRACTING AND INDEXING SERVICES

General Science Index. H. W. Wilson Co., 950 University Ave., Bronx, New York 10452. 1978-. Monthly, also issued in annual cumulation. Cumulative subject index to English language periodicals in the subject fields of astronomy, botany, chemistry, earth science, environment and conservation, food and nutrition, genetics, mathematics, medicine and health, microbiology, oceanography, physics, physiology and zoology.

Physics Briefs. Physikalische Berichte. Physik Verlag, Pappapelallee 3, Postfach 101161, Weinheim, Germany D-6940. 1979-. Semimonthly. In English. Volumes for 1979- issued by the Deutsche Physikalische Gesellschaft and the Fachinformationszentrum Energie Physik, Mathematik in cooperation with the American Institute of Physics.

Science Citation Index. Institute for Scientific Information, 3501 Market St., Philadelphia, Pennsylvania 19104. 1961-.

ENCYCLOPEDIAS AND DICTIONARIES

Encyclopedia of Physical Science and Technology. Robert A. Meyers, ed. Academic Press, c/o Harcourt Brace Jovanovich Inc., 6277 Sea Harbor Dr., Orlando, Florida 32887. (800) 346-8648. Dictionary of engineering, technology and physical sciences.

Van Nostrand's Scientific Encyclopedia. Glenn D. Considine, ed. Van Nostrand Reinhold, 115 5th Ave., New York, New York 10003. (212) 254-3232. 1983. Sixth edition. Includes all broad subject areas in science.

GENERAL WORKS

Fighting Radiation with Foods, Herbs, and Vitamins. East West Health Books, 17 Station St., PO Box 1200, Brookline, Massachusetts 02147. (617) 232-1000. 1988. Documented natural remedies that protect you from radiation, X-rays, and chemical pollutants.

Grenz Rays. Daniel Graham. Pergamon Microforms International, Inc., Fairview Park, Elmsford, New York 10523. 1980. An illustrated guide to the theory and practical application of soft x-rays.

A History of X-rays and Radium, with a Chapter on Radiation Units: 1895-1937. Richard F. Mould. IPC Building & Contract Journals, Sutton, England 1980.

X-rays, Health Effects of Common Exams. John Gofman. Sierra Club Books, 100 Bush St., San Francisco, Califor-

nia 94104. (415) 291-1600. 1985. Radiography, radiation induced tumors and adverse effects of ionizing.

HANDBOOKS AND MANUALS

An Atlas of Cardiology: Electrocardiograms and Chest X-rays. Wolfe Publishing Ltd., Brook House, 2-16 Torrington Pl., London, England WC1E 7LT. 1977. Diagnosis of cardiovascular diseases, heart radiography and electrocardiography.

The X-ray Information Book: A Consumers Guide to Avoiding Unnecessary Medical and Dental X-rays. Farrar, Straus, Giroux, Inc., 19 Union Sq. W., New York, New York 10003. (212) 741-6900. 1983. Physiological effects and safety measures for using X-rays and radioscopic diagnosis.

Your Child and X-rays: A Parents' Guide to Radiation, X-rays, and Other Imaging Procedures. Lion Press, PO Box 92541, Rochester, New York 14692. (716) 381-6410. 1988.

XYLENE

ABSTRACTING AND INDEXING SERVICES

Chemical Abstracts. Chemical Abstracts Service, 2540 Olentangy River Rd., PO Box 3012, Columbus, Ohio 43210. (800) 848-6533. 1907-.

General Science Index. H. W. Wilson Co., 950 University Ave., Bronx, New York 10452. 1978-. Monthly, also issued in annual cumulation. Cumulative subject index to English language periodicals in the subject fields of astronomy, botany, chemistry, earth science, environment and conservation, food and nutrition, genetics, mathematics, medicine and health, microbiology, oceanography, physics, physiology and zoology.

Science Citation Index. Institute for Scientific Information, 3501 Market St., Philadelphia, Pennsylvania 19104. 1961-.

ENCYCLOPEDIAS AND DICTIONARIES

Van Nostrand's Scientific Encyclopedia. Glenn D. Considine, ed. Van Nostrand Reinhold, 115 5th Ave., New York, New York 10003. (212) 254-3232. 1983. Sixth edition. Includes all broad subject areas in science.

GENERAL WORKS

ASTM Standards on Benzene, Toluene, Xylene, Solvent Naptha. American Society for Testing and Materials,

1916 S. Race St., Philadelphia, Pennsylvania 19103. (215) 299-5585. 1962. Standards for carcinogenicity testing.

NIP Technical Report on the Toxicology and Carcinogenesis Studies. National Toxicology Program, U.S. Department of Health and Human Services, National Institutes of Health, 9000 Rockville Pike, Bethesda, Maryland 20892. (301) 496-4000. 1986. Dealing with carcinogenicity testing.

Recommendations for a Xylene Standard. National Institute for Occupational Safety and Health, 1600 Clifton Rd. NE, Atlanta, Georgia 30333. (404) 639-3286. 1975. Covers toxicology of xylene, industrial hygiene standards and safety.

Toluene, The Xylenes, and Their Industrial Derivatives. Elsevier Science Publishing Co., 655 Avenue of the Americas, New York, New York 10010. (212) 984-5800. 1982. Topics in chemical engineering including toluene and xylene.

ONLINE DATA BASES

Chemical Abstracts-CA. Chemical Abstracts Service, 2540 Olentangy River Rd., P.O. Box 3012, Columbus, Ohio 43210. (800) 848-6533 or (614) 421-3600. Information sources include 9000 journals, patents from 27 countries, two industrial property organizations, new books, conference proceedings, and government research reports.

Chemical Abstracts Chemical Name Directory-CHEMNAME. Chemical Abstracts Service, 2540 Olentangy River Rd., P.O. Box 3012, Columbus, Ohio 43210. (800) 848-6533 or (614) 421-3600. Listing of chemical substances in a dictionary type file. The Chemical Abstracts (CAS) Registry Number, molecular formula, Chemical Abstracts (CA) Substance Index Name, available synonyms, ring data and other chemical substance information is given for each entry.

Chemical Collection System/Request Tracking–CCS/RTS. U.S. Environmental Protection Agency, Office of Pesticides and Toxic Substances, 401 M St., SW, Washington, District of Columbia 20460. (202) 260-2090. Contains information on various properties of a number of chemicals including environmental effects, test and analysis methods, and health effects. Available from EPA.

Chemical Dictionary Online–CHEMLINE. Chemical Abstracts Service, 2540 Olentangy River Rd., Columbus, Ohio 43210. (614) 421-3600 or (800) 848-6533. Part of MEDLINE of the National Library of Medicine (NLM). File of 900,000 names for chemical substances, representing 450,000 unique compounds. It contains such information as Chemical Abstracts (CA) Service Registry Numbers, molecular formulas, preferred chemical nomenclature, and generic and ring structure information. Available on NLM's ELHILL system.

Chemical Exposure. Science Applications International Corp., Health & Environmental Information, P.O. Box 2501, Oak Ridge, Tennessee 37831. (615) 482-9031. Database of chemicals that have been identified in both human tissues and body fluids and in feral and food animals. Contains reference to journal articles, conferences, and reports. Covers the whole fields of information related to human and animal exposure to food, air, and water contaminants and pharmaceuticals. Its records include information on chemical properties, formulas, tissues measured, analytical method used, demographics and more. Available on DIALOG.

Dewitt Petrochemical Newsletter. DeWitt and Company, 16800 Greenspoint Park, North Atrium Suite 120, Houston, Texas 77060. (713) 875-5525.

Y

YEAST

ABSTRACTING AND INDEXING SERVICES

ASFA Aquaculture Abstracts. Cambridge Scientific Abstracts, Inc., 5161 River Rd., Bethesda, Maryland 20816. (301) 961-6750. 1984.

Biological Abstracts. BIOSIS, 2100 Arch St., Philadelphia, Pennsylvania 19103-1399. (215) 587-4800. 1927-.

Chemical Abstracts. Chemical Abstracts Service, 2540 Olentangy River Rd., PO Box 3012, Columbus, Ohio 43210. (800) 848-6533. 1907-.

Ecological Abstracts. Geo Abstracts Ltd. Elsevier Applied Science, Crown House, Linton Rd., Barking, England IG 11 8JU. 1974-. Derived from over 600 leading ecological and environmental journals, plus books, conference proceedings, reports and theses.

Food Science and Technology Abstracts. International Food Information Service, c/o National Food Laboratory, 6363 Clark Ave., Dublin, California 94568. (800) 336-3782. 1969-.

General Science Index. H. W. Wilson Co., 950 University Ave., Bronx, New York 10452. 1978-. Monthly, also issued in annual cumulation. Cumulative subject index to English language periodicals in the subject fields of astronomy, botany, chemistry, earth science, environment and conservation, food and nutrition, genetics, mathematics, medicine and health, microbiology, oceanography, physics, physiology and zoology.

Science Citation Index. Institute for Scientific Information, 3501 Market St., Philadelphia, Pennsylvania 19104. 1961-.

ENCYCLOPEDIAS AND DICTIONARIES

Dictionary of Microbiology and Molecular Biology. Paul Singleton and Diana Sainsbury. John Wiley & Sons, Inc., 605 3rd Ave., New York, New York 10158-0012. (212) 850-6000. 1987. Second edition. Comprehensive dictionary with "classical descriptive aspects of microbiology to current developments in related areas of bioenergetics, biochemistry and molecular biology." Entries give synonyms, cross references, and references to pertinent works. Miscellaneous appendixes. Bibliography.

The Nutrition and Health Encyclopedia. David F. Tver and Percy Russell. Van Nostrand Reinhold, 115 5th Ave., New York, New York 10003. (212) 254-3232. 1989.

Van Nostrand's Scientific Encyclopedia. Glenn D. Considine, ed. Van Nostrand Reinhold, 115 5th Ave., New York, New York 10003. (212) 254-3232. 1983. Sixth edition. Includes all broad subject areas in science.

ONLINE DATA BASES

Chemical Abstracts-CA. Chemical Abstracts Service, 2540 Olentangy River Rd., P.O. Box 3012, Columbus, Ohio 43210. (800) 848-6533 or (614) 421-3600. Information sources include 9000 journals, patents from 27 countries, two industrial property organizations, new books, conference proceedings, and government research reports.

TRADE ASSOCIATIONS AND PROFESSIONAL SOCIETIES

American Institute of Biological Sciences. 730 11th St., N.W., Washington, District of Columbia 20001-4521. (202) 628-1500.

YIELDS

See: AGRICULTURE

Z

ZERO DISCHARGE

ABSTRACTING AND INDEXING SERVICES

Science Citation Index. Institute for Scientific Information, 3501 Market St., Philadelphia, Pennsylvania 19104. 1961-.

ENCYCLOPEDIAS AND DICTIONARIES

Van Nostrand's Scientific Encyclopedia. Glenn D. Considine, ed. Van Nostrand Reinhold, 115 5th Ave., New York, New York 10003. (212) 254-3232. 1983. Sixth edition. Includes all broad subject areas in science.

ZINC

See: METALS AND METALLURGY

ZIRCONIUM

ABSTRACTING AND INDEXING SERVICES

Chemical Abstracts. Chemical Abstracts Service, 2540 Olentangy River Rd., PO Box 3012, Columbus, Ohio 43210. (800) 848-6533. 1907-.

General Science Index. H. W. Wilson Co., 950 University Ave., Bronx, New York 10452. 1978-. Monthly, also issued in annual cumulation. Cumulative subject index to English language periodicals in the subject fields of astronomy, botany, chemistry, earth science, environment and conservation, food and nutrition, genetics, mathematics, medicine and health, microbiology, oceanography, physics, physiology and zoology.

Physics Briefs. Physikalische Berichte. Physik Verlag, Pappapelallee 3, Postfach 101161, Weinheim, Germany D-6940. 1979-. Semimonthly. In English. Volumes for 1979- issued by the Deutsche Physikalische Gesellschaft and the Fachinformationszentrum Energie Physik, Mathematik in cooperation with the American Institute of Physics.

Science Citation Index. Institute for Scientific Information, 3501 Market St., Philadelphia, Pennsylvania 19104. 1961-.

BIBLIOGRAPHIES

Zirconium in Agricultural Ecosystems: A Bibliography of the Literature from 1950 through 1971. University of Illinois, Department of Agronomy, Urbana, Illinois 61801. 1973.

ENCYCLOPEDIAS AND DICTIONARIES

Van Nostrand's Scientific Encyclopedia. Glenn D. Considine, ed. Van Nostrand Reinhold, 115 5th Ave., New York, New York 10003. (212) 254-3232. 1983. Sixth edition. Includes all broad subject areas in science.

GENERAL WORKS

Industrial Applications of Titanium and Zirconium. Charles S. Young. ASTM, 1916 Race St., Philadelphia, Pennsylvania 19103-1187. (215) 299-5400. 1986.

Standard for the Protection, Processing, Handling and Storage of Zirconium. National Fire Protection Association, 1 Battery Park, PO Box 9101, Quincy, Massachusetts 02269-9101. (617) 770-3000. 1987. Standards of fire protection

HANDBOOKS AND MANUALS

Tables of Physical and Chemical Constants and Some Mathematical Functions. G. W. C. Kaye, et al. Longman Group Ltd., Longman House, Burnt Mill, Harlow, England CM20 2J6. 0279 426721. 1988. Fifteenth edition. Includes tables on mechanical properties, density, elasticity, viscosity, surface tension, temperature and heat. Also covers radiation, optics, chemistry, electrochemistry, astrophysics, and chemical thermodynamics.

ONLINE DATA BASES

CAS Source Index–CASSI. Chemical Abstracts Service, 2540 Olentangy River Rd., P.O. Box 3012, Columbus, Ohio 43210. (800) 848-6533 or (614) 421-3600. A listing of bibliographic and library holdings information for scientific and technical primary literature relevant to the chemical sciences.

Chemical Abstracts-CA. Chemical Abstracts Service, 2540 Olentangy River Rd., P.O. Box 3012, Columbus, Ohio 43210. (800) 848-6533 or (614) 421-3600. Information sources include 9000 journals, patents from 27 countries, two industrial property organizations, new books, conference proceedings, and government research reports.

STATISTICS SOURCES

Minerals Yearbook: Hafnium and Zirconium. U.S. Department of the Interior, Bureau of Mines, Cochrans Mill Rd., Pittsburgh, Pennsylvania 15236. (412) 892-6400. Annual. Statistics on hafnium and zirconium.

ZOOGEOGRAPHY
See: BIOGEOGRAPHY

ZOOPLANKTON
See: PLANKTON

Sources Cited

13C NMR Spectroscopy: A Working Manual with Exercises. E. Breitmaier. Harwood Academic Publishers, PO Box 786, Cooper Sta., New York, NY 10276. (212) 206-8900. 1984.

Water Quality Implications of Conservation Tillage: A Reference Guide. The Center, West Lafayette, IN 1986.

33 Metal Producing–Buyer's Guide Issue. Penton Publishing Co., 1100 Superior Ave., Cleveland, OH 44114. (216) 696-7000.

50 Simple Things You Can Do to Save the Earth. G.K. Hall & Co., 70 Lincoln St., Boston, MA 02111. (617) 423-3990. 1991. Citizen participation in environmental protection.

An A-Z of Offshore Oil and Gas: An Illustrated International Glossary and Reference Guide to the Offshore Oil & Gas Industries and their Technology. Harry Whitehead. Gulf Publishing Co., Book Division, PO Box 2608, Houston, TX 77252. (713) 529-4301. Second edition. Defines and explains some 4000 specialized terms in current use in the oil and gas industries. Second edition includes 900 new entries in the key areas of new terminology, components, rig construction, new technologies, new discoveries, drilling technology, drilling fluid and med technology and key offshore locations.

Abalone Alliance. 2940 16th St., Suite 310, San Francisco, CA 94103. (415) 861-0592.

Aboveground Storage Tank Management: A Practical Guide. Joyce A. Rizzo and Albert D. Young. Government Institutes, Inc., 4 Research Pl., Suite 200, Rockville, MD 20850. (301) 921-2300. 1990. Describes how to design, build, manage, and operate above ground storage tanks in compliance with federal and state regulations.

Absorption Engineering. Motoyuki Suzuki. Elsevier Science Publishing Co., 655 Avenue of the Americas, New York, NY 10010. (212) 984-5800. 1990.

Abstracts of Air and Water Conservation Literature. American Petroleum Institute. Central Abstracting and Indexing Service, 275 Madison Avenue, New York, NY 10016. 1972.

Abstracts on Health Effects of Environmental Pollutants. BIOSIS, 2100 Arch St., Philadelphia, PA 19103. (215) 587-4800; (800) 523-4806.

Academy of Hazard Control Management. 5010A Nicholson Ln., Rockville, MD 20852. (301) 984-8969.

Academy of Natural Sciences of Philadelphia, Division of Environmental Research. 19th Street and the Parkway, Philadelphia, PA 19103. (215) 299-1081.

Acceptable Risk?: Making Decisions in a Toxic Environment. Lee Clarke. University of California Press, 2120 Berkeley Way, Berkeley, CA 94720. (415) 642-4247 (800) 822-6657. 1991. 1991

Access America: An Atlas and Guide to the National Parks for Visitors with Disabilities. Northern Cartographic, Box 133, Burlington, VT 05402. (802) 860-2886. 1992. Irregular. National parks with facilities for visitors with mobility impairments, and hearing, visual, or developmental disabilities.

Access EPA. Environmental Protection Agency. Office of Information Resources Management, National Technical Information Service, 5285 Port Royal Rd., Springfield, VA 22161. (703) 487-4650. 1991. This is a series of directories that provides contact information and descriptions of services offered by EPA's libraries, databases, information centers, clearinghouses, hotlines, dockets, record management programs and related information sources. At the present time there are seven directories in the series and one consolidated volume entitled ACCESS EPA. PB91–151563. The seven directories are Public Information Tools (PB91-151571); Major EPA Dockets (PB91-151589; Clearinghouses and Hotlines (PB91-151597); Records Management Programs (PB91-151605); Major Environmental Databases (PB91-151613); Libraries and Information Services (PB91-151621); State Environmental Libraries (PB91-151639). Note there is a contact for each state even though there is not an "environmental Library" in each state.

Accessions List. Environmental Science Information Center. Library and Information Services Division. National Oceanic and Atmospheric Administration, U.S. Department of Commerce, Washington, DC 20230. (202) 377-2985. Monthly.

Accidental Nuclear War Prevention Project. 1187 Coast Village Rd., Suite 123, Santa Barbara, CA 93108. (805) 965-3443.

ACEC Engineering Services Directory for Waste Management. American Consulting Engineering Council Research & Management Foundation, 1015 15th St., N.W., Washington, DC 20005. (202) 347-7575.

Acesulfame-K. D. G. Mayer, ed. Marcel Dekker, Inc., 270 Madison Ave., New York, NY 10016. (212) 696-9000; (800) 228-1160. 1991. Food and Science Technology series, vol. 47

Acid Aerosols Issue Paper: Health Effects and Aerometrics. U.S. Environmental Protection Agency. U.S. G.P.O., Washington, DC 20401. (202) 512-0000. 1989. Data from 1930 to present on airborne compounds resulting from fossil fuel burning.

Acid Deposition. Allan H. Legge. Lewis Publishers, 2000 Corporate Blvd., N.W., Boca Raton, FL 33431. (407) 994-0555 or (800) 272-7737. 1990. Acidic deposition is described in great detail using the results of a major holistic, interdisciplinary research program carried out with scientific input from both the U.S. and Canada.

Acid Mine Water. U.S. Department of the Interior, Office of Water Research and Technology, Water Resources Scientific Information Center, 1849 C. St. NW, Washington, DC 20240. (202) 208-3171.

Acid Politics: Environmental and Energy Policies in Britain and Germany. S. Boehmer-Christiansen and J. Skea. Belhaven Press, 136 S. Broadway, Irvington, NY 10533. (914) 591-9111. 1991. Studies the differences in Britain's and Germany's recognition of and policy reaction to the acid rain issue to exemplify the different political attitudes to "green" issues between the two countries.

Acid Precipitation. Sandra Hicks, ed. Technical Information Center, U.S. Dept. of Energy, National Technical Information Service, 5285 Port Royal Rd., Springfield, VA 37831. (703) 487-4650. 1983. Annual. Distributed in microfiche by the U.S. Dept. of Energy, Technical Information Center, #EDB-500200 and DE83 008750.

Acid Precipitation. Springer-Verlag, 175 5th Ave., New York, NY 10010. (212) 460-1500; (800) 777-4643. 1989-. 5 volume set. Deals with various aspects of acidic precipitations such as: biological and ecological effects; sources, deposition and canopy interactions; soils aquatic processes and lake acidification. Also includes case studies and an international overview and assessment.

Acid Precipitation. National Technical Information Service, 5285 Port Royal Rd., Springfield, VA 22161. (703) 487-4650. Monthly. Abstracts and indexes information on deposition transport and effects of acid precipitation.

Acid Precipitation: A Bibliography; A Compilation of Worldwide Literature. U.S. Department of Energy, Technical Information Center, PO Box 62, Oak Ridge, TN 37831. (615) 576-1223. 1983.

Acid Precipitation: An Annotated Bibliography. Denise A. Wiltshire and Margaret L. Evans. Department of the Interior, U.S. Geological Survey, Distribution Branch, Text Products Section, 119 National Center, Reston, VA 22092. (703) 648-4460. 1984. Geological Survey circular 923.

Acid Precipitation Digest. Acid Rain Information Clearinghouse, Center for Environmental Information, 46 Prince St., Rochester, NY 14607. (716) 271-3550. Monthly. A summary of current news, research, and events related to acidic deposition and transboundary air pollution, atmospheric science, aquatic and terrestrial biology and chemistry, forestry and agriculture, materials science and engineering, and pollutants emissions and control.

Acid Rain. Pauline Hollman. Library of Congress, Science and Technology Division, Science Reference Section, Washington, DC (202) 738-3238. 1986. This is part of LC Science Trace Bulletin ISSN 0090-5232 TB 86-11. It supersedes TB 80-13. Shipping list no. 87-92-P.

Acid Rain. Robert W. Lockerby. Vance Bibliographies, 112 N. Charter St., PO Box 229, Monticello, IL 61856. (217) 762-3831. 1982. Public Administration series–Bibliography: P-928.

Acid Rain. Michael Bright. Gloucester Press, 95 Madison Ave., New York, NY 10016. (212) 447-7788. 1991. Describes what acid rain is, what causes it, and how it affects the environment. Also examines ways in which pollution levels can be reduced or minimized.

Acid Rain. R. R. Bowker Co., Bowker Electronic Publishing, 121 Chanlon Rd., New Providence, NJ 07974. (800) 521-8110.

Acid Rain, 1980-1984: A Selected Bibliography. P. J. Koshy. Vance Bibliographies, 112 North Charter St., PO Box 229, Monticello, IL 61856. (217) 762-3831. 1986. Public Administration series–Bibliography: P1881

Acid Rain 1983-85. Sheldon Cheney. U.S. Department of Agriculture, National Agricultural Library, 10301 Baltimore Blvd., Beltsville, MD 20705-2351. (301) 504-5755. 1985. Part of Quick Bibliography series, #NAL-BIBL QB 86-23. The database searched is AGRICOLA and it updates QB 83-18. Shipping list 86-10-P.

Acid Rain, 1986. Sheldon Cheney. U.S. Department of Agriculture, National Agricultural Library, 10301 Baltimore Blvd., Beltsville, MD 20705-2351. (301) 504-5755. 1987. Irregular. Includes 223 citations. Quick Bibliography series: NAL-BIBL QB 87-11. It updates an earlier bibliography, QB 86-23.

Acid Rain 1986: A Handbook for States and Provinces. Acid Rain Foundation, 1410 Varsity Dr., Raleigh, NC 27606-2010. (919) 828-9443. 1986. Proceedings of Wingspread Conference sponsored by the Johnson Foundation Inc., dealing with environmental aspects of acid rain in the United States.

Acid Rain: A Bibliography of Canadian Federal and Provincial Government Documents. Albert H. Joy. Meckler, 11 Ferry Ln., W., Westport, CT 06880. (203) 226-6967. 1991. Contains Canadian Federal and provincial government documents. Includes bibliographical references and index. Approximately 1,100 documents covering diverse topics including environmental effects, air and atmospheric processes, socioeconomic aspects, and migration and corrective measures.

Acid Rain: A Bibliography of Research Annotated for Easy Access. Harry G. Stopp, Jr. Scarecrow Press, 52 Liberty St., Box 4167, Metuchen, NJ 08840. (201) 548-8600 or (800) 537-7107. 1985.

Acid Rain: A Legal and Political Perspective. Karen Fair Harrell. Vance Bibliographies, 112 N. Charter St., PO Box 229, Monticello, IL 61856. (217) 762-3831. 1983. Public Administration series–Bibliography: P-1319

Acid Rain: A Student's First Sourcebook. Beth Ann Kyle and Mary Deardorff. U.S. Environmental Protection Agency, Office of Environmental Processes and Effects Research, Office of Research and Development, 401 M St. SW, Washington, DC 20460. (202) 260-2090. 1990.

Acid Rain: A Survey of Data and Current Analyses. U.S. G.P.O., Washington, DC 20401. (202) 521-0000. 1984.

Acid Rain Abstracts. EIC/Intelligence Inc., 121 Chanlon Rd., New Providence, NJ 07974. (908) 464-6800. Bimonthly.

Acid Rain Abstracts Annual. Bowker A & I Publishing, 121 Chanlon Rd., New Providence, NJ 07974. (908) 464-6800. 1990-. Annual. Includes key retrospective research issues covered in the year. The book identifies and locates timely information in areas of rapidly developing science and technology as well as social and government policy issues. Each annual edition also contains two articles that highlight key issues and events of the year covered.

Acid Rain: An Annotated Bibliography of Selected References. University of Central Florida, Orlando, FL 32816. 1980. Library bibliography series no. 8.

Acid Rain and Dry Deposition. Larry W. Canter. Lewis Publishers, 200 Corporate Blvd. NW, Boca Raton, FL 33431. (407) 994-0555 or (800)272-7737. 1986.

Acid Rain and Emissions Trading: Implementing a Market Approach to Pollution Control. Roger K. Raufer and Stephen L. Feldman. Rowman & Littlefield, Publishers, Inc., 8705 Bollman Pl., Savage, MD 20763. (301) 306-0400. 1987. Methodological approach to the acid rain issue whereby emissions trading could be performed through a controlled leasing policy instead of outright trades. A comprehensive examination of the concerns surrounding the implementation of the market approach for dealing with acid rain.

Acid Rain and Ozone Layer Depletion. Jutta Brunnee. Transnational Publishers, PO Box 7282, Ardsley-on-Hudson, NY 10503. (914) 693-0089. 1988. International law and regulation relating to air pollution.

Acid Rain and the Environment, 1980-1984. Penny Farmer. Technical Communications, British Lib. Sci. Inf. Services, 100 High Ave., Letchworth, England SG6 3RR. 1984. Reviews a selection of the literature on acid rain. Current and projected research are summarized.

Acid Rain and the Environment, 1984-1988. Lesley Grayson, comp. and ed. Technical Communications, British Lib. Sci. Inf. Services, 100 High Ave., Letchworth, England SG6 3RR. Herts 1989. Updates the 1980-84 edition.

Acid Rain Bibliography. Charlene S. Sayers. U.S. Environmental Protection Agency, 401 M St. SW, Washington, DC 20460. (202) 260-2090. 1983. Part of EPA bibliography series no. EPA-840-83-022

The Acid Rain Controversy. James L. Regens and Robert W. Rycroft. University of Pittsburgh Press, 127 N. Bellefield Ave., Pittsburgh, PA 15260. (412) 624-4110. 1988. Examines various aspects of the U.S. government's response to the problem. Covers the emergence of acid rain as a public policy issue. Also covers acid rain's causes, effects, severity, control technologies, economic costs and benefits and alternatives for financing emissions control.

The Acid Rain Debate: Scientific, Economic, and Political Dimensions. Ernest J. Yanarella and Randal H. Ihara. Westview, 6065 Mission Gorge Rd., Suite 425, San Diego, CA 92120. 1985. Examines public policy issues relating to the environment, with special reference to acid rain in the U.S., Canada and Europe.

Acid Rain: Effects, Measurement and Monitoring, 1980. Tennessee Valley Authority, Technical Library. Tennessee Valley Authority, 400 W. Summit Hill Dr., Knoxville, TN 37902. (615) 632-2101. 1977. TVA bibliography, no. 1535 supplement

Acid Rain Foundation Speakers Bureau Directory. Acid Rain Foundation, Inc., 1410 Varsity Dr., Raleigh, NC 27606. (919) 828-9443.

Acid Rain: Impacts on Agriculture, 1975-1982. Sheldon Cheney. U.S. Department of Agriculture, National Agricultural Library, 10301 Baltimore Blvd., Beltsville, MD 20705-2351. (301) 504-5755. 1983. National Agricultural Library Quick Bibliography series 83-18. It updates QB 81-29.

Acid Rain in Canada: A Selected Bibliography. John Miletich. CPL Bibliographies, 1313 E. 60th St., Chicago, IL 60637-2897. (312) 942-2163. 1983. Council of Planning Librarians Bibliography No. 124.

Acid Rain: Industrial Pollution. Elaine Gray. Council of Planning Librarians, 1313 E. 60th St., Chicago, IL 60637-2897. (312) 942-2163. 1988. Part of Council of Planning Librarians Bibliography Series no. 223.

Acid Rain Information Book. David V. Bubenick. Noyes Publications, 120 Mill Rd., Park Ridge, NJ 07656. (201) 391-8484. 2nd ed.

Acid Rain: January 1987-March 1990. Sheldon Cheney. U.S. Department of Agriculture, National Agricultural Library, 10301 Baltimore Blvd., Beltsville, MD 20705-2351. (301) 504-5755. 1990. Contains 417 citations from AGRICOLA and is Quick Bibliography series QB 90-54. Includes an index.

Acid Rain: Measurement and Monitoring, 1970-1976. Tennessee Valley Authority, Technical Library. Tennessee Valley Authority, 400 W. Summit Hill Dr., Knoxville, TN 37902. (615) 632-2101. 1977. TVA bibliography, no. 1535

Acid Rain Publications by the U.S. Fish and Wildlife Service. Rita F. Villella. U.S. Department of the Interior, Fish and Wildlife Service, Washington, DC 20240. (202) 208-5634. 1989. Part of Air Pollution and Acid Rain Report no. 28. Also part of Biological Report 80 (40.28).

Acid Rain Resources Directory. Acid Rain Foundation, 1410 Varsity Dr., Raleigh, NC 27606-2010. (919) 828-9443. 1986. Irregular. Third edition. Lists state, national, and international governments, public and private companies, corporations and organizations actively involved in the subject area of acid rain.

The Acid Rain Sourcebook. Thomas C. Elliott and Robert G. Schwieger, eds. McGraw-Hill Science & Engineering Books, 11 W. 19th St., New York, NY 10011. (212) 337-6010. 1984. Organized under several sections dealing with the acid rain problem and legislative solutions; International mitigation programs; U.S. programs; emission reduction before, during, and after contamination; and engineering solutions under development. Text is based on papers presented at the first International Conference on Acid Rain held in Washington, DC, on March 27-28, 1984.

Acid Rain: Suggested Background Readings. Air Resources Information Clearinghouse, 99 Court St., Rochester, NY 14604. (716) 546-3796.

Acidic Deposition and Aquatic Ecosystems. D. F. Charles and S. Christie, eds. Springer-Verlag, 175 5th Ave., New York, NY 10010. (212) 460-1500. 1991. Comprehensive integrated synthesis of available information on current and potential effects of acidic precipitation on lakes and streams in different geographic regions of the U.S. Examines the current status of water chemistry.

Acidic Deposition and Forest Soils. Dan Binkley. Springer-Verlag, 175 Fifth Ave., New York, NY 10010. (212) 460-1500 or (800) 777-4643. 1990. Environmental aspects of acid deposition, forest soils and soil acidity.

Acidity Functions. Colin H. Rochester. Academic Press, c/o Harcourt Brace Jovanovich Inc., 6277 Sea Harbor Dr., Orlando, FL 32887. (800) 346-8648. 1970. Deals with acid-base equilibrium, acids and solution chemistry.

ACOPS Yearbook 1986-87. Advisory Committee on Pollution of the Sea, eds. Pergamon Microforms International, Inc., Fairview Park, Elmsford, NY 10523. (914) 592-7720. 1987. An annual review of activities by governmental and non-governmental organizations concerning remedies for global pollution, together with scientific and technical reports containing surveys of pollution in the marine environment.

Acoustical Contractors. 5711 S. 86th Circle, Omaha, NE 68127. (402) 593-4600. Annual.

Acoustical Society of America. 500 Sunnyside Blvd., Woodbury, NY 11797. (516) 349-7800.

Acoustical Society of America–Biennial Membership List. Acoustical Society of America, 500 Sunnyside Blvd., Woodbury, NY 11797. (516) 349-7800.

Acoustics Abstracts. Multi-Science Publishing Co. Ltd., 107 High St., Brentwood, England CM14 4RX. Essex (0277) 224632. Monthly. Covers the world's major periodical literature, conference proceedings, unpublished reports, and book notices on acoustics.

Acrylamide Producers Association. 1330 Connecticut Ave., N.W., Washington, DC 20036. (202) 659-0060.

Acrylic Acid Markets. FIND/SVP, 625 Avenue of the Americas, New York, NY 10011. (212) 645-4500. 1991. U.S. capacity, production, foreign trade and demand for acrylic acid, as well as acrylate esters and acrylic acid polymers.

The Acrylonitrile Group. c/o Joseph E. Hadley Jr., 1815 H St., N.W., Suite 1000, Washington, DC 20006. (202) 296-6300.

Action Alert. Rainforest Action Network, 301 Broadway, Suite A, San Francisco, CA 94133. (415) 398-4404. Monthly. Bulletin on issues requiring immediate public attention.

Action Bulletin. Citizen's Clearing House for Hazardous Wastes, Box 926, Arlington, VA 22216. (703) 276-7070. 1982-. Quarterly. Environmental hazards and neighborhood organizations faced with toxic problems.

Action Society for the Protection of New Hampshire Forests. The Forest Society, 54 Portsmouth St., Concord, NH 03301. (603) 224-9945. 1971-. Quarterly. Contains current news on New Hampshire environmental/conservation issues.

Activated Charcoal: Antidotal and Other Medical Uses. David O. Cooney. Marcel Dekker, Inc., 270 Madison Ave., New York, NY 10016. (212) 696-9000; (800) 228-1160. 1980. Therapeutic use of activated carbon, specifically as an antidote.

Activated Sludge; Theory and Practice. N.F. Gray. Oxford University Press, 200 Madison Ave., New York, NY 10016. (212) 679-7300 or (800) 334-4249. 1990. Microbial theory and kinetics, process control, modes of operation and aeration methods, trouble shooting, bulking problems, and nutrient removal.

Active and Passive Smoking Hazards in the Workplace. Judith A. Douville. Van Nostrand Reinhold, 115 5th Ave., 10003. (212) 254-3232. 1990.

Active Well Data On-Line. Petroleum Information Cooperation, 4100 E. Dry Creek Road, Littleton, CO 80122. (800) 525-5569.

Activist Newsletter. Defenders of Wildlife, 1244 19th St. NW, Washington, DC 20036. (202) 659-9510. Quarterly.

Acute and Sub-Acute Toxicology. Vernon K. Brown. E. Arnold, 41 Bedford Square, London, England WC1B 3DQ. 1988. Explains the effect of toxicants on vertebrate species, including man.

Acute Lethality Data for Ontario's Petroleum Refinery Effluents Covering the Period from December 1988 to May 1989. Ontario Ministry of Environment, c/o National Technical Information Service, 5285 Port Royal Rd., Springfield, VA 22161. (703) 487-4650. 1990. Order number MIC-91-02537 LDM.

Acute Lethality Data for Ontario's Petroleum Refinery Effluents covering the Period June 1989 to November 1989. J. T. Lee. Ontario Ministry of the Environment, c/o National Technical Information Service, 5285 Port Royal Rd., Springfield, VA 22161. (703) 487-4650. 1989. Order number MIC-91-02523 LDM.

Acute Toxicology Testing: Perspectives and Horizons. Shayne C. Gad and Christopher P. Chengelis. Telford Press, PO Box 287, West Caldwell, NJ 07006. (201) 228-7744. 1989.

Adaptations to Climatic Changes. P. Revet, ed. Karger, 26 W. Avon Rd., Box 529, Farmington, CT 06085. (203) 675-7834. 1987. Issued by the "8th Conference of the European Society for Comparative Physiology and Biochemistry, Strasbourg, August 31-September 2, 1986."

Adhesion and Adhesives. Y. Y. Liu. Library of Congress, Science and Technology Division, Reference Section, Washington, DC 20540. (202) 738-3238. 1979. LC tracer bullet TB 79-1.

Adhesion Society. c/o T.L. St. Clair, M.S. 226, NASA-Langely Research Center, Hamptong, VA 23665. (804) 864-4273.

Adhesives Age Directory. 6255 Barfield Rd., Atlanta, GA 30328. (404) 256-9800. Annual.

Adhesives/Sealants Guide. FIND/SVP, 625 Avenue of the Americas, New York, NY 10011. (212) 645-4500. 1990. Analyzes the structure of the U.S. adhesives and sealants industry and covers the overall outlook to 1994.

Adirondack Lakes Survey Corporation. New York State Dept. of Environmental Conservation, Ray Brook, NY 12977. (518) 891-2758.

Administration of the Toxic Substances Control Act. U.S. Environmental Protection Agency. Washington, DC Annual. Law and legislation regarding hazardous substances, chemicals, and poisons.

Adsorption of Energy-Related Organic Pollutants. K. A. Reinbold, et al. National Technical Information Service, 5285 Port Royal Rd., Springfield, VA 22161. (703) 487-4650. 1979. Research reporting series #3, Ecological Research; EPA-600/3-79-086.

Adsorption of Trace Metals by Hydrous Ferric Oxide in Seawater. K.C. Swallow. National Technical Information Service, 5285 Port Royal Rd., Springfield, VA 22161. (703) 487-4650. Water purification and trace elements in water.

Adsorption Science & Technology. Multi-Science Publishing Co. Ltd., 107 High St., Brentwood, Essex, England CM14 4RX. 0277-224632.

Adsorption Studies Evaluating Codisposal of Coal Gasification Ash with PAH-Containing Wastewater Sludges. John William Kilmer. University of Illinois at Urbana-Champaign, Urbana, IL 61801. 1986.

Adsorption Technology for Air and Water Pollution Control. Kenneth E. Noll. Lewis Publishers, 200 Corporate Blvd. NW, Boca Raton, FL 33431. (407) 994-0555 or (800)272-7737. 1991. Contains useful information on adsorption technology which can be applied in both air and water pollution.

Advanced Coatings & Surface Technology. NewsNet, Inc., 945 Haverford Rd., Bryn Mawr, PA 19010. (800) 345-1301.

Advanced Composites Bulletin. Elsevier Advanced Technology Publications, Mayfield House, 256 Banbury Rd., Oxford, England OX2 7DH. 44 (865) 512242.

Advanced Desiccant Materials Assessment. Gas Research Institute, 8600 W. Bryn Mawr Ave., Chicago, IL 60631. (312) 399-8100. 1988. Deals with air conditioning and gas appliances.

Advanced Environmental Technology Research Center. University of Illinois at Urbana-Champaign, Urbana, IL 61801. (217) 333-3822.

Advanced Fossil Energy Technologies. National Technical Information Service, 5285 Port Royal Road, Springfield, VA 22161. (703) 487-4650. Bimonthly. Department of Energy-sponsored reports in the field of fossil energy technology.

Advanced Oil and Gas Recovery Technologies. National Technical Information Service, 5285 Port Royal Road, Springfield, VA 22161. (703) 487-4650. Monthly. Enhanced and unconventional recovery of petroleum and natural gas, oil shales and tar sands, natural gas production from coal mines, gas hydrates, and geopressured systems.

Advanced Pollution Abatement Technology in the Pulp and Paper Industry. Environment Directorate. OECD Publication and Information Centre, 2 rue Andre Pascal, Paris, France F-75775. 1973. Waste disposal in the paper and wood-pulp industry.

Advanced Sciences Research and Development Corporation. P.O. Box 127, Lakemont, GA 30552. (404) 782-2092.

Advanced Transit Association. 1200 18th St., N.W., Suite 610, Washington, DC 20036. (703) 591-8328.

Advances in Air Sampling. Lewis Publishers, 2000 Corporate Blvd., N.W., Boca Raton, FL 33431. (407) 994-0555 or (800) 272-7737. 1988. Summary of the ACGIH Symposium on Advances in Air Sampling held February 16-18, 1987 at Pacific Grove, California. Includes topics such as particle size selective sampling, sampling gases and vapors for analysis, real-time aerosol samplers, and sampling strategy.

Advances in Analytical Toxicology. Biomedical Publications, PO Box 8209, Foster City, CA 94404. (415) 573-6224. Annual. Analysis of toxins and poisons.

Advances in Cement Research. Scholium International, Inc., 99 Seaview Blvd., Port Washington, NY 11050-4610. (516) 484-3290. Covers fundamentals of cement science.

Advances in Coating Materials, Techniques & Equipment. FIND/SVP, 625 Avenue of the Americas, New York, NY 10011. (212) 645-4500. 1991. Development of sophisticated materials, operating systems and surface modification techniques in areas as diverse as aerospace, lawn-mower components and microelectrics.

Advances in Ecological Research. Academic Press, c/o Harcourt Brace Jovanovich Inc., 6277 Sea Harbor Dr., Orlando, FL 32887. (800) 346-8648.

Advances in Environment, Behavior, and Design. Plenum Press, 233 Spring St., New York, NY 10013. (212) 620-8000; (800) 221-9369.

Advances in Environmental Science and Engineering. Gordon and Breach Science Publishers, Inc., 270 8th Ave., New York, NY 10011. (212) 206-8900. Annual.

Advances in Food Emulsions and Foams. Elsevier Science Publishing Co., 655 Avenue of the Americas, New York, NY 10010. (212) 984-5800. 1989.

Advances in Microbial Ecology. Plenum Press, 233 Spring St., New York, NY 10013-1578. (212) 620-8000; (800) 221-9369. Annual.

Advances in Neurobehavioral Toxicology: Applications in Environmental and Occupational Health. Barry L. Johnson, et al. Lewis Publishers, 2000 Corporate Blvd., N.W., Boca Raton, FL 33431. (407) 994-0555 or (800) 272-7737. 1991. Focuses on neurobehavioral methods and their development and application in environmental and occupational health. Includes new methods to assess human neurotoxicity; human exposure to, and health effects of, neurotoxic substances; and animal methods that model human toxicity.

Advances in Separation Technologies. Technical Insights, PO Box 1304, Fort Lee, NJ 07024-9967. (201) 568-4744. 1988.

Advances in Surface Enhancement Technology. FIND/SVP, 625 Avenue of the Americas, New York, NY 10011. (212) 645-4500. 1991.

Advances in Water Treatment and Environmental Management. George Thomas. Elsevier Science Publishing Co., 655 Avenue of the Americas, New York, NY 10010. (212) 984-5800. 1991. Measurement and control of groundwater quality, rivers, river management, estuaries, and beaches.

Advances on Chromatography. Marcel Dekker, Inc., 270 Madison Ave., New York, NY 10016. (212) 696-9000; (800) 228-1160.

Adverse Effects of Air Pollutants. Lillian Sheridan. ABBE Publishers Association of Washington DC, 4111 Gallows Rd., Annandale, VA 22003-1862. 1985. Medical subject analysis and research bibliography.

Adverse Effects of Aluminum. U.S. Department of Health and Human Services, Public Health Services, National Institutes of Health, 9000 Rockville Pike, Bethesda, MD 20892. (301) 496-4000. 1984. Covers toxicology of aluminum and occupational diseases.

Advisor. Great Lakes Commission, 2200 North Bonisteel Blvd., Ann Arbor, MI 48109. (313) 665-9135. 1956-. Monthly. Concerns current developments relating to activities of the Great Lakes Commission and its eight member states. Includes environment, economy, and Great Lakes related issues.

The AEE Directory of Energy Professionals. Fairmont Press, 700 Indian Trail, Lilburn, GA 30247. (404) 925-9388. 1980-. Annual. Lists members of the Association of Energy Engineers and their specialties. The membership consists of individuals who represent all facets of energy engineering/management. Also includes geographic listing and government references.

Aerial Photography and Image Interpretation for Resource Management. David P. Paine. John Wiley & Sons, Inc., 605 3rd Ave., New York, NY 10158-0012. (212) 850-6000. 1981. Photographic interpretation and aerial photography in forestry.

Aerial Photography and Remote Sensing for Soil Survey. Leslie Paul White. Clarendon Press, Oxford, England 1977.

Aerial Photography: Monographs. Mary A. Vance. Vance Bibliographies, PO Box 229, 112 N. Charter St., Monticello, IL 61856. (217) 762-3831. 1984.

Aerometric Information Retrieval System. U.S. Environmental Protection Agency, Office of Air Quality Planning and Standards, National Air Data Branch, 401 M St. SW, Washington, DC 20460. (202) 260-2090. Contains data reported by more than 5000 air monitoring stations located throughout the United States.

Aerosol Age–Buyer's Guide Issue. 389 Passaic Ave., Fairfield, NJ 07006. (201) 227-5151. Annual.

Aerosol Review. Grampion Press, London, England Annual.

Aerosol Sampling: Science and Practice. J. H. Vincent. John Wiley & Sons, Inc., 605 3rd Ave., New York, NY 10158-0012. (212) 850-6000. 1989. Details the sampling of aerosols with a "real world" approach. Makes the connection between theory and practice.

Aerosol Science. Pergamon Microforms International, Inc., Fairview Park, Elmsford, NY 10523. (914) 592-7720. 1991. Radioactive pollution of the atmosphere, nuclear reactor accidents and radioactive aerosols.

Aerosol Science and Technology. Elsevier Science Publishing Co., 655 Avenue of the Americas, New York, NY 10010. (212) 989-5800. 1982-. Bimonthly. Journal of American Association for Aerosol Research dealing with aerosol filtration and effects on climate, etc.

Aerosols. FIND/SVP, 625 Avenue of the Americas, New York, NY 10011. (212) 645-4500. 1990.

Affinity Membranes. Elias Klein. John Wiley & Sons, Inc., 605 3rd Ave., New York, NY (212) 850-6000. 1991. The chemistry and performance of affinity membranes in absorptive separation processes.

Affordable Passive Solar Homes. Richard Crowther. American Solar Energy Society, 2400 Central Ave., No. B-1, Boulder, CO 80301. (303) 443-3130. 1983. Passive systems in solar energy.

Aflatoxin Contamination. Rebecca Thompson. U.S. Department of Agriculture, National Agriculture Library, 10301 Baltimore Blvd., Beltsville, MD 20705-2351. (301) 504-5755. 1989.

Aflatoxins: Chemical and Biological Aspects. John Godfrey Heathcote and J. R. Hibbert. Elsevier Science Publishing Co., 655 Avenue of the Americas, New York, NY 10010. (212) 989-5800. 1978. Discusses the properties of aflatoxins, their toxicology and physiological effects.

African Wildlife Foundation. 1717 Massachusetts Avenue, NW, Washington, DC 20036. (202) 265-8393.

Aftermath Catalytic Convertors: Guide to Their Purchase, Installation, and Use. Illinois Environmental Protection Agency, 2200 Churchill Rd., P.O. Box 19276, Springfield, IL 62794-9276. (217) 782-2829. 1989.

AgBiotech News and Information. C. A. B. International, 845 North Park Ave., Tucson, AZ 85719. (602) 621-7897 or (800) 528-4841. 1989-. Bimonthly. Includes news items on topics such as research, companies, products, patents, books, education, diary, people, equipment, and legal issues. Also reviews articles and conference reports. Abstracts journal articles, reports, conferences, and books. Also includes biological control, bioenvironmental interactions and stress resistance and genetics.

Agency of Natural Resources: Air Quality. Director, Air Pollution Control Division, 103 South Wissell, Waterbury, VT 05676. (802) 244-8731.

Agency of Natural Resources: Environmental Protection. Secretary, 103 South Wissell, Waterbury, VT 05676. (802) 244-7347.

Agency of Natural Resources: Fish and Wildlife. Commissioner, Department of Fish and Wildlife, 103 South Wissell, Waterbury, VT 05676. (802) 224-7331.

Agency of Natural Resources: Natural Resources. Secretary, 103 South Wissell, Waterbury, VT 05676. (802) 244-7347.

Agency of Natural Resources: Solid Waste Management. Director, Solid Waste Programs, 103 South Wissell, Waterbury, VT 05676. (802) 244-7831.

Agent Orange and Vietnam: An Annotated Bibliography. Scarecrow Press, 52 Liberty St., Metuchen, NJ 08840. (908) 548-8600. Ethical and political aspects of man's relationship to the environment.

Agent Orange Dioxin, TCDD. Trellis C. Wright. Library of Congress, Science and Technology Division, Reference Section, Washington, DC 20540. (202) 738-3238. 1979.

Agent Orange Review: Information for Veterans Who Served in Vietnam. Veterans Administration, Washington, DC Quarterly. Medical care of veterans related to Agent Orange.

Aging and Environmental Toxicology: Biological and Behavioral Perspectives. Ralph L. Cooper, Jerome M. Goldman, and Thomas J. Harbin. Johns Hopkins University Press, 701 W. 40th St., Ste. 275, Baltimore, MD 21211. (410) 516-6900. 1991. Physiological aspects of adaptation.

Aging, Genetics and the Environment. Dept. of Health, Education, and Welfare, Public Health Service, National Institutes of Health, 9000 Rockville Pike, Bethesda, MD 20892. (301) 496-4000. 1979. Covers metals in the body.

SOURCES CITED

Agrarian Advocate. California Action Network, Box 464, Davis, CA 95617. (916) 756-8518. 1978-. Quarterly. Includes issues of concern to rural California residents such as groundwater pollution, pesticides, and sustainable agriculture.

Agrartechnik: Mehrsprachen-Bildworterbuch. Agricultural Engineering: Multilingual Illustrated Dictionary Magraf Scientific Publishers, Weikersheim, Germany 1987.

Agrichemical Age Magazine. HBJ Farm Publications, 731 Market Street, San Francisco, CA 94103-2011. (415) 495-3340. Eleven times a year. Use and application of agricultural chemicals.

AGRICOLA. U.S. Department of Agriculture, Office of Public Affairs, 14 Independence Ave., S.W., Washington, DC 20250. (202) 447-7454.

Agricultural and Animal Sciences Journals and Serials: An Analytical Guide. Richard D. Jensen. Greenwood Publishing Group, Inc., 88 Post Rd. W., PO Box 5007, Westport, CT 06881. (212) 226-3571. 1986.

Agricultural and Environmental Policies: Opportunities for Integration. OECD Publications and Information Center, 2001 L St. N.W., Suite 700, Washington, DC 20036. (202) 785-OECD. 1989. Describes a broad range of approaches by OECD countries to integrating environmental and agricultural policies and argues that eventual cuts in economic support for agriculture and withdrawal of land from production could produce important benefits for the environment.

Agricultural Chemicals. William Thomas Thomson. Thomson Publications, Box 9335, Fresno, CA 93791. (209) 435-2163. 1991. Book 1: Insecticides and acaricides. Book 2: Herbicides. Book 3: Fumigants, growth regulators, repellents and rodenticides. Book 4: Fungicides.

Agricultural Chemicals Hazard Response Handbook. Euan Wallace. Agro-Research Enterprises, P.O. Box 264, Haverlock North, New Zealand 64-70-65-950. 1987. Agricultural chemicals and related compounds are listed by trade names in alphabetical order, coupled to the common names or the abbreviated names of the active ingredient contained in the trade-named product.

Agricultural Conservation Program Statistical Summary. U.S. Agricultural Stabilization and Conservation Service, Dept. of Agriculture, Washington, DC 20013. (202) 512-0000. Annual. Deals with soil erosion control, water conservation, water quality and costs by state and county.

Agricultural Cooperative Development International. 50 F St., N.W., Suite 900, Washington, DC 20001. (202) 638-4661.

Agricultural Ecology. Joy Tivy. John Wiley & Sons, Inc., 605 3rd Ave., New York, NY 10158-0012. (212) 850-6000. 1990. Analyzes the nature of relationships between crops, livestock, and the biophysical environment, and the extent to which man has modified the products and environment to suit his own needs.

Agricultural Energy Conservation Project: Final Report. University of Nebraska, Cooperative Extension, Institute of Agriculture and Natural Resources, 214 Agricultural Hall, Lincoln, NE 68583-0703. (402) 472-7211. 1989.

Agricultural Engineering Abstracts. C. A. B. International, 845 North Park Ave., Tucson, AZ 85719. (602) 621-7897 or (800) 528-4841. 1976-. Monthly. Informs about significant research developments in agricultural engineering and instrumentation. Some of the topics scanned for the abstracts include mechanical power, crop production, crop harvesting and threshing, crop processing and storage, aquaculture, land improvement, protected cultivation, handling and transport, and farm buildings and equipment.

Agricultural Engineering Conference 1990. EA Books/Accents Pubs., 1990. Conference sponsored by the Institute of Engineers, Australia and co-sponsored by the American Society of Agricultural Engineers, held in Toowoomba, Australia, November 1990. Topics cover a wide range of agricultural engineering topics, including soil and water, processing of biological materials, structures and environment, power and machinery, systems and modeling, instrumentation and measurement, education, and international perspectives.

Agricultural Engineering Magazine. American Society of Agricultural Engineers, 2950 Niles Road, St Joseph, MI 49085. (616) 429-0300. Bimonthly. Irrigation and other large scale projects with environmental significance.

The Agricultural Handbook: A Guide to Terminology. Martin Whitley, et al. BSP Professional Books, 3 Cambridge Center, Suite 208, Cambridge, MA 02142. 1988. Provides an introductory reference source of definitions and explanations for agricultural terms. All areas of agriculture are covered including animal and crop production, farm management, policy and institutions.

Agricultural Information Resource Centers, a World Directory 1990. Rita C. Fisher. IAALD World Directory Working Group, 716 W. Indiana Ave., Urbana, IL 61801-4836. (217) 333-7687. 1990. Includes 3,971 information resource centers that have agriculture related collection and/or information services.

The Agricultural Notebook. Primrose McConnell; R. J. Halley, ed. Butterworth-Heinemann, 80 Montvale Ave., Stoneham, MA 02180. (617) 438-8464 or (800) 366-2665. 1982. Seventeenth edition. Includes data on the business of farming. Topics discussed include soils, drainage, crop physiology, crop nutrition, arable crops, grassland, trees on the farm, weed control, diseases of crops, pests of crops, grain preservation and storage, animal production, farm equipment, farm management, agricultural law, health and safety, and agricultural computers.

Agricultural Periodicals Published in Canada. Dorothy Mary Duke. Canada Dept. of Agriculture, Canada 1962.

Agricultural Pesticide Use Trends and Policy Issues. U.S. G.P.O, Washington, DC 20402-9325. (202) 512-0000. Irregular. Farm use of pesticides and potential impact of alternative environmental protection.

Agricultural Research Institute. 9650 Rockville Pike, Bethesda, MD 20814. (301) 530-7122.

Agricultural Research Service. Washington, DC 20250.

Agricultural Resource Conservation Program: For State and Country Offices, Short Reference. U.S. Deptartment of Agriculture, Agricultural Stabilization and Conservation Service, 14 Independence Ave., SW, Washington, DC 20250. (202) 447-7454. Guide to local conservation in the United States.

Agricultural Waste Utilization and Management. American Society of Agricultural Engineers, 2950 Niles Rd., St. Joseph, MI 49085-9659. (616) 429-0300. 1985. Proceedings of the Fifth International Symposium on Agricultural Wastes, December 16-17, 1985, Chicago, IL. Covers topics such as liquid manure storage and transportation, energy recovery from wastes, digester types and design, recycling for feed, fuel and fertilizer, land applications and odor control.

Agriculture and Fertilizers. Oluf Chr. Bockman. Agricultural Group, Norsk Hydro, Oslo, Norway 1990. Fertilizers in perspective, their role in feeding the world, environmental challenges, and alternatives.

Agriculture and Natural Resources: Planning for Educational Priorities for the Twenty-First Century. Wava G. Haney, ed. Conservation of Natural Resources, 5500 Central Ave., Boulder, CO 80301. 1991. A volume in the Social Behavior and Natural Resources Series. Text details the priorities in planning for the 21st century while conserving natural resources and the environment.

The Agriculture Dictionary. Ray V. Herren and Roy L. Donahue. Delmar Publishers Inc., 2 Computer Dr. W., Albany, NY 12212. (518) 459-1150. 1991. Covers all the agricultural areas including acid rain, acid mine drainage, food additives, agricultural engineering, conservation of the natural resources, microorganisms, triticale and other related topics.

Agriculture, Ecosystems & Environment. Elsevier Science Publishing Co., 655 Avenue of the Americas, New York, NY 10010. (212) 989-5800. Eight times a year. This journal is concerned with the interaction of methods of agricultural production, ecosystems and the environment.

Agrindex. AGRIS Coordinating Center, Via delle Terme di Caracalla, Rome, Italy I-00100. 61 0181-FA01. 1975-.

AGRIS. Food and Agriculture Organization of the United Nations, Via delle Terme di Caracalla, Rome, Italy 00100. 61 0181-FA01.

Agro-Ecosystems. Elsevier Science Publishing Co., 655 Avenue of the Americas, New York, NY 10010. (212) 989-5800. 1982-. Quarterly. Journal of International Association for Ecology featuring ecological interactions between agricultural and managed forest systems.

The Agrochemicals Handbook. H. Kidd and D. Hartlet, eds. Royal Society of Chemistry, c/o CRC Press, 2000 Corporate Blvd., N.W., Boca Raton, FL 33431-9868. (800) 272-7737. 1991. 3rd ed. Contains comprehensive worldwide information and data on substances which are active components of agriculture chemical products currently used in crop protection and pest control.

Agroecology and Small Farm Development. Miguel A. Altieri. CRC Press, 2000 Corporate Blvd. N.W., Boca Raton, FL 33431. (800) 272-7737. 1989. Reviews physical and social context of small farm agriculture, small farm development approaches, production systems, the dynamics of traditional agriculture, and research methodologies.

Agroecology: Researching the Ecological Basis for Sustainable Agriculture. Stephen R. Gliessman, ed. Springer-Verlag, 175 5th Ave., New York, NY 10010. (212) 460-1500; (800) 777-4643. 1990. Demonstrates in a series of international case studies how to combine the more production-oriented focus of the agronomist with the more systems-oriented viewpoint of the ecologist. Methodology for evaluating and quantifying agroecosystem is presented.

Agroforestry Abstracts. C. A. B. International, 845 North Park Ave., Tucson, AZ 85719. (602) 621-7897 or (800) 528-4841. 1988-. Quarterly. Abstracts journal articles, reports, conferences and books. Focuses on subjects areas such as agroforestry in general; agroforestry systems; trees, animals and crops; conservation; human ecology; social and economic aspects; development, research and methodology.

AIBC Bulletin. American Institute of Biomedical Climatology, 312 Saint St., Richland, WA 19115. (509) 375-0873. 1977-. Quarterly. Disseminates articles and news on effects of weather, climate, and the atmosphere on arts and the environment.

AIChE Journal. American Institute of Chemical Engineers, 345 East 47th Street, New York, NY 10017. (212) 705-7338. Monthly. Papers on all areas of chemical engineering.

AIPE Facilities: The Journal of Plant and Facilities Management & Engineering. American Institute of Plant Engineers, 3975 Erie Avenue, Cincinnati, OH 45208. (513) 561-6000. Bimonthly. Articles about the management of manufacturing facilities.

Air and Waste Management Association. Box 2861, Pittsburgh, PA 15230. (412) 232-3444.

Air and Waste Management Association Directory and Resource Book. Air and Waste Management Association, PO Box 2861, Pittsburgh, PA 15230. (412) 232-3444. Annual.

Air and Water Pollution Control. Bureau of National Affairs, 1231 25th St. N.W., Washington, DC 20037. (202) 452-4200. 1986-. Biweekly. Review of developments in pollution laws, regulations and trends in government and industry.

Air-Conditioning and Refrigeration Institute. 1501 Wilson Blvd., 6th Fl., Arlington, VA 22209. (703) 524-8800.

Air Conditioning, Heating, and Refrigeration News: 1990 Statistical Panorama. Business News Publishing Co., PO Box 2600, Troy, MI 48007. (313) 362-3700; (800) 247-2160. Shipments of air conditioning, refrigeration, home heating, and related products.

Air Conditioning, Heating & Refrigeration News. Directory Issue. Business News Publishing Co., PO Box 2600, Troy, MI 48007. (313) 362-3700 or (800) 247-2160. Annual.

Air Contaminants: Permissible Exposure Limits. U.S. Occupational Safety and Health Administration. U.S. G.P.O., Washington, DC 20401. (202) 512-0000. 1989. Irregular. Data on OSHA legal limits on occupational air contaminants.

Air Control Board: Air Quality. Executive Director, 6330 Highway 290 E., Austin, TX 78723. (512) 451-5711.

Air Cooled Heat Exchanger Manufacturers Association. 25 N. Broadway, Tarrytown, NY 10591. (914) 332-0040.

Air Currents. Bay Area Air Quality Management District, 939 Ellis St., San Francisco, CA 94109. (415) 771-6000. 1959-. Monthly. Describes regulation changes and other information of interest to the air pollution control community.

Air Emissions from Municipal Solid Waste Landfills. Environmental Protection Agency. National Technical Information Service, 5285 Port Royal Rd., Springfield, VA 22161. (703) 487-4650. 1991. Background information for proposed standards and guidelines. Order number PB91-197061LDM.

Air Monitoring for Toxic Exposure. Shirley A. Ness. Van Nostrand Reinhold, 115 5th Ave., New York, NY 10003. (212) 354-3232. 1991. Explains the procedures for evaluating potentially harmful exposure to people from hazardous materials including chemicals, radon and bioaerosols. Presents practical information on how to perform air sampling, collect biological and bulk samples, evaluate dermal exposures, and determine the advantages and limitations of a given method.

Air Pollution. Arthur C. Stern, ed. Academic Press, c/o Harcourt Brace Jovanovich Inc., 6277 Sea Harbor Dr., Orlando, FL 32887. (800) 346-8648. Annual.

Air Pollution, Acid Rain, and the Future of Forests. Sandra Postel. Worldwatch Institute, 1776 Massachusetts Ave., N.W., Washington, DC 20036-1904. 1984.

Air Pollution and Acid Rain Reports. National Technical Information Service, 5285 Port Royal Rd., Springfield, VA 22161. (703) 487-4650. Annual. Air pollution and acid rain environmental effects and controls.

Air Pollution by Photochemical Oxidants. Robert Guderian. Springer-Verlag, 175 5th Ave., New York, NY 10010. (212) 460-1500. 1985. Formation, transport, control, and effects on plants of photochemical oxidants.

Air Pollution Control. Howard E. Hesketh. Technomic Publishing Co., 851 New Holland Ave., Box 3535, Lancaster, PA 17604. (717) 291-5609. 1991. Presents both theory and application data. Provides a background relevant to behavior theories and control techniques for capturing gaseous and particulate air pollutants.

Air Pollution Control. Bureau of National Affairs, 1231 25th St. NW, Washington, DC 20037. (202) 452-4200. Biweekly. A reference and advisory service on the control of air pollution, designed to meet the information needs of individuals responsible for complying with EPA and state air pollution control regulations.

Air Pollution Control Commission: Air Quality. Director, 1558 Washington St., E., Charleston, WV 25311. (304) 348-4022.

Air Pollution Control Equipment & Services Market. FIND/SVP, 625 Avenue of the Americas, New York, NY 10011. (212) 645-4500. 1991. Technologies currently used to combat particulate and gaseous pollutants–gravity settlers, centrifugal separators, electrostatic precipitators, fabric filters, wet scrubbers, adsorption and absorption devices, and incinerators.

Air Pollution Damage to Man-Made Materials: Physical and Economic Estimates. A.R. Stankunas. Electric Power Research Institute, 3412 Hillview Ave., Palo Alto, CA 94304. (415) 965-4081. 1983. Environmental aspects of paint, galvanized steel and concrete.

Air Pollution Emission Standards and Guidelines for Municipal Waste Combustors: Economic Analysis of Materials Separation Requirement. B. J. Morton, et al. National Technical Information Service, 5285 Port Royal Rd., Springfield, VA 22161. (703) 487-4650. 1990. Final report prepared by the Research Triangle Institute for the Center for Economics Research.

Air Pollution: EPA's Strategy to Control Emissions of Benzene and Gasoline Vapor. U.S. General Accounting Office. Washington, DC 1985. Environmental aspects of benzene.

Air Pollution Modeling; Theories, Computational Methods, and Available Software. Paolo Zannetti. Van Nostrand Reinhold, 115 5th Ave., New York, NY 10003. (212) 254-3232. 1990. Introduces relevant historical and recently developed examples of modeling techniques for traditional problems including point source dispersion, plume rise, windfield estimation, and surface deposition.

Air Pollution Monitoring and Sampling Newsletter. McIlvaine Co., 2970 Maria Ave., Northbrook, IL 60062. (708) 272-0010. 1980-. Monthly. Information on air pollution monitoring and sampling equipment and service.

Air Pollution Research Laboratory. University of Florida, 408 Black Hall, Gainsville, FL 32611. (904) 392-0845.

Air Pollution Technical Information Center File. U.S. Environmental Protection Agency, Library Services Office, Air Information Center (MD-35), 401 M St. SW, Washington, DC 20460. (202) 260-2090. Citations and abstracts of the world's literature on air quality and air pollution prevention and control.

Air Pollution Technical Publications of the United States Environmental Protection Agency. U.S. Environmental Protection Agency, Mail Drop 75, Research Triangle Park, NC 27711. (919) 541-2184. 1976. Quarterly.

Air Pollution Titles. Pennsylvania State University, Center for Air Environmental Studies, 226 Fenske Laboratory, University Park, PA 16802. (814) 865-1415. 1965. Bibliographic guide to current research literature on air environment, including monitoring and control of air pollution, health effects, effects on agriculture, forests, toxic air contaminants, and global atmospheric pro cases.

Air Pollution Translations. A Bibliography With Abstracts. U.S. Environmental Protection Agency, MD 75, Research Triangle Park, NC 27711. (919) 541-2184. 1969.

Air Pollution's Toll on Forests and Crops. James J. MacKenzie and Mohamed T. El-Ashry, eds. Yale University Press, 92 A Yale St., 302 Temple St., New Haven, CT 06520. (203) 432-0960. 1992. Proposes an integrated strategy to reduce pollution levels based on improved energy efficiency, abatement technology, and the use of nonfossil energy technologies. This strategy takes into account other critical problems such as increasing oil imports, failure to attain clean air goals in U.S. cities, and the greenhouse effect.

Air Quality. Lewis Publishers, 200 Corporate Blvd. NW, Boca Raton, FL 33431. (407) 994-0555 or (800)272-7737. 2nd edition. Air pollution and control, stratosphere O3 depletion, global warming, and indoor air pollution.

Air Quality Criteria for Ozone and Other Photochemical Oxidants. U.S. Environmental Protection Agency, MD 75, Research Triangle Park, NC 27711. 1986. Physiological effect of atmospheric ozone and effect of air pollution on plants.

Air Quality Digest. South Coast Air Quality Management District, 9150 Flair Dr., El Monet, CA 91731. (818) 572-6200. 1971-. Quarterly. Reports developments of significance in air pollution control. Centers on program administered by LA County ARCD.

Air Quality Group. University of California, Davis, Crocker Nuclear Laboratories, Davis, CA 95616. (510) 752-1124.

Air Resources Agency: Air Quality. Director, Health and Welfare Building, 22 Hazen Dr., Concord, NH 03301. (603) 271-4582.

Air Resources Information Clearinghouse. 99 Court St., Rochester, NY 14604. (716) 546-3796.

Air Risk Information Support Center: Assistance for State and Local Agencies. U.S. Environmental Protection Agency, Public Information Center, 401 M St., SW, Washington, DC 20460. (202) 260-2090. 1988.

Air/Superfund National Technical Guidance Study Series. Database of Emission Rate Measurement Projects. B. Eklund, et al. U.S. Environmental Protection Agency, 401 M St. SW, Washington, DC 20460. (202) 260-2090. 1991. Emission rate measurements of polluted air conducted at different projects and compiled into a database.

Air/Superfund National Technical Guidance Study Series. Emission Factors for Superfund Remediation Technologies. P. Thompson, et al. Radian Corporation, Austin, TX., National Technical Information Service, 5285 Port Royal Rd., Springfield, VA 22161. (703) 487-4650. Order number PB 91-190975 LDM.

Air-to-Air Heat Exchangers: Directory and Buyers' Guide. 1100 Massachusetts Ave., Arlington, MA 02174. (617) 648-8700. Irregular.

Air Toxics and Risk Assessment. Edward J. Calabrese and Elaina M. Kenyon. Lewis Publishers, 200 Corporate Blvd. NW, Boca Raton, FL 33431. (407) 994-0555 or (800)272-7737. 1991. Does risk assessments for more than 110 chemicals that are confirmed or probable air toxics. All chemicals are analyzed with a scientifically sound methodology to assess public health risks.

Air Toxics Report. Business Publishers, Inc., 951 Pershing Dr., Silver Spring, MD 20910-4464. (301) 587-6300. 1988-. Monthly. Directed towards organizations and facilities that are or may be affected by regulations under the Clean Air Act and National Emission Standards for Hazardous Air Pollutants, with articles on government regulation, studies, compliance, violations and legal actions. Also available online.

Air Toxics Report. Business Publishers, Inc., 951 Pershing Dr., Silver Spring, MD 20910. (301) 587-6300. Online version of periodical of the same name.

Air Transport, 1990. Air Transport Association of America, 1709 New York Ave., NW, Washington, DC 20006-5206. Annual. Statistics on finances and operations of scheduled air carriers.

Air/Water Pollution Report. Business Publishers, Inc., 951 Pershing Dr., Silver Spring, MD 20910-4464. (301) 587-6300. 1963-. Weekly. Reports on the hard news and in-depth features for practical use by environmental managers. It keeps readers informed on the latest news from government and industry. Also available online.

Air/Water Pollution Report. NewsNet, Inc., 945 Haverford Rd., Bryn Mawr, PA 19010. (800) 345-1301. Online version of periodical of same name.

Airliner Cabin Environment: Contaminant, Measurements, Health Risks, and Mitigation Options. U.S. G.P.O, Washington, DC 20402-9325. (202) 512-0000. 1990. Cabin air quality tests conducted on smoking and nonsmoking flights for smoke-related contaminants (nicotine, respirable suspended particles, carbon monoxide) as well as ozone carbon dioxide, and various bacteria and fungi.

Alabama Conservation. Alabama Department of Conservation, 64 N. Union St., Montgomery, AL 36130. (205) 242-3151. 1929-. Bimonthly. Promotes the wise use of natural resources.

Alabama Department of Conservation Report. Alabama Department of Conservation, 64 N. Union St., Montgomery, AL 36130. (205) 242-3151. Annually.

Alabama Law Handbook. Government Institutes, Inc., 4 Research Pl., Ste. 200, Rockville, MD 20850. (301) 921-2300. 1990.

Alabama Pesticide News. Auburn University, Cooperative Extension Service, Extension Hall, Auburn, AL 36849. (205) 844-1592. Monthly.

The Alan Guttmacher Institute. 111 5th Avenue, New York, NY 10003. (212) 254-5656.

ALAPCO Washington Update. Association of Local Air Pollution Control Officials, 444 North Capitol Street, NW, Washington, DC 20001. (202) 624-7864. Monthly. Air pollution control in Washington, DC.

Alaska Center for the Environment Center News. Alaska Center for the Environment, 700 H St., #4, Anchorage, AK 99501. (907) 274-3621. 1972-. Bimonthly. Topics deal with environmental education and Alaskan issues, land use, hazardous waste, etc.

The Alaska Conservation Directory. Alaska Conservation Foundation, 430 W. 7th Ave.,Ste. 215, Anchorage, AK 99501. (907) 276-1917. 1990.

Alaska Conservation Foundation. 430 West 7th St., Suite 215, Anchorage, AK 99501. (907) 276-1917.

Alaska Cooperative Fishery and Wildlife Research Unit. 138 Arctic Health Research Unit, University of Alaska-Fairbanks, Fairbanks, AK 99775-0110. (907) 474-7661.

Alaska Fisheries Science Center. 7600 Sand Point Way NE, BIN C15700, Seattle, WA 98115. (206) 526-4000.

Alaska Fishery and Fur. U.S. Department of the Interior, 1849 C St. NW, Washington, DC 20240. (202) 208-3171. Annually.

Alaskan Marine Contaminants Database. National Oceanic and Atmospheric Administration, National Ocean Service, 222 W. 8th Ave., Box 56, Anchorage, AK 99513. (907) 271-3033. Contains data on the occurrence of contaminants in faunal tissue and sediments in Alaskan marine waters.

Alberta Naturalist. Federation of Alberta Naturalists, Box 1472, Edmonton, ON, Canada T5J 2N5 1971-. Quarterly.

Albion College, Whitehouse Nature Center. Albion, MI 49224. (517) 629-2030.

Alcohol and Health Research World. National Institute on Alcohol Abuse and Alcoholism. U.S. G.P.O., Washington, DC 20401. (202) 512-0000. Quarterly. Research articles on prevention and treatment of alcoholism.

Alcohol as a Fuel for Farm and Construction Equipment. G.L. Borman. National Technical Information Service, 5285 Port Royal Rd., Springfield, VA 22161. (703) 487-4650. 1982. Fuels utilization by farm and construction equipment.

Alcohol Fuels. Vivian O. Sammons. Library of Congress, Science and Technology Division, Reference Section, Washington, DC 1980.

Alcohol Health and Research World. U.S. G.P.O, Washington, DC 20402-9325. (202) 512-0000. Quarterly. Original research on treatment and prevention of alcoholism and alcohol abuse.

Aldrin and Endrin in Water: A Bibliography. National Technical Information Service, 5285 Port Royal Rd., Springfield, VA 22161. (703) 487-4650. 1972. Water Resources Scientific Information Center Bibliography series, WRSIC 72-203.

Alert. Missouri Coalition for the Environment Foundation, 6267 Delmar Blvd., St. Louis, MO 63130. (314) 727-0600. 1969-. Quarterly. Published for the statewide environmental citizen activist organization.

Algae Abstracts: A Guide to the Literature. IFI/Plenum, 233 Spring St., New York, NY 10013. (800) 221-9369. Covers algology, water pollution and eutrophication.

Alice L. Kibbe Life Science Station. Western Illinois University, Department of Biological Sciences, Macomb, IL 61455. (309) 298-1553.

Alkali Metals: An Update. F.S. Messiha. ANKHO International, Syracuse, NY (315) 463-0182. 1984.

Alkalinity, pH Changes with Temperature for Waters in Industrial Systems. A.G.D. Emerson. Halsted Press, 605 3rd Ave., New York, NY 10158. (212) 850-6000. 1986. Water and wastewater technology topics.

Alkyl Amines Council. 1330 Connecticut Ave., N.W., Washington, DC 20036. (202) 659-0060.

Allergy Products Directory. Allergy Publications, Inc., Box 640, Menlo Park, CA 94026. (415) 322-1663.

Alliance Exchange. Alliance for Environmental Education Inc., Box 1040, 3421 M. St., N.W., Washington, DC 20007. (202) 797-4530. Quarterly. Publishes material relating to environmental education. Reports on national conferences held and acts as an information base to help efforts of self-supporting education and teacher training centers for environmental education.

Alliance for Acid Rain Control. 444 N. Capitol St., Suite 526, Washington, DC 20001. (202) 624-5475.

Alliance for Clean Energy. 1901 N. Ft. Myer Dr., 12th Fl., Roslyn, VA 22209. (703) 841-0626.

Alliance for Clean Energy Newsletter. Alliance for Clean Energy, 1901 N. Ft. Myer Dr., 12th Fl., Roslyn, VA 22209. (703) 841-0626. Weekly.

Alliance for Environmental Education, Inc. 10751 Ambassador Dr., No. 201, Manassas, VA 22110. (703) 335-1025. A coalition of organizations that works at the regional, state, and national level to promote environmental education.

Alliance for Responsible Chlorofluorocarbon Policy. 1901 N. Fort Myer Dr., Suite 1200, Rosslyn, VA 22209. (703) 243-0344.

The Alliance to Save Energy. 1725 K St., N.W., Suite 914, Washington, DC 20006. (202) 857-0666.

Alluvial Fans, Mudflows, and Mud Floods. Association of State Floodplain Managers, PO Box 2051, Madison, WI 53701-2051. (608) 266-1926. 1988.

Alpha Olefins Applications Handbook. George R. Lappin. Marcel Dekker, Inc., 270 Madison Ave., New York, NY 10016. (212) 696-9000; (800) 228-1160. 1989.

Altering the Earth's Chemistry: Assessing the Risks. Sandra Postel. Worldwatch Institute, 1776 Massachusetts Avenue, N.W., Washington, DC 20036-1904. 1986.

Alternate Energy Transportation. Campbell Publishing, EV Consultants, Inc., PO Box 20041, New York, NY 10025. (212) 222-0160. Monthly. Vehicles powered by natural gas, methanol, hydrogen, or direct energy from the sun.

Alternative Agriculture. National Academy of Sciences, National Research Council, 2101 Constitution Ave., NW, Washington, DC 20418. (202) 334-2000. 1989. Economic potential of alternative farming systems, methods that emphasize natural processes, limited pesticide use, and conservation of resources.

Alternative Energy. AE Publications, 205 S. Beverly Dr., Suite 208, Beverly Hills, CA 90212. (310) 273-3486. Monthly. Biomass, solar photovoltaic, solar thermal, hydrogen fuel, nuclear fusion, battery systems, and cogeneration.

Alternative Energy Digests. International Academy at Santa Barbara, 800 Garden St., Suite D, Santa Barbara, CA 93101. (805) 965-5010.

Alternative Energy Resources Organization. 44 N. Last Chance Gulch, Helena, MT 59601. (406) 443-7272.

Alternative Energy Retailer–Solid Fuel Industry Buyer's Guide Issue. Zackin Publications, Inc., 70 Edwin Ave., Waterbury, CT 06722. (203) 755-0158.

Alternative Formulations and Packaging to Reduce Use of Chlorofluorocarbons. Thomas P. Nelson. Noyes Publications, 120 Mill Rd., Park Ridge, NJ 07656. (201) 391-8484. 1990. Pressure packaging and aerosol propellants.

Alternative Fuels: Chemical Energy Resources. E.M. Goodger. John Wiley & Sons, Inc., 605 3rd Ave., New York, NY (212) 850-6000. 1980. Covers synthetic fuels.

Alternative Fuels Research Guidebook. Michael E. Crouse. U.S. Department of Energy, 1000 Independence Ave. SW, Washington, DC 20585. (202) 252-1760. 1985. Fuel characterization, instrumentation, engine and vehicle testing.

Alternative Sources of Energy. Barbara K. Harrah. Scarecrow Press, 52 Liberty St., Metuchen, NJ 08840. (908) 548-8600. 1975. A bibliography of solar, geothermal, wind, and tidal energy, and environmental architecture.

Alternative Sources of Energy. 620 Central Ave. N., Milaca, MN 56353. (612) 983-6892. An association.

Alternative Transportation Fuels. Daniel Sperling. Quorum Books, Div. of Greenwood Press, Inc., 88 Post Rd. W., Box 5007, Westport, CT 06881. (203) 226-3571. 1989. An environmental and energy solution involving synthetic fuels.

Alternatives. University of Waterloo, Environmental Studies, ES1, Rm. 325, Waterloo, ON, Canada N2L 3G1. (519) 746-2031. 1971-. Quarterly. Perspectives on society, technology, and the environment. Professional and academic level information and theory.

Alternatives for Solid Waste and Sewage Sludge Disposal. Carel C. DeWinkel. Institute for Environmental Studies, University of Wisconsin, Madison, WI 53706. 1973. Environmental specifications of refuse and refuse disposal.

Alternatives in Regulated River Management. J. A. Gore and G. E. Petts, eds. CRC Press, 2000 Corporate Blvd. N.W., Boca Raton, FL 33431. (800) 272-7737. 1989. Provides an alternative to the emphasis on ecological effects of river regulation and is a source of alternatives for managerial decision making.

Alternatives to Deforestation: Steps Toward Sustainable Use of the Amazon Rain Forest. Anthony B. Anderson, ed. Columbia University Press, 562 W. 113th St., New York, NY 10025. (212) 316-7100. 1992. Based on papers presented at an international conference in Belem, Brazil, for scientists in several fields, as well as government policy makers and representatives from foundations who are interested in exploring possible sustainable use of the world's largest rain forest, the Amazon, which is now being destroyed on an unprecedented scale.

Alternatives to the Automobile: Transport for Livable Cities. Marcia D. Lowe. Worldwatch Institute, 1776 Massachusetts Ave., N.W., Washington, DC 20036-1904. 1990.

Aluminum in Food and the Environment. Robert C. Massey. Royal Society of Chemistry, c/o CRC Press, 2000 Corporate Blvd. N.W., Boca Raton, FL 33431-9868. (800)272-7737. 1990. Looks at the adverse health effects associated with aluminum. The evidence of aluminum's involvement in both dialysis dementia and Alzheimer's disease is reviewed and biochemical mechanisms by which aluminum may exert its detrimental effects on brain tissue are discussed.

Aluminum Recycling Association. 1000 16th St., N.W., Washington, DC 20036. (202) 785-0951.

Aluminum Situation. Aluminum Association, Publications Department, 900 19th St., NW, Washington, DC 20006. Monthly. Estimated quarterly aluminum production, shipments, order, inventories, and foreign trade.

Aluminum Statistical Review. Aluminum Association, Publications Department, 900 19th St., NW, Washington, DC 20006. Annual. Ingot and mill product shipments, end-use markets, capacity, plants, scrap recovery, foreign trade, and supply and demand.

AMA Handbook of Poisonous and Injurious Plants. American Medical Association, 515 N. State St., Chicago, IL 60610. (312) 464-4818. 1985. Toxicology of poisonous plants and skin inflammation.

An Amazonian Forest. C. F. Jordan. Parthenon Pub., Casterton Hall, Carnforth, England LA6 2LA. 1990. Volume 2 in the Man and the Biosphere series published jointly with UNESCO.

Ambient Air Pollutants from Industrial Sources: A Reference Handbook. Michael J. Suess. Elsevier Science Publishing Co., 655 Avenue of the Americas, New York, NY 10010. (212) 984-5800. 1985. Adverse effects of occupational air pollutants.

Ambient Water Quality Criteria for 2, 4-Dichlorophenol. U. S. Environmental Protection Agency. National Technical Information Service, 5285 Port Royal Rd., Springfield, VA 22161. (703) 487-4650. 1980. Describes the regulations and standards criteria set by the EPA.

Ambient Water Quality Criteria for Carbon Tetrachloride. Office of Water Regulations and Standards. U.S. Environmental Protection Agency, 401 M St., SW, Washington, DC 20460. (202) 260-2090. 1980.

Ambient Water Quality Criteria for Chlorinated Naphthalene. National Technical Information Service, 5285 Port Royal Rd., Springfield, VA 22161. (703) 487-4650. 1980. Covers toxicology of naphthalene and water quality standards.

Ambient Water Quality Criteria for Endrin. U.S. Environmental Protection Agency. National Technical Information Service, 5285 Port Royal Rd., Springfield, VA 22161. (703) 487-4650. 1980.

Ambient Water Quality Criteria for Thallium. National Technical Information Service, 5285 Port Royal Rd., Springfield, VA 22161. (703) 487-4650. 1980. Covers thallium and water quality standards.

Ambio: A Journal of the Human Environment. Royal Swedish Academy of Sciences. Pergamon Microforms International, Inc., Fairview Park, Elmsford, NY 10523. (914) 592-7720. 1971-. Monthly. Publishes recent work in the interrelated fields of environmental management, technology and the natural sciences.

America in the 21st Century: The Demographic Dimension: Environmental Concerns. Population Reference Bureau, P.O. Box 96152, Washington, DC 20090-6152. Distribution of pollution by source.

America The Beautiful Fund. 219 Shoreham Bldg., N.W., Washington, DC 20005. (202) 638-1649.

American Academy of Allergy & Immunology–Membership Directory. American Academy of Allergy & Immunology, 611 E. Wells St., Milwaukee, WI 53202. (414) 272-6071.

American Academy of Clinical Toxicology. Comparative Toxicology Laboratories, Kansas State University, Manhattan, KS 66506. (913) 532-5679.

American Academy of Environmental Engineers. 130 Holiday Court, #100, Annapolis, MD 21404. (301) 266-3311.

American Academy of Environmental Medicine. Box 16106, Denver, CO 80216. (313) 622-9755.

American Academy of Environmental Medicine Newsletter. American Academy of Environmental Medicine, Box 16106, Denver, CO 80216. (303) 622-9755. Quarterly.

American Academy of Otolaryngic Allergy. 8455 Colesville Rd., Suite 745, Silver Spring, MD 20910-9998. (301) 588-1800.

American Academy of Sanitarians. 14151 91st Ct., N.E., Bothell, WA 98011. (206) 823-5810.

American Agricultural Economics Association. 80 Heady Hall, Iowa State University, Ames, IA 50011-1070. (515) 294-8700.

American Allergy Association. P.O. Box 7273, Menlo Park, CA 94026. (415) 322-1663.

American Association for Aerosol Research. 4330 East West Hwy., Ste. 1117, Bethesda, MD 20814. (301) 718-6508.

American Association for Aerosol Research Indoor Environment Program. Lawrence Berkeley Library, 1 Cyclotron Rd., Berkeley, CA 94720. (919) 541-6736. Prog. 90-3058

American Association for Cancer Education. Box 700, UAB Station, Birmingham, AL 35294. (205) 934-3054.

American Association for the Advancement of Science. 1333 H St., N.W., Washington, DC 20005. (202) 326-6400.

American Association of Avian Pathologists. University of Pennsylvania, New Bolton Center, Kennett Square, PA 19348. (215) 444-4282.

American Association of Botanical Gardens and Arboreta. 786 Church Rd., Wayne, PA 19087. (215) 688-1120.

American Association of Petroleum Geologists. Box 979, Tulsa, OK 74101. (918) 584-2555.

American Association of Petroleum Landmen. 4100 Fossil Creek Blvd., Fort Worth, TX 76137. (817) 847-7700.

American Association of Poison Control Centers. Arizona Poison and Drug Information Center, Health Sciences Center, Rm. 3204K, 1501 N. Campbell, Tucson, AZ 85725. (602) 626-7899.

American Association of State Climatologists. c/o Dr. Ken Kunkel, Midwest Region Climate Center, 2204 Griffith Dr., Champaign, IL 61820. (217) 244-8226.

American Association of Textile Chemists and Colorists–Membership Directory. Box 12215, Research Triangle Park, NC 27709. (919) 549-8141. Annual.

American Association of Zoo Keepers. Topeka Zoo, 635 Gage Blvd., Topeka, KS 66606. (913) 272-5821.

American Association of Zoological Parks and Aquariums. Rt. 88, Oglebay Park, Wheeling, WV 26003. (304) 242-2160.

American Board of Allergy and Immunology. University City Science Center, 3624 Market St., Philadelphia, PA 19104. (215) 349-9466.

American Board of Medical Toxicology. Primary Children Center, 320 12th Ave., Salt Lake City, UT 84103. (801) 521-1536.

American Board of Radiology. 300 Park, Suite 440, Birmingham, MI 48009. (313) 645-0600.

American Bureau of Metal Statistics. P.O. Box 1405, 400 Plaza Dr., Secaucus, NJ 07094. (201) 863-6900.

American Cancer Society. 1599 Clifton Rd., N.E., Atlanta, GA 30329. (404) 320-3333.

American Cancer Society Cancer Book. Doubleday & Company, Inc., 666 Fifth Ave., New York, NY 10103. (212) 765-6500.

American Cave Conservation Association. 131 Main and Cave Sts., P.O. Box 409, Horse Cave, KY 42749. (502) 786-1466.

American Cement Directory. 123 S. Third St., Allentown, PA 18105. (215) 434-5191. Annual.

American Cetacean Society. P.O. Box 2639, San Pedro, CA 90731. (213) 548-6279.

American Chemical Society. 1155 16th St., N.W., Washington, DC 20036. (202) 872-4600.

American Clean Water Association. 7308 Birch Ave., Tacoma Park, MD 20912. (301) 495-0746.

American Coal Ash Association. 1913 I St. N.W., Washington, DC 20006. (202) 659-2303.

American Coke and Coal Chemicals Institute. 1255 23rd St., N.W., Washington, DC 20037. (202) 452-1140.

American Coke and Coal Chemicals Institute–Directory and By-Laws. 1255 23rd St., N.W., Washington, DC 20037. (202) 452-1140. Annual.

American College of Allergy and Immunology. 800 E. Northwest Hwy., Suite 1080, Palatine, IL 60067. (708) 359-2800.

American College of Radiology. 1891 Preston White Dr., Reston, VA 22091. (703) 648-8900.

American College of Toxicology. 9650 Rockville Pike, Bethesda, MD 20814. (301) 571-1840.

American College of Toxicology Newsletter. American College of Toxicology, 9650 Rockville Pike, Rockville, MD 20814. (301) 571-1840. Quarterly. Information on toxicology.

American Committee for International Conservation. c/o Roger McManus, Secretary, Center for Marine Conservation, 1725 DeSales St., N.W., Washington, DC 20036. (202) 429-5609.

American Concrete Institute. P.O. Box 19150, Detroit, MI 48219. (303) 532-2600.

American Council for an Energy Efficient Economy. 1001 Connecticut Ave., N.W., Suite 535, Washington, DC 20036. (202) 429-8873.

American Council on Science and Health. 1995 Broadway, 16th Floor, New York, NY 10023. (212) 362-7044.

American Council on the Environment. 1301 20th St., N.W., Suite 113, Washington, DC 20036. (202) 659-1900.

American Dietetic Association. 216 W. Jackson Blvd., Suite 800, Chicago, IL 60606. (312) 899-0040.

American Dyestuff Reporter–Process Controls Buyers' Guide Issue. Harmon Cove Towers, Promenade A, Suite 2, Secaucus, NJ 07094. (201) 867-4200. Annual.

American Entomological Society. 1900 Race St., Philadelphia, PA 19103. (215) 561-3978.

American Environmental Laboratory. American Laboratory Postcard Deck, 30 Controls Dr., Box 870, Shelton, CT 06484-0870. (203) 926-9310. 1989-. Bimonthly. Articles dealing with the collection and analysis of environmental samples, the development of instruments and the laboratories that use them.

American Epidemiological Society. Emory University School of Medicine, Division of Public Health, 1599 Clifton Rd., N.E., Atlanta, GA 30329. (404) 727-0199.

American Farmland Trust. 1920 N St., N.W., Suite 400, Washington, DC 20036. (202) 659-5170.

American Fertilizer. Ware Bros., Philadelphia, PA Biweekly.

American Fisheries Society. 5410 Grosvenor Ln., Suite 110, Bethesda, MD 20814. (301) 897-8616.

American Forage and Grassland Council. P.O. Box 891, Georgetown, TX 78627.

American Forest Council. 1250 Connecticut Ave., N.W., Suite 320, Washington, DC 20036. (202) 463-2455.

American Forestry Association. PO Box 2000, Washington, DC 20013. (202) 667-3300. A citizen conservation organization, that was founded in 1875, to foster the protection, wise management, and enjoyment of forest resources in America and throughout the world.

American Forests: The Magazine of Trees & Forests. American Forestry Association, 1516 P St. N.W., Washington, DC 20005. (202) 667-3300. Bimonthly.

American Gas Association. 1515 Wilson Blvd., Arlington, VA 22209. (703) 841-8400.

American Genetic Association. P.O. Box 39, Buckeystown, MD 21717. (301) 695-9292.

American Geographical Society. 156 5th Ave., Suite 600, New York, NY 10010-7002. (212) 242-0214.

American Geological Institute. 4220 King St., Alexandria, VA 22302. (703) 379-2480.

American Geophysical Union. 2000 Florida Ave., N.W., Washington, DC 20009. (202) 462-6900.

American Glass Review–Glass Factory Directory Issue. 1115 Clifton Ave., Clifton, NJ 07013. (201) 779-1600. Annual.

American Heart Association. 7320 Greenville Ave., Dallas, TX 75231. (214) 373-6300.

American In-Vitro Allergy/Immunology Society. P.O. Box 459, Lake Jackson, TX 77566. (409) 297-5636.

American Independent Refiners Association. 649 S. Olive St., Suite 500, Los Angeles, CA 20005. (202) 682-8000.

American Industrial Health Council. 1330 Connecticut Ave., N.W., Suite 300, Washington, DC 20036. (202) 659-0060.

American Industrial Hygiene Association. 345 White Pond Dr., PO Box 8390, Akron, OH 44320. (216) 873-2442.

American Industrial Hygiene Association Journal. American Industrial Hygiene Association, 345 White Pond Drive, Akron, OH 44320. (216) 873-2442. Monthly. Reports relating to occupational and environmental health hazards.

American Industrial Hygiene Council Quarterly. American Industrial Health Council, 1330 Connecticut Avenue, NW, Suite 300, Washington, DC 20036. (202) 659-0060. Quarterly. Scientific issues related to proposed standards for regulating products.

American Insects: A Handbook of the Insects of America North of Mexico. Ross H. Arnett. Van Nostrand Reinhold, 1115 5th Ave., New York, NY 10030. (212) 254-3232. 1985. General taxonomic introduction and includes classification of insects by common name, families, genus, generic name, distribution and pest species.

American Institute of Biological Sciences. 730 11th St., N.W., Washington, DC 20001-4521. (202) 628-1500.

American Institute of Biomedical Climatology. 1023 Welsh Rd., Philadelphia, PA 19115. (215) 673-8368.

American Institute of Certified Planners. 1776 Massachusetts Ave., N.W., Washington, DC 20036. (202) 872-0611.

American Institute of Chemical Engineers. 345 East 47th St., New York, NY 10017. (212) 705-7338.

American Institute of Chemists. 7315 Wisconsin Ave., Bethesda, MD 20814. (301) 652-2447.

American Institute of Hydrology. 3416 University Ave., S.E., Suite 200, Minneapolis, MN 55414. (612) 379-1030.

American Institute of Mining, Metallurgical and Petroleum Engineers. 345 E. 47th St., 14th Fl., New York, NY 10017. (212) 705-7695.

American Institute of Nutrition. 9650 Rockville Pike, Bethesda, MD 20814. (301) 530-7050.

American Institute of Physics. 335 E. 45th St., New York, NY 10017. (212) 661-9404.

American Institute of Professional Geologists. 7828 Vance Dr., Suite 103, Arvada, CO 80003. (303) 431-0831.

American Iron & Steel Institute. 1101 17th St., N.W., Washington, DC 20036-4700. (202) 463-6573.

American Iron Ore Association. 915 Rockefeller Bldg., 614 Superior Ave., N.W., Cleveland, OH 44113. (216) 241-8261.

American Journal of Epidemiology. Society for Epidemiologic Research, 20007 E. Monument Street, Baltimore, MD 21205. (301) 955-3441. Biweekly. Reporting of epidemiologic studies in the U.S.

American Journal of Public Health. American Public Health Association, 1015 15th St., NW, Washington, DC 20005. (202) 789-5600. Monthly. Current news and events of the public health field.

The American Land. American Land Resource Association, Washington, DC Five times a year. Covers topics in land use and conservation.

American Land Forum. American Land Forum, Bethesda, MD Quarterly. Research and opinion on land use and conservation of natural resources.

American Land Resource Association. 1516 P St., N.W., Washington, DC 20033. (202) 265-5000.

American Littoral Society. Sandy Hook, Highlands, NJ 07732. (908) 291-0055.

American Lung Association. 1740 Broadway, New York, NY 10019. (212) 315-8700.

American Medical Association. 515 N. State St., Chicago, IL 60610. (312) 645-4818.

American Meteorological Society. 45 Beacon St., Boston, MA 02108. (617) 227-2425.

American Midland Naturalist. University of Notre Dame, Notre Dame, IN 46556. (219) 239-7481. Quarterly. Basic research in biology including animal and plant ecology, systematics and entomology, mammalogy, ichthyology, parasitology, invertebrate zoology, and limnology.

American Mining Congress. 1920 N St., N.W., Suite 300, Washington, DC 20036. (202) 861-2800.

American Mosquito Control Association. Box 5416, Lake Charles, LA 70606. (318) 474-2723.

American National Standard, Criticality Safety Criteria for the Handling, Storage and Transportation of LWR Fuel Outside Reactors. American Nuclear Society. American Nuclear Society, 555 N. Kensington Ave., La Grange Park, IL 60525. (708) 352-6611. 1984. Safety measures and standards relating to nuclear fuels.

American National Standard Guidelines for Establishing Site-Related Parameters for Site Selection and Design of an Independent Spent Fuel Storage Installation. American National Standards Institute. American Nuclear Society, 555 N. Kensington Ave., La Grange Park, IL 60525. (708) 352-6611. 1981.

American Natural Soda Ash Corporation. Eight Wright St., Westport, CT 06880. (203) 226-9056.

The American Naturalist. Americana Society of Naturalists, Business Sciences, University of Kansas, Lawrence, KS 66045. (913) 864-3763. Monthly. Contains information by professionals of the biological sciences.

American Nature Study Society. 5881 Cold Brook Rd., Homer, NY 13077. (607) 749-3655.

American Nuclear Energy Council. 410 First St., S.E., Washington, DC 20003. (202) 484-2670.

American Nuclear Society. 555 N. Kensington Ave., La Grange Park, IL 60525. (708) 352-6611.

American Oceanic Organization. National Ocean Service, Herbert C. Hoover Bldg., Rm. 4021, 14th St. and Constitution Ave., Washington, DC 20230.

American Oil and Gas Reporter–American Drilling Rig Directory Issues. National Publishers Group, Inc., Box 343, Derby, KS 67037. (316) 681-3560.

American Oil and Gas Reporter–American Well Servicing Rig Directory Issues. National Publishers Group, Inc., Box 343, Derby, KS 63037. (316) 681-3560.

American Oil Chemists Society. P.O. Box 3489, Champaign, IL 61820. (217) 359-2344.

American Oil Chemists Society Journal. The American Oil Chemists Society, P.O. Box 3489, Champaign, IL 61820. (217) 359-2344. 1917-. Monthly.

American Ornithologists' Union. Smithsonian Institution, National Museum of Natural History, Washington, DC 20560. (202) 357-1970.

American Paint and Coatings Journal–Directory of Raw Material Distributors & Manufacturers' Agents Issue. 2911 Washington Ave., St. Louis, MO 63103. (314) 534-0301. Annual.

American Paper Institute. 260 Madison Ave., New York, NY 10016. (212) 340-0600.

American Papermaker–Mill and Personnel Directory Issue. 6 Piedmont Center, Suite 300, Atlanta, GA 30305. (404) 841-3333. Annual.

American Petroleum Institute. 1220 L St., N.W., Washington, DC 20005. (202) 682-8000.

American Pharmaceutical Association. 2215 Constitution Ave., N.W., Washington, DC 20037. (202) 628-4410.

American Pheasant and Waterfowl Society. c/o Lloyd Ure, R.R. 1, Box 164-A, Granton, WI 54436. (715) 238-7291.

American Physical Society. 335 E. 45th St., New York, NY 10017. (212) 682-7341.

American Planning Association. 1776 Massachusetts Ave., N.W., Suite 704, Washington, DC 20036. (202) 872-0611.

American Plywood Association. P.O. Box 11700, Tacoma, WA 98411. (206) 565-6600.

American Plywood Association–Member and Product Directory. American Plywood Association, PO Box 11700, Tacoma, WA 98411. (206) 565-6600.

American Psychological Association. Division 34, Department of Psychology, University of Utah, Salt Lake City, UT 84112.

American Public Gas Association. 11094-D Lee Hwy., Ste. 102, Fairfax, VA 22030. (703) 352-3890.

American Public Health Association. 1015 15th St., N.W., Washington, DC 20005. (202) 789-5600.

American Public Works Association. 106 W. 11th St., Ste. 1800, Kansas City, MO 64105-1806. (816) 472-6100.

American Public Works Association Reporter. American Public Works Association, 106 W. 11th St., Ste. 1800, Kansas City, MO 64105-1806. (816 472-6100. Monthly. Articles for public works officials.

American Pulpwood Association. 1025 Vermont Ave., N.W., Suite 1020, Washington, DC 20005. (202) 347-2900.

American Radium Society. 1101 Market St., Philadelphia, PA 19107. (215) 574-3179.

American Railway Engineering Association. 50 F St., N.W., Suite 7702, Washington, DC 20001. (202) 639-2190.

American Recreation Coalition. 1331 Pennsylvania Ave., N.W., Suite 726, Washington, DC 20004. (202) 662-7420.

American Recycling Market Directory/Reference Manual. Recoup Publishing Ltd., PO Box 577, Ogdensburg, NY 13669. (315) 471-0707. Companies, centers, state and federal government agencies responsible for recycling, and industry associations.

American Registry of Certified Professionals in Agronomy, Crops and Soils. c/o American Society of Agronomy, 677 S. Segoe Rd., Madison, WI 53711. (608) 273-8080.

American Registry of Professional Entomologists. 9301 Annapolis Rd., Lanham, MD 20706. (301) 731-4541.

American Resources Group. Signet Bank Bldg., Suite 210, 374 Maple Ave. E., Vienna, VA 22180. (703) 255-2700.

American Rivers. American Rivers, 801 Pennsylvania Ave. S.E., #303, Washington, DC 20003. (202) 547-6900. 1970-. Semiannually. Reports on the activities of American Rivers, the nation's principal river-saving organization.

American Rivers, Inc. 801 Pennsylvania Ave., S.E., Suite 303, Washington, DC 20003. (202) 547-6900.

The American Rivers Outstanding Rivers List. Matthew H. Huntington. American Rivers, Inc., 801 Pennsylvania Ave. S.E., Suite 303, Washington, DC 20003. (202) 547-6900. 1991. 2d ed. A compilation of rivers across the United States which possess outstanding ecological, recreational, natural, cultural or scientific value.

American Seed Research Foundation. 601 13th N.W., Suite 570 S., Washington, DC 20005. (202) 638-3128.

American Shore and Beach Preservation Association. P.O. 279, Middletown, CA 95461. (707) 987-2385.

American Shore and Beach Preservation Association Newsletter. American Shore and Beach Preservation Association, PO Box 279, Middletown, CA 95461. (707) 987-2385. 1955-. Quarterly.

American Society for Biochemistry and Molecular Biology. 9650 Rockville Pike, Bethesda, MD 20814. (301) 530-7145.

American Society for Engineering Education. 11 Dupont Circle, Suite 200, Washington, DC 20036. (202) 293-7080.

American Society for Engineering Management. P.O. Box 820, Rolla, MO 65401. (314) 341-2101.

American Society for Environmental Education. 1592 Union St., Suite 210, San Francisco, CA 94123. (415) 931-7000.

American Society for Environmental History. Center for Technical Studies, New Jersey Institute of Technology, Newark, NJ 07102. (201) 596-3270.

American Society for Healthcare Risk Management. American Hospital Association, 840 N. Lake Shore Dr., Chicago, IL 60611. (312) 280-6425.

American Society for Microbiology. 1325 Massachusetts Ave., N.W., Washington, DC 20005. (202) 737-3600.

American Society for Surface Mining and Reclamation. 21 Grandview Dr., Princeton, NJ 24740. (304) 425-8332.

The American Society for the Prevention of Cruelty to Animals. 441 East 92nd St., New York, NY 10128. (212) 876-7700.

American Society of Agricultural Consultants. Enterprise Center, 8301 Greensboro Dr., Suite 260, McLean, VA 22102. (703) 356-2455.

American Society of Agricultural Engineers. 2950 Niles Rd., St Joseph, MI 49085. (616) 429-0300.

American Society of Agronomy. 677 South Segoe Rd., Madison, WI 53711. (608) 273-8080.

American Society of Animal Science. c/o Carl D. Johnson, 309 W. Clark St., Champaign, IL 61820. (217) 356-3182.

American Society of Civil Engineers. 345 East 47th St., New York, NY 10017. (212) 705-7496.

American Society of Consulting Arborists. 3895 Upham, No. 12, Wheatridge, CO 80033. (303) 420-9554.

American Society of Consulting Planners–Membership Directory. 1015 15th St., N.W., Suite 600, Washington, DC 20005. (202) 789-2200.

American Society of Electroplated Plastics–Directory. 1101 14th St., N.W., Suite 1100, Washington, DC 20005. (202) 371-1323. Annual.

American Society of Heating, Refrigerating and Air-Conditioning Engineers. 1791 Tullie Circle, N.E., Atlanta, GA 30329. (404) 636-8400.

American Society of Irrigation Consultants. Four Union Sq., Suite C, Union City, CA 94587. (415) 471-9244.

American Society of Landscape Architects. 4401 Connecticut Ave., N.W., Washington, DC 20008. (202) 686-2752.

American Society of Limnology and Oceanography. Virginia Institute of Marine Science, College of William and Mary, Gloucester Point, VA 23062. (804) 642-7242.

American Society of Mechanical Engineers, Solid Waste Processing Division. 345 E. 47th St., New York, NY 10017. (212) 705-7722.

American Society of Naturalists. Department of Ecology and Evolation, State University of New York, Stony Brook, NY 11794. (516) 632-8589.

American Society of Naval Engineers. 1452 Duke St., Alexandria, VA 22314. (703) 836-6727.

American Society of Parasitologists. Department of Biological Sciences, 500 W. University Ave., University of Texas, El Paso, El Paso, TX 79968. (915) 747-5844.

American Society of Petroleum Operations Engineers. PO Box 956, Richmond, VA 23207. (703) 768-4159.

American Society of Plant Physiologists. 15501 Monona Dr., Rockville, MD 20855. (301) 251-0560.

American Society of Plant Taxonomists. c/o Dr. Samuel Jones, Dept. of Botany, University of Georgia, Athens, GA 30602. (404) 542-1802.

American Society of Plumbing Engineers. 3617 Thousand Oaks Blvd., #210, Westlake, CA 91362. (805) 495-7120.

American Society of Radiologic Technologists. 15000 Central Ave., S.E., Albuquerque, NM 87123. (505) 298-4500.

American Society of Sanitary Engineering. Box 40362, Bay Village, OH 44140. (216) 835-3040.

American Solar Energy Association. 1667 K St., N.W., Suite 395, Washington, DC 20006. (202) 347-2000.

American Solar Energy Society. 2400 Central Ave. B-1, Boulder, CO 80301. (303) 443-3130.

American Trucking Associations. 2200 Mill Rd., Alexandria, VA 22314. (703) 838-1700.

American Type Culture Collection. 12301 Parklawn Drive, Rockville, MD 20852. (301) 881-2600.

American Water Resources Association. 5410 Grosvenor Lane, Suite 220, Bethesda, MD 20814. (301) 493-8600.

American Water Works Association. 6666 W. Quincy Ave., Denver, CO 80235. (303) 794-7711.

American Water Works Association–Buyers' Guide Issue. American Water Works Association, 6666 W. Quincy Ave., Denver, CO 80235. (303) 794-7711.

American Water Works Association Directory. The Association, 6666 W. Quincy Ave., Denver, CO 80235. (303) 794-7711. Annual.

American Water Works Association Encyclopedia. American Water Works Association, 6666 W. Quincy Ave., Denver, CO 80235. (303) 794-7711. 1985. Subject headings used in water resources research and literature.

American Water Works Association Journal. American Water Works Association, 6666 W. Quincy Avenue, Denver, CO 80235. (303) 794-7711. Monthly. Articles on public water supply systems.

American Water Works Association Standard for Caustic Soda. American Water Works Association, 6666 W. Quincy Ave., Denver, CO 80235. (303) 794-7711. 1988. Standards for water purification using caustic soda.

American Water Works Association Washington Report. American Water Works Association, 6666 W. Quincy Ave., Denver, CO 80235. (303) 794-7711. Monthly. News and developments affecting the water supply industry.

American Welding Institute. 10628 Dutchtown Rd., Knoxville, TN 37932. (615) 675-2150.

American Welding Society. P.O. Box 351040, 550 LeJeune Rd., N.W., Miami, FL 33135. (305) 443-9353.

American Wilderness Alliance. 7500 E. Arapahoe Rd., Suite 355, Englewood, CO 80112. (303) 694-9047.

American Wilderness Leadership School. c/o 4800 Gates Pass Rd., Tucson, AZ 85745. (606) 620-1220.

American Wind Energy Association. 777 North Capitol, NE, Suite 805, Washington, DC 20002. (202) 408-8988.

American Wood Council. 1250 Connecticut Ave., N.W., Suite 230, Washington, DC 20036. (202) 833-1595.

Americans for Nuclear Energy. 2525 Wilson Blvd., Arlington, VA 22201. (703) 528-4430.

Americans for the Environment. 1400 16th St. N.W., Washington, DC 20036. (202) 797-6665.

Americans United for a Smoke Free Society. 8701 Georgia Ave., Silver Spring, MD 20910. (202) 667-6653.

Americans United to Combat Fluoridation. 915 Stone Rd., Laurel Springs, NJ 08021. (609) 783-0013.

America's Downtowns: Growth, Politics, and Preservation. Richard C. Collins. Preservation Press, National Trust for Historic Preservation, 1785 Massachusetts Ave. NW, Washington, DC 20036. (202) 673-4058. 1991. Examines the efforts of 10 major American cities to integrate preservation values into the local policies that shape downtown growth and development.

America's Seashore Wonderlands. National Geographic Society, 17th & M Sts. NW, Washington, DC 20036. (202) 857-7000. 1985. A guide to North American coasts and seashore ecology.

America's Soil and Water. U.S. Department of Agriculture, Soil Conservation Service, 14 Independence Ave. SW, Washington, DC 20250. (202) 447-7454. 1981. Covers water supply, land use, soil ecology, soil management, and water resources development.

The Amicus Journal. Natural Resources Defense Council, 40 West 20th Street, New York, NY 10011. (212) 727-2700. Quarterly. Articles on environmental affairs.

Amine-Enhanced Photodegradation of Polychlorinated Biphenyls. J. M. Meuser. Electric Power Research Institute, 3412 Hillview Ave., Palo Alto, CA 94304. (415) 965-4081. 1982. Capacitors, soil pollution testing and electric transformers.

Ammo Operations in the Desert. Headquarters, Dept. of the Army, Washington, DC 20310. (202) 695-6153. 1990. Safety measures in the military relating to ammunition and explosives.

AMS Food Purchases. Weekly Summary. U.S. Deptartment of Agriculture, Agricultural Marketing Service, 14 Independence Ave., SW, Washington, DC 20250. (202) 447-7454. Weekly. Food industry trade, quality control and food adulteration and inspection.

AMUSE-News. Amuse, Pearringron Post, Pittsboro, NC 27312-8548. (919) 732-7306. 1982-. Quarterly. Medium for current information on arts and the environment.

Anaerobic Digestion: A Waste Treatment Technology. Elsevier Science Publishing Co., 655 Avenue of the Americas, New York, NY 10010. (212) 984-5800. 1991. Refuse and refuse disposal, biodegradation, anaerobic bacteria and sewage sludges digestion.

Analyses of Hazardous Substances in Air. A. Kettrup, ed. VCH Publishers, 303 NW 12th Ave., Deerfield Beach, FL 33442-1788. (305) 428-5566. 1991. Proceedings from the Commission for the Investigation of Health Hazards of Chemical Compounds in the Work Area. Included are 16 analytical methods for determining organic compounds and heavy metals in the air of work areas by high pressure liquid chromatography, gas chromatography, infrared spectroscopy and atomic absorption spectrometry.

Analyses of Hazardous Substances in Biological Materials. J. Angere, ed. VCH Publishers, 303 NW 12th Ave., Deerfield Beach, FL 33442-1788. (305) 428-5566. 1991. Discusses industrial hygiene and the various toxic substances involved.

Analysis and Development of a Solar Energy Regenerated Desiccant Crop Drying Facility: Phase I, Final Report. S. M. Ko, et al. Lockheed Missiles and Space Co., available from National Technical Information Service, 5285 Port Royal Rd, Springfield, VA 22161. (703) 487-4650. 1977.

Analysis and Development of Regenerated Desiccant Systems for Industrial and Agricultural Drying. D. V. Merrifield and J. W. Fletcher. National Technical Information Center, 5285 Port Royal Rd., Springfield, VA 22161. (703) 487-4650. 1977. Prepared by Lockheed Missiles and Space Company Inc., Huntsville Research Engineering Center, Huntsville, AL, under subcontract 7296, LMSC-HREC TR D568133, for Oak Ridge National Laboratory, Oak Ridge, TN.

Analysis of Army Hazardous Waste Disposal Cost Data. B. J. Kim, et al. Construction Engineering Research Lab (Army), c/o National Technical Information Service, 5185 Port Royal Rd., Springfield, VA 22161. 1991. Order number: AD-A236 654/0LDM.

Analysis of Insecticides and Acaricides. Francis A. Gunther. Interscience Publishers, New York, NY 1955. A treatise on sampling isolation, and determination, including residue methods.

Analysis of Marine Ecosystems. A. R. Longhurst. Academic Press, c/o Harcourt Brace Jovanovich Inc., 6277 Sea Harbor Dr., Orlando, FL 32887. (800) 346-8648. 1981. Topics in marine ecology.

Analysis of Pollution Controls for Bridge Painting Contracts. Lloyd Smith. National Technical Information Service, 5285 Port Royal Rd., Springfield, VA 22161. (703) 487-4650. 1991. Monitoring pollution caused by structural painting.

Analysis of Seawater. Thomas Roy Crompton. Butterworth-Heinemann, 80 Montvale Ave., Stoneham, MA 02180. (617) 438-8464. 1989.

Analysis of State Superfund Programs: 50 State Study. U.S. G.P.O., Washington, DC 20401. (202) 512-0000. 1989. Report on state Superfund hazardous waste cleanup programs.

Analysis of Urban Solid Waste Services. Ann Arbor Science, 230 Collingwood, Ann Arbor, MI 48106. 1978. System analysis and mathematical models in refuse and refuse disposal.

Analytical Aspects of Mercury and Other Heavy Metals in the Environment. R. W. Frei. Gordon and Breach Science Publishers, Inc., 270 8th Ave., New York, NY 10011. (212) 206-8900. 1975. Heavy metals and pollution measurement.

Analytical Bibliography for Water Supply and Conservation Techniques. John Boland. U.S. Army Corps of Engineers, Institute for Water Resources, Fort Belvoir, VA 22060. (703) 780-2155. 1982.

Analytical Biochemistry. Academic Press, 111 Fifth Ave., New York, NY 10003. (800) 346-8648. Covers biological and chemical topics relating to the environment.

Analytical Chemistry. American Chemical Society, 1155 16th St. N.W., Washington, DC 20036. (800) 227-5558. 1929-. Bimonthly. Articles for chemists, life scientists and engineers.

Analytical Instrumentation for the Water Industry. T. R. Crompton. Butterworth-Heinemann, Linacre House, Jordan Hill, Oxford, England OX2 8DP. Surrey (0865) 310366. 1990.

Analytical Procedures for Determining Organic Priority Pollutants in Municipal Sludges. J.S. Warner. National Technical Information Service, 5285 Port Royal Rd., Springfield, VA 22161. (703) 487-4650. Topics in water pollution abatement.

Ancient Forests of the Pacific Northwest. Elliot A. Norse. Island Press, 1718 Connecticut Ave. N.W., Suite 300, Washington, DC 20009. (202) 232-7933. 1990. Comprehensive assessment of the biological value of the ancient forests, information about how logging and atmospheric changes threaten the forests, and convincing arguments that replicated ecosystems are too weak to support biodiversity.

And the Poor Get Children: Radical Perspectives on Population Dynamics. Karen L. Michaelson. Monthly Review Press, 122 W. 27th St., New York, NY 10001. (212) 691-2555. 1981. Population, family size, and internal migration.

And Two if by Sea: Fighting the Attack on America's Coasts. Coast Alliance, Washington, DC 1986. A citizen's guide to the Coastal Zone Management Act and other coastal laws

Andrews School Asbestos Alert. Andrews Publications, Inc., PO Box 200, Edgemont, PA 19028. (215) 353-2565. Monthly. Legal proceedings, construction, and medical problems relating to exposure to asbestos in schools.

ANEUPLOIDY. Oak Ridge National Laboratory, Environmental Mutagen Information Center, Building 2001, P.O. Box 2008, Oak Ridge, TN 37831-6050. (615) 574-7871.

Aniline Association. 1330 Connecticut Ave., N.W., Washington, DC 20036. (202) 659-0060.

Animal Breeding Abstracts. C. A. B. International, 845 North Park Ave., Tucson, AZ 85719. (602) 621-7897 or (800) 528-4841. 1933-. Monthly. Abstracts covers the literature on animal breeding, genetics, reproduction and production. Includes areas of biological research such as immunogenetics, genetic engineering and fertility improvement.

Animal Disease Occurrence. C. A. B. International, Wallingford, England OX110 8DE. 44 (491) 32111.

Animal Feed Science and Technology. Elsevier Science Publishing Co., 655 Avenue of the Americas, New York, NY 10010. (212) 984-5800.

Animal Organizations and Services Directory. Kathleen A. Reece. Animal Stories Pub., 16787 Beach Blvd., Huntington Beach, CA 92647. 1990-91. Fourth edition. Devoted to animals, pets and wildlife.

Animal Protection Institute of America. 2831 Fruitridge Road, P.O. Box 22505, Sacramento, CA 95822. (916) 731-5521.

Animal Remains in Archaeology. Rosemary-Margaret Luff. Shire Publications, Cromwell House, Church St., Princes Risborough, Aylesbury, England HP17 9AJ. Bucks 1984. Methodology of archaeology relating to animal remains.

Animal Rights International. PO Box 214, Planetarium Station, New York, NY 10024. (212) 873-3674.

Animal Rights League of America. PO Box 474, New Albany, OH 43054. (614) 855-2494.

Animal Welfare Institute. P.O. Box 3650, Georgetown Sta., Washington, DC 20007. (202) 337-2333.

Animal Welfare Institute Quarterly. Animal Welfare Institute, Box 3650, Washington, DC 20007. (202) 337-2333. 1951-. Quarterly. Promotes the reduction of total pain and fear inflicted on animals by man.

Animals' Agenda. Animal Rights Networks, 456 Monroe Tpke., Monroe, CT 06468. (203) 452-9543. 1979-. Ten times a year. Magazine of animal rights and ecology. Featured are a wide range of subjects about humanity's exploitation of animals and the environment.

Animals and Alternatives in Toxicology: Present Status and Future Prospects. Michael Balls. VCH Publishers, 303 NW 12th Ave., Deerfield Beach, FL 33442-1788. (305) 428-5566. 1991. Animals and Alternatives in Toxicology conference where invited speakers gathered to recommend and discuss the alternatives.

Animals International. World Society for the Protection of Animals, 29 Perkins St., PO Box 190, Boston, MA 02130. (617) 522-7000. Monthly. Programs and issues related to animal protection and wildlife conservation.

ANJEC Report. Association of New Jersey Environmental Commissions, Box 157, Mendham, NJ 07945. (201) 539-7547. 1969-. Quarterly. Informs environmental commissioners and interested citizens about environmental issues, laws and regulations, particularly those that effect New Jersey.

An Annotated Bibliography of Coastal Zone Management Work Products. Center for Natural Areas, 1983. A compilation of State, Territory, and Federal work products via funding from the Coastal Zone Management Act of 1972, as amended by Center for Natural Areas.

Annotated Bibliography of Literature on Flue Gas Conditioning. U.S. Environmental Protection Agency, Division of Stationary Source Enforcement. U.S. Environmental Protection Agency, 401 M St., SW, Washington, DC (202) 260-2090. 1981. Covers flue gases and fly ash.

An Annotated Bibliography of Patents Related to Coastal Engineering. Robert E. Ray. National Technical Information Service, 5285 Port Royal Rd., Springfield, VA 22161. (703) 487-4650. 1979.

An Annotated Bibliography of Remote Sensing for Highway Planning and Natural Resources. Daniel L. Civco. Storrs Agricultural Experiment Station, University of Connecticut, Storrs, CT 06268. 1980.

Annotated Bibliography on Hydrology and Sedimentation. Carroll E. Bradberry. U.S. G.P.O., Washington, DC 20401. (202) 512-0000. Annual.

An Annotated Bibliography on Water Conservation. National Technical Information Service, 5285 Port Royal Rd., Springfield, VA 22161. (703) 487-4650. 1979.

An Annotated Wetland Bibliography. Wetlands Project, Massachusetts Audubon Society, South Great Rd., Lincoln, MA 01773. (617) 259-9500. 1976.

Annual Book of ASTM Standards. American Society for Testing and Materials, 1916 S. Race St., Philadelphia, PA 19103. (215) 299-5585. 1991.

Annual Data: Copper, Brass, Bronze; Copper Supply and Consumption. Copper Development Association, Greenwich Office Park 2, Box 1840, Greenwich, CT 06836-1840. Annual. Supply and consumption of copper and copper alloy.

Annual Editions: Environment. Dushkin Publishing Group, Sluice Dock, Guilford, CT 06437. (203) 453-4351. 9th ed. This volume consists of articles compiled from the public press relating to the specific subject area.

Annual Meeting Proceedings. Institute of Environmental Sciences, 940 E. Northwest Highway, Mt. Prospect, IL 60056. (708) 255-1561. Annual. Environmental simulation and environmental contamination control.

Annual Report. U.S. Environmental Protection Agency. U.S. G.P.O., Washington, DC 20401. (202) 512-0000. Annual. Data on the activities under the Superfund legislation.

Annual Report–Inhalation Toxicology Research Institute. Lovelace Foundation for Medical Education and Research, 5400 Gibson S.E., Albuquerque, NM 87108. (505) 262-7000. Annual.

Annual Report of Abandoned or Uncontrolled Hazardous Waste Disposal Sites and Hazardous Waste Remedial Fund, 1990 Appendix. Iowa Dept. of Natural Resources. National Technical Information Service, 5285 Port Royal Rd., Springfield, VA 22161. (703) 487-4650. 1991. Annual.

Annual Report of the Inhalation Toxicology Research Institute. Inhalation Toxicology Research Institute. Lovelace Biomedical and Environmental Research Institute, 5285 Port Royal Rd., Springfield, VA 22161. (703) 487-4650. 1972/73-. Annual. Deals with aerosols, poisonous gases and radioactive substances. Describes the impact on inhalation of these hazardous substances.

Annual Report of the Marine Mammal Commission. U.S. G.P.O., Washington, DC 20401. (202) 512-0000. Annual. Research on marine mammals and actions for marine mammal conservation, including international agreements.

Annual Report of the Surface Air Sampling Program. National Technical Information Service, 5285 Port Royal Rd., Springfield, VA 22161. (703) 487-4650. Annual. Results of the Environmental Measurements Laboratory (EML) sampling program for radionucleides in surface air, by month and week, used to study the effects of nuclear weapons testing and other nuclear events.

Annual Report on Abandonment or Uncontrolled Hazardous Waste Disposal Sites and Hazardous Waste Remedial Fund. Iowa Dept. of Natural Resources. National Technical Information Service, 5285 Port Royal Rd., Springfield, VA 22161. (703) 487-4650. Annual.

Annual Report on Carcinogens. Summary. U.S. Department of Health and Human Services, Public Health Service, 9000 Rockville Pike, Bethesda, MD 20892. (301) 496-4000. Annual.

Annual Report on Hazardous Materials Transportation. U.S. Department of Transportation, Research and Transportation Bureau. U.S. G.P.O., Washington, DC Annual.

Annual Report to Congress on Federal Government Energy Management and Conservation Programs, FY89. U.S. Dept. of Energy. National Technical Information Service, 5285 Port Royal Rd., Springfield, VA 22161. (703) 487-4650. Federal agency energy use and progress in meeting conservation goals.

Annual Review of Ecology and Systematics. Annual Reviews Inc., 4139 El Camino Way, Palo Alto, CA 94303-0897. (800) 523-8635. 1970-. Annual. Original articles critically assessing the significant research literature in ecology and systematics.

Annual Review of Energy. Annual Reviews Inc., 4139 El Camino Way, Palo Alto, CA 94303-0897. (800) 523-8635. Annual.

Annual Review of Pharmacology and Toxicology. Annual Reviews Inc., 4139 El Camino Way, Palo Alto, CA 94303-0897. (800) 523-8635. Annual.

Annual Statistical Report, American Iron and Steel Institute. American Iron and Steel Institute, 1133 15th St., NW, Washington, DC 20005. Annual. Industry production, finances, employment, shipments, and foreign trade.

Annual Tropical Cyclone Report. U.S. G.P.O, Washington, DC 20402-9325. (202) 512-0000. Annual. Tropical storm activity in the western Pacific and the Indian Ocean.

Antarctic Ecosystems: Ecological Change and Conservation. K.R. Kerry, ed. Springer-Verlag, 175 5th Ave., New York, NY 10010. (212) 460-1500 or (800) 777-4643. 1990. Papers from a Symposium held in the University of Tasmania, Hobart, Australia, August-September 1988. Deals with conservation of nature in the antarctic.

Antarctic Icebergs as a Global Fresh Water Resource. John Hult. RAND, 1700 Main St., Santa Monica, CA 90401. (310) 393-0411. 1973. Water supply in Antarctic regions.

Antarctica and Global Climatic Change. Colin M. Harris. Lewis Publishers, 2000 Corporate Blvd., NW, Boca Raton, FL 33431. (800) 272-7737. 1991. A guide to recent literature on climatic changes and environmental monitoring.

The Antarctica Project. 218 D St., S.E., Washington, DC 20003. (202) 544-2600.

Anthracite Industry Association. 1275 K St., N.W., Suite 1000, Washington, DC 20005. (202) 289-3223.

Anthrozoos. University Press of New England, 17 1/2 Lebanon St., Hanover, NH 03755. (603) 643-7100. 1987-. Quarterly. A multidisciplinary journal on the interactions of people, animals, and environment.

Antioch University, Environmental Studies Center. Yellow Springs, OH 45387. (513) 767-7331.

The Ants. Bert Holldobler and Edward O. Wilson. Harvard University Press, 79 Garden St., Cambridge, MA 02138. (617) 495-2600. 1990. Reviews the anatomy, physiology, social organization, ecology and natural history of ants. Illustrates each of 292 living genera of ants and provides taxonomic keys to them.

APCA Messenger. Mid Atlantic States Section, Air and Waste Management Assn., Box 2861, Pittsburgh, PA 15230. (412) 621-1090. 1970-. Three times a year.

APILIT. American Petroleum Institute, 1220 L St. N.W., Washington, DC 20005. (202) 682-8000.

APIPAT. American Petroleum Institute, 1220 L St. N.W., Washington, DC 20005. (202) 682-8000.

Appalachian Hardwood Manufacturers. Box 427, High Point, NC 27261. (919) 885-8315.

Appalachian Underground Corrosion Short Course, Proceedings. Comer, Comer Bldg., West Virginia Univ., Morgantown, WV 26506-6070. (304) 293-5695. 1956-. Annually. Provides the practical and theoretical aspects of the causes of corrosion, instrumentation, corrosion surveys, cathodic protection pipe coatings, and miscellaneous methods of corrosion control.

Application of Environmental Impact Assessment: Highways and Dams. United Nations, 2 United Nations Plaza, Salis Section Rm. DC 2-853, New York, NY 10017. (800) 553-3210. 1987.

Application of Lidar Techniques to Estimating Atmospheric Dispersion. Edward T. Uthe. National Technical Information Service, 5285 Port Royal Rd., Springfield, VA 22161. (703) 487-4650. 1980.

Applied Acoustics. Elsevier Science Publishing Co., 655 Avenue of the Americas, New York, NY 10010. (212) 989-5800. Quarterly. Acoustics of musical instruments and of sound propagation through the atmosphere and underwater.

Applied and Environmental Microbiology Journal. American Society for Microbiology, 1325 Massachusetts Avenue N.W., Washington, DC 20005. (202) 737-3600. Monthly. Articles on industrial and food microbiology and ecological studies.

Applied Catalysts. Elsevier Science Publishing Co., 655 Avenue of the Americas, New York, NY 10010. (212) 989-5800. Bimonthly. An international journal devoted to catalytic science and its applications.

Applied Ecology Abstracts Studies in Renewable Natural Resources. Information Retrieval Ltd., 1911 Jefferson Davis Highway, Arlington, VA 22202. 1975-. Monthly.

Applied Genetics News. NewsNet, Inc., 945 Haverford Rd., Bryn Mawr, PA 19010. (800) 345-1301.

Applied Isotope Hydrogeology: A Case Study in Northern Switzerland. F. J. Pearson, Jr., et al. Elsevier Science Publishing Co., Inc, 655 Avenue of the Americas, New York, NY 10010. (212) 989-5800. 1991. This is a case study in northern Switzerland about radioactive waste disposal in the ground. Includes bibliographical references and an index.

Applied Math for Wastewater Plant Operators. Joanne Kilpatrick Price. Technomic Publishing Co., 851 New Holland Ave., Box 3535, Lancaster, PA 17604. (717) 291-5609. 1991.

Applied Microbiology and Biotechnology. Springer International, 44 Hartz Way, Seacaucus, NJ 07094. (201) 348-4033. Six times a year. Covers biotechnology, biochemical engineering, applied genetics and regulation, applied microbial and cell physiology, food biotechnology, and environmental biotechnology.

Applied Science and Technology Index. H.W. Wilson Co., 950 University Ave., Bronx, NY 10452. (800) 367-6770. Formerly Industrial Arts Index.

Applied Social Sciences Index & Abstracts. Bowker-Saur Ltd. Abstracts & Indexes, 59/60 Grosvenor St., London, England W1X 9DA. 44(71)493-5841.

Applied Solar Energy. Allerton Press Inc., 150 5th Ave., New York, NY 10011. (212) 924-3950. 1965-. Six times a year.

Applying for a Permit to Destroy PCB Waste Oil. S. G. Zelenski. Center for Environmental Research Information, U.S. Environmental Protection Agency, 26 W. Martin Luther King Dr., Cincinnati, OH 45268. (513) 569-7931. 1981. Covers hazardous wastes, incineration licenses, and polychlorinated biphenyls.

Appropriate Sanitation Alternatives. John M. Kalbermatten. Johns Hopkins University Press, 701 W. 40th St., Ste. 275, Baltimore, MD 21211. (410) 516-6900. 1983. Sanitary engineering in developing countries.

APTIC. U.S. Environmental Protection Agency, CIS Project, 401 M St., S.W., Washington, DC 20460. (202) 260-2090.

Aqua II. Institution of Chemical Engineers, PPDS Department, George E. Davis Building, 165-171 Railway Terrace, Rugby, England CV21 3HQ. Warwickshire 44 (788) 78214.

Aquaculture. National Oceanic and Atmospheric Administration, National Environmental Data Referral Service, 1825 Connecticut Ave., N.W., Washington, DC 20235. (202) 673-5548.

Aquaculture Techniques: Water Use and Discharge Quality. George W. Klontz. Idaho Water Research Institute, University of Idaho, Moscow, ID 83843. Covers aquaculture techniques, fish culture, and effluent quality.

Aqualine. Water Research Center, Medmenham Laboratory, Marlow, Buckinghamshire, England SL7 2HD. Literature on water and wastewater technology.

Aqualine Abstracts. Water Research Centre. c/o Pergamon Microforms International, Inc., Fairview Park, Elmsford, NY 10523. (914) 592-7720. 1927-. Contains some 8,000 records annually on water and wastewater technology. Covers all aspects of water, wastewater, associated engineering services and the aquatic environment. Over 600 periodicals, as well as books, reports and conference proceedings and other publications from water related institutions worldwide are scanned. Also available online.

Aqualine Thesaurus 2. Joyce G. Smith and Peter G. Jennings. Water Research Centre, Ellis Horwood, Market Cross House, Cooper St., Chichester, England PO19 1EB. West Sussex 1987.

Aquanotes. Louisiana State University, Office of Sea Grant Development Center for Wetland Resources, Baton Rouge, LA 70803. (504) 385-6449. 1972-. Quarterly. Wetlands related topics covering Louisiana Sea Grant College Program research.

AQUAREF. Environment Canada, WATDOC, Inland Waters Directorate, Ottawa, ON, Canada K1A OH3. (819) 997-2324.

The Aquarium Encyclopedia. Gunther Sterba. MIT Press, 55 Hayward St., Cambridge, MA 02142. (617) 253-2884 or (800) 356-0343. 1983.

Aquasphere. New England Aquarium, Central Wharf, Boston, MA 02110. (617) 742-8830. 1963. Articles on any subject related to the world of water. Emphasis on ecology, environment, and aquatic animals.

Aquatic Botany. Elsevier, Box 211, Amsterdam, Netherlands 1000 AE. (020) 5803-911. Monthly. Covers aquatic plants and ecology.

Aquatic Chemistry Concepts. James F. Pankow. Lewis Publishers, 2000 Corporate Blvd., N.W., Boca Raton, FL 33431. (407) 994-0555 or (800) 272-7737. 1991. A basic book on water chemistry and the concepts accompanying it. Discusses thermodynamic principles, quantitative equilibrium calculations, pH as a master variable, titration of acids and bases, and other related areas.

Aquatic Cycling of Selenium. Fish and Wildlife Service. U.S. Department of the Interior, 1849 C St., NW, Washington, DC 20240. (202) 208-3171. 1988. Implications for fish and wildlife from selenium in the environment.

Aquatic Humic Substances. I. H. Suffet. American Chemical Society, 1155 16th St. N.W., Washington, DC 20036. (800) 227-5558. 1989. Influence on fate and treatment of pollutants.

Aquatic Information Retrieval. Chemical Information Systems, Inc., 7215 York Rd., Baltimore, MD 21212. (301) 321-8440. Toxic effects of more than 5000 chemicals on 2400 freshwater and saltwater organisms, with the exclusion of bacteria, birds, and aquatic mammals.

Aquatic Plant Identification and Herbicide Use Guide: Aquatic Plants and Susceptibility to `Herbicides. Howard E. Westerdahl. National Technical Information Service, 5285 Port Royal Rd., Springfield, VA 22161. (703) 487-4650. 1988.

Aquatic Plant Management Society. P.O. Box 2695, Washington, DC 20013. (301) 330-8831.

Aquatic Research Institute. 2242 Davis Court, Hayward, CA 94545. (415) 782-4058.

Aquatic Sciences and Fisheries Abstracts. Cambridge Scientific Abstracts, 5161 River Rd., Bethesda, MD 20816. (301) 961-6750. Monthly. Compiled by the United Nations Dept. of Economic and Social Affairs, the Food and Agriculture Organization of the United Nations and the Intergovernmental Oceanographic Commission with the collaboration of other agencies. Includes the broad subject areas of ecology, fisheries, marine biology, public policy, aquatic biology, and aquatic ecology.

Aquatic Station. Southwest Texas State University, H. M. Freeman Aquatic Biology Building, San Marcos, TX 78666-4616. (512) 245-2284.

Aquatic Toxicology. Elsevier Science Publishing Co., 655 Avenue of the Americas, New York, NY 10010. (212) 989-5800. 1981-. 6/year.

Aquatic Toxicology. Jerome O. Nriagu. John Wiley & Sons, Inc., 605 3rd Ave., New York, NY 10158-0012. (212) 850-6000. 1989.

Aquatic Toxicology and Risk Assessment. ASTM, 1916 Race St., Philadelphia, PA 19103. (215) 299-5400. Annual. Covers aquatic animals, aquatic plants, water pollution, and water quality bioassay.

Arboretum. University of California, Davis, Davis, CA 95616. (916) 752-2498.

The Archaeological Conservancy. 415 Orchard Dr., Santa Fe, NM 87501. (505) 982-3278.

Archbold Biological Station. P.O. Box 2057, Lake Placid, FL 33852. (813) 465-2571.

Archeological Inundation Studies: Manual for Reservoir Managers. John A. Ware. National Technical Information Service, 5285 Port Royal Rd., Springfield, VA 22161. (703) 487-4650. 1989. Excavation safety and protection measures.

Archie Carr Center for Sea Turtle Research. University of Florida, Department of Zoology, Gainesville, FL 32611. (904) 392-5194.

Architecture of Docks, Harbor Buildings, Harbors and Marinas: A Bibliography. Coppa & Avery Consultants. Vance Bibliographies, PO Box 229, 112 N. Charter St., Monticello, IL 61856. (217) 762-3831. 1984.

Archives of Clinical Ecology Journal. Clinical Ecology Publications, 3069 South Detroit Way, Denver, CO 80210. (303) 756-7880. Quarterly. Effects of the environment on human health.

Archives of Environmental Contamination. Springer-Verlag, 175 5th Ave., New York, NY 10010. (212) 460-1500. 1972-. Bimonthly.

Archives of Environmental Health: An International Journal. Heldref Publications, Helen Dwight Reid Educational Foundation, 4000 Albemarle St., NW, Washington, DC 20016-1851. Bimonthly. Documentation on the effects of environmental agents on human health.

Archives of Toxicology. Springer-Verlag, 175 5th Ave., New York, NY 10010. (212) 460-1500.

Arctic Animal Ecology. Hermann Remmert. Springer-Verlag, 175 5th Ave., New York, NY 10010. (212) 460-1500. 1980. Animal ecology in the Arctic regions.

Arctic Arthropods. H.V. Danks. Entomological Society of Canada, 393 Winston Ave., Ottawa, ON, Canada K2A 1Y8. (613) 725-2619. 1981.

Arctic Environmental Data Directory. Diane Weixler and A.C. Brown. U.S. Geological Survey, National Center, 12201 Sunrise Valley Drive, Reston, VA 22092. (703) 648-4460. 1990.

Arctic Environmental Problems. Lassi Heininen. Tampere Peace Research Institute, Tampere, Finland 1990.

Arctic Institute of North America. 2500 University Dr., N.W., University of Calgary, Calgary, AB, Canada T2N 1N4. (403) 220-7515.

Arctic Science and Technology Information System. Arctic Institute of North America, University of Calgary, 2500 University Dr., N.W., Calgary, AB, Canada T2N 1N4. (403) 220-4036.

AREAL-RTP Acid Rain System–SAD. U.S. Environmental Protection Agency, MD 75, Research Triangle Park, NC 27711. (919) 541-2184. Data collected during the course of a study of acid precipitations in the United States, Canada, and other foreign countries.

Areas of Concern. Areas of Concern, Box 47, Bryn Mawr, PA 19010. (215) 525-1129. 1971-. Monthly. Consumer, environmental and public affairs.

Arid Land Irrigation in Developing Countries. E. Barton Worthington. Pergamon Microforms International, Inc., Fairview Park, Elmsford, NY 10523. (914) 592-7720. 1977. Environmental problems and effects.

Arid Lands Newsletter. University of Arizona, 845 N. Park Ave., Tucson, AZ 85719. (602) 621-1955. 1975-. Semiannually. Brief articles on world desert problems.

Arid Lands Research Institutions: A World Directory. Barbara S. Hutchinson. Allerton Press, Inc., 150 5th Ave., New York, NY 10011. (212) 924-3950. 1988. 3d ed.

Arid Soil Research and Rehabilitation. Taylor & Francis, 1900 Frost Rd., Ste. 101, Bristol, PA 19007. (215) 785-5800. Quarterly. Scientific studies on desert, arid, and semi-arid soil research and recovery.

Aridland Watershed Management Research Unit. 2000 East Allen Road, Tucson, AZ 85719. (602) 629-6381.

ARIDLANDS. University of Arizona, Office of Arid Lands Studies, Tucson, AZ 85719. (602) 621-1955.

Arizona Environmental Law Letter. Lee Smith Publishers & Printers, Nashville, TN

Arizona Laws Relating to Environmental Quality. Michie Co., PO Box 7587, Charlottesville, VA 22906. (804) 972-7600. 1990.

Arizona-Sonora Desert Museum. 2021 N. Kinney Road, Tucson, AZ 85743. (602) 883-1380.

Arizona State University, Center for the Study of Early Events in Photosynthesis. Department of Chemistry, Tempe, AZ 85278-1604. (602) 965-1963.

Arizona Wildlife News. Arizona Wildlife Federation, 4330 N. 62nd St., #102, Scottsdale, AZ 85251. (602) 946-6160. 1965-. Monthly.

Arkansas Biotechnology Center. University of Arkansas, Biomass Research Center, Fayetteville, AR 72701. (501) 575-2651.

Arkansas Handbook on Environmental Laws. Government Institutes, Inc., 4 Research Pl., Ste. 200, Rockville, MD 20850. (301) 921-2300. 1990.

Arkansas Water Resources Research Center. University of Arkansas, 113 Ozark Hall, Fayetteville, AR 72701. (501) 575-4403.

Armstrong Oil Directories. Armstrong Oil Directory, 1606 Jackson St., Amarillo, TX 79102. (806) 374-1818.

Arnoldia. Arnold Arboretum, Harvard University, Jamaica Plain, MA 02130-2795. (617) 524-1718. 1941-. Quarterly.

The Art & Science of Composting. BioCycle, 419 State Ave., Emmaus, PA 18049. (215) 967-4135. 1988. Composting principles, processes, management, materials, and markets.

Arthropods as Final Hosts of Nematodes and Nematomorphs: An Annotated Bibliography. M.R.N. Shepard. Commonwealth Agricultural Bureaux, Wallingford, England OX10 8DE. 1974.

The Arthur Young Guide to Water and Wastewater Finance and Pricing. George A. Raftelis. Lewis Publishers, 121 S. Main St., Chelsea, MI 48118. (313) 475-8619; (800) 525-7894. 1989. Covers virtually all aspects of establishing a financial planning and management program for a water or wastewater utility. Examines the development of capital plans, alternatives for securing capital funding and the options for a user charge system.

Asbestos Abatement Report. Buraff Publications, 1350 Connecticut Ave. N.W., Washington, DC 20036. (202) 862-0990. 1987-. Biweekly. News about developments in asbestos control.

Asbestos Abatement: Risks & Responsibilities. Bureau of National Affairs, BNA PLUS, 1231 25th Street, N.W., Rm. 215, Washington, DC 20037. (800) 452-7773.

Asbestos and Silicate Pollution: Citations from the Engineering Index Data Base. Diane M. Cavagnaro. National Technical Information Service, 5285 Port Royal Rd., Springfield, VA 22161. (703) 487-4650. 1980. Deals with asbestos pollution and silicate pollution and their effects on the environment.

Asbestos Control Report. Business Publishers, Inc., 951 Pershing Drive, Silver Spring, MD 20910-4464. (301) 587-6300. Biweekly. Information on asbestos control techniques, research, and regulations. Also available online.

Asbestos Control Report. Business Publishers, Inc., 951 Pershing Dr., Silver Spring, MD 20910-4464. (301) 587-6300. Covers industry ramifications of the Asbestos Hazard Emergency Response Act of 1986, with technical information on control techniques, worksite health and safety. Online version of periodical of the same name.

Asbestos Engineering, Management and Control. Ken Cherry. Lewis Publishers, 2000 Corporate Blvd., N.W., Boca Raton, FL 33431. (407) 994-0555 or (800) 272-7737. 1988. Details of major legal issues and cost estimating methods. Also includes every aspect of abatement work from initial survey through final cleanup. In addition medical aspects, respirator use, training, sample contracts and other topics coupled with a practical approach are covered.

Asbestos in Air. Federation of American Societies for Experimental Biology, 9650 Rockville Pike, Bethesda, MD 20814. (301) 530-7000. 1980. Bibliography of environmental aspects of asbestos.

Asbestos Information Association of North America. 1745 Jefferson Davis Highway, Suite 509, Arlington, VA 22202. (703) 979-1150.

Asbestos Information Association of North American Newsletter. Asbestos Information Association/North America, 1745 Jefferson Davis Highway, Suite 509, Arlington, VA 22202. (703) 979-1150. Monthly. Issues pertaining to asbestos and health.

Asbestos Information System–AIS. U.S. Environmental Protection Agency, Office of Pesticides and Toxic Substances, 401 M St., SW, Washington, DC 20460. (202) 260-2090. Information on asbestos including chemical use, exposure, manufacturing, the human population, and environmental releases.

Asbestos Issues. PH Publishing, Inc., 760 Whalers Way Sta., 100-A., Fort Collins, CO 80525. (303) 229-0029. 1988-. Monthly. Provides coverage of the asbestos control field. Improves awareness of management issues and informs readers of risks, insurance, etc.

Asbestos: the Hazardous Fiber. Melvin A. Bernade. CRC Press, 2000 Corporate Blvd. N.W., Boca Raton, FL 33431. (800) 272-7737. 1990. An overview of the state-of-the-art of asbestos and its problems in the environment.

Asbestos Toxicity. Geraldine Nowak. National Institutes of Health, Department of Health and Human Services, 8600 Rockville Pike, Bethesda, MD 20894. (301) 496-6308. 1977.

ASFA Aquaculture Abstracts. Cambridge Scientific Abstracts, Inc., 5161 River Rd., Bethesda, MD 20816. (301) 961-6750. 1984.

Ash at Work. American Coal Ash Association, 1000 16th Street, NW, Suite 507, Washington, DC 20036. (202) 659-2303. Quarterly. Information on fly ash from the combustion of coal.

ASM International. 9639 Kinsman, Materials Park, OH 44073. (216) 338-5151.

Asphalt/Asphalt Products Directory. 5711 S. 86th Circle, Omaha, NE 68127. (402) 593-4600.

Asphalt Emulsion Manufacturers Association–Membership Directory. Three Church Circle, Suite 250, Annapolis, MD 21401. (301) 267-0023. Annual.

Asphalt Emulsions. Harold W. Muncy, ed. ASTM, 1916 Race St., Philadelphia, PA 19103-1187. (215) 299-5400. 1990. Presents practical information on asphalt emulsions technology, from laboratory methods, to mix designs, to application of materials.

Asphalt Paving Technologists. 1404 Concordia Ave., St. Paul, MN 55104. (612) 642-1350. Annual.

Asphalt Recycling & Reclaiming Association. 3 Church Cir., Suite 250, Annapolis, MD 21401. (301) 267-0023.

Assessing Ecological Risks of Biotechnology. Lev R. Ginzburg. Butterworth-Heinemann, 80 Montvale Ave., Stoneham, MA 02180. (617) 438-8464; (800) 366-2665. 1991. Presents an analysis of the ecological risk associated with genetically engineered microorganisms, organisms that, through gene splicing, have obtained additional genetic information.

An Assessment Methodology for the Environmental Impact of Water Resource Projects. Maurice L. Warner. U.S. G.P.O., Washington, DC 20401. (202) 512-0000. 1974. Environmental aspects of flood dams and reservoirs.

Assessment of Environmental Fate and Effects of Discharges from Offshore Oil and Gas Operations. U.S. Environmental Protection Agency, Office of Water Regulations and Standards, 401 M St., S.W., Washington, DC 20460. (202) 260-2090. 1985. Environmental aspects of offshore oil and gas industry.

An Assessment of Hydroelectric Pumped Storage. Dames and Moore Co. Institute for Water Resources, c/o American Public Works Association, 1313 E. 60th St., Chicago, IL 60637. (312) 667-2200. 1982. National hydroelectric power resources study.

Assessment of the Adequacy of the Calibrations Performed by Commercial Calibration Services for Ionizing Radiation Survey Instruments. R.H. Cooke. U.S. Nuclear Regulatory Commission, Washington, DC 20555. (301) 492-7000. 1986.

Assessment of the Effects of Chlorinated Seawater from Power Plants on Aquatic Organisms. R. Sung. National Technical Information Service, 5285 Port Royal Rd., Springfield, VA 22161. (703) 487-4650. Physiological effects of marine pollution and chlorine on aquatic animals.

Assistant Attorney General: Environment and Resources Division, Department of Justice. Room 2143, 10th St. and Constitution Ave., N.W., Washington, DC 20530. (202) 514-2701.

Assistant Secretary for Natural Resources and Environment. Administrative Building, 12th St. and Jefferson Dr., S.W., Washington, DC 20250. (202) 447-7173.

Associated Laboratories. 500 S. Vermont St., Palatine, IL 60067. (708) 358-7400.

Association for Arid Land Studies. c/o International Center for Arid and Semi-Arid Land Studies, Texas Tech. University, P.O. Box 41036, Lubbock, TX 79409-1036. (806) 742-2218.

Association for Composite Tanks. 3000 Chestnut St., Suite 331, Baltimore, MD 21211. (301) 235-6000.

Association for Conservation. c/o Rod Green, Missouri Dept. of Conservation, 408 S. Polk, Albany, MO 64402. (816) 726-3677.

Association for Conservation Information. PO Box 10678, Reno, NV 89520. (702) 688-1500.

Association for Rational Environmental Alternatives. 256 Alpine Rd., West Palm Beach, FL 33405. (407) 585-7841.

Association for the Care of Asthma. Jefferson Medical College, 1025 Walnut St., Rm. 727, Philadelphia, PA 19107. (215) 955-8912.

Association for the Study of Man-Environment Relations. Box 57, Orangeburg, NY 10962. (914) 634-8221.

Association of American Cancer Institutes. 666 Elm St., Buffalo, NY 14263. (716) 845-3028.

Association of American Geographers. 1710 16th St., N.W., Washington, DC 20009-3198. (202) 234-1450.

Association of American Pesticide Control Officials. Office of the Secretary, P.O. Box 1249, Hardwick, VT 05843. (802) 472-6956.

Association of American Plant Food Control Officals. Division of Reg. Services, University of Kentucky, 103 Regional Services Bldg., Lexington, KY 40546. (606) 257-2668.

Association of American Railroads. 50 F St., N.W., Washington, DC 20001. (202) 639-2333.

Association of Applied Insect Ecologists. 1008 10th St., Ste. 549, Sacramento, CA 95814. (916) 392-5721.

Association of Asbestos Cement Pipe Producers. 1745 Jefferson Davis Hwy., Suite 509, Arlington, VA 22202. (703) 979-1026.

Association of Asphalt Paving Technologists. 1404 Concordia Ave., St. Paul, MN 55104. (612) 642-1350.

Association of Biotechnology Companies. 1666 Connecticut Ave. N.W., Suite 330, Washington, DC 20009-1039. (202) 234-3330.

Association of Bituminous Contractors. 1747 Pennsylvania Ave. N.W., Suite 1050, Washington, DC 20006. (202) 785-4440.

Association of Conservation Engineers. c/o Terry N. Boyd, Alabama Dept. of Conservation, 64 N. Union St., Montgomery, AL 36130. (205) 242-3476.

Association of Conservation Engineers–Membership Directory. Association of Conservation Engineers, c/o William P. Allinder, Engineering Section, Alabama Department of Conservation and Natural Resources, 64 N. Union St., Montgomery, AL 36130. (205) 242-3476.

Association of Consulting Foresters. 5410 Grosvenor Ln., Suite 205, Bethesda, MD 20814. (301) 530-6795.

Association of Consulting Foresters–Membership Specialization Directory. Association of Consulting Foresters, 5410 Grosvenor Lane, Suite 205, Bethesda, MD 20814. (301) 530-6795.

Association of Diesel Specialists. 9140 Ward Pkwy., Kansas City, MO 64114. (816) 444-3500.

Association of Ecosystem Research Centers. Ecology Center, Logan, UT 84322-5205. (801) 750-2555.

Association of Engineering Geologists. 323 Boston Post Rd., Suite 2D, Sudbury, MA 01776. (508) 443-4639.

Association of Environmental and Resource Economists. 1616 P St., N.W., Washington, DC 20036. (202) 328-5000.

Association of Environmental and Resource Economists Newsletter. Association of Environmental and Resource Economists, 1616 P St. NW, Washington, DC 20036. (202) 328-5000. Semiannual.

Association of Environmental Engineering Professors. Department of Civil Engineering, Virginia Polytechnic Institute and State University, Blacksburg, VA 24061. (703) 231-6021.

Association of Environmental Engineering Professors Newsletter. Association of Environmental Engineering Professors, c/o Prof. Bruce Rittmann, University of Illinois, 3221 Newmark CE Laboratory, 208 N. Romine, Urbana, IL 61801. (217) 333-6964. Three/year.

Association of Federal Safety and Health Professionals. 7549 Wilhelm Dr., Lanham, MD 20706-3737. (301) 552-2104.

Association of Field Ornithologists, Inc. c/o Elissa Landre, Broadmoor Wildlife Sanctuary, Massachusetts Audubon Society, 280 Eliot St., South Natick, MA 01760. (508) 655-2296.

Association of Food Industries. 177 Main St., P.O. Box 776, Matawan, NJ 07747. (201) 583-8188.

Association of Ground Water Scientists and Engineers. PO Box 1248, Hardwick, VT 05843. (803) 472-6956.

Association of Interpretive Naturalists. P.O. Box 1892, Ft. Collins, CO 80522. (303) 491-6434.

Association of Iron and Steel Engineers. Three Gateway Center, Suite 2350, Pittsburgh, PA 15222. (412) 281-6323.

Association of Local Air Pollution Control Officials. 444 North Capitol St., N.W., Washington, DC 20001 (202) 624-7864.

Association of Metropolitan Sewerage Agencies. 1000 Connecticut Ave., N.W., Suite 1006, Washington, DC 20036. (202) 833-4653.

Association of Metropolitan Sewerage Agencies Monthly Report. Association of Metropolitan Sewerage Agencies, 1000 Connecticut Avenue, NW, Suite 1006, Washington, DC 20005. (202) 833-4653. Monthly. Data on environmental and regulatory matters.

Association of Metropolitan Water Agencies. 1717 K St., N.W., Suite 1102, Washington, DC 20036. (202) 331-2820.

Association of Midwest Fish and Wildlife Agencies. c/o John Urbain, Michigan Dept. of Natural Resources, Box 30028, Lansing, MI 48909. (517) 373-1263.

Association of Midwest Fish and Wildlife Agencies Proceedings. Michigan Department of Natural Resources, Box 30028, Lansing, MI 48909. (517) 373-1263. Annual.

Association of New Jersey Environmental Commissions. PO Box 157, 300 Mendham Rd., Mendham, NJ 07945. (201) 539-7547.

Association of Official Analytical Chemists. 2200 Wilson Blvd., Suite 400, Arlington, VA 22201-3301. (703) 522-3032.

Association of Refrigerant and Desuperheating Manufacturing. P.O. Box 180458, Casselberry, FL 32718. (407) 260-1313.

Association of Soil & Foundation Engineers. 8811 Colesville Rd., Suite G106, Silver Spring, MD 20910. (301) 563-2733.

Association of State and Interstate Water Pollution Control Administrators. 444 N. Capitol St., N.W., Suite 330, Washington, DC 20001. (202) 624-7782.

Association of State and Territorial Solid Waste Management Officials. 444 North Capitol St., N.W., Suite 388, Washington, DC 20001. (202) 624-5828.

Association of State Drinking Water Administrators. 1911 N. Fort Myer Dr., Suite 400, Arlington, VA 22209. (703) 524-2428.

Association of State Floodplain Managers. P.O. Box 2051, Madison, WI 53701-2051. (608) 266-1926.

Association of State Wetland Managers. P.O. Box 2463, Berne, NY 12023. (518) 872-1804.

Association of the State and Interstate Water Pollution Control Administrators. 444 North Capitol St., N.W., Suite 330, Washington, DC 20001. (202) 624-7782.

Association of University Environmental Health. Institute of Environmental Medicine, NYU Medical Center, 550 First Ave., New York, NY 10016. (212) 340-5280.

Association of University Fisheries and Wildlife Program Administrators. Department of Wildlife and Fisheries Sciences, Texas A & M University, College Station, TX 77843-2258. (409) 845-1261.

Asthma and Allergy Foundation of America. 1717 Massachusetts Ave., Suite 305, Washington, DC 20036. (202) 265-0265.

ASTM Standards on Benzene, Toluene, Xylene, Solvent Naptha. American Society for Testing and Materials, 1916 S. Race St., Philadelphia, PA 19103. (215) 299-5585. 1962. Standards for carcinogenicity testing.

ASTM Standards on Chromatography. ASTM, 1916 Race St., Philadelphia, PA 19103-1187. (215) 299-5400. 1989. Gas chromatography, liquid chromatography, thin-layer chromatography and stearic exclusion chromatography.

The Atlantic Barrier Reef Ecosystem at Carrie Bow Cay, Belize, I: Structure and Communities. Klaus Rutzler and Ian G. MacIntyre. Smithsonian Institution Press, 470 L'Enfant Plaza, No. 7100, Washington, DC 20560. (800) 782-4612. 1982.

Atlantic Center for the Environment. 39 S. Main St., Ipswich, MA 01938. (508) 356-0038.

Atlantic Estuarine Research Society. c/o Michael Ewing, Old Dominion University, Applied Marine Research Lab, Norfolk, VA 23529-0456. (804) 683-4195.

Atlantic Salmon Federation. P.O. Box 429, St. Andrews, NB, Canada E0G 2X0. (506) 529-4581.

Atlantic Salmon Journal. Atlantic Salmon Federation, 1435 St. Alexandre, Rm. 1030, Montreal, PQ, Canada H3A 2G4 (514) 842-8059. 1951-. Quarterly.

Atlantic Waterfowl Council. Division of Fish and Wildlife, P.O. Box 1401, Dover, DE 19903. (302) 739-5295.

An Atlas of Cardiology: Electrocardiograms and Chest X-rays. Wolfe Publishing Ltd., Brook House, 2-16 Torrington Pl., London, England WC1E 7LT. 1977. Diagnosis of cardiovascular diseases, heart radiography and electrocardiography.

The Atlas of Endangered Species. John A. Burton. Macmillan Publishing Co., 866 Third Ave., New York, NY 10022. (212) 702-2000. 1991. Animal and plant survival and the steps to save their extinction.

Atlas of Environmental Issues. Nick Middleton. Facts on File, Inc., 460 Park Ave. S., New York, NY 10016. (212) 683-2244. 1989. Includes soil erosion, deforestation, mechanized agriculture, oil pollution of the oceans, acid rain, overfishing, and nuclear power.

Atlas of Odor Character Profiles. Andrew Dravnieks. ASTM, 1916 Race St., Philadelphia, PA 19103-1187. (215) 299-5400. Analytic chemistry and odor control.

Atlas of the Environment. Geoffrey Lean, et al. Prentice Hall, Rte. 9W, Englewood Cliffs, NY 07632. (201) 592-2000. 1990. Guide to the major environmental issues around the world that makes good use of numerous maps and diagrams to present the increasing amount of information available in this field. Covers related subjects such as indigenous people and refugees, the education gap, natural and human induced disasters, wildlife trade, and migration routes.

Atlas of the United States Environmental Issues. Robert J. Mason. Maxwell Macmillan International, 866 3rd Ave., New York, NY 10022. (212) 702-2000. Describes the texture of our environmental health using maps, photographs, charts, graphs, and diagrams.

Atmosphere. Friends of the Earth, 701-251 Laurier Ave. W., Ste. 701, Ottawa, ON, Canada K1P 5J6. (613) 230-3352. 1988-. Quarterly. News and developments on stratospheric ozone depletion and ozone protection measures.

Atmosphere and Ocean: Our Fluid Environments. John G. Harvey. Artemis Press, Sedgwick Park, Horsham, England RH13 6QH. 1976. Ocean-atmosphere interaction and oceanography.

Atmosphere-Ocean Dynamics. Adrian, E. Gill. Academic Press, c/o Harcourt Brace Jovanovich Inc., 6277 Sea Harbor Dr., Orlando, FL 32887. (800) 346-8648. 1982. Geophysical topics covering ocean-atmosphere interaction.

Atmospheres. Friends of the Earth, 218 D St. SE, Washington, DC 20003. (202) 544-2600. Quarterly. Reports on ozone depletion.

Atmospheric Carbon Dioxide and the Global Carbon Cycle. U.S. Department of Energy, Office of Energy Research, Carbon Dioxide Research Division, 1000 Independence Ave., S.W., Washington, DC 20535. (202) 252-1760. Research on atmospheric carbon dioxide.

Atmospheric Chemistry: Models and Predictions for Climate and Air Quality. C. S. Sloane and T. W. Tesche. Lewis Publishers, 2000 Corporate Blvd., N.W., Boca Raton, FL 33431. (407) 994-0555 or (800) 272-7737. 1991. Discusses the chemistry of stratospheric ozone depletion and its impact and related topics.

Atmospheric Diffusion. Frank Pasquill. Halsted Press, 605 3rd Ave., New York, NY 10158. (212) 850-6000. 1983.

Atmospheric Environment. Pergamon Microforms International, Inc., Fairview Park, Elmsford, NY 10523. (914) 592-7720. 1966-. Publishes papers on all aspects of man's interactions with his atmospheric environment, including the administrative, economic and political aspects of these interactions. Air pollution research and its applications are covered, taking into account changes in the atmospheric flow patterns, temperature distributions and chemical constitution caused by natural and artificial variations in the earth's surface.

Atmospheric Motion and Air Pollution: An Introduction for Students of Engineering and Science. Richard A. Dobbins. John Wiley & Sons, Inc., 605 3rd Ave., New York, NY 10158-0012. (212) 850-6000. 1979. Atmospheric diffusion and circulation.

Atmospheric Temperature, Density and Pressure. Allen E. Cole. Meteorology Division, Air Force Geophysics Laboratory, Hanscom Air Force Base, MA 01731. (617) 377-3237. 1983. Includes atmospheric density, atmospheric pressure, and atmospheric temperature.

Atmospheric Transmission, Emission, and Scattering. Thomas G. Kyle. Pergamon Microforms International Inc., Fairview Park, Elmsford, NY 10523. (914) 592-7720.

Atomic Energy Clearing House. Congressional Information Bureau, Inc., 1325 G St., NW, Suite 1005, Washington, DC 20005. (202) 347-2275. Weekly. Peaceful uses of nuclear energy, licensing, inspection, and legislation, waste legislation, medical uses of radioactive isotopes, and new plant construction.

Atoms and Light: Interactions. John N. Dodd. Plenum Press, 233 Spring St., New York, NY 10013-1578. (212) 620-8000. 1991. Deals with electromagnetic radiation, electromagnetic interactions, light and atoms.

Auburn University, Alabama Cooperative Fish and Wildlife Research Unit. 331 Funchess Hall, Auburn, AL 36849. (205) 844-4796.

Auburn University, International Center for Aquaculture. Auburn, AL 36849-5124. (205) 826-4786.

Auburn University, Water Resources Research Institute. 202 Hargis Hall, Auburn University, AL 36849-5124. (205) 844-5080.

Audubon. National Audubon Society, 950 3rd Ave., New York, NY 10022. (212) 832-3200. 1899-. Bimonthly.

Audubon Activist. National Audubon Society, 950 3rd Ave., New York, NY 10022. (212) 832-3200. 1986-. Bimonthly. Provide the latest information on important environmental issues throughout the country.

The Audubon Society Encyclopedia of North American Birds. Alfred A. Knopf, Inc., 201 E. 50th St., New York, NY 10022. (212) 726-0600. 1980.

The Audubon Society Handbook for Butterfly Watchers. Robert Michael Pyle. Scribner Educational Publishers, 866 3d Ave., New York, NY 10022. (212) 702-2000 or (800) 257-5755. 1984. Generously illustrated includes line drawings as well as color photography. Includes information on: the size, species, life cycle, flight, habitat and range of existence of the butterflies.

Audubon Society of Rhode Island Report. Audubon Society of Rhode Island, 12 Sanderson Rd., Smithfield, RI 02917. (401) 231-6444. 1966. Bimonthly. Covers current and historical natural history and ecology topics.

Automated Biomonitoring: Living Sensors as Environmental Monitors. D. Gruber. John Wiley & Sons, Inc., 605 3rd Ave., New York, NY 10158. (212) 850-6000. 1988. Papers presented deal with conceptual and historical issues of biological early warning systems. Studies using fish as sensors are presented as well as studies using other biological sensors. Not limited to water quality monitoring alone.

Automobile Air Conditioning Equipment Directory. 5711 S. 86th Circle, Omaha, NE 68127. (402) 593-4600. Annual.

Automobile Catalytic Converters. Kathleen C. Taylor. Agency for Toxic Substances and Disease Registry, U.S. Public Health Service, 1600 Clifton Rd. NE, Atlanta, GA 30333. (404) 452-4111. 1984.

Automotive Air Pollution. U.S. Department of Health and Human Services, 200 Independence Ave. SW, Washington, DC 20201. (202) 619-0257. 1965-. Concerns automotive air pollution.

Automotive & Industrial Lubricants. FIND/SVP, 625 Avenue of the Americas, New York, NY 10011. (212) 645-4500. 1990.

Automotive Chemical Manufacturers Council. 300 Sylvan Ave., P.O. Box 1638, Englewood Cliffs, NJ 07632-0638. (201) 569-8500.

Automotive Dismantlers and Recyclers Association. 10400 Eaton Pl., Suite 203, Fairfax, VA 22030-2208. (703) 385-1001.

Automotive Exhaust Systems Manufacturers Council. 300 Sylvan Ave., Englewood Cliffs, NJ 07632. (201) 569-8500.

Automotive Fluids & Chemicals. FIND/SVP, 625 Avenue of the Americas, New York, NY 10011. (212) 645-4500. 1990.

Automotive Industry Action Group. 20200 Lahser, Suite 200, Southfield, MI 48075. (313) 358-3570.

Automotive Products Emissions Committee. 300 Sylvan Ave., Englewood Cliffs, NJ 07632. (201) 569-8500.

Automotive Refrigeration Products Institute. 5100 Forbes Blvd., Lanham, MD 20706. (301) 731-5195.

Avian Ecology. Christopher M. Perrins. Chapman & Hall, 29 W. 35th St., New York, NY 10001-2291. (212) 244-3336. 1983.

AWWA Standard for Liquid Chlorine: American National Standard. American National Standards Institute. American Water Works Association, 6666 W. Quincy Ave., Denver, CO 80235. (303) 794-7711. 1987.

B. C. Sportsmen. British Columbia Wildlife Federation, 5659 176th St., Surrey, BC, Canada V3S 4C5. Quarterly.

The Background of Ecology. Robert P. McIntosh. Carolina Biological Supply Company, 2700 York Road, Burlington, NC 27215. (919) 584-0381. 1985.

Backyard Wildlife Habitat. National Wildlife Federation, 1400 16th St. N.W., Washington, DC 20036-2266. (202) 797-6800. 1989. Backyard Wildlife Habitat program run by the National Wildlife Federation. Participants in the program create backyard havens for native fauna.

Bacteria. L. R. Hill and B. E. Kirsop, eds. Cambridge University Press, 40 W. 20th St., New York, NY 10011. (212) 924-3900; (800) 227-0247. 1991. Directory and collection of bacteria type specimens.

Bacteria in Nature. Edward R. Leadbetter. Plenum Press, 233 Spring St., New York, NY 10013-1578. (212) 620-8000. 1989.

Bacteria in Their Natural Environments. Madilyn Fletcher, ed. Academic Press Ltd., 24-28 Oval Rd., London, England NW1 7DX. (071) 2674466. 1985.

Bacterial Genetic Systems. Jeffrey H. Miller, ed. Academic Press, c/o Harcourt Brace Jovanovich Inc., 6277 Sea Harbor Dr., Orlando, FL 32887. (800) 346-8648. 1991. A volume in the Methods in Enzymology series, no. 204.

Bacterial Toxins. W. E. Van Heyningen. Charles C. Thomas Publisher, 2600 S. First St., Springfield, IL 62794-9265. (217) 789-8980. Covers bacterial toxins and antitoxins.

BAKER. St. Baker Inc., 222 Red School Lane, Phillipsburg, NJ 08865. (201) 859-2151.

Balance. National Environmental Development Association, 1440 New York Avenue, NW, Suite 300, Washington, DC 20005. (202) 638-1230. Quarterly. Impact of environmental legislation on business and industry.

Balance Report. Population Environment Balance, 1325 6th St. N.W., #1003, Washington, DC 20005. (202) 879-3000. Quarterly.

The Balance Wheel. Association for Conservation Information, c/o Roy Edwards, Virginia Game Department, 4010 W. Broad St., Richmond, VA 23230-3916. (804) 367-1000. Quarterly.

Balancing on the Brink of Extinction: The Endangered Species Act and Lessons for the Future. Kathryn A. Kohm, ed. Island Press, 1718 Connecticut Ave. N.W., Suite 300, Washington, DC 20009. (202) 232-7933. 1991. Twenty essays providing an overview of the law's conception and history and its potential for protecting the remaining endangered species.

Banishing Tobacco. William U. Chandler. Worldwatch Institute, 1776 Massachusetts Ave., N.W., Washington, DC 20036-1904. 1986.

Barrier Island Newsletter. National Wildlife Federation, 1400 16th St. N.W., Washington, DC 20036-2266. (202) 797-6800. 1980-. Quarterly. Newsletter for activists interested in the protection of America's four coasts, through the expansion of the Coastal Barrier Resources system and improvement of the National Flood Insurance Program.

Barrier Islands Coalition. 40 W. 20th St., 11th Fl., New York, NY 10011. (212) 727-2700.

Barriers to a Better Environment: What Stops Us Solving Environmental Problems?. Stephen Trudgill. Belhaven Press, 136 S. Broadway, Irvington, NY 10533. (914) 591-9111. 1990. Postulates several types of barriers that one may come across while dealing with environmental problems: technological, and economic, social, and political barriers. Suggests the importance of holistic framework for the successful development and implementation of environmental solutions.

Bartlett Arboretum. University of Connecticut, 151 Brookdale Rd., Stamford, CT 06903. (203) 322-6971.

Baseline. W. S. Dept. of Ecology, Mail stop PV-11, Olympia, WA 98504. (206) 459-6145. 1982-. Monthly. General information about ecology programs.

Baseline Data on Utilization of Low-Grade Fuels in Gas Turbine Applications. Electric Power Research Institute, 3412 Hillview Ave., Palo Alto, CA 94304. (415) 965-4081. 1981. Economic comparisons, hot component corrosion, and emissions evaluation.

Basic Acrylic Monomer Manufacturers Association. 1330 Connecticut Ave., N.W., Washington, DC 20036. (202) 659-0060.

Basic Cloning Techniques: A Manual of Experimental Procedures. R.H. Pritchard. Blackwell Scientific Publications, PO Box 87, Oxford, England OX2 0DT. 44 0865 791155. 1985.

Basic Coastal Engineering. R. M. Sorensen. John Wiley & Sons, Inc., 605 3rd Ave., New York, NY 10158-0012. (212) 850-6000. 1978. Covers ocean engineering, hydraulic structures and ocean waves.

A Basic Comparison of Lidar and Radar for Remote Sensing of Clouds. V.E. Derr. Environmental Research Laboratories, 325 Broadway, Boulder, CO 80303. 1978.

Basic Foundation. PO Box 47012, St. Petersburg, FL 33743. (813) 526-9562. Non-profit corporation that was founded to augment efforts at balancing population growth with natural resources.

Basic Lubrication Theory. Alastair Cameron. Halsted Press, 605 3rd Ave., New York, NY 10158. (212) 850-6000. 1981.

Basic Math Concepts for Water and Wastewater Plant Operators. Joanne Kirkpatrick Price. Technomic Publishing Co., 851 New Holland Ave., Box 3535, Lancaster, PA 17604. (717) 291-5609. 1991.

Basic Mechanical Maintenance Procedures at Water and Wastewater Plants. Glenn M. Tillman. Lewis Publishers, 2000 Corporate Blvd., Boca Raton, FL 33431. (407) 994-0555 or (800) 272-7737. 1991. Part Operator's Guide series. Includes standard mechanical drawing symbols for valves, gates, gate equipment, equipment lockout procedures, centrifugal pumps, positive displacement pumps, rotary pumps, coupling alignment, pumping systems, macerator blades, shear pins, lubrication, and appendices.

Basic Petroleum Data Book: Petroleum Industry Statistics. American Petroleum Institute, 1220 L St. N.W., Washington, DC 20005. (202) 682-8000. Three times a year. Oil and gas industry exploration, production, refining, demand, financial condition, prices, and reserves.

Basic Procedures for Soil Sampling and Core Drilling. W.L. Acker. Acker Drill Co., PO Box 830, Scranton, PA 18501. (717) 586-2061. 1974. Covers soil testing procedures.

Basic Science Forcing Laws & Regulatory Case Studies. Devra Lee Lewis. Environmental Law Institute, 1616 P St., NW, Suite 200, Washington, DC 20036. (202) 328-5150. 1980. Environmental aspects and toxicology of pesticides.

Bat Conservation International. PO Box 162603, Austin, TX 78716. (512) 327-9721. Bat Conservation International was established to educate people about the important role that bats play in the environment.

Battery & EV Technology. Business Communications Company, Inc., 25 Van Zant St., Norwalk, CT 06855. (203) 853-4266. Applications in the battery and electric vehicle industries.

Battling Smog: A Plan for Action. Kenneth Chilton. Center for the Study of American Business, Washington University, Campus Box 1208, One Brookings Dr., St. Louis, MO 63130-4899. (314) 935-5630. 1989.

Baylor University, Institute of Environmental Studies. B.U. Box 7266, Waco, TX 76798-7266. (817) 755-3406.

Be Your Own Power Company. David J. Morris. Rodale Press, 33 E. Minor St., Emmaus, PA 18098. (215) 967-5171; (800) 322-6333. 1983. This book is a technical aid to those entering the power production business. Stresses that conservation is cheaper than production. Includes bibliography.

Bear News. Great Bear Foundation, Box 2699, Missoula, MT 59806. (406) 721-3009. Quarterly. Covers all topics about the world's wild bears and the lands necessary for their survival. Topics include climate change, pandas, mothers and cubs, forests, and economic conflict in bear habitats.

Beaver Defenders. Unexpected Wildlife Refuge, Box 765, Newfield, NJ 08344. (609) 697-3541. 1971-. Quarterly. Newsletter about the unexpected wildlife refuge and about issues regarding beavers everywhere.

Before the Well Runs Dry. U.S. Geological Survey, 12201 Sunrise Valley Dr., Reston, VA 22092. (703) 648-4460. 1981. A handbook for designing a local water conservation plan.

Behavioral Ecology and Sociobiology. Springer-Verlag, 175 5th Ave., New York, NY 10010. (212) 460-1500. 1976-. Eight times a year. Environmental studies.

Beilstein Online. Beilstein Institute, Varrentrappsstrasse 40-42, 6000 Frankfurt am Main 90, Germany 49 (69) 79171.

Bemidji State University, Center for Environmental Studies. Bemidji, MN 56601. (218) 755-2910.

The Bench Sheet. Water Pollution Control Federation, 601 Wythe Street, Alexandria, VA 22314-1994. (703) 684-2400. Bimonthly. Articles on water and wastewater laboratory analysis.

Beneath the Bottom Line: Agricultural Approaches to Reduce Agrichemical Contamination of Groundwater. Office of Technology Assessment, U.S. Congress, Washington, DC 20510-8025. (202) 224-8996. 1991. Identifies ways to minimize contamination of ground water by agricultural chemicals.

Benedict Estuarine Research Laboratory. Academy of Natural Sciences, Benedict Avenue, Benedict, MD 20612. (301) 274-3134.

Beneficial Use of Waste Solids. Water Pollution Control Federation, 601 Wythe St., Alexandria, VA 22314-9990. (703) 684-2400. 1989. Topics in recycling examined by the Task Force on the beneficial use of waste solids.

Benzene Toxicology. S. Jackson. U.S. Department of Health and Human Services, Public Health Services, National Institutes of Health, 9000 Rockville Pike, Bethesda, MD 20892. (301) 496-4000. 1980.

Best's Safety Directory. Ambest Rd., Oldwick, NJ 08858. (201) 439-2200. Annual.

Better Times. America the Beautiful Fund, 219 Shoreham Bldg., Washington, DC 20005. (202) 638-1649. Semiannual. Local volunteer environmental action projects involving environmental design, land preservation, green plantings, and historical and cultural preservation.

Better Trout Habitat. Christopher J. Hunter. Island Press, 1718 Connecticut Ave. N.W., Suite 300, Washington, DC 20009. (202) 232-7933. 1991. Explains the physical, chemical and biological needs of trout, and shows how climate, geology, vegetation, and flowing water all help to create trout habitats. Book includes 14 detailed case studies of successful trout stream restoration projects.

Better World Society. 1100 17th St., NW, Suite 502, Washington, DC 20036. (202) 331-3770. International non-profit membership organization that attempts to increase individual awareness of global issues related to the sustainability of life on earth.

Between the Issues. Ecology Action Center, 1657 Barrington St., #520, Halifax, NS, Canada B3J 2A1. (506) 422-4311. 1975-. Bimonthly. Newsletter that deals with environmental protection, uranium mining, waste, energy, agriculture, forestry, pesticides, and urban planning.

Between Two Worlds: Science, the Environmental Movement, and Policy Choice. Lynton Keith Caldwell. Cambridge University Press, 40 W. 20th St., New York, NY 10011. (212) 924-3900; (800) 227-0247. 1990. Focuses on international and political communication regarding the environment.

Beyond 25 Percent: Materials Recovery Comes of Age. Theresa Allan, Brenda Platt, and David Morris. Institute for Local Self-Reliance, 2425 18th St, NW, Washington, DC 20009. (202) 232-4108. 1989.

Beyond 40 Percent: Record-Setting Recycling and Composting Programs. Brenda Platt, et al. Island Press, 1718 Connecticut Ave. N.W., Suite 300, Washington, DC 20009. (202) 232-7933. 1991. Produced by the Institute for Local Self-Reliance, this volume documents the operating experience of 17 U.S. communities, from small rural towns to large cities, that are recovering between 32 and 57 percent of their waste.

Beyond Cholesterol. Peter Kwiterovich. Knightsbridge Pub. Co., 701 W. 40th St., Suite 275, Baltimore, MD 21211. (410) 516-6900. 1991. Coronary heart disease prevention.

Beyond the Green Revolution. Kenneth A. Dahlberg. Plenum Press, 233 Spring St., New York, NY 10013-1578. (212) 620-8000; (800) 221-9369. 1979. The ecology and politics of global agricultural development.

Beyond Waste. Oregon Department of Environmental Quality, 811 S.W. 6th Ave., Portland, OR 97204. (503) 229-6044. Monthly.

A Bibliographic Guide to Population Geography. Wilbur Zelinsky. University of Chicago Press, 5801 Ellis Ave., 4th Fl., Chicago, IL 60637. (312) 702-7700; (800) 621-2736. 1976.

A Bibliographic Guide to Recent Research in Environmental Geology and Natural Hazards. Mark E. Richner. Vance Bibliographies, PO Box 229, 112 N. Charter St., Monticello, IL 61856. (217) 762-3831. 1981. Covers natural disasters, land use planning, and water resource development.

Bibliography and Index of Geology. American Geological Institute, 4220 King St., Alexandria, VA 22302. Monthly. Includes environmental geology and hydrogeology.

Bibliography, Environmental Geomorphology. Susan Caris. Council of Planning Librarians, 1313 E. 60th St., Chicago, IL 60637-2897. (312) 942-2163. 1975.

Bibliography of Agricultural Engineering Books. Carl W. Hall. American Society of Agricultural Engineers, 2950 Niles Rd., St. Joseph, MI 49085-9659. (616) 429-0300. 1976.

A Bibliography of Documents Issued by the GAO on Matters Related to Environmental Protection. U.S. General Accounting Office, 441 G St., NW, Washington, DC 20548. 1985.

Bibliography of Dryland Agriculture. S. Reihl. Dryland Agricultural Technical Committee, Administration Bldg. A 422, Corvallis, OR 97331. (503) 737-2513. 1980. Covers arid regions agriculture.

A Bibliography of Forest and Rangeland as Nonpoint Sources of Pollution. John M. Fowler. New Mexico State University, Cooperative Extension Service, PO Box 30001, Las Cruces, NM 88003. 1980. Covers erosion, water pollution, sedimentation, deposition, and forest and range management.

Bibliography of Liquid Column Chromatography, 1971-1973, and Survey of Applications. Elsevier Science Publishing Co., 655 Avenue of the Americas, New York, NY 10010. (212) 984-5800. 1976.

Bibliography of Livestock Waste Management. U.S. Government Printing Office, Washington, DC 20402-9325. (202) 783-3238. 1972. Covers agricultural and animal waste, manure handling, and feedlots.

Bibliography of Living Marine Resources. Food and Agriculture Organization of the United Nations, Fishery Resources and Environment Division. Research Information Unit, Fishery and Environment Division, Rome, Italy 1976.

A Bibliography of Numerical Models for Tidal Rivers, Estuaries, and Coastal Waters. University of Rhode Island, International Center for Marine Resource Development, 126 Woodward Hall, Kingston, RI 20881. (401) 792-2479.

Bibliography of Publications of the Coastal Engineering Research Center and the Beach Erosion Board. Andre Szuwalski. National Technical Information Service, 5285 Port Royal Rd., Springfield, VA 22161. (703) 487-4650. 1981. Covers coastal engineering, oceanography, and ecology.

Bibliography of the Beneficial Uses/Sewage Sludge Irradiation Project. P.S. Homann. National Technical Information Service, 5285 Port Royal Rd., Springfield, VA 22161. (703) 487-4650. 1982. Wastewater treatment by disinfection.

Bibliography of the Computer in Environmental Design. Kaiman Lee. Environmental Design and Research Center, 26799 Elena Rd., Los Altos Hills, CA 94022. 1973.

Bibliography on Coagulation and Sedimentation in Water and Sewage Treatment. U.S. Works Project Administration for the City of New York, New York, NY 1939. Selected problems in sewage treatment.

Bibliography on Disposal of Refuse from Coal Mines and Coal Cleaning Plants. Virginia E. Gleason. Industrial Environmental Research Laboratory, Office of Research and Development, U.S. Environmental Protection Agency, 242 Atlantic Ave., Raleigh, NC 27604. (919) 834-4015. 1978.

Bibliography on Regulation of Development for Stormwater Management. Bruce K. Ferguson. Vance Bibliographies, PO Box 229, 112 N. Charter St., Monticello, IL 61856. (217) 762-3831. 1978. Covers storm sewers, runoff, and drainage.

Bibliography on the Economics and Technology of Mined Land Reclamation. Henry N. McCarl. Vance Bibliographies, PO Box 229, 112 N. Charter St., Monticello, IL 61856. (217) 762-3831. 1983.

Bibliography on the International Network of Biosphere Reserves. U.S. MAB Coordinating Committee for Biosphere Reserves. United States Man and the Biosphere Program, Available from National Technical Information Service, 5285 Port Royal Rd., Springfield, VA 22161. (703) 487-4650. 1990.

The Bicycle: Vehicle for a Small Planet. Marcia D. Lowe. Worldwatch Institute, 1776 Massachusetts Ave., N.W., Washington, DC 20036-1904. 1989.

Big Bend Bulletin. Sea Grant Extension Program, 615 Paul Russell Rd., Tallahassee, FL 32301. (904) 487-3007. Quarterly. Current issues regarding fisheries, coastal processes, and marine education.

Bigelow Laboratory for Ocean Sciences, Division of Northeast Research Foundation, Inc. Mckown Point, West Boothbay Harbor, ME 04575. (207) 633-2173.

Billboards, Glass Houses, and the Law, and Other Land Use Fables: Zoning and Land Use Reflections. Richard F. Babcock. Shepard's Citations, 555 Middlecreek Pkwy., Colorado Springs, CO 80901. 1977. Citizen participation in preventing visual pollution.

Bio-Integral Resource Center. P.O. Box 7414, Berkeley, CA 94707. (415) 524-2567.

Bioanalytical Center. Washington State University, Troy Hall, Pullman, WA 99164. (509) 335-5126.

Bioassay of Endrin for Possible Carcinogenicity. National Cancer Institute, Div. of Cancer Cause and Prevention, Carcinogenesis Testing Program, NIH Bldg. 31, Room 10A 24, 9030 Old Georgetown Rd., Bethesda, MD 20892. (301) 496-7403. 1978.

Bioassay of Fenthion for Possible Carcinogenicity. Department of Health and Human Services, 200 Independence Ave. SW, Washington, DC 20201. (202) 619-0257. 1979. Covers carcinogens and organophosphorus compounds and toxicology of insecticides.

Bioassay of Hexachlorophene for Possible Carcinogenicity. National Cancer Institute, Cancer Cause and Prevention Division, 9030 Old Georgetown Rd., Bethesda, MD 20892. (301) 496-7403. 1978.

Bioassay of Malathion for Possible Carcinogenicity. National Cancer Institute, Division of Cancer Cause and Prevention, 9030 Old Georgetown Rd., Bethesda, MD 20892. (301) 496-7403. 1979. Adverse effects of malathion and carcinogens.

BioBusiness. Dialog Information Services, Inc., Marketing Dept., 3460 Hillview Avenue, Palo Alto, CA 94304. (800) 334-2564 or (415) 858-3810. Provides information based on evaluations of the economic and business aspects of biological and biomedical research.

Biocatalysis; Fundamentals of Enzyme Deactivation Kinetics. Ajit Sadana. Prentice Hall, Rte. 9 W., Englewood Cliffs, NJ 07632. (201) 592-2000; (800) 634-2863. 1991. Focuses on the chemical kinetics of enzymes in bioreactions as used in the biotechnology and chemical industries.

Biocatalysts for Industry. Jonathan S. Dordick, ed. Plenum Press, 233 Spring St., New York, NY 10013-1578. (212) 620-8000; (800) 221-9369. 1991. Contributed papers address the applications of enzymes or whole cells to carry out selective transformations of commercial importance, as biocatalysts in the food, pharmaceutical, and chemical industries. Includes general uses of biocatalysts, biocatalysts without chemical competition, emerging biocatalysts for conventional chemical processing, and future directions of biocatalysts.

Biochemical and Physiological Aspects of Ethylene Production in Lower and Higher Plants. H. Clijsters. Kluwer Academic Publishers, 101 Philip Dr., Assinippi Park, Norwell, MA 02061. (617) 871-6600. 1989. Covers ethylene synthesis and metabolism.

Biochemical Engineering and Biotechnology Handbook. Bernard Atkinson and Ferda Mavituna. Stockton Press, 257 Park Ave. S., New York, NY 10010. (212) 673-4400. 1991. Second edition. Features an increased emphasis on biotechnology. Includes data for the pharmaceutical industry, dairy and beverage industries, and the treatment of effluent water.

Biochemical Mechanisms of Paraquat Toxicity. Anne Pomeroy Autor, ed. Academic Press, c/o Harcourt Brace Jovanovich Inc., 6277 Sea Harbor Dr., Orlando, FL 32887. (800) 346-8648. 1977. Proceedings of the Iowa Symposium on Toxic Mechanisms, 1st, 1976, Iowa City, IA.

Biochemical Oxygen Demand. National Technical Information Service, 5285 Port Royal Rd., Springfield, VA 22161. (703) 487-4650. 1973.

The Biochemistry and Uses of Pesticides: Structure, Metabolism, Mode of Action, and Uses in Crop Protection. Kenneth A. Hassall. VCH Publishers, 303 NW 12th Ave., Deerfield Beach, FL 33442-1788. (305) 428-5566. 1990. Reports the progress that has been made in the last few years towards an understanding of how pesticides function, how metabolism contributes to selectivity and safety and how the development of resistance is linked to biochemistry and molecular biology.

Biocontrol of Medical and Veterinary Pests. Marshall Laird. Praeger Publishers, 1 Madison Ave., New York, NY 10010-3603. (212) 685-5300. 1981.

Bioconversion of Waste Materials to Industrial Products. A. M. Martin, ed. Elsevier Science Publishing Co., 655 Avenue of the Americas, New York, NY 10010. (212) 984-5800. 1991. Biodegradation of refuse, refuse disposal and recycling of materials.

The Biocycle Guide to Composting Municipal Wastes. JG Press, Box 351, Emmaus, PA 18049. (215) 967-4010. 1989. Covers compost, compost plants, refuse, refuse disposal, and the recycling of waste.

The Biocycle Guide to Yard Waste Composting. The Staff of Biocycle, Journal of Waste Recycling. JG Press, Box 351, Emmaus, PA 18049. (215)967-4010. 1989. Contains chapters on: planning yard waste utilization programs; collection-evaluation options and methods; cost and economics; composting yard waste with other materials; waste reduction implemented backyard composting; and collection and composting equipment.

BioCycle-Journal of Waste Recycling. The J.G. Press, Inc., Box 351, Emmaus, PA 18049. (215) 967-4135. Monthly. Articles on the reuse of sludge, waste water, and recycled products.

Biodegradability of Organic Substances in the Aquatic Environment. Pavel Pitter, et al. CRC Press, 2000 Corporate Blvd. N.W., Boca Raton, FL 33431. (800) 272-7737. 1990. Explains the principles and theories of biodegradation, primarily from an ecological standpoint. Current techniques used to evaluate the biodegradability of individual chemicals are reviewed.

Biodegradable Containers for Use in Revegetation of Highway Right-of-Way. Russell N. Rosenthal. Washington State Department of Transportation, PO Box 47300, Olympia, WA 98504-7300. (206) 705-7000. 1981. Roadside flora and roadside improvement.

Biodegradation. Kluwer Academic Publishers, 101 Philip Dr., Assinippi Park, Norwell, MA 02061-0358. (617) 871-6600. 1990-. Quarterly. Covers all aspects of science pertaining to the detoxification, recycling, amelioration or treatment of waste materials and pollutants by naturally occurring microbial strains, associations, or recombinant microorganisms.

Biodegradation of Oil Spills: Citations from the NTIS Bibliographic Database. National Technical Information Service, 5285 Port Royal Road, Springfield, VA 22161. (703) 487-4650. 1990.

Biodegradation of PCBs Sorbed to Sewage Sludge Lagoon Sediments in an Aerobic Digester. William Amdor Chantry. University of Wisconsin Press, 114 N. Murray St., Madison, WI 53715. (608) 262-8782. 1989.

Biodegradation of Toxic Wastes: Citations from the Energy Database. National Technical Information Service, 5285 Port Royal Road, Springfield, VA 22161. (703) 487-4650. 1990.

Biodeterioration Abstracts. Farnham Royal, Slough, England SL2 3BN. Quarterly.

Biodeterioration Research Titles. Biodeterioration Information Centre, University of Aston in Birmingham, Birmingham, England

Biodiversity. E. O. Wilson. National Academy Press, 2101 Constitution Ave. N.W., PO Box 285, Washington, DC 20418. (202) 334-3313. 1988.

Biodiversity in Sub-Saharan Africa and Its Islands. Simon N. Stuart, et al. International Union for Conservation of Nature and Natural Resources, Avenue du Mont-Blanc, Gland, Switzerland CH-1196. 1990. Contains a broadly based environmental strategy and outlines actions that are necessary at political, economic, social, ecological, biological, and developmental levels. Focuses on the conservation of wild species and natural ecosystems.

Biodiversity: Scientific Issues and Collaborative Research Proposals. Otto T. Solbrig. UNESCO, 7, place de Fontenoy, Paris, France F-75700. (331) 45 68 40 67. 1991. MAB Digest 9. Overview of key scientific issues and questions related to biological diversity and its functional significance.

The Biodynamic Farm. Herbert H. Koepf. Anthroposophic Press, RR 4 Box 94 A1, Hudson, NY 12534. (518) 851-2054. 1989. Deals with agricultural ecology and with the conservation of natural resources.

Biodynamics. Bio Dynamic Farming and Gardening Association, PO Box 550, Kimberton, PA 19442-0550. (215) 935-7797. Quarterly. Soil conservation and organic agriculture.

Bioenergetics of Wild Herbivores. Robert J. Hudson. CRC Press, 2000 Corporate Blvd. N.W., Boca Raton, FL 33431. (800) 272-7737. 1985. Includes ungulata, bioenergetics, and mammals.

Bioenergy and the Environment. Janos Pasztor and Lars A. Kristoferson, eds. Westview Press, 5500 Central Ave., Boulder, CO 80301. (303) 444-3541. 1990. Includes 14 contributions which addresses issues such as the demand for biomass fuels including wood, charcoal, agricultural residues, and alcohol.

Bioengineering for Land Reclamation and Conservation. University of Alberta Press, Edmonton, AB, Canada T6G 2G2. (403) 432-3254. 1980.

Bioenvironmental Systems. Donald L. Wise, ed. CRC Press, 2000 Corporate Blvd. N.W., Boca Raton, FL 33431. (407) 994-0555; (800) 272-7737. 1987. 4 vols.

Biofouling. Harwood Academic Publishers, PO Box 786, Cooper Sta., New York, NY 10276. (212) 206-8900. Quarterly.

Biofouling and Biocorrosion in Industrial Water Systems. Hans C. Flemming, ed. Springer-Verlag, 175 5th Ave., New York, NY 10010. (212) 460-1500. 1991.

Biogas and Alcohols from Biomass: January 1986-September 1990. Jean A. Larson. National Agricultural Library, 10301 Baltimore Blvd., Beltsville, MD 20705-2351. (301) 504-5755. 1990. Covers biogas and biomass chemicals.

Biogenic Amines. Pergamon Microforms International, Inc., Fairview Park, Elmsford, NY 10523. (914) 592-7720. 1984-. Bimonthly. Journal including of all aspects of research on biogenic amines and amino acid transmitters, their relating compounds and their interaction phenomena.

Biogeochemical Processes at the Land-Sea Boundary. Pierre Lasserre. Elsevier Science Publishing Co., 655 Avenue of the Americas, New York, NY 10010. (212) 989-5800. 1988. Covers biogeochemical cycles, and seashore and coastal ecology.

Biogeochemistry: An Analysis of Global Change. William H. Schlesinger. Academic Press, c/o Harcourt Brace Jovanovich Inc., 6277 Sea Harbor Dr., Orlando, FL 32887. (800) 346-8648. 1991. Examines global changes that have occurred and are occurring in our water, air, and on land, relates them to the global cycles of water, carbon, nitrogen, phosphorous, and sulfur.

The Biogeochemistry of Lead in the Environment. J. O. Nriagu. North-Holland, 655 Avenue of the Americas, New York, NY 10010. (212) 989-5800. 1978. Topics in environmental health, ecological cycles and biological effects.

Biogeochemistry of Major World Rivers. Egon T. Degens, et al. John Wiley & Sons, Inc., 605 3rd Ave., New York, NY 10158-0012. (212) 850-6000. 1991.

The Biogeochemistry of Mercury in the Environment. J.O. Nriagu. Elsevier Science Publishing Co., 655 Avenue of the Americas, New York, NY 10010. (212) 984-5800. 1979. Environmental aspects and toxicology of mercury.

Biogeography. Joy Tivy. Longman Publishing Group, 10 Bonk St., White Plains, NY 10606. (914) 993-5000. 1982. A study of plants in the ecosphere and phytogeography.

The Biogeography of Ground Beetles. G. R. Noonan, et al., eds. VCH Publishers, 303 NW 12th Ave., Deerfield Beach, FL 33442-1788. (305) 428-5566. 1991. Book summarizes knowledge about the biogeography of ground beetles of mountains and islands. It describes a diverse group of ecologically divergent species from areas of special interest to biogeographers.

Bioindications of Chemical Radioactive Pollution. D. A. Krivolutsky. Lewis Publishers, 2000 Corporate Blvd. N.W., Boca Raton, FL 33431. (800) 272-7737. 1991. Part of the Advances in Science and Technology in the USSR series.

Bioinstrumentation and Biosensors. Donald L. Wise, ed. Marcel Dekker, Inc., 270 Madison Ave., New York, NY 10016. (212) 696-9000; (800) 228-1160. 1991. Presents novel biotechnology-based microelectronic instruments, such as those used for detection of very low levels of hazardous chemicals, as well as new medical diagnostic instruments.

The Biologic and Economic Assessment of Lindane. U.S. Department of Agriculture, 14th St. & Independence Ave., SW, Washington, DC 20250. (202) 447-2791. 1980.

The Biologic and Economic Assessment of Pentachlorophenol, Inorganic Arsenicals, Creosote. U.S. Department of Agriculture, 14 Independence Ave. SW, Washington, DC 20250. (202) 447-7454. 1980. Covers wood preservative standards.

Biologic Environmental Protection by Design. David Wann. Johnson Books, PO Box 990, Boulder, CO 80306. (800) 662-2665. 1990. Provides a compendium of ideas and strategies for various environmental problems.

Biologic Markers of Air-Pollution Stress and Damage in Forests. National Academy Press, 2101 Constitution Ave, NW, PO Box 285, Washington, DC 20418. (202) 334-3313. 1989.

Biological Abstracts. BIOSIS, 2100 Arch St., Philadelphia, PA 19103-1399. (215) 587-4800. 1927-.

The Biological Alkylation of Heavy Elements. P. J. Craig and F. Glockling. Royal Society of Chemistry, Thomas Graham House Science Park, Milton Rd., Cambridge, England CB4 4WF. 1988. Covers alkylation, heavy elements, and organic compounds.

Biological and Agricultural Index. H.W. Wilson Co., 950 University Ave., Bronx, NY 10452. (800) 367-6770. 1916-. Monthly.

Biological and Electrical Effects of Power Lines: A Worldwide Research Compilation. Interdisciplinary Environmental Associates, Minneapolis, MN 1984.

The Biological Aspects of Rare Plant Conservation. Hugh Synge. John Wiley & Sons, Inc., 605 3rd Ave., New York, NY 10158-0012. (212) 850-6000. 1981.

Biological Assessment of Toxicity Caused by Chemical Constituents Eluted from Site Soils Collected at the Drake Chemical Superfund Site, Lock Haven, Clinton Co., Pennsylvania. J. Greene. National Technical Information Service, 5285 Port Royal Rd., Springfield, VA 22161. (703) 487-4650. 1991. Order number PB91-186965 LDM

Biological Conservation. David W. Ehrenfeld. Holt, Rinehart and Winston, 6277 Sea Harbor Dr., Orlando, FL 32887. (407) 345-2500. 1970.

Biological Conservation. Applied Science Publishers, 655 Avenue of the Americas, PO Box 5399, New York, NY 10163. (718) 756-6440. Quarterly. Conservation of biological and allied natural resources, plants and animals and their habitats.

Biological Control by Natural Enemies. Paul Debach and David Rosen. Cambridge University Press, 40 W. 20th St., New York, NY 10011. (212) 924-3900. 1991. Second edition. Traces the historical background of biological control and examines in detail some of the most famous examples of the discovery of natural enemies and their implementation as active successful biological control agents.

Biological Diversity: A Selected Bibliography. Beth Clewis. Vance Bibliographies, PO Box 229, 112 N. Charter St., Monticello, IL 61856. (217) 762-3831. 1990.

Biological Effects of Effluent From a Desalination Plant at Key West, Florida. William D. Clarke, et al. Federal Water Quality Administration, U.S. Dept. of the Interior, 1849 C St. NW, Washington, DC 20240. (202) 208-3171. 1970.

Biological Effects of Electromagnetic Radiation. James W. Frazer. John Wiley & Sons, Inc., 605 3rd Ave., New York, NY 10158-0012. (212) 850-6000. 1983.

Biological Effects of Heavy Metals. E. C. Foulkes. CRC Press, 2000 Corporate Blvd. N.W., Boca Raton, FL 33431. (800) 272-7737. 1990. Two volumes. Reviews general mechanisms of metal carcinogenesis. It illustrates this effect by detailed reference to some specific metals, including Cd, Co and Ni. The material illustrates the common threads running through the field of metal carcinogenesis.

Biological Effects of Oil Pollution: A Comprehensive Bibliography with Abstracts. Melvin Light. U.S. Coast Guard, Office of Research and Development, 2100 Second St., N.W., R,. 5410 C, Springfield, VA 20593. (202) 267-1042. 1978.

Biological Effects of Ultraviolet Radiation. Cambridge University Press, 40 W. 20th St., New York, NY 10011. (212) 924-3900. 1980. Physiological effect of ultraviolet radiation and radiogenetics.

Biological Husbandry. Bernard Stonehouse. Butterworth-Heinemann, 80 Montvale Ave., Stoneham, MA 02180. (617) 438-8464. 1981. A scientific approach to organic farming.

Biological Institute of Tropical America. P.O. Box 2585, Menlo Park, CA 94026. (415) 593-9024.

Biological Monitoring Techniques for Human Exposure to Industrial Chemicals. L. Sheldon. Noyes Publications, 120 Mill Rd., Park Ridge, NJ 07656. (201) 391-8484. 1986.

Biological Oceanography. Crane, Russak & Co., 70 Madison Ave., Suite 101, New York, NY 10016. (212) 725-1999. Quarterly. Marine ecology, biology, natural products, and biochemistry.

Biological Reclamation of Solid Wastes. Clarence G. Golueke. Rodale Press, 33 E. Minor St., Emmaus, PA 18098. (215) 967-5171. 1977. Compost, refuse, refuse disposal, and biological treatment of sewage.

Biological Surveys of Estuaries and Coasts. Cambridge University Press, 40 W. 20th St., New York, NY 10011. (212) 924-3900. Coastal ecology, ecological surveys, and estuarine biology.

Biological Wastewater Treatment Systems. N. J. Horan. John Wiley & Sons, Inc., 605 3rd Ave., New York, NY 10158-0012. (212) 850-6000. 1990. Introduces basic concepts of microbial growth and reactor engineering required to fully understand the design and operation of wastewater treatment systems. Topics include wastewater characteristics, microorganisms exploited in wastewater treatment, and microbial energy generation.

Biologically Active Natural Products: Potential Use in Agriculture. Horace G. Culter and Richard B. Russell, eds. American Chemical Society, 1155 16th St. N.W., Washington, DC 20036. (202) 872-4600; (800) 227-5558. 1988. Describes natural products and their potential use in agriculture.

Biology and Fertility of Soils. Springer International, 44 Hartz Way, Seacaucus, NJ 07094. (201) 348-4033. Quarterly. Biological functions, processes and interactions in soils, agriculture, deforestation and industrialization.

Biology Digest. Data Courier, Plexus Pub Inc., 143 Old Marlton Pike, Medford, NJ 08055. 1974-. Monthly. Abstracts biology periodicals.

Biology of Freshwater Pollution. C. F. Mason. Longman, Burnt Mill, Harlow, England CM20 2J6. Essex (0279) 26721. 1991. Second edition. Deals with biological effects of pollution in water and the environment.

The Biology of Marine Plants. M. J. Dring. E. Arnold, 41 Bedford Sq., London, England 1982. Deals with marine flora.

The Biology of Particles in Aquatic Systems. Roger S. Wotton, ed. CRC Press, 2000 Corporate Blvd. N.W., Boca Raton, FL 33431. (407) 994-0555; (800) 272-7737. 1990. Discusses the classification of particulate and dissolved material and sampling for these materials.

The Biology of Respiration. Christopher Bryant. E. Arnold, 41 Bedford Sq., London, England 1980. Studies in biology relating to tissue respiration.

The Biology of Seaweeds. Christopher S. Lobban. Blackwell Scientific Publications, 3 Cambridge Ctr., Ste. 208, Boston, MA 02142. (617) 225-0401. 1981. Topics in botany with special reference to marine algae.

Bioluminescence and Chemiluminescence: Instruments and Applications. Academic Press, c/o Harcourt Brace Jovanovich Inc., 6277 Sea Harbor Dr., Orlando, FL 32887. (800) 346-8648. 1986.

Biomarkers, Genetics, and Cancer. Hoda Anton-Guirgis. Van Nostrand Reinhold, 115 5th Ave., New York, NY 10003. (212) 254-3232. 1985. Covers genetic markers and familial & genetic neoplasms.

Biomarkers of Environmental Contamination. John F. McCarthy and Lee R. Shugart. Lewis Publishers, 2000 Corporate Blvd., Boca Raton, FL 33431. (800) 272-7737. 1990. Reviews the use of biological markers in animals and plants as an innovative approach to evaluating the ecological and physiological effects of environmental contamination.

Biomarkers: The 10 Determinants of Aging You Can Control. William Evans. Simon & Schuster, 1230 Avenue of the Americas, New York, NY 10020. (212) 689-7000. 1991. Covers longevity, aging and health.

Biomass and Bioenergy. Pergamon Microforms International, Inc., Fairview Park, Elmsford, NY 10523. (914) 592-7720. 1991-. Monthly. Key areas covered by this journal are: Biomass-sources, energy, crop production processes, genetic improvements, composition; biological residues: wastes from agricultural production and forestry, processing industries, and municipal sources; bioenergy processes: fermentations, thermochemical conversions, liquid and gaseous fuels, and petrochemical substitutes; bioenergy utilization: direct combustion gasification, electricity production, chemical processes, and by-product remediation. Also includes environmental management and economic aspects of biomass and bioenergy.

Biomass Bulletin. Multi-Science Publishing Co. Ltd., 107 High Street, Brentwood, Essex, England CM14 4RX. 0277-224632. Quarterly.

Biomass, Catalysts and Liquid Fuels. Technomic Publishing Co., 851 New Holland Ave., Box 3535, Lancaster, PA 17604. (717) 291-5609.

Biomass Determination–a New Technique for Activated Sludge Control. U.S. Environmental Protection Agency, 401 M St. SW, Washington, DC 20460. (202) 260-2090. 1972. Includes an analysis of sewage sludge analysis by biomass determination. Also describes sewage disposal.

Biomass Directory. Stockton Press, 257 Park Ave. S, New York, NY 10010. (212) 673-4400 or (800)221-2123.

Biomass Energy Research Association. 1825 K St., N.W., Suite 503, Washington, DC 20006. (202) 785-2856.

Biomass Handbook. Osamu Kitani and Carl W. Hall. Gordon and Breach Science Publishers, Inc., 270 8th Ave., New York, NY 10011. (212) 206-8900. 1989. Provides knowledge of biomass and related systems. Includes biomass development from the biotechnology point of view as well as recent facts on biomass.

Biomass Production Anaerobic Digestion and Nutrient Recycling of Small Benthic or Floating Seaweeds. John H. Ryther. National Technical Information Service, 5285 Port Royal Rd., Springfield, VA 22161. (703) 487-4650. Environmental aspects of aquaculture.

Biomass Research Center. University of Arkansas, Fayetteville, AR 72701. (501) 575-6299.

Biomass Yields and Geography of Large Marine Ecosystems. Kenneth Sherman. Westview Press, 5500 Central AVe., Boulder, CO 80301. (303) 444-3541. 1989. Environmental aspects of marine pollution, marine productivity, and marine ecology.

Biomaterials. FIND/SVP, 625 Avenue of the Americas, New York, NY 10011. (212) 645-4500. 1991. Examines the U.S. and worldwide markets for the following biomaterials segments–recombinant DNA pharmaceuticals; hyaluronic acid; collagen; biosensors; human skin and organ replacement; knee prosthetic devices; and new-drug delivery systems.

Biomedical and Environmental Sciences. Academic Press, 1250 6th Ave., San Diego, CA 92101. (619) 699-6742. 1988-. Quarterly. International Journal with special emphasis on scientific data and information from China.

Biomedical Engineering Society. P.O. Box 2399, Culver City, CA 90231. (213) 206-6443.

Biomedical Materials. Elsevier Advanced Technology Publications, Mayfield House, 256 Banbury Rd., Oxford, England OX2 1OH. 44 (865) 512242.

BioPatents. BIOSIS, 2100 Arch St., Philadelphia, PA 19103. (800) 523-4806.

Biophysical and Biochemical Aspects of Fluorescence Spectroscopy. Plenum Press, 233 Spring St., New York, NY 10013-1578. (212) 620-8000. 1991. Topics in biochemistry and molecular biology.

Biophysics and Physiology of Carbon Dioxide. C. Bauer. Springer-Verlag, 175 Fifth Ave., New York, NY 10010. (212) 460-1500. Carbon dioxide in the body.

Bioprocessing Technology. Mead Data Central, Inc., P.O. Box 933, Dayton, OH 45401. (800) 227-4908.

BIOQUIP. DECHEMA Deutsche Gesellschaft fuer Chemisches Apparatewesen, Chemische Technik und Biotechnologie e.V., I & D Information Systems and Databanks, Theodor-Heuss-Allee 25, 6000 Frankfurt am Main 97, Germany 970146. 49 (69) 7564-248.

Bioremediation for Marine Oil Spills. U.S. Congress, Office of Technology Assessment, 600 Pennsylvania Ave. SE, Washington, DC 20003. (202) 224-8996. 1991.

The Bioremediation Report. Bioremediation Report, 2330 Circadian Way, Santa Rosa, CA 95407. (707) 576-6222. Monthly. Devoted solely to new technical and business developments in the field of bioremediation. Incudes profiles of companies that are applying bioremediation successfully; articles on technologies; a calendar of forthcoming meetings; and summaries of recent developments.

BIOREP. Royal Netherlands Academy of Arts & Sciences, Kloveniersburgwal 29, Amsterdam, Netherlands 1011 JV. 31 (20) 222902.

Bioresource Technology. Elsevier Science Publishing Co., 655 Avenue of the Americas, New York, NY 10010. (212) 989-5800. Monthly. Disseminates knowledge in the related areas of biomass, biological waste treatment, bioscience systems analysis and in the technologies associated with production or conversion.

BioScan: The Biotechnology Corporate Directory Service. Oryx Press, 4041 N. Central at Indian School Rd., Ste. 700, Phoenix, AZ 85012-3397. (602) 265-2651.

BioScience Journal. American Institute of Biological Sciences, 730 11th Street, Nw, Washington, DC 20001-4521. (202) 628-1500. Eleven times a year. Current research, feature articles, book reviews, and new products.

Biosensors. Elizabeth A. H. Hall. Prentice Hall, Rte. 9W, Englewood Cliffs, NJ 07632. (201) 592-2000; (800) 634-2863. 1991. A basic theoretical and practical approach to understanding of biosensors.

BIOSIS Previews. BIOSIS, 2100 Arch St., Philadelphia, PA 19103-1399. (215) 587-4800. Largest and most comprehensive database of research in the life sciences. Contains citations for nearly 9000 primary research journals, monographs, reviews, symposia, preliminary reports, semi-popular journals, selected institutional reports, government reports and research communications.

Biosorption of Heavy Metals. Bohumil Volesky. CRC Press, 2000 Corporate Blvd., N.W., Boca Raton, FL 33431. (407) 994-0555; (800) 272-7737. 1990. Comprehensive multidisciplinary review of the phenomenon of biosorption and of the state of development of biosorbent materials.

Biosphere. International Society for Environmental Education, Ohio State University, 210 Kottman Hall, 2021 Coffey Rd., Columbus, OH 43210. (614) 292-2265. Three times a year. International environmental education.

Biosphere 2: The Human Experiment. John Allen. Viking, 375 Hudson St., New York, NY 10014. (212) 366-2000. 1991.

Biosphere Politics: A New Consciousness for a New Century. Jeremy Rifkin. Crown Publishing Group, 201 E. 50th St., New York, NY 10022. (212) 751-2600. 1991. Covers human ecology, nonrenewable natural resources and environmental policy.

Biosynthesis and Biodegradation of Cellulose. Candace H. Haigler and Paul J. Weimer. Marcel Dekker, Inc., 270 Madison Ave., New York, NY 10016. (212) 696-9000; (800) 228-1160. 1991. Brings together knowledge of both the synthesis and degradation of cellulose.

Biota of Freshwater Ecosystems Identification Manual. U.S. Environmental Protection Agency, 401 M St., SW, Washington, DC 20460. (202) 260-2090. 1972. Water pollution control research relating to fresh-water fauna.

BIOTECH Business. NewsNet, Inc., 945 Haverford Rd., Bryn Mawr, PA 19010. (800) 345-1301.

Biotechnological Innovations in Food Processing. Butterworth-Heinemann, 80 Montvale Ave., Stoneham, MA 02180. (617) 438-8464. 1991.

Biotechnological Slurry Process for the Decontamination of Excavated Polluted Soils. R. Kleijintjens. National Technical Information Service, 5285 Port Royal Rd., Springfield, VA 22161. (703) 487-4650. 1991.

Biotechnologie-Informations-Knoten fuer Europa. Gesellschaft fuer Biotechnologische Forschung mbH, Mascheroder Weg 1, Braunschweig-Stoeckheim, Germany 49 (531) 6181-640.

Biotechnology Abstracts. Derwent Publications Ltd., 6845 Elm St., McLean, VA 22101. (703) 790-0400. Includes material on genetic manipulation, biochemical engineering, fermentation, biocatalysis, cell hybridization, in vitro plant propagation and industrial waste management.

Biotechnology and Bioengineering. John Wiley & Sons, Inc., 605 3rd Ave., New York, NY 10158. (212) 850-6000. Monthly. Aerobic and anaerobic processes, systems involving biofilms, algal systems, detoxification and bioremediation and genetic aspects, biosensors, and cellular systems.

Biotechnology and Food Safety. Donald D. Bills. Butterworth-Heinemann, 80 Montvale Ave., Stoneham, MA 02180. (617) 438-8464. Natural control of microorganisms, detection of microorganisms, relation of the biological control of pests to food safety, and ingredients and food safety.

Biotechnology and the Environment. J. Gibbs, et al. Stockton Press, 257 Park Ave. S, New York, NY 10010. (212) 673-4400 or (800) 221-2123. 1987. Overview of the regulatory legislation in biotechnology.

Biotechnology Application in Hazardous Waste Treatment. Gordon Lewandowski. Engineering Foundation, 345 E. 47th St., New York, NY 10017. (212) 705-7835. 1989. Trends in hazardous waste treatment using biotechnological methods.

Biotechnology Center. University of Connecticut, 184 Auditorium Rd., Storrs, CT 06269-3149. (203) 486-5011.

The Biotechnology Directory. J. Coombs and Y. R. Alston. Stockton Press, 257 Park Ave. S., New York, NY 10010. (212) 673-4400. 1992. Provides information on more than 10,000 companies, research centers, and academic institutions involved in new and established technologies, more than 2500 of which are in U.S. and Canada. There are 500 product codes to locate companies and a useful index of organizations.

Biotechnology Engineers: Biographical Directory. OMEC International, Inc., 727 15th St.,N.W., Washington, DC 20005. (202) 639-8900.

Biotechnology for Biological Control of Pests and Vectors. Karl Maramorosch. CRC Press, 2000 Corporate Blvd. N.W., Boca Raton, FL 33431. (407) 994-0555; (800) 272-7737. 1991.

Biotechnology Glossary. Elsevier Science Publishing Co., 655 Avenue of the Americas, New York, NY 10010. (212) 989-5800. 1990. Glossary originally conceived as an aid to translators faced with technical texts relating to biotechnology. Text in nine languages including English, French, German, Italian, Nedelandse, Dansk, Spanish, Portuguese, and Greek. Deals with sections on molecular biology, physiology, biochemistry, and biochemical techniques, genetic engineering, enzymology, pharmacology, immunology, plant genetics, biomass, and scientific and technical applications.

Biotechnology Guide Japan. Stockton Press, 257 Park Ave. S, New York, NY 10010. (212) 673-4400 or (800) 221-2123. 1990. Source of Who's Who and What's What in Japanese biotechnology industry.

Biotechnology Newswatch. McGraw-Hill Science & Engineering Books, 11 W. 19th St., New York, NY 10011. (212) 337-6010.

Biotechnology Perspective. FIND/SVP, 625 Avenue of the Americas, New York, NY 10011. (212) 645-4500. 1991. Analyzes 1990 sales and indicates companies receiving the most revenues from product sales and R&D.

Biotechnology Research Abstracts. Cambridge Scientific Abstracts, 5161 River Rd., Bethesda, MD 20816. (301) 961-6750. Monthly. Includes such broad areas as genetic intervention, biochemical genetics, and microbiological techniques.

Bioworld. BioWorld, 217 S. B St., San Mateo, CA 94401-9805. (800) 879-8790. Bioworld is a division of Bio Publishing, Inc.

Bird Conservation. University of Wisconsin Press, 114 N. Murray St., Madison, WI 53715. (608) 262-8782. Annual. Topics relating to the protection of birds of the United States, including endangered species.

Birds and Power Lines: A Bibliography. Charles A. Goulty. Council of Planning Librarians, 1313 E. 60th St., Chicago, IL 60637-2897. (312) 942-2163. 1988. Bird mortality due to electric lines.

Bismuth Toxicology. National Institutes of Health, National Library of Medicine, Department of Health and Human Services, 8600 Rockville Pike, Bethesda, MD 20894. (301) 496-6308. 1977.

Black Carbon in the Environment. John Wiley and Sons, 605 Third Ave., New York, NY 10158-0012. (212) 850-6000. Environmental chemistry and environmental aspects of soot.

Blandy Experimental Farm and Orland E. White Arboretum. State Arboretum of Virginia, P.O. Box 175, Boyce, VA 22620. (703) 837-1758.

Blastfurnace and Steel Slag. A.R. Lee. John Wiley & Sons, Inc., 605 3rd Ave., New York, NY 10158-0012. (212) 850-6000. 1974. Covers production, properties and uses of slag.

Blodgett Forest Research Station. University of California, Berkeley, 4531 Blodgett Forest Road, Georgetown, CA 95634. (916) 333-4475.

Blue Book and Catalog Edition of Soap and Chemical Specialties. McNairr-Dorland Co., 101 W. 31st, New York, NY 10001. 1955-. Annually.

Blue Goose Flyer. National Wildlife Refuge, Box 124, Winona, MN 55987. (612) 447-5586. 1975-. Quarterly. Wildlife refuge system management news.

Blueprint for a Green Economy: A Report. David William Pearce. Earthscan, 3 Endsleigh St., London, England 071-388 2117. 1989. Covers environmental policy, natural resources, and economic policy.

Blueprint for a Green Planet: Your Practical Guide to Restoring the World's Environment. John Seymour and Herbert Giraardet. Prentice Hall, Rte. 9W, Englewood Cliffs, NJ 07632. (201) 592-2000; (800) 634-2863. 1987. Background information and analysis of the root causes of pollution and waste in contemporary society.

Blueprint for the Environment: A Plan for Federal Action. T. Alan, ed. Howe Brothers, Box 6394, Salt Lake City, UT 84106. (801) 485-7409. 1989.

BNA Environment Daily. Bureau of National Affairs, BNA PLUS, 1231 25th St., N.W., Rm. 215, Washington, DC 20037. (800) 452-7773.

BNA International Environment Report. Bureau of National Affairs, BNA PLUS, 1231 25th St., N.W., Rm. 215, Washington, DC 20037. (800) 452-7773.

BNA Toxics Law Daily. Bureau of National Affairs, BNA PLUS, 1231 25th St., N.W., Rm. 215, Washington, DC 20037. (800) 454-7773.

BNA's National Environmental Watch. Bureau of National Affairs, BNA Plus, 1231 25th St, NW, Washington, DC 20037. (202) 452-4200. Weekly. News, technological reviews, and regulatory information regarding industry's impact on the environment.

Board of Certified Hazard Control Management. 8009 Carita Ct., Bethesda, MD 20817. (301) 984-8969.

Board of Land and Natural Resources: Natural Resources. Chairman, 1151 Punchbowl St., Honolulu, HI 96813. (808) 548-6550.

Bodega Marine Laboratory. University of California, PO Box 247, Bodega Bay, CA 94923. (707) 875-2010.

Bolton Institute for a Sustainable Future, Inc. 4 Linden Square, Wellesley, MA 02181. (617) 235-5320.

Book of Lists for Regulated Hazardous Substances. Government Institutes, Inc., 4 Research Pl., Ste. 200, Rockville, MD 20850. (301) 921-2300. 1991. Convenient source of the most frequently referenced lists for environmental compliance and regulatory information.

Boone and Crockett Club. 241 S. Farley Blvd., Dumfries, VA 22026. (703) 221-1888.

Born Free News. Elsa Wild Animal Appeal, U.S.A., Box 4572, North Hollywood, CA 91617-0572. (818) 761-8387. 1969-. News about wildlife.

Borrowed Earth, Borrowed Time: Healing America's Chemical Wounds. Glenn E. Schweitzer. Plenum Press, 233 Spring St., New York, NY 10013-1578. (212) 620-8000; (800) 221-9369. 1991. Deals with chemical contamination and the problem of industrial dumping.

Boston College Environmental Affairs Law Review. Boston College Law School, 885 Centre Street, Newton Centre, MA 02159. (617) 552-8000. Quarterly. Forum for diversity of environmental issues.

Boston University, Center for Energy and Environmental Studies. 675 Commonwealth Avenue, Boston, MA 02215. (617) 353-3083.

Boston University, Marine Program. Marine Biology Laboratory, Woods Hole, MA 02543. (508) 548-3705.

Botanical Herbarium. University of Cincinnati, Department of Biological Sciences, Cincinnati, OH 45221-0006. (513) 556-9761.

Botanical Society of America. c/o Christopher Haufler, Department of Botany, University of Kansas, Lawrence, KS 66045-2106. (913) 864-4301.

Bottle/Can Recycling Update. Resource Recycling, Box 10540, Portland, OR 97210. (503) 227-1319. 1990-. Monthly. Includes all recycling such as glass and plastic bottles, and steel and aluminum cans. Also covers market trends, economics collection processes, equipment news, and industry actions.

Bound Pesticide Residues. Shahamat U. Khan. CRC Press, 2000 Corporate Blvd. N.W., Boca Raton, FL 33431. (800) 272-7737. 1991. Overview of pesticide residues in soils and plants, its bioavailability, isolation and identification, toxicological significance and the regulatory aspects.

Bounty News. Bounty Information Service, Stephens College Post Office, Columbia, MO 65215. (314) 876-7186. Biannual. Wildlife bounties in North America and methods for removing bounties.

Bowdoin College, Marine Station. Department of Chemistry, Brunswick, ME 04011. (207) 725-3166.

Boyce Thompson Institute for Plant Research. Cornell University, Tower Road, Ithaca, NY 14853. (607) 254-1234.

Brandeis University, Photobiology Group. Biology Department, Waltham, MA 02254. (617) 736-2685.

Breaking New Ground. Gifford Pinchot. Island Press, 1718 Connecticut Ave. N.W., Suite 300, Washington, DC 20009. (202) 232-7933. 1987. Expounds the views that our precious forests should be managed for maximum yield with minimum long-term negative impact.

Breathe-Free Plan to Stop Smoking. 12501 Old Columbia Pike, Silver Spring, MD 20904-6600.

Breeders Directory. American Minor Breeds Conservancy, PO Box 477, Pittsboro, NC 27312. (919) 542-5704. Member breeders of endangered and uncommon livestock varieties.

Breeding Plants for Less Favorable Environments. M. N. Christiansen. R.E. Krieger, 605 3rd Ave., New York, NY 10158-0012. (212) 850-6000. 1990. Effects of stress on plants.

Bretherick's Handbook of Reactive Chemical Hazards. L. Bretherick. Butterworth-Heinemann, 80 Montvale Ave., Stoneham, MA 02180. (617) 438-8464; (800) 366-2665. 1990. Lists compounds or elements in order by Hill chemical formula: to aid verification, the International Union of Pure and Applied Chemistry systematic name and the Chemical Abstracts Service Registry Number are recorded. Also lists chemicals that react in some violent fashion with the main chemical cited. A brief description of the type of reaction and citations to the literature in which the reaction was reported are included.

Briefing. National Association of Manufacturers, 1331 Pennsylvania Avenue, NW, Suite 1500 North, Washington, DC 20004. (202) 637-3000. Weekly. Environmental issues as they relate to manufacturing.

Brine Shrimp and Their Habitat: An Environmental Investigation. National Wildlife Federation, 1400 16th St. NW, Washington, DC 20036-2266. (202) 797-6800. 1972.

British Columbia Ministry of Environment, Annual Report. British Columbia, Ministry of Environment, 810 Blanchard, 1st Fl., Victoria, BC, Canada V8V 1X5 (604) 387-9418. 1976-. Annually. Review of work carried out during the year by the Ministry of the Environment, including fish, wildlife, water management, and parks.

Brooks Bird Club. 707 Warwood Ave., Wheeling, WV 26003. (304) 547-5253.

Brown's Directory of North American & International Gas Companies. Energy Publications Division/Edgell Communications, Inc., 10300 N. Central Expressway, Building V-58, Dallas, TX 75231. (214) 691-3911.

Bugs, Slugs and Other Thugs: Controlling Garden Pests Organically. Rhonda Massingham Hart. Garden Way Pub., Schoolhouse Rd., Pownal, VT 05261. (802) 823-5811; (800) 441-5700. 1991.

Building a Healthy Lawn. Stuart Franklin. Garden Way Pub., Storey Communications Inc., Schoolhouse Rd., Pownal, VT 05261. (802) 823-5811; (800) 827-8673. 1988.

Building Design and Construction Handbook. Frank S. Merritt. McGraw-Hill, 1221 Avenue of the Americas, New York, NY 10020. (212) 512-2000 or (800) 262-4729. 1982. Compendium of current building design and construction practices. Data for selection of building materials and construction methods are included.

Building Sustainable Communities: An Environmental Guide for Local Governments. The Global Cities Project. Center for the Study of Law and Politics, 2962 Filmore St., San Francisco, CA 94123. (415) 775-0791. 1991. Series of handbooks provide local government with a variety of cost-effective options for developing strategies and programs addressing local environmental problems. The first four reports in this series are: 1. Water: Conservation and Reclamation. 2. Solid Waste: Reduction, Reuse and Recycling. 3. Toxics: Management and Reduction. 4. Transportation: Efficiency and Alternatives. Additional titles to be released in 1991 and 1992 will include: Energy and Alternatives, Urban Forestry, Air Quality, Pollution Prevention and Mitigation, Greenhouse Gases: Reduction and Ozone Protection, Land Use: Stewardship and the Planning Process, Open Space: Preservation and Acquisition, Water Quality: Pollution Prevention and Mitigation, and Environmental Management: Making Your Policies Stick.

Buildings Energy Technology. National Technical Information Service, 5285 Port Royal Rd., Springfield, VA 22161. (703) 487-4650. Monthly. Technology required for energy conservation in buildings and communities.

Bulk Liquid Terminals Directory. 1133 15th St., N.W., Washington, DC 20005. (202) 659-2301. Annual.

Bulletin. U.S. Department of Health and Human Services, Public Health Service, Food and Drug Administration, 9000 Rockville Pike, Bethesda, MD 20892. (301) 496-4000. Safety measures and physiological effects of poisons.

Bulletin Board. National Council of the Paper Industry for Air and Stream Improvements, 260 Madison Avenue, New York, NY 10016. (212) 532-9000. Biweekly. Issues of interest to the paper industry.

Bulletin l'Environnement. Societe pour Vaincre la Pollution, 445 rue St. Francois Xavier, Montreal, PQ, Canada H3H 2T1. 1973-. Quarterly.

Bulletin of American Meteorological Society. American Meteorological Society, 45 Beacon Street, Boston, MA 02108. (617) 227-2425. Monthly. Bulletin which certifies consulting meteorologists.

Bulletin of Environmental Contamination and Toxicology. Springer-Verlag, 175 5th Ave., New York, NY 10010. (212) 460-1500; (800) 777-4643. 1966-. Frequency varies. Disseminates advances and discoveries in the areas of soil, air and food contamination and pollution.

Bulletin of Marine Science. Rosenstiel School of Marine and Atmospheric Science, 4600 Rickenbacker Causeway, Miami, FL 33149-1098. (305) 361-4000. Bimonthly.

Bulletin of Society of Vector Ecologists. Society of Vector Ecologists, Box 87, Santa Ana, CA 92702. (714) 971-2421. Twice a year. Covers disease prevention and control measures.

Bulletin of the California Water Pollution Control Association. California Water Pollution Control Association, Box 575, Lafayette, CA 94549. (415) 284-1778. 1954-. Quarterly. Membership activity reports, environmental concerns and papers.

Bulletin of the Ecological Society of America. Arizona State University, Center for Environmental Studies, Tempe, AZ 85287. (602) 965-3000.

Bulletin Signaletique: Eau et Assainissement, Pollution Atmospherique, Droit des Pollutions. Centre de Documentation, Centre National de la Recherche Scientifique, 15, quai Anatole France, Paris, France 75700. (1) 45 55 92 25. 1983-. Monthly. Indexes pollution periodicals including water, atmospheric and related pollutions.

Bumper Recycling Association of North America–Membership Directory. Bumper Recycling Association of North America, 216 Country Club Rd., South Glastonbury, CT 06073. (203) 659-1762.

Buraff Asbestos Abatement Report. Buraff Publications, 1350 Connecticut Ave., N.W., Washington, DC 20036. (202) 862-0990.

Bureau of Economic Analysis: Environmental Economics Division. 1404 K St., N.W., Washington, DC 20230. (202) 523-0687.

Bureau of Hazardous Waste: Hazardous Waste Management. Deputy Commissioner, Compliance and Enforcement, 6 Hazen Drive, Concord, NH 03301. (603) 271-4608.

Bureau of Marine Resources: Coastal Zone Management. Director, 2620 W. Beach Blvd., Biloxi, MS 39531. (601) 864-4602.

Bureau of Oceans and International Environmental and Scientific Affairs. 2201 C St., N.W., Washington, DC 20520. (202) 647-1554.

Bureau of Solid and Hazardous Waste Management: Waste Minimization and Pollution Prevention. Director, PO Box 7921, Madison, WI 53707. (608) 266-2111.

Bureau of Solid Waste: Solid Waste Management. Director, Compliance and Enforcement, 6 Hazen Drive, Concord, NH 03301. (603) 271-4586.

Bureau of Underground Storage Tanks: Underground Storage Tanks. Chief, Division of Water Resources, 401 East State St., CN029, Trenton, NJ 08625. (609) 984-3156.

Burning and Empire, the Story of American Forest Fires. Stewart Hall Holbrook. Macmillan Publishing Co., 866 3rd Ave., New York, NY 10022. (212) 702-2000. 1943.

Burning Garbage in the U.S.: Practice vs. State of the Art. Marjorie J. Clarke. INFORM, 381 Park Ave. S, New York, NY 10016. (212) 689-4040. 1991. Deals with the state of the art in waste disposal methods.

Business and the Environment. Cutter Information Corp., 37 Broadway, Arlington, MA 02174. (617) 648-8700. Semimonthly. Global news and analysis on environmental trends. Also available online.

Business and the Environment. Cutter Information Corp., 37 Broadway, Arlington, MA 02174-4439. (617) 648-8700. Online version of periodical of the same name.

Business Associate. Western Pennsylvania Conservancy, 316 4th Ave., Pittsburgh, PA 15222. (412) 288-2777. 1984-. Semiannually. Reports on land conservation projects of the Western Pennsylvania Conservancy.

Butylated Hydroxanisole of Butylates Hydroxytoluene. Philip Wexler. U.S. Department of Health and Human Services, Public Health Services, National Institutes of Health, 9000 Rockville Pike, Bethesda, MD 20892. (301) 496-4000. 1984.

Buyer Guide and Publications Catalog of American Water Works Association. American Water Works Association, 6666 W. Quincy Ave., Denver, CO 80235. (303) 794-7711. 1991. Includes directories of AWWA agent, representative and distributor members; AWWA manufacturers agents and distributor members; AWWA contract members; consultant members; and the supplier catalog.

Buzzworm: The Environmental Journal. Buzzworm Inc., 2305 Canyon Blvd., No. 206, Boulder, CO 80302-5655. (303) 442-1969. 1988-. Quarterly. An independent environmental journal for the reader interested in nature, adventure, travel, the natural environment and the issues of conservation.

BWR Cobalt Source Identification. C.F. Falk. General Electric Co., P.O. Box 861, Gainesville, FL 32602-0861. (904) 462-3911. 1982. Safety measures in boiling water reactors.

Bypassing Bypass: The New Technique of Chelation Therapy. Elmer M. Cranton. Stein and Day, New York, NY 1984. Therapeutic use of ethylenediaminetetraacetic acid.

C. A. B. International Serials Checklist. C. A. B. International, Wallingford, England OX10 8DE. 44 0491 32111. 1988. Periodical literature relating to agriculture.

C. E. C. Member's Report. Community Environmental Council, 930 Miramonte Dr., Santa Barbara, CA 93109. Monthly. Newsletter about the community, its problems with environmental matters, etc.

C13 Nuclear Magnetic Resonance/Infrared Data Base. BASF AG, D-ZHV-B9, Ludwigshafen, Germany D-6700. 49 (621) 6028401.

CA Search. Chemical Abstracts Service, 2540 Olentangy River Rd., P.O. Box 3012, Columbus, OH 43210. (800) 848-6533.

CA Selects: Air Pollution (Books and Reviews). Chemical Abstracts Services, 2540 Olentangy River Rd., Box 3012, Columbus, OH 43210. (800) 848-6533. Biweekly. Abstracts on pollution in the atmosphere by fixed and mobile sources; effects of air pollution on animals and vegetation.

CA Selects: Carcinogens, Mutagens & Teratogens. Chemical Abstracts Services, 2540 Olentangy River Rd., Columbus, OH 43210. (800) 848-6533. Irregular.

CA Selects: Chemiluminescence. Chemical Abstracts Services, 2540 Olentangy River Rd., Box 3012, Columbus, OH 43210. (800) 848-6533. Biweekly.

CA Selects: Environment Pollution. Chemical Abstracts Services, 2540 Olentangy River Rd., Box 3012, Columbus, OH 43210. (800) 848-6533. 1978-. Biweekly. Abstracts on pollution of the environment by gaseous, liquid, solid and radioactive wastes.

CA Selects: Pollution Monitoring. Chemical Abstracts Services, 2540 Olentangy River Rd., Box 3012, Columbus, OH 43210. (800) 848-6533. 1978-. Biweekly. Abstracts on the analytical techniques and equipment relating to monitoring pollution.

CA Selects: Solar Energy. Chemical Abstracts Services, 2540 Olentangy River Rd., Box 3012, Columbus, OH 43210. (800) 848-6533. 1978-. Biweekly. Abstracts on solar energy conversion devices, materials and processes.

CAB Abstracts. C. A. B. International, Wallingford, England OX11 8DE. 44 (491) 32111.

CAB Serials Checklist. The Bureaux, Slough, England 1983. A consolidated list of the serials regularly scanned by the commonwealth agricultural bureaux with a guide to their location.

Cache la Poudre: The Natural History of Rocky Mountain River. Howard Ensign Evans and Mary Alice Evans. University Press of Colorado, PO Box 849, Niwot, CO 80544. (303) 530-5337. 1991. Includes a summary of the ecological and cultural values of the river corridor. Describes the corridor's flora, fauna, geology, insects, people and history.

Caffeine. LeRoy Werley. University of North Carolina, P.O. Box 2288, Chapel Hill, NC 27515-2288. 1981.

Caffeine: A Medical and Scientific Subject Analysis and Research Index with Bibliography. Hanna U. Tyler. ABBE Publishers Association of Washington DC, 4111 Gallows Rd., Annandale, VA 22003-1862. Bibliography of caffeine toxicology and caffeine habits and their physiological effects.

The Caffeine Book. Frances Sheridan Goulart. Mead Publishing Corp., 1515 S. Commerce St., Las Vegas, NV 81902-2703. (702) 387-8750. 1984.

Caffeine: Perspectives from Recent Research. P.B. Dews, ed. Springer-Verlag, 175 5th Ave., New York, NY 10010. (212) 460-1500. 1984.

Calcium, Cell Cycles, and Cancer. James F. Whitfield. CRC Press, 2000 Corporate Blvd. N.W., Boca Raton, FL 33431. (800) 272-7737. 1990.

Calcium Channels: Structure and Function. New York Academy of Sciences, Marketing Dept., 2E 63rd St., New York, NY 10021. (212) 838-0230. 1989.

Calcium in Biological Systems. Ronald P. Rubin. Plenum Press, 233 Spring St., New York, NY 10013-1578. (212) 620-8000. 1985. Covers calcification and calcium channel blockers.

Calcium Magnesium Acetate: An Emerging Bulk Chemical for Environmental Applications. D.L. Wise. Elsevier Science Publishing Co., 655 Avenue of the Americas, New York, NY 10010. (212) 989-5800. 1991.

Calcium, Membranes, Aging, and Alzheimer's Disease. New York Academy of Sciences, Marketing Dept., 2E 63rd St., New York, NY 10021. (212) 838-0230. 1989. Discusses calcium in the body.

Calcium Oxide and Hydroxide. Environmental Protection Service, 425 St. Joseph Blvd., 3rd Fl., Hull, PQ, Canada K1A 0H3. (613) 953-5921. 1984. Covers environmental and technical information for problem spills.

Calibration Handbook. G. Lalos. U.S. G.P.O, Washington, DC 20401. (202) 512-0000. 1983. Covers ionizing radiation measuring instruments.

California Air Environment. Statewide Air Pollution Research Center, University of California, Riverside, CA 92502. 1969-. Quarterly.

California Air Resources Board Bulletin. California Air Resources Board, 1102 Q. St., Sacramento, CA 95814. (916) 322-2990. 1962-. Monthly. Government newsletter concerning Air Resources Board activities, and air pollution control news.

California: An Environmental Atlas and Guide. Bern Kreissman and Barbara Lekisch. Bear Klaw Press, 1100 Industrial Rd. #9, San Carlos, CA 94071. (916) 753-7788. 1991. Devoted primarily to "natural features such as rivers, faultlines, habitat, and sanctuaries." An ensuing second volume will show man-made elements such as "power transmission lines, energy-generating plants, and toxic dump sites."

California Environmental Directory. California Institute of Public Affairs, Box 189040, Sacramento, CA 95818. (916) 442-2472. 1973-. Irregular. Directory of public, private and academic organizations located in California that are concerned with environmental protection.

California Environmental Law Handbook. Government Institutes, Inc., 4 Research Pl., Ste. 200, Rockville, MD 20850. (301) 921-2300. 1991.

California Hazardous Waste Directory 1991-1992: A Comprehensive Guide to the Environmental Services Marketplace. In Media Res, 848 California St., San Francisco, CA 94108. (415) 772-8949 or (800) 675-1945. 1991. An alphabetical list of companies dealing with hazardous wastes.

California Institute of Public Affairs. P.O. Box 10, Claremont, CA 91711. (714) 624-5212.

California Sea Grant College Program. University of California, La Jolla, CA 92093. (619) 534-4440.

California Solid Waste Market. FIND/SVP, 625 Avenue of the Americas, New York, NY 10011. (800) 346-3787. 1991. Cites market structure, landfill capacity, primary market participants and other primary assets.

California State Parks Foundation. 800 College Ave., P.O. Box 548, Kentfield, CA 94914. (415) 258-9975.

California Today. 909 12th St., #203, Sacramento, CA 95814-2931. (916) 448-8726. 1965-. Bimonthly. Review of California environmental legislation and activities of PCL.

California Tomorrow. California Tomorrow, Ft. Mason Ctr., Building B, #315, San Francisco, CA 94123. (415) 441-7631. 1965-. Quarterly. Illustrates need for system of comprehensive state/regional planning to protect and improve the Californian environment.

California Water Resources Center. University of California, Riverside, CA 92521. (714) 787-4327.

California Water Resources Directory: A Guide to Organizations and Information Sources. Roberta Childers, ed. California Institute of Public Affairs, PO Box 189040, Sacramento, CA 95818. (916) 442-2472. 1991. Second edition. Describes water-related activities of national executive and independent government agencies in the state. Also includes details on the California state government.

Call to Action: Handbook for Ecology, Peace, and Justice. Sierra Club Books, 100 Bush St., San Francisco, CA 94104. (415) 291-1600. 1990. Covers environmental policy and international relations.

Calypso Log. Cousteau Society Membership Center, 930 W 21st St., Norfolk, VA 23517. 6 issues a year. Presents articles for members about Cousteau Society expeditions, ecology, conservation, oceans and marine mammals.

Cambridge Dictionary of Biology. Peter M. B. Walker. Cambridge University Press, 40 W. 20th St., New York, NY 10011. (212) 924-3900 or (800) 227-0247. 1989. Includes 10,000 terms in zoology, botany, biochemistry, molecular biology and genetics. Previously published under the title Chambers Biology Dictionary.

Cambridge Encyclopedia of Life Sciences. A. E. Friday and David S. Ingram. Cambridge University Press, 40 W 20th St., New York, NY 10011. (212) 924-3900 or (800) 227-0247. 1985. Includes all topics under biology and ecology.

The Cambridge Encyclopedia of Ornithology. Michael Brooke. Cambridge University Press, 40 W. 20th St., Cambridge, NY 10011. (212) 924-3900 or (800) 227-0247. 1991. Covers all aspects of avian biology with a text-like treatise. Includes bird anatomy, physiology, reproduction, evolution, behavior, migration, ecology, conservation, and more.

Cambridge Scientific Abstracts Life Science–CSAL. Cambridge Scientific Abstracts, 5161 River Rd., Bethesda, MD 20816. (301) 961-6750. Provides access to the following abstracting services: "Life Sciences Collection," "Aquatic Sciences and Fisheries Abstracts," "Oceanic Abstracts," and "Pollution Abstracts."

Campaign California Report. Campaign California, 926 J. St. #300, Sacramento, CA 95814. (213) 393-3701. 1978-. Quarterly. Focuses on progressive politics in California, emphasis on reform of environmental laws.

Can Manufacturers Institute. 1625 Massachusetts Ave., N.W., Washington, DC 20036. (202) 232-4677.

Can the Whales Be Saved?. Philip Whitfield. Viking Kestrel, 40 W 23rd St., New York, NY 10010. (212) 337-5200. 1989.

Can We Delay a Greenhouse Warming?. U.S. G.P.O., Washington, DC 20401. (202) 512-0000. The effectiveness and feasibility of options to slow a build-up of carbon dioxide in the atmosphere.

Canada-United States Environmental Council. c/o Defenders of Wildlife, 1244 19th St., N.W., Washington, DC 20036. (202) 659-9510.

Canadian Association of Recycling Industries, Newsletter. Canadian Association of Recycling Industries, 415 Yonge St., #1620, Toronto, ON, Canada M5B 2E7. 1976-. Monthly.

Canadian Conservation Directory. Canadian Nature Federation, 453 Sussex Dr., Ottawa, ON, Canada K1N 6Z4. (613) 238-6154. 1973-. Directory of over 800 natural history, environment and conservation organizations of Canada.

Canadian Conservation Institute Technical Bulletin National. Museums of Canada, Quebec, ON, Canada K1A 0MB. (613) 776-7000. 1973-. Irregular. Deals with a variety of subjects on conservation of collections.

Canadian Environmental Control Newsletter. 6 Garamond Ct., Don Mills, ON, Canada M3C 1Z5. (416) 441-2992. 1945-. Covers the general topic of pollution and the environmental control measures designed to fight it.

Canadian Environmental Directory. Canadian Almanac & Directory Publishing Co. Ltd., 134 Adelaide St. E., Ste. 27, Toronto, ON, Canada M5C 1K9. (416) 362-4088. 1992. Includes individuals, agencies, firms, and associations.

Canadian Environmental Mediation Newsletter. Conflict Management Resources, Osgoode Law School, York Univ., 4700 Keely St., Downsview, ON, Canada M3J 2R5. 1986-. Quarterly. Deals with environmental resources development dispute resolution.

Canadian Society of Environmental Biologists Newsletter. Canadian Society of Environmental Biologists, PO Box 962, Sta. F, Toronto, ON, Canada M4Y 2N9. 1962-. Quarterly.

Cancer Control Objectives for the Nation: 1985-2000. National Cancer Institute, 9030 Old Georgetown Rd., Bethesda, MD 20892. (301) 496-7403. 1986.

Cancer Facts and Figures. American Cancer Society, 1599 Clifton Rd., NE, Atlanta, GA 30329. Annual. Discusses cancer incidence and mortality, by state, country, and sex; and survival rates.

Cancer in Populations Living Near Nuclear Facilities. U.S. G.P.O., Washington, DC 20401. (202) 512-0000. 1990.

Cancer Sourcebook: Basic Information on Cancer Types, Symptoms, Diagnostic Methods, and Treatments. Frank E. Bair, ed. Omnigraphics, Inc., 2500 Penobscot Bldg., Detroit, MI 48226. (313) 961-1340. 1990. Includes statistics of cancer occurrences worldwide and the risks associated with known carcinogens and activities.

Cancer Statistics Review. U.S. G.P.O., Washington, DC 20401. (202) 512-0000. Annual. Cancer incidence, deaths, and relative survival rates.

Cancergram. U.S. Department of Health and Human Services, 200 Independence Ave. SW, Washington, DC 20201. (202) 619-0257. 1988. Monthly. International Cancer Research Data Bank relating to molecular biology and DNA.

Cancerlit. U.S. National Institutes of Health, National Eye Institute, Building 31, Rm. 6A32, Bethesda, MD 20892. (301) 496-5248.

Cancerquest Online. CDC AIDS Weekly/NCI Cancer Weekly, 206 Roger St, N.E., Suite 104, Atlanta, GA 30317. (404) 377-8895.

Canned Food Information Council. 500 N. Michigan Ave., Suite 300, Chicago, IL 60611. (312) 836-7279.

The Canopy. Rainforest Alliance, 270 Lafayette St., Suite 512, New York, NY 10012. (212) 941-1900. Quarterly.

Canvasback Society. P.O. Box 101, Gates Mills, OH 44040. (216) 443-2340.

Canyon Explorers Club. 1223 Frances Ave., Fullerton, CA 92631. Non-profit corporation that was started in 1972 whose purpose is to explore remote areas of the world. Members believe in the preservation of wilderness areas and respect the dignity of native cultures.

Car Trouble. James J. MacKenzie, et al. World Resources Institute, 1709 New York Ave., N.W., Washington, DC 20006. 1992. Reviews the technical options for air purification, cleaner fuels, more flexible transportation systems, and more intelligent city planning, among others.

Carbon. Pergamon Microforms International, Inc., Fairview Park, Elmsford, NY 10523. (914) 592-7720. Monthly. Covers environmental aspects of carbon.

Carbon & High Performance Fibres Directory. Box 51305, Raleigh, NC 27609. (919) 847-0262. Irregular.

The Carbon Cycle and Atmospheric CO2: Natural Variations, Archean to Present. E.T. Sundquist. American Geophysical Union, 2000 Florida Ave. N.W., Washington, DC 20009. (202) 462-6900. 1985. Deals with carbon cycle, atmospheric carbon dioxide, and paleothermometry.

Carbon Dioxide and Climate: A Bibliography. National Technical Information Service, 5285 Port Royal Rd., Springfield, VA 22161. (703) 487-4650. 1981.

Carbon Dioxide and Global Change: Earth in Transition. Sherwood B. Idso. IBR Press, 631 E. Laguna Dr., Tempe, AZ 85282. (602) 966-8693. 1989. Discusses environmental aspects of greenhouse effect.

Carbon Dioxide and Other Greenhouse Gases. Kluwer Academic Publishers, 101 Philip Dr., Assinippi Pk, Norwell, MA 02061. (617) 871-6600. Looks at environmental aspects of greenhouse effects.

Carbon Dioxide Effects: Research and Assessment Program. National Technical Information Service, 5285 Port Royal Rd., Springfield, VA 22161. (703) 487-4650. 1990. Covers the effects of increasing atmospheric carbon dioxide on the physical environment and living organisms.

Carbon Dioxide: Friend or Foe?. IBR Press, 631 E. Laguna Dr., Tempe, AZ 85282. (802) 966-8693. An inquiry into the climatic and agricultural consequences of the rapidly rising CO2 content of earth's atmosphere.

Carbon Dioxide Review. Oxford University Press, 200 Madison Ave., New York, NY 10016. (212) 679-7300. 1982. Cites atmospheric carbon dioxide research.

Carbon Dioxide, the Climate and Man. John R. Gribbin. International Institute for Environment and Development, 3 Endsleigh St., London, England CB2 1ER. 1981. Influence on nature of atmospheric carbon dioxide.

Carbon Dioxide, the Greenhouse Effect, and Climate. John R. Justus. U.S. G.P.O., Washington, DC 20401. (202) 521-0000. 1984.

Carbon Monoxide. R. W. Cargill. Pergamon Microforms International, Inc., Fairview Park, Elmsford, NY 10523. (914) 592-7720. 1990. Contains tabulated collections and critical evaluations of original data for the solubility of carbon monoxide in a variety of liquid solvents.

Carbon Monoxide, the Silent Killer. Charles C. Thomas Publishers, 2600 S. First St., Springfield, IL 62794-9265. (217) 789-8980. Covers physiological effects and toxicology of carbon monoxide.

Carbon, Nitrogen, and Sulfur Pollutants and Their Determination in Air and Water. Jerome C. Greyson. Marcel Dekker, Inc., 270 Madison Ave., New York, NY 10016. (212) 696-9000; (800) 228-1160. 1990. Measurement of air and water pollution and environmental aspects of sulphur and nitrogens.

Carbon Nitrogen Sulfur: Human Interference in Grand Biospheric Cycles. Vaclay Smil. Plenum Press, 233 Spring St., New York, NY 10013-1578. (212) 620-8000. 1985.

Carbon, Nutrient and Water Balances of Tropical Rain Forest Ecosystems Subject to Disturbance: Management Implications and Research Proposals. Jonathan M. Anderson and Thomas Spencer. UNESCO, 7, place de Fontenoy, Paris, France F-75700. (331) 45 68 40 67. 1991. MAB Digest 7.

Carcinogenic, Mutagenic, and Teratogenic Marine Pollutants. Portfolio Publishing Co., P.O. Box 7802, The Woodlands, TX 77381. (713) 363-3577. 1990. Effects of marine pollution on aquatic organisms as well as human beings.

Carcinogenic Risk Assessment. Curtis C. Travis. Plenum Press, 233 Spring St., New York, NY 10013-1578. (212) 620-8000; (800) 221-9369. 1988.

Carcinogenically-Active Chemicals: A Reference Guide. Richard J. Lewis, Sr. Global Professional Publications, 2805 McGraw Ave., PO Box 19539, Irvine, CA 92713-9539. (800) 854-7179. 1990. Includes 3,400 verified or suspected carcinogens, classified as confirmed, suspected, or questionable.

Carcinogenicity and Pesticides. Nancy N. Ragsdale and Robert E. Menzer, eds. American Chemical Society, 1155 16th St. N.W., Washington, DC 20036. (202) 872-4600; (800) 227-5558. 1989. Discusses the role of structure activity relationship analysis in evaluation of pesticides for potential carcinogenicity. Also traces the background, pesticide regulations, assessment of hazard and risk, and epidemiological studies of cancer and pesticide exposure.

Carcinogenicity Assessment of Chlordane and Heptachlor/ Heptachlor Epoxide. Carcinogen Assessment Group, Office of Health and Environmental Assessment, U.S. Environmental Protection Agency, 401 Elm St. SW, Washington, DC 20460. (202) 260-7317. 1986.

Carcinogens and Mutagens in the Environment. Hans F. Stich, ed. CRC Press, 2000 Corporate Blvd. N.W., Boca Raton, FL 33431. (800) 272-7737. 1982-. Naturally occurring compounds, endogenous modulation.

Carcinogens in Industry and the Environment. James M. Sontag, ed. M. Dekker, 270 Madison Ave., New York, NY 10016. (212) 696-9000. 1981. Environmentally induced diseases and industrial hygiene.

Caribbean Conservation Corporation. PO Box 2866, Gainsville, FL 32602. (904) 373-6441.

Caring for the Earth: A Strategy for Sustainable Living. IUCN. Earthscan, 3 Endsleigh St., London, England WC1H 0DD 071-388 2117. 1991. Discusses the sustainable living methods to protect the environment.

Carrying Capacity News. Carrying Capacity Network, 1325 G St. NW, Suite 1003, Washington, DC 20005-3104. (202) 879-3044. Irregular. Discusses links between environmental, population, resources, and economic issues.

Cartons, Cans, and Orange Peels–Where Does Your Garbage Go?. Joanna Foster. Clarion Books, 215 Park Avenue, S, New York, NY 10003. (212) 420-5800. 1991. Discusses composition of garbage and trash, methods of disposal, and recycling.

CAS Source Index–CASSI. Chemical Abstracts Service, 2540 Olentangy River Rd., P.O. Box 3012, Columbus, OH 43210. (800) 848-6533 or (614) 421-3600. A listing of bibliographic and library holdings information for scientific and technical primary literature relevant to the chemical sciences.

Casarett and Doull's Toxicology. Pergamon Microforms International, Inc., Fairview Park, Elmsford, NY 10523. (914) 592-7720. 1991. Covers toxicology, poisoning and poisons.

Cascade Holistic Economic Consultants. 14417 S.E. Laurie Ave., Oak Grove, OR 97207. (503) 652-7049.

Case Studies of Waste-to-Energy Facilities. Illinois Department of Energy and Natural Resources, Office of Research and Planning, 325 W. Adams St., Rm. 300, Springfield, IL 62706. (217) 785-2800. 1989. Covers incinerators, resource recovery facilities, waste products as fuel and salvage of wastes.

CASREACT. Chemical Abstracts Service, 2540 Olentangy River Rd., P.O. Box 3012, Columbus, OH 43210. (800) 848-6533.

CASSI. Chemical Abstracts Service, 2540 Olentangy River Rd., P.O. Box 3012, Columbus, OH 43210. (800) 848-6533.

Catalog Handbook of Fine Chemicals. Aldrich Chemical Co., 1001 W. St. Paul Ave., Milwaukee, WI 53233. (414) 273-3850 or (800) 558-9160. 1990/1991. Contains more than 27,000 products of which over 4,000 are new. Includes: chemicals, equipment, glassware, books, software, research products, bulk quantities, new products, custom synthesis and rare chemicals.

A Catalog of Hazardous and Solid Waste Publications. U.S. Environmental Protection Agency, 401 M St., S.W., Washington, DC 20460. (202) 260-2090. 1990. Covers hazardous wastes, refuse, and refuse disposal.

Catalog of Teratogenic Agents. Thomas H. Shephard. Johns Hopkins University Press, 701 W. 40th St., Ste. 275, Baltimore, MD 21211. (410) 516-6900. 1992. Drug-induced abnormalities and teratogens.

Catalysis Society. c/o Dr. William J. Linn, E.I. DuPont, P.O. Box 80402, Wilmington, DE 80402. (302) 695-4655.

Catalyst Deactivation. Calvin H. Bartholomew and John B. Butt, eds. Elsevier Science Publishing Co., 655 Avenue of the Americas, New York, NY 10010. (212) 989-5800. 1991. Proceedings of the fifth International Symposium, Evanston, IL, June 24-26, 1991.

Catalyst Design: Progress and Perspectives. John Wiley & Sons, Inc., 605 Third Ave., New York, NY 10158-0012. (212) 850-6000.

Catalyst: Economics for the Living Earth. Catalyst Investing in Social Change, 64 Main St., Montpelier, VT 05602. (802) 223-7943. 1983-. Quarterly. Discusses grassroots enterprises working for social change and a humane economy. Focuses on ecological balance, articles on forest destruction, energy issues, native peoples issues and community- based economics.

Catalyst for Environment/Energy. Catalyst for Environment/ Energy, New York, NY 1970-. Irregular. Dedicated to efficient energy and environmental management.

Catalyst for Environmental Quality. Catalyst for Environmental/Energy, New York, NY

Catalyst Manufacture: Laboratory and Commercial Preparations. Marcel Dekker, Inc., 270 Madison Ave., New York, NY 10016. (212) 696-9000.

Cattle in the Cold Desert. James A. Young. Utah State University Press, Logan, UT 84322. (801)750-13620017064. 1985. Covers history of grazing, ranch life and beef cattle in the Great Basin.

Cause for Concern. R.D. 1, Box 570, Stewartsville, NJ 08886. (201) 479-4110.

Caution, Inorganic Metal Cleaners Can Be Dangerous. National Institute for Occupational Safety and Health. U.S. Department of Health and Human Services, National Institute for Occupational Safety and Health, 200 Independence Ave. SW, Washington, DC 20201. (202)619-1296. 1975.

Caves and Other Groundwater Features. JLM Visuals, 1208 Bridge St., Grafton, WI 53024. (414) 377-7775. 1979. Slides of sinkholes, stalactites, stalagmites and caves.

CAW Waste Watch. Californians Against Waste, Box 289, Sacramento, CA 95802. (916) 443-5422. 1978-. Quarterly. Newsletter about natural resources conservation, recycling, anti-litter issues in California and other related topics.

CBE Environmental Review. Citizens for Better Environment, 407 S. Dearborn, Ste. 1775, Chicago, IL 60605. (312) 939-1530. 1975-. Quarterly. Documentation of environmental matters.

CCPS/AIChE Directory of Chemical Process Safety Services. American Institute of Chemical Engineers, 345 E. 47th St., New York, NY 10017. (212) 705-7338. 1991. Lists providers of various chemical process safety services. It is compiled from questionnaires returned by the service providers. Company profiles are included.

CDC Interference in Dioxin Water Standards. Committee on Government Operations. U.S. G.P.O., Washington, DC 20401. (202) 512-0000. 1991. Hearing before the Human Resources and Intergovernmental Relations Subcommittee of the Committee on Government Operations, House of Representatives, 101st Congress, 2d session, July 26, 1991. Provides the basic standards for dioxin content in water.

CEH On-Line. SRI International, Chemical Economics Handbook Program, 333 Ravenwood Ave., Menlo Park, CA 14025. (415) 859-5039.

CEHINDEX. SRI International, Chemical Economics Handbook Program, 333 Ravenwood Ave., Menlo Park, CA 14025. (415) 859-5039.

CEIP Fund. 68 Harrison Ave., 5th Fl., Boston, MA 02111. (617) 426-4375.

Cell ATP. William A. Bridger. John Wiley & Sons, Inc., 605 3rd Ave., New York, NY 10158-0012. (212) 850-6000. 1983. Discusses the metabolism of adenosine triphosphate including cell metabolism.

Cell Calcium. Churchill Livingstone, Inc., 650 Avenue of the Americas, New York, NY 10011. (212) 206-5000. Bimonthly. The international interdisciplinary forum for research on calcium.

Cell Regulation Group. University of Calgary, Medical Biochemistry, Faculty of Medicine, 330 Hospital Dr., N.W., Calgary, AB, Canada T2N 4N1. (403) 220-3018.

Cellular Chemiluminescence. CRC Press, 2000 Corporate Blvd. N.W., Boca Raton, FL 33431. (800) 272-7737. 1987.

CEM Report. Center for Environmental Management, U.S. Environmental Protection Agency, 26 W. Martin Luther King Dr., Cincinnati, OH 45268. (617) 381-3486. Quarterly. Articles on the activities of CEM.

Cement and Concrete Research. Pergamon Microforms International, Inc., Fairview Pk., Elmsford, NY 10523. (914) 592-7720.

Cement, Concrete and Aggregates. American Society for Testing and Materials, 1916 S. Race St., Philadelphia, PA 19103. (215) 299-5585. Semiannual. Covers cement, concrete and other building materials.

Cement-Data-Book. Walter H. Duda. Bauverlag, Wittelsbacherstr. 10, Postfach 1460, Wiesbaden, Germany D-6200. 1977. Covers process engineering in the cement industry, including methods of calculation, formulas, diagrams, numerical tables.

Cement Engineers' Handbook. Otto Labahn. Bauverlag, Wittelsbacherstr. 10, Postfach 1460, Weisbaden, Germany D-6200. 1983.

Cement Manufacturer's Handbook. Kurt E. Peray. Chemical Publishing Co., 80 Eighth Ave., New York, NY 10011. (212) 255-1950. 1979.

Cements Research Progress. American Ceramic Society, 757 Brookside Plaza Dr., Westerville, OH 43081. (614) 890-4700. Annual. Bibliography of cement manufacturing.

Census of manufacturers. Preliminary report. Industry Series. Explosives. U.S. G.P.O., Washington, DC 20401. (202) 512-0000. 1987. Quinquennial. Industrial data published as part of current Industrial Reports Series.

Center for Advanced Decision Support for Water and Environmental Systems. University of Colorado-Boulder, 2945 Center Green Court, Suite B, Boulder, CO 80301. (303) 492-3972.

Center for Advanced Invertebrate Molecular Sciences. Texas A & M University, College Station, TX 77843-2475. (409) 845-9730.

Center for Air Pollution Impact and Trend Analysis. Washington University, Campus Box 1124, 319 Urbauer, St. Louis, MO 63130. (314) 889-6099.

Center for Alternative Mining Development Policy. 210 Avon St., #9, La Crosse, WI 54603. (608) 784-4399.

Center for Aquatic Plants. University of Florida, 7922 N.W. 71st Street, Gainesville, FL 32606. (904) 392-1799.

Center for Chemical Process Safety. c/o American Institute of Chemical Engineers, 345 E. 47th St., 12th Floor, New York, NY 10017. (212) 705-7319.

Center for Clean Air Policy. 444 N. Capitol St., Suite 526, Washington, DC 20001. (202) 624-7709.

Center for Coastal Studies. 59 Commercial St., P.O. Box 1036, Provincetown, MA 02657. (508) 487-3622.

Center for Conservation Biology. Department of Biological Sciences, Stanford University, Stanford, CA 94305. (415) 723-5924.

Center for Earth and Environmental Science. State University of New York, Plattsburgh, NY 12901.

Center for Energy Policy and Research. c/o New York Institute of Technology, Old Westbury, NY 11568. (516) 686-7578.

Center for Environmental Education and Research. University of Colorado-Boulder, College of Environmental Design, Boulder, CO 80309. (303) 492-7711.

Center for Environmental Information, Inc. 99 Court St., Rochester, NY 14604. (716) 546-3796.

Center for Environmental Management. Tufts University, Curtis Hall, 474 Boston Ave., Medford, MA 02155. (617) 381-3486.

Center for Environmental Research. Cornell University, 470 Hollister Hall, Ithaca, NY 14853-3501. (607) 255-7535.

Center for Environmental Sciences. University of Colorado-Denver, P.O. Box 173364, Denver, CO 80217-3364. (303) 5556-4277.

Center for Field Research. P.O. Box 403, 608 Mt. Auburn St., Watertown, MA 02272. (617) 926-8200.

Center for Hazardous Materials Research. 320 William Pitt Way, University of Pittsburgh Applied Research Center, Pittsburgh, PA 15238. (412) 826-5320.

Center for Health Action. P.O. Box 270, Forest Park Station, Springfield, MA 01108. (413) 782-2115.

Center for Holistic Resource Management. P.O. Box 7128, Albuquerque, NM 87194. (505) 344-3445.

Center for Interfacial Microbial Process Engineering. Montana State University, College of Engineering, 409 Cobleigh Hall, Bozeman, MT 59717-0007. (406) 994-4770.

Center for International Development and Environment. 1709 New York Ave., N.W., Washington, DC 20006. (202) 462-0900.

Center for Law in the Public Interest. 5750 Wilshire Blvd., Suite 561, Los Angeles, CA 90036. (213) 470-3000.

Center for Limnology. University of Colorado-Boulder, Department of EPO Biology, Boulder, CO 80309-0334. (303) 492-6379.

Center for Marine Conservation. 1725 DeSales St., NW, Suite 500, Washington, DC 20036. (202) 429-5609.

Center for Molecular Biology. Wayne State University, 5047 Gullen Mall, Detroit, MI 48202. (313) 577-0616.

Center for Molecular Genetics. University of California, San Diego, 9500 Gilman Dr., La Jolla, CA 92093. (619) 534-0396.

Center for Natural Resources. University of Florida, 1066 McCarty Hall, Gainesville, FL 32611. (904) 392-7622.

Center for Oceans Law and Policy. School of Law, University of Virginia, Charlottesville, VA 22901. (804) 924-7441.

Center for Plant Conservation. 3115 S. Grand, P.O. Box 299, St. Louis, MO 63166. (314) 577-9450.

Center for Population Options. 1025 Vermont Ave., NW, Suite 210, Washington, DC 20005. (202) 347-5700.

Center for Religion, Ethics and Social Policy. Anabel Taylor Hall, Cornell University, Ithaca, NY 14853. (607) 255-6486.

Center for Remote Sensing. University of Delaware, College of Marine Studies, Newark, DE 19711. (302) 451-2336.

Center for Research and Technology Development. 1825 K Street, N.W., Washington, DC 20006-1202. (202) 785-3756.

Center for Science in the Public Interest. 1875 Connecticut Ave., NW, Suite 300, Washington, DC 20009. (202) 332-9110.

Center for Short Lived Phenomena. P.O. Box 199, Harvard Sq. Station, Cambridge, MA 02238. (617) 492-3310.

Center for Strategic Wildland Management Studies. University of Michigan, School of Natural Resources, Ann Arbor, MI 48109. (313) 763-2200.

Center for Study of Marine Policy. University of Delaware, Newark, DE 19711. (302) 831-8086.

Center for Technology, Environment, and Development. Clark University, 16 Claremont St., Worcester, MA 01610. (508) 751-4606.

Center for Urban Pest Management. Purdue University, Ag Research Building, West Lafayette, IN 47907. (317) 494-4554.

Center for Waste Minimization and Management. Department of Chemical Engineering, North Carolina State University, PO Box 7905, Raleigh, NC 27695-7905. (919) 737-2325.

Center for Waste Reduction Technologies. American Institute of Chemical Engineers, 345 East 47th St., New York, NY 10017. (212) 705-7407.

Center for Wetlands. University of Florida, Phelps Laboratory, Gainesville, FL 32611. (904) 392-2424.

Center for Whale Research. P.O. Box 1577, Friday Harbor, WA 98250. (206) 378-5835.

Centers for Disease Control: National Institute for Occupational Safety and Health. D-36, 1600 Clifton Rd. N.E., Atlanta, GA 30333. (404) 639-3771.

Centre for Atmospheric Chemistry. York University, 4700 Keele St., Downsview, ON, Canada M3J 1P3. (416) 736-5586.

The Centre for Our Common Future. Palais Wilson, 52, rue des Paquis, 1201, Geneva, Switzerland (41) 2-732-7117.

CENYC Environmental Bulletin. CENYC, 51 Cahmbers St., New York, NY 10007. (212) 566-0990. 1971-. Bimonthly. Environmental briefs of interest in New York City area residents.

CERCLIS. Chemical Information Systems, Inc., 7215 York Rd., Baltimore, MD 21212. (301) 321-8440. Information on hazardous waste disposal sites that have either been listed by the EPA on the National Priority List (NPL) or nominated for consideration for the NPL.

The CERCular. U.S. Army Corps. of Engineers, Waterways Experiment Station, PO Box 631, Vicksburg, MS 39180. (601) 634-3774. Quarterly. Army Coastal Engineering Research Center and its work on shore and beach erosion; flood and storm protection; navigation improvements; and the design, construction, operation and maintenance of coastal structures.

CERP. Dana Silk, ed. UNESCO, 7, place de Fontenoy, Paris, France F-75700. (331) 45 68 40 67. Discusses forest and agroforestry ecosystems, urban development and planning.

Certified Professional Erosion and Sediment Control Specialists– Directory. Office of the Registry/Certified Professional Erosion and Sediment Control Specialists, 677 S. Segoe Rd., Madison, WI 53711. (503) 326-2826.

CESARS. State of Michigan, Department of Natural Resources, Great Lakes & Environmental Assessment Section, P.O. Box 30028, Lansing, MI 45909. (517) 373-2190.

The CFC Handbook. Carl Salas. Fairmont Press, 700 Indian Trail, Lilburn, GA 30247. (404) 925-9388. 1990. Discusses use of chlorofluorocarbons (CFCs), CFC recycling, reclamation and reuse for refrigeration.

CFCs & Replacements. FIND/SVP, 625 Avenue of the Americas, New York, NY 10011. (212) 645-4500. 1991. Assesses the U.S. market for chlorofluorocarbon compounds (CFCs), with a special focus on CFC replacements.

CFCs & the Polyurethane Industry: A Compilation of Technical Publications. Society of the Plastics Industry, Polyurethane Division, 355 Lexington Ave., New York, NY 10017. (212)351-5425. 1992. Bibliography of plastic foams, chlorofluorocarbons and polyurethanes.

Chainsaws in Tropical Forests: A Manual. Food and Agriculture Organization of the United Nations, Via delle Terme di Caracalla, Rome, Italy 00100. 61 0181-FA01. 1980. Tree felling-equipment and supplies and logging machinery.

The Challenge of Arctic Shipping. David L. VanderZwaag. McGill-Queen's University Press, 3430 McTavish St., Montreal, PQ, Canada H3A 1X9. (514) 398-3750. 1990. Science, environmental assessment, and human values.

The Challenge of Global Warming. Dean Edwin Abrahamson, ed. Island Press, 1718 Connecticut Ave. N.W., Suite 300, Washington, DC 20009. (202) 232-7933. 1989. Focuses on the causes, effects, policy implications, and possible solutions to global warming

The Challenging Carbon Cycle: A Global Analysis. Springer-Verlag, 175 Fifth Ave., New York, NY 10010. (212) 460-1500. 1986. Looks at environmental aspects of carbon cycle, biogeochemistry.

Chamber of Commerce of the United States. 1615 H St., N.W., Washington, DC 20062. (202) 659-6000.

The Changing Atmosphere: A Global Challenge. John Firor. Yale University Press, 302 Temple St., 92 A Yale Sta., New Haven, CT 06520. (203) 432-0960. 1990. Examines three atmospheric problems: Acid rain, ozone depletion, and climate heating.

The Changing Climate: Responses of the Natural Fauna and Flora. Michael J. Ford. G. Allen and Unwin, 8 Winchester Pl., Winchester, MA 01890. (617) 729-0830. 1982. Describes the climate changes and the acclimatization of the flora and fauna.

Changing Landscapes: An Ecological Perspective. Isaak Samuel Zonneveld and Richard T. T. Forman. Springer-Verlag, 175 5th Ave, New York, NY 10010. (212) 460-1500 or (800) 777-4643. 1990. Ecology and landscape protection.

Changing Wilderness Values, 1930-1990: An Annotated Bibliography. Joan S. Elbers. Greenwood Publishing Group, Inc., 88 Post Rd. W., Box 5007, Westport, CT 06881. (203) 226-3571. 1991. "Encompasses the different values Americans have sought in or attributed to the wilderness." Most of the entries fall into the areas of "wilderness experience."

Characteristics of Potential Repository Wastes. National Technical Information Service, 5285 Port Royal Rd., Springfield, VA 22161. (703) 487-4650. 1990. Inventories and selected characteristics of commercial light- water reactors (LWR) and non-LWR spent fuel, immobilized high-level radioactive waste (HLW), and other wastes likely to be placed in permanent geologic repositories.

Characterization of Hazardous Waste Generation and Disposal in Yukon. Moneco Consultants Ltd., Calgary (Alberta). National Technical Information Service, 5285 Port Royal Rd., Springfield, VA 22161. (703) 487-4650. 1990.

Characterization of Heterogeneous Catalysts. Francis Delannay. Marcel Dekker, Inc., 270 Madison Ave., New York, NY 10016. (212) 696-9000. 1984.

Characterization of Municipal Waste Combustor Ashes and Leachates from Municipal Solid Waste Landfills, Monofills, and Codisposal Sites. U.S. Environmental Protection Agency, Office of Solid Waste, 401 M St., S.W., Washington, DC 20460. (202) 260-2090. 1987.

Characterization of Urban and Rural Inhalable Particulates. Donald F. Gatz. Illinois Department of Energy and Natural Resources, 325 W. Adams St., Rm. 300, Springfield, IL 62706. (217) 785-2800. 1983. Covers the measurement of dust and environmental monitoring of air pollution.

Chelated Mineral Nutrition in Plants, Animals, and Man. Charles C. Thomas Publishers, 2600 S. First, Springfield, IL 62794-9265. (217) 789-8980. 217-789-8980.

Chelates in Analytical Chemistry. M. Dekker, 270 Madison Ave., New York, NY 10016. (212) 696-9000. Annual. Chemical tests and reagents.

Chelates in Nutrition. F. Howard Kratzer. CRC Press, 2000 Corporate Blvd. N.W., Boca Raton, FL 33431. (800) 272-7737. 1986. Mineral in human nutrition and chelation therapy.

Chelating Agents and Metal Chelates. Academic Press, c/o Harcourt Brace Jovanovich Inc., 6277 Sea Harbor Dr., Orlando, FL 32887. (800) 346-8648. 1964. Organic chemistry and chelating agents.

Chelonia Institute. P.O. Box 9174, Arlington, VA 22209. (703) 524-4900.

Chem Address Book. F. W. Derz, ed. Walter De Gruyter, New York, NY 1974. Includes over 180000 names (synonyms) in alphabetical order for chemical compounds and chemicals, radioactive labelled compounds, isotopes, dyes, polymers, etc. and their molecular formulas.

Chem-Bank. SilverPlatter Information, Inc., 37 Walnut St., Wellesley Hills, MA 02181. 617-239-0306. Registry of Toxic Effects of Chemical Substances; Oil and Hazardous Materials Technical Assistance Data System; Chemical Hazard Response Information System; and the Toxic Substances Control Act Initial Inventory.

CHEM-INTELL–Chemical Trade and Production Statistics Database. Chemical Intelligence Services, 39A Bowling Green Lane, London, England EC1R. OBJ 44 (71) 833-3812.

Chem Sources–International. Directories Publishing Co., Box 1824, Clemson, SC 29633. (803) 646-7840.

Chem Sources–USA. Chemical Sources International Inc., PO Box 1884, Ormond Beach, FL 32175-1884. Annual. Includes chemical nomenclature of some 130,000 chemicals of all classifications, trade name index, classified/trade name, company directory, and company index. Also includes paid advertising.

Chemcyclopedia. American Chemical Society, 1155 16th St. N.W., Washington, DC 20036. (800) 227-5558.

ChemEcology. Chemical Manufacturers Association, 2501 M St. NW, Washington, DC 20037. (202) 887-1100. Monthly. Articles on how the chemical industry deals with environmental issues.

Chemest. Technical Database Services, Inc., 10 Columbus Circle, New York, NY 10019. (212) 245-0044. Covers methods of estimating 11 important properties: water solubility, soil adsorption coefficient, bioconcentration factor, acid dissociation constant, activity coefficient, boiling point, vapor pressure, water volatilization rate, Henry's Law Constant, melting point, and liquid viscosity.

Chemical Abstracts-CA. Chemical Abstracts Service, 2540 Olentangy River Rd., P.O. Box 3012, Columbus, OH 43210. (800) 848-6533 or (614) 421-3600. Information sources include 9000 journals, patents from 27 countries, two industrial property organizations, new books, conference proceedings, and government research reports.

Chemical Abstracts Chemical Name Directory-CHEMNAME. Chemical Abstracts Service, 2540 Olentangy River Rd., P.O. Box 3012, Columbus, OH 43210. (800) 848-6533 or (614) 421-3600. Listing of chemical substances in a dictionary type file. The Chemical Abstracts (CAS) Registry Number, molecular formula, Chemical Abstracts (CA) Substance Index Name, available synonyms, ring data and other chemical substance information is given for each entry.

Chemical Age Project File. MBC Information Services Ltd., Paulton House, 8 Shepherdess Walk, London, England N1 7LB. 44 (71) 490-0049.

Chemical Analysis of Ecological Materials. Stewart E. Allen. John Wiley & Sons, Inc., 605 3rd Ave., New York, NY 10158-0012. (212) 850-6000. 1974.

The Chemical Analysis of Foods: A Practical Treatise on the Examination of Foodstuffs and the Detection of Adulterants. Henry Edward Cox. J. & A. Churchill, Rover Stevenson House, 1-3 Banter's Place, Leith Walk, Edinburgh, England EH1 3AF. (031) 556-2424. 1977.

Chemical Analysis of Inorganic Constituents of Water. CRC Press, 2000 Corporate Blvd. N.W., Boca Raton, FL 33431. (800) 272-7737. 1982.

The Chemical Analysis of Water: General Principles and Techniques. D. T. E. Hunt and A. L. Wilson. Royal Society of Chemistry, c/o CRC Press, 2000 Corporate Blvd. N.W., Boca Raton, FL 33431-9868. (800) 272-7737. 1986. 2d ed. 2d reprint. Covers the measurement of water quality with particular reference to methods for estimating and controlling possible errors in analytical results.

Chemical and Biological Characterization of Municipal Sludges, Sediments, Dredge Spoils, and Drilling Muds. James L. Lichtenberg, et al. American Society for Testing and Materials, 1916 S. Race St., Philadelphia, PA 19103. (215) 299-5585. 1988. Deals with the environmental aspects of sewage disposal, analysis, health risk assessment, biological purification of sludge, and water quality management.

Chemical & Engineering News. American Chemical Society, 1155 16th St. N.W., Washington, DC 20036. (800) 227-5558. Weekly. Cites technical and business developments in the chemical process industry.

Chemical & Radiation Waste Litigation Reporter. Chemical & Radiation Waste Litigation Reporter, Inc., 1980-. Monthly.

Chemical & Radionuclide Food Contamination. MSS Information Corp., Edison, NJ 1973. Covers radioactive contamination of food.

Chemical Business Newsbase. Royal Society of Chemistry, Thomas Graham House, Science Park, Milton Rd., Cambridge, England CB4 4WF. 44 (223) 420066.

Chemical Carcinogenesis Research Information System-CCRIS. National Library of Medicine, 8600 Rockville Pike, Bethesda, MD 20894. (800) 638-8480. Individual assay results and test conditions for 1,451 chemicals in the areas of carcinogenicity, mutagenicity, tumor promotion, and cocarcinogenicity.

Chemical Coaters Association. P.O. Box 44275, Cincinnati, OH 45244. (513) 232-5055.

Chemical Collection System/Request Tracking-CCS/RTS. U.S. Environmental Protection Agency, Office of Pesticides and Toxic Substances, 401 M St., SW, Washington, DC 20460. (202) 260-2090. Contains information on various properties of a number of chemicals including environmental effects, test and analysis methods, and health effects. Available from EPA.

Chemical Communications Association. c/o Fleishman-Hilliard, Inc., 40 W. 57th St., New York, NY 10019. (212) 265-9150.

Chemical Compatability & Environmental Stress Crack Resistance. Plastics Design Library, 345 E. 54th St., Ste. 5E, New York, NY 10022. (212) 838-2817. 1990. Plastics deterioration and biodegradation.

Chemical Concepts in Pollutant Behavior. Ian J. Tinsley. John Wiley & Sons, Inc., 605 3rd Ave., New York, NY 10158-0012. (212) 850-6000. 1979.

Chemical Contamination and Its Victims: Medical Remedies, Legal Redress, and Public Policy. David W. Schnare, ed. Greenwood Publishing Group, Inc., 88 Post Rd., W., Box 5007, Westport, CT 06881. (203) 226-3571. 1989. Covers toxicology, hazardous waste, and liability for hazardous substances pollution damages.

Chemical Contamination in the Human Environment. Morton Lippmann. Oxford University Press, 200 Madison Ave., New York, NY 10016. (212) 679-7300. 1979. Deals with pollution and environmental health.

Chemical Dictionary Online–CHEMLINE. Chemical Abstracts Service, 2540 Olentangy River Rd., Columbus, OH 43210. (614) 421-3600 or (800) 848-6533. Part of MEDLINE of the National Library of Medicine (NLM). File of 900,000 names for chemical substances, representing 450,000 unique compounds. It contains such information as Chemical Abstracts (CA) Service Registry Numbers, molecular formulas, preferred chemical nomenclature, and generic and ring structure information. Available on NLM's ELHILL system.

Chemical Ecology of Insects. William J. Bell. Chapman & Hall, 29 W. 35th St., New York, NY 10001-2291. (212) 244-3336. 1984.

Chemical Economics Handbook. SRI International, 333 Rovenswood Ave., Menlo Park, CA 14025-3493. (415) 859-4771. 1983-. 33 vols. Provides an in-depth evaluation of the present and future economic status of major chemical substances

Chemical Ecotoxicology. Jaakko Paasivirta. Lewis Publishers, 200 Corporate Blvd. NW, Boca Raton, FL 33431. (407) 994-0555 or (800)272-7737. 1991. Presents an in-depth discussion of risk assessment, chemical cycles, structure-activity relationships, organohalogens, oil residues, mercury, sampling and analysis of trace chemicals, and emissions from the forest industry. Outlines the chemical basis for applied research in environmental protection and provides important data regarding the fate and effects of various chemicals on wildlife.

Chemical Engineering. McGraw-Hill Science & Engineering Books, 11 W. 19th St., New York, NY 10011. (212) 337-6010. Online version of periodical of the same name.

Chemical Engineering. McGraw-Hill Science & Engineering Books, 11 W. 19th St., New York, NY 10011. (212) 337-6010. Monthly. Articles on new engineering techniques and equipment. Also available online.

Chemical Engineering and Biotechnology Abstracts–CEBA. Orbit Search Service, Maxwell Online Inc., 8000 W. Park Dr., McLean, VA 22102. (703) 442-0900 or (800) 456-7248. Monthly. Covers theoretical, practical and commercial material on all aspects of processing safety, and the environment. Also covers process and reaction engineering, measurement and process control, environmental protection and safety, plant design and equipment used in chemical engineering and biotechnology. More than 400 of the world's major primary chemical and process engineering journals are scanned to compile the database. Available from ORBIT.

Chemical Engineering Bibliography. Martyn S. Ray. Noyes Publications, 120 Mill Rd., Park Ridge, NJ 07656. (201) 391-8484. Contains 20,000 references from 40 journals published over the period 1967-1988. Some of the topics covered include: energy conservation, environmental management, biotechnology, plant operations, absorption and cooling towers, membrane separation and other chemical engineering areas.

Chemical Engineering Catalog. 600 Summer St., Stamford, CT 06904. (203) 348-7531. Annual.

Chemical Engineering Progress Magazine. American Institute of Chemical Engineers, 345 E. 47th St., New York, NY 10017. (212) 705-7338. Monthly. Articles covering environmental controls for chemical and petrochemical industrial plants.

Chemical Evaluation Search and Retrieval System. Michigan State Department of Natural Resources, Surface Water Quality Division, Great Lakes and Environmental Assessment Section, Knapp's Office Center, PO Box 30028, Lansing, MI 48909. (517) 373-2190. Covers toxicology information on compounds of environmental concern, providing acute and chronic toxicity data for aquatic and terrestrial life as well as information on carcinogenicity, mutagenicity, and reproductive and developmental effects, bioconcentration, and environmental fate.

Chemical Evolution. Stephen Finney Mason. Oxford University Press, 200 Madison Ave., New York, NY 10016. (212) 679-7300; (800) 334-4249. 1991. Describes the history of ideas in the study of chemistry and the development of modern theories on chemical evolution. Relates the history of chemicals.

Chemical Exposure. Science Applications International Corp., Health & Environmental Information, P.O. Box 2501, Oak Ridge, TN 37831. (615) 482-9031. Database of chemicals that have been identified in both human tissues and body fluids and in feral and food animals. Contains reference to journal articles, conferences, and reports. Covers the whole fields of information related to human and animal exposure to food, air, and water contaminants and pharmaceuticals. Its records include information on chemical properties, formulas, tissues measured, analytical method used, demographics and more. Available on DIALOG.

The Chemical Free Lawn. Warren Schultz. Rodale Press, 33 E. Minor St., Emmaus, PA 18098. (215) 967-5171; (800) 322-6333. 1989. Describes how to grow lush hardy grass without pesticides, herbicides or chemical fertilizers.

Chemical Guide to the United States. Noyes Publications, 120 Mill Rd., Park Ridge, NJ 07656. (201) 391-8484.

Chemical Hazard Communication Guidebook: OSHA, EPA, and DOT Requirements. Andrew B. Waldo and Richard D. Hinds. PennWell Books, PO Box 21288, Tulsa, OK 74121. (918) 831-9421; (800) 752-9764. 1991. Covers how to comply with hazard communication requirements applicable to chemicals in the workplace, how to meet reporting responsibilities imposed by emergency planning and community right to know requirements and how to comply with restrictions on the transportation of hazardous materials.

Chemical Hazard Response Information System–CHRIS. U.S. Coast Guard. Office of Research and Development, 2100 2d St., NW., Rm. 5410 C, Washington, DC 20593. (202) 783-3238. Contains information needed to respond to emergencies that occur during the transport of hazardous chemicals, as well as information that can help prevent emergency situations. Each of the approximately 1,300 records include information on physical and chemical properties, health and fire hazards, labeling, chemical reactivity, hazard classification and water pollution. Available on CIS and on Microdex's TOMES Plus series.

Chemical Hazards in the Workplace. Ronald M. Scott. Lewis Publishers, 200 Corporate Blvd. NW, Boca Raton, FL 33431. (407) 994-0555 or (800)272-7737. 1989. Presents basics of toxicology. Reports a sampling of the accumulated knowledge of the hazards of specific compounds in the workplace. Also discusses the federal regulatory agencies charged with worker protection and the specific practices involved in maintaining safety and regulatory compliance.

Chemical Hazards of the Work Place. Nick H. Proctor and edited by Gloria J. Hathaway, et al. Van Nostrand Reinhold, 115 5th Ave., New York, NY 10003. (212) 254-3232. 1991. 3d ed.

Chemical Industry Institute of Toxicology. P.O. Box 12137, Research Triangle Park, NC 27709. (919) 541-2070.

Chemical Industry Notes–CHEMSIS. Chemical Abstracts Service, PO Box 3012, 2540 Olentangy River, Columbus, OH 43210. (614) 421-3600 or (800) 848-6533. Contains citations to business-oriented literature relating to the chemical processing industries. Includes pricing, production, products and processes, corporate and government activities, facilities and people from more than 80 worldwide business periodicals published since 1974. Available on DIALOG and ORBIT.

Chemical Information File. OSHA Salt Lake City Analytical Laboratory, 1781 S. 300 W., Salt Lake City, UT 84165-0200. (801) 524-5287. Database is part of the OSHA Computerized Information System (OCIS) and contains chemical substances found in the workplace with current information on identification, exposure limits, compliance sampling methods, and analytical methods.

Chemical Information Manual. Government Institutes, Inc., 4 Research Pl., Ste. 200, Rockville, MD 20850. (301) 921-2300. 1991. Handbook presenting a variety of useful data on each chemical substances, including proper identification, OSHA exposure limits, description and physical properties, carcinogenic status, health effects and toxicology, sampling and analysis.

Chemical Kinetics and Process Dynamics in Aquatic Systems. Patrick L. Brezonik. Lewis Publishers, 2000 Corporate Blvd., N.W., Boca Raton, FL 33431. (407) 994-0555 or (800) 272-7737. 1993. Discusses natural waters as nonequilibrium systems, rate expressions for chemical reactions, reactors, mass transport and process models.

Chemical Manufacturers Association. 2501 M St., N.W., Washington, DC 20037. (202) 887-1100.

Chemical Market Associates Petrochemical Market Reports. Chemical Market Associates, Inc., 11757 Daty Freeway, Suite 750, Houston, TX 77079. (713) 531-4660.

The Chemical Monitor. NewsNet, Inc., 945 Haverford Rd., Bryn Mawr, PA 19010. (800) 345-1301.

Chemical, Physical, and Biological Properties of Compounds Present at Hazardous Waste Sites: Final Report. U.S. Environmental Protection Agency. Clement Associates Inc., Arlington, VA 1985.

Chemical Plant Database. Chemical Intelligence Services, 39A Bowling Green Lane, London, England EC 1R OBJ. 44 (71) 833-3812.

Chemical Plant Wastes: A Bibliography. Vance Bibliographies, PO Box 229, 112 N. Charter St., Monticello, IL 61856. (217) 762-3831.

Chemical Primary Sludge Thickening and Dewatering. Di Gregorio, David. National Technical Information Service, 5285 Port Royal Rd., Springfield, VA 22161. (703) 487-4650. 1979.

Chemical Processes in Wastewater Treatment. W. J. Eilbeck and G. Mattock. John Wiley & Sons, Inc., 605 3rd Ave., New York, NY 10185-0012. (212) 850-6000. 1984.

Chemical Producers and Distributors Association. 1220 19th St., N.W., Suite 202, Washington, DC 20036. (202) 785-2732.

Chemical Products Desk Reference. Michael and Irene Ash. Chemical Publishing Co., 80 Eighth Ave., New York, NY 10011. (212) 255-1950. Contains over 32,000 entries of currently marketed commercial chemical trademark products.

Chemical Protective Clothing. American Industrial Hygiene Association, 345 White Pond Dr., Akron, OH 44320. (216) 873-2442. 1990. 2 vols. Volume 1 reviews basic polymer chemistry and permeation theory and types, construction, and use of protective materials; specific test methods, selection guidelines and decontamination. Volume 2 contains product performance evaluation data and information on physical property test methods, permeation data, chemicals, products and vendors, and encapsulating suit ensembles.

Chemical Protective Clothing Performance in Chemical Emergency Response. J.L. Perkins. Association for Testing and Materials (ASTM), 1916 Race St., Philadelphia, PA 19103-1187. (215) 299-5400. 1989. Chemical engineering safety measures relating to protective clothing.

Chemical Protective Clothing Performance Index Book. Krister Fosberg. John Wiley & Sons, Inc., 605 3rd Ave., New York, NY 10158-0012. (212) 850-6000. 1989.

Chemical Quality of Water and the Hydrologic Cycle. Robert C. Averett and Diane M. McKnight. Lewis Publishers, 2000 Corporate Blvd. N.W., Boca Raton, FL 33431. (407) 994-0555 or (800) 272-7737. 1987. Organized collection of papers dealing with changes in the quality of water as it moves through the world's hydrologic cycle.

Chemical Referral Center. c/o Chemical Manufacturers Association, 2501 M St., N.W., Washington, DC 20037. (202) 887-1100.

Chemical Regulation Reporter. Bureau of National Affairs, BNA PLUS, 1231 25th St., N.W., Room 215, Washington, DC 20037. (800) 452-7773. Online version of periodicals of the same name.

Chemical Regulation Reporter. Bureau of National Affairs, 1231 25th St. NW, Washington, DC 20037. (202) 452-4200. Weekly. Periodical covering legislative, regulatory, and industry action affecting controls on pesticides. Also available online.

Chemical Regulations and Guidelines System–CRGS. Network Management, 11242 Waples Mill Rd., Fairfax, VA 22030. (703) 359-9400. Maintains bibliographical information on the state of regulatory material, October 1982 to the present, on control of selected chemical substances or classes. It contains U.S. Statutes, promulgated regulations, available government standards and guidelines, and support documents. CRGS follows the regulatory cycle and includes a reference to each document including main documents and revisions in the Federal Register. Available on DIALOG.

Chemical Research in Toxicology. American Chemical Society, 1155 16th St. N.W., Washington, DC 20036. (800) 227-5558. Bimonthly. Deals with chemical analysis and reactive intermediates.

Chemical Retorts. FIND/SVP, 625 Avenue of the Americas, New York, NY 10011. (212) 645-4500. 1991. Profiles the collapse of selected commodity petrochemical margins including, VCM, PVC, ethylene, polyethylene and chlorine.

Chemical Safety Newsbase. Royal Society of Chemistry, Thomas Graham House, Science Park, Milton Rd., Cambridge, England CB4 4WF. 44 (223) 420066.

Chemical Specialties Manufacturers Association. 1913 I St., N.W., Washington, DC 20006. (202) 872-8110.

Chemical Spill Uncertainty Analysis. W. J. Shields. Electric Power Research Institute, 3412 Hillview Ave., Palo Alto, CA 94304. (415) 965-4081. 1989. Covers mathematical models to deal with chemical spills.

Chemical Spills: A Bibliography. Vance Bibliographies, PO Box 229, 112 N. Charter St., Monticello, IL 61856. (217) 762-3831. Looks at hazardous substances and environmental chemistry.

Chemical Substance Control. Bureau of National Affairs, BNA PLUS, 1231 25th ST., N.W., Rm. 215, Washington, DC 20037. (800) 452-7773. Online version of periodical of the same name.

Chemical Substances Control. Bureau of National Affairs, 1231 25th St. NW, Washington, DC 20037. (202) 452-4200. Biweekly. Periodical covering regulatory compliance and management of chemicals. Also available online.

Chemical Times & Trends. Chemical Specialties Manufacturers Association, 1913 Eye Street, NW, Washington, DC 20006. (202) 872-8110. Quarterly. Discusses trends in manufacturing/selling of industrial, household, and personal care products.

Chemical Times & Trends–Directory of Toxicology Testing Laboratories Issue. Chemical Specialties Manufacturers Association, 1913 Eye St. N.W., Washington, DC 20006. (202) 872-8110.

Chemical Waste Disposal: Chemicals Identified in Terrestrial and Aquatic Waste Disposal Processes; a Selected Bibliography with Abstracts, 1964-1979. J. G. Pruett. Federation of American Societies for Experimental Biology, 9650 Rockville Pike, Bethesda, MD 20814. (301) 530-7000. 1980.

Chemical Waste: Handling and Treatment. Springer-Verlag, 175 5th Ave., New York, NY 10010. (212) 460-1500. 1986.

Chemical Waste Transportation Council. 1730 Rhode Island Ave., N.W., Suite 1000, Washington, DC 20036. (202) 659-4613.

Chemical Waste Transportation Institute. c/o National Solid Wastes Management Association, 1730 Rhode Island Ave., N.W., 10th Floor, Washington, DC 20036. (202) 659-4613.

Chemical Week. Chemical Week Associates, 816 7th Ave., New York, NY 10019. (212) 586-3430.

Chemical Week. Chemical Week Associates, 816 7th Ave., New York, NY 10019. (212) 586-3430. Online version of the periodical of the same name.

Chemical Week–Financial Survey of the 300 Largest Companies in the U.S. Chemical Process Industries Issue. 816 7th Ave., New York, NY 10019. (212) 586-3430. Annual.

Chemical Wholesalers Directory. American Business Directories, Inc., 5711 S. 86th Circle, Omaha, NE 68127. (402) 593-4600.

Chemicals Directory. Kevin R. Fitzgerald. Cahners Publishing Co., 249 W. 17th St., New York, NY 10011. (212) 645-0067. 1991. Covers manufacturers and suppliers of chemicals and raw materials, containers and packaging, transportation services and storage facilities, and environmental services companies.

Chemicals in the Environment. Selper, 33 Westville Grange, Westbury Road, Ealing, London, England W5 2LJ. Cites environmental chemistry and chemical and technical aspects of environmental pollutants.

Chemicals in the Human Food Chain. Carl K. Winter, et al. Van Nostrand Reinhold, 115 5th Ave., New York, NY 10003. (212) 254-3232. 1990. Deals with prevention of food contamination by pesticides and other toxic chemicals.

Chemicals Quarterly Industry Report. United States. Business and Defense Services Administration. U.S. Deptartment of Commerce, Washington, DC 20230. (202)377-2000. Covers chemicals, rubber, and Allied products.

Chemicals Tested as Acaricides to Control One-Host Ticks, U.S. Livestock Insects Laboratory, 1962-77. R. O. Drummond. U.S. Livestock Insects Laboratory, PO Box 232, Kerrville, TX 78029-0232. (512) 257-3566. 1979.

ChemID. National Library of Medicine, Toxicology Information Program, 8600 Rockville Pike, Bethesda, MD 20894. (800) 638-8480.

Chemiluminescence: Principles and Applications in Biology and Medicine. CCH Publishers, Inc., 220 E. 23rd St., Suite 909, New York, NY 10010-4606. (212) 683-8333. 1988.

CHEMINFO. Canadian Centre for Occupational Health & Safety, 250 Main St., East, Hamilton, ON, Canada L8N 1H6. (800) 263-8276.

Chemist. American Institute of Chemists, 7315 Wisconsin Avenue, Bethesda, MD 20814. (301) 652-2447. Monthly. Covers topics of professional interest to chemists and chemical engineers.

Chemistry, Agriculture and the Environment. Mervyn L. Richardson. Royal Society of Chemistry, Thomas Graham House, Science Park, Milton Rd., Cambridge, England CB4 4WF. 44(0)223420066. 1991. Provides an overview of the chemical pollution of the environment caused by modern agricultural practices worldwide, and describes the effects of agrochemicals used in intensive animal and crop production on the air, water, soil, plants, and animals including humans. Also available through CRC Press.

Chemistry and Physics of Lipids. North Holland Pub. Co., Amsterdam, Netherlands Bimonthly.

The Chemistry and Technology of Gypsum. Richard A. Kuntze. American Society for Testing and Materials, 1916 S. Race St., Philadelphia, PA 19103. (215) 299-5585. 1984.

Chemistry and Technology of Lime and Limestone. John Wiley & Sons, Inc., 605 3rd Ave., New York, NY 10158-0012. (212) 850-6000. 1980.

The Chemistry of Aluminium, Gallium, Indium and Thallium. Kenneth Wade. Pergamon Press, Headington Hill Hall, Oxford, England OX3 0BW. 1975.

Chemistry of Carbon Compounds: A Modern Comprehensive Treatise. M. F. Ansell, ed. Elsevier Science Publishing Co., 655 Avenue of the Americas, New York, NY 10010. (212) 984-5800. Irregular.

The Chemistry of Chlorine and Chlorination. Frank Nickols. State of Illinois Environmental Protection Agency, 2200 Churchill Rd., Springfield, IL 62706. (217) 782-2829. 1990.

Chemistry of Coal Weathering. Elsevier Science Publishing Co., 655 Avenue of the Americas, New York, NY 10010. (212) 984-5800. 1989. Discusses topics in coal science and technology.

The Chemistry of Gallium. Ivan Arsenevich Sheka. Elsevier Science Publishing Co., 655 Avenue of the Americas, New York, NY 10010. (212) 984-5800. 1966.

The Chemistry of Lithium, Sodium, Potassium, Rubidium, Cesium and Francium. William A. Hart. Pergamon Microforms International, Inc., Fairview Park, Elmsford, NY 10523. (914) 592-7720. 1973.

The Chemistry of Manganese, Technetium and Rhenium. R. D. W. Kemmitt. Pergamon Microforms International, Inc., Fairview Park, Elmsford, NY 10523. (914) 592-7720. 1975.

The Chemistry of PCBs. O. Hutzinger, et al. CRC Press, 2000 Corporate Blvd. N.W., Boca Raton, FL 33431. (407) 994-0555; (800) 272-7737. 1983.

Chemistry of Pesticides. K. H. Buchel, ed. John Wiley & Sons, Inc., 605 3rd Ave., New York, NY 10158-0012. (212) 850-6000. 1983.

The Chemistry of Ruthenium. Elaine A. Seddon. Elsevier Science Publishing Co., 655 Avenue of the Americas, New York, NY 10010. (212) 984-5800. 1984.

The Chemistry of Silica. Ralph K. Iler. John Wiley & Sons, Inc., 605 3rd Ave., New York, NY 10158-0012. (212) 850-6000. 1979. Solubility, polymerization, colloid and surface properties, and biochemistry.

The Chemistry of Sulphur, Selenium, Tellurium and Polonium. M. Schmidt. Pergamon Microforms International, Inc., Fairview Park, Elmsford, NY 10523. (914) 592-7720. 1975.

CHEMLINE. National Library of Medicine, Toxicology Information Program, 8600 Rockville Pike, Bethesda, MD 20894. (800) 638-8480.

CHEMLIST. American Petroleum Institute, Central Abstracting & Indexing Service, 275 7th Ave., New York, NY 10001. (212) 366-4040.

Chemoecology. Thieme Medical Publishers, 381 Park Ave. S., New York, NY 10016. (212) 683-5088. Quarterly. Topics in environmental chemistry.

Chemosphere: Chemistry, Biology and Toxicology as Related to Environmental Problems. Pergamon Microforms International, Inc., Fairview Park, Elmsford, NY 10523. (914) 592-7720. 1970-. Offers maximum dissemination of investigations related to the health and safety of every aspect of life. Environmental protection encompasses a very wide field and relies on scientific research in chemistry, biology, physics, toxicology and inter-related disciplines.

ChemQuest. Molecular Design Ltd., 2132 Farrallon Dr., San Leandro, CA 94577. (415) 895-1313.

CHEMSAFE. DECHEMA, Chemische Technick und Biotechnologie e.V., I & D Information Systems and Data Banks, Theodor-Heuss-Alle 25, Postfach 97 01 46, Frankfurt, Germany D-6000. 49 (69) 7564-248.

CHEMTRAN. ChemShare Corporation, P.O. Box 1885, Houston, TX 77251. (713) 627-8945.

Chesapeake Bay Foundation. 162 Prince George St., Annapolis, MD 21401. (301) 268-8816.

Chicorel Index to Urban Planning and Environmental Design. Marietta Chicorel. Chicorel Library Pub. Corp., New York, NY Irregular. Covers cities and towns planning.

Chihuahuan Desert Newsbriefs. Chihuahuan Desert Research Institute, Box 1334, Alpine, TX 79831. 1983-. Semiannually.

Chihuahuan Desert Research Institute. P.O. Box 1334, Alpine, TX 79831. (915) 837-8370.

Children of the Green Earth. P.O. Box 95219, Seattle, WA 98145. (503) 229-4721.

Children's Environment Quarterly. Center for Human Environments, 33 W. 42nd St., New York, NY 10036. (212) 790-4550. 1974-. Quarterly.

Chlorinated Dioxins and Dibenzofurans in Perspective. Christoffer Rappe, et al. Lewis Publishers, 2000 Corporate Blvd., N.W., Boca Raton, FL 33431. (407) 994-0555 or (800) 272-7737. 1986. Gives the latest human exposure data and the most advanced analytical techniques developed in the continuing effort against contamination by chlorinated dioxins and dibenzofurans.

Chlorinated Dioxins and Dibenzofurans in the Total Environment. Gangadhar Chordhary, Lawrence H. Keith, and Christoffer Rappe. Butterworth-Heinemann, 80 Montvale Ave., Stoneham, MA 02180. (617) 438-8464. 1985. Environmental aspects and toxicology of tetrachlorodibenzodioxin and dibenzofurans.

Chlorinated Paraffins Industry Association. 655 15th St., N.W., Suite 1200, Washington, DC 20005. (202) 879-5130.

Chlorine and Hydrogen Chloride. National Academy of Sciences, 2101 Constitution Ave., NW, Washington, DC 20418. (202) 334-2000. 1976. Medical and biologic effects of environmental pollutants.

The Chlorine Institute. 2001 L St., N.W., Suite 506, Washington, DC 20036. (202) 775-2790.

Chlorobenzene Producers Association. 1330 Connecticut Ave., N.W., Washington, DC 20036. (202) 659-0060.

Chlorofluorocarbons. FIND/SVP, 625 Avenue of the Americas, New York, NY 10011. (212) 645-4500. 1991. Markets for commercial fluorine compounds as represented by the chlorofluorocarbons, fluoropolymers, fluoroelastomers, membranes, hydrogen fluoride, other inorganic and organic chemicals containing fluorine, and the alternatives to CFCs.

Chlorofluoromethanes and the Stratosphere. Robert D. Hudson, ed. National Technical Information Service, 5285 Port Royal Rd., Springfield, VA 22161. (703) 487-4650. 1977.

Chloroform, Carbon Tetrachloride, and Other Halomethanes. National Academy of Sciences, 2101 Constitution Ave, N.W., Washington, DC 20418. (202) 334-2000. 1978.

Chlorophenols Other than Pentachlorophenol. World Health Organization, Ave. Appia, Geneva, Switzerland CH-1211. (518) 436-9686. 1989.

Choices: Realistic Alternatives in Cancer Treatment. Avon Books, 105 Madison Ave., New York, NY 10016. (212) 481-5600.

Cholesterol Handbook. Beekman Publishers Inc., P.O. Box 888, Woodstock, NY 12498. (914) 679-2300. 1989.

Cholesterol in Foods and Its Effects on Animals and Humans. National Technical Information Service, 5285 Port Royal Rd., Springfield, VA 22161. (703) 487-4650.

Cholesterol Metabolism, LDL, and the LDL Receptor. N.B. Myant. Academic Press, c/o Harcourt Brace Jovanovich Inc., 6277 Sea Harbor Dr., Orlando, FL 32887. (800) 346-8648. 1990.

CHRIS: A Condensed Guide to Chemical Hazards. Washington, DC 1985. Covers chemical hazard response information system.

Chromatographic Analysis of Pharmaceuticals. Marcel Dekker, Inc., 270 Madison Ave., New York, NY 10016. (212) 696-9000; (800) 228-1160. Analysis of drugs.

Chromatography: A Laboratory Handbook of Chromatographic and Electrophoretic Methods. Van Nostrand Reinhold, 115 Fifth Ave., New York, NY 10003. (212) 254-3232.

Chromatography of Environmental Hazards. Elsevier Science Publishing Co., 655 Avenue of the Americas, New York, NY 10010. (212) 984-5800. Covers carcinogens, mutagens, and teratogens, metals, gaseous and industrial pollutants, pesticides, and drugs of abuse.

CISDOC. International Occupational Safety & Health Information Centre, International Labour Office, Geneva 22, Switzerland CH-1211. 41 (22) 996740.

Citizen Alert Newsletter. Citizen Alert, Box 5391, Reno, NV 89513. (702) 827-4200. 1975-. Quarterly. Raises awareness and about nuclear, military and environmental issues facing Nevada.

Citizens Against Throwaways. Florida Conservation Foundation, Inc., 1251-B Miller Ave., Winter Park, FL 32789. (305) 644-5377.

Citizens Against Tobacco Smoke. P.O. Box 36236, Cincinnati, OH 45236. (513) 984-8833.

Citizen's Bulletin. Connecticut Dept. of Environmental Protection, 165 Capitol Ave., Hartford, CT 06106. (203) 566-3489. Monthly. Information on departmental programs and environmental issues.

Citizen's Call. P.O. Box 1722, Cedar City, UT 84720. (801) 586-4808.

Citizen's Clearinghouse for Hazardous Wastes, Inc. P.O. Box 6806, Falls Church, VA 22040. (703) 237-2249.

Citizen's Directory for Water Quality Abuses. Karen Firehock. Izaak Walton League of America, 1401 Wilson Dr., Level B, Arlington, VA 22209. (703) 528-1818. Annual. Environmental agencies, including state and regional offices interested in providing quality control by eliminating pollution and dumping of wastes into water resources.

Citizen's Energy Council. 77 Homewood Ave., Allendale, NJ 07401. (201) 327-3914.

Citizens for a Better Environment. 33 E. Congress, Suite 523, Chicago, IL 60605. (312) 939-1530.

Citizens for a Quieter City. 300 E. 42nd St., New York, NY 10017. (212) 986-6590.

The Citizen's Guide to Lead: Uncovering a Hidden Health Hazard. Barbara Wallace. NC Press, 345 Adelaide St. W., Ste. 400, Toronto, ON, Canada M5V 1R5. (416) 593-6284. 1986. Guide to the serious problems of environmental lead contamination. Describes how we are all exposed to lead and what can be done to reduce personal health risks and further environmental contamination.

A Citizen's Guide to Plastics in the Ocean. Kathryn J. O'Hara and Suzanne Iudicello. Center for Marine Conservation, 1725 DeSales St, NW, Suite 500, Washington, DC 20036. (202) 429-5609. 1988.

A Citizen's Guide to Promoting Toxic Waste Reduction. Lauren Kenworthy and Eric Schaeffer. INFORM, 381 Park Ave. S., New York, NY 10016. (212) 689-4040. 1990. The how-to manual describes source reduction and its benefits, five strategies plants can use to reduce their hazardous wastes at the source, a step-by-step process for gathering background facts, and interviewing company representatives and analyzing data.

City Currents-Resource Recovery Activities Issue. Ronald W. Musselwhite. HCI Publications, 410 Archibald St., Kansas City, MO 64111. (816) 931-1311. Annual. Operating or proposed resource recovery plants.

City Sierran. Sierra Club-NYC Group, 625 Broadway, 2nd Fl., New York, NY 10012. (212) 473-7841. 1984-. Quarterly. Reports environmental news to Sierra Club members in New York City. Writers are activists and experts on acid rain, pollution, toxic wastes, recycling, endangered species, etc.

Civic Public Works-Waste Management Reference Manual and Buyers Guide Issue. Maclean-Hunter Ltd., 777 Bay St., Toronto, ON, Canada M5W 1A7. (416) 596-5953.

Civil Engineering ASCE. American Society of Civil Engineers, 345 E 47th St., New York, NY 10017. (212) 705-7288; (800) 548-2723. Monthly. Professional journal that offers a forum for free exchange of ideas relevant to the profession of civil engineering. Covers in regular columns, engineering news, legal trends in engineering, calendar of events, membership news, publications and other items of interest to civil engineers. Formerly, Civil Engineering.

Civil Engineering Database. American Society of Civil Engineers, 345 E. 47th St., New York, NY 10017. (800) 548-2723.

Civil Engineering Hydraulic Abstracts. BHRA Fluid Engineering, Air Science Co., PO Box 143, Corning, NY 14830. (607) 962-5591. Monthly. Abstracts of periodicals that publish in the areas of hydraulic engineering and other related topics.

CJACS: Chemical Journals of the American Chemical Society. American Chemical Society, 1155 16th St. N.W., Washington, DC 20036. (800) 227-5558.

CJAOAC: Chemical Journals of the Association of Official Analytical Chemists. Association of Official Analytical Chemists, 2200 Wilson Blvd., Suite 400-P, Arlington, VA 22201-3301. (703) 522-3032.

CJELSEVIER. Elsevier Science Publishing Co., Excerpta Medica, Molemverf 1, 1014 AG Amsterdam, Netherlands 31 (20) 5803507.

Clam Mariculture in North America. J. J. Manzi. Elsevier Science Publishing Co., 655 Avenue of the Americas, New York, NY 10010. (212) 984-5800. 1989.

Clark University, Program for International Development and Social Change. 950 Main St., Worcester, MA 01610.

Classification of Floating CHRIS Chemicals for the Development of a Spill Response Manual. A. T. Szhula. National Technical Information Service, 5285 Port Royal Rd, Springfield, VA 22161. (703) 487-4650. Covers classification of chemical spills.

Classification of Plant Communities. Robert H. Whittaker. W. Junk, 101 Phelps Dr., Norwell, MA 02061. (617) 871-6600. 1978. Handbook of vegetation science, with emphasis on vegetation classification.

Clay Liners for Waste Management Facilities; Design, Construction, and Evaluation. L. J. Goldman, et al. Noyes Publications, 120 Mill Rd., Park Ridge, NJ 07656. (201) 391-8484. 1990. Compilation of all of the available information on the design, construction, and evaluation of clay liners for waste landfills, surface impoundments, and wastepiles.

Clay Minerals Society. P.O. Box 12210, Boulder, CO 80303. (303) 444-6405.

Clean Air Act 1990 Amendments: Law and Practice. J. M. Stensvaag. John Wiley & Sons, Inc., 605 3rd Ave., New York, NY 10158-0012. (212) 850-6000. 1991. In-depth practical analysis of the 1990 Amendments to the Clean Air Act that includes compliance requirements, the new operating permit system, the enhanced enforcement provisions and criminal penalties, potential for citizen enforcement, and the increased reporting requirements.

Clean Air Act: A Primer and Glossary. Clean Air Working Group, 818 Connecticut Ave., NW, Suite 900, Washington, DC 20006. (202) 857-0370. 1990.

The Clean Air Act Amendments of 1990: Summary Materials. U.S. Environmental Protection Agency, Office of Air and Radiation, 401 M St. SW, Washington, DC 20460. (202) 260-2090. 1990.

Clean Air Act Policy Compendium. Government Institutes, Inc., 4 Research Pl., Ste. 200, Rockville, MD 20850. (301) 921-2300. 1985. Gives detailed insight into both compliance and enforcement of the Clean Air Act.

Clean Air Handbook. Government Institutes, Inc., 4 Research Pl., Ste. 200, Rockville, MD 20850. (301) 921-2300. Analyzes the requirements of the Clean Air Act and its 1990 amendments, as well as what can be expected in terms of new regulation.

Clean Air News. Industrial Gas Cleaning Institute, 1707 L St. N.W., #570, Washington, DC 20036. (202) 457-0911. 1960-. Bimonthly. Industrial air pollution control.

Clean Air Permits. Thompson Publishing Group, 1725 K St., N.W., Suite 200, Washington, DC 20006. (202) 872-4000. Monthly. Manager's guide to the 1990 Clean Air Act.

Clean Air Report. National Environmental Development Assn., 1440 New York Ave., NW, Suite 300, Washington, DC 20005. (202) 638-1230. Quarterly.

Clean Air Working Group. 818 Connecticut Ave., N.W., Suite 900, Washington, DC 20006. (202) 857-0370.

Clean-Coal/Synfuels Letter. McGraw-Hill Science & Engineering Books, 11 W. 19th St., New York, NY 10011. (212) 337-6010.

Clean Coal Technologies. National Technical Information Service, 5285 Port Royal Road, Springfield, VA 22161. (703) 487-4650. Monthly. Desulfurization, coal gasification and liquefaction, flue gas cleanup, and advanced coal combustion.

Clean Coal Technology: Programmes and Issues. International Energy Agency. OECD Publications and Information Centre, 2, rue Andre-Pascal, Paris Cedex 16, France F-75775. (1) 4524 8200. 1987. Analyses the number of issues that will affect future coal use. Both economic and environmental points of view are taken into consideration.

Clean Coal Today. U.S. Department of Energy, 1000 Independence Ave., S.W., Washington, DC 20585. (202) 252-1760. 1990-. Quarterly.

Clean Fuels Development Coalition. 1129 20th St., N.W., Suite 500, Washington, DC 20036. (202) 822-1715.

The Clean Fuels Report. J. E. Sinor Consultants, Inc., 6964 North 79th Street, Suite 1, PO Box 649, Niwot, CO 80544. (303) 652-2632. Deals with new fuel choices, costs, and regulations.

Clean Harbors Cooperative. P.O. Box 1375, 1200 State St., Perth Amboy, NJ 08862. (201) 738-2438.

Clean Sites Annual Report. Clean Sites, Inc., 1199 N. Fairfax St., Alexandria, VA 22314. (703) 683-8522.

Clean Sites, Inc. 1199 N. Fairfax St., Alexandria, VA 22314. (703) 683-8522.

Clean Water. The Water Quality Bureau of the Division of Environment, Idaho Dept. of Health and Welfare, 450 W. State St., Boise, ID 83720. (208) 334-5855. Quarterly. Water quality and water pollution control in Idaho.

Clean Water Action News. Clean Water Action Project, 317 Pennsylvania Ave. S.E., Washington, DC 20003. (202) 547-1196. 1976-. Quarterly. Features news and articles on environmental political issues.

Clean Water Action Project. c/o David Zwick, 1320 18th St. N.W., Washington, DC 20003. (202) 457-1286.

Clean Water Handbook. Government Institutes, Inc., 4 Research Pl., Ste. 200, Rockville, MD 20850. (301) 921-2300. 1990. Offers straightforward explanation on enforcement, toxics, water quality standards, efficient limitations, NPDES, stormwater and nonpoint discharge control.

Clean Water Report. Business Publishers, Inc., 951 Pershing Dr., Silver Spring, MD 20910-4464. (301) 587-6300. 1964-. Biweekly. Key information source for environmental professionals, covering the important issues: groundwater, drinking water, wastewater treatment, drought, wetlands, coastal protection, dioxin, non-point source pollution, agrichemical contamination, cleanup versus prevention issues, and related topics.

The Cleaning Products Competitive Intelligence Database. Strategic Intelligence Systems, Inc., 404 Park Ave., South, New York, NY 10016. (212) 725-5954.

Cleaning Up Great Lakes Areas of Concern: How Much Will it Cost?. Northeast-Midwest Institute, Publications Office, 218 D St., SE, Washington, DC 20003. 1989.

Cleanup of Petroleum Contaminated Soils at Underground Storage Tanks. Warren J. Lyman, et al. Noyes Publications, 120 Mill Rd., Park Ridge, NJ 07656. (201) 391-8484. Describes soil venting, biorestoration, soil flushing, hydraulic barriers, and vacuum extraction of non-aqueous phase liquids, and biorestoration for saturated zones.

Clearing House Newsletter. National Inst. on Park and Grounds Management, PO Box 1936, Appleton, WI 54913. (414) 733-2301. Bimonthly. Management of large outdoor areas such as parks, campuses, and industrial areas.

Clearing Magazine. Environmental Education Project, 19600 S. Molalla Ave., Oregon City, OR 97045. (503) 656-0155. Five times a year. Resource materials, teaching ideas, and information for those interested in providing environmental education.

Clearing the Air: Perspectives on Environmental Tobacco Smoke. Robert D. Tollison. Lexington Books, 866 3rd Ave., New York, NY 10022. (212) 702-2000. 1988. Smoking and air pollution, environmental air pollutants resulting from tobacco smoke.

Clearwaters. New York Water Pollution Control Association, 90 Presidential Plaza, Suite 122, Syracuse, NY 13202. (315) 422-7811. 1971-. Quarterly. Articles on design methods, legislation, and innovations on wastewater treatment plants.

Climate and Man: From the Ice Age to the Global Greenhouse. Fred Pearce. Vision Books in Association with LWT, The Forum 74-80, Camden St., London, England NW1 OEG. 071-388-8811. 1989.

Climate Assessment Database. National Weather Service, National Meteorological Center, Climate Analysis Center, Room 808 World Weather Building, Washington, DC 20233. (301) 763-4670.

Climate Change and Society: Consequences of Increasing Atmospheric Carbon Dioxide. Westview Press, 5500 Central Ave., Boulder, CO 80301. (303) 444-3541. 1982.

Climate Change and U.S. Water Resources. P. E. Waggoner, ed. John Wiley & Sons, Inc., 605 3rd Ave., New York, NY 10158-0012. (212) 850-6000. 1990. Covers latest research in climate changes and subsequent effects on water supply. Topics include future water use, statistics in forecasting, vulnerability of water systems, irrigation, urban water systems, and reallocation by markets and prices.

Climate Change and World Agriculture. Martin Parry. Earthscan Pub. Ltd., 3 Endsleigh St., London, England WC1H ODD. (071)388-2117. 1990. Describes the effects on agriculture, estimating the impacts on plant and animal growth and looking at the geographical limits to different types of farming.

Climate Change–Evaluating the Socio-Economic Impacts. OECD, UNIPUB, 4611-F Assembly Dr., Lanham, MD 20706. (301) 459-7666 or (800) 274-4888. 1991. Describes various approaches to better understand the climate change and the socio-economic disruptions associated with it.

Climate Change: The IPCC Response Strategies. World Meteorological Organization/United Nations Env. Program, Intergovernmental Panel on Climate Change. Island Press, 1718 Connecticut Ave. N.W., Suite 300, Washington, DC 20009. (202) 232-7933. 1991. Identifies and evaluates a wide range of international strategies for limiting or adapting to climate change, and to review available mechanisms for implementing those strategies.

Climate, Fertilizers, and Soil Fertility: January 1981 - February 1991. Susan Whitmore. National Agricultural Library, 10301 Baltimore Blvd., Beltsville, MD 20705-2351. (301) 504-5755. 1991.

Climate Institute. 316 Pennsylvania Ave., S.E., Suite 403, Washington, DC 20003. (202) 547-0104.

Climate Research. Inter-Research, PO Box 1120, W-2124 Amelinghausen, Germany D-2124. 04132. 1990. Three times a year. Presents both basic and applied research as research articles. Reviews and notes concerned with the interactions of climate with organisms, ecosystems and human societies are presented.

Climates of the States. Gale Research Inc., 835 Penobscot Bldg., Detroit, MI 48226-4094. (313) 961-2242. 1986. State-by-state summaries of climate based on first order weather reporting stations for the period 1951-1980.

Climatic Change and Plant Genetic Resources. M. T. Jackson, et al., eds. Belhaven Press, 136 S. Broadway, Irvington, NY 10533. (914) 591-9111. 1990. Cities concerns about the effect of global warming on biological diversity of species is the main thrust of this text. Major portion of the book comes from the second international workshop on plant genetic resources held in 1989.

Climatic Change and Society: Consequences of Increasing Atmospheric Carbon Dioxide. Westview Press, 5500 Central Ave., Boulder, CO 80301. (303) 444-3541. 1982. Social aspects of climatic changes.

Clinical Abstracts. Medical Information Systems, Reference & Index Services, Inc., 3845 N. Meridian St., Indianapolis, IN 46208. (317) 923-1575.

Clinical Toxicology. Marcel Dekker, Inc., 270 Madison Ave., New York, NY 10016. (212) 696-9000; (800) 228-1160. Quarterly. Toxicology and poison related topics.

CLINPROT: CLINical cancer PROTocols. U.S. National Institutes of Health, National Eye Institute, Building 31, Rm. 6A32, Bethesda, MD 20892. (301) 496-5248.

Closed Waste Site Evaluation: Emsdale Landfill: Report. Ontario Waste Management Branch. Waste Site Evaluation Unit, Toronto. National Technical Information Service, 5285 Port Royal Rd., Springfield, VA 22161. (703) 487-4650. 1989. Order number MIC-91-03061LDM.

CMI Descriptions of Pathogenic Fungi and Bacteria. Commonwealth Mycological Institute, Ferry Lane, Kew, Richmond, England TW9 3AF. 1964-. Four sets a year.

Co-Op America. 2100 M St., NW, Suite 403, Washington, DC 20063. (202) 872-5307.

Co-Op America's Business and Organizational Member Directory. Co-Op America, 2100 M St. NW, No. 403, Washington, DC 20063. (202) 872-5307. Annual. Small businesses, co-operatives, and nonprofit organizations that produce environmentally benign products such as nontoxic household products, plant based paints, organic foods, and energy saving devices.

Coagulation and Lipids. CRC Press, 2000 Corporate Blvd. N.W., Boca Raton, FL 33431. (800) 272-7737. 1989. Physiological effect of phospholipids.

Coal Age Operating Handbook of Underground Mining. Coal Age Mining Informational Services, New York, NY 1978. Coal mines and mining method manual.

Coal and Slurry Technology Association. 1156 15th St., N.W., Suite 525, Washington, DC 20005. (202) 296-1133.

Coal Ash Disposal: Solid Waste Impacts. Raymond A. Tripodi and Paul N. Cheremisinoff. Technomic Publishing Co., 851 New Holland Ave., Box 3535, Lancaster, PA 17604. (717) 291-5609. 1980.

Coal Data. National Coal Association, 1130 17th St., N.W., Washington, DC 20036. (202) 463-2631.

Coal Desulfurization: A Bibliography. M. Catherine Grissom, ed. United States Department of Energy, Technical Information Center, 1000 Independence Ave. SW, Oak Ridge, TN 20585. (202) 586-5000. 1983.

Coal Distribution. U.S. Department of Energy, Energy Information Administration, Coal Division, 1000 Independence Ave. SW, Washington, DC 20585. (202) 586-5000.

Coal Exporters Association of the United States. 1130 17th St., N.W., Washington, DC 20036. (202) 463-2654.

Coal Information. International Energy Agency. OECD Publications and Information Center, 2001 L St., N.W., Washington, DC 20036. (202) 785-6323. 1986-. Annually. Reports on world coal market trends and long-term prospects. Contains analysis on country-specific statistics for OECD member countries and selected non-OECD countries on coal prices, demand, trade, production, and emission standards for coal-fired boilers. Essential facts on coal importing and exporting ports and coal- fired power stations in coal importing regions are also included.

Coal Outlook. Pasha Publications, Inc., 1401 Wilson Blvd., Suite 900, Arlington, VA 22209. (800) 424-2908.

Coal Preparation Plant Association–Buyer's Guide. 5711 S. 86th Circle, Omaha, NE 68127. (402) 593-4600. Annual.

Coal Refuse Inspection Manual. U.S. Mining Enforcement and Safety Administration, Washington, DC 1976. Covers earthwork fills and coal mining waste.

Coal Week. McGraw-Hill Science & Engineering Books, 11 W. 19th St., New York, NY 10011. (212) 337-6010.

COALDATA. DECHEMA, Chemische Technik und Biotechnologie e.V., I & D Information Systems and Data Banks, Theodor-Heuss-Allee 25, Postfach 970146, Frankfurt, Germany D-6000. 49 (69) 7564-248.

Coalition for Environmentally Responsible Economics. 711 Atlantic Ave., Boston, MA 02111. (617) 451-0927.

Coalition for Responsible Waste Incineration. 1330 Connecticut Ave., NW, Suite 300, Washington, DC 20036. (202) 659-0060.

Coalition on Resource Recovery and the Environment. c/o Dr. Walter M. Shaub, U.S. Conference of Mayors, 1620 I St. NW, Suite 600, Washington, DC 20006. (202) 293-7330.

Coalition on Smoking or Health. 1607 New Hampshire Ave., N.W., Washington, DC 20009. (202) 234-9375.

Coalition to Keep Alaska Oil. 1667 K St., N.W., Suite 660, Washington, DC 20006. (202) 775-1796.

Coalition to Protect Animals in Parks and Refuges. Coalition to Protect Animals in Parks and Refuges, Box 26, Swain, NY 14884. (607) 545-6213. 1983-. Quarterly. Primary concern is to eliminate the killing of wild animals for fun and profit in parks and National Wildlife refuges. Also covers more general wildlife and ecological issues.

COALPRO: Coal Research Projects. IEA Coal Research, 14/15 Lower Grosvenor Place, London, England SW 1W OEX. 44 (71) 828-4661.

Coast Alert: Scientists Speak Out. Daniel W. Anderson. Coast Alliance by Friends of the Earth, San Francisco, CA 1981. Coastal ecology and oil pollution of water.

Coast Alliance. 235 Pennsylvania Ave., SE, Washington, DC 20003. (202) 546-9554.

Coast Guard. Information Office, 2100 Second St., S.W., Washington, DC 20593. (202) 267-2229.

Coast Guard Enforcement of Environmental Laws. House Committee on Merchant Marine and Fisheries. U.S. G.P.O., Washington, DC 20401. (202) 512-0000. 1990.

Coastal Alert: Ecosystems, Energy, and Offshore Oil Drilling. Dwight Holing. Island Press, 1718 Connecticut Ave. N.W., Suite 300, Washington, DC 20009. (202) 232-7933. 1990. Describes how offshore drilling affects environment and quality of life, how the government auctions our coast to the oil industry, how the lease sale process works, how energy alternatives can replace offshore drilling; how citizen action works and how to become involved.

Coastal Commission: Coastal Zone Management. Chairman, 631 Howard St., 4th Floor, San Francisco, CA 94105. (415) 543-8555.

Coastal Conservation Association. 4801 Woodway, Suite 220 W., Houston, TX 77056. (713) 626-4222.

Coastal Ecosystem Management. John Ray Clark. John Wiley & Sons, Inc., 605 3rd Ave., New York, NY 10158-0012. (212) 850-6000. 1983. A technical manual for the conservation of coastal resources.

Coastal Ecosystems: Ecological Considerations for Management of the Coastal Zone. John R. Clark. Conservation Foundation, 1250 24th St. NW, Washington, DC 20037. (202) 203-4800. 1974.

Coastal Engineering. Elsevier, Box 211, Amsterdam, Netherlands 1000 AE. (020) 5803-911. 1977. An international journal for coastal, harbor and offshore engineers, covering hydraulic engineering, ocean waves, coast changes, and shore protection.

Coastal Engineering Research Council. Coastal Engineering Research Council, 215 E. Bay St., Suite 302A, Charleston, SC 29401. (803) 723-4864.

Coastal Land Use. Council of Planning Librarians, 1313 E. 60th St., Chicago, IL 60637-2897. (312) 942-2163. Bibliography of shore protection.

Coastal Management. Taylor & Francis, 1900 Frost Rd., Ste. 101, Bristol, PA 19007. (215) 785-5800. 1973-. Quarterly. Journal dealing with environmental resources and law.

Coastal Marshes: Ecology and Wildlife Management. R. H. Charbreck. University of Minnesota Press, 2037 University Ave., SE, Minneapolis, MN 55414. (612) 624-2516. 1988. Tidemarsh ecology and wildlife management.

Coastal Ocean Pollution Assessment News. Marine Sciences Research Center, State University of New York, Stony Brook, NY 11790. Frequency varies. Man and the marine environment.

Coastal Reporter Newsletter. American Littoral Society, Sandy Hook, Highlands, NJ 07732. (201) 291-0055. Quarterly. Promotes study and conservation of the coastal zone habitat.

Coastal Research. Geology Dept., Florida State University, Tallahassee, FL 32306-3026. (904) 644-3208. Three times a year. Sea level, meteorology, coastal and near shore environments, coastal geology, sedimentary research, coastal engineering, and pollution.

Coastal Sedimentation and Dredging. Naval Facilities Engineering Command. U.S. Department of the Navy, The Pentagon, Washington, DC 20350. (703) 545-6700. 1981. Design manual for dredging, sedimentation and deposition.

The Coastal Society. P.O. Box 2081, Glouster, MA 01930-2081. (508) 281-9209.

Coastal States Organization. 444 N. Capitol St., N.W., Suite 312, Washington, DC 20001. (202) 628-9636.

Coastal Wetlands of the United States. Donald W. Field. U.S. Department of Commerce, National Oceanic and Atmospheric Administration, Washington, DC 20230. (202) 377-2985. 1991. A special NOAA 20th anniversary report published in cooperation with the National Wetlands Inventory.

Coastal Zone Division: Coastal Zone Management. Sub-Secretary, Puerta de Tierra, PO Box 5887, San Juan, PR 00904. (809) 725-2769.

Coastal Zone Management. Taylor & Francis, 1900 Frost Road, Suite 101, Bristol, PA 19007. (800) 821-8312. Quarterly. Covers social, political, legal, and cultural issues of coastal resources.

Coastal Zone Management. Mary A. Vance. Vance Bibliographies, PO Box 229, 112 N. Charter St., Monticello, IL 61856. (217) 762-3831. 1985.

Coastlines. New York State Sea Grant Inst., Duchess Hall, SUNY at Stony Brook, Stony Brook, NY 11794-5001. (516) 632-6905. Quarterly. Marine and Great Lakes activities of New York Sea Grant Institute's research and extension programs.

Coastlines. Executive Office of Environmental Affairs, Massachusetts Coastal Zone Management Office, Saltonstall State Office Bldg., Rm. 2006, 100 Cambridge St., Boston, MA 02202. (617) 727-9530. Nine times a year. Coastal land and water management, port and harbor development, water quality, recreation, public access, and coastal development.

Coastlines. League for Coastal Protection, PO Box 421698, San Francisco, CA 94142-1698. Bimonthly. Legislation and planning issues affecting the California coastline.

Coasts: An Introduction to Coastal Geomorphology. B. Blackwell, 3 Cambridge Ctr., Suite 208, Cambridge, MA 02142. (617) 225-0401. 1984.

Coasts in Crisis. U.S. Department of the Interior, 1849 C St. NW, Washington, DC 20240. (202) 208-3171. 1991.

Coastwatch. Sea Grant College Program, University of North Carolina, PO Box 8605, Raleigh, NC 27695-8605. (919) 737-2454. Monthly. Shellfish contamination, beach erosion, and hurricanes.

Coastwatch. Center for Coastal Studies, 59 Commercial St., PO Box 1036, Provincetown, MA 02657. (508) 487-3622. Bimonthly. Coastal ecology and biology, whale research, and conservation issues.

Cobalt and Cobalt Alloys, a Bibliography of Allotropy and Alloy Systems. Facundo Rolf Morral. Cobalt Information Center, Columbus, OH 1967.

Cobalt + Cobalt Abstracts. Cobalt Information Center, Columbus, OH

Cobalt in Agricultural Ecosystems: A Bibliography of the Literature 1950 Through 1971. Robert Lewis Jones. Department of Agronomy, University of Illinois, Urbana, IL 61801. 1973.

Cobalt Reduction Guidelines. Electric Power Research Institute, 3412 Hillview Ave., Palo Alto, CA 94304. (415) 965-4081. 1990. Deals with nuclear power plants, hard-facing alloys, stress corrosion, and cobalt alloys.

Codisposal of Garbage and Sewage Sludge–a Promising Solution to Two Problems. U.S. General Accounting Office. U.S. G.P.O., Washington, DC 20401. (202) 512-0000. 1979.

Codisposal of Municipal Solid Waste and Sewage Sludge: An Analysis of Constraints. Dick Baldwin. National Technical Information Service, 5285 Port Royal Rd., Springfield, VA 22161. (703) 487-4650. 1980.

The Codisposal of Sewage Sludge and Refuse in the Purox System. Union Carbide Corporation. Municipal Environmental Research Laboratory, Office of Research and Development, U.S. Environmental Protection Agency, Cincinnati, OH 1978.

Cogeneration and Independent Power Coalition of America. 1025 Thomas Jefferson St., N.W., Box 1, Washington, DC 20007. (202) 965-1134.

The Cogeneration Journal. Cogeneration Journal, PO Box 14227, Atlanta, GA 30324. 1985-. Quarterly. Provides facts and data needed to evaluate the market, assess technologies, develop new projects and make key decisions.

The Cogeneration Letter: The Monthly Newsletter on Cogeneration. Energy Engineering, 700 Indian Trail, Lilburn, GA 30247. 1985-. Monthly. Covers the information of importance to the power generation industry.

Cold. U.S. Army Corps of Engineers, Cold Regions Research and Engineering Laboratory, 22 Lyme Rd., Hanover, NH 03755-1290. (603) 646-4221.

Cold Regions. Library of Congress, Science & Technology Division, Cold Regions Bibliography Project, Washington, DC 20540. (202) 707-1181.

College of Marine Studies. University of Delaware, Newark, DE 19716. (302) 451-2841.

Collins Guide to the Rare Mammals of the World. John A. Burton and Vivian G. Burton. Collins, 77/85 Fulham Palace Rd., London, England W6 8JB. W1X 3LA 071-493 7070. 1988. Includes all the mammal species which might be considered threatened.

Color Association of the United States. 343 Lexington Ave., New York, NY 10016. (212) 683-9531.

Colorado Environmental Law Handbook. Government Institutes, Inc., 4 Research Pl., Ste. 200, Rockville, MD 20850. (301) 921-2300. 1991.

The Colorado Front Range: A Century of Ecological Change. University of Utah Press, 401 Kendall D. Graff Building, Salt Lake City, UT 84112. (801) 581-7274. 1991.

Colorado River Wildlife Council. 1596 W. North Temple, Salt Lake City, UT 84116. (801) 533-9333.

Colorado Wildlife. Colorado Wildlife Federation, 1560 Broadway, Denver, CO 80202. (303) 830-2557. 1973-. Monthly.

A Colour Atlas of Poisonous Fungi: A Handbook for Pharmacists, Doctors, and Biologists. Andreas Bresinsky. Wolfe Publishing Ltd., Brook House, 2-16 Torrington Pl., London, England WC1E 7LT. 1990.

Columbia Basin Fish & Wildlife Authority. 2000 SW First Ave., Suite 170, Portland, OR 97201. (503) 294-7031.

Combustion Efficiency Tables. Harry Taplin. The Association of Energy Engineers, 4025 Pleasantdale Rd, Suite 420, Atlanta, GA 30340. (404) 925-9558. 1991. The tables are based on ASME/ANSI Power Test Code 4.1 and are designed to systematically illustrate how different variables impact the combustion process.

Combustion Modification Controls for Stationary Gas Turbine. R. Larkin. U.S. Environmental Protection Agency, Industrial Environmental Research Laboratory, MD 75, Research Triangle Park, NC 27711. 1982. Environmental monitoring of gas turbines.

Combustion Toxicology. Shane C. Gad and Rosalind C. Anderson. CRC Press, 2000 Corporate Blvd., N.W., Boca Raton, FL 33431. (407) 994-0555; (800) 272-7737. 1990. Evaluates the health hazards of the decomposition products formed when plastics are heated. Coverage includes the basics of inhalation toxicology and heat stress physiology, toxicity of smoke and combustion gases, combustion toxicity testing, regulations, toxicity of polymers by class, flame retardants and other additives, current issues and directions.

Commercial Fertilizers. Tennessee Valley Authority. U.S. G.P.O., Washington, DC 20401. (202) 512-0000. Annual. Deals with commercial fertilizer consumption by state and type of nutrient.

Commercial Nuclear Power. U.S. G.P.O, Washington, DC 20402-9325. (202) 512-0000. Annual. Current status, and future development of commercial nuclear power plants.

Commercial Refrigerator Manufacturers. 1101 Connecticut Ave., N.W., Suite 700, Washington, DC 20036. (202) 857-1145.

Commission of Environmental Quality: Air Quality. Director, Pollution Control Bureau, PO Box 10385, Jackson, MS 39289-0385. (601) 961-5104.

Commission of Environmental Quality: Water Quality. Director, Pollution Control Bureau, PO Box 10385, Jackson, MS 39289-0385. (601) 961-5100.

Committee for Better Transit. P.O. Box 3106, Long Island, NY 11103. (718) 278-0650.

Committee for Sustainable Agriculture-Ecological Farming Directory. Otis Wollan. Committee for Sustainable Agriculture, Box 1300, Colfax, CA 95713. (916) 346-2777. Annual. Organic farmers, farm suppliers and consultants, produce handlers, researchers, extension agents, students, organization representatives.

Committee for the Preservation of the Tule Elk. P.O. Box 3696, San Diego, CA 92103. (619) 485-0626.

Committee of Atomic Bomb Survivors in the U.S. 1109 Shellgate Pl., Alameda, CA 94501. (415) 523-5617.

Committee on Evolutionary Biology. University of Chicago, 915 East 57th Street, Chicago, IL 60637. (312) 702-8940.

Common Sense Pest Control. William Olkowski, et al. Tauton Pr., 63 South Main St., Box 5506, Newton, CT 06740-5506. 1991. Discusses ways to manage other living organisms that are regarded as pests.

Common Sense Pest Control Quarterly. Bio-Integral Resource Center, PO Box 7414, Berkeley, CA 94707. (415) 524-2567. Four times a year. Least-toxic management of pests on indoor plants, pests that damage paper, controlling fleas and ticks on pets, and garden pests.

Common Synonyms for Chemicals Listed Under Section 313 of the Emergency Planning and Community Right to Know Act. Washington, DC 1991. Toxic chemical release inventory, glossary of synonyms, covering hazardous substances and chemicals.

The Commonwealth Forestry Review. Commonwealth Forestry Association, c/o Oxford Forestry Institute, South Parks Rd., Oxford, England OX1 3RB. 1921-. Quarterly. Covers forestry practices.

Communications in Soil Science and Plant Analysis. M. Dekker, 270 Madison Ave., New York, NY 10016. (212) 696-9000; (800) 228-1160. 1970-.

Community and Worker Right-to-Know News. Thompson Publishing Group, 1725 K St. NW, Washington, DC 20006. (800) 424-2959. Bimonthly. Reports on chemical disclosure requirements and industrial liability.

Community Environmental Council. 930 Miramonte Drive, Santa Barbara, CA 93109. (805) 963-0583.

Community Guide to Cholesterol Resources. U.S. G.P.O., Washington, DC 20401. (202) 512-0000. 1988. Directory of low-cholesterol diet and community health services.

A Community Researcher's Guide to Rural Data. Priscilla Salant. Island Press, 1718 Connecticut Ave. N.W., Suite 300, Washington, DC 20009. (202) 232-7933. 1990. Comprehensive manual intended for those less familiar with statistical data on rural America. Identifies a wealth of data sources such as the decennial census of population and housing, population reports and surveys, and labor market information.

Community Right-to-Know and Small Business. U.S. Environmental Protection Agency, Office of Solid Waste and Emergency Response, 401 M St., S.W., Washington, DC 20460. (202) 260-2090. 1988. Interprets the community Right-to-Know Act of 1986, especially Sections 311 and 312.

Compact Heat Exchangers. R. K. Shah. American Society of Mechanical Engineers, 345 E. 47th St., New York, NY 10017. (212) 705-7722. 1992. History, technological advancement, and mechanical design problems.

Compact School and College Administrator's Guide for Compliance with Federal and State Right-to-Know Regulations. Forum for Scientific Excellence. J. B. Lippincott, 227 E. Washington Sq., Philadelphia, PA 19105. (215) 238-4200; (800) 982-4377. 1989. Presents the legal and technical language of current hazardous chemical regulations in meaningful, easily understandable terms. Provides a simplified, step-by-step program for compliance.

Comparative Analysis of Ecosystems Patterns, Mechanisms, and Theories. Jonathan Cole, ed. Springer-Verlag, 175 5th Ave., New York, NY 10010. (212) 460-1500; (800) 777-4643. 1991. Includes papers from a conference held in Milbrook, New York, 1989.

Comparative Behavior Laboratory. University of Florida, Florida Museum of Natural History, Gainesville, FL 32611. (904) 392-6570.

Comparative Chemical Mutagenesis. De Serres, Frederick J. Plenum Press, 233 Spring St., New York, NY 10013-1578. (212) 620-8000; (800) 221-9369. 1981. Mutagenicity tests and analysis of mutagens.

Comparative Climatic Data for the U.S. U.S. G.P.O, Washington, DC 20402-9325. (202) 512-0000. Annual. Monthly averages of surface weather data for U.S. and outlying areas.

Comparative Dosimetry of Radon in Mines and Homes. Commission on Life Science, National Research Council. National Academy Press, 2101 Constitution Ave. N.W., PO Box 285, Washington, DC 20418. (202) 334-3313. 1991.

Comparative Ecology of Microorganisms and Macroorganisms. John H. Andrews. Springer-Verlag, 175 5th Ave., New York, NY 10010. (212) 460-1500. 1991. Constructs a format in which to compare the ecologies of large and small plant and animal organisms. Examines the differences between the sizes, and explores what similarities or parallels can be identified, and where they don't seem to exist. The ideas are illustrated by applying evolutionary principles to the individual organism.

Comparative Urbanization: Divergent Paths in the Twentieth Century. Brian J. L. Berry. St. Martin's Press, 175 5th Ave., New York, NY 10010. (212) 674-5151. 1981.

A Comparison of Disposable and Reusable Diapers. Kristin Rahenkamp. National Conference of State Legislatures, 1050 17th St., Suite 2100, Denver, CO 80265-2101. (303) 623-7800. 1990. Economics, environmental impacts and legislative options relating to diapers.

Comparison of Serum Levels of 2,3,7,8- Tetrachlorodibenzo-p-Dioxin with Indirect Estimates of Agent Orange Exposure Among Vietnam Veterans. U.S. Center for Disease Control, c/o U.S. Government Printing Office, Washington, DC 20401. (202) 512-0000. 1989. Results of a study on blood serum dioxin concentration of army combat veterans exposed to Agent Orange while serving in Vietnam.

The Compendium Newsletter. Educational Communications, Box 351419, Los Angeles, CA 90035. (310) 559-9160. 1972-. Bimonthly. Comprehensive summary of environmental issues and activities. National emphasis lists radio and TV shows produced by Educational Communications.

Compendium of ERT Soil Sampling and Surface Geophysics Procedures. National Technical Information Service, 5285 Port Royal Rd., Springfield, VA 22161. (703) 487-4650. Sampling of soil air and hazardous waste sites.

Compendium of Hazardous Chemicals in Schools and Colleges. Forum for Scientific Excellence. J. B. Lippincott, 227 E. Washington Sq., Philadelphia, PA 19105. (215) 238-4200; (800) 982-4377. 1990. Encyclopedia of more than 950 hazardous chemicals found in academic institutions. Contains all the data necessary for identifying these chemicals and their hazardous effects.

Compendium of Safety Data Sheets for Research and Industrial Chemicals. L. H. Keith and D. B. Walters, eds. VCH Publishers, 303 NW 12th Ave., Deerfield Beach, FL 33442-1788. (305) 428-5566. 1985. Seven volumes. Provides information of safety-oriented needs involving chemicals.

Compendium on Solid Waste Management by Vermicomposting. National Technical Information Service, 5285 Port Royal Rd., Springfield, VA 22161. (703) 487-4650. 1980. Covers compost, refuse and refuse disposal, and earthworms.

Compendium on Water Supply, Drought, and Conservation. National Regulatory Research Institute. U.S. G.P.O, Washington, DC 20402-9325. (202) 512-0000. 1989. Water supply and demand, drought, conservation, utility ratemaking and regulatory issues.

Compilation of EPA's Sampling and Analysis Methods. William Mueller, et al. Lewis Publishers, 2000 Corporate Blvd., N.W., Boca Raton, FL 33431. (407) 994-0555 or (800) 272-7737. 1991. Aids with rapid searching of sampling and analytical method summaries. More than 650 method/ analytical summaries from the database are included in this volume.

The Complete Book of Vitamins. Rodale Press, 33 E. Minor St., Emmaus, PA 18098. (215) 967-5171. 1984.

The Complete Encyclopedia of the Animal World. David M.Burn, ed. Octopus Books, 59 Grosvenor St., London, England W1. 1980. Consists of 6 parts in one volume includes: the distribution of animals, animal names and classification, the animal kingdom, the way of animals, the conservation of animals, and where to see animals.

Complete Guide to America's National Parks: The Official Visitor's Guide of the National Park Foundation. National Park Foundation, 1101 17th St. NW, Suite 1008, Washington, DC 20036. (202) 785-4500. Biennial.

The Complete Guide to Environmental Careers. CEIP Fund. Island Press, 1718 Connecticut Ave. N.W., Suite 300, Washington, DC 20009. (202) 232-7933. 1989. Presents information needed to plan any career search. Case studies discuss how environmental organizations, government, and industry are working to manage and protect natural resources.

The Complete Guide to Hazardous Waste Regulations. Travis P. Wagner. Global Professional Publications, 2805 McGraw Ave., PO Box 19539, Irvine, CA 92713-9539. (800) 854-7179. A comprehensive, step-by-step guide to the regulation of hazardous wastes under RCRA, TSCA, HMTA, and Superfund.

Complete Guide to Recycling at Home. Gary D. Branson. Betterway Publications, Inc., PO Box 219, Crozet, VA 22932. (804) 823-5661. 1991. Major areas covered include recycling, paper, lawn and garden, plastics, water conservation, alternative energy, etc.

Complete Guide to Vitamins, Minerals and Supplements. H. Winter Griffith. Fisher Books, 3499 N. Campbell Ave., Suite 909, Tucson, AZ 85712. (602) 325-5263. 1988. Includes name, brand name, reasons to use, who should use, recommended daily allowance, and other related data in the form of a chart.

The Completely Illustrated Atlas of Reptiles and Amphibians for the Terrarium. Jerry G. Walls, ed. TFH Publications, One TFH Plaza, Union and 3rd Pl., Neptune City, NJ 07753. (908) 988-8400. 1988. Includes care and feeding, breeding and natural history of snakes, lizards, turtles, frogs, toads, salamanders, newts, and all other terrarium animals. Also includes additional references and a list of common names.

Compost Engineering: Principles and Practice. Robert Tim Haug. Ann Arbor Science, 230 Collingwood, Ann Arbor, MI 48106. 1980.

Compost Science/Land Utilization. JG Press, Box 351, Emmaus, PA 18049. (215) 967-4010. Journal of waste recycling.

Compost Toilets: A Guide for Owner-Builders. National Center for Appropriate Technology, PO Box 3838, Butte, MT 59702. (406) 494-4572. Covers sewage and refuse disposal facilities and toilets.

Composting Municipal Sludge: A Technology Evaluation. Noyes Publications, 120 Mill Rd., Park Ridge, NJ 07656. (201) 391-8484. 1988. Looks at sewage sludge as fertilizer, compost evaluation and activated sludge process.

Composting: the Organic Natural Way. Dick Kitto. Thornsons Publishing Ltd., Wellingborough, Northamptonshire, England NN82RQ. 1988. Covers principles of compost making and its uses.

Composting: Theory and Practice for City, Industry and Farm. JG Press, Box 351, Emmaus, PA 18049. (215) 967-4010. 1981. Covers compost science and land utilization.

Composts and Composting of Organic Wastes. Jayne T. Maclean. U.S. Department of Agriculture, National Agricultural Library, 10301 Baltimore Blvd., Beltsville, MD 20705-2351. (301) 504-5755. 1991.

Comprehensive Bibliography. Outer Continental Shelf Environmental Assessment Program. U.S. Department of the Interior, 1849 C St., NW, Washington, DC 20240. (202) 208-3171. 1986.

Comprehensive Bibliography of Cement and Concrete, 1925-1947. Floyd O. Slate. Purdue University Press, 1131 S. Campus Cts.-B, Lafayette, IN 47907. (317) 494-2038. 1952.

Comprehensive Bibliography of Drying References: Covering Bulletins, Booklets, Books, Chapters, Bibliographies. Carl W. Hall. American Society of Agricultural Engineers, 2950 Niles Rd., St. Joseph, MI 49085-9659. (616) 429-0300. 1980.

The Comprehensive Handbook of Hazardous Materials: Regulations, Handling, Monitoring, and Safety. Hildegarde L. A. Sacarello. Lewis Publishers, 2000 Corporate Blvd., N.W., Boca Raton, FL 33431. (407) 994-0555 or (800) 272-7737. 1991. Includes major governmental environmental and training regulations, chemical properties of hazardous materials toxicology, medical program and record keeping, safety planning and principles,personal protective equipment, respiratory protection and fit testing, and other related areas.

Comprehensive Report to Congress: Clean Coal Technology Program. U.S. DOE Office of Clean Coal Technology. National Technical Information Service, 5285 Port Royal Rd., Springfield, VA 22161. (703) 487-4650. Demonstration of selective catalytic reduction technology for the control of nitrogen oxide emissions from high-sulphur coal- fired boilers.

Compressed Air & Gas Institute. c/o John H. Addington, Thomas Associates, Inc., 1300 Sumner Ave., Cleveland, OH 44115. (216) 241-7333.

Compressed Gas Association. Crystal Gateway #1, Suite 501, 1235 Jefferson Davis Hwy., Arlington, VA 22202. (703) 979-0900.

Computer-Aided Environmental Legislative Data Systems–CELDS. U.S. Army Corps of Engineers, Planning Information Programs (PIP), Dept. of Urban and Regional Planning, University of Illinois, 1003 West Nevada, Urbana, IL 61801. (217) 333-1369. Federal and state environmental regulations and standards.

Computer Aided Systems for Environmental Engineering Decision Making. Jehng-Jung Kao. University of Illinois at Urbana-Champaign, Urbana, IL 61801. 1990.

Computer Graphics and Environmental Planning. Prentice-Hall, Rte. 9 W, Englewood Cliffs, NJ 07632. (201) 592-2000. 1983.

Computer Models in Environmental Planning. Steven I. Gordon. Van Nostrand Reinhold, 115 5th Ave., New York, NY 10003. (212) 254-3232. 1985.

Computerized Engineering Index–COMPENDEX. Engineering Information Inc., 345 E. 47th St., New York, NY 10017. (212) 705-7600.

Computers in Health and Safety. American Industrial Hygiene Association, 345 White Pond Dr., Akron, OH 44320. (216) 873-2442. 1990. Presents state-of-the-art computer applications specifically directed toward highlighting better ways of maintaining, manipulating, and disseminating information in the field of industrial hygiene.

Concentrated Mine Drainage Disposal into Sewage Treatment Systems. Environmental Protection Agency, 401 M St. SW, Washington, DC 20460. (202) 382-5480. 1971. Covers acid mine drainage and sewage purification.

Concentrations of Indoor Pollutants–CIP. CIP Database Coordinator, Building 90, Rm 3058, Lawrence Berkeley Lab., 1 Cyclotron Rd., Berkeley, CA 94720. (415) 486-6591. Contains field data from studies monitoring indoor air quality in occupied buildings in U.S. and Canada.

CONCERN, Inc. 1794 Columbia Rd, NW, Washington, DC 20009. (202) 328-8160.

Concerned Citizens for the Nuclear Breeder. P.O. Box 3, Ross, OH 45061. (513) 738-6750.

Concerned Neighbor in Action. P.O. Box 3847, Riverside, CA 92519.

A Concise Dictionary of Biology. Elizabeth Martin, ed. Oxford University Press, 200 Madison Ave., New York, NY 10016. (212) 679-7300 or (800) 334-4249. 1990. New edition. Derived from the Concise Science Dictionary, published in 1984.

Concise Encyclopedia of Biological & Biomedical Measurement Systems. Peter A. Payne. Pergamon Microforms International Inc., Fairview Park, Elmsford, NY 10523. (914) 592-7720. Comprehensive survey of the measurement systems and descriptions of the biological systems and subsystems.

Concise Encyclopedia of Industrial Chemical Additives. Michael Ash. VCH Publishers, 303 NW 12th Ave., Deerfield Beach, FL 33442-1788. (305) 428-5566.

Concise Encyclopedia of Polymer Processing & Applications. P. J. Corish. Pergamon Microforms International Inc., Fairview Park, Elmsford, NY 10523. (914) 592-7720.

Concise Encyclopedia of Solid State Physics. Rita G. Lerner and George L. Trigg. Addison-Wesley Longman, Rte. 128, Reading, MA 01867. (617) 944-3700. 1983. "Articles chosen for this volume have been selected from the encyclopedia of physics."

Concise Manual of Chemical and Environmental Safety in Schools and Colleges. Forum for Scientific Excellence. J. B. Lippincott, 227 E. Washington Sq., Philadelphia, PA 19105. (215) 238-4200; (800) 982-4377. 1991.

The Concise Russian-English Chemical Glossary: Acids, Esters, Ethers, and Salts. James F. Shipp. Wychwood Press, PO Box 10, College Park, MD 20740. 1983. Lists four of the basic substances commonly occurring in chemical and environmental literature: acids, esters, ethers and salts.

Concrete Contractors Directory. 5711 S. 86th Circle, Omaha, NE 68127. (402) 593-4600. Annual.

Concrete Products–Wholesale. 5711 S. 86th Circle, Omaha, NE 68127. (402) 593-4600. Annual.

Concrete–Ready Mix Directory. 5711 S. 86th Circle, Omaha, NE 68127. (402) 593-4600. Annual.

The Condensed Chemical Dictionary. Gessner G. Hawley. Van Nostrand Reinhold, 115 5th Ave., New York, NY 10003. (212) 254-3232. 1981. 10th ed.

The Condensed Encyclopedia of Surfactants. Michael and Irene Ash. Chemical Publishing Co., 80 Eighth Ave., New York, NY 10011. (212) 255-1950. Contains over 12,000 entries with the first section devoted to trademarks containing short entries that appear in volumes 1-4. Also includes chemical component and manufacturer cross reference.

Conference of Local Environmental Health Administrators. 1395 Blue Tent Ct., Cool, CA 95614-2120. (916) 823-1736.

Conference of Radiation Control Program Directors. 205 Capital Ave., Frankfort, KY 40601. (502) 227-4543.

Conference of State Health and Environmental Managers. c/o David Cochran, 3909 Cresthill Dr., Austin, TX 78731. (512) 453-6723.

Conference on Safe Transportation of Hazardous Articles. c/o Lawrence W. Bierlein, 2300 N. St., N.W., Washington, DC 20037. (202) 663-9245.

Conference on Use of Icebergs. International Glaciological Society, 700 Lensfield Rd., Cambridge, England CB2 1ER. 1980.

Conifers. D.M. van Gelderen. Timber Press, 9999 SW Wilshire, Portland, OR 97225. (800) 327-5680. 1989. Deals with ornamental conifers.

Conifers. Keith Rushforth. Facts on File, Inc., 460 Park Ave. S., New York, NY 10016. (212) 683-2244. 1987. Dictionary of conifers and ornamental conifers.

Connecticut Environmental Law Handbook. Government Institutes, Inc., 4 Research Pl., Ste. 200, Rockville, MD 20850. (301) 921-2300. 1990.

Connecticut River Watershed Council, Inc. 125 Combs Rd., Easthampton, MA 01027. (413) 584-0057.

Connecticut Sea Grant College Program. University of Connecticut at Avery Point, 1084 Schennecossett Rd., Groton, CT 06340. (203) 445-5108.

Connections: A Guide to Marine Resources, Living Systems, and Field Trips. Sea Grant College Program, Sea Grant College Program, North Carolina State University at Raleigh, Box 8605, Raleigh, NC 27695. (919) 737-2454.

Conservation. National Wildlife Federation, 1400 16th St. N.W., Washington, DC 20036-2266. (202) 797-6800. 1939-. Biweekly. Covers digest of natural conservation legislation, published when Congress is in session. This newsletter is available to members only.

Conservation and Heat Transfer. Nejat T. Veziroglu, ed. Nova Science Publishers Inc., 283 Commack Rd., Suite 300, Commack, NY 11725-3104. (516) 499-3103; (516) 499-3106. 1991. Describes methods of conservation and heat transfer.

Conservation and Natural Resources Department: Air Quality. Administrator, Environmental Protection Division, 201 South Fall St., Carson City, NV 89710. (702) 885-4670.

Conservation and Natural Resources Department: Environmental Protection. Administrator, Environmental Protection Division, 201 South Fall St., Carson City, NV 89710. (702) 885-4670.

Conservation and Natural Resources Department: Fish and Wildlife. Commissioner, 64 North Union St., Room 702, Montgomery, AL 36130. (205) 242-3465.

Conservation and Natural Resources Department: Groundwater Management. Chief, Groundwater Section, Division of Water Resources, 201 South Fall St., Carson City, NV 89710. (702) 885-4380.

Conservation and Natural Resources Department: Hazardous Waste Management. Administrator, Environmental Protection Division, 201 South Fall St., Carson City, NV 89710. (702) 885-4670.

Conservation and Natural Resources Department: Natural Resources. Commissioner, 64 North Union St., Room 702, Montgomery, AL 36130. (205) 242-3486.

Conservation and Natural Resources Department: Natural Resources. Director, 201 South Fall St., Carson City, NV 89710. (702) 885-4360.

Conservation and Natural Resources Department: Solid Waste Management. Administrator, Environmental Protection Division, 201 South Fall St., Carson City, NV 89710. (702) 885-4670.

Conservation and Natural Resources Department: Underground Storage Tanks. Administrator, Environmental Protection Division, 201 South Fall St., Carson City, NV 89710. (702) 885-4670.

Conservation and Natural Resources Department: Water Quality. Administrator, Environmental Protection Division, 201 South Fall St., Carson City, NV 89710. (702) 885-4670.

Conservation and Renewable Energy: Guide to Sources of Information. Robert Argue. Energy Mines and Resources Canada, 580 Booth, Ottawa, ON, Canada KIA OE4. 1980.

Conservation and Renewable Energy Inquiry and Referral Service. P.O. Box 8900, Silver Spring, MD 20907. (800) 523-2929.

Conservation and Research Foundation Inc. 240 Arapahal E., Lake Quivira, KS 66106. (913) 268-0076.

Conservation and Service Corps Profiles. Human Environment Center, 1001 Connecticut Ave NW, Suite 827, Washington, DC 20036. (202) 331-8387. Semiannual.

The Conservation Atlas of Tropical Forests. N. Mark Collins. Simon & Schuster, 1230 Avenue of the Americas, New York, NY 10020. (212) 689-7000. 1991. Detailed and authoritative study of the issues surrounding deforestation-and the first complete visual analysis in country-by- country maps.

The Conservation Atlas of Tropical Forests: Asia and the Pacific. N. Mark Collins, Jeffery A. Sayer, and Timothy C. Whitmore. Simon & Schuster, 1230 Avenue of the Americas, New York, NY 10020. (212) 689-7000. 1991. Focuses on closed canopy, and true rain forests. This Asian volume is the first of a set of three–tropical America and Africa being the next. Address such regional subjects as forest wildlife, human impacts on forest lands, and the tropical timber trade; and includes a "Tropical Forestry Action Plan" to conserve and protect important remaining stands. The second part of the atlas gives a detailed survey of 17 countries plus the island groups of Fiji and the Solomons, but not those of New Caledonia, New Hebrides, or Micronesia.

Conservation Biology. Blackwell Scientific Publications, 3 Cambridge Ctr., Suite 208, Cambridge, MA 02142. (617) 225-0401. 1987-. Quarterly. Covers conservation and development, wildlife management the economics, ethics and agroforestry of the extinction crisis.

Conservation Bits and Bytes. National Association of Conservation Districts, 509 Capitol St. NE, Washington, DC 20002. (202) 547-6223. Quarterly.

Conservation Commission News. New Hampshire Association of Conservation Commissions, 54 Portsmouth St., Concord, NH 03301. (603) 224-7867. 1968-. Quarterly. Concerns national, state, local information and issues dealing with natural resources and the environment.

Conservation Directory. National Wildlife Federation, 1400 16th St. N.W., Washington, DC 20036-2266. (202) 797-6800. 1956-. Annually. Contains information on organizations, agencies, officials, and education programs in the natural resources management field.

Conservation Districts Foundation, Inc. Conservation Film Service, Davis Conservation Library. 404 E. Main, P.O. Box 776, League City, TX 77573. (713) 332-3404.

The Conservation Easement in California. Thomas S. Barrett & Putnam Livermore for the Trust for Public Land. Island Press, 1718 Connecticut Ave. N.W., Suite 300, Washington, DC 20009. (202) 232-7933. 1983. Conservation lawyers discuss techniques, tax implications and solutions to potential problems.

Conservation Education Association Newsletter. Conservation Education Association, c/o Conservation Education Center, RR 1, Box 153, Guthrie Center, IA 50115. (515) 747-8383. Quarterly. Promotes environmental conservation education.

Conservation Foundation. 1250 24th St., N.W., Washington, DC 20037. (202) 293-4800. The World Wildlife Fund absorbed the Conservation Foundation in 1990.

Conservation Foundation Letter. Conservation Foundation, 1250 24th St. N.W., Washington, DC 20037. (202) 293-4800. 1966-. Bimonthly. Provides in-depth examinations of environmental issues.

Conservation Information Network. The Getty Conservation Institute, 4503 Glencoe Ave., Marina del Rey, CA 90292-6537. (213) 822-2287.

Conservation International. 1015 18th St. N.W., Suite 1002, Washington, DC 20036. (202) 429-5660. Non-profit organization established in 1987. Provides resources and expertise to private organizations, government agencies and universities of Latin America and Caribbean countries in an effort to develop the capacity and preserve critical habitats.

Conservation Law Foundation of New England, Inc. 3 Joy St., Boston, MA 02108. (617) 742-2540.

Conservation News Digest. American Resources Group, 374 Maple Ave., E, Suite 204, Vienna, VA 22180. (703) 255-2700. Bimonthly. Non-industrial private forestry and conservation and natural resources.

Conservation of Living Nature and Resources: Problems, Trends, and Prospects. A. V. Yablokov. Springer-Verlag, 175 5th Ave., New York, NY 10010. (212) 460-1500 or (800) 777-4643. 1991. Deals with wildlife conservation, the associated problems, solutions, and its future.

Conservation of Medicinal Plants. O. Akerele. World Conservation Union, IUCN Publications Services Unit, 181a Huntingdon Road, Cambridge, England CB3 0DJ. (0223) 277894. 1991. Plants identified as having medicinal properties.

Conservation of Natural Resources. Gary A. Klee. Prentice-Hall, Rte. 9W, Englewood Cliffs, NJ 07632. (201) 592-2000; (800) 634-2863. 1991. Draws together current and useful tools, techniques, and policy strategies for students training to be natural resource managers.

Conservation of Tidal Marshes. Franklin C. Daiber. Van Nostrand Reinhold, 115 Fifth Ave., New York, NY 10003. (212) 254-3232. 1986. Topics in wetland conservation.

Conservation of Water and Related Land Resources. Peter E. Black. Rowman & Littlefield, Publishers, Inc., 8705 Bollman Pl., Savage, MD 20763. (301) 306-0400. 1988. 2d ed. Analysis of the current status of water and land-water resources policy and programming in the United States.

A Conservation Strategy for the Northern Spotted Owl. Jack Ward Thomas. U.S. Interagency Scientific Committee, Portland, OR 1990. Includes topics in endangered species and wildlife management.

Conservation Voter. California League of Conservation Voters, 965 Mission St. #705, San Francisco, CA 94103-2928. (415) 896-5330. 1974-. Quarterly. Environmental political affairs analysis.

Conservationist. New York State Dept. of Environmental Conservation, 50 Wolf Rd., Albany, NY 12233. (518) 457-6668. 1946-. Bimonthly. Covers all aspects of conservation and outdoor recreation, scientific information, art and history of New York State.

Conservative Contractor. Conservative Contractor, 214 Suncrest Dr., PO Box 45, Port Lavaca, TX 77979. 1962-. Bimonthly. Official publication of Conservation Contractors of Texas, Inc.

Conserve. Western Pennsylvania Conservancy, 316 4th Ave., Pittsburgh, PA 15222. (412) 288-2777. 1971-. Semiannually. Reports on land conservation projects of the western Pennsylvania Conservancy.

Conserving the Polar Regions. Barbara James. Steck-Vaughn Co., PO Box 26015, Austin, TX 78755. (512) 343-8227. 1991. Focuses on the Arctic and the Antarctic, their uniqueness, relation to world climate, development and conservation.

Conserving the World's Biological Diversity. Jeffrey A. McNeely, et al. World Resources Institute, 1709 New York Ave. N.W., Washington, DC 20006. (800) 822-0504. 1990. Provides a clear concise and well illustrated guide to the meaning and importance of biological diversity. Discusses a broad range of practical approaches to biodiversity preservation, including policy changes, integrated land-use management, species and habitat protection, and pollution control.

Conserving Water: The Untapped Alternative. Postel, Sandra. Worldwatch Institute, 1776 Massachusetts Ave., N.W., Washington, DC 20036-1904. 1985.

Conservogram. Soil and Water Conservation Society, 7515 NE Ankeny Rd., Ankeny, IA 50021. (515) 289-2331. Bimonthly.

CONSO. Canadian Conservation Institute, 1030 Innes Rd., Ottawa, ON, Canada K1A OC8. (613) 998-3721.

Consolidated List of Products Whose Consumption and/or Sale Have Been Banned, Withdrawn, Severely Restricted or not Approved by Governments. United Nations, 2 United Nations Plaza, Salis Section Rm. DC 2-853, New York, NY 10017. (800) 553-3210. Biennial.

Consolidated List of Products Whose Consumption and/or Sale Have Been Banned, Withdrawn, Severely Restricted or Not Approved by Governments. United Nations, 2 United Nations Plaza, Salis Section Rm. DC 2-853, New York, NY 10017. (800) 553-3210. Biennial. International legislation against hazardous substances.

Constructed Wetlands for Wastewater Treatment. Donald A. Hammer. Lewis Publishers, 200 Corporate Blvd. NW, Boca Raton, FL 33431. (407) 994-0555 or (800)272-7737. 1989. Presents general principles of wetland ecology, hydrology, soil chemistry, vegetation, microbiology, and wildlife dependence on wetlands. It provides management guidelines, beginning with policies and regulations, and including siting and construction and operations and monitoring of constructed wetland systems.

Constructed Wetlands in Water Pollution Control. Pergamon Microforms International, Inc., Fairview Park, Elmsford, NY 10523. (914) 592-7720. 1990.

Construction and Environmental Insurance Case Digests. Wiley Law Publications Editorial Staff. John Wiley & Sons, Inc., 605 3rd Ave., New York, NY 10158-0012. (212) 850-6000. 1991. Quick reference to help construction industry practitioners and environmental practitioners determine the prevailing legal interpretation in the field of construction and environmental insurance coverage.

Construction, Installation, and Handling Procedure for National Marine Fisheries Service's Sea Turtle Excluder Device. U.S. Department of Commerce, National Oceanic and Atmospheric Administration, National Marine Service, Southeast Fisheries Center, 3209 Frederick St., Pascagoula, MS 39568. (601) 762-4591. 1981. Covers equipment and supplies of trawls and trawling.

Construction of Dams and Aircraft Overflights in National Park Units. U.S. Congress. House Committee on Interior and Insular Affairs. U.S. G.P.O., Washington, DC 20401. Covers national parks and reserves, environmental aspects of dams, airplane noise and air traffic rules.

Consultant Directory. American Academy of Environmental Engineers, 132 Holiday Ct., #100, Annapolis, MD 21401. (301) 266-3311. 1985-. Annually.

Consumer and Regulatory Affairs Department: Groundwater Management. Administrator, Housing and Environmental Regulations, 614 H St., N.W., Washington, DC 20001. (202) 727-7395.

Consumer Drug Information. American Society of Hospital Pharmacists, Database Services Division, 4630 Montgomery Ave., Bethesda, MD 20814. (301) 657-3000.

Consumer Energy Research: An Annotated Bibliography. C. Dennis Anderson and Gordon H. G. McDougall. Consumer Research and Evaluation Branch, Consumer and Corporate Affairs, Ottawa, ON, Canada 1984. Two volumes, revised. Prefatory material in English and French. Bibliography dealing with energy consumed in the residential sector and for most part is limited to annotations of empirical studies.

The Consumer Guide to Home Energy Savings. The American Council for an Energy Efficient Economy, 1001 Connecticut Ave., N.W., #535, Washington, DC 20036. (202) 429-8873. 1991.

Consumer Health and Nutrition Index. Oryx Press, 4041 N. Central at Indian School Rd., Ste. 700, Phoenix, AZ 85012-3397. (602) 265-2651. Quarterly. Includes articles in 35 popular level health and nutrition magazines and newsletters. Many of these periodicals are not indexed elsewhere. Includes articles in nutrition, health and related areas.

A Consumer's Guide to Kerosene Heaters. Consumer Information Center, 18 F St. NW, Rm. G-142, Washington, DC 20405. (202) 501-1794. 1982.

Contaminant Hydrogeology: A Practical Guide. Chris Palmer and Gettler-Ryan. Lewis Publishers, 2000 Corporate Blvd., N.W., Boca Raton, FL 33431. (407) 994-0555 or (800) 272-7737. 1991. Contains geologic frameworks for contaminant hydrogeology investigations. Also includes subsurface exploration, sampling and mapping techniques, ground-water monitoring well installation, ground water monitoring and well sampling.

Contaminant Transport in Groundwater. H.E. Kobus and W. Kinzelbach. A. A. Balkema, Old Post Rd., Brookfield, VT 05036. (802) 276-3162. 1989. Describes physical and chemical processes, model building and application as well as remedial action.

Contaminated Communities. Michael R. Edelstein. Island Press, 1718 Connecticut Ave., NW, Suite 300, Washington, DC 20036. (202) 232-7933. 1988. The social and psychological impacts of residential toxic exposure.

Contamination of Animal Feedstuffs: Chemicals, Mycotoxins, Heavy Metals. U.S. Department of Health and Human Services, Public Health Services, National Institutes of Health, 9000 Rockville Pike, Bethesda, MD 20892. (301) 496-4000. 1981.

Contamination of Ground Water Prevention, Assessment, Restoration. Michael Barcelona, et al. Noyes Publications, 120 Mill Rd., Park Ridge, NJ 07656. (201) 391-8484. 1990. Provides regulatory agencies and industry a convenient source of technical information on the management of contaminated ground water.

Contingency Planning for Industrial Emergencies. Piero Armenante. Global Professional Publications, 2805 McGraw Ave., PO Box 19539, Irvine, CA 92713-9539. (800) 854-7179. 1991. Addresses the potential environmental and human risks from large chemical industrial accidents, as well as emergency medical planning and long-term environmental monitoring following such an occurrence.

Contracts for Field Projects and Supporting Research on Enhanced Oil Recovery and Improved Drilling Technology. Bartlesville Energy Technology Center, Box 1398, Bartlesville, OK 74005. (918) 336-2400.

Contributing to Sustained Resource Use in the Humid and Sub-Humid Tropics: Some Research Approaches and Insights. Malcolm Hadley and Kathrin Schreckenberg. UNESCO, 7, place de Fontenoy, Paris, France F-75700. (331)45 68 40 67. 1989. Overview of recent, ongoing and planned activities with in the framework of MAB relating to the ecology of humid and sub-humid tropical ecosystems, principally forests and savannas.

Control of Asbestos Exposure During Brake Drum Service. U.S. G.P.O, Washington, DC 20402-9325. (202) 512-0000. Annual. Airborne asbestos control technologies used in the motor vehicle brake drum service industry.

The Control of Eutrophication of Lakes and Reservoirs. S. O. Ryding and W. Rast, eds. Parthenon Pub., Casterton Hall, Carnforth, England LA6 2LA. Lancs. 1990. Volume 1 of the Man and the Biosphere series published jointly with UNESCO.

Control of Fugitive and Hazardous Dusts. C. Cowherd, et al. Noyes Publications, 120 Mill Rd., Park Ridge, NJ 07656. (201) 391-8484. 1990. Coverage is of source identification, magnitude estimation, selection and evaluation of control measures, and control plan formulation. Among the sources discussed: paved and unpaved roads, open waste piles and staging areas, dry surface impoundments, landfills, land treatment, and waste stabilization.

The Control of Nature. John A. McPhee. Noonday Pr., 19 Union Sq. W, New York, NY 10003. (212) 741-6900. 1990. Describes the strategies and tactics through which people attempt to control nature.

Control of Respiration. D. J. Pallot. Oxford University Press, 200 Madison Ave., New York, NY 10016. (212) 679-7300. 1983. Peripheral arterial and central chemoreceptors, lung and airway receptors and tissue oxygen transport in health and disease.

Control of the Thyroid Gland: Regulation of its Normal Function and Growth. Plenum Press, 233 Spring St., New York, NY 10013-1578. (212) 620-8000; (800) 221-9369. 1989. Physiology of thyroid hormones and receptors.

Control Strategies for Photochemical Oxidants Across Europe. OECD Publications and Information Center, 2001 L St. N.W., Suite 700, Washington, DC 20036. (202) 785-OECD. 1990. Describes the emissions causing high photochemical oxidant levels, analyzes possible emission control technologies and their costs, evaluates the impact of economically feasible control scenarios.

Controlled Air Incineration. Frank L. Cross, Jr. and Howard E. Hesketh. Technomic Publishing Co., 851 New Holland Ave., Box 3535, Lancaster, PA 17604. (717) 291-5609. 1985.

Controlling Chemical Hazards: Fundamentals of the Management of Toxic Chemicals. Raymond P. Cote and Peter G. Wells, eds. Unwin Hyman, 77/85 Fulham Palace Rd., London, England W6 8JB. 081 741 7070. 1991. Gives an overview of the properties, fate of, and dilemmas involving hazardous chemicals.

Controlling Indoor Radon. Kenneth Q. Lao. Global Professional Publications, 2805 McGraw Ave., PO Box 19539, Irvine, CA 92713-9539. (800) 854-7179.

Controlling Nonprofit-Source Water Pollution. National Audubon Society, 950 3rd Ave., New York, NY 10022. (212) 832-3200. 1988. Guide to citizen participation in water quality management.

Controlling Toxic Substances in Agricultural Drainage. U.S. Committee on Irrigation and Drainage, PO Box 15326, Denver, CO 80215. 1990. Looks at current technology on toxic substances and water treatment processes and techniques.

Controlling Vegetable Pests. Cynthia Putnam. Ortho Information Services, PO Box 5047, San Ramon, CA 94583. (415) 842-5537. 1991. Describes pest control in horticultural crops.

Controlling Volatile Organic Compound Emissions From Industrial Wastewater. Jeffrey Elliott and Sheryl Watkins. Noyes Publications, 120 Mill Rd., Park Ridge, NJ 07656. (201) 391-8484. 1990. Describes sources of organic containing wastewater, volatile organic compound emission estimation procedures for treatment and collection system units, and available volatile organic compound emission control strategies. Secondary impacts and the control costs associated with steam stripping are also presented.

Convention on International Trade in Endangered Species of Wild Fauna and Flora. Federal Wildlife Permit Office, Washington, DC Annual. Covers endangered species and wild animal trade.

Conversations on Chelation and Mineral Nutrition. H. DeWayne Ashmead. Keats Publishing, Inc., P.O. Box 876, New Canaan, CT 06840. (203) 966-8721. 1989.

Conversations on Chelation and Mineral Nutrition. H. DeWayne Ashmead. Keats Publishing Inc., P.O. Box 876, New Canaan, CT 06840. (203) 966-8721. 1989. Physiological effect of malnutrition.

Converting Transit to Methanol. Stephenie Frederick. Institute of Transportation Studies, University of California, Irvine, CA 92717. (714) 833-5989. 1987. Costs and benefits for California's South Coast Air Basin.

Cool Energy: The Renewable Solution to Global Warming. Michael Brower. Union of Concerned Scientists, 26 Church St., Cambridge, MA 02238. (617) 547-5552. 1990. Describes how fossil fuel and renewable energy sources could be used to avoid global warming and air pollution.

Coolidge Center for Environmental Leadership. 1675 Massachusetts Ave., Suite 4, Cambridge, MA 02138. (617) 864-5085.

Cooling Tower Institute. 530 Wells Fargo Dr., Suite 113, Houston, TX 77273. (713) 583-4087.

Cooling Tower Technology: Maintenance, Upgrading and Rebuilding. Robert Burger. The Association of Energy Engineers, 4025 Pleasantdale Rd., Suite 420, Atlanta, GA 30340. (404) 925-9558. 1990. Second edition. Provides a compendium of successful, readily applicable techniques which can be utilized to improve the performance of any cooling tower.

Cooperative National Park Resources Studies Unit. University of California, Davis, Institute of Ecology, Davis, CA 95616. (916) 752-7119.

Coping with an Oiled Sea: An Analysis of Oil Spill Response Technologies. U.S. Government Printing Office, Washington, DC 20402-9325. (202) 512-0000. 1990. Oil spill volume, date, location, cause, and vessel or other spill source, for individual major spills.

COPIRG Outlook. Colorado Public Interest Research Group, 1724 Gilpin St., Denver, CO 80218. (303) 355-1861. Quarterly. Covers consumer rights, environmental protection, and citizen action organization.

Coral Reefs of Florida. Gilbert L. Voss. Pineapple Press, PO Drawer 16008, Sarasota, FL 34239. (813) 952-1085. 1988.

Coral Reefs of the World. Susan M. Wells. World Conservation Union, IUCN Publications Services Unit, 181a Huntingdon Rd., Cambridge, England CB3 0DJ. (0223) 277894. 1991. Catalogues for the first time the significant coral reefs of the world, their geographical context and ecology, their current condition and status in legislation, and prescriptions for their conservation and sustainable use.

The Coral Seas. Hans W. Fricke. Putman Berkley Group, 200 Madison Ave., New York, NY 10016. (212) 951-8400. 1976. Wonders and mysteries of underwater life, includes coral reef ecology.

Core Arboretum. West Virginia University, PO Box 6057, Morgantown, WV 26506-6057. (304) 293-5201.

Corporation Commission: Underground Storage Tanks. Chairman, Jim Thorpe Building, Oklahoma City, OK 73105. (405) 521-2264.

Corrective Action Response Guide for Leaking Underground Storage Tanks. Albert D. Young, Jr. Government Institutes, Inc., 4 Research Pl., Suite 200, Rockville, MD 20850. (301) 921-2300. 1990. Comprehensive resource for preparing for or preventing an uncontrolled release in underground storage tanks.

Corrosion. Orbit Search Service, 8000 Westpark Dr., Suite 400, McLean, VA 22102. (800) 456-7248.

Cosanti Foundation. HC 74, Box 4136, Mayer, AZ 86333. (602) 632-7135.

Cosmetics/Household Products Advertising Trends. FIND/ SVP, 625 Avenue of the Americas, New York, NY 10011. (212) 645-4500. 1991. Media expenditures by the personal care industry, highlighting product areas which are experiencing extremes in the level of competitive activity and the scope of each company's efforts.

Costing the Earth. Frances Cairncross. The Economist Books, PO Box 87, Osney Mead, Oxford, England OX2 0DT. (44) 865 791155/794376.

Council for Agricultural Science & Technology. 137 Lynn Ave., Ames, IA 50010. (515) 292-2125.

Council for Tobacco Research–U.S.A. 900 Third Ave., New York, NY 10022. (212) 421-8885.

Council of Chemical Association Executives. c/o CMA, 2501 M St., N.W., Washington, DC 20037. (202) 887-1265.

Council of Pollution Control Financing Agencies. 1225 I. St., N.W., Suite 300, Washington, DC 20005. (202) 682-3996.

Council of Soil Testing and Plant Analysis. P.O. Box 2007, Georgia University Station, Athens, GA 30612. (404) 542-0782.

Council on Alternate Fuels. 1225 Eye St., Suite 320, Washington, DC 20005. (202) 898-0711.

Council on Economic Priorities. 30 Irving Place, New York, NY 10003. (212) 420-1133.

Council on Ocean Law. 1709 New York Ave., NW, Suite 700, Washington, DC 20006. (202) 347-3766.

Council on Plastics and Packaging in the Environment. 1001 Connecticut Ave., N.W., Suite 401, Washington, DC 20036. (202) 331-0099.

Council on the Environment: Coastal Zone Management. Administrator, Ninth Street Office Bldg., Room 903, Richmond, VA 23219. (804) 786-4500.

Council on the Environment: Environmental Protection. Administrator, Ninth Street Office Bldg., Room 903, Richmond, VA 23219. (804) 786-4500.

Countermeasures to Airborne Hazardous Chemicals. J. M. Holmes and C. H. Byers. Noyes Publications, 120 Mill Rd., Park Ridge, NJ 07656. (201) 391-8484. 1990. Presents a study of major incidents involving the release of hazardous chemicals and reviews the entire spectrum of activities, recommends appropriate action and gives technical guidance.

Cousteau Society. Cousteau Society Membership Center, 930 W 21st St., Norfolk, VA 23517. In addition to carrying on the many research projects and explorations made famous by Jacques-Yves Cousteau, the Society publishes educational materials and numerous Technical publications as well as Calypso Log (monthly) and Dolphin Log (bimonthly children's publication).

Cover Crops for Clean Water. W. L. Hargrove, ed. Soil and Water Conservation Society, 7515 Northeast Ankeny Rd., Ankeny, IA 50021-9764. (515) 289-2331; (800) THE-SOIL. 1991. Includes the latest information on the role of cover crops in water quality management, including means of reducing water runoff, soil erosion, agrichemical loss in runoff, and nitrate leaching to groundwater.

CPSC Warns of Carbon Monoxide Hazard with Oil/Wood Combination Furnaces. U.S. Consumer Product Safety Commission, 5401 Westbard Ave., Bethesda, MD 20207. (301) 492-6580. 1984. Safety measures relating to carbon monoxide and product safety of furnaces.

CRC Critical Reviews in Environmental Control. CRC Press, 2000 Corporate Blvd. N.W., Boca Raton, FL 33431. (800) 272-7737. 1970-. Quarterly. Provides qualitative reviews of scientific literature published in the discipline.

CRC Critical Reviews of Food Science and Nutrition. Chemical Rubber Company. CRC Press, 2000 Corporate Blvd. N.W., Boca Raton, FL 33431. (800) 272-7737. 1979. Food, nutrition, and food-processing industry.

CRC Handbook of Biological Effects of Electromagnetic Fields. Charles Polk. CRC Press, 2000 Corporate Blvd. N.W., Boca Raton, FL 33431. (800) 272-7737. 1986. Presents current knowledge about the effects of electromagnetic fields on living matter.

CRC Handbook of Chemistry and Physics. CRC Press, 2000 Corporate Blvd. N.W., Boca Raton, FL 33431. (407) 994-0555; (800) 272-7737. 1988. 67th ed.

CRC Handbook of Chromatography. CRC Press, 2000 Corporate Blvd. N.W., Boca Raton, FL 33431. (800) 272-7737. Pesticides and related organic chemicals.

CRC Handbook of Data on Organic Compounds. Robert C. Weast. CRC Press, 2000 Corporate Blvd. N.W., Boca Raton, FL 33431. (800) 272-7737. 1985.

CRC Handbook of Endocrinology. George H. Gass. CRC Press, 2000 Corporate Blvd. N.W., Boca Raton, FL 33431. (800) 272-7737. 1987. Endocrine glands and hormones.

CRC Handbook of EPR Spectra from Quinones and Quinols. J.A. Pedersen. CRC Press, 200 Corporate Blvd. N.W., Boca Raton, FL 33431. (800) 272-7737. 1985. Topics in electron paramagnetic resonance spectroscopy.

CRC Handbook of Hormones, Vitamins, and Radiopaques. Matthew Verderame. CRC Press, 2000 Corporate Blvd. N.W., Boca Raton, FL 33431. (800) 272-7737. 1986. Covers contrast media, hormones, and vitamins.

CRC Handbook of Identified Carcinogens and Noncarcinogens: Carcinogenicity-Mutagenicity Database. Jean V. Soderman, ed. CRC Press, 2000 Corporate Blvd. N.W., Boca Raton, FL 33431. (800) 272-7737. 1982.

CRC Handbook of Incineration of Hazardous Wastes. William S. Rickman, ed. CRC Press, 2000 Corporate Blvd. N.W., Boca Raton, FL 33431. (800) 272-7737. 1991.

CRC Handbook of Laser Science and Technology. Marvin Weber. CRC Press, 2000 Corporate Blvd. N.W., Boca Raton, FL 33431. (800) 272-7737. 1982.

CRC Handbook of Mariculture. CRC Press, 2000 Corporate Blvd. N.W., Boca Raton, FL 33431. (800) 272-7737. 1993. Covers crustacean aquaculture.

CRC Handbook of Marine Science. F. G. Walton Smith. CRC Press, 2000 Corporate Blvd. N.W., Boca Raton, FL 33431. (800) 272-7737. 1976. Topics in oceanography and ocean engineering.

CRC Handbook of Mass Spectra of Environmental Contaminants. R.A. Hites. CRC Press, 2000 Corporate Blvd. N.W., Boca Raton, FL 33431. (800) 272-7737. 1985. Pollutants spectra and mass spectrometry.

CRC Handbook of Natural Pesticides. Volume V: Microbial Insecticides. Carlo M. Ignoffo. CRC Press, 2000 Corporate Blvd. N.W., Boca Raton, FL 33431. (800) 272-7737. 1991. Review of the use of entomopathogenic microorganisms to control insects and other arthropod pests.

CRC Handbook of Naturally Occurring Food Toxicants. Miloslav Rechcigal, Jr. CRC Press, 2000 Corporate Blvd. N.W., Boca Raton, FL 33431. (800) 272-7737. 1983. Covers food contamination and poisoning and their adverse effects.

CRC Handbook of Pest Management in Agriculture. David Pimentel. CRC Press, 2000 Corporate Blvd. N.W., Boca Raton, FL 33431. (800) 272-7737. 1991. 2d ed. Examines the interdependency of agricultural pest management strategies.

CRC Handbook of Phosphorus-31 Nuclear Magnetic Resonance Data. John C. Tebby. CRC Press, 2000 Corporate Blvd. N.W., Boca Raton, FL 33431. (800) 272-7737. 1991.

CRC Handbook of Radiation Chemistry. Yoneho Tabata, ed. CRC Press, 2000 Corporate Blvd. N.W., Boca Raton, FL 33431. (800) 272-7737. 1991. Covers broad fields from basic to applied in radiation chemistry and its related fields.

CRC Handbook of Radiobiology. K. N. Prasad. CRC Press, 2000 Corporate Blvd. N.W., Boca Raton, FL 33431. (800) 272-7737. 1984. Covers ionizing radiation, radiology and dose response relationship.

CRC Handbook of Techniques for Aquatic Sediments Sampling. Alena Murdoch and Scott D. MacKnight. CRC Press, 2000 Corporate Blvd., N.W., Boca Raton, FL 33431. (407) 994-0555 or (800) 272-7737. 1991. Contents includes: selection of bottom sediment sampling stations, bottom sediment sampling, sampling the settling and suspended particulate matter, sediment sample handling process, and sampling sediment pore water.

CRDS. Orbit Search Service, 8000 Westpark Dr., Suite 400, McLean, VA 22102. (800) 456-7248.

Creating Freshwater Wetlands. Donald A. Hammer. Lewis Publishers, 2000 Corporate Blvd., N.W., Boca Raton, FL 33431. (407) 994-0555 or (800) 272-7737. 1992. Includes marshes, bogs, swamps, sloughs, fens, tules, bayous. Also describes methods for creating wetlands and a history of creation and restoration.

Creating Successful Communities. Michael A. Mantelli, et al. Island Press, 1718 Connecticut Ave. N.W., Suite 300, Washington, DC 20009. (202) 232-7933. 1990. Compendium of techniques for effective land use and growth management to help communities retain their individuality in the face of rapid growth.

CRIS/USDA. U.S. Department of Agriculture, Cooperative State Research Service, Current Research Information System, National Agricultural Library Building, 5th Fl., 10301 Baltimore Blvd., Beltsville, MD 20705. (301) 344-3850. Agricultural, food and nutrition, and forestry research projects.

Criteria for a Recommended Standard: Occupational Exposure to Carbon Tetrachloride. National Institute for Occupational Safety and Health, 1600 Clifton Rd. NE, Atlanta, GA 30333. (404) 639-3286. 1976.

Criteria for a Recommended Standard: Occupational Exposure to Hydrogen Flouride. U.S. G.P.O., Washington, DC 20401. (202) 512-0000. 1976.

Criteria for a Recommended Standard, Occupational Exposure to Malathion. U.S. Department of Health and Human Services, Public Health Service, National Institute for Occupational Safety and Health, Robert A. Taft Lab, 4676 Columbia Pkwy., Cincinnati, OH 45226. (513) 684-8465. 1976.

Criteria for Controlling Occupational Exposure to Cobalt. U.S. Department of Health and Human Services, 200 Independence Ave., SW, Room 34AF, Washington, DC 20201. (202) 472-5543. 1982.

Criteria Pollutant Point Source Directory. North American Water Office, Box 174, Lake Elmo, MN 55042. (612) 770-3861. Biennial. Utilities, smelters, refineries, and other facilities that emit more than 1000 tons of particulates, sulfur oxides, nitrogen oxides, volatile organic compounds, or carbon monoxide.

Critical Issues in Biological Control. Simon Fraser, et al., eds. VCH Publishers, 303 NW 12th Ave., Deerfield Beach, FL 33442-1788. (305) 428-5566. 1990. Analyzes the current concerns about the risks that synthetic pesticides pose to the environment and human health. As a potentially powerful forum of pest control that has few environmental disadvantages, biological control is an attractive alternative which has increased the urgency for more research into non-chemical methods of crop and food production.

Critical Mass Energy Bulletin. Public Citizen Critical Mass Energy Project, 215 Pennsylvania Ave, SE, Washington, DC 20003. (202) 546-4996. Bimonthly. Nuclear power, nuclear waste, nuclear weapons facilities, renewable energy, solar technologies, energy conservation and energy efficiency, and global warming.

Critical Mass Energy Project of Public Citizen. 215 Pennsylvania Ave., S.E., Washington, DC 20003. (202) 546-4996.

Critical Reviews in Environmental Control. CRC Press, 2000 Corporate Blvd. N.W., Boca Raton, FL 33431. (800) 272-7737. Four times a year. Articles on environment and environmental control.

A Critique for Ecology. Robert Henry Peters. Cambridge University Press, 40 W. 20th St., New York, NY 10011. (212) 924-3900. Offers examples of scientific criticism of contemporary ecology.

Crop Physiology Abstracts. C. A. B. International, 845 North Park Ave., Tucson, AZ 85719. (602) 621-7897 or (800) 528-4841. 1975-. Monthly. Abstracts focus on the physiology of all higher plants of economic importance. Aspects include germination, reproductive development, nitrogen fixation, metabolic inhibitors, salinity, radiobiology, enzymes, membranes and other related areas.

Crop Protection Chemical Reference. Chemical and Pharmaceutical Press/Wiley, 605 3rd Ave., New York, NY 10158-0012. (212) 850-6000. 1991. 7th ed. Updated annual edition of a standard reference on label information on crop protection chemicals contains the complete text of some 540 product labels, which provide detailed information concerning what products can be used to treat a certain crop for certain problems, using what quantities of the chemical and under what restrictions and precautions. Appendices provide useful information on such matters as coding required when transporting products, safety practices, calibrations, etc.

Crop Protection Chemicals. B. G. Lever. E. Horwood, 1230 Avenue of the Americas, New York, NY 10020. (212) 698-7000; (800) 223-2348. 1990. Overview of crop protection technology. Traces the evolution of pest control as an integral part of crop production. Focuses on the requirements of governments and society regarding the safety of products to users, food consumers and the environment.

Crop Residue Management for Conservation. Soil and Water Conservation Society, 7515 Northeast Ankeny Rd., Ankeny, IA 50021-9764. (515) 289-2331 or (800) THE-SOIL. 1991. Proceedings of a National Conference sponsored by the Soil and Water Conservation Society, Lexington, KY, August, 1991. State of the art on crop residue management techniques from the experts in the field. It of major consequence for agricultural conservationists and a major component of the conservation compliance provision in the 1985 Food Security Act and the Food, Agriculture, Conservation, and Trade Act of 1990.

Crop Science Society of America. 677 S. Segoe Rd., Madison, WI 53711. (608) 273-8080.

Cross-Reference Index of Hazardous Chemicals, Synonyms, and CAS Registry Numbers. The Forum for Scientific Excellence. J. B. Lippincott, 227 E. Washington Sq., Philadelphia, PA 19105. (215) 238-4200; (800) 982-4377. 1990. Contains more than 50,000 synonyms for the hazardous chemicals and environmental pollutants identified. Comprehensive resource title available for properly identifying common names, chemical names and product names associated with these chemicals.

Crossroads: Environmental Priorities for the Future. Peter Borrelli, ed. Island Press, 1718 Connecticut Ave. N.W., Suite 300, Washington, DC 20009. (202) 232-7933. 1988. An assessment of the environmental movement written by some of the country's top environmental leaders, activists and authors.

Crow's Buyers and Sellers Guide of the Forest Products Industries. C. C. Crow Publications, Inc., Box 25749, Portland, OR 97225. (503) 646-8075.

Cryobiology. Academic Press, c/o Harcourt Brace Jovanovich Inc., 6277 Sea Harbor Dr., Orlando, FL 32887. (800) 346-8648. Bimonthly.

The CSIRO Family Key to Hardwood Identification. C. J. Ilic. Commonwealth Scientific and Industrial Research Organisation, Private Bag 10, Clayton, Australia 3168. 1987. Describes the anatomical data of 152 families of Angiosperms for the identification of hardwoods using the microscope and the computer.

CTCP. Dartmouth Medical School, Department of Pharmacology and Toxicology, Hanover, NH 03755.

Cure Formaldehyde Poisoning Association. 9255 Lynnwood Rd., Waconia, MN 55387. (612) 442-4665.

Current Advances in Ecological and Environmental Science. Pergamon Microforms International, Inc., Fairview Park, Elmsford, NY 10523. (914) 592-7720. 1989-. Monthly. Current literature searching service including journals, reports, abstracts, etc. This service is available online as part of the CABS database on the hosts BRS and ORBIT search service.

Current Advances in Pharmacology & Toxicology. Pergamon Microforms International, Inc., Fairview Park, Elmsford, NY 10523. (914) 592-7720. 1984. Current awareness in biological sciences including toxicology and pharmacology.

Current Advances in Plant Science. Pergamon Microforms International, Inc., Fairview Park, Elmsford, NY 10523. (914) 592-7720. 1984-. Monthly. Current literature searching service including journals, reports, abstracts, etc. This service is available online as part of the CABS database on the hosts BRS and ORBIT search service.

Current Awareness in Particle Technology. Particle Technology Information Service, University of Technology, Loughborough, England LE11 3TU. Leics. (0509) 222528. Monthly. Includes particles, sampling, instrumentation, occupational health, powder and compact properties, handling and mixing, sintering, porous media flow gas filtration, drying, colloids, and other related subjects. Scans over 292 journals on the subjects and retrieves relevant citations on the subject.

Current Cancer Research on Molecular Biology of DNA Tumor Viruses: Replication and Genetics. National Cancer Institute. U.S. Department of Health and Human Services, Public Health Service, National Institutes of Health, 9000 Rockville Pike, Bethesda, MD 20892. (301) 496-4000. 1980. Annual.

Current Cancer Research on Role of Hormones in Carcinogenesis and Related Studies of Hormone Receptors. National Technical Information Service, 5285 Port Royal Rd., Springfield, VA 22161. (703) 487-4650. 1980.

Current Contents. Agriculture, Biology and Environmental Sciences. Institute for Scientific Information, 3501 Market St., Philadelphia, PA 19104. (800) 523-1857. 1973-. Previous title: Current Contents. Agricultural, Food & Veterinary Sciences. Gives the table of contents of periodicals in the fields of agriculture, biology, environmental and related areas.

Current Contents Search. Institute for Scientific Information, 3501 Market St., Philadelphia, PA 19104. (800) 523-1857.

Current Federal Aid Research Report: Wildlife. Claude Stephens. Department of the Interior, Fish & Wildlife Service, 1849 C St. NW, Washington, DC 20240. (202) 208-5634. Annual. Wildlife research projects funded by the Pittman-Robertson grant program.

Current Fisheries Statistics. U.S. G.P.O., Washington, DC 20401. (202) 512-0000. Annual. Production and trade of fish products, including fresh, frozen, canned, cured, and nonedible products.

Current Industrial Reports. U.S. G.P.O., Washington, DC 20401. (202) 512-0000. Annual. Statistical data on air pollution control industry.

Current Ornithology. Richard F. Johnston. Plenum Press, 233 Spring St., New York, NY 10013-1578. (212) 620-8000; (800) 221-9369. 1983.

Current Paleoethnobotany: Analytical Methods and Cultural Interpretations of Archaeological Plant Remains. Christine A. Hastorf and Virginia S. Popper. University of Chicago Press, 5801 Ellis Ave., 4th Floor, Chicago, IL 60637. (800) 621-2736. 1988. Prehistoric archeology and ecology.

Current Perspectives on Energy Conservation in Architecture: A Selected Bibliography. Robert Bartlett Harmon. Vance Bibliographies, PO Box 229, 112 N. Charter St., Monticello, IL 61856. (217) 762-3831. 1980.

Current Research in the Pleistocene. Center for the Study of Early Man, University of Maine at Orono, Orono, ME 04473. 1985-.

Current Research Information System–CRIS/USDA. U.S. Department of Agriculture, National Agricultural Library, 10301 Baltimore Blvd., 5th Floor, Beltsville, MD 20705-2351. (301) 504-5755. Looks at current research projects in agriculture and allied sciences covering the biological, physical, social and behavioral sciences related to agriculture.

The Current State of Atmospheric Fluidized-Bed Combustion Technology. Electric Power Research Institute. The World Bank, Washington, DC 1989.

Curtailing Usage of De-icing Agents in Winter Maintenance: Report. OECD Scientific Expert Group. OECD Publications and Information Centre, 2, rue Andre-Pascal, Paris Cedex 16, France F-75775. (1) 4524 8200. 1989. Discusses snow and ice control over the roads using deicing chemicals.

Cutting Chemical Wastes. David J. Sarokin, et al. INFORM, 381 Park Ave. S., New York, NY 10016. (212) 689-4040. 1985. Describes the activities of 29 organic chemical plants that are trying to reduce hazardous chemical wastes.

Cutting Our Losses: Policy Reform to Sustain Tropical Forest Resources. Charles V. Barber. World Resources Institute, 1709 New York Ave. N.W., Washington, DC 20006. (800) 822-0504. 1991. Focuses on the underlying economic social and political forces that drive forest conversation and exploitation.

Cycad Society. c/o David S. Mayo, 1161 Phyllis Ct., Mountain View, CA 94040. (415) 964-7898.

Cycle/The Waste Paper. Environmental Action Coalition, 625 Broadway, New York, NY 10012. (212) 677-1601. Irregular. Disposal of solid waste materials, such as paper, used containers, metal and garbage.

Cycles of Soil: Carbon, Nitrogen, Phosphorus, Sulfur, Micronutrients. F.J. Stevenson. John Wiley & Sons Inc., 605 3rd Ave., New York, NY 10158-0012. (212) 850-6000. 1986.

Cystic Fibrosis Foundation. 6931 Arlington Rd., #200, Bethesda, MD 20814. (301) 951-4422.

Dams and the Environment. John A. Dixon. The World Bank, 1818 H. St., N.W., Washington, DC 20433. 1989.

Dangerous Premises: An Insider's View of OSHA Enforcement. ILR Press, Cornell University, Ithaca, NY 14851. (607) 255-3061. Grouped by hazard: asbestos, solvents, lead, noise, carbon monoxide, and formaldehyde.

Dangerous Properties of Industrial Materials. Irving Newton Sax. Van Nostrand Reinhold, 115 5th Ave., New York, NY 10003. (212) 254-3232. 1989. 7th ed. Deals with hazardous substances and chemically induced occupational diseases.

Dangerous Properties of Industrial Materials Report. Van Nostrand Reinhold, 115 5th Avenue, New York, NY 10003. (212) 254-3232. Bimonthly. Chemical and environmental review of hazardous industrial materials.

Database for Hydrocarbon-Contaminated Site Remediation: Software and Manual. C.E. Spear. Electric Power Research Institute, 3412 Hillview Ave., Palo Alto, CA 94304. (415) 965-4081. 1990. Waste disposal, gas manufacture and works, and hazardous waste sites.

DC Water Resources Research Center. University of District of Columbia, 4200 Connecticut Avenue, NW, MB5004, Washington, DC 20008. (202) 673-3442.

Dead Heat. M. Oppenheimer and R. Boyle. IB Tauris, 110 Gloucester Ave., London, England NW1 8JA. 071 483 2681. 1990. Guide to global warming and some possible solutions.

Deadly Brew: Advanced Improvised Explosives. Seymour Lecker. Paladin Press, 2523 Broadway, Boulder, CO 80304. (303) 443-7250. 1987.

Deadly Dust: Silicosis and the Politics of Occupational Disease in Twentieth-Century America. David Rosner and Gerald Markowitz. Princeton University Press, 41 Williams St., Princeton, NJ 08540. (609) 258-4900. 1991. Case study of how occupational diseases are defined and addressed.

Death in the Marsh. Tom Harris. Island Press, 1718 Connecticut Ave. N.W., Suite 300, Washington, DC 20009. (202) 232-7933. 1991. Explains how federal irrigation projects have altered the selenium's circulation in the environment, allowing it to accumulate in marshes, killing ecosystems and wildlife, and causing deformities in some animals.

Death Rush: Poppers & AIDS: With Annotated Bibliography. John Lauritsen. Pagan Press, 26 St. Mark's Pl., New York, NY 10003. (212) 674-3321. 1986. Chemically induced substance abuse including nitrites.

Debt-for-Nature Exchanges and Biosphere Reserves: Experiences and Potential. Peter Dogse and Bernd von Droste. UNESCO, 7, place de Fontenoy, Paris, France F-75700. (331) 45 68 40 67. 1990. MAB Digest 6.

DECHEMA Environmental Technology Equipment Data–DETEQ. STN International, c/o Chemical Abstracts Service, 2540 Olentangy River Road, P.O. Box 3012, Columbus, OH 43210. Information on the manufacturers of apparatus and technical equipment in the field of environmental engineering. Corresponds to the "ACHEMA Handbook Pollution Control."

Deciduous Tree Fruit Disease Workers. c/o David Sugar, Southern Oregon Expt. Sta., 569 Hanley Rd., Medford, OR 97502. (503) 772-5165.

Decline of the Sea Turtles: Causes and Prevention. National Research Council, Committee on Sea Turtle Conservation. National Academy Press, 2101 Constitution Ave., NW, PO Box 285, Washington, DC 20055. (202) 334-3313. 1990. Conservation of endangered species, especially sea turtles.

Decommissioning: Nuclear Power's Missing Link. Cynthia Pollock. Worldwatch Institute, 1776 Massachusetts Ave., N.W., Washington, DC 20036-1904. 1986.

Deep Coal Mining: Waste Disposal Technology. William S. Doyle. Noyes Publications, 120 Mill Rd., Park Ridge, NJ 07656. (201) 391-8484. 1976. Pollution technology review covering waste disposal in coal mining.

Deep Ecology. Bill Devall and George Sessions. G. M. Smith, PO Box 667, Layton, UT 84041. (801) 554-9800; (800) 421-8714. 1985. Explores the philosophical, psychological and sociological roots of today's environmental movement and offers specific direct action suggestions for individuals to practice.

Deep Ecology and Environmental Ethics: A Selected and Annotated Bibliography of Materials Published Since 1980. Teresa DeGroh. Council of Planning Librarians, 1313 E. 60th St., Chicago, IL 60637-2897. (312) 942-2163. 1987. Covers human ecology and environmental protection.

Deer Unlimited of America. P.O. Box 1129, Abbeville, SC 29620. (803) 391-2300.

Defenders. Defenders of Wildlife, 1244 19th St. NW, Washington, DC 20036. (202) 659-9510. Bimonthly. Wildlife and conservation.

Defenders of Wildlife. 1244 19th St., NW, Washington, DC 20036. (202) 659-9510.

Defending the Earth. South End Press, 116 St. Botolph St., Boston, MA 02115. (800) 533-8478. 1991.

Defense Cleanup. Pasha Publications, 1401 Wilson Blvd., Suite 900, Arlington, VA 22209. (703) 528-1244. Weekly. Reports on projects to analyze, recycle, and dispose of defense weapons.

Definition for Asbestos and Other Health-Related Silicates. American Society for Testing and Materials, 1916 S. Race St., Philadelphia, PA 19103. (215) 299-5585. 1984. Toxicology of asbestos and silicates.

Defusing the Toxics Threat: Controlling Pesticides and Industrial Waste. Sandra Postel. Worldwatch Institute, 1776 Massachusetts Ave., N.W., Washington, DC 20036-1904. 1987.

Degradable Materials: Perspectives, Issues, and Opportunities. Sumner A. Barenberg, et al. CRC Press, 2000 Corporate Blvd. N.W., Boca Raton, FL 33431. (800) 272-7737. 1990. State-of-the-art of degradable materials including plastics.

Degradation and Stabilization of Polyolefins. Norman S. Allen. Applied Science Publications, 655 Avenue of the Americas, New York, NY 10010. (212) 989-5800. 1983.

Degradation of Chemical Carcinogens: An Annotated Bibliography. M.W. Slein. Van Nostrand Reinhold, 115 Fifth Ave., New York, NY 10003. (212) 254-3232. 1980.

Degradation of Synthetic Organic Molecules in the Biosphere. National Academy of Sciences, 2101 Constitution Ave. N.W., Washington, DC 20418. (202) 334-2000. 1972. Proceedings of conference, San Francisco, CA, June 12-13, 1971, under the aegis of the National Research Council.

Degradation, Retention and Dispersion of Pollutants in Groundwater. E. Arvin, ed. Pergamon Microforms International, Inc., Fairview Park, Elmsford, NY 10523. (914) 592-7720. 1985. Proceedings of the IAWPRC Seminar held in Copenhagen, Denmark, September 12-14, 1984.

Dehumidification Handbook. Cargocaire Engineering Corp., PO Box 640, Amesbury, MA 01913. 1982.

Delaware Conservationist. Delaware Dept. of Natural Resources, 89 Kings Hwy., Box 1401, Dover, DE 19903. (302) 736-4506. Quarterly. Natural resources in the state.

Delaware River Basin Commission. 1100 L St., N.W., Room 5113, Washington, DC 20240. (202) 343-5761.

Delaware's Environmental Legacy: Shaping Tomorrow's Environment Today: Report to the Governor and the People of Delaware. Delaware Department of Natural Resources and Environmental Control, Information and Education Section, Office of the Secretary, PO Box 1401, Dover, DE 19903. (302) 739-4506. 1988.

The Delicate Balance. National Center for Environmental Health Strategies, 1100 Rural Ave., Voorhers, NJ 08043. (609) 429-5358. 1990. Quarterly.

Demanding Clean Food and Water. Plenum Press, 233 Spring St., New York, NY 10013. (212) 620-8000. Details specific chemicals to avoid in foods and discusses approaches for eradicating pests without polluting the environment.

Demography as an Interdiscipline. J. Mayone Stycos, ed. Transaction Pub., Rutgers University, New Brunswick, NJ 08903. (201) 932-2280. 1989. Deals with social sciences and the population problem; fertility transition: Europe and the third world compared; migration and social structure; proximate determination of fertility and mortality.

Demography for Agricultural Planners. D. S. Baldwin. Food and Agriculture Organization of the United Nations, 4611-F, Assembly Dr., Lanham, MD 20706-4391. (301) 459-7666; (800) 274-4888. 1975. Deals with the rural population demography and agricultural economics.

Demonstrations of Vapor Control Technology for Gasoline Loading of Barges. S. S. Gross. U.S. Environmental Protection Agency, Industrial Environmental Research Laboratory, MD 75, Research Triangle Park, NC 27711. 1984. Air pollution in the United States caused by gasoline.

Denitrification, Nitrification, and Atmospheric Nitrous Oxide. C.C. Delwiche. John Wiley & Sons, Inc., 605 3rd Ave., New York, NY 10158-0012. (212) 850-6000. 1981. Covers nitrification, nitrogen cycle, and nitrous oxide.

Dentrification in Soil and Sediment. Niels Peter Revsbech and Jan Sorensen, eds. Plenum Press, 233 Spring St., New York, NY 10013-1578. (212) 620-8000; (800) 221-9369. 1991. The process, its measurement, and its significance are analyzed in 20 papers from a June 1989 symposium in Ahrus, Denmark. Topics included are: biochemistry, genetics, ecophysiology, and the emission of nitrogen-oxygen compounds.

Department of Administration: Coastal Zone Management. Director, Coastal Management Section, PO Box 7864, Madison, WI 53707. (608) 266-3687.

Department of Agriculture and Commerce: Pesticide Registration. State Entomologist/Director, Plant Industry Division, PO Box 5207, Mississippi State University, MS 39762. (601) 325-3390.

Department of Agriculture and Consumer Affairs: Pesticide Registration. Director, Division of Inspection, 3125 Conner Blvd., Tallahassee, FL 32399-1650. (904) 488-3731.

Department of Agriculture and Consumer Services: Pesticide Registration. Supervisor, Office of Pesticide Registration, PO Box 1163, Richmond, VA 23209. (804) 786-3162.

Department of Agriculture and Industry: Pesticide Registration. Director, Division of Agricultural Chemistry and Plant/Plant Industry, PO Box 3336, 1445 Federal Dr., Montgomery, AL 36193. (205) 261-2656.

Department of Agriculture: Occupational Safety. Chief, Division of Plant Industry, 8995 East Main St., Reynoldsburg, OH 43068-3399. (614) 866-6361, Ext. 285.

Department of Agriculture: Pesticide Bureau. Chief, Bureau of Plant Industry, Division of Agronomic Services, 2301 North Cameron St., Harrisburg, PA 17110-9408. (717) 787-4843.

Department of Agriculture: Pesticide Registration. Director, Division of Plant Industry, 4th Floor, 1525 Sherman St., Denver, CO 80203. (303) 866-2838.

Department of Agriculture: Pesticide Registration. Pesticide Compliance Supervisor, 2320 South Dupont Highway, Dover, DE 19901. (302) 736-4817.

Department of Agriculture: Pesticide Registration. Assistant Commissioner, Entomology and Pesticide Division, 19 Martin Luther King Pkwy., S.W., Atlanta, GA 30334. (404) 656-4958.

Department of Agriculture: Pesticide Registration. Administrator, Plant Industry Division, 1428 South King St., Honolulu, HI 96814. (808) 548-7119.

Department of Agriculture: Pesticide Registration. Chief, Bureau of Pesticides, 2270 Old Penitentiary Rd., Boise, ID 83712. (208) 334-3243.

Department of Agriculture: Pesticide Registration. Bureau Chief, Plant and Apiary Protection, PO Box 19281, Springfield, IL 62794-9281. (217) 785-2427.

Department of Agriculture: Pesticide Registration. Secretary of Agriculture, Wallace State Office Building, Des Moines, IA 50319. (515) 281-5321.

Department of Agriculture: Pesticide Registration. Director, Plant Health Division, 109 S.W. 9th St., Topeka, KS 66612-1281. (913) 292-2263.

Department of Agriculture: Pesticide Registration. Director, Division of Pesticides, 109 S.W. 9th St., Frankfurt, KY 66612-1281. (502) 564-7274.

Department of Agriculture: Pesticide Registration. Director, Pesticide and Environmental Programs, PO Box 44153, Capitol Station, Baton Rouge, LA 70804-4153. (504) 925-3763.

Department of Agriculture: Pesticide Registration. Director, Board of Pesticide Control, State House Station #28, Augusta, ME 04333. (207) 289-2731.

Department of Agriculture: Pesticide Registration. Assistant Secretary, Office of Plant Industries and Pest Management, 50 Harry S. Truman Pkwy., Annapolis, MD 21401. (301) 841-5870.

Department of Agriculture: Pesticide Registration. Director, Agronomy Services Division, 90 West Plato Blvd., St Paul, MN 55107. (612) 297-2530.

Department of Agriculture: Pesticide Registration. Director, Plant Industries Division, PO Box 630, Jefferson City, MO 65102. (314) 751-2462.

Department of Agriculture: Pesticide Registration. Administrator, Environmental Management Division, Agriculture/Livestock Building, Capitol Station, 6th and Roberts, Helena, MT 59620-0201. (406) 444-2944.

Department of Agriculture: Pesticide Registration. Director, Bureau of Plant Industry, 301 Centennial Mall S., Lincoln, NE 68509. (402) 471-2394.

Department of Agriculture: Pesticide Registration. Director, Division of Plant Industry, 350 Capitol Hill Ave., PO Box 11100, Reno, NV 89510-1100. (702) 789-0180.

Department of Agriculture: Pesticide Registration. Director, Division of Pesticide Control, Caller Box 2042, Concord, NH 03301. (603) 271-3550.

Department of Agriculture: Pesticide Registration. Director, Division of Agricultural and Environmental Services, Department 3150, PO Box 30005, New Mexico State University, Las Cruces, NM 88003-0005. (505) 646-2674.

Department of Agriculture: Pesticide Registration. Pesticide Administrator, Food and Drug Protection Division, PO Box 27647, Raleigh, NC 27611-0647. (919) 733-3556.

Department of Agriculture: Pesticide Registration. Pesticide Regulation, 8995 East Main St., Reynoldsburg, OH 43068. (614) 866-6361.

Department of Agriculture: Pesticide Registration. Director, Plant Industry Division, 2800 North Lincoln Blvd., Oklahoma City, OK 73105. (405) 521-3864.

Department of Agriculture: Pesticide Registration. Administrator, Plant Division, 635 Capitol St., N.E., Salem, OR 97310. (503) 378-3776.

Department of Agriculture: Pesticide Registration. Director, Analysis and Registration of Agricultural Materials, PO Box 10163, Santurce, PR 00908. (809) 796-1710.

Department of Agriculture: Pesticide Registration. Administrator, Feed, Fertilizer and Pesticide Program, Division of Regulatory Services, Joe Foss Building, 523 E. Capital, Pierre, SD 57501. (605) 773-3724.

Department of Agriculture: Pesticide Registration. Director, Division of Plant Industries, PO Box 40627, Melrose Station, Nashville, TN 37204. (615) 360-0130.

Department of Agriculture: Pesticide Registration. Director, Agriculture and Environmental Sciences Division, PO Box 12847, Austin, TX 78711. (512) 463-7534.

Department of Agriculture: Pesticide Registration. Director, Division of Plant Industry, 350 North Redwood Rd., Salt Lake City, UT 84116. (801) 538-7128.

Department of Agriculture: Pesticide Registration. Director, Plant Industry, Laboratory and Standards Division, 116 State St., Montpelier, VT 05602. (802) 828-2431.

Department of Agriculture: Pesticide Registration. Director, Chemical and Plant Division, 406 General Administration Bldg., GT-12, Olympia, WA 98504. (206) 753-5062.

Department of Agriculture: Pesticide Registration. Administrator, Regulatory and Inspection Division, Capitol Building, Charleston, WV 25305. (304) 348-2208.

Department of Agriculture: Pesticide Registration. Manager, Pesticide Control Division, 2219 Carey Ave., Cheyenne, WY 82002-0100. (307) 777-6590.

Department of Agriculture, Trade and Consumer Protection: Pesticide Registration. Assistant Administrator, Agricultural Resources Management Division, Bureau of Plant Division, 801 West Badger Rd., Madison, WI 53708. (608) 266-7131.

Department of Arkansas Heritage: Natural Resources. Director, 225 East Markham St., #200, Little Rock, AR 72201. (501) 371-1639.

Department of Commerce: Underground Storage Tanks. State Fire Marshal, Division of State Fire Marshal, 8895 East Main St., Reynoldsburg, OH 43068. (614) 466-2416.

Department of Community Affairs: Emergency Preparedness and Community Right-to-Know. Chair, Emergency Response Commission, 2740 Centerview Dr., Tallahassee, FL 32399-2149. (904) 488-1472.

Department of Community Development: Emergency Preparedness and Community Right-to-Know. Emergency Response Commission, 9th and Columbia Bldg., Olympia, WA 98504. (206) 459-9191.

Department of Conservation: Fish and Wildlife. Director, Lincoln Tower Plaza, 524 South 2nd St., Springfield, IL 62701. (217) 782-6302.

Department of Conservation: Fish and Wildlife. Director, PO Box 180, Jefferson City, MO 65102-0180. (314) 751-4115.

Department of Conservation: Natural Resources. Director, 1416 Ninth St., Room 1320, Sacramento, CA 95814. (916) 322-1080.

Department of Conservation: Natural Resources. Commissioner, 701 Broadway, Nashville, TN 37243-0345. (615) 742-6747.

Department of Consumer and Regulatory Affairs: Air Quality. Administrator, Housing and Environmental Regulations, 614 H St., N.W., Washington, DC 20001. (202) 727-7395.

Department of Consumer and Regulatory Affairs: Environmental Protection. Administrator, Housing and Environmental Regulations, 614 H St., N.W., Washington, DC 20001. (202) 727-7395.

Department of Consumer and Regulatory Affairs: Fish and Wildlife. Administrator, Housing and Environmental Regulations, 614 H St., N.W., Washington, DC 20001. (202) 727-7395.

Department of Consumer and Regulatory Affairs: Hazardous Waste Management. Administrator, Housing and Environmental Regulations, 614 H St., N.W., Washington, DC 20001. (202) 727-7395.

Department of Consumer and Regulatory Affairs: Natural Resources. Administrator, Housing and Environmental Regulations, 614 H St., N.W., Washington, DC 20001. (202) 727-7395.

Department of Consumer and Regulatory Affairs: Pesticide Registration. Branch Chief, Pesticides and Hazardous Waste Management Branch, Environmental Control Division, Suite 114, 5010 Overlook Ave., S.W., Washington, DC 20032-5397. (202) 783-3194.

Department of Consumer and Regulatory Affairs: Underground Storage Tanks. Pesticides and Hazardous Waste Management Branch, 5010 Overlook Ave., S.W., Room 114, Washington, DC 20032. (202) 783-3190.

Department of Consumer and Regulatory Affairs: Water Quality. Administrator, Housing and Environmental Regulations, 614 H St., N.W., Washington, DC 20001. (202) 727-7395.

Department of Ecology: Air Quality. Air Program Manager, Air Program Division, Mail Stop PV-11, Olympia, WA 98504. (206) 459-6255.

Department of Ecology: Environmental Protection. Director, Mail Stop PV-11, Olympia, WA 98504. (206) 459-6168.

Department of Ecology: Hazardous Waste Management. Program Manager, Solid and Hazardous Waste, Mail Stop PV-11, Olympia, WA 98504. (206) 459-6316.

Department of Ecology: Solid Waste Management. Section Head, Solid Waste Support, 4224 Sixth Ave., S.E., Row 6, Building 4, Mail Stop PV-11, Lacey, WA 98503. (206) 459-6259.

Department of Ecology: Underground Storage Tanks. Unit Supervisor, Underground Storage Tank Program, 4224 Sixth Ave., S.E., Mail Stop PV-11, Lacey, WA 98504. (206) 459-6272.

Department of Ecology: Waste Minimization and Pollution Prevention. Program Manager, Hazardous Waste Section, 4424 6th Ave., S.E., Olympia, WA 98504-8711. (206) 459-6322.

Department of Ecology: Water Quality. Assistant Director, Water and Shorelands, Mail Stop PV-11, Olympia, WA 98504-8711. (206) 438-7090.

Department of Employment Services: Occupational Safety. Associate Director, Occupational Safety and Health Office, 950 Upshur St., N.W., Washington, DC 20011. (202) 576-6651.

Department of Employment Services: Occupational Services. Administrator, Occupational Safety and Health Administration, 1000 East Grand, Des Moines, IA 50319. (515) 281-3606.

Department of Energy and Natural Resources: Natural Resources. Director, 325 West Adams St., Springfield, IL 62704. (217) 785-2002.

Department of Energy and Natural Resources: Solid Waste Management. Director, 325 West Adams St., Springfield, IL 62704. (217) 785-2800.

Department of Energy and Natural Resources: Waste Minimization and Pollution Prevention. Director, Hazardous Waste Research and Information Center, 1 East Hazlewood Dr., Champaign, IL 61820. (217) 333-8940.

Department of Energy, Minerals, and Natural Resources: Natural Resources. Director, 525 Camino de los Marcos, Santa Fe, NM 87503. (505) 827-7835.

Department of Environment: Air Quality. Director, Air Management Association, 2500 Broening Highway, Baltimore, MD 21224. (301) 631-3225.

Department of Environment: Environmental Protection. Secretary, 2500 Broening Highway, Annapolis, MD 21224. (301) 631-3084.

Department of Environment: Hazardous Waste Management. Director, Hazardous and Solid Waste Management, 2500 Broening Highway, Baltimore, MD 21224. (301) 631-3304.

Department of Environment: Solid Waste Management. Director, Hazardous and Solid Waste Management, 2500 Broening Highway, Baltimore, MD 21224. (301) 631-3304.

Department of Environmental Affairs: Air Quality. Secretary, 1102 Q St., Sacramento, CA 95814. (916) 322-5840.

Department of Environmental Affairs: Environmental Protection. Secretary, 1102 Q St., Sacramento, CA 95814. (916) 322-5840.

Department of Environmental Conservation: Air Quality. Commissioner, 50 Wolf Rd., Albany, NY 12233. (518) 457-7230.

Department of Environmental Conservation: Emergency Preparedness and Community Right-to-Know. Deputy Director, Emergency Response Commission, Bureau of Spill Response, 50 Wolf Rd., Room 326, Albany, NY 12233-3510. (518) 457-4107.

Department of Environmental Conservation: Environmental Protection. Commissioner, 50 Wolf Rd., Albany, NY 12233. (518) 457-3446.

Department of Environmental Conservation: Fish and Wildlife. Commissioner, 50 Wolf Rd., Albany, NY 12233. (518) 457-5690.

Department of Environmental Conservation: Groundwater Management. Commissioner, 50 Wolf Rd., Albany, NY 12233. (518) 457-3446.

Department of Environmental Conservation: Groundwater Management. Commissioner, Agency of Natural Resources, 103 South Wissell, Waterbury, VT 05676. (802) 244-8755.

Department of Environmental Conservation: Hazardous Waste Management. Commissioner, 50 Wolf Rd., Albany, NY 12233. (518) 457-6943.

Department of Environmental Conservation: Hazardous Waste Management. Commissioner, 103 South Wissell, Waterbury, VT 05676. (802) 244-5141.

Department of Environmental Conservation: Natural Resources. Commissioner, 50 Wolf Rd., Albany, NY 12233. (518) 457-3446.

Department of Environmental Conservation: Pesticide Registration. Director, Environmental Health, 3132 Channel Dr., Room 135, Juneau, AK 99811. (907) 465-2696.

Department of Environmental Conservation: Pesticide Registration. Director, Bureau of Pesticides, Room 404, 50 Wolf Rd., Albany, NY 12233-0001. (518) 457-7842.

Department of Environmental Conservation: Solid Waste Management. Commissioner, 50 Wolf Rd., Albany, NY 12233. (518) 457-6603.

Department of Environmental Conservation: Underground Storage Tanks. Commissioner, 50 Wolf Rd., Albany, NY 12233. (518) 457-3446.

Department of Environmental Conservation: Underground Storage Tanks. Commissioner, Agency of Natural Resources, 103 South Wissell, Waterbury, VT 05676. (802) 244-8755.

Department of Environmental Conservation: Water Quality. Commissioner, 50 Wolf Rd., Albany, NY 12233. (518) 457-6674.

Department of Environmental Conservation: Water Quality. Director, Water Quality Division, 103 South Wissell, Waterbury, VT 05676. (802) 244-6951.

Department of Environmental Control: Air Quality. Chief, Air Pollution Control Division, PO Box 98922, Lincoln, NE 68509-8922. (402) 471-2189.

Department of Environmental Control: Emergency Preparedness and Community Right-to-Know. Coordinator, Emergency Response Commission, PO Box 98922, State House Station, Lincoln, NE 68509-8922. (402) 471-2186.

Department of Environmental Control: Environmental Protection. Director, 301 Centennial Mall S., Box 94877, Lincoln, NE 68509-4877. (402) 471-2186.

Department of Environmental Control: Solid Waste Management. Director, 301 Centennial Mall S., Box 94877, Lincoln, NE 68509-4877. (402) 471-2186.

Department of Environmental Control: Water Quality. Director, 301 Centennial Mall S., PO Box 98922, Lincoln, NE 68509-8922. (402) 471-4220.

Department of Environmental Management: Air Quality. Chief, Air and Hazardous Materials Division, 75 Davis St., Providence, RI 02908. (401) 277-2808.

Department of Environmental Management: Coastal Zone Management. Chairman, Coastal Resources Management Council, 9 Hayes St., Providence, RI 02903. (401) 277-2476.

Department of Environmental Management: Emergency Preparedness and Community Right-to-Know. 291 Promenade St., Providence, RI 02908. (401) 277-2808.

Department of Environmental Management: Environmental Protection. Commissioner, 105 South Meridan St., Indianapolis, IN 46206. (317) 232-8162.

Department of Environmental Management: Environmental Protection. Director, 9 Hayes St., Providence, RI 02908-5003. (401) 277-2771.

Department of Environmental Management: Fish and Wildlife. Chief, Fish and Wildlife Division, Washington County Government Center, South Kingstown, RI 02903. (401) 789-3094.

Department of Environmental Management: Groundwater Management. Deputy Commissioner, 105 South Meridan St., Indianapolis, IN 46206. (317) 232-8595.

Department of Environmental Management: Groundwater Management. Director, Water Resources, 100 Cambridge St., Boston, MA 02202. (617) 727-3267.

Department of Environmental Management: Hazardous Waste Management. Branch Chief, Hazardous Waste Management Branch, 105 South Meridan St., Indianapolis, IN 46206. (317) 232-4458.

Department of Environmental Management: Hazardous Waste Management. Chief, Air and Hazardous Materials Division, 75 Davis St., Providence, RI 02908. (401) 277-2808.

Department of Environmental Management: Natural Resources. Director, 9 Hayes St., Providence, RI 02908. (401) 277-2771.

Department of Environmental Management: Pesticide Registration. Chief, Division of Agriculture, 22 Hayes St., Providence, RI 02908. (401) 277-2782.

Department of Environmental Management: Solid Waste Management. Chief, Solid Waste Management Branch, 105 South Meridan St., Indianapolis, IN 46206. (317) 232-4473.

Department of Environmental Management: Solid Waste Management. Director, Division of Solid Waste Disposal, 100 Cambridge St., Boston, MA 02202. (617) 727-3260.

Department of Environmental Management: Solid Waste Management. Executive Director, Solid Waste Management Corporation, 75 Davis St., Providence, RI 02908. (401) 277-2808.

Department of Environmental Management: Waste Minimization and Pollution Prevention. Program Director, Office of Safe Waste Management, 100 Cambridge St., Room 1904, Boston, MA 02202. (617) 727-3260.

Department of Environmental Management: Waste Minimization and Pollution Prevention. Chief, Office of Environmental Coordination, Ocean State Cleanup and Recycling Program and Hazardous Waste Reduction Program, 9 Hayes St., Providence, RI 02908-5003. (401) 277-3434.

Department of Environmental Protection: Air Quality. Director, Environmental Quality, 401 East State St., 2nd Floor, Trenton, NJ 08625. (609) 292-5383.

Department of Environmental Protection: Emergency Preparedness and Community Right-to-Know. Chair, 18 Reilly Rd., Frankfurt, KY 40601. (502) 564-2150.

Department of Environmental Protection: Environmental Protection. Commissioner, State House Station #17, Augusta, ME 04333. (207) 289-2812.

Department of Environmental Protection: Groundwater Management. Commissioner, State House Station #17, Augusta, ME 04333. (207) 289-2811.

Department of Environmental Protection: Hazardous Waste Management. Director, Hazardous Waste Management, State Office Building, 165 Capitol Ave., Hartford, CT 06106. (203) 566-4924.

Department of Environmental Protection: Natural Resources. Commissioner, State House Station #17, Augusta, ME 04333. (207) 289-2811.

Department of Environmental Protection: Solid Waste Disposal. Director, Division of Solid Waste Management, 401 East State St., CN 402, Trenton, NJ 08625. (609) 530-8591.

Department of Environmental Protection: Solid Waste Management. Commissioner, State House Station #17, Augusta, ME 04333. (207) 289-2811.

Department of Environmental Protection: Underground Storage Tanks. Commissioner, State House Station #17, Augusta, ME 04333. (207) 289-2811.

Department of Environmental Protection: Water Quality. Director, Division of Water Resources, 401 East State St., CN402, Trenton, NJ 08625. (609) 292-1637.

Department of Environmental Protection: Water Quality Control Bureau. Commissioner, State House Station #17, Augusta, ME 04333. (207) 289-3901.

Department of Environmental Quality: Air Quality. Director, 2005 North Central, Room 701, Phoenix, AZ 85004. (602) 257-2308.

Department of Environmental Quality: Air Quality. Assistant Secretary, Office of Air Quality, PO Box 44096, Baton Rouge, LA 70804-7096. (504) 342-9047.

Department of Environmental Quality: Air Quality. Director, 811 S.W. Sixth Ave., Portland, OR 97204. (503) 229-5397.

Department of Environmental Quality: Air Quality. Administrator, Air Quality Division, Herschler Building, Cheyenne, WY (307) 777-7391.

Department of Environmental Quality: Emergency Preparedness and Community Right-to-Know. Emergency Response Coordinator, PO Box 44066, 333 Laurel St., Baton Rouge, LA 70804-4066. (504) 342-8617.

Department of Environmental Quality Engineering: Air Quality. Commissioner, One Winter St., Boston, MA 02108. (617) 292-5856.

Department of Environmental Quality Engineering: Emergency Preparedness and Community Right-to-Know. Title III Emergency Response Commission, One Winter St., 10th Floor, Boston, MA 02108. (617) 292-5993.

Department of Environmental Quality Engineering: Underground Storage Tanks. Program Director, Underground Storage Tank Program, 1 Winter St., Boston, MA 02108. (617) 292-5500.

Department of Environmental Quality: Environmental Protection. Director, 2005 North Central, Room 701, Phoenix, AZ 85004. (602) 257-6917.

Department of Environmental Quality: Environmental Protection. Secretary, PO Box 15570, Baton Rouge, LA 70895. (504) 342-1266.

Department of Environmental Quality: Environmental Protection. Director, 811 S.W. Sixth Ave., Portland, OR 97204. (503) 229-5696.

Department of Environmental Quality: Environmental Protection. Director, Herschler Building, 4W, Cheyenne, WY 82002. (307) 777-7938.

Department of Environmental Quality: Groundwater Management. Assistant Secretary, Office of Water Resources, PO Box 44091, Baton Rouge, LA 70804-4066. (504) 342-6363.

Department of Environmental Quality: Hazardous Waste Management. Administrator, Hazardous Waste Division, 438 Main St., Baton Rouge, LA 70804. (504) 342-1216.

Department of Environmental Quality: Hazardous Waste Management. Executive Director, Southport Mall, Jackson, MS 39209. (601) 961-5000.

Department of Environmental Quality: Hazardous Waste Management. Director, 811 S.W. Sixth Ave., Portland, OR 97204. (503) 229-5696.

Department of Environmental Quality: Natural Resources. Executive Director, Southport Mall, Jackson, MS 39209. (601) 961-5000.

Department of Environmental Quality: Pesticide Registration. Director, Division of Environmental Quality, 401 East State St., CN027, Trenton, NJ 08625. (609) 292-5383.

Department of Environmental Quality: Solid Waste Management. Director, 2005 North Central, Room 701, Phoenix, AZ 85004. (602) 257-6917.

Department of Environmental Quality: Solid Waste Management. Administrator of Solid Waste, Hazardous and Solid Waste Office, PO Box 44307, Baton Rouge, LA 70804-4307. (504) 342-1216.

Department of Environmental Quality: Solid Waste Management. Director, 811 S.W. Sixth Ave., Portland, OR 97204. (503) 229-5696.

Department of Environmental Quality: Solid Waste Management. Supervisor, Solid Waste Program, Herschler Building, Cheyenne, WY 82002. (307) 777-7090.

Department of Environmental Quality: Underground Storage Tanks. Director, 811 S.W. Sixth Ave., Portland, OR 97204. (503) 229-5696.

Department of Environmental Quality: Underground Storage Tanks. Engineering Supervisor, Water Quality Division, Herschler Building, Cheyenne, WY 82002. (307) 777-7090.

Department of Environmental Quality: Waste Minimization and Pollution Prevention. Waste Reduction Manager, Hazardous Waste Reduction Program, 811 Southwest Sixth Ave., Portland, OR 97204. (503) 229-5913.

Department of Environmental Quality: Waste Minimization and Pollution Prevention. Program Manager, Solid Waste Management Program, Herschler Building, 4th Floor, West Wing, 122 West 25th St., Cheyenne, WY 82002. (307) 777-7752.

Department of Environmental Quality: Water Quality. Director, 2005 North Central, Room 701, Phoenix, AZ 85004. (602) 257-2305.

Department of Environmental Quality: Water Quality. Assistant Secretary, Office of Water Resources, PO Box 44091, Baton Rouge, LA 70804-4066. (504) 342-6363.

Department of Environmental Quality: Water Quality. Director, 811 S.W. Sixth Ave., Portland, OR 97204. (503) 229-5324.

Department of Environmental Quality: Water Quality. Administrator, Water Quality Division, Herschler Building, Cheyenne, WY 82002. (307) 777-7781.

Department of Environmental Services: Environmental Protection. Commissioner, 6 Hazen Dr., Concord, NH 03301. (603) 271-3503.

Department of Environmental Services: Underground Storage Tanks. Commissioner, 6 Hazen Dr., Concord, NH 03301. (603) 271-3503.

Department of Environmental Services: Water Quality. Commissioner, 6 Hazen Dr., Concord, NH 03301. (603) 271-3503.

Department of Fish and Game: Fish and Wildlife. Commissioner, PO Box 3-2000, Juneau, AK 99802-2000. (907) 465-4100.

Department of Fish and Game: Fish and Wildlife. Director, 1416 Ninth St., 12th Floor, Sacramento, CA 95814. (916) 445-3535.

Department of Fish and Game: Fish and Wildlife. Director, 600 South Walnut St., PO Box 25, Boise, ID 83707. (203) 334-5159.

Department of Fish and Game: Fish and Wildlife. Director, PO Box 59, Portland, OR 97207. (503) 229-6339.

Department of Fish, Game and Parks: Fish and Wildlife. Secretary, Joe Foss Building, 523 E. Capital, Pierre, SD 57501. (605) 773-3387.

Department of Fisheries, Wildlife and Environmental Law Enforcement. Director, 100 Cambridge St., Boston, MA 02202. (617) 727-1614.

Department of Food and Agriculture: Pesticide Registration. Associate Director, Division of Pest Management, Environmental Protection and Worker Safety, PO Box 942871, Sacramento, CA 94271-0001. (916) 322-6315.

Department of Food and Agriculture: Pesticide Registration. Chief, Pesticide Bureau, 100 Cambridge St., 21st Floor, Boston, MA 02202. (617) 727-7712.

Department of Forest Resources. University of Arkansas at Monticello, Monticello, AR 71655. (501) 460-1052.

Department of Health: Air Quality. Director, Air Pollution Control Division, 4210 East 11th Ave., Denver, CO 80220. (303) 331-8500.

Department of Health: Air Quality. Deputy Director, Environmental Protection and Health Services Division, 1250 Punchbowl St., PO Box 3378, Honolulu, HI 96813. (808) 548-4139.

Department of Health: Air Quality. Chief, Air Quality Service, 1000 N.E. 10th St., PO Box 53551, Oklahoma City, OK 73152. (405) 271-4468.

Department of Health: Air Quality. Director, Bureau of Air Quality, 288 North 1460 West, Salt Lake City, UT 84116. (801) 538-6108.

Department of Health and Consolidated Laboratories: Air Quality. Director, Environmental Engineering Division, 1200 Missouri Ave., Bismarck, ND 58501. (701) 224-2348.

Department of Health and Consolidated Laboratories: Emergency Preparedness and Community Right-to-Know. Coordinator, SARA Title III Coordinator, 1200 Missouri Ave., PO Box 5520, Bismark, ND 58502-5520. (701) 224-2374.

Department of Health and Consolidated Laboratories: Pesticide Registration. Assistant Director, PO Box 937, Bismark, ND 58505-0020. (701) 221-6146.

Department of Health and Environment: Air Quality. Director, Air and Waste Management, Forbes Field, Building 740, Topeka, KS 66620. (913) 926-1593.

Department of Health and Environment: Air Quality. Bureau Chief, Air Quality Bureau, 725 St. Michael Dr., Santa Fe, NM 87503. (505) 827-0070.

Department of Health and Environment: Air Quality. Director, Air Pollution Control Board, TERRA Building, 150 Ninth Ave., N., Nashville, TN 37247-3001. (615) 741-3931.

Department of Health and Environment: Emergency Preparedness and Community Right-to-Know. Manager, Right-to-Know Program, Forbes Field, Building 740, Topeka, KS 66620. (913) 296-1690.

Department of Health And Environment: Environmental Protection. Director, Division of Environment, Forbes Field, Building 740, Topeka, KS 66620. (913) 296-1535.

Department of Health and Environment: Environmental Protection. Director, Environmental Improvement Division, PO Box 968, Santa Fe, NM 87504. (505) 827-0020.

Department of Health and Environment: Environmental Protection. Assistant Commissioner, Bureau of Environment, 4th Floor, Customs House, Nashville, TN 37203. (615) 741-3424.

Department of Health and Environment: Groundwater Management. Deputy Director, Environmental Protection Division, PO Box 968, Santa Fe, NM 87504-0968. (505) 827-2850.

Department of Health and Environment: Hazardous Waste Management. Director, Environmental Improvement Division, PO Box 968, Santa Fe, NM 87504-0968. (505) 827-2850.

Department of Health and Environment: Hazardous Waste Management. Director, Solid Waste Management Division, 4th Floor, Customs House, Nashville, TN 37203. (615) 741-3424.

Department of Health and Environment: Natural Resources. Director, Division of Environment, Forbes Field, Building 740, Topeka, KS 66620. (913) 296-1535.

Department of Health and Environment: Occupational Safety. Bureau Chief, Occupational Health and Safety Bureau, PO Box 968, Santa Fe, NM 87504-0968. (505) 827-2877.

Department of Health and Environment: Solid Waste Management. Director, Division of Environment, Forbes Field, Building 740, Topeka, KS 66620. (913) 296-1535.

Department of Health and Environment: Solid Waste Management. Deputy Director, Environmental Improvement Division, PO Box 968, Santa Fe, NM 87504-0968. (505) 827-2850.

Department of Health and Environment: Solid Waste Management. Director, Solid Waste Management Division, 4th Floor, Customs House, Nashville, TN 37203. (615) 741-3424.

Department of Health and Environment: Underground Storage Electronics. Director, Underground Storage Tank Program, 150 Ninth Ave., N., Nashville, TN 37219. (615) 741-0690.

Department of Health and Environment: Waste Minimization and Pollution Prevention. Chief, Bureau of Air and Waste Management, Forbes Field, Building 740, Topeka, KS 66620. (913) 296-1607.

Department of Health and Environment: Water Quality. Director, Division of Environment, Forbes Field, Building 740, Topeka, KS 66620. (913) 296-5500.

Department of Health and Environment: Water Quality. Chief, Surface Water Quality Bureau, PO Box 968, Santa Fe, NM 87504-0968. (505) 827-2793.

Department of Health and Environment: Water Quality. Administrator, Water Quality Control Bureau, TERRA Building, 150 Ninth St., N., Nashville, TN 37204. (615) 741-4608.

Department of Health and Welfare: Environmental Protection. Division Administrator, Division of the Environment, 450 West State St., Boise, ID 83720. (208) 334-5840.

Department of Health and Welfare: Water Quality. Chief, Bureau of Water Quality, 450 West State St., Boise, ID 83720. (208) 334-4250.

Department of Health: Emergency Preparedness and Community Right-to-Know. Emergency Planning Commission, 4210 East 11th Ave., Denver, CO 80220. (303) 331-4858.

Department of Health: Emergency Preparedness and Community Right-to-Know. Chair, State Emergency Response Commission, PO Box 3378, Honolulu, HI 96801-9904. (808) 548-6505.

Department of Health: Emergency Preparedness and Community Right-to-Know. Director, PO Box 53504, Oklahoma City, OK 73152. (405) 271-4468.

Department of Health: Emergency Preparedness and Community Right-to-Know. Commissioner, 60 Main St., PO Box 70, Montpelier, VT 05402. (802) 863-7281.

Department of Health: Environmental Protection. Director, Air Pollution Control Division, 4210 East 11th Ave., Denver, CO 80220. (303) 331-8500.

Department of Health: Environmental Protection. Deputy Director, Environmental Protection and Health Services, 1250 Punchbowl St., Honolulu, HI 96813. (808) 548-4139.

Department of Health: Environmental Protection. Director, Environmental Health Section, 1200 Missouri Ave., Bismark, ND 58501. (701) 224-2374.

Department of Health: Environmental Protection. Associate Commissioner, Environment and Consumer Health Protection, 100 West 49th St., Austin, TX 78756. (512) 458-7541.

Department of Health: Environmental Protection. Director, Division of Environmental Health, 288 North 1460 W., PO Box 16690, Salt Lake City, UT 84116-1690. (801) 538-0700.

Department of Health: Hazardous Waste Management. Deputy Director, Environmental Protection and Health Services, 1250 Punchbowl St., Honolulu, HI 96813. (808) 548-4139.

Department of Health: Hazardous Waste Management. Chief, Solid and Hazardous Waste Bureau, State Capitol, Helena, MT 59620. (406) 444-2821.

Department of Health: Hazardous Waste Management. Chief, Waste Management Service, 1000 N.E. 10th St., PO Box 53551, Oklahoma City, OK 73152. (405) 271-5338.

Department of Health: Occupational Safety. Director, Occupational Safety and Health, 4443 I-55 North, Jackson, MS 39211. (601) 982-6315.

Department of Health: Occupational Safety. Commissioner, 1100 West 49th St., Austin, TX 78756. (512) 458-7375.

Department of Health Services: Underground Storage Tanks. Director, 1740 W. Adams St., Room 407, Phoenix, AZ 85007. (602) 542-1024.

Department of Health: Solid Waste Management. Deputy Director, Environmental Protection and Health Services Division, 1250 Punchbowl St., Honolulu, HI 96813. (808) 548-4139.

Department of Health: Solid Waste Management. Chief, Solid and Hazardous Waste Bureau, State Capitol, Helena, MT 59620. (406) 444-2821.

Department of Health: Solid Waste Management. Chief, Waste Management Service, 1000 N.E. 10th St., PO Box 53551, Oklahoma City, OK 73152. (405) 271-5338.

Department of Health: Solid Waste Management. Director, Division of Solid Waste Management, 1100 West 49th St., Austin, TX 78756. (512) 458-7271.

Department of Health: Underground Storage Tanks. Chief, Solid and Hazardous Waste Bureau, State Capitol, Helena, MT 59620. (406) 444-2821.

Department of Health: Waste Minimization and Pollution Prevention. Service Chief, Waste Minimization Service, PO Box 53551, Oklahoma City, OK 73152. (405) 271-7047.

Department of Health: Water Quality. Director, Water Quality Control Commission, 4210 East 11th Ave., Denver, CO 80220. (303) 331-4534.

Department of Health: Water Quality. Deputy Director, Environmental Protection and Health Services Division, 1250 Punchbowl St., Honolulu, HI 96813. (808) 548-4139.

Department of Health: Water Quality. Director, Drinking Water/Sanitation Bureau, 288 North 1460 W., PO Box 16690, Salt Lake City, UT 84116-0700. (801) 538-6159.

Department of Human Resources: Hazardous Waste Management. Chief, Solid Waste Management Section, 401 Oberlin Rd., Raleigh, NC 27605. (919) 733-4996.

Department of Human Resources: Occupational Safety. Director, Employment Standards and Labor Relations, 430 S.W. Topeka, 3rd Floor, Topeka, KS 66603. (913) 296-7475.

Department of Human Resources: Solid Waste Management. Chief, Solid Waste Management Section, 401 Oberlin Rd., Raleigh, NC 27605. (919) 733-4966.

Department of Industrial Relations: Occupational Safety. Chief, Occupational Safety and Health, 525 Golden Gate Ave., San Francisco, CA 94102. (415) 557-1946.

Department of Industrial Relations: Occupational Safety. Administrator, Occupational Safety and Health, 1370 South Curry St., Carson City, NV 89710. (702) 885-5270.

Department of Inland Fisheries and Wildlife: Fish and Wildlife. Commissioner, State House Station #41, Augusta, ME 04333. (207) 289-4471.

Department of Insurance and Finance: Occupational Safety. Administrator, Accident Prevention Division, 21 Labor and Industries Bldg., Salem, OR 97310. (503) 378-3272.

Department of Labor and Human Resources: Occupational Safety. Secretary, 505 Munoz Rivera Ave., Hato Rey, PR 00918. (809) 754-5353.

Department of Labor and Industry: Occupational Safety. Director, Division of Industrial Safety, 100 Cambridge St., Boston, MA 02202. (617) 727-3567.

Department of Labor and Industry: Occupational Safety. Director, Occupational Safety and Health Administration, 444 Lafayette Rd., St Paul, MN 55101. (612) 296-2116.

Department of Labor and Industry: Occupational Safety. Director, Occupational and Industry Safety, 1529 Labor and Industry Bldg., Harrisburg, PA 17120. (717) 787-3323.

Department of Labor and Industry: Occupational Safety. Manager, VOSHA Division, 5 Court St., Montpelier, VT 05602. (802) 828-2765.

Department of Labor and Industry: Occupational Safety. Commissioner, PO Box 12064, Richmond, VA 23219. (804) 786-2377.

Department of Labor and Industry: Occupational Safety. Assistant Director, Industrial Safety and Health, 805 Plum St., S.E., Mail Stop HC-402, Olympia, WA 98504

Department of Labor and Statistics: Occupational Safety. Commissioner, Occupational Health and Safety, Herschler Building, Cheyenne, WY 82002. (307) 777-7261.

Department of Labor: Emergency Preparedness and Community Right-to-Know. Depository of Documents, 10421 West Markham, Little Rock, AR 72205. (501) 681-4534.

Department of Labor: Occupational Safety. Assistant Commissioner, 64 North Union St., Room 600, Montgomery, AL 36130. (205) 242-3460

Department of Labor: Occupational Safety. Deputy Director, Occupational Safety and Health Division, PO Box 1149, Juneau, AK 99802. (907) 465-4855.

Department of Labor: Occupational Safety. Director, 10421 W. Markham, #100, Little Rock, AR 72205. (501) 682-4500.

Department of Labor: Occupational Safety. Director, Occupational Safety and Health, 200 Folly Brook Blvd., Wethersfield, CT 06109. (203) 566-4550.

Department of Labor: Occupational Safety. Director, Division of Industrial Affairs, 820 North French St., Wilmington, DE 19801. (302) 571-2877.

Department of Labor: Occupational Safety. Assistant Commissioner, Field Services, 254 Washington St., S.W., Atlanta, GA 30334. (404) 656-3014.

Department of Labor: Occupational Safety. Manager, #1 W. Old State Capitol Plaza, Springfield, IL 62706. (217) 782-9386.

Department of Labor: Occupational Safety. Secretary, The 127 Building, U.S. 127 South, Frankfurt, KY 40601. (502) 564-2300.

Department of Labor: Occupational Safety. Assistant Secretary, Office of Labor, PO Box 94094, Baton Rouge, LA 70804-9094. (504) 925-4221.

Department of Labor: Occupational Safety. Director, Bureau of Labor Statistics, State House Station #45, Augusta, ME 04333. (207) 289-2015.

Department of Labor: Occupational Safety. Director, Bureau of Safety and Regulation, PO Box 30015, Lansing, MI 48909. (517) 322-1814.

Department of Labor: Occupational Safety. Safety Bureau Chief, Worker's Compensation Division, 5 S. Last Chance Gulch, Helena, MT 59601. (406) 444-6401.

Department of Labor: Occupational Safety. Director, Division of Safety, PO Box 95024, Lincoln, NE 68509-5024. (402) 471-2239.

Department of Labor: Occupational Safety. Commissioner, 19 Pillsbury St., Concord, NH 03301. (603) 271-3171.

Department of Labor: Occupational Safety. Assistant Commissioner, Division of Workplace Standards, John Fitch Plaza, CN386, Trenton, NJ 08625. (609) 292-2313.

Department of Labor: Occupational Safety. Commissioner, Campus, State Office Building, Albany, NY 12240. (518) 457-2741.

Department of Labor: Occupational Safety. Commissioner, 4 West Edenton St., Raleigh, NC 27601-1092. (919) 733-7166.

Department of Labor: Occupational Safety. Supervisor, Safety Standards Division, 1315 Broadway Place, Oklahoma City, OK 73103. (405) 521-2461.

Department of Labor: Occupational Safety. Administrator, Occupational Safety and Health, 220 Elmwood Ave., Providence, RI 02907. (401) 457-1800.

Department of Labor: Occupational Safety. Director, Occupational Safety and Health, PO Box 11329, Columbia, SC 29211. (803) 734-9644.

Department of Labor: Occupational Safety. Occupational Safety Division, 501 Union Bldg., Nashville, TN 37219. (615) 741-2793.

Department of Labor, Occupational Safety and Health Administration: Docket Room. 200 Constitution Ave., N.W., Room N3670, Washington, DC 20210. (202) 523-7894.

Department of Labor: Technical Data Center. 200 Constitution Ave., N.W., Washington, DC 20210. (202) 523-9700.

Department of Land and Natural Resources: Groundwater Management. Deputy Director, Water and Land Development Division, 1151 Punchbowl St., Honolulu, HI 96813. (808) 548-7533.

Department of Land Conservation and Development: Coastal Zone Management. Director, 1175 Court St., N.E., Salem, OR 97310. (503) 378-4928.

Department of Lands: Underground Storage Tanks. Petroleum Engineer, Water Quality Bureau, Oil and Gas Commission, 701 River Ave., Coeur d'Alene, ID 83814. (208) 664-2171.

Department of Natural Resources: Air Quality. Air Protection Branch Chief, Environmental Protection Division, Floyd Towers East, Room 1162, 205 Butler St., S.E., Atlanta, GA 30334. (404) 656-6900.

Department of Natural Resources: Air Quality. Director, Air Quality and Solid Waste Protection Bureau, Wallace State Office Building, Des Moines, IA 50319. (515) 281-8852.

Department of Natural Resources: Air Quality. Air Quality Division, 4th Floor Mason Bldg., PO Box 30028, Lansing, MI 48909. (517) 373-7023.

Department of Natural Resources: Air Quality. Staff Director, Air Pollution Control Program, PO Box 176, Jefferson City, MO 65102. (314) 751-4817.

Department of Natural Resources: Air Quality. Director, Bureau of Natural Resources, PO Box 7921, Madison, WI 53707. (608) 266-0603.

Department of Natural Resources and Community Development: Underground Storage Tanks. Director, Environmental Management, 512 North Salisbury St., Raleigh, NC 27604-1148. (919) 733-7015.

Department of Natural Resources and Conservation: Natural Resources. Director, 1520 E. Sixth St., Helena, MT 59620. (406) 444-6699.

Department of Natural Resources and Energy: Fish and Wildlife. Director, Division of Wildlife Resources, 1596 N.W. Temple, Salt Lake City, UT 84116. (801) 530-4700.

Department of Natural Resources and Energy: Natural Resources. Executive Director, 1636 N.W. Temple, Room 316, Salt Lake City, UT 84116. (801) 538-7200.

Department of Natural Resources and Environmental Control: Air Quality. Secretary, 89 Kings Highway, P.O. Box 1401, Dover, DE 19903. (302) 739-4764.

Department of Natural Resources and Environmental Control: Coastal Zone Management. Secretary, 89 Kings Highway, Dover, DE 19903. (302) 736-4403.

Department of Natural Resources and Environmental Control: Emergency Preparedness and Community Right-to-Know. Chief Program Administrator, Air Resource Section, PO Box 1401, Dover, DE 19903. (302) 736-4791.

Department of Natural Resources and Environmental Control: Environmental Protection. Secretary, 89 Kings Highway, Box 1401, Dover, DE 19903. (302) 736-4403.

Department of Natural Resources: Coastal Zone Management. Director, Coastal Resources Division, 1200 Glynn Ave., Brunswick, GA 31523-9990. (912) 264-7221.

Department of Natural Resources: Coastal Zone Management. Assistant Director, Division of Water, 2475 Director's Row, Indianapolis, IN 46241. (317) 232-4221.

Department of Natural Resources: Coastal Zone Management. Director, Office of Coastal Management, PO Box 44124, Baton Rouge, LA 70804-4487. (504) 342-7591.

Department of Natural Resources: Coastal Zone Management. Administrator, Tidewater Administration, Tawes State Office Bldg., Annapolis, MD 21401. (301) 974-2926.

Department of Natural Resources: Coastal Zone Management. Chief, Great Lakes Shoreland Section, PO Box 30028, Lansing, MI 48909. (517) 373-1950.

Department of Natural Resources: Coastal Zone Management. Director, Water Division, 500 Lafayette Rd., St Paul, MN 55155-4001. (612) 296-4810.

Department of Natural Resources: Coastal Zone Management. Chief, Division of Water, Fountain Square, Building E, Columbus, OH 43224. (614) 265-6712.

Department of Natural Resources: Emergency Preparedness and Community Right-to-Know. Chair, Records Department, 900 East Grand Ave., Des Moines, IA 50319. (515) 281-8852.

Department of Natural Resources: Emergency Preparedness and Community Right-to-Know. Title III Coordinator, Environmental Response Division, Title III Notification, PO Box 30028, Lansing, MI 48909. (517) 373-8481.

Department of Natural Resources: Emergency Preparedness and Community Right-to-Know. Emergency Response Commission, PO Box 3133, Jefferson City, MO, 65102. (314) 751-7929.

Department of Natural Resources: Emergency Preparedness and Community Right-to-Know. Director, PO Box 7921, Madison, WI 53707. (608) 266-9255.

Department of Natural Resources: Environmental Protection. Commissioner, 205 Butler St., S.E., Floyd Towers, Suite 1252, Atlanta, GA 30334. (404) 656-4713.

Department of Natural Resources: Environmental Protection. Deputy Director, Environmental Protection Bureau, PO Box 30028, Lansing, MI 48909. (517) 373-7917.

Department of Natural Resources: Environmental Protection. Director, Pollution Control Bureau, Southport Mall, Jackson, MS 39289-0385. (601) 961-5100.

Department of Natural Resources: Environmental Protection. Director, Division of Environmental Quality, PO Box 176, Jefferson City, MO 65102. (314) 751-4810.

Department of Natural Resources: Environmental Quality. Administrator, Division of Environmental Quality, PO Box 7921, Madison, WI 53707. (608) 266-1099.

Department of Natural Resources: Fish and Wildlife. Director, Division of Wildlife, 6060 Broadway, Denver, CO 80216. (303) 297-1192.

Department of Natural Resources: Fish and Wildlife. Director, Game and Fish Division, 205 Butler St., S.E., Floyd Towers East, Suite 1362, Atlanta, GA 30334. (404) 656-3523.

Department of Natural Resources: Fish and Wildlife. Director, Fish and Wildlife Division, 607 State Office Building, Indianapolis, IN 46204. (317) 232-4091.

Department of Natural Resources: Fish and Wildlife. Administrator, Fish and Wildlife Division, Wallace State Office Building, Des Moines, IA 50319. (515) 281-5918.

Department of Natural Resources: Fish and Wildlife. Director, Tidewater Administration, Tawes State Office Building, Annapolis, MD 21401. (301) 974-2926.

Department of Natural Resources: Fish and Wildlife. Director, Mason Building, PO Box 30028, Lansing, MI 48909. (517) 373-1263.

Department of Natural Resources: Fish and Wildlife. Director, Division of Fish and Wildlife, 500 Lafayette Rd., St Paul, MN 55155-4001. (612) 296-1308.

Department of Natural Resources: Fish and Wildlife. Clayton Lakes, Chief, Division of Wildlife, Fountain Square, Building C-4, Columbus, OH 43224. (614) 265-6305.

Department of Natural Resources: Fish and Wildlife. Secretary, PO Box 5887, San Juan, PR 00906. (809) 724-8774.

Department of Natural Resources: Fish and Wildlife. Chief, Division of Wildlife Resources, State Capitol Complex, Building 3, Room 669, Charleston, WV 25305. (304) 348-2771.

Department of Natural Resources: Fish and Wildlife. Director, Bureau of Wildlife Management, PO Box 7921, Madison, WI 53707. (608) 266-2193.

Department of Natural Resources: Groundwater Management. Manager, State Groundwater Program, 205 Butler St., S.E., Atlanta, GA 30334. (404) 656-5660.

Department of Natural Resources: Groundwater Management. Chief, Division of Law Enforcement, Wallace State Office Building, Des Moines, IA 50319. (515) 281-5385.

Department of Natural Resources: Groundwater Management. Division Director, Water Supply Division, 580 Taylor Ave., Annapolis, MD 21401. (301) 974-3675.

Department of Natural Resources: Groundwater Management. Director and State Geologist, Division of Geology and Land Survey, PO Box 250, Rolla, MO 65401. (314) 364-1752.

Department of Natural Resources: Groundwater Management. State Engineer, Division of Water Rights, 1636 N.W. Temple, Salt Lake City, UT 84116. (801) 538-7240.

Department of Natural Resources: Groundwater Management. Director, Bureau of Water Resources Management, PO Box 7921, Madison, WI 53707. (608) 266-8631.

Department of Natural Resources: Hazardous Waste Management. Bureau Chief, Solid Waste Protection Bureau, Wallace State Office Building, Des Moines, IA 50319. (515) 281-8693.

Department of Natural Resources: Hazardous Waste Management. Chief, Waste Management Division, PO Box 30028, Lansing, MI 48909. (517) 373-2730.

Department of Natural Resources: Hazardous Waste Management. Director, Bureau of Solid Waste Management, PO Box 7921, Madison, WI 53707. (608) 266-1327.

Department of Natural Resources: Natural Resources. Commissioner, PO Box M, Juneau, AK 99802. (907) 465-2400.

Department of Natural Resources: Natural Resources. Executive Director, 1313 Sherman St., Room 718, Denver, CO 80203. (303) 866-3311.

Department of Natural Resources: Natural Resources. Executive Director, 3900 Commonwealth Blvd., Tallahassee, FL 32399-3000. (904) 488-1554.

Department of Natural Resources: Natural Resources. Commissioner, 205 Butler St., S.E., Floyd Towers, Suite 1252, Atlanta, GA 30334. (404) 656-3500.

Department of Natural Resources: Natural Resources. Director, 608 State Office Building, Indianapolis, IN 46204. (317) 232-4020.

Department of Natural Resources: Natural Resources. Chief, Division of Law Enforcement, Wallace State Office Building, Des Moines, IA 50319. (515) 281-5385.

Department of Natural Resources: Natural Resources. Secretary, PO Box 94396, Baton Rouge, LA 70804-9396. (504) 342-4500.

Department of Natural Resources: Natural Resources. Secretary, Tawes State Office Bldg., Annapolis, MD 21401. (301) 974-3041.

Department of Natural Resources: Natural Resources. Director, Mason Building, PO Box 30028, Lansing, MI 48909. (517) 373-2329.

Department of Natural Resources: Natural Resources. Commissioner, 500 Lafayette Rd., St Paul, MN 55155-4001. (612) 296-2549.

Department of Natural Resources: Natural Resources. Director, Jefferson State Office Building, 205 Jefferson St., Jefferson City, MO 65102. (314) 751-4422.

Department of Natural Resources: Natural Resources. Director, Fountain Square, Building D-3, Columbus, OH 43224. (614) 265-6875.

Department of Natural Resources: Natural Resources. Secretary, PO Box 5887, San Juan, PR 00906. (809) 724-8774.

Department of Natural Resources: Natural Resources. Commissioner of Public Lands, 201 John A. Cherburg Bldg., Mail Stop QW-21, Olympia, WA 98504. (206) 753-5317.

Department of Natural Resources: Natural Resources. Secretary, PO Box 7921, Madison, WI 53707. (608) 266-2121.

Department of Natural Resources: Solid Waste Department. Chief, Air Quality and Solid Waste Protection Bureau, Wallace State Office Building, Des Moines, IA 50319. (515) 281-8693.

Department of Natural Resources: Solid Waste Management. Deputy Director, Environmental Protection Bureau, PO Box 30028, Lansing, MI 48909. (517) 373-7917.

Department of Natural Resources: Solid Waste Management. Chief, Division Director, Solid Waste Management Superfund, PO Box 40485, Jackson, MS 39209. (601) 961-5062.

Department of Natural Resources: Solid Waste Management. Director, Bureau of Solid Waste Management, PO Box 7921, Madison, WI 53707. (608) 266-1327.

Department of Natural Resources: Underground Storage Tanks. Petroleum Manager, PO Box 7034, Anchorage, AK 99510-0734. (907) 561-2020.

Department of Natural Resources: Underground Storage Tanks. Assistant Director, Environmental Protection Division, 205 Butler St., S.W., Floyd Towers East, Suite 1152, Atlanta, GA 30334. (404) 656-3500.

Department of Natural Resources: Underground Storage Tanks. Director, Air Quality and Solid Waste Bureau, Wallace State Office Building, Des Moines, IA 50319. (515) 281-8852.

Department of Natural Resources: Underground Storage Tanks. Director, Oil Control Division, 580 Taylor Ave., Annapolis, MD 21401. (301) 974-3551.

Department of Natural Resources: Waste Minimization and Pollution Control. Division Chief, Waste Management Division, Resource Recovery Division, PO Box 30241, Lansing, MI 48909. (517) 373-0540.

Department of Natural Resources: Waste Minimization and Pollution Prevention. Director, Air Quality and Solid Waste Protection Bureau, Wallace State Office Building, 900 East 9th and Grand Ave., Des Moines, IA 50319-0034. (515) 281-8690.

Department of Natural Resources: Waste Minimization and Pollution Prevention. Director, Environmental Quality Program, Waste Management Program, PO Box 176, Jefferson City, MO 65102. (314) 751-4919.

Department of Natural Resources: Water Quality. Branch Chief, 205 Butler St., S.E., Floyd Towers East, Suite 1252, Atlanta, GA 30334. (404) 656-4708.

Department of Natural Resources: Water Quality. Director, Mason Building, PO Box 30028, Lansing, MI 48909. (517) 373-2329.

Department of Natural Resources: Water Quality. Director, Waters Division, 500 Lafayette Rd., St. Paul, MN 55155-4810. (612) 296-4800.

Department of Natural Resources: Water Quality. Director, Bureau of Water Resources Management, PO Box 7921, Madison, WI 53707. (608) 266-8631.

Department of Pollution Control and Ecology: Air Quality. Director, 8001 National Dr., Little Rock, AR 72219. (501) 562-7444.

Department of Pollution Control and Ecology: Environmental Protection. Director, 8001 National Dr., Little Rock, AR 72219. (501) 570-2121.

Department of Pollution Control and Ecology: Hazardous Waste Management. Director, 8001 National Dr., Little Rock, AR 72219. (501) 570-2872.

Department of Pollution Control and Ecology: Solid Waste Management. Director, 8001 National Dr., Little Rock, AR 72219. (501) 570-2858.

Department of Pollution Control and Ecology: Underground Storage Tanks. 8001 National Dr., Little Rock, AR 72219. (501) 562-7444.

Department of Pollution Control and Ecology: Waste Minimization and Pollution Prevention. Directors, Solid Waste & Hazardous Waste Division, 1 Capitol Mall, Little Rock, AR 72201. (501) 562-7444.

Department of Pollution Control and Ecology: Water Quality. Director, 8001 National Dr., Little Rock, AR 72219. (501) 570-2114.

Department of Pollution Control: Environmental Protection. Director, 1000 N.E. 10th St., PO Box 53504, Oklahoma City, OK 73152. (405) 271-4677.

Department of Public Safety: Emergency Preparedness and Community Right-to- Know. Director, Emergency Response Commission, PO Box 1628, Santa Fe, NM 87504-1628. (505) 827-9226.

Department of Public Works: Solid Waste Management. Administrator, Public Space Maintenance Administration, 4701 Shephard Pkwy., S.W., Washington, DC 20032. (202) 767-8512.

Department of Regulation: Pesticide Registration. Director, Pesticide and Plant Management Division, PO Box 30017, Lansing, MI 48909. (517) 373-4540.

Department of Resources and Economic Development: Natural Resources. Commissioner, PO Box 856, Concord, NH 03301. (603) 271-2411.

Department of State: Coastal Zone Management. Secretary of State, 162 Washington Ave., Albany, NY 12231. (518) 474-4750.

Department of the Environment: Emergency Preparedness and Community Right-to-Know. State Emergency Response Commission, Department of the Environment, Toxics Information Center, 2500 Broening Highway, Baltimore, MD 21224. (301) 631-3800.

Department of Waste Management: Air Quality. Director, Emergency Response Council, James Monroe Building, 14th Floor, 101 North 14th St., Richmond, VA 23219. (804) 225-2997.

Department of Waste Management: Emergency Preparedness and Community Right-to-Know. State Emergency Response Council, James Monroe Bldg., 11th Floor, 101 North 14th St., Richmond, VA 23219. (804) 225-2667.

Department of Waste Management: Hazardous Waste Management. Executive Director, 101 North 14th St., 11th Floor, Richmond, VA 23219. (804) 225-2667.

Department of Waste Management: Solid Waste Management. Executive Director, 101 North 14th St., 11th Floor, Richmond, VA 23219. (804) 225-2667.

Department of Waste Management: Waste Minimization and Pollution Prevention. Director, Office of Policy and Planning, 11th Floor, Monroe Bldg., 101 North 14th St., Richmond, VA 23219. (804) 225-2667.

Department of Water and Natural Resources: Emergency Preparedness and Community Right-to-Know. Emergency Response Commission, Joe Foss Building, 523 East Capitol, Pierre, SD 57501-3181. (605) 773-3153.

Department of Water Resources: Groundwater Management. Director, 15 S. 15th Ave., Phoenix, AZ 85007. (602) 542-1540.

Department of Water Resources: Groundwater Management. Chief, Planning Division, 1416 9th St., Sacramento, CA 95814. (916) 445-9610.

Department of Water Resources: Groundwater Management. Administrator, Water Management Division, 1301 N. Orchard St., Boise, ID 83720. (208) 327-7902.

Department of Water Resources: Groundwater Management. Director, 301 Centennial Mall S., PO Box 94676, Lincoln, NE 68509-4676. (402) 471-2363.

Department of Wildlife and Parks: Fish and Wildlife. Secretary, Landon State Office Building, 900 S.W. Jackson St., Room 502, Topeka, KS 66612-1220. (913) 296-2281.

Department of Wildlife Conservation: Fish and Wildlife. Director, PO Box 53476, Oklahoma City, OK 73152. (405) 521-3851.

Department of Wildlife: Fish and Wildlife. Director, PO Box 10678, Reno, NV 89520. (702) 688-1500.

Department of Wildlife: Fish and Wildlife. Director, 600 North Capitol Way, Olympia, WA 98501-1091. (206) 753-5710.

Department of Wildlife, Fisheries and Parks: Fish and Wildlife. Director, Division of Wildlife and Fisheries, PO Box 451, Jackson, MS 39205. (601) 364-2015.

Dermal Absorption. U.S. Environmental Protection Agency, Office of Pesticides and Toxic Substances, 401 M St., SW, Washington, DC 20460. (202) 260-2090. Toxic effects, absorption, distribution, metabolism, and excretion relation to the dermal absorption of 655 chemicals.

Dermatotoxicology. Francis N. Marzulli and Howard I. Maibach, eds. Hemisphere Publishing Co., 79 Madison Ave., Suite 1110, New York, NY 10016. (212) 725-1999; (800) 821-8312. 1991. 4th ed. Provides information on theoretical aspects and practical test methods, including both in vitro and in vivo approaches. Pays attention to the worldwide movement for the development of suitable alternatives to animals when feasible.

Desalination. Elsevier, Box 211, Amsterdam, Netherlands 1000 AE. 020-5803-911. 1966-. Forty-two times a year. The international journal on the science and technology of desalting and water purification. Formed by the merger of the Journal of Membrane Science and Desalination.

Desalination Abstracts. National Center for Scientific and Technological Information, PO Box 20125, Tel-Aviv, Israel 1966-. Quarterly.

Desalination and Water Re-Use. Miriam Balaban, ed. Institution of Chemical Engineers, c/o Hemisphere Pub., 1900 Frost Rd., Suite 101, Bristol, PA 19007-1598. (215) 785-5800. 1991. Four volumes. Includes the papers presented at a four-day symposium organized by the Institution of Chemical Engineers (UK) on behalf of the European Federation of Chemical Engineers Working Parties on Desalination and Water Technology and the Membrane Society.

Desalination and Water Re-Use Technologies in Japan. Annual Report. Water Re-Use Promotion Center, Landix Akasaka Bldg, 2-3-4, Akasaka, Minato-ku, Tokyo, Japan 107 1981-. Annual.

Desalination Directory: Desalination and Water Purification. Elsevier Science Publishing Co., 655 Avenue of the Americas, New York, NY 10010. (212) 989-5800. 1981-.

Desalination Materials Manual. Dow Chemical Company. Office of Water Research and Technology, U.S. Dept. of the Interior, Washington, DC 20240. 1975.

Desalination Processes and Multistage Flash Distillation Practice. Arshad Hassan Khan. Elsevier Science Publishing Co., 655 Avenue of the Americas, New York, NY 10010. (212) 984-5800. 1986. Saline water conservation through flash distillation process.

Desalination Technology. Vance Bibliographies, PO Box 229, 112 N. Charter St., Monticello, IL 61856. (217) 762-3831. 1981.

Desalting Handbook for Planners. Catalytic Inc. U.S. Department of the Interior, Office of Water Research and Technology, Washington, DC 20240. 1979. 2d ed.

Description of Manganese Nodule Processing Activities for Environmental Studies. Dames & Moore. National Technical Information Service, 5285 Port Royal Rd., Springfield, VA 22161. (703) 487-4650. 1977. Technical analysis of transportation and waste disposal.

Description of the Ecoregions of the United States. Robert G. Bailey. Forest Service, U.S. Dept. of Agriculture, PO Box 96090, Washington, DC 20090. (202) 720-3760. 1980. Biotic communities in the United States.

Desert Bighorn Council. P.O. Box 5430, Riverside, CA 92517. (714) 683-7523.

Desert Botanical Garden. 1201 N. Galvin Pkwy., Phoenix, AZ 85008. (602) 941-1225.

Desert Protective Council. P.O. Box 4294, Palm Springs, CA 92263. (619) 397-4264.

Desert Tortoise Council. P.O. Box 1738, Palm Desert, CA 92261-1738. (619) 341-8449.

Desert Turfgrass Research Facility. University of Arizona, Forbes Building, Tucson, AZ 85721. (602) 621-1851.

Desiccants and Humectants. Ronald W. James. Noyes Publications, 120 Mill Rd., Park Ridge, NJ 07656. (201) 391-8484. 1973. Patents relative to humectants and drying agents.

Design and Operation of Sewage Treatment Plants in Coastal Tourist Areas. M. Nicolaou and I. Hadjivassilis, eds. Pergamon Microforms International, Inc., Fairview Park, Elmsford, NY 10523. (914) 592-7720. 1989. Proceedings of the IAWPRC Conference held in Limassol, Cyprus, November 3-4, 1987. Discusses problems associated with all aspects of water pollution prevention and control in coastal tourist areas. Also covers the reuse of treated wastewater, as shortage of freshwater is a problem in some countries which have a large seasonal demand for water through tourism.

Design Bases for Facilities for LMFBR Spent Fuel Storage in Liquid Metal Outside the Primary Coolant Boundary. American National Standards Institute. American Nuclear Society, 555 N. Kensington Ave., La Grange Park, IL 60525. (708) 352-6611. 1985. Spent reactor fuel storage standards.

The Design Connection. Ralph W. Crump. Van Nostrand Reinhold, 115 5th Ave., New York, NY 10003. (212) 254-3232. 1981. Energy and technology in architecture.

Design, Construction, and Monitoring of Sanitary Landfill. Amalendu Bagchi. John Wiley & Sons, Inc., 605 3rd Ave., New York, NY 10158-0012. (212) 850-6000. 1990. Handbook of theory, practice, and mathematical models of sanitary landfill technology and how they apply to waste disposal.

Design, Construction, and Operation of Hazardous and Non-Hazardous Waste Surface Impoundments. R. P. Hartley. National Technical Information Service, 5285 Port Royal Rd., Springfield, VA 22161. (703) 487-4650. 1991.

Design for a Livable Planet: How You Can Help Clean Up the Environment. Jon Naar. Perennial Library, 10 E. 53d St., New York, NY 10022. (212) 207-7000; (800) 242-7737. 1990. Explains the dangers we present to our environment and what we can do about it. Also available from Carolina Biological Supply Co., 2700 York Rd., Burlington, NC.

Design Handbook for Automation of Activated Sludge Wastewater Treatment Plants. Alan W. Manning. National Technical Information Service, 5285 Port Royal Rd., Springfield, VA 22161. (703) 487-4650. 1980. Sewage purification and activated sludge process.

Design Manual: Neutralization of Acid Mine Drainage. U.S. Environmental Protection Agency, Office of Research and Development, Industrial Environmental Research Laboratory, 26 W. Martin Luther King Dr., Cincinnati, OH 45268. (513) 569-7931. 1983. Acid mine drainage and the chemistry of neutralization.

Design of Industrial Catalysts. Elsevier Science Publishing Co., 655 Avenue of the Americas, New York, NY 10010. (212) 989-5800.

Design of Warning Labels and Instructions. Joseph P. Ryan. Global Professional Publications, 2805 McGraw Ave., PO Box 19539, Irvine, CA 92713-9539. (800) 854-7179. 1990. Describes the techniques for design and writing crucial cautionary, safety, hazard and other kinds of labels.

Design of Water Quality Monitoring Systems. Robert C. Ward. Van Nostrand Reinhold, 115 5th Ave., New York, NY 10003. (212) 254-3232. 1990. Describes the essential tools to design a system that gets consistently valid results. Features the latest methods of sampling and lab analysis, data handling and analysis, reporting, and information utilization, and includes case studies of system design projects.

Design Research News. Environmental Design Research Assn., PO Box 24083, Oklahoma City, OK 73124. (405) 232-2655. Quarterly. Environmental policy, planning, design, and education; human behavior and implications for environmental designing.

Destruction of Chemical Weapons and Defense Equipment to Prevent Enemy Use. Headquarters, Dept. of the Army, Washington, DC 20310. (202) 695-6153. 1992. Deals with demolition in the military and explosive ordnance disposal.

Destruction of VOCs by a Catalytic Paint Drying Device. C. David Cooper. U.S. Environmental Protection Agency, Air and Energy Engineering Research Laboratory, MD 75, Research Triangle Park, NC 27711. 1985. Environmental aspects of drying paint and infrared drying equipment.

Desulphurisation 2: Technologies and Strategies for Reducing Sulphur Emissions. Hemisphere Publishing Co., 79 Madison Ave., Suite 1110, New York, NY 10016. (212) 725-1999. 1991. Proceedings of a Symposium held in Sheffield, March 1991.

Desulphurization in Coal Combustion Systems. Hemisphere Publishing Co., 79 Madison Ave., Suite 1110, New York, NY 10016. (212) 725-1999. 1989.

Detecting the Climatic Effects of Increasing Carbon Dioxide. National Technical Information Service, 5285 Port Royal Rd., Springfield, VA 22161. (703) 487-4650. Carbon dioxide and air pollution measurement.

Detection of Subsurface Hazardous Waste Containers by Nondestructive Techniques. Arthur E. Lord and Robert M. Koerner. Noyes Publications, 120 Mill Rd., Park Ridge, NJ 07656. (201) 391-8484. 1990. Describes a study undertaken to identify and assess the best possible NDT techniques for detecting and delineating hazardous waste, particularly in steel and plastic containers buried beneath soil or water.

Detergent Chemicals. FIND/SVP, 625 Avenue of the Americas, New York, NY 10011. (212) 645-4500. 1990.

Determination of TCDD in Industrial and Municipal Wastewaters. U.S. Environmental Protection Agency, Environmental Monitoring and Support Laboratory, Center for Environmental Research Information, 26 W. Martin Luther King Dr., Cincinnati, OH 45268. (513) 569-7931. 1982. Covers sewage purification through chlorination, particularly tetrachlorodibenzodioxin.

Determining Wastewater Treatment Costs for Your Community. U.S. Environmental Protection Agency, Office of Water Program Operations, 401 M St., S.W., Washington, DC 20460. (202) 260-2090. 1979. Economic aspects of sewage disposal plants.

Developing Document for Effluent Limitations Guidelines, New Source Performance Standards and Pretreatment Standards for the Metal Molding and Casting Point Source Category. Industrial Technology Division, Office of Water Regulations and Standards, U.S. Environmental Protection Agency., 401 M St. SW, Washington, DC 20460. (202) 260-5400. 1986. Environmental aspects of metal work, effluent quality and water use.

Developing with Recreational Amenities: Golf, Tennis, Skiing, Marinas. Patrick L. Phillips. Urban Land Institute, 625 Indiana Ave., N.W., Washington, DC 20004. (202) 624-7000. 1986. Recreation areas, resorts, retirement communities, condominiums, and vacation homes.

Development Concept Plan Environmental Assessment: Gulf Coast, Everglades National Park, Florida. U.S. National Park Service, Department of the Interior, PO Box 37127, Washington, DC 20013. (202) 208-6843. 1990. Land use concepts in the Everglades National Park.

Development Document for Proposed Effluent Limitations Guidelines, New Source Performance Standards and Pretreatment Standards for the Iron and Steel Manufacturing Point Source Category. U.S. Environmental Protection Agency, Office of Water and Waste Management, Effluent Guidelines Division, 401 M St. SW, Washington, DC 20460. (202) 260-2090. 1981.

Development Document for the Effluent Monitoring Regulation for the Metal Casting Sector. Ontario Ministry of the Environment, Toronto. National Technical Information Service, 5285 Port Royal Rd., Springfield, VA 22161. (703) 487-4650. 1990.

Development of a Chemical Toxicity Assay for Pulp Mill Effluents. J.M. Leach. U.S. Environmental Protection Agency, 401 M St., S.W., Washington, DC 20460. (202) 260-2090. 1981. Sulphate pulping process and effect of water pollution on fishes.

Development of a Solar Desiccant Dehumidifier: Second Technical Progress Report. M. E. Gunderson, et al. National Technical Information Services, 5285 Port Royal Rd., Springfield, VA 22161. (703) 487-4650. 1980.

Development of Circadian Rhythmicity and Photoperiodism in Mammals. Steven M. Reppert. Perinatology Press, 507 Cayuga Heights Rd., Ithaca, NY 14850. (607) 257-3278. 1989. Comparative physiology of mammals development.

Development of Sinkholes Resulting from Man's Activities in the Eastern United States. John G. Newton. U.S. Geological Survey, 12201 Sunrise Valley Dr., Reston, VA 22092. (703) 648-4460. 1987. Causes and environmental aspects of sinkholes.

Development without Destruction: Evolving Environmental Perceptions. M. Tolba. Cassell PLC, Publishers Distribution Center, PO Box C831, Rutherford, NJ 07070. (201) 939-6064/5. 1982.

Developmental Biology Center. University of California, Irvine, Irvine, CA 92717. (714) 856-5957.

Developments in Agricultural and Managed Forest Ecology. Elsevier Science Publishing Co., 655 Avenue of the Americas, New York, NY 10010. (212) 984-5800. Annual.

Developments in Design and Operation of Large Wastewater Treatment Plants. P. Benedek, et al., eds. Pergamon Microforms International, Inc., Fairview Park, Elmsford, NY 10523. (914) 592-7720. 1988. Proceedings of an IAWPRC Workshop held in Budapest, Hungary, September 14-18, 1987. Covers a wide range of topics of interest to designers, operators and researchers in the field of wastewater treatment plants. Includes practical applications of research work.

Dewitt Petrochemical Newsletter. DeWitt and Company, 16800 Greenspoint Park, North Atrium Suite 120, Houston, TX 77060. (713) 875-5525.

Diagnosis. George Thieme Verlag, Ruedigerstrasse 14, Stuttgart 30, Germany D-7000.

Dickey Data. W.S. Dickey Clay Mfg. Co., Box 6, Pittsburgh, KS 66762. (316) 231-1400. Quarterly. Waste-water facilities, drainage, plumbing, pollution control and building materials industry.

Dictionary of Agricultural and Food Engineering. Arthur W. Farrall. Interstate Publishers, 510 N. Vermillion St., PO Box 50, Danville, IL 61834-0050. (217) 446-0500. 1979.

Dictionary of Agriculture. Gunther Haensch and G. H. Deanton. Elsevier Science Publishing Co., 655 Avenue of the Americas, New York, NY 10010. (212) 984-5800. 1986.

A Dictionary of Air Pollution Terms. Air & Waste Management Association, P.O. Box 2861, Pittsburgh, PA 15230. (412) 233-3444. 1989.

Dictionary of Alkaloids. J. Buckingham Southon. Chapman & Hall, 29 West 35th St., New York, NY 10001-2291. (212) 244-3336. 1989.

Dictionary of Animals. Michael Chinery, ed. Arco Pub. Inc., 215 Park Ave. S., New York, NY 10003. 1984.

Dictionary of Antibiotics and Related Substances. Chapman & Hall, 29 West 35th St., New York, NY 10001-2291. (212) 244-3336. 1988.

Dictionary of Biotechnology. J. Coombs. Elsevier Science Publishing Co., 655 Avenue of the Americas, New York, NY 10010. (212) 984-5800. 1986. Areas covered in this dictionary include: fermentation; brewing; vaccines; plant tissue; culture; antibiotic production; production and use of enzymes; biomass; byproduct recovery and effluent treatment; equipment; processes; micro-organisms and biochemicals.

Dictionary of Biotechnology English-German. W. Babel, et al., ed. Elsevier Science Publishing Co., 655 Avenue of the Americas, New York, NY 10010. (212) 984-5800. 1989. Presents over 7300 terms in the area of biotechnology from many academic disciplines and treats biotechnology as more than just a bioscience.

Dictionary of Biotechnology in English-Japanese and German. R. Schmid and Saburo Fukui. Springer Verlag, 175 5th Ave., New York, NY 10010. (212) 460-1500 or (800) 777-4643. 1986.

A Dictionary of Birds. Bruce Campbell. Buteo Books, PO Box 425, Friday Harbor, WA 98250. (206) 378-6146. 1985.

Dictionary of Blasting Technology. Barbara Student-Bilharz. VCH Publishers, 303 NW 12th Ave., Deerfield Beach, FL 33442-1788. (305) 428-5566. 1988. Polyglot dictionary in German, French and English covering explosives and blasting.

The Dictionary of Cell Biology. J. M. Lackie and J. A. T. Dow, eds. Academic Press, c/o Harcourt Brace Jovanovich Inc., 6277 Sea Harbor Dr., Orlando, FL 32887. (800) 346-8648. 1989. Covers the broad subject area of cell biology including lipid, vitamins, amino acid, lectins, proteins, and other related topics.

A Dictionary of Chromatography. Macmillan Publishing Co., 866 Third Ave., New York, NY 10022. (212) 702-2000. 1982.

Dictionary of Civil Engineering. John S. Scott. Halsted Press, Division of J. Wiley, 605 3rd Ave., New York, NY 10158. (212) 850-6000. 1981. Third edition.

Dictionary of Colloid and Surface Science. Paul Becher. Marcel Dekker, Inc., 270 Madison Ave., New York, NY 10016. (212) 696-9000; (800) 228-1160. 1990. Dictionary deals with the areas of colloids, surface chemistry, and the physics and technology involved with surfaces.

Dictionary of Dangerous Pollutants, Ecology, and Environment. David F. Tver. Industrial Press, 200 Madison Ave., New York, NY 10016. (212) 889-6330. 1981.

Dictionary of Demography: Terms, Concepts and Institutions. William Petersen and Renee Petersen. Greenwood Publishing Group, Inc., 88 Post Rd. W., PO Box 5007, Westport, CT 06881. (212) 226-3571. 1986. 2 vols.

Dictionary of Drying. Carl W. Hall. Marcel Dekker Inc., 270 Madison Ave., New York, NY 10016. (212) 696-9000 or (800) 228-1160. 1979.

A Dictionary of Dyes and Dying. K. G. Ponting. Bell & Hyman Ltd., Denmark House, 37-39 Queen Elizabeth St., London, England SE1 2QB. 1981.

Dictionary of Ecology and Environment. P. H. Collin. Collin Pub., 8 The Causeway, Teddington, England TW11 0HE. 1988. Vocabulary of 5,000 words and expressions covering a range of topics relating to ecology, including: climate, vegetation, pollution, waste disposal, and energy conservation.

A Dictionary of Ecology, Evolution and Systematics. R. J. Lincoln, G. A. Boxshall and P. F. Clark. Cambridge University Press, 40 W 20th St., New York, NY 10011. (212) 924-3900; (800) 227-0247. 1984.

Dictionary of Energy. Malcolm Slesser. Nichols Pub., PO Box 96, New York, NY 10024. 1988. Provides information on concepts, ideas, definitions and explanations in areas of interdisciplinary nature connected with energy.

Dictionary of Environment and Development. Earthscan, 3 Endsleigh St., London, England 071-388 2117. 1991.

Dictionary of Environmental Engineering and Related Sciences: English-Spanish, Spanish-English. Jose T. Villate. Ediciones Universal, 3090 SW 8th St., Miami, FL 33135. (305) 642-3355. 1979.

Dictionary of Environmental Protection. Otto E. Tutzauer. Fred B. Rothman, 10368 W. Centennial Rd., Littleton, CA 80127. (303) 979-5657. 1979.

Dictionary of Environmental Protection Technology: In Four Languages, English, German, French, Russian. Egon Seidel. Elsevier Science Publishing Co., 655 Avenue of the Americas, New York, NY 10010. (212) 984-5800. 1988.

A Dictionary of Environmental Quotations. Barbara K. Rodes and Rice Odell. Simon and Schuster, 15 Columbus Circle, New York, NY 10023. (212) 373-7342. 1992. Collection of nearly 3000 quotations arranged by topic, such as air, noise, energy, nature, pollution, forests, oceans, and other subjects on the environment.

Dictionary of Environmental Science and Technology. Andrew Porteous. John Wiley & Sons, Inc., 605 3rd Ave., New York, NY 10158-0012. (212) 850-6000. 1992.

Dictionary of Environmental Terms. Alan Gilpin. Routledge, 29 W 35th St., New York, NY 10001-2291. (212) 244-3336. 1978. Covers human ecology and includes a bibliography.

A Dictionary of Ethology. Colin Beer. Harvard University Press, 79 Garden St., Cambridge, MA 02138. (617) 495-2600. 1992. Dictionary of animal behavior and related terms.

The Dictionary of Ethology and Animal Learning. Romano Harre and Roger Lamb. Blackwell Scientific Publications, PO Box 87, Oxford, England OX2 0DT. 44 0865 791155. 1986. The biological study of animal behavior dictionary.

Dictionary of Evolutionary Fish Osteology. Alfonso L. Rojo. CRC Press, 2000 Corporate Blvd. NW, Boca Raton, FL 33431. (407) 994-0555 or (800) 272-7737. 1991. Describes the preparation of fish skeletons and gives the translation of each term in five languages (French, German, Latin, Russian, and Spanish). Offers a rationale for the understanding of nomenclature of all fish skeletal structures.

Dictionary of Forest Structural Terminology. C.J. Geldenhuys, ed. Foundation for Research Development, Pretoria, Republic of #South Africa 1988.

Dictionary of Forest Terminology. Society of American Foresters, 5400 Grosvenor Ln., Bethesda, MD 20814. (301) 897-8720. 1987.

Dictionary of Forestry in Five Languages. Johannes Weck, et al. Elsevier Science Publishing Co., 655 Avenue of the Americas, New York, NY 10010. (212) 989-5800. 1966. Contains definitions in German, English, French, Spanish, and Russian.

A Dictionary of Genetics. Robert C. King and William A. Stansfield. Oxford University Press, 200 Madison Ave., New York, NY 10016. (212) 679-7300 or (800) 334-4249. 1991. Fourth edition. Includes 7,100 definitions with 250 illustrations. Also includes bibliography of major sources.

Dictionary of Genetics and Cell Biology. Norman Maclean. New York University Press, 70 Washington Sq. S., New York, NY 10012. (212) 998-2575. 1987. Includes the subject areas of cytology and genetics.

Dictionary of Inorganic Compounds. Chapman & Hall, 29 West 35th St., New York, NY 10001-2291. (212) 244-3336. 1991. Arranged by formula but not divided into element sections.

A Dictionary of Landscape: A Dictionary of Terms Used in the Description of the World's Land Surface. George A. Goulty. Avebury Technical, c/o Gower, Gower House, Croft Rd., Aldershot, England GU11 3HR. (0252) 331551. 1991. Earth sciences dictionary. Covers architecture, building construction, horticulture, and town planning.

Dictionary of Microbiology and Molecular Biology. Paul Singleton and Diana Sainsbury. John Wiley & Sons, Inc., 605 3rd Ave., New York, NY 10158-0012. (212) 850-6000. 1987. Second edition. Comprehensive dictionary with "classical descriptive aspects of microbiology to current developments in related areas of bioenergetics, biochemistry and molecular biology." Entries give synonyms, cross references, and references to pertinent works. Miscellaneous appendixes. Bibliography.

Dictionary of Nutrition. R. Ashley and H. Duggal. St. Martin's Press, 175 5th Ave., New York, NY 10010. (212) 674-5151. 1975.

Dictionary of Nutrition and Food Technology. Arnold E. Bender. Butterworth-Heinemann, 80 Montvale Ave., Stoneham, MA 02180. (617) 438-8464. Equipment and techniques, abbreviations, proper names, and the composition of common foods; covers agriculture, engineering, microbiology, biochemistry, and aspects of medicine.

Dictionary of Organic Compounds. Chapman & Hall, 29 West 35th St, New York, NY 10001-2291. (212) 244-3336. 1991. Continually updated system of information on most important inorganic chemical substances.

Dictionary of Organometallic Compounds. Chapman & Hall, 29 West 35th St., New York, NY 10001-2291. (212) 244-3336. 1989. Entries arranged by molecular formula within separate element section according to the Hill Convention.

Dictionary of Organophosphorus Compounds. Chapman & Hall, 29 West 35th St., New York, NY 10001-2291. (212) 244-3336. 1988.

The Dictionary of Pest Control. Sandra K. Kraft. Pinto, 914 Hillcrest Dr., Vienna, VA 22180. 1985. Deals with terms that relate to household, structural, industrial, commercial, and institutional pest control.

Dictionary of Pesticides. Meister Publishing Co., 37733 Euclid Ave., Willoughby, OH 44094. (216) 942-2000. 1972.

Dictionary of Petroleum Technology: English/French and French/English. M. Moureau and G. Brace. Editions Technip, 27 rue Giroux, Paris, France F-75737. Cedex 15 1979. Second edition. Includes approximately 50,000 terms and expressions. Multidisciplinary dictionary dealing with subject areas of: geology, geophysics, drilling, production, reservoir engineering, refining, petrochemicals, transportation, applications, engines, pollution economics, safety data processing and alternative energies.

A Dictionary of Petroleum Terms. Jodie Leecraft, ed. Petroleum Extension Service, Division of Continuing Education, The University of Texas at Austin, Austin, TX 78712. 1983. Third edition.

Dictionary of Refrigeration and Air Conditioning. K. M. Booth. Elsevier Science Publishing Co., 655 Avenue of the Americas, New York, NY 10010. (212) 989-5800. 1970.

The Dictionary of Sodium, Fats, and Cholesterol. Barbara Kraus. Putnam Berkley Group, 200 Madison Ave., New York, NY 10016. (212) 951-8400. 1990. Food composition, fat, cholesterol, and sodium.

Dictionary of Surfactants. Kurt Siekmann, J. Falbe, ed. Springer Verlag, 175 5th Ave., New York, NY 10010. (212) 460-1500 or (800) 777-4643. 1986. Supplement to Surfactants in Consumer Products.

Dictionary of the Environment. Michael Allaby. New York University Press, 70 Washington Sq. S., New York, NY 10012. (212) 998-2575. 1989.

Dictionary of Waste and Water Treatment. Butterworth-Heinemann, 80 Montvale Ave., Stoneham, MA 02180. (617) 438-8464. 1981. Dictionary of sanitary engineering.

Dictionary of Water and Sewage Engineering. Fritz Meinck and Helmut Mohle. Elsevier Science Publishing Co., 655 Avenue of the Americas, New York, NY 10010. (212) 984-5800. 1977. Text is in German, English, French and Italian. Deals with water management engineering and sewage.

Diesel & Gas Turbine Catalog. 13555 Bishop's Court, Brookfield, WI 53005. (414) 784-9177. Annual.

Diesel Fuel–Wholesale. 5711 S. 86th Circle, Omaha, NE 68127. (402) 593-4600. Annual.

Diesels in Underground Mining. U.S. Department of the Interior, Bureau of Mines, Avondale, MD 1984. Investigation of diesel motor safety measures, diesel motor exhaust gas, mine ventilation, air quality measurement, coal mines and mining, equipment and supplies.

Dietary Cholesterol: Health Concerns and the Food Industry. National Technical Information Service, 5285 Port Royal Rd., Springfield, VA 22161. (703) 487-4650. 1989.

Diethylenetriamine Producers Importers Alliance. 1330 Connecticut Ave., N.W., Washington, DC 20036. (202) 659-0060.

Digester/Over the Spillway. Illinois Environmental Protection Agency, 2200 Churchill Rd., Box 19276, Springfield, IL 62794-9276. (217) 782-5562. Bimonthly. Water & wastewater operators.

Digests of Environmental Impact Statements. Cambridge Scientific Abstracts, 5161 River Rd., Bethesda, MD 20816. (301) 961-6750. Abstracts and indexes of approximately 500 environmental impact studies.

Dimension Buyer's Guide to Forest Products Industry. 1000 Johnson Ferry Rd., Suite A-130, Marietta, GA 30068. (404) 565-6660. Annual.

Dioxin Bibliography. Kay Flowers. TCT Engineers, 1908 Inner Belt Business Center Dr., St. Louis, MO 63114-5700. (314) 426-0880. 1984.

Dioxin Contamination of Milk. Committee on Energy and Commerce. Subcommittee on Health and Environment. U.S. G.P.O., Washington, DC 20401. (202) 512-0000. 1990. Hearing before the subcommittee on Health and the Environment of the Committee on Energy and Commerce, House of Representatives, 101st Congress, 1st session, September 8, 1989. Contains facts about dioxin contamination of milk and the health effects on the environment.

The Diplomate. American Academy of Environmental Engineers, 130 Holiday Court, Ste. 100, Annapolis, MD 21401. (301) 266-3311. Quarterly. Issues and happenings in the environmental field.

Direct Effects of Increasing Carbon Dioxide on Vegetation. National Technical Information Service, 5285 Port Royal Rd., Springfield, VA 22161. (703) 487-4650. Covers carbon dioxide, vegetation and climate.

Direct Energy Conversion. Stanley W. Angrist. Allyn and Bacon, 160 Gould St., Needham Heights, MA 02194. (617) 455-1250; (800) 852-8024. 1982. Techniques in mechanical engineering and applied mechanics.

Direct Solar Energy. T. Nejat Veziroglu, ed. Nova Science Publishers. Inc, 283 Commack Rd., Suite 300, Commack, NY 11725-3104. (516) 499-3103; (516) 499-3106. 1991. Examines direct solar energy aspects such as solar radiation, greenhouses, water heaters, heat pumps, distillation/potable water and energy storage.

Directory, Fertilizer Research in the U.S. Victor L. Sheldon. National Fertilizer Development Center, Muscle Shoals, AL 35660. 1981.

Directory of Astacologists. International Association of Astacology, c/o Jay V. Huner, Secretary-Treasurer, University of Southwestern Louisiana, Box 44650, Lafayette, LA 70504. (318) 231-5239.

Directory of Behavior and Environmental Design. Research and Design Institute, Providence, RI Includes experts in human ecology and environmental engineering.

Directory of Biomass Installations in 13 Southeastern States. Philip C. Badger. Southeastern Regional Biomass Energy Program, Tennessee Valley Authority, CEB 1C, Muscle Shoals, AL 35660. (205) 386-3086. 1986. Irregular. Energy and alcohol and methane production facilities in Alabama, Arkansas, Florida, Georgia, Kentucky, Louisiana, Missouri, Mississippi, North Carolina, South Carolina, Tennessee, Virginia, and West Virginia.

Directory of Biotechnology Centers. North Carolina Biotechnology Center, 79 Alexander Dr., P.O. Box 13547, Research Triangle Park, NC 27709-3547. (919) 541-9366.

Directory of Biotechnology Information Resources. National Library of Medicine, Specialized Information Services Division, 8600 Rockville Pike, Bethesda, MD 20894. (301) 496-6531.

Directory of Certificates of Compliance for Radioactive Materials Packages. Office of Nuclear Material Safety and Safeguards, U.S. Nuclear Regulatory Commission, Washington, DC 20555. (301) 492-7000.

Directory of Certified Petroleum Geologists. American Association of Petroleum Geologists, Box 979, Tulsa, OK 74101. (918) 584-2555.

Directory of Chemical Producers. Chemical Information Services, Inc., Stanford Research Institute, Menlo Park, CA 94305-2235. 1973-. Lists both plants and products for 1,300 companies and approximately 10,000 commercial chemicals. Some information on capacity, process, and raw materials is included for major chemicals.

Directory of Chemical Waste Transporters. Chemical Waste Transport Institute. National Solid Waste Management Association, 1730 Rhode Island Ave. N.W., Suite 1000, Washington, DC 20036. (202) 659-4613. 1989.

Directory of Commercial Hazardous Waste Treatment and Recycling Facilities. Office of Solid Waste, Environmental Protection Agency, Washington, DC 20460. (202) 475-8710.

Directory of Companies Producing Salt in the United States. Department of the Interior, 810 7th St. NW, Washington, DC 20241. (202) 501-9649.

Directory of Computer Software Applications. Environmental Pollution and Control. National Technical Information Service, 5285 Port Royal Rd., Springfield, VA 22161. (703) 487-4650. 1977-1980.

The Directory of Consultants in Energy Technologies. Research Publications, 12 Lunar Drive, Woodbridge, CT 06525. (203) 397-2600. 1985. Scientists and engineers in the fields of air, land and water projects; environmental and agricultural analysis.

Directory of Country Environmental Studies: An Annotated Bibliography of Environmental and Natural Resources Profiles and Assessments. World Resources Institute, 1709 New York Ave., NW, Washington, DC 20006. 1990. Concentrates on studies of developing countries. Reports on the condition and trends of the major natural resources of a country and their condition and relationship to economic development.

Directory of Energy Alternatives. Energy Research Inst., 6850 Rattlesnake Hammock Rd., Naples, FL 33962. (813) 793-1922. Semimonthly. Individuals and companies interested in development of alternative energy sources, including alcohol, wind, methane, solar, biomass, waste, and hydrogen.

Directory of Engineering Societies and Related Organizations. Hemisphere Publishing Co., 79 Madison Ave., Suite 1110, New York, NY 10016. (212) 725-1999 or (800) 821-8312. Irregular.

Directory of Environmental/Health Protection Professionals. National Environmental Health Association, 720 S. Colorado Blvd., Suite 970, Denver, CO 80222. (303) 756-9090.

Directory of Environmental Information Sources. Thomas F. P. Sullivan, ed. Government Institutes, Inc., 4 Research Pl., Ste. 200, Rockville, MD 20850. (301) 921-2300. 1992. 3d ed.

Directory of Environmental Investing. Michael Silverstein. Environmental Economics, 1026 Irving st., Philadelphia, PA 19107. (215) 925-7168. Annual. Publicly-traded companies, plus Fortune 500 firms involved in environmental services.

Directory of Environmental Journals & Media Contacts. Tom Cairns. Council for Environmental Conservation, 80 York Way, London, England N1 9AG. 1985.

Directory of Environmental Organizations. Educational Communications, Box 35473, Los Angeles, CA 90035. (213) 559-9160. Semiannual. Environmental organizations names, addresses, & phone numbers.

Directory of Environmental Scientists in Agriculture. Roland D. Hauck. Council for Agricultural Science and Technology, Memorial Union, Iowa State University, Ames, IA 50011. 1979. Second edition. Special publication no.6. Pt.1 is organized by environmental topics which the scientists included in this directory are qualified to discuss. pt.2. lists administrators and liaison officers of state and federal research, extension, and regulatory organizations. pt.3. alphabetical listing of the scientists with address and telephone numbers.

Directory of Federal Contacts on Environmental Protection. Naval Energy and Environmental Support Activity/Department of Navy, Code 112, Port Hueneme, CA 93043. (805) 982-5667.

Directory of Federal Environmental Research and Development Programs. William G. Margetts, et al., eds. Government R & D Report, MIT Branch, PO Box 85, Cambridge, MA 02139. (617) 356-2424. 1978. Provides information on environmental programs supported by various agencies/departments of the federal government. Budget data are also provided.

Directory of Food and Nutrition Information Services and Resources. Robyn C. Frank, ed. Oryx Press, 4041 N. Central at Indian School Rd., Ste. 700, Phoenix, AZ 85012-3397. (602) 265-2651. 1984. Focuses on nutrition education, food science, food service management, and related aspects of applied nutrition.

Directory of Global Climate Change Organizations. Janet Wright. National Agricultural Library, 10301 Baltimore Blvd., Beltsville, MD 20705. (301) 504-5755. 1991. Identifies organizations that provide information regarding global climate change issues to the general public.

Directory of Hardwood Plywood Manufacturers in the United States and Canada. 1825 Michail Faraday Dr., Reston, VA 22090. (703) 435-2900. Irregular.

Directory of Hydrogen Energy Products and Services. Pergamon Microforms International Inc., Fairview Park, Elmsford, NY 10523. (914) 592-7720. 1980.

Directory of Institutions and Individuals Active in Environmentally-Sound and Appropriate Technologies. Pergamon Press, Headington Hill Hall, Headington, Oxford, England OX3 0BW. 1979.

Directory of Intermediate Biomass Energy Combustion Equipment. Council of Great Lake Governors, 310 S. Michigan, 10th Fl., Chicago, IL 60604. (312) 427-0092.

Directory of Medical Specialists. Marquis Who's Who/Macmillan Directory Division, 3002 Glenview Rd., Wilmette, IL 60091. (312) 441-2387.

A Directory of Natural Resources Management Organizations in Latin America and the Caribbean. Julie Buckley-Ess, ed. Tinker Foundation, Inc., 55 East 59th St., New York, NY 10022. 1988. Lists the public and private organizations working in each country. Describes their activities, whom they work with, their funding sources and contact people.

Directory of Oil Refineries: Construction, Engineers, Petrochemical and Natural Gas Processing Plants. Midwest Oil Register, 15 W. 6th St., Ste. 1308, Tulsa, OK 74119-1505. (918) 582-2000. Annual.

Directory of Oil Well Drilling Contractors. Midwest Register, Inc., 15 W. 6th St., Suite 1308, Tulsa, OK 74119-1505. (918) 582-2000.

Directory of On-Going Research in Cancer Epidemiology. International Agency for Research on Cancer, 150, Cours Albert Thomas, Cedex 08, Lyons, France F-69372. 78 72738485.

Directory of Plastics Recycling Companies. Resource Recycling, Box 10540, Portland, OR 97210. (503) 227-1319.

Directory of Professional Services. Professional Services Institute/National Solid Wastes Management Association, 1730 Rhode Island Ave, N.W., Suite 1000, Washington, DC 20036. (202) 659-4613.

Directory of Published Proceedings. Interdok Corp., 173 Halstead Ave., Harrison, NY 10528. (914) 835-3506. 1990. Monthly. This is a listing of published proceedings including the series SEMTE (Science/Medicine/Engineering/Technology) and the series SSH (Social Science/Humanities).

Directory of Resource Recovery Projects and Services. Julie C. Grady. Institute of Resource Recovery, National Solid Wastes Management Association, 1730 Rhode Island Ave., NW, Suite 1000, Washington, DC 20036. (202) 659-4613. Annual. Firms active in recovering energy from solid waste materials.

Directory of Selected U.S. Cogeneration, Small Power, and Industrial Power Plants. Utility Data Institute, 1700 K St., N.W., Suite 400, Washington, DC 20006. (202) 466-3660.

Directory of Solar Rating and Certificating Corporation Certified Collectors and Solar Water Heating Systems Ratings. Solar Rating & Certification Corp., 777 N. Capital St., NE, Suite 805, Washington, DC 20002. (202) 408-0306. 1991. Manufacturers of solar collectors and water heaters certified by the organization.

Directory of State Certification Officers for Drinking Water Laboratories. Association of State Drinking Water Administrators, 1911 N. Fort Myer Dr., Arlington, VA 22209. (703) 524-2428.

Directory of State Environmental Agencies. Kathyrn Hubler and Timothy R. Henderson, eds. Environmental Law Institute in cooperation with the Natural Resources Committee of the American Bar Association General Practice Section, 1616 P St. N.W. #200, Washington, DC 20036. (202) 328-5150. 1985.

Directory of State Environmental Libraries. U.S. Environmental Protection Agency, Office of Information Resources Management, 401 M St., SW, Washington, DC 20460. (202) 260-2090. 1988-. Annually.

Directory of State Environmental Planning Agencies. United States Air Force Directorate of Engineering and Services. The Directorate, 1616 P St. N.W., No. 200, Washington, DC 20036. 1977. On microfiche.

Directory of State Waste Management Program Officials. Association of State Territorial Solid Waste Management Officials, 444 N. Capitol St., Suite 388, Washington, DC 20001. (202) 624-5828.

Directory of the Forest Products Industry. Miller Freeman Publications, Inc., 500 Howard St., San Francisco, CA 94105. (415) 397-1881.

Directory of the Paint and Coatings Industry. Communication Channels, 6255 Barfield Rd., Atlanta, GA 30328. (404) 256-9800. 1987. Annual.

Directory of the Transportation Research Board. Jewelene Gaskins, ed. Transportation Research Board, National Research Council, 2101 Constitution Ave. NW, Washington, DC 20418. (202) 334-2934. 1991. Gives information on committees and membership. Includes alphabetical listing of (U.S. and foreign) committee members and associates, and a list of TRB awards and recipients.

Directory of Toxicological and Related Testing Laboratories. Regulatory Assistance Corporation. Taylor & Francis, 1900 Frost Road, Suite 101, Bristol, PA 19007-1598. (800) 821-8312. 1991. Lists toxicology, ecotoxicology, environmental, analytical, and support service laboratories in the United States.

Directory of U.S. and Canadian Scrap Plastics Processors and Buyers. Jerry Powell. Resource Recycling, Box 10540, Portland, OR 97210. (503) 227-1319. Annual. Recycled plastics processors and end users.

Directory of U.S. Cogeneration, Small Power & Industrial Power Plants. FIND/SVP, 625 Avenue of the Americas, New York, NY 10011. (212) 645-4500. Semiannual. More than 4800 cogeneration, small power and industrial power projects, refuse-to-energy plants, gas turbine and combined-cycle facilities, geothermal units, coal and wood-fired plants, wind and solar installations and a variety of other plant types.

Directory of Urban Forestry Professionals. Urban Forestry Professionals, PO Box 2000, Washington, DC 20013.

Directory of Used Oil Collectors Handlers and Recyclers Serving the Southeast. Project ROSE, Box 870203, University of Alabama, Tuscaloosa, AL 35487-0203. (205) 348-4878. Covers the states of Alabama, Florida, Georgia, Kentucky, Mississippi, North Carolina, South Carolina, and Tennessee.

Directory of Waste Equipment Manufacturers. Waste Equipment Manufacturers Institute/National Solid Wastes Management Association, 1730 Rhode Island Ave., N.W., Suite 1000, Washington, DC 20036. (202) 659-4613.

Directory of Waste Utilization Technologies in Europe and the United States. Institute for Local Self-Reliance, 2425 18th St., N.W., Washington, DC 20009. (202) 232-4108.

Directory of Water Resources Expertise. California Water Resources Center, Rubidoux Hall, University of California, Riverside, CA 92521. (714) 787-4327.

A Directory of Wetlands of International Importance. World Conservation Monitoring Centre. World Conservation Union, IUCN Publications Services Unit, 181a Huntingdon Road, Cambridge, England CB3 0DJ. (0223) 277894. 1990. Sites designated for the list of Wetlands of International Importance.

Directory of World Chemical Producers. Chemical Information Services, Inc., PO Box 8344, University Station, Dallas, TX 75205. (214) 340-4345. 1991. Contains 48,355 alphabetically listed product titles (including cross-references), manufactured by 5,152 chemical producers in 60 countries on five continents.

The Disappearing Russian Forest: A Dilemma in Soviet Resource Management. Brenton M. Barr and Kathleen Braden. Rowman & Littlefield, Publishers, Inc., 8705 Bollman Pl., Savage, MD 20763. (301) 306-0400. 1988. Focuses on the crisis in the Soviet forest industry caused by the resource depletion and regional imbalance in the supply and demand for commercial timber. It emphasizes how Soviet decision-makers actually deal with management and day-to-day operations in utilization of that country's timber stocks.

Discarding the Throwaway Society. John E. Young. Worldwatch Institute, 1776 Massachusetts Ave., N.W., Washington, DC 20036-1904. 1991.

Disposable Paper Products. FIND/SVP, 625 Avenue of the Americas, New York, NY 10011. (212) 645-4500. 1990. Addresses the problems and questions facing marketers of disposable paper products–facial tissue, paper towels, toilet paper and paper napkins.

Disposal of Brines Produced in Renovation of Municipal Wastewater. Burns and Roe. Federal Water Quality Administration, U.S. Dept. of the Interior, 1849 C St. NW, Washington, DC 20240. (202) 208-3171. 1970.

Disposal of Flue Gas Cleaning Water. R.B. Fling. National Technical Information Service, 5285 Port Royal Rd., Springfield, VA 22161. (703) 487-4650. Annual.

Disposal of Flue Gas Desulfurization Wastes. P.R. Hurt. U.S. Environmental Protection Agency, 401 M St. SW, Washington, DC 20460. (202) 260-2090. 1981.

Distillate Fuel. Howard L. Chesneau. ASTM, 1916 Race St., Philadelphia, PA 19103-1187. (215) 299-5400. 1988. Contamination, storage, and handling.

Encyclopedia of Environmental Information Sources

Distillation Bibliography. Dr. Frank C. Vibrandt. Newman Library, Rm. 6030, Virginia Polytechnic Institute, Blacksburg, VA 24061. (703) 961-5593.

Distillation Operations. Henry Z. Kister. McGraw-Hill, 1221 Avenue of the Americas, New York, NY 10020. (212) 512-2000 or (800) 262-4729.

Distribution and Taxonomy of Birds of the World. Charles G. Sibley and Burt L. Monroe. Yale University Press, 92 A Yale Station, 302 Temple St., New Haven, CT 06520. (203) 432-0960. 1990. An up-to-date delineation of the present distribution of the species of birds arranged in a classification based primarily on evidence of phytogenetic relationships from comparison of the DNAs. Includes a list of scientific and English names of species.

Distribution, Transport, and Fate of the Insecticides Malathion and Parathion in the Environment. Mir S. Mulla. Springer-Verlag, 175 5th Ave., New York, NY 10010. (212) 460-1500. 1981. Environmental health problems caused by insecticides.

Distributional Aspects of Human Fertility: A Global Comparative Study. Wolfgang Lutz. Academic Press, c/o Harcourt Brace Jovanovich Inc., 6277 Sea Harbor Dr., Orlando, FL 32887. (800) 346-8648. 1989. Studies in population dealing with family characteristics, population growth, birth intervals, fertility and maternal age.

Diversity and Pattern in Plant Communities. H. J. During. SPB Academic Publishing, Postbus 97747, The Hague, Netherlands 1988. Vegetation dynamics and plant communities.

Diversity of Environmental Biogeochemistry. J. Berthelin, ed. Elsevier Science Publishing Co., 655 Avenue of the Americas, New York, NY 10010. (212) 989-5800. 1991.

Diversity of Marine Plants. Bobby N. Irby. University Press of Mississippi, 3825 Ridgewood Rd., Jackson, MS 39211. (601) 982-6205. 1984. Various marine plants, their adaptive characteristics, and the interdependence of flora and fauna.

Divining Rod. New Mexico Water Resources Research Institute, Box 30001, Dept. 3167, Las Cruces, NM 88003-0001. (505) 646-1813. Quarterly. Water issues & water research in New Mexico.

Division of Air Pollution Control: Emergency Preparedness and Community Right-to-Know. Coordinator, 1800 Watermark Dr., Columbus, OH 43215. (614) 644-2266.

Division of Emergency Management: Emergency Preparedness and Community Right-to-Know. Chair, 2525 South Carson St., Carson City, NV 89710. (702) 885-4240.

Division of Emergency Management: Emergency Preparedness and Community Right-to-Know. Chair, Emergency Response Commission, 116 West Jones St., Raleigh, NC 27603-1335. (919) 733-3867.

Division of Environmental Health: Emergency Preparedness and Community Right-to-Know. Director, Division of Wildlife Resources, 1596 N.W. Temple, Salt Lake City, UT 84116. (801) 530-1245.

Division of Environmental Health: Hazardous Waste Management. Director, Bureau of Hazardous Waste Management, 288 North 1460 W., PO Box 16690, Salt Lake City, UT 84116-0700. (801) 538-6170.

Division of Environmental Health: Solid Waste Management. Director, Bureau of Hazardous Waste Management, 288 North 1460 W., Box 16690, Salt Lake City, UT 84116-0700. (801) 538-6170.

Division of Environmental Health: Underground Storage Tanks. Director, Bureau of Hazardous Waste Management, 288 North 1460 W., PO Box 16690, Salt Lake City, UT 84116-0700. (801) 538-6170.

Division of Environmental Quality: Air Quality. Administrator, 450 West State St., Boise, ID 83720. (208) 334-5840.

Division of Environmental Quality: Hazardous Waste Management. Director, Solid Waste Program, PO Box 176, Jefferson City, MO 65102. (314) 751-3176.

Division of Environmental Quality: Solid Waste Management. Director, Solid Waste Program, PO Box 176, Jefferson City, MO 65102. (314) 751-3176.

Division of Environmental Quality: Underground Storage Tanks. Director, Water Pollution Control Program, PO Box 176, Jefferson City, MO 65102. (314) 751-1300.

Division of Environmental Quality: Water Quality. Director, Water Pollution Control Program, PO Box 176, Jefferson City, MO 65102. (314) 751-1300.

Division of Hazardous Waste Management and Special Studies: Hazardous Waste Management. Director, 1200 Missouri Ave., Bismark, ND 58502-5520. (701) 224-2366.

Division of Hazardous Waste Management and Special Studies: Solid Waste Management. Director, 1200 Missouri Ave., Bismark, ND 58502-5520. (701) 224-2366.

Division of Hazardous Waste Management and Special Studies: Underground Storage Tanks. Director, 1200 Missouri Ave., Bismark, ND 58502-5502. (701) 224-2366.

Division of Health: Water Quality. Chief, Environmental Engineering Division, State Capital Complex, Building 3, Charleston, WV 25305. (304) 348-2981.

Division of Labor: Occupational Safety. Commissioner, 1013 State Office Building, Indianapolis, IN 46204. (317) 232-2663.

Division of Labor: Occupational Safety. Commissioner, State Capitol Complex, Building 3, Charleston, WV 25305. (304) 348-7890.

Division of Natural Resources: Environmental Protection. Director, State Capital Complex, Building 3, Room 669, Charleston, WV 25305. (304) 348-2754.

Division of Natural Resources: Groundwater Management. Chairman, Groundwater Policy and Technical Advisory Commission, State Capital Complex, Charleston, WV 25305. (304) 348-2754.

Division of Natural Resources: Natural Resources. Director, State Capital Complex, Building 3, Room 669, Charleston, WV 25305. (304) 348-2754.

Division of Safety and Buildings: Occupational Safety. Administrator, Industry, Labor, and Human Relations, PO Box 7969, Madison, WI 53707. (608) 266-1816.

Division of the Environment: Hazardous Waste Management. Chief, Bureau of Hazardous Materials, 450 West State St., Boise, ID 83720. (208) 334-5879.

Division of the Environment: Solid Waste Management. Chief, Bureau of Hazardous Materials, 450 West State St., Boise, ID 83720. (208) 334-5879.

Division of Waste Disposal: Hazardous Waste Management. Director, 100 Cambridge St., Boston, MA 02202. (617) 727-3260.

Division of Waste Management: Hazardous Waste Management. Division Chief, Solid Waste Management Section, 1201 Greenbrier St., Charleston, WV 25311. (304) 348-5929.

Division of Waste Management: Solid Waste Management. Division Chief, Solid Waste Management Section, 1201 Greenbrier St., Charleston, WV 25311. (304) 348-5929.

Division of Waste Management: Underground Storage Tanks. Division Chief, Solid Waste Management Section, 1201 Greenbrier St., Charleston, WV 25311. (304) 348-5929.

Division of Water Resources: Coastal Zone Management. Section Chief, Lake Michigan Management Section, Division of Water Resources, 310 South Michigan, Room 1606, Chicago, IL 60604. (312) 793-3123.

Division of Water Resources: Groundwater Management. Manager, Groundwater Management Section, 89 Kings Highway, Dover, DE 19901. (302) 736-5722.

Division of Water Resources: Groundwater Management. Chief, Groundwater Quality Management, 401 East State St., Trenton, NJ 08625. (609) 292-0424.

Division of Waters: Groundwater Management. Groundwater Division, 500 Lafayette Rd., St Paul, MN 55155-4001. (612) 296-0436.

DNA and Cell Biology. Mary Ann Liebert, Inc., 1651 3rd Ave., New York, NY 10128. (212) 289-2300. 1981-. Ten times a year. Covers eukaryotic or prokaryotic gene structure, organization, expression and evolution. Papers, short communications, reviews, and editorials. Includes studies of genetics at RNA or protein levels.

DNA and Protein Engineering Techniques. Alan R. Liss, 41 E. 11th St., New York, NY 10003. (212) 475-7700. 1988-. Six times a year. Covers recombinant DNA, Genetic intervention methods, proteins, and recombinant proteins.

Documentation of the Threshold Limit Values. American Conference of Governmental Industrial Hygienists, 6500 Glenway, Building D-5, Cincinnati, OH 45211. 1991. Provides threshold limit value documentation for any physical phenomenon in the environment, including chemical substances and physical agents.

DOE Model Conference on Waste Management and Environmental Restoration: Proceedings. National Technical Information Service, 5285 Port Royal Rd., Springfield, VA 22161. (703) 487-4650. 1990.

Dolphin Log. Cousteau Society Inc., 8440 Santa Monica Blvd., Los Angeles, CA 90069. (804) 627-1144. Six issues a year. Covers marine animals, the oceans, science, natural history, and the arts as they relate to global water system. Magazine is for ages 7-15.

Dolphins, Porpoises and Whales of the World: The IUCN Red Data Book. M. Klinowska. The World Conservation Union, IUCN Publications Services Unit, 181a Huntingdon Road, Cambridge, England CB3 0DJ. (0223) 277894. 1991. Reviews the status of all cetacean species. Detailed accounts are provided for each species, describing their distribution, population, threats, and the conservation measures required to ensure their survival.

Domestication: The Decline of Environmental Appreciation. Helmut Hemmer. Cambridge University Press, 40 W. 20th St., New York, NY 10011. (212) 924-3900; (800) 227-0247. 1990. The books proposes the thesis that domestication must lead to reduced environmental appreciation. The origins of domesticated mammals, their scientific nomenclature, the relationships between feral mammals and their wild progenitors, and modern attempts at domestication are also covered.

DOMIS. ECHO Service, BP 2373, Luxembourg L-1023. (352) 488041.

Down by the River: The Impact of Federal Water Projects and Policies on Biological Diversity. Constance Elizabeth Hunt with Verne Huser. Island Press, 1718 Connecticut Ave. N.W., Suite 300, Washington, DC 20009. (202) 232-7933. 1988. Presents case studies of development projects on seven river systems, including the Columbia, the Delaware, the Missouri, and the rivers of Maine ,to illustrate their effect on biological diversity.

Down to Earth. Montana Environmental Information Center, Box 1184, Helena, MT 59624. (406) 443-2520. Quarterly. Montana environmental news & concerns.

Dr. Axelrod's Atlas of Freshwater Aquarium Fishes. H. R. Axelrod, ed. TFH Publications, 1 TFH Plaza, Neptune City, NJ 07753. (908) 988-8400. 1989. Third edition. Identifies fish, their common names, scientific name, range, habitat, water condition, size and food requirement. Includes colored illustrations and 4500 photos in full color.

Dr. Burgess's Atlas of Marine Aquarium Fishes. W. E. Burgess, et al. TFH Publications, 1 TFH Plaza, Neptune City, NJ 07753. (908) 988-8400. 1988. Pictorial aid for identification of marine fishes. More than 400 photos in full color are included. Also includes scientific name and common name, food habits, size and habitat.

Draft Report: Fossil Ridge Wilderness Study Area: Grand Mesa, Uncompahgre and Gunnison National Forests, Taylor River Ranger District, Gunnison County, Colorado. U.S. Department of Agriculture, Forest Service, PO Box 25127, Lakewood, CO 80225. 1982.

The Draize Eye-Irritancy Test. Janice C. Swanson. National Agricultural Library, 10301 Baltimore Blvd., Beltsville, MD 20705-2351. (301) 504-5755. 1990. Citations in the area of toxicity testing using rabbits as laboratory animals and the resulting eye diseases due to toxicity. This bibliography updates an earlier publications numbered SRB 89- 02.

Dream–Analytical Ground Water Flow Programs. Bernadine A. Bonn and Stewart A. Rounds. Lewis Publishers, 2000 Corporate Blvd., N.W., Boca Raton, FL 33431. (407) 994-0555 or (800) 272-7737. 1990. Software for basic field work, including the first-cut evaluation of remediation design.

The Dream of the Earth. Thomas Berry. Sierra Club Books, 100 Bush St., San Francisco, CA 94104. (415) 291-1600. 1988. Describes the ecological fate from a species perspective.

Drinking Water: A Community Action Guide. Concern, Inc., 1794 Columbia Rd., NW, Washington, DC 20009. (202) 328-8160. 1990.

Drinking Water & Backflow Prevention. Elizabeth Gold, PO Box 33209, Northglenn, CO 80233. (303) 451-0980. Monthly. Safety standards, water system protection, training programs, cross-connection control, and issues related to preventing the contamination of potable drinking water supplies with backflow prevention devices.

Drinking Water and Groundwater Remediation Cost Evaluation: Air Stripping. Robert M. Clark and Jeffrey Q. Adams. Lewis Publishers, 2000 Corporate Blvd. N.W., Boca Raton, FL 33431. (800) 272-7737. 1991. The new software program shows air stripping costs and performance of the remediation of hazardous waste sites or drinking water treatment. The program helps do cost comparisons of the technology against other available technologies.

Drinking Water and Groundwater Remediation Cost Evaluation: Granular Activated Carbon. Robert M. Clark and Jeffrey Q. Adams. Lewis Publishers, 2000 Corporate Blvd. N.W., Boca Raton, FL 33431. (800) 272-7737. 1991. Shows GAC costs and performance forthe remediation of hazardous waste sites or drinking watertreatment. Compares the cost of the technology against other available technologies.

The Drinking Water Book: A Complete Guide to Safe Drinking Water. Colin Ingram. Ten Speed Press, P.O. Box 7123, Berkeley, CA 94707. (800) 841-2665. 1991. Discusses potential pollutants and their sources in drinking water. Includes water testing and methods for reducing pollutants in the home water supply.

Drinking Water Hazards: How to Know If There Are Toxic Chemicals in Your Water and What to Do If There Are. John Cary Stewart. Envirographics, PO Box 334, Hiram, OH 44234. (216) 527-5207. 1990. Documents the increase of cancer and other diseases that may be environmentally induced. Discusses the increases in the use of synthetic organic chemicals, and covers each group of drinking water contaminants in some detail: inorganic chemicals, heavy metals, bacteria and viruses, radionuclides, nitrates, and organic chemicals, including pesticides.

Drinking Water Health Advisory: Volatile Organic Compounds. United States Environmental Protection Agency Office of Drinking Water. Lewis Publishers, 2000 Corporate Blvd., N.W., Boca Raton, FL 33431. (407) 994-0555 or (800) 272-7737. 1991. Provides technical guidance to public health officials on health effects, analytical methodologies, and treatment technologies associated with drinking water contamination.

Drinking Water News. Business Publishers, Inc., PO Box 1067, Blair Station, Silver Spring, MD 20910. (301) 587-6300. 1977-.

Drinking Water Treatment. P. Toft, et al., eds. Pergamon Microforms International, Inc., Fairview Park, Elmsford, NY 10523. (914) 592-7720. 1989. Proceedings of the 3d National Conference on Drinking Water, St. John's Newfoundland, Canada, June 12-14, 1988. Discussions concerned all aspects of design, construction and operation of small systems for the provision and treatment of drinking water.

Drinking Water Treatment Technologies: Comparative Health Effects Assessments. Government Institutes, Inc., 4 Research Pl., Ste. 200, Rockville, MD 20850. (301) 921-2300. 1990. Evaluates the relative benefits and risks of each of the common types of drinking water treatment technologies.

Drive for Clean Air: Natural Gas and Methane Vehicles. James Spencer Cannon. INFORM, 381 Park Ave. S., New York, NY 10016. (212) 689-4040. 1989.

Driving Forces: Motor Vehicle Trends and Their Implications for Global Warming, Energy Strategies, and Transportation. James J. MacKenzie and Michael P. Walsh. World Resources Institute, 1709 New York Ave., Washington, DC 20006. (800) 822-0504. 1990. Overview of new-vehicle fuel efficiency, reductions in air pollution emissions, and overall improvements in transportation and land-use as they relate to global warming planning. Also available through State University of New York Press.

Drowning the National Heritage: Climate Change and Coastal Biodiversity in the United States. Walter V. C. Reid and Mark C. Trexler. World Resources Institute, 1709 New York Ave. N.W., Washington, DC 20006. (800) 822 0504. 1991. Examines erosion, flooding, and salt-water intrusion into groundwater, rivers, bays, and estuaries as well as receding coastlines and altered coastal current and upwelling patterns. Evaluates various policy responses and recommends specific changes to protect the biological wealth of these vital ecosystems.

Drug and Chemical Toxicology. Marcel Dekker, Inc., 270 Madison Ave., New York, NY 10016. (212) 696-9000. Quarterly. Covers safety evaluations of drugs and chemicals.

The Dry Cell Battery Market. FIND/SVP, 625 Avenue of the Americas, New York, NY 10011. (212) 645-4500. 1990. Analyzes the $3 billion dry-cell battery market and its four major product categories–carbon zinc, alkaline, rechargeable and lithium ultralife batteries.

Dry Color Manufacturers Association. P.O. Box 20839, Alexandria, VA 22320. (703) 684-4044.

Drying '89. Arun S. Mujumdar and Michel Roques. Hemisphere Publishing Co., 79 Madison Ave., Suite 1110, New York, NY 10016. (212) 725-1999. 1990. Papers from the 10th International Drying Symposium held at Versailles, France, Sept. 5-8, 1988.

Dryland Agriculture. H.E. Dregne. American Society of Agronomy, 677 S. Segoe Rd., Madison, WI 53711-1086. (608) 273-8080. 1983.

Dryland Farming. Henry Gilbert. U.S. Department of Agriculture, 10301 Baltimore Blvd., Beltsville, MD 20705-2351. (301) 504-5755. 1987.

Duckological. Ducks Unlimited, 1 Waterfowl Way, Long Grove, IL 60047. (708) 438-4300. Bimonthly. Protection of ducks.

Ducks Unlimited. 1 Waterfowl Way, Long Grove, IL 60047. (708) 438-4300.

Dwarf Conifers; A Handbook on Low and Slow-Growing Evergreens. Brooklyn Botanic Garden, 1000 Washington Ave., Brooklyn, NY 11225. (718) 622-4433. 1984.

Dyes & Organic Pigments to 1994. FIND/SVP, 625 Avenue of the Americas, New York, NY 10011. (212) 645-4500. 1990.

Dying Oceans. Paula Hogan. Gareth Stevens, Inc., 7317 W. Green Tree Rd., Milwaukee, WI 53223. (414) 466-7550. 1991. Ecological balance of life in the oceans endangered by pollution.

Dying Planet; The Extinction of Species. Jon Erickson. Tab Books, PO Box 40, Blue Ridge Summit, PA 17294-0850. (717) 794-2191. 1991.

Dynamic Modeling and Expert Systems in Wastewater Engineering. Giles G. Patry and David Chapman. Lewis Publishers, 200 Corporate Blvd. NW, Boca Raton, FL 33431. (407) 994-0555 or (800)272-7737. 1988. Result of a workshop held at McMaster University (May 19-20, 1988). Brings together current work on dynamic modelling and expert systems as applied to the design, operation and control of waste- water treatment systems.

A Dynamic Nutrient Cycle Model for Waste Stabilization Ponds. R.A. Ferrara. MIT Department of Civil Engineering, 77 Massachusetts Ave., Cambridge, MA 02137. 1978. Hydraulic models pf sewage lagoons.

E Magazine. Earth Action Network, 28 Knight St., Norwalk, CT 06851. (203) 854-5559. Bimonthly. News, information, and commentary on environmental issues.

E/MJ Operating Handbook of Mineral Underground Mining. E/MJ Mining Informational Services, New York, NY 1978.

The Eagle Foundation Inc. 300 E. Hickory St., Apple River, IL 61001. (815) 594-2259.

Eagle Lake Field Station. Department of Biological Sciences, California State University, Chico, Chico, CA 95929-0515. (916) 898-4490.

EARR: Environment and Natural Resources. Academic Publishers, Box 786, Cooper Station, New York, NY 10276. (212) 206-8900. Monthly. All aspects of environmental and natural resources.

The Earth Care Annual. Russell Wild, ed. Rodale Press, 33 E. Minon St., Emmaus, PA 18098. (215) 967-5171; (800) 322-6333. 1990-. Annually. Organized in alphabetical sections such as garbage, greenhouse effect, oceans, ozone, toxic waste, and wildlife, the annual presents environmental problems and offers innovative working solutions.

Earth Communications Office. 1925 Century Park East, Suite 2300, Los Angeles, CA 90067. (213) 277-1665.

Earth Ecology Foundation. 612 N. 2nd St., Fresno, CA 93702. (209) 442-3034.

Earth Education: A New Beginning. Steve Van Matre. Institute for Earth Education, PO Box 288, Warrenville, IL 60555. (708) 393-3096. 1990. Describes environmental education which adopts an alternative foundation for improving awareness about the environment through changes in attitudes and life styles.

Earth First!. PO Box 5176, Missoula, MT 59806.

Earth First! Journal in Defense of Wilderness and Biodiversity. Earth First!, PO Box 5176, Missoula, MT 59806. Eight/year.

Earth Island Institute. 300 Broadway, Suite 28, San Francisco, CA 94133. (415) 788-3666.

Earth Island Journal. Earth Island Institute, 300 Broadway, #28, San Francisco, CA 94133-3312. (415) 788-3666. Quarterly. Local news from around the world on environmental issues.

The Earth Manual. Malcolm Margolin. Heyday Books, PO Box 9145, Berkeley, CA 94709. (510) 549-3564. 1985. How to work on wild land without taming it.

Earth Ponds: The Country Pond Maker's Guide. Tim Matson. Countryman Press, PO Box 175, Woodstock, VT 05091-0175. (802) 457-1049. 1991. How-to manual regarding pond making.

Earth Quest. University Corp. for Atmospheric Research, PO Box 3000, Boulder, CO 80307. (303) 497-1682. Quarterly. National and international programs addressing global environmental change.

Earth Regeneration Society. 1442A Walnut St., #57, Berkeley, CA 94709. (415) 525-7723.

The Earth Report. Edward Goldsmith. Price Stern Sloan, Inc., 360 N. La Cienega Blvd., Los Angeles, CA 90048. (213) 657-6100. 1988.

Earth Science. American Geological Institute, 4220 King Street, Alexandria, VA 22302. (703) 379-2480. Quarterly. Covers geological issues.

Earth Sciences Centre. University of Toronto, 33 Willcocks St., Toronto, ON, Canada M5S 3B3. (416) 978-3248.

Earth-Sheltered Habitat. Gideon Golany. Van Nostrand Reinhold, 115 5th Ave., New York, NY 10003. (212) 254-3232. 1983. History, architecture, urban design, and underground architecture.

Earth Society Foundation. 585 Fifth Ave., New York, NY 10017. (718) 574-3059.

Earth Words. Friends of the Earth, 701-251 Laurier Ave., W., Ottawa, ON, Canada K1P 5J6. (613) 230-3352. Quarterly. Informs citizens and decision makers about environmental issues.

Earth Work. The Student Conservation Association Inc., PO Box 550, Charlestown, NH 03603-0550. (603) 826-4301. 1991-. Monthly. Articles focus on the people, agencies, and the nonprofit organizations that protect our parks, refuges, forests and other lands. Carries a special feature entitled JobScan which provides the most comprehensive listing of natural resource and environmental job opportunities anywhere.

Earthcare Network. c/o Michael McCloskey, 408 C St., N.E., Washington, DC 20002. (202) 547-1141.

Earthquake Engineering and Structural Dynamics. John Wiley & Sons, Inc., 605 3rd Ave., New York, NY 10158-0012. (212) 850-6000. 1978-. Bimonthly.

Earthquake Engineering Research Institute. 6431 Fairmont, Suite 7, El Cerrito, CA 94530. (415) 525-3668.

Earthquake Prediction. David A. Tyckoson. Oryx Press, 4041 N. Central at Indian School Rd., Ste. 700, Phoenix, AZ 85012-3397. (602) 265-2651. 1986.

Earthquakes & Volcanos. Geological Survey. U.S. Geological Survey, 12201 Sunrise Valley Dr., Reston, VA 22092. (703) 648-4460. Bimonthly. Earthquake information bulletin.

Earthright. H. Patricia Hynes. St. Martin's Press, 175 5th Ave., New York, NY 10010. (212) 674-5151. 1990. Guide to practical ways to resolve problems with pesticides, water pollution, garbage disposal, the ozone layer and global warming.

EarthSave. 706 Frederick St., Santa Cruz, CA 95062. (408) 423-4069.

Earthstewards Network News. Holyearth Foundation, Box 10697, Winslow, WA 98110. (206) 842-7986. Bimonthly.

Earthwatch. 680 Mt. Auburn St., P.O. Box 403, Watertown, MA 02272. (617) 926-8200.

Earthwatch Magazine. Earthwatch Expeditions, 680 Mt. Auburn St., Box 403, Watertown, MA 02272. (617) 926-8200. Bimonthly. Worldwide research expeditions, endangered species, cultures, and world health.

Earthwatch Oregon. Oregon Environmental Council, 2637 S. W. Water Ave., Portland, OR 97201. 1969-. Monthly.

Earthwatch: The Climate from Space. John E. Harries. E. Horwood, 200 Old Tappan Rd., Old Tappan, NJ 07675. (800) 223-2348. 1990. Surveys theories of climate and specifically concentrates on current concerns: ozone holes, the greenhouse effect and El Nino.

East End Environment. Southampton College, Natural Science Division, Southampton, NY 11968. 1970-. Quarterly.

EBIB. Texas A & M University, Sterling C. Evans Library, Reference Division, College Station, TX 77843. (409) 845-5741.

Eco-Humane Letter. International Ecology Society, 1471 Barcly St., St. Paul, MN 55106-1405. (612) 774-4971. Irregular. Issues concerning animals, wildlife, and the environment.

Eco-Justice Project and Network. Cornell University, Anabel Taylor Hall, Ithaca, NY 14850. 1990.

Eco-Log. California Conservation Council, Box 5572, Pasadena, CA 91107.

Eco/Log Week. Southam Business Information, 1450 Don Mills Rd., Don Mills, ON, Canada M3D 2X7. (416) 445-6641. Weekly. Effluent treatment, emission controls, waste disposal, and land use and reclamation.

Eco-News. Environmental Action Coalition, 625 Broadway, 2nd Fl., New York, NY 10012. (212) 677-1601. Monthly. Children's environmental newsletter on pollution, nature, and ecology.

Eco Newsletter. Antarctica Project, 218 D St., SE, Washington, DC 20003. (202) 544-2600. Quarterly. Conservation news.

Eco-Politics. California League of Conservation Voters, 965 Mission St., # 705, San Francisco, CA 94103-2928. (415) 397-7780. Quarterly. News of citizen action on environmental issues.

ECO Technics: International Pollution Control Directory. ECO-Verlags A G, Josefstrasse 8, Zurich, Switzerland CH-8021.

Eco-Warriors: Understanding the Radical Environmental Movement. Rik Scarce. Noble Pr., 111 E. Chestnut, Suite 48 A, Chicago, IL 60611. (312) 880-0439. 1990. Recounts escapades of pro-ecology sabotage by self styled eco-warriors. Episodes such as the sinking of two whaling ships in Iceland, the botched attempt to hang a banner on Mt. Rushmore, a national tree-sitting week, and raids on research facilities by animal liberation activists.

ECOAlert. CCNB, 180 St. John St., Fredericton, NB, Canada E3B 4A9. (506) 458-8747. Bimonthly. Conservation news and developments.

ECOL News. Environmental Conservation Library, 300 Nicollet Mall, Minneapolis, MN 55401. (612) 372-6570. Semiannual. Environmental update on the library.

Ecolert. Orba Information Ltd., 265 Cray St. W., Montreal, PQ, Canada H2Z 1H6 1971-. Weekly.

Ecological Abstracts. Geo Abstracts Ltd. Elsevier Applied Science, Crown House, Linton Rd., Barking, England IG 11 8JU. Essex 1974-. Derived from over 600 leading ecological and environmental journals, plus books, conference proceedings, reports and theses.

Ecological Applications. Ecological Society of America, Center for Environmental Studies, Arizona State University, Tempe, AZ 85287. (602) 965-3000. 1991-. Quarterly. Emphasizes the application of basic ecological concepts to a wide range of problems.

Ecological Approach to Pest Management. David J. Horn. Guilford Press, 72 Spring St., New York, NY 10012. (212) 431-9800. 1987. Insect pests, food production and natural resources.

Ecological Aspects of Social Evolution. Daniel I. Rubenstein. Princeton University Press, 41 Williams St., Princeton, NJ 08540. (609) 258-4900. 1986. Behavior of birds and mammals.

Ecological Aspects of the Reclamation of Derelict and Disturbed Land: An Annotated Bibliography. Gordon T. Goodman. Geo Abstracts Ltd., c/o Elsevier Science Publishers, Crown House, Linton Rd., Barking, England 1G11 8JU. 1975.

Ecological Communities. Donald R. Strong. Princeton University Press, 41 Williams St., Princeton, NJ 08540. (609) 258-4900. 1984. Conceptual issues and the evidence relating to biotic communities.

Ecological Economics. Robert Costanza. Columbia University Press, 562 W. 113th Street, New York, NY 10025. (212) 316-7100. 1991. The science and management of sustainability.

Ecological Effects of Thermal Discharges. T.E. Langford. Elsevier Science Publishing Co., 655 Avenue of the Americas, New York, NY 10010. (212) 984-5800. 1990. Review of the biological studies which have been carried out in various habitats and in response to a variety of problems related to cooling water usage, particularly on the large scale such as in thermal power stations.

Ecological Engineering: An Introduction to Ecotechnology. William J. Mitsch and Sven Erik Jorgensen, eds. John Wiley & Sons, Inc., 605 3rd Ave., New York, NY 10158-0012. (212) 850-6000. 1989. Presents 12 international case studies of ecological engineering. The case studies survey problems and existing methodologies indicate where methods are ecologically sound, and illustrate examples of the use of ecological engineering.

Ecological Engineering. The Journal of Ecotechnology. Elsevier Science Publishing Co., 655 Avenue of the Americas, New York, NY 10010. (212) 984-5800. 1992. Quarterly. Specific areas of coverage will include habitat reconstruction, rehabilitation, biomanipulation, restoration and conservation.

Ecological Fruit Production in the North. Bart Hall-Beyer, and Jean Richard. B. Hall-Beyer, RR #3, Scotstown, PQ, Canada J0B 3J0. 1983. Deals with the production of tree fruits and small fruits in North America. Discusses methods of ecological agriculture.

Ecological Genetics and Air Pollution. George E. Taylor, Jr., ed. Springer-Verlag, 175 5th Ave., New York, NY 10010. (212) 460-1500; (800) 777-4643. 1991. Describes role of air pollution in governing the genetic structure and evolution of plant species.

Ecological Heterogeneity. Jurek Kolasa, et al., eds. Springer-Verlag, 175 5th Ave., New York, NY 10010. (212) 460-1500. 1991. Examines the meaning of heterogeneity in a particular environment and its consequences for individuals, populations, and communities of plants and animals. Among the topics of the 14 papers are the causes of heterogeneity, system and observer dependence, dimension and scale, ecosystem organization, temporal and spatial changes, new models of competition and landscape patterns, and applications in desert, temperate, and marine areas.

Ecological Impact of Parathion in Soybeans. U.S. Department of Agriculture, Agricultural Research Service, 14 Independence Ave. SW, Washington, DC 20250. (202) 447-7454. 1982.

Ecological Implications of Contemporary Agriculture. H. Eijsackers and A. Quispel, eds. Munksgaard International, PO Box 2148, Copenhagen K, Denmark DK-1016. 1988. Proceedings of the 4th European Symposium, September 7-12, 1986, Wageningen. Ecological bulletins are published in cooperation with ecological journals; holarctic ecology and Oikos. They consist of monographs, reports, and symposium proceedings on topics of international interest.

Ecological Modeling. Elsevier Science Publishing Co., Inc., Journal Information Ctr., 655 Ave. of the Americas, New York, NY 10010. Computer models used in environmentalist issues.

Ecological Monographs. Business Office of the Ecological Society of America, Center of Environmental Studies, Arizona State University, Tempe, AZ 85287-1201. (602) 965-3000. Quarterly. Scientific journal of ecological issues.

Ecological Physical Chemistry. C. Rossi, ed. Elsevier Science Publishing Co., 655 Avenue of the Americas, New York, NY 10010. (212) 989-5800. 1991. Proceedings of a workshop held in Sienna, Italy, November 1990. Papers deal mostly with physical and environmental chemistry.

Ecological Processes and Cumulative Impacts Illustrated by Bottomland Harwood Wetland Ecosystems. James G. Gosselink, et al. Lewis Publishers, 2000 Corporate Blvd., N.W., Boca Raton, FL 33431. (407) 994-0555 or (800) 272-7737. 1990. Covers the ecological processes in bottomland hardwood forests and relates these processes to human activities.

Ecological Restoration of Prince William Sound and the Gulf of Alaska: An Annotated Bibliography of Relevant Literature: Preliminary Draft. Restoration Planning Work Group, Oregon State University, Corvallis, OR 97311. 1990.

The Ecological Self. Freya Mathews. Rowman & Littlefield, Publishers, Inc., 8705 Bollman Pl., Savage, MD 20763. (301) 306-0400. 1991. Considers the metaphysical foundations of ecological ethics.

Ecological Society of America. Arizona State University, Center for Environmental Studies, Tempe, AZ 85287. (602) 965-3000.

Ecological Society of America Bulletin. Ecological Society of America, Center of Environmental Studies, Arizona State University, Tempe, AZ 85287-1201. (602) 965-3000. Quarterly. Study of living things in relation to their environments.

Ecological Society of America Bulletin–Directory of Members Issue. Ecological Society of America, c/o Dr. Duncan Patten, Center for Environmental Studies, Arizona State University, Tempe, AZ 85287. (602) 965-3000.

Ecological Studies; Analysis and Synthesis. Springer-Verlag, 175 5th Ave., New York, NY 10010. (212) 460-1500. Quarterly.

Ecological Studies of Six Endangered Butterflies (Lepidoptera, Lycaenidea). Richard Arthur Arnold. University of California Press, 2120 Berkeley Way, Berkeley, CA 94720. (415) 642-4247 (800) 822-6657. 1983. Island biogeography, patch dynamics, and the design of habitat preserves.

Ecological Systems of the Geo-Biosphere. Heinrich Walter. Springer-Verlag, 175 5th Ave., New York, NY 10010. (212) 460-1500. 1985-. Ecological principles in global perspective and tropical and subtropical zonobiomes.

Ecological Theory and Integrated Pest Management Practice. Marcos Kogan. John Wiley & Sons, Inc., 605 3rd Ave., New York, NY 10158-0012. (212) 850-6000. 1986.

Ecologie. Les Editions Humus, Inc., 4545 Pierre-de-Coubertin, Montreal, PQ, Canada H1V 3R2. (514) 252-3148. Bimonthly. Environmental scientific and international information.

Ecologist. Tycooly Publishing International, Box C-166, Riverton, NJ 08077. Bimonthly. Magazine for environment and development.

Ecologist. MIT Press, 55 Hayward St., Cambridge, MA 02142. (617) 253-2889. Bimonthly. Man's impact on the biosphere and social, economic and political barriers.

The Ecologist. Ecosystems Ltd., Wadebridge, England Covers human ecology, pollution, and natural resources.

Ecologue: The Environmental Catalogue and Consumer's Guide for a Safe Earth. Bruce N. Anderson, ed. Prentice Hall, Rte. 9W, Englewood Cliffs, NY 07632. (201) 592-2000. 1990. Compares and evaluates the cost, performance, energy efficiency and effect on the environment of a wide range of products used in everyday settings. The book is arranged according to the products used: groceries, household cleaners, clothing, personal care items, baby care, appliances and transportation.

Ecology. Ecological Society of America, Center of Environmental Studies, Arizona State University, Tempe, AZ 85287-1201. (602) 965-3000. Bimonthly. Information on the study of living things.

Ecology Abstracts. Cambridge Scientific Abstracts, 5161 River Rd., Bethesda, MD 20816. (301) 961-6750. Monthly.

Ecology Action Educational Institute. Box 3895, Modesto, CA 95352. (209) 576-0739.

Ecology and Land Management in Amazonia. Michael J. Eden. Belhaven Press, 136 S. Broadway, Irvington, NY 10533. (914) 591-9111. 1990. Deals with three major areas: the rain forest as a global resource and its role in sustaining life on the planet as a whole; needs of the countries with large tracts of tropical rain forest (including the factors that relate to how one can utilize land, the climate, geomorphology, hydrology, soils and ecology); and how the Amazonia rain forest can be conserved, including the role of national parks and management at the regional level.

The Ecology and Management of Aquatic Terrestrial Ecotones. R. J. Naiman and H. Decamps, eds. Parthenon Pub., Casterton Hall, Carnforth, England LA6 2LA. Lancs. 1990.

Ecology and Management of Food Industry Pests. J. Richard Gorham. AOAC International, 2200 Wilson Blvd., Suite 400, Arlington, VA 22201-3301. (703) 522-3032.

Ecology and Paleoecology of Benthic Foraminifera. John Williams Murray. John Wiley & Sons, Inc., 605 3rd Ave., New York, NY (212) 850-6000. 1991.

Ecology: Balance and Imbalance in Nature. Shirley Fung. Longman Cheshire, 95 Coventry St., South Melbourne, VIC, Australia 3205. Victoria 1991.

Ecology Center. 2530 San Pablo Ave., Berkeley, CA 94702. (510) 548-2220.

Ecology Center Newsletter. Ecology Center, 2530 San Pablo Ave., Berkeley, CA 94702. (510) 548-2220. Monthly. Politics and philosophy of the environment.

Ecology, Community, and Lifestyle: Outline of an Ecosophy. David Rothenberg. Cambridge University Press, 40 W. 20th St., New York, NY 10011. (212) 924-3900. 1989. Handbook on strategy and tactics for environmentalists.

Ecology: Community Profiles. U.S. Fish and Wildlife Service. National Technical Information Service, 5285 Port Royal Road, Springfield, VA 22161. (703) 487-4650. Irregular. Data on coastal and inland ecosystems, including wetlands, tidal-flats, near-shore seagrasses, sand dunes, drilling platforms, oyster reefs, estuaries, rivers and streams.

Ecology Digest. Ecology Digest, Box 60961, Sacramento, CA 95860. (916) 961-2942. Quarterly. Articles on environmental and political issues.

Ecology, Economics, Ethics: The Broken Circle. Herbert R. Bormann and Stephen R. Kellert, eds. Yale University Press, 302 Temple St., New Haven, CT 06520. (203) 432-0960. 1991. Addresses a wide range of concerns and offers practical remedies including: economic incentives for conservation, technical adaptations to use resources effectively; better accounting procedures for measuring the environmental system that better explains our responsibility to the environment.

Ecology for Beginners. Stephen Croall. Pantheon Books, 201 E 50th St., New York, NY 10022. (212) 751-2600. 1981. The story of man's struggle with the environment.

Ecology International. INTECOL–International Association for Ecology, c/o Institute of Ecology, University of Georgia, Athens, GA 30602. (404) 542-2968. Semiannual.

Ecology Law Quarterly. School of Law of the University of California, Berkeley, Boalt Hall, Rm. 20, Berkeley, CA 94720. (510)642-0457. Quarterly. Environmental law in the United States.

The Ecology of a Garden: The First Fifteen Years. Jennifer Owen. Cambridge University Press, 40 W. 20th St., New York, NY 10011. (212) 924-3900; (800) 227-0247. 1991.

Ecology of a Subarctic Mire. Swedish Natural Science Research Council, PO Box 6711, Stockholm, Sweden S-113 85. 08-15-1580. 1980. Topics in tundra ecology.

The Ecology of a Tropical Forest. Egbert J. Leigh, Jr., et al., eds. Smithsonian Institution Press, 470 L'Enfant Plaza, No. 7100, Washington, DC 20560. (800) 782-4612. 1983. Describes the rhythm of plant reproduction through the seasons and how it affects animal population.

The Ecology of Aquatic Insects. Vincent H. Resh. Praeger Publishers, 1 Madison Ave., New York, NY 10010-3603. (212) 685-5300. 1984.

Ecology of Arable Land. Olof Andersen, et al., eds. Munksgaard International, PO Box 2148, Copenhagen K, Denmark DK-1016. 1990. Investigates and synthesizes the contributions of the soil organisms and nitrogen and carbon circulation in four contrasting cropping systems. Also looks into future challenges of agroecosystem research.

Ecology of Biological Invasions of North America and Hawaii. H. G. Baker, et al. Springer-Verlag, 175 5th Ave., New York, NY 10010. (212) 460-1500; (800) 777-4643. 1986.

The Ecology of Bird Communities. John A. Wiens. Cambridge University Press, 40 W. 20th St., New York, NY 10011. (212) 924-3900. 1989. Foundations, patterns, processes, and variations in birds.

The Ecology of Desert Communities. Gary A. Polis, ed. University of Arizona Press, 1230 N. Park, No. 102, Tucson, AZ 85719. (602) 621-1441. 1991. Presents the relatively new ideas and syntheses of this beta generation of desert biologists. Focuses on the structure of desert communities since the early 1970s. Synthesizes new ideas on desert communities.

Ecology of Estuaries: Anthropogenic Effects. CRC Press, 2000 Corporate Blvd. N.W., Boca Raton, FL 33431. (800) 272-7737. 1992. Covers estuarine ecology and environmental aspects of estuarine pollution.

The Ecology of Fishes on Coral Reefs. Peter F. Sale. Academic Press, 1250 Sixth Ave., San Diego, CA 92101. (619) 231-0926. 1991.

Ecology of Food and Nutrition. Gordon & Breach Science Publishers, Inc., 270 8th Ave., New York, NY 10011. (212) 206-8900. Quarterly.

The Ecology of Giant Kelp Forests in California. Michael S. Foster. U.S. Department of the Interior, U.S. Fish and Wildlife Service, Washington, DC 20240. (202) 343-5634. 1985. Macrocystis pyrifera, marine ecology and kelp bed ecology.

Ecology of Marine Benthos. Bruce C. Coull. University of South Carolina Press, Columbia, SC 29208. (803) 777-5243. 1977. Papers on marine science, marine biological and coastal research.

The Ecology of Marine Sediments. John S. Gray. Cambridge University Press, 40 W. 20th St., New York, NY 10011. (212) 924-3900. 1981. An introduction to the structure and function of benthic communities.

Ecology of Photosynthesis in Sun and Shade. J. R. Evans, et al. CSIRO, PO Box 89, East Melbourne, VIC, Australia 3002. 1988. The popular topic of function analysis of the photosynthetic apparatus in response to irradiance, and problems of acclimation and photoinhibition are also discussed.

Ecology of Salt Marshes and Sand Dunes. D. S. Ranwell. Chapman & Hall, 2-6 Boundary Row, London, England SE1 8HN. 1975. Seashore ecology, sand dunes, and tidemarsh ecology.

Ecology of Sandy Shores. A. C. Brown and A. Mclachlan. Elsevier Science Publishing Co., 655 Avenue of the Americas, New York, NY 10010. (212) 989-5800. 1990. Deals with the biological study of sandy beaches.

Ecology of Soil Organisms. Brown Alison Leadley. Heinemann Educational, Holley Court, Jordan Hill, Oxford, England OX2 8EJ. 1978.

The Ecology of the Ancient Greek World. Robert Sallares. Cornell University Press, 124 Roberts Place, Ithaca, NY 14850. 1991. Synthesis of ancient history and biological or physical anthropology. Includes chapters on demography and on agriculture in ancient Greece and Egypt. Also includes extensive notes and bibliographies.

The Ecology of Urban Habitats. O.L. Gilbert. Chapman & Hall, 29 W. 35th St., New York, NY 10001-2291. (212) 244-3336. 1989.

Ecology Reports. Ecology Center of Ann Arbor, 417 Detroit St., Ann Arbor, MI 48104. (313) 461-3186. Ten times a year. Environmental awareness through local and state research and education.

Ecology USA. Business Publishers, Inc., 951 Pershing Dr., Silver Spring, MD 20910-4464. (301) 587-6300. 1972-. Biweekly. Contains all the legislation, regulation, and litigation affecting efforts to conserve and protect America's unique environmental and ecological heritage.

Ecolution: The Eco Home Newsletter. Eco Home Network, 4344 Russell Ave., Los Angeles, CA 90027. (213) 662-5207. Bimonthly. News of pollution and abatement.

Ecomod. ISEM–North America Chapter, Water Quality Division, South Florida Water Management District, P.O. Box 24608, West Palm Beach, FL 33416. (407) 686-8800. Monthly. Current events in ecological and environmental modeling.

ECON; Environmental Contractor. Duane Enterprises, 319 West St., Braintree, MA 02184. (914) 737-2676. Monthly. Information in the asbestos industry.

Econews. Northcoast Environmental Center, 879 Ninth St., Arcata, CA 95521. (707) 822-6918. Eleven times a year. Environmental news focusing on northwestern California.

Econometric and Dynamic Modelling–Exemplified by Caesium in Lakes after Chernobyl. Lars Hakanson. Springer-Verlag, 175 5th Ave., New York, NY 10010. (212) 460-1500 or (800) 777-4643. 1991. Details methods to establish representative and compatible lake data models and load after the Chernobyl accident. Deals with ecotoxicology and hydrogeology.

Economic Analysis of Proposed Revised Effluent Guidelines and Standards for the Inorganic Chemicals Industry. National Technical Information Service, 5285 Port Royal Rd., Springfield, VA 22161. (703) 487-4650. 1980. Covers effluent quality and sewage purification technology.

An Economic Analysis of the Environmental Impact of Highway Deicing. Donald M. Murray and Ulrich F. W. Ernst. U.S. Environmental Protection Agency, Office of Research and Development, Municipal Environmental Laboratory, 401 M St., SW, Washington, DC 20460. (202) 260-2090. 1976.

Economic and Ecological Sustainability of Tropical Rain Forest Management. Kathrin Schreckenberg and Malcolm Hadley, eds. UNESCO, 7, place de Fontenoy, Paris, France F-75700. (331) 45 68 40 67. 1991.

Economic and Technical Adjustments in Irrigation Due to Declining Ground Water. U.S. G.P.O, Washington, DC 20402-9325. (202) 512-0000. 1990. Impact of declining ground water levels on irrigation use and costs.

Economic Instruments for Environmental Protection. OECD Publications and Information Center, 2001 L St. N.W., Suite 700, Washington, DC 20036. (202) 785-OECD. 1989. Reviews the current role of economic instruments and assesses their effectiveness and future potential. Discusses charges and taxes on effluents, user and product charges, tax relief and subsidies for anti-pollution investments, and trading of pollution rights. Problems of enforcement, and implications for the polluter pays principle are also covered.

Economic News Notes. National Association of Home Builders, 15th & M St., N.W., Washington, DC 20005. (202) 822-0434. Monthly.

Economic Poisons Report. New Mexico Dept. of Agriculture, Las Cruces, NM 1979. Annual. Covers pesticides, pest control, and pesticides industry.

Economics and Biological Diversity: Developing and Using Economic Incentives to Conserve Biological Resources. Jeffrey A. McNeely. Pinter Pub., 136 S. Broadway, Irvington, NY 10533. (914) 591-9111. 1991. Explains how economic incentives can be applied to conservation while complementing development efforts.

SOURCES CITED

Economics and the Environment: A Reconciliation. Walter Block. Fraser Institute, 626 Bute St., Vancouver, BC, Canada V6E3M1. (604) 688-0221. 1990. Environmental policy and how it impacts on the national economy.

The Economics of Agricultural Pest Control. U.S. Department of Agriculture, Economics and Statistics Service, 14 Independence Ave. SW, Washington, DC 20250. (202) 447-7454. 1981.

The Economics of Coastal Zone Management: A Manual of Assessment Techniques. Edmund Penning-Rowsell, ed. Belhaven Press, 136 S. Broadway, Irvington, NY 10533. (914) 591-9111. 1991. Manual for assessing and pricing the procedures that protect vulnerable coastlines against flood, storm, high tide and other environmental damage.

The Economics of "Green Consumerism": A Bibliography. Leslie Anderson Morales. Public Affairs Information Service, 521 W. 43rd St., New York, NY 10036. (212) 736-6629. 1991. Economic impact of environmentally safe products and services from the perspectives of the consumer, wholesaler, and provider.

The Economics of Improved Estuarine Water Quality: An NEP Manual for Measuring Benefits. U.S. Environmental Protection Agency, Office of Marine and Estuarine Protection, 401 M St., S.W., Washington, DC 20460. (202) 260-2090. 1990. Covers wetland conservation and estuarine ecology.

The Economics of Managing Chlorofluorocarbons: Stratospheric Ozone and Climatic Issues. Johns Hopkins University Press, 701 W. 40th St., Suite 275, Baltimore, MD 21211. (410) 516-6900. 1982.

Economics of Natural Resources and the Environment. David W. Pearce. Johns Hopkins University Press, 701 W. 40th St., Suite 275, Baltimore, MD 21211. (410) 516-6900. 1990.

Economics of Protected Areas: A New Look at Benefits and Costs. John A. Dixon and Paul B. Sherman. Island Press, 1718 Connecticut Ave. N.W., Suite 300, Washington, DC 20009. (202) 232-7933. 1990. Represents a ground-breaking effort to help government examine the costs and benefits of maintaining protected areas. Provides a methodology for assigning monetary values to nature and explains the economic techniques involved.

The Economics of Salt. FIND/SVP, 625 Avenue of the Americas, New York, NY 10011. (212) 645-4500. 1991. Salt markets, the main influences on salt prices, the impact of environmental pressure on chlorine manufacturing, consumption by end use, international trade, prices, costs and freights, methods of recovery, occurrence and reserves and world production.

The Economics of Uranium 1991. FIND/SVP, 625 Avenue of the Americas, New York, NY 10011. (212) 645-4500. 1991. Analyzes uranium and nuclear activities within 39 countries with subsections on the roles played by 28 leading companies.

Ecophilosophy: A Field Guide to the Literature. Donald Edward Davis. R. & E. Miles Publishers, International Sales, PO Box 1916, San Pedro, CA 90733. 1989.

The Ecopolitics of Development in the Third World: Politics and Environment in Brazil. Roberto Pereira Guimaraes. L. Rienner Publishers, 1800 30th St, Suite 314, Boulder, CO 80301. (303) 444-6684. 1991. History of environmental policy in Brazil.

Ecopreneuring: The Complete Guide to Small Business Opportunities from the Environmental Revolution. Steven J. Bennett. John Wiley & Sons, Inc., 605 3rd Ave., New York, NY 10158-0012. (212) 850-6000. 1991. Covers opportunities in recycling, energy conservation, personal care products, safe foods, and investment services. Offers practical information, including market size, growth potential, and capital requirement. Provides a directory of resources.

Ecosphere. Forum International, 91 Gregory Ln., Ste. 21, Pleasant Hill, CA 94523. (510) 671-2900. Bimonthly. Eco-development, ecology, ecosystems, interface between culture-environment-tourism.

Ecosystems Experiments. H. A. Mooney, et al., eds. John Wiley & Sons, Inc., 605 3rd Ave., New York, NY 10158-0012. (212) 850-6000. 1991. Explores the potential ecosystem experimentation as a tool for understanding and predicting changes in the biosphere. Areas investigated include deforestation, desertification, El Nino phenomenon, acid rain, watersheds, wetlands, and aquatic and climatic changes.

Ecosystems of Florida. Ronald L. Myers and John J. Ewel, eds. Central Florida University, Dist. by Univ. Presses of Florida, 15 N.W. 15th St., Gainesville, FL 32603. (904) 392-1351. 1990. Presents an ecosystem setting with geology, geography and soils, climate, and 13 ecosystems in a broad human context of historical biogeography and current human influences. Also presents community vulnerability and management techniques and issues in conservation.

Ecotoxicology and Climate. Philippe Bordeaux, et al., eds. John Wiley & Sons, Inc., 605 3rd Ave., New York, NY 10158-0012. (212) 850-6000. 1989. Describes environmental chemistry of toxic pollutants in hot and cold climates. Includes bibliographical references and an index.

Ecotoxicology and Environmental Safety. Academic Press, c/o Harcourt Brace Jovanovich Inc., 6277 Sea Harbor Dr., Orlando, FL 32887. (800) 346-8648. 1977-. Bimonthly.

Ecotoxicology of Metals: Current Concepts and Applications. Michael C. Newman and Alan W. McIntosh. Lewis Publishers, 2000 Corporate Blvd., N.W., Boca Raton, FL 33431. (407) 994-0555 or (800) 272-7737. 1991. Examines the influence of water chemistry on metal toxicity. Also includes a review of toxic effects on fish and other biological forms that exist in the water. Analyzes and presents alternatives to standard techniques. Describes present and future needs in sediment toxicity and community level response of stream organisms to heavy metals.

ECRI. 5200 Butler Pike, Plymouth Meeting, PA 19462. (215) 825-6000.

EDF Letter. Environmental Defense Fund, 257 Park Ave. S., 16th Fl., New York, NY 10010-7304. (212) 505-2100. Bimonthly. Reports environmental quality & public health.

Edison Electric Institute. 701 Pennsylvania Ave., N.W., Washington, DC 20004-2696. (202) 508-5000.

Editorially Speaking about Ground Water: Its First Quarter Century. Jay H. Lehr and Anita B. Stanley. National Water Well Association, 6375 Riverside Dr., Dublin, OH 43017. (614) 761-1711. 1988. A collection of editorials from the Journal of Ground Water which traces the evolution of ground water science during the journal's first 25 years of publication.

Educational Materials for Animal Rights. International Society for Animal Rights, Inc., 421 S. State St., Clarks Summit, PA 18411. (717) 586-2200. Annual.

Edwards Aquifer Research and Data Center. 248 Freeman Building, Southwest Texas State University, San Marcos, TX 78666-4616. (512) 245-2329.

Effect of Air Pollution on Pinus Strobus L. and Genetic Resistance. Henry D. Gerhold. U.S. Corvallis Environmental Research Laboratory, 200 SW 35th St., Corvallis, OR 97333. (503) 754-4600. 1977. Effect of air pollution on white pine.

Effect of Hydrogen Sulfide on Fish and Invertebrates. National Technical Information Service, 5285 Port Royal Rd., Springfield, VA 22161. (703) 487-4650. 1976. Effect of water pollution on fish and freshwater invertebrates.

Effects of Acid Rain on Soil and Water. E.C. Krug. Connecticut Agricultural Extension Station, PO Box 1106, New Haven, CT 06504. (203) 789-7272. 1983. Topics in soil and water pollution.

Effects of Aerosols and Surface Shadowing on Bidirectional Reflectance Measurements of Deserts Microform. David E. Bowker. National Aeronautics and Space Administration, Scientific and Technical Information Office, 5285 Port Royal Rd., Springfield, VA 22161. (703) 487-4805. 1987. NASA technical paper; #2756.

The Effects of Agri-SC Soil Conditioner on Soil Physical Properties. Bryan C. Fitch. Southern Illinois University, Carbondale, IL 62901. 1988.

Effects of Air Pollution and Acid Rain on Agriculture. Joseph R. Barse, Walter Ferguson, and Virgil Whetzel. U.S. Department of Agriculture, Economic Research Service, Natural Resources Division, 14th St. and Independence Ave. S.W., Washington, DC (202) 447-7454. 1985. Series no. ERS Staff Report: No AGES 850702. It is distributed to depository libraries in microfiche. The bibliography is annotated. It is also available to the research community outside the United States for limited distribution.

The Effects of Air Pollution and Acid Rain on Fish, Wildlife, and Their Habitats: Forests. Louis Borghi. Fish and Wildlife Service, Department of the Interior, Washington, DC 20240. (202) 653-8750. 1982. Effect of acid precipitation on plants and forest ecology.

The Effects of Air Pollution and Acid Rain on Fish, Wildlife, and Their Habitats: Grasslands. M.A. Peterson. U.S. G.P.O, Washington, DC 20401. (202) 512-0000. 1982. Effects of acid precipitation on plants and grassland ecology.

Effects of Bank Stabilization on the Physical and Chemical Characteristics of Streams and Small Rivers: An Annotated Bibliography. Daniel H. Stern. U.S. G.P.O., Washington, DC 20401. (202) 512-0000. 1980. Covers stream channelization, rivers, streambank planting, erosion and turbidity.

Effects of Environment on Microhardness of Magnesium Oxide. Hiroyuki Ishigaki. National Technical Information Service, 5285 Port Royal Rd., Springfield, VA 22161. (703) 487-4650. 1982. Testing of magnesia.

The Effects of Environmental Chemicals on the Immune System: A Selected Bibliography with Abstracts. Federation of American Societies for Experimental Biology, 9650 Rockville Pike, Bethesda, MD 20814. (301) 530-7000. 1981. Chemically induced immunologic diseases and environmental carcinogens.

The Effects of Fire and Other Disturbances on Small Mammals and Their Predators. Catherine H. Ream. U.S. Department of Agriculture, Forest Service, 324 25th St., Ogden, UT 84401. 1981. Includes mammal populations, predatory animals, fire ecology, and animal ecology.

Effects of Fuel Additives on Air Pollutant Emissions from Distillated-Oil-Fired Furnaces. G. B. Martin. U.S. Environmental Protection Agency, Office of Air Programs, MD 75, Research Triangle Park, NC 27711. 1971. Air pollution caused by oil burners and petroleum additives.

Effects of Highways on Wildlife. National Technical Information Service, 5285 Port Royal Rd., Springfield, VA 22161. (703) 487-4650. 1982. Wildlife conservation and environmental aspects of roads and highways.

Efficiency in Environmental Regulation: A Benefit-Cost Analysis of Alternative Approaches. Kluwer Academic Publishers, 101 Philip Dr., Assinippi Park, Norwell, MA 02061-0358. (617) 871-6600. Quantitative assessment of the efficiency of the EPA's regulation of conventional air and water pollutants from the pulp and paper industry.

Effluent Treatment and Waste Disposal. Institution of Chemical Engineers. Hemisphere Publishing Corp., 79 Madison Ave., Suite 1110, New York, NY 10016. (212) 725-1999. 1990. Provides a detailed analysis of the strides which industry has taken to address the pollution of waterways.

Effluents from Livestock. J. K. R. Gasser, et al., eds. Applied Science Publications, PO Box 5399, New York, NY 10163. (718) 756-6440. 1980. Proceedings of a seminar to discuss work carried out within the EEC under the programme Effluents from Intensive Livestock, organized by Prof. H. Vetter and held at Bad Zwischenahn, 2-5 October, 1979.

The Egg-An Eco-Justice Quarterly. Eco-Justice Project and Network, Cornell University, Anabel Taylor Hall, Ithaca, NY 14850. Quarterly.

EHP, Environmental Health Perspectives. National Institute of Environmental Health Sciences, National Institutes of Health, Dept. of Health Education and Welfare, Box 12233, Bldg. 101, Rm. A 259, Research Triangle Park, NC 27709. (919) 541-3406. 1972-. Bimonthly.

EI Digest. Environmental Information Ltd., 7400 Metro Blvd., Ste. 400, Minneapolis, MN 55435. (612) 831-2473. Monthly. Industrial and hazardous waste management regulations & technologies.

EIS: Digests of Environmental Impact Statements. Cambridge Scientific Abstracts, 5161 River Rd., Bethesda, MD 20816. (301) 951-1400. 1970-. Bimonthly. Provides detailed abstracts of all the environmental impact statements issued by the federal government each year and indexes them. Also extracts the key issues from the complex government released environmental impact statements. Contents include areas such as: air transportation, defense programs, energy, hazardous substances, land use, manufacturing, parks, refuges, forests, research and development, roads and railroads, urban and social programs, wastes, and water.

EIS, Key to Environmental Impact Statements. Information Resources Press, 2100 M St., NW, Suite 316, Washington, DC 20037.

El Environmental Services Directory. Environmental Information Ltd., 4801 W. 81st St., No. 119, Minneapolis, MN 55437-1111. (612) 831-2473.

El Paisano. Desert Protective Council, Inc., PO Box 4294, Palm Springs, CA 92263. (619) 670-7127. Quarterly. Environmental study of the desert.

Electric Energy Systems. National Technical Information Service, 5285 Port Royal Rd., Springfield, VA 22161. (703) 487-4650. Monthly. Fossil and hydroelectric power generation, transmission, environmental control technology, and policy.

Electric Perspectives. Edison Electric Institute, 1111 19th St., NW, Washington, DC 20036-3691. Bimonthly. Business, regulatory, and technological developments concerning electric utilities.

Electric Power Industry Abstracts. Utility Data Institute, 1700 K St., N.W., Suite 400, Washington, DC 20006. (800) 466-3660.

Electric Power Research Institute. 3412 Hillview Ave., Palo Alto, CA 94304. (415) 855-2000.

Electric Utility Power Disturbances in the U.S. by Geographic Region. FIND/SVP, 625 Avenue of the Americas, New York, NY 10011. (212) 645-4500. Voltage spikes, surges, sustained over voltages, EMI and RFI noise, glitches, sags, brownouts, outages, harmonic distortion, and frequency drifts.

Electrical Energy in Agriculture. Kenneth L. McFate. Elsevier Science Publishing Co., 655 Avenue of the Americas, New York, NY 10010. (212) 984-5800. 1989.

Electrical Hazards and Accidents: Their Cause and Prevention. E. K. Greenwald, ed. Global Professional Publications, 2805 McGraw Ave., PO Box 19539, Irvine, CA 92713-9539. (800) 854-7179. 1991. Workplace hazards associated with electricity and proven design, maintenance, and operating procedures for preventing them.

Electricity and the Environment. International Atomic Energy Agency, Wagramerstrasse 5, Vienna, Austria Discusses the health environmental factors, and the economic factors involved in supplying electrical services.

Electricity End-Use Efficiency. OECD Publications and Information Centre, 2, rue Andre-Pascal, Paris Cedex 16, France F-75775. 1989. Government policy on electric utilities, electric power conservation, household appliances and energy consumption in industry.

Electricity Supply and Demand. North American Electric Reliability Council, 101 College Rd., E., Princeton, NJ 08540-6601. Annual. Forecasts of electricity supply and demand by region and subregion.

Electrochemical Synthesis of Inorganic Compounds: A Bibliography. Zoltan Nagy. Plenum Press, 233 Spring St., New York, NY 10013-1578. (212) 620-8000; (800) 221-9369. 1985.

Electron Beam Wastewater Treatment Removes Organics. FIND/SVP, 625 Avenue of the Americas, New York, NY 10011. (212) 645-4500. New low-cost, high-capacity method of effectively treating low-level contamination; the uses of electron-beam radiation (EBR); EBR potential in effluent lines of waste-producing factories; EBR treatment of low-level concentration and disinfection of sewage.

Electronic Information Exchange System. Office of Research and Development, U.S. Environmental Protection Agency, RD-618, 401 M St., Washington, DC 20460. Legislative Tracking System, which tracks the status of both state and federal legislation pertaining to source reduction and recycling; and National Waste Exchange.

Electronic Pest Control Association. 710 E. Ogden, Suite 113, Naperville, IL 60563. (708) 369-2406.

Electronic System Design: Interference and Noise Control Techniques. John R. Barnes. Prentice Hall, Rte. 9W, Englewood Cliffs, NJ 07632. (201) 592-2000. 1987. Deals with electronic circuit design and electromagnetic noise.

Electroplating & Metal Finishing. Wheatland Journals Ltd., Penn House, Penn Place, Rickmansworth, England WD3 1FN.

Electroplating Wastewater Pollution Control Technology. George C. Cushnie. Noyes Publications, 120 Mill Rd., Park Ridge, NJ 07656. (201) 391-8484. 1985. Environmental aspects of electroplating waste disposal and sewage purification.

Elements of Marine Ecology. Ronald Victor Tait. Butterworth-Heinemann, 80 Montvale Ave., Stoneham, MA 02180. (617) 438-8464. 1981.

The Elements: Their Origin, Abundance, and Distribution. P.A. Cox. Oxford University Press, 200 Madison Ave., New York, NY 10016. (212) 679-7300. 1989.

Elephant Interest Group. 106 E. Hickory Grove, Bloomfield Hills, MI 48013. (313) 540-3947.

Eleventh Commandment Fellowship. P.O. Box 14667, San Francisco, CA 94114. (415) 626-6064.

The Eleventh Commandment: Toward an Ethic of Ecology. Eleventh Commandment Fellowship, PO Box 14667, San Francisco, CA 94114. (415) 626-6064. Semiannual.

Elmwood Institute. P.O. Box 5805, Berkeley, CA 94705. (510) 845-4595.

Elsa Clubs of America. PO Box 4572, North Hollywood, CA 91617-0572. (818) 761-8387.

Elsa Wild Animal Appeal-USA. P.O. Box 675, Elmhurst, IL 60126. (708) 833-8896.

Elsevier's Dictionary of Building Construction. James Maclean. Elsevier Science Publishing Co., 655 Avenue of the Americas, New York, NY 10010. (212) 989-5800. 1989. Terms cover the basic vocabulary of the building construction industry, with particular emphasis on mechanical and electrical services.

Elsevier's Dictionary of Horticultural and Agricultural Plant Production in Ten Languages. Elsevier Science Publishing Co., 655 Avenue of Americas, New York, NY 10010. (212) 989-5800. 1990. Language of the text: English, Dutch, French, German, Danish, Swedish, Italian, Spanish, Portuguese and Latin.

Elsevier's Dictionary of Hydrology and Water Quality Management. J. D. Van der Tuin. Elsevier Science Publishing Co., 655 Avenue of the Americas, New York, NY 10010. (212) 989-5800. 1991. The languages are English, French, Spanish, Dutch, and German. Freshwater environment constitutes the main subject of this dictionary. Defines more than 37,000 terms.

Elsevier's Dictionary of Metallurgy and Metal Working in Six Languages. W. E. Clason. Elsevier Science Publishing Co., 655 Avenue of the Americas, New York, NY 10010. (212) 989-5800. 1978. Text in English/American, French, Spanish, Italian, Dutch, and German.

Elsevier's Dictionary of Soil Mechanics and Geotechnical Engineering. J. D. Van Der Tuin. Elsevier Science Publishing Co., 655 Avenue of the Americas, New York, NY 10010. (212) 989-5800. 1989. The text is in English, French, Spanish, Dutch, and German.

Elsevier's Dictionary of Solar Technology. K. Neutwig. Elsevier Science Publishing Co., 655 Avenue of the Americas, New York, NY 10010. (212) 989-5800. 1985. Text in English, German, French, Spanish and Italian. Specialized terms from the field of solar technology.

Elsevier's Dictionary of the World's Game and Wildlife. G. Ferlin. Elsevier Science Publishing Co., 655 Avenue of the Americas, New York, NY 10010. (212) 989-5800. 1989. The languages included are English, Latin, French, German, Dutch, Spanish.

Elsevier's Dictionary of Water and Hydraulic Engineering. J. D. Van Der Tuin. Elsevier Science Publishing Co., 655 Avenue of the Americas, New York, NY 10010. (212) 989-5800. 1987. The text is in English, Spanish, French, Dutch and German.

Elsevier's Dictionary of Wild and Cultivated Plants in Latin, English, French, Italian, Dutch, and German. W. E. Clason. Elsevier Science Publishing Co., 655 Avenue of the Americas, New York, NY 10010. (212) 989-5800. 1989. This dictionary consists of the scientific names of wild and cultivated plants found in Europe.

Elsevier's Oil and Gas Field Dictionary. L. Y. Caballe, et al, eds. Elsevier Science Publishing Co., 655 Avenue of the Americas, New York, NY 10010. (212) 989-5800. 1980. The text is in English/American, French, Spanish, Italian, Dutch, German, Arabic supplement. Includes terms used in oil and gas field operations.

Elton's Ecologists: A History of the Bureau of Animal Population. Peter Crowcroft. University of Chicago Press, 5801 Ellis Ave., 4th Fl., Chicago, IL 60637. (312) 702-7700. 1991. The story of a smallish university department chronicles an enterprise that appreciably shaped the history of ecology during the mid-decades of the 20th century.

Embankment Dam Instruction Manual. Charles L. Bartholomew. U.S. G.P.O., Washington, DC 20401. 1987. Measurement of earth dams.

EMBASE Drug Information. Elsevier Science Publishing Co., Excerpta Medica, Molenwerf 1, 1014 AG Amsterdam, Netherlands 31 (20) 5803507.

EMBL Nucleotide Sequence Database. European Molecular Biology Laboratory, EMBL Data Library, Meyerhofstrasse 1, 6900 Heidelberg, Germany 49 (6221) 387258.

EMCANCER. Elsevier Science Publishing Co., Excerpta Medica, Molenwerf 1, 1014 AG Amsterdam, Netherlands 31 (20) 5803507.

EMDRUGS. Elsevier Science Publishing Co., Excerpta Medica, Molenwerf 1, 1014 AG Amsterdam, Netherlands 31 (20) 5803507.

Emergence: The New Science of Becoming. Lindisfarne Press, RR4, Box 94A-1, Hudson, NY 12534. (518) 851-9155. Covers ecology and philosophy of biology.

Emergency Committee to Save America's Marine Resources. c/o Allan J. Ristori, 1552 Osprey Ct., Manasquan Park, NJ 08736. (201) 223-5729.

Emergency Fuels Utilization Guidebook: Alternative Fuels Utilization Program. National Technical Information Service, 5285 Port Royal Rd., Springfield, VA 22161. (703) 487-4650. 1980.

Emergency Management Agency: Emergency Preparedness and Community Right-to-Know. Emergency Response Commission, PO Box 4501, Fondren Station, Jackson, MS 39296-4501. (601) 960-9973.

Emergency Management Agency: Emergency Preparedness and Community Right-to-Know. Emergency Response Commission, Comprehensive Emergency Management, 5500 Bishop Blvd., Cheyenne, WY 82009. (307) 777-7566.

Emergency Planning and Community Right to Know. Sarith Guerra. Management Information Service, 777 N. Capitol St., NE, Ste. 500, Washington, DC 20002-420. (800) 745-8780. 1991. Covers the reporting of health risks from hazardous substances.

Emergency Preparedness and Community Right-to-Know. Director, 290 Bigclow Bldg., 450 North Syndicate, St Paul, MN 55104. (612) 643-3000.

Emergency Preparedness News. Business Publishers, Inc., 951 Pershing Drive, Silver Spring, MD 20910. (301) 587-6300. Biweekly. Emergency management techniques and technologies.

Emergency Response Commission: Emergency Preparedness and Community Right-to-Know. Chair, PO Box O, Juneau, AK 99811. (907) 465-2600.

Emergency Response Commission: Emergency Preparedness and Community Right-to-Know. Division of Emergency Services, Building 341, 5036 East McDowell Rd., Phoenix, AZ 85008. (602) 231-6326.

Emergency Response Commission: Emergency Preparedness and Community Right-to-Know. SARA Title III Coordinator, State Office Building, Room 161, 165 Capitol Ave., Hartford, CT 06106. (203) 566-4856.

Emergency Response Commission: Emergency Preparedness and Community Right-to-Know. Chair, 205 Butler St., S.E., Floyd Towers East, 11th Floor, Suite 1166, Atlanta, GA 30334. (404) 656-6905.

Emergency Response Commission: Emergency Preparedness and Community Right-to-Know. Chair, State House, Boise, ID 83720. (208) 334-5888.

Emergency Response Commission: Emergency Preparedness and Community Right-to-Know. Director, 5500 West Bradbury Ave., Indianapolis, IN 46241. (317) 243-5176.

Emergency Response Commission: Emergency Preparedness and Community Right-to-Know. Chairman, Statehouse Station #11, 157 Capitol Street, Augusta, ME 04333. (207) 289-4080.

Emergency Response Commission: Emergency Preparedness and Community Right-to-Know. Department of Environmental Protection, Division of Environmental Quality, Bureau of Hazardous Substances Information, Trenton, NJ 08625. (609) 292-6714.

Emergency Response Commission: Emergency Preparedness and Community Right-to-Know. Director, c/o State Fire Marshal, 3000 Market Street Plaza, Suite 534, Salem, OR 97310. (503) 378-2885.

Emergency Response Commission: Emergency Preparedness and Community Right-to-Know. Chair, 3041 Sidco, Nashville, TN 37204. (615) 252-3300.

Emergency Response Commission: Emergency Preparedness and Community Right-to-Know. Director, Office of Emergency Services, State Capitol Bldg. 1, Room EB-80, Charlestown, WV 25305. (304) 348-5380.

Emergency Response Directory for Hazardous Materials Accidents. Pamela Lawrence. Odin Press, PO Box 536, Lenox Hill Sta., New York, NY 10021. (212) 744-2538. Biennial. Governmental agencies, chemical manufacturers and transporters, hotlines and strike teams, burn care centers, civil defense and disaster centers concerned with the containment and cleanup of chemical spills and other hazardous material accidents.

Emergency Response Planning Guidelines Set 5. American Industrial Hygiene Association, 345 White Pond Dr., Akron, OH 44320. (216) 873-2442. 1991. Includes guidelines for acrylic acid, 1,3-butadiene, epichlorohydrin, tetrafluoroethylene, and vinyl acetate.

Emerging Technologies in Hazardous Waste Management. D. William Tedder and Frederick G. Pohland, eds. American Chemical Society, 1155 16th St. N.W., Washington, DC 20036. (202) 872-4600; (800) 227-5558. 1990. Hazardous waste management technology.

Emerging Technologies in Hazardous Waste Management II. D. William Tedder and Frederick G. Pohland, eds. American Chemical Society, 1155 16th St. N.W., Washington, DC 20036. (202) 872-4600; (800) 227-5558. 1991. Developed from a symposium sponsored by the Division of Industrial and Engineering Chemistry, Inc. of the American Chemical Society at the Industrial and Engineering Chemistry Special Symposium, Atlantic City, NJ, June 4-7, 1990.

EMFORENSIC. Elsevier Science Publishing Co., Excerpta Medica, Molenwerf 1, 1014 AG Amsterdam, Netherlands 31 (20) 5803507.

EMICBACK. Oak Ridge National Laboratory, Environmental Teratology Information Center, Building 2001, P.O. Box 2008, Oak Ridge, TN 37831-6050. (615) 574-7871.

EMIS. TECNON (U.K.) Limited, 12 Calico House, Plantation Wharf, York Place, Battersea, London, England SW11 3TN. 44 (71) 924-3955.

Emission Control in Electricity Generation and Industry. OECD Publications and Information Center, 2001 L St., N.W., Suite 700, Washington, DC 20036. (202) 785-OECD. 1989. Describes progress in IEA countries in reducing the impact of fossil fuel burning on the environment; systems in place for SO2 and NOx control; economic and energy security implications of the various emissions control strategies; of more rational use of energy; the development of combined heat and power and district heating.

Emissions from Combustion Processes–Origin, Measurement, Control. R. E. Clement and R. O. Kagel, eds. Lewis Publishers, 2000 Corporate Blvd., N.W., Boca Raton, FL 33431. (407) 994-0555 or (800) 272-7737. 1990. Topics discussed include all aspects of combustion from the mechanics, formation, and disposal to emission abatement and risk assessment.

Emissions: Misfueling, Catalytic Deactivation and Alternative Catalyst. Society of Automotive Engineers, 400 Commonwealth Dr., Warrendale, PA 15096. (412) 776-4841. 1985. Automobile catalytic converters, internal combustion engines, spark ignition, and alternative fuels.

Emissions of Reactive Volatile Organic Compounds from Utility Broilers. National Technical Information Service, 5285 Port Royal Rd., Springfield, VA 22161. (703) 487-4650. 1980. Air pollution management, electrical power plants, and flue gases.

Emphysema Anonymous. P.O. Box 3224, Seminole, FL 34642. (813) 391-9977.

Employers and the Environmental Challenge. Harry Z. Evan. International Labour Organization, H, rue des Morillons, Geneva, Switzerland CH-1211. 1986. Industrial hygiene, industrial safety and environmental health.

Emulsifiers & Detergents–International Edition. McCutcheon's Publications, 175 Rock Rd., Glen Rock, NJ 07452. (201) 652-2655.

Encyclopaedia Coniferae. H. N. Moldenke and A. L. Moldenke, Corvallis, OR 1986.

An Encyclopaedia of Metallurgy and Materials. C. R. Tottle. Institute of Metals, MacDonald and Evans, Estover, England PL6 7PZ. 1984. Deals with thermoelectric properties and other related data on metals.

Encyclopedia of Allergy and Environmental Illness: A Self-Help Approach. Ellen Rothera. Sterling Pub. Co., 387 Park Ave, South, New York, NY 10016-8810. (212) 532-7160 or (800) 367-9692. 1991. Presents the problem of multiple environmental allergies and deals with allergic reactions to such things as foods, food additives, household cleaners, molds, cooking gas, and air pollution.

The Encyclopedia of Animal Ecology. Peter D. Moore. Facts on File, Inc., 460 Park Ave. S., New York, NY 10016. (212) 683-2244. 1987.

The Encyclopedia of Atmospheric Sciences and Astrogeology. Rhodes Whitmore Fairbridge. Reinhold Pub. Co., 115 5th Ave., New York, NY 10003. (212) 254-3232. 1967.

The Encyclopedia of Beaches and Coastal Environments. Maurice L. Schwartz. Hutchinson Ross Pub. Co., Stroudsburg, PA 1982.

Encyclopedia of Bioethics. Warren T. Reich, ed. Free Press, 866 3rd Ave., New York, NY 10022. (212) 702-2004 or (800) 257-5755. 1978. Four volumes. Includes review articles in the field of bioethics by 330 reviewers representing fields such as: surgery, Islamic studies, pediatrics, philosophy, environmental sciences, theology, psychiatry, etc.

Encyclopedia of Building and Construction Terms. Hugh Brooks. Prentice Hall, Rte. 9W, Englewood Cliffs, NJ 07632. (201) 592-2000 or (800) 634-2863. 1983. Includes construction terminology. Also contains index by function, list of construction associations classed under their functions and general conditions of the contract for construction.

Encyclopedia of Chemical Processing and Design. John J. Mcketta and W. A. Cunningham. Marcel Dekker, Inc., 270 Madison Ave., New York, NY 10016. (212) 696-9000; (800) 228-1160. 1992. Thirty-eight volumes.

Encyclopedia of Chemical Technology. Raymond E. Kirk. John Wiley & Sons, Inc., 605 3rd Ave., New York, NY 10158-0012. (212) 850-6000. 1991-. 4th ed. Also known as Kirk Othmer Encyclopedia of Chemical Technology; consists of 26 volumes.

The Encyclopedia of Climatology. John E. Oliver and Rhodes W. Fairbridge, eds. Van Nostrand Reinhold, 115 5th Ave., New York, NY 10003. (212) 254-3232. 1987. Belongs in the series Encyclopedia of Earth Sciences, v.11.

Encyclopedia of Common Natural Ingredients Used in Foods, Drugs, and Cosmetics. John Wiley & Sons, Inc., 605 3rd Ave., New York, NY 10158-0012. (212) 850-6000. 1980. Includes 300 natural ingredients used in food, cosmetics and drugs. Each entry lists genus and species, synonyms, general description, chemical composition, pharmacologic and biological activity, uses, commercial preparation, regulatory status and references.

Encyclopedia of Community Planning and Environmental Management. Marilyn Spigel Schultz. Facts on File, Inc., 460 Park Ave. S., New York, NY 10016. (212) 683-2244. 1984.

Encyclopedia of Electrochemistry of Elements. A. J. Bard. Marcel Dekker, Inc., 270 Madison Ave., New York, NY 10016. (212) 696-9000 or (800) 228-1160. Encyclopedic treatment of the subject area of electrochemistry and related subjects.

Encyclopedia of Energy-Efficient Building Design. Kaiman Lee. Environmental Design & Research Center, 26799 Elena Rd., Los Altos Hills, CA 94022. 1977. Covers architecture and energy consumption, designs and plans, and environmental engineering of buildings.

Encyclopedia of Environmental Control Technology. Paul N. Cheremisinoff, ed. Gulf Publishing Co., Book Division, PO Box 2608, Houston, TX 77252. (713) 529-4301 or (800) 231-6275. 1992. Volume 1: Thermal Treatment of Hazardous Wastes; volume 2: Air Pollution Control; volume 3: Wastewater Treatment Technology; volume 4: Hazardous Waste Containment and Treatment; volumes 5 through 8 in progress. Provides in-depth coverage of specialized topics related to environmental and industrial pollution control problems and state-of-the-art information on technology and research as well as projections of future trends in the field.

Encyclopedia of Environmental Science and Engineering. J.R. Pfafflin. Gordon and Breach Science Publishers, Inc., 270 8th Ave., New York, NY 10011. (212) 206-8900. 1992.

Encyclopedia of Environmental Studies. William Ashworth. Facts on File, Inc., 460 Park Ave. S., New York, NY 10016. (212) 683-2244. 1991.

Encyclopedia of Explosives and Related Items. Seymour M. Kaye. National Technical Information Service, 5285 Port Royal Rd., Springfield, VA 22161. (703) 487-4650. 1978.

Encyclopedia of Food Engineering. C. W. Hall, et al. AVI Pub. Co., 250 Post Rd. E., PO Box 831, Westport, CT 06881. 1986. Presents technical data on the application of modern engineering to the food processing industry. Entries are alphabetically arranged and include equipment, facilities, machinery, processes, relevant engineering concepts, and physical properties of selected foods.

Encyclopedia of Food Science. Y. H. Hui, ed. John Wiley & Sons, Inc., 605 3rd Ave., New York, NY 10158-0012. (212) 850-6000. 1991. Deals with the properties, analysis and processing of foods including: grains and bakery products, beans, nuts, seeds, fruits and vegetables, dairy products, meat products, poultry and fish products, and alcoholic beverages. Emphasis is placed on issues associated with food additives and food spoilage.

Encyclopedia of Food Science. M. S. Peterson and A. H. Johnson. The AVI Pub. Co., 250 Post Rd. E., PO Box 831, Westport, CT 06881. 1978. Consists of short individually authored articles in an alphabetical arrangement, each with a brief bibliography. A section entitled "Food Science Around the World" includes information on food science and the food industries in various countries.

The Encyclopedia of Geochemistry and Environmental Sciences. Rhodes Whitmore Fairbridge. Van Nostrand Reinhold Co., 115 5th Ave., New York, NY 10003. (212) 254-3232. 1972.

Encyclopedia of Georgia Law. Harrison Co., 3110 Crossing Park, Norcross, GA 30071. (404) 447-9150.

Encyclopedia of Human Biology. Renato Dulbecco, ed. Academic Press, c/o Harcourt Brace Jovanovich Inc., 6277 Sea Harbor Dr., Orlando, FL 32887. (800) 346-8648. 1991. Eight volumes.

Encyclopedia of Industrial Chemical Additives. Michael and Irene Ash. Chemical Publishing Co., 80 Eighth Ave., New York, NY 10011. (212) 255-1950. 1984-87. Four volumes. Comprehensive compilation of tradename products that function as additives in enhancing the properties of various major industrial products.

Encyclopedia of Marine Invertebrates. Jerry G. Walls, ed. TFH Publications, 1 TFH Plaza, Union and 3rd Plaza, Neptune, NJ 07753. (908) 998-8400. 1982.

The Encyclopedia of Mineralogy. Hutchinson Ross Pub. Co., Stroudsburg, PA 1981.

Encyclopedia of Minerals. Willard Lincoln Roberts, et al. Van Nostrand Reinhold, 115 5th Ave., New York, NY 10003. (212) 254-3232 or (800) 926-2665. 1990. Second edition. Gives information on rare minerals, those minerals widely known and collected and those that are most attractive or visually diagnostic.

The Encyclopedia of Mushrooms. Colin Dickinson and John Lucas, eds. Putnam Berkley Group, 200 Madison Ave., New York, NY 10016. (212) 951-8400. 1979. First American edition. Traces many different common kinds of fungi. Emphasis is placed on larger fungi.

The Encyclopedia of North American Wildlife. Stanley Klein. Facts on File, Inc., 460 Park Ave. S., New York, NY 10016. (212) 683-2244. 1983. Includes mammals, birds, reptiles, amphibians, and fish. Appendices include information on wildlife conservation organizations, a bibliographical list of endangered species and an index of Latin names.

Encyclopedia of Occupational Health and Safety. Luigi Parmeggiani. International Labour Office, 49 Sheridan Ave., Albany, NY 12210. (518) 436-9686. 1983. Reference work concerned with workers' safety and health, information for those with no specialized medical or with technical knowledge.

The Encyclopedia of Oceanography. Rhodes Whitmore Fairbridge. Reinhold Pub. Co., 115 5th Ave., New York, NY 10003. (212) 254-3232. 1966.

Encyclopedia of Physical Science and Technology. Robert A. Meyers, ed. Academic Press, c/o Harcourt Brace Jovanovich Inc., 6277 Sea Harbor Dr., Orlando, FL 32887. (800) 346-8648. Dictionary of engineering, technology and physical sciences.

Encyclopedia of Physics. Rita G. Lerner and George L. Trigg. VCH Publishers, 303 NW 12th Ave., Deerfield Beach, FL 33442-1788. (305) 428-5566. 1991. Second edition.

Encyclopedia of Polymer Science and Engineering. Herman F. Mark, et al., eds. John Wiley & Sons, Inc., 605 3rd Ave., New York, NY 10158-0012. (212) 850-6000. 1985-. Seventeen volumes and two supplements.

The Encyclopedia of Sedimentology. Rhodes W. Fairbridge. Van Nostrand Reinhold, Information Services, 115 5th Ave., New York, NY 10003. (212) 254-3232. 1978.

The Encyclopedia of Soil Science. Rhodes W. Fairbridge. Academic Press, c/o Harcourt Brace Jovanovich Inc., 6277 Sea Harbor Dr., Orlando, FL 32887. (800) 346-8648. 1979-. Includes soil physics, soil chemistry, soil biology, soil fertility and plant nutrition, soil genesis, classification and cartography.

Encyclopedia of Surfactants. Michael Ash and Irene Ash. Chemical Pub. Co., 80 8th Ave., New York, NY 10011. (212) 255-1950. 1980-1985. Four volumes. Provides information on each trade name product including chemical ingredients, properties, form and applications.

Encyclopedia of Terpenoids. John S. Glasby. John Wiley & Sons, Inc., 605 3rd Ave., New York, NY 10158-0012. (212) 850-6000. 1982. Two volumes. Compendium of organic compounds found in nature, embracing a wide range of substances from the simple monoterpenoids to the highly complex triterpenoids and cartenoids, which are used in perfumes, antibiotics, cytotoxic agents and antifeedeants. Covers literature to the end of 1979.

Encyclopedia of the Alkaloids. Johns S. Glasby. Plenum Press, 233 Spring St., New York, NY 10013-1578. (212) 620-8000 or (800) 221-9369. 1975-. Compendium of plant alkaloids, with their origin and structure, molecular formula, and toxic properties. Also includes references to original papers. Covers the literature to the end of 1981.

The Encyclopedia of the Chemical Elements. Clifford A. Hampel. Reinhold Pub. Co., 115 5th Ave., New York, NY 10003. (212)254-3232. 1968.

Encyclopedia of Trademarks and Synonyms. H. Bennett, ed. Chemical Publishing Co., 80 Eighth Ave., New York, NY 10011. (212) 255-1950. 1981. Three volumes. Includes chemical compounds, compositions consisting of one or more chemicals and other products. Also included are abbreviated names and WHO free names.

Encyclopedic Dictionary of Genetics: With German Term Equivalents and Extensive German/English Index. R. C. King and W. D. Stansfield. VCH Publishers, 303 NW 12th Ave., Deerfield Beach, FL 33442-1788. (305) 428-5566. 1990. 4th ed. Revised edition of: A Dictionary of Genetics, third edition.

The End of Nature. Bill McKibben. Anchor Books, 666 5th Ave., New York, NY 10103. (212) 765-6500; (800) 223-6834. 1990.

Endangered Coral Reefs of the World. Beth Clewis. Vance Bibliographies, 112 N. Charter St., PO Box 229, Monticello, IL 61856. (217) 762-3831. 1990. Coral reef conservation and coral reef ecology.

The Endangered Kingdom: The Struggle to Save America's Wildlife. Roger L. DiSilvestro. John Wiley & Sons, Inc., 605 3rd Ave., New York, NY 10158-0012. (212) 850-6000. 1989. Describes the historical perspective and overview of present-day wildlife conservation. Included are game animals, endangered species, and nongame species.

Endangered Plant Species of the World and Their Endangered Habitats: A Compilation of the Literature. Meryl A. Miasek. New York Botanical Garden Library, 200th St. & Southern Blvd., Bronx, NY 10458. (718)817-8705. 1985. Bibliography of plant conservation and endangered species.

Endangered Species Act Reauthorization Coordinating Committee. 900 17th St. N.W., Washington, DC 20006-2596. (202) 833-2300.

Endangered Species Listing Handbook. U.S. Department of the Interior, U.S. Fish and Wildlife Service, Washington, DC 20240. (202) 343-5634. 1989. Looseleaf format.

Endangered Species Report. Defenders of Wildlife, 1244 19th St. NW, Washington, DC 20036. (202) 659-9510. Annual.

Endangered Vertebrates: a Selected Annotated Bibliography, 1981-1988. Sylva Baker. Garland Publishing, Inc., 1000A Sherman Ave., Hamden, CT 06514. (203) 281-4487. 1990. Covers scientific literature, legislative activity, organizations active in the field, and periodicals devoted to the subject.

Energy, Agriculture, and Natural Resources: Natural Resources. Director, Governor's Office, 1205 Pendleton St., Columbia, SC 29201. (803) 734-0445.

Energy: An Abstract Newsletter. National Technical Information Service, 5285 Port Royal Rd., Springfield, VA 22161. (703) 487-4650. Weekly. Energy use, supply, and demand; power and heat generation; energy conservation, transmission, and storage; fuel conversion processes; energy policies, regulations, engines, and fuels.

Energy and Architecture. Christopher Flavin. Worldwatch Institute, 1776 Massachusetts Ave. NW, Washington, DC 20036. 1980. Solar energy and conservation potential.

Energy and Climate Change. Lewis Publishers, 2000 Corporate Blvd., N.W., Boca Raton, FL 33431. (407) 994-0555 or (800) 272-7737. 1990. Includes energy scenarios, cost and risk analysis, energy emissions, atmospheric chemistry, and climate effects.

Energy & Environment. Multi-Science Publishing Co. Ltd., 107 High St., Brentwood, Essex, England CM14 4RX. 0277-224632. Quarterly.

Energy & Environment Alert. National Council for Environmental Balance, Inc., 4169 Westport Rd., Box 7732, Louisville, KY 40207. (502) 896-8731. Quarterly. Energy environment, agriculture, chemistry, entomology, and mineral resources.

Energy and Environmental Strategies for the 1990's. Mary Jo Winer and Marilyn Jackson, eds. Fairmont Pr., 700 Indian Trail, Lilburn, GA 30247. (404) 925-9388. 1991. Papers from the 13th World Energy Engineering Congress and the World Environmental Engineering Congress organized by the Association of Energy Engineers and sponsored by the U.S. Department of Energy, Office of Institutional Programs.

Energy and Housing Report. Business Publishers, Inc., 951 Pershing Dr., Silver Spring, MD 20910. (301) 587-6300. Monthly. Energy conservation problems; developments in home energy products.

Energy and the Environment. J. Dunderdale, ed. Royal Society of Chemistry, c/o CRC Press, 2000 Corporate Blvd. N.W., Boca Raton, FL 33431-9868. (800) 272-7737. 1990. Compares the environmental impact of the various energy producing and using processes. The book covers the types and quantities of pollutants produced by these processes, looks at the interaction of these pollutants with the atmosphere, and reviews the use of renewable sources as possible alternatives.

Energy and the Environment in the 21st Century. Jefferson W. Tester, et al., eds. MIT Press, 55 Hayward St., Cambridge, MA 02142. (617) 253-2884; (800) 356-0343. 1991. Proceedings of the conference held at the Massachusetts Institute of Technology, Cambridge, MA, March 26-28, 1990. Compendium of more than 80 original contributions, providing the basis for an international agenda of energy and environmental technology policy.

Energy and the Environment Policy Overview. OECD Publications and Information Center, 2001 L St. N.W., Suite 700, Washington, DC 20036. (202) 785-OECD. 1990. Analyzes the way energy policies can be adapted to environmental concerns.

Energy and the Social Sciences: A Bibliographic Guide to the Literature. E. J. Yanarella and Ann-Marie Yanarella. Westview Press, 5500 Central Ave., Boulder, CO 80301. (303) 444-3541. 1983. Focuses on the needs of social scientists entering the "miasma of energy policy studies."

Energy Conservation and Management Consultants. American Business Directories, Inc., 5711 S. 86th Circle, Omaha, NE 68127. (402) 593-4600.

Energy Conservation Digest. Editorial Resources, Inc., PO Box 21133, Washington, DC 20009. (202) 332-2267. Semimonthly. Commercial, residential, and industrial energy conservation issues and policy developments.

Energy Conservation in Existing Buildings. Albert Thumann. The Association of Energy Engineers, 4025 Pleasantdale Rd., Suite 420, Atlanta, GA 30340. (404) 925-9558. 1991. Step-by-step guide to implement a comprehensive energy conservation program in existing buildings. Includes figures to calculate energy efficient opportunities.

Energy Conservation News. Business Communications Company, Inc., 25 Van Zant St., Norwalk, CT 06855. (203) 853-4266. Technology and economics of energy conservation at industrial, commercial, and institutional facilities.

Energy Conservation Products Retail Directory. American Business Directories, Inc., 5711 S. 86th Circle, Omaha, NE 68127. (402) 593-4600. Annual.

Energy Conversion and Management. Pergamon Microforms International, Inc., Fairview Park, Elmsford, NY 10523. (914) 592-7720. 1980. Quarterly. Topics in direct energy conversion and thermoelectricity.

Energy Conversion Systems. Harry A. Sorensen. John Wiley & Sons, Inc., 605 3rd Ave., New York, NY 10158-0012. (212) 850-6000. 1983. Includes power and power plants.

Energy Deskbook. Samuel Glasstone. Van Nostrand Reinhold, 115 5th Ave., New York, NY 10020. (212) 254-3232. 1983. Single volume reference covering all energy resources.

Energy Dictionary. V. Daniel Hunt. Van Nostrand Reinhold, 115 5th Ave., New York, NY 10003. (212) 254-3232. 1979. Covers the broad field of energy including fossil, nuclear, solar, geothermal, ocean, and wind energy.

Energy-Environment-Quality of Life. Inderscience Enterprises Ltd., World Trade Center Bldg., 110 Avenue Louis Casai, Case Postale 306, Geneva-Airport, Switzerland CH1215. (44) 908-314248. 1991. A special publication of the International Journal of Global Energy. Contains the proceedings of the 13th annual International Scientific Forum on Energy (ISFE) held at the UNESCO building, Paris, France, December 4-7, 1989. Focuses on important energy issues facing the planet, their likely impact on the environment and their effects on the quality of life.

Energy: Facts and Future. Herbert F. Matare. CRC Press, 2000 Corporate Blvd. N.W., Boca Raton, FL 33431. (800) 272-7737. 1989. Data on power resources and power mechanics.

Energy for a Habitable World: A Call for Action. Pierre Elliott Trudeau. Crane Russak & Co., 1900 Frost Rd., Suite 101, Bristol, PA 19007-1598. (215) 785-5800. 1991. Summary of the report of the InterAction Council, a group of some 30 former heads of state founded in 1983. Discusses the need for cogent energy policies to deal with the world crisis.

Energy from Biomass and Municipal Wastes. National Technical Information Service, 5285 Port Royal Rd., Springfield, VA 22161. (703) 487-4650. Monthly. Biomass production, conversion, and utilization for energy.

Energy Guide: A Directory of Information Resources. Virginia Bemis, et al. Garland Publishers, 136 Madison Ave., New York, NY 10016. (212) 686-7492 or (800) 627-6273. 1977.

Energy Handbook. Robert L. Loftness. Van Nostrand Reinhold, 115 5th Ave., New York, NY 10003. (212) 254-3232. 1984. Second edition. Resource book on energy with current data taking into consideration the environmental control technologies. Includes an appendix with an energy conversion factor, a glossary and a general index.

Energy in Plant Nutrition and Pest Control. Zane R. Helsel. Elsevier Science Publishing Co., 655 Avenue of the Americas, New York, NY 10010. (212) 984-5800. 1987. Fertilizer and pesticides industry energy consumption.

Energy Information Abstracts Annual 1987 in Retrospect. EIC/ Intelligence Inc., 121 Chanlon Rd., New Providence, NJ 07974. (908) 464-6800. 1988. Annual. Cumulative edition of the monthly Energy Information Abstracts. Monitors sources in the field of energy including the scientific, technical and business journal literature, conference and symposia proceedings, corporate, government and academic reports.

Energy Information Administration. James Forrestal Building, 1000 Independence Ave., S.W., Washington, DC 20585. (202) 586-5830.

Energy Information Centers Directory. U.S. Council for Energy Awareness, 1776 I St., N.W., Suite 400, Washington, DC 20006-2495. (202) 293-0770.

Energy Information Guide. R. David Weber. ABC-CLIO, PO Box 1911, Santa Barbara, CA 93116-1911. (805) 963-4221. 1982. Three volumes. Includes more than 2000 reference works on energy and energy related topics. Volume 1: General and Alternative Energy Sources; volume 2: Nuclear and Electric Power: volume 3: Fossil Fuels.

Energy Options. John Bockris. John Wiley & Sons, Inc., 605 3rd Ave., New York, NY 10158-0012. (212) 850-6000. 1980.

Energy Policy Implications of Global Warming. U.S. G.P.O., Washington, DC 20401. (202) 512-0000. 1989. Energy policy implications of the global warming trend and other climatic changes resulting from atmospheric concentrations of heat-retaining gases.

Energy Regulation: Hydropower Impacts on Fish Should be Adequately Considered. U.S. General Accounting Office, 441 G St., NW, Washington, DC (202) 275-5067. 1986.

Energy Research Guide Journals, Indexes and Abstracts. John Viola, et al. Ballinger Publishing Co., 10 E. 53rd St., New York, NY 10022. (212) 207-7581. 1983. Covers over 500 periodicals, indexes and abstracts covering energy or related fields. Section one: an alphabetical master list of all titles; section 2: subject list; section 3: description of each publication.

Energy Research Institute. 6850 Rattlesnake Hammock Rd., Hwy. 951, Naples, FL 33962. (813) 793-1922.

Energy Research Office. James Forrestal Building, 1000 Independence Ave., S.W., Washington, DC 20585. (202) 586-5430.

Energy Research Reports. ER Publications Inc., PO Box 157, 17 Langdon Ave., Watertown, MA 02172. (508) 872-8200. Twenty-two issues a year.

Energy Resource Institute–Directory of Energy Alternatives. Energy Research Institute, 6850 Rattlesnake Hammock Rd., Hwy. 951, Naples, FL 33962. (813) 793-1922.

Energy, Resources and Environment. John Blunden and Alan Reddish, eds. Hodder & Stoughton, PO Box 257, North Pomfret, VT 05053. (802) 457-1911. 1991.

Energy Statistics: Definitions, Units of Measure, and Conversion Factors. Department of International Economic and Social Affairs, Statistical Office. United Nations, 2 United Nations Plz., Salis Section, Rm. DC 2-853, New York, NY 10017. (800) 553-3210. 1987. Terminology of statistical methods in power resources.

Energy Storage Systems. National Technical Information Service, 5285 Port Royal Rd., Springfield, VA 22161. (703) 487-4650. Bimonthly.

Energy Technologies and the Environment. U.S. Department of Energy, 1000 Independence Avenue, SW, Washington, DC 20585. (202) 586-5000. 1988.

Energy Technologies for Reducing Emissions of Greenhouse Gases. OECD Publications and Information Center, 2001 L St. N.W., Suite 700, Washington, DC 20036. (202) 785-OECD. 1989. Gives suggestions for dealing with the emissions of gases that can produce a change in the global climate.

Energy Technology Characterizations Handbook. National Technical Information Service, 5285 Port Royal Rd., Springfield, VA 22161. (703) 487-4650. 1983. Environmental pollution and control factors.

Energy Terminology: A Multilingual Glossary. Pergamon Microforms International, Inc., Fairview Park, Elmsford, NY 10523. (914) 592-7720. 1986. Second edition. Contains 1500 defined terms and concepts related to the field of energy together with an index of several thousand undefined keywords used in the definitions of these terms and concepts. Contents appear in four languages: English, French, German and Spanish.

Energy, the Environment, and Public Policy: Issues for the 1990s. David L. McKee, ed. Praeger Publishers, 1 Madison Ave., New York, NY 10010-3603. (212) 685-5300. 1991. Addresses the extent and gravity of our environmental situation, from industrial waste to acid rain, from the Alaskan oil spill to the destruction of the rain forests.

Energy Today. Trends Publishing, Inc., 1079 National Press Bldg., Washington, DC 20045. (202) 393-0031. 1973-. Semimonthly.

Energy Update: A Guide to Current Literature. R. David Weber. Energy Information Press, 1100 Industrial Suite 9, San Carlos, CA 94070. (415) 594-0743. 1991. Some 1000 reference works are fully identified as well as 75 databases available for purchase or use on an online system. All forms of conventional and alternate energy sources are covered with consideration given to conservation and environmental impact.

Energy User News–Directory of Energy Consultants Issue. Fairchild Publications/Capitol Cities Media, Inc., 7 E. 12th St., New York, NY 10003. (212) 741-4428.

Enflex Info. ERM Computer Services, Inc., 855 Springdale Dr., Exton, PA 19341. (215) 524-3600. Text of all U.S. federal and state environmental regulations, including those covering hazardous materials, the transportation of hazardous materials, health and safety.

ENFO. 1251-B Miller Ave., Winter Park, FL 32789-4827. (407) 644-5377. Bimonthly. Water resources, parks, wildlife air quality, growth management, government and private actions.

Engine Manufacturers Association. 111 E. Wacker Dr., Chicago, IL 60601. (312) 644-6610.

Engineer Construction Equipment Repairer. U.S. Army Training Support Center, Reserve Schools Division, Fort Eusitis, VA 23604. (804) 878-5251. 1987.

Engineered Materials Abstracts. The Institute of Metals, Materials Information, 1 Carlton House Terrace, London, England SW1 Y5DB. 44 (71) 839-4071.

Engineered Plastics to 1995. FIND/SVP, 625 Avenue of the Americas, New York, NY 10011. (212) 645-4500. 1991. Market for engineered plastics, historical data, and forecasts by type and market.

Engineering and Mining Journal. Maclean Hunter Publishing Company, 29 N. Wacker Dr., Chicago, IL 60606. (312) 726-2802.

Engineering and Mining Journal–Buying Directory Issue. Maclean Hunter Publishing Company, 29 North Wacker Dr., Chicago, IL 60606. (312) 726-2802.

Engineering Field Manual. U.S. Soil Conservation Service, PO Box 2890, Washington, DC 20013. (202) 205-0027. 1984. Procedures recommended for water and soil conservation.

Engineering Index. The Engineering Index Inc., 345 E. 47th St., New York, NY 10017. 1962-.

Engineering Manual. Robert H. Perry. McGraw-Hill Science & Engineering Books, New York, NY 1976. A practical reference of design methods and data in building systems, chemical, civil, electrical, mechanical, and environmental engineering and energy conservation.

Engineering Research Center for Hazardous Substances Control. University of California, Los Angeles, 6722 Boelter Hall, Los Angeles, CA 90024. (213) 206-3071.

The Engineer's Clean Air Handbook. P. D. Osborn. Butterworth-Heinemann, Linacre House, Jordan Hill, Oxford, England OX2 8DP. (0865) 310366. 1989. Deals with the causes of various types of air pollution and the complicated nature of many of the pollutants. Also describes methods and necessary instrumentation for pollution removal. Includes a list of useful references.

English-Russian Dictionary of Environmental Protection: About 14,000 Terms. E.L. Milovanov. Pergamon Microforms International, Inc., Fairview Park, Elmsford, NY 10523. (914) 592-7720. 1981.

Enhanced Biodegradation of Pesticides in the Environment. Kenneth D. Racke and Joel R. Coats, eds. American Chemical Society, 1155 16th St. N.W., Washington, DC 20036. (202) 872-4600; (800) 227-5558. 1990. Discusses pesticides in the soil, microbial ecosystems, and the effects of long term application of herbicides on the soil.

Enhanced Recovery Week. Pasha Publications, Inc., 1401 Wilson Blvd., Suite 900, Arlington, VA 22209. (800) 424-2908.

Enquete Annuelle d'Entreprises dans l'Industrie. McGraw-Hill Science & Engineering Books, 11 W. 19th St., New York, NY 10011. (212) 337-6010.

ENREP. Commission of the European Communities, Database Distribution Service, 200 Rue de le Loi, Brussels, Belgium 1049. 32 (2) 2350001.

ENSDF-NSR. Brookhaven National Laboratory, National Nuclear Data Center, Building 197D, Upton, NY 11973. (516) 282-2901.

ENSI. Asian Institute of Technology, Environmental Sanitation Information Center, P.O. Box 2754, Bangkok, Thailand 10501. 66 (2) 5290100-13-X2870.

Entanglement Network Coalition. c/o Dr. Albert Manville II, Defenders of Wildlife, 1244 19th St. NW, Washington, DC 20036. (202) 659-9510.

Entering Adulthood. Creating a Healthy Environment: A Curriculum for Grades 9-12. Donna Lloyd-Kolkin. Network Publications, PO Box 1830, Santa Cruz, CA 95061-1830. (408) 438-4060. 1990.

Entomogenous Nematodes. George O. Polnar. Brill, Plantijnstraat 2, Postbus 9000, Leiden, Netherlands 2321 JC. 31 071 312 624. 1975. A manual and host list of insect-nematode associations.

Entomological Society of America. 9301 Annapolis Rd., Lanham, MD 20706-3115. (301) 731-4535.

Entropy: Into the Greenhouse World. Jeremy Rifkin. Bantam Books, 666 Fifth Ave., New York, NY 10103. (212) 765-6500. 1989.

Enumeration of Scientific Terms and Concepts Used in the Establishment of National Ambient Air Quality Standards. Patricia A. Porter. U.S. National Commission on Air Quality, Washington, DC 1980. Terminology of air quality.

Enviro/Energyline Abstracts Plus. R. R. Bowker Co., 121 Chanlon Rd., New Providence, NJ 07974. (908) 464-6800.

Enviroline. R. R. Bowker Co., Bowker Electronic Publishing, 121 Chanlon Rd., New Providence, NJ 07974. (800) 521-8110.

Environ: A Magazine for Ecological Living & Health Wary. Canary Press, Box 2204, Ft. Collins, CO 80522. (303) 224-0083. Quarterly. Consumer alternatives for ecologically sound lifestyles.

Environews. New York State Dept. of Law Environmental Protection Bureau, 2 World Trade Center, Rm. 4772, New York, NY 10048. (212) 341-2246. Bimonthly. News of environmental issues.

Environic Foundation International. 916 St. Vincent St., South Bend, IN 46617. (219) 259-9976.

Environment. Scientists Institute for Public Information, 560 Trinity Ave., St. Louis, MO 63130. 1958-. Monthly. Formerly Scientist and Citizen.

Environment. Newsbank, Inc., 58 Pine St., New Canaan, CT 06840. (203)966-1100. Monthly.

Environment. Heldref Publications, 4000 Albemarle Street, NW, Washington, DC 20016. (202) 362-6445. Ten a year. Covers science and science policy.

Environment Abstracts. Bowker A & I Publishing, 121 Chanlon Rd., New Providence, NJ 07974. (908) 464-6800. 1974-.

Environment and Energy. T. Nejat Veziroglu, ed. Nova Science Publishers, Inc., 283 Commack Rd., Ste. 300, Commack, NY 11725. (516) 499-3103. 1991. Based on a conference and a volume in the series Energy and Environmental Progress–I, Vol F. Deals mostly with environmental pollution engineering and the energy technology involved in the process.

Environment and Health: Themes in Medical Geography. Rais Akhtar, ed. Ashish Pub. House, Box 502, Columbia, MO 65205. (314) 474-0116. 1991. Discusses environmental health.

Environment and Plant Ecology. John Wiley & Sons Inc., 605 3rd Ave., New York, NY 10158-0012. (212) 850-6000. 1982. Topics in botanical ecology.

Environment and Quality of Life. OECD Publications and Information Center, 2001 L St., N.W., Suite 700, Washington, DC 20036. (202) 785-OECD. International comparisons of environmental data and environmental indicators, as well as more specific studies on water policy, energy policy, noise reduction and transportation in 24 member countries.

Environment Careers. PH Publishing, Inc., 760 Whalers Way, STE. 100-A, Fort Collins, CO 80525. (303) 229-0029. Monthly. Career opportunities in the field.

Environment Control for Animals and Plants. Louis D. Albright. American Society of Agricultural Engineers, 2950 Niles Rd., St. Joseph, MI 49085-9659. (616) 429-0300. 1990. Deals with the physical aspects of environmental control with some attention to biological factors relevant to successful environment control. Includes 10 executable computer programs that allow the user to explore design options.

Environment Daily. Pasha Publications Inc., 1401 Wilson Blvd., Suite 900, Arlington, VA 22209-9970. (703) 528-1244. 1991-. Daily. Reports brief wrap-up of the previous day's highlights from: Committee agendas and reports; Congressional Record; Federal Register; Agency Audits; CBD business opportunities; GAO, CBO, and OTA studies; Budget documents; court decisions; advocacy groups.

Environment-Employment-New Industrial Societies. Maryse Gaudier. International Labour Organization, H4, rue des Morillons, Geneva 22, Switzerland CH-1211. 1991. Situates environmental issues within the context of industrial societies at the threshold of the 21st century; critically evaluates the harmonization of ecology, modern technology and human resources.

Environment-Employment–New Industrial Societies: A Bibliographic Map. International Labor Organization, 4, rue des Morillons, Geneva 22, Switzerland CH-1211. 1991.

Environment, Energy, and Society. Craig R. Humphrey. Wadsworth Pub. Co., 10 Davis Dr., Belmont, CA 94002. (415) 595-2350. 1982. Social aspects of environmental and population policy and the green revolution.

Environment Hawaii. Environment Hawaii Pub., Honolulu, HI

Environment, Health and Natural Resources Department: Air Quality. Director, Environmental Management, PO Box 27687, Raleigh, NC 27611. (919) 733-7015.

Environment, Health and Natural Resources Department: Coastal Zone Management. Director, Coastal Management Division, PO Box 27687, Raleigh, NC 27611. (919) 733-2293.

Environment, Health and Natural Resources Department: Environmental Protection. Secretary, PO Box 27687, Raleigh, NC 27611. (919) 733-4984.

Environment, Health and Natural Resources Department: Fish and Wildlife. Executive Director, Wildlife Resources Division, PO Box 27687, Raleigh, NC 27611. (919) 733-3391.

Environment, Health and Natural Resources Department: Groundwater Management. Groundwater Chief, Division of Environment Management, PO Box 27687, Raleigh, NC 27611. (919) 733-3221.

Environment, Health and Natural Resources Department: Natural Resources. Secretary, PO Box 27687, Raleigh, NC 27611. (919) 733-4984.

Environment, Health and Natural Resources Department: Waste Minimization and Pollution Prevention. Information Officer, Pollution Prevention Pays Program, PO Box 27687, Raleigh, NC 27611. (919) 733-7015.

Environment, Health and Natural Resources Department: Water Quality. Director, Environmental Management, 512 North Salisbury St., Raleigh, NC 27604-1148. (919) 733-7015.

Environment Ideology and Policy. Frances Sandbach. Rowman & Littlefield, Publishers, Inc., 8705 Bollman Pl., Savage, MD 20763. (301) 306-0400. 1980. Describes the environmental movement, behavioral assessments, alternative technologies, environmental evaluation, economic analysis, environmental policies and other environment related areas.

Environment Impact of Nonpoint Source Pollution. Michael R. Overcash and James M. Davidson, eds. Ann Arbor Science, 230 Collingwood, Ann Arbor, MI 48106. 1980.

Environment in Key Words: A Multilingual Handbook of the Environment: English-French-German-Russian. Isaac Paenson. Pergamon Microforms International, Inc., Fairview Park, Elmsford, NY 10523. (914) 592-7720. 1990. Two volumes. Terminology in the areas of ecology, environmental protection, pollution, conservation of natural resources and related areas.

Environment in Peril. Anthony B. Wolbarst, ed. Smithsonian Institution Press, 470 L'Enfant Plaza, No. 7100, Washington, DC 20560. (800) 782-4612. 1991. Brings together in one volume the primary concerns of eleven of the world's leaders in conservation, ecology and public policy. Broad environmental issues covered are: ozone depletion, overpopulation, global warming, thinning forests, extinction of species, spreading deserts, toxic chemicals, and various pollutants.

Environment Index. Environment Information Center, Index Research Department, 124 E. 39th St., New York, NY 10016. 1971-. Annual.

Environment International: A Journal of Science, Technology, Health, Monitoring and Policy. Pergamon Microforms International, Inc., Fairview Park, Elmsford, NY 10523. (914) 592-7720. 1974-. Bimonthly. Includes vital data, causes of pollution, and methods for protection, covering the entire field of environmental protection.

Environment Library. OCLC Online Computer Library Center, Inc., 6565 Frantz Rd., Dublin, OH 43017. (614) 764-6000. Bibliographic and cataloging information for English and foreign-language materials on the topic of environmental issues.

Environment Midwest. U.S. Environmental Protection Agency, 230 S. Dearborn, Chicago, IL 60604. (312) 353-2072. Monthly. Programs for fighting air and water pollution, hazardous and solid wastes, toxicants, pesticides, noise, and radiation.

Environment Ohio. Ohio Environmental Protection Agency, PO Box 1049, Columbus, OH 43216. (614) 644-2160. Bimonthly. Air, water, land pollution, and public water supply.

Environment Periodicals Bibliography. Environmental Studies Institute, International Academy at Santa Barbara, 800 Garden St., Suite D, Santa Barbara, CA 993101. (805) 965-5010. 6 issues plus a cumulative annual index. Indexes journal articles relevant to environmental issues. Includes broad subject areas such as: air, energy, land resources, agriculture, marine and fresh water resources, water pollution, water management, effluents, sewage and pollution, nutrition and health, acid rain. Covers over 350 journal titles.

The Environment: Problems and Solutions. Stuart Bruchey, ed. Garland Publishing, Inc., 1000A Sherman Ave., Hamden, CT 06514. (203) 281-4487. 1991. Topics covered: forested wetlands and agriculture, the political economy of smog in southern California, environmental limits to growth in world agriculture, the tradeoff between cost and risk in hazardous waste management, and the protection of groundwater from agricultural pollution.

Environment Report. Trends Publishing, Inc., 1079 National Press Bldg., Washington, DC 20045. (202) 393-0031. Semimonthly. Developments in environment, ecology and pollution abatement, with emphasis on policy, research, and development.

Environment Reporter. Bureau of National Affairs, 1231 25th St., N.W., Rm. 215, Washington, DC 20037. (800) 372-1033. Online version of periodical of the same name.

Environment Reporter. Bureau of National Affairs, 1231 25th St. NW, Washington, DC 20037. (800) 372-1033. Weekly. Issues of pollution control and environmental activity. Also available online.

Environment Research. Academic Press, c/o Harcourt Brace Jovanovich Inc., 6277 Sea Harbor Dr., Orlando, FL 32887. (800) 346-8648. Bimonthly. Journal of environmental medicine and sciences.

Environment, Resources, and Conservation. Susan Owens and Peter L. Owens. Cambridge University Press, 40 W 20th St., New York, NY 10011. (212) 924-3900 or (800) 227-0247. 1991. The book studies three cases illuminating problems and policy responses at three levels of geographic scale–international, national, and local. The case of acid rain is used to illustrate a pollution problem with international dimensions; the British coal industry is analyzed as an example of national nonrenewable resource depletion; and renewable wetland ecosystem management illustrates a local concern by analyzing conservation measures.

Environment, Safety and Health Office: Department of Energy. James Forrestal Building, 1000 Independence Ave., S.W., Washington, DC 20585. (202) 586-6151.

Environment Today. Enterprise Communications Inc., 1483 Chain Bridge Rd., Suite 202, McLean, VA 22101-4599. (703) 448-0322. Nine times a year. Magazine for environmental professionals, including corporate waste generators, municipal utilities managers, and governmental decision makers.

Environment Week. King Communications Group, Inc., 627 National Press Bldg., Washington, DC 20045. (202) 638-4260. Weekly. Covers acid rain, solid waste and disposal, clean coal, nuclear and hazardous waste. Also available online.

Environment Week. NewsNet, Inc., 945 Haverford Rd., Bryn Mawr, PA 19010. (800) 345-1301. Online version of periodical of same name.

Environmental Action. Environmental Action Foundation, 6930 Carroll Ave., Ste. 600, Takoma Park, MD 20912. (301) 891-1100. Bimonthly. Impact of humans and industry on the environment.

Environmental Action Coalition. 625 Broadway, 2nd Fl., New York, NY 10012. (212) 677-1601.

Environmental Action Foundation. 6930 Carroll Ave., 6th Fl., Takoma Park, MD 20912. (202) 745-4870.

Environmental Action, Inc. 1525 New Hampshire Ave., NW, Washington, DC 20036. (202) 745-4870.

The Environmental Address Book: How to Reach the Environment's Greatest Champions and Worst Offenders. Michael Levine. Perigee Books, 200 Madison Ave., New York, NY 10016. (800) 631-8571. 1991. Names and addresses of organizations, agencies, celebrities, political figures, and businesses (local, state, national, and international level) concerned with the state of the world's environment.

Environmental Affairs. Boston College Law School, 885 Centre St., Newton Center, MA 02159. Quarterly. Legal issues regarding the environment.

Environmental Affairs Agency: Hazardous Waste Management. Chairman, Waste Management Board, 1020 Ninth St., Suite 300, Sacramento, CA 95814. (916) 322-3330.

Environmental Affairs Agency: Solid Waste Management. Chairman, Waste Management Board, 1020 Ninth St., Suite 300, Sacramento, CA 95814. (916) 322-3330.

An Environmental Agenda for the Future. John H. Adams, et al. Island Press, 1718 Connecticut Ave. N.W., Washington, DC 20009. (202) 232-7933. 1985. Contains articles by the CEOs of the 10 largest environmental organizations in the United States.

Environmental Almanac. World Resources Institute. Houghton Mifflin, 1 Beacon St., Boston, MA 02108. (617) 725-5000; (800) 225-3362. 1991. Covers consumer products, energy, endangered species, food safety, global warming, solid wastes, toxics, wetlands and other related areas. Also included are the names and addresses of the chief environmental executives for all 50 states.

Environmental America. D.J. Herda. Millbrook Press, 2 Old New Milford Rd., PO Box 335, Brookfield, CT 06804-0335. (203) 740-2220. 1991. Focuses on environmental issues, concerns and steps being taken to counteract damage.

Environmental Analysis: For Land Use and Site Planning. McGraw-Hill Science & Engineering Books, 11 W. 19th St., New York, NY 10011. (212) 337-6010. 1978.

The Environmental and Biological Behavior of Plutonium and Some Other Transuranium Elements. NEA Group of Experts. OECD Publications and Information Center, 2 rue Andre Pascal, Paris, France F-75775. 1981. Environmental aspects of transuranium elements and transuranium and plutonium elements in the body.

Environmental & Ecological Services. American Business Directories, Inc., 5711 S. 86th Circle, Omaha, NE 68127. (402) 593-4600.

Environmental and Energy Study Institute. 122 C St., N.W., Suite 700, Washington, DC 20001. (202) 628-1400.

Environmental & Energy Study Institute. 122 C St., N.W., Suite 700, Washington, DC 20001. (202) 628-1400.

Environmental and Experimental Botany. Pergamon Microforms International, Inc., Fairview Park, Elmsford, NY 10523. (914) 592-7720. 1960-. An international journal covering radiation botany, photobotany, chemical mutagenesis, anatomy and morphology, cytogenetics and somatic cell genetics.

Environmental and Functional Engineering of Agricultural Buildings. Henry J. Barre. Van Nostrand Reinhold, 115 5th Ave., New York, NY 10003. (212) 254-3232. 1988.

Environmental and Metabolic Animal Physiology. C. Ladd Prosser, ed. John Wiley & Sons, Inc., Wiley-Liss Division, 605 3rd Ave., New York, NY 10158-0012. (212) 850-6000. 1991. 4th ed. Focuses on the various aspects of adaptive physiology, including environmental, biochemical, and regulatory topics. Examines the theory of adaptation, water and ions, temperature and hydrostatic pressure, nutrition, digestion, nitrogen metabolism, and energy transfer, respiration, O2 and CO2 transport and circulation.

Environmental and Molecular Mutagenesis. Wiley-Liss, 605 3rd Ave., New York, NY 10158-0012. (212) 850-6000. 1974-. Eight issues per year. Provides an international forum for research on basic mechanisms of mutation, the detection of mutagens, and the implications of environmental mutagens for human health.

Environmental and Urban Issues. FAU/FIU Joint Center for Environmental and Urban Problems, Florida Atlantic University, Fort Lauderdale, FL 33301. Quarterly. Environmental policy and regional planning in Florida.

Environmental Aspects of Applied Biology. Association of Applied Biologists, Institute of Horticultural Research, Littlehampton, England BN17 6LP. Warwick 1988. Volume 1 contains environmental impacts of crop protection and practices within the agricultural ecosystem (crop protection topics). Volume 2 includes environmental aspects of post-harvest practices, the plant response to the combined stresses of pollution, climate and soil conditions, and the straw problem. Includes bibliographies.

Environmental Aspects of Artificial Aeration and Oxygenation of Reservoirs: A Review of Theory, Techniques, and Experiences. Robert A. Pastorok. National Technical Information Service, 5285 Port Royal Rd., Springfield, VA 22161. (703) 487-4650. 1982. Environmental and water quality operation studies, and impact analysis relating to aeration treatment of wastewater.

Environmental Aspects of Coasts and Islands. BAR, Oxford, England 1981. Maritime anthropology, coastal ecology and environmental ecology.

Environmental Aspects of Iron and Steel Production: A Technical Review. Industry & Environment Office, United Nations Environment Programme, Paris, France 1986. Waste disposal in the iron and steel industry.

Environmental Aspects of Irrigation and Drainage. American Society of Civil Engineers, 345 E. 47th St., New York, NY 10017. (212) 705-7288. 1976.

Environmental Aspects of Plantation Forestry in Wales. J. E. G. Good, ed. Institute of Terrestrial Ecology, Merlewood Research Station, Grange-Over-Sands, England LA11 6JU. Cumbria 1987. Proceedings of a symposium held at the Snowdonia National Park Study Centre, Plas Tan-Y-Bwlch, Maentwrog, Gwynedd, North Wales, 20-21 November 1986.

Environmental Aspects of Potential Petroleum Exploration and Exploitation in Antarctica. Katherine A. Green Hammond. National Technical Information Service, 5285 Port Royal Rd., Springfield, VA 22161. (703) 487-4650. 1982. Forecasting and evaluating risks.

Environmental Assessment of a Reciprocating Engine Retrofitted with Selective Catalytic Reduction. C. Castaldini. National Technical Information Service, 5285 Port Royal Rd., Springfield, VA 22161. (703) 487-4650. Measurement of flue gases and environmental aspects of internal combustion engines.

An Environmental Assessment of Potential Gas and Leachate Problems at Land Disposal Sites. U.S. Environmental Protection Agency, 401 M St. SW, Washington, DC 20460. (202) 260-2090. 1975.

Environmental Assessment of Waste-to-Energy Processes. National Technical Information Service, 5285 Port Royal Rd., Springfield, VA 22161. (703) 487-4650. 1977. Environmental aspects of refuse as fuel.

Environmental Auditor: Compliance-Risk Assessment-Resource Management. Springer-Verlag, 175 5th Ave., New York, NY 10010. (212) 460-1500. Quarterly.

Environmental Audits. Government Institutes Inc., 4 Research Place, #200, Rockville, MD 20850. (301) 921-2300. 6th edition. Contains guidance for conducting and managing environmental audit.

The Environmental Behaviour of Radium. International Atomic Energy Agency, Vienna International Centre, Wagromerstrasse 5, Postfach 100, Vienna, Austria A-1400. 1990. Covers radium measurement, environmental monitoring and impact analysis.

Environmental Bibliography. Environmental Studies Institute, International Academy at Santa Barbara, 800 Garden St., Ste. D, Santa Barbara, CA 93101. (805) 965-5010. International periodical literature dealing with environmental topics such as air pollution, water treatment, energy conservation, noise abatement, soil mechanics, wildlife preservation, and chemical wastes.

Environmental Biogeochemistry. R. Hallberg. Publishing House/FRN, P.O. Box 6711, Stockholm, Sweden S-113 85. 08-15-1580. 1983. Biogeochemistry and environmental engineering.

Environmental Biology. E. J. W. Barrington. John Wiley & Sons, Inc., 605 3rd Ave., New York, NY 10158-0012. (212) 850-6000. 1980. Resource and Environmental Series.

Environmental Biology for Engineers. George Camougis. McGraw-Hill Science & Engineering Books, 11 West 19th St., New York, NY 10011. (212) 337-6010. 1981. Deals with environmental impact analysis, ecology, environmental engineering and environmental legislation.

Environmental Biology of Fishes. Dr. W. Junk Publishers, Postbus 163, Dordrecht, Netherlands 3300 AD. 1976-.

Environmental Biotechnology. A. Balaozej and V. Prnivarovna, eds. Elsevier Science Publishing Co., 655 Avenue of the Americas, New York, NY 10010. (212) 989-5800. 1991. Proceedings of the International Symposium on Biotechnology, Bratislava, Czechoslovakia, June 27-29, 1990.

Environmental Biotechnology for Waste Treatment. Gary S. Sayler, et al., eds. Plenum Press, 233 Spring St., New York, NY 10013-1578. (212) 620-8000. 1991. Symposium on Environmental Biotechnology: Moving from the Flask to the Field. Knoxville, TN, 1990.

Environmental Biotechnology: Reducing Risks from Environmental Chemicals through Biotechnology. Gilbert S. Omenn. Plenum Press, 233 Spring St., New York, NY 10013-1578. (212) 620-8000. Covers environmental aspects of the chemical and biological treatment of sewage.

Environmental Bulletin. New Jersey Conservation Foundation, 300 Mendham Rd., Morristown, NJ 07960. (201) 539-7540. Monthly. State environmental legislation bulletin.

Environmental Business Journal. EnviroQuest, PO Box 371769, San Diego, CA 92137. (619) 295-7685. Monthly. Products relating to environmental protection.

Environmental Business Journal. EnviroQuest, PO Box 371769, San Diego, CA 92137. (619) 295-7685. Online access.

Environmental Career Guide: Job Opportunities with the Earth in Mind. Nicholas Basta. John Wiley & Sons, Inc., 605 3rd Ave., New York, NY 10158-0012. (212) 850-6000. 1991. Complete guide to the many career options in the growing environmental field. Shows how to find employers engaged in environmental activity, and how to get the job. Lists key environmental businesses–manufacturing, government agencies, engineering consulting firms, waste handling firms, and others. Lists key professional careers in environmental conservation and maps career strategies.

The Environmental Challenge of the 1990's. U.S. Environmental Protection Agency, 401 M St. SW, Washington, DC 20460. (202) 260-2090. 1991. Provides an overview of past and present projects for pollution prevention, focusing on the promotion of clean technologies and clean products in both the public and private sectors. Covers new prevention ideas relating to solid and hazardous wastes, pesticides, drinking water, wastewater and toxic substances.

Environmental Change in Iceland: Past and Present. Judith K. Maizels and Chris Caseldine, eds. Kluwer Academic Publishers, 101 Philip Dr., Assinippi Park, Norwell, MA 02061. (617) 871-6600. 1991. Describes the glacial landforms and paleoclimatology in Iceland. Volume 7 of the Glaciology and Quaternary Geology Series.

Environmental Chemistry. Stanley E. Manahan. Lewis Publishers, 2000 Corporate Blvd., N.W., Boca Raton, FL 33431. (407) 994-0555 or (800) 272-7737. 1991. Fifth edition. Deals with environmental chemistry and chemical hazards.

Environmental Chemistry. Royal Society of Chemistry, Burlington House, Piccadilly, London, England W1V 0BN. 71 4378656. Biennial. A review of recent literature concerning the organic chemistry of environments.

Environmental Chemistry and Toxicology of Aluminum. Timothy E. Lewis. Lewis Publishers, 2000 Corporate Blvd., N.W., Boca Raton, FL 33431. (407) 994-0555 or (800) 272-7737. 1989. Examines the sources, fate, transport, and health effects of aluminum in aquatic and terrestrial environments. Also includes the latest advances in the study of aluminum in the environment; toxicity research–aquatic and terrestrial biota; neurotoxicity and possible links to Alzheimer's disease; different forms of aluminum in soils and soil water; coordination chemistry; specification and analytical methods.

Environmental Chemistry: Australian Perspective. Greg Laidler. Longman Cheshire, South Melbourne, Australia 1991.

The Environmental Chemistry of Aluminum. Garrison Sposito. CRC Press, 2000 Corporate Blvd. N.W., Boca Raton, FL 33431. (800) 272-7737. 1989. Environmental aspects of aluminum content in water, soil and acid deposition.

Environmental Chemistry of Herbicides. Raj Grover and Alan J. Cessna. CRC Press, 2000 Corporate Blvd. N.W., Boca Raton, FL 33431. (800) 272-7737. 1990. Vol. 1: Adsorption and bioavailability. Mass flow and dispersion, herbicides in surface waters. Evaporation from soils and crops. Dissipation from soil. Transformations in soil. Vol. 2: Dissipation of transformations in water and sediment. Nature, transport, and fate of airborne residues, absorption and transport in plants. Transformations in biosphere. Bioaccumulation and food chain accumulation. Photochemical transformations. Bound residues. Predictability and environmental chemistry.

Environmental Claims Journal. Executive Enterprises Publications Co., Inc., 22 W. 21st St., New York, NY 10010-6990. (212) 645-7880. Quarterly. News of environmental professionals, risk managers, and insurance executives.

Environmental Coalition on Nuclear Power. 433 Orlando Ave., State College, PA 16803. (814) 237-3900.

Environmental Combination by Lead and Other Heavy Metals. University of Illinois, Institute for Environmental Studies, Urbana, IL 61801. 1977.

Environmental Communication and Public Relations Handbook. Government Institutes, Inc., 4 Research Pl., Ste. 200, Rockville, MD 20850. (301) 921-2300. Managing the environmental disclosure requirements of OSHA and SARA.

Environmental Communicator. North American Association for Environmental Education, P.O. Box 400, Troy, OH 45373. (513) 339-6835. Bimonthly. Information on environmental topics and teaching methods.

Environmental Compliance in your State. Business and Legal Reports, 64 Wall St., Madison, CT 06443. (203) 245-7448. Monthly. Environmental law at the national and state levels.

Environmental Compliance Institute. Aetna Bldg., Suite 850, 2350 Lakeside Blvd., Richardson, TX 75082-4342. (214) 644-8971.

Environmental Compliance Letter. Ste. 850, 2350 Lakeside Blvd., Richardson, TX 75085. (214) 644-8971. Regulatory issues on environment.

Environmental Compliance Update. High Tech Publishing Co., Ridge, NY

Environmental Conference. TAPPI Press, Technology Park/ Atlanta, PO Box 105113, Atlanta, GA 30348. (404) 446-1400. 1980-. Annually. Conference papers include topics relating to the environment such as: landfill permitting; bleach plant emissions; environmental control; sludge dewatering; air toxics regulations and risk assessment as they relate to pulp and paper industry; water reuse and load control; water toxins; air modeling; and other pertinent environmental topics.

Environmental Consequences of and Control Processes for Energy Technologies. Argonne National Laboratory. Noyes Publications, 120 Mill Rd., Park Ridge, NJ 07656. (201) 391-8484. 1990. Describes energy technologies which will be in use in the United States during the next 20 years.

Environmental Conservation Department: Air Quality. Chief, Air and Hazardous Waste Management Science, PO Box O, Juneau, AK 99811-1800. (907) 465-2666.

Environmental Conservation Department: Environmental Protection. Commissioner, PO Box O, Juneau, AK 99811-1800. (907) 465-4100.

Environmental Conservation Department: Groundwater Management. Chief, Water Quality Management, PO Box O, Juneau, AK 99811-1800. (907) 465-2634.

Environmental Conservation Department: Hazardous Waste Management. Chief, Hazardous Waste Management Section, PO Box O, Juneau, AK 99811-1800. (907) 465-2666.

Environmental Conservation Department: Solid Waste Management. Chief, Hazardous Waste Management Section, PO Box O, Juneau, AK 99811-1800. (907) 465-2666.

Environmental Conservation Department: Water Quality. Chief, Water Quality Management, PO Box O, Juneau, AK 99811. (907) 465-2634.

Environmental Conservation: The Oil and Gas Industries: An Overview. National Petroleum Council, 1625 K St., NW, Washington, DC 20006. (202) 393-6100. 1981.

Environmental Contamination Following a Major Nuclear Accident. STI/PUB, UNIPUB, 4611-F Assembly Dr., Lanham, MD 20706. (301) 459-7666 or (800) 274-4888. 1991. Two volumes. Reviews the extent and magnitude of environmental contamination occurring after a massive release of radioactive materials.

Environmental Contamination of Lead and Other Heavy Metals. G. L. Rolfe. Institute for Environmental Studies, University of Illinois at Urbana- Champaign, Urbana-Champaign, IL 61801. 1977. Environmental aspects of lead pollution.

Environmental Control Department: Underground Storage Tanks. Division Chief, Land Quality Division, 301 Centennial Mall S., PO Box 94877, Lincoln, NE 68509. (402) 471-2186.

Environmental Control for Agricultural Buildings. Merle L. Esmay. AVI Pub. Co., 250 Post Rd. E., PO Box 831, Westport, CT 06881. 1986.

Environmental Control for Confinement Livestock Housing. Don D. Jones. Purdue University, Cooperative Extension Service, West Lafayette, IN 47907. (317) 494-8489. 1980. Heating and ventilation of livestock housing.

Environmental Control for Pulp and Paper Mills. Howard Edde. Noyes Publications, 120 Mill Rd., Park Ridge, NJ 07656. (201) 391-8484. 1984. Pollution technology review of pulp and paper making and trade.

Environmental Control News. E.F. Williams, 3637 Park Ave. #224, Memphis, TN 38111. (901) 458-4696. Monthly. Regulatory, legislative, environmental, and technical developments.

Environmental Costs of Electricity. Richard L. Ottinger, et al. Oceana Publications Inc., 75 Main St., Dobbs Ferry, NY 10522. (914) 693-8100. 1990. Report reviews and analyzes the studies that have been made to quantify the external costs of environmental damages caused by electric supply and demand-reduction technologies. It reviews ways to incorporate these costs in electric utility planning, bid evaluation and resource selection procedures.

Environmental Crimes at DOE's Nuclear Weapons Facilities. House Committee on Energy and Commerce. U.S. G.P.O., Washington, DC 20401. (202) 512-0000. 1990. Management of nuclear facilities, safety regulations, and environmental health.

Environmental Data Bases: Design, Implementation, and Maintenance. Gene Y. Michael. Lewis Publishers, 2000 Corporate Blvd., N.W., Boca Raton, FL 33431. (407) 994-0555 or (800) 272-7737. 1991. Describes how the data bases for environmental information came into existence. Includes data requirements, design, software, hardware configurations, PC system management, and other related matters.

Environmental Data Compendium. OECD Publications and Information Center, 2001 L St., N.W., Suite 700, Washington, DC 20036. (202) 785-6323. 1989.

Environmental Defense Fund. 257 Park Ave., S., New York, NY 10010. (212) 505-2100. Non-profit organization that was established more than 20 years ago. Its goals are to protect the earth's environment by providing lasting solutions to global environmental problems.

Environmental Defense Fund Letter. Environmental Defense Fund, 257 Park Avenue South, New York, NY 10010. (212) 505-2100. 1971-. Bimonthly. Environmental issues of concern.

Environmental Degradation and Crisis in India. S. S. Negi. Indus Pub. Co. (South Asia Books), Box 502, Columbia, MO 65205. (314) 474-0116. 1991. Discusses environmental planning and management in the conservation of natural resources.

Environmental Design Research Association. P.O. Box 24083, Oklahoma City, OK 73124. (405) 843-4863.

Environmental Determinism in Twentieth Century American Geography: Reflection in the Professional Journals. Joanna Eunice Beck. University of California Press, 2120 Berkeley Way, Berkeley, CA 94720. (510) 642-4262; (800) 822-6657. 1985. Covers human ecology and man's influence on the environment.

The Environmental Dictionary. James J. King. PennWell Books, PO Box 21288, Tulsa, OK 74121. (918) 831-9421; (800) 752-9764. 1989. Gives more than 5,000 definitions of terms used and applied by the EPA.

Environmental Dispute Handbook: Liability and Claims. Robert E. Carpenter, et al. John Wiley & Sons, Inc., 605 3rd Ave., New York, NY 10158-0012. (212) 850-6000. 1991. Two volumes. Explains as clearly as possible the claims and liabilities arising from environmental litigation. Covers environmental liability; parties potentially liable for environmental damage, such as property owners, insurers, transporters, etc.; remedies; and procedural considerations.

Environmental Disputes: Community Involvement in Conflict Resolution. James E. Crowfoot and Julia M. Wondolleck, eds. Island Press, 1718 Connecticut Ave. N.W., Suite 300, Washington, DC 20009. (202) 232-7933. 1990. Set of procedures for settling disputes over environmental policies without litigation.

Environmental Economics: A Guide to Information Sources. Barry C. Field and Cleve E. Willis. Gale Research Co., 835 Penobscot Bldg., Detroit, MI 48226-4094. (313) 961-2242. 1979. Man and the Environment Information Guide Series; v.8

Environmental Economics and Management: Pollution and Natural Resources. Finn R. Forsund. Croom Helm, 51 Washington St., Dover, NH 03820. (603) 749-5038. 1988. Covers environmental policy, pollution, human ecology, and natural resources.

Environmental Education: A Guide to Information Sources. William B. Stapp. Gale Research Co., 835 Penobscot Bldg., Detroit, MI 48226-4094. (313) 961-2242. 1975. Man and the Environment Information Guide Series; v.1.

Environmental Education Report and Newsletter. American Society for Environmental Education, P.O. Box 800, White River, NH 03755. (603) 448-6697. Quarterly. Contemporary environmental issues.

Environmental Effects of Dredging. U.S. Army Corps of Engineers, Waterways Experiment Station, PO Box 631, Vicksburg, MS 39180. (601) 634-3774. Quarterly. Effects of dredging and dredged material disposal operations and the development of technically, environmentally, and economically feasible dredging and disposal alternatives.

Environmental Effects of Energy Systems: The OECD COMPASS Project. OECD Publications and Information Center, 2 rue Andre Pascal, Paris, France F-75775. 1983. Environmental aspects of energy development.

Environmental Effects of the Uranium Fuel Cycle; A Review of Data for Technetium. J. E. Till. U.S. Nuclear Regulatory Commission, Office for Nuclear Reactor Regulation, Division of Systems Integration, Washington, DC 20555. (301) 492-7000. 1985. Environmental aspects of the uranium industry, particularly technetium.

Environmental Encyclopedia. William P. Cunningham, Terence Ball, et. al. Gale Research Inc., 835 Penobscot Bldg., Detroit, MI 48226-4094. (313) 961-2242. 1993.

Environmental Engineering. Mary A. Vance. Vance Bibliographies, PO Box 229, 112 N. Charter St., Monticello, IL 61856. (217) 762-3831. 1983.

Environmental Engineering and Sanitation. Joseph A. Salvato. John Wiley & Sons, Inc., 605 3rd Ave., New York, NY 10158-0012. (212) 850-6000. 1992. 3d ed. Applies principles of sanitary science and engineering to sanitation and environmental health. It includes design, construction, maintenance, and operations of sanitation plants and structures. Provides state-of-the-art information on environmental factors associated with chronic and non-infectious diseases; environmental engineering planning and impact analysis; waste management and control; food sanitation; administration of health and sanitation programs; acid rain; noise control; campground sanitation, etc.

Environmental Engineering and Sciences Department. Virginia Polytech Institute and State University, 330 Norris Hall, Department of Civil Engineering, Blacksburg, VA 24061. (703) 961-6635.

Environmental Engineering Dictionary. C. C. Lee. Government Institutes, Inc., 4 Research Pl., Ste. 200, Rockville, MD 20850. (301) 921-2300. 1989. Defines over 6000 engineering terms relating to pollutioncontrol technologies, monitoring, risk assessment, sampling andanalysis, quality control, permitting, and environmentally-regulated engineering and science. Includes bibliographical references (p. 612-627).

Environmental Engineering News. Purdue University, School of Civil Engineering, Lafayette, IN 47907. (317) 494-2194. Monthly. Trends in environmental engineering.

Environmental Engineering Science Research Laboratory. University of Florida, College of Engineering, 217 Black Hall, Gainesville, FL 32611. (904) 392-0841.

Environmental Engineering Selection Guide. American Academy of Environmental Engineers, 132 Holiday Ct., # 206, Annapolis, MD 21401. (301) 266-3311. Annual. Certified environmental engineers in consulting, education, and manufacturing.

Environmental Entomology. Entomological Society of America, 9301 Annapolis Road, Lanham, MD 20706. (301) 731-4538. Bimonthly. Covers ecology and population dynamics.

Environmental Ethics. Environmental Ethics, Department of Philosophy, University of North Texas, P.O. Box 13496, Denton, TX 76203-3496. (817) 565-2727. Quarterly. Covers philosophical aspects of environmental problems.

Environmental Ethics. Holmes Tolston. Temple University Press, 1601 N. Broad St., USB 306, Philadelphia, PA 19122. (215) 787-8787. 1988.

Environmental Ethics: A Selected Bibliography for the Environmental Professional. Deborah A. Simmons. Council of Planning Librarians, 1313 E. 60th St., Chicago, IL 60637-2897. (312) 942-2163. 1988. Moral and ethical aspects of human ecology.

Environmental Ethics for Engineers. Alistairs Gunn and P. Aarne Veslind. Lewis Publishers, 2000 Corporate Blvd.,N.W., Boca Raton, FL 33431. (407) 994-0555 or (800) 272-7737. 1986. Consists of two parts. The first part is a primer on professional ethics as applied to the environment. The second part is comprised of various articles. Some are written to foster a development ofenvironmental ethics, while others deal with controversial issues and professional approaches to ethics.

Environmental Fact Sheet: EPA's Endangered Species Protection Program. U.S. Environmental Protection Agency, Office of Pesticides and Toxic Substances, 401 M St. SW, Washington, DC 20460. (202) 260-2090. 1990.

Environmental Fact Sheet: Mercury Biocides in Paint. U.S. Environmental Protection Agency, Office of Pesticides and Toxic Substances, 401 M St. SW, Washington, DC 20460. (202) 260-2090. 1990.

Environmental Fact Sheet: Pesticide Reregistration. U.S. Environmental Protection Agency, Office of Pesticides and Toxic Substances, 401 M St. SW, Washington, DC 20460. (202) 260-2090. 1990.

Environmental Fact Sheet: Pesticide Tolerances. U.S. Environmental Protection Agency, Office of Pesticides and Toxic Substances, 401 M St. SW, Washington, DC 20460. (202) 260-2090. 1990.

Environmental Fact Sheet: Risk/Benefit Balancing Under the Federal Insecticide, Fungicide, and Rodenticide Act. U.S. Environmental Protection Agency, Office of Pesticides and Toxic Substances, 401 M St. SW, Washington, DC 20460. (202) 260-2090. 1990.

Environmental Fact Sheet: The Delaney Paradox and Negligible Risk. U.S. Environmental Protection Agency, Office of Pesticides and Toxic Substances, 401 M St. SW, Washington, DC 20460. (202) 260-2090. 1990.

Environmental Fate Databases. Syracuse Research Cooperation, Merrill Lane, Syracuse, NY 13210. (312) 426-3200. Environmental fate of chemicals.

Environmental Forum. Environmental Law Institute, 1616 P St., N.W., # 200, Washington, DC 20036. (202) 328-5150. Bimonthly. Policy on environmental protection.

Environmental Fund. Population-Environment Balance, 1325 6th St., N.W., #1003, Washington, DC 20005. Population-environment balance.

The Environmental Gardener: The Solution to Pollution for Lawns and Gardens. Laurence Sombke. MasterMedia, 17 E. 89th St., New York, NY 10128. (212) 348-2020. 1991.

Environmental Geochemistry and Health. Society for Environmental Geochemistry and Health, c/o Willard R. Chappell, University of Colorado, Denver, Center for Environmental Sciences, Campus Box 136, Denver, CO 80204. (303) 556-3460. Quarterly.

Environmental Geography: A Handbook for Teachers. Keith Wheeler. Hart-Davis Educational, St. Albans, England 1976. Study and teaching of human ecology.

Environmental Geology. Ronald W. Tank. Oxford University Press, 200 Madison Ave., New York, NY 10016. (212) 679-7300. 1983. Mines, mineral resources, natural disasters and conservation of natural resources.

Environmental Geology & Water Sciences. Springer-Verlag, 175 Fifth Avenue, New York, NY 10010. (212) 460-1500. Bimonthly. Covers interactions between humanity and Earth.

Environmental Grantmaking Foundations. Environmental Data Research Institute, 797 Elmwood Avenue, Rochester, NY 14620-2946. (800) 724-0968. 1992. Fund raising for regional, state, and local organizations that work on environmental issues.

The Environmental Handbook for Property Transfer and Financing. Michael K. Prescott. Lewis Publishers, 200 Corporate Blvd. NW, Boca Raton, FL 33431. (407) 994-0555 or (800)272-7737. 1990. Covers liability for environmental damages in the United States.

Environmental Hazard Assessment of Effluents. Pergamon Microforms International, Inc., Fairview Park, Elmsford, NY 10523. (914) 592-7720. Concepts of effluent testing, biomonitoring, hazard assessment, and disposal.

Environmental Hazards Air Pollution: A Reference Handbook. ABC-CLIO, PO Box 1911, Santa Barbara, CA 93116-1911. (805) 968-1911.

Environmental Hazards of War: Releasing Dangerous Forces in an Industrialized World. Arthur H. Westing. SAGE Pub., 2111 W. Hillcrest Dr., Newbury Park, CA 91320. (805) 499-0721. 1990. Population living downstream from hydrologic facilities, and near or adjacent to chemical and nuclear plants, greatly increases the potential risk to civilians from collateral damage by war. This book examines such a situation.

Environmental Hazards: Radioactive Materials and Wastes: A Reference Handbook. E. Willard Miller and Ruby M. Miller. ABC-Clio, 130 Cremona Dr., PO Box 1911, Santa Barbara, CA 93116-1911. (805) 968-1911; (800) 422-2546. 1990. Information source on radioactive materials and wastes. Introductory chapters describe the nature and characteristics of both natural and manufactured radioactive materials. Also provides information on laws, regulations, and treaties about waste materials. Including a directory of private, governmental, and international organizations that deal with radioactive wastes.

Environmental Health Administration: Environmental Protection. Director, Room 251, State Office Building, Montgomery, AL 36130. (205) 242-5004.

Environmental Health and Safety Division: Waste Minimization and Pollution Prevention. Director, Hazardous Waste Treatment Assistance Program, Georgia Institute of Technology, O'Keefe Building, Room 037, Atlanta, GA 30332. (404) 894-3806.

Environmental Health and Safety Manager's Handbook, 2nd edition. Government Institutes, Inc., 4 Research Pl., Ste. 200, Rockville, MD 20850. (301) 921-2300. Organization and management of environmental programs, criteria for developing a program, human resources, communication; information management; government inspections and enforcement.

Environmental Health and Toxicology. Centers for Disease Control, Center for Environmental Health and Injury Control, Chamblee 27 F-29, Atlanta, GA 30333. (404) 488-4588. 1991. A selected bibliography of printed information sources.

Environmental Health Components for Water Supply, Sanitation and Urban Projects. James A. Listorti. World Bank, 1818 H. St., N.W., Washington, DC 20433. (202) 477-1234. 1990. Sanitary engineering, with special reference to health related aspects of the water supply.

Environmental Health Letter. Business Publishers, Inc., 951 Pershing Dr., Silver Spring, MD 20910-4464. (301) 587-6300. 1961-. Biweekly. Covers areas such as: indoor air, asbestos health effects, toxic substances testing, health problems at wastewater plants, risk-based sludge rules, medical waste, developmental toxicity risk assessment, animal carcinogen tests, pesticide risk, air toxics, aerospace chemicals, lead, radionuclide emissions, state right-to-know statutes, and incinerator emissions.

Environmental Health News. University of Washington, School of Public Health, Dept. of Environmental Health, Seattle, WA 98195. (206) 543-3222. Quarterly. Occupational health, air pollution and safety.

Environmental Health News. Occupational Health Services, Inc., 450 7th Ave., New York, NY 10123. (212) 967-1100. Online access to court decisions, regulatory changes, and medical and scientific news related to hazardous substances.

Environmental Health Perspectives. National Institute of Environmental Health Sciences, P.O. Box 12233, Research Triangle Park, NC 27709. (919) 541-3406. Bimonthly. Proceedings from science conferences and issues on target organisms.

Environmental Health-Related Information: A Bibliographic Guide to Federal Sources for the Health Professional. Interagency Education Program Liaison Group, Task Force on Environmental Cancer and Heart and Lung Disease, MD 1984.

Environmental Health Report. S.D. Gregory, Box 7955, Dallas, TX 75209. (214) 725-6492. Monthly. Physicians, environmental scientists, and public health practitioners concerned with environmental health.

Environmental Health Trends Report. National Environmental Health Assn., South Tower, 720 S. Colorado Blvd., Ste. 970, Denver, CO 80222. (303) 756-9090. Quarterly.

Environmental History Newsletter. American Society for Environmental History, 6727 College Station, Duke University, History Dept., Durham, NC 27708. (303) 871-2347. Quarterly.

Environmental Hotline. U.S. Environmental Protection Agency, Region V, Office of Public Information, 230 S. Dearborn St., Chicago, IL 60604. Annual.

Environmental Hotline. Devel Associated, Inc., 7208 Jefferson St., N.E., Albuquerque, NM 87109. (505) 345-8732. Monthly. Regulations and analysis of key environmental issues.

Environmental Impact and Health Effects of Wastewater Chlorination. Gary R. Brenniman. Institute of Natural Resources, Chicago, IL 1981. Physiological and environmental aspects of chlorination.

Environmental Impact Assessment: A Bibliography with Abstracts. B. Clark, et al. Cassell PLC, Publishers Distribution Center, PO Box C831, Rutherford, NJ 07070. (201) 939-6064/5. 1980.

Environmental Impact Assessment for Developing Countries. A. K. Biswas and Q. Geping, eds. Cassell PLC, Publishers Distribution Center, PO Box C831, Rutherford, NJ 07070. (201) 939-6064; (201) 939-6065. 1987.

Environmental Impact Assessment Review. Elsevier Science Publishing Co., 655 Avenue of the Americas, New York, NY 10010. (212) 989-5800. Quarterly.

The Environmental Impact of Electrical Power Generation: Nuclear and Fossil. Pennsylvania Department of Education. U.S. G.P.O., Washington, DC 20401. (202) 512-0000. 1975. Environmental aspects of electric power production.

Environmental Impact of Nonpoint Source Pollution. Ann Arbor Science, 230 Collingwood, Ann Arbor, MI 48106. 1980.

Environmental Impact of Soft Drink Delivery System. National Association for Plastic Container Recovery, 4828 Pkwy. Plaza Blvd., Suite 260, Charlotte, NC 28217. (704) 357-3250. Irregular.

Environmental Impact Statement Directory: The National Network of EIS- Related Agencies and Organizations. Marc Landy, ed. IFI/Plenum, 233 Spring Street, New York, NY 10013. (800) 221-9369. 1981. Environmental impact statements classified as general, physical and cultural. Includes general directories, physical directories and cultural directories. Not available online.

Environmental Impacts from Offshore Exploration and Production of Oil and Gas. OECD Publications and Information Center, 2 rue Andre Pascal, Paris, France F-75775. 1977. Oil pollution of water and petroleum in submerged lands.

Environmental Impacts of Agricultural Production Activities. Larry W. Canter. Lewis Publishers, 200 Corporate Blvd. NW, Boca Raton, FL 33431. (407) 994-0555 or (800)272-7737. Volume in general deals with agricultural production technologies and its environmental impacts. It includes case studies and has chapters that separately deal with water and soil impacts; air quality impacts; noise and solid waste impacts. Most importantly it evaluates emerging agricultural technologies and includes a bibliography on the subject.

Environmental Impacts of Artificial Ice Nucleating Agents. Donald A. Klein. Van Nostrand Reinhold, Information Services, 115 5th Ave., New York, NY 10003. (212) 254-3232. 1978. Environmental aspects of silver and silver compounds.

Environmental Impacts of Coal Mining and Utilization. M. J. Chadwick, et al., eds. Pergamon Microforms International, Inc., Fairview Park, Elmsford, NY 10523. (914) 592-7720. 1987. Presents an up-to-date account of the whole coal fuel cycle and the recent developments to combat and control them.

Environmental Impacts of Hazardous Waste Treatment, Storage and Disposal Facilities. Rodolfo N. Salcedo, et al. Technomic Publishing Co., 851 New Holland Ave., Box 3535, Lancaster, PA 17604. (717) 291-5609. 1989. Provides guidance in dealing with the many obstacles and preliminary requirements in siting TSD facilities.

The Environmental Impacts of Marinas and Their Boats. Gail L. Chmura. Marine Advisory Service, University of Rhode Island, Narragansett, RI 02882. 1978. Environmental aspects of marinas, boats, and boating.

The Environmental Impacts of Production and Use of Energy: An Assessment. Essam E. el-Hinnawi. Tycooly Press, Dublin, Ireland 1981. Environmental aspects of energy consumption.

Environmental Impacts of Smelters. Jerome O. Nriagu. John Wiley & Sons, Inc., 605 3rd Ave., New York, NY 10158-0012. (212) 850-6000. 1984. Toxicity of water pollutants and environmental aspects of smelting furnaces.

The Environmental Index. UMI Data Courier, 620 South Third St., Louisville, KY 40202-2475. (800) 626-2823 or (502) 583-4111. 1992. Quarterly updates. Provides citations to articles in nearly 1,000 U.S. publications including New York Times, USA Today, and other popular journals like Time, Newsweek, Consumer Reports, Environment, Business Week and National Geographic. Covers topics such as global warming, overflowing landfills, waste management companies, city-wide recycling program, green consumers, buildings with asbestos, rivers full of toxins and other environmental issues.

Environmental Indicators. OECD Publication and Information Center, 2001 L St. N.W., Suite 700, Washington, DC 20036. (202) 785-OECD. 1991. Comprehensive assessments of environmental issues in industrialized countries. Charts the progress achieved over the past 20 years, and points to problems still remaining and sets an agenda of environmental issues to be dealt with in the 1990s.

Environmental Industries Marketplace. Karen Napoleone Meech. Gale Research Inc., 835 Penobscot Bldg., Detroit, 48226-4904. (313) 961-2242. 1992.

Environmental Industry Council. 1825 K St., N.W., Suite 210, Washington, DC 20006. (202) 331-7706.

Environmental Information Connection–EIC. Planning Information Program, Dept. of Urban and Regional Planning, University of Illinois, 1003 West Nevada, Urbana, IL 61801. (217) 333-1369. Also available online.

Environmental Inorganic Chemistry. Pergamon Microforms International, Inc., Fairview Park, Elmsford, NY 10523. (914) 592-7720. Environmentally important physiochemical properties of inorganic chemicals.

Environmental Investigations During Manganese Nodule Mining Tests in the North Equatorial Pacific. E. Ozturgut. Environmental Research Laboratories, Marine Ecosystems Analysis Program, 325 Broadway, Boulder, CO 80303. 1980. Environmental aspects of submarine manganese mines and mining.

Environmental Investments: The Costs of a Clean Government. Island Press, 1718 Connecticut Ave. N.W., Suite 300, Washington, DC 20009. (202) 232-7933. 1991. Report tells industry what to expect in direct expenses for implementing pollution control measures and undertaking compliance activities for environmental laws.

Environmental Issues: An Anthology of 1989. Thomas W. Joyce, ed. TAPPI Press, Technology Park/Atlanta, PO Box 105113, Atlanta, GA 30348. (404) 446-1400. 1990. Contains 39 papers on environmental, safety and occupational health concerns from 11 TAPPI, CPPA and AIChE meetings held during 1989. Also included is a literature review of over 200 papers published in 1989.

Environmental Issues in the Third World: A Bibliography. Joan Nordquist. Reference and Research Services, 511 Lincoln St., Santa Cruz, CA 95060. (408) 426-4479. 1991.

Environmental Lab. Mediacom, Inc., 760 Whalers Way, Suite 100, Bldg. A, Fort Collins, CO 80525. (303) 229-0029. Monthly.

Environmental Labelling in OECD Countries. OECD, UNIPUB, 4611-F Assembly Dr., Lanham, MD 20706. (301) 459-7666 or (800) 274-4888. 1991. Describes the origin and aims of the existing government sponsored labelling programs in the OECD countries.

Environmental Law: A Guide to Information Sources. Mortimer D. Schwartz. Gale Research Co., 835 Penobscot Bldg., Detroit, MI 48226-4094. (313) 961-2242. 1977. Man and the Environment Information Guide Series, v.6.

Environmental Law and the Siting of Facilities: Issues in Land Use and Coastal Zone Management. Michael S. Baram. Ballinger Publishing Co., 10 E. 53rd St., New York, NY 10022. (212) 207-7581. 1976. Law and legislation in the United States relative to coastal zone management.

The Environmental Law Digest. Environmental Law Institute, 1616 P St., NW, Suite 200, Washington, DC 20036. (202) 328-5150. 1984. Monthly.

Environmental Law for Oregon Practitioners. Oregon Law Institute, 921 SW Morrison St., Ste. 409, Portland, OR 97205. (503) 243-3326. 1991.

Environmental Law Handbook. Government Institutes, Inc., 4 Research Pl., Ste. 200, Rockville, MD 20850. (301) 921-2300. Current compliance information on Environmental Law Fundamentals; Enforcement and Liabilities; RCRA; UST; SARA Title III; CERCLA; Water; Air; TSCA; OSHA/Noise; SDWA; NEPA; Pesticides; and Asbestos.

Environmental Law in Louisiana. The Cambridge Institute, 1964 Gallows Rd., Vienna, VA 22182. (703) 893-8500. 1989.

Environmental Law in New York. Berle, Kass & Case, 45 Rockefeller Plaza, New York, NY 10111. (212) 765-1800. Bimonthly. Covers environmental law decisions by state and federal courts .

Environmental Law Institute. 1616 P St., N.W., Suite 200, Washington, DC 20036. (202) 328-5150.

Environmental Law Reporter. Environmental Law Institute, 1616 P St., N.W., Suite 200, Washington, DC 20036. (202) 328-5150. News, analysis, commentary, primary documents, and other materials dealing with environmental law, including statutes and regulations, pending litigation, and Superfund cases.

Environmental Law Update from Various Perspectives. Oklahoma Bar Association, Dept. of Continuing Education, PO Box 53036, Oklahoma City, OK 73152. 1990.

Environmental Lender Liability. O. T. Smith. John Wiley & Sons, Inc., 605 3rd Ave., New York, NY 10158-0012. (212) 850-6000. 1991. Covers the leaders' aspects of environmental law. Focuses on the liability of lenders for hazardous waste cleanup. Also discusses other provisions of federal environmental law statutes and the impact of bankruptcy on environmental obligations. Analyzes the newly proposed EPA guidelines on lender liability and includes relevant forms, checklists, and working documents.

Environmental Liability and Real Property Transactions. Joel S. Moskowitz. John Wiley & Sons, Inc., 605 3rd Ave., New York, NY 10158-0012. (212) 850-6000. 1989. Examines the growing body of environmental laws and regulations, and outlines ways to avoid liability. Appendix contains numerous sample forms which can be used for negotiating the purchase or sale of contaminated property.

The Environmental Liability Handbook for Property Transfer and Financing. Michael K. Prescott and Douglas S. Brossman. Lewis Publishers, 2000 Corporate Blvd., N.W., Boca Raton, FL 33431. (407) 994-0555 or (800) 272-7737. 1990. Provides an analysis of existing environmental legislation and trends that demonstrate the importance of the environmental site assessment in today's transactional market.

Environmental Liability Monitor. Business Publishers, Inc., 951 Pershing Dr., Silver Spring, MD 20910-4464. (301) 587-6300. 1990-. Monthly. Reports about environmental liability in all areas.

Environmental Litigation News. Environmental Compliance Inst., Aetna Bldg., Suite 850, 2350 Lakeside Blvd., Richardson, TX 75082-4342. (214) 644-8971. Monthly. Environmental compliance legislation.

Environmental Management. Springer-Verlag, 175 5th Ave., New York, NY 10010. (212) 460-1500. Six times a year.

Environmental Management and Education Program: Waste Minimization and Pollution Prevention. Office Director, Civil Engineering Boulevard, Room 2129, Purdue University, West Lafayette, IN 47907. (317) 494-5036.

Environmental Management Association. 255 Detroit St., Suite 200, Denver, CO 80206. (303) 320-7855.

Environmental Management Department: Air Quality. Chief, Air Division, 1751 Congressman W. L. Dickinson Dr., Montgomery, AL 36130. (205) 271-7861.

Environmental Management Department: Coastal Zone Management. Chief of Field Operations, 1751 Congressman W. L. Dickinson Dr., Montgomery, AL 36130. (205) 271-7700.

Environmental Management Department: Emergency Preparedness and Community Right-to-Know. Chief of Operations, Emergency Response Commission, 1751 Congressman W. L. Dickinson Dr., Montgomery, AL 36109. (205) 271-7700.

Environmental Management Department: Hazardous Waste Management. Chief, Hazardous Waste Branch, Land Division, 1751 Congressman W.L. Dickinson Dr., Montgomery, AL 36130. (205) 271-7736.

Environmental Management Department: Water Quality. Acting Director, Water Quality, 1751 Congressman W.L. Dickinson Dr., Montgomery, AL 36130. (205) 271-7823.

Environmental Management Division: Solid Waste Management. Chief, Division of Solid Waste, 1751 Congressman W.L. Dickinson Dr., Montgomery, AL 36130. (205) 271-7823.

Environmental Management Handbook: Toxic Chemical Materials and Waste. Leopold C. Kokoszka. Marcel Dekker, Inc., 270 Madison Ave., New York, NY 10016. (212) 696-9000; (800) 228-1160. 1989.

Environmental Management in Developing Countries. OECD, UNIPUB, 4611-F Assembly Dr., Lanham, MD 20706. (301) 459-7666 or (800) 274-4888. 1991. Comprised of papers from a conference which looks at environmental management in a developmental context.

Environmental Management: Journal of Industrial Sanitation and Facilities Management. Environmental Management Assn., 255 Detroit St., Suite 200, Denver, CO 80206. (303) 320-7855. Quarterly.

Environmental Management News. Stevens Publishing Co., PO Box 1604, Waco, TX 76710. (817) 776-9000. Semimonthly. Legal issues, technological advances and trends in the environmental arena.

Environmental Management Review. Government Institutes, Inc., 4 Research Pl., Ste. 200, Rockville, MD 20850. (301) 921-2300. Quarterly. Environmental risk assessment, enforcement priorities, regulatory requirements, and organizing and managing compliance programs.

Environmental Manager. Executive Enterprises Publications Co., Inc., 22 W. 21st St., 10th Fl., New York, NY 10010-6990. (212) 645-7880. Monthly. Toxic waste cleanups, waste minimization, and underground storage tank leaks.

Environmental Manager's Compliance Advisor. Business & Legal Reports, Inc., 64 Wall St., Madison, CT 06443-1513. (203) 245-7448. Biweekly. Integrated environmental compliance system. Also available online.

Environmental Manager's Compliance Advisor. Business & Legal Reports, Inc., 64 Wall St., Madison, CT 06443. (203) 245-7448. Online version of periodical of same name.

Environmental Media Association. 10536 Culver Blvd., Culver City, CA 90232. (213) 559-9334.

Environmental Mediation International. 1775 Pennsylvania Ave., N.W., Suite 1000, Washington, DC 20036. (202) 457-0457.

Environmental Modelling for Developing Countries. Asit K. Biswas, et al., eds. Cassell PLC, Publishers Distribution Center, PO Box C831, Rutherford, NJ 07070. (201) 939-6064/5. 1990. Explores how mathematical models can be effectively used in developing countries to improve environmental planning and management processes, with emphasis on modelling applications rather than knowledge accumulation.

Environmental Monitoring & Assessment. Kluwer Academic Publishers, 101 Philip Dr., Assinippi Pk., Norwell, MA 02061. (617) 871-6600. Monthly. Legislation, enforcement, and technology.

Environmental Monitoring and Disposal of Radioactive Wastes from U.S. Naval Nuclear-Powered Ships and their Support Facilities. U.S. G.P.O, Washington, DC 20402-9325. (202) 512-0000. Annual. Generation and disposal of radioactive waste from pressurized water reactors aboard nuclear-powered submarines and surface ships, and estimated public radiation exposure.

Environmental Monitoring and Evaluation of Calcium Magnesium Acetate. Richard Ray Horner. Transportation Research Board, National Research Council, 2101 Constitution Ave. NW, Washington, DC 20418. 1988. Deicing chemicals and snow and ice control of roads.

Environmental Monitoring: Meeting the Technical Challenge. E. M. Cashell, ed. American Institute of Physics, 335 E 45th St., New York, NY 10017. (212) 661-9404. 1990. Proceedings of the International Conference organized by ISA International and held in Cork, Ireland, May 1990. Examines the current state of the technology and methodology employed by industry to fulfill its legal and public responsibilities, and looks at new innovative technologies which are likely to figure prominently in environmental monitoring in the future.

Environmental Monitoring, Restoration, and Assessment: What Have We Learned?. Handord Symposium on Health and Environment, 28th, 1989, Richmond, WA. Battelle Press, 505 King Ave., Columbus, OH 43201. (614) 424-6393. 1990. Evaluates some of the monitoring and assessment programs that have been conducted or are currently in place. Focuses on radiological monitoring and its expenditures.

Environmental Mutagen Information Center. U.S. Department of Energy, Oak Ridge National Laboratory, Environmental Mutagen Information Center, Bldg. 9224, PO Box Y, Oak Ridge, TN 37830. (615) 574-7871. Chemical, biological and physical agents tested for mutagenicity.

Environmental Mutagen Society. 1600 Wilson Blvd., Suite 905, Arlington, VA 22209. (703) 525-1191.

Environmental Mutagen Society Newsletter. Dr. Virginia Houk. U.S. Environmental Protection Agency, M/D-68, Research Triangle Park, NC 27711. (919) 541-2815. Twice a year. Studies of mutagens.

Environmental Mutagenesis, Carcinogenesis, and Plant Biology. Edward Klekowski. Praeger Publishers, 1 Madison Ave., New York, NY 10010-3603. (212) 685-5300. 1982. Plant metabolism and plant metabolites.

Environmental News. Environmental Studies Unit, University of Waikato, Hamilton, New Zealand 1980-. Deals with a comprehensive treatment of environmental issues such as protection, policy research and related areas.

Environmental News. N.J. Department of Environmental Protection, 401 E. State St., CN 402, Trenton, NJ 08625. (609) 984-6773. Bimonthly. News of state programs relating to cleaner air, water, land management, conservation and preservation of natural resources.

Environmental Notice Bulletin. New York State Dept. of Environmental Conservation, 50 Wolf Rd., Albany, NY 12233. (518) 457-6668. Weekly. Information on state environmental quality review actions.

Environmental Nutrition. Environmental Nutrition, Inc., 52 Riverside Dr., 15th Fl., New York, NY 10024. (212) 362-0424. Monthly.

An Environmental Odyssey: People, Pollution and Politics in the Life of a Practical Scientist. Merril Eisenbud. University of Washington Press, PO Box 50096, Seattle, WA 98145-5096. (206) 543-4050 or (800) 441-4115. 1990. A professional biography where Eisenbud writes about a number of environmental challenges. He concludes with a 54-year perspective on the development of his field, on current environmental hazards, on the political pitfalls confronting environmentalists, and on the harmful effects of technology on human health.

Environmental Organization Computer Readable Directory. Environmental Research Information, Inc., 575 8th Ave., New York, NY 10018-3011. (212) 465-1060. Also available online.

Environmental Organization Computer Readable Directory Database. Environmental Research Information, Inc., 575 8th Ave., New York, NY 10018-3011. (212) 465-1060. Federal, state, and local agencies, legislative committees, public and private organizations, and individuals concerned with environmental issues. Online version of directory of same name.

Environmental Outlook. Institute for Environmental Studies, University of Washington, FM-12, Seattle, WA 98105. (206) 543-1812. Monthly. Regional and local environmental education.

Environmental Pathways of Selected Chemicals in Freshwater Systems. J. H. Smit. U.S. Environmental Protection Agency, Office of Research and Development, 960 College Sation Rd., Athens, GA 30605. (706) 546-3154. 1978. Mathematical models of water pollution, fresh water analysis and photochemistry.

Environmental Periodicals Bibliography. National Information Services Corp., Ste. 6, Wyman Towers, 3100 St. Paul St., Baltimore, MD 21218. (410)243-0797. Online version of abstract of same name.

Environmental Periodicals Bibliography. Environmental Studies Institute, International Academy at Santa Barbara, 800 Garden St., Suite D, Santa Barbara, CA 93101. (805) 965-5010. Also available online.

Environmental Physics in Construction. Granada, 717 E. Jericho Tpke., Ste. 281, Huntington Station, NY 11746. 1982. Applications in architectural design.

Environmental Physiology and Biochemistry of Insects. Klaus Hoffman. Springer-Verlag, 175 5th Ave., New York, NY 10010. (212) 460-1500. 1987. Physiology and ecology of insects.

Environmental Physiology of Plants. A. H. Fitter and R. K. M. Hay. Academic Press, c/o Harcourt Brace Jovanovich Inc., 6277 Sea Harbor Dr., Orlando, FL 32887. (800) 346-8648. 1987. 2d ed. Discusses the interaction of plants with the environment. Also outlines the adaptation of plants to the environment and concepts such as optimization. Covers geographical areas of North America and Europe. Has an extensive reference section.

Environmental Planning: A Guide to Information Sources. Michael J. Meshenberg. Gale Research Co., 835 Penobscot Bldg., Detroit, MI 48226-4094. (313) 961-2242. 1976. Focuses on environmental engineering and planning. Part of the series Man and the Environment Information Guide Series, v.3.

Environmental Policies for Cities in the 1990s. OECD Publications and Information Center, 2001 L St. N.W., Suite 700, Washington, DC 20036. (202) 785-OECD. 1991. Examines existing urban environmental improvement policies and suggests practical solutions to urban renewal, urban transportation and urban energy management.

Environmental Policy Alert. Inside Washington Publishers, P.O. Box 7167, Ben Franklin Station, Washington, DC 20044. Biweekly. Deals with environmental policy news.

Environmental Policy Benefits: Monetary Valuation. OECD Publications and Information Center, 2001 L St., N.W., Suite 700, Washington, DC 20036. (202) 785-OECD. 1989. Report explores monetary evaluations for benefits in the environmental policies decision making process.

Environmental Policy Institute. 218 D St., S.E., Washington, DC 20003. (202) 544-2600.

Environmental Politics and Policy. Congressional Quarterly, Inc., 1414 22nd St., N.W., Washington, DC 20037. (202) 887-8500.

Environmental Pollution. Inderscience Enterprises Ltd., World Trade Center Bldg., 110 Avenue Louis Casai, Case Postale 306, Geneva-Airport, Switzerland CH-1215. (44) 908-314248. 1991. Special issue of the International Journal of Environment and Pollution. Proceedings of the 1st International Conference on Environmental Pollution held at the Congress Centre, Lisbon, April 15-19, 1991.

Environmental Pollution. Applied Science Publications, PO Box 5399, New York, NY 10163. (718) 756-6440. 1987-.

Environmental Pollution. National Technical Information Service, 5285 Port Royal Road, Springfield, VA 22161. (703) 487-4650. Monthly.

Environmental Pollution and Control. P. Aarne Vesiling, et al. Butterworth-Heinemann, 80 Montvale Ave., Stoneham, MA 02180. (617) 438-8468; (800) 366-2665. 1990. Describes the more important aspects of environmental engineering science and technology.

Environmental Pollution & Control. National Technical Information Service, 5285 Port Royal Rd., Springfield, VA 22161. (703) 487-4650. Weekly. Covers air, noise, solid waste, water pollution, radiation, environmental health and safety, pesticide pollution and control.

Environmental Problem Solving Using Gas and Liquid Chromatography. Elsevier Science Publishing Co., 655 Avenue of the Americas, New York, NY 10010. (212) 984-5800. Covers environmental chemistry and chromatographic analysis.

Environmental Problems at the Department of Energy's Nuclear Weapons Complex. J. Dexter Peach. U.S. General Accounting Office, 441 G St., NW, Washington, DC 20548. (202) 275-5067. 1989. Environmental aspects of nuclear weapons industry and nuclear facilities.

Environmental Problems: Nature, Economy and State. R. J. Johnston. Belhaven Press, 136 S. Broadway, Irvington, NY 10533. (914) 591-9111. 1990. Argues that environmental studies should be regarded as a unified social and natural science, central to the survival of the human species.

Environmental Professional. National Association of Environmental Professionals, P.O. Box 15210, Alexandria, VA 22309-0210. (703) 660-2364. Quarterly. Covers effective impact assessment, regulation, and environmental protection.

Environmental Progress. American Institute of Chemical Engineers, 345 E. 47th St., New York, NY 10017. (212) 705-7338. Quarterly. Deals with environmental policies, protection and management-especially relating to chemicals.

The Environmental Properties of Polonium-218. Scott D. Goldstein. University of Illinois at Urbana-Champaign, Urbana, IL 61801. 1984.

Environmental Protection. Carol Mouche, ed. Stevens Publishing Co., PO Box 2604, Waco, TX 76706. (817) 776-9000. Nine times a year. Trade journal devoted to the areas of waste water; hazardous materials; risk assessment; environmental audits.

Environmental Protection. U.S. General Accounting Office, Resources, Community, and Economic Development Division, 441 G St., NW, Washington, DC 20548. (202) 275-5067. 1990. Bibliography of GAO documents of environmental protection.

Environmental Protection Agency: Air Quality. Director, 2200 Churchill Rd., Springfield, IL 62708. (217) 782-3397.

Environmental Protection Agency: Air Quality. Chief, Air Pollution Control Division, 1800 Watermark Dr., Columbus, OH 43266-0149. (614) 644-2270.

Environmental Protection Agency: Environmental Protection. Director, 2200 Churchill Rd., Springfield, IL 62708. (217) 782-3397.

Environmental Protection Agency: Environmental Protection. Director, 1800 Watermark Dr., Columbus, OH 43266-0149. (614) 481-7050.

Environmental Protection Agency: Groundwater Management. Director, 2200 Churchill Rd., Springfield, IL 62708. (217) 782-3397.

Environmental Protection Agency: Groundwater Management. Chief, Division of Groundwater, 1800 Watermark Dr., Columbus, OH 43266-0149. (614) 644-2905.

Environmental Protection Agency: Hazardous Waste Management. Chief, Division of Solid and Hazardous Waste Management, 1800 Watermark Dr., Columbus, OH 43266-0149. (614) 644-2917.

Environmental Protection Agency Journal. U.S. Environmental Protection Agency MC A-107, 401 M St. SW, Washington, DC 20460. (202) 260-2090. Bimonthly. Addresses environmental matters of interest.

Environmental Protection Agency: Office of Atmospheric and Indoor Air Programs. Waterside West Building, 401 M St., S.W., Washington, DC 20460. (202) 382-7404.

Environmental Protection Agency: Public Information Center. 401 M St., S.W., Washington, DC 20460. (202) 382-2080.

Environmental Protection Agency Regulatory Agenda. U.S. Environmental Protection Agency, 401 M St. SW, Washington, DC 20460. (202) 260-2090. Twice a year. Information on the status of proposed regulations.

Environmental Protection Agency: Small Business Ombudsman Office. 401 M St., S.W., 1A49C-1108, Washington, DC 20460. (202) 557-7777.

Environmental Protection Agency: Solid Waste Management. Chief, Division of Solid and Hazardous Waste, 1800 Watermark Dr., Columbus, OH 43266-0149. (614) 644-2917.

Environmental Protection Agency: Waste Minimization and Pollution Protection. Chief, Solid Waste Section, PO Box 1049, 1800 Watermark Dr., Columbus, OH 43266-0149. (614) 644-2917.

Environmental Protection Agency: Water Quality. Director, 2200 Churchill Rd., Springfield, IL 62708. (217) 782-3397.

Environmental Protection Agency: Water Quality. Chief, 1800 Watermark Dr., Columbus, OH 43266-0149. (614) 644-2856.

Environmental Protection and Biological Forms of Control of Pest Organisms. B. Lundholm. Swedish National Science Research Council, Editorial Service, P.O. Box 6711, Stockholm, Sweden S-113 85. 08-15-1580. 1980. Environmental aspects of pests and natural pesticides.

Environmental Protection Careers Guidebook. U.S. Department of Labor, Employment and Training Administration, 200 Constitution Ave., NW, Washington, DC 20210. (202) 523-8165. 1980. Includes information on education in environmental protection field.

Environmental Protection Department: Air Quality. Commissioner, Division of Environmental Quality, 165 Capitol Ave., Hartford, CT 06106. (203) 566-2506.

Environmental Protection Department: Coastal Zone Management. Director, Planning and Coastal Area Management, 18-20 Trinity St., Hartford, CT 06106. (203) 566-7404.

Environmental Protection Department: Coastal Zone Management. Director, Division of Control Resources, 401 East State St., CN401, Trenton, NJ 08625. (609) 292-2795.

Environmental Protection Department: Environmental Protection. Commissioner, Department of Environmental Quality, 165 Capitol Ave., Room 161, Hartford, CT 06106. (203) 566-2110.

Environmental Protection Department: Environmental Protection. Commissioner, CN 402, 401 E. State St., Trenton, NJ 08625. (609) 292-2885.

Environmental Protection Department: Fish and Wildlife. Chief, Fish and Wildlife, State Office Building, Room 254, 165 Capitol Ave., Hartford, CT 06106. (203) 566-2287.

Environmental Protection Department: Fish and Wildlife. Director, Fish, Game, and Wildlife Division, CN 400, Trenton, NJ 08625. (609) 292-9410.

Environmental Protection Department: Groundwater Management. Director, Water Compliance Unit, 122 Washington St., Hartford, CT 06106. (203) 566-3245.

Environmental Protection Department: Hazardous Waste Management. Director, Division of Hazardous Waste Management, 401 East State St., Trenton, NJ 08625. (609) 633-1408.

Environmental Protection Department: Natural Resources. Commissioner, Division of Environmental Quality, 165 Capitol Ave., Room 161, Hartford, CT 06106. (203) 566-2110.

Environmental Protection Department: Natural Resources. Assistant Commissioner, Natural Resources, John Fitch Plaza, CN 402, Trenton, NJ 08625. (609) 292-3541.

Environmental Protection Department: Pesticide Registration. Hazardous Materials Management Unit, State Office Building, 165 Capitol Ave., Hartford, CT 06106. (203) 566-4924.

Environmental Protection Department: Solid Waste Department. Director, Solid Waste Management Unit, 122 Washington St., Hartford, CT 06106. (203) 566-5847.

Environmental Protection Department: Underground Storage Tanks. Director, Hazardous Waste Management, State Office Building, 165 Capitol Ave., Hartford, CT 06106. (203) 566-4924.

Environmental Protection Department: Water Quality. Director, Water Compliance Unit, 122 Washington St., Hartford, CT 06106. (203) 566-3245.

Environmental Protection Division: Air Quality. Bureau of Air Quality Control, State House Station #17, Augusta, ME 04333. (207) 289-2437.

Environmental Protection Division: Hazardous Waste Management. Land Protection Branch Chief, Industrial and Hazardous Waste Program, 205 Butler St., S.W., Floyd Towers East, Suite 1252, Atlanta, GA 30334. (404) 656-2833.

Environmental Protection Division: Solid Waste Management. Land Protection Branch Chief, Industrial and Hazardous Waste Program, 205 Butler St., S.E., Floyd Towers East, Atlanta, GA 30334. (404) 656-2833.

Environmental Protection Magazine. Stevens Publishing Co., 225 New Road, PO Box 2604, Waco, TX 76702-2573. (817) 776-9000. Air and water pollution, wastewater and hazardous materials.

Environmental Protection: Meeting Public Expectations with Limited Resources. U.S. General Accounting Office, 441 G St., NW, Washington, DC 20548. (202) 275-5067. 1991. Monthly.

Environmental Protection News. Stevens Publishing Co., PO Box 2604, Waco, TX 76706. (817) 776-9000. 1990-. Weekly. Covers topics such as: The EPA looking at the Endangered Species Act; The Indoor Air Bill debate intensifies in Congress; Capitol Hill considers new Hazmat Trade Laws; The EPA turns to the media to help prosecute polluters; The Superfund fiasco is not the fault of contractors?; and other environmental topics.

Environmental Quality. U.S. Joint Publication Research Service, 1000 N. Glebe Rd., Arlington, VA 22201. (703) 557-4630. Semimonthly. Policy issues relating to environmental protection.

Environmental Quality. Council on Environmental Quality. U.S. G.P.O., Washington, DC 20401. (202) 512-0000. Annual.

Environmental Quality and the Law. Michigan House of Representatives, Conservation, Recreation and Environment Committee, PO Box 30014, Lansing, MI 48909. (517)373-0135. 1990.

Environmental Quality Board: Air Quality. Chairman, PO Box 11488, Santurce, PR 00910. (809) 767-8056.

Environmental Quality Board: Environmental Protection. Chairman, PO Box 11488, Santurce, PR 00910. (809) 725-5140.

Environmental Quality Board: Hazardous Waste Management. Chairman, PO Box 11488, Santurce, PR 00910. (809) 725-5140.

Environmental Quality Board: Water Quality. Chairman, PO Box 11488, Santurce, PR 00910. (809) 725-5140.

Environmental Quality Engineering: Water Quality. Director, Water Pollution, 1 Winter St., Boston, MA 02108. (617) 292-5636.

Environmental Quality Index. National Wildlife Federation, 1400 16th St. NW, Washington, DC 20036-2266. (202) 797-6800. Annual.

Environmental Quality Industrial Resources Center. The Ohio State University, 1200 Chambers Rd., Room 310, Columbus, OH 43212. (614) 292-6717.

Environmental Regulation Department: Air Quality. Division Director, Division of Air Resources Management, 2600 Blairstone Rd., Tallahassee, FL 32399-2400. (904) 488-1344.

Environmental Regulation Department: Coastal Zone Management. Environmental Administrator, Coastal Zone Management, 2600 Blairstone Rd., Tallahassee, FL 32399-2400. (904) 488-6221.

Environmental Regulation Department: Environmental Protection. Secretary, Twin Towers, 2600 Blairstone Rd., Tallahassee, FL 32399-2400. (904) 488-4805.

Environmental Regulation Department: Groundwater Management. Chief, Bureau of Groundwater Management, 2600 Blairstone Rd., Tallahassee, FL 32399-2400. (904) 488-3601.

Environmental Regulation Department: Hazardous Waste Management. Chief, Bureau of Groundwater Protection, 2600 Blairstone Rd., Tallahassee, FL 32399-2400. (904) 488-3601.

Environmental Regulation Department: Solid Waste Management. Director, 2600 Blairstone Rd., Tallahassee, FL 32399-2400. (904) 488-0190.

Environmental Regulation Department: Underground Storage Tanks. Division Director, Environmental Operations Division, 2600 Blairstone Rd., Tallahassee, FL 32399-2400. (904) 487-3299.

Environmental Regulation Department: Water Quality. Chief, Surface Water Management, 2600 Blairstone Rd., Tallahassee, FL 32399-2400. (904) 488-6221.

Environmental Regulation From the State Capital: Waste Disposal and Pollution Control. Wakeman/Walworth, 300 N. Washington St., Alexandria, VA 22314. (703) 549-8606. Legislative action concerning pollution control.

Environmental Regulatory Glossary. G. William Frick and Thomas P. Sullivan. Government Institutes, Inc., 4 Research Pl., Rockville, MD 20850. (301) 921-2300. 1990. Over 4,000 entries. Definitions were gathered from the Code of Federal Regulations, EPA documents, and Federal Environmental Statutes.

Environmental Reporting and Recordkeeping Requirements. Government Institutes, Inc., 4 Research Pl., Ste. 200, Rockville, MD 20850. (301) 921-2300. Reporting and recordkeeping under Clean Air, Clean Water, RCRA, CERCLA, SARA, TSCA, and OSHA.

Environmental Research. Academic Press, 1250 6th Ave., San Diego, CA 92101. (619) 231-0926. Bimonthly. Toxic effects of environmental agents in humans and animals.

Environmental Research Center. Washington State University, 305 Troy Hall, Pullman, WA 99164-4430. (509) 335-8536.

Environmental Research Foundation. PO Box 3541, Princeton, NJ 08543-3541. (609) 683-0707.

Environmental Research Institute for Hazardous Materials and Wastes. University of Connecticut, Rt. 44, Langley Bldg., Box U210, Storrs, CT 06269-3210. (203) 486-4015.

Environmental Research Laboratories Publication Abstracts. National Oceanic and Atmospheric Administration. Environmental Research Laboratories, 325 Broadway, Boulder, CO 80303. 1990. Annual. Sixth annual bibliography of NOAA Environmental Research Laboratories staff publications, FY 89. Covers journal articles, official ERL reports, conference papers, and publications released in cooperation with universities and by ERL funded contractors.

Environmental Resource Center. Crowder College, Neosho, MO 64850. (417) 451-3583.

Environmental Resources Conservation, and Economic Aspects of Used Oil Recycling. D. W. Brinkman. Bartlesville Energy Technology Center, Box 1398, Bartlesville, OK 74005. (918) 336-2400. 1981. Recycling of petroleum waste and lubricating oils.

Environmental Resources Department: Air Quality. Director, Bureau of Air Quality Control, PO Box 2063, Harrisburg, PA 17105. (717) 787-9702.

Environmental Resources Department: Coastal Zone Management. Director, Bureau of Water Resources Management, Room 208, Evangelical Press Building, Harrisburg, PA 17120. (717) 787-6750.

Environmental Resources Department: Natural Resources. Secretary, PO Box 2063, Harrisburg, PA 17105. (717) 787-2814.

Environmental Resources Department: Solid Waste Management. Director, Bureau of Solid Waste Management, PO Box 2063, Harrisburg, PA 17105. (717) 787-9870.

Environmental Resources Department: Underground Storage Tanks. Director, Bureau of Water Quality Management, PO Box 2063, Harrisburg, PA 17105. (717) 787-2666.

Environmental Resources Department: Water Quality. Director, Bureau of Water Quality Management, PO Box 2063, Harrisburg, PA 17105. (717) 787-2666.

Environmental Resources Research Institute, Newsletter. Environmental Resources Research Institute, Pennsylvania State University, University Park, PA 16802. (814) 863-0291. Quarterly. Land, water, air, and mining.

Environmental Restoration: Science and Strategies for Restoring the Earth. John J. Berger. Island Press, 1718 Connecticut Ave. N.W., Suite 300, Washington, DC 20009. (202) 232-7933. 1990. Overview techniques of restoration.

Environmental Review. Citizens for a Better Environment, 407 S. Dearborn, Ste. 1775, Chicago, IL 60605. (312) 939-1530. Quarterly. Environmental policy and environmental protection issues in the Midwest.

Environmental Review. American Society for Environmental History, Department of History, University of Oregon, Corvallis, OR 97331. Quarterly. Covers human ecology as seen through history and the humanities.

Environmental Risk: Evaluation and Finance in Real Estate. Albert R. Wilson. Lewis Publishers, 2000 Corporate Blvd., N.W., Boca Raton, FL 33431. (407) 994-0555 or (800) 272-7737. 1991. Deals with the ownership of hazardous materials effected property, types of environmental audits, property evaluation, and legal implications.

Environmental Role of Nitrogen-Fixing Blue-Green Algae and Asymbiotic Bacteria. U. Granhall. Swedish Natural Science Research Council, P.O. Box 6711, Stockholm, Sweden S-113 85. 08-15-1580. 1978. Deals with nitrogen-fixing microorganisms, nitrogen-fixing algae and cyanobacteria.

Environmental Safety. 1700 N. More St., Suite 1920, Arlington, VA 22209. (703) 527-8300.

Environmental Sampling and Analysis. Lawrence H. Keith. Lewis Publishers, 2000 Corporate Blvd., N.W., Boca Raton, FL 33431. (407) 994-0555 or (800) 272-7737. 1991. Provides a basis for understanding the principles that affect the choices made in environmental sampling and analysis.

Environmental Sampling and Analysis: A Practical Guide. Lewis Publishers, 200 Corporate Blvd. NW, Boca Raton, FL 33431. (407) 994-0555 or (800)272-7737. 1991. Topics in environmental monitoring and environmental chemistry.

Environmental Scene. Arizona Dept. of Environmental Quality, 2005 N. Central, Phoenix, AZ 85004. (602) 257-6940. Quarterly. State programs in areas of air quality, water quality and waste programs.

Environmental Science and Engineering. Davcom Communications Inc., 10 Petch Circle, Aurora, ON, Canada L4G 5N7. (416) 727-4666. Bimonthly. Water, sewage, and pollution control.

Environmental Science and Technology. American Chemical Society, 1155 16th St. N.W., Washington, DC 20036. (800) 227-5558. 1967-. Monthly. Contains research articles on various aspects of environmental chemistry, interpretative articles by invited experts and commentary on the scientific aspects of environmental management.

Environmental Science & Technology. American Chemical Society, 1155 16th St. N.W., Washington, DC 20036. (800) 227-5558. Covers pollution, sanitary chemistry and environmental engineering.

Environmental Science Handbook for Architects and Builders. S.V. Szokolay. John Wiley & Sons, Inc., 605 3rd Ave., New York, NY 10158-0012. (212) 850-6000. 1980. Topics in the environmental engineering of buildings.

Environmental Sensors & Monitoring. FIND/SVP, 625 Avenue of the Americas, New York, NY 10011. (212) 645-4500. Step-by-step guide to a group of biosensor, optic sensor and mass sensor technologies, patents and regulations.

Environmental Services Department: Groundwater Management. Administrator, Groundwater Protection Bureau, Box 95, 6 Hazen Drive, Concord, NH 03301. (603) 271-3503.

Environmental Software. Computational Mechanics Publications Inc., Suite 6200, 400 W. Cummings Park, Woburn, MA 01801. Quarterly. Computer programs for environmental monitoring.

Environmental Software Directory. Donley Technology, PO Box 335, Garrisonville, VA 22463. (703) 659-1954. 1989-. Annually. Provides descriptive access to commercial and government databases, software and online systems related to hazardous materials management, water and wastewater, groundwater, soils, mapping, air pollution and ecology.

The Environmental Sourcebook. Edith Carol Stein. Lyons & Burford, 31 W. 21st St., New York, NY 10010. (212) 620-9580. 1992. Provides information on 11 specific environmental issues, including population; agriculture; energy; climate and atmosphere; biodiversity; water; oceans; solid waste; hazardous substances and waste; endangered lands; and development.

Environmental Spectrum. New Jersey Cooperative Extension Service, Cook College, Rutgers University, P.O. Box 231, New Brunswick, NJ 08903. 1968-. Bimonthly. Emphasis on air/noise pollution, energy, water and other environmental topics.

Environmental Statistics Handbook: Europe. Allan Foster, Oksana Newman. Gale Research Inc., 835 Penobscot Bldg., Detroit, MI 48226-4094. (313) 961-2242. 1993.

Environmental Statutes. Government Institutes, Inc., 4 Research Pl., Ste. 200, Rockville, MD 20850. (301) 921-2300. Annual. Complete text of twelve major environmental statutes.

Environmental Studies & Practice: An Educational Resource and Forum. Yale School of Forestry and Environmental Studies, 205 Prospect St., New Haven, CT 06511. (203) 432-5132. 1991. Bimonthly. Subject matters range widely from air pollution to wildlife biology. Each issue contains a selection of recent publications, from all subject areas of environmental and natural resources management.

Environmental Studies Institute. 800 Garden St., Suite D, Santa Barbara, CA 93101. (805) 965-5010.

Environmental Studies to Natural Resources Management: An Annotated Guide to University and Government Training Programs in the United States. Sierra Club. International Earthcare Center, 802 2nd Ave., New York, NY 10017. 1980.

Environmental Systems Engineering Institute. University of Central Florida, Department of Civil Engineering and Environmental Science, PO Box 25000, Orlando, FL 32816. (305) 275-2785.

Environmental Systems Library. Washington, DC 1963-1979. Consists of design and installation manuals and worksheets published by the National Environmental Systems Contractors Association and the Air Conditioning Contractors of America.

Environmental Task Force. 6930 Carroll Ave., 6th Floor, Takoma Park, MD 20912. (202) 745-4870.

Environmental Technical Information System. U.S. Army Corps of Engineers, Construction Engineering Research Laboratory, ETIS Support Program, 1003 W. Nevada St., Urbana, IL 61801. (217) 333-1369. The environmental effects of activities by the U.S. Department of Defense activities and other major governmental programs.

Environmental Technology. Park Publishing Co., 333 Hudson St., New York, NY 10013. (212) 255-1500. Semimonthly. Research on pollution abatement.

Environmental Technology and Economics. Technomic Publishing Co., 750 Summer St., Stamford, CT 06902. (717) 291-5609. 1966-. Semimonthly.

Environmental Technology Seminar. P.O. Box 391, Bethpage, NY 11714. (516) 931-3200.

Environmental Telephone Directory. Government Institutes, Inc., 4 Research Pl., Ste. 200, Rockville, MD 20850. (301) 921-2300.

Environmental Telephone Directory. Government Institutes, Inc., 4 Research Pl., Ste. 200, Rockville, MD 20850. (301) 921-2300. 1990-1991. Complete addresses and phone numbers for Senators and Representatives with their Environmental Aides, full information on Senate and House Committees and Subcommittees and Federal and Executive agencies dealing with environmental issues, and detailed information on state environmental agencies.

Environmental Tobacco Smoke: A Guide to Workplace Smoking Policies. U.S. Environmental Protection Agency, 401 M St. SW, Washington, DC 20460. (202) 260-2090. 1990. Tobacco smoke pollution effects on atmospheric air, and indoor air and air radiation.

Environmental Tobacco Smoke and Cancer. William Weiss. U.S. G.P.O., Washington, DC 20401. (202) 512-0000. 1989. Passive smoking and lungs–cancer.

Environmental Tobacco Smoke in the Workplace: Lung Cancer and Other Health Effects. National Institute for Occupational Safety and Health, 1600 Clifton Rd. NE, Atlanta, GA 30333. (404) 639-3286. 1992. Current Intelligence Bulletin No. 54. DHHS (NIOSH) Publication No. 91-108.

Environmental Toxicology. J. K. Fawell and S. Hunt. John Wiley & Sons, Inc., 605 3rd Ave., New York, NY 10158. (212) 850-6000. 1988. Information on the toxicology of contaminants in drinking water, upland surface water and ground water. Analysis is done using gas chromatography and mass spectrometry.

Environmental Toxicology. Robert L. Rudd. Gale Research Co., 835 Penobscot Bldg., Detroit, MI 48226-4094. (313) 961-2242. 1977. Includes the broad areas of pollution, pesticides, and their effects. This bibliography is part of the series entitled Man and the Environment Information Guide Series, v.7.

Environmental Toxicology and Chemistry. Society of Environmental Toxicology and Chemistry. Pergamon Microforms International, Inc., Fairview Park, Elmsford, NY 10523. (914) 592-7720. 1981-. Monthly. Contains information on environmental toxicology, and chemistry, including the application of science to hazard assessment.

Environmental Toxicology and Water Quality. John Wiley & Sons, Inc., 605 3rd Ave., New York, NY 10158-0012. (212) 850-6000. Quarterly. Covers water pollution toxicology, microbiological assay, water quality bioassay and toxicity testing.

Environmental Toxins. Cheryl Brown Travis. American Physiological Society, 9650 Rockville Pike, Bethesda, MD 20814. (301) 530-7164. 1989. Bibliography of toxicity in environmental pollutants.

Environmental Values, 1860-1972: A Guide to Information Sources. Loren C. Owings. Gale Research Co., 835 Penobscot Bldg., Detroit, MI 48226-4094. (313) 961-2242. 1976. This bibliography includes the broad areas of human ecology, nature and outdoor life. It belongs in the series entitled Man and the Environment Information Guide Series, v.4.

Environmental Viewpoints. Marie Lazzari. Gale Research Inc., 835 Penobscot Bldg., Detroit, MI 48226-4094. (313) 961-2242. 1992.

Environmentally Acceptable Incineration of Chlorinated Chemical Waste. Martin A. de Zeeuw. Coronet Books, 311 Bainbridge St., Philadelphia, PA 19147. (215) 925-2762. 1987.

Environments. Faculty of Environmental Studies, University of Waterloo, Waterloo, ON, Canada N2L 3G1. (519) 885-1211. Three times a year. People in man-made and natural environments.

Environs. King Hall School of Law, University of California, Environmental Law Society, King Hall, University of California, Davis, CA 95616. (916) 752-6703. Environmental law and natural resource management in the western United States.

Envirosoft 86. P. Zanetti, ed. Computational Mechanics Inc., 25 Bridge St., Billerica, MA 01821. 1986. Environmental software part of the proceedings of the International Conference on Development and Applications of Computer Techniques to Environmental Studies, Los Angeles, 1986.

Envirosoft 88: Computer Techniques in Environmental Studies. P. Zannetti, ed. Computational Mechanics Inc., 25 Bridge St., Billerica, MA 01821. (508) 667-5841. 1988. Proceedings of the 2nd International Conference, Envirosoft 88, covering the development and application of computer techniques to environmental problems.

Enzyme Handbook. D. Schomburg and M. Salzmann, eds. Springer-Verlag, 175 5th Ave., New York, NY 10010. (212) 460-1500; (800) 777-4643. 1990. The enzymes are arranged in accord with the 1984 Enzyme Commission list of enzymes and follow-up supplements. Information contained for each enzyme is organized in seven basic sections.

Enzyme Nomenclature 1984. Edwin C. Webb. Academic Press, c/o Harcourt Brace Jovanovich Inc., 6277 Sea Harbor Dr., Orlando, FL 32887. (800) 346-8648. 1992. Fifth edition. "This edition is a revision of the Recommendations (1978) of the Nomenclature Committee of IUB, and has been approved for publication by the Executive Committee of the International Union of Biochemistry." Includes 2728 enzymes. It considers classification and nomenclature, their units of activity and standard methods of assay, together with symbols used in the description of enzyme kinetics.

EPA Bulletin. U.S. Environmental Protection Agency, 401 M St., S.W., A-107, Washington, DC 20460. (202) 755-0890. Monthly. News of conservation and legislation.

EPA Fact Sheet Program. National Pesticide Information Retrieval System (NPIRS) Services Manager, Purdue University, Entomology Hall, West Lafayette, IN 47907. (317) 494-6616.

EPA Hazardous Waste Numbers for Waste Streams Commonly Generated by Small Quantity Generators. U.S. Environmental Protection Agency, 401 M St., SW, Washington, DC 20460. (202) 260-2090. 1986. Identification of hazardous wastes.

EPA Headquarters Telephone Directory. Government Institutes, Inc., 4 Research Pl., Ste. 200, Rockville, MD 20850. (301) 921-2300. Key to converting the Federal Telecommunications System phone numbers to outside commercial numbers.

EPA Index: A Key to U.S. Environmental Protection Agency Reports and Superintendent of Documents and NTIS Numbers. Cynthia E. Bower and Mary L. Rhoads, eds. Oryx Press, 4041 N. Central at Indian School Rd., Ste. 700, Phoenix, AZ 85012-3397. (602) 265-2651. 1983. Identifies and locates certain numbered EPA reports published prior to 1982. The list is not comprehensive. Arranged by report number and by title.

EPA Journal. U.S. Environmental Protection Agency, 401 M St., S.W., A-107, Washington, DC 20460. (202) 382-4393. Bimonthly. Air and water pollution, pesticides, noise, solid waste.

The EPA Manual for Waste Minimization Opportunity Assessments. U.S. Environmental Protection Agency. Technomic Publishing Co., 851 New Holland Ave., Box 3535, Lancaster, PA 17604. (717) 291-5609. 1990.

EPA Organization and Functions Manual. Government Institutes, Inc., 4 Research Pl., Ste. 200, Rockville, MD 20850. (301) 921-2300. Detailed descriptions of exactly which office, division or support staff lab, within the EPA is responsible for various functions; includes a comprehensive organization chart for each office.

EPA Policy Alert. Inside Washington Publishers, 1235 Jefferson Davis Hwy., #1206, Arlington, VA 22202. (703) 892-8500. Biweekly. News of legislation and enforcement.

EPA Product Data Base. National Pesticide Information Retrieval System (NPIRS) Services Manager, Purdue University, Entomology Hall, West Lafayette, IN 47907. (317) 494-6616.

EPA Publications Bibliography. U.S. Environmental Protection Agency, Library Systems Branch, 401 M St., SW, Washington, DC 20460. (202) 260-2090. Quarterly.

EPA Publications Bibliography Quarterly. 5285 Port Royal Rd., Springfield, VA 22161. (703) 487-4650. Quarterly. Literary reviews of books and articles.

EPA RCRA/OUST Superfund Hotline. EPA: Office of Solid Waste (OS305), 401 M St. SW, WA, DC 20460. (800) 424-9346; (800) 346-5009.

EPA's Final PCB Ban Rule. U.S. Environmental Protection Agency, Industrial Assistance Office and Chemical Control Division, Office of Toxic Substances, 401 M St., S.W., Washington, DC 20460. (202) 260-2090. 1980.

EPA's Handbook Responding to Sinking Hazardous Substances. Pudvan Publishing Co., Inc., 1935 Shermer Rd., Northbrook, IL 60062. (312) 498-9840. 1988. Prepared by the U.S. Environmental Protection Agency and the United States Coast Guard.

EPA's RCRA/Superfund & EPCRA Hotlines: Questions and Answers. Government Institutes, Inc., 4 Research Pl., Suite 200, Rockville, MD 20850. (301) 921-2300. 1991. Actual test of the Significant Questions and Resolved Issues internal EPA reports released each month by the RCRA/Superfund Industrial assistance Hotline, and the Emergency Planning and Community Right-to-Know Industrial Hotline covering 1989 and 1990.

EPA's Sampling and Analysis Methods Database. William Mueller, et al. Lewis Publishers, 2000 Corporate Blvd., N.W., Boca Raton, FL 33431. (407) 994-0555 or (800) 272-7737. 1990. Three volumes, five diskettes. Compiled by EPA chemists. Permits rapid searches of sampling and analytical method summaries: v.1. Industrial chemicals; v.2. Pesticides, Herbicides, Dioxins, and PCBs; v.3. Elements and Water Quality Parameters.

EPB Online Vocabulary Aid. Environmental Studies Institute, International Academy at Santa Barbara, 800 Garden St., Ste. D, Dept. ADWL-R, Santa Barbara, CA 93101. (805) 965-5010. Annual. Deals with human ecology and environmental protection terminology.

EPI Environmental Products Index. Duane Enterprises, 319 West St., Braintree, MA 02184. (617) 848-6150. Product and technology for testing, monitoring, transportation.

EPICOR-II Resin Waste Form Testing. R. M. Neilson. Division of Waste Management, U.S. Nuclear Regulatory Commission, Washington, DC 20555. (301) 492-7000. 1986. Leaching radioactive waste disposal, and ion exchange resins.

Epidemiology Information System. Oak Ridge National Laboratory, Toxicology Information Response Center, Building 2001, P.O. Box 2008, Oak Ridge, TN 37831-6050. (615) 576-1746.

Eradication of Marijuana with Paraquat. U.S. G.P.O., Washington, DC 20401. (202) 512-0000. 1985. Hearings before the Subcommittee on Crime of the Judiciary Committee, House of Representatives, 98th Congress, 1st session, October 5 and November 17, 1983.

ERDA Research Abstracts. U.S. ERDA Technical Information Center, Box 62, Oak Ridge, TN 37830.

Ergonomics Abstracts. Taylor & Francis, 4 John St., London, England WC1N 2ET. 1990-. Bimonthly. Provides details on recent additions to the international literature on human factors in human-machine systems and physical environmental influences.

ERIC Clearinghouse for Science, Mathematics, and Environmental Education. Ohio State University, 1200 Chambers Rd., 3rd Floor, Columbus, OH 43212. (614) 292-6717.

Erie the Lake that Survived. Noel M. Burns. Rowman & Littlefield, Publishers, Inc., 8705 Bollman Pl., Savage, MD 20763. (301) 306-0400. 1985. Describes a model for anyone concerned with large lakes.

ERMD Directory. Special Libraries Association, Environmental Resources Management Division, Forest Resources Lib., AQ-15, Seattle, WA 98195. Irregular. Listing of membership, services, contact persons, and consultants in environmental areas.

ERT Handbook on Requirements for Industrial Facilities under the Clear Air Act: New–Information on Toxic Air Pollutants. Environmental Research & Technology, Concord, MA 1984. Air pollution law and legislation in the United States and environmental aspects of industry.

Escaping the Heat Trap. Irving Mintzer and William R. Moomaw. World Resources Institute, 1709 New York Ave. N.W., Washington, DC 20006. (800) 822-0504. 1991. Report is based on a series of scenarios developed using WRI's Model of Warming Commitment. Investigates the potential of societies to dramatically limit the rate of future greenhouse gas buildup and reduce to zero annual commitment to global warming.

Escheria Coli and Salmonella Typherium: Cellular and Molecular Biology. Frederick C. Neidhardt. American Society for Microbiology, 1325 Massachusetts Ave., N.W., Washington, DC 20005. (202) 737-3600. 1987.

ESE Notes. UNC Dept. of Environmental Science & Engineering School of Public Health, CB# 7400, Chapel Hill, NC 27599-7400. (919) 966-1171. Quarterly. Research and training activities of the EPA.

The Essential Whole Earth Catalog. The Point Foundation. Doubleday, 666 5th Ave., New York, NY 10103. (212) 765-6500; (800) 223-6834. 1986.

Estimates of Biofuels Consumption in the U.S. U.S. G.P.O, Washington, DC 20402-9325. (202) 512-0000. 1990. Consumption of energy from biofuels, including wood, solid waste, and ethanol. Waste energy types include mass burning, manufacturing wastes, refuse derived fuel and methane gas form landfills.

Estimating Costs of Air Pollution Control. William M. Vatavuk. Lewis Publishers, 2000 Corporate Blvd., N.W., Boca Raton, FL 33431. (407) 994-0555 or (800) 272-7737. 1990. Deals with information to select, size, and estimate budget/ study level capital and annual costs for a variety of air pollution control equipment.

Estuaries. Chesapeake Biological Laboratory, 1 William St., Solomons, MD 20688-0038. (410) 326-4281. Quarterly. Journal of the Estuarine Research Federation dealing with estuaries and estuarine biology.

Estuaries and Tidal Marshes. National Institute for Urban Wildlife, 10921 Trotting Ridge Way, Columbia, MD 21044. (301) 596-3311. 1986. Topics in estaurine and tidemarsh ecology.

Estuaries of the United States: Vital Statistics of a National Resource Base. U.S. Ocean Assessments Division, Coastal and Estuaries Assessment Branch, Rockville, MD 1990. Data on nation's estuaries, coasts, and marine resources conservation.

Estuarine Pollution, a Bibliography. Water Resources Scientific Information Center. National Technical Information Service, 5285 Port Royal Rd., Springfield, VA 22161. (703) 487-4650. 1976.

Estuarine Research Federation. P.O. Box 544, Crownsville, MD 21032-0544. (301) 266-5489.

Ethanol Fuels Reference Guide. Technical Information Branch, Solar Energy Research Institute, 1617 Cole Blvd., Golden, CO 80401. 1982. A decision-maker's guide to ethanol fuels like biomass energy and gasohol.

An Ethnobiology Source Book. Richard I. Ford. Garland Publishers, 136 Madison Ave., New York, NY 10016. (212) 686-7492 or (800) 627-6273. 1986. The uses of plants and animals by, and the food habits of, American Indians.

Ethnobotany Specialist Group. c/o Prof. Richard Evans Schultes, Botanical Museum, Oxford St., Harvard University, Cambridgc, MA 02138. (617) 495-2326.

Ethyl Alcohol Production and Use as a Motor Fuel. Noyes Publications, 120 Mill Rd., Park Ridge, NJ 07656. (201) 391-8484. 1979. Patents relating to alcohol.

Ethylene Dibromide Toxicology. U.S. Department of Health and Human Services, Public Health Services, National Institutes of Health, 9000 Rockville Pike, Bethesda, MD 20892. (301) 496-4000. 1984.

Ethylene Oxide Industry Council. 2501 M St., N.W., Suite 330, Washington, DC 20037. (202) 887-1100.

Ethylmercury: Formation in Plant Tissues and Relation to Methylmercury Formation. L. Fortmann. National Technical Information Service, 5285 Port Royal Rd., Springfield, VA 22161. (703) 487-4650. 1978. Environmental aspects of mercury and botanical chemistry.

ETICBACK: Environmental Teratology Information Center Backfile. Oak Ridge National Laboratory, Environmental Teratology Information Center, Building 2001, P.O. Box 2008, Oak Ridge, TN 37831-6050. (615) 574-7871.

European Directory of Agrochemical Products. Royal Society of Chemistry, Thomas Graham House, Science Park, Milton Rd., Cambridge, England CB4 4WF. 1990. 4th ed. Volume 1: Fungicides. Volume 2: Herbicides. Volume 3: Insecticides. Volume 4: Growth regulators including rodenticides; molluscicides; nematicides; repellents and synerists.

European Directory of Agrochemical Products. H. Kidd and D. James, eds. Royal Society of Chemistry, c/o CRC Press, 2000 Corporate Blvd. N.W., Boca Raton, FL 33431-9868. (800) 272-7737. 1990. Provides comprehensive information on over 26,000 agrochemical products currently manufactured, marketed or used in 25 European countries.

European Environment Review. European Environment Review, 23, Ave. Gen. Eisenhower, B-1030, Brussels, Belgium Quarterly. Environmental policy and law in the European Economic Community countries.

European Environmental Yearbook, 1991. Doctor Institute of Environmental Studies. BNA Books, 1250 23rd St. NW, Washington, DC 20037. (202) 452-4276. 1991. The yearbook has been prepared with the cooperation of and financial assistance from the Commission of the European Communities/Brussels. It is a comprehensive guide to the environmental policies, laws, and regulations of the European Economic Community. Compares countries' responses to air and water pollution, nuclear safety, toxic and hazardous waste, land reclamation and other issues.

European Federation of Chemical Engineering. Working Party on Distillation. Six-Language Vocabulary of Distillation Terms. Institution of Chemical Engineers for the European Federation of Chemical Engineering, London, England Text in English, French, Spanish, Russian, Italian, and German.

European Journal of Population. North-Holland, 655 Avenue of the Americas, New York, NY 10010. (212) 989-5800. 1985-. Quarterly. Published under the auspices of the European Association for Population Studies.

European Water Pollution Control. European Water Pollution Control Association, Elsevier Science Pub., PO Box 211, 1000 AE, Amsterdam, Netherlands 1991-. Bimonthly. Discussion of views, policies, strategies, directives and guidelines, design procedures, technical ideas and solutions, performance and experience in construction, maintenance and operation of water pollution control.

Europhysics Study Conference on Induced Critical Conditions in the Atmosphere. A. Tartaglia. World Scientific, 687 Hartwell St., Teaneck, NJ 07666. (800) 227-7562. 1990. Deals with climatology, nuclear winter, ozone layer depletion, and the greenhouse effect.

Eutrophication: A Bimonthly Summary of Current Literature. University of Wisconsin-Madison, Water Resources Information Program, 1513 University Ave., Madison, WI 53706.

Eutrophication Management Framework for the Policy-Maker. Walter Rast, et al. UNESCO, 7, place de Fontenoy, Paris, France F-75700. (331) 45 68 40 67. 1989. MAB Digest 1.

Eutrophication of Fresh Waters. David Harper. Chapman & Hall, 29 West 35th St., New York, NY 10001-2291. (212) 244-3336. 1992. Principles, problems, and restoration of marine ecosystems.

Evaluating Soil Contamination. W. Nelson Beyer. U.S. Department of the Interior, Fish and Wildlife Service, Washington, DC 20240. (202) 343-5634. 1990. Biological analysis of soil pollution.

Evaluating the Benefits of Environmental Resources with Special Reference to Scenic Resources. John V. Krutilla. Centre for Resource Development, University of Guelph, Guelph, ON, Canada 1971. Economic measurement of natural resources.

Evaluation of a Pulsed Bed Filter for Filtration of Municipal Primary Effluent. Donald S. Brown. U.S. Environmental Protection Agency, 401 M St. SW, Washington, DC 20460. (202) 260-2090. Water treatment and purification plants.

Evaluation of Environmental Data for Regulatory and Impact Assessment. S. Ramamoorthy and E. Baddaloo. Elsevier Science Publishing Co., 655 Avenue of the Americas, New York, NY 10010. (212) 984-5800. 1991.

An Evaluation of Formaldehyde Problems in Residential Mobile Homes. Geomet Inc. U.S. Department of Housing and Urban Development, Office of Policy Development and Research, 451 7th St. SW, Washington, DC 20410. (202) 708-1422. 1981. Environmental safety measures relating to formaldehyde in mobile homes.

Evaluation of Longitudinal Dispersivity from Tracer Test Data. Claire Welty and Lynn W. Gelhar. Ralph M. Parsons Laboratory for Water Resources and Hydrodynamics, Massachusetts Institute of Technology, Cambridge, MA 02139. 1989. Groundwater flow, tracers, and diffusion in hydrology.

An Evaluation of Streaming Current Detectors. Steven Keith Dentel. AWWA Research Foundation, 6666 W. Quincy Ave., Denver, CO 80235. (303) 794-7711. 1988. Evaluation of water current meters.

Evaluation of the Report on Interceptor Sewers and Suburban Sprawl. U.S. Environmental Protection Agency, Office of Planning and Evaluation, 401 M St. SW, Washington, DC 20460. (202) 260-2090. 1975.

Evaluation of the Role of Ozone, Acid Deposition, and Other Airborne Pollutants in the Forests of Eastern North America. J.H.B. Garner. U.S. G.P.O., Washington, DC 20401. (202) 512-0000. 1989. Effects of air pollution on forests in the eastern U.S. and Canada, based on a review of field studies conducted primarily during 1960-1989. Pollutants studied include sulfur dioxide (SO_2), nitrogen oxides, ozone and other photochemical oxidants, and acid precipitation components.

Evaluation of Treatment Technologies for Listed Petroleum Refinery Wastes. R. Rowe. American Petroleum Institute, 1220 L St. N.W., Washington, DC 20005. (202) 682-8000. 1987. Field studies conducted by the API Waste Technology Task Force on petroleum waste.

Everglades National Park Protection and Expansion Act of 1989. U.S. House Committee on Interior and Insular Affairs. U.S. G.P.O., Washington, DC 20401. (202) 512-0000. 1991. Law and legislation relating to national parks and reserves and the conservation of natural resources with special reference to Everglades National Park.

The Everglades Reporter. Friends of the Everglades, 202 Park St., #4, Miami, FL 33166. (305) 888-1230. Five times a year. Ecology and nature conservation of the Florida Everglades.

Every Day is Earth Day: Simple Practical Things You Can Do to Help Clean Up the Planet. Peggy Taylor and Laura Danylin Duprez. New Age Journal, 342 Western Ave., Brighton, MA 02135. 1990.

Everyone's Back Yard. Citizen's Clearinghouse for Hazardous Wastes, P.O. Box 926, Arlington, VA 22216. (703) 276-7070. Bimonthly. Contains news, views, and resources for grassroots environmental activists.

Evolutionary Ecology. Chapman & Hall, 2-6 Boundary Row, London, England SE1 8HN. 1987-. Evolution of biotic communities and ecology.

Evolutionary Genetics and Environmental Stress. Ary A. Hoffmann. Oxford University Press, 200 Madison Ave., New York, NY 10016. (212) 679-7300 or (800) 334-4249. 1991. Outlines the results of numerous laboratory experiments and field studies from such diverse disciplines as agriculture, biochemistry, developmental biology, ecology, molecular biology, and genetics.

Evolutionary Trends in Plants. Evolutionary Trends in Plants, Zurich, Switzerland Quarterly.

Examining Your Environment. Daniel F. Wentworth. Holt, Rinehart & Winston of Canada, 55 Horner Ave., Toronto, ON, Canada M8Z 4X6. 1971-1976. Ecology program designed for use in grades 4-8 covering astronomy, birds, dandelions, ecology, mapping, mini-climates, pollution, running water, small animals, snow, ice, and trees.

Excerpta Botanica. Section A. Taxonomica et Chorologica. G. Fischer, 220E 23d St., Ste. 909, New York, NY 10010-4606. (212) 683-8333 or (800) 422-8824. 1959-.

Executive Office of Environmental Affairs: Coastal Zone Management. Director, Coastal Zone Management, 100 Cambridge St., Boston, MA 02202. (617) 727-9530.

Executive Office of Environmental Affairs: Environmental Protection. Secretary, 100 Cambridge St., 20th Floor, Boston, MA 02202. (617) 727-9800.

Executive Office of Environmental Affairs: Natural Resources. Commissioner, Department of Environmental Management, 100 Cambridge St., Boston, MA 02202. (617) 727-3163.

Exotic Species and the Shipping Industry. Great Lakes Fishery Commission, 2200 North Bonisteel Blvd., Ann Arbor, MI 481009. (313) 665-9135. 1990. The Great Lakes-St. Lawrence ecosystem at risk: a special report to the governments of the United States and Canada.

The Expandable Future. Richard J. Tobin. Duke University Press, College Sta., Box 6697, Durham, NC 27708. (919) 684-2173. 1990. Politics and the protection of biological diversity.

Expanded Shale, Clay & Slate Institute–Roster of Members. 2225 E. Murray Holladay Rd., Suite 102, Salt Lake City, UT 84117. (801) 272-7070. Annual.

Experimental Ecological Reserves. U.S. G.P.O, Washington, DC 20401. (202) 512-0000. 1977. Ecological research on natural areas.

Experimental Toxicology: The Basic Issues. Diana Anderson and D. M. Conning, eds. Royal Society of Chemistry, c/o CRC Press, 2000 Corporate Blvd. N.W., Boca Raton, FL 33431-9868. (800) 272-7737. 1988. Addresses the basic issues concerned with the practice of experimental toxicology.

Expert Systems for Environmental Applications. Judith M. Hushon, ed. American Chemical Society, 1155 16th St. N.W., Washington, DC 20036. (202) 872-4600; (800) 227-5558. 1990. Overview of environmental expert systems and its future applications for environmental protection.

Exploring the Tropical Rain Forest. D. Lamb. Parthenon Pub., Casterton Hall, Carnforth, England LA6 2LA. 1990. Volume 3 of the Man and the Biosphere series published jointly with UNESCO.

Explosives. Rudolf Meyer. VCH Publishers, 303 NW 12th Ave., Deerfield Beach, FL 33442-1788. (305) 428-5566. 1992.

Explosives Detection. National Technical Information Service, 5285 Port Royal Rd., Springfield, VA 22161. (703) 487-4650. 1986. Bibliography of explosives taken from COMPENDEX.

The Explosives Engineer. Hercules Inc., Hercules Plaza, 313 N. Market St., Wilmington, DE 19894-0001. (302) 594-5000. Bimonthly. Articles dealing with design, manufacturers and safety measures involving explosives and blasting.

Explosives Incidents Report. Bureau of Alcohol, Tobacco, and Firearms, 650 Massachusetts Ave. NW, Washington, DC 20226. (202) 927-8500. Annual. Data on offenses against property.

Explosives, Propellants and Pyrotechnics. A. Bailey. Brassey's Defense Publishers, 8000 Westpark Dr., 1st Fl., McLean, VA 22102. (703) 442-4535. 1989. Military fireworks and explosives.

Explosives Usage Policy. United States. Bureau of Alcohol, Tobacco, and Firearms. Department of Treasury, Bureau of Alcohol, Tobacco, and Firearms, 650 Massachusetts Ave. NW, Washington, DC 20226. (202) 927-8500. Transportation and safety measures relating to explosives.

Exposure Assessment for Epidemiology and Hazard Control. Lewis Publishers, 2000 Corporate Blvd., N.W., Boca Raton, FL 33431. (407) 994-0555 or (800) 272-7737. 1991. Examines the various approaches to answering questions on the topic. Includes measurement of current exposures, the application of toxicological relationships including biological markers and sample models; an epidemiological evaluation of exposure-effect relationships, including new methods for evaluation and models for population exposure estimates, and strategies for exposure assessments.

Exposure Factors Handbook. U.S. Environmental Protection Agency, Office of Health and Environmental Assessment, Exposure Assessment Group, 401 M St. SW, Washington, DC 20460. (202) 382-5480. 1989. Assessing human exposure including drinking water consumption, consumption rates of broad classes of food including fruits, vegetables, beef, dairy products, and fish; soil ingestion; inhalation rate; skin area; activity patterns and body weight.

Extension of the Principles of Radiation Protection to ... International Atomic Energy Agency. UNIPUB, 4611-F Assembly Dr., Lanham, MD 20706-4391. (301) 459-7666; (800) 274-4888. 1990.

Extinct Species of the World. Jean Christophe Balouet. Barron's, 200 Liberty St., New York, NY 10281. (212) 416-2700. 1990. Deals with extinction and nature conservation.

Extra High Voltage A.C. Transmission Engineering. John Wiley & Sons, Inc., 605 3rd Ave., New York, NY (212) 850-6000. 1986. High tension electric power distribution.

Extractive Bioconversions. Marcel Dekker, Inc., 270 Madison Ave., New York, NY 10016. (212) 696-9000; (800) 228-1160. Integration of downstream processing and bioconversion, separation technologies, cultivation of eukaryotic and prokaryotic cells, and the separation of the bioproducts.

Extremely Hazardous Substances: Superfund Chemical Profiles. U. S. Environment Protection Agency. Noyes Publications, 120 Mill Rd., Park Ridge, NJ 07656. (201) 391-8484. 1988. Contains chemical profiles for each of the 366 chemicals listed as extremely hazardous substances by the USEPA in 1988. The EPA developed this set of documents for use in dealing with Section 302 of Title III of the Superfund Amendments and Reauthorization Act (SARA). Each profile contains a summary of documented information which has been reviewed for accuracy and completeness.

Exxon Oil Spill: Hearing Before the Committee on Commerce, Science, Transportation, U. S. Senate, 101st Congress, First Session on Exxon Valdez Oil Spill and Its Environmental and Maritime Implications. U.S. G.P.O., Washington, DC 20401. (202) 512-0000. 1989.

Exxon Oil Spill: Hearing Before the National Ocean Policy Study and the Subcommittee on Merchant Marine of the Committee on Commerce, Science, and Transportation, U. S. Senate 101st Congress First Session on Cleanup,... U.S. G.P.O., Washington, DC 20401. (202) 512-0000. 1989.

The Eyas. Institute for Wildlife Research, National Wildlife Federation, 1412 16th St., NW, Washington, DC 20036-2266. (202) 797-6800. Semiannual. Research, education, and management programs about birds of prey in the United states, Canada, and Latin America.

F*A*C*T: Facility for the Analysis of Chemical Thermodynamics. Thermfact, Ltd., 447 Berwick Ave., Mont-Royal, PQ, Canada H3R 1Z8.

FAA Aviation Forecasts. U.S. Federal Aviation Administration. U.S. G.P.O., Washington, DC 20401. (202) 512-0000. Annual. Data on air traffic activity at major hubs projected to 2005.

FAA Statistical Handbook of Aviation. U.S. G.P.O., Washington, DC 20401. (202) 512-0000. Annual. Detailed and comprehensive data on all phases of aviation- related regulated by the FAA.

Facets of Freshwater. Freshwater Biological Research Foundation, 2500 Shadywood Rd., Box 90, Navarre, MN 55392. (612) 471-8407. 1970-. Quarterly. Topics in freshwater biological research.

Facets of Modern Biogeochemistry. V. Ittekkott, et al. Springer-Verlag, 175 5th Ave., New York, NY 10010. (212) 460-1500; (800) 777-4643. 1990. Deals with the geochemistry of marine sediments and related areas.

Facilities Evaluation Manual: Safety Fire Protection and Environmental Compliance. K. L. Petrocelly. The Association of Energy Engineers, 4025 Pleasantdale Rd., Suite 420, Atlanta, GA 30340. (404) 925-9558. 1991. Guide to help plant and facility managers conduct thorough inspections and evaluations of their facilities in order to pinpoint and solve problems in the areas of maintenance, safety, energy efficiency and environmental compliance.

Facility for Advanced Instrumentation. University of California Davis, Davis, CA 95616. (916) 752-0284.

Facing America's Trash: What Next for Municipal Solid Waste?. U.S. Office of Technology Assessment. Van Nostrand Reinhold, Washington, DC 20401. (202) 512-0000. 1991. Generation, composition and cost of recycling municipal solid waste.

FACTS. Institute of Scrap Recycling Industries, 1627 K St., NW, Suite 700, Washington, DC 20006. (202) 466-4050. Annual. Scrap production, consumption, prices, and foreign trade, for ferrous and nonferrous metals, paper, and textiles.

Facts and Figures of the U.S. Plastics Industry. Society of the Plastics Industry, Statistical Department, 1275 K St., NW, Suite 400, Washington, DC 20005. (202) 371-5200. Annual. Capacity, production, sales, markets, and foreign trade, by resin type.

The Facts on File Dictionary of Environmental Science. L. Harold Stevenson and Bruce Wyman. Facts on File, Inc., 460 Park Ave. S., New York, NY 10016. (212) 683-2244. 1991.

FAO Conservation Guide. Food and Agriculture Organization of the United Nations, Via delle Terme di Caracalla, Rome, Italy 00100. 61 0181-FA01. Annual. Covers soil and water conservation.

FAO Fertilizer and Plant Nutrition Bulletin. Food and Agriculture Organization of the United Nations, Via delle Terme di Caracalla, Rome, Italy 00100. 61 0181-FA01. 1981-.

Farm Building Series Circular. Michigan State University, Cooperative Extension Service, East Lansing, MI 48824. Irregular.

Farm Chemical Handbook. Meister Publishing Co., 37733 Euclid Ave., Willoughby, OH 44094. (216) 942-2000. Annual. Covers fertilizers and manures.

Farm Chemicals Magazine. Meister Publishing Co., 37733 Euclid Avenue, Willoughby, OH 44094. (216) 942-2000. Monthly. Covers the production, marketing and application of fertilizers and crop protection chemicals.

Farmer's Own Network for Education. Rodale Institute, 222 Main St., Emmaus, PA 18098. (215) 967-5171. Efforts/results of farmers who have cut chemical use, diversified their farms, and adopted other regenerative agricultural techniques.

Farming in Nature's Image. Judith A. Soule. Island Press, 1718 Connecticut Ave. N.W., Suite 300, Washington, DC 20009. (202) 232-7933. 1992. Gives a detailed look into the pioneering work of the Land Institute, the leading educational and research organization for sustainable agriculture.

Farming on the Edge: Saving Family Farms in Marin County, California. John Hart. University of California Press, 2120 Berkeley Way, Berkeley, CA 94720. (415) 642-4262; (800) 822-6657. 1991. Case study in successful land-use planning.

Farmland. American Farmland Trust, 1920 N St., NW, Suite 400, Washington, DC 20036. (202) 659-5170. Quarterly. Voluntary land protection programs to protect farmland from conversion pressures, soil erosion, and other environmental impacts.

Farmland Industries. 3315 N. Oak Trafficway, P.O. Box 7305, Kansas City, MO 64116. (816) 459-6000.

Farmland of Wasteland. Rodale Press, 33 E. Minor St., Emmaus, PA 18098. (215) 967-5171. 1981. Deals with soil conservation, agricultural water supply and land use.

Farms of Tomorrow. Trauger Groh. Bio-Dynamic Farming and Gardening Association, PO Box 550, Kimberton, PA 19442. (215) 935-7797. 1990. Describes a new approach to farming called community supported agriculture (CSA). It is built upon the solid foundation of organic and biodynamic cultivation, but it focuses on the social and economic conditions that make farming possible.

Fate of Pesticides and Chemicals in the Environment. Jerald L. Schnoor, ed. John Wiley & Sons, Inc., 605 3rd Ave., New York, NY 10158-0012. (212) 850-6000. 1992. Focuses on the necessity to improve our deteriorating standards of public health, environmental science and technology with a total systems approach through the pooled talents of scientists and engineers.

Fate of Trace Metals in a Rotary Kiln Incinerator with a Single-Stage Ionizing Wet Scrubber. D. J. Fournier and L. R. Waterland. National Technical Information Service, 5285 Port Royal Rd., Springfield, VA 22161. (703) 487-4650. 1991. Two volumes. Vol. 1 Technical results. vol. 2. Appendices.

Fates and Biological Effects of Polycyclic Aromatic Hydrocarbons in Aquatic Systems. John P. Giesy. U.S. Environmental Protection Agency, Center for Environmental Research Information, 26 W. Martin Luther King Dr., Cincinnati, OH 45268. (513) 569-7931. 1983. Aquatic biology, water pollution, and environmental aspects of hydrocarbons.

FDA Enforcement Report. Food and Drug Administration, 5600 Fishers Ln., Rockville, MD 20857. (301)443-1544. Weekly. Legal actions covering food adulteration and inspection.

FDA Food Additives Analytical Manual. C. Warner, et al., eds. Association of Official Analytical Chemists, 2200 Wilson Blvd., Suite 400-P, Arlington, VA 22201-3301. (703) 522-3032. 1983-1987. 2 vols. Provides methodology for determining compliance with food additive regulations. Contains analytical methods that have been evaluated by the FDA or found to operate satisfactorily in at least two laboratories.

FDA Inspection Operation Manual. U.S. Dept. of Health and Human Services, Public Health Service, Food and Drug Administration. U.S. G.P.O., Washington, DC 20401. (202) 512-0000. Food and drug adulteration and inspection. Looseleaf format.

FDA Surveillance Index for Pesticides. National Technical Information Service, 5285 Port Royal Rd., Springfield, VA 22161. (703) 487-4650. Monthly. Health risks of individual pesticides from a dietary exposure standpoint; FDA monitoring; chemical, biological, and toxicological data.

Feasibility of Disposal of High-Level Radioactive Waste into the Seabed. Nuclear Energy Agency. OECD Publication and Information Centre, 2 rue Andre Pascal, Paris, France F-75775. 1988. Radiological assessment, geoscience characterization, deep-sea biology, radiological processes and radiobiology, migration through deep-sea sediments and the review of the processes near a buried waste canister.

Feasibility of Environmental Monitoring and Exposure Assessment for a Municipal Waste Combustor. C. Sonich-Mullin. U.S. Environmental Protection Agency, 401 M St., SW, Washington, DC 20460. (202) 260-2090. 1991.

The Feasibility of Methods and Systems for Reducing LNG Tanker Fire Hazards. Arthur D. Little, Inc. U.S. Department of Energy, Division of Environmental Safety and Engineering, Washington, DC 1980. Liquefied natural gas accidents.

The Feasibility of Using Computer Graphics in Environmental Evaluations. Daniel D. McGeehan. National Technical Information Service, 5285 Port Royal Rd., Springfield, VA 22161. (703) 487-4650. 1981.

Feather in the Wind. Last Chance Forever, 506 Ave. A, San Antonio, TX 78215. (512) 224-7228. Semiannual. Birds of prey and their relation to the environment.

Federal Biotechnology Funding Sources. Oskar R. Zaborsky and B. K. Young. OMEC International Inc., 727 15th St., NW, Washington, DC 20005. (202) 639-8400. 1984.

Federal Biotechnology Information Resources Directory. OMEC International Inc., 727 15th St. NW, Washington, DC 20005. (202) 639-8400. 1987. Directory of federal government information resources relevant to biotechnology. Covers federal programs and provides comprehensive access to federal information resources in biotechnology.

Federal Biotechnology Programs Directory. OMEC International Inc., 727 15th St., NW, Washington, DC 20005. (202) 639-8400. 1987. Describes federal programs relevant to biotechnology. Provides composite information gleaned from various sources such as program announcements, annual reports, reports to Congress, and OMEC International Inc. extensive contact files.

Federal Facilities Environmental Journal. Executive Enterprises Publications Co., Inc., 22 W. 21st St., New York, NY 10010-6990. (212) 645-7880. Quarterly. Environmental issues at federal facilities.

Federal Guidelines for Dam Safety. United States Ad Hoc Interagency Committee on Dam Safety. U.S. G.P.O., Washington, DC 20401. 1979. Deals with dam safety and dam inspection.

Federal Highway Administration: Right-of-Way and Environment. 400 7th St., S.W., Washington, DC 20590. (202) 366-0342.

Federal Lands: A Guide to Planning, Management, and State Revenues. Sally K. Fairfax. Island Press, 1718 Connecticut Ave. N.W., Suite 300, Washington, DC 20009. (202) 232-7933. 1987. Comprehensive reference on the management and allocation of revenues from public lands.

Federal Offshore Statistics. U.S. Dept. of Interior. Minerals Management Service. U.S. G.P.O., Washington, DC 20401. (202) 512-0000. Annual. Oil, gas and mineral exploration, production, well blowouts and spills.

Federal Parks and Recreation. Resources Publishing Co., 1010 Vermont Ave., NW, Suite 708, Washington, DC 20005. (202) 638-7529. Biweekly. Policy changes affecting national parks and federal, state, and local park and recreation areas.

Federal Register Search System. Chemical Information Systems, Inc., 7215 York Rd., Baltimore, MD 21212. (301) 321-8440. Regulations, rules, standards, and guidelines involving chemical substances and cross-referencing to other citations on related substances.

Federal Regulation of Hazardous Wastes: A Guide to RCRA. John Quaries. Environmental Law Institute, 1616 P St., NW, Suite 200, Washington, DC 20036. (202) 328-5150. 1982. Law and legislation in connection with hazardous wastes.

Federal Water Quality Association. PO Box 44163, Washington, DC 20026. (202) 447-4925.

Federal Water Quality Association Newsletter. Federal Water Quality Association, P.O. Box 44163, Washington, DC 20026. (202) 447-4925. Seven times a year. Concerns sewage and industrial waste treatment and disposal.

Federation Highlights. Water Pollution Control Federation, 601 Wythe St., Alexandria, VA 22314-1994. (703) 684-2400. Monthly. News and trends in water pollution control.

Federation of American Societies for Experimental Biology. 9650 Rockville Pike, Bethesda, MD 20814. (301) 530-7090.

Federation of Environmental Technologists. P.O. Box 185, Milwaukee, WI 53201. (414) 251-8163.

Federation of Western Outdoor Clubs. 365 K St. N.W., Ste. 400, Seattle, WA 98102. (206) 322-3050.

Feed from Animal Wastes: Feeding Manual. Z.O. Muller. Food and Agriculture Organization of the United Nations, Via delle Terme di Caracalla, Rome, Italy 00100. 61 0181-FA01. 1982. Organic wastes as feed and animal waste.

Feed from Animal Wastes: State of Knowledge. Z.O. Muller. Food and Agriculture Organization of the United Nations, Via delle Terme di Caralla, Rome, Italy 00100. 61 0181-FA01. 1980.

Feeding Tomorrow's World. Albert Sasson. Centre for Agriculture and Rural Cooperation and UNESCO, 7 Place de Fontenoy, Paris, France 75700 1990. Analyzes Green Revolution and biotechnological revolution and tries to answer other pressing questions through a pluridisciplinary approach to human nutrition and food production. Synthesizes the scientific, economic, socioeconomic and environmental aspects of nutrition throughout the world.

Felicidades Wildlife Foundation. P.O. Box 490, Waynesville, NC 28786. (704) 926-0192.

The Feminine Hygiene Market. FIND/SVP, 625 Avenue of the Americas, New York, NY 10011. (212) 645-4500. 1990. Feminine hygiene market, including: tampons; napkins; douches, washes and wipes; and feminine deodorant sprays.

Ferro–Alloy Directory and Databook. 220 5th Ave., 10th Fl., New York, NY 10001. (212) 213-6202. Irregular.

Ferrous Scrap Consumers Coalition. c/o Collier, Shannon, Rill, & Scott, 1055 Thomas Jefferson St., N.W., Suite 308, Washington, DC 20007. (202) 342-8485.

Fertile Soil: A Grower's Guide to Organic and Inorganic Fertilizers. Robert Parnes. AgAccess, PO Box 2008, Davis, CA 95617. (916) 756-7177. 1990. Comprehensive technical resource on creating fertile soils using a balanced program that does not rely on chemical fertilizers.

Fertility and Sterility. American Fertility Society, 2140 11th Ave. S., Birmingham, AL 35205-2800. (205) 933-8494. Monthly.

Fertility of American Women. U.S. Bureau of the Census, Department of Commerce, Washington, DC 20233. (301) 763-4040. Annual. Data on fertility, childbirth and birth rate.

Fertilizer Abstracts. National Fertilizer Development Center, Muscle Shoals, AL 35660. Contains information on fertilizers technology, marketing use, and related research.

Fertilizer Institute. 501 2nd Ave., N.E., Washington, DC 20002. (202) 675-8250.

Fertilizer Progress. Clear Window, Inc., 15444 Clayton Road, #314, St. Louis, MO 63011. (202) 861-4900. Bimonthly. Covers business and management of fertilizers and farm chemicals.

Fertilizer Research: An International Journal on Fertilizer Use and Technology. Kluwer Academic Publishers, 101 Philip Dr., Assinippi Park, Norwell, MA 02061. (617) 871-6600. Monthly. Soils, soil fertility, soil chemistry, crop and animal production and husbandry, crop quality and environment.

Fertilizer Trade Statistics, 1970-88. Harry Vroomen. U.S. Deptartment of Agriculture, Economic Research Service, 14 Independence Ave., SW, Washington, DC 20250. (202) 447-7454. 1989.

FGD Newsletter. McIlvaine Co., 2970 Maria Ave., Northbrook, IL 60062. (708) 272-0010. Monthly. Desulphurization and flue gases, purification of fluidized-bed furnaces, and coal-fired power plants.

FGD Quarterly Report. The Laboratory, Highway 54 and Alexander Dr., Research Triangle Park, NC 27711. (919) 541-2821. Quarterly.

Fiber Organon–Directory of U.S. Manufactured Fiber Products Issue. 101 Eisenhower Parkway, Roseland, NJ 07068. (201) 228-1107. Annual.

Fibre Box Association. 2850 Golf Rd., Rolling Meadows, IL 60008. (708) 364-9600.

Fibre Market News–Directory of Paper Stock Dealers Issue. 4012 Bridge Ave., Cleveland, OH 44113. (216) 961-4130. Annual.

Field Comparison of Ground-Water Sampling Methods. Ronald Paul Blegen. National Technical Information Service, 5285 Port Royal, Springfield, VA 22161. (703) 487-4650. 1988. Thesis (M.S.)–Geoscience, University of Nevada, Las Vegas, 1988.

Field Crop Abstracts. C. A. B. International, 845 North Park Ave., Tucson, AZ 85719. (602) 621-7897 or (800) 528-4841. 1948-. Monthly. Covers literature on agronomy, field production, crop botany and physiology of all annual field crops, both temperate and tropical.

Fields, Currents, and Aerosols in the Lower Troposphere. A. A. Balkema, Rotterdam, Netherlands 1986.

FIFRA and TSCA Enforcement System–FATES. U.S. Environmental Protection Agency, Office of Compliance and Monitoring, 401 M St., S.W., Washington, DC 20460. (202) 260-2090.

Fighting Noise in 1990s. Organisation for Economic Cooperation and Development. OECD Publication and Information Center, 2001 L. St. N.W., Suite 700, Washington, DC 20036. (202) 785-6323. 1991. Deals with transportation noise pollution. Includes the economic impacts and relevant legislation.

Fighting Radiation with Foods, Herbs, and Vitamins. East West Health Books, 17 Station St., PO Box 1200, Brookline, MA 02147. (617) 232-1000. 1988. Documented natural remedies that protect you from radiation, X-rays, and chemical pollutants.

Fighting Toxics. Gary Cohen and John O'Connor, eds. Island Press, 1718 Connecticut Ave. N.W., Suite 300, Washington, DC 20009. (202) 232-7933. 1990. Investigates the toxic hazards in the community, determining the health risks they pose, and launching an effective campaign to eliminate them.

Filters–Air & Gas-Retail. 5711 S. 86th Circle, Omaha, NE 68127. (402) 593-4600. Annual.

Filters and Filtration Handbook. R.H. Warring. Gulf Publishing Co., Book Division, PO Box 2608, Houston, TX 77252. (713) 529-4301. 1981.

Filtration and Separation. Elsevier Science Publishing Co., 655 Avenue of the Americas, New York, NY 10010. (212) 984-5800. Bimonthly. Filtration, separation dust control, air filtration or gas cleaning equipment; manufacturers of such equipment and designers.

Filtration News. Eagle Publication, Inc., 42400 Nine Mile Road, Suite B, Novi, MI 48375. (313) 347-3486. Bimonthly. Information on equipment and components used for particulate removal.

Final Covers on Hazardous Waste Landfills and Surface Impoundments. Office of Solid Waste and Emergency Response, U.S. Environment Protection Agency, U.S. G.P.O., Washington, DC 20402-9325. (202) 783-3238. 1989. Technical Guidance Document series EPA/530-SW-89-047. Shipping list no. 89-483-P.

Financial Times Who's Who in World Oil and Gas. Longman Group UK Ltd., Westgate House, 6th Fl., The High, Harlow, England CM20 1NE. 279 442601.

Financing the Cleanup of Hazardous Wastes: The National Environmental Trust Fund. American International Group, New York, NY 1989.

Finding the Rx for Managing Medical Wastes. U.S. G.P.O., Washington, DC 20401. (202) 512-0000. 1990. Medical waste composition and management technologies. Includes human and animal products, discarded medical equipment and parts, radioactive waste, and wastes from surgery and selected clinical and laboratory procedures, including chemotherapy and dialysis.

Fine Chemical Database. Chemron, Inc., 3038 Orchard Hill, San Antonio, TX 78230-3057. (512) 493-2247.

Fine Chemicals. FIND/SVP, 625 Avenue of the Americas, New York, NY 10011. (212) 645-4500. 1990.

Fine Chemicals Directory. Molecular Design Ltd., 2132 Farrallon Dr., San Leandro, CA 94577. (415) 895-1313.

Fine Hardwoods-American Walnut Association. 5603 W. Raymond St., Suite O, Indianapolis, IN 46241. (317) 244-3311.

Fine Pore Aeration for Wastewater Treatment. W. C. Boyle, et al. Noyes Publications, 120 Mill Rd., Park Ridge, NJ 07656. (201) 391-8484. 1990. Presents information from Design Manual prepared for the U.S. Environmental Protection Agency, Sept. 1989. Includes the following devices: porous ceramic plates, discs, domes, tubes, perforated membrane tubes and discs.

Fire and Ice: The Nuclear Winter. Michael Rowan-Robinson. Longman Group Ltd., Longman House, Burnt Mill, Harlow, England CM20 2J6. (0279) 426721. 1985.

Fire Ecology, United States and Southern Canada. Henry A. Wright. John Wiley & Sons, Inc., 605 3rd Ave., New York, NY 10158-0012. (212) 850-6000. 1982. Procedures in prescribed burning.

Fire in North America Wetland Ecosystems and Fire-Wildlife Relations: An Annotated Bibliography. Ronald E. Kirby. Fish and Wildlife Service, Department of the Interior, 18th & C Sts., N.W., Washington, DC 20240. (202) 653-8750. 1988.

Fire in the Rain. Peter Gould. Carolina Biological Supply Company, 2700 York Rd., Burlington, NC 27215. (919) 584-0381. 1990. Describes the Chernobyl accident.

Fire in the Tropical Biota: Ecosystem Processes and Global Challenges. J.G. Goldammer. Springer-Verlag, 175 5th Ave., New York, NY 10010. (212) 460-1500. 1990. Covers fire ecology, wildfires, botany, tropical fires, and biotic communities.

Fire Protection Management for Hazardous Materials. Byron L. Briese, ed. Government Institutes, Inc., 4 Research Pl., Suite 200, Rockville, MD 20850. (301) 921-2300. 1991. Designed as a guide to the industry, this manual gives standard fire and building codes and a framework needed to manage the federal, state and local requirements and the specific technical needs of the individual facility.

Fire Safety of LPG in Marine Transportation. Applied Technology Corp. National Technical Information Service, 5285 Port Royal Rd., Springfield, VA 22161. (703) 487-4650. 1980. Fire prevention in shipping LPG.

FIREDOC Vocabulary List. Nora H. Jason. National Institute of Standards and Technology, Rte. I-270 & Quince Orchard Rd., Gaithersburg, MD 20899. (301) 975-2000. 1985. Terminology of FIREDOC computer program.

Firefighter's Hazardous Materials Reference Book. Daniel J. Davis and Grant T. Christianson. Van Nostrand Reinhold, 115 5th Ave., New York, NY 10003. (212) 254-3232. 1991. List of hazardous materials. For quick reference, each hazardous material is given its own page with material's name in bold at the top.

Firewood-Retail. American Business Directories, Inc., 5711 S. 86th Circle, Omaha, NE 68127. (402) 593-4600.

Fish and Fish Egg Distribution Report. U.S. Fish and Wildlife Service. U.S. G.P.O., Washington, DC 20401. (202) 512-0000. Annual. Propagation and distribution activities of the National Fish Hatchery System.

Fish and Game Department: Fish and Wildlife. Director, 34 Bridge St., Concord, NH 03301. (603) 271-3512.

Fish and Wildlife Department: Fish and Wildlife. Commissioner, Tourism Cabinet, #1 Game Farm Rd., Frankfort, KY 40601. (502) 564-3400.

Fish and Wildlife Reference Service Database. U.S. Fish and Wildlife Service, The Maxima Corporation, 5430 Grosvenor Lane, Suite 110, Bethesda, MD 20814. (301) 492-6403. State fish and game agency technical reports covering American fish and wildlife.

Fish and Wildlife Reference Service Newsletter. U.S. Fish and Wildlife Reference Service, 5430 Grosvenor Lane, Suite 110, Bethesda, MD 20814. (800) 582-3421. Quarterly. Federal Aid in Fish and Wildlife Program.

Fish: Five Language Dictionary of Fish, Crustaceans, and Mollusks. Willibad Krane. Behr's Verlag, c/o Van Nostrand Reinhold, 115 5th Ave., New York, NY 10003. 1986.

Fish Habitat Improvement Handbook. Monte E. Seehorn. U.S. Department of Agriculture, Forest Service, Southern Region, 1720 Peachtree Rd., NW, Atlanta, GA 30367. 1985.

Fish Oil: Role of Omega-3S in Health and Nutrition: January 1979-December 1990. Deborah Hanfman. National Agricultural Library, 10301 Baltimore Blvd., Beltsville, MD 20705-2351. (301) 504-5755. 1991. Health aspects of fish oils in human nutrition.

Fish Oils: January 1989 through July 1990: 653 Citations. Jacqueline Van De Kamp. U.S. Department of Health and Human Services, 200 Independence Ave. SW, Washington, DC 20201. (202) 619-0257. 1990. Therapeutic use of fatty acids and fish oils.

Fish Quality Control by Computer Vision. L. F. Pau and R. Olafsson, eds. Marcel Dekker, Inc., 270 Madison Ave., New York, NY 10016. (212) 696-9000; (800) 228-1160. 1991. Explores how computer vision and image processing can be applied to such aspects of the fishing industry as the quality inspection of fish and fish products for defects; the measurement and sorting by length, weight, species, shape, orientation, etc. in the processes of packaging, handling, selection, registration and pricing.

Fish, Wildlife, and Parks Department: Fish and Wildlife. Director, 1420 E. Sixth Ave., Helena, MT 59620. (406) 444-3186.

Fish, Wildlife, and Parks Department: Groundwater Management. Boating Law Administrator, 1420 E. Sixth Ave., Helena, MT 59620. (406) 444-3186.

FishAmerica Foundation. c/o Sport Fishing Institute, 1010 Massachusetts Ave., N.W., Suite 320, Washington, DC 20001. (202) 898-0869.

Fisheries of the U.S. U.S. G.P.O., Washington, DC 20401. (202) 512-0000. Annual. Fish landings, fish trade, prices, consumption, production of fishery products, and industry employment.

Fisheries Review. U.S. Fish and Wildlife Service. U.S. G.P.O., Washington, DC 20401. (202) 512-0000. Quarterly. Abstracting service dealing with fisheries and ichthyology.

Fisheries Socio-Economic Data Locator. Office of Fisheries Management/National Marine Fisheries Service, 1335 East-West Highway, Silver Spring, MD 20910. (202) 634-7218.

Fishing Vessel Safety: Blueprint for a National Program. National Research Council. Committee on Fishing Vessel Safety. National Academy Press, 2101 Constitution Ave. NW, PO Box 285, Washington, DC 20055. (202) 334-3313. 1991. Comprehensive assessment of vessel and personnel safety in the U.S. commercial fishing fleet. Includes a chronology of safety efforts and summarizes various parameters of commercial fishing industry.

FISHNET. Aquatic Data Center, 1100 Gentry St., North Kansas City, MO 64116. (816) 842-5936.

Flagellates in Freshwater Ecosystems. R. I. Jones. Kluwer Academic Publishers, 101 Philip Dr., Assinippi Park, Norwell, MA 02061. (617) 871-6600. 1988. Developments in hydrobiology and freshwater invertebrates.

Flashpoint. National Association of Solvent Recyclers, 1333 New Hampshire Ave., N.W., No. 1100, Washington, DC 20036. (202) 463-6956. Biweekly. Overview of recycling hazardous waste fuel blending & related industries.

Flavor and Extract Manufacturers Association of the United States. 1620 I St., N.W., Suite 925, Washington, DC 20006. (202) 293-5800.

Flexible Packaging Association. 1090 Vermont Ave., N.W., Suite 500, Washington, DC 20005. (202) 842-3880.

Flexible Pavements. P.O. Box 16186, Columbus, OH 43216. (614) 221-5402.

Florida Conservation News. Florida Department of Natural Resources, 3900 Commonwealth Blvd., Tallahassee, FL 32303. (904)488-1234. 1965-. Monthly.

Florida Environments. Florida Environments Pub., 215 N. Main St., PO Box 1617, High Springs, FL 32643. (904) 454-2007. Monthly. Florida's hazardous materials/wastes, wildlife, regulation, drinking/ground/surface waters, air, and solid waste.

Florida Fish & Wildlife News. Florida Wildlife Federation, Box 6870, Tallahassee, FL 32314-6870. (904) 656-7113. Monthly. Conservation news concerning fish & wildlife.

Florida Medical Entomology Laboratory. University of Florida, Institute of Food and Agricultural Sciences, 200 9th Street, S.E., Vero Beach, FL 32962. (407) 778-7200.

Florida Naturalist. Florida Audubon Society, PO Drawer 7, Maitland, FL 32751. 1917-. Bimonthly.

Florida Sea Grant College Program. University of Florida, Building 803, Room 4, Gainesville, FL 32611-0341. (904) 392-5870.

Florida Wildlife. Florida Game and Fresh Water Fish Commission, Florida State Game, 620 S. Meridian St., Tallahassee, FL 32399-1600. (904) 488-5563. 1976-. Bimonthly. State wildlife conservation magazine.

Flue Gas Cleaning Wastes Disposal and Utilization. D. Khoury. Noyes Publications, 120 Mill Rd., Park Ridge, NJ 07656. (201) 391-8484. 1981. Pollution technology relating to flue gases, purification, and waste disposal.

FLUIDEX. STI, a subsidiary of BHR Group Limited, Cranfield, Bedfordshire, England MK43 OAJ. 44 (234) 750422.

Fluidized Bed Combustion and Applied Technology. Hemisphere Publishing Co., 79 Madison Ave., Suite 1110, New York, NY 10016. (212) 725-1999. 1984.

A Fluorescence Standard Reference Material, Quinine Sulfate Dihydrate. R.A. Velapoldi. National Bureau of Standards, Gaithersburg, MD 20899. (301)975-2000. 1980. Standards for fluorescence, quinine sulfate optical properties, and materials.

Fluorine, Its Compounds, and Air Pollution: A Bibliography with Abstracts. U.S. Environmental Protection Agency, Office of Air Quality Planning Standards, MD 75, Research Triangle Park, NC 27711. 1976.

Fly Ash Utilization in Soil-Bentonite Slurry Trench Cutoff Walls. University Microfilms International, 300 N. Zeeb Rd., Ann Arbor, MI 48106. (313) 761-4700. 1990.

Foamed Plastics Market. FIND/SVP, 625 Avenue of the Americas, New York, NY 10011. (212) 645-4500. 1991. Historical (1980, 1985, 1990) and forecast (1995 and 2000) data for foamed urethanes, foamed styrenes and other foamed types.

Foams: Physics, Chemistry, and Structure. A. J. Wilson. Springer-Verlag, 175 5th Ave., New York, NY 10010. (212) 460-1500. 1989.

Focus. Hazardous Materials Control Research Institute, 9300 Columbia Blvd, Silver Spring, MD 20910-1702. (301) 587-9390. Monthly. Covers hazardous materials technology and legislation.

Focus on International Joint Commission Activities. IJC Great Lakes Regional Office, PO Box 32869, Detroit, MI 48232. (313) 226-2170. 1986-. Three issues a year. Provides information on Great Lakes water quality and quantity issues.

Focus: Quarterly Report on the Nuclear Fuel Cycle. Nuclear Assurance Corp., 6251 Crooked Creek Road, Norcross, GA 30092. Quarterly. Data on nuclear reactor and fuel cycle operations; uranium project profile and Fuel-Trac summary.

Food Additives and Contaminants. Taylor & Francis, 1900 Frost Rd., Suite 101, Bristol, PA 19007. (215) 785-5580. Bimonthly.

Food Additives and Their Impact on Health. Oryx Press, 4041 N. Central at Indian School Rd., Ste. 700, Phoenix, AZ 85012-3397. (602) 265-2651. 1988. Bibliography of health aspects and toxicology of food additives.

Food Additives Handbook. Van Nostrand Reinhold, 115 Fifth Ave., New York, NY 10003. (212) 254-3232. 1989. Toxicology of food additives.

Food Additives Tables. Food Law Research Centre, Univ. of Brussels. Elsevier Science Publishing Co., 655 Avenue of the Americas, New York, NY 10010. (212) 984-5800. 1988. Three volumes. Data on the regulatory status of food additives used in specific foods from 19 countries is included. Arrangement is by class of food.

Food and Agriculture Organization. Liaison Office for North America, 1001 22nd St., N.W., Washington, DC 20437. (202) 653-2402.

Food and Agriculture Organization of the United Nations. CN Index of Agricultural Research Institutions in Europe. AGRIS Coordinating Center, Via delle Terme di Caracalla, Rome, Italy I-00100. Directory of agriculture and agricultural experiment stations.

Food and Chemical Toxicology. Pergamon Microforms International Inc., Fairview Park, Elmsford, NY 10523. (914) 592-7720. Monthly. Information and risks of food and chemicals.

Food & Drug Law Institute. 1000 Vermont Ave., N.W., Suite 1200, Washington, DC 20036. (202) 371-1420.

Food and Nutrition Encyclopedia. A. H. Ensminger, et al. Pegus Press, 648 W. Sierra Ave, Clovis, CA 93612. 1983. Two volumes. Covers commodities, nutrients, concepts, nutrition disorders and simple nutritional biochemistry with both brief and extensive entries.

Food and Nutrition Information Guide. Paula Szilard. Libraries Unlimited, Inc., PO Box 6633, Englewood, CO 80155-6633. (303) 770-1220. 1987. Focuses on reference materials on human nutrition dietetics, food science and technology, and related subjects such as food service. It covers chiefly English-language materials published in the last ten years.

Food and Nutrition Quarterly Index. Oryx Press, 4041 N. Central at Indian School Rd., Ste. 700, Phoenix, AZ 85012-3397. (602) 265-2651. 1985-. Quarterly. Abstracting service succeeds the Food and Nutrition Bibliography which was issued from 1980-1984 and covered the literature from 1978-1980, and was a continuation of the FNIC catalog and its supplements.

Food & Water, Inc. 225 Lafayette St., Suite 612, New York, NY 10012. (212) 941-9340.

Food Chain Yields, Models, and Management of Large Marine Ecosystems. Kenneth Sherman, et al., eds. Westview Press, 5500 Central Ave., Boulder, CO 80301. (303) 444-3541. 1991. Describes marine ecology, its productive resources and its management.

Food Contamination from Environmental Sources. J. O. Nriagu and M. S. Simmons, eds. John Wiley & Sons, Inc., 605 3rd Ave., New York, NY 10158-0012. (212) 850-6000. 1990. Discusses the accumulation and transfer of contaminants through the food chain to the consumer.

Food, Cosmetics & Drug Packaging. Elsevier Advanced Technology Publications, Mayfield House, 256 Banbury Rd., Oxford, England OX2 7DH. 44 (865) 512242.

Food Flavourings, Ingredients, Processing, Packaging. United Trade Press Ltd, London, England Monthly.

Food, Fuel, and Fertilizer from Organic Wastes. National Research Council. National Academy Press, 2101 Constitution Ave. NW, PO Box 285, Washington, DC 20418. (202) 334-3313. 1981. Recycling of organic wastes.

Food Industry Wastes: Disposal and Recovery. A. Herzka. Applied Science Publishers, Crown House, Linton Rd., Barking, England IG 11 8JU. 1981.

Food Irradiation. Walter M. Urbain. Academic Press, c/o Harcourt Brace Jovanovich Inc., 6277 Sea Harbor Dr., Orlando, FL 32887. (800) 346-8648. 1986. Food science and technology relating to food preservation.

Food News for Consumers. U.S. Deptartment of Agriculture, Food Safety and Quality Service, 14 Independence Ave., SW, Washington, DC 20250. (202) 447-7454. Quarterly. Consumer protection in the area of food adulteration.

Food Pollution: A Bibliography. Joan Nordquist. Reference and Research Services, 511 Lincoln St., Santa Cruz, CA 95060. (408) 426-4479. 1990. Bibliography of food adulteration and inspection, food additives and toxicology.

Food Processing. Techpress (FPI) Ltd., Bromley, England Kent Quarterly.

Food Production Management–Advertisers Buyers Guide Issue. 2619 Maryland Ave., Baltimore, MD 21218. (301) 467-3338. Annual.

Food Protection Technology. Charles W. Felix. Lewis Publishers, 2000 Corporate Blvd., N.W., Boca Raton, FL 33431. (407) 994-0555 or (800) 272-7737. 1987. Updates the new and proven techniques and methods in food protection technology.

Food Safety, 1990: An Annotated Bibliography of the Literature. Dorothy C. Gosting, et al. Butterworth-Heinemann, 80 Montvale Ave., Stoneham, MA 02180. (617) 438-8464 or (800) 366-2665. 1991. Deals with the areas of environmental health and toxicology in relation to food safety and preservation. The bibliography is divided into three major parts headed "Diet and Health," "Safety of Food Components," and "Foodborne Microbial Illness." The appendix is titled "Food-and-Water-Associated Viruses."

Food Science. Gordon Gerard Birch. Pergamon Microforms International, Inc., Fairview Park, Elmsford, NY 10523. (914) 592-7720. 1977. Science, technology, engineering of food.

Food Science. Helen Charley. John Wiley & Sons, Inc., 605 3rd Ave., New York, NY 10158-0012. (212) 850-6000. 1982. Second edition.

Food Science and Nutrition: Current Issues and Answers. Fergus Clydesdale. Prentice-Hall, Rte. 9W, Englewood Cliffs, NJ 07632. (201) 592-2000. 1979. Food additives and food-processing industry.

Food, Science, and Technology: A Bibliography of Recommended Materials. Richard E. Wallace. National Agricultural Library, 10301 Baltimore Blvd., Beltsville, MD 20705-2351. (301) 504-5755. 1978.

Food Science and Technology Abstracts. International Food Information Service, c/o National Food Laboratory, 6363 Clark Ave., Dublin, CA 94568. (800) 336-3782. 1969-.

Foods ADLIBRA. General Mills, Inc., Foods Adlibra Publications, 9000 Plymouth Ave., North, Minneapolis, MN 55427. (612) 540-3463. Online version of periodical of same name.

Foods ADLIBRA. K & M Pub. Inc., 2000 Frankfort Ave., Louisville, KY 40206. Semimonthly. Contains abstracts of current literature concerning the food industry. Topics covered include: food technology, food packaging, new food products, world food economics, nutrition, patents, and marketing.

Foods and Food Production Encyclopedia. D. M. Considine and G. D. Considine, eds. Van Nostrand Reinhold, 115 5th Ave., New York, NY 10020. (212) 254-3232. 1982. Three fundamental stages of food production are discussed: the start or initiation; the nurture; and the processing.

Foodservice and Packaging Institute. 1025 Connecticut Ave., N.W., Washington, DC 20036. (202) 822-6420.

For Earth's Sake: The Life and Times of David Brower. David R. Brower. Gibbs Smith, PO Box 667, Layton, UT 84041. (801) 554-9800; (800) 421-8714. 1990. Personal reflections that catalog events and commentary and provides explanatory insight into several events of America's contemporary environmental history.

The Forbidden Fuel. Hal Bernton. Boyd Griffin, 714 Stratfield Rd., Fairfield, CT 06432. (203) 335-0229. 1982. Power alcohol in the twentieth century.

Forensic Science Database. Home Office Forensic Science Service, Central Research and Support Establishment, Aldermaston, Reading, Berkshire, England RG7 4PN. 44 (734) 814100.

FOREST. Forest Products Research Society, 2801 Marshall Court, Madison, WI 53705. (608) 231-1361.

Forest and Conservation History. Forest History Society, 701 Vickers Ave., Durham, NC 27701. (919) 682-9319. Quarterly.

The Forest and the Trees: A Guide to Excellent Forestry. Gordon Robinson. Island Press, 1718 Connecticut Ave. N.W., Suite 300, Washington, DC 20009. (202) 232-7933. 1988. Gives concerned citizens who are not foresters the technical information they need to compete with the experts when commenting on how our national forests should be managed.

Forest Conservation. Forestry Range Club, Washington State University, Pullman, WA 99164-3200. 1958-. Annually. None published in 1974. Deals with forest conservation and related topics.

Forest Conservation Communications Association. Hall of the States, 444 N. Capitol St., N.W., Washington, DC 20001.

Forest Environmental Resource Planning: A Selective Bibliography. Lizbeth Ann Jones. Council of Planning Librarians, 1313 E. 60th St., Chicago, IL 60637-2897. (312) 942-2163. 1977.

Forest Farmers Association. 4 Executive Park, Box 95385, Atlanta, GA 30347. (404) 325-2954.

The Forest Farmer's Handbook. Orville Camp. Sky River Press, 2466 Virginia St., #205, Berkeley, CA 94709. (510) 841-1368. 1984. A guide to natural selection forest management and tree crops.

Forest History Society, Inc. 701 Vickers Ave., Durham, NC 27701. (919) 682-9319.

Forest Industries. Forest Industries, 500 Howard St., San Francisco, CA 94105. Monthly. Concerned with logging, pulpwood and forest management, and the manufacture oflumber, plywood, board, and pulp.

Forest Industries Council. 1250 Connecticut Ave., N.W., Suite 320, Washington, DC 20036. (202) 833-1596.

Forest Industries–Equipment Catalog & Buyers Guide Issue. Miller Freeman Publications, Inc., 500 Howard St., San Francisco, CA 94105. (415) 397-1881.

Forest Industry Wastewaters Biological Treatment. A. A. O. Luonsi and P. K. Rantala, eds. Pergamon Microforms International, Inc., Fairview Park, Elmsford, NY 10523. (914) 592-7720. 1988. First volume of the proceedings of an IAWPRC Symposium held at the University of Technology, Finland, June 9-12, 1987. Includes a wide range of research and practical results in the field of biological treatment of various pulp and paper mill effluents and sludges. Includes reports from various parts of the world including discussions on the choice of internal and external measures in pollution control.

Forest Insect and Disease Conditions in Alaska. Alaska, Dept. of Agriculture, Forest Service, Alaska Region, Division of State and Private Forestry, 201 E. 9th St., Suite 303, Anchorage, AK 99501. (907) 271-2583. 1978-. Annual.

Forest Insect and Disease Conditions in the Intermountain Region. Intermountain Region, Forest Insect and Disease Management, State and Private, USDA Forest Service, 324 25th St., Ogden, UT 84401. (801) 625-5431. 1979-. Annual.

Forest Insect and Disease Conditions in the Northern Region. U.S. Department of Agriculture, Forest Service, Northern Region, PO Box 8089, Missoula, MT 59807. (406) 721-5694. 1978-. Annual.

Forest Insect and Disease Conditions in the Pacific Northwest. U.S. Department of Agriculture, Forest Service, Pacific Northwest Region, 319 S. W. Pine St., PO Box 3890, Portland, OR 97208. (503) 294-5640. 1978-. Annual.

Forest Insect and Disease Conditions in the United States. U.S. Department of Agriculture, Forest Service, 14th St. and Independence Ave. S.W., Washington, DC 20250. (202) 447-7454. 1971-. Annual.

Forest Management Chemicals. Forest Pest Management, Forest Service, U.S. Department of Agriculture. U.S. G.P.O., Washington, DC 20401. (202) 512-0000. Annual. Use of pesticides and insect control.

Forest Nature Conservation Guidelines. HMSO, UNIPUB, 4611-F Assembly Dr., Lanham, MD 20706. (301) 459-7666 or (800) 274-4888. 1991. Contains practical conservation advice to those involved in forestry.

Forest Notes. Society for the Protection of New Hampshire Forests, 54 Portsmouth St., Concord, NH 03301. (603) 224-9945. 1937-. Quarterly. Devoted to forestry, land protection and other issues affecting New Hampshire natural resources.

Forest Products Abstracts. C. A. B. International, 845 North Park Ave., Tucson, AZ 85719. (602) 621-7897 or (800) 528-4841. Bimonthly. Contains abstracts in the area of forest product industry; wood properties; timber extraction; conversion and measurement; damage to timber and timber production; utilization of wood; pulp industries and the chemical utilization of wood and other related areas.

Forest Products Laboratory. University of California, Berkeley, 1301 South 46th Street, Richmond, CA 94804. (510) 231-9452.

Forest Products Research Society. 2801 Marshall Ct., Madison, WI 53705. (608) 231-1361.

Forest Regeneration Manual. Mary L. Duryea. Kluwer Academic Publishers, 101 Philip Dr., Assinippi Park, Norwell, MA 02061. (617) 871-6600. 1991. Volume 36 in the series entitled Forestry Sciences.

Forest Science. Society of American Foresters, 5400 Grosvenor Ln., Bethesda, MD 20814-2198. (301) 897-8720. Quarterly. Silviculture, soils, biometry, diseases, recreation, photosynthesis, tree physiology, management, harvesting, and policy analysis.

Forest Stand Dynamics. Chadwick Dearing Oliver and Bruce C. Larson. McGraw-Hill Science & Engineering Books, 11 W. 19th St., New York, NY 10011. (212) 337-6010. 1990. Offers a unique synthesis of information from the fields of silviculture, ecology, and physiology that shows how different types of forest develop and outlines appropriate forest management techniques for each type.

Forest Trust. PO Box 519, Santa Fe, NM 87504-0519. (505) 983-8992.

Forest Watch: The Citizen's Forestry Magazine. Cascade Holistic Economic Consultants, 14417 SE Laurie Ave., Oak Grove, OR 97207. (503) 652-7049. Eleven times a year.

Forest World. World Forestry Center, 4033 SW Canyon Rd., Portland, OR 97221. (503) 228-1367. Quarterly. Forest and natural resource issues.

Forestry Abstracts. C. A. B. International, Wallingford, England OX10 8DE. (0491) 3211. 1939/40-. Monthly. Journal of abstracts of journal articles, conferences, technical reports in the subject areas of: silviculture, forest mensuration and management, physical environment, fire, plant biology, genetics and breeding, mycology and pathology, game and wildlife, fish, protection of forests and other related matter.

Forestry, Conservation Communications Association. c/o Donald W. Pfohl, P.O. Box 1466, Mesa, AZ 85211-1466. (602) 644-3166.

Forestry Research: A Mandate for Change. National Research Council (U.S.) Board on Biology. National Academy Press, 2101 Constitution Ave. N.W., PO Box 285, Washington, DC 20418. (202) 334-3313. 1990. Begins with a general look at societal needs and concerns for the forest; it then explores the gap between society's requirements and the status of forestry research. Specific research needs by field are then addressed and conclusions and recommendations are supplied.

Forests and Forestry in China. S. D. Richardson. Island Press, 1718 Connecticut Ave. N.W., Suite 300, Washington, DC 20009. (202) 232-7933. 1990. In-depth look at current forest practice in China, including how China manages forest resources.

Forests and People. Louisiana Forestry Assn., PO Drawer 5067, Alexandria, LA 71307-5067. (318) 443-2558. Quarterly.

Forests for Whom and for What?. Marion Clawson. Johns Hopkins University Press, 701 W. 40th St., Ste. 275, Baltimore, MD 21211. (410) 516-6900. 1975. Policy relative to forests and forestry.

The Forever Fuel: The Story of Hydrogen. Peter Hoffman. Westview Press, 5500 Central Ave., Boulder, CO 80301. (303) 444-3541. 1981.

Formaldehyde. World Health Organization, Ave. Appia, Geneva, Switzerland CH-1211. 1989. Physiological effects and toxicology of formaldehyde.

Formaldehyde: Analytical Chemistry and Toxicology. Victor Turoski. American Chemical Society, 1155 16th St. N.W., Washington, DC 20036. (800) 227-5558. 1985.

Formaldehyde: Environmental and Technical Information for Problem Spills. Technical Services Branch, Environment Protection Programs Directorate, Environmental Protection Service, 425 St. Joseph Blvd., 3rd Fl., Hull, PQ, Canada K1A 0H3. (613) 953-5921. 1985.

Formaldehyde: Evidence of Carcinogenicity. U.S. Department of Health and Human Services, Public Health Service, 200 Independence Ave. SW, Washington, DC 20201. (202) 619-1296. 1981.

Formaldehyde Institute. 1330 Connecticut Ave., N.W., Suite 300, Washington, DC 20036. (202) 659-0060.

Formaldehyde Sensitivity and Toxicity. Susan E. Feinman. CRC Press, 2000 Corporate Blvd. N.W., Boca Raton, FL 33431. (800) 272-7737. 1988. Covers allergy, contact dermatitis, and allergenicity.

Formaldehyde Toxicology. Siles Jackson. National Institutes of Health, Bethesda, MD 1982. Adverse effects of formaldehyde.

Forum for Applied Research and Public Policy. University of Tennessee, Energy, Environment and Resources Center, Knoxville, TN 37996-0710. (919) 966-3561. 1986-. Quarterly. Presents a discussion of options by academic, government and corporate experts in energy, environment and economic development.

Foundation for Field Research. PO Box 2010, Alpine, CA 92001-0020. (619) 445-9264.

Foundation for North American Wild Sheep. 720 Allen Ave., Cody, WY 82414-3402. (307) 527-6261.

Foundations of Ecology. Leslie A. Real. University of Chicago Press, 5801 Ellis Ave., 4th Fl., Chicago, IL 60637. (312) 568-1550 or (800) 621-2736. Forty classic papers that have laid the foundation of modern ecology and are ideal for graduate courses that deal with the development of ecological ideas.

FPIRG Citizen Agenda. Florida Public Interest Research Group, 1441 E Fletcher Ave., Ste. 2200-3, Tampa, FL 33612. (813) 971-7564. Citizen actions for environmental protection.

The Fragile Environment. Laurie Friday and Ronald Laskey, eds. Cambridge University Press, 40 W. 20th St., New York, NY 10011. (212) 924-3900; (800) 227-0247. 1989. The fragile environment brings together a team of distinguished authors to consider areas of urgent environmental concern.

The Fragile South Pacific: An Ecological Odyssey. Andrew Mitchell. University of Texas Press, PO Box 7819, Austin, TX 78713-7819. (512) 471-7233 or (800) 252-3206. 1991. Narrative of the ecology and natural history of the major South Pacific islands, the story of their human inhabitants, how they got there, and human impacts on those islands.

The Fragrant Path. Louise Wilder. Collier Books, 866 3rd Ave., New York, NY 10022. (212) 702-2000. 1990. Aromatic plants and flower odor as well as fragrant gardens.

Franc Nord. Union Quebecoise pour la conservation de la nature, 160, 76 rue est, 2nd fl., Charlesbourg, PQ, Canada H1K 7H6. (418) 628-9600. 1984-. Quarterly. Devoted to the conservation of natural resources, and the pollution free environment.

Free Market Environmentalism. Terry L. Anderson and Donald R. Leal. Westview Press, 5500 Central Ave., Boulder, CO 80301. (303) 444-3541. 1991. Examines the prospects and pitfalls of improving natural resource allocation and environmental quality through market processes.

Freshwater and Terrestrial Radioecology: A Selected Bibliography. Alfred W. Klement. Hutchinson & Ross, Stroudsburg, PA 1980. Bibliography of ecology and environmental pollution.

Freshwater Biology. Blackwell Scientific Publications, PO Box 87, Oxford, England OX2 0DT. 44 0865 791155. Quarterly.

Freshwater Ecology: Principles and Applications. Michael Jeffries and Derek Mills. Belhaven Press, 136 S. Broadway, Irvington, NY 10533. (914) 591-9111. 1991. Explains and illustrates the principles of freshwater ecology and their application to the management and conservation of plant and animal life, and the impact of human actions on lakes, rivers and streams.

Freshwater Foundation. spring Hill Center, 728 County Rd. 6, Wayzata, NM 55391. (612) 449-0092.

Freshwater Marshes: Ecology and Wildlife Management. Milton Webster Weller. University of Minnesota Press, 2037 University Ave., SE, Minneapolis, MN 55414. (612) 624-2516. 1987.

Friend O'Wildlife. North Carolina Wildlife Federation,Inc., Box 10626, Raleigh, NC 27605. (919) 833-1923. 1959-. Bimonthly. Covers North Carolina wildlife conservation and related hunting, fishing and boating activities and other environmental issues.

Friends of Africa in America. 330 S. Broadway, Tarrytown, NY 10591. (914) 631-5168.

Friends of Animals, Inc. Box 1244, Norwalk, CT 06856. (203) 866-5223.

Friends of the Earth. 218 D St., SE, Washington, DC 20003. (202) 544-2600.

The Friends of the Everglades. 101 Westward Dr., No. 2, Miami Springs, FL 33166. (305) 888-1230.

Friends of the National Zoo. National Zoological Park, Washington, DC 20008. (202) 673-4950.

Friends of the River Foundation. Fort Mason Center, Bldg. C, San Francisco, CA 94123. (415) 771-0400.

Friends of the Trees...Yearbook. Friends of the Trees, PO Box 1466, Chelan, WA 98816. 1986-. Annually. Devoted to the care of trees and citizen participation in such activities.

Friends of the U.S. National Arboretum. 3501 New York Ave., N.E., Washington, DC 20002. (202) 544-8733.

Friends of the United Nations Environment Programme. 2013 Q St., N.W., Washington, DC 20009. (202) 234-3600.

From Cell to Clone: the Story of Genetic Engineering. Margery Facklam. Harcourt Brace Jovanovich, Inc., 1250 6th Ave., San Diego, CA 92101. (800) 346-8648. 1979.

From Clone to Clinic. D.J.A. Crommelin, ed. Kluwer Academic Publishers, 101 Philip Dr., Assinippi Pk., Norwell, MA 02061. (617) 871-6600. 1990.

From the Land. Nancy P. Pittman, ed. Island Press, 1718 Connecticut Ave. N.W., Suite 300, Washington, DC 20009. (202) 232-7933. 1988. Anthology comes from 13 years of the Land–a journal of conservation writings from the '40s and '50s. Through fiction, essay, poetry, and philosophy we learn how our small farms have given way to today's agribusiness.

From the State Capitals: Parks and Recreation Trends. Wakeman/Walworth, PO Box 1939, New Haven, CT 06509. (203) 562-8518. Monthly. What states and municipalities are doing in conservation, land management and development, parks and recreational programs, wildlife preserves, state fisheries, river management, poaching and game restrictions, and systems of licensing and fees.

FROSTI: Food RA Online Scientific and Technical Information. Leatherhead Food Research Association, Randalls Rd., Leatherhead, Surrey, England KT22 7RY. 44 (372) 376761.

The Frozen Foods Industry Competitive Intelligence Database. Strategic Intelligence Systems, Inc., 404 Park Ave., South, Suite 1301, New York, NY 10016. (212) 725-5954.

FSTA: Food Science and Technology Abstracts. International Food Information Service, Melibocusstrasse 52, 6000 Frankfurt, Germany 49 (69) 669007-8.

Fuel from Farms. National Agricultural Library. National Technical Information Service, 5285 Port Royal Rd., Springfield, VA 22161. (703) 487-4650. 1982. A guide to small-scale ethanol production, and biomass energy.

Fuel Handling and Storage Systems in Nuclear Power Plants: A Safety Guide. International Atomic Energy Agency. UNIPUB, 1984. Safety measures relating to nuclear fuels and atomic power plants.

Fuel Oil News–Source Book Issue. IIunter Publishing Company, Inc., 950 Lee St., Des Plaines, IL 60016. (708) 296-0770.

Fuels and Fuel Additives for Highway Vehicles and Their Combustion Products. National Research Council, Committee on Toxicology. National Academy of Sciences, 2101 Constitution Ave., NW, Washington, DC 20418. (202) 334-2000. 1976. Evaluation of the potential effects of fuels and fuel additives on health.

Fully Halogenated Chlorofluorocarbons. World Health Organization, Ave. Appia, Geneva, Switzerland CH-1211. (518) 436-9686. 1990. Environmental aspects of chlorofluorocarbons.

Function of Glutathione. Agne Larsson. Raven Press, 1185 Avenue of the Americas, New York, NY 10036. (212) 930-9500. 1983. Biochemical, physiological, toxicological, and clinical aspects.

A Functional Biology of Marine Gastropods. Roger N. Hughes. Johns Hopkins University Press, 701 W. 40th St., Ste. 275, Baltimore, MD 21211. (410) 516-6900. 1986. Covers marine invertebrates.

The Functioning of Freshwater Ecosystems. E. D. Le Cren and R. H. Lowe-McConnell. Cambridge University Press, 40 W. 20th St., New York, NY 10011. (212) 924-3900. 1979. Freshwater ecology and freshwater productivity.

Fund for Animals, Inc. 200 W. 57th St., New York, NY 10019. (212) 246-2096.

Fund for Renewable Energy & the Environment. 1400 16th St., N.W., Suite 710, Washington, DC 20036. (202) 232-2252.

Fundamentals & Applied Toxicology. Academic Press, c/o Marcourt Brace, PO Box 6250, 6277 Sea Harbor Dr., Orlando, FL 32887. (218) 723-9828. 8/year. Covers risk assessment and safety studies of toxic agents.

Fundamentals of Environmental Compliance Inspections. Government Institutes Inc., 4 Research Place, #200, Rockville, MD 20850. (301) 921-2300. Developed by EPA for their inspector training course. Gives technical and procedural insight into compliance inspections.

Fundamentals of Hazardous Materials Incidents. Reginald L. Campbell and Roland E. Langford. Lewis Publishers, 2000 Corporate Blvd., N.W., Boca Raton, FL 33431. (407) 994-0555 or (800) 272-7737. 1990. Gives basic introduction to anatomy and physiology, toxicology. Discusses hazardous materials and workers protection, environmental protection, hazard communication and medical surveillance, factors affecting personnel, personal protection equipment and other related topics.

Fundamentals of Laboratory Safety: Physical Hazards in the Academic Laboratory. William J. Mahn. Van Nostrand Reinhold, 115 5th Ave., New York, NY 10003. (212) 254-3232. 1991. Discusses safety methods in chemical laboratories, accident prevention and the various hazardous materials in use in the labs.

Fundamentals of Soil Science. Henry D. Foth. John Wiley & Sons, Inc., 605 3rd Ave., New York, NY 10158-0012. (212) 850-6000. 1992.

Fungal Genetics Stock Center. Department of Microbiology, University of Kansas Medical Center, Kansas City, KS 66103. (913) 588-7044.

Fungi Without Gills. Martin B. Ellis. Chapman & Hall, 29 W. 35th St., New York, NY 10001-2291. (212) 244-3336. 1990. Identification of gastromycetes and hymenomycetes.

Fungicides, Insecticides & Nematicides Used of Sugar Beet. FIND/SVP, 625 Avenue of the Americas, New York, NY 10011. (800) 346-3787. 1991. Focuses on the diseases and pests that attack the sugar-beet crop in Western developed countries.

Fusion Facilities Directory. Fusion Power Associates, 2 Professional Dr., Suite 248, Gaithersburg, MD 20879. (301) 258-0545. Biennial. Government and private institutions and laboratories involved in atomic fusion research.

Fusion Power Associates. Two Professional Dr., Suite 248, Gaithersburg, MD 20879. (301) 258-0545.

Fusion Power Report. Business Publishers, Inc., 951 Pershing Dr., Silver Spring, MD 20910. (301) 587-6300. Monthly. Scientific, engineering, economic, and political developments in the field of fusion energy.

Future Fisherman Foundation. 1250 Grove Ave., Ste. 300, Barrington, IL 60010. (708) 381-4061.

The Future of Urbanization: Facing the Ecological and Economic Constraints. Lester R. Brown, Jodi L. Jacobson. Worldwatch Institute, 1776 Massachusetts Ave., N.W., Washington, DC 20036-1904. 1987.

The Future of Wetlands: Assessing Visual-Cultural Values. Richard C. Smardon, ed. Rowman & Littlefield, Publishers, Inc., 8705 Bollman Pl., Savage, MD 20763. (301) 306-0400. 1983. Attempts to provide a systematic basis for incorporating migrational, aesthetic, social, and educational values into the decision-making processes involved in land-use allocation.

Future Risk: Research Strategies for the 1990's. The Science Advisory Board, U.S. Environmental Protection Agency, 401 M St. SW, Washington, DC 20460. (202) 260-2090. 1988. Strategies for sources, transport and fate research, strategies for exposure assessment research, and ecological effects research.

GAIA: A New Look at Life on Earth. J. E. Lovelock. Oxford University Press, 200 Madison Ave., New York, NY 10016. (212) 679-7300; (800) 334-4249. 1988. Explores the idea that life on earth functions as a single organism which actually defines and maintains conditions necessary for its survival.

GAIA, an Atlas of Planet Management. Norman Myers. Anchor Pr./Doubleday, 666 5th Ave., New York, NY 10103. (212) 765-6500; (800) 223-6834. Resource atlas including a wealth of data on the environment with text by authoritative environmentalists.

GAIA Connections: An Introduction to Ecology, Ecoethics and Economics. Alan S. Miller. Rowman & Littlefield, Publishers, Inc., 8705 Bollman Pl., Savage, MD 20763. (301) 306-0400. 1991. Synthesis of humanity's ethical and economic options in coping with the global environmental crisis.

Gale Environmental Almanac. Russ Hoyle. Gale Research Inc., 835 Penobscot Bldg., Detroit, MI 48226-4094. (313) 961-2242. 1993. Focuses on the U.S. and Canada, although worldwide and transboundary issues are discussed.

Gale Environmental Sourcebook. Karen Hill. Gale Research Co., 835 Penobscot Bldg., Detroit, MI 48226-4094. (313) 961-2242. Contacts, information sources, or general information on environmental topics.

Gallium Bibliography. M. W. Brennecke. ALCOA-Aluminum Company of America, Alcoa Bldg., Pittsburgh, PA 15219. (412) 553-4545. 1959.

Game and Fish Commission: Fish and Wildlife. Director, #2 Natural Resources Dr., Little Rock, AR 72205. (501) 223-6305.

Game and Fish Commission: Fish and Wildlife. Director, 5400 Bishop Blvd., Cheyenne, WY 82002. (307) 777-7632.

Game and Fish Department: Fish and Wildlife. Director, 2221 W. Greenway Rd., Phoenix, AZ 85023. (602) 942-3000.

Game and Fish Department: Fish and Wildlife. Director, Villagra Building, Santa Fe, NM 87503. (505) 827-7899.

Game and Fish Department: Fish and Wildlife. Commissioner, 100 North Bismark Expressway, Bismark, ND 58501. (701) 221-6300.

Game and Fresh Water Fish Commission: Fish and Wildlife. Executive Director, 620 South Meridan St., Tallahassee, FL 32399-1600. (904) 488-2975.

Game and Inland Fisheries Department: Fish and Wildlife. Executive Director, Fresh Water, 4010 W. Broad St., Richmond, VA 23230. (804) 367-9231.

Game and Park Commission: Fish and Wildlife. Director, 2200 North 33rd St., PO Box 30370, Lincoln, NE 68503-0370. (402) 464-0641.

Game Conservation International. P.O. Box 17444, San Antonio, TX 78217. (512) 824-7509.

Game Wars: The Undercover Pursuit of Wildlife Poachers. Marc Reisner. Academic Marketing, Penguin USA, 375 Hudson St., New York, NY 10014. (212) 366-2000; (800) 253-2304. 1991. Provides a first hand account of the life and dangers encountered by federal wildlife agents working for U.S. Fish and Wildlife Service: the elaborate covers they devise; the meticulous preparation necessary to pull off a successful sting; the weeks, months, even years they spend putting together their traps and cases; and the dangers they face as they impersonate big game hunters, ivory trades; and professional smugglers.

Garbage and Recycling. Judith Woodburn. Gareth Stevens, Inc., 7317 W. Green Tree Rd., Milwaukee, WI 53223. (414) 466-7550. 1991. Solid waste crisis, landfill crowding, and recycling.

Garbage and Recycling. Kathlyn Gay. Enslow Publishers, Bloy St. & Ramsey Ave., PO Box 777, Hillside, NJ 07205. (908) 964-4116. 1991. Garbage accumulation and different recycling solutions which may prevent the situation from getting worse.

The Garbage Dilemma: A Community Guide to Solid Waste Management. Marilyn Rosenzweig. League of Women Voters of Illinois Education Fund, 332 S. Michigan Ave., Chicago, IL 60604. (312) 939-5935. 1990. Refuse and refuse disposal, hazardous wastes and recycling of waste.

Garbage in the Cities: Refuse, Reform, and the Environment, 1880-1980. Martin V. Melosi. Texas A & M University Press, College Station, TX 77843. 1981. Environmental history of refuse and refuse disposal in the United States.

Garbage: The History and Future of Garbage in America. Katie Kelly. Saturday Review Press, 201 Park Ave. S., Rm. 1305, New York, NY 10017. 1973. Refuse and refuse disposal in the United States.

Garbage: The Practical Journal for the Environment. Old House Journal Corp., 2 Main St., Gloucester, MA 01930. (508) 283-4629. Bimonthly. Issues in municipal wastes.

Gas Appliance Manufacturers Association. 1901 N. Moore St., Ste. 1100, Arlington, VA 22209. (703) 525-9565.

Gas Chromatography in Air Pollution Analysis. Viktor G. Berezkin and Yuri S. Drugov. Elsevier Science Publishing Co., 655 Avenue of the Americas, New York, NY 10010. (212) 989-5800. 1991.

Gas Facts, 1988 Data: A Statistical Record of the Gas Utility Industry. American Gas Association, 1515 Wilson Blvd., Arlington, VA 22209. 1989. Annual. Transmission, distribution, consumption, finances, and prices.

Gas Liquified Petroleum Directory. American Business Directories, Inc., 5711 S. 86th Circle, Omaha, NE 68127. (402) 593-4600.

Gas Mileage Guide. U.S. Dept. of Energy. U.S. G.P.O, Washington, DC 20402-9325. (202) 512-0000. Annual. Fuel economy results for cars and light-duty trucks tested by EPA and meeting EPA emissions standards.

Gas Processors Association. 6526 E. 60th St., Tulsa, OK 74145. (918) 493-3872.

Gas Research Institute. 8600 W. Bryn Mawr Ave., Chicago, IL 60631. (312) 399-8100.

Gaseous Pollutants: Characterization and Cycling. Jerome O. Nriagu, ed. J. Wiley, 605 3rd Ave., New York, NY 10158-0012. (800) CALL-WILEY. 1992. Focuses on various methods of sampling and analyzing gaseous pollutants in the atmosphere with emphasis on understanding the chemical and physical processes that occur.

Gasohol: Energy from Agriculture. Robert W. Lockerby. Vance Bibliographies, PO Box 229, 112 N. Charter St., Monticello, IL 61856. (217) 762-3831. 1980.

Gasohol-One Answer to the Energy Crisis. Joseph Lee Cook. Vance Bibliographies, PO Box 229, 112 N. Charter St., Monticello, IL 61856. (217) 762-3831. 1979.

Gasohol Sourcebook: Literature Survey and Abstracts. N. P. Cheremisinoff and P. N. Cheremisinoff. Ann Arbor Science, 230 Collingwood, PO Box 1425, Ann Arbor, MI 48106. 1981. Volume includes: biotechnology and bioconversion; ethanol and methanol production; automotive and other fuels; production of chemical feedstocks; and economics of alcohol production.

Gasoline and Diesel Fuel Additives. K. Owen. John Wiley & Sons Inc., 605 3rd Ave., New York, NY 10158-0012. (212) 850-6000. 1989. Environmental effects of motor fuels-additives and diesel fuels- additives.

Gel Electrophoresis of Proteins. M.J. Dunn. IOP Pub. Ltd., Techno House, Radcliffe Way, Bristol, England BS1 6NX. 1990. Techniques of analytical gel electrophoresis.

GEM Notes: an Update of the Groundwater Education in Michigan Program. Groundwater Education in Michigan, Institute of Water Research, Michigan State University, 25 Manly Miles Bldg., 1405 S. Harrison Rd., East Lansing, MI 48824. (517) 355-9543. 1988-. Irregular.

General Energetics; Energy in the Biosphere and Civilization. Vaclav Smil. John Wiley & Sons, Inc., 605 3rd Ave., New York, NY 10158-0012. (212) 850-6000. 1991. Provides an integrated framework for analyzing planetary energetics (solar radiation and gemorphic processes), bioenergetics (photosynthesis), and human energetics (metabolism and thermoregulation) traced from hunting-gathering and agricultural societies through modern day industrial civilization, concluding with the impact of modern energy use on environment and society.

General Science Index. H. W. Wilson Co., 950 University Ave., Bronx, NY 10452. 1978-. Monthly, also issued in annual cumulation. Cumulative subject index to English language periodicals in the subject fields of astronomy, botany, chemistry, earth science, environment and conservation, food and nutrition, genetics, mathematics, medicine and health, microbiology, oceanography, physics, physiology and zoology.

Generating Energy Alternatives. Investor Responsibility Research Center, 1755 Massachusetts Ave., N.W., Suite 600, Washington, DC 20036. (202) 939-7500.

The Generator's Guide to Hazardous Materials/Waste Management. Leo H. Traverse. Van Nostrand Reinhold, 115 5th Ave., New York, NY 10003. (212) 254-3232. 1991. Comprehensive information source for hazardous waste and hazardous materials management.

Generic Facilities Plan for a Small Community: Stabilization Pond and Oxidation Ditch. Elaine Stanley. U.S. Environmental Protection Agency, 401 M St., S.W., Washington, DC 20460. (202) 260-2090. 1981. Design and construction of sewage disposal plants.

Genetic Aspects of Plant Mineral Nutrition. N. El Bassam, et al., eds. Kluwer Academic Publishers, 101 Philip Dr., Assinippi Park, Norwell, MA 02061. (617) 871-6600. 1990. Proceedings of the 3rd International Symposium on Genetic Aspects of Plant Mineral Nutritions, Braunschweig, 1988. Papers discuss the fact that many nutritional characteristics are independently inherited and could be selected for a breeding program. Discusses development of plant breeding techniques. Special features include papers on genetic variation in symbiotic systems and a timely section on the creation of genotypes with increased efficiency of ion absorption under conditions of low input agriculture.

Genetic Engineering, DNA, and Cloning: A Bibliography in the Future of Genetics. Joseph Menditto. Whitston Publishing Co., P.O. Box 958, Troy, NY 12181. (518) 283-4363. 1983.

Genetic Engineering Letter. Environews, Inc., 952 National Press Bldg., Washington, DC 20045. (202) 662-7299. Twice a month. Covers developments in the field of biotechnology.

Genetic Engineering of Plants: An Agricultural Perspective. Isune Kosuge. Plenum Press, 233 Spring St., New York, NY 10013-1578. (212) 620-8000. 1983. Plant breeding techniques and plant genetic engineering.

Genetic Resistance to Pesticides. Biological Sciences Curriculum Study, Pleasantville, NY Study and teaching of biology and genetics.

Genetic Stock Center for Cockroaches. Virginia Polytech Institute and State University, Blacksburg, VA 24061. (703) 961-5844.

Genetic Toxicity. U.S. Environmental Protection Agency, Office of Pesticides and Toxic Substances, 401 M St. SW, Washington, DC 20460. (202) 260-2090. Mutagenicity information on more than 2600 chemicals tested on 38 biological systems.

Genetic Toxicology Association. c/o Kerry Dearfield, USEPA, 401 M St., S.W., Washington, DC 20460. (703) 557-9780.

Genetically Altered Viruses and the Environment. Bernard Fields. Cold Spring Harbor Laboratory Press, PO Box 100, Cold Spring Harbor, NY 11724. (800) 843-4388. 1985. Covers virology, viral genetics, environmental microbiology, and genetic engineering.

Genetics Abstracts. Cambridge Scientific Abstracts, 5161 River Rd., Bethesda, MD 20816. (301) 961-6750. 1968-. Monthly. Formerly published by Information Retrieval Ltd., London England. Published by Cambridge Scientific Abstracts since 1982.

Genetics and Conservation: A Reference for Managing Wild Animal and Plant Populations. Christine M. Schonewald-Cox. Benjamin/Cummings Publishing Co., 390 Bridge Pkwy., Redwood City, CA 94065. (415) 594-4400. 1983. Germplasm resources and population genetics.

Genetics and Developmental Biology Program. West Virginia University, Division of Plant and Soil Science, College of Agriculture, Morgantown, WV 26506. (304) 293-6256.

Genetics Society of America. 9650 Rockville Pike, Bethesda, MD 20814. (301) 571-1825.

Geo Abstracts, Social Geography and Cartography. Geo Abstracts Ltd., c/o Elsevier Science Pub., Crown House, Linton Rd., Barking, England 1611 8JU.

GEOBASE. Elsevier/GEO Abstracts, Regency House, 34 Duke St., Norwich, England NR3 3AP. 44 (603) 626327.

Geochemical Biomarkers. T. F. Yen. Hardwood Academic Publishers, PO Box 786, Cooper Station, New York, NY 10276. (212) 206-8900. 1988. Topics in organic geochemistry and biological markers.

Geochemical Modeling of Ground Water. William J. Deutsch and Stanley R. Peterson. Lewis Publishers, 2000 Corporate Blvd., N.W., Boca Raton, FL 33431. (407) 994-0555 or (800) 272-7737. 1991. Explains the natural chemical system, geochemical processes, development of, conceptual model, computer codes and geochemical models.

Geochemistry of Marine Humic Compounds. Mohammed A. Rashid. Springer-Verlag, 175 5th Ave., New York, NY 10010. (212) 460-1500. 1985.

Geographical Abstracts. London School of Economics, Dept. of Geography, Regency House, 34 Duke St., London, England 1966-. Continued by Geo Abstracts issued in 6 parts: Pt. A. Landforms and the quaternary; Pt. B. Biogeography and Climatology; Pt. C. Economic geography; Pt. D. Social geography and cartography; Pt. E. Sedimentology; Pt. F. Regional and community planning.

Geojourney. Florida Department of Natural Resources, 3900 Commonwealth Blvd., Tallahassee, FL 32303. (904) 488-1234. 1980-. Quarterly. Covers activities on resource management, marine resources, parks and recreation, and subjects related to fishing, boating and all uses of Florida's natural resources.

GEOLINE. Informationszentrum Rohstoffgewinnung, Geowissenschaften Wasserwirtschaft, Bundesanstalt fuer Geowissenschaften und Rohstoffe (BGR), Postfach 510153, Stilleweg 2, Hannover 51, Germany D-3000. 49 (511) 643-2819.

Geological Society of America. P.O. Box 9140, 3300 Penrose Pl., Boulder, CO 80301. (303) 447-2020.

Geomechanics Abstracts. Rockmechanics Information Service, Imperial College of Science, Technology and Medicine, Department of Mineral Resources Engineering, Royal School of Mines, Prince Consort Rd., London, England SW7 2BP. 44 (71) 589-5111, x6436.

The Geophysical Directory Regional and Worldwide Coverage. Geophysical Directory Inc., 2200 Welch Ave., PO Box 130508, Houston, TX 77219. (713) 529-8789. 1988. Annual. Forty-third edition. Gives addresses and company profiles classified by their function. Also includes a list of U.S. Government agencies utilizing geophysics.

GeoRef. American Geological Institute, 4220 King St., Alexandria, VA 22302. (703) 379-2480.

Georgia Conservancy Newsletter. Georgia Conservancy, 3376 Peachtree Rd., NE, Suite 44, Atlanta, GA 30326. 1967-. Monthly.

Georgia Environmental Law Handbook. Government Institutes, Inc., 4 Research Pl., Ste. 200, Rockville, MD 20850. (301) 921-2300. 1990.

Georgia Environmental Law Letter. Georgia Law Letter Pub., 10 Park Place South, PO Box 1597, Atlanta, GA 30301-1597. 1989-. Monthly.

Georgia Operator. Georgia Water and Pollution Control Association, 2532 Bolton Rd. N.W., Atlanta, GA 30318. 1963-. Quarterly.

The Geostationary Applications Satellite. Peter Berlin. Cambridge University Press, 40 W. 20th St., New York, NY 10011. (212) 924-3900. 1988. Environmental applications of satellite technology.

Geosynthetic Testing for Waste Containment Applications. Robert M. Koerner, ed. ASTM, 1916 Race St., Philadelphia, PA 19103-1187. (215) 299-5400. 1990. Contains papers presented at the symposium held in Las Vegas, January 1990. Examines the selection, testing design, and use of geosynthetics.

Geotechnical and Environmental Geophysics. Stanley H. Ward. Society of Exploration Geophysicists, PO Box 702740, Tulsa, OK 74170-2740. (918) 493-3516. 1990.

Geotechnical Engineering of Ocean Waste Disposal. Kenneth R. Demars and Ronald C. Chaney. ASTM, 1916 Race St., Philadelphia, PA 19103-1187. (215) 299-5400. 1990. Proceedings of the symposium held in Orlando, FL, Jan 1989. Reviews geotechnical test methods and procedures for site evaluation, design, construction, and monitoring of both contaminated areas and waste disposal facilities in the marine environment.

Geothermal Energy. National Technical Information Service, 5285 Port Royal Rd., Springfield, VA 22161. (703) 487-4650. Bimonthly. Technology required for economic recovery of geothermal energy and its use.

Geothermal Energy. Diana Niskern. Library of Congress, Science and Technology Division, Reference Section, Washington, DC 20540. (202) 207-1181. 1983.

Geothermal Heating: A Handbook of Engineering Economics. R. Harrison. Pergamon Microforms International, Inc., Fairview Park, Elmsford, NY 10523. (914) 592-7720. 1990.

Geothermal Progress Monitor Report. National Technical Information Service, 5285 Port Royal Rd., Springfield, VA 22161. (703) 487-4650. Annual. Statistics on the development of geothermal resources.

Geothermal Resources Council. P.O. Box 1350, Davis, CA 95617. (916) 758-2360.

Geothermal Resources Exploration and Exploitation. U.S. Energy Research and Development Administration, Technical Information Center, PO Box 2001, Oak Ridge, TN 37831. (615) 576-4444. 1976.

Geraghty & Miller's Groundwater Bibliography. Frits Van Der Leeden. Lewis Publishers, 200 Corporate Blvd. NW, Boca Raton, FL 33431. (407) 994-0555 or (800)272-7737. 1991. 5th ed. Since the last edition, this essential research aid reflects increased interest in areas such as ground water contamination, modeling, and legal issues. Contains a listing of general bibliographies, periodicals, and books, followed by a subject section covering 3 specific aspects of hydrogeology.

Get Oil Out. P.O. Box 1513, Santa Barbara, CA 93102. (805) 965-1519.

Glaciological Data. U.S. National Environmental Satellite, Data and Info Service. U.S. G.P.O., Washington, DC 20401. (202) 512-0000. Irregular. Covers occurrence, properties, processes, and effects of snow, ice and glaciers.

Glass Factory Directory. National Glass Budget, Box 7138, Pittsburgh, PA 15213. (412) 682-5136. Annual.

Glass Magazine–Directory of Suppliers Section. 8200 Greensboro Dr., Suite 302, McLean, VA 22102. (703) 442-4890. Monthly.

Glass Materials & Chemicals. FIND/SVP, 625 Avenue of the Americas, New York, NY 10011. (212) 645-4500. 1991.

Glass Packaging Institute. 1801 K St., N.W., Suite 1105L, Washington, DC 20006. (202) 887-4850.

Glass, Pottery, Plastics, & Allied Workers International Union. 608 E. Baltimore Pike, Box 607, Media, PA 19063. (215) 565-5051.

Glass, Science and Technology. Academic Press, c/o Harcourt Brace Jovanovich Inc., 6277 Sea Harbor Dr., Orlando, FL 32887. (800) 346-8648. Annual. Structure, microstructure, and properties of glass.

Glass Technical Institute. 12653 Portada Pl., San Diego, CA 92130. (619) 481-1277.

Global Air Pollution: Problems for the 1990s. Howard Bridgman. Belhaven Press, 136 S. Broadway, Irvington, NY 10533. (914) 591-9111. 1990. Addresses the environmental problems caused by human activities resulting in change and deterioration of the earth's atmosphere.

Global Biodiversity 1992: Status of the Earth's Living Resources. World Conservation Monitoring Centre. World Conservation Union, IUCN Publications Services Unit, 181a Huntingdon Road, Cambridge, England CB3 0DJ. (0223) 277894. Describes diversity at the genetic, species, and ecosystem levels; the trends and rates of change; "in situ" and "ex situ" management; the benefits and values of biodiversity; gap analysis for data priorities; and data requirements for monitoring.

Global Biomass Burning. Joel S. Levine. MIT Press, 55 Hayward St., Cambridge, MA 02142. (617) 253-2884 or (800) 356-0343. 1991. Atmospheric, climatic, and biospheric implications.

Global Catastrophes in Earth History. Virgil L. Sharpton and Peter Douglas Ward. Geological Society of America, 3300 Penrose Pl., PO Box 9140, Boulder, CO 80301. (303) 447-2020. 1990. Covers Extinction (Biology), Cretaceous/Tertiary boundary and Volcanism.

Global Change Information Packet. National Agricultural Library, Reference Section, Room 111, 10301 Baltimore Blvd., Beltsville, MD 20705-2351. (301) 504-5755. 1991. Books and journal articles on the effects of global climate change.

Global Climate Change Digest. Elsevier Science Publishing Co., 655 Avenue of the Americas, New York, NY 10010. (212) 984-5800. Monthly. Topics dealing with ozone depletion and the large-scale climatic changes linked to industrial activity, industrial by-products, and man-made substances.

Global Climate Change: Human and Natural Influences. Paragon House Publishers, 90 5th Ave., New York, NY 10011. (212) 620-2820. Carbon dioxide, methane, chlorofluorocarbons and ozone in the atmosphere; acid rain and water pollution in the hydrosphere; oceanographic and meteorological processes, nuclear war, volcanoes, asteroids, and meteorites.

Global Climate Change: Recent Publications. Library of the Department of State. The Library, 2201 C St. N.W., Washington, DC 20520. 1989.

Global Ecology. Colin Tudge. Oxford University Press, 200 Madison Ave., New York, NY 10016. (212) 679-7300 or (800) 334-4249. Overview of ecological science including climate and habitats of our planet while emphasizing the global unity of earth's ecosystem.

Global Ecology and Biogeography Letter. Blackwell Scientific Publications, 3 Cambridge Ctr., Suite 208, Cambridge, MA 02142. (617) 225-0401. 1991. Bimonthly. Global Ecology and Biogeography Letters is a sister publication of Journal of Biogeography and is only available with a subscription to the Journal. Provides a fast-track outlet for short research papers, news items, editorials, and book reviews. Topics related to the major scientific concerns of our present era, such as global warming, world sea-level rises, environmental acidification, development and conservation, biodiversity, and important new theories and themes in biogeography and ecology.

The Global Ecology Handbook: What You Can Do about the Environmental Crisis. Walter H. Corson, ed. The Global Tomorrow Coalition, Beacon Pr., 25 Beacon St., Boston, MA 02108-2800. (617) 742-2110. 1990. Covers environment, energy policy, population growth and other issues. It includes chapters on tropical rain forests, garbage, oceans and coasts, global warming, population growth, agriculture, biological diversity, fresh water, hazardous wastes, and environment and development.

Global Energy Futures and the Carbon Dioxide Problem. Council on Environmental Quality, Old Executive Office Bldg., Rm. 154, Washington, DC 20500. (202) 395-5080. 1981. Fossil fuels and energy policy.

Global Environment Issues. E. El-Hinnawi and M. Hashmi, eds. Cassell PLC, Publishers Distribution Center, Rutherford, NJ 07070. (201) 939-6064; (201) 939-6065. 1982.

Global Environmental Change: Human and Policy Dimensions. James K. Mitchell, ed. Department of Geography, Lucy Stone Hall, Kilmer Campus, New Brunswick, NJ 08903. (201) 932-4103. 1991. Five issues a year. Produced in cooperation with the United Nations University, including its International Human Dimensions of Global Change Programme. Addresses the human, ecological and public policy aspects of environmental processes that might affect the sustainability of life on Earth.

Global Environmental Change Report. Cutter Information Corp., 37 Broadway, Arlington, MA 02174-5539. (617) 648-8700. Online access to environmental issues worldwide, including global warming, ozone depletion, deforestation, and acid rain. Online version of periodical of the same name.

Global Environmental Change Report. Cutter Information Corp., 37 Broadway, Arlington, MA 02174-5539. (617) 648-8700. Biweekly. Focus on global warming, ozone depletion, deforestation, and acid rain. Also available online.

Global Environmental Issues; a Climatological Approach. David D. Kemp. Routledge, 29 W. 35th St., New York, NY 10001-2291. (212) 244-3336. 1990. A textbook for an introductory college course in geography or environmental studies, but interdisciplinary enough for use in other courses with an environmental approach. Bridges the gulf between technical reports and popular articles on such topics as the greenhouse effect, ozone depletion, nuclear winter, atmospheric turbidity, and drought.

Global Forest Resources. Alexander S. Mather. Timber Press, 9999 S.W. Wilshire, Portland, OR 97225. (503) 292-0745; (800) 327-5680. 1990. Covers all major aspects, from the extent and distribution of the resource base to the control, management, and use of forests. Historical, environmental, and sociological features are blended into the coverage. Numerous maps, figures, and tables are supplied.

Global Forests. Roger A. Sedjo and Marion Clawson. Resources for the Future, 1616 P. St. N.W., Rm. 532, Washington, DC 20036. (202) 328-5086. 1988.

Global Indexing System. U.S. Environmental Protection Agency, 401 M St., S.W., Washington, DC 20460. (202) 260-2090. International information on various qualities of chemicals.

Global Marine Pollution Bibliography: Ocean Dumping of Municipal and Industrial Wastes. Michael A. Champ. IFI/Plenum, 233 Spring St., New York, NY 10013. (800) 221-9369. 1982.

Global Patterns; Climate, Vegetation, and Soils. Wallace E. Akin. University of Oklahoma Press, 1005 Asp Ave., Norman, OK 73019. (405) 325-5111. 1991. Maps the three systems that dominate and shape life on earth in such a way as to clarify their interaction and combined effect.

Global Pollution and Health: Results of Health-Related Environmental Monitoring. World Health Organization, Ave. Appia, Geneva, Switzerland CH-1211. 1987. International cooperation in environmental monitoring.

Global Tomorrow Coalition. 1325 G St., N.W., Suite 915, Washington, DC 20005-3103. (202) 628-4016.

Global Warming. Stephen Henry Schneider. Sierra Club Books, 100 Bush St., San Francisco, CA 94104. (415) 291-1600. 1989. Climatic changes due to the greenhouse effect.

Global Warming: Do We Know Enough to Act?. S. Fred Singer. Center for the Study of American Business, Washington University, Campus Box 1208, One Brookings Dr., St. Louis, MO 63130-4899. (314) 935-5630. 1991.

Global Warming: The Greenpeace Report. Jeremy Leggett. Oxford University Press, 200 Madison Ave., New York, NY 10016. (800) 334-4249. 1990. Climate change and consequences of global warming, and means for abating and even halting global warming.

Glossary of Geology. Robert Latimer Bates and Julia A. Jackson, eds. American Geological Institute, 4220 King St., Alexandria, VA 22302-1507. (703) 379-2480 or (800) 336-4764. 1987. Third edition.

Glossary of Pesticide Toxicology and Related Terms. Naeem Eesa. Thomson Publications, PO Box 9335, Fresno, CA 93791. (209) 435-2163. 1984.

Glossary of Terms in Nuclear Science and Technology. American Nuclear Society, 555 North Kensington Ave., La Grange Park, IL 60525. (708) 352-6611. 1986. Prepared by the American Nuclear Society Standards Committee. Subcommittee ANS-9.

A Glossary of Terms Used in Range Management. Peter W. Jacoby. Society for Range Management, 1839 York St., Denver, CO 80206. (303) 355-7070. 1989. A definition of terms commonly used in range management.

The Glutamate Association–U.S. 5775 Peachtree-Dunwoody Rd., Suite 500-D, Atlanta, GA 30342. (404) 252-3663.

Glutathione: Chemical, Biochemical, and Medical Aspects. David Dolphin. John Wiley & Sons, Inc., 605 3rd Ave., New York, NY 10158-0012. (212) 850-6000. 1989. Covers derivatives, metabolism, and physiological effect of glutathione.

Glutathione Conjugation. Helmut Sies. Academic Press, 1250 Sixth Ave., San Diego, CA 92101. (619) 231-0926. 1988. Glutathione transferases and their mechanisms and biological significance.

Glutathione: Metabolism and Physiological Functions. Jose Vina. CRC Press, 2000 Corporate Blvd. N.W., Boca Raton, FL 33431. (800) 272-7737. 1990. Metabolism and physiological effects of glutathione.

Gmelin Formula Index. Gmelin Institut fuer Anorganische Chemie der Max-Planck- Gellschaft zur Foerderung der Wissenschaften, Varrentrappstrasse 40-42, Frankfurt, Germany D-6000. 49 (69) 7917-577.

Gnomic: A Dictionary of Genetic Codes. Edward N. Trifonov. Balaban, 220 E. 23rd St., Suite 909, New York, NY 10010-4606. (212) 683-8333 or (800) 422-8824. 1986. Deals with DNA and nucleotide sequence.

God's Own Junkyard; The Planned Deterioration of America's Landscape. Peter Blake. Holt, Rinehart and Winston, 6277 Sea Harbor Dr., Orlando, FL 32887. (407) 345-2500. 1964. Billboards and national monuments in the United States.

Gold Dust. McIlvaine Co., 2970 Maria Ave., Northbrook, IL 60062. (708) 272-0010. Monthly. Air pollution control & equipment service companies.

Goldman Environmental Foundation. 1160 Battery St., Suite 400, San Francisco, CA 94111. (415) 788-1090.

Good Laboratory Practice Compliance Inspection Manual. Government Institutes, Inc., 4 Research Pl., Ste. 200, Rockville, MD 20850. (301) 921-2300. Laboratory inspection procedures to comply with TSCA and FIFRA.

Goodbye to the Flush Toilet. Rodale Press, 33 E. Minor St., Emmaus, PA 18098. (215) 967-5171. 1977.

Government Institutes, Inc. 966 Hungerford Dr., #24, Rockville, MD 20850. (301) 251-9250.

Government Refuse Collection & Disposal Association. 8750 Georgia Ave., Ste. 140, PO Box 7219, Silver Spring, MD 20910. (301) 585-2898.

Governmental Management of Chemical Risk. Rae Zimmerman. Lewis Publishers, 2000 Corporate Blvd., N.W., Boca Raton, FL 33431. (407) 994-0555 or (800) 272-7737. 1990. Covers managerial, legal and financial strategies that are or can be employed to manage the health risks posed by technology.

Governor's Office of Budget and Planning: Coastal Zone Management. Director, Box 12428, Capitol Station, Austin, TX 78711. (512) 463-1778.

Grain Dust Abstracts. Fang S. Lai. U.S. Dept. of Agriculture, Science and Education Administration, 14 Independence Ave., SW, Washington, DC 20250. (202) 447-7454. 1981. Topics in grain dust explosions.

Grain Dust, Problems and Utilization. L. D. Schnake. U.S. Department of Agriculture, 14 Independence Ave., S.W., Washington, DC 20250. (202) 447-7454. 1981. Safety measures relating to grain elevators.

Grain Industry Dust Explosions and Fires. Occupational Safety and Health Branch, Labour Canada, Phase 2 Place du Porpage, 165 Hotel de Ville, Ottawa, ON, Canada K1AOJ2. (613) 997-3520. 1984.

Graphite Fluorides and Carbon-Fluorine Compounds. Tsuyoshi Nakajima. CRC Press, 2000 Corporate Blvd. N.W., Boca Raton, FL 33431. (800) 272-7737. 1991.

Grass Productivity. A. Voisin. Island Press, 1718 Connecticut Ave. N.W., Suite 300, Washington, DC 20009. (202) 232-7933. 1988. Textbook of scientific information concerning every aspect of management "where the cow and the grass meet." Voisin's "rational grazing" method maximizes productivity in both grass and cattle operations.

Grassland Heritage Foundation. P.O. Box 344, Shawnee Mission, KS 66201-0394. (913) 677-3326.

Grazing Management: An Ecological Perspective. R.K. Heitschmidt. Timber Press, 9999 SW Wilshire, Portland, OR 97225. (800) 327-5680. 1991. Environmental aspects of grazing and range management.

Great American Bridges and Dams. Preservation Press, 1785 Massachusetts Ave. N.W., Washington, DC 20036. (202) 673-4058. 1988. A national trust guide to bridges and dams in the United States.

Great Basin Drama. Darwin Lambert. Roberts Rinehart Pub., PO Box 666, Niwot, CO 80544. (303) 652-2921. 1991. Deals with conservation of natural resources and parks.

The Great Basin Naturalist. Brigham Young University, 290 Life Science Museum, Provo, UT 84602. (801) 378-5053.

The Great Dying. Kenneth J. Hsu. Harcourt Brace Jovanovich, Inc., 1250 6th Ave., San Diego, CA 92101. (800) 346-8648. 1986. Deals with paleontology, extinction, and periodicity in geology.

Great Lakes Commission. The Argus II Bldg., 400 4th St., Ann Arbor, MI 48103-4816. (313) 665-9135.

The Great Lakes Directory of the Natural Resources Agencies and Organizations. Fresh Water Society. Center for the Great Lakes, 435 N Michigan Ave., Suite 1408, Chicago, IL 60611. 1984-. Biennially. Profiles hundreds of organizations working on natural resource management around the Great Lakes.

Great Lakes Exchange. Waste Systems Institute of Michigan, Inc., 470 Market, SW, Suite 100-A, Grand Rapids, MI 49503. (616) 363-3262. Bimonthly. Information on waste management and pollution control .

Great Lakes News Letter. Great Lakes Commission, The Argus II Bldg., 400 S. Fourth St., Ann Arbor, MI 48109. (313) 665-9135. 1956-. Bimonthly.

Great Lakes Red Book. Fishwater Press, Inc., 1701 E. 12th St., Suite 3KW, Cleveland, OH 44114. (216) 241-0373.

Great Lakes Region Biomass Energy Facilities Directory. Council of Great Lakes Governors, 310 S. Michigan, 10th Fl., Chicago, IL 60604. (312) 427-0092.

Great Lakes Sport Fishing Council. c/o Dan Thomas, 293 Berteau, Elmhurst, IL 60126. (708) 941-1351.

Great Lakes Troller. District Extension Sea Grant Agent, 333 Clinton, Grand Haven, MI 49417. (616) 846-8250. Quarterly. Issues concerning Great Lakes fisheries.

Great Lakes United. Cassety Hall, 1300 Elmwood Ave., State University College at Buffalo, Buffalo, NY 14222. (716) 886-0142.

Great Lakes Unlimited. 24 Agassiz Circle, Buffalo, NY 14214. (716) 886-0142.

Great Lakes Water Quality Data Base. U.S. Environmental Protection Agency, Office of Research and Development, Large Lakes Research Station, 401 M St. SW, Washington, DC 20460. (202) 260-2090. Water data related to the Great Lakes and related tributaries and watersheds.

Great Swamp Research Institute. Lycoming College, Dean of the College, Washington Blvd., Williamsport, PA 17701-5192. (717) 321-4102.

Greater Yellowstone Coalition. 13 S. Wilson, Bozeman, MT 59715. (406) 586-1593.

The Greater Yellowstone Ecosystem. Robert B. Keiter and Mark S. Boyce, eds. Yale University Press, 302 Temple St., New Haven, CT 06520. (203) 432-0960. 1991. Discusses key resource management issues in the greater Yellowstone ecosystem, using them as starting points to debate the manner in which humans should interact with the environment of this area.

The Green Activity Book. Meryl Doney. Lion Publishing Corp., 1705 Hubbard Ave., Batavia, IL 60510. (708) 879-0707. 1991. Environmental problems and relevant activities and projects.

Green Alternative Information for Action. Earth Island Inst., 300 Broadway, Suite 28, San Francisco, CA 94133. (415) 788-3666. Monthly.

Green Committees of Correspondence. P.O. Box 30208, Kansas City, MO 64112. (816) 931-9366.

The Green Consumer. John Elkington, Julia Hailes, and Joel Makower. Penguin Books, 375 Hudson St., New York, NY 10014. (212) 366-2000. 1990. Shoppers guide to purchasing ecological products and services.

The Green Consumer Supermarket Guide. Joel Makower, et al. Penguin Books, 375 Hudson St., New York, NY 10014. (212) 366-2000; (800) 253-2304. 1991. A buying guide to products that don't cost the earth.

Green Earth Resource Guide: A Comprehensive Guide About Environmentally Friendly Services and Products Books, Clean Air... Cheryl Gorder. Blue Bird Pub., 1713 East Broadway #306, Tempe, AZ 85282. (602) 968-4088; (800) 654-1993. 1991. Book emphasizes positive steps we can take to help planets. Consists of two parts. Part one profiles people or businesses that are environmentally-friendly and are actively involved with projects and products; part two has resources listings of things concerned with environmental problems. Includes a company index with addresses and phone numbers.

The Green Encyclopedia. Irene Franck, David Brownstone. Prentice-Hall, Rte. 9W, Englewood Cliffs, NY 07632. (201) 592-2000. 1992. Covers environmental organizations.

Green Engineering: A Current Awareness Bulletin. Institution of Mechanical Engineers, 1 Birdcage Walk, Westminster, London, England SW1H 9JJ. 71973 1266/7. 1991. Monthly. Covers acid rain, aerosol technology, biotechnology chlorofluorocarbons, chemical and process engineering, environmental protection, energy conservation, energy generation, greenhouse effect, materials, pollution, recycling, waste disposal, and other environmental topics.

Green Fields Forever. Charles E. Little. Island Press, 1718 Connecticut Ave. N.W., Suite 300, Washington, DC 20009. (202) 232-7933. 1987. An objective look at the costs and benefits of conservation tillage, a promising solution to agricultural problems such as decreased yields, soil erosion and reliance on pesticides and herbicides.

Green Index: A State-by-State Guide to the Nation's Environmental Health. Island Press, 1718 Connecticut Ave. N.W., Suite 300, Washington, DC 20009. (202) 232-7933. 1991-. Biennially. Compares state by state more than 250 environmental categories. Includes an overall environmental quality score for each state.

The Green Index: Directory of Environmental Organisations in Britain and Ireland. Cassell PLC, Publishers Distribution Center, PO Box C831, Rutherford, NJ 07070. (201) 939-6064; (201) 939-6065. 1990.

Green Letter. Green Letter, Box 9242, Berkeley, CA 94709. Bimonthly. Information about the worldwide green movement.

Green Library Journal: Environmental Topics in the Information World. Maria A. Jankowska, ed. Green Library, University of Idaho Library, Moscow, ID 83843. (208) 885-6260. Jan 1992-. Scope of the journal would include information sources about: conservation, ecologically balanced regional development, environmental protection, natural resources management, environmental issues in libraries, publishing industries, and information science.

The Green Lifestyle Handbook. Jeremy Rifkin. Henry Holt & Co., 115 W. 18th St., 6th Fl., New York, NY 10011. (212) 886-9200. 1990. Citizen participation in environmental protection.

Green Light News. Green Light News, Box 12, Liberty Sq., Ellenville, NY 12428. (914) 647-3300. Monthly. Ecology news.

Green-Line Parks. Library of Congress-Environmental Policy Division. U.S. G.P.O., Washington, DC 20401. (202) 512-0000. 1975. An approach to preserving recreational landscapes in urban areas.

The Green Machine: Ecology and the Balance of Nature. Wallace Arthur. B. Blackwell, 3 Cambridge Ctr., Suite 208, Cambridge, MA 02142. (617) 225-0401. 1990. Provides an overview of most topics routinely included in ecology courses. Includes trophic dynamics, predator-prey theory, competition coevolution, and species diversity. Evolutionary topics such as plate tectonics, geologic time, speciation, extinction, and natural selection are also included.

Green Marketing Report. Business Publishers, Inc., 951 Pershing Dr., Silver Spring, MD 20910-4464. (301) 587-6300. 1990-. Monthly. Looks at the steps taken by product manufacturers and advertisers to address consumers' environmental concerns as well as government examination of (and challenges to) some companies' environmental claims. Also available online.

Green Marketing Report. Business Publishers, Inc., 951 Pershing Dr., Silver Spring, MD 20910. (301) 587-6300. Online version of periodical of the same name.

Green Markets. McGraw-Hill Science & Engineering Books, 11 W. 19th St., New York, NY 10011. (212) 337-6010.

The Green Pages: Your Everyday Shopping Guide to Environmentally Safe Products. Random House, Inc., 201 E. 50th St., New York, NY 10022. (212) 751-2600. 1990.

Green Party News. Green Party of B.C., 831 Commercial Dr., Vancouver, BC, Canada V5L. (604) 254-8165. Quarterly. Covers environmental politics in British Columbia.

Green Perspectives. Green Perspectives, Box 111, Vermont, VT 05402. Monthly. News and information on the Green Program Project.

The Green Revolution. T. R. Liao. Library of Congress, Science and Technology Division, Reference Sectiion, Washington, DC 20540. (202) 707-1181. 1980. Agricultural innovations in developing countries.

The Green Revolution: An International Bibliography. M. Bazlui Karim. Greenwood Publishing Group, Inc., 88 Post Rd. W., PO Box 5007, New York, NY 06881. (212) 226-3571. 1986. Covers economic aspects of agriculture, food supply, green revolution, and agricultural innovations.

The Green Revolution Revisited: Critique and Alternatives. Bernhard Glaeser. Unwin Hyman, c/o Routledge Chapman & Hall Inc., 29 W. 35th St., New York, NY 10001. (212) 244-6412. 1987. Economic aspects of agricultural innovations in developing countries.

The Green Shopping Revolution. Food Marketing Institute, Research Department, 1750 K St., NW, Washington, DC 20006. 1990. How solid wastes are affecting consumer behavior and citizen participation in packaging and waste minimization.

Green Warriors. Fred Pearce. Bodley Head, Random Century House, 20 Vauxhall Bridge Rd., London, England SW1V 2SA. 071-973-9730. 1990.

Greenhouse Crisis Foundation. 1130 17th St., NW, Suite 630, Washington, DC 20036. (202) 466-2823.

The Greenhouse Effect and Ozone Layer. Philip Neal. Dryad, 15 Sherman Ave., Takoma Park, MD 20912. (301) 891-3729. 1989. Covers atmospheric carbon dioxide and effects of carbon dioxide on climate.

Greenhouse Effect: Life on a Warmer Planet. Rebecca Johnson. Carolina Biological Supply Company, 2700 York Rd., Burlington, NC 27215. (919) 584-0381. 1990. Discusses the effects of what may be the most serious environmental problem ever. Suggests steps everyone can take to reduce the impact of global warming.

Greenhouse Effect Report. Business Publishers, Inc., 951 Pershing Dr., Silver Spring, MD 20910-4464. (301)587-6300. 1988-. Biweekly. This is a newsletter on international, governmental, regulatory, business and technological actions on global warming and the greenhouse effect. Also available online.

Greenhouse Effect Report. Business Publishers, Inc., 951 Pershing Dr., Silver Spring, MD 20910-4464. (301) 587-6300. Access to regulatory, legislative, business, and technological news and developments. Online version of periodical of same name.

Greenhouse Effect, Sea Level Rise, and Coastal Wetlands. U.S. Environmental Protection Agency, 401 M St., S.W., Washington, DC 20460. (202) 260-2090. 1988. Deals with wetland conservation and atmospheric greenhouse effect.

Greenhouse Gas Emissions–The Energy Dimension. OECD Publications and Information Center, 2001 L St., N.W., Suite 700, Washington, DC 20036. (202) 785-OECD. Source for a comprehensive discussion on the relationship between energy use and greenhouse emissions as they relate to the energy used by geographical and regional sectors.

The Greenhouse Trap: What We're Doing to the Atmosphere and How We Can Slow Global Warming. Francesca Lyman and James J. MacKenzie. World Resources Institute, 1709 New York Ave. N.W., Washington, DC 20006. (800) 822-0504. 1990. Traces the history of the greenhouse effect and show how the current crisis has come about. Possible future consequences, based on the most credible scientific research available, are described and assessed.

Greenhouse Warming: Negotiating a Global Regime. Jessica Tuchman Mathews, ed. World Resources Institute, 1709 New York Ave. N.W., Washington, DC 20006. (800) 822-0504. 1991. Offers specific suggestions for formulating, implementing, and enforcing a global regime to combat greenhouse warming.

Greenletter. Woodstock Resort, Woodstock Inn, Woodstock, VT 05091-1298. (802) 457-1100. Quarterly. Ecological and environmental topics.

Greenpeace. 1436 U St., NW, Washington, DC 20009. (202) 462-1177.

The Greenpeace Guide to Paper. Greenpeace, 1436 U St., NW, Washington, DC 20009. (202) 462-1177. 1990. Waste paper recycling and environmental aspects of paper industry.

Greenpeace Magazine. Greenpeace, 1436 U St., NW, Washington, DC 20009. (202) 462-1177. Bimonthly. Deals with nature and wildlife conservation, and environmental protection.

The Greenpeace Story. Michael Brown. Prentice-Hall, 1870 Birchmount Rd., Scarborough, ON, Canada M1P 2J7. (416) 293-3621. 1989. History of Greenpeace Foundation and its work towards nature and conservation.

Greensward Foundation. 104 Prospect Park, W., Brooklyn, NY 11215.

Greenwire. American Political Network, 282 North Washington St., Falls Church, VA 22046. (703) 237-5130. 1991. Daily. Daily electronic 12-page summary of the last 24 hours of news coverage of environmental issues worldwide. Monday through Friday at 10 am EST, it can be accessed by a PC, modem and an 800 number contains issues on environmental protection, energy/natural resources, business science, 50-state news, worldwide headlines, TV monitor, daily calendar, marketplace battles, Capitol Hill, spotlight story, global issues, environment and the law, solid waste and focus interviews.

Grenz Rays. Daniel Graham. Pergamon Microforms International, Inc., Fairview Park, Elmsford, NY 10523. 1980. An illustrated guide to the theory and practical application of soft x-rays.

Grocery Shopping Guide: A Consumer's Manual for Selecting Foods Lower in Dietary Saturated Fat and Cholesterol. Nelda Mercer. University of Michigan Medical Center, 1500 E. Medical Center Dr., Ann Arbor, MI 48109. (313) 936-4000. 1989. Fat content, sodium content, and cholesterol content of food.

Ground Beetles: Their Role in Ecological and Environmental Studies. Nigel E. Stork, ed. VCH Publishers, 303 NW 12th Ave., Deerfield Beach, FL 33442-1788. (305) 428-5566. 1990. Summarizes the latest advances in the use of beetles in a range of ecological studies.

Ground Water. Water Well Journal Publishing Co., 6375 Riverside Dr., Dublin, OH 43017. (614) 761-3222. Bimonthly. Contains technical papers for NWWA.

Ground Water. H. M. Raghunath. John Wiley & Sons, Inc., 605 3rd Ave., New York, NY 10158-0012. (212) 850-6000. 1987. Hydrogeology, ground water survey and pumping tests, rural water supply and irrigation systems.

Ground Water Age. National Trade Publications, Inc., 13 Century Hill, Latham, NY 12110. (518) 783-1281. Monthly. Covers product and literature developments and industry news.

Ground Water Age–Directory of Manufacturers. National Trade Publications, Inc., 13 Century Hill, Latham, NY 12110. (518) 783-1281.

Ground Water Age–Handbook Issue. National Trade Publications, Inc., 13 Century Hill, Latham, NY 12110. (518) 783-1281.

Ground Water and Toxicological Risk. Jenifer S. Heath. Lewis Publishers, 2000 Corporate Blvd., N.W., Boca Raton, FL 33431. (407) 994-0555 or (800) 272-7737. 1991. Discusses the nature of ground water, the nature of toxicology, risk assessment, basics of risk perception and two case studies of reaction.

Ground Water and Vadose Zone Monitoring. David M. Nielsen and A. Ivan Johnson, eds. PennWell Books, PO Box 21288, Tulsa, OK 74121. (918) 831-9421; (800) 752-9764. 1988. Contains 22 papers presented at the symposium on standards and development for ground water and Vadose Zone monitoring investigations.

Ground Water Federal Register Notices. National Ground Water Information Center, National Water Well Association, 6375 Riverside Dr., Dublin, OH 43017. (614) 761-1711.

Ground Water Handbook. Government Institutes, Inc., 4 Research Pl., Ste 200, Rockville, MD 20850. (301) 921-2300. 1989. Includes highlights of chapters on ground water contamination, use of models in managing ground water protection programs, ground water restoration, ground water quality investigations, basic hydrogeology, monitoring well design and construction, ground water sampling, ground water tracers and basic geology.

Ground Water Industry Standards. National Ground Water Information Center, National Water Well Association, 6375 Riverside Dr., Dublin, OH 43017. (614) 761-1711.

Ground Water Institute. P.O. Box 580981, Minneapolis, MN 55458-0981. (612) 636-3204.

Ground Water Job Mart. National Ground Water Information Center, National Water Well Association, 6375 Riverside Dr., Dublin, OH 43017. (614) 761-1711.

Ground Water Manual: A Guide for the Investigation, Development, and Management of Ground Water Resources. U.S. G.P.O., Washington, DC 20401. (202) 512-0000. 1981. Underground water resources in the water states.

Ground Water Monitor. Business Publishers, Inc., 951 Pershing Dr., Silver Spring, MD 20910-4464. (301) 587-6300. Biweekly. Legislation, litigation, regulations and quality problems on ground water. Also available online.

Ground Water Monitor. Business Publishers, Inc., 951 Pershing Dr., Silver Spring, MD 20910. (301) 587-6300. Online version of periodical of the same name.

Ground Water Monitoring Review. Water Well Journal Publishing Co. National Water Well Association, 6375 Riverside Drive, Dublin, OH 43017. (614) 761-3222. Quarterly. Covers protection and restoration of ground water.

Ground Water Monitoring Review–Buyers Guide Issue. Water Well Journal Publishing Company/National Water Well Association, 6375 Riverside Dr., Dublin, OH 43017. (614) 761-3222.

Ground Water Monitoring Review–Consultant and Contractor Directory Issue. Water Well Journal Publishing Co., National Water Well Association, 6375 Riverside Dr., Dublin, OH 43017. (614) 761-3222.

Ground Water Newsletter. Water Information Center, Inc., 125 East Bethpage Road, Plainview, NY 11803. (516) 249-7634. Biweekly. Covers ground water exploration, development, and management.

Ground Water On-Line. National Water Well Association, National Ground Water Information Center, 6375 Riverside Dr., Dublin, OH 43017. (614) 761-1711. Technical literature covering all aspects of groundwater and well technology.

Ground Water Pollution News. Buraff Publications, 1350 Connecticut Ave., NW, Washington, DC 20036. (202) 862-0990. Biweekly. Legislation, regulation and litigation concerning ground water pollution.

Ground Water Regulations. National Ground Water Information Center, National Water Well Association, 6375 Riverside Dr., Dublin, OH 43017. (614) 761-1711.

Ground Water Sampling Devices. National Ground Water Information Center, National Well Water Association, 6375 Riverside Dr., Dublin, OH 43017. (614) 761-1711.

Groundswell. Nuclear Information and Resource Service, Inc., 1424 16th St., NW, No. 601, Washington, DC 20036. (202) 328-0002. Quarterly. Hazards of nuclear energy and safe alternative sources; legislative and regulatory trends, policies of utility corporations, and funding.

Groundwater and Soil Contamination Remediation. Water Science and Technology Board. National Academy Press, Washington, DC (202) 334-3343. 1990. Science, policy and public perception.

Groundwater Chemicals Desk Reference. John H. Montgomery. Lewis Publishers, 2000 Corporate Blvd. NW, Boca Raton, FL 33431. (407) 994-0555 or (800)272-7737. 1990. Protection and remediation of the groundwater environment. Includes profiles of chemical compounds promulgated by the EPA under the Clean Water Act of 1977.

Groundwater Chemicals Desk Reference, Volume II. John Montgomery. Lewis Publishers, 2000 Corporate Blvd., N.W., Boca Raton, FL 33431. (407) 994-0555 or (800) 272-7737. 1991. Contains abbreviations, symbols, chemicals, conversion factors, CAS index, RTECS number index empirical formula, and synonym index.

Groundwater Contamination. J. H. Guswa, et al. Noyes Publications, 120 Mill Rd., Park Ridge, NJ 07656. (201) 391-8484. 1984. A technology review of equipment, methods, and field techniques; an overview of groundwater hydrology and a methodology for estimating groundwater contamination under emergency response conditions.

Groundwater Contamination: Sources, Control, and Preventive Measures. Chester D. Rail. Technomic Publishing Co., 851 New Holland Ave., Box 3535, Lancaster, PA 17604. (717) 291-5609. 1989. Reviews the presently known sources of groundwater contamination and its many complex interactions, including managerial and political implications.

Groundwater Management Caucus. Box 637, White Deer, TX 79097. (806) 883-2501.

Groundwater Management Districts Association. 1125 Maize Rd., Colby, KS 67701. (913) 462-3915.

The Groundwater Newsletter. Water Information Center, Inc., 125 E. Bethpage Rd., Plainview, NY 11803. (516) 249-7634. Semimonthly.

Groundwater Protection: Local Success Stories. Milou Carolan. Internal City Management Association, 777 N. Capital St., NE, Suite 500, Washington, DC 20002-4201. (800) 745-8780. 1990. Case studies from local governments that have created effective programs for protecting the local water supply by evaluating contamination sources and developing community support.

Groundwater Remediation and Petroleum: A Guide for Underground Storage Tanks. David C. Noonan and James T. Curtis. PennWell Books, PO Box 21288, Tulsa, OK 74121. (918) 831-9421; (800) 752-9764. 1990. Guide for personnel charged with the responsibility of addressing contamination caused by leaking underground storage tanks.

Groundwater Research Center. University of Cincinnati, College of Engineering, Mail Location 18, Cincinnati, OH 45221-0018. (513) 475-2933.

Groundwater Residue Sampling Design. Ralph G. Nash and Anne R. Leslie, eds. American Chemical Society, 1155 16th St. N.W., Washington, DC 20036. (202) 872-4600; (800) 227-5558. 1991. Gives an overview of the approach taken by government agencies and discusses in great detail the various techniques in sampling and analysis of groundwater.

Group Against Smokers' Pollution. P.O. Box 632, College Park, MD 20740. (301) 459-4791.

Grzimek's Animal Life Encyclopedia. Van Nostrand Reinhold, 115 5th Ave., New York, NY 10003. (212) 254-3232. 1975. Thirteen volumes. Includes lower animals, insects, mollusks, fishes, amphibians, reptiles, birds, and mammals.

Grzimek's Encyclopedia of Ecology. Bernhard Grzimek. Van Nostrand Reinhold, 115 5th Ave., New York, NY 10003. (212) 254-3232. 1976.

Grzimek's Encyclopedia of Ethology. Bernard Grzimek. Van Nostrand Reinhold, 115 5th Ave., New York, NY 10003. (212) 254-3232. 1977. Comprehensive detailed coverage on animal behavior.

Guidance and Procedures for Administering and Enforcing the Oily Waste Reception Facility Program. U.S. Coast Guard, 2100 Second St., N.W., Rm. 5410 C, Washington, DC 20593. (202) 267-1042. 1985. Oil pollution of the sea and law relating to ship waste disposal.

Guidance for the Reregistration of Pesticide Products Containing Lindane as the Active Ingredient. U.S. Environmental Protection Agency, Office of the Pesticides and Toxic Substances, 401 M St., SW, Washington, DC 20460. (202) 260-2090. 1985. The Federal Insecticide, Fungicide, Rodenticide Act directs EPA to reregister all pesticides as expeditiously as possible. The guide helps the user to carry out this task and to participate in the EPA's registration standard program. Includes extensive tabular data to the pesticides and an extensive bibliography.

Guidance Manual for Aluminum, Copper, and Nonferrous Metals Forming and Metal Powders Pretreatment Standards. U.S. Environmental Protection Agency, 401 M St. SW, Washington, DC 20460. (202) 260-2090. Environmental aspects of metallurgy and nonferrous metals.

Guidance Manual for Compliance with the Filtration and Disinfection Requirements for Public Water Systems Using Surface Water Sources. American Water Works Association, 6666 W. Quincy Ave., Denver, CO 80235. (303) 794-7711. 1991.

Guidance Manual for Electroplating and Metal Finishing Pretreatment Standards. U.S. Environmental Protection Agency, 401 M St., SW, Washington, DC 20460. (202) 260-2090. 1984. Environmental aspects of electroplating and metal finishing.

Guidance Manual for Sewerless Sanitary Devices and Recycling Methods. U.S. Department of Housing and Urban Development, 451 7th St. SW, Washington, DC 20410. (202) 708-1422. 1983. Sanitary engineering relating to rural sewage disposal.

Guidance to State and Local Agencies in Preparing Regulations to Control Volatile Organic Compounds from Ten Stationary Source Categories. National Technical Information Service, 5285 Port Royal Rd., Springfield, VA 22161. (703) 487-4650. 1979. Environmental aspects of organic compounds and air pollution standards.

Guide for Air Pollution Episode Avoidance. U.S. G.P.O., Washington, DC 20401. (202) 512-0000. 1971.

Guide to Energy Specialists. Porter B. Bennett, ed. Center for International Environment Information, 300 E 42d St., New York, NY 10017. (212) 697-3232. 1979. Lists energy specialists who are willing to answer questions in the area of their expertise.

Guide to EPA Hotlines, Clearinghouses, Libraries, and Dockets. United States Environmental Protection Agency. U.S. G.P.O., Washington, DC 20401. (202) 512-0000. 1990.

Guide to Experts in Forestry and Natural Resources. Northeastern Forest Experimentation Service/Forest Service/ U.S. Department of Agriculture, 5 Radnor Corporate Center, Suite 200, Radnor, PA 19087. (215) 975-4229.

Guide to Hazardous Products Around the Home: A Personal Action Manual for Protecting Your Health and Environment. Household Hazardous Waste Project, 901 S. National Ave., Box 87, Springfield, MO 65804. 1989. Covers hazardous substances, safety measures, home accidents, and prevention.

Guide to Information on Research in the Marine Science and Engineering. U.S. Department of Commerce, National Oceanic and Atmospheric Administration, Office of Ocean Engineering, 6010 Executive Blvd., Rockville, MD 20852. (301) 443-8344. 1978.

Guide to Natural Gas Cogeneration. Nelson E. Hay. The Association of Energy Engineers, 4025 Pleasantdale Rd., Suite 420, Atlanta, GA 30340. (404) 925-9558. 1991. Second edition. Details the engineering and economic aspects of gas fired cogeneration systems. Includes examination of equipment considerations and applications strategies for gas engines, gas turbines, steam engines, and electrical switch gear. Guidelines show you how to select the prime mover which is best suited for a specific type of application.

Guide to Oil Waste Management Alternatives for Used Oil, Oily Wastewater, Oily Sludge, and Other Wastes Resulting from the Use of Oil Products. Robert H. Salvesen Associates. Energy and Environmental Research Corporation, Irvine, CA 1988. Recycling of hazardous and petroleum waste.

Guide to Refrigeration CFCs. Carl Salas and Marianne Salas. The American Association of Energy Engineers, 4025 Pleasantdale Rd., Suite 420, Atlanta, GA 30340. (404) 925-9558. 1992. Information needed to assess CFC-related alternatives, requirements and restrictions is included. The information presented will enable to assess how the mandated phase out of chlorofluocarbons will impact operations.

Guide to Sources for Agricultural and Biological Research. University of California Press, 2120 Berkeley Way, Berkeley, CA (415) 642-4262; (800) 822-6657. 1981.

Guide to State Environmental Programs. Bureau of National Affairs, 1231 25th St., NW, Washington, DC 20037. (800) 372-1033. 1990.

Guide to the Management of Hazardous Waste: A Handbook for the Businessman and the Concerned Citizen. J. William Haun. Fulcrum Publishing, 350 Indiana St., Ste. 350, Golden, CO 80401. (303) 277-1623. 1991. Fact book on hazardous waste management, including factory and trade waste, and hazardous waste law and legislation in the United States.

Guide to the Petroleum Reference Literature. Barbara C. Pearson and Katharine B. Ellwood. Libraries Unlimited, Inc., PO Box 6633, Englewood, CO 80155-6633. (303) 770-1220. 1987. Focuses on petroleum sources, also includes some major works in these related disciplines as they apply to the petroleum industry.

A Guide to the Safe Handling of Hazardous Materials Accidents. ASTM, 1916 Race St., Philadelphia, PA 19103-1187. (215) 299-5400. 1990. 2d ed. Planning and training document to assure the safest, most effective handling of a hazardous material accident.

A Guide to the Study of Animal Ecology. Charles Christopher Adams. Arno Press, PO Box 958, Salem, NH 03079. (603) 669-5933. 1977.

Guide to the U.S. Paint Industry. FIND/SVP, 625 Avenue of the Americas, New York, NY 10011. (212) 645-4500. 1991. Shipment trends/forecasts; company performances; profitability; prices; productivity; geographical patterns; transportation; distribution; foreign trade; and world production/trade.

Guide to U.S. Produced Water Well Drilling Rigs and Support Vehicles. National Water Well Association, 6375 Riverside Dr., Dublin, OH 43017. (614) 761-1711.

Guidebook on Spent Fuel Storage. International Atomic Energy Agency, Wagramerstrasse 5, Vienna, Austria A-1400. 222 23606198. 1991. Radioactive waste disposal.

Guidelines for Can Manufacturers and Food Canners: Prevention of Metal Contamination of Canned Foods. Food and Agricultural Organization of the United Nations, Via delle Terme di Caracalla, Rome, Italy 00100. 61 0181 FAO1. 1986. Canned foods industry and food contamination.

Guidelines for Environmental Pollution Controls for Bridge Painting Contracts. Lloyd Smith. Department of Transportation, Office of Research & Special Studies, 400 7th St. SW, Washington, DC 20590. (202) 366-4433. 1991. Environmental aspects of protective coatings and structural painting.

Guidelines for Evaluation of Potential Product Contamination and Procedures for Withdrawal and/or Recall of Food Products. American Meat Institute, PO Box 3556, Washington, DC 20007. (703) 841-2400. 1981. Food contamination, product recall and food handling.

Guidelines for Handling Excavated Acid-Producing Materials. Federal Lands Highway Programs. U.S. Federal Highway Administration, 400 7th St., S.W., Washington, DC 20590. (202) 366-0630. 1990. Soil acidification, leaching and environmental aspects of sulphide minerals.

Guidelines for Mastering the Properties of Molecular Sieves. Plenum Press, 233 Spring St., New York, NY 10013-1578. (212) 620-8000. Relationship between the physiochemical properties of zeolitic systems and their low dimensionality.

Guidelines for Protected Areas Legislation. Barbara J. Lausche. International Union for Conservation of Nature and Natural Resources, Avenue du Mont-Blanc, Gland, Switzerland CH-1196. 1985. Manual on environmental policy and law.

Guidelines for the Control of Insect and Mite Pest of Foods, Fibers, Feeds, Ornamentals, Livestock, and Households. Agricultural Research Service. U.S. G.P.O., Washington, DC 20401. (202) 7512-0000. 1982. Plant diseases and pests, mites, and insect control.

Guidelines for the Management of Highway Runoff on Wetlands. N. P. Kobriger. Transportation Research Board, National Research Council, 2101 Constitution Ave. NW, Washington, DC 20418. 1983. Wetland conversion and environmental aspects of road and runoffs.

Guidelines for the Radiation Protection of Workers in Industry, Ionising Radiations. International Labour Office, 49 Sheridan Ave., Albany, NY 12210. (518) 436-9686. 1989. Provides technical information on protection against radiation in specific installations and for specific equipment. Designed to be used in conjunction with the ILO code of practice Radiation Protection of Workers (ionising rations), they describe the requirements of workers engaged in radiation work with external sources and unsealed sources.

Guidelines for the Selection of Chemical Protective Clothing. Arthur D. Little Inc. U.S. Coast Guard, 2100 Second St., N.W., Rm. 5410 C, Washington, DC 20593. (202) 267-1042. 1987. A field guide and a technical and reference manual.

Guides to Pollution Prevention. U.S. Environmental Protection Agency, 26 W. Martin Luther King Dr., Cincinnati, OH 45220. 1990. Waste disposal in the paint industry and trade and U.S. environmental aspects.

Gulf & Caribbean Fisheries Institute. Sea Grant Consortium, 287 Meeting St., Charleston, SC 29401. (803) 727-2078.

Gypsum. U.S. Department of the Interior, Bureau of Mines, 810 7th St., NW, Washington, DC 20241. (202) 501-9649. Monthly. Statistics on the gypsum industry.

Gypsum Association. 801 First St. N.W., No. 510, Washington, DC 20002. (202) 289-5440.

Habitat. Pergamon Microforms International, Inc., Fairview Park, Elmsford, NY 10523. (914) 592-7720. Quarterly. An international multidisciplinary journal concerning all aspects of human settlements, both urban and rural.

Habitat Destruction. Tony Hare. Gloucester Press, 95 Madison Ave., New York, NY 10016. (212) 447-7788. 1991. Factors threatening animal and plant habitats, such as pollution and depletion of our natural resources.

Habitat Structure. Susan S. Bell. Chapman & Hall, 29 W. 35th St., New York, NY 10001-2291. (212) 244-3336. 1991. The physical arrangement of objects in space, animal population, biotic communities and habitat ecology.

Hach Water Analysis Handbook. Hach Chemical Co., P.O. Box 907, Ames, IA 50010. (515) 232-2533. 1973.

HADB. National Library of Medicine, Toxicology Information Program, 8600 Rockville Pike, Bethesda, MD 20894. (800) 638-8480.

Halocarbons and the Stratospheric Ozone Layer. George D. Havas. Science Reference Section, Science and Technology Division, Library of Congress, 101 Independence Ave. SE, Washington, DC 20540. (202)707-5000. 1989.

Halocarbons: Environmental Effects of Chlorofluoromethane Release. National Research Council. Committee on Impacts of Stratospheric Change. National Academy of Sciences, 2101 Constitution Ave., NW, Washington, DC 20418. (202) 334-2000. 1976.

Halogenated Biphenyls, Terphenyls, Naphthalenes, Dibenzodioxins, and Related Products. Elsevier Science Publishing Co., 655 Avenue of the Americas, New York, NY 10010. (212) 984-5800. 1989. Toxicology and environmental aspects of halocarbons.

Halogenated Solvent Industry Alliance Newsletter. Halogenated Solvent Industry Alliance, 1225 19th Street, NW, Suite 300, Washington, DC 20036. (202) 223-5890. Bimonthly. Covers legislative and regulatory problems involving halogenated solvents.

Halogenated Solvents Industry Alliance. 1225 19th St., N.W., Suite 300, Washington, DC 20036. (202) 223-5890.

Handbook: Control Technologies for Hazardous Air Pollutants. Air and Energy Research Laboratory, U.S. Environmental Protection Agency, Research Triangle Park, NC 27711. (919) 541-2350. 1986. Environmental research information relative to hazardous wastes.

Handbook for Flue Gas Desulfurization Scrubbing with Limestone. D.S. Henzel. Noyes Publications, 120 Mill Rd., Park Ridge, NJ 07656. (201) 391-8484. 1982. Chemical technology of scrubbers.

Handbook for Identification and Correction of Typical Design Deficiencies at Municipal Wastewater Treatment Facilities. U.S. Environmental Protection Agency, Office of Research and Development, Municipal Environmental Research Laboratory, 26 W. Martin Luther King Dr., Cincinnati, OH 45268. (513) 569-7931. 1982. Sewage purification and sewage disposal plants.

Handbook for Oil Spill Protection and Cleanup Priorities. Municipal Environmental Research Laboratory, U.S. Environmental Protection Agency, 26 W Martin Luther King Dr., Cincinnati, OH 45268. (513) 569-7931. 1981. Environmental aspects of oil pollution of water and oil spills.

Handbook for Preparing Office of Marine Assessment Reports. Rosa Lee Echard. National Oceanic and Atmospheric Administration, U.S. Department of Commerce, Washington, DC 20230. (202) 377-2895. 1982.

Handbook for State/EPA Agreements. U.S. Environmental Protection Agency. U.S. Environmental Protection Agency, 401 M St. SW, Washington, DC 20460. (202) 260-2090. Annual. Environmental protection and policy in the United States.

Handbook for the Identification, Location and Investigation of Pollution Sources Affecting Ground Water. National Water Well Association, 6375 Riverside Dr., Dublin, OH 43017. (614) 761-1711. 1989.

Handbook for Water Analysis for the Food Industry: Industrial, Potable, and Wastewater Systems for the Use of Food Processors and Packers. Avery Publishing Corp., 120 Old Broadway, Garden City Park, NY 11040. (201) 696-3359. 1982. A manual for water analysis for use in the food industry and trade.

Handbook of Acid-Proof Construction. Friedrich Karl Flacke. VCH Publishers, 303 NW 12th Ave., Deerfield Beach, FL 33442-1788. (305) 428-5566. 1985. Details the equipment and supplies used in chemical plants and how corrosion affects them.

Handbook of Acoustical Measurements and Noise Control. Cyril M. Harris. McGraw-Hill Science & Engineering Books, 11 W. 19th St., New York, NY 10011. (212) 337-6010. 1991.

Handbook of Acute Toxicity of Chemicals to Fish and Aquatic Invertebrates. Waynon W. Johnson and Mack T. Finley. U.S. Department of the Interior, Fish and Wildlife Service, Washington, DC 20240. (202) 208-5634. 1980. Fisheries Research Laboratory, 1965-78; Resource publication/U.S. Fish and Wildlife Service, no. 137.

Handbook of Air Pollution Analysis. Roy M. Harrison. Chapman & Hall, 29 W. 35th St., New York, NY 10001-2291. (212) 244-3336. 1986. Topics in environmental chemistry and measurement of air pollution.

Handbook of Analytical Chemistry. Louis Meites, ed. McGraw-Hill Science & Engineering Books, 11 W. 19th St., New York, NY 10011. (212) 337-6010. 1963.

Handbook of Analytical Toxicology. Irving Sunshine, ed. CRC Press, 2000 Corporate Blvd. N.W., Boca Raton, FL 33431. (407) 994-0555; (800) 272-7737. 1969.

Handbook of Biological Wastewater Treatment. Garland Publishing, Inc., 1000A Sherman Ave., Hamden, CT 06514. (203) 281-4487. 1980.

Handbook of Carcinogen Testing. Harry A. Milman. Noyes Publications, 120 Mill Rd., Park Ridge, NJ 07656. (201) 391-8484. 1985. Biological assay, carcinogens and carcinogenicity testing.

Handbook of Carcinogens and Hazardous Substances: Chemical and Trace Analysis. Malcolm C. Bowman, ed. M. Dekker, 270 Madison Ave., New York, NY 10016. (212) 696-9000. 1982. Alkylating agents, aromatic amines and azo compounds, estrogens, mycotoxins, N-nitrosamines and n-nitroso compounds, pesticides and related substances and hydrocarbons.

Handbook of Catalyst Manufacture. Noyes Publications, 120 Mill Rd., Park Ridge, NJ 07656. (201) 391-8484. Contains patents of catalysts.

Handbook of Chemical and Environmental Safety in Schools and Colleges. Forum for Scientific Excellence, Inc. J. B. Lippincott, 227 E. Washington Sq., Philadelphia, PA 19105. (215) 238-4200. 1990. Hazardous substances safety measures and school plant management. A single resource book containing all of the information outlined in a 5 volume training manual.

Handbook of Chemical Property Estimation Methods. Warren J. Lyman, et al. McGraw-Hill Science & Engineering Books, 11 W. 19th St., New York, NY 10011. (212) 337-6010. 1982.

Handbook of Chemistry and Physics. CRC Press, 2000 Corporate Blvd. N.W., Boca Raton, FL 33431. (800) 272-7737. Annually.

The Handbook of Chlorination. George Clifford White. Van Nostrand Reinhold Co., 115 Fifth Ave., New York, NY 10003. (212) 254-3232. 1986. Water purification through chlorination.

Handbook of Coastal and Ocean Engineering. John B. Herbich. Gulf Publishing Co., Book Division, PO Box 2608, Houston, TX 77252. (713) 529-4301. 1991. Wave phenomena in coastal structures.

Handbook of Control Technologies for Hazardous Air Pollutants. Robert Y. Purcell. Science Information Resource Center, Cambridge, MA 1988. Evaluation of control technologies for hazardous air pollutants.

Handbook of Dangerous Materials. N. Irving Sax. Reinhold Pub. Co., 115 5th Ave., New York, NY 10003. (212)254-3232. 1951. Covers medical mycology and safety measures relating to chemicals, explosives, and radioactivity.

Handbook of Dehumidification Technology. G. W. Brundrett. Butterworth-Heinemann, 80 Montvale Ave., Stoneham, MA 02180. (617) 438-8464 or (800) 366-2665. 1987.

Handbook of Deltaic Facies. Donald C. Swanson. Swanson Petroleum Enterprises, Lafayette, IN 1980. A collection of practical and useful information and exercises for the subsurface geologist.

Handbook of Drinking Water Quality: Standards and Controls. John De Zuane. Van Nostrand Reinhold, 115 5th Ave., New York, NY 10003. (212) 254-3232. 1990. Aids in evaluating water quality control at every stage of the water path, from source to treatment plant, from distribution system to consumer.

Handbook of Emergency Management: Programs and Policies Dealing With Major Hazards and Disasters. William L. Waugh, Jr., and Ronald John Hy, eds. Greenwood Publishing Group, Inc., 88 Post Rd. W., Box 5007, Westport, CT 06881. (203) 226-3571. 1990.

Handbook of Energy Technology Trends and Perspectives. V. Daniel Hunt. Van Nostrand Reinhold, 115 5th Ave., New York, NY 10003. (212) 254-3232. 1982.

Handbook of Engineering Control Methods for Occupational Radiation Protection. Michael K. Orn. Prentice Hall, Rte 9W, Englewood Cliffs, NJ 07632. (201) 592-2000 or (800) 922-0579. 1992. Deals with radiological safety in the workplace.

The Handbook of Environmental Chemistry. O. Hutzinger. Springer-Verlag, 175 5th Ave., New York, NY 10010. (212) 460-1500. Irregular. Distribution and equilibria between environmental compartments, pathways, thermodynamics and kinetics.

Handbook of Environmental Data on Organic Chemicals. Karel Verschueren. Van Nostrand Reinhold, 115 5th Ave., New York, NY 10003. (212) 254-3232. 1983. Covers individual substances as well as mixtures and preparations. The profiles include: properties, air pollution factors, water pollution factors, and biological effects.

Handbook of Environmental Degradation Rates. Philip H. Howard, et al. Lewis Publishers, 2000 Corporate Blvd., N.W., Boca Raton, FL 33431. (407) 994-0555 or (800) 272-7737. 1991. Provides rate constant and half-life ranges for various processes and combines them into ranges for different media (air, groundwater, surface water, soils) which can be directly entered into various models.

Handbook of Environmental Genotoxicology. Eugene Sawicki. CRC Press, 2000 Corporate Blvd. N.W., Boca Raton, FL 33431. (800) 272-7737. 1982. Human chromosome abnormalities, mutagenesis, carcinogenesis, and environmentally induced diseases.

Handbook of Environmental Health and Safety, Principles and Practices. Herman Koren. Lewis Publishers, 2000 Corporate Blvd., N.W., Boca Raton, FL 33431. (800) 272-7737. 1991. Two volumes. Current issues and regulations are presented. The broad spectrum of topics is presented outlining the relationship of the environment to humans and also environmental health emergencies and how to deal with them.

Handbook of Evaporation Technology. Paul E. Minton. Noyes Publications, 120 Mill Rd., Park Ridge, NJ 07656. (201) 391-8484. 1986.

Handbook of Fiberglass and Advanced Plastics Composites. George Lubin. Van Nostrand Reinhold, 115 5th Ave., New York, NY 10003. (212) 254-3232. 1969. Deals with reinforced plastics, fibrous composites, and glass fibers.

Handbook of Food Additives. T. E. Furia, ed. CRC Press, 2000 Corporate Blvd. N.W., Boca Raton, FL 33431. (800) 272-7737. 1972-1980. Second edition. Two volumes. Additives are discussed by broad categories and a table indicates the regulatory status of food additives, giving pertinent FEMA numbers and FDA regulation numbers. Volume 2 updates volume 1.

Handbook of Geophysics and the Space Environment. Adolph S. Jursa, ed. Air Force Geophysics Laboratory, Air Force Systems Command, United States Air Force, c/o National Technical Information Service, 5285 Port Royal Rd., Springfield, VA 22161. (703) 487-4650. 1985. Two volumes. Broad subject areas covered are space, atmosphere, and terrestrial environment. Includes topics such as solar radiation, sunspots, solar wind, geomagnetic fields, radiation belts, cosmic radiation, atmospheric gases, etc.

Handbook of Geothermal Energy. L.M. Edwards. Gulf Publishing Co., Book Division, PO Box 2608, Houston, TX 77252. (713) 529-4301. 1982. Methods relating to use of geothermal resources.

Handbook of Ground Water Development. The Roscoe Moss Company. John Wiley & Sons, Inc., 605 3rd Ave., New York, NY 10158-0012. (212) 850-6000. 1989. Guide to current theories and techniques for the exploration, extraction, use and management of ground water. Covers the physical geology and hydrodynamics of water in the ground, the exploitation of ground water and well design and construction, and the management of wells and well field operations.

Handbook of Hazardous Chemicals and Carcinogens. Marshall Sittig. Noyes Publications, 120 Mill Rd., Park Ridge, NJ 07656. (201) 391-8484. 1985.

Handbook of Hazardous Waste Management for Small Quantity Generators. Russell W. Phifer and William R. McTigue, Jr. Lewis Publishers, 2000 Corporate Blvd., N.W., Boca Raton, FL 33431. (407) 994-0555 or (800) 272-7737. 1988. Includes practical "how to" instructions, state/federal regulations, overview, lab waste management, interpretations of regulation, enforcement, generator checklist, etc.

Handbook of Highway Engineering. Robert F. Baker, ed. R. E. Krieger Publishing Co., 115 5th Ave., New York, NY 10003. (212) 254-3232. 1982. Provides reference data on the application of technology to highway transportation.

Handbook of Holocene Palaeoecology and Palaeohydrology. B.E. Berglund. John Wiley & Sons, Inc., 605 3rd Ave., New York, NY 10158-0012. (212) 850-6000. 1986. Topics in straligraphic geology.

Handbook of In Vivo Toxicity Testing. Academic Press, c/o Harcourt Brace Jovanovich Inc., 6277 Sea Harbor Dr., Orlando, FL 32887. (800) 346-8648. 1990.

Handbook of Incineration Systems. Calvin R. Brunner. McGraw-Hill Science & Engineering Books, 11 West 19th St., New York, NY 10011. (212) 337-6010. 1991. Examines every type of modern incinerator, describes the analytical techniques required to utilize the equipment, explains the basic scientific principles involved, and defines the regulations that apply to various incineration facilities and procedures for upgrading existing facilities to conform to new, stricter operating standards.

Handbook of Industrial Drying. Arun S. Majumdar, ed. Marcel Dekker Inc., 270 Madison Ave., New York, NY 10016. (212) 696-9000 or (800) 228-1160. 1987.

Handbook of Insect Pheromones and Sex Attractants. Marion S. Meyer and John R. McLaughlin. CRC Press, 2000 Corporate Blvd., N.W., Boca Raton, FL 33431. (800) 272-7737. 1991. Guide to the literature published before 1988 on chemicals that effect aggregation for mating and/or elicit sexual behavior in insects, mites and ticks.

Handbook of Laboratory Distillation. Erich Kreel. 655 Avenue of the Americas, New York, NY 10010. (212) 989-5800. An introduction into the pilot plant distillation.

Handbook of Limnology. J. Schwoerbel. John Wiley & Sons, Inc., 605 3rd Ave., New York, NY 10158. (212) 850-6000. 1987. Gives an evaluation of response to environmental problems relating to surface water systems, water quality pollution control and environmental concern.

Handbook of Lipid Research. Plenum Press, 233 Spring St., New York, NY 10013-1578. (212) 620-8000; (800) 221-9369. 1978.

Handbook of Livestock Management Techniques. Richard Battaglia. Burgess Publishing Co., 7110 Ohms Ln., Minneapolis, MN 55439-2143. (612) 831-1344. 1981.

Handbook of Marine Mammals. Sam H. Ridgway. Academic Press, c/o Harcourt Brace Jovanovich Inc., 6277 Sea Harbor Dr., Orlando, FL 32887. (800) 346-8648. 1989. Covers walruses, sea lions, fur seals, sea otters, seals, and the sirenians and baleen whales.

Handbook of Methods for Acid Deposition Studies: Field Methods for Surface Water Chemistry. D. J. Chaloud, et al. U.S. Environmental Protection Agency, Office of Modeling, Monitoring Systems, and Quality Assurance, 401 M St., SW, Washington, DC 20460. (202) 260-2090. 1990-.

Handbook of Methods for Acid Deposition Studies: Laboratory Analyses for Soil Chemistry. L.J. Blume. Environmental Monitoring Systems Laboratory, PO Box 15027, Las Vegas, NV 89104. (702) 798-2000. 1990.

Handbook of Methods for the Evaluation of Water Conservation for Municipal and Industrial Water Supply. Institute for Water Resources, c/o American Public Works Association, 1313 E. 60th St., Chicago, IL 60637. (312) 667-2200. 1985.

Handbook of Oil Industry Terms and Phrases. R. D. Langenkamp. PennWell Books, PO Box 1260, Tulsa, OK 74101. (918) 835-3161. 1984. Fourth edition. Includes more than 700 new entries relating to geology, new equipment, advances in drilling technology and operating methods, investment funds, operating interests, royalty interests, nondrilling leases, top leases, joint leases, implied covenants and "escape clauses" and other related topics.

Handbook of Pest Control: The Behavior, Life History, and Control of Household Pests. Arnold Mallis. Franzak & Foster, 4012 Bridge Ave., Cleveland, OH 44113. (216) 961-4134. 1982. Covers injurious and beneficial insects.

Handbook of Pesticide Toxicology. Wayland J. Hayes and Edward R. Laws, eds. Academic Press, c/o Harcourt Brace Jovanovich Inc., 6277 Sea Harbor Dr., Orlando, FL 32887. (800) 346-8648. 1991. Three volumes. Covers various types of toxicity, nature of injury, reversibility, various methods of quantitating dose response, metabolism of toxins, factors affecting toxicity, absorption, and elimination.

Handbook of Photon Interaction Coefficients in Radioisotope-Excited X-Ray Fluorescence Analysis. O.S. Marenkov. Nova Science Publishers, Inc., 283 Commack Rd., Ste. 300, Commack, NY 11725. (516) 499-3103. 1991.

Handbook of Poisoning: Prevention, Diagnosis, and Treatment. Lange Medical Publications, Los Altos, CA 1983.

Handbook of Protein Sequence Analysis. L.R. Croft. John Wiley & Sons, Inc., 605 3rd Ave., New York, NY 10158-0012. (212) 850-6000. 1980. A compilation of amino acid sequences with an introduction to the methodology.

Handbook of Protoctista. Lynn Margulis. Jones and Bartlett Publishers, 20 Park Plaza, Boston, MA 02116. (617) 482-5243. 1990. The structure, cultivation, habitats, and life histories of the eukaryotic microorganisms and their descendants exclusive of animals, plants, and fungi. A guide to the algae, ciliates, foraminifera, sporozoa, water molds, slime molds, and the other protoctists.

Handbook of Suggested Practices for the Design and Installation of Ground-Water Monitoring Wells. Linda Aller. Environmental Monitoring Systems Laboratory, PO Box 15027, Las Vegas, NV 89104. (702) 798-2000. 1991.

Handbook of the Elements. Samuel Ruben. Open Court Pub. Co., 407 S. Dearborn, #1300, Chicago, IL 60605. (312) 939-1500. 1990. Third edition. Provides essential information on the 108 known chemical elements.

Handbook of Thermal Insulation Design Economics for Pipes and Equipment. William Turner. Krieger Publishing Co., Inc., PO Box 9542, Melbourne, FL 32902. (407) 724-9542. 1980. Topics in energy conservation.

Handbook of Toxic and Hazardous Chemicals and Carcinogens. Marshall Sittig. Noyes Publications, 120 Mill Rd., Park Ridge, NJ 07656. (201) 391-8484. 1991.

Handbook of Toxic Fungal Metabolites. Richard J. Cole and Richard H. Cox. Academic Press, c/o Harcourt Brace Jovanovich Inc., 6277 Sea Harbor Dr., Orlando, FL 32887. (800) 346-8648. Oriented toward fungal metabolites that elicit a toxic response in vertebrate animals. Also includes metabolites that show little or no known acute toxicity.

Handbook of Toxicity of Pesticides to Wildlife. U.S. Department of the Interior, Fish and Wildlife Service, 1849 C St. NW, Washington, DC 20240. (202) 208-3171. 1984.

Handbook of Toxicologic Pathology. Wanda M. Haschek and Colin G. Rosseaux, eds. Academic Press, c/o Harcourt Brace Jovanovich Inc., 6277 Sea Harbor Dr., Orlando, FL 32887. (800) 346-8648. 1991. Handbook describing experimental methods and animal models for toxicological assessment.

Handbook of Toxicology. W. Thomas Shier and Dietrich Mebs. Marcel Dekker, Inc., 270 Madison Ave., New York, NY 10016. (212) 696-9000; (800) 228-1160. 1990. Covers most toxins for which sufficient research has been done to clearly establish the identity and characteristics of the toxin.

Handbook of Underground Storage Tank Safety and Correction Technology. Hemisphere Publishing Co., Science Information Resource Center, 79 Madison Ave., Ste. 1110, New York, NY 10016. (212) 725-1999. 1988.

Handbook of Vapor Pressures and Heats of Vaporization of Hydrocarbons and Related Compounds. Randolph C. Wilhoit. Thermodynamics Research Center, Dept. of Chemistry, Texas A & M Univ., Drawer C, Lewis St., University Campus, College Station, TX 77843. (409) 845-1436. 1971. Covers data on vapor liquid equilibrium tables and hydrocarbon tables.

Handbook of Vitamins. Lawrence J. Machlin. Marcel Dekker, Inc., 270 Madison Ave., New York, NY 10016. (212) 696-9000; (800) 228-1160. 1991. Food science and technology of vitamins in human nutrition.

Handbook of Vitamins, Minerals, and Hormones. Roman J. Kutsky. Van Nostrand Reinhold, 115 5th Ave., New York, NY 10003. (212) 254-3232. 1981. Covers vitamins, hormones and minerals in the body.

Handbook of Wastewater Collection and Treatment: Principles and Practice. Garland Publishing, Inc., 1000A Sherman Ave., Hamden, CT 06514. (203) 281-4487. 1980. Sewage disposal and sewage purification.

Handbook of Water Purification. Walter Lorch. Halsted Press, 605 3rd Ave., New York, NY 10158. (212) 850-6000.

Handbook of Water Quality Management Planning. Van Nostrand Reinhold, 115 Fifth Ave., New York, NY 10003. (212) 254-3232. 1977. Topics in environmental engineering including water purification and water supply.

Handbook of Water Resources and Pollution Control. Harry W. Gehm. Van Nostrand Reinhold, 115 Fifth Ave., New York, NY 10003. (212) 254-3232. 1976. Covers sewage disposal, water pollution, and water supply engineering.

Handbook on Aerosols. National Defense Research Committee. Atomic Energy Commission, Washington, DC 20555. (301) 492-7000. 1950.

Handbook on Atmospheric Diffusion. Steven R. Hanna. Technical Information Center, U.S. Dept. of Energy, PO Box 62, Oak Ridge, TN 37831. (615)576-2268. 1982. Includes cooling towers, climatic factors, and smoke plumes.

Handbook on Environmental Aspects of Fertilizer Use. Martinus Nijhoff/W. Junk, 101 Philips Dr., Boston, MA 02061. (617) 871-6600. 1983.

Handbook on International Food Regulatory Toxicology. SP Medical & Scientific Books, New York, NY 1980-. Toxicity of food additives and pesticide residues, as well as food-contamination prevention and control.

Handbook on Marine Pollution. Edgar Gold. Assuranceforeningen Gard, Postboks 1563 Myrene, Arendal, Norway N-4801. 1985. Law and legislation relative to marine pollution.

Handbook on Procedures for Implementing the National Environmental Policy Act. U.S. Office of Surface Mining Reclamation and Enforcement. Office of Surface Mining Reclamation and Enforcement, Washington, DC Environmental law in the United States.

Handbook on the Toxicology of Metals. Lars Friberg. Elsevier Science Publishing Co., 655 Avenue of the Americas, New York, NY 10010. (212) 984-5800. 1986. Pharmacodynamics and toxicity of metals.

Handbook on Toxicity of Inorganic Compounds. Marcel Dekker Inc., 270 Madison Ave., New York, NY 10016. (212) 696-9000; (800) 228-1160. 1988. Environmental aspects of inorganic compounds.

Handbook on Toxicity of Organic Compounds. Marcel Dekker, Inc., 270 Madison Ave., New York, NY 10016. (212) 696-9000; (800) 228-1160. 1988.

Handbook: Operation and Maintenance of Hospital Medical Waste Incinerators. U.S. Environmental Protection Agency, MD 75, Research Triangle Park, NC 27711. 1990.

Handbook: Responding to Discharges of Sinking Hazardous Substances. K. R. Boyer. National Technical Information Service, 5285 Port Royal Rd., Springfield, VA 22161. (703) 487-4650. 1987.

Hands-On Ecology. Children's Press, 5440 N. Cumberland Ave., Chicago, IL 60656. (312) 693-0800. 1991. Practical ways of conserving the environment.

The Harbinger File: A Directory of Citizen Groups, Government Agencies and Environmental Education Programs Concerned with California Environmental Issues. Harbinger Communications, 50 Rustic Lane, Santa Cruz, CA 95060. (415) 429-8727. 1990/91.

Hardwood Manufacturers Association. 400 Penn Center Bldv., Pittsburgh, PA 15235. (901) 346-2222.

Hardwood Plywood Manufacturers Association. 1825 Michael Faraday Dr., P.O. Box 2789, Reston, VA 22090. (703) 435-2900.

Hardwood Plywood Manufacturers Association–Face Veneer Manufacturers List. Hardwood Plywood Manufacturers Association, 1825 Michael Faraday Dr., P.O. Box 2789, Reston, VA 22090. (703) 435-2900.

Hardwood Plywood Manufacturers Association–Lists of Manufacturers. Hardwood Plywood Manufacturers Association, 1825 Michael Faraday Dr., P.O. Box 2789, Reston, VA 22090. (703) 435-2900.

Hardwood Research Council. Box 34518, Memphis, TN 38184. (901) 377-1824.

Harnessing Science for Environmental Regulation. John D. Graham. Praeger Publishers, 1 Madison Ave., New York, NY 10010-3603. (212) 685-5300. 1991. Environmental law in the United States relating to hazardous substances.

Harvard Environmental Law Review. Environmental Law Review, c/o Publication Center, Harvard Law School, 202 Austin Hall, Cambridge, MA 02138. (617) 495-3110. Semiannual. Law reviews of cases involving the environment.

The Harvard Environmental Law Review: HELR. Harvard Environmental Law Review, 202 Austin Hall, Harvard Law Review, Cambridge, MA 02138. (617) 495-3110. Semiannual.

Harvard Environmental Law Society. 202 Austin Hall, Harvard Law School, Cambridge, MA 02138. (617) 495-3125.

Harvest of Hope. Jennifer Curtis, et al. Natural Resources Defense Council, 40 W. 20th St., New York, NY 10011. (212) 727-2700. 1991. Details potential reductions in pesticide use and offers recommendations for reform in research, farm programs, marketing policy and water pricing.

Hastings Natural History Reservation. University of California, Berkeley, 38601 E. Carmel Valley Rd., Carmel Valley, CA 93924. (408) 659-2664.

Hawaii Environmental Resources 1990 Directory. Office of Environmental Control, State of Hawaii, 220 S King St., 4th Fl., Honolulu, HI 96813. (808) 586-4185. 1990.

Hazard Assessment and Control Technology in Semiconductor Manufacturing. The American Conference of Governmental Industrial Hygienists. Lewis Publishers, 2000 Corporate Blvd., N.W., Boca Raton, FL 33431. (407) 994-0555 or (800) 272-7737. 1989. Covers health studies, hazard control technology of manufacturing processes, catastrophic releases, and emerging technologies.

Hazard Assessment of Chemicals. Academic Press, c/o Harcourt Brace Jovanovich Inc., 6277 Sea Harbor Dr., Orlando, FL 32887. (800) 346-8648. 1981-. Annually. Presents comprehensive authoritative reviews of new and significant developments in the area of hazard assessment of chemicals or chemical classes.

Hazard Communication Compliance Manual Database. Bureau of National Affairs, BNA PLUS, 1231 25th St., N.W., Rm. 215, Washington, DC 20037. (800) 452-7773.

Hazard Communication Guide: Federal & State Right-to-Know Standards. J. J. Keller & Associates, Inc., 3003 W. Breezewood, PO Box 368, Neenah, WI 54957-0368. (414) 722-2848. 1985. Deals with legal aspects of industrial hygiene, hazardous substances, and industrial safety.

Hazard Communication Standard Inspection Manual. Government Institutes, Inc., 4 Research Pl., Ste. 200, Rockville, MD 20850. (301) 921-2300. 1991. Includes detailed inspection procedures. Covers hazard communication program, hazard determination procedures, new enforcement guidance on the construction industry, employee information and training, labeling, trade secrets, MSDS completeness, and the instances in which OSHA inspectors are instructed to issue citations.

Hazard Monthly. Research Alternatives, Inc., 1401 Rockville Pike, Rockville, MD 20852. (301) 424-2803. Monthly. Covers natural disasters and hazardous substances.

Hazardline. Occupational Health Services, Inc., 450 7th Ave., Ste. 2407, New York, NY 10123. (212) 967-1100. More than 3600 dangerous materials, including physical and chemical descriptions, standards and regulations, and safety precautions for handling.

Hazardous and Industrial Wastes, 1990. Joseph P. Martin, et al., eds. Technomic Publishing Co., 851 Holland Ave., Box 3535, Lancaster, PA 17604. (717) 291-5609. 1990. Proceedings of the 22nd Mid-Atlantic Industrial Waste Conference, June 24-27, 1990, Drexel University, Philadelphia, PA. Fifty-one new reports on developments in industrial and hazardouswaste management, technology and regulation were presented.

Hazardous and Industrial Wastes, 1991. Technomic Publishing Co., 851 New Holland Ave., Box 3535, Lancaster, PA 17604. (717) 291-5609. 1991. Proceedings of the 23rd Mid-Atlantic Industrial Waste Conference held at Drexel University, 1991.

Hazardous and Toxic Effects of Industrial Chemicals. Marshall Sittig. Noyes Publications, 120 Mill Rd., Park Ridge, NJ 07656. (201) 391-8484. 1979. Dictionary of poisons and industrial toxicology.

Hazardous and Toxic Waste Management January 1979-May 1989. Louise Reynnells. U.S. Department of Agriculture Library, Beltsville, MD 1989.

Hazardous Chemicals Data Book. G. Weiss, ed. Noyes Publications, 120 Mill Rd., Park Ridge, NJ 07656. (201) 391-8484. 1986. 2d ed. Supplies instant information on 1015 hazardous chemicals. The data will provide rapid assistance to personnel involved with handling of hazardous chemical materials and related accidents.

Hazardous Chemicals Desk Reference. Richard J. Lewis. Van Nostrand Reinhold, 115 Fifth Ave., New York, NY 10003. (212) 254-3232. 1991. Information on the hazardous properties of some 5500 chemicals commonly encountered in industry, laboratories, environment, and the workplace.

Hazardous Chemicals Information Annual. Van Nostrand Reinhold, Information Services, 115 5th Ave., New York, NY 10003. (212) 254-3232. 1987. Annual.

The Hazardous Chemicals on File Collection. Craig T. Norback. Facts on File, Inc., 460 Park Ave. S., New York, NY 10016. (212) 683-2244. A guide for the general public seeking up-to-date, authoritative information on the characteristics of, and protection against, hazardous materials in the workplace

Hazardous Laboratory Chemicals; Disposal Guide. M. A. Armour. CRC Press, 2000 Corporate Blvd., N.W., Suite 700, Boca Raton, FL 33431. (407) 994-0555; (800) 272-7737. 1991. Chemical disposal procedures are designed to enable chemicals to be recycled or disposed of inhouse, eliminating the need to incinerate them or take them to a landfill. Disposal methods for heavy metals, salts, explosive chemicals such as picric acid, and toxic organic materials are included.

Hazardous Location Equipment Directory [UL label]. 333 Pfingsten Rd., Northbrook, IL 60062-2096. (708) 272-8800. Annual.

Hazardous Materials Advisory Council. 1110 Vermont Ave. N.W., Ste. 250, Washington, DC 20005. (202) 728-1460.

Hazardous Materials Advisory Council–Directory. Hazardous Materials Advisory Council, 1110 Vermont Ave., N.W., Suite 250, Washington, DC 20005. (202) 728-1460.

Hazardous Materials Control. Hazardous Materials Control Research Institute, 9300 Columbia Blvd., Silver Spring, MD 20910-1702. (301) 587-9390. Bimonthly. Information, innovations and articles in the hazardous materials field.

Hazardous Materials Control Directory. Hazardous Materials Control Research Institute, 9300 Columbia Blvd., Silver Spring, MD 20910. (301) 587-9390.

Hazardous Materials Control Research Institute. 7237 Hanover Pkwy., Greenbelt, MD 20770. (301) 982-9500.

Hazardous Materials Dictionary. Ronny J. Coleman and Kara Hewson Williams. Technomic Publishing Co., 851 New Holland Ave., Box 3535, Lancaster, PA 17604. (717) 291-5609. 1988. Defines more than 2600 specialized words which are critical for communication, especially under the stressful circumstances of an emergency. Identifies many of the unique terms that apply to the handling of hazardous materials emergencies.

Hazardous Materials Exposure; Emergency Response and Patient Care. Jonathan Borak, et al. Prentice-Hall, Rte. 9W, Englewood Cliffs, NJ 07632. (201) 592-2000; (800) 634-2863. 1991. Focuses on the emergency medical service sector and hazardous materials releases. Provides EMS personnel and other first responders with an education and training program for improving medical knowledge and performance skills.

Hazardous Materials Guide: Shipping, Materials Handling, and Transportation. J. J. Keller & Associates, Inc., 3003 W. Breezewood, PO Box 368, Neenah, WI 54957-0368. (414) 722-2848. Laws and procedures relating to the packing and transportation of hazardous substances.

Hazardous Materials Intelligence Report. World Information Systems, P.O. Box 535, Harvard Square Station, Cambridge, MA 02238. (617) 491-5100. Weekly. Timely information on hazardous substances rules and procedures.

Hazardous Materials Intelligence Report. World Information Systems, PO Box 535, Cambridge, MA 02238. (617) 491-5100. Online access to federal, state, and local legislation, regulations, and programs related to hazardous waste and hazardous material management. Online version of the periodical of the same name.

Hazardous Materials Management. Canadian Hazardous Materials Mgmt., 12 Salem Ave., Toronto, ON, Canada M6H 3C2. (416) 536-5974. Biweekly. All aspects of pollution control, including air quality, water treatment, and solid waste.

Hazardous Materials: Sources of Information on Their Transportation. Nigel Lees. British Library Science Reference and Information Service, London, England 1990.

Hazardous Materials Spills Emergency Handbook. American Water Works Association, 6666 W. Quincy Ave., Denver, CO 80235. (303) 794-7711. Covers chemical safety measures, water pollution, and water purification.

Hazardous Materials Transportation. Department of California Highway Patrol, PO Box 94298, Sacramento, CA 94298-0001. (916) 445-1865. 1985. Hazardous substances transportation law and legislation in California.

Hazardous Materials Transportation. Bureau of National Affairs, 1231 25th St. NW, Washington, DC 20037. (202) 452-4200. Monthly. Covers rules and regulations governing the shipment of hazardous materials in the U.S.

Hazardous Materials Transportation Accidents. National Fire Protection Association, 1 Battery Park, Quincy, MA 02269. (617) 770-3000; (800) 344-3555. 1978. Compilation of articles from Fire Journal and Fire Command. Deals with transportation of hazardous substances, their combustibility during accidents and preventive measures.

Hazardous Materials World. HazMat World, Circulation Dept., P.O. Box 3021, Wheaton, IL 60137. (708) 858-1888. Monthly. Covers biobusiness, hazardous wastes management, and hazardous substance safety measures.

Hazardous Substances. Melvin Berger. Enslow Publishers, Bloy St. & Ramsey Ave., PO Box 777, Hillside, NJ 07205. (908) 964-4116. 1986.

Hazardous Substances Advisor. J. J. Keller & Associates, Inc., 3003 W. Breezewood, PO Box 368, Neenah, WA 54957-0368. (414) 722-2848. Monthly. Report on Congressional and regulatory activity to control or eliminate situations created by hazardous and toxic substances.

Hazardous Substances and Public Health: A Publication of the Agency for Toxic Substances and Disease Registry. Agency for Toxic Substances and Disease Registry, Department of Health and Human Services, 1600 Clifton Rd. NE, M/S E33, Atlanta, GA 30333. (404) 639-0727. Quarterly.

Hazardous Substances Resource Guide. Richard Pohanish, Stanley Greene. Gale Research Inc., 835 Penobscot Bldg., Detroit, MI 48226-4094. (313) 961-2242. 1993.

Hazardous Waste. U.S. General Accounting Office. U.S. G.P.O., Washington, DC 20401. (202) 512-0000. 1989. Expenditures on and enforcement actions relating to clean-up.

Hazardous Waste and Hazardous Materials. Mary Ann Liebert, Inc., 1651 3rd Avenue, New York, NY 10128. (212) 289-2300. Quarterly. Industrial waste technology.

Hazardous Waste and Toxic Torts. Leader Publications, 111 Eighth Ave., New York, NY 10011. (212) 463-5709. Monthly.

Hazardous Waste Audit Program: A Regulatory & Safety Compliance System: Evaluation Guidelines, Monitoring Procedures, Checklists, Forms. J. J. Keller & Associates, Inc., 3003 W. Breezewood, PO Box 368, Neenah, WI 54957-0368. (414) 722-2848. 1986.

Hazardous Waste Bibliography. National Institute for Occupational Safety and Health, Washington, DC 1989.

Hazardous Waste Center: Hazardous Waste Management. Director, 1808 Woodfield Dr., Savoy, IL 61874. (217) 333-8941.

Hazardous Waste Chemistry, Toxicology and Treatment. Stanley E. Manahan. Lewis Publishers, 2000 Corporate Blvd., N.W., Boca Raton, FL 33431. (407) 994-0555 or (800) 272-7737. 1990. Reviews hazardous wastes, their chemistry and toxicology. Gives a basic coverage of chemistry and biochemistry, environmental chemical processes, and toxicology.

Hazardous Waste Consultant. McCoy & Associates, 13701 West Jewell Avenue, Suite 202, Lakewood, CO 80228. (303) 987-0333. Bimonthly. Information on hazardous and toxic waste issues.

Hazardous Waste Consultant–Directory of Commercial Hazardous Waste Management Facilities Issue. McCoy and Associates, Inc., 13701 W. Jewel Ave., No. 252, Lakewood, CO 80228. (303) 987-0333.

Hazardous Waste Containment and Treatment. Paul N. Cheremisnoff. Gulf Publishing Co., Book Division, PO Box 2608, Houston, TX 77252. (713) 529-4301. 1990. Environmental control technology relating to hazardous wastes and hazardous waste sites.

Hazardous Waste Database. U.S. Environmental Protection Agency, Office of Administration and Resources Management, 401 M St., S.W., Washington, DC 20460. (202) 260-2090. Hazardous waste directives, treatment and disposal of hazardous waste, and its storage.

Hazardous Waste: Efforts to Address Problems at Federal Prisons. U.S. General Accounting Office, 441 G St., NW, Washington, DC 20548. (202) 275-5067. 1990.

Hazardous Waste Extension Program: Waste Minimization and Pollution Prevention. Program Director, Center for Industrial Services, 226 Capitol Boulevard Bldg., Suite 401, University of Tennessee, Nashville, TN 37219-1804. (615) 242-2456.

Hazardous Waste Facilities Siting Board: Waste Minimization and Pollution Prevention. Director, 60 West St., Suite 200 A, Annapolis, MD 21401. (301) 974-3432.

Hazardous Waste Facilities Siting Commission: Waste Minimization and Pollution Prevention. Director, Room 514, 28 West State St., CN028, Trenton, NJ 08625-0406. (609) 292-1459.

Hazardous Waste from Small Quantity Generators. Seymour I. Schwartz, et al. Island Press, 1718 Connecticut Ave. N.W., Suite 300, Washington, DC 20009. (202) 232-7933. 1990. Examines the role small businesses play in degrading the environment. Includes information on the extent and seriousness of the problem, regulations; and liability issues; national, state, and local programs for SQ Gas in California, analysis of methods for managing SQG waste; policy options for promoting legal methods; and discouraging illegal methods.

Hazardous Waste Identification and Classification Manual. Travis P. Wagner. Global Professional Publications, 2805 McGraw Ave., PO Box 19539, Irvine, CA 92713-9539. (800) 854-7179.

Hazardous Waste Incineration Calculations. Joseph P. Reynolds. John Wiley & Sons, Inc., 605 3rd Ave., New York, NY 10158-0012. (212) 850-6000. 1991.

Hazardous Waste Land Treatment. Municipal Environmental Research Laboratory, Office of Research and Development, U.S. Environmental Protection Agency, 26 W. Martin Luther King Dr., Cincinnati, OH 45268. (513) 569-7931. 1983. Covers hazardous wastes, sanitary landfills and waste disposal in the ground.

Hazardous Waste Law and Practice. John-Mark Stensvaag. John Wiley & Sons, Inc., 605 3rd Ave., New York, NY 10158-0012. (212) 850-6000. 1986-1989. 2 vols. Discusses the intricacies of defining hazardous wastes and shows potentially regulated entities how to make that determination. Guides the user through the listed hazardous wastes under the EPA's Subtitle C, discussing commercial chemical products, specific and nonspecific source wastes, derivative wastes, delisted wastes, and exclusions.

Hazardous Waste Laws, Regulations, and Taxes for the U.S. Petroleum Refining Industry: An Overview. David E. Fenster. PennWell Books, PO Box 21288, Tulsa, OK 74121. (918) 831-9421; (800) 752-9764. 1990. Describes the impact of hazardous waste legislation on the petroleum refining industry.

Hazardous Waste Litigation Reporter. Andrews Communications, Inc., 1646 Westchester Pike, Westtown, PA 19395. (215) 399-6600. Biweekly.

Hazardous Waste Management. S. Maltezou, et al., eds. Cassell PLC, Publishers Distribution Center, PO Box C831, Rutherford, NJ 07070. (201) 939-6064; (201) 939-6065. 1989.

Hazardous Waste Management. H. M. Freeman. Global Professional Publications, 2805 McGraw Ave., PO Box 19539, Irvine, CA 92713-9539. (800) 854-7179.

Hazardous Waste Management. FIND/SVP, 625 Avenue of the Americas, New York, NY 10011. (212) 645-4500. 1990. Hazardous materials handling costs and the potential threat of increased state and federal regulation.

Hazardous Waste Management Engineering. Edward J. Martin and James H. Johnson. PennWell Books, PO Box 21288, Tulsa, OK 74121. (918) 831-9421; (800) 752-9764. 1986. Covers the basic principles and applications of the most current hazardous waste technologies. Provides a wealth of data and techniques that can be immediately applied to analyzing, designing and developing effective hazardous waste management solutions.

Hazardous Waste Management Facilities Directory: Treatment, Storage, Disposal and Recycling. U. S. Environmental Protection Agency. Noyes Publications, 120 Mill Rd., Park Ridge, NJ 07656. (201) 391-8484. 1990. Provides geographical listings of 1045 commercial hazardous waste management facilities, along with information on the types of commercial services offered and types of wastes managed. It is a compilation of recent data from EPA data bases and includes the facility name, address, contact person, and phone number.

Hazardous Waste Management Guide. California Safety Council, Sacramento, CA 1988. Covers California law and legislation relating to hazardous wastes.

Hazardous Waste Management: New Regulation and New Technology. Brian Price. Financial Times Bus. Info. Ltd., 50-64 Broadway, 7th Fl., London, England SW1H 0DB 071-799 2002. 1990.

Hazardous Waste Management: Recent Changes and Policy Alternatives. Daniel Carol. Congress of the United States, Congressional Budget Office, c/o U.S. Government Printing Office, N. Capitol & H Sts. NW, Washington, DC 20401. (202) 512-0000. 1985. Describes the economic aspects of hazardous wastes. Also includes the law and legislation in the United States regarding hazardous wastes aa well as government policy.

Hazardous Waste Management: Reducing the Risk. Council on Economic Priorities. Island Press, 1718 Connecticut Ave. N.W., Suite 300, Washington, DC 20009. (202) 232-7933. 1986. Includes information for regulatory agencies, waste generators, host communities, and public officials. Topics include compliance, liabilities, technologies, corporate and public relations, groundwater monitoring, key laws and recommendations.

Hazardous Waste Management Service: Waste Minimization and Pollution Prevention. Chair, Executive Office, 865 Brook St., Rocky Hill, CT 06067. (203) 244-2007.

Hazardous Waste Management Strategies for Health Care Facilities. Nelson S. Slavik. American Hospital Association, 840 North Lake Shore Dr., Chicago, IL 60611. 1987. Contains helpful information for health care facilities in the management of their chemical, cytotoxic, infectious, and radiological wastes.

Hazardous Waste Management: The Basics, the Issues and the Controversy: Proceedings of the Commission on the Arizona Environment's Summer Conference. Commission on the Arizona Environment, Phoenix, AZ

Hazardous Waste Materials and Waste Management Division: Hazardous Waste Management. Director, 4210 East 11th Ave., Denver, CO 80220. (303) 331-4830.

Hazardous Waste Materials and Waste Management Division: Solid Waste Management. Director, 4210 East 11th Ave., Denver, CO 80220. (303) 331-4830.

Hazardous Waste Measurements. Milagros S. Simmons, ed. Lewis Publishers, 200 Corporate Blvd. NW, Boca Raton, FL 33431. (407) 994-0555 or (800)272-7737. 1991. Focuses on recent developments in field testing methods and quality assurance.

Hazardous Waste Minimization Assessment, Fort Carson, CO. Seshasayi Dharmavaram, et al. National Technical Information Service, 5285 Port Royal Rd., Springfield, VA 22161. (703) 487-4650. 1991.

Hazardous Waste Minimization Assessment, Fort Meade, MD. Seshasayi Dharmavaram and Bernard A. Donahue. National Technical Information Service, 5285 Port Royal Rd., Springfield, VA 22161. (703) 487-4650. 1991.

Hazardous Waste Minimization Audit Studies on the Paint Manufacturing Industry. Jacobs Engineering Group, Inc., S. Lake Ave., Pasadena, CA 91171. (818)449-2171. 1987. Factory and trade wastes and disposal in the paint industry.

Hazardous Waste Minimization Bibliography. Waste Programs Planning Section, Office of Waste Programs, Arizona Dept. of Environmental Quality, 3033 N. Central, Phoenix, AZ 85012. (602) 207-2381. 1990.

Hazardous Waste Minimization Handbook. Thomas E. Higgins, et al. Lewis Publishers, 2000 Corporate Blvd., Boca Raton, FL 33431. (407) 994-0555 or (800) 272-7737. 1989. Describes how to make changes in waste handling, manufacturing, and purchasing to reduce costs and liabilities of waste disposal.

Hazardous Waste Minimization Manual for Small Quantity Generators. Center for Hazardous Materials Research, University of Pittsburgh, 320 William Pitt Way, Pittsburgh, PA 15238. (412) 826-5320. 1989. Recycling of hazardous waste and its legal aspects.

Hazardous Waste News. Business Publishers, Inc., 951 Pershing Drive, Silver Spring, MD 20910-4464. (301) 587-6300. Weekly. Covers legislative, regulatory and judicial decisions on hazardous waste. Also available online.

Hazardous Waste News. Business Publishers, Inc., 951 Pershing Dr., Silver Spring, MD 20910-4464. (301) 587-6300. Online access to legislative, regulatory, and judicial decisions at the federal and state levels relating to the field of hazardous waste management. Online version of the periodical of the same name.

Hazardous Waste Practitioners Directory. Hazardous Waste Action Coalition, c/o American Consulting Engineers Council, 1015 15th St. NW, No. 802, Washington, DC 20005. (202) 347-7474. Annual. Engineering firms responsible for designing cleanup solutions for hazardous waste sites.

Hazardous Waste Regulatory Guide: State Waste Management Programs. J. J. Keller & Associates, Inc., 3003 W. Breezewood, PO Box 368, Neenah, WI 54957-0368. (414) 722-2848. 1992. State by state guide to laws relating to hazardous wastes.

Hazardous Waste Services Directory: Transporters, Disposal Sites, Laboratories, Consultants, and Specialized Services. George McDowell. J. J. Keller & Associates, Inc., 3003 W. Breezewood, PO Box 368, Neenah, WI 54957-0368. (414) 722-2848. Semiannual. Guide to various services available in the field of hazardous waste.

Hazardous Waste Site Data Base. U.S. Environmental Protection Agency, Environmental Monitoring Systems Lab, PO Box 93478, Las Vegas, NV 89193-3478. (702) 798-2525. Identifies a total of 944 chemical constituents for more than 5000 wells at over 350 hazardous waste sites nationwide.

Hazardous Waste Sites: Descriptions of Sites on Current National Priorities List. Office of Emergency and Remedial Response, U.S. Environmental Protection Agency, 401 M St., S.W., Washington, DC 20460. (202) 382-2090.

The Hazardous Waste System. U.S. Environmental Protection Agency, Office of Solid Waste and Emergency Response, 401 M St., SW April 9, 1992, Washington, DC 20460. (202) 382-4610. 1987. Hazardous wastes law and legislation in the United States.

Hazardous Waste Treatment Council. 1440 New York Ave., Suite 310, Washington, DC 20005. (202) 783-0870.

Hazardous Waste Treatment Technologies: Biological Treatment, Wet Air Oxidation, Chemical Fixation, Chemical Oxidation. Alan P. Jackman. Noyes Publications, 120 Mill Rd., Park Ridge, NJ 07656. (201) 391-8484. 1991. Purification of hazardous wastes.

Hazardous Waste TSDF: Background Information for Proposed RCRA Air Emission Standards. National Technical Information Service, 5285 Port Royal Rd., Springfield, VA 22161. (703) 487-4650. 1991.

Hazardous Wastes and Hazardous Materials. Hazardous Materials Control Research Institute, 9300 Columbia Blvd., Silver Spring, MD 20910. (301) 587-9390. 1987.

Hazardous Water Federation. Div. 3314, P.O. Box 5800, Albuquerque, NM 87185. (505) 846-2655.

Hazards in Reuse of Disposable Dialysis Devices. Committee on Aging, United States Senate. U.S. G.P.O., Washington, DC 20401. (202) 512-0000. 1986.

Hazards in the Chemical Laboratory. L. Bretherick, ed. Royal Society of Chemistry, c/o CRC Press, 2000 Corporate Blvd. N.W., Boca Raton, FL 33431-9868. (800) 272-7737. 1986. 4th ed. Handbook of safety practices, measures and toxic effects for laboratories handling dangerous chemicals.

Hazards to Nuclear Power Plants from Large Liquefied Natural Gas Spills on Water. C.A. Kot. U.S. G.P.O., Washington, DC 20401. (202)512-0000. 1981.

HAZCHEM Alert. Van Nostrand Reinhold, 115 Fifth Ave., New York, NY 10003. (212) 254-3232. Biweekly. Covers hazardous chemical news and information.

HAZINF. University of Alberta, Department of Chemistry, Edmonton, AB, Canada T6G 2G2. (403) 432-3254.

Hazmat Emergency Response Contracting. FIND/SVP, 625 Avenue of the Americas, New York, NY 10011. (800) 346-3787. 1991. Challenges facing existing contractors and the business strategies required for continued success in the market.

Hazmat News: The Authoritative News Resource for Hazardous Control and Waste Management. Stevens Publishing Co., PO Box 2604, Waco, TX 76702-2604. (817) 776-9000. Semimonthly. Hazardous materials transportation, storage, and disposal.

Hazmat World. Tower-Borner Publishing, Inc., Bldg. C, Suite 206, 800 Roosevelt Rd., Glen Ellyn, IL 60137. (708) 858-1888. Monthly. Covers hazardous management issues and technology.

HazTech News. Business Publishers, Inc., 951 Pershing Drive, Silver Spring, MD 20910. (301) 587-6300. Biweekly. Covers developments and discoveries in waste management.

Headwaters. Friends of the River, Bldg. C, Ft. Mason Center, San Francisco, CA 94123. (415) 771-0400. Biweekly. River conservation, recreation, and water politics.

Healing the Environment. R. Nicole Warner. Center for Clean Air Policy, 444 N. Capitol St., Ste. 526, Washington, DC 20001. (202) 624-7709. 1991. A look at coalbed methane as a cost-effective means of addressing global climate change.

Health and Administrative Sciences Department: Emergency Preparedness And Community Right-to-Know. Co-Chair, Emergency Response Commission, Environmental Sciences Division, Cogswell Building, A-107, Helena, MT 59620. (406) 444-6911.

Health and Ecological Assessment of Polynuclear Aromatic Hydrocarbons. Si Duk Lee and Lester Grant, eds. Chem-Orbital, PO Box 134, Park Forest, IL 60466. (708) 748-0440. 1981.

Health and Energy Institute. 615 Kenevec, Takoma Park, MD 20912. (301) 585-5541.

Health and Environment Department: Underground Storage Tanks. Bureau Chief, Underground Storage Tanks Bureau, PO Box 968, Runnels Building, Santa Fe, NM 87503. (505) 827-2894.

Health & Environment Digest. Freshwater Biological Research Foundation, 2500 Shadywood Road, Box 90, Navarre, MN 55392. (612) 471-8407. Monthly. Public health effects of environmental contaminants of water, air, and soil.

Health and Environmental Control Department: Underground Storage Tanks. Director, Groundwater Protection, 2600 Bull St., Columbia, SC 29201. (803) 734-5331.

Health and Environmental Control: Groundwater Management. Director, Groundwater Protection, 2600 Bull St., Columbia, SC 29201. (803) 734-5331.

Health and Environmental Control: Hazardous Waste Management. Chief, Solid and Hazardous Waste Management, 2600 Bull St., Columbia, SC 29201. (803) 734-5213.

Health and Environmental Control: Solid Waste Management. Chief, Solid and Hazardous Waste Management, 2600 Bull St., Columbia, SC 29201. (803) 734-5200.

Health and Environmental Control: Water Quality. Deputy Commissioner, Division of Environmental Quality Control, 2600 Bull St., Columbia, SC 29201. (803) 734-5360.

Health and Environmental Effects Document for Boron and Boron Compounds. National Technical Information Service, 5285 Port Royal Rd., Springfield, VA 22161. (703) 487-4650. 1991.

Health and Environmental Effects of Acid Rain: An Abstracted Literature Collection, 1966-1979. Nancy S. Dale. Federation of American Societies for Experimental Biology, 9650 Rockville Pike, Bethesda, MD 20814. (301) 530-7000. 1980. Prepared in cooperation with the National Library of Medicine as a response to the chemical crises project of the Federation of American Societies for Experimental Biology. Covers the years 1966-1979.

Health and Environmental Sciences: Air Quality. Chief, Air Quality Bureau, Cogswell Building, Helena, MT 59620. (406) 444-3454.

Health and Environmental Sciences: Environmental Protection. Administrator, Environmental Sciences Division, Cogswell Building, Helena, MT 59620. (406) 444-3948.

Health and Environmental Sciences: Water Quality. Chief, Water Quality Bureau, Capitol Station, Helena, MT 59620. (406) 444-2406.

Health & Medical Aspects of Chemical Industries. ABBE Publishers Association of Washington DC, 4111 Gallows Rd., Annandale, VA 22003-1862. 1984. Health aspects of chemical industries, industrial waste, and chemically enforced occupational diseases.

Health and the Global Environment. Ross Hume Hall. B. Blackwell, 3 Cambridge Ctr., Suite 208, Cambridge, MA 02142. (617) 225-0401. 1990.

Health Aspects of Chloroform. National Technical Information Center, 5285 Port Royal Rd., Springfield, VA 22161. (703) 487-4650. 1977.

Health Aspects of Urea-formaldehyde Compounds: A Selected Bibliography with Abstracts. Federation of American Societies for Experimental Biology, 9650 Rockville Pike, Bethesda, MD 20814. (301) 530-7000. 1980. Covers urea-formaldehyde resins and insulating materials.

Health Assessment Document for Carbon Tetrachloride. U.S. Environmental Protection Agency, 401 M St., SW, Washington, DC 20460. (202) 260-2090. 1984.

Health Assessment Document for Chloroform. U.S. Environmental Protection Agency, Office of Research and Development, MD 75, Research Triangle Park, NC 27711. (919) 541-2184. 1985.

Health Effects Due to the Cessation of Chlorination of Wastewater Treatment Plant Effluent. Janet A. Holden. Institute of Natural Resources, Chicago, IL 1981.

Health Effects from Hazardous Waste Sites. Julian B. Andelman and Dwight W. Underhill. Lewis Publishers, 2000 Corporate Blvd., N.W., Boca Raton, FL 33431. (407) 994-0555 or (800) 272-7737. 1987.

Health Effects of Airborne Particles. Harvard University, 79 John F. Kennedy St., Cambridge, MA 02130.

The Health Effects of Caffeine. American Council on Science and Health. The Council, Summit, NJ 1981.

Health Effects of Diesel Engine Emissions. Silas Jackson. U.S. Department of Health and Human Services, Public Health Services, National Institutes of Health, 9000 Rockville Pike, Bethesda, MD 20892. (301) 496-4000. 1984.

Health Effects of Drinking Water Treatment Technologies. Lewis Publishers, 200 Corporate Blvd. NW, Boca Raton, FL 33431. (407) 994-0555 or (800)272-7737. 1989. Evaluates the public health impact from the most widespread drinking water treatment technologies, with particular emphasis on disinfection. Focuses solely on the most common treatment technologies and practices used today.

Health Effects of Municipal Waste Incineration. Holly A. Hattemer-Frey and C. C. Travis. CRC Press, 2000 Corporate Blvd. N.W., Boca Raton, FL 33431. (800) 272-7737. 1991.

Health Hazards of Nitrite Inhalants. Harry W. Haverkos and John A. Dougherty. National Institute on Drug Abuse, 5600 Fishers Ln., Rm. 10-15, Rockville, MD 20857. (301) 443-6487. 1988. Toxicology of nitrites.

Health Periodicals Database. Information Access Company, 362 Lakeside Dr., Foster City, CA 94404. (800) 227-8431.

Health Physics Society. 8000 Westpark Dr., Suite 400, McLean, VA 22102. (703) 790-1745.

Health Risks of Toxic Emissions from a Coal-Fired Power Plant. J.G. Bolten. RAND, 1700 Main St., Santa Monica, CA 90401. (310) 393-0411. 1987. Toxicology of selenium and beryllium used in coal-fired power plants.

HealthNet. HealthNet, Ltd., 716 E. Carlisle, Milwaukee, WI 53217. (414) 963-8829.

Healthy Harvest II: A Directory of Sustainable Agriculture and Horticulture Organizations 1987-1988. Susan J. Sanzone, et al., eds. Potomac Valley Press, Suite 105, 1424 16th St. NW, Washington, DC 20036. 1987.

Healthy Homes, Healthy Kids. Joyce M. Schoemaker and Charity Y. Vitale. Island Press, 1718 Connecticut Ave. N.W., Suite 300, Washington, DC 20009. (202) 232-7933. 1991. Identifies many hazards that parents tend to overlook. It translates technical, scientific information into an accessible how-to guide to help parents protect children from even the most toxic substances.

Hearing Conservation Programs: Practical Guidelines for Success. Julia D. Royster and Larry H. Royster. Lewis Publishers, 2000 Corporate Blvd., N.W., Boca Raton, FL 33431. (407) 994-0555 or (800) 272-7737. 1990. Essentials for creating an effective hearing conservation program, details how to best organize to get the job done, and identifies the specific aspects within each phase of the program that spell the difference between success and failure.

Heat and Water Transport Properties in Conifer Duff and Humus. Michael A. Fosberg. Department of Agriculture Forest Service, Rocky Mountain Forest Experiment Station, 240 W Prospect Rd., Fort Collins, CO 80526-2098. (303) 498-1100. 1977. Forest soils and soil permeability.

Heat Exchange Institute. c/o Christine M. Devor, Thomas Associates, Inc., 1230 Keith Bldg., Cleveland, OH 44115. (216) 241-7333.

Heat Exchangers. S. Kakac. Hemisphere Publishing Co., 79 Madison Ave., Suite 1110, New York, NY 10016. (212) 725-1999. 1981. Thermal-hydraulic fundamentals and design.

Heat Exchangers: Design and Theory Sourcebook. Naim Afgan. Scripta Book Co., Washington, DC 1974.

Heat Exchangers–Theory and Practice. J. Taborek. McGraw-Hill Science & Engineering Books, 11 W. 19th St., New York, NY 10011. (212) 337-6010. 1983.

Heating, Cooling, Lighting. John Wiley & Sons, Inc., 605 3rd Ave., New York, NY 10158-0012. (212) 850-6000. 1991.

Heating Equipment Dealers & Contractors Directory. 5711 S. 86th Circle, Omaha, NE 68127. (402) 593-4600. Annual.

Heating-Plumbing Air Conditioning–Buyers' Guide Issue. 1450 Don Mills Rd., Don Mills, ON, Canada M3B 2X7. (416) 445-6641. Annual.

Heating, Ventilating, Refrigeration & Air Conditioning Year Book and Daily Buyers' Guide. 34 Palace Court, ESCA House, Bayswater, England W2 4JG. London (71) 292488. Annual.

Heating, Ventilation, and Air-Conditioning Systems Estimating Manual. A. M. Khashab. McGraw-Hill Science & Engineering Books, 11 W. 19th St., New York, NY 10011. (212) 337-6010. 1984.

Heaven is Under Our Feet. Don Henley, ed. Longmeadow Press, 201 High Ridge Rd, PO Box 10218, Stamford, CT 06904. (203) 352-2110. 1991. Describes the conservation of natural resources.

The Heavy-Duty Detergent Market. FIND/SVP, 625 Avenue of the Americas, New York, NY 10011. (800) 346-3787. 1992. Technological developments, total sales in retail dollars, local and state regulations, sales projections to 1996, and market composition.

The Heavy Elements: Chemistry, Environmental Impact and Health Effects. Jack E. Fergusson. Pergamon Microforms International, Inc., Fairview Park, Elmsford, NY 10523. (914) 592-7720. 1990. Provides a broad survey of the heavy elements, their relevant chemistry, environmental impacts and health effects.

Heavy Metals in Natural Waters. James W. Moore. Springer-Verlag, 175 5th Ave., New York, NY 10010. (212) 460-1500. 1984. Applied monitoring and impact assessment.

Heavy Metals in the Environment: International Conference. J. P. Vernet. CEP Consultants, 26 Albany St., Edinburgh, Scotland EH1 3QH. 1989.

Heavy Metals in the Marine Environment. Robert W. Furness and Philip S. Rainbow. CRC Press, 2000 Corporate Blvd. N.W., Boca Raton, FL 33431. (800) 272-7737. 1990. Includes heavy metals in the marine environment, trace metals in sea water, metals in the marine atmosphere, processes affecting metal concentration in estuarine and coastal marine sediments, heavy metal levels in marine invertebrates, use of microalgae and invertebrates to monitor metal levels in estuaries and coastal waters, toxic effects of metals, and the incidence of metal pollution in marine ecosystems.

Heavy Metals in Water: A Bibliography. Water Resources Scientific Information Center, Office of Water Research and Technology, Washington, DC 1977.

Helminthological Abstracts. C. A. B. International, 845 North Park Ave., Tucson, AZ 85719. (602) 621-7897 or (800) 528-4841. 1969. Monthly. Continues Helminthological Abstracts and Series A: Animal and Human Helminthology. Covers the literature on parasitic helminths such as gastrointestinal nematodes, liver flukes, hydatid, trichinella, and other related areas.

Helping Nature Heal: An Introduction to Environmental Restoration. Richard Nilsen, ed. Ten Speed Press, P.O. Box 7123, Berkeley, CA 94707. (800) 841-2665. 1991.

Heptachlor. World Health Organization, Q Corp., 49 Sheridan Ave., Albany, NY 12221. (518) 436-9686. 1984. Toxicity and environmental physiological effects.

Heptachlor Contamination. Jerry Rafats. National Agricultural Library, 10301 Baltimore Blvd., Beltsville, MD 20705-2351. (301) 504-5755. 1986. Environmental aspects of pesticides.

Heptachlor Health and Safety Guide. World Health Organization, Ave. Appia, Geneva, Switzerland CH-1211. 1988. Toxicology and safety measures relative to heptachlor.

Herbage Abstracts. C. A. B. International, 845 North Park Ave., Tucson, AZ 85719. (602) 621-7897 or (800) 528-4841. 1931-. Monthly. Covers management, productivity and economics of grasslands, rangelands and fodder crops, grassland ecology, seed production, toxic plants, land use and farming systems, weed control, agricultural meteorology, and other related areas.

Herbarium. University of California, Los Angeles, 405 Hilgard Avenue, Los Angeles, CA 90024. (213) 825-3620.

Herbarium. University of Colorado, Campus Box 350, Boulder, CO 80309. (303) 492-5074.

Herbarium. University of Florida, 209 Rolfs Hall, Gainesville, FL 32611. (904) 392-1767.

Herbarium. West Virginia University, Brooks Hall, Morgantown, WV 26506. (304) 293-5201.

Herbarium. William Jewell College, Liberty, MO 64068. (816) 781-7700.

Herbarium. Yale University, 550 Osborn Memorial Laboratory, Biology Department, PO Box 6666, New Haven, CT 06511. (203) 432-3904.

Herbicide Manual. Gary W. Hansen. U.S. G.P.O., Washington, DC 20401. (202) 512-0000. 1984. A guide to supervise pest management and to train personnel.

Herbicides: Chemistry, Degradation, and Mode of Action. P. C. Kearney and D. D. Kaufman, eds. Marcel Dekker, Inc., 270 Madison Ave., New York, NY 10016. (212) 696-9000; (800) 228-1160. 1988. 2d ed.

Herbicides, Ecological Effects, 1982-1987. Jayne T. Maclean. National Agricultural Library, 10301 Baltimore Blvd., Beltsville, MD 20705-2351. (301) 504-5755. 1988.

Herbivory, the Dynamics of Animal-Plant Interactions. Michael J. Crawley. University of California Press, 2120 Berkeley Way, Berkeley, CA 94720. (415) 642-4247; (800) 822-6657. 1983. The dynamics of animal-plant interactions.

Herman Wildlife Database. Julie Moore & Assoc., Box 5156, Riverside, CA 92517. (714) 943-3863.

Hexachlorobenzene Distribution in Domestic Animals. Dennis Wayne Wilson. University of Illinois at Urbana-Champaign, Urbana-Champaign, IL 61801. 1979.

Hexachlorophene: January 1969 through March 1972. Geraldine D. Nowak. National Institutes of Health, Department of Health and Human Services, Bethesda, MD 1972.

Hickory Stump. Middle Tennessee Land Trust, 8070 Regency Dr., Nashville, TN 37221. (615) 645-6245. Quarterly. Land trusts and ecologically oriented lifestyles.

Hidden Dangers: Environmental Consequences of Preparing for War. Anne H. Ehrlich and John W. Birks, eds. Sierra Club Books, 100 Bush St., San Francisco, CA 94104. (415) 291-1600. 1991. Considers a number of questions concerning the dangers–health-related, environmental, psychological, economic, etc.–that have been and are still being engendered by the U.S. and other nations, since the 1940s, to manufacture, store, and dispose of nuclear, chemical, and biological weapons.

A Hierarchial Concept of Ecosystems. R.V. O'Neill. Princeton University Press, 41 Williams St., Princeton, NJ 08540. (609) 258-4900. 1986. Covers population biology including ecology and biotic communities.

High Country News. High Country Foundation, 124 Grand Ave., Box 1090, Paonia, CO 81428-1090. (303) 527-4898. Biweekly. Environmental and public-lands issues in the Rocky Mountain region.

High Explosives and Propellants. Stanley Fordham. Pergamon Microforms International, Inc., Fairview Park, New York, NY 10523. (914) 592-7720. 1980. Science and technology of explosives.

High Level Radioactive Waste Management. American Society of Civil Engineers, 345 E. 47th St., New York, NY 10017. (212) 705-7288; (800) 548-2723. 1991. Proceedings of International Topical Meeting hosted by the University of Nevada Las Vegas, April 8-12, 1990.

High Level Radioactive Waste Management. American Society of Civil Engineers, 345 E. 47th St., New York, NY 10017. (212) 705-7288; (800) 548-2723. 1992. Proceedings of the 2nd Annual International Conference, Las Vegas, Nevada, April 28-May 3, 1991.

High-Performance Liquid Chromatography. Academic Press, c/o Harcourt Brace Jovanovich Inc., 6277 Sea Harbor Dr., Orlando, FL 32887. (800) 346-8648.

High-Quality Industrial Water Management Manual. Paul N. Garay and Franklin M. Chn. The Association of Energy Engineers, 4025 Pleasantdale Rd., Suite 420, Atlanta, GA 30340. (404) 925-9558. 1992. Guide to managing water resources.

The Highlands Voice. West Virginia Highlands, 1205 Quarrier St. Lower Level, Charleston, WV 25301. Monthly. Covers environmental topics in the Appalachian area of West Virginia.

Highway and Heavy Construction. Dun Donnelley Pub. Corp., 1350 E. Touhy Ave., Box 5080, Des Plaines, IL 60017-8800. (708) 635-8800. 1892-. Fifteen times a year. Features on-site reports of current construction projects nationwide and advises senior personnel on the changing needs and demands of the market.

Highway Beautification: The Environmental Movement's Greatest Failure. Charles F. Floyd. Westview Press, 5500 Central AVe., Boulder, CO 80301. (303) 444-3541. 1979. Roadside improvement and law and legislation relating to signs and billboards.

Highway Drainage Guidelines. Federal Highway Administration, 400 7th St. SW, Washington, DC 20590. (202) 366-0630. 1987. Hydraulic considerations in highway planning and location, highway construction, and hydraulic design of culverts.

Highway Research Abstracts. Transportation Research Board, National Research Council, 2101 Constitution Ave. NW., Washington, DC 20418. 1931-. Monthly. Provides information about highway and nonrail mass transit. It also deals with related environmental issues such as energy and environment, environmental design, climate, safety, human factors, and soils.

Highway-Wildlife Relationships. Urban Wildlife Research Center, Inc. National Technical Information Service, 5285 Port Royal Rd., Springfield, VA 22161. (703) 487-4650. 1975. Design and construction and environmental aspects of roads and wildlife conservation.

Highways and the Environment. D. J. Coleman. Council of Planning Librarians, 1313 E. 60th St., Chicago, IL 60637-2897. (312) 942-2163. 1973. Features the effects of highways on the physical, biological, recreational and aesthetic environments and of techniques for the analysis ofthese effects.

Highways and Transportation: Journal of the Institution of Highways and Transportation & HTTA. The Institution of Highways and Transportation, 3 Lygon Place, Elbury St., London, England SW1 0JS. (01) 730-5245. 1983-. Monthly. Information on roads and traffic for highway and transportation engineers.

Highways and Wetlands: Annotated Bibliography. Paul A. Erickson. Federal Highway Administration, Office of Development, 400 7th St. SW, Washington, DC 20590. (202) 366-0630. 1980.

Hilgardia: A Journal of Agricultural Science. California Agricultural Experiment Station, 2120 University Ave., Berkeley, CA 94720. 1925-.

Historical Plant Cost and Annual Production Expenses for Selected Electric Plants. Department of Energy, 1000 Independence Ave., N.W., Washington, DC 20585. (202) 586-8800. Annual.

History of Concrete, 30 B.C. to 1926 A.D.: Annotated. American Concrete Institute, 22400 W. Seven Mile Rd., P.O. Box 19150, Detroit, MI 48219. (313) 532-2600. 1982.

History of Polyolefins. Raymond B. Seymour. Kluwer Academic Publishers, 101 Philip Dr., Assinippi Park, Norwell, MA 02061. (617) 871-6600. 1987.

A History of X-rays and Radium, with a Chapter on Radiation Units: 1895-1937. Richard F. Mould. IPC Building & Contract Journals, Sutton, England 1980.

HODOC: Handbook of Data on Organic Compounds. CRC Press, 2000 Corporate Blvd. N.W., Boca Raton, FL 33431. (800) 727-7737.

The Hole in the Sky: Man's Threat to the Ozone Layer. John R. Gribbin. Bantam Books, 666 5th Ave., New York, NY 10103. (212) 765-6500; (800) 223-6834. 1988. Scientific revelations about the ozone layer and global warming.

Holistic Resource Management. Allan Savory. Island Press, 1718 Connecticut Ave. N.W., Suite 300, Washington, DC 20009. (202) 232-7933. 1988. Presents a comprehensive planning model that treats people and their environment as a whole. Discusses the scientific and management principles of the model, followed by detailed descriptions of each tool and guideline.

Holistic Resource Management Work Book. Sam Bingham and Allan Savory. Island Press, 1718 Connecticut Ave. N.W., Suite 300, Washington, DC 20009. (202) 232-7933. 1989. Provides practical instruction in financial, biological, and land planning segments necessary to apply the holistic management model.

The Holocene: An Interdisciplinary Journal Focusing on Recent Environmental Change. Edward Arnold, c/o Cambridge University Press, 40 W. 20th St., New York, NY 10011-4211. (212) 924-3900. Three times a year.

Home Composting. Seattle Tilth Association, Dept. NA, 4649 Sunnyside Ave. N., Seattle, WA 98103. 1990.

Home Ecology. Karen Christensen. Fulcrum Publishing, 350 Indiana St., Ste. 350, Golden, CO 80401. (303) 277-1623. 1990. Simple and practical ways to green homes.

Home Energy. Energy Auditor & Retrofitter, Inc., 2124 Kittredge St., Suite 95, Berkeley, CA 94704. Bimonthly. Deals with building retrofits to save on energy consumption.

Home Ventilating Institute Division of the Air Movement Control Association. 30 W. University Drive, Arlington Heights, IL 60004. (312) 394-0150.

Home, Yard and Garden Pest Newsletter. Agriculture Newsletter Service, University of Illinois, 116 Mumford Hall, 1301 W. Gregory Dr., Urbana, IL 61801. Twenty times a year. Pest controls, application equipment and methods, and storage and disposal of pesticides for the yard and garden.

The Homeowner's Guide to Coalburning Stoves and Furnaces. James Warner Morrison. Arco Pub. Inc., 215 Park Ave. S., New York, NY 10003. 1981.

A Homeowners Guide to Recycling Yard Wastes: How to Improve the Health and Quality of Your Yard and Garden by Using Grass Clippings, Leaves and Wood Chips. Illinois Cooperative Extension Service, 1715 W. Springfield Ave., Champaign, IL 61821. (217) 333-7672. 1989. Compost, waste, recycling and refuse collection.

Hormones, Drugs, and Aggression. Eden Medical Research, St. Albans, VT 05481. Annual.

Horticultural Abstracts. C. A. B. International, 845 North Park Ave., Tucson, AZ 85719. (602) 621-7897 or (800) 528-4841. 1931-. Monthly. Covers the literature on fruits, vegetables, ornamental plants, nuts, and plantation crops.

Hot Flue Gas Spiking and Recovery Study for Tetrachlorodibenzodioxins Using Modified Method 5 and SASS Sampling with a Simulated Incinerator. Marcus Cooke. U.S. Environmental Protection Agency, Industrial Environmental Research Laboratory, MD 75, Research Triangle Park, NC 27711. 1984. Covers environmental aspects of flue gases, steamboilers, and tetrachlorodibenzodioxin.

Hot Topics from the Tropics. Rainforest Alliance, 270 Lafayette St., Suite 512, New York, NY 10012. (212) 941-1900. Bimonthly.

Hotline. Ohio Environmental Council, 22 E. Gay St., #300, Columbus, OH 43215. (614) 486-4055. Ten times a year. Breaking news relating to environmental protection.

Housatonic Current. Housatonic Valley Assn., Box 28, Cornwall Bridge, CT 06754. (203) 672-6678. Quarterly. Environmental programs and land planning throughout the Housatonic River Watershed.

Household Cleaners. FIND/SVP, 625 Avenue of the Americas, New York, NY 10011. (212) 645-4500. 1991. Covers all-purpose cleaners, bathroom cleaners, scouring powders and liquids, and disinfectants.

Household Hazardous Waste: Solving the Disposal Dilemma. Golden Empire Health Planning Center, c/o Local Government Commission, 909 12th St., Suite 205, Sacramento, CA 95814. (916) 448-1198.

Household Hazards: a Guide to Detoxifying Your Home. League of Women Voters of Albany County, 119 Washington Ave., Albany, NY 12207. 1988. Covers household supplies and appliances safety measures.

Household Specialty Cleaners. FIND/SVP, 625 Avenue of the Americas, New York, NY 10011. (212) 645-4500. 1992. Analyzes the household specialty cleaners market including toilet-bowl cleaners, window/glass cleaners, oven cleaners, and drain cleaners.

How Green Are You?. David Bellamy. Clarkson N. Potter, Inc., 225 Park Ave., S., New York, NY 10003. (212) 254-1600. 1991. Information and projects about ecology and environmental concerns that teach how to conserve energy, protect wildlife, and reduce pollution.

How on Earth Do We Recycle Glass?. Joanna Randolph Rott. Millbrook Press, 2 Old New Milford Rd., PO Box 335, Brookfield, CT 06804-0335. (203) 740-2220. 1992. Making of glass and the problems causes by glass waste; ways of using discarded glass.

How on Earth Do We Recycle Metal?. Rudy Kouhoupt. Millbrook Press, 2 Old New Milford Rd., PO Box 335, New York, NY 06804-0335. (203) 740-2220. 1992. Disposal and recycling of metal waste by creating objects such as jewelry, weather vanes, and Christmas ornaments.

How on Earth Do We Recycle Paper?. Helen Jill Fletcher. Millbrook Press, 2 Old New Milford Rd., PO Box 335, Brookfield, CT 06804-0335. (203) 740-2220. 1992. How paper is produced and recycled. Presents crafts projects using paper discards.

How on Earth Do We Recycle Plastic?. Janet D'Amato. Millbrook Press, 2 Old New Milford Rd., PO Box 335, Brookfield, CT 06804-0335. (203) 740-2220. 1992. Manufacture and disposal of plastic and how it can be recycled.

How Serious is the Threat of Asbestos?. Institute of Real Estate Management, PO Box 109025, Chicago, IL 60610-9025. (312) 661-1953. 1989. Harvard Symposium on Health Aspects of Exposure to Asbestos in Buildings.

How Solid Waste Issues Are Affecting Consumer Behavior. Food Marketing Institute, Research Department, 1750 K St., NW, Washington, DC 20006. 1990. Consumer attitudes and practices regarding solid waste disposal.

How the Environmental Legal & Regulatory System Works: A Business Primer. Government Institutes, Inc., 4 Research Pl., Ste. 200, Rockville, MD 20850. (301) 921-2300. Explains where environmental laws originates; conflicts between federal, state, and local laws; how laws and regulations are made; how the regulated community can affect the development of regulations; the environmental regulatory agencies; how the laws are enforced; and what regulations apply to what business activities.

How to Bottle Rainstorms. Bauer Engineering Inc. Metropolitan Water Reclamation District of Greater Chicago, 100 E. Erie, Chicago, IL 60611. (312) 751-5600. 1974. Urban runoff, sewage disposal and sanitation.

How to Identify and Control Noninfectious Diseases of Trees. Forest Service, North Central Forest Exp. Sta. The Station, 1992 Folwell Ave., St. Paul, MN 55108. (612) 642-5207. 1990. Revised edition. Deals with defoliation of conifers and the diseases and the pests that affect them.

How to Implement Waste-to-Energy Projects. Noyes Publications, 120 Mill Rd., Park Ridge, NJ 07656. (201) 391-8484. 1987. Refuse and waste products as fuel.

How to Live with Low-Level Radiation: A Nutritional Protection Plan. Leon Chaitow. Healing Arts Pr., 1 Park St., Rochester, VT 05767. (802) 767-3174. 1988. Discusses the problem of low-level radiation in depth and offers safe, nutritional measures to counteract this invisible hazard.

How to Meet Requirements for Hazardous Waste Landfill Design, Construction and Closure. U. S. Environmental Protection Agency. Noyes Publications, 120 Mill Rd., Park Ridge, NJ 07656. (201) 391-8484. 1990. Outlines in detail the provisions of the minimum technology guidance regulations, and offers practical and detailed technology transfer information on the construction of hazardous waste facilities that comply with these requirements.

How to Predict the Spread and Intensity of Forest and Range Fires. Richard C. Rothermel. U.S. Department of Agriculture, Forest Service, Intermountain Forest and Range Experiment Station, 324 25th St., Ogden, UT 84401. 1983. Detection, prevention, and control of forest fires.

How to Protect Your Child Against Pesticides in Food. Anne Witte Garland. Natural Resources Defense Council, 40 W. 20th St., New York, NY 10011. (212) 727-2700. 1989. Food contamination, pesticide residues in food, and children's health and hygiene.

How to Respond to Hazardous Chemical Spills. W. Unterberg, et al. Noyes Publications, 120 Mill Rd., Park Ridge, NJ 07656. (201) 391-8484. 1988. Reference manual of countermeasures is designed to assist responders to spills of hazardous substances.

How to Save the World: Strategy for World Conservation. Robert Allen. Rowman & Littlefield, Publishers, Inc., 8705 Bollman Pl., Savage, MD 20763. (301) 306-0400. 1980. Based on the Global Conservation Strategy prepared in Switzerland in 1980 by the United Nations Environment Program, the World Wildlife Fund and the International Union for Conservation. Presents strategies in four critical areas: food supply, forest, the sea, and endangered species. Sets priorities, identifies obstacles, and recommends cost effective ways of overcoming those obstacles.

How to Select Hazardous Waste Treatment Technologies for Soil and Sludges: Alternative, Innovative and Emerging Technologies. Tim Holden, et al. Noyes Publications, 120 Mill Rd., Park Ridge, NJ 07656. (201) 391-8484. 1989. Guide for screening feasible alternative, innovative and emerging treatment technologies for contaminated soils and sludges at CERCLA (Superfund) sites. The technology data were selected from individual treatment technology vendors.

The Hudson Valley Green Times. Hudson Valley Grass Roots Energy and Environment Network, 30 E. Market St., P.O. Box 208, Red Hook, NY 12571. (914) 758-4484. Bimonthly. Energy and environment news with emphasis on Hudson Valley.

Hudsonia LTD. Bard College Field Station, Annadale, NY 12504. (914) 758-1881.

Human Aspects of Urban Form: Towards a Man-Environment Approach to Urban Form and Design. Pergamon Microforms International, Inc., Fairview Park, Elmsford, NY 10523. (914) 592-7720. 1977. Human factors in city planning, geographical perception and environmental aspects of architecture.

Human Ecology: A Guide to Information Sources. Frederick Sargent. Gale Research Co., 835 Penobscot Bldg., Detroit, MI 48226-4094. (313) 961-2242 or (800) 877-4253. 1983.

The Human Ecology Action League, Inc. P.O. Box 49126, Atlanta, GA 30359-1126. (404) 248-1898.

Human Ecology Forum. New York State College of Human Ecology, Cornell University, Martha Van Rensselaer Hall, Ithaca, NY 14853. Quarterly.

Human Ecology: Monographs Published in the 1980's. Mary A. Vance. Vance Bibliographies, PO Box 229, 112 N. Charter St., Monticello, IL 61856. (217) 762-3831. 1987.

Human Environment Center. 1001 Connecticut Ave., N.W., Ste. 827, Washington, DC 20003. (202) 331-8387.

Human Exposure Assessment for Airborne Pollutants: Advances and Opportunities. National Research Council (U.S.) Board of Environmental Studies and Toxicology. National Academy of Sciences, 2101 Constitution Ave. NW., Washington, DC 20418. (202) 334-2000 or (800) 624-6242. 1991. Provides a technical account of the principles and methodology of exposure assessment applied to air pollutants. Also provides valuable information for students on how to study air pollutant exposure and health effects through questionnaires, through air sampling, and through modeling.

Human Factors. Human Factors Society, Publications Division, Box 1369, Santa Monica, CA 90406-1369. (310) 394-1811. Bimonthly. Deals with human engineering and human factors.

Human Factors Design Handbook: Information and Guidelines for the Design of Systems, Facilities, Equipment, and Products for Human Use. Wesley E. Woodson, et al. McGraw-Hill, 1221 Avenue of Americas, New York, NY 10020. (212) 512-2000 or (800) 262-4729. 1992. Second edition. Provides a general reference to key human factors questions and human-product interface design suggestions in a form that engineers and designers can utilize with a minimum of searching or study. Includes a selective bibliography.

Human Factors Society Bulletin. Human Factors Society, PO Box 1369, Santa Monica, CA 90406-1369. (310) 394-1811. Monthly.

Human Health Damages from Mobile Source Air Pollution. Steve Leung. National Technical Information Service, 5285 Port Royal Rd., Springfield, VA 22161. (703) 487-4650. A delphi analysis of smog, air pollution, carbon monoxide and nitrogen dioxide poisoning.

Human Health Risks from Chemical Exposure: The Great Lakes Ecosystem. R. Warren Flint. Lewis Publishers, 2000 Corporate Blvd., N.W., Boca Raton, FL 33431. (407) 994-0555 or (800) 272-7737. 1991. Gives background on toxic chemicals in the Great Lakes. Also describes the toxicology and environmental chemistry of exposure to toxic chemicals, environmental and wildlife toxicology, epidemiology, public health and other related areas.

The Human Impact on the Natural Environment. Andrew Goudie. MIT Press, 55 Hayward St., Cambridge, MA 02142. (617) 253-2884. 1986. Discusses man's influence on nature.

Human Investment and Resource Use: A New Research Orientation at the Environment/Economics Interface. Michael Young and Natarajan Ishwaran, eds. UNESCO, 7, place de Fontenoy, Paris, France F-75700. (331) 45 68 40 67. 1989. Explores the issue of the environment/economics interface, parcularly the effect of the level and nature of human investments in determining the manner in which natural resources are utilized.

Human Performance in the Cold. Gary A. Laursen. Undersea and Hyperbaric Medical Society, 9650 Rockville Pike, Bethesda, MD 20814. (301) 571-1818. 1982.

Human Performance Physiology and Environmental Medicine Atterrestrial Extremes. Kent B. Pandolf, et al., eds. WCB Brown and Benchmark Pr., 2460 Kerper Blvd., Dubuque, IA 52001. (800) 338-5578. 1988. Includes the most current information available on the physiological and medical responses to heat, cold, altitude, poor air quality and hyperbaric conditions.

Human Population Exposures to Mirex and Kepone. Benjamin E. Suta. National Technical Information Service, 5285 Port Royal Rd., Springfield, VA 22161. (703) 487-4650. 1978. Environmental aspects of pesticides, organochlorine, insecticides, and chlordecone.

Human T Cell Clones: A New Approach to Immune Regulation. Marc Feldmann, ed. Humana Press, P.O. Box 2148, Clifton, NJ 07015. (201) 773-4389. 1984.

Human Toxicology of Pesticides. Fina P. Kaloyanova and Mostafa A. El Batawi. CRC Press, 2000 Corporate Blvd. NW, Boca Raton, FL 33431. (407) 994-0555; (800) 272-7737. 1991. Describes how pesticides affect humans.

Humane Society of the United States. 2100 L St., NW, Washington, DC 20037. (202) 452-1100.

Humus Acids of Soils. Dmitrii Sergeevich Orlov. National Technical Information Service, 5285 Port Royal Rd., Springfield, VA 22161. (703) 487-4650. 1985. Topics in soil chemistry.

Humus Chemistry: Genesis, Composition, Reactions. F. J. Stevenson. John Wiley & Sons, Inc., 605 3rd Ave., New York, NY 10158-0012. (212) 850-6000. 1982. Covers soil biochemistry.

Hydata News and Views. American Water Resources Association, 5410 Grosvenor Lane, Suite 220, Bethesda, MD 20814. (301) 493-8600. Six times a year. Research, planning and management in water resources.

Hydraulic Data for Shallow Open-Channel Flow in a High-Gradient Flume with Large Bed Material. Fred J. Watts. Deptartment of the Interior, U.S. Geological Survey, 119 National Center, Reston, VA 22092. (703) 648-4460. 1989. Hydraulic engineering channels and flumes.

Hydro Review–Industry Directory Issue. HCI Publications, 410 Archibald St., Kansas City, MO 64111. (816) 931-1311.

Hydrobiological Journal. John Wiley & Sons, Inc., Periodicals Division, 605 Third Ave., New York, NY 10158-0012. (212) 850-6000. Six times a year. Deals with fisheries in various water resources.

Hydrocarbon Contaminated Soils and Groundwater: Analysis, Fate, Environmental and Public Health Effects, and Remediation. Paul T. Kostecki and Edward J. Calabrese. Lewis Publishers, 2000 Corporate Blvd.,N.W., Boca Raton, FL 33431. (407) 994-0555 or (800) 272-7737. 1991. Describes perspectives and emerging issues, analytical techniques and site assessments, environmental fate and modeling.

Hydrocarbon Control Strategies for Gasoline Marketing Operations. R. L. Norton. U.S. Environmental Protection Agency, Office of Air and Waste Management, MD 75, Research Triangle Park, NC 27711. 1978. Pollution control of motor vehicle exhaust.

Hydrodynamic Forces. Eduard Naudascher. A. A. Balkema, Old Post Rd., Brookfield, VT 05036. (802) 276-3162. 1991. Covers fluctuating and mean hydrodynamic forces, hydrodynamic forces on high-head gates, and hydrodynamic forces on low-head gates and other related information.

Hydroelectric and Pumped Storage Plants. M.G. Jog. John Wiley & Sons, Inc., 605 3rd Ave., New York, NY 10158-0012. (212) 850-6000. 1989. Design and construction of hydroelectric plants.

Hydroelectric Construction. American Society of Civil Engineers, 345 E. 47th St., New York, NY 10017. (212) 705-7288. 1981-. Monthly.

Hydroelectric Power Resources of the United States, Developed and Underdeveloped. Federal Energy Regulatory Commission, 825 N. Capital St. NE, Washington, DC 20426. (202) 208-0200. 1980.

Hydrogen as a Fuel: A Bibliography. Vance Bibliographies, PO Box 229, 112 N. Charter St., Monticello, IL 61856. (217) 762-3831. 1988.

Hydrogen Chloride and Hydrogen Flouride Emission Factors for the NAPAP Emission Inventory. U.S. Environmental Protection Agency, MD 75, Research Triangle Park, NC 27711. 1986. Environmental aspects of chlorides, acid disposition and hydrogen flouride.

Hydrogen Energy: A Bibliography with Abstracts. University of New Mexico, Albuquerque, NM 87131. Annual.

Hydrogen Energy and Power Generation. T. Nejat Veziroglu, ed. Nova Science Publishers Inc., 283 Commack Rd., Suite 300, Commack, NY 11725-3104. (516) 499-3103; (516) 499-3106. 1991. Deals with clean energy and with other new and increasingly significant forms of energy generation, i.e. cogeneration, waste energy. Defines the role of hydrogen energy in the upcoming decade.

Hydrogen Energy Coordinating Committee Annual Report: Summary of Department of Energy Hydrogen Programs. Department of Energy, 1000 Independence Ave., S.W., Washington, DC 20585. (202) 586-5000.

Hydrogen Fuels: A Bibliography. National Technical Information Service, 5285 Port Royal Rd., Springfield, VA 22161. (703) 487-4650.

Hydrogen, Its Technology and Implications. Kenneth Cox. CRC Press, 2000 Corporate Blvd. N.W., Boca Raton, FL 33431. (800) 272-7737. 1979. Production technology, transmissions, and storage.

Hydrogen Peroxide in Organic Chemistry. Jean-Pierre Schirmann. Edition et Documentation Industrielle, 5 rue Jules Lefelvre, Paris, France 75009. 1979.

Hydrogen Peroxide-Use or Abuse?. The Academy, Chicago, IL 1988.

Hydrogen Sulfide. World Health Organization, Ave. Appia, Geneva, Switzerland CH-1211. 1988. Environmental health criteria relating to hydrogen sulfide.

Hydrogeological Assessment of the Closed Coboconk Landfill. Gartner Lee Ltd. Toronto (Ontario). National Technical Information Service, 5285 Port Royal Rd., Springfield, VA 22161. (703) 487-4650. 1989.

Hydrological Application of Weather Radar. I. D. Cluckie and C. G. Collier, eds. E. Horwood, 66 Wood Lane End, Hemel Hempstead, England HP2 4RG. 1991.

Hydrological Problems of Surface Mining. Peter Wood. IEA Coal Research, 14/15 Lower Grosvenor Place, London, England SW 1W OEX. 44 (71) 828-4661. 1981.

Hydroponic Society of America. P.O. Box 6067, Concord, CA 94524. (415) 682-4193.

Hydropower Engineering Handbook. John S. Gulliver. McGraw-Hill Science & Engineering Books, 11 W. 19th St., New York, NY 10011. (212) 337-6010. 1991. Hydroelectric power plants and hydraulic engineering.

Hydrosoft. Computational Mechanics Publications Inc., 400 W. Cummings Park, Suite 6200, Woburn, MA 01801. Quarterly. Covers software for hydraulics, hydrology and hydrodynamics.

Hydrowire. HCI Publications, 410 Archibald St., Kansas City, MO 64111. (816) 931-1311.

Hygiene Guide Series. American Industrial Hygiene Association, 345 White Pond Dr., Akron, OH 44320. (216) 873-2442. 1955-. 1 v. (loose-leaf).

Hypothermia and Cold Stress. Evan L. Lloyd. Aspen Systems Corp., 1600 Research Blvd., Rockville, MD 20850. (301) 251-5554. 1986. Cold therapy, body temperature regulation and adverse effects of cold.

Hypothermia, Causes, Effects, Prevention. Robert S. Pozos. New Win Publishing, Inc., RR 1 Box 384C, Rte. 173 W., Hampton, NJ 08827. (201) 735-9701. 1982. Covers physiological effects of cold.

Hypothermia, Frostbite, and Other Cold Injuries: Prevention, Recognition, and Prehospital Treatment. James A. Wilkerson. The Mountaineers, 306 Second Ave. W, Seattle, WA 98119. (206) 285-2665. 1986. Adverse effects of cold, frostbite and hypothermia.

Hypothermia: Recognition and Prevention. Alice D. Zimmerman. University of Wyoming, P.O. Box 3315, University Station, Laramie, WY 82071. (307) 766-2379. 1983.

Hypothermia: The Facts. Kenneth John Collins. Oxford University Press, Walton St., Oxford, England OX2 6DP. 1983.

IAFWA Newsletter. International Association of Fish and Wildlife Agencies, 444 N. Capitol St., NW, #534, Washington, DC 20001. (202) 624-7890. Bimonthly. Fish & wildlife conservation, fishing, wildlife management.

IARC Monographs on the Evaluation of the Carcinogenic Risk of Chemicals to Man. International Agency for Research on Cancer, Q Corp., 49 Sheridan Ave., Albany, NY 12221. (518) 436-9686. 1972-. Irregular.

IBSEDEX. Building Services Research & Information Association, Old Bracknell Lane West, Bracknell, Berkshire, England RG12 4AH. 44 (344) 426511.

ICWM Directory of Hazardous Waste Treatment and Disposal Facilities. Institute of Chemical Waste Management/National Solid Wastes Management Association, 1730 Rhode Island Ave., N.W., Suite 1000, Washington, DC 20036. (202) 659-4613.

ICWP Policy Statement & Bylaws. Interstate Conference on Water Problems, 5300 M Street, NW, Suite 800, Washington, DC 20037. (202) 466-7287. Annual. Covers conservation and administration of water.

Idaho and Wyoming: Endangered and Sensitive Plant Field Guide. U.S. Department of Agriculture, Forest Service, Intermountain Region, 324 25th St., Ogden, UT 84401. 1990. Manual for identification of rare plants in Idaho and Wyoming as well as endangered species. Also covers plant conservation.

Idaho Wildlife. Idaho Dept. of Fish and Game, P.O. Box 25, 600 S. Walnut, Boise, ID 83712. (208) 334-3746. Bimonthly. Covers conservation, wildlife management, fish and game operations and policies.

Identification and Analysis of Organic Pollutants in Air. Lawrence Keith. Butterworth-Heinemann, 80 Montvale Ave., Stoneham, MA 02180. (617) 438-8464. 1984. Analysis of organic compounds and air pollution measurement.

Identification Manual. Peter Drollinger. Convention on International Trade in Endangered Species of Wild Fauna and Flora, Lausanne, Switzerland 1987. Identification of rare animals, endangered species and fur.

Identification of Pure Organic Compounds. Ernest Hamlin Huntress. John Wiley & Sons, Inc., 605 Third Ave., New York, NY 10158-0012. (212) 850-6000. 1941. Tables of data on selected compounds of order I (compounds of carbon with hydrogen or with hydrogen and oxygen).

Identification of Selected Federal Activities Directed to Chemicals Near- Term Concern. U.S. Environmental Protection Agency, Office of Toxic Substances, 401 M St., S.W., Washington, DC 20460. (202) 260-2090. 1976.

Identifying and Regulating Carcinogens. M. Dekker, 270 Madison Ave., New York, NY 10016. (212) 696-9000. 1989. Health risk assessment and testing.

IECA Report. International Erosion Control Association, P.O. Box 195, Pinole, CA 94564. (415) 223-2134. Bimonthly. Covers urban erosion and sediment control.

IEEE Engineering in Medicine and Biology Society. c/o Inst. of Electrical and Electronics Engineers, 345 E. 47th St., New York, NY 10017. (212) 705-7867.

IEEE Transactions on Energy Conversion. Institute of Electrical and Electronics Engineers, 345 E. 47th St., New York, NY 10017. (212) 705-7900. Quarterly. Deals with power apparatus and systems.

Ill Winds. James J. Mackenzie. State University of New York Press, State University Plaza, Albany, NY 12246. (518) 472-5000. 1988. Airborne pollution's toll on trees and crops.

Illinois Environmental Law Handbook. Government Institutes, Inc., 4 Research Pl., Ste. 200, Rockville, MD 20850. (301) 921-2300. 1989.

Illinois EPA: Emergency Preparedness and Community Right-to-Know. Chair, Emergency Planning Unit, PO Box 19276, 2200 Churchill Rd., Springfield, IL 62794-9276. (217) 782-3637.

Illinois Hazardous Waste Research and Information Center. One East Hazelwood Dr., Champaign, IL 61820. (217) 333-8940.

Illinois Homeowner's Guide to Reduction of Indoor Radon. Illinois Department of Energy and Natural Resources, Office of Research and Planning, 325 W. Adams St., Rm. 300, Springfield, IL 62706. (217) 785-2800. 1989. Environmental and health aspects of indoor air pollution.

Illinois Wildlife. Illinois Wildlife Federation, 123 S. Chicago St., Rossville, IL 60963. (217) 748-6365. Bimonthly. Deals with outdoor recreational trends.

The Illustrated Encyclopedia of Birds: The Definitive Reference to Birds of the World. Prentice Hall, Rte. 9W, Englewood Cliffs, NY 07632. (201) 592-2000. 1991. Includes a short summary of basic bird biology, an illustrated catalog of about 1,200 species representing all living orders and families, and a checklist of all 9,300-plus currently recognized species.

Illustrated Encyclopedia of Science and the Future. Mike Biscare, et al., ed. Marshall Cavendish, 58 Old Compton St., London, England 0W1V5 PA. 01-734 6710. 1983. Twenty volumes. Each volume has 5 sections: Frontiers, Electronics in Action, Medical Science, Military Technology, and Resources.

The Illustrated Petroleum Reference Dictionary. Robert D. Langenkamp. PennWell Books, PO Box 1260, Tulsa, OK 74101. (918) 835-3161. 1985. Third edition. Includes terms relating to petroleum. Special features of this dictionary include: D & D Standard Oil abbreviator and Universal Conversion Factor list.

IMAGE, An Integrated Model to Assess the Greenhouse Effect. Jan Rotmans. Kluwer Academic Publishers, 101 Philip Dr., Assinippi Park, Norwell, MA 02061. (617) 871-6600. 1990. Explains how the computer simulation model IMAGE is constructed, the fundamental assumptions on which it is based, the ways in which it has been verified, and how to use it.

IMI Descriptions of Fungi and Bacteria. International Mycological Institute, Kew, England Four sets a year. Identification of pathogenic bacteria and pathogenic fungi.

Imidazolinone Herbicides. Dale L. Shaner, ed. CRC Press, 2000 Corporate Blvd. N.W., Boca Raton, FL 33431. (407) 994-0555 or (800) 272-7737. 1991.

IMMAGE. Institution of Mining & Metallurgy Library and Information Services, 44 Portland Place, London, England W1N 4BR. 44 (71) 580-3802.

Immunoassays for Trace Chemical Analysis; Monitoring Toxic Chemicals in Humans, Food, and the Environment. Martin Vandelaan, et al. American Chemical Society, 1155 16th St., N.W., Washington, DC 20036. (202) 872-4600; (800) 227-5558. Deals with the use of immunoassays as alternative methods for conducting sampling for chemical residues in food and the environment, for natural toxins, and for monitoring human exposure to toxic chemicals.

Immunochemical Methods for Environmental Analysis. Jeanette M. Van Emon and Ralph O. Mumma, eds. American Chemical Society, 1155 16th St. N.W., Washington, DC 20036. (202) 872-4600; (800) 227-5558. 1990. Describes antibodies used as analytical tools to study environmentally important compounds. Discusses various applications in food industry, environmental analysis, and applications in agriculture.

Immunotoxicology of Drugs and Chemicals. Elsevier Science Publishing Co., 655 Avenue of the Americas, New York, NY 10010. (212) 984-5800. 1988.

Impact Assessment Bulletin. Center for Technology Assessment and Policy Studies, Rose Hulman Institute of Technology, Georgia Institute of Technology, Terra Haute, IN 47803-3999. (812) 877-1511. Quarterly. Covers the assessment of environmental and technical impact.

Impact Models to Assess Regional Acidification. Juha Kamari. Kluwer Academic Publishers, 101 Philip Dr., Assinippi Park, Norwell, MA 02061. (617) 871-6600. 1990. Contains a description of the development and use of the Regional Acidification Information and Simulation (RAINS) model, an integrated assessment model of developing and determining control strategies to reduce regional acidification in Europe.

The Impact of Denitrification on In-Stream Dissolved Oxygen Concentration. Ayoub V. Torkian. University of Texas Press, PO Box 7819, Austin, TX 78713-7819. (512) 471-7233 or (800) 252-3206. 1989. Thesis submitted to University of Texas at Dallas, 1989. Describes water purification by nitrogen removal.

The Impact of Green Consumerism on Food & Beverage Industries. FIND/SVP, 625 Avenue of the Americas, New York, NY 10011. (212) 645-4500. 1991/92.

The Impact of Inorganic Phosphates in the Environment. Justine Welch. U.S. Environmental Protection Agency, Office of Pesticides and Toxic Substances, 401 M St., SW, Washington, DC 20460. (202) 260-2090. 1978. Eutrophication of phosphorus in the environment.

Impact of NOx Selective Catalytic Reduction Process on Flue Gas Cleaning Systems. G.D. Jones. Industrial Environmental Research Laboratory, Environmental Protection Agency, Raleigh, NC 27604. (919) 834-4015. 1982. Covers catalytic cracking, efficiency of boilers, purification of flue gases and pollution control equipment.

Imperiled Planet: Restoring Our Endangered Ecosystems. Edward Goldsmith, et al. MIT Press, 55 Hayward St., Cambridge, MA 02142. (617) 253-2884; (800) 356-0343. 1990. Presentation of a wide range of ecosystems, showing how they work, the traditional forms of human use, threats and losses, causes of destruction, and preservation attempts.

Implementation Strategy for the Clean Air Act Amendments of 1990. U.S. Environmental Protection Agency, Office of Air and Radiation, 401 M St. SW, Washington, DC 20460. (202) 260-2090. 1991.

Impounded Rivers: Perspectives for Ecological Management. Geoffrey E. Petts. John Wiley & Sons, Inc., 605 3rd Ave., New York, NY 10158. (212) 850-6000. 1984. Environmental aspects of dams, stream ecology and stream conservation.

Improved Fire Protection for Underground Fuel Storage and Fuel Transfer Areas. William H. Pomroy. U.S. Department of the Interior, Bureau of Mines, Pittsburgh, PA 1985. Prevention and control of mine fires and underground storage of petroleum products.

In-line Aeration and Treatment of Acid Mine Drainage. U.S. Department of the Interior, Bureau of Mines, 810 7th St. NW, Washington, DC 20241. (202) 501-9649. 1984. Water and oxidation methods.

In One Barn: Efficient Livestock Housing and Management. Lee Pelley. Countryman Press, PO Box 175, Woodstock, VT 05091-0175. (802) 457-1049. 1984.

In Search of Environmental Excellence: Moving Beyond Blame. Bruce Piasecki and Peter Asmus. Simon and Schuster, 1230 Avenue of the Americas, New York, NY 10020. (212) 689-7000. 1990. Analyses of the roles and motivations of government, business/industry, and the general public in solving environmental problems.

In Search of Safety: Chemicals and Cancer Risk. J. D. Graham. Harvard University Press, 79 Garden St., Cambridge, MA 02138. (617) 495-2600. 1988.

In Situ Immobilization of Heavy-Metal-Contaminated Soils. G. Czupyrna, et al. Noyes Publications, 120 Mill Rd., Park Ridge, NJ 07656. (201) 391-8484. 1989. Reports on an evaluation of various treatment chemicals for the in situ immobilization of heavy-metal-contaminated soils.

In Situ Vitrification of PCB-Contaminated Soils. Battelle, Pacific Northwest Laboratories. Electric Power Research Institute, 3412 Hillview Ave., Palo Alto, CA 94304. (415) 965-4081. 1986. Covers polychlorinated biphenyls and soil contamination.

In Situ Vitrification of Transuranic Wastes. K. H. Oma, et al. Pacific Northwest Laboratory, National Technical Information Service, 5285 Port Royal Rd., Springfield, VA 22161. (703) 487-4650. 1983. Prepared for the U.S. Department of Energy under contract by Pacific Northwest Laboratory, Richland, WA.

In the U.S. Interest: Resources, Growth, and Security in the Developing World. Janet Welsh Brown, ed. World Resources Institute, 1709 New York Ave. N.W., Washington, DC 20006. (800) 822-0504. 1990.

In the Wake of the Exxon Valdez: Devastating Impact of Alaska's Oil Spill. Art Davidson. Sierra Club Books, 100 Bush St., San Francisco, CA 94104. (415) 291-1600. 1990. Story of environmental risk and the consequences that arise.

Incinerating Hazardous Wastes. Harry M. Freeman, ed. Technomic Publishing Co., 851 New Holland Ave., Box 3535, Lancaster, PA 17604. (717) 291-5609. 1988. Book provides the essence of the thermal destruction research program at the EPA Lab in Cincinnati, Ohio. Highlights papers that have represented significant contributions to the field of incineration research. Provides a general overview of the role of incineration in the United States today.

Incinerating Municipal and Industrial Waste; Fireside Problems and Prospects for Improvement. Richard W. Bryers. Hemisphere, 79 Madison Ave., Suite 1110, New York, NY 10016. (212) 725-1999; (800) 821-8312. 1991. Addresses the causes and possible cures for corrosion and deposits due to impurities in the combustion of industrial and municipal refuse.

Incineration for Site Cleanup and Destruction of Hazardous Wastes. Howard E. Hesketh. Technomic Publishing Co., 851 New Holland Ave., Box 3535, Lancaster, PA 17604. (717) 291-5609; (800) 233-9936. 1990.

Incineration of Industrial Wastes. FIND/SVP, 625 Avenue of the Americas, New York, NY 10011. (212) 645-4500. 1990. Present state of incineration technology–liquid injection, fume, fixed hearth, multiple hearth, rotary kiln, fluidized bed, circulating bed, infrared, plasma-arc, mobile/transportable, oxygen-enhanced, auxiliary systems–as well as emerging technologies.

The Incredible Heap: A Guide to Compost Gardening. Chris Catton. St. Martin's Press, 175 5th Ave., New York, NY 10010. (212) 674-5151. 1984. Covers organic gardening and compost.

Independent Energy–Industry Directory Issue. Alternative Sources of Energy, Inc., 107 S. Central Ave., Milaca, MN 56353. (612) 983-6892.

Index Hortensis: A Modern Nomenclator for Botanists, Horticulturalists, Plantsmen, and the Serious Gardener. Piers Trehane. Quarterjack Publishing, Hampreston Manor Farm, Wimborne, England BH21 7LX. 1989-. List of plants alphabetically arranged by genus indicating the correct name, hybrid species, botanical epithet and the family name and other related information. Volume 1 contains: perennials, including border plants, herbs, bulbous plants, non-woody alpines, aquatic plants, outdoor ferns and ornamental grasses.

Index of Fungi. C. A. B. International, 845 North Park Ave., Tucson, AZ 85719. (602) 621-7897 or (800) 528-4841. 1947-. Semiannual. A list of names of new genera, species and intraspeific taxa, new names of fungi and lichens.

Index of Hazardous Contents of Commercial Products in Schools and Colleges. The Forum for Scientific Excellence. J. B. Lippincott, 227 E. Washington Sq., Philadelphia, PA 19105. (215) 238-4200; (800) 982-4377. 1990. Lists the hazardous components found in thousands of commercial products used in educational institutions.

Index of Publications on Biological Effects of Electromagnetic Radiation. James B. Kinn. U.S. Environmental Protection Agency, Health Effects Research Laboratory, 401 M St., SW, Washington, DC 20460. (202) 260-2090. 1981.

Index of Selected Aerial Photography of the United States. U.S. Fish and Wildlife Service, Office of Biological Services. U.S. Department of the Interior, Fish and Wildlife Service, 1849 C St. NW, Washington, DC 20240. (202) 208-5634. 1976.

Index to Scientific Book Contents. Institute for Scientific Information, 3501 Market St., Philadelphia, PA 19104. (800) 523-1857. 1985-. Annual. Gives contents of science books published.

Index Veterinarius. C. A. B. International, 845 North Park Ave., Tucson, AZ 85719. (602) 621-7897 or (800) 528-4841. 1933-. Monthly. A monthly subject and author index to the world's veterinary literature. References are given to abstracts published in Veterinary Bulletin. Animals included in the index are: cattle, horses, sheep, goats, pigs, poultry, cats, dogs, rabbits, cagebirds, laboratory animals, wildlife, zoo animals, fish and other domestic animals.

Indirect Solar, Geothermal, and Nuclear Energy. T. Nejat Veziroglu, ed. Nova Science Publishers Inc., 283 Commack Rd., Suite 300, Commack, NY 11725-3401. (516) 499-3103; (516) 499-3106. 1991. Presents several focussed sectors of the energy spectrum: wind energy, ocean energy, gravitational energy, I.C. engines, and fluidized beds and looks at nuclear energy.

Indoor Air Pollution: A Health Perspective. Jonathan M. Samet and John D. Spengler. Johns Hopkins University Press, 701 W. 40th St., Ste. 275, Baltimore, MD 21211. (212) 516-6900. 1991. Explores the relationship between air pollution and health. Provides a wealth of useful information including epidemiologic results and standards or requirements that influence air quality both indoor and out.

Indoor Air Pollution Control. Thad Godish. Lewis Publishers, 2000 Corporate Blvd., N.W., Boca Raton, FL 33431. (407) 994-0555 or (800) 272-7737. 1989. Provides practical information and data needed for indoor air pollution control. Deals with how to conduct indoor air quality investigations in both residences and public access buildings; indoor air quality mitigation practice, and case histories.

Indoor Air Pollution: Radon, Bioaerosols, and VOCs. Jack G. Kay, et al. Lewis Publishers, 2000 Corporate Blvd., N.W., Boca Raton, FL 33431. (407) 994-0555 or (800) 272-7737. 1991. Consists of two parts: Overview of the ACS Symposium on Indoor Air Pollution, and Radon overview

Indoor Air Quality. Bradford O. Brooks. CRC Press, 2000 Corporate Blvd. N.W., Boca Raton, FL 33431. (800) 272-7737. 1991. Traces history in context of indoor air quality, measurement, quality improvement and regulations and current philosophy of litigation.

Indoor Air Quality Control Techniques: Radon, Formaldehyde, Combustion Products. W.J. Fisk. Noyes Publications, 120 Mill Rd., Park Ridge, NJ 07656. (201) 391-8484. 1987. Air quality in the United States.

Indoor Air Quality Design Guidebook. Milton Meckler. Fairmont Press, 700 Indian Trail, Lilburn, GA 30247. (404) 925-9388. 1991. Air cleaning systems, the carbon dioxide method, health lead/lag procedure, desiccants, contaminant absorption, effects of sick buildings, assessment of measurement techniques, indoor air quality simulation with computer models, and system design and maintenance techniques. Also available through the Association of Energy Engineers.

Indoor Air: Reference Bibliography. U.S. Environmental Protection Agency, 401 M St., S.W., Washington, DC 20460. (202) 260-2090.

Indoor Air Review. IAQ Pub. Inc., 5335 Wisconsin Ave., NW., Suite 440, Washington, DC 20015. (202) 686-2626. 1991. Monthly. Gives the latest news and information on the topic of indoor air quality. Special sections are devoted to updates of legislation, research and development, technology, liability and insurance issues, state and federal governments reports, industry and business forecasts and reports, meetings, conferences, training, standards and accreditation.

Indoor Environment. S. Karger Publishing, Inc., 26 West Avon Rd., PO Box 529, Farmington, CT 06085. Bimonthly. The quality of the indoor environment at home and in the workplace, building design, materials, ventilation and air conditioning, and chemistry.

Indoor Pollution Law Report. Leader Publications, New York Law Publishing Co., 111 Eighth Ave., New York, NY 10011. (212) 463-5709. Monthly.

Indoor Pollution News. Buraff Publications, 1350 Connecticut Ave., NW, Suite 100, Washington, DC 20036. (202) 862-0990. Biweekly. Air quality in buildings (including radon, formaldehyde, solvents and asbestos) or other air pollutions, such as lead in pipes.

Industrial Air Pollution Control Equipment. FIND/SVP, 625 Avenue of the Americas, New York, NY 10011. (212) 645-4500. 1991.

Industrial and Federal Environmental Markets Report. Government Institutes, Inc., 4 Research Pl., Ste. 200, Rockville, MD 20850. (301) 921-2300. Environmental industry developments and environmental laws and policies.

Industrial and Hazardous Waste Management Firms. Environmental Information Ltd., 4801 W. 81st St., No. 119, Minneapolis, MN 55437-1111. (612) 831-2473.

Industrial and Hazardous Waste Treatment. Nelson Leonard Nemerow and Avijit Dasgupta. Van Nostrand Reinhold, 115 5th Ave., New York, NY 10003. (212) 254-3232. 1991. Factory and trade waste, and hazardous waste purification.

Industrial Applications of Titanium and Zirconium. Charles S. Young. ASTM, 1916 Race St., Philadelphia, PA 19103-1187. (215) 299-5400. 1986.

Industrial Biotechnology Association. 1625 K St., N.W., Suite 1100, Washington, DC 20006-1604. (202) 857-0244.

Industrial Chemical Research Association. 1811 Monroe St., Dearborn, MI 48124. (313) 563-0360.

Industrial Commission: Occupational Safety. Director, 800 W. Washington, Phoenix, AZ 85007. (602) 542-4411.

Industrial Commission: Occupational Safety. Administrator, Occupational Safety and Health Division, 160 East 300 S., Salt Lake City, UT 84110-5800. (801) 530-6901.

Industrial Energy Conservation. Federal Energy Administration, Conservation and Environment, Office of Industrial Programs, 1000 Independence Ave. SW, Washington, DC 20585. (202) 586-5000. 1975. Petroleum waste and petroleum recycling in the U.S.

Industrial Environmental Control. A. M. Springer. John Wiley & Sons, Inc., 605 3rd Ave., New York, NY 10158-0012. (212) 850-6000. 1986. Covers in great detail all the basic information regarding industrial pollution and its treatment.

Industrial Explosives Markets. FIND/SVP, 625 Avenue of the Americas, New York, NY 10011. (212) 645-4500. 1990.

Industrial Gas Clearing Institute. 1707 L St., N.W., Suite 570, Washington, DC 20036. (202) 457-0911.

Industrial Health & Hazards Update. Merton Allen Associates, P.O. Box 15640, Plantation, FL 33318-5640. (305) 473-9560.

Industrial Health Foundation. 34 Penn Cir. W., Pittsburgh, PA 15206. (412) 363-6600.

Industrial Heat Exchangers. Graham Walker. Hemisphere Publishing Co., 79 Madison Ave., Suite 1110, New York, NY 10016. (212) 725-1999. 1982.

Industrial Heating Equipment Association. 1901 N. Moore St., Arlington, VA 22209. (703) 525-2513.

Industrial Hygiene News. Rimbach Publishing, Inc., 8650 Babcock Boulevard, Pittsburgh, PA 15237. (412) 364-5366. Bimonthly. Covers new products, literature, and product briefs.

Industrial Labor and Human Relations: Underground Storage Tanks. Director, Bureau of Petroleum Inspection, PO Box 7969, Madison, WI 53707. (608) 266-7605.

Industrial Lubrication. Michael Billett. Pergamon Microforms International, Inc., Fairview Park, Elmsford, NY 10523. (914) 592-7720. 1979. A practical handbook for lubrication and production engineers.

Industrial Metal Containers Section of the Material Handling Institute. c/o Material Handling Inst., IMC, 8720 Red Oak Blvd., Suite 201, Charlotte, NC 28217. (704) 522-8644.

Industrial Minerals Directory: World Guide to Producers and Processors. Metal Bulletin, Inc., 220 5th Ave., 10th Fl., New York, NY 10001. (212) 213-6202. Includes mineral processing companies in addition to those which own and operate mines or quarries.

Industrial Organic Chemicals in Perspective. Harold A. Wittcoff. John Wiley & Sons, Inc., 605 3rd Ave., New York, NY 10158-0012. (212) 850-6000. 1980. Raw materials and manufacturing in the chemicals industry.

Industrial Safety and Hygiene News. Chilton Book Co., 201 King of Prussia Rd., Radnor, PA 19089. (215) 964-4000. Monthly. Covers fire protection, security, and emergency first aid equipment.

Industrial Safety Equipment Association. 1901 N. Moore St., Arlington, VA 22209. (703) 525-1695.

Industrial Specialty Chemical Association. c/o Sigmund Domanski, 1520 Locust St., 5th Floor, Philadelphia, PA 19102. (215) 546-9608.

Industrial Studies Data Base–ISDB. U.S. Environmental Protection Agency, Office of Solid Waste, 401 M St., N.W., Washington, DC 20460. (202) 260-2090.

Industrial Ventilation Workbook; Indoor Air Quality Workbook; Laboratory Ventilation Workbook. American Industrial Hygiene Association, 345 White Pond Dr., Akron, OH 44320. (216) 873-2442. 1990-1991. Includes expanded coverage of introductory concepts through advanced materials and discussions of the state-of-the-art hood and duct design, loss factors, dilution ventilation, etc. Also describes HVAC in simple understandable terms. The Lab workbook describes lab hood exhaust systems and associated HVAC systems.

Industrial Waste Gases: Utilization and Minimization. RCG/ Hagler Bailly Inc. Technomic Publishing Co., 851 New Holland Ave., Box 3535, Lancaster, PA 17604. (717) 291-5609. 1990. Also released under title Industrial Waste Gas Management. Deals with factory and trade waste and the effluents that are released into the atmosphere.

Industrial Wastewater Heavy Metal Removal. Robert W. Peters. CRC Press, 2000 Corporate Blvd. N.W., Boca Raton, FL 33431. (800) 272-7737. 1991. Includes heavy metal contamination episodes, metal speciation complexation, brief review of various unit operation processes used for removal of heavy metals from solution with approximate percentage of installations employing each technology. Also discusses the various technologies used and the new emerging techniques.

Industrial Wastewater Source Control: An Inspection Guide. Nancy Rukonen. Technomic Pub. Co., 851 New Holland Ave., Box 3535, Lancaster, PA 17604. (800) 233-9936. 1992. Comprehensive guide for industrial waste inspectors.

Industrial Water Conditioning Institute. c/o J.J. Jewett, III, One James Center, 6th Fl., Richmond, VA 23219. (804) 775-1005.

Infectious and Medical Waste Management. Peter A. Rinehardt and Judith G. Gordon. Lewis Publishers, 2000 Corporate Blvd., N.W., Boca Raton, FL 33431. (407) 994-0555 or (800) 272-7737. 1991. Explains in detail how to safely comply with the complex regulations and how to set up an effective infectious and medical waste program (including AIDS and Hepatitis B viruses) so the right decisions can be made.

Infectious Disease Society of America. c/o Vincent T. Andriole, M.D., 333 Cedar St., 201-202 LCI, New Haven, CT 06510. (203) 785-8782.

Infectious Waste Management. Frank L. Cross. Technomic Publishing Co., 851 New Holland Ave., Box 3535, Lancaster, PA 17604. (717) 291-5609; (800) 233-9936. 1990.

Infectious Wastes News. Richard H. Freeman, Washington Sq., PO Box 65686, Washington, DC 20035-5686. (202) 861-0708. Biweekly. Disposal of infectious wastes, new methods and technologies, sterilization and incineration of waste, and environmental standards.

Infiltration and Recharge of Stormwater. Bruce K. Ferguson. Vance Bibliographies, 112 N. Charters St., PO Box 229, Monticello, IL 61856. (217) 762-3831. 1984. A resource conserving alternative for the urban infrastructure.

Influence and Removal of Organics in Drinking Water. Joel Mallevialle and Mel Suffet. Lewis Publishers, 2000 Corporate Blvd., N.W., Boca Raton, FL 33431. (407) 994-0555 or (800) 272-7737. 1992. Includes fundamentals and applications of adsorption phenomena, different aspects of coagulation process, recent developments in oxidations and disinfection and new technologies.

Influence of Environmental Factors on the Control of Grape, Pests, Diseases and Weeds. R. Cavalloro. A. A. Balkema, Old Post Rd., Brookfield, VT 05036. (802) 276-3162. 1989. Influence of environmental factors on cultivation of vines, and impact of insects, mites, diseases and weeds and pesticides.

INFORM. 381 Park Avenue S., New York, NY 10016. (212) 689-4040.

INFORM Reports. INFORM Inc., 381 Park Ave., So., New York, NY 10016. (212) 689-4040. Quarterly. INFORM is a nonprofit environmental research & education organization for the preservation and conservation of natural resources and public health.

Information and Communications: Extension Service. 14th and Independence Ave., S.W., Washington, DC 20250. (202) 447-3029.

Information Division: Statistical Reporting Service. Room 209, JSM Building, 15th and Independence Ave., S.W., Washington, DC 20250. (202) 447-4230.

Information Kit. Coalition for Responsible Waste Incineration, 1330 Connecticut Ave. NW, Suite 300, Washington, DC 20036. (202) 659-0060. Irregular.

Information Office: Forest Service. PO Box 2417, Washington, DC 20013. (202) 447-3760.

Information Resources in Toxicology. Elsevier Science Publishing Co., 655 Avenue of the Americas, New York, NY 10010. (212) 984-5800. 1988. Toxicology directory, bibliography and societies.

Information Sources in Agriculture and Food Science. G. P. Lilley. Butterworth-Heinemann, 80 Montvale Ave., Stoneham, MA 02180. (617) 438-8464. 1981.

Information Sources in Biotechnology. A. Crafts-Lighty. Stockton Press, New York, NY 10010. (212) 673-4400. 1986. Describes information sources in the field of biotechnology.

Information System for Hazardous Organics in Water. U.S. Environmental Protection Agency, Office of Pesticides & Toxic Substances, 401 M St., S.W., Washington, DC 20460. (202) 260-2090.

INFOTERRA–World Directory of Environmental Expertise. United States National Focal Point for UNEP/INFOTERRA, Environmental Protection Agency, 401 M St., S.W., Rm 2903, Washington, DC 20460. (202) 382-5917.

INFOTOX. Centre de Documentation, Commission de la Sante et de la Securite du Travail (CSST), 1199 rue de Bueury, 4th Floor, C.P. 6067 succ "A", Montreal, PQ, Canada H3C 4E2. (514) 873-2297.

The Infrared Spectra Handbook of Adhesives and Sealants. Sadtler Research Laboratories, 3316 Spring Garden St., Philadelphia, PA 19104. (215)382-7800. 1988. Contains 520 adhesives and sealants.

The Infrared Spectra Handbook of Priority Pollutants and Toxic Chemicals. Sadtler Research Laboratories, 3316 Spring Garden St., Philadelphia, PA 19104. (215) 382-7800. 1982. Chemicals spectra, hazardous substances spectra, gases spectra, and toxic chemicals.

Inhalation Toxicology. D. Dungworth. Springer-Verlag, 175 5th Ave., New York, NY 10010. (212) 460-1500. 1988.

Inhalation Toxicology of Air Pollution. Robert Frank. ASTM, 1916 Race St., Philadelphia, PA 19103-1187. (215) 299-5400. 1985.

INIS Atomindex. International Atomic Energy Agency, Wagramerstrasse 5, Vienna, Austria A-1400. 222 23606198. 1988-. Semiannual. Abstracts nuclear energy and nuclear physics topics from journals, conferences, technical reports and other related publications. Issued in 6 parts: Personal Author, Corporate Entry, Subject, Report, Standard Patent, Conference (by place), Conference (by date).

Inland Bird Banding Association. RD 2, Box 26, Wisner, NE 68791. (402) 529-6679.

Inland Commercial Fisheries Association. c/o Green Island Fishing Co., Inc., 11 Ogden St., Marinette, WI 54143. (715) 732-1313.

Inland River Ports & Terminals. 204 E. High St., Jefferson City, MO 65101. (314) 634-2028.

Innovation and Environmental Risk. Lewis Roberts and Albert Wheale. Belhaven Press, 136 S. Broadway, Irvington, NY 10533. (914) 591-9111. 1991. Debates public policies and scientific issues concerning environmental problems. Stresses energy, radiological protection, biotechnology and the role of the media.

Innovative/Alternative Pollution Control Technology Facility File–IADB. U.S. Environmental Protection Agency, Office of Water Program Operations, 401 M St., S.W., Washington, DC 20460. (202) 260-2090.

Innovative Thermal Hazardous Organic Waste Treatment Processes. Noyes Publications, 120 Mill Rd., Park Ridge, NJ 07656. (201) 391-8484. 1985. Technological innovations in hazardous waste treatment.

Inorganic & Fertilizer Chemical Forecast Database. Probe Economics, Inc., 241 Lexington Ave., Mt. Kisco, NY 10549. (914) 241-0744.

Inorganic & Fertilizer Chemicals. Sage Data, Inc., 104 Carnegie Ctr., Princeton, NJ 08540. (609) 924-3000.

Inorganic Arsenic Emissions from Primary Copper Smelters and Arsenic Plants. Office of Air Quality Planning and Standards. U.S. Environmental Protection Agency, 401 M St., S.W., Washington, DC 20460. (202) 260-2090. 1986. Background information for promulgated standards.

Inorganic Contaminants in the Vadose Zone. Springer-Verlag, 175 5th Ave., New York, NY 10010. (212) 460-1500. 1989. Soil pollution and zone of aeration.

Inorganic Contaminants of Surface Water; Research and Monitoring Priorities. James W. Moore. Springer-Verlag, 175 Fifth Ave., New York, NY 10010. (212) 460-1500 or (800) 777-4643. 1991. Inorganic contaminants of surface water in terms of production, sources, and residues, chemistry, bioacculation, toxic effects to aquatic organisms, health effects and drinking water.

Inorganic Crystal Structure Database. Institute of Inorganic Chemistry, University of Bonn, Gerhard-Domagk-Strasse-1, Bonn 1, Germany D-5300. 49 (228) 732657.

Insect Pest Management. David Dent. C. A. B. International, Oxon, Wallingford, England OX10 8DE. (44) 0491 3211. 1991.

Insect Photoperiodism. Stanley Beck. Academic Press, c/o Harcourt Brace Jovanovich Inc., 6277 Sea Harbor Dr., Orlando, FL 32887. (800) 346-8648. 1980.

The Insect Repellent Market. FIND/SVP, 625 Avenue of the Americas, New York, NY 10011. (212) 645-4500. 1991. Insect repellents marketed as aerosols, lotions and roll-on sticks.

Insecticide and Acaricide Tests. Entomological Society of America, 9301 Annapolis Rd., Lanham, MD 20706-3115. (301) 731-4538. Irregular.

The Insecticide, Herbicide, Fungicide Quick Guide and Data Book. B. G. Page and N. T. Thomson. Thomson Publications, PO Box 9335, Fresno, CA 93791. (209) 435-2163. 1984. Annually.

Insecticides, Mechanisms of Action and Resistance. D. Otto and B. Weber, eds. VCH Publishers, 303 NW 12th Ave., Deerfield Beach, FL 33442-1788. (305) 428-5566. 1991. Covers development of new concepts for ecologically-oriented plant protection. Latest applied research on commercial insecticides and pesticides. Reports on worldwide research.

Insecticides of Plant Origin. J. T. Armason, et al., eds. American Chemical Society, 1155 16th St. N.W., Washington, DC 20036. (202) 872-4600; (800) 227-5558. 1989. Describes all about biochemical pesticides past, present and future.

Inside E.P.A. Weekly Report. Inside Washington Publishers, P.O. Box 7167, Ban Franklin Station, Washington, DC 20044. Weekly. Environmental policy trends.

Inside the Environmental Movement: Meeting the Leadership Challenge. Donald Snow, ed. Island Press, 1718 Connecticut Ave. N.W., Suite 300, Washington, DC 20009. (202) 232-7933. 1992. Book offers recommendations and concrete solutions which will make it an invaluable resource as the conservation community prepares to meet the formidable challenges that lie ahead.

Inside the EPA'S Superfund Report. Inside Washington Publishers, PO Box 7167, Ben Franklin Station, Washington, DC 20044. Biweekly. Liability for hazardous substances pollution and damages.

Inside the Poison Trade. Coronet/MTI Film & Video, 108 Wilmot Rd., Deerfield, IL 60015. 1990. This video shows what the Greenpeace organization is doing to stop chemical waste export to Africa, as well as the efforts of other organizations.

Inspecting Incoming Food Materials. U.S. Dept. of Health and Human Services, Public Health Service, Food and Drug Administration. U.S. G.P.O., Washington, DC 20401. (202) 512-0000. 1990. Covers food adulteration and inspection procedures.

Inspection System Guide (ISG). U.S. Deptartment of Agriculture, Food Safety and Inspection Service, 14 Independence Ave., SW, Washington, DC 20250. (202) 447-7454. Food adulteration and inspection as well as standards for food safety measures. Looseleaf format.

Inspector's Guide: To Be Used in the Evaluation of Municipal Wastewater Treatment Plants. U.S. G.P.O., Washington, DC 20401. (202) 512-0000. 1979. Sewage disposal plant evaluation and sewage purification.

Institute for 21st Century Studies. 1611 N. Kent St., Suite 610, Arlington, VA 22209. (703) 841-0048.

Institute for Alternative Agriculture. 9200 Edmonston Rd., Suite 117, Greenbelt, MD 20770. (301) 441-8777.

Institute for Community Design Analysis. 66 Clover Dr., Great Neck, NY 11021. (516) 773-4727.

Institute for Community Economic and Ecological Development. 1807 2nd St., Santa Fe, NM 87501. (505) 986-1401.

Institute for Earth Education. PO Box 288, Warrenville, IL 60555. (708) 393-3096.

Institute for Environmental Auditing. PO Box 23686, L'Enfant Plaza Station, Washington, DC 20026-3686. (703) 818-1000.

Institute for Environmental Management. Western Illinois University, College of Arts and Sciences, Macomb, IL 61455. (309) 298-1266.

Institute for Local Self-Reliance. 2425 18th St., N.W., Washington, DC 20009. (202) 232-4108.

Institute for Molecular Biology and Nutrition. Biology Department, MH 282, California State University, Fullerton, Fullerton, CA 92634. (714) 773-3637.

Institute for Polyacrylate Absorbents. 1330 Connecticut Ave., N.W., Suite 300, Washington, DC 20036. (202) 659-0060.

Institute for Research on Land and Water Resources. Newsletter. Institute for Research on Land and Water Resources, Pennsylvania State University, University Park, PA 16802. 1970-. Bimonthly.

Institute for Resource Management. 262 S. 200 W., Salt Lake City, UT 84101. (801) 322-0530.

Institute for the Human Environment. c/o Institute of International Education, 41 Sutter No. 510, San Francisco, CA 94104. (415) 362-6520.

Institute for Wildlife Research. c/o National Wildlife Fed., 1400 16th St., N.W., Washington, DC 20036. (703) 790-4483.

Institute of Arthropodology and Parasitology. Georgia Southern University, Biology Department, Landrum Box 8042, Statesboro, GA 30460-8042. (912) 681-5564.

Institute of Biological Chemistry. Washington State University, Clark Hall, Pullman, WA 99164. (509) 335-3412.

Institute of Biomedical Aquatic Studies. University of Florida, Box J-144, Gainesville, FL 32610. (904) 392-0921.

Institute of Chemical Waste Management. 1730 Rhode Island Ave., N.W., Suite 1000, Washington, DC 20036. (202) 659-4613.

Institute of Ecology. University of California, Davis, Davis, CA 95616. (916) 752-3026.

Institute of Ecosystem Studies. Box AB, Millbrook, NY 12545-0129. (914) 677-5976.

Institute of Environmental Sciences. 940 E. Northwest Hwy., Mount Prospect, IL 60056. (708) 255-1561.

Institute of Environmental Sciences' National Conference and Workshop, Environmental Stress Screening of Electronic Hardware Proceedings. The Institute of Environmental Sciences, 940 E. Northwest Highway, Mt. Prospect, IL 60056. (708) 255-1561. Environmental testing and environmental stress screening of electronic hardware.

Institute of Food Technologists. 221 N. LaSalle St., Chicago, IL 60601. (312) 782-8424.

Institute of Gas Technology. 1225 I. St., N.W., Suite 320, Washington, DC 20005. (202) 898-0711.

Institute of Marine Resources. University of California, La Jolla, CA 92093-0228. (619) 534-2868.

Institute of Marine Sciences. University of California, Santa Cruz, Applied Sciences, Room 272, Santa Cruz, CA 95064. (408) 459-4730.

The Institute of Metals. North American Publications Center, Old Post Rd., Brookfield, VT 05036. (802) 276-3162.

Institute of Noise Control Engineering. Box 3206, Arlington Branch, Poughkeepsie, NY 12603. (914) 462-4006.

Institute of Nuclear Materials Management. 60 Revere Dr., Suite 500, Northbrook, IL 60062. (708) 480-9080.

Institute of Nuclear Power Operations. 1100 Circle 75 Pkwy., Suite 1500, Atlanta, GA 30339. (040) 953-3600.

Institute of Paper Chemistry. 1043 E. South River St., Appleton, WI 54915. (414) 734-9251.

Institute of Resource Recovery. 1730 Rhode Island Ave., N.W., Suite 1000, Washington, DC 20036. (202) 659-4613.

Institute of Scrap Recycling Industries. 1627 K St., N.W., Suite 700, Washington, DC 20006. (202) 466-4050.

Institute of Scrap Recycling Industries–Membership Directory. Institute of Scrap Recycling Industries, 1627 K St., N.W., Suite 700, Washington, DC 20006. (202) 466-4050.

The Institute of the North American West. 110 Cherry St., Suite 202, Seattle, WA 98104. (206) 623-9597.

Institute of Transportation Engineers. 525 School St., S.W., Suite 410, Washington, DC 20024. (202) 554-8050.

Institute of Waste Equipment Distributors. 1730 Rhode Island Ave., N.W., Suite 1000, Washington, DC 20036. (202) 659-4613.

Institute of Water Resources. University of Connecticut, U-18, Storrs, CT 06269-4018. (203) 486-0335.

Instructional Resources Information System. Ohio State University, Environmental Quality Instructional Resources Center, 1200 Chambers Rd., Room 310, Columbus, OH 43212. (614) 292-6717. Training materials in the area of water resources, water quality, solid wastes, hazardous wastes, and toxic materials.

Instructions, Drainway. U.S. Department of the Interior, Bureau of Mines, 810 7th St., NW, Washington, DC 20241. (202) 501-9649. 1988. Problems and exercises relating to mine drainage.

Instrumental Analysis of Pollutants. C. N. Hewitt, ed. Elsevier Science Publishing Co., 655 Avenue of the Americas, New York, NY 10010. (212) 989-5800. 1991.

Instrumental Methods for Quality Assurance in Foods. Daniel Y. C. Fung and Richard F. Matthews. Marcell Dekker Inc., 270 Madison Ave., New York, NY 10016. (212) 696-9000; (800) 228-1160. 1991.

Instrumentation Handbook for Water & Wastewater Treatment Plants. Lewis Publishers, 121 S. Main St., Chelsea, MI 48118. (313) 475-8619. 1988. Water and sewage purification equipment and supplies.

Insulating Livestock and Other Farm Buildings. Don D. Jones. Purdue University, Cooperative Extension Service, AGAD Bldg., West Lafayette, IN 47907. (317) 494-8489. 1979.

Insulating Materials and Insulation. Mary Vance. Vance Bibliographies, PO Box 229, 112 N. Charter St., Monticello, IL 61856. (217) 762-3831. 1981.

Insurance Claims for Environmental Damages. Lynne M. Miller, ed. PennWell Books, PO Box 21288, Tulsa, OK 74121. (918) 831-9421; (800) 752-9764. 1989. Case management and technical strategies are presented for effectively handling environmental claims.

INTECOL–International Association for Ecology. Drawer E, Aiken, SC 29802. (803) 725-2472.

Integrated Approaches to Water Pollution. Joao Bau. Elsevier Science Publishing Co., 655 Avenue of the Americas, New York, NY 10010. (212) 984-5800. 1991. Integrated management strategies, policies for pollution control, groundwater pollution resulting from industrial, agricultural and urban sources, data and measurement.

Integrated Design of Water Treatment Facilities. Susumu Kawamura. John Wiley & Sons, Inc., 605 3rd Ave., New York, NY 10158-0012. (212) 850-6000. 1991. Covers research pilot studies and preliminary design studies, as well as the actual design, construction and plant management. Covers the entire project sequence, describing not only very basic and essential design criteria, but also how to design each phase to maximize overall efficiency while minimizing operation and maintenance costs.

Integrated Environmental Management. John Cairns, Jr. and Todd V. Crawford. Lewis Publishers, 2000 Corporate Blvd., N.W., Boca Raton, FL 33431. (407) 994-0555 or (800) 272-7737. 1991. Discusses the need for integrated environmental systems management, managing environmental risks, applied ecology, a strategy for the long-term management of the Savannah River site lands, and the role of the endangered species act in the conservation of biological diversity.

Integrated Pest Management. ANR Publications, University of California, 6701 San Pablo Ave., Oakland, CA 94608-1239. (510) 642-2431. 1990-. Irregular. Provides and orderly, scientifically based system for diagnosing, recording, evaluating, preventing, and treating pest problems in a variety of crops.

Integrated Pest Management. Jayne T. Maclean. National Agricultural Library, 10301 Baltimore Blvd., Beltsville, MD 20705-2351. (301) 504-5755. 1985.

Integrated Pest Management for the Home and Garden. Robert L. Metcalf. University of Illinois, Urbana, IL 61801. 1980.

Integrated Physical, Socio-Economic and Environmental Planning. Y. Ahmad and F. Muller, eds. Cassell PLC, Publishers Distribution Center, PO Box C831, Rutherford, NJ 07070. (201) 939-6064; (201) 939-6065. 1983.

Integrated Pollution Control in Europe and North America. Nigel Haigh. World Wildlife Fund, The Conservation Foundation, Publications Dept., 1250 Twenty-Fourth St., NW, Washington, DC 20037. (202) 203-4800. 1990.

Integrated Risk Information System - IRIS. US Environomental Protection Agency. Toxicology Data Network (TOXNET), 8600 Rockville Pike, Bethesda, MD 20894. (301) 496-1131. Quarterly. Effects of chemicals on human health and information on reference doses and carcinogen assessments.

Integrated Water Management. Bruce Mitchell, ed. Belhaven Press, 136 S. Broadway, Irvington, NY 10533. (914) 591-9111. 1990. Using case studies from the United States, New Zealand, Canada, Japan, England, Poland and Nigeria, this book surveys the principles and the practice of water management.

Integrating Environment into Business: A Guide to Policy Making and Implementation. Environment Council. Environment Council and 3M United Kingdom PLC, 80 York Way, London, England N1 9AG. 071 278 4736. 1990. Outcome of the Environmental Policy Workshop which was held in February 1990. Addresses the issues to help businesses and other organizations to implement environmental legislations and other behavioral changes that might affect their operations.

Intelligent Buildings. Michelle D. Gouin. Dow Jones-Irwin, Homewood, IL 1986. Strategies for technology and architecture in office buildings .

Inter-American Association of Sanitary Engineering and Environmental Sciences. 18729 Considine Dr., Brookeville, MD 20833. (301) 492-7686.

Interactions of Aquaculture, Marine Coastal Ecosystems, and Near-Shore Waters: A Bibliography. Deborah T. Hanfman. National Agricultural Library, 10301 Baltimore Blvd., Beltsville, MD 20705-2351. (301) 504-5755. Covers coastal ecology.

Interactions of Food Proteins. Nicholas Parris and Robert Bradford, eds. American Chemical Society, 1155 16th St. N.W., Washington, DC 20036. (202) 872-4600; (800) 227-5558. 1991. Discusses food proteins in great detail such as their composition, functionality, stability, properties, and other useful features.

Interceptor Sewers and Suburban Sprawl. National Technical Information Service, 5285 Port Royal Rd., Springfield, VA 22161. (703) 487-4650. 1974. The impact of construction grants on residential land use.

Interceptor Sewers and Urban Sprawl. Clark Binkley. Lexington Books, 866 3rd Ave., New York, NY 10022. (212) 702-2000. 1975.

An Interdisciplinary Bibliography of Freshwater Crayfishes. C. W. Hart, Jr. and Janice Clark. Smithsonian Institution Press, 470 L'Enfant Plaza, No. 7100, Washington, DC 20560. (800) 782-4612. 1987.

Interim Procedures for Estimating Risks Associated with Exposures to Mixtures of Chlorinated Dibenzo-RHO-Dioxins-and- Dibenzofurans. Judith S. Bellin. U.S. Environmental Protection Agency, 401 M St., SW, Washington, DC 20460. (202) 260-2090.

Internal Nutrition. University of Iowa Hospitals and Clinics. Iowa State University Press, 2121 S. State Ave., Ames, IA 50010. (515) 292-0140. 1990. A handbook for dieticians and health professionals.

International Air Data Base. U.S. Environmental Protection Agency, Office of Monitoring Systems and Quality Assurance, 401 M St., S.W., Washington, DC 20460. (202) 260-2090. Ambient air data from the World Health Organization and precipitation data from the World Meteorological Organization.

International Antarctic Glaciological Project. Geophysical and Polar Research Center, University of Wisconsin, Madison, WI 53706. (608) 262-1921.

International Aquaculture Foundation. 2440 Virginia Ave., N.W., No. D305, Washington, DC 20037. (202) 785-8215.

International Association for Bear Research and Management. ADF&G, 333 Raspberry Rd., Anchorage, AK 99518-1599. (907) 344-0541.

International Association for Ecology. Institute of Ecology, University of Georgia, Athens, GA 30606. (404) 542-2968.

International Association for Great Lakes Research. 2200 Bonisteel Blvd., University of Michigan, Ann Arbor, MI 48109-2099. (313) 747-1673.

International Association for the Advancement of Earth & Environmental Sciences. Northeastern Illinois University, Geography & Environmental Studies, 5500 N. St. Louis Ave., Chicago, IL 60625. (312) 794-2628.

International Association for the Physical Sciences of the Ocean. P.O. Box 1161, Del Mar, CA 92014-1161. (619) 481-0850.

International Association of Environmental Testing Laboratories. 1911 Ft. Myer Dr., Arlington, VA 22209. (703) 524-2427.

International Association of Fish & Wildlife Agencies. 444 N. Capitol St., N.W., Suite 534, Washington, DC 20001. (202) 624-7890.

International Association of Heat & Frost Insulators & Asbestos Workers. 1300 Connecticut Ave., N.W., Suite 505, Washington, DC 20036. (202) 785-2388.

International Association of Milk, Food, & Environmental Sanitarians. 502 E. Lincoln Way, Ames, IA 50010. (515) 232-6699.

International Association of Theoretical and Applied Limnology. c/o Dr. Robert G. Wetzel, Dept. of Biology, University of Michigan, Ann Arbor, MI 48109. (313) 936-3193.

International Bibliography of Acid Rain, 1977-1986. BIOSIS, 2100 Arch St., Philadelphia, PA 19103-1399. (215) 587-4800. 1987. Contains more than 3,900 references to literature dating from 1977 through 1986.

International Bio-Energy Directory and Handbook. P. F. Bente, Jr. , ed. The Bio-Energy Council, Suite 825 A, 1625 Eye St. NW, Washington, DC 20006. 1984.

International Bio-Environmental Foundation. 15300 Ventura Blvd., Suite 405, Sherman Oaks, CA 91403. (818) 907-5483.

International Bird Research Center. 699 Potter St., Berkeley, CA 94710. (415) 841-9086.

International Board of Environmental Medicine. 2114 Martingale Dr., Norman, OK 73072. (405) 329-8437.

International Bottled Water Association. 113 N. Henry St., Alexandria, VA 22314. (703) 683-5213.

An International Census of the Coniferae, I. John Silba. Moldenke, Plainfield, NJ 1984.

International Center for the Solution of Environmental Problems. 535 Lovett Blvd., Houston, TX 77006. (713) 527-8711.

International Clearinghouse for Environmental Technologies. 12600 West Colfax Ave., Suite C-310, Lakewood, CO 80215. (303) 233-1248.

International Co-ordinating Council of the Programme on Man and the Biosphere, 11th session. Final Report. UNESCO, 7, place de Fontenoy, Paris, France F-75700. (331) 45 68 40 67. 1990. MAB Report series no. 62. Report of the Council session held in Paris 12-16, November 1990.

International Commission on Human Ecology and Ethnology. Box 3495, Grand Central Station, New York, NY 10163.

International Commission on Radiation Units and Measurements. 7910 Woodmont Ave., Suite 800, Bethesda, MD 20814. (301) 657-2652.

International Committee for Coal Petrology. Energy and Fuels Res. Center, 517 Deike Bldg., Pennsylvania State University, University Park, PA 16802. (814) 865-6544.

International Conservation Institute. 45 Elm St., Byfield, MA 01922. (617) 465-5389.

The International Control of Marine Pollution. J. Tiamgenis. Oceana Publications Inc., 75 Main St., Dobbs Ferry, NY 10522. (914) 693-8100. 1990. 2 vols. Focuses on conventional law on marine pollution, particularly from dumping and ships, within the context of a wider law-making process. The main body of the book is devoted to an analysis of international conventions, with reference to some 450 books and articles on the subject.

International Council for Bird Preservation, U.S. Section. c/o World Wildlife Fund, 1250 24th St. N.W., Washington, DC 20037. (202) 778-9563.

International Crane Foundation. E-11376 Shady Lane Rd., Baraboo, WI 53913-9778. (608) 356-9462.

International Desalination Association. P.O. Box 387, Topsfield, MA 01983. (508) 356-2727.

International Directory for Sources of Environmental Information. United States National Focal Point for UNEP/INFOTERRA, Environmental Protection Agency, 401 M St., S.W., Rm 2903, Washington, DC 20460. (202) 382-5917.

International Directory of Acid Deposition Researchers. National Technical Information Service, 5285 Port Royal Rd., Springfield, VA 22161. (703) 487-4650. Irregular.

International Directory of Contract Laboratories. Edward M. Jackson. Marcel Dekker, Inc., 270 Madison Ave., New York, NY 10016. (212) 696-9000; (800) 228-1160. 1989. List of toxicology laboratories that list specific tests conducted on chemicals, foods, prescription drugs, over-the-counter drugs, cosmetics, and household products. Alphabetical arrangement by names of laboratories. Each entry gives address, year founded, and tests. Contains geographical listing. Miscellaneous indexes.

International Directory of Human Ecologists. Richard J. Borden. Society for Human Ecology, College of the Atlantic, Bar Harbor, MA 04609. (207) 288-5015. 1989.

International Directory of New and Renewable Energy: Information Sources and Research Centres. UNESCO, 7 place de Fontenoy, 75700 Paris, France F-75700. 1986. Second edition. Contains a total of 3,956 entries representing 156 countries. Profiles of the organizations associated with new and renewable energy areas are included.

International Directory of Occupational Safety and Health Institutions. International Labour Office, 49 Sheridan Ave., Albany, NY 12210. (518) 436-9686. 1990.

International Ecology Society. 1471 Barclay St., St. Paul, MN 55106. (612) 774-4971.

International Environment Reporter. Bureau of National Affairs, 1231 25th St. N.W., Washington, DC 20037. (202) 452-4200. Monthly. International environment law and policy in the major industrial nations.

International Environmental Affairs. University Press of New England, 17 1/2 Lebanon Street, Hanover, NH 03755. (603) 646-3340. Quarterly. Issues on management of natural resources.

International Environmental Bureau. 61, route de Chene, CH-1208, Geneva, Switzerland (412) 2786-5111.

International Environmental Diplomacy. John E. Carroll. Cambridge University Press, 40 W. 20th St., New York, NY 10011. (212) 924-3900. 1988.

International Environmental Information Sources. Pira, Randalls Rd., Leatherhead, England KT22 7RU. 0372 376161. 1990. Contains valuable business and technical contacts for environmental information sources worldwide. Information sources cover the following subjects: Air, noise, water and land pollution; waste control and disposal; recycling; energy recovery; nature conservation. Informational sources include associations, research organizations, legislative/regulatory agencies, directories, statistics, on-line databases, magazines and news letters in 24 countries.

International Environmental Law. Robert J. Munro. Oceana Publications Inc., 75 Main St., Dobbs Ferry, NY 10522. (914) 693-8100. 1990. This international law bibliography extends beyond the usual legal sources, and includes a diverse array of law-related and non- law publications that discuss the topic of the world's environment and international law.

International Environmental Law and Regulation. Butterworth Legal Publishers, 289 E. 5th St., St. Paul, MN 55101. (612) 227-4200. Covers issues in environmental law. Looseleaf format.

International Environmental Policy: Emergence and Dimensions. Lynton Keith Caldwell. Duke University Press, College Sta., Box 6697, Durham, NC 27708. (919) 684-2173. 1990.

International Erosion Control Association. Box 4904, Steamboat Springs, CO 80477. (303) 879-3010.

International Federation of Professional & Technical Engineers. 8701 Georgia Ave., Suite 701, Silver Spring, MD 20910. (301) 565-9016.

International Food Additives Council. 5775 Peachtree-Dunwoody Rd., Suite 500-D, Atlanta, GA 30342. (404) 252-3663.

International Food Information Council. 1100 Connecticut Ave., N.W., Suite 430, Washington, DC 20036. (202) 296-6540.

International Genetics Federation. c/o Prof. Peter R. Day, Center for Agricultural Molecular Biology, Cook College, P.O. Box 231, Rutgers University, New Brunswick, NJ 08903. (908) 932-8165.

International Green Front Report. Michael Pilarski. Friends of the Trees, PO Box 1064, Tonasket, WA 98855. (509) 486-4726. 1988. Irregular. Organizations and periodicals dealing with sustainable forestry and agriculture.

International Institute for Energy Conservation. 420 C St., N.E., Washington, DC 20002. (202) 546-3388.

International Joint Commission Report. International Joint Commission, 2001 S St. NW, 2nd floor, Washington, DC 20440. (202) 673-6222. Information on water quality in the Great Lakes system.

International Journal of Antimicrobial Agents. Elsevier Science Publishing Co., 655 Avenue of the Americas, New York, NY 10010. (212) 984-5800. Bimonthly. Physical, chemical, pharmacological, in vitro and clinical properties of individual antimicrobial agents, antiviral agents, antiparasitic agents, antibacterial agents, antifungal agents, and immunotherapy.

International Journal of Biosocial and Medical Research. Life Sciences Press, P.O. Box 1174, Takoma, WA 98401-1174. (206) 922-0442. Semiannual. Deals with psychological and psychobiological aspects of environments.

International Journal of Biotechnology. Inderscience Enterprises Ltd., World Trade Center Building, 110 Avenue Louis Casai, Case Postale 306, Geneva-Aeroport, Switzerland CH 1215. (44) 908-314248. Quarterly. Authoritative source of information in the field of biotechnology which establishes channels of communication between policy makers, executives in industry.

International Journal of Energy, Environment, Economics. Nova Science Publishers, Inc., 283 Commack Rd., Ste. 300, Commack, NY 11725. (516) 499-3103. 1991-. Quarterly. Aims to provide a vehicle for the multidisciplinary field of energy-environment economics between research scientists, engineers and economists. The areas covered would be technological, environmental, economic and social feasibility.

International Journal of Environment and Pollution. Inderscience Enterprises Ltd., World Trade Center Bldg., 110 Avenue Louis Casai, Case Postale 306, Geneva-Airport, Switzerland CH-1215. (44) 908-314248. 1991-. Publishes original state-of-the-art articles, book reviews, and technical papers in the areas of: Environmental policies, protection, institutional aspects of pollution, risk assessments of all forms of pollution, protection of soil and ground water, waste disposal strategies, ecological impact of pollutants and other related topics.

International Journal of Environmental Studies. Gordon and Breach Science Publishers, Inc., 270 8th Ave., New York, NY 10011. (212) 206-8900. Irregular. Science, technology and policy relating to the environment.

International Journal of Food Science & Technology. Blackwell Scientific Publications, PO Box 87, Oxford, England OX2 0DT. 44 0865 79115. Quarterly.

The International Journal of Global Energy Issues. Inderscience Enterprises Ltd., World Trade Center Building, 110 Avenue Louis Casai, Case Postale 306, Geneva-Airport, Switzerland CH-1215 (44) 908-314248. 1989-. Quarterly. Provides a forum and an authoritative source of information in the field of energy issues and related topics.

International Journal of Hydrogen Energy. Pergamon Microforms International, Inc., Fairview Park, Elmsford, NY 10523. (914) 592-7720. Monthly.

International Journal of Plant Nutrition, Plant Chemistry, Soil Microbiology and Soil-Bourne Plant Diseases. Kluwer Academic Publishers, 101 Philip Dr., Assinippi Park, Norwell, MA 02061. (617) 871-6600. 1948-.

International Journal of Sustainable Development. Inderscience Enterprises Ltd., World Trade Center Building, 110 Avenue Louis Casai, Case Postale 306, Geneva-Aeroport, Switzerland CH 1215. (44) 908-314248. Quarterly. Forum to provide and authoritative source of information in the field of sustainable development and related fields.

International Lead Zinc Research Organization. 2525 Meridian Pkwy., P.O. Box 12036, Research Triangle Park, NC 27709. (919) 361-4647.

International Marinelife Alliance. 94 Station St., Suite 645, Hingham, MA 02043. (617) 383-1209.

International Nuclear Information System. International Atomic Energy Agency, INIS Section, Vienna International Centre, P.O. Box 100, Vienna, Austria A-1400. 43 (222) 23602882.

International Ocean Pollution Symposium. Department of Chemical and Environmental Engineering, Florida Institute of Tech., Melbourne, FL 32901. (407) 768-8000.

International Oceanographic Foundation. 4600 Rickenbacker Causeway, P.O. Box 499900, Miami, FL 33149-9900. (305) 361-4888.

International Oil Spill Control Directory. Cutter Information Corp., 37 Broadway, Arlington, MA 02174-5537. (617) 648-8700.

The International Osprey Foundation. P.O. Box 250, Sanibel, FL 33957. (813) 472-5218.

International Oxygen Manufacturers Association. P.O. Box 16248, Cleveland, OH 44116-0248. (216) 228-2166.

International Ozone Association. Pan American Committee, 83 Oakwood Ave., Norwalk, CT 06850. (203) 847-8169.

International Permaculture Solutions Journal. Yankee Permaculture, P.O. Box 16683, Wichita, KS 67216. Irregular. Tools for sustainable lifestyles, extensive green pages, and resources directory.

International Pesticide Applicators Association. Box 1377, Milton, WA 98354. (206) 922-9437.

International Petroleum Abstracts. John Wiley & Sons, Ltd., Baffers Lane, Chichester, Sussex, England PO1 91UD. 44 (243) 770215.

International Petroleum Annual. U.S. Department of Energy, Integrated Technical Information System, P.O. Box 62, Oak Ridge, TN 37831. (615) 576-1222.

International Plant Biotech Network. c/o TCCP, Dept. of Biology, Colorado State University, Fort Collins, CO 80523. (303) 491-6996.

International Pollution Control. Scranton Pub. Co., 434 S. Wabash Ave., Chicago, IL 60605. 1972-. Quarterly.

International Protection of the Environment. Bernard Ruster and Bruno Simma. Oceana Publications Inc., 75 Main St., Dobbs Ferry, NY 10522. (914) 693-8100. 1990. The 31 volume set is now in a loose-leaf format that will bring and keep the document up-to-date. Contains the documents of environmental law in the world.

International Regulation of Whaling. Patricia Birnie. Oceana Publications Inc., 75 Main St., Dobbs Ferry, NY 10522. (914) 693-8100. 1985. A chronological account of the development of international law pertaining to the regulation of whaling. Traces the growing relationship of the regulation of whaling to the development of other relevant laws and institutions for the conservation of migratory species.

International Research Expeditions. 140 University Dr., Menlo Park, CA 94025. (415) 323-4228.

International Resource Management. S. Anderssen and Willy Ostreng, eds. Belhaven Press, 136 S. Broadway, Irvington, NY 10533. (914) 591-9111. 1990. Analyzes the relationship between scientific knowledge and policy in the management of natural resources at the international level. Presents current practice and problems. Problems such as ozone layer protection, whaling, and air pollution.

International Rivers Network. 301 Broadway, Suite B, San Francisco, CA 94133. (415) 986-4694.

International Sanitary Supply Association–Membership Directory. 7373 N. Lincoln Ave., Lincolnwood, IL 60646. (708) 982-0800. Annual.

International Snow Leopard Trust. 16463 S.E. 35th St., Bellevue, WA 98008.

International Society for Animal Rights Support. International Society for Animal Rights, Inc., 421 S. State St., Clarks Summit, PA 18411. (717) 586-2200. Bimonthly.

International Society for Ecological Modeling/North American Chapter. Water Quality Division, South Florida Water Management District, PO Box 24680, West Palm Beach, FL 33416. (407) 686-8800.

International Society for Environmental Toxicology and Cancer. P.O. Box 134, Park Forest, IL 60466. (312) 755-2080.

International Society for Fluoride Research. P.O. Box 692, Warren, MI 48090. (313) 375-5544.

International Society for Plant Molecular Biology. Biochemistry Dept., University of Georgia, Athens, GA 30602. (404) 542-3239.

International Society for the Preservation of the Tropical Rainforest. 3931 Camino de la Cumbre, Sherman Oaks, CA 91423. (818) 788-2002.

International Society for the Protection of Mustangs and Burros. c/o Helen A. Reilly, 11790 Deodar Way, Reno, NV 89506. (702) 972-1989.

International Society of Animal Rights. 421 S. State St., Clark's Summit, PA 18411. (715) 586-2200.

International Society of Arboriculture. P.O. Box 908, 303 W. University Ave., Urbana, IL 61801. (217) 328-2032.

International Society of Chemical Ecology. University of South Florida, Dept. of Biology, Tampa, FL 33620. (813) 974-2336.

International Society of Toxinology. Dept. of Pharmacology and Toxicology, School of Pharmacy, University of Connecticut, Storrs, CT 06269. (203) 486-2213.

International Society of Tropical Foresters, Inc. 5400 Grosvenor Ln., Bethesda, MD 20814. (301) 897-8720.

International Solar Energy Intelligence Report. Business Publishers, Inc., 951 Pershing Dr., Silver Spring, MD 20910. (301) 587-6300.

International Technologies for Hazardous Waste Site Cleanup. Thomas Nunno, et al. Noyes Publications, 120 Mill Rd., Park Ridge, NJ 07656. (201) 391-8484. 1990. Identifies 95 international technologies that could be utilized for hazardous waste site remediation within the United States.

International Trade in Endangered Species of Wild Fauna and Flora: Amendment to the Convention of March 3, 1973, Done at Bonn June 22, 1979. United States Dept. of State. U.S. G.P.O., Washington, DC 20401. (202) 512-0000. 1991. Law and legislation relating to endangered species and wild animal trade.

International Tree Crops Institute U.S.A. P.O. Box 4460, Davis, CA 95617. (916) 753-4535.

International Union for the Conservation of Nature, Natural Resources Primate Specialists Group. Dept. of Anatomical Sciences, HSC, State University of New York, Stony Brook, NY 11794. (516) 444-3132.

International Union of Petroleum & Industrial Workers. 8131 E. Rosencrans Ave., Paramount, CA 90723. (213) 630-6232.

International Water Power and Dam Construction. Reed Business Pub., 205 E. 42d St., New York, NY 10017. 1949-. Monthly. Formerly Water Power and includes practical and theoretical articles and news concerning all aspects of hydro-electric developments and large dam construction throughout the world. Coverage of research into hydraulic machinery, wave and tidal power.

International Water Report. Water Information Center, Inc., 125 East Bethpage Road, Plainview, NY 11803. (516) 249-7634. Quarterly. Covers water works and topics done in Europe, Asia, South America.

International Water Resources Association. 205 N. Mathews Ave., University of Illinois, Urbana, IL 61801. (217) 333-0536.

International Who's Who in Energy and Nuclear Sciences. Longman Editorial Team. Longman, c/o Gale Research Inc., 835 Penobscot Bldg., Detroit, MI 48226-4094. (313) 961-2242. 1983. Deals with the subject areas of energy and nuclear science. Gives professional biographical profiles of over 3800 individuals arranged by surname from A to Z. Also includes a country and topic list of the same people.

International Wild Waterfowl Association. c/o Nancy Collins, Hidden Lake Waterfowl, 5614 River Styx Rd., Medina, OH 44256. (216) 725-8782.

International Wildlife. National Wildlife Federation, 1400 16th Street, NW, Washington, DC 20036. (202) 797-6800. Bimonthly. Covers international conservation activities.

International Wildlife Coalition. 634 N. Falmouth Hwy., P.O. Box 388, Falmouth, MA 02556. (508) 564-9980.

International Wildlife Rehabilitation Council. 1171 Kellog St., Suisun, CA 94585. (707) 428-IWRC.

International Wildlife Trade: Whose Business Is It?. Sarah Fitzgerald. World Wildlife Fund, The Conservation Foundation, Publications Dept., 1250 Twenty-Fourth St., NW, Washington, DC 20037. (202) 293-4800. 1989.

Interprofessional Council on Environmental Design. c/o Israel Stallman, American Institute of Certified Planners, 1776 Massachusetts Ave., N.W., Washington, DC 20036. (202) 872-0611.

Intersections. Center for Urban Environment Studies, Rensselaer Polytechnic Institute, Troy, NY 12180-3590. Annual. Urban and environmental studies.

Intersociety Committee on Methods for Air Sampling and Analysis. 12113 Shropshire Blvd., Austin, TX 78753. (512) 835-5118.

Interstate Conference on Water Policy. 955 L'Enfant Plaza, 6th Floor, Washington, DC 20024. (202) 466-7287.

Interstate Natural Gas Association of America. 555 13thSt., N.W., Ste. 300 W., Washington, DC 20004. (202) 626-3200.

Interstate Oil Compact Commission. Box 53127, Oklahoma City, OK 73152. (405) 525-3556 OR (800) 822-4015.

Interstate Oil Compact Commission 1990 Directory. Interstate Oil and Gas Compact Commission, 990 NE 23d St., PO Box 53127, Oklahoma City, OK 73152. (405) 525-3556 or (800) 822-4015. 1990. Includes addresses and telephone numbers of members.

Interstate Solar Coordination Council. 900 American Center Bldg., ST. Paul, MN 55101. (612) 296-4737.

Into Adolescence. Caring for Our Planet and Our Health: A Curriculum for Grades 5-8. Lisa K. Hunter. Network Publications, PO Box 1830, Santa Cruz, CA 95061-1830. (408) 438-4060. 1991.

Into Harmony with the Planet: The Delicate Balance Between Industry and the Environment. Michael Allaby. Bloomsbury Pub., 2 Soho Sq., London, England W1V 5DE. SW15 1990. Describes the ecosystem and its delicate balance. Also discusses the effect industry and its pollutants on the environment.

Into the Amazon: The Struggle for the Rain Forest. Augusta Dwyer. Sierra Club Books, 100 Bush St., San Francisco, CA 94104. (415) 291-1600. 1991. Summarizes the life-styles of the various socioeconomic classes of people who live in the Amazon Basin.

Introduction of High Performance Liquid Chromatography. John Wiley & Sons, Inc., 605 Third Ave., New York, NY 10158-0012. (212) 850-0660.

Introduction to Characterization and Testing of Catalysts. Academic Press, c/o Harcourt Brace Jovanovich Inc., 6277 Sea Harbor Dr., Orlando, FL 32887. (800) 346-8648. Analysis and industrial applications of catalysts.

Introduction to Environmental Engineering and Science. Gilbert M. Masters. Prentice-Hall, Rte. 9W, Englewood Cliffs, NJ 07632. (201) 592-2000; (800) 639-2863. 1991. An introduction to the fundamental principles common to most environmental problems is followed by major sections on water pollution, hazardous waste and risk assessment, waste treatment technologies, air pollution, global climate change, hazardous substances, and risk analysis, includes problems.

Introduction to Environmental Management. Elsevier Science Publishing Co., 655 Avenue of the Americas, New York, NY 10010. (212) 984-5800. 1991. Environmental protection and environmental aspects of agriculture.

An Introduction to Environmental Pattern Analysis. P. J. A. Howard. Parthenon Group Inc., 120 Mill Rd., Park Ridge, NJ 07656. (201) 391-6796. 1991. Explains the basic mathematics of the most widely used ordination and cluster analysis methods, types of data to which they are suited and their advantages and disadvantages.

An Introduction to LP-Gases. W.W. Clark. Butane-Propane News, 338 W. Foothill Blvd., Arcadia, CA 91006. (818) 357-2168. 1983.

Introduction to Thermal Analysis: Techniques and Applications. Michael E. Brown. Chapman & Hall, 29 W. 35th St., New York, NY 10001-2291. (212) 244-3336. 1988.

An Introduction to Tropical Rain Forests. T. C. Whitmore. Oxford University Press, 200 Madison Ave., New York, NY 10016. (212) 679-7300; (800) 334-4249. 1990. Describes the world's tropical rainforests, their structure and functioning, their value to humans, and what is being done to them.

Introduction to Water Quality Standards. U.S. Environmental Protection Agency, Office of Water, 401 M St. SW, Washington, DC 20460. (202) 260-2090. 1988.

Introductory Chemistry for the Environmental Sciences. S. J. de Mora, et al. Cambridge University Press, 40 W. 20th St., New York, NY 10011. (212) 924-3900; (800) 227-0247. 1991.

An Introductory Guide to the New Hampshire Department of Environmental Services. New Hampshire Dept. of Environmental Services, PO Box 95, Concord, NH 03301. (603)271-3503. 1988.

Inventory of Open Dumps. Office of Solid Waste, Environmental Protection Agency, Washington, DC 20460. (202) 475-8710. 1984. Covers factory and trade waste and refuse and refuse disposal.

Inventory of Power Plants in the United States. Department of Energy, 1000 Independence Ave., N.W., Washington, DC 20585. (202) 586-8800. Annual. Inventory of individual electric power plants operating, added, and retired and planned for operation. Includes information on ownership, capacity, and energy source.

Inventory of Reports. National Technical Information Service, 5285 Port Royal Rd., Washington, DC 22161. (703) 487-4650. Annual. Environmental impact analysis.

Investigating Hydrocarbon Spills. James M. Davidson. Lewis Publishers, 2000 Corporate Blvd., N.W., Boca Raton, FL 33431. (407) 994-0555 or (800) 272-7737. 1991. Includes regulatory reviews, scope of investigations, identification of a problem, phased approach and preparation for remediation.

Investigation of Shredded Pesticide Containers for Recycling. Materials and Testing Department, Alberta Research Council for Alberta Environment, National Technical Information Service, 5285 Port Royal Rd., Springfield, VA 22161. (703) 487-4650. 1990.

An Investigation of the International Toxic Waste Trade. Christoph Hilz. Van Nostrand Reinhold, 115 Fifth Ave., New York, NY 10003. (212) 254-3232. 1992. Hazardous waste management industry, environmental aspects, and law and legislation.

Investigations in Fish Control. Verdel K. Dawson. U.S. Department of the Interior, Fish and Wildlife Service, Washington, DC 20240. (202) 343-5634. 1982. Effect of lampricides and rotenone on fishes.

Investing in Biological Diversity: U.S. Research and Conservation Efforts in Developing Countries. Janet A. Abramovitz. World Resources Institute, 1709 New York Ave. N.W., Washington, DC 20006. (800) 822-0504. 1991. Analyzes funding for 1,093 projects in 100 developing countries. Special features of the report include multiyear funding comparisons by region and country, type of conservation activity, funder, and implementor. Also examines the funding for areas identified as priorities for biodiversity conservation.

Investor's Environmental Report. Investor Responsibility Research Center, 1755 Massachusetts Ave., NW, Suite 600, Washington, DC 20036. (202) 234-7500. Quarterly. Environmental topics of particular relevance to the investment and corporate communities.

Iodine Species in Reactor Effluents and in the Environment. Paul Voillegue. Electric Power Research Institute, 3412 Hillview Ave., Palo Alto, CA 94304. (415) 965-4081. 1979. Environmental aspects of radioactive waste disposal.

Iowa 1990 Environmental Resource Handbook. Environmental Advocates, Iowa City, IA 1990.

Iowa Conservationist. Iowa Dept. of Natural Resources, Wallace St. Office Building, Des Moines, IA 50319-0034. (515) 281-6159. Monthly. Outdoor recreation opportunities, fish, wildlife, parks and environmental issues.

Iron and Steel Society. 410 Commonwealth Dr., Warrendale, PA 15086. (412) 776-1535.

Irrigation and Drainage Abstracts. C. A. B. International, 845 North Park Ave., Tucson, AZ 85719. (602) 621-7897 or (800) 258-4841. 1975-. Quarterly. Subject areas scanned are: water management, irrigation of crop plants, drainage, soil water relations, plant water relations, salinity and toxicity problems, soil condition, evaporotranspiration, evaporation, land use, streams, water quality, and other related areas.

Irrigation Association. 1911 N. Fort Myer Dr., Suite 1009, Arlington, VA 22209. (703) 524-1200.

Irrigation-Induced Water Quality Problems. National Academy Press, 2101 Constitution Ave. NW, PO Box 285, Washington, DC 20418. (202) 334-3313. 1989.

Irrigation: International Guide to Organizations and Institutions. International Irrigation Information Center, Distr: Pergamon Press, Maxwell House, Fairview Park, Elmsford, NY 10523. (914) 592-7720. 1980. Includes 864 organizations from 109 countries concerned with irrigation.

Irrigation Science. Springer International, 44 Hartz Way, Seacaucus, NJ 07094. (201) 348-4033.

Irrigation with Treated Sewage Effluent: Management for Environmental Protection. A. Feigin. Springer-Verlag, 175 5th Ave., New York, NY 10010. (212) 460-1500 or (800) 777-4643. 1991. Use of treated sewage effluent as an irrigation source for agriculture.

IRSS. U.S. Environmental Protection Agency, CIS Project, 401 M St., S.w., Washington, DC 20460. (202) 260-2090.

Is Paraquat Sprayed Marihuana Harmful or Not?. U.S. G.P.O., Washington, DC 20401. (202) 512-0000. 1980. Hearing before the select committee on Narcotics and Abuse Control, House of Representatives, 96th Congress, first session, November 29, 1979. Discusses the effects of sprayed marihuana effects on humans.

Is Your Water Safe to Drink?. Raymond Gabler. Consumer Union U.S., New York, NY 1988. Health, microbial, inorganic, and organic hazards in drinking water, chlorination, bottled water, and water shortages.

Islands under Siege: National Parks and the Politics of External Threats. John C. Freemuth. University Press of Kansas, 329 Carruth, Lawrence, KS 66045. (913) 864-4154. 1991. Outlines a diverse set of political strategies, evaluating each in terms of environmental effectiveness and political feasibility.

Isolating Organic Water Pollutants: XAD Resins, Urethane Foams, Solvent Extraction. Ronald G. Webb. National Environmental Research Center, Corvallis, OR 1975. Isolation and purification of water pollutants.

Issues in Food Irradiation. Susan Mills. Science Council of Canada, Publications Office, Ottawa, ON, Canada 1987.

It's Time to Go Wild. American Wildlands, 7600 E. Arapahoe Rd., Suite 114, Englewood, CO 80112. (303) 771-0380. Quarterly. Protection and proper use of wilderness lands and rivers.

It's Your Choice: Small-Community Wastewater Options. U.S. Environmental Protection Agency, Office of Water, 401 M St. SW, Washington, DC 20460. (202) 260-2090. 1989.

IUCN Amphibia-Reptilia Red Data Book. B. Groombridge. World Conservation Union, IUCN Publications Services Unit, 181a Huntingdon Road, Cambridge, England CB3 0DJ. (0223) 277894. 1982.

IUCN Bulletin. World Conservation Union, IUCN Publications Services Unit, 181a Huntingdon Road, Cambridge, England CB3 0DJ. (0223) 277894. Quarterly. News and information from the world's largest and most influential network of governmental and independent conservation interests.

IUCN Invertebrate Red Data Book. S.M. Wells. World Conservation Union, IUCN Publications Services Unit, 181a Huntingdon Road, Cambridge, England CB3 0DJ. (0223) 277894. 1983.

IUCN Mammal Red Data Book: The Americas and Australasia. J. Thornback. World Conservation Union, IUCN Publications Services Unit, 181a Huntingdon Road, Cambridge, England CB3 0DJ. (0223) 277894. 1982.

IUCN Plant Red Data Book. G. Lucas. World Conservation Union, IUCN Publications Services Unit, 181a Huntingdon Road, Cambridge, England CB3 0DJ. (0223) 277894. 1978.

IUCN Red List of Threatened Animals. IUCN Conservation Monitoring Centre. World Conservation Union, Ave. du Mont-Blanc, CH-1196, Gland, Sweden 022-647181. 1988. Details on rare animals and endangered species.

IUCN Red List of Threatened Animals. World Conservation Monitoring Centre. World Conservation Union, IUCN Publications Services Unit, 181a Huntingdon Road, Cambridge, England CB3 0DJ. (0223) 277894. 1990. Aims to focus attention of the plight of the earth's vanishing wildlife.

IWED Guide to Waste Management Distributors. Institute of Waste Equipment Distributors, National Solid Wastes Management Association, 1730 Rhode Island Ave., N.W., Suite 1000, Washington, DC 20036. (202) 659-4613.

The Izaak Walton League of America. 1401 Wilson Boulevard, Level B, Arlington, VA 22209. (703) 528-1818.

J. N. "Ding" Darling Foundation. P.O. Box 703, Des Moines, IA 50303. (305) 361-9788.

Jamie Whitten Delta States Research Center. PO Box 225, Stoneville, MS 3877-0225. (601) 686-5231.

The Jane Goodall Institute for Wildlife Research, Education and Conservation. P.O. Box 41720, Tucson, AZ 85717. (602) 325-1211.

Japanese Biotechnology. R. T. Yuan and M. Dibner. Stockton Press, 257 Park Ave. S, New York, NY 10010. (212) 673-4400 or (800) 221-2123. 1991. Comprehensive study of the development of biotechnology in Japan. Covers a broad spectrum of topics including government policy, the biological R & D establishment, industrial activities in biotechnology, technological transfer, and finance.

The Jessie Smith Noyes Foundation. 16 E. 34th St., New York, NY 10016. (212) 684-6577.

Job Safety and Health. Bureau of National Affairs, 1231 25th St. NW, Washington, DC 20037. (202) 452-4200. Biweekly. Covers job safety and health laws.

John Muir Institute for Environmental Studies. 743 Wilson St., Napa, CA 94559. (707) 252-8333.

Joint Facility for Regional Ecosystem Analysis. University of Colorado-Boulder, Boulder, CO 80309. (303) 492-7303.

Joseph M. Long Marine Laboratory. University of California, Santa Cruz, 100 Shaffer, Santa Cruz, CA 95060. (408) 459-2464.

Journal - American Water Works Association. American Water Works Association, 6666 W. Quincy Ave., Denver, CO 80235. (303) 794-7711. Monthly. Includes regulatory summaries, conference information and job listings. Has state chapters, annual meetings, and special publications.

The Journal of Adhesion. Gordon and Breach Science Publishers, Inc., 270 8th Ave., New York, NY 10011. (212) 206-8900. Quarterly. Phenomenon of adhesion and its practical applications.

Journal of Adhesion Science and Technology. VNU Science Press, VSP BV., PO Box 346, Zeist, Netherlands 3700 A H. (03404)25790. Quarterly. Focus on theories of adhesion; surface energetics; fracture mechanics. Development and application of surface-sensitive methods to study adhesion phenomena, and other related topics.

Journal of Agricultural and Food Chemistry. American Chemical Society, 1155 16th St. N.W., Washington, DC 20036. (202) 872-4600; (800) 227-5558. 1953-. Monthly. Contains documentation of significant advances in the science of agriculture and food chemistry.

Journal of Agricultural Engineering Research. Academic Press, c/o Harcourt Brace Jovanovich Inc., 6277 Sea Harbor Dr., Orlando, FL 32887. (800) 346-8648. Eight times a year.

Journal of Air and Waste Management Association. Air and Waste Management Association, P.O. Box 2861, Pittsburgh, PA 15230. (412) 232-3444. Monthly. Current events in air pollution control and hazardous wastes.

Journal of American Mining Congress. American Mining Congress, 1920 N Street, NW, Suite 300, Washington, DC 20036. (202) 861-2800. Monthly. Contains information on the mining industry.

Journal of American Planning Association. American Planning Association, 1776 Massachusetts Avenue, NW, Suite 704, Washington, DC 20036. (202) 872-0611. Quarterly. Represents the interests of professional urban and regional planners.

Journal of Analytical Toxicology. Preston Publications, PO Box 48312, 7800 Merrimac, Niles, IL 60648. (708) 965-0566. Bimonthly. Articles on industrial toxicology, environmental pollution and pharmaceuticals.

The Journal of Animal Ecology. Blackwell Scientific Publications, PO Box 87, Oxford, England OX2 0DT. 44 0865 791155. Three times a year.

The Journal of Applied Bacteriology. Academic Press, c/o Harcourt Brace Jovanovich Inc., 6277 Sea Harbor Dr., Orlando, FL 32887. (800) 346-8648. Monthly. Deals with agricultural, biological and environmental aspects of bacteriology.

Journal of Applied Meteorology. American Meteorological Society, 45 Beacon Street, Boston, MA 02108. (617) 227-2425. Monthly. Articles on the relationship between weather and environment.

Journal of Applied Physiology. American Physiology Society, 9650 Rockville Pike, Bethesda, MD 20814-3991. Monthly. Covers physiological aspects of exercise, adaption, respiration, and exertion.

Journal of Arboriculture. Society of Arboriculture, 303 W. University Ave., PO Box 908, Urbana, IL 61801. (217) 328-2032. 1975-. Monthly.

Journal of Arid Environmentals. Academic Press, c/o Harcourt Brace Jovanovich Inc., 6277 Sea Harbor Dr., Orlando, FL 32887. (800) 346-8648. Quarterly. Ecology of deserts and arid zones.

Journal of Atmospheric Sciences. American Meteorology Society, 45 Beacon Street, Boston, MA 02108. (617) 227-2425. Biweekly. Articles on the atmosphere of the earth and other planets.

Journal of Biochemical Toxicology. VCH Publishers, 303 NW 12th Ave., Deerfield Beach, FL 33442-1788. (305) 428-5566. 1986. Topics in biochemistry and biochemical toxicology.

Journal of Biogeography. Blackwell Scientific Publications Inc., 3 Cambridge Ctr., Suite 208, Cambridge, MA 02142. (617) 225-0401.

The Journal of Biological Chemistry. American Society of Biological Chemists, 428 E. Preston St., Baltimore, MD 21202. Three times a month. Biological, agricultural, and energy aspects of the environment.

Journal of Chemical and Engineering Data. American Chemical Society, 1155 16th St. N.W., Washington, DC 20036. (202) 872-4600; (800) 227-5558. 1959-. Quarterly.

Journal of Chemical Ecology. Plenum Press, 233 Spring St., New York, NY 10013-1578. (212) 620-8000. Monthly. Articles on the origin, function, and significance of natural chemicals.

Journal of Chromatographic Science. Preston Publications, PO Box 48312, Niles, IL 60648. (312) 965-0566. Covers chromatography and electrophoresis.

Journal of Chromatography: Biomedical Applications. Elsevier Science Publishing Co., 655 Avenue of the Americas, New York, NY 10010. (212) 984-5800. Covers chromatography, electrophoresis and biology.

Journal of Colloid and Interface Science. Academic Press, c/o Harcourt Brace Jovanovich Inc., 6277 Sea Harbor Dr., Orlando, FL 32887. (800) 346-8648. 1946-. Fourteen times a year.

Journal of Energy, Natural Resources & Environmental Law. College of Law, University of Utah, Salt Lake City, UT 84112. Semiannual. Legal aspects of energy development, natural resources, and environment.

Journal of Engineering Mechanics. American Society of Civil Engineers, 345 E. 47th St., New York, NY 10017. (212) 705-7288; (800) 548-2723. Bimonthly. Covers activity and development in the field of applied mechanics as it relates to civil engineering, research on bioengineering, computational mechanics, computer aided engineering, dynamics of structures, elasticity, experimental analysis and instrumentation, fluid mechanics, flow of granular media, inelastic behavior of solids and structures, probablistic methods, properties of materials, stability of structural elements and systems, and turbulence.

Journal of Environmental Biology. Academy of Environmental Biology, 657-5 Civil Lines (south), Muzaffarnagar, India 251001. 1980-. Quarterly. An international journal concerned with toxicology and the interrelations of organisms and their environment.

Journal of Environmental Economics and Management. Academic Press, c/o Harcourt Brace Jovanovich Inc., 6277 Sea Harbor Dr., Orlando, FL 32887. (800) 346-8648. Quarterly. Linkages between economic & environmental systems.

The Journal of Environmental Education. Heldref Publications, 4000 Albemarle Street, NW, Washington, DC 20016. (202) 362-6445. Quarterly. Teaching methods, case studies, and evaluations of new research.

Journal of Environmental Engineering. American Society for Civil Engineers, 345 East 47th Street, New York, NY 10017. (212) 705-7496. Bimonthly. Covers problems in the environment and sanitation.

Journal of Environmental Health. National Environmental Health Association, 720 South Colorado Boulevard, Suite 970, Denver, CO 80222. (303) 756-9090. Bimonthly. Covers phases in environmental health.

Journal of Environmental Pathology, Toxicology, and Oncology. Chem-Orbital, PO Box 134, Park Forest, IL 60466. (708) 748-0440. Six times a year. Official organ of the International Society for Environmental Toxicology and Cancer, covering environmentally induced diseases and carcinogenes.

Journal of Environmental Planning and Management. Carfax Publishing Company, P.O. Box 2025, Dunnellon, FL 32630. Biannual. Covers issues of environmental policy, planning, management, land-use, impact assessment, valuation, audits, regulatory aspects of natural resources, environmental protection, conservation and human-environment interactions.

Journal of Environmental Quality. American Society of Agronomy, 677 S. Segoe Rd., Madison, WI 53711-1086. (608) 273-8080. 1972-. Quarterly. Reports and brief reviews of agricultural ecology, environmental engineering and pollution.

Journal of Environmental Science and Health. Marcel Dekker, Inc., 270 Madison Ave., New York, NY 10016. (212) 696-9000. Bimonthly. Concerns pesticides, food contaminants, chemical carcinogens, and agricultural wastes.

Journal of Environmental Sciences. Institute of Environmental Sciences, 940 East Northwest Highway, Mt. Prospect, IL 60656. (312) 255-1561. Bimonthly. Covers research, controlling and teaching of environmental sciences.

Journal of Environmental Systems. Baywood Pub. Co., Inc., 26 Austin Ave., Box 337, Amityville, NY 11701. (516) 691-1270. Quarterly. Analysis, design, and management of our environment.

Journal of Ethnobiology. Center for Western Studies, Flagstaff, AZ Semiannual. Covers archaeology and ethnozoology of plant and animal remains.

Journal of Fish Biology. Academic Press, c/o Harcourt Brace Jovanovich Inc., 6277 Sea Harbor Dr., Orlando, FL 32887. (800) 346-8648. Quarterly.

Journal of Fluorine Chemistry. Elsevier Science Publishing Co., 655 Avenue of the Americas, New York, NY 10010. (212) 984-5800. Quarterly.

Journal of Food Processing and Preservation. Food and Nutrition Press, 2 Corporation Dr., PO Box 374, Trumbull, CT 06611. (203) 261-8587. Quarterly.

Journal of Food Protection. International Association of Milk, Food, and Environmental Sanitarians, 502 E. Lincoln Way, Ames, IA 50010-6666. (515) 232-6699. Covers milk hygiene and food adulteration and inspection procedures.

The Journal of Freshwater. Freshwater Biological Research Foundation, 2500 Shadywood Rd., Box 90, Navarre, MN 55392. (612) 471-8407. 1977-. Quarterly.

Journal of General Microbiology. Society for General Microbiology, Harvest House, 62 London Rd., Reading, England RG1 5AS.

Journal of Geotechnical Engineering. American Society of Civil Engineers, 345 E. 47th St., New York, NY 10017. (212) 705-7288. 1956-. Monthly. Covers the field of soil mechanics and foundations with emphasis on the relationship between the geologic and man-made works.

Journal of Great Lakes Research. International Association for Great Lakes Research, University of Michigan, 2200 Bonisteel Blvd., Ann Arbor, MI 48109-2099. (313) 763-1520. Quarterly. Research on lakes of the world.

Journal of Groundwater. Association of Ground Water Scientists and Engineers, Division of National Water Well Association, 6375 Riverside Dr., Dublin, OH 43017. (614) 761-1711. 1963-. Bimonthly. Serial dealing with all forms of ground water and its quality.

Journal of Hydraulic Engineering. American Society of Civil Engineers, 345 E. 47th St., New York, NY 10017. (212) 705-7288; (800) 548-2723. 1983-. Monthly. Papers describe the analysis and solutions of problems in hydraulic engineering, hydrology and water resources. Emphasizes concepts, methods, techniques and results that advance knowledge in the hydraulic engineering profession.

Journal of Insect Behavior. Plenum Press, 233 Spring St., New York, NY 0013-1578. (212) 620-8000. Quarterly. Agricultural and biological aspects of insect behavior.

Journal of Lipid Research. Federation of American Societies for Experimental Biology, 9650 Rockville Pike, Bethesda, MD 20814-3998. (301) 530-7000. Monthly. Chemistry, biochemistry, and metabolism of lipids. Includes morphological and clinical studies.

Journal of Low Frequency Noise & Vibration. Multi-Science Publishing Co. Ltd., 107 High St., Brentwood, Essex, England CM14 4RX. 0277-224632. Quarterly.

Journal of Occupational Medicine. Williams & Wilkins, P.O. Box 64380, Baltimore, MD 21264. (301) 528-4105. Monthly. Issues on the maintenance and improvement of the health of workers.

Journal of Organic Chemistry. American Chemical Society, 1155 16th St. N.W., Washington, DC 20036. (202) 872-4600; (800) 227-5558. 1936-.

Journal of Pesticide Science. Elsevier Science Publishing Co., Journal Information Center, 655 Avenue of the Americas, New York, NY 10010. (212) 989-5800. Quarterly. Pesticide science in general, agrochemistry and chemistry of biologically active natural products.

Journal of Plant Growth Regulation. Springer-Verlag, 175 5th Ave., New York, NY 10010. (212) 460-1500. Quarterly. Growth and development of plants.

Journal of Plant Nutrition. Marcel Dekker, Inc., 270 Madison Ave., New York, NY 10016. (212) 696-9000; (800) 228-1160. Quarterly.

Journal of Reproduction and Fertility. Abstract Series. Journals of Reproduction and Fertility, Ltd., Cambridge, England Monthly.

Journal of Shoreline Management. Elsevier Science Publishing Co., 655 Avenue of the Americas, New York, NY 10010. (212) 989-5800. Two issues a year. Deals with coastal ecology, coastal zone management, and ocean and shoreline management.

The Journal of Social Ecology. Institute for Social Ecology, P.O. Box 89, Plainfield, VT 05667. 1983-. Issues relating to human ecology.

Journal of Soil and Water Conservation. Soil and Water Conservation Society, 7515 Northeast Ankeny Road, Ankeny, IA 50021. (515) 289-2331. Bimonthly. Promotes better land and water use and management.

The Journal of Soil Science. Clarendon Press, Walton St., Oxford, England OX2 6DP. Quarterly.

The Journal of the Acoustical Society of America. American Institute of Physics for the Acoustical Society of America, 500 Sunnyside Boulevard, Woodbury, NY 11797-2999. (516) 349-7800. Monthly.

Journal of the Air Pollution Control Association Directory Issue. Air Pollution Control Association, P.O. Box 2861, Pittsburgh, PA 15230. (412) 232-3444. Annual.

Journal of the American Chemical Society. American Chemical Society, 1155 16th St. N.W., Washington, DC 20036. (202) 872-4600; (800) 227-5558. 1879-. Biweekly.

Journal of the American College of Toxicology. Mary Ann Liebert, Inc. Publishers, 1651 Third Avenue, New York, NY 10128. (202) 289-2300. Bimonthly. Issues and events that influence the field of toxicology.

Journal of the American Mosquito Control Association. American Mosquito Control Association, PO Box 5416, Lake Charles, LA 70606. (318) 474-2723. Quarterly.

Journal of the American Veterinary Medical Association. American Veterinary Medical Association, 930 N. Meacham Rd., Schaumburg, IL 60196-1074. Semimonthly. Professional developments, research and clinical reports.

Journal of the Association of Environmental Scientists and Engineers. Association of Environmental Scientists and Engineers, 2718 S.W. Kelly, # C-190, Portland, OR 97201. (503) 635-5129. Quarterly. Technical aspects of environmental management.

Journal of the National Cancer Institute. National Institute of Health. U.S. G.P.O., Washington, DC 20401. (202) 512-0000. Semi-monthly. Covers epidemiology and biochemistry of cancer.

Journal of the Royal Society of New Zealand. The Royal Society of New Zealand, Wellington, New Zealand 1971-. Quarterly. Formed by the union of: Transactions of the Royal Society of New Zealand. Earth Sciences; Transactions of the Royal Society of New Zealand. General, and Biological Sciences.

Journal of the Transportation Research Forum. Transportation Research Forum, 103 S. Howard St., Box 405, Oxford, IN 47971. 1962-. Annual. Continues Transportation Research Forum Proceedings.

Journal of the Water Pollution Control Federation. Water Pollution Control Federation, 801 Wythe St., Alexandria, VA 22314-1994. (703) 684-2400. Monthly. Deals with sewage and pollution.

Journal of the World Mariculture Society. Louisiana State University, Division of Continuing Education, Baton Rouge, LA Quarterly.

Journal of Thermal Analysis. Akademiai Kiado, Prielle Kornelia ut 19-35, Budapest, Hungary H-1117. 36 01 181 21 31. An international forum for communications on thermal investigations.

Journal of Toxicology. Marcel Dekker, Inc., 270 Madison Ave., New York, NY 10016. (212) 696-9000; (800) 228-1160. Ten times a year.

Journal of Toxicology and Environmental Health. Taylor & Francis, 1900 Frost Road, Suite 101, Bristol, PA 19007. (800) 821-8312. Monthly. Covers toxilogical effects of environmental pollution.

Journal of Toxicology: Clinical Toxicology. Marcel Dekker, Inc., 270 Madison Ave., New York, NY 10016. (212) 696-9000. Bimonthly. Covers all facets of medical toxicology.

Journal of Toxicology: Cutaneous and Ocular Toxicology. Marcel Dekker, Inc., 270 Madison Ave., New York, NY 10016. (212) 696-9000. Quarterly. Covers dermatological, toxicological, and ophthalmological studies.

Journal of Toxicology: Toxin Reviews. Marcel Dekker, Inc., 270 Madison Ave., New York, NY 10016. (212) 696-9000. Three times a year. Covers new underutilized substances.

Journal of Tribology. American Society of Mechanical Engineers, 345 E. 47th St., New York, NY 10017. (212) 705-7722. Quarterly. Topics in lubrication and lubricants.

Journal of Waste Recycling. Chemical Abstracts Service, PO Box 3012, Columbus, OH 43210. (614) 421-3600. Bimonthly. Covers compost science, land utilization, waste disposal in the ground and recycling.

Journal of Water Resources Planning and Management. American Society of Civil Engineers, Resource Planning and Management Division, 345 E. 47th St., New York, NY 10017. (212) 705-7288; (800) 548-2723. 1983-. Quarterly. Reports on all phases of planning and management of water resources. Examines social, economic, environmental, and administrative concerns relating to the use and conservation of water.

Journal of Wild Culture. Society for the Preservation of Wild Culture, 158 Crawford St., Toronto, ON, Canada M6J 2V4. (416) 588-8266. Quarterly. Deals with wildlife preservation.

The Journal of Wildlife Management. The Wildlife Society, 5410 Grosvenor Ln., Bethesda, MD 20814. (301) 897-9770. Quarterly. Covers wildlife management and research.

The Journal of World Forest Management. A B Academic Publishers, Herts, England Quarterly.

Junkyards: The Highway and Visual Quality. Randolph F. Blum. U.S. G.P.O., Washington, DC 20401. (202) 512-0000. 1979. Abandonment of automobiles and the environmental impact.

Kaiman's Encyclopedia of Energy Topics. Lee Kaiman and J. Masloff. Environmental Design and Research Center, 26799 Elena Rd., Los Altos Hills, CA 94022. 1983. Two volumes. Coverage of topics range from natural energy sources that are renewable to nonrenewable, and the application of these energy sources.

Kansas Environmental Law Handbook. Government Institutes, Inc., 4 Research Pl., Ste. 200, Rockville, MD 20850. (301) 921-2300. 1990.

Kansas Water News. Kansas Water Resources Board, Mills Bldg., 4th Floor, 109 West 9th, Topeka, KS 66612.

Katherine Ordway Preserve and the Swisher Memorial Sanctuary. University of Florida, School of Forest Resources and Conservation, Gainesville, FL 32611. (904) 392-1721.

Keep America Beautiful, Inc. 9 W. Broad St., Stamford, CT 06902. (203) 323-8987.

Keep Tahoe Blue. League to Save Lake Tahoe, 2197 Lake Tahoe Rd., Box 10110, S. Lake Tahoe, CA 95731. (916) 541-5388. Quarterly. Environmental balance, recreational opportunities, and scenic beauty of Tahoe Basin.

Keeping It Green: Tropical Forestry and the Mitigation of Global Warming. Mark C. Trexler. World Resources Institute, 1709 New York Ave. N.W., Washington, DC 20006. (800) 822-0504. 1991. Report links knowledge gained from past tropical forestry initiatives with expectations for their future effectiveness in the mitigation of global warming.

Keeping Options Alive: The Scientific Basis for Conserving Biodiversity. Walter V. C. Reid and Kenton R. Miller. World Resources Institute, 1709 New York Ave. N.W., Washington, DC 20006. (800) 822-0504. 1989. Examines the fundamental questions and recommends policies based on the best available scientific information for conserving biodiversity.

Kelp Biomass Production. M. Neushul. Gas Research Institute, National Technical Information Service, 5285 Port Royal Rd., Springfield, VA 22161. (703) 487-4650. Annual.

Kelp Forests. Judith Connor. Monterey Bay Aquarium Foundation, Monterey, CA (408) 648-4888. 1989.

KEMI-INFO. Danish National Institute of Occupational Health, Produktregestret, Lerso Parkalle 105, Copenhagen 0, Denmark 45 (31) 299711.

Kentucky Environmental Law Handbook. Government Institutes, Inc., 4 Research Pl., Ste. 200, Rockville, MD 20850. (301) 921-2300. 1991.

Kentucky Soil and Water News. Kentucky Division of Soil, 628 Teton Trail, Frankfort, KY 40601. (502) 564-3080. Monthly. Water management issues and erosion in the state.

Kepone: A Literature Summary. James Edward Huff. National Technical Information Service, 5285 Port Royal Rd., Springfield, VA 22161. (703) 487-4650. 1977.

Kepone, Mirex, Hexachlorocyclopentadine: An Environmental Assessment. National Research Council, National Academy of Sciences, 2101 Constitution Ave., NW, Washington, DC 20418. (202) 334-2000. 1978. Toxicology and environmental aspects of pesticides.

Kepone Toxicology. Silas Jackson. U.S. Department of Health and Human Services, Public Health Services, National Institutes of Health, 9000 Rockville Pike, Bethesda, MD 20892. (301) 496-4000. 1983.

Kerosene Heaters. U.S. Consumer Product Safety Commission, 5401 Westbord Ave., Bethesda, MD 20207. (301) 492-6580. 1984. Product safety fact sheet.

Kerosine-Retail. American Business Directories, Inc., 5711 S. 86th Circle, Omaha, NE 68127. (402) 593-4600.

Keyguide to Information Sources in Agricultural Engineering. Bryan Morgan. Mansell Publishing Ltd., 387 Park Ave. S., 5th Fl., New York, NY 10016. (212) 779-1822. 1985.

The Keystone Center. P.O. Box 8606, Keystone, CO 80435. (303) 468-5822.

Keystone Coal Industry Manual. Maclean Hunter Publishing Company, 29 N. Wacker Dr., Chicago, IL 60606. (312) 726-2802.

Kids for a Clean Environment. P.O. Box 158254, Nashville, TN 37215. (615) 331-0708.

Kinetic Model for Orthophosphate Reactions in Mineral Soils. Carl George Enfield. U.S. G.P.O., Washington, DC 20401. (202) 512-0000.

Kirk-Othmer Encyclopedia of Chemical Technology. John Wiley & Sons, Inc., 605 3rd Ave., 5th Floor, New York, NY 10158. (212) 850-6000. Online version of the publication of the same name.

Kirk-Othmer Encyclopedia of Chemical Technology. J. I. Kroschwitz, ed. John Wiley & Sons, Inc., 605 3rd Ave., New York, NY 10158-0012. (212) 850-6000. 1992-. All articles in the new edition have been rewritten and updated adding new subjects such as biotechnology, computer topics, analytical techniques and instrumentation, environmental concerns, fuels and energy, inorganic and solid state chemistry; composite materials and material science in general, and pharmaceuticals. Also available online.

Labor and Industrial Relations Department: Occupational Safety. Administrator, Occupational Safety and Health Division, 830 Punchbowl St., Room 423, Honolulu, HI 96813. (808) 548-4155.

Labor and Industrial Relations Department: Occupational Safety. Director, Division of Labor Standards, PO Box 449, Jefferson City, MO 65102. (314) 751-3403.

Labor and Industrial Services Department: Occupational Safety. Director, 317 Main St., Boise, ID 83720. (208) 334-3950.

Laboratory Chemical Standards: The Complete OSHA Compliance Manual. Bureau of National Affairs, 1231 25th St. N.W., Washington, DC 20037. (800) 372-1033. 1990. OSHA's new lab standard applies to laboratories that use hazardous chemicals and requires a written plan that satisfies federal guidelines.

Laboratory for Environmental Studies. Ohio Agricultural R & D Center, Ohio State University, Madison, OH 44691. (216) 263-3720.

Laboratory for Marine Animal Husbandry. University of Connecticut, Noank, CT 06340.

Laboratory Manual of General Ecology. George W. Cox. Carolina Biological Supply Company, 2700 York Rd., Burlington, NC 27215. (919) 584-0381. 1989. 6th ed. Provides a good section on activities, exercises and references in the field of ecology as a whole.

Laboratory of Chemical Biodynamics. University of California, Berkeley, Berkeley, CA 64720. (415) 486-4311.

Lagoon Information Source Book. E. J. Middlebrooks, et al. Ann Arbor Science, 230 Collingwood, Ann Arbor, MI 48106. 1978. Presents information on all aspects of lagoon performance, operation, maintenance, upgrading, construction, construction techniques and problems associated with this method of wastewater treatment. Includes abstracts of the articles reviewed.

Lake and Reservoir Restoration. Butterworth-Heinemann, 80 Montvale Ave., Stoneham, MA 02180. (617) 438-8464. 1986. Covers lake renewal, reservoirs, water quality management and eutrophication.

Lake Line. North American Lake Management Society, 1000 Connecticut Ave., NW, Suite 300, Washington, DC 20036. (202) 466-8550. Bimonthly. Articles on developments in limnology and lake management.

The Lake Michigan Pollution Case. Cliff Mortimer. University of Wisconsin, Center for Great Lake Studies, 3203 N. Downer Ave., Milwaukee, WI 53211. 1981.

Lake Studies: An Annotated Bibliography of Social Science Research on Lakes. Vance Bibliographies, PO Box 229, 112 N. Charter St., Monticello, IL 61856. (217) 762-3831. 1986.

Land and Natural Resources Department: Fish and Wildlife. Acting Administrator, Division of Forestry and Wildlife, 1151 Punchbowl St., Honolulu, HI 96813. (808) 548-8850.

Land & Water. Land & Water, Route 3, P.O. Box 1197, Fort Dodge, IA 50501. (515) 576-3191. Eight times a year. Covers soil conservation, new machines and products.

Land and Water Contracting. A. B. Morse Co., 200 James St., Barrington, IL 60010. Monthly.

Land Areas of the National Forest System. U.S. Forest Service. U.S. G.P.O., Washington, DC 20401. (202) 512-0000. Annual. Data on wilderness, scenic-research, monument and recreation areas, and game refuges.

Land Clearing and Leveling. 5711 S. 86th Circle, Omaha, NE 68127. (402) 248-9510. Irregular.

Land Degradation: Development and Breakdown of Terrestrial Environments. C. J. Barrow. Cambridge University Press, 40 W. 20th St., New York, NY 10011. (212) 924-3900; (800) 227-0247. 1991.

Land Disposal of Hazardous Waste: Engineering and Environmental Issues. J.R. Gronow. John Wiley & Sons, Inc., 605 3rd Ave., New York, NY 10158-0012. (212) 850-6000. 1988. Waste disposal and teaching at hazardous waste sites.

Land Disposal of Hexachlorobenzene Wastes: Controlling Vapor Movement in Soil. Walter J. Farmer. National Technical Information Service, 5285 Port Royal Rd., Springfield, VA 22161. (703) 487-4650. 1980. Hazardous substances and soil chemistry.

Land Disposal of Municipal and Industrial Wastes. Robert W. Lockerby. Vance Bibliographies, PO Box 229, 112 N. Charter St., Monticello, IL 61856. (217) 762-3831. 1982. Bibliography of sewage irrigation.

Land Husbandry. T.F. Shaxson. Soil and Water Conservation Society, 7515 NE Ankeny Rd., Ankeney, IA (515) 289-2331. 1989. A framework for hill farming, soil and water conservation.

Land Improvement Contractors of America. P.O. Box 9, 1300 Maybrook Dr., Maywood, IL 60153. (708) 344-0700.

Land Improvement Contractors of America News. LICA Service Corp., LICA News, 1300 Maybrook Dr., Maybrook, IL 60153. Monthly. Deals with erosion control, land use and improvement.

Land/Leaf Newsletter. Land Educational Association, 3368 Oak Ave., Stevens Point, WI 54481. (715) 344-6158. Bimonthly. Nuclear weapons and the environment.

Land Letter. The Conservation Fund, 1800 N. Kent St., Suite 1120, Arlington, VA 22209. (703) 522-8008. Thirty four times a year. National land use and conservation policy; legislative, regulatory, and legal developments; use of private and public lands.

Land Management & Environmental Report. John Wiley & Sons, Inc., Box 1239, Brooklandville, MD 21022. Legal aspects of land use.

Land Planning in National Parks and Forests: A Selective Bibliography. Julia Johnson. Council of Planning Librarians, 1313 E. 60th St., Chicago, IL 60637-2897. (312) 942-2163. 1977. Covers forest reserves, rural land use, and national parks reserves.

Land Reclamation: An End to Dereliction?. M. C. R. Davies, ed. Elsevier Applied Science, Crown House, Linton Rd., Barking, England IG11. (081) 594-7272. 1991. Proceedings of the 3rd International Conference on Land Reclamation held at Cardiff, Wales.

Land Reclamation and Biomass Production with Municipal Wastewater and Sludge. Pennsylvania State University Press, Barbara Bldg., Ste. C, University Park, PA 16802. (814) 865-1372. 1982. Sewage and sewage sludge as fertilizer.

Land Reclamation in Cities: A Guide to Methods of Establishment of Vegetation on Urban Waste Land. R. A. Dutton. HMSO, PO Box 276, London, England SW8 5DT. 1982.

Land-Saving Action. Russell L. Brenneman and Sarah M. Bates, eds. Island Press, 1718 Connecticut Ave. N.W., Suite 300, Washington, DC 20009. (202) 232-7933. 1984. Guide to saving land and an explanation of the conservation tools and techniques developed by individuals and organizations across the country.

Land Treatment of an Oily Waste–Degradation, Immobilization, and Bioaccumulation. R.C. Loehr. U.S. Environmental Protection Agency, Robert S. Kerr Environmental Research Laboratory, Ada, OK 1985. Refuse and refuse disposal, factory and trade waste, and sewage irrigation.

Land Trust Alliance. 900 17th St., NW, Suite 410, Washington, DC 20006. (202) 785-1410.

Land Trust Exchange. 1017 Duke St., Alexandria, VA 22314. (703) 683-7778.

Land Use and Environmental Law Review. Clark Boardman Callaghan, 155 Pfingsten Rd., Deerfield, IL 60015. (800) 221-9428. Annual. Reprints of articles that appear in law reviews.

Land Use Digest. Urban Land Institute, 625 Indiana Avenue, NW, Suite 400, Washington, DC 20004. (202) 624-7000. Monthly. Information for planners and developers.

Land Use Planning Abstracts. Environmental Information Center, Land Use Reference Dept., 292 Madison Ave., New York, NY 10017.

Land Use Planning and Coal Refuse Disposal. Robert P. Larkin. Oxford University Press, Gipsy Ln., Headington, Oxford, England OX3 0BP. 1980. Covers land use, coal mines and mining, and waste disposal.

Land Use Planning Report. Business Publishers, Inc., 951 Pershing Dr., Silver Spring, MD 20910-4464. (301) 587-6300. Biweekly. Issues affecting urban, suburban, agricultural, and natural resource land jurisdictions .

Landfill Capacity in the U.S.: How Much Do We Really Have?. National Solid Wastes Management Association, 1730 Rhode Island Ave., NW, Suite 1000, Washington, DC 20036. 1988. Future landfill capacity needs, household/neighborhood business solid waste recycled, recovered through waste-to-energy combustion, and requiring landfill disposal.

Landfill Capacity in the Year 2000. National Solid Waste Management Association, 1730 Rhode Island Ave., NW, Ste. 1000, Washington, DC 20036. (202) 659-4613. 1989.

Landfill Management. Salvadore J. Lucido. Management Information Service, Suite 500, 777 N. Capitol St., N.E., Washington, DC 20002-420. (800) 745-8780. 1990.

The Lands Nobody Wanted: Policy for National Forests in the Eastern United States. William E. Shands. Conservation Foundation, 1250 24th St. NW, Washington, DC 20037. (202) 293-4800. 1977. Forest conservation, forest reserves, and forest policy.

Landscape Architecture and Energy Conservation. Coppa & Avery Consultants. Vance Bibliographies, PO Box 229, 112 N. Charter St., Monticello, IL 61856. (217) 762-3831. 1980.

Landscape Linkages and Biodiversity. Wendy E. Hudson, ed. Island Press, 1718 Connecticut Ave. N.W., Suite 300, Washington, DC 20009. (202) 232-7933. 1991. Explains biological diversity conservation, focusing on the need for protecting large areas of the most diverse ecosystems, and connecting these ecosystems with land corridors to allow species to move among them more easily.

Landscape Planning: Environmental Applications. William M. Marsh. John Wiley & Sons, Inc., 605 3rd Ave., New York, NY 10158-0012. (212) 850-6000. 1991. Second edition. Discusses landscape protection and the effective use of land and its environmental aspects.

Lange's Handbook of Chemistry. John A. Dean, ed. McGraw-Hill Science & Engineering Books, 11 W. 19th St., New York, NY 10011. (212) 337-6010. 1973-. 11th ed.

Large Experimental Aquifer Program. Oregon Graduate Institute of Science and Technology, 19600 N.W. Von Neumann Dr., Beaverton, OR 97006. (503) 690-1193.

Large Marine Ecosystems: Patterns, Processes, and Yields. Kenneth Sherman, et al., eds. American Association for the Advancement of Science, 1333 H St. N.W., 8th Flr., Washington, DC 20005. (202) 326-6400. 1990. Deals with the conservation and management of vitally important components of the ecosphere.

Large Power Plant Effluent Study. Francis A. Schiermeier. U.S. National Air Pollution Control Administration, Raleigh, NC 1970. Electric power plants and air pollution in the United States.

Large-Scale Water Transfers: Emerging Environmental and Social Experiences. G. Golubev and A. Biswas, eds. Cassell PLC, Publishers Distribution Center, PO Box C831, Rutherford, NJ 07070. (201) 939-6064; (201) 939-6065. 1986.

Laser Association of America. 72 Mars St., San Francisco, CA 94114. (415) 621-5776.

Laser Focus/World Buyers' Guide. Advanced Technology Group/Penwell Publishing Company, One Technology Park Dr., Westford, MA 01886. (508) 692-0700.

The Laser Guidebook. McGraw-Hill Science & Engineering Books, 11 W. 19th St., New York, NY 10011. (212) 337-6010. 1992. Topics in optical and electro-optical engineering.

The Laser Handbook. McGraw-Hill Science & Engineering Books, 11 W. 19th St., New York, NY 10011. (212) 337-6010. 1986.

Laser Institute of America. 12424 Research Pkwy., Suite 130, Orlando, FL 32826. (407) 380-1553.

Lasers & Optronics Buying Guide. Elsevier Communications, 301 Gibraltar Dr., Morris Plains, NJ 07950. (201) 292-5100.

Lasers in Materials Processing–A Summary and Forecast. Tech Tran Consultants, Box 220, Lake Geneva, WI 53147. (414) 248-9510. Irregular.

Last Chance Forever. 506 Avenue A, San Antonio, TX 78215. (512) 224-7228.

The Last Rain Forests: A World Conservation Atlas. Mark Collins, ed. Oxford University Press, 200 Madison Ave., New York, NY 10016. (212) 679-7300; (800) 334-4249. 1990. Containing more than 200 full color photos and maps, this is a guide to the people, flora and fauna of the richest habitats on earth. Maps the world's rain forests, spells out the problems facing these regions, and proposes concrete, realistic strategies for ensuring their survival.

Last Stand of the Red Spruce. Robert A. Mello. Island Press, 1718 Connecticut Ave. N.W., Suite 300, Washington, DC 20009. (202) 232-7933. 1987. Hypothesizes that acid rain is the most likely culprit that is killing the trees.

The Last Tree: Reclaiming the Environment in Tropical Asia. James Rush. Asia Society, Distr: Westview, 5500 Central Ave., Boulder, CO 80301. (303) 444-3541. 1991. Traces the history of tropical Asia to make the point that "without an alternative, people will cut the last tree." Also describes the many nongovernmental agencies and grass-roots organizations that are working to conserve tropical forests.

Law and Practice Relating to Oil Pollution from Ships. D.W. Abecassis. Stevens & Sons, South Quay Plaza, 183 Marsh Wall, London, England E14 9FT. 1985. International, United Kingdom, and United States law and practice.

Law Digest. Association of Metropolitan Sewerage Agencies, 1000 Connecticut Avenue, NW, Suite 1006, Washington, DC 20036. (202) 833-2672. Monthly. Legal issues on environmental and regulatory matters.

The Law of Hazardous Waste. Susan M. Cooke. Matthew Bender, DM Dept., 1275 Broadway, Albany, NY 12204. (800) 833-3630. 1992. Management, cleanup, liability, and litigation.

Law of Wetlands Regulation. Clark Boardman Callaghan, 155 Pfingsten Rd., Deerfield, IL 60015. (800) 221-9428. 1990. Law and legislation in United States relating to wetlands.

Law, Policy, Planning, and Administration in Forestry. Judith L. Schwab. Vance Bibliographies, PO Box 229, 112 N. Charter St., Monticello, IL 61856. (217) 762-3831. 1982.

Lawrence Berkeley Laboratory, Chemical Biodynamics Division. One Cyclotron Road, Berkeley, CA 94720. (415) 486-4355.

LC GC: Magazine of Liquid and Gas Chromatography. Aster Publishing Co., 859 Willamette St., PO Box 10460, Eugene, OR 97440. (503) 343-1200.

The LD50 and LC50 Toxicity Tests, January 1980-August 1990. Karen J. Clingerman. National Agricultural Library, 10301 Baltimore Blvd., Beltsville, MD 20705-2351. (301) 504-5755. 1990.

Leaching and Hydraulic Properties of Retorted Oil Shale Including Effects from Codisposal of Wastewater. David B. McWhorter. U.S. Environmental Protection Agency, Air and Energy Engineering Research Laboratory, MD 75, Research Triangle Park, NC 27711. (919) 541-2184. 1987.

Lead Abatement News. FIND/SVP, 625 Avenue of the Americas, New York, NY 10011. (800) 346-3787. Monthly. Government and business news involving the nationwide effort to remove lead from homes, drinking water, the air and the workplace.

Lead Acoustical Products and Suppliers. 295 Madison Ave., New York, NY 10017. (212) 578-4750. Annual.

Lead and Its Alloys. D. R. Blaskett. E. Horwood, 200 Old Tappan Rd., Old Tappan, NJ 07675. (800) 223-2348. 1990. Presents a comprehensive account of the historical evolution of the extraction, smelting, and refining of lead. Also covers its working and shaping, and its corrion behavior.

Lead Based Paint Abatement. FIND/SVP, 625 Avenue of the Americas, New York, NY 10011. (800) 346-3787. 1991. Analyzes and forecasts to 1995 the market for lead-based paint abatement, focusing on the market potential for both contractors and consultants.

Lead Contractors and Materials Suppliers. 295 Madison Ave., New York, NY 10017. (212) 578-4750. Irregular.

Lead Exposure: Public and Occupational Health Hazards. National Technical Information Service, 5285 Port Royal Rd., Springfield, VA 22161. (703) 487-4650. 1990. Bibliography of lead toxicology and pollution.

Lead in Agricultural Ecosystems. Robert Lewis Jones. University of Illinois, Department of Agronomy, Urbana, IL 61801. 1973.

Lead in the Marine Environment. M. Branica and Z. Konrad, eds. Pergamon Microforms International, Inc., Fairview Park, Elmsford, NY 10523. (914) 592-7720. 1980. Proceedings of the International Experts Discussion, Rovinj, Yugoslavia, October 1977.

Lead Industries Association. 292 Madison Ave., New York, NY 10017. (212) 578-4750.

Lead, Mercury, Cadmium, and Arsenic in the Environment. T.C. Hutchinson. John Wiley & Sons, Inc., 605 3rd Ave., New York, NY 10158-0012. (212) 850-6000. 1987. Environmental aspects of mercury, lead and arsenic.

Lead Paint Poisoning in Urban Children. Council of Planning Librarians, 1313 E. 60th St., Chicago, IL 60637-2897. (312) 942-2163. 1976.

Lead Poisoning. National Park Service Housing, Washington, DC 20013. (202) 208-6843. 1991. Lead toxicology, health aspects of paints and children's health safety.

Lead Poisoning: A Selected Bibliography. Vance Bibliographies, PO Box 229, 112 N. Charter St., Monticello, IL 61856. (217) 762-3831. 1988. Bibliography of lead toxicology.

Lead Pollution from Motor Vehicles. Penny Farmer. Elsevier Science Publishing Co., 655 Avenue of the Americas, New York, NY 10010. (212) 984-5800. 1987.

Lead Pollution Prevention. U.S. G.P.O, Washington, DC 20401. (202) 512-0000. 1991. Toxicology of lead, hazardous substances, and chemicals. Also covers pediatric toxicology.

Lead Versus Health. Michael Rutter. John Wiley & Sons, Inc., 605 3rd Ave., New York, NY 10158-0012. (212) 850-6000. 1983.

League for Ecological Democracy. P.O. Box 1858, San Pedro, CA 90733. (213) 833-2633.

League Leader. Izaak Walton League of America, 1401 Wilson Blvd., Level B, Arlington, VA 22209. (703) 528-1818. Bimonthly. Soil, forest, water, & other natural resources.

League of Conservation Voters. 1150 Connecticut, N.W., Suite 201, Washington, DC 20002. (202) 785-8683.

Leak Detection Technology Association. 1801 K St., N.W., Suite 800, Washington, DC 20006. (202) 835-2355.

Leak Prevention and Corrective Action Technology for Underground Storage Tanks. Noyes Publications, 120 Mill Rd., Park Ridge, NJ 07656. (201) 391-8484. 1988. Oil storage tanks safety measures and tcchnology.

Leakage and Loss in Fluid Systems. Scientific and Technical Information Ltd., 4 Kings Meadow, Ferry Hinksey Rd., Oxford, England OX2 0DU. (0865) 798898. 1990. A bibliography of leak detection, monitoring, control and modelling in pipelines, dams, reservoirs, and associated pumping systems.

Leaking Underground Gasoline Storage Tanks. Better Government Association, 230 N. Michigan Ave., Chicago, IL 60601. (312) 641-1181. 1988. Water, pollution, and environmental aspects of gasoline storage.

Leaking Underground Storage Tanks Containing Motor Fuels: A Chemical Advisory. U.S. Environmental Protection Agency, Office of Toxic Substances, 401 M St., S.W., Washington, DC 20460. (202) 260-2090. 1984. Underground storage of petroleum products.

Learning Alliance. 494 Broadway, New York, NY 10012. (212) 226-7171.

Least-Cost Energy: Solving the CO2 Problem. Amory B. Levins. Brick House Publishing Co., Inc., Francestown Tpke., New Boston, NH 03070. (603) 487-3718. 1982. Energy conservation and environmental aspects of carbon dioxide.

Legacy. 1100 Revere Dr., Olonomowoc, WI 53066. (414) 567-3454.

Legal Environmental Assistance Foundation. 1115 N. Gadsden St., Tallahassee, FL 32303. (904) 681-2591.

Legal Handbook on Sign Control. Scenic America, 216 7th St. SE, Washington, DC 20003. (202) 546-1100. 1990.

The Legal Regime of the Protection of the Mediterranean against Pollution from Land-Based Sources. S. Kuwabara. Cassell PLC, Publishers Distribution Center, PO Box C831, Rutherford, NJ 07070. (201) 939-6064; (201) 939-6065. 1984.

Legal Responses to Indoor Air Pollution. Frank B. Cross. Quorum Books, Div. of Greenwood Publishing Group, Inc., 88 Post Rd. W., Box 5007, Westport, CT 06881. (203) 226-3571. 1990. Examines the under-recognized risks of indoor air pollution and the shortcomings of regulatory and judicial responses to these risks.

Legal Risk Mitigation for the Environmental Professional. Jack V. Matson. Lewis Publishers, 2000 Corporate Blvd., N.W., Boca Raton, FL 33431. (407) 994-0555 or (800) 272-7737. 1991. Describes environmental statutes concerning civil and criminal provisions. Differentiates civil and criminal activities, professional practice, mitigating professional risks, and case studies.

Lehigh University, Bioprocessing Institute. 111 Research Drive, Mountaintop Campus, Bethlehem, PA 18015. (215) 758-4258.

Lehigh University, Center for Molecular Bioscience and Biotechnology. Mountaintop Campus, Building 111, Bethlehem, PA 18015. (215) 758-5426.

Lessons Learned in Global Environmental Governance. Peter H. Sand. World Resources Institute, 1709 New York Ave. N.W., Washington, DC 20006. (800) 822-0504. 1990. Takes stock of significant international environmental initiatives to date and highlights innovative features of transnational regimes for setting and implementing standards.

Let it Rot! The Home Gardener's Guide to Composting. Stu Campbell. Storey Communications, School House Rd., Pownal, VT 05261. (802) 823-5811. 1990.

Lewes Marine Studies Complex. University of Delaware, Lewes, DE 19958. (302) 645-4212.

LEXIS Admiralty and Maritime Library. Mead Data Central, Inc., P.O. Box 933, Dayton, OH 45401. (800) 227-4908.

LEXIS Environmental Library. Mead Data Central, Inc., P.O. Box 933, Dayton, OH 45401. (800) 227-4908.

Liaison Conservation Directory. U.S. Office of Endangered Species, Fish & Wildlife Service, Int., Washington, DC 20240. (703) 235-2407.

Licensing and Regulation Department: Occupational Safety. Assistant Commissioner, Occupational Safety and Health, 501 St. Paul Place, Baltimore, MD 21202-272. (301) 333-4195.

Lichen Ecology. Mark Seaward. Academic Press, c/o Harcourt Brace Jovanovich Inc., 6277 Sea Harbor Dr., Orlando, FL 32887. (800) 346-8648. 1977. Topics in botanical ecology.

Lichens and Air Pollution. Kenneth Metzler. State Geological and Natural History Survey of Connecticut, Hartford, CT 1980.

Lichens as Pollution Monitors. D.L. Hawksworth. E. Arnold, 41 Bedford Sq., London, England 1976.

Life History and Ecology of the Slider Turtle. J. Whitfield Gibbons. Smithsonian Institution Press, 470 L'Enfant Plaza #7100, Washington, DC 20560. (800) 782-4612. 1990. Deals with all that is known about a species, its taxonomic status and genetics, reproduction and growth, population structure and demography, population ecology, and bioenergetics.

Life History of a Fossil: An Introduction to Taphonomy and Paleoecology. Harvard University Press, 79 Garden St., Cambridge, MA 02138. (617) 495-2600. 1981.

Life In and Around the Salt Marshes. Michael Ursin. Crowell, New York, NY 1972. A handbook of plant and animal life in and around the temperate Atlantic coastal marshes.

The Life of Prairies and Plains. Durward Leon Allen. McGraw-Hill Science & Engineering Books, 11 W. 19th St., New York, NY 10011. (212) 337-6010. 1967.

The Life of the African Plains. Leslie Brown. McGraw-Hill Science & Engineering Books, 11 W. 19th St., New York, NY 10011. (212) 337-6010. 1972.

Life Sciences from NTIS. National Technical Information Center for the Utilization of Federal Technology, 5285 Port Royal Rd., Springfield, VA 22161. (703) 487-4650.

Life Sciences on File. Diagram Group. Facts on File, Inc., 460 Park Ave. S., New York, NY 10016. (212) 683-2244. 1986. Encyclopedia of pictorial collection in life sciences. Deals with all major topics in life sciences including ecology.

Life, Space, and Time: A Course in Environmental Biology. Howard Barraclough Fell. Harper & Row, 10 E. 53rd St., New York, NY 10022. (212) 207-7000; (800) 242-7737. 1974. Deals with natural history and ecological matters.

Lime Use in Wastewater Treatment. Denny Parker. National Technical Information Service, 5285 Port Royal Rd., Springfield, VA 22161. (703) 487-4650. 1975.

Limnology and Oceanography. American Society of Limnology and Oceanography, Inc., PO Box 1897, Lawrence, KS 66044-8897. (913) 843-1221. Topics in aquatic disciplines.

Lindane Health and Safety Guide. World Health Organization, Ave. Appia, Geneva, Switzerland CH-1211. 1991. Chemical safety and toxicology of hexachlorobenzene.

Linking the Natural Environment and the Economy: Essays the Eco-Eco Group. Carl Folke, ed. Kluwer Academic Publishers, 101 Philip Dr., Assinippi Park, Norwell, MA 02061. (617) 871-6600. 1991. Volume 1 of the series entitled Ecology, Economy and Environment.

Linscott's Directory of Immunological & Biological Reagents. William D. Linscott, 40 Glen Dr., Mill Valley, CA 94941. (415) 383-2666.

Lipid Analysis. William W. Christie. Pergamon Microforms International, Inc., Fairview Park, Elmsford, NY 10523. (914) 592-7720. 1982. Isolation, separation, identification, and structural analysis of lipids.

Lipid Manual: Methodology Appropriate for Fatty Acid-Cholesterol Analysis. Alan J. Sheppard. U.S. Food and Drug Administration, Division of Nutrition, 5600 Fishers Ln., Rockville, MD 20857. (301) 443-1544. 1989. Analysis of oils, fats, and cholesterol.

Lipids. American Oil Chemists' Society, PO Box 3489, 1608 Broadmoor Dr., Champaign, IL 61826-3489. (217) 359-2344. 1966-. Monthly.

Lipids. Helmut K. Mangold. CRC Press, 2000 Corporate Blvd. N.W., Boca Raton, FL 33431. (800) 272-7737. 1984. Chromatographic analysis of lipids.

Liquid Chromatography/Mass Spectrometry: Applications in Agricultural, Pharmaceutical and Environmental Chemistry. Mark A. Brown, ed. American Chemical Society, 1155 16th St. N.W., Washington, DC 20036. (202) 872-4600; (800) 227-5558. 1990. Review of the development of LC/MS techniques for enhancing structural information for high-performance LC/MS.

Liquid Filtration Newsletter. McIlvanine Co., 2970 Maria Ave., Northbrook, IL 60062. (708) 272-0010. Monthly. Industry information and product comparisons.

Liquified Petroleum Gas. I.P. Sharp Associates, a Reuter Company, Suite 1900, Exchange Tower, 2 First Canadian Place, Toronto, ON, Canada M5X 1E3. (800) 387-1588.

List of Chemical Compounds, Authorized for Use and Under USDA Inspection and Grading Programs. U.S. Dept. of Agriculture, Food Safety and Quality Service. U.S. G.P.O., Washington, DC 20401. (202) 512-0000. Annual. Covers food adulteration and inspection, egg products industry, equipment and supplies, and meat industry trade.

List of Lists of Worldwide Hazardous Chemicals and Pollutants. The Forum of Scientific Excellence. J. B. Lippincott, 227 E. Washington Sq., Philadelphia, PA 19105. (215) 238-4200; (800) 982-4377. 1990. Extensive compilation of regulated hazardous chemicals and environmental pollutants in existence. Includes separate lists of substances that are regulated by more than 40 states, as well as federal and international agencies. A master list of the regulated material is also included in both alphabetical and CAS number sequence.

List of National Wildlife Refuges. U.S. Dept. of Interior, Fish, Interior Dept., Washington, DC 20240. (202) 343-5634.

List of Periodicals and Serials in the Forestry Library. Commonwealth Forestry Association, c/o Oxford Forestry Institute, Oxford, England OX1 3RB. 1968. Covers agriculture and forests and forestry.

List of PET Recyclers in the United States and Canada. National Assn. for Plastic Container Recovery, 4828 Pkwy. Plaza Blvd., Suite 260, Charlotte, NC 28217. (704) 357-3250. Monthly.

List of Proprietary Substances and Nonfood Compounds Authorized for Use Under USDA Inspection and Grading Programs: microform. U.S. Dept. of Agriculture, Food Safety and Inspection Service. U.S. G.P.O., Washington, DC 20401. (202) 512-0000. Annual. Food adulteration and inspection, meat industry and trade, and egg products industry.

A List of Publications Issued by the Consortium for Integrated Pest Management. Perry Adkisson. Consortium for Integrated Pest Management, New York, NY 1988.

List of Publications of the U.S. Army Engineer Waterways Experiment Station. U.S. Army Corps of Engineers, Waterways Experiment Station, PO Box 631, Vicksburg, MS 39180. (601) 634-3774. Annual. Covers hydraulic and environmental engineering, coastal engineering, soil mechanics, concrete, and pavements.

List of Publications on Agricultural Engineering Subjects. University of Illinois, Dept. of Agricultural Engineering, Urbana, IL 61801. 1964.

List of Publications Sent to Government Depository Libraries. U.S. National Commission on Air Quality, Washington, DC 1980.

List of Water Pollution Control Administrators. Association of State and Interstate Water Pollution Control Administrators, 444 N. Capitol St., N.W., Suite 330N, Washington, DC 20001. (202) 624-7782.

Literature on the Revegetation of Coal-Mined Lands. David L. Veith. U.S. Department of the Interior, Bureau of Mines, Cochrans Mill Rd., 15236. (412) 892-6400. 1985.

Literature Review. Water Pollution Control Federation, 601 Wythe St., Alexandria, VA 22314-1994. (703) 684-2400.

Literature Review of Wetland Evaluation Methodologies. U.S. Environmental Protection Agency, 401 M St., S.W., Washington, DC 20460. (202) 260-2090. 1984.

Lithium and Animal Behavior. Eden Press, Montreal, PQ, Canada Annual. Toxicology and therapeutic use of lithium.

Littoral Drift. University of Wisconsin Sea Grant Institute, 1800 University Ave., Madison, WI 53705. (608) 263-3259. Ten times a year. National Sea Grant program and current Great Lakes issues.

Livable Cities. Marcia D. Lowe. Worldwatch Institute, 1776 Massachusetts Ave., N.W., Washington, DC 20036-1904.

Livable Cities Almanac. J.T. Marlin. Harper Perennial, New York, NY 1992. How over 100 metropolitan areas compare in economic health, air quality, water quality, life expectancy and health services.

Livestock Conservation Institute. 6414 Copps Ave. #116, Madison, WI 53716. (608) 221-4848.

Livestock Feedlot Runoff Control by Vegetative Filters. Robert S. Kerr. National Technical Information Service, 5285 Port Royal Rd., Springfield, VA 22161. (703) 487-4650. 1979. Environmental protection technology relating to filters and filtration.

Livestock Grazing Strategies: Environmental Considerations, January 1980 - May 1991. Janet E. Dombrowski. National Agricultural Library, 10301 Baltimore Blvd., Beltsville, MD 20705-2351. (301) 504-5755. 1991.

Livestock Health Housing. David Sainsbury. Bailliere Tindall, 24-28 Oval Rd., London, England NW1 7DX. 1988. Prevention and control of animal disease.

Livestock Waste, a Renewable Resource. American Society of Agricultural Engineers, 2950 Niles Rd., St. Joseph, MI 49085-9659. (616) 429-0300. 1981. Papers presented at the 4th International Symposium on Livestock Wastes, Amarillo, TX, 1980. Topics covered include: processing manure for feed, methane production, land application, lagoons, runoff, odors, economics, stabilization, treatment, collection and transport, storage and solid-liquid separation.

Livestock Waste Facilities Handbook. Midwest Plan Service, Ames, IA 1985. Deals with agricultural waste management and manure handling in livestock waste facilities.

The Living Landscape: An Ecological Approach to Landscape Planning. Frederick R. Steiner. McGraw-Hill, 1221 Avenue of the Americas, New York, NY 10020. (212) 512-2000 or (800) 262-4729. 1991. An ecological approach to landscape planning and landscape protection. Discusses the ways in which land could be effectively used taking into consideration the fragility of the environment.

The Living Ocean. Boyce Thorne-Miller. Island Press, 1718 Connecticut Ave. N.W., Suite 300, Washington, DC 20009. (202) 232-7933. 1991. Discusses all marine ecosystems, including coastal benthic, shore systems, estuaries, wetlands, and coral reefs, coastal pelagic, deep-sea benthic, hydrothermal vents and others.

Living Without Oxygen: Closed and Open Systems in Hypoxia Tolerance. Peter W. Hochachka. Harvard University Press, 79 Garden St., Cambridge, MA 02138. (617) 495-2600. 1980. Covers anaerobiosis, anoxemia glycolysis, anoxia and glycolysis.

Local Climatological Data. National Environmental Satellite, Data, and Information Service, 2069 Federal Bldg. 4, Washington, DC 20233. (301) 763-7190. Monthly.

Locating and Estimating Air Emission from Sources of Polychlorinated Biphenyls. U.S. Environmental Protection Agency, MD 75, Research Triangle Park, NC 27711. 1987. Environmental aspects of Polychlorinated Biphenyls.

Locating and Estimating Air Emissions from Sources of Carbon Tetrachloride [microform]. U.S. Environmental Protection Agency, 401 M St., SW, MD 75, Research Triangle Park, NC 27711. (919) 541-2184. 1984.

Locating and Estimating Air Emissions from Sources of Chloroform. U.S. Environmental Protection Agency, Office of Air and Radiation, MD 75, Research Triangle Park, NC 27711. (919) 541-2184. 1984.

Lockwood-Post's Directory of the Pulp, Paper and Allied Trades. Miller Freeman Publications, 370 Lexington Ave., New York, NY 10017. (212) 683-9294. 1987. Annual.

LOGAN Workplace Exposure Evaluation System. American Industrial Hygiene Association, 345 White Pond Dr., Akron, OH 44320. (216) 873-2442. 1987. A computerized software package, presents statistical method for characterizing employee exposure to chemicals, noise, and other environmental hazards.

The Long-Range Atmospheric Transport of Natural and Containment Substances. Anthony H. Knap. Kluwer Academic Publishers, 101 Philip Dr., Assinippi Pk., Norwell, MA 02061. (617) 871-6600. Transport of sulphur and nitrogen, organic compounds, mineral aerosols and trace elements.

Long Range Transport of Pesticides. David A. Kurtz. Lewis Publishers, 2000 Corporate Blvd., N.W., Boca Raton, FL 33431. (407) 994-0555 or (800) 272-7737. 1990. Presents the latest vital information on long range transport of pesticides. Includes sources of pesticides from lakes, oceans, and soil, circulation on global and regional basis, deposition, and fate of pesticides.

Long-Term Ecological Research: An International Perspective. Paul G. Risser, ed. John Wiley & Sons, Inc., 605 3rd Ave., New York, NY 10158-0012. (212) 850-6000. 1991. Describes and analyzes research programs in various ecosystems such as temperate forests, arid steppes, deserts, temperate and tropical grasslands, aquatic systems from countries including Scotland, Kenya, USA, Australia, Canada, Germany, and France.

Long-Term Ecological Research Project. University of Colorado-Boulder, CB 450, Boulder, CO 80309. (303) 492-6198.

Long-Term Neurotoxic Effects of Paint Solvents. Royal Society of Chemistry, c/o CRC Press, 2000 Corporate Blvd. N.W., Boca Raton, FL 33431-9868. (800) 272-7737. 1990. Various components of oil-based decorative paints are described, as are studies that have been made on the neurotoxicity of the individual solvents. The relative advantages and disadvantages of oil-based and water-based paints are described.

Longevity, Senescence, and the Genome. Caleb Ellicott Finch. University of Chicago Press, 5801 Ellis Ave., 4th Floor, Chicago, IL 60637. (800) 621-2736. 1990. Genetic aspects of aging and longevity.

Longman Illustrated Dictionary of Food Science. Nicholas Light. Longman, Burnt Hill, Harlow, England CM20 2J6. (0279) 26721. 1989. Food, its components, nutrition, preparation and preservation.

Los Angeles Catalytic Study–LACS. U.S. Environmental Protection Agency, Office of Monitoring Systems and Quality Assurance, 401 M St., S.W., Washington, DC 20460. (202) 260-2090.

Louisiana Conservationist. Louisiana Department of Wildlife & Fisheries, 2000 Quail Dr., Baton Rouge, LA 70808. (504) 765-2916. Bimonthly. Conservation education, outdoor recreation, and commercial utilization of fish and wildlife resources.

Louisiana State University, Mycological Herbarium. Department of Botany, Room 305, Life Sciences Building, Baton Rouge, LA 70803. (504) 388-8487.

Louisiana State University, Office of Sea Grant Development. Center for Wetland Resources, Baton Rouge, LA 70803. (504) 388-6710.

Louisiana Universities Marine Consortium. Chauvin, LA 70344. (504) 851-2800.

Low-Cost Technology Options for Sanitation. W. Rybczynski. The World Bank, 1818 H. St., N.W., Washington, DC 20433. 1982. A state of the art review of toilets and sanitary engineering in underdeveloped countries.

Low-Level Radioactive Waste: From Cradle to Grave. E. L. Gershey. Global Professional Publications, 2805 McGraw Ave., PO Box 19539, Irvine, CA 92713-9539. (800) 854-7179.

LPG Land Transportation and Storage Safety. Applied Technology Corp. National Technical Information Service, 5285 Port Royal Rd., Springfield, VA 22161. (703) 487-4650. 1981. Storage and transportation of liquid petroleum gas.

LPG Tanks, Inspection and Safety. U.S. Customs Service, Office of Inspection and Control, 1301 Constitution Ave. NW, Washington, DC 20229. (202) 927-2095. 1986. A handbook for the safe, effective inspection of liquefied petroleum gas fuel tanks in cars and pick-up trucks.

Lubrication in Practice. W. S. Robertson. Macmillan Publishers Ltd., 4 Little Essex St., London, England WC2R 3LF. 1983.

Lumber Retailers Directory. 5711 S. 86th Circle, Omaha, NE 68127. (402) 593-4600. Annual.

Lumbermens Red Book. Lumbermens Credit Association, 111 W. Jackson Blvd., 10th Fl., Chicago, IL 60604. (312) 427-0733.

Macmillan Dictionary of Toxicology. Ernest Hodgson, et al. Van Nostrand Reinhold, 115 5th Ave., New York, NY 10003. (212) 254-3232. 1988. Intended as a "starting point" to the literature of toxicology. American spelling is used with cross references to British version of words. Contains a list of references. Signed entries give explanatory definitions and cross references.

Macmillan Illustrated Animal Encyclopedia. Philip Whitfield, ed. Macmillan Publishing Co., 866 3rd Ave., New York, NY 10022. (212) 702-2000. 1984. Provides a comprehensive catalog of the staggering range of animal types within the vertebrate group. Also the IUCN endangered species are noted and includes common names, range and habitat. Includes mammals, birds, reptiles, amphibians, and fish.

Macrocosm U.S.A. Sandra L. Brockway. Macrocosm U.S.A., Box 969, Cambria, CA 93428-0969. (805) 927-8030. Annual. Covers organizations, businesses, publishers, and publications concerned with various global and humanitarian issues including ecology.

Madison Conference of Applied Research & Practice on Municipal & Industrial Waste. Dept. of Engineering Professional Development, University of Wisconsin-Madison, Madison, WI 53706. 1990. Annual. Sewage disposal, factory and trade waste, soil liners, ground water clean up, landfill leachate treatment, groundwater monitary systems, evaluation of groundwater and soil gas remedial action; leachate generation estimates and landfills.

Magill's Survey of Science. Earth Science Series. Frank N. Magill. Salem Press, PO Box 50062, Pasadena, CA 91105. 1990-. Five volumes. Includes information on earth's crust, hot spots and volcanic island chains, physical properties of minerals, rock magnetism, physical properties of rocks, and index.

Magill's Survey of Science. Life Science Series. Frank N. Magill, ed. Salem Press, PO Box 50062, Pasadena, CA 91105. 1991. Six volumes. Contents: v.1. A-Central and peripheral nervous system functions; v.2. Central metabolism regulation - eukaryotic transcriptional control; v.3. Positive and negative eukaryotic transcriptional control - mammalian hormones; v.4. Hormones and behavior - muscular contraction; v.5. Muscular contraction and relaxation - sexual reproduction in plants; v.6. Reproductive behavior and mating - X inactivation and the Lyon hypothesis.

Mailing of Biological Toxins and Etiologic Agents. Washington, DC 1990. Hazardous substances transportation through the postal service.

Maine Audubon News. Maine Audubon Society, Old Route 1, Falmouth, ME 04105. (207) 781-2330. Monthly. Wild life conservation, energy conservation, and alternative sources of energy.

Maine Department of Inland Fisheries and Wildlife, Fishery Research Management Division. Fisheries Laboratory, P.O. Box 1298, Bangor, ME 04401. (207) 941-4461.

Maine Environment. Natural Resource Council of Maine, 20 Willow St., Augusta, ME 04330. 1974-. Monthly. Environmental activities and problems in Maine.

Maine Environment Systems. A.S.M.E.R., PO Box 57, Orangeburg, NY 10962. (914) 634-8221. Bimonthly. Synergy between behavioral researchers and the design profession.

Maine Environmental Law Handbook. Government Institutes, Inc., 4 Research Pl., Ste. 200, Rockville, MD 20850. (301) 921-2300. 1990.

Maine Fish. Maine Fish, 284 State St., Sta. 41, Augusta, ME 04333. (207) 289-2871. Quarterly. Fish & wildlife research & management.

Maine Legacy. Nature Conservancy, 1815 N Lynn St., Arlington, VA 22209. (207) 729-5181. Bimonthly. Nature conservancy projects in Maine.

Maine Times/Maine Environmental Weekly. Maine Times, Maine Environmental Weekly, 41 Main St., Topsham, ME 04086. 1968-. Weekly.

Maine's Coastal Program Newsletter. Maine State Planning Office, Station 38, State House, Augusta, ME 04333. (207) 289-3261. Quarterly. Gulf of Maine resources.

Mainstream. Animal Protection Institute of America, 2831 Frutridge Rd., PO Box 22505, Sacramento, CA 95822. (916) 731-5521. Quarterly. Covers animal welfare problems.

Maintaining a Satisfactory Environment: At What Price?. N. Akerman, ed. Westview Press, 5500 Central Ave., Boulder, CO 80301. (303) 444-3541. 1990.

Making Peace with the Planet. Barry Commoner. Pantheon Books, 201 E. 50th St., New York, NY 10220. (212) 751-2000. 1990. Reviews the vast efforts made in the public and private sphere to address and control damage to the environment.

Making the Switch. Sacramento League of Women Voters. Golden Empire Health Planning Center, P.O. Box 649, Sacramento, CA 98120. (916) 448-1198. 1988. Alternatives to using toxic chemicals in the home.

Making Things Happen: How to Be an Effective Volunteer. Joan Wolfe. Island Press, 1718 Connecticut Ave. N.W., Suite 300, Washington, DC 20009. (202) 232-7933. 1991. Environmental movement is nurtured by volunteers. This book teaches volunteers the basic skills they need to make a stronger impact.

Man and Animals in Hot Environments. Douglas Leslie Ingram. Springer-Verlag, 175 5th Ave., New York, NY 10010. (212) 460-1500; (800) 777-4643. 1975. Describes the physiological effect of heat on man and animals. Includes extensive bibliography.

Man and the Biosphere Series. J. N. R. Jeffers, ed. Parthenon Pub., Casterton Hall, Carnforth, England LA6 2LA. (05242) 72084. 1990-. Contents: v.1. The Control of Eutrophication of Lakes and Reservoirs; v.2. An Amazonian Rain Forest; v.3. Exploiting the Tropical Rain Forest; v.4. The Ecology and Management of Aquatic-Terrestrial Ecotones; v.5. Sustainable Development and Environmental Management of Small Islands; v.6. Rain Forest Regeneration and Management; v.7. Reproductive Ecology of Tropical Forest Plants; v.8. Redevelopment of Degraded Ecosystems; v.9. Pastoralism in Transition.

Man at High Altitude: the Pathophysiology of Acclimatization and Adaptation. Donald Heath and David Reid Williams. Churchill Livingstone, Inc., 650 Avenue of the Americas, New York, NY 10011. (212) 206-5000. 1981.

Man Belongs to the Earth. International Co-operation in Environmental Research, UNESCO's Man and the Biosphere Programme. UNESCO, 7, place de Fontenoy, Paris, France F-75700. (331) 45 68 40 67. 1988. Provides an account of the MAB programme as it stood in 1987.

Man-Environment Systems. Association for the Study of Man-Environment Relations, PO Box 57, Orangeburg, NY 10962. (914) 634-8221. Bimonthly.

Man in the Cold Environment: A Bibliography with Informative Abstracts. Charles W. Shilling. Undersea and Hyperbaric Medical Society, 9650 Rockville Pike, Bethesda, MD 20814. (301) 571-1818. 1981. Bibliography of hypothermia.

Man-made Carbon Dioxide and Climatic Change. Geo Abstracts Ltd., c/o Elsevier Science Pub., Crown House, Linton Rd., Barking, England IG11 8JU. 1983.

Man-Made Lakes and Human Health. N. F. Stanley. Academic Press, c/o Harcourt Brace Jovanovich Inc., 6277 Sea Harbor Dr., Orlando, FL 32887. (800) 346-8648. 1975. Environmental and hygienic aspects of reservoirs.

Managed Area Basic Record. The Nature Conservancy, 1815 N. Lynn St., Arlington, VA 22209. (703) 841-5300. Database of about 3,100 nature preserves.

Management and Control of Invertebrate Crop Pests. Gordon E. Russell, ed. VCH Publishers, 303 NW 12th Ave., Deerfield Beach, FL 33442-1788. (305) 428-5566. 1989. Review articles covering important aspects of the management and control of several important insect and nematode pests of crop plants, selected from the multi-disciplinary series of annual review books Agricultural Zoology Reviews and Biotechnology & Genetic Engineering Reviews.

Management and Restoration of Human-Impacted Resources: Approaches to Ecosystem Rehabilitation. Kathrin Schreckenberg, et al, eds. UNESCO, 7, place de Fontenoy, Paris, France F-75700. (331) 45 68 40 67. 1990. MAB Digest 5.

The Management of Radioactive Waste. Uranium Institute, 12th Floor, Bowater House, 68 Knightsbridge, London, England SW1X 7LT. 071-225 0303. 1991. Discusses methods of disposal of radioactive wastes and the hazards involved.

Management of Radioactive Waste: The Issues for Local Authorities. Stuart Kemp, ed. Telford, Telford House, 1 Heron Quay, London, England E14 9XF. (071) 987-6999. 1991. Proceedings of the conference organized by the National Steering Committee, Nuclear Free Local Authorities, and held in Manchester on February 12, 1991.

Management of World Wastes. Communication Channels, 6255 Barfield Road, Atlanta, GA 30328. (404) 256-9800. Monthly. Covers public and private waste operations.

Management of World Wastes–Buyers' Guide Issue. Communication Channels, 6255 Barfield Rd., Atlanta, GA 30328. (404) 256-9800.

Management Strategies for Landscape Waste: Collection, Composting, and Marketing. Illinois Department of Energy and Natural Resources, Office of Solid Waste and Renewable Resources, 325 W. Adams St., Rm. 300, Springfield, IL 62706. (217) 785-2800. 1989. Compost, waste, recycling, and refuse collection.

Managing Environmental Risks. Air & Waste Management Association, PO Box 2861, Pittsburgh, PA 15230. (412) 232-3444. 1990. Papers presented at the Air & Waste Management Association International Specialty Conference, held in October 1989 in Quebec City, contains topics such as risks related to hazardous waste sites, chemical contaminants, and biotechnology.

Managing Health Care Hazards. Linda F. Chaff. Labelmaster, 574 N. Pulaski Rd., Chicago, IL 60646. (312) 478-0900. 1988.

Managing Indoor Air Quality. Shirely J. Hansen. The Association of Energy Engineers, 4025 Pleasantdale Rd., Suite 420, Atlanta, GA 30340. (404) 925-9558. 1991. Includes readily applicable air quality control measures and preventive strategies that can head off the economic and legal problems.

Managing Industrial Hazardous Waste–Practical Handbook. Gary F. Lindgren. Lewis Publishers, 2000 Corporate Blvd., N.W., Boca Raton, FL 33431. (407) 994-0555 or (800) 272-7737. 1989. Explains the regulations regarding identification and listing of hazardous wastes.

Managing Interior Northwest Rangelands. U.S. G.P.O, Washington, DC 20402-9325. (202) 512-0000. Irregular. Grazing management practices and their effects on herbage production, water resources, and local economic conditions.

Managing Marine Environments. Richard A. Kenchington. Taylor & Francis, 1900 Frost Rd., Ste. 101, Bristol, PA 19007. (215) 785-5800. 1990. Contemporary issues of multiple-use planning and management of marine environments and natural resources.

Managing Marine Protected Areas: An Action Plan. Nancy Foster. U.S. Man and the Biosphere Program, Washington, DC 1988. Management of marine parks and reserves.

Managing our Wildlife Resources. Stanley H. Anderson. Prentice-Hall, Rte. 9W, Englewood Cliffs, NJ 07632. (201) 592-2000; (800) 634-2863. 1991. Reviews wildlife management, history, population characteristic, and habitat intervention; emphasizes planning, developing programs, and the impact of pollutants.

Managing Resistance to Agrochemicals: From Fundamental Research to Practical Strategies. Maurice B. Green, et al., eds. American Chemical Society, 1155 16th St. N.W., Washington, DC 20036. (800) 227-5558. 1990. A compilation of chapters written by some of the foremost scientists in pesticide and pest management research today.

Managing the Heavy Metals on the Land. Geoffrey Winthrop Leeper. Marcel Dekker, Inc., 270 Madison Ave., New York, NY 10016. (212) 696-9000; (800) 228-1160. 1978. Effect of heavy metals on plants, sewage irrigation, and soil pollution.

Managing the Nation's Public Lands. U.S. Bureau of Land Management. U.S. G.P.O., Washington, DC 20401. (202) 512-0000. Annual. Data on wilderness, wildlife, recreational resources, rangeland and forests.

Managing Troubled Water. National Academy Press, 2101 Constitution Ave., NW, PO Box 285, Washington, DC 20418. (202) 334-3313. 1990.

Mandatory Deposit Legislation and Alternatives for Managing Solid Waste: A Review of the Evidence. Joan Rohlfs. University of Maryland, College Park, Institute for Governmental Service, College Park, MD 20742. 1988.

Mangone's Concise Marine Almanac. Gerard J. Mangone. Taylor & Francis, 1900 Frost Rd., Ste. 101, Bristol, PA 19007. (215) 785-5800. 1991. Covers oceanography, marine resources, merchant marine, and fisheries.

Manomet Bird Observatory. P.O. Box 1770, Manomet, MA 02345. (508) 224-6521.

Man's Impact of the Troposphere: Lectures in Tropospheric Chemistry. National Technical Information Service, 5285 Port Royal Rd., Springfield, VA 22161. (703) 487-4650. 1978. Man's influence on nature and air pollution and atmospheric chemistry.

Man's Impact on Vegetation. Kluwer Academic Publishers, 101 Philip Dr., Assinippi Park, Norwell, Canada 02061. (617) 871-6600. 1983. Man's influence on nature and botanical ecology.

Mansfield University, Fisheries Program. Grant Science Center, Mansfield, PA 16933. (717) 662-4539.

Manual for Preventing Spills of Hazardous Substances at Fixed Facilities. Hemisphere Publishing Co., 79 Madison Ave., Suite 1110, New York, NY 10016. (212) 725-1999. Environmental monitoring of chemical spills and hazardous substances.

Manual for Review and Update of Hospital Department Safety, Environmental and Infection Control Policies. Frank D. Murphy. G.K. Hall & Co., 70 Lincoln St., Boston, MA 02111. (617) 423-3990. 1980. Administrative manuals for health care institutions, hospital departments relating to accident prevention and cross infection.

The Manual for the Home and Farm Production of Alcohol Fuel. Stephen W. Mathewson. Ten Speed Press, P.O. Box 7123, Berkeley, CA 94707. (800) 841-2665. 1980.

Manual of Acute Pesticide Toxicity. Guidotti. CRC Press, 2000 Corporate Blvd. N.W., Boca Raton, FL 33431. (800) 272-7737. 1991.

Manual of Aerial Photography. Ron Graham. Focal Press, 80 Montvale Ave., Stoneham, MA 02180. (617) 438-8464. 1986.

Manual of Clinical Endocrinology & Metabolism. James E. Griffin. McGraw-Hill Science & Engineering Books, 11 W. 19th St., New York, NY 10011. (212) 337-6010. 1982. Metabolism disorders and diseases of endocrine glands.

Manual of Cultivated Conifers. Gerd Krussmann. Timber Press, 9999 SW Wilshire, Portland, OR 97225. (800) 327-5680. 1985.

Manual of Determination of Volatile Organic Compounds in Paints, Inks, and Related Coating Products. J. John Brezinski. ASTM, 1916 Race St., Philadelphia, PA 19103-1187. (215) 299-5400. 1989. Analysis of solvents.

Manual of Fumigation for Insect Control. E. J. Bond. Food and Agriculture Organization of the United Nations, Via delle Terme di Caracalla, Rome, Italy 00100. 61 0181-FA01. 1984.

Manual of Pesticide Residue Analysis. Hans-Peter Thier and Hans Zeumer, eds. VCH Publishers, 303 NW 12th Ave., Deerfield Beach, FL 33442-1788. (305) 428-5566. 1989. Describes methods for analyzing pesticide residues representing those proven methods that are of the most value to the analyst. It presents 23 compound specific analytical methods.

Manual on Disposal of Refinery Wastes: Volume on Solid Wastes. American Petroleum Institute, 1220 L St. N.W., Washington, DC 20005. (202) 682-8000. 1980. Covers sewage disposal and petroleum waste.

A Manual on Ground Applications of Forestry Herbicides. James H. Miller. U.S. Department of Agriculture, Forest Service, 1720 Peachtree Rd. NW, Atlanta, GA 30367. 1990.

Manual on the Causes and Control of Activated Sludge Bulking and Foaming. David Jenkins. Water Research Commission, PO Box 824, Pretoria, Republic of #South Africa 0001. 1992. Handbook on sludge characterization.

Manuals of Food Quality Control. Food and Agriculture Organization of the United Nations. Food and Agriculture Organization of the United Nations, Via delle Terme di Caracalla, Rome, Italy 00100. 61 0181-FA01. 1986. Food and nutrition, and adulteration and inspection guidelines.

The Manufacture of Soaps and other Detergents, and Glycerine. Halsted Press, 605 3rd Ave., New York, NY 10158. (212) 850-6000. 1985. Ellis Horwood series in applied science and industrial technology.

Manufacturers List. Synerjy, Box 1854, Cathedral Station, New York, NY 10025. (212) 865-9595.

Manufacturers of Emission Controls Association. 1707 L St., N.W., Suite 570, Washington, DC 20036. (202) 296-4797.

Manure: Uses, Costs and Benefits, January 1984-May 1990. Jayne T. Maclean. National Agricultural Library, 10301 Baltimore Blvd., Beltsville, MD 20705-2351. (301) 504-5755. 1990. Topics in manures, fertilizers and organic wastes as fertilizers.

Mapping Insect Defoliation in Eastern Hardwood Forests with Color-IR Aerial Photos. J. D. Ward, et al. U.S. Department of Agriculture, Forest Service, Forest Pest Management, Methods Applications Group, 240 W. Prospect Rd., Fort Collins, CO 80526. (303) 224-1100. 1986. An infrared photo interpretation guide of the insect defoliation in the hardwood forests.

Marinas: A Working Guide to Their Development and Design. Donald W. Adie. Nichols Publishing Co., PO Box 96, New York, NY 10024. 1984.

Marine and Coastal Protected Areas: A Guide for Planners and Managers. Rodney V. Salm. International Union for Conservation of Nature and Natural Resources, Avenue du Mont-Blanc, Gland, Switzerland CH-1196. 1984. Case studies in coastal zone management and marine resources conservation.

Marine and Estuarine Protection: Programs and Activities. U.S. Environmental Protection Agency, Office of Water, 401 M St. SW, Washington, DC 20460. (202) 260-2090. 1989.

Marine Biological Laboratory. Woods Hole, MA 02543. (508) 548-3705.

Marine Biology. Springer-Verlag, 175 5th Ave., New York, NY 10010. (212) 461-1500; (800) 777-4643. Sixteen/year. Life in oceans and coastal waters.

Marine Biology. Matthew Lerman. Benjamin/Cummings Publishing Co., 390 Bridge Pkwy., Redwood City, CA 94065. (415) 594-4400. 1986. Environment, diversity and ecology.

Marine Biotechnology Center. University of California, Santa Barbara, Marine Science Institute, Santa Barbara, CA 93106. (805) 893-3765.

Marine Bulletin. National Coalition for Marine Conservation, Box 23298, Savannah, GA 31403. (912) 234-8062. Monthly. Marine fisheries, biological research, marine environmental pollution, and the prevention of the over-exploitation of ocean fish.

Marine Conservation News. Center for Marine Conservation, 1725 Desales St., N.W., Suite 500, Washington, DC 20036. (202) 429-5609. Quarterly. Marine conservation issues: whales, seals, sea turtles, and habitat.

Marine Cooperative Fish and Wildlife Research Unit. U.S. Fish and Wildlife Service, 240 Nutting Hall, University of Maine, Orono, ME 04469. (207) 581-2870.

Marine Debris Newsletter. Center for Marine Conservation, 1725 DeSales St, NW, Suite 500, Washington, DC 20036. (202) 429-5609. Quarterly. Plastic debris and other nondegradable trash in oceans and waterways.

Marine Ecological Institute. 1200 Chesapeake Drive, Redwood City, CA 94063. (415) 364-2760.

Marine Ecology. Paul Parey Scientific Publishers, P.O. Box 236, 150 East 27th Street, Suite 1A, New York, NY 10016. (212) 730-0518. Quarterly. Information on specific organisms in the environment.

Marine Ecology. Jeffery S. Levinton. Prentice-Hall, Rte. 9W, Englewood Cliffs, NJ 07632. (201) 592-2000. 1982.

Marine Ecology Research Highlights. U.S. Environmental Protection Agency, South Ferry Rd., Narragansett, RI 02882. Semiannual. Ocean research news.

Marine Ecology: Selected Readings. J. Stanley Cobb. University Park Press, Baltimore, MD 1976.

Marine Environment Law in the United Nations Environment Programme: An Emergent Ecoregime. P. H. Sand, ed. Cassell PLC, Publishers Distribution Center, PO Box C831, Rutherford, NJ 07070. (201) 939-6064; (201) 939-6065. 1988.

Marine Environmental Engineering Handbook. Frank L. Cross. Technomic Publishing, Co., 265 Post Rd. W, PO Box 8, Saug Station, Westport, CT 06880. 1974. Marine pollution abatement technology.

Marine Environmental Research. ASP Ltd., Ripple Road, Barking, Essex, England Monthly. Covers marine pollution and marine ecology.

Marine Equipment and Supplies. 5711 S. 86th Circle, Omaha, NE 68127. (402) 593-4600. Annual.

Marine Equipment Catalog. Maritime Activity Reports, Inc., 118 E. 25th St., New York, NY 10010. (212) 477-6700. 1984. Annual.

Marine Fish Management. Nautillus Press Inc., 1056 National Press Bldg., Washington, DC 20045. Monthly.

Marine Fisheries Review. U.S. G.P.O, Washington, DC 20402-9325. (202) 512-0000. Quarterly. Marine fishery resources, development, and management. Covers fish, shellfish, and marine mammal populations.

Marine/Freshwater Biomedical Center. Oregon State University, Department of Food Science, Corvallis, OR 97331. (503) 737-4193.

Marine Industry Fax Directory. National Marine Representatives' Association, Box 957075, Hoffman Estates, IL 60195. (708) 213-0606. 1988. Annual.

Marine Interfaces Ecohydrodynamics. J.C.J. Nihoul. Elsevier Science Publishing Co., 655 Avenue of the Americas, New York, NY 10010. (212) 984-5800. 1986. Ocean-atmosphere interaction and marine ecology.

Marine Invertebrates and Plants of the Living Reef. Patrick Lynn Colin. TFH Publications, 1 TFH Plaza, Neptune City, NJ 07753. (908) 988-8400. 1988. Identification of coral reef flora and marine invertebrates.

Marine Laboratory. University of Florida, 313 Carr, Gainesville, FL 32611. (904) 392-1097.

Marine Mammal News. Nautilus Press Inc., National Press Bldg., 1056 National Press Bldg., Washington, DC 20045. 1971-. Monthly.

Marine Mammal Science. Society for Marine Mammology, Lawrence, KS Quarterly. Covers marine mammal fossil and marine mammals.

Marine Mineral Exploration. H. Kunzendorf. Elsevier Science Publishing Co., 655 Avenue of the Americas, New York, NY 10010. (212) 984-5800. 1986. Geochemical prospecting, marine mineral resources, ore-deposits, and geophysical methods prospecting.

Marine Organisms as Indicators. Dorothy F. Soule. Springer-Verlag, 175 5th Ave., New York, NY 10010. (212) 460-1500. 1988. Environmental aspects of marine ecology and marine pollution.

Marine Photosynthesis: With Special Emphasis on the Ecological Aspects. E. Steema Nielsne. Elsevier Science Publishing Co., 655 Avenue of the Americas, New York, NY 10010. (212) 984-5800. 1975. Marine ecology and primary productivity.

Marine Plankton Ecology. Paul Bougis. Elsevier Science Publishing Co., 655 Ave. of the Americas, New York, NY 10010. (212) 989-5800. 1976.

Marine Policy Center. Crowell House, Woods Hole Oceanographic Institution, Woods Hole, MA 02543. (508) 548-1400.

Marine Policy Reports. Center for the Study of Marine Policy, College of Marine Studies, University of Delaware, Newark, DE 19716. (302) 451-8086. Bimonthly. Ocean research.

Marine Pollution Bulletin: The International Journal for Marine Environmentalists, Scientists, Engineers, Administrators, Politicians and Lawyers. Pergamon Microforms International, Inc., Fairview Park, Elmsford, NY 10523. (914) 592-7720. 1969-. Monthly. Concerned with the rational use of maritime and marine resources in estuaries, the seas and oceans. Covers pollution control, management and productivity of the marine environment in general.

Marine Pollution: Monographs. Mary A. Vance. Vance Bibliographies, PO Box 229, 112 N. Charter St., Monticello, IL 61856. (217) 762-3831. 1985.

Marine Products Directory. Underwriters' Laboratory, 333 Pfingston Rd., Northbrook, IL 60062-2096. (708) 272-8800. Annual.

Marine Resource Economics. Taylor & Francis, 1900 Frost Road, Suite 101, Bristol, PA 19007. (800) 821-8312. Quarterly. Issues related to the economics of marine resources.

Marine Resource Mapping: An Introductory Manual. M. J. A. Butler. Food and Agriculture Organization of the United Nations, Via delle Terme di Caracalla, Rome, Italy 00100. 61 0181-FA01. 1987. Topics in cartography relative to marine resources.

Marine Resources Development Foundation. Koblick Marine Center, 51 Shoreland Drive, P.O. Box 787, Key Largo, FL 33037. (305) 451-1139.

Marine Resources Research Institute. South Carolina Wildlife and Marine Resources Dept., Charleston, SC 29412. (803) 795-6350.

Marine Sanctuaries News. Center for Marine Conservation, 1725 DeSales St., NW, Suite 500, Washington, DC 20036. (202) 429-5609. Quarterly. Current issues regarding marine sanctuaries.

Marine Science Center. Educational Service District 114, State Superintendent of Public Instruction, 18743 Front St., N.E., P.O. Box 2079, Poulsbo, WA 98370. (206) 779-5549.

Marine Science Institute. University of California, Santa Barbara, Santa Barbara, CA 93106. (805) 893-3764.

Marine Science Newsletters–1977: An Annotated Bibliography. Charlotte M. Ashby. National Oceanic and Atmospheric Administration, National Environmental Data Referral Service, Washington, DC 1977. NOAA Technical Memorandum EDS NODC; 5.

Marine Sciences Institute. University of Connecticut at Avery Point, Groton, CT 06340. (203) 445-4714.

Marine Station. Walla Walla College, 174 Rosario Beach, Anacortes, WA 98221. (206) 293-2326.

Marine Technology. Society of Naval Architects and Marine Engineers, 601 Pavonia Ave., Jersey City, NJ 07306. (201) 498-4800. 1964-1987.

Marine Technology Society. 1825 K. St., N.W., Suite 218, Washington, DC 20006. (202) 775-5966.

Marine Toxins: Origin, Structure, and Molecular Pharmacology. Sherwood Hall and Gary Strichartz, eds. American Chemical Society, 1155 16th St. N.W., Washington, DC 20036. (202) 872-4600; (800) 227-5558. 1990. Describes the history of marine toxins and their various properties and effects on the environment.

Marine Treatment of Sewage Sludge. Telford House, 1 Heron Quay, London, England E14 9XF. 1988.

Marine World Africa USA. Marine World Foundation, Marine World Parkway, Vallejo, CA 94589. (707) 644-4000.

MARINELINE. Informationszentrum Rohstoffgewinnwig Geowissenschaften Wasserwirtschaft, Bundesanstalt fuer Geowissenschaften und Rohstoffe, Postfach 510153, Stilleweg 2, Hanover 51, Germany D-3000. 49 (511) 643-2819.

Marion Ownbey Herbarium. Washington State University, Pullman, WA 99164-4309. (509) 335-3250.

Maritime Center. 10 North Water Street, South Norwalk, CT 06854. (203) 852-0700.

The Market for Agricultural Chemicals. FIND/SVP, 625 Avenue of the Americas, New York, NY 10011. (212) 645-4500. 1990. Covers the markets for three types of agricultural chemicals: fertilizers, pesticide and natural and biotechnology products.

The Market for Cancer Therapeutics and Diagnostics. FIND/SVP, 625 Avenue of the Americas, New York, NY 10011. (212) 645-4500. 1991/92.

The Market for Disposable Hospital Products. FIND/SVP, 625 Avenue of the Americas, New York, NY 10011. (212) 645-4500. 1991. Covers the disposable products: prepackaged kits and trays; surgical and examination gloves; syringes; intravenous IV disposables; catheters; and nebulizers.

The Market for Hazardous Waste Site Remediation Services. FIND/SVP, 625 Avenue of the Americas, New York, NY 10011. (212) 645-4500. 1991/92. Market for hazardous waste site remediation equipment and services. These include biological, thermal, and physical techniques as well as solidification/vitrification.

The Market for Plastics Recycling & Degradable Products. FIND/SVP, 625 Avenue of the Americas, New York, NY 10011. (212) 645-4500. 1990. The market for all types of degradable products, including bio-and photodegradable; and the complex distribution channel that includes collection, hailing, sorting, bailing and transporting by type of plastic.

The Market for Water Pollution Control Equipment & Services. FIND/SVP, 625 Avenue of the Americas, New York, NY 10011. (212) 645-4500. Chemicals and supplies; equipment and instruments; engineering and analytical services.

Marsh Botanical Garden. Yale University, PO Box 6666, Biology Department, New Haven, CT 06511-8112. (203) 432-3906.

The Marshall Cavendish Encyclopedia of Gardening. Marshall Cavendish, 58 Old Compton St., London, England W1V 5PA. 01-734 6710. 1971. Seven volumes. Encyclopedic treatment of garden plants and advise on how to grow them.

The Marshall Cavendish Illustrated Encyclopedia of Plants and Earth Sciences. Marshall Cavendish Corp., 2415 Jerusalem Ave., North Bellmore, NY 11710. (516) 826-4200. 1988.

Marshes of the Ocean Shore: Development of an Ecological Ethic. Joseph Vincent Siry. Texas A & M University Press, College Station, TX 77843. 1984. Coastal zone management and tidemarsh ecology.

Mary B. Trotten Center for Biosystematics Technology. University of Nebraska, 436 Nebraska Hall, Lincoln, NE 68588-0514. (402) 472-6606.

Maryland Conservationist. Department of Natural Resources, Tawes State Office Bldg., C-2, Annapolis, MD 21401. 1924-. Bimonthly.

Maryland Guide to Environmental Law. Maryland Chamber of Commerce, Annapolis St., Annapolis, MD 21401. (410)268-7676. 1989.

Mass Mortality of Bottlenose Dolphins. U.S. House. Committee on Merchant Marine and Fisheries. U.S. G.P.O., Washington, DC 20401. (202) 512-0000. 1989. Dolphin deaths caused by brevetoxin produced by red-tide algae.

Mass Spectrometry of Priority Pollutants. Brian S. Middleditch. Plenum Press, 233 Spring St., New York, NY 10013-1578. (212) 620-8000 or (800) 221-9369. 1981. Spectra relating to organic water pollutants.

Massachusetts Audubon Newsletter. Massachusetts Audubon Society, S. Great Rd., Lincoln, MA 01773. (617) 259-9500. 1962-. Ten times a year.

Massachusetts College of Pharmacy and Allied Health Sciences, Herbarium. 179 Longwood Avenue, Boston, MA 02115. (617) 732-2960.

Massachusetts Institute of Technology Biotechnology Process Engineering Center. Room 20A-207, Cambridge, MA 02139. (617) 253-0805.

Massachusetts Institute of Technology, Center for Fisheries Engineering Research. Sea Grant College Program, Building E38-376, 292 Main Street, Cambridge, MA 02139. (617) 253-7079.

Massachusetts Institute of Technology, Comprehensive NMR Center for Biomedical Research. Francis Bitter National Magnet Laboratory, NW 14-5121, 170 Albany Street, Cambridge, MA 02139. (617) 253-5592.

Massachusetts Institute of Technology, MIT Sea Grant College Program. E38-300, 292 Main St., Cambridge, MA 02139. (617) 253-7041.

Massachusetts Solid Waste Market. FIND/SVP, 625 Avenue of the Americas, New York, NY 10011. (800) 346-3787. 1991. Market structure, landfill capacity, primary market participants and other primary assets.

The Master Handbook of All Home Heating Systems. Billy L. Price. Tab Books, PO Box 40, Blue Ridge Summit, PA 17294-2191. (717) 794-2191. 1979. Tune up, repair, installation, and maintenance as well as heating equipment and supplies.

Master Index for the Carbon Dioxide Research State-of-the-Art Report. Michael P. Farrell. U.S. Department of Energy, Carbon Dioxide Research Division, Washington, DC 1987. Covers atmospheric carbon dioxide and the global carbon cycle and the effects of increasing carbon dioxide on vegetation the climate.

Master Water Data Index. U.S. Geological Survey, Water Resources Division, National Water Data Exchange, 12201 Sunrise Valley Dr., Reston, VA 22092. (703) 648-4460. Information on more than 450,000 water data collection sites.

Material Safety Data Sheets Reference Files–MSDS. NPIRS (National Pesticide Information Retrieval System) User Services Manager, Entomology Hall, Purdue University, West Lafayette, IN 47907. (317) 494-6614.

Materials Evaluated as Insecticides and Acaricides at Brownsville, TX, September, 1955 to June, 1961. B. A. Butt and J. C. Keller. Agricultural Research Service, U.S. Dept. of Agriculture, PO Box 96456, Washington, DC 20250. (202) 720-8999. 1964.

Materials Technology Institute of the Chemical Process Industries. 12747 Olive Blvd., Suite 203, St. Louis, MO 63141. (314) 576-7712.

A Matrix Approach to Biological Investigation of Synthetic Fuels. U.S. Environmental Protection Agency, Health Effects Research Laboratory, Office of Research and Development, MD 75, Research Triangle Park, NC (919) 541-2184. Covers toxicology of shale oils, diesel fuels, jet planes, and synthetic fuels.

Maurice T. James Entomological Collection. Washington State University, Department of Entomology, Pullman, WA 99164-6432. (509) 335-5504.

Max McGraw Wildlife Foundation. P.O. Box 9, Dundee, IL 60118. (708) 741-8000.

Mazingira: The World Forum for Environment and Development. UNIPUB, 4611-F Assembly Dr., Lanham, MD 20706-4391. (301) 459-7666 or (800) 274-4888. Quarterly. Impact of economic growth on environment.

McCutcheon's Functional Materials. Manufacturing Confectioner Publishing Co., 175 Rock Rd., Glen Rock, NJ 07451. (201) 652-2655. 1985. Annual.

McGraw Hill Encyclopedia of Energy. Sybil P. Parker. McGraw-Hill Science & Engineering Books, 1221 Avenue of Americas, New York, NY 10020. (212) 512-2000 or (800) 262-4729. 1981. Second edition. Major issues in energy are discussed in six feature articles. The second section has 300 alphabetically arranged entries relating to energy.

McGraw-Hill Encyclopedia of Environmental Science. Sybil P. Parker. McGraw-Hill Science & Engineering Books, 11 W. 19th St., New York, NY 10011. (212) 337-6010. 1980. Covers ecology, man's influence on nature, and environmental protection.

McGraw-Hill Encyclopedia of Science and Technology. McGraw-Hill, 1221 Avenue of the Americas, New York, NY 10020. (212) 512-2000 or (800) 262-4729. 1992. Seventh edition. Issued in multiple volumes including index. Includes all science and technology broad subject areas.

McGraw-Hill Encyclopedia of the Geological Sciences. Sybil P. Parker, ed. McGraw-Hill, 1221 Avenue of the Americas, New York, NY 10020. (212) 512-2000 or (800) 262-4729. 1988. Second edition. Published previously in the McGraw-Hill Encyclopedia of Science and Technology.

Meadowcreek Project, Inc. Fox, AK 72051. (501) 363-4500.

Means Illustrated Construction Dictionary. Kornelis Smit, ed. R. S. Means Co., 100 Construction Plaza, PO Box 800, Kingston, MA 02364-0800. (617) 747-1270. 1991. Focuses on every-day language used by the construction trades and professions in the United States. Includes illustrations.

Measurement of PCB Emissions from Combustion Sources. Philip L. Levins. National Technical Information Service, 5285 Port Royal Rd., Springfield, VA 22161. (703) 487-4650. 1979. Covers combustion measurement, polychlorinated biphenyls and emission spectroscopy.

Measurement Techniques for Carcinogenic Agents in Workplace Air. Royal Society of Chemistry, c/o CRC Press, 2000 Corporate Blvd. N.W., Boca Raton, FL 33431-9868. (800) 272-7737. 1989. Covers 31 substances with known or suspected carcinogenic properties and describes recommended analytical methods for each substance when present in workplace air. It provides information including CAS Registry number, synonyms, manufacture, uses and determination (with recommended sampling and measuring procedures, and performance characteristics), plus a review of other methods used.

Mecca News. Minnesota Environmental Control Citizens Association, PO Box 80089, St. Paul, MN 55108. Monthly.

Mechanics of Sediment Transportation and Alluvial Stream Problems. R.J. Garde. John Wiley & Sons, Inc., 605 3rd Ave., New York, NY 10158-0012. (212) 850-6000. 1985.

Media and the Environment. Craig L. LaMay and Everette E. Dennis. Island Press, 1718 Connecticut Ave. N.W., Suite 300, Washington, DC 20009. (202) 232-7933. 1992. Explores environmental reporting.

Medical and Biomedical Waste Management Markets. FIND/SVP, 625 Avenue of the Americas, New York, NY 10011. (212) 645-4500. 1990. Discusses the increasing amount of waste as a result of the trend toward disposable instruments and clothing, and the establishment of more small clinics and health facilities.

Medical Gynaecology and Fertility Abstracts. Family Centre Ltd., London, England Monthly.

A Medical Monitoring Program for the Marine Hazardous Chemical Worker. R.J. Prevost. U.S. Coast Guard, Office of Research and Development, 2100 Second St., N.W., Rm. 5410 C, Washington, DC 20593. (202) 267-1042. 1985. Safety measures and environmental effects of hazardous substances transportation.

Medical Toxicology and Environmental Health. Department of Health and Social Security, Medical Toxiclogy & Environmental Health Division, Hannibal House, Rm. 719, Elephant and Castle, London, England SE1 6TE. 44 (71) 972-2162.

Medical Waste Handling for Health Care Facilities. John H. Keene. American Society for Healthcare Environmental Services of the American Hospital Association., 840 N. Lake Shore Dr., Chicago, IL 60611. (312) 280-6245. 1989. Covers medical waste, refuse disposal, environmental exposure, accident prevention, and health facilities.

Medical Waste Incineration Handbook. C. C. Lee. Government Institutes, Inc., 4 Research Pl., Suite 200, Rockville, MD 20850. (301) 921-2300. 1990. Covers incineration, equipment, measurement techniques, potential emissions, maintenance, safety guidance, operational problems and solutions, and the federal and state regulatory framework. Includes a list of addresses and phone numbers of manufacturers of medical waste incinerators and manufacturers of air pollution control equipment.

Medical Waste News. Business Publishers, Inc., 951 Pershing Dr., Silver Spring, MD 20910-4464. (301) 587-6300. 1989-. Biweekly. Covers EPA regulations and actions, state and nationwide changes in the laws, which management firms are landing big contracts, and also reports on technology such as: incineration, autoclaving, microwaves, etc. Also available online.

Medical Waste News. Business Publishers, Inc., 951 Pershing Dr., Silver Spring, MD 20910-4464. (301) 587-6300. Online access to regulation, legislation, and technological news and developments related to medical waste management and disposal. Online version of the periodical of the same name.

MEDIS. Mead Data Central, Inc., P.O. Box 933, Dayton, OH 45401. (800) 227-4908.

MEDITEC. FIZ Technik, Ostbahnhofstrasse 13, Postfach 600547, Frankfurt, Germany D-6000. 49 (69) 4308-225.

Mediterranean-Type Ecosystems: A Data Source Book. Kluwer Academic Publishers, 101 Philip Dr., Assinippi Park, Norwell, MA 02061. (617) 871-6600. 1988. Covers ecology and bioclimatology.

Meeting Environmental Work Force Needs. Information Dynamics, 111 Claybrook Dr., Silver Spring, MD 20902. 1985. Proceedings of the Second National Conference on Meeting Environmental Workforce Needs, April 1-3, 1985: Education and Training to Assure a Qualified Work Force.

Megaherbivores. R. Norman Owen-Smith. Cambridge University Press, 40 W. 20th St., New York, NY 10011. (212) 924-3900. 1988. The influence of very large body size on ecology; cover ungulata and mammals.

Membrane & Separation Technology News. NewsNet, Inc., 945 Haverford Rd., Bryn Mawr, PA 19010. (800) 345-1301.

The Merck Index. Merck Co., Inc., Box 2000, Rahway, NJ 07065. (201) 855-4558. Data on chemicals, drugs, and biological substances.

The Merck Index Online. Merck & Company, Inc., Box 2000, Building 86-0900, Rahway, NJ 07065-0900. (201) 855-4558.

Mercury: Environmental Aspects. World Health Organization, Ave. Appia, Geneva, Switzerland CH-1211. Environmental health criteria relating to toxicology of mercury.

Metabolic Maps of Pesticides. Hiroyasu Aizawa. Academic Press, c/o Harcourt Brace Jovanovich Inc., 6277 Sea Harbor Dr., Orlando, FL 32887. (800) 346-8648. 1982. Ecotoxicology and environmental quality of pesticides metabolism.

The Metabolism and Toxicity of Fluoride. Gary M. Whitford. Karger, 26 W. Avon Rd., Box 529, Farmington, CT 06085. (203) 675-7834. 1989.

Metal-Bearing Waste Streams: Mining, Recycling, and Treatment. Michael Meltzer, et al. Noyes Publications, 120 Mill Rd., Park Ridge, NJ 07656. (201) 391-8484. 1990. Examines the management of metal-bearing wastes. Covers an in-depth industry study of the generation of metal-bearing waste streams. Summaries of waste management practices in various metal operations, including foundry activities, metal cleaning and stripping, surface treatment and plating, coating, and auxiliary operations, are provided.

Metal Bulletin Prices and Data. Metal Bulletin Books Ltd., 220 5th St, 10th Fl, New York, NY 10001. (212) 213-6202. 1987-. Annual.

Metal Casting Industry Directory. 1100 Superior Ave., Cleveland, OH 44114. (216) 696-7000. Annual.

Metal Contamination of Food. Conor Reilly. Elsevier Science Publishing Co., 655 Avenue of the Americas, New York, NY 10010. (212) 984-5800. 1991. Analysis of testing of metals in food.

Metal Finishing Guidebook Directory. Metals and Plastics Publications, Inc., 3 University Plaza, Hackensack, NJ 07601. (201) 487-3700. Annual. Covers electroplating and metal finishing.

Metal Recovery from Industrial Waste. Clyde S. Brooks. Lewis Publishers, 2000 Corporate Blvd., N.W., Boca Raton, FL 33431. (407) 994-0555 or (800) 272-7737. 1991. Gives details of industrial waste recycling in particular nonferrous metals.

Metals Abstracts. ASM International, 9639 Kinsman, Materials Park, OH 44073. (216) 338-5151. 1968-. Published jointly by the Institute of Metals, London and the American Society for Metals. Formed by the Union of Metallurgical Abstracts and Review of Metal Literature.

Metals and Their Compounds in the Environment. Ernest Merian, ed. VCH Publishers, 303 NW 12th Ave., Deerfield Beach, FL 33442-1788. (305) 428-5566. 1990.

Metals in Groundwater. Herbert E. Allen. Lewis Publishers, 2000 Corporate Blvd., N.W., Boca Raton, FL 33431. (407) 994-0555 or (800) 272-7737. 1991. Discusses in depth the state of the knowledge of metal sorption by aquifer materials. The status of chemical partitioning, hydrologic transport models is also considered. Includes agricultural, wastewater, and mining field-site examples.

Metals Week. McGraw-Hill Financial Services Company, 25 Broadway, New York, NY 10004. (212) 208-8880.

Meteorological and Geoastrophysical Abstracts. American Meteorological Society, 45 Beacon St., Boston, MA 02108. (617) 227-2425.

Meteorology of Air Pollution: Implications for the Environment and Its Future. R. S. Scorer. E. Horwood, 66 Wood Lane End, Hemel Hempstead, England HP2 4RG. 1990. Discusses methods of air pollution measurement and future expectations.

Methane Recovery from Landfill Yearbook. Robert N. Gould. Government Advisory Associates, 177 E. 87th St., Suite 404, New York, NY 10128. (212) 410-4165. Biennial.

Methanol. Environmental Protection Services, Environment Canada, 425 St. Joseph Blvd., 3rd Fl., Hull, PQ, Canada K1A 0H3. (613) 953-5921. 1985. Environmental and technical information for problem spills.

Methods for Assessing Exposure of Human and Non-Human Biota. R. G. Tardiff and B. D. Goldstein, eds. John Wiley & Sons, Inc., 605 3rd Ave., New York, NY 10158-0012. (212) 850-6000. 1991. Provides a critical and collective evaluation of approaches to chemical exposure assessment.

Methods for Determination of Toxic Organic Compounds in Air; EPA Methods. William T. Winberry, et al. Noyes Publications, 120 Mill Rd., Park Ridge, NJ 07656. (201) 391-8484. 1990. Contains 14 procedures in a standardized format; five were selected to cover as many compounds as possible, and the others are targeted toward specific compounds.

Methods for Measuring the Acute Toxicity of Effluents to Freshwater and Marine Organisms. William H. Peltier. Environmental Monitoring and Support Laboratory, Office of Research and Development, U.S. Environmental Protection Agency, 401 M St. SW, Washington, DC 20024. (202) 260-2090. 1985. Measurement of water pollution in the United States.

Methods for the Analysis of Mineral Chromites and Ferrochrome Slag. Delbert A. Baker. U.S. Department of the Interior, 1849 C St., NW, Washington, DC 20240. (202) 208-3171. 1989. Analysis of chromium ores.

Methods for Toxicity Tests of Single Substances and Liquid Complex Wastes With Marine Unicellular Algae. Gerald E. Walsh. Environmental Protection Agency, U.S. Environmental Research Laboratory, 401 M St. SW, Washington, DC 20460. (202) 260-2090. 1988. Deals with the impact of factory and trade waste on the marine environment, especially on algae and other biological forms.

Methods in Enzymology. Sidney P. Colowick and Nathan O. Kaplan, eds. Academic Press, c/o Harcourt Brace Jovanovich Inc., 6277 Sea Harbor Dr., Orlando, FL 32887. (800) 346-8648. 1955-. Series of volumes in enzymology. Each volume has a distinct title.

Methods of Air Sampling and Analysis. James P. Lodge, Jr. Lewis Publishers, 2000 Corporate Blvd., N.W., Boca Raton, FL 33431. (407) 994-0555 or (800) 272-7737. 1989. Third edition. Includes all contaminants analyzed or monitored with a given method. Includes information on how to deal with indoor and outdoor air pollution, industrial hygiene, and other related topics.

Methods of Protein Analysis. Istavan Kerese. Halsted Press, 605 Third Ave., New York, NY 10158. (212) 850-6000. 1984. Deals with electrophoresis, proteins and chromatography.

Methods of Protein Microcharacterization. John E. Shiveley. Humana Press, PO Box 2148, Clifton, NJ 07015. (201) 773-4389. 1986. Peptides analysis, trace analysis and amino acid sequences.

Methods of Soil Analysis. Arnold Klute. Soil Science Society of America, 677 S. Segoe Rd., Madison, WI 53611. (608) 273-8080. 1986. Physical and mineralogical methods and chemical and microbiological properties of soil.

Methyl Chloride Industry Alliance. c/o Latham and Watkins, 1001 Pennsylvania Ave., N.W., #130, Washington, DC 20004. (202) 637-2200.

Methylmercury. World Health Organization, Ave. Appia, Geneva, Switzerland CH-1211. 1990. Environmental health criteria relating to methylmercury.

Metracom Data. Metracom, Inc., P.O. Box 23498, Oklahoma City, OK 73132. (415) 721-0207.

Metropolitan Tree Improvement Alliance. c/o Andrew Todd, Division of Forestry, Ohio Dept. of Natural Resources, Fountain Square Bldg. B-3, Columbus, OH 43224. (614) 265-6707.

MHIDAS. U.K. Atomic Energy Authority, Safety and Reliability Directorate, Wiashaw Lane, Culcheta, Warrington, England WA3 4NE. 44 (925) 31244.

Michigan Environmental Law Letter. M. Lee Smith Publishers & Printers, 162 4th Ave., N., Box 2678, Arcade Sta., Nashville, TN 37219. (615) 242-7395.

Michigan Environmental Management Directory. Michigan Waste Report, Inc., 400 Ann, SW, Ste. 204, Grand Rapids, MI 49504. (616) 363-3262. 1989.

Michigan Environmental Statutes and Regulations. State Bar of Michigan, 306 Townsend, Lansing, MI 48933. (517)372-9030. 1990.

Michigan State University, Center for Environmental Toxicology. C 231 Holden Hall, East Lansing, MI 48824. (517) 353-6469.

Michigan State University, Center for Genetic and Biochemical Alteration of Plant Lipids and Starch. c/o Department of Botany and Plant Pathology, East Lansing, MI 48824. (517) 353-0611.

Michigan State University, Department of Fisheries and Wildlife. East Lansing, MI 48824. (517) 353-0647.

Michigan State University. Dept. of Resource Development. Water Bulletin. Dept. of Resource Development, Michigan State University, 302 Natural Resources Bldg., East Lansing, MI 48824-1222. (517) 355-0100. Monthly.

Michigan State University, Dunbar Forest Experiment Station. Route 1, Box 179, Sault Ste. Marie, MI 49783. (906) 632-3932.

Michigan State University, Fred Russ Research Forest. 20673 Marcellis Highway, Decatur, MI 49045. (616) 782-5652.

Michigan State University, Inland Lakes Research and Study Center. 334 Natural Resources Building, East Lansing, MI 48824. (517) 353-3742.

Michigan State University, Institute of Water Research. 334 Natural Resources Building, East Lansing, MI 48824. (517) 353-3742.

Michigan State University, Microbial Ecology Center. 540 Plant and Soil Sciences Building, East Lansing, MI 48824-1325. (517) 353-9021.

Michigan State University, MSU-DOE Plant Research Laboratory. 106 Plant Biology Building, East Lansing, MI 48824-1312. (517) 353-2270.

Michigan State University, W.J. Beal Botanical Garden. 412 Olds Hall, East Lansing, MI 48824-1047. (517) 355-9582.

Michigan State University, W.K. Kellogg Biological Station. 3700 East Gull Lake Drive, Hickory Corners, MI 49060. (616) 671-5117.

Michigan State University, W.K. Kellogg Forest. 7060 N. 42nd St., Augusta, MI 49012. (616) 731-4597.

Michigan Technological University, Center for Intensive Forestry in Northern Regions. School of Forestry and Wood Products, Houghton, MI 49931. (906) 487-2897.

Michigan Technological University, Environmental Engineering Center for Water and Waste Management. 1400 Townsend Rd., Houghton, MI 49931. (906) 487-2194.

Michigan Technological University, Ford Forestry Center. Route 2, Box 7361, Lansing, MI 49946. (906) 487-2454.

Michigan Technological University, Great Lakes Area Resource Studies Unit. Department of Biological Sciences, Houghton, MI 49931. (906) 487-2478.

Michigan Waste Report. Michigan Waste Report, Inc., 400 Ann, SW, Suite 204, Grand Rapids, MI 49504. (616) 363-3262. Biweekly. Covers information about waste management.

Micro-Organisms. Lilian E. Hawker. E. Arnold, 41 Bedford Sq., London, England 1979. Function, form, and environment of microbiology.

Microbes and Microbial Products as Herbicides. Robert E. Hoagland, ed. American Chemical Society, 1155 16th St. N.W., Washington, DC 20036. (202) 872-4600; (800) 227-5558. 1990. Discusses the suitability of host specific phytotoxins, synthetic derivatives of abcisic acid, phytoalexins, pathogens, soilborne fungi, its biochemistry and other potential microbial product herbicides.

Microbial Control of Weeds. David O. TeBeest, ed. Chapman & Hall, 29 W. 35th St., New York, NY 10001-2291. (212) 244-3336. 1991. Summarizes the progress that has been made over the last 20 years in the biological control of weeds.

Microbial Ecology. Richard Campbell. Blackwell Scientific Publication, 3 Cambridge Ctr., Suite 208, Cambridge, MA 02142. (617) 225-0401. 1983.

Microbial Ecology. Morris A. Levin. McGraw-Hill Science & Engineering Books, 11 W. 19th St., New York, NY 10011. (212) 337-6010. 1992. Principles, methods, and applications.

Microbial Enzymes in Aquatic Environments. Ryszard J. Chrost. Springer-Varlag, 175 5th Ave., New York, NY 10010. (212) 460-1500. 1991. Brings together studies on enzymatic degradation processes from disciplines as diverse as water and sediment research, bacterial and algal aquatic ecophysiology, eutrophication, nutrient cycling, and biogeochemistry, in both freshwater and marine ecosystem.

Microbial Hydrocarbon Degradation in Sediments Impacted by the Exxon Valdez Oil Spill; Final Report. Water Research Center, University of Alaska, Fairbanks, 460 Duckering Bldg., Fairbanks, AK 99775. (907) 474-7350. 1990.

Microbial Mats. Yehuda Cohen. American Society of Microbiology, 1325 Massachusetts Ave. NW, Washington, DC 20005. (202) 737-3600. 1989. Physiological ecology of benthic microbial communities.

Microbial Toxins in Focus and Feeds. Albert E. Pohland, et al., eds. Plenum Press, 233 Spring St., New York, NY 10013. (212) 620-8000; (800) 221-9369. 1990. Proceedings of a Symposium on Cellular and Molecular Mode of Action of Selected Microbial Toxins in Foods and Feeds, Oct. 31- Nov. 2, 1988, Chevy Chase, MD.

Microbiology Abstracts. Section A. Industrial and Applied Microbiology. Cambridge Scientific Abstracts, 5161 River Rd., Bethesda, MD 20816. (301) 961-6750. 1972-.

Microcomputer Applications in Occupational Health and Safety. Lewis Publishers, 2000 Corporate Blvd., N.W., Boca Raton, FL 33431. (407) 994-0555 or (800) 272-7737. 1987. Practical software use in the "real world" of occupational health and safety is the main theme of this book.

Microcomputer Applications in Water Resources. Otto J. Helweg. Prentice Hall, Rte. 9W, Englewood Cliffs, NJ 07632. (201) 592-2000; (800) 634-2863. 1991. Presents 14 programs for solving a range of water resource engineering problems on microcomputers. Includes a 5 1/4 inch disk containing the problems described in the text. Also includes a basic introduction to computers and to BASIC, in which the programs are written.

Microcomputers in Environmental Biology. J. N. R. Jeffers, ed. Parthenon Pub., Casterton Hall, Carnforth, England LA6 2LA. Lancs. 1991. Contains extensive lists of programs written specially to show the ways in which microcomputers can be most usefully employed in the analysis of experiments and surveys, the analysis of multivariate data, radio tagging and the analysis of animal movement, and in modeling complex systems.

Micromolar Evolution, Systematics, and Ecology. Otto Richard Gottlieb. Springer-Verlag, 175 5th Ave., New York, NY 10010. (212) 460-1500. 1982. Evolution of plants, plant chemotaxonomy, botanical chemistry, classification, and ecology of botany.

Microwave Energy Applications Newsletter. International Microwave Power Institute. R. V. Decareau, PO Box 241, Amherst, NH 03031. (603) 673-2245. Irregular.

Mid-Continent Oil & Gas Association. 801 Pennsylvania Ave. N.W., Ste. 840, Washington, DC 20004-2604. (202) 638-4400.

The Mid-Net Zipper Ridge a Possible Cause of Unobserved Porpoise Mortality. David B. Holts. National Oceanic and Atmospheric Administration, U.S. Department of Commerce, Washington, DC 20230. (202) 377-2985. 1980. Effects of purse seining.

Middle States Independent Power. 320 Walnut St., Suite 105, Philadelphia, PA 19106. (215) 627-0307.

The Mighty Rain Forest. John Nicol. Sterling Pub. Co. Inc., 387 Park Ave. S., New York, NY 10016. (212) 532-7160; (800) 367-9692. 1990. Focuses on the emotive debate on the environment regarding rainforests and the paper manufacturers. Includes a bibliography and a list of organizations working in rainforest conservation.

Migration Processes in the Soil and Groundwater Zone. Ludwig Luckner. Lewis Publishers, 2000 Corporate Blvd., N.W., Boca Raton, FL 33431. (407) 994-0555 or (800) 272-7737. 1991. Discusses the significance of migration main objectives of migration simulation and some methods of mathematical modelling.

MILDOS-a Computer Program for Calculating Environmental Radiation Doses from Uranium Recovery Operations. D. L. Strenge. National Technical Information Service, 5285 Port Royal Rd., Springfield, VA 22161. (703) 487-4650. 1981.

Military Explosives. Headquarters, Dept. of the Army, Washington, DC 20310. (202) 695-6153. 1990. Army manual dealing with handling explosives.

Military Standard: Activated Desiccants. U.S. Department of Defense, The Pentagon, Washington, DC 20301-1155. (703) 545-6700. Looseleaf; standards for drying agents in the United States.

Mind and Nature: A Necessary Unit. Gregory Bateson. Bantam Books, 666 5th Ave., New York, NY 10103. (212) 765-6500; (800) 223-6834. 1988. Reveals the pattern which connects man and nature.

Minding the Carbon Store: Weighing U.S. Forestry Strategies to Slow Global Warming. Mark C. Trexler. World Resources Institute, 1709 New York Ave. N.W., Washington, DC 20006. (800) 833 0504. 1991. Assesses the strengths and weaknesses of each of the major domestic forestry options, including their costs and carbon benefits.

Minding the Earth. Latham Foundation, Latham Plaza Bldg., Clement & Shiller Sts., Alameda, CA 94501. (206) 463-9773. Quarterly. Environmental ethics.

Mine Drainage Bibliography. V.E. Gleason. National Technical Information Service, 5285 Port Royal Rd., Springfield, VA 22161. (703) 487-4650. Formation and effects of acid mine drainage; erosion and sedimentation; sediment control technology effects of coal mining on ground water quality and on hydrology; and drainage from coal storage piles.

Mineral Acids. FIND/SVP, 625 Avenue of the Americas, New York, NY 10011. (212) 645-4500. 1991. Historical data and forecasts of demand and market for sulfuric; phosphoric; nitric; hydrochloric; and hydrofluoric.

Mineral Commodity Summaries. U.S. Bureau of Mines. U.S. G.P.O., Washington, DC 20401. (202) 512-0000. Annual. Market profiles of mineral commodities.

Mineral Industry Location System. Department of the Interior, 810 7th St. NW, Washington, DC 20241. (202) 501-9649.

Mineral Industry Surveys. U.S. G.P.O, Washington, DC 20402-9325. (202) 512-0000. Annual. Mineral production, consumption, trade, and industry operations, by commodity.

Mineralization Center. University of South Alabama, Department of Biological Sciences, LSB, Room 214, Mobile, AL 36688. (205) 460-6331.

Mineralogical Abstracts. Mineralogical Society, 41 Queen's Gate, London, England SW7 5HR. 71 5847916. Quarterly. Abstracts of journal articles, conferences, technical reports and specialized books in the areas of minerals, clay minerals, economic minerals, ore deposits, environmental studies, experimental mineralogy, gemstones, geochemistry, petrology, lunar and planetary studies and other related areas in mineralogy.

Mineralogical Society of America. 1130 17th St., N.W., Suite 330, Washington, DC 20036. (202) 775-4344.

Minerals Availability System. Bureau of Mines, Department of the Interior, Box 25086, Denver, CO 80225. (303) 236-5210.

Minerals Data System & Rock Analysis Storage System. Geological Information Systems, c/o University of Oklahoma, 830 Van Fleet Oval, Norman, OK 73019. (405) 325-3031.

Minerals Management Service. Room 1442, M5612, 18th and C St., N.W., Washington, DC 20240. (202) 208-3500.

Minerals, Metals, and Materials Society. 420 Commonwealth Dr., Warrendale, PA 15086. (412) 776-9000.

Minerals Yearbook. Department of the Interior, 810 7th St. NW, Washington, DC 20241. (202) 501-9649.

Minerals Yearbook: Gallium. U.S. Department of the Interior, Bureau of Mines, 810 7th St. NW, Washington, DC 20241. (202) 501-9649. Annual.

Minerals Yearbook: Hafnium and Zirconium. U.S. Department of the Interior, Bureau of Mines, Cochrans Mill Rd., Pittsburgh, PA 15236. (412) 892-6400. Annual. Statistics on hafnium and zirconium.

Minesearch. Metals Economics Group, Ltd., 1722 14th St., Boulder, CO 80302. (303) 442-7501.

The Minimizer. Center for Hazardous Materials Research, University of Pittsburgh Applied Research Center, 320 William Pitt Way, Pittsburgh, PA 15238. (412) 826-5320. Quarterly. Environmental and regulatory information regarding solid and hazardous waste.

Mining and Metallurgical Society of America. 9 Escalle Lane, Larkspur, CA 94939. (415) 924-7441.

Mining in National Forests. U.S. Department of Agriculture, Forest Service, 14 Independence Ave., S.W., Washington, DC 20250. (202) 447-7454. 1974. Forest reserves, mines and minerals in the U.S.

Mining Urban Wastes: The Potential for Recycling. Cynthia Pollock. Worldwatch Institute, 1776 Massachusetts Ave., N.W., Washington, DC 20036-1904. 1987.

Minnesota Division of Game & Fish, Technical Bulletin. Minnesota Dept. of Conservation, 90 W. Plato Blvd., St. Paul, MN 55107. Irregular.

Minnesota Environmental Law Handbook. Government Institutes, Inc., 4 Research Pl., Ste. 200, Rockville, MD 20850. (301) 921-2300. 1990.

Minnesota Out-of-Doors. Minnesota Conservation Federation, 1036-B Cleveland Ave., S., St. Paul, MN 55116. (612) 690-3077. Monthly. Conservation, natural resources, hunting & fishing.

Minnesota Transgenic Fish Group. University of Minnesota, Department of Animal Science, 1988 Fitch Ave., St. Paul, MN 55108. (612) 624-4277.

Minnesota Volunteer. Minnesota Dept. of Natural Resources, 500 Lafayette Rd., St. Paul, MN 55155-4046. (612) 296-3336. Bimonthly. Natural resources & conservation education.

Minnesota Wildlife Reports. Minnesota Dept. of Natural Resources, 500 Lafayette Rd., St. Paul, MN 55155-4046. (612) 296-3344. Irregular. Wildlife research & surveys.

Mirex. World Health Organization, Ave. Appia, Geneva, Switzerland CH-1211. 1984. Toxicology of mirex and insecticides.

Mirex Hazards to Fish, Wildlife, and Invertebrates: A Synoptic Review. Ronald Eisler. Fish and Wildlife Service, Department of the Interior, 18th and C Sts., NW, Washington, DC 20240. (202) 653-8750. 1985. Effect of water pollution on fish and wildlife and environmental aspects of mirex.

Mississippi-Alabama Sea Grant Consortium. Caylor Building, Gulf Coast Research Laboratory, P.O. Box 7000, Ocean Springs, MS 39564-7000. (601) 875-9341.

Mississippi Cooperative Fish & Wildlife Research Unit. Mississippi State University, P.O. Box BX, Mississippi State, MS 39762. (601) 325-2643.

Mississippi Forest Products Utilization Laboratory. Mississippi State University, P.O. Drawer FP, Mississippi State, MS 39762. (601) 325-2116.

Mississippi State Chemical Laboratory. Mississippi State University, P.O. Box CR, Mississippi State, MS 39762. (601) 325-3324.

Mississippi State University, Mississippi Remote Sensing Center. P.O. Box FR, Mississippi State, MS 39762. (601) 325-3279.

Mississippi State University, Research Center. John C. Stennis Space Center, Stennis Space Center, MS 39529-6000. (601) 688-3227.

Mississippi State University, Water Resources Research Institute. P.O. Drawer AD, Mississippi State, MS 39762. (601) 325-3620.

Missouri Botanical Garden. P.O. Box 299, St. Louis, MO 63166-0299. (314) 577-5100.

Missouri Conservationist. Missouri Deptartment of Conservation, Box 180, Jefferson City, MO 65102. (314) 751-4115. Monthly. Game, fish, and forestry management and hunting and fishing techniques.

Missouri Cooperative Fish and Wildlife Research Unit. University of Missouri, 112 Stephens Hall, Columbia, MO 65211. (314) 882-3524.

Missouri Environmental Law Handbook. Government Institutes, Inc., 4 Research Pl., Ste. 200, Rockville, MD 20850. (301) 921-2300. 1990.

Missouri Wildlife. Conservation Federation of Missouri, 728 W. Main St., Jefferson City, MO 65101. (314) 634-2322. Bimonthly. Conservation & environmental news and features.

MIT Sea Grant Quarterly Report. Sea Grant College Program, Bldg. E38-320, Cambridge, MA 02139. (617) 235-3461. Quarterly. Ocean related research.

The Mode in Furs. Ruth Turner Wilcox. Scribner Educational Publishers, 866 3rd Ave., New York, NY 10022. (212) 702-2000. 1951. The history of furred costume of the world from the earliest times to the present.

Modeling of the Seepage Flux of Ground Water from Coastal Landfills. D. A. Colden. National Technical Information Service, 5285 Port Royal Rd., Springfield, VA 22161. (703) 487-4650. 1990. Master's Thesis, Rhode Island University, Kingston.

Modeling of Total Acid Precipitation Impacts. Jerald L. Schnoor. Butterworth-Heinemann, 80 Montvale Ave., Stoneham, MA 02180. (617) 438-8464. 1984.

Modeling the Environmental Fate of Microorganisms. Criston J. Hurst. American Society for Microbiology, 1325 Massachusetts Ave. NW, Washington, DC 20005. (202) 737-3600. 1991. Mathematical models of microbial ecology.

Modern and Ancient Fluvial Systems. J.D. Collinson. Blackwell Scientific Publications, 3 Cambridge Ctr., Ste. 208, Boston, MA 02142. (617) 225-0401. 1983. Topics in sediment transport in rivers.

Modern Plastics. Modern Plastics, Circulation Department, 777 14th St., NW, Suite 8000, Washington, DC 20005. (202) 639-8040. Monthly. Plastics manufacturing, management, R&D, marketing, and consumption.

Modern Plastics Encyclopedia. Modern Plastics Encyclopedia, PO Box 602, Highstown, NJ 08520-9955. 1992. Contains information on a broad range of topics from resin manufacture to semi finished materials. Includes environmental and safety regulations, on manufacture, use,and recycling and related matter.

Modern Selective Fungicides. H. Lyr. John Wiley & Sons, Inc., 605 3rd Ave., New York, NY 10158-0012. (212) 850-6000. 1987. Properties, applications, mechanisms of action.

Modern Sewer Design. American Iron and Steel Institute, 1133 15th St., NW, Washington, DC 20005. 1980. Manual for sheet steel producers.

Modifying the Root Environment to Reduce Crop Stress. G. F. Arkin and H. M. Taylor, eds. American Society of Agricultural Engineers, 2950 Niles Rd., St. Joseph, MI 49085-9659. (616) 429-0300. 1981. Emphasizes the development and understanding of relationship between the plant and its subterranean environment and effect of modification of that environment on plant response.

Molecular and Cellular Endocrinology. North-Holland, Shannon, Ireland Monthly.

Molecular Aspects of Monooxygenases and Bioactivation of Toxic Compounds. Emel Arinc, ed. Plenum Press, 233 Spring St., New York, NY 10013-1578. (212) 620-8000 or (800) 221-9369. 1991. Proceedings of the NATO Advanced Study Institute on Molecular Aspects of Monooxgenases and Bioactivation held in August-September, 1989.

Molecular Biology Institute. University of California, Los Angeles, 405 Hilgard Avenue, Los Angeles, CA 90024. (213) 825-1018.

Molecular Industrial Mycology; Systems and Applications for Filamentous Fungi. Marcel Dekker, Inc., 270 Madison Ave., New York, NY 10016. (212) 696-9000; (800) 228-1160. Genetics and molecular biology of fungus species that are economically significant in industry.

Molecular Strategies of Pathogens and Host Plants. Suresh S. Patil, et al., eds. Springer-Verlag, 175 5th Ave, New York, NY 10010. (212) 460-1500. 1991. Papers from an April seminar in Honolulu discusses the molecular interactions between plant pathogens and their hosts, considering the strategies of various bacteria and fungi, the plant's response, and an approach to breeding disease-resistant plants.

Molybdenum Catalyst Bibliography. Climax Molybdenum Co., 101 Merritt 7 Corporate Park, Norvalk, CT 06851. (203) 845-3000. Irregular. Bibliography of catalysts.

Molybdenum in Agricultural Ecosystems: A Bibliography of the Literature 1950 through 1971. Robert L. Jones. Department of Agronomy, University of Illinois, Urbana, IL 61801. 1973. Environmental aspects of molybdenum and sewage sludge.

Molybdenum in the Environment. Willard R. Chappell. Marcel Dekker, Inc., 270 Madison Ave., New York, NY 10016. (212) 696-9000; (800) 228-1160. 1976. Physiological environmental and toxicological effects.

Molybdenum Removal from Concentration Waste Water. R. D. Dannenberg. U.S. Department of the Interior, Bureau of Mines, 810 7th St., NW, Washington, DC 20241. (202) 501-9649. 1982. Waste disposal and water purification relating to molybdenum.

Monitor Consortium. 1506 19th St., N.W., Washington, DC 20036. (202) 234-6576.

Monitoring and Integrated Management of Arthropod Pests of Small Fruit Crops. N. J. Bostanian, et al., eds. VCH Publishers, 303 NW 12th Ave., Deerfield Beach, FL 33442-1788. (305) 428-5566. 1990. Examines the population models, pest management and insect- natural enemy interactions of pests of small fruit crops. It covers topics of major importance to those who grow strawberries, cranberries and other fruit crops.

Monitoring for Conservation and Ecology. Barrie Goldsmith, ed. Chapman & Hall, 29 W 35th St., New York, NY 10001-2291. (212) 244-3336. 1991. Focuses on an audience of those practicing ecology, nature conservation, or other similar land-based sciences. The differences between surveying and monitoring are discussed and emphasis is placed on the nature of monitoring as being purpose- oriented dynamic in philosophy, and often providing a baseline for recording possible changes in the future.

Monitoring Human Tissues for Toxic Substances. National Academy Press, 2101 Constitution Ave. N.W., PO Box 285, Washington, DC 20418. (202) 334-3313. 1991. Evaluates the National Human Monitoring Program.

Montana Outdoors. Montana Dept. of Fish, Wildlife, and Parks, 930 Custer Ave., W., Helena, MT 59620. (406) 444-2474. Bimonthly. Wildlife and fisheries management.

Montana State University, Herbarium. Bozeman, MT 59717. (406) 994-4424.

Montana State University, Montana Cooperative Fishery Research Unit. Biology Department, Bozeman, MT 59715. (406) 994-3491.

Montana State University, Plant Growth Center. Bozeman, MT 59717-0002. (406) 994-4821.

Montana State University, Reclamation Research Unit. Animal & Range Science Department, Bozeman, MT 59717. (406) 994-4821.

Montana University System Water Resources Center. 412 Cobleigh Hall, Bozeman, MT 59715. (406) 994-6690.

Monteverde Institute. Tropical Biology Program, Council on International Educational Exchange, 205 E. 42nd St., New York, NY 10017.

Monthly Catalog of United States Government Publications. U.S. G.P.O., Supt. of Docs., PO Box 371954, Pittsburgh, PA 15250-7954. (202) 512-0000.

Monthly Completion Report: Report on Well Completions in the U.S. American Petroleum Institute, 1220 L St. N.W., Washington, DC 20005. (202) 682-8000. Monthly. Exploratory and development oil and gas well drilling.

Monthly Report. Association of Metropolitan Water Agencies, 1717 K St. NW, Suite 1006, Washington, DC 20036. (202) 331-2820.

Monthly Rubber Consumption Report. Rubber Manufacturers Association, 1400 K St., NW, Washington, DC 20005. Monthly. Production, trade, consumption and stock.

Monthly Statistical Report, Estimated U.S. Petroleum Balance. American Petroleum Institute, 1220 L St. N.W., Washington, DC 20005. (202) 682-8000. Monthly. Petroleum supply and demand.

Monthly Tire Report. Rubber Manufacturers Association, 1400 K St., NW, Washington, DC 20005. Monthly. Tire and inner tube shipments, production, trade, and inventories.

MoPIRG Reports. Missouri Public Interest Research Group, Box 8276, St. Louis, MO 63156. (314) 534-7474. Quarterly. Consumer/environmental citizen advocacy.

More?. League of Women Voters of the United States, 1730 M St., NW, Washington, DC 20036. (202) 429-1965. 1972. The interfaces between population, economic growth, and the environment.

More About Leaking Underground Storage Tanks: A Background Booklet for the Chemical Advisory. U.S. Environmental Protection Agency, 401 M St., S.W., Washington, DC 20460. (202) 260-2090. 1984. Covers underground storage and drinking water contamination.

More Protection from Microwave Radiation Hazards Needed. U.S. General Accounting Office, 441 G St., NW, Washington, DC 1978. Health, environmental, and physiological effects of microwave devices.

Morton Arboretum. Route 53, Lisle, IL 60532. (708) 968-0074.

Mosquito Control Research Laboratory. University of California, Berkeley, 9240 S. Riverbend Ave., Parlier, CA 93648. (209) 891-2581.

Mosquito Research Program. University of California, Department of Entomology, Davis, CA 95616. (916) 752-6983.

Mote Marine Laboratory. 1600 Thompson Park, Sarasota, FL 34236. (813) 388-4441.

The Mother Earth News Alcohol Fuel Handbook. Michael R. Kerley. Mother Earth News, PO Box 801, Arden, NC 28704-0801. (704) 693-0211. 1980.

Motor Emission Control Manual. Michael J. Kromida. Hearst Books, 105 Madison Ave., New York, NY 10016. (212) 889-3050. 1989. Ninth edition. Revised edition of Motor's Emission Control Manual. Describes the effects of emission from automobile exhausts and the consequent problems.

The Motor Gasoline Industry: Past, Present, and the Future. Energy Information Administration. U.S. G.P.O., Washington, DC 20401. (202) 512-0000. 1991. Includes a great deal of historical and current statistical information. The book is grouped under topics such as history, chemistry (and combustion), supply constraints, distribution, pricing, alternative fuels, and future outlook.

Mount Evans Field Station. University of Denver, 16 Colorado Highway 5, Idaho Springs, CO 80452. (303) 871-3540.

Mountain Research and Development. University of California Press, 2120 Berkeley Way, Berkeley, CA 94720. (415) 642-7485; (800) 822-6657. Quarterly. Environmental & land use problems.

Mountain Research Station. University of Colorado-Boulder, 818 County Road 116, Nederland, CO 80466. (303) 492-8841.

MSDS Reference for Crop Protection Chemicals. John Wiley & Sons, Inc., 605 3rd Ave., New York, NY 10158-0012. (212) 850-6000. 1990. 3d ed. Covering over 650 brand name pesticides and related products from 19 manufacturers, their reference reproduces the manufacturers' information exactly, in a standardized typeset format.

MSDS Solution/Suspect Chemicals Sourcebook Database. Logical Technology, Inc., PO Box 3655, 1422 W. Main, Peoria, IL 61614. (309) 655-0223.

Mt. Desert Island Biological Laboratory. Salsbury Cove, ME 04672. (207) 288-3605.

Muir & Friends. John Muir Institute of Environmental Studies, 2118 C. Vine St., Berkeley, CA 94709. 1970-. Monthly.

Multi-Media Compliance Inspection Manual, 4th edition. Government Institutes, Inc., 4 Research Pl., Ste. 200, Rockville, MD 20850. (301) 921-2300. Multimedia compliance audit inspection of facilities that result in effluents, emissions, wastes or materials regulated under several laws such as Clean Water Act, Clean Air Act, RCRA and TSCA.

Multimedia Environmental Models: The Fugacity Approach. Donald Mackay. Lewis Publishers, 2000 Corporate Blvd., N.W., Boca Raton, FL 33431. (407) 994-0555 or (800) 272-7737. 1991. Discusses basic concepts, environmental chemicals and their properties, and the nature of the environmental media.

Multimedia Index to Ecology. National Information Center for Educational Media, University of Southern California, Los Angeles, CA 90007.

Multinational Environmental Outlook. Business Publishers, Inc., 951 Pershing Dr., Silver Spring, MD 20910-4464. (301) 587-6300. 1974-. Biweekly. Covers developments in world environmental problems such as acid rain, deforestation, soil erosion, overfishing, threats to health, animal extinction, population growth, diminishing water supply and other related matters. Also available online.

Multinational Environmental Outlook. Business Publishers, Inc., 951 Pershing Dr., Silver Spring, MD 20910-4464. (301) 587-6300. Environmental problems and solutions in countries outside the United States and their impact on the United States.

Multispecies Toxicity Testing. John Cairns, Jr. Pergamon Microforms International, Inc., Fairview Park, Clumsford, NY 10523. (914) 592-7720. Toxicity tests in the safety assessments of chemicals.

Multispectral Scanner and Photographic Imagery. U.S. Environmental Protection Agency, Office of Modeling and Monitoring Systems and Quality Assurance, 401 M St., S.W., Washington, DC 20460. (202) 260-2090. An index for various data tapes containing multispectral imagery from aircraft and satellites relating to sources of pollution.

Multivariate Methods in Drug and Agrochemical Research. David W. Salt and Martyn G. Ford. E. Horwood, 1230 Avenue of the Americas, New York, NY 10020. (212) 698-7000; (800) 223-2348. 1990. Comprehensive reference that provides users with the scope and application of multivariate analysis for researchers in the agrochemical and drug industries.

Municipal Composting: Resources for Local Officials and Communities Organizations. Institute for Local Self-Reliance, 2425 18th St., NW, Washington, DC 20009. (202) 232-4108. 1980. Deals with refuse and refuse disposal, and compost.

Municipal Solid Waste Incinerator Ash Management and Disposal Data Entries. The Institute, 2425 18th St., N.W., Washington, DC 20009. (202) 232-4108. Database on solid waste resources recovery and economic development, including municipal solid waste ash.

The Municipal Solid Waste Market. FIND/SVP, 625 Avenue of the Americas, New York, NY 10011. (212) 645-4500. 1991. Existing and emerging technologies (de-inking newsprint, recycling plastics, fluidized bed combustion, etc.) as well as applications and business opportunities in recycling and materials recovery, new waste-to-energy plant design, improved incineration technology, transportation of waste, compliance and landfill management.

Municipal Waste Combustion Study: Assessment of Health Risks Associated with Municipal Waste Combustion Emissions. U.S. Environmental Protection Agency, 401 M St., S.W., 20460. (202) 260-2090. 1987.

Municipal Waste Disposal. Bela Liptak. Chilton Book Co., 201 King of Prussia Rd., Radnor, PA 19089. (215) 964-4000. 1991.

Municipal Wastewater Stabilization Ponds. Office of Water Program Operations. U.S. Environmental Protection Agency, 401 M St., S.W., Washington, DC 20460. (202) 260-2090. 1983. Design manual for sewage lagoons and aeration purification of sewage.

Municipal Water Conservation. Vance Bibliographies, PO Box 229, 112 N. Charter St., Monticello, IL 61856. (217) 762-3831. 1982.

Murray State University, Center of Excellence for Reservoir Research. College of Science, Murray, KY 42071. (502) 762-2886.

Murray State University, Handcock Biological Station. Murray, KY 42071. (502) 474-2272.

Muscles, Molecules and Movement: An Essay in the Contraction of Muscles. J. R. Bendall. Heinemann Educational, Hanover St., Portsmouth, NH 03801-3959. (603) 431-7894. 1969. Discusses muscle proteins and also the effects of adenosine triphosphate.

Museum of Comparative Zoology. Harvard University, 26 Oxford Street, Cambridge, MA 02138. (617) 495-2460.

Mushrooms and Toadstools: A Color Field Guide. U. Nonis. Hippocrene Books, 171 Madison Ave., New York, NY 10016. (212) 685-4371. 1982. Includes 168 species of fungi reproduced and described that were selected from 1500 which were studied. The specimens were actually tested for edibility, toxicity, and are guaranteed.

Mushrooms Demystified: A Comprehensive Guide to the Fleshy Fungi of the Central California Coast. David Arora. Ten Speed Press, P.O. Box 7123, Berkeley, CA 94707. (800) 841-2665. 1979. Second edition. Covers covers the United States and Canada. Generously illustrated and includes lots of information on geography, climate and other related details for the growth of mushrooms.

Mutagenicity, Carcinogenicity, and Teratogenicity of Industrial Pollutants. Micheline Krisch-Volders. Plenum Press, 233 Spring St., New York, NY 10013-1578. (212) 620-8000; (800) 221-9369. 1984. Industrial toxicology of teratogenic agents.

Mycological Herbarium. Washington State University, 345 Johnson Hall, Pullman, WA 99164-6430. (509) 335-9541.

The Mycologist. C.U.P., Cambridge, MA Quarterly. Bulletin of the British Mycological Society.

Mycotoxic Fungi, Mycotoxins, Mycotoxicoses: An Encyclopedic Handbook. Thomas D. Wyllie and Lawrence G. Morehouse. Marcel Dekker, Inc., 270 Madison Ave., New York, NY 10016. (212) 696-9000; (800) 228-1160. 1977. Covers mycotoxic fungi and chemistry of mycotoxins, mycotoxicoses of domestic and laboratory animals, and mycotoxicoses of man and plants.

Mycotoxins. Vladimir Betina. Elsevier Science Publishing Co., 655 Avenue of the Americas, New York, NY 10010. (212) 984-5800. 1989. Chemical, biological, and environmental aspects of toxigenic fungi.

Mystic Marinelife Aquarium. 55 Coogan Boulevard, Exit 90, I-95, Mystic, CT 06355-1997. (203) 536-9631.

N.A.E.E. Newsletter. National Association for Environmental Education, Box 1295, Miami, FL 33143. 1972-. Monthly.

NAEP Newsletter. National Association of Environmental Professionals, P.O. Box 15210, Alexandria, VA 22309-0210. (703) 660-2364. Monthly. Covers environmental planning, management, review and research.

Naphthalene: Registration Standard. U.S. Environmental Protection Agency, Office of Pesticides and Toxic Substances, 401 M St., SW, Washington, DC 20460. (202) 260-2090. 1981. Naphthalene and pesticides law and legislation in the United States.

National Aerosol Association. 584 Bellerive Dr., Suite 3D, Annapolis, MD 21401. (301) 974-4472.

National Agricultural Aviation Association. 1005 E St., S.E., Washington, DC 20003. (202) 546-5722.

National Agricultural Chemicals Association. 1155 15th St., N.W., Madison Building, Suite 900, Washington, DC 20005. (202) 296-1585.

National Agricultural Library. Route 1, Beltsville, MD 20705. (301) 344-4348.

National Agricultural Plastics Association. P.O. Box 860238, St. Augustine, FL 32086. (904) 829-1667.

National Air Pollutant Emission Estimates. U.S. Environmental Protection Agency, 401 M St., S.W., Washington, DC 20460. (202) 260-2090. Annual. Estimates of nationwide emissions of particulates, sulfur oxides, nitrogen oxides, volatile organic compounds, carbon monoxide, and lead, by source.

National Air Quality and Emissions Trends Report. U.S. Environmental Protection Agency, 401 M St., S.W., Washington, DC 20460. (202) 260-2090. Annual. Status of air pollution in selected MSAs, 10 EPA regions, and nationwide for each pollutant, pollutant concentrations, and average annual emissions by source (transportation, fuel combustion, industrial processes, and solid waste).

National Air Toxics Information Clearinghouse. Research Triangle Park, NC 27711. (919) 541-0850.

National Air Toxics Information Clearinghouse Newsletter. National Air Toxic Information Clearinghouse, P.O. Box 13000, Research Triangle Park, NC 27709. (919) 541-9100. Bimonthly. Covers noncriteria pollutant emissions.

National Air Transportation Association. 4226 King St., Alexandria, VA 22302. (703) 845-9000.

National Ambient Volatile Organic Compounds. U.S. Environmental Protection Agency, Atmospheric Sciences Research Laboratory, MD 75, Research Triangle Park, NC 27711. 1988.

National Animal Damage Control Association. Rte. 1, Box 37, Shell Lake, WI 54871. (715) 468-2038.

National Arbor Day Foundation. 100 Arbor Ave., Nebraska City, NE 68410. (402) 474-5655.

National Arborist Association. The Meeting Place Mall, Rt. 101, P.O. Box 1094, Amherst, NH 03031. (603) 673-3311.

National Asbestos Council. 1777 N.E. Expressway, Suite 150, Atlanta, GA 30329. (404) 633-2622.

National Asphalt Pavement Association. Calvert Bldg., Suite 620, 6811 Kenilworth Ave., Riverdale, MD 20737. (301) 779-4880.

National Association for Plastic Container Recovery. 4828 Parkway Plaza Blvd., Suite 260, Charlotte, NC 28217. (704) 357-3250.

National Association of Agricultural Employees. c/o Eric White, Box B, U.S. Aid Bridgetown, FPO Miami, FL 34054.

National Association of Conservation Districts. 509 Capitol Court, N.E., Washington, DC 20002. (202) 547-6223.

National Association of Conservation Districts, Tuesday Letter. National Association of Conservation Districts, 509 Capitol Ct., N.E., Washington, DC 20002. (202) 347-5995. Weekly. Conservation policy at national, state, and local levels.

National Association of Corrosion Engineers. P.O. Box 218340, Houston, TX 77218. (713) 492-0535.

National Association of Counties, Committee on Environment, Energy and Land Use. Solid and Hazardous Waste Subcommittee, 440 First St., N.W., Washington, DC 20001. (202) 393-6226.

National Association of County Agricultural Agents. 1575 Northside Dr., 200 ATC, Ste. 170, Atlanta, GA 30318. (404) 730-7004.

National Association of Energy Service Companies. 1440 New York Ave. N.W., Washington, DC 20005. (202) 371-7000.

National Association of Environmental Professionals. PO Box 15210, Alexandria, VA 22309-0210. (703) 660-2364.

National Association of Environmental Risk Auditors. 4211 East Third St., Bloomington, IN 47401. (812) 333-0077.

National Association of Fruits, Flavors and Syrups. P.O. Box 776, 177 Main St., Matawan, NJ 07747. (201) 583-8272.

National Association of Insect Electrocutor Manufacturers. P.O. Box 439, Medina, NY 14103-0439.

National Association of Local Governments on Hazardous Wastes.

National Association of Manufacturers. 1331 Pennsylvania Ave., N.W., Suite 1500 North, Washington, DC 20004. (202) 637-3000.

National Association of Metal Finishers. 401 N. Michigan Ave., Chicago, IL 60611-4267. (312) 644-6610.

National Association of Noise Control Officials. 53 Cubberly Rd., Trenton, NJ 08690. (609) 984-4161.

National Association of Pharmaceutical Manufacturers. 747 Third Ave., New York, NY 10017. (212) 838-3720.

National Association of Power Engineers. 2350 E. Devon Ave., Suite 115, Des Plaines, IL 60018. (718) 298-0600.

National Association of Radiation Survivors. P.O. Box 20749, Oakland, CA 94620. (415) 655-4886.

National Association of Sewer Service Companies. 101 Wymore Rd., Suite 521, Altamonte, FL 32714. (407) 774-0304.

National Association of Solvent Recyclers. 1875 Connecticut Ave., N.W., Suite 1200, Washington, DC 20009. (202) 986-8150.

National Association of Solvent Recyclers–Membership List. National Association of Solvent Recyclers, 1875 Connecticut Ave., NW, Suite 1200, Washington, DC 20009. (202) 986-8150.

National Association of State Departments of Agriculture. 1616 H St., N.W., Suite 704, Washington, DC 20006. (202) 628-1566.

National Association of State Foresters. 444 Capitol St., N.W., Hall of the States, Washington, DC 20001. (202) 624-5415.

National Association of State Land Reclamationists. 459 B Carlisle Dr., Herndon, VA 22070. (703) 709-8654.

National Association of State Outdoor Recreation Liaison Officers. c/o Ney C. Landrum, 126 Mill Branch Rd., Tallahassee, FL 32312. (904) 893-4959.

National Association of State Park Directors. 126 Mill Branch Rd., Tallahassee, FL 32312. (904) 893-4959.

National Association of State Recreation Planners. c/o Dick Westfall, Illinois Dept. of Conversation, Division of Planning, 524 S. 2nd St., Room 310, Springfield, IL 62701-1787. (217) 782-3715.

National Association of Water Companies. 1725 K St., N.W., Suite 1212, Washington, DC 20006. (202) 833-8383.

National Association of Water Institute Directors. Water Resources Research Center, Blaisdell House, University of Massachusetts, Amherst, MA 01003. (413) 545-2842.

National Audubon Society. 950 Third Ave., New York, NY 10022. (212) 832-3200.

National Automotive Muffler Association. P.O. Box 1857, West Covina, CA 91793. (213) 338-2417.

National Bark and Soil Producers Association. 13542 Union Village Circle, Clifton, VA 22024. (703) 830-5367.

National Campaign for Radioactive Waste Safety. 105 Stanford SE, PO Box 4524, Albuquerque, NM 87106. (505) 262-1862.

National Campground Owners Association. 11307 Sunset Hills Rd., Ste. B7, Reston, VA 22090. (703) 471-0143.

National Center for Atmospheric Research. National Science Foundation, 1800 G. St., N.W., Room 520, Washington, DC 20550. (202) 357-9498.

National Center for Environmental Health Strategies. 1100 Rural Ave., Voorhees, NJ 08043. (609) 429-5358.

National Center for Ground Water Research. University of Oklahoma, 200 Telgar St., Rm. 127, Norman, OK 73019-0470. (405) 325-5202.

National Center for Health Statistics: Public Health Service. 6525 Belcrest Rd., Hyattsville, MD 20782. (301) 436-7016.

National Center for Intermedia Transport Research. University of California, Los Angeles, 5531 Boelter, Department of Chemical Engineering, Los Angeles, CA 90024-1592. (213) 825-9741.

National Center for Toxicological Research Associated Universities, Inc. 4301 W. Markham, UAMS 522, Little Rock, AR 72205. (501) 686-6501.

National Center for Urban Environmental Studies. 516 N. Charles St., Suite 501, Baltimore, MD 21201. (301) 727-6212.

National Cholesterol Education Program Coordinating Committee Members Activities and Materials Directory. U.S. Department of Health and Human Services, 200 Independence Ave. SW, Washington, DC 20201. (202) 619-0257. 1991. Heart disease prevention and health promotion directories.

National Clean Air Coalition. 1400 16th St., N.W., Washington, DC 20036. (202) 797-5496.

National Coal Association. 1130 17th St., N.W., Washington, DC 20036. (202) 463-2625.

National Coalition Against the Misuse of Pesticides. 701 E St., SE, Suite 200, Washington, DC 20003. (202) 543-5450.

National Coalition for Marine Conservation, Inc. P.O. Box 23298, Savannah, GA 31403. (912) 234-8062.

National Coalition to Stop Food and Water Irradiation. 225 Lafayette St., Ste. 613, New York, NY 10012. (212) 941-9340.

National Coastal Resources Research and Development Institute. Hatfield Marine Science Center, 2030 South Marine Science Dr., Newport, OR 97365. (503) 867-0131.

National Committee for Radiation Victims. 6935 Laurel Ave., Takoma Park, MD 20912. (301) 891-3990.

A National Compendium of Freshwater Fish and Water Temperature Data. Kenneth E. Biesinger. U.S. Environmental Protection Agency, Environmental Research Laboratory, Office of Research and Development, 6201 Congdon Blvd., Duluth, MN 55804. (218) 720-5500. 1979. River temperature, thermal pollution of rivers and lakes, and freshwater fishes.

National Concrete Masonry Association. P.O. Box 781, Herndon, VA 22070. (703) 435-4900.

National Conference of Local Environmental Health Administrators. 1395 Blue Tent Ct., Cool, CA 95614-2120. (916) 823-1736.

National Council for Environmental Balance. 4169 Westport Rd., P.O. Box 7732, Louisville, KY 40207. (502) 896-8731.

National Council of Acoustical Consultants. 66 Morris Ave., Springfield, NJ 07081. (201) 379-1100.

National Council of Acoustical Consultants–Directory. 66 Morris Ave., Springfield, NJ 07081. (201) 379-1100. Biennial.

National Council of Commercial Plant Breeders. 601 13th St., N.W., Suite 570, Washington, DC 20005. (202) 638-3128.

National Council of Forestry Association. c/o Northeastern Loggers Assn., Rt. 28, Box 69, Old Forge, NY 13420. (315) 369-3078.

National Council of the Paper Industry for Air and Stream Improvements. 260 Madison Ave., New York, NY 10016. (212) 532-9000.

National Council on Radiation Protection and Measurements. 7910 Woodmont Ave., Suite 800, Bethesda, MD 20814. (301) 657-2652.

National Council on Refrigeration Sales Association–Membership Directory. c/o Fernley & Fernley, Inc., 1900 Arch St., Philadelphia, PA 19103. (215) 564-3484. Annual.

National Defense Transportation Association. 50 S. Pickett St., Suite 220, Alexandria, VA 22304-3008. (703) 571-5011.

National Demonstration Water Project. Rural Community Assistance Program, 602 King St., Suite 402, Leesburg, VA 22075. (703) 771-8636.

National Directory of Citizen Volunteer Environmental Monitoring Programs. Virginia Lee and Eleanor Lee. Rhode Island Sea Grant College Program, Narragansett Bay Campus, Narragansett, RI 02882. (401) 792-6842. 1990.

National Directory of Conservation Land Trusts. Land Trust Exchange, 1017 Duke St., Alexandria, VA 22314. (207) 288-9751.

National Directory of Farmland Protection Organizations. Nancy Bushwick. NASDA Research Foundation, Farmland Project, 14 Independence Ave. SW, Washington, DC 20250. (202)720-8732. 1983. Organizations which deal with soil conservation and rural land use.

National Directory of Floodplain Managers. Association of State Floodplain Managers, Box 2051, Madison, WI 53701-2051. (608) 266-1926.

National Directory of Safe Energy Organizations. Public Citizen's Critical Mass Energy Project, 215 Pennsylvania Ave., S.E., Washington, DC 20003. (202) 546-4996.

National Drilling Contractors Association. 3008 Millwood Ave., Columbia, SC 29205. (803) 252-5646.

National Drosophila Species Resource Center. Department of Biological Sciences, Bowling Green State University, Bowling Green, OH 43403-0212. (419) 372-2096.

National Electrical Manufacturers Association. 2101 L St., N.W., Washington, DC 20037. (202) 457-8400.

National Emergency Training Guide. Emergency Response Institute, 4537 Foxhall Drive, NW, Olympia, WA 98506. (206) 491-7785. Annual. Covers topics of emergency search and rescue.

National Emissions Data System. U.S. Environmental Protection Agency, Office of Air Quality Planning and Standards, National Air Data Branch, 401 M St. SW, Washington, DC 20460. (202) 260-2090. Pollutant emissions and 10,000 sources in 3,300 areas across the United States and territories.

National Emissions Standards for Hazardous Air Pollutants, Benzene Emissions. U.S. Environmental Protection Agency, 401 M St., S.W., Washington, DC 20460. (202) 260-2090. 1989.

National Engineering Handbook. Section 3, Sedimentation. U.S. Department of Agriculture, Soil Conservation Service, 14 Independence Ave., SW, Washington, DC 20250. (202) 447-7454. 1983. Deals with sedimentation, deposition, and erosion in the United States.

National Environmental Balancing Bureau. 8224 Old Courthouse Rd., Vienna, VA 19103. (215) 564-3484.

National Environmental Data Referral Service. National Oceanic and Atmospheric Administration, Department of Commerce, 1825 Connecticut Ave., N.W., Washington, DC 20235. (202) 673-5548. Also available online.

National Environmental Data Referral Service Database. National Oceanic & Atmospheric Administration, Department of Commerce, 1825 Connecticut Ave., N.W., Washington, DC 20235. (202) 673-5548. Data files, published data sources, documentation references, and organizations that make environmental data available.

National Environmental Development Association. 1440 New York Ave., N.W., Suite 300, Washington, DC 20005. (202) 638-1230.

National Environmental Enforcement Journal. National Association of Attorneys General, 444 N. Capitol, N.W., Suite 403, Washington, DC 20001. Monthly. Litigation and inventive settlements in cases of waste dumping and pollution.

National Environmental Health Association. South Tower, 720 S. Colorado Blvd., #970, Denver, CO 80222. (303) 756-9090.

National Environmental Policy Act Handbook. U.S. Bureau of Reclamation. U.S. Department of the Interior, Bureau of Reclamation, Washington, DC 20240. (202) 208-4662. 1990. Covers environmental law and environmental impact statements.

National Environmental Satellite, Data, and Information Service. 1825 Connecticut Ave., N.W., Washington, DC 20235. (301) 763-7190.

National Environmental Training Association. 2930 E. Camelback Rd., Phoenix, AZ 85016. (602) 956-6099.

National Environmental Training Association Newsletter. National Environmental Training Association, 2930 E. Camelback Rd., Phoenix, AZ 85016. (602) 956-6099. Bimonthly. Covers environmental training programs and training materials.

National Eutrophication Study Data Base. U.S. Environmental Protection Agency, Environmental Monitoring Systems Laboratory, Las Vegas, 401 M St. SW, Washington, DC 20460. (202) 260-2090. Water quality data collected over a one-year period for each of some 800 lakes and their tributaries in 48 states.

National Farmers Union. 10065 E. Harvard Ave., Denver, CO 80231. (303) 337-5500.

National Feed Ingredients Association. One Corporate Pl., Suite 375, West Des Moines, IA 50265. (515) 225-9611.

National Fertilizer Solutions Association. 339 Consort Dr., Manchester, MO 63011. (314) 256-4900.

National Fish & Wildlife Federation. 18th & C Streets, N.W., Rm 2626, Washington, DC 20240. (202) 343-1040.

National Fisheries Containment Research Center. Fish and Wildlife Service, U.S. Dept. of the Interior, 4200 New Haven Rd., Columbia, MO 65201. (314) 875-5399.

National Fisheries Education & Research Foundation, Inc. 1525 Wilson Blvd., Ste. 500, Arlington, VA 22209. (703) 524-9216.

National Fisheries Institute. 1525 Wilson Blvd., Suite 500, Arlington, VA 22209. (703) 524-8880.

National Fluid Power Association–Membership Directory. 3333 N. Mayfair Rd., Suite 311, Milwaukee, WI 53222. (414) 259-0990. Annual.

National Food and Conservation Through Swine. c/o Ronie Polen, Fox Run Rd., R.R. 4, Box 397, Sewell, NJ 08080. (609) 468-5447.

National Food & Energy Council. 409 VanDiver West, Suite 202, Columbia, MO 65202. (314) 875-7155.

National Food Processors Association. 1401 New York Ave., N.W., 4th Floor, Washington, DC 20005. (202) 639-5900.

National Forest Association. 1250 Connecticut Ave.,N.W., Suite 200, Washington, DC 20036. (202) 463-2700.

National Forest Recreation Association. Rt. 3, Box 210, Hwy. 89 N., Flagstaff, AZ 86004. (602) 526-4330.

National Forests Fire Report. U.S. Department of Agriculture, Forest Service, 14 Independence Ave., S.W., Washington, DC 20250. (202) 447-7454. Annual.

National Foundation for Asthma. P.O. Box 30069, Tucson, AZ 85751. (602) 323-6046.

National Future Farmers of America. P.O. Box 15160, National FFA Center, Alexandria, VA 22309. (703) 360-3600.

National Gardening Association. 180 Flynn Ave., Burlington, VT 05401. (802) 863-1308.

National Geographic. National Geographic Society, 17th & M Sts. NW, Washington, DC 20036. (202) 857-7000. Monthly. Articles on geography, culture, natural history, and the environment.

National Geographic Society. 17th and M Streets, NW, Washington, DC 20036. (202) 857-7000.

National Governors Association. Hall of the States, Suite 250, 444 N. Capitol St., N.W., Washington, DC 20001-1572. (202) 624-5300.

National Hardwood Lumber Association. Box 34518, Memphis, TN 38184. (901) 377-1818.

National Hardwood Lumber Association–Members. Box 34518, Memphis, TN 38184. (901) 377-1818. Annual.

National Health Council. 1730 M St. N.W., Ste. 500, Washington, DC 20036. (202) 785-3913.

National Hearing Conservation Association. 900 Des Moines St., Suite 200, Des Moines, IA 50309. (515) 266-2189.

National Hydropower Association. 555 13th St., N.W., Suite 900 E., Washington, DC 20004. (202) 637-8115.

National Independent Coal Operators Association. Box 354, Richland, VA 24641. (703) 963-9011.

National Industrial Transportation League. 1700 N. Moore St., Suite 1900, Arlington, VA 22209-1904. (703) 524-5011.

National Information Service for Earthquake Engineering. Earthquake Engineering Research Center, 1301 S. 46th St., University of California, Richmond, CA 94804. (415) 231-9554.

National Institute for Chemical Studies. 2300 MacCorkle Ave., S.E., Charleston, WV 25304. (304) 346-6264.

National Institute for Urban Wildlife. 10921 Trotting Ridge Way, Columbia, MD 21044. (301) 596-3311.

National Institute of Building Sciences. 1201 L. St., N.W., Suite 400, Washington, DC 20005. (202) 289-7800.

National Institute of Environmental Health Science. PO Box 12233, Research Triangle Park, NC 27709. (919) 541-3345.

National Institute on Park & Grounds Management. Box 1936, Appleton, WI 54913. (414) 733-2301.

National Insulation and Abatement Contractors Association–Membership Directory and Buyer's Guide. 99 Canal Center Plaza, No. 222, Alexandria, VA 22314. (703) 683-6422. Annual.

National Inventory of Sources and Emissions of Carbon Dioxide. A.P. Jaques. Environmental Canada, 425 St. Joseph Blvd., 3rd Fl., Hull, PQ, Canada K1A OH3. (613) 953-5921. 1987. Covers environmental aspects of carbon dioxide.

National Kerosene Heater Association. First American Center, #15, Nashville, TN 37238. (615) 254-1961.

National Landscape Association. 1250 I St., N.W., Ste. 500, Washington, DC 20005. (202) 789-2900.

National Leaders of American Conservation. Richard H. Stroud, ed. Smithsonian Institution Press, 470 L'Enfant Plaza, Suite 7100, Washington, DC 20560. (800) 782-4612. 1985. 2nd ed. Sponsored by the Natural Resources Council of America. The book identifies national conservation leaders in the United States.

National League of Cities, Natural Resources Committee. 1301 Pennsylvania Ave., N.W., 6th Floor, Washington, DC 20004. (202) 626-3000.

National Lime Association. 3601 N. Fairfax Dr., Arlington, VA 22201. (703) 243-5463.

National Listing of Fisheries Offices. Fish and Wildlife Service, Department of the Interior, 18th & C Sts., N.W., Washington, DC 20240. (202) 653-8750.

National Lubricating Grease Institute. 4635 Wyandotte St., Kansas City, MO 64112. (816) 931-9480.

National Lumber Exporters Association. 1250 Connecticut Ave., N.W., Suite 200, Washington, DC 20036. (202) 463-2723.

National Marine Educators Association. P.O. Box 51215, Pacific Beach, CA 93950. (408) 648-4841.

National Marine Fisheries Service. 1825 Connecticut Ave., N.W., Washington, DC 20235. (202) 673-5450.

National Marine Manufacturers Association. 401 N. Michigan Ave., Chicago, IL 60611. (312) 836-4747.

National Marine Pollution Program. U.S. G.P.O, Washington, DC 20402-9325. (202) 512-0000. Annual. Federally funded programs for development, or monitoring activities related to marine pollution.

National Marine Pollution Program Plan, Federal Plan for Ocean Pollution Research, Development and Monitoring. Fiscal Years 1988-1992. National Oceanic and Atmospheric Administration, U.S. Dept. of Commerce, Washington, DC 20230. (202) 377-2985. 1988.

National Marine Pollution Program. Summary of Federal Programs and Projects, FY 1988 Update. National Marine Pollution Program Office, National Oceanic and Atmospheric Administration, 11400 Rockville Pike, Rockville, MD 20852. 1990.

National Marine Sanctuary Program: Program Development Plan. Sanctuary Programs Office, Office of Coastal Zone Management, National Oceanic and Atmospheric Administration, Department of Commerce, Washington, DC 20230. 1982. Marine parks and reserves in the United States.

National Military Fish & Wildlife Association. c/o Slader G. Buck, P.O. Box 230128, Encinitas, CA 92023. (619) 725-4540.

National News Report. Sierra Club Books, 100 Bush St., San Francisco, CA 94104. (415) 291-1600. 1969-. Weekly.

National Ocean Industries Association. 1120 G St., N.W., Suite 900, Washington, DC 20005. (202) 347-6900.

National Oil Recyclers Association. 805 15th St., N.W., Suite 900, Washington, DC 20005. (202) 962-3020.

National Organization for River Sports. 314 N. 20th St., P.O. Box 6847, Colorado Springs, CO 80934. (719) 473-2466.

National Organization of Test, Research, & Training Reactors. c/o Francis DiMeglio, Rhode Island Nuclear Science Center, S. Ferry Rd., Narragansett, RI 02882-1197. (401) 789-9391.

National Organization to Insure a Sound-Controlled Environment. 1620 I St., N.W., Suite 300, Washington, DC 20006. (202) 429-0166.

National Paperbox and Packaging Association. 1201 E. Abingdon Dr., Ste. 203, Alexandria, VA 22314. (703) 684-2212.

National Park Foundation. 1101 17th St. N.W., Ste. 1102, Washington, DC 20036. (202) 785-4500.

National Park Service Cooperative Park Studies Unit. University of Washington, College of Forest Resources AR-10, Seattle, WA 98195. (206) 543-1587.

National Park Service Cooperative Unit. Institute of Ecology, University of Georgia, Athens, GA 30602. (404) 542-8301.

National Park Service Integrated Pest Management Information Packages. National Park Service, Biological Research Division, Washington, DC 20013. (202) 208-6843. 1984.

National Park Service Statistical Abstract. U.S. G.P.O., Washington, DC 20401. (202) 512-0000. Annual. Recreation visits, acreages, areas administered visits and visitor use and overnight stays.

National Parks and Conservation Association. 1015 31st St., N.W., Washington, DC 20007. (202) 944-8530.

National Pest Control Association. 8100 Oak St., Dunn Loring, VA 22027. (703) 573-8330.

National Pesticide Information Retrieval System. Entomology Hall, Purdue University, West Lafayette, IN 47907. (317) 494-6616. Pesticide products registered with the Environmental Protection Agency, as well as similar information from 36 states.

National Pesticide Survey: Fact Sheets. U.S. Environmental Protection Agency, Office of Pesticides and Toxic Substances, 401 M St. SW, Washington, DC 20460. (202) 260-2090. 1990.

National Pesticide Survey: Phase I Report. U.S. Environmental Protection Agency, Office of Pesticides and Toxic Substances, 401 M St. SW, Washington, DC 20460. (202) 260-2090. 1990.

National Pesticide Survey: Project Summary. U.S. Environmental Protection Agency, Office of Pesticides and Toxic Substances, 401 M St. SW, Washington, DC 20460. (202) 260-2090. 1990.

National Pesticide Survey: Summary Results of EPA's National Survey of Pesticides in Drinking Water Wells. U.S. Environmental Protection Agency, Office of Pesticides and Toxic Substances, 401 M St. SW, Washington, DC 20460. (202) 260-2090. 1990.

National Petroleum Council. 1625 K St., N.W., Suite 601, Washington, DC 20006. (202) 393-6100.

National Petroleum Refiners Association. 1899 L St., N.W., Suite 1000, Washington, DC 20036. (202) 457-0480.

National Planning Association. 1424 16th St., N.W., Suite 700, Washington, DC 20036. (202) 265-7685.

National Plant Material Manual. U.S. Soil Conservation Service, PO Box 2890, Washington, DC 20013. (202) 205-0027. 1984. Looseleaf.

National Precast Association. 825 E. 64th St., Indianapolis, IN 46220. (317) 253-0486.

National Priorities List. U.S. G.P.O., Washington, DC 20401. (202) 512-0000. Annual. Inventories of hazardous waste sites included in the EPA National Priorities List (NPL) and proposed for addition to and removal from the list.

National Propane Gas Association. 1600 Eisenhower Ln., Lisle, IL 60532. (708) 515-0600.

National Ready Mixed Concrete Association. 900 Spring St., Silver Springs, MD 20910. (301) 587-1400.

National Recreation & Park Association. 3101 Park Center Dr., Alexandria, VA 22302. (703) 820-4940.

National Recycling Coalition. 1101 30th St., N.W., Washington, DC 20007. (202) 625-6406.

National Registry of Laboratories Certified to Test for Drinking Water Parameters. Association of State Drinking Water Administrators, 1911 N. Fort Myer Dr., Arlington, VA 22209. (703) 524-2428. 1990. Annual.

National Research Council. 2101 Constitution Ave., N.W., Washington, DC 20418. (202) 334-2000.

National Resource Recovery Association. 1620 Eye St., N.W., Washington, DC 20006. (202) 293-7330.

National Rural Electric Cooperative Association. 1800 Massachusetts Ave., N.W., Washington, DC 20036. (202) 857-9500.

National Safety Council. 444 N. Michigan Ave., Chicago, IL 60611. (312) 527-4800.

National Sanitation Foundation. 3475 Plymouth Rd., P.O. Box 130140, Ann Arbor, MI 48105. (313) 769-8010.

National Science Foundation. 1800 G St., N.W., Washington, DC 20550. (202) 357-9498.

National Sea Grant Depository. Pell Library Building, University of Rhode Island, Narragansett, RI 02882. (401) 792-6114.

National Slag Association. 300 S. Washington St., Alexandria, VA 22314. (703) 549-3111.

National Society of Professional Engineers. 1420 King St., Alexandria, VA 22314. (703) 684-2800.

National Society of Professional Sanitarians. 1224 Hoffman Dr., Jefferson City, MO 65101. (314) 751-6095.

National Solid Wastes Management Association. 1730 Rhode Island Ave., N.W., Suite 1000, Washington, DC 20036. (202) 659-4613.

National Speleological Society. Cave Ave., Huntsville, AL 35810. (205) 852-1300.

National Stream Quality Accounting Network. National Water Data Exchange, U.S. Geological Survey, 421 National Center, Reston, VA 22092. (703) 648-4000. 150 hydrologic measurements collected at daily, monthly and quarterly intervals from more than 500 monitoring stations in the U.S.

National Stripper Well Association. 801 Petroleum Bldg., Wichita, TX 76301. (817) 766-3870.

National Survey of Hazardous Waste Generators and Treatment, Storage, and Disposal Facilities Regulated Under RCRA in 1981. U.S. Environmental Protection Agency, Office of Solid Waste and Emergency Response, 401 M St., S.W., Washington, DC 20460. (202) 260-2090. 1984. Environmental aspects of hazardous substances and waste disposal in the ground.

National Tank Truck Carriers. 2200 Mill Rd., Alexandria, VA 22314. (703) 838-1960.

National Technical Information Service. U.S. Department of Commerce, National Technical Information Service, Office of Data Base Services, 5285 Port Royal Rd., Springfield, VA 22161. (703) 487-4807. Bibliographic database of government sponsored research and technical reports.

National Toxicology Program. U.S. G.P.O., Washington, DC 20401. (202) 512-0000. Annual. Effort to strengthen and coordinate research and testing of toxic chemicals.

National Toxics Campaign. 1168 Commonwealth Ave., Boston, MA 02134. (617) 232-0327.

National Trails Council. Box 493, Brookings, SD 57006.

National Transportation Safety Board Marine Accident Report: Prince William Sound, Alaska, March 24, 1989 Grounding of the U.S. Tankship Exxon Valdez. National Transportation Safety Board, 800 Independence Avenue, SW, Washington, DC 20544. (202) 382-6600. 1990.

National Trappers Association. P.O. Box 3667, Bloomington, IL 61702. (309) 829-2422.

National Undersea Research Center. University of Connecticut at Avery Point, Groton, CT 06340. (203) 445-4714.

National Urban Mass Transportation Statistics. U.S. Urban Mass Transportation Administration. U.S. G.P.O., Washington, DC 20401. (202) 512-0000. Annual. Data on public transit use by type, including car and van pools.

National Utility Contractors Association. 1235 Jefferson Davis Hwy., Suite 606, Arlington, VA 22202. (703) 486-2100.

National Waste Exchange Data Base. Northeast Industrial Waste Exchange, 90 Presidential Plaza, Ste. 122, Syracuse, NY 13202. (315) 422-6572. Computerized catalog of waste materials listed with the Northeast Industrial Exchange.

National Water Alliance. 1225 I St., N.W., Suite 300, Washington, DC 20005. (202) 646-0917.

National Water Center. P.O. Box 264, Eureka Springs, AR 72632. (510) 253-9755.

National Water Data Exchange. National Water Data Exchange, U.S. Geological Survey, 421 National Center, Reston, VA 22092. (703) 648-4000. Identification, location, and acquisition of water data.

National Water Data Storage and Retrieval System. U.S. Geological Survey, Water Resources Division, 12201 Sunrise Valley Dr., Reston, VA 22092. (703) 648-4460. Surface and underground water resources of the United States.

National Water Line. National Water Resources Association, 3800 North Fairfax Drive, #4, Arlington, VA 22203. (703) 524-1544. Monthly. Covers water resource development projects.

National Water Quality Inventory. U.S. G.P.O., Washington, DC 20401. (202) 512-0000. Biennial. Water pollution problems and control activities by states.

National Water Resources Association. 3800 N. Fairfax Dr., Suite 4, Arlington, VA 22203. (703) 524-1544.

National Water Summary. U.S. G.P.O, Washington, DC 20402-9325. (202) 512-0000. Annual. Hydrological events and issues, including floods, drought, inland oil spills, and water supply and use.

National Water Supply Improvement Association. P.O. Box 102, St. Leonard, MD 20865. (301) 855-1173.

National Water Well Association. 6375 Riverside Dr., Dublin, OH 43107. (614) 761-1711.

National Water Well Association–Membership Directory. National Water Well Association, 6375 Riverside Dr., Dublin, OH 43017. (614) 761-1711.

National Waterfowl Alliance. Box 50, Waterfowl Bldg., Edgefield, SC 29824. (803) 637-5767.

National Waterfowl Council. c/o Roger Holmes, Minnestoa Dept. of Natural Resources, 500 Lafayette Rd., St. Paul, MN 55155. (612) 297-1308.

National Watershed Congress. c/o National Assn. of Conservation Districts, 509 Capital Ct., Washington, DC 20002. (202) 547-6223.

National Waterways Conference. 1130 17th St. N.W., Washington, DC 20036. (202) 296-4415.

National Weather Service. 8060 13th St., Silver Spring, MD 20910. (301) 443-8910.

National Wetlands Newsletter. Environmental Law Institute, 1616 P St., NW, Suite 200, Washington, DC 20036. (202) 328-5150. Bimonthly. Federal, state, and local laws, policies, and programs concerning wetlands, floodplains, and coastal water resources.

National Wetlands Technical Council. 1616 P St., N.W., 2nd floor, Washington, DC 20036. (202) 328-5150.

National Wild Turkey Federation. P.O. Box 530, Edgefield, SC 29824. (803) 637-3106.

National Wildlife. National Wildlife Federation, 1400 16th Street, NW, Washington, DC 20036. (202) 797-6800. Bimonthly. Covers all forms of conservation activities.

National Wildlife Federation. 1400 16th St., N.W., Washington, DC 20036. (202) 797-6800.

National Wildlife Federation Corporate Conservation Council. 1400 16th St., N.W., Washington, DC 20036. (202) 797-6800.

National Wildlife Health Foundation. c/o James L. Naviaux, 606 El Pintado Rd., Danville, CA 94526. (415) 939-3456.

National Wildlife Newsletter. Sierra Club Books, 100 Bush St., San Francisco, CA 94104. (415) 291-1600. 1976-. Monthly.

National Wildlife Refuge Association. 10824 Fox Hunt Ln., Potomac, MD 20854. (301) 983-1238.

National Wildlife Refuges: A Visitor's Guide. Fish and Wildlife Service, Department of the Interior, 18th and C Sts., N.W., Washington, DC 20240. (202) 653-8750.

National Wildlife Rehabilitators Association. c/o Carpenter Nature Center, 12805 St. Croix Trail, Hastings, MN 55033. (612) 437-9194.

National Wildlife Rescue Team. 160 N.E. 165th St., North Miami Beach, FL 33162.

National Wood Energy Association. 777 N. Capitol St. N.W., Suite 805, Washington, DC 20002. (202) 408-0664.

National Woodland Owners Association. 374 Maple Ave., E., Suite 210, Vienna, VA 22180. (703) 255-2300.

Nation's Business. Chamber of Commerce of the United States, 1615 H Street , NW, Washington, DC 20062. (202) 659-6000. Monthly.

Native Americans for a Clean Environment. P.O. Box 40, Marble City, OK 74945. (918) 458-4322.

Native Seeds/Search. 2509 N. Campbell Ave., No. 325, Tucson, AZ 85719. (602) 327-9123.

Natural and Anthropogenic Sources of Oxides of Nitrogen for the Troposphere. National Technical Information Service, 5285 Port Royal Rd., Springfield, VA 22161. (703) 487-4650. 1982. Covers nitrogen oxides, troposphere, and aircraft exhaust emissions.

Natural Area Council. 219 Shoreham Bldg., N.W., Washington, DC 20005. (202) 638-1649.

Natural Areas Association. 320 S. Third St., Rockford, IL 61104. (815) 964-6666.

Natural Areas Journal. Natural Areas Association, 320 S. Third St., Rockford, IL 61104. (815) 964-6666. Quarterly. Information of interest to natural areas professionals.

Natural Disaster Studies. National Academy Press, 2101 Constitution Ave. N.W., PO Box 285, Washington, DC 20418. (202) 334-3313. 1991. An investigative series of the Committee on Natural Disasters issued by the National Research Council, Committee on Natural Disasters.

Natural Fire: Its Ecology in Forests. Laurence Pringle. William Morrow & Co., 1350 Avenue of the Americas, New York, NY 10019. (212) 261-6500. 1979. Explains the beneficial effects of periodic fires to forests and their wildlife.

Natural Gas and the Environment: New Issues, New Opportunities. Gas Research Institute, National Technical Information Service, 5285 Port Royal Rd., Springfield, VA 22161. (703) 487-4650. 1987.

Natural Gas Applications for Air Pollution Control. Nelson E. Hay. Fairmont Press, 700 Indian Trail, Lilburn, GA 30247. (404) 925-9388. 1987. Natural gas-induced air pollution.

Natural Gas Supply Association. 1129 20th St., N.W., Suite 300, Washington, DC 20036. (202) 331-8900.

Natural Hazards Observer. University of Colorado, Hazards Res. & Apl. Info. Ctr., Campus Box 482, Boulder, CO 80309. (303) 492-6818. Bimonthly. Hazards-legislation at federal, state, and local levels.

Natural Hazards Research and Applications Information Center. Campus Box 482, University of Colorado, Boulder, CO 80309. (303) 492-6818.

A Natural History of Marine Mammals. Victor B. Scheffer. Scribner Educational Publishers, 866 3rd Ave., New York, NY 10022. (212) 702-2000. 1976.

The Natural History of Nematodes. George O. Polanr. Prentice-Hall, Rte. 9W, Englewood Cliffs, NJ 07632. (201) 592-2000. 1983.

A Natural History of the Coral Reef. Blandford Press, Villiers House, 41/47 Strand, London, England WC2N 5JE. 071-839 4900. 1983. Coral reef biology and ecology.

Natural Landscaping: Designing with Native Plant Communities. John Diekelmann. McGraw-Hill Science & Engineering Books, 11 W. 19th St., New York, NY 10011. (212) 337-6010. 1982. Wild flower and landscape gardening.

Natural Microbial Communities: Ecological and Physiological Features. Tomomichi Yanagita. Springer-Verlag, 175 5th Ave., New York, NY 10010. (212) 460-1500; (800) 777-4643. 1990. Translation of a work which originally appeared in Japanese entitled Microbial Ecology.

Natural POWWER. 5420 Mayfield Rd., Cleveland, OH 44124. (216) 442-5600.

Natural Resource Conservation: An Ecological Approach. Oliver S. Owen. Macmillan Publishing Co., 866 3rd Ave., New York, NY 10022. (212) 702-2000. 1990. Covers environmental protection, conservation of natural resources and ecology.

Natural Resource Management and Protection: A New Hampshire State Development Plan. Office of State Planning, 2 1/2 Beacon St., Concord, CT 03301. (603)271-2155. 1988.

Natural Resources & Earth Sciences. NTIS, 5285 Port Royal Rd., Springfield, VA 22161. (703) 487-4650. Weekly. Mineral industry, natural resources management, hydrology, limnology, soil conservation, watershed management, forestry, soil sciences, & geology.

Natural Resources and Environmental Control Department: Fish and Wildlife. Director, Division of Fish and Wildlife, 89 Kings Highway, Box 1401, Dover, DE 19903. (302) 739-5295.

Natural Resources and Environmental Control Department: Hazardous Waste Management. Administrator, Waste Management Section, 89 Kings Highway, Box 1401, Dover, DE 19903. (302) 736-4781.

Natural Resources and Environmental Control Department: Natural Resources. Secretary, 89 Kings Highway, Box 1401, Dover, DE 19903. (302) 736-4403.

Natural Resources and Environmental Control Department: Underground Storage Tanks. Administrator, UST Office, Division of Air and Waste Management, 89 Kings Highway, Dover, DE 19903. (302) 736-4764.

Natural Resources and Environmental Control Department: Water Quality. Director, Soil and Water Conservation Division, 89 Kings Highway, Box 1401, Dover, DE 19903. (302) 736-4764.

Natural Resources and Environmental Protection: Air Quality. Director, Air Pollution Control Division, 18 Reilly Rd., Frankfurt, KY 40601. (502) 564-3382.

Natural Resources and Environmental Protection Cabinet: Solid Waste Management. Director, Division of Waste Management, 18 Reilly Rd., Frankfurt, KY 40601. (502) 564-6716.

Natural Resources and Environmental Protection Cabinet: Waste Minimization and Pollution Prevention. Public Information Officer, Division of Waste Management, 18 Reilly Rd., Frankfurt, KY 40601. (502) 564-6716.

Natural Resources and Environmental Protection: Environmental Protection. Secretary, Capital Plaza Tower, 5th Floor, Frankfurt, KY 40601. (502) 564-3350.

Natural Resources and Environmental Protection: Groundwater Management. Secretary, Capital Plaza, 5th Floor, Frankfurt, KY 40601. (502) 564-3350.

Natural Resources and Environmental Protection: Hazardous Waste Management. Secretary, Capital Plaza, 5th Floor, Frankfurt, KY 40601. (502) 564-3350.

Natural Resources and Environmental Protection: Natural Resources. Secretary, 107 Mero St., Frankfurt, KY 40601. (502) 564-2184.

Natural Resources and Environmental Protection: Underground Storage Tanks. Secretary, Capitol Plaza Tower, 5th Floor, Frankfurt, KY 40601. (502) 564-3350.

Natural Resources and Environmental Protection: Water Quality. Director, Division of Water, 18 Reilly Rd., Frankfurt, KY 40601. (502) 564-3410.

Natural Resources Commission: Natural Resources. Director, 301 Centennial Mall S., Box 94876, Lincoln, NE 68509-4876. (402) 471-2081.

Natural Resources Council of America. 801 Pennsylvania Ave., SE, Suite 410, Washington, DC 20003. (202) 547-7553.

Natural Resources Defense Council. 40 W. 20th St., New York, NY 10011. (212) 727-2700.

Natural Resources for the 21st Century. R. Neil Sampson and Dwight Hair, eds. Island Press, 1718 Connecticut Ave. N.W., Suite 300, Washington, DC 20009. (202) 232-7933. 1990. Looks at lost or diminished resources, as well as those that appear to be rebounding. It offers a reliable status report on water, croplands, soil, forests, wetlands, rangelands, fisheries, wildlife, and wilderness.

Natural Resources Glossary. Government Institutes, Inc., 4 Research Pl., Ste. 200, Rockville, MD 20850. (301) 921-2300. Defines and standardizes over 2,500 terms, abbreviations, and acronyms, all compiled directly from the Natural Resources Statutes and the code of Federal Regulations.

Natural Resources Journal. University of New Mexico School of Law, 1117 Stanford, NE, Albuquerque, NM 87131. (505) 277-4820. Quarterly. Study of natural and environmental research.

Natural Resources Law Center. University of Colorado-Boulder, Campus Box 401, Boulder, CO 80309-0401. (303) 492-1288.

Natural Resources Law Handbook. Government Institutes, Inc., 4 Research Pl., Ste. 200, Rockville, MD 20850. (301) 921-2300. Laws governing public lands, wildlife, forests, mining, fisheries, oil, gas and coal resources, and water rights.

Natural Resources Law Update. University of Mississippi Law Center, Natural Resources Law Program, University, MS 38677.

Natural Resources Metabase. National Information Services Corporation, Ste. 6, Wyman Towers, 3100 St. Paul St., Baltimore, MD 21218. (301) 243-0797. Published and unpublished reports and other materials dealing with natural resources and environmental issues released by U.S. and Canadian government agencies and organizations.

Natural Resources Statutes. Government Institutes, Inc., 4 Research Pl., Ste. 200, Rockville, MD 20850. (301) 921-2300. Includes the statutes covering coastal zones, federal islands, fish and wildlife, forestry, minerals, soil and water, and endangered species.

Natural Resources Technical Bulletin. Earthcare Network, c/o Douglas Wheeler, 730 Polk St., San Francisco, CA 94109. (415) 981-8634. Quarterly.

The Natural Selection of Populations and Communities. David Sloan Wilson. Benjamin/Cummings Publishing Co., 390 Bridge Pkwy., Redwood City, CA 94065. (415) 594-4400. 1980. Evolutionary biology, biotic communities and population genetics.

Natural Ventilation, Passive Cooling, and Human Comfort in Buildings: A Comprehensive Technical Bibliography. The Associates, Washington, DC

Naturally Occurring Pest Bioregulators. Paul A. Hedin. American Chemical Society, 1155 16th St. NW, Washington, DC 20036. (202) 872-4600; (800) 227-5558. 1991. Symposium papers on naturally occurring biologically active chemicals grouped in five general sections: bioregulation of insect behavior and development; allelochemicals for control of insects and other animals; phytoalexins and phototoxins in plant pest control; mechanisms of plant resistance to insects; and allelochemicals as plant disease control agents.

Naturally Occurring Quinones. Ronald Hunter Thomson. Chapman & Hall, 29 W. 35th St., New York, NY 10001-2291. (212) 244-3336. 1987. Recent advances in quinone derivatives and spectra.

Nature and Resources. Elsevier Science Publishing Co., 655 Avenue of the Americas, New York, NY 10010. (212) 989-5800. 1965-. Quarterly. Provides in-depth reviews of contemporary environmental issues from an international perspective.

The Nature and Treatment of Hypothermia. University of Minnesota Press, 2037 University Ave., SE, Minneapolis, MN 55414. (612) 624-2516. 1983. Therapy relating to hypothermia.

Nature Center News. National Audubon Society, Nature Center Planning Division, 950, 3d Ave., New York, NY 10022. (212) 832-3200. 1971-. Monthly.

The Nature Conservancy. 1815 N. Lynn St., Arlington, VA 22209. (703) 841-5300.

Nature Conservancy Magazine. The Nature Conservancy, 1815 North Lynn St., Arlington, VA 22209. (703) 841-5300. 1951-. Bimonthly. Membership magazine covering biotic diversity and related conservation issues.

Nature in America Your A-Z Guide to Our Country's Animals, Plants, Landforms and Other Natural Features. Readers Digest Association, 260 Madison Ave., New York, NY 10016. 1991. Reference guide of nature in North America. Explores plants, animals, weather, land forms, and wildlife habitats. Includes over 1000 photographs and illustrations for some 1200 entries.

Nature in Cities: The Natural Environment in the Design and Development of Urban Green Space. John Wiley & Sons, Inc., 605 3rd Ave., New York, NY 10158-0012. (212) 850-6000. 1979. Urban ecology, city planning, and urban beautification.

Nature Reserves: Island Theory and Conservation Practice. Craig L. Shafer. Smithsonian Institution Press, 470 L'Enfant Plaza, No. 7100, Washington, DC 20560. (800) 782-4612. 1991. Encompasses ecology, biogeography, evolutionary biology, genetics, paleobiology, as well as legal, social, and economic issues.

Nature Tourism: Managing for the Environment. Tensie Whelan. Island Press, 1718 Connecticut Ave. N.W., Suite 300, Washington, DC 20009. (202) 232-7933. 1991. Provides practical advice and models for planning and developing a nature tourism industry, evaluating economic benefits and marketing nature tourism.

NBS Crystal Data Identification File. National Institute of Standards & Technology, Office of Standard Reference Data, A323 Physics Building, Gaithersburg, MD 20899. (301) 975-2208.

NBSFLUIDS. National Institute of Standards & Technology, Office of Standard Reference Data, A323 Physics Building, Gaithersburg, MD 20899. (301) 975-2208.

NCAMP's Technical Report. National Coalition Against the Misuse of Pesticides, 530 7th St., S.E., Washington, DC 20003. (202) 543-5450. Monthly. Actions on state & federal levels, legislation & litigation.

NCI Cancer Weekly. CANCERQUEST, 206 Rogers St., N.E., suite 104, Atlanta, GA 30317. (404) 377-8895.

NCLEHA Newsletter. National Conference of Local Environmental Health Administrators, Allegheny County Health Department, Bureau of Environmental Health, 33333 Forbes Avenue, Pittsburgh, PA 15213. (412) 578-8030. Twice a year. Covers local environmental health programs.

NCSHPO Newsletter. National Conference of State Historic Preservation Offices, 444 North Capitol Street, NW, Suite 332, Washington, DC 20001. (202) 624-5465. Monthly. Covers state and federal historic preservation programs.

Nebraska Resources. Nebraska Natural Resources Commission, 301 Centennial Mall South, Lincoln, NE 68508. 1970-. Quarterly.

NEG (Nordic Expert Group for Documentation of Occupational Exposure Limits) and NIOSH Basis for an Occupational Safety and Health Standard: Propylene Glycol Ethers and Their Acetates. National Institute for Occupation Safety and Health, 4676 Columbia Parkway, Cincinnati, OH 45226-1998. (513) 533-8287. 1991. DHHS (NIOSH) Publication No. 91-103.

Negative Population Growth, Inc. 210 The Plaza, P.O. Box 1206, Teaneck, NJ 07666. (201) 837-3555.

NEIWPCC Aqua News. New England Interstate Water Pollution Control Commission, 607 Boylston St., Boston, MA 02116. 1970-. Quarterly.

Nematodes in Soil Ecosystems. Diana W. Freckman. University of Texas Press, PO Box 7819, Austin, TX 78713-7819. (512) 471-7233 or (800) 252-3206. 1982.

Nematological Abstracts. C. A. B. International, 845 North Park Ave., Tucson, AZ 85719. (602) 621-7897 or (800) 528-4841. 1932-. Quarterly. Abstracts of the world literature on: nematode parasitic on plants; free-living and marine nematodes; nematodes parasitic on insects or other invertebrates.

Nemesis: The Death-Star and Other Theories of Mass Extinction. Donald Goldsmith. Walker & Co., New York, NY 1985.

Neotropical Wildlife Use and Conservation. John R. Robinson, ed. University of Chicago Press, 5801 Ellis Ave., 4th Fl., Chicago, IL 60637. (800) 621-2736. 1991. The importance of wildlife to people, impact of the use of wildlife on population or biological communities.

Network News. World Environment Center, 419 Park Avenue South, Suite 1403, New York, NY 10016. (212) 683-4700. Quarterly. Covers international environmental issues.

Neuroscience Research Institute. University of California, Santa Barbara, Santa Barbara, CA 93106. (805) 893-3637.

New Abolitionist. Nuclear Free America, 325 E. 25th St., Baltimore, MA 21218. (301) 235-3575. Quarterly. Nuclear free zone movement.

New Alchemy Institute. 237 Hatchville Rd., East Falmouth, MA 02536. (508) 564-6301.

The New Alchemy Quarterly. New Alchemy Inst., Inc., 237 Hatchville Rd., East Falmouth, MA 02536. (508) 564-6301. Quarterly. Sustainable technologies for providing food, energy, shelter, landscape design, and bioshelters.

New Careers: A Directory of Jobs and Internship in Technology and Society. R. Hefland, ed. Student Pugeash USA, 1638 R St. NW, Suite 32, Washington, DC 20009. (202) 328-6555. 1990-. Third edition. Includes organizations from 15 major cities nationwide including Washington, DC, Boston, New York, San Francisco, and Chicago. An index to organizations is provided.

The New Cubicle: A Magazine about Man and his Environment. De Young Press, Rte. 1, Box 76, Stark, KS 66775. (316) 754-3203. Monthly. Environmental magazine covering political, sociological, and legal issues.

New Developments in Industrial Wastewater Treatment. Aysen Turkman, ed. Kluwer Academic Publishers, 101 Philip Dr., Assinippi Park, Norwell, MA 02061-0358. (617) 871-6600. 1991. NATO Advanced Research Workshop, Oct-Nov. 1989.

New Directions in Transportation Fuels. FIND/SVP, 625 Avenue of the Americas, New York, NY 10011. (212) 645-4500. 1991. Covers the following modes of transport: cars, buses, trucks, jet aircraft and railroads.

New England Aquarium, Harold E. Edgerton Research Laboratory. Central Wharf, Boston, MA 02110. (617) 973-5252.

New England Association of Environmental Biologists. 25 Nashua Rd., Bedford, NH 03102. (603) 472-5191.

New England Environmental Network News. Lincoln Filene Center for Citizenship, Civic Education Foundation/Tufts, Medford, MA 02155. (617) 381-3451. Quarterly. State environmental news.

New England Forestry Foundation, Inc. 85 Newbury St., Boston, MA 02116. (617) 437-1441.

New England Interstate Water Pollution Control Commission. 85 Merrimac St., Boston, MA 02114. (617) 367-8522.

New England Natural Resources Center. 200 Lincoln St., Boston, MA 02111. (617) 541-3670.

New England Network of Light Directory. Sirius Community, Box 388, Amherst, MA 01004. (413) 256-8015. Annual. New age communities, holistic health centers, and ashrams.

New Environmental Bulletin. New Environment Association, 270 Fenway Dr., Syracuse, NY 13224. (315) 446-8009. Monthly. New pattern of living.

New Forests. Martinus Nijhoff Publishers, 101 Philips Dr., Boston, MA 02061. (617) 871-6600. Quarterly. Topics in biology, biotechnology, and management of afforestation and reforestation.

New Forests Project. 731 8th St., SE, Washington, DC 20003. (202) 547-3800.

New Generation Guide to the Birds of Britain and Europe. Christopher Perrins, ed. University of Texas Press, PO Box 7819, Austin, TX 78713-7819. (512) 471-7233 or (800) 252-3206. 1987.

New Generation Guide to the Fungi of Britain and Europe. Stefan Buczacki, ed. University of Texas Press, PO Box 7819, Austin, TX 78713-7819. (512) 471-7233 or (800) 252-3206. 1989. This directory includes over 1,350 species of fungi, representative of all major groups.

New Hampshire Audubon News. Audubon Society of New Hampshire, 3 Silk Farm Rd., Concord, NH 03301. 1966-. Monthly.

New Hampshire Conservation News. New Hampshire Association of Conservation Commissions, 54 Portsmouth St., Concord, NH 03301. (603) 224-7867. 1967-. Quarterly.

New Health Considerations in Water Treatment. Roger Holdsworth, ed. Avebury Technical, Gower House, Croft Rd., Aldershot, England GU11 3HR. Hants (0252) 331551. 1991.

The New International Wildlife Encyclopedia. Maurice Burton and Robert Burton, eds. N. C. L. S. Ltd., 150 Southampton Row, London, England WC1. 1980. Two volumes.

New Jersey Air, Water, & Waste Management Times. New Jersey State Department of Health, Division of Clean Air & Water, John Fitch Plaza, Trenton, NJ 08625. Bimonthly.

New Jersey Environmental Directory. Youth Environmental Society, Box 441, Cranbury, NJ 08512. (609) 655-8030. Annual. Annotated listings of organizations which affect environmental issues.

New Jersey Environmental Law Handbook. Government Institutes, Inc., 4 Research Pl., Ste. 200, Rockville, MD 20850. (301) 921-2300. 1990.

New Jersey Institute of Technology, Air Pollution Research Laboratory. 323 Martin Luther King Boulevard, Newark, NJ 07102. (201) 596-3459.

New Jersey Marine Sciences Consortium. Building 22, Fort Hancock, NJ 07732. (201) 872-1300.

New Mexico Environmental Law Handbook. Government Institutes, Inc., 4 Research Pl., Ste. 200, Rockville, MD 20850. (301) 921-2300. 1990.

New Mexico State University, Center for Biochemical Engineering Research. Department of Chemical Engineering, Box 30001, Dept. 3805, Las Cruces, NM 88003-0001. (505) 646-1214.

New Mexico State University, Water Resources Research Institute. P.O. Box 30001 Dept. 3167, Las Cruces, NM 88003. (505) 646-4337.

New Mexico Wildlife Magazine. N.M. Dept. of Game & Fish, Villagra Bldg., 408 Galisteo, Santa Fe, NM 87503. (505) 827-7911. Irregular. Hunting, fishing, and wildlife management.

The New Organic Grower. Eliot Coleman. Chelsea Green Publishing, PO Box 130, Post Mills, VT 05058-0130. (802) 333-9073. 1989. Covers crop rotation, green manures, tillage, seeding, transplanting, cultivation, and garden pests.

New Perspectives on Silvicultural Management of Northern Hardwoods. U.S. G.P.O, Washington, DC 20402-9325. (202) 512-0000. 1989. Timber stand condition and other factors involved in selecting management strategies for northern U.S. and Canada hardwood forests.

New Publications: Bureau of Mines. U.S. Department of the Interior, 1849 C St. NW, Washington, DC 20240. (202) 208-3171. 1910-. Monthly. Subject areas included are mines and mineral resources, mining engineering and related areas.

New Publications of the Geological Survey. U.S. Department of the Interior, Geological Survey, 119 National Center, Reston, VA 22092. (703) 648-4460. 1984-. Monthly. Bibliography of geological publications and related government documents published by the Geological Survey.

New Separation Chemistry Techniques for Radioactive Waste and Other Specific Applications. L. Cecille. Elsevier Science Publishing Co., 655 Avenue of the Americas, New York, NY 10010. (212) 989-5800. 1991. Purification technology relating to radioactive wastes and sewage. Proceedings of a technical seminar jointly organized by the Commission of the European Communities, Directorate General for Science, Research and Development and the Italian Commission.

The New Superfund: What It Is, How It Works. U.S. Environmental Protection Agency, 401 M St. SW, Washington, DC 20460. (202) 260-2090. 1987.

New Technologies in Urban Drainage. C. Maksimovic. Elsevier Science Publishing Co., 655 Avenue of the Americas, New York, NY 10010. (212) 984-5800. 1991. Advances in rainfall-runoff modelling, hydrodynamics and quality modelling of receiving waters, and urban drainage in specific climates.

New Trends in CO Activation. L. Guczi, ed. Elsevier Science Publishing Co., 655 Avenue of the Americas, New York, NY 10010. (212) 989-5800. 1991.

New Trends in the Chemistry of Nitrogen Fixation. J. Chatt. Academic Press, c/o Harcourt Brace Jovanovich Inc., 6277 Sea Harbor Dr., Orlando, FL 32887. (800) 346-8648. 1980.

New World New Mind: Moving toward Conscious Evolution. Robert E. Ornstein. Simon & Schuster, 1230 Avenue of the Americas, New York, NY 10020. (212) 698-7000; (800) 223-2348. 1990. Proposes revolutionary new ways to close the dangerous gap between our current mind set and the high-tech world of today.

New World Parrots in Crisis. Steven R. Beissinger and Noel F. R. Snyder, eds. Smithsonian Institution Press, 470 L'Enfant Plaza, No. 7100, Washington, DC 20560. (800) 782-4612. 1991. Provides an overview of the hazards facing neotropical parrots one of the world's most threatened group of birds, as well as a detailed discussion of a range of possible conservation solutions.

New York Botanical Garden, Institute of Economic Botany. Bronx, NY 10458-5126. (212) 220-8763.

New York City Environmental Bulletin. Council on the Environment of New York City, 51 Chambers St., New York, NY 10007. (212) 566-0990. Bimonthly. Environmental briefs of interest to city residents.

The New York Environment Book. Eric A. Goldstein. Island Press, 1718 Connecticut Ave. N.W., Suite 300, Washington, DC 20009. (202) 232-7933. 1990. Provides an in-depth analysis of New York City's environment. The five areas surveyed are: solid waste disposal, hazardous substances, water pollution, air quality, and drinking water quality. Discusses past clean-up efforts, and offers an agenda for the future. Describes and analyzes the general environment of urban areas, and offers solutions for their special environmental problems.

New York Environmental Law Handbook. Government Institutes, Inc., 4 Research Pl., Ste. 200, Rockville, MD 20850. (301) 921-2300. 1990.

New York Fish and Game Journal. Dept. of Fish and Wildlife, Environmental Conservation, Albany, NY 12233-4750. Semiannual. Fish and game management studies in New York.

New York Sea Grant Institute. Duchess Hall, State University of New York, Stony Brook, NY 11794-5001. (516) 632-6905.

New York State Center for Hazardous Waste Management. State University of New York at Buffalo, Jarvis Hall 207, Buffalo, NY 14260. (716) 636-3446.

New York State Environment. New York State Journal for Health Physical Education, Dutchess Community College, Poughkeepsie, NY 12601. Semimonthly. State environmental news.

The New York Times Encyclopedic Dictionary of the Environment. Paul Sarnoff. Quadrangle Books, New York, NY 1971. Focuses on state-of-the-art methods of pollution control, abatement, prevention and removal.

New York University, Laboratory of Cellular Biology. Biology Department, 109 Main Building, Washington Square, New York, NY 10003. (212) 998-820.

New York University, Laboratory of Microbial Ecology. 735 Brown Building, New York, NY 10003. (212) 998-8268.

New York Zoological Society. The Zoological Park, Bronx, NY 10460. (212) 220-5100.

New York's Waters. New York State Department of Health, 84 Holland Ave., Albany, NY 12208. Quarterly.

Newfound Harbor Marine Institute. Route 3, Box 170, Big Pine Key, FL 33043. (305) 872-2331.

News & Notes. National Food & Energy Council, Inc., 409 Vandiver W., Suite 202, Columbia, MO 65202. (314) 875-7155. Bimonthly. Efficient use and management of electricity on farms and assurance of continuing energy for the food system.

News Net. UN-NGLS, 2 UN Plaza, #DC2-1103, New York, NY 10017. (212) 963-3125. Environment & development issues.

News Release From The Air-Conditioning and Refrigeration Institute. Air Conditioning and Refrigeration Institute, 1501 Wilson Blvd., Suite 600, Arlington, VA 22209. Monthly. Unitary air conditioner/heat pump domestic shipments.

Newsletter. American Shore and Beach Preservation Association, PO Box 279, Middletown, CA 95461. (707) 987-2385. Quarterly. Coastal management projects, news, conservation issues, and government policies.

Newsletter. Americans for Energy Independence, 1629 K St., NW, Washington, DC 20006. (202) 466-2105. Quarterly. Developments in energy policy; legislative, educational, and media strategies.

Newsletter. Association of Battery Recyclers, Sanders Lead Co. Corp., Sanders Rd., PO Drawer 707, Troy, AL 36081. (205) 566-1563. Bimonthly.

Newsletter. Association of Conservation Engineers, c/o William P. Allinder, Alabama Department of Conservation, 64 N. Union St., Montgomery, AL 36130. (205) 261-3476. Semiannual.

Newsletter. Coalition on Resource Recovery and the Environment, c/o Dr. Walter M. Schaub, U.S. Conference of Mayors, 1620 I St. NW, Suite 600, Washington, DC 20006. (202) 293-7330. Monthly.

Newsletter. Spill Control Association of America, 400 Renaissance Center, Suite 1900, Detroit, MI 48243-1509. (313) 567-0500. Biweekly. Oil and hazardous substance spill control technology.

Newsletter of Association of Ground Water Scientists and Engineers. Association of Groundwater Scientists and Engineers, 6375 Riverside Drive, Dublin, OH 43017. (614) 761-1711. Bimonthly. Reports on events, activities, courses and conferences of AGSE.

Newsletter (U.S. Forest Insect and Disease Management, Methods Application Group). The Group, PO Box 2417, Washington, DC 20013. (703) 235-8065. 1972-. Irregular.

Newsprint Division Monthly Statistical Report. American Paper Institute, 260 Madison Ave., New York, NY 10016. Monthly. Newsprint production, shipments, inventory, and plant capacity.

The Next One Hundred Years: Shaping the Fate of Our Living Earth. Jonathan Weiner. Bantam Books, 666 5th Ave., New York, NY 10103. (212) 765-6500; (800) 223-6834. 1991. Explores the following issues: the greenhouse effect, deforestation, the destruction of the ozone layer, the human population explosion and the onset of mass extinctions.

NIOSH Certified Equipment List as of December 31, 1991. National Institute for Occupational Safety and Health, 1600 Clifton Rd. NE, Atlanta, GA 30333. (404) 639-3286. 1991. DHHS (NIOSH) Publication No. 91-105. This list of personal equipment that has been tested, approved and certified as safe by NIOSH is updated on an annual basis. Users should request the new list annually if they are not currently on the NIOSH publications mailing list.

NIOSH Pocket Guide to Chemical Hazards. National Institute for Occupational Safety and Health, 1600 Clifton Rd. NE, Atlanta, GA 30333. (404) 639-3286. 1990. Presents sources of general industrial hygiene and medical surveillance information for workers, employees and others. Presents key information and data in an abbreviated format for 398 individual chemicals or chemical types.

NIOSHTIC. U.S. Department of Health and Human Services, Centers for Disease Control, National Institute for Occupational Safety and Health, 4676 Columbia Parkway, Cincinnati, OH 45226. (513) 533-8317.

NIP Technical Report on the Toxicology and Carcinogenesis Studies. National Toxicology Program, U.S. Department of Health and Human Services, National Institutes of Health, 9000 Rockville Pike, Bethesda, MD 20892. (301) 496-4000. 1986. Dealing with carcinogenicity testing.

Nitrate and Drinking Water. European Chemical Industry Ecology & Toxicology Centre, Brussels, Belgium 1988. Physiological effect of nitrites and water nitrogen content.

Nitrate and Nitrite in Vegetables. W. J. Corre. Centre for Agricultural Publishing and Documentation, Wageningen, Netherlands 1979. Toxicology and physiological effect of nitrates, minerals in the body and minerals in animal nutrition.

Nitrification. J.I. Prosser, ed. IRL, Southfield Rd., Eynsham, Oxford, England OX8 1JJ. (0865) 88283. 1987.

Nitrification Inhibition Biokinetics. R.D. Neufeld. U.S. Environmental Protection Agency, Industrial Environmental Research Laboratory, MD 75, Research Triangle Park, NC 27711. 1984. Water purification by biological treatment.

Nitrogen Fixation. W. J. Broughton. Oxford University Press, 200 Madison Ave., New York, NY 10016. (212) 679-7300. 1981. Covers ecology, rhizobium, legumes, and molecular biology.

Nitrogen Fixing Tree Association. P.O. Box 680, 41-698 Ahiki St., Waimanalo, HI 96795. (808) 259-8555.

Nitrogen in Organic Wastes Applied to Soils. Academic Press, c/o Harcourt Brace Jovanovich Inc., 6277 Sea Harbor Dr., Orlando, FL 32887. (800) 346-8648. 1989. Nitrogen fertilizers and organic wastes as fertilizer.

Nitrogen in the Environment. Donald R. Nielsen. Academic Press, c/o Harcourt Brace Jovanovich Inc., 6277 Sea Harbor Dr., Orlando, FL 32887. (800) 346-8648. 1978. Nitrogen behavior in field soil and soil plant nitrogen relationship.

Nitrogen, Public Health, and the Environment: Some Tools for Critical Thought. John H. Timothy Winneberger. Ann Arbor Science, 230 Collingwood, Ann Arbor, MI 48106. 1982. Environmental aspects of nitrogen removal in sewage.

Nitrosamines and Human Cancer. Peter N. Magee. Cold Spring Harbor Laboratory Press, PO Box 100, Cold Spring Harbor, NY 11724. (800) 843-4388. 1982. Cover carcinogenesis, nitrosamines, neoplasms, and drug dose response relationships.

Nitrous Oxide/N20. Edmond I. Eger. Elsevier Science Publishing Co., 655 Avenue of the Americas, New York, NY 10010. (212) 984-5800. 1985.

NJPIRG. New Jersey Public Interest Research Group, 99 Bayard St., New Brunswick, NJ 08901-2120. Semiannual. Consumer & environmental advocacy actions.

NMPIS Database. U.S. National Environmental Satellite, Data, and Information Service, National Oceanographic Data Center, 1825 Connecticut Ave., N.W., Suite 406, Washington, DC 20235. (202) 673-5594. Marine pollution research, development, or monitoring projects conducted or funded by federal agencies.

NOAA Earth Systems Data Directory. National Oceanic and Atmospheric Administration, National Environmental Data Referral Service, 1825 Connecticut Ave., N.W., Washington, DC 20235. (202) 673-5548.

NOAA Environmental Digest. National Oceanic and Atmospheric Administration, U.S. Department of Commerce, Washington, DC 20230. (202) 377-2985. Irregular. Selected environmental indicators of the United States and the global environment.

NOAA Weather Service. National Oceanic and Atmospheric Administration, National Environmental Data Referral Service, 1825 Connecticut Ave., N.W., Washington, DC 20235. (202) 673-5548.

NODC Data Inventory Data Base. U.S. National Environmental Satellite, Data, and Information Service, National Oceanographic Data Center, 1825 Connecticut Ave., N.W., Suite 406, Washington, DC 20235. (202) 673-5594. Information on National Oceanographic Data Center holdings.

Noise and Vibration Bulletin. Multi-Science Publishing Co. Ltd., 1070 High St., Brentwood, Essex, England CM14 4RX. 0227-224632. Monthly. Effects of noise on the human and animal organism, instrumentation, standards and regulations; mechanisms involved in road and rail transport, aircraft, domestic and other sources, reduction and control.

Noise and Vibration in Industry. Multi-Science Publishing Co. Ltd., 107 High St., Brentwood, Essex, England CM14 4RX. 0227-224632. Quarterly. Effects of noise and vibration on individuals at work, the effects of vibration on machines and buildings, the impact of industrially-generated noise on the community, hearing protection, audiology and audiometry.

Noise, Buildings, and People. Derek J. Croome. Pergamon Microforms International, Inc., Fairview Park, Elmsford, NY 10523. (914) 592-7720. 1977. Soundproofing techniques in buildings.

Noise Control Engineering Journal. Institute of Noise Control Engineering, Department of M.E., Auburn University, Auburn, AL 36849. (205) 826-4820. Bimonthly. Covers local, state and federal standards for noise control.

Noise Control in Building Services. Pergamon Microforms International, Inc., Fairview Park, Elmsford, NY 10523. (914) 592-7720. 1988. Soundproofing techniques in buildings.

Noise Control Manual. David A. Harris. Van Nostrand Reinhold, 115 5th Ave., New York, NY 10003. (212) 254-3232. 1991. Guidelines for problem-solving in the industrial/commercial acoustical environment.

Noise Control Products and Materials Association. 104 Cresta Verde Dr., Rolling Hills, CA 90274. (213) 377-9958.

Noise Levels. Canadian Centre for Occupational Health & Safety, 250 Main St., East, Hamilton, ON, Canada L8N 1H6. (800) 263-8276.

Noise/News. Institute of Noise Control Engineering, PO Box 1758, Poughkeepsie, NY 12601. 1972-. Bimonthly.

Noise Pollution: A Guide to Information Sources. Clifford R. Bragdon. Gale Research Co., 835 Penobscot Bldg., Detroit, MI 48226-4094. (313) 961-2242. 1979. Part of the series entitled Man and the Environment Information Guides series, v.5.

Noise Regulation Report. Business Publishers, Inc., 951 Pershing Dr., Silver Spring, MD 20910-4464. (301) 587-6300. 1974-. Biweekly. Focuses exclusively on noise abatement and control. Covers developments in this field, news from the federal government including regulatory activities at key federal agencies such as FAA and OSHA. Also covers hard to find information on which state and local governments are doing to enforce noise abatement laws.

Nomenclature Pertaining to Environmental Sanitation. Wilhelmena C. Carey. National Institute of Mental Health, 5600 Fishers Ln., Rm. 15CO5, Rockville, MD 20857. (301) 493-3877. 1980. Institutional housekeeping manual.

Non-Ferrous Metal Data. American Bureau of Metal Statistics, 400 Plaza Dr. (Harmon Meadow), P.O. Box 1405, Secaucus, NJ 07094-0405. Annual. Production and consumption, imports and exports, and exchange prices.

Non-Ionizing Radiation Levels. Canadian Centre for Occupational Health & Safety, 250 Main St. E., Hamilton, ON, Canada L8N 1H6. (800) 263-8276.

Nonferrous Metals Abstracts. British Non-Ferrous Metals Technology Centre, Grove Laboratories, Denchworth Rd., Wantage, Oxfordshire, England OX12 9BJ. 44 (2357) 2992.

Nonferrous Metals: Industry Structure. U.S. G.P.O., Washington, DC 20401. (202) 512-0000. 1990. Nonferrous metal production facilities and copper facility sales and aluminum production and sales.

Nonindustrial Private Forest Ownership Studies: A Bibliography. William B. Kurtz. CPL Bibliographies, 1313 E. 60th St., Chicago, IL 60637-2897. (312) 942-2163. 1981.

Nonpoint Source Pollution. Bruce W. Vigon. American Water Resources Association, 5410 Grosvenor Lane, Suite 220, Bethesda, MD 20814. (301) 493-8600. 1985. Water quality management and water pollution in the U.S.

Nonpoint Source Pollution, an Agricultural Concern, 1983-1987. National Agricultural Library, 10301 Baltimore Blvd., Beltsville, MD 20705-2351. (301) 504-5755. 1986.

Nonpoint Source Pollution: Land Use and Water Quality. Anne Weinberg. University of Wisconsin-Extension, 432 N. Lake St., Madison, WI 53706. 1979. Covers water pollution and water quality management.

Nonprofit Sample and Core Repositories Open to the Public in the United States. Branch of Sedimentary Processes/U.S. Geological Survey, Department of the Interior, Box 25046, Denver Federal Center, MS975, Denver, CO 80225-0046. (303) 236-1930. 1984.

Nontoxic, Natural and Earthwise: How to Protect Yourself and Your Family from Harmful Products and Live in Harmony with the Earth. Debra Lynn Dadd. Jeremy P. Tarcher, 5858 Wilshire Blvd., Ste. 200, Los Angeles, CA 90036. (213) 935-9980. 1990. Evaluation of household products and recommendations as to natural and homemade alternatives.

Nonwoven Disposables in 1990s. FIND/SVP, 625 Avenue of the Americas, New York, NY 10011. (212) 645-4500. 1990. Analyzes to the years 1995 and 2000 for the market of nonwoven disposables.

North American Association for Environmental Education. 1255 23rd St., N.W., Suite 400, Washington, DC 20037. (202) 862-1991.

North American Association for Environmental Education Magazine. North American Association for Environmental Education, Box 400, Troy, OH 45373. (513) 339-6835. Bimonthly.

North American Benthological Society. c/o Cheryl R. Black, Savannah River Ecology Laboratory, Drawer E, Aiken, SC 29802. (803) 925-7425.

North American Bluebird Society. Box 6295, Silver Spring, MD 20906. (301) 384-2798.

The North American Directory of Aquaculture. Kevin Gordon, ed. Kevgor Aquasystems, PO Box 48851, 595 Burrard St., Vancouver, BC, Canada V7X 1A8. (604) 681-2377. 1989/1990. Annual. Lists buyers and sellers of seafood in general. Includes participation listings, province/state listings, company listings, and future conferences.

North American Directory of Non-Ferrous Foundries. 455 State St., Suite 100, Des Plaines, IL 60061. (708) 299-0950. Biennial.

North American Falconers Association. 820 Jay Pl., Berthoud, CO 80513.

North American Family Campers Association. 16 Evergreen Terr., North Reading, MA 01864. (508) 664-4294.

North American Gamebird Association. Box 2105, Cayce-West Columbia, SC 29171. (803) 796-8163.

North American Lake Management Society. 1 Progress Blvd., Box 27, Alachua, FL 32615-9536. (904) 462-2554.

North American Native Fishers Association. 123 W. Mt. Airy Ave., Philadelphia, PA 19119. (215) 247-0384.

North American Radon Association. 8441 River Birch, Roswell, GA 30075. (404) 993-5033.

North American Reference Encyclopedia of Ecology and Pollution. William White. North American Pub. Co., 401 N. Broad St., Philadelphia, PA 19108. (215) 238-5300. 1972.

North American Wholesale Lumber Association–Distribution Directory. 2340 S. Arlington Heights Rd., Suite 680, Arlington Heights, IL 60005. (708) 981-8630. Annual.

North American Wildlife and Natural Resources Conference, Transactions. Wildlife Management Institute, 1101 14th St., N.W., Ste. 725, Washington, DC 20005. (202) 371-1808. Annual. Natural resource conservation.

North American Wildlife Foundation. 102 Wilmot Rd., Suite 410, Deerfield, IL 60015. (708) 940-7776.

North American Wildlife Park Foundation. Wolf Park, Battle Ground, IN 47920. (317) 567-2265.

North American Wolf Society. P.O. Box 82950, Fairbanks, AK 99708. (907) 474-6117.

North Atlantic Ports Association. 31 Coventry Dr., Lewes, DE 19958. (302) 654-9732.

North Carolina Aquarium at Pine Knoll Shores. Atlantic Beach, NC 28512. (919) 247-4003.

North Carolina Aquarium/Roanoke Island. P.O. Box 967, Airport Road, Manteo, NC 27954. (919) 473-3493.

North Carolina Cooperative Fish and Wildlife Unit. North Carolina State University, Raleigh, NC 27695-7617. (919) 737-2631.

North Carolina Environmental and Natural Resources Law Directory. Radian Corp., PO Box 13000, Research Triangle Park, NC 27709. (919) 481-0212. 1990.

North Carolina Environmental Bulletin. North Carolina Office of Intergovernmental Relations, 116 W. Jones St., Raleigh, NC 27603. Monthly. State environmental news.

North Carolina Environmental Law Letter. M. Lee Smith Pub. & Printers, 162 4th Ave., N., Box 2678, Arcade Sta., Nashville, TN 37219. (615) 242-7395. Monthly. Environmental law developments that affect North Carolina companies.

North Carolina State University Cooperative Tree Improvement Programs. P.O. Box 8002, Raleigh, NC 27695. (919) 515-3168.

North Carolina State University, Herbarium. Box 7612, Raleigh, NC 27695. (919) 515-2700.

North Carolina State University, Hope Valley Forest. Department of Forestry, Box 8002, Raleigh, NC 27695. (919) 737-2891.

North Carolina State University, Natural Resources Research Center. Box 8210, Raleigh, NC 27695. (919) 515-5100.

North Carolina State University, Pulp and Paper Laboratory. College of Forest Resources, Box 8005, Raleigh, NC 247695. (919) 737-2888.

North Carolina State University, Southeastern Plant Environment Laboratory. Box 7618, Gardner, Raleigh, NC 27695. (919) 737-2778.

North Carolina State University, Wood Products Laboratory. Box 8005, Raleigh, NC 27695. (919) 737-2881.

North Central Soil Conservation Research Laboratory. North Iowa Avenue, Morris, MN 56267. (612) 589-3411.

North Central Weed Science Society. Research Report. Michael Barrett, ed. North Central Weed Science Society, 309 W. Clark St., Champaign, IL 61820. (217) 356-3182. 1990.

North Country Almanac: Journal of the Adirondack Seasons. Robert F. Hall. Purple Mountain Press, PO Box E-3, Fleischmanns, NY 12430. (914)254-4062. 1990. Essays on the conservation of nature and its resources.

North Dakota State University, Herbarium. State University Station, Fargo, ND 58102. (701) 237-7222.

North Dakota Water Resources Research Institute. North Dakota State University, Box 5626, Fargo, ND 58105. (701) 237-7193.

North Woods Call-Charlevoix. North Woods Call, 00509 Turkey Run, Charlevoix, MI 49720. (616) 547-9797. Biweekly. Issues involving natural resources.

Northeast Association of Fish & Wildlife Resource Agencies. Division of Fish & Wildlife, Dept. of Environmental Conservation, 50 Wolf Rd., Albany, NY 12233. (518) 457-5691.

Northeast Conservation Law Enforcement Chiefs' Association. Dept. of Natural Resources, 1800 Washington St., S.E., Charleston, WV 25305. (304) 348-2784.

Northeast Industrial Waste Exchange Listings Catalog. 90 Presidential Plaza, Suite 122, Syracuse, NY 13202. (315) 422-6572. Quarterly.

Northeast Louisiana University, Soil-Plant Analysis Laboratory. Room 117, Chemistry and Natural Sciences Building, Monroe, LA 71209-0505. (318) 342-1948.

Northeast Watershed Research Center. 111 Research Building A, Pennsylvania State University, University Park, PA 16802. (814) 865-2048.

Northeastern Environmental Science. Northeastern Science Foundation, Box 746, Troy, NY 12181. (518) 273-3247. Semiannual. Environmental research & policies.

Northeastern Lumber Manufacturers Association. 272 Tuttle Rd., P.O. Box 87 A, Cumberland Center, ME 04021. (207) 829-6901.

Northeastern Research Center for Wildlife Diseases. University of Connecticut, Box U-89, CT 06268. (203) 486-3737.

Northeastern University, Marine Science Center. East Point, Nahant, MA 01908. (617) 581-7370.

Northern Illinois University, Center for Biochemical and Biophysical Studies. Faraday Hall, DeKalb, IL 60115. (815) 753-6866.

Northern Illinois University, Plant Molecular Biology Center. Department of Biological Sciences, Montgomery Hall, DeKalb, IL 60115-2861. (815) 753-7841.

Northern Line. Northern Alaska Environmental Center, 218 Driveway, Fairbanks, AK 99701. (907) 452-5021. Quarterly. State environmental news.

Northern Plains Resource Council. 419 Stapleton Bldg., Billings, MT 59101. (406) 248-1154.

Northern Sun News. Northern Sun Alliance, 1519 E. Franklin Ave., Minneapolis, MN 55404. (612) 874-1540. Ten times a year. Alternatives in energy.

Northwest Conifers: A Photographic Key. Dale N. Bever. Binford and Mort Publishing, 1202 Northwest 17th Ave., Portland, OR 97209. (503) 221-0866. 1981. Identification of Pacific Northwest conifers.

Northwest Environmental Journal. Institute for Environmental Studies, University of Washington, Seattle, WA 98195. (206) 543-1812. Biannual. Covers environmental issues in the Northwest states and Canada.

Northwest Fisheries Science Center. 2725 Montlake Boulevard East, Seattle, WA 98112. (206) 553-1872.

Northwest Forestry Association. 1500 S.W. First Ave., Suite 770, Portland, OR 97201. (503) 222-9505.

The Northwest Greenbook. Jonathan King. Sasquatch Books, 1931 2nd Ave., Seattle, WA 98101. (206) 441-5555. 1991.

Not Man Apart. Friends of the Earth, 218 D St. SE, Washington, DC 20003. (202) 544-2600. Bimonthly.

Notes on Sedimentation Activities. U.S. Geological Survey, 12201 Sunrise Valley Dr., Reston, VA 22092. (703) 648-4460. 1967-. Annual. Monitoring of suspended sediments, measurement of sediment loads and deposition, studies of erosion and sedimentation damage, and sediment removal projects.

Notes on Water Research. Water Research Centre, Stevenage Laboratory, Elder Way, Stevenage, England SG1 1TH. Herts 1975-. Bimonthly. Notes on water pollution.

Nova University, Institute of Marine and Coastal Studies. 8000 North Ocean Drive, Dania, FL 33004. (305) 920-1909.

Nova University, Oceanographic Center. 8000 North Ocean Drive, Dania, FL 33004. (305) 920-1909.

NPDES Compliance Inspection Manual. Government Institutes, Inc., 4 Research Pl., Ste. 200, Rockville, MD 20850. (301) 921-2300. 1988. Provides basic guidance on inspection procedures, and gives a wealth of specific technical information for accurate compliance.

NPDES Permit Handbook. Government Institutes, Inc., 4 Research Pl., Ste. 200, Rockville, MD 20850. (301) 921-2300. 1989. Gives details on what a permit is, who needs one, how to apply and renew, establishing efficient limits, compliance deadlines and schedules, special provisions, permitting procedures, and enforcement.

NPIRS Pesticide and Hazardous Chemical Databases. National Pesticide Information Retrieval System, Purdue University, Entomology Hall, West Lafayette, IN 47907. (317) 494-6616. Covers more than 60,000 pesticides registered with the Environmental Protection Agency and with state government agencies.

NRDC Newsline. Natural Resources Defense Council, 40 W. 20th St., 11th Fl., New York, NY 10011. (212) 949-0049. Bimonthly. Enforcement news.

NSCA Environmental Glossary. J. Dunmore. National Society for Clean Air, 136 North Street, Brighton, England BN1 1RG. 1905. Covers air pollution, noise, water pollution, wastes and radiation.

NTP Technical Report on the Toxicology and Carcinogenesis Studies of Trichloroethylene. National Technical Information Service, 5285 Port Royal Rd., Springfield, VA 22161. (703)487-4650. 1988. Deals with toxicology of trichloroethylene and ethylene.

NTP Technical Report on the Toxicology and Carcinogenesis Studies of Two Pentachlorophenol Technical-Grade Mixtures. National Toxicology Program, U.S. Dept. of Health and Human Services, 9000 Rockville Pike, Research Triangle Park, NC 20892. (301)496-4000. 1989.

Nuclear Action Project. 2020 Pennsylvania Ave., Suite 103, Washington, DC 20006. (202) 331-9831.

Nuclear Criticality Information Systems. Lawrence Livermore National Laboratory, Criticality Safety Office, Box 808, Livermore, CA 94550. (415) 422-9799.

The Nuclear Energy Option: An Alternative for the 90s. Bernard L. Cohen. Plenum Press, 233 Spring St., New York, NY 10013-1578. (212) 620-8000; (800) 221-9369. 1990. Sets out to redress what is perceived as unbalanced negative media reporting on the risks of nuclear power.

Nuclear Facility Decommissioning and Site Remedial Actions. Oak Ridge National Laboratory, Remedial Action Program Information Center, PO Box 2008, Bldg. 2001, Oak Ridge, TN 37831-6050. (615) 576-0568. Radioactively contaminated facilities and site remedial actions.

Nuclear Facility Decommissioning and Site Remedial Actions: A Selected Bibliography. National Technical Information Service, 5285 Port Royal Rd., Springfield, VA 22161. (703) 487-4650. Annual. Nuclear facility decommissioning, uranium mill tailings management, and radioactive waste site remedial actions.

Nuclear Free America. 325 E. 25th St., Baltimore, MD 21218. (301) 235-3575.

Nuclear Free: The New Zealand Way. David Lange. Penguin Books, 375 Hudson St., New York, NY 10014. (212) 366-2000; (800) 253-2304. 1990. Provides a first-hand account of the behind-the-scenes story of how one small country in the South Pacific found the political will to say "no" to nuclear weapons.

Nuclear Fuel. McGraw-Hill Science & Engineering Books, 11 W. 19th St., New York, NY 10011. (212) 337-6010.

The Nuclear Fuel Cycle Information System. International Atomic Energy Agency, Wagramerstrasse 5, Vienna, Austria A-1400. 222 2360 6198.

Nuclear Fusion–World Survey of Activities in Controlled Fusion Research Special Supplement. International Atomic Energy Agency, Wagramerstrasse 5, Vienna, Austria A-1400. 222 23606198.

Nuclear Information and Records Management. 210 Fifth Ave., New York, NY 10010. (212) 683-9221.

Nuclear Information and Resource Service. 1424 16th St., N.W., #601, Washington, DC 20036. (202) 328-0002.

Nuclear Magnetic Resonance Facility. University of California, Davis, Davis, CA 95616. (916) 752-7677.

Nuclear Management and Resources Council. 1776 I St., N.W., Suite 300, Washington, DC 20006. (202) 872-1280.

The Nuclear Monitor. Nuclear Information and Resource Service, Inc., 1424 16th St., NW, No. 601, Washington, DC 20036. (202) 328-0002. Biweekly. Tracks the records of nuclear utilities in both operation and construction.

Nuclear News. American Nuclear Society, 555 N. Kensington Ave., LaGrange Park, IL 60525. (708) 352-6611.

Nuclear News–World List of Nuclear Power Plants Issues. American Nuclear Society, 555 N. Kensington Ave., La Grange Park, IL 60525. (708) 352-6611.

Nuclear Power Plant Construction Activity. Energy Information Administration, Department of Energy, EI 231, 1000 Independence Ave., S.W., Washington, DC 20585. (202) 586-8800. 1985.

Nuclear Power Plants Worldwide. Peter D. Dresser. Gale Research Inc., 835 Penobscot Bldg., Detroit, MI 48226-4094. (313) 961-1242. 1993.

Nuclear Reactions in Heavy Elements: A Data Handbook. V.M. Gorbachev. Pergamon Microforms International, Inc., Fairview Park, Elmsford, NY 10523. (914) 592-7720. 1979. Covers nuclear reactions, nuclear fission and heavy elements.

Nuclear Reactors Built, Being Built, or Planned in the United States. Office of Scientific and Technological Information, Department of Energy, Box 62, Oak Ridge, TN 37831. (615) 576-5637.

Nuclear Recycling Consultants. P.O. Box 819, Provincetown, MA 02657. (508) 487-1930.

Nuclear Regulatory Commission: General Information, Addresses, Phone Numbers, and Personnel Listing. Nuclear Regulatory Commission, 1717 H St., N.W., Washington, DC 20555. (301) 492-7000. 1980.

Nuclear Science Abstracts. U.S. Department of Energy, Office of Scientific & Technical Information, P.O. Box 62, Oak Ridge, TN 37831. (615) 576-6299.

Nuclear Waste Disposal Under the Seabed. Edward L. Miles. Institute of International Studies, University of California, 215 Moses Hall, Berkeley, CA 94720. (510) 642-2472. 1985. Assessment of government policy regarding the disposal in the ocean of radioactive waste.

Nuclear Waste Fund Fee Adequacy: An Assessment. National Technical Information Service, 5285 Port Royal Rd., Springfield, VA 22161. (703) 487-4650. 1990. User fees paid by nuclear-generated electric utilities into the Nuclear Waste Fund.

Nuclear Waste News. Business Publishers, Inc., 951 Pershing Dr., Silver Spring, MD 20910-4464. (301) 587-6300. 1981-. Weekly. Covers up-to-the-minute information on radioactive wastes management. Includes facts on all aspects of radioactive wastes such as generation, packaging, transportation, processing, storage and disposal.

Nuclear Waste News–Online. Business Publishers, Inc., 951 Pershing Dr., Silver Spring, MD 20910-4464. (301) 587-6300. Federal and legislation regulation and research and development activities concerning the generation, packaging, transportation, processing, and disposal of nuclear wastes.

Nuclear Waste Project. 218 D St., S.E., Washington, DC 20003. (202) 544-2600.

The Nuclear Weapons Complex. National Research Council. National Academy Press, 2101 Constitution Ave., NW, PO Box 285, Washington, DC 20418. (202) 334-3313. 1989. Management for health, safety, and the environment.

Nuclear Winter: A Bibliography. Robert W. Lockerby. Vance Bibliographies, PO Box 229, 112 N. Charter St., Monticello, IL 61856. (217) 762-3831. 1986.

Nuclear Winter: The Evidence and the Risks. Owen Greene. B. Blackwell, 3 Cambridge Ctr., Suite 208, Cambridge, MA 02142. (617) 225-0401. 1985. Environmental aspects of nuclear warfare.

Nucleic Acid Sequences Handbook. Christian Gautier. Greenwood Publishing Group, Inc., 88 Post Rd., W., P. O. Box 5007, Westport, CT 06881. (203) 226-3571. 1981-.

Nucleic Acids and Molecular Biology. Fritz Eckstein. Springer-Verlag, 175 5th Ave., New York, NY 10010. (212) 460-1500 or (800) 777-4643. 1987. Annual.

Nucleic Acids and Related Compounds. CRC Press, 2000 Corporate Blvd. N.W., Boca Raton, FL 33431. (800) 272-7737. 1987. Annual. A manual of chromatographic analysis.

Nucleus. Union of Concerned Scientists, 26 Church St., Cambridge, MA 02238. (617) 547-5552. Quarterly. Global warming, renewable energy, energy efficiency, nuclear reactor safety, and radioactive waste disposal.

Nukewatch. P.O. Box 2658, Madison, WI 53701-2658. (608) 256-4146.

Nutrient Cycling in Terrestrial Ecosystems Field Methods. A. F. Harrison, et al. Elsevier Science Publishing Co., 655 Avenue of the Americas, New York, NY 10010. (212) 984-5800. 1990. Describes a wide range of methods for the estimation of nutrient fluxes. The book is divided into sections dealing with inputs, turnover, losses and plant uptake processes.

The Nutrition and Health Encyclopedia. David F. Tver and Percy Russell. Van Nostrand Reinhold, 115 5th Ave., New York, NY 10003. (212) 254-3232. 1989.

Nutrition Education Resource Guide: An Annotated Bibliography of Education Materials. Food and Nutrition Information Center. National Agricultural Library, 10301 Baltimore Blvd., Beltsville, MD 20705-2351. (301) 504-5755. 1991.

NYS Environment. New York State Dept. of Environmental Conservation, 50 Wolf Rd., Albany, NY 12233. (518) 457-2344. Biweekly. Controversial environmental issues in legislation.

Oberlin College, Herbarium. Kettering Hall, Oberlin, OH 44074. (216) 775-8315.

Observed Behavior of Cesium, Iodine, and Tellurium in the ORNL Fission Product Release Program. J.L. Collins. U.S. Nuclear Regulatory Commission, Office of Nuclear Regulatory Research, Washington, DC 20555. (301) 492-7000. 1985.

Occupational Epidemiology. Richard R. Monson. CRC Press, 2000 Corporate Blvd. N.W., Boca Raton, FL 33431. (800) 272-7737. 1990. 2d ed. Updates and extends the first edition. Includes basic introduction to epidemiology in the occupational context and introduces new analytic methods.

Occupational Exposure Limits for Airborne Toxic Substances. International Labour Office, 49 Sheridan Ave., Albany, NY 12210. (518) 436-9686. 1991.

Occupational Exposure to Hydrogen Sulfide. National Institute for Occupational Safety and Health. U.S. G.P.O., Washington, DC 20401. (202) 512-0000. 1976.

Occupational Exposure to Malathion. National Institute for Occupational Safety and Health, 1600 Clifton Rd. NE, Atlanta, GA 30333. (404) 639-3286. 1976. Occupational diseases and environmental exposure to malathion.

Occupational Exposure to Silica and Cancer Risk. L. Simonato, et al., eds. International Agency for Research on Cancer, Distributed by Oxford Univ. Press, 200 Madison Ave., New York, NY 10016. (212) 679-7300. 1990. IARC Scientific Publications: No. 97. Deals with toxicology of silica in the workplace and the incidents of cancer.

Occupational Exposures to Diisocyanates. National Institute for Occupational Safety and Health. Department of Health and Human Services, Public Health Service, Center for Disease Control, National Institute for Occupational Safety and Health, 200 Independence Ave. SW, Cincinnati, OH 20201. (202) 619-1296. 1978. Discusses toxicology of isocyanates and safety measures that are in practice.

Occupational Hazards. Penton Publishing Co., 1100 Superior Ave., Cleveland, OH 44114. (216) 696-7000. Monthly. Covers safety management and plant protection.

Occupational Health and Safety. Stevens Publishing Co., P.O. Box 2604, Waco, TX 76714. (817) 776-9000. Monthly. Covers occupational health and safety.

Occupational Health and Safety: Seven Critical Issues. Bureau of National Affairs, BNA PLUS, 1231 25th St., N.W., Rm. 215, Washington, DC 20037. (800) 452-7773.

Occupational Radiation Exposure from U.S. Naval Nuclear Propulsion Plants and Their Support Facilities. U.S. G.P.O, Washington, DC 20401. (202) 512-0000. Annual. Radiation exposure for personnel engaged in operation and maintenance of pressurized water reactors aboard nuclear-powered submarines and surface ships, on duty aboard tenders, and at support facilities.

Occupational Safety and Health. National Institute for Occupational Safety and Health, Standards Development and Technology Transfer Division, 4676 Columbia Pkwy., Cincinnati, OH 45226. (513) 684-8326. Hazardous agents and waste, unsafe workplace environment, toxicology, chemistry,and control technology.

Occupational Safety and Health Administration: Assistant Secretary for Occupational Safety and Health. 200 Constitution Ave., N.W., Washington, DC 20210. (202) 523-7162.

Occupational Safety and Health Administration: Directorate for Policy. 200 Constitution Ave., N.W., Washington, DC 20210. (202) 523-8021.

Occupational Safety and Health Administration: Directorate of Administrative Programs. 200 Constitution Ave., N.W., Washington, DC 20210. (202) 523-8576.

Occupational Safety and Health Administration: Directorate of Compliance Programs. 200 Constitution Ave., N.W., Washington, DC 20210. (202) 523-9308.

Occupational Safety and Health Administration: Directorate of Federal- State Operations. 200 Constitution Ave., N.W., Washington, DC 20210. (202) 523-7251.

Occupational Safety and Health Administration: Directorate of Health Standards Programs. 200 Constitution Ave., N.W., Washington, DC 20210. (202) 523-7075.

Occupational Safety and Health Administration: Directorate of Safety Standards Programs. 200 Constitution Ave., N.W., Washington, DC 20210. (202) 523-8063.

Occupational Safety and Health Administration: Directorate of Technical Support. 200 Constitution Ave., N.W., Washington, DC 20210. (202) 523-7031.

Occupational Safety and Health Administration: Information, Consumer Affairs and Freedom of Information. 200 Constitution Ave., N.W., Washington, DC 20210. (202) 523-8148.

Occupational Safety and Health Administration: Office and Field Operations. 3rd St. and Constitution Ave., N.W., Washington, DC 20210. (202) 523-7725.

Occupational Safety and Health Administration: Publications Office. 200 Constitution Ave., N.W., Room N3101, Washington, DC 20210. (202) 523-9668.

Occupational Safety and Health Administration: Region 1 Office. 133 Portland St., Boston, MA 02114. (617) 565-7164.

Occupational Safety and Health Administration: Region 10 Office. 1111 Third Ave., Suite 715, Seattle, WA 98101-3212. (206) 442-5930.

Occupational Safety and Health Administration: Region 2 Office. 201 Varick St., New York, NY 10014. (212) 337-2378.

Occupational Safety and Health Administration: Region 3 Office. 3535 Market St., Philadelphia, PA 19104. (215) 596-1201.

Occupational Safety and Health Administration: Region 4 Office. 1375 Peachtree St., N.E., Suite 587, Atlanta, GA (404) 347-3573.

Occupational Safety and Health Administration: Region 5 Office. 230 S. Dearborn St., Room 3244, Chicago, IL 60604. (312) 353-2220.

Occupational Safety and Health Administration: Region 6 Office. Federal Building, 525 Griffen St., Dallas, TX 75202. (214) 767-4764.

Occupational Safety and Health Administration: Region 7 Office. 911 Walnut St., Kansas City, MO 64106. (816) 426-5861.

Occupational Safety and Health Administration: Region 8 Office. Federal Building, 1961 Stout St., Room 1576, Denver, CO 80294. (303) 844-3061.

Occupational Safety and Health Administration: Region 9 Office. 71 Stevenson St., Suite 415, San Francisco, CA 94105. (415) 744-7102.

Occupational Safety and Health Reporter. Bureau of National Affairs, BNA PLUS, 1231 25th St., N.W., Rm. 215, Washington, DC 20037. (800) 452-7773. Online version of the periodical of the same name.

Occupational Safety and Health Reporter. Bureau of National Affairs, 1231 25th St. NW, Washington, DC 20037. (202) 452-4200. Weekly. Covers federal safety and health standards, regulations, and policies. Also available online.

Occupational Safety Equipment. FIND/SVP, 625 Avenue of the Americas, New York, NY 10011. (212) 645-4500.

Occupational Toxicants. VCH Publishers, 303 NW 12th Ave., Deerfield Beach, FL 33442-1788. (305) 428-5566. 1991. Contains critical data evaluation for MAK values and classification of carcinogens. Also has standards for hazardous chemical compounds in the work area.

Occurrence, Characteristics, and Genesis of Carbonate, Gypsum, and Silica Accumulations in Soils. W. D. Nettleton. Soil Science Society of America, 677 S. Segoe Rd., Madison, WI 53611. (608) 273-8080. 1991.

Ocean & Shoreline Management. Elsevier Science Publishing Co., 655 Avenue of the Americas, New York, NY 10010. (212) 989-5800. Bimonthly.

Ocean Development and International Law Journal. Crane, Russak & Co., 79 Madison Ave., New York, NY 10016. (212) 725-1999. Quarterly. International law of marine resources.

Ocean Dumping and Marine Pollution. Van Nostrand Reinhold, Information Services, 115 5th Ave., New York, NY 10003. (212) 254-3232. 1979. Geological aspects of waste disposal in the ocean and marine pollution.

The Ocean Dumping Quandary. Donald Fleming Squires. State University of New York Press, State University Plaza, Albany, NY 12246. (518) 472-5000. 1983. Waste disposal in the New York Bight.

The Ocean in Human Affairs. S. Fred Singer, ed. Paragon House Publishers, 90 5th Ave., New York, NY 10011. (212) 620-2820. 1990. Describes the role of the oceans on climate, its resources, energy and water projects in the eastern Mediterranean and other related essays on marine topics.

Ocean Industry–Marine Drilling Rigs Directory Issue. Gulf Publishing Co., Book Division, PO Box 2608, Houston, TX 77252. (713) 529-4301.

Ocean Outlook. 1230 31st St., N.W., #5, Washington, DC 20007. (202) 333-1188.

Ocean Physics and Engineering. Marcel Dekker, Inc., 270 Madison Ave., New York, NY 10016. (212) 696-9000; (800) 228-1160. Quarterly.

Ocean Science News. Nautilus Press Inc., 1056 National Press Bldg., Washington, DC 20045. 1970-. Weekly.

Ocean Studies Institute. PH1-114, California State University, Long Beach, Long Beach, CA 90840. (310) 985-5343.

Ocean Wave and Tidal Energy. National Technical Information Service, 5285 Port Royal Rd., Springfield, VA 22161. (703) 487-4650. 1988. Bimonthly. Ocean thermal energy conversion systems; salinity gradient power systems.

Ocean Yearbook. The University of Chicago Press, Journals Division, PO Box 37005, Chicago, IL 60637. 1978-. Annual. A comprehensive guide to current research and data on living and nonliving resources, marine science and technological environmental, and coastal management.

Oceanic Abstracts. UMI Data Courier, 620 S. 3rd St., Louisville, KY 40202. (800) 626-2823. Formerly: Oceanic Index and Oceanic Citation Journal.

Oceanic Abstracts. Cambridge Scientific Abstracts, 5161 River Rd., Bethesda, MD 20816. (301) 961-6750. Online access.

Oceanic Society. 218 D St., S.E., Washington, DC 20003. (202) 544-2600.

Oceanic Society Expeditions. Ft. Mason Center, Bldg. E, San Francisco, CA 94123. (415) 441-1106.

Oceanographic Literature Review. Woods Hole Data Base, Inc., PO Box 712, Woods Hole, MA 02574. (508) 548-2743. International periodical literature dealing with oceanography, ocean waste disposal and pollution.

Oceans under Threat. Phillip Neal. London Dryad Press, Essex, England 1990. Marine pollution and marine ecology.

OCS Directory: Federal and State Agencies Involved in the Outer Continental Shelf Oil and Gas Program. Minerals Management Science, Department of the Interior, 381 Elden St., Herndon, VA 22070. (703) 787-1028.

Odor and Corrosion Control in Sanitary Sewerage Systems and Treatment Plants: Design Manual. U.S. Environmental Protection Agency, 401 M St., S.W., Washington, DC 20460. (202) 260-2090. 1985. Sewage disposal plants and odor control.

Odor Control and Olfaction: A Handbook. James P. Cox. Pollution Sciences Publishing Company, Lynden, WA 1975.

OECD Environmental Data Compendium 1989. OECD Publications and Information Center, 2001 L St. N.W., Suite 700, Washington, DC 20036. (202) 785-OECD. 1989. Provides statistical data for OECD countries on air pollution, water pollution, the marine environment, land use, forests, wildlife, solid waste, noise and radioactivity. Also provides data on the underlying pressures on the environment such as energy use, transportation, industrial activity and agriculture.

Oecologia. Springer-Verlag, 175 5th Ave., New York, NY 10010. (212) 460-1500. Monthly. Devoted to aquatic ecology.

Office of Emergency Preparedness: Emergency Preparedness and Community Right-to-Know. Chair, Emergency Response Commission for Title III, 2000 14th St., N.W., Frank Reeves Center for Municipal Affairs, Washington, DC 20009. (202) 727-6161.

Office of Environmental Affairs: Bureau of Reclamation. 18th and C St., N.W., Washington, DC 20240. (202) 343-4662.

Office of Environmental Affairs: Emergency Preparedness and Community Right-to-Know. Section 313 Reports, PO Box 2815, Sacramento, CA 95832. (916) 427-4287.

Office of Hazardous Materials Transportation. 400 7th St., S.W., Washington, DC 20590. (202) 366-0656.

Office of Pipeline Safety Regulation. 400 7th St., S.W., Washington, DC 20590. (202) 366-4595.

Office of Public Affairs. 1717 H St., N.W., Washington, DC 20555. (301) 492-7715.

Office of Public Affairs: Bureau of Land Management. 18th and C St., N.W., Washington, DC 20240. (202) 208-3435.

Office of Public Affairs: Fish and Wildlife Service. 18th and C St., N.W., Washington, DC 20240. (202) 343-5634.

Office of Public Affairs: National Ocean Service. 6013 Herbert C. Hoover Building, 14th and Constitution Avenues, N.W., Washington, DC 20230. (202) 673-5111.

Office of Public Affairs: National Oceanic and Atmospheric Administration. 14th and Constitution Avenues, N.W., Washington, DC 20230. (202) 377-2985.

Office of Public Information: Bureau of Mines. 2401 E St., N.W., Washington, DC 20241. (202) 501-9650.

Office of Public Information: Federal Energy Regulatory Commission. 825 North Capitol St., N.E., Washington, DC 20426. (202) 357-8055.

Office of State Chemist: Pesticide Registration. State Chemist, PO Box 1586, Phoenix, AZ 85211-1586. (602) 833-5442.

Office of State Planning: Coastal Zone Management. Chief, State Capitol, PO Box 2359, Honolulu, HI 96813. (808) 548-3026.

Office of State Planning: Coastal Zone Management. Director, 2-1/2 Beacon St., Concord, NH 03301. (603) 271-2155.

Office of the Governor: Coastal Zone Management. Director, Division of Governmental Coordination, PO Box AW, Juneau, AK 99811. (907) 762-4355.

Office of the Governor: Natural Resources. 160 State Capitol, Salem, OR 97310. (503) 378-3548.

Office of the Governor: Natural Resources. Natural Resources Analyst, State Planning Coordinator's Office, Herschler Building, Cheyenne, WY 82002. (307) 777-7574.

Office of the Secretary of Natural Resources: Natural Resources. Secretary, 733 Ninth St., Richmond, VA 23212. (804) 786-0044.

Office of Waste Management: Hazardous Waste Management. Director, 1350 Energy Lane, St Paul, MN 55108. (612) 649-5741.

Office of Water Resources Management: Groundwater Management. Groundwater Management Program, State Water Control Board, PO Box 11143, Richmond, VA 23230. (804) 367-6387.

Official Bulletin of the North Dakota Water and Pollution Control Conference. North Dakota State Health Dept., Bismarck, ND 58501. (701) 224-2354. Quarterly. Municipal water and waste systems and industrial wastes.

Official Guide for the Transportation of Hazardous Materials. K III Press, 424 W. 33rd St., 11th Fl., New York, NY 10001. (212) 714-3100. Directory of services available to transport hazardous material.

The Official World Wildlife Fund Guide to Endangered Species of North America. David W. Lowe, ed. Beacham Publishing, Inc., 2100 S. St. NW, Washington, DC 20008. (202) 234-0877. 1990. Two volumes. Guide to endangered plants and animals. Describes 540 endangered or threatened species including their habitat, behavior and, recovery. Includes: directories of the Offices of the U.S. Fish and Wildlife Service, Offices ofthe National Marine Fisheries Service, State Heritage Programs, Bureau of Land Management Offices, National Forest Service Offices, National Wildlife Refuges, Canadian agencies, and state offices.

Offshore Contractors and Equipment Worldwide Directory. PennWell Books, Box 1260, Tulsa, OK 74101. (918) 831-3161. 1984.

Offshore: Incorporating the Oilman. Offshore, P.O. Box 2895, Tulsa, OK 74101. Monthly. Offshore oil and gas exploration, production, transportation, and finance.

Offshore Marine Service Association. 1440 Canal St., Suite 1709, New Orleans, LA 70112. (504) 566-4577.

Offshore Rig Owners Personnel Directory. Offshore Data Services, Inc., Box 19909, Houston, TX 77224. (713) 781-2713.

Offshore Services and Equipment Directory. Greene Dot, Inc., Box 28663, San Diego, CA 92128. (619) 485-7237.

Ohio Biological Survey. Biological Sciences Building, Ohio State University, 1315 Kinnear Rd., Columbus, OH 43212-1192. (614) 292-9645.

Ohio Environmental Law Handbook. Government Institutes, Inc., 4 Research Pl., Ste. 200, Rockville, MD 20850. (301) 921-2300. 1990.

Ohio Environmental Report. Ohio Environmental Council, 22 E. Gay St., # 300, Columbus, OH 43215. (614) 224-4900. Monthly. News on environmental issues and projects in Ohio.

Ohio Fish and Wildlife Reports. Ohio Dept. of Natural Resources, Division of Wildlife, 1500 Dublin Rd., Columbus, OH 43215. (614) 265-7036. Irregular. Administration of fish and wildlife conservation.

Ohio Solid Waste Market. FIND/SVP, 625 Avenue of the Americas, New York, NY 10011. (800) 346-3787. 1991. Market structure, landfill capacity, primary market participants and other primary assets.

Ohio State University, Acarology Laboratory. 484 West 12th Avenue, Columbus, OH 43210. (614) 292-7180.

Ohio State University, Biotechnology Center. Rightmire Hall, 1060 Carmack Road, Columbus, OH 43210. (614) 292-5670.

Ohio State University, Franz Theodore Stone Laboratory. 1541 Research Center, 1314 Kinnear Road, Columbus, OH 43212. (614) 292-8949.

Ohio State University, Museum of Zoology. 1315 Kinnear Rd., Columbus, OH 43212. (614) 422-8560.

Ohio State University, Ohio Cooperative Fish and Wildlife Research Unit. 1735 Neil Avenue, Columbus, OH 43210. (614) 292-6112.

Ohio State University, Ohio Sea Grant College Program. 1541 Research Center, 1314 Kinnear Road, Columbus, OH 43212. (614) 292-8949.

Ohio State University, Secrest Arboretum. 1680 Madison Avenue, Wooster, OH 44691. (216) 263-3761.

Ohio State University, Water Resources Center. 262 Agriculture Building, 590 Woody Hayes Drive, Columbus, OH 43210. (614) 292-2334.

Ohio University, Edison Animal Biotechnology Center. West Green, Athens, OH 45701. (614) 593-4713.

OHM-TADS (Oil and Hazardous Materials-Technical Assistance Data System). U.S. Environmental Protection Agency, Emergency Response Division, 410 M St., S.W., Washington, DC 20460. (800) 479-2449.

Oil and Chemical Pollution. Elsevier Science Publishing Co., 655 Avenue of the Americas, New York, NY 10010. (212) 989-5800. Technology of spills and cleanups.

The Oil and Gas Directory; Regional and Worldwide. Oil and Gas Directory, 2200 Welch Ave., PO Box 13508, Houston, TX 77219. (713) 529-8789. 1987-88. Eighteenth edition. Comprehensive listing of all companies and individuals directly connected with or engaged in petroleum exploration, drilling, and production.

Oil and Gas Exploration and Development. American Business Directories, Inc., 5711 S. 86th Circle, Omaha, NE 68127. (402) 593-4600.

Oil and Gas Information. International Energy Agency. OECD Pub., Suite 700, 2001 L St. N.W., Washington, DC 20036-4905. (202) 785-6323. 1989-. Annually. IEA's annual statistical reference (in French and English) on oil and gas supply and demand. Contains statistics for OECD member countries on production, trade, demand, prices, refining capacity, and reserves. Data on world production, trade, and consumption of major oil products and natural gas are shown in summary tables.

Oil & Gas Journal Energy Database. PennWell Books, PO Box 1260, Tulsa, OK 74101. (918) 835-3161.

Oil and Gas Law: The North Sea Exploration. Kenneth R. Simmonds. Oceana Publications Inc., 75 Main St., Dobbs Ferry, NY 10522. (914) 693-8100. 1988. Surveys the legal framework within which operators have to carry out the exploration and exploitation of North Sea oil and gas resources.

Oil and Hazardous Materials Technical Assistance Data System. U.S. Environmental Protection Agency, Office of Solid Waste and Emergency Response, 401 M St., S.W., Washington, DC 20460. (202) 260-2090. Hazardous substances and their deleterious effects on water quality and other environmental media.

Oil, Chemical, & Atomic Workers International Union. Box 2812, Denver, CO 80201. (303) 987-2229.

Oil Field Haulers Association. 700 E. 11th St., Box 1669, Austin, TX 78767. (512) 478-2541.

Oil Pollution Abstracts. Industrial Environmental Research Laboratory, Office of Research and Development, U.S. Environmental Protection Agency, 2412 Atlantic Ave., Raleigh, NC 27604. (919) 834-4015. 1979.

Oil Pollution Act of 1990: Special Report. Government Institutes, Inc., 4 Research Pl., Ste. 200, Rockville, MD 20850. (301) 921-2300. 1991. Gives complete coverage of the Oil Pollution Act for the Government Institutes' conference.

Oil Pollution from Tanker Operations; Causes, Costs, Controls. W.G. Waters. Centre for Transportation Studies, University of British Columbia, 1924 W. Mall, Rm. 100, Vancouver, BC, Canada V6I 1Z2. (604) 822-4977. 1980. Tanker safety measures, costs, and oil pollution of the sea.

Oil Spill Data Base. Center for Short-Lived Phenomena, Box 199, Harvard Square Station, Cambridge, MA 02238. (617) 492-3310.

Oil Spill Intelligence Report. Cahners Publishing Co., 249 W. 17th St., New York, NY 10011. (212) 645-0067. Irregular. Global information on oil spill cleanup, prevention control.

Oil Spill Intelligence Report. Cutter Information Corp., 37 Broadway, Arlington, MA 02174-5539. (617) 648-8700. Oil spills and cleanup efforts, contingency planning and response, legislative and regulatory developments and technologies. Online version of periodical of same name.

Oil Spill Response Guide. Robert J. Meyers & Associates and Research Planning Institute, Inc. Noyes Publications, 120 Mill Rd., Park Ridge, NJ 07656. (201) 391-8484. 1989. Describes equipment, techniques and logistics for responding to oil spills. It is designed to serve as a planning guide which will help the on-scene coordinator (OSC) identify the steps and priorities for responding to major oil spill, or oil well blowouts associated with petroleum activity.

Oil Terms: A Dictionary of Terms Used in Oil Exploration and Development. Leo Crook. International Pub Service, 114 E 32d St., New York, NY 10016. 1975.

Oil Transportation by Tankers. United States Congress Office of Technology Assessment. U.S. G.P.O., Washington, DC 20401. (202) 512-0000. 1975. An analysis of marine pollution and safety measures.

Oil/Water Separation: State-of-the-Art. Fidelis A. Osamor. National Technical Information Service, 5285 Port Royal Rd., Springfield, VA 22161. (703) 487-4650. 1978. Oil pollution of water, rivers, and harbors and the technology of abatement.

Okeanos Ocean Research Foundation, Inc. P.O. Box 776, Hamptons Bays, NY 11946. (516) 728-4522.

Oklahoma Fishery Research Laboratory. 500 East Constellation, Norman, OK 73072. (405) 325-7288.

Oklahoma State University, Herbarium. Stillwater, OK 74078. (405) 744-9558.

Oklahoma State University, Oklahoma Cooperative Fish and Wildlife Research Unit. 404 Life Sciences Building, Stillwater, OK 74078. (405) 744-6342.

Oklahoma State University, Oklahoma Water Resources Research Institute. University Center for Water Research, 003 Life Science East, Stillwater, OK 74078. (405) 744-9994.

Oklahoma State University, Plant Disease Diagnostic Laboratory. Department of Plant Pathology, 119 Noble Research Center, Stillwater, OK 74078. (405) 744-9961.

Oklahoma State University, University Center for Water Research. 003 Life Sciences East, Stillwater, OK 74078. (405) 744-9995.

Oklahoma State University, Water Quality Research Laboratory. Stillwater, OK 74078-0459. (405) 744-5551.

Old Dominion University, Applied Marine Research Laboratory. Norfolk, VA 23529-0456. (804) 683-4195.

Olefins: Manufacture and Derivatives. Marshall Sittig. Noyes Publications, 120 Mill Rd., Park Ridge, NJ 07656. (201) 391-8484. 1968.

Olsen's Biomass Energy Report. G. V. Olsen Associates, 170 Broadway, Room 201, New York, NY 10038. (212) 866-5034. Literature relating to biodegradable renewable energy sources and uses.

On Methuselah's Trail: Living Fossils and the Great Extinctions. Peter Douglas Ward. W. H. Freeman, 41 Madison Ave., New York, NY 10010. (212) 576-9400. 1992. Biological aspects of extinction.

On Possible Changes in Global Sealevel and Their Potential Causes. T.P. Barnett. National Technical Information Service, 5285 Port Royal Rd., Springfield, VA 22161. (703) 487-4650. A Scripps Institute of Oceanography study on climatic changes, global warming, etc.

On the Brink of Extinction: Conserving the Diversity of Life. Edward C. Wolf. Worldwatch Institute, 1776 Massachusetts Ave., N.W., Washington, DC 20036-1904. 1987.

On the Edge. Wildlife Preservation Trust International, 34th St. & Girard Ave., Philadelphia, PA 19104. (215) 222-2191. Semiannual. Animal conservation, endangered species and captive breeding.

On the Linkage of Solar Ultraviolet Radiation to Skin Cancer. Department of Transportation, Federal Aviation Administration, Office of Environmental Quality, 800 Independence Ave. SW, Washington, DC 20591. (202) 267-3484. 1978. Effect of radiation on the skin.

One World. Trans-Species Unlimited, Box 1553, Williamsport, PA 17703. (717) 322-3252. Irregular. Vegetarianism and animal rights.

OPD Chemical Buyer's Directory. Chemical Marketing Reporter, Schnell Pub. Co., 80 Broad St., New York, NY 10004-2203. (212) 248-4177. 1992. Seventy-ninth edition. Known as the "Green Book", this buyer's directory includes an index of chemical suppliers, branch offices, a glossary, an 800 phone directory for quick supplier reference. Also includes the chemfile folio of company catalogs, chemicals and related materials listings, and other related data.

Open Space Institute. 145 Main St., Ossining, NY 10562. (914) 762-4630.

Operating Research Plan. Interagency Task Force on Acid Precipitation. The Task Force, Washington, DC 1984. Volume One covers research framework. Volume Two contains an inventory of research under the National Acid Precipitation Assessment Program.

Operation and Maintenance Experiences of Pumped-Storage Plants. A. Borenstadt. Electric Power Research Institute, 3412 Hillview Ave., Palo Alto, CA 94304. (415) 965-4081. 1991. Repair and maintenance of hydroelectric power plants.

Operation and Maintenance of Hospital Medical Waste Incinerators. U.S. Environmental Protection Agency–Office of Air Quality Planning and Standards. U.S. G.P.O, Washington, DC 20401. (202) 512-0000. 1990. A manual covering incineration of hazardous and medical wastes.

Operation, Maintenance and Management of Wastewater Treatment Facilities. Municipal Operations Branch, Office of Water Program Operations, U.S. Environmental Protection Agency, 401 M St. SW, Washington, DC 20460. (202) 260-5856. 1978. Bibliography of operations and maintenance of wastewater treatment plants.

Operation of Municipal Wastewater Treatment Plants. Water Pollution Control Federation, 601 Wythe St., Alexandria, VA 22314. (800) 556-8700. 2nd ed.

Operations Forum. Water Pollution Control Federation, 601 Wythe Street, Alexandria, VA 22314-1994. (703) 684-2400. Monthly. Covers the advancement of practical knowledge in water quality control systems.

Operator's Organizational, DS, GS, and Depot Maintenance Manual. U.S. G.P.O, Washington, DC 20401. (202) 512-0000. 1988. Covers repair parts and special tools list for dehumidifier, desiccant, electric and air distribution manifolds.

Optoelectronics for Environmental Science. S. Martellucci and A. N. Chester, eds. Plenum Press, 233 Spring St., New York, NY 10013-1578. (212) 620-8000; (800) 221-9369. 1991. Contribution of lasers and the optical sciences to specific problems, in situ measurements, atmospheric ozone, lidar detection, wind velocity, oceanographic measurements, heavy metal detection, toxic metals, and trace analysis. Proceedings of the 14th course of the International School of Quantum Electronics on Optoelectronics for Environmental Sciences, held September 3-12, 1989, in Erice, Italy.

OPTS Regulation Tracking System. U.S. Environmental Protection Agency, Office of Pesticides and Toxic Substances, 401 M St., S.W., Washington, DC 20460. (202) 260-2090. Histories of various regulations, as well as compliance.

Oregon Cooperative Park Studies Unit. College of Forestry, Oregon State University, Corvallis, OR 97331. (503) 737-2056.

Oregon Department of Fish and Wildlife Research & Development Section. 850 S.W. 15th Street, Oregon State University, Corvallis, OR 97333. (503) 737-3241.

Oregon Natural Resources Council. Yeon Building, Suite 1050, 522 Southwest Fifth Ave., Portland, OR 97204. (503) 223-9001.

Oregon State University, Center for Gene Research and Biotechnology. Cordley 3096, Corvallis, OR 97331. (503) 737-3347.

Oregon State University, Environmental Remote Sensing Applications Laboratory. Peavy Hall 108, College of Forestry, Corvallis, OR 97331. (503) 737-3056.

Oregon State University, Forest Research Laboratory. College of Forestry, Corvallis, OR 97331. (503) 737-2221.

Oregon State University, Hatfield Marine Science Center. Marine Science Drive, Newport, OR 97365. (503) 867-3011.

Oregon State University, Herbarium. Corvallis, OR 97331-2910. (503) 737-4106.

Oregon State University, Laboratory for Nitrogen Fixation Research. Corvallis, OR 97331. (503) 737-4214.

Oregon State University, Oak Creek Laboratory of Biology. Department of Fisheries and Wildlife, 104 Nash Hall, Corvallis, OR 97331. (503) 737-3503.

Oregon State University, Oceanographic & Geophysics Research Program. College of Oceanography, Oceanography Administration Building 104, Corvallis, OR 97331-5503. (503) 737-3504.

Oregon State University, Oregon Cooperative Fishery Research Unit. 104 Nash Hall, Corvallis, OR 97331. (503) 737-4531.

Oregon State University, Oregon Sea Grant College Program. Administrative Services Building-A 500, Corvallis, OR 97331. (503) 737-2714.

Oregon State University, Seafoods Laboratory. 250 36th Street, Astoria, OR 97103. (503) 325-4531.

Oregon State University, Water Resources Research Institute. 210 Strand Agriculture Hall, Corvallis, OR 97331-2208. (503) 737-4022.

Oregon Wildlife. Oregon State Dept. of Fish, Box 59, Portland, OR 97207. (503) 229-5403. Bimonthly.

Organic Chemistry of the Earth's Atmosphere. Valerii A. Isidorov. Springer-Verlag, 175 5th Ave., New York, NY 10010. (212) 460-1500; (800) 777-4643. 1990. Describes the composition of atmosphere; distribution of organic components in space and time; natural sources; human-created sources; atmosphere organic reactions methods of analysis.

Organic Farming: A Bibliography. CPL Bibliographies, 1313 E. 60th St., Chicago, IL 60637-2897. (312) 942-2163. 1984.

Organic Farming and Gardening. Jayne T. MacLean. National Agricultural Library, 10301 Baltimore Blvd., Beltsville, MD 20705-2351. (301) 504-5755. 1987.

Organic Garden Vegetables. George F. Van Patten. Van Patten Pub., PO Box 82009, Portland, OR 97202. (503) 775-3815. 1991.

Organic Gardening. Rodale Press, 33 E. Minor St., Emmaus, PA 18098. (215) 967-5171.

Organic Reactions Catalysis Society. c/o R.L. Augustine, Dept. of Chemistry, Seton Hall University, South Orange, NJ 07079. (201) 761-9033.

Organic Solvents: Physical Properties and Methods of Solvents. John A. Riddick, et al. John Wiley & Sons, Inc., 605 3rd Ave., New York, NY 10158-0012. (212) 850-6000. 1986. 4th ed.

Organic Substances and Sediment in Water. Robert A. Baker. Lewis Publishers, 2000 Corporate Blvd., Boca Raton, FL 33431. (407) 994-0555 or (800) 272-7737. 1991. vol. 1-3.

Organic Waste Recycling. Chongrak Polprasert. John Wiley & Sons, Inc., 605 Third Ave., New York, NY 10158. (212) 850-6000. 1989. Covers technologies for treating human waste, animal manure, agricultural residues and wastewater, sludge, algae, aquatic weeds and others.

Organization for Flora Neotropica. New York Botanical Garden, Kazimirov Boulevard and 200th Street, Bronx, NY 10458. (212) 220-8742.

Organization for Tropical Studies, Inc. P.O. Box DM, Duke Station, Durham, NC 27706. (919) 684-5774.

Organization of Biological Field Stations. Box 351, Eureka, MO 63025. (314) 938-5346.

Organization of Wildlife Planners. 1420 E. 6th Ave., Helena, MT 59620. (406) 444-4758.

Organometallic Compounds of Aluminum, Gallium, Indium, and Thallium. A. McKillog. Chapman & Hall, 29 W. 35th St., New York, NY 10001-2291. (212) 244-3336. 1985. Covers organoaluminum, organogallium and organothallium compounds.

Orion Nature Quarterly. Myrin Institute, Inc., 136 E. 64th St., New York, NY 10021. (212) 758-6475. Quarterly. Natural world and man's relation to it.

Osborn Laboratories of Marine Sciences. New York Aquarium, Boardwalk and West 8th, Brooklyn, NY 11224. (718) 265-3400.

OSHA Field Operations Manual. Government Institutes, Inc., 4 Research Pl., Ste. 200, Rockville, MD 20850. (301) 921-2300. 4th edition. Step-by-step manual, developed by OSHA for use by its own compliance safety and health officers in carrying out inspections.

OSHA Regulated Hazardous Substances: Health, Toxicity, Economic, and Technological Data. U.S. Occupational Safety and Health Administration. Noyes Publications, 120 Mill Rd., Park Ridge, NJ 07656. (201) 391-8484. 1990. Provides industrial exposure data and control technologies for more than 650 substances currently regulated, or candidates for regulation, by the Occupational Safety and Health Administration.

OSHA Systems Safety Inspection Guide. Government Institutes, Inc., 4 Research Pl., Ste. 200, Rockville, MD 20850. (301) 921-2300. 1989. Focuses on overall management of any operation in which hazardous chemicals are handled.

OSHA Technical Manual. Government Institutes, Inc., 4 Research Pl., Ste. 200, Rockville, MD 20850. (301) 921-2300. 1991. Covers both health and safety inspections and procedures.

OSPIRG Citizen Agenda. Oregon State Public Interest Research Group, 027 SW Arthur St., Portland, OR 97201. (503) 222-9641. Quarterly. Consumer rights, environmental protection, & citizen action.

Our Common Future. World Commission on Environment and Development. Oxford University Press, 200 Madison Ave., New York, NY 10016. (212) 679-7300; (800) 334-4249. 1987. Cautions that it is time that economy and ecology worked hand in hand, so that governments and their people can take responsibility not just for environmental damage, but for the policies that cause the damage.

Our Common Lands: Defending the National Parks. David J. Simon, ed. Island Press, 1718 Connecticut Ave. N.W., Suite 300, Washington, DC 20009. (202) 232-7933. 1988. Explains the complexities of key environmental laws and how they can be used to protect our national parks. Includes discussion of successful and unsuccessful attempts to use the laws and how the courts interpret them.

Our Earth, Ourselves: The Action-Oriented Guide to Help You Protect and Preserve Our Planet. Ruth Caplan and the Staff of Environmental Action. Bantam Books, 666 5th Ave., New York, NY 10103. (212) 765-6500; (800) 223-6834. 1990. Provides practical advice on what we can do to reverse the damage already done to our air, water, and land.

Our National Wetland Heritage. Jon A. Kusler. Environmental Law Institute, 1616 P St., NW, Suite 200, Washington, DC 20036. (202) 328-5150. 1983. Discusses practical ways to preserve and protect wetlands and their benefits, which include recreation, wildlife habitat, pollution and flood control, scientific research and groundwater recharge.

Our Public Lands. Superintendent of Documents, U.S. Government Printing Office, Washington, DC 20402. 1951-. Quarterly.

Out of the Channel: The Exxon Valdez Oil Spill in Prince William Sound. John Keeble. Harper & Row, 10 E. 53rd St., New York, NY 10022. (212) 207-7000. 1991. Presents a detailed account of the disaster, its implications and ramifications.

Outdoor America. Izaak Walton League of America, 1401 Wilson Blvd., Level B, Arlington, VA 22209. (703) 528-1818. Quarterly. Outdoor recreation and natural resource conservation.

Outdoor California. California State Dept. of Fish & Game, 1416 9th St., Sacramento, CA 95814. (916) 445-3531. Bimonthly. Wildlife conservation.

Outdoor Ethics Guild. c/o Bruce Bandurski, General Delivery, Bucks Harbor, ME 04618.

Outdoor Indiana. Indiana State Dept. of Natural Resources, Box 6113, Indianapolis, IN 46204. (317) 232-4004. Ten times a year. Facilities, services, and state programs.

Outdoor News Bulletin. Wildlife Management Institute, 1101 14th St., N.W., Suite 725, Washington, DC 20005. (202) 371-1808. Biweekly. Conservation and wildlife.

Outdoor Oklahoma. Oklahoma Dept. Wildlife Conservation, Box 53465, 1801 N. Lincoln, Oklahoma City, OK 73152. Bimonthly. Hunting, fishing, and outdoor activities.

Outdoor Writers Association of America. 2017 Cato Ave., Suite 101, State College, PA 16801. (814) 234-1011.

Outdoors Forum. CompuServe Information Service, 5000 Arlington Centre Blvd., PO Box 20212, Columbus, OH 43220. (614) 457-8600. Outdoor sports, hobbies, and entertainment. Includes search and rescue, nature, wildlife, equipment, and park and campground information.

Outdoors Unlimited. Outdoor Writers Association of America, 4141 West Bradley Rd., Milwaukee, WI 53209. 1940-. Monthly.

Outdoors Unlittered Pitch-In News. Outdoors Unlittered, 200-1676 Martin Dr., White Rock, BC, Canada V4A 6E7. (403) 429-0517. Semiannually. Solid waste and litter problems

Outer Continental Shelf Environmental Assessment Program. U.S. NOAA. National Ocean Service. U.S. G.P.O., Washington, DC 20401. (202) 512-0000. 1991. Irregular. Environmental impacts of pollutants, including petroleum hydrocarbons and trace metals in marine biota, sediments and water.

Outer Continental Shelf Oil and Gas Activities. U.S. Dept. of Interior. Mineral Management Service. U.S. G.P.O., Washington, DC 20401. (202) 512-0000. 1980. Annual. Data on oil and gas drilling, production and reserves.

The Overall Diaper Market. FIND/SVP, 625 Avenue of the Americas, New York, NY 10011. (212) 645-4500. 1990. Market for disposable and cloth diapers and diaper services.

Overtapped Oasis: Reform or Revolution for Western Water. Marc Reisner and Sarah Bates. Island Press, 1718 Connecticut Ave. N.W., Suite 300, Washington, DC 20009. (202) 232-7933. 1990. Comprehensive critique of the cardinal dogma of the American West: that the region is always running out of water and therefore must build more and more dams.

Oxidation Communications. Elsevier, Box 211, Amsterdam, Netherlands 1000 AE. 020-5803-911. Quarterly.

Oxygen Depletion and Associated Benthic Mortalities in New York Bight. R. Lawrence Swanson. National Oceanic and Atmospheric Administration, U.S. Department of Commerce, Washington, DC 20230. (202) 377-2985. 1980. Covers anoxemia, marine pollution, and dissolved oxygen in water.

Oxygenated Fuels Association. 1330 Connecticut Ave., N.W., #300, Washington, DC 20036. (202) 822-6750.

Ozone. Kathryn Gay. Franklin Watts, 387 Park Ave. S., New York, NY 10016. (212) 686-7070. 1989. Environmental aspects of chlorofluorocarbons.

Ozone and Carbon Monoxide Air Quality Design Values. U.S. G.P.O., Washington, DC 20401. (202) 512-0000. Annual. National Ambient Air Quality Standards for Ozone and Carbon Monoxide Concentrations.

Ozone and Chlorine Dioxide Technology for Disinfection of Drinking Water. J. Katz. Noyes Publications, 120 Mill Rd., Park Ridge, NJ 07656. (201) 391-8484. 1980. Purification of drinking water through oxidation, chlorination, and ozonization.

Ozone and Ultraviolet Radiation Disinfection for Small Community Water Systems. Municipal Environmental Research Laboratory, Office of Research and Development, U.S. Environmental Protection Agency, 26 W. Martin Luther King Dr., Cincinnati, OH 45268. 1979. Water purification through ultraviolet treatment, water quality management and water purification ozonization.

Ozone Crisis: The 15-Year Evolution of a Sudden Global Emergency. Sharon L. Roan. John Wiley & Sons, Inc., 605 3rd Ave., New York, NY 10158-0012. (212) 850-6000. 1989. Chronicles the experiences of F. Sherwood Rowland and Mario Molina, the scientists who first made the ozone depletion discovery.

Ozone Depletion: Health and Environmental Consequences. John Wiley & Sons, Inc., 605 3rd Ave., New York, NY 10158-0012. (212) 850-6000. 1989.

Ozone Drinking Water Treatment Handbook. Rip G. Rice. Lewis Publishers, 2000 Corporate Blvd., N.W., Boca Raton, FL 33431. (407) 994-0555 or (800) 272-7737. 1991. Explains how ozone can be used to provide primary disinfection, while minimizing halogenated by-products.

Ozone in the Atmosphere: Proceedings of the Quadrennial Ozone Symposium 1988 and Tropospheric Ozone Workshop, Gottingen, Germany, August 4-13, 1988. Rumen D. Bojkov and Peter Fabian, eds. A. Deepak, 101 Research Dr., Hampton, VA 23666-1340. 1989. Covers the topics: tropospheric ozone, polar ozone, ozone observations (from ground and space), observations of relevant trace constituents, reaction kinetics, mesospheric ozone, chemical- radiative-dynamic models, and new observational techniques.

Ozone in the Troposphere and the Stratosphere. Council of Planning Librarians, 1313 E. 60th St., Chicago, IL 60637-2897. (312) 942-2163. 1988. Atmospheric ozone bibliography.

Ozone in Water Treatment; Application and Engineering. Lewis Publishers, 200 Corporate Blvd. NW, Boca Raton, FL 33431. (407) 994-0555 or (800)272-7737. 1991. Ozone technology as it is applied to drinking water production.

The Ozone Layer. Jane Duden. Crestwood House, Inc., c/o Macmillan Publishing Co., Front & Brown Streets, Riverside, NJ 08075. (609) 461-6500. 1990. Describes the ozone layer and its important function in protecting the earth from dangerous ultraviolet rays. Also examines the threats posed to the ozone layer by chlorofluorocarbons and other pollutants.

Ozone Risk Communication and Management. Edward J. Calabrese and Charles Gilbert. Lewis Publishers, 2000 Corporate Blvd., N.W., Boca Raton, FL 33431. (407) 994-0555 or (800) 272-7737. 1990. Covers the non-attainment of EPS goals for ozone. Targets specific examples of environmental, agricultural, and public health implications of this non-compliance.

Ozone: Science and Engineering. Rip G. Rice, ed. Lewis Publishers, 2000 Corporate Blvd., N.W., Boca Raton, FL 33431. (407) 994-0555 or (800) 272-7737. 1979-. Six times a year. Exchanges information concerning ozone and other oxygen-related species between scientific disciplines.

Ozone, Smog and You. Office of Public Information. Illinois Environmental Protection Agency, 2200 Churchill Rd., PO Box 19276, Springfield, IL 62794-9276. (217) 782-2829. 1987. Physiological effects of air pollution.

Pacific Basin Consortium for Hazardous Waste Research. Environmental and Policy Institute, 1777 East-West Rd., Honolulu, HI 96848. (808) 944-7555.

Pacific Institute for Studies in Development, Environment, and Security. 1681 Shattuck Ave., Suite H, Berkeley, CA 94709. (415) 843-9550.

Pacific Logging Congress. 4494 River Rd., N., Salem, OR 97303. (503) 393-6754.

Pacific Whale Foundation. Kealia Beach Plaza, Ste. 25, 101 N. Kihei Rd., Kihei, HI 96753. (808) 879-8811.

Pacific Wildlife Project. P.O. Box 7673, Laguna Niguel, CA 92607. (714) 831-1178.

Pack & Paddie. Ozark Society, Box 2914, Little Rock, AR 72203. (501) 225-1795. Quarterly. Regional conservation.

Packaging. Cahners Publishing Co., 249 W. 17th St., New York, NY 10011. (212) 645-0067. Monthly. Manufacturing, R&D, marketing, and consumption.

Packaging and the Environment: Alternatives, Trends, and Solutions. Susan E. M. Selke. Technomic Publishing Co., 851 New Holland Ave., Box 3535, Lancaster, PA 17604. (717) 291-5609. 1990. Review of the contribution of packaging to various environmental problems.

Packaging Institute International. Institute of Packaging Professionals, 481 Carlisle Dr., Herndon, VA 22070. (703) 318-8970.

Paddy Drying Manual. N. C. Teter. Food and Agriculture Organization of the United Nations, 4611-F Assembly Dr., Lanham, MD 20706-4391. (301) 459-7666 or (800) 274-4888. 1987.

Paint & Coatings Industry–Raw Materials & Equipment Source Directory & Buyers Guide Issue. Business News, 60 Industrial Way, Brisbane, CA 94005. (415) 468-7786.

Paint & Resin. Wheatland Journals Ltd., Penn House, Penn Place, Rickmansworth, England WD3 1FN. 1981.

Paint, Body & Equipment Association–Membership Roster. Paint, Body & Equipment Association, 9140 Ward Parkway, Kansas City, MO 64114. (816) 444-3500.

Paint Formulation: Principles and Practice. J. Boxall. Industrial Press, 200 Madison Ave., New York, NY 10016. (212) 889-6330. 1981.

Paint Handbook. McGraw-Hill Science & Engineering Books, 11 W. 19th St., New York, NY 10011. (212) 337-6010. 1981. Covers industrial painting and paint.

Paint Manual. U.S. G.P.O., Washington, DC 20401. (202) 512-0000. 1976. Covers protective coatings and industrial painting.

Paleobotany, Paleoecology, and Evolution. Praeger Publishers, 1 Madison Ave., New York, NY 10010-3603. (212) 685-5300. 1981.

Paleoecology, Concepts and Applications. John Wiley & Sons, Inc., 605 3rd Ave., New York, NY 10158-0012. (212) 850-6000. 1990.

Paleoenvironments in the Namib Desert: The Lower Tumas Basin in the Late Cenozoic. Justin Wilkinson. University of Chicago Press, Committee on Geographical Studies, 5801 Ellis Ave., 4th Floor, Chicago, IL 60637. (800) 621-2736. 1990. Focuses on the great coastal desert of Southwestern Africa the Namib, and explores the complex changes in depositional environments throughout the Cenozoic.

Panel Report on Ozone. United Nations Environment Program. United Nations Environment Programme, Box 30552, Nairobi, Kenya 1991.

Paper Industry Management Association. 2400 E. Oakton St., Suite 100, Arlington Hts., IL 60005. (708) 956-0250.

Paper, Paperboard, and Wood Pulp: Monthly Statistical Summary. American Paper Institute, 260 Madison Ave., New York, NY 10016. Monthly.

Paper Production and Processing. Robert Soklow. U.S. Environmental Protection Agency, Industrial Environmental Research Laboratory, 26 W. Martin Luther King Dr., Cincinnati, OH 45268. (513) 569-7931. 1984. Occupational exposure and environmental release study.

Paper Products–Wholesale. American Business Directories, Inc., 5711 S. 86th Circle, Omaha, NE 68127. (402) 593-4600.

Paper Stock Report. McEntee Media Corp., 13727 Holland Rd., Cleveland, OH 44142-3920. (216) 362-7979. Weekly. Paper recycling markets and prices of various grades of waste paper.

Paper Year Book. Edgell Communications, Inc., 7500 Old Oak Blvd., Cleveland, OH 44130. (218) 243-8100.

PaperBase: Paper Industry Information Service. Communication & Information Services, 2399 Eugene Court, Concord, CA 94518. (415) 687-4303.

Paperboard Packaging Council. 1101 Vermont Ave., N.W., Suite 411, Washington, DC 20005. (202) 289-4100.

PAPERCHEM. Institute of Paper Science & Technology, Inc., 575 14th St., N.W., Atlanta, GA 30318. (404) 853-9500.

Parameter Estimation in Ecology. O. Richter and D. Sondgerath. VCH Publishers, 303 NW 12th Ave., Deerfield Beach, FL 33442-1788. (305) 428-5566. 1990. Brings together the different aspects of biological modelling, in particular ecological modelling using both stochastic and deterministic models.

Paraquat and Diquat. World Health Organization, Ave. Appia, Geneva, Switzerland CH-1211. 1984. Covers toxicology and environmental aspects of herbicides and heterocyclic compounds.

Paraquat Hazards to Fish, Wildlife, and Invertebrates. U.S. Department of the Interior, Fish and Wildlife Service, 1849 C St. NW, Washington, DC 20240. (202) 208-3171. 1990.

Parks. Science Reviews Inc., 707 Foulk Road, Suite 102, Wilmington, DE 19803. Three times a year. The international magazine dedicated to the protected areas of the world.

Parks and Wildlife Department: Fish and Wildlife. Executive Director, 4200 Smith School Rd., Austin, TX 78744. (512) 389-4800.

Participatory Rural Appraisal Handbook. World Resources Institute, 1709 New York Ave. N.W., Washington, DC 20006. (800) 822-0504. 1990. A practical guide to resource management in rural African communities, the handbook offers proven methodologies for defining problems, ranking priorities and implementing a village based plan to manage the local natural resource base.

Particle Technology. Chapman & Hall, 29 W. 35th St., New York, NY 10001-2291. (212) 244-3336. 1990. Preparation, separation, mixing, agglomeration, crushing, storing, and conveying of particulate matter and bulk solids.

Particulate Carbon, Atmospheric Life Cycle. Plenum Press, 233 Spring St., New York, NY 10013-1578. (212) 620-8000. 1982.

Particulates and Air Pollution: An Annotated Bibliography. U.S. Environmental Protection Agency, Office of Air Quality Planning Standards, Research Triangle Park, NC 27711. 1977.

Particulates and Fine Dust Removal: Processes and Equipment. Marshall Sittig. Noyes Publications, 120 Mill Rd., Park Ridge, NJ 07656. (201) 391-8484. 1977. Exhaust systems and dust removal.

Particulates in Water. Michael Kavanaugh. American Chemical Society, 1155 16th St. N.W., Washington, DC 20036. (800) 227-5558. 1980. Characterizations, fate, effects, and removal.

Partners for Liveable Places. 1429 21st St., N.W., Washington, DC 20036. (202) 887-5990.

Partners of the Americas. 1424 K St., N.W., #700, Washington, DC 20005. (202) 628-3300.

Passive Solar Industries Council. 1090 Vermont Ave., N.W., Suite 1200, Washington, DC 20005. (202) 371-0357.

Passive Solar Institute. P.O. Box 722, Bascom, OH 44809. (419) 937-2225.

Pastures: Their Ecology and Management. R. H. M. Langer, ed. Oxford University Press, 200 Madison Ave., New York, NY 10016. (212) 679-7300; (800) 334-4249. 1990. Covers such areas as the grasslands of New Zealand, pasture plants, pasture as an ecosystem, pasture establishment, soil fertility, management, assessment, livestock production, animal disorders, high country pastures, hay or silage, seed production, weeds, pests, and plant diseases.

A Path Where No Man Thought. Carl Sagan. Random House Inc., 201 E. 50th St., New York, NY 10022. (212) 751-2600. 1990.

The Pathfinder Fund. 9 Galen St., Suite 217, Watertown, MA 02172. (617) 924-7200.

Patterns of Primary Production in the Biosphere. Helmut F. H. Lieth. Van Nostrand Reinhold, Information Services, 115 5th Ave., New York, NY 10003. (212) 254-3232. 1978.

Paying the Farm Bill: U.S. Agricultural Policy and the Transition to Sustainable Agriculture. Paul Faeth, et al. World Resources Institute, 1709 New York Ave. N.W., Washington, DC 20006. (800) 822-0504. 1991. Demonstrates that resource conserving agricultural systems are environmentally and economically superior to conventional systems over the long term.

PCB Compliance Guide for Electrical Equipment. John W. Coryell. Bureau of National Affairs, 1231 25th St. N.W., Washington, DC 20037. (202) 452-4200. 1991.

PCB Regulation Manual. Glenn Kuntz. PennWell Books, PO Box 21288, Tulsa, OK 74121. (918) 831-9421; (800) 752-9764. 1990. 3rd ed. Provides the corporate environmental manager or plant engineer with a practical guide to compliance with PCB regulations.

PCBs and the Environment. John S. Waid, ed. CRC Press, 2000 Corporate Blvd. N.W., Boca Raton, FL 33431. (407) 994-0555; (800) 272-7737. 1987. 3 vols.

PCBs: Human and Environmental Hazards. Frank M. D'itri and Michael A. Kamrin, eds. Ann Arbor Science, 230 Collingwood, Ann Arbor, MI 48106. 1983.

PDQ. International Cancer Information Center, National Cancer Institute, R.A. Bloch Building, Bethesda, MD 20892. (301) 496-7403.

Peace Corps. 1990 K St., N.W., Washington, DC 20526. (800) 424-8580.

Peat and Water: Aspects of Water Retention and Dewatering in Peat. Elsevier Science Publishing Co., 655 Avenue of the Americas, New York, NY 10010. (212) 984-5800. 1986. Covers peat, peat bogs, and soil moisture.

Peat, Industrial Chemistry and Technology. Charles H. Fuchsman. Academic Press, c/o Harcourt Brace Jovanovich Inc., 6277 Sea Harbor Dr., Orlando, FL 32887. (800) 346-8648. 1980.

Peat Producers in the United States. U.S. Department of the Interior, Bureau of Mines, 810 7th St. NW, Washington, DC 20241. (202) 501-9649. Annual. Statistical data in the peat industry in the United States.

Pedestrian Research. American Pedestrian Assn., PO Box 624, Forest Hills, NY 11375. Quarterly. Pedestrian environment and protection against vehicular encroachments.

Peninsula Conservation Center. 2448 Watson Ct., Palo Alto, CA 94303. (415) 494-9301.

Pennsylvania Econotes. Pennsylvania Department on Environmental Resources, Box 1467, Harrisburg, PA 17120. 1972-. Monthly.

Pennsylvania Environmental Law Handbook. Government Institutes, Inc., 4 Research Pl., Ste. 200, Rockville, MD 20850. (301) 921-2300. 1991.

Pennsylvania Environmental Law Letter. Andrews Communications, Inc., 1646 Westchester Pike, Westtown, PA 19395. (215) 399-6600. Monthly.

Pennsylvania State University, Bioprocessing Resource Center. Biotechnology Institute, 519 Wartik Laboratory, University Park, PA 16802. (814) 863-3650.

Pennsylvania State University, Center for Statistical Ecology and Environmental Statistics. Department of Statistics, 303 Pond Laboratory, University Park, PA 16802. (814) 865-9442.

Pennsylvania State University, Deer Research Center. Department of Dairy & Animal Science, 324 Henning Building, University Park, PA 16802. (814) 865-1362.

Pennsylvania State University, Environmental Resources Research Institute. 100 Land and Water Resource Building, University Park, PA 16802. (814) 863-0291.

Pennsylvania State University, Frost Entomological Museum. Patterson Building, Department of Entomology, University Park, PA 16802. (814) 863-2863.

Pennsylvania State University, Mushroom Research Center. Department of Plant Pathology, 211 Buckhorn, University Park, PA 16802. (814) 863-2168.

Pennsylvania State University, Office of Hazardous and Toxic Waste Management. Environmental Resources Research Institute, University Park, PA 16802. (814) 863-0291.

Pennsylvania State University, Pennsylvania Cooperative Fish and Wildlife Research Unit. Ferguson Building, University Park, PA 16802. (814) 865-6592.

Pennsylvania State University, Pesticide Research Laboratory and Graduate Study Center. Department of Entomology, University Park, PA 16802. (814) 863-7345.

Pentachlorophenol. World Health Organization, Ave. Appia, Geneva, Switzerland CH-1211. (518) 436-9686. 1987.

Pentachlorophenol: Chemistry, Pharmacology, and Environmental Toxicology. K. Ranga Rao. Plenum Press, 233 Spring St., New York, NY 10013-1578. (212) 620-8000; (800) 221-9369. 1978.

Pentachlorophenol Hazards to Fish, Wildlife, and Invertebrates: A Synoptic Review. Ronald Eisler. U.S. Department of the Interior, Fish and Wildlife Service, 1849 C St. NW, 20240. (202)208-5634. 1989. Covers organochlorine compounds, herbicide toxicology, and pesticides and wildlife.

Pentachlorophenol Health and Safety Guide. World Health Organization, Ave. Appia, Geneva, Switzerland CH-1221. (518) 436-9686. 1989.

People, Food. People Food, 35751 Oak Springs Dr., Tollhouse, CA 93667. (209) 855-3710. Annual.

People for Ethical Treatment of Animals. Box 42516, Washington, DC 20015. (301) 770-7444.

Performance of RCRA Method 8280 for the Analysis of Dibenzo-P- Dioxins and Dibenzofurans in Hazardous Waste Samples. J.M. Ballard. U.S. Environmental Protection Agency, Environmental Monitoring Systems Laboratory, 944 E. Harmon, Las Vegas, NV 89119. (702) 798-2100. 1986.

Performance Tests of Four Selected Oil Spill Skimmers. Robert W. Urban. National Technical Information Service, 5285 Port Royal Rd., Springfield, VA 22161. (703) 487-4650. 1978.

Permaculture: A Practical Guide for a Sustainable Future. B. C. Mollison. Island Press, 1718 Connecticut Ave. N.W., Suite 300, Washington, DC 20009. (202) 232-7933. 1990.

The Permafrost Environment. Stuart A. Harris. Rowman & Littlefield, Publishers, Inc., 8705 Bollman Pl., Savage, MD 20763. (301) 306-0400. 1986. Contains the scientific and engineering facets of permafrost.

Persistent Pollutants: Economics and Policy. Hans Opschoor, ed. Kluwer Academic Publishers, 101 Philip Dr., Assinippi Park, Norwell, MA 02061. (617) 871-6600. 1991. Discusses environmental pollution and the studies conducted in that area.

Perspectives in Grassland Ecology: Results and Applications of the US/IBP Grassland Biome Study. Norman R. French. Springer-Verlag, 175 5th Ave., New York, NY 10010. (212) 460-1500. 1979. Covers range management and grassland ecology.

Pest and Disease Control Handbook. Nigel Scopes. BCPC Publications, Bear Farm, Binfield, Brocknell, England RG12 5QE. 1983. Covers pest control and plant diseases.

Pest Control Literature Documentation. Derwent Publications, Ltd., 6845 Elm St., McLean, VA 22101. (703) 790-0400.

Pest Control Technology. Gei, Inc., 4012 Bridge Ave., Cleveland, OH 44113. (316) 961-4130. Monthly. Articles on pests and pesticides.

Pest Management in Rice. B. T. Grayson, et al., eds. Elsevier Science Publishing Co., 655 Avenue of the Americas, New York, NY 10010. (212) 989-5800. 1990.

Pest Management Research Information System. Agriculture Canada Research Branch, K.W. Neatby Building, Rm. 1135, Ottawa, ON, Canada K1A OC6. (613) 995-7084 x7254.

PESTDOC. Derwent Publications, Ltd., Rochdale House, 128 Theobalds Rd., London, England WC1X BRP. 44 (71) 242-5823.

PESTDOC II. Derwent Publications, Ltd., Rochdale House, 128 Theobalds Rd., London, England WC1X BRP. 44 (71) 242-5823.

Pesticide. U.S. Department of the Interior, Natural Resource Library, 1849 C St. NW, Washington, DC 20240. (202) 208-3171. Annual.

Pesticide Action Network. North America Regional Center, 965 Mission St., Suite 514, San Francisco, CA 94103. (415) 541-9140.

Pesticide Alert. Lawrie Mott, Karen Snyder. Sierra Club Books, 100 Bush St., San Francisco, CA 94104. (415) 291-1600. 1987.

Pesticide & Toxic Chemical News. Food Chemical News, Inc., 1101 Pennsylvania Ave., S.E., Washington, DC 20003. (202) 544-1980. Online version of the periodical of the same name.

Pesticide & Toxic Chemical News. Food Chemical News, Inc., 1101 Pennsylvania Avenue, SE, Washington, DC 20003. (202) 544-1980. Weekly. Covers government regulations of chemical pollution, transportation, disposal and occupational health. Also available online.

Pesticide Applicator Training Materials: A Bibliography. Barbara O. Stommel. National Agricultural Library, 10301 Baltimore Blvd, Beltsville, MD 20705-2351. (301) 504-5755. 1991.

Pesticide Background Statements. Volume II, Fungicides and Fumigants. J.F. Sassaman. Forest Service, U.S. Department of Agriculture, PO Box 96090, Washington, DC 20090. (202) 720-3760. 1986.

Pesticide Bioassays with Arthropods. Jacqueline Robertson. Lewis Publishers, 2000 Corporate Blvd., N.W., Boca Raton, FL 33431. (407) 994-0555 or (800) 272-7737. 1992. Describes the experimental design of pesticide bioassays, tests with pesticides in an arthropod's natural environment, with unnatural environments, and international quarantine regulations.

Pesticide Biochemistry and Physiology. Academic Press, c/o Harcourt Brace Jovanovich Inc., 6277 Sea Harbor Dr., Orlando, FL 32887. (800) 346-8648. Nine times a year. Covers biochemistry and physiology of insecticides, herbicides and similar compounds.

Pesticide Chemistry: Advances in International Research, Development, and Legislation. Helmut Frehse. VCH Publishers, 303 NW 12th Ave., Deerfield Beach, FL 33442-1788. (305) 428-5566.

Pesticide Development: Structure Activity Relationships. Wilfried Draber and Toshio Fujita. Lewis Publishers, 2000 Corporate Blvd., N.W., Boca Raton, FL 33431. (407) 994-0555 or (800) 272-7737. 1991. Describes the physiochemical approach, biorational approach and the design of herbicides, fungicides, and insecticides.

The Pesticide Directory. Lori Thomson Harvey and W. T. Thomson. Thomson Publications, PO Box 9335, Fresno, CA 93791. (209) 435-2163. 1990. A guide to producers and products, regulators, researchers, and associations in the U.S. Detailed listings (name, addresses, telephone numbers, key personnel, products or services) in four sections: chemicals, research, regulatory and miscellaneous.

Pesticide Fact Handbook. U. S. Environmental Protection Agency. Noyes Publications, 120 Mill Rd., Park Ridge, NJ 07656. (201) 391-8484. 1988-1990. Two volumes. Contains over 217 currently available pesticide fact sheets issued by the EPA. Each listing includes a description of the chemical use patterns and formulations, scientific findings, a summary of the Agency's regulatory position/rationale, toxicology, and a summary of major data gaps. Also covers trade name pesticides.

Pesticide Formulations and Application Systems. ASTM, 1916 Race St., Philadelphia, PA 19103-1187. (215) 299-5400. Perspectives on pesticide risks, formulation technology and characteristics of uptake, and application systems.

Pesticide Handbook. Peter Hurst. Journeyman Press, 955 Massachusetts Ave., Cambridge, MA 02139. (617) 868-3305. 1990.

Pesticide Handbook–Entoma. Entomological Society of America, 9301 Annapolis Rd., Lanham, MD 20706. (301) 731-4538. 1965-. Annual.

The Pesticide Handbook: Profiles for Action. International Organization of Consumers Unions, Emmastraat 9, The Hague, Netherlands 2595 EG. 1989.

Pesticide Index. H. Kidd and D. Hartley, eds. Royal Society of Chemistry, c/o CRC Press, 2000 Corporate Blvd. N.W., Boca Raton, FL 33431-9868. (800) 272-7737. 1988. A quick guide to chemical, common and trade names of pesticides and related crop-protection products world-wide. About 800 active-ingredients are included with about 25,000 trade names of pesticides containing these ingredients.

Pesticide Management for Local Governments. Anne R. Leslie. International City Management Association, 777 N. Capital St., NE, Suite 500, Washington, DC 20002-4201. (800) 745-8780. 1989. Case studies of integrated pest management and its application in local government operations. Includes turf grass management and mosquito control.

Pesticide Poisonings Handbook: Recognition and Management of Pesticide Poisonings. Government Institutes, Inc., 4 Research Pl., Ste. 200, Rockville, MD 20850. (301) 921-2300. Provides current information on health hazards of pesticides and consensus recommendation for management of poisonings.

Pesticide Producers Association. c/o Robert Bor, Bishop, Cook, Purcell, and Reynolds, 1400 L St., N.W., Suite 800, Washington, DC 20005. (202) 371-5700.

Pesticide Residue Analysis with Special Reference to Ion Pairing Techniques. Malin Akerblom. National Laboratory for Agricultural Chemistry, Uppsala, Sweden 1990. Analysis of pesticides and pesticide residues in food.

Pesticide Residues and Food Safety: A Harvest of Viewpoints. B. G. Tweedy, et al., eds. American Chemical Society, 1155 16th St. N.W., Washington, DC 20036. (202) 872-4600; (800) 227-5558. 1991. Discusses all the issues raised in connection with the use of pesticides in the United States. Some of the issues are the economic and social aspects, impact assessment programs, food safety, consumer attitude, pesticide free fruit crops, integrated pest management, EPA's program for validation of pesticides, and other related matters.

Pesticide Residues in Food. Food and Agriculture Organization of the United Nations, 4611-F Assembly Dr., Lanham, MD 20706-4391. (800) 274-4888. 1990.

Pesticide Science: An International Journal on Crop Protection and Pest Control. Elsevier Science Publishing Co., 655 Avenue of the Americas, New York, NY 10010. (212) 989-5800. 1970-. Monthly. Topics covered: Synthesis, screening, structure/activity and biochemical mode of action studies of compounds; physicochemical properties of new compounds; metabolism, degradation, field performance, environmental studies and safety in use of new and existing products; synthetic and naturally occurring insecticides; ecological implications of pesticide applications.

Pesticide Tolerance Legislation. U.S. G.P.O., Washington, DC 20401. (202) 512-0000. 1984.

Pesticide Transformation Products: Fate and Significance in the Environment: Papers. L. Somasundaram and Joel R. Coats, eds. American Chemical Society, 1155 16th St. N.W., Washington, DC 20036. (202) 872-4600; (800) 227-5558. 1991. The significance and impact of pesticide products on the environment is discussed.

Pesticide Waste Disposal Technology. James S. Bridges and Clyde R. Dempsey, eds. Noyes Publications, 120 Mill Rd., Park Ridge, NJ 07656. (201) 391-8484. 1988. Defines practical solutions to pesticide users' disposal problems.

Pesticides: A Community Action Guide. Concern, Inc., 1794 Columbia Rd., N.W., Washington, DC 20009. (202) 328-8160.

Pesticides Abstracts. U.S. Environmental Protection Agency, Office of Pesticides Programs, 345 Curtland, Atlanta, GA 30365. (404) 347-2864. 1981. Monthly. Formerly: Health Aspects of Pesticides Abstracts Bulletin.

Pesticides and Non-Target Invertebrates. Paul C. Jepson, ed. VCH Publishers, 303 NW 12th Ave., Deerfield Beach, FL 33442-1788. (305) 428-5566. 1990. Current state of research into the side-effects of pesticides on non-target insects.

Pesticides and You. National Coalition Against the Misuse of Pesticides, 701 E St., S.E., Washington, DC 20003. (202) 543-5450. Five times a year. Analysis of pesticides and issues concerning urban and rural uses.

Pesticides Inspection Manual. Government Institutes, Inc., 4 Research Pl., Ste. 200, Rockville, MD 20850. (301) 921-2300. Provides all of the necessary guidance to carry out the standard field procedures including Pesticide law and definitions.

Petrochemical Energy Group. 1100 15th St., N.W., Suite 1200, Washington, DC 20005. (202) 452-1880.

Petroleum Contaminated Soils: Remediation Techniques, Environmental Fate and Risk Assessment. Paul T. Kostecki and Edward J. Calabrese. Lewis Publishers, 200 Corporate Blvd. NW, Boca Raton, FL 33431. (407) 994-0555 or (800)272-7737. 1991. Three volumes. Provides valuable information to determine feasible solutions to petroleum contaminated soils.

Petroleum Contaminated Soils, Volume 2. Edward J. Calabrese and Paul T. Kostecki. Lewis Publishers, 200 Corporate Blvd. NW, Boca Raton, FL 33431. (407) 994-0555 or (800)272-7737. 1989. Proceedings of the Third National Conference on Petroleum Contaminated Soils held at the University of Massachusetts-Amherst, September 19-21, 1988.

Petroleum Engineering and Technology School. Society of Petroleum Engineers, PO Box 833836, Richardson, TX 75083-3836. (214) 669-3377. 1987. Resource document for educational institutions and petroleum companies. Includes information about students, courses of study and institutional size and other related data.

Petroleum Engineering Handbook. Howard B. Bradley, ed. Society of Petroleum Engineers, PO Box 833836, Richardson, TX 75083-3836. (214) 669-3377. 1987. Revised edition. Compilation of practical information and data covering production equipment and reservoir engineering.

Petroleum Marketer–Self-Service Equipment Directory. McKeand Publications, Inc., 636 First Ave., West Haven, CT 06516. (203) 934-5288.

Petroleum Transportation and Production: Oil Spill and Pollution Control. Marshall Sittig. Noyes Publications, 120 Mill Rd., Park Ridge, NJ 07656. (201) 391-8484. 1978. Environmental aspects of petroleum industry and trade; oil spills and petroleum transportation.

Pharmaceutical and Healthcare Industries News Database. PJB Publications Ltd., 18-20 Hill Rise, Richmond, Surrey, England TW10 6UA. 44 (81) 948-0751.

Pharmaceutical Industry: Hazardous Waste Generation, Treatment, and Disposal. U.S. Environmental Protection Agency, 401 M St., S.W., Washington, DC 20460. (202) 260-2090. 1976. Pollutants in the pharmaceutical industry.

Pharmaceutical Manufacturers Association. 110 15th St., N.W., Washington, DC 20005. (202) 835-3400.

Pharmaceutical Manufacturers of the U.S. Noyes Publications, 120 Mill Rd., Park Ridge, NJ 07656. (201) 391-8484. 1977.

Pharmaceutical Products–Wholesalers & Manufacturers. American Business Directories, Inc., 5711 S. 86th Circle, Omaha, NE 68127. (402) 593-4600.

Philip L. Boyd Deep Canyon Desert Research Center. University of California, Riverside, PO Box 1738, Palm Desert, CA 92261. (619) 341-3655.

The Philosophy and Practice of Wildlife Management. Frederick F. Gilbert and Donald G. Dodds. Krieger Publishing Co., Inc., PO Box 9542, Melbourne, FL 32902-9542. (407) 724-9542. 1992. Shows the mechanisms and historical foundations of wildlife management and traces the evolution of increasingly sophisticated approaches to the management of our natural fauna.

Phosphate Chemicals Export Association. 8750 W. Bryn Mawr Ave., Suite 1200, Chicago, IL 60631. (312) 399-1010.

Phosphate Slag Risk. U.S. Congress, Senate Committee on Environment and Public Works, Subcommittee on Nuclear Regulation. U.S. G.P.O., Washington, DC 20401. (202) 512-0000. 1990.

Phosphates and Phosphoric Acid: Raw Materials, Technology, and Economics of the Wet Process. Pierre Becker. Marcel Dekker, Inc., 270 Madison Ave., New York, NY 10016. (212) 696-9000; (800) 228-1160. 1983.

Phosphorous Removal From Wastewater. Robert P. G. Bowker and H. David Stensel. Noyes Publications, 120 Mill Rd., Park Ridge, NJ 07656. (201) 391-8484. 1990. Oriented toward design methods and operating procedures. Cost information from actual phosphorous removing installations is presented when available. Planning level cost estimates are also included.

Phosphorus: An Outline of Its Chemistry, Biochemistry, and Technology. Elsevier Science Publishing Co., 655 Avenue of the Americas, New York, NY 10010. (212) 984-5800. 1985. Covers organophosphorus and phosphorus compounds.

Phosphorus Chemistry in Everyday Living. Arthur Dock Fon Toy. American Chemical Society, 1155 16th St. N.W., Washington, DC 20036. (800) 227-5558. 1987.

Phosphorus in Agriculture. C. A. B. International, 845 North Park Ave., Tucson, AZ 85719. (602) 621-7897 or (800) 528-4841. 1991. Two volumes. Contains 1,100 citations.

Photo Chemical Machining Institute. 4113 Barberry Dr., Lafayette Hills, PA 19444. (215) 825-2506.

Photochemical Oxidants. World Health Organization, Ave. Appia, Geneva, Switzerland CH-1211. 1979.

Photochemical Smog and Ozone Reaction. American Chemical Society, 1155 16th St. N.W., Washington, DC 20036. (800) 227-5558. 1972.

Photochemical Smog: Contribution of Volatile Organic Compounds. OECD Publications and Information Center, 2001 L St., NW, Washington, DC 20036. (202) 785-6323. 1982. Covers smog resulting from hydrocarbons and gasoline.

Photochemistry of Environmental Aquatic Systems. Rod G. Zika. American Chemical Society, 1155 16th St. N.W., Washington, DC 20036. (800) 227-5558. 1987.

Photoperiodism in Plants and Animals. William S. Hillman. Scientific Publications Division, Carolina Biological Supply Co., 2700 York Rd., Burlington, NC 27215. (919) 584-0381. 1979.

Photosynthesis. Academic Press, c/o Harcourt Brace Jovanovich Inc., 6277 Sea Harbor Dr., Orlando, FL 32887. (800) 346-8648. 1982.

Phreatophytes; A Bibliography. Patricia Paylore. Water Resources Scientific Information Center, Washington, DC 1974.

PHTM. Bureau of Hygiene and Tropical Diseases, Keppel St., London, England WC1E 7HT. 44 (71) 636-8636.

Physical and Chemical Characteristics of Aquatic Humus. Egil T. Gjessing. Ann Arbor Science, 230 Collingwood, Ann Arbor, MI 48106. 1976.

Physical and Chemical Properties. W.W. Clark. Butane-Propane News, 338 W. Foothill Blvd., Arcadia, CA 91006. (818) 357-2168. 1983. Covers LP-gas, propane and butane.

Physical Behavior of PCBs in the Great Lakes. Donald Mackay. Ann Arbor Science, 230 Collingwood, Ann Arbor, MI 48106. 1983.

Physical, Chemical and Biological Changes in Food Caused by Thermal Processing. Tore Hoyem. Applied Science Publishers, Crown House, Linton Rd., Barking, England IG 11 8JU. 1977.

Physical-Chemical Treatment of Raw Municipal Wastewater. Dolloff Bishop. U.S. G.P.O., Washington, DC 20401. (202) 512-0000. 1974.

Physical Chemistry of Magmas. Leonid L. Perchuk. Springer-Verlag, 175 5th Ave., New York, NY 10010. (212) 460-1500. 1991.

Physical Impacts of Small-Scale Hydroelectric Facilities and their Effects on Fish and Wildlife. Haydon Rochester. Fish and Wildlife Service, Department of the Interior, 18th and C Sts., NW, Washington, DC 20240. (202) 653-8750. 1984.

Physical Oceanography of Coastal Waters. K. F. Bowden. John Wiley & Sons, Inc., 605 3rd Ave., New York, NY 10158-0012. (212) 850-6000. 1984.

Physicians' Desk Reference. Medical Economics Company, 680 Kinderkamack Rd., Oradell, NJ 07649. (201) 262-3030. 1974-.

Physicians for Social Responsibility. 1000 16th St., NW, Suite 810, Washington, DC 20036. (202) 785-3777.

Physicochemical and Biological Detoxification of Hazardous Wastes. Yeun C. Wu, ed. Technomic Publishing Co., 851 New Holland Ave., Box 3535, Lancaster, PA 17604. (717) 291-5609. 1989. 2 volume set. Proceedings of the International Conference of Physicochemical and Biological Detoxification of Hazardous Wastes, May 3-5, 1988, Atlantic City, NJ. Provides new information on a variety of established, new and in-development methods for treating a wide range of industrial and municipal hazardous wastes.

Physics Briefs. Physikalische Berichte. Physik Verlag, Pappapelallee 3, Postfach 101161, Weinheim, Germany D-,6940. 1979-. Semimonthly. In English. Volumes for 1979- issued by the Deutsche Physikalische Gesellschaft and the Fachinformationszentrum Energie Physik, Mathematik in cooperation with the American Institute of Physics.

The Physiological Ecology of Seaweeds. Christopher S. Lobban. Cambridge University Press, 40 W. 20th St., New York, NY 10011. (212) 924-3900. 1985.

Physiological Plant Ecology. O. L. Lange, et al., eds. Springer-Verlag, 175 5th Ave., New York, NY 10010. (212) 460-1500; (800) 777-4643. 1981-1983. Contents: Volume 1 - Responses to the physical environment; Volume 2 - Water relations and carbon assimilation; Volume 3 - Responses to the chemical and biological environment; Volume 4 - Ecosystem processes (mineral cycling, productivity, and man's influence).

PHYTOMED. Biologische Bundesanstalt fuer Land-und Forstwirtschaft, Dokumentationstelle fuer Phytomedizin, Koeingn-Luise-Strasse 19, Berlin, Germany D-1000. 49 (30) 83041.

Phytotoxicity of Insecticides and Acaricides to Anthuriums. Trent Y. Hata. HITAHR, College of Tropical Agriculture and Human Resources, University of Hawaii, 2840 Kolowalu St., Honolulu, HI 96822. (808) 948-8255. 1988.

Pictorial Handbook of Medically Important Fungi and Aerobic Actinomycetes. Michael R. McGinnis. Praeger Publishers, 1 Madison Ave., New York, NY 10010-3603. (212) 685-5300. 1982.

Pinacea: Being a Handbook of the Firs and Pines. Senilis. Bishen Singh Mahendra Pal Singh, 23A Connaught Pl., P.B. 137, Dehra Dun, India 1984.

Pipe Line Industries. American Business Directories, Inc., 5711 S. 86th Circle, Omaha, NE 68127. (402) 593-4600.

Pipeline & Gas Journal–Buyer's Guide Issue. Energy Publications Division/Edgell Communications, Inc., 10300 N. Central Expressway, Building V-580, Dallas, TX 75231. (214) 691-3911.

Pipeline & Gas Journal–P&GJ 500 Issue. Energy Publications Division/Edgell Communications, Inc., 10300 N. Central Expressway, Building V-580, Dallas, TX 75231. (214) 691-3911.

Pipeline–Directory of Pipelines and Equipment Issue. Oildom Publishing Company of Texas, Inc., 3314 Mercer, Houston, TX 77027. (713) 622-0676.

Pipelines and the Environment. J. N. H. Tiratsoo. Pipeline Industries Guild, 17 Grosvenor Crescent, London, England SW1X 7ES. 1984.

Pira's International Environmental Information Sources. Pira, Randalls Rd., Leatherhead, England KT22 7RU. Surrey 0372 376161. 1990. Sourcebook includes over 2,000 entries from more than 20 countries, including Australia, Finland, Germany, the United Kingdom, and the United States. Entries are from organizations, research centers, legislative and regulatory bodies, directories, online databases and periodicals. Subject areas covered are: air, noise, water and land pollution, waste control and disposal, recycling, energy recovery and nature conservation.

PIRGIM Citizen Connection. Public Interest Research Group on Michigan, 212 S. 4th Ave. #207, Ann Arbor, MI 48104. (313) 662-6597. Quarterly. Environmental and consumer protection.

Pit & Quarry–Buyers' Guide Issue. Edgell Communications, Inc., 7500 Old Oak Blvd., Cleveland, OH 44130. (216) 243-8100.

Pitless Adapter Division of Water Council. 600 S. Federal St., Suite 400, Chicago, IL 60605. (312) 922-6222.

Plan Sheet M. University of Minnesota, Agricultural Extension Service, 1444 Cleveland Ave. N., St. Paul, MN 55108. Irregular.

Planet Drum. Box 31251, San Francisco, CA 94131. (415) 285-6556.

Planet Earth. Planetary Citizens, Box 1509, Mt. Shasta, CA 96067. (415) 325-2939.

Planet under Stress: The Challenge of Global Change. Constance Mungall and Digby J. McLaren, eds. Oxford University Press, 200 Madison Ave., New York, NY 10016. (212) 679-7300; (800) 334-4249. 1991.

Planetary Biology and Microbial Ecology. Lynn Margulis. National Aeronautics and Space Administration, Scientific and Technical Information Office, 5285 Port Royal Rd., Springfield, VA 22161. (703) 487-4650. 1983.

Plankton and Productivity in the Oceans. John E. G. Raymont. Pergamon Microforms International, Inc., Fairview Park, Elmsford, NY 10523. (914) 592-7720. 1980. Covers phytoplankton and zooplankton.

Planning and Conservation League. 909 12th St., Suite 203, Sacramento, CA 95814. (916) 444-8726.

Planning for an Urban World. MIT Press, 55 Hayward St., Cambridge, MA 02142. (617) 253-2884. 1974.

Planning for Change. Columbia University, Teachers College, 525 W. 120th St., New York, NY 10027. (212) 678-3000. 1982.

Planning Pollution Prevention: Anticipatory Controls Over Air Pollution Sources. Christopher Wood. Heinemann Newnes, Halley Court, Jordan Hill, Oxford, England OX2 8EJ. 1991. Presents a comparative evaluation of two very different approaches to environmental regulation: the British controls based on 'best practicable means' and the American controls based upon air quality standards.

Plant-Animal Interactions; Evolutionary Ecology in Tropical and Temperate Regions. Peter W. Price, et al. John Wiley & Sons, Inc., 605 3rd Ave., New York, NY 10158-0012. (212) 850-6000. 1991. Comprises a comparative analysis of the existing ecological systems of temperate and tropical regions.

Plant Demography in Vegetation Succession. Krystyna Falinska. Kluwer Academic Publishers, 101 Philip Dr., Assinippi Park, Norwell, MA 02061. (617) 871-6600. 1991.

Plant Energy Management. Walker-Davis Pub. Inc., 2500 Office Center, Willow Grove, PA 19090. Quarterly.

Plant Engineering. Cahners Publishing Co., 249 W. 17th St., New York, NY 10011. (212) 645-0067. Twenty-one times a year. Covers operating and maintaining industrial plant systems.

Plant Engineers and Managers Guide to Energy Conservation. Albert Thumann. The Association of Energy Engineers, 4025 Pleasantdale Rd., Suite 420, Atlanta, GA 30340. (404) 925-9558. 1991. Fifth edition. Covers both management and technical strategies which can be utilized to conserve energy.

Plant Engineers' Pollution Control Handbook. Richard A. Young. American Institute of Plant Engineers, 3975 Erie Ave., Cincinnati, OH 45208. (513) 561-6000. 1973.

Plant Food Review. The Fertilizer Institute, 501 2nd Ave. NE, Washington, DC (202)675-8250. Quarterly.

Plant Genetic Resources: A Conservation Imperative. Christopher W. Yeatman. Westview Press, 5500 Central Ave., Boulder, CO 80301. (303) 444-3541. 1984.

Plant Growth: Interactions with Nutrition and Environment. J.R. Porter. Cambridge University Press, 40 W. 20th St., New York, NY 10011. (212) 924-3900. 1991. Plant growth, nutrition, and ecology.

Plant Growth Regulator Abstracts. Plant Growth Regulator Society of America, Boyce Thompson Institute, Tower Rd., Ithaca, NY 14850. Quarterly. Papers on applied and basic aspects of plant growth regulation by either natural or synthetic substances are accepted for publication.

Plant Molecular Biology Manual. Stanton B. Gelvin. Kluwer Academic Publishers, 101 Philip Dr., Assinippi Park, Norwell, MA 02061. (617) 871-6600. 1988.

Plant Toxicity Data. University of Oklahoma, Department of Botany & Microbiology, 770 Van Fleet Oval, Room 135, Norman, OK 73019. (405) 325-3174.

Plants in Danger: What Do We Know?. Stephen Davis. World Conservation Union, IUCN Publications Services Unit, 181a Huntingdon Road, Cambridge, England CB3 0DJ. (0223) 277894. 1988. Indicates which plants are known to be threatened, where further information can be found, and which organizations can be contacted.

Plastic Bag Association. 505 White Plains Rd., #206, Tarrytown, NY 10591. (914) 631-0909.

Plastic Bottle Institute. 1275 K St., N.W., Suite 400, Washington, DC 20005. (202) 371-5244.

Plastic Bottle Recycling Directory and Reference Guide. Plastic Bottle Information Bureau, 1275 K St. N.W., Suite 400, Washington, DC 20005. (202) 371-5200.

The Plastic Bottle Reporter. Plastic Bottle Information Bureau, 1275 K St. NW, Suite 400, Washington, DC 20005. (202) 371-5200. Quarterly. Recycling technology and plastic bottle applications.

Plastic Waste Strategies. Washington Business Information, Inc., 1117 N. 19th St., Suite 200, Arlington, VA 22209-1798. (703) 247-3422. Monthly. Recycling, degradability, incineration, and alternative methods of handling solid and plastic waste.

Plastics: America's Packaging Dilemma. Nancy A. Wolf and Ellen D. Feldman. Island Press, 1718 Connecticut Ave. N.W., Ste. 300, Washington, DC 20009. (202) 232-7933. 1991. Source books on plastics deal with packaging, building materials, consumer goods, electrical products, transportation, industrial machinery, adhesives, legislative and regulatory issues. Also covers the controversies over plastics incineration, degradability, and recyclability.

Plastics Compounding Redbook. Edgell Communications, Inc., 7500 Old Oak Blvd., Cleveland, OH 44130. (216) 243-8100.

Plastics Education Foundation. 14 Fairfield Dr., Brookfield Center, CT 06804. (203) 775-0471.

Plastics Engineering Dictionary German/English. M. S. Welling. Hanser International, Scientific and Technical Books, Macmillan Pub. Co, 866 3d Ave., New York, NY 10022. 1982.

Plastics–Fabricating, Finishing & Decor. American Business Directories, Inc., 5711 S. 86th Circle, Omaha, NE 68127. (402) 593-4600.

Plastics Recycling Foundation. 1275 K St., N.W., Suite 400, Washington, DC 20005. (202) 371-5200.

Plastics Recycling in the Industrial Sector. National Technical Information Service, 5285 Port Royal Rd., Springfield, VA 22161. (703) 487-4650. Potential for development of plastic waste recycling industry, with projections to 2000 and background data from 1973.

Plastics Recycling Institute. Rutgers Univ., PO Box 909, Piscataway, NJ 08854. (201) 932-4420.

Plastics Recycling Update. Resource Recycling, Box 10540, Portland, OR 97210. (503) 227-1319. Monthly.

Plastics Technology Manufacturing Handbook and Buyers' Guide. Bill Communications, Inc., 633 Third Ave., New York, NY 10017. (212) 986-4800.

Plating. American Electroplaters and Surface Finishers Society, 12644 Research Pkwy., Orlando, FL 32826. (407) 281-6441. Monthly.

Plating. American Business Directories, Inc., 5711 S. 86th Circle, Omaha, NE 68127. (402) 593-4600.

Plating and Surface Finishing-American Electroplaters' and Surface Finishers Society Branch Directory. American Electroplaters' and Surface Finishers Society, 12644 Research Parkway, Orlando, FL 32826. (407) 281-6441.

Plating and Surface Finishing–Directory of American Electroplaters' and Surface Finishers Society of Boards and Committees Issue. American Electroplaters' and Surface Finishers Society, 12644 Research Parkway, Orlando, FL 32826. (407) 281-6441.

Plowman's Folly. Edward H. Faulkner. Island Press, 1718 Connecticut Ave. N.W., Suite 300, Washington, DC 20009. (202) 232-7933. 1987.

Plumbing and Drainage Institute. c/o Sol Baker, 1106 W. 77th St., South Dr., Indianapolis, IN 46260. (317) 251-6970.

Plumbing Manufacturers Institute. Bldg. C, Suite 20, 800 Roosevelt Rd., Glen Ellyn, IL 60137. (312) 858-9172.

Plutonium in the Environment. U.S. Energy Research and Development Administration, Office of Public Affairs, 1000 Independence Ave. SW, Washington, DC 20585. (202) 586-4940. 1976. Safety and environmental aspects of plutonium.

Plywood & Panel World–Directory and Buyers' Guide Issue. Hatten-Brown Publishers, Inc., P.O. Box 2268, Montgomery, AL 36102-2268. (205) 834-1170.

PMS Blue Book. Department of Health and Human Services, Food and Drug Administration, Public Health Service, 5600 Fishers Ln., Rockville, MD 20857. (301) 443-1544. Annual.

PNI. UMI Data Courier, 620 S. 3rd St., Louisville, KY 40202-2475. (502) 583-4111; 800 626-2823.

Pocket Flora of the Redwood Forest. Rudolf Willem Becking. Island Press, 1718 Connecticut Ave. N.W., Suite 300, Washington, DC 20009. (202) 232-7933. 1982. Guide to 212 of the most frequently seen plants in the Redwood Forest of the Pacific Coast. It is interspersed with accurate drawing color photographs and systematic keys to plant identification.

Point Foundation. 27 Gate Five Rd., Sausalito, CA 94965. (415) 332-1716.

Point-of-Use/Entry Treatment of Drinking Water. Noyes Publications, 120 Mill Rd., Park Ridge, NJ 07656. (201) 391-8484. 1990. Covers the administrative and technical aspects of utilizing POU/POE systems to solve individual and small community drinking water problems.

Point Reyes Bird Observatory. 4990 Shoreline Highway, Stinson Beach, CA 94970. (415) 868-1221.

Poison Runoff: A Guide to State and Local Control of Nonpoint Source Water Pollution. Paul Thompson. Natural Resources Defense Council, 40 W. 20th St., New York, NY 10011. (212) 727-2700. 1989. How-to-book addressing pollution in agricultural lands, urban development and construction, logging, mining and grazing.

The Poisoned Well: New Strategies for Groundwater Protection. Eric P. Jorgensen, ed. Island Press, 1718 Connecticut Ave. N.W., Suite 300, Washington, DC 20009. (202) 232-7933. 1989. Explains how individuals can work with agencies and the courts to enforce water laws, how the major federal water laws, work what remedies exist for each type of groundwater contamination, and what state and local programs may be helpful.

Poisonous Plants of Eastern North America. Randy G. Westbrooks and James W. Preacher. University of South Carolina Press, Columbia, SC 29208. (803) 777-5243. 1986. List of poisonous plants which include species of plants, the plant part (leaf, root, fruit), the amount of plant material involved, the stage of development of the plant, and the soil type and growing conditions.

Polar and Glaciological Abstracts. Cambridge University Press, 40 W. 20th St., New York, NY 10011. (212) 924-3900. 1990. Quarterly. Contains abstracts selected from the SPRILIB bibliographic database maintained by the Library of the Scott Polar Research Institute.

Polar Geography and Geology. V. H. Winston, Washington, DC Quarterly.

Polar Lands. Lawrence Williams. Marshall Cavendish Corp., 2415 Jerusalem Ave., North Bellmore, NY 11710. (516) 546-4200. 1990. Living and working in the polar regions without destroying the environment.

Polar Oceanography. Walker O. Smith. Academic Press, c/o Harcourt Brace Jovanovich Inc., 6277 Sea Harbor Dr., Orlando, FL 32887. (800) 346-8648. 1990.

Policies and Systems of Environmental Impact Assessment. UNIPUB, 4611-F Assembly Dr., Lanham, MD 20706. (301) 459-7666 or (800) 274-4888. 1991. Describes current trends and experience gained regarding policies and systems of environmental impact assessment (EIA) in the ECE region.

Policies For Maximizing Nature Tourism's Contribution to Sustainable Development. Kreg Lindberg. World Resources Institute, 1709 New York Ave. N.W., Washington, DC 20006. (800) 822-0504. 1991. Examines how better economic management of nature tourism can promote development and conservation without degrading the natural resources on which development depends.

Policy Implication of Greenhouse Warming. National Academy Press, 2101 Constitution Ave. N.W., PO Box 285, Washington, DC 20418. (202) 334-3313. 1991. Identifies what could be done to counter potential greenhouse warming. It has a helpful section on question and answers about greenhouse warming.

Policy Options for Stabilizing Global Climate. Daniel A. Lashof and Dennis A. Tirpak. Hemisphere Publishing Co., 79 Madison Ave., Suite 1110, New York, NY 10016. (212) 725-1999. 1990. Covers climatic changes, environmental policy and protection and atmospheric greenhouse effect.

Political Economy of Smog in Southern California. Jeffry Fawcett. Garland Publishers, 136 Madison Ave., New York, NY 10016. (212) 686-7492; (800) 627-6273. 1990.

The Politics of Park Design. MIT Press, 55 Hayward St., Cambridge, MA 02142. (617) 253-2884. 1982. Lists history, design and construction of parks in the United States.

Pollutant Effects on Marine Organisms. C. S. Giam. Lexington Books, 866 3rd Ave., New York, NY 10022. (212) 702-2000. 1977. Effect of water pollution on aquatic animals.

Pollution Abstracts. Cambridge Scientific Abstracts, 5161 River Rd., Bethesda, MD 20816. (301) 961-6750. Six/year. Indexes worldwide technical literature on environmental pollution. Covers air pollution, marine and freshwater pollution, sewage and wastewater treatment, waste management, toxicology and health, noise pollution, radiation, land pollution, and environmental policies, programs, legislation, and education. Also available online.

Pollution and Its Containment. Institution of Civil Engineers Infrastructure Policy Group. Telford, 1 Heron Quay, London, England E14 9XF. (071) 987-6999. 1990.

Pollution: Causes, Effects and Control. Roy Michael Harrison. Royal Society of Chemistry, c/o CRC Press, 2000 Corporate Blvd. N.W., Boca Raton, FL 33431. (800) 272-7737. 1990. 2nd ed. Deals with environmental pollution and its associated problems and legal ramifications.

Pollution Control. FIND/SVP, 625 Avenue of the Americas, New York, NY 10011. (212) 645-4500. 1991.

Pollution Control Agency: Air Quality. Director, Division of Air Quality, 520 Lafayette Rd., St Paul, MN 55155. (612) 296-7731.

Pollution Control Agency: Environmental Protection. Commissioner, 520 Lafayette Rd., St Paul, MN 55155. (612) 296-7301.

Pollution Control Agency: Solid Waste Management. Director, Solid and Hazardous Waste Division, 520 Lafayette Rd., St Paul, MN 55155. (612) 643-3402.

Pollution Control Agency: Underground Storage Tanks. Director, Solid and Hazardous Waste Division, 520 Lafayette Rd., St Paul, MN 55155. (612) 296-7282.

Pollution Control Agency: Waste Minimization and Pollution Prevention. Director, Solid and Hazardous Waste Minimization Division, 520 Lafayette Rd., St Paul, MN 55155. (612) 296-6300.

Pollution Control and Conservation. M. Kovacs, ed. John Wiley & Sons, Inc., 605 3rd Ave., New York, NY 10158. (212) 850-6000. 1985. Comprehensive view on current knowledge and research in the area of effective protection of air, water, soil and living matter and pollution control.

Pollution Control Guide. Commerce Clearing House, 4205 W Peterson Ave., Chicago, IL 60646. (312) 583-8500. 1973-1985. National environmental policy: Water standards, effluent limitations, permit programs, solid-waste-radiation, noise, pesticides, toxic substances, air standards-emission limitations, and state implementation plans.

Pollution Control Newsletter. Arizona State Dept. of Health Services, Bureau of Air Quality Control, 1740 W. Adams St., Phoenix, AZ 85007. (602) 542-1000. Eight times a year.

Pollution Engineering. Cahners Publishing Co., 249 W. 17th St., New York, NY 10011. (212) 645-0067. 1969-. Monthly.

Pollution Engineering Locator. Cahners Publishing Co., 249 W. 17th St., New York, NY 10011. (212) 645-0067.

Pollution Engineering–Yellow Pages Telephone Directory Issue. Pudvan Publishing Company, Inc., 1935 Shermer Rd., Northbrook, IL 60062. (708) 498-9840.

Pollution Equipment News. Rimbach Publishing, Inc., 8650 Babcock Boulevard, Pittsburgh, PA 15237. (412) 364-5366. Bimonthly. Covers new products, techniques, and literature.

Pollution Equipment News–Buyer's Guide Issue. Rimbach Publishing, Inc., 8650 Babcock Blvd., Pittsburgh, PA 15237. (412) 364-5366.

Pollution Equipment News Catalog and Buyers' Guide. Rimbach Publishing, Inc., 8650 Babcock Blvd., Pittsburgh, PA 15237. (412) 364-5366. Annual. Product/service supplier information including specification, purchase, installation, and maintenance of pollution control equipment.

Pollution Law Handbook. Sidney M. Wolf. Quorum Books, Div. of Greenwood Press, Inc., 88 Post Rd. W., Box 5007, Westport, CT 06881. (203) 226-3571. 1988. A guide to federal environmental laws.

Pollution Liability Insurance Association. 1333 Butterfield Rd., Suite 100, Downers Grove, IL 60515. (312) 969-5300.

Pollution Prevention. Executive Enterprises Publications Co., Inc., 22 W. 21st St., New York, NY 10010-6990. (212) 645-7880 or (800) 332-8804. 1991. Quarterly. Includes practical approaches to reducing waste, case studies of successful waste reduction programs and the saving they provide, analyses of new technologies and their efficacy in reducing waste, and updates of federal and state legislative initiatives and their impacts on industries.

Pollution Prevention Pays: An Overview by the 3M Company of Low- and Non-Pollution Technology. World Environment Center, 419 Park Ave. S, Suite 1404, New York, NY 10016. (212) 683-4700. Covers natural resources, pollution and control.

Pollution Research Index: A Guide to World Research in Environment Pollution. A. I. Sors and D. Coleman. Francis Hodgson, Longman House, Burnt Mill, Harlow, England CM20 2JE. Essex 1979. Second edition. Provides a detailed insight of pollution research. Includes over 2000 entries related to government departments, universities, research institutions and manufacturing industry from over 100 countries throughout the world.

POLYMAT. Deutsches Kunststoff-Institut, Schlossgartenstrasse 6, D-6100 Darmstadt, Germany 49 (6151) 162106.

Polymeric Reagents and Catalysts. American Chemical Society, 1155 16th St. N.W., Washington, DC 20036. (800) 227-5558. Covers chemical tests and reagents, polymers and polymerization.

Polypropylene in North America. FIND/SVP, 625 Avenue of the Americas, New York, NY 10011. (212) 645-4500. 1991. Market for polypropylene to the years 1995 and 2000; analyzes pricing and capacity data, recent developments in manufacturing technology and production processes.

Polyurethane Division, Society of the Plastics Industry. 355 Lexington Ave., New York, NY 10017. (212) 351-5425.

Polyurethane Foam Association. P.O. Box 1459, Wayne, NJ 07470. (201) 633-9044.

Polyurethane Manufacturers Association. 800 Roosevelt Rd., Bldg. C, Suite 20, Glen Ellyn, IL 61037. (708) 858-2670.

POPLINE. Johns Hopkins University, Population Information Program, 701 W. 40th St., Ste. 275, Baltimore, MD 21211. (410) 516-6900.

Popping the Plastics Question: Plastics Recycling and Bans on Plastics - Contacts, Resources and Legislation. Joan Mullany. National League of Cities, 1301 Pennsylvania Ave. N.W., Washington, DC 20004. (202) 626-3150. 1990.

Population Communication. 1489 E. Colorado Blvd., Suite 202, Pasadena, CA 91106. (818) 793-4750.

The Population Council. 1 Dag Hammarskjold Plaza, New York, NY 10017. (212) 644-1300.

Population Crisis Committee. 1120 19th St., N.W., Washington, DC 20036. (202) 659-1833.

Population Dose Commitments Due to Radioactive Releases from Nuclear Power Plant Sites. U.S. G.P.O, Washington, DC 20402-9325. (202) 512-0000. Annual.

Population Dynamics of Forest Insects. VCH Publishers, 303 NW 12th Ave., Deerfield Beach, FL 33442-1788. (305) 428-5566. 1990. Reviews the current research from an international Congress of delegates which covers population models, pest management and insect natural enemy interaction on forest insects. Topics include the effects of industrial air pollutants and acid rain as well as reviews of the biology and population dynamics of most major forest insects.

Population Education: Sources and Resources. Judith Seltzer and John Robinson. Population Reference Bureau, 777 14th St. N.W., Washington, DC 20005. (202) 639-8040. 1979.

Population-Environment Balance. 1325 G St., N.W., Suite 1003, Washington, DC 20005. (202) 879-3000.

Population Growth Estimation: A Handbook of Vital Statistics Measurement. Eli Samplin Marks. Population Council, 1 Dag Hammarskjold Plaza, New York, NY 10017. (212) 644-1300. 1974. Handbook covers population forecasting and other vital statistics.

Population Institute. 110 Maryland Ave., N.E., Washington, DC 20002. (202) 544-3300.

Population Reference Bureau. 1875 Connecticut Ave., Suite 520, Washington, DC 20009. (202) 483-1100.

The Population Reference Bureau's Population Handbook. Arthur Haupt. Population Reference Bureau, 1875 Connecticut Ave., Ste. 520, Washington, DC 20009. (202) 483-1100. 1991. A quick guide to population dynamics for journalists, policymakers, teachers, students, and other people interested in population.

Population Resource Center. 500 E. 62nd St., New York, NY 10021. (212) 888-2820.

Population Risks from Uranium Ore Bodies. U.S. Environmental Protection Agency, Office of Radiation Programs, 401 M St., S.W., Washington, DC 20460. (202) 260-2090. 1980.

Population Today. Population Reference Bureau, Circulation Department, 777 14th St., NW, Suite 800, Washington, DC 20005. (202) 639-8040. Monthly. Data on international population size and growth.

Porpoise, Dolphin and Small Whale Fisheries of the World: Status and Problems. Edward Mitchell. International Union for Conservation of Nature and Natural Resources, Avenue du Mont-Blanc, Gland, Switzerland CH-1196. 1975.

Port Planning. Paul D. Marr. Council of Planning Librarians, 1313 E. 60th St., Chicago, IL 60637-2897. (312) 942-2163. 1987.

Portable Electric Air Cleaners/Purifiers. FIND/SVP, 625 Avenue of the Americas, New York, NY 10011. (212) 645-4500. 1991. Projects ownership incidence and the market size of portable electric oil cleaners/purifiers, delineated brand shares, prices paid, types of filtration, types of outlet.

Portable Sanitation Association International. 7800 Metro Pkwy., Suite 104, Bloomington, MN 55420. (612) 854-8300.

Portland Cement Association. 5320 Old Orchard Rd., Skokie, IL 60077. (708) 966-6200.

Portraits of the Rainforest. Adrian Forsyth. Firefly Books, PO Box 1325, Ellicot Sta., Buffalo, NY 14205. 1990. Explores the precarious contingencies that determine the nature of tropical life.

Position Statements. Association of State and Interstate Water Pollution Control Administrators, 444 N. Capitol St., NW, Suite 330, Washington, DC 20001. (202) 624-7782.

Post-Accident Procedures for Chemicals and Propellants. Deborah K. Shaver. Noyes Publications, 120 Mill Rd., Park Ridge, NJ 07656. (201) 391-8484. 1984. Covers accidents occurring during transportation of hazardous substances.

Potash and Phosphate Institute. c/o R.T. Roberts, 2801 Buford Hwy., N.E., No. 401, Atlanta, GA 30329. (404) 634-4274.

Potassium, its Biologic Significance. Robert Whang. CRC Press, 2000 Corporate Blvd. N.W., Boca Raton, FL 33431. (800) 272-7737. 1983.

Potassium: Keeping a Delicate Balance. U.S. Department of Health and Human Services, Public Health Service, Food and Drug Administration, 900 Rockville Pike, Rockville, MD 20892. (301) 406-4000. 1984.

Potential Effects of Climate Change in the United Kingdom. HMSO, UNIPUB, 4611-F Assembly Dr., Lanham, MD 20706. (301) 459-7666 or (800) 274-4888. 1991. Considers the potential impacts of climate change in the UK in a wide variety of environmental and socioeconomic areas.

The Potential Effects of Global Climate Change on the United States. Joel B. Smith and Dennis A. Tirpak, eds. Hemisphere Publishing Co., 79 Madison Ave., Suite 1110, New York, NY 10016. (212) 725-1999; (800) 821-8312. 1990. Addresses the effects of climate change in vital areas such as water resources, agriculture, sea levels and forests. Also focuses on wetlands, human health, rivers and lakes and analyzes policy options for mitigating the effects of global warming.

Potential Industrial Carcinogens and Mutagens. Lawrence Fishbein. Elsevier Science Publishing Co., 655 Avenue of the Americas, New York, NY 10010. (212) 984-5800. 1979.

Potential Salmonella Virulence Factors. Suraj B. Baloda. College of Veterinary Medicine, Swedish University of Agricultural Sciences, Uppasal, Sweden 1987. Studies on toxins, cell-surface adhesions, enterotoxins and cell membranes.

Powder/Bulk Solids Guide and Directory. Gordon Publications, 301 Gibraltar Dr., Morris Plains, NJ 07950. (201) 292-5100.

Powder Coatings. FIND/SVP, 625 Avenue of the Americas, New York, NY 10011. (212) 645-4500. 1991. Comprehensive of the U.S. market for powder coatings by material type.

Powder Metallurgy Consultant's Directory. Metal Powder Industries Federation, 105 College Rd. East, Princeton, NJ 08540. (609) 452-7700.

Powder Metallurgy Equipment Directory. Powder Metallurgy Equipment Association, 105 College Rd. East, Princeton, NJ 08540. (609) 452-7700.

POWER. U.S. Department of Energy, Energy Library, MA-232.2, Washington, DC 20585. (202) 586-9534. Monographs, proceedings, and other materials related to the energy field, including conservation and environmental aspects.

Power Energy Ecology. Taylor & Francis, 1900 Frost Rd., Suite 101, Bristol, PA 19007. (215) 785-5800. Quarterly. Energy conservation, power efficiency, renewable energy development, and global environment protection.

Power Generation and the Environment. P. S. Liss and P. A. H. Saunders. Oxford University Press, 200 Madison Ave., New York, NY 10016. (212) 679-7300; (800) 334-4249. 1990. Analyses the problems and possibilities inherent in producing electricity on a large scale.

Power Generation, Energy Management and Environmental Sourcebook. Marilyn Jackson. The Association of Energy Engineers, 4025 Pleasantdale Rd., Suite 420, Atlanta, GA 30340. (404) 925-9558. 1992. Includes practical solutions to energy and environmental problems.

Power Line. Utility Action Foundation, 724 Dupont Circle Bldg., Washington, DC 20036. 1977-. Monthly.

Power Line. Environmental Action Foundation, 6930 Carroll Ave., Ste. 600, Takoma Park, MD 20912. (301) 891-1100. Biannual.

Power Plants: Effects on Fish and Shellfish Behavior. Charles H. Hocutt. Academic Press, c/o Harcourt Brace Jovanovich Inc., 6277 Sea Harbor Dr., Orlando, FL 32887. (800) 346-8648. 1980.

Power Transmission Equipment–Wholesale. American Business Directories, Inc., 5711 S. 86th Circle, Omaha, NE 68127. (402) 593-4600.

PPI International Pulp & Paper Directory. Miller Freeman Publications, Inc., 500 Howard St., San Francisco, CA 94105. (415) 397-1881.

Practical Aspects of Groundwater Modeling. William Clarence Walton. National Water Well Association, 6375 Riverside Dr., Dublin, OH 43017. (614) 761-1711. 1985. Practical aspects of groundwater computer models. Deals with flow, mass and heat transport and subsidence.

Practical Electroplating Handbook. N.V. Parthasaradhy. Prentice Hall, Rte. 9W, Englewood Cliffs, NJ 07632. (201) 592-2000. 1989.

Practical Handbook of Ground Water Monitoring. David M. Nielsen. Lewis Publishers, 2000 Corporate Blvd., N.W., Boca Raton, FL 33431. (407) 994-0555 or (800) 272-7737. 1991. Covers the complete spectrum of state-of-the-science technology applied to investigations of ground water quality. Emphasis is placed on the practical application of current technology, and minimum theory is discussed.

Practical Manual for Groundwater Microbiology. D. Roy Cullimore. Lewis Publishers, 2000 Corporate Blvd., N.W., Boca Raton, FL 33431. (407) 994-0555 or (800) 272-7737. 1991. Describes the direct observation of microbial activities in groundwater, sampling procedures, indirect and direct microbiological examinations.

Practical Pedology. Stuart Gordon McRae. Halsted Press, 605 3rd Ave., New York, NY 10158. (212) 850-6000. 1988. Handbook for studying soils in the field.

Practical Protein Chemistry. A. Darbre. John Wiley & Sons, Inc., 605 3rd Ave., New York, NY 10158-0012. (212) 850-6000. 1986. A handbook on proteins.

Practices and Problems of Land Reclamation in Western North America. Mohan K. Wali. University of North Dakota, Grand Forks, ND 1975. Environmental aspects of stripmining and coal mines and mining.

The Practitioner's Approach to Indoor Air Quality Investigations. American Industrial Hygiene Association, 345 White Pond Dr., Akron, OH 44320. (216) 873-2442. 1990. Presents pragmatic advice for approaching and conducting an investigation and describes the range and causes of complaints that fall into categories of acute to subchronic adverse health effects.

The Prairie Club. 940 Lee St., Suite 204, Des Plaines, IL 60016. (708) 299-8402.

Prairie Wetland Drainage Regulations. North Dakota State University, Agricultural Experiment Station, Fargo, ND 58105. 1981.

Precambrian Paleobiology Research Group. Geology Building, Center for the Study of Evolution and Origin of Life, University of California, Los Angeles, Los Angeles, CA 90024. (213) 825-1170.

Precious Metal Databook. Metal Bulletin Inc., 220 5th Ave., 10th Floor, New York, NY 10001. (212) 213-6202.

Preclinical Drug Disposition: A Laboratory Handbook. Francis L.S. Tse. Marcel Dekker, Inc., 270 Madison Ave., New York, NY 10016. (212) 696-9000; (800) 228-1160. 1991. Covers drug metabolism and pharmacokinetics.

Predicting Nuclear and Other Technological Disasters. Christopher Lampton. F. Watts, 387 Park Ave. S., New York, NY 10016. (800) 672-6672. 1989. Discusses risks involved in state-of-the-art technology.

Predicting Photosynthesis for Ecosystem Models. J. D. Hesketh. CRC Press, 2000 Corporate Blvd. N.W., Boca Raton, FL 33431. (800) 272-7737. 1980. Simulation methods in photosynthesis.

Prediction and Regulation of Air Pollution. M. E. Berlyand. Kluwer Academic Publishers, 101 Philip Dr., Assinippi Park, Norwell, MA 02061-0358. (617) 871-6600. 1991. Revised and updated version of Prognoz i regulirovanie, 1985.

The Prentice-Hall Dictionary of Nutrition and Health. K. Anderson and L. Harmon. Prentice Hall, Rte 9 W, Englewood Cliffs, NJ 07632. (201) 592-2000 or (800) 634-2863. 1985. Focuses on health rather than nutrition. Includes 900 to 1000 entries.

Preparing for Emergency Planning. National Association of Manufacturers, 1331 Pennsylvania Ave., NW, Suite 1500 N., Washington, DC 20004. (202) 637-3000. 1987. Explains the Emergency Planning and Community Right-to-Know Act under the Superfund Law.

Present State of Knowledge of the Upper Atmosphere. R.T. Watson. National Aeronautics and Space Administration, Scientific and Technical Information Office, 5285 Port Royal Rd., Springfield, VA 22161. (703) 487-4805. 1988. Atmospheric ozone and atmospheric chemistry.

Preservation of Food by Ionizing Radiation. Edward S. Josephson. CRC Press, 2000 Corporate Blvd. N.W., Boca Raton, FL 33431. (800) 272-7737.

Preserving Communities and Corridors. Gay Mackintosh, ed. Defenders of Wildlife, 1244 19th St. N.W., Washington, DC 20036. (202) 659-9510. 1989.

Preserving the Global Environment: The Challenge of Shared Leadership. Jessica Tuchman Mathews, ed. World Resources Institute, 1709 New York Ave. N.W., Washington, DC 20006. (800) 822-0504. 1990. Includes findings on population growth, deforestation and the loss of biological diversity, the ozone layer, energy and climate change, economics, and other critical trends spell out new approaches to international cooperation and regulation in response to the shift from traditional security concerns to a focus on collective global security.

PressNet Environmental Reports. Chemical Information Systems, Inc., 7215 York Rd., Baltimore, MD 21212. (301) 321-8440.

Preventing Pollution Through Technical Assistance: One State's Experience. Mark H. Dorfman, et al. INFORM Inc., 381 Park Ave. S., New York, NY 10016. (212) 689-4040. 1990. Examines the state of North Carolina's voluntary program aimed at assisting the industry in pollution prevention. It also includes a glossary, a bibliography of information sources and helpful statistical tables of data collected.

Prevention and Control of Wildlife Damage. Nebraska Cooperative Extension Service, Institute of Agricultural and Natural Resources, University of Nebraska, 211 Agricultural Hall, Lincoln, NE 68583-0703. (402) 472-7211. 1983. Published in cooperation with Great Plains Agricultural Council Wildlife Resources Committee.

Prevention of Major Industrial Accidents. International Labour Office, 49 Sheridan Ave., Albany, NY 12210. (518) 436-9686. 1992. Provides guidance in setting up an administrative, legal and technical system for the control of installations producing, storing or using hazardous substances. Covers siting, analysis of risks, prevention, safe operation, emergency planning, and the duties and responsibilities of all those involved.

Prevention Reference Manual: Control Technologies. Daniel S. Davis. Air and Energy Research Laboratory, U.S. Environmental Protection Agency, Research Triangle Park, NC 27711. (919) 541-2350. 1987-. Accidents caused by hazardous substances and chemicals.

Pricing of Water Services. OECD Publications and Information Center, 2001 L St., N.W., Suite 700, Washington, DC 20036. (202) 785-OECD. 1987. Reviews existing practices in various OECD countries and presents options for economically rational pricing practices which would also lead to environmentally acceptable results.

Primary Aluminium Smelters and Producers of the World. Aluminium-Verlag GmbH, P.O. Box 1207, Dusseldorf 1, Germany D-4000. 211 320821.

Primary Aluminum Plants, Worldwide. Department of the Interior, 810 7th St. NW, Washington, DC 20241. (202) 501-9649.

Primary Productivity in the Sea. Paul G. Falkowski. Plenum Press, 233 Spring St., New York, NY 10013-1578. (212) 620-8000; (800) 221-9369. 1980.

Primary Productivity of the Biosphere. Helmut Lieth. Springer-Verlag, 175 5th Ave., New York, NY 10010. (212) 460-1500. 1975. Covers biometry and ecology.

Primate Responses to Environmental Change. Hillary O. Box, ed. Chapman & Hall, 29 W. 35th St., New York, NY 10001-2291. (212) 244-3336. 1991. Contributions of 24 authors grouped around the subject area of behavioral and physiological responses by primates to environmental change.

A Primer on Greenhouse Effect Gases. Donald J. Wuebbles and Jae Edmonds. Lewis Publishers, 200 Corporate Blvd. NW, Boca Raton, FL 33431. (407) 994-0555 or (800)272-7737. 1991. Brings together the most current information available on greenhouse gases. Reveals information critical to developing an understanding of the role of energy and atmospheric chemical and radiative processes in determining atmospheric concentrations of greenhouse gases.

Principles and Measurements in Environmental Biology. F. I. Woodward and J. E. Sheehy. Butterworth-Heinemann, 80 Montvale Ave., Stoneham, MA 02180. (617) 438-8464. 1983.

Principles of Air Pollution Meteorology. T. J. Lyons and W. D. Scott. CRC Press, 2000 Corporate Blvd., N.W., Boca Raton, FL 33431. (800) 272-7737. 1990. Describes atmospheric boundary layer, atmospheric diffusion, pollutants and their properties, and environmental monitoring and impact.

Principles of Air Toxics. Roger D. Griffin. Lewis Publishers, 2000 Corporate Blvd., N.W., Boca Raton, FL 33431. (407) 994-0555 or (800) 272-7737. 1991. Includes health effects of air pollutants, meteorology, pollutant transport and dispersion, types and definitions, sources and emissions, air emission characteristics, control and mitigation approaches, stationary source control technology, mobile source control, ambient air quality, and regulatory approaches.

Principles of Animal Extrapolation. Edward J. Calabrese. Lewis Publishers, 2000 Corporate Blvd., Boca Raton, FL 33431. (800) 272-7737. 1991. Animal models for toxicity testing are described. Also includes statistical methods in experimental toxicology.

Principles of Environmental Health Science. K. H. Mancy and Robert Gray. Lewis Publishers, 2000 Corporate Blvd., N.W., Boca Raton, FL 33431. (407) 994-0555 or (800) 272-7737. 1991. Discusses global environmental changes and the related issues and controversies, environmental contaminants, food and water, community air and indoor pollution, radiological health and solid waste, and nimby syndrome.

Principles of Environmental Sampling. Lawrence H. Keith, ed. American Chemical Society, 1155 16th St. N.W., Washington, DC 20036. (202) 872-4600; (800) 227-5558. 1988. Overview of the sampling process and its various applications.

Principles of Hazardous Materials Management. Roger D. Griffin. Lewis Publishers, 2000 Corporate Blvd., N.W., Boca Raton, FL 33431. (407) 994-0555 or (800) 272-7737. 1988. Gives basic understanding of the principles involved in each major topic represented: risk assessment, air toxics, groundwater, management methods, federal laws, transportation, waste minimization, treatment and disposal, toxicology, and analytical methods.

Principles of Plant Nutrition. Konrad Mengel. International Potash Institute, Postfach 121, Worblaufen, Bern, Switzerland CH-3048. 1978. Eight volumes.

Principles of Sampling. B. G. Kratochvil and J. K. Taylor. Lewis Publishers, 2000 Corporate Blvd., N.W., Boca Raton, FL 33431. (407) 994-0555 or (800) 272-7737. 1991. Contents include: sample modeling, sample planning, calibration sampling, mechanism of sampling, sub-sampling, statistics of sampling, sample quality assurance, uncertainty of sampling, validation of samples, general sampling, acceptance sampling, and special sampling topics.

Principles of Water Quality Management. William Wesley Eckenfelder. CBI, Boston, MA 1980.

Principles of Weed Control in California. Thomson Publications, PO Box 9335, Fresno, CA 93791. (209) 435-2163. 1989. 2d ed. Describes irrigated or California-type agricultural weed control methods. Also includes growers, chemical company reps, pest control advisors, extension people, etc.

Priorities For Long Life and Good Health. American Council on Health and Science, 1995 Broadway, 16th Floor, New York, NY 10023. (212) 362-7044. Quarterly. Covers evaluations of food, chemicals, and health.

Priority Issue Reporting Service–PIRS. Information for Public Affairs, Inc., Client Services Dept., 1900 14th St., Sacramento, CA 95814.

Private Options: Tools and Concepts for Land Conservation. Montana Land Reliance, Land Trust Exchange. Island Press, 1718 Connecticut Ave. N.W., Suite 300, Washington, DC 20009. (202) 232-7933. 1982. Private land conservation experts offer their expertise on how individuals can help contain urban sprawl, conserve wetlands, and protect wildlife. This book covers estate planning, tax incentives, purchase options, conservation easements and land management.

Probe Post. Pollution Probe Foundation, 12 Madison Ave., Toronto, ON, Canada M5R 2S1. (416) 926-1647. Quarterly. Acid rain, toxic waste, renewable energy, deep ecology, land use, and greenhouse effect.

The Problem of Sulphur. Butterworth-Heinemann, 80 Montvale Ave., Stoneham, MA 02180. (617) 438-8464. 1989.

Problems in Assessing the Cancer Risks of Low-Level Ionizing Radiation Exposure. U.S. General Accounting office, 441 G St., NW, Washington, DC 20548. (202) 275-5067. 1981. Toxicology of radiation and radiation-induced neoplasms.

Problems of Desert Development. Allerton Press, Inc., 150 Fifth Ave., New York, NY 10011. (212) 924-3950. Bimonthly.

Problems of Hydroelectric Development at Existing Dams. R.J. Taylor. Department of Energy, 5285 Port Royal Rd, Springfield, VA 22161. 1979. An analysis of institutional, economic, and environmental restraints.

Procedures for the Preparation of Emission Inventories for Volatile Organic Compounds. National Technical Information Service, 5285 Port Royal Rd., Springfield, VA 22161. (703) 487-4650. 1980. Air pollution measurement and air quality management.

Procedures Pertaining to Environmental Sanitation. Wilhelmina C. Carey. U.S. G.P.O., Washington, DC 20401. (202) 512-0000. 1976. A manual on hospital housekeeping procedures.

Proceedings. Conservation Education Association, c/o Dennis Bryan, Rte. #1, New Franken, WI 54229. (414) 465-2397.

Proceedings Digests. Air and Waste Management Association, PO Box 2861, Pittsburgh, PA 15230. (412) 232-3444. Annual.

Proceedings, North Central Weed Science Society Conference. North Central Weed Science Society, 309 W. Clark St., Champaign, IL 61820. (217) 356-3182. 1989. Forty-Fourth North Central Weed Science Society Conference held December 5-7, 1989 in Lexington, Kentucky. Topics included are: cereals and oilseeds; computers; maize and sorghum; edaphic factors; environmental and health; equipment and application methods; extension; forage and range weed control; forests, rights- of-ways and industrial weed control; herbicide physiology; horticulture and aquatics; resident eduction; soybeans and annual legumes and; weed ecology and biology.

Proceedings of the 44th Industrial Waste Conference May 1989, Purdue University. John W. Bell, ed. Lewis Publishers, 2000 Corporate Blvd., N.W., Boca Raton, FL 33431. (407) 994-0555 or (800) 272-7737. 1990. Includes new research, case histories and operating data, on every conceivable facet of today's big problem with unparalleled appropriate, usable information and data for current industrial waste problems.

Proceedings of the 45th Industrial Waste Conference, May 1990 at Purdue University. Ross A. Duckworth. Lewis Publishers, 2000 Corporate Blvd., N.W., Boca Raton, FL 33431. (407) 994-0555 or (800) 272-7737. 1991. Subject areas included in the conference were: site remediation, hazardous waste minimization and treatment, biological systems, aerobic processes, anaerobic processes, sludge treatment, respirometry, new processes, equipment, and applications.

Proceedings of the 4th National Symposium on Individual and Small Community Sewage Systems. American Society of Agricultural Engineers, 2950 Niles Rd., St. Joseph, MI 49085-9659. (616) 429-0300. 1985. Includes current trends such as design, planning, management, and performance of large systems, the use of computers for on-site technology, site evaluation, etc. The 5th National Symposium held in 1987 further includes environmental effects of on-site disposal soil absorption/system siting requirement and groundwater impact.

Proceedings of WAFWA. Western Association of Fish, 1416 9th St., Sacramento, CA 95814. (916) 445-9880. Annual. Research and management of fish and wildlife.

Process Design Manual for Sulfide Control in Sanitary Sewerage Systems. Richard D. Pomeroy. U.S. Environmental Protection Agency, 401 M St., SW, Washington, DC 20460. (202) 260-2090. 1974.

Process Drying Practice. Edward M. Cook and Harman D. Dumont. McGraw-Hill, 1221 Avenue of the Americas, New York, NY 10020. (212) 512-2000 or (800) 262-4729. 1991.

Process Safety & Environmental Protection. Taylor & Francis, 1900 Frost Rd., Ste. 101, Bristol, PA 19007. (215) 785-5800. Quarterly.

Proctor and Hughes' Chemical Hazards of the Workplace. G. J. Hathaway, et al. Global Professional Publications, 2805 McGraw Ave., PO Box 19539, Irvine, CA 92713-9539. (800) 854-7179. 1991. Third edition. Includes 100 new chemicals and the new 1991 Threshold Limit Values. Gives a practical easy-to-use introduction to toxicology and hazards of over 600 chemicals most likely to be encountered in the workplace.

Product Risk Reduction in the Chemical Industry. Leonard A. Miller. Executive Enterprises Publications Co., Inc., 22 W. 21st St., New York, NY 10010-6990. (212) 645-7880. 1985. A handbook for managing product and regulatory liability.

Product Safety Evaluation Handbook. Shayne Cox Gad. Dekker, 270 Madison Ave., New York, NY 10016. (212) 696-9000 or (800) 228-1160. 1988. Discusses toxicity testing of products such as drugs, chemicals, etc. Gives an evaluation of their safety for the consumer.

Product Tankers and Their Market Role. Michael Grey. Fairplay, London, England 1982. Economic aspects of petroleum transportation and tankers.

Production and Processing of U.S. Tar Sands, An Environmental Assessment. N.A. Frazier. National Technical Information Service, 5285 Port Royal Rd., Springfield, VA 22161. (703) 487-4650. 1980. Bitumen geology and environmental aspects of oil sands.

Production and Utilization of Products from Commercial Seaweeds. Dennis J. McHugh. Food and Agriculture Organization of the United Nations, Via delle Terme di Caracalla, Rome, Italy 00100. 61 0181-FA01. 1987. Marine algae as feed and food.

Production Response of Illinois Farmers to Premiums for Low-Temperature Dried Corn. Lowell D. Hill, et al. Dept. of Agricultural Economics, Agricultural Experiment Station, University of Illinois at Urbana-Champaign, Urbana, IL 61801. 1987. Describes the procedure for drying of corn and its prices.

Professional Engineers in Private Practice. 1420 King St., Alexandria, VA 22314. (703) 684-2862.

Professional Grounds Management Society. 120 Cockeysville Rd., Ste. 104, Hunt Valley, MD 21031. (410) 667-1833.

Professional Reactor Operators Society. Box 181, Mishicot, WI 54288. (414) 755-2725.

Program Guide to Used Oil Recycling. National Technical Information Service, 5285 Port Royal Rd., Springfield, VA 22161. (703) 487-4650. 1982.

Progress in Chemical Fibrinolysis. Raven Press, 1185 Ave. of the Americas, New York, NY 10036. (212) 930-9500.

Progress in Hormone Biochemistry and Pharmacology. Eden Medical Research, St. Albans, VT Annual.

Progress in Hydrogen Energy. Kluwer Academic Publishers, 101 Philip Dr., Assinippi Park, Norwell, MA 02061. (617) 871-6600. 1987.

Progress in Lipid Research. Pergamon Microforms International, Inc., Fairview Park, Elmsford, NY 10523. (914) 592-7720. Quarterly. Covers topics in the chemistry of fats and other lipids.

Progress in Organic Coatings. Elsevier Sequoia, 50, ave. de la Gare, PO Box 564, Lausanne, Switzerland CH-1001. Covers protective coatings, polymers and polymerization.

Progress in Physical Geography. Cambridge University Press, 40 W. 20th St., New York, NY 10011. (212) 924-3900. Quarterly. Studies on animate and inanimate aspects of the earth, ocean, and atmosphere with interest in man-environment interaction .

Progress in Protein-Lipid Interactions. Elsevier Science Publishing Co., 655 Avenue of the Americas, New York, NY 10010. (212) 984-5800. Annual. Review designed to critically evaluate actively developing areas of research in protein-lipid interactions.

Progress in the Prevention and Control of Air Pollution. U.S. Environmental Protection Agency. National Technical Information Service, Springfield, VA 22161. (703) 487-4650. Annual. Covers air quality trends and control of radon, suspended particulates, sulfur and nitrogen oxides, carbon monoxide, ozone and lead.

Project Circle. Marine World Africa USA, Marine World Parkway, Vallejo, CA 94589. (707) 644-4000.

Project in Conservation Science. University of California, San Diego, Department of Biology C-016, La Jolla, CA 92093. (619) 534-2375.

Project Lighthawk. P.O. Box 8163, Santa Fe, NM 87504. (505) 982-9656.

Projecting Future Sealevel Rise. John S. Hoffman. Office of Policy and Resource Management, U.S. Environmental Protection Agency, 401 M St. SW, Washington, DC 20460. (202) 260-2090. 1983. Methodology, estimates of sealevel rise to the year 2100 and research needs on solar radiation and climatic change.

Projecting the Climatic Effects of Increasing Carbon Dioxide. Michael C. MacCracken. National Technical Information Service, 5285 Port Royal Rd., Springfield, VA 22161. (703) 487-4650. 1985.

The Prokaryotes: A Handbook on Habitats, Isolation, and Identification of Bacteria. M. P. Starr. Springer-Verlag, 175 5th Ave., New York, NY 10010. (212) 460-1500. 1981. Identification of bacteria and cultures and culture media of bacteriology.

Promoting Environmentally Sound Economic Progress: What the North Can Do. Robert Repetto. World Resources Institute, 1709 New York Ave. N.W., Washington, DC 20006. (800) 822-0504. 1990. Spells out actions that must be taken if the world economy is going to continue to develop and yet avoid the environmental degradation that threatens to undermine living standards.

Promoting Recycling to the Public. National Soft Drink Association, 1101 16th St., N.W., Washington, DC 20036. (202) 463-6770.

Promotion of Women's Participation in Water Resources Development. UNIPUB, 4611-F Assembly Dr., Lanham, MD 20706-4391. (301) 459-7666; (800) 274-4888. 1990.

Proof of Causation and Damages in Toxic Chemical, Hazardous Waste, and Drug Cases. Sheila L. Birnbaum. Practicing Law Institute, 810 7th Ave., New York, NY 10019. (212) 765-5700. 1987.

Propellants, Explosives, Pyrotechnics. VCH Publishers, 303 NW 12th Ave., Deerfield Beach, FL 33442-1788. (305) 428-5566. Quarterly.

Proposed Federal Radiation Protection Guidance for Occupational Exposure. Office of radiation Programs. USEPA, Washington, DC 1981. Safety measures in the nuclear industry.

Propylene Oxide. Environmental Protection Service, 425 St. Joseph Blvd., 3rd Fl., Hull, PQ, Canada K1A 0H3. (613) 953-5921. 1985. Environmental aspects of oxides.

Propylene Oxide & Derivatives. FIND/SVP, 625 Avenue of the Americas, New York, NY 10011. (212) 645-4500. 1991.

Prospects for Future Climate: A Special US/USSR Report on Climate and Climate Change. Michael C. MacCracken, et al. Lewis Publishers, 2000 Corporate Blvd., N.W., Boca Raton, FL 33431. (407) 994-0555 or (800) 272-7737. 1990. Describes the effects of the increasing concentration of greenhouse gases and the potential for climate change and impact on agriculture and hydrology. Projections are based on insights from both numerical models and empirical methods.

Prosperity without Pollution. Joel S. Hirschhorn and Kirsten U. Oldenburg. Van Nostrand Reinhold, 115 5th Ave., New York, NY 10003. (212) 254-3232. 1991. Explains how to decrease pollution without making a sacrifice in our standard of living.

Protect. Tennessee Environmental Council, 1725 Church St., Nashville, TN 37203-2921. (615) 321-5075. Bimonthly.

Protecting America's Wetlands. Conservation Foundation, 1250 24th St. NW, Washington, DC 20037. (202) 293-4800. 1988. Final report of the National Wetlands Policy Forum.

Protecting Ground Water: The Hidden Resource. U.S. Environmental Protection Agency, Office of Public Affairs, 401 M St. SW, Washington, DC 20460. (202) 260-2090. 1984.

Protecting Life on Earth: Steps to Save the Ozone Layer. Cynthia Pollock Shea. Worldwatch Institute, 1776 Massachusetts Ave., N.W., Washington, DC 20036-1904. 1988. Reduction of air pollution and atmospheric ozone.

Protecting Nontidal Wetlands. David G. Burke, et al. American Planning Association, 1776 Massachusetts Ave. N.W., Washington, DC 20036. (202) 872-0611. 1988. Describes wetlands types and values, looks at the current status of U.S. wetlands, and reviews federal, state, and local regulations to protect nontidal wetlands.

Protecting Our Ground Water. U.S. Environmental Protection Agency, Office of Public Affairs, 401 M St. SW, Washington, DC 20460. (202) 260-2090. 1990.

Protecting the Nation's Groundwater from Contamination. U.S. G.P.O., Washington, DC 20401. 1984-. Covers underground water quality and pollution.

The Protection and Management of Our Natural Resources, Wildlife and Habitat. W. Jack Grosse. Oceana Publications Inc., 75 Main St., Dobbs Ferry, NY 10522. (914) 693-8100. 1992. Covers question of overall management, control and protection of wildlife and habitat. Additionally, as the federal government has recently created numerous acts which serve to control wildlife and habitat, many questions have emerged over shared and conflicting power with the states.

Protection Ecology. Elsevier Science Publishing Co., Journal Information Center, 655 Avenue of the Americas, New York, NY 10010. (212) 989-5800. Livestock and agricultural ecology and pest control.

The Protection of Lawn and Turf Grasses, 1979-April 1991. Charles N. Bebee. National Agricultural Library, 10301 Baltimore Blvd., Beltsville, MD 20705-2351. (301) 504-5755. 1991. Citations from AGRICOLA concerning diseases and other environmental considerations. Volume 107 of Bibliographies and literature of Agriculture.

The Protection of Peanuts. Charles N. Bebee. National Agricultural Library, 10301 Baltimore Blvd., Beltsville, MD 20705-2351. (301) 504-5755. 1991. Citations from AGRICOLA concerning diseases and other environmental considerations.

Protection of River Basins, Lakes, and Estuaries. Robert C. Ryans. American Fisheries Society, 5410 Grosvenor Lane, Bethesda, MD 20814. (301) 897-8616. 1988. Fifteen years of cooperation toward solving environmental problems in the USSR and USA.

The Protection of Tomatoes, Egg Plants and Peppers. Charles N. Bebee. National Agricultural Library, 10301 Baltimore Blvd., Beltsville, MD 20705-2351. (301) 504-5755. 1991. Citations from AGRICOLA concerning diseases and other environmental considerations.

Protective Clothing for Hazardous Materials Incidents. National Fire Protection Association. Burclan Productions, Batterymarch Park, PO Box 9101, Quincy, MA 02269. (617) 770-3000. 1984. A sound cassette, slide and technical manual relating to protective clothing.

Protein Production by Biotechnology. T. J. R. Harris, ed. Elsevier Science Publishing Co., 655 Avenue of the Americas, New York, NY 10010. (212) 984-5800. 1990. Describes the use of recombinant DNA techniques to produce proteins of therapeutic or other importance.

Protein Purification: Design and Scale Up of Downstreams Processing. Scott M. Wheelwright. Oxford University Press, 200 Madison Ave., New York, NY 10016. (212) 679-7300; (800) 334-4249. 1991.

Protein Refolding. George Georgiou and Eliana De Barnardez-Clark, eds. American Chemical Society, 1155 16th St. N.W., Washington, DC 20036. (202) 872-4600; (800) 227-5558. 1991. Studies protein recovery, aggregation, formation, structure, and other features.

Provasoli-Guillard Center for Culture of Marine Phytoplankton. Bigelow Laboratory for Ocean Sciences, McKown Point, West Boothbay Harbor, ME 04575. (207) 633-2173.

Public Affairs Office. James Forrestal Building, 1000 Independence Ave., S.W., Washington, DC 20585. (202) 586-6250.

Public Affairs Office: Environmental Research Laboratories. 3100 Marine St., Boulder, CO 80303. (303) 497-6286.

Public Affairs Office: U.S. Army Corps of Engineers. Room 8137, 20 Massachusetts Ave., N.W., Washington, DC 20314. (202) 272-0010.

Public Affairs Office: U.S. Geological Survey. 119 National Center, 12201 Sunrise Valley Dr., Reston, VA 22092. (703) 648-4460.

Public and Private Water Utility Treatment: Metals and Organics in Raw and Finished Waters. Vance Bibliographies, PO Box 229, 112 N. Charter St., Monticello, IL 61856. (217) 762-3831. 1980. Bibliography of water analysis, environmental aspects of metals and organic compounds.

Public Attitudes Toward Garbage Disposal. National Solid Wastes Management Association, 1730 Rhode Island Ave., NW, Ste. 1000, Washington, DC 20036. (202) 659-4613. 1990.

Public Citizen. PO Box 19404, Washington, DC 20036. (202) 293-9142.

Public Citizen Health Research Group. 2000 P St., N.W., Suite 700, Washington, DC 20036. (202) 872-0320.

The Public Environment Center. 1 Milligan Pl., New York, NY 10011. (212) 691-4877.

Public Health Consequences of Disasters. U.S. G.P.O., Washington, DC 20401. (202) 512-0000. 1989. Natural and human-generated disasters impact on public health.

Public Health Engineer. Institution of Public Health Engineers, Municipal Publications, 32 Eccleston Square, London, England SW1V IP3. 1895-. Monthly.

Public Health Engineering Abstracts. U.S. G.P.O., Washington, DC 20401. (202) 512-0000. Monthly.

The Public Health Implications of Medical Waste: A Report to Congress. U.S. Department of Health and Human Services, Public Health Service, 200 Independence Ave. SW, Washington, DC 20201. (202) 619-1296. 1990. Covers infectious wastes and medical wastes.

Public Information Office: Federal Highway Administration. 400 7th St., S.W., Washington, DC 20590. (202) 366-0660.

Public Information Office: Soil Conservation Service. 12th and Independence Ave., S.W., PO Box 2890, Washington, DC 20013. (202) 447-4543.

Public Interest Research Group. 215 Pennsylvania Ave. S.E., Washington, DC 20003. (202) 546-9707.

Public Involvement Manual: Involving the Public in Water and Power Resources Decisions. James L. Creighton. U.S. G.P.O., Washington, DC 20401. (202) 512-0000. Citizen participation in power development.

Public Land News. Resources Publishing Co., 1010 Vermont Avenue, NW, Suite 708, Washington, DC 20005. (202) 638-7529. Biweekly. Covers land use and land development.

Public Lands Council-Washington Highlight Report. Public Lands Council, 1301 Penn Ave., NW, #300, Washington, DC 20004. (202) 347-5355. Quarterly.

Public Policies and the Misuse of Forest Resources. Robert Repetto and Malcolm Gillis, eds. Cambridge University Press, 40 W. 20th St., New York, NY 10011. (212) 924-3900; (800) 227-0247. 1988. Case studies of forest policies in developing countries. Also deals with deforestation problems from the environmental point of view.

Public Policy for Chemicals: National and International Issues. Conservation Foundation, 1250 24th St., NW, Washington, DC 20037. (202) 293-4800. 1980. Legal aspects of chemicals and hazardous substances.

Public Power Directory of Local Publicly Owned Electric Utilities. American Public Power Association, 2301 M St., N.W., Washington, DC 20037. (202) 467-2900.

Public Use of National Wildlife Refugees. U.S. Department of the Interior, Fish and Wildlife Service, 1849 C St. NW, Washington, DC 20240. (202) 208-5634. Annual.

Public Water Supply. FIND/SVP, 625 Avenue of the Americas, New York, NY 10011. (212) 645-4500. 1991. Market for equipment, supplies and services sold to public water utilities.

Publications. Argonne National Laboratory. Energy and Environmental Systems Division. National Technical Information Service, 5285 Port Royal Rd., Springfield, VA 22161. (703) 487-4650. Annual. Covers topics in environmental engineering.

Publications Index. U.S. G.P.O., Washington, DC 20401. (202) 512-0000. Annual. Covers radiation toxicology and radiation management.

Puerto Rico Environmental Law Handbook. Government Institutes, Inc., 4 Research Pl., Ste. 200, Rockville, MD 20850. (301) 921-2300. 1990.

Puerto Rico Environmental Quality Board: Emergency Preparedness and Community Right-to-Know. SERC Commissioner, Title III-SARA Section 313, PO Box 11488, Sernades Juncos Station, Santurce, PR 00910. (809) 722-0077.

Puerto Rico Water Resources Research Institute. College of Engineering, University of Puerto Rico, P.O. Box 5000, Mayaguez, PR 00709-5000. (809) 834-4040.

Pulp and Paper. James P. Casey. John Wiley & Sons, Inc., 605 3rd Ave., New York, NY 10158-0012. (212) 850-6000. 1980. Chemistry and chemical technology relating to paper making and wood-pulp.

Pulp and Paper. Forest Industries, 500 Howard St., San Francisco, CA 94105. Monthly. Production, engineering/maintenance, management, and marketing.

Pulp and Paper–Buyer's Guide Issue. Miller Freeman Publications, Inc., 500 Howard Street, San Francisco, CA 94105. (415) 397-1881.

Pulp and Paper Data Bank. Resource Information Systems, 110 Great Rd., Bedford, MA 01730. (617) 271-0030.

Pulp and Paper Industry Corrosion Problems. National Association of Corrosion Engineers, P.O. Box 218340, Houston, TX 77218. (713) 492-0535. 1982.

Pulp Chemicals Association. P.O. Box 105113, Atlanta, GA 30348. (404) 446-1290.

Pulp Technology and Treatment for Paper. James Clark. Freeman Publications, 600 Harrison St., San Francisco, CA 94107. (415) 905-2200. 1985.

Pumped-Storage Planning and Evaluation Guide. H.H. Chen. Electric Power Research Institute, 3412 Hillview Ave., Palo Alto, CA 94304. (415) 965-4081. 1990. Economic aspects of electric power production.

Purdue University, Arthur Herbarium. Department of Botany and Plant Pathology, 115 S. Lilly Hall, Rm. 1-423, West Lafayette, IN 47907. (317) 494-4623.

Purdue University, Great Lakes Coastal Research Laboratory. School of Civil Engineering, West Lafayette, IN 47907. (317) 494-3713.

Pure Water from the Sea. International Desalination Association, Box 328, Englewood, NJ 07631. (201) 567-0188. Bimonthly.

Purification of Laboratory Chemicals. Douglas Dalzell Perrin. Pergamon Microforms International, Inc., Fairview Park, Elmsford, NY 10523. (914) 592-7720. Deals with chemical purification technology.

The Pyrethroid Insecticides. John P. Leahey. Taylor & Francis, 1900 Frost Rd., Ste. 101, Philadelphia, PA 19007. (215) 785-5800. 1985. Toxicology and environmental aspects of pyrethroids.

Pyrethroids Residues, Immunoassays for Low Molecular Weight Compounds. Wolfgang Blass. Springer-Verlag, 175 5th Ave., New York, NY 10010. (212) 460-1500. 1990. Chemistry of plant protection, and pesticide residues in food.

Quality Assurance Data for Routine Water Analysis. U.S. Geological Survey. U.S. G.P.O., Washington, DC 20401. (202) 512-0000. Annual. Test results determining alkalinity, inorganic ion, trace metal and organic nutrients.

Quality Assurance of Environmental Measurements. H. G. Nowicki. Lewis Publishers, 2000 Corporate Blvd., N.W., Boca Raton, FL 33431. (407) 994-0555 or (800) 272-7737. 1991. Includes an overview of costs/benefits of quality assurance, sample plans to match quality objectives, statistics for evaluating the numbers, agency required sample containers, program data for inorganic analysis, and designing and implementing and monitoring a quality assurance program.

Quality Assurance/Quality Control Procedures for Hazardous Waste Incineration. Center for Environmental Research Information. U.S. Environmental Protection Agency, 26 W. Martin Luther King Dr., Cincinnati, OH 45628. (513) 569-7931. 1990.

Quarterly. Council on Plastics and Packaging in the Environment, 1275 K St. NW, Suite 900, Washington, DC 20005. (202) 789-1310. Quarterly.

Quarterly Literature Review of the Remote Sensing of Natural Resources. Technology Application Center, University of New Mexico, Albuquerque, NM 87131. Quarterly.

Queens College of City University of New York, Center for Environmental Teaching and Research. Queens College of City University of New York, Center for Environmental Teaching and Research, Caumsett State Park, 31 Lloyd Harper Rd., Huntington, NY 11743. (516) 421-3526.

Queens College of City University of New York, Center for the Biology of Natural Systems. Flushing, NY 11367. (718) 670-4180.

Quetico-Superior Wilderness Research Center. Box 479, MN

R. M. Bohart Museum of Entomology. University of California, Davis, Department of Entomology, Davis, CA 95616. (916) 752-0493.

Race to Save the Tropics. Robert Goodland, ed. Island Press, 1718 Connecticut Ave. N.W., Suite 300, Washington, DC 20009. (202) 232-7933. 1990. Documents the conflict between economic development and protection of biological diversity in tropical countries.

Rachel Carson Council. 8940 Jones Mill Rd., Chevy Chase, MD 20815. (301) 652-1877.

Rachel's Hazardous Waste News. Environmental Research Foundation, PO Box 3541, Princeton, NJ 08543-3541. (609) 683-0707. Weekly. Topics include landfills, toxins, incinerators, health and the environment, grassroots lobbying, and community energy conservation.

Radial Growth of Grand Fir and Douglas Fir Ten Years after Defoliation by the Douglas Fir Tussock Moth in the Blue Mountains Outbreak. Boyd E. Wickman. U.S. Department of Agriculture, Forest Service, Pacific Northwest Research Station, 319 S. W. Pine St., PO Box 3890, Portland, OR 97208. (503) 294-5640. 1986.

Radiation Exposure and Occupational Risks. G. Keller, et al. Springer-Verlag, 175 5th Ave., New York, NY 10010. (212) 460-1500; (800) 777-4643. 1990. Discusses radiation exposure injuries in the workplace and prevention.

Radiation Protection Research Training Programme. European Community Information Service (UNIPUB), 4611-F Assembly Dr., Lanham, MD 20706-4391. (800) 274-4888. 1990. Review of the radiation protection programme, 1960-89. Gives a synopsis of results 1985-89. Includes radiation safety and decontamination procedures.

Radiation Research Society. American College of Radiology, 1101 Market St., 14th Fl., Philadelphia, PA 19107. (215) 574-3153.

Radiation Safety in Shelters. Federal Emergency Management Agency, 500 C St. SW, Washington, DC 20472. (202) 646-4600. 1983. A handbook for finding and providing the best protection in shelters with the use of nuclear radiation-detecting instruments.

Radioactive Aerosols. A. C. Chamberlin. Cambridge University Press, 40 W 20th St., New York, NY 10011. (212) 924-3900; (800) 227-0247. 1991. Describes radioactive gases and particles which are dispersed in the environment, either from natural causes or following nuclear test and accidental emissions.

Radioactive Heaven and Earth. The Apex Press, c/o Council on International and Public Affairs, 777 United Nations Plaza, Suite 3C, New York, NY 10017. (212) 953-6920. 1991. The health and environmental effects of nuclear weapons testing in, on, and above the Earth.

Radioactive Material Released from Nuclear Power Plants. U.S. Nuclear Regulatory Commission. U.S. G.P.O., Washington, DC 20401. (202) 512-0000. Annual. Data on radioactive content of airborne and liquid effluents and solid wastes from nuclear power plants.

Radioactive Waste as a Social and Political Issue: A Bibliography. Frederick Frankena. AMS Press, 56 E. 13th St., New York, NY 10003. (212) 777-4700. 1991.

Radioactive Waste Campaign. 625 Broadway, 2nd Fl., New York, NY 10012-2611. (212) 473-7390.

Radioactive Waste Management. National Technical Information Service, 5285 Port Royal Rd., Springfield, VA 22161. (703) 487-4650. Monthly. Topics include spent-fuel transport and storage; radioactive effluents from nuclear facilities; and techniques of processing wastes, their storage, and ultimate disposal.

Radiocarbon Dating. Sheridan Bowman. British Museum Publications, 46 Bloomsbury St., London, England WC1B 3QQ. 44 071 323 1234. 1990.

Radiocarbon Dating Literature: The First 21 Years. Dilette Polach. Academic Press Inc., 24-28 Oval Rd., London, England NW1 7DX. 071-267 4466. 1988.

Radioecology. Whicker F.Ward. CRC Press, 2000 Corporate Blvd. N.W., Boca Raton, FL 33431. (800) 272-7737. 1982. Topics in nuclear energy and its environmental impact.

Radiological Society of North America. 1415 W. 22nd St., Tower B, Oak Brook, IL 60521. (312) 571-2670.

Radon and Its Decay in Indoor Air. William W. Nazaroff and Anthony V. Nero. John Wiley & Sons, Inc., 605 3rd Ave., New York, NY 10158-0012. (212) 850-6000. 1988. Radon isotopes toxicology and hygienic aspects of indoor air pollution.

Radon Attenuation Handbook for Uranium Mill Tailings Cover Design. U.S. Nuclear Regulatory Commission, Division of Health, Siting and Waste Management, Office of Nuclear Regulatory Research, Washington, DC 20555. (301) 492-7000. 1984.

Radon Directory. Radon Press, Inc., 500 N. Washington St., Alexandria, VA 22314. (703) 548-2756.

Radon in the Environment. M. Wilkening. Elsevier Science Publishing Co., 655 Avenue of the Americas, New York, NY 10010. (212) 989-5800. 1990. Describes the discovery of radon, its characteristics, and sources in the environment methods of control, as well as possible health effects.

Radon News Digest. Hoosier Environmental Pubs., Box 709, Carmel, IN 46032. (317) 843-0788. Monthly. Testing, mitigation, legislation and market trends.

Radon, Radium, and Uranium in Drinking Water. C. Richard Cothern and Paul Rebers. Lewis Publishers, 2000 Corporate Blvd., N.W., Boca Raton, FL 33431. (407) 994-0555 or (800) 272-7737. 1990. Covers most aspects of radionuclides in drinking water.

Railroad Commission: Underground Storage Tanks. Assistant Director, Oil and Gas Division, PO Box 12967, Capitol Station, Austin, TX 78711. (512) 463-6922.

Rails-to-Trails Conservancy. 1400 16th St., NW, Washington, DC 20036. (202) 797-5400.

Railway Fuel & Operating Officers Association. Box 8496, Springfield, IL 62791. (217) 544-7834.

Rain Forest Regeneration and Management. G. Pompa, et al., eds. Parthenon Group Inc., 120 Mill Rd., Park Ridge, NJ 07656. (201) 391-6796. 1991. Explores the management implications of present scientific knowledge on rain forest generation. Providing case studies.

Rainforest Action Network. 301 Broadway, Suite 28, San Francisco, CA 94133. (415) 398-4404.

Rainforest Alliance. 270 Lafayette St., Suite 512, New York, NY 10012. (212) 941-1900.

Rainforest Health Alliance. Fort Mason, Building E, San Francisco, CA 94123. (415) 921-1203.

Raise the Stakes–North America Plus Issue. Planet Drum Foundation, Box 31251, San Francisco, CA 94131. (415) 285-6556.

Rancho Santa Ana Botanic Garden. 1500 North College Avenue, Claremont, CA 91711. (714) 626-3922.

Range and Pasture Research. U.S. Agricultural Research Service, Washington, DC 1986.

Rangelands. Bruce A. Buchanan. University of New Mexico Press, 1720 Lomas Blvd., NE, Albuquerque, NM 87131. (505) 277-2346. 1988. Profiles range ecology and range management in the West.

RAPRA Abstracts. RAPRA Technology Limited, Shawbury, Shrewsbury, England SY4 4NR. 44 (939) 250383.

Rare and Endangered Native Plant Exchange. Biology Dept., County College of Morris, Rt. 10 and Center Grove Rd., Randolph, NJ 07869. (201) 361-5000.

RARE Center for Tropical Bird Conservation. 15290 Walnut St., Philadelphia, PA 19102. (215) 568-0420.

Rare, Inc. 1601 Connecticut Ave., N.W., Washington, DC 20009.

Rare Plant Conservation: Geographical Data Organization. Larry E. Morse. New York Botanical Garden, Scientific Publications Dept., Bronx, NY 10458-5126. (212) 220-8721. 1981.

Rating Forest Stands for Gypsy Moth Defoliation. Owen W. Herrick and David A. Ganser. U.S. Department of Agriculture, Northeastern Forest Experiment Station, 370 Reed Rd., Broomall, PA 19008. (215) 461-3104. 1986.

Rauch Guide to the U.S. Plastics Industry. Rauch Associates, P.O. Box 6802, Bridgewater, NJ 08807. Recurring. Economic structure, production of basic materials, processing, and end use markets.

RCDC Bibliographic Database. University of Notre Dame, Radiation Chemistry Data Center, Radiation Laboratory, Notre Dame, IN 46556. (219) 239-6527.

RCRA Compliance Implementation Guide. Mary P. Bauer and Elizabeth J. Kellar. Government Institutes, Inc., 4 Research Pl., Suite 200, Rockville, MD 20850. (301) 921-2300. 1990. Interprets how a particular situation fits into the whole compliance process. Step-by-step directions are given to satisfy the compliance program. Also included are copies of EPA reports, manifests and forms.

RCRA Hazardous Wastes Handbook. Crowell & Moring. Government Institutes, Inc., 4 Research Place, Suite 200, Rockville, MD 20850. (301) 921-2300. 1989. 8th ed. Analyzes the impact of the Resource Conservation and Recovery Act on the business, while incorporating the most recent regulatory changes to the RCRA. These include the final 1988 underground storage tank rules, the medical waste regulations, permit modification regulations, amendments regarding corrective action and closures, the exemption for "treatability tests," waste export rules, etc. Includes the complete test of the RCRA statute as currently amended.

RCRA Inspection Manual. Environment Protection Agency. Government Institutes, Inc., 4 Research Pl., Suite 200, Rockville, MD 20850. (301) 921-2300. 1989. 2nd ed. Developed by EPA to support its inspectors in conducting complex field inspections. It covers the key topics that will help eliminate deficiencies, satisfy inspections and avoid civil and criminal penalties.

Reactions and Processes. P.B. Barraclough. Springer-Verlag, 175 5th Ave., New York, NY 10010. (212) 460-1500. 1988. Covers natural environment and the biological cycles, reaction and processes, anthropogenic compounds, air and water pollution.

Reactor Accidents: Nuclear Safety and the Role of Institutional Failure. David Mosey. Nuclear Engineering International Special Publications, c/o Butterworth-Heinemann, 80 Montvale Ave., Stoneham, MA 02180. (617) 438-8464; (800) 366-2665. 1990.

Real Estate Transactions and Environmental Risks: A Practical Guide. Donald C. Nanney. PennWell Books, PO Box 21288, Tulsa, OK 74121. (918) 831-9421; (800) 752-9764. 1990. Presents general principles used when approaching environmental issues from a real estate agent's point of view.

Real-Time Atmospheric Monitoring. Kavouras, Inc., 6301 34th Ave. S, Minneapolis, MN 554540. (612) 726-9515.

Real Time Control of Urban Drainage Systems, the State-of-the-Art. Wolfgang Schilling, ed. Pergamon Microforms International, Inc., Fairview Park, Elmsford, NY 10523. (914) 592-7720. 1989. Report by the IAWPRC Task Group on real-time control of drainage systems.

Reassessing Nuclear Power: The Fallout from Chernobyl. Christopher Flavin. Worldwatch Institute, 1776 Massachusetts Ave., N.W., Washington, DC 20036-1904. 1987.

Receptor Model Source Composition Library. U.S. Environmental Protection Agency, MD 75, Research Triangle Park, NC 27711. (919) 541-2184. 1984. Covers air management technology, monitoring and data analysis.

Reclamation & Revegetation Research. Elsevier, Box 211, Amsterdam, Netherlands 1000 AE. 020-5803-911. Quarterly.

Recombinant DNA Research and Viruses: Cloning and Expression of Viral Genes. Yechiel Becker, ed. Martinus Nijoff/W. Junk, 101 Philips Dr., Norwell, MA 02061. (617) 871-6600. 1985.

Recommendations for a Xylene Standard. National Institute for Occupational Safety and Health, 1600 Clifton Rd. NE, Atlanta, GA 30333. (404) 639-3286. 1975. Covers toxicology of xylene, industrial hygiene standards and safety.

Recommendations of the Transport of Dangerous Goods: Test and Criteria. United Nations Publications, Sales Section, Room DC2-0853, Department 733, New York, NY 10017. (800) 253-9646. Companion to the ORANGE BOOK which provides technical guidelines on the transport of dangerous explosive substances and organic peroxides.

Recommended Research on LNG Safety. R & D Associates. National Technical Information Service, 5285 Port Royal Rd., Springfield, VA 22161. (703) 487-4650. 1981.

Record Retention Requirements in the CFRs. Superintendent of Documents, U.S. Government Printing Office, Washington, DC 20402. (202) 783-3238. Irregular. Covers federal regulations relating to public records.

Recoverable Materials and Energy from Industrial Waste Streams. Fran V. Kremer. American Water Works Association, 6666 W. Quincy Ave., Denver, CO 80235. (303) 794-7711. 1987.

Recreation Vehicle Industry Association. 1896 Preston White Dr., Reston, VA 22090. (703) 620-6003.

Recycler's Handbook: Everything You Need to Make Recycling a Part of Your Life. Earthworks Press, 1400 Shattuck Ave., No. 25, Berkeley, CA 94709. (510) 652-8533. 1990.

Recycling. HMSO, UNIPUB, 4611-F Assembly Dr., Lanham, MD 20706. (301) 459-7666 or (800) 274-4888. 1991. Provides guidance for devising and implementing statutory recycling strategies in Great Britain. Gives advice to waste collection authorities on recycling plant design and current ideology.

Recycling and Incineration: Evaluating Choices. Richard A. Denison and John Ruston. Island Press, 1718 Connecticut Ave. N.W., Suite 300, Washington, DC 20009. (202) 232-7933. 1990. Presents the technology, economics, environmental concerns, and legal intricacies behind these two approaches. Includes basics of waste reduction, recycling, and incineration; cost comparisons of the two approaches; an evaluation of the health and environmental impacts.

Recycling Centers Directory. American Business Directories, Inc., 5711 S. 86th Circle, Omaha, NE 68127. (402) 593-4600.

Recycling in America. Debi Kimball. ABC-CLIO, PO Box 1911, 130 Cremona Dr., Santa Barbara, CA 93116-1911. (805) 963-4221. 1992. Includes a history of the recycling movement, a chronology, and biographies of people in the field of recycling. Also contains descriptions of widely recycled materials.

Recycling Organic Wastes on the Land: A Bibliography. Diane E. Kirtz. Institute for Environmental Studies, University of Wisconsin, Madison, WI 53706. 1975.

Recycling Paper: From Fiber to Finished Product. Matthew J. Coleman. TAPPI Press, Technology Park/Atlanta, PO Box 105113, Atlanta, GA 30348. (404) 446-1400. 1991.

Recycling Solid Waste. Milou Carolan. International City Management Association, 777 N. Capital St., NE, Suite 500, Washington, DC 20002-4201. (800) 745-8780. 1989. Integrated approach to waste management, focussing on the components of a successful recycling program.

Recycling Sourcebook. Thomas J. Cichonski, Karen Hill. Gale Research Inc., 835 Penobscot Bldg., Detroit, MI 48226-4094. (313) 961-2242. 1992. Covers 3,000 U.S. recycling organizations, agencies, publications, etc.

Recycling Times. Recycling Times, 5616 W. Cermak Road, Cicero, IL 60650. (202) 861-0708. Biweekly. Covers major recycled commodities markets in the U.S.

Recycling Today. GIE Incorporated Publisher, 4012 Bridge Ave., Cleveland, OH 44113-3320. (216) 961-4130. Monthly. Covers recycling of secondary raw materials and solid waste management. Formerly, entitled Secondary Raw Materials.

Recycling Today–Equipment and Services Directory Issue. GIE Incorporated Publisher, 4012 Bridge Ave., Cleveland, OH 44113. (216) 961-4130.

Recycling Update. Illinois Department of Energy and Natural Resources, 325 W. Adams, Room 300, Springfield, IL 62704-9950. (217) 785-0310 or (800) 252-8955. Weekly. Features articles and announces the availability of publications, videos and fact sheets on recycling.

Redevelopment of Degraded Ecosystems. H. Regier, et al., eds. Parthenon Pub., Casterton Hall, Carnforth, England LA6 2LA. Lancs. 1991. Volume 8 in the "Man and the Biosphere" series published jointly with UNESCO.

Reducing Methane Emissions from Livestock. U.S. Environmental Protection Agency. U.S. G.P.O., Washington, DC 20401. (202) 512-0000. 1989.

Reference Directory to Asbestos Removal Contractors, Consultants and Laboratories. Rimbach Publishing, Inc., 8650 Babcock Blvd., Pittsburgh, PA 15237. (412) 364-5366.

Reference Directory to Hazardous, Toxic, and Superfund Services. Rimbach Publishing, Inc., 8650 Babcock Blvd., Pittsburgh, PA 15237. (412) 364-5366.

A Reference Guide to Clean Air. Cass Sandak. Carolina Biological Supply Company, 2700 York Rd., Burlington, NC 27215. (919) 584-0381. 1990. A collection of references and a glossary.

Reference Method for Source Testing. Environment Canada, WATDOC, Inland Waters Directorate, Ottawa, ON, Canada K1A 0H3. (819) 997-2324. 1991.

Refinery System Safety for Contractors: A Six Volume Set. Fluke & Associates, Inc. PennWell Books, PO Box 21288, Tulsa, OK 74121. (918) 831-9421; (800) 752-9764. 1991. Employee-training and documentation manuals that comply with the safety regulations of OSHA and insurance carriers.

Refining, Construction, Petrochemical & Natural Gas Processing Plants of the World. Midwest Register, Inc., 15 W. 6th St., Suite 1308, Tulsa, OK 74119-1501. (918) 582-2000.

Reforesting the Earth. Sandra Postel, Lori Heise. Worldwatch Institute, 1776 Massachusetts Ave., N.W., Washington, DC 20036-1904. 1988.

Reforming the Forest Service. Randal O'Toole. Island Press, 1718 Connecticut Ave. N.W., Suite 300, Washington, DC 20009. (202) 232-7933. 1988. Investigates possible economic inefficiencies and environmental consequences of the agency and proposes sweeping reforms to make the forest service more environmentally sensitive and efficient.

Refrigerating Engineers and Technicians Association. c/o Smith-Bucklin Associates, 401 N. Michigan Ave., Chicago, IL 60611. (312) 644-6610.

Regenerative Agriculture Association. 222 Main St., Emmaus, PA 18098. (215) 967-5171.

Region 8 Office. One Denver Place, 999 18th St., Suite 500, Denver, CO 80202. (303) 293-1603.

Regional Tide and Tidal Current Tables. U.S. G.P.O, Washington, DC 20402-9325. (202) 512-0000. Annual.

Register of Environmental Engineering Graduate Programs. W. R. Knocke and G. L. Amy. Association of Environmental Engineering Professors, c/o Prof. Bruce Rittman, University of Illinois, 3221 Newmark CE Laboratory, 208 N. Romine, Urbana, IL 61801. (217) 333-6964. 1989. Two volumes. Catalog of environmental engineering graduate programs in the United States and Canada. Includes a brief description of the program, university, tuition and fees, support mechanisms, and geographical location.

Registry of Toxic Effects of Chemical Substances. Doris V. Sweet, ed. U.S. Department of Health and Human Services, National Institute for Occupational Safety and Health, Washington, DC 20402-9325. (202) 783-3238. 1988. Contains information on over 35,000 chemicals.

Registry of Toxic Effects of Chemical Substances–Online1. US Department of Health and Human Services, National Institute for Occupational Safety and Health, Washington, DC 20402-9325. (202) 783-3238. Tests on chemical substances: Substance Identification, Toxicity/Biomedical Effects, Toxicology and Carcinogenicity Review, and Exposure Standards and Regulations.

Regulating Chlorofluorocarbon Emissions. Kathleen A. Wolf. RAND, 1700 Main St., Santa Monica, CA 90401. (310) 393-0411. 1980. Effects on chemical production.

Regulating the Environment: An Overview of Federal Environmental Laws. Neil Stoloff. Oceana Publications Inc., 75 Main St., Dobbs Ferry, NY 10522. (914) 693-8100. 1991. An overview of federal environmental laws.

Regulation of Agrochemicals: A Driving Force in Their Evolution. Gino J. Marco, et al., eds. American Chemical Society, 1155 16th St. N.W., Washington, DC 20036. (800) 227-5558. 1991. Agrochemicals and the regulatory process before 1970, subsequent regulations and their impact on pesticide chemistry.

Regulation of Pesticides: Science, Law and the Media. Government Institutes, Inc., 4 Research Pl., Ste. 200, Rockville, MD 20850. (301) 921-2300. Includes regulatory process, risk perception and risk communication, laboratory practices, and the weighing of risks and benefits.

Regulatory and Public Service Programs: Pesticide Registration. Director, 212 Barre Hall, Clemson University, Clemson, SC 29634-2775. (803) 656-3005.

Regulatory Management: A Guide to Conducting Environmental Affairs and Minimizing Liability. James T. Egan. Lewis Publishers, 2000 Corporate Blvd., Boca Raton, FL 33431. (800) 272-7737. 1991.

Regulatory Protection of Critical Transitional Areas Within Freshwater Wetlands Ecosystems. Curtis R. LaPierre. University of Illinois, Urbana-Champaign, IL 61801. 1990. Law and legislation relating to watershed management.

Reinforced Concrete Research Council. 205 N. Mathews Ave., Urbana, IL 61801. (217) 333-7384.

The Relative Role of Methane and Carbon Dioxide in the Greenhouse Effect: Final Report. Robert R. Gamache. American Gas Association, 1515 Wilson Blvd., Arlington, VA 22209. 1990.

Release Detection for Underground Storage Tank Piping System. Roy F. Weston Inc. Electric Power Research Institute, 3412 Hillview Ave., Palo Alto, CA 94304. (415) 965-4081. 1990. Discusses leak detection systems for suction and pressurized piping.

Release of Formaldehyde from Various Consumer Products. John A. Pickrell. Inhalation Toxicology Research Institute, Lovelace Biomedical and Environmental Research Institute, PO Box 5890, Albuquerque, NM 87185. (505) 845-1183. 1982. Environmental aspects of formaldehyde.

Reliability Engineering and Management Institute. 7340 N. La Oesta Ave., Tucson, AZ 85704. (602) 297-2679.

Remarkable Animals: A Unique Encyclopedia of Wildlife Wonders. Guinness Books, 33 London Rd., Enfield, England EN2 6DJ. Middlesex 1987. Includes mammals, birds, fishes, amphibians, reptiles, insects, and arachnids.

Remote Sensing Center. Rutgers University, Department of Environmental Resources, Cook College, PO Box 231, New Brunswick, NJ 08903. (908) 932-9631.

Remote Sensing of Biosphere Functioning. Springer-Verlag, 175 5th Ave., New York, NY 10010. (212) 460-1500. 1990. Ecological studies relating to biosphere sensing and biological aspects of remote sensing.

Remote Sensing of Natural Resources. Technology Application Center, University of New Mexico, Albuquerque, NM 87131.

Removal and Recovery of Metals and Phosphates from Municipal Sewage Sludge. Donald S. Scott. U.S. Environmental Protection Agency, Office of Research and Development, Municipal Environmental Research Laboratory, 26 W. Martin Luther King Dr., Cincinnati, OH 45268. (513) 569-7931. 1980.

Removal of Heavy Metals from Groundwaters. Robert W. Peters. Lewis Publishers, 2000 Corporate Blvd., N.W., Boca Raton, FL 33431. (407) 994-0555 or (800) 272-7737. 1991. Describes the sources of heavy metal contamination, classification of metals by industry, extent of the contamination problem, toxicity associated with various heavy metals, effects of heavy metals in biological wastewater treatment operations, leaching of heavy metals from sludges, modeling of heavy metals in the saturated and unsaturated zones, and other related areas.

Removal of Heavy Metals from Wastewaters. Stephen Beszedits. B and L Information Services, PO Box 458, Station L, Toronto, ON, Canada M6E 2W4. (416) 657-1197. 1980. Covers wastewater treatment, electrodialysis, heavy metals, ultrafication, ozonization, foam separation, and ion exchange process.

Removal of Soluble Manganese from Water by Oxide-Coated Filter Media. William R. Knocke. AWWA Research Foundation, 6666 W. Quincy Ave., Denver, CO 80235. (303) 794-7711. 1990. Covers water purification and manganese removal.

Rene Dubos Center for Human Environments. 100 E. 85th St., New York, NY 10028. (212) 249-7745.

Renew America. 17 16th Street, N. W., Suite 710, Washington, DC 20036. (202) 232-2252.

Renewable Energy: An International Journal. Pergamon Microforms International, Inc., Fairview Park, Elmsford, NY 10523. (914) 592-7720. 1991-. Six issues a year. Topics include environmental protection and renewable sources of energy.

Renewable Energy Bulletin. Multi-Science Publishing Co. Ltd., 107 High St., Brentwood, Essex, England CM14 4RX. 0277-224632. Six times a year.

Renewable Energy Info Center. c/o Mindsight Corp., Eight W. Janss Rd., Thousand Oaks, CA 91360-3325. (805) 388-3097.

Renewable Energy Sources. M. A. Laughton. Elsevier Science Publishing Co., 655 Avenue of the Americas, New York, NY 10010. (212) 984-5800. 1990.

Renewable Energy: Today's Contribution, Tomorrow's Promise. Cynthia Pollock Shea. Worldwatch Institute, 1776 Massachusetts Ave., N.W., Washington, DC 20036-1904. 1988.

Renewable Fuels Association. 201 Massachusetts Ave., N.E., Suite C-4, Washington, DC 20002. (202) 543-3802.

Renewable Natural Resources Foundation. 5430 Grosvenor Ln., Bethesda, MD 20814. (301) 493-9101.

Rensselaer Polytechnic Institute, Rensselaer Fresh Water Institute. MRC 203, Troy, NY 12181-3590. (518) 276-6757.

Reopening the Western Frontier. Ed Marston, ed. Island Press, 1718 Connecticut Ave. N.W., Suite 300, Washington, DC 20009. (202) 232-7933. 1989. Documents the changes and challenges that lie ahead as the West's natural resource economies–oil and gas, uranium, mining, and ranching–decline.

Replacing Gasoline: Alternative Fuels for Light-Duty Vehicles. Congress of the U.S., c/o U.S. Government Printing Office, Office of Technology Assesment, N. Capitol & H Sts. NW, Washington, DC 20401. (202) 512-0000. 1990. Gives information on alternatives to standard gasoline. Some of the alternatives are: electricity, hydrogen, compressed natural gas, liquified natural gas, liquid propane gas, methanol, ethanol, and reformulated gasoline.

The Report in the Medical Waste Policy Committee. Nelson A. Rockefeller Institute of Government, State University of New York, 411 State St., Albany, NY 12203-1003. (518) 443-5258. 1989. Waste disposal for health facilities and infectious wastes.

Report on Defense Plant Wastes. Business Publishers, Inc., 951 Pershing Dr., Silver Spring, MD 20910-4464. (301) 587-6300. 1989-. Biweekly. Reports on environmental laws, regulations, cleanups, contracts and court actions affecting U.S. defense weapons production, government hospitals and other government institutions. Also available online.

Report on Defense Plant Wastes. Business Publishers, Inc., 951 Pershing Dr., Silver Spring, MD 20910-4464. (301) 587-6300. Laws, regulations, cleanup actions, contracts, and court actions affecting U.S. defense, weapons production, government hospitals and laboratories, and other government institutions. Online version of periodical of the same name.

Report on Low-Level Radioactive Waste Management Progress. U.S. Dept. of Energy. Nuclear Energy Office. National Technical Information Service, 5285 Port Royal Road, Springfield, VA 22161. (703) 487-4650. Annual. Disposal of waste generated by nuclear power plants and non-utility sources by states.

Report on Renewable Energy and Utility Regulation. National Association of Regulatory Utility Commissioners, 1102 ICC Bldg., PO Box 684, Washington, DC 20044-0684. (202) 898-2200. 1990. Recently released NARUC report that addresses some key questions and makes some basic conclusions about potential of renewable energy resources.

Report on the Design and Operation of a Full-Scale Anaerobic Dairy Manure Digester: Final Report. Elizabeth Coppinger, et al. U.S. Department of Energy, Solar Energy Research Institute, 5285 Port Royal Rd., Springfield, VA 22161. (703) 487-4650. 1979.

Report on the Nation's Renewable Resources. U.S. Forest Service. U.S. G.P.O., Washington, DC 20401. (202) 512-0000. Quinquennial. Projections of resource use and supply from 1920 to 2040, covering wilderness, wildlife, fish, range, timber, water and minerals.

Report to Congress on Automotive Technology Development Program. U.S. Dept. of Energy. Conservation and Renewable Energy Office. National Technical Information Service, 5285 Port Royal Road, Springfield, VA 22161. (703) 487-4650. Annual. Programs for improved fuel economy and multi-fuel capability.

Report to the President and Congress on the Need for Leaded Gasoline on the Farm. U.S. Environmental Protection Agency, 401 M St., SW, Washington, DC 20460. (202) 260-2090. 1988. Environmental aspects of gasoline used in farm equipment.

Reproductive Ecology of Tropical Forest Plants. K. Bawa and M. Hadley, eds. Parthenon Pub., Casterton Hall, Carnforth, England LA6 2LA. 1990. Volume 7 in the "Man and the Biosphere" series jointly published with UNESCO.

Reproductively Active Chemicals: A Reference Guide. Richard J. Lewis, Sr. Van Nostrand Reinhold, 115 5th Ave., New York, NY 10003. (212) 254-3232. 1991. Provides the dose, species exposed, a brief characterization of the exposure conditions, and a reference to the source of the data.

REPRORISK System. Micromedex, Inc., 600 Grant St., Denver, CO 80203. (800) 525-9083 or (303) 831-1400. Reproductive risks to females and males caused by drugs, chemicals, and physical and environmental agents. Includes the Teratogen Information System (TERIS), which deals with the teratogenicity of over 700 drugs and environmental agents that affect a fetus. One of the additional modules under development is the REPROTEXT database, containing a ranking system for reproductive hazards and the general toxicity of over 600 chemicals, emphasizing chronic occupational exposures.

REPROTOX. Columbia Hospital for Women, Reproductive Toxicology Center, 2440 M St., N.W., Suite 217, Washington, DC 20037-1404. (202) 293-5137. Industrial and environmental chemicals and their effects on human fertility, pregnancy, and fetal development.

Research and Development. National Technical Information Service, 5285 Port Royal Rd., Springfield, VA 22161. (703) 487-4650. 1980. Environmental effects of dichlorethylene.

Research in Radiobiology. National Technical Information Service, 5285 Port Royal Rd., Springfield, VA 22161. (703) 487-4650. Annual. Annual report of work in progress in the Internal Irradiation Program.

Research Journal of the Water Pollution Control Federation. Water Pollution Control Federation, 601 Wythe St., Alexandria, VA 22314-1994. (800) 556-8700. Bimonthly. Covers area water pollution, sewage and sewage treatment.

Research Priorities for Conservation Biology. Michael E. Soulfe and Kathryn A. Kohm, eds. Island Press, 1718 Connecticut Ave. N.W., Suite 300, Washington, DC 20009. (202) 232-7933. 1989. Proposes an urgent research agenda to improve our understanding and preservation of biological diversity.

Research, Training, Test and Production Reactor Directory: United States of America. America Nuclear Society, 555 N. Kensington Ave., La Grange Park, IL 60525. (708) 352-6611.

Reserved Water Rights Settlement Manual. Peter W. Sly. Island Press, 1718 Connecticut Ave. N.W., Suite 300, Washington, DC 20009. (202) 232-7933. 1988. Manual provides a negotiating process for settling water disputes between states and/or reservations.

Reservoir Management for Water Quality and THM Precursor Control. George Dennis Cooke. American Water Works Association, 6666 W. Quincy Ave., Denver, CO 80235. (303) 794-7711. 1989. Water quality management and environmental effects of trihalomethanes.

Residential Water Conservation. U.S. Environmental Protection Agency, 401 M St., S.W., Washington, DC 20460. (202) 260-2090. 1980. Bibliography of water supply and water consumption

Residential Water Conservation: A Selected Research Bibliography. Marc J. Rogoff. Vance Bibliographies, PO Box 229, 112 N. Charter St., Monticello, IL 61856. (217) 762-3831. 1982.

Residential Water Purification. FIND/SVP, 625 Avenue of the Americas, New York, NY 10011. (212) 645-4500. Examines equipment sales, services and supplies, as well as renting and leasing.

Residual Deposits. Blackwell Scientific Publications, 3 Cambridge Ctr., Suite 208, Cambridge, MA 02142. (617) 225-0401. 1983. Surface related weathering processes.

Resource Accounting in Costa Rica. Wilfrido Cruz and Robert Repetto. World Resources Institute, 1709 New York Ave. N.W., Washington, DC 20006. (800) 822-0504. 1991.

Resource and Environmental Consequences of Population and Economic Growth. Ronald Gene Ridker. Resources for the Future, 1616 P St., NW, Washington, DC 20036. (202) 328-5086. 1979.

Resource and Environmental Effects of U.S. Agriculture. Resources for the Future, 1616 P St., NW, Washington, DC 20036. (202) 328-5086. 1982. Soil conservation and agricultural ecology.

Resource Conservation and Recovery Act Handbook. ERT, Marketing Dept., 696 Virginia Road, Concord, MA 01742. Law relating to hazardous wastes and waste sites.

Resource Conservation and Recovery Act Inspection Manual. U.S. Environmental Protection Agency. Government Institutes, Inc., 4 Research Pl., Ste. 200, Rockville, MD 20850. (301) 921-2300. 1989.

Resource Conservation Glossary. Soil and Water Conservation Society, 7515 Northeast Ankeny Rd., Ankeny, IA 50021. (515) 289-2331. 1982. Third edition. Includes 4,000 terms commonly used in resource management. Terms from 34 technologies are represented.

Resource Exchange and News. Waste Systems Institute of Michigan, 400 Ann, NW, Suite 204, Grand Rapids, MI 49503. (616) 363-3262. Bimonthly.

Resource Policy Institute. c/o Dr. Arthur H. Purcell, 1745 Selby, Ste. 11, Los Angeles, CA 90024. (213) 475-1684.

Resource Recovery Briefs. National Center for Resource Recovery Inc., 1211 Connecticut Ave., N.W., Washington, DC 20036. Monthly.

Resource Recovery Plant Cost Estimates: A Comparative Evaluation of Four Recent Dry-Shredding Designs. U.S. Environmental Protection Agency, 401 M St., S.W., Washington, DC 20460. (202) 260-2090. 1975.

Resource Recovery Report. Frank McManus, 5313 38th St. N.W., Washington, DC 20015. (202)362-3034. Monthly.

Resource Recycling. Resource Recycling, PO Box 10540, Portland, OR 97210. (503) 227-1319. 1989-. Seven times a year.

Resource Recycling–Equipment Guide Issue. Resource Recycling, Box 10540, Portland, OR 97210. (503) 227-1319.

Resources. Resources for the Future Inc., 1616 P St., NW, Washington, DC 20036. (202) 328-5000. 1959-. Three times a year.

Resources, Conservation and Recycling. Pergamon Microforms International, Inc., Fairview Park, Elmsford, NY 10523. (914) 592-7720. 1985-. Quarterly. Contains analyses and reviews of the interdisciplinary aspects of renewable and nonrenewable resource management, particularly their conservation.

Resources for Organic Pest Control. Rodale Press, 33 E. Minor St., Emmaus, PA 18098. (215) 967-5171. Biennial.

Resources for the Future, Inc. 1616 P St., N.W., Washington, DC 20036. (202) 328-5000.

Resources for the Future, Inc. Energy and Natural Resources Division. 1616 P Street, N.W., Washington, DC 20036. (202) 328-5000.

Resources for the Future, Inc., Quality of the Environment Division. 1616 P Street, N.W., Washington, DC 20036. (202) 328-5000.

Respiratory Health Association. 55 Paramus Rd., Paramus, NJ 07652. (201) 843-4111.

Respiratory Protection: A Manual and Guideline. American Industrial Hygiene Association, 345 White Pond Dr., PO Box 8390, Akron, OH 44320. (216) 873-2442. 1991. 2d ed. Provides practical guidelines for establishing and managing respiratory protection programs. Presents guidelines for establishing chemical cartridge field service life policies and audit criteria for evaluating respiratory protection programs. Contains validated qualitative life-testing protocols, new equipment for quantitative respiratory protection, and information on use and testing of supplied-air suits.

Response Manual for Combatting Spills of Floating Hazardous CHRIS Chemicals. National Technical Information Service, 5285 Port Royal Rd., Springfield, VA 22161. (703) 487-4650. Covers chemical spills, hazardous substance accidents, and marine pollution.

Response of Marine Animals to Petroleum and Specific Petroleum Hydrocarbons. Jerry M. Neff. John Wiley & Sons, Inc., 605 3rd Ave., New York, NY 10158-0012. (212) 850-6000. 1981. Effect of water and oil pollution on marine fauna.

Responses of Plants to Environmental Stresses. J. Levitt. Academic Press, c/o Harcourt Brace Jovanovich Inc., 6277 Sea Harbor Dr., Orlando, FL 32887. (800) 346-8648. 1980. 2nd ed. Volume 1 covers chilling, freezing and high temperature. Volume 2 contains water, radiation, salt, and other stresses.

Restoration of Petroleum-Contaminated Aquifers. Stephen M. Testa and Duane L. Winegardner. Lewis Publishers, 200 Corporate Blvd. NW, Boca Raton, FL 33431. (407) 994-0555 or (800)272-7737. 1991. Presents information on restoring aquifers contaminated by petroleum products and derivatives. Discusses the regulatory environment and framework within which environmental issues are addressed and explains the geochemistry of petroleum.

Restoring Acid Waters. G. Howells. Elsevier Science Publishing Co., 655 Avenue of the Americas, New York, NY 10010. (212) 984-5800. 1992. Detailed and comprehensive accounts of pre-liming conditions, liming techniques employed, post-liming changes in water quality and fish restoration.

A Retrospective Bibliography of American Demographic History from Colonial Times to 1983. David R. Gerhan and Robert V. Wells. Greenwood Publishing Group, Inc., 88 Post Rd. W., Box 5007, Westport, CT 06881. (203) 226-3571. 1989.

Returnable Times. Environmental Action Foundation, 6930 Carroll Ave., Ste. 600, Takoma Park, MD 20912. (301) 891-1100. Quarterly.

Reuse/Recycle. Technomic Publishing Co., 851 New Holland Ave., Box 3535, Lancaster, PA 17604. (717) 291-5609. 1970-. Monthly. Monthly newsletter of resource recycling reports on new technology, uses and markets for recycled materials, advances in recycling plants and equipment, and the changing infrastructure of the plastics recycling industry.

Reverse Osmosis Technical Manual. U.S. Department of the Interior, Office of Water Research and Technology, 1849 C St. NW, Washington, DC 20240. (202) 208-3171. 1979.

Reverse Osmosis Technology. Bipin S. Parekh. Marcel Dekker, Inc., 270 Madison Ave., New York, NY 10016. (212) 696-9000; (800) 228-1160. 1988. Applications for high-purity-water production.

Reverse Osmosis Treatment of Drinking Water. Talbert N. Eisenberg. Butterworth-Heinemann, 80 Montvale Ave., Stoneham, MA 02180. (617) 438-8464. 1986.

Review and Evaluation of Urban Flood Flow Frequency. U.S. Department of the Interior, 1849 C St. NW, Washington, DC 20240. (202) 208-3171. 1980. Covers flood forecasting, flood routing and urban runoff.

Review of Agricultural Entomology. C. A. B. International, 845 North Park Ave., Tucson, AZ 85719. (602) 621-7897 or (800) 528-4841. 1990. Monthly. Abstracts of the world literature on: insects and other arthropods as pests of cultivated plants, forest trees and stored products, beneficial arthropods such as parasites and predators, slugs and snails as agricultural pests.

Review of Applied Mycology. Commonwealth Mycological Institute, Ferry Ln., Kew, Richmond, England TW9 3AF. Surrey 1969. Covers plant diseases and pathology, specifically phytopathogenic fungi.

Review of Literature on Herbicides. U.S. Veterans Health Services and Research Administration. U.S. G.P.O., Washington, DC 20401. (202) 512-0000. Annual. Health effects of agent orange, phenoxy herbicides and other dioxins.

Review of Literature Related to Engineering Aspects of Grain Dust Explosions. David F. Aldis. U.S. Department of Agriculture, Science and Education Administration, 14 Independence Ave., S.W., Washington, DC 20250. (202) 447-7454. 1979. Fires and fire prevention in grain elevators.

Review of National Emission Standards for Mercury. National Technical Information Service, 5285 Port Royal Rd., Springfield, VA 22161. (703) 487-4650. 1987.

A Review of Radiation Exposure Estimates from Normal Operations in the Management and Disposal of High-Level Radioactive Waste and Spent Nuclear Fuel. William F. Holcomb. U.S. Environmental Protection Agency, 401 M St., S.W, Washington, DC 20460. (202) 260-2090. 1980.

A Review of Thermal Plume Modeling. Lorin R. Davis. U.S. Environmental Protection Agency, Corvallis Environmental Research Laboratory, Office of Research and Development, 200 SW 35th St., Corvallis, OR 97333. (503) 754-4600. 1978. Environmental implications of electric power plants and thermal pollution of rivers and lakes.

Reviews of Environmental Contamination and Toxicology: v. 120. George W. Ware, ed. Springer-Verlag, 175 5th Ave., New York, NY 10010. (212) 460-1500; (800) 777-4643. 1991. Covers organochlorine pesticides and polychlorinated biphenyls in human adipose tissue, pesticide residues in foods imported into the U.S., and selected trace elements and the use of biomonitors in subtropical and tropical marine ecosystems.

The Revised Hazard Ranking System: Os and As. U.S. Environmental Protection Agency, Office of Solid Waste and Emergency Response, 401 M St. SW, Washington, DC 20460. (202) 260-2090. 1990.

Reynolds Homestead Agricultural Experiment Station. Virginia Polytech Institute and State University, PO Box 70, Critz, VA 24082. (703) 694-4135.

Rhode Island Environmental Law Handbook. Government Institutes, Inc., 4 Research Pl., Ste. 200, Rockville, MD 20820. (301) 921-2300. 1991.

Rhode Island Sea Grant Marine Advisory Service. Narragansett Bay Campus, University of Rhode Island, Narragansett, RI 02882. (401) 792-6211.

Riegel's Handbook of Industrial Chemistry. James A. Kent, ed. Van Nostrand Reinhold, 115 5th Ave., New York, NY 10020. (212) 254-3232. 1983. Eighth edition. Includes industries such as: wastewater technology, coal technology, phosphate fertilizers, synthetic plastics, man-made textiles, detergents, sugar, animal and vegetable oils, chemical explosives, dyes, nuclear industry, and much more.

The Rights Livelihood Awards Foundation. P.O. Box 15072, S-10465, Stockholm, Sweden (08) 702 03 04.

Riparian and Wetland Classification Review. Karl Gebhardt. U.S. Department of the Interior, Bureau of Land Management, 2850 Youngfield St., Lakewood, CO 80215. (303) 239-3700. 1990.

RISI Forest Products. Resource Information Systems, 110 Great Rd., Bedford, MA 01730. (617) 271-0030.

The Rising Tide: Global Warming and World Sea Levels. Lynne T. Edgerton. Island Press, 1718 Connecticut Ave. N.W., Suite 300, Washington, DC 20009. (202) 232-7933. 1991. Analysis of global warming and rising world sea level. Outlines state, national and international actions to respond to the effects of global warming on coastal communities and ecosystems.

Risk Assessment for Hazardous Installations. J. C. Chicken. Pergamon Microforms International, Inc., Fairview Park, Elmsford, NY 10523. (914) 592-7720. 1986.

Risk Assessment for the Chemical Process Industries. Stone & Webster Engineering Corp. Global Professional Publications, 2805 McGraw Ave., PO Box 19539, Irvine, CA 92713-9539. (800) 854-7179. 1991. Covers the performance and supervision of safety studies for chemical, petrochemical, and other process industries. Also includes hazard identification and assessment embraces methods for both detecting hazards and determining root causes.

Risk Assessment Guidelines and Information Directory. Government Institutes, Inc., 4 Research Pl., Ste. 200, Rockville, MD 20850. (301) 921-2300. Contains both EPA guidance on the conduct of EPA risk assessments, as well as information on EPA and non-EPA databases, environmental and dose response models, manuals, directories, and periodicals applicable to each element of risk assessment.

Risk Assessment in Genetic Engineering; Environmental Release of Organisms. Morris A. Levin and Harlee Strauss. McGraw-Hill, 1221 Avenue of the Americas, New York, NY 10020. (212) 512-2000; (800) 262-4729. 1991. Investigates issues such as the transport of microorganisms via air, water, and soil; the persistence and establishment of viruses, bacteria, and plants; and the genetic transfer via viruses.

Risk Assessment of Chemicals in the Environment. M. L. Richardson, ed. Royal Society of Chemistry, c/o CRC Press, 2000 Corporate Blvd. N.W., Boca Raton, FL 33431-9868. (800) 272-7737. 1990. Covers both chemical and radioactive risk acceptance approaches to the control of chemical disasters, etc.

Risk Assessment of Groundwater Pollution Control. William F. McTernan and Edward Kaplan, eds. American Society of Civil Engineers, 345 E. 47th St., New York, NY 10017. (212) 705-7288; (800) 548-2723. 1990.

Risk Factors for Cancer in the Workplace. Jack Siemia Tycki. CRC Press, 2000 Corporate Blvd., N.W., Boca Raton, FL 33431. (407) 994-0555 or (800) 272-7737. 1991. Describes occupational risks from contamination and precautions.

RISKLINE. Swedish National Chemicals Inspectorate, P.O. Box 1384, Solna, Sweden 171 27. 46 (8) 7305700.

River Conservation Directory. National Association for State River Conservation Programs, 801 Pennsylvania Ave., SE, Suite 302, Washington, DC 20003. (202) 543-2862. Biennial.

The River of the Mother of God and Other Essays. Aldo Leopold. University of Wisconsin Press, 114 N. Murray St., Madison, WI 53715. (608) 262-8782. 1991. Brings together 60 of Leopold's previously unpublished or illusive essays.

River Pollution: An Ecological Perspective. S. M. Haslam. Belhaven Press, 136 S. Broadway, Irvington, NY 10533. (914) 591-9111. 1990. Describes the impact of natural and man-made pollution in the ecosystem of freshwater streams, stressing understanding of processes and techniques of measurement.

River Protection in Montana: A Review of State Laws, Policies and Rules. Montana Department of Fish, Wildlife and Parks, 1420 E. 6th Ave., Helena, MT 59620. (406)444-2535. 1990.

Rivers and Lakes Protection Program. Office of State Planning, 2 1/2 Beacon St., Concord, CT 03301. (603)271-2155. 1988.

Rivers at Risk: The Concerned Citizen's Guide to Hydropower. John D. Echeverria. Island Press, 1718 Connecticut Ave., NW, Suite 300, Washington, DC 20009. (202) 232-7933. 1989. Offers practical understanding of how to influence government decisions about hydropower development on the nation's rivers.

Rivers, Ponds, and Lakes. Anita Ganeri. Dillon Press, Inc., 242 Portland Ave., S., Minneapolis, MN 55415. (612) 333-2691. 1992. A guide to pond, river, and lake pollution globally and conservation of indigenous endangered species.

Roads and Trails Study and Environmental Assessment. National Park Service. U.S. Department of the Interior, 1849 C St., NW, Washington, DC 20240. (202) 208-3171. 1991. Wild and scenic rivers and outdoor recreation.

Robert J. Bernard Biological Field Station. Claremont McKenna College, Claremont, CA 91711. (714) 621-5425.

Rockefeller University. 1230 York Ave., New York, NY 10021-6399. (212) 570-7661.

Rockefeller University, Field Research Center for Ecology and Ethology. Tyrrel Road, Millbrook, NY 12545. (212) 570-8628.

Rockefeller University, Laboratory of Biochemistry and Molecular Biology. 1230 York Avenue, New York, NY 10021-6399. (212) 570-8000.

Rockefeller University, Laboratory of Biophysics. 1230 York Avenue, New York, NY 10021-6399. (212) 570-8000.

Rockefeller University, Laboratory of Cell Biology. 1230 York Avenue, New York, NY 10021-6399. (212) 570-8770.

Rockefeller University, Laboratory of Genetics. 1230 York Avenue, New York, NY 10021-6399. (212) 570-8644.

Rockefeller University, Laboratory of Microbiology. 1230 York Avenue, New York, NY 10021-6399. (212) 570-8277.

Rockefeller University, Laboratory of Molecular Cell Biology. 1230 York Ave., New York, NY 10021-6399. (212) 570-8791.

Rockefeller University, Laboratory of Molecular Parasitology. 1230 York Ave., New York, NY 10021-6399. (212) 570-7571.

Rockefeller University, Laboratory of Neurobiology and Behavior. 1230 York Ave., New York, NY 10021-6399. (212) 570-8666.

Rockefeller University, Laboratory of Organic Chemistry and Physical Biochemistry. 1230 York Ave, New York, NY 10021-6399. (212) 570-8264.

Rockefeller University, Laboratory of Plant Biochemistry. 1230 York Ave, New York, NY 10021-6399. (212) 570-8000.

Rockefeller University, Laboratory of Plant Molecular Biology. 1230 York Ave, Box 301, New York, NY 10021-6399. (212) 570-8126.

Rocky Mountain Institute. 1739 Snowmass Creek Rd, Snowmass, CO 81654. (303) 927-3128.

Rodale's Environmental Action Bulletin. Rodale Press, 33 E. Minor St., Emmaus, PA 18098. (215) 967-5171. 1970-. Semimonthly.

Rodent Control in Agriculture. J. H. Greaves. Food and Agriculture Organization of the United Nations, Via delle Terme di Caracalla, Rome, Italy 00100. 61 0181-FA01. 1982. A handbook on the biology and control of commensal rodents as agricultural pests.

The Rodent Handbook. Austin M. Frishman. Frishman, Farmingdale, NY 1974. Questions and answers on rats, mice, and other pest vertebrae.

The Role of Calcium in Biological Systems. CRC Press, 2000 Corporate Blvd. N.W., Boca Raton, FL 33431. (800) 272-7737. 1982-.

The Role of Calcium in Drug Action. Pergamon Microforms International Inc., Fairview Park, Elmsford, NY 10523. (914) 592-7720. 1987. Calcium, agonists and their therapeutic use.

Role of Environment Factors. R. P. Pharis, et al. Springer-Verlag, 175 5th Ave., New York, NY 10010. (212) 460-1500 or (800) 777-4643. 1985. Encyclopedia of plant physiology.

The Role of Environmental Impact Assessment in the Planning Process. M. Clark and J. Herington, eds. Cassell PLC, Publishers Distribution Center, PO Box C831, Rutherford, NJ 07070. (201) 939-6064; (201) 939-6065. 1988.

The Role of Fire in the Ecosystems of Forests and Grasslands. Glenna Dunning. Vance Bibliographies, PO Box 229, 112 N. Charter St., Monticello, IL 61856. (217) 762-3831. 1990.

The Role of Ground Beetles in Ecological and Environmental Studies. Nigel E. Stork. Intercept, PO Box 716, Andover, England SP10 1YG. Ecology of carabidae and beetles.

The Role of Land/Inland Water Ecotones in Landscape Management and Restoration. Robert J. Naiman, et al, eds. UNESCO, 7, place de Fontenoy, Paris, France F-75700. (331) 45 68 40 67. 1989. MAB Digest 4. This is a proposal for collaborative research dealing with land management and restoration.

The Role of Surfactants in U.S., W. European & Japanese Household/Personal Care Market. FIND/SVP, 625 Avenue of the Americas, New York, NY 10011. (212) 645-4500. 1991.

The Roles of Gypsum in Agriculture. Adolph Mehlich. United States Gypsum, Chemicals Division, 101 S. Wacker Dr., Chicago, IL 60606. (312) 606-4000. 1974. Effect of gypsum, fertilizers and manures on plants.

The Room Deodorizer Market. FIND/SVP, 625 Avenue of the Americas, New York, NY 10011. (212) 645-4500. 1991. Retail market for room deodorizers, primarily air fresheners and carpet deodorizers, but also toilet bowl deodorizers.

Room to Grow. Diana Stevenson. Office of Planning and Research, 1400 10th St., Sacramento, CA 95814. (916)322-2318. 1983. Issues in agricultural land conservation and conversion.

Rose Lake Wildlife Research Center. Michigan Department of Natural Resources, Wildlife Division, 8562 East Stoll Road, East Lansing, MI 48823. (517) 373-9358.

Roster of State Dam Safety Officials Contacts. Association of State Dam Safety Officials, P.O. Box 55270, Lexington, KY 40555. (606) 257-5140.

Rubber Red Book. Communication Channels, 6255 Barfield Rd., Atlanta, GA 30328. (404) 256-9800.

Rubber World. Lippincott & Peto, Inc., 1867 W. Market St., Akron, OH 44313. (216) 864-2122. Monthly. Tire, hose, carbon black, and other major rubber and rubber chemical industry sectors.

Rubber World Blue Book: Materials, Compounding Ingredients and Machinery for Rubber. Lippincott & Peto, Inc., 1867 W. Market St., Akron, OH 44313. (216) 864-2122.

Rubber World–Custom Mixers Directory Issue. Lippincott and Peto, Inc., 1867 W. Market St., Akron, OH 44313. (216) 864-2122.

Rubber World–Machinery Suppliers Issue. Lippincott & Peto, Inc., 1867 W. Market St., Akron, OH 44313. (216) 864-2122.

Rules and Regulations, Department of Environmental Quality, Land Quality Division, State of Wyoming. Dept. of Environmental Quality, 122 W. 25th St., Hersler Bldg., 3rd Fl., Cheyenne, WY 82002. (307) 777-7756. 1989.

Rural Advancement Fund International (*RAFI-USA*). P.O. Box 655, Pittsboro, NC 27312. (919) 542-1396.

Rural Environment Planning for Sustainable Communities. Frederic O. Sargent, et al. Island Press, 1718 Connecticut Ave. N.W., Ste. 300, Washington, DC 20009. (202) 232-7933. 1991.

Rural Water Supply and Sanitation: Time for a Change. Anthony A. Churchill. World Bank, 1818 H. St., N.W., 20433. (202) 477-1234. 1987. Rural water supplies in developing countries.

Rush to Burn: Solving America's Garbage Crisis?. Island Press, 1718 Connecticut Ave. N.W., Suite 300, Washington, DC 20009. (202) 232-7933. 1989. Describes incineration, refuse and refuse disposal.

Rutgers University, Center for Agricultural Molecular Biology. Cook College, P.O. Box 231, New Brunswick, NJ 08903. (908) 932-8165.

Rutgers University, Center for Coastal and Environmental Studies. 104 Doolittle Building, Busch Campus, New Brunswick, NJ 08903. (201) 932-3738.

Rutgers University, Fisheries and Aquaculture Technology Extension Center. P.O. Box 231, New Brunswick, NJ 08903. (908) 932-8959.

Rutgers University, Little Egg Inlet Marine Field Station. Great Bay Blvd., PO Box 278, Tuckerton, NJ 08087. (609) 296-5260.

Rutgers University, Mosquito Research and Control. P.O. Box 231, New Jersey Agricultural Experiment Station, New Brunswick, NJ 08903. (908) 932-9437.

Rutgers University, Rutgers Shellfish Research Laboratory. P.O. Box 06230, Port North Norris, NJ 08349. (609) 785-0074.

Rutgers University, Waksman Institute. P.O. Box 759, Piscataway, NJ 08855. (908) 932-4257.

Ruthenium: Its Behavior in Plant and Soil Systems. K. W. Brown. National Technical Information Service, 5285 Port Royal Rd., Springfield, VA 22161. (703) 487-4650. 1976. Effect of radioactive pollution on plants and radioactive substances in soils.

The Sadtler Standard Gas Chromatography Retention Index Library. Sadtler Research Laboratories, 3316 Spring Garden St., Philadelphia, PA 19104. (215) 382-7800. 1986. Annual.

SAE. 400 Commonwealth Dr., Warrendale, PA 15096-0001. (412) 776-4841.

Safari Club International. 4800 W. Gates Pass Rd., Tucson, AZ 85745. (602) 620-1220.

The Safe and Effective Use of Pesticides. Patrick J. Marer, et al. University of California Statewide Integrated Pest Management Project, Division of Agriculture and Natural Resources, Dist: Thomson Pub., PO Box 9335, Fresno, CA 93791, Oakland, CA (209) 435-2163. 1988. Includes general information on pesticides, chemical pest control, and other pest management methods. Can be used as a study guide for the pest applicator test.

Safe Disposal of Hazardous Wastes. Roger Batstone, ed. The World Bank, 1818 H. St. N.W., Washington, DC 20433. 1990. Describes the special needs and problem of the management of hazardous wastes in developing countries.

Safe Energy Communication Council. 1717 Massachusetts Ave., N.W., LL215, Washington, DC 20036. (202) 483-8491.

Safe Food Handling. Michael Jacob. World Health Organization, Ave. Appia, Geneva, Switzerland CH-1211. 1989. A training guide for managers of food service establishments.

Safe Handling of Chemical Carcinogens, Mutagens, and Highly Toxic Substances. Douglas B. Walters, ed. Ann Arbor Science, 230 Collingwood, Ann Arbor, MI 48106. 1980-. Prevention and control of occupational accidents.

Safe Water Coalition. 150 Woodland Ave., San Anselmo, CA 94960. (415) 453-0158.

Safeguarding the Land: Women at Work in Parks, Forests, and Rangelands. Harcourt Brace Jovanovich, Inc., 1250 6th Ave., San Diego, CA 92101. (800) 346-8648. 1981.

Safer Insecticides: Development and Use. Marcel Dekker, Inc., 270 Madison Ave., New York, NY 10016. (212) 696-9000; (800) 228-1160. 1990. Communicates practical data for designing new insecticides, nontoxic to the environment and the public, and emphasizes optimal food production with safer insecticides.

Safety and Health for Engineers. Roger L. Brauer. Global Professional Publications, 2805 McGraw Ave., PO Box 19539, Irvine, CA 92713-9539. (800) 854-7179. 1990. Discusses the ethical, technical, legal, social and economic considerations involving safety and health in engineering planning and practice.

Safety & Health–Safety Equipment Buyers' Guide Issue. National Safety Council, 444 N. Michigan Ave., Chicago, IL 60611. (312) 527-4800.

Safety and Health Standards Applicable to Underground Metal and Nonmetal Mining and Milling Operations. U.S. G.P.O., Washington, DC 20401. (202) 512-0000. 1985. Mine safety law and legislation in the United States.

Safety Equipment Distributors Association–Membership Roster. Safety Equipment Distributors Association, c/o Smith, Bucklin & Associates, Inc., 111 E. Wacker Dr., Chicago, IL 60601. (312) 644-6610.

Safety in the Process Industries. Butterworth-Heinemann, 80 Montvale Ave., Stoneham, MA 02180. (617) 438-8464. 1990. Hazards of process plants, and causes of accidents and how they may be controlled.

Safety in the Use of Asbestos. International Labour Office, 49 Sheridan Ave., Albany, NY 12210. (518) 436-9686. 1990. An ILO code of practice. The first part of the code includes monitoring in the work place, preventive measures, the protection and supervision of the workers' health, and the packaging, handling, transport and disposal of asbestos waste. More detailed guidance on the limitation of exposure to asbestos in specific activities is given in the second part of the code, which includes sections on mining and milling, asbestos cement, textiles, friction materials, and the removal of asbestos-containing materials.

Safety in the Use of Mineral and Synthetic Fibers. International Labour Office, 49 Sheridan Ave., Albany, NY 12210. (518) 436-9686. 1990. Working document for, and report of, a meeting of experts set up by the ILO to study the questions contained in this book, including discussions of man-made fibers, natural mineral fibers other than asbestos, and synthetic organic fibers. The meeting defined certain preventive measures based on adopting safe working methods, controlling the working environment and the exposure of workers to mineral and synthetic fibers, and monitoring the health of the workers.

Saline Water Processing: Desalination and Treatment of Seawater, Brackish Water, and Industrial Waste Water. Hans-Gunter Heitmann, ed. VCH Publishers, 303 NW 12th Ave., Deerfield Beach, FL 33442-1788. (305) 428-5566. 1990. Desalination and treatment of seawater, brackish water, and industrial waste water.

The Salmonella Investigation. Lee Daniels. Illinois. House Republican Committee, Illinois Secretary's State's Office, Springfield, IL 1985. An agenda for governmental action to combat salmonella incidents.

Salmonellas in Laboratory Animals. Kevin Engler. National Agricultural Library, 10301 Baltimore Blvd., Beltsville, MD 20705-2351. (301) 504-5755. 1988.

Salt and the Environment. Salt Institute, 206 North Washington St., Alexandria, VA 23314.

Salt, Evaporites, and Brines: An Annotated Bibliography. Vivian S. Hall and Mary R. Spencer. Oryx Press, 4041 N. Central Ave., #700, Phoenix, AZ 85012. (602) 265-2651; (800) 279-6799. 1984.

The Salt Storage Handbook. The Salt Institute, Fairfax Plaza, Ste. 600, 700 N. Fairfax, Alexandria, VA 22314. (703) 549-4648. 1987. A practical guide for storing and handling de-icing salt.

Saltmarsh Ecology. Paul Adam. Cambridge University Press, 40 W. 20th St., New York, NY 10011. (212) 924-3900. 1991. Flora, fauna, vegetation, how saltmarsh biota copes with this stressful environment, life history studies, marshes as ecosystems.

Sampling and Analysis of Wastes Generated by Gray Iron Foundries. W.F. Beckert. Center for Environmental Research Information, U.S. Environmental Protection Agency, 26 W. Martin Luther King Dr., Cincinnati, OH 45268. (513) 569-7931. 1981.

San Diego State University, Center for Marine Studies. San Diego, CA 92182. (619) 594-6523.

San Diego State University, Systems Ecology Research Group. San Diego, CA 92182. (619) 594-5976.

Sand Dune Ecology and Formation. Jan Gumprecht. Educational Images Ltd., PO Box 3456, Elmira, NY 14905. (607) 732-1090. 1986. Filmstrip describing the animate and inanimate composition of sand dunes.

Sanitary Engineering and Environmental Health Research Laboratory. University of California, Berkeley, 1301 South 46th, Building 112, Richmond, CA 94804. (415) 231-9449.

Sanitation Compliance and Enforcement Ratings of Interstate Milk Shippers. Milk Safety Branch/Food and Drug Administration, Department of Health and Human Services, Washington, DC 20204. (208) 485-0175. 1974.

Sanitation Safety & Environmental Standards. Lewis J. Minor. AVI Pub. Co., 250 Post Rd., PO Box 831, Westport, CT 06881. 1983. Environmental aspects of food industry and trade.

SARA Title III: Intent and Implementation of Hazardous Materials Regulations. Frank L. Fire and Nancy K. Grant. PennWell Books, PO Box 21288, Tulsa, OK 74121. (918) 831-9421; (800) 752-9764. 1990. Addresses what is required for implementation of hazardous materials regulations.

Saskatchewan Fisheries Laboratory. Saskatchewan Parks and Renewable Resources, 112 Research Drive, Saskatoon, SK, Canada S7K 2H6. (306) 933-5776.

The Satellite as Microscope. R. S. Scorer. E. Horwood, 66 Wood Lane End, Hemel Hempstead, England HP2 4RG. 1990. Describes the use of artificial satellites in air pollution control.

Satellite Surveying. Gregory J. Hoar. Magnavox Advanced Products & Systems Co., 2529 Maricopa St., Torrance, CA 90503. (310) 618-1200. 1982. Theory, geodesy, map projections, applications, equipment and operations.

SATIVA Opportunities Directory. Society for Agricultural Training through Integrated Voluntary Activities, Route 2, Viola, WI 54664. (608) 625-2217. Annual. Training programs and work opportunities in organic farming and homesteading.

Save a Landfill: Compost Instead of Bag. Illinois Environmental Protection Agency, 2200 Churchill Rd., PO Box 19276, Springfield, IL 62794-9276. (217) 782-2829. 1990. Compost and waste recycling.

Save L.A.: An Environmental Resource Directory: The Thinking and Caring Person's Directory of Environmental Products, Services, and Resources for the Los Angeles Area. Tricia R. Hoffman and Nan Kathryn Fuchs. Chronicle Books, 275 5th St., San Francisco, CA 94103. (415) 777-7240; (800) 722-6657. 1990. This comprehensive guidebook opens with a brief overview of the most pressing ecological issues peculiar to the Los Angeles area and then goes on to provide a list of some 1000 resources targeted for the environmental challenges the city Angelenos faces.

Save Oregon: An Environmental Resource Directory. Chronicle Books, 275 5th Ave., San Francisco, CA 94103. (415) 777-7240. 1991.

Save Our Planet: 750 Everyday Ways You Can Help Clean Up the Earth. Diane MacEachern. Dell Pub., 666 5th Ave., New York, NY 10103. (212) 765-6500; (800) 255-4133. 1990. Practical guide to ways in which everyone can help clean up the earth.

Save Our Shores. PO Box 103, North Quincy, MA 02171. (508) 888-4694.

Save the Bay. 434 Smith St., Providence, RI 02908. (401) 272-3540.

Save the Dunes Council. PO Box 114, Beverly Shores, IN 46301. (219) 879-3937.

Save the Redwoods League. 114 Sansome St., Rm. 605, San Francisco, CA 94104. (415) 362-2352.

Save the Tall Grass Prairie, Inc. PO Box 557, Topeka, KS 66601. (913) 357-4681.

Saving America's Countryside: A Guide to Rural Conservation. Samuel N. Stokes. Johns Hopkins University Press, 701 W. 40th St., Suite 275, Baltimore, MD 21211. (410) 516-6900. 1989.

Saving America's Wildlife. Thomas R. Dunlap. Princeton University Press, 41 Williams St., Princeton, NJ 08540. (609) 258-4900. 1988. Explores how we have deepened our commitment to and broadened the scope of animal conservation through the 1980s.

Saving the Earth: A Citizen's Guide to Environmental Action. Will Steger. Knopf, 201 E. 50th St., New York, NY 10022. (301) 848-1900; (800) 733-3000. 1990. Describes the causes and effects of the major environmental threats, and offers practical solutions. A complete resource guide, providing specific information to aid individuals and organizations wanting to take action.

Saving the Mediterranean: The Politics of International Environmental Cooperation. Peter M. Haas. Columbia University Press, 562 W. 113th St., New York, NY 10025. (212) 316-7100. 1990. Focuses on the international pollution management of the Mediterranean. Ninety scientists and international officials were interviewed to ascertain how the international community responded to this particular threat.

Saving the Tropical Forests. Judith Gradwohl and Russell Greenberg. Island Press, 1718 Connecticut Ave. N.W., Suite 300, Washington, DC 20009. (202) 232-7933. 1988. Sourcebook about the causes and effects of tropical deforestation, with case studies, examples of sustainable agriculture and forestry, and a section on the restoration of tropical rain forests.

Scenic America. 216 Seventh St., S.E., Washington, DC 20003. (202) 546-1100.

School for Field Studies. 16 Broadway, Box S, Beverly, MA 01915. (508) 927-7777.

Science Citation Index. Institute for Scientific Information, 3501 Market St., Philadelphia, PA 19104. 1961-.

The Science of Food. P. Gaman. Pergamon Microforms International, Inc., Fairview Park, Elmsford, NY 10523. (914) 592-7720. 1977. An introduction to food science, nutrition, and microbiology.

The Science of Food. Marion Bennion. John Wiley & Sons, Inc., 605 3rd Ave., New York, NY 10158-0012. (800) 225-5945. 1980.

A Science of Impurity: Water Analysis in Nineteenth Century Britain. Christopher Hamlin. University of California Press, Berkeley, CA 94720. (510) 642-4247. 1990. Presents a series of biographies of scientists and government officials responsible for London's water quality during a period of pressing need and sparse scientific knowledge. Also presents some chemical information, placing chemical and epidemiological concepts in perspective, which is needed to grasp the inconsistencies of water analysis in 19th-century Britain.

Scientific Basis for Nuclear Waste Management XII. Werner Lutze, ed. Materials Research Society, 9800 McKnight Rd., Pittsburgh, PA 15237. (412) 367-3003. 1989. Symposium held in Berlin Germany October 1988. Volume 127 of the Materials Research society Symposium Proceedings.

Scientists' Institute for Public Information. 355 Lexington Ave., New York, NY 10017. (212) 661-9110.

SCISEARCH. Institute for Scientific Information, University City Science Center, 3501 Market St., Philadelphia, PA 19104. (215) 386-0100.

Scrap Age. Three Sons Pub. Co., 6311 Gross Point Rd., Niles, IL 60648. Monthly.

Scrap Processing and Recycling. Institute of Scrap Recycling Industries, 1627 K Street, NW, Washington, DC 20006. (202) 466-4050. Bimonthly. Issues in the field of scrap processing and recycling.

Screening Equipment Handbook: For Industrial and Municipal Water and Wastewater Treatment. Tom M. Pankratz. Technomic Publishing Co., Lancaster, PA 1988. Covers the water purification equipment industry, fish screens, and filters and filtration.

Screening Techniques for Determining Compliance with Environmental Standards. National Council on Radiation Protection and Measurements, 7910 Woodmont Ave., Ste. 800, Bethesda, MD 20814. (301) 657-2652. 1986. Commentary on the release of radionuclides in the atmosphere.

Scripps Institution of Oceanography. University of California, San Diego, Mail Code 0210, La Jolla, CA 92093. (619) 534-3624.

Scripps Institution of Oceanography, Center for Coastal Studies. University of California, San Diego, 9500 Gilman Dr., La Jolla, CA 92093. (619) 534-4333.

Scripps Institution of Oceanography, Division of Ship Operations and Marine Technical Support. University of California, San Diego, Mail Code A-010, La Jolla, CA 92093. (619) 534-2853.

Scripps Institution of Oceanography, Hydrolics Laboratory. University of California, San Diego, 9500 Gilman Dr., La Jolla, CA 92093. (619) 534-0595.

Scripps Institution of Oceanography, Marine Biology Research Division. University of California, San Diego, A-0202, San Diego, CA 92093-0202. (619) 534-7378.

Scripps Institution of Oceanography, Marine Life Research Group. University of California, San Diego, A-027, La Jolla, CA 92093-0227. (619) 534-3565.

Scripps Institution of Oceanography, Marine Physical Laboratory. University of California, San Diego, San Diego, CA 92152-6400. (619) 534-1789.

Scripps Institution of Oceanography, Physical Oceanography Research Division. University of California, San Diego, La Jolla, CA 92093. (619) 534-1876.

Scripps Institution of Oceanography, Physiological Research Laboratory. University of California, San Diego, A-0204, La Jolla, CA 92093. (714) 534-2934.

Scripps Institution of Oceanography, Scripps Aquarium-Museum. University of California, San Diego, 8602 La Jolla Shores Drive, La Jolla, CA 92093-6933. (619) 534-4084.

Sea Fog. Pin-hau Wang. Springer-Verlag, 175 5th Ave., New York, NY 10010. (212) 460-1500. 1985. Deals with meteorology.

Sea Grant Abstracts. National Sea Grant Depository, Pell Laboratory Bldg., Bay Campus, University of Rhode Island, Narragansett, RI 02882. (401) 792-6114. 1986-. Quarterly. Published by the National Sea Grant Programs, this collection includes annual reports, serials and newsletters, charts and maps.

Sea Grant Association. c/o Dr. Christopher F. D'Elia, Maryland Sea Grant College, 1123 Taliaferro Hall, UMCP, College Park, MD 20742. (301) 405-6371.

Sea Grant College Program. University of Delaware, 196 South College Avenue, Newark, DE 19716. (302) 451-8182.

Sea Level Variation for the United States, 1855-1980. Steacy D. Hicks. National Oceanic and Atmospheric Administration, Department of Commerce, 20230. (202) 377-2985. 1983. Changes in tides and water levels over the years.

Sea Mammals and Oil: Confronting the Risks. Joseph R. Geraci and David J. St. Aubin, eds. Academic Press, c/o Harcourt Brace Jovanovich Inc., 6277 Sea Harbor Dr., Orlando, FL 32887. (800) 346-8648. 1990. Explores the effects of spilled petroleum on seals, whales, dolphins, sea otters, polar bears, and manatees, which inhabit the coastal water of North America where spills occur. They consider the constant low-level leakage of urban and industrial oil, large spills, and long-term as well as immediate effects.

Sea Shepherd Conservation Society. 1314 2nd St., Santa Monica, CA 90401. (213) 394-3198.

Sea-Slug Gastropods. Wesley M. Farmer. W.M. Farmer Enterprises, Tempe, AZ 1980. Gastropods and mollusks in the Pacific coast.

Sea Turtle Conservation and the Shrimp Industry. Congress Committee on Merchant Marine and Fisheries. U.S. G.P.O., Washington, DC 20401. (202) 512-0000. 1990. Equipment and supplies used in the shrimp industry.

Sea World Research Institute. 1700 south Shores Road, San Diego, CA 92109. (619) 226-3870.

Seabed Disposal of High-Level Radioactive Waste. Nuclear Energy Agency. OECD Publication and Information Centre, 2 rue Andre Pascal, Paris, France F-75775. 1984. A status report on the NEA-coordinated research program on the radioactive pollution of the ocean.

Seabirds of the Farallon Islands: Ecology, Dynamics, and Structure of an Upwelling-System Community. David G. Ainley and Robert J. Boekelheide, eds. Stanford University, Stanford, CA 94305-2235. (415) 723-9434. 1990. History of seabird populations at the Farallons, a general discussion of patterns in the marine environment, and the general feeding ecology of Farallon seabirds.

Seacoast Anti-Pollution League. Five Market St., Portsmouth, NH 03801. (603) 431-5089.

Seafloor Geosciences Division. John C. Stennis Space Center, Bay St. Louis, MS 39529-5004. (601) 688-4657.

The Seavegetable Book. Judith Cooper Madlener. Crown Publishing Group, 201 E. 50th St., New York, NY 10022. (212) 751-2600. 1977. Marine algae as food.

Seawater and Desalting. A. Delyannis. Springer-Verlag, 175 5th Ave., New York, NY 10010. (212) 460-1500. 1980. Topics in saline water conversion.

Secondary Lead Smelters Association. 6000 Lake Forest Dr., Suite 350, Atlanta, GA 30328. (404) 257-9634.

Secondary Metabolism in Microorganisms, Plants and Animals. Martin Luckner. Springer-Verlag, 175 5th Ave., New York, NY 10010. (212) 460-1500. 1990. Includes reviews of the latest results on the biosynthesis for age and degradation of secondary metabolites and characteristics of compounds of specialized cells from all groups of organisms. Has new chapters on: the transport of secondary compounds with the producer organism; the significance of colored and toxic secondary products; and on the improvement of secondary product biosynthesis by genetical means.

Secondary Reclamation of Plastics Waste. Plastics Institute of America, Stevens Institute of Technology, Castle Point, Hoboken, NJ 07030. (201) 420-5553. 1987. Research report on Phase I development of techniques for preparation and formulation for recycling plastic scrap.

Sediment Oxygen Demand in Streams Receiving Sewage Effluent. Eastern Illinois University, Department of Botany, Charleston, IL 61920. 1984. Covers sewage irrigation and sediment control.

Sedimentary Dynamics of Continental Shelves. C.A. Nittrouer. Elsevier, Amsterdam, 1000 AE. 020-5803-911. 1981. Developments in sedimentology and marine sediments.

Sedimentation Engineering. Vito A. Vanoni. American Society of Civil Engineers, 345 E. 47th St., New York, NY 10017. (212) 705-7288; (800) 548-2723. 1975. Hydraulic engineering aspects of sedimentation and deposition.

Sedimentology and Geochemistry of Dolostones. Vijai Shukla. The Society of Economic Paleontologists and Mineralogists, P.O. Box 4756, Tulsa, OK 74159-0756. (918) 743-9765. 1988.

Sediments: Chemistry and Toxicity of In-Place Pollutants. Renato Baudo, et al., eds. Lewis Publishers, 200 Corporate Blvd. NW, Boca Raton, FL 33431. (407) 994-0555 or (800)272-7737. 1990.

Seismological Society of America. El Cerrito Professional Bldg., Suite 201, El Cerrito, CA 94530. (415) 525-5474.

Select Use of Gas: Regulator's Perspective. Ruth K. Kretschmer. Illinois Commerce Commission, 527 E. Capitol Ave., PO Box 14280, Springfield, IL 62794-9280. (217) 782-7295. 1985. Economic and environmental aspects of the natural gas industry.

Selected Abstracts on Aflatoxins and other Mycotoxins Carcinogenesis. U.S. Dept. of Health Education and Welfare. National Technical Information Service, 5285 Port Royal Rd., Springfield, VA 22161. (703) 487-4650. 1978. Prepared for the ICRDB Program by the Cancer Information Dissemination and Analysis Center for Carcinogenesis Information.

Selected Abstracts on DNA Viral Transforming Proteins. International Cancer Research Data Bank. U.S. Department of Health and Human Services, Public Health Service, National Institutes of Health, 9000 Rockville Pike, Bethesda, MD 20892. (301) 496-4000.

Selected Abstracts on Rearrangements of DNA Sequences as They Occur in Nature. William C. Summers. U.S. Department of Health and Human Services, Public Health Service, National Institutes of Health, 9000 Rockville Pike, Bethesda, MD 20892. (301) 496-4000. 1983. Potential models for differentiation and tumorigenesis.

Selected Abstracts on Short-Term Test Systems for Potential Mutagens and Carcinogens. Vincent F. Simmon. National Technical Information Service, 5285 Port Royal Rd., Springfield, VA 22161. (703) 487-4650. 1981.

Selected Abstracts on the Role of Dietary Nitrate and Nitrite in Human Carcinogenesis. Steven R. Tannenbaum. National Technical Information Service, 5285 Port Royal Rd., Springfield, VA 22161. (703) 487-4650. 1982.

A Selected Annotated Bibliography of 1989 Hazards Publications. Dave Morton. Natural Hazards Center, Campus Box 482, University of Colorado, Boulder, CO 80309-0482. (303) 492-6819. 1990. Contains 292 entries in 12 categories: earthquakes and tsunamis; floods, hurricanes, cyclones, tornados and severe storms, volcanoes; technological hazards; health and medical hazards; miscellaneous hazards; coastal zone management and planning; landslides and other mass earth movements; water resources and wetland management and climate and drought.

A Selected Annotated Bibliography on Ecological Planning Resources. Fredrick Steiner. Vance Bibliographies, PO Box 229, 112 N. Charter St., Monticello, IL 61856. (217) 762-3831. 1983.

A Selected Bibliography on Alcohol Fuels. Solar Energy Research Institute, 1617 Cole Blvd., Golden, CO 80401. 1982. Covers literature written about biomass derived ethyl and methyl alcohols, including production processes, economics, use as fuel, engine conversion, feedstocks, financing, government regulations, coproducts, environmental effects and safety. The main focus is on alcohol fuels.

A Selected Bibliography on Mercury in the Environment, with Subject Listing. Susan Robinson. Royal Ontario Museum, 100 Queens Park, Toronto, ON, Canada M5S 2C6. (416) 586-5581. 1974.

Selected Highway Statistics and Charts. U.S. Federal Highway Administration. U.S. G.P.O., Washington, DC 20401. (202) 512-0000. Annual. Travel mileage on public roads and motor fuel use.

Selected References on Environmental Quality as It Relates to Health. National Library of Medicine, 8600 Rockville Pike, Bethesda, MD 20894. (800) 638-8480. 1977.

Selected Water Abstracts on Dioxins and Dibenzofurans in Carcinogenesis, 1980-1986. Anthony J. Girardi. National Cancer Institute, U. S. Dept. of Health and Human Services, Public Health Service, National Institutes of Health, Washington, DC 20402-9325. (202) 783-3238. 1987.

Selenium. Charles Grady Wilber. Charles C. Thomas Publishing Co., 2600 S. First St., Springfield, IL 62794-9265. (217) 789-8980. 1983. A potential environmental poison and a necessary food constituent.

Selenium in Agricultural Ecosystems. Robert Lewis Jones. Department of Agronomy, University of Illinois, Urbana, IL 61801. 1971. A bibliography of literature, 1950 through 1971, covering environmental aspects of sewage sludge.

Selenium Pretreatment Study. Lisa H. Rowley. Bureau of Reclamation, U.S. Department of the Interior, Washington, DC 202400. (202) 208-4662. 1991. Water purification using agricultural chemicals, especially selenium.

Selenium-Tellurium Development Association. 301 Borgtstraat, B1850 Brimbergen, Belgium

Seminar on Emissions and Air Quality at Natural Gas Pipeline Installations. American Gas Association, 1515 Wilson Blvd., Arlington, VA 22209. 1981. Compressor emissions, nitrogen oxides, and natural gas pipelines.

Senescence and Aging in Plants. L.C. Nooden. Academic Press, c/o Harcourt Brace Jovanovich Inc., 6277 Sea Harbor Dr., Orlando, FL 32887. (800) 346-8648. 1988.

Sensitive Biochemical and Behavioral Indicators of Trace Substance Exposure. Edward J. Massaro. Center for Environmental Research Information, U.S. Environmental Protection Agency, 26 W. Martin Luther King Dr., Cincinnati, OH 45268. (518) 569-7931. 1981.

Separation and Purification. Edmond S. Perry. John Wiley & Sons, Inc., 605 3rd Ave., New York, NY 10158-0012. (212) 850-6000. 1978. Techniques of chemistry and separation technology.

Separation and Purification Methods. Marcel Dekker, Inc., 270 Madison Ave., New York, NY 10016. (212) 696-9000. 1972. Technology of separation and chemical purification.

Septic Systems Handbook. O. Benjamin Kaplan. Lewis Publishers, 2000 Corporate Blvd., N.W., Boca Raton, FL 33431. (407) 994-0555 or (800) 272-7737. 1991. Discusses why public health agencies control the disposal of domestic sewage. The septic system, economics of leachfield size, soils at a glance, soil water movement, the percolation test, size of leachline, factors affecting failure of leachlines, size of seepage pits, various onsite sewage disposal technologies, degradation of groundwater by septic systems and related matters.

Serial Publications Indexed in Bibliography of Agriculture. National Agricultural Library, 10301 Baltimore Blvd., Washington, DC 20705-2351. (301) 504-5755. 1963.

Serious Reduction of Hazardous Waste: Summary. Congress of the U.S., c/o U.S. Government Printing Office, Office of Technology Assessment, N. Capitol & H Sts. NW, Washington, DC 20401. (202) 512-0000. 1986. Deals with waste reduction from factories and air pollution control.

Sewage and the Bacterial Purification of Sewage. Samuel Rideal. John Wiley & Sons, Inc., 605 3rd Ave., New York, NY 10158-0012. (212) 850-6000. 1906. Publication on sewage purification with illustrations and colored plates.

Sewage and Waste Disposal. Sewage and Waste Disposal, 321 Sunset Ave., Asbury Park, NJ 07712. 1946-. Fourteen times a year.

Sewage Lagoons in Cold Climates. Environmental Protection Service, Technical Service Branch, 425 St. Joseph Blvd., 3rd Fl., Hull, PQ, Canada K1A 0H3. (613) 953-5921. 1985. Cold weather conditions in sewage lagoons.

Sewer and Water–Main Design Tables. L. B. Escrit. Maclaren and Sons Ltd., 7 Grape St., London, England WC2. 1969. Includes tables of flow in sewers, drains and water-mains in British and Metric units. Also includes tables of rainfall, run-off, repayment of loans, etc.

Shading Our Cities. Gary Moll and Sara Ebenreck, eds. Island Press, 1718 Connecticut Ave. N.W., Suite 300, Washington, DC 20009. (202)232-7933. 1989. Handbook to help neighborhood groups, local officials, and planners develop urban forestry projects, not only to beautify their cities, but also to help reduce energy demand, improve air quality, protect water supplies, and contribute to healthier living conditions.

Shannon Point Marine Center. Western Washington University, 1900 Shannon Point Rd., Anacortes, WA 98221. (206) 293-2188.

The Shaping of Environmentalism in America. Victor B. Scheffer. University of Washington Press, PO Box 50096, Seattle, WA 98145-5096. (206) 543-4050; (800) 441-4115. 1991. History of environmental policy and protection in the United States.

Sharing Environmental Risks: How to Control Governments' Losses in Natural Disasters. Raymond J. Burby, et al. Westview Press, 5500 Central Ave., Boulder, CO 80301. (303) 444-3541. 1991. Deals with ways and means to control costs in the aftermath of a disaster. Explains risk insurance and how it can help.

Sharks in Question: The Smithsonian Answer Book. Victor G. Springer and Joy P. Gold. Smithsonian Institution Press, 470 L'Enfant Plaza #7100, Washington, DC 20560. (800) 782-4612. 1989.

Shattering: Food, Politics, and the Loss of Genetic Diversity. Cary Fowler. University of Arizona Press, 1230 N. Park, No. 102, Tucson, AZ 85719. (602) 621-1441. 1990. Reviews the development of genetic diversity over 10,000 years of human agriculture and its loss in our lifetimes.

Sheet Metal Workers' International Association. 1750 New York Ave., N.W., Washington, DC 20006. (202) 783-5880.

Sheldon Biotechnology Centre. McGill University, 3773 University St., Montreal, PQ, Canada H3A 2B4. (514) 398-3998.

Sherbrooke University, Centre for Remote Sensing Research and Applications. 2500 Boulevard Universite, Sherbrooke, PQ, Canada J1K 2R1. (819) 821-7180.

Shippensburg University, Vertebrate Museum. Franklin Science Center, Shippensburg, PA 17257. (714) 532-1407.

Shopping for a Better Environment. Laurence Tasaday. Meadowbrook Press, Inc., 18318 Minnetonka Blvd., Deephaven, MN 55391. (612) 473-5400. 1991. A brand name guide to environmentally responsible shopping.

Shopping for a Better World. The Council for Economic Priorities. Ballantine Books, 201 E. 50th St., New York, NY 10022. (212) 572-2620; (800) 733-3000. 1991. Rev. ed. Investigates 206 companies and over 2,015 products.

The Shore Environment. J.H. Price. Academic Press, c/o Harcourt Brace Jovanovich Inc., 6277 Sea Harbor Dr., Orlando, FL 32887. (800) 346-8648. 1980. Seashore ecology management methods.

Shrimp Mariculture: January 1979 - January 1990. Eileen McVey. National Agricultural Library, 10301 Baltimore Blvd., Beltsville, MD 20705-2351. (301) 504-5755. 1990.

Sierra Club. 100 Bush St., San Francisco, CA 94104. (415) 291-1600.

Sierra Club Bulletin. Sierra Club Books, 100 Bush St., San Francisco, CA 94104. (415) 291-1600. 1893-. Ten times a year.

Sierra Club Legal Defense Fund. 180 Montgomery St., Ste. 1400, San Francisco, CA 94104. (415) 627-6700.

Sierra Magazine. Sierra Club Books, 100 Bush St., San Francisco, CA 94104. (415) 291-1600. Bimonthly. Covers the environment and ecological systems.

The Sierra Nevada: A Mountain Journey. Tim Palmer. Island Press, 1718 Connecticut Ave. N.W., Suite 300, Washington, DC 20009. (202) 232-7933. 1988. This natural history of the Sierra Nevadas deals with the range, the people, and the surrounding communities to life. It describes development from the Gold Rush days to modern battles over preservation, water quality, wildlife protection and logging.

The Sigma-Aldrich Handbook of Stains, Dyes and Indicators. Floyd J. Green. Aldrich Chemical Co., 1001 W. St. Paul Ave., Milwaukee, WI 53233. (414) 273-3850 or (800) 558-9160. 1990.

Sign Control News. Scenic America, 216 7th St. SE, Washington, DC 20003. (202) 546-1100. Bimonthly.

Significance and Treatment of Volatile Organic Compounds in Water Supplies. Neil M. Ram, et al. Lewis Publishers, 2000 Corporate Blvd., N.W., Boca Raton, FL 33431. (407) 994-0555 or (800) 272-7737. 1990. Includes EPA approved analytical methods for VOC analysis, QA/QC, data quality objectives and limits of detection. Covers current methods for the assessment of health effects, including toxicity and carcinogenicity.

Signs of Hope: Working towards Our Common Future. Linda Starke. Oxford University Press, Walton St., Oxford, England OX2 6DP 1990. Sequel to the report of the World Commission on Environment and Development Commissioned by the Centre For Our Common Future. Records the progress made in the implementation of the recommendations of Our Common Future and looks at initiatives being taken by governments, industry, scientists, non-governmental organizations and the media.

Silent Running Society. P.O. Box 529, Howell, NJ 07731. (201) 364-0539.

Silent Spring. Rachel Carson. Carolina Biological Supply Company, 2700 York Rd., Burlington, NC 27215. (919) 584-0381. 1987.

Silent Spring Revisited. Gino J. Marco, et al., eds. American Chemical Society, 1155 16th St. N.W., Washington, DC 20036. (202) 872-4600; (800) 227-5558. 1987. Discusses Rachel Carson's vision and legacy. Traces the evolution of government regulations and the current pesticide registration criteria. Critically appraises the existing conditions and evaluates hazards.

Silica, Silicosis, and Cancer: Controversy in Occupational Medicine. Praeger Publishers, 1 Madison Ave., New York, NY 10010-3603. (212) 685-5300. Covers lung cancer and the toxicology of silica.

Silicones Health Council. 1330 Connecticut Ave., N.W., Suite 300, Washington, DC 20036. (202) 659-0060.

Silver in Agricultural Ecosystems: A Bibliography of the Literature 1950 through 1971. Robert L. Jones. Department of Agronomy, University of Illinois, Urbana, IL 61801. 1973.

Simon Fraser University, Centre for Pest Management. Burnaby Mountain, Burnaby, BC, Canada V5 A1S6. (607) 291-3705.

The Simple Act of Planting a Tree: A Citizen Forester's Guide to Healing Your Neighborhood, Your City, and Your World. Andy Lipkis. Jeremy P. Tarcher, 5858 Wilshire Blvd., Ste. 200, Los Angeles, CA 90036. (213) 935-9980. 1990. Covers tree planting and urban forestry.

Simulating the Environmental Impact of a Large Hydroelectric Project. Normand Therien. Society for Computer Simulation, 4838 Ronson Ct., San Diego, CA 92111. (619) 277-3888. 1981. Environmental aspects of hydroelectric power plants.

Simulations and Economic Analyses of Desiccant Cooling Systems. Benjamin Shelpuk, et al. Solar Energy Research Institute, available from National Technical Information Services, 5285 Port Royal Rd., Springfield, VA 22161. (703) 487-4650. 1979.

Sinkhole Type, Development and Distribution in Florida. William C. Sinclair. Department of Natural Resources, Bureau of Geology, 3900 Commonwealth Blvd., Tallahassee, FL 32399. (904) 488-7131. 1985. Maps giving locations and descriptions of Florida sinkholes.

Sinkholes. Barry F. Beck. A. A. Balkema, Boston, MA 1984. Sinkhole geology, engineering and environmental impact.

The Siren: News from UNEP's Regional Seas Programme (English Ed.). United Nations Environment Programme, Regional Seas Programme Activity Centre, Geneva, Switzerland 1978-. Three issues yearly since 1983. Covers marine pollution, environmental policy, and coastal zone management.

SIRS Science CD-ROM. Social Issues Resources Series, Inc., PO Box 2348, Boca Raton, FL 33427-2348. (407) 994-0079. Climatology, ecology, and oceanography.

SIRS Social Issues and Critical Issues CD-ROM. Social Issues Resources Series, Inc., PO Box 2348, Boca Raton, FL 33427-2348. (407) 994-0079. Pollution, population, and the atmosphere.

Site-Directed Mutagenesis and Protein Engineering. M. Rafaat El-Gewely. Elsevier Science Publishing Co., 655 Avenue of the Americas, New York, NY 10010. (212) 989-5800. 1991.

Site-Specific Risk Assessments. Frank A. Jones. Lewis Publishers, 2000 Corporate Blvd., N.W., Boca Raton, FL 33431. (407) 994-0555 or (800) 272-7737. 1991. Describes site characterization, hazard characterization, exposure characterization, risk characterization, uncertainties and case studies.

Siting Hazardous Waste Treatment Facilities; the Nimby Syndrome. Kent E. Portney. Auburn House, 14 Dedham St., Dover, MA 02030-0658. (800) 223-2665. 1991. Advice to producers of hazardous waste on how to overcome people's reluctance to have it shipped into their neighborhood.

Siting of Power Lines and Communication Towers. Lynne De Merritt. Council of Planning Librarians, 1313 E. 60th St., Chicago, IL 60637-2897. (312) 942-2163. 1990. A bibliography on the potential health effects of electric and magnetic fields.

Skidaway Institute of Oceanography. P.O. Box 13687, McWhorter Drive, Skidaway Island, Savannah, GA 31416. (912) 356-2453.

Skin Penetration; Hazardous Chemicals at Work. Philippe Grandjean. Taylor & Francis, 79 Madison Ave., New York, NY 10016. (212) 725-1999 or (800) 821-8312. 1990. Mechanisms of percutaneous absorption and methods of evaluating its significance. Reviews different classes of chemicals, emphasizing those considered major skin hazards.

The Sky is the Limit: Strategies for Protecting the Ozone Layer. Alan S. Miller. World Resources Institute, 1709 New York Ave., N.W., Washington, DC 20006. (800) 822-0504. 1986. Law and legislation relating to chlorofluorocarbons and atmospheric ozone reduction.

Slowing Global Warming: A Worldwide Strategy. Christopher Flavin. Worldwatch Institute, 1776 Massachusetts Ave. N.W., Washington, DC 20036. How to cope with environmental warming as an environmental threat.

Sludge. Business Publishers, Inc., 951 Pershing Dr., Silver Spring, MD 20910-4464. (301) 587-6300. Management of sludge residuals and byproducts generated by industrial and municipal air and water pollution control measures.

Sludge Management. W. F. Garber and D. R. Anderson, eds. Pergamon Microforms International, Inc., Fairview Park, Elmsford, NY 10523. (914) 592-7720. 1990. Proceedings of the IAWPRC Conference on Sludge Management, held at Loyola Marymount University, Los Angeles, California, 8-12 January 1990. Offers an insight into sludge management. Topics include: treatment plant planning and management, sludge melting, incineration, drying and dewatering, aerobic and anaerobic digestion, heavy metal contaminants, and the use of sludge products as construction materials.

Sludge Newsletter. Business Publishers, Inc., 951 Pershing Dr., Silver Spring, MD 20910-4464. (301) 587-6300. 1976-. Biweekly. Reports on continuing changes at EPA, plus an array of new hazardous waste management and industrial pretreatment requirements that will affect municipal sludge.

Sludge Treatment. W.W. Eckenfelder. Marcel Dekker Inc., 270 Madison Ave., New York, NY 10016. (212) 696-9000; (800) 228-1160. 1981. Design and construction of sewage disposal plants and sewage purification.

Slurry Technology Association. 1156 15th St., N.W., Suite 525, Washington, DC 20005. (202) 296-1133.

Small Water Purification Systems. Richard B. Case. U.S. Department of the Interior, Bureau of Land Management, 2850 Youngfield St., Denver, CO 80215. (303) 239-3700. 1981. Covers water, purification, equipment, supplies, and drinking water standards.

Smithells Metals Reference Book. Eric A. Brandes, ed. Butterworth-Heinemann, 80 Montvale Ave., Stoneham, MA 02180. (617) 438-8464 or (800) 366-2665. 1983. Sixth edition. Contains data, pertaining to metals, such as: thermochemical data, physical properties of molten salts, metallography, equilibrium diagrams, gas-metal systems, diffusion in metals, general physical properties, elastic properties, temperature measurement and other related data.

Smithsonian Institution. National Museum of Natural History, NHB-106, Washington, DC 20560. (202) 786-2821.

Smoking and Health. U.S. Department of Health & Human Services. Center for Disease Control, Center for Chronic Disease Prevention & Health Promotion, Office on Smoking and Health, Technical Information Center, Park Building, Rm. 1-16, 5600 Fishers Lane, Rockville, MD 20857. (301) 443-1690.

Smoking and Health, A National Status Report. U.S. Centers for Disease Control, c/o U.S. Government Printing Office, Washington, DC 20401. (202) 512-0000. 1986. Biennial. Smoking and health research, education, legislative and other intervention efforts, program outcomes, and smoking prevalence.

Smoking Guns. Nuclear Regulatory Commission, Advisory Committee on Nuclear Facility Safety, 1717 H St., NW, Washington, DC 20555. (301) 492-7000. 1991. Deals with the Energy Department's campaign to improve safety and environmental compliance at its nuclear weapons plants.

Smoking in the Workplace: 1987 Update. Society for Human Resource Management, 606 N. Washington St., Alexandria, VA 22314. (703) 548-3440.

Smoking Policy Institute. 218 Broadway E., Seattle, WA 98102. (206) 324-4444.

Smoking, Tobacco, and Health: A Fact Book. U.S. Centers for Disease Control. U.S. G.P.O., Washington, DC 20401. (202) 512-0000. 1987. Irregular. Smoking related death and illness rates, nicotine absorption and exposure levels.

The Snake River: Window to the West. Tim Palmer. Island Press, 1718 Connecticut Ave. N.W., Suite 300, Washington, DC 20009. (202) 232-7933. 1991. Offers information about instream flows for fish and wildlife; groundwater management and quality; water conservation and efficiency; pollution of streams from agriculture and logging; small hydroelectric development; and reclamation of riparian habitat.

Soap and Detergent Association. 475 Park Ave., S., New York, NY 10016. (212) 725-1262.

Soap, Cosmetics, Chemical Specialties. MacNair-Dorland Co., 101 W. 31st, New York, NY 10001. 1925-. Monthly. Formerly entitled Soap and Chemical Specialties

The Social and Environmental Effects of Large Dams. Edward Goldsmith. Sierra Club Books, 100 Bush St., San Francisco, CA 94104. (415) 291-1600. 1986. History of irrigation and the impact of dams on the environment.

Social Ecology: Monographs. Mary A. Vance. Vance Bibliographies, PO Box 229, 112 N. Charter St., Monticello, IL 61856. (217) 762-3831. 1987.

Social Insects and the Environment. G. K. Veeresh, et al., eds. E. J. Brill, PO Box 9000, Leiden, Netherlands 2300 PA. NL-2300 PA 1990. Proceedings of the 11th International Congress of IUSSI, 1990. Includes 370 papers presented, and topics covered include: evolution of sociality, polygyny, social polymorphism, kin-recognition, foraging strategies, reproductive strategies, the biogeography and phycogenetics of bees and ants, pollination ecology and the management of pestiferous social insects.

Social Network Analysis: A Man/Environment Approach to Urban Design and Planning. Council of Planning Librarians, 1313 E. 60th St., Chicago, IL 60637-2897. (312) 942-2163. 1978. Bibliography of city planning and social structure.

Societal Issues and Economics of Energy and the Environment. T. Nejat Veziroglu, ed. Nova Science Publishers Inc., 283 Commack Rd., Suite 300, Commack, NY 11725-3401. (516) 499-3103; (516) 499-3106. 1990. Deals with important societal issues and the economics of energy and the environment. Focuses on why the environment, as a resource, must be protected at all cost.

Society and Natural Resources: An International Journal. Taylor & Francis, 1900 Frost Rd., Suite 101, Bristol, PA 19007. (215) 785-5800. Quarterly. Social science research and the environment.

Society for Animal Protective Legislation. PO Box 3719, Georgetown Station, Washington, DC 20007. (202) 337-2334.

Society for Conservation Biology. Department of Wildlife Ecology, University of Wisconsin, Madison, WI 53706. (608) 262-2671.

Society for Ecological Restoration. 1207 Seminole Hwy., Madison, WI 53711. (608) 262-9547.

Society for Environmental Geochemistry and Health. c/o Wilard R. Chappell, University of Colorado, Denver Center for Environmental Sciences, P.O. Box 136, Denver, CO 80217-3364. (303) 556-3460.

Society for Epidemiologic Research. Colorada State University, Department of Health, Microbiology Bldg., Room B107, Ft. Collins, CO 80523. (303) 491-6156.

Society for Industrial Microbiology. Box 12534, Arlington, VA 22209. (703) 941-5373.

The Society for Marine Mammology. National Marine Fisheries Service, SW Fisheries Center, PO Box 271, La Jolla, CA 92038. (619) 546-7096.

Society for Mining, Metallurgy, and Exploration, Inc. P.O. Box 625005, Littleton, CO 80162. (303) 973-9550.

Society for Occupational & Environmental Health. 6728 Old McLeen Village Dr., McLean, VA 22101. (703) 556-9222.

Society for Range Management. 1839 York St., Denver, CO 80206. (303) 355-7070.

Society for Vector Ecology. Box 87, Santa Ana, CA 92702. (714) 971-2421.

Society Meeting (194th, 1987). American Chemical Society, 1155 16th St. N.W., Washington, DC 20036. (800) 227-5558.

Society of American Foresters. 5400 Grosvenor Lane, Bethesda, MD 20814. (301) 897-8720.

Society of American Wood Preservers. 7297 Lee Hwy., Unit P, Falls Church, VA 22042. (703) 237-0900.

Society of Automotive Engineers. 400 Commonwealth Dr., Warrendale, PA 15096. (412) 776-4841.

Society of Commercial Seed Technologists. c/o Accu-Test Seed Lab., P.O. Box 1712, Brandon, MB, Canada R7A 6S3. (204) 328-5313.

Society of Environmental Graphic Designers–Corporate Directory. Society of Environmental Graphic Designers, 47 Third St., Cambridge, MA 02141. (617) 577-8225.

Society of Environmental Graphic Designers–Professional Firm Directory. Society of Environmental Graphic Designers, 47 Third St., Cambridge, MA 02141. (617) 577-8225.

Society of Exploration Geo-Physicists. P.O. Box 702740, Tulsa, OK 74170. (918) 493-3516.

Society of Flavor Chemists. c/o Denise McCafferty, McCormick and Co., 204 Wright Ave., Hunt Valley, MD 21031. (301) 771-7491.

Society of Forensic Toxicologists. 1013 Three Mile Dr., Grosse Pointe Park, MI 48230. (313) 884-4718.

Society of Manufacturing Engineers. 1 SME Dr., Box 930, Dearborn, MI 48121. (313) 271-1500.

Society of Marine Port Engineers. P.O. Box 466, Avenel, NJ 07001. (908) 381-7673.

Society of Mineral Analysts. P.O. Box 5416, Elko, NV 89802. (801) 569-7159.

Society of Mining Engineers. PO Box 625005, Littleton, CO 80162. (303) 973-9550.

Society of Nematologists. c/o R.N. Huehel, Ph.D., USDA, ARS, Nematology Laboratory, Bldg. 011A BARC-W, Beetsville, MD 20705. (301) 344-3081.

Society of Petroleum Engineers. P.O. Box 833836, Richardson, TX 75083. (214) 669-3377.

Society of Plastics Engineers. 14 Fairfield Dr., Brookfield Center, CT 06805. (203) 775-0471.

Society of Risk Analysis. Plenum Press, 233 Spring St., New York, NY 10013-1578. (212) 620-8000; (800) 221-9369. 1990. Proceedings of the Annual Meeting of the Society for Risk Analysis, held November 9-12, 1986, in Boston, MA.

Society of the Plastics Industry. 1275 K St., N.W., Suite 400, Washington, DC 20005. (202) 371-5200.

Society of the Plastics Industry–Membership Directory and Buyers' Guide. Society of the Plastics Industry, Inc., 1275 K St.,N.W., Washington, DC 20005. (202) 371-5200.

Society of Toxicology. 1101 14th St., N.W., Suite 1100, Washington, DC 20005. (202) 371-1393.

Society of Vector Ecologists. Box 87, Santa Anna, CA 92702. (714) 971-2421.

Society of Women Engineers. 345 E. 47th St., Rm. 305, New York, NY 10017. (212) 705-7855.

Society of Wood Science and Technology. One Gifford Pinchot Dr., Madison, WI 53705. (608) 231-9347.

Socioeconomic Values of Wetlands: Concepts, Research Methods, and Annotated Bibliography. North Dakota State University, Agricultural Experiment Station, Fargo, ND 58105. 1981. Bibliography of wetland ecology; its economic aspects and recreational uses.

The Sociology of Range Management: A Bibliography. Jere Lee Gilles. CPL Bibliographies, 1313 E. 60th St., Chicago, IL 60637-2897. (312) 942-2163. 1982.

Sodium Chemicals. FIND/SVP, 625 Avenue of the Americas, New York, NY 10011. (212) 645-4500. 1991. Historical production and demand data with forecasts to 1995 and 2000 for caustic soda; sodium chlorate; sodium bichromate; soda ash; sodium bicarbonate; STPP; silicates; and other chemicals.

Sodium Chloride. Environmental Protection Programs Directorate. Environmental Protection Service, 425 St. Joseph Blvd., 3rd Fl., Hull, PQ, Canada K1A 0H3. (613) 953-5921. 1984. Environmental and technical information for problem spills.

Sodium Hydroxide. Environmental Protection Service, 425 St. Joseph Blvd., 3rd Fl., Hull, PQ, Canada K1A 0H3. (613) 953-5921. 1984. Environmental and technical information for problem spills manuals.

Sodium, Its Biologic Significance. Solomon Papper. CRC Press, 2000 Corporate Blvd. N.W., Boca Raton, FL 33431. (800) 272-7737. 1982. Sodium in the body, sodium metabolism disorders, complications and sequelae.

Sodium: Think About It. U.S. Department of Agriculture, Washington, DC 1982. Deals with sodium in the body.

Soil Analysis: Modern Instrumental Techniques. Keith A. Smith, ed. Marcel Dekker, Inc., 270 Madison Ave., New York, NY 10016. (212) 696-9000; (800) 228-1160. 1991. Covers instrumental analysis for soil chemists. The second edition combines the underlying principles of current techniques with discussions of sample preparation and matrix problems which critically reviewing applications in modern soil science and related disciplines.

Soil and Environmental Chemistry Lab. Pennsylvania State University, 104 Research Unit A, University Park, PA 16802. (814) 865-1221.

Soil and Water Conservation. Frederick R. Troeh, et al. Prentice-Hall, Rte. 9W, Englewood Cliffs, NJ 07632. (201) 592-2000; (800) 634-2863. 1991. 2d ed. Describes the hazards of erosion, sedimentation, and pollution, and the techniques needed to conserve soil and maintain environmental quality.

Soil and Water Conservation Engineering. John Wiley & Sons, Inc., 605 3rd Ave., New York, NY 10158-0012. (212) 850-6000. 1981. Agricultural engineering and soil and water conservation.

Soil and Water Conservation News. U.S. Soil Conservation Service, PO Box 2890, Washington, DC 20013. (202) 205-0027. Monthly.

Soil & Water Conservation Society. 7515 Northeast Ankeny Rd., Ankeny, IA 50021. (515) 289-2331.

Soil and Water Conservation Society of America. 7515 N.E. Ankeny Rd., Ankeny, IA 50021. (515) 289-2331.

Soil Biology and Biochemistry. Pergamon Microforms International, Inc., Fairview Park, Elmsford, NY 10523. (914) 592-7720. Eight times a year. Soil biology, soil biochemistry, nitrogen fixation, nitrogenase activity, sampling microorganisms in soil, soil compaction, and nutrient release in soils.

The Soil Chemistry of Hazardous Materials. James Dragun. Hazardous Material Control Research Institute, 7737 Hanover Pkwy., Greenbelt, MD 20770. (301) 982-9500. 1988. Hazardous substances, soil absorption and adsorption.

Soil Erosion by Water as Related to Management of Tillage and Surface Residues, Terracing, and Contouring in Eastern Oregon. R. R. Allmaras. U.S. Department of Agriculture, Science and Education Administration, Agricultural Research, 800 Buchanan St., Albany, CA 94710. (510) 559-6082. 1980. Covers soil erosion and soil management and tillage.

Soil Erosion: Quiet Crisis in the World Economy. Lester R. Brown, Edward C. Wolf. Worldwatch Institute, 1776 Massachusetts Ave., N.W., Washington, DC 20036-1904. 1984.

Soil Fumigation: How and Why It Works. Harry S. Fenwick. University of Idaho, College of Agriculture, Moscow, ID 83843. 1971.

Soil Fungicides. A. P. Sinha. CRC Press, 2000 Corporate Blvd. N.W., Boca Raton, FL 33431. (800) 272-7737. 1988.

Soil, Humus and Health: An Organic Guide. Wilfred Edward Shewell-Cooper. David & Charles, Inc., PO Box 257, North Pomfret, VT 05053. (802) 457-1911. 1975.

Soil Management for Sustainability. R. Lal and F. J. Pierce, eds. Soil and Water Conservation Society, 7515 NE Ankeny Rd., Ankeny, IA 50021-9764. (515) 289-2331. 1991. Topics discussed in the book include: soil structure, soil compaction, and predicting soil erosion and its effects on crop productivity. Also covered are the basic processes, management options, and policy issues and priorities. Published in cooperation with the World Association of Soil and Water Conservation and the Soil Science Society of America

Soil Mineral Weathering. Van Nostrand Reinhold, 115 Fifth Ave., New York, NY 10003. (212) 254-3232. 1986. Topics in soil science and soil mineralogy.

Soil Organisms as Components of Ecosystems. U. Lohm. Swedish Natural Science Research Council, P.O. Box 6711, Stockholm, Sweden S-113 85. 08-15-1580. 1977. Covers soil ecology and soil fauna.

Soil Sampling and Analysis for Volatile Organic Compounds. U.S. Environmental Protection Agency Center for Environmental Research Information, 26 W. Martin Luther King Dr., Cincinnati, OH 45268. (513) 569-7931. 1991. Organic compounds in the underground water and their testing.

Soil Sampling and Soil Description. J.M. Hodgson. Clarendon Press, Walton St., Oxford, England OX2 6DP. 1978. Topics in conducting soil surveys.

Soil Science Society of America. 677 S. Segoe Rd., Madison, WI 53711. (608) 273-8080.

Soil Testing and Plant Analysis. R. L. Westerman, et al., eds. Crop Science Society of America, 677 South Segoe Rd., Madison, WI 53711. (608) 273-8080. 1990. 3d ed. Standard source on the subject of soil testing. Summarizes current knowledge and experience as diagnostic tool for assessing nutritional requirements of crops, efficient fertilizer use, saline-sodic conditions, and toxicity of metals.

Soil Vapor Extraction Technology. Tom A. Pedersen. Noyes Publications, 120 Mill Rd., Park Ridge, NJ 07656. (201) 391-8484. 1991. Environmental aspects of hydrocarbons.

Soils and Fertilizers. C. A. B. International, 845 North Park Ave., Tucson, AZ 85719. (602) 621-7897 or (800) 528-4841. 1937-. Monthly. Focuses on soil chemistry, soil physics, soil biology, soil fertility, soil management, soil classification, soil formation, soil conservation, land reclamation, irrigation and damage, fertilizer technology, fertilizer use, plant nutrition, plant water relations, and environmental aspects.

Soils and the Greenhouse Effect. A. F. Bouwman, ed. John Wiley & Sons, Inc., 605 3rd Ave., New York, NY 10158-0012. (212) 850-6000. 1990. Proceedings of the International Conference on Soils and the Greenhouse Effect, Wageningen, Netherlands, 1989. Covers the present status and future trends concerning the effect of soils and vegetation on the fluxes of greenhouse gases, the surface energy balance, and the water balance. Discusses the role of deforestation and management practices such as mulching, wetlands, agriculture and livestock.

Soils, Microbiology and Chemistry of Prairie Wetlands. North Dakota State University, Agricultural Experiment Station, Fargo, ND 58105. 1981. Annotated bibliography of soil science and wetlands.

Solar Buildings Technology. National Technical Information Service, 5285 Port Royal Road, Springfield, VA 22161. (703) 487-4650. 1988-. Bimonthly. Solar energy use in buildings, including desulfurization, photovoltaic systems, solar thermal, solar collectors, and heat storage.

The Solar Collector. Florida Solar Energy Center, 300 State Rd., 401, Cape Canaveral, FL 32920-4099. (407) 783-0300. Quarterly. Renewable energy research and technology.

Solar Dictionary. C. Breuning and F. F. Evangel. Energy Store, PO Box 1120, San Juan Pueblo, NM 87566. 1983. "Terms defined in the dictionary relate to solar energy and associated fields."

The Solar Energy Almanac. Facts on File, Inc., 460 Park Ave. S., New York, NY 10016. (212) 683-2244. 1983. " Basic book about the use of solar energy by individuals, communities, and nations."

Solar Energy Application, Bioconversion and Synfuels. T. Nejat Veziroglu, ed. Nova Science Publishers Inc., 283 Commack Rd., Suite 300, Commack, NY 11725-3401. (516) 499-3103; (516) 499-3106. 1990. Deals with solar energy applications such as heating and cooking, energy transmission, photovoltaics and industrial applications. Also includes chapters on bioconversion and synfuels.

Solar Energy Directory. Sandra Oddo, ed. Grey House Pub., 229 E. 79th St., Suite 3E, New York, NY 10010. 1983. Lists those U.S. organizations, institutions, agencies and industries working with the direct use of solar energy.

Solar Energy in Agriculture. Blaine F. Parker, ed. Elsevier Science Publishing Co., 655 Avenue of the Americas, New York, NY 10010. (212) 989-5800. 1991.

Solar Energy in Housing and Architecture: A Bibliography. Kathleen Ann Lodl. Vance Bibliographies, PO Box 229, 112 N. Charter St., Monticello, IL 61856. (217) 762-3831. 1987.

Solar Energy Index: The Arizona State University Solar Energy Collection. George Machovic. Pergamon Microforms International, Inc., Fairview Park, Elmsford, NY 10523. (914) 592-7720. 1980. Includes over 10,500 citations covering from the late 1800's to 1979. Aimed primarily at researchers, graduate students and advanced undergraduates.

Solar Energy Industries Association. 1730 N. Lynn St., Suite 610, Arlington, VA 22209. (703) 524-6100.

Solar Energy: Official Journal of the International Solar Energy Society. Pergamon Microforms International Inc., Fairview Park, Elmsford, NY 10523. (914) 592-7720. Monthly. Science and technology of solar energy applications.

Solar Energy Sourcebook for the Home Owner, Commercial Builder and Manufacturer. Christopher Wells Martz. Solar Energy Institute of America, 1110 6th St. NW, Washington, DC 20001. (202) 667-6611. 1978. Second edition. Gives profiles of companies and their services in connection with the application of solar energy in everyday life.

Solar-Hydrogen Energy Systems. Tokio Ohta. Pergamon Microforms International, Inc., Fairview Park, Elmsford, NY 10523. (914) 592-7720. 1979.

Solar Hydrogen: Moving Beyond Fossil Fuels. Joan M. Ogden and Robert H. Williams. World Resources Institute, 1709 New York Ave. N.W., Washington, DC 20006. (800) 822-0504. 1989. Traces the technical breakthroughs associated with solar hydrogen. Assesses the new fuel's potential as a replacement for oil, compares its costs and uses with those of both traditional and synthetic fuels, and charts a path for developing solar hydrogen markets.

The Solar Jobs Book. Katharine Ericson. Brick House Publishing Co., Inc., Francestown Tpke., New Boston, NH 03070. (603) 487-3718. 1980. How-to book that covers educational programs that teach how to participate in the new movement towards energy self-sufficiency.

Solar Primer One: Solar Energy in Architecture: A Guide for the Designer. Quinton M. Bradley. SOLARC, 2300 Cliff Dr., Newport Beach, CA 92263. (714)631-3182. 1975. Architecture and solar radiation, and energy conservation.

Solar Thermal Directory. Solar Energy Industries Association, 1730 N. Lynn St., Suite 610, Arlington, VA 22209. (703) 524-6100.

Solar Thermal Energy Technology. National Technical Information Service, 5285 Port Royal Road, Springfield, VA 22161. (703) 487-4650. 1983-. Bimonthly. Advanced concepts in materials research, concentrator and receiver technology, and salinity-gradient solar pond technology.

The Solar Thermal Report. Solar Liaison, Chicago, IL Quarterly. Covers solar energy and geothermal resources.

Solartherm. 1315 Apple Ave., Silver Spring, MD 20910. (301) 587-8686.

Solid Fuel Advisory Council of America. Star Rt. 104, Bristol, NH 03222. (603) 744-8627.

Solid State and Superconductivity Abstracts. Cambridge Scientific Abstracts, 5161 River Rd., Bethesda, MD 20816. (301) 961-6750.

Solid Waste and Power: The Waste-To-Energy Magazine. HCI Publications, 410 Archibald St., Suite 100, Kansas City, MO 64111. (816) 931-1311. Six times a year. Environmental considerations and proven approaches for dealing with concerns and requirements.

Solid Waste & Power–Waste-to-Energy Industry Directory Issue. HCI Publications, 410 Archibald St., Kansas City, MO 64111. (816) 931-1311.

Solid Waste Authority: Solid Waste Management. General Manager, PO Box 455, Dover, DE 19903. (302) 736-5361.

Solid Waste Authority: Solid Waste Management. Executive Director, PO Box 40285, Minallas Station, San Juan, PR 00940. (809) 765-7584.

The Solid Waste Dilemma: An Agenda for Action. U.S. Environmental Protection Agency, Office of Solid Waste and Emergency Response, 401 M St. SW, Washington, DC 20460. (202) 260-2090. 1989.

Solid Waste Education Recycling Directory. Teresa Jones, et al. Lewis Publishers, 200 Corporate Blvd. NW, Boca Raton, FL 33431. (407) 994-0555 or (800)272-7737. 1990. Summarizes recycling education curricula for each state covering all levels, K-12. Provides names, addresses, phone numbers, information about the availability of materials, how you collect them, and how much they cost.

The Solid Waste Handbook: A Practical Guide. William D. Robinson, ed. John Wiley & Sons, Inc., 605 3rd Ave., New York, NY 10158-0012. (212) 850-6000. 1986. Covers the field of solid waste management, including legislation, regulation, planning, finance, technologies, operations, economics administration, and future trends.

Solid Waste Management and the Environment: The Mounting Garbage and Trash Crisis. Homer A. Neal. Prentice-Hall, Rte. 9W, Englewood Cliffs, NJ 07632. (201) 592-2000. 1987. Environmental aspects of refuse and refuse disposal.

Solid Waste Management in the Food Distribution Industry. Food Marketing Institute, Research Department, 1750 K St., NW, Washington, DC 20006. 1990.

Solid Waste Management Newsletter. Cook College, Rutgers University, New Brunswick, NJ 08903. Bimonthly.

The Solid Waste Management Newsletter. Office of Technology Transfer (M/C 922), School of Public Health, University of Illinois at Chicago, Box 6998, Chicago, IL 60680. (312) 996-6927. Monthly. Provides a summary of important aspects in solid waste management. Subject matter for the newsletter reflects the hierarchy of methods for waste management specified in the Illinois Solid Waste Management Act of 1986.

Solid Waste Recycling; The Complete Resource Guide. Bureau of National Affairs, 1231 25th St. N.W., Washington, DC 20037. (800) 372-1033. 1990. Details federal and state laws and regulations, legal issues and local initiatives relating to waste crisis. Includes case studies of programs, surveys, studies, reports guidelines, recommendations, resources and references.

Solid Waste Report. Business Publishers, Inc., 951 Pershing Dr., Silver Spring, MD 20910-4464. (301) 587-6300. 1970-. Weekly. Covers the generation, collection, transportation, processing, resource recovery, recycling and ultimate disposal of municipal, commercial, agricultural and nonhazardous industrial refuse. Also available online.

Solid Waste Report. NewsNet, Inc., 945 Haverford Rd., Bryn Mawr, PA 19010. (800) 345-1301. Online version of the periodical of the same name.

Solid Waste Shredding and Shredder Selection. Harvey W. Rogers. U.S. Environmental Protection Agency, 401 M St., S.W., Washington, DC 20460. (202) 260-2090. 1974. Refuse and refuse disposal in the United States.

Solid Waste Systems. Government Refuse Collection and Disposal Association, 444 North LaBrea Ave., Los Angeles, CA 90036. Bimonthly.

Solubilities of Inorganic and Organic Compounds. H. Stephen and T. Stephen, eds. Macmillan Publishing Co., 866 3rd Ave., New York, NY 10022. (212) 702-2000; (800) 257-5755. 1963-67.

The Solution to Pollution in the Workplace. Laurence Sombke, et al. MasterMedia, 17 E. 89th St., New York, NY 10028. (212) 348-2020. 1991. Non-technical guidebook for cost-effective, practical tips and actions to help businesses, big and small, take a proactive role in solving pollution problems.

Solvent Waste Reduction. Noyes Publications, 120 Mill Rd., Park Ridge, NJ 07656. (201) 391-8484. 1990. Alternatives for reducing or eliminating environmental risk from waste solvents, either by internal practices or processes, or by the treatment, reuse, or recycling of the material before its final disposition.

Solvents & the Environment. FIND/SVP, 625 Avenue of the Americas, New York, NY 10011. (212) 645-4500. 1991. Demand forecasts on hydrocarbons for 1995 and 2000; chlorinated, ketones, alcohols and alcohol esters, ethers, glycols and other esters, and recycled solvents.

Solvents in Common Use: Health Risks to Workers. Royal Society of Chemistry, c/o CRC Press, 2000 Corporate Blvd. N.W., Boca Raton, FL 33431-9868. (800) 272-7737. 1988. 1st reprint 1990. Handbook contains essential information on ten of the most commonly used solvents.

Solvents Update. Halogenated Solvents Industry Alliance, 1225 19th Street, NW, Suite 300, Washington, DC 20036. (202) 223-5890. Monthly. Regulations and standards of state and national agencies.

Some Applications of Satellite Radiation Observations to Climate Studies. T.S. Chen. National Technical Information Service, 5285 Port Royal Rd., Springfield, VA 22161. (703) 487-4650. Detection of atmospheric radiation by meteorological satellites.

Some Aspects of the Environment and Electric Power Generation. Sylvain Denis. RAND, 1700 Main St., Santa Monica, CA 90401. (310) 393-0411. 1972. Thermal pollution of rivers, lakes, and electric power-plants.

Some Economic Impacts of Freshwater Stream Effluent Discharge Limits on Selected Small Communities in Mississippi. Leo R. Cheatham. Water Resources Research Institute, Mississippi State University, Mississippi State, MS 39762. Water supply, water pollution and drinking water contamination.

Some Publicly Available Sources of Computerized Information on Environmental Health and Toxicology. Kathy Deck. Centers for Disease Control, 1600 Clifton Rd., N.E., Atlanta, GA 30333. (404) 488-4588. 1991.

Sorbent Material for Spills & Other Liquid Pickups. FIND/SVP, 625 Avenue of the Americas, New York, NY 10011. (800) 346-3787. 1991. Analysis of regulations, economic variables, players, technologies, manufacturing processes and market strategies.

Sorghum and Millets Abstracts. C. A. B. International, 845 North Park Ave., Tucson, AZ 85719. (602) 621-7897 or (800) 528-4841. 1976-. Bimonthly. Covers studies from throughout the world in areas such as sorghum bicolor, eleusine coracana, panicum miliaceum, pennisetum americanum, and minor millets and related crops.

Sound Analysis and Noise Control. Van Nostrand Reinhold, 115 Fifth Ave., New York, NY 10003. (212) 254-3232. 1990. Discusses the physics of sound, the mechanism of hearing and the application of those principles to specific problems.

The Sounds Conservancy, Inc. c/o Marine Sciences Institute, University of Connecticut, Groton, CT 06340. (203) 445-1868.

A Source Book on Integrated Pest Management. Mary Louise Flint. U.S. G.P.O., Washington, DC 20401. (202) 512-0000. 1977.

Source of Water Supply. National Ground Water Information Center, National Water Well Association, 6375 Riverside Dr., Dublin, OH 43017. (614) 761-1711.

Sourcebook of Methods of Analysis for Biomass and Biomass Conversion Processes. T. A. Milne, et al. Elsevier Applied Science, 655 Avenue of the Americas, New York, NY 10010. 1990. Presents titles and abstracts of methods relevant to biomass conversion, from analyzing feedstocks to evaluating the performance of biofuels.

Sources and Applications of Ultraviolet Radiation. Academic Press, c/o Harcourt Brace Jovanovich Inc., 6277 Sea Harbor Dr., Orlando, FL 32887. (800) 346-8648. 1983. Topics in photochemistry.

Sources and Distribution of Nitrate in Ground Water at a Farmed Field Irrigated With Sewage Treatment Plant Effluent. Marian P. Berndt. Department of the Interior, U.S. Geological Survey, 119 National Center, Reston, VA 22092. (703) 648-4460. 1990. Covers underground water, sewage sludge as fertilizer, and nitrates.

Sources for Metal Castings: A Buyers Guide and Directory of Members. American Cast Metals Association, 455 State St., Des Plaines, IL 60016. (312) 299-9160.

Sources for the Future. Wallace Oates. Resources for the Future, 1616 P St., NW, Washington, DC 20036. (202) 328-5086. Examines emissions taxes, abatement subsides, and transferable emission permits in a national, regional, and global context.

Sources of Coastal Engineering Information. Yen-hsi Chu. National Technical Information Service, 5285 Port Royal Rd., Springfield, VA 22161. (703) 487-4650. 1987.

Sources of Concentrations of Dissolved Solids and Selenium in the San Joaquin River and its Tributaries, California, October 1985 to March 1987. Daphne G. Clifton and Robert J. Gilliom. Department of the Interior, U.S. Geological Survey, 119 National Center, Reston, VA 22092. (703) 648-4460. 1989. Report describes sediment transportation in rivers and tributaries.

Sources of Ignition: Flammability Characteristics of Chemicals and Products. John Bond. Butterworth-Heinemann, 80 Montvale Ave., Stoneham, MA 02180. (617) 438-8464; (800) 366-2665. 1991.

Sources of Radioiodine at Pressurized Water Reactors. Charles A. Pelletier. Electric Power Research Institute, 3412 Hillview Ave., Palo Alto, CA 94304. (415) 965-4081. 1978.

Sources of Supply/Buyers Guide. Advertisers & Publishers Service, Inc., 300 N. Prospect Ave., Park Ridge, IL 60068. (708) 823-3145.

South Carolina Environmental & Social Action Directory. Carolina Peace Resource Center, Columbia, SC (803) 799-3640.

South Carolina Environmental Law Reporter. Environmental Law Society, University of South Carolina Law Center, 1244 Blossom St., Columbia, SC 29208.

South Carolina Sea Grant Consortium. 287 Meeting Street, Charleston, SC 29401. (803) 727-2078.

South Dakota State University, South Dakota Cooperative Fish and Wildlife Research Unit. P.O. Box 2206, Brookings, SD 57007. (605) 688-6121.

South Dakota State University, Water Resources Institute. Brookings, SD 57007. (605) 688-4910.

Southeast California Research Station. 2140 Eastman Avenue, Suite 100, Ventura, CA 93003. (805) 644-1766.

Southeastern Association of Fish & Wildlife Agencies. c/o Joe L. Herring, 102 Rodney Dr., Baton Rouge, LA 70808. (504) 766-0519.

Southeastern Cooperative Wildlife & Fisheries Statistics Project. Institute of Statistics, North Carolina State University, Box 8203, Raleigh, NC 27695. (919) 737-2531.

Southeastern Cooperative Wildlife Disease Study. College of Veterinary Medicine, University of Georgia, Athens, GA 30602. (404) 548-1032.

Southeastern Fishes Council. 1300 Blue Spruce Dr., Ft. Collins, CO 80524. (303) 493-4855.

Southeastern Massachusetts University, Southeastern New England Clinical Microbiology Research Group. North Dartmouth, MA 02747. (508) 999-8320.

Southern Exposure: Deciding Antarctica's Future. Lee A. Kimball. World Resources Institute, 1709 New York Ave. N.W., Washington, DC 20006. (800) 822-0504. 1990. Reviews Antarctica's importance from a global perspective.

Southern Forest Products Association. Box 52468, New Orleans, LA 70152. (504) 443-4464.

Southern Illinois University at Carbondale, Cooperative Fisheries Research Laboratory. Carbondale, IL 62901. (618) 536-7761.

Southern Illinois University at Carbondale, Cooperative Wildlife Research Laboratory. Carbondale, IL 62901-6504. (618) 536-7766.

Southern Methodist University, Herbarium. Science Information Center, Dallas, TX (214) 692-2257.

Southwest Consortium on Plant Genetics and Water Resources. New Mexico State University, Box 3GL, Las Cruces, NM 88003. (505) 646-5453.

Southwest Research and Information Center. P.O. Box 4524, Albuquerque, NM 87106. (505) 262-1862.

Southwestern Research Station. American Museum of Natural History, Portal, AZ 85632. (602) 558-2396.

SPC Soap Perfumery & Cosmetics. United Trade Press Ltd., UTP House, 33-35 Bowling Green Ln., London, England EC1R 0DA. (01) 837 1212. 1928-. Monthly.

Specialty Household Chemicals. FIND/SVP, 625 Avenue of the Americas, New York, NY 10011. (212) 645-4500. 1991.

Specialty Vehicle Institute of America. 2 Jenner St., Ste. 150, Irvine, CA 92718. (714) 727-3727.

Species Conservation: A Population Biological Approach. A. Seitz, ed. Birkhauser Verlag, 675 Massachusetts Ave., Cambridge, MA 02139. (800) 777-4643. 1991.

Species Profiles: Life Histories and Environmental Requirements of Coastal Fishes and Invertebrates. U.S. G.P.O, Washington, DC 20402-9325. (202) 512-0000. Annual. Life cycle and environmental requirements of selected fish and shellfish species, by coastal region.

Species Profiles: Life Histories and Environmental Requirements of Coastal Fishes and Invertebrates, Pink Shrimp. Lourdes M. Bielsa. U.S. Department of the Interior, Fish and Wildlife Service, Washington, DC 20240. (202) 343-5634. 1983. Anatomy of invertebrates, fish, and shrimps.

Spent Fuel Storage. National Technical Information Service, 5285 Port Royal Rd., Springfield, VA 22161. (703) 487-4650. 1984. Bibliography of spent reactor fuel storage and reactor fuel reprocessing.

Spent Fuel Storage Requirements. U.S. Dept. of Energy. Nuclear Energy Office. National Technical Information Service, 5285 Port Royal Road, Springfield, VA 22161. (703) 487-4650. 1980. Annual. Required storage capacity for spent fuel discharges to the year 2020.

Spent Nuclear Fuel Discharges from U.S. Reactors. U.S. G.P.O., Washington, DC 20402-9325. (202) 512-0000. 1991. Commercial nuclear power plant spent fuel discharges, shipments, storage capacity, and inventory.

SPI/ERS Plastics Data Base. Ernst & Young, 1225 Connecticut Ave., N.W., Washington, DC 20036. (202) 862-6042. Time series on the production and sales of plastic resins in the United States.

Spill Control Association of America. 400 Renaissance Center, Suite 1900, Detroit, MI 48243. (313) 567-0500.

Spill Control Association of America News Brief. Spill Control Association of America, 400 Renaissance Center, Suite 1900, Detroit, MI 48243. (313) 567-0500. Monthly. Covers spill control, clean-up, and protection.

Spill Reporting Procedures Guide. Robert E. Abbott. Bureau of National Affairs, 1231 25th St. N.W., Washington, DC 20037. (202) 452-4200. 1990. This aid to fulfilling the requisite federal, state, and local reporting requirements contains the verbal and written reporting requirements for oil, hazardous substances, hazardous wastes, hazardous materials, excess air emissions, wastewater excursions, underground tank leaks, and SARA Title III.

Sport Fishing Institute. 1010 Massachusetts Ave., N.W., Washington, DC 20001. (202) 898-0770.

Sprinkle and Trickle Irrigation. Jack Keller and Ron D. Bliesner. Van Nostrand Reinhold, 115 5th Ave., New York, NY 10003. (212) 254-3232. 1990. Analyses environmental demands (evaporotranspiration, leaching, and irrigation water requirements) with moisture and infiltration characteristics of the soil and the various hydraulic, economic, and physical constraints of pressurized systems.

St. Catherine's Island Research Program. Office of Grants and Fellowships, American Museum of Natural History, Central Park West at 79th Street, New York, NY 10024. (212) 873-1300.

St. Joseph's University, Organic Synthesis Research Laboratory. 5600 City Ave., Philadelphia, PA 19131. (215) 660-1788.

Stabilization, Disinfection, and Odor Control in Sewage Sludge Treatment: An Annotated Bibliography Covering the Period 1950-1983. E. S. Connor. E. Horwood, 1230 Avenue of the Americas, New York, NY 10020. (212) 698-7000. 1984.

Stable Isotopes: Natural and Anthropogenic Sulphur in the Environment. R. R. Krouse and V. H. Grinenko, eds. John Wiley & Sons, Inc., 605 3rd Ave., New York, NY 10158-0012. (212) 850-6000. 1991. Published on behalf of the Scientific Committee on Problems of the Environment (SCOPE) of the International Council of Scientific Unions (ICSU) in collaboration with the United Nations Environment Programme. Addresses the important question of differentiating natural and anthropogenic sulphur in the environment. International experts explain how stable isotopes of sulphur and oxygen have been used to study the origin and transformations of sulphur in ecosystems.

Stainless Steel Databook. Metal Bulletin Inc., 220 5th St, 10th Fl., New York, NY 10001. (212) 213-6202. 1988.

Standard for Flame Arrestors for Use on Vents of Storage Tanks for Petroleum Oil and Gasoline. American National Standards Institute. Underwriters' Laboratories, 333 Pfingsten Rd., Northbrook, IL 60062. (708) 272-8800. 1984. Standards for fire prevention in oil and gasoline storage tanks.

Standard for the Protection, Processing, Handling and Storage of Zirconium. National Fire Protection Association, 1 Battery Park, PO Box 9101, Quincy, MA 02269-9101. (617) 770-3000. 1987. Standards of fire protection

Standard Handbook of Environmental Engineering. Robert A. Corbitt. McGraw-Hill, 1221 Ave. of the Americas, New York, NY 10020. (212) 512-2000 or (800) 262-4729. 1990. Hands-on reference to understand environmental engineering technology. Covers air quality control, water supply, wastewater disposal, waste management, stormwater and hazardous wastes.

Standard Handbook of Hazardous Waste Treatment and Disposal. Harry M. Freeman, ed. McGraw-Hill Science & Engineering Books, 11 West 19th St., New York, NY 10011. (212) 337-6010. 1989. A reference of alternatives and innovative technologies for managing hazardous waste and cleaning up abandoned disposal sites.

Standard Pesticide File. Derwent Publications, Ltd., 6845 Elm St., McLean, VA 22101. (703) 790-0400.

The Standard Pesticide User's Guide. Bert L. Bohmont. Prentice Hall, Rte. 9W, Englewood Cliffs, NJ 07632. (201) 592-2000. 1990. Includes material on laws and requirements, labeling, soil, groundwater, and endangered species. Covers new equipment, pumps, and techniques, as well as transportation, storage, decontamination, and disposal. Also covers integrated pest management.

Standard Reference Method for Ambient Testing. Environmental Protection Service, 425 St. Joseph Blvd., 3rd Fl., Hull, PQ, Canada K1A 0H3. (613) 953-5921. 1984.

Standard Tests for Toughened Resin Composites. National Technical Information Service, 5285 Port Royal Rd., Springfield, VA 22161. (703) 487-4650. 1983. Composite materials testing.

Stanford Environmental Law Journal. Stanford Environmental Law Society, Stanford Law School, Stanford, CA 94305. (415)723-4421. Annual.

Stanford University, Center for Conservation Biology. Department of Biological Sciences, Sanford, CA 94305-5020. (415) 723-5924.

Stanford University, Hopkins Marine Station. Pacific Grove, CA 93950. (408) 655-6200.

Stanford University, Jasper Ridge-Herrin Labs. Room 223, Stanford, CA 94305. (415) 723-1589.

Stat/EPA Indoor Radon Survey. U.S. G.P.O., Washington, DC 20401. (202) 512-0000. Annual. Indoor radon levels in houses in selected states.

State and Local Government Solid Waste Management. James T. O'Reilly. Clark Boardman Callaghan, 155 Pfingsten Rd., Deerfield, IL 60015. (800) 221-9428. 1991. To be revised annually. Focuses on municipal solid waste issues.

State and Private Forestry Learning System: Quick Reference Guide. U.S. Department of Agriculture, Forest Service, 14 Independence Ave., SW, Washington, DC 20250. 1983. Forestry schools and education in the United States.

State and Territorial Air Pollution Program Administrators. 444 North Capitol St., Washington, DC 20001. (202) 624-7864.

State Board of Health: Air Quality. Acting Assistant Commissioner, Air Pollution Control Division, 105 South Meridan St., Indianapolis, IN 46206. (317) 232-8217.

State Chemist Office: Pesticide Registration. State Chemist, Purdue University, Department of Biochemistry, West Lafayette, IN 47907. (317) 494-1585.

State Emergency Management Agency: Emergency Preparedness and Community Right-to-Know. Director, Title III Program, State Office Park South, 107 Pleasant St., Concord, NH 03301. (603) 271-2231.

State Environment Report: Toxic Substances & Hazardous Wastes. Business Publishers, Inc., 951 Pershing Drive, Silver Spring, MD 20910. (301) 587-6300. Weekly. Covers state legislative and regulatory initiatives.

State Environmental Facilities Corporation: Waste Minimization and Pollution Prevention. President, 50 Wolf Rd., Albany, NY 12205. (518) 457-4222.

State Environmental Law Special Report. Government Institutes, Inc., 4 Research Pl., Ste. 200, Rockville, MD 20850. (301) 921-2300. 1991. Provides a nationwide perspective of state environmental trends from 43 states. Highlights are included from recent and forthcoming major events in hazardous and solid waste control, underground storage tanks, state superfunds, special land use regulations, etc.

State Environmental Report. NewsNet, Inc., 945 Haverford Rd., Bryn Mawr, PA 19010. (800) 345-1301.

State Fire Marshal: Underground Storage Tanks. 3150 Executive Park Dr., Springfield, IL 62703. (217) 785-0969.

State Land Commissioner and Forester: Natural Resources. 1616 West Adams St., Room 329, Phoenix, AZ 85007. (602) 542-4621.

State of California Resources Agency News and Views. State of California Resources Agency, Department of Parks and Recreation, 1416 9th St., Sacramento, CA 95814. 1943-. Monthly.

State of the Art of Energy-Efficiency: Future Directions. Edward Vine and Drury Crawley, eds. University-Wide Energy Research Group, University of California, 2120 Berkeley Way, Berkeley, CA 94720. (415) 642-4262; (800) 822-6657. 1991. Practical compilation of energy-efficient technologies and programs, resource planning, and data collection and analysis for buildings, which account for more than half of all U.S. energy.

State-of-the-Art of the Pulp and Paper Industry. Neil McCubbin. Environmental Protection Service, 425 St. Joseph Blvd., 3rd Fl., Hull, PQ, Canada K1A 0H3. (613) 953-5921. 1984. Control technology of the wood-pulp industry; paper making and trade.

The State of the Earth Atlas. Joni Seger, ed. Touchstone/Simon and Schuster, Rockefeller Center, 1230 Avenue of the Americas, New York, NY 10020. 1990. Deals with environmental issues such as air quality, urban sprawl, toxic waste, tropical forests and tourism from a socioeconomic perspective.

The State of the Environment. OECD Publications and Information Center, 2001 L St., N.W., Suite 700, Washington, DC 20036. (202) 785-6323. 1991.

State of the Environment and Supplement: Environmental Indicators. UNIPUB, 4611-F Assembly Dr., Lanham, MD 20706. (301) 459-7666 or (800) 274-4888. 1991. Reviews the recent progress of OECD countries regarding environmental objectives by analyzing world ecological and economic independence and the need for sustainable development.

The State of the Environment with Supplement: Environmental Indicators. A. Preliminary Set. Organization for Economic Co-Operation and Development. OECD Publications and Information Centre, 2001 L. St. NW, Suite 700, Washington, DC 20036-4095. (202) 785-6323. 1991. Provides a review of the environment today for the purpose of assessing the "progress achieved over the past two decades...the lifetime of environmental policies and institutions in most member countries."

State of Washington Water Research Center. Washington State University, Pullman, WA 99164-3002. (509) 335-5531.

State Planning Office: Coastal Zone Management. Director, State House Station #38, Augusta, ME 04333. (207) 289-3261.

State Plant Board: Pesticide Registration. Director, Division of Feeds, Fertilizer and Pesticides, PO Box 1069, Little Rock, AR 72205. (501) 225-1598.

State Regulation Report: Toxics. NewsNet, Inc., 945 Haverford Rd., Bryn Mawr, PA 19010. (215) 527-8030. Toxic substances control and hazardous waste management at the state level.

State Univeristy of New York College of Environmental Science and Forestry. Adirondak Ecological Center, Huntington Forest, Newcomb, NY 12852. (518) 582-4551.

State University of New York at Albany, Center for Biological Macromolecules. Chemistry Department, 1400 Washington Avenue, Albany, NY 12222. (518) 422-4454.

State University of New York at Albany, Institute of Hemoproteins. Chemistry 131 A, 1400 Washington Avenue, Albany, NY 12222. (518) 442-4420.

State University of New York at Buffalo, Center for Applied Molecular Biology and Immunology. Vice President of Sponsored Programs, Department of Biochemistry, Cary Hall, Buffalo, NY 14260. (716) 636-3321.

State University of New York at Buffalo, Great Lakes Laboratory. 1300 Elmwood Avenue, Buffalo, NY 14222. (716) 878-5422.

State University of New York at Buffalo, Toxicology Research Center. 102 Faber Hall, Buffalo, NY 14214. (716) 831-2125.

State University of New York at Oneonta, Biological Field Station. RD 2, Box 1066, Cooperstown, NY 13326. (607) 547-8778.

State University of New York at Oswego, Research Center. King Hall, Oswego, NY 13126. (315) 341-3639.

State University of New York at Plattsburg, Biochemistry/ Biophysics Program. Plattsburg, NY 12901. (518) 564-3159.

State University of New York at Plattsburg, Center for Earth and Environmental Science. Plattsburg, NY 12901. (518) 564-2028.

State University of New York at Plattsburg, In Vitro Cell Biology and Biotechnology Program. Department of Biological Science, Plattsburg, NY 12901. (518) 846-7144.

State University of New York at Stony Brook, Ecology Laboratory. Stony Brook, NY 11797-5245. (516) 623-8600.

State University of New York at Stony Brook, Marine Sciences Research Center. Stony Brook, NY 11794. (516) 632-8700.

State University of New York College of Environmental Science and Forestry. Cellulose Research Institute, Baker Laboratory, Syracuse, NY 13210. (315) 470-6851.

State University of New York College of Environmental Science and Forestry. Institute for Environmental Policy and Planning, Bray Hall, Room 320, Syracuse, NY 13210. (315) 470-6636.

State University of New York College of Environmental Science and Forestry. Roosevelt Wildlife Institute, Syracuse, NY 13210. (315) 470-6741.

State University of New York College of Environmental Science and Forestry. Syracuse Forest Experiment Station, 452 Lafayette Rd., Syracuse, NY 13205. (315) 469-3053.

State University of New York College of Environmental Science and Forestry. Tropical Timber Information Center, 1 Forestry Dr., Syracuse, NY 13210-2786. (315) 470-6879.

State Water Commission: Groundwater Management. State Office Building, 900 East Blvd., Bismark, ND 58505. (701) 224-2750.

State Water Control Board: Underground Storage Tanks. Director, Office of Water Resources Management, PO Box 11143, Richmond, VA 23230. (804) 367-6383.

State Water Control Board: Water Quality. Executive Director, PO Box 11143, Richmond, VA 23230. (804) 257-6384.

The Statehouse Effect: State Policies to Cool the Greenhouse. Daniel A. Lashof and Eric L. Washburn. Natural Resources Defense Council, 40 W. 20th St., New York, NY 10011. (212) 727-2700. 1990. Discusses the need for states to take the initiative in controlling CO2 emissions. Details the sources of greenhouse gases and explains how greenhouse emissions can be reduced through energy efficiency, renewable energy strategies, recycling, and taxation and reforms in transportation, agriculture and forests.

Statewide Air Pollution Research Center. University of California, Riverside, Riverside, CA 92521. (714) 787-5124.

Statistical Methods for the Environmental Sciences. A.H. El-Shaarwi, ed. Kluwer Academic Publishers, 101 Philip Dr., Assinippi Pk., Norwell, MA 02061. (617) 871-6600. 1991.

Statistical Methods in Soil and Land Resource Survey. R. Webster and M. A. Oliver. Oxford University Press, 200 Madison Ave., New York, NY 10016. (212) 679-7300; (800) 334-4249. 1990. Describes methods for making quantitative surveys, stressing the need for sound sampling, sensible and efficient estimation and proper planning.

Statistical Record of the Environment. Arsen J. Darnay. Gale Research Inc., 835 Penobscot Bldg., Detroit, MI 48226-4094. (313) 961-2242. 1992.

Statistical Report. Potash and Phosphate Institute, 2801 Buford Hwy., NE, Suite 401, Atlanta, GA 30329-2199. Monthly. Production, sales, imports, and exports.

Statistical Roundup. National Forest Products Association, 1250 Connecticut Ave., NW, Suite 200, Washington, DC 20036. 1980-. Monthly. Production and shipments, orders, consumption, foreign trade, and employment.

Statistical Summary of Fish and Wildlife Restoration. U.S. Fish and Wildlife Service. U.S. G.P.O., Washington, DC 20401. (202) 512-0000. Annual. Data on hunting, fishing activities, and restoration.

Statistical Yearbook. Edison Electric Institute, 1111 19th St., NW, Washington, DC 20036-3691. Annual. Electric utility industry financial and operating data.

Status Assessment of Toxic Chemicals: Hexachlorobenzene. T. R. Blackwood. National Technical Information Service, 5285 Port Royal Rd., Springfield, VA 22161. (703) 487-4650. 1980.

Status Assessment of Toxic Chemicals: Phosphates. J. C. Ochsner. National Technical Information Service, 5285 Port Royal Rd., Springfield, VA 22161. (703) 487-4650. 1980.

Status of the Fishery Resources Off the Northeastern U.S. U.S. National Marine Fisheries Service. National Technical Information Service, Springfield, VA 22161. (703) 487-4650. Annual. Covers Atlantic ocean finfish and shellfish landings.

Staying Out of Trouble: What You Should Know about the New Hazardous Waste Law. National Association of Manufacturers, 1331 Pennsylvania Ave., NW, Suite 1500 N., Washington, DC 20004. (202) 637-3000. 1985. Hazardous waste laws and legislation in the United States. Also covers refuse and disposal.

Steady-State Economics. Herman E. Daly. Island Press, 1718 Connecticut Ave. N.W., Suite 300, Washington, DC 20009. (202) 232-7933. 1991.

Steam-Electric Plant Air and Water Quality Control Data for the Year Ended...Summary Report. Federal Energy Regulatory Commission, Office of Electrical Power Regulation, 825 N. Capitol St. NE, Washington, DC 20426. (202) 208-0200. 1969-1973. Covers electric power-plants, air quality, and water quality.

Steel Can Recycling Institute. Foster Plaza X, 680 Anderson Dr., Pittsburgh, PA 15220. (412) 922-2772.

Steel Shot and Lead Poisoning in Waterfowl. National Wildlife Federation, Resources Conservation Department, 1400 16th St. NW, Washington, DC 20036-2266. (202) 797-6800. 1983. Covers waterfowl shooting, veterinary toxicology and lead poisoning.

Steering a New Course: Transportation, Energy and the Environment. Deborah Gordon. Island Press, 1718 Connecticut Ave. N.W., Suite 300, Washington, DC 20009. (202) 232-7933. 1991. Includes a history of modern American transportation, an overview of the U.S. transportation sector, and an in-depth discussion of the strategies that hold the most promise for the future. Also has information on alternative fuels, advances in mass transit, ultra fuel efficient vehicles, high-occupancy vehicle facilities and telecommuting and alternative work schedules.

Steering Committee for Sustainable Agriculture. P.O. Box 1300, Colfax, CA 95713. (916) 346-2777.

Stella Duncan Memorial Research Institute. University of Montana, Missoula, MT 59812. (406) 243-6676.

Steroids. CRC Press, 2000 Corporate Blvd. N.W., Boca Raton, FL 33431. (800) 272-7737. 1986. Chromatographic analysis of steroids.

A Stillness in the Pines: The Ecology of the Red-Cockaded Woodpecker. Robert W. McFarlane. Norton, 500 5th Ave., New York, NY 10110. (800) 223-2584 or (212) 354-5500. 1992. Tells the story of the decline of the red-cockaded woodpecker, a specialized inhabitant of mature Southeastern pine forests.

Stochastic Hydrology and Hydraulics. Springer-Verlag, 175 5th Ave., New York, NY 10010. (212) 460-1500. Four times a year. Statistical methods in hydraulics.

Stochastic Processes in Demography and Applications. Suddhendu Biswas. John Wiley & Sons, Inc., 605 3rd Ave., New York, NY 10158-0012. (212) 850-6000. 1989. Describes statistical methods applied in demography.

Stones in a Glass House: CFCs and Ozone Depletion. Douglas G. Cogan. Investor Responsibility Research Center, 1755 Massachusetts Ave., NW, Suite 600, Washington, DC 20036. (202) 234-7500. 1988. Environmental aspects of air pollution.

Stopping Acid Mine Drainage: A New Approach. West Virginia Geological and Economic Survey, PO Box 879, Morgantown, WV 26507. (304) 594-2331. 1985.

Storage of Water Reactor Spent Fuel in Water Pools: Survey of World Experience. International Atomic Energy and the Nuclear Energy Agency. UNIPUB, 4611-F Assembly Dr., Lanham Seabrook, MD 20706-4391. (301) 459-7666. 1982. Nuclear fuels storage techniques.

Storage, Shipment, Handling, and Disposal of Chemical Agents and Hazardous Chemicals. Department of the Army, The Pentagon, Washington, DC 20310. (202) 545-6700. 1989. Safety measures and transportation of chemicals.

STORET. U.S. Environmental Protection Agency, Office of Information Resources Management, 401 M St., S.W., Washington, DC 20460. (202) 260-2090. Water pollution measurement data collected from more than 700,000 observation stations across the United States.

Storm Data. National Environmental Satellite, Data, and Information Service, 2069 Federal Bldg. 4, Washington, DC 20233. (301) 763-7190. Monthly.

Storm Sewers: Monographs. Mary A. Vance. Vance Bibliographies, 112 N. Charter St., PO Box 229, Monticello, IL 61856. (217) 762-3831. 1984.

Storm Water: Guidance Manual for the Preparation of NPDES Permit Applications for Storm Water Discharges Associated with Industrial Activity. Government Institutes, Inc., 4 Research Pl., Ste. 200, Rockville, MD 20850. (301) 921-2300. 1991. Provides an overview of the new EPA regulations; contains an overview of the permitting process and information regarding the permit application requirements.

Strategic Planning for Energy and the Environment Journal. Energy Engineering, 700 Indian Trail, Lilburn, GA 30247. 1990-. Quarterly. Concentrates on the background, new developments and policy issues which impact corporate planning for energy and environmental issues.

Strategic Planning for Waste Minimization. FIND/SVP, 625 Avenue of the Americas, New York, NY 10011. (212) 645-4500. 1990.

Strategies for Human Settlements: Habitat and Environment. Gwen Bell. University of Hawaii Press, 840 Kolowalu St., Honolulu, HI 96822. (808) 956-8257. 1076. Community development and environmental policy.

A Strategy for Occupational Exposure Assessment. American Industrial Hygiene Association, 345 White Pond Dr., Akron, OH 44320. (216) 873-2442. 1991. Highlights the considerations to be made in determining priorities for monitoring work exposures.

Stray Voltage. American Society of Agricultural Engineers, 2950 Niles Rd., St. Joseph, MI 49085-9659. (616) 429-0300. 1985. Proceedings of the National Stray Voltage Symposium, October 10-12, 1984, New York. Includes animal sensitivity, electrical system characteristics and source identification and mitigation and protection.

Stray Voltage. Robert J. Gustafson. Energy Research and Development Division, Energy and Environmental Policy Department, National Rural Electric Cooperative Association, 1800 Massachusetts Ave., NW, Washington, DC 20036. (202) 857-9500. 1988. Seasonal variations in grounding and primary neutral-to-earth voltages.

Stray Voltages in Agriculture: Workshop. American Society of Agricultural Engineers, 2950 Niles Rd., St. Joseph, MI 49085-9659. (616) 429-0300. 1983. Includes the effects of stray voltage on animals, source of stray voltage, diagnostic procedures for detection and measurement and treatments or corrective procedure for stray voltage problem. The workshop was sponsored by the National Rural Electric Cooperative Association in Minneapolis, MN.

Stream, Lake, Estuary, and Ocean Pollution. Nelson Leonard Nemerow. Van Nostrand Reinhold, 115 5th Ave., New York, NY 10003. (800) 926-2665. 1991.

Strengthening Environmental Cooperation with Developing Countries. OECD Publications and Information Center, 2001 L St. N.W., Ste. 700, Washington, DC 20036. (202) 785-OECD. 1989. Report from an OECD seminar involving developing countries, aid and environmental agencies, multinational financing institutions, and non-governmental organizations concludes that early environmental assessment of development assistance projects and programs can play a key role in improving international cooperation for sustainable development.

Stress Responses in Plants: Adaptation and Acclimation Mechanisms. Ruth G. Alscher. Wiley-Liss, 605 3rd Ave., New York, NY 10158-0012. (212) 850-6000. 1990. Effect of stress on plant adaptation and acclimatization.

Stroud Water Research Center. 512 Spencer Road, Avondale, PA 19311. (215) 268-2153.

Structural Cement-Fiber Products Association. 5028 Wisconsin Ave., N.W., Washington, DC 20016. (301) 961-9800.

Student Conservation Association. P.O. Box 550, Charlestown, NH 03603. (603) 826-4301.

Student Conservation Association Evaluation Report. Student Conservation Assn., Box 550, Charlestown, NH 03603. (603) 826-4301. Annual.

The Student Environmental Action Guide. The Student Environmental Action Coalition. Earthworks Press, 1400 Shattuck Ave., No. 25, Berkeley, CA 94709. (510) 652-8533. 1991. The coalition in collaboration with Earth Works has made adaptations to student lifestyles.

Studies in Surface Science and Catalysis. Elsevier Science Publishing Co., 655 Avenue of the Americas, New York, NY 10010. (212) 989-5800. 1991.

A Study of Enzymes. Stephen Kuby, ed. CRC Press, 2000 Corporate Blvd. N.W., Boca Raton, FL 33431. (407) 994-0555; (800) 272-7737. 1991. 2 vols. Deals in detail with selected topics in enzyme mechanisms.

A Study of the Photodegradation of Commercial Dyes. John J. Porter. U.S. G.P.O., Washington, DC 20401. (202) 512-0000. 1973. Textile waste, dyes and dyeing in terms of their chemistry and waste disposal.

Styrene and Ethylbenzene Association. c/o SOCMA, 1330 Connecticut Ave., N.W., Suite 300, Washington, DC 20036. (202) 659-0060.

Styrene Information and Research Center. 1275 K St., N.W., Suite 400, Washington, DC 20036. (202) 371-5314.

Subantarctic Macquarie Island: Environment and Biology. P. M. Selkirk, et al. Cambridge University Press, 40 W. 20th St., New York, NY 10011. (212) 924-3900; (800) 227-0247. 1990. Review of environmental and biologic research on the Macquarie Island. It presents summary of studies done in the last 15 years by Australian scientists. Contains a sequence of 12 chapters that concern the island's discovery and history; situation in the Southern ocean; tectonics and geology; landforms and Quaternary history; vegetation; lakes; birds; mammals; anthropoids; microbiology; near shore environments; and human impact.

Sublittoral Ecology. R. Earll. Oxford University Press, Inc., 200 Madison Ave., New York, NY 10016. (212) 679-7300. 1983. The ecology of the shadow sublittoral benthos.

Submersible Wastewater Pump Association. 600 Federal St., Suite 400, Chicago, IL 60605. (312) 922-6222.

Subsidence from Underground Mining. U.S. Geological Survey, 12201 Sunrise Valley Dr., Reston, VA 22092. (703) 648-4460. 1983. Environmental aspects of mine subsidence.

Substitute Fuels for Road Transport: A Technology Assessment. OECD Publications and Information Center, 2001 L. St., N.W., Suite 700, Washington, DC 20036. (202) 785-OECD. 1990. Report analyzes the availability, economics, technical problems and effects on the environment from the use of substitute fuels.

Substituted Anilines Task Force. 1330 Connecticut Ave., N.W., Suite 300, Washington, DC 20036. (202) 659-0060.

Subsurface Contamination Reference Guide. Office of Emergency and Remedial Response, U.S. Environmental Protection Agency, 401 M St.,S.W., Washington, DC 1991. Underground water pollution and hazardous substances.

Subsurface Migration of Hazardous Wastes. Joseph S. Devinny. Van Nostrand Reinhold, 115 5th Ave., New York, NY 10003. (212) 254-3232. 1990. Environmental aspects of underground water pollution.

Subterranean Termites. Raymond H. Beal. U.S. Department of Agriculture, c/o U.S. Government Printing Office, Washington, DC 20401. (202) 512-0000. 1989.

Success and Dominance in Ecosystems. Edward O. Wilson. Ecology Institute, Nordbunte 23, Oldendorf/Luhe, Germany D-2124 1990. Proposes that the success of a species is measured by its evolutionary longevity and its dominance by its ability to dominate or control the appropriation of biomass and energy in ecosystems. Explores how and why social insects, representing only 2 percent of insect species but accounting for one-half of insect biomass, became the ecological center of terrestrial ecosystems. Much of the social insects success is attributed to their ability to function as highly structured superorganisms.

Sul Ross State University Herbarium. Alpine, TX 79830. (915) 837-8112.

Sulphur Institute. 1725 K St., N.W., Suite 508, Washington, DC 20006. (202) 331-9660.

Summaries of DOE Hydrogen Programs. Hydrogen Energy Coordinating Committee/Office of Conservation and Renewable Energy, Department of Energy, 1000 Independence Ave., S.W., Washington, DC 20585. (202) 586-6104.

Summaries of Foreign Government Environmental Reports. U.S. Environmental Protection Agency, 401 M St., S.W., Washington, DC 20460. (202) 260-2090.

A Summary of Current Forest Insect and Disease Problems for New York State. Society of American Foresters, 5400 Grosvenor Ln., Bethesda, MD 20814. (301) 897-8720. 1969/70-.

Summary of Federal Programs and Projects. National Marine Pollution Program Office, National Oceanic and Atmospheric Administration, 11400 Rockville Pike, Rm. 610, Rockville, MD 20852. (301) 443-8823. 1969.

A Summary of the NBS Literature Reviews on the Chemical Nature and Toxicity of the Pyrolysis and Combustion Products from Seven Plastics. Barbara C. Levin. National Technical Information Service, 5285 Port Royal Rd., Springfield, VA 22161. (703) 487-4650. 1986. Acrylonitrile-butadiene-styrenes (ABS), nylons, polyesters, polyethylenes, polystyrenes, poly(vinyl chlorides), and rigid polyurethane foams.

Summary of the U.S. Geological Survey and U.S. Bureau of Land Management National Coal-Hydrology Program. L.J. Britton. U.S. G.P.O., Washington, DC 20401. (202) 512-0000. 1990. Environmental aspects of coal and coal mining.

Summary Review of Health Effects Associated with Hydrogen Flouride. U.S. Environmental Protection Agency, MD 75, Research Triangle Park, NC 27711. 1989.

Sump and Sewage Pump Association. P.O. Box 298, Winnetka, IL 60093. (312) 835-8911.

Sun/Earth: Alternative Energy Design for Architecture. Richard L. Crowther. Van Nostrand Reinhold, 115 Fifth Ave., New York, NY 10003. (212) 254-3232. 1983. Renewable energy sources and energy conservation in dwellings.

Sun Power: A Bibliography of United States Government Documents on Solar Energy. Sandra McAninch. Greenwood Publishing Group, Inc., 88 Post Rd. W., PO Box 5007, Westport, CT 06881. (212) 226-3571. 1981. Has over 3600 citations.

Sunken Nuclear Submarines: A Threat to the Environment?. Viking Oliver Eriksen. Norwegian Univ. Pr., Oxford Univ. Pr., 200 Madison Ave., New York, NY 10016. (212) 679-7300; (800) 334-4249. 1990. Part 1 is a survey of existing submarines, based upon surmise and extrapolation from public knowledge of civilian terrestrial and nautical reactors. Part 2 describes potential accident scenarios and their potential for nuclide release, and Part 3 briefly sketches the oceanographic factors governing dispersion of radioactive nuclides.

Sunlight, Ultraviolet Radiation, and the Skin. U.S. Department of Health and Human Services, Public Health Services, National Institutes of Health, 9000 Rockville Pike, Bethesda, MD 20892. (301) 496-4000. 1989. Bibliography of the physiological effects of solar and ultraviolet radiation.

Sunrise. International Ecology Society, 1471 Barclay St., St. Paul, MN 55106-1405. (612) 774-4971. Monthly.

Superconductor Week. NewsNet, Inc., 945 Haverford Rd., Bryn Mawr, PA 19010. (800) 345-1301.

Superfund. NewsNet, Inc., 945 Haverford Rd., Bryn Mawr, PA 19010. (800) 345-1301.

SUPERFUND: A More Vigorous and Better Managed Enforcement Program Is Needed. U.S. G.P.O., Washington, DC 20401. (202) 512-0000. 1989. Irregular. Superfund hazardous waste site cleanup enforcement and cost recovery activities.

Superfund Handbook. Sidley & Austin, 696 Virginia Road, Concord, MA 01742. 1987. Law and legislation relating to refuse, refuse disposal, and its environmental aspects.

Superfund Manual: Legal and Management Strategies. Crowell & Moring. Government Institutes, Inc., 4 Research Pl., Suite 200, Rockville, MD 20850. (301) 921-2300. 1990. 4th ed. Industrial liability for hazardous waste and pollution damage at hazardous waste sites are explained. Explains the latest developments in the Superfund program. Includes the interrelationships between Superfund and RCRA; new regulations to implement Emergency Planning and the Community Right-to-Know Act; revisions to the National Contingency Plan; new EPA guidance documents relating to cleanup standards, site studies, and settlement procedures; court decisions and the special problems.

Supplier Notification Requirements. U.S. Environmental Protection Agency, Office of Pesticides and Toxic Substances, 401 M St., SW, Washington, DC 20460. (202) 260-2090. 1990. Legal aspects of reporting on chemicals and hazardous wastes.

Supplying Water and Saving the Environment for Six Billion People. Udai P. Singh and Otto J. Helweg, eds. American Society of Civil Engineers, 345 E. 47th St., New York, NY 10017. (212) 705-7288; (800) 548-2723. 1990. Proceedings of selected sessions from the 1990 ASCE Convention, San Francisco, CA, Nov. 5-8, 1990. Sponsored by the Environmental Engineering Division, Irrigation and Drainage Division, Water Resources Planning and Management Division of the American Society of Civil Engineers.

Support Senate NOx Ozone Non-Attainment Provision: White Paper. American Gas Association, 1515 Wilson Blvd., Arlington, VA 22209. 1990. Covers environmental aspects of the gas industry, nitric oxide, and ozone layer depletion-law and legislation.

Surface-Level Ozone Exposures and Their Effects on Vegetation. A. S. Lefohn. Lewis Publishers, 2000 Corporate Blvd., N.W., Boca Raton, FL 33431. (407) 994-0555 or (800) 272-7737. 1992. Discusses the tropospheric ozone, the characterization of ambient ozone exposures, experimental methodology, and effects on crops, trees and vegetation.

Surface Mining of Non-Coal Minerals: Appendix II, Mining and Processing of Oil Shale and Tar Sands. National Research Council. National Academy of Sciences, 2101 Constitution Ave., NW, Washington, DC 20418. (202) 334-2000. 1980. Environmental aspects of oil shale industry, strip mining, and mining law.

Surface Mining Water Diversion Manual. Li Simons & Associates, Inc. U.S. G.P.O., Washington, DC 20401. (202) 512-0000. 1982.

The Surface Water Acidification Programme. B. J. Mason, ed. Cambridge University Press, 40 W. 20th St., New York, NY 10011. (212) 924-3900; (800) 227-0247. 1991. Proceedings of the final Conference of the Surface Water Acidification Programme, held at the Royal Society in March 1990. Deals with the acid pollution of rivers and lakes and presents research results on watersheds in Great Britain and Scandinavia.

Surfactants to 1995. FIND/SVP, 625 Avenue of the Americas, New York, NY 10011. (212) 645-4500. 1991. Analyzes four major types of surfactants used in over a dozen markets.

Surveillance of Drinking Water Quality in Rural Areas. Barry Lloyd. John Wiley & Sons, Inc., 605 3rd Ave, New York, NY 10158-0012. (212) 850-6000. 1991. Examines the human and technical resources required for monitoring, maintaining and improving the safety of rural water supply services. A practical guide to improving the quality of service from small water supplies, it describes the essential minimum of reliable methods of monitoring water quality and discusses new cost effective approaches to sanitary inspection of community water supplies.

Surveillance of Items Important to Safety in Nuclear Power Plants. International Atomic Energy Agency. UNIPUB, 4611-F Assembly Dr., Lanham, MD 20706-4391. (301) 459-7666; (800) 270-4888. 1990. Discusses the safety measures observed at atomic power plants.

Survey of Alternatives to the Use of Chlorides for Highway Deicing. Joseph A. Zenewitz. Department of Transportation, Federal Highway Administration, National Technical Information Service, 5285 Port Royal Rd., Springfield, VA 22161. (703) 487-4650. 1977.

Survey of Carbon Tetrachloride Emission Sources. National Technical Information Service, 5285 Port Royal Rd., Springfield, VA 22161. (703) 487-4650. 1985.

Survey of Chemicals Tested for Carcinogenicity. Science Resource Center, Kensington, MD 1976. Entries from scientific literature from approximately 1913 to 1973, reporting on groups of animals treated with any chemical compounds and subsequently examined for tumors.

Survey of Compounds Which Have Been Tested for Carcinogenic Activity. National Cancer Institute. National Institutes of Health, National Cancer Institute, 9000 Rockville Pike, Bethesda, MD 20892. (301) 496-4000. 1976. Series of books with extracted data from scientific literature regarding the test of chemical compounds in experimental animals. Over 4,500 compounds are identified.

Survey of Household Hazardous Wastes and Related Collection Programs. Waste Management Division/Office of Solid Waste, U.S. Environmental Protection Agency, 401 M St., S.W., Washington, DC 20460. (202) 382-2090.

A Survey of the Market, Supply, and Availability of Gallium. Fred D. Rosi. National Technical Information Service, 5285 Port Royal Rd., Springfield, VA 22161. (703) 487-4650. 1980.

Suspect Chemicals Sourcebook. Roytech Publications, Inc., 7910 Woodmont Ave., Ste. 902, Bethesda, MD 20814. (301) 654-4281. References to U.S. federal regulations and precautionary data pertaining to the manufacture, sale, storage, use, and transportation of more than 5,000 industrial chemical substances. Online version of handbook of the same name.

Suspect Chemicals Sourcebook. Roytech Publications, Inc., 7910 Woodmont Ave., Ste. 902, Bethesda, MD 20814. (301) 654-4281. 1985-. Includes: chemical name index, CAS registry numbers; OSHA Chemical Hazard chemical name; Summary and full text of OSHA Chemical Hazard Communication Standard and history and overview. Also available online.

Suspected Carcinogens: A Subfile of the NIOSH Toxic Substance List. Herbert E. Christensen and Thomas T. Luginbyh, eds. U.S. Department of Health and Human Services, 200 Independence Ave. SW, Washington, DC 20201. (202) 619-0257. 1975.

Suspended, Cancelled, and Restricted Pesticides. U.S. Environmental Protection Agency, Office of Pesticides and Toxic Substances, 401 M St. SW, Washington, DC 20460. (202) 260-2090. 1990.

Susquehanna River Basin Commission. Department of Interior Building, 1100 L St., N.W., Room 5113, Washington, DC 20240. (202) 343-4091.

Susquehanna River Tri-State Association. Stark Learning Center, Rm. 441, Wilkes College, Wilkes-Barre, PA 18702. (717) 824-5193.

Sustainable Development and Environmental Management of Small Islands. W. Beller, et al., eds. Parthenon Pub., Casterton Hall, Carnforth, England LA6 2LA. Lancs. 1990. Volume 5 in the Man and the Biosphere series published jointly with UNESCO.

Symposium on Regeneration Research (1975: Gatlinburg, Tenn.) Proceedings. American Society of Civil Engineers, 345 E. 47th St., New York, NY 10017. (212) 705-7288. 1979. Papers presented dealt with water quality and dissolved oxygen in water and the water aeration process.

SYNERJY: A Directory of Renewable Energy. SYNERJY, Box 1854, Cathedral Station, New York, NY 10025. (212) 865-9595.

Synfuels Handbook. Including the Yellow Pages of Synfuels. McGraw-Hill Science & Engineering Books, 1221 Avenue of the Americas, New York, NY 10020. (212) 512-2000 or (800) 262-4729. 1980. Specific aspects included in this handbook are: coal gasification and liquefaction, oil shale, overview, process development, materials, synfuels, and other products, mining and environmental aspects.

Synthesis and Chemistry of Agrochemicals II. Don R. Baker, et al., eds. American Chemical Society, 1155 16th St. N.W., Washington, DC 20036. (202) 872-4600; (800) 227-5558. 1991. Trends in synthesis and chemistry of agrochemicals.

Synthesis of Effects of Oil on Marine Mammals. U.S. Dept. of Interior. Mineral Management Service. National Technical Information Service, 5285 Port Royal Road, Springfield, VA 22161. (703) 487-4650. 1988. Impacts of spills and spill-treating agents on marine and arctic land mammals.

Synthesis of Fluorinated Hydrocarbons: A Compilation. U.S. National Aeronautics and Space Administration, Technology Utilization Division. Technology Utilization Division, Office of Technology Utilization, NASA, Washington, DC 1968.

Synthetic Amorphous Silica an Silicates Industry Association. 1226 Cardinal Ave., Pittsburgh, PA 15243. (201) 807-3173.

Synthetic Fuels and Alternate Energy Worldwide Directory. PennWell Books, PO Box 1260, Tulsa, OK 74101. (918) 663-4225. 1984. Third edition. Provides a complete list of companies, organizations, individuals, government agencies and educational institutions involved in the development of and the application of synthetic fuels and alternate energy sources.

Synthetic Organic Chemical Manufacturers Association. 1330 Connecticut Ave., N.W., Suite 300, Washington, DC 20036. (202) 659-0060.

Synthetic Organic Chemical Manufacturers Association Newsletter. Synthetic Organic Chemical Manufacturers Association, 1330 Connecticut Avenue, NW, Washington, DC 20036. (202) 659-0060. Biweekly. Covers trade, environmental and safety issues.

Synthetic Organic Chemicals. U.S. G.P.O., Washington, DC 20401. (202) 512-0000. 1967. An annual publication on production and sales in the U.S. for all synthetic organic chemicals produced commercially. About 800 chemicals and 800 manufacturers are included in the USITC surveys, but because of confidentiality requirements only parts of the data are published. U.S. Tariff Commission acts under the provisions of Section 332 of the Tariff Act of 1930, as amended.

Synthetic Organic Chemicals: U.S. Production and Sales. United States International Trade Commission, 500 E St., S.W., Washington, DC 20436. (202) 523-0161.

Synthetic Pyrethroid Insecticides. Klaus Naumann. Springer-Verlag, 175 5th Ave., New York, NY 10010. (212) 460-1500. 1990. Structure and properties of pyrethroids and their synthesis.

Synthetically Useful Dipole-Stabilized Carbonions from Thioesters and Thiocarbamates. Peter Donald Becker. University of Illinois, Urbana, IL 61801. 1982.

Syracuse University, Biological Research Laboratories. 130 College Place, Syracuse, NY 13210. (315) 423-3186.

System Analysis Applied to Management of Water Resource. M. Jellali, ed. Pergamon Microforms International, Inc., Fairview Park, Elmsford, NY 10523. (914) 592-7720. 1989. Proceedings of the Fourth IFAC Symposium, Rabat, Morocco, 11- 13 October 1988. Illustrates aspects of the application of systems analysis to water resource management. Also included are theoretical discussions on mathematical modelling and the potential role of expert systems.

Systems Ecology. Howard T. Odum. John Wiley & Sons, Inc., 605 3rd Ave., New York, NY (212) 850-6000. 1983. Simulation methods in ecology and biotic communities and bioenergetics.

T Cell Clones. Year Book Medical Publishers, Inc., 200 N. LaSalle St., Chicago, IL 60601. (800) 622-5410. 1981.

Tables of Physical and Chemical Constants and Some Mathematical Functions. G. W. C. Kaye, et al. Longman Group Ltd., Longman House, Burnt Mill, Harlow, England CM20 2J6. 0279 426721. 1988. Fifteenth edition. Includes tables on mechanical properties, density, elasticity, viscosity, surface tension, temperature and heat. Also covers radiation, optics, chemistry, electrochemistry, astrophysics, and chemical thermodynamics.

Taking Stock: The Tropical Forestry Action Plan After Five Years. Robert Winterbottom. World Resources Institute, 1709 New York Ave. N.W., Washington, DC 20006. (800) 822-0504. 1990. Analyzes Tropical Forestry Action Plan's accomplishments and shortcomings, drawing on the biannual meetings of the TFAP Forestry Advisors' groups, assessments by FAO, various aid agencies, and by such organizations as the World Rainforest Movement, Friends of the Earth, and World Life Fund.

Talking Leaves. Institute for Earth Education, PO Box 288, Warrenville, IL 60555. (708) 393-3096. Quarterly. Programs and events dealing with earth and ecology education.

Talking Trash: Municipal Solid Waste Mismanagement. Kenneth Chilton. Center for the Study of American Business, Washington University, Campus Box 1208, One Brookings Dr., St. Louis, MO 63130-4899. (314) 935-5630. 1990.

Tall Timbers Research Station. R.R. 1, Box 678, Tallahassee, FL 32312. (904) 893-4153.

Tallgrass Prairie Alliance. 4101 W. 54th Terrance, Shawnee Mission, KS 66205.

TAPPI Environmental Conference Proceedings, Seattle, WA, April 9-11, 1990. TAPPI Press, Technology Park/Atlanta, PO Box 105113, Atlanta, GA 30348. (404) 446-1400. 1990. Contains 11 papers presented at the conference covering industrial pollution and its remedies.

TAPPI Journal. Technical Association of the Pulp and Paper Industry, Box 105113, Atlanta, GA 30348-5113. (404) 446-1400. Monthly. Covers new technology and advancements in the pulp and paper industry.

Tar Sands and Oil Shales. Walter Ruhl. Enke, Rudigerstr. 14, Stuttgart, Germany D-7000. 1982. Deals with the geology of petroleum.

Target Marketing Directory: U.S. Paint and Coating Manufacturers. Mannsville Chemical Products Corporation, Box 271, Asbury Park, NJ 07712. (908) 776-7888.

Task Force Against Nuclear Pollution. P.O. Box 1817, Washington, DC 20013. (301) 474-8311.

Teaching Population Geography: An Interdisciplinary Ecological Approach. George Warren Carey. Teachers College Pr., 1234 Amsterdam Ave., New York, NY 10027. (212) 678-3929. 1969. Bibliography on human ecology and demography.

Technical Additions to Methods for Chemical Analysis of Water and Wastes. U.S. Environmental Protection Agency, Environmental Monitoring and Support Laboratory, 26 W. Martin Luther King Dr., Cincinnati, OH 45268. (513) 569-7931. 1983. Analysis of sewage and water.

A Technical Assessment of Portable Explosives Vapor Detection Devices. Marc R. Nyden. U.S. Department of Justice, Office of Justice Programs, National Institute of Justice, Constitution Ave. & 10th St. NW, Washington, DC 20530. (202) 514-2000. 1990. Evaluation of technology relating to explosives detectors.

Technical Assistance Program: Waste Minimization and Pollution Prevention. Chief, Technical Assistance Program, 248 Calder Way, 307 University Park, PA 16810. (814) 865-0427.

Technical Association of the Pulp and Paper Industry. Box 105113, Atlanta, GA 30348-5113. (404) 446-1400.

Technical Dictionary of Chromatography. Pergamon Microforms International Inc., Fairview Park, Elmsford, NY 10523. (914) 592-7720. 1970.

A Technical Framework for Life-Cycle Assessment. Society of Environmental Toxicology and Chemistry and the SETAC Foundation for Environmental Education, 1101 14th St, NW, Washington, DC 20005. (202) 371-1275. 1991. Evaluates the environmental burdens associated with a product, process or activity.

Technical Guidance Manual for Performing Waste Load Allocations. U.S. Environmental Protection Agency, 401 M St., S.W., Washington, DC 20460. (202) 260-2090. 1984-.

Technical Paper-Agricultural Experiment Station. University of California Press, 2120 Berkeley Way, Berkeley, CA 94720. (510) 642-4247. 1924-. Monthly (irregularly).

Technical Report. National Coalition Against the Misuse of Pesticides, 701 E St., SE, Washington, DC 20003. (202) 543-5450. Monthly. Congressional rulings and legislative action taken on pesticides.

Techniques for Hazardous Chemical and Waste Spill Control. L. Albert Weaver. L.A. Weaver, 308 E. Jones St., Raleigh, NC 27601. 1983.

Techniques for Measuring Indoor Air. John Y. Yocom and Sharon M. McCarthy. John Wiley & Sons, Inc., 605 3rd Ave., New York, NY 10158-0012. (212) 850-6000. 1991. Addresses the recent, rapid expansion of interest in indoor air quality and its contribution to total human exposure to air pollutants by presenting past and present developments and also the directions that the field seems to be taking.

Techniques in Calcium Research. M.V. Thomas. Academic Press, c/o Harcourt Brace Jovanovich Inc., 6277 Sea Harbor Dr., Orlando, FL 32887. (800) 346-8648. 1982. Calcium analysis and physiological effect.

Technological Responses to the Greenhouse Effect. George Thurlow, ed. Elsevier Science Publishing Co., 655 Avenue of the Americas, New York, NY 10010. (212) 989-5800. 1990. Watt Committee on Energy (London) working with 23 British experts has reported on various greenhouse gases, their sources and sinks, followed by an analysis of the release of these gases in "energy conversion" primarily in electric power production.

Technologies for Small Water and Wastewater Systems. Edward J. Martin and Edward T. Martin. Van Nostrand Reinhold, 115 5th Ave., New York, NY 10003. (212) 254-3232. 1991. Addresses how to exploit different water treatment technologies according to available resources. Includes extensive sections on costs and design of both established and new technologies with vital data on limitations, operations and maintenance, control and special factors.

Technologies for Upgrading Existing or Designing New Drinking Water Treatment Facilities. Office of Drinking Water, Center for Environmental Research Information, U.S. Environmental Protection Agency. Technomic Publishing Co., 851 New Holland Ave., Box 3535, Lancaster, PA 17604. (717) 291-5609. 1991. Discusses drinking water treatment technologies that address contamination and contaminant categories regulated under the Safe Drinking Water Act and its 1986 amendments.

Technology, Law, and the Working Environment. Nicholas A. Ashford and Charles C. Caldart. Global Professional Publications, 2805 McGraw Ave., PO Box 19539, Irvine, CA 92713-9539. (800) 854-7179. 1991. Discusses how to improve safety and health conditions through creative uses of workplace technology and application of relevant health and safety laws.

Technology of Environmental Pollution Control. Esber I. Shaheen. PennWell Books, PO Box 21288, Tulsa, OK 74121. (918) 831-9421; (800) 752-9764. 1992. 2d ed. Covers the environmental spectrum in an attempt to update the reader on new technologies and topics regarding pollution control.

Telegen Reporter Annual. Bowker A & I Publishing. 245 W 17th St., New York, NY 10011. 1989. Provides up-to-date reviews of the pharmaceutical, agricultural, industrial and energy applications of the products, processes, and markets of genetic engineering and biotechnology. Also addresses economic, social, regulatory, patent, and public policy issues. This annual cumulation abstracts and indexes information from scientific, technical, and business journals, conference and symposium proceedings, and academic government, and corporate reports.

Temephos. U.S. Environmental Protection Agency, Office of Pesticides and Toxic Substances, 401 M St., S.W., Washington, DC 20460. (202) 260-2090. 1981. Covers mosquito control and pesticide law and legislation.

The Temperate Forest Ecosystem. Yang Hanxi. Institute of Terrestrial Ecology, Merlewood Research Station, Grange-over-Sands, England LA11 6JU. 1987. Topics in forest ecology.

Temperature and Environmental Effects on the Testis. Plenum Press, 233 Spring St., New York, NY 10013-1578. (212) 620-8000; (800) 221-9369. 1991. Role of intrinsic and extrinsic temperature alterations in testis physiology and male fertility.

Temple University, Insect Biocontrol Center. Department of Biology, Philadelphia, PA 19122. (215) 787-8843.

Ten-Year List of Publications on Agricultural Engineering Subjects. University of Illinois, Agricultural Engineering Dept., Urbana, IL 61801. 1973.

Tennessee Environmental Council Newsletter. Tennessee Environmental Council, 1725 Church St., Nashville, TN 37203-2921. (615) 321-5075.

Tennessee Environmental Law Letter. Lee Smith Publishers & Printers, Nashville, TN 1989.

Tennessee Technological University, Tennessee Cooperative Fishery Research Unit. TTU Box 5114, Cookeville, TN 38505. (615) 372-3094.

Teratologic Assessment of Butylene Oxide, Styrene Oxide and Methyl Bromide. Melvin R. Sikov. U.S. G.P.O., Washington, DC 20401. (202) 512-0000. 1981. Toxicology aspects of the following: butene, styrene, bromomethane, teratogenic agents, hydrocarbons, and ethers.

Terrestrial and Aquatic Ecosystems: Perturbation and Recovery. Oscar Ravera, ed. E. Horwood, 1230 Avenue of the Americas, New York, NY 10020. (800) 223-2348. 1991. Presented at the 5th European Ecological Symposium held at Siena, Italy in 1989. Some of the topics included: biological responses to the changing ecosystem; anthropogenic perturbations of the community and ecosystem; restoration of degraded ecosystems; environmental management and strategies.

Test and Evaluation of Potassium Sensors in Fresh and Saltwater. Gary K. Ward. National Ocean Survey, National Oceanic and Atmospheric Administration, 11400 Rockville Pike, Rockville, MD 20852. (301) 443-8823. 1979.

Texas A & M University, Schubot Exotic Bird Health Center. 119 VMS Building, College Station, TX 77843-4467. (409) 845-5941.

Texas A & M University, Separation and Ingredient Sciences Laboratory. Food Protein Research and Development Center, College Station, TX 77843-2476. (409) 845-2741.

Texas A&I University, Caesar Kleberg Wildlife Research Institute. College of Agriculture & Home Economics, Campus Box 218, Kingsville, TX 78363. (512) 595-3922.

Texas A&I University, Herbarium. Kingsville, TX 78363. (512) 595-3803.

Texas A&I University, South Texas Plant Materials Center. Caesar Kleberg Wildlife Research Institute, Campus Box 218, Kingsville, TX 78363. (512) 595-3960.

Texas A&M University at Galveston Coastal Zone Laboratory. P.O. Box 1675, Galveston, TX 77553. (409) 740-4465.

Texas A&M University, Faculty of Genetics. College Station, TX 77843. (409) 845-8877.

Texas A&M University, Forest Genetics Laboratory. College Station, TX 77843. (409) 845-1325.

Texas A&M University, Lipid Research Laboratory. Department of Biochemistry, College Station, TX 77843. (409) 845-5616.

Texas A&M University, Paleoethnobotanical Laboratory. Department of Anthropology, College Station, TX 77843. (409) 845-9334.

Texas A&M University, Pecan Insect Laboratory. Department of Entomology, College Station, TX 77843. (409) 845-9757.

Texas A&M University, S.M. Tracy Herbarium. College Station, TX 77843. (409) 845-4328.

Texas A&M University, Sea Grant College Program. 1716 Briarcrest Dr., Ste. 702, College Station, TX 77802. (409) 845-3854.

Texas A&M University, Texas Cooperative Wildlife Collection. Maple Hall, Rm. 210, Mail Stop 2258, College Station, TX 77843. (409) 845-5777.

Texas A&M University Texas Water Resources Institute. College Station, TX 77843-2118. (409) 845-1851.

Texas Environmental Law Handbook. Government Institutes, Inc., 4 Research Pl., Ste. 200, Rockville, MD 20850. (301) 921-2300. 1990.

Texas Forest Products Laboratory. Texas A&M University, P.O. Box 310, Lafkin, TX 75901. (409) 639-8180.

Texas Pollution Report. Report Publications, P.O. Box 12368, Austin, TX 78711. (512) 478-5663. Weekly. Covers regulatory activity, court decisions and legislation.

Texas Solid Waste Market. FIND/SVP, 625 Avenue of the Americas, New York, NY 10011. (800) 346-3787. 1991. Market structure, landfill capacity, primary market participants and other primary assets.

Texas Tech University, Brush Control Research Center. Goddard Range and Wildlife Building, Lubbock, TX 79409. (806) 742-2841.

Texas Tech University, Herbarium. Texas Tech Museum, P.O. Box 4149, Lubbock, TX 79409. (806) 742-3222.

Texas Tech University, International Center for Arid and Semiarid Land Studies. P.O. Box 4620, Lubbock, TX 79409. (806) 742-2218.

Texas Tech University, Water Resources Center. Box 4630, Lubbock, TX 79409. (806) 742-3597.

Texas Water Commission: Emergency Preparedness and Community Right-to-Know. Supervisor, Emergency Response Unit, PO Box 13087 Capitol Station, 1100 West 49th St., Austin, TX 78756. (512) 458-7410.

Texas Water Development Board: Water Quality. Executive Director, Box 13231, Austin, TX 78711. (512) 463-7847.

Texas Water Report. Report Publications, P.O. Box 12368, Austin, TX 78711. (512) 478-5663. Weekly. Covers water pollution, waste, and conservation.

Texas Woman's University, Biology Science Research Laboratory. Denton, TX 76204. (817) 898-2351.

Textile Bay & Packaging Association. 1024 W. Kinzie Ave., Chicago, IL 60622. (312) 733-3660.

Textile Chemist and Colorist–Buyer's Guide Issue. American Association of Textile Chemists and Colorists, Box 12215, Research Triangle Park, NC 27709. (919) 549-8141.

Textile Processors, Service Trades, Health Care, Professional & Technical Employees International Union. 303 E. Wacker Dr., Suite 1109, Chicago, IL 60601. (312) 946-0450.

Thallium Toxicology. S. Jackson. Department of Health and Human Services, Public Health Service, National Institutes of Health, National Library of Medicine, 9000 Rockville Pike, Bethesda, MD 20892. (301) 496-4000. 1977.

The Thee Generation: Reflections on the Coming Revolution. Tom Regan. Temple University Press, 1601 N. Broad St., Philadelphia, PA 19122. (215) 787-8787. 1991. Topics in animal rights and ecology.

Theories of Populations in Biological Communities. F.B. Christiansen. Springer-Verlag, 175 5th Ave., New York, NY 10010. (212) 460-1500. 1977. Ecological studies in biotic communities and population biology.

Thermal Analysis. W. W. Wendlandt. Halsted Press, 605 3rd Ave., New York, NY 10158. (212) 850-6000. 1976. Topics in analytical chemistry.

Thermal Analysis Research Program Reference Manual. George N. Walton. National Technical Information Service, 5285 Port Royal Rd., Springfield, VA 22161. (703) 487-4650. 1983. Mathematical models in heat transmission.

Thermal Generation of Aromas. Thomas H. Parliment. American Chemical Society, 1155 16th St. N.W., Washington, DC 20036. (800) 227-5558. 1989. Food odor and effect of heat on food.

Thermal Insulation Handbook. William Turner. McGraw-Hill Science & Engineering Books, 11 W. 19th St., New York, NY 10011. (212) 337-6010. 1981.

Thiamin Pyrophosphate Biochemistry. Alfred Schellenberger. CRC Press, 2000 Corporate Blvd. N.W., Boca Raton, FL 33431. (800) 272-7737. 1988. Fundamentals of pyruvate decarboxylase and transketolase and pyruvate dehydrogenace complex.

Thorne Ecological Institute. 5398 Manhattan Circle, Boulder, CO 80303. (303) 499-3647.

Threatened Birds of Africa and Related Islands. N. Collar. World Conservation Union, IUCN Publications Services Unit, 181a Huntingdon Road, Cambridge, England CB3 0DJ. (0223) 277894. 1985.

Threatened Primates of Africa: The IUCN Red Data Book. Phyllis C. Lee. World Conservation Union, IUCN Publications Services Unit, 181a Huntingdon Road, Cambridge, England CB3 0DJ. (0223) 277894. 1988. Comprehensive review of the conservation status of African primates.

Threatened Swallowtail Butterflies of the World. N. Mark Collins. World Conservation Union, IUCN Publications Services Unit, 181a Huntingdon Road, Cambridge, England CB3 0DJ. (0223) 277894. 1988.

Three Men and a Forester. Ian S. Mahood. Harbour Pub., PO Box 219, Madeira Park, BC, Canada V0N 2H0. 1990. Describes forest management in British Columbia and the forest products industry.

Three Mile Island Alert. 315 Peffer St., Harrisburg, PA 17102. (717) 233-3072.

Threshold, International Center for Environmental Renewal. Drawer CU, Bisbee, AZ 85603. (602) 432-7353.

Thyroid Function and Disease. W. B. Saunders, Curtis Center, Independence Sq. W., Philadelphia, PA 19106. (215) 238-7800. 1989. Physiology of thyroid gland.

Tide. Coastal Conservation Assn., 4801 Woodway, Suite 220 W., Houston, TX 77056. (713) 626-4222. Bimonthly.

Tide Tables 1991, High and Low Water Predictions. U.S. G.P.O, Washington, DC 20402-9325. (202) 512-0000. Annual. Daily tide heights and times for 200 reference ports worldwide.

Timber & Timberland Companies. American Business Directories, Inc., 5711 S. 86th Circle, Omaha, NE 68127. (402) 593-4600.

Timber Operators Council. 6825 S.W. Sandburg St., Tigard, OR 97223. (503) 620-1710.

Timber Products Manufacturers. 951 E. Third Ave., Spokane, WA 99202. (509) 535-4646.

Timber Sale Administration Handbook. U.S. Department of Agriculture, Forest Service, 324 25th St., Ogden, UT 84401. 1984. Economic aspects of forest management.

The Times Atlas and Encyclopedia of the Sea. A.D. Couper. Harper & Row, 10 E. 53rd St., New York, NY 10022. (212) 207-7000; (800) 242-7737. 1990.

Tire and Rim Association. 175 Montrose Ave., W., Copely, OH 44321. (216) 666-8121.

The Tire & Rubber Industry. FIND/SVP, 625 Avenue of the Americas, New York, NY 10011. (212) 645-4500. Covers pricing, demand and market share, the replacement and retread markets, the supply side, distribution and foreign producers.

Tire Industry Safety Council. National Press Bldg., Suite 844, Washington, DC 20045. (202) 783-1022.

Titanium Development Association. 4141 Arapahoe Ave., Ste. 100, Boulder, CO 80303. (303) 443-7515.

Titanium Development Association–Buyers Guide. Titanium Development Association, 4141 Arapahoe Ave., Ste. 100, Boulder, CO 80303. (303) 443-7515. 1984-.

To Heal the Earth: The Case for an Earth Ethic. Robert F. Harrington. Hancock House, 1431 Harrison Ave., Blaine, WA 98230. 1990. Moral and ethical aspects of human ecology and environmental protection.

Tobacco Institute. 1875 I St., N.W., Suite 800, Washington, DC 20006. (202) 457-4800.

The Toilet Papers: Designs to Recycle Human Waste and Water. Capra Press, PO Box 2068, Santa Barbara, CA 93120. (805) 966-4590. 1980. Environmental aspects of toilets and sewage disposal, privies, and sewage irrigation.

The Toilet Soap Market. FIND/SVP, 625 Avenue of the Americas, New York, NY 10011. (212) 645-4500. 1992. Market for toilet soaps, including: deodorant, antibacterial, medicated, beauty, liquid, moisturizing, specialty, multipurpose and "pure".

Tolerance Database. NPIRS (National Pesticide Information Retrieval System) User Services Manager, Entomology Hall, Purdue University, West Lafayette, IN 47907. (317) 494-6614.

Toluene, The Xylenes, and Their Industrial Derivatives. Elsevier Science Publishing Co., 655 Avenue of the Americas, New York, NY 10010. (212) 984-5800. 1982. Topics in chemical engineering including toluene and xylene.

The Top Fifty Industrial Chemicals. Raymond Chang. Random House, Inc., 201 E. 50th St., New York, NY 10022. (212) 751-2600. 1988. Technical chemistry and chemical engineering.

Topics in Carbon-13 NMR Spectroscopy. John Wiley & Sons Inc., 605 3rd Ave., New York, NY 10158-0012. (212) 850-6000. 1974-. Irregular.

Tort Liability In Emergency Planning. John C. Pine. U.S. Environmental Protection Agency, 401 M St. SW, Washington, DC 20460. (202) 260-2090. 1988.

Tortricid Pests: Their Biology, Natural Enemies, and Control. L.P.S. van der Geest. Elsevier Science Publishing Co., 655 Avenue of the Americas, New York, NY 10010. (212) 989-5800. 1991.

Totem. Department of Natural Resources, Public Lands Bldg., Olympia, WA 98504. Monthly.

Tourism Planning: An Integrated and Sustainable Development Approach. Van Nostrand Reinhold, 115 5th Ave., New York, NY 10003. (212) 254-3232. 1991. Provides guidelines and approaches for developing tourism that take environmental, socioeconomic and institutional issues into account.

Towards a Green Scotland: Contributions to the Debate. Karen Allan and Nick Radcliffe, eds. Scottish Green Party, 11 Forth St., Edinburgh, Scotland EH1 3LE 1990.

Towards Sustainable Agricultural Development. Michael D. Young. Belhaven Press, 136 S. Broadway, Irvington, NY 10533. (914) 591-9111. 1991. Organisation of Economic Cooperation and Development commissioned experts to examine how sustainability can be achieved for food, industrial crops, and livestock in the developed and developing world. This report provides some sources on the current world status of sustainable agriculture.

Towards Wiser Use of Our Forests and Rangelands. U.S. Forest Service, PO Box 96090, Washington, DC 20090. (202) 720-3760. 1982. Forest management in the United States.

TOXALL. National Library of Medicine, Specialized Information Services Division, 8600 Rockville Pike, Bethesda, MD 20894. (301) 496-6531.

Toxic Air Pollutant Emission Factors. U.S. Environmental Protection Agency. National Technical Information Service, Springfield, VA 22161. (703) 487-4650. 1990. Irregular. Data on emissions by source, SIC code, combustion material and pollutant process.

Toxic Air Pollution–A Comprehensive Study of Non-Criteria Air Pollutants. Paul J. Lioy and Joan M. Daisey. Lewis Publishers, 2000 Corporate Blvd., N.W., Boca Raton, FL 33431. (407) 994-0555 or (800) 272-7737. 1987. Provides historical data base of ambient toxic air pollution measurements for future trend analysis, assessment of total exposure and indoor air pollution relationships.

Toxic and Hazardous Materials: A Sourcebook and Guide to Information Sources. James K. Webster. Greenwood Publishing Group, Inc., 88 Post Rd. W., PO Box 5007, New York, NY 06881. (212) 226-3571. 1987.

Toxic Chemical Release Inventory. U.S. National Library of Medicine/Toxicology Information Program, 8600 Rockville Pike, Bethesda, MD 20894. (301) 496-1131.

Toxic Chemical Release Inventory. Office of Research and Development, U.S. Environmental Protection Agency, RD-689, 401 M St., S.W., Washington, DC 20460. Releases of toxic chemicals to the environment. Includes names and addresses of the facilities and the amount of certain toxic chemicals they release to the air, water, or land.

Toxic Chemical Releases and Your "Right-To-Know". U.S. Environmental Protection Agency, 401 M St. SW, Washington, DC 20460. (202) 260-2090. 1988.

Toxic Chemicals. Earon S. Davis. Farmworker Justice Fund, Inc., 2001 S St., NW, Ste. 210, Washington, DC 20009. (202) 462-8192. 1980. The interface between law and science: an introduction to scientific methods of demonstrating causation of diseases.

Toxic Chemicals and Public Protection. Toxic Substances Strategy Committee. U.S. G.P.O., Washington, DC 20201. (202) 512-0000. 1980.

Toxic Hazard Assessment of Chemicals. M. L. Richardson. Royal Society of Chemistry, c/o CRC Press, 2000 Corporate Blvd. N.W., Boca Raton, FL 33431-9868. (800) 272-7737. 1989. Provides basic guidance on means of retrieving, validating, and interpreting data in order to make a toxicological hazard assessment upon a chemical.

Toxic Hazards of Certain Pesticides to Man, Together with a Select Bibliography on the Toxicology of Pesticides in Man and Mammals. World Health Organization, Ave. Appia, Geneva, Switzerland CH-1211. 1953. Toxicology and toxicity of pesticides and insecticides.

Toxic Marine Phytoplankton. Edna Graneli. Elsevier Science Publishing Co., 655 Avenue of the Americas, New York, NY 10010. (212) 984-5800. 1990. Covers toxicology of marine phytoplankton.

Toxic Materials News. Business Publishers, Inc., 951 Pershing Dr., Silver Spring, MD 20910-4464. (301) 587-6300. 1974-. Weekly. Informs on regulations governing the manufacture, handling, transport, distribution and disposal of toxic chemicals and pesticides. Also available online.

Toxic Materials News. Business Publishers, Inc., 951 Pershing Dr., Silver Spring, MD 20910-4464. (301) 587-6300. Legislation, regulations, and litigation concerning toxic substances. Online version of periodical of the same name.

Toxic Materials Transport. Business Publishers, Inc., 951 Pershing Dr., Silver Spring, MD 20910. (301) 587-6300. Biweekly. Covers new laws and regulations at federal, state and local levels.

Toxic Politics: Responding to Chemical Disasters. Cornell University Press, 124 Roberts Place, Ithaca, NY 14850. 1991.

Toxic Release Inventory CD-ROM Retrieval User Guide. Environmental Protection Agency. U.S. G.P.O, Washington, DC 20402-9325. (202) 512-0000. 1990. Data on industrial facilities that intentionally or accidently release toxic chemicals into the environment.

Toxic Residues in Foods, 1979-March 1987. Charles N. Bebee. National Agricultural Library, 10301 Baltimore Blvd., Beltsville, MD 20705-2351. (301) 504-5755. 1987. Quick bibliography series: NAL-BIBL. QB 87-70

The Toxic Substances Control Act. U.S. G.P.O., Washington, DC 20401. (202) 512-0000. 1981.

Toxic Substances Control Act Chemical Substances Inventory. U.S. Environmental Protection Agency, Office of Pesticides and Toxic Substances, 401 M St., S.W., Washington, DC 20460. (202) 260-2090. Lists chemical substances manufactured, imported, or processed in the United States for commercial purposes.

Toxic Substances Control Act Test Submissions. Chemical Information Systems, Inc., 7215 York Rd., Baltimore, MD 21212. (301) 321-8440. An index of unpublished health and safety studies submitted to the U.S. Environmental Protection Agency under the Toxic Substances Control Act.

Toxic Substances Control Program: Waste Minimization and Pollution Prevention. Supervising Waste Management Engineer, Alternative Technology Division, 714/744 P St., Sacramento, CA 94234-7320. (916) 322-5347.

Toxic Substances Journal. Hemisphere Publishing Co., 79 Madison Ave., Suite 1110, New York, NY 10016. (212) 725-1999. Quarterly. Legislation, testing, and guidelines relating to toxic substances.

Toxic Substances Sourcebook. Environment Information Center, 124 E. 39th St., New York, NY 10016. 1980. Includes hazardous substances, poisons, and pollution.

The Toxicities of Selected Bridge Painting Materials and Guidelines for Bridge Painting Projects. Harold G. Hunt. National Technical Information Service, 5285 Port Royal Rd., Springfield, VA 22161. (703) 487-4650. 1990. Environmental aspects of maintenance and repair of bridges.

Toxicity and Metabolism of Explosives. Jehuda Yinon. CRC Press, 2000 Corporate Blvd. N.W., Boca Raton, FL 33431. (800) 272-7737. 1990. Safety measures relating to military explosives.

Toxicity and Metabolism of Industrial Solvents. Ethel Browning. Elsevier Science Publishing Co., 655 Avenue of the Americas, New York, NY 10010. (212) 984-5800. 1965.

Toxicity of Heavy Metals in the Environment. Frederick W. Oehme. Marcel Dekker, Inc., 270 Madison Ave., New York, NY 10016. (212) 696-9000; (800) 228-1160. 1978. Toxicology and environmental aspects of heavy metals.

Toxicity of Industrial Metals. Ethel Browning. Butterworth-Heinemann, 80 Montvale Ave., Stoneham, MA 02180. (617) 438-8464; (800) 366-2665. 1969. 2d ed.

The Toxicity of Methyl Mercury. Christine U. Eccles. Johns Hopkins University Press, 701 W. 40th St., Ste. 275, Baltimore, MD 21211. (410) 516-6900. 1987. Toxicology and physiological effects of methylmercury.

Toxicity Reduction in Industrial Effluents. Perry W. Lanford, et al. Van Nostrand Reinhold, 115 5th Ave., New York, NY 10003. (212) 254-3232. 1990. Overview of aquatic toxicology and toxicity reduction. Specific treatment technologies that can be used to reduce toxicity, such as aerobic and anaerobic biological treatment, air and steam stripping of volatile organics, granulated carbon absorption, powdered activated carbon treatment and chemical oxidation, are discussed in detail.

Toxicity Reduction through Chemical and Biological Modification of Spent Pulp Bleaching Liquors. Carlton W. Dence. National Technical Information Service, 5285 Port Royal Rd., Springfield, VA 22161. (703) 487-4650. 1980. Chlorophenol toxicology, chemical reactions and biological assay.

Toxicological and Environmental Chemistry. Gordon and Breach Science Publishers, Inc., 270 8th Ave., New York, NY 10011. (212) 206-8900. Quarterly.

Toxicological and Teratogenic Studies with Paraquat. Northern Illinois University, Department of Biological Sciences, Dekalb, IL 60115. 1984.

Toxicological Chemistry: A Guide to Toxic Substances in Chemistry. Stanley E. Manahan. Lewis Publishers, 200 Corporate Blvd. NW, Boca Raton, FL 33431. (407) 994-0555 or (800)272-7737. 1989. Defines toxicological chemistry and gives information on its origin and use. Emphasizes the chemical formulas, structures, and reactions of toxic substances.

Toxicological / Environmental Health Information Source Update. Centers for Disease Control, 1600 Clifton Rd. NE, Atlanta, GA 30333. (404) 488-4588. Lists recent online bibliographic databases relating to environmental health and toxicology.

Toxicological Evaluation of Parathion and Azinphosmethyl in Freshwater Model Ecosystems. Centre for Agricultural Publishing and Documentation, Wageningen, Netherlands 1980. Covers water pollution and environmental aspects of pesticides.

Toxicological Evaluations. Volume 1: Potential Health Hazards of Existing Chemicals. B. G. Chemie, ed. Springer-Verlag, 115 5th Ave., New York, NY 10010. (212) 460-1500; (800) 777-4643. 1990. Identifies thousands of compounds which might possibly be toxic and to date several hundreds that have been investigated. Contains results of the first 57 reviews of the literature.

Toxicological Profile for Carbon Tetrachloride. Agency for Toxic Substances and Disease Registry, U.S. Public Health Service, 1600 Clifton Rd. NE, Atlanta, GA 30333. (404) 452-4111. 1989.

Toxicological Profile for Chloroform. National Technical Information Service, 5285 Port Royal Rd., Springfield, VA 22161. (703) 487-4650. 1989.

Toxicological Profile for Heptachlor/Heptachlor Epoxide. Dynamac Corporation. Oak Ridge National Laboratory, PO Box 2008, Oak Ridge, TN 37831-6050. (615) 576-1746. 1989. Adverse effects and toxicity of heptachlor.

Toxicological Profile for Naphthalene and 2-Methylnaphthalene. Life System, Inc. Agency for Toxic Substances and Disease Registry, U.S. Public Health Service, 1600 Clifton Rd. NE, Atlanta, GA 30333. (404) 452-4111. 1990. Toxicology and physiological effect of methylnaphthalenes.

Toxicological Profile for Silver. Clement International Corporation. Agency for Toxic Substances and Disease Registry, U.S. Public Health Service, 1600 Clifton Rd. NE, Atlanta, GA 30333. (404) 452-4111. 1990. Toxicology and physiological effects and environmental aspects of silver.

Toxicological Profile for Uranium. Agency for Toxic Substances and Disease Registry, U.S. Public Health Service, 1600 Clifton Rd. NE, Atlanta, GA 30333. (404) 452-4111. 1990. Physiological effects, environmental aspects and toxicology of uranium compounds.

Toxicological Profile of Radium. Life Systems Inc. Agency for Toxic Substances and Disease Registry, U.S. Public Health Service, 1600 Clifton Rd. NE, Atlanta, GA 30333. (404) 452-4111. 1990. Toxicology, physiological and environmental aspects of radium.

Toxicological Risk in Aquatic Ecosystems. Steven M. Bartell, et al. Lewis Publishers, 2000 Corporate Blvd., N.W., Boca Raton, FL 33431. (407) 994-0555 or (800) 272-7737. 1991. Describes the development, application, and analysis of a methodology for forecasting probable effects of toxic chemicals on the production dynamics of a generalized aquatic ecosystem.

Toxicology & Applied Pharmacology. Academic Press, P.O. Box 6250, c/o Harcourt Brace, 6277 Sea Harbor Dr., Orlando, FL 32887. (218) 723-9828. Fifteen times a year. Covers the effects of chemicals on living organisms.

Toxicology and Environmental Chemistry. Gordon and Breach Science Publishers, Inc., 270 8th Ave., New York, NY 10011. (212) 206-8900. 1984.

Toxicology Forum. 1575 I St., N.W., 5th Fl., Washington, DC 20005. (202) 659-0030.

Toxicology Handbook. Government Institutes, Inc., 4 Research Pl., Ste. 200, Rockville, MD 20850. (301) 921-2300. 1986. Contains a list of key acronyms, glossary of terms, and chapters on Fundamental Concepts; Toxicity Assessments; Protocols in Toxicology Studies; Exposure Assessment; Risk Assessment and dioxing.

Toxicology Letters. Elsevier, PO Box 211, Amsterdam, Netherlands 1000 AE. 020-5803-911. 1977.

Toxicology Methods. Raven Press, 1185 Avenue of the Americas, New York, NY 10036. (212) 930-9500. Quarterly.

Toxicology of Halogenated Hydrocarbons. M. A. Q. Khan. Pergamon Microforms International, Inc., Fairview Park, Elmsford, NY 10523. (914) 592-7720. 1981. Environmental health and ecological effects.

Toxicology of Inhaled Materials. I.Y.R. Adamson. Springer-Verlag, 175 5th Ave., New York, NY 10010. (212) 460-1500. 1985. General principles of inhalation toxicology.

The Toxicology of Paraquat, Diquat and Morfamquat. Aurelio Pasi. Hans Huber, Langgasstr. 76, Bern, Switzerland D-3000. 1978. The toxicology of paraquat and pyridinium compounds is described.

Toxicology of Polychlorinated Biphenyl Compounds. S. Jackson. U.S. Department of Health and Human Services, Public Health Services, National Institutes of Health, 9000 Rockville Pike, Bethesda, MD 20892. (301) 496-4000. 1981.

Toxicology Research Projects Directory. Toxicology Information Subcommittee of the DHEW. National Technical Information Service, 5285 Port Royal Rd., Springfield, VA 22161. (703) 487-4650. 1976-. Monthly, with annual cumulation. Monthly publication containing selections from the Smithsonian Science Information Exchange data base. Provides on going project summaries related to toxicology manuals.

Toxics A to Z: A Guide to Everyday Pollution Hazards. University of California Press, 2120 Berkeley Way, Berkeley, CA 94720. (510) 642-4247 (900) 822-6657. 1991. A consumer guide to toxicology and poisons.

Toxics in the Community: National and Local Perspectives. U.S. Environmental Protection Agency, Offices of Pesticides and Toxic Substances, 401 M St. SW, Washington, DC 20460. (202) 260-2090. 1990.

Toxics Law Reporter. Bureau of National Affairs, 1231 25th St. NW, Washington, DC 20037. (202) 452-4200. Weekly. Covers legal developments of toxic tort.

Toxics/Organics. Arthur D. Little, Inc. U.S. G.P.O., Washington, DC 204021. (202) 512-0000. 1979. Environmental considerations of selected energy conserving manufacturing process options.

The Toxics Release Inventory: Executive Summary. U.S. Environmental Protection Agency, Office of Pesticides and Toxic Substances, 401 M St. SW, Washington, DC 20460. (202) 260-2090. 1989.

TOXLIT. National Library of Medicine, Toxicology Information Program, 8600 Rockville Pike, Bethesda, MD 20894. (800) 638-8480.

Trace Elements in Health and Disease. A. Aitio, et al., eds. Royal Society of Chemistry, c/o CRC Press, 2000 Corporate Blvd. N.W., Boca Raton, FL 33431-9868. (800) 272-7737. 1991. Reviews the newest data available on both nutritional and toxicological aspects of trace elements. Assesses the current state of knowledge on the relationship between trace elements and human health and disease.

Trace Elements in Soils and Plants. Alina Kabata-Pendias and Henryk Pendias. CRC Press, 2000 Corporate Blvd. N.W., Boca Raton, FL 33431. (800) 272-7737. 1991. 2d ed. Discusses the pollution of air, water, soil and plants, all about soil processes, and the involvement of trace elements in the soil and plants.

Trace Metal Concentrations in Marine Organisms. Ronald Eisler. Pergamon Microforms International, Inc., Fairview Park, Elmsford, NY 10523. (914) 592-7720. 1981. Physiology of marine flora and fauna as well as trace elements in the body.

Trace Residue Analysis. David A. Kurtz. American Chemical Society, 1155 16th St. N.W., Washington, DC 20036. (800) 227-5558. 1985. Chemometric estimations of sampling, amount and error.

Tracking Toxic Substances at Industrial Facilities: Engineering Mass Balance Versus Materials Accounting. National Research Council–Committee to Evaluate Mass Balance Information for Facilities Handling Toxic Substances. National Academy Press, 2101 Constitution Ave., NW, Washington, DC 20418. (202) 334-3343. 1990. Covers measurement of factory and trade waste and hazardous substances.

The Tradeoff Between Cost and Risk in Hazardous Waste Management. Kenneth S. Sewall. Garland Publishers, 136 Madison Ave., New York, NY 10016. (212) 686-7492 or (800) 627-6273. 1990. Management and risk assessment of hazardous waste sites.

TRAFFIC. World Wildlife Fund, 1250 24th St., NW, Washington, DC 20037. (202) 293-4800. Quarterly. International trade in wild plants and animals, with emphasis on endangered and threatened species; information on Convention on International Trade in Endangered Species.

TRAFFIC, USA. c/o World Wildlife Fund, 1250 24th St., N.W., Washington, DC 20037. (202) 293-4800.

Training Manual on Food Irradiation Technology and Techniques. UNIPUB, 1982. Technical reports on radiation preservation of foods.

The Trans-Alaska Pipeline Controversy: Technology, Conservation, and the Frontier. Peter A. Coates. Lehigh University Press, 302 Linderman Library 30, Bethlehem, PA 18015-3067. (215) 758-3933. 1991. Question of oil extraction from the Arctic National Wildlife Refuge.

Transforming Technology: An Agenda for Environmentally Sustainable Growth in the Twenty-First Century. George Heaton, et al. World Resources Institute, 1709 New York Ave. N.W., Washington, DC 20006. (800) 822-0504. 1991. Explores the extraordinarily rich potential of new technologies to resolve environmental and economic problems.

Transit Fact Book. American Public Transit Association, 1201 New York Ave., NW, Suite 400, Washington, DC 20005. 1975-. Annual. Mass transportation systems finances, operations, equipment, employment, energy use, and governmental assistance.

Transmission Line Design Manual. Holland H. Farr. Water and Power Resources Service, Engineering and Research Center, P.O. Box 25007, Denver Federal Center, Denver, CO 80225. 1980.

Transport and the Environment. OECD Publications and Information Center, 2001 L St., N.W., Suite 700, Washington, DC 20036. (202) 785-OECD. 1988. Comprehensive overview of the impact on the environment of road transport. Assesses the efficacy of technical changes to motor vehicles to reduce air pollution and noise and evaluates innovations in the management of the transport systems of ten large cities in OECD countries.

Transport of Oil under Smooth Ice. M. S. Ozuner. Corvallis Environmental Research Laboratory, 200 S.W. 35th, Corvallis, OR 97333. (503) 754-4600. 1979. Environmental aspects of oil spills in polar regions.

Transport Policy and the Environment. OECD Publications and Information Center, 2001 L St., N.W., Suite 700, Washington, DC 20036. (202) 785-OECD. 1990. Describes how the government is addressing the adverse environmental effects of transport and the challenges that lie ahead.

Transport Statistics in the United States. U.S. Interstate Commerce Commission. U.S. GPO, Washington, DC 20401. (202) 512-0000. Annual. Data on intercity motor carriers and railroads and water services.

Transportation Alternatives. 494 Broadway, New York, NY 10012. (212) 941-4600.

Transportation and Development Department: Underground Storage Tanks. Materials Division, PO Box 9425, Baton Rouge, LA 70804. (504) 929-9131.

Transportation Energy Data Book. Stacy C. Davis and Patricia S. Hu. Oak Ridge National Laboratory, Transportation Energy Group, PO Box 2008, Oak Ridge, TN 37831-6050. (615) 576-1746. 1991. Eleventh edition. Data book represents an assembly and display of statistics that characterize transportation activity and presents data on other factors that influence transportation energy use.

Transportation Energy Research. National Technical Information Service, 5285 Port Royal Rd., Springfield, VA 22161. (703) 487-4650. 1986-. Monthly. Engineering and design of energy-efficient advanced automotive propulsion systems and other aspects of energy conservation measures involving transportation .

Transportation Institute. 5201 Auth Way, Camp Springs, MD 20746. (301) 423-3335.

Transportation Legislative Data Base. Battelle Memorial Institute, Office of Transportation Systems and Planning, 505 King Ave., Columbus, OH 43201-2693. (614) 424-5606. Shipment of radioactive materials which have been introduced, enacted, or denied at U.S. federal, state, or local levels of government.

The Transportation of Hazardous Materials. Joseph Lee Cook. Vance Bibliographies, PO Box 229, 112 N. Charter St., Monticello, IL 61856. (217) 762-3831. 1986.

Transportation of Hazardous Materials: A Management Guide for Generators and Manufactuerers. William E. Kenworthy. Government Institutes, Inc., 4 Research Pl., Suite 200, Rockville, MD 20850. (301) 921-2300. 1989. A management guide for generators of hazardous waste. Covers of hazardous materials regulation, alternative shipping methods for generators, and useful approaches for achieving compliance.

Transportation of Urban Radionuclides in Urban Environs. Nancy C. Finlay. Nuclear Regulatory Commission, 1717 H St. NW, Washington, DC 20555. (301) 492-7000. 1980. Environmental aspects of transportation of radioactive substances.

Transportation Research Board. Box 289, Washington, DC 20055. (202) 334-3213.

Transportation Research Forum. 1600 Wilson Blvd., #905, Arlington, VA 22209. (703) 525-1191.

Transportation Research Information Service–TRIS. Transportation Research Board, Box 289, Washington, DC 20055. (202) 334-3213.

Transportation Research News. National Academy of Science, Transportation Research Board, Box 289, Washington, DC 20055. (202) 334-3213. 1982. Monthly.

Transportation Science. Operations Research Society of America, Mount Royal and Guilford Ave., Baltimore, MD 21202. (301) 528-4146. 1967-. Quarterly.

Transuranic Elements in the Environment. Wayne C. Hanson. National Technical Information Service, 5285 Port Royal Rd., Springfield, VA 22161. (703) 487-4650. A summary of environmental research on transuranium radionuclides funded by USDOE.

Trash & Garbage Removal Directory. American Business Directories, Inc., 5711 S. 86th Circle, Omaha, NE 68127. (402) 593-4600.

Treatability Manual. U.S. Environmental Protection Agency, Office of Research and Development, 401 M St., SW, Washington, DC 20460. (202) 260-2090. 1983-. V.1 Treatability data. v.2 Change 2. Industrial Descriptions. v.3 Change 2. Technology for Control/removal of pollutants. v.4. Cost estimating. v.5. Change 2 summary.

Treatability Studies for Hazardous Waste Sites. Hazardous Waste Action Coalition, 1015 15th St. N.W., Suite 802, Washington, DC 20005. (202) 347-7474. 1990. Assesses the use of treatability studies for evaluating the effectiveness and cost of treatment technologies performed at hazardous waste sites.

Treatability Studies for the Inorganic Chemicals Manufacturing Point Source Category. United States Environmental Protection Agency. Environmental Protection Agency, Effluent Guidelines Division, 401 M. St., SW, Washington, DC 20460. (202) 260-2090. 1980. Topics in sewage purification.

Treatise on Adhesion and Adhesives. Marcel Dekker, Inc., 270 Madison Ave., New York, NY 10016. (212) 696-9000; (800) 228-1160. Irregular. Each volume is devoted to a special topic in adhesion and adhesives.

Treatment and Conditioning of Radioactive Incinerator Ashes. L. Crecille, ed. Elsevier Science Publishing Co., 655 Avenue of the Americas, New York, NY 10010. (212) 989-5800. 1991. Incineration of radioactive wastes and purification of fly ash.

Treatment of Volatile Organic Compounds in Drinking Water. U.S. Environmental Protection Agency, Municipal Environmental Research Laboratory, Office of Research and Development, 26 W. Martin Luther King Dr., Cincinnati, OH 45268. (513) 569-7931. 1983. Drinking water purification methods.

Treatment Potential for 56 EPA Listed Hazardous Chemicals in Soil. Ronald C. Sims, et al. Robert S. Kerr Environmental Research Laboratory, U.S. Environmental Protection Agency, PO Box 1198, Ada, OK 74820. (405) 332-8800. 1988.

Treatment Technologies. Environment Protection Agency. Government Institutes, Inc., 4 Research Pl., Ste. 200, Rockville, MD 20850. (301)921-2300. 1991. 2nd ed. Provides a clear explanation of 24 treatment technologies and evaluates the effectiveness of the design and operations of each type of treatment. This new edition has more supporting numerical data, examples for a better understanding of the technology and an updated reference for specific industrial wastes.

Tree Crops: A Permanent Agriculture. J. Russell Smith. Island Press, 1718 Connecticut Ave. N.W., Suite 300, Washington, DC 20009. (202) 232-7933. 1987. Most complete reference for growing high yield fruit and nut bearing trees. First published in 1929, this guide to the development of successful tree crops illustrates that vast, untapped food sources can be harvested from common species of trees.

Tree-Ring Society. Tree-Ring Research Laboratory, University of Arizona, Tucson, AZ 85721. (602) 621-2191.

Tree Talk: The People and Politics of Timber. Ray Raphael. Island Press, 1718 Connecticut Ave. N.W., Suite 300, Washington, DC 20009. (202) 232-7933. Looks at the forest industry from the perspective of environmentalists, loggers, old-time woodsmen and young pioneers.

TreePeople. 12601 Mulholland Dr., Beverly Hills, CA 90210. (818) 753-4600.

Trees. Springer-Verlag, Heidelberger Platz, Berlin, Germany 33 030-8207-1. 1987-. Quarterly.

Trees for Tomorrow. 611 Sheridan St., P.O. Box 609, Eagle River, WI 54521. (715) 479-6456.

Trees in Urban Design. Van Nostrand Reinhold, 115 Fifth Ave., New York, NY 10003. (212) 254-3232. 1993. Trees in cities and urban beautification.

Trees of Life: Saving Tropical Forests and their Biological Wealth. Kenton Miller and Laura Tangley. World Resources Institute, 1709 New York Ave. N.W., Washington, DC 20006. (800) 822-0504. 1991. Explains what deforestation is doing to the global environment and why rainforest preservation is valid to human welfare around the world.

Trees of North America. Christian Frank Brockman. Western Publishing Co., 1220 Mound Ave., Racine, WI 53404. (414) 633-2431. 1986. A field guide to the major native and introduced species of North America.

Trees, Why Do You Wait? America's Changing Rural Culture. Richard Critchfield. Island Press, 1718 Connecticut Ave. N.W., Suite 300, Washington, DC 20009. (202) 232-7933. 1991. Oral history chronicling the changes taking place in rural America.

Trends '90: A Compendium of Data on Global Change. Thomas A. Boden, et al. Carbon Dioxide Information Analysis Center, Environmental Sciences Division, Oak Ridge National Laboratory, Oak Ridge, TN 37831-6335. 1990. Source of frequently used global change data. Includes estimates of global and national CO_2 emissions from the burning of fossil fuels and from the production of cement and other pollutants.

Trends in Cell Biology. Elsevier Science Publishing Co., 655 Avenue of the Americas, New York, NY 10010. (212) 984-5800. Monthly. Includes current opinion in the field such as comments, letters and also includes headlines and short subject reviews as well as book reviews. A calendar events and the job trends are also outlined.

Trends in Food Science and Technology. Elsevier Science Publishing Co., 655 Avenue of the Americas, New York, NY 10010. (212) 984-5800. Monthly. A news and reviews journal that discusses recent developments in all areas of the food science and technology field. It includes feature articles, view points, book reviews, conference calendar and job trends.

Tri-State Bird Rescue and Research, Inc. 110 Possum Hollow Road, Wilmington, DE 19711. (302) 737-9543.

Triangle Universities Consortium for Research and Education in Plant Molecular Biology. North Carolina Biotechnology Center, P.O. Box 13547, Research Triangle Park, NC 27709. (919) 541-9366.

Trihalomethane Removal by Coagulation Techniques in a Softening Process. U.S. Environmental Protection Agency, Municipal Environmental Research Laboratory, 26 W. Martin Luther King Dr., Cincinnati, OH 45268. (513) 569-7931. 1983. Sewage purification through chlorination.

Tritium Deposition in the Continental U.S. U.S. G.P.O, Washington, DC 20402-9325. (202) 512-0000. Irregular. Showing precipitation and tritium deposition, by location.

Tropical Deforestation and Species Extinction. T.C. Whitmore. World Conservation Union, IUCN Publications Services Unit, 181a Huntingdon Road, Cambridge, England CB3 0DJ. (0223) 277894. 1992. Conservationist's perception of how fast tropical forests are being lost and what the consequences are for biological diversity.

Tropical Forest and Its Environment. Kenneth Alan Longman. Longman Scientific & Technical, 1560 Broadway, New York, NY 10036. (212) 819-5400. 1990. Rain forest and tropical ecology, ecosystems, and cycles.

Tropical Forests Forever. PO Box 69583, Portland, OR 97201. (503) 227-4127.

Tropical Forests Working Group. 1350 New York Ave., N.W., Washington, DC 20005.

Tropical Rain Forests and the World Atmosphere. T. Ghillean. Westview Press, 5500 Central Ave., Boulder, CO 80301. (303) 444-3541. 1986. Deals with vegetation and climate in the tropics. Also describes the weather patterns in that part of the world.

Tropical Rainforest: A World Survey of Our Most Valuable Endangered Habitat With a Blueprint for its Survival. Arnold Newman. Facts on File, Inc., 460 Park Ave. S., New York, NY 10016. (212) 683-2244; (800) 322-8755. 1990. Considers threats to rain forests, including logging and slash and burn agricultural practices. Presents a variety of measures to preserve our valuable rain forests.

Tropical Resources: Ecology and Development. Jose I. Furtado, et al., eds. Harwood Academic Publishers, PO Box 786, Cooper Sta., New York, NY 10276. (212) 206-8900. 1990. Overview of global tropical resources, both terrestrial and aquatic. Subjects discussed include forest resources, wildlife resources, general land use, pasture resources, economic development, fisheries, marine resources, and aquaculture.

Tropical Resources Institute. Yale University, School of Forestry and Environmental Studies, 205 Prospect St., New Haven, CT 06511. (203) 432-5109.

Troubled Skies, Troubled Waters: The Story of Acid Rain. Jon R. Loma. Viking, 375 Hudson St., New York, NY 10014. (212) 366-2000 or (800) 631-3577. 1984.

Trout Unlimited. 800 Folin Ln., S.E., Ste. 250, Vienna, VA 22180. (703) 281-1100.

Trumpeter Swan Society. 3800 County Rd. 24, Maple Plain, MN 55359. (612) 476-4663.

Trust for Public Land. 116 New Montgomery St., 4th Floor, San Francisco, CA 94105. (415) 495-5660.

The Truth About Chernobyl. Evelyn Rossiter. Basic Books, 10 E. 53rd St., New York, NY 10022. (212) 207-7057. 1991. Describes how bureaucratic mistakes caused the disaster.

TSCA Chemical Substances Inventory. U.S. Environmental Protection Agency, Office of Pesticides and Toxic Substances, 401 M St., S.W., Washington, DC 20460. (202) 260-2090.

TSCA Chemicals on Progress Bulletin. TSCA Assistance Office, Office of Pesticide & Toxic Substances, U.S. EPA, Washington, DC 20460. (202) 554-1404. Quarterly. Covers happenings in the EPA.

TSCA Compliance/Enforcement Guidance Manual. Government Institutes, Inc., 4 Research Pl., Ste. 200, Rockville, MD 20850. (301) 921-2300. 1984. Includes analyzing evidence collected during a compliance inspection.

TSCA Handbook. Government Institutes, Inc., 4 Research Pl., Ste. 200, Rockville, MD 20850. (301) 921-2300. 1989. 2nd edition. Details existing chemical regulation under TSCA; EPA's program for evaluating and regulating new chemical substances; PMN preparations and follow through; civil and criminal liability; inspections and audits; required testing of chemical substances and mixtures and exemptions from PMN requirements.

TSCA Inspection Manual. Government Institutes, Inc., 4 Research Pl., Ste. 200, Rockville, MD 20850. (301) 921-2300. Forms and procedures to ensure your compliance with the Toxic Substances Control Act.

TSCA Plant and Production Data. Chemical Information Systems, Inc., 7215 York Rd., Baltimore, MD 21212. (301) 321-8440. Unique substances data, which represents the non-confidential portion of reports received by the Environmental Protection Agency as a result of the U.S. Toxic Substances Control Act.

TSCA Policy Compendium. Government Institutes, Inc., 4 Research Pl., Ste. 200, Rockville, MD 20850. (301) 921-2300. 1985. Clarifies inspection and enforcement requirements with the official EPA supporting documents.

TSCATS. U.S. Environmental Protection Agency, Office of Pesticides and Toxic Substances, 401 M St., S.W., Washington, DC 20460. (202) 382-3524.

Tucker Wildlife Sanctuary. Star Route, Box 858, Orange, CA 92667. (714) 649-2760.

Tufts University. Curtis Hall, 474 Boston Avenue, Medford, MA 02155. (617) 381-3486.

Tundra Ecosystems: A Comparative Analysis. Cambridge University Press, 40 W. 20th St., New York, NY 10011. (212) 924-3900. 1981. Report of the International Biological Programme on tundra ecology.

Turf and Ornamental Chemicals Reference. John Wiley & Sons, Inc., 605 3rd Ave., New York, NY 10158-0012. (212) 850-6000. 1990. Provides with a consolidated and fully cross-indexed set of chemical product labels and material safety data sheets (MSDA's) in one easily accessible source. Products are indexed in 6 separate color coded indexes as follows: Brand name quick reference; manufacturer; product category; common and chemical name; and plant and site use and pet use.

Turning the Tide: Saving the Chesapeake Bay. Tom Horton. Island Press, 1718 Connecticut Ave. N.W., Suite 300, Washington, DC 20009. (202) 232-7933. 1991. Presents a comprehensive look at two decades of efforts to save the Chesapeake Bay. It outlines which methods have worked, and which have not. Sets a new strategy for the future, calling for greater political coverage, environmental leadership and vision.

Turtles of the World. Carl H. Ernst and Roger W. Barbour. Smithsonian Institution Press, 470 L'Enfant Plaza #7100, Washington, DC 20560. (800) 782-4612. 1989. Comprehensive coverage of the world's 257 turtle species.

TVA Public Information Office. 400 West Summit Hill Dr., Knoxville, TN 37902. (615) 632-8000.

U.S. Air Force Geophysics Laboratory. Adolph S. Jursa. Phillips Laboratory, 29 Randolph Rd., Hanscom Air Force Base, Bedford, MA 01731-3010. (617) 377-5191. 1985.

U.S. Antarctic Research Program. Polar Information Program, National Science Foundation, Washington, DC 20550. (202) 357-7817.

U.S. Arctic Research Commission. Geophysical Institute, University of Alaska, Fairbanks, AK 99775-0800. (202) 371-9631.

U. S. Bureau of Land Management. Information Bulletins. Superintendent of Documents, U.S. Government Printing Office, Washington, DC 20402. Irregular.

U.S. Committee on Irrigation and Drainage. P.O. Box 15326, Denver, CO 80215. (303) 236-6960.

U.S. Council for Energy Awareness. 1776 I St., N.W., Suite 400, Washington, DC 20006. (202) 293-0770.

U.S. Department of Labor: Mine Safety and Health Administration. 4015 Wilson Blvd., Arlington, VA 22203. (703) 235-1452.

U. S. Department of the Interior. Conservation Bulletins. Superintendent of Documents, U.S. Government Printing Office, Washington, DC 20402. Irregular.

U. S. Energy and Environmental Interest Groups: Institutional Profiles. Lettie McSpadden Wenner. Greenwood Publishing Group, Inc., 88 Post Rd. W., PO Box 5007, Westport, CT 06881. (212) 226-3571. 1990. Included are organizations that lobby in the energy and environmental policy areas including business corporations and trade associations, not-for-profit public interest groups, and professional research groups, and governmental organizations.

U.S. Environmental Protection Agency. 401 M St., S.W., Washington, DC 20460. (202) 382-7400.

U.S. Environmental Protection Agency: Air Emission Factor Clearinghouse. Research Triangle Park, NC 27711. (919) 541-0888.

U.S. Environmental Protection Agency: Air Risk Information Support Center. Research Triangle Park, NC 27711. (919) 541-0888.

U.S. Environmental Protection Agency: Assistant Administrator for Enforcement. 401 M St., S.W., Washington, DC 20460. (202) 382-4134.

U.S. Environmental Protection Agency: Assistant Administrator for Pesticides and Toxic Substances. 401 M St., S.W., Washington, DC 20460. (202) 382-2902.

U.S. Environmental Protection Agency: Assistant Administrator for Policy, Planning and Evaluation. 401 M St., S.W., Washington, DC 20460. (202) 382-4332.

U.S. Environmental Protection Agency: Assistant Administrator for Research and Development. 401 M St., S.W., Washington, DC 20460. (202) 382-7676.

U.S. Environmental Protection Agency: Assistant Administrator for Solid Waste and Emergency Response. 401 M St., S.W., Washington, DC 20460. (202) 382-4610.

U.S. Environmental Protection Agency: Assistant Administrator for Water. 401 M St., S.W., Washington, DC 20460. (202) 382-5700.

U.S. Environmental Protection Agency: CERCLA Enforcement Division. 401 M St., S.W., Washington, DC 20460. (202) 382-4812.

U.S. Environmental Protection Agency: Communications and Public Affairs Office. 401 M St., S.W., Washington, DC 20460. (202) 382-4361.

U.S. Environmental Protection Agency: Cooperative Environmental Management Office. Room 605, 499 South Capitol St., S.W., Washington, DC 20460. (202) 475-9741.

U.S. Environmental Protection Agency: Dockets. 401 M St., S.W., Washington, DC 20460. (202) 382-5926.

U.S. Environmental Protection Agency: Freedom of Information Office. 401 M St., S.W., Washington, DC 20460. (202) 382-4048.

U.S. Environmental Protection Agency: Library, Room 2404. 401 M St., S.W., Washington, DC 20460. (202) 382-5921.

U.S. Environmental Protection Agency Library System Book Catalog. U.S. Environmental Protection Agency, Library Systems Branch. U.S. G.P.O., Washington, DC 20401. (202) 512-0000. Annual. Includes the monographic collection of the 28 libraries comprising the library system of the Environmental Protection Agency.

U.S. Environmental Protection Agency: National Enforcement Investigations Center. Building 53, Box 25227, Denver, CO 80225. (303) 236-5100.

U.S. Environmental Protection Agency: Office of Air Quality Planning and Standards. Research Triangle Park, NC 27711. (919) 541-5615.

U.S. Environmental Protection Agency: Office of Civil Enforcement. 401 M St., S.W., Washington, DC 20460. (202) 382-4544.

U.S. Environmental Protection Agency: Office of Compliance Monitoring. 401 M St., S.W., Washington, DC 20460. (202) 382-3807.

U.S. Environmental Protection Agency: Office of Criminal Enforcement. 401 M St., S.W., Washington, DC 20460. (202) 475-9660.

U.S. Environmental Protection Agency: Office of Drinking Water. 401 M St., S.W., Washington, DC 20460. (202) 382-5543.

U.S. Environmental Protection Agency: Office of Emergency and Remedial Response. Emergency Response Division, 401 M St., S.W., Washington, DC 20460. (202) 382-2180.

U.S. Environmental Protection Agency: Office of Environmental Engineering and Technology. 401 M St., S.W., Washington, DC 20460. (202) 382-2600.

U.S. Environmental Protection Agency: Office of Environmental Processes and Effects Research. 401 M St., S.W., Washington, DC 20460. (202) 382-5950.

U.S. Environmental Protection Agency: Office of Exploratory Research. 401 M St., S.W., Washington, DC 20460. (202) 382-5750.

U.S. Environmental Protection Agency: Office of Federal Activities. 401 M St., S.W., Washington, DC 20460. (202) 382-5053.

U.S. Environmental Protection Agency: Office of Ground Water Protection. 401 M St., S.W., Washington, DC 20460. (202) 382-7077.

U.S. Environmental Protection Agency: Office of Health and Environmental Assessment. 401 M St., S.W., Washington, DC 20460. (202) 382-7317.

U.S. Environmental Protection Agency: Office of Health Research. 401 M St., S.W., Washington, DC 20460. (202) 382-5900.

U.S. Environmental Protection Agency: Office of Marine and Estuarine Protection. 401 M St., S.W., Washington, DC 20460. (202) 382-8580.

U.S. Environmental Protection Agency: Office of Mobile Services. 401 M St., S.W., Washington, DC 20460. (202) 382-7645.

U.S. Environmental Protection Agency: Office of Modeling and Monitoring Systems and Quality Assurance. 401 M St., S.W., Washington, DC 20460. (202) 382-5767.

U.S. Environmental Protection Agency: Office of Municipal Pollution Control. 401 M St., S.W., Washington, DC 20460. (202) 382-5850.

U.S. Environmental Protection Agency: Office of Pesticide Programs. 401 M St., S.W., Washington, DC 20460. (202) 557-7090.

U.S. Environmental Protection Agency: Office of Policy Analysis. 401 M St., S.W., Washington, DC 20460. (202) 382-4034.

U.S. Environmental Protection Agency: Office of Pollution Prevention. 401 M St., S.W., Washington, DC 20460.

U.S. Environmental Protection Agency: Office of Radiation Programs. 401 M St., S.W., Washington, DC 20460. (202) 557-9710.

U.S. Environmental Protection Agency: Office of Regulatory Management and Evaluation. 401 M St., S.W., Washington, DC 20460. (202) 382-4028.

U.S. Environmental Protection Agency: Office of Research Program Management. 401 M St., S.W., Washington, DC 20460. (202) 382-7500.

U.S. Environmental Protection Agency: Office of Solid Waste. 401 M St., S.W., Washington, DC 20460. (202) 382-4627.

U.S. Environmental Protection Agency: Office of Technology Transfer and Regulatory Support. 401 M St., S.W., Washington, DC 20460.

U.S. Environmental Protection Agency: Office of Toxic Substances. 401 M St., S.W., Washington, DC 20460. (202) 382-3813.

U.S. Environmental Protection Agency: Office of Underground Storage Tanks. 401 M St., S.W., Washington, DC 20460. (202) 382-4517.

U.S. Environmental Protection Agency: Office of Waste Programs Enforcement. 401 M St., S.W., Washington, DC 20460. (202) 382-4814.

U.S. Environmental Protection Agency: Office of Water Enforcement and Permits. 401 M St., S.W., Washington, DC 20460. (202) 475-8488.

U.S. Environmental Protection Agency: Office of Water Regulations and Standards. 401 M St., S.W., Washington, DC 20460. (202) 382-5400.

U.S. Environmental Protection Agency: Office of Wetlands Protection. 401 M St., S.W., Washington, DC 20460. (202) 382-7946.

U.S. Environmental Protection Agency, PM-233: EPA Regulatory Agenda. 401 M St., S.W., Washington, DC 20460. (202) 382-5480.

U.S. Environmental Protection Agency: RCRA Enforcement Division. 401 M St., S.W., Washington, DC 20460. (202) 382-4808.

U.S. Environmental Protection Agency: RCRA/Superfund Hotline. 401 M St., S.W., Washington, DC 20460. (202) 382-9346.

U.S. Environmental Protection Agency, TS-799: Toxic Assistance Office. 401 M St., S.W., Washington, DC 20460. (202) 382-3790.

U.S. EPA Region 1: Pollution Prevention. Program Manager, JFK Federal Building, Boston, MA 02203. (617) 565-3715.

U.S. EPA Region 10: Pollution Prevention. Chief, Hazardous Waste Policy Office, 1200 Sixth Ave., Seattle, WA 98101. (206) 442-5810.

U.S. EPA Region 2: Pollution Prevention. Regional Contact, 26 Federal Plaza, New York, NY 10278. (212) 264-2525.

U.S. EPA Region 3: Pollution Prevention. Program Manager, 841 Chestnut St., Philadelphia, PA 19107. (215) 597-9800.

U.S. EPA Region 4: Pollution Prevention. Program Manager, 345 Courtland St., N.E., Atlanta, GA 30365. (404) 347-7109.

U.S. EPA Region 5: Emergency Preparedness and Community Right-to-Know. Pesticides and Toxic Substances Branch, 230 South Dearborn St., Chicago, IL 60604. (312) 353-2000.

U.S. EPA Region 5: Pollution Prevention. 230 South Dearborn St., Chicago, IL 60604. (312) 353-2000.

U.S. EPA Region 6: Pollution Prevention. Coordinator, 1445 Ross Ave., Suite 1200, Dallas, TX 75202-2733. (214) 655-6444.

U.S. EPA Region 7: Pollution Prevention. Section Chief, State Programs Section, 726 Minnesota Ave., Kansas City, MO 66101. (913) 551-7006.

U.S. EPA Region 8: Pollution Prevention. Senior Policy Advisor, 999 18th St., Suite 500, Denver, CO 80202-2405. (303) 293-1603.

U.S. EPA Region 9: Pollution Prevention. Deputy Director, Hazardous Waste, 215 Fremont St., San Francisco, CA 94105. (415) 556-6322.

U.S. EPA Test and Evaluation Facility. 26 W. Martin Luther King Dr., Cincinnati, OH 45268. (513) 684-2621.

U.S. Forest Planting Report. U.S. Department of Agriculture, Forest Service, 14 Independence Ave. SW, Washington, DC 20250. (202) 447-7454. Annual. Covers afforestation, strip mining and reclamation of land in the United States.

U.S. Forest Service, Aquatic Ecosystem Analysis Laboratory. 105 Page, Brigham Young University, Provo, UT 84602. (801) 378-4928.

U.S. Forest Service, Forest Engineering Research Project. George W. Andrews Forestry Sciences Laboratory, Auburn University, Devall Street, Auburn, AL 36849. (205) 826-8700.

U.S. Forest Service, Forest Hydrology Laboratory. Southern Forest Experiment Station, P.O. Box 947, Oxford, MS 38655. (601) 234-2744.

U.S. Forest Service, Forest Products Laboratory. One Gifford Pinchot Drive, Madison, WI 53705-2398. (608) 231-9200.

U.S. Forest Service, Forest Tree Seed Laboratory. P.O. Box 906, Starkville, MS 39759. (601) 323-8160.

U.S. Forest Service, Forestry Sciences Laboratory. Carlton Street, Athens, GA 30602. (404) 546-2441.

U.S. Forest Service, Forestry Sciences Laboratory. Montana State University, Bozeman, MT 59717. (406) 994-4852.

U.S. Forest Service, Forestry Sciences Laboratory. Southern Illinois University at Carbondale, Carbondale, IL 62901-4630. (618) 453-2318.

U.S. Forest Service, Forestry Sciences Laboratory. I-26 Agricultural Building, University of Missouri- Columbia, Columbia, MO 65211. (314) 875-5341.

U.S. Forest Service, Forestry Sciences Laboratory. Forest Hill Road, Houghton, MI 49931. (906) 482-6303.

U.S. Forest Service, Forestry Sciences Laboratory. 222 South 22nd Street, Laramie, WY 82070. (307) 742-6621.

U.S. Forest Service, Forestry Sciences Laboratory. 860 North 1200 East, Logan, UT 84321. (801) 752-1311.

U.S. Forest Service, Forestry Sciences Laboratory. 1221 South Main Street, Moscow, ID 83843. (208) 882-3557.

U.S. Forest Service, Forestry Sciences Laboratory. South Dakota School of Mines and Technology, Rapid City, SD 57701. (605) 394-1960.

U.S. Forest Service, Forestry Sciences Laboratory. Arizona State University, Temple, AZ 85287. (602) 379-4365.

U.S. Forest Service Grazing and Rangelands: A History. William D. Rowley. Texas A & M University Press, College Station, TX 1985. Forest and range policy, forest reserves and grazing history.

U.S. Forest Service, Institute of Forest Genetics. 2480 Carson Road, Placerville, CA 95667. (916) 622-1225.

U.S. Forest Service, Institute of Northern Forestry. 308 Tanana Drive, University of Alaska, Fairbanks, AK 99775-5500. (907) 474-8163.

U.S. Forest Service, Institute of Tropical Forestry. Call Box 25000, Rio Piedras, PR 00928-2500. (809) 766-5335.

U.S. Forest Service, Intermountain Fire Sciences. P.O. Box 8089, Missoula, MT 59807. (406) 329-3495.

U.S. Forest Service, Intermountain Research Station. 324 25th Street, Ogden, UT 84401. (801) 625-5431.

U.S. Forest Service, North Central Forest Experiment Station. 1407 South Harrison Road, Suite 220, East Lansing, MI 48823. (517) 355-7740.

U.S. Forest Service, Northeastern Forest Experiment Station. 5 Godfrey Dr., Orono, ME 04473. (207) 866-4140.

U.S. Forest Service, Pacific Southwest Forest and Range Experiment Station. P.O. Box 245, 1960 Addison Street, Berkeley, CA 94701. (415) 486-3292.

U.S. Forest Service, Redwood Science Laboratory. 1700 Bayview Dr., Arcata, CA 95521. (707) 822-3691.

U.S. Forest Service, Rocky Mountain Forest and Range Experiment Station. 240 West Prospect Road, Fort Collins, CO 80526-2098. (303) 498-1126.

U.S. Forest Service, San Joaquin Experimental Range. 24075 Highway 41, Coarsegold, CA 93614. (209) 868-3349.

U.S. Forest Service, Shrub Sciences Laboratory. 735 N. 500 E., Provo, UT 84606. (801) 377-5717.

U.S. Forest Service, Sierra Field Station. c/o Center for Environmental Studies, Arizona State University, Temple, AZ 85287-3211. (602) 965-2975.

U.S. Forest Service, Timber Management Research Project. George W. Andrews Forestry Sciences Laboratory, DeVall Drive, Auburn University, AL 36849. (205) 826-8700.

U.S. Forest Service, Wildlife Habitat and Silviculture Laboratory. Box 7600, SFA Sta., Nacogdoches, TX 75962. (409) 569-7981.

U. S. Geological Survey. Water Supply Papers. Superintendent of Documents, U.S. Government Printing Office, Washington, DC 20402. 1896-. Irregular.

U.S. National Committee for the Scientific Committee on Oceanic Research. Ocean Studies Blvd., 2001 Wisconsin Ave., N.W., Rm. MH550, Washington, DC 20007. (202) 334-2714.

U.S. Petroleum Strategies in the Decade of the Environment. Bob Williams. PennWell Books, PO Box 21288, Tulsa, OK 74121. (918) 831-9421; (800) 752-9764. 1991.

The U.S. Plastics Industry. FIND/SVP, 625 Avenue of the Americas, New York, NY 10011. (212) 645-4500. 1990. Data on plastics additives production and use of major polymers, including engineering plastics, and processing equipment.

U.S. Timber Production, Trade, Consumption and Price Statistics. U.S. Forest Service. U.S. G.P.O., Washington, DC 20402-9325. (202) 783-3238. 1987. Annual. Covers the period from 1950 to present. Includes measures of economic growth.

U.S. Tundra Biome Publication List. U.S. Army Corps of Engineers, Cold Regions Research and Engineering Laboratory, 22 Lyme Rd., Hanover, NH 03755-1290. (603) 646-4221. 1983. Bibliography of the U.S. Tundra Biome International Biological Program

UC IPM Pest Management Guidelines. ANR Publications, University of California, 6701 San Pablo Avenue, Oakland, CA 94608-1239. (510) 642-2431. Official guidelines for monitoring techniques, pesticide use, and alternatives in agricultural crops.

UK Pesticides for Farmers and Growers. H. Kidd and D. Hartley, eds. Royal Society of Chemistry, c/o CRC Press, 2000 Corporate Blvd. N.W., Boca Raton, FL 33431-9868. (800) 272-7737. 1987. Practical guide to pesticides designed specifically to meet the needs of farmers and growers.

ULI–The Urban Land Institute. 625 Indiana Ave., N.W., Washington, DC 20004. (202) 624-7000.

Ullmanns Encyclopedia of Industrial Chemistry. Hans Jurgen Arpe and Wolfgang Gerhartz, eds. VCH Publishers, 303 NW 12th Ave., Deerfield Beach, FL 33442-1788. (305) 428-5566. 1990. Designed to keep up with the broad spectrum of chemical technology. Thirty-six volumes of the encyclopedia have been divided into two sets: the 28 A volumes contain alphabetically arranged articles on chemicals, product groups, processes and technological concepts; and the 8 B volumes are compendia of basic knowledge in industrial chemistry.

Ultra-violet Rays: Factors & Adverse Effects. ABBE Publishers Association of Washington DC, 4111 Gallows Rd., Annandale, VA 22003-1862. 1987. Bibliography of the physiological effects of ultraviolet radiation.

Ultrafiltration Handbook. Munir Cheryan. Technomic Publishing Co., 851 New Holland Ave., Box 3535, Lancaster, PA 17604. (717) 291-5609. 1986. Covers filters and filtration, and membranes technology.

Ultrapurity; Methods and Techniques. Marcel Dekker, Inc., 270 Madison Ave., New York, NY 10016. (212) 696-9000. 1972. Purification of chemicals and chemical storage.

Ultraviolet Radiation. American Industrial Hygiene Association, 345 White Pond Dr., Akron, OH 44320. (216) 873-2442. 1991. Offers updated and expanded information on ultraviolet radiations' physical characteristics; generation, uses, and sources; interaction with matter; biological effects; exposure criteria; instrumentation; evaluation and measurement; and controls and their practical applications.

Under the Influence: A History of Nitrous Oxide and Oxygen Anaesthesia. W.D.A. Smith. Wood Library-Museum of Anesthesiology, 515 Busse Hwy., Park Ridge, IL 60068. (708) 825-5586. 1982.

Underground Injection Practices Council. 525 Central Park Dr., Suite 304, Oklahoma City, OK 73105. (405) 525-6146.

Underground Mining Methods Handbook. Society for Mining, Metallurgy and Exploration Inc., PO Box 625005, Littleton, CO 80162. (303) 973-9550. 1982. A manual of mining engineering.

Underground Storage of Gaseous Fuels. American Gas Association, 1515 Wilson Blvd., Arlington, VA 22209. 1981. Underground storage of natural gas and petroleum products.

Underground Storage of Natural Gas: Theory and Practice. Kluwer Academic Publishers, 101 Philip Dr., Assinippi Park, Norwell, MA 02061. (617) 871-6600. 1989.

Underground Storage of Oil and Gas in Salt Deposits and Other Non-Hard Rocks. Wolfgang Dreyer. Enke, Rudigerstr. 14, Stuttgart, Germany D-7000. 1982. Petroleum and natural gas underground storage and salt deposits.

Underground Storage Tank Compliance Manual. IMA and Rooks, Pitts and Poust, Chicago, IL 1988. Underground storage, maintenance and repair, and waste disposal.

Underground Storage Tank Guide. Jeffrey L. Leiter, ed. PennWell Books, PO Box 21288, Tulsa, OK 74121. (918) 831-9421; (800) 752-9764. Monthly. Describes exactly what EPA's underground storage tank regulations require. Lists contacts and requirements for each state's underground storage tank program.

Underground Storage Tank Management: A Practical Guide. Hart Environmental Management Corp. Government Institutes Inc., 4 Research Place, Suite 200, Rockville, MD 20850. (301) 921-2300. 1991. 3rd ed. Presents the latest in the state-of-the-art tank design, how to predict tank leaks, test tank integrity, avoid costly tank replacement through low-cost retrofit and maintenance techniques, and how to respond to leaks.

Underground Storage Tanks: A Primer on the New Federal Regulatory Program. American Bar Association, 750 N. Lake Shore Dr., Chicago, IL 60611. (312) 988-5000. 1989. Environmental law relative to hazardous waste sites, waste disposal sites and underground storage.

Understanding Cell Toxicology: Principles and Practice. Erik Walum, Kjell Stenberg and Dag Jenssen. E. Horwood, 200 Old Tappan Rd., Old Tappan, NJ 07675. (800) 223-2348. 1990. Surveys the uses of mammalian cell assays to evaluate the toxic actions of chemical and physical agents.

Understanding Ground-Water Contamination: An Orientation Manual. Paul E. Bailey and William D. Ward, eds. PennWell Books, PO Box 21288, Tulsa, OK 74121. (918) 831-9421; (800) 752-9764. 1990. Orientation manual for businesses, their counsel, local and regional officials, and government agencies, that must make decisions regarding groundwater.

Underwater and Marine Parks: An Indexed Bibliography. Don Huff. Vance Bibliographies, PO Box 229, 112 N. Charter St., Monticello, IL 61856. (217) 762-3831. 1983.

Underwater Naturalist. American Littoral Society, Sandy Hook, Highlands, NJ 07732. (201) 291-0055. Monthly. Covers issues relating to coastal areas.

The UNESCO Courier. UNESCO, 7 place de Fontenoy, Paris, France F-75700. 75015 1948-. Monthly. Each issue deals with a theme of universal interest including regular features on the environment, world heritage and UNESCO activities.

Unfulfilled Promises: A Citizen Review of the International Water Quality Agreement. Great Lakes United, State University College at Buffalo, Cassety Hall, 1300 Elmwood Ave., Buffalo, NY 14222. (716) 886-0142. 1990.

Union of Concerned Scientists. 26 Church St., Cambridge, MA 02238. (617) 547-5552.

United Association of Journeymen & Apprentices of the Plumbing & Pipe Fitting Industry of the United States & Canada. P.O. Box 37800, Washington, DC 20013. (202) 628-5823.

United Cancer Council. 4010 W. 86th St., Suite H, Indianapolis, IN 46268. (317) 879-9900.

United Citizens Coastal Protection League. P.O. Box 46, Cardiff by the Sea, CA 92007. (619) 753-7477.

United Mine Workers of America. 900 15th St., N.W., Washington, DC 20005. (202) 842-7200.

United Nations Environment Programme. DC2-0803 United Nations, New York, NY 10017. (212) 963-8093.

United Nations Information Centre. 1889 F St. N.W., Ground Floor, Washington, DC 20006. (202) 289-8670.

United Nations List of National Parks and Protected Areas. World Conservation Monitoring Centre. World Conservation Union, IUCN Publications Services Unit, 181a Huntingdon Road, Cambridge, England CB3 0DJ. (0223) 277894. 1990. Standard list of national parks and other protected areas. Includes lists of world heritage sites, biosphere reserves and wetlands of international importance.

United New Conservationists. P.O. Box 362, Campbell, CA 95009. (408) 241-5769.

United Paperworkers International Union. PO Box 1475, Nashville, TN 37202. (615) 834-8590.

United Pesticide Formulators & Distributors Association. Prentiss Drug & Chemical, 3609 Shallowford Rd., Atlanta, GA 30340. (404) 458-1055.

United Rubber, Cork, Linoleum, & Plastic Workers of America. 570 White Pond Dr., Akron, OH 44320. (216) 376-6181.

The United States and the Global Environment: A Guide to American Organizations Concerned with International Environmental Issues. Thaddeus C. Trzyna. California Institute of Public Affairs, PO Box 10, Claremont, CA 91711. (714) 624-5212. 1983. A guide to American organizations concerned with international environmental issues.

United States Animal Health Association. P.O. Box K227, 1610 Forest Ave., Ste. 114, Richmond, VA 23228. (804) 266-3275.

United States Committee for UNICEF. 333 E. 38th St., New York, NY 10016. (212) 686-5522.

United States Committee on Large Dams. P.O. Box 15103, Denver, CO 80215. (303) 236-6960.

United States Conference of Mayors National Resource Recovery Association. 1620 Eye St., N.W., 4th Fl., Washington, DC 20006. (202) 293-7330.

United States Energy Association. 1620 I St., N.W., Suite 615, Washington, DC 20006. (202) 331-0415.

United States Man and the Biosphere Program: Directory of Biosphere Reserves in the United States. National Technical Information Service, 5285 Port Royal Rd., Springfield, VA 22161. (703) 487-4650. 1991. Research on biosphere, natural areas, and national parks and reserves.

United States National Committee of the International Peat Society. P.O. Box 441, Eveleth, MN 55734. (218) 744-2993.

United States Operating Committee on ETAD. 1330 Connecticut Ave., N.W., Suite 300, Washington, DC 20036-1702. (202) 659-0060.

United States Public Interest Research Group. 215 Pennsylvania Ave., SE, Washington, DC 20003. (202) 546-9707.

United States Sources of Information in the Area of Decertification. United States. U.S. Environmental Protection Agency, Assistant Administrator for Planning and Management, Office of Administration, Washington, DC 1977.

United Steelworkers of America. 5 Gateway Center, Pittsburgh, PA 15222. (412) 562-2400.

Universities Council on Water Resources. 4543 Faner Hall, Dept. of Geography, Southern Illinois University, Carbondale, IL 62901. (618) 536-7571.

Universities Council on Water Resources Update. Universities Council on Water Resources, 4543 Faner Hall, Dept. of Geography, Southern Illinois University, Carbondale, IL 62901-4526. (618) 536-7571. Three times a year. Covers education, research, and legislation on water resources.

University and Jepson Herbaria. University of California, Berkeley, Berkeley, CA 94720. (415) 642-2463.

University Center for Environmental and Hazardous Materials Studies. Virginia Polytech Institute and State University, 1020 Derring Hall, Blacksburg, VA 24061. (703) 951-5538.

University Corporation for Atmospheric Research. P.O. Box 3000, Boulder, CO 80307-3000. (303) 497-1650.

University Forest. West Virginia University, Morgantown, WV 26506. (304) 293-2941.

University of Alabama, Alabama Waste Exchange. P.O. Box 870203, Tuscaloosa, AL 35487. (205) 348-5889.

University of Alabama, Arboretum. Box 870344, Tuscaloosa, AL 35487-0344. (205) 553-3278.

University of Alabama, Environmental Institute for Waste Management Studies. P.O. Box 870203, Tuscaloosa, AL 35487-0203. (205) 348-8401.

University of Alabama, Hazardous Materials Management Resource Recovery. Department of Chemical Engineering, P.O. Box 870203, Tuscaloosa, AL 35487-0203. (205) 348-8401.

University of Alabama, Project Rose. P.O. Box 870203, Tuscaloosa, AL 35487-0203. (205) 348-4878.

University of Alaska Anchorage, Arctic Environmental Information and Data Center. 707 A Street, Anchorage, AK 99501. (907) 257-2733.

University of Alaska Fairbanks, Alaska Sea Grant College Program. 138 Irving II, Fairbanks, AK 99775-5040. (907) 474-7086.

University of Alaska Fairbanks, Forestry Soils Laboratory. Fairbanks, AK 99775. (907) 474-7114.

University of Alaska Fairbanks, Institute of Arctic Biology. Fairbanks, AK 99775. (907) 474-7648.

University of Alaska Fairbanks, Seward Marine Center. P.O.Box 730, Seward, AK 99664. (907) 224-5261.

University of Alaska Fairbanks, Water Research Center. Fairbanks, AK 99775. (907) 474-7350.

University of Arizona, Arizona Cooperative Fish and Wildlife Research Unit. 210 Biological Sciences Building, Tucson, AZ 85721. (602) 621-1959.

University of Arizona, Arizona Remote Sensing Center. Office of Arid Lands Studies, 845 North Park Avenue, Tucson, AZ 85719. (602) 621-7896.

University of Arizona, Arizona Research Laboratories Division of Neurobiology. 611 Gould-Simpson Science Building, Tucson, AZ 85721. (602) 621-6628.

University of Arizona, Boyce Thompson Arboretum. P.O. Box AB, Superior, AZ 85723. (602) 689-2811.

University of Arizona, Center for Insect Science. Tucson, AZ 85721. (602) 621-5769.

University of Arizona, Environmental Engineering Laboratory. Civil Engineering Department, Room 206, Tucson, AZ 85721. (602) 621-6586.

University of Arizona, Environmental Research Laboratory. Tucson International Airport, 2601 East Airport Drive, Tucson, AZ 85706. (602) 741-1990.

University of Arizona, Herbarium. 113 Shantz Building, Tucson, AZ 85721. (602) 621-7243.

University of Arizona, Laboratory of Tree-Ring Research. Tucson, AZ 85721. (602) 621-2191.

University of Florida, Water Resources Research Center. 424 Black Hall, Gainesville, FL 32611. (904) 471-0684.

University of Florida, Whitney Laboratory. 9505 Ocean Shore Boulevard, St. Augustine, FL 32086-8623. (904) 461-4000.

University of Georgia, Center for Advanced Ultrastructural Research. Barrow Hall, Athens, GA 30602. (404) 542-4080.

University of Georgia, Complex Carbohydrate Research Center. 220 Riverbend Road, Athens, GA 30602. (404) 542-4401.

University of Georgia, Herbarium. Athens, GA 30602. (404) 542-1823.

University of Georgia, Institute for Natural Products Research. Chemistry Building, Athens, GA 30602. (404) 542-5800.

University of Georgia, Institute of Ecology. 103 Ecology Building, Athens, GA 30602. (404) 542-2968.

University of Georgia, Julian H. Miller Mycological Herbarium. Department of Plant Pathology, Plant Sciences Building, Athens, GA 30602. (404) 542-1280.

University of Georgia, Marine Extension Service. P.O. Box 13687, Savannah, GA 31416. (912) 356-2496.

University of Georgia, Marine Institute. Sapelo, GA (912) 485-2221.

University of Georgia, Marine Sciences Program. Athens, GA 30602 (404) 542-7671.

University of Georgia, Savanna River Ecology Laboratory. P.O. Box Drawer E, Aiken, SC 29801. (803) 725-2472.

University of Georgia, Southeastern Cooperative Wildlife Disease. College of Veterinary Medicine, Athens, GA 30602. (404) 542-3000.

University of Georgia, State Botanical Garden of Georgia. 2450 South Milledge Avenue, Athens, GA 30605. (404) 542-1244.

University of Georgia, Zooarchaelogy Laboratory. Baldwin Hall, Athens, GA 30602. (404) 542-3922.

University of Guam. Marine Laboratory, UOG Station, GU 96923. (671) 734-2421.

University of Hawaii at Manoa, Environmental Center. 2550 Campus Road, Honolulu, HI 96822. (808) 956-7361.

University of Hawaii at Manoa Harold L. Lyon Center. 3860 Manoa Road, Honolulu, HI 96822. (808) 988-3177.

University of Hawaii at Manoa Hawaii Cooperative Fishery Research Unit. 2538 The Mall, Honolulu, HI 96822. (808) 956-8350.

University of Hawaii at Manoa Hawaii Institute of Marine Biology. Coconut Island, P.O. Box 1346, Kaneohe, HI 96744-1346. (808) 236-7401.

University of Hawaii at Manoa Hawaii Undersea Research Laboratory. 1000 Pope Road, MSB 303, Honolulu, HI 96822. (808) 956-6335.

University of Hawaii at Manoa Kewalo Basin Marine Mammal Laboratory. 1129 Ala Moana Boulevard, Honolulu, HI 96814. (808) 538-0067.

University of Hawaii at Manoa Sea Grant College Program. 1000 Pope Road, MSB 220, Honolulu, HI 96822. (808) 948-7031.

University of Hawaii at Manoa, Water Resources Research Center. 2540 Dole Street, Honolulu, HI 96822. (808) 956-7847.

University of Houston Coastal Center. c/o Office of the Senior Vice President, Houston, TX 77204-5502. (713) 749-2351.

University of Houston, Environmental Liability Law Program. Law Center, 4800 Calhoun, Houston, TX 77204-6381. (208) 749-1393.

University of Idaho Cooperative Park Studies Unit. College of Forestry, Wildlife and Range Sciences, Moscow, ID 83843. (208) 885-7990.

University of Idaho Forest, Wildlife and Range Experiment Station. Moscow, ID 83843. (208) 885-6441.

University of Idaho Herbarium. Department of Biological Sciences, Moscow, ID 83843. (208) 885-6798.

University of Idaho, Idaho Cooperative Fish and Wildlife Research Unit. College of Forestry, Wildlife and Range Sciences, Moscow, ID 83843. (208) 885-6336.

University of Idaho, Idaho Water Resources Research Institute. Morrill Hall 106, Moscow, ID 83843. (208) 885-6429.

University of Idaho, Remote Sensing Center. College of Forestry, Wildlife and Range Sciences, Moscow, ID 83843. (208) 885-7209.

University of Idaho, Wilderness Research Center. Moscow, ID 83843. (208) 885-7911.

University of Illinois, Biotechnology Center. 105 Observatory, 901 South Matthews, Urbana, IL 61801. (217) 333-1695.

University of Illinois, Herbarium. Department of Plant Biology, 505 S. Goodwin Ave., Urbana, IL 61801. (217) 333-2522.

University of Illinois, Institute for Environmental Studies. 408 South Goodwin Avenue, Urbana, IL 61801. (217) 333-4178.

University of Illinois, Laboratory of Plant Pigment Biochemistry and Photobiology. 1302 West Pennsylvania, Urbana, IL 61801. (217) 333-1968.

University of Illinois, Water Resources Center. 2535 Hydrosystems Laboratory, 205 North Matthews Avenue, Urbana, IL 61801. (217) 333-0536.

University of Iowa, Herbarium. Department of Botany, Iowa City, IA 52242. (319) 335-1320.

University of Iowa, High Field Nuclear Magnetic Resonance Facility. Department of Chemistry, Room 77 Chemistry-Botany Building, Iowa City, IA 52242. (319) 335-3669.

University of Iowa, Iowa Lakeside Laboratory. R.R. 2, Box 305, Milford, IA 51351. (712) 337-3669.

University of Iowa, University Large Scale Fermentation Facility. Department of Microbiology, Iowa City, IA 52242. (319) 335-7780.

University of Kansas, Fitch Natural History Reservation. Lawrence, KS 66044. (913) 843-3612.

University of Kansas, John H. Nelson Environmental Study Area. Division of Biological Sciences, Lawrence, KS 66045. (913) 864-3236.

University of Kansas, Kansas Biological Survey. 2041 Constant Avenue-Foley Hall, Lawrence, KS 66047-2906. (913) 864-7725.

University of Kansas, Kansas Ecological Reserves. Lawrence, KS 66045. (913) 864-3236.

University of Kansas, McGregor Herbarium. Joseph S. Bridwell Botanical Research Laboratory, 2045 Constant Ave., Campus West, Lawrence, KS 66047. (913) 864-4493.

University of Kansas, Museum of Natural History. Dyche Hall, Lawrence, KS 66045. (913) 864-4541.

University of Kansas, Snow Entomological Museum. Snow Hall, Lawrence, KS 66045. (913) 864-3065.

University of Kansas, Water Resources Institute. Lawrence, KS 66045. (913) 864-3807.

University of Kentucky, Herbarium. School of Biological Science, Room 216 Funkhouser, Morgan 101, Lexington, KY 40506. (606) 257-3240.

University of Kentucky, Kentucky Water Resources Research Institute. 219 Anderson Hall, Lexington, KY 40506-0046. (606) 257-1832.

University of Louisville, Water Resource Laboratory. Louisville, KY 40292. (502) 588-6731.

University of Maine, Center for Marine Studies. 14 Coburn Hall, Orono, ME 04469. (207) 581-1435.

University of Maine, Cooperative Forestry Research Unit. College of Forest Resources, Orono, ME 04469. (207) 581-2893.

University of Maine, Dwight D. Demeritt Forest. College of Forest Resources, 206 Nutting Hall, Orono, ME 04469. (207) 827-7804.

University of Maine, Environmental Studies Center. Coburn Hall #11, Orono, ME 04469. (207) 581-1490.

University of Maine, Herbarium. Department of Botany & Plant Pathology, Orono, ME 04469. (207) 581-2976.

University of Maine, Ira C. Darling Center for Research Teaching and Service. Walpole, ME 04573. (207) 563-3146.

University of Maine, Maine Sea Grant College Program. 14 Coburn Hall, University of Maine, Orono, ME 04469-0114. (207) 581-1435.

University of Maine, Migratory Fish Research Institute. Department of Zoology, Orono, ME 04469. (207) 581-2548.

University of Maryland, Bioprocess Scale-Up Facility. Engineering Research Center, College Park, MD 20742. (301) 405-3908.

University of Maryland, Center for Environmental and Estuarine Studies. Center Operations, Horn Point, P.O.Box 775, Cambridge, MD 21613. (410) 228-9250.

University of Maryland, Center of Marine Biotechnology. 600 East Lombard Street, Baltimore, MD 21202. (301) 783-4800.

University of Maryland, Sea Grant College. 1123 Taliaferro Hall, College Park, MD 20742. (301) 405-6371.

University of Maryland, Water Resources Research Center. 3101 Chemistry Bldg., College Park, MD 20742. (301) 405-6829.

University of Massachusetts At Boston, Urban Harbors Institute. Harbor Campus, Boston, MA 02125. (617) 287-5570.

University of Massachusetts, Cooperative Marine Research Program. The Environmental Institute, Blaisdell House, Amherst, MA 01003-0040. (413) 545-2842.

University of Massachusetts, Environmental Institute. Blaisdell House, Amherst, MA 01003-0040. (413) 545-2842.

University of Massachusetts, Herbarium. Amherst, MA 01003. (413) 545-2775.

University of Massachusetts, Marine Station. P.O. Box 7125, Lanesville Station, 932 Washington Street, Gloucester, MA 01930. (508) 281-1930.

University of Massachusetts, Massachusetts Cooperative Fish and Wildlife Unit. Holdworth Hall, Amherst, MA 01003. (413) 545-0398.

University of Massachusetts, Massachusetts Water Resources Research Center. Blaisdell House, Amherst, MA 01003. (413) 545-2842.

University of Massachusetts, Museum of Zoology. Department of Zoology, Amherst, MA 01003. (413) 545-2287.

University of Miami, Cooperative Institute for Marine and Atmospheric Studies. 4600 Rickenbacker Causeway, Miami, FL 33149. (305) 361-4159.

University of Miami, Institute for Molecular Cellular Evolution. 12500 SW 152 Street, Miami, FL 33177. (305) 284-7366.

University of Miami, Morton Collectanea. Box 8204, Coral Gables, FL 33124. (305) 284-3741.

University of Miami, Research Collections. Department of Biology, Coral Gables, FL 33124. (305) 284-3973.

University of Miami, Rosenstiel School of Marine and Atmospheric Science. 4600 Rickenbacker Causeway, Miami, FL 33149. (305) 361-4000.

University of Michigan, Biochemical Engineering Laboratory. Department of Chemical Engineering, Ann Arbor, MI 48109. (313) 763-1178.

University of Michigan, Biological Station. Pellston, MI 49769. (616) 539-8406.

University of Michigan, Biophysics Research Division. Institute of Science and Technology, 2200 Bonisteel Boulevard, Ann Arbor, MI 48109-2099. (313) 764-5218.

University of Michigan, Cell Biology Laboratories. Department of Anatomy & Cell Biology, 4747 Medical Science II, Box 0616, 1301 Catherine Road, Ann Arbor, MI 48109. (313) 764-4360.

University of Michigan, Center for Great Lakes and Aquatic Sciences. 2200 Bonisteel Boulevard, Ann Arbor, MI 48109-2099. (313) 763-3515.

University of Michigan, Herbarium. North University Building, Ann Arbor, MI 48109-1057. (313) 764-2407.

University of Michigan, Marine Geochemistry Laboratory. Department of Geological Sciences, 1006 C.C. Little Building, Ann Arbor, MI 48109. (313) 763-4593.

University of Michigan, Marine Geology Laboratory. Department of Geological Sciences, Ann Arbor, MI 48109-1063. (313) 936-0521.

University of Michigan, Matthaei Botanical Gardens. 1800 North Dixboro Road, Ann Arbor, MI 48105. (313) 763-7060.

University of Michigan, Michigan Atmospheric Deposition Laboratory. 2126 Space Research Building, Ann Arbor, MI 48109-2143. (313) 763-6213.

University of Michigan, Museum of Zoology. 1082 University Museums, Ann Arbor, MI 48109. (313) 764-0476.

University of Michigan, Nichols Arboretum. Ann Arbor, MI 48109-1115. (313) 763-9315.

University of Michigan, Protein Sequencing Facility. Department of Biological Chemistry, 1301 Catherine Road, Ann Arbor, MI 48109-0606. (313) 763-0289.

University of Michigan, Radiation Safety Service. North University Building, Room 1101, Ann Arbor, MI 48109-1057. (313) 764-4420.

University of Michigan, School of Natural Resources, Research Service. 430 East University, Ann Arbor, MI 48109. (313) 764-6823.

University of Michigan, Wetland Ecosystem Research Group. Department of Chemical Engineering, 3094 Dow Building, Ann Arbor, MI 48109. (313) 764-3362.

University of Michigan, Wildland Management Center. School of Natural Resources, 430 East University, Ann Arbor, MI 48109-1115. (313) 763-1312.

University of Minnesota, All University Council on Environmental Quality. 330 Humphrey Center, 301 19th Avenue South, Minneapolis, MN 55455. (612) 625-1551.

University of Minnesota, Bell Museum of Natural History. 10 Church St., S.E., Minneapolis, MN 55455. (612) 624-4112.

University of Minnesota, Cedar Creek Natural History Area. 2660 Fawn Lake Drive NE, Bethel, MN 55005. (612) 434-5131.

University of Minnesota, Center for Natural Resource Policy and Management. 110 Green Hall, 1530 North Cleveland Avenue, St. Paul, MN 55108. (612) 624-9796.

University of Minnesota, Cloquet Forestry Center. 175 University Road, Cloquet, MN 55720. (218) 879-0850.

University of Minnesota, Duluth, Center for Water and The Environment. Natural Resources Research Institute, 5103 Miller Trunk Highway, Duluth, MN 55811. (218) 720-4270.

University of Minnesota, Duluth, Natural Resources Research Institute. 5013 Miller Trunk Highway, Duluth, MN 55811. (218) 720-4294.

University of Minnesota, Gray Freshwater Biological Institute. P.O. Box 100, Navarre, MN 55392. (612) 471-8476.

University of Minnesota, Herbarium. St. Paul, MN 55108. (612) 625-1234.

University of Minnesota, Industry/University Cooperative Research Center for Biocatalytic Processing. 240 Gortner Laboratory, 1479 Gortner Avenue, St. Paul, MN 55108. (612) 624-6774.

University of Minnesota, Institute for Advanced Studies In Biological Process Technology. 240 Gortner Laboratory, 1479 Gortner Avenue, St. Paul, MN 55108. (612) 624-6774.

University of Minnesota, Lake Itasca Forestry and Biological Station. Post Office, Lake Itasca, MN 56460. (218) 266-3345.

University of Minnesota, Limnological Research Center. Pillsbury Hall 220, 310 Pillsbury Drive Southeast, Minneapolis, MN 55455. (612) 624-7005.

University of Minnesota, Minnesota Sea Grant College Program. 1518 Cleveland Ave., Ste. 302, St. Paul, MN 55108. (612) 625-9288.

University of Minnesota, Remote Sensing Laboratory. 1530 North Cleveland Avenue, St. Paul, MN 55108. (612) 624-3400.

University of Minnesota, Water Resources Research Center. 1518 Cleveland Ave., Ste. 302, St. Paul, MN 55108. (612) 624-9282.

University of Mississippi, Biological Field Station. Department of Biology, University, MS 38677. (601) 232-5479.

University of Mississippi, Biological Museum. Department of Biology, University, MS 38677. (601) 232-7204.

University of Mississippi, Herbarium. Department of Biology, University, MS 38677. (601) 232-7215.

University of Missouri-Columbia, Clair L. Kucera Research Station At Tucker Prairie. Columbia, MO 65211. (314) 882-7541.

University of Missouri-Columbia, Gaylord Memorial Laboratory. Puxico, MO 63960. (314) 222-3531.

University of Missouri-Columbia, Herbarium. 226 Tucker Hall, Columbia, MO 65211. (314) 882-6519.

University of Missouri-Columbia, Missouri Water Resources Research Center. 0056 Engineering Complex, Columbia, MO 65211. (314) 882-3132.

University of Missouri-Columbia, Schnabel Woods. 1-30 Agricultural Building, Columbia, MO 65211. (314) 882-6446.

University of Missouri-Columbia, Thomas S. Baskett Wildlife Research and Education Center. 112 Stephens Hall, Columbia, MO 65201. (314) 882-3436.

University of Missouri-Columbia, University Forest. 1-30 Agriculture Building, Columbia, MO 65211. (314) 222-8373.

University of Missouri-Columbia, Wilber R. Enns Entomology Museum. 1-87 Agriculture Building, Department of Entomology, Columbia, MO 65211. (314) 882-2410.

University of Missouri, Environmental Trace Substances Research Center. 5450 South Sinclair Road, Columbia, MO 65203. (314) 882-2151.

University of Missouri-Rolla, Environmental Research Center. Rolla, MO 65401. (314) 341-4485.

University of Missouri-Rolla, Institute of River Studies. 111 Civil Engineering, Rolla, MO 65401. (314) 341-4476.

University of Montana, Flathead Lake Biological Station. 311 Bio Station Lane, Polson, MT 59860. (406) 982-3301.

University of Montana, Montana Cooperative Wildlife Research Unit. Missoula, MT 59812. (406) 243-5372.

University of Montana, Montana Forest and Conservation Experiment Station. Missoula, MT 59812. (406) 243-5521.

University of Montana, Wilderness Institute. Forestry Building, Room 207, Missoula, MT 59812. (406) 243-5361.

University of Montana, Wood Chemistry Laboratory. Missoula, MT 59812. (406) 243-6212.

University of Nebraska-Lincoln, Center for Biotechnology. 101 Manter Hall, Lincoln, NE 68588-0159. (402) 472-2635.

University of Nebraska-Lincoln, Center for Microbial Ecology. Lincoln, NE 68588-0343. (402) 472-2253.

University of Nebraska-Lincoln, Harold W. Manter Laboratory of Parasitology. W529 Nebraska Hall West, Lincoln, NE 68588-0514. (402) 472-3334.

University of Nebraska-Lincoln, Water Center. 103 Natural Resources Hall, Lincoln, NE 68503-0844. (402) 472-3305.

University of Nevada-Las Vegas, Environmental Research Center. 4505 S. Maryland Parkway, Las Vegas, NV 89154-4009. (702) 739-3382.

University of Nevada-Las Vegas, Lake Mead Limnological Research Center. 4505 Maryland Parkway, Las Vegas, NV 89154. (702) 798-0580.

University of Nevada-Las Vegas, Marjorie Barrick Museum of Natural History. Las Vegas, NV 89154. (702) 739-3381.

University of Nevada-Reno, Desert Research Institute, Biological Sciences Center. P.O. Box 60220, Reno, NV 89506. (702) 673-7321.

University of Nevada-Reno, Desert Research Institute, Energy and Environmental Engineering Center. P.O. Box 60220, Reno, NV 89506. (702) 677-3107.

University of Nevada-Reno, Desert Research Institute, Water Resources Center. P.O. Box 60220, Reno, NV 89506-0220. (703) 673-7365.

University of Nevada-Reno, Knudtsen Renewable Resources Center. Department of Range, Wildlife and Forestry, 1000 Valley Road, Reno, NV 89512. (702) 784-4000.

University of Nevada-Reno, S-S Field Laboratory. Box 10, Wadsworth, NV 89442. (702) 575-1057.

University of New Hampshire, Anadromous Fish and Aquatic Invertebrate Research Facility. Marine Institute, Department of Zoology, Durham, NH 03824. (603) 862-2103.

University of New Hampshire, Coastal Marine Laboratory. Department of Zoology, Durham, NH 03824. (603) 862-2100.

University of New Hampshire, Complex Systems Research Center. Science and Engineering Research Building, Durham, NH 03824. (603) 862-1792.

University of New Hampshire, Diamond Island Engineering Center. Marine Systems Engineering Lab, Science and Engineering Building, Durham, NH 03824. (603) 862-4600.

University of New Hampshire, Institute of Marine Science and Ocean Engineering. Marine Programs Building, Durham, NH 03824. (603) 862-2995.

University of New Hampshire, Jackson Estuarine Laboratory. 85 Adams Point Road, Durham, NH 03824-3406. (603) 862-2175.

University of New Hampshire, New Hampshire Sea Grant College Program. Marine Programs Building, Durham, NH 03824-3512. (603) 749-1565.

University of New Hampshire, Ocean Process Analysis Laboratory. Science and Engineering Research Building, Durham, NH 03824. (603) 862-3505.

University of New Hampshire, Water Resources Research Center. 218 Science & Engineering Research Building, Durham, NH 08324. (603) 862-2144.

University of New Haven, Institute of Analytical and Environmental Chemistry. 300 Orange Avenue, West Haven, CT 06516. (203) 932-7171.

University of New Mexico, Institute of Southwestern Biology. Biology Building, Albuquerque, NM 87131. (505) 277-5340.

University of North Carolina at Chapel Hill, Herbarium. 401 Coker Hall 010A, CB 3280, Chapel Hill, NC 27599-3280. (919) 962-6931.

University of North Carolina at Chapel Hill, Institute for Environmental Studies. CB #7410, 311 Pittsboro Street, Chapel Hill, NC 27599-7410. (919) 966-2358.

University of North Carolina at Chapel Hill, North Carolina Botanical Garden. CB #3375 Totten Center, Chapel Hill, NC 27599. (919) 962-0522.

University of North Carolina at Charlotte, Southeast Waste Exchange. Charlotte, NC 28223. (704) 547-2307.

University of North Carolina at Wilmington, Center for Marine Research. 601 South College Road, Wilmington, NC 28406. (919) 256-3721.

University of North Carolina at Wilmington, NOAA National Undersea Research Center. 7205 Wrightsville Avenue, Wilmington, NC 28403. (919) 256-5133.

University of North Carolina, Institute of Marine Sciences. 3407 Arendell Street, Morehead City, NC 28577. (919) 726-6841.

University of North Carolina, North Carolina Water Resources Research Institute. North Carolina State University, Box 7912, Raleigh, NC 27695-7912. (919) 737-2815.

University of North Dakota, Devil's Lake Biological Station. Grand Forks, ND 58202-8238. (701) 777-2621.

University of North Dakota, Institute for Ecological Studies. Box 8278, University Station, Grand Forks, ND 58202. (701) 777-2851.

University of North Dakota, Institute for Remote Sensing. Geography Department, Grand Folks, ND 58202. (701) 777-4246.

University of North Texas, Institute of Applied Sciences. P.O. Box 13078, Denton, TX 76203. (817) 565-2694.

University of Notre Dame, Environmental Research Center. Department of Biological Sciences, Notre Dame, IN 46556. (219) 239-7186.

University of Notre Dame, Greene-Nieuwland Herbarium. Department of Biological Sciences, Notre Dame, IN 46556. (219) 239-6684.

University of Notre Dame, Vector Biology Laboratory. Notre Dame, IN 46556. (219) 239-7366.

University of Oklahoma, Aquatic Biology Center. Zoology Department, 730 Van Vleet Oval, Norman, OK 73019. (405) 325-1058.

University of Oklahoma, Aquatic Ecology and Fisheries Research Center. 730 Van Vleet Oval, Room 314, Richards Hall, Norman, OK 73019. (405) 325-4821.

University of Oklahoma, Biological Station. Star Route B, Kingston, OK 73439. (405) 564-2463.

University of Oklahoma, Bureau of Water and Environmental Resources Research. P.O. Box 2850, Norman, OK 73070. (405) 325-2960.

University of Oklahoma, Environmental & Ground Water Institute. 200 Felgar Street, Room 127, Norman, OK 73019-0470. (405) 325-5202.

University of Oklahoma, Hebb Herbarium. Department of Botany and Microbiology, 770 Van Vleet Oval, Norman, OK 73019-0245. (405) 325-6443.

University of Oklahoma, Oklahoma Biological Survey. Sutton Hall, Room 303, 625 Elm Avenue, Norman, OK 73019. (405) 325-4034.

University of Oregon, Environmental Studies Center. Room 104, Condon Hall, Eugene, OR 97403. (503) 686-5006.

University of Oregon, Herbarium. Department of Biology, Eugene, OR 97403. (503) 346-3033.

University of Oregon, Institute of Molecular Biology. Eugene, OR 97403. (503) 686-5151.

University of Oregon, Oregon Institute of Marine Biology. Charleston, OR 97420. (503) 888-2581.

University of Oregon, Program in Cellular Biology. Institute of Molecular Biology, Eugene, OR 97403. (503) 346-5151.

University of Pennsylvania, Morris Arboretum. 9414 Meadowbrook Avenue, Philadelphia, PA 19118. (215) 247-5777.

University of Pittsburgh, Pymatuning Laboratory of Ecology. R.R. #1, Box 7, Linesville, PA 16424. (814) 683-5813.

University of Puerto Rico, Central Analytical Laboratory. P.O. Box 21360, Rio Piedras, PR 00928. (809) 767-9705.

University of Puerto Rico, Sea Grant College Program. Department of Marine Sciences, P.O. Box 5000, Mayaguez, PR 00681-5000. (809) 832-3585.

University of Rhode Island, Coastal Resources Center. Narragansett, RI 02882. (401) 792-6224.

University of Rhode Island, Graduate School of Oceanography. Narragansett Bay Campus, Narragansett, RI 02882-1197. (401) 792-6222.

University of Rhode Island, International Center for Marine Resource Development (*ICMRD*). 126 Woodward Hall, Kingston, RI 02881. (401) 792-2479.

University of Rhode Island, Marine Ecosystems Research Laboratory. Graduate School of Oceanography, Narragansett, RI 02882. (401) 792-6104.

University of Rhode Island, Sea Grant College Program. Graduate School of Oceanography, Narragansett, RI 02882-1197. (401) 792-6800.

University of Rhode Island, Water Resources Center. 202 Bliss Hall, Kingston, RI 02881. (401) 792-2297.

University of San Francisco, Institute of Chemical Biology. Ignarian Heights, Room H342, San Francisco, CA 94117-1080. (415) 666-6415.

University of South Carolina at Columbia, Belle W. Baruch Institute for Marine Biology and Coastal Research. Columbia, SC 29208. (803) 777-5288.

University of South Carolina at Columbia, International Center for Public Health Research. Wedge Plantation, P.O. Box 699, McClellanville, SC 29458. (803) 527-1371.

University of South Dakota, South Dakota Herbarium. Biology Department, Vermillion, SD 57069. (605) 677-6176.

University of South Florida, Herbarium. Biology Department, Tampa, FL 33620. (813) 974-2359.

University of Southern California, Catalina Marine Science Center. P.O. Box 398, Avalon, CA 90704. (213) 743-6792.

University of Southern California, Fish Harbor Marine Research Laboratory. 820 South Seaside Avenue, Terminal Island, CA 90731. (310) 830-4570.

University of Southern California, Hancock Institute for Marine Studies. University Park, Los Angeles, CA 90089-0373. (213) 740-6276.

University of Southern California, Sea Grant Program. University Park, Los Angeles, CA 90089-1231. (213) 740-1961.

University of Southern Mississippi, Center for Marine Science. John C. Stennis Space Center, Stennis Space Center, MS 39529. (601) 688-3177.

University of Southwestern Louisiana, Crawfish Research Center. P.O. Box 44650, Lafayette, LA 70504. (318) 231-5239.

University of Tennessee at Knoxville, Biology Consortium. M303 Walters Life Sciences Building, Knoxville, TN 37996. (615) 974-6841.

University of Tennessee at Knoxville, Center for Environmental Biotechnology. 10515 Research Drive, Knoxville, TN 37932. (615) 675-9450.

University of Tennessee at Knoxville, Energy Environment and Resource Center. 327 South Stadium Hall, Knoxville, TN 37996. (615) 974-4251.

University of Tennessee at Knoxville, Forestry Experiment Stations and Arboretum. 901 Kerr Hollow Road, Oak Ridge, TN 37830. (615) 483-3571.

University of Tennessee at Knoxville, Tennessee State Herbarium. Knoxville, TN 37916. (615) 974-6212.

University of Tennessee at Knoxville, Waste Management Research and Education Institute. 327 South Stadium Hall, Knoxville, TN 37996-0710. (615) 974-4251.

University of Tennessee at Knoxville, Water Resources Research Center. Knoxville, TN 37996. (615) 974-2151.

University of Texas at Arlington, Center for Corbicula Research. Department of Biology, P.O.Box 19498, Arlington, TX 76019. (817) 273-2412.

University of Texas at Arlington, Center for Parasitology. Box 19498, Arlington, TX 76019. (817) 273-2423.

University of Texas at Austin, Brackenridge Field Laboratory. Lake Austin Boulevard, Austin, TX 78712. (512) 471-7131.

University of Texas at Austin, Brues-Wheeler-Sellards Archives for Entomology and Paleoentomology. Texas Memorial Museum, 2400 Trinity Street, Austin, TX 78705. (512) 471-4823.

University of Texas at Austin, Cell Research Institute. Austin, TX 78713-7640. (512) 471-1431.

University of Texas at Austin, Center for Research in Water Resources. Balcones Research Center, Building 119, Austin, TX 78712. (512) 471-3131.

University of Texas at Austin, Culture Collection of Algae. Department of Botany, Austin, TX 78713. (512) 471-4019.

University of Texas at Austin, Genetics Institute. Department of Zoology, 528 Patterson Laboratories, Austin, TX 78712. (512) 471-6268.

University of Texas at Austin, Marine Science Institute. Port Aransas, TX 78373. (512) 749-6711.

University of Texas at Austin, Plant Resources Center. Department of Botany, Main Building 228, Austin, TX 78712. (512) 471-5128.

University of Texas at Austin, Texas Natural History Laboratory. Texas Memorial Museum, 2400 Trinity, Austin, TX 78705. (512) 471-5302.

University of Texas at El Paso, Laboratory for Environmental Biology. Department of Biology, EL Paso, TX 79968. (915) 747-5164.

University of Texas Health Science Center at Houston, Cryobiology Research Center. 3606 A. Suite 1, Research Forest Drive, Woodlands, TX 77381. (713) 221-8000.

University of Texas-Pan American, Coastal Studies Laboratory. P.O. Box 2591, South Padre Island, TX 78597. (512) 761-2644.

University of the Virgin Islands, Environmental Research Center. St. Thomas, VI 00802. (809) 776-9200.

University of Utah, Entomology Research Collections. Utah Museum of Natural History, President Circle, Salt Lake City, UT 84112. (801) 581-6927.

University of Vermont, Pringle Herbarium. Burlington, VT 05405. (802) 656-3221.

University of Vermont, Vermont Water Resources Research Center. Aiken Center for Natural Resources, Burlington, VT 05405. (802) 656-4057.

University of Virginia, Center for Bioprocess/Product Development. Department of Chemical Engineering, Thornton Hall, Charlottesville, VA 22901. (804) 924-6278.

University of Virginia, Mountain Lake Biological Station. Room 251, Gilmer Hall, Charlottesville, VA 22901. (804) 982-5486.

University of Washington, Center for Quantitative Science in Forestry, Fisheries and Wildlife. 3737 Fifteenth Avenue N.E., HR-20, Seattle, WA 98195. (206) 543-1191.

University of Washington, Center for Urban Horticulture. Seattle, WA 98195. (206) 543-8616.

University of Washington, Fisheries Research Institute. School of Fisheries, WH-10, Seattle, WA 98195. (206) 543-4650.

University of Washington, Friday Harbor Laboratories. 620 University Road, Friday Harbor, WA 98250. (206) 378-2165.

University of Washington, Herbarium. Seattle, WA 98195. (206) 543-8850.

University of Washington, Institute for Environmental Studies. Engineering Annex FM-12, Seattle, WA 98195. (206) 543-1812.

University of Washington, Institute for Marine Studies. College of Ocean and Fishery Science, 3707 Brooklyn Avenue, N.E., Seattle, WA 98195. (206) 543-7004.

University of Washington, Institute of Forest Resources. 216 Anderson Hall, College of Forest Resources, Seattle, WA 98195. (206) 685-1928.

University of Washington, Laboratory of Radiation Ecology. Fisheries Research Center, College of Fisheries, Seattle, WA 98195. (206) 543-4259.

University of Washington, Washington Sea Grant College Program. 3716 Brooklyn Avenue N.E., Seattle, WA 98195. (206) 543-6600.

University of Wisconsin-Madison, Biology & Biomaterial Specimen Preparation Laboratory. Room B22, Veterinary Science Building, 1665 Linden Drive, Madison, WI 53706. (608) 263-3952.

University of Wisconsin-Madison, Biotechnology Center. 1710 University Avenue, Madison, WI 53705. (608) 262-8606.

University of Wisconsin-Madison, Biotron. 2115 Observatory Drive, Madison, WI 53706. (608) 262-4900.

University of Wisconsin-Madison, Center for Biotic Systems. 1042 WARF Office Building, 610 Walnut Street, Madison, WI 53705. (608) 262-9937.

University of Wisconsin-Madison, Center for Human Systems. 1042 WARF Building, 610 North Walnut Street, Madison, WI 53705. (608) 262-9937.

University of Wisconsin-Madison, Center for Limnology. 680 North Park Street, Madison, WI 53706. (608) 262-3014.

University of Wisconsin-Madison, Center for Restoration Ecology. Arboretum, 1207 Seminole Highway, Madison, WI 53711. (608) 263-7889.

University of Wisconsin-Madison, Center for the Study of Nitrogen Fixation. 420 Henry Mall, Department of Biochemistry, Madison, WI 53706. (608) 262-6859.

University of Wisconsin-Madison, Drosophila Mutagenesis Laboratory. Zoology Department, Madison, WI 53706. (608) 263-7875.

University of Wisconsin-Madison, Environmental Remote Sensing Center. 1225 West Dayton Street, Madison, WI 53706. (608) 263-3251.

University of Wisconsin-Madison, Herbarium. Birge Hall, Madison, WI 53706. (608) 262-2792.

University of Wisconsin-Madison, Institute for Environmental Studies. 1017 WARF Office Building, 610 Walnut Street, Madison, WI 53705. (608) 262-5957.

University of Wisconsin-Madison, Institute for Enzyme Research. 1710 University Avenue, Madison, WI 53705. (608) 262-2140.

University of Wisconsin-Madison, Institute of Plant Development. B121 Birge Hall, Department of Botany, Madison, WI 53706. (608) 262-9997.

University of Wisconsin-Madison, Integrated Microscopy Resource for Biomedical Research. Animal Science Building, 1675 Observatory Drive, Madison, WI 53706. (608) 263-6288.

University of Wisconsin-Madison, Kemp Natural Resources Station. Agricultural Research Station, 620 Babcock Drive, Madison, WI 53706. (608) 262-2969.

University of Wisconsin-Madison, Laboratory of Molecular Biology. 1525 Linden Drive, Madison, WI 53706. (608) 262-3203.

University of Wisconsin-Madison, Marine Studies Center. 1269 Engineering Building, 1415 Johnson Drive, Madison, WI 53706. (608) 262-3883.

University of Wisconsin-Madison, Marine Studies Centers. Department of Botany, 132 Birge Hall, Madison, WI 53706. (608) 262-1057.

University of Wisconsin-Madison, Sea Grant Advisory Services. Walkway Mall, 522 Bayshore Drive, Sister Bay, WI 54234. (414) 854-5329.

University of Wisconsin-Madison, Water Chemistry Program. 660 North Park Street, Madison, WI 53706. (608) 262-2470.

University of Wisconsin-Madison, Water Resources Center. 1975 Willow Drive, Madison, WI 53706. (608) 262-3577.

University of Wisconsin-Madison, Zoological Museum. Lowell Noland Building, 225 North Mills, Madison, WI 53706. (608) 262-3766.

University of Wisconsin-Milwaukee, Center for Great Lakes Studies. Milwaukee, WI 53201. (414) 649-3000.

University of Wisconsin-Milwaukee, Field Station. 3095 Blue Goose Road, Saukville, WI 53080. (414) 675-6844.

University of Wisconsin-Milwaukee, Herbarium. Department of Biological Sciences, Box 413, Milwaukee, WI 53201. (414) 229-6728.

University of Wisconsin, River Studies Center. 4032 Cowley Hall, La Crosse, WI 54601. (608) 785-8232.

University of Wisconsin-Stevens Point, Wisconsin Cooperative Fishery Research Unit. College of Natural Resources, Stevens Point, WI 54481. (715) 346-2178.

University of Wisconsin-Superior, Center for Lake Superior Environmental Studies. 1800 Grand Avenue, Superior, WI 54880. (715) 394-8315.

University of Wisconsin, University of Wisconsin Sea Grant Institute. 1800 University Avenue, Madison, WI 53705. (608) 262-0905.

University of Wyoming, High Altitude Balloon Research Group. Physics and Astronomy Department, Box 3905, Laramie, WY 82071. (307) 766-4323.

University of Wyoming, National Park Service Research Center. Box 3166, University Station, Laramie, WY 82071. (307) 766-4227.

University of Wyoming, Red Buttes Environmental Biology Laboratory. Box 3166, University Station, Laramie, WY 82071. (307) 745-8504.

University of Wyoming, Rocky Mountain Herbarium. Aven Nelson Building, 3165 University Station, Laramie, WY 82071. (307) 766-2236.

University of Wyoming, Wilhelm G. Solheim Mycological Herbarium. 3165 University Station, Laramie, WY 82071. (307) 766-2236.

University of Wyoming, Wyoming Water Research Center. Box 3067, University Station, Laramie, WY 82071. (307) 766-2143.

Update. Council on Plastics and Packaging in the Environment, 1275 K St. NW, Suite 900, Washington, DC 20005. (202) 789-1310. Recycling research and legislation.

An Update on Formaldehyde. U.S. Consumer Product Safety Commission, 5401 Westbard Ave., Bethesda, MD 20207. (301) 492-6580. 1990.

An Updated World Review of Interactions between Marine Mammals and Fisheries. Simon P. Northridge. Food and Agriculture Organization of the United Nations, Via delle Terme di Caracalla, Rome, Italy 00100. 61 0181-FA01. 1991.

Upgrading Lagoons. U.S. Environmental Protection Agency, Technology Transfer, 401 M St. SW, Washington, DC 20460. (202) 382-5480. 1973.

Upper Cumberland Biological Station at Tech Aqua. Tennessee Technological University, Box 5063, Edison, NJ 38505. (615) 372-3129.

Upper Mississippi River Conservation Committee. 1830 Second Ave., Rock Island, IL 61201. (309) 793-5800.

Upstream/Downstream: Issues in Environmental Ethics. Donald Scherer, ed. Temple University, Broad & Oxford Sts., University Services Bldg., Room 305, Philadelphia, PA 19122. (215) 787-8787. 1991. Assesses effects of pollution and global warming. Predicts environmental damage scientifically. Provides property owners with information on modifications to satisfy environmental requirements and cost-benefit analysis.

Uranium Industry Annual. U.S. G.P.O, Washington, DC 20402-9325. (202) 512-0000. 1984. Annual. Reserves, exploration, mining and milling operations, prices, and marketing.

Uranium Series Disequilibrium. Clarendon Press, Walton St., Oxford, England OX2 6DP. 1982. Environmental aspects of uranium isotopes decay.

Urban Affairs Abstracts. National League of Cities, 1301 Pennsylvania Ave., NW, Washington, DC 20004. (202) 626-3150. 1977-. Weekly.

Urban Design. Vance Bibliographies, PO Box 229, 112 N. Charter St., Monticello, IL 61856. (217) 762-3831. 1983.

Urban Discharges and Receiving Water Quality Impacts. J. B. Ellis, ed. Pergamon Microforms International, Inc., Fairview Park, Elmsford, NY 10523. (914) 592-7720. 1989. Proceedings of a seminar organized by the IAWPRC/IAHR Sub Committee for Urban Runoff Quality Data, as part of the IAWPRC 14th biennial conference, Brighton, UK, July 18-21, 1988.

Urban Ecology. Elsevier, Box 211, Amsterdam, Netherlands 1000 AE. (020) 5803-911. Quarterly.

Urban Environment Conference. 7620 Morningside Dr., N.W., Washington, DC 20012. (202) 726-8111.

Urban Forests: A Selected Bibliography. Anthony G. White. Council of Planning Librarians, 1313 E. 60th St., Chicago, IL 60637-2897. (312) 942-2163. 1977. Covers trees in cities.

Urban Initiatives. 530 W. 25th St., New York, NY 10001. (212) 620-9773.

Urban Land Institute. 625 Indiana Ave., N.W., Washington, DC 20004. (202) 624-7000.

Urban Land: News and Trends in Land Development. Urban Land Institute, 1200 18th St. N.W., Washington, DC 20036. 1941-. Ten times a year.

Urban Patterns: Studies in Human Ecology. George A. Theodorson. Pennsylvania State University Press, Barbara Bldg., Ste. C, University Park, PA 16802. (814) 865-1372. 1982.

Urban Pest Control Research Group. Virginia Polytech Institute and State University, Department of Entomology, Glade Road, Blacksburg, VA 24061. (703) 961-4045.

Urban Rail Transit Projects. U.S. Urban Mass Transportation Administration. U.S. G.P.O., Washington, DC 20401. (202) 512-0000. 1989. Data on actual ridership, costs, mileage, areas served and impacts.

Urban Runoff Treatment Methods. National Technical Information Service, 5285 Port Royal Rd., Springfield, VA 22161. (703) 487-4650. 1977. Environmental protection technology related to non-structural wetland treatment.

Urban Stormwater Management and Technology. John A. Lager. U.S. G.P.O., Washington, DC 20401. (202) 512-0000. 1975. Technology relating to runoff and combined sewers.

Urban Stormwater Runoff. Gary T. Fisher. U.S. Geological Survey, 12201 Sunrise Valley Dr., Reston, VA 22092. (703) 648-4460. 1989. Selected background information and techniques for problem assessment.

Urban Vegetation Laboratory. Morton Arboretum, Route 53, Lisle, IL 60532. (708) 968-0074.

Urban Wastes in Coastal Marine Environments. Krieger Publishing Co., Inc., PO Box 9542, Melbourne, FL 32902. (407) 724-9542. 1988. Deals with marine pollution, refuse and refuse disposal, factory and trade waste and waste disposal in the ocean.

Urban Wildlife Research Center. 10921 Trotting Ridge Way, Columbia, MD 21044. (301) 596-3311.

Urbanization and Changing Land Uses: A Bibliography of Selected References, 1950-58. Elizabeth Gould Davis. U.S. Department of Agriculture, 14 Independence Ave. SW, Washington, DC 20250. (202) 447-7454. 1960. Bibliography of land utilization and urban growth.

Urbanization and Cities: Historical and Comparative Perspectives in Our Urbanizing World. Hilda H. Golden. D. C. Heath, 125 Spring St., Lexington, MA 02173. (617) 862-6650. 1991. Urban sociology and urbanization.

Urbanization and Environmental Quality. Isao Orishimo. Kluwer Academic Publishers, 101 Philip Dr., Assinippi Park, Norwell, MA 02061. (617) 871-6600. 1982. Covers central places, pollution, quality of life, residential mobility, and urbanization.

USDA Biological Control of Insects Research Laboratory. P.O. Box 7629, Columbia, MO 65205. (314) 875-5361.

USDA National Sedimentation Laboratory. P.O.Box 1157, Oxford, MO 38655. (601) 232-2900.

USDA Plant Gene Expression Center. 800 Buchanan Street, Albany, CA 94710. (510) 559-5900.

USDA Water Conservation Laboratory. 4331 East Broadway, Phoenix, AZ 85040. (602) 379-4356.

USDA Wind Erosion Research Unit. Room 105-B, East Waters Hall, Kansas State University, Manhattan, KS 66506. (913) 532-6807.

The Use of Macrophytes in Water Pollution Control. D. Athie and C. C. Cerri, eds. Pergamon Microforms International, Inc., Fairview Park, Elmsford, NY 10523. (914) 592-7720. 1988. Proceedings of an IAWPRC specialized seminar held in Piracicaba, Brazil, August 24-28,1986. Describes the problem of river pollution, caused mainly by sewage and industrial effluents.

The Use of Paraquat to Eradicate Illicit Marihuana Crops and the Health Implications of Paraquat-Contaminated Marihuana on the U.S. Market. Select Committee on Narcotics and Abuse Control, U.S. Government Printing Office, Washington, DC 2042-9325. (202) 783-3238. 1980. A report of the Select Committee on Narcotics and Abuse Control, 96th Congress, 2nd session.

Use of Pathogens in Scarab Pest Management. Trevor A. Jackson and Travis R. Glare, eds. VCH Publishers, 303 NW 12th Ave., Deerfield Beach, FL 33442-1788. (305) 428-5566. 1991. Provides a concise up-to-date reference on alternate controls such as pathogens in pest management.

Use of Soil for Treatment and Final Disposal of Effluents and Sludge. P. R. C. Oliveira and S. A. S. Almeida, eds. Pergamon Microforms International, Inc., Fairview Park, Elmsford, NY 10523. (914) 592-7720. 1988. Proceedings of an IAWPRC Seminar held in Salvador, Bahia, Brazil, August 13-15, 1986. Contains a broad scope of topics regarding the treatment and final disposal of effluents and sludge on land.

Use of the Environmental Impact Computer System. Thomas M. Whiteside. Department of Urban and Regional Planning, University of Illinois at Urbana-Champaign, Urbana, IL 61801. 1988.

Used Oil: Disposal Options, Management Practices and Potential Liability. John J. Nolan, et al. Government Institutes, Inc., 4 Research Pl., Suite 200, Rockville, MD 20850. (301) 921-2300. 1990. 3d ed. Helps with developing a plan to store and manage the handling of used oil that affects thousands of generators, collectors, processors, marketers and burners.

User Manual for Two-Dimensional Multi-Class Phytoplankton Model with Internal Nutrient Pool Kinetics. U.S. Environmental Protection Agency, Office of Research and Development, Environmental Research Laboratory, 401 M St. SW, Washington, DC 20460. (202) 260-2090. 1986. Covers phytoplankton and eutrophication.

User's Guide for the Handling, Treatment, and Disposal of Oily Sludge. U.S. Naval Facilities Engineering Command, 200 Stovel St., Alexandria, VA 22332-2300. (703) 325-0589. 1986. Manual for waste disposal in the ocean.

User's Guide to the EPA PCB Spill Cleanup Policy. Glenn Kuntz. National Rural Electric Cooperative Assoc., 1800 Massachusetts Ave., NW, Washington, DC 20036. (202) 857-9598. 1988. Guide for PCB spill cleanup. Includes detailed review of published and unpublished information on the subject. This is NRECA research project 87-3.

The Uses of Ecology: Lake Washington and Beyond. W. T. Edmondson. University of Washington Press, PO Box 50096, Seattle, WA 98145-5096. (206) 543-4050; (800) 441-4115. 1991. Author delivered most of the contents of this book as a Danz lecture at the University of Washington. Gives an account of the pollution and recovery of Lake Washington and describes how communities worked and applied lessons learned from Lake Washington cleanup. Includes extensive documentation and bibliographies.

USSR Report. Human Resources. Foreign Broadcast Information Service. National Technical Information Service, 5285 Port Royal Rd., Springfield, VA 22161. (703) 487-4650. 1980-. Irregular.

Utah Environmental News. Utah State Division of Health, 44 Medical Drive, Salt Lake City, UT 84113.

Utah State University, Bear Lake Biological Laboratory. c/o Department of Fisheries and Wildlife, Logan, UT 84322-5210. (801) 753-2459.

Utah State University, Biotechnology Center. Logan, UT 84322-4430. (801) 750-2730.

Utah State University, Center for Bio-Catalysis Science and Technology. Logan, UT 84322-4630. (801) 750-2033.

Utah State University, Ecology Center. Logan, UT 84322-5200. (801) 750-2555.

Utah State University, Institute for Land Rehabilitation. College of Natural Resources, Logan, UT 84322-5230. (801) 750-2547.

Utah State University, Intermountain Herbarium. UMC 55, Department of Biology, Logan, UT 84322. (801) 750-1586.

Utah State University, Utah Cooperative Fish and Wildlife Research Unit. Logan, UT 84322. (801) 750-2509.

Utah State University, Utah Water Research Laboratory. Logan, UT 84322-8200. (801) 750-3200.

Utah State University, Watershed Science Unit. Range Science Department, Logan, UT 84322-5250. (801) 750-2759.

Utility Reporter. Merton Allen Associates, PO Box 15640, Plantation, FL 33318-5640. (305)473-9560. Monthly. Covers current activities in power generation and energy conservation.

Utilization of Sewage Sludge Compost as a Soil Conditioner and Fertilizer for Plant Growth. Agricultural Research service. U.S. G.P.O., Washington, DC 1984.

Values for the Environment–A Guide to the Economic Appraisal. HMSO, UNIPUB, 4611 - F Assembly Dr., Lanham, MD 20706. (301) 459-7666 or (800) 274-4888. 1991. Practical guide to the economic treatment of the environment in project appraisal using cost benefit analysis as the decision framework.

Valuing Wildlife: Economic and Social Perspectives. Daniel J. Decker and Gary R. Goff, eds. Westview Press, 5500 Central Ave., Boulder, CO 80301. (303) 444-3541. 1987. State of the art guide to determining the value of wildlife, the application for environmental impact assessment, and strategies in wildlife planning and policy.

Van Nostrand's Scientific Encyclopedia. Glenn D. Considine, ed. Van Nostrand Reinhold, 115 5th Ave., New York, NY 10003. (212) 254-3232. 1983. Sixth edition. Includes all broad subject areas in science.

Vancouver Aquarium Research Department. Van Dusen Aquatic Science Centre, P.O.Box 3232, Vancouver, BC, Canada V6B 3X8. (604) 685-3364.

The Vanishing Lichens. David Richardson. David & Charles, Brunel House, Newton Abbot, England TQ12 4PU. 1975.

Vapor-Phase Organic Pollutants: Volatile Hydrocarbons and Oxidation Products. National Research Council. National Academy of Sciences, 2101 Constitution Ave., NW, Washington, DC 20418. (202) 334-2000. 1976. Medical and biologic effects of environmental pollutants.

Vapor Pressure Database. Texas A & M University, Thermodynamics Research Center, College Station, TX 77843-3111. (409) 845-4940.

Variability and Management of Large Marine Ecosystems. Kenneth Sherman. Westview Press, 5500 Central Ave., Boulder, CO 80301. (303) 444-3541. 1986. Managing marine resources and marine ecology.

Vegetables from the Sea. Seibin Arasaki. Kodansha International/USA, 114 5th Ave., New York, NY 10011. (212) 727-6460. 1983.

Vegetation and Environmental Features of Forest and Range Ecosystems. Garrison, George A. U.S. Forest Service, Box 96090, Washington, DC 20090. (202) 720-3760. 1977. Range and forest ecology and classification of vegetation.

Vegetation and Production Ecology of the Alaskan Arctic Tundra. Larry L. Tieszen. Springer-Verlag, 175 5th Ave., New York, NY 10010. (212) 460-1500. 1978. Primary productivity, tundra ecology, and tundra flora.

Verhandlungen. Larry L. Tieszen. Springer-Verlag, 175 5th Ave., New York, NY 10010. (212) 460-1500. 1978.

Vermicomposting, Selected Articles. Flowerfield Enterprises, 10332 Shaver Rd., Kalamazoo, MI 49002. (616) 327-0108. 1982.

Vermont Environmental Law Handbook. Vermont Bar Association, PO Box 100, Montpelier, VT 05601. (802) 223-2020. 1990.

Vermont Environmental Services Directory. Putney Press, PO Box 935, Brattleboro, VT 05302. (802)257-7305. 1991.

Vermont Institute of Natural Science. Church Hill, Woodstock, VT 05091. (802) 457-2779.

Vertebrate Ecology in Northern Neotropics. John F. Esenberg, ed. Smithsonian Institution Press, 470 L'Enfant Plaza, No. 7100, Washington, DC 20560. (800) 782-4612. 1979. Comparison of faunas found in tropical forests covering several mammalian species, including the red howler monkey, crab-eating fox, cebus monkey, and the didelphid marsupials.

Veterinary and Human Toxicology. College of Veterinary Medicine, Drawer V, Mississippi State, MS 39762. (601) 325-1106.

Vibration Institute. 6262 S. Kingery Hwy., Suite 212, Willowbrook, IL 60514. (708) 654-2254.

Vibrations. National Association of Noise Control Officials, 53 Cubberly Rd., Trenton, NJ 08690. (609) 984-4161. Monthly. Covers technical advancements in the environmental noise control area.

Vineyard Environmental Research Institute. RFD 862, Martha's Vineyard Airport, Tisbury, MA 02568. (508) 693-4632.

Vinyl Chloride Toxicology. U.S. Department of Health and Human Services, Public Health Services, National Institutes of Health, 9000 Rockville Pike, Bethesda, MD 20892. (301) 496-4000. 1980.

The Violence of Green Revolution. Vandana Shiva. Humanities Pr. Intl., 171 1st Ave., Atlantic Highlands, NJ 07716-1289. (201) 872-1441; (800) 221-3845. 1991.

Virgin Islands Conservation Society Inc., Newsletter. Virgin Island Conservation Society Inc., Box 226, Cruz Bay, St. John, VI 00830. Quarterly.

Virginair. Virginia State Air Pollution Control Board, Room 1106, 9th St., Office Bldg., Richmond, VA 23219. 1972-. Quarterly.

Virginia Cooperative Fish and Wildlife Research Unit. Virginia Polytech Institute and State University, 106 Cheatham Hall, Blacksburg, VA 24061. (703) 231-5927.

Virginia Environmental Law Handbook. Government Institutes, Inc., 4 Research Pl., Ste. 200, Rockville, MD 20850. (301) 921-2300. 1990.

Virginia Polytechnic Institute and State University, Anaerobe Laboratory. Department of Anaerobic Microbiology, Blacksburg, VA 24061-0305. (703) 231-6935.

Virginia Polytechnic Institute and State University, Biobased Materials Technology Development Center. Thomas M. Brooks Forest Products Center, Blacksburg, VA 24061-0503. (703) 231-4403.

Virginia Water Resources Research Center. Virginia Polytech Institute and State University, 617 North Main Street, Blacksburg, VA 24060. (703) 231-5624.

Virus Laboratory. University of California, Berkeley, 229 Stanley Hall, Berkeley, CA 94720. (510) 642-1722.

Visual Amenity Aspects of High Voltage Transmission. George A. Goulty. John Wiley & Sons, Inc., 605 3rd Ave., New York, NY (212) 850-6000. 1990. High tension electric power distribution, overhead electric lines, and location of poles and towers.

Visual Pollution and Sign Control: A Legal Handbook on Billboard Reform. Southern Environmental Law Center, 201 W. Main St., Ste. 14, Charlottesville, VA 22901. (804) 977-4090. 1988.

Vitamin E Abstracts. Max K. Horwitt. VERIS–Vitamin E Research & Information Service, 5325 S. 9th Ave., La Grange, IL 60525. (800) 328-6199. 1980-. Annual. Gives information of current interest on Vitamin E. Answers to questions about Vitamin E; Vitamin E related research findings; Annual comprehensive Vitamin E research Abstracts; and Vitamin E for university research.

Vitamins and "Health" Foods. Victor Herbert. George F. Stickley Co., Philadelphia, PA 1981. Vitamins, dietary supplements and nutrition as well as inherent dangers of quackery.

Vitamins and Minerals: Help or Harm?. Charles W. Marshall. George F. Stickley Co., Philadelphia, PA 1983.

Vitamins in Human Biology and Medicine. Michael H. Briggs. CRC Press, 2000 Corporate Blvd. N.W., Boca Raton, FL 33431. (800) 272-7737. 1981. Deals with physiological effects of vitamins and vitamins in human nutrition.

VNRC Legislative Bulletin. Vermont Natural Resources Council, 9 Bailey Ave., Montpelier, VT 05602. (802) 223-2328.

Vocabulaire sur les Precipitations Acides et la Pollution Atmosphrique. Vocabulary of Acid Precipitation and Air Pollution Denis Rivard. Dept. of the Secretary of State of Canada, 200 W. Rene Levesque, Tower West, Rm 401, Montreal, PQ, Canada H2Z 1X4. (514) 283-0289. 1987.

Volatile Organic Compound Species Data Manual. National Technical Information Service, 5285 Port Royal Rd., Springfield, VA 22161. (703) 487-4650. 1980. Covers air pollution standards in the United States.

Volatile Organic Compounds. Lewis Publishers, 200 Corporate Blvd. NW, Boca Raton, FL 33431. (407) 994-0555 or (800)272-7737. 1991. Covers health aspects of drinking water, organic water pollutants, water purification and organic compounds removal.

Volcanoes. Susanna Van Rose and Ian Mercer. Harvard University Press, 79 Garden St., Cambridge, MA 02138. (617) 495-2600. 1991. Second edition.

Volumetric Leak Detection Methods for Underground Fuel Storage Tanks. Joseph E. Maresca, et al. Noyes Publications, 120 Mill Rd., Park Ridge, NJ 07656. (201) 391-8484. 1990. Summarizes the results of the USEPA's research program to evaluate the current performance of commercially available volumetric test methods for the detection of small leaks in underground fuel storage tanks.

Walker's Mammals of the World. Ronald M. Nowak. Johns Hopkins University Press, 701 W. 40th St., Ste. 275, Baltimore, MD 21211-2190. (410) 516-6900. 1991. Fifth edition 2 vols. Describes: monotremata; massupialia; insectivora; macroscelida; dermoptra; chiroptra; scandentia; primates; xenarthra; pholidota; langomorpha; rodentia; cetacea; carnivora; pemipedia; tubulidentata; proboscidea; hyracoidia; sirenia; perissodactyla; and artiodactyla. Includes a bibliography of literature cited.

War on Waste: Can America Win its Battle With Garbage?. Louis Blumberg and Robert Gottlieb. Island Press, 1718 Connecticut Ave. N.W., Suite 300, Washington, DC 20009. (202) 232-7933. 1989. In-depth analysis of the waste disposal crisis.

Warriors of the Rainbow. Robert Hunter. Holt, Rinehart and Winston, 6277 Sea Harbor Dr., Orlando, FL 32887. (407) 345-2500. 1979. Chronicles the Greenpeace movement.

Washington Bulletin. Water Pollution Control Federation, 601 Wythe Street, Alexandria, VA 22314-1994. (703) 684-2400. Monthly. Covers legislative issues in the water control industry.

The Washington Conference on Underground Storage, July 15-16, 1985, Stouffer Concourse. Center for Energy and Environmental Management, Washington, DC (202) 543-3939.

Washington Cooperative Fishery and Wildlife Research Unit. University of Washington, School of Fisheries, WH-10, Seattle, WA 98195. (206) 543-6475.

Washington Department of Wildlife, Fisheries Management Division. 600 Capitol Way North, Olympia, WA 98504-1091. (206) 753-5713.

Washington Environmental Law Handbook. Government Institutes, Inc., 4 Research Pl., Ste. 200, Rockville, MD 20850. (301) 921-2300. 1990.

Washington Environmental Protection Report. Callahan Publication, P.O. Box 3751, Washington, DC 20007. (703) 356-1925. Biweekly.

Washington Report. Interstate Conference on Water Policy, 955 L'Enfant Plaza, 6th Floor, Washington, DC 20024. (202) 466-7287. Every six weeks. Covers water conservation, development and administration.

Washington Update. Association of Local Air Pollution Control Officials, 444 N. Capitol St, NW, Suite 306, Washington, DC 20001. (202) 624-7864. Monthly. Congressional and Environmental Protection Agency activities, and current issues related to air pollution.

Washington Waterline. Environmental Communication Corp., Box 1824, Washington, DC 20013. 1967-. Weekly.

Waste Age. National Solid Waste Management Association, 1730 Rhode Island Avenue, NW, Ste. 1000, Washington, DC 20036. (202) 659-4613. Monthly. Covers control and use of solid, hazardous and liquid wastes.

Waste Age–Directory to Waste Systems and Services Supplement. National Solid Waste Management Association, 1730 Rhode Island Ave., NW, Suite 1000, Washington, DC 20036. (202) 659-4613.

Waste Containment Systems: Construction, Regulation and Performance. Rudolph Bonaparte, ed. American Society of Civil Engineers, 345 E. 47th St., New York, NY 10017. (212) 705-7288; (800) 548-2723. 1990. Proceedings of a symposium sponsored by the Committee on Soil Improvement and Geosynthetics and the Committee on Soil properties of the Geotechnical Engineering Division, American Society of Civil Engineers in conjunction with the ASCE National Convention, San Francisco, CA, November 6-7, 1990.

Waste Disposal and Pollution Control. Wakeman/Walworth, P.O. Box 1939, New Haven, CT 06509. (203) 562-8518. Monthly. Covers air and water pollution, toxic waste, and acid rain.

Waste Disposal and Treatment in the Food Processing Industry: Citations for the BioBusiness Database. National Technical Information Service, 5285 Port Royal Rd., Springfield, VA 22161. (703) 487-4650. 1989.

Waste Disposal in Academic Institutions. James A. Kaufman. Lewis Publishers, 2000 Corporate Blvd., N.W., Boca Raton, FL 33431. (407) 994-0555 or (800) 272-7737. 1990. Discusses academic waste disposal programs, identifies unknown chemicals, discusses methods for handling and treating wastes, and waste disposal practices.

Waste Equipment Manufacturers Institute. National Solid Waste, Mgmt. Association, 1730 Rhode Island Ave., N.W., Washington, DC 20036. (202) 659-4613.

Waste Industry Buyer Guide. National Solid Wastes Management Association, 1730 Rhode Island Ave., N.W., Suite 1000, Washington, DC 20036. (202) 659-4613.

Waste Information Digest. Environmental Studies Institute, International Academy at Santa Barbara, 800 Garden St., Suite D, Santa Barbara, CA 93101-1552. (805) 965-5010. Online version of the periodical of the same name.

Waste Information Digests. Environmental Studies Institute, International Academy at Santa Barbara, 800 Garden St., Suite D, Santa Barbara, CA 93101-1552. (805) 965-5010. Eight times a year. Covers waste collection, management and recycling.

Waste Management and Resource Recovery. International Research & Evaluation, 21098 IRE Control Center, Eagan, MN 55121. (612) 888-9635.

Waste Management Control Handbook for Dairy Food Plants. W. J. Harper. U.S. Environmental Protection Agency, Office of Research and Development, 26 W. Martin Luther King Dr., Cincinnati, OH 45268. (513) 569-7931. 1984. Waste disposal in the food processing plants.

Waste Management in Petrochemical Complexes. S. A. S. Almeida, et al., eds. Pergamon Microforms International, Inc., Fairview Park, Elmsford, NY 10523. (914) 592-7720. 1989. Proceedings of an IAWPRC Seminar held in Porto Alegre, Rio Grande do Sul, Brazil, October 26-28, 1987. Covers a wide range of topics related to the processing and final disposal of effluents derived from the chemical and petrochemical industries.

Waste Management: Nuclear, Chemical, Biological, Municipal. Pergamon Microforms International, Inc., Fairview Park, Elmsford, NY 10523. (914) 592-7720. 1980-. Quarterly. Formerly Nuclear and Chemical Waste Management. Presents information encompassing the entire field of waste disposal, including radioactive and transuranic waste.

Waste Management Research and Education Institute Newsletter. Waste Management Research and Education Institute, University of Tennessee at Knoxville, 327 S. Stadium Hall, Knoxville, TN 37996-0710. (615) 974-4251. Quarterly. Environmental biotechnology research.

Waste Management: Towards A Sustainable Society. Om Prakash Kharbanda and E. A. Stallworthy. Auburn House, 14 Dedham St., Dover, MA 02030-0658. (505) 785-2220; (800) 223-2665. 1990. Describes the generation of various types of hazardous and nonhazardous wastes, with a whole chapter devoted to acid rain.

Waste Minimization and Pollution Prevention. Director, Hazardous Material Management and Resource Recovery Program, PO Box 872203, Tuscaloosa, AL 35487-0203. (205) 348-8401.

Waste Minimization & Recycling Report. Government Institutes, Inc., 4 Research Pl., Ste. 200, Rockville, MD 20850. (301) 921-2300. Monthly. Covers waste minimization, reduction and recycling strategies.

Waste Minimization Manual. Government Institutes, Inc., 4 Research Pl., Ste. 200, Rockville, MD 20850. (301) 921-2300.

Waste Minimization: Manufacturer's Strategies for Success. National Association of Manufacturers, 1331 Pennsylvania Ave., NW, Suite 1500 N., Washington, DC 20004. (202) 637-3000. 1989.

Waste Minimization Opportunity Assessment Manual. Government Institutes, Inc., 4 Research Pl., Ste. 200, Rockville, MD 20850. (301) 921-2300. 1988. Deals with managing hazardous waste and its minimization.

Waste Not, Want Not. Northeast-Midwest Institute, Publications Office, 218 D St., SE, Washington, DC 20003. 1989. State and federal roles in source reduction and recycling of solid waste.

Waste Oil: Reclaiming Technology, Utilization and Disposal. Mueller Associates Inc. Noyes Publications, 120 Mill Rd., Park Ridge, NJ 07656. (201) 391-8484. 1989. Describes and assesses the current status of the technologies and environmental information associated with the waste oil industry.

Waste Oil Recovery and Disposal. Noyes Publications, 120 Mill Rd., Park Ridge, NJ 07656. (201) 391-8484. 1975.

Waste Recovery Report. ICON, Inc., 211 S. 45th St., Philadelphia, PA 19104. (215) 349-6500. Monthly. Recycling, waste-to-energy, and other resource recovery fields.

Waste Reduction Assistance Program: Waste Minimization and Pollution Program. Executive Director, 431 West Seventh Ave., Anchorage, AK 99501. (907) 276-2864.

Waste Reduction: Policy and Practice. Waste Management Inc. and Piper & Marbury. Executive Enterprises Publications Co., Inc., 22 W. 21st St., New York, NY 10010-6990. (212) 645-7880. 1990. Examines waste reduction on a national level. Gives an overview of the makeup of hazardous waste and municipal solid waste streams and different means of reducing the generation of those streams. Case studies of waste reduction in industry are described.

Waste Service Industry Review. FIND/SVP, 625 Avenue of the Americas, New York, NY 10011. (800) 346-3787. 1991. Major components and current and future industry fundamentals and opportunities within each sector of the waste services industry.

Waste Systems Institute of Michigan, Inc. 400 Ann, N.W., Suite 204, Grand Rapids, MI 49504. (616) 363-3262.

Waste-to-Energy. The American Public Power Association, 2301 M St., NW, Washington, DC 20037. (202) 467-2900. 1986. Waste products as fuel and electric power production.

Waste-to-Energy Commercial Facilities Profiles; Technical, Operational, and Economic Perspectives. Dick Richards, et al. Noyes Publications, 120 Mill Rd., Park Ridge, NJ 07656. (201) 391-8484. 1990. Presents profiles of all commercial-scale facilities in the U.S. that are processing municipal solid waste to recover energy, as well as case studies for three of the facilities. Information comes from Waste-to-Energy revised edition 1988 prepared for the U.S. Dept. of Energy Dec 1988 and Case Studies of Waste-to-Energy Facilities prepared by the Illinois Dept. of Energy and Natural Resources, May 1989.

Waste-to-Energy Compendium. National Technical Information Service, 5285 Port Royal Rd., Springfield, VA 22161. (703) 487-4650. 1988. Deals with refuse and refuse disposal, waste product as fuel and factory and trade waste.

Waste-to-Energy Facilities. National Publishing, Alexandria, VA 1986. Covers refuse as fuel and refuse disposal facilities in the United States.

Waste-to-Energy Industry. FIND/SVP, 625 Avenue of the Americas, New York, NY 10011. (212) 645-4500. Environment regulation of waste-to-energy; and competing means of solid waste disposal.

Waste Treatment Technology News. Business Communications Company, Inc., 25 Van Zant Street, Norwalk, CT 06855. (203) 853-4266. Monthly. Covers effective management and handling of hazardous wastes.

Waste Watch. P.O. Box 298, Livingston, KY 40445.

Waste Watch Magazine. Massachusetts Department of Environmental Quality Control, Division of Solid Waste Management, 1 Winter Street, 4th Floor, Boston, MA 02108. (617) 292-5989. Quarterly. Covers issues and events in solid waste disposal.

WasteInfo. Waste Management Information Bureau, United Kingdom Atomic Energy Authority, Building 46J, Harwell Laboratory, Harwell, Oxfordshire, England OX11 ORB. 44 (235) 24141.

Wastewater Engineering: Treatment, Disposal, and Reuse. Metcalf & Eddy, Inc. McGraw-Hill Science & Engineering Books, 11 West 19th St., New York, NY 10011. (212) 337-6010. 1991. Reflects the impact of changing federal legislation on environmental quality control and sludge management. Gives a solid overall perspective on wastewater engineering.

Wastewater Management: A Guide to Information Sources. George Tchobanoglous, et al. Gale Research Co., 835 Penobscot Bldg., Detroit, MI 48226-4094. (313) 961-2242. 1976.

Wastewater Treatment Plant Instrumentation Handbook. National Technical Information Service, 5285 Port Royal Rd., Springfield, VA 22161. (703) 487-4650. 1985.

Wastewater Treatment: Pocket Handbook. Pudvan Publishing Co., Inc., 1935 Shermer Rd., Northbrook, IL 60062. (312) 498-9840. 1987. Covers sewage purification methods.

Wastewater Treatment Using Flocculation, Coagulation, and Flotation; Citations from the American Petroleum Institute Data Base. National Technical Information Service, 5285 Port Royal Rd., Springfield, VA 22161. (703) 487-4650.

Wastewater Works News. Michigan Department of Health, Wastewater Section, Division of Engineering, Lansing, MI 48914. Bimonthly.

Wasting Assets: Natural Resources in the National Income Accounts. Robert Repetto and William B. Magrath. World Resources Institute, 1709 New York Ave. N.W., Washington, DC 20006. (800) 822-0504. 1989. Using Indonesia's timber, petroleum and soils as examples, this report tests and applies a new methodology for integrating natural resource depletion into a revised national accounting system that can more accurately reflect economic reality.

Water. Hans Silvester. Thomasson-Grant, 1 Morton Dr., Suite 500, Charlottesville, VA 22901. (804) 977-1780. 1990. Details the dangers posed by the industrial society to the flow of clean water

Water, Air, and Soil Pollution. Kluwer Academic Publishers, 101 Philip Dr., Assinippi Park, Norwell, MA 02061. (617) 871-6600. Bimonthly. Covers water, soil, and air pollution. This is an international journal on environmental pollution dealing with all types of pollution including acid rain.

Water Analysis. Academic Press, c/o Harcourt Brace Jovanovich Inc., 6277 Sea Harbor Dr., Orlando, FL 32887. (800) 346-8648. 1982. Analysis of inorganic species in water.

Water and Air Resources in North Carolina. Department of Natural and Economic Resources, PO Box 27687, Raleigh, NC 27611.

Water and Energy Research Institute of the Western Pacific (*WERI*). University of Guam, UOG Station, GU 96923. (617) 734-3132.

Water and Natural Resources Building: Natural Resources. Secretary, 2nd Floor, Joe Foss Building, 523 E. Capital, Pierre, SD 57501. (605) 773-3151.

Water and Natural Resources Department: Air Quality. Administrator, Air Quality and Solid Waste, Joe Foss Building, 523 E. Capital, Pierre, SD 57501. (605) 773-3329.

Water and Natural Resources Department: Environmental Protection. Director, Division of Environmental Health, Joe Foss Building, 523 E. Capital, Pierre, SD 57501. (605) 773-3151.

Water and Natural Resources Department: Groundwater Management. Director, Division of Environmental Health, Joe Foss Building, 523 E. Capital, Pierre, SD 57501. (605) 773-3151.

Water and Natural Resources Department: Hazardous Waste Management. Administrator, Air Quality and Solid Waste, Joe Foss Building, 523 E. Capital, Pierre, SD 57501. (605) 773-3329.

Water and Natural Resources Department: Solid Waste Management. Director, Division of Environmental Health, Joe Foss Building, 523 E. Capital, Pierre, SD 57501. (605) 773-3151.

Water and Natural Resources Department: Underground Storage Tanks. Director, Division of Environmental Health, Joe Foss Building, 523 E. Capital, Pierre, SD 57501. (605) 773-3151.

Water and Natural Resources Department: Water Quality. Director, Division of Environmental Health, Joe Foss Building, 523 E. Capital, Pierre, SD 57501. (605) 773-3751.

Water and Pollution Control. Southam Business Pub. Inc., 1450 Don Mills Rd., Don Mills, ON, Canada M3B 2X7. M3B 2X7 1893-. Monthly. Formerly Canada Municipal Utilities.

Water & Waste Treatment. D.R. Publications, Faversham House, 111 St. James's Rd., Croydon, England CR9 2TH. Monthly. Covers water-supply engineering, sewage and sanitary engineering.

Water and Waste Treatment Journal. D.R. Publications, Faversham House, 111 St. James's Rd., Croydon, England CR9 2TH. Monthly. Sewage and water supply engineering topics.

Water and Wastes Digest. Scranton Gillette Communications, Inc., 380 Northwest Highway, Des Plaines, IL 60016. (708) 298-6622. Bimonthly. Covers publicly and privately owned water and sewage systems.

Water & Wastewater Equipment Manufacturers Association. Box 17402, Dulles International Airport, Washington, DC 20041. (703) 444-1777.

Water and Wastewater Examination Manual. V. Dean Adams. Lewis Publishers, 2000 Corporate Blvd., N.W., Boca Raton, FL 33431. (407) 994-0555 or (800) 272-7737. 1990. Guide and reference for water/wastewater quality analysis. Includes procedures for parameters frequently used in water quality analysis.

Water Chlorination: Chemistry, Environmental Impact and Health Effects. Robert L. Jolley, et al., eds. Lewis Publishers, 2000 Corporate Blvd., N.W., Boca Raton, FL 33431. (407) 994-0555 or (800) 272-7737. 1990. Proceedings of the 6th conference on Water Contamination held in Oak Ridge, Tennessee, May 3-8, 1987. Includes all the ramifications of water chlorination practice and presents the most significant original research and developments of recent occurrence.

Water Commission: Groundwater Management. Chief, Groundwater Management, Box 13087, Capitol Station, Austin, TX 78711. (512) 463-4969.

Water Commission: Hazardous Waste Management. Director, Hazardous and Solid Waste Management, PO Box 13087, Capitol Station, Austin, TX 78711. (512) 463-7760.

Water Commission: Natural Resources. Executive Director, Box 13087, Capitol Station, Austin, TX 78711. (512) 463-7898.

Water Conditioning and Purification. Publicom Inc., 4651 N. 1st Ave., Suite 101, Tucson, AZ 85718. (602) 293-5446. Monthly.

Water Conditioning & Purification–Buyers Guide Issue. Publicom, Inc., 4651 N. First Ave., Suite 101, Tucson, AZ 85718. (602) 293-5446.

Water Contamination by Viruses: Occurrence, Detection, Treatment. Charles P. Gerba, et al. Lewis Publishers, 2000 Corporate Blvd., N.W., Boca Raton, FL 33431. (407) 994-0555 or (800) 272-7737. 1991. Describes the occurrence of viruses in the environment such as soil, sludge, drinking water, and rivers. Also gives details on how these viruses are detected, and their elimination by adsorption, irradiation, and other related methods.

Water Desalination. Headquarters, Dept. of the Army, Washington, DC 20310. (202) 695-6153. 1986-.

The Water Encyclopedia. Lewis Publishers, 2000 Corporate Blvd. N.W., Boca Raton, FL 33431. (800) 272-7737. 1990. 2d ed. Includes groundwater contamination, drinking water, floods, waterborne diseases, global warming, climate change, irrigation, water agencies and organizations, precipitation, oceans and seas, and river, lakes and waterfalls.

Water Engineering and Landscape: Water Control and Landscape Transformation in the Modern Period. D. Cosgrove and G. Petts, eds. Belhaven Press, 136 S. Broadway, Irvington, NY 10533. (914) 591-9111. 1990. Examines the role played by water management in the environment.

Water Engineering & Management. Scranton Gillette Communications, Inc., 380 E. Northwest Hwy., Des Plaines, IL 60016-2282. (708) 298-6622. 1986-. Monthly. A professional trade publication which includes latest legislative news in the area of water quality, EPA criteria for drinking water, pesticides, and related standards. Includes articles of interest by water professionals and has regular news features such as forthcoming conferences, products at work, surveys, company profiles, etc.

Water Engineering & Management–Reference Handbook/ Buyer's Guide Issue. Scranton Gillette Communications, Inc., 380 E. Northwest Hwy., Des Plaines, IL 60016. (708) 298-6622.

Water, Environment, and Technology. Water Pollution Control Federation, 601 Wythe St., Alexandria, VA 22314-1994. (703) 684-2400. Monthly.

Water Environment & Technology–Buyer's Guide and Yearbook. Water Pollution Control Federation, 601 Wythe St., Alexandria, VA 22314-1994. (703) 684-2400.

Water Environment Federation. 601 Wythe St., Alexandria, VA 22314-1994. (703) 684-2400. Formerly, Water Pollution Control Federation.

Water in the News. Soap and Detergent Association, 457 Park Ave. S., New York, NY 10016. (212) 725-1262. 1965-. Bimonthly.

Water Law. William Goldfarb. Lewis Publishers, 200 Corporate Blvd. NW, Boca Raton, FL 33431. (407) 994-0555 or (800)272-7737. 1988. Explains all legal terms and covers all aspects of water laws, including water pollution law.

Water Management Association: Water Quality. Health and Mental Hygiene Department, 201 West Preston St., 5th Floor, Baltimore, MD 21201. (301) 225-6300.

Water Management Chemicals. FIND/SVP, 625 Avenue of the Americas, New York, NY 10011. (212) 645-4500. 1991. Analyzes U.S. consumption of water management chemicals.

Water Newsletter. Water Information Center Inc., 7 High St., Huntington, NY 11743. 1958-. Semimonthly. Includes news about water supply, waste, disposal, conservation and pollution.

Water Pollution: A Guide to Information Sources. Allen W. Knight and Mary Ann Simmons. Gale Research Co., 835 Penobscot Bldg., Detroit, MI 48226-4094. (313) 961-2242. 1980. Brings together a diverse set of information sources in the subject area of water pollution from the physical, social and natural sciences in the economic context of the environment planning and management process.

Water Pollution Biology. P. D. Abel. John Wiley & Sons, Inc., 605 3rd Ave., New York, NY 10158. (212) 850-6000. 1988. State-of-the-art information on methods of investigating water pollution problems and critically assesses the literature on water pollution. Also included is a discussion on the role of toxicological studies in the monitoring and control of water pollution.

Water Pollution Biology: A Laboratory/Field Handbook. Robert A. Coler, John P. Rockwood. Technomic Publishing Co., 851 New Holland Ave., PO Box 3535, Lancaster, PA 17604. (717) 291-5609. 1989. Overview of the types of surface water quality problems and the types of field and laboratory methodologies used to assess the impacts of those problems on aquatic biota.

Water Pollution Control Federation Research Foundation. 601 Wythe St., Alexandria, VA 22314-1994. (703) 684-2400.

Water Pollution: Modelling, Measuring and Prediction. L.C. Wrobel. Elsevier Science Publishing Co., 655 Avenue of the Americas, New York, NY 10010. (212) 984-5800. 1991. Mathematical modelling data acquisition waste disposal and wastewater treatment chemical and biological problems.

Water Pollution Newsletter. Water Information Center Inc., 7 High St., Huntington, NY 11743.

Water Pollution Research and Control. L. Lijklema, ed. Pergamon Microforms International, Inc., Fairview Park, Elmsford, NY 10523. (914) 592-7720. 1989. Proceedings of the 14th biennial conference of the International Association on Water Pollution Research and Control held in Brighton, UK, July 18-21, 1988. Incorporates aspects of both research and practice in water pollution control, and contains valuable information for the abatement of water pollution and the enhancement of the quality of the water environment worldwide.

Water Power and Dam Construction Handbook. Richard Taylor, ed. Reed Business Pub., Quadrant House, The Quadrant, Sutton, England SM2 5AS. 1990.

Water Purification and Filteration Equipment. American Business Directories, Inc., 5711 S. 86th Circle, Omaha, NE 68127. (402) 593-4600.

The Water Purification Market. FIND/SVP, 625 Avenue of the Americas, New York, NY 10011. (212) 645-4500. 1991. State-of-the-art technologies and equipment sold into each market sector, and the cost effectiveness of various treatment methods.

Water Quality and Forestry. Jodee Kuske. National Agricultural Library, 10301 Baltimore Blvd., Beltsville, MD 20705-2351. (301) 504-5755. 1991.

Water Quality and Management for Recreation and Tourism. B. Rigden and L. Henry, eds. Pergamon Microforms International, Inc., Fairview Park, Elmsford, NY 10523. (914) 592-7720. 1989. Proceedings of the IAWPRC Conference held in Brisbane, Australia, July 10-15, 1988. Describes the problems associated with water quality and management for recreation tourism.

Water Quality and Treatment: A Handbook of Community Water Supplies. McGraw-Hill Science & Engineering Books, 11 W. 19th St., New York, NY 10011. (212) 337-6010. 1990. Covers water purification and water supply in the United States.

Water Quality and Treatment; A Handbook of Public Water Supplies. American Water Works Association. McGraw-Hill, 1221 Avenue of the Americas, New York, NY 10020. (212) 512-2000; (800) 262-4729. 1990. 4th ed. Revised and updated to reflect recent developments in the field. Addresses water quality issues for both municipal and industrial water supply, reports on the source of contaminants and other problems, and describes the treatment methods of choice.

Water Quality Assessment. W. B. Mills, et al. U.S. Environmental Protection Agency, Office of Research and Development, Environmental Research Laboratory, 401 M St. SW, Washington, DC 20460. (202) 260-2090. 1985. 2 vols.

Water Quality Association. 4151 Naperville Rd., Lisle, IL 60532. (708) 505-0160.

Water Quality Association Directory. Water Quality Association, 4151 Naperville Rd., Lisle, IL 60532. (708) 505-0160. Annual.

Water Quality Branch: Water Quality. Chief, 105 South Meridian St., Box 6015, Indianapolis, IN 46206. (317) 245-5028.

Water Quality in Agriculture. National Agricultural Library, 10301 Baltimore Blvd., Beltsville, MD 20705-2351. (301) 504-5755. 1990.

Water Quality International. Pergamon Microforms International, Inc., Fairview Park, Elmsford, NY 10523. (914) 592-7720. 1990-. Quarterly. Contains news and information from IAWPRC conferences and Specialist and Task Groups, and other news.

Water Quality Laboratory. Western Illinois University, Department of Chemistry, Macomb, IL 61455. (309) 298-1356.

Water Quality Modeling. Brian Henderson-Sellere, et al. CRC Press, 2000 Corporate Blvd. N.W., Boca Raton, FL 33431. (407) 994-0555; (800) 272-7737. 1990. Issues in four volumes. Discusses water supply and treatment and water resources engineering.

Water Quality Research Council. 4151 Naperville Rd., Lisle, IL 60532. (708) 505-0160.

Water Quality Standards Criteria Summaries. National Technical Information Service, 5285 Port Royal Rd., Springfield, VA 22161. (703) 487-4650. Maximum allowable pollutant concentrations, and limits for other properties. Includes agricultural chemicals, trace metals, and bacteria; or physical or chemical properties including acidity, temperature, and turbidity.

Water Quality Standards Handbook. U.S. Environmental Protection Agency, Office of Water Regulations and Standards, 401 M St., S.W., Washington, DC 20460. (202) 260-2090. 1982. Covers water quality management in the United States.

Water Research. International Association on Water Pollution Research and Control. Pergamon Microforms International, Inc., Fairview Park, Elmsford, NY 10523. (914) 592-7720. 1966-. Monthly. Covers all aspects of the pollution of marine and fresh water and the management of water quality as well as water resources.

Water Research Institute. West Virginia University, Morgantown, WV 26506. (304) 293-2757.

Water Resource Management: Integrated Policies. OECD Publications and Information Center, 2001 L St., N.W., Suite 700, Washington, DC 20036. (202) 785-OECD. 1989. Report underlines the need for more effective policy integration within the water sector itself (in order to improve water quality and quantity, demand management, surface and groundwater supply).

Water Resources Abstracts. U.S. Department of the Interior, Geological Survey, Water Resources Scientific Information Center, 119 National Center, Reston, VA 22092. (703) 648-4460.

Water Resources Association of the Delaware River Basin. Box 867, Davis Road, Valley Forge, PA 19481. (215) 783-0634.

Water Resources Board: Water Quality. Chief, Water Quality Division, 1000 N.E. 10th St., PO Box 53585, Oklahoma City, OK 73152. (405) 271-2540.

Water Resources Center. University of Delaware, 210 Hullihen Hall, Newark, DE 19716. (302) 451-2191.

Water Resources Congress. Courthouse Plaza II, 2300 Clarendon Blvd., Suite 404, Arlington, VA 22201. (703) 525-4881.

Water Resources Control Board: Water Quality. Chief, Division of Water Quality, 901 P St., PO Box 100, Sacramento, CA 95801. (916) 445-9552.

Water Resources Data. U.S. Geological Survey. U.S. G.P.O., Washington, DC 20401. (202) 512-0000. Annual. Data on water supply and quality of streams, lakes and reservoirs for individual states by water year.

Water Resources Department: Groundwater Management. Manager, Groundwater Division, 3850 Portland Rd., N.E., Salem, OR 97310. (503) 378-3671.

Water Resources Development. U.S. Army Core of Engineers. U.S. G.P.O., Washington, DC 20401. (202) 512-0000. Biennial. Data on the corporation's activities relating to flood control, erosion, shore protection and disaster relief.

Water Resources Institute. Grand Valley State University, Allendale, MI 49401. (616) 895-3749.

Water Resources Planning. Andrew A. Dzurik. Rowman & Littlefield, Publishers, Inc., 8705 Bollman Pl., Savage, MD 20763. (301) 306-0400. 1990. Offers a comprehensive survey of all aspects of water resources planning and management.

Water Resources Protection Technology. J. Toby Tourbier. Urban Land Institute, 625 Indiana Ave., NW, Ste. 400, Washington, DC 20004. (202) 624-7000. 1981. Covers urbanization and water resources development.

Water Resources Research Center. University of Arizona, Geology Building, Room 314, Tucson, AZ 85721. (602) 621-7607.

Water: Rethinking Management in an Age of Scarcity. Sandra Postel. Worldwatch Institute, 1776 Massachusetts Ave., N.W., Washington, DC 20036-1904. 1984.

Water Science and Technology. Pergamon Microforms International Inc., Fairview Park, Elmsford, NY 10523. (914) 592-7720. Monthly. Covers water, pollution, sewage, purification, and water quality management.

Water Softening Equipment Service Directory. American Business Directories, Inc., 5711 S. 86th Circle, Omaha, NE 68127. (402) 593-4600.

Water Supply and Pollution Control Division: Water Quality. Director, 1200 Missouri Ave., Bismark, ND 58501. (701) 224-2354.

Water Supply and Treatment. Jack G. Walters, ed. TAPPI Press, Technology Park/Atlanta, PO Box 105113, Atlanta, GA 30348. (404) 446-1400. 1989. In-depth study of water use in the pulp and paper industry. Covers selection of equipment for a water treatment system, raw water treatment, clarification, lime soda softening, filtration, demineralizers, cooling systems and cooling water treatment and pumping systems.

Water Supply and Wastewater Disposal International Almanac. A. Kepinske and W. A. S. Kepinski. Vulkan-Verlag, Dr. W. Classen Nacht, Gooiland 11, Netherlands 1976-1985. Seven volumes. Deals with all problems and aspects in the domain of water supply and wastewater disposal.

Water Supply (from the State Capitals). Bethune Jones, 321 Sunset Ave., Asbury Park, NJ 07712. 1946-. Fourteen times a year. Provides water resource information from state capitals.

Water Supply Management. A. B. Morse Co., 200 James St., Barrington, IL 60010. 1927-. Monthly.

Water Systems Council. 600 S. Federal St., Suite 400, Chicago, IL 60605. (312) 922-6222.

Water Systems Council and Pitless Adapter Division–Membership Directory. Pitless Adapter Division/ Water Systems Council, 600 S. Federal St., Suite 400, Chicago, IL 60605. (312) 922-6222.

Water Technology. National Trade Publications, Inc., 13 Century Hill Dr., Latham, NY 12110. (518) 783-1281. Monthly.

Water Technology–Directory of Manufacturers and Suppliers Issue. National Trade Publications, Inc., 13 Century Hill Dr., Latham, NY 12110. (518) 783-1281.

Water Technology–Planning & Purchasing Handbook Issue. National Trade Publications, Inc., 13 Century Hill Dr., Latham, NY 12110. (518) 783-1281.

Water Treatability. National Ground Water Information Center, National Well Water Association, 6375 Riverside Dr., Dublin, OH 43017. (614) 761-1711.

Water Treatment Equipment Service/Supplies. American Business Directories, Inc., 5711 S. 86th Circle, Omaha, NE 68127. (402) 593-4600.

Water Treatment Handbook. Degremont s.a., 184, ave. du 18-Juin-1940, Rueil-Malmaison, France F-92500. 1991. Sixth edition. Part 1 is a general survey of water and its action on the materials with which it comes into contact, and theoretical principles of separation and correction processes used in water treatment. Part 2 describes the process and the treatment plant beginning with the separation process.

Water Treatment: Principles and Design. James M. Montgomery. John Wiley & Sons, Inc., 605 3rd Ave., New York, NY 10158-0012. (212) 850-6000. 1985. Offers a comprehensive coverage of the principles and design of water quality and treatment programs, plus plant operations.

Water Vapor, Precipitation, Clouds and Fog. D. D. Grantham. Meteorology Division, Air Force Geophysics Laboratory, Hanscom Air Force Base, MA 01731. (617) 377-3237. 1983. Covers precipitation, atmospheric water vapor, fog and clouds.

Water Well Drilling Directory. American Business Directories, Inc., 5711 S. 86th Circle, Omaha, NE 68127. (402) 593-4600.

Water Well Regulations Data Base. National Water Well Association, 6375 Riverside Dr., Dublin, OH 43017. (614) 761-1711.

Waterborne Commerce of the U.S.: Waterways and Harbors. U.S. G.P.O, Washington, DC 20402-9325. (202) 512-0000. 1959. Annual. Freight, passengers, and vessels within or between coastal and noncontiguous U.S. ports, on inland waterways, and on the Great Lakes.

Waternet. American Water Works Association, Technical Library, 6666 W. Quincy Ave., Denver, CO 80235. (303) 794-7711.

Watershed Management Field Manual. Food and Agriculture Organization of the United Nations, 46110F Assembly Dr., Lanham, MD 20706-4391. (800) 274-4888. 1986.

Waterways and Wetlands. British Trust for Conservation Volunteers, Berkshire, Reading, England 1976. Covers conservation of natural resources, with special reference to wetlands.

Waterworld News. American Water Works Association, 6666 West Quincy Ave., Denver, CO 80235. (303) 794-7711. Bimonthly. Articles on technological developments in the water industry.

Wear Control Handbook. M. B. Peterson. American Society of Mechanical Engineers, 345 E. 47th St., New York, NY 10017. (212) 705-7722. 1980. Mechanical wear remediation through lubrication and lubricants.

The Weather Almanac. Frank E. Bair, ed. Gale Research Co., 835 Penobscot Bldg., Detroit, MI 48226-4094. (313) 961-2242. 1992. Sixth edition. A reference guide to weather, climate, and air quality in the United States and its key cities, compromising statistics, principles, and terminology.

Weather from Above: America's Meteorological Satellites. Janice Hill. Smithsonian Institution Press, 470 L'Enfant Plaza, #7100, Washington, DC 20560. (800) 782-4612. 1991. Covers global weather systems. Describes instruments the satellites carried as well as images they returned to earth analyses how meteorological data are used to predict weather.

Weather of U.S. Cities. Frank E. Bair. Gale Research Inc., 835 Penobscot Bldg., Detroit, MI 48226-4094. (313) 961-2242. 1992. Compilation of U.S. government weather data on 281 cities and weather observation stations.

Weathering. Longman Scientific & Technical, 1560 Broadway, New York, NY 10036. (212) 819-5400. 1984. Topics in geomorphology.

Weathering and Erosion. Butterworth-Heinemann, 80 Montvale Ave., Stoneham, MA 02180. (617) 438-8464. 1983. Techniques and methods used in weathering and the prevention of erosion.

Weed Abstracts. C. A. B. International, 845 North Park Ave., Tucson, AZ 85719. (602) 621-7897 or (800) 528-4841. 1954-. Monthly. Abstracts the world literature on weeds, weed control and allied subjects.

Weed Research. Blackwell Scientific Publications, 3 Cambridge Ctr., Suite 208, Cambridge, MA 02142. (617) 225-0401. 1974-. Six times a year.

Weed Science Society of America. 309 W. Clark St., Champaign, IL 61820. (217) 356-3182.

Weed Technology. Weed Science Society of America, 309 W. Clark St., Champaign, IL 61820. (217) 356-3182. Quarterly. Weed control and herbicides.

Weekly Statistical Bulletin. American Petroleum Institute, 1220 L St. N.W., Washington, DC 20005. (202) 682-8000. 1962-. Weekly. Crude oil and refined product daily average production and imports, and end-of-week stocks.

Welded Steel Tanks for Oil Storage. American Petroleum Institute, 1220 L St. N.W., Washington, DC 20005. (202) 682-8000. 1980. Petroleum storage and standards for design and construction for oil storage tanks.

Welding Research Council. 345 E. 47th St., New York, NY 10017. (212) 705-7956.

Well Drilling. American Business Directories, Inc., 5711 S. 86th Circle, Omaha, NE 68127. (402) 593-4600.

Well Log. National Water Well Association, 500 W. Wilson Bridge Rd., Worthington, OH 43085. (614) 761-1711. Eight numbers a year. Newsletter of the National Water Well Association

West Coast Fisheries Development Foundation. 812 S.W. Washington, Suite 900, Portland, OR 97205. (503) 222-3518.

West Virginia Environmental Law Handbook. Government Institutes, Inc., 4 Research Pl., Ste. 200, Rockville, MD 20850. (301) 921-2300. 1990.

Western Agricultural Chemicals Association. 930 G St., Suite 210, Sacramento, CA 95815. (916) 446-9222.

Western Association of Fish & Wildlife Agencies. Dept. of Fish & Game, 1416 Ninth St., Sacramento, CA 95814. (916) 323-7319.

Western Fertilizer Handbook. California Fertilizer Association, Soil Improvement Committee. Interstate Publishers, 510 Vermillion St., PO Box 50, Danville, IL 61834-0050. (217) 446-0500. 1990. Covers soil management and crops nutrition.

Western Forestry & Conservation Association. 4033 SW Canyon Rd., Portland, OR 97221. (503) 226-4562.

Western Lands and Waters Series. Arthur H. Clark Co., 1264 S. Central Ave., Glendale, CA 91204. 1959-. Irregular.

Western Oil & Gas Association. 505 N. Brand Ave., Suite 1400, Glendale, CA 91203. (818) 545-4105.

Western Regional Environmental Education Council. c/o Idaho Dept. of Fish & Game, 600 S. Walnut, Box 25, Boise, ID 83707. (208) 334-3747.

Western Snow Conference. P.O. Box 2646, Portland, OR 97208. (503) 326-2843.

Western Timber Association. California Forestry Association, 1311 I St., Ste. 1000, Sacramento, CA 95814. (916) 444-6592.

Western Water. Western Water Education Foundation, 717 K St., Ste. 517, Sacramento, CA 95814. (916) 444-6240. Bimonthly.

Western Water Education Foundation. 717 K St., Ste. 517, Sacramento, CA 95814-3406. (916) 444-6240.

Western Water Made Simple. Ed Marston, ed. Island Press, 1718 Connecticut Ave. N.W., Suite 300, Washington, DC 20009. (202) 232-7933. 1987.

WESTLAW Environmental Law Library. West Publishing Company, 50 W. Kellogg Blvd., PO Box 64526, St. Paul, MN 55164-0526. (612) 228-2500. Text of U.S. federal court decisions, statutes and regulations, administrative law publications, specialized files, and texts and periodicals dealing with the environmental law.

Wet Scrubber Newsletter. McIlvaine Co., 2970 Maria Ave., Northbrook, IL 60062. (708) 272-0010. 1974-. Monthly.

Wetland Center. Duke University, School of Forestry and Environmental Studies, Durham, NC 27706. (919) 684-8741.

Wetland Creation and Restoration: The Status of the Science. Jon A. Kusler and Mary E. Kentula, eds. Island Press, 1718 Connecticut Ave. N.W., Suite 300, Washington, DC 20009. (202) 232-7933. 1990. Eighty papers from leading scientists and technicians draw upon important new information and provide assessment by region of the capacity to implement a goal of no-net-loss of wetlands.

Wetland Economics and Assessment. Garland Publishing Inc., 1000A Sherman Ave., Hamden, CT 06514. (203) 281-4487. 1989. Bibliography of the social and economic aspects of wetland conservation.

Wetland Hydrology. North Dakota State University, Agricultural Experiment Station, Fargo, ND 58105. 1981. Bibliography of hydrology of wetlands.

Wetland Losses in the United States. U.S. Department of the Interior, Fish and Wildlife Service, 1849 C St. NW, Washington, DC 20240. (202) 208-5634. 1990. A National Wetlands Inventory Group report on wetland conservation.

Wetland Modelling. Elsevier Science Publishing Co., 655 Avenue of the Americas, New York, NY 10010. (212) 984-5800. 1988. Simulation methods in wetland ecology and wetlands.

Wetland News. Association of State Wetland Managers, PO Box 2463, Berne, NY 12023. (518) 872-1804. Quarterly.

Wetland Values Bibliographic Database. U.S. Army Corps of Engineers, Waterways Experiment Station, Environmental Lab, P.O. Box 631, Vicksburg, MS 39180. (601) 634-3774.

Wetlands. Council of Planning Librarians, 1313 E. 60th St., Chicago, IL 60637-2897. (312) 942-2163. 1991. Bibliography of wetland conservation.

Wetlands. Society of the Wetlands Scientists, Wilmington, NC Annual.

Wetlands: A Threatened Landscape. Michael Williams. B. Blackwell, 3 Cambridge Ctr., Suite 208, Cambridge, MA 02142. (617) 225-0401. 1990. Explores the evolution and composition of wetlands and their physical and biological dynamics, considers the impact of agriculture, industry, urbanization, and recreation upon them, and examines what steps we are taking and what steps should be considered to manage and preserve wetlands.

Wetlands for Wildlife, Inc. PO Box 344, West Bend, WI 53095. (414) 334-0327.

Wetlands Institute. Stone Harbor Boulevard, Stone Harbor, NJ 08247. (609) 368-1211.

Wetlands: Mitigating and Regulating Development Impacts. David Salvesen. The Urban Land Institute, 1090 Vermont Ave. N.W., Washington, DC 20005. (202) 289-8500; (800) 237-9196. 1990. Presents the latest examination of the conflicts surrounding development of wetlands. Explains both federal and state wetland regulations. Included is an up-to-date review of important wetlands case law and a detailed look at six of the toughest state programs.

Wetlands of North America. William A. Niering. Thomasson-Grant, 1 Morton Dr., Suite 500, Charlottesville, VA 22901. (804) 977-1780 or (800) 999-1780. 1991. Deals with wetlands ecology and the methods of its preservation.

Wetlands of the California Central Valley: Status and Trends 1939 to Mid-1980's. U.S. G.P.O., Washington, DC 20401. (202) 512-0000. 1989. Report on area of current wetlands, and former wetlands converted to other uses, in the California Central Valley.

Wetlands of the United States. National Wetlands Inventory, U.S. Department of the Interior, Fish and Wildlife Service, 1849 C St. NW, Washington, DC 20240. (202) 208-3171.

Wetlands Protection: The Role of Economics. Paul F. Scodari. Environmental Law Institute, 1616 P St. N.W., Suite 200, Washington, DC 20036. (202) 328-5150. 1990. Discussion of market economics as applied to wetland functions and values. Key features include the science of wetland valuation, principles and methods of wetland valuation, principles and methods for valuing wetland goods, the implementation of wetland valuation, and the natural resource damage assessment.

Wetlands Research Area. Unity College, Unity, ME 04988. (207) 948-3131.

Wetlands, Their Use and Regulation. Congress of the U.S., Office of Technology Assessment, c/o U.S. Government Printing Office, N. Capitol & H Sts. NW, Washington, DC 20401. (202) 512-0000. 1984. Legal aspects of wetland conservation.

Whale Center. 3929 Piedmont Ave., Oakland, CA 94611. (415) 654-6692.

The Whale War. David Day. Sierra Club Books, 100 Bush St., San Francisco, CA 94104. (415) 291-1600. 1987.

What Farmers Need to Know About Environmental Law. Drake University Agricultural Law Center, Des Moines, IA 50311. (515) 271-2065. 1990.

Wheat, Barley, and Triticale. C. A. B. International, 845 North Park Ave., Tucson, AZ 85719. (602) 621-7897 or (800) 528-4841. 1984-. Bimonthly. Abstracts the world literature in the areas of: Plant breeding and genetics; plant physiology; soil science; pests and diseases; agriculture engineering and other related areas focusing on wheat barley and triticale.

When All Else Fails!: Enforcement of The Emergency Planning and Community Right-To-Know Act; A Self Help Manual for Local Emergency Planning Committees. U.S. Environmental Protection Agency, Office of Solid Waste and Emergency Response, 401 M St. SW, Washington, DC 20460. (202) 260-2090. 1990.

Where Did That Chemical Go? A Practical Guide to Chemical Fate and Transport in the Environment. Ronald E. Ney. Van Nostrand Reinhold, 115 Fifth Ave., New York, NY 10003. (212) 254-3232. 1990. Offers predictive techniques for determining what happens to a chemical once it is accidently released, or intentionally placed, in air, water, soil, plants, and animals.

Where Have All the Birds Gone?. John Terborgh. Princeton University Press, 41 Williams St., Princeton, NJ 08540. (609) 258-4900. 1989. Includes topics such as: population monitoring, ecological consequences of fragmentation, evolution of migration, social and territorial behaviors of wintering songbirds.

Where There's Smoke: Problems and Policies Concerning Smoking in the Workplace. Bureau of National Affairs, 1231 25th St., N.W., Rm. 215, Washington, DC 20037. (800) 452-7773.

Whiteflies: Their Bionomics, Pest Status and Management. Dan Gerling, ed. VCH Publishers, 303 NW 12th Ave., Deerfield Beach, FL 33442-1788. (305) 428-5566. 1990. Covers the many aspects of whitefly study from evolution and morphology, to biology, natural enemies, sampling, modeling and control.

Who Should Take Out the Trash?. Kenneth Chilton. Center for the Study of American Business, Washington University, Campus Box 1208, One Brookings Dr., St. Louis, MO 63130-4899. (314) 935-5630. 1991.

Whole Earth Ecolog: The Best of Environmental Tools and Ideas. J. Baldwin, ed. Harmony Books, 201 E. 50th St., New York, NY 10022. (212) 572-6120. 1990. Provides in-depth reviews of materials that have been meticulously reviewed by the staff of Whole Earth Access. Lists hundreds of materials that have the potential for making things a little easier on the planet.

Whole Earth Lectronic Link. The Well, 25 Gate Five Rd., Sausalito, CA 94965. (415) 332-1716.

Whooping Crane Conservation Association, Inc. 1007 Carmel Ave., Lafayette, LA 70501. (318) 234-6339.

Who's Who in Energy Recovery from Waste. Biofuels and Municipal Waste Technology Division/Office of Renewable Energy Technologies, Office of Conservation and Renewable Energy, Department of Energy, Washington, DC 20585. (202) 586-6750. 1982.

Who's Who in Environmental Engineering. American Academy of Environmental Engineers, 132 Holiday Court, Suite 206, Annapolis, MD 21401. (301) 266-3311. 1980. Annual. Directory of environmental engineers who are certified by the academy.

Who's Who in Industrial Woodworking Machinery Distribution. Woodworking Machinery Distributors' Association, 251 W. DeKalb Pike, King of Prussia, PA 19406. (215) 265-6658.

Who's Who in Ozone. International Ozone Association, c/o Wasserversorgung Zurich, Hardhaf 9, Postfach, Zurich, Switzerland CH-8023. 1 4352112.

Who's Who in the Plumbing-Heating-Cooling Industry. National Association of Plumbing-Heating-Cooling Contractors, 180 S. Washington St., P.O. Box 6808, Falls Church, VA 22046. (703) 237-8100.

Who's Who in World Agriculture. Longman Group Ltd., 6th Floor, Westgate House, The High, Harlow, England CM20 1NE. 1985. Second edition. Profiles 12,000 senior agricultural and veterinary scientists.

A Who's Who of American Ozone Depleters: A Guide to 3,014 Factories Emitting Three Ozone-Depleting Chemicals. Natural Resources Defense Council, 40 W. 20th St., New York, NY 10011. (212) 727-2700. 1990.

Wild America Magazine. American Wildlands, 7500 E. Arapahoe Rd., Suite 355, Englewood, CO 80112. (303) 771-0380. Annual.

Wild and Scenic River Economics. Richard D. Walsh. American Wildlands, 7600 E. Arapahoe Rd., Ste. 114, Englewood, CO 80112. (303) 771-0380. 1985. Economic aspects, recreation use and preservation values relating to reserves.

Wilderness. The Wilderness Society, 900 17th St. NW, Washington, DC 20006. (202) 833-2300. Quarterly. Preserving wilderness and wildlife, protecting America's prime forests, parks, rivers, shorelands, and fostering an American land ethic.

Wilderness Flyers. c/o Seaplane Pilots Association, 421 Aviation Way, Frederick, MD 21701. (301) 695-2082.

Wilderness Management. John C. Hendee, et al. North American Press, 350 Indiana St., Ste. 350, Golden, CO 80401. (303) 277-1623. 1990. 2d ed. rev. The expertise of the main authors has been combined with that of 10 other authorities in wilderness related fields, and nearly 100 wilderness managers, scientists, educators, and citizen conservationists, to make this book a valuable tool of practical information.

Wilderness Preservation and the Sagebrush Rebellions. William L. Graf. Rowman & Littlefield, Publishers, Inc., 8705 Bollman Pl., Savage, MD 20763. (301) 306-0400. 1990. Narrates the emergence of wilderness preservation as part of American public land policy from the 1880s to the 1980s.

Wilderness Society. 900 17th St., NW, Washington, DC 20006. (202) 833-2300.

Wilderness Watch. P.O. Box 782, Sturgeon Bay, WI 54235. (414) 743-1238.

Wildland Resources Center. University of California, 145 Walter Mulford Hall, Berkeley, CA 94720. (415) 642-0263.

Wildlife and Fisheries Department: Fish and Wildlife. Secretary, PO Box 98000, Baton Rouge, LA 70898-2803. (504) 765-2803.

Wildlife and Fisheries Habitat Improvement Handbook. Neil F. Payne. Wildlife and Fisheries, Department of the Interior, 18th and C Sts. NW, Washington, DC 20240. (202) 653-8750. 1990.

Wildlife and Habitat Law. Jack W. Grosse. Oceana Publications Inc., 75 Main St., Dobbs Ferry, NY 10522. (914) 693-8100. 1991. Covers questions of overall management, control and protection of wildlife and habitat. Issues of shared and conflicting power with the states are covered.

Wildlife and Marine Resources Department: Fish and Wildlife. Executive Director, PO Box 167, Columbia, SC 29202. (803) 734-4007.

Wildlife and Protected Areas: An Overview. United Nations Environment Program. UNIPUB, 1980.

Wildlife Conservation. Wildlife Conservation International, c/o New York Zoological Society, Bronx, NY 10460. (212) 220-5155. Bimonthly.

Wildlife Conservation Fund of America. 801 Kingsmill Pkwy., Columbus, OH 43229-1137. (614) 888-4868.

Wildlife Conservation International. c/o New York Zoological Society, Bronx, NY 10460. (212) 220-5155.

Wildlife Data Base. Julie Moore & Associates, 9956 N. Highway 85, Los Cruces, NM 88005. Scientific literature on wildlife, including North American waterfowl, shore and marsh birds, upland game birds, birds of prey, rodents and lagomorphs, carnivores and ungulates; international oceanic birds, marine mammals including whales, and bats.

Wildlife Disease Association. Box 886, Ames, IA 50010. (515) 233-1931.

Wildlife Disease Association Journal. Wildlife Disease Assn., PO Box 886, Ames, IA 50010. (515) 233-1931. Quarterly.

Wildlife Extinction. Charles L. Cadieux. Stone Wall Pr., 1241 30th St. N.W., Washington, DC 20007. (202) 333-1860. 1991. Presents a worldwide picture of animals in danger of extinction and addresses controversial issues such as exploding human population, the role of zoos and wildlife parks, hunting and poaching.

Wildlife, Forests, and Forestry. Malcolm L. Hunter, Jr. Prentice Hall, Rte 9W, Englewood Cliffs, NJ 07632. (201) 592-2000. 1990. Presents new ideas that will form the basis of forest wildlife management in years to come. It looks at the costs of managing wildlife, as well as national policies on forest wildlife management and quantitative techniques for measuring diversity.

Wildlife Habitat Enhancement Council. 1010 Wayne Ave., Suite 1240, Silver Spring, MD 20910. (301) 588-8994.

Wildlife Information Center, Inc. 629 Green St., Allentown, PA 18102. (215) 434-1637.

Wildlife Legislative Fund of America & The Wildlife Conservation. 50 W. Broad St., Columbus, OH 43215. (614) 221-2684.

Wildlife Management Institute. 1101 14th Street, N.W., Suite 725, Washington, DC 20005. (202) 371-1808.

Wildlife of the Florida Keys: A Natural History. James D. Lazell, Jr. Island Press, 1718 Connecticut Ave. N.W., Suite 300, Washington, DC 20009. (202) 232-7933. 1989. Identifies habits, behaviors, and histories of most of the species indigenous to the Keys.

Wildlife Preservation Trust International. 34th St. and Girard Ave., Philadelphia, PA 19104. (215) 222-3636.

Wildlife Research Institute, Inc. Box 4446, Arcata, CA 95521. (208) 456-2246.

Wildlife Reserves and Corridors in the Urban Environment. Lowell W. Adams. National Institute for Urban Wildlife, 10921 Trotting Ridge Way, Columbia, MD 21044. (301) 596-3311. 1989. Reviews the knowledge base on wildlife habitat reserves and corridors in urban and urbanizing areas. Provides guidelines and approaches to ecological landscape planning and wildlife conservation in these regions.

Wildlife Resources Agency: Fish and Wildlife. Executive Director, PO Box 40747, Nashville, TN 37204. (615) 781-6552.

Wildlife Society. 5410 Grosvenor Lane, Bethesda, MD 20814. (301) 897-9770.

Wildlife Society Bulletin. The Wildlife Society, 5410 Grosvenor Lane, Bethesda, MD 20814. (301) 897-9770. Quarterly. Covers wildlife management and conservation education.

Wildlife Toxicology. Tony J. Peterle. Van Nostrand Reinhold, 115 5th Ave., New York, NY 10003. (212) 354-3232. 1991. Presents an historical overview of the toxicology problem and summarizes the principal laws, testing protocols, and roles of leading U.S. federal agencies, especially EPA. Examines state and local issues, monitoring programs, and contains an unique section on the regulation of toxic substances overseas.

The Wildlifer. The Wildlife Society, 5410 Grosvenor Lane, Bethesda, MD 20814. (301) 897-9770. Bimonthly. Covers protection of wildlife resources.

Willowwood Arboretum. PO Box 1295, Morristown, NJ 07962-1295. (201) 326-7600.

Wilson Ornithological Society. Dept. of Internal Medicine, Gastroenterology Division, University of Texas, Medical Branch, Galveston, TX 77550.